P9-DZY-599

The Concise Oxford Dictionary

The Concise Oxford Dictionary

of Current English

First edited by

H. W. Fowler and F. G. Fowler

NINTH EDITION

Edited by

Della Thompson

CLARENDON PRESS · OXFORD

Oxford University Press, Walton Street, Oxford OX2 6DP
Oxford New York
Athens Auckland Bangkok Bombay
Calcutta Cape Town Dar es Salaam Delhi
Florence Hong Kong Istanbul Karachi
Kuala Lumpur Madras Madrid Melbourne
Mexico City Nairobi Paris Singapore
Taipei Tokyo Toronto
and associated companies in
Berlin Ibadan

Published in the United States by
Oxford University Press Inc., New York

First edition 1911
New edition (revised) 1929
Third edition (with Addenda) 1934
Fourth edition 1951
Fifth edition 1964
Sixth edition 1976
Seventh edition 1982
Eighth edition 1990
Ninth edition 1995

British Library Cataloguing in Publication Data
The Concise Oxford Dictionary of Current English.—9th ed.
1. English language—Dictionaries
I. Thompson, Della
ISBN 0-19-861320-2 thumb index
ISBN 0-19-861319-9 plain

Library of Congress Cataloging in Publication Data
The Concise Oxford Dictionary of Current English.—9th ed./edited by Della Thompson.
p. cm.
'First edited by H. W. Fowler and F. G. Fowler.'
ISBN 0-19-861319-9—ISBN 0-19-861320-2 (thumb index)
1. English language—Dictionaries. I. Thompson, Della. II. Fowler, H. W. (Henry Watson), 1858-1933. III. Fowler, F. G. (Francis George), 1870-1918.
PE1628.C68 1990
423—dc20 89-72114 CIP

10 9 8 7 6 5 4 3 2

Printed in the United States of America
on acid-free paper

Contents

The Concise Oxford Dictionary

Appendices

Editorial Staff

Managing Editor
Della Thompson

Senior Editor (incl. Science)
Jeremy Marshall

Senior Assistant Editor
Glynnis Chantrell

Assistant Editor
Andrew Hodgson

Keyboarding Manager
Anne Whear

Keyboarding Assistants
Pam Marjara, Kay Pepler

Other Contributors
Frank Abate (US Usage)
Robert Allen (*English over Fifteen Centuries*)
Katherine Barber (Canadian Usage)
Sam Howard
Louise Jones
Richard Lindsay
Fred McDonald (Etymologies)
Bernadette Paton
Robert Ritter
Anne St John-Hall
Joanna Thompson
Clive Upton (Pronunciations)
Sandy Vaughan

Chief Editor, Current English Dictionaries
Patrick Hanks

Preface

The ninth edition of the *Concise Oxford Dictionary* is 14 per cent larger than the eighth and it takes further the changes in methodology and presentation that were introduced in its predecessor. These changes were in two main areas: firstly, the use of computer technology; and secondly, the aim of making the information contained in the dictionary more accessible to the user.

With regard to the use of computer technology, the *COD* has benefited in this edition not only from the availability of the previous edition in the form of an electronically tagged database, but from access to large bodies of corpus and citational evidence. The British National Corpus, a database containing over 100,000,000 words of text, has been the most significant of these, together with the OUP Dictionary Department's vast computerized collection of selected citations and its other computerized dictionary texts including the twenty-volume *Oxford English Dictionary*. The gathering of evidence for new words and usages has been greatly enhanced by electronic access to these sources, and the dictionary is now able to incorporate more quickly and reflect more accurately changes that have arisen in the language since the previous edition, with additions being made to the text right up to the time of printing. As a result, this edition contains over 7,000 new words and senses in a wide variety of areas. For example, the growing availability of international cuisine in Britain and elsewhere is reflected by the use in English of terms such as *bhaji, fajita, gravlax, penne, sharon fruit,* and many others; in the field of politics we have *dream ticket, Euro-rebel, placeman, rainbow coalition,* and *spin doctor*; in ecology new terms such as *arcology, carr, ecocide, greening,* and *wind farm* have arisen; in science and medicine, *blue box, bronchodilator, Creutzfeldt-Jakob disease, Feynman diagram, hyperspace, nicad, packet switching, repetitive strain injury,* and *wormhole.*

Access to large corpora has also facilitated the statistical evaluation of disputed spellings, a reassessment of the hyphenation of compound nouns and a review of the italicization or otherwise of foreign words and phrases. The general trends away from the hyphenating of compound nouns and away from the italicization of foreign words and phrases are now recorded in the dictionary. For example, instead of being hyphenated, *aftercare, postdoctoral,* and *teardrop* are now usually written as one word, while *boiler room, hand grenade,* and *taxi driver* are usually found as separate words. Similarly, *en route, hoi polloi,* and *tour de force* now tend to be written in roman rather than italic script, reflecting their increased assimilation into English. In addition to these changes, some proprietary terms are now recorded in the dictionary with a lower case initial letter, also reflecting general usage (but not affecting their legal proprietary status).

Another important feature of this edition has been the enlisting of special consultants for North American usage, which has enabled us to improve our coverage of this area and to apply geographical labels more accurately. Examples of new North American entries are *antsy, badass, ditzy, drywall, all-wheel drive, Latino, pork barrel, road kill, sweat sock,* and *upchuck.*

Special attention has been given to the improvement of coverage in science and technology. Many terms which have become familiar outside the pages of technical books and journals have been added, especially in life sciences (including natural history) and computing, such as *accelerator board, biocide, client-server, flash memory,* and *ketamine,* and their definitions seek to balance comprehensibility and precision.

The aim to make the information contained in the dictionary more accessible to the user has resulted firstly in extending the policy of 'denesting' begun in the eighth edition. In this edition all compound nouns have been given their own entries rather than being 'nested' under their first element. This makes them easier to find and results in fewer extremely long entries. Attention has also been given to making etymologies clearer by minimizing the use of abbreviations and bracketed information and by the use of clearer punctuation. Usage Notes, which were previously buried within entries, have been extracted, expanded, and placed at the end of entries. A clearer style of explanation has been adopted and many more illustrative examples given.

Finally, the pronunciations have been thoroughly revised, giving a more up-to-date representation of the standard British English accent (Received Pronunciation) by means of the International Phonetic Alphabet, in line with the system introduced into the *New Shorter Oxford English Dictionary*.

Many people were involved in the preparation of this new edition. In addition to the editorial staff already listed on page v, we would like to thank the following for sundry advice and contributions and for help with proofreading: Judy Pearsall, David Shirt, Catherine Soanes, Angus Stevenson, Bill Trumble, Rachel Unsworth, and Maurice Waite.

D. J. T.

March 1995

English over Fifteen Centuries

Fifteen centuries of English cannot easily be summarized, but this brief account may afford some perspective to the information given in the dictionary, and help to make more sense of the strange and often unpredictable ways in which words seem to behave.

ORIGINS

English belongs to the Indo-European family of languages, a vast group with many branches, thought to be derived from a common ancestor-language called Proto-Indo-European. The words we use in English are derived from a wide range of sources, mostly within this family. The earliest sources are Germanic, Norse, and Romanic; more recently, with the growth and decline of the British Empire and the rapid development of communications, they have been worldwide.

It is difficult to be sure exactly what we mean by an 'English' word. Most obviously, words are English if they can be traced back to the Germanic language of the Anglo-Saxons, who settled in Britain from the fifth century. From this time are derived many common words such as *eat, drink, speak, work, house, door, man, woman, husband, wife*. The Anglo-Saxons displaced the Celtic peoples, whose speech survives in Scottish and Irish Gaelic, Welsh, Manx, and Cornish. Little Celtic influence remains in English, except in names of places and rivers.

Anglo-Saxon Britain continued to have contact with the Roman Empire, of which Britain had formerly been a part, and with Latin, which was the official language throughout the Empire and survived as a language of ritual (and for a time also of learning and communication) in the Western Christian Church. After the mission of St Augustine in AD 597, the Christianized Anglo-Saxons built churches and monasteries, and there were considerable advances in art and learning. At this time English was enriched by many words from Latin, some of which are still in use, such as *angel, disciple, martyr,* and *shrine*. Other words were derived from Latin via the Germanic languages, for example *copper, mint* (in the sense of coinage), *pound, sack,* and *tile,* and others were ultimately of oriental origin, for example *camel* and *pepper*.

The next important influence on the vocabulary of English was the Old Norse language of the Danish and other Scandinavian invaders of the ninth and tenth centuries, collectively called Vikings. They occupied much of the east side of England, and under Cnut (Canute) ruled the whole country for a time. Because Old Norse was also a Germanic language (of a different branch from English) many words were similar to the Anglo-Saxon ones, and it is difficult to establish the extent of the Old Norse influence. However, a number of Norse words are identifiable and are still in use, such as *call, take,* and *law,* names of parts of the body such as *leg,* and other basic words such as *egg, root,* and *window*. Many more Norse words are preserved in some dialects of the east side of England, and especially in place names.

In the Saxon kingdom of Wessex, King Alfred (871–99) and his successors did much to keep English alive by using it (rather than Latin) as the language of education and learning; by the tenth century there was a considerable amount of English prose and verse literature. Saxon and Danish kingdoms existed side by side for several generations, and there was much linguistic interaction. One very important effect on English was the gradual disappearance of many word-endings, or inflections, leading to a simpler grammar. This was partly because the stems of English and Norse words were often very close in form (for example, *stan* and *steinn,* meaning *'stone'*), and only the inflections differed as an impediment to mutual understanding. So forms such as *stāne, stānes,* etc., began to be simplified and, eventually, eliminated. The process continued for hundreds of years into Middle English (see below).

THE NORMAN CONQUEST

In 1066 William of Normandy was crowned King of England. The arrival of the French-speaking Normans as a ruling nobility brought a transforming influence on the language. French, as one of the Romance languages, has its roots in the spoken or 'vulgar' Latin that continued in use until about AD 600. For two hundred years after the Norman Conquest, French (in its regional Norman form) was the language of the aristocracy, the lawcourts, and the Church hierarchy in England. During these years many French words were adopted into English. Some were connected with law and government, such as *justice, council,* and *tax,* and some were abstract terms such as *liberty, charity,* and *conflict.* The Normans also had an important effect on the spelling of English words. The combination of letters *cw-*, for example, was standardized in the Norman manner to *qu-*, so that *cwēn* became *queen* and *cwic* became *quik* (later *quick*).

This mixture of conquering peoples and their languages—Germanic, Scandinavian, and Romance—has had a decisive effect on the forms of words in modern English. The three elements make up the basic stock of English vocabulary, and different practices of putting sounds into writing are reflected in each. The different grammatical characteristics of each element can be seen in the structure and endings of many words. Many of the variable endings such as *-ant* and *-ent, -er* and *-or, -able* and *-ible* exist because the Latin words on which they are based belonged to different classes of verbs and nouns, each of which had a different ending. For example, *important* comes from the Latin verb *portare,* meaning 'to carry' (which belongs to one class or conjugation) while *repellent* comes from the Latin verb *pellere,* meaning 'to drive' (which belongs to another). *Capable* comes from a Latin word ending in *-abilis,* while *sensible* comes from one ending in *-ibilis,* and so on.

MIDDLE ENGLISH

Middle English, as the English of c.1100–1500 is called, emerged as the spoken and written form of the language under these influences. By the reign of Henry II (1154–89) many of the aristocracy spoke English and the use of French diminished, especially after King John (1199–1216) lost possession of Normandy in 1204. Many Anglo-Saxon words had disappeared altogether: for example, *niman* was replaced by the Old Norse (Scandinavian) *taka* (meaning 'take), and the Old English *sige* was replaced by a word derived from Old French, *victory.* Other Old English words that disappeared are *ādl* (disease), *lof* (praise), and *lyft* (air: compare German *Luft*).

Hundreds of the Romance words were short simple words that would now be distinguished with difficulty from Old English words if their origin were not known: for example, *bar, cry, fool, mean, pity, stuff, touch,* and *tender.* Sometimes new and old words continued in use side by side, in some cases on a roughly equal footing and in others with a distinction in meaning (as with *doom* and *judgement,* and *stench* and *smell*). This has produced pairs of words which are both in use today, such as *shut* and *close,* and *buy* and *purchase,* in which the second word of each pair is Romance in origin and often more formal in connotation. This mixture of types of words is a feature especially of modern English. For many meanings we now have a choice of less formal or more formal words, the more formal ones in some cases being used only in very specific circumstances. For example, the word *vendor* is used instead of *seller* only in the context of buying or selling property. Many technical words derived from or ultimately from Latin, such as *estop* and *usucaption,* survive only in legal contexts, to the great confusion of the layman.

PRINTING

There was much regional variation in the spelling and pronunciation of Middle English, although a good measure of uniformity was imposed by the development of printing from the fifteenth century. This uniformity was based as much on practical considerations of the printing process as on what seemed most 'correct' or suitable. It became common practice, for example, to add a final *e* to words to fill a line of print. The printers—many of whom were foreign—used rules from their own languages, especially Dutch and Flemish, when setting English into type. William Caxton, the first English printer (1422–91), exercised an important but not always beneficial influence. The unnecessary insertion of *h* in *ghost,* for example, is due to Caxton (who learned the business of printing on the Continent), and the change had its effect on other words such as *ghastly* and (perhaps) *ghetto.* In general, Caxton used the form of English prevalent in the south-east of England, although the East Midland dialect was the more extensive. This choice, together with the growing importance of London as the English capital, gave the dialect of the South-East a special importance that survives to the present day.

PRONUNCIATION

At roughly the same time as the early development of printing, the pronunciation of English was also undergoing major changes. The main change, which began in the fourteenth century during the lifetime of the poet Chaucer, was in the pronunciation of vowel sounds. The so-called 'great vowel shift' resulted in the reduction of the number of long vowels (for example, in *deed* as distinct from *dead*) from seven to the five which we know today (discernible in the words *bean, barn, born, boon,* and *burn*). It also affected the pronunciation of other vowels: the word *life,* for example, was once pronounced as we now pronounce *leaf,* and *name* was pronounced as two syllables to rhyme with *farmer.* In many cases, as with *name,* the form of the word did not change, and this accounts for many of the 'silent' vowels at the ends of words. The result of these developments was a growing difference between what was spoken and what was written.

THE RENAISSANCE

The rediscovery in Europe of the culture and history of the ancient Greek and Roman worlds exercised a further romanizing influence on English which blossomed in the Renaissance of the fifteenth to seventeenth centuries. Scholarship flourished, and the language used by scholars and writers was Latin. During the Renaissance, words such as *arena, dexterity, excision, genius, habitual, malignant, specimen,* and *stimulus* came into use in English. They are familiar and useful words but their Latin origins sometimes make them awkward to handle, as, for example, when we use *arena, genius,* and *stimulus* in the plural. There was also a tendency in the Renaissance to try to emphasize the Greek or Latin origins of words when writing them. This accounts for the *b* in *debt* (the earlier English word was *det;* in Latin it is *debitum*), and *l* in *fault* (earlier *faut;* the Latin source is *fallere* fail), the *s* in *isle* (earlier *ile; insula* in Latin), and the *p* in *receipt* (earlier *receit; recepta* in Latin). Some words that had gone out of use were reintroduced, usually with changed meanings, for example *artificial, disc* (originally the same as *dish*), and *fastidious.*

LATER INFLUENCES

The development of technology from the eighteenth century onwards has also played a part in continuing the influence of Latin. New technical terms have come into use, formed on Latin or Greek source-words because these can convey precise ideas in easily combinable forms, for example *bacteriology, microscope, radioactive,* and *semiconductor.* Combinations of Germanic elements are also used, as in *software, splashdown,* and *take-off.* This process has sometimes produced odd mixtures, such as *television,* which is half Greek and half Latin, and *microchip,* which is half Greek and half Germanic.

In recent times English speakers have come into contact with people from other parts of the world, through trade, colonization, and improved communications. This contact has produced a rich supply of new words that are often strange in form. India, where the British first had major dealings in the seventeenth century, is the source of words such a *bungalow, jodhpurs,* and *khaki.* Usually these words have been altered or assimilated to make them look more natural in English (e.g. *bungalow* from Gujarati *bangalo*). Examples from other parts of the world are *harem* and *mufti* (from Arabic), *bazaar* (from Persian), *kiosk* (from Turkish), and *anorak* (from Eskimo). From European countries we have acquired *balcony* (from Italian), *envelope* (from French), and *yacht* (from Dutch).

Thousands of such words, though not English in the Germanic sense, are regarded as fully absorbed into English. In addition, many words and phrases are used in English contexts but are generally regarded as 'foreign', and are conventionally printed in italics to distinguish them when used in an English context. Very many of these are French, for example *accouchement* (childbirth), *bagarre* (a scuffle), *chanson* (a French song), *flânerie* (idleness), and *rangé* (domesticated), but other languages are represented, as with *echt* (genuine) and *Machtpolitik* (power politics) from German, and *mañana* (tomorrow) from Spanish (see also *Italicization,* Appendix XIII D).

Usage often recognizes the difficulties of absorbing words from various sources by assimilating them into forms that are already familiar. The word *picturesque* which came into use in the eighteenth century, is a compromise between its French source *pittoresque* and the existing Middle English word *picture,* to which it is obviously related. The English word *cockroach* is a conversion of the Spanish word *cucaracha* into a pair of familiar words *cock* (a bird) and *roach* (a fish). Cockroaches have nothing to do with cocks or roaches, and the association is simply a matter of linguistic convenience.

Problems of inflection arise with words taken from other languages. The ending *-i* in particular is very unnatural in English, and usage varies between *-is* and *-ies* in the plural. A similar difficulty occurs with the many adopted nouns ending in *-o,* some of which come from Italian (*solo*), some from Spanish (*armadillo*), and some from Latin (*hero*); here usage varies between *-os* and *-oes.* Verbs often need special treatment, as for example *bivouac* (from French, and before that probably from Swiss German) which needs a *k* in the past tense (*bivouacked,* not *bivouaced* which might be mispronounced), and *ski* (from Norwegian) where the past form *skied* is not really satisfactory, and *ski'd* was once popular as an alternative. In this dictionary extensive help is given with these and other difficulties of inflection.

DICTIONARIES

One obvious consequence of the development of printing in the fifteenth century was that it allowed the language to be recorded in glossaries and dictionaries, and this might be expected to have had a considerable effect on the way words were used and spelt. However, listing all the words in the language systematically in alphabetical order with their spellings and meanings is a relatively recent idea. In 1580, when Shakespeare was sixteen, a schoolmaster named William Bullokar published a manual for the 'ease, speed, and perfect reading and writing of English', and he called for the writing of an English dictionary. Such a dictionary, the work of Robert Cawdrey (another schoolmaster), was not published until 1604. Like the dictionaries that followed in quick succession (including Bullokar's own *English Expositor*), its purpose was described as being for the understanding of 'hard words'. It was not until the eighteenth century that dictionaries systematically listed all the words in general use at the time regardless of how 'easy' or 'hard' they were; the most notable of these were compiled by Nathaniel Bailey (1721) and, especially, Samuel Johnson (1755). They were partly a response to a call, expressed by Swift, Pope, Addison, and other writers, for the language to be fixed and stabilized, and for the establishment of an English Academy to monitor it. None of these hopes as such were realized, but the dictionaries played an important role in settling the form and senses of English words.

The systematic investigation and recording of words in all their aspects and on a historical basis is first and exclusively represented in the *Oxford English Dictionary,* began by the Scottish schoolmaster James A. H. Murray in 1879. This describes historically the spelling, inflection, origin, and meaning of words, and is supported by citations from printed literature and other sources as evidence from Old English to the present day. To take account of more recent changes and developments in the language, a four-volume *Supplement* was added to the work from 1972 to 1986, and a new edition integrating the original dictionary and its *Supplement* appeared in 1989. Because of its depth of scholarship, the *Oxford English Dictionary* forms a major basis of all English dictionaries produced since. Smaller concise and other household dictionaries that aim at recording the main vocabulary in current use began to appear early this century and in recent years the number has grown remarkably.

Dictionaries of current English, as distinct from historical dictionaries, generally record the language as it is being used at the time, and with usage constantly changing the distinction between 'right' and 'wrong' is sometimes difficult to establish. Unlike French, which is guided by the rulings of the *Académie française,* English is not monitored by any single authority; established usage is the principal criterion. One result of this is that English tolerates many more alternative spellings than other languages. The alternatives are based on certain patterns of word formation and variation in the different languages through which they have passed before reaching ours.

It should also be remembered that the smaller dictionaries, such as this one, provide a selection, based on currency, of a recorded stock of over half a million words; that is to say, they represent about 15–20 per cent of what is attested to exist by printed sources and other materials. Dictionaries therefore differ in the selection they make, beyond the core of vocabulary and idiom that can be expected to be found in any dictionary.

DIALECT

Within the British Isles, regional forms and dialects, with varying accents and usage, have continued to exist since the Middle Ages, although in recent times, especially with the emergence of mass communications, they have been in decline. A special feature of a dialect is its vocabulary of words (often for everyday things) that are understood only locally. It is not possible in a small dictionary to treat this kind of vocabulary in any detail, but its influence can be seen in the origins of words that have achieved a more general currency, for example *boss-eyed* (from a dialect word *boss* meaning 'miss', 'bungle'), *fad, scrounge* (from a dialect *scrunge* meaning 'steal') and *shoddy.* Far more information on dialect words is available in *The English Dialect Dictionary* (ed. J. Wright, London, 1898–1905), in the *Oxford English Dictionary,* and in numerous glossaries published by dialect societies.

ENGLISH WORLDWIDE

Usage in modern times is greatly influenced by rapid worldwide communications, by newspapers and, in particular, by television and radio. Speakers of British English are brought into daily contact with alternative forms of the language, especially American English. This influence is often regarded as unsettling or harmful but it has had a considerable effect on the vocabulary, idiom, and spelling of British English, and continues to do so. Among the many words and idioms in use in British English, usually without any awareness of or concern about their American origin, are *OK, to fall for, to fly off the handle, round trip,* and *to snoop.* American English often has more regular spellings, as outlined in *Spelling Rules,* Appendix XIII B.

English is now used all over the world; as a result, there are many varieties of English, with varying accents, vocabulary, and usage. Varieties in use in Southern Africa, India, Australia, New Zealand, Canada, and elsewhere have an equal claim to be regarded as 'English' and, although learners of English may look to British English as the centre of an English-speaking world, or British and American English as the two poles of such a world, it is very important that dictionaries should take account of English overseas, especially as it affects usage in Britain. The process is a strengthening and enriching one, and is the mark of a living and flourishing language.

FURTHER READING

This survey has had to be brief, and restricted to those aspects of English that are of immediate concern to the users of a dictionary. Those who are interested in exploring further will find a host of books on the history and development of English. Good general accounts are A. C. Baugh and T. Cable, *A History of the English Language* (3rd edn., New Jersey and London, 1978) and B. M. H. Strang, *A History of English* (London, 1970). At a more popular level, and more up to date on recent trends, are R. W. Burchfield, *The English Language* (Oxford, 1985) and R. McCrum et al., *The Story of English* (London, 1986). *The Oxford Companion to the English Language* (ed. T. McArthur, Oxford, 1992) contains much that will interest those who want to know more about the English of today and its place among the languages of the world.

Using this Dictionary

1. STRUCTURE OF ENTRIES

The following pages aim to illustrate the presentation of information in entries in the dictionary. The use of special conventions has been kept to a minimum. A reference list of abbreviations used may be found on p. xx; for additional information on the use of labels see p. xix.

1.1 The Headword

(a) Its Forms

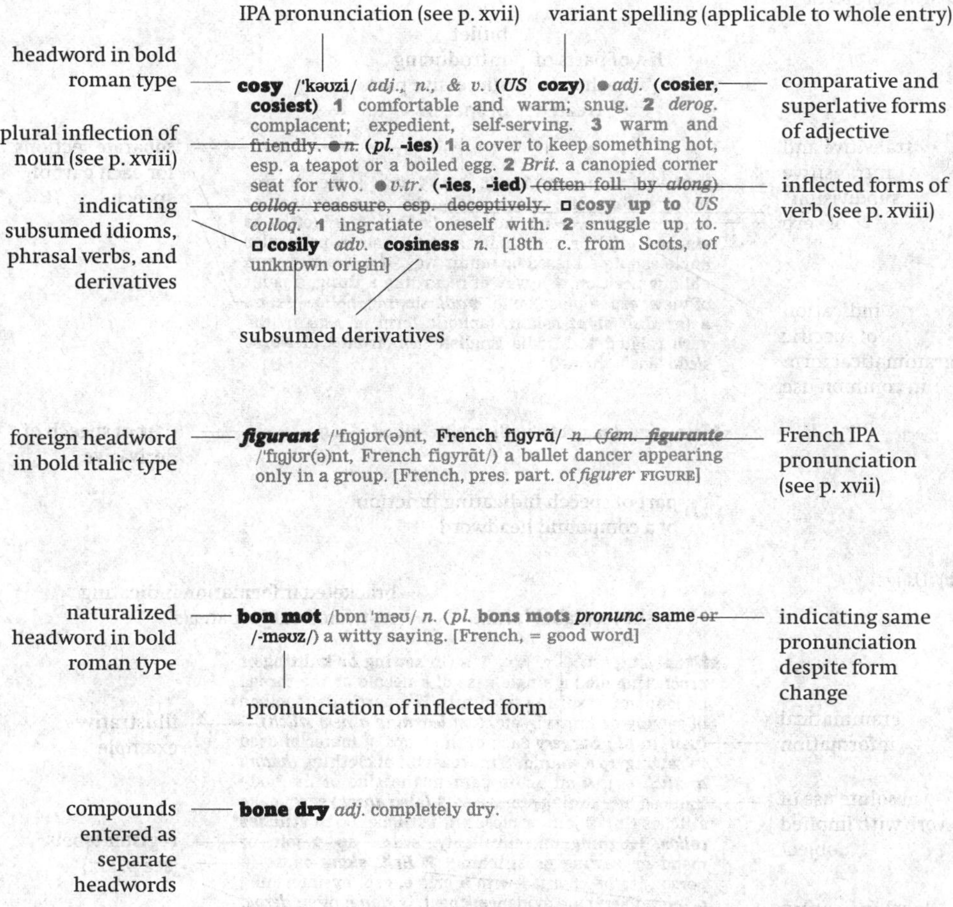

IPA pronunciation (see p. xvii)
variant spelling (applicable to whole entry)
headword in bold roman type
cosy /ˈkəʊzi/ *adj., n., & v.* (**US cozy**) ● *adj.* (**cosier, cosiest**) **1** comfortable and warm; snug. **2** *derog.* complacent; expedient, self-serving. **3** warm and friendly. ● *n.* (*pl.* **-ies**) **1** a cover to keep something hot, esp. a teapot or a boiled egg. **2** *Brit.* a canopied corner seat for two. ● *v.tr.* (**-ies, -ied**) (often foll. by *along*) *colloq.* reassure, esp. deceptively. □ **cosy up to** *US colloq.* **1** ingratiate oneself with. **2** snuggle up to. □ **cosily** *adv.* **cosiness** *n.* [18th c. from Scots, of unknown origin]
comparative and superlative forms of adjective
plural inflection of noun (see p. xviii)
inflected forms of verb (see p. xviii)
indicating subsumed idioms, phrasal verbs, and derivatives
subsumed derivatives
foreign headword in bold italic type
figurant /ˈfɪgjʊr(ə)nt, French figyrɑ̃/ *n.* (*fem.* ***figurante*** /ˈfɪgjʊr(ə)nt, French figyrɑ̃t/) a ballet dancer appearing only in a group. [French, pres. part. of *figurer* FIGURE]
French IPA pronunciation (see p. xvii)
naturalized headword in bold roman type
bon mot /bɒn ˈməʊ/ *n.* (*pl.* **bons mots** *pronunc.* same or /-məʊz/) a witty saying. [French, = good word]
indicating same pronunciation despite form change
pronunciation of inflected form
compounds entered as separate headwords
bone dry *adj.* completely dry.

It should be noted that proper names are not listed as such in the dictionary, but only the general vocabulary items to which they have given rise—hence, for example, the format of the entry for *Jesus.*

(*b*) *Sense Division*

superior numeral to distinguish a homograph

numbered sequence of senses by currency or comparative significance

letters used for closely-related or dependent subdivisions

definition

beaver[1] /'bi:və/ *n. & v.* ● *n.* (*pl.* same or **beavers**) **1 a** **any large amphibious broad-tailed rodent of the genus *Castor*, native to N. America, Europe, and Asia, and able to gnaw through tree trunks and make dams.** **b** its soft light brown fur. **c** a hat of this. **2** (in full **beaver cloth**) a heavy woollen cloth like beaver fur. **3** (**Beaver**) a boy aged six or seven who is an affiliate member of the Scout Association. ● *v.intr.* (usu. foll. by *away*) *colloq.* work hard. [Old English *be(o)for*, from Germanic]

alternative form only applicable to specific sense

different spelling (capital initial), applicable to specific sense

1.2 Labelling

(*a*) *Parts of Speech*

list of parts of speech to be treated

bullet introducing successive parts of speech

separate sections for each part of speech

transitive and intransitive subdivisions of verb

slant /slɑ:nt/ *v., n., & adj.* ● *v.* **1** *intr.* slope; diverge from a line; lie or go obliquely to a vertical or horizontal line. **2** *tr.* cause to do this. **3** *tr.* (**often as slanted** *adj.*) present (information) from a particular angle esp. in a biased or unfair way. ● *n.* **1** a slope; an oblique position. **2** a way of regarding a thing; a point of view, esp. a biased one. ● *adj.* sloping, oblique. □ **on a** (or **the**) **slant** aslant. [aphetic form of ASLANT: the verb related to Middle English *slent* from Old Norse *sletta* 'dash, throw']

indication of specific grammatical form in common use

blue blood *n.* noble birth. □ **blue-blooded** *adj.*

part of speech of derivative

part of speech indicating function of a compound headword

(*b*) *Usage*

subject label (p. xix)

bracketed information indicating restricted subject area(s)

stitch /stɪtʃ/ *n. & v.* ● *n.* **1 a** (**in sewing or knitting or crocheting etc.**) a single pass of a needle or the thread or loop etc. resulting from this. **b** a particular method of sewing or knitting etc. (***am learning a new stitch***). **2** (**usu. in *pl.***) ***Surgery*** each of the loops of material used in sewing up a wound. **3** the least bit of clothing (*hadn't a stitch on*). **4** an acute pain in the side of the body induced by running etc. ● *v.tr.* **1** (**also *absol.***) sew; make stitches (in). **2** join or close with stitches. □ **in stitches** ***colloq.*** laughing uncontrollably. **stitch up 1** join or mend by sewing or stitching. **2** ***Brit. slang*** cause (a person) to be charged with a crime, esp. by informing or manufacturing evidence; cheat. **3** *slang*; often ***derog.*** = *sew up* 2. □ **stitcher** *n.* **stitchery** *n.* **stitchless** *adj.* [Old English *stice* from Germanic: related to STICK[2]]

grammatical information

illustrative example

absolute use of verb with implied object

register labels (see p. xix)

label indicating restricted geographical area (cf. next sample) bracketed comment referring to an institution associated with the country named — **FBI** *abbr.* **(in the US)** Federal Bureau of Investigation.

conscious /ˈkɒnʃəs/ *adj.* & *n.* ● *adj.* **1** awake and aware of one's surroundings and identity. **2 (usu. foll. by *of*, or *that* + clause)** aware, knowing (*conscious of his inferiority*). **3 (of actions, emotions, etc.)** realized or recognized by the doer; intentional (*made a conscious effort not to laugh*). **4 (in *comb.*)** aware of; concerned with (*fashion-conscious*). ● *n.* **(prec. by *the*)** the conscious mind. □ **consciously** *adv.* [Latin *conscius* 'knowing with others or in oneself' from *conscire* (as COM-, *scire* 'know')]

delimiter; headword productive in combinations of elements joined usu. by a hyphen; formula for grammatical construction; specific construction

lunchtime /ˈlʌn(t)ʃtʌɪm/ *n.* the time when lunch is eaten **(often *attrib.*: *lunchtime drinking*)**.

noun used attributively

use restricted to predicative position

fond *adj.* **1 (*predic.*;** foll. by *of*) having affection or a liking for. **2 (*attrib.*)** affectionate, loving, doting. **3 (*attrib.*)** (of beliefs etc.) foolishly optimistic or credulous; naive. □ **fondly** *adv.* **fondness** *n.* [Middle English from obsolete *fon* 'fool, be foolish']

adjective used attributively in these senses

1.3 Cross-reference

small capitals indicating a headword entry elsewhere

statics /ˈstatɪks/ *n.pl.* (usu. treated as *sing.*) **1** the science of bodies at rest or of forces in equilibrium **(opp. DYNAMICS 1a)**. **2 = STATIC *n.*** [from STATIC *n.* + -S[1]: **see -ICS**]

antonym for consultation; more information at headword -ics; cross-reference to noun sense of the headword **static**

cum grano salis /kʌm ˌɡrɑːnəʊ ˈsɑːlɪs/ *adv.* with a grain of salt **(cf. *take with a pinch of salt* (see SALT))**. [Latin]

cross-reference to information for comparison or classification; italic script indicating subsumed idiom; information to be found at headword named

variant entered in headword list — **'mongst** *poet.* **var.** of AMONGST (see AMONG).

calves *pl.* of CALF[1], CALF[2].

irregular forms in headword list (when 3 or more entries from headword indicated)

trodden *past part.* of TREAD.

1.4 Etymology

boomslang /ˈbuːmslaŋ/ *n.* a venomous tree-snake, *Dispholidus typus*, native to southern Africa. **[Afrikaans from *boom* 'tree' + *slang* 'snake']**

no etymology given where headword is composed of elements explained elsewhere — **boom town** *n.* a town undergoing sudden growth due to a boom.

boon[1] /buːn/ *n.* **1** an advantage; a blessing. **2** *archaic* **a** a thing asked for; a request. **b** a gift; a favour. **[Middle English, originally = prayer, via Old Norse *bón* from Germanic]**

immediate source language given first

boon[2] /buːn/ *adj.* close, intimate, favourite (usu. *boon companion*). **[Middle English (originally = jolly, congenial) via Old French *bon* from Latin *bonus* 'good']**

boondock /ˈbuːndɒk/ *n.* (usu. in *pl.*) *N. Amer. slang* rough or isolated country. **[Tagalog *bundok* 'mountain']**

boondoggle /ˈbuːndɒg(ə)l/ *n.* & *v. N. Amer. colloq.* ● *n.* **1** a trivial or useless undertaking. **2** a dishonest undertaking; a fraud. ● *v.intr.* take part in a trivial, useless, or dishonest undertaking. **[20th c.: origin uncertain]**

various types of etymology showing the origin of the headword, placed in square brackets at the end of an entry

1.5 Usage Notes

aggravate /ˈagrəveɪt/ *v.tr.* **1** increase the gravity of (an illness, offence, etc.) (*the war was aggravating the situation*). **2** *disp.* annoy, exasperate (a person). □ **aggravating** *adj. disp.* **aggravation** /-ˈveɪʃ(ə)n/ *n.* [Latin *aggravare aggravat-* 'make heavy' from *gravis* 'heavy']

Usage Note, placed between horizontal lines after main part of the entry — ■ **Usage** The use of *aggravate* in sense 2, to mean 'annoy, exasperate', is regarded by some people as incorrect but is common in informal use and dates back to the 17th century. *Aggravating* meaning 'annoying' is similarly frowned upon.

2. PRONUNCIATION

Guidance on pronunciation follows the system of the International Phonetic Alphabet (IPA), and is based on the pronunciation associated especially with southern England (sometimes called 'Received Pronunciation').

It is not possible in a dictionary of this size to show the many variations heard in educated speech in other parts of the English-speaking world.

The symbols used, with their values, are as follows:

Consonants

b, d, f, h, k, l, m, n, p, r, s, t, v, w, and *z* have their usual English values. Other symbols are used as follows:

g *get*	x lo*ch*	ð *this*	j *yes*
tʃ *chip*	ŋ ri*ng*	ʃ *she*	
dʒ *jar*	θ *thin*	ʒ deci*s*ion	

Vowels

short vowels	*long vowels* (ː *indicates length*)	*diphthongs*
a *cat*	ɑː *arm*	ʌɪ *my*
ɛ *bed*	ɛː *hair*	aʊ *how*
ə *ago*	əː *her*	eɪ *day*
ɪ *sit*	iː *see*	əʊ *no*
i *cosy*	ɔː *saw*	ɪə *near*
ɒ *hot*	uː *too*	ɔɪ *boy*
ʌ *run*		ʊə *poor*
ʊ *put*		ʌɪə *fire*
		aʊə *sour*

(ə) signifies the indeterminate sound as in gard*e*n, carn*a*l, and rhyth*m*.

(r) indicates an *r* that is sometimes sounded when a vowel follows as in drawer, cha-chaing.

The additional symbols used to represent foreign pronunciations, with their values, are as follows:

Consonants

ç (German) e*ch*t

ɲ (French) Monsei*gn*eur

Vowels

Short vowels	*long vowels* (ː *indicates length*)	*nasalized vowels* (~ *indicates nasality*)	*diphthongs*
ɑ (French) crime passionnel		*naturalized* { ã p*in*cette; õ cord*on* bleu } ɑ̃ (French) accouche*men*t	aɪ (German) Gl*ei*chschaltung
e (French) d*é*mod*é* (German) e*ch*t (Italian) dolc*e* vita	eː (German) W*eh*rmacht (Italian) comm*e*dia dell'arte	ɛ̃ (French) dist*in*gué	
o (French) *au*berge (German) Bildungsr*o*man (Italian) am*o*retto	oː (German) verb*o*ten (Italian) calz*o*ne		
ɔ (French) b*o*rné (German) durchk*o*mponiert (Italian) c*o*n am*o*re		ɔ̃ (French) c*on*gé	
œ (French) accouch*eu*r	ɜː (German) Gasth*ö*fe		
ø (French) berc*eu*se			
u (French) bij*ou* (Italian) fig*u*rante			
y (French) cr*u*	yː (German) gem*ü*tlich		ɥi (French) à h*ui*s clos

- The main or primary stress is shown by ' preceding the relevant syllable in disyllabic or polysyllabic words; any secondary stress is shown by ˌ in certain polysyllabic words to avoid doubt.
- Pronunciations are given enclosed in oblique strokes / /. Where more than one pronunciation is given, that given first is generally the preferred pronunciation. The label *disp.* indicates that some people consider the variant incorrect.
- In the case of hyphenated headwords or headwords consisting of separate words the pronunciation is given only for elements that do not appear individually elsewhere in the dictionary.
- Pronunciations for variant forms are given at the main entry where the pronunciation differs from that of the headword.
- Pronunciation of derivatives listed at the end of the entries is only given when there is a change of stress (as with many words in *-ation*) or some other significant change.
- In the case of inflected forms, a pronunciation is given when this differs significantly from the pronunciation of the headword.
- The pronunciation given for a prefix, suffix, or combining form is an approximate one for purposes of articulating (and in some cases identifying) the headword; pronunciation and stress may change considerably when they form part of a word.
- If a word is not naturalized in English and therefore in italics as a headword, a standard pronunciation in English is given, followed in many cases, by guidance to the foreign pronunciation.

3. INFLECTION

The inflection of nouns, verbs, adjectives, and adverbs is given when it is irregular, or when, though regular, it causes difficulty (as with forms such as **budgeted, coos,** and **taxis**). See also Appendix XIII B.

3.1 Plurals of nouns

For nouns that form their plural regularly by adding *-s* (or *-es* when they end in *-s, -x, -z, -sh,* or soft *-ch*), the inflection is not shown. Other plural forms are given, notably for:

- nouns ending in *-i* or *-o*, e.g. **agouti**, **gazebo**, or nouns ending in Latinate forms such as *-a* and *-um*, e.g. **tunica, adytum**.
- nouns ending in the suffix *-y*, e.g. **colloquy**.
- nouns with more than one plural form, e.g. **fish, aquarium**.
- nouns with plurals showing a change in the stem, e.g. **foot, feet**.
- nouns with a plural form unchanged from the singular form, e.g. **sheep**.
- nouns in *-ful*, e.g. **handful**.

3.2 Forms of verbs

The following forms are regarded as regular:

(*a*) third person singular present forms adding *-s* to the stem (or *-es* to stems ending in *-s, -x, -z, -sh,* or soft *-ch*).

(*b*) past tenses and past participles dropping a final silent *e* and adding *-ed* to the stem (e.g. **changed, danced**).

(*c*) present participles dropping a final silent *e* and adding *-ing* to the stem(e.g. **changing, dancing**).

Other forms are given, notably for:

- verbs which inflect by doubling a consonant e.g. **batted, batting.**
- verbs with strong and irregular forms showing a change in the stem, e.g. *go, went, gone*
- verbs ending in *-y* which inflect by changing *-y* to *-i*, e.g. *try, tries, tried*

3.3 Comparative and superlative of adjectives

For the following regular forms, inflections are not given:

(*a*) Words of one syllable adding *-er* and *-est* (e.g. *greater, greatest*).

(*b*) Words of one syllable ending in silent *e*, which drop the *e* and add *-er* and *-est* (e.g. *braver, bravest*). Most one-syllable words have these forms, but participial adjectives (e.g. **pleased**) do not.

Other forms are given, notably for:

- Those adjectives that double a final consonant (e.g. **hot, hotter, hottest**)
- Two-syllable words that have comparative and superlative forms in *-er* and *-est* (of which very many are forms ending in *-y*, e.g. **happy, happier, happiest**), and their negative forms (e.g. **unhappy, unhappier, unhappiest**).

Specification of the above forms indicates only that they are available; it is usually also possible to form comparatives with *more* and superlatives with *most* (as in *more happy, most unhappy*), which is the standard formation in the case of those adjectives and adverbs that do not inflect.

Adjectives in -able

These are given as derivatives when there is sufficient evidence of their currency, and as headwords when further definition is called for. In general they are formed as follows:

- Verbs drop silent final *-e* except after *c* and g (e.g. **movable, bridgeable**).
- Verbs of more than one syllable ending in *-y* (preceded by a consonant or *qu*) change *y* to *i* (e.g. **enviable, undeniable**).

A final consonant is often doubled as in normal inflection (e.g. **conferrable, regrettable**).

4. PREFIXES, SUFFIXES, AND COMBINING FORMS

A large selection of these is given in the main body of the text; prefixes are given in the form *ex-*, *re-*, etc., and suffixes in the form *-ion*, *-ness*, etc. These entries should be consulted to explain the many routinely formed derivatives given at the end of entries.

For a usage note on combining forms see the entry COMBINING FORM in the dictionary.

5. LABELS

These are used to clarify the particular context in which a word or phrase is normally used.

5.1 Subject

Some subject labels are used to indicate the particular relevance of a term or subject which which it is associated (e.g. *Mus.*, *Law*, *Physics*). They are not used when this is sufficiently clear from the definition itself.

5.2 Geographical

The geographical label *Brit.* indicates that the use of a word or phrase is found chiefly in British English (and often in other parts of the Commonwealth) but not in American English. *US* indicates that the use is found chiefly in American English but not in British English except as a conscious Americanism. Other geographical labels (e.g. *Austral.*, *Canad.*, *S. Afr.*) show that use is generally restricted to the area named.

5.3 Register

formal, colloq., slang

Words and phrases more common in formal (esp. written English) are labelled *formal*. Those more common in informal spoken English are labelled *colloq.* (colloquial) or, especially if very informal or restricted to a particular social group, *slang*.

coarse slang, offens.

Two categories of deprecated usage are indicated by special markings: *coarse slang* indicates a word that, although widely found, is still unacceptable to many people; *offens.* (offensive) indicates a use that is regarded as offensive by members of a particular ethnic, religious, or other group. It is our policy not to exclude from the dictionary words which are regarded as offensive but to include and mark them for the information of the reader as basic guidance. What is perhaps acceptable in one context may be unacceptable in another. (See also Appendix XIII F.)

disp.

Where usage is disputed or controversial, *disp.* alerts the user to a danger or difficulty; any further information is given in a usage note at the end of the entry.

joc., derog.

Where use is intended to be humorous, the label *joc.* is given; *derog.* denotes the intentionally disparaging use of the word or phrase.

literary, poet.

Words or phrases found mainly in literature are indicated by *literary* whereas *poet.* indicates that use is confined generally to poetry or other contexts with romantic connotations.

archaic, hist.

For words that have lost currency except perhaps in special contexts such as legal or religious use, *archaic* is given; *hist.* denotes a word or use that is confined to historical reference, normally because the thing referred to no longer exists.

propr.

The label *propr.* indicates a term that has the status of a trademark (see the Note on Proprietary Status, p. xxi).

Abbreviations used in the Dictionary

Most abbreviations appear in italics. Abbreviations in general use (such as *etc.*, *i.e.*, and those for books of the Bible) are explained in the dictionary itself.

abbr.	abbreviation
absol.	absolute
adj.	adjective
adv.	adverb
Aeron.	Aeronautics
Amer.	American
Anat.	Anatomy
Anglo-Ind.	Anglo-Indian
Anthropol.	Anthropology
Antiq.	Antiquities, Antiquity
Archaeol.	Archaeology
Archit.	Architecture
assim.	assimilated
Astrol.	Astrology
Astron.	Astronomy
attrib.	attributive(ly)
attrib. adj.	attributive adjective
Austral.	Australian
aux.	auxiliary
Bibl.	Biblical
Biochem.	Biochemistry
Biol.	Biology
Bot.	Botany
Brit.	British
Canad.	Canadian
Chem.	Chemistry, chemical
Cinematog.	Cinematography
collect.	collective
colloq.	colloquial
comb.	combination; combining
compar.	comparative
compl.	complement
conj.	conjunction
contr.	contraction
Criminol.	Criminology
Crystallog.	Crystallography
derog.	derogatory
det.	determiner
dial.	dialect
disp.	disputed
Eccl.	Ecclesiastical
Ecol.	Ecology

Econ.	Economics
Electr.	Electricity
ellipt.	elliptical(ly)
emphat.	emphatic
Engin.	Engineering
esp.	especially
euphem.	euphemistic
fem.	feminine
foll.	followed
Geog.	Geography
Geol.	Geology
Geom.	Geometry
Gk	Greek
Gram.	Grammar
Hist.	History
hist.	with historical reference
imper.	imperative
infin.	infinitive
int.	interjection
interrog.	interrogative
interrog. determiner	interrogative determiner
interrog. pron.	interrogative pronoun
intr.	intransitive
Ir.	Irish
iron.	ironical
joc.	jocular
masc.	masculine
Math.	Mathematics
Mech.	Mechanics
Med.	Medicine
Meteorol.	Meteorology
Mil.	Military
Mineral.	Mineralogy
Mus.	Music
Mythol.	Mythology
n.	noun
N. Amer.	North American
Naut.	Nautical

neg.	negative
N. Engl.	Northern English
neut.	neuter
n.pl.	noun plural
NZ	New Zealand
offens.	offensive
opp.	opposite; (as) opposed (to)
orig.	originally
Parl.	Parliament
part.	participle
past part.	past participle
Pharm.	Pharmacy; Pharmacology
Philol.	Philology
Philos.	Philosophy
Phonet.	Phonetics
Photog.	Photography
phr.	phrase
phrs.	phrases
Physiol.	Physiology
pl.	plural
poet.	poetical
Polit.	Politics
poss.	possessive
prec.	preceded
predet.	predeterminer
predic.	predicate; predicative(ly)
predic. adj.	predicative adjective
prep.	preposition
pres. part.	present participle
pron.	pronoun
pronunc.	pronunciation
propr.	proprietary term
Psychol.	Psychology
RC Ch.	Roman Catholic Church
refl.	reflexive
rel. adj.	relative adjective
rel. adv.	relative adverb
rel. det.	relative determiner
Relig.	Religion
rel.pron.	relative pronoun
Rhet.	Rhetoric
Rom.	Roman
S. Afr.	South African
Sc.	Scottish
Sci.	Science
sing.	singular
Stock Exch.	Stock Exchange
superl.	superlative
symb.	symbol
Telev.	Television
Theatr.	Theatre
Theol.	Theology
tr.	transitive
US	American, United States
usu.	usually
v.	verb
var.	variant(s)
v. aux	auxiliary verb
v. intr.	intransitive verb
v. refl.	reflexive verb
v. tr.	transitive verb
W. Ind.	West Indian
Zool.	Zoology
●	introduces a new part of speech
□	introduces a section containing phrases or derivatives
■	introduces a Usage Note

Note on Proprietary Status

This dictionary includes some words which have, or are asserted to have, proprietary status as trade marks or otherwise. Their inclusion does not imply that they have acquired for legal purposes a non-proprietary or general significance, nor any other judgement concerning their legal status. In cases where the editorial staff have some evidence that a word has proprietary status this is indicated in the entry for that word by the abbreviation *propr.*, but no judgement concerning the legal status of such words is made or implied thereby.

Aa

A[1] /eɪ/ *n.* (also **a**) (*pl.* **As** or **A's**) **1** the first letter of the alphabet. **2** *Mus.* the sixth note of the diatonic scale of C major. **3** the first hypothetical person or example. **4** the highest class or category (of roads, academic marks, etc.). **5** (usu. ***a***) *Algebra* the first known quantity. **6** a human blood type of the ABO system. □ **from A to B** from one place to another (*a means of getting from A to B*). **from A to Z** over the entire range; completely.

A[2] /eɪ/ *abbr.* (also **A.**) **1** ace. **2** = A LEVEL. **3** answer. **4** atomic (*A-bomb*).

A[3] /eɪ/ *symb.* **1** ampere(s). **2** *Brit. hist.* (of films) classified as suitable for an adult audience but not necessarily for children.

Å *abbr.* ångström(s).

a[1] /ə, eɪ/ *det.* (also **an** before a vowel) (called *the indefinite article*) **1** one, some, any (used when referring to something for the first time in a text or conversation) (cf. THE). **2** one like (*a Judas*). **3** one single (*not a thing in sight*). **4** the same (*all of a size*). **5** in, to, or for each (*twice a year*; *£20 a man*; *seven a side*). [weakening of Old English *ān* 'one'; sense 5 originally = A[2]]

■ **Usage** See Usage Note at AN.

a[2] /ə/ *prep.* (usu. as *prefix*) **1** to, towards (*ashore*; *aside*). **2** (with verb in pres. part. or infin.) in the process of; in a specified state (*a-hunting*; *a-wandering*; *abuzz*; *aflutter*). **3** on (*afire*; *afoot*). **4** in (*nowadays*). [weakening of Old English prep. *an*, *on* (see ON)]

a[3] *abbr.* (also **a.**) **1** arrives. **2** before. [sense 2 from Latin *ante*]

a[4] *symb.* **1** atto-. **2** acceleration. **3** are(s) (measure of area).

a-[1] /ə, eɪ, a/ *prefix* not, without (*amoral*; *agnostic*; *apetalous*). [Greek *a-*, or Latin from Greek, or French via Latin from Greek]

a-[2] /ə/ *prefix* implying motion onward or away, adding intensity to verbs of motion (*arise*; *awake*). [Old English *a-*, originally *ar-*]

a-[3] /ə/ *prefix* to, at, or into a state (*adroit*; *agree*; *amass*; *avenge*). [Middle English *a-* (= Old French prefix *a-*), from Latin *ad-* 'to, at': in later words sometimes via French]

a-[4] /ə/ *prefix* **1** from, away (*abridge*). **2** of (*akin*; *anew*). **3** out, utterly (*abash*; *affray*). **4** in, on, engaged in, etc. (see A[2]). [sense 1 from Middle English *a-*, Old French *a-*, from Latin *ab*; sense 2 from Middle English *a-*, from Old English *of* (*prep.*); sense 3 from Middle English, Anglo-French *a-* = Old French *e-*, *es-*, from Latin *ex*]

a-[5] /ə/ *prefix* assim. form of AD- before *sc*, *sp*, *st*.

-a[1] /ə/ *suffix* forming nouns from Greek, Latin, and Romanic feminine singular, esp.: **1** ancient or Latinized modern names of animals and plants (*amoeba*; *campanula*). **2** oxides (*alumina*). **3** geographical names (*Africa*). **4** ancient or Latinized modern feminine names (*Lydia*; *Hilda*).

-a[2] /ə/ *suffix* forming plural nouns from Greek and Latin neuter plural, esp. corresponding to a singular in *-um* or *-on* (*addenda*; *phenomena*), and in names (often from modern Latin) of zoological groups (*Carnivora*).

-a[3] /ə/ *suffix colloq.* **1** of (*kinda*; *coupla*). **2** have (*mighta*; *coulda*). **3** to (*oughta*).

A1 *n. & adj.* ● *n. Naut.* a first-class vessel in Lloyd's Register of Shipping. ● *adj. colloq.* **1** excellent; first-rate. **2** fit; in excellent health.

A3 *n.* **1** a standard European size of paper, 420 × 297 mm. **2** paper of this size (often *attrib.*: *A3 sheets*).

A4 *n.* **1** a standard European size of paper, 210 × 297 mm. **2** paper of this size (often *attrib.*: *A4 sketchpad*).

A5 *n.* **1** a standard European size of paper, 210 × 148 mm. **2** paper of this size (often *attrib.*: *A5 pages*).

AA *abbr.* **1** (in the UK) Automobile Association. **2** Alcoholics Anonymous. **3** *Mil.* anti-aircraft. **4** *Brit. hist.* (of films) classified as suitable for persons of over 14 years.

aa /'ɑːɑː/ *n. Geol.* lava forming very rough, jagged, light-textured masses (cf. PAHOEHOE). [Hawaiian *'a-'a*]

AAA *abbr.* **1** (in the UK) Amateur Athletic Association. **2** American Automobile Association. **3** Australian Automobile Association.

A. & M. *abbr.* (Hymns) Ancient and Modern.

A. & R. *abbr.* **1** artists and recording. **2** artists and repertoire.

aardvark /'ɑːdvɑːk/ *n.* a nocturnal mammal of southern Africa, *Orycteropus afer*, with a tubular snout and a long extensible tongue, that feeds on termites. Also called *ant-bear*, *earth-pig*. [Afrikaans from *aarde* 'earth' + *vark* 'pig']

aardwolf /'ɑːdwʊlf/ *n.* (*pl.* **aardwolves** /-wʊlvz/) an African mammal, *Proteles cristatus*, of the hyena family, with grey fur and black stripes, that feeds on insects. [Afrikaans from *aarde* 'earth' + *wolf* 'wolf']

Aaron's beard /'ɛːr(ə)nz/ *n.* any of several plants, esp. rose of Sharon (*Hypericum calycinum*). [with reference to Ps. 133:2]

Aaron's rod /'ɛːr(ə)nz/ *n.* any of several tall plants, esp. the great mullein (*Verbascum thapsus*). [with reference to Num. 17:8]

A'asia *abbr.* Australasia.

aasvogel /'ɑːsfəʊg(ə)l/ *n. S.Afr.* a vulture. [Afrikaans from *aas* 'carrion' + *vogel* 'bird']

AAU *abbr.* (in the US) Amateur Athletic Union.

AB[1] *n.* a human blood type of the ABO system.

AB[2] *abbr.* **1** able rating or seaman. **2** *US* Bachelor of Arts. [sense 1 from *able-bodied*; sense 2 from Latin *Artium Baccalaureus*]

Ab *abbr.* antibody.

ab- /əb, ab/ *prefix* off, away, from (*abduct*; *abnormal*; *abuse*). [French or Latin]

abaca /'abəkə/ *n.* **1** Manila hemp. **2** the plant, *Musa textilis*, yielding this. [Spanish *abacá*]

aback /ə'bak/ *adv.* **1** *archaic* backwards, behind. **2** *Naut.* (of a sail) pressed against the mast by a headwind. □ **take aback 1** surprise, disconcert (*your request took me aback*; *I was greatly taken aback by the news*). **2** (as **taken aback** *adj.*) (of a ship) with the sails pressed against the mast by a headwind. [Old English *on bæc* (as A[2], BACK)]

abacus /'abəkəs/ *n.* (*pl.* **abacuses**) **1** an oblong frame with rows of wires or grooves along which beads are slid, used for calculating. **2** *Archit.* the flat slab on top of a capital, supporting the architrave. [Latin via Greek *abax abakos* 'slab, drawing board' originally in the sense 'a board strewn with sand, for writing on', from Hebrew *'āḇāk* 'dust']

Abaddon /ə'bad(ə)n/ *n.* **1** hell. **2** the Devil (Rev. 9:11). [Hebrew, = destruction]

abaft /ə'bɑːft/ *adv. & prep. Naut.* ● *adv.* in the stern half of a ship. ● *prep.* nearer the stern than; aft of. [A[2] +

-baft from Old English *beæftan* from *be* BY + *æftan* 'behind']

abalone /abə'ləʊni/ *n.* a mollusc of the genus *Haliotis*, with a shallow ear-shaped shell having respiratory holes, and lined with mother-of-pearl, e.g. the ormer. [Latin American Spanish *abulón*, from Shoshonean *aulun*]

abandon /ə'band(ə)n/ *v. & n.* ● *v.tr.* **1** give up completely or before completion (*abandoned hope*; *abandoned the game*). **2 a** forsake or desert (a person or a post of responsibility). **b** leave or desert (a motor vehicle, ship, building, etc.). **3 a** give up to another's control or mercy. **b** *refl.* yield oneself completely to a passion or impulse. ● *n.* lack of inhibition or restraint; reckless freedom of manner. □ **abandonment** *n.* [Middle English, in the sense 'bring under control', from Old French *abandoner* from *à bandon* 'under control', ultimately from Late Latin *bannus, -um* BAN]

abandoned /ə'band(ə)nd/ *adj.* **1 a** (of a person or animal) deserted, forsaken (*an abandoned child*). **b** (of a building, vehicle, etc.) left empty or unused (*an abandoned cottage*; *an abandoned ship*). **2** (of a person or behaviour) unrestrained, profligate.

abase /ə'beɪs/ *v.tr. & refl.* humiliate or degrade (another person or oneself). □ **abasement** *n.* [Middle English from Old French *abaissier* (as A-[3], *baissier* 'to lower', ultimately from Late Latin *bassus* 'short of stature'): influenced by BASE[2]]

abash /ə'baʃ/ *v.tr.* (usu. as **abashed** *adj.*) embarrass, disconcert. □ **abashment** *n.* [Middle English from Old French *esbaïr* (*es-* = A-[4] 3, *baïr* 'astound' or *baer* 'yawn')]

abate /ə'beɪt/ *v.* **1** *tr. & intr.* make or become less strong, severe, intense, etc. **2** *tr. Law* **a** quash (a writ or action). **b** put an end to (a nuisance). □ **abatement** *n.* [Middle English via Old French *abatre* from Romanic (as A-[3], Latin *batt(u)ere* 'beat')]

abatis /'abətɪs/ *n.* (also **abattis**) (*pl.* same or **abatises**, **abattises**) *hist.* a defence made of felled trees with the boughs pointing outwards. [French from Old French *abatre* 'fell': see ABATE]

abattoir /'abətwɑː/ *n.* a slaughterhouse. [French (as ABATIS, -ORY[1])]

abaxial /ab'aksɪəl/ *adj. Bot.* facing away from the stem of a plant, esp. designating the lower surface of a leaf (cf. ADAXIAL). [AB- + AXIAL]

abaya /ə'beɪjə/ *n.* a sleeveless outer garment worn by Arabs. [Arabic *'abā'*]

abbacy /'abəsi/ *n.* (*pl.* **-ies**) the office, jurisdiction, or period of office of an abbot or abbess. [Middle English from ecclesiastical Latin *abbacia*, from *abbat-* ABBOT]

Abbasid /ə'basɪd, 'abəsɪd/ *n. & adj.* ● *n.* a member of a dynasty of caliphs ruling in Baghdad 750–1258. ● *adj.* of this dynasty. [*Abbas*, Muhammad's uncle d. 652]

abbatial /ə'beɪʃ(ə)l/ *adj.* of an abbey, abbot, or abbess. [French *abbatial* or medieval Latin *abbatialis* (as ABBOT)]

abbé /'abeɪ/ *n.* (in France) an abbot; a man entitled to wear ecclesiastical dress. [French, from ecclesiastical Latin *abbas abbatis* ABBOT]

abbess /'abɛs/ *n.* a woman who is the head of certain communities of nuns. [Middle English via Old French *abbesse* from ecclesiastical Latin *abbatissa* (as ABBOT)]

Abbevillian /ab'vɪlɪən/ *n. & adj.* ● *n.* the culture of the earliest palaeolithic period in Europe. ● *adj.* of this culture. [French *Abbevillien* from *Abbeville* in N. France, where tools from this period were discovered]

abbey /'abi/ *n.* (*pl.* **-eys**) **1** the building(s) occupied by a community of monks or nuns. **2** the community itself. **3** a church or house that was once an abbey. [Middle English via Old French *ab(b)eïe* from medieval Latin *abbatia* ABBACY]

abbot /'abət/ *n.* a man who is the head of an abbey of monks. □ **abbotship** *n.* [Old English *abbod* via ecclesiastical Latin *abbas -atis* from Greek *abbas* 'father', from Aramaic *'abbā*]

abbreviate /ə'briːvɪeɪt/ *v.tr.* shorten, esp. represent (a word etc.) by a part of it. [Middle English via Late Latin *abbreviare* 'shorten' from Latin *brevis* 'short': cf. ABRIDGE]

abbreviation /əbriːvɪ'eɪʃ(ə)n/ *n.* **1** an abbreviated form, esp. a shortened form of a word or phrase. **2** the process or result of abbreviating.

ABC[1] *n.* **1** the alphabet. **2** the rudiments of any subject. **3** an alphabetical guide.

ABC[2] *abbr.* **1** Australian Broadcasting Corporation. **2** American Broadcasting Company.

abdicate /'abdɪkeɪt/ *v.tr.* **1** (usu. *absol.*) give up or renounce (the throne). **2** renounce (a responsibility, duty, etc.). □ **abdication** /-'keɪʃ(ə)n/ *n.*, **abdicator** *n.* [Latin *abdicare abdicat-* (as AB-, *dicare* 'declare')]

abdomen /'abdəmən, ab'dəʊmən/ *n.* **1** the part of the body containing the stomach, bowels, reproductive organs, etc. **2** *Zool.* the hinder part of an insect, crustacean, spider, etc. □ **abdominal** /ab'dɒmɪn(ə)l/ *adj.* [Latin]

abduct /əb'dʌkt/ *v.tr.* **1** carry off or kidnap (a person) illegally by force or deception. **2** (of a muscle etc.) draw (a limb etc.) away from the midline of the body. □ **abduction** *n.* **abductor** *n.* [Latin *abducere abduct-* (as AB-, *ducere* 'draw')]

abeam /ə'biːm/ *adv.* **1** on a line at right angles to a ship's or an aircraft's length. **2** (foll. by *of*) opposite the middle of (a ship etc.). [A[2] + BEAM]

abed /ə'bɛd/ *adv. archaic* in bed. [Old English (as A[2], BED)]

abele /ə'biːl, 'eɪb(ə)l/ *n.* the white poplar, *Populus alba*. [Dutch *abeel* from Old French *abel, aubel*, ultimately from Latin *albus* 'white']

abelia /ə'biːlɪə/ *n.* a hardy evergreen shrub of the genus *Abelia* (honeysuckle family). [C. *Abel*, English botanist d. 1826]

abelian /ə'biːlɪən/ *adj. Math.* (of a group) having members related by a commutative operation (i.e. $a*b = b*a$). [named after Niels H. *Abel*, Norwegian mathematician d. 1829]

Aberdeen Angus /ˌabədiːn 'aŋgəs/ *n.* **1** an animal of a Scottish breed of hornless black beef cattle. **2** this breed. [*Aberdeenshire* and *Angus*, former Scottish counties, where the breed originated]

Aberdonian /abə'dəʊnɪən/ *adj. & n.* ● *adj.* of Aberdeen. ● *n.* a native or citizen of Aberdeen. [medieval Latin *Aberdonia*]

aberrant /ə'bɛr(ə)nt/ *adj.* **1** esp. *Biol.* diverging from the normal type. **2** departing from an accepted standard. □ **aberrance** *n.* **aberrancy** *n.* [Latin *aberrare aberrant-* (as AB-, *errare* 'stray')]

aberration /abə'reɪʃ(ə)n/ *n.* **1** a departure from what is normal or accepted or regarded as right. **2** a moral or mental lapse. **3** *Biol.* deviation from a normal type. **4** *Optics* the failure of rays to converge at one focus because of a defect in a lens or mirror. **5** *Astron.* the apparent displacement of a celestial object from its true position caused by the observer's relative motion. [Latin *aberratio* (as ABERRANT)]

abet /ə'bɛt/ *v.tr.* (**abetted**, **abetting**) (usu. in **aid and abet**) encourage or assist (an offender or offence). □ **abetment** *n.* [Middle English, from Old French *abeter* from *à* 'to' + *beter* BAIT]

abetter /ə'bɛtə/ *n.* (also **abettor**) a person who abets.

abeyance /ə'beɪəns/ *n.* (usu. prec. by *in, into*) a state of temporary disuse or suspension. □ **abeyant** *adj.* [Anglo-French *abeiance*, from Old French *abeer*, from *à* 'to' + *beer*, from medieval Latin *batare* 'gape']

ABH *abbr.* actual bodily harm.

abhor /əb'hɔː/ *v.tr.* (**abhorred**, **abhorring**) detest; regard with disgust and hatred. □ **abhorrer** *n.* [Middle English, from French *abhorrer* or from Latin *abhorrēre* (as AB-, *horrēre* 'shudder')]

abhorrence /əb'hɒr(ə)ns/ *n.* **1** disgust; detestation. **2** a detested thing.

abhorrent /əbˈhɒr(ə)nt/ *adj.* **1** (often foll. by *to*) (of conduct etc.) inspiring disgust; repugnant, hateful, detestable. **2** (foll. by *to*) not in accordance with; strongly conflicting with (*abhorrent to the spirit of the law*).

abide /əˈbʌɪd/ *v.* (*past* and *past part.* **abided** or rarely **abode** /əˈbəʊd/) **1** *tr.* (usu. in *neg.* or *interrog.*) tolerate, endure (*can't abide him*). **2** *intr.* (foll. by *by*) **a** act in accordance with (*abide by the rules*). **b** remain faithful to (a promise). **3** *intr. archaic* **a** remain, continue. **b** dwell. □ **abidance** *n.* [Old English *ābīdan* (as A-², *bidan* BIDE)]

abiding /əˈbʌɪdɪŋ/ *adj.* enduring, permanent (*an abiding sense of loss*). □ **abidingly** *adv.*

ability /əˈbɪlɪti/ *n.* (*pl.* **-ies**) **1** (often foll. by *to* + infin.) capacity or power (*has the ability to write songs*). **2** cleverness, talent; mental power (*a person of great ability*; *has many abilities*). [Middle English via Old French *ablete* from Latin *habilitas -tatis*, from *habilis* 'able']

-ability /əˈbɪlɪti/ *suffix* forming nouns of quality from, or corresponding to, adjectives in *-able* (*capability*; *vulnerability*). [French *-abilité* or Latin *-abilitas*: cf. -ITY]

ab initio /ab ɪˈnɪʃɪəʊ/ *adv.* from the beginning. [Latin]

abiogenesis /ˌeɪbʌɪəˈdʒɛnɪsɪs/ *n.* **1** the formation of organic matter without the action of living organisms. **2** the supposed spontaneous generation of living organisms. □ **abiogenic** *adj.* [A-¹ + Greek *bios* 'life' + GENESIS]

abiotic /eɪbʌɪˈɒtɪk/ *adj.* inanimate, non-living, not of a biological nature. [A-¹ + BIOTIC]

abject /ˈabdʒɛkt/ *adj.* **1** miserable, wretched. **2** degraded, self-abasing, humble. **3** despicable. □ **abjectly** *adv.* **abjectness** *n.* [Middle English from Latin *abjectus*, past part. of *abicere* (as AB-, *jacere* 'throw')]

abjection /abˈdʒɛkʃ(ə)n/ *n.* a state of misery or degradation. [Middle English from Old French *abjection* or Latin *abjectio* (as ABJECT)]

abjure /əbˈdʒʊə/ *v.tr.* **1** renounce on oath (an opinion, cause, claim, etc.). **2** swear perpetual absence from (one's country etc.). □ **abjuration** /abdʒʊˈreɪʃ(ə)n/ *n.* [Latin *abjurare* (as AB-, *jurare* 'swear')]

Abkhazian /əbˈkɑːzɪən, əbˈkeɪzjən/ *n.* & *adj.* ● *n.* **1** a native or inhabitant of Abkhazia, an autonomous republic in NW Georgia. **2** the Caucasian language of Abkhazia. ● *adj.* of or relating to Abkhazia, its people, or its language.

ablation /əˈbleɪʃ(ə)n/ *n.* **1** the surgical removal of body tissue. **2** *Geol.* the wasting or erosion of a glacier, iceberg, or rock by melting or the action of water. **3** *Astron.* the loss of surface material from a spacecraft, meteorite, etc. through evaporation or melting caused by friction with the atmosphere. □ **ablate** *v.tr.* [French *ablation* or Late Latin *ablatio*, from Latin *ablat-* (as AB-, *lat-*, past part. stem of *ferre* 'carry')]

ablative /ˈablətɪv/ *n.* & *adj. Gram.* ● *n.* the case (esp. in Latin) of nouns and pronouns (and words in grammatical agreement with them) indicating an agent, instrument, or location. ● *adj.* of or in the ablative. [Middle English from Old French *ablatif -ive* or Latin *ablativus* (as ABLATION)]

ablative absolute *n.* an absolute construction in Latin with a noun and participle or adjective in the ablative case (see ABSOLUTE *adj.* 5).

ablaut /ˈablaʊt/ *n.* a change of vowel in related words or forms, esp. in Indo-European languages, arising from differences of accent and stress in the parent language, e.g. in *sing, sang, sung*. [German, from *ab* 'off' + *Laut* 'sound']

ablaze /əˈbleɪz/ *predic.adj.* & *adv.* **1** on fire (*set it ablaze*; *the house was ablaze*). **2** (often foll. by *with*) glittering, glowing, radiant. **3** (often foll. by *with*) greatly excited.

able /ˈeɪb(ə)l/ *adj.* (**abler**, **ablest**) **1** (often foll. by *to* + infin.; used esp. in *is able, will be able, was able*, etc., replacing tenses of *can*) having the capacity or power (*was not able to come*). **2** having great ability; clever, skilful. [Middle English via Old French *hable*, *able* from Latin *habilis* 'handy', from *habēre* 'hold']

-able /əb(ə)l/ *suffix* forming adjectives meaning: **1** that may or must be (*eatable*; *forgivable*; *payable*). **2** that can be made the subject of (*dutiable*; *objectionable*). **3** that is relevant to or in accordance with (*fashionable*; *seasonable*). **4** (with active sense, in earlier word-formations) that may (*comfortable*; *suitable*). [French *-able*, or Latin *-abilis* forming verbal adjectives from verbs of first conjugation]

able-bodied *adj.* fit, healthy.

able-bodied rating *n.* (also **able-bodied seaman**) *Naut.* a rating able to perform all duties.

abled /ˈeɪb(ə)ld/ *adj.* having a full range of physical or mental abilities; able-bodied.

ableism /ˈeɪblɪz(ə)m/ *n.* (also **ablism**) discrimination in favour of able-bodied people.

able rating *n.* (also **able seaman**) *Naut.* = ABLE-BODIED RATING.

abloom /əˈbluːm/ *predic.adj.* blooming; in flower.

ablush /əˈblʌʃ/ *predic.adj.* blushing.

ablution /əˈbluːʃ(ə)n/ *n.* (usu. in *pl.*) **1** the ceremonial washing of parts of the body or of sacred vessels etc. **2** *colloq.* the ordinary washing of the body. **3** *Brit.* a building containing washing places etc. in a camp, ship, etc. □ **ablutionary** *adj.* [Middle English from Old French *ablution* or Latin *ablutio* (as AB-, *lutio* from *luere lut-* 'wash')]

ably /ˈeɪbli/ *adv.* capably, cleverly, competently.

-ably /əbli/ *suffix* forming adverbs corresponding to adjectives in *-able*.

ABM *abbr.* anti-ballistic missile.

abnegate /ˈabnɪgeɪt/ *v.tr.* **1** give up or deny oneself (a pleasure etc.). **2** renounce or reject (a right or belief). □ **abnegator** *n.* [Latin *abnegare abnegat-* (as AB-, *negare* 'deny')]

abnegation /abnɪˈgeɪʃ(ə)n/ *n.* **1** denial; the rejection or renunciation of a doctrine. **2** = SELF-DENIAL. [Old French *abnegation* or Late Latin *abnegatio* (as ABNEGATE)]

abnormal /əbˈnɔːm(ə)l/ *adj.* **1** deviating from what is normal or usual; exceptional. **2** relating to or dealing with what is abnormal (*abnormal psychology*). □ **abnormally** *adv.* [earlier *anormal*, *anomal*, via French from Greek *anōmalos* ANOMALOUS, associated with Latin *abnormis* 'abnormality, monstrosity']

abnormality /abnɔːˈmalɪti, -nəˈmalɪti/ *n.* (*pl.* **-ies**) **1 a** an abnormal quality, occurrence, etc. **b** the state of being abnormal. **2** a physical irregularity.

Abo /ˈabəʊ/ *n.* & *adj.* (also **abo**) *Austral. slang offens.* ● *n.* (*pl.* **Abos**) an Aborigine. ● *adj.* Aboriginal. [abbreviation]

aboard /əˈbɔːd/ *adv.* & *prep.* **1** on or into (a ship, aircraft, train, etc.). **2** alongside. □ **all aboard!** a call that warns of the imminent departure of a ship, train, etc. [Middle English, from A² + BOARD and French *à bord*]

abode¹ /əˈbəʊd/ *n.* **1** habitual residence; a house or home. **2** *archaic* a stay or sojourn. [verbal noun of ABIDE: cf. *ride, rode, road*]

abode² *past* of ABIDE.

abolish /əˈbɒlɪʃ/ *v.tr.* put an end to the existence or practice of (esp. a custom or institution). □ **abolishable** *adj.* **abolisher** *n.* **abolishment** *n.* [Middle English via French *abolir* from Latin *abolēre* 'destroy']

abolition /abəˈlɪʃ(ə)n/ *n.* **1** the act or process of abolishing or being abolished. **2** an instance of this. [French *abolition* or Latin *abolitio* (as ABOLISH)]

abolitionist /abəˈlɪʃ(ə)nɪst/ *n.* a person who favours the abolition of a practice or institution, esp. of capital punishment or (formerly) of slavery. □ **abolitionism** *n.*

abomasum /abəʊˈmeɪsəm/ *n.* (*pl.* **abomasa** /-sə/) the fourth stomach of a ruminant. [modern Latin from AB- + OMASUM]

A-bomb /ˈeɪbɒm/ *n.* = ATOM BOMB. [A² 4 + BOMB]

abominable /ə'bɒm(ə)nəb(ə)l/ *adj.* **1** detestable; loathsome; morally reprehensible. **2** *colloq.* very bad or unpleasant (*abominable weather*). □ **abominably** *adv.* [Middle English via Old French from Latin *abominabilis*, from *abominari* 'deprecate' (as AB-, *ominari* from OMEN)]

Abominable Snowman *n.* an unidentified manlike or bearlike animal said to exist in the Himalayas; a yeti.

abominate /ə'bɒmɪneɪt/ *v.tr.* detest, loathe. □ **abominator** *n.* [Latin *abominari* (as ABOMINABLE)]

abomination /əbɒmɪ'neɪʃ(ə)n/ *n.* **1** an object of disgust. **2** an odious or degrading habit or act. **3** loathing. [Middle English from Old French (as ABOMINATE)]

aboral /ab'ɔːr(ə)l/ *adj.* furthest from or opposite the mouth. [AB- + ORAL]

aboriginal /abə'rɪdʒɪn(ə)l/ *adj.* & *n.* ● *adj.* **1** (of races and natural phenomena) inhabiting or existing in a land from the earliest times or from before the arrival of colonists. **2** (**Aboriginal**) of the Australian Aboriginals or their languages. ● *n.* **1** an aboriginal inhabitant. **2** (**Aboriginal**) = ABORIGINE 2. **3** (**Aboriginal**) any of the Australian Aboriginal languages. [as ABORIGINE + -AL]

■ **Usage** With reference to indigenous Australians, some people prefer *Aborigine* and others *Aboriginal* as the noun. The adjective is always *Aboriginal*.

aborigine /abə'rɪdʒɪniː/ *n.* (usu. in *pl.*) **1** an aboriginal inhabitant. **2** (**Aborigine**) an aboriginal inhabitant of Australia. **3** an aboriginal plant or animal. [back-formation from pl. *aborigines* from Latin, probably from the phrase *ab origine* 'from the beginning']

■ **Usage** See Usage Note at ABORIGINAL.

aborning /ə'bɔːnɪŋ/ *adv.* & *adj.* esp. *N. Amer.* ● *adv.* (esp. in phr. **die aborning**) while being born or produced. ● *predic. adj.* being born or produced. [A-[4] 4 + *borning* verbal noun from *born* 'be born']

abort /ə'bɔːt/ *v.* & *n.* ● *v.* **1** *intr.* **a** (of a woman) undergo abortion; miscarry. **b** (of a foetus) suffer abortion. **2** *tr.* **a** effect the abortion of (a foetus). **b** effect abortion in (a mother). **3 a** *tr.* cause to end fruitlessly or prematurely; stop in the early stages. **b** *intr.* end unsuccessfully or prematurely. **4 a** *tr.* abandon or terminate (a space flight or other technical project) before its completion, usu. because of a fault. **b** *intr.* terminate or fail to complete such an undertaking. **5** *Biol.* **a** *intr.* (of an organ or embryo) remain undeveloped; shrink away. **b** *tr.* cause to do this. ● *n.* **1** a prematurely terminated space flight or other undertaking. **2** the termination of such an undertaking. [Latin *aboriri* 'miscarry' (as AB-, *oriri ort-* 'be born')]

abortifacient /əbɔːtɪ'feɪʃ(ə)nt/ *adj.* & *n.* ● *adj.* effecting abortion. ● *n.* a drug or other agent that effects abortion.

abortion /ə'bɔːʃ(ə)n/ *n.* **1** the expulsion of a foetus (naturally or esp. by medical induction) from the womb before it is able to survive independently, esp. in the first 28 weeks of a human pregnancy. **2** a stunted or deformed creature or thing. **3** the failure of a project or an action. **4** *Biol.* the arrest of the development of an organ or embryo. [Latin *abortio* (as ABORT)]

abortionist /ə'bɔːʃ(ə)nɪst/ *n.* **1** a person who carries out abortions, esp. illegally. **2** a person who favours the legalization of abortion.

abortive /ə'bɔːtɪv/ *adj.* **1** fruitless, unsuccessful, unfinished. **2** resulting in abortion. **3** *Biol.* (of an organ etc.) rudimentary; arrested in development. □ **abortively** *adv.* [Middle English via Old French *abortif -ive* from Latin *abortivus* (as ABORT)]

ABO system *n.* a system of four types (A, AB, B, and O) by which human blood may be classified, based on the presence or absence of certain inherited antigens.

aboulia /ə'buːlɪə/ *n.* (also **abulia**) the loss of will-power as a mental disorder. □ **aboulic** *adj.* [Greek *a-* 'not' + *boulē* 'will']

abound /ə'baʊnd/ *v.intr.* **1** be plentiful. **2** (foll. by *in*, *with*) be rich; teem or be infested. [Middle English from Old French *abunder* etc. from Latin *abundare* 'overflow' (as AB-, *undare* from *unda* 'wave')]

about /ə'baʊt/ *prep.* & *adv.* ● *prep.* **1 a** on the subject of; in connection with (*a book about birds*; *what are you talking about?*; *argued about money*). **b** relating to (*something funny about this*). **c** in relation to (*symmetry about a plane*). **d** so as to affect (*what are you going to do about it?*). **2** at a time near to (*come about four*). **3 a** in, round, surrounding (*wandered about the town*; *a scarf about her neck*). **b** all round from a centre (*look about you*). **4** here and there in; at points throughout (*toys lying about the house*). **5** at a point or points near to (*fighting going on about us*). **6** carried with (*have no money about me*). **7** occupied with (*what are you about?*). ● *adv.* **1 a** approximately (*costs about a pound*; *is about right*). **b** *colloq.* used to indicate understatement (*just about had enough*; *it's about time they came*). **2** here and there; at points nearby (*a lot of flu about*; *I've seen him about recently*). **3** all round; in every direction (*look about*). **4** on the move; in action (*out and about*). **5** in partial rotation or alteration from a given position (*the wrong way about*). **6** in rotation or succession (*turn and turn about*). **7** *Naut.* on or to the opposite tack (*go about*; *put about*). □ **be about** *colloq.* have as its most important aim (*putting on the play was not about making money but having fun*). **be about to 1** be on the point of (doing something) (*was about to laugh*). **2** (with *neg.*) *colloq.* intending to; prepared to (*we're not about to give in*). [Old English *onbūtan* (*on* = A[2], *būtan* BUT[1])]

about-face *n.*, *v.*, & *int.* ● *n.* & *v.intr.* esp. *US* = ABOUT-TURN *n.* & *v.* ● *int.* = ABOUT TURN *int.*

about-turn *n.*, *v.*, & *int.* ● *n.* **1** a turn made so as to face the opposite direction. **2** a change of opinion or policy etc. ● *v.intr.* make an about-turn. ● *int.* (**about turn**) *Mil.* a command to make an about-turn. [originally as int.]

above /ə'bʌv/ *prep.*, *adv.*, *adj.*, & *n.* ● *prep.* **1** over; on the top of; higher (vertically, up a slope or stream etc.) than; over the surface of (*head above water*; *above the din*). **2** more than (*above twenty people*; *above average*). **3** higher in rank, position, importance, etc., than (*thwarted by those above him*). **4 a** too great or good for (*above one's station*; *is not above cheating at cards*). **b** beyond the reach of; not affected by (*above my understanding*; *above suspicion*). **5** *archaic* to an earlier time than (*not traced above the third century*). ● *adv.* **1** at or to a higher point; overhead (*the floor above*; *the clouds above*). **2 a** upstairs (*lives above*). **b** upstream. **3** (of a text reference) further back on a page or in a book (*as noted above*). **4** on the upper side (*looks similar above and below*). **5** in addition (*over and above*). **6** *literary* in heaven (*Lord above!*). ● *adj.* mentioned earlier; preceding (*the above argument*). ● *n.* (prec. by *the*) what is mentioned above (*the above shows*). □ **above all** more than anything else; most of all. **above ground** alive. **above one's head** see HEAD. **above oneself** conceited, arrogant. [A[2] + Old English *bufan*, from *be* = BY + *ufan* 'above']

above board *adj.* & *adv.* without concealment; fair or fairly; open or openly.

ab ovo /ab 'əʊvəʊ/ *adv.* from the very beginning. [Latin, = from the egg]

Abp. *abbr.* Archbishop.

abracadabra /abrəkə'dabrə/ *int.* & *n.* ● *int.* a supposedly magic word used by conjurors in performing a trick. ● *n.* **1** a spell or charm. **2** jargon or gibberish. [a mystical word engraved and used as a charm: Latin from Greek]

abrade /ə'breɪd/ *v.tr.* scrape or wear away (skin, rock, etc.) by rubbing. □ **abrader** *n.* [Latin from AB-, *radere ras-* 'scrape']

abrasion /ə'breɪʒ(ə)n/ *n.* **1** the scraping or wearing away (of skin, rock, etc.). **2** a damaged area resulting from this. [Latin *abrasio* (as ABRADE)]

abrasive /ə'breɪsɪv/ *adj.* & *n.* ● *adj.* **1 a** tending to rub or graze. **b** capable of polishing by rubbing or grinding. **2** harsh or hurtful in manner. ● *n.* an abrasive substance. [as ABRADE + -IVE]

abreact /abrɪ'akt/ *v.tr. Psychol.* release (an emotion) by abreaction. [back-formation from ABREACTION]

abreaction /abrɪ'akʃ(ə)n/ *n. Psychol.* the free expression and consequent release of a previously repressed emotion. □ **abreactive** *adj.* [AB- + REACTION, influenced by German *Abreagierung*]

abreast /ə'brɛst/ *adv.* **1** side by side and facing the same way. **2 a** (often foll. by *with*) up to date. **b** (foll. by *of*) well informed (*abreast of all the changes*). [Middle English, from A² + BREAST]

abridge /ə'brɪdʒ/ *v.tr.* **1** shorten (a book, film, etc.) by using fewer words or making deletions. **2** curtail (liberty). □ **abridgeable** *adj.* **abridger** *n.* [Middle English via Old French *abreg(i)er* from Late Latin *abbreviare* ABBREVIATE]

abridgement /ə'brɪdʒm(ə)nt/ *n.* (also **abridgment**) **1 a** a shortened version, esp. of a book; an abstract. **b** the process of producing this. **2** a curtailment (of rights). [French *abrégement* (as ABRIDGE)]

abroad /ə'brɔːd/ *adv.* **1** in or to a foreign country or countries. **2** over a wide area; in different directions; everywhere (*scatter abroad*). **3** at large; freely moving about; in circulation (*there is a rumour abroad*). **4** *archaic* in or into the open; out of doors. **5** *archaic* wide of the mark; erring. □ **from abroad** from another country. [Middle English, from A² + BROAD]

abrogate /'abrəgeɪt/ *v.tr.* repeal, annul, or abolish (a law or custom). □ **abrogation** /abrə'geɪʃ(ə)n/ *n.* **abrogator** *n.* [Latin *abrogare* (as AB-, *rogare* 'propose a law')]

abrupt /ə'brʌpt/ *adj.* **1** sudden and unexpected; hasty (*his abrupt departure*). **2** (of speech, manner, etc.) uneven; lacking continuity; curt. **3** steep, precipitous. **4** *Bot.* truncated. □ **abruptly** *adv.* **abruptness** *n.* [Latin *abruptus*, past part. of *abrumpere* (as AB-, *rumpere* 'break')]

ABS *abbr.* anti-lock braking system (for motor vehicles).

abs- /əbs, abs/ *prefix* = AB-. [variant of Latin *ab-* used before *c*, *q*, *t*]

abscess /'absɪs, -sɛs/ *n.* a swollen area accumulating pus within a body tissue. □ **abscessed** *adj.* [Latin *abscessus* 'a going away' (as AB-, *cedere cess-* 'go'): from the elimination of bad matter via the pus]

abscisic acid /ab'sɪsɪk/ *n.* a plant hormone which promotes leaf detachment and bud dormancy and inhibits germination. [Latin *abscis-* past part. stem of *abscindere* (as AB-, *scindere* 'cut')]

abscissa /ab'sɪsə/ *n.* (*pl.* **abscissae** /-siː/ or **abscissas**) *Math.* **1** (in a system of coordinates) the shortest distance from a point to the vertical or *y*-axis, measured parallel to the horizontal or *x*-axis; the Cartesian *x*-coordinate of a point (cf. ORDINATE). **2** the part of a line between a fixed point on it and an ordinate drawn to it from any other point. [modern Latin *abscissa* (*linea*) 'cut-off (line)', fem. past part. of *abscindere abscissa-* (as AB-, *scindere* 'cut')]

abscission /əb'sɪʃ(ə)n/ *n.* **1** the act or an instance of cutting off. **2** *Bot.* the natural detachment of leaves, branches, flowers, etc. [Latin *abscissio* (as ABSCISSA)]

abscond /əb'skɒnd/ *v.intr.* depart hurriedly and furtively, esp. unlawfully or to avoid arrest. □ **absconder** *n.* [originally in the sense 'hide, conceal (oneself)': Latin *abscondere* 'hide, put away' (as AB-, *condere* 'stow')]

abseil /'abseɪl, -zʌɪl/ *v.* & *n.* esp. *Brit.* ● *v.intr.* descend a steep rock face etc. by using a doubled rope coiled round the body and fixed at a higher point. ● *n.* a descent made by abseiling. □ **abseiler** *n.* [German *abseilen* from *ab* 'down' + *Seil* 'rope']

absence /'abs(ə)ns/ *n.* **1** the state of being away from a place or person. **2** the time or duration of being away. **3** (foll. by *of*) the non-existence or lack of. □ **absence of mind** inattentiveness. [Middle English via Old French from Latin *absentia* (as ABSENT)]

absent *adj.* & *v.* ● *adj.* /'abs(ə)nt/ **1 a** not present. **b** (foll. by *from*) not present at or in. **2** not existing. **3** inattentive to the matter in hand. ● *v.refl.* /ab'sɛnt/ **1** stay away. **2** withdraw. □ **absently** *adv.* (in sense 3 of *adj.*). [Middle English, ultimately from Latin *absent-*, pres. part. of *abesse* 'be absent']

absentee /abs(ə)n'tiː/ *n.* a person not present, esp. one who is absent from work or school.

absenteeism /abs(ə)n'tiːɪz(ə)m/ *n.* the practice of absenting oneself from work or school etc., esp. frequently or illicitly.

absentee landlord *n.* a landlord who lets a property while living elsewhere.

absent-minded /abs(ə)nt'mʌɪndɪd/ *adj.* habitually forgetful or inattentive; with one's mind on other things. □ **absent-mindedly** *adv.* **absent-mindedness** *n.*

absinth /'absɪnθ/ *n.* **1** the shrub wormwood, *Artemisia absinthium*, or an essence from it. **2** (usu. **absinthe**) a green aniseed-flavoured potent liqueur turning milky when water is added, originally made with wormwood. [French *absinthe* via Latin *absinthium* from Greek *apsinthion* 'wormwood']

absit omen /'absɪt 'əʊmən/ *int.* may what is threatened not become fact. [Latin, = may this (evil) omen be absent]

absolute /'absəluːt/ *adj.* & *n.* ● *adj.* **1** complete, utter, perfect (*an absolute fool*; *absolute bliss*). **2** unconditional, unlimited (*absolute authority*). **3** despotic; ruling arbitrarily or with unrestricted power (*an absolute monarch*). **4** (of a standard or other concept) universally valid; not admitting exceptions; not relative or comparative. **5** *Gram.* **a** (of a construction) syntactically independent of the rest of the sentence, as in *dinner being over, we left the table*; *let us toss for it, loser to pay*. **b** (of an adjective or transitive verb) used or usable without an expressed noun or object (e.g. *the deaf*, *guns kill*). **6** (of a legal decree etc.) final. ● *n. Philos.* **1** a value, standard, etc., which is objective and universally valid, not subjective or relative. **2** (prec. by *the*) **a** *Philos.* that which can exist without being related to anything else. **b** *Theol.* ultimate reality; God. □ **absoluteness** *n.* [Middle English from Latin *absolutus*, past part. of *absolvere*: see ABSOLVE]

absolute alcohol *n. Chem.* ethanol which is at least 99 per cent pure.

absolutely /'absəluːtli/ *adv.* **1** completely, utterly, perfectly (*absolutely marvellous*; *he absolutely denies it*). **2** independently; in an absolute sense (*God exists absolutely*). **3** (foll. by *neg.*) (no or none) at all (*absolutely no chance of winning*; *absolutely nowhere*). **4** *colloq.* in actual fact; positively (*it absolutely exploded*). **5** *Gram.* in an absolute way, esp. (of a verb) without a stated object. **6** /-'luːtli, -'ljuːtli/ *colloq.* (used in reply) quite so; yes.

absolute magnitude *n.* the magnitude, i.e. brightness, of a celestial object as it would be seen at a standard distance of 10 parsecs (opp. APPARENT MAGNITUDE).

absolute majority *n.* **1** a majority over all others combined. **2** more than half.

absolute pitch *n. Mus.* **1** the ability to recognize the pitch of a note or produce any given note; perfect pitch. **2** a fixed standard of pitch defined by the rate of vibration.

absolute temperature *n.* a temperature measured from absolute zero.

absolute zero *n.* a theoretical lowest possible temperature, at which the particles whose motion constitutes heat would be minimal, calculated as −273.15°C (or zero on the Kelvin scale).

absolution /absə'luːʃ(ə)n/ *n.* **1** a formal release from guilt, obligation, or punishment. **2** an ecclesiastical declaration of forgiveness of sins. **3** a remission of penance. **4** forgiveness. [Middle English via Old French from Latin *absolutio -onis* (as ABSOLVE)]

absolutism /ˈabsəluːtɪz(ə)m/ *n.* the acceptance of or belief in absolute principles in political, philosophical, ethical, or theological matters. □ **absolutist** *n. & adj.*

absolve /əbˈzɒlv/ *v.tr.* **1** (often foll. by *from, of*) **a** set or pronounce free from blame or obligation etc. **b** acquit; pronounce not guilty. **2** pardon or give absolution for (a sin etc.). [Latin *absolvere* (as AB-, *solvere solut-* 'loosen')]

absorb /əbˈzɔːb, -ˈsɔːb/ *v.tr.* **1** include or incorporate as part of itself or oneself (*the country successfully absorbed its immigrants*). **2** take in; suck up (liquid, heat, knowledge, etc.) (*she quickly absorbed all she was taught*). **3** reduce the effect or intensity of; deal easily with (an impact, sound, difficulty, etc.). **4** consume (income, time, resources, etc.) (*his debts absorbed half his income*). **5** engross the attention of (*television absorbs them completely*). □ **absorbable** *adj.* **absorbability** /-ˈbɪlɪti/ *n.* **absorber** *n.* [Middle English, from French *absorber* or Latin *absorbēre absorpt-* (as AB-, *sorbēre* 'suck in')]

absorbance /əbˈzɔːb(ə)ns, -ˈsɔːb(ə)ns/ *n. Physics* a measure of the capacity of a substance to absorb light etc., equal to the logarithm of the reciprocal of the transmittance.

absorbed /əbˈzɔːbd, -ˈsɔːbd/ *predic.adj.* intensely engaged or interested (*he was absorbed in his work*). □ **absorbedly** /-bɪdli/ *adv.*

absorbent /əbˈzɔːb(ə)nt, -ˈsɔːb-/ *adj. & n.* ● *adj.* having a tendency to absorb (esp. liquids). ● *n.* an absorbent substance or thing. □ **absorbency** *n.* [Latin *absorbent-* from *absorbēre* ABSORB]

absorbing /əbˈzɔːbɪŋ, -ˈsɔːbɪŋ/ *adj.* engrossing; intensely interesting. □ **absorbingly** *adv.*

absorption /əbˈzɔːpʃ(ə)n, -ˈsɔːp-/ *n.* **1** the process or action of absorbing or being absorbed. **2** disappearance through incorporation into something else. **3** mental engrossment. □ **absorptive** /-ˈzɔːptɪv, -ˈsɔːb-/ *adj.* [Latin *absorptio* (as ABSORB)]

absorption spectrum *n.* a spectrum of electromagnetic radiation transmitted through a substance, with dark lines or bands showing absorption at specific wavelengths.

abstain /əbˈsteɪn/ *v.intr.* **1 a** (usu. foll. by *from*) restrain oneself; refrain from indulging in (*abstained from cakes and sweets; abstained from mentioning it*). **b** refrain from drinking alcohol. **2** formally decline to use one's vote. □ **abstainer** *n.* [Middle English via Anglo-French *astener* and Old French *abstenir* from Latin *abstinēre abstent-* (as AB-, *tenēre* 'hold')]

abstemious /əbˈstiːmɪəs/ *adj.* (of a person, habit, etc.) moderate, not self-indulgent, esp. in eating and drinking. □ **abstemiously** *adv.* **abstemiousness** *n.* [Latin *abstemius* (as AB-, *temetum* 'strong drink')]

abstention /əbˈstɛnʃ(ə)n/ *n.* the act or an instance of abstaining, esp. from voting. □ **abstentionism** *n.* [French *abstention* or Late Latin *abstentio -onis* (as ABSTAIN)]

abstinence /ˈabstɪnəns/ *n.* the act of abstaining, esp. from food, alcohol, or sexual activity. [Middle English via Old French from Latin *abstinentia* (as ABSTINENT)]

abstinent /ˈabstɪnənt/ *adj.* practising abstinence. □ **abstinently** *adv.* [Middle English via Old French from Latin (as ABSTAIN)]

abstract *adj., v., & n.* ● *adj.* /ˈabstrakt/ **1 a** to do with or existing in thought rather than matter, or in theory rather than practice; not tangible or concrete (*abstract questions rarely concerned him*). **b** (of a word, esp. a noun) denoting a quality or condition or intangible thing rather than a concrete object. **2** (of art) achieving its effect by grouping shapes and colours in satisfying patterns rather than by the recognizable representation of physical reality. ● *v.* /əbˈstrakt/ **1** *tr.* (often foll. by *from*) take out of; extract; remove. **2 a** *tr.* summarize (an article, book, etc.). **b** *intr.* do this as an occupation. **3** *tr. & refl.* (often foll. by *from*) disengage (a person's attention etc.); distract. **4** *tr.* (foll. by *from*) consider abstractly or separately from something else. **5** *tr. euphem.* steal. ● *n.* /ˈabstrakt/ **1** a summary or statement of the contents of a book etc. **2** an abstract work of art. **3** an abstraction or abstract term. □ **in the abstract** in theory rather than in practice. □ **abstractly** /ˈabstraktli/ *adv.* **abstractor** /əbˈstraktə/ *n.* (in sense 2 of *v.*). [Middle English from Old French or Latin *abstractus*, past part. of *abstrahere* (as AB-, *trahere* 'draw')]

abstracted /əbˈstraktɪd/ *adj.* inattentive to the matter in hand; preoccupied. □ **abstractedly** *adv.*

abstract expressionism *n.* a development of abstract art which aims at a subjective emotional expression of an ideal rather than a picture of a physical object.

abstraction /əbˈstrakʃ(ə)n/ *n.* **1** the act or an instance of abstracting or taking away. **2 a** an abstract or visionary idea. **b** the formation of abstract ideas. **3 a** abstract qualities (esp. in art). **b** an abstract work of art. **4** absent-mindedness. [French *abstraction* or Latin *abstractio* (as ABSTRACT)]

abstractionism /əbˈstrakʃ(ə)nɪz(ə)m/ *n.* **1** the principles and practice of abstract art. **2** the pursuit or cult of abstract ideas. □ **abstractionist** *n.*

abstruse /əbˈstruːs/ *adj.* hard to understand; obscure; profound. □ **abstrusely** *adv.* **abstruseness** *n.* [French *abstruse* or Latin *abstrusus* 'put away, hidden' (as AB-, *trusus*, past part. of *trudere* 'push')]

absurd /əbˈsəːd/ *adj. & n.* ● *adj.* **1** (of an idea, suggestion, etc.) wildly unreasonable, illogical, or inappropriate. **2** (of a person) unreasonable or ridiculous in manner. **3** (of a thing) ludicrous, incongruous (*an absurd hat; the situation was becoming absurd*). ● *n.* (**the absurd**) that which is absurd, esp. human existence in a purposeless chaotic universe. □ **absurdly** *adv.* **absurdness** *n.* [French *absurde* or Latin *absurdus* (as AB-, *surdus* 'deaf, dull')]

absurdism /əbˈsəːdɪz(ə)m/ *n.* the belief that human beings exist in a purposeless chaotic universe. □ **absurdist** *adj. & n.*

absurdity /əbˈsəːdɪti/ *n.* (*pl.* **-ies**) **1** wild inappropriateness or incongruity. **2** extreme unreasonableness. **3** an absurd statement or act. [French *absurdité* or Late Latin *absurditas* (as ABSURD)]

ABTA /ˈabtə/ *abbr.* Association of British Travel Agents.

abulia var. of ABOULIA.

abundance /əˈbʌnd(ə)ns/ *n.* **1** a very great quantity, usu. considered to be more than enough. **2** wealth, affluence. **3** wealth of emotion (*abundance of heart*). **4** a call in solo whist undertaking to make nine tricks. [Middle English via Old French *abundance* from Latin *abundantia* (as ABUNDANT)]

abundant /əˈbʌnd(ə)nt/ *adj.* **1** existing or available in large quantities; plentiful. **2** (foll. by *in*) having an abundance of (*a country abundant in fruit*). □ **abundantly** *adv.* [Middle English from Latin, pres. part. of *abundare* ABOUND]

abuse *v. & n.* ● *v.tr.* /əˈbjuːz/ **1** use to bad effect or for a bad purpose; misuse (*abused his position of power*). **2** insult verbally. **3** maltreat; assault (esp. sexually). ● *n.* /əˈbjuːs/ **1 a** incorrect or improper use (*the abuse of power*). **b** an instance of this. **2** insulting language (*a torrent of abuse*). **3** unjust or corrupt practice. **4** maltreatment or (esp. sexual) assault of a person (*child abuse*). □ **abuser** /əˈbjuːzə/ *n.* [Middle English via Old French *abus* (*n.*), *abuser* (*v.*) from Latin *abusus, abuti* (as AB-, *uti us-* USE)]

abusive /əˈbjuːsɪv/ *adj.* **1** using or containing insulting language. **2** (of language) insulting. □ **abusively** *adv.* **abusiveness** *n.*

abut /əˈbʌt/ *v.* (**abutted**, **abutting**) **1** *intr.* (foll. by *on*) (of estates, countries, etc.) adjoin (another). **2** *intr.* (foll. by *on, against*) (of part of a building) touch or lean upon (another) with a projecting end or point (*the shed abutted on the side of the house*). **3** *tr.* abut on. [Old French *abouter* (BUTT[1]) and Anglo-Latin *abuttare*, from Old French *but* 'end']

abutment /ə'bʌtm(ə)nt/ *n.* **1** the lateral supporting structure of a bridge, arch, etc. **2** the point of junction between such a support and the thing supported.

abutter /ə'bʌtə/ *n. Law* the owner of an adjoining property.

abuzz /ə'bʌz/ *adv. & adj.* in a 'buzz' (see BUZZ *n.* 3); in a state of excitement or activity.

abysmal /ə'bɪzm(ə)l/ *adj.* **1** *colloq.* extremely bad (*abysmal weather*; *the standard is abysmal*). **2** profound, utter (*abysmal ignorance*). □ **abysmally** *adv.* [archaic or poet. *abysm* = ABYSS, via Old French *abi(s)me* from medieval Latin *abysmus*]

abyss /ə'bɪs/ *n.* **1** a deep or seemingly bottomless chasm. **2 a** an immeasurable depth (*abyss of despair*). **b** a catastrophic situation as contemplated or feared (*his loss brought him a step nearer the abyss*). **3** (prec. by *the*) primal chaos; hell. [Middle English via Late Latin *abyssus* from Greek *abussos* 'bottomless' (as A-[1], *bussos* 'depth')]

abyssal /ə'bɪs(ə)l/ *adj.* **1** at or of the ocean depths or floor. **2** *Geol.* at or from a great depth in the earth's crust; plutonic.

AC *abbr.* **1** (also **ac**) alternating current. **2** aircraftman. **3** before Christ. **4** Companion of the Order of Australia. **5** *appellation contrôlée*. [sense 3 from Latin *ante Christum*]

Ac *symb. Chem.* the element actinium.

ac- /ak, ək/ *prefix* assim. form of AD- before *c*, *k*, *q*.

a/c *abbr.* account. [*account current*: see ACCOUNT *n.* 2, 3]

-ac /ak/ *suffix* forming adjectives which are often also (or only) used as nouns (*cardiac*; *maniac*) (see also -ACAL). [French *-aque*, Latin *-acus*, or Greek *-akos* adjectival suffix]

acacia /ə'keɪʃə, -sjə/ *n.* **1** (also **acacia tree**) a leguminous tree of the genus *Acacia*, with yellow or white flowers, esp. *A. senegal* yielding gum arabic. **2** (also **false acacia**) the locust tree, *Robinia pseudoacacia*, grown for ornament. [Latin, from Greek *akakia*]

academe /'akədi:m/ *n.* **1 a** the world of learning. **b** universities collectively. **2** *literary* a college or university. [Greek *Akadēmos* (see ACADEMY): used by Shakespeare (*Love's Labour's Lost* I. i. 13) and Milton (*Paradise Regained* iv. 244)]

academia /akə'di:mɪə/ *n.* the academic world; scholastic life. [modern Latin: see ACADEMY]

academic /akə'dɛmɪk/ *adj. & n.* ● *adj.* **1 a** scholarly; to do with learning. **b** of or relating to a scholarly institution (*academic dress*). **2** abstract; theoretical; not of practical relevance. **3** *Art* conventional, over-formal. **4 a** of or concerning Plato's philosophy. **b** sceptical. ● *n.* a teacher or scholar in a university or institute of higher education. □ **academically** *adv.* [French *académique* or Latin *academicus* (as ACADEMY)]

academical /akə'dɛmɪk(ə)l/ *adj. & n.* ● *adj.* belonging to a college or university. ● *n.* (in *pl.*) *Brit.* formal university attire.

academician /əkadə'mɪʃ(ə)n/ *n.* **1** a member of an Academy, esp. of the Royal Academy of Arts, the Académie française, or the Russian Academy of Sciences. **2** *US* an academic; an intellectual. [French *académicien* (as ACADEMIC)]

academicism /akə'dɛmɪsɪz(ə)m/ *n.* (also **academism** /ə'kadəmɪz(ə)m/) academic principles or their application in art.

academic year *n.* a period of nearly a year reckoned from the time of the main student intake, usu. from the beginning of the autumn term to the end of the summer term.

academy /ə'kadəmi/ *n.* (*pl.* **-ies**) **1 a** a place of study or training in a special field (*military academy*; *academy of dance*). **b** *hist.* a place of study. **2** (usu. **Academy**) a society or institution of distinguished scholars, artists, scientists, etc. (*Royal Academy*). **3** *US* & *Sc.* a secondary school, esp. (*US*) a private one. **4 a** Plato's followers or philosophical system. **b** the garden near Athens where Plato taught. [French *académie* or Latin *academia* from Greek *akadēmeia*, from *Akadēmos* the hero after whom Plato's garden was named]

Acadian /ə'keɪdɪən/ *n. & adj.* ● *n.* **1 a** *hist.* a native or inhabitant of the 17th-c. French colony of Acadia on the east coast of Canada. **b** esp. *Canad.* a French-speaking descendant of the early French settlers in Acadia. **2** *US* a descendant of the Acadians deported to Louisiana in the 18th c. (see CAJUN). ● *adj.* of or relating to Acadia or its people. [*Acadie*, the French name for Nova Scotia]

-acal /ək(ə)l/ *suffix* forming adjectives, often used to distinguish them from nouns in *-ac* (*heliacal*; *maniacal*).

acanthus /ə'kanθəs/ *n.* **1** any herbaceous plant or shrub of the genus *Acanthus*, with spiny leaves. **2** *Archit.* a conventionalized representation of an acanthus leaf, used esp. as a decoration for Corinthian column capitals. [Latin from Greek *akanthos*, from *akantha* 'thorn', perhaps from *akē* 'sharp point']

a cappella /a kə'pɛlə, ɑ:/ *adj. & adv.* (also **alla cappella** /alə/) *Mus.* (of choral music) unaccompanied. [Italian, = in church style]

acaricide /'akərɪsʌɪd/ *n.* a preparation for destroying mites.

acarid /'akərɪd/ *n.* any small arachnid of the order Acarina, including mites and ticks. □ **acarology** /akə'rɒlədʒi/ *n.* [modern Latin *acarus* + -ID[3], from Greek *akari* 'mite']

ACAS /'eɪkas/ *abbr.* (in the UK) Advisory, Conciliation, and Arbitration Service.

acausal /eɪ'kɔ:z(ə)l, a-/ *adj.* not causal; not causally related.

Accadian var. of AKKADIAN.

accede /ək'si:d/ *v.intr.* (often foll. by *to*) **1** take office, esp. become monarch. **2** assent or agree (*acceded to the proposal*). **3** (foll. by *to*) formally subscribe to a treaty or other agreement. [Middle English from Latin *accedere* (as AC-, *cedere cess-* 'go')]

accelerando /əksɛlə'randəʊ, ətʃɛl-/ *adv., adj., & n. Mus.* ● *adj. & adv.* with a gradual increase of speed. ● *n.* (*pl.* **accelerandos** or **accelerandi** /-di/) a passage performed accelerando. [Italian]

accelerate /ək'sɛləreɪt/ *v.* **1** *intr.* **a** (of a moving body, esp. a vehicle) move or begin to move more quickly; increase speed. **b** (of a process) happen or reach completion more quickly. **2** *tr.* **a** cause to increase speed. **b** cause (a process) to happen more quickly. [Latin *accelerare* (as AC-, *celerare* from *celer* 'swift')]

acceleration /əksɛlə'reɪʃ(ə)n/ *n.* **1** the process or act of accelerating or being accelerated. **2** an instance of this. **3** (of a vehicle etc.) the capacity to gain speed (*the car has good acceleration*). **4** *Physics* the rate of change of velocity measured in terms of a unit of time. [French *accélération* or Latin *acceleratio* (as ACCELERATE)]

accelerative /ək'sɛlərətɪv/ *adj.* tending to increase speed; quickening.

accelerator /ək'sɛləreɪtə/ *n.* **1** a device for increasing speed, esp. the pedal that controls the speed of a vehicle's engine. **2** *Physics* an apparatus for imparting high speeds to charged particles. **3** *Chem.* a substance that speeds up a chemical reaction.

accelerator board *n.* (also **accelerator card**) *Computing* an accessory circuit board which can be plugged into a small computer to increase its speed of operation.

accelerometer /əksɛlə'rɒmɪtə/ *n.* an instrument for measuring acceleration esp. of rockets. [ACCELERATE + -METER]

accent *n. & v.* ● *n.* /'aks(ə)nt, -sɛnt/ **1** a particular mode of pronunciation, esp. one associated with a particular region or group (*Liverpool accent*; *German accent*; *upper-class accent*). **2** prominence given to a syllable by stress or pitch. **3** a mark on a letter or word to indicate pitch, stress, or the quality of a vowel. **4** a distinctive feature or emphasis (*an accent on comfort*). **5** *Mus.* emphasis on a particular note or chord. ● *v.tr.* /ak'sɛnt/ **1** pronounce with an accent; emphasize (a word or syllable). **2** write or print accents on (words etc.). **3** accentuate. **4** *Mus.* play (a note etc.) with an accent. □ **accentual** /ək'sɛntjʊəl/ *adj.* [Latin *accentus* (as AC-, *cantus* 'song') representing Greek *prosōidia* (PROSODY), or through French *accent, accenter*]

accentor /ək'sɛntə/ *n.* a songbird of the Eurasian genus *Prunella* (formerly *Accentor*), e.g. the hedge sparrow or dunnock. [medieval Latin *accentor* from Latin *ad* 'to' + *cantor* 'singer']

accentuate /ək'sɛntjʊeɪt/ *v.tr.* emphasize; make prominent. □ **accentuation** /əksɛntjʊ'eɪʃ(ə)n/ *n.* [medieval Latin *accentuare accentuat-* (as ACCENT)]

accept /ək'sɛpt/ *v.tr.* **1** (also *absol.*) consent to receive (a thing offered). **2** (also *absol.*) give an affirmative answer to (an offer or proposal). **3** regard favourably; treat as welcome (*her mother-in-law never accepted her*). **4 a** believe or receive (an opinion, explanation, etc.) as adequate, valid, or correct. **b** be prepared to subscribe to (a belief, philosophy, etc.). **5** receive as suitable (*the hotel accepts traveller's cheques; the machine only accepts tokens*). **6 a** tolerate; submit to (*accepted the umpire's decision*). **b** (often foll. by *that* + clause) esp. *Brit.* be willing to believe (*we accept that you meant well*). **7** undertake (an office or responsibility). **8** agree to meet (a draft or bill of exchange). □ **accepter** *n.* [Middle English from Old French *accepter* or Latin *acceptare*, from *accipere* (as AC-, *capere* 'take')]

acceptable /ək'sɛptəb(ə)l/ *adj.* **1 a** worthy of being accepted. **b** pleasing, welcome. **2** adequate, satisfactory. **3** tolerable (*an acceptable risk*). □ **acceptability** /əksɛptə'bɪlɪti/ *n.* **acceptableness** *n.* **acceptably** *adv.* [Middle English via Old French from Late Latin *acceptabilis* (as ACCEPT)]

acceptance /ək'sɛpt(ə)ns/ *n.* **1** willingness to receive (a gift, payment, duty, etc.). **2** an affirmative answer to an invitation or proposal. **3** (often foll. by *of*) a willingness to accept (conditions, a circumstance, etc.). **4 a** approval, belief (*found wide acceptance*). **b** willingness or ability to tolerate. **5 a** agreement to meet a bill of exchange. **b** a bill so accepted. [French from *accepter* (as ACCEPT)]

acceptant /ək'sɛpt(ə)nt/ *adj.* (foll. by *of*) willingly accepting. [French (as ACCEPTANCE)]

acceptation /aksɛp'teɪʃ(ə)n/ *n.* a particular sense, or the generally recognized meaning, of a word or phrase. [Middle English via Old French from medieval Latin *acceptatio* (as ACCEPT)]

acceptor /ək'sɛptə/ *n.* **1** *Commerce* a person who accepts a bill. **2** *Physics* an atom or molecule able to receive an extra electron, esp. an impurity in a semiconductor. **3** *Chem.* a molecule or ion etc. to which electrons are donated in the formation of a bond. **4** *Electr.* a circuit tuned to resonate at a particular frequency.

access /'aksɛs/ *n.* & *v.* ● *n.* **1** a way of approaching or reaching or entering (*a building with rear access*). **2 a** (often foll. by *to*) the right or opportunity to reach, use, or visit; admittance (*has access to secret files; was granted access to the prisoner*). **b** the condition of being readily approached; accessibility. **3** (often foll. by *of*) an attack or outburst (*an access of anger*). **4** (*attrib.*) *Brit.* (of broadcasting) given over to minority or special-interest groups (*access television*). ● *v.tr.* esp. *Computing* gain access to (data, a file, etc.). [Middle English from Old French *acces* or Latin *accessus*, from *accedere* (as AC-, *cedere cess-* 'go')]

■ **Usage** The use of the verb to mean 'gain access to' in contexts other than computing (as in *The kitchen can be accessed from the dining room*) is considered incorrect by some people.

accessary var. of ACCESSORY.

accessible /ək'sɛsɪb(ə)l/ *adj.* (often foll. by *to*) **1** that can readily be reached, entered, or used. **2** (of a person) readily available (esp. to subordinates). **3** (in a form) easy to understand. □ **accessibility** /əksɛsɪ'bɪlɪti/ *n.* **accessibly** *adv.* [French *accessible* or Late Latin *accessibilis* (as ACCEDE)]

accession /ək'sɛʃ(ə)n/ *n.* & *v.* ● *n.* **1** entering upon an office (esp. the throne) or a condition (as manhood). **2** (often foll. by *to*) a thing added (e.g. a book to a library); increase, addition. **3** *Law* the incorporation of one item of property in another. **4** assent; the formal acceptance of a treaty etc. ● *v.tr.* record the addition of (a new item) to a library or museum. [French *accession* or Latin *accessio -onis* (as ACCEDE)]

accessorize /ək'sɛsərʌɪz/ *v.tr.* (also **-ise**) provide (an outfit etc.) with accessories.

accessory /ək'sɛs(ə)ri/ *n.* & *adj.* (also **accessary**) ● *n.* (*pl.* **-ies**) **1** an additional or extra thing. **2** (usu. in *pl.*) **a** a small attachment or fitting. **b** a small item of (esp. a woman's) dress (e.g. shoes, gloves, handbag). **3** (often foll. by *to*) a person who helps in or knows the details of an (esp. illegal) act, without taking part in it. ● *adj.* additional; contributing or aiding in a minor way; dispensable. □ **accessory before** (or **after**) **the fact** a person who incites (or assists) another to commit a crime. □ **accessorial** /aksɛ'sɔːrɪəl/ *adj.* [medieval Latin *accessorius* (as ACCEDE)]

access road *n.* **1** a road giving access to a place, site, or buildings. **2** a slip road.

access time *n. Computing* the time taken to retrieve data from storage.

acciaccatura /ətʃakə'tʊərə/ *n. Mus.* a grace note performed as quickly as possible before an essential note of a melody. [Italian, from *acciacare* 'to crush']

accidence /'aksɪd(ə)ns/ *n.* the part of grammar that deals with the variable parts or inflections of words. [medieval Latin sense of Latin *accidentia* (translation of Greek *parepomena* 'accompanying things'), neut. pl. of *accidens* (as ACCIDENT)]

accident /'aksɪd(ə)nt/ *n.* **1** an event that is without apparent cause, or is unexpected (*their early arrival was just an accident*). **2** an unfortunate event, esp. one causing physical harm or damage, brought about unintentionally. **3** occurrence of things by chance; the working of fortune (*accident accounts for much in life*). **4** *colloq.* an occurrence of involuntary urination or defecation. **5** an irregularity in structure. □ **by accident** unintentionally. [Middle English via Old French and Late Latin *accidens* from Latin *accidere* (as AC-, *cadere* 'fall')]

accidental /aksɪ'dɛnt(ə)l/ *adj.* & *n.* ● *adj.* **1** happening by chance, unintentionally, or unexpectedly. **2** not essential to a conception; subsidiary. ● *n.* **1** *Mus.* a sign indicating a momentary departure from the key signature by raising or lowering a note. **2** something not essential to a conception. **3** = VAGRANT *n.* 3. □ **accidentally** *adv.* [Middle English from Late Latin *accidentalis* (as ACCIDENT)]

accident-prone *adj.* (of a person) subject to frequent accidents.

accidie /'aksɪdi/ *n.* **1** laziness, sloth, apathy. **2** black despair. [Middle English via Anglo-French *accidie* and Old French *accide* from medieval Latin *accidia*, alteration of Late Latin ACEDIA]

accipiter /ak'sɪpɪtə/ *n.* a short-winged, long-legged hawk of the genus *Accipiter*, e.g. a sparrowhawk, a goshawk. [Latin, = hawk, bird of prey]

acclaim /ə'kleɪm/ *v.* & *n.* ● *v.tr.* **1** welcome or applaud enthusiastically; praise publicly. **2** (foll. by compl.) hail as (*acclaimed him king; was acclaimed the winner*). ● *n.* **1** applause; welcome; public praise. **2** a shout of acclaim. [Middle English from Latin *acclamare* (as AC-, *clamare* 'shout': spelling assimilated to *claim*)]

acclamation /aklə'meɪʃ(ə)n/ *n.* **1** loud and eager assent to a proposal. **2** (usu. in *pl.*) shouting in a person's honour. **3** the act or process of acclaiming. □ **by acclamation** *Polit.* **1** *US* by overwhelming vocal approval and without ballot. **2** *Canad.* by virtue of being the sole candidate. [Latin *acclamatio* (as ACCLAIM)]

acclimate /ə'klʌɪmət/ *v.tr.* **1** esp. *N. Amer.* acclimatize. **2** *Biol.* adapt physiologically to environmental stress. [French *acclimater* (as A-[3] + *climat* CLIMATE)]

acclimation /aklɪ'meɪʃ(ə)n, əklʌɪ-/ *n.* **1** esp. *N. Amer.* acclimatization. **2** *Biol.* physiological adaptation to environmental stress. [formed irregularly from ACCLIMATE]

acclimatize /ə'klʌɪmətʌɪz/ *v.* (also **-ise**) **1** *tr.* accustom to a new climate or to new conditions. **2** *intr.* become acclimatized. □ **acclimatization** /-'zeɪʃ(ə)n/ *n.* [French *acclimater*: see ACCLIMATE]

acclivity /ə'klɪvɪti/ *n.* (*pl.* **-ies**) an upward slope. □ **acclivitous** *adj.* [Latin *acclivitas* from *acclivis* (as AC-, *clivis* from *clivus* 'slope')]

accolade /'akəleɪd, akə'lɑ:d, -kəʊl-/ *n.* **1** the awarding of praise; an acknowledgement of merit. **2** a touch made with a sword at the bestowing of a knighthood. [French from Provençal *acolada* (as AC-, Latin *collum* 'neck')]

accommodate /ə'kɒmədeɪt/ *v.tr.* **1** provide lodging or room for (*the flat accommodates three people*). **2** adapt, harmonize, reconcile (*must accommodate ourselves to new surroundings*; *cannot accommodate your needs to mine*). **3 a** do a service or favour to; oblige (a person). **b** (foll. by *with*) supply (a person) with. [Latin *accommodare* (as AC-, *commodus* 'fitting')]

accommodating /ə'kɒmədeɪtɪŋ/ *adj.* obliging, compliant. □ **accommodatingly** *adv.*

accommodation /əkɒmə'deɪʃ(ə)n/ *n.* **1** (in *sing.* or *US* in *pl.*) room for receiving people, esp. a place to live or lodgings. **2** an adjustment or adaptation to suit a special or different purpose. **3** a convenient arrangement; a settlement or compromise. **4** the automatic adjustment of the focus of the eye by flattening or thickening of the lens. [French *accommodation* or Latin *accommodatio -onis* (as ACCOMMODATE)]

accommodation address *n. Brit.* an address used on letters to a person who is unable or unwilling to give a permanent address.

accommodation bill *n.* a bill to raise money on credit.

accommodationist /əkɒmə'deɪʃ(ə)nɪst/ *n. US* a person who seeks esp. political compromise.

accommodation ladder *n.* a ladder up the side of a ship from a small boat.

accommodation road *n. Brit.* a road for access to a place not on a public road.

accompaniment /ə'kʌmp(ə)nɪm(ə)nt/ *n.* **1** *Mus.* an instrumental or orchestral part supporting or partnering a solo instrument, voice, or group. **2** an accompanying thing; an appendage. [French *accompagnement* (as ACCOMPANY)]

accompanist /ə'kʌmpənɪst/ *n.* a person who provides a musical accompaniment.

accompany /ə'kʌmpəni/ *v.tr.* (**-ies, -ied**) **1** go with; escort, attend. **2** (usu. in *passive*; foll. by *with, by*) **a** be done or found with; supplement (*speech accompanied with gestures*). **b** have as a result (*pills accompanied by side effects*). **3** *Mus.* support or partner with accompaniment. [Middle English from French *accompagner* (as A-[3] + Old French *compaing* COMPANION[1]): assimilated to COMPANY]

accomplice /ə'kʌmplɪs, ə'kɒm-/ *n.* a partner or helper, esp. in a crime or wrongdoing. [Middle English and French *complice* (probably by association with ACCOMPANY), from Late Latin *complex complicis* 'confederate': cf. COMPLICATE]

accomplish /ə'kʌmplɪʃ, ə'kɒm-/ *v.tr.* perform; complete; succeed in doing. [Middle English via Old French *acomplir* from Latin *complēre* COMPLETE]

accomplished /ə'kʌmplɪʃt, ə'kɒm-/ *adj.* clever, skilled; well trained or educated.

accomplishment /ə'kʌmplɪʃm(ə)nt, ə'kɒm-/ *n.* **1** the fulfilment or completion (of a task etc.). **2** an acquired skill, esp. a social one. **3** a thing done or achieved.

accord /ə'kɔ:d/ *v.* & *n.* ● *v.* **1** *intr.* (often foll. by *with*) (esp. of a thing) be in harmony; be consistent. **2** *tr.* **a** grant (permission, a request, etc.). **b** give (a welcome etc.). ● *n.* **1** agreement, consent. **2** harmony or harmonious correspondence in pitch, tone, colour, etc. □ **in accord** of one mind; united; in harmony. **of one's own accord** on one's own initiative; voluntarily. **with one accord** unanimously; in a united way. [Middle English via Old French *acord*, *acorder* from Latin *cor cordis* 'heart']

accordance /ə'kɔ:d(ə)ns/ *n.* harmony, agreement. □ **in accordance with** in a manner corresponding to (*we acted in accordance with your wishes*). [Middle English from Old French *acordance* (as ACCORD)]

accordant /ə'kɔ:d(ə)nt/ *adj.* (often foll. by *with*) in tune; agreeing. [Middle English from Old French *acordant* (as ACCORD)]

according /ə'kɔ:dɪŋ/ *adv.* **1** (foll. by *to*) **a** as stated by or in (*according to my sister*; *according to their statement*). **b** in a manner corresponding to; in proportion to (*he lives according to his principles*). **2** (foll. by *as* + clause) in a manner or to a degree that varies as (*he pays according as he is able*).

accordingly /ə'kɔ:dɪŋli/ *adv.* **1** as suggested or required by the (stated) circumstances (*silence is vital so please act accordingly*). **2** consequently, therefore (*accordingly, he left the room*).

accordion /ə'kɔ:dɪən/ *n.* **1** a portable musical instrument with metal reeds blown by bellows, played by means of keys and buttons. **2** (*attrib.*) folding like the bellows of an accordion (*accordion pleat*; *accordion wall*). □ **accordionist** *n.* [German *Akkordion* from Italian *accordare* 'to tune']

accost /ə'kɒst/ *v.tr.* **1** approach and address (a person), esp. boldly. **2** (of a prostitute) solicit. [originally in the sense 'lie or go alongside': French *accoster* from Italian *accostare*, ultimately from Latin *costa* 'rib, side']

accouchement /a'ku:ʃmɒ̃, French akuʃmɑ̃/ *n.* **1** childbirth. **2** the period of childbirth. [French from *accoucher* 'act as midwife']

accoucheur /aku:'ʃə:, French akuʃœr/ *n.* a male midwife. [French (as ACCOUCHEMENT)]

account /ə'kaʊnt/ *n.* & *v.* ● *n.* **1** a narration or description (*gave a long account of the ordeal*). **2 a** an arrangement or facility at a bank or building society etc. for commercial or financial transactions, esp. for depositing and withdrawing money (*opened an account*). **b** the assets credited by such an arrangement (*has a large account*; *paid the money into her account*). **c** esp. *Brit.* an arrangement at a shop for buying goods on credit (*has an account at the newsagent's*). **3 a** (often in *pl.*) a record or statement of money, goods, or services received or expended, with the balance (*firms must keep detailed accounts*). **b** (in *pl.*) the practice of accounting or reckoning (*is good at accounts*). **4** a statement of the administration of money in trust (*demand an account*). **5** *Brit.* the period during which transactions take place on a stock exchange; the period from one account day to the next. **6** counting, reckoning. ● *v.tr.* (foll. by *to be* or compl.) consider, regard as (*account it a misfortune*; *account him wise*; *account him to be guilty*). □ **account for 1** serve as or provide an explanation or reason for (*that accounts for their misbehaviour*). **2 a** give a reckoning of or answer for (money etc. entrusted). **b** answer for (one's conduct). **3** succeed in killing, destroying, disposing of, or defeating. **4** supply or make up a specified amount or proportion of (*rent accounts for 50% of expenditure*). **by all accounts** in everyone's opinion. **call to account** require an explanation from (a person). **give a good** (or **bad**) **account of oneself** make a favourable (or unfavourable) impression; be successful (or unsuccessful). **keep account of** keep a record of; follow closely. **leave out of account** fail or decline to consider. **money of account** denominations of money used in reckoning, but not current as coins. **of no account** unimportant. **of some account** important. **on account 1** (of goods) to be paid for later. **2** (of money) in part payment. **on one's account** for one's benefit (*don't do it on my account*). **on account of** because of. **on no account** under no circumstances; certainly not. **on one's own account** for one's own purposes; at one's own risk. **settle** (or **square**) **accounts with 1** receive or pay money etc. owed to. **2** have revenge on. **take account of** (or **take into account**) consider along with other factors (*took their age into account*). **turn to account** (or **good account**) turn to one's advantage. [Middle English from Old French *acont, aconter* (as AC-, *conter* COUNT[1])]

■ **Usage** The use of the verb with *as* (e.g. *We accounted him as wise*) is considered incorrect in standard English.

accountable /əˈkaʊntəb(ə)l/ *adj.* **1** responsible; required to account for one's conduct (*accountable for one's actions*). **2** explicable, understandable. □ **accountability** /-ˈbɪlɪti/ *n.* **accountably** *adv.*

accountancy /əˈkaʊnt(ə)nsi/ *n.* the profession or duties of an accountant.

accountant /əˈkaʊnt(ə)nt/ *n.* a professional keeper or inspector of accounts. [legal French from pres. part. of Old French *aconter* ACCOUNT]

account day *n. Brit.* a day of periodic settlement of stock exchange accounts.

account executive *n.* a business executive, esp. in advertising, who manages a client's account.

accounting /əˈkaʊntɪŋ/ *n.* **1** the process of or skill in keeping and verifying accounts. **2** in senses of ACCOUNT *v.*

account rendered *n.* a bill which has been sent but is not yet paid.

accounts payable *n.pl.* money owed by a company.

accounts receivable *n.pl.* money owed to a company.

accoutre /əˈkuːtə/ *v.tr.* (*US* **accouter**) (usu. as **accoutred**, *US* **-tered** *adj.*) attire, equip, esp. with a special outfit. [French *accoutrer* from Old French *acoustrer* (as A-[3], *cousture* 'sewing')]

accoutrement /əˈkuːtəm(ə)nt, -trə-/ *n.* (*US* also **accouterment** /-təm(ə)nt/) (usu. in *pl.*) **1** equipment, trappings. **2** *Mil.* a soldier's outfit other than weapons and garments. [French (as ACCOUTRE)]

accredit /əˈkrɛdɪt/ *v.tr.* (**accredited**, **accrediting**) **1** (foll. by *to*) attribute (a saying etc.) to (a person). **2** (foll. by *with*) credit (a person) with (a saying etc.). **3** (usu. foll. by *to* or *at*) send (an ambassador etc.) with credentials; recommend by documents as an envoy (*was accredited to the sovereign*). **4** gain belief or influence for or make credible (an adviser, a statement, etc.). □ **accreditation** /-ˈteɪʃ(ə)n/ *n.* [French *accréditer* (as AC-, *crédit* CREDIT)]

accredited /əˈkrɛdɪtɪd/ *adj.* **1** (of a person or organization) officially recognized. **2** (of a belief) generally accepted; orthodox. **3** (of cattle, milk, etc.) having guaranteed quality.

accrete /əˈkriːt/ *v.* **1** *intr.* grow together or into one. **2** *intr.* (often foll. by *to*) form round or on, as round a nucleus. **3** *tr.* attract (such additions). [Latin *accrescere* (as AC-, *crescere cret-* 'grow')]

accretion /əˈkriːʃ(ə)n/ *n.* **1 a** the addition of external matter or things. **b** growth by this means. **c** a thing formed by such growth. **2** an extraneous addition to something. **3** the growing together or cohesion of separate things to form one. **4** growth by organic enlargement. **5** *Law* **a** = ACCESSION *n.* 3. **b** the increase of a legacy etc. by the share of a failing co-legatee. □ **accretive** *adj.* [Latin *accretio* (as ACCRETE)]

accrue /əˈkruː/ *v.* (**accrues**, **accrued**, **accruing**) **1** *intr.* (often foll. by *to*) come as a natural increase or advantage, esp. financial. **2** *tr.* accumulate; collect. □ **accrual** *n.* **accrued** *adj.* [Middle English from Anglo-French *acru(e)*, past part. of *acreistre* 'increase', from Latin *accrescere* ACCRETE]

acculturate /əˈkʌltʃəreɪt/ *v.* **1** *intr.* adapt to or adopt a different culture. **2** *tr.* cause to do this. □ **acculturation** /-ˈreɪʃ(ə)n/ *n.* **acculturative** /-rətɪv/ *adj.*

accumulate /əˈkjuːmjʊleɪt/ *v.* **1** *tr.* **a** acquire an increasing number or quantity of; heap up. **b** produce or acquire (a resulting whole) in this way. **2** *intr.* grow numerous or considerable; form an increasing mass or quantity. [Latin *accumulare* (as AC-, *cumulus* 'heap')]

accumulation /əkjuːmjʊˈleɪʃ(ə)n/ *n.* **1** the act or process of accumulating or being accumulated. **2** an accumulated mass. **3** the growth of capital by continued interest. [Latin *accumulatio* (as ACCUMULATE)]

accumulative /əˈkjuːmjʊlətɪv/ *adj.* **1** arising from accumulation; cumulative (*accumulative evidence*). **2** arranged so as to accumulate. **3** acquisitive; given to hoarding. □ **accumulatively** *adv.*

accumulator /əˈkjuːmjʊleɪtə/ *n.* **1** *Brit.* a rechargeable electric cell. **2** *Brit.* a bet placed on a sequence of events, the winnings and stake from each being placed on the next. **3** a register in a computer used to contain the results of an operation. **4** a person who accumulates things.

accuracy /ˈakjʊrəsi/ *n.* (*pl.* **-ies**) **1** exactness or precision, esp. arising from careful effort. **2** the degree of refinement in measurement or specification.

accurate /ˈakjʊrət/ *adj.* **1** careful, precise; lacking errors. **2** conforming exactly with the truth or with a given standard. □ **accurately** *adv.* [Latin *accuratus* 'done carefully', past part. of *accurare* (as AC-, *cura* 'care')]

accursed /əˈkəːsɪd, əˈkəːst/ *adj.* (*archaic* **accurst** /əˈkəːst/) **1** lying under a curse; ill-fated. **2** *colloq.* detestable, annoying. [past part. of *accurse*, from A-[2] + CURSE]

accusal /əˈkjuːz(ə)l/ *n.* accusation.

accusation /akjʊˈzeɪʃ(ə)n/ *n.* **1** the act or process of accusing or being accused. **2** a statement charging a person with an offence or crime. [Middle English via Old French from Latin *accusatio -onis* (as ACCUSE)]

accusative /əˈkjuːzətɪv/ *n.* & *adj. Gram.* ● *n.* the case of nouns, pronouns, and adjectives, expressing the object of an action or the goal of motion. ● *adj.* of or in this case. [Middle English, from Old French *accusatif -ive* or Latin (*casus*) *accusativus*, translation of Greek (*ptōsis*) *aitiatikē* '(the case) showing cause']

accusatorial /əkjuːzəˈtɔːrɪəl/ *adj. Law* (of proceedings) involving accusation by a prosecutor and a verdict reached by an impartial judge or jury (opp. INQUISITORIAL 3). [Latin *accusatorius* (as ACCUSE)]

accusatory /əˈkjuːzət(ə)ri/ *adj.* (of language, manner, etc.) of or implying accusation.

accuse /əˈkjuːz/ *v.tr.* **1** (foll. by *of*) charge (a person etc.) with a fault or crime; indict (*accused them of murder*; *was accused of stealing a car*). **2** lay the blame on. □ **the accused** the person or persons charged with a crime. □ **accuser** *n.* **accusingly** *adv.* [Middle English *acuse* via Old French *ac(c)user* from Latin *accusare* (as AC-, CAUSE)]

accustom /əˈkʌstəm/ *v.tr.* & *refl.* (foll. by *to*) make (a person or thing or oneself) used to (*the army accustomed him to discipline*; *was accustomed to their strange ways*). [Middle English from Old French *acostumer* (as AC-, *costume* CUSTOM)]

accustomed /əˈkʌstəmd/ *adj.* **1** (usu. foll. by *to*) used (*accustomed to hard work*). **2** customary, usual.

AC/DC *abbr.* **1** alternating current/direct current. **2** *slang* bisexual.

ace /eɪs/ *n.* & *adj.* ● *n.* **1 a** a playing card, domino, etc., with a single spot and generally having the value 'one' or in card games the highest value in each suit. **b** a single spot on a playing card etc. **2 a** a person who excels in some activity. **b** a pilot who has shot down many enemy aircraft. **3** *Tennis* etc. **a** a service that is too good for the opponent to return. **b** a point scored in this way. **4** *Golf* a hole in one. ● *adj. slang* excellent. □ **ace up one's sleeve** (or *N. Amer.* **in the hole**) something effective kept in reserve. **play one's ace** use one's best resource. **within an ace of** on the verge of. [Middle English via Old French from Latin *as* 'unity', AS[2]]

-acea /'eɪʃə/ *suffix* forming the plural names of orders and classes of animals (*Crustacea*) (cf. -ACEAN). [neut. pl. of Latin adjectival suffix *-aceus* 'of the nature of']

-aceae /'eɪsɪi:/ *suffix* forming the plural names of families of plants (*Rosaceae*). [fem. pl. of Latin adjectival suffix *-aceus* 'of the nature of']

-acean /'eɪʃ(ə)n/ *suffix* **1** forming adjectives, = -ACEOUS. **2** forming nouns as the sing. of names in *-acea* (*crustacean*). [Latin *-aceus*: see -ACEA]

acedia /ə'si:dɪə/ *n.* = ACCIDIE. [Late Latin *acedia* from Greek *akēdia* 'listlessness']

acellular /eɪ'sɛljʊlə/ *adj. Biol.* **1** having no cells; not consisting of cells. **2** (esp. of protozoa) consisting of one cell only; unicellular.

-aceous /'eɪʃəs/ *suffix* forming adjectives, esp. from nouns in *-acea*, *-aceae* (*herbaceous*; *rosaceous*). [Latin *-aceus*: see -ACEA]

acephalous /eɪ'sɛf(ə)ləs, -'kɛf-/ *adj.* **1** headless. **2** having no chief. **3** *Zool.* having no part of the body specially organized as a head. **4** *Prosody* lacking a syllable or syllables in the first foot. [medieval Latin *acephalus* from Greek *akephalos* 'headless' (as A-[1], *kephalē* 'head')]

acer /'eɪsə/ *n.* a tree or shrub of the genus *Acer*, which includes maples and the European sycamore. [Latin, = maple]

acerbic /ə'sə:bɪk/ *adj.* **1** astringently sour; harsh-tasting. **2** bitter in speech, manner, or temper. □ **acerbically** *adv.* **acerbity** *n.* (*pl.* **-ies**). [Latin *acerbus* 'sour-tasting']

acetabulum /asɪ'tabjʊləm/ *n.* (*pl.* **acetabula** /-lə/) **1** *Anat.* the socket of the hip bone, into which the head of the femur fits. **2** a cup-shaped sucker in tapeworms, cuttlefish, and other animals. [Middle English from Latin, = vinegar cup, from *acetum* 'vinegar' + *-abulum*, diminutive of *-abrum* 'holder']

acetal /'asɪtal/ *n. Chem.* any of a class of organic compounds formed by the condensation of two alcohol molecules with an aldehyde molecule. [as ACETIC + -AL]

acetaldehyde /asɪt'aldɪhʌɪd/ *n.* a colourless volatile liquid aldehyde. Also called *ethanal*. Chem. formula: CH_3CHO. [ACETIC + ALDEHYDE]

acetaminophen /əsetə'mɪnəfɛn, ˌasɪt-/ *n. N. Amer.* = PARACETAMOL. [para-*acetylaminophenol* (cf. PARACETAMOL]

acetate /'asɪteɪt/ *n.* **1** a salt or ester of acetic acid, esp. the cellulose ester used to make textiles, gramophone records, etc.; also called *ethanoate*. **2** a fabric made from cellulose acetate. [ACETIC + -ATE[1]]

acetate fibre *n.* (also **acetate silk**) fibre (or silk) made artificially from cellulose acetate.

acetic /ə'si:tɪk, ə'sɛt-/ *adj.* of or like vinegar or acetic acid. [French *acétique* from Latin *acetum* 'vinegar']

acetic acid *n.* the clear liquid acid that gives vinegar its characteristic taste. Also called *ethanoic acid*. Chem. formula: CH_3COOH.

aceto- /ə'si:təʊ, 'asɪtəʊ/ *comb. form Chem.* acetic, acetyl.

acetone /'asɪtəʊn/ *n.* a colourless volatile liquid ketone valuable as a solvent of organic compounds esp. paints, varnishes, etc. Also called *propanone*. Chem. formula: CH_3COCH_3. [ACETO- + -ONE]

acetous /ə'si:təs/ *adj.* **1** having the qualities of vinegar. **2** producing vinegar. **3** sour. [Late Latin *acetosus* 'sour' (as ACETIC)]

acetyl /'asɪtʌɪl, -tɪl/ *n. Chem.* the monovalent radical of acetic acid, CH_3CO–. [ACETIC + -YL]

acetylcholine /asɪtɪl'kəʊli:n, asɪtʌɪl-/ *n.* a compound serving to transmit impulses from nerve fibres. [ACETYL + CHOLINE]

acetylene /ə'sɛtɪli:n/ *n.* a colourless hydrocarbon gas, burning with a bright flame, used esp. in welding and formerly in lighting. Also called *ethyne*. Chem. formula: C_2H_2. [ACETIC + -YL + -ENE]

acetylide /ə'sɛtɪlʌɪd/ *n.* any of a class of salts formed from acetylene and a metal.

acetylsalicylic acid /ˌasɪtʌɪlˌsalɪ'sɪlɪk/ *n.* = ASPIRIN. [ACETYL + SALICYLIC ACID]

acetyl silk *n.* = ACETATE FIBRE.

Achaean /ə'ki:ən/ *adj.* & *n.* ● *adj.* **1** of or relating to Achaea in ancient Greece. **2** *literary* (esp. in Homeric contexts) Greek. ● *n.* **1** an inhabitant of Achaea. **2** (usu. in *pl.*) *literary* a Greek. [Latin *Achaeus* from Greek *Akhaios*]

Achaemenid /ə'ki:mənɪd/ *adj.* & *n.* (also **Achaemenian** /akɪ'mi:nɪən/) ● *adj.* of or relating to the dynasty ruling in Persia from Cyrus I to Darius III (553–330 BC). ● *n.* a member of this dynasty. [Latin *Achaemenius* from Greek *Akhaimenēs*, the name of the ancestor of the dynasty]

acharnement /ə'ʃɑ:nmɒ̃, French aʃarnəmɑ̃/ *n.* **1** bloodthirsty fury; ferocity. **2** gusto. [French]

ache /eɪk/ *n.* & *v.* ● *n.* **1** a continuous or prolonged dull pain. **2** mental distress. ● *v.intr.* **1** suffer from or be the source of an ache (*I ached all over*; *my left leg ached*). **2** (foll. by *to* + infin.) desire greatly (*we ached to be at home again*). □ **achingly** *adv.* [Old English *œce* (*n.*), *acan* (*v.*)]

achene /ə'ki:n/ *n. Bot.* a small dry one-seeded fruit that does not open to liberate the seed (e.g. a strawberry pip). [modern Latin *achaenium* (as A-[1], Greek *khainō* 'gape')]

Acheulian /ə'ʃu:lɪən/ *adj.* & *n.* (also **Acheulean**) ● *adj.* of the palaeolithic period in Europe etc. following the Abbevillian and preceding the Mousterian. ● *n.* the culture of this period. [French *acheuléen* from St-*Acheul* in N. France, where remains dating from this period were found]

achieve /ə'tʃi:v/ *v.tr.* **1 a** reach or attain by effort (*achieved victory*). **b** acquire, gain, earn (*achieved notoriety*). **2** accomplish or carry out (a feat or task). **3** *absol.* be successful; attain a desired level of performance. □ **achievable** *adj.* **achiever** *n.* [Middle English from Old French *achever* 'come or bring to a head' from *a chief* 'to a head']

achievement /ə'tʃi:vm(ə)nt/ *n.* **1** something achieved. **2 a** the act or process of achieving. **b** an instance of this. **3** *Psychol.* performance in a standardized test. **4** *Heraldry* a representation of a coat of arms with all the adjuncts to which a bearer of arms is entitled.

achillea /akɪ'li:ə, a'kɪlɪə/ *n.* any plant of the genus *Achillea* (daisy family), usu. aromatic with heads of small white or yellow flowers, e.g. common yarrow or milfoil. [Latin, from Greek *Akhilleios*, a plant supposed to have been used medicinally by Achilles]

Achilles heel /ə'kɪli:z/ *n.* a person's weak or vulnerable point. [Latin *Achilles* from Greek *Akhilleus*, a hero in the *Iliad*, invulnerable except in the heel]

Achilles tendon /ə'kɪli:z/ *n.* the tendon connecting the heel with the calf muscles.

achiral /eɪ'kʌɪər(ə)l/ *adj. Chem.* (of a crystal or molecule) not chiral.

achondroplasia /əkɒndrə'pleɪzjə, eɪˌkɒn-/ *n. Med.* a hereditary condition in which the growth of long bones by ossification of cartilage is retarded, resulting in very short limbs and often a small face. □ **achondroplasic** *adj.* **achondroplastic** /-'plastɪk/ *adj.* [A-[1] + Greek *khondros* 'cartilage' + *plasis* 'moulding' + -IA[1]]

achromat /'akrə(ʊ)mat/ *n.* a lens made achromatic by correction.

achromatic /akrə(ʊ)'matɪk/ *adj. Optics* **1** that transmits light without separating it into constituent colours (*achromatic lens*). **2** without colour (*achromatic fringe*). □ **achromatically** *adv.* **achromaticity** /əkrəʊmə'tɪsɪti/ *n.* **achromatism** /ə'krəʊmətɪz(ə)m/ *n.* [French *achromatique* from Greek *akhromatos* (as A-[1], CHROMATIC)]

achy /'eɪki/ *adj.* full of or suffering from aches.

acid /'asɪd/ *n.* & *adj.* ● *n.* **1** *Chem.* **a** any of a class of substances that liberate hydrogen ions in water, are usu. sour and corrosive, turn litmus red, and have a pH of less than 7. **b** any compound or atom donating protons. **2** (in general use) any sour substance. **3** *slang* the drug LSD. ● *adj.* **1** sharp-tasting; sour. **2** biting, sharp (*an acid wit*). **3** *Chem.* having the essential properties of an acid. **4** *Geol.* containing much silica. **5** (of a colour) intense, bright. □ **put the acid on** *Austral. slang* seek to extract a loan or favour etc. from. □ **acidic** /əˈsɪdɪk/ *adj.* **acidimetry** /asɪˈdɪmɪtri/ *n.* **acidly** *adv.* **acidness** *n.* [French *acide* or Latin *acidus*, from *acēre* 'be sour']

acid drop *n. Brit.* a kind of sweet with a sharp taste.

acid head *n. slang* a user of the drug LSD.

acid house *n.* a kind of synthesized music with a simple repetitive beat, often associated with the taking of hallucinogenic drugs (often *attrib.*: *acid house parties*).

acidify /əˈsɪdɪfʌɪ/ *v.tr. & intr.* (**-ies**, **-ied**) make or become acid. □ **acidification** /-fɪˈkeɪʃ(ə)n/ *n.*

acidity /əˈsɪdɪti/ *n.* (*pl.* **-ies**) an acid quality or state, esp. an excessively acid condition of the stomach.

acidophilic /asɪdəˈfɪlɪk, əsɪd-/ *adj.* **1** *Biol.* (of a cell etc.) readily stained with acid dyes. **2** esp. *Bot.* growing best in acidic conditions. [ACID + -PHILIC (see -PHILIA)]

acidophilus /asɪˈdɒfɪləs/ *n.* a bacterium, *Lactobacillus acidophilus*, used to make yogurt and to supplement the intestinal flora. [modern Latin, = acid-loving]

acidosis /asɪˈdəʊsɪs/ *n.* an over-acid condition of the body fluids or tissues. □ **acidotic** /-ˈdɒtɪk/ *adj.*

acid radical *n.* a radical formed by the removal of hydrogen ions from an acid.

acid rain *n.* rain containing acid formed in the atmosphere esp. from industrial waste gases.

acid test *n.* **1** a severe or conclusive test. **2** a test in which acid is used to test for gold etc.

acidulate /əˈsɪdjʊleɪt/ *v.tr.* make somewhat acid. □ **acidulation** /-ˈleɪʃ(ə)n/ *n.* [Latin *acidulus*, diminutive of *acidus* 'sour']

acidulous /əˈsɪdjʊləs/ *adj.* somewhat acid.

acinus /ˈasɪnəs/ *n.* (*pl.* **acini** /-nʌɪ/) *Anat.* a small saclike cavity, esp. one in a gland surrounded by secretory cells. [Latin, = berry, kernel]

-acious /ˈeɪʃəs/ *suffix* forming adjectives meaning 'inclined to, full of' (*vivacious*; *pugnacious*; *voracious*; *capacious*). [Latin *-ax -acis*, added chiefly to verbal stems to form adjectives + -OUS]

-acity /ˈasɪti/ *suffix* forming nouns of quality or state corresponding to adjectives in *-acious*. [French *-acité* or Latin *-acitas -tatis*]

ack-ack /akˈak/ *adj. & n. colloq.* ● *adj.* anti-aircraft. ● *n.* an anti-aircraft gun etc. [formerly signallers' name for the letters *AA*]

ackee /ˈaki/ *n.* (also **akee**) **1** a tropical tree, *Blighia sapida*. **2** its fruit, edible when cooked. [Kru *ākee*]

ack emma /ak ˈɛmə/ *adv. & n. Brit. colloq.* = A.M. [formerly signallers' name for the letters *AM*]

acknowledge /əkˈnɒlɪdʒ/ *v.tr.* **1 a** recognize; accept; admit the truth of (*acknowledged the failure of the plan*). **b** (often foll. by *to be* + compl.) recognize as (*acknowledged it to be a great success*). **c** (often foll. by *that* + clause or *to* + infin.) admit that something is so (*acknowledged that he was wrong*; *acknowledged him to be wrong*). **2** confirm the receipt of (*acknowledged her letter*). **3 a** show that one has noticed (*acknowledged my arrival with a grunt*). **b** express appreciation of (a service etc.). **4** own; recognize the validity of (*the acknowledged king*). □ **acknowledgeable** *adj.* [obsolete verb *knowledge*, influenced by obsolete *acknow* (as A-[4], KNOW), or from obsolete noun *acknowledge*: see KNOWLEDGE]

acknowledgement /əkˈnɒlɪdʒm(ə)nt/ *n.* (also **acknowledgment**) **1** the act or an instance of acknowledging. **2 a** a thing given or done in return for a service etc. **b** a letter confirming receipt of something. **3** (usu. in *pl.*) an author's statement of indebtedness to others.

aclinic line /əˈklɪnɪk/ *n.* = MAGNETIC EQUATOR. [Greek *aklinēs* (as A-[1], *klinō* 'bend')]

acme /ˈakmi/ *n.* the highest point or period (of achievement, success, etc.); the peak of perfection (*displayed the acme of good taste*). [Greek, = highest point]

acne /ˈakni/ *n.* a skin condition, usu. of the face, characterized by red pimples. □ **acned** *adj.* [modern Latin, from erroneous Greek *aknas* for *akmas*, accusative pl. of *akmē* 'facial eruption': cf. ACME]

acolyte /ˈakəlʌɪt/ *n.* **1** a person assisting a priest in a service or procession. **2** an assistant; a beginner. [Middle English via Old French *acolyt* or ecclesiastical Latin *acolytus*, from Greek *akolouthos* 'follower']

aconite /ˈakənʌɪt/ *n.* **1 a** any poisonous plant of the genus *Aconitum* (buttercup family), esp. monkshood or wolfsbane. **b** = ACONITINE. **2** (in full **winter aconite**) any related plant of the genus *Eranthis*, with yellow flowers. [French *aconit* or Latin *aconitum*, from Greek *akoniton*]

aconitine /əˈkɒnɪtiːn/ *n. Chem.* a poisonous alkaloid obtained from the aconite.

acorn /ˈeɪkɔːn/ *n.* the fruit of the oak, a smooth nut in a rough cuplike base. [Old English *æcern*, related to *æcer* ACRE, later associated with OAK and CORN[1]]

acorn barnacle *n.* any stalkless barnacle of the family Balanidae, forming a sharp-edged encrustation on rocks by the sea.

acorn worm *n.* any wormlike burrowing marine animal of the phylum Hemichordata, having a proboscis and gill slits, and inhabiting seashores.

acotyledon /əkɒtɪˈliːd(ə)n/ *n.* a plant with no distinct seed-leaves. □ **acotyledonous** *adj.* [modern Latin *acotyledones* pl. (as A-[1], COTYLEDON)]

acoustic /əˈkuːstɪk/ *adj. & n.* ● *adj.* **1** relating to sound or the sense of hearing. **2** (of a musical instrument, gramophone, or recording) not having electrical amplification (*acoustic guitar*). **3** (of building materials) used for soundproofing or modifying sound. **4** *Mil.* (of a mine) that can be exploded by sound waves transmitted under water. ● *n.* **1** (usu. in *pl.*) the properties or qualities (esp. of a room or hall etc.) in transmitting sound (*good acoustics*; *a poor acoustic*). **2** (in *pl.*; usu. treated as *sing.*) the science of sound (*acoustics is not widely taught*). □ **acoustical** *adj.* **acoustically** *adv.* [Greek *akoustikos* from *akouō* 'hear']

acoustic coupler *n. Computing* a modem which converts digital signals into audible signals and vice versa, so that the former can be transmitted and received over telephone lines.

acoustician /akuːˈstɪʃ(ə)n/ *n.* an expert in acoustics.

acquaint /əˈkweɪnt/ *v.tr. & refl.* (usu. foll. by *with*) make (a person or oneself) aware of or familiar with (*acquaint me with the facts*). □ **be acquainted with** have personal knowledge of (a person or thing). [Middle English via Old French *acointier* from Late Latin *accognitare* (as AC-, *cognoscere cognit-* 'come to know')]

acquaintance /əˈkweɪnt(ə)ns/ *n.* **1** (usu. foll. by *with*) slight knowledge (of a person or thing). **2** the fact or process of being acquainted (*our acquaintance lasted a year*). **3** a person one knows slightly. □ **make one's acquaintance** first meet or introduce oneself to another person. **make the acquaintance of** (or **make a person's acquaintance**) meet (a person) for the first time; come to know. □ **acquaintanceship** *n.* [Middle English from Old French *acointance* (as ACQUAINT)]

acquaintance rape *n.* the rape of a girl or woman by a person known to her.

acquiesce /akwɪˈɛs/ *v.intr.* **1** (often foll. by *in*) agree, esp. tacitly; accept (an arrangement). **2** (often foll. by *to*) raise no objection. □ **acquiescence** *n.* **acquiescent** *adj.* [Latin *acquiescere* (as AC-, *quiescere* 'rest')]

acquire /əˈkwʌɪə/ *v.tr.* **1** gain by and for oneself; obtain. **2** come into possession of (*acquired fame*; *acquired much property*). □ **acquirable** *adj.* **acquirer** *n.* [Middle English from Old French *aquerre*, ultimately from Latin *acquirere* (as AC-, *quaerere* 'seek')]

acquired characteristic *n. Biol.* a characteristic caused by the environment, not inherited.

acquired immune deficiency syndrome see AIDS.

acquired taste *n.* **1** a liking gained by experience. **2** the object of such a liking.

acquirement /əˈkwʌɪəm(ə)nt/ *n.* **1** something acquired, esp. a mental attainment. **2** the act or an instance of acquiring.

acquisition /akwɪˈzɪʃ(ə)n/ *n.* **1** something acquired, esp. if regarded as useful. **2** the act or an instance of acquiring. [Latin *acquisitio* (as ACQUIRE)]

acquisitive /əˈkwɪzɪtɪv/ *adj.* keen to acquire things; avaricious; materialistic. □ **acquisitively** *adv.* **acquisitiveness** *n.* [French *acquisitive* or Late Latin *acquisitivus* (as ACQUIRE)]

acquit /əˈkwɪt/ *v.* (**acquitted**, **acquitting**) **1** *tr.* (often foll. by *of*) declare (a person) not guilty (*were acquitted of the offence*). **2** *refl.* **a** conduct oneself or perform in a specified way (*we acquitted ourselves well*). **b** (foll. by *of*) discharge (a duty or responsibility). [Middle English via Old French *aquiter* from medieval Latin *acquitare* 'pay a debt' (as AC-, QUIT)]

acquittal /əˈkwɪt(ə)l/ *n.* **1** the process of freeing or being freed from a charge, esp. by a judgement of not guilty. **2** performance of a duty.

acquittance /əˈkwɪt(ə)ns/ *n.* **1** payment of or release from a debt. **2** a written receipt attesting settlement of a debt. [Middle English from Old French *aquitance* (as ACQUIT)]

acre /ˈeɪkə/ *n.* **1** a measure of land, 4,840 sq. yards, 0.405 hectare. **2** (in *pl.*; usu. foll. by *of*) a large area or amount. □ **acred** *adj.* (esp. in *comb.*). [Old English *æcer*, from Germanic]

acreage /ˈeɪk(ə)rɪdʒ/ *n.* **1** a number of acres. **2** an extent of land.

acrid /ˈakrɪd/ *adj.* **1** bitterly pungent; irritating; corrosive. **2** bitter in temper or manner. □ **acridity** /əˈkrɪdɪti/ *n.* **acridly** *adv.* [formed irregularly from Latin *acer acris* 'keen' + -ID[1], probably influenced by *acid*]

acridine /ˈakrɪdiːn/ *n.* a solid colourless organic compound used in the manufacture of dyes and drugs. [ACRID + -INE[4]]

acriflavine /akrɪˈfleɪvɪn, -iːn/ *n.* a reddish powder used as an antiseptic. [formed irregularly from ACRIDINE + FLAVINE]

acrimonious /akrɪˈməʊnɪəs/ *adj.* bitter in manner or temper. □ **acrimoniously** *adv.* [French *acrimonieux*, *-euse* via medieval Latin *acrimoniosus* from Latin *acrimonia* ACRIMONY]

acrimony /ˈakrɪməni/ *n.* (*pl.* **-ies**) bitterness of temper or manner; ill feeling. [French *acrimonie* or Latin *acrimonia* 'pungency' (as ACRID)]

acrobat /ˈakrəbat/ *n.* **1** a performer of spectacular gymnastic feats. **2** a person noted for constant change of mind, allegiance, etc. □ **acrobatic** /akrəˈbatɪk/ *adj.* **acrobatically** /akrəˈbatɪk(ə)li/ *adv.* [French *acrobate* from Greek *akrobatēs*, from *akron* 'summit' + *bainō* 'walk']

acrobatics /akrəˈbatɪks/ *n.pl.* **1** acrobatic feats. **2** (treated as *sing.*) the art of performing these. **3** a skill requiring ingenuity (*mental acrobatics*).

acromegaly /akrə(ʊ)ˈmɛɡəli/ *n. Med.* abnormal growth of the hands, feet, and face, caused by overproduction of growth hormone by the pituitary gland. □ **acromegalic** /-mɪˈɡalɪk/ *adj.* [French *acromégalie*, from Greek *akron* 'extremity' + *megas megal-* 'great']

acronym /ˈakrənɪm/ *n.* a word, usu. pronounced as such, formed from the initial letters of other words (e.g. *Ernie, laser, Nato*). [Greek *akron* 'end' + *onuma* = *onoma* 'name']

acropetal /əˈkrɒpɪt(ə)l/ *adj. Bot.* developing from below upwards. □ **acropetally** *adv.* [Greek *akron* 'tip' + Latin *petere* 'seek']

acrophobia /akrəˈfəʊbɪə/ *n. Psychol.* an abnormal dread of heights. □ **acrophobic** *adj.* [Greek *akron* 'peak' + -PHOBIA]

acropolis /əˈkrɒpəlɪs/ *n.* **1** a citadel or upper fortified part of an ancient Greek city. **2** (**Acropolis**) the ancient citadel at Athens. [Greek *akropolis* from *akron* 'summit' + *polis* 'city']

across /əˈkrɒs/ *prep.* & *adv.* ● *prep.* **1** to or on the other side of (*walked across the road*; *lives across the river*). **2** from one side to another side of (*the cover stretched across the opening*; *a bridge across the river*). **3** at or forming an angle (esp. a right angle) with (*deep cuts across his legs*). ● *adv.* **1** to or on the other side (*ran across*; *shall soon be across*). **2** from one side to another (*a blanket stretched across*). **3** forming a cross (*with cuts across*). **4** (of a crossword clue or answer) read horizontally (*cannot do nine across*). □ **across the board** general; generally; applying to all. [Middle English from Old French *a croix*, *en croix* 'in, on a cross', later regarded as from A[2] + CROSS]

acrostic /əˈkrɒstɪk/ *n.* **1** a poem or other composition in which certain letters in each line form a word or words. **2** a word-puzzle constructed in this way. [French *acrostiche* or Greek *akrostikhis*, from *akron* 'end' + *stikhos* 'row, line of verse', assimilated to -IC]

acrylic /əˈkrɪlɪk/ *adj.* & *n.* ● *adj.* **1** made with a synthetic polymer derived from acrylic acid. **2** *Chem.* of or derived from acrylic acid. ● *n.* **1** an acrylic textile fibre. **2** (also in *pl.*) acrylic paint. [*acrolein* (from Latin *acer acris* 'pungent' + *olēre* 'to smell') + -YL + -IC]

acrylic acid *n.* a pungent liquid organic acid. Chem. formula: $C_3H_4O_2$.

acrylic resin *n.* any of various transparent colourless polymers of acrylic acid.

ACT *abbr.* Australian Capital Territory.

act /akt/ *n.* & *v.* ● *n.* **1** something done; a deed; an action. **2** the process of doing something (*caught in the act*). **3 a** a piece of entertainment, usu. one of a series in a programme. **b** the performer(s) of this. **4** a pretence; behaviour intended to deceive or impress (*it was all an act*). **5** a main division of a play or opera. **6 a** (also **Act**) a written ordinance of a parliament or other legislative body. **b** a document attesting a legal transaction. **7** (often in *pl.*) the recorded decisions or proceedings of a committee, an academic body, etc. **8** (**Acts**) (in full **Acts of the Apostles**) the New Testament book relating the growth of the early Church. ● *v.* **1** *intr.* behave (*see how they act under stress*). **2** *intr.* perform actions or functions; operate effectively; take action (*act as referee*; *the brakes failed to act*; *we must act quickly*). **3** *intr.* (also foll. by *on*) exert energy or influence (*the medicine soon began to act*; *alcohol acts on the brain*). **4** *intr.* **a** perform a part in a play, film, etc. **b** pretend. **5** *tr.* **a** perform the part of (*acted Othello*; *acts the fool*). **b** perform (a play etc.). **c** portray (an incident) by actions. **d** feign (*we acted indifference*). □ **act for** be the (esp. legal) representative of. **act of God** an instance of uncontrollable natural forces in operation. **act of grace** a privilege or concession that cannot be claimed as a right. **act on** (or **upon**) perform or carry out; put into operation (*acted on my advice*). **act out 1** translate (ideas etc.) into action. **2** *Psychol.* represent (one's subconscious desires etc.) in action. **act up** *colloq.* misbehave; give trouble (*my car is acting up again*). **get one's act together** *slang* become properly organized; make preparations for an undertaking etc. **get in on the act** *slang* become a participant (esp. for profit). **put on an act** *colloq.* carry out a pretence. □ **actable** *adj.* (in sense 5 of *v.*). **actability** /-ˈbɪlɪti/ *n.* (in sense 5 of *v.*). [Middle English, ultimately from Latin *agere act-* 'do']

ACTH *abbr.* adrenocorticotrophic hormone.

actin /ˈaktɪn/ *n.* a protein which with myosin forms the contractile filaments of muscle fibres. [Greek *aktis -inos* 'ray' + -IN]

acting /ˈaktɪŋ/ *n.* & *adj.* ● *n.* **1** the art or occupation of performing parts in plays, films, etc. **2** in senses of ACT *v.* ● *attrib.adj.* serving temporarily or on behalf of another or others (*acting manager*; *Acting Captain*).

acting pilot officer *n.* a rank in the RAF above warrant officer and below pilot officer.

actinia /ak'tɪnɪə/ *n.* (*pl.* **actiniae** /-nɪiː/) a sea anemone, esp. of the genus *Actinia*. [modern Latin, from Greek *aktis -inos* 'ray']

actinide /'aktɪnʌɪd/ *n.* (also **actinoid** /'aktɪnɔɪd/) *Chem.* any of the series of 15 radioactive elements of increasing atomic number from actinium (no. 89) to lawrencium (no. 103). [ACTINIUM + -IDE on the pattern of *lanthanide*]

actinide series *n. Chem.* the series of 15 radioactive elements from actinium to lawrencium.

actinism /'aktɪnɪz(ə)m/ *n.* the property of short-wave radiation that produces chemical changes, as in photography. □ **actinic** /ak'tɪnɪk/ *adj.* [Greek *aktis -inos* 'ray']

actinium /ak'tɪnɪəm/ *n. Chem.* a radioactive metallic element of the actinide series, occurring naturally in pitchblende (symbol **Ac**). [Greek *aktis -inos* 'ray' + -IUM]

actinoid var. of ACTINIDE.

actinometer /aktɪ'nɒmɪtə/ *n.* an instrument for measuring the intensity of radiation, esp. ultraviolet radiation. [Greek *aktis -inos* 'ray' + -METER]

actinomorphic /ˌaktɪnə'mɔːfɪk/ *adj. Biol.* radially symmetrical. [Greek *aktis, -inos* 'ray' + Greek *morphē* 'form']

actinomycete /ˌaktɪnə(ʊ)'mʌɪsiːt/ *n.* any of the usu. non-motile filamentous anaerobic bacteria of the order Actinomycetales. [Greek *aktis, -inos* 'ray' + *-mycetes* from Greek *mukēs -ētos* 'fungus']

action /'akʃ(ə)n/ *n. & v.* ● *n.* **1** the fact or process of doing or acting (*demanded action*; *put ideas into action*). **2** forcefulness or energy as a characteristic (*a woman of action*). **3** the exertion of energy or influence (*the action of acid on metal*). **4** something done; a deed or act (*not aware of his own actions*). **5 a** a series of events represented in a story, play, etc. **b** *slang* exciting activity (*arrived late and missed the action*; *want some action*). **6 a** armed conflict; fighting (*killed in action*). **b** an occurrence of this, esp. a minor military engagement. **7 a** the way in which a machine, instrument, etc. works (*explain the action of an air pump*). **b** the mechanism that makes a machine, instrument, etc. (e.g. a musical instrument, a gun, etc.) work. **c** the mode or style of movement of an animal or human (usu. described in some way) (*a runner with good action*). **8** a legal process; a lawsuit (*bring an action*). **9** (in *imper.*) a word of command to begin, esp. used by a film director etc. ● *v.tr.* bring a legal action against. □ **go into action** start work. **out of action** not working. **take action** begin to act (esp. energetically in protest). [Middle English via Old French from Latin *actio -onis* (as ACT)]

actionable /'akʃ(ə)nəb(ə)l/ *adj.* giving cause for legal action.

action committee *n.* (also **action group** etc.) a body formed to take active steps, esp. in politics.

action-packed *adj. colloq.* full of action or excitement.

action painting *n.* an aspect of abstract expressionism with paint applied by the artist's random or spontaneous gestures.

action point *n.* a proposal for action, esp. arising from a discussion etc.

action replay *n. Brit.* a playback of part of a television broadcast, esp. a sporting event, often in slow motion.

action research *n.* research carried out in the course of an activity or occupation, esp. education, to improve the methods and approach of those involved.

action stations *n.pl.* esp. *Brit.* positions taken up in readiness for action, esp. by troops preparing for battle.

activate /'aktɪveɪt/ *v.tr.* **1** make active; bring into action. **2** *Chem.* cause reaction in; excite (a substance, molecules, etc.). **3** *Physics* make radioactive. □ **activation** /-'veɪʃ(ə)n/ *n.* **activator** *n.*

activated carbon *n.* carbon, esp. charcoal, treated to increase its adsorptive power.

activated sludge *n.* aerated sewage containing aerobic micro-organisms to break it down.

active /'aktɪv/ *adj. & n.* ● *adj.* **1 a** consisting in or marked by action; energetic; diligent (*leads an active life*; *an active helper*). **b** able to move about or accomplish practical tasks (*infirmity made him less active*). **2** working, operative (*an active volcano*). **3** originating action; not merely passive or inert (*active support*; *active ingredients*). **4** radioactive. **5** *Gram.* designating the voice that attributes the action of a verb to the person or thing from which it logically proceeds (e.g. of the verbs in *guns kill*; *we saw him*). ● *n. Gram.* the active form or voice of a verb. □ **actively** *adv.* **activeness** *n.* [Middle English from Old French *actif -ive* or Latin *activus* (as ACT *v.*)]

active birth *n.* childbirth during which the mother is encouraged to be as active as possible, mainly by moving around freely and assuming any position which feels comfortable.

active carbon *n.* = ACTIVATED CARBON.

active citizen *n.* a person who plays an active role in the community, esp. by participating in crime prevention, self-help schemes, etc.

active duty *n.* participation in policing or military operational activities.

active matrix *n. Electronics* a display system in which each pixel is individually controlled (also *attrib.*: *active matrix LCD*).

active service *n.* participation in warfare as a member of the armed forces.

active transport *n. Biol.* the movement of ions or molecules across a cell membrane into a region of higher concentration, assisted by enzymes and requiring energy.

activism /'aktɪvɪz(ə)m/ *n.* a policy of vigorous action in a cause, esp. in politics. □ **activist** *n.*

activity /ak'tɪvɪti/ *n.* (*pl.* **-ies**) **1 a** the condition of being active or moving about. **b** the exertion of energy; vigorous action. **2** (often in *pl.*) a particular occupation or pursuit (*outdoor activities*). **3** = RADIOACTIVITY. [French *activité* or Late Latin *activitas* (as ACTIVE)]

Act of Supremacy *n. Brit. hist.* an act securing ecclesiastical supremacy to the Crown and excluding the authority of the Pope.

Act of Uniformity *n. Brit. hist.* any of four acts (esp. that of 1662) for securing uniformity in public worship and the use of a particular Book of Common Prayer.

actor /'aktə/ *n.* **1 a** a person who acts a part in a play etc. **b** a person whose profession is performing such parts. **2** a person who pretends to be something he or she is not. [Latin, = doer, actor (as ACT, -OR[1])]

actor-manager *n.* a person who is both manager of and actor in a theatre company.

actress /'aktrɪs/ *n.* a female actor.

actual /'aktjʊəl, -tʃʊəl/ *adj.* (usu. *attrib.*) **1** existing in fact; real (often as distinct from ideal). **2** existing now; current. □ **actualize** *v.tr.* (also **-ise**). **actualization** /-'zeɪʃ(ə)n/ *n.* [Middle English via Old French *actuel* from Late Latin *actualis*, from *actus* ACT *n.*]

■ **Usage** Redundant use, as in *Tell me the actual facts*, is common but to be avoided in formal contexts.

actual bodily harm *n.* injury, such as bruising, broken bones, etc., inflicted intentionally on a person but less serious than grievous bodily harm.

actuality /aktjʊ'alɪti, -tʃʊ-/ *n.* (*pl.* **-ies**) **1** reality; what is the case. **2** (in *pl.*) existing conditions. [Middle English from Old French *actualité* 'entity' or medieval Latin *actualitas* (as ACTUAL)]

actually /'aktjʊəli, -tʃʊ-/ *adv.* **1** as a fact, really (*I asked for ten, but actually got nine*). **2** as a matter of fact, even (strange as it may seem) (*he actually refused!*). **3** at present; for the time being.

actuary /'aktjʊəri, -tʃʊ-/ *n.* (*pl.* **-ies**) an expert in statistics and probability theory, esp. one who calculates insurance risks and premiums. □ **actuarial** /-'ɛːrɪəl/ *adj.* **actuarially** /-'ɛːrɪəli/ *adv.* [Latin *actuarius* 'bookkeeper' from *actus* ACT *n.*]

actuate /'aktjʊeɪt, -tʃʊ-/ *v.tr.* **1** communicate motion to (a machine etc.). **2** cause the operation of (an electrical device etc.). **3** cause (a person) to act. ▫ **actuation** /-'eɪʃ(ə)n/ *n.* **actuator** *n.* [medieval Latin *actuare* from Latin *actus* ACT *n.*]

acuity /ə'kju:ɪti/ *n.* sharpness, acuteness (of a needle, senses, understanding). [French *acuité* or medieval Latin *acuitas*, from *acuere* 'sharpen': see ACUTE]

aculeate /ə'kju:lɪət/ *adj. & n.* ● *adj.* **1** *Zool.* having a sting. **2** pointed, incisive. ● *n. Zool.* any hymenopteran insect of the section Aculeata, including bees, wasps, and ants. [Latin *aculeatus* from *aculeus* 'sting', diminutive of *acus* 'needle']

acumen /'akjʊmən, ə'kju:mən/ *n.* keen insight or discernment; penetration. [Latin *acumen -minis* 'point, acuteress' from *acuere* 'sharpen': see ACUTE]

acuminate /ə'kju:mɪnət/ *adj. Biol.* tapering to a point. [Latin *acuminatus* 'pointed' (as ACUMEN)]

acupressure /'akjʊprɛʃə/ *n.* = SHIATSU. [portmanteau word from ACUPUNCTURE + PRESSURE]

acupuncture /'akjʊpʌŋktʃə/ *n.* a method (originally Chinese) of treating various medical conditions by pricking the skin or tissues with needles. ▫ **acupuncturist** *n.* [Latin *acu* 'with a needle' + PUNCTURE]

acushla /ə'kʊʃlə/ *n. Ir.* darling. [Irish *a chuisle* (*moi chroi*) 'O pulse (of my heart)!']

acute /ə'kju:t/ *adj. & n.* ● *adj.* (**acuter**, **acutest**) **1** (of sensation or senses) keen, penetrating. **2** shrewd, perceptive (*an acute critic*). **3** (of a disease) coming sharply to a crisis; severe, not chronic. **4** (of a difficulty or controversy) critical, serious. **5 a** (of an angle) less than 90°. **b** sharp, pointed. **6** (of a sound) high, shrill. ● *n.* = ACUTE ACCENT. ▫ **acutely** *adv.* **acuteness** *n.* [Latin *acutus*, past part. of *acuere* 'sharpen' from *acus* 'needle']

acute accent *n.* a mark (´) placed over letters in some languages to show quality, vowel length, pronunciation (e.g. *maté*), etc.

acute rheumatism *n.* = RHEUMATIC FEVER.

ACW *abbr.* Aircraftwoman.

-acy /əsi/ *suffix* forming nouns of state or quality (*accuracy*; *piracy*; *supremacy*), or an instance of it (*conspiracy*; *fallacy*) (see also -CRACY). [a branch of the suffix -CY from or influenced by French *-acie*, Latin *-acia* or *-atia*, or Greek *-ateia*]

acyclovir /eɪ'sʌɪkləvʌɪə/ *n. Pharm.* an antiviral drug used esp. in the treatment of herpes and Aids.

acyl /'eɪsʌɪl, 'asɪl/ *n. Chem.* the monovalent radical of a carboxylic acid. [German (as ACID, -YL)]

AD *abbr.* (of a date) of the Christian era. [*Anno Domini*, 'in the year of the Lord']

■ **Usage** Strictly, AD should precede a date (e.g. AD 410), but uses such as *the tenth century* AD are well established.

ad /ad/ *n. colloq.* an advertisement. [abbreviation]

ad- /ad, əd/ *prefix* (also **a-** before *sc*, *sp*, *st*, **ac-** before *c*, *k*, *q*, **af-** before *f*, **ag-** before *g*, **al-** before *l*, **an-** before *n*, **ap-** before *p*, **ar-** before *r*, **as-** before *s*, **at-** before *t*) **1** with the sense of motion or direction to, reduction or change into, addition, adherence, increase, or intensification. **2** formed by assimilation of other prefixes (*accurse*; *admiral*; *advance*; *affray*). [(sense 1) (via Old French *a-*) from Latin *ad* 'to': (sense 2) *a-* representing various prefixes other than *ad-*]

-ad[1] /ad, əd/ *suffix* forming nouns: **1** in collective numerals (*myriad*; *triad*). **2** in fem. patronymics (*Dryad*). **3** in names of poems and similar compositions (*Iliad*; *Dunciad*; *jeremiad*). [Greek *-as -ada*]

-ad[2] /əd/ *suffix* forming nouns (*ballad*; *salad*) (cf. -ADE[1]). [French *-ade*]

adage /'adɪdʒ/ *n.* a traditional maxim; a proverb. [French from Latin *adagium* (as AD-, root of *aio* 'say')]

adagio /ə'dɑ:dʒɪəʊ/ *adv., adj., & n. Mus.* ● *adv. & adj.* in slow time. ● *n.* (*pl.* **-os**) an adagio movement or passage. [Italian, from *ad agio* 'at ease']

Adam[1] /'adəm/ *n.* the first man, in the biblical and Koranic traditions. ▫ **not know a person from Adam** be unable to recognize the person in question. [Hebrew *'ādām* 'man']

Adam[2] /'adəm/ *adj.* of the style of architecture, furniture, and design created by the Scottish brothers Robert and James Adam (18th c.).

adamant /'adəm(ə)nt/ *adj. & n.* ● *adj.* stubbornly resolute; resistant to persuasion. ● *n. archaic* diamond or other hard substance. ▫ **adamance** *n.* **adamantine** /-'mantʌɪn/ *adj.* **adamantly** *adv.* [Old French *adamaunt* via Latin *adamas adamant-* 'untameable' from Greek (as A-[1], *damaō* 'to tame')]

Adam's ale *n.* water.

Adam's apple *n.* the projection at the front of the neck formed by the thyroid cartilage of the larynx.

adapt /ə'dapt/ *v.* **1** *tr.* **a** (foll. by *to*) fit, adjust (one thing to another). **b** (foll. by *to*, *for*) make suitable for a purpose. **c** alter or modify (esp. a text). **d** arrange for broadcasting etc. **2** *intr. & refl.* (usu. foll. by *to*) become adjusted to new conditions. ▫ **adaptive** *adj.* [French *adapter* from Latin *adaptare* (as AD-, *aptare* from *aptus* 'fit')]

adaptable /ə'daptəb(ə)l/ *adj.* **1** able to adapt oneself to new conditions. **2** that can be adapted. ▫ **adaptability** /-'bɪlɪti/ *n.* **adaptably** *adv.*

adaptation /adəp'teɪʃ(ə)n/ *n.* **1** the act or process of adapting or being adapted. **2** a thing that has been adapted. **3** *Biol.* the process by which an organism or species becomes suited to its environment. [French, from Late Latin *adaptatio -onis* (as ADAPT)]

adaptive radiation *n. Biol.* the diversification of a group of organisms into forms filling different ecological niches.

adaptor /ə'daptə/ *n.* (also **adapter**) **1** a device for making equipment compatible. **2** *Brit.* a device for connecting several electrical plugs to one socket. **3** a person who adapts.

adaxial /a'daksɪəl/ *adj. Bot.* facing toward the stem of a plant, esp. designating the upper side of a leaf (cf. ABAXIAL). [AD- + AXIAL]

ADC *abbr.* **1** aide-de-camp. **2** analogue-digital converter.

add /ad/ *v.tr.* **1** join (one thing to another) as an increase or supplement (*add your efforts to mine*; *add insult to injury*). **2** put together (two or more numbers) to find a number denoting their combined value. **3** say in addition (*added a remark*; *added that I was wrong*; *'What's more, I don't like it,' he added*). ▫ **add in** include. **add to** increase; be a further item among (*this adds to our difficulties*). **add up 1** find the total of. **2** (foll. by *to*) amount to; constitute (*adds up to a disaster*). **3** *colloq.* make sense; be understandable. ▫ **added** *adj.* [Middle English from Latin *addere* (as AD-, *dare* 'put')]

addax /'adaks/ *n.* a large antelope, *Addax nasomaculatus*, of N. Africa, with twisted horns. [Latin, from an African word]

addendum /ə'dɛndəm/ *n.* (*pl.* **addenda** /-də/) **1** a thing (usu. something omitted) to be added, esp. (in *pl.*) as additional matter at the end of a book. **2** an appendix; an addition. [Latin, gerundive of *addere* ADD]

adder /'adə/ *n.* a small often venomous snake, esp. the common viper, *Vipera berus*, the only poisonous snake in Britain. [Old English *nædre*: *n* lost in Middle English by wrong division of *a naddre*: cf. APRON, AUGER, UMPIRE]

adder's tongue *n.* any of several plants, esp. a fern of the genus *Ophioglossum* or (*N. Amer.*) the dog's tooth violet.

addict *v. & n.* ● *v.tr. & refl.* /ə'dɪkt/ (usu. foll. by *to*) devote or apply habitually or compulsively; make addicted. ● *n.* /'adɪkt/ **1** a person addicted to a habit, esp. one dependent on a (specified) drug (*drug addict*; *heroin addict*). **2** *colloq.* an enthusiastic devotee of a sport or pastime (*film addict*). [originally as *adj.*, in the sense 'formally assigned or bound to': Latin *addicere* 'assign' (as AD-, *dicere dict-* 'say')]

addicted /ə'dɪktɪd/ *adj.* (often foll. by *to*) **1** dependent on as a habit; unable to do without a thing (*addicted to heroin*; *found he was addicted*). **2** devoted (*addicted to football*).

addiction /ə'dɪkʃ(ə)n/ *n.* the fact or process of being addicted, esp. the condition of taking a drug habitually and being unable to give it up without incurring adverse effects. [Latin *addictio*: see ADDICT]

addictive /ə'dɪktɪv/ *adj.* (of a drug, habit, etc.) causing addiction or dependence.

Addison's disease /'adɪs(ə)nz dɪˌzi:z/ *n.* a condition caused by an adrenal deficiency and marked by weakness, low blood pressure, and brown discoloration of the skin. [named after T. *Addison*, English physician d. 1860, who first recognized it]

addition /ə'dɪʃ(ə)n/ *n.* **1** the act or process of adding or being added. **2** a person or thing added (*a useful addition to the team*). □ **in addition** (often foll. by *to*) as something added. [Middle English from Old French *addition* or from Latin *additio* (as ADD)]

additional /ə'dɪʃ(ə)n(ə)l/ *adj.* added, extra, supplementary. □ **additionally** *adv.*

additive /'adɪtɪv/ *n.* & *adj.* ● *n.* a thing added, esp. a substance added to another so as to give it specific qualities (*food additive*). ● *adj.* **1** characterized by addition (*additive process*). **2** to be added. [Late Latin *additivus* (as ADD)]

addle /'ad(ə)l/ *v.* & *adj.* ● *v.* **1** *tr.* muddle, confuse. **2** *intr.* (of an egg) become addled. ● *adj.* **1** (in *comb.*) muddled, unsound (*addle-brained*; *addle-head*). **2** empty, vain. **3** (of an egg) addled. [Old English *adela* 'filth', used as adj., then as verb]

addled /'ad(ə)ld/ *adj.* **1** (of an egg) rotten, producing no chick. **2** muddled. [ADDLE *adj.*, assimilated to past part. form]

add-on *n.* something added to an existing object or quantity (also *attrib.*: *several add-on features are available*).

address /ə'drɛs/ *n.* & *v.* ● *n.* **1 a** the place where a person lives or an organization is situated. **b** particulars of this, esp. for postal purposes. **c** *Computing* the location of an item of stored information. **2** a discourse delivered to an audience. **3** skill, dexterity, readiness. **4** (in *pl.*) a courteous approach; courtship (*pay one's addresses to*). **5** *archaic* manner in conversation. ● *v.tr.* **1** write directions for delivery (esp. the name and address of the intended recipient) on (an envelope, packet, etc.). **2** direct in speech or writing (remarks, a protest, etc.). **3** speak or write to, esp. formally (*addressed the audience*; *asked me how to address a duke*). **4** direct one's attention to. **5** *Golf* take aim at or prepare to hit (the ball). □ **address oneself to 1** speak or write to. **2** attend to. □ **addressable** *adj.* **addresser** *n.* [Middle English from Old French *adresser*, ultimately from Latin (as AD-, *directus* DIRECT): the noun perhaps from French *adresse*]

addressee /adrɛ'si:/ *n.* the person to whom something (esp. a letter) is addressed.

Addressograph /ə'drɛsəgrɑ:f/ *n. propr.* a machine for printing addresses on envelopes.

adduce /ə'dju:s/ *v.tr.* cite as an instance or as proof or evidence. □ **adducible** *adj.* [Latin *adducere adduct-* (as AD-, *ducere* 'lead')]

adduct /ə'dʌkt/ *v.tr.* draw towards a middle line, esp. draw (a limb) towards the midline of the body. □ **adduction** *n.* **adductor** *n.*

-ade[1] /eɪd/ *suffix* forming nouns: **1** an action done (*blockade*; *tirade*). **2** the body concerned in an action or process (*cavalcade*). **3** the product or result of a material or action (*arcade*; *lemonade*; *masquerade*). [from or influenced by French *-ade*, via Provençal, Spanish, or Portuguese *-ada* or Italian *-ata* from Latin *-ata*, fem. sing. past part. of verbs ending in *-are*]

-ade[2] /eɪd/ *suffix* forming nouns (*decade*) (cf. -AD[1]). [French *-ade* from Greek *-as -ada*]

-ade[3] /eɪd/ *suffix* forming nouns: **1** = -ADE[1] (*brocade*). **2** a person concerned (*renegade*). [Spanish or Portuguese *-ado*, masc. form of *-ada*: see -ADE[1]]

adenine /'adɪni:n/ *n.* a purine derivative found in all living tissue as a component base of DNA or RNA. [German *Adenin* from Greek *adēn* 'gland': see -INE[4]]

adenoids /'adɪnɔɪdz/ *n.pl. Med.* a mass of enlarged lymphatic tissue between the back of the nose and the throat, often hindering speaking and breathing in the young. □ **adenoidal** /-'nɔɪd(ə)l/ *adj.* [Greek *adēn* 'gland' + -OID]

adenoma /adɪ'nəʊmə/ *n.* (*pl.* **adenomas** or **adenomata** /-mətə/) a glandlike benign tumour. [modern Latin from Greek *adēn* 'gland' + -OMA]

adenosine /ə'dɛnəʊsi:n/ *n.* a nucleoside of adenine and ribose present in all living tissue in combined form. [ADENINE + RIBOSE]

adenosine triphosphate *n.* a nucleotide important in living cells, whose breakdown to the diphosphate provides energy for physiological processes (abbr.: ATP).

adept *adj.* & *n.* ● *adj.* /'adɛpt, ə'dɛpt/ (foll. by *at*, *in*) thoroughly proficient. ● *n.* /'adɛpt/ a skilled performer; an expert. □ **adeptly** *adv.* **adeptness** *n.* [Latin *adeptus*, past part. of *adipisci* 'attain']

adequate /'adɪkwət/ *adj.* **1** sufficient, satisfactory (often with the implication of being barely so). **2** (foll. by *to*) proportionate. **3** barely sufficient. □ **adequacy** *n.* **adequately** *adv.* [Latin *adaequatus*, past part. of *adaequare* 'make equal' (as AD-, *aequus* 'equal')]

à deux /ɑ: 'də:, French a dø/ *adv.* & *adj.* **1** for two. **2** between two. [French]

ad fin. /ad 'fɪn/ *abbr.* at or near the end. [Latin *ad finem*]

adhere /əd'hɪə/ *v.intr.* **1** (usu. foll. by *to*) (of a substance) stick fast to a surface, another substance, etc. **2** (foll. by *to*) behave according to; follow in detail (*adhered to our plan*). **3** (foll. by *to*) give support or allegiance to. [French *adhérer* or Latin *adhaerēre* (as AD-, *haerēre haes-* 'stick')]

adherent /əd'hɪər(ə)nt/ *n.* & *adj.* ● *n.* **1** a supporter of a party, person, etc. **2** a devotee of an activity. ● *adj.* **1** (foll. by *to*) faithfully observing a rule etc. **2** (often foll. by *to*) (of a substance) sticking fast. □ **adherence** *n.* [French *adhérent* (as ADHERE)]

■ **Usage** See Usage Note at ADHESION.

adhesion /əd'hi:ʒ(ə)n/ *n.* **1** the act or process of adhering. **2** the capacity of a substance to stick fast. **3** *Med.* an abnormal union of surfaces due to inflammation or injury. **4** the maintenance of contact between the wheels of a vehicle and the road. **5** the giving of support or allegiance. [French *adhésion* or Latin *adhaesio* (as ADHERE)]

■ **Usage** Adhesion is more common in physical senses (e.g. *The glue has good adhesion*), with *adherence* used in abstract senses (e.g. *adherence to principles*).

adhesive /əd'hi:sɪv, -zɪv/ *adj.* & *n.* ● *adj.* sticky, enabling surfaces or substances to adhere to one another. ● *n.* an adhesive substance, esp. one used to stick other substances together. □ **adhesively** *adv.* **adhesiveness** *n.* [French *adhésif -ive* (as ADHERE)]

adhibit /əd'hɪbɪt/ *v.tr.* (**adhibited**, **adhibiting**) **1** affix. **2** apply or administer (a remedy). □ **adhibition** /adhɪ'bɪʃ(ə)n/ *n.* [Latin *adhibēre adhibit-* (as AD-, *habēre* 'have')]

ad hoc /ad 'hɒk/ *adv.* & *adj.* for a particular (usu. exclusive) purpose (*an ad hoc appointment*). [Latin, = to this]

ad hominem /ad 'hɒmɪnɛm/ *adv.* & *adj.* **1** relating to or associated with a particular person. **2** (of an argument) appealing to the emotions and not to reason. [Latin, = to the person]

adiabatic /ˌeɪdʌɪə'batɪk, ˌadɪə-/ *adj.* & *n. Physics* ● *adj.* **1** impassable to heat. **2** occurring without heat entering or leaving the system. ● *n.* a curve or formula for adiabatic phenomena. ◻ **adiabatically** *adv.* [Greek *adiabatos* 'impassable' (as A-[1], *diabainō* 'pass')]

adieu /ə'dju:/ *int. & n.* ● *int.* goodbye. ● *n.* (*pl.* **adieus** or **adieux** /ə'dju:z/) a goodbye. [Middle English from Old French, from *à* 'to' + *Dieu* 'God']

ad infinitum /ad ɪnfɪ'nʌɪtəm/ *adv.* without limit; for ever. [Latin, = to infinity]

ad interim /ad 'ɪntərɪm/ *adv. & adj.* for the meantime. [Latin]

adios /adɪ'ɒs/ *int.* goodbye. [Spanish *adiós*, from *a* 'to' + *Dios* 'God']

adipocere /adɪpə(ʊ)'sɪə/ *n.* a greyish fatty or soapy substance generated in dead bodies subjected to moisture. [French *adipocire*, from Latin *adeps adipis* 'fat' + French *cire* 'wax' from Latin *cera*]

adipose /'adɪpəʊs, -z/ *adj.* of or characterized by fat, esp. as stored in the body tissues; fatty. ◻ **adiposity** /-'pɒsɪti/ *n.* [modern Latin *adiposus* from *adeps adipis* 'fat']

adit /'adɪt/ *n.* **1** a horizontal entrance or passage in a mine. **2** a means of approach. [Latin *aditus* (as AD-, *itus* from *ire it-* 'go')]

Adivasi /ɑ:dɪ'vɑ:si/ *n.* (*pl.* **Adivasis**) a member of the aboriginal tribal peoples of India. [Hindi *ādivāsī* 'original inhabitant']

Adj. /adʒ/ *abbr.* (preceding a name) Adjutant.

adjacent /ə'dʒeɪs(ə)nt/ *adj.* (often foll. by *to*) lying near or adjoining. ◻ **adjacency** *n.* [Middle English from Latin *adjacēre* (as AD-, *jacēre* 'lie')]

adjective /'adʒɪktɪv/ *n. & adj.* ● *n.* a word or phrase naming an attribute, added to or grammatically related to a noun to modify it or describe it. ● *adj.* additional; not standing by itself; dependent. ◻ **adjectival** /adʒɪk'tʌɪv(ə)l/ *adj.* **adjectivally** /adʒɪk'tʌɪv(ə)li/ *adv.* [Middle English from Old French *adjectif -ive*, ultimately from Latin *adjicere adject-* 'throw to, add, attribute' in the phrase *nomen adjectivus* 'attributive noun' (as AD-, *jacere* 'throw')]

adjoin /ə'dʒɔɪn/ *v.tr.* **1** be next to and joined with. **2** *archaic* = ADD 1. [Middle English via Old French *ajoindre, ajoign-* from Latin *adjungere adjunct-* (as AD-, *jungere* 'join')]

adjourn /ə'dʒə:n/ *v.* **1** *tr.* **a** put off; postpone. **b** break off (a meeting, discussion, etc.) with the intention of resuming later. **2** *intr.* of persons at a meeting: **a** break off proceedings and disperse. **b** (foll. by *to*) transfer the meeting to another place. [Middle English from Old French *ajorner* (as AD-, *jorn* 'day', ultimately from Latin *diurnus* DIURNAL): cf. JOURNAL, JOURNEY]

adjournment /ə'dʒə:nm(ə)nt/ *n.* adjourning or being adjourned.

adjournment debate *n. Brit.* a debate in the House of Commons on the motion that the House be adjourned, used as an opportunity for raising various matters.

adjudge /ə'dʒʌdʒ/ *v.tr.* **1** adjudicate (a matter). **2** (often foll. by *that* + clause, or *to* + infin.) pronounce judicially. **3** (foll. by *to*) award judicially. **4** *archaic* condemn. ◻ **adjudgement** *n.* (also **adjudgment**). [Middle English via Old French *ajuger* from Latin *adjudicare*: see ADJUDICATE]

adjudicate /ə'dʒu:dɪkeɪt/ *v.* **1** *intr.* act as judge in a competition, court, tribunal, etc. **2** *tr.* **a** decide judicially regarding (a claim etc.). **b** (foll. by *to be* + compl.) pronounce (*was adjudicated to be bankrupt*). ◻ **adjudication** /-'keɪʃ(ə)n/ *n.* **adjudicative** *adj.* **adjudicator** *n.* [Latin *adjudicare* (as AD-, *judicare* from *judex -icis* 'judge')]

adjunct /'adʒʌŋ(k)t/ *n.* **1** (foll. by *to, of*) a subordinate or incidental thing. **2** an assistant; a subordinate person, esp. one with temporary appointment only. **3** *Gram.* a word or phrase used to amplify or modify the meaning of another word or words in a sentence. ◻ **adjunctive** /ə'dʒʌŋ(k)tɪv/ *adj.* [Latin *adjunctus*: see ADJOIN]

adjure /ə'dʒʊə/ *v.tr.* (usu. foll. by *to* + infin.) charge or request (a person) solemnly or earnestly, esp. under oath. ◻ **adjuration** /adʒʊə'reɪʃ(ə)n/ *n.* **adjuratory** /-rət(ə)ri/ *adj.* [Middle English from Latin *adjurare* (as AD-, *jurare* 'swear') in Late Latin sense 'put a person to an oath']

adjust /ə'dʒʌst/ *v.* **1** *tr.* **a** arrange; put in the correct order or position. **b** regulate, esp. by a small amount. **2** *tr.* (usu. foll. by *to*) make suitable. **3** *tr.* harmonize (discrepancies). **4** *tr.* assess (loss or damages). **5** *intr.* (usu. foll. by *to*) make oneself suited to; become familiar with (*adjust to one's surroundings*). ◻ **adjustable** *adj.* **adjustability** /-'bɪlɪti/ *n.* **adjuster** *n.* **adjustment** *n.* [French *adjuster* from Old French *ajoster*, ultimately from Latin *juxta* 'near']

adjutant /'adʒʊt(ə)nt/ *n.* **1 a** *Mil.* an officer who assists superior officers by communicating orders, conducting correspondence, etc. **b** an assistant. **2** (in full **adjutant bird**) a large black and white S. Asian stork of the genus *Leptoptilos*. ◻ **adjutancy** *n.* [Latin *adjutare*, frequentative of *adjuvare*: see ADJUVANT]

Adjutant General *n.* (*pl.* **Adjutant Generals**) a high-ranking army administrative officer.

adjuvant /'adʒʊv(ə)nt/ *adj. & n.* ● *adj.* **1** helpful, auxiliary. **2** *Med.* (of therapy) applied after initial treatment for cancer, esp. to suppress secondary tumour formation. ● *n.* **1** an adjuvant person or thing. **2** *Med.* a substance which enhances the body's immune response to an antigen. [French *adjuvant* or Latin *adjuvare* (as AD-, *juvare jut-* 'help')]

Adlerian /ad'lɪərɪən/ *adj.* of or relating to A. Adler, Austrian psychologist d. 1937, or his system of psychology.

ad lib /ad 'lɪb/ *v., adj., adv., & n.* ● *v.intr.* (**ad libbed, ad libbing**) speak or perform without formal preparation; improvise. ● *adj.* improvised. ● *adv.* as one pleases; to any desired extent. ● *n.* something spoken or played extempore. [abbreviation of AD LIBITUM]

ad libitum /ad 'lɪbɪtəm/ *adv.* = AD LIB *adv.* [Latin, = according to pleasure]

ad litem /ad 'lʌɪtɛm/ *adj.* (of a guardian etc.) appointed for a lawsuit. [Latin]

Adm. *abbr.* (preceding a name) Admiral.

adman /'adman/ *n.* (*pl.* **admen**) *colloq.* a person who produces advertisements commercially.

admass /'admas/ *n.* esp. *Brit.* the section of the community that is regarded as readily influenced by advertising and mass communication.

admeasure /əd'mɛʒə/ *v.tr. archaic* apportion; assign in due shares. ◻ **admeasurement** *n.* [Middle English via Old French *amesurer* from medieval Latin *admensurare* (as AD-, MEASURE)]

admin /'admɪn/ *n. Brit. colloq.* administration. [abbreviation]

adminicle /əd'mɪnɪk(ə)l/ *n.* **1** a thing that helps. **2** (in Scottish law) collateral evidence of the contents of a missing document. ◻ **adminicular** /admɪ'nɪkjʊlə/ *adj.* [Latin *adminiculum* 'prop']

administer /əd'mɪnɪstə/ *v.* **1** *tr.* attend to the running of (business affairs etc.); manage. **2** *tr.* **a** be responsible for the implementation of (the law, justice, punishment, etc.). **b** *Eccl.* give out, or perform the rites of (a sacrament). **c** (usu. foll. by *to*) direct the taking of (an oath). **3** *tr.* **a** provide, apply (a remedy). **b** give, deliver (a rebuke). **4** *intr.* act as administrator. ◻ **administrable** *adj.* [Middle English via Old French *aministrer* from Latin *administrare* (as AD-, MINISTER)]

administrate /əd'mɪnɪstreɪt/ *v.tr. & intr.* administer (esp. business affairs); act as an administrator. [Latin *administrare* (as ADMINISTER)]

administration /ədmɪnɪ'streɪʃ(ə)n/ *n.* **1 a** management of a business, institution, etc. **b** (prec. by *the*) *N. Amer.* the people responsible for this, regarded collectively. **2** the management of public affairs; government. **3** the government in power; the ministry. **4** *N. Amer.* the term of office of a political leader or government. **5** (**Administration**) (in the US) a government agency (*the Food and Drug Administration*). **6** *Law* the management of another person's estate. **7** (foll. by *of*) **a** the administering of justice, an oath, etc. **b** application of remedies. [Middle English, from Old French *administration* or Latin *administratio* (as ADMINISTRATE)]

administrative /əd'mɪnɪstrətɪv/ *adj.* concerning or relating to the management of affairs. □ **administratively** *adv.* [French *administratif -ive* or Latin *administrativus* (as ADMINISTRATION)]

administrator /əd'mɪnɪstreɪtə/ *n.* **1** a person who administers a business or public affairs. **2** a person capable of organizing (*is no administrator*). **3** *Law* a person appointed to manage the estate of a person who has died intestate. **4** a person who performs official duties in some sphere, e.g. in religion or justice. □ **administratorship** *n.* **administratrix** *n.* [Latin (as ADMINISTER)]

admirable /'adm(ə)rəb(ə)l/ *adj.* **1** deserving admiration. **2** excellent. □ **admirably** *adv.* [French, from Latin *admirabilis* (as ADMIRE)]

admiral /'adm(ə)r(ə)l/ *n.* **1 a** the commander-in-chief of a country's navy. **b** a naval officer of high rank; the commander of a fleet or naval squadron. **c** (**Admiral**) an admiral of the second grade. **2** a boldly patterned nymphalid butterfly (*red admiral*; *white admiral*). □ **admiralship** *n.* [Middle English via Old French *a(d)mira(i)l* etc. and medieval Latin *a(d)miralis* etc., from Arabic *'amīr* 'commander' (cf. AMIR), associated with ADMIRABLE]

Admiral of the Fleet *n.* an admiral of the first grade.

Admiralty /'adm(ə)r(ə)lti/ *n.* (*pl.* **-ies**) **1** (*hist.* except in titles) (in the UK) the department administering the Royal Navy. **2** (**admiralty**) *Law* the maritime branch of the administration of justice. [Middle English from Old French *admiral(i)té* (as ADMIRAL)]

Admiralty Board *n. Brit. hist.* a committee of the Ministry of Defence superintending the Royal Navy.

admiration /admə'reɪʃ(ə)n/ *n.* **1** pleased contemplation. **2** respect; warm approval. **3** an object of this (*was the admiration of the whole town*). [French *admiration* or Latin *admiratio* (as ADMIRE)]

admire /əd'mʌɪə/ *v.tr.* **1** regard with approval, respect, or satisfaction. **2** express one's admiration of. [French *admirer* or Latin *admirari* (as AD-, *mirari* 'wonder at')]

admirer /əd'mʌɪərə/ *n.* **1** a woman's suitor. **2** a person who admires, esp. a devotee of an able or famous person.

admiring /əd'mʌɪərɪŋ/ *adj.* showing or feeling admiration (*an admiring follower*; *admiring glances*). □ **admiringly** *adv.*

admissible /əd'mɪsɪb(ə)l/ *adj.* **1** (of an idea or plan) worth accepting or considering. **2** *Law* allowable as evidence. **3** (foll. by *to*) capable of being admitted. □ **admissibility** /-'bɪlɪti/ *n.* [French *admissible* or medieval Latin *admissibilis* (as ADMIT)]

admission /əd'mɪʃ(ə)n/ *n.* **1** an acknowledgement (*admission of error*; *admission that he was wrong*). **2 a** the process or right of entering or being admitted. **b** a charge for this (*admission is £5*). **3** a person admitted to a hospital. [Middle English from Latin *admissio* (as ADMIT)]

admit /əd'mɪt/ *v.* (**admitted**, **admitting**) **1** *tr.* **a** (often foll. by *to be*, or *that* + clause) acknowledge; recognize as true. **b** accept as valid or true. **2** *intr.* (foll. by *to*) acknowledge responsibility for (a deed, fault, etc.). **3** *tr.* **a** allow (a person) entrance or access. **b** allow (a person) to be a member of (a class, group, etc.) or to share in (a privilege etc.). **c** (of a hospital etc.) bring in (a person) for residential treatment. **4** *tr.* (of an enclosed space) have room for; accommodate. **5** *intr.* (foll. by *of*) allow as possible. [Middle English from Latin *admittere admiss-* (as AD-, *mittere* 'send')]

admittance /əd'mɪt(ə)ns/ *n.* **1** the right or process of admitting or being admitted, usu. to a place (*no admittance except on business*). **2** *Electr.* a measure of electrical conduction, the reciprocal of impedance.

admittedly /əd'mɪtɪdli/ *adv.* as an acknowledged fact (*admittedly there are problems*).

admix /'admɪks/ *v.* **1** *tr. & intr.* (foll. by *with*) mingle. **2** *tr.* add as an ingredient.

admixture /əd'mɪkstʃə/ *n.* **1** a thing added, esp. a minor ingredient. **2** the act of adding this. [Latin *admixtus*, past part. of *admiscēre* (as AD-, *miscēre* 'mix')]

admonish /əd'mɒnɪʃ/ *v.tr.* **1** reprove. **2** (foll. by *to* + infin., or *that* + clause) urge. **3** give earnest advice to. **4** (foll. by *of*) warn. □ **admonishment** *n.* **admonition** /admə'nɪʃ(ə)n/ *n.* **admonitory** *adj.* [Middle English from Old French *amonester*, ultimately from Latin *admonēre* (as AD-, *monēre monit-* 'warn')]

ad nauseam /ad 'nɔːzɪam, -sɪam/ *adv.* to an excessive or disgusting degree. [Latin, = to sickness]

adnominal /əd'nɒmɪn(ə)l/ *adj. Gram.* attached to a noun. [Latin *adnomen -minis* 'added name']

Adnyamathanha /'adnjəmʌdənə/ *n.* an Aboriginal language of S. Australia.

ado /ə'duː/ *n.* busy activity; fuss, trouble, difficulty. □ **without more** (or **further**) **ado** immediately. [originally in *much ado* = much to do, from northern Middle English *at do* (= to do), from Old Norse *at* AT (used to mark an infinitive) + DO[1]]

-ado /'eɪdəʊ, 'ɑː-/ *suffix* forming nouns (*desperado*) (cf. -ADE[3]). [Spanish or Portuguese *-ado* from Latin *-atus*, past part. of verbs ending in *-are*]

adobe /ə'dəʊbi, ə'dəʊb/ *n.* **1** an unburnt sun-dried brick. **2** the clay used for making such bricks. [Spanish from Arabic]

adolescent /adə'lɛs(ə)nt/ *adj. & n.* ● *adj.* between childhood and adulthood. ● *n.* an adolescent person. □ **adolescence** *n.* [Middle English via Old French from Latin *adolescere* 'grow up']

Adonis /ə'dəʊnɪs/ *n.* a handsome young man. [the name of a youth loved by Venus: Latin via Greek from Phoenician *adōn* 'lord']

Adonis blue *n.* a European butterfly, *Lysandra bellargus*.

adopt /ə'dɒpt/ *v.tr.* **1** take (a person) into a relationship, esp. another's child as one's own. **2** choose to follow (a course of action etc.). **3** take over (an idea etc.) from another person. **4** *Brit.* choose as a candidate for office. **5** *Brit.* (of a local authority) accept responsibility for the maintenance of (a road etc.). **6** accept; formally approve (a report, accounts, etc.). □ **adoption** /-pʃ(ə)n/ *n.* [French *adopter* or Latin *adoptare* (as AD-, *optare* 'choose')]

adoptive /ə'dɒptɪv/ *attrib.adj.* as a result of adoption (*adoptive son*; *adoptive father*). □ **adoptively** *adv.* [Middle English via Old French *adoptif -ive* from Latin *adoptivus* (as ADOPT)]

adorable /ə'dɔːrəb(ə)l/ *adj.* **1** deserving adoration. **2** *colloq.* delightful, charming. □ **adorably** *adv.* [French from Latin *adorabilis* (as ADORE)]

adore /ə'dɔː/ *v.tr.* **1** regard with honour and deep affection. **2 a** worship as divine. **b** *RC Ch.* offer reverence to (the Host etc.). **3** *colloq.* like very much. □ **adoration** /adə'reɪʃ(ə)n/ *n.* **adoring** *adj.* **adoringly** *adv.* [Middle English via Old French *ao(u)rer* from Latin *adorare* 'worship' (as AD-, *orare* 'speak, pray')]

adorer /ə'dɔːrə/ *n.* **1** a worshipper. **2** an ardent admirer.

adorn /ə'dɔːn/ *v.tr.* **1** add beauty or lustre to; be an ornament to. **2** furnish with ornaments; decorate. □ **adornment** *n.* [Middle English via Old French *ao(u)rner* from Latin *adornare* (as AD-, *ornare* 'furnish, deck')]

ADP *abbr.* **1** adenosine diphosphate. **2** automatic data processing.

ad personam /ad pəː'səʊnam/ *adv. & adj.* ● *adv.* to the person. ● *adj.* personal. [Latin]

ad rem /ad 'rɛm/ *adv. & adj.* to the point; to the purpose. [Latin, = to the matter]

adrenal /ə'driːn(ə)l/ *adj. & n.* ● *adj.* **1** at or near the kidneys. **2** of the adrenal glands. ● *n.* (in full **adrenal**

gland) either of two ductless glands above the kidneys, secreting adrenalin, corticosteroids, etc. [AD- + RENAL]

adrenal cortex *n. Anat.* the outer part of the adrenal glands, secreting corticosteroids etc.

adrenalin /əˈdrɛn(ə)lɪn/ *n.* (also **adrenaline**) **1** a hormone secreted by the adrenal glands, affecting circulation and muscular action, and causing excitement and stimulation. **2** the same substance obtained from animals or by synthesis, used as a stimulant.

adrenocorticotrophic hormone /əˌdriːnəˌkɔːtɪkəˈtrɒfɪk/ *n.* (also **adrenocorticotropic hormone** /-ˈtrɒpɪk/) a hormone secreted by the pituitary gland and stimulating the adrenal cortex (abbr.: **ACTH**). [ADRENAL + CORTEX + -TROPHIC, -TROPIC]

adrenocorticotrophin /əˌdriːnəˌkɔːtɪkəˈtrɒfɪn/ *n.* (also **adrenocorticotropin** /-pɪn/) = ADRENOCORTICOTROPHIC HORMONE. [ADRENOCORTICOTROPHIC (HORMONE) + -IN]

adrift /əˈdrɪft/ *adv. & predic.adj.* **1** drifting. **2** at the mercy of circumstances. **3** *Brit. colloq.* **a** unfastened. **b** out of touch. **c** absent without leave. **d** (often foll. by *of*) failing to reach a target. **e** out of order. **f** ill-informed. [A[2] + DRIFT]

adroit /əˈdrɔɪt/ *adj.* dexterous, skilful. □ **adroitly** *adv.* **adroitness** *n.* [French from *à droit* 'according to right, properly']

adsorb /ədˈsɔːb, -ˈzɔːb/ *v.tr.* (usu. of a solid) hold (molecules of a gas or liquid or solute) to its surface, causing a thin film to form. □ **adsorbable** *adj.* **adsorbent** *adj. & n.* **adsorption** /-ˈsɔːpʃ(ə)n, -ˈzɔːpʃ(ə)n/ *n.* (also **adsorbtion**). **adsorptive** *adj.* [AD-, on the pattern of ABSORB]

adsorbate /adˈsɔːbeɪt/ *n.* a substance adsorbed.

adsuki var. of ADZUKI.

ADT *abbr.* Atlantic Daylight Time (one hour ahead of Atlantic Standard Time).

aduki var. of ADZUKI.

adulate /ˈadjʊleɪt/ *v.tr.* flatter obsequiously. □ **adulation** /-ˈleɪʃ(ə)n/ *n.* **adulator** *n.* **adulatory** *adj.* [Latin *adulari adulat-* 'fawn on']

adult /ˈadʌlt, əˈdʌlt/ *adj. & n.* ● *adj.* **1** mature, grown-up. **2 a** of or for adults (*adult education*). **b** *euphem.* sexually explicit; indecent (*adult films*). ● *n.* **1** an adult person. **2** *Law* a person who has reached the age of majority. □ **adulthood** *n.* **adultly** *adv.* [Latin *adultus*, past part. of *adolescere* 'grow up': cf. ADOLESCENT]

adulterant /əˈdʌlt(ə)r(ə)nt/ *adj. & n.* ● *adj.* used in adulterating. ● *n.* an adulterant substance.

adulterate *v. & adj.* ● *v.tr.* /əˈdʌltəreɪt/ debase (esp. foods) by adding other or inferior substances. ● *adj.* /əˈdʌlt(ə)rət/ spurious, debased, counterfeit. □ **adulteration** /-ˈreɪʃ(ə)n/ *n.* **adulterator** *n.* [Latin *adulterare adulterat-* 'corrupt']

adulterer /əˈdʌlt(ə)rə/ *n.* (*fem.* **adulteress** /-(ə)rɪs/) a person who commits adultery. [obsolete verb *adulter* via Old French *avoutrer* from Latin *adulterare*: see ADULTERATE]

adulterine /əˈdʌlt(ə)rʌɪn/ *adj.* **1** illegal, unlicensed. **2** spurious. **3** born of adultery. [Latin *adulterinus* from *adulter* 'adulterous': see ADULTERY]

adulterous /əˈdʌlt(ə)rəs/ *adj.* of or involved in adultery. □ **adulterously** *adv.* [Middle English from obsolete noun *adulter*, from Old French *avoutrer*: see ADULTERER]

adultery /əˈdʌlt(ə)ri/ *n.* (*pl.* **-ies**) **1** voluntary sexual intercourse between a married person and a person (married or not) other than his or her spouse. **2** an instance of this. [Middle English from Old French *avout(e)rie*, from *avoutre* 'adulterer' from Latin *adulter*, assimilated to Latin *adulterium*]

adumbrate /ˈadʌmbreɪt/ *v.tr.* **1** indicate faintly. **2** represent in outline. **3** foreshadow, typify. **4** overshadow. □ **adumbration** /-ˈbreɪʃ(ə)n/ *n.* **adumbrative** /əˈdʌmbrətɪv/ *adj.* [Latin *adumbrare* (as AD-, *umbrare* from *umbra* 'shade')]

ad valorem /ad vəˈlɔːrɛm/ *adv. & adj.* (of taxes) in proportion to the estimated value of the goods concerned. [Latin, = according to the value]

advance /ədˈvɑːns/ *v., n., & adj.* ● *v.* **1** *tr. & intr.* move or put forward. **2** *intr.* make progress. **3** *tr.* **a** pay (money) before it is due. **b** lend (money). **4** *tr.* give active support to; promote (a person, cause, or plan). **5** *tr.* put forward (a claim or suggestion). **6** *tr.* cause (an event) to occur at an earlier date (*advanced the meeting three hours*). **7** *tr.* raise (a price). **8** *intr.* rise (in price). **9** *tr.* (as **advanced** *adj.*) **a** far on in progress (*the work is well advanced*). **b** ahead of the times (*advanced ideas*). ● *n.* **1** an act of going forward. **2** progress. **3** a payment made before the due time. **4** a loan. **5** (esp. in *pl.*; often foll. by *to*) an amorous or friendly approach. **6** a rise in price. ● *attrib.adj.* done or supplied beforehand (*advance warning*; *advance copy*). □ **advance on** approach threateningly. **in advance** ahead in place or time. □ **advancer** *n.* [Middle English via Old French *avancer* and Late Latin *abante* 'in front' from Latin *ab* 'away' + *ante* 'before': the noun partly through French *avance*]

advanced level *n.* (in the UK except Scotland) a GCE examination of a standard higher than ordinary level and GCSE.

advanced supplementary level *n.* (in the UK except Scotland) a GCE examination with a smaller syllabus than A levels.

advance guard *n.* a body of soldiers preceding the main body of an army.

advance man *n.* esp. *N. Amer.* a person who visits a location ahead of a dignitary etc. to make appropriate arrangements.

advancement /ədˈvɑːnsm(ə)nt/ *n.* the promotion of a person, cause, or plan. [Middle English from French *avancement*, from *avancer* (as ADVANCE)]

advantage /ədˈvɑːntɪdʒ/ *n. & v.* ● *n.* **1** a beneficial feature; a favourable circumstance. **2** benefit, profit (*is not to your advantage*). **3** (often foll. by *over*) a better position; superiority in a particular respect. **4** *Tennis* the next point won after deuce. ● *v.tr.* **1** be beneficial or favourable to. **2** further, promote. □ **have the advantage of** be in a better position in some respect than. **take advantage of 1** make good use of (a favourable circumstance). **2** exploit or outwit (a person), esp. unfairly. **3** *euphem.* seduce. **to advantage** in a way which exhibits the merits (*was seen to advantage*). **turn to advantage** benefit from. □ **advantageous** /adv(ə)nˈteɪdʒəs/ *adj.* **advantageously** /adv(ə)nˈteɪdʒəsli/ *adv.* [Middle English from Old French *avantage*, *avantager*, from *avant* 'in front' from Late Latin *abante*: see ADVANCE]

advection /ədˈvɛkʃ(ə)n/ *n. Meteorol.* transfer of heat by the horizontal flow of air. □ **advective** *adj.* [Latin *advectio* from *advehere* (as AD-, *vehere vect-* 'carry')]

Advent /ˈadv(ə)nt, -vɛnt/ *n.* **1** the season before Christmas, including the four preceding Sundays. **2** the coming or second coming of Christ. **3** (**advent**) the arrival of esp. an important person or thing. [Old English via Old French *advent*, *auvent* from Latin *adventus* 'arrival', from *advenire* (as AD-, *venire vent-* 'come')]

Advent calendar *n.* a calendar for Advent, usu. made of card with flaps to open each day to reveal a picture, scene, or small gift.

Adventist /ˈadv(ə)ntɪst/ *n.* a member of a Christian sect that believes in the imminent second coming of Christ. □ **Adventism** *n.*

adventitious /adv(ə)nˈtɪʃəs/ *adj.* **1** accidental, casual. **2** added from outside. **3** *Biol.* formed accidentally or in an unusual anatomical position. **4** *Law* (of property) coming from a stranger or by collateral succession rather than directly. □ **adventitiously** *adv.* [Latin *adventicius* (as ADVENT)]

Advent Sunday *n.* the first Sunday in Advent.

adventure /ədˈvɛntʃə/ *n. & v.* ● *n.* **1** an unusual and exciting experience. **2** a daring enterprise; a hazardous activity. **3** enterprise (*the spirit of adventure*). **4** a commercial speculation. ● *v.intr.* **1** (often foll. by *into, upon*) dare to go or come. **2** (foll. by *on, upon*) dare to undertake. **3** incur risk; engage in adventure. □ **adventuresome** *adj.* [Middle English via Old French *aventure* (*n.*), *aventurer* (*v.*) from Latin *adventurus* 'about to happen' (as ADVENT)]

adventure playground *n. Brit.* a playground where children are provided with functional materials for climbing on, building with, etc.

adventurer /əd'ventʃ(ə)rə/ *n.* (*fem.* **adventuress** /-(ə)rɪs/) **1** a person who seeks adventure, esp. for personal gain or enjoyment. **2** a financial speculator. [French *aventurier* (as ADVENTURE)]

adventurism /əd'ventʃərɪz(ə)m/ *n.* a tendency to take risks, esp. in foreign policy. □ **adventurist** *n.*

adventurous /əd'ventʃ(ə)rəs/ *adj.* **1** rash, venturesome; enterprising. **2** characterized by adventures. □ **adventurously** *adv.* **adventurousness** *n.* [Middle English from Old French *aventuros* (as ADVENTURE)]

adverb /'ædvɜːb/ *n.* a word or phrase that modifies or qualifies another word (esp. an adjective, verb, or other adverb) or a word-group, expressing a relation of place, time, circumstance, manner, cause, degree, etc. (e.g. *gently, quite, then, there*). □ **adverbial** /əd'vɜːbɪəl/ *adj.* [French *adverbe* or Latin *adverbium* (as AD-, VERB)]

adversarial /ædvə'seːrɪəl/ *adj.* **1** involving conflict or opposition. **2** opposed, hostile. [ADVERSARY + -IAL]

adversary /'ædvəs(ə)ri/ *n.* (*pl.* **-ies**) **1** an enemy. **2** an opponent in a sport or game; an antagonist. [Middle English via Old French *adversarie* from Latin *adversarius*, from *adversus*: see ADVERSE]

adversative /əd'vɜːsətɪv/ *adj.* (of words etc.) expressing opposition or antithesis. [French *adversatif -ive* or Late Latin *adversativus*, from *adversari* 'oppose' from *adversus*: see ADVERSE]

adverse /'ædvɜːs/ *adj.* (often foll. by *to*) **1** contrary, hostile. **2** hurtful, injurious. □ **adversely** *adv.* **adverseness** *n.* [Middle English via Old French *advers* from Latin *adversus*, past part. of *advertere* (as AD-, *vertere vers-* 'turn')]

adversity /əd'vɜːsɪti/ *n.* (*pl.* **-ies**) **1** the condition of adverse fortune. **2** a misfortune. [Middle English via Old French *adversité* from Latin *adversitas -tatis* (as ADVERSE)]

advert[1] /'ædvɜːt/ *n. Brit. colloq.* an advertisement. [abbreviation]

advert[2] /əd'vɜːt/ *v.intr.* (foll. by *to*) *literary* refer in speaking or writing. [Middle English via Old French *a(d)vertir* from Latin *advertere*: see ADVERSE]

advertise /'ædvətʌɪz/ *v.* **1** *tr.* (also *absol.*) draw attention to or describe favourably (goods, services, or vacant positions) in a public medium in order to sell, promote sales, or seek employees. **2** *tr.* make generally or publicly known. **3** *intr.* (foll. by *for*) seek by public notice, esp. in a newspaper. **4** *tr.* (usu. foll. by *of*, or *that* + clause) notify. □ **advertiser** *n.* [Middle English from Old French *a(d)vertir* (stem *advertiss-*): see ADVERT[2]]

advertisement /əd'vɜːtɪzm(ə)nt, -tɪs-/ *n.* **1 a** a public notice or announcement, esp. one advertising goods or services in newspapers, on posters, or in broadcasts. **b** (usu. foll. by *for*) *colloq.* a person or thing regarded as a means of conveying the merits or demerits of something (*he's a good advertisement for a healthy lifestyle*). **2** the act or process of advertising. **3** *archaic* a notice to readers in a book etc. [earlier *avert-* from French *avertissement* (as ADVERTISE)]

advertorial /ædvɜː'tɔːrɪəl/ *n.* an advertisement in the style of editorial comment. [blend of ADVERTISEMENT and EDITORIAL]

advice /əd'vʌɪs/ *n.* **1** words given or offered as an opinion or recommendation about future action or behaviour. **2** information given; news. **3** formal notice of a transaction. **4** (in *pl.*) communications from a distance. □ **take advice 1** obtain advice, esp. from an expert. **2** act according to advice given. [Middle English, in the sense 'point of view, opinion (given)', via Old French *avis* from Latin *ad* 'to' + *visum*, past part. of *vidēre* 'see']

advisable /əd'vʌɪzəb(ə)l/ *adj.* (of a course of action etc.) to be recommended; expedient. □ **advisability** /-'bɪlɪti/ *n.* **advisably** *adv.*

advise /əd'vʌɪz/ *v.* **1** *tr.* (also *absol.*) give advice to. **2** *tr.* recommend; offer as advice (*they advise caution*; *advised me to rest*). **3** *tr.* (usu. foll. by *of*, or *that* + clause) inform, notify. **4** *intr.* (foll. by *with*) *US* consult. [Middle English, in the sense 'look at, consider', via Old French *aviser* from Latin (as AD- + *visare*, frequentative of *vidēre* 'see')]

advised /əd'vʌɪzd/ *adj.* **1** judicious, prudent. **2** deliberate, considered. □ **advisedly** /-zɪdli/ *adv.*

adviser /əd'vʌɪzə/ *n.* (also *disp.* **advisor**) a person who advises, esp. one appointed to do so and regularly consulted.

■ **Usage** The variant form *advisor* is fairly common, but is considered incorrect by some people. Its spelling is probably influenced by the adjective *advisory*.

advisory /əd'vʌɪz(ə)ri/ *adj.* & *n.* ● *adj.* **1** giving advice; constituted to give advice (*an advisory body*). **2** consisting in giving advice. ● *n.* (*pl.* **-ies**) *N. Amer.* an advisory statement, esp. a warning about bad weather or potential danger.

advocaat /'ædvəkɑː, -kɑːt/ *n.* a liqueur of eggs, sugar, and brandy. [Dutch, = ADVOCATE (being originally an advocate's drink)]

advocacy /'ædvəkəsi/ *n.* **1** (usu. foll. by *of*) verbal support or argument for a cause, policy, etc. **2** the function of an advocate. [Middle English via Old French *a(d)vocacie* from medieval Latin *advocatia* (as ADVOCATE)]

advocate *n.* & *v.* ● *n.* /'ædvəkət/ **1** (foll. by *of*) a person who supports or speaks in favour. **2** a person who pleads for another. **3 a** a professional pleader in a court of justice. **b** *Sc.* a barrister. ● *v.tr.* /'ædvəkeɪt/ **1** recommend or support by argument (a cause, policy, etc.). **2** plead for, defend. □ **advocateship** *n.* [Middle English via Old French *avocat* from Latin *advocatus*, past part. of *advocare* (as AD-, *vocare* 'call')]

advowson /əd'vaʊz(ə)n/ *n. Brit.* (in ecclesiastical law) the right of recommending a member of the Anglican clergy for a vacant benefice, or of making the appointment. [Middle English via Anglo-French *a(d)voweson* and Old French *avoeson* from Latin *advocatio -onis* (as ADVOCATE)]

advt. *abbr.* advertisement.

adytum /'ædɪtəm/ *n.* (*pl.* **adyta** /-tə/) the innermost part of an ancient temple. [Latin from Greek *aduton*, neut. of *adutos* 'impenetrable' (as A-[1], *duō* 'enter')]

adze /ædz/ *n.* & *v.* (*US* also **adz**) ● *n.* a tool like an axe with an arched blade at right angles to the handle, used for cutting away the surface of wood. ● *v.tr.* dress or cut with an adze. [Old English *adesa*]

adzuki /əd'zuːki/ *n.* (in full **adzuki bean**) (also **adsuki**, **aduki** /ə'duːki/, **azuki** /ə'zuːki/) **1** an annual leguminous plant, *Vigna angularis*, native to China and Japan. **2** the small round dark red edible bean of this plant. [Japanese *azuki*]

-ae /iː/ *suffix* forming plural nouns, used in names of animal and plant families, tribes, etc. (*Felidae*; *Rosaceae*) and instead of *-as* in the plural of many non-naturalized or unfamiliar nouns in *-a* derived from Latin or Greek (*larvae*; *actiniae*). [pl. *-ae* of Latin nouns ending in *-a* or pl. ending *-ai* of some Greek nouns]

aedile /'iːdʌɪl/ *n. Rom.Hist.* either of a pair of Roman magistrates who administered public works, maintenance of roads, public games, the corn-supply, etc. □ **aedileship** *n.* [Latin *aedilis* 'concerned with buildings' from *aedes* 'building']

AEEU *abbr.* Amalgamated Engineering and Electrical Union.

aegis /'i:dʒɪs/ *n.* a protection; an impregnable defence. □ **under the aegis of** under the auspices of. [Latin from Greek *aigis*, the mythical shield of Zeus or Athene]

aegrotat /ʌɪ'grə(ʊ)tat, 'i:-, i:'grə(ʊ)-/ *n. Brit.* **1** a certificate that a university student is too ill to attend an examination. **2** an examination pass awarded in such circumstances. [Latin, = is sick from *aeger* 'sick']

-aemia /'i:mɪə/ *comb. form* (also **-haemia** /'hi:mɪə/, *US* **-emia**, **-hemia** /'hi:mɪə/) forming nouns denoting that a substance is (esp. excessively) present in the blood (*bacteriaemia*; *pyaemia*). [modern Latin, from Greek *-aimia* from *haima* 'blood']

aeolian /i:'əʊlɪən/ *adj.* (*US* **eolian**) wind-borne. [Latin *Aeolius* from *Aeolus*, the name of the god of the winds, from Greek *Aiolos*]

aeolian harp *n.* a stringed instrument or toy that produces musical sounds when the wind passes through it.

Aeolian mode /i:'əʊlɪən/ *n. Mus.* the mode represented by the natural diatonic scale A–A. [Latin *Aeolius* 'from *Aeolis*' (in Asia Minor), from Greek *Aiolis*]

aeon /'i:ən/ *n.* (also **eon**) **1** a very long or indefinite period. **2** an age of the universe. **3** *Astron.* a thousand million years. **4** an eternity. **5** *Philos.* (in Neoplatonism, Platonism, and Gnosticism) a power existing from eternity; an emanation or phase of the supreme deity. [ecclesiastical Latin from Greek *aiōn* 'age']

aerate /'ɛ:reɪt/ *v.tr.* **1** charge (a liquid) with a gas, esp. carbon dioxide, e.g. to produce effervescence. **2** expose to the mechanical or chemical action of the air. □ **aeration** /-'reɪʃ(ə)n/ *n.* **aerator** *n.* [Latin *aer* AIR + -ATE[3], influenced by French *aérer*]

aerenchyma /ɛ:'rɛŋkɪmə/ *n. Bot.* a soft plant tissue containing air spaces, found esp. in many aquatic plants. [Greek *aēr* 'air' + *egkhuma* 'infusion']

aerial /'ɛ:rɪəl/ *n. & adj.* ● *n.* a metal rod, wire, or other structure by which signals are transmitted or received as part of a radio or television transmission or receiving system. ● *adj.* **1** by or from or involving aircraft (*aerial navigation*; *aerial photography*). **2 a** existing, moving, or happening in the air. **b** of or in the atmosphere; atmospheric. **3 a** thin as air; ethereal. **b** immaterial, imaginary. **c** of air; gaseous. □ **aeriality** /-'alɪti/ *n.* **aerially** *adv.* [Latin *aerius* from Greek *aerios*, from *aēr* 'air']

aerialist /'ɛ:rɪəlɪst/ *n.* a high-wire or trapeze artist.

aerial torpedo see TORPEDO *n.* 1b.

aerie var. of EYRIE.

aero- /'ɛ:rəʊ/ *comb. form* **1** air. **2** aircraft. [Greek *aero-* from *aēr* 'air']

aerobatics /ɛ:rə'batɪks/ *n.pl.* feats of expert and usu. spectacular flying and manoeuvring of aircraft. [AERO- + ACROBATICS]

aerobe /'ɛ:rəʊb/ *n.* a micro-organism usu. growing in the presence of air, or needing oxygen for growth. [French *aérobie* (as AERO-, Greek *bios* 'life')]

aerobic /ɛ:'rəʊbɪk/ *adj.* **1** of or relating to aerobics. **2** *Biol.* relating to or requiring free oxygen.

aerobics /ɛ:'rəʊbɪks/ *n.pl.* (often treated as *sing.*) vigorous exercises designed to increase the body's oxygen intake.

aerobiology /ˌɛ:rə(ʊ)bʌɪ'ɒlədʒi/ *n.* the study of airborne micro-organisms, pollen, spores, etc., esp. as agents of infection.

aerodrome /'ɛ:rədrəʊm/ *n. Brit.* a small airport or airfield.

■ **Usage** *Aerodrome* has now been largely replaced by *airfield* and *airport*.

aerodynamics /ˌɛ:rə(ʊ)dʌɪ'namɪks/ *n.pl.* (usu. treated as *sing.*) the study of the interaction between the air and solid bodies moving through it. □ **aerodynamic** *adj.* **aerodynamically** *adv.* **aerodynamicist** /-sɪst/ *n.*

aero-engine /'ɛ:rəʊˌɛndʒɪn/ *n. Brit.* an engine used to power an aircraft.

aerofoil /'ɛ:rəfɔɪl/ *n. Brit.* a structure with curved surfaces (e.g. a wing, fin, or tailplane) designed to give lift in flight.

aerogramme /'ɛ:rəgram/ *n.* (also **aerogram**) an air letter in the form of a single sheet that is folded and sealed.

aerolite /'ɛ:rəlʌɪt/ *n.* a stony meteorite.

aerology /ɛ:'rɒlədʒi/ *n.* the study of the atmosphere, esp. away from ground level. □ **aerological** /-ə'lɒdʒɪk(ə)l/ *adj.*

aeronautics /ɛ:rə'nɔ:tɪks/ *n.pl.* (usu. treated as *sing.*) the science or practice of motion or travel in the air. □ **aeronautic** *adj.* **aeronautical** *adj.* [modern Latin *aeronautica* (as AERO-, NAUTICAL)]

aeronomy /ɛ:'rɒnəmi/ *n.* the science of the upper atmosphere.

aeroplane /'ɛ:rəpleɪn/ *n.* esp. *Brit.* a powered heavier-than-air flying vehicle with fixed wings. [French *aéroplane* (as AERO-, PLANE[1])]

aerosol /'ɛ:rəsɒl/ *n.* **1 a** a substance packed under pressure, usu. with a propellant gas, and able to be released as a fine spray. **b** a container holding such a substance. **2** a system of colloidal particles dispersed in a gas (e.g. fog or smoke). [AERO- + SOL[2]]

aerospace /'ɛ:rəspeɪs/ *n.* **1** the earth's atmosphere and outer space. **2** the technology of aviation in this region.

aerostat /'ɛ:rəstat/ *n.* an airship or balloon, esp. a tethered balloon. [French *aérostat* (as AERO- + Greek *statos* 'standing')]

aerotowing /'ɛ:rəʊˌtəʊɪŋ/ *n.* the towing of a glider etc. by a powered aircraft.

aerotrain /'ɛ:rəʊˌtreɪn/ *n.* a train that is supported on an air cushion and guided by a track. [French *aérotrain* (as AERO-, TRAIN)]

Aesculapian /i:skjʊ'leɪpɪən/ *adj.* of or relating to medicine or physicians. [Latin *Aesculapius* from Greek *Asklēpios*, the name of the god of medicine]

aesthete /'i:sθi:t, 'ɛs-/ *n.* (*US* also **esthete**) a person who has or professes to have a special appreciation of beauty. [Greek *aisthētēs* 'a person who perceives', or from AESTHETIC]

aesthetic /i:s'θɛtɪk, ɛs-/ *adj. & n.* (*US* also **esthetic**) ● *adj.* **1** concerned with beauty or the appreciation of beauty. **2** having such appreciation; sensitive to beauty. **3** in accordance with the principles of good taste. ● *n.* **1** (in *pl.*) the philosophy of the beautiful, esp. in art. **2** a set of principles of good taste and the appreciation of beauty. □ **aesthetically** *adv.* **aestheticism** /-sɪz(ə)m/ *n.* [Greek *aisthētikos* from *aisthanomai* 'perceive']

aesthetician /i:sθə'tɪʃ(ə)n, ɛs-/ *n.* (*US* also **esthetician**) **1** a person versed in or devoted to aesthetics. **2** *N. Amer.* a beautician.

aestival /'i:stɪv(ə)l, i:'stʌɪv(ə)l; 'ɛ-, ɛ-/ *adj.* (*US* **estival**) *formal* belonging to or appearing in summer. [Middle English via Old French *estival* from Latin *aestivalis*, from *aestivus* from *aestus* 'heat']

aestivate /'i:stɪveɪt, 'ɛst-/ *v.intr.* (*US* **estivate**) **1** *Zool.* spend the summer or dry season in a state of torpor. **2** *formal* pass the summer. [Latin *aestivare aestivat-*]

aestivation /i:stɪ'veɪʃ(ə)n, ɛst-/ *n.* (*US* **estivation**) **1** *Bot.* the arrangement of petals in a flower bud before it opens (cf. VERNATION). **2** *Zool.* spending the summer or dry season in a state of torpor.

aet. *abbr.* (also ***aetat.***) *aetatis*.

aetatis /ʌɪ'tɑ:tɪs, i:-/ *adj.* of or at the age of. [Latin]

aether var. of ETHER 2, 3.

aetiology /i:tɪ'ɒlədʒi/ *n.* (*US* **etiology**) **1** the assignment of a cause or reason. **2** the study of causation. **3** *Med.* the causation of diseases and disorders, esp. of a specific disease, as a subject of investigation. □ **aetiologic** /-ə'lɒdʒɪk/ *adj.* **aetiological** /-ə'lɒdʒɪk(ə)l/ *adj.* **aetiologically** /-ə'lɒdʒɪk(ə)li/ *adv.* [Late Latin *aetiologia* from Greek *aitiologia*, from *aitia* 'cause']

AEU *abbr. hist.* (in the UK) Amalgamated Engineering Union.

AF *abbr.* audio frequency.

af- /af, əf/ *prefix* assim. form of AD- before *f*.

afar /əˈfɑː/ *adv.* at or to a distance. □ **from afar** from a distance. [Middle English from A-[2], A-[4] + FAR]

AFC *abbr.* **1** (in the UK) Air Force Cross. **2** (in the UK) Association Football Club.

AFDCS *abbr.* (in the UK) Association of First Division Civil Servants (cf. FDA).

affable /ˈafəb(ə)l/ *adj.* friendly, good-natured. □ **affability** /-ˈbɪlɪti/ *n.* **affably** *adv.* [French from Latin *affabilis*, from *affari* (as AD-, *fari* 'speak')]

affair /əˈfɛː/ *n.* **1** a concern; a business; a matter to be attended to (*that is my affair*). **2 a** a celebrated or notorious happening or sequence of events. **b** *colloq.* a noteworthy thing or event (*was a puzzling affair*). **3** = LOVE AFFAIR. **4** (in *pl.*) **a** ordinary pursuits of life. **b** business dealings. **c** public matters (*current affairs*). [Middle English via Anglo-French *afere* from Old French *afaire*, from *à faire* 'to do': cf. ADO]

affaire /afɛːr/ *n.* (also **affaire de** or **du cœur** /a,fɛː də, dy ˈkəː/) a love affair. [French]

affairé /aˈfɛːreɪ, French afere/ *adj.* busy; involved. [French]

affect[1] /əˈfɛkt/ *v.tr.* **1 a** produce an effect on (*their business was not affected by the recession*). **b** (of a disease etc.) attack (*his liver is affected*). **2** move; touch the feelings of (*affected me deeply*). □ **affecting** *adj.* **affectingly** *adv.* [French *affecter* or Latin *afficere affect-* 'influence' (as AD-, *facere* 'do')]

■ **Usage** *Affect* should not be confused with *effect* which means 'to bring about, to accomplish', e.g. *The government effected great changes.* Note also that *effect* is commonly used as a noun as well as a verb.

affect[2] /əˈfɛkt/ *v.tr.* **1** pretend to have or feel (*affected indifference*). **2** (foll. by *to* + infin.) pretend. **3** assume the character or manner of; pose as (*affect the freethinker*). **4** make a show of liking or using (*she affects fancy hats*). [French *affecter* or Latin *affectare* 'aim at', frequentative of *afficere* (as AFFECT[1])]

affect[3] /ˈafɛkt/ *n. Psychol.* an emotion, a feeling, or a desire, esp. as leading to action. [German *Affekt* from Latin *affectus* 'disposition', from *afficere* (as AFFECT[1])]

affectation /afɛkˈteɪʃ(ə)n/ *n.* **1** an assumed or contrived manner of behaviour, esp. in order to impress. **2** (foll. by *of*) a studied display. **3** pretence. [French *affectation* or Latin *affectatio* (as AFFECT[2])]

affected /əˈfɛktɪd/ *adj.* **1** in senses of AFFECT[1], AFFECT[2]. **2** artificially assumed or displayed; pretended (*an affected air of innocence*). **3** (of a person) full of affectation; artificial. **4** (prec. by adv.; often foll. by *towards*) *archaic* disposed, inclined. □ **affectedly** *adv.*

affection /əˈfɛkʃ(ə)n/ *n.* **1** (often foll. by *for*, *towards*) goodwill; fond or kindly feeling. **2** a disease; a diseased condition. **3** a mental state; an emotion. **4** a mental disposition. **5** the act or process of affecting or being affected. □ **affectional** *adj.* (in sense 3). [Middle English via Old French from Latin *affectio -onis* (as AFFECT[1])]

affectionate /əˈfɛkʃ(ə)nət/ *adj.* loving, fond; showing love or tenderness. □ **affectionately** *adv.* [French *affectionné* or medieval Latin *affectionatus* (as AFFECTION)]

affective /əˈfɛktɪv/ *adj.* **1** concerning the affections; emotional. **2** *Psychol.* relating to affects. □ **affectivity** /afɛkˈtɪvɪti/ *n.* [French *affectif -ive* from Late Latin *affectivus* (as AFFECT[1])]

affenpinscher /ˈafənpɪnʃə/ *n.* **1** a dog of a small breed resembling the griffon. **2** this breed. [German from *Affe* 'monkey' + *Pinscher* 'terrier']

afferent /ˈaf(ə)r(ə)nt/ *adj. Physiol.* conducting inwards or towards (*afferent nerves; afferent vessels*) (opp. EFFERENT). [Latin *afferre* (as AD-, *ferre* 'bring')]

affiance /əˈfʌɪəns/ *v.tr.* (usu. in *passive*) *literary* promise solemnly to give (a person) in marriage. [Middle English via Old French *afiancer* from medieval Latin *affidare* (as AD-, *fidus* 'trusty')]

affiant /əˈfʌɪənt/ *n. N. Amer.* a person who makes an affidavit. [French: see -ANT]

affidavit /afɪˈdeɪvɪt/ *n.* a written statement confirmed by oath, for use as evidence in court. [medieval Latin, = has stated on oath, from *affidare*: see AFFIANCE]

affiliate *v. & n.* ● *v.* /əˈfɪlɪeɪt/ **1** *tr.* (usu. in *passive*; foll. by *to*, *with*) attach or connect (a person or society) with a larger organization. **2** *tr.* (of an institution) adopt (persons as members, societies as branches). **3** *intr.* **a** (foll. by *to*) associate oneself with a society. **b** (foll. by *with*) associate oneself with a political party. ● *n.* /əˈfɪlɪət/ an affiliated person or organization. □ **affiliative** /əˈfɪlɪətɪv/ *adj.* [medieval Latin *affiliare* 'adopt' (as AD-, *filius* 'son')]

affiliation /əfɪlɪˈeɪʃ(ə)n/ *n.* the act or process of affiliating or being affiliated. [French from medieval Latin *affiliatio*, from *affiliare*: see AFFILIATE]

affiliation order *n. Brit.* a legal order that the man judged to be the father of an illegitimate child must help to support it.

affined /əˈfʌɪnd/ *adj.* related, connected. [*affine* (*adj.*) from Latin *affinis* 'related': see AFFINITY]

affinity /əˈfɪnɪti/ *n.* (*pl.* **-ies**) **1** (often foll. by *between*, *for*, or *with*) a spontaneous or natural liking for or attraction to a person or thing. **2** relationship, esp. by marriage. **3** resemblance in structure between animals, plants, or languages. **4** a similarity of characteristics suggesting a relationship; family likeness. **5** *Chem.* the tendency of certain substances to combine with others. [Middle English via Old French *afinité* from Latin *affinitas -tatis*, from *affinis* 'related', literally 'bordering on' (as AD- + *finis* 'border')]

affinity card *n.* **1** a discount card issued to members of an affinity group. **2** (in the UK) a bank card for which the bank donates to a specific charity etc. a portion of the money spent using the card.

affinity group *n.* a group of people linked by a common interest or purpose.

affirm /əˈfəːm/ *v.* **1** *tr.* assert strongly; state as a fact. **2** *intr.* **a** *Law* make an affirmation. **b** make a formal declaration. **3** *tr. Law* confirm, ratify (a judgement). □ **affirmatory** *adj.* **affirmer** *n.* [Middle English via Old French *afermer* from Latin *affirmare* (as AD-, *firmus* 'strong')]

affirmation /afəˈmeɪʃ(ə)n/ *n.* **1** the act or process of affirming or being affirmed. **2** *Law* a solemn declaration by a person who conscientiously declines to take an oath. [French *affirmation* or Latin *affirmatio* (as AFFIRM)]

affirmative /əˈfəːmətɪv/ *adj., n., & int.* ● *adj.* **1 a** affirming; asserting that a thing is so. **b** *Gram.* (of a word, clause, etc.) stating that a fact is so; answering 'yes' to a question. **2** (of a vote) expressing approval. ● *n.* **1** an affirmative statement or reply. **2** *Gram.* a word or particle expressing affirmation. **3** (prec. by *the*) a positive or affirming position. ● *int.* esp. *N. Amer.* yes. □ **in the affirmative** with affirmative effect; so as to accept or agree to a proposal; yes (*the answer was in the affirmative*). □ **affirmatively** *adv.* [Middle English via Old French *affirmatif -ive* from Late Latin *affirmativus* (as AFFIRM)]

affirmative action *n.* esp. *N. Amer.* action favouring those who tend to suffer from discrimination; positive discrimination, esp. in recuitment to jobs.

affix *v. & n.* ● *v.tr.* /əˈfɪks/ **1** (usu. foll. by *to*, *on*) attach, fasten. **2** add in writing (a signature or postscript). **3** impress (a seal or stamp). ● *n.* /ˈafɪks/ **1** an appendage; an addition. **2** *Gram.* an addition or element placed at the beginning (*prefix*) or end (*suffix*) of a root, stem, or word, or in the body of a word (*infix*), to modify its meaning. □ **affixation** /afɪkˈseɪʃ(ə)n/ *n.* [French *affixer*, *affixe* or medieval Latin *affixare*, frequentative of Latin *affigere* (as AD-, *figere fix-* 'fix')]

afflatus /əˈfleɪtəs/ *n.* a divine creative impulse; inspiration. [Latin, from *afflare* (as AD-, *flare flat-* 'to blow')]

afflict /ə'flɪkt/ *v.tr.* inflict bodily or mental suffering on. □ **afflicted with** suffering from. □ **afflictive** *adj.* [Middle English, from Latin *afflictare* or from Latin *afflict-*, past part. stem of *affligere* (as AD-, *fligere flict-* 'dash')]

■ **Usage** See Usage Note at INFLICT.

affliction /ə'flɪkʃ(ə)n/ *n.* **1** physical or mental distress, esp. pain or illness. **2** a cause of this. [Middle English via Old French from Latin *afflictio -onis* (as AFFLICT)]

affluence /'aflʊəns/ *n.* an abundant supply of money, commodities, etc.; wealth. [Middle English via Old French from Latin *affluentia*, from *affluere*: see AFFLUENT]

affluent /'aflʊənt/ *adj.* & *n.* ● *adj.* **1** wealthy, rich. **2** abundant. **3** flowing freely or copiously. ● *n.* a tributary stream. □ **affluently** *adv.* [Middle English via Old French from Latin *affluere* (as AD-, *fluere flux-* 'flow')]

afflux /'aflʌks/ *n.* a flow towards a point; an influx. [medieval Latin *affluxus* from Latin *affluere*: see AFFLUENT]

afford /ə'fɔːd/ *v.tr.* **1** (prec. by *can* or *be able to*; often foll. by *to* + infin.) **a** have enough money, means, time, etc., for; be able to spare (*can afford £50*; *could not afford a holiday*; *can we afford to buy a new television?*). **b** be in a position to do something (esp. without risk of adverse consequences) (*can't afford to let him think so*). **2** yield a supply of. **3** provide (*affords a view of the sea*). □ **affordable** *adj.* **affordability** /-'bɪlɪti/ *n.* [Old English *geforthian* 'promote' (as Y-, FORTH), assimilated to words in AF-]

afforest /ə'fɒrɪst/ *v.tr.* **1** convert into forest. **2** plant with trees. □ **afforestation** /-'steɪʃ(ə)n/ *n.* [medieval Latin *afforestare* (as AD-, *foresta* FOREST)]

affranchise /ə'fran(t)ʃʌɪz/ *v.tr.* release from servitude or an obligation. [Old French *afranchir* (as ENFRANCHISE, with prefix A-[3])]

affray /ə'freɪ/ *n.* a breach of the peace by fighting or rioting in public. [Middle English via Anglo-French *afrayer* (*v.*) and Old French *esfreer* from Romanic]

affricate /'afrɪkət/ *n. Phonet.* a combination of a plosive with an immediately following fricative or spirant, e.g. *ch* as in *chair*. [Latin *affricare* (as AD-, *fricare* 'rub')]

affront /ə'frʌnt/ *n.* & *v.* ● *n.* an open insult (*feel it an affront*; *offer an affront to*). ● *v.tr.* **1** insult openly. **2** offend the modesty or self-respect of. **3** face, confront. [Middle English from Old French *afronter* 'slap in the face, insult', ultimately from Latin *frons frontis* 'face']

Afghan /'afgan/ *n.* & *adj.* ● *n.* **1 a** a native or national of Afghanistan. **b** a person of Afghan descent. **2** the official language of Afghanistan; also called PASHTO. **3** (**afghan**) a knitted and sewn woollen blanket or shawl. **4** (in full **Afghan coat**) *Brit.* a kind of sheepskin coat with the skin outside and usu. with a shaggy border. ● *adj.* of or relating to Afghanistan, its people, or its language. [Pashto *afghānī*]

Afghan hound *n.* **1** a tall hunting dog of a breed with long silky hair. **2** this breed.

afghani /af'gɑːni/ *n.* (*pl.* **afghanis**) the chief monetary unit of Afghanistan. [Pashto]

aficionado /afɪsjə'nɑːdəʊ/ *n.* (*pl.* **-os**) a devotee of a sport or pastime (originally of bullfighting). [Spanish]

afield /ə'fiːld/ *adv.* **1** away from home; to or at a distance (esp. in phr. **far afield**). **2** in the field. [Old English (as A[2], FIELD)]

afire /ə'fʌɪə/ *adv.* & *predic.adj.* **1** on fire. **2** intensely roused or excited.

aflame /ə'fleɪm/ *adv.* & *predic.adj.* **1** in flames. **2** = AFIRE 2.

aflatoxin /aflə'tɒksɪn/ *n. Chem.* any of a class of toxic compounds produced by the mould *Aspergillus flavus*, which cause liver damage and cancer. [*Aspergillus* + *flavus* + TOXIN]

AFL-CIO *abbr.* American Federation of Labor and Congress of Industrial Organizations.

afloat /ə'fləʊt/ *adv.* & *predic.adj.* **1** floating in water or air. **2** at sea; on board ship. **3** out of debt or difficulty. **4** in general circulation; current. **5** full of or covered with a liquid. **6** in full swing. [Old English (as A[2], FLOAT)]

AFM *abbr.* (in the UK) Air Force Medal.

afoot /ə'fʊt/ *adv.* & *predic.adj.* **1** in operation; progressing. **2** astir; on the move. **3** *N. Amer.* **a** on foot (*dismounted and went afoot*). **b** on one's feet (*slow afoot*).

afore /ə'fɔː/ *prep., conj.,* & *adv. archaic* or *dial.* before; previously; in front (of). [Old English *onforan* (as A[2], FORE)]

afore- /ə'fɔː/ *prefix* before, previously (*aforementioned*; *aforesaid*).

aforethought /ə'fɔːθɔːt/ *adj.* premeditated (following a noun: *malice aforethought*).

a fortiori /eɪ fɔːtɪ'ɔːrʌɪ/ *adv.* & *adj.* with a yet stronger reason (than a conclusion already accepted); more conclusively. [Latin]

afoul /ə'faʊl/ *adv.* (in phrs. **fall afoul of**, **run afoul of**) *N. Amer.* foul (see FALL, RUN).

afraid /ə'freɪd/ *predic.adj.* **1** (often foll. by *of*, or *that* or *lest* + clause) alarmed, frightened. **2** (foll. by *to* + infin.) unwilling or reluctant for fear of the consequences (*was afraid to go in*). □ **be afraid** (foll. by *that* + clause) *colloq.* admit or declare with (real or politely simulated) regret (*I'm afraid there's none left*). [Middle English (past part. of obsolete verb *affray*), via Anglo-French *afrayer* from Old French *esfreer*]

A-frame /'eɪfreɪm/ *n.* **1** (often *attrib.*) a frame shaped like a capital letter A. **2** *N. Amer.* an A-frame house. [A[1] + FRAME]

afreet /'afriːt/ *n.* (also **afrit**) a demon in Arabian mythology. [Arabic *'ifrīt*]

afresh /ə'frɛʃ/ *adv.* anew; with a fresh beginning. [A-[2] + FRESH]

African /'afrɪk(ə)n/ *n.* & *adj.* ● *n.* **1** a native of Africa (esp. a dark-skinned person). **2** a person of African descent. ● *adj.* of or relating to Africa. [Latin *Africanus*]

Africana /afrɪ'kɑːnə/ *n.pl.* things connected with Africa.

African-American *n.* & *adj.* ● *n.* a black American. ● *adj.* of or relating to black Americans.

Africander /afrɪ'kandə/ *n.* (also **Afrikander**) one of a S. African breed of sheep or longhorn cattle. [Afrikaans *Afrikaander*, alteration of Dutch *Afrikaner* on the pattern of *Hollander* etc.]

African elephant *n.* the elephant, *Loxodonta africana*, of Africa, which is larger than the Indian elephant.

Africanize /'afrɪk(ə)nʌɪz/ *v.tr.* (also **-ise**) **1** make African in character. **2** place under the control of African blacks. **3** (usu. as **Africanized** *adj.*) hybridize (honey bees) with African stock producing an aggressive strain. □ **Africanization** /-'zeɪʃ(ə)n/ *n.*

African violet *n.* a small E. African plant of the genus *Saintpaulia*, with heart-shaped velvety leaves and blue, purple, or pink flowers, esp. *S. ionantha*, a popular house plant. Also called *saintpaulia*.

Afrikaans /afrɪ'kɑːns/ *n.* the language of the Afrikaner people developed from Dutch, an official language of the Republic of South Africa. [Dutch, = African]

Afrikander var. of AFRICANDER.

Afrikaner /afrɪ'kɑːnə/ *n.* **1** an Afrikaans-speaking white person in S. Africa, esp. one of Dutch descent. **2** a S. African species of *Gladiolus* or *Homoglossum*. [Afrikaans from Dutch: see AFRICANDER]

afrit var. of AFREET.

Afro /'afrəʊ/ *adj.* & *n.* ● *adj.* (of a hairstyle) long and bushy, as naturally grown by some blacks. ● *n.* (*pl.* **-os**) an Afro hairstyle. [AFRO-, or abbreviation of AFRICAN]

Afro- /'afrəʊ/ *comb. form* African (*Afro-Asian*). [Latin *Afer Afr-* 'African']

Afro-American /afrəʊə'mɛrɪk(ə)n/ *adj.* & *n.* = AFRICAN-AMERICAN.

Afro-Caribbean /ˌafrəʊkarɪ'biːən, -kə'rɪbɪən/ *n.* & *adj.* ● *n.* a person of African descent living in or coming from the Caribbean. ● *adj.* of or relating to Afro-Caribbeans.

Afrocentric /afrəʊ'sɛntrɪk/ *adj.* centring on African or Afro-American culture; regarding African or black culture as pre-eminent. [AFRO- + -CENTRIC]

afrormosia /afrɔː'məʊzɪə/ *n.* **1** an African tree, *Pericopsis* (formerly *Afrormosia*) *elata*, yielding a hardwood resembling teak and used for furniture. **2** this wood. [modern Latin from AFRO- + *Ormosia*, a related genus]

aft /ɑːft/ *adv. Naut.* & *Aeron.* at or towards the stern or tail. [probably from Middle English *baft*: see ABAFT]

after /'ɑːftə/ *prep., conj., adv., & adj.* ● *prep.* **1 a** following in time; later than (*after six months*; *after midnight*; *day after day*). **b** *N. Amer.* in specifying time (*a quarter after eight*). **2** (with causal force) in view of (something that happened shortly before) (*after your behaviour tonight what do you expect?*). **3** (with concessive force) in spite of (*after all my efforts I'm no better off*). **4** behind (*shut the door after you*). **5** in pursuit or quest of (*run after them*; *enquire after him*; *hanker after it*; *is after a job*). **6** about, concerning (*asked after her*; *asked after her health*). **7** in allusion to (*named him William after the prince*). **8** in imitation of (a person, word, etc.) (*a painting after Rubens*; *'aesthete' is formed after 'athlete'*). **9** next in importance to (*the best book on the subject after mine*). **10** according to (*after a fashion*). ● *conj.* in or at a time later than that when (*left after they arrived*). ● *adv.* **1** later in time (*soon after*; *a week after*). **2** behind in place (*followed on after*; *look before and after*). ● *adj.* **1** later, following (*in after years*). **2** *Naut.* nearer the stern (*after cabins*; *after mast*; *after-peak*). □ **after all 1** in spite of all that has happened or has been said etc. (*after all, what does it matter?*). **2** in spite of one's exertions, expectations, etc. (*they tried for an hour and failed after all*; *so you have come after all!*). **after one's own heart** see HEART. **after you** a formula used in offering precedence. [Old English *æfter*, from Germanic]

afterbirth /'ɑːftəbəːθ/ *n.* the placenta and foetal membranes discharged from the womb after the birth of offspring.

afterburner /'ɑːftəˌbəːnə/ *n.* an auxiliary burner in a jet engine to increase thrust.

aftercare /'ɑːftəkɛː/ *n.* **1** care of a patient after a stay in hospital or of a person on release from prison. **2 a** subsequent care or maintenance (*tips for aftercare*). **b** support or advice offered to a customer following the purchase of a product or service.

afterdamp /'ɑːftədamp/ *n.* choking gas left after an explosion of firedamp in a mine.

after-effect *n.* an effect that follows after an interval or after the primary action of something.

afterglow /'ɑːftəgləʊ/ *n.* **1** a light or radiance remaining after its source has disappeared or been removed. **2** a pleasant feeling remaining after a pleasurable experience.

after-hours *attrib.adj.* taking place after normal hours.

after-image *n.* an image retained by a sense organ, esp. the eye, and producing a sensation after the cessation of the stimulus.

afterlife /'ɑːftəlʌɪf/ *n.* **1** *Relig.* life after death. **2** life at a later time.

aftermarket /'ɑːftəˌmɑːkɪt/ *n.* **1** a market in spare parts and components. **2** *Stock Exch.* a market in shares after their original issue.

aftermath /'ɑːftəmaθ/ *n.* **1** consequences or after-effects, esp. when unpleasant (*the aftermath of war*). **2** *dial.* new grass growing after mowing or after a harvest. [AFTER *adj.* + *math* 'mowing' (Old English *mæth*, from Germanic)]

aftermost /'ɑːftəməʊst/ *adj. Naut.* furthest aft. [AFTER *adj.* + -MOST]

afternoon /ɑːftə'nuːn/ *n. & int.* ● *n.* **1** the time from noon or lunchtime to evening (*this afternoon*; *during the afternoon*; *afternoon tea*). **2** this time spent in a particular way (*had a lazy afternoon*). **3** a time compared with this, esp. the later part of something (*the afternoon of life*). ● *int. colloq.* = *good afternoon* (see GOOD *adj.* 14).

afterpains /'ɑːftəpeɪnz/ *n.pl.* pains caused by contraction of the womb after childbirth.

afters /'ɑːftəz/ *n.pl. Brit. colloq.* the course following the main course of a meal; dessert.

after-school *attrib.adj.* taking place after normal school hours.

aftershave /'ɑːftəʃeɪv/ *n.* an astringent lotion for use after shaving.

aftershock /'ɑːftəʃɒk/ *n.* a lesser shock following the main shock of an earthquake.

aftertaste /'ɑːftəteɪst/ *n.* a taste remaining or recurring after eating or drinking.

afterthought /'ɑːftəθɔːt/ *n.* an item or thing that is thought of or added later.

afterwards /'ɑːftəwədz/ *adv.* (*US* also **afterward** /-wəd/) later, subsequently. [Old English *æfterwearde* (*adj.*) from *æftan* AFT + -WARD]

afterword /'ɑːftəwəːd/ *n.* concluding remarks in a book, esp. by a person other than its author.

Ag[1] /ag / *symb. Chem.* the element silver. [Latin *argentum*]

Ag[2] *abbr.* antigen.

ag- /ag, əg/ *prefix* assim. form of AD- before *g*.

Aga /'ɑːgə/ *n. Brit. propr.* a type of heavy heat-retaining cooking stove or range burning solid fuel or powered by gas, oil, or electricity, and intended for continuous heating. [Swedish, from Svenska *A*ktienbolaget *Ga*s*a*ckumulator (Swedish Gas Accumulator Company), the original manufacturer]

aga /'ɑːgə/ *n.* (in Muslim countries, esp. under the Ottoman Empire) a commander; a chief. [Turkish *ağa* 'master']

again /ə'gɛn, ə'geɪn/ *adv.* **1** another time; once more. **2** as in a previous position or condition (*back again*; *home again*; *quite well again*). **3** in addition (*as much again*; *half as many again*). **4** further, besides (*again, what about the children?*). **5** on the other hand (*I might, and again I might not*). □ **again and again** repeatedly. [Old English *ongēan*, *ongægn*, etc., from Germanic]

against /ə'gɛnst, ə'geɪnst/ *prep.* **1** in opposition to (*fight against the invaders*; *am against hanging*; *arson is against the law*). **2** into collision or in contact with (*ran against a rock*; *lean against the wall*; *up against a problem*). **3** to the disadvantage of (*his age is against him*). **4** in contrast to (*against a dark background*; *99 as against 102 yesterday*). **5** in anticipation of or preparation for (*against his coming*; *against a rainy day*; *protected against the cold*; *warned against pickpockets*). **6** as a compensating factor to (*income against expenditure*). **7** in return for (*issued against payment of the fee*). □ **against the clock** see CLOCK[1] 3. **against the grain** see GRAIN. **against time** see TIME. [Middle English *ayenes* etc., from *ayen* AGAIN + adverbial genitive *-s* + *-t* as in *amongst*]

Aga Khan /ɑːgə 'kɑːn/ *n.* the spiritual leader of the Nizari sect of Ismaili Muslims.

agal /a'gɑːl/ *n.* a fillet worn by Bedouin Arabs to keep the keffiyeh in place. [Arabic *'iḳāl* 'bond, rope']

agama /ə'gɑːmə/ *n.* an iguana-like Old World lizard of the genus *Agama* or a related genus. [Carib]

agamic /ə'gamɪk/ *adj.* characterized by asexual reproduction. [Greek *agamos* 'unmarried' + -IC]

agamospermy /'agəməˌspəːmi/ *n. Bot.* asexual reproduction by division of an unfertilized ovule. [Greek *agamos* 'unmarried' + *sperma* 'seed']

agapanthus /agə'panθəs/ *n.* any lilylike plant of the African genus *Agapanthus*. [modern Latin, from Greek *agapē* 'love' + *anthos* 'flower']

agape[1] /ə'geɪp/ *adv. & predic.adj.* gaping, open-mouthed, esp. with wonder or expectation.

agape[2] /'agəpi/ *n.* **1** a Christian feast in token of fellowship, esp. one held by early Christians in commemoration of the Last Supper. **2** *Theol.* Christian love, esp. as distinct from erotic love. [Greek, = brotherly love]

agar /ˈeɪgɑː/ *n.* (also **agar-agar** /eɪgɑːrˈeɪgɑː/) a gelatinous substance obtained from various kinds of red seaweed and used in making soups, biological culture media, etc. [Malay]

agaric /ˈag(ə)rɪk, əˈgɑːrɪk/ *n.* any fungus of the family Agaricaceae, with cap and stalk, including the common edible mushroom. [Latin *agaricum* from Greek *agarikon*]

agate /ˈagət/ *n.* **1** a hard usu. banded variety of chalcedony. **2** a coloured toy marble resembling this. [French *agate, -the,* via Latin *achates* from Greek *akhatēs*]

agave /əˈgeɪvi/ *n.* any plant of the genus *Agave,* with rosettes of narrow spiny leaves, and tall inflorescences, e.g. the American aloe. [Latin from Greek *Agauē,* a proper name in mythology, from *agauos* 'illustrious']

agaze /əˈgeɪz/ *adv. poet.* gazing.

age /eɪdʒ/ *n. & v.* ● *n.* **1 a** the length of time that a person or thing has existed or is likely to exist. **b** a particular point in or part of one's life, often as a qualification (*old age; voting age*). **2 a** (often in *pl.*) *colloq.* a long time (*took an age to answer; have been waiting for ages*). **b** a distinct period of the past (*golden age; Bronze Age; Middle Ages*). **c** *Geol.* a period of time. **d** a generation. **3** the latter part of life; old age (*the peevishness of age*). ● *v.* (*pres. part.* **ageing, aging**) **1** *intr.* show signs of advancing age (*has aged a lot recently*). **2** *intr.* grow old. **3** *intr.* mature. **4** *tr.* cause or allow to age. □ **come of age** reach adult status (esp. in Law at 18, formerly 21). [Middle English from Old French, ultimately from Latin *aetas -atis* 'age']

-age /ɪdʒ, ɑːʒ/ *suffix* forming nouns denoting: **1** an action (*breakage; spillage*). **2** a condition or function (*bondage; a peerage*). **3** an aggregate or number of (*coverage; the peerage; acreage*). **4** fees payable for; the cost of using (*postage*). **5** the product of an action (*dosage; wreckage*). **6** a place; an abode (*anchorage; orphanage; parsonage*). [Old French, ultimately from Latin *-aticum,* neut. of adjectival suffix *-aticus* -ATIC]

aged *adj.* **1** /eɪdʒd/ **a** of the age of (*aged ten*). **b** that has been subjected to ageing. **c** (of a horse) over six years old. **2** /ˈeɪdʒɪd/ having lived long; old.

age group *n.* a number of persons or things classed together as of similar age.

ageing /ˈeɪdʒɪŋ/ *n.* (also **aging**) **1** growing old. **2** giving the appearance of advancing age. **3** a change of properties occurring in some metals after heat treatment or cold working.

ageism /ˈeɪdʒɪz(ə)m/ *n.* prejudice or discrimination on the grounds of age. □ **ageist** *adj. & n.*

ageless /ˈeɪdʒlɪs/ *adj.* **1** never growing or appearing old or outmoded. **2** eternal, timeless.

age-long *adj.* lasting for a very long time.

agency /ˈeɪdʒ(ə)nsi/ *n.* (*pl.* **-ies**) **1 a** the business or establishment of an agent (*employment agency*). **b** the function of an agent. **2 a** active operation; action (*free agency*). **b** intervening action; means (*fertilized by the agency of insects*). **c** action personified (*an invisible agency*). **3** (also **Agency**) a department or body providing a specific service for a government, political union, etc. (*United Nations relief agency; News Agency*). [medieval Latin *agentia* from Latin *agere* 'do']

agenda /əˈdʒendə/ *n.* **1** (*pl.* **agendas**) **a** a list of items of business to be considered at a meeting. **b** a series of things to be done; a plan of activities or action. **2** (*sing.* **agendum**) (treated as *pl.*) **a** items of business to be considered. **b** things to be done. [Latin, neut. pl. of gerundive of *agere* 'do']

■ **Usage** *Agenda* is now usually treated as a singular noun (with plural *agendas*), as in sense 1 above, e.g. *The agenda for the meeting was very long; Today's agenda includes a visit to the old town; Anticipate what hidden agendas others may have.* It is occasionally found in sense 2 (its original sense) meaning 'items to be considered' or 'things to be done'. Cf. DATA, MEDIA[1].

agent /ˈeɪdʒ(ə)nt/ *n.* **1 a** a person who acts for another in business, politics, etc. (*literary agent*). **b** a person or company that acts as broker and provides a specified service (*estate agent; travel agent*). **c** a travelling salesman or saleswoman. **d** a spy. **2 a** a person or thing that exerts power or produces an effect. **b** the cause of a natural force or effect on matter (*oxidizing agent*). **c** such a force or effect. [Latin *agent-,* part. stem of *agere* 'do']

agent-general *n.* (*pl.* **agents-general**) a representative of an Australian state or Canadian province.

agent noun *n.* a noun denoting an agent or agency (e.g. *lawyer, accelerator*).

agent provocateur /ˌaʒɒ̃ prəˌvɒkəˈtəː/ *n.* (*pl.* **agents provocateurs** *pronunc.* same) a person employed to detect suspected offenders by tempting them to overt self-incriminating action. [French, = provocative agent]

age of consent *n.* the age at which consent to sexual intercourse is valid in law.

age of discretion see DISCRETION.

age of puberty *n.* the age at which puberty begins, in law usu. 14 in boys and 12 in girls.

age-old *adj.* having existed for a very long time.

age range *n.* a range of ages.

agglomerate *v., n., & adj.* ● *v.tr. & intr.* /əˈglɒməreɪt/ **1** collect into a mass. **2** accumulate in a disorderly way. ● *n.* /əˈglɒmərət/ **1** a mass or collection of things. **2** *Geol.* a mass of large volcanic fragments bonded under heat (cf. CONGLOMERATE *adj.* 2, *n.* 3). ● *adj.* /əˈglɒmərət/ collected into a mass. □ **agglomeration** /-ˈreɪʃ(ə)n/ *n.* **agglomerative** /əˈglɒmərətɪv/ *adj.* [Latin *agglomerare* (as AD-, *glomerare* from *glomus -meris* 'ball')]

agglutinate /əˈgluːtɪnət/ *v.* **1** *tr.* unite as with glue. **2** *tr. & intr. Biol.* cause or undergo rapid clumping (of bacteria, erythrocytes, etc.). **3** *tr.* (of language) combine (simple words) without change of form to express compound ideas. □ **agglutination** /-ˈneɪʃ(ə)n/ *n.* **agglutinative** /əˈgluːtɪnətɪv/ *adj.* [Latin *agglutinare* (as AD-, *glutinare* from *gluten -tinis* 'glue')]

agglutinin /əˈgluːtɪnɪn/ *n. Biol.* an antibody, lectin, or other substance causing agglutination. [AGGLUTINATE + -IN]

aggrandize /əˈgrandʌɪz/ *v.tr.* (also **-ise**) **1** increase the power, rank, or wealth of (a person or state). **2** cause to appear greater than is the case. □ **aggrandizement** /-dɪzm(ə)nt/ *n.* **aggrandizer** *n.* [French *agrandir* (stem *agrandiss-*), probably via Italian *aggrandire* from Latin *grandis* large: assimilated to verbs in -IZE]

aggravate /ˈagrəveɪt/ *v.tr.* **1** increase the gravity of (an illness, offence, etc.) (*the war was aggravating the situation*). **2** *disp.* annoy, exasperate (a person). □ **aggravating** *adj. disp.* **aggravation** /-ˈveɪʃ(ə)n/ *n.* [Latin *aggravare aggravat-* 'make heavy' from *gravis* 'heavy']

■ **Usage** The use of *aggravate* in sense 2, to mean 'annoy, exasperate', is regarded by some people as incorrect but is common in informal use and dates back to the 17th century. *Aggravating* meaning 'annoying' is similarly frowned upon.

aggregate *n., adj., & v.* ● *n.* /ˈagrɪgət/ **1** a collection of, or the total of, disparate elements. **2** pieces of crushed stone, gravel, etc., used in making concrete. **3 a** *Geol.* a mass of minerals formed into solid rock. **b** a mass of particles. ● *adj.* /ˈagrɪgət/ **1** (of disparate elements) collected into one mass. **2** constituted by the collection of many units into one body. **3** *Bot.* (of a group of species) comprising several very similar species formerly regarded as a single species. ● *v.tr. & intr.* /ˈagrɪgeɪt/ collect together; combine into a whole. □ **in the aggregate** as a whole. □ **aggregation** /-ˈgeɪʃ(ə)n/ *n.* **aggregative** /ˈagrɪgətɪv/ *adj.* [Latin *aggregare aggregat-* 'herd together' (as AD-, *grex gregis* 'flock')]

aggregate fruit *n. Bot.* a fruit formed from several carpels derived from the same flower (e.g. raspberry).

aggression /əˈɡrɛʃ(ə)n/ *n.* **1** the act or practice of attacking without provocation, esp. beginning a quarrel or war. **2** an unprovoked attack. **3** self-assertiveness; forcefulness. **4** *Psychol.* a hostile or destructive tendency; such behaviour. [French *agression* or Latin *aggressio* 'attack', from *aggredi aggress-* (as AD-, *gradi* 'walk')]

aggressive /əˈɡrɛsɪv/ *adj.* **1** of a person: **a** given to aggression; openly hostile. **b** forceful; self-assertive. **2** (of an act) offensive, hostile. **3** of aggression. ▫ **aggressively** *adv.* **aggressiveness** *n.*

aggressor /əˈɡrɛsə/ *n.* a person who attacks without provocation. [Latin (as AGGRESSION)]

aggrieved /əˈɡriːvd/ *adj.* having a grievance. ▫ **aggrievedly** /-vɪdli/ *adv.* [Middle English, past part. of *aggrieve*, from Old French *agrever* 'make heavier' (as AD-, GRIEVE[1])]

aggro /ˈaɡrəʊ/ *n. Brit. slang* **1** aggressive trouble-making. **2** trouble, difficulty. [abbreviation of AGGRAVATION (see AGGRAVATE) or AGGRESSION]

aghast /əˈɡɑːst/ *predic.adj.* (often foll. by *at*) filled with dismay or consternation. [Middle English, past part. of obsolete *agast*, *gast* 'frighten': see GHASTLY]

agile /ˈadʒʌɪl/ *adj.* quick-moving, nimble, active. ▫ **agilely** *adv.* **agility** /əˈdʒɪlɪti/ *n.* [French from Latin *agilis*, from *agere* 'do']

agin /əˈɡɪn/ *prep. colloq.* or *dial.* against. [corruption of AGAINST or obsolete prep. *again*, with the same meaning]

aging var. of AGEING.

agio /ˈadʒɪəʊ/ *n.* (*pl.* **agios**) **1** the percentage charged on the exchange of one currency, or one form of money, into another more valuable. **2** the excess value of one currency over another. **3** money-exchange business. [Italian *aggio*]

agist /əˈdʒɪst/ *v.tr.* take in and feed (livestock) for payment. ▫ **agistment** *n.*

agitate /ˈadʒɪteɪt/ *v.* **1** *tr.* disturb or excite (a person or feelings). **2** *intr.* (often foll. by *for, against*) stir up interest or concern, esp. publicly (*agitated for tax reform*). **3** *tr.* shake or move, esp. briskly. ▫ **agitatedly** *adv.* [Latin *agitare agitat-*, frequentative of *agere* 'drive']

agitation /adʒɪˈteɪʃ(ə)n/ *n.* **1** the act or process of agitating or being agitated. **2** mental anxiety or concern. [French *agitation* or Latin *agitatio* (as AGITATE)]

agitato /adʒɪˈtɑːtəʊ/ *adv. & adj. Mus.* in an agitated manner. [Italian]

agitator /ˈadʒɪteɪtə/ *n.* **1** a person who agitates, esp. publicly for a cause. **2** an apparatus for shaking or mixing liquid etc. [Latin (as AGITATE)]

agitprop /ˈadʒɪtprɒp, ˈaɡ-/ *n. hist.* the dissemination of Communist political propaganda, esp. in plays, films, books, etc. [Russian (as AGITATION, PROPAGANDA)]

aglet /ˈaɡlət/ *n.* **1** a metal tag attached to each end of a shoelace etc. **2** = AIGUILLETTE. [Middle English from French *aiguillette* 'small needle', ultimately from Latin *acus* 'needle']

agley /əˈɡleɪ, əˈɡliː/ *adv. Sc.* askew, awry. [A[2] + Scots *gley* 'squint']

aglow /əˈɡləʊ/ *adv. & predic.adj.* glowing; in a glow (of warmth, excitement, etc.).

AGM *abbr. Brit.* annual general meeting.

agma /ˈaɡmə/ *n.* **1** the speech sound of 'ng' as in *thing*, represented by the symbol /ŋ/. **2** this symbol. [Greek, literally 'fragment']

agnail /ˈaɡneɪl/ *n.* **1** a piece of torn skin at the root of a fingernail. **2** the soreness resulting from this. [Old English *angnægl* from *nægl* NAIL *n.* 2a: cf. HANGNAIL]

agnate /ˈaɡneɪt/ *adj. & n.* ● *adj.* **1** descended esp. by male line from the same male ancestor (cf. COGNATE *adj.* 1). **2** descended from the same forefather; of the same clan or nation. **3** of the same nature; akin. ● *n.* a person who is descended esp. by male line from the same male ancestor. ▫ **agnatic** /-ˈnatɪk/ *adj.* **agnation** /-ˈneɪʃ(ə)n/ *n.* [Latin *agnatus*, from *ad* AG- + (*g*)*natus* 'born']

agnolotti /anjəˈlɒti/ *n.* small pasta shapes containing meat stuffing. [Italian]

agnosia /əɡˈnəʊsɪə/ *n. Med.* the loss of the ability to interpret sensations. [modern Latin from Greek *agnōsia* 'ignorance']

agnostic /aɡˈnɒstɪk/ *n. & adj.* ● *n.* **1** a person who believes that nothing is known, or can be known, of the existence or nature of God or of anything beyond material phenomena. **2** a person who is uncertain or non-committal about a certain thing. ● *adj.* of or relating to agnostics or agnosticism. ▫ **agnosticism** /-sɪz(ə)m/ *n.* [A-[1] + GNOSTIC]

Agnus Dei /ˈaɡnʊs ˈdeɪiː/ *n.* **1** a figure of a lamb bearing a cross or flag, as an emblem of Christ. **2** the part of the Roman Catholic Mass beginning with the words 'Lamb of God'. [Latin, = Lamb of God]

ago /əˈɡəʊ/ *adv.* earlier; before the present (*ten years ago*; *long ago*). [Middle English (*ago*, *agone*), past part. of obsolete verb *ago* (as A-[2], GO[1])]

■ **Usage** Note the construction *it is ten years ago that* (not *since*) *I saw them.*

agog /əˈɡɒɡ/ *adv. & adj.* ● *adv.* eagerly, expectantly. ● *predic.adj.* eager, expectant. [French *en gogues*, from *en* 'in' + pl. of *gogue* 'fun']

agogic /əˈɡɒdʒɪk/ *adj. & n. Mus.* ● *adj.* designating or relating to an accent effected by lengthening the time value of a note. ● *n.* (in *pl.*, usu. treated as *sing.*) the use of agogic accents; the deliberate modification of time values in a musical performance. [German *agogisch*, from Greek *agogos* 'leading']

à gogo /ə ˈɡəʊɡəʊ/ *adv.* in abundance (*whisky à gogo*). [French]

agonic line /əˈɡɒnɪk/ *n.* a line passing through both the north pole and the north magnetic pole and joining places at which a compass needle points to true north (i.e. without declination). [Greek *agōn(i)os*, from *a-* A-[1] + *gonia* 'angle' + -IC]

agonist /ˈaɡənɪst/ *n.* **1** *Physiol.* a muscle whose contraction moves a part directly. **2** *Biochem.* a substance which initiates a physiological response when combined with a receptor. **3** = PROTAGONIST 1, 2. [Greek *agōnistēs* 'contestant', from *agōn* 'contest']

agonistic /aɡəˈnɪstɪk/ *adj.* **1** polemical, combative. **2** *Zool.* (of animal behaviour) associated with conflict. **3** *Biochem.* of or relating to an agonist; acting as an agonist. ▫ **agonistically** *adv.* [Late Latin *agonisticus* from Greek *agōnistikos*, via *agōnistēs* 'contestant' from *agōn* 'contest']

agonize /ˈaɡənʌɪz/ *v.* (also **-ise**) **1** *intr.* (often foll. by *over*) undergo (esp. mental) anguish; suffer agony. **2** *tr.* cause agony to. **3** *tr.* (as **agonized** *adj.*) expressing agony (*an agonized look*). **4** *intr.* struggle, contend. ▫ **agonizingly** *adv.* [French *agoniser* or Late Latin *agonizare* from Greek *agōnizomai* 'contend', from *agōn* 'contest']

agony /ˈaɡəni/ *n.* (*pl.* **-ies**) **1** extreme mental or physical suffering. **2** a severe struggle. [Middle English via Old French *agonie* or Late Latin from Greek *agōnia*, from *agōn* 'contest']

agony aunt *n.* (*masc.* **agony uncle**) *Brit. colloq.* a person who answers letters in an agony column.

agony column *n. Brit. colloq.* **1** a column in a newspaper or magazine offering personal advice to readers who write in. **2** = PERSONAL COLUMN.

agoraphobe /ˈaɡ(ə)rəfəʊb/ *n.* a person who suffers from agoraphobia.

agoraphobia /aɡ(ə)rəˈfəʊbɪə/ *n. Psychol.* an abnormal fear of open spaces or public places. ▫ **agoraphobic** *adj. & n.* [modern Latin from Greek *agora* 'place of assembly, market place' + -PHOBIA]

agouti /əˈɡuːti/ *n.* (also **aguti**) (*pl.* **-tis**) **1** a burrowing rodent of the genus *Dasyprocta* or *Myoprocta* of Central and S. America, related to the guinea pig. **2** any animal whose fur has each hair banded dark and light. [French *agouti* or Spanish *aguti*, from Tupi *aguti*]

AGR *abbr.* advanced gas-cooled (nuclear) reactor.

agrarian /əˈgrɛːrɪən/ *adj. & n.* ● *adj.* **1** of or relating to the land or its cultivation. **2** relating to landed property. ● *n.* a person who advocates a redistribution of landed property. [Latin *agrarius*, from *ager agri* 'field']

agree /əˈgriː/ *v.* (**agrees**, **agreed**, **agreeing**) **1** *intr.* hold a similar opinion (*I agree with you about that; they agreed that it would rain*). **2** *intr.* (often foll. by *to*, or *to* + infin.) consent (*agreed to the arrangement; agreed to go*). **3** *intr.* (often foll. by *with*) **a** become or be in harmony. **b** suit; be good for (*caviar didn't agree with him*). **c** *Gram.* have the same number, gender, case, or person as. **4** *tr. Brit.* reach agreement about (*agreed a price*). **5** *tr. Brit.* consent to or approve of (terms, a proposal, etc.). **6** *tr. Brit.* bring (things, esp. accounts) into harmony. **7** *intr.* (foll. by *on*) decide by mutual consent (*agreed on a compromise*). □ **agree to differ** leave a difference of opinion unresolved. **be agreed** have reached the same opinion. [Middle English from Old French *agreer*, ultimately from Latin *gratus* 'pleasing']

agreeable /əˈgriːəb(ə)l/ *adj.* **1** (often foll. by *to*) pleasing. **2** (often foll. by *to*) (of a person) willing to agree (*was agreeable to going*). **3** (foll. by *to*) conformable. □ **agreeableness** *n.* **agreeably** *adv.* [Middle English from Old French *agreable*, from *agreer* AGREE]

agreement /əˈgriːm(ə)nt/ *n.* **1** the act of agreeing; the holding of the same opinion (*reached agreement*). **2** mutual understanding. **3** an arrangement between parties as to a course of action etc. **4** *Gram.* having the same number, gender, case, or person. **5** mutual conformity of things; harmony. [Middle English from Old French (as AGREE)]

agribusiness /ˈagrɪbɪznɪs/ *n.* **1** agriculture conducted on strictly commercial principles, esp. using advanced technology. **2** an organization engaged in this. **3** the group of industries dealing with the produce of, and services to, farming. □ **agribusinessman** /-ˈbɪznɪsmən/ *n.* (*pl.* **-men**). [AGRICULTURE + BUSINESS]

agriculture /ˈagrɪkʌltʃə/ *n.* the science or practice of cultivating the soil and rearing animals. □ **agricultural** /-ˈkʌltʃ(ə)r(ə)l/ *adj.* **agriculturalist** /-ˈkʌltʃ(ə)r(ə)lɪst/ *n.* **agriculturally** /-ˈkʌltʃ(ə)r(ə)li/ *adv.* **agriculturist** /-ˈkʌltʃ(ə)rɪst/ *n.* [French *agriculture* or Latin *agricultura*, from *ager agri* 'field' + *cultura* CULTURE]

agrimony /ˈagrɪməni/ *n.* (*pl.* **-ies**) any perennial plant of the genus *Agrimonia*, esp. *A. eupatoria* with small yellow flowers. [Middle English via Old French *aigremoine* from Latin *agrimonia*, alteration of *argemonia*, from Greek *argemōnē* 'poppy']

agro- /ˈagrəʊ/ *comb. form* agricultural (*agro-climatic; agro-ecological*). [Greek *agros* 'field']

agrochemical /agrəʊˈkɛmɪk(ə)l/ *n.* a chemical used in agriculture.

agroforestry /agrəʊˈfɒrɪstri/ *n.* agriculture incorporating the cultivation and conservation of trees.

agronomy /əˈgrɒnəmi/ *n.* the science of soil management and crop production. □ **agronomic** /agrəˈnɒmɪk/ *adj.* **agronomical** /agrəˈnɒmɪk(ə)l/ *adj.* **agronomically** /agrəˈnɒmɪk(ə)li/ *adv.* **agronomist** *n.* [French *agronomie* from *agronome* 'agriculturist', from Greek *agros* 'field' + *-nomos* from *nemō* 'arrange']

aground /əˈgraʊnd/ *predic.adj. & adv.* (of a ship) on or on to the bottom of shallow water (*be aground; run aground*). [Middle English from A[2] + GROUND[1]]

ague /ˈeɪgjuː/ *n.* **1** *hist.* a malarial fever, with cold, hot, and sweating stages. **2** a shivering fit. □ **agued** *adj.* **aguish** *adj.* [Middle English via Old French from medieval Latin *acuta* (*febris*) 'acute (fever)']

aguti var. of AGOUTI.

AH *abbr.* in the year of the Hegira (AD 622); of the Muslim era. [Latin *anno Hegirae*]

ah /ɑː/ *int.* expressing surprise, pleasure, sudden realization, resignation, etc. [Middle English from Old French *a*]

■ **Usage** See Usage Note at AHA.

aha /əˈhɑː, ɑːˈhɑː/ *int.* expressing surprise, triumph, mockery, irony, etc. [Middle English from AH + HA[1]]

■ **Usage** As with many exclamations, sense depends much on intonation.

ahead /əˈhɛd/ *adv.* **1** further forward in space or time. **2** in the lead; further advanced (*ahead on points*). **3** in the line of one's forward motion (*roadworks ahead*). **4** straight forwards. □ **ahead of 1** further forward or advanced than. **2** in the line of the forward motion of. [originally nautical, from A[2] + HEAD]

ahem /əˈhɛm/ (not usu. clearly articulated) *int.* used to attract attention, gain time, or express disapproval. [lengthened form of HEM[2]]

ahimsa /əˈhɪmsɑː/ *n.* (in the Hindu, Buddhist, and Jainist tradition) respect for all living things and avoidance of violence towards others both in thought and deed. [Sanskrit, from *a* 'without' + *himsa* 'injury']

ahoy /əˈhɔɪ/ *int. Naut.* a call used in hailing. [AH + HOY[1]]

à huis clos /ɑː wiː ˈkləʊ, French a ɥi klo/ *adv.* in private. [French, = with closed doors]

AI *abbr.* **1** artificial insemination. **2** artificial intelligence.

ai /ˈɑːɪ/ *n.* (*pl.* **ais**) the three-toed sloth of S. America, of the genus *Bradypus*. [Tupi *ai*, representing its cry]

AID *abbr.* artificial insemination by donor.

aid /eɪd/ *n. & v.* ● *n.* **1** help. **2** financial or material help, esp. given by one country to another. **3** a material source of help (*teaching aid*). **4** a person or thing that helps. **5** (as second element in *comb.*) esp. *Brit.* denoting an organization or event that raises money for charity (*Band Aid*). **6** *hist.* a grant of subsidy or tax to a king. ● *v.tr.* **1** (often foll. by *in* + gerund) help. **2** promote or encourage (*sleep will aid recovery*). □ **in aid of** *Brit.* in support of. **what's this** (or **all this**) **in aid of?** *Brit. colloq.* what is the purpose of this? [Middle English from Old French *aïde* (*n.*), *aïdier* (*v.*), ultimately from Latin *adjuvare* (as AD-, *juvare jut-* 'help')]

aide /eɪd/ *n.* **1** an aide-de-camp. **2** an assistant. [abbreviation]

aide-de-camp /eɪddəˈkɒ̃/ *n.* (*pl.* **aides-de-camp** *pronunc.* same) an officer acting as a confidential assistant to a senior officer. [French, = camp adjutant]

aide-mémoire /ˌeɪdmɛmˈwɑː/ *n.* (*pl.* **aides-mémoires** or **aides-mémoire** *pronunc.* same) **1 a** an aid to the memory. **b** a book or document meant to aid the memory. **2** *Diplomacy* a memorandum. [French, from *aider* 'to help' + *mémoire* 'memory']

Aids /eɪdz/ *n.* (also **AIDS**) acquired immune deficiency syndrome, a condition caused by a virus transmitted in the body fluids, marked by severe loss of resistance to infection and so ultimately fatal. [acronym]

Aids-related complex *n.* the symptoms of a person who is affected with the Aids virus but does not necessarily develop the disease.

aigrette /ˈeɪgrɛt, eɪˈgrɛt/ *n.* **1** a white plume from an egret. **2** a tuft of feathers or hair. **3** a spray of gems or similar ornament. [French: see EGRET]

aiguille /ˈeɪgwiːl/ *n.* a sharp peak of rock, esp. in the Alps. [French: see AGLET]

aiguillette /eɪgwɪˈlɛt/ *n.* a tagged point hanging from the shoulder on the breast of some uniforms. [French: see AGLET]

AIH *abbr.* artificial insemination by husband.

aikido /ʌɪˈkiːdəʊ/ *n.* a Japanese form of self-defence and martial art, using locks, holds, throws, and the opponent's own movements. [Japanese, from *ai* 'together, unify' + *ki* 'spirit' + *dō* 'way']

ail /eɪl/ *v.* **1** *tr.* (only in 3rd person interrog. or indefinite constructions) *archaic* trouble or afflict in mind or body (*what ails him?*). **2** *intr.* (usu. **be ailing**) be ill. [Old English *egl(i)an*, from *egle* 'troublesome']

ailanthus /eɪˈlanθəs/ *n.* a tall deciduous tree of the genus *Ailanthus*, native to Asia and Australasia, esp. the tree of heaven, *A. altissima.* [modern Latin, via French *ailante* from Amboinese *aylanto*: ending influenced by *-anthus* = Greek *anthos* 'flower']

aileron /ˈeɪlərɒn/ *n.* a hinged surface in the trailing edge of an aeroplane wing, used to control lateral balance. [French, diminutive of *aile* 'wing', from Latin *ala*]

ailing /ˈeɪlɪŋ/ *adj.* **1** ill, esp. chronically. **2** in poor condition.

ailment /ˈeɪlm(ə)nt/ *n.* an illness, esp. a minor one.

aim /eɪm/ *v. & n.* ● *v.* **1** *intr.* (foll. by *at* + verbal noun, or *to* + infin.) intend or try (*aim at winning*; *aim to win*). **2** *tr.* (usu. foll. by *at*) direct or point (a weapon, remark, etc.). **3** *intr.* take aim. **4** *intr.* (foll. by *at*, *for*) seek to attain or achieve. ● *n.* **1** a purpose or design; an object aimed at. **2** the directing of a weapon, missile, etc., at an object. □ **take aim** direct a weapon etc. at an object. [Middle English from Old French, ultimately from Latin *aestimare* 'reckon']

aimless /ˈeɪmlɪs/ *adj.* without aim or purpose. □ **aimlessly** *adv.* **aimlessness** *n.*

ain't /eɪnt/ *contr. colloq.* **1** am not; are not; is not (*you ain't doing it right*; *she ain't nice*). **2** has not; have not (*we ain't seen him*). [contraction of *are not*]

■ **Usage** *Ain't* is usually regarded as an uneducated use, and unacceptable in spoken and written English, except in representations of dialect speech.

aioli /ʌɪˈəʊli/ *n.* (also **aïoli**) mayonnaise seasoned with garlic. [French, from Provençal *ai* 'garlic' + *oli* 'oil']

air /ɛː/ *n. & v.* ● *n.* **1** an invisible gaseous substance surrounding the earth, a mixture mainly of oxygen and nitrogen. **2 a** the earth's atmosphere. **b** the free or unconfined space in the atmosphere (*birds of the air*; *in the open air*). **c** the atmosphere as a place where aircraft operate or as a medium for transmitting radio waves. **3 a** a distinctive impression or characteristic (*an air of absurdity*). **b** one's manner or bearing, esp. a confident one (*with a triumphant air*; *does things with an air*). **c** (esp. in *pl.*) an affected manner; pretentiousness (*gave himself airs*). **4** *Mus.* a tune or melody; a melodious composition. **5** a breeze or light wind. ● *v.tr.* **1** *Brit.* warm (washed laundry) to remove damp, esp. at a fire or in a heated cupboard. **2** expose (a room etc.) to the open air; ventilate. **3** express publicly (an opinion, grievance, etc.). **4** parade; show ostentatiously (esp. qualities). **5** *refl.* go out in the fresh air. □ **airs and graces** affected elegance designed to attract or impress. **by air** by aircraft; in an aircraft. **in the air** (of opinions or feelings) prevalent; gaining currency. **on** (or **off**) **the air** in (or not in) the process of broadcasting. **take the air** go out of doors. **tread** (or **walk**) **on air** feel elated. **up in the air** (of projects etc.) uncertain; not decided. [Middle English via French and Latin from Greek *aēr*]

air bag *n.* a safety device that fills with air or nitrogen on impact to protect the occupants of a vehicle in a collision.

airbase /ˈɛːbeɪs/ *n.* a base for the operation of military aircraft.

air-bed *n. Brit.* an inflatable mattress.

air bladder *n.* a bladder or sac filled with air in fish or some plants (cf. SWIM-BLADDER).

airborne /ˈɛːbɔːn/ *adj.* **1** transported by air. **2** (of aircraft) in the air after taking off.

air brake *n.* **1** a brake worked by air pressure. **2** a movable flap or other device on an aircraft to reduce its speed.

airbrick /ˈɛːbrɪk/ *n. Brit.* a brick perforated with small holes for ventilation.

air bridge *n. Brit.* a portable bridge or walkway put against an aircraft door.

airbrush /ˈɛːbrʌʃ/ *n. & v.* ● *n.* an artist's device for spraying paint by means of compressed air. ● *v.tr.* paint or paint over with an airbrush esp. for the purpose of enhancement.

Airbus /ˈɛːbʌs/ *n. propr.* an aircraft designed to carry a large number of passengers economically, esp. over relatively short routes.

Air Chief Marshal *n.* an RAF officer of high rank, below Marshal of the RAF and above Air Marshal.

Air Commodore *n.* an RAF officer next above Group Captain.

air-conditioning *n.* **1** a system for regulating the humidity, ventilation, and temperature in a building or vehicle. **2** the apparatus for this. □ **air-conditioned** *adj.* **air-conditioner** *n.*

air-cooled *adj.* cooled by means of a current of air.

air corridor *n.* = CORRIDOR 4.

aircraft /ˈɛːkrɑːft/ *n.* (*pl.* same) a machine capable of flight, esp. an aeroplane or helicopter.

aircraft carrier *n.* a warship that carries and serves as a base for aeroplanes.

aircraftman /ˈɛːkrɑːftmən/ *n.* (*pl.* **-men**; *fem.* **aircraftwoman** /ˈɛːkrɑːftˌwʊmən/, *pl.* **-women**) the lowest rank in the RAF.

aircrew /ˈɛːkruː/ *n.* **1** the crew manning an aircraft. **2** (*pl.* same) a member of such a crew.

air cushion *n.* **1** an inflatable cushion. **2** the layer of air supporting a hovercraft or similar vehicle.

airdrop /ˈɛːdrɒp/ *n. & v.* ● *n.* the act or an instance of dropping supplies, troops, etc. by parachute. ● *v.tr.* (**-dropped**, **-dropping**) drop (supplies etc.) by parachute.

Airedale /ˈɛːdeɪl/ *n.* **1** a large terrier of a rough-coated breed. **2** this breed. [*Airedale*, a district in Yorkshire]

airer /ˈɛːrə/ *n. Brit.* a frame or stand for airing or drying clothes etc.

airfield /ˈɛːfiːld/ *n.* an area of land where aircraft take off and land, are maintained, etc.

airflow /ˈɛːfləʊ/ *n.* the flow of air, esp. that encountered by a moving aircraft or vehicle.

airfoil /ˈɛːfɔɪl/ *n. N. Amer.* = AEROFOIL. [AIR + FOIL[2]]

air force *n.* a branch of the armed forces concerned with fighting or defence in the air.

airframe /ˈɛːfreɪm/ *n.* the body of an aircraft as distinct from its engine(s).

airglow /ˈɛːgləʊ/ *n.* radiation from the upper atmosphere, detectable at night.

airgun /ˈɛːgʌn/ *n.* a gun using compressed air to propel pellets.

airhead /ˈɛːhɛd/ *n.* **1** *Mil.* a forward base for aircraft in enemy territory. **2** *slang* a silly or foolish person. [sense 1 on the pattern of *bridgehead*]

air hostess *n. Brit.* a stewardess in a passenger aircraft.

airing /ˈɛːrɪŋ/ *n.* **1** exposure to fresh air, esp. for exercise or an excursion. **2** *Brit.* exposure (of laundry etc.) to warm air. **3** public expression of an opinion etc. (*the idea will get an airing at tomorrow's meeting*).

air lane *n.* a path or course regularly used by aircraft (cf. LANE 4).

airless /ˈɛːlɪs/ *adj.* **1** stuffy; not ventilated. **2** without wind or breeze; still. □ **airlessness** *n.*

air letter *n.* a sheet of light paper forming a letter for sending by airmail.

airlift /ˈɛːlɪft/ *n. & v.* ● *n.* the transport of troops and supplies by air, esp. in a blockade or other emergency. ● *v.tr.* transport in this way.

airline /ˈɛːlʌɪn/ *n.* **1** an organization providing a regular public service of air transport on one or more routes. **2** a pipe supplying air, esp. to a diver.

airliner /ˈɛːlʌɪnə/ *n.* a large passenger aircraft.

airlock /ˈɛːlɒk/ *n.* **1** a stoppage of the flow in a pump or pipe, caused by an air bubble. **2** a compartment with controlled pressure and parallel sets of doors, to permit movement between areas at different pressures.

airmail /ˈɛːmeɪl/ *n. & v.* ● *n.* **1** a system of transporting mail by air. **2** mail carried by air. ● *v.tr.* send by airmail.
airman /ˈɛːmən/ *n.* (*pl.* **-men**) **1** a pilot or member of the crew of an aircraft, esp. in an air force. **2** a member of the RAF below commissioned rank.
Air Marshal *n.* an RAF officer of high rank, below Air Chief Marshal and above Air Vice-Marshal.
air mattress *n. N. Amer.* = AIR-BED.
air mile *n.* **1** a nautical mile used as a measure of distance flown by aircraft. **2** (**Air Miles**) *pl. propr.* points (equivalent to miles of free air travel) accumulated by buyers of airline tickets and other products.
airmiss /ˈɛːmɪs/ *n. Brit.* a circumstance in which two or more aircraft in flight on different routes are less than a prescribed distance apart.
airmobile /ɛːˈməʊbʌɪl/ *adj.* (of troops) that can be moved about by air.
Air Officer *n.* any RAF officer above the rank of Group Captain.
airplane /ˈɛːpleɪn/ *n. N. Amer.* = AEROPLANE.
air plant *n.* a plant growing naturally without soil.
airplay /ˈɛːpleɪ/ *n.* broadcasting (of recorded music).
air pocket *n.* **1** a cavity containing air. **2** a region of low pressure etc. causing an aircraft to lose height suddenly.
airport /ˈɛːpɔːt/ *n.* a complex of runways and buildings for the take-off, landing, and maintenance of civil aircraft, with facilities for passengers.
air power *n.* the ability to defend and attack by means of aircraft, missiles, etc.
air pump *n.* a device for pumping air into or out of an enclosed space.
air raid *n.* an attack by aircraft.
air rifle *n.* a rifle using compressed air to propel pellets.
air sac *n.* an extension of the lungs in birds or of the tracheae in insects.
airscrew /ˈɛːskruː/ *n. Brit.* an aircraft propeller.
air-sea rescue *n.* rescue from the sea by aircraft.
airship /ˈɛːʃɪp/ *n.* a power-driven aircraft that is lighter than air.
air show *n.* a show at which aircraft are on view and perform aerial displays.
airsick /ˈɛːsɪk/ *adj.* affected with nausea due to travel in an aircraft. □ **airsickness** *n.*
airside /ˈɛːsʌɪd/ *n.* the side of an airport terminal from which aircraft can be observed; the area beyond passport and customs control (opp. LANDSIDE).
airspace /ˈɛːspeɪs/ *n.* the air available to aircraft to fly in, esp. the part subject to the jurisdiction of a particular country.
air speed *n.* the speed of an aircraft relative to the air through which it is moving.
airstream /ˈɛːstriːm/ *n.* **1** a current of air. **2** = AIRFLOW.
airstrip /ˈɛːstrɪp/ *n.* a strip of ground suitable for the take-off and landing of aircraft.
air terminal *n.* **1** *Brit.* an airline office in a town to which passengers report and which serves as a base for transport to and from an airport. **2** = TERMINAL *n.* 3.
airtight /ˈɛːtʌɪt/ *adj.* not allowing air to pass through.
airtime /ˈɛːtʌɪm/ *n.* time allotted for a broadcast.
air-to-air *attrib.adj.* from one aircraft to another in flight (*air-to-air refuelling*; *air-to-air missile*).
air traffic control *n.* the control of air traffic by giving radio instructions to pilots concerning route, altitude, take-off, and landing. □ **air traffic controller** *n.*
Air Vice-Marshal *n.* an RAF officer of high rank, just below Air Marshal.
airwaves /ˈɛːweɪvz/ *n.pl.* radio waves used in broadcasting.
airway /ˈɛːweɪ/ *n.* **1** a natural or artificial passage by which air reaches the lungs. **2 a** a recognized route followed by aircraft. **b** (often in *pl.*) = AIRLINE 1. **3** a ventilating passage in a mine.
airwoman /ˈɛːwʊmən/ *n.* (*pl.* **-women**) **1** a woman pilot or member of the crew of an aircraft, esp. in an air force. **2** a female member of the RAF below commissioned rank.
airworthy /ˈɛːwəːði/ *adj.* (of an aircraft) fit to fly. □ **airworthiness** *n.*
airy /ˈɛːri/ *adj.* (**airier**, **airiest**) **1** well-ventilated, breezy. **2** flippant, superficial. **3 a** light as air. **b** graceful, delicate. **4** insubstantial, ethereal, immaterial. □ **airily** *adv.* **airiness** *n.*
airy-fairy *adj. colloq.* unrealistic, impractical, foolishly idealistic.
aisle /ʌɪl/ *n.* **1** part of a church, esp. one parallel to and divided by pillars from the nave, choir, or transept. **2 a** a passage between rows of pews, seats, etc. **b** a passage between cabinets and shelves of goods in a supermarket etc. □ **aisled** *adj.* [Middle English *ele, ile* via Old French *ele* from Latin *ala* 'wing': spelling influenced by confusion with *isle* and French *aile* 'wing']
ait /eɪt/ *n.* (also **eyot**) *Brit.* a small island, esp. in a river. [Old English *iggath* etc., from *īeg* ISLAND + diminutive suffix]
aitch /eɪtʃ/ *n.* the name of the letter H. □ **drop one's aitches** fail to pronounce the initial *h* in words. [Old French *ache*]
aitchbone /ˈeɪtʃbəʊn/ *n.* **1** the buttock or rump bone of cattle. **2** a cut of beef lying over this. [Middle English *nage-, nache-bone* 'buttock', ultimately from Latin *natis, -es* 'buttock(s)': for loss of *n* cf. ADDER]
ajar[1] /əˈdʒɑː/ *adv. & predic.adj.* (of a door) slightly open. [A[2] + obsolete *char* from Old English *cerr* 'a turn']
ajar[2] /əˈdʒɑː/ *adv.* out of harmony. [A[2] + JAR[2]]
AK *abbr. US* Alaska (in official postal use).
aka *abbr.* also known as.
akee var. of ACKEE.
Akela /ɑːˈkeɪlə/ *n. colloq.* the adult leader of a group of Cub Scouts, officially termed Cub Scout Leader. [name of the leader of a wolf pack in Kipling's *Jungle Book* (1894–5)]
akimbo /əˈkɪmbəʊ/ *adv.* (of the arms) with hands on the hips and elbows turned outwards. [Middle English *in kenebowe*, probably from Old Norse]
akin /əˈkɪn/ *predic.adj.* **1** related by blood. **2** (often foll. by *to*) of similar or kindred character. [A-[4] + KIN]
Akkadian /əˈkeɪdɪən/ *adj. & n.* (also **Accadian**) *hist.* ● *adj.* of or relating to Akkad in ancient Babylonia or its language. ● *n.* **1** the Semitic language of Akkad. **2** an inhabitant of Akkad.
akvavit var. of AQUAVIT.
AL *abbr. US* Alabama (in official postal use).
Al *symb. Chem.* the element aluminium.
al- /al/ *prefix* assim. form of AD- before *-l.*
-al /əl/ *suffix* **1** forming adjectives meaning 'relating to, of the kind of': **a** from Latin or Greek words (*central*; *regimental*; *colossal*; *tropical*) (cf. -IAL, -ICAL). **b** from English nouns (*tidal*). **2** forming nouns, esp. of verbal action (*animal*; *rival*; *arrival*; *proposal*; *trial*). [sense 1 from French *-el* or Latin *-alis*, adjectival suffix related to *-aris* (-AR[1]); sense 2 from French *-aille* or from (or influenced by) Latin *-alis* used as a noun]
Ala. *abbr.* Alabama.
à la /ɑː lɑː, French a la/ *prep.* after the manner of (*à la russe*). [French, from À LA MODE]
alabaster /ˈaləbɑːstə, -bastə/ *n. & adj.* ● *n.* a translucent usu. white form of gypsum, often carved into ornaments. ● *adj.* **1** of alabaster. **2** like alabaster in whiteness or smoothness. □ **alabastrine** /-ˈbɑːstrɪn, -ˈbastrɪn, -ʌɪn/ *adj.* [Middle English via Old French *alabastre* from Latin *alabaster*, *-trum*, from Greek *alabast(r)os*]
à la carte /ɑː lɑː ˈkɑːt/ *adv. & adj.* ordered as separately priced item(s) from a menu, not as part of a set meal. [French, = according to the card (menu)]
alack /əˈlak/ *int.* (also **alack-a-day**) *archaic* an expression of regret or surprise. [probably from AH + LACK]

alacrity /ə'lakrɪti/ *n.* briskness or cheerful readiness. [Latin *alacritas*, from *alacer* 'brisk']

Aladdin's cave /ə'ladɪnz/ *n.* a place of great riches. [*Aladdin* in the *Arabian Nights' Entertainments*, a collection of oriental folk tales]

Aladdin's lamp /ə'ladɪnz/ *n.* a talisman enabling its holder to gratify any wish.

à la mode /ɑ: lɑ: 'məʊd/ *adv.* & *adj.* **1** in fashion; fashionable. **2 a** (of beef) braised in wine. **b** *N. Amer.* served with ice cream. [French, = in the fashion]

alanine /'aləni:n/ *n. Biochem.* a hydrophobic amino acid present in proteins. [German *Alanin*]

Alar /'eɪlɑ:/ *n. propr.* a growth retardant sprayed on fruit and vegetables to enhance the quality of the crop. [20th c.: origin unknown]

alar /'eɪlə/ *adj.* **1** relating to wings. **2** winglike or wing-shaped. **3** axillary. [Latin *alaris*, from *ala* 'wing']

alarm /ə'lɑ:m/ *n.* & *v.* ● *n.* **1** a warning of danger etc. (*gave the alarm*). **2 a** a warning sound or device (*the burglar alarm was set off accidentally*). **b** = ALARM CLOCK. **3** frightened expectation of danger or difficulty (*were filled with alarm*). ● *v.tr.* **1** frighten or disturb. **2** arouse to a sense of danger. [Middle English via Old French *alarme* from Italian *allarme*, from *all'arme!* 'to arms']

alarm clock *n.* a clock with a device that can be made to sound at the time set in advance.

alarming /ə'lɑ:mɪŋ/ *adj.* disturbing, frightening. □ **alarmingly** *adv.*

alarmist /ə'lɑ:mɪst/ *n.* & *adj.* ● *n.* a person given to spreading needless alarm. ● *adj.* creating needless alarm. □ **alarmism** *n.*

alarum /ə'lɑ:rəm/ *n. archaic* = ALARM. □ **alarums and excursions** *joc.* confused noise and bustle.

Alas. *abbr.* Alaska.

alas /ə'las, ə'lɑ:s/ *int.* an expression of grief, pity, or concern. [Middle English from Old French *a las(se)*, from *a* 'ah' + *las(se)* from Latin *lassus* 'weary']

alate /'eɪleɪt/ *adj.* having wings or winglike appendages. [Latin *alatus*, from *ala* 'wing']

alb /alb/ *n.* a white vestment reaching to the feet, worn by clergy and servers in some Christian Churches. [Old English *albe* from ecclesiastical Latin *alba*, fem. of Latin *albus* 'white']

albacore /'albəkɔ:/ *n.* **1** a long-finned tunny, *Thunnus alalunga*; also called *germon*. **2** any of various other related fish. [Portuguese *albacor*, *-cora*, from Arabic *al* 'the' + *bakr* 'young camel' or *bakūr* 'premature, precocious']

Albanian /al'beɪmɪən/ *n.* & *adj.* ● *n.* **1 a** a native or national of Albania in SE Europe. **b** a person of Albanian descent. **2** the language of Albania. ● *adj.* of or relating to Albania, its people, or its language.

albatross /'albətrɒs/ *n.* **1 a** any long-winged stout-bodied bird of the family Diomedeidae related to petrels, inhabiting the Pacific and Southern Oceans. **b** a source of frustration or guilt; an encumbrance (in allusion to Coleridge's *The Rime of the Ancient Mariner*). **2** *Brit. Golf* a score of three strokes under par at any hole. [alteration (influenced by Latin *albus* 'white') of 17th-c. *alcatras*, applied to various seabirds including the pelican, from Spanish and Portuguese *alcatraz*, from Arabic *alkādūs* 'the pitcher' (probably from the belief that the pelican carried water in its bill)]

albedo /al'bi:dəʊ/ *n.* (*pl.* **-os**) the proportion of light or radiation reflected by a surface, esp. of a planet or moon. [ecclesiastical Latin, = whiteness, from Latin *albus* 'white']

albeit /ɔ:l'bi:ɪt/ *conj.* though (*he tried, albeit without success*). [ALL *adv.* + BE + IT[1] *pron.*, = although it be (that)]

albert /'albət/ *n. Brit.* a watch-chain with a bar at one end for attaching to a buttonhole. [named after Prince *Albert*, consort of Queen Victoria, d. 1861]

albescent /al'bɛs(ə)nt/ *adj.* growing or shading into white. [Latin *albescere albescent-*, from *albus* 'white']

Albigenses /albɪ'gɛnsi:z, -'dʒɛn-/ *n.pl.* the members of a heretic sect in southern France in the 12th–13th c. □ **Albigensian** *adj.* [Latin, from *Albi* in S. France]

albino /al'bi:nəʊ/ *n.* (*pl.* **-os**) **1** a person or animal having a congenital absence of pigment in the skin and hair (which are white), and the eyes (which are usu. pink). **2** a plant lacking normal colouring. □ **albinism** /'albɪnɪz(ə)m/ *n.* **albinotic** /albɪ'nɒtɪk/ *adj.* [Spanish & Portuguese (originally of albinos among African blacks), from Latin *albo* from *albus* 'white' + *-ino* = -INE[1]]

Albion /'albɪən/ *n.* (also **perfidious Albion**) Britain or England. [Old English via Latin from Celtic, probably related to Latin *albus* 'white', with reference to the white cliffs of Dover: French *la perfide Albion* with reference to alleged treachery to other nations]

albite /'albʌɪt/ *n. Mineral.* a feldspar, usu. white, rich in sodium. [Latin *albus* 'white' + -ITE[1]]

album /'albəm/ *n.* **1** a blank book for the insertion of photographs, stamps, etc. **2 a** a long-playing gramophone record. **b** a set of recordings issued together. [Latin, = a blank tablet, neut. of *albus* 'white']

albumen /'albjʊmɪn/ *n.* **1** egg white. **2** *Bot.* the substance found between the skin and germ of many seeds, usu. the edible part; = ENDOSPERM. [Latin *albumen -minis* 'white of egg', from *albus* 'white']

albumin /'albjʊmɪn/ *n.* any of a class of water-soluble proteins found in egg white, milk, blood, etc. □ **albuminous** /al'bju:mɪnəs/ *adj.* [French *albumine* from Latin *albumin-*: see ALBUMEN]

albuminoid /al'bju:mɪnɔɪd/ *n.* = SCLEROPROTEIN.

albuminuria /ˌalbjʊmɪ'njʊərɪə/ *n.* the presence of albumin in the urine, usu. a symptom of kidney disease.

alburnum /al'bə:nəm/ *n.* = SAPWOOD. [Latin, from *albus* 'white']

alcahest var. of ALKAHEST.

alcaic /al'keɪɪk/ *adj.* & *n.* ● *adj.* of the verse metre invented by Alcaeus, lyric poet of Mytilene *c.*600 BC, occurring in four-line stanzas. ● *n.* (in *pl.*) alcaic verses. [Late Latin *alcaicus* from Greek *alkaikos*, from *Alkaios* 'Alcaeus']

alcalde /al'kaldi/ *n.* a magistrate or mayor in a Spanish, Portuguese, or Latin American town. [Spanish from Arabic *al-kāḍī* 'the judge': see CADI]

alchemy /'alkɪmi/ *n.* (*pl.* **-ies**) **1** the medieval forerunner of chemistry, esp. seeking to turn base metals into gold or silver. **2** a miraculous transformation or the means of achieving this. □ **alchemic** /al'kɛmɪk/ *adj.* **alchemical** /al'kɛmɪk(ə)l/ *adj.* **alchemist** *n.* **alchemize** *v.tr.* (also **-ise**). [Middle English via Old French *alkemie*, *alkamie* and medieval Latin *alchimia*, *-emia* from Arabic *alkīmiyā'*, from *al* 'the' + *kīmiyā'* from Greek *khēmia*, *-meia* 'art of transmuting metals']

alcheringa /altʃə'rɪŋgə/ *n.* (in the mythology of some Australian Aboriginals) the 'golden age' when the first ancestors were created. [Aranda *aljerre-nge* 'in the dreamtime']

alcid /'alsɪd/ *n.* a bird of the auk family, Alcidae. [modern Latin *Alcidae* from genus name *Alca*: cf. AUK]

alcohol /'alkəhɒl/ *n.* **1** (in full **ethyl alcohol**) a colourless volatile inflammable liquid forming the intoxicating element in wine, beer, spirits, etc., and also used as a solvent, as fuel, etc.; also called *ethanol*. Chem. formula: C_2H_5OH. **2** drink containing this (*had always enjoyed food and alcohol*). **3** *Chem.* any of a large class of organic compounds that contain one or more hydroxyl groups attached to carbon atoms. [earlier applied to powders, specifically kohl, and esp. those obtained by sublimation; hence, a distilled or rectified spirit: French or medieval Latin from Arabic *al-kuḥl*, from *al* 'the' + *kuḥl* KOHL]

alcohol-free *adj.* **1** not containing alcohol. **2** where, or during which, alcoholic drinks are not consumed.

alcoholic /alkəˈhɒlɪk/ *adj.* & *n.* ● *adj.* of, relating to, containing, or caused by alcohol. ● *n.* a person suffering from alcoholism.

alcoholism /ˈalkəhɒlɪz(ə)m/ *n.* **1** an addiction to the consumption of alcoholic liquor. **2** the diseased condition resulting from this. [modern Latin *alcoholismus* (as ALCOHOL)]

alcoholometer /alkəhɒˈlɒmɪtə/ *n.* an instrument for measuring alcoholic concentration. □ **alcoholometry** *n.*

alcove /ˈalkəʊv/ *n.* a recess, esp. in the wall of a room or of a garden. [French via Spanish *alcoba* from Arabic *al-ḳubba*, from *al* 'the' + *ḳubba* 'vault']

aldehyde /ˈaldɪhʌɪd/ *n. Chem.* any of a class of compounds formed by the oxidation of alcohols (and containing the group -CHO). □ **aldehydic** /aldɪˈhɪdɪk/ *adj.* [abbreviation of modern Latin *alcohol dehydrogenatum* 'alcohol deprived of hydrogen']

al dente /al ˈdɛnti/ *adj.* & *adv.* (of pasta etc.) (cooked) so as to be still firm when bitten. [Italian, literally 'to the tooth']

alder /ˈɔːldə/ *n.* **1** (also **alder tree**) a tree of the genus *Alnus*, related to the birch, bearing catkins and toothed leaves, esp. *A. glutinosa*, common in damp ground. **2** the wood of this tree. [Old English *alor*, *aler*, related to Latin *alnus*, with euphonic *d*]

alder buckthorn *n.* a shrub, *Frangula alnus*, related to the buckthorn.

alder fly *n.* a neuropterous insect of the genus *Sialis*, found near streams.

alderman /ˈɔːldəmən/ *n.* (*pl.* **-men**) **1** esp. *hist.* a co-opted member of an English county or borough council, next in dignity to the Mayor. **2** (*fem.* **alderwoman**, *pl.***-women**) *N. Amer.* & *Austral.* an elected member of a city council. □ **aldermanic** /-ˈmanɪk/ *adj.* **aldermanship** *n.* [Old English *aldor* 'patriarch', from *ald* 'old' + MAN]

alderperson /ˈɔːldəpəːs(ə)n/ *n. N. Amer.* an alderman or alderwoman (used as a neutral alternative).

Aldis lamp /ˈɔːldɪs/ *n. propr.* a hand-held lamp for signalling in Morse code. [A. C. W. *Aldis* d. 1953, its inventor]

aldosterone /alˈdɒstərəʊn/ *n. Physiol.* a corticosteroid hormone which stimulates absorption of sodium by the kidneys and so regulates water and salt balance. [ALDEHYDE + STEROID + -ONE]

aldrin /ˈɔːldrɪn/ *n.* a white crystalline chlorinated hydrocarbon formerly used as an insecticide. [K. *Alder*, German chemist d. 1958 + -IN]

ale /eɪl/ *n.* **1** esp. *Brit.* beer (now usu. as a trade word). **2** *N. Amer.* a type of beer fermented rapidly at high temperatures. [Old English *alu*, from Germanic]

aleatoric /eɪlɪəˈtɒrɪk, al-/ *adj.* **1** depending on the throw of a die or on chance. **2** *Mus.* & *Art* involving random choice by a performer or artist. [Latin *aleatorius aleator* 'dice-player', from *alea* 'die']

aleatory /ˈeɪlɪət(ə)ri, ˈal-/ *adj.* = ALEATORIC. [as ALEATORIC]

alec /ˈalɪk/ *n.* (also **aleck**) *Austral. slang* a stupid person. [shortening of SMART ALEC]

alee /əˈliː/ *adv.* & *predic.adj.* **1** on the lee or sheltered side of a ship. **2** to leeward. [Middle English, from A[2] + LEE]

alehouse /ˈeɪlhaʊs/ *n. hist.* a tavern.

alembic /əˈlɛmbɪk/ *n.* **1** *hist.* an apparatus formerly used in distilling. **2** a means of refining or extracting. [Middle English via Old French and medieval Latin *alembicus* from Arabic *al-'anbīḳ*, from *al* 'the' + *'anbīḳ* 'still', from Greek *ambix*, *-ikos* 'cup, cap of a still']

aleph /ˈɑːlɛf/ *n.* the first letter of the Hebrew alphabet. [Hebrew *'ālep*, literally 'ox']

alert /əˈləːt/ *adj.*, *n.*, & *v.* ● *adj.* **1** watchful or vigilant; ready to take action. **2** nimble (esp. of mental faculties); attentive. ● *n.* **1** a warning call or alarm. **2 a** a warning of an air raid. **b** the duration of this. ● *v.tr.* (often foll. by *to*) make alert; warn (*were alerted to the danger*). □ **on the alert** on the lookout against danger or attack. □ **alertly** *adv.* **alertness** *n.* [French *alerte* from Italian *all' erta* 'to the watchtower']

-ales /ˈeɪliːz/ *suffix* forming the plural names of orders of plants (*Rosales*). [pl. of Latin adjectival suffix *-alis*: see -AL]

aleurone /əˈljʊərəʊn/ *n.* (also **aleuron** /-rən/) *Biochem.* protein stored as granules in the seeds of plants etc. [Greek *aleuron* 'flour']

A level *n. Brit.* = ADVANCED LEVEL. [abbreviation]

alewife /ˈeɪlwʌɪf/ *n.* (*pl.* **alewives**) a fish of the NW Atlantic, *Alosa pseudoharengus*, related to the herring. [17th-c.: origin uncertain]

alexanders /alɪgˈzɑːndəz/ *n.* an umbelliferous plant, *Smyrnium olusatrum*, formerly used in salads but superseded by celery. [Old English, from medieval Latin *alexandrum*]

Alexander technique /alɪgˈzɑːndə/ *n.* a system of body awareness designed to promote well-being by ensuring minimum effort in maintaining postures and carrying out movements. [F. M. *Alexander*, Australian-born physiotherapist d. 1955]

Alexandrian /alɪgˈzɑːndrɪən/ *adj.* **1** of or characteristic of Alexandria in Egypt. **2 a** belonging to or akin to the schools of literature and philosophy of Alexandria. **b** (of a writer) derivative or imitative; fond of recondite learning.

alexandrine /alɪgˈzɑːndrɪn, -ʌɪn/ *adj.* & *n.* ● *adj.* (of a line of verse) having six iambic feet. ● *n.* an alexandrine line. [French *alexandrin*, from *Alexandre* = Alexander the Great, the subject of an Old French poem in this metre]

alexandrite /alɪgˈzɑːndrʌɪt/ *n. Mineral.* a green variety of chrysoberyl, originally found in the Ural Mountains. [named after Tsar *Alexander* I of Russia: see -ITE[1]]

alexia /əˈlɛksɪə, eɪ-/ *n.* the inability to see words or to read, caused by a defect of the brain. Cf. DYSLEXIA. [modern Latin, A-[1] + Greek *lexis* 'speech' from *legein* 'speak', confused with Latin *legere* 'read']

alfalfa /alˈfalfə/ *n.* a leguminous plant, *Medicago sativa*, with clover-like leaves and flowers, grown for fodder and as a salad vegetable. Also called LUCERNE. [Spanish, from Arabic *al-faṣfaṣa*, a green fodder]

alfresco /alˈfrɛskəʊ/ *adv.* & *adj.* in the open air (*we lunched alfresco; an alfresco lunch*). [Italian *al fresco* 'in the fresh (air)']

alga /ˈalgə/ *n.* (*pl.* **algae** /ˈaldʒiː, ˈalgiː/) (usu. in *pl.*) a non-flowering stemless usu. aquatic plant, esp. a seaweed or a single-celled plant. □ **algal** *adj.* [Latin]

algebra /ˈaldʒɪbrə/ *n.* **1** the branch of mathematics that uses letters and other general symbols to represent numbers and quantities in formulae and equations. **2** a system of this based on given axioms (*linear algebra; the algebra of logic*). □ **algebraic** /aldʒɪˈbreɪɪk/ *adj.* **algebraical** /aldʒɪˈbreɪɪk(ə)l/ *adj.* **algebraically** /aldʒɪˈbreɪɪk(ə)li/ *adv.* **algebraist** /aldʒɪˈbreɪɪst/ *n.* [Italian, Spanish, and medieval Latin, from Arabic *al-jabr* from *al* 'the' + *jabr* 'reunion of broken parts' from *jabara* 'reunite']

-algia /ˈaldʒə/ *comb. form Med.* denoting pain in a part specified by the first element (*neuralgia*). □ **-algic** *comb. form* forming adjectives. [Greek from *algos* 'pain']

algicide /ˈaldʒɪsʌɪd, ˈalgɪ-/ *n.* a preparation for destroying algae.

alginate /ˈaldʒɪneɪt/ *n. Chem.* a salt or ester of alginic acid, e.g. the sodium salt, used as a thickener. [ALGA + -IN + -ATE[1]]

alginic acid /alˈdʒɪnɪk/ *n. Chem.* an insoluble carbohydrate found (chiefly as salts) in many brown seaweeds. [ALGA + -IN + -IC]

Algol /ˈalgɒl/ *n.* a high-level computer programming language. [ALGORITHMIC (see ALGORITHM) + LANGUAGE]

algolagnia /algəʊˈlagnɪə/ *n.* sexual pleasure derived from inflicting pain on oneself or others; masochism or sadism. □ **algolagnic** *adj.* & *n.* [modern Latin from German *Algolagnie*, from Greek *algos* 'pain' + *lagneia* 'lust']

algology /əl'gɒlədʒi/ *n.* the study of algae. ▫ **algological** /-'lɒdʒɪk(ə)l/ *adj.* **algologist** *n.*

Algonquian /al'gɒŋkwɪən, -kɪ-/ *n.* & *adj.* (also **Algonkian** /-kɪən/) ● *n.* **1** a member of any of a large group of scattered N. American Indian peoples. **2** any of the family of languages used by them, including Cree and Ojibwa. ● *adj.* of or relating to these peoples or their languages. [*Algonquin*, N. American tribal name, + -IAN]

Algonquin /al'gɒŋkwɪn/ *n.* & *adj.* ● *n.* **1** a member of a N. American Indian people living in Canada along the Ottawa River and its tributaries. **2** the dialect of Ojibwa spoken by this people. **3** = ALGONQUIAN *n.* 1, 2. ● *adj.* **1** of or relating to the Algonquins or their language. **2** = ALGONQUIAN *adj.* [French from an Algonquian word meaning 'at the place of spearing fish and eels']

■ **Usage** The use of *Algonquin* to refer to the Algonquian peoples or their languages (sense 3 above) is widespread but strictly incorrect.

algorithm /'algərɪð(ə)m/ *n.* **1** *Math.* a process or set of rules used for calculation or problem-solving, esp. with a computer. **2** *hist.* the Arabic or decimal notation of numbers. ▫ **algorithmic** /-'rɪðmɪk/ *adj.* **algorithmically** /-'rɪðmɪk(ə)li/ *adv.* [Middle English *algorism*, ultimately from Arabic *al-Ḵuwārizmī*, the cognomen of a 9th-c. mathematician: *algorithm* influenced by Greek *arithmos* 'number' (cf. French *algorithme*)]

alguacil /algwə'sɪl/ *n.* (also **alguazil** /algwə'zɪl/) **1** a mounted official at a bullfight. **2** a constable or an officer of justice in Spain or Spanish-speaking countries. [Spanish, from Arabic *al-wazīr* from *al* 'the' + *wazīr*: see VIZIER]

alias /'eɪlɪəs/ *adv.* & *n.* ● *adv.* also named or known as. ● *n.* a false or assumed name. [Latin, = at another time, otherwise]

alibi /'alɪbʌɪ/ *n.* & *v.* ● *n.* (*pl.* **alibis**) **1** a claim, or the evidence supporting it, that when an alleged act took place one was elsewhere. **2** *disp.* an excuse of any kind; a pretext or justification. ● *v.* (**alibis, alibied, alibiing**) *colloq.* **1** *tr.* provide an alibi or offer an excuse for (a person). **2** *intr.* provide an alibi. [Latin, = elsewhere]

■ **Usage** The use of the noun *alibi* in sense 2, meaning 'an excuse', is informal and to some people unacceptable.

alicyclic /alɪ'sʌɪklɪk, -'sɪk-/ *adj. Chem.* of, denoting, or relating to organic compounds combining a cyclic structure with aliphatic properties, e.g. cyclohexane. [German *alicyclisch* (as ALIPHATIC, CYCLIC)]

alidade /'alɪdeɪd/ *n. Surveying* & *Astron.* a sighting device or pointer for determining directions or measuring angles. [French via medieval Latin from Arabic *al-'idāda* 'the revolving radius', from *'adud* 'upper arm']

alien /'eɪlɪən/ *adj.* & *n.* ● *adj.* **1 a** (often foll. by *to*) unfamiliar; not in accordance or harmony; unfriendly, hostile; unacceptable or repugnant (*army discipline was alien to him; struck an alien note*). **b** (often foll. by *from*) different or separated. **2** foreign; from a foreign country (*help from alien powers*). **3** of or relating to beings supposedly from other worlds; extraterrestrial. **4** *Bot.* (of a plant or animal species) introduced from elsewhere and naturalized. ● *n.* **1** a foreigner, esp. one who is not a naturalized citizen of the country where he or she is living. **2** a being from another world. **3** an alien plant or animal species. ▫ **alienness** /'eɪlɪənnɪs/ *n.* [Middle English via Old French from Latin *alienus* 'belonging to another', from *alius* 'other']

alienable /'eɪlɪənəb(ə)l/ *adj. Law* able to be transferred to new ownership. ▫ **alienability** /-'bɪlɪti/ *n.*

alienage /'eɪlɪənɪdʒ/ *n.* the state or condition of being an alien.

alienate /'eɪlɪəneɪt/ *v.tr.* **1 a** cause (a person) to become unfriendly or hostile. **b** (often foll. by *from*) cause (a person) to feel isolated or estranged from (friends, society, etc.). **2** transfer ownership of (property) to another person etc. ▫ **alienator** *n.* [Middle English from Latin *alienare alienat-* (as ALIEN)]

alienation /eɪlɪə'neɪʃ(ə)n/ *n.* **1** the act or result of alienating. **2** (in full **alienation effect**) *Theatr.* a dramatic effect whereby an audience remains objective, not identifying with the characters or action of a play. [in sense 2 a translation of German *Verfremdungseffekt*]

alienist /'eɪlɪənɪst/ *n. US* a psychiatrist, esp. a legal adviser on psychiatric problems. [French *aliéniste* (as ALIEN)]

aliform /'eɪlɪfɔːm/ *adj.* wing-shaped. [modern Latin *aliformis*, from Latin *ala* 'wing': see -FORM]

alight[1] /ə'lʌɪt/ *v.intr.* (**alighted**) **1** esp. *Brit.* **a** (often foll. by *from*) descend from a vehicle. **b** dismount from a horse. **2** descend and settle; come to earth from the air. **3** (foll. by *on*) find by chance; notice. [Old English *ālīhtan* (as A-[2], *līhtan* LIGHT[2] *v.*)]

alight[2] /ə'lʌɪt/ *adv.* & *predic.adj.* **1** on fire; burning (*they set the old shed alight; is the fire still alight?*). **2** lit up; excited (*eyes alight with expectation*). [Middle English, probably from the phrase *on a light* (= lighted) *fire*]

align /ə'lʌɪn/ *v.tr.* **1** put in a straight line or bring into line (*three books were neatly aligned on the shelf*). **2** esp. *Polit.* (usu. foll. by *with*) bring (oneself etc.) into agreement or alliance with (a cause, policy, political party, etc.). ▫ **alignment** *n.* [French *aligner* from the phrase *à ligne* 'into line': see LINE[1]]

alike /ə'lʌɪk/ *adj.* & *adv.* ● *adj.* (usu. *predic.*) similar, like one another; indistinguishable. ● *adv.* in a similar way or manner (*all were treated alike*). [Old English *gelīc* and Old Norse *glíkr* (LIKE[1])]

aliment /'alɪm(ə)nt/ *n. formal* **1** food. **2** support or mental sustenance. ▫ **alimental** /-'mɛnt(ə)l/ *adj.* [Middle English from French *aliment* or Latin *alimentum*, from *alere* 'nourish']

alimentary /alɪ'mɛnt(ə)ri/ *adj.* of, relating to, or providing nourishment or sustenance. [Latin *alimentarius* (as ALIMENT)]

alimentary canal *n. Anat.* the whole passage along which food passes through the body from mouth to anus during digestion.

alimentation /ˌalɪm(ə)n'teɪʃ(ə)n/ *n.* **1** nourishment; feeding. **2** maintenance, support; supplying with the necessities of life. [French *alimentation* or medieval Latin *alimentatio*, from *alimentare* (as ALIMENT)]

alimony /'alɪməni/ *n.* esp. *US* money payable by a man to his wife or former wife or by a woman to her husband or former husband after they are separated or divorced (in UK use now replaced by *maintenance*). [Latin *alimonia* 'nutriment', from *alere* 'nourish']

A-line /'eɪlʌɪn/ *adj.* (of a garment) having a narrow waist or shoulders and a slightly flared skirt.

aliphatic /alɪ'fatɪk/ *adj. Chem.* of, denoting, or relating to organic compounds in which carbon atoms form open chains, not aromatic rings. [Greek *aleiphar -atos* 'fat']

aliquot /'alɪkwɒt/ *adj.* & *n.* ● *adj. Math.* (of a part or portion) contained by the whole an integral or whole number of times (*4 is an aliquot part of 12*). ● *n.* **1** *Math.* an aliquot part; an integral factor. **2** a known fraction of a whole; a sample. [French *aliquote*, from Latin *aliquot* 'some, so many']

alive /ə'lʌɪv/ *adj.* (usu. *predic.*) **1** (of a person, animal, plant, etc.) living, not dead. **2 a** (of a thing) existing; continuing; in operation or action (*kept his interest alive*). **b** under discussion; provoking interest (*the topic is still very much alive today*). **3** (of a person or animal) lively, active. **4** charged with an electric current; connected to a source of electricity. **5** (foll. by *to*) aware of; alert or responsive to. **6** (foll. by *with*) **a** swarming or teeming with. **b** full of. ▫ **alive and kicking** *colloq.* very active; lively. **alive and well** still alive or active (esp. despite contrary assumptions or rumours). ▫ **aliveness** *n.* [Old English *on līfe* (as A[2], LIFE)]

alizarin /ə'lɪz(ə)rɪn/ *n.* **1** the red colouring matter of madder root, used in dyeing. **2** (*attrib.*) (of a dye) derived from or similar to this pigment. [French *alizarine* from *alizari* 'madder', from Arabic *al-'iṣāra* 'pressed juice' from *'aṣara* 'to press fruit']

alkahest /'alkəhɛst/ *n.* (also **alcahest**) the universal solvent sought by alchemists. [sham Arabic, probably invented by Paracelsus]

alkali /'alkəlʌɪ/ *n.* (*pl.* **alkalis**) **1** *Chem.* any of a class of substances which neutralize acids and turn litmus blue, typically dissolving in water to form often caustic solutions with a pH of more than 7, containing free hydroxide ions; a soluble base. **2** any soluble salt present in excess in the soil. □ **alkalimeter** /alkə'lɪmɪtə/ *n.* **alkalimetry** /alkə'lɪmɪtri/ *n.* [Middle English, applied to a saline substance derived from the ashes of various plants: from medieval Latin, from Arabic *al-ḳalī* 'calcined ashes' of the glasswort etc., from *ḳala* 'fry']

alkali metal *n.* any of the group of monovalent metals, lithium, sodium, potassium, rubidium, and caesium, whose hydroxides are alkalis.

alkaline /'alkəlʌɪn/ *adj.* of, relating to, or having the nature of an alkali; rich in alkali. □ **alkalinity** /alkə'lɪnɪti/ *n.*

alkaline earth *n.* **1** (in full **alkaline earth metal**) any of the group of divalent metals, beryllium, magnesium, calcium, strontium, barium, and radium. **2** a basic oxide of an element of this group.

alkaloid /'alkəlɔɪd/ *n.* *Chem.* any of a series of nitrogenous organic compounds of plant origin, many of which are used as drugs, e.g. morphine, quinine. [German (as ALKALI)]

alkalosis /alkə'ləʊsɪs/ *n.* *Med.* an excessive alkaline condition of the body fluids or tissues.

alkane /'alkeɪn/ *n.* *Chem.* any of a series of saturated aliphatic hydrocarbons having the general formula C_nH_{2n+2}, including methane, ethane, and propane. [ALKYL + -ANE²]

alkanet /'alkənɛt/ *n.* **1 a** any plant of the genus *Alkanna*, esp. *A. tinctoria*, yielding a red dye from its roots. **b** the dye itself. **2** any of various similar plants. [Middle English from Spanish *alcaneta*, diminutive of *alcana*, from Arabic *al-ḥinnā'* = the henna shrub]

alkene /'alki:n/ *n.* *Chem.* any of a series of unsaturated aliphatic hydrocarbons containing a double bond and having the general formula C_nH_{2n}, including ethylene and propene. [ALKYL + -ENE]

alky /'alki/ *n.* (also **alkie**) (*pl.* **-ies**) *slang* an alcoholic.

alkyd /'alkɪd/ *n.* (usu. *attrib.*) *Chem.* any of a group of synthetic resins derived from various alcohols and acids. [ALKYL + ACID]

alkyl /'alkʌɪl, -kɪl/ *n.* (usu. *attrib.*) *Chem.* a radical derived from an alkane by the removal of a hydrogen atom. [German *Alkohol* ALCOHOL + -YL]

alkylate /'alkɪleɪt/ *v.tr.* *Chem.* introduce an alkyl radical into (a compound).

alkyne /'alkʌɪn/ *n.* *Chem.* any of a series of unsaturated aliphatic hydrocarbons containing a triple bond and having the general formula C_nH_{2n-2}, including acetylene. [ALKYL + -YNE]

all /ɔ:l/ *predet., pron., n., & adv.* ● *predet.* **1 a** the whole amount, quantity, or extent of (*all the upheaveal; all this clutter; waited all day; all his life*). **b** (with *pl.*) the entire number of (*all the others left; all ten men*). **2** any whatever (*beyond all doubt*). **3** greatest possible (*with all speed*). ● *pron.* **1 a** all the persons or things concerned (*all were present; all were thrown away*). **b** everything (*all is lost; that is all*). **2** (foll. by *of*) **a** the whole of (*take all of it*). **b** every one of (*all of us*). **c** *colloq.* as much as (*all of six feet tall*). **d** *colloq.* affected by; in a state of (*all of a dither*). ● *n.* (prec. by *my, your,* etc.) one's whole strength or resources (*gave his all*). ● *adv.* **1 a** entirely, quite (*dressed all in black; all round the room*). **b** as an intensifier (*a book all about ships; stop all this grumbling; it was all too clear*). **2** *Brit. colloq.* very (*went all shy*). **3** (foll. by *the* + *compar.*) **a** by so much; to that extent (*if they go, all the better*). **b** in the full degree to be expected (*that makes it all the worse*). **4** (in games) on both sides (*two goals all*). □ **all along** all the time (*he was joking all along*). **all and sundry** everyone. **all but** very nearly (*it was all but impossible; he was all but drowned*). **all for** *colloq.* strongly in favour of. **all in** *colloq.* exhausted. **all in all** everything considered. **all manner of** see MANNER. **all of a sudden** see SUDDEN. **all one** (or **the same**) (usu. foll. by *to*) a matter of indifference (*it's all one to me*). **all out** involving all one's strength or resources; at full speed (also, with hyphen, *attrib.*: *an all-out effort*). **all over 1** completely finished. **2** in or on all parts of (esp. the body) (*went hot and cold all over; mud all over the carpet*). **3** *colloq.* typically (*that is you all over*). **4** *slang* effusively attentive to (a person). **all right** *predic.adj.* satisfactory; safe and sound; in good condition; adequate. ● *adv.* **1** satisfactorily, as desired (*it worked out all right*). **2** as an intensifier (*that's the one all right*). ● *int.* an interjection expressing consent or assent to a proposal or order. **all round** (*US* also **all around**) **1** in all respects (*a good performance all round*). **2** for each person (*he bought drinks all round*). **all the same** nevertheless, in spite of this (*he was innocent but was punished all the same*). **all set** *colloq.* ready to start. **all standing 1** *Naut.* without time to lower the sails. **2** taken by surprise. **all there** (usu. in *neg.*) *colloq.* mentally alert; not mentally deficient. **all the time** see TIME. **all together** all at once; all in one place or in a group (*they came all together*) (cf. ALTOGETHER). **all told** in all. **all very well** *colloq.* an expression used to reject or to imply scepticism about a favourable or consoling remark. **all the way** the whole distance; completely. **at all** (with *neg.* or *interrog.*) in any way; to any extent (*did not swim at all; did you like it at all?*). **be all up with** see UP. **in all** in total number; altogether (*there were 10 people in all*). **on all fours** see FOUR. [Old English *all, eall*, probably from Germanic]

■ **Usage** *All of* meaning 'the whole of, every one of' is usual before pronouns (e.g. *all of it, all of us*) and emphatically, often paralleling *none of, some of,* etc., before nouns (e.g. *all of the advantages but none of the disadvantages*). Otherwise, *all* + noun is normal, e.g. *phoned all his friends, ate all the bread*). See also Usage Notes at ALRIGHT and ALTOGETHER.

alla breve /alə 'breɪvi/ *n.* *Mus.* a time signature indicating 2 or 4 minim beats in a bar. [Italian, = at the BREVE]

alla cappella var. of A CAPPELLA.

Allah /'alə, ə'lɑ:/ *n.* the name of God among Arabs and Muslims. [Arabic *'allāh*, contraction of *al-'ilāh*, from *al* 'the' + *'ilāh* 'god']

all-American *adj. & n.* ● *adj.* **1** representing the whole of (or only) America or the US. **2** truly American (*all-American boy*). **3** (also **all-America**) *US* honoured as one of the best amateur sportsmen in the US. ● *n.* (also **all-America**) *US* an all-American sportsman.

allantois /ə'lantəʊɪs/ *n.* (*pl.* **allantoides** /-ɪdi:z/) *Biol.* the foetal membrane lying below the chorion in embryonic reptiles, birds, and mammals. □ **allantoic** /alən'təʊɪk/ *adj.* [modern Latin from Greek *allantoeidēs* 'sausage-shaped']

all-around *attrib.adj.* *US* = ALL-ROUND.

allay /ə'leɪ/ *v.tr.* **1** diminish (fear, suspicion, etc.). **2** relieve or alleviate (pain, hunger, etc.). [Old English *ālecgan* (as A-², LAY¹)]

All Blacks *n.pl.* *colloq.* the New Zealand international Rugby Union football team. [from their black strip]

all-clear *n.* (usu. prec. by *the*) a signal that danger or difficulty is over (*had further tests and was given the all-clear*).

all comers *n.pl.* any applicants (with reference to a position, or esp. a challenge to a champion, that is unrestricted in entry).

all-day *attrib.adj.* lasting or available throughout the day.

allegation /alɪ'geɪʃ(ə)n/ *n.* **1** an assertion, esp. an unproved one; an accusation. **2** the act or an instance of alleging or accusing. [Middle English from French *allégation* or Latin *allegatio*, from *allegare* 'allege']

allege /əˈlɛdʒ/ *v.tr.* **1** (often foll. by *that* + clause, or *to* + infin.) declare to be the case, esp. without proof. **2** advance as an argument or excuse. □ **alleged** *adj.* [Middle English from Anglo-French *alegier*, Old French *esligier* 'clear at law'; confused in sense with Latin *allegare*: see ALLEGATION]

allegedly /əˈlɛdʒɪdli/ *adv.* as is alleged or said to be the case.

allegiance /əˈliːdʒ(ə)ns/ *n.* **1** loyalty (to a person or cause etc.). **2** the duty of a subject to his or her sovereign or government. [Middle English via Anglo-French from Old French *ligeance* (as LIEGE): perhaps associated with ALLIANCE]

allegorical /alɪˈgɒrɪk(ə)l/ *adj.* (also **allegoric** /-rɪk/) consisting of or relating to allegory; by means of allegory. □ **allegorically** *adv.*

allegorize /ˈalɪg(ə)rʌɪz/ *v.tr.* (also **-ise**) treat as or by means of an allegory. □ **allegorization** /-ˈzeɪʃ(ə)n/ *n.*

allegory /ˈalɪg(ə)ri/ *n.* (*pl.* **-ies**) **1** a story, play, poem, picture, etc., in which the meaning or message is represented symbolically. **2** the use of such symbols. **3** a symbol. □ **allegorist** *n.* [Middle English via Old French *allegorie* and Latin *allegoria* from Greek *allēgoria*, from *allos* 'other' + *-agoria* 'speaking']

allegretto /alɪˈgrɛtəʊ/ *adv., adj., & n. Mus.* ● *adv. & adj.* in a fairly brisk tempo. ● *n.* (*pl.* **-os**) an allegretto passage or movement. [Italian, diminutive of ALLEGRO]

allegro /əˈleɪgrəʊ, -ˈlɛg-/ *adv., adj., & n. Mus.* ● *adv. & adj.* in a brisk tempo. ● *n.* (*pl.* **-os**) an allegro passage or movement. [Italian, = lively, gay]

allele /ˈaliːl/ *n.* (also **allel** /ˈalɛl/) one of the (usu. two) alternative forms of a gene, found at the same place on a chromosome. □ **allelic** /əˈliːlɪk/ *adj.* [German *Allel*, abbreviation of ALLELOMORPH]

allelomorph /əˈliːləʊmɔːf/ *n.* = ALLELE. □ **allelomorphic** /-ˈmɔːfɪk/ *adj.* [Greek *allēl-* 'one another' + *morphē* 'form']

alleluia /alɪˈluːjə/ *int. & n.* (also **alleluya**, **hallelujah** /hal-/) ● *int.* God be praised. ● *n.* **1** praise to God. **2** a song of praise to God. **3** *RC Ch.* the part of the Mass including this. [Middle English via ecclesiastical Latin and Greek *allēlouia* (in the Septuagint), from Hebrew *hallĕlūyāh* 'praise ye the Lord']

allemande /ˈalmɑːnd, almɒ̃d/ *n.* **1 a** the name of several German dances. **b** the music for any of these, esp. as a movement of a suite. **2** a figure in a country dance. [French, = German (dance)]

all-embracing *adj.* embracing or including much or all; comprehensive.

Allen key /ˈalən/ *n. propr.* a spanner designed to fit into and turn an Allen screw. [*Allen*, the name of the US manufacturer]

Allen screw /ˈalən/ *n. propr.* a screw with a hexagonal socket in the head. [as ALLEN KEY]

allergen /ˈalədʒ(ə)n/ *n.* any substance that causes an allergic reaction. □ **allergenic** /aləˈdʒɛnɪk/ *adj.* [ALLERGY + -GEN]

allergic /əˈləːdʒɪk/ *adj.* **1** (foll. by *to*) **a** having an allergy to. **b** *colloq.* having a strong dislike for (a person or thing). **2** caused by or relating to an allergy.

allergy /ˈalədʒi/ *n.* (*pl.* **-ies**) **1** *Med.* a damaging immune response by the body to a substance (esp. a particular food, pollen, fur, or dust) to which it has become hypersensitive. **2** *colloq.* an antipathy. □ **allergist** *n.* [German *Allergie*, on the pattern of *Energie* ENERGY, from Greek *allos* 'other']

alleviate /əˈliːvɪeɪt/ *v.tr.* lessen or make less severe (pain, suffering, etc.). □ **alleviation** /-ˈeɪʃ(ə)n/ *n.* **alleviative** /-vɪətɪv/ *adj.* **alleviator** *n.* **alleviatory** /-vɪət(ə)ri/ *adj.* [Late Latin *alleviare* 'lighten', from Latin *allevare* (as AD-, *levare* 'raise')]

alley[1] /ˈali/ *n.* (*pl.* **-eys**) **1** (also **alleyway**) **a** a narrow street. **b** a narrow passageway, esp. between or behind buildings. **2** a path or walk in a park or garden. **3** an enclosure for skittles, bowling, etc. [Middle English, from Old French *alee* 'walking, passage' from *aler* 'go', from Latin *ambulare* 'walk']

alley[2] var. of ALLY[2].

alley cat *n.* a stray town cat, often mangy or half wild.

all flesh *n.* all human and animal creation.

All Fools' Day var. of APRIL FOOL'S DAY.

All Hallows /ˈhaləʊz/ *n.* All Saints' Day, 1 Nov.

alliaceous /alɪˈeɪʃəs/ *adj.* **1** of or relating to the genus *Allium*, which includes onion, garlic, leek, etc. **2** tasting or smelling like onion or garlic. [modern Latin *alliaceus*, from Latin *allium* 'garlic']

alliance /əˈlʌɪəns/ *n.* **1 a** union or agreement to cooperate, esp. of states by treaty or families by marriage. **b** the parties involved. **2** (**Alliance**) a political party formed by the allying of separate parties. **3** a relationship resulting from an affinity in nature or qualities etc. (*the old alliance between logic and metaphysics*). **4** *Bot.* a group of allied families. [Middle English from Old French *aliance* (as ALLY[1])]

allicin /ˈalɪsɪn/ *n. Biochem.* a pungent oily liquid with antibacterial properties, present in garlic. [Latin *allium* 'garlic']

allied /ˈalʌɪd, əˈlʌɪd/ *adj.* **1 a** united or associated in an alliance. **b** (**Allied**) of or relating to Britain and her allies in the First and Second World Wars. **2** connected or related (*studied medicine and allied subjects*). [past part. of ALLY[1]]

alligator /ˈalɪgeɪtə/ *n.* **1** a large reptile of the order Crocodilia native to the Americas and China, with upper teeth that lie outside the lower teeth and a head broader and shorter than that of the crocodile. **2** (in general use) any of several large members of this order. **3 a** the skin of such an animal or material resembling it. **b** (in *pl.*) shoes of this. [Spanish *el lagarto* 'the lizard', from Latin *lacerta*]

alligator clip *n.* a clip with teeth for gripping.

alligator pear *n.* esp. *N. Amer.* an avocado.

alligator snapper *n.* (also **alligator tortoise**) a large freshwater snapping turtle found around the Gulf of Mexico.

all-important *adj.* crucial; vitally important.

all-in *attrib.adj. Brit.* inclusive of all.

all-inclusive *adj.* including all or everything.

all-in-one *adj.* combining two or more items in a single unit (*all-in-one shampoo and conditioner*).

all-in wrestling *n.* esp. *Brit.* wrestling with few or no restrictions.

alliterate /əˈlɪtəreɪt/ *v.* **1** *intr.* **a** contain alliteration. **b** use alliteration in speech or writing. **2** *tr.* **a** construct (a phrase etc.) with alliteration. **b** speak or pronounce with alliteration. □ **alliterative** /əˈlɪt(ə)rətɪv/ *adj.* [back-formation from ALLITERATION]

alliteration /əlɪtəˈreɪʃ(ə)n/ *n.* the occurrence of the same letter or sound at the beginning of adjacent or closely connected words (e.g. *cool, calm, and collected*). [modern Latin *alliteratio* (as AD-, *littera* 'letter')]

allium /ˈalɪəm/ *n.* any plant of the genus *Allium*, usu. bulbous and strong-smelling, e.g. onion and garlic. [Latin, = garlic]

all-night *attrib.adj.* lasting or available throughout the night.

allo- /ˈaləʊ/ *comb. form* other (*allophone*; *allogamy*). [Greek *allos* 'other']

allocate /ˈaləkeɪt/ *v.tr.* (usu. foll. by *to*) assign or devote to (a purpose, person, or place). □ **allocable** /ˈaləkəb(ə)l/ *adj.* **allocation** /aləˈkeɪʃ(ə)n/ *n.* **allocator** *n.* [medieval Latin *allocare* (as AL-, *locus* 'place')]

allochthonous /əˈlɒkθənəs/ *adj. Geol.* (of a deposit) formed at a distance from its present position (cf. AUTOCHTHONOUS 3). [ALLO- + Greek *khthōn -onos* 'earth']

allocution /aləˈkjuːʃ(ə)n/ *n.* a formal or hortatory speech or manner of address. [Latin *allocutio*, from *alloqui allocut-* 'speak to' (as AL-, *loqui* 'speak')]

allogamy /əˈlɒgəmi/ *n. Bot.* cross-fertilization in plants. [ALLO- + Greek *-gamia*, from *gamos* 'marriage']

allograft /'aləgrɑːft/ *n.* a tissue graft from a donor of the same species as the recipient but not genetically identical (cf. HOMOGRAFT). [ALLO- + GRAFT[1]]

allomorph /'aləmɔːf/ *n. Linguistics* any of two or more alternative forms of a morpheme. □ **allomorphic** /alə'mɔːfɪk/ *adj.* [ALLO- + MORPHEME]

allopath /'aləpaθ/ *n.* a person who practises allopathy. [French *allopathe*, back-formation from *allopathie* = ALLOPATHY]

allopathy /ə'lɒpəθi/ *n.* the treatment of disease by conventional means, i.e. with drugs having opposite effects to the symptoms (cf. HOMOEOPATHY). □ **allopathic** /alə'paθɪk/ *adj.* **allopathist** *n.* [German *Allopathie* (as ALLO-, -PATHY)]

allopatric /alə'patrɪk/ *adj. Biol.* occurring in separate geographical areas. [ALLO- + Greek *patra* 'fatherland']

allophone /'aləfəʊn/ *n. Linguistics* any of the variant sounds forming a single phoneme. □ **allophonic** /alə'fɒnɪk/ *adj.* [ALLO- + PHONEME]

allot /ə'lɒt/ *v.tr.* (**allotted**, **allotting**) **1** give or apportion to (a person) as a share or task; distribute officially to (*they allotted us each a pair of boots; the men were allotted duties*). **2** (foll. by *to*) give or distribute officially to (*a sum was allotted to each charity*). [Old French *aloter* (as A-[3] + LOT)]

allotment /ə'lɒtm(ə)nt/ *n.* **1** *Brit.* a small piece of land rented (usu. from a local authority) for cultivation. **2** a share allotted. **3** the action of allotting.

allotrope /'alətrəʊp/ *n.* each of two or more different physical forms in which an element can exist (*graphite, charcoal, and diamond are all allotropes of carbon*). [back-formation from ALLOTROPY]

allotropy /ə'lɒtrəpi/ *n.* the existence of two or more different physical forms of a chemical element. □ **allotropic** /alə'trɒpɪk/ *adj.* **allotropical** /alə'trɒpɪk(ə)l/ *adj.* [Greek *allotropos* 'of another form', (as ALLO- + *tropos* 'manner' from *trepō* 'turn')]

allottee /əlɒ'tiː/ *n.* a person to whom something is allotted.

all-out see *all out* (ALL).

all-over *attrib.adj.* covering the whole of something (*an all-over tan*).

allow /ə'laʊ/ *v.* **1** *tr.* permit (a practice, a person to do something, a thing to happen or be done, etc.) (*smoking is not allowed; we allowed them to speak*). **2** *tr.* give or provide; permit (a person) to have (a limited quantity or sum) (*we were allowed £500 a year*). **3** *tr.* provide or set aside for a purpose; add or deduct in consideration of something (*allow 10% for inflation*). **4** *tr.* **a** admit, agree, concede (*he allowed that it was so; 'You know best,' he allowed*). **b** *dial.* assert; be of the opinion. **5** *refl.* permit oneself, indulge oneself in (conduct) (*allowed herself to be persuaded; allowed myself a few angry words*). **6** *intr.* (foll. by *of*) admit of. **7** *intr.* (foll. by *for*) take into consideration or account; make addition or deduction corresponding to (*allowing for wastage*). □ **allowable** *adj.* **allowably** *adv.* [Middle English, originally = 'praise, assign as a right', from Old French *alouer*, partly from Latin *allaudare* 'to praise', partly from medieval Latin *allocare* 'to place': see ALLOCATE]

allowance /ə'laʊəns/ *n.* & *v.* ● *n.* **1** **a** an amount or sum allowed to a person, esp. regularly for a stated purpose. **b** *N. Amer.* = POCKET MONEY 2. **2** an amount allowed in reckoning. **3** a deduction or discount (*an allowance on your old cooker*). **4** (foll. by *of*) tolerance of. ● *v.tr.* **1** make an allowance to (a person). **2** supply in limited quantities. □ **make allowances** (often foll. by *for*) **1** take into consideration (mitigating circumstances) (*made allowances for his demented state*). **2** look with tolerance upon; make excuses for (a person, bad behaviour, etc.). [Middle English from Old French *alouance* (as ALLOW)]

allowedly /ə'laʊɪdli/ *adv.* as is generally allowed or acknowledged.

alloy *n.* & *v.* ● *n.* /'alɔɪ/ **1** a mixture of two or more chemical elements at least one of which is a metal, e.g. brass (a mixture of copper and zinc). **2** an inferior metal mixed esp. with gold or silver. ● *v.tr.* /ə'lɔɪ/ **1** mix (metals). **2** **a** debase (a pure substance) by admixture. **b** reduce the quality or spoil the character of a thing by adding something else. **3** moderate. [French *aloi* (*n.*), *aloyer* (*v.*) via Old French *aloier*, *aleier* 'combine' from Latin *alligare* 'bind']

all-party *attrib.adj.* involving all (esp. political) parties.

all-pervading *adj.* (also **all-pervasive**) pervading everything.

all-points bulletin *n. US* a general alert issued among police officers, esp. one giving information for the capture of a suspected criminal.

all-powerful *adj.* having complete power; almighty.

all-purpose *adj.* suitable for many uses.

all-right *attrib.adj. colloq.* fine, acceptable (*an all-right guy*).

all right see ALL.

all-round *attrib.adj.* (of a person) versatile.

all-rounder *n. Brit.* a versatile person or thing.

All Saints' Day *n.* a Christian festival in honour of the saints, 1 Nov.

all-seater *adj.* (usu. *attrib.*) (of a sports stadium etc.) providing only seats and no standing places.

allseed /'ɔːlsiːd/ *n.* any of various plants producing much seed, esp. *Radiola linoides*.

All Souls' Day *n.* a Roman Catholic festival with prayers for the souls of the dead, 2 Nov.

allspice /'ɔːlspʌɪs/ *n.* **1** **a** the aromatic spice obtained from the ground berry of the W. Indian tree *Pimenta dioica*. **b** this plant. Also called PIMENTO. **2** any of various other aromatic shrubs.

all-star *adj.* & *n.* ● *adj.* composed wholly of outstanding performers. ● *n. N. Amer.* a member of an all-star group or team.

all-ticket *adj.* (usu. *attrib.*) (of an event) that may be attended only by those with tickets bought in advance.

all-time *attrib.adj.* (of a record etc.) hitherto unsurpassed.

allude /ə'luːd, ə'ljuːd/ *v.intr.* (foll. by *to*) **1** refer to indirectly or covertly. **2** *disp.* mention. [Latin *alludere* (as AD-, *ludere lus-* 'play')]

■ **Usage** *Allude to* should not be used simply as a synonym for *mention*. The sentence *Mr Smith was alluded to several times, though not actually mentioned by name, in the president's speech* illustrates the difference.

all-up weight *n. Brit.* the total weight of an aircraft with passengers, cargo, etc. when airborne.

allure /ə'ljʊə/ *v.* & *n.* ● *v.tr.* attract, charm, or fascinate. ● *n.* attractiveness, personal charm; fascination. □ **allurement** *n.* [Middle English from Old French *alurer* 'attract' (as AD-, *luere* LURE[1] *v.* 1)]

allusion /ə'luːʒ(ə)n, -'ljuː-/ *n.* (often foll. by *to*) an indirect or passing reference. [French *allusion* or Late Latin *allusio* (as ALLUDE)]

■ **Usage** Care should be taken not to confuse *allusion* with *illusion*. See also Usage Note at ALLUDE.

allusive /ə'luːsɪv, -'ljuː-/ *adj.* **1** (often foll. by *to*) containing an allusion. **2** containing many allusions. □ **allusively** *adv.* **allusiveness** *n.*

alluvial /ə'luːvɪəl, -'ljuː-/ *adj.* & *n.* ● *adj.* of or relating to alluvium. ● *n.* alluvium, esp. containing a precious metal.

alluvion /ə'luːvɪən, -'ljuː-/ *n. Law* the formation of new land by the movement of the sea or of a river. [French from Latin *alluvio -onis*, from *luere* 'wash']

alluvium /ə'luːvɪəm, -'ljuː-/ *n.* (*pl.* **alluvia** /-vɪə/ or **alluviums**) a deposit of usu. fine fertile soil left during a time of flood, esp. in a river valley or delta. [Latin, neut. of *alluvius* (*adj.*), from *luere* 'wash']

all-weather *adj.* of, relating to, or suitable for all types of weather (usu. *attrib.*: *all-weather track*).

all-wheel drive *n. N. Amer.* = FOUR-WHEEL DRIVE.

ally[1] /'alʌɪ/ *n.* & *v.* ● *n.* (*pl.* **-ies**) **1** a state formally cooperating or united with another for a special purpose, esp. by a treaty. **2** a person or organization that cooperates with or helps another. ● *v.tr.* /also ə'lʌɪ/ (**-ies**, **-ied**) (often foll. by *with*) combine or unite in alliance. [Middle English via Old French *al(e)ier* from Latin *alligare* 'bind': cf. ALLOY]

ally[2] /'ali/ *n.* (also **alley**) (*pl.* **-ies** or **-eys**) a choice playing-marble made of marble, alabaster, or glass. [perhaps diminutive of ALABASTER]

-ally /əli/ *suffix* forming adverbs from adjectives in *-al* (cf. -AL, -LY[2], -ICALLY).

allyl /'alʌɪl, -lɪl/ *n.* (usu. *attrib.*) *Chem.* the unsaturated monovalent radical CH_2=CH-CH_2-. [Latin *allium* 'garlic' + -YL]

almacantar var. of ALMUCANTAR.

Alma Mater /ˌalmə 'mɑːtə, 'meɪt-/ *n.* (also **alma mater**) the university, school, or college one attends or attended. [Latin, = bounteous mother]

almanac /'ɔːlmənak, 'ɒl-/ *n.* (also **almanack**) **1** an annual table, or book of tables, containing a calendar of months and days and usu. astronomical data and other information. **2** a usu. annual directory or handbook containing statistical and other information of either general or specialist interest. [Middle English via medieval Latin *almanac(h)* from Greek *almenikhiaka*]

almandine /'almәndiːn, -dʌɪn/ *n.* a kind of garnet with a violet tint. [French, alteration of obsolete *alabandine* from medieval Latin *alabandina*, from *Alabanda*, an ancient city in Asia Minor, where these stones were cut]

almighty /ɔːl'mʌɪti/ *adj.* & *adv.* ● *adj.* **1** having complete power; omnipotent. **2** (**the Almighty**) God. **3** *slang* very great (*an almighty crash*). ● *adv. slang* extremely; very much. [Old English *ælmihtig* (as ALL, MIGHTY)]

almond /'ɑːmənd/ *n.* **1** the oval nutlike seed (kernel) of the stone fruit from the tree *Prunus dulcis*, of which there are sweet and bitter varieties. **2** (in full **almond tree**) the tree itself, of the rose family and allied to the peach and plum. [Middle English via Old French *alemande* etc., medieval Latin *amandula*, and Latin *amygdala* from Greek *amugdalē*]

almond eyes *n.pl.* narrow almond-shaped eyes.

almond oil *n.* the oil expressed from the seed of the almond (esp. the bitter variety), used for toilet preparations, flavouring, and medicinal purposes.

almond paste *n.* = MARZIPAN.

almoner /'ɑːmənə, 'alm-/ *n. hist.* **1** *Brit.* = HOSPITAL SOCIAL WORKER. **2** an official distributor of alms. [Middle English from Anglo-French *aumoner*, Old French *aumonier*, ultimately from medieval Latin *eleēmosynarius* (as ALMS)]

almost /'ɔːlməʊst/ *adv.* all but; very nearly. [Old English *ælmǣst* 'for the most part' (as ALL, MOST)]

alms /ɑːmz/ *n.pl. hist.* charitable donations of money or food to the poor. [Old English *ælmysse*, *-messe* from Germanic, ultimately from Greek *eleēmosunē* 'compassionateness' via *eleēmōn* (*adj.*) from *eleos* 'compassion']

almshouse /'ɑːmzhaʊs/ *n. hist.* a house founded by charity for the poor.

almucantar /almə'kantə/ *n.* (also **almacantar**) *Astron.* a line of constant altitude above the horizon. [Middle English via medieval Latin *almucantarath* or French *almucantara* etc. from Arabic *almukanṭarāt* (*pl.*) 'lines of celestial latitude', from *ḳanṭara* 'arch']

aloe /'aləʊ/ *n.* **1** any plant of the genus *Aloe*, usu. having toothed fleshy leaves. **2** (in *pl.*) (in full **bitter aloes**) a strong laxative obtained from the bitter juice of various species of aloe. **3** (also **American aloe**) an agave native to Central America, which flowers only once in many years, and from whose sap tequila is made; also called *century plant*. [Old English *al(e)we* via Latin *aloē* from Greek]

aloe vera /'vɪərə/ *n.* **1** a Caribbean aloe, *Aloe vera*, yielding a gelatinous substance used esp. in cosmetics as an emollient. **2** this substance. [modern Latin, = true aloe]

aloft /ə'lɒft/ *predic.adj.* & *adv.* **1** high up; overhead. **2** upwards. [Middle English from Old Norse *á lopt(i)*, from *á* 'in, on, to' + *lopt* 'air': cf. LIFT, LOFT]

alogical /eɪ'lɒdʒɪk(ə)l/ *adj.* **1** not logical. **2** opposed to logic.

aloha /ə'ləʊhə/ *int.* & *n.* a Hawaiian expression of love or affection, used as a greeting and at parting.

aloha shirt *n.* a loose brightly coloured Hawaiian shirt.

alone /ə'ləʊn/ *predic.adj.* & *adv.* **1 a** without others present (*they wanted to be alone*; *the tree stood alone*). **b** without others' help (*succeeded alone*). **c** lonely and wretched (*felt alone*). **2** (often foll. by *in*) standing by oneself in an opinion etc. (*was alone in thinking this*). **3** only, exclusively (*you alone can help me*). □ **go it alone** act by oneself without assistance. □ **aloneness** *n.* [Middle English from ALL + ONE]

along /ə'lɒŋ/ *prep.* & *adv.* ● *prep.* **1** from one end to the other end of (*a handkerchief with lace along the edge*). **2** on or through any part of the length of (*was walking along the road*). **3** beside or through the length of (*shelves stood along the wall*). ● *adv.* **1** onward; into a more advanced state (*come along*; *getting along nicely*). **2** at or to a particular place; arriving (*I'll be along soon*). **3** in company with a person, esp. oneself (*bring a book along*). **4** beside or through part or the whole length of a thing. □ **along with** in addition to; together with. [Old English *andlang* from West Germanic, related to LONG[1]]

alongshore /əlɒŋ'ʃɔː/ *adv.* along or by the shore.

alongside /əlɒŋ'sʌɪd/ *adv.* & *prep.* ● *adv.* at or to the side (of a ship, pier, etc.). ● *prep.* close to the side of; next to. □ **alongside of** side by side with; together or simultaneously with.

aloof /ə'luːf/ *adj.* & *adv.* ● *adj.* distant, unsympathetic. ● *adv.* away, apart (*he kept aloof from his colleagues*). □ **aloofly** *adv.* **aloofness** *n.* [originally nautical, from A[2] + LUFF]

alopecia /alə'piːʃə/ *n. Med.* the absence (complete or partial) of hair from areas of the body where it normally grows; baldness. [Latin, from Greek *alōpekia* 'fox-mange' from *alōpēx* 'fox']

aloud /ə'laʊd/ *adv.* **1** audibly; not silently or in a whisper. **2** *archaic* loudly. [A[2] + LOUD]

alow /ə'ləʊ/ *adv.* & *predic.adj. Naut.* in or into the lower part of a ship. [A[2] + LOW[1]]

alp /alp/ *n.* **1 a** a high mountain. **b** (**the Alps**) the high range of mountains in Switzerland and adjoining countries. **2** (in Switzerland) pastureland on a mountainside. [originally pl., from French via Latin *Alpes* from Greek *Alpeis*]

alpaca /al'pakə/ *n.* **1** a S. American mammal, *Lama pacos*, related to the llama, with long shaggy hair. **2** wool from this animal. **3** fabric made from the wool, with or without other fibres. [Spanish, from Aymara or Quechua]

alpargata /alpɑː'gɑːtə/ *n.* a light canvas shoe with a plaited fibre sole; an espadrille. [Spanish]

alpenhorn /'alpənhɔːn/ *n.* a long wooden horn used by Alpine herdsmen to call their cattle. [German, = Alp-horn]

alpenstock /'alpənstɒk/ *n.* a long iron-tipped staff used in hillwalking. [German, = Alp-stick]

alpha /'alfə/ *n.* **1** the first letter of the Greek alphabet (Α, α). **2** *Brit.* a first-class mark given for a piece of work or in an examination. **3** (**Alpha**) *Astron.* the first (usu. brightest) star in a constellation (foll. by Latin genitive: *Alpha Centauri*). □ **alpha and omega** the beginning and the end; the most important features. [Middle English, via Latin from Greek]

alphabet /'alfəbɛt/ *n.* **1** the set of letters used in writing a language (*the Russian alphabet*). **2** a set of symbols or signs representing letters. [Late Latin *alphabetum* from Greek *alpha, bēta*, the first two letters of the alphabet]

alphabetical /alfə'bɛtɪk(ə)l/ *adj.* (also **alphabetic** /-'bɛtɪk/) **1** of or relating to an alphabet. **2** in the order of the letters of the alphabet. □ **alphabetically** *adv.*

alphabetize /'alfəbətʌɪz/ *v.tr.* (also **-ise**) arrange (words, names, etc.) in alphabetical order. □ **alphabetization** /-'zeɪʃ(ə)n/ *n.*

alphabet soup *n. colloq.* a confusing variety of acronyms or symbols. [alluding to a kind of clear soup containing pasta in the shapes of letters]

alpha decay *n.* radioactive decay in which an alpha particle is emitted.

alphanumeric /alfənju:'mɛrɪk/ *adj.* (also **alphanumerical**) containing both alphabetical and numerical symbols. [ALPHABETIC + NUMERICAL]

alpha particle *n.* (also **alpha ray**) a helium nucleus emitted by a radioactive substance, originally regarded as a ray.

alpha rhythm *n.* (also **alpha waves**) *Physiol.* the normal electrical activity of the brain when conscious and relaxed, with a frequency of approx. 8 to 13 hertz.

alpha test *n. & v.* ● *n.* a test of machinery, software, etc. carried out by the developer before the product is made available for beta testing. ● *v.tr.* subject (a product) to an alpha test.

alpine /'alpʌɪn/ *adj. & n.* ● *adj.* **1 a** of or relating to high mountains. **b** growing or found on high mountains. **2** (**Alpine**) of or relating to the Alps. **3** (**Alpine**) (of skiing) involving fast downhill racing. ● *n.* **1** a plant native to mountain districts. **2** a plant suited to rock gardens. [Latin *Alpinus*: see ALP]

Alpinist /'alpɪnɪst/ *n.* (also **alpinist**) a climber of high mountains, esp. in the Alps. [French *alpiniste* (as ALPINE; see -IST)]

already /ɔ:l'rɛdi/ *adv.* **1** before the time in question (*I knew that already*). **2** as early or as soon as this (*already at the age of six*). **3** *N. Amer. colloq.* as an intensive at the end of a phrase, to express impatience (*enough already!*). [ALL *adv.* + READY: sense 3 influenced by Yiddish use]

alright /ɔ:l'rʌɪt/ *adj., adv., & int. disp.* = *all right* (see ALL).

■ **Usage** Although widely used, *alright* is still non-standard and considered incorrect by many people.

Alsatian /al'seɪʃ(ə)n/ *n. & adj.* ● *n.* **1** *Brit.* **a** a large dog of a breed used as guard dogs etc. and for police work. **b** this breed. Also called *German shepherd (dog)*. **2** a native of Alsace, a region of eastern France. ● *adj.* of or relating to Alsace or its inhabitants. [*Alsatia* (the ancient name of Alsace) + -AN]

alsike /'alsɪk/ *n.* a species of clover, *Trifolium hybridum*. [named after *Alsike* in Sweden]

also /'ɔ:lsəʊ/ *adv.* in addition; likewise; besides. [Old English *alswā* (as ALL *adv.*, SO[1])]

also-ran *n.* **1** a horse or dog etc. not among the winners in a race. **2** an undistinguished person.

alstroemeria /alstrə'mɪərɪə/ *n.* an ornamental plant of the S. American genus *Alstroemeria* (lily family), with showy lily-like flowers. [modern Latin, named after K. von *Alstroemer*, Swedish naturalist d. 1796]

Alta. *abbr.* Alberta.

altar /'ɔ:ltə, 'ɒl-/ *n.* **1** a table or flat-topped block, often of stone, for making sacrifices or offerings to a deity. **2** a Communion table. □ **lead to the altar** marry (a woman). [Old English *altar -er*, Germanic adoption of Late Latin *altar, altarium*, from Latin *altaria* (pl.) 'burnt offerings, altar', probably related to *adolēre* 'burn in sacrifice']

altar boy *n.* a boy who serves as a priest's assistant in a service.

altarpiece /'ɔ:ltəpi:s, 'ɒl-/ *n.* a piece of art, esp. a painting, set above or behind an altar.

altazimuth /al'tazɪməθ/ *n.* an instrument for measuring altitude and azimuth in astronomy and navigation, or vertical and horizontal angles in surveying (usu. *attrib.*: *altazimuth mount*). [ALTITUDE + AZIMUTH]

alter /'ɔ:ltə, 'ɒl-/ *v.* **1** *tr. & intr.* make or become different; change. **2** *tr. US & Austral.* castrate or spay. □ **alterable** *adj.* **alteration** /-'reɪʃ(ə)n/ *n.* [Middle English via Old French *alterer* and Late Latin *alterare* from Latin *alter* 'other']

alterative /'ɔ:lt(ə)rətɪv, 'ɒl-/ *adj.* tending to produce alteration. [Middle English, from medieval Latin *alterativus* (as ALTER)]

altercate /'ɔ:ltəkeɪt, 'ɒl-/ *v.intr.* (often foll. by *with*) dispute hotly; wrangle. □ **altercation** /-'keɪʃ(ə)n/ *n.* [Latin *altercari altercat-*]

alter ego /ˌaltər 'ɛgəʊ, ˌɒlt-, 'i:g-/ *n.* (*pl.* **alter egos**) **1** a person's secondary or alternative personality. **2** an intimate and trusted friend. [Latin, = other self]

alternate *v., adj., & n.* ● *v.* /'ɔ:ltəneɪt, 'ɒl-/ **1** *intr.* (often foll. by *with*) (of two things) succeed each other by turns (*rain and sunshine alternated; elation alternated with depression*). **2** *intr.* (foll. by *between*) change repeatedly (between two conditions) (*the patient alternated between hot and cold fevers*). **3** *tr.* (often foll. by *with*) cause (two things) to succeed each other by turns (*the band alternated fast and slow tunes; we alternated criticism with reassurance*). ● *adj.* /ɔ:l'tə:nət, ɒl-/ **1** (with noun in *pl.*) every other (*comes on alternate days*). **2** (of things of two kinds) each following and succeeded by one of the other kind (*alternate joy and misery*). **3** (of a sequence etc.) consisting of alternate things. **4** *Bot.* (of leaves etc.) placed alternately on the two sides of the stem. **5** esp. *N. Amer.* = ALTERNATIVE (*an alternate route*). ● *n.* /ɔ:l'tə:nət, ɒl-/ esp. *N. Amer.* a deputy or substitute. □ **alternately** /ɔ:l'tə:nətli, ɒl-/ *adv.* [Latin *alternatus*, past part. of *alternare* 'do things by turns', from *alternus* 'every other' from *alter* 'other']

■ **Usage** See Usage Note at ALTERNATIVE.

alternate angles *n.pl.* two angles, not adjoining one another, that are formed on opposite sides of a line that intersects two other lines.

alternating current *n.* an electric current that reverses its direction at regular intervals (abbr. **AC**, **ac**).

alternation /ɔ:ltə'neɪʃ(ə)n, ɒl-/ *n.* the action or result of alternating.

alternation of generations *n. Biol.* a reproductive pattern in which two different forms (often sexual and asexual or haploid and diploid) alternate in the life cycle, as in ferns and some jellyfish.

alternative /ɔ:l'tə:nətɪv, ɒl-/ *adj. & n.* ● *adj.* **1** (of one or more things) available or usable instead of another (*an alternative route*). **2** (of two things) mutually exclusive. **3** of or relating to practices that offer a substitute for the conventional ones (*alternative theatre*). ● *n.* **1** any of two or more possibilities. **2** the freedom or opportunity to choose between two or more things (*I had no alternative but to go*). □ **alternatively** *adv.* [French *alternatif -ive* or medieval Latin *alternativus* (as ALTERNATE)]

■ **Usage** Use of the adjective in sense 1 with reference to more than two options (e.g. *many alternative methods*) is common and acceptable. *Alternative* should not be used in place of *alternate* in the sense 'every other', e.g. *There was a dance on alternate Saturdays*.

alternative birth *n.* (also **alternative birthing**) any method of childbirth in which the delivery occurs at home or in a similar environment, often with minimal medical intervention.

alternative comedy *n.* a style of comedy which seeks to reject established (esp. racist or sexist) stereotypes.

alternative energy *n.* energy fuelled in ways that do not use up the earth's natural resources or otherwise harm the enviroment.

alternative fuel *n.* a fuel other than petrol for powering motor vehicles.

alternative medicine *n.* any of a range of medical therapies not regarded as orthodox by the medical profession, e.g. chiropractic, faith healing, herbalism, homoeopathy, and reflexology. Also called *complementary medicine*.

alternative society *n.* (usu. prec. by *the*) esp. *Brit.* a group of people dissociating themselves from conventional society and its values.

alternator /ˈɔːltəneɪtə, ˈɒl-/ *n.* a dynamo that generates an alternating current.

althorn /ˈalthɔːn/ *n. Mus.* an instrument of the saxhorn family, esp. the alto or tenor saxhorn in E flat. [German, from *alt* 'high' (from Latin *altus*) + HORN]

although /ɔːlˈðəʊ, ɒl-/ *conj.* = THOUGH *conj.* 1, 3, 4. [Middle English from ALL *adv.* + THOUGH]

altimeter /ˈaltɪmiːtə/ *n.* an instrument for showing height above sea or ground level, esp. one fitted to an aircraft. [Latin *altus* 'high' + -METER]

altitude /ˈaltɪtjuːd/ *n.* **1** the height of an object in relation to a given point, esp. sea level or the horizon. **2** *Geom.* the length of the perpendicular from a vertex to the opposite side of a figure. **3** a high or exalted position (*a social altitude*). □ **altitudinal** /altɪˈtjuːdɪn(ə)l/ *adj.* [Middle English, from Latin *altitudo* from *altus* 'high']

altitude sickness *n.* a sickness experienced at high altitudes.

alto /ˈaltəʊ/ *n.* (*pl.* **-os**) **1** = CONTRALTO. **2 a** the highest adult male singing voice, above tenor. **b** a singer with this voice. **c** a part written for it. **3 a** (*attrib.*) denoting the member of a family of instruments pitched second or third highest. **b** an alto instrument, esp. an alto saxophone. [Italian *alto* (*canto*) 'high (singing)']

alto clef *n.* a clef placing middle C on the middle line of the staff, used chiefly for viola music.

altocumulus /altəʊˈkjuːmjʊləs/ *n. Meteorol.* cloud formed at medium altitude as a layer of rounded masses with a level base. [modern Latin, from Latin *altus* 'high' + CUMULUS]

altogether /ɔːltəˈgɛðə, ɒl-/ *adv.* **1** totally, completely (*you are altogether wrong*). **2** on the whole (*altogether it had been a good day*). **3** in total. □ **in the altogether** *colloq.* naked. [Old English, (as ALL + TOGETHER)]

■ **Usage** Note that *altogether* means 'in total', as in *there are six bedrooms altogether*, whereas *all together* is used to mean 'all in one place' or 'all at once', as in *there are six bedrooms all together; they came in all together*.

alto-relievo /ˌaltəʊrɪˈliːvəʊ/ *n.* (also **alto-rilievo** /-rɪˈljeɪvəʊ/) (*pl.* **-os**) *Sculpture* **1** = *high relief* (see RELIEF 6a). **2** a sculpture, carving, etc. in high relief. [Italian *alto-rilievo*]

altostratus /altəʊˈstrɑːtəs, -ˈstreɪtəs/ *n. Meteorol.* cloud formed as a continuous uniform layer at medium altitude. [modern Latin, from Latin *altus* 'high' + STRATUS]

altricial /alˈtrɪʃ(ə)l/ *adj. & n.* ● *adj.* **1** (of a young bird or animal) requiring care and feeding by the parents after hatching or birth. **2** having such young. ● *n.* an altricial bird (cf. PRECOCIAL). [Latin *altrix altricis* fem. of *altor* 'nourisher', from *alere* 'nourish']

altruism /ˈaltrʊɪz(ə)m/ *n.* **1** regard for others as a principle of action. **2** unselfishness; concern for other people. □ **altruist** *n.* **altruistic** /altrʊˈɪstɪk/ *adj.* **altruistically** /altrʊˈɪstɪk(ə)li/ *adv.* [French *altruisme* from Italian *altrui* 'somebody else' (influenced by Latin *alter* 'other')]

alum /ˈaləm/ *n. Chem.* **1** a double sulphate of aluminium and potassium. **2** any of a group of crystalline salts which are double sulphates of a monovalent metal (or group) and a trivalent metal. [Middle English via Old French from Latin *alumen aluminis*]

alumina /əˈluːmɪnə/ *n.* the compound aluminium oxide occurring naturally as corundum and emery. Chem. formula: Al_2O_3. [Latin *alumen* 'alum', on the pattern of *soda* etc.]

aluminium /aljʊˈmɪnɪəm/ *n.* (*N. Amer.* **aluminum** /əˈluːmɪnəm/) a silvery light and malleable metallic element resistant to tarnishing by air (symbol **Al**). [*aluminium*, alteration (on the pattern of *sodium* etc.) from *aluminum*, earlier *alumium*, from ALUM + -IUM]

aluminium bronze *n.* an alloy of copper and aluminium.

aluminize /əˈluːmɪnʌɪz/ *v.tr.* (also **-ise**) coat with aluminium. □ **aluminization** /-ˈzeɪʃ(ə)n/ *n.*

aluminosilicate /əˌluːmɪnəʊˈsɪlɪkeɪt/ *n. Mineral.* a silicate containing aluminium, esp. a rock-forming mineral of this kind, e.g. a feldspar, a clay mineral. [ALUMINIUM + -O- + SILICATE]

alumnus /əˈlʌmnəs/ *n.* (*pl.* **alumni** /-ni/; *fem.* **alumna**, *pl.* **alumnae** /-ni/) a former pupil or student of a particular school, college, or university. [Latin, = 'nursling, pupil' from *alere* 'nourish']

alveolar /alˈvɪələ/ *adj.* **1** of an alveolus. **2** *Phonet.* (of a consonant) pronounced with the tip of the tongue in contact with the ridge of the upper teeth, e.g. *n, s, t*. [ALVEOLUS + -AR[1]]

alveolus /alˈvɪələs, alvɪˈəʊləs/ *n.* (*pl.* **alveoli** /-lʌɪ, -liː/) **1** a small cavity, pit, or hollow. **2** any of the many tiny air sacs of the lungs which allow for rapid gaseous exchange. **3** the bony socket for the root of a tooth. **4** the cell of a honeycomb. □ **alveolate** /alˈvɪələt/ *adj.* [Latin, diminutive of *alveus* 'cavity']

always /ˈɔːlweɪz, -ɪz/ *adv.* **1** at all times; on all occasions (*they are always late*). **2** whatever the circumstances (*I can always sleep on the floor*). **3** repeatedly; often (*they are always complaining*). **4** for ever; for all time (*he will always be a fool*). [Middle English, probably distributive genitive from ALL + WAY + -'S[1]]

alyssum /ˈalɪs(ə)m, əˈlɪs(ə)m/ *n.* **1** a cruciferous plant of the genus *Alyssum*, widely cultivated and usu. having yellow or white flowers. **2** (in full **sweet alyssum**) a small Mediterranean cruciferous plant, *Lobularia maritima*, with fragrant white flowers. [Latin, from Greek *alusson*]

Alzheimer's disease /ˈaltshʌɪməz/ *n.* a serious disorder of the brain manifesting itself in premature senility. [named after A. *Alzheimer*, German neurologist (d. 1915), who first identified it]

AM *abbr.* **1** amplitude modulation. **2** *US* Master of Arts. **3** Member of the Order of Australia. [(sense 2) Latin *artium Magister*]

Am *symb. Chem.* the element americium.

am *1st person sing. present* of BE.

a.m. *abbr.* before noon. [Latin *ante meridiem*]

amadavat var. of AVADAVAT.

amadou /ˈamədu:/ *n.* a spongy and combustible tinder prepared from dry fungi. [French from modern Provençal, literally 'lover' (because quickly kindled) from Latin (as AMATEUR)]

amah /ˈɑːmə/ *n.* (in the Far East and India) a nursemaid or maid. [Portuguese *ama* 'nurse']

amalgam /əˈmalgəm/ *n.* **1** a mixture or blend. **2** an alloy of mercury with one or more other metals, used esp. in dentistry. [Middle English via French *amalgame* or medieval Latin *amalgama* from Greek *malagma* 'an emollient']

amalgamate /əˈmalgəmeɪt/ *v.* **1** *tr. & intr.* combine or unite to form one structure, organization, etc. **2** *intr.* (of metals) alloy with mercury. □ **amalgamation** /-ˈmeɪʃ(ə)n/ *n.* [medieval Latin *amalgamare amalgamat-* (as AMALGAM)]

amanuensis /əˌmanjʊˈɛnsɪs/ *n.* (*pl.* **amanuenses** /-siːz/) **1** a person who writes from dictation or copies manuscripts. **2** a literary assistant. [Latin from (*servus*) *a manu* '(slave) at hand(writing), secretary' + *-ensis* 'belonging to']

amaranth /ˈamərانθ/ *n.* **1** any plant of the genus *Amaranthus*, usu. having small green, red, or purple tinted flowers, e.g. prince's feather. **2** an imaginary flower that never fades. **3** a purple colour. □ **amaranthine** /aməˈranθʌɪn/ *adj.* [French *amarante* or modern Latin *amaranthus* via Latin from Greek *amarantos* 'everlasting', (as A-[1] + *marainō* 'wither'), alteration influenced by *polyanthus* etc.]

amaretto /amə'rɛtəʊ/ *n.* (*pl.* **amaretti** /-ti/) **1** an Italian almond-flavoured liqueur. **2** (in *pl.*) Italian almond-flavoured biscuits. [Italian, diminutive of *amaro* 'bitter' (with reference to bitter almonds)]

■ **Usage** Care should be taken not to confuse *amaretto*/*amaretti* 'a liqueur; almond-flavoured biscuits' with *amoretto* 'a Cupid'.

amaryllis /amə'rɪlɪs/ *n.* **1** a bulbous lily-like plant, *Amaryllis belladonna*, native to S. Africa, with white or rose-pink flowers; also called *belladonna lily*. **2** a related plant formerly of this genus, esp. one of the genus *Hippeastrum*. [Latin, from Greek *Amarullis*, a name for a country girl in pastoral poetry]

amass /ə'mas/ *v.tr.* **1** gather or heap together. **2** accumulate (esp. riches). □ **amasser** *n.* [French *amasser* or medieval Latin *amassare*, ultimately from Latin *massa* MASS]

amateur /'amətə, -tjʊə/ *n.* **1 a** a person who engages in a pursuit (e.g. an art or sport) as a pastime rather than a profession. **b** *derog.* a person who does something unskilfully or amateurishly. **2** (*attrib.*) for or done by amateurs (*amateur athletics*). **3** (foll. by *of*) a person who is fond of (a thing). □ **amateurism** *n.* [French, via Italian *amatore* from Latin *amator -oris* 'lover', from *amare* 'love']

amateurish /'amətərɪʃ/ *adj.* characteristic of an amateur, esp. *derog.* one who is unskilful or inept. □ **amateurishly** *adv.* **amateurishness** *n.*

amatory /'amət(ə)ri/ *adj.* of or relating to sexual love or desire. [Latin *amatorius*, from *amare* 'love']

amaurosis /amɔː'rəʊsɪs/ *n. Med.* partial or total loss of sight, from disease of the optic nerve, retina, spinal cord, or brain. □ **amaurotic** /-'rɒtɪk/ *adj.* [modern Latin from Greek, from *amauroō* 'darken' from *amauros* 'dim']

amaze /ə'meɪz/ *v.tr.* (often foll. by *at*, or *that* + clause, or *to* + infin.) surprise greatly; overwhelm with wonder (*am amazed at your indifference*; *was amazed to find them alive*). □ **amazement** *n.* **amazing** *adj.* **amazingly** *adv.* **amazingness** *n.* [Old English *āmasian*, of uncertain origin]

Amazon /'aməz(ə)n/ *n.* **1** a member of a legendary race of female warriors in Scythia and elsewhere. **2** (**amazon**) a very tall, strong, or athletic woman. □ **Amazonian** /amə'zəʊnɪən/ *adj.* [Middle English via Latin from Greek: explained by the Greeks as 'breastless' (as if A-[1] + *mazos* 'breast'), but probably of foreign origin]

amazon ant *n.* an ant of the genus *Polyergus*, which captures pupae of other ant species to raise as slaves.

ambassador /am'basədə/ *n.* **1** an accredited diplomat sent by a state on a mission to, or as its permanent representative in, a foreign country. **2** a representative or promoter of a specified thing (*an ambassador of peace*). □ **ambassadorial** /ambasə'dɔːrɪəl, am'bas-/ *adj.* **ambassadorship** *n.* [Middle English via French *ambassadeur* from Italian *ambasciator*, ultimately from Latin *ambactus* 'servant']

ambassador-at-large *n. N. Amer.* an ambassador with special duties, not appointed to a particular country.

ambassadress /am'basədrɪs/ *n.* **1** a female ambassador. **2** an ambassador's wife.

ambatch /'ambatʃ/ *n.* an African tree, *Aeschynomene elaphroxylon*, with very light spongy wood. [Ethiopic]

amber /'ambə/ *n.* & *adj.* ● *n.* **1 a** a yellowish translucent fossilized resin deriving from extinct (esp. coniferous) trees and used in jewellery. **b** the honey-yellow colour of this. **2** a cautionary yellow light, esp. a traffic light showing between green for 'go' and red for 'stop'. ● *adj.* made of or coloured like amber. [Middle English via Old French *ambre* from Arabic *'anbar* 'ambergris, amber']

ambergris /'ambəgrɪs, -iːs/ *n.* a strong-smelling waxlike secretion of the intestine of the sperm whale, found floating in tropical seas and used in perfume manufacture. [Middle English, from Old French *ambre gris* 'grey' AMBER]

amberjack /'ambədʒak/ *n.* esp. *N. Amer.* any large brightly coloured marine fish of the genus *Seriola* found in tropical and subtropical Atlantic waters.

ambiance /ɑ̃bjɑ̃s/ *n.* = AMBIENCE. [French]

ambidextrous /ambɪ'dɛkstrəs/ *adj.* **1** able to use the right and left hands equally well. **2** working skilfully in more than one medium. □ **ambidexterity** /-'stɛrɪti/ *n.* **ambidextrously** *adv.* **ambidextrousness** *n.* [Late Latin *ambidexter*, from Latin *ambi-* 'on both sides' + *dexter* 'right-handed']

ambience /'ambɪəns/ *n.* **1** the surroundings or atmosphere of a place. **2** background noise added to a musical recording to give the impression that it was recorded live. [AMBIENT + -ENCE or French *ambiance*]

ambient /'ambɪənt/ *adj.* surrounding; of the surroundings (*ambient temperature*). [French *ambiant* or Latin *ambiens -entis*, pres. part. of *ambire* 'go round']

ambient music *n.* background music used to create atmosphere.

ambiguity /ambɪ'gjuːɪti/ *n.* (*pl.* **-ies**) **1 a** double meaning, either deliberate or caused by inexactness of expression (*tried to avoid ambiguity in setting out the rules*). **b** an example of this. **2** an expression able to be interpreted in more than one way (e.g. *dogs must be carried*). [Middle English, from Old French *ambiguité* or Latin *ambiguitas* (as AMBIGUOUS)]

ambiguous /am'bɪgjʊəs/ *adj.* **1** having an obscure or double meaning. **2** difficult to classify. □ **ambiguously** *adv.* **ambiguousness** *n.* [Latin *ambiguus* 'doubtful' from *ambigere*, from *ambi-* 'both ways' + *agere* 'drive']

ambisonics /ambɪ'sɒnɪks/ *n.pl.* (treated as *sing.*) a system of high-fidelity sound reproduction designed to reproduce the directional and acoustic properties of the sound source using two or more channels. [Latin *ambi-* 'on both sides' + SONIC]

ambit /'ambɪt/ *n.* **1** the scope, extent, or bounds of something. **2** precincts or environs. [Middle English from Latin *ambitus* 'circuit', from *ambire*: see AMBIENT]

ambition /am'bɪʃ(ə)n/ *n.* (often foll. by *to* + infin.) **1** drive to succeed or progress (*was full of ambition to succeed*). **2** a strong desire or aspiration (*her ambition to be a doctor*; *an ambition to visit Rome*). [Middle English via Old French from Latin *ambitio -onis*, from *ambire ambit-* 'canvass for votes': see AMBIENT]

ambitious /am'bɪʃəs/ *adj.* **1 a** full of ambition. **b** showing ambition (*an ambitious attempt*). **2** (foll. by *of*, or *to* + infin.) strongly determined. □ **ambitiously** *adv.* **ambitiousness** *n.* [Middle English via Old French *ambitieux* from Latin *ambitiosus* (as AMBITION)]

ambivalence /am'bɪv(ə)l(ə)ns/ *n.* (also **ambivalency** /-ənsi/) the coexistence in one person's mind of opposing feelings, esp. love and hate, in a single context. □ **ambivalent** *adj.* **ambivalently** *adv.* [German *Ambivalenz* from Latin *ambo* 'both', on the pattern of *Äquivalenz* 'equivalence': cf. EQUIVALENT]

ambivert /'ambɪvəːt/ *n. Psychol.* a person who fluctuates between being an introvert and an extrovert. □ **ambiversion** /ambɪ'vəːʃ(ə)n/ *n.* [Latin *ambi-* 'on both sides' + *-vert* from Latin *vertere* 'to turn', on the pattern of EXTROVERT, INTROVERT]

amble /'amb(ə)l/ *v.* & *n.* ● *v.intr.* **1** move at an easy pace, in a way suggesting an ambling horse. **2** (of a horse etc.) move by lifting the two feet on one side together. **3** ride an ambling horse; ride at an easy pace. ● *n.* **1** an easy pace. **2** the gait of an ambling horse. [Middle English via Old French *ambler* from Latin *ambulare* 'walk']

amblyopia /amblɪ'əʊpɪə/ *n.* dimness of vision without obvious defect or change in the eye. □ **amblyopic** /-'ɒpɪk/ *adj.* [Greek from *ambluōpos* (*adj.*), from *amblus* 'dull' + *ōps*, *ōpos* 'eye']

ambo /ˈambəʊ/ *n.* (*pl.* **-os** or **ambones** /-ˈbəʊniːz/) a stand for reading the lesson in an early Christian church etc. [medieval Latin from Greek *ambōn* 'rim' (in medieval Greek = pulpit)]

amboyna /amˈbɔɪnə/ *n.* the decorative wood of the SE Asian tree *Pterocarpus indicus.* [named after *Amboina* Island in Indonesia]

ambrosia /amˈbrəʊzjə/ *n.* **1** (in Greek and Roman mythology) the food of the gods; the elixir of life. **2** anything very pleasing to taste or smell. **3 a** a fungal product used as food by pinhole borers. **b** = BEE-BREAD. □ **ambrosial** *adj.* **ambrosian** *adj.* [Latin from Greek, = elixir of life, from *ambrotos* 'immortal']

ambrosia beetle *n.* a small beetle of the family Scolytidae or Platypodidae, whose larvae are pinhole borers.

ambry var. of AUMBRY.

ambulance /ˈambjʊl(ə)ns/ *n.* **1** a vehicle specially equipped for conveying the sick or injured to and from hospital, esp. in emergencies. **2** a mobile hospital following an army. [French (as AMBULANT)]

ambulance chaser *n. N. Amer. colloq. derog.* **1** a lawyer who specializes in personal injury litigation. **2** a person seeking to profit from others' misfortunes. [from the reputation gained by certain lawyers for attending accidents and encouraging victims to sue]

ambulance man *n.* (*fem.* **ambulance woman**) a member of an ambulance crew.

ambulant /ˈambjʊl(ə)nt/ *adj. Med.* **1** (of a patient) able to walk about; not confined to bed. **2** (of treatment) not confining a patient to bed. [Latin *ambulare ambulant-* 'walk']

ambulatory /ˈambjʊlət(ə)ri/ *adj.* & *n.* ● *adj.* **1** = AMBULANT. **2** of or adapted for walking. **3 a** movable. **b** not permanent. ● *n.* (*pl.* **-ies**) a place for walking, esp. an aisle or cloister in a church or monastery. [Latin *ambulatorius*, from *ambulare* 'walk']

ambuscade /ambəˈskeɪd/ *n.* & *v.* ● *n.* an ambush. ● *v.* **1** *tr.* attack by means of an ambush. **2** *intr.* lie in ambush. **3** *tr.* conceal in an ambush. [French *embuscade* via Italian *imboscata* or Spanish *emboscada* from Latin *imboscare*: see AMBUSH, -ADE[1]]

ambush /ˈambʊʃ/ *n.* & *v.* ● *n.* **1** a surprise attack by persons (e.g. troops) in a concealed position. **2 a** the concealment of troops etc. to make such an attack. **b** the place where they are concealed. **c** the troops etc. concealed. ● *v.tr.* **1** attack by means of an ambush. **2** lie in wait for. [Middle English, in the sense 'set (troops) to ambush': via Old French *embusche*, *embuschier*, from a Romanic form = 'put in a wood': related to BUSH[1]]

ameba *US* var. of AMOEBA. □ **amebic** *adj.* **ameboid** *adj.*

ameer var. of AMIR.

ameliorate /əˈmiːlɪəreɪt/ *v.tr.* & *intr. formal* make or become better; improve. □ **amelioration** /əˌmiːlɪəˈreɪʃ(ə)n/ *n.* **ameliorative** *adj.* **ameliorator** *n.* [alteration of MELIORATE, influenced by French *améliorer*]

amen /ɑːˈmɛn, eɪ-/ *int.* & *n.* ● *int.* **1** uttered at the end of a prayer or hymn etc., meaning 'so be it'. **2** (foll. by *to*) expressing agreement or assent (*amen to that*). ● *n.* an utterance of 'amen'. [Old English via ecclesiastical Latin and Greek from Hebrew *'āmēn* 'certainly']

amenable /əˈmiːnəb(ə)l/ *adj.* **1** responsive, tractable. **2** (often foll. by *to*) (of a person) responsible to law. **3** (foll. by *to*) (of a thing) subject or liable. □ **amenability** /-ˈbɪlɪti/ *n.* **amenableness** *n.* **amenably** *adv.* [Anglo-French (*Law*) via French *amener* 'bring to' (as A-[3] + *mener* 'bring') via Late Latin *minare* 'drive (animals)' from Latin *minari* 'threaten']

amend /əˈmɛnd/ *v.tr.* **1** make minor improvements in (a text or a written proposal). **2** correct an error or errors in (a document). **3** make better; improve. □ **amendable** *adj.* **amender** *n.* [Middle English, from Old French *amender*, ultimately from Latin *emendare* EMEND]

■ **Usage** *Amend* should not be confused with *emend*, a more technical word used in the context of textual correction.

amende honorable /əˌmɒ̃d ɒnɔːˈrɑːb(ə)l, French amɑ̃d ɔnɔrabl/ *n.* (*pl.* ***amendes honorables*** *pronunc.* same) a public or open apology, often with some form of reparation. [French, = honourable reparation]

amendment /əˈmɛn(d)m(ə)nt/ *n.* **1** a minor improvement in a document (esp. a legal or statutory one). **2** an article added to the US Constitution. [AMEND + -MENT]

amends /əˈmɛn(d)z/ *n.* □ **make amends** (often foll. by *for*) compensate or make up (for). [Middle English from Old French *amendes* 'penalties, fine', pl. of *amende* 'reparation', from *amender* AMEND]

amenity /əˈmiːnɪti, -ˈmɛn-/ *n.* (*pl.* **-ies**) **1** (usu. in *pl.*) a pleasant or useful feature. **2** pleasantness (of a place, person, etc.). [Middle English from Old French *amenité* or Latin *amoenitas*, from *amoenus* 'pleasant']

amenity bed *n. Brit.* a bed available in a hospital to give more privacy for a small payment.

amenorrhoea /əmɛnəˈriːə/ *n.* (*US* **amenorrhea**) *Med.* an abnormal absence of menstruation. [A-[1] + MENORRHOEA]

ament /ˈeɪmɛnt, əˈmɛnt/ *n.* (also **amentum** /-təm/) (*pl.* **aments** or **amenta** /-tə/) *Bot.* a catkin. [Latin, = thong]

amentia /eɪˈmɛnʃə, ə-/ *n. Med.* severe congenital mental handicap. [Latin from *amens ament-* 'mad' (as A-[1], *mens* 'mind')]

Amerasian /aməˈreɪʃ(ə)n, -ʒ(ə)n/ *adj.* & *n.* ● *adj.* of mixed American and Asian parentage. ● *n.* an Amerasian person, esp. a child fathered by an American serviceman in Asia. [portmanteau word from AMERICAN + ASIAN]

amerce /əˈməːs/ *v.tr.* **1** *Law* punish by fine. **2** punish arbitrarily. □ **amercement** *n.* **amerciable** /-sɪəb(ə)l/ *adj.* [Middle English *amercy* from Anglo-French *amercier* from *à merci* 'at (the) mercy']

American /əˈmɛrɪk(ə)n/ *adj.* & *n.* ● *adj.* **1** of, relating to, or characteristic of the United States or its inhabitants. **2** (usu. in *comb.*) of or relating to the continents of America (*Latin American*). ● *n.* **1** a native or citizen of the United States. **2** (usu. in *comb.*) a native or inhabitant of the continents of America (*North Americans*). **3** the English language as it is used in the United States. [modern Latin *Americanus* from *America*, from the Latinized form of the name of *Amerigo* Vespucci, Italian navigator (d. 1512), who made several voyages to the New World]

Americana /əmɛrɪˈkɑːnə/ *n.pl.* things connected with America, esp. with the United States.

American aloe var. of ALOE 3.

American dream *n.* the traditional social ideals of the American people, such as equality, democracy, and material prosperity.

American football *n.* a kind of football played with an oval ball, evolved from rugby.

American Indian *n.* a member of a group of indigenous peoples of N. and S. America and the Caribbean.

■ **Usage** The term *Native American* is now often, though not universally, preferred.

Americanism /əˈmɛrɪk(ə)nɪz(ə)m/ *n.* **1 a** a word, sense, or phrase peculiar to or originating from the United States. **b** a thing or feature characteristic of or peculiar to the United States. **2** attachment to or sympathy for the United States.

Americanize /əˈmɛrɪk(ə)nʌɪz/ *v.* (also **-ise**) **1** *tr.* **a** make American in character. **b** naturalize as an American. **2** *intr.* become American in character. □ **Americanization** /-ˈzeɪʃ(ə)n/ *n.*

American Legion *n.* (in the US) an association of ex-servicemen formed in 1919.

American plaice see PLAICE 2.

American plan *n. N. Amer.* a system of charging for a hotel room and meals (cf. EUROPEAN PLAN).

americium /amə'rɪsjəm/ *n. Chem.* an artificially made transuranic radioactive metallic element (symbol **Am**). [*America* (where it was first made) + -IUM]

Amerind /'amərmd/ *adj. & n.* (also **Amerindian** /amə'rɪndɪən/) = AMERICAN INDIAN. [portmanteau word from AMERICAN + INDIAN]

amethyst /'aməθɪst/ *n.* a precious stone of a violet or purple variety of quartz. ◻ **amethystine** /-'θɪsti:n/ *adj.* [Middle English via Old French *ametiste* and Latin *amethystus* from Greek *amethustos* 'not drunken', the stone being supposed to prevent intoxication]

Amex /'amɛks/ *abbr.* **1** *propr.* American Express. **2** American Stock Exchange.

Amharic /am'harɪk/ *n. & adj.* ● *n.* the official and commercial language of Ethiopia. ● *adj.* of or relating to this language. [*Amhara*, Ethiopian province + -IC]

amiable /'eɪmɪəb(ə)l/ *adj.* friendly and pleasant in temperament; likeable. ◻ **amiability** /eɪmɪə'bɪlɪti/ *n.* **amiableness** *n.* **amiably** *adv.* [Middle English via Old French from Late Latin *amicabilis* 'amicable': the spelling from confusion with French *aimable* 'lovable']

amianthus /amɪ'anθəs/ *n.* (also **amiantus** /-təs/) a fine silky-fibred variety of asbestos. [Latin from Greek *amiantos* 'undefiled' from *a-* 'not' + *miainō* 'defile' (i.e. purified by fire, being incombustible): for *-h-* cf. AMARANTH]

amicable /'amɪkəb(ə)l/ *adj.* showing or done in a friendly spirit (*an amicable meeting*). ◻ **amicability** /amɪkə'bɪlɪti/ *n.* **amicableness** *n.* **amicably** *adv.* [Late Latin *amicabilis*, from Latin *amicus* 'friend']

amice[1] /'amɪs/ *n.* a white linen cloth worn on the neck and shoulders by a priest celebrating the Eucharist. [Middle English via medieval Latin *amicia*, *-sia* from Latin *amictus* 'outer garment']

amice[2] /'amɪs/ *n.* a cap, hood, or cape worn by members of certain religious orders. [Middle English via Old French *aumusse* from medieval Latin *almucia* etc., of unknown origin]

amicus curiae /a,mʌɪkəs 'kjʊərii:/ *n.* (*pl.* **amici curiae** /-si/) *Law* an impartial adviser in a court of law. [modern Latin, = friend of the court]

amid /ə'mɪd/ *prep.* (also **amidst** /ə'mɪdst/) **1** in the middle of. **2** in the course of. [Middle English *amidde(s)* (as A[2] + MID)]

amide /'eɪmʌɪd, 'amʌɪd/ *n. Chem.* a compound formed from ammonia by replacement of one (or sometimes more than one) hydrogen atom by a metal or an acyl radical. [AMMONIA + -IDE]

amidships /ə'mɪdʃɪps/ *adv.* (*US* also **amidship**) in or into the middle of a ship. [MIDSHIP, influenced by AMID]

amidst var. of AMID.

amigo /ə'mi:gəʊ/ *n.* (*pl.* **-os**) esp. *N. Amer. colloq.* (often as a form of address) a friend or comrade, esp. in Spanish-speaking areas. [Spanish]

amine /'eɪmi:n/ *n. Chem.* a compound formed from ammonia by replacement of one or more hydrogen atoms by an organic radical or radicals. [AMMONIA + -INE[4]]

amino /ə'mi:nəʊ/ *n.* (used *attrib.*) *Chem.* the monovalent group $-NH_2$. [AMINE]

amino acid /ə,mi:nəʊ 'asɪd, ə,mʌɪn-/ *n. Biochem.* any of a group of simple organic compounds containing both the carboxyl (COOH) and amino (NH_2) group, many occurring naturally in plant and animal tissues and forming the basic constituents of proteins.

amir /ə'mi:ə/ *n.* (also **ameer**) the title of some Arab rulers. [Arabic *'amīr* 'commander' from *amara* 'command': cf. EMIR]

Amish /'amɪʃ, 'ɑ:-, 'eɪ-/ *adj. & n.* ● *adj.* belonging to a strict US Mennonite sect. ● *n.pl.* (prec. by *the*) the members of this sect. [probably from German *Amisch*, from J. *Amen* 17th-c. Swiss Mennonite preacher]

amiss /ə'mɪs/ *adj. & adv.* ● *predic.adj.* wrong; out of order; faulty (*knew something was amiss*). ● *adv.* wrong; wrongly; inappropriately (*everything went amiss*). ◻ **take amiss** be offended by (*took my words amiss*). [Middle English, probably from Old Norse *à mis* 'so as to miss', from *à* 'on' + *mis* related to MISS[1]]

amitosis /amɪ'təʊsɪs, eɪmʌɪ-/ *n. Biol.* a form of nuclear division that does not involve mitosis. [A-[1] + MITOSIS]

amitriptyline /amɪ'trɪptɪli:n/ *n. Pharm.* an antidepressant drug that has a mild tranquillizing action. [AMINE + TRI- + *heptyl* (see HEPTANE) + -INE[4]]

amity /'amɪti/ *n.* friendship; friendly relations. [Middle English from Old French *amitié*, ultimately from Latin *amicus* 'friend']

ammeter /'amɪtə/ *n.* an instrument for measuring electric current in amperes. [AMPERE + -METER]

ammo /'aməʊ/ *n. colloq.* ammunition. [abbreviation]

ammonia /ə'məʊnɪə/ *n. Chem.* **1** a colourless gas with a characteristic pungent smell. Chem. formula: NH_3. **2** (in general use) a strongly alkaline solution of ammonia gas in water. [modern Latin from SAL AMMONIAC]

ammoniacal /amə(ʊ)'nʌɪək(ə)l/ *adj.* of, relating to, or containing ammonia or sal ammoniac. [Middle English *ammoniac* via Old French and Latin from Greek *ammōniakos* 'of Ammon', used as a noun for the salt and gum obtained near the temple of Jupiter Ammon (the Greek name for the Egyptian deity Amen) at Siwain Egypt (cf. SAL AMMONIAC)]

ammoniated /ə'məʊnɪeɪtɪd/ *adj.* combined or treated with ammonia.

ammonite /'amənʌɪt/ *n.* an extinct cephalopod mollusc of the order Ammonoidea, with a flat coiled spiral shell found as a fossil. [modern Latin *ammonites*, from medieval Latin *cornu Ammonis* 'horn of Ammon' (see AMMONIACAL), from the fossil's resemblance to the ram's horn associated with Ammon]

ammonium /ə'məʊnɪəm/ *n.* the monovalent ion NH_4^+, formed from ammonia. [modern Latin (as AMMONIA)]

ammunition /amjʊ'nɪʃ(ə)n/ *n.* **1** a supply of projectiles (esp. bullets, shells, and grenades). **2** points used or usable to advantage in an argument. [obsolete French *amunition*, corruption of (*la*) *munition* '(the) MUNITION']

amnesia /am'ni:zjə/ *n.* a partial or total loss of memory. ◻ **amnesiac** /-zɪak/ *n.* **amnesic** *adj. & n.* [modern Latin from Greek, = forgetfulness]

amnesty /'amnɪsti/ *n. & v.* ● *n.* (*pl.* **-ies**) a general pardon, esp. for political offences. ● *v.tr.* (**-ies**, **-ied**) grant an amnesty to. [French *amnestie*, or Latin from Greek *amnēstia* 'oblivion']

Amnesty International *n.* an independent international organization in support of human rights, esp. for prisoners of conscience.

amnio /'amnɪəʊ/ *n.* (*pl.* **-os**) *colloq.* amniocentesis. [abbreviation]

amniocentesis /,amnɪəʊsɛn'ti:sɪs/ *n.* (*pl.* **amniocenteses** /-si:z/) *Med.* the sampling of amniotic fluid by insertion of a hollow needle into the uterus to determine the condition of a foetus. [AMNION + Greek *kentēsis* 'pricking', from *kentō* 'to prick']

amnion /'amnɪən/ *n.* (*pl.* **amnia**) *Zool. & Physiol.* the innermost membrane that encloses the embryo of a reptile, bird, or mammal. ◻ **amniotic** /amnɪ'ɒtɪk/ *adj.* [Greek, = caul (diminutive of *amnos* 'lamb')]

amniote /'amnɪəʊt/ *n. & adj. Zool.* ● *n.* an animal whose embryo develops in an amnion. ● *adj.* of or relating to such animals. [back-formation from AMNIOTIC (see AMNION)]

amniotic fluid *n.* the fluid surrounding a foetus within the amnion.

amoeba /ə'mi:bə/ *n.* (*US* also **ameba**) (*pl.* **amoebas** or **amoebae** /-bi:/) any usu. aquatic protozoan of the genus *Amoeba*, esp. *A. proteus*, capable of changing shape. ◻ **amoebic** *adj.* **amoeboid** *adj.* [modern Latin, from Greek *amoibē* 'change']

amoebiasis /amiːˈbʌɪəsɪs/ *n.* (*US* **amebiasis**) (*pl.* **amoebiases**) *Med.* infection with amoebas, esp. as causing dysentery. [AMOEBA + -ASIS]

amoebic dysentery *n.* (*US* also **amebic dysentery**) dysentery caused by infection of the gut with certain amoebae.

amok /əˈmɒk/ *adv.* (also **amuck** /əˈmʌk/) □ **run amok** run about wildly in an uncontrollable violent rage. [Malay *amok* 'rushing in a frenzy']

among /əˈmʌŋ/ *prep.* (also esp. *Brit.* **amongst** /əˈmʌŋst/, *poet.* **'mongst** /mʌŋst/) **1** surrounded by; in the company of (*lived among the trees*; *be among friends*). **2** in the number of (*among us were those who disagreed*). **3** an example of; in the class or category of (*is among the richest men alive*). **4 a** between; within the limits of (collectively or distributively); shared by (*had £5 among us*; *divide it among you*). **b** by the joint action or from the joint resources of (*among us we can manage it*). **5** with one another; by the reciprocal action of (*was decided among the participants*; *talked among themselves*). **6** as distinguished from; pre-eminent in the category of (*she is one among many*). [Old English *ongemang*, (as A[2] + *gemang* 'assemblage'): *-st* = adverbial genitive *-s* + *-t* as in AGAINST]

amontillado /əmɒntɪˈlɑːdəʊ, -ˈljɑː-/ *n.* (*pl.* **-os**) a medium dry sherry. [Spanish, from *Montilla* in Spain + *-ado* = -ATE[2]]

amoral /eɪˈmɒr(ə)l/ *adj.* **1** not concerned with or outside the scope of morality (cf. IMMORAL). **2** having no moral principles. □ **amoralism** *n.* **amoralist** *n.* **amorality** /-ˈralɪti/ *n.*

amoretto /aməˈrɛtəʊ, Italian amoˈretto/ *n.* (*pl.* ***amoretti*** /-tiː/) a Cupid. [Italian, diminutive of *amore* 'love', from Latin *amor*]

■ **Usage** See Usage Note at AMARETTO.

amorist /ˈamərɪst/ *n.* a person who professes or writes of (esp. sexual) love. [Latin *amor* or French *amour* + -IST]

amoroso[1] /aməˈrəʊzəʊ/ *adv.* & *adj. Mus.* in a loving or tender manner. [Italian]

amoroso[2] /aməˈrəʊzəʊ/ *n.* (*pl.* **-os**) a full rich type of sherry. [Spanish, = amorous]

amorous /ˈam(ə)rəs/ *adj.* **1** showing, feeling, or inclined to sexual love. **2** of or relating to sexual love. □ **amorously** *adv.* **amorousness** *n.* [Middle English via Old French and medieval Latin *amorosus* from Latin *amor* 'love']

amorphous /əˈmɔːfəs/ *adj.* **1** shapeless. **2** vague, ill-organized. **3** *Mineral.* & *Chem.* non-crystalline; having neither definite form nor structure. □ **amorphously** *adv.* **amorphousness** *n.* [medieval Latin *amorphus* from Greek *amorphos* 'shapeless' (as A-[1] + *morphē* 'form')]

amortize /əˈmɔːtʌɪz/ *v.tr.* (also **-ise**) *Commerce* **1** gradually extinguish (a debt) by money regularly put aside. **2** gradually write off the initial cost of (assets). **3** *hist.* transfer (land) to a corporation in mortmain. □ **amortization** /-ˈzeɪʃ(ə)n/ *n.* [Middle English from Old French *amortir* (stem *amortiss-*), ultimately from Latin *ad* 'to' + *mors mort-* 'death']

amount /əˈmaʊnt/ *n.* & *v.* ● *n.* a quantity, esp. the total of a thing or things in number, size, value, extent, etc. (*a large amount of money*; *came to a considerable amount*). ● *v.intr.* (foll. by *to*) be equivalent to in number, size, significance, etc. (*amounted to £100*; *amounted to a disaster*). □ **any amount of** a great deal of. **no amount of** not even the greatest possible amount of. [Middle English via Old French *amunter* from *amont* 'upward', literally 'uphill', from Latin *ad montem*]

amour /əˈmʊə/ *n.* a love affair, esp. a secret one. [French, = love, from Latin *amor amoris*]

amour propre /aˌmʊə ˈprɒpr(ə), French amur prɔpr/ *n.* self-respect. [French]

AMP *abbr.* adenosine monophosphate.

amp[1] /amp/ *n. Electr.* an ampere. [abbreviation]

amp[2] /amp/ *n. colloq.* an amplifier. [abbreviation]

ampelopsis /ampɪˈlɒpsɪs/ *n.* (*pl.* same) any plant of the genus *Ampelopsis* or *Parthenocissus*, usu. a climber supporting itself by twining tendrils, e.g. Virginia creeper. [modern Latin from Greek *ampelos* 'vine' + *opsis* 'appearance']

amperage /ˈamp(ə)rɪdʒ/ *n. Electr.* the strength of an electric current in amperes.

ampere /ˈampɛː/ *n. Electr.* the SI base unit of electric current (symbol **A**). [named after A. M. *Ampère*, French physicist d. 1836]

ampersand /ˈampəsand/ *n.* the sign & (= *and*, Latin *et*). [corruption of *and per se and* ('&' by itself is 'and'), chanted as an aid to learning the sign]

amphetamine /amˈfɛtəmiːn, -ɪn/ *n.* a synthetic drug used esp. as a stimulant. [abbreviation of chemical name *a*lpha-*m*ethyl *phe*ne*t*hyl*amine*]

amphi- /ˈamfi/ *comb. form* **1** both. **2** of both kinds. **3** on both sides. **4** around. [Greek]

amphibian /amˈfɪbɪən/ *adj.* & *n.* ● *adj.* **1** living both on land and in water. **2** *Zool.* of or relating to the class Amphibia. **3** (of a vehicle) able to operate on land and water. ● *n.* **1** *Zool.* any vertebrate of the class Amphibia, with a life history of an aquatic gill-breathing larval stage followed by a terrestrial lung-breathing adult stage, including frogs, toads, newts, and salamanders. **2** (in general use) a creature living both on land and in water. **3** an amphibian vehicle. [modern Latin *amphibium* from Greek *amphibion*, from AMPHI- + *bios* 'life']

amphibious /amˈfɪbɪəs/ *adj.* **1** living both on land and in water. **2** of or relating to or suited for both land and water. **3** *Mil.* **a** (of a military operation) involving forces landed from the sea. **b** (of forces) trained for such operations. **4** having a twofold nature; occupying two positions. □ **amphibiously** *adv.*

amphibole /ˈamfɪbəʊl/ *n. Mineral.* any of a class of rock-forming silicate and aluminosilicate minerals with fibrous or columnar crystals. [French from Latin *amphibolus* 'ambiguous', so called because of the varied structure of these minerals]

amphibolite /amˈfɪbəlʌɪt/ *n. Geol.* a granular metamorphic rock consisting mainly of hornblende and plagioclase.

amphibology /amfɪˈbɒlədʒi/ *n.* (*pl.* **-ies**) **1** a quibble. **2** an ambiguous wording. [Middle English via Old French and Late Latin from Latin, from Greek *amphibolia* 'ambiguity']

amphimixis /amfɪˈmɪksɪs/ *n. Biol.* true sexual reproduction with the fusion of gametes from two individuals (cf. APOMIXIS). □ **amphimictic** *adj.* [modern Latin (as AMPHI- + Greek *mixis* 'mingling')]

amphioxus /amfɪˈɒksəs/ *n.* any lancelet of the genus *Branchiostoma* (formerly *Amphioxus*). [modern Latin (as AMPHI- + Greek *oxus* 'sharp')]

amphipathic /amfɪˈpaθɪk/ *adj. Chem.* **1** (of a molecule) having both hydrophilic and hydrophobic parts. **2** consisting of such molecules. [AMPHI- + Greek *pathikos* (as PATHOS)]

amphipod /ˈamfɪpɒd/ *n.* any crustacean of the largely marine order Amphipoda, having a laterally compressed abdomen with two kinds of limb, e.g. the freshwater shrimp (*Gammarus pulex*). [AMPHI- + Greek *pous podos* 'foot']

amphiprostyle /amˈfɪprəstʌɪl/ *n.* & *adj.* ● *n.* a classical building with a portico at each end. ● *adj.* of or in this style. [Latin *amphiprostylus* from Greek *amphiprostulos* (as AMPHI-, *prostulos* PROSTYLE)]

amphisbaena /amfɪsˈbiːnə/ *n.* **1** *Mythol.* & *poet.* a fabulous serpent with a head at each end. **2** *Zool.* a burrowing wormlike lizard of the genus *Amphisbaena*, having no apparent division of head from body, making both ends look similar. [Middle English via Latin from Greek *amphisbaina*, from *amphis* 'both ways' + *bainō* 'go']

amphitheatre /ˈamfɪθiːətə/ *n.* (*US* **amphitheater**) **1** a round, usu. unroofed building with tiers of seats surrounding a central space. **2** a semicircular gallery in a theatre. **3** a large circular hollow. **4** the scene of a contest. [Latin *amphitheatrum* from Greek *amphitheatron* (as AMPHI-, THEATRE)]

amphora /ˈamf(ə)rə/ *n.* (*pl.* **amphorae** /-riː/ or **amphoras**) a Greek or Roman vessel with two handles and a narrow neck. [Latin, from Greek *amphoreus*]

amphoteric /amfəˈtɛrɪk/ *adj. Chem.* able to react as a base and an acid. [Greek *amphoteros*, comparative of *amphō* 'both']

ampicillin /ampɪˈsɪlɪn/ *n. Pharm.* a semi-synthetic penicillin used esp. in treating infections of the urinary and respiratory tracts. [*amino* + *penicillin*]

ample /ˈamp(ə)l/ *adj.* (**ampler**, **amplest**) **1 a** plentiful, abundant, extensive. **b** *euphem.* (esp. of a person) large, stout. **2** enough or more than enough. □ **ampleness** *n.* **amply** *adv.* [French, from Latin *amplus*]

amplifier /ˈamplɪfʌɪə/ *n.* **1** an electronic device for increasing the strength of electrical signals, used esp. in sound reproduction. **2** this combined with a loudspeaker and used to amplify musical instruments etc.

amplify /ˈamplɪfʌɪ/ *v.* (**-ies**, **-ied**) **1** *tr.* increase the volume or strength of (sound, electrical signals, etc.). **2** *tr.* enlarge upon or add detail to (a story etc.). **3** *intr.* expand what is said or written. □ **amplification** /-fɪˈkeɪʃ(ə)n/ *n.* [Middle English via Old French *amplifier* from Latin *amplificare* (as AMPLE, -FY)]

amplitude /ˈamplɪtjuːd/ *n.* **1 a** *Physics* the maximum extent of a vibration or oscillation from the position of equilibrium. **b** *Electr.* the maximum departure of the value of an alternating current or wave from the average value. **2 a** spaciousness, breadth; wide range. **b** abundance. [French *amplitude* or Latin *amplitudo* (as AMPLE)]

amplitude modulation *n. Electr.* the modulation of a wave by variation of its amplitude, esp. as a means of carrying an audio signal by radio (abbr. **AM**).

ampoule /ˈampuːl/ *n.* (also esp. *US* **ampul** or **ampule** /ˈampjuːl/) a small capsule in which measured quantities of liquids or solids, esp. for injecting, are sealed ready for use. [French, from Latin AMPULLA]

ampulla /amˈpʊlə/ *n.* (*pl.* **ampullae** /-liː/) **1 a** a Roman globular flask with two handles. **b** a vessel for sacred uses. **2** *Anat.* the dilated end of a vessel or duct. [Latin]

amputate /ˈampjʊteɪt/ *v.tr.* cut off by surgical operation (a part of the body, esp. a limb), usu. because of injury or disease. □ **amputation** /-ˈteɪʃ(ə)n/ *n.* **amputator** *n.* [Latin *amputare*, from *amb-* 'about' + *putare* 'prune']

amputee /ampjʊˈtiː/ *n.* a person who has lost a limb etc. by amputation.

amtrac /ˈamtrak/ *n.* (also **amtrak**) *US* an amphibious tracked vehicle used for landing assault troops on a shore. [*am*phibious + *trac*tor]

amu *abbr.* atomic mass unit.

amuck var. of AMOK.

amulet /ˈamjʊlɪt/ *n.* **1** an ornament or small piece of jewellery worn as a charm against evil. **2** something which is thought to give such protection. [Latin *amuletum*, of unknown origin]

amuse /əˈmjuːz/ *v.tr.* **1** cause (a person) to laugh or smile. **2** (also *refl.*; often foll. by *with*, *by*) interest or occupy; keep (a person) entertained. □ **amusing** *adj.* **amusingly** *adv.* [Middle English from Old French *amuser* 'cause to muse'(see MUSE[2]) from causal, *a* 'to' + *muser* 'stare']

amusement /əˈmjuːzm(ə)nt/ *n.* **1** something that amuses, esp. a pleasant diversion, game, or pastime. **2 a** the state of being amused. **b** the act of amusing. **3** *Brit.* a mechanical device (e.g. a roundabout) for entertainment at a fairground etc. [French from *amuser*: see AMUSE, -MENT]

amusement arcade *n. Brit.* an indoor area for entertainment with automatic game machines.

amusement park *n.* a large outdoor area with fairground amusements etc.

amygdaloid /əˈmɪɡdəlɔɪd/ *adj.* shaped like an almond. [Latin *amygdala*, from Greek *amugdalē* 'almond']

amygdaloid nucleus *n.* a roughly almond-shaped mass of grey matter deep inside each cerebral hemisphere, associated with the sense of smell.

amyl /ˈeɪmʌɪl, ˈamɪl/ *n.* (used *attrib.*) *Chem.* the monovalent group C_5H_{11}–, derived from pentane. Also called *pentyl*. [Latin *amylum* 'starch']

amylase /ˈamɪleɪz/ *n. Biochem.* an enzyme that converts starch and glycogen into simple sugars. [AMYL + -ASE]

amyloid /ˈamɪlɔɪd/ *n. & adj. Med.* ● *n.* a glycoprotein deposited in connective tissue in certain diseases. ● *adj.* of or involving this substance. [AMYL + -OID]

amylopsin /amɪˈlɒpsɪn/ *n. Biochem.* a digestive enzyme, secreted by the pancreas, that converts starch into maltose. [AMYL, on the pattern of *pepsin*]

Amytal /ˈamɪt(ə)l/ *n. propr.* a barbiturate drug used as a sedative and a hypnotic. [AMYL + BARBITAL]

an /an, ən/ *det.* the form of the indefinite article (see A[1]) used before words beginning with a vowel sound (*an egg*; *an hour*; *an MP*).

■ **Usage** Some people retain the use of *an* before words beginning with a sounded *h* e.g. *an hotel, an historian.* Historically this was justifiable because the *h-* was dropped in these words, but today this is not the case and *a hotel, a historian* are now the preferred forms.

an-[1] /an/ *prefix* not, without (*anarchy*) (cf. A-[1]). [Greek *an-*]

an-[2] /ən, an/ assim. form of AD- before *n*.

-an *suffix* **1** /(ə)n/ (also **-ean**, **-ian**) forming adjectives and nouns, esp. from names of places, systems, zoological classes or orders, and founders (*Mexican*; *Anglican*; *crustacean*; *European*; *Lutheran*; *Georgian*; *theologian*). **2** /an/ *Chem.* forming names of organic compounds (*dextran*). [ultimately from Latin adjectival endings *-(i)anus, -aeus*: cf. Greek *-aios, -eios*]

ana /ˈɑːnə/ *n.* **1** (treated as *pl.*) anecdotes or literary gossip about a person. **2** (treated as *sing.*) a collection of a person's memorable sayings. [= -ANA]

ana- /ˈanə/ *prefix* (usu. **an-** before a vowel) **1** up (*anadromous*). **2** back (*anamnesis*). **3** again (*anabaptism*). [Greek *ana* 'up']

-ana /ˈɑːnə/ *suffix* forming plural nouns meaning 'things associated with' (*Victoriana*; *Americana*). [neut. pl. of Latin adjectival ending *-anus*]

Anabaptism /anəˈbaptɪz(ə)m/ *n.* the doctrine that baptism should only be administered to believing adults. □ **Anabaptist** *n.* [ecclesiastical Latin *anabaptismus* from Greek *anabaptismos* (as ANA-, BAPTISM)]

anabas /ˈanəbas/ *n.* = CLIMBING PERCH. [modern Latin from Greek, past part. of *anabainō* 'walk up']

anabasis /aˈnabəsɪs/ *n.* (*pl.* **anabases** /-siːz/) **1** the march of Cyrus the Younger into Asia in 401 BC as narrated by Xenophon in his work *Anabasis*. **2** a military up-country march. [Greek, = ascent, from *anabainō* (as ANA-, *bainō* 'go')]

anabatic /anəˈbatɪk/ *adj. Meteorol.* (of a wind) caused by local upward motion of warm air (cf. KATABATIC). [Greek *anabatikos* 'ascending' (as ANABASIS)]

anabiosis /anəbʌɪˈəʊsɪs/ *n. Biol.* **1** a temporary state of suspended animation or greatly reduced metabolism. **2** the ability to revive from this. □ **anabiotic** /-ˈɒtɪk/ *adj.* [medieval Latin from Greek *anabiōsis*, from *anabioō* 'return to life']

anabolic /anəˈbɒlɪk/ *adj. Biochem.* of or relating to anabolism.

anabolic steroid *n.* a synthetic steroid hormone used to increase muscle size.

anabolism /aˈnabəlɪz(ə)m/ *n. Biochem.* the synthesis of complex molecules in living organisms from simpler ones together with the storage of energy; constructive metabolism (opp. CATABOLISM). [Greek *anabolē* 'ascent' (as ANA-, *ballō* 'throw')]

anabranch /'anəbrɑːn(t)ʃ/ *n.* esp. *Austral.* a stream that leaves a river and re-enters it lower down. [ANASTOMOSE + BRANCH]

anachronism /ə'nakrənɪz(ə)m/ *n.* **1 a** the attribution of a custom, event, etc. to a period to which it does not belong. **b** a thing attributed in this way. **2 a** anything out of harmony with its period. **b** an old-fashioned or out-of-date person or thing. □ **anachronistic** /-'nɪstɪk/ *adj.* **anachronistically** /-'nɪstɪk(ə)li/ *adv.* [French *anachronisme* or Greek *anakhronismos* (as ANA-, *khronos* 'time')]

anacoluthon /anəkə'luːθɒn, -θ(ə)n/ *n.* (*pl.* **anacolutha** /-θə/) a sentence or construction which lacks grammatical sequence (e.g. *while in the garden the door banged shut*). □ **anacoluthic** *adj.* [Late Latin, from Greek *anakolouthon* (as AN-[1], *akolouthos* 'following')]

anaconda /anə'kɒndə/ *n.* a S. American boa of the genus *Eunectes*, esp. the very large semiaquatic *E. murinus*. [alteration of Latin *anacandaia* 'python' from Sinhalese *henakandayā* 'whip snake', from *hena* 'lightning' + *kanda* 'stem': originally the name of a snake in Sri Lanka]

anacreontic /ənakrɪ'ɒntɪk/ *n.* & *adj.* ● *n.* a poem written after the manner of Anacreon, a Greek lyric poet (d. 478 BC). ● *adj.* **1** after the manner of Anacreon. **2** convivial and amatory in tone. [Late Latin *anacreonticus* from Greek *Anakreōn*]

anacrusis /anə'kruːsɪs/ *n.* (*pl.* **anacruses** /-siːz/) **1** (in poetry) an unstressed syllable at the beginning of a verse. **2** *Mus.* an unstressed note or notes before the first bar line. [modern Latin from Greek *anakrousis* 'prelude' (as ANA-, *krousis* from *krouō* 'strike')]

anadromous /ə'nadrəməs/ *adj.* (of a fish, e.g. the salmon) that swims up a river from the sea to spawn (opp. CATADROMOUS). [Greek *anadromos* (as ANA-, *dromos* 'running')]

anaemia /ə'niːmɪə/ *n.* (*US* **anemia**) a deficiency in the blood, usu. of red cells or their haemoglobin, resulting in pallor and weariness. [modern Latin from Greek *anaimia* (as AN-[1], -AEMIA)]

anaemic /ə'niːmɪk/ *adj.* (*US* **anemic**) **1** relating to or suffering from anaemia. **2** pale; lacking in vitality.

anaerobe /'anərəʊb, ə'nɛːrəʊb/ *n.* an organism that grows without air, or requires oxygen-free conditions to live. □ **anaerobic** /anɛː'rəʊbɪk/ *adj.* [French *anaérobie* (as AN-[1] + AEROBE)]

anaesthesia /anɪs'θiːzjə/ *n.* (*US* **anesthesia**) the absence of sensation, esp. artificially induced insensitivity to pain, usu. achieved by the administration of gases or the injection of drugs. □ **anaesthesiology** /-'ɒlədʒi/ *n.* [modern Latin from Greek *anaisthēsia* (as AN-[1], *aisthēsis* 'sensation')]

anaesthetic /anɪs'θɛtɪk/ *adj.* & *n.* (*US* **anesthetic**) ● *n.* a substance that produces insensibility to pain etc. ● *adj.* producing partial or complete insensibility to pain etc. [Greek *anaisthētos* 'insensible' (as ANAESTHESIA)]

anaesthetist /ə'niːsθətɪst/ *n.* a specialist in the administration of anaesthetics.

anaesthetize /ə'niːsθətʌɪz/ *v.tr.* (also **-ise**, *US* **anesthetize**) **1** administer an anaesthetic to. **2** deprive of physical or mental sensation. □ **anaesthetization** /-'zeɪʃ(ə)n/ *n.*

anaglyph /'anəglɪf/ *n.* **1** *Photog.* a composite stereoscopic photograph printed in superimposed complementary colours. **2** an embossed object cut in low relief. □ **anaglyphic** /-'glɪfɪk/ *adj.* [Greek *anagluphē* (as ANA-, *gluphē* from *gluphō* 'carve')]

Anaglypta /anə'glɪptə/ *n. propr.* a type of thick embossed wallpaper, usu. for painting over. [Latin *anaglypta* 'work in low relief': cf. ANAGLYPH]

anagram /'anəgram/ *n.* a word or phrase formed by transposing the letters of another word or phrase. □ **anagrammatic** /-grə'matɪk/ *adj.* **anagrammatical** /-grə'matɪk(ə)l/ *adj.* **anagrammatize** /-'gramətʌɪz/ *v.tr.* (also **-ise**). [French *anagramme* or modern Latin *anagramma*, from Greek ANA- + *gramma -atos* 'letter': cf. -GRAM]

anal /'eɪn(ə)l/ *adj.* relating to or situated near the anus. □ **anally** *adv.* [modern Latin *analis* (as ANUS)]

analects /'anəlɛkts/ *n.pl.* (also **analecta** /anə'lɛktə/) a collection of short literary extracts. [Latin from Greek *analekta* 'things gathered', from *analegō* 'pick up']

analeptic /anə'lɛptɪk/ *adj.* & *n.* ● *adj.* (of a drug etc.) restorative. ● *n.* a restorative medicine or drug. [Greek *analēptikos* from *analambanō* 'take back']

analgesia /an(ə)l'dʒiːzjə/ *n.* the absence or relief of pain. [modern Latin from Greek, = painlessness]

analgesic /an(ə)l'dʒiːsɪk, -zɪk/ *adj.* & *n.* ● *adj.* relieving pain. ● *n.* an analgesic drug.

analog *US* var. of ANALOGUE.

analogize /ə'nalədʒʌɪz/ *v.* (also **-ise**) **1** *tr.* represent or explain by analogy. **2** *intr.* use analogy.

analogous /ə'naləgəs/ *adj.* (often foll. by *to*) **1** partially similar or parallel; showing analogy. **2** *Biol.* performing a similar function but having a different evolutionary origin (opp. HOMOLOGOUS 2). □ **analogously** *adv.* [Latin *analogus* from Greek *analogos* 'proportionate']

■ **Usage** *Analogous* means 'similar in certain respects'. It should not be used as a mere synonym for *similar*.

---

analogue /'anəlɒg/ *n.* & *adj.* (*US* also **analog**) ● *n.* **1** an analogous or parallel thing. **2** *Chem.* a compound with a molecular structure closely similar to that of another. **3** a synthetic food product resembling a natural food in taste and texture. ● *adj.* (usu. **analog**) **1** relating to or using signals or information represented by a continuously variable quantity such as spatial position, voltage, etc. **2** (of a watch etc.) showing the time by means of hands or a pointer rather than displayed digits. Cf. DIGITAL *adj.* 2. [French from Greek *analogon* neut. adj.: see ANALOGOUS]

analogy /ə'nalədʒi/ *n.* (*pl.* **-ies**) **1** (usu. foll. by *to*, *with*, *between*) correspondence or partial similarity. **2** *Logic* a process of arguing from similarity in known respects to similarity in other respects. **3** *Philol.* the imitation of existing words in forming inflections or constructions of others, without the existence of corresponding intermediate stages. **4** *Biol.* the resemblance of function between organs essentially different. **5** an analogue. □ **analogical** /anə'lɒdʒɪk(ə)l/ *adj.* **analogically** /anə'lɒdʒɪk(ə)li/ *adv.* [French *analogie* or Latin *analogia* 'proportion', from Greek (as ANALOGOUS)]

anal-retentive *adj.* (of a person) excessively orderly and fussy (supposedly owing to conflict over toilet-training in infancy). □ **anal retention** *n.* **anal retentiveness** *n.*

analysand /ə'nalɪsand/ *n.* a person undergoing psychoanalysis.

analyse /'an(ə)lʌɪz/ *v.tr.* (*US* **analyze**) **1** examine in detail the constitution or structure of. **2** *Chem.* ascertain the constituents of (a sample of a mixture or compound). **3** find or show the essence or structure of (a book, music, etc.). **4** *Gram.* resolve (a sentence) into its grammatical elements. **5** psychoanalyse. □ **analysable** *adj.* **analyser** *n.* [obsolete *analyse* (*n.*) or French *analyser* (*v.*), from medieval Latin ANALYSIS]

analysis /ə'nalɪsɪs/ *n.* (*pl.* **analyses** /-siːz/) **1 a** a detailed examination of the elements or structure of a substance etc. **b** a statement of the result of this. **2 a** *Chem.* the determination of the constituent parts of a mixture or compound. **b** the act or process of breaking something down into its constituent parts. **3** psychoanalysis. **4** *Math.* the use of algebra and calculus in problem-solving. **5** *Cricket* a statement of the performance of a bowler, usu. giving the numbers of overs and maiden overs bowled, runs conceded, and wickets taken. □ **in the final** (or **last** or **ultimate**) **analysis** after all due consideration; in the end. [medieval Latin from Greek *analusis* (as ANA-, *luō* 'set free')]

analyst /ˈan(ə)lɪst/ *n.* **1** a person skilled in (esp. chemical) analysis. **2** a psychoanalyst. [French *analyste*]

analytic /anəˈlɪtɪk/ *adj.* **1** of or relating to analysis. **2** *Philol.* analytical. **3** *Logic* (of a statement etc.) such that its denial is self-contradictory; true by definition (cf. SYNTHETIC *adj.* 3). [Late Latin, from Greek *analutikos* (as ANALYSIS)]

analytical /anəˈlɪtɪk(ə)l/ *adj.* **1** using analytic methods. **2** *Philol.* using separate words instead of inflections (cf. SYNTHETIC *adj.* 4). □ **analytically** *adv.*

analytical geometry *n.* geometry using coordinates.

analyze *US* var. of ANALYSE.

anamnesis /anəmˈniːsɪs/ *n.* (*pl.* **anamneses** /-siːz/) **1** recollection (esp. of a supposed previous existence). **2** a patient's account of his or her medical history. **3** *Eccl.* the part of the anaphora recalling the Passion, Resurrection, and Ascension of Christ. [Greek, = remembrance]

anamorphosis /anəˈmɔːfəsɪs/ *n.* a distorted projection or drawing which appears normal when viewed from a particular point or in a suitable mirror. □ **anamorphic** *adj.* [Greek *anamorphōsis* 'transformation']

anandrous /əˈnandrəs/ *adj. Bot.* having no stamens. [Greek *anandros* 'without males' (as AN-[1] + *anēr andros* 'male')]

anapaest /ˈanəpiːst, -pɛst/ *n.* (*US* **anapest**) *Prosody* a foot consisting of two short or unstressed syllables followed by one long or stressed syllable. □ **anapaestic** /-ˈpiːstɪk/ *adj.* [Latin *anapaestus* from Greek *anapaistos* 'reversed' (because the reverse of a dactyl)]

anaphase /ˈanəfeɪz/ *n. Biol.* the stage of meiotic or mitotic cell division when the chromosomes move away from one another to opposite poles of the spindle. [ANA- + PHASE]

anaphora /əˈnaf(ə)rə/ *n.* **1** *Rhet.* the repetition of a word or phrase at the beginning of successive clauses. **2** *Gram.* the use of a word referring to or replacing a word used earlier in a sentence, to avoid repetition (e.g. *do* in *I like it and so do they*). **3** *Eccl.* the part of the Eucharist which contains the consecration, anamnesis, and Communion. □ **anaphoric** /anəˈfɒrɪk/ *adj.* [Latin from Greek, = repetition (as ANA-, *pherō* 'to bear')]

anaphrodisiac /ənafrəˈdɪzɪak/ *adj.* & *n.* ● *adj.* tending to reduce sexual desire. ● *n.* an anaphrodisiac drug.

anaphylaxis /anəfɪˈlaksɪs/ *n. Med.* an extreme, often life-threatening reaction to an antigen, e.g. to a bee sting, due to hypersensitivity following an earlier dose. □ **anaphylactic** *adj.* [modern Latin from French *anaphylaxie* (as ANA- + Greek *phulaxis* 'guarding')]

anaptyxis /anəpˈtɪksɪs/ *n. Phonet.* the insertion of a vowel between two consonants to aid pronunciation (as in *went thataway*). □ **anaptyctic** *adj.* [modern Latin from Greek *anaptuxis* (as ANA-, *ptussō* 'fold')]

anarchism /ˈanəkɪz(ə)m/ *n.* the doctrine that all government should be abolished. [French *anarchisme* (as ANARCHY)]

anarchist /ˈanəkɪst/ *n.* & *adj.* ● *n.* an advocate of anarchism or of political disorder. ● *adj.* relating to anarchism or its advocates. □ **anarchistic** /-ˈkɪstɪk/ *adj.* [French *anarchiste* (as ANARCHY)]

anarchy /ˈanəki/ *n.* **1** disorder, esp. political or social. **2** lack of government in a society. □ **anarchic** /əˈnɑːkɪk/ *adj.* **anarchical** /əˈnɑːkɪk(ə)l/ *adj.* **anarchically** /əˈnɑːkɪk(ə)li/ *adv.* [medieval Latin from Greek *anarkhia* (as AN-[1], *arkhē* 'rule')]

anastigmat /əˈnastɪgmat/ *n.* a lens or lens system made free from astigmatism by correction. [German from *anastigmatisch* ANASTIGMATIC]

anastigmatic /anəstɪgˈmatɪk/ *adj.* (of a lens) free from astigmatism. [AN-[1] + ASTIGMATIC (see ASTIGMATISM)]

anastomose /əˈnastəməʊz/ *v.intr.* link by anastomosis. [French *anastomoser* (as ANASTOMOSIS)]

anastomosis /ənastəˈməʊsɪs/ *n.* (*pl.* **anastomoses** /-siːz/) a cross-connection of arteries, branches, rivers, etc. [modern Latin from Greek, from *anastomoō* 'provide with a mouth' (as ANA-, *stoma* 'mouth')]

anastrophe /əˈnastrəfi/ *n. Rhet.* the inversion of the usual order of words or clauses. [Greek *anastrophē* 'turning back' (as ANA-, *strephō* 'to turn')]

anathema /əˈnaθəmə/ *n.* (*pl.* **anathemas**) **1** a detested thing or person (*is anathema to me*). **2 a** a curse of the Church, excommunicating a person or denouncing a doctrine. **b** a cursed thing or person. **c** a strong curse. [ecclesiastical Latin, = excommunicated person, excommunication, from Greek *anathema* 'thing devoted', (later) 'accursed thing', from *anatithēmi* 'set up']

anathematize /əˈnaθəmətʌɪz/ *v.tr.* & *intr.* (also **-ise**) curse. [French *anathématiser* via Latin *anathematizare* from Greek *anathematizo* (as ANATHEMA)]

anatomical /anəˈtɒmɪk(ə)l/ *adj.* **1** of or relating to anatomy. **2** of or relating to bodily structure. □ **anatomically** *adv.* [French *anatomique* or Late Latin *anatomicus* (as ANATOMY)]

anatomist /əˈnatəmɪst/ *n.* a person skilled in anatomy. [French *anatomiste* or medieval Latin *anatomista* (as ANATOMIZE)]

anatomize /əˈnatəmʌɪz/ *v.tr.* (also **-ise**) **1** examine in detail. **2** dissect. [French *anatomiser* or medieval Latin *anatomizare*, from *anatomia* (as ANATOMY)]

anatomy /əˈnatəmi/ *n.* (*pl.* **-ies**) **1** the science of the bodily structure of animals and plants. **2** this structure. **3** *colloq.* a human body. **4** analysis. **5** the dissection of the human body, animals, or plants. [French *anatomie* or Late Latin *anatomia*, from Greek (as ANA-, -TOMY)]

anatta (also **anatto**) var. of ANNATTO.

ANC *abbr.* African National Congress.

-ance /(ə)ns/ *suffix* forming nouns expressing: **1** a quality or state or an instance of one (*arrogance*; *protuberance*; *relevance*; *resemblance*). **2** an action (*assistance*; *furtherance*; *penance*). [from or on the pattern of French *-ance*, from Latin *-antia*, *-entia* (cf. -ENCE), from pres. part. stem *-ant-*, *-ent-*]

ancestor /ˈansɛstə/ *n.* (*fem.* **ancestress** /-strɪs/) **1** any (esp. remote) person from whom one is descended. **2** an early type of animal or plant from which others have evolved. **3** an early prototype or forerunner (*ancestor of the computer*). [Middle English via Old French *ancestre* from Latin *antecessor -oris*, from *antecedere* (as ANTE-, *cedere cess-* 'go')]

ancestral /anˈsɛstr(ə)l/ *adj.* belonging to or inherited from one's ancestors. [French *ancestrel* (as ANCESTOR)]

ancestry /ˈansɛstri/ *n.* (*pl.* **-ies**) **1** one's (esp. remote) family descent. **2** one's ancestors collectively. [Middle English alteration of Old French *ancesserie* (as ANCESTOR)]

anchor /ˈaŋkə/ *n.* & *v.* ● *n.* **1** a metal device designed to dig into the seabed and moor a ship when lowered from it on a long chain. **2** a thing affording stability. **3** a source of confidence. **4** = ANCHORPERSON. ● *v.* **1** *tr.* secure (a ship) by means of an anchor. **2** *tr.* fix firmly. **3** *intr.* cast anchor. **4** *intr.* be moored by means of an anchor. □ **at anchor** moored by means of an anchor. **cast** (or **come to**) **anchor** let down the anchor. **weigh anchor** take up the anchor. [Old English *ancor* via Latin *anchora* from Greek *agkura*]

anchorage /ˈaŋk(ə)rɪdʒ/ *n.* **1** a place where a ship may be anchored. **2** the act of anchoring or lying at anchor. **3** anything dependable.

anchorite /ˈaŋkərʌɪt/ *n.* (also **anchoret** /-rɪt/) (*fem.* **anchoress** /-rɪs/) **1** a hermit; a religious recluse. **2** a person of secluded habits. □ **anchoretic** /-ˈrɛtɪk/ *adj.* **anchoritic** /-ˈrɪtɪk/ *adj.* [Middle English via medieval Latin *anc(h)orita*, ecclesiastical Latin *anchoreta* from ecclesiastical Greek *anakhōrētēs*, from *anakhōreō* 'retire']

anchorman /ˈaŋkəmən/ *n.* (*pl.* **-men**; *fem.* **anchorwoman**, *pl.* **-women**) **1** a person who coordinates activities, esp. as compère in a broadcast. **2** a person who plays a crucial part, esp. at the back of a tug-of-war team or as the last runner in a relay race.

anchorperson /'aŋkəpə:s(ə)n/ *n.* (*pl.* **anchorpersons** or **anchorpeople**) an anchorman or anchorwoman (used as a neutral alternative).

anchor plate *n.* a heavy piece of timber or metal, e.g. as support for suspension bridge cables.

anchoveta /antʃə'vɛtə/ *n.* a small Pacific anchovy caught for use as bait or to make fishmeal. [Spanish, diminutive of *anchova*: cf. ANCHOVY]

anchovy /'antʃəvi, an'tʃəʊvi/ *n.* (*pl.* **-ies**) any of various small silvery fish of the herring family, usu. preserved in salt and oil and having a strong taste. [Spanish & Portuguese *ancho(v)a*, of uncertain origin]

anchovy pear *n.* a W. Indian fruit like a mango.

anchovy toast *n.* toast spread with paste made from anchovies.

anchusa /əŋ'kju:zə, an'tʃu:zə/ *n.* any plant of the genus *Anchusa*, akin to borage. [Latin from Greek *agkhousa*]

anchylose var. of ANKYLOSE.

anchylosis var. of ANKYLOSIS.

ancien régime /ˌɒnsɪən reɪ'ʒi:m, French ɑ̃sjɛ̃ reʒim/ *n.* (*pl.* ***anciens régimes*** *pronunc.* same) **1** the political and social system in France before the Revolution of 1789. **2** any superseded regime. [French, = old rule]

ancient[1] /'eɪnʃ(ə)nt/ *adj.* & *n.* ● *adj.* **1** of long ago. **2** having lived or existed long. ● *n.* *archaic* an old man. □ **the ancients** the people of ancient times, esp. the Greeks and Romans. □ **ancientness** *n.* [Middle English via Anglo-French *auncien* from Old French *ancien*, ultimately from Latin *ante* 'before']

ancient[2] /'eɪnʃ(ə)nt/ *n.* *archaic* = ENSIGN 1, 2. [corruption of form *ensyne* etc. by association with *ancien* = ANCIENT[1]]

ancient history *n.* **1** the history of the ancient civilizations of the Mediterranean area and the Near East before the fall of the Western Roman Empire in 476. **2** something already long familiar.

ancient lights *n.pl.* *Brit.* a window that a neighbour may not deprive of light by erecting a building.

anciently /'eɪnʃ(ə)ntli/ *adv.* long ago.

ancient monument *n.* *Brit.* an old building etc. preserved usu. under Government control.

ancient world *n.* the region around the Mediterranean and the Near East before the fall of the Roman Empire in AD 476.

ancillary /an'sɪləri/ *adj.* & *n.* ● *adj.* **1** (of a person, activity, or service) providing essential support to a central service or industry, esp. the medical service. **2** (often foll. by *to*) subordinate, subservient. ● *n.* (*pl.* **-ies**) **1** an ancillary worker. **2** something which is ancillary; an auxiliary or accessory. [Latin *ancillaris*, from *ancilla* 'maidservant']

ancon /'aŋkɒn, -k(ə)n/ *n.* (*pl.* **ancones** /aŋ'kəʊni:z/) *Archit.* **1** a console, usu. of two volutes, supporting or appearing to support a cornice. **2** each of a pair of projections on either side of a block of stone etc. for lifting or repositioning. [Latin, from Greek *agkōn* 'elbow']

-ancy /(ə)nsi/ *suffix* forming nouns denoting a quality (*constancy; relevancy*) or state (*expectancy; infancy*) (cf. -ANCE). [from or on the pattern of Latin *-antia*: cf. -ENCY]

and /ənd, (ə)n, and/ *conj.* **1 a** connecting words, clauses, or sentences, that are to be taken jointly (*cakes and buns*; *white and brown bread*; *buy and sell*; *two hundred and forty*). **b** implying progression (*better and better*). **c** implying causation (*do that and I'll hit you*; *she hit him and he cried*). **d** implying great duration (*he cried and cried*). **e** implying a great number (*miles and miles*). **f** implying addition (*two and two are four*). **g** implying variety (*there are books and books*). **h** implying succession (*walking two and two*). **2** *colloq.* to (*try and open it*). **3** in relation to (*Britain and the EEC*). □ **and/or** either or both of two stated possibilities (usually restricted to legal and commercial use). [Old English]

-and /and/ *suffix* forming nouns meaning 'a person or thing to be treated in a specified way' (*analysand*; *ordinand*). [Latin gerundive ending *-andus*]

Andalusian /andə'lu:zjən, -sjən/ *adj.* & *n.* ● *adj.* of or relating to Andalusia in southern Spain, its inhabitants, or its language. ● *n.* **1** a native or inhabitant of Andalusia. **2** the variety of Spanish spoken in Andalusia.

andante /an'danti/ *adv., adj., & n.* *Mus.* ● *adv.* & *adj.* in a moderately slow tempo. ● *n.* an andante passage or movement. [Italian, pres. part. of *andare* 'go']

andantino /andan'ti:nəʊ/ *adv., adj., & n.* *Mus.* ● *adv.* & *adj.* rather quicker (originally slower) than andante. ● *n.* (*pl.* **-os**) an andantino passage or movement. [Italian, diminutive of ANDANTE]

Andean /'andɪən/ *adj.* of or relating to the region of the Andes, a high mountain range in western S. America.

Andean condor see CONDOR 1.

andesite /'andɪzʌɪt/ *n.* a fine-grained brown or greyish intermediate volcanic rock. [named after the *Andes* mountain chain in S. America (where it is found) + -ITE[1]]

andiron /'andʌɪən/ *n.* a metal stand (usu. one of a pair) for supporting burning wood in a fireplace; a firedog. [Middle English from Old French *andier*, of unknown origin: assimilated to IRON]

androecium /an'dri:sjəm/ *n.* (*pl.* **androecia** /-sɪə/) *Bot.* the stamens taken collectively. [modern Latin, from Greek *andro-* 'male' + *oikion* 'house']

androgen /'andrədʒ(ə)n/ *n.* any of a group of male sex hormones, esp testosterone, involved in developing and maintaining certain male sexual characteristics. □ **androgenic** /-'dʒɛnɪk/ *adj.* [Greek *andro-* 'male' + -GEN]

androgyne /'andrədʒʌɪn/ *adj.* & *n.* ● *adj.* = ANDROGYNOUS. ● *n.* an androgynous person. [Old French *androgyne* or Latin *androgynus*, from Greek *androgunos* (*anēr andros* 'male', *gunē* 'woman')]

androgynous /an'drɒdʒɪnəs/ *adj.* **1** having a partly male, partly female appearance; of ambiguous gender. **2** *Bot.* with stamens and pistils in the same flower or inflorescence. **3** = HERMAPHRODITE. [as ANDROGYNE]

androgyny /an'drɒdʒɪni/ *n.* **1** androgynous character. **2** *Biol.* hermaphroditism.

android /'andrɔɪd/ *n.* a robot with a human appearance. [Greek *andro-* 'male, man' + -OID]

-androus /'andrəs/ *comb. form* *Bot.* forming adjectives meaning 'having specified male organs or stamens' (*monandrous*). [modern Latin from Greek *-andros*, from *anēr andros* 'male' + -OUS]

-ane[1] /eɪn/ *suffix* var. of -AN; usu. with distinction of sense (*germane; humane; urbane*) but sometimes with no corresponding form in *-an* (*mundane*).

-ane[2] /eɪn/ *suffix* *Chem.* forming names of saturated hydrocarbons (*methane*; *propane*). [on the pattern of *-ene*, *-ine*, etc.]

anecdotage /'anɪkdəʊtɪdʒ/ *n.* **1** *joc.* garrulous old age. **2** anecdotes. [ANECDOTE + -AGE: sense 1 DOTAGE]

anecdote /'anɪkdəʊt/ *n.* a short account (or painting etc.) of an entertaining or interesting incident. □ **anecdotal** /-'dəʊt(ə)l/ *adj.* **anecdotalist** /-'dəʊt(ə)lɪst/ *n.* **anecdotic** /-'dɒtɪk/ *adj.* **anecdotist** *n.* [French or modern Latin, from Greek *anekdota* 'things unpublished' (as AN-[1], *ekdotos* from *ekdidōmi* 'publish')]

anechoic /anɪ'kəʊɪk/ *adj.* free from echo.

anele /ə'ni:l/ *v.tr.* *archaic* anoint, esp. in extreme unction. [Middle English from AN-[2] + *elien*, from Old English *ele* 'oil' from Latin *oleum*]

anemia *US* var. of ANAEMIA.

anemic *US* var. of ANAEMIC.

anemograph /ə'nɛməgrɑ:f/ *n.* an instrument for recording on paper the direction and force of the wind. □ **anemographic** /-'grafɪk/ *adj.* [Greek *anemos* 'wind' + -GRAPH]

anemometer /ænɪˈmɒmɪtə/ *n.* an instrument for measuring or indicating the force of the wind. [Greek *anemos* 'wind' + -METER]

anemometry /ænɪˈmɒmɪtri/ *n.* the measurement of the force of the wind. □ **anemometric** /-məˈmɛtrɪk/ *adj.* [Greek *anemos* 'wind' + -METRY]

anemone /əˈnɛməni/ *n.* **1** any plant of the genus *Anemone*, akin to the buttercup, with flowers of various vivid colours. **2** = SEA ANEMONE. [Latin from Greek *anemōnē* 'windflower', from *anemos* 'wind']

anemophilous /ænɪˈmɒfɪləs/ *adj.* wind-pollinated. [Greek *anemos* 'wind' + *-philous* (see -PHILIA)]

anent /əˈnɛnt/ *prep. archaic* or *Sc.* or *N. Amer.* concerning. [Old English *on efen* 'in line with, in company with']

-aneous /ˈeɪnɪəs/ *suffix* forming adjectives (*cutaneous*; *miscellaneous*). [Latin *-aneus* + -OUS]

aneroid /ˈænərɔɪd/ *adj.* & *n.* ● *adj.* (of a barometer) that measures air pressure by its action on the elastic lid of an evacuated box. ● *n.* an aneroid barometer. [French *anéroïde* (as A-[1] + Greek *nēros* 'water')]

anesthesia etc. *US* var. of ANAESTHESIA etc.

aneurin /əˈnjʊərɪn, ˈænjʊrɪn/ *n.* (also **aneurine** /-riːn/) = THIAMINE. [*a*nti + poly*neur*itis + vitam*in*]

aneurysm /ˈænjʊrɪz(ə)m/ *n.* (also **aneurism**) an excessive localized enlargement of an artery. □ **aneurysmal** /-ˈrɪzm(ə)l/ *adj.* (also **aneurismal**). [Greek *aneurusma* from *aneurunō* 'widen out', from *eurus* 'wide']

anew /əˈnjuː/ *adv.* **1** again. **2** in a different way. [Middle English, from A-[4] + NEW]

anfractuosity /ænfræktjʊˈɒsɪti/ *n.* **1** circuitousness. **2** intricacy. [French *anfractuosité* via Late Latin *anfractuosus* from Latin *anfractus* 'a bending']

angary /ˈæŋɡəri/ *n. Law* the right of a belligerent (subject to compensation for loss) to seize or destroy neutral property under military necessity. [French *angarie*, via Italian or Latin *angaria* 'forced service' from Greek *aggareia*, from *aggaros* 'courier']

angel /ˈeɪndʒ(ə)l/ *n.* **1 a** an attendant or messenger of God. **b** a conventional representation of this in human form with wings. **c** an attendant spirit (*evil angel*; *guardian angel*). **d** a member of the lowest order of the ninefold celestial hierarchy (see ORDER *n.* 19). **2 a** a very virtuous person. **b** an obliging person (*be an angel and answer the door*). **3** a messenger or bringer of something (*angel of death*; *angel of mercy*). **4** an old English coin bearing the figure of the archangel Michael piercing the dragon. **5** *slang* a financial backer of an enterprise, esp. in the theatre. **6** an unexplained radar echo. [Old English *engel* or Old French *angele*, via ecclesiastical Latin *angelus* from Greek *aggelos* 'messenger']

angel cake *n.* (also **angel food cake**) a very light sponge cake of flour and egg whites and no fat.

angel dust *n. slang* the hallucinogenic drug phencyclidine hydrochloride.

Angeleno /ændʒəˈliːnəʊ/ *n.* (in full **Los Angeleno** /lɒs/) (*pl.* **-os**) esp. *US* a native or inhabitant of Los Angeles in California. [American Spanish]

angelfish /ˈeɪndʒ(ə)lfɪʃ/ *n.* (*pl.* usu. same) any of various fish, esp. *Pterophyllum scalare*, with large dorsal and ventral fins.

angelic /ænˈdʒɛlɪk/ *adj.* **1** like or relating to angels. **2** having characteristics attributed to angels, esp. sublime beauty or innocence. □ **angelical** *adj.* **angelically** *adv.* [Middle English via French *angélique* or Late Latin *angelicus* from Greek *aggelikos* (as ANGEL)]

angelica /ænˈdʒɛlɪkə/ *n.* **1** an aromatic umbelliferous plant, *Angelica archangelica*, used in cooking and medicine. **2** its candied stalks. [medieval Latin (*herba*) *angelica* 'angelic (herb)']

angel-shark *n.* = MONKFISH 2.

angels-on-horseback *n. Brit.* a savoury of oysters wrapped in slices of bacon.

angelus /ˈændʒ(ə)ləs/ *n.* **1** a Roman Catholic devotion commemorating the Incarnation, said at morning, noon, and sunset. **2** a bell announcing this. [from the opening words *Angelus domini* (Latin, = the angel of the Lord)]

anger /ˈæŋɡə/ *n.* & *v.* ● *n.* extreme or passionate displeasure. ● *v.tr.* make angry; enrage. [Middle English from Old Norse *angr* 'grief', *angra* 'vex']

Angevin /ˈændʒəvɪn/ *n.* & *adj.* ● *n.* **1** a native or inhabitant of Anjou. **2** a Plantagenet, esp. any of the English kings from Henry II to John. ● *adj.* **1** of Anjou. **2** of the Plantagenets. [French]

angina /ænˈdʒʌɪnə/ *n.* **1** (in full **angina pectoris** /ˈpɛkt(ə)rɪs/) pain in the chest brought on by exertion, owing to an inadequate blood supply to the heart. **2** an attack of intense constricting pain, esp. in the throat, often causing suffocation. [Latin, = quinsy (the earliest use in English), from Greek *agkhonē* 'strangling' (+ Latin *pectoris* 'of the chest' in sense 1)]

angiogram /ˈændʒɪə(ʊ)ɡræm/ *n.* a radiograph of blood and lymph vessels, made by introducing a substance opaque to X-rays. □ **angiography** *n.* [Greek *aggeion* 'vessel' + -GRAM]

angioma /ændʒɪˈəʊmə/ *n.* (*pl.* **angiomata** /-mətə/) an abnormal growth produced by the dilatation or new formation of blood vessels. [modern Latin, from Greek *aggeion* 'vessel']

angioplasty /ˈændʒɪə(ʊ)plæsti/ *n.* an operation to repair a damaged blood vessel or to unblock a coronary artery. [Greek *aggeion* 'vessel' + -PLASTY]

angiosperm /ˈændʒɪə(ʊ)spəːm/ *n.* a plant of the subdivision Angiospermae producing flowers and reproducing by seeds enclosed within a carpel, including herbaceous plants, herbs, shrubs, grasses, and most trees (opp. GYMNOSPERM). □ **angiospermous** /ændʒɪə(ʊ)ˈspəːməs/ *adj.* [Greek *aggeion* 'vessel' + *sperma* 'seed']

Angle /ˈæŋɡ(ə)l/ *n.* (usu. in *pl.*) a member of a tribe from Schleswig that settled in eastern Britain in the 5th c. □ **Anglian** *adj.* [Latin *Anglus* from Germanic (Old English *Engle*: cf. ENGLISH), from *Angul* a district of Schleswig (now in N. Germany) (as ANGLE[2], so called from its shape)]

angle[1] /ˈæŋɡ(ə)l/ *n.* & *v.* ● *n.* **1 a** the space between two meeting lines or surfaces. **b** the inclination of two lines or surfaces to each other. **2 a** a corner. **b** a sharp projection. **3 a** the direction from which a photograph etc. is taken. **b** the aspect from which a matter is considered. ● *v.* **1** *tr.* & *intr.* move or place obliquely. **2** *tr.* present (information) from a particular point of view (*was angled in favour of the victim*). [Middle English from Old French *angle* or from Latin *angulus* 'corner']

angle[2] /ˈæŋɡ(ə)l/ *v.* & *n.* ● *v.intr.* **1** (often foll. by *for*) fish with hook and line. **2** (foll. by *for*) seek an objective by devious or calculated means (*angled for a pay rise*). ● *n. archaic* a fish-hook. [Old English *angul*]

angle brackets *n.pl.* brackets in the form < > (see BRACKET *n.* 3).

angled /ˈæŋɡ(ə)ld/ *adj.* **1** placed at an angle to something else. **2** presented to suit a particular point of view. **3** having an angle.

angle-iron *n.* a piece of iron or steel with an L-shaped cross-section, used to strengthen a framework.

angle of attack *n.* the angle between the chord of an aerofoil etc. and the direction of the surrounding undisturbed flow of air, water, etc.

angle of incidence see INCIDENCE.

angle of reflection see REFLECTION.

angle of refraction see REFRACTION.

angle of repose *n.* the steepest angle at which a sloping surface formed of loose material is stable.

anglepoise /ˈæŋɡ(ə)lpɔɪz/ *n.* (often *attrib.*) *propr.* a type of desk lamp with a sprung and jointed adjustable arm.

angler /ˈæŋɡlə/ *n.* **1** a person who fishes with a hook and line. **2** = ANGLER FISH.

angler fish *n.* any of various fishes that prey upon small fish, attracting them by filaments arising from the dorsal fin. Also called *frogfish*.

Anglican /ˈaŋglɪk(ə)n/ *adj. & n.* ● *adj.* of or relating to the Church of England or any Church in communion with it. ● *n.* a member of an Anglican Church. □ **Anglicanism** *n.* [medieval Latin *Anglicanus* (Magna Carta) from *Anglicus* (Bede) from *Anglus* ANGLE]

anglice /ˈaŋglɪsi/ *adv.* in English. [medieval Latin]

Anglicism /ˈaŋglɪsɪz(ə)m/ *n.* **1** a peculiarly English word or custom. **2** Englishness. **3** preference for what is English. [Latin *Anglicus* (see ANGLICAN) + -ISM]

Anglicize /ˈaŋglɪsʌɪz/ *v.tr.* (also **-ise**) make English in form or character.

Anglist /ˈaŋglɪst/ *n.* a student of or scholar in English language or literature. □ **Anglistics** /-ˈglɪstɪks/ *n.* [German from Latin *Anglus* 'English']

Anglo /ˈaŋgləʊ/ *n. & adj.* ● *n.*(*pl.* **Anglos**) **1** esp. *N. Amer.* **a** a person of British or northern European origin, esp. (*US*) as distinct from a Hispanic American. **b** an English-speaking person, esp. a white N. American who is not (*US*) of Hispanic descent or (*Canad.*) of French descent. **2** *Brit.* a Scottish, Irish, or Welsh sports player who plays for an English club. ● *adj.* of or relating to Anglos. [abbreviation of ANGLO-SAXON]

Anglo- /ˈaŋgləʊ/ *comb. form* **1** English (*Anglo-Catholic*). **2** of English origin (*an Anglo-American*). **3** English or British and (*an Anglo-American agreement*). [modern Latin from Latin *Anglus* 'English']

Anglo-Catholic /aŋgləʊˈkaθ(ə)lɪk/ *adj. & n.* ● *adj.* of a High Church Anglican group which emphasizes its Catholic tradition. ● *n.* a member of this group.

Anglocentric /aŋgləʊˈsɛntrɪk/ *adj.* centred on or considered in terms of England.

Anglo-French /aŋgləʊˈfrɛn(t)ʃ/ *adj. & n.* ● *adj.* **1** English (or British) and French. **2** of Anglo-French. ● *n.* the French language as retained and separately developed in England after the Norman Conquest.

Anglo-Indian /aŋgləʊˈɪndɪən/ *adj. & n.* ● *adj.* **1** of or relating to England and India. **2 a** of British descent or birth but living or having lived long in India. **b** of mixed British and Indian parentage. **3** (of a word) adopted into English from an Indian language. ● *n.* an Anglo-Indian person.

Anglo-Irish /aŋgləʊˈʌɪrɪʃ/ *adj. & n.* ● *adj.* **1** of English descent but born or resident in Ireland. **2** of mixed English and Irish parentage. **3** of or belonging to both Britain and the Republic of Ireland. ● *n.* **1** (prec. by *the*; treated as *pl.*) Anglo-Irish people. **2** the English language as used in Ireland.

Anglo-Latin /aŋgləʊˈlatɪn/ *adj. & n.* ● *adj.* of Latin as used in medieval England. ● *n.* this form of Latin.

Anglomania /aŋgləʊˈmeɪnɪə/ *n.* excessive admiration of English customs.

Anglo-Norman /aŋgləʊˈnɔːmən/ *adj. & n.* ● *adj.* **1** English and Norman. **2** of the Normans in England after the Norman Conquest. **3** = ANGLO-FRENCH *adj.* 2. ● *n.* = ANGLO-FRENCH *n.*

Anglophile /ˈaŋglə(ʊ)fʌɪl/ *n. & adj.* ● *n.* a person who is fond of or greatly admires England or the English. ● *adj.* being or characteristic of an Anglophile.

Anglophobe /ˈaŋglə(ʊ)fəʊb/ *n. & adj.* ● *n.* a person who greatly hates or fears England or the English. ● *adj.* being or characteristic of an Anglophobe.

Anglophobia /aŋglə(ʊ)ˈfəʊbɪə/ *n.* intense hatred or fear of England or the English.

anglophone /ˈaŋglə(ʊ)fəʊn/ *adj. & n.* ● *adj.* English-speaking. ● *n.* an English-speaking person. [ANGLO-, on the pattern of FRANCOPHONE]

Anglo-Saxon /aŋgləʊˈsaks(ə)n/ *adj. & n.* ● *adj.* **1** of the English Saxons (as distinct from the Old Saxons of the Continent, and from the Angles) before the Norman Conquest. **2** of the Old English people as a whole before the Norman Conquest. **3** of English descent. ● *n.* **1** an Anglo-Saxon person. **2** the Old English language. **3** *colloq.* plain (esp. crude) English. **4** *US* the modern English language. [modern Latin *Anglo-Saxones*, medieval Latin *Angli Saxones*, translating Old English *Angulseaxe, -an*]

angora /aŋˈgɔːrə/ *n.* (often *attrib.*) **1** a fabric made from the hair of the angora goat or rabbit. **2** a long-haired variety of cat, goat, or rabbit. [*Angora* (the former name of Ankara in Turkey)]

angora wool *n.* a mixture of sheep's wool and angora rabbit hair.

angostura /aŋgəˈstjʊərə/ *n.* (in full **angostura bark**) an aromatic bitter bark used as a flavouring, and formerly used as a tonic and to reduce fever. [*Angostura*, a town in Venezuela on the Orinoco, now Ciudad Bolívar]

Angostura Bitters *n.pl. propr.* a kind of tonic first made in Angostura.

angry /ˈaŋgri/ *adj.* (**angrier**, **angriest**) **1** feeling or showing anger; extremely displeased or resentful. **2** (of a wound, sore, etc.) inflamed, painful. **3** suggesting or seeming to show anger (*an angry sky*). □ **angrily** *adv.* [Middle English, from ANGER + -Y[1]]

angst /aŋst/ *n.* **1** anxiety. **2** a feeling of guilt or remorse. [German]

angstrom /ˈaŋstrəm/ *n.* (also **ångström** /ˈɒŋstrəːm/) a unit of length equal to 10^{-10} metre (symbol Å). [named after A.J. *Ångström*, Swedish physicist d. 1874]

anguine /ˈaŋgwɪn/ *adj.* of or resembling a snake. [Latin *anguinus* from *anguis* 'snake']

anguish /ˈaŋgwɪʃ/ *n.* severe mental or physical pain or suffering. [Middle English via Old French *anguisse* 'choking' from Latin *angustia* 'tightness', from *angustus* 'narrow']

anguished /ˈaŋgwɪʃt/ *adj.* suffering or expressing anguish. [past part. of *anguish* via Old French *anguissier* from ecclesiastical Latin *angustiare* 'to distress': see ANGUISH]

angular /ˈaŋgjʊlə/ *adj.* **1 a** having angles or sharp corners. **b** (of a person) having sharp features; lean and bony. **c** awkward in manner. **2** forming an angle. **3** measured by angle (*angular distance*). □ **angularity** /-ˈlarɪti/ *n.* **angularly** *adv.* [Latin *angularis* from *angulus* ANGLE[1]]

angular momentum *n.* the quantity of rotation of a body, the product of its moment of inertia and angular velocity.

angular velocity *n.* the rate of change of angular position of a rotating body.

angwantibo /əŋˈgwɒntɪbəʊ/ *n.* (*pl.* **-os**) a small rare primate, *Arctocebus calabarensis* of west central Africa, related to the potto. [Efik]

anhedral /anˈhiːdr(ə)l, -ˈhɛd-/ *n. & adj. Aeron.* ● *n.* the angle between the wing of an aircraft and the horizontal when the wing is inclined downwards. ● *adj.* of or having an anhedral. [AN-[1] + *-hedral* (see -HEDRON)]

anhinga /anˈhɪŋgə/ *n. US* a darter, esp. *Anhinga anhinga* of America. Also called *snake bird*. [Portuguese, from Tupi *áyinga*]

anhydride /anˈhʌɪdrʌɪd/ *n. Chem.* a compound obtained by removing the elements of water from another compound, esp. from an acid. [as ANHYDROUS + -IDE]

anhydrite /anˈhʌɪdrʌɪt/ *n.* a naturally occurring usu. rock-forming anhydrous mineral form of calcium sulphate. [as ANHYDROUS + -ITE[1]]

anhydrous /anˈhʌɪdrəs/ *adj. Chem.* without water, esp. water of crystallization. [Greek *anudros* (as AN-[1], *hudōr* 'water')]

ani /ˈɑːni/ *n.* (*pl.* **anis**) any of various glossy black large-billed birds of the genus *Crotophaga*, of the cuckoo family, found in Central and S. America. [Spanish *aní*, Portuguese *anum*, from Tupi *anū*]

aniline /ˈanɪliːn, -lɪn/ *n.* a colourless oily liquid, used in the manufacture of dyes, drugs, and plastics. Chem. formula: $C_6H_5NH_2$. [German *Anilin* from *Anil* 'indigo' (from which it was originally obtained), ultimately from Arabic *an-nīl*]

aniline dye *n.* a synthetic dye, esp. one made from aniline.

anima /ˈanɪmə/ *n. Psychol.* **1** the inner personality (opp. PERSONA 1). **2** Jung's term for the feminine part of a man's personality (opp. ANIMUS 4). [Latin, = mind, soul]

animadvert /ˌanɪmədˈvəːt/ *v.intr.* (foll. by *on*) criticize, censure (conduct, a fault, etc.). □ **animadversion** *n.* [Latin *animadvertere* from *animus* 'mind' + *advertere* (as AD-, *vertere vers-* 'turn')]

animal /ˈanɪm(ə)l/ *n. & adj.* ● *n.* **1** a living organism which feeds on organic matter, usu. with specialized sense organs and nervous system, and able to respond rapidly to stimuli. **2 a** such an organism other than a human. **b** a quadruped. **3** a brutish or uncivilized person. **4** *colloq.* a person or thing of any kind (*there is no such animal*). ● *adj.* **1** characteristic of animals. **2** of animals as distinct from plants (*animal charcoal*). **3** characteristic of the physical needs of animals; carnal, sensual. [Latin from *animale*, neut. of *animalis* 'having breath' from *anima* 'breath']

animalcule /anɪˈmalkjuːl/ *n. archaic* a microscopic animal. □ **animalcular** *adj.* [modern Latin *animalculum* (as ANIMAL, -CULE)]

animal husbandry *n.* the science of breeding and caring for farm animals.

animalism /ˈanɪm(ə)lɪz(ə)m/ *n.* **1** the nature and activity of animals. **2** the belief that humans are not superior to other animals. **3** concern with physical matters; sensuality.

animality /anɪˈmalɪti/ *n.* **1** the animal world. **2** the nature or behaviour of animals. [French *animalité* from *animal* (*adj.*)]

animalize /ˈanɪm(ə)lʌɪz/ *v.tr.* (also **-ise**) **1** make (a person) bestial; sensualize. **2** convert to animal substance. □ **animalization** /-ˈzeɪʃ(ə)n/ *n.*

animal liberation *n.* the liberation of animals from exploitation by humans.

animal magnetism *n.* **1** *hist.* mesmerism. **2** sexual attraction.

animal rights *n.pl.* the natural right of animals to live free from human exploitation (often *attrib.*: *animal rights activists*).

animal spirits *n.pl.* natural exuberance.

animate *adj. & v.* ● *adj.* /ˈanɪmət/ **1** having life. **2** lively. ● *v.tr.* /ˈanɪmeɪt/ **1** enliven, make lively. **2** give life to. **3** inspire, actuate; encourage. **4** (esp. as **animated** *adj.*) *Cinematog.* give (a film, cartoon figure, etc.) the appearance of movement using animation techniques. [Latin *animatus*, past part. of *animare* 'give life to', from *anima* 'life, soul']

animated /ˈanɪmeɪtɪd/ *adj.* **1** lively, vigorous. **2** having life. □ **animatedly** *adv.*

animateur /anɪməˈtəː/ *n.* a person who enlivens or encourages something, esp. a promoter of artistic projects. [French]

animation /anɪˈmeɪʃ(ə)n/ *n.* **1** vivacity, ardour. **2** the state of being alive. **3** *Cinematog.* the technique of filming successive drawings or positions of puppets or models to create an illusion of movement when the film is shown as a sequence.

animator /ˈanɪmeɪtə/ *n.* **1** an artist who prepares animated films, esp. cartoons. **2** a person who animates something, esp. who facilitates a discussion.

animatronics /ˌanɪməˈtrɒnɪks/ *n.pl.* (treated as *sing.*) the technique of making and operating lifelike robots. □ **animatronic** *adj.* [portmanteau word from ANIMATED + ELECTRONICS]

animé /ˈanɪmeɪ/ *n.* any of various resins, esp. a W. Indian resin used in making varnish. [French, from Tupi *wana'ni*]

animism /ˈanɪmɪz(ə)m/ *n.* **1** the attribution of a living soul to plants, inanimate objects, and natural phenomena. **2** the belief in a supernatural power that organizes and animates the material universe. □ **animist** *n.* **animistic** /-ˈmɪstɪk/ *adj.* [Latin *anima* 'life, soul' + -ISM]

animosity /anɪˈmɒsɪti/ *n.* (*pl.* **-ies**) a spirit or feeling of strong hostility. [Middle English from Old French *animosité* or Late Latin *animositas*, from *animosus* 'spirited', formed as ANIMUS]

animus /ˈanɪməs/ *n.* **1** a display of animosity. **2** ill feeling. **3** a motivating spirit or feeling. **4** *Psychol.* Jung's term for the masculine part of a woman's personality (opp. ANIMA 2). [Latin, = spirit, mind]

anion /ˈanʌɪən/ *n. Chem.* a negatively charged ion; an ion that is attracted to the anode in electrolysis (opp. CATION). [ANA- + ION]

anionic /anʌɪˈɒnɪk/ *adj. Chem.* **1** of an anion or anions. **2** having an active anion.

anise /ˈanɪs/ *n.* an umbelliferous plant, *Pimpinella anisum*, having aromatic seeds (see ANISEED). [Middle English via Old French *anis* and Latin from Greek *anison* 'anise, dill']

aniseed /ˈanɪsiːd/ *n.* the seed of the anise, used to flavour liqueurs and sweets. [Middle English from ANISE + SEED]

anisette /anɪˈzɛt/ *n.* a liqueur flavoured with aniseed. [French, diminutive of *anis* ANISE]

anisotropic /ˌanʌɪsəˈtrəʊpɪk, -ˈtrɒp-/ *adj.* having physical properties that are different in different directions, e.g. the strength of wood along the grain differing from that across the grain (opp. ISOTROPIC). □ **anisotropy** /-ˈsɒtrəpi/ *n.* [AN-[1] + ISOTROPIC]

ankh /aŋk/ *n.* a device consisting of a looped bar with a shorter crossbar, used in ancient Egypt as a symbol of life. [Egyptian, = life, soul]

ankle /ˈaŋk(ə)l/ *n. & v.* ● *n.* **1** the joint connecting the foot with the leg. **2** the part of the leg between this and the calf. ● *v.intr.* **1** *slang* walk. **2** flex the ankles while cycling to increase pedalling efficiency. [Old English and Old Norse, from Germanic: related to ANGLE[1]]

ankle-biter *n. N. Amer. & Austral. slang* a child.

ankle-bone *n.* a bone forming the ankle.

ankle sock *n.* a short sock just covering the ankle.

anklet /ˈaŋklɪt/ *n.* **1** an ornament or fetter worn round the ankle. **2** esp. *US* = ANKLE SOCK. [ANKLE + -LET, on the pattern of BRACELET]

ankylosaur /ˈaŋkɪləsɔː/ *n.* a member of the suborder Ankylosauria of heavily armoured quadrupedal herbivorous dinosaurs. [modern Latin *Ankylosaurus* genus name, from Greek *agkulōsis* ANKYLOSIS + *sauros* 'lizard']

ankylose /ˈaŋkɪləʊz/ *v.tr. & intr.* (also **anchylose**) (of bones or a joint) stiffen or unite by ankylosis. [back-formation from ANKYLOSIS, on the pattern of *anastomose* etc.]

ankylosis /aŋkɪˈləʊsɪs/ *n.* (also **anchylosis**) **1** the abnormal stiffening and immobility of a joint by fusion of the bones. **2** such fusion. □ **ankylotic** *adj.* [modern Latin from Greek *agkulōsis*, from *agkuloō* 'crook']

anna /ˈanə/ *n.* a former monetary unit of India and Pakistan, one-sixteenth of a rupee. [Hindustani *ānā*]

annal /ˈan(ə)l/ *n.* **1** the annals of one year. **2** a record of one item in a chronicle. [back-formation from ANNALS]

annalist /ˈan(ə)lɪst/ *n.* a writer of annals. □ **annalistic** /-ˈlɪstɪk/ *adj.* **annalistically** /-ˈlɪstɪk(ə)li/ *adv.*

annals /ˈan(ə)lz/ *n.pl.* **1** a narrative of events year by year. **2** historical records. [French *annales* or Latin *annales* (*libri*) 'yearly (books)', from *annus* 'year']

annates /ˈaneɪts/ *n.pl. RC Ch.* the first year's revenue of a see or benefice, paid to the Pope. [French *annate* from medieval Latin *annata* 'year's proceeds', from *annus* 'year']

annatto /əˈnatəʊ/ *n.* (also **anatta** /-tə/, **anatto**) an orange-red dye from the pulp of a tropical fruit, used for colouring foods. [Carib name of the fruit tree]

anneal /əˈniːl/ *v. & n.* ● *v.* **1** *tr.* heat (metal or glass) and allow it to cool slowly, esp. to toughen it. **2** *tr.* toughen. **3** *Biochem.* **a** *tr.* recombine (DNA) in the double-stranded form. **b** *intr.* undergo this process. ● *n.* treatment by annealing. □ **annealer** *n.* [Old English *onǣlan*, from *on* + *ǣlan* 'burn, bake' from *āl* 'fire']

annelid /ˈan(ə)lɪd/ *n.* a segmented worm of the phylum Annelida, which includes earthworms, lugworms, etc.

[French *annélide* or modern Latin *annelida* (*pl.*), from French *annelés* 'ringed animals' via Old French *anel* 'ring' from Latin *anellus*, diminutive of *anulus* 'ring']

annelidan /ə'nɛlɪd(ə)n/ *adj. & n.* ● *adj.* of the annelids. ● *n.* an annelid.

annex *v. & n.* ● *v.tr.* /ə'nɛks/ **1 a** add as a subordinate part. **b** (often foll. by *to*) append to a book etc. **2** incorporate (territory of another) into one's own. **3** add as a condition or consequence. **4** *colloq.* take without right. ● *n.* /'anɛks/ = ANNEXE. □ **annexation** /-'seɪʃ(ə)n/ *n.* [Middle English via Old French *annexer* from Latin *annectere* (as AN-[2], *nectere nex-* 'bind')]

annexe /'anɛks/ *n.* esp. *Brit.* **1** a separate or added building, esp. for extra accommodation. **2** an addition to a document. [French *annexe* from Latin *annexum*, past part. of *annectere* 'bind': see ANNEX]

annihilate /ə'nʌɪɪleɪt/ *v.tr.* **1** completely destroy. **2** defeat utterly; make insignificant or powerless. □ **annihilator** *n.* [Late Latin *annihilare* (as AN-[2], *nihil* 'nothing')]

annihilation /ənʌɪɪ'leɪʃ(ə)n/ *n.* **1** the act or process of annihilating. **2** *Physics* the conversion of a particle and an antiparticle into radiation. [French *annihilation* or Late Latin *annihilatio* (as ANNIHILATE)]

anniversary /anɪ'vəːs(ə)ri/ *n.* (*pl.* **-ies**) **1** the date on which an event took place in a previous year. **2** the celebration of this. [Middle English from Latin *anniversarius*, from *annus* 'year' + *versus* 'turned']

Anno Domini /ˌanəʊ 'dɒmɪnʌɪ/ *adv. & n.* ● *adv.* in the year of our Lord, in the year of the Christian era. ● *n.* *colloq.* advancing age (*suffering from Anno Domini*). [Latin, = in the year of the Lord]

annotate /'anəteɪt/ *v.tr.* add explanatory notes to (a book, document, etc.). □ **annotatable** *adj.* **annotation** /-'teɪʃ(ə)n/ *n.* **annotative** *adj.* **annotator** *n.* [Latin *annotare* (as AD-, *nota* 'mark')]

announce /ə'naʊns/ *v.tr.* **1** (often foll. by *that*) make publicly known. **2** make known the arrival or imminence of (a guest, dinner, etc.). **3** make known (without words) to the senses or the mind; be a sign of. □ **announcement** *n.* [Middle English via Old French *annoncer* from Latin *annuntiare* (as AD-, *nuntius* 'messenger')]

announcer /ə'naʊnsə/ *n.* a person who announces, esp. introducing programmes in broadcasting.

annoy /ə'nɔɪ/ *v.tr.* **1** cause slight anger or mental distress to. **2** (in *passive*) be somewhat angry (*am annoyed with you*; *was annoyed at my remarks*). **3** molest; harass repeatedly. □ **annoyance** *n.* **annoyer** *n.* [Middle English from Old French *anuier*, *anui*, *anoi*, etc., ultimately from Latin *in odio* 'hateful']

annual /'anjʊəl/ *adj. & n.* ● *adj.* **1** reckoned by the year. **2** occurring every year. **3** living or lasting for one year. ● *n.* **1** a book etc. published once a year; a yearbook. **2** a plant that lives only for a year or less. □ **annually** *adv.* [Middle English via Old French *annuel* and Late Latin *annualis* from Latin *annalis*, from *annus* 'year']

annual general meeting *n. Brit.* a yearly meeting of members or shareholders, esp. for holding elections and reporting on the year's events.

annualized /'anjʊəlʌɪzd/ *adj.* (of rates of interest, inflation, etc.) calculated on an annual basis, as a projection from figures obtained for a shorter period.

annual ring *n.* a ring in the cross-section of a plant, esp. a tree, produced by one year's growth.

annuitant /ə'njuːɪt(ə)nt/ *n.* a person who holds or receives an annuity. [ANNUITY + -ANT, by assimilation to *accountant* etc.]

annuity /ə'njuːɪti/ *n.* (*pl.* **-ies**) **1** a yearly grant or allowance. **2** an investment of money entitling the investor to a series of equal annual sums over a stated period. **3** a sum payable in respect of a particular year. [Middle English via French *annuité* and medieval Latin *annuitas -tatis* from Latin *annuus* 'yearly' (as ANNUAL)]

annul /ə'nʌl/ *v.tr.* (**annulled**, **annulling**) **1** declare (a marriage etc.) invalid. **2** cancel, abolish. □ **annulment** *n.* [Middle English via Old French *anuller* from Late Latin *annullare* (as AD-, *nullus* 'none')]

annular /'anjʊlə/ *adj.* ring-shaped; forming a ring. □ **annularly** *adv.* [French *annulaire* or Latin *annularis*, from *an(n)ulus* 'ring']

annular eclipse *n.* an eclipse of the sun in which the edge of the sun remains visible as a bright ring around the moon.

annulate /'anjʊlət/ *adj.* having rings; marked with or formed of rings. □ **annulation** /-'leɪʃ(ə)n/ *n.* [Latin *annulatus* (as ANNULUS)]

annulet /'anjʊlɪt/ *n.* **1** *Archit.* a small fillet or band encircling a column. **2** a small ring. [Latin *annulus* 'ring' + -ET[1]]

annulus /'anjʊləs/ *n.* (*pl.* **annuli** /-lʌɪ, -liː/) esp. *Math.* & *Biol.* a ring. [Latin *an(n)ulus*]

annunciate /ə'nʌnsɪeɪt/ *v.tr.* **1** proclaim. **2** indicate as coming or ready. [Late Latin *annunciare* from Latin *annuntiare annuntiat-* 'announce']

annunciation /ənʌnsɪ'eɪʃ(ə)n/ *n.* **1** (**Annunciation**) **a** the announcing of the Incarnation, made by the angel Gabriel to Mary, related in Luke 1:26–38. **b** the festival commemorating this (Lady Day) on 25 March. **2 a** the act or process of announcing. **b** an announcement. [Middle English via Old French *annonciation* from Late Latin *annuntiatio -onis* (as ANNUNCIATE)]

annunciator /ə'nʌnsɪeɪtə/ *n.* **1** a device giving an audible or visible indication of which of several electrical circuits has been activated, of the position of a train, etc. **2** an announcer. [Late Latin *annuntiator* (as ANNUNCIATE)]

annus horribilis /ˌanəs hɒ'riːbɪlɪs/ *n.* a horrible year. [modern Latin]

annus mirabilis /ˌanəs mɪ'rɑːbɪlɪs/ *n.* a remarkable or auspicious year. [modern Latin, = wonderful year]

anoa /ə'nəʊə/ *n.* any of several small deerlike water buffalo of the genus *Bubalus*, native to Sulawesi. [its name in Sulawesi]

anode /'anəʊd/ *n. Electr.* **1** the negative terminal of an electrical device (opp. CATHODE). **2** the terminal or electrode by which electric current enters a device. □ **anodal** /ə'nəʊd(ə)l/ *adj.* **anodic** /ə'nɒdɪk/ *adj.* [Greek *anodos* 'way up', from *ana* 'up' + *hodos* 'way']

anodize /'anədʌɪz/ *v.tr.* (also **-ise**) coat (a metal, esp. aluminium) with a protective oxide layer by electrolysis. □ **anodizer** *n.* [ANODE + -IZE]

anodyne /'anədʌɪn/ *adj. & n.* ● *adj.* **1** able to relieve pain. **2** mentally soothing. ● *n.* an anodyne drug or medicine. [Latin *anodynus* from Greek *anōdunos* 'painless' (as AN-[1], *odunē* 'pain')]

anoesis /anəʊ'iːsɪs/ *n. Psychol.* consciousness with sensation but without thought. □ **anoetic** /-'ɛtɪk/ *adj.* [A-[1] + Greek *noēsis* 'understanding']

anoint /ə'nɔɪnt/ *v.tr.* **1** apply oil or ointment to, esp. as a religious ceremony (e.g. at baptism, or the consecration of a priest or king, or in ministering to the sick). **2** (usu. foll. by *with*) smear, rub. □ **Anointing of the Sick** esp. *RC Ch.* the sacramental anointing of the ill or infirm with blessed oil; unction. □ **anointer** *n.* [Middle English via Anglo-French *anoint* (*adj.*) from Old French *enoint*, past part. of *enoindre*, from Latin *inungere* (as IN-[2], *ungere unct-* 'smear with oil')]

anole /ə'nəʊli/ *n.* a lizard of the American genus *Anolis*, esp. the green *A. carolinensis*. [Carib]

anomalistic /ənɒmə'lɪstɪk/ *adj. Astron.* of or relating to the anomaly of a planet etc.

anomalistic month *n.* a month measured between successive perigees of the moon.

anomalistic year *n.* a year measured between successive perihelia of the earth.

anomalous /ə'nɒm(ə)ləs/ *adj.* having an irregular or deviant feature; abnormal. □ **anomalously** *adv.* **anomalousness** *n.* [Late Latin *anomalus* from Greek *anōmalos* (as AN-[1], *homalos* 'even')]

anomalure /ə'nɒməljʊə/ *n.* any of the squirrel-like rodents of the family Anomaluridae, having tails with rough overlapping scales on the underside. [modern Latin *anomalurus*, from Greek *anōmalos* ANOMALOUS + *oura* 'tail']

anomaly /əˈnɒm(ə)li/ *n.* (*pl.* **-ies**) **1** an anomalous circumstance or thing; an irregularity. **2** irregularity of motion, behaviour, etc. **3** *Astron.* the angular distance of a planet or satellite from its last perihelion or perigee. [Latin from Greek *anōmalia*, from *anōmalos* ANOMALOUS]

anomie /ˈanəmi/ *n.* (also **anomy**) lack of the usual social or ethical standards in an individual or group. □ **anomic** /əˈnɒmɪk/ *adj.* [Greek *anomia* from *anomos* 'lawless': *-ie* from French]

anon /əˈnɒn/ *adv. archaic* or *literary* soon, shortly (*will say more of this anon*). [originally = in or into one state, course, etc., later = at once: Old English *on ān* 'into one', *on āne* 'in one']

anon. /əˈnɒn/ *abbr.* anonymous; an anonymous author.

anonym /ˈanənɪm/ *n.* **1** an anonymous person or publication. **2** a pseudonym. [French *anonyme* from Greek *anōnumos*: see ANONYMOUS]

anonymous /əˈnɒnɪməs/ *adj.* **1** of unknown name. **2** of unknown or undeclared source or authorship. **3** without character; featureless, impersonal. □ **anonymity** /anəˈnɪmɪti/ *n.* **anonymously** *adv.* [Late Latin *anonymus* from Greek *anōnumos* 'nameless' (as AN-[1], *onoma* 'name')]

anopheles /əˈnɒfɪliːz/ *n.* a mosquito of the genus *Anopheles*, which includes many that are carriers of the malarial parasite. [modern Latin from Greek *anōphelēs* 'unprofitable']

anorak /ˈanərak/ *n.* **1** a waterproof jacket of cloth or plastic, usu. with a hood, of a kind originally used in polar regions. **2** *colloq. derog.* a boring, studious, or socially inept person with unfashionable and solitary interests. [Greenland Eskimo *anoraq*]

anorexia /anəˈrɛksɪə/ *n.* **1** a lack or loss of appetite for food. **2** (in full **anorexia nervosa** /nəːˈvəʊsə/) a psychological illness, esp. in young women, characterized by an obsessive desire to lose weight by refusing to eat. [Late Latin from Greek (as AN-[1] + *orexis* 'appetite')]

anorexic /anəˈrɛksɪk/ *adj. & n.* (also **anorectic** /-ˈrɛktɪk/) ● *adj.* **1** involving, producing, or characterized by a lack of appetite, esp. in anorexia nervosa. **2** *colloq.* extremely thin. ● *n.* **1** an anorexic agent. **2** a person with anorexia. [French *anoréxique*: *anorectic* from Greek *anorektos* 'without appetite' (as ANOREXIA)]

anorthosite /əˈnɔːθəsʌɪt/ *n. Geol.* a granular igneous rock composed largely of plagioclase. [French *anorthose* 'plagioclase' + -ITE[1]]

anosmia /aˈnɒzmɪə/ *n.* the loss of the sense of smell. □ **anosmic** *adj.* [Late Latin from Greek (as AN-[2] + *osmē* 'smell')]

another /əˈnʌðə/ *det. & pron.* ● *det.* **1** an additional; one more (*have another cake*; *after another six months*). **2** a person like or comparable to (*another Callas*). **3** a different (*quite another matter*). **4** some or any other (*will not do another man's work*). ● *pron.* **1** an additional one (*have another*). **2** a different one (*take this book away and bring me another*). **3** some or any other one (*I love another*). **4** *Brit.* an unnamed additional party to a legal action (*X versus Y and another*). **5** (usu. **A. N. Other** /eɪ ɛn ˈʌðə/) *Brit.* a player unnamed or not yet selected. □ **such another** another of the same sort. [Middle English from AN + OTHER]

another place *n. Brit.* the other House of Parliament (used in the Commons to refer to the Lords, and vice versa).

ANOVA /ˈanəvɑː/ *n.* analysis of variance, a statistical method in which the variation in a set of observations is divided into distinct components. [acronym]

anovulant /aˈnɒvjʊlənt/ *n. & adj. Pharm.* ● *n.* a drug preventing ovulation. ● *adj.* preventing ovulation. [AN-[1] + *ovulation* (see OVULATE) + -ANT]

anoxia /aˈnɒksɪə/ *n. Med.* an absence or deficiency of oxygen reaching the tissues; severe hypoxia. □ **anoxic** *adj.* [AN-[1] + OXYGEN + -IA[1]]

anschluss /ˈanʃlʊs/ *n.* a unification, esp. (***Anschluss***) the annexation of Austria by Germany in 1938. [German from *anschliessen* 'join']

anserine /ˈansərʌɪn/ *adj.* **1** of or like a goose. **2** silly. [Latin *anserinus*, from *anser* 'goose']

ANSI *abbr.* American National Standards Institute.

answer /ˈɑːnsə/ *n. & v.* ● *n.* **1** something said or done to deal with or in reaction to a question, statement, or circumstance. **2** the solution to a problem. ● *v.* **1** *tr.* make an answer to (*answer me*; *answer my question*). **2** *intr.* (often foll. by *to*) make an answer. **3** *tr.* respond to the summons or signal of (*answer the door*; *answer the telephone*). **4** *tr.* be satisfactory for (a purpose or need). **5** *intr.* (foll. by *for, to*) be responsible (*you will answer to me for your conduct*). **6** *intr.* (foll. by *to*) correspond, esp. to a description. **7** *intr.* be satisfactory or successful. □ **answer back** answer a rebuke etc. impudently. **answer to the name of** be called. [Old English *andswaru, andswarian* from Germanic, = swear against (charge)]

answerable /ˈɑːns(ə)rəb(ə)l/ *adj.* **1** (usu. foll. by *to, for*) responsible (*answerable to them for any accident*). **2** that can be answered.

answering machine *n.* a tape recorder which supplies a recorded answer to a telephone call.

answering service *n.* a business that receives and answers telephone calls for its clients.

answerphone /ˈɑːnsəfəʊn/ *n. Brit.* a telephone answering machine.

ant /ant/ *n. & v.* ● *n.* any small insect of the widely distributed hymenopterous family Formicidae, living in complex social colonies, wingless (except for adults at the time of mating), and proverbial for industry. ● *v.intr. & refl.* (usu. as **anting** *n.*) (of a bird) place or rub ants on the feathers to repel parasites. □ **have ants in one's pants** *colloq.* be fidgety or restless. [Old English *ǣmet(t)e*, *ēmete* (see EMMET), from West Germanic]

ant- /ant/ assim. form of ANTI- before a vowel or *h* (*Antarctic*).

-ant /(ə)nt/ *suffix* **1** forming adjectives denoting attribution of an action (*pendant*; *repentant*) or state (*arrogant*; *expectant*). **2** forming nouns denoting an agent (*assistant*; *celebrant*; *deodorant*). [French *-ant* or Latin *-ant-*, *-ent-*, pres. part. stem of verbs: cf. -ENT]

antacid /antˈasɪd/ *n. & adj.* ● *n.* a substance that prevents or corrects acidity esp. in the stomach. ● *adj.* having these properties.

antagonism /anˈtag(ə)nɪz(ə)m/ *n.* active opposition or hostility. [French *antagonisme* (as ANTAGONIST)]

antagonist /anˈtag(ə)nɪst/ *n.* **1** an opponent or adversary. **2** *Biol.* a substance or organ that partially or completely opposes the action of another. □ **antagonistic** /-ˈnɪstɪk/ *adj.* **antagonistically** /-ˈnɪstɪk(ə)li/ *adv.* [French *antagoniste* or Late Latin *antagonista*, from Greek *antagōnistēs* (as ANTAGONIZE)]

antagonize /anˈtag(ə)nʌɪz/ *v.tr.* (also **-ise**) **1** evoke hostility or opposition or enmity in. **2** (of one force etc.) counteract or tend to neutralize (another). □ **antagonization** /-ˈzeɪʃ(ə)n/ *n.* [Greek *antagōnizomai* (as ANTI-, *agōnizomai* from *agōn* 'contest')]

Antarctic /anˈtɑːktɪk/ *adj. & n.* ● *adj.* of the south polar regions. ● *n.* these regions. [Middle English via Old French *antartique* or Latin *antarcticus* from Greek *antarktikos* (as ANTI-, *arktikos* ARCTIC)]

Antarctic Circle *n.* the parallel of latitude 66° 33′ S., forming an imaginary line round the Antarctic regions.

Antarctic Ocean *n.* = SOUTHERN OCEAN.

ant-bear *n.* = AARDVARK.

ante /ˈanti/ *n. & v.* ● *n.* **1** a stake put up by a player in poker etc. before receiving cards. **2** (esp. in phr. **up the ante**) an amount to be paid in advance; a stake. ● *v.tr.*

(**antes**, **anted**) **1** put up as an ante. **2 a** bet, stake. **b** (foll. by *up*) pay. [Latin, = before]

ante- /'anti/ *prefix* forming nouns and adjectives meaning 'before, preceding' (*ante-room*; *antenatal*; *ante-post*). [Latin *ante* (prep. & adv.), = before]

anteater /'anti:tə/ *n.* a mammal that feeds on ants and termites, esp. one of the edentate family Myrmecophagidae, with a long snout and sticky tongue.

ante-bellum /antɪ'bɛləm/ *attrib.adj.* occurring or existing before a particular war, esp. the US Civil War. [Latin, from *ante* 'before' + *bellum* 'war']

antecedent /antɪ'si:d(ə)nt/ *n. & adj.* ● *n.* **1** a preceding thing or circumstance. **2** *Gram.* a word, phrase, clause, or sentence, to which another word (esp. a relative pronoun, usu. following) refers. **3** (in *pl.*) past history, esp. of a person. **4** *Logic* the statement contained in the 'if' clause of a conditional proposition. ● *adj.* **1** (often foll. by *to*) previous. **2** presumptive, a priori. □ **antecedence** *n.* **antecedently** *adv.* [Middle English, from French *antécédent* or Latin *antecedere* (as ANTE-, *cedere* 'go')]

antechamber /'antɪtʃeɪmbə/ *n.* a small room leading to a main one. [earlier *anti-*: French *antichambre* from Italian *anticamera* (as ANTE-, CHAMBER)]

antechapel /'antɪˌtʃap(ə)l/ *n.* the outer part at the west end of a college chapel.

antedate *v. & n.* ● *v.tr.* /antɪ'deɪt, 'antɪdeɪt/ **1** exist or occur at a date earlier than. **2** assign an earlier date to (a document, event, etc.), esp. one earlier than its actual date. ● *n.* /'antɪdeɪt/ a date earlier than the actual one.

antediluvian /ˌantɪdɪ'lu:vɪən/ *adj.* **1** of or belonging to the time before the biblical Flood. **2** *colloq.* very old or out of date. [ANTE- + Latin *diluvium* DELUGE + -AN]

antelope /'antɪləʊp/ *n.* (*pl.* same or **antelopes**) **1** a deerlike ruminant of the family Bovidae, mainly found in Africa, typically tall, slender, graceful, and swift-moving with smooth hair and upward-pointing horns, e.g. gazelles, gnus, kudus, and impala. **2** leather made from the skin of any of these. **3** *N. Amer.* = PRONGHORN. [Middle English via Old French *antelop* or medieval Latin *ant(h)alopus* from late Greek *antholops*, of unknown origin]

antenatal /antɪ'neɪt(ə)l/ *adj.* esp. *Brit.* **1** existing or occurring before birth. **2** relating to the period of pregnancy.

antenna /an'tɛnə/ *n.* **1** (*pl.* **antennae** /-ni:/) *Zool.* each of a pair of mobile appendages on the heads of insects, crustaceans, etc., sensitive to touch and taste; a feeler. **2** (*pl.* **antennas**) = AERIAL *n.* □ **antennal** *adj.* (in sense 1). **antennary** *adj.* (in sense 1). [Latin, = yard (of a ship), used in pl. to translate Greek *keraioi* 'horns' of insects]

antenuptial /antɪ'nʌpʃ(ə)l/ *adj.* esp. *Brit.* existing or occurring before marriage. [Late Latin *antenuptialis* (as ANTE-, NUPTIAL)]

antenuptial contract *n. S.Afr.* a contract between two persons intending to marry each other, setting out the terms and conditions of their marriage.

antepenult /ˌantɪpɪ'nʌlt/ *n.* the last syllable but two in a word. [abbreviation of Late Latin *antepaenultimus* (as ANTE-, *paenultimus* PENULT)]

antepenultimate /ˌantɪpɪ'nʌltɪmət/ *adj. & n.* ● *adj.* last but two. ● *n.* anything that is last but two.

ante-post /antɪ'pəʊst/ *adj. Brit.* (of betting) done at odds determined at the time of betting, in advance of the event concerned. [ANTE- + POST[1]]

anterior /an'tɪərɪə/ *adj.* **1** nearer the front. **2** (often foll. by *to*) earlier, prior. □ **anteriority** /-rɪ'ɒrɪti/ *n.* **anteriorly** *adv.* [French *antérieur* or Latin *anterior*, from *ante* 'before']

ante-room /'antɪru:m, -rʊm/ *n.* **1** a small room leading to a main one. **2** *Mil.* a sitting room in an officers' mess.

antheap /'anthi:p/ *n.* = ANTHILL.

anthelion /ant'hi:lɪən, an'θi:l-/ *n.* (*pl.* **anthelia** /-lɪə/) a luminous halo projected on a cloud or fog bank opposite to the sun. [Greek, neut. of *anthēlios* 'opposite to the sun' (as ANTI-, *hēlios* 'sun')]

anthelmintic /anθ(ə)l'mɪntɪk/ *n. & adj.* (also **anthelminthic** /-θɪk/) ● *n.* any drug or agent used to destroy parasitic, esp. intestinal, worms, e.g. tapeworms, roundworms, and flukes. ● *adj.* having the power to eliminate or destroy parasitic worms. [ANTI- + Greek *helmins helminthos* 'worm']

anthem /'anθəm/ *n.* **1** an elaborate choral composition usu. based on a passage of scripture for church use. **2 a** a solemn hymn of praise etc., esp. = NATIONAL ANTHEM. **b** a popular song that is identified with a person, group, etc. (*rock anthem*). **3** a composition sung antiphonally. [Old English *antefn*, *antifne* from Late Latin *antiphona* ANTIPHON]

anthemion /an'θi:mɪən/ *n.* (*pl.* **anthemia** /-mɪə/) a flower-like ornament used in art. [Greek, = flower]

anther /'anθə/ *n. Bot.* the apical portion of a stamen containing pollen. □ **antheral** *adj.* [French *anthère* or modern Latin *anthera*, in Latin 'medicine extracted from flowers', from Greek *anthēra* 'flowery', fem. adj. from *anthos* 'flower']

antheridium /anθə'rɪdɪəm/ *n.* (*pl.* **antheridia** /-dɪə/) *Bot.* the male sex organ of algae, mosses, ferns, etc. [modern Latin from *anthera* (as ANTHER) + Greek *-idion* diminutive suffix]

anthill /'anthɪl/ *n.* **1** a moundlike nest built by ants or termites. **2** a community teeming with people.

anthologize /an'θɒlədʒʌɪz/ *v.tr. & intr.* (also **-ise**) compile or include in an anthology.

anthology /an'θɒlədʒi/ *n.* (*pl.* **-ies**) a published collection of passages from literature (esp. poems), songs, reproductions of paintings, etc. □ **anthologist** *n.* [French *anthologie* or medieval Latin from Greek *anthologia*, from *anthos* 'flower' + *-logia* 'collection' from *legō* 'gather']

anthozoan /anθə'zəʊən/ *n. & adj.* ● *n.* a sessile marine coelenterate of the class Anthozoa which includes sea anemones and corals. ● *adj.* of or relating to this class. [modern Latin *Anthozoa*, from Greek *anthos* 'flower' + *zōia* 'animals']

anthracene /'anθrəsi:n/ *n.* a colourless crystalline aromatic hydrocarbon obtained by the distillation of crude oils and used in the manufacture of chemicals. [Greek *anthrax -akos* 'coal' + -ENE]

anthracite /'anθrəsʌɪt/ *n.* coal of a hard variety containing relatively pure carbon and burning with little flame and smoke. □ **anthracitic** /-'sɪtɪk/ *adj.* [Greek *anthrakitis* a kind of coal (as ANTHRACENE)]

anthracnose /an'θraknəʊs/ *n.* a fungal disease of plants causing dark lesions. [French from Greek *anthrak- anthrax* 'coal' + *nosos* 'disease']

anthrax /'anθraks/ *n.* a fatal bacterial disease of sheep and cattle, transmissible to humans, usu. affecting the skin and lungs. [Late Latin from Greek, = carbuncle (the earliest sense in English)]

anthropic principle /an'θrɒpɪk/ *n.* the cosmological principle that theories of the origin of the universe are constrained by the necessity to allow individual human existence. [Greek *anthrōpikos*, from *anthrōpos* 'human being']

anthropo- /'anθrəpəʊ/ *comb. form* human, humankind. [Greek *anthrōpos* 'human being']

anthropocentric /anθrəpə'sɛntrɪk/ *adj.* regarding humankind as the centre of existence. □ **anthropocentrically** *adv.* **anthropocentrism** *n.*

anthropogenesis /anθrəpə'dʒɛnɪsɪs/ *n.* = ANTHROPOGENY.

anthropogenic /anθrəpə'dʒɛnɪk/ *adj.* **1** relating to anthropogeny. **2** *Ecol.* originating in human activity.

anthropogeny /anθrə'pɒdʒɪni/ *n.* the study of the origin of man.

anthropoid /'anθrəpɔɪd/ *adj. & n.* ● *adj.* **1** resembling a human being in form, esp. (of an ape) tailless and often bipedal. **2** of or relating to the primate suborder Anthropoidea, which includes monkeys, apes, and humans. *colloq.* (of a person) apelike. ● *n.* a being that is human in form only, esp. an anthropoid ape. [Greek *anthrōpoeidēs* (as ANTHROPO-, -OID)]

anthropology /anθrəˈpɒlədʒi/ *n.* **1** the study of humankind, esp. of its societies and customs. **2** the study of the structure and evolution of humans as animals. □ **anthropological** /-pəˈlɒdʒɪk(ə)l/ *adj.* **anthropologist** *n.*

anthropometry /anθrəˈpɒmɪtri/ *n.* the scientific study of the measurements of the human body. □ **anthropometric** /-pəˈmɛtrɪk/ *adj.*

anthropomorphic /anθrəpəˈmɔːfɪk/ *adj.* of or characterized by anthropomorphism. □ **anthropomorphically** *adv.* [as ANTHROPOMORPHOUS + -IC]

anthropomorphism /anθrəpəˈmɔːfɪz(ə)m/ *n.* the attribution of a human form or personality to a god, animal, or thing. □ **anthropomorphize** *v.tr.* (also **-ise**).

anthropomorphous /anθrəpəˈmɔːfəs/ *adj.* human in form. [Greek *anthrōpomorphos* (as ANTHROPO-, *morphē* 'form')]

anthropophagy /anθrəˈpɒfədʒi/ *n.* the eating of human flesh; cannibalism. □ **anthropophagous** /-gəs/ *adj.* [Greek *anthrōpophagia* (as ANTHROPO-, *phagō* 'eat')]

anthroposophy /anθrəˈpɒsəfi/ *n.* **1** the knowledge of the nature of humans; human wisdom. **2** a movement inaugurated by Rudolf Steiner to develop the faculty of cognition and the realization of spiritual reality. [ANTHROPO- + Greek *sophos* 'wise']

anti /ˈanti/ *prep. & n.* ● *prep.* (also *absol.*) opposed to (*is anti everything*; *seems to be rather anti*). ● *n.* (*pl.* **antis**) a person opposed to a particular policy etc. [ANTI-]

anti- /ˈanti/ *prefix* (also **ant-** before a vowel or *h*) forming nouns and adjectives meaning: **1** opposed to; against (*antivivisectionism*). **2** preventing (*antiscorbutic*). **3** the opposite of (*anticlimax*). **4** rival (*antipope*). **5** unlike the conventional form (*anti-hero*; *anti-novel*). **6** *Physics* the antiparticle of a specified particle (*antineutrino*; *antiproton*). [from or influenced by Greek *anti-* 'against']

anti-abortion /ˌantɪəˈbɔːʃ(ə)n/ *attrib.adj.* opposing abortion. □ **anti-abortionist** *n.*

anti-aircraft /antɪˈɛːkrɑːft/ *attrib.adj.* (of a gun, missile, etc.) used to attack enemy aircraft.

anti-apartheid /ˌantɪəˈpɑːteɪt, -tʌɪt/ *attrib.adj.* opposed to the policy or system of apartheid.

antibacterial /ˌantɪbakˈtɪərɪəl/ *adj.* active against bacteria.

antibiosis /ˌantɪbʌɪˈəʊsɪs/ *n.* an antagonistic association between two organisms (esp. micro-organisms), in which one is adversely affected (cf. SYMBIOSIS). [French *antibiose* (as ANTI-, SYMBIOSIS)]

antibiotic /ˌantɪbʌɪˈɒtɪk/ *n. & adj. Pharm.* ● *n.* any of various substances (e.g. penicillin) produced by micro-organisms or made synthetically, that can inhibit or destroy susceptible micro-organisms. ● *adj.* functioning as an antibiotic. [French *antibiotique* (as ANTI-, Greek *biōtikos* 'fit for life' from *bios* 'life')]

antibody /ˈantɪbɒdi/ *n.* (*pl.* **-ies**) any of a class of blood proteins (immunoglobulins) produced in response to and counteracting antigens. [translation of German *Antikörper* (as ANTI-, *Körper* 'body')]

antic /ˈantɪk/ *n. & adj.* ● *n.* **1** (usu. in *pl.*) absurd or foolish behaviour. **2** an absurd or silly action. ● *adj. archaic* grotesque, bizarre. [Italian *antico* ANTIQUE, used to mean 'grotesque']

anticathode /antɪˈkaθəʊd/ *n.* the target (or anode) of an X-ray tube on which the electrons from the cathode impinge and from which X-rays are emitted.

Antichrist /ˈantɪkrʌɪst/ *n.* **1** an arch-enemy of Christ. **2** a postulated personal opponent of Christ expected by the early Church to appear before the end of the world. [Middle English from Old French *antecrist* from ecclesiastical Latin *antichristus* from Greek *antikhristos* (as ANTI-, *Khristos* CHRIST)]

antichristian /antɪˈkrɪstʃ(ə)n, -tɪən/ *adj.* **1** opposed to Christianity. **2** concerning the Antichrist.

anticipate /anˈtɪsɪpeɪt/ *v.tr.* **1** be aware of (a thing) in advance and act accordingly; forestall (an action) (*anticipated his opponent's moves*; *anticipated the hard winter ahead*; *anticipates my every need*). **2** *disp.* expect, foresee; regard as probable (*did not anticipate any difficulty*). **3** take action before (another person); forestall (*was about to announce the discovery but was anticipated by his pupil*). **4** look forward to (*I anticipated the interview with pleasure*). **5** cause (a future event) to happen earlier; accelerate. □ **anticipative** *adj.* **anticipator** *n.* **anticipatory** *adj.* [Latin *anticipare* (as ANTE- + *-cipare* from *capere* 'take')]

■ **Usage** The use of *anticipate* in sense 2 above is well established in informal use, but is regarded as incorrect by some people.

anticipation /antɪsɪˈpeɪʃ(ə)n/ *n.* **1** the act or process of anticipating. **2** *Mus.* the introduction beforehand of part of a chord which is about to follow. [French *anticipation* or Latin *anticipatio* (as ANTICIPATE)]

anticlerical /antɪˈklɛrɪk(ə)l/ *adj. & n.* ● *adj.* opposed to the influence of the clergy, esp. in politics. ● *n.* an anticlerical person. □ **anticlericalism** *n.*

anticlimax /antɪˈklʌɪmaks/ *n.* a trivial conclusion to something significant or impressive, esp. where a climax was expected. □ **anticlimactic** /-ˈmaktɪk/ *adj.* **anticlimactically** /-ˈmaktɪk(ə)li/ *adv.*

anticline /ˈantɪklʌɪn/ *n. Geol.* a ridge or fold of stratified rock in which the strata slope down from the crest (opp. SYNCLINE). □ **anticlinal** /-ˈklʌɪn(ə)l/ *adj.* [ANTI- + Greek *klinō* 'lean', on the pattern of INCLINE]

anticlockwise /antɪˈklɒkwʌɪz/ *adv. & adj. Brit.* ● *adv.* in a curve opposite in direction to the movement of the hands of a clock. ● *adj.* moving anticlockwise.

anticoagulant /ˌantɪkəʊˈagjʊl(ə)nt/ *n. & adj.* ● *n.* any drug or agent that retards or inhibits coagulation, esp. of the blood. ● *adj.* retarding or inhibiting coagulation.

anticodon /antɪˈkəʊdɒn/ *n. Biochem.* a sequence of three nucleotides forming a unit of genetic code in a transfer RNA molecule, corresponding to a complementary codon in messenger RNA.

anti-communist /antɪˈkɒmjʊnɪst/ *adj.* against communism or communists.

anticonstitutional /ˌantɪkɒnstɪˈtjuːʃ(ə)n(ə)l/ *adj.* violating a political constitution.

anticonvulsant /ˌantɪkənˈvʌls(ə)nt/ *n. & adj.* ● *n.* any drug or agent that prevents or reduces the severity of convulsions, esp. epileptic fits. ● *adj.* preventing or reducing convulsions.

anticyclone /antɪˈsʌɪkləʊn/ *n.* a system of winds rotating outwards from an area of high barometric pressure, producing fine weather. □ **anticyclonic** /-ˈklɒnɪk/ *adj.*

antidepressant /ˌantɪdɪˈprɛs(ə)nt/ *n. & adj.* ● *n.* any drug or agent that alleviates depression. ● *adj.* alleviating depression.

antidiuretic hormone /ˌantɪdʌɪjʊˈrɛtɪk/ *n.* = VASOPRESSIN. [ANTI- + DIURETIC]

antidote /ˈantɪdəʊt/ *n.* (often foll. by *to, for, against*) **1** a medicine etc. taken or given to counteract poison. **2** anything that counteracts something unpleasant or evil (*antidote to jet lag*). □ **antidotal** *adj.* [French *antidote* or Latin *antidotum* from Greek *antidoton*, neut. of *antidotos* 'given against' (as ANTI- + stem of *didonai* 'give')]

anti-establishment /ˌantɪɪˈstablɪʃm(ə)nt/ *adj.* (also **anti-Establishment**) against the Establishment or established authority.

antifreeze /ˈantɪfriːz/ *n.* a substance (usu. ethylene glycol) added to water to lower its freezing point, esp. in the radiator of a motor vehicle.

anti-g /antɪˈdʒiː/ *adj.* (of clothing for an astronaut etc.) designed to counteract the effects of high acceleration. [ANTI- + *g* (symbol for acceleration due to gravity)]

antigen /'æntɪdʒ(ə)n/ *n.* a foreign substance (e.g. a toxin) which induces an immune response in the body, esp. the production of antibodies. □ **antigenic** /-'dʒɛnɪk/ *adj.* [German (as ANTIBODY, -GEN)]

anti-government /æntɪ'gʌv(ə)nm(ə)nt/ *adj.* (also **anti-Government**) against a government or the ministry in office.

anti-gravity /æntɪ'grævɪtɪ/ *n. & adj.* ● *n. Physics* a hypothetical force opposing gravity. ● *adj.* = ANTI-G.

anti-hero /'æntɪ,hɪərəʊ/ *n.* (*pl.* **-oes**) a central character in a story or drama who noticeably lacks conventional heroic attributes.

antihistamine /æntɪ'hɪstəmɪn, -miːn/ *n.* a substance that counteracts the effects of histamine, used esp. in the treatment of allergies.

anti-inflammatory /,æntɪɪn'flæmət(ə)rɪ/ *adj. & n.* ● *adj.* (of a drug etc.) reducing inflammation. ● *n.* (*pl.* **-ies**) an anti-inflammatory drug.

antiknock /'æntɪnɒk/ *n.* (usu. *attrib.*) a substance added to motor fuel to prevent premature combustion.

anti-lock /'æntɪlɒk/ *attrib.adj.* (of brakes) set up so as to prevent locking and skidding if applied suddenly.

antilog /'æntɪlɒg/ *n.* = ANTILOGARITHM. [abbreviation]

antilogarithm /æntɪ'lɒgərɪð(ə)m/ *n.* the number to which a logarithm belongs (*100 is the common antilogarithm of 2*).

antilogy /æn'tɪlədʒɪ/ *n.* (*pl.* **-ies**) a contradiction in terms. [French *antilogie* from Greek *antilogia* (as ANTI-, -LOGY)]

antimacassar /,æntɪmə'kæsə/ *n.* a covering put over furniture, esp. over the back of a chair, as a protection from grease in the hair or as an ornament. [ANTI- + MACASSAR]

antimatter /'æntɪ,mætə/ *n. Physics* matter composed solely of antiparticles.

antimetabolite /,æntɪmɪ'tæbəlaɪt/ *n. Pharm.* a drug that interferes with the normal metabolic processes within cells, usu. by combining with enzymes.

antimony /'æntɪmənɪ/ *n. Chem.* a brittle silvery-white metallic element used esp. in alloys with lead (symbol Sb). □ **antimonial** /-'məʊnɪəl/ *adj.* **antimonic** /-'mɒnɪk/ *adj.* **antimonious** /-'məʊnɪəs/ *adj.* [Middle English from medieval Latin *antimonium* (11th c.), of unknown origin]

antinode /'æntɪnəʊd/ *n. Physics* the position of maximum displacement in a standing wave system.

antinomian /æntɪ'nəʊmɪən/ *adj. & n.* ● *adj.* of or relating to the view that Christians are released from the obligation of observing the moral law. ● *n.* (**Antinomian**) *hist.* a person who holds this view. □ **antinomianism** *n.* [medieval Latin *Antinomi*, name of a sect in Germany (1535) alleged to hold this view (as ANTI-, Greek *nomos* 'law')]

antinomy /æn'tɪnəmɪ/ *n.* (*pl.* **-ies**) **1** a contradiction between two beliefs or conclusions that are in themselves reasonable; a paradox. **2** a conflict between two laws or authorities. [Latin *antinomia* from Greek (as ANTI-, *nomos* 'law')]

antinovel /'æntɪ,nɒv(ə)l/ *n.* a novel in which the conventions of the form are studiously avoided.

anti-nuclear /æntɪ'njuːklɪə/ *adj.* opposed to the development of nuclear weapons or nuclear power.

antioxidant /æntɪ'ɒksɪd(ə)nt/ *n.* **1** *Chem.* an agent that inhibits oxidation, esp. used to counteract deterioration of stored food products. **2** *Biol.* a substance (e.g. vitamin C or E) that removes potentially damaging oxidizing agents in a living organism.

antiparticle /'æntɪ,pɑːtɪk(ə)l/ *n. Physics* a subatomic particle having the same mass as a given particle but opposite electric or magnetic properties.

antipasto /æntɪ'pɑːstəʊ/ *n.* (*pl.* **antipasti** /-tɪ/) an hors d'oeuvre, esp. in an Italian meal. [Italian (as ANTE- + Latin *pastus* 'food')]

antipathetic /,æntɪpə'θɛtɪk/ *adj.* (usu. foll. by *to*) having a strong aversion or natural opposition. □ **antipathetical** *adj.* **antipathetically** *adv.* [as ANTIPATHY, on the pattern of PATHETIC]

antipathic /æntɪ'pæθɪk/ *adj.* of a contrary nature or character.

antipathy /æn'tɪpəθɪ/ *n.* (*pl.* **-ies**) (often foll. by *to, for, between*) a strong or deep-seated aversion or dislike. [French *antipathie* or Latin *antipathia* from Greek *antipatheia*, from *antipathēs* 'opposed in feeling' (as ANTI-, *pathos -eos* 'feeling')]

anti-personnel /,æntɪpɜːsə'nɛl/ *attrib.adj.* (of a bomb, mine, etc.) designed to kill or injure people rather than to damage buildings or equipment.

antiperspirant /æntɪ'pɜːspɪrənt/ *n. & adj.* ● *n.* a substance applied to the skin to prevent or reduce perspiration. ● *adj.* that acts as an antiperspirant.

antiphon /'æntɪf(ə)n/ *n.* **1** a hymn or psalm, the parts of which are sung or recited alternately by two groups. **2** a versicle or phrase from this. **3** a sentence sung or recited before or after a psalm or canticle. **4** a response. [ecclesiastical Latin *antiphona* from Greek (as ANTI-, *phōnē* 'sound')]

antiphonal /æn'tɪfən(ə)l/ *adj. & n.* ● *adj.* **1** sung or recited alternately by two groups. **2** responsive, answering. ● *n.* a collection of antiphons. □ **antiphonally** *adv.*

antiphonary /æn'tɪf(ə)nərɪ/ *n.* (*pl.* **-ies**) a book of antiphons. [ecclesiastical Latin *antiphonarium* (as ANTIPHON)]

antiphony /æn'tɪf(ə)nɪ/ *n.* (*pl.* **-ies**) **1** antiphonal singing or chanting. **2** a response or echo.

antipode /'æntɪpəʊd/ *n.* (usu. foll. by *of, to*) the exact opposite. [back-formation from ANTIPODES]

antipodes /æn'tɪpədiːz/ *n.pl.* **1 a** (also **Antipodes**) a place diametrically opposite to another, esp. Australasia as the region on the opposite side of the earth to Europe. **b** places diametrically opposite to each other. **2** (usu. foll. by *of, to*) the exact opposite. □ **antipodal** *adj.* **antipodean** /-'diːən/ *adj. & n.* [French or Late Latin, from Greek *antipodes* 'having the feet opposite' (as ANTI-, *pous podos* 'foot')]

antipope /'æntɪpəʊp/ *n.* a person set up as pope in opposition to one (held by others to be) canonically chosen. [French *antipape* from medieval Latin *antipapa*, assimilated to POPE[1]]

antiproton /æntɪ'prəʊtɒn/ *n. Physics* the negatively charged antiparticle of a proton.

antipruritic /,æntɪprʊə'rɪtɪk/ *adj. & n.* ● *adj.* relieving itching. ● *n.* an antipruritic drug or agent. [ANTI- + PRURITUS + -IC]

antipyretic /,æntɪpaɪ'rɛtɪk. -pɪ-/ *adj. & n.* ● *adj.* preventing or reducing fever. ● *n.* an antipyretic drug or agent.

antiquarian /æntɪ'kwɛːrɪən/ *adj. & n.* ● *adj.* **1** of or dealing in antiques or rare books. **2** of the study of antiquities. ● *n.* an antiquary. □ **antiquarianism** *n.* [see ANTIQUARY]

antiquary /'æntɪkwərɪ/ *n.* (*pl.* **-ies**) a student or collector of antiques or antiquities. [Latin *antiquarius* from *antiquus* 'ancient']

antiquated /'æntɪkweɪtɪd/ *adj.* old-fashioned; out of date. [ecclesiastical Latin *antiquare antiquat-* 'make old']

antique /æn'tiːk/ *n., adj., & v.* ● *n.* an object of considerable age, esp. an item of furniture or the decorative arts having a high value. ● *adj.* **1** of or existing from an early date. **2** old-fashioned, archaic. **3** of ancient times. ● *v.tr.* (**antiques**, **antiqued**, **antiquing**) give an antique appearance to (furniture etc.) by artificial means. [French *antique* or Latin *antiquus, anticus* 'former, ancient', from *ante* 'before']

antiquity /æn'tɪkwɪtɪ/ *n.* (*pl.* **-ies**) **1** ancient times, esp. the period before the Middle Ages. **2** great age (*a city of great antiquity*). **3** (usu. in *pl.*) physical remains or relics from ancient times, esp. buildings and works of art. **4** (in *pl.*) customs, events, etc., of ancient times. **5** the people of ancient times regarded collectively.

[Middle English via Old French *antiquité* from Latin *antiquitas -tatis*, from *antiquus*: see ANTIQUE]

anti-racism /antɪˈreɪsɪz(ə)m/ *n.* the policy or practice of opposing racism and promoting racial tolerance. ▫ **anti-racist** *n. & adj.*

antirrhinum /antɪˈrʌɪnəm/ *n.* a plant of the genus *Antirrhinum* (figwort family), with tubular two-lipped flowers, esp. the snapdragon. [Latin from Greek *antirrhinon*, from *anti* 'counterfeiting' + *rhis rhinos* 'nose' (from the resemblance of the flower to an animal's snout)]

antiscorbutic /ˌantɪskɔːˈbjuːtɪk/ *adj. & n.* ● *adj.* preventing or curing scurvy. ● *n.* an antiscorbutic agent or drug.

anti-Semite /antɪˈsiːmʌɪt, -ˈsɛmʌɪt/ *n.* a person hostile to or prejudiced against Jews. ▫ **anti-Semitic** /-sɪˈmɪtɪk/ *adj.* **anti-Semitism** /-ˈsɛmɪtɪz(ə)m/ *n.*

antisepsis /antɪˈsɛpsɪs/ *n.* the process of using antiseptics to eliminate undesirable micro-organisms such as bacteria, viruses, and fungi that cause disease. [modern Latin (as ANTI-, SEPSIS)]

antiseptic /antɪˈsɛptɪk/ *adj. & n.* ● *adj.* **1** counteracting sepsis esp. by preventing the growth of disease-causing micro-organisms. **2** sterile or free from contamination. **3** lacking character. ● *n.* an antiseptic agent. ▫ **antiseptically** *adv.*

antiserum /ˈantɪˌsɪərəm/ *n.* (*pl.* **antisera** /-rə/) a blood serum containing antibodies against specific antigens, injected to treat or protect against specific diseases.

antisocial /antɪˈsəʊʃ(ə)l/ *adj.* **1** contrary to or harmful to the existing social order (*antisocial behaviour*). **2** not sociable.

■ **Usage** See Usage Note at UNSOCIABLE.

antistatic /antɪˈstatɪk/ *adj.* that counteracts the effects of static electricity.

antistrophe /anˈtɪstrəfi/ *n.* the second section of an ancient Greek choral ode or of one division of it (see STROPHE 1c). [Late Latin from Greek *antistrophē*, from *antistrephō* 'turn against']

anti-tank /antɪˈtaŋk/ *attrib.adj.* for use against tanks.

antitetanus /antɪˈtɛtənəs/ *adj.* effective against tetanus.

antithesis /anˈtɪθəsɪs/ *n.* (*pl.* **antitheses** /-siːz/) **1** (foll. by *of, to*) the direct opposite. **2** (usu. foll. by *of, between*) contrast or opposition between two things. **3** a contrast of ideas expressed by parallelism of strongly contrasted words. [Late Latin, from Greek *antitithēmi* 'set against' (as ANTI-, *tithēmi* 'place')]

antithetical /antɪˈθɛtɪk(ə)l/ *adj.* (also **antithetic**) **1** contrasted, opposite. **2** connected with, containing, or using antithesis. ▫ **antithetically** *adv.* [Greek *antithetikos* (as ANTITHESIS)]

antitoxin /antɪˈtɒksɪn/ *n.* an antibody that counteracts a toxin. ▫ **antitoxic** *adj.*

antitrades /antɪˈtreɪdz, ˈantɪ-/ *n.pl.* winds that blow in the opposite direction to (and usu. above) a trade wind.

antitrust /antɪˈtrʌst/ *attrib.adj.* *US* (of a law etc.) opposed to or controlling trusts or other monopolies (see TRUST *n.* 8c).

antitype /ˈantɪtʌɪp/ *n.* **1** that which is represented by a type or symbol. **2** a person or thing of the opposite type. ▫ **antitypical** /-ˈtɪpɪk(ə)l/ *adj.* [Greek *antitupos* 'corresponding as an impression to the die' (as ANTI-, *tupos* 'stamp')]

antivenin /antɪˈvɛnɪn/ *n.* (also **antivenom** /-ˈvɛnəm/) an antiserum containing antibodies against specific poisons in the venom of snakes, spiders, scorpions, etc. [ANTI- + VENOM + -IN]

antiviral /antɪˈvʌɪər(ə)l/ *adj.* effective against viruses.

antivivisectionism /ˌantɪˌvɪvɪˈsɛkʃ(ə)nɪz(ə)m/ *n.* opposition to vivisection. ▫ **antivivisectionist** *n. & adj.*

antler /ˈantlə/ *n.* **1** each of the branched horns of a stag or other (usu. male) deer. **2** a branch of this. ▫ **antlered** *adj.* [Middle English from Anglo-French, variant of Old French *antoillier*, of unknown origin]

ant-lion *n.* a dragonfly-like neuropterous insect with predatory larvae which trap other insects in conical pits.

Antonine /ˈantənʌɪn/ *adj. & n.* ● *adj.* of or relating to the Roman emperors Antoninus Pius and Marcus Aurelius or their rules (AD 137–80). ● *n.* either of the Antonine emperors.

antonomasia /antənəˈmeɪzɪə/ *n.* **1** the substitution of an epithet or title etc. for a proper name (e.g. *the Maid of Orleans* for Joan of Arc, *his Grace* for an archbishop). **2** the use of a proper name to express a general idea (e.g. *a Scrooge* for a miser). [Latin, from Greek from *antonomazō* 'name instead' (as ANTI-, + *onoma* 'name')]

antonym /ˈantənɪm/ *n.* a word opposite in meaning to another in the same language (e.g. *bad* and *good*) (opp. SYNONYM 1). ▫ **antonymous** /anˈtɒnɪməs/ *adj.* [French *antonyme* (as ANTI-, SYNONYM)]

antrum /ˈantrəm/ *n.* (*pl.* **antra** /-trə/) *Anat.* **1** a natural chamber or cavity in the body, esp. in a bone. **2** the part of the stomach just inside the pylorus. ▫ **antral** *adj.* [Latin, from Greek *antron* 'cave']

ant's eggs *n.pl. colloq.* the pupae of ants.

antsy /ˈantsi/ *adj. N. Amer. colloq.* agitated, impatient, fidgety. [from the phrase *have ants in one's pants*: see ANT]

anuran /əˈnjʊər(ə)n/ *n. & adj.* ● *n.* any tailless amphibian of the order Anura, including frogs and toads. ● *adj.* of or relating to this order. [modern Latin *Anura* (AN-[1] + Greek *oura* 'tail')]

anus /ˈeɪnəs/ *n. Anat.* the excretory opening at the end of the alimentary canal. [Latin]

anvil /ˈanvɪl/ *n.* **1** a block (usu. of iron) with a flat top, concave sides, and often a pointed end, on which metals are worked in forging. **2** *Anat.* a bone of the ear; the incus. [Old English *anfilte*, from the Germanic base of ON *prep.* + a verbal stem meaning 'beat']

anxiety /aŋˈzʌɪəti/ *n.* (*pl.* **-ies**) **1** the state of being anxious. **2** concern about an imminent danger, difficulty, etc. **3** (foll. by *for*, or *to* + infin.) anxious desire. **4** a thing that causes anxiety (*my greatest anxiety is that I shall fall ill*). **5** *Psychol.* a nervous disorder characterized by a state of excessive uneasiness. [French *anxieté* or Latin *anxietas -tatis* (as ANXIOUS)]

anxiolytic /ˌaŋzɪəˈlɪtɪk/ *n. & adj. Pharm.* ● *n.* a drug reducing anxiety. ● *adj.* reducing anxiety. [ANXIETY + -LYTIC]

anxious /ˈaŋ(k)ʃəs/ *adj.* **1** troubled; uneasy in the mind. **2** causing or marked by anxiety (*an anxious moment*). **3** (foll. by *for*, or *to* + infin.) earnestly or uneasily wanting or trying (*anxious to please*; *anxious for you to succeed*). ▫ **anxiously** *adv.* **anxiousness** *n.* [Latin *anxius* from *angere* 'choke']

any /ˈɛni/ *det., pron., & adv.* ● *det.* **1** (with *interrog.*, *neg.*, or conditional expressed or implied) **a** one, no matter which, of several (*cannot find any answer*; *are there any good films on?*). **b** some, no matter how much or many or of what sort (*if any books arrive*; *have you any sugar?*). **2** a minimal amount of (*hardly any difference*). **3** whichever might be chosen (*any fool knows that*). **4 a** an appreciable or significant (*did not stay for any length of time*). **b** a very large (*has any amount of money*). ● *pron.* **1** any one (*did not know any of them*; *is any of these films worth seeing?*). **2** any number (*are any of them yours?*). **3** any amount (*is there any left?*). ● *adv.* (usu. with *neg.* or *interrog.*) at all; in some degree (*is that any good?*; *do not make it any larger*; *without being any the wiser*). ▫ **any more** to any further extent; any longer (*don't like you any more*). **any time** *colloq.* at any time. **any time** (or **day** or **minute** etc.) **now** *colloq.* at any time in the near future. **not having any** *colloq.*

unwilling to participate. [Old English *ǣnig*, from Germanic (as ONE, -Y[1])]

■ **Usage** The pronoun *any* can be used with either a singular or plural verb depending on the context (see examples above).

anybody /'ɛnɪbɒdi/ *n. & pron.* **1 a** a person, no matter who. **b** a person of any kind. **c** whatever person is chosen. **2** a person of importance (*are you anybody?*). □ **anybody's** (of a contest) evenly balanced (*it was anybody's game*). **anybody's guess** see GUESS.

anyhow /'ɛnɪhaʊ/ *adv.* **1** anyway. **2** in a disorderly manner or state (*does his work anyhow; things are all anyhow*).

anymore /ɛnɪ'mɔː/ *adv.* esp. *N. Amer.* = *any more* (see ANY).

anyone /'ɛnɪwʌn/ *pron.* anybody.

■ **Usage** *Anyone* is written as two words to imply a numerical sense, as in *Any one of us can do it*.

anyplace /'ɛnɪpleɪs/ *adv. N. Amer. colloq.* anywhere.

any road *adv.* esp. *N.Engl.* = ANYWAY 2, 3.

anything /'ɛnɪθɪŋ/ *pron.* **1** a thing, no matter which. **2** a thing of any kind. **3** whatever thing is chosen. □ **anything but** not at all (*was anything but honest*). **like anything** *colloq.* with great vigour, intensity, etc.

anytime /'ɛnɪtʌɪm/ *adv.* esp. *N. Amer. colloq.* = *any time* (see ANY).

anyway /'ɛnɪweɪ/ *adv.* **1** (also **any way**) in any way or manner. **2** at any rate; in any case. **3** to resume (*anyway, as I was saying*).

anyways /'ɛnɪweɪz/ *adv. N. Amer. colloq.* or *dial.* = ANYWAY.

anywhere /'ɛnɪwɛː/ *adv. & pron.* ● *adv.* in or to any place. ● *pron.* any place (*anywhere will do*).

anywise /'ɛnɪwʌɪz/ *adv. archaic* in any manner. [Old English *on ǣnige wīsan* 'in any wise']

Anzac /'anzak/ *n.* **1** a soldier in the Australian and New Zealand Army Corps (1914–18). **2** a person, esp. a member of the armed services, from Australia or New Zealand. [acronym]

Anzac Day *n.* (in Australia and New Zealand) the day (25 April) commemorating the Anzac landing at Gallipoli in 1915.

Anzus /'anzəs/ *n.* (also **ANZUS**) Australia, New Zealand, and the US, as an alliance for the Pacific area.

AO *abbr.* Officer of the Order of Australia.

AOB *abbr. Brit.* any other business.

AOC *abbr. appellation d'origine contrôlée.*

A-OK *abbr. N. Amer. colloq.* excellent; in good order. [*a*ll systems *OK*]

aorist /'eɪərɪst, 'ɛːr-/ *n. & adj. Gram.* ● *n.* an unqualified past tense of a verb (esp. in Greek), without reference to duration or completion. ● *adj.* of or designating this tense. □ **aoristic** /eɪə'rɪstɪk, ɛː'r-/ *adj.* [Greek *aoristos* 'indefinite' (as A-[1] + *horizō* 'define, limit')]

aorta /eɪ'ɔːtə/ *n.* (*pl.* **aortas**) the main artery of the body, supplying oxygenated blood to the circulatory system, in humans passing over the heart from the left ventricle and running down in front of the backbone. □ **aortic** *adj.* [Greek *aortē*, from *a(e)irō* 'raise']

à outrance /ɑː 'uːtrɒns, French a utrɑ̃s/ *adv.* **1** to the death. **2** to the bitter end. [French, = to the utmost]

ap-[1] /əp, ap/ *prefix* assim. form of AD- before *p*.

ap-[2] /əp, ap/ *prefix* assim. form of APO- before a vowel or *h*.

apace /ə'peɪs/ *adv. literary* swiftly, quickly. [Old French *à pas* 'at (a considerable) pace']

Apache *n. & adj.* ● *n.* **1** /ə'patʃi/ **a** (*pl.* same or **Apaches**) a member of a N. American Indian people of New Mexico and Arizona. **b** the language of this people. **2** (**apache** /ə'paʃ/) (*pl.* **apaches** *pronunc.* same) a violent street ruffian, originally in Paris. ● *adj.* /ə'patʃi/ of or relating to the Apache or their langauge. [Mexican Spanish]

apanage /'ap(ə)nɪdʒ/ *n.* (also **appanage**) **1** provision for the maintenance of the younger children of kings etc. **2** a perquisite. **3** a natural accompaniment or attribute. [French, ultimately from medieval Latin *appanare* 'endow']

apart /ə'pɑːt/ *adv.* **1** separately; not together (*keep your feet apart*). **2** into pieces (*came apart in my hands*). **3 a** to or on one side. **b** out of consideration (placed after noun: *joking apart*). **4** to or at a distance. □ **apart from 1** excepting; not considering. **2** in addition to (*apart from roses we grow irises*). □ **apartness** *n.* [Middle English from Old French, from *à* 'to' + *part* 'side']

apartheid /ə'pɑːtheɪt/ *n.* **1** *hist.* (esp. in S. Africa) a policy or system of segregation or discrimination on grounds of race. **2** segregation in other contexts. [Afrikaans (as APART, -HOOD)]

apartment /ə'pɑːtm(ə)nt/ *n.* **1** (in *pl.*) a suite of rooms, usu. furnished and rented. **2** a single room in a house. **3** *N. Amer.* **a** a flat. **b** = APARTMENT BUILDING. [French *appartement* from Italian *appartamento*, from *appartare* 'to separate' from *a parte* 'apart']

apartment building *n. N. Amer.* a block of flats.

apartment hotel *n. N. Amer.* a hotel with furnished suites of rooms including kitchen facilities, available for long-term or short-term rental.

apartment house *n.* esp. *US* = APARTMENT BUILDING.

apathetic /apə'θɛtɪk/ *adj.* having or showing no emotion or interest. □ **apathetically** *adv.* [APATHY, after PATHETIC]

apathy /'apəθi/ *n.* (often foll. by *towards*) lack of interest or feeling; indifference. [French *apathie* via Latin *apathia* from Greek *apatheia*, from *apathēs* 'without feeling' (as A-[1] + *pathos* 'suffering')]

apatite /'apətʌɪt/ *n.* a mineral consisting of calcium phosphate with other elements, esp. fluorine, used in the manufacture of fertilizers. [German *Apatit* from Greek *apatē* 'deceit' (from its deceptive similarity to other substances)]

apatosaurus /əpatə'sɔːrəs/ *n.* a huge plant-eating dinosaur of the genus *Apatosaurus* (formerly *Brontosaurus*), of the Jurassic and Cretaceous periods, with a long tail and trunklike legs. Also called *brontosaurus*. [modern Latin, from Greek *apatē* 'deceit' + *sauros* 'lizard']

APB *n. US* an all points bulletin. [abbreviation]

ape /eɪp/ *n. & v.* ● *n.* **1** any of the various primates of the family Pongidae characterized by the absence of a tail, e.g. the gorilla, chimpanzee, orang-utan, and gibbon. **2** (in general use) any monkey. **3 a** an imitator. **b** an apelike person. ● *v.tr.* imitate, mimic. □ **go ape** *slang* become crazy. [Old English *apa*, from Germanic]

apeman /'eɪpmən/ *n.* (*pl.* **-men**) any of various extinct apelike primates held to be related to present-day humans.

aperçu /apɛː'sjuː/ *n.* **1** a summary or survey. **2** an insight. [French, past part. of *apercevoir* 'perceive']

aperient /ə'pɪərɪənt/ *adj. & n.* ● *adj.* laxative. ● *n.* a laxative medicine. [Latin *aperire aperient-* 'to open']

aperiodic /ˌeɪpɪərɪ'ɒdɪk/ *adj.* **1** not periodic; irregular. **2** *Physics* (of a potentially oscillating or vibrating system, e.g. an instrument with a pointer) that is adequately damped to prevent oscillation or vibration. **3** (of an oscillation or vibration) without a regular period. □ **aperiodicity** /-rɪə'dɪsɪti/ *n.*

aperitif /ə'pɛrɪtiːf, əpɛrɪ'tiːf/ *n.* an alcoholic drink taken before a meal to stimulate the appetite. [French *apéritif* via medieval Latin *aperitivus* from Latin *aperire* 'to open']

aperture /'apətjʊə, -tʃ(ʊ)ə/ *n.* **1** an opening; a gap. **2** a space through which light passes in an optical or photographic instrument, esp. a variable opening by which light enters a camera. [Latin *apertura* (as APERITIF)]

apery /'eɪpəri/ *n.* pretentious or silly mimicry.

apetalous /eɪˈpɛt(ə)ləs, ə-/ *adj. Bot.* (of flowers) having no petals. [modern Latin *apetalus* from Greek *apetalos* 'leafless', from *a-* 'not' + *petalon* 'leaf']

APEX /ˈeɪpɛks/ *abbr.* (in the UK) Association of Professional, Executive, Clerical, and Computer Staff.

Apex /ˈeɪpɛks/ *n.* (also **APEX**) (often *attrib.*) a system of reduced fares for scheduled airline flights when paid for before a certain period in advance of departure. [*A*dvance *P*urchase *Ex*cursion]

apex /ˈeɪpɛks/ *n.* (*pl.* **apexes** or **apices** /ˈeɪpɪsiːz/) **1** the highest point. **2** a climax; a high point of achievement etc. **3** the vertex of a triangle or cone. **4** a tip or pointed end. [Latin, = peak, tip]

apfelstrudel /ˈapf(ə)lʃtruːd(ə)l/ *n.* an originally Austrian confection of flaky pastry filled with spiced apple. [German, from *Apfel* 'apple' + STRUDEL]

aphaeresis /əˈfɪərɪsɪs/ *n.* the omission of a letter or syllable at the beginning of a word as a morphological development (e.g. in the derivation of *adder*). [Late Latin, from Greek *aphairesis* (as APO-, *haireō* 'take')]

aphasia /əˈfeɪzɪə/ *n. Med.* the loss of ability to understand or express speech, owing to brain damage. ◻ **aphasic** *adj. & n.* [Greek, from *aphatos* 'speechless' (as A-[1] + *pha-* 'speak')]

aphelion /apˈhiːlɪən, əˈfiːlɪən/ *n.* (*pl.* **aphelia** /-lɪə/) the point in the orbit of a planet, comet, etc., at which it is furthest from the sun (opp. PERIHELION) (symbol **Q**). [Graecized from modern Latin *aphelium*, from Greek *aph' hēliou* 'from the sun']

aphesis /ˈafɪsɪs/ *n.* the gradual loss of an unstressed vowel at the beginning of a word (e.g. of *e* from *esquire* to form *squire*). ◻ **aphetic** /əˈfɛtɪk/ *adj.* **aphetically** /əˈfɛtɪk(ə)li/ *adv.* [Greek, = letting go (as APO-, *hiēmi* 'send')]

aphid /ˈeɪfɪd/ *n.* a small homopterous insect of the family Aphididae, feeding by sucking sap from leaves, stems, or roots of plants, e.g. a greenfly, a blackfly. [back-formation from *aphides*: see APHIS]

aphis /ˈeɪfɪs/ *n.* (*pl.* **aphides** /-diːz/) an aphid, esp. of the genus *Aphis* which includes the greenfly. [modern Latin from Greek, perhaps a misreading (αφ *aph* for κορ *kor*) of *koris* 'bug']

aphonia /eɪˈfəʊnɪə, ə-/ *n.* (also **aphony** /ˈaf(ə)ni/) *Med.* the loss or absence of the voice through a disease of the larynx or mouth. [modern Latin *aphonia* from Greek, from *aphōnos* 'voiceless' (as A-[1] + *phōnē* 'voice')]

aphorism /ˈafərɪz(ə)m/ *n.* **1** a short pithy maxim. **2** a brief statement of a principle. ◻ **aphorist** *n.* **aphoristic** /-ˈrɪstɪk/ *adj.* **aphoristically** /-ˈrɪstɪk(ə)li/ *adv.* **aphorize** *v.intr.* (also **-ise**). [French *aphorisme* or Late Latin from Greek *aphorismos* 'definition', from *aphorizō* (as APO-, *horos* 'boundary')]

aphrodisiac /afrəˈdɪzɪak/ *adj. & n.* ● *adj.* that arouses sexual desire. ● *n.* an aphrodisiac drug. [Greek *aphrodisiakos* from *aphrodisios*, from *Aphroditē*, the name of the Greek goddess of love]

aphyllous /əˈfɪləs/ *adj. Bot.* (of plants) having no leaves. [modern Latin from Greek *aphullos* (as A-[1] + *phullon* 'leaf')]

apian /ˈeɪpɪən/ *adj.* of or relating to bees. [Latin *apianus* from *apis* 'bee']

apiary /ˈeɪpɪəri/ *n.* (*pl.* **-ies**) a place where bees are kept. ◻ **apiarist** *n.* [Latin *apiarium* from *apis* 'bee']

apical /ˈeɪpɪk(ə)l, ˈap-/ *adj.* of, at, or forming an apex. [Latin *apex apicis*: see APEX]

apices *pl.* of APEX.

apiculture /ˈeɪpɪkʌltʃə/ *n.* bee-keeping. ◻ **apicultural** /-ˈkʌltʃ(ə)r(ə)l/ *adj.* **apiculturist** /-ˈkʌltʃərɪst/ *n.* [Latin *apis* 'bee', on the pattern of AGRICULTURE]

apiece /əˈpiːs/ *adv.* for each one; severally (*had five pounds apiece*). [A[2] + PIECE]

apish /ˈeɪpɪʃ/ *adj.* **1** of or like an ape. **2** silly; affected. ◻ **apishly** *adv.* **apishness** *n.*

aplanat /ˈaplənat/ *n.* a reflecting or refracting surface made aplanatic by correction. [German]

aplanatic /apləˈnatɪk/ *adj.* (of a reflecting or refracting surface) free from spherical aberration. [Greek *aplanētos* 'free from error' (as A-[1] + *planaō* 'wander')]

aplasia /əˈpleɪzɪə/ *n. Med.* total or partial failure of development of an organ or tissue. ◻ **aplastic** /əˈplastɪk/ *adj.* [Greek (as A-[1] + *plasis* 'formation')]

aplenty /əˈplɛnti/ *adv.* in plenty.

aplomb /əˈplɒm/ *n.* assurance; self-confidence. [French, = perpendicularity, from *à plomb* 'according to a plummet']

apnoea /apˈniːə/ *n.* (*US* **apnea**) *Med.* a temporary cessation of breathing. [modern Latin from Greek *apnoia*, from *apnous* 'breathless']

apo- /ˈapəʊ/ *prefix* **1** away from (*apogee*). **2** separate (*apocarpous*). [Greek *apo* 'from, away, un-, quite']

Apoc. *abbr.* **1** Apocalypse (New Testament). **2** Apocrypha.

apocalypse /əˈpɒkəlɪps/ *n.* **1** (**the Apocalypse**) = REVELATION 3. **2** a revelation, esp. of the end of the world. **3** a grand or violent event resembling those described in the Apocalypse. [Middle English from Old French, ultimately from Greek *apokalupsis* from *apokaluptō* 'uncover, reveal']

apocalyptic /əpɒkəˈlɪptɪk/ *adj.* **1** of or resembling the Apocalypse. **2** revelatory, prophetic. ◻ **apocalyptically** *adv.* [Greek *apokaluptikos* (as APOCALYPSE)]

apocarpous /apəˈkɑːpəs/ *adj. Bot.* (of ovaries) having distinct carpels not joined together (opp. SYNCARPOUS). [APO- + Greek *karpos* 'fruit']

apochromat /ˈapəkrəmat/ *n.* a lens or lens system that reduces spherical and chromatic aberrations. ◻ **apochromatic** /-krəˈmatɪk/ *adj.* [APO- + CHROMATIC]

apocope /əˈpɒkəpi/ *n.* the omission of a letter or letters at the end of a word as a morphological development (e.g. in the derivation of *curio*). [Late Latin from Greek *apokopē* (as APO-, *koptō* 'cut')]

Apocr. *abbr.* Apocrypha.

apocrine /ˈapəkrʌɪn, -krɪn/ *adj. Biol.* (of a multicellular gland, e.g. the mammary gland) releasing parts of its cells with its secretion. [APO- + Greek *krinō* 'sift']

Apocrypha /əˈpɒkrɪfə/ *n.pl.* (also treated as *sing.*) **1** biblical writings not forming part of the accepted canon. **2** (**apocrypha**) writings or reports not considered genuine. [Middle English via ecclesiastical Latin *apocrypha (scripta)* 'hidden (writings)' from Greek *apokruphos*, from *apokruptō* 'hide away']

■ **Usage** The Old Testament Apocrypha include those writings appearing in the Septuagint and Vulgate versions but not in the Hebrew Bible; they are accepted by the Roman Catholic Church as the 'deuterocanonical' books.

apocryphal /əˈpɒkrɪf(ə)l/ *adj.* **1** of doubtful authenticity (originally of some early Christian texts resembling those of the New Testament). **2** invented, mythical (*an apocryphal story*). **3** of or belonging to the Apocrypha.

apodal /ˈapəd(ə)l/ *adj. Zool.* **1** without (or with undeveloped) feet. **2** (of fish) without ventral fins. [obsolete *apod* 'apodal creature' from Greek *apous* 'footless' (as A-[1] + *pous podos* 'foot')]

apodictic /apəˈdɪktɪk/ *adj.* (also **apodeictic** /-ˈdʌɪktɪk/) **1** clearly established. **2** of clear demonstration. [Latin *apodicticus* from Greek *apodeiktikos* (as APO-, *deiknumi* 'show')]

apodosis /əˈpɒdəsɪs/ *n.* (*pl.* **apodoses** /-ˌsiːz/) the main (consequent) clause of a conditional sentence (e.g. *I would agree* in *if you asked me I would agree*). [Late Latin, from Greek from *apodidōmi* 'give back' (as APO-, *didōmi* 'give')]

apogee /ˈapədʒiː/ *n.* **1** the point in a body's orbit at which it is furthest from the earth (opp. PERIGEE). **2** the most distant or highest point. ◻ **apogean** /apəˈdʒiːən/ *adj.* [French *apogée* or modern Latin *apogaeum*, from Greek *apogeion* 'away from earth' (as APO-, *gē* 'earth')]

apolitical /eɪpəˈlɪtɪk(ə)l/ *adj.* not interested in or concerned with politics.

Apollinaris /əpɒlɪ'nɛ:rɪs/ *n.* an effervescent mineral water from Apollinarisburg. [*Apollinarisburg* in the Rhineland of Germany]

Apollonian /apə'ləʊnɪən/ *adj.* **1** of or relating to Apollo, the Greek and Roman sun-god, patron of music and poetry. **2** orderly, rational, self-disciplined. [Latin *Apollonius* from Greek *Apollōnios*]

apologetic /əpɒlə'dʒɛtɪk/ *adj. & n.* ● *adj.* **1** regretfully acknowledging or excusing an offence or failure. **2** diffident. **3** of reasoned defence or vindication. ● *n.* (usu. in *pl.*) a reasoned defence, esp. of Christianity. □ **apologetically** *adv.* [French *apologétique* via Late Latin *apologeticus* from Greek *apologētikos*, from *apologeomai* 'speak in defence']

apologia /apə'ləʊdʒɪə/ *n.* a formal defence of one's opinions or conduct. [Latin: see APOLOGY]

apologist /ə'pɒlədʒɪst/ *n.* a person who defends something by argument. [French *apologiste* from Greek *apologizomai* 'render account', from *apologos* 'account']

apologize /ə'pɒlədʒʌɪz/ *v.intr.* (also **-ise**) make an apology; express regret. [Greek *apologizomai*: see APOLOGIST]

apologue /'apəlɒg/ *n.* a moral fable. [French *apologue* or Latin *apologus*, from Greek *apologos* 'story' (as APO-, *logos* 'discourse')]

apology /ə'pɒlədʒi/ *n.* (*pl.* **-ies**) **1** a regretful acknowledgement of an offence or failure. **2** an assurance that no offence was intended. **3** an explanation or defence. **4** (foll. by *for*) a poor or scanty specimen of (*this apology for a letter*). [French *apologie* or Late Latin *apologia* from Greek (as APOLOGETIC)]

apolune /'apə(ʊ)lu:n/ *n.* the point in a body's lunar orbit at which it is furthest from the moon (opp. PERILUNE). [APO- + Latin *luna* 'moon', on the pattern of *apogee*]

apomixis /apə'mɪksɪs/ *n.* (*pl.* **apomixes** /-si:z/) *Biol.* asexual reproduction, esp. agamospermy (cf. AMPHIMIXIS). □ **apomictic** *adj.* [modern Latin (as APO- + Greek *mixis* 'mingling')]

apophthegm /'apəθɛm/ *n.* (*US* also **apothegm**) a terse saying or maxim, an aphorism. □ **apophthegmatic** /-θɛg'matɪk/ *adj.* [French *apophthegme* or modern Latin *apothegma* from Greek *apophthegma -matos*, from *apophtheggomai* 'speak out']

apoplectic /apə'plɛktɪk/ *adj.* **1** of, causing, suffering, or liable to apoplexy. **2** *colloq.* enraged. □ **apoplectically** *adv.* [French *apoplectique* or Late Latin *apoplecticus* from Greek *apoplēktikos*, from *apoplēssō* 'strike completely' (as APO-, *plēssō* 'strike')]

apoplexy /'apəplɛksi/ *n.* **1** *Med.* = STROKE *n.* 2. **2** *colloq.* a rush of extreme emotion, esp. anger. [Middle English via Old French *apoplexie* and Late Latin *apoplexia* from Greek *apoplēxia* (as APOPLECTIC)]

apoptosis /apəp'təʊsɪs/ *n. Biol.* the controlled death of cells as part of an organism's normal growth, development, etc. □ **apoptotic** /-'tɒtɪk/ *adj.* [Greek *apoptōsis* 'falling off' (as APO- + PTOSIS)]

aporia /ə'pɔ:rɪə, ə'pɒrɪə/ *n.* **1** *Rhet.* an expression of doubt. **2** a doubtful matter; a perplexing difficulty. [Late Latin from Greek, from *aporos* 'impassable' (as A-[1] + *poros* 'passage')]

aposematic /ˌapəʊsɪ'matɪk/ *adj. Zool.* (of coloration, markings, etc.) serving to warn or repel predators. [APO- + Greek *sēma sēmatos* 'sign']

apostasy /ə'pɒstəsi/ *n.* (*pl.* **-ies**) **1** renunciation of a belief or faith, esp. religious. **2** abandonment of principles or of a party. **3** an instance of apostasy. [Middle English via ecclesiastical Latin and NT Greek *apostasia* from *apostasis* 'defection' (as APO-, *stat-* 'stand')]

apostate /'apəsteɪt/ *n. & adj.* ● *n.* a person who renounces a belief, adherence, etc. ● *adj.* engaged in apostasy. □ **apostatical** /apə'statɪk(ə)l/ *adj.* [Middle English via Old French *apostate* or ecclesiastical Latin *apostata* from Greek *apostatēs* 'deserter' (as APOSTASY)]

apostatize /ə'pɒstətʌɪz/ *v.intr.* (also **-ise**) renounce a former belief, adherence, etc. [medieval Latin *apostatizare* from *apostata*: see APOSTATE]

a posteriori /eɪ, ɑ:, pɒˌstɛrɪ'ɔ:rʌɪ, pɒˌstɪə-/ *adj. & adv.* ● *adj.* (of reasoning) inductive, empirical; proceeding from effects to causes. ● *adv.* inductively, empirically; from effects to causes (opp. A PRIORI). [Latin, = from what comes after]

apostle /ə'pɒs(ə)l/ *n.* **1 a** (**Apostle**) each of the twelve chief disciples of Jesus Christ. **b** any of a number of early Christian teachers ranked with these, esp. St Paul. **c** the first successful Christian missionary in a country or to a people. **2** a leader or outstanding figure, esp. of a reform movement (*apostle of temperance*). **3** a messenger or representative. □ **apostleship** *n.* [Old English *apostol* via ecclesiastical Latin *apostolus* from Greek *apostolos* 'messenger' (as APO-, *stellō* 'send forth')]

apostle-bird *n.* any of various Australian birds, forming flocks of about a dozen.

Apostles' Creed *n.* an early form of the Christian creed, traditionally ascribed to the Apostles.

apostolate /ə'pɒstəleɪt/ *n.* **1** the position or authority of an Apostle. **2** leadership in reform. [ecclesiastical Latin *apostolatus* (as APOSTLE)]

apostolic /apə'stɒlɪk/ *adj.* **1** of or relating to the Apostles. **2** of the Pope regarded as the successor of St Peter. **3** of the character of an Apostle. [French *apostolique* or ecclesiastical Latin *apostolicus*, from Greek *apostolikos* (as APOSTLE)]

Apostolic Fathers *n.pl.* the Christian leaders immediately succeeding the Apostles.

apostolic succession *n.* the uninterrupted transmission of spiritual authority from the Apostles through successive popes and bishops.

apostrophe[1] /ə'pɒstrəfi/ *n.* a punctuation mark used to indicate: **1** the omission of letters or numbers (e.g. *can't*; *he's*; *1 Jan. '92*). **2** the possessive case (e.g. *Harry's book*; *boys' coats*). [French *apostrophe* or Late Latin *apostrophus* from Greek *apostrophos* 'accent of elision', from *apostrephō* 'turn away' (as APO-, *strephō* 'turn')]

apostrophe[2] /ə'pɒstrəfi/ *n.* an exclamatory passage in a speech or poem, addressed to a person (often dead or absent) or thing (often personified). □ **apostrophize** *v.tr. & intr.* (also **-ise**). [Latin from Greek, literally 'turning away' (as APOSTROPHE[1])]

apothecaries' measure *n.* (also **apothecaries' weight**) *hist.* units of weight and liquid volume formerly used in pharmacy (12 ounces = one pound; 20 fluid ounces = one pint).

apothecary /ə'pɒθɪk(ə)ri/ *n.* (*pl.* **-ies**) *archaic* a chemist licensed to dispense medicines and drugs. [Middle English via Old French *apotecaire*, Late Latin *apothecarius*, and Latin *apotheca* from Greek *apothēkē* 'storehouse']

apothegm *US* var. of APOPHTHEGM.

apothem /'apəθɛm/ *n. Geom.* a line from the centre of a regular polygon at right angles to any of its sides. [Greek *apotithēmi* 'put aside' (as APO-, *tithēmi* 'place')]

apotheosis /əpɒθɪ'əʊsɪs/ *n.* (*pl.* **apotheoses** /-si:z/) **1** elevation to divine status; deification. **2** a glorification of a thing; a sublime example (*apotheosis of the dance*). **3** a deified ideal. [ecclesiastical Latin, from Greek *apotheoō* 'make a god of' (as APO-, *theos* 'god')]

apotheosize /ə'pɒθɪəsʌɪz/ *v.tr.* (also **-ise**) **1** make divine; deify. **2** idealize, glorify.

apotropaic /apətrə'peɪɪk/ *adj.* supposedly having the power to avert an evil influence or bad luck. [Greek *apotropaios* (as APO-, *trepō* 'turn')]

app /ap/ *n.* esp. *N. Amer. Computing* application. [abbreviation]

appal /ə'pɔ:l/ *v.tr.* (*US* **appall**) (**appalled**, **appalling**) **1** greatly dismay or horrify. **2** (as **appalling** *adj.*) *colloq.* shocking; unpleasant; bad. □ **appallingly** *adv.* [Middle English from Old French *apalir* 'grow pale']

Appaloosa /apə'lu:sə/ *n.* **1** a horse of a N. American breed having dark spots on a light background. **2** this breed. [*Opelousas* in Louisiana, or *Palouse*, a river in Idaho]

appanage var. of APANAGE.

apparat /apəˈrɑːt/ *n.* esp. *hist.* the administrative system of a Communist party, esp. in a Communist country. [Russian from German, = apparatus]

apparatchik /apəˈratʃɪk/ *n.* (*pl.* **apparatchiks** or **apparatchiki** /-ˌkiː/) **1 a** esp. *hist.* a member of a Communist apparat. **b** a Communist agent or spy. **2 a** a member of a political party in any country who executes policy; a zealous functionary. **b** an official of a public or private organization. [Russian: see APPARAT]

apparatus /apəˈreɪtəs/ *n.* **1** the equipment needed for a particular purpose or function, esp. scientific or technical. **2** a political or other complex organization. **3** *Anat.* the organs used to perform a particular process. **4** (in full **apparatus criticus** /ˈkrɪtɪkəs/) a collection of variants and annotations accompanying a printed text and usu. appearing below it. [Latin, from *apparare apparat-* 'make ready for']

apparel /əˈpar(ə)l/ *n.* & *v.* ● *n.* **1** *US* or *formal* clothing, dress. **2** embroidered ornamentation on some ecclesiastical vestments. ● *v.tr.* (**apparelled, apparelling**; *US* **appareled, appareling**) *archaic* clothe. [Middle English *aparailen*, in the sense 'make ready or fit', from Old French *apareillier*, ultimately from Latin *par* 'equal']

apparent /əˈpar(ə)nt/ *adj.* **1** readily visible or perceivable. **2** seeming. □ **apparently** *adv.* [Middle English via Old French *aparant* from Latin (as APPEAR)]

apparent horizon see HORIZON 1b.

apparent magnitude *n.* the magnitude, i.e. brightness, of a celestial object as seen from the earth (opp. ABSOLUTE MAGNITUDE).

apparent time *n.* solar time (see SOLAR *adj.*).

apparition /apəˈrɪʃ(ə)n/ *n.* a sudden or dramatic appearance, esp. of a ghost or phantom; a visible ghost. [Middle English from French *apparition* or from Latin *apparitio* 'attendance' (as APPEAR)]

appeal /əˈpiːl/ *v.* & *n.* ● *v.* **1** *intr.* make an earnest or formal request; plead (*appealed for calm*; *appealed to us not to leave*). **2** *intr.* (usu. foll. by *to*) be attractive or of interest; be pleasing. **3** *intr.* (foll. by *to*) resort to or cite for support. **4** *Law* **a** *intr.* (often foll. by *to*) apply (to a higher court) for a reconsideration of the decision of a lower court. **b** *tr.* refer to a higher court to review (a case). **c** *intr.* (foll. by *against*) apply to a higher court to reconsider (a verdict or sentence). **5** *intr. Cricket* call on the umpire for a decision on whether a batsman is out. ● *n.* **1** the act or an instance of appealing. **2** a formal or urgent request for public support, esp. financial, for a cause. **3** *Law* the referral of a case to a higher court. **4** attractiveness; appealing quality (*sex appeal*). □ **appealer** *n.* [Middle English via Old French *apel, apeler* from Latin *appellare* 'to address']

appealable /əˈpiːləb(ə)l/ *adj. Law* (of a case) that can be referred to a higher court for review.

appealing /əˈpiːlɪŋ/ *adj.* attractive, likeable. □ **appealingly** *adv.*

appear /əˈpɪə/ *v.intr.* **1** become or be visible. **2** be evident (*a new problem then appeared*). **3** seem; have the appearance of being (*appeared unwell*; *you appear to be right*). **4** present oneself publicly or formally, esp. on stage or as the accused or counsel in a law court. **5** be published (*it appeared in the papers*; *a new edition will appear*). [Middle English via Old French *apareir* from Latin *apparēre apparit-* 'come in sight']

appearance /əˈpɪər(ə)ns/ *n.* **1** the act or an instance of appearing. **2** an outward form as perceived (whether correctly or not), esp. visually (*smartened up his appearance*; *gives an appearance of scalded skin*). **3** a semblance (*lend an appearance of legitimacy*). □ **keep up appearances** maintain an impression or pretence of virtue, affluence, etc. **make** (or **put in**) **an appearance** be present, esp. briefly. **to all appearances** as far as can be seen; apparently. [Middle English via Old French *aparance, -ence* from Late Latin *apparentia* (as APPEAR, -ANCE)]

appease /əˈpiːz/ *v.tr.* **1** make calm or quiet, esp. conciliate (a potential aggressor) by making concessions. **2** satisfy (an appetite, scruples). □ **appeasement** *n.* **appeaser** *n.* [Middle English from Anglo-French *apeser*, Old French *apaisier* from *à* 'to' + *pais* PEACE]

appellant /əˈpɛl(ə)nt/ *n. Law* a person who appeals to a higher court. [Middle English from French (as APPEAL, -ANT)]

appellate /əˈpɛlət/ *adj. Law* (esp. of a court) concerned with or dealing with appeals. [Latin *appellatus* (as APPEAL, -ATE[2])]

appellation /apəˈleɪʃ(ə)n/ *n. formal* a name or title; nomenclature. [Middle English via Old French from Latin *appellatio -onis* (as APPEAL, -ATION)]

appellation contrôlée /apəˌlasjɒn kənˈtrɒleɪ, French apɛlasjɔ̃ kɔ̃trole/ *n.* (also ***appellation d'origine*** /dɒriʒin/ ***contrôlée***) a guarantee of the description of a bottle of French wine or of a foodstuff as to its origin, in conformity with statutory regulations. [French, = controlled appellation]

appellative /əˈpɛlətɪv/ *adj.* **1** naming. **2** *Gram.* (of a noun) that designates a class; common. [Late Latin *appellativus* (as APPEAL, -ATIVE)]

append /əˈpɛnd/ *v.tr.* (usu. foll. by *to*) attach, affix, add, esp. to a written document etc. [Latin *appendere* 'hang']

appendage /əˈpɛndɪdʒ/ *n.* **1** something attached; an addition. **2** *Zool.* a leg or other projecting part of an arthropod.

appendant /əˈpɛnd(ə)nt/ *adj.* & *n.* ● *adj.* (usu. foll. by *to*) attached in a subordinate capacity. ● *n.* an appendant person or thing. [Old French *apendant* from *apendre* (as APPEND, -ANT)]

appendectomy /ap(ə)nˈdɛktəmi/ *n.* (also *Brit.* **appendicectomy** /əpɛndɪˈsɛktəmi/) (*pl.* **-ies**) the surgical removal of the appendix. [APPENDIX + -ECTOMY]

appendicitis /əpɛndɪˈsʌɪtɪs/ *n.* inflammation of the appendix. [APPENDIX + -ITIS]

appendix /əˈpɛndɪks/ *n.* (*pl.* **appendices** /-siːz/; **appendixes**) **1** (in full **vermiform appendix**) *Anat.* a small outgrowth of tissue forming a tube-shaped sac attached to the lower end of the large intestine. **2** subsidiary matter at the end of a book or document. [Latin *appendix -icis* from *appendere* APPEND]

apperceive /apəˈsiːv/ *v.tr.* **1** be conscious of perceiving. **2** *Psychol.* compare (a perception) to previously held ideas so as to extract meaning from it. □ **apperception** /-ˈsɛpʃ(ə)n/ *n.* **apperceptive** /-ˈsɛptɪv/ *adj.* [Middle English (in obsolete sense 'observe') from Old French *aperceveir*, ultimately from Latin *percipere* PERCEIVE]

appertain /apəˈteɪn/ *v.intr.* (foll. by *to*) **1** relate. **2** belong as a possession or right. **3** be appropriate. [Middle English via Old French *apertenir* and Late Latin *appertinēre* from Latin *pertinēre* PERTAIN]

appetence /ˈapɪt(ə)ns/ *n.* (also **appetency** /-(ə)nsi/) (*pl.* **-ces** or **-cies**) (foll. by *for*) longing or desire. [French *appétence* or Latin *appetentia*, from *appetere* 'seek after']

appetite /ˈapɪtʌɪt/ *n.* **1** a natural desire to satisfy bodily needs, esp. for food or sexual activity. **2** (usu. foll. by *for*) an inclination or desire. □ **appetitive** /əˈpɛtɪtɪv/ *adj.* [Middle English via Old French *apetit* from Latin *appetitus*, from *appetere* 'seek after']

appetizer /ˈapɪtʌɪzə/ *n.* (also **-iser**) a small amount, esp. of food or drink, to stimulate an appetite. [*appetize* (back-formation from APPETIZING)]

appetizing /ˈapɪtʌɪzɪŋ/ *adj.* (also **-ising**) stimulating an appetite, esp. for food. □ **appetizingly** *adv.* [French *appétissant*, irregular formation from *appétit* (as APPETITE)]

applaud /əˈplɔːd/ *v.* **1** *intr.* express strong approval or praise, esp. by clapping. **2** *tr.* express approval of (a person or action) verbally or by clapping. [Latin *applaudere applaus-* 'clap hands']

applause /əˈplɔːz/ *n.* **1** an expression of approbation, esp. from an audience etc. by clapping. **2** emphatic approval. [medieval Latin *applausus* (as APPLAUD)]

apple /ˈap(ə)l/ *n.* **1** the fruit of a tree of the genus *Malus*, rounded in form and with a crisp flesh. **2** (in full **apple tree**) the tree bearing this. □ **apple of one's eye** (prec. by *the*) a cherished person or thing. **she's apples** *Austral. slang* everything is fine. **upset the apple-cart** spoil careful plans. [Old English *æppel*, from Germanic]

apple-cheeked *adj.* having round rosy cheeks.

applejack /ˈap(ə)ldʒak/ *n. N. Amer.* a spirit distilled from fermented apple juice. [APPLE + JACK[1]]

apple-pie bed *n.* a bed made (as a joke) with the sheets folded short, so that the legs cannot be accommodated.

apple-pie order *n.* perfect order; extreme neatness.

appliance /əˈplʌɪəns/ *n.* a device or piece of equipment used for a specific task, esp. a machine for domestic use. [APPLY + -ANCE]

applicable /əˈplɪkəb(ə)l, ˈaplɪk-/ *adj.* (often foll. by *to*) **1** that may be applied. **2** having reference; appropriate. □ **applicability** /-ˈbɪlɪti/ *n.* **applicably** *adv.* [Old French *applicable* or medieval Latin *applicabilis* (as APPLY, -ABLE)]

applicant /ˈaplɪk(ə)nt/ *n.* a person who applies for something, esp. a job. [APPLICATION + -ANT]

application /aplɪˈkeɪʃ(ə)n/ *n.* **1** the act of applying, esp. medicinal ointment to the skin. **2** a formal request, usu. in writing, for employment, membership, etc. **3 a** relevance. **b** the use to which something can or should be put. **4** sustained or concentrated effort; diligence. [Middle English via Old French from Latin *applicatio -onis* (as APPLY, -ATION)]

application program *n.* a computer program designed and written to fulfil a particular purpose of the user.

applicator /ˈaplɪkeɪtə/ *n.* a device for applying a substance to a surface, esp. the skin, or for inserting something into a cavity, esp. into the body. [APPLICATION + -OR[1]]

applied /əˈplʌɪd/ *adj.* (of a subject of study) put to practical use as opposed to being theoretical (cf. PURE *adj.* 9).

applied mathematics see MATHEMATICS.

appliqué /əˈpliːkeɪ/ *n., adj., & v.* ● *n.* ornamental work in which fabric is cut out and attached, usu. sewn, to the surface of another fabric to form pictures or patterns. ● *adj.* executed in appliqué. ● *v.tr.* (**appliqués, appliquéd, appliquéing**) decorate with appliqué; make using appliqué technique. [French, past part. of *appliquer* 'apply' from Latin *applicare*: see APPLY]

apply /əˈplʌɪ/ *v.* (**-ies, -ied**) **1** *intr.* (often foll. by *for, to*, or *to* + infin.) make a formal request for something to be done, given, etc. (*apply for a job*; *apply for help to the governors*; *applied to be sent overseas*). **2** *intr.* (often foll. by *to*) have relevance (*does not apply in this case*). **3** *tr.* **a** make use of as relevant or suitable; employ (*apply the rules*). **b** operate (*apply the handbrake*). **4** *tr.* (often foll. by *to*) **a** put or spread on (*applied the ointment to the cut*). **b** administer (*applied the remedy*; *applied common sense to the problem*). **5** *refl.* (often foll. by *to*) devote oneself (*applied myself to the task*). □ **applier** *n.* [Middle English via Old French *aplier* from Latin *applicare* 'fold, fasten to']

appoggiatura /əpɒdʒəˈtʊərə/ *n. Mus.* a grace note performed before an essential note of a melody and normally taking half its time value. [Italian, = lean upon, rest]

appoint /əˈpɔɪnt/ *v.tr.* **1** assign a post or office to (*appoint him governor*; *appoint him to govern*; *appointed to the post*). **2** (often foll. by *for*) fix, decide on (a time, place, etc.) (*Wednesday was appointed for the meeting*; *8.30 was the appointed time*). **3** prescribe; ordain (*Holy Writ appointed by the Church*). **4** *Law* **a** (also *absol.*) declare the destination of (property etc.). **b** declare (a person) as having an interest in property etc. (*Jones was appointed in the will*). **5** (as **appointed** *adj.*) equipped, furnished (*a badly appointed hotel*). □ **appointee** /-ˈtiː/ *n.* **appointer** *n.* **appointive** *adj.* esp. *N. Amer.* (in sense 1 of *v.*). [Middle English from Old French *apointer*, from *à point* 'to a point']

appointment /əˈpɔɪntm(ə)nt/ *n.* **1** an arrangement to meet at a specific time and place. **2 a** a post or office available for applicants, or recently filled (*took up the appointment on Monday*). **b** a person appointed. **3** (usu. in *pl.*) **a** furniture, fittings. **b** equipment. [Middle English from Old French *apointement* (as APPOINT, -MENT)]

apport /əˈpɔːt/ *n.* **1** the production of material objects by supposedly occult means at a seance. **2** an object so produced. [Middle English, in the sense 'something brought', from Old French *aport* from *aporter*, from *à* 'to' + *porter* 'bring']

apportion /əˈpɔːʃ(ə)n/ *v.tr.* (often foll. by *to*) share out; assign as a share. □ **apportionable** *adj.* [French *apportionner* or medieval Latin *apportionare* (as AD-, PORTION)]

apportionment /əˈpɔːʃənm(ə)nt/ *n.* **1** the act or an instance of apportioning. **2** *US* the determination of the proportional number of members each state sends to the House of Representatives (based on population figures).

apposite /ˈapəzɪt/ *adj.* (often foll. by *to*) **1** apt; well chosen. **2** well expressed. □ **appositely** *adv.* **appositeness** *n.* [Latin *appositus* past part. of *apponere* (as AD-, *ponere* 'put')]

apposition /apəˈzɪʃ(ə)n/ *n.* **1** placing side by side; juxtaposition. **2** *Gram.* the placing of a word next to another, esp. the addition of one noun to another, in order to qualify or explain the first (e.g. *William the Conqueror*; *my friend Sue*). □ **appositional** *adj.* [Middle English from French *apposition* or Late Latin *appositio* (as APPOSITE, -ITION)]

appraisal /əˈpreɪz(ə)l/ *n.* **1** the act or an instance of appraising. **2** a formal evaluation of the performance of an employee over a particular period.

appraise /əˈpreɪz/ *v.tr.* **1** estimate the value or quality of (*appraised her skills*). **2** (esp. of an official valuer) set a price on; value. **3** evaluate the performance of (an employee) formally. □ **appraisable** *adj.* **appraisee** /-ˈziː/ *n.* **appraiser** *n.* **appraisingly** *adv.* **appraisive** *adj.* [from APPRIZE, by assimilation to PRAISE]

appreciable /əˈpriːʃəb(ə)l, -ʃɪə-/ *adj.* large enough to be noticed; significant; considerable (*appreciable progress has been made*). □ **appreciably** *adv.* [French, from *apprécier* (as APPRECIATE)]

appreciate /əˈpriːʃɪeɪt, -sɪ-/ *v.* **1** *tr.* **a** esteem highly; value. **b** be grateful for (*we appreciate your sympathy*). **c** be sensitive to (*appreciate the nuances*). **2** *tr.* (often foll. by *that* + clause) understand; recognize (*I appreciate that I may be wrong*). **3 a** *intr.* (of property etc.) rise in value. **b** *tr.* raise in value. □ **appreciative** /-ʃ(ɪ)ətɪv/ *adj.* **appreciatively** /-ʃətɪvli/ *adv.* **appreciativeness** /-ʃətɪvnɪs/ *n.* **appreciator** *n.* **appreciatory** /-ʃ(ɪ)ət(ə)ri/ *adj.* [Late Latin *appretiare* 'appraise' (as AD-, *pretium* 'price')]

appreciation /əpriːʃɪˈeɪʃ(ə)n, -sɪ-/ *n.* **1** favourable or grateful recognition. **2** an estimation or judgement; sensitive understanding of or reaction to (*a quick appreciation of the problem*). **3** an increase in value. **4** a (usu. favourable) review of a book, film, etc. [French, from Late Latin *appretiatio -onis* (as APPRECIATE, -ATION)]

apprehend /aprɪˈhɛnd/ *v.tr.* **1** understand, perceive (*apprehend your meaning*). **2** seize, arrest (*apprehended the criminal*). **3** anticipate with uneasiness or fear (*apprehending the results*). [French *appréhender* or Latin *apprehendere* (as AD-, *prehendere prehens-* 'lay hold of')]

apprehensible /aprɪˈhɛnsɪb(ə)l/ *adj.* capable of being apprehended by the senses or the intellect (*an apprehensible theory*; *an apprehensible change in her expression*). □ **apprehensibility** /-ˈbɪlɪti/ *n.* [Late Latin *apprehensibilis* (as APPREHEND, -IBLE)]

apprehension /aprɪ'hɛnʃ(ə)n/ *n.* **1** uneasiness; a sense of foreboding. **2** understanding, grasp. **3** arrest, capture (*apprehension of the suspect*). **4** an idea; a conception. [French *appréhension* or Late Latin *apprehensio* (as APPREHEND, -ION)]

apprehensive /aprɪ'hɛnsɪv/ *adj.* **1** (often foll. by *about, of, for*) uneasily fearful; anxious. **2** relating to perception by the senses or the intellect. **3** *archaic* perceptive; intelligent. □ **apprehensively** *adv.* **apprehensiveness** *n.* [French *appréhensif* or medieval Latin *apprehensivus* (as APPREHEND, -IVE)]

apprentice /ə'prɛntɪs/ *n. & v.* ● *n.* **1** a person who is learning a trade by being employed in it for an agreed period at low wages. **2** a beginner; a novice. ● *v.* **1** *tr.* (usu. foll. by *to*) engage or bind as an apprentice (*was apprenticed to a builder*). **2** *intr. N. Amer.* serve as an apprentice (*she apprenticed at a hairdresser's*). □ **apprenticeship** *n.* [Middle English from Old French *aprentis*, from *apprendre* 'learn' (as APPREHEND), on the pattern of words ending in *-tis, -tif*, from Latin *-tivus*: see -IVE]

apprise /ə'prʌɪz/ *v.tr.* (foll. by *of*) inform. □ **be apprised of** be aware of. [French *appris -ise*, past part. of *apprendre* 'learn, teach' (as APPREHEND)]

apprize /ə'prʌɪz/ *v.tr.* (also **-ise**) *archaic* **1** esteem highly. **2** appraise. [Middle English from Old French *aprisier*, from *à* 'to' + *pris* PRICE]

appro /'aprəʊ/ *n. Brit. colloq.* □ **on appro** = *on approval* (see APPROVAL). [abbreviation of *approval* or *approbation*]

approach /ə'prəʊtʃ/ *v. & n.* ● *v.* **1** *tr.* come near or nearer to (a place or time). **2** *intr.* come near or nearer in space or time (*the hour approaches*). **3** *tr.* make a tentative proposal or suggestion to (*approached me about a loan*). **4** *tr.* **a** be similar in character, quality, etc., to (*doesn't approach her for artistic skill*). **b** approximate to (*a population approaching 5 million*). **5** *tr.* attempt to influence or bribe. **6** *tr.* set about (a task etc.). **7** *intr. Golf* play an approach shot. **8** *intr. Aeron.* prepare to land. **9** *tr. archaic* bring near. ● *n.* **1** an act or means of approaching (*made an approach; an approach lined with trees*). **2** an approximation (*an approach to an apology*). **3** a way of dealing with a person or thing (*needs a new approach*). **4** (usu. in *pl.*) a sexual advance. **5** *Golf* a stroke from the fairway to the green. **6** *Aeron.* the final part of a flight before landing. **7** *Bridge* a bidding method with a gradual advance to a final contract. [Middle English via Old French *aproch(i)er* from ecclesiastical Latin *appropiare* 'draw near' (as AD-, *propius*, comparative of *prope* 'near')]

approachable /ə'prəʊtʃəb(ə)l/ *adj.* **1** friendly; easy to talk to. **2** able to be approached. □ **approachability** /-'bɪlɪti/ *n.*

approach road *n. Brit.* a road by which traffic enters a motorway.

approbate /'aprəbeɪt/ *v.tr. US* approve formally; sanction. [Middle English from Latin *approbare* (as AD-, *probare* 'test' from *probus* 'good')]

approbation /aprə'beɪʃ(ə)n/ *n.* approval, consent. □ **approbative** /'aprəbeɪtɪv/ *adj.* **approbatory** *adj.* [Middle English via Old French from Latin *approbatio -onis* (as APPROBATE, -ATION)]

appropriate *adj. & v.* ● *adj.* /ə'prəʊprɪət/ (often foll. by *to, for*) **1** suitable or proper. **2** *formal* belonging or particular. ● *v.tr.* /ə'prəʊprɪeɪt/ **1** take possession of, esp. without authority. **2** devote (money etc.) to special purposes. □ **appropriately** *adv.* **appropriateness** *n.* **appropriation** /əprəʊprɪ'eɪʃ(ə)n/ *n.* **appropriator** /-eɪtə/ *n.* [Late Latin *appropriatus*, past part. of *appropriare* (as AD-, *proprius* 'own')]

approval /ə'pru:v(ə)l/ *n.* **1** the act of approving. **2** an instance of this; consent; a favourable opinion (*with your approval; looked at him with approval*). □ **on approval** (of goods supplied) to be returned if not satisfactory.

approve /ə'pru:v/ *v.* **1** *tr.* confirm; sanction (*approved his application*). **2** *intr.* give or have a favourable opinion. **3** *tr.* commend (*approved the new hat*). **4** *tr.* (usu. *refl.*) *archaic* demonstrate oneself to be (*approved himself a coward*). □ **approve of** pronounce or consider good or satisfactory; commend. □ **approvingly** *adv.* [Middle English via Old French *aprover* from Latin (as APPROBATE)]

approved school *n. Brit. hist.* a residential place of training for young offenders.

approx. *abbr.* **1** approximate. **2** approximately.

approximate *adj. & v.* ● *adj.* /ə'prɒksɪmət/ **1** fairly correct or accurate; near to the actual (*the approximate time of arrival; an approximate guess*). **2** near or next (*your approximate neighbour*). ● *v.tr. & intr.* /ə'prɒksɪmeɪt/ (often foll. by *to*) bring or come near (esp. in quality, number, etc.), but not exactly (*approximates to the truth; approximates the amount required*). □ **approximately** /-mətli/ *adv.* **approximation** /-'meɪʃ(ə)n/ *n.* [Late Latin *approximatus*, past part. of *approximare* (as AD-, *proximus* 'very near')]

appurtenance /ə'pə:t(ɪ)nəns/ *n.* (usu. in *pl.*) a belonging; an appendage; an accessory. [Middle English from Anglo-French *apurtenaunce*, Old French *apertenance* (as APPERTAIN, -ANCE)]

appurtenant /ə'pə:t(ɪ)nənt/ *adj.* (often foll. by *to*) belonging or appertaining; pertinent. [Middle English from Old French *apartenant* pres. part. (as APPERTAIN)]

APR *abbr.* annual or annualized percentage rate (esp. of interest on loans or credit).

Apr. *abbr.* April.

après-ski /apreɪ'ski:/ *n. & adj.* ● *n.* the evening, esp. its social activities, following a day's skiing. ● *attrib.adj.* (of clothes, drinks, etc.) appropriate to social activities following skiing. [French]

apricot /'eɪprɪkɒt/ *n. & adj.* ● *n.* **1 a** a juicy soft fruit, smaller than a peach, of an orange-yellow colour. **b** (in full **apricot tree**) the tree, *Prunus armeniaca*, bearing it. **2** the ripe fruit's orange-yellow colour. ● *adj.* of an orange-yellow colour (*apricot dress*). [Portuguese *albricoque* or Spanish *albaricoque* via Arabic *al* 'the' + *barḳūḳ* and late Greek *praikokion* from Latin *praecoquum*, variant of *praecox* 'early-ripe': *apri-* influenced by Latin *apricus* 'ripe', *-cot* by French *abricot*]

April /'eɪpr(ɪ)l/ *n.* the fourth month of the year. [Middle English from Latin *Aprilis*]

April Fool *n.* a person successfully tricked on 1 April.

April Fool's Day *n.* (also **April Fools' Day**, **All Fools' Day**) 1 April.

a priori /eɪ prʌɪ'ɔ:rʌɪ, ɑ: prɪ'ɔ:ri/ *adj. & adv.* ● *adj.* **1** (of reasoning) deductive; proceeding from causes to effects (opp. A POSTERIORI). **2** (of concepts, knowledge, etc.) logically independent of experience; not derived from experience (opp. EMPIRICAL). **3** not submitted to critical investigation (*an a priori conjecture*). ● *adv.* **1** in an a priori manner. **2** as far as one knows; presumptively. □ **apriorism** /eɪ'prʌɪərɪz(ə)m/ *n.* [Latin, = from what is before]

apron /'eɪpr(ə)n/ *n.* **1 a** a garment covering and protecting the front of a person's clothes, either from chest or waist level, and tied at the back. **b** official clothing of this kind (*bishop's apron*). **c** anything resembling an apron in shape or function. **2** *Theatr.* the part of a stage in front of the curtain. **3** the hard-surfaced area on an airfield used for manoeuvring or loading aircraft. **4** an endless conveyor belt. □ **tied to a person's apron strings** dominated by or dependent on that person (usu. a woman). □ **aproned** *adj.* **apronful** *n.* (*pl.* **-fuls**). [Middle English *naperon* etc. from Old French, diminutive of *nape* 'tablecloth' from Latin *mappa*: for loss of *n* cf. ADDER]

apropos /aprə'pəʊ, 'aprəpəʊ/ *adj., prep., & adv.* ● *adj.* to the point or purpose; appropriate (*his comment was apropos*). ● *prep.* (often foll. by *of*) *colloq.* in respect of; concerning (*apropos the meeting; apropos of the talk*). ● *adv.* **1** appropriately (*spoke apropos*). **2** (*absol.*) by the way; incidentally (*apropos, she's not going*). [French *à propos* from *à* 'to' + *propos* PURPOSE]

apse /aps/ *n.* **1** a large semicircular or polygonal recess, arched or with a domed roof, esp. at the eastern end of a church. **2** = APSIS. □ **apsidal** /'apsɪd(ə)l/ *adj.* [Latin APSIS]

apsis /'apsɪs/ *n.* (*pl.* **apsides** /-di:z/) either of two points on the orbit of a planet or satellite that are nearest to or furthest from the body round which it moves. □ **apsidal** *adj.* [Latin, from Greek (*h*)*apsis, -idos* 'arch, vault']

apt /apt/ *adj.* **1** appropriate, suitable (*an apt moment*). **2** (foll. by *to* + infin.) having a tendency; prone, likely (*apt to lose his temper*). **3** clever; quick to learn (*an apt pupil; apt at the work*). □ **aptly** *adv.* **aptness** *n.* [Middle English from Latin *aptus* 'fitted', past part. of *apere* 'fasten']

apterous /'apt(ə)rəs/ *adj.* **1** *Zool.* (of insects) without wings. **2** *Bot.* (of seeds or fruits) having no winglike expansions. [Greek *apteros* (as A-[1] + *pteron* 'wing')]

apteryx /'aptərɪks/ *n.* = KIWI. [modern Latin, from Greek (as A-[1] + *pterux* 'wing')]

aptitude /'aptɪtju:d/ *n.* **1** a natural propensity or talent (*shows an aptitude for drawing*). **2** ability or fitness, esp. to acquire a particular skill. [French from Late Latin *aptitudo -inis* (as APT, -TUDE)]

aqua /'akwə/ *n. & adj.* ● *n.* the colour aquamarine. ● *adj.* of this colour. [abbreviation]

aquaculture /'akwəkʌltʃə/ *n.* the cultivation or rearing of aquatic plants or animals. [Latin *aqua* 'water' + CULTURE, on the pattern of *agriculture*]

aqua fortis /ˌakwə 'fɔ:tɪs/ *n. Chem.* nitric acid. [Latin, = strong water]

Aqua Libra /ˌakwə 'li:brə/ *n. propr.* a drink made from mineral water and fruit juices.

aqualung /'akwəlʌŋ/ *n. & v.* ● *n.* a portable breathing apparatus for divers, consisting of cylinders of compressed air strapped on the back, feeding air automatically through a mask or mouthpiece. ● *v.intr.* use an aqualung. [Latin *aqua* 'water' + LUNG]

aquamarine /ˌakwəmə'ri:n/ *n. & adj.* ● *n.* **1** a light bluish-green beryl. **2** its colour. ● *adj.* of bluish-green colour. [Latin *aqua marina* 'sea water']

aquanaut /'akwənɔ:t/ *n.* an underwater swimmer or explorer. [Latin *aqua* 'water' + Greek *nautēs* 'sailor']

aquaplane /'akwəpleɪn/ *n. & v.* ● *n.* a board for riding on water, pulled by a speedboat. ● *v.intr.* **1** ride on an aquaplane. **2** (of a vehicle) glide uncontrollably on the wet surface of a road. [Latin *aqua* 'water' + PLANE[1]]

aqua regia /ˌakwə 'ri:dʒə/ *n. Chem.* a mixture of concentrated nitric and hydrochloric acids, a highly corrosive liquid attacking many substances unaffected by other reagents. [Latin, = royal water]

aquarelle /akwə'rɛl/ *n.* a painting in thin, usu. transparent, watercolours. [French from Italian *acquarella* 'watercolour', diminutive of *acqua*, from Latin *aqua* 'water']

aquarium /ə'kwɛ:rɪəm/ *n.* (*pl.* **aquaria** /-rɪə/ or **aquariums**) an artificial environment designed for keeping live aquatic plants and animals for study or exhibition, esp. a tank of water with transparent sides. [neut. of Latin *aquarius* 'of water' (*aqua*), on the pattern of *vivarium*]

Aquarius /ə'kwɛ:rɪəs/ *n.* **1** *Astron.* a large constellation (the Water-carrier or Water-bearer), said to represent a man pouring water from a jar. **2** *Astrol.* **a** the eleventh sign of the zodiac, which the sun enters about 21 Jan. **b** a person born when the sun is in this sign. □ **Aquarian** *adj. & n.* [Middle English from Latin (as AQUARIUM)]

aquatic /ə'kwatɪk, -'kwɒt-/ *adj. & n.* ● *adj.* **1** growing or living in or near water. **2** (of a sport) played in or on water. ● *n.* **1** an aquatic plant or animal. **2** (in *pl.*) aquatic sports. [Middle English from French *aquatique* or Latin *aquaticus*, from *aqua* 'water']

aquatint /'akwətɪnt/ *n.* **1** a print resembling a watercolour, produced from a copper plate etched with nitric acid. **2** the process of producing this. [French *aquatinte* from Italian *acqua tinta* 'coloured water']

aquavit /akwə'vi:t/ *n.* (also **akvavit** /'akvə-/) an alcoholic spirit made from potatoes etc. [Norwegian, Swedish, Danish *akvavit* AQUA VITAE]

aqua vitae /ˌakwə 'vʌɪti:, 'vi:tʌɪ/ *n.* a strong alcoholic spirit, esp. brandy. [Latin = water of life]

aqueduct /'akwɪdʌkt/ *n.* **1** an artificial channel for conveying water, esp. in the form of a bridge supported by tall columns across a valley. **2** *Physiol.* a small canal, esp. in the head of mammals. [Latin *aquae ductus* 'conduit', from *aqua* 'water' + *ducere duct-* 'to lead']

aqueous /'eɪkwɪəs/ *adj.* **1** of, containing, or like water. **2** *Geol.* produced by water (*aqueous rocks*). [medieval Latin *aqueus* from Latin *aqua* 'water']

aqueous humour *n. Anat.* the clear fluid in the eye between the lens and the cornea.

aquifer /'akwɪfə/ *n. Geol.* a layer of rock or soil able to hold or transmit much water. [Latin *aqui-* from *aqua* 'water' + *-fer* 'bearing' from *ferre* 'bear']

aquilegia /akwɪ'li:dʒə/ *n.* a plant of the genus *Aquilegia* (buttercup family) with (often blue) flowers having backward-pointing spurs. Also called COLUMBINE. [medieval Latin, probably from Latin *aquilegus* 'water-collecting']

aquiline /'akwɪlʌɪn/ *adj.* **1** of or like an eagle. **2** (of a nose) curved like an eagle's beak. [Latin *aquilinus*, from *aquila* 'eagle']

AR *abbr.* **1** *US* Arkansas (in official postal use). **2** Autonomous Republic.

Ar *symb. Chem.* the element argon.

ar- /ar, ər/ *prefix* assim. form of AD- before *r*.

-ar[1] /ə/ *suffix* **1** forming adjectives (*angular*; *linear*; *nuclear*; *titular*). **2** forming nouns (*scholar*). [Old French *-aire* or *-ier*, or Latin *-aris*]

-ar[2] /ə/ *suffix* forming nouns (*pillar*). [French *-er* or Latin *-ar*, *-are*, neut. of *-aris*]

-ar[3] /ə/ *suffix* forming nouns (*bursar*; *exemplar*; *mortar*; *vicar*). [Old French *-aire* or *-ier*, or Latin *-arius*, *-arium*]

-ar[4] /ə/ *suffix* assim. form of -ER[1], -OR[1] (*liar*; *pedlar*).

ARA *abbr.* Associate of the Royal Academy.

Arab /'arəb/ *n. & adj.* ● *n.* **1** a member of a Semitic people inhabiting originally Saudi Arabia and the neighbouring countries, now the Middle East generally. **2** a horse of a breed originally native to Arabia. ● *adj.* of or relating to Arabia or the Arabs (esp. with ethnic reference). [French *Arabe* via Latin *Arabs Arabis* and Greek *Araps -abos* from Arabic *'arab*]

arabesque /arə'bɛsk/ *n.* **1** *Ballet* a posture with one leg extended horizontally backwards, torso extended forwards, and arms outstretched. **2** a design of intertwined leaves, scrolls, etc. **3** *Mus.* a florid melodic section or composition. [French from Italian *arabesco* 'in the Arabic style', from *arabo* 'Arab']

Arabian /ə'reɪbɪən/ *adj. & n.* ● *adj.* of or relating to Arabia (esp. with geographical reference) (*the Arabian desert*). ● *n.* **1** a native of Arabia. **2** *US*= ARAB *n.* 2. [Middle English from Old French *arabi*, probably from Arabic *'arabī*, or via Latin *Arabus*, *Arabius* from Greek *Arabios*]

■ **Usage** In the sense 'a native of Arabia', the usual term is now *Arab*.

Arabian camel *n.* a domesticated one-humped camel, *Camelus dromedarius*, native to the deserts of N. Africa and the Near East. Also called *dromedary*.

Arabic /'arəbɪk/ *n. & adj.* ● *n.* the Semitic language of the Arabs, now spoken in much of N. Africa and the Middle East. ● *adj.* of or relating to Arabia (esp. with reference to language or literature). [Middle English via Old French *arabic* and Latin *arabicus* from Greek *arabikos*]

arabica /ə'rabɪkə/ *n.* **1** coffee or coffee beans from the most widely grown species of the coffee plant, *Coffea arabica*. **2** the plant itself (cf. ROBUSTA). [modern Latin, from Latin *arabicus* ARABIC]

Arabic numeral *n.* any of the numerals 0, 1, 2, 3, 4, 5, 6, 7, 8, and 9 (cf. ROMAN NUMERAL).

arabis /'arəbɪs/ *n.* a low-growing cruciferous plant of the genus *Arabis*, with toothed leaves and usu. white flowers. Also called *rock cress, wall cress.* [medieval Latin from Greek, = Arabian]

Arabist /'arəbɪst/ *n.* a student of Arabic civilization, language, etc.

arable /'arəb(ə)l/ *adj. & n.* ● *adj.* **1** (of land) ploughed, or suitable for ploughing and crop production. **2** (of crops) that can be grown on arable land. ● *n.* arable land or crops. [French *arable* or Latin *arabilis*, from *arare* 'to plough']

Araby /'arəbi/ *n. poet.* Arabia. [Old French *Arabie* via Latin *Arabia* from Greek]

arachnid /ə'raknɪd/ *n.* any arthropod of the class Arachnida, having four pairs of legs, simple eyes, and usu. pincers or fangs e.g. scorpions, spiders, mites, and ticks. □ **arachnidan** *adj. & n.* [French *arachnide* or modern Latin *arachnida*, from Greek *arakhnē* 'spider']

arachnoid /ə'raknɔɪd/ *n. & adj.* ● *n.* (in full **arachnoid membrane**) *Anat.* one of the three membranes (see MENINX) that surround the brain and spinal cord of vertebrates. ● *adj. Bot.* covered with long cobweb-like hairs. [modern Latin *arachnoides* from Greek *arakhnoeidēs* 'like a cobweb', from *arakhnē*: see ARACHNID]

arachnophobia /əraknə(ʊ)'fəʊbɪə/ *n.* an abnormal fear of spiders. □ **arachnophobe** /ə'raknəfəʊb/ *n.* **arachnophobic** *adj.* [modern Latin, from Greek *arakhnē* 'spider' + -PHOBIA]

arak var. of ARRACK.

Araldite /'ar(ə)ldʌɪt/ *n. Brit. propr.* an epoxy resin used as a strong heatproof cement to mend china, plastic, etc. [20th c.: origin uncertain]

Aramaic /arə'meɪɪk/ *n. & adj.* ● *n.* a branch of the Semitic family of languages, esp. the language of Syria used as a lingua franca in the Near East from the sixth century BC, later dividing into varieties one of which included Syriac and Mandaean. ● *adj.* of or in Aramaic. [Latin *Aramaeus* from Greek *Aramaios* 'of Aram' (biblical name of Syria)]

Aran /'ar(ə)n/ *attrib.adj.* designating a type of knitwear or garment with traditional patterns, esp. involving raised cable stitch and large diamond designs. [from the *Aran* islands off the W. coast of Ireland]

Aranda /ə'randə/ *n. & adj.* ● *n.* (also **Arunta** /ə'rʌntə/) (*pl.* same or **-s**) **1** a member of an Aboriginal people of central Australia. **2** the language spoken by this people. ● *adj.* of or relating to the Aranda or their language. [Aboriginal]

arapaima /arə'pʌɪmə/ *n.* a very large edible S. American freshwater fish, *Arapaima gigas*. [Tupi]

arational /eɪ'raʃ(ə)n(ə)l/ *adj.* that does not purport to be rational.

araucaria /arə'kɛːrɪə/ *n.* an evergreen conifer of the genus *Araucaria*, native to the southern hemisphere, e.g. the monkey-puzzle tree. [modern Latin from *Arauco*, the name of a province in Chile]

Arawak /'arəwak/ *n.* (*pl.* same or **Arawaks**) **1** any of several related languages spoken by American Indian peoples of the Caribbean and parts of S. America. **2** a member of one of these peoples.

arb /ɑːb/ *n. colloq.* = ARBITRAGEUR. [abbreviation]

arbalest /'ɑːbəlɛst/ *n.* (also **arblast** /'ɑːblɑːst/) *hist.* a crossbow with a mechanism for drawing the string. [Old English *arblast* via Old French *arbaleste* and Late Latin *arcubalista* from Latin *arcus* 'bow' + BALLISTA]

arbiter /'ɑːbɪtə/ *n.* (*fem.* **arbitress** /-trɪs/) **1 a** an arbitrator in a dispute. **b** a judge; an authority (*arbiter of taste*). **2** (often foll. by *of*) a person who has entire control of something. [Latin]

arbiter elegantiarum /ˌɛlɪgantɪ'ɑːrəm/ *n.* (also **arbiter elegantiae** /ɛlɪ'gantɪʌɪ/) a judge of artistic taste and etiquette.

arbitrage /'ɑːbɪtrɪdʒ, ɑːbɪ'trɑːʒ/ *n.* the buying and selling of stocks or bills of exchange to take advantage of varying prices in different markets. [French, from *arbitrer* (as ARBITRATE)]

arbitrageur /ˌɑːbɪtrɑː'ʒəː/ *n.* (also **arbitrager** /'ɑːbɪtrɪdʒə/) a person who engages in arbitrage. [French]

arbitral /'ɑːbɪtr(ə)l/ *adj.* concerning arbitration. [French *arbitral* or Late Latin *arbitralis*: see ARBITER]

arbitrament /ɑː'bɪtrəm(ə)nt/ *n.* **1** the deciding of a dispute by an arbiter. **2** an authoritative decision made by an arbiter. [Middle English via Old French *arbitrement* from medieval Latin *arbitramentum* (as ARBITRATE, -MENT)]

arbitrary /'ɑːbɪt(rə)ri/ *adj.* **1** based on or derived from uninformed opinion or random choice; capricious. **2** despotic. □ **arbitrarily** *adv.* **arbitrariness** *n.* [Latin *arbitrarius* or French *arbitraire* (as ARBITER, -ARY[1])]

arbitrate /'ɑːbɪtreɪt/ *v.tr. & intr.* decide by arbitration. [Latin *arbitrari* 'judge']

arbitration /ɑːbɪ'treɪʃ(ə)n/ *n.* the settlement of a dispute by an arbitrator. [Middle English via Old French from Latin *arbitratio -onis* (as ARBITER, -ATION)]

arbitrator /'ɑːbɪtreɪtə/ *n.* a person appointed to settle a dispute; an arbiter. □ **arbitratorship** *n.* [Middle English from Late Latin (as ARBITRATION, -OR[1])]

arbitress see ARBITER.

arblast var. of ARBALEST.

arbor[1] /'ɑːbə/ *n.* **1** an axle or spindle on which something revolves. **2** a device holding a tool in a lathe etc. [French *arbre* 'tree, axis', from Latin *arbor*]

arbor[2] *US* var. of ARBOUR.

arboraceous /ɑːbə'reɪʃəs/ *adj.* **1** treelike. **2** wooded. [Latin *arbor* 'tree' + -ACEOUS]

Arbor Day /'ɑːbə/ *n.* a day dedicated annually to public tree-planting in the US, Australia, and other countries. [Latin *arbor* 'tree']

arboreal /ɑː'bɔːrɪəl/ *adj.* of, living in, or connected with trees. [Latin *arboreus*, from *arbor* 'tree']

arboreous /ɑː'bɔːrɪəs/ *adj.* **1** wooded. **2** arboreal.

arborescent /ɑːbə'rɛs(ə)nt/ *adj.* treelike in growth or general appearance. □ **arborescence** *n.* [Latin *arborescere* 'grow into a tree', from *arbor* 'tree']

arboretum /ɑːbə'riːtəm/ *n.* (*pl.* **arboretums** or **arboreta** /-tə/) a botanical garden devoted to trees. [Latin, from *arbor* 'tree']

arboriculture /'ɑːb(ə)rɪkʌltʃə, ɑː'bɔːr-/ *n.* the cultivation of trees and shrubs. □ **arboricultural** /-'kʌltʃ(ə)r(ə)l/ *adj.* **arboriculturist** /-'kʌltʃ(ə)rɪst/ *n.* [Latin *arbor -oris* 'tree', on the pattern of *agriculture*]

arborization /ɑːb(ə)rʌɪ'zeɪʃ(ə)n/ *n.* (also **-isation**) a treelike arrangement esp. in anatomy.

arbor vitae /ˌɑːbə 'vʌɪtiː, 'viːtʌɪ/ *n.* = THUJA. [Latin, = tree of life]

arbour /'ɑːbə/ *n.* (*US* **arbor**) a shady garden alcove with the sides and roof formed by trees or climbing plants; a bower. □ **arboured** *adj.* [Middle English via Anglo-French *erber* and Old French *erbier*, from *erbe* 'herb', from Latin *herba*: phonetic change to *ar-* assisted by association with Latin *arbor* 'tree']

arbovirus /'ɑːbəvʌɪrəs/ *n. Med.* any of a group of viruses transmitted by mosquitoes, ticks, etc., and causing disease, e.g. yellow fever. [*ar*thropod-*bo*rne + VIRUS]

arbutus /ɑː'bjuːtəs, 'ɑːbjʊtəs/ *n.* **1** an evergreen tree or shrub of the genus *Arbutus* (heath family), with white or pink clusters of flowers and reddish berries, esp. the strawberry tree, *A. unedo*. **2** *US* = TRAILING ARBUTUS. [Latin]

ARC *abbr.* **1** *hist.* (in the UK) Agricultural Research Council. **2** Aids-related complex.

arc /ɑːk/ *n. & v.* ● *n.* **1** part of the circumference of a circle or any other curve. **2** *Electr.* a luminous discharge between two electrodes. ● *v.intr.* (**arced** /ɑːkt/; **arcing** /'ɑːkɪŋ/) form an arc. [Middle English via Old French from Latin *arcus* 'bow, curve']

arcade /ɑː'keɪd/ *n.* **1** a passage with an arched roof. **2** esp. *Brit.* any covered walk, esp. with shops along one or both sides. **3** *Archit.* a series of arches supporting or set along a wall. **4** = AMUSEMENT ARCADE. ▫ **arcaded** *adj.* **arcading** *n.* [French via Provençal *arcada* or Italian *arcata* from Romanic: related to ARCH[1]]

Arcadian /ɑːˈkeɪdɪən/ *n.* & *adj.* ● *n.* an idealized peasant or country dweller, esp. in poetry. ● *adj. poet.* of or relating to Arcady; ideally rustic. ▫ **Arcadianism** *n.* [Latin *Arcadius* from Greek *Arkadia*, a mountain district in the Peloponnese]

Arcady /ˈɑːkədi/ *n. poet.* an ideal rustic paradise. [Greek *Arkadia*: see ARCADIAN]

arcane /ɑːˈkeɪn/ *adj.* mysterious, secret; understood by few. ▫ **arcanely** *adv.* [French *arcane* or Latin *arcanus*, from *arcēre* 'shut up' from *arca* 'chest']

arcanum /ɑːˈkeɪnəm/ *n.* (*pl.* **arcana** /-nə/) (usu. in *pl.*) a mystery; a profound secret. [Latin, neut. of *arcanus*: see ARCANE]

arch[1] /ɑːtʃ/ *n.* & *v.* ● *n.* **1 a** a curved structure as an opening or a support for a bridge, roof, floor, etc. **b** an arch used in building as an ornament. **2** any arch-shaped curve, e.g. as on the inner side of the foot, the eyebrows, etc. ● *v.* **1** *tr.* provide with or form into an arch. **2** *tr.* span like an arch. **3** *intr.* form an arch. [Middle English from Old French *arche*, ultimately from Latin *arcus* 'arc']

arch[2] /ɑːtʃ/ *adj.* self-consciously or affectedly playful or teasing. ▫ **archly** *adv.* **archness** *n.* [ARCH-, originally in *arch rogue* etc.]

arch- /ɑːtʃ/ *comb. form* **1** chief, superior (*archbishop*; *archdiocese*; *archduke*). **2** pre-eminent of its kind (esp. in unfavourable senses) (*arch-enemy*). [Old English *arce-* or Old French *arche-*, ultimately from Greek *arkhos* 'chief']

Archaean /ɑːˈkiːən/ *adj.* & *n.* (*US* **Archean**) ● *adj.* of or relating to the earlier part of the Precambrian era, characterized by the absence of life (cf. PROTEROZOIC). ● *n.* this period. [Greek *arkhaios* 'ancient', from *arkhē* 'beginning']

archaeology /ɑːkɪˈɒlədʒi/ *n.* (*US* also **archeology**) the study of human history and prehistory through the excavation of sites and the analysis of physical remains. ▫ **archaeologic** /-ˈlɒdʒɪk/ *adj.* **archaeological** /-ˈlɒdʒɪk(ə)l/ *adj.* **archaeologically** /-ˈlɒdʒɪk(ə)li/ *adv.* **archaeologist** *n.* **archaeologize** *v.intr.* (also **-ise**). [modern Latin *archaeologia* from Greek *arkhaiologia* 'ancient history' (as ARCHAEAN, -LOGY)]

archaeopteryx /ɑːkɪˈɒptərɪks/ *n.* the oldest known fossil bird, *Archaeopteryx lithographica*, of the late Jurassic period, which has wings and feathers like a bird, but teeth and a bony tail like a reptile. [Greek *arkhaios* 'ancient' + *pterux* 'wing']

archaic /ɑːˈkeɪɪk/ *adj.* **1 a** antiquated. **b** (of a word etc.) no longer in ordinary use, though retained for special purposes. **2** primitive. **3** of an early period of art or culture, esp. the 7th–6th c. BC in Greece. ▫ **archaically** *adv.* [French *archaïque* from Greek *arkhaïkos* (as ARCHAEAN)]

archaism /ˈɑːkeɪɪz(ə)m/ *n.* **1** the retention or imitation of the old or obsolete, esp. in language or art. **2** an archaic word or expression. ▫ **archaistic** /-ˈɪstɪk/ *adj.* [modern Latin from Greek *arkhaïsmos*, from *arkhaïzō* (as ARCHAIZE, -ISM)]

archaize /ˈɑːkeɪʌɪz/ *v.* (also **-ise**) **1** *intr.* imitate archaic style, expression, etc. **2** *tr.* make (a work of art, literature, etc.) imitate the archaic in style etc. [Greek *arkhaïzō* 'be old-fashioned', from *arkhaios* 'ancient']

archangel /ˈɑːkeɪndʒ(ə)l, ɑːˈkeɪn-/ *n.* **1** an angel of the highest rank. **2** a member of the eighth order of the nine ranks of heavenly beings (see ORDER *n.* 19). ▫ **archangelic** /-anˈdʒɛlɪk/ *adj.* [Old English via Anglo-French *archangele* and ecclesiastical Latin *archangelus* from ecclesiastical Greek *arkhaggelos* (as ARCH-, ANGEL)]

archbishop /ɑːtʃˈbɪʃəp, *esp. in titles* ˈɑːtʃ-/ *n.* the chief bishop of a province. [Old English (as ARCH-, BISHOP)]

archbishopric /ɑːtʃˈbɪʃəprɪk/ *n.* the office or diocese of an archbishop. [Old English (as ARCH-, BISHOPRIC)]

archdeacon /ɑːtʃˈdiːkən, *esp. in titles* ˈɑːtʃ-/ *n.* **1** an Anglican cleric ranking below a bishop. **2** a member of the clergy of similar rank in other Churches. ▫ **archdeaconry** *n.* (*pl.* **-ies**). **archdeaconship** *n.* [Old English *arce-*, *ercediacon*, via ecclesiastical Latin *archidiaconus* from ecclesiastical Greek *arkhidiakonos* (as ARCH-, DEACON)]

archdiocese /ɑːtʃˈdʌɪəsɪs/ *n.* the diocese of an archbishop. ▫ **archdiocesan** /ɑːtʃdʌɪˈɒsɪs(ə)n/ *adj.*

archduke /ˈɑːtʃdjuːk/ *n.* (*fem.* **archduchess** /-dʌtʃɪs/) *hist.* the chief duke (esp. as the title of a son of the Emperor of Austria). ▫ **archducal** *adj.* **archduchy** /-dʌtʃi/ *n.* (*pl.* **-ies**). [Old French *archeduc* from medieval Latin *archidux -ducis* (as ARCH-, DUKE)]

Archean *US* var. of ARCHAEAN.

archegonium /ɑːkɪˈgəʊnɪəm/ *n.* (*pl.* **archegonia** /-ɪə/) *Bot.* the female sex organ in mosses, ferns, conifers, etc. [Latin, diminutive of Greek *arkhegonos* from *arkhe-* 'chief' + *gonos* 'race']

arch-enemy /ɑːtʃˈɛnəmi/ *n.* (*pl.* **-ies**) **1** a chief enemy. **2** the Devil.

archeology *US* var. of ARCHAEOLOGY.

archer /ˈɑːtʃə/ *n.* **1** a person who shoots with a bow and arrows. **2** (**the Archer**) the zodiacal sign or constellation Sagittarius. [Anglo-French from Old French *archier*, ultimately from Latin *arcus* 'bow']

archer fish *n.* a SE Asian fish that catches flying insects by shooting water at them from its mouth.

archery /ˈɑːtʃəri/ *n.* shooting with a bow and arrows, esp. as a sport. [Old French *archerie* from *archier* (as ARCHER, -ERY)]

archetype /ˈɑːkɪtʌɪp/ *n.* **1 a** an original model; a prototype. **b** a typical specimen. **2** (in Jungian psychology) a primitive mental image inherited from man's earliest ancestors, and supposed to be present in the collective unconscious. **3** a recurrent symbol or motif in literature, art, etc. ▫ **archetypal** /-ˈtʌɪp(ə)l/ *adj.* **archetypical** /-ˈtɪpɪk(ə)l/ *adj.* [Latin *archetypum* from Greek *arkhetupon* (as ARCH-, *tupos* 'stamp')]

archidiaconal /ˌɑːkɪdʌɪˈak(ə)n(ə)l/ *adj.* of or relating to an archdeacon. ▫ **archidiaconate** /-nət, -neɪt/ *n.* [medieval Latin *archidiaconalis* (as ARCH-, DIACONAL)]

archiepiscopal /ˌɑːkɪɪˈpɪskəp(ə)l/ *adj.* of or relating to an archbishop. ▫ **archiepiscopate** /-pət, -peɪt/ *n.* [ecclesiastical Latin *archiepiscopus* from Greek *arkhiepiskopos* 'archbishop']

archil var. of ORCHIL.

archimandrite /ɑːkɪˈmandrʌɪt/ *n.* **1** the superior of a large monastery or group of monasteries in the Orthodox Church. **2** an honorary title given to a monastic priest. [French *archimandrite* or ecclesiastical Latin *archimandrita*, from ecclesiastical Greek *arkhimandritēs* (as ARCH-, *mandra* 'monastery')]

Archimedean /ɑːkɪˈmiːdɪən/ *adj.* of or associated with the Greek mathematician Archimedes (d. 212 BC).

Archimedean screw *n.* a device of ancient origin for raising water by means of a spiral within a tube.

Archimedes' principle /ɑːkɪˈmiːdiːz/ *n.* the law that a body totally or partially immersed in a fluid is subject to an upward force equal in magnitude to the weight of fluid it displaces.

archipelago /ɑːkɪˈpɛləgəʊ/ *n.* (*pl.* **-os** or **-oes**) **1** a group of islands. **2** a sea with many islands. [Italian *arcipelago*, from Greek *arkhi-* 'chief' + *pelagos* 'sea' (originally = the Aegean Sea)]

architect /ˈɑːkɪtɛkt/ *n.* **1** a designer who prepares plans for buildings, ships, etc., and supervises their construction. **2** (foll. by *of*) a person who brings about a specified thing (*the architect of his own fortune*). [French *architecte* from Italian *architetto*, or their source Latin *architectus* from Greek *arkhitektōn* (as ARCH-, *tektōn* 'builder')]

architectonic /ˌɑːkɪtɛkˈtɒnɪk/ *adj.* & *n.* ● *adj.* **1** of or relating to architecture or architects. **2** of or relating to the systematization of knowledge. ● *n.* (in *pl.*; usu. treated as *sing.*) **1** the scientific study of architecture. **2**

the study of the systematization of knowledge. [Latin *architectonicus* from Greek *arkhitektonikos* (as ARCHITECT)]

architecture /ˈɑːkɪtɛktʃə/ *n.* **1** the art or science of designing and constructing buildings. **2** the style of a building as regards design and construction. **3** buildings or other structures collectively. **4** the conceptual structure and logical organization of a computer or computer-based system. □ **architectural** /-ˈtɛktʃ(ə)r(ə)l/ *adj.* **architecturally** /-ˈtɛktʃ(ə)r(ə)li/ *adv.* [French *architecture* or Latin *architectura*, from *architectus* (as ARCHITECT)]

architrave /ˈɑːkɪtreɪv/ *n.* **1** (in classical architecture) a main beam resting across the tops of columns. **2** the moulded frame around a doorway or window. **3** a moulding round the exterior of an arch. [French from Italian (as ARCH-, *trave* from Latin *trabs trabis* 'beam')]

archive /ˈɑːkʌɪv/ *n.* & *v.* ● *n.* (usu. in *pl.*) **1** a collection of esp. public or corporate documents or records. **2** the place where these are kept. ● *v.tr.* **1** place or store in an archive. **2** *Computing* transfer (data) to a less frequently used file, e.g. from disc to tape. □ **archival** /ɑːˈkʌɪv(ə)l/ *adj.* [French *archives* (pl.) via Latin *archi(v)a* from Greek *arkheia* 'public records', from *arkhē* 'government']

archivist /ˈɑːkɪvɪst/ *n.* a person who maintains and is in charge of archives.

archivolt /ˈɑːkɪvəʊlt/ *n.* **1** a band of mouldings round the lower curve of an arch. **2** the lower curve itself from impost to impost of the columns. [French *archivolte* or Italian *archivolto* (as ARC, VAULT)]

archlute /ˈɑːtʃl(j)uːt/ *n.* a bass lute with an extended neck and unstopped bass strings. [French *archiluth* (as ARCH-, LUTE¹)]

archon /ˈɑːkən/ *n.* each of the nine chief magistrates in ancient Athens. □ **archonship** *n.* [Greek *arkhōn* 'ruler' (pres. part. of *arkhō* 'rule') used as a noun]

archway /ˈɑːtʃweɪ/ *n.* **1** a vaulted passage. **2** an arched entrance.

arc lamp *n.* (also **arc light**) a light source using an electric arc.

arcology /ɑːˈkɒlədʒi/ *n.* (*pl.* **-ies**) an ideal city that is fully integrated with its natural environment. [blend of ARCHITECTURE and ECOLOGY]

Arctic /ˈɑːktɪk/ *adj.* & *n.* ● *adj.* **1** of or relating to the north polar regions. **2** (**arctic**) *colloq.* (esp. of weather) very cold. **3** (**arctic**) designed for use in arctic conditions (*arctic clothing*). ● *n.* **1** the regions north of the Arctic Circle. **2** (**arctic**) esp. *US* a thick waterproof overshoe. [Middle English via Old French *artique* and Latin *ar(c)ticus* from Greek *arktikos*, from *arktos* 'bear, Ursa Major, pole star']

Arctic Circle *n.* the parallel of latitude 66° 33′ N., forming an imaginary line round the Arctic regions.

Arctic Ocean *n.* the partly ice-covered expanse of ocean surrounding the North Pole.

arcuate /ˈɑːkjʊət/ *adj.* shaped like a bow; curved. [Latin *arcuatus*, past part. of *arcuare* 'curve', from *arcus* 'bow, curve']

arcus senilis /ˌɑːkʊs sɛˈniːlɪs/ *n.* a narrow opaque band commonly encircling the cornea in old age. [Latin, literally 'senile bow']

arc welding *n.* a method of welding using an electric arc to melt metals to be welded.

-ard /əd, ɑːd/ *suffix* **1** forming nouns in depreciatory senses (*drunkard*; *sluggard*). **2** forming nouns in other senses (*bollard*; *Spaniard*; *wizard*). [Middle English & Old French from German *-hard* 'hard, hardy']

ardent /ˈɑːd(ə)nt/ *adj.* **1** eager, zealous; (of persons or feelings) fervent, passionate. **2** burning. □ **ardency** *n.* **ardently** *adv.* [Middle English via Old French *ardant* from Latin *ardens -entis*, from *ardēre* 'burn']

ardour /ˈɑːdə/ *n.* (*US* **ardor**) zeal; burning enthusiasm; passion. [Middle English via Old French from Latin *ardor -oris*, from *ardēre* 'burn']

arduous /ˈɑːdjʊəs/ *adj.* **1** hard to achieve or overcome; laborious, strenuous. **2** steep, difficult (*an arduous path*). □ **arduously** *adv.* **arduousness** *n.* [Latin *arduus* 'steep, difficult']

are¹ /ɑː/ *2nd sing. present* & *1st, 2nd, 3rd pl. present* of BE.

are² /ɑː/ *n.* a metric unit of measure, equal to 100 square metres. [French, from Latin AREA]

area /ˈɛːrɪə/ *n.* **1** the extent or measure of a surface (*over a large area*; *3 acres in area*; *the area of a triangle*). **2** a region or tract (*the southern area*). **3** a space allocated for a specific purpose (*dining area*; *camping area*). **4** the scope or range of an activity or study. **5** a sunken enclosure giving access to the basement of a building. **6** (prec. by *the*) *Football* = PENALTY AREA. □ **areal** *adj.* [Latin, = vacant piece of level ground]

areaway /ˈɛːrɪəweɪ/ *n. N. Amer.* = AREA 5.

areca /ˈarɪkə, əˈriːkə/ *n.* a tropical Asian palm of the genus *Areca*. [Portuguese from Malayalam *ádekka*]

areca nut *n.* the astringent seed of a species of areca, *A. catechu*. Also called *betel-nut*.

areg *pl.* of ERG²

arena /əˈriːnə/ *n.* **1** the central part of an amphitheatre etc., where contests take place. **2** a scene of conflict; a sphere of action or discussion. [Latin *(h)arena* 'sand, sand-strewn place of combat']

arenaceous /arɪˈneɪʃəs/ *adj.* **1** (of rocks) containing sand; having a sandy texture. **2** sandlike. **3** (of plants) growing in sand. [Latin *arenaceus* (as ARENA, -ACEOUS)]

arena stage *n.* a stage situated with the audience all round it.

aren't /ɑːnt/ *contr.* **1** are not. **2** (in *interrog.*) am not (*aren't I coming too?*).

areola /əˈriːələ/ *n.* (*pl.* **areolae** /-liː/) **1** *Anat.* a circular pigmented area, esp. that surrounding a nipple. **2** any of the spaces between lines on a surface, e.g. of a leaf or an insect's wing. □ **areolar** *adj.* [Latin, diminutive of *area* AREA]

arête /əˈrɛt, əˈreɪt/ *n.* a sharp mountain ridge. [French, from Latin *arista* 'ear of corn, fishbone, spine']

argali /ˈɑːg(ə)li/ *n.* (*pl.* same) a large Asiatic wild sheep, *Ovis ammon*, with massive horns. [Mongolian]

argent /ˈɑːdʒ(ə)nt/ *n.* & *adj.* *Heraldry* silver; silvery white. [French, from Latin *argentum*]

argentiferous /ɑːdʒ(ə)nˈtɪf(ə)rəs/ *adj.* containing natural deposits of silver. [Latin *argentum* + -FEROUS]

Argentine /ˈɑːdʒ(ə)ntʌɪn/ *adj.* & *n.* (also **Argentinian** /-ˈtɪnɪən/) ● *adj.* of or relating to Argentina in S. America. ● *n.* **1** a native or national of Argentina. **2** a person of Argentine descent. □ **the Argentine** Argentina. [Spanish *Argentina* from Latin *argentum* 'silver' (a major historical export)]

argentine /ˈɑːdʒ(ə)ntʌɪn/ *adj.* of silver; silvery. [French *argentin* from *argent* 'silver']

argil /ˈɑːdʒɪl/ *n.* clay, esp. that used in pottery. □ **argillaceous** *adj.* [French *argille* via Latin *argilla* from Greek *argillos*, from *argos* 'white']

arginine /ˈɑːdʒɪniːn/ *n.* a basic amino acid present in many animal proteins and an essential nutrient in the vertebrate diet. [German *Arginin*, perhaps from Greek *arginoeis* 'bright-shining, white']

Argive /ˈɑːgʌɪv, -dʒʌɪv/ *adj.* & *n.* ● *adj.* **1** of Argos in ancient Greece. **2** *literary* (esp. in Homeric contexts) Greek. ● *n.* **1** a citizen of Argos. **2** (usu. in *pl.*) *literary* a Greek. [Latin *Argivus* from Greek *Argeios*]

argol /ˈɑːg(ə)l/ *n.* crude potassium hydrogen tartrate. [Middle English from Anglo-French *argoile*, of unknown origin]

argon /ˈɑːgɒn/ *n.* *Chem.* an inert gaseous element of the noble gas group, forming almost 1 per cent of the earth's atmosphere (symbol Ar). [Greek, neut. of *argos* 'idle' (as A-¹ + *ergon* 'work')]

argosy /ˈɑːgəsi/ *n.* (*pl.* **-ies**) *poet.* a large merchant ship, originally esp. from Ragusa (now Dubrovnik) or Venice. [probably Italian *Ragusea* (*nave*) 'Ragusan (vessel)']

argot /ˈɑːgəʊ/ *n.* the jargon of a group or class, formerly esp. of criminals. [French: ultimate origin unknown]

arguable /ˈɑːɡjʊəb(ə)l/ *adj.* open to argument or disagreement; debatable. □ **arguably** *adv.*

argue /ˈɑːɡjuː/ *v.* (**argues**, **argued**, **arguing**) **1** *intr.* (often foll. by *with*, *about*, etc.) exchange views or opinions, especially heatedly or contentiously (with a person). **2** *tr.* & *intr.* (often foll. by *that* + clause) indicate; maintain by reasoning. **3** *intr.* (foll. by *for*, *against*) reason (*argued against joining*). **4** *tr.* treat by reasoning (*argue the point*). **5** *tr.* (foll. by *into*, *out of*) persuade (*argued me into going*). □ **argue the toss** esp. *Brit. colloq.* dispute a decision or choice already made. □ **arguer** *n.* [Middle English via Old French *arguer* from Latin *argutari* 'prattle', frequentative of *arguere* 'make clear, prove, accuse']

argufy /ˈɑːɡjʊfʌɪ/ *v.intr.* (**-ies**, **-ied**) *colloq.* argue excessively or tediously. [fanciful from ARGUE: cf. SPEECHIFY]

argument /ˈɑːɡjʊm(ə)nt/ *n.* **1** an exchange of views, esp. a contentious or prolonged one. **2** (often foll. by *for*, *against*) a reason advanced; a reasoning process (*an argument for abolition*). **3** a summary of the subject matter or line of reasoning of a book. **4** *Math.* an independent variable determining the value of a function. [Middle English via Old French from Latin *argumentum*, from *arguere* (as ARGUE, -MENT)]

argumentation /ˌɑːɡjʊmɛnˈteɪʃ(ə)n/ *n.* **1** methodical reasoning. **2** debate or argument. [French from Latin *argumentatio*, from *argumentari* (as ARGUMENT, -ATION)]

argumentative /ɑːɡjʊˈmɛntətɪv/ *adj.* **1** fond of arguing; quarrelsome. **2** using methodical reasoning. □ **argumentatively** *adv.* **argumentativeness** *n.* [French *argumentatif -ive* or Late Latin *argumentativus* (as ARGUMENT, -ATIVE)]

argument from design *n.* (in Christian theology) the argument that God's existence is provable by the evidence of design in the universe.

Argus /ˈɑːɡəs/ *n.* **1** a watchful guardian. **2** an Asiatic pheasant having markings on its tail resembling eyes. **3** a butterfly having markings resembling eyes. [Middle English via Latin from Greek *Argos*, the name of a mythical watchman with a hundred eyes]

Argus-eyed *adj.* vigilant.

argute /ɑːˈɡjuːt/ *adj. literary* **1** sharp or shrewd. **2** (of sounds) shrill. [Middle English from Latin *argutus*, past part. of *arguere*: see ARGUE]

argy-bargy /ˌɑːdʒɪˈbɑːdʒi, ˌɑːɡɪˈbɑːɡi/ *n.* & *v. joc.* esp. *Brit.* ● *n.* (*pl.* **-ies**) a dispute or wrangle. ● *v.intr.* (**-ies**, **-ied**) quarrel, esp. loudly. [originally Scots]

aria /ˈɑːrɪə/ *n. Mus.* a long accompanied song for solo voice in an opera, oratorio, etc. [Italian, = tune, air]

Arian /ˈɛːrɪən/ *n.* & *adj.* ● *n.* an adherent of the doctrine of Arius of Alexandria (4th c.), who denied the divinity of Christ. ● *adj.* of or concerning this doctrine. □ **Arianism** *n.*

-arian /ˈɛːrɪən/ *suffix* forming adjectives and nouns meaning '(one) concerned with or believing in' (*agrarian*; *antiquarian*; *humanitarian*; *vegetarian*). [Latin *-arius* (see -ARY[1])]

arid /ˈarɪd/ *adj.* **1** **a** (of ground, climate, etc.) dry, parched. **b** too dry to support vegetation; barren. **2** uninteresting (*arid verse*). □ **aridity** /əˈrɪdɪti/ *n.* **aridly** *adv.* **aridness** *n.* [French *aride* or Latin *aridus*, from *arēre* 'be dry']

ariel /ˈɛːrɪəl/ *n.* a Middle Eastern and African gazelle, *Gazella arabica*. [Arabic *'aryal*]

Aries /ˈɛːriːz/ *n.* (*pl.* same) **1** *Astron.* a small constellation (the Ram), said to represent the ram whose Golden Fleece was sought by Jason and the Argonauts. **2** *Astrol.* **a** the first sign of the zodiac, which the sun enters at the vernal equinox (about 20 Mar.). **b** a person born when the sun is in this sign. □ **Arian** /-rɪən/ *adj.* & *n.* [Middle English from Latin, = ram]

aright /əˈrʌɪt/ *adv.* rightly. [Old English (as A[2], RIGHT)]

aril /ˈarɪl/ *n. Bot.* an extra seed-covering, often coloured and hairy or fleshy, e.g. the red fleshy cup around a yew seed. □ **arillate** *adj.* [modern Latin *arillus*, of unknown origin: cf. medieval Latin *arilli* 'dried grape-stones']

arioso /arɪˈəʊzəʊ, ɑː-/ *adj.*, *adv.*, & *n. Mus.* ● *adj.* & *adv.* in a melodious songlike style. ● *n.* (*pl.* **-os**) a piece of music to be performed in this way. [Italian, from ARIA]

-arious /ˈɛːrɪəs/ *suffix* forming adjectives (*gregarious*; *vicarious*). [Latin *-arius* (see -ARY[1]) + -OUS]

arise /əˈrʌɪz/ *v.intr.* (*past* **arose** /əˈrəʊz/; *past part.* **arisen** /əˈrɪz(ə)n/) **1** begin to exist; originate. **2** (usu. foll. by *from*, *out of*) result (*accidents can arise from carelessness*). **3** come to one's notice; emerge (*the question of payment arose*). **4** *archaic* or *poet.* rise or get up. [Old English *ārīsan* (as A-[2], RISE)]

arisings /əˈrʌɪzɪŋz/ *n.pl.* materials forming the secondary or waste products of industrial operations.

aristocracy /arɪˈstɒkrəsi/ *n.* (*pl.* **-ies**) **1** **a** the highest class in society; the nobility. **b** the nobility as a ruling class. **2** **a** government by the nobility or a privileged group. **b** a state governed in this way. **3** **a** (often foll. by *of*) the best representatives or upper echelons (*aristocracy of intellect*; *aristocracy of labour*). **b** any group which is privileged or is regarded as superior. [French *aristocratie* from Greek *aristokratia*, from *aristos* 'best' + *kratia* (as -CRACY)]

aristocrat /ˈarɪstəkrat, əˈrɪst-/ *n.* a member of the nobility. [French *aristocrate* (as ARISTOCRATIC)]

aristocratic /ˌarɪstəˈkratɪk/ *adj.* **1** of or relating to the aristocracy. **2** **a** distinguished in manners or bearing. **b** grand; stylish. □ **aristocratically** *adv.* [French *aristocratique* from Greek *aristokratikos* (as ARISTOCRACY)]

Aristotelian /ˌarɪstəˈtiːlɪən/ *n.* & *adj.* ● *n.* a disciple or student of the Greek philosopher Aristotle (d. 322 BC). ● *adj.* of or concerning Aristotle or his ideas.

Aristotle's lantern /ˈarɪstɒt(ə)lz/ *n. Zool.* a conical structure of calcareous plates and muscles supporting the rasping teeth of a sea urchin.

Arita /əˈriːtə/ *n.* (usu. *attrib.*) a type of Japanese porcelain characterized by asymmetric decoration. [the town of *Arita* in Japan, where it is made]

arithmetic *n.* & *adj.* ● *n.* /əˈrɪθmətɪk/ **1** **a** the science of numbers. **b** one's knowledge of this (*have improved my arithmetic*). **2** the use of numbers; computation (*a problem involving arithmetic*). ● *adj.* /arɪθˈmɛtɪk/ (also **arithmetical** /-ˈmɛtɪk(ə)l/) of or concerning arithmetic. □ **arithmetician** /ərɪθməˈtɪʃ(ə)n/ *n.* [Middle English via Old French *arismetique* and Latin *arithmetica* from Greek *arithmētikē* (*tekhnē*) 'art of counting', from *arithmos* 'number']

arithmetic mean *n.* the central number in an arithmetic progression.

arithmetic progression *n.* **1** an increase or decrease by a constant quantity (e.g. 1, 2, 3, 4, etc., 9, 7, 5, 3, etc.). **2** a sequence of numbers showing this.

arithmetic series *n.* a series in arithmetic progression.

-arium /ˈɛːrɪəm/ *suffix* forming nouns usu. denoting a place (*aquarium*; *planetarium*). [Latin, neut. of adjs. ending in *-arius*: see -ARY[1]]

Ariz. *abbr.* Arizona.

Ark. *abbr.* Arkansas.

ark /ɑːk/ *n.* **1** = NOAH'S ARK 1. **2** *archaic* a chest or box. □ **out of the ark** *colloq.* very antiquated. [Old English *ærc* from Latin *arca* 'chest']

Ark of the Covenant *n.* (also **Ark of the Testimony**) a chest or cupboard containing the scrolls or tables of Jewish Law.

arm[1] /ɑːm/ *n.* **1** each of the two upper limbs of the human body from the shoulder to the hand. **2** **a** the forelimb of an animal. **b** the flexible limb of an invertebrate animal (e.g. an octopus). **3** **a** the sleeve of a garment. **b** the side part of a chair etc., used to support a sitter's arm. **c** a thing resembling an arm in branching from a main stem (*an arm of the sea*). **d** a large branch of a tree. **4** a control; a means of reaching (*arm of the law*). **5** a subsidiary company or specialist branch of a business, institution, etc. □ **an arm and a leg** *colloq.* a large sum of money. **arm in arm** (of two or more persons) with arms linked. **as long as your** (or **my**) **arm** *colloq.* very long. **at arm's length 1** as far as an arm can reach. **2** far enough to avoid undue familiarity. **in arms** (of a baby) too young to walk. **in a person's arms** embraced. **on one's arm** supported by one's arm. **under one's arm** between the arm and the body. **within arm's reach** reachable without moving one's position. **with open arms** cordially. □ **armful** *n.* (*pl.* **-fuls**). **armless** *adj.* [Old English, from Germanic]

arm[2] /ɑːm/ *n. & v.* ● *n.* **1** (usu. in *pl.*) **a** a weapon. **b** = FIREARM. **2** (in *pl.*) the military profession. **3** a branch of the military, of the armed forces, or other organization. **4** (in *pl.*) heraldic devices (*coat of arms*). ● *v.tr. & refl.* **1** supply with weapons. **2** supply with tools or other requisites or advantages (*armed with the truth*). **3** make (a bomb etc.) able to explode. □ **in arms** armed. **lay down one's arms** cease fighting. **take up arms** begin fighting. **under arms** ready for war or battle. **up in arms** (usu. foll. by *against, about*) actively rebelling. □ **armless** *adj.* [Middle English via Old French *armes* (*pl.*), *armer* (*v.*), from Latin *arma* 'arms, fittings']

armada /ɑːˈmɑːdə/ *n.* a fleet of warships, esp. that sent by Spain against England in 1588. [Spanish, from Romanic *armata* 'army']

armadillo /ɑːməˈdɪləʊ/ *n.* (*pl.* **-os**) a nocturnal insect-eating edentate mammal of the family Dasypodidae, native to Central and S. America, with large claws for digging and a body covered in bony plates, often rolling itself into a ball when threatened. [Spanish, diminutive of *armado* 'armed man' from Latin *armatus*, past part. of *armare* 'to arm']

Armageddon /ɑːməˈgɛd(ə)n/ *n.* **1** (in the New Testament): **a** the last battle between good and evil before the Day of Judgement. **b** the place where this will be fought. **2** a bloody battle or struggle on a huge scale. [Greek, from Hebrew *har megiddōn* 'hill of Megiddo': see Rev. 16:16]

armament /ˈɑːməm(ə)nt/ *n.* **1** (often in *pl.*) military weapons and equipment, esp. guns on a warship. **2** the process of equipping for war. **3** *archaic* a force equipped for war. [Latin *armamentum* (as ARM[2], -MENT)]

armamentarium /ɑːməmenˈtɛːrɪəm/ *n.* (*pl.* **armamentaria** /-rɪə/) **1** a set of medical equipment or drugs. **2** the resources available to a person engaged in a task. [Latin, = arsenal]

armature /ˈɑːmətʃə, -tjə/ *n.* **1 a** the rotating coil or coils of a dynamo or electric motor. **b** any moving part of an electrical machine in which a voltage is induced by a magnetic field. **2** = KEEPER 6. **3** *Biol.* the protective covering of an animal or plant. **4** a metal framework on which a sculpture is moulded with clay or similar material. **5** *archaic* arms; armour. [French, from Latin *armatura* 'armour' (as ARM[2], -URE)]

armband /ˈɑːmband/ *n.* a band worn around the upper arm to hold up a shirtsleeve or as a form of identification etc.

armchair *n.* **1** /ɑːmˈtʃɛː, ˈɑːm-/ a comfortable, usu. upholstered, chair with side supports for the arms. **2** /ˈɑːmtʃɛː/ (*attrib.*) theoretical rather than active or practical (*an armchair critic*).

armed forces *n.pl.* the army, navy, and air force as fighting resources.

Armenian /ɑːˈmiːnɪən/ *n. & adj.* ● *n.* **1 a** a native of Armenia in the Caucasus. **b** a person of Armenian descent. **2** the language of Armenia. ● *adj.* of or relating to Armenia, its language, or the Christian Church established there *c.*300.

armhole /ˈɑːmhəʊl/ *n.* each of two holes in a garment through which the arms are put, usu. into a sleeve.

armiger /ˈɑːmɪdʒə/ *n.* a person entitled to heraldic arms. [Latin, = bearing arms, from *arma* 'arms' + *gerere* 'bear']

armillary sphere *n. hist.* a representation of the celestial globe constructed from metal rings and showing the equator, the tropics, etc. [modern Latin *armillaris* from *armilla* 'bracelet']

Arminian /ɑːˈmɪnɪən/ *adj. & n.* ● *adj.* relating to the doctrine of Arminius, a Dutch Protestant theologian (d. 1609), who opposed the views of Calvin, esp. on predestination. ● *n.* an adherent of this doctrine. □ **Arminianism** *n.*

armistice /ˈɑːmɪstɪs/ *n.* a stopping of hostilities by common agreement of the opposing sides; a truce. [French *armistice* or modern Latin *armistitium*, from *arma* 'arms' (ARM[2]) + *-stitium* 'stoppage']

Armistice Day *n.* the anniversary of the armistice of 11 Nov. 1918 (cf. REMEMBRANCE SUNDAY).

armlet /ˈɑːmlɪt/ *n.* **1** a band worn round the arm. **2** a small inlet of the sea, or branch of a river.

armlock /ˈɑːmlɒk/ *n.* a close hold by the arm in wrestling or judo.

armoire /ɑːˈmwɑː/ *n.* a cupboard or wardrobe, esp. one that is ornate or antique. [French: see AUMBRY]

armor *US* var. of ARMOUR.

armorer *US* var. of ARMOURER.

armory[1] /ˈɑːməri/ *n.* (*pl.* **-ies**) heraldry. □ **armorial** /ɑːˈmɔːrɪəl/ *adj.* [Old French *armoierie*: see ARMOURY]

armory[2] *US* var. of ARMOURY.

armour /ˈɑːmə/ *n. & v.* (*US* **armor**) ● *n.* **1** a defensive covering, usu. of metal, formerly worn to protect the body in fighting. **2 a** (in full **armour-plate**) a protective metal covering for an armed vehicle, ship, etc. **b** armoured fighting vehicles collectively. **3** a protective covering or shell on certain animals and plants. **4** heraldic devices. ● *v.tr.* (usu. as **armoured** *adj.*) provide with a protective covering, and often with guns (*armoured car*; *armoured train*). [Middle English via Old French *armure* from Latin *armatura*: see ARMATURE]

armourer /ˈɑːmərə/ *n.* (*US* **armorer**) **1** a maker or repairer of arms or armour. **2** an official in charge of a ship's or a regiment's arms. [Anglo-French *armurer*, Old French *-urier* (as ARMOUR, -ER[5])]

armoury /ˈɑːməri/ *n.* (*US* also **armory**) (*pl.* **-ies**) **1** a place where arms are kept; an arsenal. **2** an array of weapons, defensive resources, usable material, etc. **3** *US* a place where arms are manufactured. **4** (in *pl.*) (in Canada) a place where militia units drill and train. [Middle English from Old French *armoirie, armoierie* from *armoier* 'to blazon', from *arme* ARM[2]: assimilated to ARMOUR]

armpit /ˈɑːmpɪt/ *n.* **1** the hollow under the arm at the shoulder; also called AXILLA. **2** *N. Amer. colloq.* a place or part considered disgusting or contemptible (*the armpit of the world*).

armrest /ˈɑːmrɛst/ *n.* = ARM[1] 3b.

arms control *n.* international disarmament or arms limitation, esp. by mutual agreement.

arms race *n.* (usu. prec. by *the*) competition between nations for superiority in the development and accumulation of weapons.

arm-twisting *n. colloq.* persuasion by the use of physical force or (esp.) moral pressure.

arm-wrestling *n.* a trial of strength in which each party tries to force the other's arm down on to a table on which their elbows rest.

army /ˈɑːmi/ *n.* (*pl.* **-ies**) **1** an organized force armed for fighting on land. **2** (prec. by *the*) the military profession. **3** (often foll. by *of*) a very large number (*an army of locusts*; *an army of helpers*). **4** an organized body regarded as fighting for a particular cause (*Salvation Army*). [Middle English via Old French *armee* from Romanic *armata*, fem. past part. of *armare* 'arm']

army ant *n.* any ant of the subfamily Dorylinae, foraging in large groups.

Army List *n.* (in the UK) an official list of commissioned officers.

army worm *n.* any of various moth or fly larvae occurring in destructive swarms.

arnica /ˈɑːnɪkə/ *n.* **1** a plant of the genus *Arnica* (daisy family), having erect stems bearing yellow daisy-like flower heads, e.g. mountain tobacco. **2** a medicine prepared from this, used for bruises etc. [modern Latin: ultimate origin unknown]

aroid /ˈɛːrɔɪd/ *adj.* of or relating to the family Araceae, including arums. [ARUM + -OID]

aroma /əˈrəʊmə/ *n.* **1** a fragrance; a distinctive and pleasing smell, often of food. **2** a subtle pervasive quality. [Latin, from Greek *arōma -atos* 'spice']

aromatherapy /ərəʊməˈθɛrəpi/ *n.* the use of aromatic plant extracts and essential oils in massage or other treatment. □ **aromatherapeutic** /-ˈpjuːtɪk/ *adj.* **aromatherapist** *n.*

aromatic /arəˈmatɪk/ *adj. & n.* ● *adj.* **1** fragrant, spicy; (of a smell) pleasantly pungent. **2** *Chem.* (of an organic compound) having an unsaturated ring, esp. a benzene ring. ● *n.* an aromatic substance. □ **aromatically** *adv.* **aromaticity** /arəməˈtɪsɪti/ *n.* [Middle English via Old French *aromatique* and Late Latin *aromaticus* from Greek *arōmatikos* (as AROMA, -IC)]

aromatize /əˈrəʊmətʌɪz/ *v.tr.* (also **-ise**) *Chem.* convert (a compound) into an aromatic structure. □ **aromatization** /-ˈzeɪʃ(ə)n/ *n.*

arose *past* of ARISE.

around /əˈraʊnd/ *adv. & prep.* ● *adv.* **1** on every side; all round; round about. **2** in various places; here and there; at random (*fool around*; *shop around*). **3** *colloq.* **a** in existence; available (*has been around for weeks*). **b** near at hand (*it's good to have you around*). **4** approximately (*around 400 people attended*). ● *prep.* **1** on or along the circuit of. **2** on every side of; enveloping. **3** here and there in; here and there near (*chairs around the room*). **4** *N. Amer.* (and increasingly *Brit.*) **a** round (*the church around the corner*). **b** approximately at; at a time near to (*come around four o'clock*; *happened around June*). □ **have been around** *colloq.* be widely experienced. [A² + ROUND]

arouse /əˈraʊz/ *v.tr.* **1** induce; call into existence (esp. a feeling, emotion, etc.). **2** awake from sleep. **3** stir into activity. **4** stimulate sexually. □ **arousable** *adj.* **arousal** *n.* [A-² + ROUSE]

arpeggio /ɑːˈpɛdʒɪəʊ/ *n.* (*pl.* **-os**) *Mus.* the notes of a chord played in succession, either ascending or descending. [Italian, from *arpeggiare* 'play the harp' from *arpa* 'harp']

arquebus var. of HARQUEBUS.

arr. *abbr.* **1** *Mus.* arranged by. **2** arrives.

arrack /ˈarək/ *n.* (also **arak** /əˈrak/) an alcoholic spirit, esp. distilled from coco sap or rice. [Arabic *ʻarak* 'sweat', *ʻarak al-tamr* 'alcoholic spirit from dates']

arraign /əˈreɪn/ *v.tr.* **1** indict before a tribunal; accuse. **2** find fault with; call into question (an action or statement). □ **arraignment** *n.* [Middle English via Anglo-French *arainer* from Old French *araisnier* (ultimately as AD-, Latin *ratio -onis* 'reason, account')]

arrange /əˈreɪn(d)ʒ/ *v.* **1** *tr.* put into the required order; classify. **2** *tr.* plan or provide for; cause to occur (*arranged a meeting*). **3** *tr.* settle beforehand the order or manner of. **4** *intr.* take measures; form plans; give instructions (*arrange to be there at eight; arranged for a taxi to come*; *will you arrange about the cake?*). **5** *intr.* come to an agreement (*arranged with her to meet later*). **6** *tr.* **a** *Mus.* adapt (a composition) for performance with instruments or voices other than those originally specified. **b** adapt (a play etc.) for broadcasting. **7** *tr. archaic* settle (a dispute, claim, etc.). □ **arrangeable** *adj.* **arranger** *n.* (esp. in sense 6). [Middle English from Old French *arangier*, from *à* 'to' + *rangier* RANGE]

arrangement /əˈreɪn(d)ʒm(ə)nt/ *n.* **1** the act or process of arranging or being arranged. **2** the condition of being arranged; the manner in which a thing is arranged. **3** something arranged. **4** (in *pl.*) plans, measures (*make your own arrangements*). **5** *Mus.* a composition arranged for performance by different instruments or voices (see ARRANGE 6a). **6** settlement of a dispute etc. [French (as ARRANGE, -MENT)]

arrant /ˈar(ə)nt/ *attrib.adj.* downright, utter, notorious (*arrant liar*; *arrant nonsense*). □ **arrantly** *adv.* [Middle English, variant of ERRANT, originally in phrases like *arrant* (= outlawed, roving) *thief*]

arras /ˈarəs/ *n. hist.* a rich tapestry, often hung on the walls of a room, or to conceal an alcove. [from *Arras*, a town in NE France famous for the fabric]

array /əˈreɪ/ *n. & v.* ● *n.* **1** an imposing or well-ordered series or display. **2** an ordered arrangement, esp. of troops (*battle array*). **3** *poet.* an outfit or dress (*in fine array*). **4 a** *Math.* an arrangement of quantities or symbols in rows and columns; a matrix. **b** *Computing* an ordered set of related elements. **5** *Law* a list of jurors empanelled. ● *v.tr.* **1** deck, adorn. **2** set in order; marshal (forces). **3** *Law* empanel (a jury). [Middle English from Anglo-French *araier*, Old French *areer*, ultimately from Latin *ad* AR- + a Germanic root meaning 'prepare']

arrears /əˈrɪəz/ *n.pl.* an amount still outstanding or uncompleted, esp. work undone or a debt unpaid. □ **in arrears** (or **arrear**) behindhand, esp. in payment. □ **arrearage** *n.* [Middle English (originally as *adv.*) via Old French *arere* from medieval Latin *adretro* (as AD-, *retro* 'backwards'): first used in the phrase *in arrear*]

arrest /əˈrɛst/ *v. & n.* ● *v.tr.* **1 a** seize (a person) and take into custody, esp. by legal authority. **b** seize (a ship) by legal authority. **2** stop or check (esp. a process or moving thing). **3 a** attract (a person's attention). **b** attract the attention of (a person). ● *n.* **1** the act of arresting or being arrested, esp. the legal seizure of a person. **2** a stoppage or check (*cardiac arrest*). □ **arrest of judgement** *Law* the staying of proceedings, notwithstanding a verdict, on the grounds of a material irregularity in the course of the trial. □ **arrestingly** *adv.* [Middle English from Old French *arester*, ultimately from Latin *restare* 'remain, stop']

arrestable /əˈrɛstəb(ə)l/ *adj.* **1** susceptible of arrest. **2** *Law* (esp. of an offence) such that the offender may be arrested without a warrant.

arrester /əˈrɛstə/ *n.* (also **arrestor**) a device, esp. on an aircraft carrier, for slowing an aircraft by means of a hook and cable after landing.

arrestment /əˈrɛs(t)m(ə)nt/ *n.* esp. *Sc.* attachment of property for the satisfaction of a debt.

arrhythmia /əˈrɪðmɪə/ *n. Med.* deviation from the normal rhythm of the heart. [Greek *arruthmia* 'lack of rhythm' (as A-¹, RHYTHM, -IA¹)]

arrière-pensée /arɪɛːˈpɒnseɪ, French arjɛrpɑ̃se/ *n.* **1** an undisclosed motive. **2** a mental reservation. [French, = behind thought]

arris /ˈarɪs/ *n. Archit.* a sharp edge formed by the meeting of two flat or curved surfaces. [corruption from French *areste*, modern ARÊTE]

arrival /əˈrʌɪv(ə)l/ *n.* **1 a** the act or an instance of arriving. **b** an appearance on the scene. **2** a person or thing that has arrived. [Middle English from Anglo-French *arrivaille* (as ARRIVE, -AL)]

arrive /əˈrʌɪv/ *v.intr.* (often foll. by *at*, *in*) **1** reach a destination; come to the end of a journey or a specified part of a journey (*arrived in Tibet*; *arrived at the station*; *arrived late*). **2** (foll. by *at*) reach (a conclusion, decision, etc.). **3** *colloq.* establish one's reputation or position. **4** *colloq.* (of a child) be born. **5** (of a thing) be brought (*the flowers have arrived*). **6** (of a time) come (*her birthday arrived at last*). [Middle English, in the sense 'reach the end of a voyage', from Old French *ariver*, ultimately as AD- + Latin *ripa* 'shore']

arriviste /ariːˈviːst/ *n.* an ambitious or ruthlessly self-seeking person. [French from *arriver* (as ARRIVE, -IST)]

arrogant /ˈarəg(ə)nt/ *adj.* (of a person, attitude, etc.) aggressively assertive or presumptuous; overbearing. □ **arrogance** *n.* **arrogantly** *adv.* [Middle English from Old French (as ARROGATE, -ANT)]

arrogate /ˈarəgeɪt/ *v.tr.* **1** (often foll. by *to* oneself) claim (power, responsibility, etc.) without justification. **2**

(often foll. by *to*) attribute unjustly (to a person). □ **arrogation** /-'geɪʃ(ə)n/ *n.* [Latin *arrogare arrogat-* (as AD-, *rogare* 'ask')]

arrondissement /a'rɒndi:smɑ̃, arɒn'di:smɑ̃/ *n.* **1** a subdivision of a French department, for local government administration purposes. **2** an administrative district of a large city, esp. Paris. [French]

arrow /'arəʊ/ *n.* & *v.* ● *n.* **1** a sharp pointed wooden or metal stick shot from a bow as a weapon. **2** a drawn or printed etc. representation of an arrow indicating a direction; a pointer. ● *v.* **1** *intr.* move like an arrow; move swiftly. **2** *tr.* (as **arrowed** *adj.*) provided or marked with an arrow or arrows. □ **arrowy** *adj.* [Old English *ar(e)we* via Old Norse *ör* from Germanic]

arrow-grass *n.* a marsh plant of the genus *Triglochin.*

arrowhead /'arəʊhɛd/ *n.* **1** the pointed end of an arrow. **2** a water plant, *Sagittaria sagittaria*, with arrow-shaped leaves. **3** a decorative device resembling an arrowhead.

arrowroot /'arə(ʊ)ru:t/ *n.* a plant of the family Marantaceae, esp *Maranta arundinacea* of the W. Indies, from which a starch is prepared and used for nutritional and medicinal purposes. [alteration of Arawak *aru-aru* (literally 'meal of meals') by assimilation to ARROW and ROOT[1], the tubers having been used to absorb poison from arrow wounds]

arrow worm *n.* = CHAETOGNATH.

arroyo /ə'rɔɪəʊ/ *n.* (*pl.* **-os**) esp. *US* **1** a usu. dry gully cut by a stream, esp. in arid regions. **2** a brook or stream. [Spanish]

arse /ɑ:s/ *n.* & *v.* (*N. Amer.* **ass** /as/) *coarse slang* ● *n.* the buttocks. ● *v.intr.* (usu. foll. by *about, around*) play the fool. [Old English *ærs*]

arsehole /'ɑ:shəʊl/ *n.* (*N. Amer.* **asshole** /'as-/) *coarse slang* **1** the anus. **2** *offens.* a term of contempt for a person.

arse-licking *n.* (*N. Amer.* **ass-licking**) *coarse slang* obsequiousness for the purpose of gaining favour; toadying. □ **arse-licker** *n.*

arsenal /'ɑ:s(ə)n(ə)l/ *n.* **1** a store of weapons. **2** a government establishment for the storage and manufacture of weapons and ammunition. **3** resources of anything compared with weapons (e.g. abuse), regarded collectively. [obsolete French *arsenal* or Italian *arzanale* from Arabic *dārṣinā'a*, from *dār* 'house' + *sinā'a* 'art, industry' from *ṣana'a* 'fabricate']

arsenic *n.* & *adj.* ● *n.* /'ɑ:s(ə)nɪk/ **1** (in full **white arsenic**) a non-scientific name for arsenic trioxide, a highly poisonous white powdery substance used in weedkillers, rat poison, etc. **2** *Chem.* a brittle semi-metallic element, used in semiconductors and alloys (symbol As). ● *adj.* /ɑ:'sɛnɪk/ **1** of or concerning arsenic. **2** *Chem.* containing arsenic with its higher valency of five. [Middle English via Old French and Latin *arsenicum* from Greek *arsenikon* 'yellow orpiment', identified with *arsenikos* 'male', but in fact from Arabic *al-zarnīk*, from *al* 'the' + *zarnīk* 'orpiment', ultimately from Persian *zar* 'gold']

arsenical /ɑ:'sɛnɪk(ə)l/ *adj.* & *n.* ● *adj.* of or containing arsenic. ● *n.* a drug containing arsenic.

arsenious /ɑ:'si:nɪəs/ *adj.* *Chem.* containing arsenic with its lower valency of three.

arsine /'ɑ:si:n/ *n.* *Chem.* arsenic trihydride, a colourless poisonous gas smelling slightly of garlic. [ARSENIC on the pattern of *amine*]

arsis /'ɑ:sɪs/ *n.* (*pl.* **arses** /-si:z/) a stressed syllable or part of a metrical foot in Greek or Latin verse (opp. THESIS 3). [Middle English via Late Latin from Greek, = lifting, from *airō* 'raise']

arson /'ɑ:s(ə)n/ *n.* the act of maliciously setting fire to property. □ **arsonist** *n.* [legal Anglo-French, Old French, via medieval Latin *arsio -onis* from Latin *ardēre ars-* 'burn']

arsphenamine /ɑ:s'fɛnəmi:n, -ɪn/ *n.* a drug formerly used in the treatment of syphilis and parasitic diseases. [ARSENIC + PHENYL + AMINE]

art[1] /ɑ:t/ *n.* **1 a** human creative skill or its application. **b** work exhibiting this. **2 a** (in *pl.*; prec. by *the*) the various branches of creative activity concerned with the production of imaginative designs, sounds, or ideas, e.g. painting, music, writing, considered collectively. **b** any one of these branches. **3** creative activity, esp. painting and drawing, resulting in visual representation (*interested in music but not art*). **4** human skill or workmanship as opposed to the work of nature (*art and nature had combined to make her a great beauty*). **5** (often foll. by *of*) a skill, aptitude, or knack (*the art of writing clearly*; *keeping people happy is quite an art*). **6** (in *pl.*; usu. prec. by *the*) those branches of learning (esp. languages, literature, and history) associated with creative skill as opposed to scientific, technical, or vocational skills. [Middle English via Old French from Latin *ars artis*]

art[2] /ɑ:t/ *archaic* or *dial. 2nd sing. present* of BE.

art. *abbr.* article.

art deco /'dɛkəʊ/ *n.* the predominant decorative art style of the period 1910–30, characterized by precise and boldly delineated geometric motifs, shapes, and strong colours. [shortened from French *art décoratif*, from the 1925 *Exposition des Arts décoratifs* in Paris]

artefact /'ɑ:tɪfakt/ *n.* (*US* **artifact**) **1** a product of human art and workmanship. **2** *Archaeol.* a product of prehistoric or aboriginal workmanship as distinguished from a similar object naturally produced. **3** *Biol.* etc. a feature not naturally present, introduced during preparation or investigation (e.g. in the preparation of a microscope specimen). □ **artefactual** *adj.* (in senses 1 and 2). [Latin *arte* (ablative of *ars* 'art') + *factum* (neut. past part. of *facere* 'make')]

artel /ɑ:'tɛl/ *n.* an association of craftsmen, peasants, etc., in Russia and other countries of the former Soviet Union. [Russian]

artemisia /ɑ:tɪ'mɪzjə/ *n.* an aromatic or bitter-tasting plant of the genus *Artemisia* (daisy family), which includes wormwood, mugwort, sagebrush, etc. [Latin from Greek, = wormwood, from *Artemis*, the name of a goddess, to whom it was sacred]

arterial /ɑ:'tɪərɪəl/ *adj.* **1** of or relating to an artery (*arterial blood*). **2** (esp. of a road) main, important, esp. linking large cities or towns. [French *artériel* from *artère* ARTERY]

arterialize /ɑ:'tɪərɪəlʌɪz/ *v.tr.* (also **-ise**) **1** convert venous into arterial (blood) by reoxygenation esp. in the lungs. **2** provide with an arterial system. □ **arterialization** /-'zeɪʃ(ə)n/ *n.*

arteriole /ɑ:'tɪərɪəʊl/ *n.* a small branch of an artery leading into capillaries. [French *artériole*, diminutive of *artère* ARTERY]

arteriosclerosis /ɑ:ˌtɪərɪəʊsklɪə'rəʊsɪs, -sklə-/ *n.* the loss of elasticity and thickening of the walls of the arteries, esp. in old age; hardening of the arteries. □ **arteriosclerotic** /-'rɒtɪk/ *adj.* [ARTERY + SCLEROSIS]

artery /'ɑ:təri/ *n.* (*pl.* **-ies**) **1** any of the muscular-walled tubes forming part of the blood circulation system of the body, carrying usu. oxygen-enriched blood from the heart (cf. VEIN 1a). **2** a main road or railway line. □ **arteritis** /-'rʌɪtɪs/ *n.* [Middle English via Latin *arteria* from Greek *artēria*, probably from *airō* 'raise']

artesian well /ɑ:'ti:zɪən, -ʒ(ə)n/ *n.* a well bored perpendicularly, esp. through rock, into water-bearing strata lying at an angle, so that natural pressure produces a constant supply of water with little or no pumping. [French *artésien* from *Artois*, an old French province, where such wells were first made]

Artex /'ɑ:tɛks/ *n. propr.* a kind of plaster applied to give a textured finish, often in decorative patterns, to walls and ceilings. [ART[1] + TEXTURE]

art form *n.* **1** any medium of artistic expression. **2** an established form of composition (e.g. the novel, sonata, sonnet, etc.).

artful /ˈɑːtfʊl, -f(ə)l/ *adj.* **1** (of a person or action) crafty, deceitful. **2** skilful, clever. □ **artfully** *adv.* **artfulness** *n.*

arthritis /ɑːˈθrʌɪtɪs/ *n.* any of various diseases, esp. rheumatoid arthritis and osteoarthritis, involving pain and stiffness of the joints. □ **arthritic** /-ˈθrɪtɪk/ *adj. & n.* [Latin from Greek, from *arthron* 'joint']

arthropod /ˈɑːθrəpɒd/ *n. Zool.* any invertebrate animal of the phylum Arthropoda, with a segmented body, jointed limbs, and an external skeleton, e.g. an insect, spider, or crustacean. [Greek *arthron* 'joint' + *pous podos* 'foot']

Arthurian /ɑːˈθjʊərɪən/ *adj.* relating to or associated with King Arthur, the legendary British ruler, or his court.

artichoke /ˈɑːtɪtʃəʊk/ *n.* **1** a European plant, *Cynara scolymus*, allied to the thistle. **2** (in full **globe artichoke**) the flower head of the artichoke, the bracts of which have edible bases (see also JERUSALEM ARTICHOKE). [Italian *articiocco* from Arabic *al-ḵaršūfa*]

article /ˈɑːtɪk(ə)l/ *n. & v.* ● *n.* **1** (often in *pl.*) an item or commodity, usu. not further distinguished (*a collection of odd articles*). **2** a non-fictional essay, esp. one included with others in a newspaper, magazine, journal, etc. **3 a** a particular part (*an article of faith*). **b** a separate clause or portion of any document (*articles of apprenticeship*). **4** *Gram.* the definite or indefinite article. ● *v.tr.* bind by articles of apprenticeship. [Middle English via Old French from Latin *articulus*, diminutive of *artus* 'joint']

articled clerk *n.* a trainee solicitor.

article of virtu *n.* an article interesting because of its workmanship, antiquity, rarity, etc.

articular /ɑːˈtɪkjʊlə/ *adj.* of or relating to the joints. [Middle English from Latin *articularis* (as ARTICLE, -AR[1])]

articulate *adj. & v.* ● *adj.* /ɑːˈtɪkjʊlət/ **1** able to speak fluently and coherently. **2** (of sound or speech) having clearly distinguishable parts. **3** having joints. ● *v.* /ɑːˈtɪkjʊleɪt/ **1** *tr.* **a** pronounce (words, syllables, etc.) clearly and distinctly. **b** express (an idea etc.) coherently. **2** *intr.* speak distinctly (*was quite unable to articulate*). **3** *tr.* (usu. in *passive*) connect by joints. **4** *tr.* mark with apparent joints. **5** *intr.* (often foll. by *with*) form a joint. □ **articulacy** *n.* **articulately** *adv.* **articulateness** *n.* **articulator** *n.* [Latin *articulatus* (as ARTICLE, -ATE[2])]

articulated lorry *n. Brit.* a lorry consisting of two or more sections connected by a flexible joint.

articulation /ɑːˌtɪkjʊˈleɪʃ(ə)n/ *n.* **1 a** the act of speaking. **b** articulate utterance; speech. **2 a** the act or a mode of jointing. **b** a joint. [French *articulation* or Latin *articulatio*, from *articulare* 'joint' (as ARTICLE, -ATION)]

artifact *US* var. of ARTEFACT.

artifice /ˈɑːtɪfɪs/ *n.* **1** a clever device; a contrivance. **2 a** cunning. **b** an instance of this. **3** skill, dexterity. [French from Latin *artificium*, from *ars artis* 'art' + *-ficium* 'making' from *facere* 'make']

artificer /ɑːˈtɪfɪsə/ *n.* **1** an inventor. **2** a craftsman. **3** a skilled mechanic in the armed forces. [Middle English from Anglo-French, probably alteration of Old French *artificien*]

artificial /ɑːtɪˈfɪʃ(ə)l/ *adj.* **1** produced by human art or effort rather than originating naturally (*an artificial lake*). **2** not real; imitation, fake (*artificial flowers*). **3** affected, insincere (*an artificial smile*). □ **artificiality** /-ʃɪˈalɪti/ *n.* **artificially** *adv.* [Middle English from Old French *artificiel* or Latin *artificialis* (as ARTIFICE, -AL)]

artificial insemination *n.* the injection of semen into the vagina or uterus other than by sexual intercourse.

artificial intelligence *n.* the theory and development of computer systems able to perform tasks normally requiring human intelligence, such as decision-making and speech recognition.

artificial kidney *n.* an apparatus that performs the functions of the human kidney (outside the body), when one or both organs are damaged. Also called *kidney machine*.

artificial respiration *n.* the restoration or initiation of breathing by manual or mechanical or mouth-to-mouth methods.

artificial silk *n.* rayon.

artillery /ɑːˈtɪləri/ *n.* (*pl.* **-ies**) **1** large-calibre guns used in warfare on land. **2** a branch of the armed forces that uses these. □ **artillerist** *n.* [Middle English from Old French *artillerie* from *artiller*, alteration of *atillier*, *atirier* 'equip, arm']

artilleryman /ɑːˈtɪlərɪmən/ *n.* (*pl.* **-men**) a member of the artillery.

artiodactyl /ɑːtɪə(ʊ)ˈdaktɪl/ *adj. & n. Zool.* ● *adj.* of or relating to the order Artiodactyla of ungulate mammals with two main toes on each foot, including camels, pigs, and ruminants. ● *n.* an animal of this order. [modern Latin *Artiodactyla*, from Greek *artios* 'even' + *daktulos* 'finger, toe']

artisan /ɑːtɪˈzan, ˈɑːtɪzan/ *n.* a skilled (esp. manual) worker; a craftsman. [French from Italian *artigiano*, ultimately from Latin *artitus*, past part. of *artire* 'instruct in the arts']

artist /ˈɑːtɪst/ *n.* **1** a painter. **2** a person who practises any of the arts. **3** an artiste. **4** a person who works with the dedication and attributes associated with an artist (*an artist in crime*). **5** *colloq.* a devotee; a habitual practiser of a specified (usu. reprehensible) activity (*con artist*). □ **artistry** *n.* [French *artiste* from Italian *artista* (as ART[1], -IST)]

artiste /ɑːˈtiːst/ *n.* a professional performer, esp. a singer or dancer. [French: see ARTIST]

artistic /ɑːˈtɪstɪk/ *adj.* **1** having natural skill in art. **2** made or done with art. **3** of art or artists. □ **artistically** *adv.*

artless /ˈɑːtlɪs/ *adj.* **1** guileless, ingenuous. **2** not resulting from or displaying art. **3** clumsy. □ **artlessly** *adv.*

art nouveau /ɑː nuːˈvəʊ/ *n.* a European art style of the late 19th c. characterized by flowing lines and natural organic forms. [French, = new art]

art of war *n.* strategy and tactics.

art paper *n. Brit.* smooth-coated high-quality paper.

arts and crafts *n.pl.* decorative design and handicraft.

artwork /ˈɑːtwəːk/ *n.* the illustrations in a printed work.

arty /ˈɑːti/ *adj.* (also esp. *N. Amer.* **artsy** /ˈɑːtsi/) (**-ier**, **-iest**) *colloq.* pretentiously or affectedly artistic. □ **artiness** *n.*

arty-crafty *adj.* esp. *Brit.* **1** quaintly artistic. **2** (of furniture etc.) seeking stylistic effect rather than usefulness or comfort.

arty-farty *adj.* (also **artsy-fartsy**) *colloq.* pretentiously artistic.

arugula /əˈruːgjʊlə/ *n. N. Amer.* = ROCKET[2] 2. [Italian dialect, ultimately diminutive of Latin *eruca*]

arum /ˈɛːrəm/ *n.* **1** a plant of the European genus *Arum*, usu. stemless with arrow-shaped leaves and a white spathe, e.g. cuckoo-pint. **2** any of several other plants of the family Araceae. [Latin, from Greek *aron*]

arum lily *n.* esp. *Brit.* a tall lily-like aroid plant of the African genus *Zantedeschia*. Also called *calla lily*.

Arunta var. of ARANDA.

arvo /ˈɑːvəʊ/ *n.* (*pl.* **-os**) *Austral. slang* afternoon. [abbreviation]

-ary[1] /əri/ *suffix* **1** forming adjectives (*budgetary*; *contrary*; *primary*; *unitary*). **2** forming nouns (*dictionary*; *fritillary*; *granary*; *January*). [French *-aire* or Latin *-arius* 'connected with']

-ary[2] /əri/ *suffix* forming adjectives (*military*). [French *-aire* or from Latin *-aris* 'belonging to']

Aryan /ˈɛːrɪən/ *n. & adj.* ● *n.* **1** a member of the peoples speaking any of the languages of the Indo-European (esp. Indo-Iranian) family. **2** the parent language of this family. **3** (in Nazi ideology) a Caucasian not of Jewish descent. ● *adj.* of or relating to Aryan or the Aryans. [Sanskrit *āryas* 'noble']

aryl /'ærʌɪl, -rɪl/ *n. Chem.* a radical derived from an aromatic hydrocarbon by removal of a hydrogen atom. [German *Aryl* (as AROMATIC, -YL)]

AS *abbr.* Anglo-Saxon.

As *symb. Chem.* the element arsenic.

as[1] /æz, əz/ *adv., conj., & pron.* ● *adv. & conj.* (*adv.* as antecedent in main sentence; *conj.* in relative clause expressed or implied) ... to the extent to which ... is or does etc. (*I am as tall as he; am as tall as he is; am not so tall as he; (colloq.) am as tall as him; as many as six; as recently as last week; it is not as easy as you think*). ● *conj.* (with relative clause expressed or implied) **1** (with antecedent *so*) expressing result or purpose (*came early so as to meet us; we so arranged matters as to avoid a long wait; so good as to exceed all hopes*). **2** (with antecedent adverb omitted) having concessive force (*good as it is* = although it is good; *try as he might* = although he might try). **3** (without antecedent adverb) **a** in the manner in which (*do as you like; was regarded as a mistake; they rose as one man*). **b** in the capacity or form of (*I speak as your friend; Olivier as Hamlet; as a matter of fact*). **c** during or at the time that (*came up as I was speaking; fell just as I reached the door*). **d** for the reason that; seeing that (*as you are here, we can talk*). **e** for instance (*cathedral cities, as York*). ● *rel.pron.* (with verb of relative clause expressed or implied) **1** that, who, which (*I had the same trouble as you; he is a writer, as is his wife; such money as you have; such countries as France*). **2** (with sentence as antecedent) a fact that (*he lost, as you know*). □ **as and when** to the extent and at the time that (*I'll do it as and when I want to*). **as for** with regard to (*as for you, I think you are wrong*). **as from** esp. *Brit.* on and after (a specified date). **as if** (or **though**) as would be the case if (*acts as if he were in charge; as if you didn't know!; looks as though we've won*). **as it is** (or **as is**) in the existing circumstances or state. **as it were** in a way; to a certain extent (*he is, as it were, infatuated*). **as long as** see LONG[1]. **as much** see MUCH. **as of 1** = *as from*. **2** as at (a specified time). **as per** see PER 3. **as regards** see REGARD. **as soon as** see SOON. **as such** see SUCH. **as though** see *as if*. **as to** with respect to; concerning (*said nothing as to money; as to you, I think you are wrong*). **as was** *Brit.* in the previously existing circumstances or state. **as well** see WELL[1]. **as yet** until now or a particular time in the past (usu. with *neg.* and with implied reserve about the future: *have received no news as yet*). [reduced form of Old English *alswá* ALSO]

■ **Usage** In comparisions expressed by *as ... as*, the pronoun standing for the subject of the second half of the phrase should, strictly, be in the nominative case, i.e. *I am not as wealthy as he/she/they*. However, in all but very formal contexts, the accusative or object case is now acceptable, i.e. *I am not as wealthy as her/him/them*.

These comments also apply to *so ... as* and *the same ... as*, e.g. *We're not so eager as them*/(formal)*they*; *I live in the same street as her*/(formal)*she*.

As from and *as of*, meaning 'from' or 'after' should be followed by a particular date, e.g. *as from 15 October*. Phrases such as *as of now, as of yesterday*, etc. should be used only in informal contexts.

as[2] /æs/ *n.* (*pl.* **asses**) a Roman copper coin. [Latin: see ACE]

as- /æs, əs/ *prefix* assim. form of AD- before *s*.

ASA *abbr.* **1** Amateur Swimming Association. **2** American Standards Association (esp. in film-speed specification, as *200 ASA*).

asafoetida /æsə'fiːtɪdə, -'fɛt-/ *n.* (*US* **asafetida**) a resinous plant gum with a fetid ammoniac smell, formerly used in medicine, now as a herbal remedy and in Indian cooking. [Middle English from medieval Latin, from *asa* (from Persian *azā* 'mastic') + *fetida* (as FETID)]

a.s.a.p. *abbr.* as soon as possible.

asbestos /æz'bɛstɒs, æs-, -təs/ *n.* **1** a fibrous silicate mineral that is incombustible. **2** this used as a heat-resistant or insulating material. □ **asbestine** /-tɪn/ *adj.* [Middle English from Old French *albeston*, ultimately from Greek *asbestos* 'unquenchable' (as A-[1] + *sbestos* from *sbennumi* 'quench')]

asbestosis /æzbɛ'stəʊsɪs, æs-/ *n.* a lung disease resulting from the inhalation of asbestos particles.

ascarid /'æskərɪd/ *n.* (also **ascaris** /-rɪs/) a parasitic nematode worm of the genus *Ascaris*, e.g. the intestinal roundworm of humans and pigs. [modern Latin *ascaris* from Greek *askaris*]

ascend /ə'sɛnd/ *v.* **1** *intr.* move upwards; rise. **2** *intr.* **a** slope upwards. **b** lie along an ascending slope. **3** *tr.* climb; go up. **4** *intr.* rise in rank or status. **5** *tr.* mount upon. **6** *intr.* (of sound) rise in pitch. **7** *tr.* go along (a river) to its source. **8** *intr. Printing* (of a letter) have part projecting upwards. □ **ascend the throne** become king or queen. [Middle English from Latin *ascendere* (as AD-, *scandere* 'climb')]

ascendancy /ə'sɛnd(ə)nsi/ *n.* (also **ascendency**) (often foll. by *over*) a superior or dominant condition or position.

ascendant /ə'sɛnd(ə)nt/ *adj. & n.* ● *adj.* **1** rising. **2** *Astron.* rising towards the zenith. **3** *Astrol.* just above the eastern horizon. **4** predominant. ● *n. Astrol.* the point of the sun's apparent path that is ascendant at a given time (*Aries in the ascendant*). □ **in the ascendant 1** supreme or dominating. **2** rising; gaining power or authority. [Middle English via Old French from Latin (as ASCEND, -ANT)]

ascender /ə'sɛndə/ *n.* **1 a** a part of a letter that extends above the main part (as in *b* and *d*). **b** a letter having this. **2** a person or thing that ascends.

ascension /ə'sɛnʃ(ə)n/ *n.* **1** the act or an instance of ascending. **2** (**Ascension**) the ascent of Christ into heaven on the fortieth day after the Resurrection. □ **ascensional** *adj.* [Middle English via Old French from Latin *ascensio -onis* (as ASCEND, -ION)]

Ascension Day *n.* the Thursday forty days after Easter on which Christ's ascension is celebrated.

Ascensiontide /ə'sɛnʃ(ə)ntʌɪd/ *n.* the period of ten days from Ascension Day to Whitsun Eve.

ascent /ə'sɛnt/ *n.* **1** the act or an instance of ascending. **2 a** an upward movement or rise. **b** advancement or progress (*the ascent of man*). **3** a way by which one may ascend; an upward slope. [ASCEND, on the pattern of *descent*]

ascertain /æsə'teɪn/ *v.tr.* **1** find out as a definite fact. **2** get to know. □ **ascertainable** *adj.* **ascertainment** *n.* [Middle English from Old French *acertener*, stem *acertain-*, from *à* 'to' + CERTAIN]

ascesis /ə'siːsɪs/ *n.* the practice of self-discipline. [Greek *askēsis* 'training', from *askeō* 'exercise']

ascetic /ə'sɛtɪk/ *n. & adj.* ● *n.* a person who practises severe self-discipline and abstains from all forms of pleasure, esp. for religious or spiritual reasons. ● *adj.* relating to or characteristic of ascetics or asceticism; abstaining from pleasure. □ **ascetically** *adv.* **asceticism** /-tɪsɪz(ə)m/ *n.* [medieval Latin *asceticus* or Greek *askētikos* from *askētēs* 'monk', from *askeō* 'exercise']

ascidian /ə'sɪdɪən/ *n. Zool.* a tunicate animal of the class Ascidiacea, the adults of which are sedentary on rocks or seaweeds often in colonies, e.g. the sea squirt. [modern Latin *Ascidia* from Greek *askidion*, diminutive of *askos* 'wineskin']

ASCII /'æski/ *abbr. Computing* American Standard Code for Information Interchange.

ascites /ə'sʌɪtiːz/ *n.* (*pl.* same) *Med.* the accumulation of fluid in the abdominal cavity, causing swelling. [Middle English via Late Latin from Greek, from *askitēs* from *askos* 'wineskin']

ascorbic acid /ə'skɔːbɪk/ *n.* a vitamin found in citrus fruits and green vegetables, essential in maintaining healthy connective tissue, and a deficiency of which results in scurvy. Also called *vitamin C.* [A-[1] + medieval Latin *scorbutus* 'scurvy' + -IC]

ascribe /ə'skrʌɪb/ *v.tr.* (usu. foll. by *to*) **1** attribute or impute (*ascribes his well-being to a sound constitution*). **2** regard as belonging. ◻ **ascribable** *adj.* [Middle English from Latin *ascribere* (as AD-, *scribere script-* 'write')]

ascription /ə'skrɪpʃ(ə)n/ *n.* **1** the act or an instance of ascribing. **2** a preacher's words ascribing praise to God at the end of a sermon. [Latin *ascriptio -onis* (as ASCRIBE)]

asdic /'azdɪk/ *n.* esp. *Brit.* an early form of echo sounder. [acronym from *A*llied *S*ubmarine *D*etection *I*nvestigation *C*ommittee]

-ase /eɪz/ *suffix Biochem.* forming the name of an enzyme (*amylase*). [DIASTASE]

ASEAN /'asɪən/ *abbr.* Association of South East Asian Nations.

asepsis /eɪ'sɛpsɪs/ *n.* **1** the absence of harmful bacteria, viruses, or other micro-organisms. **2** a method of achieving asepsis in surgery.

aseptic /eɪ'sɛptɪk/ *adj.* **1** free from contamination caused by harmful bacteria, viruses, or other micro-organisms. **2** (of a wound, instrument, or dressing) surgically sterile or sterilized. **3** (of a surgical method etc.) aiming at the elimination of harmful micro-organisms, rather than counteraction (cf. ANTISEPTIC).

asexual /eɪ'sɛksjʊəl, -ʃʊəl/ *adj.* **1** *Biol.* without sex or sexual organs. **2** *Biol.* (of reproduction) not involving the fusion of gametes. **3** without sexuality. ◻ **asexuality** /-'alɪti/ *n.* **asexually** *adv.*

ASH /aʃ/ *abbr.* (in the UK) Action on Smoking and Health.

ash[1] /aʃ/ *n.* **1 a** (often in *pl.*) the powdery residue left after the burning of any substance. **b** *Chem.* such residue used in chemical analysis, e.g. to assess mineral content. **2** (in *pl.*) the remains of the human body after cremation or disintegration. **3** (**the Ashes**) *Cricket* a trophy competed for regularly by Australia and England. **4** ashlike material thrown out by a volcano. [Old English *æsce*]

ash[2] /aʃ/ *n.* **1** (also **ash tree**) any forest tree of the genus *Fraxinus*, with silver-grey bark, compound leaves, and hard, tough, pale wood. **2** its wood. **3** an Old English runic letter, = ᚫ (named from a word of which it was the first letter). [Old English *æsc*, from Germanic]

ashamed /ə'ʃeɪmd/ *adj.* (usu. *predic.*) **1** (often foll. by *of* (= with regard to), *for* (= on account of), or *to* + infin.) embarrassed or disconcerted by shame (*ashamed of his aunt*; *ashamed of having lied*; *ashamed for you*; *ashamed to be seen with him*). **2** (foll. by *to* + infin.) hesitant, reluctant (but usu. not actually refusing or declining) (*am ashamed to admit that I was wrong*). ◻ **ashamedly** /-mɪdli/ *adv.* [Old English *āscamod*, past part. of *āscamian* 'feel shame' (as A-[2], SHAME)]

ash blonde *n.* & *adj.* (*US* also **ash blond**) ● *n.* **1** a very pale blonde colour. **2** a person with hair of this colour. ● *adj.* (hyphenated when *attrib.*) very pale blonde.

ashcan /'aʃkan/ *n. US* a dustbin.

ashen[1] /'aʃ(ə)n/ *adj.* **1** of or resembling ashes. **2** ash-coloured; grey or pale.

ashen[2] /'aʃ(ə)n/ *adj.* **1** of or relating to the ash tree. **2** *archaic* made of ashwood.

ashen-faced *adj.* very pale, esp. from shock or exhaustion.

ashet /'aʃɪt/ *n. Sc.* & *NZ* a large plate or dish. [French *assiette*]

Ashkenazi /aʃkə'nɑːzi/ *n.* (*pl.* **Ashkenazim** /-zɪm/) **1** an East European Jew. **2** a Jew of East European ancestry (cf. SEPHARDI). ◻ **Ashkenazic** *adj.* [modern Hebrew, from *Ashkenaz* (Gen. 10:3)]

ash-key *n. Brit.* the winged seed of the ash tree, growing in clusters resembling keys.

ashlar /'aʃlə/ *n.* **1** a large square-cut stone used in building. **2** masonry made of ashlars. **3** such masonry used as a facing on a rough rubble or brick wall. [Middle English via Old French *aisselier* from Latin *axilla*, diminutive of *axis* 'board']

ashlaring /'aʃlərɪŋ/ *n.* **1** ashlar masonry. **2** the short upright boarding in a garret which cuts off the acute angle between the roof and the floor.

ashore /ə'ʃɔː/ *adv.* towards or on the shore or land (*sailed ashore*; *stayed ashore*).

ashpan /'aʃpan/ *n.* a tray under a grate to catch the ash.

ashplant /'aʃplɑːnt/ *n.* a sapling from an ash tree, used as a walking stick etc.

ashram /'aʃrəm/ *n.* **1** (in the Indian subcontinent) a place of religious retreat; a hermitage. **2** any place of religious retreat or community life modelled on the Indian ashram. [Sanskrit *āshrama* 'hermitage']

ashtray /'aʃtreɪ/ *n.* a small receptacle for cigarette ash, stubs, etc.

Ash Wednesday *n.* the first day of Lent. [from the custom of marking the foreheads of penitents with ashes on that day]

ashy /'aʃi/ *adj.* **1** = ASHEN[1]. **2** covered with ashes.

Asian /'eɪʃ(ə)n, -ʒ(ə)n/ *n.* & *adj.* ● *n.* **1** a native of Asia. **2** a person of Asian descent. ● *adj.* of or relating to Asia or its people, customs, or languages. [Latin *Asianus* from Greek *Asianos*, from *Asia*]

▪ **Usage** *Asian* is the preferred term when referring to people, with *Asiatic* now widely considered derogatory. In Britain it is the usual term for people who come from (or whose parents came from) the Indian subcontinent, while in North America it commonly also includes people from the Far East.

Asiatic /eɪʃɪ'atɪk, eɪz-/ *n.* & *adj.* ● *n. offens.* an Asian. ● *adj.* (*offens.* if used of people) Asian. [Latin *Asiaticus* from Greek *Asiatikos*]

▪ **Usage** *Asiatic* is now acceptable only as an adjective, and is found chiefly in geographical, zoological, and medical contexts, e.g. *Asiatic coastal regions*; *Asiatic golden plover*; *Asiatic cholera*. See also Usage Note as ASIAN.

A-side /'eɪsʌɪd/ *n.* the side of a gramophone record regarded as the main one.

aside /ə'sʌɪd/ *adv.* & *n.* ● *adv.* **1** to or on one side; away. **2** out of consideration (placed after noun: *joking aside*). ● *n.* **1** words spoken in a play for the audience to hear, but supposed not to be heard by the other characters. **2** an incidental remark. ◻ **aside from** apart from. **set aside 1** put to one side. **2** keep for a special purpose or future use. **3** reject or disregard. **4** annul. **5** remove (land) from agricultural production for fallow, forestry, or other use. **take aside** engage (a person) esp. for a private conversation. [originally *on side*: see A[2]]

asinine /'asɪnʌɪn/ *adj.* **1** stupid. **2** of or concerning asses; like an ass. ◻ **asininity** /-'nɪnɪti/ *n.* [Latin *asininus* from *asinus* 'ass']

-asis /əsɪs/ *suffix* (usu. as **-iasis**) forming the names of diseases (*psoriasis*; *satyriasis*). [Latin, from Greek *-asis* in nouns denoting a state or condition from verbs ending in *-aō*]

ask /ɑːsk/ *v.* **1** *tr.* call for an answer to or about (*ask her about it*; *ask him his name*; *ask a question of him*). **2** *tr.* seek to obtain from another person (*ask a favour of*; *ask to be allowed*). **3** *tr.* (usu. foll. by *out* or *over*, or *to* (a function etc.)) invite; request the company of (*must ask them over*; *asked her to dinner*). **4** *intr.* (foll. by *for*) seek to obtain, meet, or be directed to (*ask for a donation*; *ask for the post office*; *asking for you*). **5** *tr. archaic* require (a thing). ◻ **ask after** enquire about (esp. a person). **ask for it** *colloq.* invite trouble. **ask me another** *colloq.* I do not know. **for the asking** (obtainable) for nothing. **I ask you!** an exclamation of disgust, surprise, etc. **if you ask me** *colloq.* in my opinion. ◻ **asker** *n.* [Old English *āscian* etc., from West Germanic]

askance /ə'skans, ə'skɑːns/ *adv.* (also **askant** /-'skant, -'skɑːnt/) sideways or squinting. □ **look askance at** regard with suspicion or disapproval. [15th c.: origin unknown]

askari /ə'skɑːri/ *n.* (*pl.* same or **askaris**) an E. African soldier or police officer. [Arabic *'askarī* 'soldier']

askew /ə'skjuː/ *adv.* & *adj.* ● *adv.* obliquely; awry. ● *predic.adj.* oblique; awry. [A[2] + SKEW]

asking price *n.* the price of an object set by the seller.

aslant /ə'slɑːnt/ *adv.* & *prep.* ● *adv.* obliquely or at a slant. ● *prep.* obliquely across (*lay aslant the path*).

asleep /ə'sliːp/ *predic.adj.* & *adv.* **1 a** in or into a state of sleep (*he fell asleep*). **b** inactive, inattentive (*the nation is asleep*). **2** (of a limb etc.) numb. **3** *euphem.* dead.

Aslef /'azlɛf/ *abbr.* (in the UK) Associated Society of Locomotive Engineers and Firemen. [acronym]

AS level *n.* = ADVANCED SUPPLEMENTARY LEVEL. [abbreviation]

aslope /ə'sləʊp/ *adv.* & *predic.adj.* sloping; crosswise. [Middle English: origin uncertain]

ASM *abbr.* air-to-surface missile.

asocial /eɪ'səʊʃ(ə)l/ *adj.* **1** not social; antisocial. **2** inconsiderate of or hostile to others.

asp /asp/ *n.* **1** a small viper, *Vipera aspis*, native to southern Europe, resembling the adder. **2** the Egyptian cobra, *Naja haje*, found throughout Africa. [Middle English via Old French *aspe* or Latin *aspis* from Greek]

asparagine /ə'sparədʒiːn/ *n. Biochem.* a hydrophilic amino acid, an amide of aspartic acid, occurring in proteins. [ASPARAGUS + -INE[4]]

asparagus /ə'sparəgəs/ *n.* **1** any plant of the genus *Asparagus*. **2** one species of this, *A. officinalis*, with edible young shoots and leaves; this as food. [Latin, from Greek *asparagos*]

asparagus fern *n.* a decorative plant, *Asparagus setaceus*.

aspartame /ə'spɑːteɪm/ *n.* a very sweet low-calorie substance used as a sweetener instead of sugar or saccharin. [chemical name *1-methyl N-*L*-aspartyl-*L*-phenylalanine*, from ASPARTIC ACID]

aspartic acid /ə'spɑːtɪk/ *n. Biochem.* an acidic amino acid present in many proteins, important in animal metabolism, and also acting as a neurotransmitter. [French *aspartique*, formed arbitrarily from ASPARAGUS]

aspect /'aspɛkt/ *n.* **1 a** a particular component or feature of a matter (*only one aspect of the problem*). **b** a particular way in which a matter may be considered. **2 a** a facial expression; a look (*a cheerful aspect*). **b** the appearance of a person or thing, esp. as presented to the mind of the viewer (*has a frightening aspect*). **3** the side of a building or location facing a particular direction (*southern aspect*). **4** *Gram.* a verbal category or form expressing inception, duration, or completion. **5** *Astrol.* the relative position of planets etc. measured by angular distance. □ **aspectual** /a'spɛktʃʊəl/ *adj.* (in sense 4). [Middle English from Latin *aspectus*, from *adspicere adspect-* 'look at' (as AD-, *specere* 'to look')]

aspect ratio *n.* **1** *Aeron.* the ratio of the span to the mean chord of an aerofoil. **2** *Telev.* the ratio of picture width to height.

aspen /'asp(ə)n/ *n.* a poplar tree, *Populus tremula*, with especially tremulous leaves. [earlier name *asp* (from Old English *æspe*) + -EN[2] forming an adjective then used as a noun]

asperity /ə'spɛrɪti/ *n.* (*pl.* **-ies**) **1** harshness or sharpness of temper or tone. **2** roughness. **3** a rough excrescence. [Middle English from Old French *asperité* or Latin *asperitas*, from *asper* 'rough']

asperse /ə'spəːs/ *v.tr.* (often foll. by *with*) attack the reputation of; calumniate. [Middle English, = besprinkle, spatter, from Latin *aspergere aspers-* (as AD-, *spargere* 'sprinkle')]

aspersion /ə'spəːʃ(ə)n/ *n.* □ **cast aspersions on** attack the reputation or integrity of. [Latin *aspersio* (as ASPERSE, -ION)]

asphalt /'asfalt, -əlt/ *n.* & *v.* ● *n.* **1** a dark bituminous pitch occurring naturally or made from petroleum. **2** a mixture of this with sand, gravel, etc., for surfacing roads etc. ● *v.tr.* surface with asphalt. □ **asphaltic** /-'faltɪk/ *adj.* [Middle English, ultimately from Late Latin *asphalton*, *-um*, from Greek *asphalton*]

asphodel /'asfədɛl/ *n.* **1** any of various plants of the genus *Asphodelus* and related genera of the lily family. **2** *poet.* an immortal flower growing in Elysium. [Latin *asphodelus* from Greek *asphodelos*: cf. DAFFODIL]

asphyxia /əs'fɪksɪə/ *n.* a lack of oxygen in the blood, causing unconsciousness or death; suffocation. □ **asphyxial** *adj.* **asphyxiant** *adj.* & *n.* [modern Latin from Greek *asphuxia* (as A-[1] + *sphuxis* 'pulse')]

asphyxiate /əs'fɪksɪeɪt/ *v.tr.* cause (a person) to have asphyxia; suffocate. □ **asphyxiation** /-'eɪʃ(ə)n/ *n.* **asphyxiator** *n.*

aspic /'aspɪk/ *n.* a savoury meat jelly used as a garnish or to contain game, eggs, etc. [French, = ASP, from the colours of the jelly (compared to those of the asp)]

aspidistra /aspɪ'dɪstrə/ *n.* a plant of the genus *Aspidistra*, with broad tapering leaves, native to the Far East and often grown as a house plant. [modern Latin, from Greek *aspis -idos* 'shield' (from the shape of the leaves)]

aspirant /ə'spʌɪər(ə)nt, 'asp(ɪ)r-/ *adj.* & *n.* (usu. foll. by *to, after, for*) ● *adj.* aspiring. ● *n.* a person who aspires. [French *aspirant* or from Latin *aspirant-* (as ASPIRE, -ANT)]

aspirate *adj., n.,* & *v.* ● *adj.* /'asp(ə)rət/ *Phonet.* **1** pronounced with an exhalation of breath. **2** blended with the sound of *h*. ● *n.* /'asp(ə)rət/ *Phonet.* **1** a consonant pronounced in this way. **2** the sound of *h*. ● *v.* /'aspəreɪt/ **1** *Phonet.* **a** *tr.* pronounce with a breath. **b** *intr.* make the sound of *h*. **2** *tr.* draw (fluid) by suction from a vessel or cavity. [Latin *aspiratus*, past part. of *aspirare*: see ASPIRE]

aspiration /aspə'reɪʃ(ə)n/ *n.* **1** a strong desire to achieve an end; an ambition. **2** the act or process of drawing breath. **3** the action of aspirating. □ **aspirational** *adj.* [Middle English from Old French *aspiration* or Latin *aspiratio* (as ASPIRATE, -ATION)]

aspirator /'aspɪreɪtə/ *n.* an apparatus for aspirating fluid. [Latin *aspirare* (as ASPIRATE, -OR[1])]

aspire /ə'spʌɪə/ *v.intr.* (usu. foll. by *to, after*, or *to* + infin.) **1** have ambition or strong desire. **2** *poet.* rise high. [Middle English from French *aspirer* or Latin *aspirare* (as AD- + *spirare* 'breathe')]

aspirin /'asp(ə)rɪn/ *n.* (*pl.* same or **aspirins**) **1** a white compound, acetylsalicylic acid, used to relieve pain and fever and in the prevention of thrombosis. **2** a tablet of this. [German, formed as ACETYL + *spiraeic* (= salicylic) *acid* + -IN]

asquint /ə'skwɪnt/ *predic.adj.* & *adv.* (usu. in phr. **look asquint**) **1** to one side; from the corner of an eye. **2** with a squint. [Middle English, perhaps from Dutch *schuinte* 'slant']

ass[1] /as/ *n.* & *v.* ● *n.* **1 a** either of two kinds of four-legged long-eared mammal of the horse genus *Equus*, *E. africanus* of Africa and *E. hemionus* of Asia. **b** (in general use) a donkey. **2** a stupid person. ● *v.intr.* (foll. by *about, around*) *slang* act the fool. □ **make an ass of** make (a person) look absurd or foolish. [Old English *assa* via Celtic from Latin *asinus*]

ass[2] *N. Amer.* var. of ARSE.

assagai var. of ASSEGAI.

assai /a'sʌɪ/ *adv. Mus.* very (*adagio assai*). [Italian]

assail /ə'seɪl/ *v.tr.* **1** make a strong or concerted attack on. **2** make a resolute start on (a task). **3** make a strong or constant verbal attack on (*was assailed with angry questions*). □ **assailable** *adj.* [Middle English from Old French *asaill-*, stressed stem of *asalir*, via medieval Latin *assalire* from Latin *assilire* (as AD-, *salire salt-* 'leap')]

assailant /ə'seɪl(ə)nt/ *n.* a person who attacks another physically or verbally. [French (as ASSAIL)]

Assamese /asəˈmiːz/ *n. & adj.* ● *n.* (*pl.* same) **1** a native or inhabitant of Assam, a state of NE India. **2** the Indic (official) language of Assam. ● *adj.* of or relating to Assam, its people, or its language.

assassin /əˈsasɪn/ *n.* **1** a killer, esp. of a political or religious leader. **2** *hist.* any of a group of Muslim fanatics sent on murder missions in the time of the Crusades. [French *assassin* or via medieval Latin *assassinus* from Arabic *ḥašīšī* 'hashish-eater']

assassinate /əˈsasɪneɪt/ *v.tr.* **1** kill (esp. a political or religious leader) for political or religious motives. **2** destroy or injure (esp. a person's reputation). □ **assassination** /-ˈneɪʃ(ə)n/ *n.* **assassinator** *n.* [medieval Latin *assassinare* from *assassinus*: see ASSASSIN]

assassin bug *n.* a predatory or bloodsucking hemipterous bug of the family Reduviidae.

assault /əˈsɔːlt, əˈsɒlt/ *n. & v.* ● *n.* **1** a violent physical or verbal attack. **2 a** *Law* an act that threatens physical harm to a person (whether or not actual harm is done). **b** *euphem.* an act of rape. **3** a vigorous start made to a lengthy or difficult task. **4** a final rush on a fortified place, esp. at the end of a prolonged attack. **5** (*attrib.*) relating to or used in an assault (*assault craft*; *assault troops*). ● *v.tr.* **1** make an assault on. **2** *euphem.* rape. □ **assaulter** *n.* **assaultive** *adj.* [Middle English from Old French *asaut*, *assauter*, ultimately from Latin (as AD-, *salire salt-* 'leap')]

assault and battery *n. Law* the act of threatening a person followed by physical contact (see ASSAULT *n.* 2a, BATTERY 7).

assault course *n. Brit.* an obstacle course used in training soldiers etc.

assay /əˈseɪ/ *n. & v.* ● *n.* **1** the testing of a metal or ore to determine its ingredients and quality. **2** *Chem.* etc. the determination of the content or concentration of a substance. ● *v.* **1** *tr.* make an assay of (a metal or ore). **2** *tr. Chem.* etc. determine the concentration of (a substance). **3** *tr.* show (content) on being assayed. **4** *intr.* make an assay. **5** *tr. archaic* attempt. □ **assayer** *n.* [Middle English from Old French *assaier*, *assai*, variant of *essayer*, *essai*: see ESSAY]

assay office *n.* **1** *Brit.* an establishment which awards hallmarks. **2** esp. *N. Amer.* an office for the assaying of ores.

assegai /ˈasəgʌɪ/ *n.* (also **assagai**) a slender iron-tipped spear of hardwood, esp. as used by southern African peoples. [obsolete French *azagaie* or Portuguese *azagaia* from Arabic *az-zaġāyah*, from *al* 'the' + *zaġāyah* 'spear']

assemblage /əˈsɛmblɪdʒ/ *n.* **1** the act or an instance of bringing or coming together. **2** a collection of things or gathering of people. **3 a** the act or an instance of fitting together. **b** an object made of pieces fitted together. **4** a work of art made by grouping found or unrelated objects.

assemble /əˈsɛmb(ə)l/ *v.* **1** *tr. & intr.* gather together; collect. **2** *tr.* arrange in order. **3** *tr.* esp. *Mech.* fit together the parts of. [Middle English from Old French *asembler*, ultimately from Latin (as AD- + *simul* 'together')]

assembler /əˈsɛmblə/ *n.* **1** a person who assembles a machine or its parts. **2** *Computing* **a** a program for converting instructions written in low-level symbolic code into machine code. **b** the low-level symbolic code itself; an assembly language.

assembly /əˈsɛmbli/ *n.* (*pl.* **-ies**) **1** the act or an instance of assembling or gathering together. **2 a** a group of persons gathered together, esp. as a deliberative body or a legislative council. **b** a gathering of the entire membership or a section of a school, esp. at the start of a day. **3** the assembling of a machine or structure or its parts. **4** *Mil.* a call to assemble, given by drum or bugle. [Middle English from Old French *asemblee*, fem. past part. of *asembler*: see ASSEMBLE]

assembly language *n. Computing* the low-level symbolic code converted by an assembler.

assembly line *n.* machinery arranged in stages by which a product is progressively assembled.

assembly rooms *n.pl.* esp. *Brit.* public rooms in which meetings or social functions are held.

assembly shop *n.* (also **assembly room**) a place where a machine or its components are assembled.

assent /əˈsɛnt/ *v. & n.* ● *v.intr.* (usu. foll. by *to*) **1** express agreement (*assented to my view*). **2** consent (*assented to my request*). ● *n.* **1** mental or inward acceptance or agreement (*a nod of assent*). **2** consent or sanction, esp. official. □ **assenter** *n.* (also **assentor**). [Middle English from Old French *asenter*, *as(s)ente*, ultimately from Latin *assentari* (as AD-, *sentire* 'think')]

assentient /əˈsɛnʃ(ə)nt, -ʃɪənt/ *adj. & n.* ● *adj.* assenting. ● *n.* a person who assents. [Latin *assentire* (as ASSENT, -ENT)]

assert /əˈsəːt/ *v.* **1** *tr.* declare; state clearly (*assert one's beliefs*; *assert that it is so*). **2** *refl.* insist on one's rights or opinions; demand recognition. **3** *tr.* vindicate a claim to (*assert one's rights*). □ **assertor** *n.* (also **asserter**). [Latin *asserere* (as AD-, *serere sert-* 'join')]

assertion /əˈsəːʃ(ə)n/ *n.* **1** a declaration; a forthright statement. **2** the act or an instance of asserting. **3** (also **self-assertion**) insistence on the recognition of one's rights or claims. [Middle English from French *assertion* or Latin *assertio* (as ASSERT, -ION)]

assertive /əˈsəːtɪv/ *adj.* **1** tending to assert oneself; forthright, positive. **2** dogmatic. □ **assertively** *adv.* **assertiveness** *n.*

asses *pl.* of AS², ASS¹, ASS².

asses' bridge /ˈasɪz/ *n.* = PONS ASINORUM.

assess /əˈsɛs/ *v.tr.* **1 a** estimate the size or quality of. **b** estimate the value of (a property) for taxation etc. **2 a** (usu. foll. by *on*) fix the amount of (a tax etc.) and impose it on a person or community. **b** (usu. foll. by *in*, *at*) fine or tax (a person, community, etc.) in or at a specific amount (*assessed them at £100*). □ **assessable** *adj.* **assessment** *n.* [Middle English via French *assesser* from Latin *assidēre* (as AD-, *sedēre* 'sit')]

assessor /əˈsɛsə/ *n.* **1** a person who assesses taxes or estimates the value of property for taxation or *Brit.* insurance purposes. **2** a person called upon to advise a judge, committee of inquiry, etc., on technical questions. [Middle English via Old French *assessour* from Latin *assessor -oris* 'assistant-judge' (as ASSESS, -OR¹): sense 1 from medieval Latin]

asset /ˈasɛt/ *n.* **1 a** a useful or valuable quality. **b** a person or thing possessing such a quality or qualities (*is an asset to the firm*). **2** (usu. in *pl.*) **a** property and possessions, esp. regarded as having value in meeting debts, commitments, etc. **b** any possession having value. [*assets* (taken as pl.), via Anglo-French *asetz* from Old French *asez* enough, ultimately from Latin (as AD + *satis* 'enough')]

asset-stripping *n.* the practice of taking over a company and selling off its assets to make a profit. □ **asset-stripper** *n.*

asseverate /əˈsɛvəreɪt/ *v.tr.* declare solemnly or emphatically. □ **asseveration** /-ˈreɪʃ(ə)n/ *n.* [Latin *asseverare* (as AD-, *severus* 'serious')]

asshole *N. Amer.* var. of ARSEHOLE.

assibilate /əˈsɪbɪleɪt/ *v.tr. Phonet.* **1** pronounce (a sound) as a sibilant or affricate ending in a sibilant. **2** alter (a syllable) to become this. □ **assibilation** /-ˈleɪʃ(ə)n/ *n.* [Latin *assibilare* (as AD-, *sibilare* 'hiss')]

assiduity /asɪˈdjuːɪti/ *n.* (*pl.* **-ies**) **1** constant or close attention to what one is doing. **2** (usu. in *pl.*) constant attentions to another person. [Latin *assiduitas* (as ASSIDUOUS, -ITY)]

assiduous /əˈsɪdjʊəs/ *adj.* **1** persevering, hard-working. **2** attending closely. □ **assiduously** *adv.* **assiduousness** *n.* [Latin *assiduus* (as ASSESS)]

assign /əˈsʌɪn/ *v. & n.* ● *v.tr.* **1** (usu. foll. by *to*) **a** allot as a share or responsibility. **b** appoint to a position, task, etc. **2** fix (a time, place, etc.) for a specific purpose. **3** (foll. by *to*) ascribe or refer to (a reason, date, etc.)

(*assigned the manuscript to 1832*). **4** (foll. by *to*) transfer formally (esp. personal property) to (another). ● *n.* a person to whom property or rights are legally transferred. □ **assignable** *adj.* **assigner** *n.* **assignor** *n.* (in sense 4 of *v.*). [Middle English via Old French *asi(g)ner* from Latin *assignare* 'mark out to' (as AD-, *signum* 'sign')]

assignation /asɪg'neɪʃ(ə)n/ *n.* **1 a** an appointment to meet. **b** a secret appointment, esp. between illicit lovers. **2** the act or an instance of assigning or being assigned. [Middle English via Old French from Latin *assignatio -onis* (as ASSIGN, -ATION)]

assignee /asɪ'niː, -sʌɪ-/ *n.* **1** a person appointed to act for another. **2** an assign. [Middle English from Old French *assigné*, past part. of *assigner* ASSIGN]

assignment /ə'sʌɪnm(ə)nt/ *n.* **1** something assigned, esp. a task allotted to a person. **2** the act or an instance of assigning or being assigned. **3 a** a legal transfer. **b** the document effecting this. [Middle English via Old French *assignement* from medieval Latin *assignamentum* (as ASSIGN, -MENT)]

assimilate /ə'sɪmɪleɪt/ *v.* **1** *tr.* **a** absorb and digest (food etc.) into the body. **b** absorb (information etc.) into the mind. **c** absorb (people) into a larger group. **2** *tr.* (usu. foll. by *to, with*) make like; cause to resemble. **3** *tr. Phonet.* make (a sound) more like another in the same or next word. **4** *intr.* be absorbed into the body, mind, or a larger group. □ **assimilable** *adj.* **assimilation** /-'leɪʃ(ə)n/ *n.* **assimilative** *adj.* **assimilator** *n.* **assimilatory** /-lət(ə)ri/ *adj.* [Middle English from Latin *assimilare* (as AD-, *similis* 'like')]

assimilationist /əsɪmɪ'leɪʃ(ə)nɪst/ *n.* & *adj.* ● *n.* a person who advocates or participates in racial or cultural integration. ● *adj.* of, relating to, or promoting the views of assimilationists.

assist /ə'sɪst/ *v.* & *n.* ● *v.* **1** *tr.* (often foll. by *in* + verbal noun) help (a person, process, etc.) (*assisted them in running the playgroup*). **2** *intr.* (often foll. by *in, at*) attend or be present (*assisted in the ceremony*). ● *n. N. Amer.* **1** a help; an act of helping. **2** *Baseball* etc. a player's action of helping to put out an opponent, score a goal, etc. □ **assistance** *n.* **assister** *n.* [Middle English via French *assister* from Latin *assistere* 'take one's stand by' (as AD-, *sistere* 'take one's stand')]

assistant /ə'sɪst(ə)nt/ *n.* **1** a helper. **2** (often *attrib.*) a person who assists, esp. as a subordinate in a particular job or role. **3** *Brit.* = SHOP ASSISTANT. [Middle English *assistent* from medieval Latin *assistent-* present participial stem of *assistere* (as ASSIST, -ANT, -ENT)]

assisted place *n.* (in the UK) a place in an independent school which is wholly or partially subsidized by the State.

assize /ə'sʌɪz/ *n.* (usu. in *pl.*) *hist.* a court sitting at intervals in each county of England and Wales to administer the civil and criminal law. [Middle English from Old French *as(s)ise*, fem. past part. of *aseeir* 'sit at', from Latin *assidēre*: cf. ASSESS]

ass-kissing *n. N. Amer. coarse slang* = ARSE-LICKING.

ass-licking *N. Amer.* var. of ARSE-LICKING.

Assoc. *abbr.* (as part of a title) Association.

associable /ə'səʊʃɪəb(ə)l, -sɪ-/ *adj.* (usu. foll. by *with*) capable of being connected in thought. □ **associability** /-'bɪlɪti/ *n.* [French, from *associer* (as ASSOCIATE, -ABLE)]

associate *v., n.,* & *adj.* ● *v.* /ə'səʊʃɪeɪt, -sɪeɪt/ **1** *tr.* connect in the mind (*associate holly with Christmas*). **2** *tr.* join or combine. **3** *refl.* make oneself a partner; declare oneself in agreement (*associate myself in your endeavour*; *did not want to associate ourselves with the plan*). **4** *intr.* combine for a common purpose. **5** *intr.* (usu. foll. by *with*) meet frequently or have dealings. ● *n.* /ə'səʊʃɪət, -sɪət/ **1** a business partner or colleague. **2** a friend or companion. **3** a subordinate member of a body, institute, etc. **4** a thing connected with another. ● *adj.* /ə'səʊʃɪət, -sɪət/ **1** joined in companionship, function, or dignity. **2** allied; in the same group or category. **3** of less than full status (*associate member*). □ **associateship** /ə'səʊʃɪətʃɪp, ə'səʊs-/ *n.* **associator** /ə'səʊʃɪeɪtə, ə'səʊs-/ *n.* [Middle English from Latin *associatus*, past part. of *associare* (as AD-, *socius* 'sharing, allied')]

association /əsəʊsɪ'eɪʃ(ə)n, -ʃɪ-/ *n.* **1** a group of people organized for a joint purpose; a society. **2** the act or an instance of associating. **3** fellowship; human contact or cooperation. **4** a mental connection between ideas. **5** *Chem.* a loose aggregation of molecules. **6** *Ecol.* a group of associated plants. □ **associational** *adj.* [French *association* or medieval Latin *associatio* (as ASSOCIATE, -ATION)]

Association Football *n. Brit.* football played by sides of 11 players with a round ball which may not be handled during play except by the goalkeepers.

associative /ə'səʊʃɪətɪv, -sɪ-/ *adj.* **1** of or involving association. **2** *Math.* & *Computing* involving the condition that a group of quantities connected by operators (see OPERATOR 4) gives the same result whatever their grouping, as long as their order remains the same, e.g. $(a \times b) \times c = a \times (b \times c)$.

assonance /'as(ə)nəns/ *n.* the resemblance of sound between two syllables in nearby words, arising from the rhyming of two or more accented vowels, but not consonants, or the use of identical consonants with different vowels, e.g. *sonnet, porridge,* and *killed, cold, culled*. □ **assonant** *adj.* **assonate** /-neɪt/ *v.intr.* [French from Latin *assonare* 'respond to' (as AD-, *sonus* 'sound')]

assort /ə'sɔːt/ *v.* **1** *tr.* (usu. foll. by *with*) classify or arrange in groups. **2** *intr.* suit; fit into; harmonize with (usu. in phrs. **assort ill** or **well with**). [Old French *assorter*, from *à* 'to' + *sorte* SORT]

assortative /ə'sɔːtətɪv/ *adj.* assorting.

assortative mating *n. Biol.* non-random mating resulting from the selection of similar partners.

assorted /ə'sɔːtɪd/ *adj.* **1** of various sorts put together; miscellaneous. **2** sorted into groups. **3** matched (*ill-assorted*; *poorly assorted*).

assortment /ə'sɔːtm(ə)nt/ *n.* a set of various sorts of things or people put together; a mixed collection.

ASSR *abbr. hist.* Autonomous Soviet Socialist Republic.

Asst. *abbr.* Assistant.

assuage /ə'sweɪdʒ/ *v.tr.* **1** calm or soothe (a person, pain, etc.). **2** appease or relieve (an appetite or desire). □ **assuagement** *n.* [Middle English from Old French *as(s)ouagier*, ultimately from Latin *suavis* 'sweet']

assume /ə'sjuːm/ *v.tr.* **1** (usu. foll. by *that* + clause) take or accept as being true, without proof, for the purpose of argument or action. **2** simulate or pretend (ignorance etc.). **3** undertake (an office or duty). **4** take or put on oneself or itself (an aspect, attribute, etc.) (*the problem assumed immense proportions*). **5** (usu. foll. by *to*) arrogate, usurp, or seize (credit, power, etc.) (*assumed to himself the right of veto*). □ **assumable** *adj.* **assumedly** /-mɪdli/ *adv.* [Middle English from Latin *assumere* (as AD-, *sumere sumpt-* 'take')]

assuming /ə'sjuːmɪŋ/ *adj.* (of a person) taking too much for granted; arrogant, presumptuous.

assumption /ə'sʌm(p)ʃ(ə)n/ *n.* **1** the act or an instance of assuming. **2 a** the act or an instance of accepting without proof. **b** a thing assumed in this way. **3** arrogance. **4** (**Assumption**) **a** the reception of the Virgin Mary bodily into heaven, according to Roman Catholic doctrine. **b** the feast in honour of this, 15 Aug. [Middle English from Old French *asompsion* or Latin *assumptio* (as ASSUME, -ION)]

assumptive /ə'sʌm(p)tɪv/ *adj.* **1** taken for granted. **2** arrogant. [Latin *assumptivus* (as ASSUME, -IVE)]

assurance /ə'ʃʊər(ə)ns/ *n.* **1** a positive declaration that a thing is true. **2** a solemn promise or guarantee. **3** esp. *Brit.* insurance, esp. life insurance. **4** certainty. **5 a** self-confidence. **b** impudence. [Middle English from Old French *aseürance* from *aseürer* (as ASSURE, -ANCE)]

assure /ə'ʃʊə/ *v.tr.* **1** (often foll. by *of*) **a** make (a person) sure; convince (*assured him of my sincerity*). **b** tell (a person) confidently (*assured him the bus went to Westminster*). **2 a** make certain of; ensure the happening etc. of (*will assure her success*). **b** make safe (against overthrow etc.). **3** esp. *Brit.* insure (esp. a life). **4** (as **assured** *adj.*) **a** guaranteed. **b** self-confident. □ **rest assured** remain confident. □ **assurer** *n.* [Middle English from Old French *aseürer*, ultimately from Latin (as AD-, *securus* 'safe', SECURE)]

assuredly /əˈʃʊərɪdli/ *adv.* certainly.

Assyrian /əˈsɪrɪən/ *n. & adj. hist.* ● *n.* **1** an inhabitant of Assyria, an ancient kingdom in Mesopotamia. **2** the Akkadian dialect of Assyria. ● *adj.* of or relating to Assyria or its dialect. [Latin *Assyrius* from Greek *Assurios* 'of Assyria']

Assyriology /əsɪrɪˈɒlədʒi/ *n.* the study of the language, history, and antiquities of Assyria. □ **Assyriologist** *n.*

AST *abbr.* Atlantic Standard Time.

astable /əˈsteɪb(ə)l, eɪ-/ *adj.* **1** not stable. **2** *Electr.* of or relating to a circuit which oscillates spontaneously between unstable states.

astatic /əˈstatɪk/ *adj.* **1** not static; unstable or unsteady. **2** *Physics* not tending to keep one position or direction. [Greek *astatos* 'unstable' (as A-[1] + *sta-* 'stand')]

astatic galvanometer *n.* a galvanometer in which the effect of the earth's magnetic field on the meter needle is greatly reduced.

astatine /ˈastətiːn/ *n. Chem.* a radioactive element, the heaviest of the halogens, which occurs naturally and can be artificially made by nuclear bombardment of bismuth (symbol **At**). [formed as ASTATIC + -INE[4]]

aster /ˈastə/ *n.* a plant of the genus *Aster* (daisy family), with bright rayed flowers, e.g. the Michaelmas daisy. [Latin, from Greek *astēr* 'star']

-aster /ˈastə/ *suffix* **1** forming nouns denoting poor quality (*criticaster*; *poetaster*). **2** *Bot.* denoting incomplete resemblance (*oleaster*; *pinaster*). [Latin]

asterisk /ˈastərɪsk/ *n. & v.* ● *n.* a symbol (*) used in printing and writing to mark words etc. for reference, to stand for omitted matter, etc. ● *v.tr.* mark with an asterisk. [Middle English via Late Latin *asteriscus* from Greek *asteriskos*, diminutive of *astēr* 'star']

asterism /ˈastərɪz(ə)m/ *n.* **1** a cluster of stars. **2** a group of three asterisks (⁂) calling attention to following text. [Greek *asterismos* (as ASTER, -ISM)]

astern /əˈstəːn/ *adv.* (often foll. by *of*) *Naut. & Aeron.* **1** aft; away to the rear. **2** backwards. [A[2] + STERN[2]]

asteroid /ˈastərɔɪd/ *n.* **1** a small rocky body orbiting the sun, mainly between the orbits of Mars and Jupiter. **2** *Zool.* a starfish. □ **asteroidal** /astəˈrɔɪd(ə)l/ *adj.* [Greek *asteroeidēs* (as ASTER, -OID)]

asthenia /əsˈθiːnɪə/ *n. Med.* loss of strength; debility. [modern Latin, from Greek *astheneia* from *asthenēs* 'weak']

asthenic /əsˈθɛnɪk/ *adj. & n.* ● *adj.* **1** of lean or long-limbed build. **2** *Med.* of or characterized by asthenia. ● *n.* a lean long-limbed person. [Greek *asthenikos* from *asthenēs* 'weak']

asthenosphere /əsˈθɛnəsfɪə/ *n. Geol.* the upper layer of the earth's mantle, whose capacity for gradual flow is thought to give rise to continental drift. [Greek *asthenēs* 'weak' + -O- + SPHERE]

asthma /ˈasmə/ *n.* a usu. allergic respiratory disease, often with paroxysms of difficult breathing. [Middle English from Greek *asthma -matos*, from *azō* 'breathe hard']

asthmatic /asˈmatɪk/ *adj. & n.* ● *adj.* relating to or suffering from asthma. ● *n.* a person suffering from asthma. □ **asthmatically** *adv.* [Latin *asthmaticus* from Greek *asthmatikos* (as ASTHMA, -IC)]

Asti /ˈasti/ *n.* (*pl.* **Astis**) an Italian white wine. [*Asti*, a province in Piedmont]

astigmatism /əˈstɪgmətɪz(ə)m/ *n.* a defect in the eye or in a lens resulting in distorted images, as light rays are prevented from meeting at a common focus. □ **astigmatic** /astɪgˈmatɪk/ *adj.* [A-[1] + Greek *stigma -matos* 'point']

astilbe /əˈstɪlbi/ *n.* a plant of the genus *Astilbe* (saxifrage family), with plumelike heads of tiny white or red flowers. [modern Latin from Greek (as A-[1] + *stilbē*, fem. of *stilbos* 'glittering'), from the inconspicuous (individual) flowers]

astir /əˈstəː/ *predic.adj. & adv.* **1** in motion. **2** awake and out of bed (*astir early*; *already astir*). **3** excited. [A[2] + STIR[1] *n.*]

Asti spumante /spuːˈmanti/ *n.* a sparkling form of Asti.

astonish /əˈstɒnɪʃ/ *v.tr.* amaze; surprise greatly. □ **astonishing** *adj.* **astonishingly** *adv.* **astonishment** *n.* [obsolete *astone* via Old French *estoner* from Gallo-Roman, ultimately from Latin (as EX-[1], *tonare* 'to thunder'): see -ISH[2]]

astound /əˈstaʊnd/ *v.tr.* shock with alarm or surprise; amaze. □ **astounding** *adj.* **astoundingly** *adv.* [obsolete *astound* (*adj.*) = *astoned*, past part. of obsolete *astone*: see ASTONISH]

astraddle /əˈstrad(ə)l/ *adv. & predic.adj.* in a straddling position.

astragal /ˈastrəg(ə)l/ *n. Archit.* a small semicircular moulding round the top or bottom of a column. [ASTRAGALUS]

astragalus /əˈstrag(ə)ləs/ *n.* (*pl.* **astragali** /-lʌɪ/) **1** *Anat.* = TALUS[1]. **2** a leguminous plant of the genus *Astragalus*, e.g. the milk-vetch. [Latin, from Greek *astragalos* 'ankle-bone, moulding, a plant']

astrakhan /astrəˈkan/ *n.* **1** the dark curly fleece of young lambs from Astrakhan. **2** a cloth imitating astrakhan. [*Astrakhan*, a city and region in Russia]

astral /ˈastr(ə)l/ *adj.* **1** of or connected with the stars. **2** consisting of stars; starry. **3** *Theosophy* relating to or arising from a supposed ethereal existence, esp. of a counterpart of the body, associated with oneself in life and surviving after death. [Late Latin *astralis* from *astrum* 'star']

astray /əˈstreɪ/ *adv. & predic.adj.* **1** in or into error or sin (esp. in phr. **lead astray**). **2** out of the right way. □ **go astray** be lost or mislaid. [Middle English from Old French *estraié*, past part. of *estraier*, ultimately from Latin *extra* 'out of bounds' + *vagari* 'wander']

astride /əˈstrʌɪd/ *adv. & prep.* ● *adv.* **1** (often foll. by *of*) with a leg on each side. **2** with legs apart. ● *prep.* with a leg on each side of; extending across.

astringent /əˈstrɪn(d)ʒ(ə)nt/ *adj. & n.* ● *adj.* **1** causing the contraction of body tissues. **2** checking bleeding. **3** severe, austere. ● *n.* an astringent substance or drug. □ **astringency** *n.* **astringently** *adv.* [French from Latin *astringere* (as AD-, *stringere* 'bind')]

astro- /ˈastrəʊ/ *comb. form* **1** relating to the stars or celestial objects. **2** relating to outer space. [Greek from *astron* 'star']

astrochemistry /astrəʊˈkɛmɪstri/ *n.* the study of molecules and radicals in interstellar space.

astrodome /ˈastrədəʊm/ *n.* **1** a domed window in an aircraft for astronomical observations. **2** esp. *US* an enclosed stadium with a domed roof.

astrohatch /ˈastrəhatʃ/ *n.* = ASTRODOME.

astroid /ˈastrɔɪd/ *n. Math.* a hypocycloid with four cusps (like a square with concave sides). [Greek *astron* 'star' + -OID]

astrolabe /ˈastrəleɪb/ *n.* an instrument, usu. consisting of a disc and pointer, formerly used to make astronomical measurements, esp. of the altitudes of celestial bodies, and as an aid in navigation. [Middle English via Old French *astrelabe* and medieval Latin *astrolabium* from Greek *astrolabon*, neut. of *astrolabos* 'star-taking']

astrology /əˈstrɒlədʒi/ *n.* the study of the movements and relative positions of celestial bodies interpreted as an influence on human affairs. □ **astrologer** *n.* **astrological** /astrəˈlɒdʒɪk(ə)l/ *adj.* **astrologist** *n.* [Middle English via Old French *astrologie* and Latin *astrologia* from Greek (as ASTRO-, -LOGY)]

astronaut /ˈastrənɔːt/ *n.* a person who is trained to travel in a spacecraft. □ **astronautical** /astrəˈnɔːtɪk(ə)l/ *adj.* [ASTRO-, on the pattern of *aeronaut*, *aquanaut*]

astronautics /astrəˈnɔːtɪks/ *n.* the science of space travel.

astronomical /astrəˈnɒmɪk(ə)l/ *adj.* (also **astronomic**) **1** of or relating to astronomy. **2** extremely large; too large to contemplate. □ **astronomically** *adv.* [Latin *astronomicus* from Greek *astronomikos*]

astronomical unit *n.* a unit of measurement in astronomy equal to the mean distance from the centre of the earth to the centre of the sun, 1.496×10^{11} metres or 92.9 million miles.

astronomical year see YEAR *n.* 1.

astronomy /əˈstrɒnəmi/ *n.* the scientific study of celestial objects, of space, and of the physical universe as a whole. □ **astronomer** *n.* [Middle English via Old French *astronomie* and Latin from Greek *astronomia*, from *astronomos* (*adj.*) ' star-arranging', from *astron* 'star', *nemō* 'arrange']

astrophysics /astrə(ʊ)ˈfɪzɪks/ *n.* a branch of astronomy concerned with the physics and chemistry of celestial bodies. □ **astrophysical** *adj.* **astrophysicist** /-sɪst/ *n.*

AstroTurf /ˈastrətəːf/ *n. propr.* an artificial grass surface, esp. for sports fields. □ **astroturfed** *adj.* [*Astro*dome, name of a sports stadium in Texas where it was first used, + TURF]

astute /əˈstjuːt/ *adj.* **1** shrewd; sagacious. **2** crafty. □ **astutely** *adv.* **astuteness** *n.* [obsolete French *astut* or Latin *astutus*, from *astus* 'craft']

asunder /əˈsʌndə/ *adv. literary* apart. [Old English *on sundran* 'into pieces': cf. SUNDER]

asylum /əˈsʌɪləm/ *n.* **1** sanctuary; protection, esp. for those pursued by the law (*seek asylum*). **2** esp. *hist.* any of various kinds of institution offering shelter and support to distressed or destitute individuals, esp. the mentally ill. [Middle English via Latin from Greek *asulon* 'refuge' (as A-[1], *sulon* 'right of seizure')]

asymmetry /aˈsɪmɪtri, eɪ-/ *n.* (*pl.* **-ies**) **1** lack of symmetry. **2** an instance of this. □ **asymmetric** /-ˈmɛtrɪk/ *adj.* **asymmetrical** /-ˈmɛtrɪk(ə)l/ *adj.* **asymmetrically** /-ˈmɛtrɪk(ə)li/ *adv.* [Greek *asummetria* (as A-[1], SYMMETRY)]

asymptomatic /əsɪmptəˈmatɪk, eɪ-/ *adj.* producing or showing no symptoms.

asymptote /ˈasɪm(p)təʊt/ *n.* a line that continually approaches a given curve but does not meet it at a finite distance. □ **asymptotic** /asɪm(p)ˈtɒtɪk/ *adj.* **asymptotically** /asɪm(p)ˈtɒtɪk(ə)li/ *adv.* [modern Latin *asymptota* (*linea* 'line') from Greek *asumptōtos* 'not falling together' (as A-[1], *sun* 'together' + *ptōtos* 'falling' from *piptō* 'fall')]

asynchronous /əˈsɪŋkrənəs, eɪ-/ *adj.* not synchronous. □ **asynchronously** *adv.*

asyndeton /əˈsɪndɪt(ə)n/ *n.* (*pl.* **asyndeta** /-tə/) the omission of a conjunction. □ **asyndetic** /asɪnˈdɛtɪk/ *adj.* [modern Latin from Greek *asundeton*, neut. adj. from A-[1] + *sundetos* 'bound together']

At *symb. Chem.* the element astatine.

at /at, ət/ *prep.* **1** expressing position, exact or approximate (*wait at the corner*; *at the top of the hill*; *met at Bath*; *is at school*; *at a distance*). **2** expressing a point in time (*see you at three*; *went at dawn*). **3** expressing a point in a scale or range (*at boiling point*; *at his best*). **4** expressing engagement or concern in a state or activity (*at war*; *at work*; *at odds*). **5** expressing a value or rate (*sell at £10 each*). **6 a** with or with reference to; in terms of (*at a disadvantage*; *annoyed at losing*; *good at cricket*; *play at fighting*; *sick at heart*; *came at a run*; *at short notice*; *work at it*). **b** in response to (*starts at a touch*). **c** by means of (*drank it at a gulp*). **7** expressing: **a** motion towards (*arrived at the station*; *went at them*). **b** aim towards or pursuit of (physically or conceptually) (*aim at the target*; *work at a solution*; *guess at the truth*; *laughed at us*; *has been at the milk again*). □ **at all** see ALL. **at hand** see HAND. **at home** see HOME. **at it 1** engaged in an activity; working hard. **2** *colloq.* repeating a habitual (usu. disapproved of) activity (*found them at it again*). **at once** see ONCE. **at that** moreover (*found one, and a good one at that*). **at times** see TIME. **where it's at** *slang* the fashionable scene or activity. [Old English *æt* from Germanic, related to Latin *ad* 'to']

at- /at, ət/ *prefix* assim. form of AD- before *t*.

Atabrine var. of ATEBRIN.

ataractic /atəˈraktɪk/ *adj. & n.* (also **ataraxic** /-ˈraksɪk/) ● *adj.* calming or tranquillizing. ● *n.* a tranquillizing drug. [Greek *ataraktos* 'calm': cf. ATARAXY]

ataraxy /ˈatəraksi/ *n.* (also **ataraxia** /atəˈraksɪə/) calmness or tranquillity; imperturbability. [French *ataraxie* from Greek *ataraxia* 'impassiveness']

atavism /ˈatəvɪz(ə)m/ *n.* **1** a resemblance to remote ancestors rather than to parents in plants or animals. **2** reversion to an earlier type. □ **atavistic** /-ˈvɪstɪk/ *adj.* **atavistically** /-ˈvɪstɪk(ə)li/ *adv.* [French *atavisme* from Latin *atavus* 'great-grandfather's grandfather']

ataxy /əˈtaksi/ *n.* (also **ataxia** /-sɪə/) *Med.* the loss of full control of bodily movements. □ **ataxic** *adj.* [modern Latin *ataxia* from Greek (as A-[1] + *taxis* 'order')]

at bat *n. & adv. Baseball* ● *n.* **1** an inning. **2** a player's turn at batting. ● *adv.* batting.

ATC *abbr.* **1** air traffic control. **2** Air Training Corps.

ate *past* of EAT.

-ate[1] /ət, eɪt/ *suffix* **1** forming nouns denoting: **a** status or office (*doctorate*; *episcopate*). **b** state or function (*curate*; *magistrate*; *mandate*). **2** forming nouns denoting a group (*electorate*). **3** *Chem.* forming nouns denoting the salt of an acid with a corresponding name ending in *-ic* (*chlorate*; *nitrate*). **4** *Chem.* forming nouns denoting a product (*condensate*; *filtrate*). [from or suggested by Old French *-at* or *é(e)*, or from Latin *-atus* noun or past part.: cf. -ATE[2]]

-ate[2] /ət, eɪt/ *suffix* **1** forming adjectives and nouns (*associate*; *delegate*; *duplicate*; *separate*). **2** forming adjectives from Latin or English nouns and adjectives (*cordate*; *insensate*; *Italianate*). [from or influenced by French *-é* or its source, Latin *-atus*, past part. of verbs ending in *-are*]

-ate[3] /eɪt/ *suffix* forming verbs (*associate*; *duplicate*; *fascinate*; *hyphenate*; *separate*). [from or influenced by French *-er* or its source, Latin *-are* (past part. *-atus*): cf. -ATE[2]]

A-team *n.* a group consisting of one's best workers, advisers, etc. [from sports terminology in which an organization's A-team is its best team]

Atebrin /ˈatɪbrɪn/ *n.* (also **Atabrine** /-briːn/) *propr.* = QUINACRINE. [20th c.: origin unknown]

atelier /əˈtɛlɪeɪ/ *n.* a workshop or studio, esp. of an artist or designer. [French]

a tempo /ɑː ˈtɛmpəʊ/ *adv. Mus.* in the previous tempo. [Italian, literally 'in time']

Athanasian Creed /aθəˈneɪʃ(ə)n/ *n.* a summary of Christian doctrine formerly attributed to Athanasius (bishop of Alexandria d. 373), but probably dating from the 5th c.

atheism /ˈeɪθɪɪz(ə)m/ *n.* the theory or belief that God does not exist. □ **atheist** *n.* **atheistic** /-ˈɪstɪk/ *adj.* **atheistical** /-ˈɪstɪk(ə)l/ *adj.* [French *athéisme* from Greek *atheos* 'without God' (as A-[1] + *theos* 'god')]

atheling /ˈaθ(ə)lɪŋ/ *n. hist.* a prince or lord in Anglo-Saxon England. [Old English *ætheling*, from a West Germanic base meaning 'race, family': see -ING[3]]

athematic /aθɪˈmatɪk, eɪ-/ *adj.* **1** *Mus.* not based on the use of themes. **2** *Gram.* (of a verb form) having a suffix attached to the stem without a connecting (thematic) vowel.

athenaeum /aθɪˈniːəm/ *n.* (*US* **atheneum**) **1** an institution for literary or scientific study. **2** a library. [Late Latin *Athenaeum* from Greek *Athēnaion* 'temple of Athene' (used as a place of teaching)]

Athenian /əˈθiːnɪən/ *n. & adj.* ● *n.* a native or inhabitant of ancient or modern Athens. ● *adj.* of or relating to Athens. [Latin *Atheniensis* from *Athenae*, from Greek *Athēnai* 'Athens', principal city of Greece]

atherosclerosis /ˌaθərəʊsklɪəˈrəʊsɪs, -sklə-/ *n.* a form of arteriosclerosis characterized by the degeneration of the arteries because of the build-up of fatty deposits. □ **atherosclerotic** /-ˈrɒtɪk/ *adj.* [German *Atherosklerose*, from Greek *athērē* 'groats' + SCLEROSIS]

athirst /əˈθəːst/ *predic.adj. poet.* **1** (usu. foll. by *for*) eager (*athirst for knowledge*). **2** thirsty. [Old English *ofthyrst* for *ofthyrsted*, past part. of *ofthyrstan* 'be thirsty']

athlete /ˈaθliːt/ *n.* **1** a skilled performer in physical exercises, esp. *Brit.* in track and field events. **2** a healthy person with natural athletic ability. [Latin *athleta* from Greek *athlētēs*, from *athlein* 'contend for a prize' from *athlon* 'prize']

athlete's foot *n.* a fungal foot condition affecting esp. the skin between the toes.

athletic /aθˈlɛtɪk/ *adj.* **1** of or relating to athletes or athletics (*an athletic competition*). **2** muscular or physically powerful. □ **athletically** *adv.* **athleticism** /-ˈlɛtɪsɪz(ə)m/ *n.* [French *athlétique* or Latin *athleticus* from Greek *athlētikos* (as ATHLETE, -IC)]

athletics /aθˈlɛtɪks/ *n.pl.* (usu. treated as *sing.*) **1** esp. *Brit.* **a** track and field events (often *attrib.*: *athletics meeting*). **b** the practice of these. **2** *N. Amer.* physical sports and games of any kind.

at-home *n.* a social reception in a person's home.

athwart /əˈθwɔːt/ *adv. & prep.* ● *adv.* **1** across from side to side (usu. obliquely). **2** perversely or in opposition. ● *prep.* **1** from side to side of. **2** in opposition to. [A[2] + THWART]

-atic /ˈatɪk/ *suffix* forming adjectives and nouns (*aquatic*; *fanatic*; *idiomatic*). [French *-atique* or Latin *-aticus*, often ultimately from Greek *-atikos*]

atilt /əˈtɪlt/ *adv.* tilted and nearly falling. [A[2] + TILT]

-ation /ˈeɪʃ(ə)n/ *suffix* **1** forming nouns denoting an action or an instance of it (*alteration*; *flirtation*; *hesitation*). **2** forming nouns denoting a result or product of action (*plantation*; *starvation*; *vexation*) (see also -FICATION). [from or suggested by French *-ation* or from Latin *-atio -ationis* from verbs ending in *-are*: see -ION]

-ative /ətɪv, ˈeɪtɪv/ *suffix* forming adjectives denoting a characteristic or propensity (*authoritative*; *imitative*; *pejorative*; *qualitative*; *talkative*). [from or suggested by French *-atif -ative* or from Latin *-ativus* from past part. stem *-at-* of verbs ending in *-are* + *-ivus* (see -IVE): cf. -ATIC]

Atlantean /atˈlantɪən, atlənˈtiːən/ *adj.* **1** *literary* of or like Atlas, esp. in physical strength. **2** of or relating to the legendary lost civilization of Atlantis. [sense 1 from Latin *Atlanteus* (as ATLAS): sense 2 from Greek *Atlantis*]

atlantes /atˈlantiːz/ *n.pl. Archit.* male figures carved in stone and used as columns to support the entablature of a Greek or Greek-style building. [Greek, pl. of *Atlas*: see ATLAS]

Atlantic /atˈlantɪk/ *n. & adj.* ● *n.* (**the Atlantic**) = ATLANTIC OCEAN. ● *adj.* of or adjoining the Atlantic. [Middle English via Latin *Atlanticus* from Greek *Atlantikos* (as ATLAS, -IC): originally of the Atlas Mountains, then of the sea near the W. African coast]

Atlanticism /atˈlantɪˌsɪz(ə)m/ *n.* belief in or support for Nato or the close relationship between western Europe and the US. □ **Atlanticist** *n. & adj.*

Atlantic Ocean *n.* the ocean between Europe and Africa to the east, and America to the west.

Atlantic Standard Time *n.* (also **Atlantic Time**) the standard time in a zone including the easternmost parts of mainland Canada, four hours behind GMT.

atlas /ˈatləs/ *n.* **1** a book of maps or charts. **2** *Anat.* the cervical vertebra of the backbone articulating with the skull at the neck. [Latin from Greek *Atlas -antos*, the name of a Titan who held up the pillars of the universe, whose picture appeared at the beginning of early atlases]

ATM *abbr.* automated teller machine.

atm *abbr. Physics* atmosphere(s).

atman /ˈɑːtmən/ *n. Hinduism* **1** the real self. **2** the supreme spiritual principle. [Sanskrit *ātmán* 'essence, breath']

atmosphere /ˈatməsfɪə/ *n.* **1 a** the envelope of gases surrounding the earth, any other planet, or any substance. **b** the air in any particular place, esp. if unpleasant. **2 a** the pervading tone or mood of a place or situation, esp. with reference to the feelings or emotions evoked. **b** the feelings or emotions evoked by a work of art, a piece of music, etc. **c** a feeling of tension between people, caused by a disagreement etc. **3** *Physics* a unit of pressure equal to mean atmospheric pressure at sea level, 101,325 pascals (abbr.: **atm**). □ **atmospheric** /-ˈfɛrɪk/ *adj.* **atmospherical** /-ˈfɛrɪk(ə)l/ *adj.* **atmospherically** /-ˈfɛrɪk(ə)li/ *adv.* [modern Latin *atmosphaera* from Greek *atmos* 'vapour': see SPHERE]

atmospherics /atməsˈfɛrɪks/ *n.pl.* **1** electrical disturbance in the atmosphere, esp. caused by lightning. **2** interference with telecommunications caused by this. **3 a** actions intended to create a particular atmosphere or mood. **b** a deliberately created atmosphere or mood.

atoll /ˈatɒl, əˈtɒl/ *n.* a ring-shaped coral reef enclosing a lagoon. [Maldivian *atolu*]

atom /ˈatəm/ *n.* **1 a** the smallest particle of a chemical element that can take part in a chemical reaction. **b** this particle as a source of nuclear energy. **2** (usu. with *neg.*) the least portion of a thing or quality (*not an atom of pity*). [Middle English via Old French *atome* and Latin *atomus* from Greek *atomos* 'indivisible']

atom bomb *n.* a bomb which derives its power from the release of energy by nuclear fission.

atomic /əˈtɒmɪk/ *adj.* **1** concerned with or using atomic energy or atom bombs. **2** of or relating to an atom or atoms. □ **atomically** *adv.* [modern Latin *atomicus* (as ATOM, -IC)]

atomic bomb *n.* = ATOM BOMB.

atomic clock *n.* a clock in which the periodic process (timescale) is regulated by the vibrations of an atomic or molecular system, such as caesium or ammonia.

atomic energy *n.* nuclear energy.

atomicity /atəˈmɪsɪti/ *n.* **1** the number of atoms in the molecules of an element. **2** the state or fact of being composed of atoms.

atomic mass *n.* the mass of an atom measured in atomic mass units.

atomic mass unit *n.* a unit of mass used to express atomic and molecular weights that is equal to one-twelfth of the mass of an atom of carbon-12 (abbr.: **amu**).

atomic number *n.* the number of protons in the nucleus of an atom, which is characteristic of a chemical element and determines its place in the periodic table (symbol **Z**).

atomic physics *n.* the branch of physics concerned with the structure of the atom and the characteristics of the subatomic particles.

atomic pile *n.* a nuclear reactor.

atomic power *n.* nuclear power.

atomic spectrum *n.* the emission or absorption spectrum arising from electron transitions inside an atom and characteristic of the element.

atomic structure *n.* the structure of an atom as being a central positively charged nucleus surrounded by negatively charged orbiting electrons.

atomic theory *n.* **1** *Physics* the theory that atoms are composed of subatomic particles. **2** the theory that all matter is made up of tiny indivisible particles called atoms, and esp. that the atoms of any one element are identical but differ from those of other elements and unite to form compounds in fixed proportions. **3** *Philos.* atomism.

atomic warfare *n.* warfare involving the use of atom bombs.

atomic weight *n.* = RELATIVE ATOMIC MASS.

atomism /ˈatəmɪz(ə)m/ *n.* **1** *Philos.* the theory that all matter consists of tiny individual particles. **2** *Psychol.* the theory that mental states are made up of elementary units. ▫ **atomist** *n.* **atomistic** /-ˈmɪstɪk/ *adj.*

atomize /ˈatəmʌɪz/ *v.tr.* (also **-ise**) **1** reduce to atoms or fine particles. **2** fragment (*atomized society*). ▫ **atomization** /-ˈzeɪʃ(ə)n/ *n.*

atomizer /ˈatəmʌɪzə/ *n.* (also **-iser**) an instrument for emitting liquids as a fine spray.

atom smasher *n. colloq.* = ACCELERATOR 2.

atomy /ˈatəmi/ *n.* (*pl.* **-ies**) *archaic* **1** a skeleton. **2** an emaciated body. [ANATOMY taken as *an atomy*]

atonal /eɪˈtəʊn(ə)l, ə-/ *adj. Mus.* not written in any key or mode. ▫ **atonality** /-ˈnalɪti/ *n.*

atone /əˈtəʊn/ *v.intr.* (usu. foll. by *for*) make amends; expiate (for a wrong). [back-formation from ATONEMENT]

atonement /əˈtəʊnm(ə)nt/ *n.* **1** expiation; reparation for a wrong or injury. **2** the reconciliation of God and man. ▫ **the Atonement** the expiation by Christ of mankind's sin. [*at one* + -MENT, influenced by medieval Latin *adunamentum* and earlier *onement* from obsolete *one* (*v.*) 'to unite']

atonic /əˈtɒnɪk/ *adj.* **1** without accent or stress. **2** *Med.* lacking bodily tone. ▫ **atony** /ˈatəni/ *n.*

atop /əˈtɒp/ *adv. & prep.* ● *adv.* (often foll. by *of*) on the top. ● *prep.* on the top of.

-ator /eɪtə/ *suffix* forming agent nouns, usu. from Latin words (sometimes via French) (*agitator*; *creator*; *equator*; *escalator*). See also -OR[1]. [Latin *-ator*]

-atory /ət(ə)ri/ *suffix* forming adjectives meaning 'relating to or involving (a verbal action)' (*amatory*; *explanatory*; *predatory*). See also -ORY[2]. [Latin *-atorius*]

ATP *abbr.* adenosine triphosphate.

atrabilious /atrəˈbɪlɪəs/ *adj. literary* melancholy; ill-tempered. [Latin *atra bilis* 'black bile', translation of Greek *melagkholia* MELANCHOLY]

atrium /ˈeɪtrɪəm/ *n.* (*pl.* **atriums** or **atria** /-trɪə/) **1 a** the central court of an ancient Roman house. **b** a usu. skylit central court rising through several storeys with galleries and rooms opening off at each level. **c** (in a modern house) a central hall or glazed court with rooms opening off it. **2** *Anat.* a cavity in the body, esp. one of the two upper cavities of the heart, receiving blood from the veins. ▫ **atrial** *adj.* [Latin]

atrocious /əˈtrəʊʃəs/ *adj.* **1** very bad or unpleasant (*atrocious weather*; *their manners were atrocious*). **2** extremely savage or wicked (*atrocious cruelty*). ▫ **atrociously** *adv.* **atrociousness** *n.* [Latin *atrox -ocis* 'cruel']

atrocity /əˈtrɒsɪti/ *n.* (*pl.* **-ies**) **1** an extremely wicked or cruel act, esp. one involving physical violence or injury. **2** extreme wickedness. [French *atrocité* or Latin *atrocitas* (as ATROCIOUS, -ITY)]

atrophy /ˈatrəfi/ *v. & n.* ● *v.* (**-ies**, **-ied**) **1** *intr.* waste away through undernourishment, ageing, or lack of use; become emaciated. **2** *tr.* cause to atrophy. ● *n.* the process of atrophying; emaciation. [French *atrophie* or Late Latin *atrophia* from Greek (as A-[1] + *trophē* 'food')]

atropine /ˈatrəpiːn, -ɪn/ *n.* a poisonous alkaloid found in deadly nightshade, used in medicine to dilate the pupil of the eye, and to treat intestinal spasm and counteract slowing of the heart. [modern Latin *Atropa belladonna* 'deadly nightshade' from Greek *Atropos* 'inflexible', the name of one of the Fates]

attach /əˈtatʃ/ *v.* **1** *tr.* fasten, affix, join. **2** *tr.* (in *passive*; foll. by *to*) be very fond of or devoted to (*am deeply attached to her*). **3** *tr.* attribute, assign (some function, quality, or characteristic) (*can you attach a name to it?*; *attaches great importance to it*). **4 a** *tr.* include; cause to form part of a thing (*no conditions are attached*). **b** *intr.* (foll. by *to*) be an attribute or characteristic (*great prestige attaches to the job*). **5** *refl.* (usu. foll. by *to*) take part in; join (*attached themselves to the expedition*). **6** *tr.* appoint for special or temporary duties. **7** *tr. Law* seize (a person or property) by legal authority. ▫ **attachable** *adj.* [Middle English via Old French *estachier* 'fasten' from Germanic: in Law sense via Old French *atachier*]

attaché /əˈtaʃeɪ/ *n.* **1** a person appointed to an ambassador's staff, usu. with a special sphere of activity (*military attaché*; *press attaché*). **2** *N. Amer.* = ATTACHÉ CASE. [French, past part. of *attacher*: see ATTACH]

attaché case *n.* a small flat rectangular case for carrying documents etc.

attachment /əˈtatʃm(ə)nt/ *n.* **1** a thing attached or to be attached, esp. to a machine, device, etc., for a special function. **2** affection, devotion. **3** a means of attaching. **4** the act of attaching or the state of being attached. **5** legal seizure. **6** *Brit.* a temporary position in, or secondment to, an organization. [Middle English from French *attachement*, from *attacher* (as ATTACH, -MENT)]

attack /əˈtak/ *v. & n.* ● *v.* **1** *tr.* act against with (esp. armed) force. **2** *tr.* seek to hurt or defeat. **3** *tr.* criticize adversely. **4** *tr.* act harmfully upon (*a virus attacking the nervous system*; *rust had attacked the metal*). **5** *tr.* vigorously apply oneself to; begin work on (*attacked his meal with gusto*). **6** *tr.* (in various games) try to score goals, points, etc. against (one's opponents). **7** *intr.* make an attack. **8** *intr.* be in a mode of attack. ● *n.* **1** an act, or the process, of acting against a person or thing with (esp. armed) force; an offensive operation or mode of behaviour. **2** a sudden occurrence of an illness. **3** gusto, vigour. **4** *Mus.* the action or manner of beginning a piece, passage, etc. **5** a player or players seeking to score goals etc. ▫ **attacker** *n.* [French *attaque*, *attaquer* from Italian *attacco* 'attack', *attaccare* ATTACH]

attain /əˈteɪn/ *v.* **1** *tr.* arrive at; reach (a goal etc.). **2** *tr.* gain, accomplish (an aim, distinction, etc.). **3** *intr.* (foll. by *to*) arrive at by conscious development or effort. ▫ **attainable** *adj.* **attainability** /-ˈbɪlɪti/ *n.* **attainableness** *n.* [Middle English via Anglo-French *atain-*, *atein-*, Old French *ataign-* 'stem of *ataindre*' from Latin *attingere* (as AD-, *tangere* 'touch')]

attainder /əˈteɪndə/ *n. hist.* the forfeiture of land and civil rights suffered as a consequence of a sentence of death for treason or felony. ▫ **act** (or **bill**) **of attainder** an item of legislation inflicting attainder without judicial process. [Middle English from Anglo-French, = Old French *ateindre* ATTAIN, used as a noun: see -ER[6]]

attainment /əˈteɪnm(ə)nt/ *n.* **1** (often in *pl.*) something attained or achieved; an accomplishment. **2** the act or an instance of attaining.

attaint /əˈteɪnt/ *v.tr.* **1** *hist.* subject to attainder. **2 a** (of disease etc.) strike, affect. **b** taint. [Middle English from obsolete *attaint* (*adj.*) from Old French *ataint*, *ateint* past part. of *ataindre* (see ATTAIN): confused in meaning with TAINT]

attar /ˈatə/ *n.* (also **otto** /ˈɒtəʊ/) a fragrant essential oil, esp. from rose petals. [Persian *'atar* from Arabic *'itr* 'perfume']

attempt /əˈtɛm(p)t/ *v. & n.* ● *v.tr.* **1** (often foll. by *to* + infin.) seek to achieve or complete (a task or action) (*attempted the exercise*; *attempted to explain*). **2** seek to climb or master (a mountain etc.). ● *n.* **1** (often foll. by *at*, or *to* + infin.) an act of attempting; an endeavour (*made an attempt at winning*; *an attempt to succeed*). **2** (foll. by *on*) an attack; an effort to overcome (*an attempt on his life*; *attempt on the world record*). ▫ **attempt the life of** *archaic* try to kill. ▫ **attemptable** *adj.* [Old French *attempter* from Latin *attemptare* (as AD-, *temptare* TEMPT)]

attend /əˈtɛnd/ *v.* **1** *tr.* **a** be present at (*attended the meeting*). **b** go regularly to (*attends the local school*). **2** *intr.* **a** be present (*many members failed to attend*). **b** be present in a serving capacity; wait. **3 a** *tr.* escort, accompany (*the king was attended by soldiers*). **b** *intr.* (foll. by *on*) wait on; serve. **4** *intr.* **a** (usu. foll. by *to*) turn or apply one's mind; focus one's attention (*attend to what I am saying*; *was not attending*). **b** (foll. by *to*) deal with (*shall attend to the matter myself*). **5** *tr.* (usu. in *passive*) follow as a result from (*the error was attended by serious consequences*). ▫ **attender** *n.* [Middle

English via Old French *atendre* from Latin *attendere* (as AD-, *tendere tent-* 'stretch')]

attendance /ə'tɛnd(ə)ns/ *n.* **1** the act of attending or being present. **2** the number of people present (*a high attendance*). [Middle English from Old French *atendance* (as ATTEND, -ANCE)]

attendance allowance *n.* (in the UK) a state benefit paid to disabled people in need of constant care at home.

attendance centre *n.* (in the UK) a place where young offenders report by order of a court as a minor penalty.

attendant /ə'tɛnd(ə)nt/ *n. & adj.* ● *n.* a person employed to wait on others or provide a service (*cloakroom attendant; museum attendant*). ● *adj.* **1** accompanying (*attendant circumstances*). **2** waiting on; serving (*ladies attendant on the queen*). [Middle English from Old French (as ATTEND, -ANT)]

attendee /atɛn'diː/ *n.* a person who attends (a meeting etc.).

attention /ə'tɛnʃ(ə)n/ *n. & int.* ● *n.* **1** the act or faculty of applying one's mind (*give me your attention; attract his attention*). **2 a** consideration (*give attention to the problem*). **b** care (*give special attention to your handwriting*). **3** (in *pl.*) **a** ceremonious politeness (*he paid his attentions to her*). **b** wooing, courting (*she was the subject of his attentions*). **4** *Mil.* an erect attitude of readiness (*stand at attention*). ● *int.* **1** (in full **stand at** or **to attention!**) *Mil.* an order to assume an attitude of attention. **2** an imperative warning, to gain attention (*attention please!*). □ **attentional** *adj.* [Middle English from Latin *attentio* (as ATTEND, -ION)]

attentive /ə'tɛntɪv/ *adj.* **1** concentrating; paying attention. **2** assiduously polite. **3** heedful. □ **attentively** *adv.* **attentiveness** *n.* [Middle English from French *attentif -ive* from *attente*, Old French *atente*, fem. past part. of *atendre* ATTEND]

attenuate *v. & adj.* ● *v.tr.* /ə'tɛnjʊeɪt/ **1** make thin. **2** reduce in force, value, or virulence. **3** *Electr.* reduce the amplitude of (a signal or current). ● *adj.* /ə'tɛnjʊət/ **1** slender. **2** tapering gradually. **3** rarefied. □ **attenuated** *adj.* **attenuation** /-'eɪʃ(ə)n/ *n.* **attenuator** *n.* [Latin *attenuare* (as AD-, *tenuis* 'thin')]

attest /ə'tɛst/ *v.* **1** *tr.* **a** certify the validity of. **b** be evidence of. **2** *intr.* (foll. by *to*) bear witness to. **3** esp. *Brit. Mil. hist.* **a** *intr.* declare oneself willing to serve if called upon. **b** *tr.* recruit by putting on oath to serve if called upon. □ **attestable** *adj.* **attestor** *n.* [French *attester* from Latin *attestari* (as AD-, *testis* 'witness')]

attestation /atɛ'steɪʃ(ə)n/ *n.* **1** the act of attesting. **2** a testimony. [French *attestation* or Late Latin *attestatio* (as ATTEST, -ATION)]

Attic /'atɪk/ *adj. & n.* ● *adj.* of or relating to ancient Athens or Attica, or the form of Greek spoken there. ● *n.* the form of Greek used by the ancient Athenians. [Latin *Atticus* from Greek *Attikos*]

attic /'atɪk/ *n.* **1** the uppermost storey in a house, usu. under the roof. **2** a room in the attic area. [French *attique*, as ATTIC: originally (*Archit.*) a small order (column and entablature) above a taller one]

atticism /'atɪsɪz(ə)m/ *n.* **1** extreme elegance of speech. **2** an instance of this. [Greek *Attikismos* (as ATTIC, -ISM)]

Attic salt *n.* (also **Attic wit**) refined wit.

attire /ə'tʌɪə/ *v. & n. formal* ● *v.tr.* dress, esp. in fine clothes or formal wear. ● *n.* clothes, esp. fine or formal. [Middle English from Old French *atir(i)er* 'equip' from *à tire* 'in order', of unknown origin]

attitude /'atɪtjuːd/ *n.* **1 a** a settled opinion or (also **attitude of mind**) way of thinking. **b** behaviour reflecting this (*I don't like his attitude*). **2 a** a bodily posture. **b** a pose adopted in a painting or a play, esp. for dramatic effect (*strike an attitude*). **3** the position of an aircraft, spacecraft, etc., in relation to specified directions. **4** esp. *N. Amer. slang* **a** truculence; a lack of cooperation; arrogance. **b** style, swagger. □ **attitudinal** /atɪ'tjuːdɪn(ə)l/ *adj.* [French via Italian *attitudine* 'fitness, posture', from Late Latin *aptitudo -dinis* from *aptus* 'fit']

attitudinize /atɪ'tjuːdɪnʌɪz/ *v.intr.* (also **-ise**) **1** practise or adopt attitudes, esp. for effect. **2** speak, write, or behave affectedly. [Italian *attitudine* from Late Latin (as ATTITUDE) + -IZE]

attn. *abbr.* **1** attention. **2** for the attention of.

atto- /'atəʊ/ *comb. form Math.* denoting a factor of 10^{-18} (*attometre*). [Danish or Norwegian *atten* 'eighteen' + -o-]

attorney /ə'təːni/ *n.* (*pl.* **-eys**) **1** a person, esp. a lawyer, appointed to act for another in business or legal matters. **2** *US* a qualified lawyer, esp. one representing a client in a law court. □ **attorneyship** *n.* [Middle English from Old French *atorné*, past part. of *atorner* 'assign', from *à* 'to' + *torner* 'turn']

Attorney-General *n.* the chief legal officer in England, the US, and other countries.

attract /ə'trakt/ *v.tr.* **1** (also *absol.*) draw or bring to oneself or itself (*attracts many admirers; attracts attention*). **2** be attractive to; fascinate. **3** (of a magnet, gravity, etc.) exert a pull on (an object). □ **attractable** *adj.* **attractor** *n.* [Latin *attrahere* (as AD-, *trahere tract-* 'draw')]

attractant /ə'trakt(ə)nt/ *n. & adj.* ● *n.* a substance which attracts (esp. insects). ● *adj.* attracting.

attraction /ə'trakʃ(ə)n/ *n.* **1 a** the act or power of attracting (*the attraction of foreign travel*). **b** a person or thing that attracts by arousing interest (*the fair is a big attraction*). **2** *Physics* the force by which bodies attract or approach each other (opp. REPULSION). **3** *Gram.* the influence exerted by one word on another which causes it to change to an incorrect form, e.g. *the wages of sin is* (for *are*) *death*. [French *attraction* or Latin *attractio* (as ATTRACT, -ION)]

attractive /ə'traktɪv/ *adj.* **1** attracting or capable of attracting; interesting (*an attractive proposition*). **2** aesthetically pleasing or appealing. □ **attractively** *adv.* **attractiveness** *n.* [French *attractif -ive* from Late Latin *attractivus* (as ATTRACT, -IVE)]

attribute *v. & n.* ● *v.tr.* /ə'trɪbjuːt/ (foll. by *to*) **1** ascribe to or regard as the effect of (a stated cause) (*the delays were attributed to the heavy traffic*). **2** regard as having been created or originated by (*a poem attributed to Shakespeare*). **3** regard as characteristic of; regard as possessing or having (*attributed magical powers to their gods; he attributes particular significance to their absence*). ● *n.* /'atrɪbjuːt/ **1 a** a quality ascribed to a person or thing. **b** a characteristic quality. **2** a material object recognized as appropriate to a person, office, or status (*a large car is an attribute of seniority*). **3** *Gram.* an attributive adjective or noun. □ **attributable** /ə'trɪbjʊtəb(ə)l/ *adj.* **attribution** /atrɪ'bjuːʃ(ə)n/ *n.* [Middle English from Latin *attribuere attribut-* (as AD-, *tribuere* 'assign'): the noun from Old French *attribut* or Latin *attributum*]

attributive /ə'trɪbjʊtɪv/ *adj. Gram.* (of an adjective or noun) preceding the word it qualifies or modifies and expressing an attribute, as *old* in *the old dog* (but not in *the dog is old*) and *expiry* in *expiry date* (opp. PREDICATIVE 1). □ **attributively** *adv.* [French *attributif -ive* (as ATTRIBUTE, -IVE)]

attrit /ə'trɪt/ *v.tr.* (**attritted**, **attritting**) *US colloq.* wear down (an opponent or enemy) by sustained action. [back-formation from ATTRITION]

attrition /ə'trɪʃ(ə)n/ *n.* **1 a** the act or process of gradually wearing out, esp. by friction. **b** abrasion. **2** *Theol.* sorrow for sin, falling short of contrition. **3** esp. *N. Amer.* & *Austral.* = WASTAGE 3. □ **attritional** *adj.* [Middle English from Late Latin *attritio*, from *atterere attrit-* 'rub']

attune /ə'tjuːn/ *v.tr.* **1** (usu. foll. by *to*) adjust (a person or thing) to a situation. **2** bring (an orchestra, instrument, etc.) into musical accord. [AT- + TUNE]

Atty. *abbr.* Attorney.

atypical /eɪ'tɪpɪk(ə)l, a-/ *adj.* not typical; not conforming to a type. □ **atypically** *adv.*

AU *abbr.* **1** (also **au.**) astronomical unit. **2** ångström unit.

Au *symb. Chem.* the element gold. [Latin *aurum*]

aubade /əʊ'bɑ:d/ *n.* a poem or piece of music appropriate to the dawn or early morning. [French from Spanish *albada*, from *alba* 'dawn']

auberge /əʊ'bɛ:ʒ, French obɛrʒ/ *n.* an inn. [French, from Provençal *alberga* 'lodging']

aubergine /'əʊbəʒi:n/ *n. & adj.* esp. *Brit.* ● *n.* **1** a tropical plant, *Solanum melongena*, having erect or spreading branches bearing white or purple egg-shaped fruit; also called EGGPLANT. **2** this fruit eaten as a vegetable. **3** the dark purple colour of this fruit. ● *adj.* of the colour of the aubergine; dark purple. [French via Catalan *alberginia*, Arabic *al-bādinjān*, and Persian *bādingān* from Sanskrit *vātiṃgaṇa*]

aubrietia /ɔ:'bri:ʃə/ *n.* (also **aubretia**) a dwarf perennial rock plant of the genus *Aubrieta*, having purple or pink flowers in spring. [alteration of modern Latin, named after Claude *Aubriet*, French botanist d. 1743]

■ **Usage** Note that the correct spelling of the Latin name is *Aubrieta*.

auburn /'ɔ:bən, -bə:n/ *adj. & n.* ● *adj.* (usu. of a person's hair) of a reddish-brown colour. ● *n.* this colour. [Middle English, originally 'yellowish white', via Old French *auborne*, *alborne*, from Latin *alburnus* 'whitish', from *albus* 'white']

AUC *abbr.* (of a date) from the foundation of the city (of Rome). [Latin *ab urbe condita*]

au courant /əʊ ku'rɒ̃/ *predic.adj.* (usu. foll. by *with*, *of*) knowing what is going on; well informed. [French, = in the (regular) course]

auction /'ɔ:kʃ(ə)n/ *n. & v.* ● *n.* **1** a sale of goods, usu. in public, in which articles are sold to the highest bidder. **2** the sequence of bids made at auction bridge. ● *v.tr.* sell by auction. [Latin *auctio* 'increase, auction' from *augēre auct-* 'increase']

auction bridge *n.* a form of bridge in which players bid for the right to name trumps.

auctioneer /ɔ:kʃə'nɪə/ *n.* a person who conducts auctions professionally, by calling for bids and declaring goods sold. □ **auctioneering** *n.*

auction house *n.* a company that runs auction sales.

auction room *n.* (often in *pl.*) the premises where auction sales take place.

auction sale *n.* = AUCTION *n.* 1.

audacious /ɔ:'deɪʃəs/ *adj.* **1** daring, bold. **2** impudent. □ **audaciously** *adv.* **audaciousness** *n.* **audacity** /ɔ:'dasɪti/ *n.* [Latin *audax -acis* 'bold' from *audēre* 'dare']

audible /'ɔ:dɪb(ə)l/ *adj.* capable of being heard. □ **audibility** /-'bɪlɪti/ *n.* **audibleness** *n.* **audibly** *adv.* [Late Latin *audibilis* from *audire* 'hear']

audience /'ɔ:dɪəns/ *n.* **1 a** the assembled listeners or spectators at an event, esp. a stage performance, concert, etc. **b** the people addressed by a film, book, play, etc. **2** a formal interview with a person in authority. **3** *archaic* a hearing (*give audience to my plea*). [Middle English via Old French from Latin *audientia*, from *audire* 'hear']

audile /'ɔ:dʌɪl/ *adj.* of or referring to the sense of hearing. [formed irregularly from Latin *audire* 'hear', on the pattern of *tactile*]

audio /'ɔ:dɪəʊ/ *n.* (usu. *attrib.*) sound or the reproduction of sound. [AUDIO-]

audio- /'ɔ:dɪəʊ/ *comb. form* hearing or sound. [Latin *audire* 'hear' + -o-]

Audio-Animatronics /ˌɔ:dɪəʊˌanɪmə'trɒnɪks/ *n.pl.* (usu. treated as *sing.*) *propr.* = ANIMATRONICS. [AUDIO- + ANIMATRONICS]

audio cassette *n.* a cassette of audiotape.

audio frequency *n.* a frequency capable of being perceived by the human ear.

audiology /ɔ:dɪ'ɒlədʒi/ *n.* the science of hearing. □ **audiologist** *n.*

audiometer /ɔ:dɪ'ɒmɪtə/ *n.* an instrument for testing hearing.

audiophile /'ɔ:dɪə(ʊ)fʌɪl/ *n.* a hi-fi enthusiast.

audiotape /'ɔ:dɪə(ʊ)teɪp/ *n. & v.* ● *n.* (also **audio tape**) **1 a** magnetic tape on which sound can be recorded. **b** a length of this, esp. an audio cassette. **2** a sound recording on tape. ● *v.tr.* record (sound, speech, etc.) on tape.

audio typist *n.* a person who types direct from a recording.

audio-visual /ɔ:dɪəʊ'vɪʒjʊəl, -'vɪzjʊəl/ *adj.* (esp. of teaching methods) using both sight and sound.

audit /'ɔ:dɪt/ *n. & v.* ● *n.* **1** an official examination of accounts. **2** a systematic review (*safety audit*). ● *v.tr.* (**audited**, **auditing**) **1** conduct an audit of. **2** *N. Amer.* attend (a class) informally, without working for credits. [Middle English from Latin *auditus* 'hearing', from *audire audit-* 'hear']

audition /ɔ:'dɪʃ(ə)n/ *n. & v.* ● *n.* **1** an interview for a role as a singer, actor, dancer, etc., consisting of a practical demonstration of suitability. **2** the power of hearing or listening. ● *v.* **1** *tr.* interview (a candidate) at an audition. **2** *intr.* be interviewed at an audition. [French *audition* or Latin *auditio*, from *audire audit-* 'hear']

auditive /'ɔ:dɪtɪv/ *adj.* concerned with hearing. [French *auditif -ive* (as AUDITION, -IVE)]

auditor /'ɔ:dɪtə/ *n.* **1** a person who conducts an audit. **2** a listener. **3** *N. Amer.* a person who audits a class. □ **auditorial** /-'tɔ:rɪəl/ *adj.* [Middle English via Anglo-French *auditour* from Latin *auditor -oris* (as AUDITIVE, -OR[1])]

auditorium /ɔ:dɪ'tɔ:rɪəm/ *n.* (*pl.* **auditoriums** or **auditoria** /-rɪə/) **1** the part of a theatre etc. in which the audience sits. **2** *N. Amer.* a large room, esp. a school hall. **3** *N. Amer.* a building incorporating a large hall for public gatherings, sports events, etc. [Latin, neut. of *auditorius* (*adj.*): see AUDITORY, -ORIUM]

auditory /'ɔ:dɪt(ə)ri/ *adj.* **1** concerned with hearing. **2** received by the ear. [Latin *auditorius* (as AUDITOR, -ORY[2])]

AUEW *abbr.* (in the UK) Amalgamated Union of Engineering Workers.

au fait /əʊ 'feɪ/ *predic.adj.* (usu. foll. by *with*) having current knowledge; conversant (*fully au fait with the arrangements*). □ **put** (or **make**) **au fait with** esp. *Brit.* instruct in. [French, literally 'to the fact, to the point']

au fond /əʊ 'fɒ̃, French o fɔ̃/ *adv.* basically; at bottom. [French]

Aug. *abbr.* August.

Augean /ɔ:'dʒi:ən/ *adj. literary* filthy; extremely dirty. [Latin *Augeas* from Greek *Augeias* (in Greek mythology, the owner of stables which Hercules cleaned by diverting a river through them)]

auger /'ɔ:gə/ *n.* **1** a tool resembling a large corkscrew, for boring holes in wood. **2** a similar larger tool for boring holes in the ground. [Old English *nafogār* from *nafu* NAVE[2], + *gār* 'pierce': for loss of *n* cf. ADDER]

aught[1] /ɔ:t/ *n.* (also **ought**) (usu. implying *neg.*) *archaic* anything at all. [Old English *āwiht*, from Germanic]

aught[2] var. of OUGHT[2].

augite /'ɔ:dʒʌɪt/ *n. Mineral.* a dark green or black mineral of the pyroxene group, occurring in many igneous rocks. [Latin *augites* from Greek *augitēs*, from *augē* 'lustre']

augment *v. & n.* ● *v.tr. & intr.* /ɔ:g'mɛnt/ make or become greater; increase. ● *n.* /'ɔ:gm(ə)nt/ *Gram.* a vowel prefixed to the past tenses in the older Indo-European languages. □ **augmenter** *n.* [Middle English from Old French *augment* (*n.*), French *augmenter* (*v.*), or Late Latin *augmentum*, *augmentare* from Latin *augēre* 'increase']

augmentation /ɔ:gmɛn'teɪʃ(ə)n/ *n.* **1** enlargement; growth; increase. **2** *Mus.* the lengthening of the time values of notes in melodic parts. [Middle English via

French from Late Latin *augmentatio -onis* from *augmentare* (as AUGMENT)]

augmentative /ɔːg'mɛntətɪv/ *adj.* **1** having the property of increasing. **2** *Gram.* (of an affix or derived word) reinforcing the idea of the original word. [French *augmentatif -ive* or medieval Latin *augmentativus* (as AUGMENT)]

augmented interval *n. Mus.* a perfect or major interval that is increased by a semitone.

au gratin /əʊ 'gratan/ *adj.* sprinkled with breadcrumbs or grated cheese and browned. [French from *gratter*, = by grating, from GRATE[1]]

augur /'ɔːgə/ *v. & n.* ● *v.* **1** *intr.* (of an event, circumstance, etc.) suggest a specified outcome (usu. **augur well** or **ill**); portend, bode (*all augured well for our success*). **2** *tr.* **a** foresee, predict. **b** portend. ● *n. hist.* an ancient Roman religious official who observed natural signs, esp. the behaviour of birds, interpreting these as an indication of divine approval or disapproval of a proposed action. □ **augural** /'ɔːgjʊr(ə)l/ *adj.* [Latin]

augury /'ɔːgjʊri/ *n.* (*pl.* **-ies**) **1** an omen; a portent. **2** the work of an augur; the interpretation of omens. [Middle English from Old French *augurie* or Latin *augurium* from AUGUR]

August /'ɔːgəst/ *n.* the eighth month of the year. [Old English from Latin *Augustus* Caesar, the first Roman emperor]

august /ɔː'gʌst/ *adj.* inspiring reverence and admiration; venerable, impressive. □ **augustly** *adv.* **augustness** *n.* [French *auguste* or Latin *augustus* 'consecrated, venerable']

Augustan /ɔː'gʌst(ə)n/ *adj. & n.* ● *adj.* **1** connected with, occurring during, or influenced by the reign of the Roman emperor Augustus, esp. as an outstanding period of Latin literature. **2** (of a nation's literature) refined and classical in style (in England of the literature of the 17th–18th c.). ● *n.* a writer of the Augustan age of any literature. [Latin *Augustanus* from *Augustus*]

Augustine /ɔː'gʌstɪn/ *n.* an Augustinian friar. [Middle English via Old French *augustin* from Latin *Augustinus* AUGUSTINIAN]

Augustinian /ɔːgə'stɪnɪən/ *adj. & n.* ● *adj.* **1** of or relating to St Augustine, a Doctor of the Church (d. 430), or his doctrines. **2** belonging to a religious order observing a rule derived from St Augustine's writings. ● *n.* **1** an adherent of the doctrines of St Augustine. **2** a member of an Augustinian order. [Latin *Augustinus* 'Augustine']

auk /ɔːk/ *n.* any marine diving bird of the family Alcidae, native to the northern oceans, with heavy body, short wings, and black and white plumage, e.g. the guillemot, puffin, and razorbill. [Old Norse *álka*]

auklet /'ɔːklɪt/ *n.* any of several small auks mainly of the N. Pacific.

auld /ɔːld, ɑːld/ *adj. Sc.* old. [Old English *ald*, Anglian form of OLD]

auld lang syne /ɔːld laŋ 'sʌɪn/ *n.* times long past. [Scots, = old long since: also as the title and refrain of a song]

aumbry /'ɔːmbri/ *n.* (also **ambry** /'ambri/) (*pl.* **-ies**) **1** a small recess in the wall of a church. **2** *hist.* a small cupboard. [Middle English via Old French *almarie*, *armarie* (modern *armoire*) from Latin *armarium* 'closet, chest', from *arma* 'utensils']

au naturel /ˌəʊ natjʊ'rɛl/ *predic.adj. & adv.* **1** uncooked; (cooked) in the most natural or simplest way. **2** in its natural state. [French, = in the natural state]

aunt /ɑːnt/ *n.* **1** the sister of one's father or mother. **2** an uncle's wife. **3** *colloq.* an unrelated woman friend of a child or children. □ **my** (or **my sainted** etc.) **aunt** esp. *Brit. slang* an exclamation of surprise, disbelief, etc. [Middle English via Anglo-French *aunte*, Old French *ante*, from Latin *amita*]

auntie /'ɑːnti/ *n.* (also **aunty**) (*pl.* **-ies**) *colloq.* **1** = AUNT. **2** (**Auntie**) *Brit.* an institution considered to be conservative or cautious, esp. the BBC.

Aunt Sally *n. Brit.* **1** a game in which players throw sticks or balls at a wooden dummy. **2** the object of unreasonable attack.

au pair /əʊ 'pɛː/ *n.* a young foreign person, esp. a woman, helping with housework etc. in exchange for room, board, and pocket money, esp. as a means of learning a language. [French, = on equal terms: earlier as adj. denoting payment by mutual services]

aura /'ɔːrə/ *n.* (*pl.* **aurae** /-riː/ or **auras**) **1** the distinctive atmosphere diffused by or attending a person, place, etc. **2** (in mystic or spiritualistic use) a supposed subtle emanation, visible as a sphere of white or coloured light, surrounding the body of a living creature. **3** a subtle emanation or aroma from flowers etc. **4** *Med.* premonitory symptom(s) in epilepsy etc. □ **aural** *adj.* **auric** *adj.* [Middle English via Latin from Greek, = breeze, breath]

aural /'ɔːr(ə)l/ *adj.* of or relating to or received by the ear. □ **aurally** *adv.* [Latin *auris* 'ear']

■ **Usage** *Aural* is sometimes pronounced /'aʊr(ə)l/ (the first syllable rhyming with *cow*), in order to distinguish it from *oral*. Some people regard this as incorrect.

aureate /'ɔːrɪət/ *adj.* **1** golden, gold-coloured. **2** resplendent. **3** (of language) highly ornamented. [Middle English via Late Latin *aureatus* from Latin *aureus* 'golden', from *aurum* 'gold']

aureole /'ɔːrɪəʊl/ *n.* (also **aureola** /ɔː'rɪələ/) **1** a halo or circle of light, esp. round the head or body of a portrayed religious figure. **2** a corona round the sun or moon. [Middle English from Latin *aureola* (*corona*) 'golden (crown)', fem. of *aureolus* (diminutive of *aureus*) from *aurum* 'gold': *aureole* via Old French from Latin *aureola*]

au revoir /əʊ rə'vwɑː/ *int. & n.* goodbye (until we meet again). [French, literally 'to the seeing again']

auric /'ɔːrɪk/ *adj.* of or relating to trivalent gold. [Latin *aurum* 'gold']

auricle /'ɔːrɪk(ə)l/ *n. Anat.* **1 a** a small muscular pouch on the surface of each atrium of the heart. **b** the atrium itself. **2** the external part of the ear; the pinna. **3** an appendage shaped like the ear. [AURICULA]

auricula /ɔː'rɪkjʊlə/ *n.* a primula, *Primula auricula*, with leaves shaped like bears' ears. Also called *bear's ear*. [Latin, diminutive of *auris* 'ear']

auricular /ɔː'rɪkjʊlə/ *adj.* **1** of or relating to the ear or hearing. **2** of or relating to the auricle of the heart. **3** shaped like an auricle. [Late Latin *auricularis* (as AURICULA)]

auriculate /ɔː'rɪkjʊlət/ *adj.* having one or more auricles or ear-shaped appendages. [Latin]

auriferous /ɔː'rɪf(ə)rəs/ *adj.* naturally bearing gold. [Latin *aurifer* from *aurum* 'gold']

Aurignacian /ɔːrɪ'njeɪʃ(ə)n, -ɪg'neɪ-/ *adj. & n.* ● *adj.* of or relating to a palaeolithic culture in Europe and the Near East, following the Mousterian and dated to *c.* 34,000–29,000 BC. ● *n.* this culture. [French *Aurignacien* from *Aurignac* in SW France, where remains were found]

aurochs /'ɔːrɒks, 'aʊ-/ *n.* (*pl.* same) an extinct wild ox, *Bos primigenius*, ancestor of domestic cattle and formerly native to many parts of the world. Also called *urus*. [German from Old High German *ūrohso* from *ūr-* 'urus' + *ohso* 'ox']

aurora /ɔː'rɔːrə/ *n.* (*pl.* **auroras** or **aurorae** /-riː/) **1** a luminous electrical atmospheric phenomenon, usu. of streamers of light in the sky above the northern or southern magnetic pole. **2** *poet.* the dawn. □ **auroral** *adj.* [Latin, = dawn, goddess of dawn]

aurora australis /ɔː'streɪlɪs/ *n.* the aurora of the southern regions. [Latin *australis* 'southern': see AUSTRAL]

aurora borealis /bɔːrɪˈeɪlɪs/ *n.* the aurora of the northern regions. [Latin *borealis* 'northern': see BOREAL]

auscultation /ɔːsk(ə)lˈteɪʃ(ə)n/ *n.* the act of listening, esp. to sounds from the heart, lungs, etc., as a part of medical diagnosis. □ **auscultatory** /-ˈskʌltət(ə)ri/ *adj.* [Latin *auscultatio* from *auscultare* 'listen to']

auspice /ˈɔːspɪs/ *n.* **1** (in *pl.*) patronage (esp. in phr. **under the auspices of**). **2** a forecast. [originally 'observation of bird-flight in divination': French *auspice* or Latin *auspicium*, from *auspex* 'observer of birds' from *avis* 'bird']

auspicious /ɔːˈspɪʃəs/ *adj.* **1** of good omen; favourable. **2** prosperous. □ **auspiciously** *adv.* **auspiciousness** *n.* [AUSPICE + -OUS]

Aussie /ˈɒzi, ˈɒsi/ *n. & adj.* (also **Ossie, Ozzie**) *colloq.* ● *n.* **1** an Australian. **2** Australia. ● *adj.* Australian. [abbreviation]

austere /ɒˈstɪə, ɔː-/ *adj.* (**austerer, austerest**) **1** severely simple. **2** morally strict. **3** harsh, stern. □ **austerely** *adv.* [Middle English via Old French and Latin *austerus* from Greek *austēros* 'severe']

austerity /ɒˈsterɪti, ɔː-/ *n.* (*pl.* **-ies**) **1** sternness; moral severity. **2** severe simplicity, e.g. of nationwide economies. **3** (esp. in *pl.*) an austere practice (*the austerities of a monk's life*).

Austin /ˈɒstɪn, ˈɔː-/ *n.* = AUGUSTINIAN. [contraction of AUGUSTINE]

austral /ˈɒstr(ə)l, ˈɔː-/ *adj.* **1** southern. **2** (**Austral**) of Australia or Australasia (*Austral English*). [Middle English from Latin *australis*, from *Auster* 'south wind']

Australasian /ɒstrəˈleɪʒ(ə)n, -ʃ(ə)n, ɔː-/ *adj.* of or relating to Australasia, a region consisting of Australia and islands of the SW Pacific. [*Australasia* from French *Australasie*, as *Australia* + *Asia*]

Australian /ɒˈstreɪlɪən, ɔː-/ *n. & adj.* ● *n.* **1** a native or national of Australia. **2** a person of Australian descent. ● *adj.* of or relating to Australia. □ **Australianism** *n.* [French *australien* from Latin (as AUSTRAL)]

Australian bear *n.* a koala bear.

Australian Rules *n.* (in full **Australian Rules football**) a form of football played with an oval ball on an oval pitch by teams of 18. Also called *Australian National Football.*

Australian salmon see SALMON 2a.

Australian terrier *n.* a wire-haired Australian breed of terrier.

Australopithecus /ˌɒstrələʊˈpɪθɪkəs, ˌɔː-/ *n.* an extinct bipedal primate of the genus *Australopithecus*, having apelike and human characteristics, found fossilized in Africa. □ **australopithecine** /-ɪsiːn/ *n. & adj.* [modern Latin, from Latin *australis* 'southern' + Greek *pithēkos* 'ape']

Austrian /ˈɒstrɪən, ˈɔː-/ *n. & adj.* ● *n.* **1** a native or national of Austria. **2** a person of Austrian descent. ● *adj.* of or relating to Austria.

Austro-[1] /ˈɒstrəʊ, ˈɔː-/ *comb. form* Austrian; Austrian and (*Austro-Hungarian*).

Austro-[2] /ˈɒstrəʊ, ˈɔː-/ *comb. form* Australian; Australian and (*Austro-Asiatic*).

Austronesian /ɒstrə(ʊ)ˈniːzjən, -ʒ(ə)n, ɔː-/ *n. & adj.* ● *n.* a family of agglutinative languages spoken widely in Malaysia, Indonesia, and other parts of SE Asia, and in the islands of the central and southern Pacific. ● *adj.* of or relating to this language family. [German *austronesisch*, from Latin *australis* 'southern' + -o- + Greek *nēsos* 'island']

AUT *abbr.* (in the UK) Association of University Teachers.

autarchy /ˈɔːtɑːki/ *n.* (*pl.* **-ies**) **1** absolute sovereignty. **2** despotism. **3** an autarchic country or society. □ **autarchic** /ɔːˈtɑːkɪk/ *adj.* **autarchical** /ɔːˈtɑːkɪk(ə)l/ *adj.* [modern Latin *autarchia* (as AUTO-, Greek *-arkhia* from *arkhō* 'rule')]

autarky /ˈɔːtɑːki/ *n.* (*pl.* **-ies**) **1** self-sufficiency, esp. as an economic system. **2** a state etc. run according to such a system. □ **autarkic** /ɔːˈtɑːkɪk/ *adj.* **autarkical** /ɔːˈtɑːkɪk(ə)l/ *adj.* **autarkist** *n.* [Greek *autarkeia* (as AUTO-, *arkeō* 'suffice')]

auteur /əʊˈtəː, ɔː-/ *n.* a film director who has such great influence on his or her films that he or she ranks as their author. [French, = author]

authentic /ɔːˈθentɪk/ *adj.* **1 a** of undisputed origin; genuine. **b** reliable or trustworthy. **2** *Mus.* (of a mode) containing notes between the final and an octave higher (cf. PLAGAL). □ **authentically** *adv.* **authenticity** /ɔːθenˈtɪsɪti/ *n.* [Middle English via Old French *autentique* and Late Latin *authenticus* from Greek *authentikos* 'principal, genuine']

authenticate /ɔːˈθentɪkeɪt/ *v.tr.* **1** establish the truth or genuineness of. **2** validate. □ **authentication** /-ˈkeɪʃ(ə)n/ *n.* **authenticator** *n.* [medieval Latin *authenticare* from Late Latin *authenticus*: see AUTHENTIC]

author /ˈɔːθə/ *n. & v.* ● *n.* (*fem.* **authoress** /ˈɔːθrɪs, ɔːθəˈres/) **1** a writer, esp. of books. **2** the originator of an event, a condition, etc. (*the author of all my woes*). ● *v.tr.* **1** *disp.* be the author of (a book, article, etc.). **2** be the originator of (an idea, condition, circumstance, etc.); bring about. □ **authorial** /ɔːˈθɔːrɪəl/ *adj.* [Middle English via Anglo-French *autour*, Old French *autor* from Latin *auctor*, from *augēre auct-* 'increase, originate, promote']

■ **Usage** *Author* can be used of both male and female writers and many women writers prefer it to *authoress.*

The use of the verb *author* as a mere synonym for *write* (as in *he authored several books on the subject*) is deplored by many people, although *author* is different from *write* in that it implies publication of the text produced. In addition, *author* is often used in contexts where the person or people responsible for the text (often a committee) did not actually write it themselves, and where the thing written is a report, article, or document, rather than a book, e.g. *The chairperson of the commission that authored the report referred to it several times in her speech.*

In the terminology of computing, *authoring* is used to mean the creation of programs, databases, etc., as in the phrases *authoring system, authoring package*, or *authoring tool.*

Unlike *author, co-author* is generally acceptable as a verb.

---

authoring /ˈɔːθərɪŋ/ *n. Computing* the creation of programs, databases, etc. for computer applications such as computer-assisted learning or multimedia products.

authoritarian /ɔːθɒrɪˈteːrɪən/ *adj. & n.* ● *adj.* **1** favouring, encouraging, or enforcing strict obedience to authority, as opposed to individual freedom. **2** tyrannical or domineering. ● *n.* a person favouring absolute obedience to a constituted authority. □ **authoritarianism** *n.*

authoritative /ɔːˈθɒrɪtətɪv, -teɪtɪv/ *adj.* **1** being recognized as true or dependable. **2** (of a person, behaviour, etc.) commanding or self-confident. **3** official; supported by authority (*an authoritative document*). □ **authoritatively** *adv.* **authoritativeness** *n.*

authority /ɔːˈθɒrɪti/ *n.* (*pl.* **-ies**) **1 a** the power or right to enforce obedience. **b** (often foll. by *for*, or *to* + infin.) delegated power. **2** (esp. in *pl.*) a person or body having authority, esp. political or administrative. **3 a** an influence exerted on opinion because of recognized knowledge or expertise. **b** such an influence expressed in a book, quotation, etc. **c** a person whose opinion is accepted, esp. an expert in a subject (*an authority on vintage cars*). **4** the weight of evidence. [Middle English via Old French *autorité* from Latin *auctoritas*, from *auctor*: see AUTHOR]

authorize /ˈɔːθərʌɪz/ *v.tr.* (also **-ise**) **1** sanction. **2** (foll. by *to* + infin.) **a** give authority. **b** commission (a person or body) (*authorized to trade*). □ **authorization** /ɔːθərʌɪˈzeɪʃ(ə)n/ *n.* [Middle English via Old French *autoriser* and medieval Latin *auctorizare* from *auctor*: see AUTHOR]

Authorized Version *n.* esp. *Brit.* an English translation of the Bible made in 1611 and still widely used. Also called *King James Bible.*

authorship /ˈɔːθəʃɪp/ *n.* **1** the origin of a book or other written work (*of unknown authorship*). **2** the occupation of writing.

autism /ˈɔːtɪz(ə)m/ *n.* a mental condition, usu. present from childhood, characterized by complete self-absorption and a reduced ability to respond to or communicate with the outside world. □ **autistic** /ɔːˈtɪstɪk/ *adj.* [modern Latin *autismus* (as AUTO-, -ISM)]

auto /ˈɔːtəʊ/ *n.* (*pl.* **-os**) (usu. *attrib.*) *N. Amer. colloq.* a motor car. [abbreviation of AUTOMOBILE]

auto- /ˈɔːtəʊ/ *comb. form* (usu. **aut-** before a vowel) **1** self (*autism*). **2** one's own (*autobiography*). **3** by oneself or spontaneous (*auto-suggestion*). **4** by itself or automatic (*automobile*). [from or on the pattern of Greek *auto-*, from *autos* 'self']

autobahn /ˈɔːtəbɑːn/ *n.* a German, Austrian, or Swiss motorway. [German from *Auto* 'motor car' + *Bahn* 'path, road']

autobiography /ɔːtəbʌɪˈɒgrəfi/ *n.* (*pl.* **-ies**) **1** a personal account of one's own life, esp. for publication. **2** this as a process or literary form. □ **autobiographer** *n.* **autobiographic** /ˌɔːtəʊbʌɪəˈgrafɪk/ *adj.* **autobiographical** /-ˈgrafɪk(ə)l/ *adj.*

autocar /ˈɔːtə(ʊ)kɑː/ *n. archaic* a motor vehicle.

autocephalous /ɔːtəʊˈsɛf(ə)ləs/ *adj.* **1** (esp. of an Eastern Church) appointing its own head. **2** (of a bishop, Church, etc.) independent. [Greek *autokephalos* (as AUTO-, *kephalē* 'head')]

autochthon /ɔːˈtɒkθ(ə)n, -θəʊn/ *n.* (*pl.* **autochthons** or **autochthones** /-θəniːz/) (usu. in *pl.*) the original or earliest known inhabitants of a country; aboriginals. [Greek, = sprung from the earth (as AUTO-, *khthōn*, *-onos* 'earth')]

autochthonous /ɔːˈtɒkθənəs/ *adj.* **1** indigenous, native. **2** of independent or local formation. **3** *Geol.* (of a deposit) formed in its present position.

autoclave /ˈɔːtəkleɪv/ *n.* **1** a strong vessel used for chemical reactions at high pressures and temperatures. **2** a sterilizer using high-pressure steam. [AUTO- + Latin *clavus* 'nail' or *clavis* 'key': so called because self-fastening]

autocracy /ɔːˈtɒkrəsi/ *n.* (*pl.* **-ies**) **1** absolute government by one person. **2** the power exercised by such a person. **3** an autocratic country or society. [Greek *autokrateia* (as AUTOCRAT)]

autocrat /ˈɔːtəkrat/ *n.* **1** an absolute ruler. **2** a dictatorial person. □ **autocratic** /-ˈkratɪk/ *adj.* **autocratically** /-ˈkratɪk(ə)li/ *adv.* [French *autocrate* from Greek *autokratēs* (as AUTO-, *kratos* 'power')]

autocross /ˈɔːtəʊkrɒs/ *n.* motor racing across country or on unmade roads. [AUTOMOBILE + CROSS- 1]

autocue /ˈɔːtəʊkjuː/ *n.* esp. *Brit. propr.* a device, unseen by the audience, displaying a television script to a speaker or performer as an aid to memory (cf. TELEPROMPTER).

auto-da-fé /ˌɔːtəʊdɑːˈfeɪ/ *n.* (*pl.* **autos-da-fé**) /ˌɔːtəʊz-/ **1** a sentence of punishment by the Spanish Inquisition. **2** the execution of such a sentence, esp. the burning of a heretic. [Portuguese, = act of the faith]

autodidact /ˈɔːtəʊdɪdakt/ *n.* a self-taught person. □ **autodidactic** /-ˈdaktɪk/ *adj.* [AUTO- + *didact* as DIDACTIC]

auto-erotism /ɔːtəʊˈɛrətɪz(ə)m/ *n.* (also **auto-eroticism** /-ɪˈrɒtɪsɪz(ə)m/) *Psychol.* sexual excitement generated by stimulating one's own body; masturbation. □ **auto-erotic** /-ɪˈrɒtɪk/ *adj.*

autofocus /ˈɔːtəʊˌfəʊkəs/ *n.* a device focusing a camera etc. automatically.

autogamy /ɔːˈtɒgəmi/ *n. Bot.* self-fertilization in plants. □ **autogamous** *adj.* [AUTO- + Greek *-gamia* from *gamos* 'marriage']

autogenous /ɔːˈtɒdʒɪnəs/ *adj.* self-produced.

autogenous welding *n.* a process of joining metal by melting the edges together, without adding material.

autogiro /ɔːtəʊˈdʒʌɪrəʊ/ *n.* (also **autogyro**) (*pl.* **-os**) a form of aircraft like a small helicopter but with freely rotating horizontal vanes and a propeller. [Spanish (as AUTO-, *giro* 'gyration')]

autograft /ˈɔːtəgrɑːft/ *n. Surgery* a graft of tissue from one point to another of the same individual's body.

autograph /ˈɔːtəgrɑːf/ *n.* & *v.* ● *n.* **1 a** a signature, esp. that of a celebrity. **b** handwriting. **2** a manuscript in an author's own handwriting. **3** a document signed by its author. ● *v.tr.* **1** sign (a photograph, autograph album, etc.). **2** write (a letter etc.) by hand. [French *autographe* or Late Latin *autographum* from Greek *autographon*, neut. of *autographos* (as AUTO-, -GRAPH)]

autography /ɔːˈtɒgrəfi/ *n.* **1** writing done with one's own hand. **2** the facsimile reproduction of writing or illustration. □ **autographic** /-ˈgrafɪk/ *adj.*

autogyro var. of AUTOGIRO.

autoharp /ˈɔːtə(ʊ)hɑːp/ *n.* a kind of zither with a mechanical device to allow the playing of chords.

autoimmune /ˌɔːtəʊɪˈmjuːn/ *adj. Med.* (of a disease) caused by antibodies or lymphocytes produced against substances naturally present in the body. □ **autoimmunity** *n.*

autointoxication /ˌɔːtəʊɪntɒksɪˈkeɪʃ(ə)n/ *n. Med.* poisoning by a toxin formed within the body itself.

autolysis /ɔːˈtɒlɪsɪs/ *n.* the destruction of cells by their own enzymes. □ **autolytic** /ɔːtəˈlɪtɪk/ *adj.* [German *Autolyse* (as AUTO-, -LYSIS)]

automat /ˈɔːtəmat/ *n. US* **1** a slot machine that dispenses goods. **2** *hist.* a cafeteria containing slot machines dispensing food and drink. [German from French *automate*, formed as AUTOMATION]

automate /ˈɔːtəmeɪt/ *v.tr.* convert to or operate by automation (*the ticket office has been automated*). [back-formation from AUTOMATION]

automatic /ɔːtəˈmatɪk/ *adj.* & *n.* ● *adj.* **1** (of a machine, device, etc., or its function) working by itself, without direct human intervention. **2 a** done spontaneously, without conscious thought or intention (*an automatic reaction*). **b** necessary and inevitable (*an automatic penalty*). **3** *Psychol.* performed unconsciously or subconsciously. **4** (of a firearm) that continues firing until the ammunition is exhausted or the pressure on the trigger is released. **5** (of a motor vehicle or its transmission) using gears that change automatically according to speed and acceleration. ● *n.* **1** an automatic device, esp. a gun or transmission. **2** *colloq.* a vehicle with automatic transmission. □ **automatically** *adv.* **automaticity** /ɔːtəməˈtɪsɪti/ *n.* [as AUTOMATON + -IC]

automatic pilot *n.* a device for keeping an aircraft on a set course.

automation /ɔːtəˈmeɪʃ(ə)n/ *n.* **1** the use of automatic equipment to save mental and manual labour. **2** the automatic control of the manufacture of a product through its successive stages. [irregular formation from AUTOMATIC + -ATION]

automatism /ɔːˈtɒmətɪz(ə)m/ *n.* **1** *Psychol.* the performance of actions unconsciously or subconsciously; such action. **2** involuntary action. **3** unthinking routine. [French *automatisme* from *automate* AUTOMATON]

automatize /ɔːˈtɒmətʌɪz/ *v.tr.* (also **-ise**) **1** make (a process etc.) automatic. **2** subject (a business, enterprise, etc.) to automation. □ **automatization** /-ˈzeɪʃ(ə)n/ *n.* [AUTOMATIC + -IZE]

automaton /ɔːˈtɒmət(ə)n/ *n.* (*pl.* **automata** /-tə/ or **automatons**) **1** a mechanism with concealed motive power. **2** a person who behaves mechanically, like an automaton. [Latin from Greek, neut. of *automatos* 'acting of itself': see AUTO-]

automobile /ˈɔːtəməbiːl/ *n.* esp. *N. Amer.* a motor car. [French (as AUTO-, MOBILE)]

automotive /ɔːtə'məʊtɪv/ *adj.* concerned with motor vehicles.

autonomic /ɔːtə'nɒmɪk/ *adj.* esp. *Physiol.* functioning involuntarily. [AUTONOMY + -IC]

autonomic nervous system *n.* the part of the nervous system responsible for control of the bodily functions not consciously directed, e.g. heartbeat.

autonomous /ɔː'tɒnəməs/ *adj.* **1** having self-government. **2** acting independently or having the freedom to do so. □ **autonomously** *adv.* [Greek *autonomos* (as AUTONOMY)]

autonomy /ɔː'tɒnəmi/ *n.* (*pl.* **-ies**) **1** the right of self-government. **2** personal freedom. **3** freedom of the will. **4** a self-governing community. □ **autonomist** *n.* [Greek *autonomia* from *autos* 'self' + *nomos* 'law']

autopilot /'ɔːtəʊˌpʌɪlət/ *n.* an automatic pilot. [abbreviation]

autopista /ɔːtə'piːstə/ *n.* a Spanish motorway. [Spanish (as AUTOMOBILE, *pista* 'track')]

autopsy /'ɔːtɒpsi, ɔː'tɒpsi/ *n. & v.* ● *n.* (*pl.* **-ies**) **1** a post-mortem examination. **2** any critical analysis. **3** a personal inspection. ● *v.tr.* perform an autopsy on (a body). [French *autopsie* or modern Latin *autopsia* from Greek, from *autoptēs* 'eye-witness']

autoradiograph /ɔːtəʊ'reɪdɪəgrɑːf/ *n.* a photograph of an object produced by radiation from radioactive material in the object. □ **autoradiographic** /ˌɔːtəreɪdɪə'grafɪk/ *adj.* **autoradiography** /ˌɔːtəreɪdɪ'ɒgrəfi/ *n.*

autorotation /ˌɔːtə(ʊ)rə(ʊ)'teɪʃ(ə)n/ *n.* **1** *Aeron.* rotation (esp. of rotor blades) not caused by engine power. **2** rotation resulting from the shape or structure of an object (e.g. a winged seed). □ **autorotate** *v.intr.*

autoroute /'ɔːtəruːt/ *n.* a French motorway. [French (as AUTOMOBILE, ROUTE)]

autostrada /'ɔːtəstrɑːdə/ *n.* an Italian motorway. [Italian (as AUTOMOBILE, *strada* 'road')]

auto-suggestion /ˌɔːtə(ʊ)sə'dʒɛstʃ(ə)n/ *n.* a self-induced or subconscious suggestion affecting reaction, behaviour, etc.

autotelic /ɔːtə(ʊ)'tɛlɪk/ *adj.* having or being a purpose in itself. [AUTO- + Greek *telos* 'end']

autotomy /ɔː'tɒtəmi/ *n. Zool.* the casting off of a part of the body, e.g. the tail of a lizard, when threatened.

autotoxin /ɔːtə(ʊ)'tɒksɪn/ *n.* a poisonous substance originating within an organism. □ **autotoxic** *adj.*

autotrophic /ɔːtə(ʊ)'trəʊfɪk, -'trɒfɪk/ *adj. Biol.* able to form complex nutritional organic substances from simple inorganic substances such as carbon dioxide (cf. HETEROTROPHIC). [AUTO- + Greek *trophos* 'feeder']

autotype /'ɔːtə(ʊ)tʌɪp/ *n.* **1** a facsimile. **2 a** a photographic printing process for monochrome reproduction. **b** a print made by this process.

autoxidation /ˌɔːtɒksɪ'deɪʃ(ə)n/ *n. Chem.* spontaneous oxidation at ambient temperatures in the presence of oxygen.

autumn /'ɔːtəm/ *n.* **1** the third season of the year, when crops and fruits are gathered, and leaves fall, in the northern hemisphere from September to November and in the southern hemisphere from March to May. **2** *Astron.* the period from the autumnal equinox to the winter solstice. **3** a time of maturity or incipient decay. [Middle English from Old French *autompne* or Latin *autumnus*]

autumnal /ɔː'tʌmn(ə)l/ *adj.* **1** of, characteristic of, or appropriate to autumn (*autumnal colours*). **2** maturing or blooming in autumn. **3** past the prime of life. [Latin *autumnalis* (as AUTUMN, -AL)]

autumn crocus *n.* a plant of the genus *Colchicum*, esp. the meadow saffron.

autumn equinox *n.* (also **autumnal equinox**) **1** the equinox in autumn, on about 22 Sept. in the northern hemisphere and 20 Mar. in the southern hemisphere. **2** *Astron.* the equinox in September.

auxiliary /ɔːg'zɪlɪəri, ɒg-/ *adj. & n.* ● *adj.* **1** (of a person or thing) that gives help. **2** (of services or equipment) subsidiary, additional. ● *n.* (*pl.* **-ies**) **1 a** an auxiliary person or thing. **b** *N. Amer.* an auxiliary group, esp. one of volunteers involved in charitable activities. **2** (in *pl.*) *Mil.* auxiliary troops. **3** *Gram.* an auxiliary verb. [Latin *auxiliarius* from *auxilium* 'help']

auxiliary troops *n.pl.* foreign or allied troops in a belligerent nation's service.

auxiliary verb *n. Gram.* a verb used in forming the tenses, moods, and voices of other verbs.

auxin /'ɔːksɪn/ *n.* any of a group of plant hormones that regulate growth. [German, from Greek *auxō* 'increase' + -IN]

AV *abbr.* **1** audio-visual (teaching aids etc.). **2** Authorized Version (of the Bible).

avadavat /'avədəvat/ *n.* (also **amadavat** /'amə-/) either of two brightly coloured S. Asian waxbills, the green *Amandava formosa* or esp. the red *A. amandava*. [named after *Ahmadabad* in India, where the birds were sold]

avail /ə'veɪl/ *v. & n.* ● *v.* **1** *tr.* help, benefit. **2** *refl.* (foll. by *of*) profit by; take advantage of. **3** *intr.* **a** provide help. **b** be of use, value, or profit. ● *n.* (usu. in *neg.* or *interrog.* phrases) use, profit (*to no avail*; *without avail*; *of what avail?*). [Middle English from obsolete *vail* (*v.*) via Old French *valoir* 'be worth' from Latin *valēre*]

available /ə'veɪləb(ə)l/ *adj.* (often foll. by *to*, *for*) **1** capable of being used; at one's disposal. **2** obtainable; within one's reach. **3 a** (of a person) free, not otherwise occupied. **b** able to be contacted. **4** sexually unattached. □ **availability** /-'bɪlɪti/ *n.* **availableness** *n.* **availably** *adv.* [Middle English from AVAIL + -ABLE]

avalanche /'avəlɑːnʃ/ *n. & v.* ● *n.* **1** a mass of snow and ice, tumbling rapidly down a mountain. **2** a sudden appearance or arrival of anything in large quantities (*faced with an avalanche of work*). ● *v.* **1** *intr.* descend like an avalanche. **2** *tr.* carry down like an avalanche. [French, alteration of dialect *lavanche*, influenced by *avaler* descend]

avant-garde /avɒ̃ː(ŋ)'gɑːd/ *n. & adj.* ● *n.* pioneers or innovators esp. in art and literature. ● *adj.* (of art, ideas, etc.) new, progressive. □ **avant-gardism** *n.* **avant-gardist** *n.* [French, = vanguard]

avarice /'av(ə)rɪs/ *n.* extreme greed for money or gain; cupidity. □ **avaricious** /avə'rɪʃəs/ *adj.* **avariciously** /-'rɪʃəsli/ *adv.* **avariciousness** /-'rɪʃəsnɪs/ *n.* [Middle English via Old French from Latin *avaritia*, from *avarus* 'greedy']

avast /ə'vɑːst/ *int. Naut.* stop, cease. [Dutch *houd vast* 'hold fast']

avatar /'avətɑː/ *n.* **1** *Hinduism* the descent of a deity or released soul to earth in bodily form. **2** incarnation; manifestation. **3** a manifestation or phase. [Sanskrit *avatāra* 'descent', from *ava* 'down' + *tar-* 'pass over']

avaunt /ə'vɔːnt/ *int. archaic* begone. [Middle English via Anglo-French from Old French *avant*, ultimately from Latin *ab* 'from' + *ante* 'before']

Ave. *abbr.* Avenue.

ave /'ɑːvi, 'ɑːveɪ/ *int. & n.* ● *int.* **1** welcome. **2** farewell. ● *n.* **1** (**Ave**; in full **Ave Maria**) a prayer to the Virgin Mary, the opening line from Luke 1:28; also called HAIL MARY. **2** a shout of welcome or farewell. [Middle English from Latin, 2nd sing. imperative of *avēre* 'fare well']

avenge /ə'vɛn(d)ʒ/ *v.tr.* **1** inflict retribution on behalf of (a person, oneself, a violated right, etc.) (*the murderer was punished and the victim avenged*). **2** take vengeance for (an injury) (*the loss of the aircraft would be avenged*). □ **be avenged** avenge oneself. □ **avenger** *n.* [Middle English from Old French *avengier*, from *à* 'to' + *vengier* from Latin *vindicare* 'vindicate']

■ **Usage** Where necessary, though uncommon, the preposition *on* (or *upon*) is used with *avenge*, to introduce the person on whom vengeance is being taken, e.g. *swore he would be avenged on their leader*; *had the power to avenge himself on them*. *Avenge* usually implies that the retribution inflicted is justifiable, whereas *revenge* often implies that the main aim of retribution is to satisfy the injured party's resentment. See also Usage Note at REVENGE.

avens /'eɪv(ə)nz/ *n.* a plant of the genus *Geum* (rose family). See also MOUNTAIN AVENS. [Middle English from Old French *avence* (medieval Latin *avencia*), of unknown origin]

aventurine /ə'vɛntʃərɪn/ *n. Mineral.* **1** brownish glass or mineral containing sparkling gold-coloured particles usu. of copper or gold. **2** a variety of spangled quartz resembling this. [French, from Italian *avventurino* from *avventura* 'chance' (because of its accidental discovery)]

avenue /'av(ə)njuː/ *n.* **1 a** a broad road or street, often with trees at regular intervals along its sides. **b** a tree-lined approach to a country house. **2** a way of approaching or dealing with something (*explored every avenue to find an answer*). **3** (in many American cities having a grid layout) a road running perpendicular to another, esp. east-west. [French, fem. past part. of *avenir*, from Latin *advenire* 'come to']

aver /ə'vəː/ *v.tr.* (**averred**, **averring**) *formal* assert, affirm. [Middle English from Old French *averer* (as AD-, Latin *verus* 'true')]

average /'av(ə)rɪdʒ/ *n., adj., & v.* ● *n.* **1 a** the usual amount, extent, or rate. **b** the ordinary standard. **2** an amount obtained by dividing the total of given amounts by the number of amounts in the set. **3** *Law* the distribution of loss resulting from damage to a ship or cargo. ● *adj.* **1 a** usual, ordinary. **b** mediocre. **2** estimated or calculated by average. ● *v.tr.* **1** amount on average to (*the sale of the product averaged one hundred a day*). **2** do on average (*averages six hours' work a day*). **3 a** estimate the average of. **b** estimate the general standard of. □ **average out** result in an average. **average out at** result in an average of. **on** (or **on an**) **average** as an average rate or estimate. □ **averagely** *adv.* [French *avarie* 'damage to ship or cargo' (see sense 3), via Italian *avaria* from Arabic *'awārīya* 'damaged goods', from *'awār* 'damage at sea, loss': *-age* on the pattern of *damage*]

average adjustment *n. Law* the apportionment of average (see AVERAGE *n.* 3).

averment /ə'vəːm(ə)nt/ *n.* a positive statement; an affirmation, esp. *Law* one with an offer of proof. [Middle English from Anglo-French, Old French *aver(r)ement* (as AVER, -MENT)]

averse /ə'vəːs/ *predic.adj.* (usu. foll. by *to*; also foll. by *from*) opposed, disinclined (*was not averse to helping me*). [Latin *aversus* (as AVERT)]

■ **Usage** Although condemned in the past as etymologically improper (the literal meaning being 'turned *from*'), *averse* is now more often followed by *to* than *from*. This can be justified by analogy with semantically related words such as *disinclined*, *hostile*, *opposed*, etc., which are also used with *to*.

aversion /ə'vəːʃ(ə)n/ *n.* **1** (usu. foll. by *to*, *from*, *for*) a dislike or unwillingness (*has an aversion to hard work*). **2** an object of dislike (*my pet aversion*). □ **aversive** *adj.* [French *aversion* or Latin *aversio* (as AVERT, -ION)]

aversion therapy *n.* therapy designed to make a patient give up an undesirable habit by associating it with an unpleasant effect.

avert /ə'vəːt/ *v.tr.* **1** (often foll. by *from*) turn away (one's eyes or thoughts). **2** prevent or ward off (an undesirable occurrence). □ **avertible** *adj.* (also **avertable**). [Middle English from Latin *avertere* (as AB-, *vertere vers-* 'turn'): partly via Old French *avertir* and Romanic]

■ **Usage** Care should be taken not to confuse sense 2 of *avert* with *avoid*, e.g. *Disaster was narrowly averted* and *He narrowly avoided being arrested. Avert* incorporates the idea of taking action to ward off an undesirable event in advance, while *avoid* means 'to escape' or 'evade'.

Avesta /ə'vɛstə/ *n.* (usu. prec. by *the*) the sacred writings of Zoroastrianism (see ZEND). [Persian]

Avestan /ə'vɛst(ə)n/ *adj. & n.* ● *adj.* of or relating to the Avesta. ● *n.* the ancient Iranian language of the Avesta.

avian /'eɪvɪən/ *adj.* of or relating to birds. [Latin *avis* 'bird']

aviary /'eɪvɪəri/ *n.* (*pl.* **-ies**) a large enclosure or building for keeping birds. [Latin *aviarium* (as AVIAN, -ARY[1])]

aviate /'eɪvɪeɪt/ *v.* **1** *intr.* pilot or fly in an aeroplane. **2** *tr.* pilot (an aeroplane). [back-formation from AVIATION]

aviation /eɪvɪ'eɪʃ(ə)n/ *n.* **1** the skill or practice of operating aircraft. **2** aircraft manufacture. [French, from Latin *avis* 'bird']

aviator /'eɪvɪeɪtə/ *n.* (*fem.* **aviatrix** /'eɪvɪətrɪks/) an airman or airwoman. [French *aviateur* from Latin *avis* 'bird']

aviculture /'eɪvɪkʌltʃə/ *n.* the rearing and keeping of birds. □ **aviculturist** /-'kʌltʃ(ə)rɪst/ *n.* [Latin *avis* 'bird', on the pattern of AGRICULTURE]

avid /'avɪd/ *adj.* (usu. foll. by *of*, *for*) eager, greedy. □ **avidly** *adv.* [French *avide* or Latin *avidus*, from *avēre* 'crave']

avidity /ə'vɪdɪti/ *n.* **1** eagerness, greed. **2** *Biochem.* the overall strength of binding between an antibody and an antigen.

avifauna /'eɪvɪfɔːnə/ *n.* birds of a region or country collectively. □ **avifaunal** *adj.* [Latin *avis* 'bird' + FAUNA]

avionics /eɪvɪ'ɒnɪks/ *n.pl.* (usu. treated as *sing.*) electronics as applied to aviation.

avitaminosis /eɪˌvɪtəmɪ'nəʊsɪs, -ˌvʌɪt-/ *n.* (*pl.* **avitaminoses** /-'nəʊsiːz/) *Med.* a condition resulting from vitamin deficiency.

avizandum /avɪ'zandəm/ *n. Sc. Law* a period of time for further consideration of a judgement. [medieval Latin, gerund of *avizare* 'consider' (as ADVISE)]

avocado /avə'kɑːdəʊ/ *n. & adj.* ● *n.* (*pl.* **-os**) **1** (in full **avocado pear**) a pear-shaped fruit with a rough leathery skin, smooth oily edible flesh, and a large stone; also called *alligator pear*. **2** the tropical evergreen tree, *Persea americana*, native to Central America, bearing this fruit. **3** the light green colour of the flesh of this fruit. ● *adj.* of the colour avocado; light green. [Spanish, = advocate (substituted for Nahuatl *ahuacatl*)]

avocation /avə'keɪʃ(ə)n/ *n.* **1** a minor occupation. **2** *colloq.* a vocation or calling. [Latin *avocatio* from *avocare* 'call away']

avocet /'avəsɛt/ *n.* a wading bird of the genus *Recurvirostra* with long legs and a long slender upward-curved bill and usu. black and white plumage. [French *avocette* from Italian *avosetta*]

Avogadro's constant /avə'gɑːdrəʊz/ *n.* (also **Avogadro's number**) *Chem.* the number of atoms or molecules in one mole of a substance (symbol **L**). [named after A. *Avogadro*, Italian physicist d. 1856]

Avogadro's law /avə'gɑːdrəʊz/ *n.* (also **Avogadro's hypothesis**) *Physics* a law stating that equal volumes of gases at the same temperature and pressure contain equal numbers of molecules.

avoid /ə'vɔɪd/ *v.tr.* **1** keep away from (a thing, person, or action); refrain from. **2** escape; evade. **3** *Law* **a** nullify (a decree or contract). **b** quash (a sentence). □ **avoidable** *adj.* **avoidably** *adv.* **avoidance** *n.* **avoider** *n.* [Anglo-French *avoider*, Old French *evuider* 'clear out, get rid of', from *vuide* 'empty', VOID]

■ **Usage** See Usage Note at AVERT.

avoirdupois /avədə'pɔɪz, ˌavwɑːdjʊ'pwɑː/ *n.* **1** (in full **avoirdupois weight**) a system of weights based on a pound of 16 ounces or 7,000 grains. **2** weight, heaviness. [Middle English from Old French *aveir de peis* 'goods of weight' from *aveir* (modern *avoir*) 'to have', used as a noun, from Latin *habēre* 'have', + *peis* (see POISE[1])]

avouch /ə'vaʊtʃ/ *v.tr. & intr. archaic* or *literary* guarantee, affirm, confess. □ **avouchment** *n.* [Middle

English via Old French *avochier* from Latin *advocare* (as AD-, *vocare* 'call')]

avow /ə'vaʊ/ *v.tr.* **1** admit, confess. **2 a** *refl.* admit that one is (*avowed himself the author*). **b** (as **avowed** *adj.*) admitted (*the avowed author*). □ **avowal** *n.* **avowedly** /ə'vaʊɪdli/ *adv.* [Middle English via Old French *avouer* 'acknowledge' from Latin *advocare* (as AD-, *vocare* 'call')]

avulsion /ə'vʌlʃ(ə)n/ *n.* **1** a tearing away. **2** *Law* a sudden removal of land by a flood etc. to another person's estate. □ **avulse** *v.tr.* [French *avulsion* or Latin *avulsio*, from *avellere avuls-* 'pluck away']

avuncular /ə'vʌŋkjʊlə/ *adj.* like or of an uncle; kind and friendly, esp. towards a younger person. [Latin *avunculus* 'maternal uncle', diminutive of *avus* 'grandfather']

aw /ɔ:/ *int.* esp. *N. Amer.* & *Sc.* expressing mild protest, entreaty, commiseration, or disapproval. [a natural exclamation]

AWACS /'eɪwaks/ *n.* a long-range airborne radar system for detecting enemy aircraft. [abbreviation of *a*irborne *w*arning *a*nd *c*ontrol *s*ystem]

await /ə'weɪt/ *v.tr.* **1** wait for. **2** (of an event or thing) be in store for (*a surprise awaits you*). [Middle English from Anglo-French *awaitier*, Old French *aguaitier* (as AD-, *waitier* WAIT)]

awake /ə'weɪk/ *v.* & *adj.* ● *v.* (*past* **awoke** /ə'wəʊk/; *past part.* **awoken** /ə'wəʊk(ə)n/) **1** *intr.* **a** cease to sleep. **b** become active. **2** *intr.* (foll. by *to*) become aware of. **3** *tr.* rouse, esp. from sleep. ● *predic.adj.* **1 a** not asleep. **b** vigilant. **2** (foll. by *to*) aware of. □ **be awake up** *Austral. colloq.* = *be a wake-up* (see WAKE[1]). [Old English *āwæcnan*, *āwacian* (as A-[2], WAKE[1])]

■ **Usage** See Usage Note at AWAKEN.

awaken /ə'weɪk(ə)n/ *v.* **1** *v.tr.* & *intr.* = AWAKE *v.* **2** *tr.* (often foll. by *to*) make aware. [Old English *onwæcnan* etc. (as A-[2], WAKEN)]

■ **Usage** *Awake* and *awaken* are largely interchangeable, but *awaken* is much rarer than *awake* as an intransitive verb, and has an extra transitive usage (sense 2 above), as in *The strike had awakened them to the possibilities of resistance.*

award /ə'wɔ:d/ *v.* & *n.* ● *v.tr.* **1** give or order to be given as a payment, compensation, or prize (*awarded him a knighthood; was awarded damages*). **2** grant, assign. ● *n.* **1** a payment, compensation, or prize awarded. **2** a judicial decision. □ **awarder** *n.* [Middle English from Anglo-French *awarder*, ultimately from Germanic: see WARD]

aware /ə'wɛ:/ *predic.adj.* **1** (often foll. by *of*, or *that* + clause) conscious; not ignorant; having knowledge. **2** well informed (often in *comb.*: *politically aware*). □ **awareness** *n.* [Old English *gewær*, from West Germanic]

■ **Usage** In popular use, *aware* is sometimes used in sense 2 to mean 'well informed', without any qualifying word, as in *she's a very aware person*. This should be avoided in formal contexts.

awash /ə'wɒʃ/ *predic.adj.* **1** level with the surface of water which just washes over; covered in water; flooded. **2** (usu. foll. by *with*, *in*) rich, overflowing, abounding.

away /ə'weɪ/ *adv.*, *adj.*, & *n.* ● *adv.* **1** to or at a distance from the place, person, or thing in question (*go away; give away; look away; they are away; 5 miles away*). **2** towards or into non-existence (*sounds die away; explain it away; idled their time away*). **3** constantly, persistently, continuously (*work away; laugh away*). **4** without hesitation (*ask away*). ● *adj. Sport* played on an opponent's ground etc. (*away match; away win*). ● *n. Sport* an away match or win. □ **away with** (as *imper.*) take away; let us be rid of. [Old English *onweg*, *aweg* 'on one's way' from A[2] + WAY]

awe /ɔ:/ *n.* & *v.* ● *n.* reverential fear or wonder (*stand in awe of*). ● *v.tr.* inspire with awe. [Old English *ege* and Old Norse *agi*, from Germanic]

aweary /ə'wɪəri/ *predic.adj.* (often foll. by *of*) *poet.* weary. [*a* (imitating A-[3]) + WEARY]

aweigh /ə'weɪ/ *predic.adj. Naut.* (of an anchor) clear of the sea or river bed; hanging. [A[2] + WEIGH[1]]

awe-inspiring *adj.* causing awe or wonder; amazing, magnificent.

awesome /'ɔ:s(ə)m/ *adj.* **1** inspiring awe; dreaded. **2** *slang* marvellous, excellent. □ **awesomely** *adv.* **awesomeness** *n.* [AWE + -SOME[1]]

awestricken /'ɔ:strɪk(ə)n/ *adj.* (also **awestruck** /-strʌk/) struck or affected by awe.

awful /'ɔ:fʊl, -f(ə)l/ *adj.* **1** *colloq.* **a** unpleasant or horrible (*awful weather*). **b** poor in quality; very bad (*has awful writing*). **c** (*attrib.*) excessive; remarkably large (*an awful lot of money*). **2** *poet.* inspiring awe. □ **awfulness** *n.* [AWE + -FUL]

awfully /'ɔ:fʊli, -fli/ *adv.* **1** *colloq.* in an unpleasant, bad, or horrible way (*he played awfully*). **2** *colloq.* very (*she's awfully pleased; thanks awfully*). **3** *poet.* reverently.

awhile /ə'wʌɪl/ *adv.* for a short time. [Old English *āne hwīle* 'a while']

awkward /'ɔ:kwəd/ *adj.* **1** ill-adapted for use; causing difficulty in use. **2** clumsy or bungling. **3 a** esp. *Brit.* embarrassed; ill at ease (*felt awkward about it*). **b** embarrassing (*an awkward situation*). **4** esp. *Brit.* difficult to deal with (*an awkward customer*). □ **the awkward age** adolescence. □ **awkwardly** *adv.* **awkwardness** *n.* [obsolete *awk* backhanded, untoward (Middle English, from Old Norse *afugr* 'turned the wrong way') + -WARD]

awl /ɔ:l/ *n.* a small pointed tool used for piercing holes, esp. in leather. [Old English *æl*]

awn /ɔ:n/ *n.* a stiff bristle, esp. one growing from the sheath around the seed of cereals and other grasses. □ **awned** *adj.* [Old English from Old Norse *ögn*]

awning /'ɔ:nɪŋ/ *n.* a sheet of canvas or similar material stretched on a frame and used to shade a shop window, doorway, ship's deck, or other area from the sun or rain. [17th c. (nautical): origin uncertain]

awoke *past* of AWAKE.

awoken *past part.* of AWAKE.

AWOL /'eɪwɒl/ *abbr. colloq.* absent without leave.

awry /ə'rʌɪ/ *adv.* & *adj.* ● *adv.* **1** crookedly or askew. **2** improperly or amiss. ● *predic.adj.* crooked; deviant or unsound (*his theory is awry*). □ **go awry** go or do wrong. [Middle English from A[2] + WRY]

aw-shucks /ɔ:'ʃʌks/ *adj. N. Amer. colloq.* characterized by a self-deprecating, self-conscious, or shy manner. [AW + *shucks*: see SHUCK]

axe /aks/ *n.* & *v.* (*US* usu. **ax**) ● *n.* **1** a chopping tool, usu. of iron with a steel edge and wooden handle. **2** (**the axe**) **a** the drastic cutting or elimination of expenditure, staff, etc. **b** the abandoning of a project. **3** *slang* a musical instrument used in jazz or pop music, esp. (originally) a saxophone, or (now) a guitar. ● *v.tr.* (**axing**) **1** cut (esp. costs, services, or staff) drastically. **2** abandon (a project). □ **an axe to grind** private ends to serve. [Old English *æx*, from Germanic]

axe-breaker *n.* an Australian tree, *Notelæa longifolia*, with very hard timber.

axel /'aks(ə)l/ *n.* a jump in skating from the forward outside edge of one skate to the backward outside edge of the other, with one and a half turns in the air. [named after *Axel* R. Paulsen, Norwegian skater d. 1938]

axeman /'aksman/ *n.* (*pl.* **-men**) **1** a person who works with or wields an axe. **2** *slang* a jazz or rock guitarist.

axes *pl.* of AXIS[1].

axial /'aksɪəl/ *adj.* **1** forming or belonging to an axis. **2** round an axis (*axial rotation; axial symmetry*). □ **axially** *adv.*

axil /'aksɪl/ *n. Bot.* the upper angle between a leaf and the stem it springs from, or between a branch and the trunk. [Latin *axilla*: see AXILLA]

axilla /ak'sɪlə/ *n.* (*pl.* **axillae** /-li:/) **1** *Anat.* the armpit. **2** *Bot.* an axil. [Latin, = armpit, diminutive of *ala* 'wing']

axillary /ak'sɪləri/ *adj.* **1** *Anat.* of or relating to the armpit. **2** *Bot.* in or growing from the axil.

axiom /'aksɪəm/ *n.* **1** an established or widely accepted principle. **2** esp. *Geom.* a self-evident truth. [French *axiome* or Latin *axioma* from Greek *axiōma axiōmat-*, from *axios* 'worthy']

axiomatic /aksɪə'matɪk/ *adj.* **1** self-evident. **2** relating to or containing axioms. □ **axiomatically** *adv.* [Greek *axiōmatikos* (as AXIOM)]

axis[1] /'aksɪs/ *n.* (*pl.* **axes** /-si:z/) **1 a** an imaginary line about which a body rotates or about which a plane figure is conceived as generating a solid. **b** a line which divides a regular figure symmetrically. **2** *Math.* a fixed reference line for the measurement of coordinates etc. **3** *Bot.* the central column of an inflorescence or other growth. **4** *Anat.* the second cervical vertebra. **5** *Physiol.* the central part of an organ or organism. **6** an agreement or alliance between two or more countries forming a centre for an eventual larger grouping of nations sharing an ideal or objective. **7** (**the Axis**) **a** the alliance of Germany and Italy formed before and during the Second World War, later extended to include Japan and other countries. **b** these countries as a group. [Latin, = axle, pivot]

axis[2] /'aksɪs/ *n.* (*pl.* same) a white-spotted deer, *Cervus axis*, of S. Asia. Also called *chital*. [Latin]

axle /'aks(ə)l/ *n.* a rod or spindle (either fixed or rotating) on which a wheel or group of wheels is fixed. [originally *axle-tree* (Middle English *axel-tre*) from Old Norse *öxull-tré*]

Axminster /'aksmɪnstə/ *n.* (in full **Axminster carpet**) a kind of machine-woven patterned carpet with a cut pile. [the town of *Axminster* in S. England, where such carpets are made]

axolotl /'aksəlɒt(ə)l/ *n.* an aquatic newtlike salamander, *Ambystoma mexicanum*, from Mexico, which in natural conditions retains its larval form for life but is able to breed. [Nahuatl, from *atl* 'water' + *xolotl* 'servant']

axon /'aksɒn/ *n.* *Anat.* & *Zool.* a long threadlike part of a nerve cell, conducting impulses from the cell body. [modern Latin, from Greek *axōn* 'axis']

axonometric /aks(ə)nə(ʊ)'mɛtrɪk/ *adj.* *Art* etc. (of a pictorial representation) using an orthographic projection of the object on a plane inclined to each of the three principal axes of the object.

ay var. of AYE[1].

ayah /'ʌɪə/ *n.* a nurse or maidservant, esp. of Europeans in India and in other former British territories abroad. [Anglo-Indian, from Portuguese *aia* 'nurse']

ayatollah /ʌɪə'tɒlə/ *n.* a Shi'ite religious leader in Iran. [Persian from Arabic, = token of God]

aye[1] /ʌɪ/ *adv.* & *n.* (also **ay**) ● *adv.* **1** *archaic* or *dial.* yes. **2** (in voting) I assent. **3** (as **aye aye**) *Naut.* a response accepting an order. ● *n.* an affirmative answer or assent, esp. in voting. □ **the ayes have it** the affirmative votes are in the majority. [16th c.: probably from first person personal pronoun expressing assent]

aye[2] /eɪ, ʌɪ/ *adv.* *archaic* ever, always. □ **for aye** for ever. [Middle English from Old Norse *ei*, *ey*, from Germanic, related to Latin *aevum* 'age', Greek *aiōn* AEON]

aye-aye /'ʌɪʌɪ/ *n.* an arboreal nocturnal lemur, *Daubentonia madagascariensis*, native to Madagascar. [French, from Malagasy *aiay*]

Aylesbury /'eɪlzb(ə)ri/ *n.* (*pl.* **Aylesburys**) **1** a bird of a breed of large white domestic ducks. **2** this breed. [the town of *Aylesbury* in S. England, where the ducks were bred]

Aymara /'ʌɪmərɑ:/ *n.* & *adj.* ● *n.* (*pl.* same or **Aymaras**) **1** a member of a S. American Indian people of Bolivia and Peru. **2** the language of this people. ● *adj.* of or relating to this people or language. [Bolivian Spanish]

Ayrshire /'ɛ:ʃə/ *n.* **1** an animal of a mainly white breed of dairy cattle. **2** this breed. [name of a former Scottish county, where the cattle were bred]

ayurveda /ɑ:jə'veɪdə, -'vi:də/ *n.* a traditional Hindu system of medicine based on the idea of balance in bodily systems and emphasizing diet, herbal treatment, yogic breathing, etc. □ **ayurvedic** *adj.* [Sanskrit *āyurveda* 'science of life' (see VEDA)]

AZ *abbr.* *US* Arizona (in official postal use).

azalea /ə'zeɪlɪə/ *n.* any of various flowering deciduous shrubs of the genus *Rhododendron*, with large pink, purple, white, or yellow flowers. [modern Latin from Greek, fem. of *azaleos* 'dry' (from the dry soil in which it was believed to flourish)]

azeotrope /'eɪzɪətrəʊp, ə'zi:ə-/ *n.* *Chem.* a mixture of liquids in which the boiling point remains constant during distillation, at a given pressure, without change in composition. □ **azeotropic** /ˌeɪʒɪə'trəʊpɪk, -'trɒpɪk, əˌzi:ə-/ *adj.* [A-[1] + Greek *zeō* 'boil' + *tropos* 'turning']

Azerbaijani /ˌazəbʌɪ'dʒɑ:ni/ *n.* & *adj.* ● *n.* (*pl.* **Azerbaijanis**) **1** a native or inhabitant of Azerbaijan in the Caucasus. **2** the Turkic language of Azerbaijan. ● *adj.* of or relating to the Azerbaijanis or their language. [*Azerbaijan* + -I[2]]

Azeri /ə'zɛ:ri/ *n.* & *adj.* ● *n.* (*pl.* **Azeris**) **1** a member of a Turkic people living mainly in Azerbaijan, Armenia, and northern Iran. **2** their language. ● *adj.* of or relating to this people or their language. [Turkish *azerî* from Persian, = fire]

azide /'eɪzʌɪd/ *n.* *Chem.* any compound containing the radical N_3^-. [French *azote* 'nitrogen' + -IDE]

Azilian /ə'zɪlɪən/ *n.* & *adj.* *Archaeol.* ● *n.* an early mesolithic culture in western Europe, dated about 10,000 to 8000 BC. ● *adj.* of or relating to this culture. [named after Mas d'*Azil* in the French Pyrenees, where remains of it were found]

azimuth /'azɪməθ/ *n.* **1** the angular distance from a north or south point of the horizon to the intersection with the horizon of a vertical circle passing through a given celestial object. **2** the horizontal angle or direction of a compass bearing. □ **azimuthal** /-'mju:θ(ə)l/ *adj.* [Middle English via Old French *azimut* from Arabic *as-sumūt*, from *al* 'the' + *sumūt*, pl. of *samt* 'way, direction']

azimuthal projection *n.* a map projection in which a region of the earth is projected on to a plane tangential to the surface, usually at the pole or equator.

azine /'eɪzi:n/ *n.* *Chem.* any organic compound with two or more nitrogen atoms in a six-atom ring. [AZO- + -INE[4]]

azo- /'eɪzəʊ/ *prefix* *Chem.* containing two adjacent nitrogen atoms between carbon atoms. [French *azote* 'nitrogen' from Greek *azōos* 'without life']

azo dye *n.* any of a number of dyes whose molecules contain two adjacent nitrogen atoms between two carbon atoms.

azoic /eɪ'zəʊɪk/ *adj.* **1** having no trace of life. **2** *Geol.* (of an age etc.) having left no organic remains. [Greek *azōos* 'without life']

AZT *abbr.* the drug zidovudine. [chemical name *azidothymidine*]

Aztec /'aztɛk/ *n.* & *adj.* ● *n.* **1** a member of the native people dominant in Mexico before the Spanish conquest of the 16th c. **2** the language of the Aztecs. ● *adj.* of or relating to the Aztecs or their language (see also NAHUATL). [French *Aztèque* or Spanish *Azteca*, from Nahuatl *aztecatl* 'men of the north']

azuki var. of ADZUKI.

azure /'aʒə, -ʒj(ʊ)ə, -zjʊə; 'eɪ-/ *n.* & *adj.* ● *n.* **1 a** a deep sky-blue colour. **b** *Heraldry* blue. **2** *poet.* the clear sky. ● *adj.* **1 a** of the colour azure. **b** *Heraldry* blue. **2** *poet.* serene, untroubled. [Middle English via Old French *asur*, *azur* and medieval Latin *azzurum*, *azolum* from Arabic *al* 'the' + *lāzaward* from Persian *lāžward* 'lapis lazuli']

azygous /ˈazɪɡəs/ *adj. & n. Anat.* ● *adj.* (of any organic structure) single; not existing in pairs. ● *n.* an organic structure occurring singly. [Greek *azugos* 'unyoked' (as A-[1] + *zugon* 'yoke')]

Bb

B[1] /biː/ *n.* (also **b**) (*pl.* **Bs** or **B's**) **1** the second letter of the alphabet. **2** *Mus.* the seventh note of the diatonic scale of C major. **3** the second hypothetical person or example. **4** the second highest class or category (of roads, academic marks, etc.). **5** (usu. ***b***) *Algebra* the second known quantity. **6** a human blood type of the ABO system.

B[2] *abbr.* (also **B.**) **1** black (pencil lead). **2** *Chess* bishop. **3** Blessed.

B[3] *symb.* **1** *Chem.* the element boron. **2** *Physics* magnetic flux density. **3** bel(s).

b[1] *abbr.* (also **b.**) **1** born. **2** *Cricket* **a** bowled by. **b** bye. **3** billion.

b[2] *symb. Physics* barn.

BA *abbr.* **1** Bachelor of Arts. **2** British Academy. **3** British Airways. **4** British Association (for the Advancement of Science).

Ba *symb. Chem.* the element barium.

BAA *abbr.* British Airports Authority.

baa /bɑː/ *v.* & *n.* ● *v.intr.* (**baas**, **baaed** or **baa'd**) (of a sheep etc.) bleat. ● *n.* (*pl.* **baas**) the cry of a sheep or lamb. [imitative]

Baagandji /ˈbɑːg(ə)ndʒi/ *n.* an Aboriginal language of SE Australia, now extinct.

baa-lamb *n.* (a child's word for) a lamb.

baas /bɑːs/ *n. S.Afr.* boss, master (often as a form of address). [Dutch: cf. BOSS[1]]

baasskap /ˈbɑːskap/ *n. S.Afr.* domination, esp. of non-whites by whites. [Afrikaans from *baas* 'master' + *-skap* 'condition']

baba /ˈbɑːbɑː/ *n.* (in full **rum baba**) a small rich sponge cake, usu. soaked in rum-flavoured syrup. [French from Polish, literally 'married peasant woman']

babacoote /ˈbabəkuːt/ *n.* = INDRI. [Malagasy *babakoto*]

Babbitt /ˈbabɪt/ *n.* a materialistic, complacent businessman. □ **Babbittry** *n.* [George *Babbitt*, a character in the novel *Babbitt* (1922) by S. Lewis]

babbitt /ˈbabɪt/ *n.* **1** (in full **babbitt metal**) any of a group of soft alloys of tin, antimony, copper, and usu. lead, used for lining bearings etc., to diminish friction. **2** a bearing-lining made of this. [I. *Babbitt*, American inventor d. 1862]

babble /ˈbab(ə)l/ *v.* & *n.* ● *v.* **1** *intr.* **a** talk in an inarticulate or incoherent manner. **b** chatter excessively or irrelevantly. **c** (of a stream etc.) murmur, trickle. **2** *tr.* repeat foolishly; divulge through chatter. ● *n.* **1 a** incoherent speech. **b** foolish, idle, or childish talk. **2** the murmur of voices, water, etc. **3** background disturbance caused by interference from conversations on other telephone lines. □ **babblement** *n.* [Middle English, from Middle Low German *babbelen*, or imitative]

babbler /ˈbablə/ *n.* **1** a chatterer. **2** a person who reveals secrets. **3** a passerine bird of the large family Timaliidae, with a loud chattering voice.

babe /beɪb/ *n.* **1** *literary* a baby. **2** an innocent or helpless person (*babes and sucklings*; *babes in the wood*). **3** *N. Amer. slang* often *offens.* a young woman (often as a form of address). [Middle English: imitative of child's *ba, ba*]

babel /ˈbeɪb(ə)l/ *n.* **1** a confused noise, esp. of voices. **2** a noisy assembly. **3** a scene of confusion. [Middle English, from Hebrew *Bāḇel* 'Babylon' from Akkadian *bāb ili* 'gate of god' (with reference to the biblical account of the tower that was built to reach heaven but ended in chaos when Jehovah confused the builders' speech: see Gen. 11)]

Babi /ˈbɑːbi/ *n.* a member of an eclectic Persian sect founded in 1844, teaching that a new prophet would follow Muhammad, and later giving rise to the Baha'i faith. □ **Babism** *n.* [Persian *Bab*, 'gate' (= intermediary), name taken by the founder]

babirusa /bɑːbɪˈruːsə/ *n.* (also **babiroussa**) a wild hog, *Babyrousa babyrussa*, with upturned tusks, native to the Malay Archipelago. [Malay, from *babi* 'hog' + *rusa* 'deer']

baboon /bəˈbuːn/ *n.* **1** any of various large Old World monkeys of the genera *Papio* and *Mandrillus*, having a long doglike snout, large teeth, and naked callosities on the buttocks. **2** an ugly or uncouth person. [Middle English, from Old French *babuin* or medieval Latin *babewynus*, perhaps from Old French *baboue* 'muzzle, grimace']

babu /ˈbɑːbuː/ *n.* **1** (in the Indian subcontinent) a title of respect, esp. to Hindus. **2** *Anglo-Ind. offens.* an Indian clerk or official who has a superficial knowledge of English. [Hindi *bābū*, literally 'father']

babushka /bəˈbʊʃkə/ *n.* **1** (in Russia) an old woman; a grandmother. **2** a headscarf tied under the chin. [Russian, = grandmother]

baby /ˈbeɪbi/ *n.* & *v.* ● *n.* (*pl.* **-ies**) **1** a very young child or infant, esp. one not yet able to walk. **2** an unduly childish person (*is a baby about injections*). **3** the youngest member of a family, team, etc. **4** (often *attrib.*) **a** a young or newly born animal. **b** a thing that is small of its kind (*baby car*; *baby rose*). **5** *slang* a young woman; a sweetheart (often as a form of address). **6** *slang* a person or thing regarded with affection or familiarity. **7** one's own responsibility, invention, concern, achievement, etc., regarded in a personal way. ● *v.tr.* (**-ies**, **-ied**) **1** treat like a baby. **2** pamper. □ **carry** (or **hold**) **the baby** bear unwelcome responsibility. **throw away** (or **out**) **the baby with the bathwater** reject the essential with the inessential. □ **babyhood** *n.* [Middle English (as BABE, -Y[2])]

baby blue *n.* & *adj.* ● *n.* a light blue colour. ● *adj.* (hyphenated when *attrib.*) of this colour.

baby boom *n. colloq.* a temporary marked increase in the birth rate.

baby boomer *n.* a person born during a baby boom, esp. after the Second World War.

baby bouncer *n. Brit.* a frame supported by elastic or springs, into which a child is harnessed to exercise its limbs.

baby buggy *n.* **1** *Brit. propr.* a kind of child's collapsible pushchair. **2** *N. Amer.* a pram.

baby carriage *n. N. Amer.* a pram.

baby face *n.* **1** a smooth round face like a baby's. **2** a person with such a face. □ **baby-faced** *adj.*

baby grand *n.* the smallest size of grand piano.

Babygro /ˈbeɪbɪgrəʊ/ *n.* (*pl.* **-os**) *Brit. propr.* a kind of all-in-one stretch garment for babies. [BABY + GROW]

babyish /ˈbeɪbɪɪʃ/ *adj.* **1** childish, simple. **2** immature. □ **babyishly** *adv.* **babyishness** *n.*

Babylonian /babɪˈləʊnɪən/ *n.* & *adj.* ● *n.* an inhabitant of Babylon, an ancient city and kingdom in Mesopotamia. ● *adj.* of or relating to Babylon. [Latin *Babylonius* via Greek *Babulonios* from *Babulon*, from Hebrew *Bāḇel*]

baby's breath *n.* any of various scented plants, esp. *Gypsophila paniculata.*

babysit /ˈbeɪbɪsɪt/ *v.intr.* (**-sitting**; *past* and *past part.* **-sat**) look after a child or children while the parents are out. ▫ **babysitter** *n.*

baby-snatcher *n. colloq.* **1** a person who abducts a very young child. **2** *Brit.* = CRADLE-SNATCHER.

baby talk *n.* childish talk used by or to young children.

baby walker *n.* a wheeled frame in which a baby learns to walk.

Bacardi /bəˈkɑːdi/ *n.* (*pl.* **Bacardis**) *propr.* a West Indian rum produced originally in Cuba. [name of the company producing it]

baccalaureate /bakəˈlɔːrɪət/ *n.* **1** an examination intended to qualify successful candidates for higher education, esp. in France and many international schools. **2** the university degree of bachelor. [French *baccalauréat* or medieval Latin *baccalaureatus*, from *baccalaureus* 'bachelor']

baccarat /ˈbakərɑː/ *n.* a gambling card game played by punters in turn against the banker. [French *baccara*, of unknown origin]

bacchanal /ˈbakən(ə)l, -nal/ *n. & adj.* ● *n.* **1** a wild and drunken revelry. **2** a drunken reveller. **3** a priest, worshipper, or follower of Bacchus, the Greek or Roman god of wine. ● *adj.* **1** of or like Bacchus or his rites. **2** riotous, roistering. [Latin *bacchanalis* from *Bacchus*, from Greek *Bakkhos*]

Bacchanalia /bakəˈneɪlɪə/ *n.pl.* **1** the Roman festival of Bacchus. **2** (**bacchanalia**) a drunken revelry. ▫ **Bacchanalian** *adj. & n.* [Latin, neut. pl. of *bacchanalis*: see BACCHANAL]

bacchant /ˈbakənt/ *n. & adj.* ● *n.* (*pl.* **bacchants** or **bacchantes** /bəˈkantiːz/; *fem.* **bacchante** /bəˈkant, bəˈkanti/) **1** a priest, priestess, or follower of Bacchus. **2** a drunken reveller. ● *adj.* **1** of or like Bacchus or his rites. **2** riotous, roistering. ▫ **bacchantic** /bəˈkantɪk/ *adj.* [French *bacchante* from Latin *bacchari* 'celebrate bacchanal rites']

Bacchic /ˈbakɪk/ *adj.* = BACCHANAL *adj.* [Latin *bacchicus* from Greek *bakkhikos* 'of Bacchus']

baccy /ˈbaki/ *n. colloq.* tobacco. [abbreviation]

bachelor /ˈbatʃələ/ *n.* **1** an unmarried man. **2** a man or woman who has taken the degree of Bachelor of Arts or Science etc. **3** *hist.* a young knight serving under another's banner. ▫ **bachelorhood** *n.* **bachelorship** *n.* [Middle English & Old French *bacheler* 'aspirant to knighthood', of uncertain origin]

bachelor girl *n.* an independent unmarried young woman.

bachelor's buttons *n.pl.* (treated as *sing.* or *pl.*) any of various button-like flowers, esp. the double buttercup.

bacillary /bəˈsɪləri/ *adj.* relating to or caused by bacilli.

bacilliform /bəˈsɪlɪfɔːm/ *adj.* rod-shaped.

bacillus /bəˈsɪləs/ *n.* (*pl.* **bacilli** /-lʌɪ, -liː/) **1** any rod-shaped bacterium. **2** (usu. in *pl.*) any pathogenic bacterium. [Late Latin, diminutive of Latin *baculus* 'stick']

back /bak/ *n., adv., v., & adj.* ● *n.* **1 a** the rear surface of the human body from the shoulders to the hips. **b** the corresponding upper surface of an animal's body. **c** the spine (*fell and broke his back*). **d** the keel of a ship. **2 a** any surface regarded as corresponding to the human back, e.g. of the head or hand, or of a chair. **b** the part of a garment that covers the back. **3 a** the less active or visible or important part of something functional, e.g. of a knife or a piece of paper (*write it on the back*). **b** the side or part normally away from the spectator or the direction of motion or attention, e.g. of a car, house, or room (*stood at the back*). **4 a** a defensive player in field games. **b** this position. **5** (**the Backs**) the grounds of Cambridge colleges which back on to the River Cam. ● *adv.* **1** to the rear; away from what is considered to be the front (*go back a bit*; *ran off without looking back*). **2 a** in or into an earlier or normal position or condition (*came back late*; *went back home*; *ran back to the car*; *put it back on the shelf*). **b** in return (*pay back*). **3** in or into the past (*back in June*; *three years back*). **4** at a distance (*stand back from the road*). **5** in check (*hold him back*). **6** (foll. by *of*) *N. Amer.* behind (*was back of the house*). ● *v.* **1** *tr.* **a** help with moral or financial support. **b** bet on the success of (a horse etc.). **2** *tr. & intr.* move, or cause (a vehicle etc.) to move, backwards. **3** *tr.* **a** put or serve as a back, background, or support to. **b** *Mus.* accompany. **4** *tr.* lie at the back of (*a beach backed by steep cliffs*). **5** *intr.* (of the wind) move round in an anticlockwise direction. ● *attrib.adj.* **1** situated behind, esp. as remote or subsidiary (*back entrance*; *back teeth*). **2** of or relating to the past; not current (*back pay*; *back issue*). **3** reversed (*back flow*). **4** *Phonet.* formed at the back of the mouth. ▫ **at a person's back** in pursuit or support. **at the back of one's mind** remembered but not consciously thought of. **back and forth** to and fro. **back down** withdraw one's claim or point of view etc.; concede defeat in an argument etc. **the back of beyond** a very remote or inaccessible place. **back off 1** draw back, retreat. **2** abandon one's intention, stand, etc. **back on to** have its back adjacent to (*the house backs on to a field*). **back out** (often foll. by *of*) withdraw from a commitment. **back up 1** give (esp. moral) support to. **2** *Computing* make a spare copy of (data, a disk, etc.). **3** (of running water) accumulate behind an obstruction. **4** reverse (a vehicle) into a desired position. **5** form a queue of vehicles etc., esp. in congested traffic. **get** (or **put**) **a person's back up** annoy or anger a person. **get off a person's back** stop troubling a person. **go back on** fail to honour (a promise or commitment). **know like the back of one's hand** be entirely familiar with. **on one's back** injured or ill in bed. **on the back burner** see BURNER. **put one's back into** approach (a task etc.) with vigour. **see the back of** see SEE[1]. **turn one's back on 1** abandon. **2** ignore. **with one's back to** (or **up against**) **the wall** in a desperate situation; hard-pressed. ▫ **backer** *n.* (in sense 1 of *v.*). **backless** *adj.* [Old English *bæc*, from Germanic]

backache /ˈbakeɪk/ *n.* a (usu. prolonged) pain in one's back.

backbar /ˈbakbɑː/ *n.* esp. *US* a structure behind a bar counter, with shelves for holding bottles etc.

backbeat /ˈbakbiːt/ *n. Mus.* a strong accent on one of the normally unaccented beats of the bar, esp. in jazz and popular music.

backbench /bakˈbɛn(t)ʃ/ *n. Brit.* a backbencher's seat in the House of Commons.

backbencher /bakˈbɛn(t)ʃə/ *n. Brit.* a Member of Parliament not holding a senior office.

backbiting /ˈbakbʌɪtɪŋ/ *n. & adj.* ● *n.* malicious talk. ● *attrib.adj.* speaking ill of another or others. ▫ **backbiter** *n.*

backblocks /ˈbakblɒks/ *n.pl. Austral. & NZ* land in the remote and sparsely inhabited interior.

backboard /ˈbakbɔːd/ *n.* **1** a board worn to support or straighten the back. **2** a board placed at or forming the back of anything. **3** *Basketball* a board behind the basket, off which the ball may rebound.

back boiler *n. Brit.* a boiler behind and integral with a domestic fire.

backbone /ˈbakbəʊn/ *n.* **1** the spine. **2** the main support of a structure. **3** firmness of character. **4** *US* the spine of a book.

back-breaking *adj.* (esp. of manual work) extremely hard.

backchat /ˈbaktʃat/ *n. Brit. colloq.* the practice of replying rudely or impudently.

backcloth /ˈbakklɒθ/ *n. Brit.* **1** *Theatr.* a painted cloth at the back of the stage as a main part of the scenery. **2** the background to a scene or situation.

backcomb /ˈbakkəʊm/ *v.tr. Brit.* comb (the hair) towards the the top of the head to make it look thicker.

backcountry /ˈbakkʌntri/ *n.* esp. *N. Amer.* an area away from settled districts.

back-crawl *n.* = BACKSTROKE.
back cross *v.tr.* & *n. Biol.* ● *v.tr.* cross (a hybrid) with one of its parents. ● *n.* an instance or the product of this.
backdate /bakˈdeɪt/ *v.tr.* **1** put an earlier date to (an agreement etc.) than the actual one. **2** *Brit.* make retrospectively valid.
back door *n.* & *adj.* ● *n.* **1** the door or entrance at the back of a building. **2** a secret or ingenious means of gaining an objective. ● *attrib.adj.* (**back-door**) (of an activity) clandestine, underhand (*back-door deal*).
backdown /ˈbakdaʊn/ *n.* an instance of backing down.
backdrop /ˈbakdrɒp/ *n.* = BACKCLOTH.
backfield /ˈbakfiːld/ *n. Amer. Football* **1** the area of play behind the line of scrimmage. **2** the players in this, or their positions.
backfill /ˈbakfɪl/ *v.tr.* refill (an excavated hole) with the material dug out of it.
backfire *v.* & *n.* ● *v.intr.* /bakˈfʌɪə/ **1** undergo a mistimed explosion in the cylinder or exhaust of an internal-combustion engine. **2** (of a plan etc.) rebound adversely on the originator; have the opposite effect to what was intended. ● *n.* /ˈbakfʌɪə/ an instance of backfiring.
backflip /ˈbakflɪp/ *n.* a backward somersault done in the air with the arms and legs stretched out straight.
back-formation *n.* **1** the formation of a word from its seeming derivative (e.g. *laze* from *lazy*). **2** a word formed in this way.
backgammon /ˈbakgamən/ *n.* **1** a game for two played on a board with pieces moved according to throws of the dice. **2** the most complete form of win in this. [BACK + GAMMON²]
background /ˈbakgraʊnd/ *n.* **1** part of a scene, picture, or description, that serves as a setting to the chief figures or objects and foreground. **2** an inconspicuous or obscure position (*kept in the background*). **3** a person's education, knowledge, or social circumstances. **4** explanatory or contributory information or circumstances. **5** *Physics* low-intensity ambient radiation from radioisotopes present in the natural environment. **6** *Electronics* unwanted signals, such as noise in the reception or recording of sound.
background music *n.* music intended as an unobtrusive accompaniment to some activity, or to provide atmosphere in a film etc.
backhand /ˈbakhand/ *n. Tennis* etc. **1** a stroke played with the back of the hand turned towards the opponent. **2** (*attrib.*) of or made with a backhand (*backhand volley*).
backhanded /bakˈhandɪd/ *adj.* **1** (of a blow etc.) delivered with the back of the hand, or in a direction opposite to the usual one. **2** indirect; ambiguous (*a backhanded compliment*). **3** = BACKHAND 2.
backhander /ˈbakhandə/ *n.* **1 a** a backhand stroke. **b** a backhanded blow. **2** *colloq.* an indirect attack. **3** *Brit. slang* a bribe.
backhoe /ˈbakhəʊ/ *n. N. Amer.* a mechanical excavator which draws towards itself a bucket attached to a hinged boom.
backing /ˈbakɪŋ/ *n.* **1 a** support. **b** a body of supporters. **c** material used to form a back or support. **2** musical accompaniment, esp. to a singer.
backing track *n.* a recorded musical accompaniment, esp. for a soloist to play or sing along with.
backlash /ˈbaklaʃ/ *n.* **1** an excessive or marked adverse reaction. **2 a** a sudden recoil or reaction between parts of a mechanism. **b** excessive play between such parts.
backlight /ˈbaklʌɪt/ *n.* illumination from behind.
backlist /ˈbaklɪst/ *n.* a publisher's list of books published before the current season and still in print.
backlit /ˈbaklɪt/ *adj.* (esp. in photography) illuminated from behind.
backlog /ˈbaklɒg/ *n.* **1** arrears of uncompleted work etc. **2** a reserve; reserves (*a backlog of goodwill*).
backmarker /ˈbakmɑːkə/ *n. Brit.* a competitor who has the least favourable handicap in a race etc.
backmost /ˈbakməʊst/ *adj.* furthest back.
back number *n.* **1** an issue of a periodical earlier than the current one. **2** *slang* an out-of-date person or thing.
backpack /ˈbakpak/ *n.* & *v.* ● *n.* a rucksack. ● *v.intr.* travel or hike with a backpack. ▫ **backpacker** *n.*
back passage *n. Brit. colloq.* the rectum.
back-pedal *v.intr.* (**-pedalled**, **-pedalling**; *US* **-pedaled**, **-pedaling**) **1** pedal backwards on a bicycle etc. **2** reverse one's previous action or opinion.
back-projection *n.* the projection of a picture from behind a translucent screen for viewing or filming.
backrest /ˈbakrɛst/ *n.* a support for the back.
back room *n.* (often, with hyphen, *attrib.*) a place where secret work is done.
backscattering /ˈbakskat(ə)rɪŋ/ *n.* the scattering of radiation in a reverse direction. ▫ **backscatter** *v.tr.* & *n.*
back-scratcher /ˈbakskratʃə/ *n.* **1** a rod terminating in a clawed hand for scratching one's own back. **2** a person who performs mutual services with another for gain. ▫ **back-scratching** *n.* & *adj.*
back seat *n.* **1** a seat at the back of a vehicle, hall, etc. **2** an inferior position or status.
back-seat driver *n.* a person who is eager to advise without responsibility (originally of a passenger in a car etc.).
backsheesh var. of BAKSHEESH.
backside /bakˈsʌɪd, ˈbaksʌɪd/ *n. colloq.* the buttocks.
backsight /ˈbaksʌɪt/ *n.* **1** the sight of a rifle etc. that is nearer the stock. **2** *Surveying* a sight or reading taken backwards or towards the point of starting.
back slang *n.* slang using words spelt backwards (e.g. *yob*).
backslapping /ˈbakslapɪŋ/ *adj.* vigorously hearty.
backslash /ˈbakslaʃ/ *n.* a backward-sloping diagonal line; a reverse solidus (\).
backslide /ˈbakslʌɪd/ *v.intr.* (*past* **-slid**; *past part.* **-slid** or **-slidden**) relapse into bad ways or error. ▫ **backslider** *n.*
backspace /ˈbakspeɪs/ *v.intr.* move a typewriter carriage or computer cursor back one or more spaces.
backspin /ˈbakspɪn/ *n.* a backward spin imparted to a ball causing it to fly off at an angle on hitting a surface.
backstage /bakˈsteɪdʒ/ *adv.* & *adj.* ● *adv.* **1** *Theatr.* out of view of the audience, esp. in the wings or dressing rooms. **2** not known to the public. ● *adj.* /also ˈbak-/ that is backstage; concealed.
backstairs /ˈbakstɛːz/ *n.pl.* **1** stairs at the back or side of a building. **2** (also **backstair**) (*attrib.*) denoting underhand or clandestine activity.
backstay /ˈbaksteɪ/ *n.* a rope etc. leading downwards and aft from the top of a mast.
backstitch /ˈbakstɪtʃ/ *n.* & *v.* ● *n.* sewing with overlapping stitches. ● *v.tr.* & *intr.* sew using backstitch.
backstop /ˈbakstɒp/ *n.* **1 a** *Cricket* etc. a fielder directly behind the wicketkeeper. **b** *Baseball* = CATCHER 2. **c** these fielding positions. **2** an emergency precaution.
backstreet /ˈbakstriːt/ *n.* **1** a street in a quiet part of a town, away from the main streets. **2** (*attrib.*) denoting illicit or illegal activity (*a backstreet abortion*).
backstroke /ˈbakstrəʊk/ *n.* a swimming stroke performed on the back with the arms lifted alternately out of the water in a backward circular motion and the legs extended in a kicking action.
back talk *n. N. Amer. colloq.* = BACKCHAT.
back-to-back *adj.*, *n.*, & *adv.* ● *attrib.adj.* **1** esp. *Brit.* (of houses) with a party wall at the rear. **2** *N. Amer.* consecutive. ● *n.* a back-to-back house. ● *adv.* (**back to back**) **1** with backs adjacent and opposite each other (*we stood back to back*). **2** *N. Amer.* consecutively.
back to front *adj.* **1** with the back at the front and the front at the back. **2** in disorder.

back-to-nature *adj.* (usu. *attrib.*) denoting a movement or enthusiast for the reversion to a simpler way of life.

backtrack /ˈbaktrak/ *v.intr.* **1** retrace one's steps. **2** reverse one's previous action or opinion.

back-up *n.* **1** moral or technical support (*called for extra back-up*). **2** a reserve. **3** (often *attrib.*) *Computing* **a** the procedure for making security copies of data (*back-up facilities*). **b** the copy itself (*made a back-up*). **4** *N. Amer.* a queue of vehicles etc., esp. in congested traffic.

backup light /ˈbakʌp/ *n. US* a reversing light.

backveld /ˈbakvɛlt/ *n. S.Afr.* remote country districts, esp. those strongly conservative. ▫ **backvelder** *n.*

backward /ˈbakwəd/ *adv. & adj.* ● *adv.* = BACKWARDS. ● *adj.* **1** directed to the rear or starting point (*a backward look*). **2** reversed. **3** mentally retarded or slow. **4** reluctant, shy, unassertive. **5** *Cricket* (of a fielding position) behind a line through the stumps at right angles to the wicket. ▫ **backwardness** *n.* [earlier *abackward*, associated with BACK]

▪ **Usage** *Backward* is both an adjective and an adverb, while *backwards* is only an adverb and more common than *backward* as such, especially in literal senses.

backwardation /bakwəˈdeɪʃ(ə)n/ *n.* esp. *Brit. Stock Exch.* the percentage paid by a person selling stock for the right of delaying the delivery of it (cf. CONTANGO).

backwards /ˈbakwədz/ *adv.* **1** away from one's front (*lean backwards*; *look backwards*). **2 a** with the back foremost (*walk backwards*). **b** in reverse of the usual way (*count backwards*; *spell backwards*). **3 a** into a worse state (*new policies are taking us backwards*). **b** into the past (*looked backwards over the years*). **c** (of a thing's motion) back towards the starting point (*rolled backwards*). ▫ **backwards and forwards** in both directions alternately; to and fro. **bend** (or **fall** or **lean**) **over backwards** (often foll. by *to* + infin.) *colloq.* make every effort, esp. to be fair or helpful. **know backwards** be entirely familiar with.

▪ **Usage** See Usage Note at BACKWARD.

backwash /ˈbakwɒʃ/ *n.* **1 a** receding waves created by the motion of a ship etc. **b** a backward current of air created by a moving aircraft. **2** repercussions.

backwater *n. & v.* ● *n.* /ˈbakwɔːtə/ **1** a place or condition remote from the centre of activity or thought. **2** stagnant water fed from a stream. ● *v.intr.* (**back water**) reverse a boat's forward motion using oars.

backwoods /ˈbakwʊdz/ *n.pl.* **1** remote uncleared forest land. **2** any remote or sparsely inhabited region.

backwoodsman /ˈbakwʊdzmən/ *n.* (*pl.* **-men**) **1** an inhabitant of backwoods. **2** an uncouth person. **3** a peer who very rarely attends the House of Lords.

backyard /bakˈjɑːd/ *n.* **1** *Brit.* a yard at the back of a house etc. **2** *N. Amer.* a back garden. ▫ **in one's own backyard** *colloq.* near one's home; in one's own area; near at hand.

baclava var. of BAKLAVA.

bacon /ˈbeɪk(ə)n/ *n.* cured meat from the back or sides of a pig. ▫ **bring home the bacon** *colloq.* **1** succeed in one's undertaking. **2** supply material provision or support. [Middle English via Old French from Frankish *bako* ham, flitch: related to BACK]

Baconian /beɪˈkəʊnɪən/ *adj. & n.* ● *adj.* of or relating to the English philosopher Sir Francis Bacon (d. 1626), or to his inductive method of reasoning and philosophy. ● *n.* **1** a supporter of the view that Bacon was the author of Shakespeare's plays. **2** a follower of Bacon.

bacteria *pl.* of BACTERIUM.

bactericide /bakˈtɪərɪsʌɪd/ *n.* a substance capable of destroying bacteria. ▫ **bactericidal** /-ˈsʌɪd(ə)l/ *adj.*

bacteriology /bak,tɪərɪˈɒlədʒi/ *n.* the study of bacteria. ▫ **bacteriological** /-əˈlɒdʒɪk(ə)l/ *adj.* **bacteriologically** /-əˈlɒdʒɪk(ə)li/ *adv.* **bacteriologist** *n.*

bacteriolysis /bak,tɪərɪˈɒlɪsɪs/ *n.* the rupture of bacterial cells.

bacteriolytic /bak,tɪərɪəˈlɪtɪk/ *adj.* capable of lysing bacteria.

bacteriophage /bakˈtɪərɪə(ʊ)feɪdʒ, -fɑːʒ/ *n.* a virus which parasitizes a bacterium by infecting it and reproducing inside it. [BACTERIUM + Greek *phagein* 'eat']

bacteriostat /bakˈtɪərɪə(ʊ)stat/ *n.* a substance which inhibits the multiplying of bacteria without destroying them. ▫ **bacteriostasis** *n.* **bacteriostatic** *adj.* [BACTERIUM + Greek *statos* 'standing']

bacterium /bakˈtɪərɪəm/ *n.* (*pl.* **bacteria** /-rɪə/) a member of a large group of unicellular micro-organisms lacking organelles and an organized nucleus, some of which can cause disease. ▫ **bacterial** *adj.* [modern Latin from Greek *baktērion*, diminutive of *baktron* 'stick']

▪ **Usage** A very common mistake is the use of *bacteria* as the singular form, e.g. *The salmonella bacteria accounts for the majority of food poisoning cases today*. This is not acceptable and the form *bacterium* should always be used in such examples.

Bactrian /ˈbaktrɪən/ *adj.* of or relating to Bactria, a region and former empire in central Asia (now northern Afghanistan). [Latin *Bactrianus* from Greek *Baktrianos*]

Bactrian camel *n.* a camel with two humps, *Camelus ferus*, native to central Asia.

bad /bad/ *adj., n., & adv.* ● *adj.* (**worse** /wəːs/; **worst** /wəːst/) **1** inferior, inadequate, defective (*bad work*; *a bad driver*; *bad light*). **2 a** unpleasant, unwelcome (*bad weather*; *bad news*). **b** unsatisfactory, unfortunate (*a bad business*). **3** harmful (*is bad for you*). **4 a** (of food) decayed, putrid. **b** (of the atmosphere) polluted, unhealthy (*bad air*). **5** *colloq.* ill, injured (*am feeling bad today*; *a bad leg*). **6** *colloq.* regretful, guilty, ashamed (*feels bad about it*). **7** (of an unwelcome thing) serious, severe (*a bad headache*; *a bad mistake*). **8 a** morally wicked or offensive (*a bad man*; *bad language*). **b** naughty; badly behaved (*a bad child*). **9** worthless; not valid (*a bad cheque*). **10** (**badder**, **baddest**) esp. *US slang* good, excellent. ● *n.* **1 a** ill fortune (*take the bad with the good*). **b** ruin; a degenerate condition (*go to the bad*). **2** the debit side of an account (*£500 to the bad*). **3** (treated as *pl.*; prec. by *the*) bad or wicked people. ● *adv. N. Amer. colloq.* badly (*took it bad*). ▫ **from bad to worse** into an even worse state. **in a bad way** ill; in trouble (*looked in a bad way*). **not** (or **not so**) **bad** *colloq.* fairly good. **too bad** *colloq.* (of circumstances etc.) regrettable but now beyond retrieval. ▫ **baddish** *adj.* **badness** *n.* [Middle English, perhaps from Old English *bǣddel* 'hermaphrodite, womanish man': for loss of *l* cf. MUCH, WENCH]

badass /ˈbadas/ *n. & adj.* esp. *N. Amer. slang* ● *n.* an aggressive, uncooperative person; a troublemaker. ● *adj.* **1** tough, aggressive. **2** bad, worthless. **3** formidable, excellent. [ASS[2]]

bad blood *n.* ill feeling.

bad books see BOOK.

bad break *n. colloq.* **1** a piece of bad luck. **2** a mistake or blunder.

bad breath *n.* unpleasant-smelling breath; halitosis.

bad company *n.* **1** a dull companion. **2** an unsuitable associate or group of friends.

bad debt *n.* a debt that is not recoverable.

baddy /ˈbadi/ *n.* (also **baddie**) (*pl.* **-ies**) *colloq.* a villain or criminal, esp. in a story, film, etc.

bade see BID.

bad egg see EGG[1] *n.* 3.

bad faith *n.* intent to deceive.

bad form *n.* an offence against current social conventions.

badge /badʒ/ *n. & v.* ● *n.* **1** a distinctive emblem worn as a mark of office, membership, achievement, licensed employment, etc. **2** any feature or sign which reveals a characteristic condition or quality. ● *v.tr.* mark with or distinguish by a badge. [Middle English: origin unknown]

badger /ˈbadʒə/ *n. & v.* ● *n.* **1 a** an omnivorous greyish-black nocturnal Eurasian mammal, *Meles meles*, of the weasel family, having a white head with two black stripes, and living in burrows called sets. **b** a related N. American animal, *Taxidea taxus*. **2** a fishing-fly, brush, etc., made of its hair. ● *v.tr.* pester, harass, tease. [16th c.: perhaps from BADGE, with reference to its white forehead mark]

badinage /ˈbadɪnɑːʒ/ *n.* humorous or playful ridicule. [French from *badiner* 'to joke']

bad job *n. Brit. colloq.* an unfortunate state of affairs.

badlands /ˈbadlandz/ *n.pl.* extensive uncultivable eroded tracts in arid areas. [translation of French *mauvaises terres*]

bad lot *n.* a person of bad character.

badly /ˈbadli/ *adv.* (**worse** /wəːs/; **worst** /wəːst/) **1** in a bad manner (*works badly*). **2** *colloq.* very much (*wants it badly*). **3** severely (*was badly defeated*).

badminton /ˈbadmɪnt(ə)n/ *n.* **1** a game with rackets in which a shuttlecock is played back and forth across a net. **2** *Brit.* a summer drink of claret, soda, and sugar. [*Badminton* in S. England, a country house where the game was first played]

bad mouth *n. & v. N. Amer. slang* ● *n.* malicious gossip or criticism. ● *v.tr.* (**bad-mouth**) criticize maliciously; abuse.

bad news *n. colloq.* an unpleasant or troublesome person or thing.

bad scran see SCRAN.

bad-tempered *adj.* having a bad temper; irritable; easily annoyed. □ **bad-temperedly** *adv.*

Baedeker /ˈbeɪdɪkə/ *n.* any of various travel guidebooks published by the firm founded by the German Karl *Baedeker* (d. 1859).

baffle /ˈbaf(ə)l/ *v. & n.* ● *v.tr.* **1** confuse or perplex (a person, one's faculties, etc.). **2 a** frustrate or hinder (plans etc.). **b** restrain or regulate the progress of (fluids, sounds, etc.). ● *n.* (also **baffle plate**) a device used to restrain the flow of fluid, gas, etc., or to limit the emission of sound, light, etc. □ **bafflement** *n.* **baffling** *adj.* **bafflingly** *adv.* [perhaps related to French *bafouer* 'ridicule', Old French *beffer* 'mock, deceive']

baffle board *n.* a device to prevent sound from spreading in different directions, esp. round a loudspeaker cone.

baffler /ˈbaflə/ *n.* = BAFFLE *n.*

BAFTA /ˈbaftə/ *abbr.* British Academy of Film and Television Arts.

bag /baɡ/ *n. & v.* ● *n.* **1** a receptacle of flexible material with an opening at the top. **2 a** (usu. in *pl.*) a piece of luggage (*put the bags in the boot*). **b** a woman's handbag. **3** (in *pl.*; usu. foll. by *of*) esp. *Brit. colloq.* a large amount; plenty (*bags of time*). **4** (in *pl.*) *Brit. colloq.* trousers. **5** *slang derog.* a woman, esp. regarded as unattractive or unpleasant. **6** an animal's sac containing poison, honey, etc. **7** an amount of game shot by a hunter. **8** (usu. in *pl.*) baggy folds of skin under the eyes. **9** *slang* a person's particular interest or preoccupation, esp. in a distinctive style or category of music (*his bag is Indian music*). ● *v.* (**bagged**, **bagging**) **1** *tr.* put in a bag. **2** *tr. colloq.* **a** secure; get hold of (*bagged the best seat*). **b** *colloq.* steal. **c** shoot (game). **d** (often in phr. **bags I**) *Brit. colloq.* claim on grounds of being the first to do so (*bagged first go*; *bags I go first*). **3 a** *intr.* hang loosely; bulge; swell. **b** *tr.* cause to do this. **4** *tr. Austral. slang* criticize, disparage. □ **bag and baggage** with all one's belongings. **bag of bones** an emaciated person or animal. **bag of nerves** a very tense or timid person. **bag** (or **whole bag**) **of tricks** *colloq.* everything; the whole lot. **in the bag** *colloq.* achieved; as good as secured. □ **bagful** *n.* (*pl.* **-fuls**). [Middle English, perhaps from Old Norse *baggi*]

bagarre /bɑːˈɡɑː, French baɡar/ *n.* a scuffle or brawl. [French]

bagasse /bəˈɡas/ *n.* the dry pulpy residue left after the extraction of juice from sugar cane, usable as fuel or to make paper etc. [French, from Spanish *bagazo*]

bagatelle /baɡəˈtɛl/ *n.* **1** a game in which small balls are struck into numbered holes on a board, with pins as obstructions. **2** a mere trifle; a negligible amount. **3** *Mus.* a short piece of music, esp. for the piano. [French from Italian *bagatella* diminutive, perhaps from *baga* BAGGAGE or Latin *baca* 'berry']

bagel /ˈbeɪɡ(ə)l/ *n.* a hard bread roll in the shape of a ring. [Yiddish *beygel*]

baggage /ˈbaɡɪdʒ/ *n.* **1** everyday belongings packed up in suitcases etc. for travelling; luggage. **2** the portable equipment of an army. **3** *joc.* or *derog.* a girl or woman. **4** mental encumbrances. [Middle English, from Old French *bagage* from *baguer* 'tie up' or *bagues* 'bundles': perhaps related to BAG]

baggy /ˈbaɡi/ *adj.* (**baggier**, **baggiest**) **1** hanging in loose folds. **2** puffed out. □ **baggily** *adv.* **bagginess** *n.*

bag lady *n.* esp. *N. Amer.* a homeless woman who carries her possessions around in shopping bags.

bagman /ˈbaɡmən/ *n.* (*pl.* **-men**) **1** *Brit. slang* a travelling salesman. **2** *Austral.* a tramp. **3** *Canad.* a political fund-raiser. **4** *US & Austral. slang* an agent who collects or distributes the proceeds of illicit activities.

bagnio /ˈbɑːnjəʊ/ *n.* (*pl.* **-os**) **1** a brothel. **2** an oriental prison. [Italian *bagno* from Latin *balneum* 'bath']

bagpipe /ˈbaɡpʌɪp/ *n.* (usu. in *pl.*) a musical instrument consisting of a windbag squeezed by the player's arm to force air into reeded pipes, usu. including a chanter with finger-holes to play the melody and one or more drones. □ **bagpiper** *n.*

baguette /baˈɡɛt/ *n.* **1** a long narrow French loaf. **2** a gem cut in a long rectangular shape. **3** *Archit.* a small moulding, semicircular in section. [French from Italian *bacchetto*, diminutive of *bacchio*, from Latin *baculum* 'staff']

bagworm /ˈbaɡwəːm/ *n. US* any of various destructive caterpillars which live in silk cases covered in plant debris.

bah /bɑː/ *int.* an expression of contempt or disbelief. [probably French]

Baha'i /bɑːˈhɑːi/ *n.* (*pl.* **Baha'is**) an adherent of a monotheistic religion founded in 1863 as a branch of Babism (see BABI), emphasizing religious unity and world peace. □ **Baha'ism** *n.* [Persian *bahá* 'splendour']

Bahamian /bəˈheɪmɪən/ *n. & adj.* ● *n.* **1** a native or national of the Bahamas in the W. Indies. **2** a person of Bahamian descent. ● *adj.* of or relating to the Bahamas.

Bahasa Indonesia /bəˌhɑːsə ˌɪndəˈniːzjə/ *n.* the official language of Indonesia. [Indonesian *bahasa* 'language' from Sanskrit *bhāṣā* 'speech, language']

baht /bɑːt/ *n.* (*pl.* same) the basic monetary unit of Thailand. [Thai *bāt*]

Bahutu *pl.* of HUTU.

bail[1] /beɪl/ *n. & v.* ● *n.* **1** money etc. required as security against the temporary release of a prisoner pending trial. **2** a person or persons giving such security. ● *v.tr.* (usu. foll. by *out*) **1** release or secure the release of (a prisoner) on payment of bail. **2** (also **bale** by association with *bale out* 1: see BALE[1]) release from a difficulty; come to the rescue of. □ **forfeit** (or *colloq.* **jump**) **bail** fail to appear for trial after being released on bail. **go** (or **stand**) **bail** (often foll. by *for*) act as surety (for an accused person). □ **bailable** *adj.* [Middle English via Old French *bail* 'custody', *bailler* 'take charge of', from Latin *bajulare* 'bear a burden']

bail[2] /beɪl/ *n. & v.* ● *n.* **1** *Cricket* either of the two crosspieces bridging the stumps. **2** the bar on a typewriter holding the paper against the platen. **3** a bar separating horses in an open stable. **4** *Austral. & NZ* a framework for securing the head of a cow during milking. ● *v.* (usu. foll. by *up*) *Austral. & NZ* **1** *tr.* secure (a cow) during milking. **2 a** *tr.* make (a person) hold up his or her arms to be robbed. **b** *intr.* surrender by throwing up one's arms. **c** *tr.* buttonhole (a person). [Middle English from Old French *bail(e)* 'enclosure', perhaps from Latin *baculum* 'stick']

bail[3] /beɪl/ *v.tr.* (also *Brit.* **bale**) **1** (usu. foll. by *out*) scoop water out of (a boat etc.). **2** scoop (water etc.) out. ▫ **bail out** var. of *bale out* 1 (see BALE[1]). ▫ **bailer** *n.* [obsolete *bail* 'bucket' from French *baille*, ultimately from Latin *bajulus* 'carrier']

bail bandit *n. colloq.* a person who commits a crime while on bail.

bailee /beɪ'li:/ *n. Law* a person or party to whom goods are committed for a purpose, e.g. custody or repair, without transfer of ownership. [BAIL[1] + -EE]

bailey /'beɪli/ *n.* (*pl.* **-eys**) **1** the outer wall of a castle. **2** a court enclosed by it. [Middle English, variant of BAIL[2]]

Bailey bridge /'beɪli/ *n.* a temporary bridge of lattice steel designed for rapid assembly from prefabricated standard parts, used esp. in military operations. [named after Sir D. *Bailey* (d. 1985), its designer]

bailie /'beɪli/ *n.* esp. *hist.* a municipal officer and magistrate in Scotland. [Middle English, from Old French *bailli(s)* BAILIFF]

bailiff /'beɪlɪf/ *n.* **1** esp. *Brit.* a sheriff's officer who executes writs and processes and carries out distraints and arrests. **2** *Brit.* the agent or steward of a landlord. **3** *N. Amer.* an official in a court of law who keeps order, looks after prisoners, etc. **4** *Brit.* (*hist.* except in formal titles) the sovereign's representative in a district, esp. the chief officer of a hundred. **5** the first civil officer in the Channel Islands. [Middle English from Old French *baillif*, ultimately from Latin *bajulus* 'carrier, manager']

bailiwick /'beɪlɪwɪk/ *n.* **1** *joc.* a person's sphere of operations or particular area of interest. **2** *Law* the district or jurisdiction of a bailie or bailiff. [BAILIE + WICK[2]]

bailment /'beɪlm(ə)nt/ *n.* the act of delivering goods etc. for a (usu. specified) purpose.

bailor /beɪ'lɔ:/ *n. Law* a person or party that entrusts goods to a bailee. [BAIL[1] + -OR[1]]

bailout /'beɪlaʊt/ *n.* financial assistance given to a failing business, economy, etc., to save it from collapse.

bailsman /'beɪlzmən/ *n.* (*pl.* **-men**) a person who stands bail for another. [BAIL[1] + MAN]

bain-marie /banmə'ri:/ *n.* (*pl.* **bains-marie** *pronunc.* same) a cooking utensil consisting of a vessel of hot water in which a receptacle containing a sauce etc. can be slowly and gently heated; a double boiler. [French, translation of medieval Latin *balneum Mariae* 'bath of Maria' (an alleged Jewish alchemist)]

Bairam /bʌɪ'rɑ:m/ *n.* either of two annual Muslim festivals, **Greater** and **Lesser Bairam**. [Turkish & Persian]

bairn /bɛ:n/ *n. Sc.* & *N.Engl.* a child. [Old English *bearn*]

bait /beɪt/ *n.* & *v.* ● *n.* **1** food used to entice a prey, esp. a fish or an animal. **2** an allurement; something intended to tempt or entice. **3** *archaic* a halt on a journey for refreshment or a rest. **4** var. of BATE. ● *v.* **1** *tr.* **a** harass or annoy (a person). **b** torment (a chained animal). **2** *tr.* put bait on (a hook, trap, etc.) to entice a prey. **3** *archaic* **a** *tr.* give food to (horses on a journey). **b** *intr.* stop on a journey to take food or a rest. [Middle English, from Old Norse *beita* 'hunt or chase']

baize /beɪz/ *n.* a coarse usu. green woollen material resembling felt used as a covering or lining, esp. on the tops of billiard tables and card tables. [French *baies* (pl.) fem. of *bai* 'chestnut-coloured' (BAY[4]), treated as sing.]

bajra /'bɑ:dʒrɑ:/ *n.* (in the Indian subcontinent) pearl millet or similar grain. [Hindi]

bake /beɪk/ *v.* & *n.* ● *v.* **1 a** *tr.* cook (food) by dry heat in an oven or on a hot surface, without direct exposure to a flame. **b** *intr.* undergo the process of being baked. **2** *intr. colloq.* **a** (usu. as **be baking**) (of weather etc.) be very hot. **b** (of a person) be hot. **3 a** *tr.* harden (clay etc.) by heat. **b** *intr.* (of clay etc.) be hardened by heat. **4 a** *tr.* (of the sun) affect by its heat, e.g. ripen (fruit). **b** *intr.* be affected by the sun's heat. ● *n.* **1** the act or an instance of baking. **2** a batch of baking. **3** *US* a social gathering at which baked food is eaten. ▫ **bake blind** see BLIND. [Old English *bacan*]

baked Alaska /ə'laskə/ *n.* sponge cake and ice cream in a meringue covering. [*Alaska*, name of a state of the US]

baked beans *n.pl.* baked haricot beans, usu. *Brit.* tinned in tomato sauce or *US* cooked with salt pork.

bakehouse /'beɪkhaʊs/ *n.* = BAKERY.

Bakelite /'beɪkəlʌɪt/ *n. propr.* any of various thermosetting resins or plastics made from formaldehyde and phenol and used for cables, buttons, plates, etc. [German *Bakelit* from L.H. *Baekeland*, its Belgian-born inventor d. 1944]

baker /'beɪkə/ *n.* a person who bakes and sells bread, cakes, etc., esp. professionally. [Old English *bæcere*]

Baker day /'beɪkə deɪ/ *n. colloq.* (in England and Wales) a day set aside for the in-service training of teachers, now usu. called *INSET day* (see INSET). [K. *Baker*, name of the Education Secretary (1986–9) who introduced the practice]

baker's dozen *n.* thirteen (so called from the former bakers' custom of adding an extra loaf to a dozen sold; the exact reason for this is unclear).

bakery /'beɪk(ə)ri/ *n.* (*pl.* **-ies**) a place where bread and cakes are made or sold.

Bakewell tart /'beɪkwɛl/ *n.* a baked open pie consisting of a pastry case lined with jam and filled with a rich almond paste. [*Bakewell* in Derbyshire]

baking powder *n.* a mixture of sodium bicarbonate, cream of tartar, etc., used instead of yeast in baking.

baking soda *n.* sodium bicarbonate.

baklava /'bɑ:kləvə/ *n.* (also **baclava**) a rich dessert of flaky pastry, honey, and nuts. [Turkish]

baksheesh /bak'ʃi:ʃ/ *n.* (also **backsheesh**) (in some oriental countries) a small sum of money given as a gratuity or as alms. [ultimately from Persian *bakšīš* from *bakšīdan* 'give']

balaclava /balə'klɑ:və/ *n.* (in full **balaclava helmet**) a tight woollen garment covering the whole head and neck except for parts of the face, worn originally by soldiers on active service in the Crimean War. [*Balaclava* in the Crimea, the site of a battle in 1854]

balalaika /balə'lʌɪkə/ *n.* a guitar-like musical instrument having a triangular body and from two to four strings, popular in Russia and other Slavonic countries. [Russian]

balance /'bal(ə)ns/ *n.* & *v.* ● *n.* **1** an apparatus for weighing, esp. one with a central pivot, beam, and two scales. **2 a** a counteracting weight or force. **b** (in full **balance wheel**) the regulating device in a clock etc. **3 a** an even distribution of weight or amount. **b** stability of body or mind (*regained his balance*). **4** a preponderating weight or amount (*the balance of opinion*). **5 a** an agreement between or the difference between credits and debits in an account. **b** the difference between an amount due and an amount paid (*will pay the balance next week*). **c** an amount left over; the rest. **6 a** *Art* harmony of design and proportion. **b** *Mus.* the relative volume of various sources of sound (*bad balance between violins and trumpets*). **7** (**the Balance**) the zodiacal sign or constellation Libra. ● *v.* **1** *tr.* (foll. by *with, against*) offset or compare (one thing) with another (*must balance the advantages with the disadvantages*). **2** *tr.* counteract, equal, or neutralize the weight or importance of. **3 a** *tr.* bring into or keep in equilibrium (*balanced a book on her head*). **b** *intr.* be in equilibrium (*balanced on one leg*). **4** *tr.* (usu. as **balanced** *adj.*) establish equal or appropriate proportions of elements in (*a balanced diet; balanced opinion*). **5** *tr.* weigh (arguments etc.) against each other. **6 a** *tr.* compare and esp. equalize debits and credits of (an account). **b** *intr.* (of an account) have credits and debits equal. ▫ **in the balance** uncertain; at a critical stage. **on balance** all things considered. **strike a balance** choose a moderate course or compromise. □ **balancer** *n.* [Middle English from Old French, ultimately from Late Latin (*libra*) *bilanx bilancis* '(balance) having two scale-pans']

balance of payments *n.* the difference in value between payments into and out of a country.

balance of power *n.* **1** a situation in which states of the world have roughly equal power. **2** the power held by a small group when larger groups are of equal strength.

balance of trade *n.* the difference in value between imports and exports.

balance sheet *n.* a written statement of the balance of assets and liabilities of an organization at a particular point in time.

balance wheel see BALANCE *n.* 2b.

balancing act *n.* an action or activity that requires achieving a delicate balance between different situations or requirements.

balata /ˈbalətə, bəˈlɑːtə/ *n.* **1** any of several latex-yielding trees of Central America, esp. *Manilkara bidentata*. **2** the dried sap of this used as a substitute for gutta-percha. [ultimately from Carib]

Balbriggan /balˈbrɪg(ə)n/ *n.* a knitted cotton fabric used for underwear etc. [*Balbriggan* in Ireland, where it was originally made]

balcony /ˈbalkəni/ *n.* (*pl.* **-ies**) **1** a usu. balustraded platform on the outside of a building, with access from an upper-floor window or door. **2 a** the tier of seats in a theatre above the dress circle. **b** the upstairs seats in a cinema etc. **c** *N. Amer.* the dress circle in a theatre. □ **balconied** *adj.* [Italian *balcone*]

bald /bɔːld/ *adj.* **1** (of a person) with the scalp wholly or partly lacking hair. **2** (of an animal, plant, etc.) not covered by the usual hair, feathers, leaves, etc. **3** *colloq.* with the surface worn away (*a bald tyre*). **4 a** blunt, unelaborated (*a bald statement*). **b** undisguised (*the bald effrontery*). **5** meagre or dull (*a bald style*). **6** marked with white, esp. on the face (*a bald horse*). □ **balding** *adj.* (in senses 1–3). **baldish** *adj.* **baldly** *adv.* (in sense 4). **baldness** *n.* [Middle English *ballede*, originally 'having a white blaze', probably from an Old English root *ball-* 'white patch']

baldachin /ˈbaldəkɪn, ˈbɔːld-/ *n.* (also **baldaquin**) **1** a ceremonial canopy over an altar, throne, etc. **2** a rich brocade. [Italian *baldacchino* from *Baldacco* 'Baghdad', the brocade's place of origin]

bald eagle *n.* a white-headed eagle, *Haliaeetus leucocephalus*, used as the emblem of the United States.

balderdash /ˈbɔːldədaʃ/ *n.* senseless talk or writing; nonsense. [17th c. in the sense 'a mixture of drinks', then 'a senseless jumble of words': origin unknown]

baldhead /ˈbɔːldhɛd/ *n.* a person with a bald head.

baldmoney /ˈbɔːldmʌni/ *n.* (*pl.* **-eys**) = SPIGNEL. [Middle English in the sense 'gentian': origin unknown]

baldric /ˈbɔːldrɪk/ *n. hist.* a belt for a sword, bugle, etc., hung from the shoulder across the body to the opposite hip. [Middle English *baudry* from Old French *baudrei*, of unknown origin]

baldy /ˈbɔːldi/ *n. & adj.* (also **baldie**) ● *n.* (*pl.* **-ies**) a bald person. ● *adj.* bald.

bale[1] /beɪl/ *n. & v.* ● *n.* **1** a bundle of merchandise or hay etc. tightly wrapped and bound with cords or hoops. **2** the quantity in a bale as a measure, esp. *US* 500 lb of cotton. ● *v.tr.* make up into bales. □ **bale** (or **bail**) **out 1** (of a pilot etc.) make an emergency parachute descent from an aircraft (cf. BAIL[3]). **2** = BAIL[1] *v.* 2. [Middle English, probably from Middle Dutch, ultimately identical with BALL[1]]

bale[2] /beɪl/ *n. archaic* or *poet.* evil, destruction, woe, pain, misery. [Old English *b(e)alu*]

bale[3] *Brit.* var. of BAIL[3].

baleen /bəˈliːn/ *n.* whalebone. [Middle English via Old French *baleine* from Latin *balaena* 'whale']

baleen whale *n.* any of various whales of the suborder Mysticeti, having plates of whalebone in the mouth for straining plankton from the water.

baleful /ˈbeɪlfʊl, -f(ə)l/ *adj.* **1** (esp. of a manner, look, etc.) gloomy, menacing. **2** harmful, malignant, destructive. □ **balefully** *adv.* **balefulness** *n.* [BALE[2] + -FUL]

baler /ˈbeɪlə/ *n.* a machine for making bales of hay, straw, metal, etc.

Balinese /bɑːlɪˈniːz/ *n. & adj.* ● *n.* (*pl.* same) **1** a native of Bali, an island in Indonesia. **2** the language of Bali. ● *adj.* of or relating to Bali or its people or language.

balk var. of BAULK.

Balkan /ˈbɒlkən, ˈbɔːl-/ *adj. & n.* ● *adj.* **1** of or relating to the region of SE Europe bounded by the Adriatic, the Aegean, and the Black Sea. **2** of or relating to its peoples or countries. ● *n.* (**the Balkans**) the Balkan countries. [Turkish]

Balkanize /ˈbɒlkənʌɪz, ˈbɔːl-/ *v.tr.* (also **-ise**) divide (an area) into smaller mutually hostile states. □ **Balkanization** /-ˈzeɪʃ(ə)n/ *n.*

balky var. of BAULKY.

ball[1] /bɔːl/ *n. & v.* ● *n.* **1** a solid or hollow sphere, esp. for use in a game. **2 a** a ball-shaped object; material forming the shape of a ball (*ball of snow*; *ball of wool*; *rolled himself into a ball*). **b** a rounded part of the body (*ball of the foot*). **3** a solid non-explosive missile for a cannon etc. **4** a single delivery of a ball in cricket, baseball, etc., or passing of a ball in football. **5** (in *pl.*) *coarse slang* **a** the testicles. **b** *Brit.* (usu. as an exclamation of contempt) nonsense, rubbish. **c** *Brit.* = BALLS-UP. **d** courage, 'guts'. ● *v.* **1** *tr.* squeeze or wind into a ball. **2** *intr.* form or gather into a ball or balls. □ **the ball is in your** etc. **court** you etc. must be next to act. **balls** (or *Brit.* **ball**) **up** *coarse slang* bungle; make a mess of. **have the ball at one's feet** have one's best opportunity. **keep the ball rolling** maintain the momentum of an activity. **on the ball** *colloq.* alert. **play ball** *colloq.* cooperate. **start** etc. **the ball rolling** set an activity in motion; make a start. [Middle English from Old Norse *bǫllr*, from Germanic]

ball[2] /bɔːl/ *n.* **1** a formal social gathering for dancing. **2** *slang* an enjoyable time (esp. *have a ball*). [French *bal* from Late Latin *ballare* 'to dance']

ballad /ˈbaləd/ *n.* **1** a poem or song narrating a popular story. **2** a slow sentimental or romantic song. [Middle English via Old French *balade* from Provençal *balada* 'dancing-song', from *balar* 'to dance']

ballade /baˈlɑːd/ *n.* **1** a poem of one or more triplets of stanzas with a repeated refrain and an envoi. **2** *Mus.* a short lyrical piece, esp. for piano. [earlier spelling and pronunciation of BALLAD]

balladeer /baləˈdɪə/ *n.* a singer or composer of ballads.

ballad metre *n.* = COMMON METRE.

balladry /ˈbalədri/ *n.* ballad poetry.

ball-and-socket joint *n.* a natural or man-made joint in which a rounded end lies in a concave cup or socket, allowing freedom of movement.

ballast /ˈbaləst/ *n. & v.* ● *n.* **1** any heavy material placed in a ship or the car of a hot-air balloon etc. to secure stability. **2** coarse stone etc. used to form the bed of a railway track or road. **3** a mixture of coarse and fine aggregate for making concrete. **4** *Electr.* any device used to stabilize the current in a circuit. **5** anything that affords stability or permanence. ● *v.tr.* **1** provide with ballast. **2** afford stability or weight to. [16th c.: from Low German or Scandinavian, of uncertain origin]

ball-bearing *n.* **1** a bearing in which the two halves are separated by a ring of small metal balls which reduce friction. **2** one of these balls.

ballboy /ˈbɔːlbɔɪ/ *n.* (*fem.* **ballgirl** /-gəːl/) a boy or girl who retrieves balls that go out of play during a game of tennis etc.

ballcock /'bɔːlkɒk/ *n.* a floating ball on a hinged arm, whose movement up and down controls the water level in a cistern etc.

ballerina /balə'riːnə/ *n.* a female ballet dancer. [Italian, fem. of *ballerino* 'dancing master' from *ballare* 'to dance' from Late Latin]

ballet /'baleɪ, -li/ *n.* **1 a** a dramatic or representational style of dancing and mime, using set steps and techniques and usu. (esp. in classical ballet) accompanied by music. **b** a particular piece or performance of ballet. **c** the music for this. **2** a company performing ballet. □ **balletic** /bə'lɛtɪk/ *adj.* [French from Italian *balletto*, diminutive of *ballo* BALL[2]]

ballet dancer *n.* a dancer who specializes in ballet.

balletomane /'balɪtəʊmeɪn/ *n.* a devotee of ballet. □ **balletomania** /-'meɪnɪə/ *n.*

ball game *n.* **1 a** any game played with a ball. **b** *N. Amer.* a game of baseball. **2** esp. *N. Amer. colloq.* a particular affair or concern (*a whole new ball game*).

ballgirl see BALLBOY.

ballista /bə'lɪstə/ *n.* (*pl.* **ballistae** /-stiː/) a catapult used in ancient warfare for hurling large stones etc. [Latin from Greek *ballō* 'throw']

ballistic /bə'lɪstɪk/ *adj.* **1** of or relating to projectiles. **2** moving under the force of gravity only. □ **go ballistic** esp. *N. Amer. slang* become furious. □ **ballistically** *adv.* [BALLISTA + -IC]

ballistic missile *n.* a missile which is initially powered and guided but falls under gravity on its target.

ballistics /bə'lɪstɪks/ *n.* the science of projectiles and firearms.

ball lightning *n.* a rare globular form of lightning.

ballocks var. of BOLLOCKS.

ballon d'essai /ba͵lɔ̃ dɛ'seɪ, French balɔ̃ desɛ/ *n.* (*pl.* ***ballons d'essai*** *pronunc.* same) = TRIAL BALLOON. [French, = trial balloon]

balloon /bə'luːn/ *n.* & *v.* ● *n.* **1** a small inflatable rubber pouch with a neck, used as a child's toy or as decoration. **2** a large usu. round bag inflatable with hot air or gas to make it rise in the air, often carrying a basket for passengers. **3** *colloq.* a balloon shape enclosing the words or thoughts of characters in a comic strip or cartoon. **4** a large globular drinking glass, usu. for brandy. ● *v.* **1** *intr.* & *tr.* swell out or cause to swell out like a balloon. **2** *intr.* travel by balloon. **3** *tr. Brit.* hit or kick (a ball etc.) high in the air. □ **when the balloon goes up** *colloq.* when the action or trouble starts. □ **balloonist** *n.* [French *ballon* or Italian *ballone* 'large ball']

ballot /'balət/ *n.* & *v.* ● *n.* **1** a process of voting, in writing and usu. secret. **2** the total of votes recorded in a ballot. **3** the drawing of lots. **4** a paper or ticket etc. used in voting. ● *v.* (**balloted**, **balloting**) **1** *intr.* (usu. foll. by *for*) **a** hold a ballot; give a vote. **b** draw lots for precedence etc. **2** *tr.* take a ballot of (*the union balloted its members*). [Italian *ballotta*, diminutive of *balla* BALL[1] (from the practice of registering votes by placing coloured balls in a container)]

ballot box *n.* a sealed box into which voters put completed ballot papers.

ballot paper *n. Brit.* a slip of paper used to register a vote.

ballpark /'bɔːlpɑːk/ *n. N. Amer.* **1** a baseball ground. **2** (*attrib.*) *colloq.* approximate, rough (*a ballpark figure*). □ **in the right ballpark** *colloq.* close to one's objective; approximately correct.

ballpoint /'bɔːlpɔɪnt/ *n.* (in full **ballpoint pen**) a pen with a tiny ball as its writing point.

ball-race *n.* **1** a ring-shaped groove in which the balls of a ball-bearing move. **2** a ball-bearing.

ballroom /'bɔːlruːm, -rʊm/ *n.* a large room or hall for dancing.

ballroom dancing *n.* formal social dancing as a recreation or performed competitively.

balls-up *n. Brit. coarse slang* a mess; a confused or bungled situation.

ballsy /'bɔːlzi/ *adj. slang* **1** manly, powerful. **2** courageous. [BALL[1] *n.* 5d]

ball valve *n.* a valve opened or closed by a ball which fits into a cup-shaped opening.

bally /'bali/ *adj.* & *adv. Brit. slang* a mild form of *bloody* (see BLOODY *adj.* 3) (*took the bally lot*). [alteration of BLOODY]

ballyhoo /balɪ'huː/ *n.* **1** a loud noise or fuss; a confused state or commotion. **2** extravagant or sensational publicity. [19th c., originally US: origin unknown]

ballyrag /'balɪrag/ *v.tr.* (also **bullyrag** /'bʊl-/) (**-ragged**, **-ragging**) *slang* play tricks on; scold, harass. [18th c.: origin unknown]

balm /bɑːm/ *n.* **1** an aromatic ointment for anointing, soothing, or healing. **2** a fragrant and medicinal exudation from certain trees and plants. **3** a healing or soothing influence or consolation. **4** a tree that yields balm, esp. an Asian and N. African tree of the genus *Commiphora*. **5** any aromatic herb, esp. one of the genus *Melissa*. **6** a pleasant perfume or fragrance. [Middle English via Old French *ba(s)me* from Latin *balsamum* BALSAM]

balm of Gilead /'gɪlɪad/ *n.* (cf. Jer. 8:22) **1 a** a fragrant resin formerly much used as an unguent. **b** a tree of the genus *Commiphora* yielding such resin. **2** the balsam fir or poplar.

balmoral /bal'mɒr(ə)l/ *n.* **1** a type of brimless boat-shaped cocked hat with a cockade or ribbons attached, usu. worn by certain Scottish regiments. **2** a heavy leather walking boot with laces up the front. [*Balmoral* Castle in Scotland]

balmy /'bɑːmi/ *adj.* (**balmier**, **balmiest**) **1** mild and fragrant; soothing. **2** yielding balm. **3** esp. *Brit. slang* = BARMY. □ **balmily** *adv.* **balminess** *n.*

balneology /balnɪ'ɒlədʒi/ *n.* the scientific study of bathing and medicinal springs. □ **balneological** /-nɪə'lɒdʒɪk(ə)l/ *adj.* **balneologist** *n.* [Latin *balneum* 'bath' + -LOGY]

baloney /bə'ləʊni/ *n.* (also **boloney**) (*pl.* **-eys**) *slang* **1** humbug, nonsense. **2** *N. Amer.* = BOLOGNA SAUSAGE. [20th c.: alteration of *Bologna* (see BOLOGNA SAUSAGE)]

BALPA /'balpə/ *abbr.* British Air Line Pilots Association.

balsa /'bɒlsə/ *n.* **1** (in full **balsa wood**) a type of tough lightweight wood used for making models, rafts, etc. **2** the tropical American tree, *Ochroma lagopus*, from which it comes. [Spanish, = raft]

balsam /'bɔːlsəm, 'bɒl-/ *n.* **1** an aromatic resinous exudation, such as balm, obtained from various trees and shrubs and used as a base for certain fragrances and medical preparations. **2** an ointment, esp. one composed of a substance dissolved in oil or turpentine. **3** any of various trees or shrubs which yield balsam. **4** any of several flowering plants of the genus *Impatiens*. **5** a healing or soothing agency. □ **balsamic** /-'samɪk/ *adj.* [Old English, from Latin *balsamum*]

balsam fir *n.* a N. American tree, *Abies balsamea*, which yields balsam.

balsamic vinegar *n.* a dark, sweet, Italian vinegar, matured in wooden barrels.

balsam poplar *n.* any of various N. American poplars, esp. *Populus balsamifera*, yielding balsam.

balsa wood see BALSA 1.

Balti /'bɔːlti, 'balti/ *n.* a type of Pakistani curry, usu. cooked and served in a dish like a shallow wok. [20th c.: origin uncertain; perhaps from *Balti* 'native or inhabitant of Baltistan']

Baltic /'bɔːltɪk, 'bɒlt-/ *n.* & *adj.* ● *n.* **1** (**the Baltic**) **a** an almost landlocked sea of northern Europe. **b** the states bordering this sea. **2** an Indo-European branch of languages including Old Prussian, Lithuanian, Latvian, and Lettish. ● *adj.* of or relating to the Baltic or the branch of languages called *Baltic*. [medieval Latin

Balticus from Late Latin *Balthae* 'dwellers near the Baltic Sea']

baluster /ˈbaləstə/ *n.* each of a series of usu. ornamental short posts or pillars supporting a rail or coping etc. [French *balustre* via Italian and Latin from Greek *balaustion* 'wild-pomegranate flower', which the baluster resembles in shape]

■ **Usage** *Baluster* is sometimes confused with *banister* because their meanings overlap. A *baluster* is usually a curved ornamental post forming part of a *balustrade* which is mainly found around a gallery, bridge, or terrace, as in *Expert craftsmen have restored stone balusters taken from the bridge and fitted plinths to the top to form bird tables.*

A *banister* is a post supporting the handrail of a staircase, e.g. *He shook the stair banisters and rail and found they were loose.* It can also mean the posts together with the rail, as in *He looked over the banister(s).* In this case it is often used in the plural.

Occasionally, a large staircase in a grand house may have ornamental carved banisters, in which case they may be called *balusters.*

balustrade /baləˈstreɪd/ *n.* a railing supported by balusters, esp. forming an ornamental parapet to a balcony, bridge, or terrace. □ **balustraded** *adj.* [French (as BALUSTER)]

bambino /bamˈbiːnəʊ/ *n.* (*pl.* **bambini** /-ni/) *colloq.* a young (esp. Italian) child. [Italian, diminutive of *bambo* 'silly']

bamboo /bamˈbuː/ *n.* **1** a giant woody grass of the mainly tropical subfamily Bambusidae. **2** its hollow jointed stem, used as a stick or to make furniture etc. [Dutch *bamboes* via Portuguese *mambu* from Malay]

bamboo shoot *n.* a young shoot of bamboo, eaten as a vegetable.

bamboozle /bamˈbuːz(ə)l/ *v.tr. colloq.* cheat, hoax, mystify. □ **bamboozler** *n.* [*c.*1700: of unknown origin]

ban /ban/ *v.* & *n.* ● *v.tr.* (**banned**, **banning**) forbid, prohibit, esp. formally. ● *n.* **1** a formal or authoritative prohibition (*a ban on smoking*). **2** a tacit prohibition by public opinion. **3** *hist.* a sentence of outlawry. **4** *archaic* a curse or execration. [originally = public proclamation or summons, from Old English *bannan* 'summon', from Germanic]

banal /bəˈnɑːl, -ˈnal/ *adj.* trite, feeble, commonplace. □ **banality** /-ˈnalɪti/ *n.* (*pl.* **-ies**). **banally** *adv.* [originally in sense 'compulsory', hence 'common to all': French from *ban* (as BAN)]

banana /bəˈnɑːnə/ *n.* **1** a long curved fruit with soft pulpy flesh and yellow skin when ripe, growing in clusters. **2** (in full **banana tree**) the tropical and subtropical treelike plant, *Musa sapientum*, bearing this. □ **go bananas** *slang* become crazy or angry. [Portuguese or Spanish, from a name in Guinea]

banana republic *n. derog.* a small state, esp. in Central America, economically dependent on usu. one trade such as banana-growing and therefore dependent on foreign capital.

banana skin *n.* **1** the skin of a banana. **2** a cause of upset or humiliation; a blunder.

banana split *n.* a sweet dish made with split bananas, ice cream, sauce, etc.

banausic /bəˈnɔːsɪk/ *adj. derog.* **1 a** uncultivated. **b** materialistic. **2** suitable only for artisans. [Greek *banausikos* 'for artisans']

Banbury cake /ˈbanb(ə)ri/ *n. Brit.* a flat pastry with a spicy currant filling. [*Banbury* in S. England, where it was originally made]

banc /baŋk/ *n.* □ **in banc** *Law* sitting as a full court. [Anglo-French (= bench) from medieval Latin (as BANK²)]

band¹ /band/ *n.* & *v.* ● *n.* **1** a flat, thin strip or loop of material (e.g. paper, metal, or cloth) put round something esp. to hold it together or decorate it (*headband*). **2 a** a strip of material forming part of a garment (*hatband*; *waistband*). **b** a stripe of a different colour or material on an object. **c** a portion of a substance or of an area in the form of a long flat strip (*a band of cloud*). **3** a range or category within which items fall (*tax band*; *top band of the fifth form*). **4 a** a range of frequencies or wavelengths in a spectrum (esp. of radio frequencies). **b** a range of values within a series. **5** a plain gold ring, esp. a gold wedding ring. **6** *Mech.* a belt connecting wheels or pulleys. **7** (in *pl.*) a collar having two hanging strips, worn by some lawyers, ministers, and academics in formal dress. **8** *archaic* a thing that restrains, binds, connects, or unites; a bond. ● *v.tr.* **1** put a band on. **2 a** mark with stripes. **b** (as **banded** *adj.*) *Bot.* & *Zool.* marked with coloured bands or stripes. **3 a** divide into, or arrange in, bands or ranges with a view to treating the bands differently. **b** group (pupils) on the basis of ability. [Middle English, from Old French *bande*, *bende* (sense 6 from Old Norse *band*), from Germanic]

band² /band/ *n.* & *v.* ● *n.* **1 a** a group of musicians who play together (usu. popular rather than classical music) (*jazz band*; *brass band*; *rock band*). **b** *colloq.* an orchestra. **2** an organized group of people having a common object, esp. of a criminal nature (*band of cut-throats*). **3** *N. Amer.* a herd or flock. ● *v.tr.* & *intr.* (usu. foll. by *together*) form into a group for a purpose (*band together for mutual protection*). [Middle English from Old French *bande* (*n.*), *bander* (*v.*), medieval Latin *banda*, probably of Germanic origin]

bandage /ˈbandɪdʒ/ *n.* & *v.* ● *n.* **1** a strip of material for binding up a wound etc. **2** a piece of material used as a blindfold. ● *v.tr.* bind (a wound etc.) with a bandage. [French from *bande* (as BAND¹)]

Band-Aid *n.* (also **band-aid**) **1** *propr.* **a** a type of sticking plaster with a gauze pad. **b** a piece of this. **2** a makeshift or temporary solution.

bandanna /banˈdanə/ *n.* a large coloured handkerchief or neckerchief, usu. of silk or cotton, and often having white spots. [probably Portuguese from Hindi]

B. & B. *abbr.* (also **b. & b.**) bed and breakfast.

bandbox /ˈban(d)bɒks/ *n.* a usu. circular cardboard box for carrying hats, used originally for neckbands. □ **out of a bandbox** extremely neat. [BAND¹ + BOX¹]

bandeau /ˈbandəʊ/ *n.* (*pl.* **bandeaux** /-dəʊz/) a narrow band worn round the head. [French]

banderilla /bandəˈrɪljə/ *n.* a decorated dart thrust into a bull's neck or shoulders during a bullfight. [Spanish, dimunitive of *bandera* 'banner']

banderole /ˈbandərəʊl/ *n.* (also **banderol**) **1 a** a long narrow flag with a cleft end, flown at a masthead. **b** an ornamental streamer on a knight's lance. **2 a** a ribbon-like scroll. **b** a stone band resembling a banderole, bearing an inscription. [French *banderole* from Italian *banderuola*, diminutive of *bandiera* 'banner']

bandicoot /ˈbandɪkuːt/ *n.* **1** any mainly insect-eating marsupial of the family Peramelidae, of Australia and New Guinea. **2** (in full **bandicoot rat**) a destructive Asian rat of the genus *Bandicota*, esp. the large *B. indica*. [Telugu *pandikokku* literally 'pig-rat']

banding /ˈbandɪŋ/ *n.* **1** the presence or formation of visible bands or stripes. **2** division into a series of categories e.g. by ability, value, tax liability, etc. **3** *Biochem.* **a** the pattern of regions on a chromosome made visible by staining. **b** the separation of molecules into bands of concentration in a gel etc. **4** the labelling of individual birds or animals with bands.

bandit /ˈbandɪt/ *n.* (*pl.* **bandits** or **banditti** /-ˈdɪti/) **1** a robber or murderer, esp. a member of a gang; a gangster. **2** an outlaw. □ **banditry** *n.* [Italian *bandito* (pl. *-iti*), past part. of *bandire* 'ban', = medieval Latin *bannire* 'proclaim': related to BAN, BANISH]

bandleader /ˈbandliːdə/ *n.* the leader of a musical band.

bandmaster /ˈban(d)mɑːstə/ *n.* the conductor of a (esp. military or brass) band. [BAND² + MASTER]

Band of Hope *n.* (in the UK) an association promoting total abstinence from alcohol.

bandog /ˈbandɒg/ *n.* a fighting dog bred for its strength and ferocity by crossing aggressive breeds. [originally = a dog kept on a chain, from BAND[1] 'fastening' + DOG]

bandolier /bandəˈlɪə/ *n.* (also **bandoleer**) a shoulder-belt with loops or pockets for cartridges. [Dutch *bandelier* or French *bandoulière*, probably formed as BANDEROLE]

bandpass /ˈban(d)pɑːs/ *n.* the range of frequencies (of sound, electrical signals, etc.) which are transmitted through a filter.

bandsaw /ˈban(d)sɔː/ *n.* an endless saw, consisting of a steel belt with a serrated edge running over wheels.

bandsman /ˈban(d)zmən/ *n.* (*pl.* **-men**) a player in a (esp. military or brass) band.

bandstand /ˈban(d)stand/ *n.* a covered outdoor platform for a band to play on, usu. in a park.

bandwagon /ˈbandwagən/ *n.* orig. *US* a wagon used for carrying a band in a parade etc. □ **climb** (or **jump**) **on the bandwagon** join a party, cause, or group that seems likely to succeed.

bandwidth /ˈbandwɪtθ, -wɪdθ/ *n.* the range of frequencies within a given band (see BAND[1] *n.* 4a).

bandy[1] /ˈbandi/ *adj.* (**bandier**, **bandiest**) **1** (of the legs) curved so as to be wide apart at the knees. **2** (also **bandy-legged**) (of a person) having bandy legs. [perhaps from obsolete *bandy* 'curved stick']

bandy[2] /ˈbandi/ *v.tr.* (**-ies**, **-ied**) **1** (often foll. by *about*) **a** pass (a story, rumour, etc.) to and fro. **b** throw or pass (a ball etc.) to and fro. **2** (often foll. by *about*) discuss disparagingly (*bandied her name about*). **3** (often foll. by *with*) exchange (blows, insults, etc.) (*don't bandy words with me*). [perhaps from French *bander* from *bande* BAND[2]]

bane /beɪn/ *n.* **1** the cause of ruin or trouble; the curse (esp. *the bane of one's life*). **2** *poet.* ruin; woe. **3** *archaic* (except in *comb.*) poison (*ratsbane*). □ **baneful** *adj.* **banefully** *adv.* [Old English *bana*, from Germanic]

baneberry /ˈbeɪnb(ə)ri/ *n.* (*pl.* **-ies**) **1** any of several plants of the genus *Actaea*. **2** the bitter poisonous berry of these plants.

bang /baŋ/ *n.*, *v.*, & *adv.* ● *n.* **1 a** a loud short sound. **b** an explosion. **c** the report of a gun. **2 a** a sharp blow. **b** the sound of this. **3** (in *pl.*) esp. *N. Amer.* a fringe of hair cut straight across the forehead. **4** *coarse slang* an act of sexual intercourse. **5** *slang* a drug injection (cf. BHANG). ● *v.* **1** *tr.* & *intr.* strike or shut noisily (*banged the door shut*; *banged on the table*). **2** *tr.* & *intr.* make or cause to make the sound of a blow or an explosion. **3** *tr.* esp. *N. Amer.* cut (hair) in bangs. **4** *coarse slang* **a** *intr.* have sexual intercourse. **b** *tr.* have sexual intercourse with. ● *adv.* **1** with a bang or sudden impact. **2** esp. *Brit. colloq.* exactly (*bang in the middle*). □ **bang off** *Brit. slang* immediately. **bang on** *Brit. colloq.* exactly right. **bang on about** talk tediously and at length about. **go bang 1** (of a door etc.) shut noisily. **2** explode. **3** *colloq.* be suddenly destroyed (*bang went their chances*). **go with a bang** go successfully. [16th c.: perhaps from Scandinavian]

banger /ˈbaŋə/ *n.* esp. *Brit.* **1** *slang* a sausage. **2** *slang* an old car, esp. a noisy one. **3** a loud firework.

Bangladeshi /baŋgləˈdeʃi/ *n.* & *adj.* ● *n.* (*pl.* same or **Bangladeshis**) a native or inhabitant of Bangladesh, in the north-east of the Indian subcontinent. ● *adj.* of or relating to Bangladesh or its people. [*Bangladesh* + -I[2]]

bangle /ˈbaŋg(ə)l/ *n.* a rigid ornamental band worn round the arm or occasionally the ankle. [Hindi *banglī* 'glass bracelet']

bangtail /ˈbaŋteɪl/ *n.* a horse, esp. with its tail cut straight across.

bangtail muster *n. Austral.* the counting of cattle involving cutting across the tufts at the tail-ends as each is counted.

bang-up *adj.* (esp. in phr. **a bang-up job**) *N. Amer. slang* first-class, excellent.

banian var. of BANYAN.

banish /ˈbanɪʃ/ *v.tr.* **1** formally expel (a person), esp. from a country. **2** dismiss from one's presence or mind. □ **banishment** *n.* [Middle English from Old English *banir*, ultimately from the Germanic base of BAN]

banister /ˈbanɪstə/ *n.* (also **bannister**) **1** (often in *pl.*) the uprights and handrail at the side of a staircase. **2** each of these uprights. [earlier *barrister*, corruption of BALUSTER]

■ **Usage** See Usage Note at BALUSTER.

banjo /ˈbandʒəʊ/ *n.* (*pl.* **-os** or **-oes**) a stringed musical instrument with a neck and head like a guitar and an open-backed body consisting of parchment stretched over a metal hoop. □ **banjoist** *n.* [US southern corruption of earlier *bandore*, ultimately from Greek *pandoura* 'three-stringed lute']

bank[1] /baŋk/ *n.* & *v.* ● *n.* **1 a** the sloping edge of land by a river. **b** the area of ground alongside a river (*had a picnic on the bank*). **2** a raised shelf of ground; a slope. **3** an elevation in the sea or a river bed. **4 a** the artificial slope of a road etc., enabling vehicles to maintain speed round a curve. **b** the sideways tilt of an aircraft when turning in flight. **5** a mass of cloud, fog, snow, etc. **6** the edge of a hollow place (e.g. the top of a mine shaft). ● *v.* **1** *tr.* & *intr.* (often foll. by *up*) heap or rise into banks. **2** *tr.* heap up (a fire) tightly so that it burns slowly. **3 a** *intr.* (of a vehicle or aircraft or its occupant) travel with one side higher than the other in rounding a curve. **b** *tr.* cause (a vehicle or aircraft) to do this. **4** *tr.* contain or confine within a bank or banks. **5** *tr.* build (a road etc.) higher at the outer edge of a bend to enable fast cornering. [Middle English from Old Norse *bakki*, from Germanic: related to BENCH]

bank[2] /baŋk/ *n.* & *v.* ● *n.* **1 a** a financial establishment which uses money deposited by customers for investment, pays it out when required, makes loans at interest, exchanges currency, etc. **b** a building in which this business takes place. **2** = PIGGY BANK. **3 a** the money or tokens held by the banker in some gambling games. **b** the banker in such games. **4** a place for storing anything for future use (*blood bank*; *data bank*). ● *v.* **1** *tr.* deposit (money or valuables) in a bank. **2** *intr.* engage in business as a banker. **3** *intr.* (often foll. by *at*, *with*) keep money (at a bank). **4** *intr.* act as banker in some gambling games. □ **bank on** rely on (*I'm banking on your help*). [originally = a money-dealers' bench or table, from French *banque* or Italian *banca* via medieval Latin *banca*, *bancus*, from Germanic: related to BANK[1], BENCH]

bank[3] /baŋk/ *n.* **1** a row of similar objects, esp. of keys, lights, or switches. **2** a tier of oars. [Middle English via Old French *banc* from Germanic: related to BANK[1], BENCH]

bankable /ˈbaŋkəb(ə)l/ *adj.* **1** certain to bring profit; good for the box office. **2** acceptable at a bank. **3** reliable (*a bankable reputation*). □ **bankability** /-əˈbɪlɪti/ *n.*

bank balance *n.* the amount of money held in a bank account at a given moment.

bank bill *n.* **1** *Brit.* a bill drawn by one bank on another. **2** esp. *US* = BANKNOTE.

bank book *n.* = PASSBOOK.

bank card *n.* = CHEQUE CARD.

banker[1] /ˈbaŋkə/ *n.* **1** a person who manages or owns a bank or group of banks. **2 a** a keeper of the bank or dealer in some gambling games. **b** a card game involving gambling. **3** *Brit.* a result forecast identically (while other forecasts differ) in several football-pool entries on one coupon. [French *banquier* from *banque* BANK[2]]

banker[2] /ˈbaŋkə/ *n.* **1 a** a fishing boat off Newfoundland. **b** a Newfoundland fisherman. **2** *Austral. colloq.* a river flooded to the top of its banks. [BANK[1] + -ER[1]]

banker's card *n. Brit.* = CHEQUE CARD.

banker's order *n. Brit.* an instruction to a bank to pay money or deliver property, signed by the owner or the owner's agent.

bank holiday *n.* a day on which banks are officially closed, (in the UK) usu. kept as a public holiday.

banking /ˈbaŋkɪŋ/ *n.* the business transactions of a bank.

bank machine *n.* = CASH DISPENSER.

bank manager *n.* a person in charge of a local branch of a bank.

banknote /ˈbaŋknəʊt/ *n.* a banker's promissory note, esp. from a central bank, payable to the bearer on demand, and serving as money.

Bank of England *n.* the central bank of England and Wales, issuing banknotes and having the British Government as its main customer.

bankroll /ˈbaŋkrəʊl/ *n. & v.* orig. *N. Amer.* ● *n.* **1** a roll of banknotes. **2** funds. ● *v.tr. colloq.* support financially.

bankrupt /ˈbaŋkrʌpt/ *adj., n., & v.* ● *adj.* **1 a** insolvent; declared in law unable to pay debts. **b** undergoing the legal process resulting from this. **2** (often foll. by *of*) exhausted or drained (of some quality etc.); deficient, lacking. ● *n.* **1 a** an insolvent person whose estate is administered and disposed of for the benefit of the creditors. **b** an insolvent debtor. **2** a person exhausted of or deficient in a certain attribute (*a moral bankrupt*). ● *v.tr.* make bankrupt. □ **bankruptcy** /-ˌrʌptsi/ *n.* (*pl.* **-ies**). [16th c.: from Italian *banca rotta* 'broken bench' (as BANK[2], Latin *rumpere rupt-* 'break')]

banksia /ˈbaŋksɪə/ *n.* an evergreen flowering shrub of the genus *Banksia*, native to Australia. [Sir J. *Banks*, English naturalist d. 1820]

banksia rose *n.* a Chinese climbing rose, *Rosa banksiae*, with small flowers.

bank statement *n.* a printed statement of transactions and balance issued periodically to the holder of a bank account.

banner /ˈbanə/ *n.* **1 a** a large rectangular sign bearing a slogan or design and usu. carried on two side-poles or a crossbar in a demonstration or procession. **b** a long strip of cloth etc. hung across a street or along the front of a building etc. and bearing a slogan. **2** a slogan or phrase used to represent a belief or principle. **3** a flag on a pole used as the standard of a king, knight, etc., esp. in battle. **4** (*attrib.*) *US* excellent, outstanding (*a banner year in sales*). □ **join** (or **follow**) **the banner of** adhere to the cause of. □ **bannered** *adj.* [Middle English via Anglo-French *banere*, Old French *baniere* from Romanic, ultimately from Germanic]

banneret /ˈbanərɪt/ *n. hist.* **1** a knight who commanded his own troops in battle under his own banner. **2** a knighthood given on the battlefield for courage. [Middle English & Old French *baneret*, from *baniere* BANNER + *-et* as -ATE[1]]

banner headline *n.* a large newspaper headline, esp. one across the top of the front page.

bannister var. of BANISTER.

bannock /ˈbanək/ *n. Sc. & N.Engl.* a round flat loaf, usu. unleavened. [Old English *bannuc*, perhaps from Celtic]

banns /banz/ *n.pl.* a notice read out on three successive Sundays in a parish church, announcing an intended marriage and giving the opportunity for objections. □ **forbid the banns** raise an objection to an intended marriage, esp. in church following the reading of the banns. [pl. of BAN]

banquet /ˈbaŋkwɪt/ *n. & v.* ● *n.* **1** an elaborate usu. extensive feast. **2** a dinner for many people followed by speeches in favour of a cause or in celebration of an event. ● *v.* (**banqueted**, **banqueting**) **1** *intr.* hold a banquet; feast. **2** *tr.* entertain with a banquet. □ **banqueter** *n.* [French, diminutive of *banc* 'bench', BANK[2]]

banquette /baŋˈkɛt/ *n.* **1** an upholstered bench along a wall, esp. in a restaurant or bar. **2** a raised step behind a rampart. [French from Italian *banchetta*, diminutive of *banca* 'bench', BANK[2]]

banshee /banˈʃiː, ˈbanʃiː/ *n. Ir. & Sc.* a female spirit whose wailing warns of a death in a house. [Irish *bean sídhe* from Old Irish *ben síde* 'woman of the fairies']

bantam /ˈbantəm/ *n.* **1** a breed of small domestic fowl, of which the cock is aggressive. **2** a small but aggressive person. [apparently from *Banten* in Java, although the fowl is not native there]

bantamweight /ˈbantəmweɪt/ *n.* **1** a weight in certain sports intermediate between flyweight and featherweight, in the amateur boxing scale 51–4 kg but differing for professional boxers, wrestlers, and weightlifters. **2** a boxer etc. of this weight.

banter /ˈbantə/ *n. & v.* ● *n.* good-humoured teasing. ● *v.* **1** *tr.* ridicule in a good-humoured way. **2** *intr.* talk humorously or teasingly. □ **banterer** *n.* [17th c.: origin unknown]

Bantu /banˈtuː, ˈbantuː/ *n. & adj.* ● *n.* (*pl.* same or **Bantus**) **1** *offens.* **a** a large group of Negroid peoples of central and southern Africa. **b** a member of any of these peoples. **2** the group of languages spoken by them. ● *adj.* of or relating to these peoples (*offens.*), or languages. [Bantu, = people]

■ **Usage** *Bantu*, originally a neutral 'scientific' term, became strongly associated with apartheid policies in South Africa and is therefore regarded as offensive with references to the peoples.

Bantustan /bantuːˈstɑːn, -ˈstan/ *n. S.Afr. colloq. derog.* = HOMELAND 2. [BANTU + *-stan* 'country', as in *Hindustan* etc.]

banyan /ˈbanɪən, -njən/ *n.* (also **banian**) **1** (also **banyan tree**) an Indian fig tree, *Ficus benghalensis*, the branches of which hang down and root themselves. **2** a Hindu trader. **3** a loose flannel jacket, shirt, or gown worn in India. [Portuguese *banian* from Gujarati *vāṇiyo* 'man of trading caste', from Sanskrit: applied originally to one such tree under which banyans had built a pagoda]

banzai /banˈzʌɪ/ *int. & adj.* ● *int.* a Japanese battle-cry. ● *attrib. adj.* reckless. [Japanese, = ten thousand years (of life to you)]

baobab /ˈbeɪəbab/ *n.* **1** an African tree, *Adansonia digitata*, with an enormously thick trunk and large edible pulpy fruit hanging down on stalks. **2** a related Australian tree, *Adansonia gregorii*. [Latin (1592), probably from an African language]

BAOR *abbr.* British Army of the Rhine.

bap /bap/ *n. Brit.* a soft flattish bread roll. [16th c.: origin unknown]

baptism /ˈbaptɪz(ə)m/ *n.* **1 a** the religious rite, symbolizing admission to the Christian Church, of sprinkling or pouring water on to the forehead, or (usu. only with adults) of immersion, generally accompanied by name-giving. **b** the act of baptizing or being baptized. **2** an initiation, e.g. into battle. **3** the naming of ships, church bells, etc. □ **baptismal** /-ˈtɪzm(ə)l/ *adj.* [Middle English via Old French *ba(p)te(s)me* and ecclesiastical Latin *baptismus* from ecclesiastical Greek *baptismos*, from *baptizō* BAPTIZE]

baptism of fire *n.* **1** initiation into battle. **2** a painful new undertaking or experience.

baptist /ˈbaptɪst/ *n.* **1** a person who baptizes, esp. John the Baptist. **2** (**Baptist**) a member of a Protestant Christian denomination advocating baptism only of adult believers by total immersion. [Middle English via Old French *baptiste* and ecclesiastical Latin *baptista* from ecclesiastical Greek *baptistēs*, from *baptizō* BAPTIZE]

baptistery /ˈbaptɪst(ə)ri/ *n.* (also **baptistry** /-tri/) (*pl.* **-ies**) **1 a** the part of a church used for baptism. **b** *hist.* a building next to a church, used for baptism. **2** (in a Baptist chapel) a sunken receptacle used for total immersion. [Middle English via Old French *baptisterie* and ecclesiastical Latin *baptisterium* from ecclesiastical Greek *baptistērion* 'bathing place', from *baptizō* BAPTIZE]

baptize /bap'tʌɪz/ *v.tr.* (also **-ise**) **1** (also *absol.*) administer baptism to. **2** give a name or nickname to; christen. [Middle English via Old French *baptiser* and ecclesiastical Latin *baptizare* from Greek *baptizō* 'immerse, baptize']

bar[1] /bɑː/ *n., v., & prep.* ● *n.* **1** a long rod or piece of rigid wood, metal, etc., esp. used as an obstruction, confinement, fastening, weapon, etc. **2 a** something resembling a bar in being (thought of as) straight, narrow, and rigid (*bar of soap*; *bar of chocolate*). **b** a band of colour or light, esp. on a flat surface. **c** the heating element of an electric fire. **d** = CROSSBAR. **e** *Brit.* a metal strip below the clasp of a medal, awarded as an extra distinction. **f** a sandbank or shoal at the mouth of a harbour or an estuary. **g** *Brit.* a rail marking the end of each chamber in the Houses of Parliament. **h** *Heraldry* a narrow horizontal stripe across a shield. **3 a** a barrier of any shape. **b** a restriction (*colour bar*; *a bar to promotion*). **4 a** a counter in a public house, restaurant, or café across which alcohol or refreshments are served. **b** a room in a public house in which customers may sit and drink. **c** a public house. **d** a small shop or stall serving refreshments (*snack bar*). **e** a specialized department in a large store (*heel bar*). **5 a** an enclosure in which a prisoner stands in a law court. **b** a public standard of acceptability, before which a person is said to be tried (*bar of conscience*). **c** a plea arresting an action or claim in a law case. **d** a particular court of law. **6** *Mus.* **a** any of the sections of usu. equal time value into which a musical composition is divided by vertical lines across the staff. **b** = BAR LINE. **7** (**the Bar**) *Law* **a** barristers collectively. **b** the profession of barrister. ● *v.tr.* (**barred**, **barring**) **1 a** fasten (a door, window, etc.) with a bar or bars. **b** (usu. foll. by *in, out*) shut or keep in or out (*barred him in*). **2** obstruct, prevent (*bar his progress*). **3 a** (usu. foll. by *from*) prohibit, exclude (*bar them from attending*). **b** exclude from consideration (cf. BARRING). **4** mark with stripes. **5** *Law* prevent or delay (an action) by objection. ● *prep.* **1** esp. *Brit.* except (*all were there bar a few*). **2** *Brit. Racing* except (the horses indicated: used in stating the odds, indicating the number of horses excluded) (*33–1 bar three*). □ **bar none** with no exceptions. **be called to the Bar** *Brit.* be admitted as a barrister. **be called within the Bar** *Brit.* be appointed a Queen's Counsel. **behind bars** in prison. [Middle English from Old French *barre* (*n.*), *barrer* (*v.*), from Romanic]

bar[2] /bɑː/ *n.* esp. *Meteorol.* a unit of pressure, 10^5 newton per square metre, approx. one atmosphere. [Greek *baros* 'weight']

barathea /barə'θiːə/ *n.* a fine woollen cloth, sometimes mixed with silk or cotton, used esp. for coats, suits, etc. [19th c.: origin unknown]

Barb /bɑːb/ *abbr.* (also **BARB**) Broadcasters' Audience Research Board. [acronym]

barb /bɑːb/ *n. & v.* ● *n.* **1** a secondary backward-facing projection from an arrow, fish-hook, etc., angled to make extraction difficult. **2** a deliberately hurtful remark. **3** a beardlike filament at the mouth of some fish, e.g. barbel and catfish. **4** any one of the fine hairlike filaments growing from the shaft of a feather, forming the vane. ● *v.tr.* **1** provide (an arrow, a fish-hook, etc.) with a barb or barbs. **2** (as **barbed** *adj.*) (of a remark etc.) deliberately hurtful. □ **barbless** *adj.* [Middle English via Old French *barbe* from Latin *barba* 'beard']

Barbadian /bɑː'beɪdɪən/ *n. & adj.* ● *n.* **1** a native or national of Barbados in the W. Indies. **2** a person of Barbadian descent. ● *adj.* of or relating to Barbados or its people.

barbarian /bɑː'bɛːrɪən/ *n. & adj.* ● *n.* **1** an uncultured or brutish person; a lout. **2** a member of a primitive community or tribe. ● *adj.* **1** rough and uncultured. **2** uncivilized. [originally of any foreigner with a different language or customs: French *barbarien* from *barbare* (as BARBAROUS)]

barbaric /bɑː'barɪk/ *adj.* **1** brutal; cruel (*flogging is a barbaric punishment*). **2** rough and uncultured; unrestrained. **3** of or like barbarians and their art or taste; primitive. □ **barbarically** *adv.* [Middle English via Old French *barbarique* or Latin *barbaricus* via Greek *barbarikos*, from *barbaros* 'foreign']

barbarism /'bɑːbərɪz(ə)m/ *n.* **1 a** the absence of culture and civilized standards; ignorance and rudeness. **b** an example of this. **2** a word or expression not considered correct; a solecism. **3** anything considered to be in bad taste. [French *barbarisme* via Latin *barbarismus* from Greek *barbarismos*, from *barbarizō* 'speak like a foreigner', from *barbaros* 'foreign']

barbarity /bɑː'barɪti/ *n.* (*pl.* **-ies**) **1** savage cruelty. **2** an example of this.

barbarize /'bɑːbərʌɪz/ *v.tr. & intr.* (also **-ise**) make or become barbarous. □ **barbarization** /-'zeɪʃ(ə)n/ *n.*

barbarous /'bɑːb(ə)rəs/ *adj.* **1** uncivilized. **2** cruel. **3** coarse and unrefined. □ **barbarously** *adv.* **barbarousness** *n.* [originally of any foreign language or people: from Latin from Greek *barbaros* 'foreign']

Barbary ape /'bɑːb(ə)ri/ *n.* a tailless macaque, *Macaca sylvana*, of N. Africa and Gibraltar. [*Barbary*, an old name of the western part of N. Africa, ultimately from Arabic *barbar* BERBER]

barbastelle /bɑːbə'stɛl, 'bɑːbəstɛl/ *n.* a bat of the genus *Barbastella*, esp. *B. barbastellus*, found rarely in W. Europe. [French from Italian *Barbastello*]

barbecue /'bɑːbɪkjuː/ *n. & v.* ● *n.* **1 a** a meal cooked on an open fire out of doors, esp. meat grilled on a metal appliance. **b** a party at which such a meal is cooked and eaten. **2 a** the metal appliance used for the preparation of a barbecue. **b** a fireplace, usu. of brick, containing such an appliance. ● *v.tr.* (**barbecues**, **barbecued**, **barbecuing**) cook (esp. meat) on a barbecue. [Spanish *barbacoa* from Arawak *barbacòa* 'wooden frame on posts']

barbecue sauce *n.* a highly seasoned sauce, usu. containing chillies, in which meat etc. may be cooked.

barbed wire *n.* wire bearing sharp pointed spikes close together and used in fencing, or in warfare as an obstruction.

barbel /'bɑːb(ə)l/ *n.* **1** any large European freshwater fish of the genus *Barbus*, with fleshy filaments hanging from its mouth. **2** such a filament growing from the mouth of any fish. [Middle English via Old French from Late Latin *barbellus*, diminutive of *barbus* 'barbel', from *barba* 'beard']

barbell /'bɑːbɛl/ *n.* an iron bar with a series of graded discs at each end, used for weightlifting exercises. [BAR[1] + BELL[1]]

barber /'bɑːbə/ *n. & v.* ● *n.* a person who cuts men's hair and shaves or trims beards as an occupation; a men's hairdresser. ● *v.tr.* **1** cut the hair of; shave or trim the beard of. **2** cut or trim closely (*barbered the grass*). [Middle English & Anglo-French, via Old French *barbeor* from medieval Latin *barbator -oris*, from *barba* 'beard']

barberry /'bɑːb(ə)ri/ *n.* (*pl.* **-ies**) **1** any shrub of the genus *Berberis*, with spiny shoots, yellow flowers, and ovoid red berries, often grown as hedges. **2** its berry. [Middle English from Old French *berberis*, of unknown origin: assimilated to BERRY]

barber-shop *n.* a popular style of close harmony singing, esp. for four male voices (often *attrib.*: *barber-shop quartet*).

barber's pole *n.* a spirally painted striped red and white pole hung outside barbers' shops as a business sign.

barbet /'bɑːbɪt/ *n.* any small brightly coloured tropical bird of the family Capitonidae, with bristles at the base of its beak. [French from *barbe* 'beard']

barbette /bɑː'bɛt/ *n.* a platform in a fort or ship from which guns can be fired over a parapet etc. without an embrasure. [French, diminutive of *barbe* 'beard']

barbican /'bɑ:bɪk(ə)n/ *n.* the outer defence of a city, castle, etc., esp. a double tower above a gate or drawbridge. [Middle English from Old French *barbacane*, of unknown origin]

barbie /'bɑ:bi/ *n.* esp. *Austral. slang* a barbecue. [abbreviation]

Barbie doll /'bɑ:bi/ *n. propr.* **1** a doll representing a conventionally attractive young woman. **2** a pretty but characterless or passive young woman. [diminutive of the name *Barbara*]

bar billiards *n. Brit.* a form of billiards in which balls are struck with a cue into holes in the table.

barbitone /'bɑ:bɪtəʊn/ *n.* (*US* **barbital** /'bɑ:bɪt(ə)l/) a sedative drug. [as BARBITURIC ACID + -ONE, *-al* as in *veronal*]

barbiturate /bɑ:'bɪtjʊrət/ *n.* any derivative of barbituric acid used in the preparation of sedative and sleep-inducing drugs.

barbituric acid /bɑ:bɪ'tjʊərɪk/ *n. Chem.* an organic acid from which various sedatives and sleep-inducing drugs are derived. [French *barbiturique* from German *Barbitursäure* (*Säure* 'acid') from the name *Barbara*]

barbola /bɑ:'bəʊlə/ *n.* (in full **barbola work**) **1** the craft of making small models of fruit, flowers, etc. from a plastic paste. **2** articles, e.g. mirrors, decorated with such models. [arbitrary formation from *barbotine* clay slip for ornamenting pottery]

Barbour /'bɑ:bə/ *n.* (in full **Barbour jacket**) *propr.* a type of green waxed jacket. [J. *Barbour*, name of a draper (d. 1918) in NE England who sold waterproof clothing]

barbule /'bɑ:bju:l/ *n.* a minute filament projecting from the barb of a feather. [Latin *barbula*, diminutive of *barba* 'beard']

barbwire /bɑ:b'wʌɪə/ *n. N. Amer.* = BARBED WIRE.

barcarole /'bɑ:kərəʊl, bɑ:kə'rəʊl/ *n.* (also **barcarolle** /-rɒl, -'rɒl/) **1** a song sung by Venetian gondoliers. **2** music in imitation of this. [French *barcarolle* from Venetian Italian *barcarola* 'boatman's song', from *barca* 'boat']

barchan /'bɑ:k(ə)n/ *n.* a crescent-shaped shifting sand dune. [Turkic *barkhan*]

bar chart *n.* (also **bar graph**) a chart or graph using bars to represent quantity.

bar code *n.* a machine-readable code in the form of a pattern of stripes printed on and identifying a commodity, used esp. for stock-control.

bard[1] /bɑ:d/ *n.* **1 a** *hist.* a Celtic minstrel. **b** the winner of a prize for Welsh verse at an Eisteddfod. **2** *poet.* a poet, esp. one treating heroic themes. ◻ **the Bard** (or **the Bard of Avon**) Shakespeare. ◻ **bardic** *adj.* [Gaelic & Irish *bárd*, Welsh *bardd*, from Celtic]

bard[2] /bɑ:d/ *n.* & *v.* ● *n.* a rasher of fat bacon placed on meat or game before roasting. ● *v.tr.* cover (meat etc.) with bards. [French *barde*, originally = horse's breastplate, ultimately from Arabic]

bardy /'bɑ:di/ *n.* (*pl.* **-ies**) *Austral.* an edible wood-boring grub. [Nyungar (and other Aboriginal languages) *bardi*]

bare /bɛ:/ *adj.* & *v.* ● *adj.* **1** (esp. of part of the body) unclothed or uncovered (*with bare head*). **2** without appropriate covering or contents: **a** (of a tree) leafless. **b** unfurnished; empty (*bare rooms*; *the cupboard was bare*). **c** (of a floor) uncarpeted. **3 a** undisguised (*the bare truth*). **b** unadorned (*bare facts*). **4** (*attrib.*) **a** scanty (*a bare majority*). **b** mere (*bare necessities*). ● *v.tr.* **1** uncover, unsheathe (*bared his teeth*). **2** reveal (*bared his soul*). ◻ **bare of** without. **with one's bare hands** without using tools or weapons. ◻ **bareness** *n.* [Old English *bær* (*n.*), *barian* (*v.*), from Germanic]

bareback /'bɛ:bak/ *adj.* & *adv.* on an unsaddled horse, donkey, etc.

barefaced /bɛ:'feɪst/ *adj.* undisguised; impudent (*barefaced cheek*). ◻ **barefacedly** /-'feɪsɪdli/ *adv.* **barefacedness** *n.*

barefoot /'bɛəfʊt/ *adj.* & *adv.* (also **barefooted** /-'fʊtɪd/) with nothing on the feet.

barefoot doctor *n.* a paramedical worker with basic medical training, esp. in China.

barège /bə'reɪʒ, French barɛʒ/ *n.* a silky gauze made from wool or other material. [French from *Barèges* in SW France, where it was originally made]

bareheaded /bɛ:'hɛdɪd/ *adj.* & *adv.* without a covering for the head.

bare-knuckle *attrib.adj.* (also **bare-knuckled**) **1** (of boxing etc.) wearing no gloves. **2** severe, implacable.

barely /'bɛ:li/ *adv.* **1** only just; scarcely (*barely escaped*). **2** scantily (*barely furnished*). **3** *archaic* openly, explicitly.

barf /bɑ:f/ *v.* & *n. slang* ● *v.intr.* vomit or retch. ● *n.* an attack of vomiting. [20th c.: origin unknown]

barfly /'bɑ:flʌɪ/ *n.* (*pl.* **-flies**) *colloq.* a person who frequents bars.

barfly jumping *n.* the sport of jumping at and sticking to a Velcro-covered wall while wearing a Velcro suit.

bargain /'bɑ:gɪn/ *n.* & *v.* ● *n.* **1 a** an agreement on the terms of a transaction or sale. **b** this seen from the buyer's viewpoint (*a bad bargain*). **2** something acquired or offered cheaply. ● *v.intr.* (often foll. by *with*, *for*) discuss the terms of a transaction (*expected him to bargain, but he paid up*; *bargained with her*; *bargained for the table*). ◻ **bargain away** part with for something worthless (*had bargained away the estate*). **bargain for** (or *colloq.* **on**) (usu. with *neg.* actual or implied) be prepared for; expect (*didn't bargain for bad weather*; *more than I bargained for*). **bargain on** rely on. **drive a hard bargain** be uncompromising in making a bargain. **into** (*US* **in**) **the bargain** moreover; in addition to what was expected. **make** (or **strike**) **a bargain** agree a transaction. ◻ **bargainer** *n.* [Middle English from Old French *bargaine* (*n.*), *bargaignier* (*v.*), probably from Germanic]

bargain basement *n.* the basement of a shop where bargains are displayed (hyphenated when *attrib.*: *bargain-basement prices*).

barge /bɑ:dʒ/ *n.* & *v.* ● *n.* **1** a long flat-bottomed boat for carrying freight on canals, rivers, etc. **2** a long ornamental boat used for pleasure or ceremony. **3** a boat used by the chief officers of a warship. ● *v.* **1** *intr.* (often foll. by *around*) lurch or rush clumsily about. **2** *intr.* (foll. by *in*, *into*) **a** intrude or interrupt rudely or awkwardly (*barged in while we were kissing*). **b** collide with (*barged into her*). **3** *tr.* convey by barge. [Middle English from Old French, perhaps via medieval Latin *barica* from Greek *baris* 'Egyptian boat']

bargeboard /'bɑ:dʒbɔ:d/ *n.* a board (often ornamental) fixed to the gable-end of a roof to hide the ends of the roof timbers. [perhaps from medieval Latin *bargus* 'gallows']

bargee /bɑ:'dʒi:/ *n. Brit.* a person in charge of or working on a barge.

bargepole /'bɑ:dʒpəʊl/ *n.* a long pole used for punting barges etc. and for fending off obstacles. ◻ **would not touch with a bargepole** *Brit.* refuse to be associated or concerned with (a person or thing).

bar graph var. of BAR CHART.

barilla /bə'rɪlə/ *n.* **1** any plant of the genus *Salsola* found chiefly in Spain and Sicily. **2** an impure alkali made by burning either this or kelp. [Spanish]

barite /'barʌɪt, 'bɛ:-/ *n.* (also **baryte**) a mineral form of barium sulphate. Also called *barytes*. [BARIUM + -ITE[1], *-yte* form influenced by *barytes*]

baritone /'barɪtəʊn/ *n.* & *adj.* ● *n.* **1 a** the second lowest adult male singing voice. **b** a singer with this voice. **c** a part written for it. **2 a** an instrument that is second lowest in pitch in its family. **b** its player. ● *adj.* second lowest in musical pitch (*baritone saxophone*). [Italian *baritono* from Greek *barutonos*, from *barus* 'heavy' + *tonos* TONE]

barium /'bɛ:rɪəm/ *n.* **1** *Chem.* a white reactive soft metallic element of the alkaline earth group (symbol Ba). **2** a mixture of barium sulphate and water, opaque to X-rays, which is given to patients requiring

barysphere /ˈbarɪsfɪə/ *n.* the dense interior of the earth, including the mantle and core, enclosed by the lithosphere. [Greek *barus* 'heavy' + *sphaira* 'sphere']

baryta /bəˈrʌɪtə/ *n.* barium oxide or hydroxide. □ **barytic** /-ˈrɪtɪk/ *adj.* [BARYTES, on the pattern of *soda* etc.]

baryte var. of BARITE.

barytes /bəˈrʌɪtiːz/ *n.* = BARITE. [Greek *barus* 'heavy', partly assimilated to mineral names in *-ites*]

basal /ˈbeɪs(ə)l/ *adj.* **1** of, at, or forming a base. **2** fundamental. [BASE[1] + -AL]

basal ganglia *n.pl. Anat.* a group of structures linked to the thalamus in the base of the brain and involved in coordination of movement.

basal metabolism *n.* the chemical processes occurring in an organism at complete rest.

basalt /ˈbasɔːlt, -(ə)lt, bəˈsɔːlt, -ˈsɒlt/ *n.* **1** a dark basic volcanic rock whose deposits sometimes form columns. **2** a kind of black stoneware resembling basalt. □ **basaltic** /bəˈsɔːltɪk/ *adj.* [Latin *basaltes*, variant of *basanites*, from Greek, from *basanos* 'touchstone']

bascule bridge /ˈbaskjuːl/ *n.* a type of drawbridge which is raised and lowered using counterweights. [French, earlier *bacule* 'see-saw' from *battre* 'bump' + *cul* 'buttocks']

base[1] /beɪs/ *n. & v.* ● *n.* **1 a** a part that supports from beneath or serves as a foundation for an object or structure. **b** a notional structure or entity on which something draws or depends (*power base*; *economic base*). **2** a principle or starting point; a basis. **3** esp. *Mil.* a place from which an operation or activity is directed. **4 a** a main or important ingredient of a mixture. **b** a substance, e.g. water, in combination with which pigment forms paint etc. **5** a substance used as a foundation for make-up. **6 a** *Chem.* a substance capable of reacting with an acid to form a salt and water, or (more broadly) of accepting or neutralizing hydrogen ions. **b** *Biochem.* a purine or pyrimidine group as in a nucleotide or nucleic acid. **7** *Math.* a number in terms of which other numbers or logarithms are expressed (see RADIX 1). **8** *Archit.* the part of a column between the shaft and pedestal or pavement. **9** *Geom.* a line or surface on which a figure is regarded as standing. **10** *Surveying* a known line used as a geometrical base for trigonometry. **11** *Electronics* the middle part of a transistor separating the emitter from the collector. **12** *Linguistics* a root or stem as the origin of a word or a derivative. **13** *Baseball* etc. one of the four stations that must be reached in turn to score a run. **14** *Bot. & Zool.* the end at which an organ is attached to the trunk or main part. **15** *Heraldry* the lowest part of a shield. ● *v.tr.* **1** (usu. foll. by *on, upon*) found or establish (*a theory based on speculation*; *his opinion was soundly based*). **2** (foll. by *at, in*, etc.) station (*troops were based in Malta*). □ **get to first base** esp. *N. Amer. slang* achieve the first step towards one's objective. **off base** esp. *N. Amer. slang* **1** mistaken. **2** unprepared, unawares. **touch base** (often foll. by *with*) esp. *N. Amer.* make (personal) contact. [French *base* or Latin *basis* 'stepping, step, pedestal', from Greek]

base[2] /beɪs/ *adj.* **1** lacking moral worth; cowardly, despicable. **2** menial. **3** not pure; alloyed (*base coin*). **4** (of a metal) not regarded as noble or precious. □ **basely** *adv.* **baseness** *n.* [Middle English in the sense 'of small height', via French *bas* from medieval Latin *bassus* 'short' (in Latin as a cognomen)]

baseball /ˈbeɪsbɔːl/ *n.* **1** a game played esp. in the US with teams of nine, a bat and ball, and a circuit of four bases which the batter must complete to score. **2** the ball used in this game.

baseboard /ˈbeɪsbɔːd/ *n. N. Amer.* a skirting board.

base camp *n.* a camp from which expeditions set out or operations are conducted.

basehead /ˈbeɪshɛd/ *n. US slang* a person who habitually takes either of the drugs freebase or crack. [FREEBASE + HEAD]

base hospital *n.* esp. *Austral.* a hospital in a rural area, or (in warfare) removed from the field of action.

BASE jump /beɪs/ *n. & v.* (also **base jump**) ● *n.* a parachute jump from a fixed point (esp. a high building or promontory) rather than an aircraft. ● *v.intr.* perform such a jump. □ **BASE jumper** *n.* [acronym from *b*uilding, *a*ntenna-tower, *s*pan, *e*arth, denoting the types of structure used]

baseless /ˈbeɪslɪs/ *adj.* unfounded, groundless. □ **baselessly** *adv.* **baselessness** *n.*

baseline /ˈbeɪslʌɪn/ *n.* **1** a line used as a base or starting point. **2** (in tennis, volleyball, etc.) the line marking each end of a court.

baseload /ˈbeɪsləʊd/ *n. Brit. Electr.* the permanent load on power supplies etc.

baseman /ˈbeɪsmən/ *n.* (*pl.* **-men**) *Baseball* a fielder stationed near a base.

basement /ˈbeɪsm(ə)nt/ *n.* the lowest floor of a building, usu. at least partly below ground level. [probably Dutch, perhaps from Italian *basamento* 'column-base']

basement membrane *n. Anat.* a thin delicate membrane separating the epithelium from underlying tissue.

basenji /bəˈsɛndʒi/ *n.* (*pl.* **basenjis**) a smallish hunting dog of a central African breed, which growls and yelps but does not bark. [Bantu]

base pairing *n. Biochem.* complementary binding by means of hydrogen bonds of a purine to a pyrimidine base in opposite strands of nucleic acids.

base rate *n. Brit.* the interest rate set by the Bank of England, used as the basis for other banks' rates.

bases *pl.* of BASE[1], BASIS.

base unit *n.* a unit that is defined arbitrarily and not by combinations of other units.

bash /baʃ/ *v. & n.* ● *v.* **1** *tr.* **a** strike bluntly or heavily. **b** (often foll. by *up*) *colloq.* attack violently. **c** (often foll. by *down, in*, etc.) damage or break by striking forcibly. **d** esp. *N. Amer.* criticize severely. **2** *intr.* (foll. by *into*) collide with. ● *n.* **1** a heavy blow. **2** *Brit. colloq.* an attempt (*had a bash at painting*). **3** *slang* a party or social event. [imitative, perhaps from *bang, smash, dash*, etc.]

bashful /ˈbaʃfʊl, -f(ə)l/ *adj.* **1** shy, diffident, self-conscious. **2** sheepish. □ **bashfully** *adv.* **bashfulness** *n.* [obsolete *bash* (*v.*), = ABASH]

basho /ˈbaʃəʊ/ *n.* (*pl.* same or **-os**) a sumo wrestling tournament. [Japanese from *ba* 'place' + *shō* 'victory, win']

BASIC /ˈbeɪsɪk/ *n.* a computer programming language using familiar English words, designed for beginners and widely used on microcomputers. [*B*eginner's *A*ll-purpose *S*ymbolic *I*nstruction *C*ode]

basic /ˈbeɪsɪk/ *adj. & n.* ● *adj.* **1** forming or serving as a base. **2** fundamental. **3 a** simplest or lowest in level (*basic pay*; *basic requirements*). **b** vulgar (*basic humour*). **4** *Chem.* having the properties of or containing a base. **5** *Geol.* (of volcanic rocks etc.) having less than 50 per cent silica. **6** *Metallurgy* designating, involving, or resulting from steel-making processes using lime-rich refractories etc. (*basic slag*). ● *n.* (usu. in *pl.*) the fundamental facts or principles. [BASE[1] + -IC]

basically /ˈbeɪsɪk(ə)li/ *adv.* **1** fundamentally, essentially. **2** (qualifying a clause) in fact, actually.

basic dye *n.* a dye consisting of salts of organic bases.

Basic English *n.* a simplified form of English limited to 850 selected words, intended for international communication.

basic industry *n.* an industry of fundamental economic importance.

basicity /beɪˈsɪsɪti/ *n. Chem.* the number of protons with which a base will combine.

basic slag *n.* slag containing phosphates formed as a by-product during steel manufacture and used as fertilizer.

basic wage *n.* **1** a minimum wage earned before possible additional payments such as overtime etc. **2**

Austral. & *NZ* the minimum living wage, fixed by industrial tribunal.

basidium /bəˈsɪdɪəm/ *n.* (*pl.* **basidia** /-dɪə/) a microscopic spore-bearing structure produced by certain fungi. [modern Latin from Greek *basidion*, diminutive of BASIS]

basil /ˈbaz(ə)l, -zɪl/ *n.* an aromatic herb of the genus *Ocimum*, esp. *O. basilicum* (in full **sweet basil**), whose leaves are used as a flavouring in savoury dishes. [Middle English via Old French *basile* and medieval Latin *basilicus* from Greek *basilikos* 'royal']

basilar /ˈbasɪlə/ *adj.* of or at the base (esp. of the skull). [modern Latin *basilaris* (as BASIS)]

basilica /bəˈsɪlɪkə, -ˈzɪl-/ *n.* **1** an ancient Roman public hall with an apse and colonnades, used as a law court and place of assembly. **2** a similar building used as a Christian church. **3** a church having special privileges from the Pope. □ **basilican** *adj.* [Latin from Greek *basilikē* (*oikia*, *stoa*) 'royal (house, portico)' from *basileus* 'king']

basilisk /ˈbazɪlɪsk/ *n.* **1** a mythical reptile with a lethal breath and look. **2** any small American lizard of the genus *Basiliscus*, with a crest from its back to its tail. **3** *Heraldry* = COCKATRICE 2. [Middle English via Latin *basiliscus* from Greek *basiliskos* 'little king, serpent']

basin /ˈbeɪs(ə)n/ *n.* **1 a** = WASHBASIN. **b** a wide round open container, esp. one for preparing food in or for holding water. **2** a hollow rounded depression. **3** any sheltered area of water where boats can moor safely. **4** a round valley. **5** an area drained by rivers and tributaries. **6** *Geol.* **a** a rock formation where the strata dip towards the centre. **b** an accumulation of rock strata formed in this dip as a result of subsidence and sedimentation. □ **basinful** *n.* (*pl.* **-fuls**). [Middle English via Old French *bacin* from medieval Latin *ba(s)cinus*, perhaps from Gaulish]

basipetal /beɪˈsɪpɪt(ə)l/ *adj. Bot.* (of each new part produced) developing nearer the base than the previous one did. □ **basipetally** *adv.* [BASIS + Latin *petere* 'seek']

basis /ˈbeɪsɪs/ *n.* (*pl.* **bases** /-siːz/) **1** the foundation or support of something, esp. an idea or argument. **2** the main or determining principle or ingredient (*on a purely friendly basis*). **3** the starting point for a discussion etc. [Latin from Greek, = BASE[1]]

bask /bɑːsk/ *v.intr.* **1** sit or lie back lazily in warmth and light (*basking in the sun*). **2** (foll. by *in*) derive great pleasure (from) (*basking in glory*). [Middle English, apparently from Old Norse: related to BATHE]

basket /ˈbɑːskɪt/ *n.* **1** a container made of interwoven cane etc. **2** a container resembling this. **3** the amount held by a basket. **4** the goal in basketball, or a goal scored. **5** *Econ.* a group or range (of currencies). **6** *Brit. euphem. colloq.* bastard. □ **basketful** *n.* (*pl.* **-fuls**). [Anglo-French & Old French *basket*, Anglo-Latin *baskettum*, of unknown origin]

basketball /ˈbɑːskɪtbɔːl/ *n.* **1** a game between two teams of five, in which goals are scored by making the ball drop through hooped nets fixed high up at each end of a court. **2** the ball used in this game.

basket case *n. colloq. offens.* **1** a person who has lost both arms and legs. **2** something regarded as hopeless, esp. a bankrupt country or a helpless person.

basket-maker *n.* a person who makes baskets. □ **basket-making** *n.*

basketry /ˈbɑːskɪtri/ *n.* **1** the art of making baskets. **2** baskets collectively.

basket weave *n.* a weave resembling that of a basket.

basketwork /ˈbɑːskɪtwəːk/ *n.* **1** material woven in the style of a basket. **2** the art of making this.

basking shark *n.* a very large shark, *Cetorhinus maximus*, which feeds on plankton and often lies near the surface of the sea.

basmati /basˈmɑːti, -z-/ *n.* (in full **basmati rice**) a kind of long-grain Indian rice, with a delicate nutty flavour. [Hindi, = fragrant]

basophilic /beɪzə(ʊ)ˈfɪlɪk/ *adj. Biol.* (of a cell etc.) readily stained with basic dyes.

Basque /bask, bɑːsk/ *n.* & *adj.* ● *n.* **1** a member of a people of the western Pyrenees. **2** the language of this people. ● *adj.* of or relating to the Basques or their language. [French from Latin *Vasco -onis*]

basque /bask, bɑːsk/ *n.* a close-fitting bodice extending from the shoulders to the waist and often with a short continuation below waist level. [origin unknown: perhaps allusively from BASQUE, referring to Basque dress]

bas-relief /ˈbasrɪliːf, ˈbɑː(s)-/ *n. Sculpture* **1** = *low relief* (see RELIEF 6a). **2** a sculpture, carving, etc. in low relief. [earlier *basse relieve* from Italian *basso-rilievo* 'low relief': later altered to French form]

bass[1] /beɪs/ *n.* & *adj.* ● *n.* **1 a** the lowest adult male singing voice. **b** a singer with this voice. **c** a part written for it. **2** the lowest part in harmonized music. **3 a** an instrument that is the lowest in pitch in its family. **b** a player of such an instrument. **4** *colloq.* **a** a bass guitar or double bass. **b** a player of this instrument. **5** the low-frequency output of a radio, record player, etc., corresponding to the bass in music. ● *adj.* **1** lowest in musical pitch. **2** deep-sounding. □ **bassist** *n.* (in sense 4b of *n.*). [alteration of BASE[2] influenced by BASSO]

bass[2] /bas/ *n.* (*pl.* same or **basses**) **1** the common European freshwater perch. **2 a** a similar marine fish, *Dicentrarchus labrax* of European waters. **b** a related N. American fish of the genus *Morone*. **3** (in full **sea bass**) a similar marine fish of the family Serranidae, esp. of the genus *Centropristis*. **4** (in full **black bass**) an American freshwater fish of the genus *Micropterus*. [earlier *barse* from Old English *bærs*]

bass[3] /bas/ *n.* = BAST. [alteration of BAST]

bass clef *n.* a clef placing F below middle C on the second highest line of the staff.

basset /ˈbasɪt/ *n.* (in full **basset-hound**) **1** a sturdy hunting dog of a breed with a long body, short legs, and big ears. **2** this breed. [French, diminutive of *bas basse* 'low': see BASE[2]]

basset-horn /ˈbasɪthɔːn/ *n.* an alto clarinet in F, with a dark tone. [German, translation of French *cor de bassette*, from Italian *corno di bassetto* from *corno* 'horn' + *bassetto*, diminutive of *basso* BASE[2]]

bassinet /basɪˈnɛt/ *n.* a child's wicker cradle, usu. with a hood. [French, diminutive of *bassin* BASIN]

basso /ˈbasəʊ/ *n.* (*pl.* **-os** or **bassi** /-si/) a singer with a bass voice. [Italian, = BASS[1]]

bassoon /bəˈsuːn/ *n.* **1 a** a bass instrument of the oboe family, with a double reed. **b** a player of this instrument. **2** an organ stop with the quality of a bassoon. □ **bassoonist** *n.* (in sense 1a). [French *basson* from *bas* BASS[1]]

basso profundo /prəˈfʌndəʊ/ *n.* (*pl.* **basso profundos** or **bassi profundi** /-di/) a bass singer with an exceptionally low range. [Italian: BASSO + *profondo* 'deep']

basso-relievo /ˌbasəʊrɪˈliːvəʊ/ *n.* (also **basso-rilievo** /-rɪˈljeɪvəʊ/) (*pl.* **-os**) *Sculpture* **1** = *low relief* (see RELIEF 6a). **2** a sculpture, carving, etc. in low relief. [Italian *basso-rilievo*]

bass viol *n.* **1 a** a viola da gamba. **b** a player of this instrument. **2** *US* a double bass.

basswood /ˈbaswʊd/ *n.* **1** the American lime, *Tilia americana*. **2** the wood of this tree. [BASS[3] + WOOD]

bast /bast/ *n.* the inner bark of lime, or other flexible fibrous bark, used as fibre in matting etc. [Old English *bæst*, from Germanic]

bastard /ˈbɑːstəd, ˈbast-/ *n.* & *adj.* ● *n.* **1** *archaic* or *offens.* a person born of parents not married to each other. **2** *coarse slang* **a** an unpleasant or despicable person. **b** a person of a specified kind (*poor bastard*; *rotten bastard*; *lucky bastard*). **3** *coarse slang* a difficult or awkward thing, undertaking, etc. ● *adj.* (usu. *attrib.*) **1** *archaic* or *offens.* born of parents not married to each other; illegitimate. **2** (of things): **a** unauthorized, counterfeit. **b** hybrid. ◻ **bastardy** *n.* (in sense 1 of *n. archaic*). [Middle English via Old French from medieval Latin *bastardus*, perhaps from *bastum* 'packsaddle': cf. Old French *fils de bas(t)* 'packsaddle son' (son of a mule driver etc. using a packsaddle for a pillow)]

bastardize /'bɑ:stədʌɪz, 'bast-/ *v.tr.* (also **-ise**) **1** declare (a person) illegitimate. **2** corrupt, debase. ◻ **bastardization** /-'zeɪʃ(ə)n/ *n.*

baste[1] /beɪst/ *v.tr.* moisten (meat) with gravy or melted fat during cooking. [15th c.: origin unknown]

baste[2] /beɪst/ *v.tr.* stitch loosely together in preparation for sewing; tack. [Middle English from Old French *bastir* 'sew lightly', ultimately from Germanic]

baste[3] /beɪst/ *v.tr.* beat soundly; thrash. [perhaps figurative use of BASTE[1]]

bastille /ba'sti:l/ *n. hist.* a fortress or prison. [Middle English via Old French from Provençal *bastir* 'build': the name of the fortress and prison in Paris, destroyed in 1789]

bastinado /bastɪ'neɪdəʊ/ *n.* & *v.* ● *n.* punishment by beating with a stick on the soles of the feet. ● *v.tr.* (**-oes**, **-oed**) punish (a person) in this way. [Spanish *bastonada* from *bastón* BATON]

bastion /'bastɪən/ *n.* **1** a projecting part of a fortification built at an angle of, or against the line of, a wall. **2** a thing regarded as protecting (*bastion of freedom*). **3** a natural rock formation resembling a bastion. [French from Italian *bastione*, from *bastire* 'build']

basuco /bə'su:kəʊ/ *n.* a highly addictive impure form of cocaine. [Colombian Spanish]

bat[1] /bat/ *n.* & *v.* ● *n.* **1** an implement with a handle, usu. of wood and with a flat or curved surface, used for hitting balls in games. **2** *Cricket* a turn at using this. **3** a batsman, esp. in cricket, usu. described in some way (*an excellent bat*). **4** (usu. in *pl.*) an object like a table tennis bat used to guide aircraft when taxiing. ● *v.* (**batted**, **batting**) **1** *tr.* hit with or as with a bat. **2** *intr.* take a turn at using a bat; have an innings at cricket, baseball, etc. ◻ **bat around 1** *slang* potter aimlessly. **2** discuss (an idea or proposal). **off one's own bat** *Brit.* unprompted, unaided. **right off the bat** *N. Amer.* immediately. [Old English *batt* 'club', perhaps partly from Old French *batte*, from *battre* 'strike']

bat[2] /bat/ *n.* **1** any mouselike nocturnal mammal of the order Chiroptera, capable of flight by means of membranous wings extending from its forelimbs. **2** (esp. in phr. **old bat**) *derog.* a woman, esp. regarded as unattractive or unpleasant. ◻ **have bats in the belfry** be eccentric or crazy. **like a bat out of hell** very fast. [16th c., alteration of Middle English *bakke* from Scandinavian]

bat[3] /bat/ *v.tr.* (**batted**, **batting**) ◻ **not** (or **never**) **bat an eyelid** (or **eye**) *colloq.* show no reaction or emotion. [variant of obsolete *bate* 'flutter']

batch /batʃ/ *n.* & *v.* ● *n.* **1** a number of things or persons forming a group or dealt with together. **2** an instalment (*have sent off the latest batch*). **3** the loaves produced at one baking. **4** (*attrib.*) using or dealt with in batches, not as a continuous flow (*batch production*). **5** *Computing* a group of records processed as a single unit. ● *v.tr.* arrange or deal with in batches. [Middle English, ultimately from Old English *bacan* BAKE]

batch processing *n.* **1** the performance of an industrial process on material in batches. **2** *Computing* the processing of previously collected data or jobs in batches, esp. automatically.

bate /beɪt/ *n.* (also **bait**) *Brit. slang* a rage; a cross mood (*is in an awful bate*). [BAIT = state of baited person]

bateau /'batəʊ/ *n.* (*pl.* **bateaux** /-əʊz/) a light riverboat, esp. of the flat-bottomed kind used in Canada. [French, = boat]

bated /'beɪtɪd/ *adj.* ◻ **with bated breath** very anxiously. [past part. of obsolete *bate* (*v.*) 'restrain', from ABATE]

bateleur /'bat(ə)lə:/ *n.* a short-tailed African eagle, *Terathopius ecaudatus*. [French, = juggler]

Batesian mimicry /'beɪtsɪən/ *n. Zool.* mimicry in which an edible animal is protected by its resemblance to one avoided by predators. [H.W. *Bates*, English naturalist d. 1892, + -IAN]

bath /bɑ:θ/ *n.* & *v.* ● *n.* (*pl.* **baths** /bɑ:ðz/) **1 a** a container for liquid, usu. water, used for immersing and washing the body. **b** this with its contents (*your bath is ready*). **2** the act or process of immersing the body for washing or therapy (*have a bath*; *take a bath*). **3 a** a vessel containing liquid in which something is immersed, esp. when undergoing a process such as film developing etc. **b** this with its contents. **4** (usu. in *pl.*) a building with baths or a swimming pool, usu. open to the public. **5** esp. *N. Amer.* a bathroom. ● *v.* **1** *tr.* wash (esp. a person) in a bath. **2** *intr.* take a bath. [Old English *bæth*, from Germanic]

Bath bun /bɑ:θ/ *n. Brit.* a round yeast bun with currants, topped with granules of sugar. [*Bath* in S. England, where it was originally made]

bath chair /bɑ:θ/ *n.* esp. *hist.* a kind of wheelchair for invalids. [*Bath* in S. England, named for its hot springs, thought to have curative powers]

bath cube *n. Brit.* a cube of compacted bath salts.

bathe /beɪð/ *v.* & *n.* ● *v.* **1** *intr.* immerse oneself in water, esp. (*Brit.*) to swim or (esp. *N. Amer.*) to wash oneself. **2** *tr.* **a** immerse in or wash or treat with liquid esp. for cleansing or medicinal purposes. **b** *N. Amer.* wash (esp. a person) in a bath. **3** *tr.* (of sunlight etc.) envelop. ● *n.* an act of immersing oneself or part of the body in liquid, esp. to swim or cleanse. [Old English *bathian*, from Germanic]

bather /'beɪðə/ *n.* **1** a person who bathes. **2** (in *pl.*) *Austral.* a bathing costume.

bathhouse /'bɑ:θhaʊs/ *n.* a building with baths for public use.

bathing suit *n.* (*Brit.* also **bathing costume**) a garment worn for swimming.

bath mat *n.* **1** a mat for standing on after getting out of the bath. **2** a rubber mat put in the bottom of a bath to prevent slipping.

batholith /'baθəlɪθ/ *n.* a dome of igneous rock extending inwards to an unknown depth. [German from Greek *bathos* 'depth' + -LITH]

Bath Oliver /bɑ:θ 'ɒlɪvə/ *n. Brit. propr.* a kind of savoury biscuit. [Dr W. *Oliver* of *Bath* (d. 1764), who invented it]

bathometer /bə'θɒmɪtə/ *n.* an instrument used to measure the depth of water. [Greek *bathos* 'depth' + -METER]

bathos /'beɪθɒs/ *n.* **1** an unintentional lapse in mood from the sublime to the absurd or trivial. **2** a commonplace or ridiculous feature offsetting an otherwise sublime situation; an anticlimax. ◻ **bathetic** /bə'θetɪk/ *adj.* **bathotic** /bə'θɒtɪk/ *adj.* [Greek, = depth]

bathrobe /'bɑ:θrəʊb/ *n.* a loose coat usu. of towelling worn esp. before and after taking a bath; a dressing gown.

bathroom /'bɑ:θru:m, -rʊm/ *n.* **1 a** a room containing a bath and usu. other washing facilities. **b** bathroom fitments or units esp. as sold together. **2** esp. *N. Amer.* a room containing a lavatory.

bath salts *n.pl.* soluble salts used for softening or scenting bathwater.

bathtub /'bɑ:θtʌb/ *n.* = BATH *n.* 1.

bathwater /'bɑ:θwɔ:tə/ *n.* the water in a bath.

bathymetry /bə'θɪmɪtri/ *n.* the measurement of depth of water in seas, lakes, etc. ◻ **bathymeter** *n.* **bathymetric** /baθɪ'mɛtrɪk/ *adj.* [Greek *bathus* 'deep' + -METRY]

bathyscaphe /'baθɪskaf/ *n.* a manned vessel for deep-sea diving. [Greek *bathus* 'deep' + *skaphos* 'ship']

bathysphere /'baθɪsfɪə/ *n.* a spherical vessel for deep-sea observation. [Greek *bathus* 'deep' + SPHERE]

batik /'batɪk, bə'ti:k/ *n.* a method (originally used in Java) of producing coloured designs on textiles by applying wax to the parts to be left uncoloured; a piece of cloth treated in this way. [Javanese, = painted]

batiste /bə'ti:st/ *n. & adj.* ● *n.* a fine linen or cotton cloth. ● *adj.* made of batiste. [French (earlier *batiche*), perhaps related to *battre* BATTER[1]]

batman /'batmən/ *n.* (*pl.* **-men**) *Mil.* (in the British forces) an attendant serving an officer. [Old French *bat*, *bast* from medieval Latin *bastum* 'packsaddle' + MAN]

baton /'bat(ə)n/ *n.* **1** a thin stick used by a conductor to direct an orchestra, choir, etc. **2** *Athletics* a short stick or tube carried and passed on by the runners in a relay race. **3** a long stick carried and twirled by a drum major. **4** a staff of office or authority, esp. a field marshal's. **5** esp. *Brit.* a police officer's truncheon. **6** *Heraldry* a narrow truncated bend. **7** a short bar replacing some figures on a clock-face etc. [French *bâton*, *baston*, ultimately from Late Latin *bastum* 'stick']

baton round *n. Brit.* a rubber or plastic bullet used esp. in riot control.

batrachian /bə'treɪkɪən/ *n. & adj.* ● *n.* a frog or toad; an anuran. ● *adj.* of or relating to frogs or toads. [Greek *batrakhos* 'frog']

bats /bats/ *predic.adj. slang* crazy. [from the phrase *have bats in the belfry*: see BAT[2]]

batsman /'batsmən/ *n.* (*pl.* **-men**) **1** a person who bats or is batting, esp. in cricket. **2** a signaller using bats to guide aircraft on the ground. □ **batsmanship** *n.* (in sense 1).

Batswana see TSWANA.

battalion /bə'talɪən/ *n.* **1** a large body of troops ready for battle, esp. an infantry unit forming part of a brigade. **2** a large group of people pursuing a common aim or sharing a major undertaking. [French *bataillon* from Italian *battaglione*, from *battaglia* BATTLE]

battels /'bat(ə)lz/ *n.pl. Brit.* an Oxford college account for expenses, esp. for board and the supply of provisions. [perhaps from obsolete *battle* (*v.*) 'fatten' from obsolete *battle* (*adj.*) 'nutritious': cf. BATTEN[2]]

batten[1] /'bat(ə)n/ *n. & v.* ● *n.* **1** a long flat strip of squared timber or metal, esp. used to hold something in place or as a fastening against a wall etc. **2** a strip of wood used for clamping the boards of a door etc. **3** *Naut.* a strip of wood or metal for securing a tarpaulin over a ship's hatchway. ● *v.tr.* strengthen or fasten with battens. □ **batten down the hatches 1** *Naut.* secure a ship's tarpaulins. **2** prepare for a difficulty or crisis. [Old French *batant*, part. of *batre* 'beat', from Latin *battuere*]

batten[2] /'bat(ə)n/ *v.intr.* (foll. by *on*) thrive or prosper at another's expense. [Old Norse *batna* 'get better' from *bati* 'advantage']

Battenberg /'bat(ə)nbə:g/ *n.* esp. *Brit.* a kind of oblong cake, usu. of two colours of sponge and covered with marzipan. [*Battenberg* in Germany]

batter[1] /'batə/ *v.* **1 a** *tr.* strike repeatedly with hard blows, esp. so as to cause visible damage. **b** *intr.* (often foll. by *against*, *at*, etc.) strike repeated blows; pound heavily and insistently (*batter at the door*). **2** *tr.* (often in *passive*) **a** handle roughly, esp. over a long period. **b** censure or criticize severely. □ **batterer** *n.* [Middle English via Anglo-French *baterer* and Old French *batre* 'beat' from Latin *battuere*]

batter[2] /'batə/ *n.* **1** a fluid mixture of flour, egg, and milk or water, used in cooking, esp. for pancakes and for coating food before frying. **2** *Printing* an area of damaged type. [Middle English via Anglo-French *batour* from Old French *bateüre*, from *batre*: see BATTER[1]]

batter[3] /'batə/ *n. Sport* a player batting, esp. in baseball.

batter[4] /'batə/ *n. & v.* ● *n.* **1** a wall etc. with a sloping face. **2** a receding slope. ● *v.intr.* have a receding slope. [16th c.: origin unknown]

battered /'batəd/ *adj.* (esp. of fish) coated in batter and deep-fried.

battered baby *n.* an infant that has suffered repeated violence from adults, esp. its parents.

battered wife *n.* a wife subjected to repeated violence by her husband.

battering ram *n.* **1 a** *hist.* a heavy beam, originally with an end in the form of a carved ram's head, used in breaching fortifications. **b** a similar object, used to break down doors. **2** a means of forceful persuasion.

battery /'bat(ə)ri/ *n.* (*pl.* **-ies**) **1** a usu. portable container of a cell or cells carrying an electric charge, as a source of current. **2** (often *attrib.*) esp. *Brit.* a series of cages for the intensive breeding and rearing of poultry or cattle. **3** a set of similar units of equipment, esp. connected. **4** (usu. foll. by *of*) an extensive series, sequence, or range. **5** a series of tests, esp. psychological. **6 a** a fortified emplacement for heavy guns. **b** an artillery unit of guns, men, and vehicles. **7** *Law* an act, including touching, inflicting unlawful personal violence on another person, even if no physical harm is done. **8** *Baseball* the pitcher and the catcher. [French *batterie* from *batre*, *battre* 'strike' from Latin *battuere*]

batting /'batɪŋ/ *n.* **1** the action of hitting with a bat. **2** cotton wadding prepared in sheets for use in quilts etc.

batting average *n.* **1** *Cricket* a batsman's runs scored per completed innings. **2** *Baseball* a batter's safe hits per time at bat.

batting order *n.* the order in which people act or take their turn, esp. of batsmen in cricket or baseball.

battle /'bat(ə)l/ *n. & v.* ● *n.* **1** a prolonged fight between large organized armed forces. **2** a contest; a prolonged or difficult struggle (*life is a constant battle*; *a battle of wits*). ● *v.* **1** *intr.* struggle; fight persistently (*battled against the elements*; *battled for women's rights*). **2** *tr.* fight (one's way etc.). **3** *tr. N. Amer.* engage in battle with. □ **half the battle** the key to the success of an undertaking. □ **battler** *n.* [Middle English from Old French *bataille*, ultimately from Late Latin *battualia* 'gladiatorial exercises', from Latin *battuere* 'beat']

battleaxe /'bat(ə)laks/ *n.* **1** a large axe used in ancient warfare. **2** *colloq.* a formidable or domineering older woman.

battlebus /'bat(ə)lbʌs/ *n.* a bus or coach used as a mobile operational centre during an election campaign.

battlecruiser /'bat(ə)lkru:zə/ *n. hist.* a heavy-gunned ship faster and more lightly armoured than a battleship.

battle-cry *n.* a cry or slogan of participants in a battle or contest.

battledore /'bat(ə)ldɔ:/ *n. hist.* **1 a** (in full **battledore and shuttlecock**) a game played with a shuttlecock and rackets. **b** the racket used in this. **2** a kind of wooden utensil like a paddle, formerly used in washing, baking, etc. [Middle English, perhaps from Provençal *batedor* 'beater' from *batre* 'beat']

battledress /'bat(ə)ldrɛs/ *n. archaic* = COMBAT DRESS.

battle fatigue *n.* = COMBAT FATIGUE.

battlefield /'bat(ə)lfi:ld/ *n.* (also **battleground** /-graʊnd/) the piece of ground on which a battle is or was fought.

battlement /'bat(ə)lm(ə)nt/ *n.* (usu. in *pl.*) **1** a parapet with recesses along the top of a wall, as part of a fortification. **2** a section of roof enclosed by this (*walking on the battlements*). □ **battlemented** *adj.* [Old French *bataillier* 'furnish with ramparts' + -MENT]

battle royal *n.* (*pl.* **battles royal**) **1** a battle in which several combatants or all available forces engage; a free fight. **2** a heated argument.

battleship /'bat(ə)lʃɪp/ *n.* a warship with the heaviest armour and the largest guns.

battue /bə't(j)u:/ *n.* **1 a** the driving of game towards hunters by beaters. **b** a shooting party arranged in this way. **2** wholesale slaughter. [French, fem. past part. of *battre* 'beat', from Latin *battuere*]

batty /'bati/ *adj.* (**battier**, **battiest**) *slang* crazy. □ **battily** *adv.* **battiness** *n.* [BAT[2] + -Y[1]]

batwing /'batwɪŋ/ *attrib.adj.* (esp. of a sleeve or a flame) shaped like the wing of a bat.

batwoman /ˈbatwʊmən/ *n.* (*pl.* **-women**) a female attendant serving an officer in the British women's services. [as BATMAN + WOMAN]

bauble /ˈbɔːb(ə)l/ *n.* **1** a showy trinket or toy of little value. **2** a baton formerly used as an emblem by jesters. [Middle English from Old French *ba(u)bel* 'child's toy', of unknown origin]

baud /bəʊd, bɔːd/ *n.* (*pl.* same or **bauds**) *Computing* etc. **1** a unit used to express the speed of electronic code-signals, corresponding to one information unit per second. **2** (loosely) a unit of data-transmission speed of one bit per second. [J. M. E. *Baudot*, French engineer d. 1903]

Bauhaus /ˈbaʊhaʊs/ *n.* **1** a German school of architectural design (1919–33). **2** its principles, based on functionalism and development of existing skills. [German from *Bau* 'building' + *Haus* 'house']

baulk /bɔːlk, bɔːk/ *v.* & *n.* (also esp. *US* **balk**) ● *v.* **1** *intr.* **a** refuse to go on. **b** (often foll. by *at*) hesitate. **2** *tr.* **a** thwart, hinder. **b** disappoint. **3** *tr.* **a** miss, let slip (a chance etc.). **b** ignore, shirk. ● *n.* **1** a hindrance; a stumbling block. **2 a** a roughly squared timber beam. **b** a tie-beam of a house. **3** *Snooker* etc. the area on the table from which a player begins a game. **4** *Baseball* an illegal action made by a pitcher. **5** a ridge left unploughed between furrows. [Old English *balc* via Old Norse *bálkr* from Germanic]

baulky /ˈbɔːlki, ˈbɔːki/ *adj.* (also esp. *US* **balky**) (**-ier**, **-iest**) reluctant, perverse. [BAULK + -Y[1]]

bauxite /ˈbɔːksʌɪt/ *n.* a claylike mineral containing varying proportions of alumina, the chief source of aluminium. □ **bauxitic** /-ˈsɪtɪk/ *adj.* [French from *Les Baux* near Arles in SE France (where it was found) + -ITE[1]]

Bavarian /bəˈvɛːrɪən/ *adj.* & *n.* ● *adj.* of or relating to Bavaria in Germany, its people, or their dialect. ● *n.* **1** a native or inhabitant of Bavaria. **2** the dialect of German used there.

bawd /bɔːd/ *n.* a woman who runs a brothel. [Middle English *bawdstrot* from Old French *baudetrot*, *baudestroyt* 'procuress']

bawdy /ˈbɔːdi/ *adj.* & *n.* ● *adj.* (**bawdier**, **bawdiest**) humorously indecent or coarse. ● *n.* bawdy talk or writing. □ **bawdily** *adv.* **bawdiness** *n.* [BAWD + -Y[1]]

bawdy house *n.* a brothel.

bawl /bɔːl/ *v.* **1** *tr.* speak or call out noisily. **2** *intr.* weep loudly. □ **bawl out** *colloq.* reprimand angrily. [imitative: cf. medieval Latin *baulare* 'bark', Icelandic *baula* (Swedish *böla*) 'to low']

bay[1] /beɪ/ *n.* **1** a broad inlet of the sea where the land curves inwards. **2** a recess in a mountain range. [Middle English via Old French *baie* from Old Spanish *bahia*]

bay[2] /beɪ/ *n.* **1** (in full **bay laurel** or **bay tree**) a laurel, *Laurus nobilis*, having deep green leaves and purple berries; also called *sweet bay*. **2** (in *pl.*) a wreath made of bay leaves, for a victor or poet. [Old French *baie* from Latin *baca* 'berry']

bay[3] /beɪ/ *n.* **1** a space created by a window-line projecting outwards from a wall. **2** a recess; a section of wall between buttresses or columns, esp. in the nave of a church etc. **3** a compartment (*bomb bay*). **4** an area specially allocated or marked off (*sickbay*; *loading bay*). **5** *Brit.* the terminus of a branch line at a railway station also having through lines, usu. at the side of an outer platform. [Middle English via Old French *baie*, from *ba(y)er* 'gape', from medieval Latin *batare*]

bay[4] /beɪ/ *adj.* & *n.* ● *adj.* (esp. of a horse) dark reddish brown. ● *n.* a bay horse with a black mane and tail. [Old French *bai* from Latin *badius*]

bay[5] /beɪ/ *v.* & *n.* ● *v.* **1** *intr.* (esp. of a large dog) bark or howl loudly and plaintively. **2** *tr.* bay at. ● *n.* the sound of baying, esp. in chorus from hounds in close pursuit. □ **at bay 1** cornered, apparently unable to escape. **2** in a desperate situation. **bring to bay** gain on in pursuit; trap. **hold** (or **keep**) **at bay** hold off (a pursuer). **stand at bay** turn to face one's pursuers. [Middle English via Old French *bai*, *baiier* 'bark' from Italian *baiare*, of imitative origin]

bayberry /ˈbeɪbɛri/ *n.* (*pl.* **-ies**) a N. American shrub, *Myrica cerifera*, having aromatic leaves and bearing berries covered in a wax coating. Also called *wax myrtle*. [BAY[2] + BERRY]

bay laurel see BAY[2] 1.

bay leaf *n.* the aromatic (usu. dried) leaf of the bay tree, used in cooking.

bayonet /ˈbeɪənɪt/ *n.* & *v.* ● *n.* **1** a stabbing blade attachable to the muzzle of a rifle. **2** an electrical or other fitting engaged by being pushed into a socket and twisted. ● *v.tr.* (**bayoneted**, **bayoneting**) stab with a bayonet. [French *baïonnette*, perhaps from *Bayonne* in SW France, where they were first made]

bayou /ˈbʌɪuː/ *n.* a marshy offshoot of a river etc. in the southern US. [Louisiana French, from Choctaw *bayuk*]

bay rum *n.* a perfume, esp. for the hair, distilled originally from bayberry leaves in rum.

Bay State *n.* *US* Massachusetts.

bay tree see BAY[2] 1.

bay window *n.* a window built into a bay.

bazaar /bəˈzɑː/ *n.* **1** a market in an oriental country. **2** a fund-raising sale of goods, esp. for charity. **3** a large shop selling fancy goods etc. [Persian *bāzār*, probably through Turkish and Italian]

bazooka /bəˈzuːkə/ *n.* **1** a tubular short-range rocket launcher used against tanks. **2** a crude trombone-like musical instrument. [apparently from *bazoo* 'mouth', of unknown origin]

BB *abbr.* *Brit.* double-black (pencil lead).

BBC *abbr.* British Broadcasting Corporation.

BBC English *n.* English as supposedly pronounced by BBC announcers.

BBFC *abbr.* British Board of Film Classification (formerly *British Board of Film Censors*).

bbl. *abbr.* barrels (esp. of oil).

BBQ *abbr.* barbecue.

BBSRC *abbr.* (in the UK) Biotechnology and Biological Sciences Research Council.

BC *abbr.* British Columbia.

BC *abbr.* (of a date) before Christ.

BCD *n.* *Computing* a code representing decimal numbers as a string of binary digits. [abbreviation of *b*inary *c*oded *d*ecimal]

BCE *abbr.* before the Common Era.

B-cell *n.* *Physiol.* = B-LYMPHOCYTE.

BCG *abbr.* Bacillus Calmette-Guérin, an anti-tuberculosis vaccine.

BD *abbr.* Bachelor of Divinity.

Bde *abbr.* Brigade.

bdellium /ˈdɛlɪəm/ *n.* **1** any of various trees, esp. of the genus *Commiphora*, yielding resin. **2** this fragrant resin used in perfumes. [Latin via Greek *bdellion* from Hebrew *bᵉdhōlaḥ*]

Bdr. *abbr.* *Brit.* (before a name) Bombardier.

BDS *abbr.* Bachelor of Dental Surgery.

BE *abbr.* **1** Bachelor of Education. **2** Bachelor of Engineering. **3** bill of exchange.

Be *symb.* *Chem.* the element beryllium.

be /biː/ *v.* & *v.aux.* (*sing. present* **am** /am, əm/; **are** /ɑː, ə/; **is** /ɪz/; *pl. present* **are**; *1st and 3rd sing. past* **was** /wɒz, wəz/; *2nd sing. past and pl. past* **were** /wəː, wə/; *present subjunctive* **be**; *past subjunctive* **were**; *pres. part.* **being**; *past part.* **been** /biːn, bɪn/) ● *v.intr.* **1** (often prec. by *there*) exist; live (*I think, therefore I am*; *there once was a man*; *there is a house on the corner*; *there was no doubt*). **2 a** occur; take place (*dinner is at eight*). **b** occupy a position in space (*he is in the garden*; *have you been to Paris?*). **3** remain, continue (*let it be*). **4** linking subject and predicate, expressing: **a** identity (*she is the person*; *today is Thursday*). **b** condition (*he is ill today*). **c** state or quality (*he is very kind*; *they are my friends*). **d** opinion (*I am against hanging*). **e** total (*two and two* *are four*). **f** cost or significance (*it is £5 to enter*; *it is nothing to me*). ● *v.aux.* **1** with a past participle to form the passive mood (*it was done*; *it is said*; *we shall be helped*). **2** with a present participle to form continuous tenses (*we are coming*; *it is being cleaned*). **3** with an infinitive to express duty or commitment, intention, possibility, destiny, or hypothesis (*I am to tell you*; *we are to wait here*; *he is to come at four*; *it was not to be found*; *they were never to meet again*; *if I were to die*). **4** *archaic* with the past participle of intransitive verbs to form perfect tenses (*the sun is set*; *Babylon is fallen*). □ **be about** occupy oneself with (*is about his business*). **be at** occupy oneself with (*what is he at?*; *mice have been at the food*). **been** (or **been and gone**) **and** *slang* an expression of protest or surprise (*he's been and taken my car!*). **be off** *colloq.* go away; leave. **be that as it may** see MAY. **-to-be** of the future (in *comb.*: *bride-to-be*). [Old English *beo(m)*, *(e)am*, *is*, *(e)aron*; past tense from Old English *wæs* from *wesan* 'to be'; there are numerous Germanic cognates]

be- /bɪ/ *prefix* forming verbs: **1** (from transitive verbs) **a** all over; all round (*beset*; *besmear*). **b** thoroughly, excessively (*begrudge*; *belabour*). **2** (from intransitive verbs) expressing transitive action (*bemoan*; *bestride*). **3** (from adjectives and nouns) expressing transitive action (*befool*; *befoul*). **4** (from nouns) **a** affect with (*befog*). **b** treat as (*befriend*). **c** (forming adjectives in *-ed*) having; covered with (*bejewelled*; *bespectacled*). [Old English *be-*, weak form of *bī* BY, as in *bygone*, *byword*, etc.]

BEA *abbr.* British Epilepsy Association.

beach /biːtʃ/ *n.* & *v.* ● *n.* a pebbly or sandy shore esp. of the sea between high and low water marks. ● *v.tr.* **1** run or haul up (a boat etc.) on to a beach. **2** (as **beached** *adj.*) (of a whale etc.) stranded out of the water. [16th c.: origin unknown]

beach ball *n.* a large inflated ball for games on the beach.

beach buggy *n.* a low wide-wheeled motor vehicle for recreational driving on sand.

beachcomber /ˈbiːtʃkəʊmə/ *n.* **1** a vagrant who lives by searching beaches for articles of value. **2** a long wave rolling in from the sea.

beachfront /ˈbiːtʃfrʌnt/ *n.* esp. *N. Amer.* = SEAFRONT.

beachhead /ˈbiːtʃhɛd/ *n.* *Mil.* a fortified position established on a beach by landing forces. [on the pattern of *bridgehead*]

Beach-la-mar /biːtʃləˈmɑː/ *n.* *Brit.* an English-based Creole language spoken in the W. Pacific. [corruption from Portuguese *bicho do mar* BÊCHE-DE-MER 'sea cucumber' (traded as a commodity: the word then applied to the language of trade)]

beach plum *n.* **1** a maritime N. American shrub, *Prunus maritima*. **2** its edible fruit.

beachside /ˈbiːtʃsʌɪd/ *attrib.adj.* next to the beach (*beachside tavernas*).

beachwear /ˈbiːtʃwɛː/ *n.* clothing suitable for wearing on the beach.

beacon /ˈbiːk(ə)n/ *n.* **1** **a** a fire or light set up in a high or prominent position as a warning etc. **b** *Brit.* (now often in place names) a hill suitable for this. **2** a visible warning or guiding point or device (e.g. a lighthouse, navigation buoy, etc.). **3** a radio transmitter whose signal helps fix the position of a ship or aircraft. **4** *Brit.* = BELISHA BEACON. [Old English *bēacn*, from West Germanic]

bead /biːd/ *n.* & *v.* ● *n.* **1** **a** a small usu. rounded and perforated piece of glass, stone, etc., for threading with others to make jewellery, or sewing on to fabric, etc. **b** (in *pl.*) a string of beads; a rosary. **2** a drop of liquid; a bubble. **3** a small knob in the foresight of a gun. **4** the inner edge of a pneumatic tyre that grips the rim of the wheel. **5** *Archit.* **a** a moulding like a series of beads. **b** a narrow moulding with a semicircular cross-section. ● *v.* **1** *tr.* furnish or decorate with beads. **2** *tr.* string together. **3** *intr.* form or grow into beads. □ **draw a bead on** take aim at. **tell one's beads** use the beads of a rosary etc. in counting prayers. □ **beaded** *adj.* [originally = 'prayer' (for which the earliest use of beads arose): Old English *gebed* from Germanic, related to BID]

beading /ˈbiːdɪŋ/ *n.* **1** decoration in the form of or resembling a row of beads, esp. lacelike looped edging. **2** *Archit.* a bead-moulding. **3** the bead of a tyre.

beadle /ˈbiːd(ə)l/ *n.* **1** *Brit.* a ceremonial officer of a church, college, etc. **2** *Sc.* a church officer attending on the minister. **3** *Brit. hist.* a minor parish officer dealing with petty offenders etc. □ **beadleship** *n.* [Old English *bydel* and Old French *bedel*, ultimately from Germanic]

beadsman /ˈbiːdzmən/ *n.* (*pl.* **-men**) *hist.* **1** a pensioner provided for by a benefactor in return for prayers. **2** an inmate of an almshouse.

beadwork /ˈbiːdwəːk/ *n.* decorative work in beads.

beady /ˈbiːdi/ *adj.* (**beadier**, **beadiest**) **1** (of the eyes) small, round, and bright. **2** covered with beads or drops. □ **beadily** *adv.* **beadiness** *n.*

beady-eyed *adj.* **1** having beady eyes. **2** observant.

beagle /ˈbiːg(ə)l/ *n.* & *v.* ● *n.* **1** **a** a small hound of a breed with a short coat, used for hunting hares. **b** this breed. **2** *hist.* an informer or spy; a constable. ● *v.intr.* (often as **beagling** *n.*) hunt with beagles. □ **beagler** *n.* [Middle English from Old French *beegueule* 'noisy person', probably from *beer* 'open wide' + *gueule* 'throat']

beak[1] /biːk/ *n.* **1** **a** a bird's horny projecting jaws; a bill. **b** the similar projecting jaw of other animals, e.g. a turtle. **2** *slang* a hooked nose. **3** *Naut. hist.* the projection at the prow of a warship. **4** a spout. □ **beaked** *adj.* **beaky** *adj.* [Middle English via Old French *bec* from Latin *beccus*, of Celtic origin]

beak[2] /biːk/ *n.* *Brit. slang* **1** a magistrate. **2** a schoolmaster. [19th c.: probably from criminals' slang]

beaker /ˈbiːkə/ *n.* **1** *Brit.* a tall drinking vessel, usu. of plastic and tumbler-shaped. **2** a lipped cylindrical glass vessel for scientific experiments. **3** *archaic* or *literary* a large drinking vessel with a wide mouth. [Middle English from Old Norse *bikarr*, perhaps from Greek *bikos* 'drinking bowl']

Beaker Folk *n.* *Archaeol.* a people thought to have come to Britain from central Europe in the early Bronze Age, named after beaker-shaped pottery found in their graves.

be-all and end-all *n.* (often foll. by *of*) *colloq.* the whole being or essence.

beam /biːm/ *n.* & *v.* ● *n.* **1** a long sturdy piece of squared timber or metal spanning an opening or room, usu. to support the structure above. **2** **a** a ray or shaft of light. **b** a directional flow of particles or radiation. **3** a bright look or smile. **4** **a** a series of radio or radar signals as a guide to a ship or aircraft. **b** the course indicated by this (*off beam*). **5** the crossbar of a balance. **6** **a** a ship's breadth at its widest point. **b** the width of a person's hips (esp. *broad in the beam*). **7** (in *pl.*) the horizontal cross-timbers of a ship supporting the deck and joining the sides. **8** the side of a ship (*land on the port beam*). **9** the chief timber of a plough. **10** the cylinder in a loom on which the warp or cloth is wound. **11** the main stem of a stag's antlers. **12** the lever in an engine connecting the piston rod and crank. **13** the shank of an anchor. ● *v.* **1** *tr.* emit or direct (light, radio waves, etc.). **2** *intr.* **a** shine. **b** look or smile radiantly. **3** (often foll. by *up*, *down*) (in science fiction) **a** *intr.* travel from one point to another along an invisible beam of energy. **b** *tr.* transport in this way. □ **a beam in one's eye** a fault that is greater in oneself than in the person one is finding fault with (see Matt. 7:3). **off** (or **off the**) **beam** *colloq.* mistaken. **on the beam** *colloq.* on the right track. **on the beam-ends** (of a ship) on its side; almost capsizing. **on one's beam-ends** near the end of one's resources. [Old English *bēam* 'tree', from West Germanic]

beam-compass *n.* (also **beam-compasses** *pl.*) compasses with a beam connecting sliding sockets, used for large circles.

beamer /ˈbiːmə/ *n. Cricket colloq.* a ball bowled at a batsman's head.

beamy /ˈbiːmi/ *adj.* (of a ship) broad-beamed.

bean /biːn/ *n. & v.* ● *n.* **1 a** any kind of leguminous plant with edible usu. kidney-shaped seeds in long pods. **b** one of these seeds. **2** a similar seed of coffee and other plants. **3** *slang* the head, esp. as a source of common sense. **4** (in *pl.*; with *neg.*) *US slang* anything at all (*doesn't know beans about it*). ● *v.tr.* esp. *N. Amer. slang* hit on the head. □ **full of beans** *colloq.* lively; in high spirits. **not a bean** *Brit. slang* no money. **old bean** *Brit. slang* a friendly form of address, usu. to a man. [Old English *bēan*, from Germanic]

beanbag /ˈbiːnbag/ *n.* **1** a small bag filled with dried beans and used esp. in children's games. **2** a large cushion filled usu. with polystyrene beads and used as a seat.

bean-counter *n.* orig. *US colloq. derog.* **1** an accountant (esp. one who is obsessed with returns on investments). **2** a penny-pincher.

bean curd *n.* jelly or paste made from beans, used esp. in Asian cookery.

beanery /ˈbiːnəri/ *n.* (*pl.* **-ies**) *N. Amer. slang* a cheap restaurant.

beanfeast /ˈbiːnfiːst/ *n. Brit. colloq.* a celebration, originally an annual dinner with colleagues; any festive occasion or merry time. [BEAN + FEAST, beans and bacon being regarded as an indispensable dish]

bean goose *n.* a grey goose, *Anser fabalis*, breeding in the Arctic.

beanie /ˈbiːni/ *n.* a small close-fitting hat worn on the back of the head. [perhaps from BEAN 'head' + -IE]

beano /ˈbiːnəʊ/ *n.* (*pl.* **-os**) *Brit. slang* a celebration; a party. [abbreviation of BEANFEAST]

beanpole /ˈbiːnpəʊl/ *n.* **1** a stick for supporting bean plants. **2** *colloq.* a tall thin person.

bean sprout *n.* a sprout of a bean seed, esp. of the mung bean, used as food.

beanstalk /ˈbiːnstɔːk/ *n.* the stem of a bean plant.

bear[1] /bɛː/ *v.* (*past* **bore** /bɔː/; *past part.* **borne**, **born** /bɔːn/) **1** *tr.* carry, bring, or take (esp. visibly) (*bear gifts*). **2** *tr.* show; be marked by; have as an attribute or characteristic (*bear marks of violence*; *bears no relation to the case*; *bore no name*). **3** *tr.* **a** produce, yield (fruit etc.). **b** give birth to (*has borne a son*; *was born last week*). **4** *tr.* **a** sustain (a weight, responsibility, cost, etc.). **b** stand, endure (an ordeal, difficulty, etc.). **5** *tr.* (usu. with *neg.* or *interrog.*) **a** tolerate; put up with (*can't bear him*; *how can you bear it?*). **b** admit of; be fit for (*does not bear thinking about*). **6** *tr.* carry in thought or memory (*bear a grudge*). **7** *intr.* veer in a given direction (*bear left*). **8** *tr.* bring or provide (something needed) (*bear him company*). **9** *refl.* behave (in a certain way). □ **bear arms 1** carry weapons; serve as a soldier. **2** wear or display heraldic devices. **bear away** (or **off**) win (a prize etc.). **bear down** exert downward pressure. **bear down on** approach rapidly or purposefully. **bear fruit** have results. **bear a hand** help. **bear hard on** oppress. **bear in mind** take into account having remembered. **bear on** (or **upon**) be relevant to. **bear out** support or confirm (an account or the person giving it). **bear repeating** be worth repetition. **bear up** raise one's spirits; not despair. **bear with** treat forbearingly; tolerate patiently. **bear witness** testify. [Old English *beran*, from Germanic]

■ **Usage** Note the difference between *borne* and *born*. *Borne* is the standard past participle of *bear* and is used in all senses above except one, e.g. *the ship that had borne me across the sea*; *the worried look she has borne since his departure*; *the findings have been borne out*. *Born* is used only in the passive with reference to birth, e.g. *was born in July*, and then not if followed by *by* and the name of the mother (e.g. *was borne by Sarah*). Compare *a son was born to Sarah* which is also correct. Although *born* is used only in one sense, this sense is so common that *born* is a more common English word than *borne*, which probably adds to the confusion.

bear[2] /bɛː/ *n. & v.* ● *n.* **1** any large heavy mammal of the family Ursidae, having thick fur and walking on its soles. **2** a rough, unmannerly, or uncouth person. **3** *Stock Exch.* a person who sells shares hoping to buy them back later at a lower price. **4** = TEDDY 1. **5** (**the Bear**) *colloq.* Russia. **6** esp. *US slang* **a** a police officer. **b** (prec. by *the*) the police. ● *v. Stock Exch.* **1** *intr.* speculate for a fall in price. **2** *tr.* produce a fall in the price of (stocks etc.). □ **like a bear with a sore head** *Brit. colloq.* very irritable. [Old English *bera*, from West Germanic]

bearable /ˈbɛːrəb(ə)l/ *adj.* that may be endured or tolerated. □ **bearability** /-ˈbɪlɪti/ *n.* **bearableness** *n.* **bearably** *adv.*

bear-baiting *n. hist.* an entertainment involving setting dogs to attack a captive bear.

bearberry /ˈbɛːb(ə)ri/ *n.* an evergreen ericaceous plant of the genus *Arctostaphylos*, esp. *A. uva-ursi*, a trailing moorland plant with pinkish flowers and bright red berries.

beard /bɪəd/ *n. & v.* ● *n.* **1** hair growing on the chin and lower cheeks of the face. **2** a tuft of hair or similar growth or marking on the face or chin of an animal (e.g. a goat). **3** the awn of a grass, sheath of barley, etc. ● *v.tr.* oppose openly; defy. □ **bearded** *adj.* **beardless** *adj.* [Old English, from West Germanic]

bearded tit *n.* a small Eurasian passerine bird, *Panurus biarmicus*, which frequents reed-beds.

beardie /ˈbɪədi/ *n. Brit. colloq.* a bearded man.

bearer /ˈbɛːrə/ *n.* **1** a person or thing that bears, carries, or brings. **2** a carrier of equipment on an expedition etc. **3** a person who presents a cheque or other order to pay money. **4** (*attrib.*) payable to the possessor (*bearer stock*). **5** *hist.* (in India etc.) a personal servant.

beargarden /ˈbɛːgɑːd(ə)n/ *n.* a rowdy or noisy scene.

bear-hug *n.* a tight embrace.

bearing /ˈbɛːrɪŋ/ *n.* **1** a person's bodily attitude or outward behaviour. **2** (foll. by *on*, *upon*) relation or relevance to (*his comments have no bearing on the subject*). **3** endurability (*beyond bearing*). **4** a part of a machine that supports a rotating or other moving part. **5** direction or position relative to a fixed point, measured esp. in degrees. **6** (in *pl.*) **a** one's position relative to one's surroundings. **b** awareness of this; a sense of one's orientation (*get one's bearings*; *lose one's bearings*). **7** *Heraldry* a device or charge. **8** = BALL-BEARING.

bearing-rein *n.* a fixed rein from bit to saddle that forces a horse to arch its neck.

bearish /ˈbɛːrɪʃ/ *adj.* **1** like a bear, esp. in temper. **2** *Stock Exch.* causing or associated with a fall in prices.

bear market *n. Stock Exch.* a market with falling prices.

Béarnaise sauce /beɪəˈneɪz/ *n.* a rich sauce thickened with egg yolks and flavoured with tarragon. [French, fem. of *béarnais* 'of *Béarn*' (in SW France)]

bearpit /ˈbɛːpɪt/ *n.* **1** a sunken enclosure in which bears are kept in a zoo etc. **2** a scene or place of rowdy disorder.

bear's breech *n.* an acanthus, esp. the Mediterranean *Acanthus mollis*.

bear's ear *n.* = AURICULA.

bear's foot *n.* a hellebore, *Helleborus fetidus*.

bearskin /ˈbɛːskɪn/ *n.* **1 a** the skin of a bear. **b** a wrap etc. made of this. **2** a tall furry hat worn ceremonially by some regiments.

beast /biːst/ *n.* **1** an animal other than a human being, esp. a wild quadruped. **2 a** a brutal person. **b** *colloq.* an objectionable or unpleasant person or thing (*he's a beast for not inviting her*; *a beast of a problem*). **3** (prec. by *the*) a human being's brutish or uncivilized characteristics (*saw the beast in him*). [Middle English via Old French *beste* and Romanic *besta* from Latin *bestia*]

beastie /ˈbiːsti/ *n. Sc.* or *joc.* a small animal.

beastly /ˈbiːstli/ *adj. & adv.* ● *adj.* (**beastlier**, **beastliest**) **1** *colloq.* objectionable, unpleasant. **2** like a beast; brutal. ● *adv. Brit. colloq.* very, extremely. □ **beastliness** *n.*

beast of burden *n.* an animal, e.g. a mule, used for carrying loads.

beast of prey *n.* an animal which hunts animals for food.

beat /biːt/ *v., n., & adj.* ● *v.* (*past* **beat**; *past part.* **beaten** /ˈbiːt(ə)n/) **1** *tr.* **a** strike (a person or animal) persistently or repeatedly, esp. to harm or punish. **b** strike (a thing) repeatedly, e.g. to remove dust from (a carpet etc.), to sound (a drum etc.). **2** *intr.* (foll. by *against, at, on*, etc.) **a** pound or knock repeatedly (*waves beat against the shore*; *beat at the door*). **b** = *beat down* 3. **3** *tr.* **a** overcome; surpass; win a victory over. **b** complete an activity before (another person etc.). **c** be too hard for; perplex. **4** *tr.* (often foll. by *up*) stir (eggs etc.) vigorously into a frothy mixture. **5** *tr.* (often foll. by *out*) fashion or shape (metal etc.) by blows. **6** *intr.* (of the heart, a drum, etc.) pulsate rhythmically. **7** *tr.* (often foll. by *out*) **a** indicate (a tempo or rhythm) by gestures, tapping, etc. **b** sound (a signal etc.) by striking a drum or other means (*beat a tattoo*). **8 a** *intr.* (of a bird's wings) move up and down. **b** *tr.* cause (wings) to move in this way. **9** *tr.* make (a path etc.) by trampling. **10** *tr.* strike (bushes etc.) to rouse game. **11** *intr. Naut.* sail in the direction from which the wind is blowing. ● *n.* **1 a** a main accent or rhythmic unit in music or verse (*three beats to the bar*; *missed a beat and came in early*). **b** the indication of rhythm by a conductor's movements (*watch the beat*). **c** (in popular music) a strong rhythm. **d** (*attrib.*) characterized by a strong rhythm (*beat music*). **2 a** a stroke or blow (e.g. on a drum). **b** a measured sequence of strokes (*the beat of the waves on the rocks*). **c** a throbbing movement or sound (*the beat of his heart*). **3 a** a route or area allocated to a police officer etc. **b** a person's habitual round. **4** *Physics* a pulsation due to the combination of two sounds or electric currents of similar but not equivalent frequencies. **5** *colloq.* = BEATNIK. ● *adj.* **1** (*predic.*) *slang* exhausted, tired out. **2** (*attrib.*) of the beat generation or its philosophy. □ **beat about** (often foll. by *for*) search (for an excuse etc.). **beat about** (or *US* **around**) **the bush** discuss a matter without coming to the point. **beat the bounds** *Brit.* mark parish boundaries by striking certain points with rods. **beat one's breast** strike one's chest in anguish or sorrow. **beat the clock** complete a task within a stated time. **beat down 1 a** bargain with (a seller) to lower the price. **b** cause a seller to lower (the price). **2** strike (a resisting object) until it falls (*beat the door down*). **3** (of the sun, rain, etc.) radiate heat or fall continuously and vigorously. **beat the drum for** publicize, promote. **beaten at the post** defeated at the last moment. **beat in** crush. **beat it** *slang* go away. **beat off** drive back (an attack etc.). **beat a retreat** withdraw; abandon an undertaking. **beat time** indicate or follow a musical tempo with a baton or other means. **beat a person to it** arrive or achieve something before another person. **beat up** give a beating to, esp. with punches and kicks. **it beats me** I do not understand (it). □ **beatable** *adj.* [Old English *bēatan*, from Germanic]

beaten /ˈbiːt(ə)n/ *adj.* **1** outwitted; defeated. **2** exhausted; dejected. **3** (of gold or any other metal) shaped by a hammer. **4** (of a path etc.) well-trodden, much used. □ **off the beaten track 1** in or into an isolated place. **2** unusual. [past part. of BEAT]

beater /ˈbiːtə/ *n.* **1** an implement used for beating (esp. a carpet or eggs). **2** a person employed to rouse game for shooting. **3** a person who beats metal. **4** *N. Amer. colloq.* an old or dilapidated vehicle.

beat generation *n.* the members of a movement of young people esp. in the 1950s who rejected conventional society in their dress, habits, and beliefs.

beatific /biːəˈtɪfɪk/ *adj.* **1** *colloq.* blissful (*a beatific smile*). **2 a** of or relating to blessedness. **b** making blessed. □ **beatifically** *adv.* [French *béatifique* or Latin *beatificus*, from *beatus* 'blessed']

beatification /bɪˌatɪfɪˈkeɪʃ(ə)n/ *n.* **1** *RC Ch.* the act of formally declaring a dead person 'blessed', often a step towards canonization. **2** making or being blessed. [French *béatification* or ecclesiastical Latin *beatificatio* (as BEATIFY)]

beatify /bɪˈatɪfʌɪ/ *v.tr.* (**-ies**, **-ied**) **1** *RC Ch.* announce the beatification of. **2** make happy. [French *béatifier* or ecclesiastical Latin *beatificare*, from Latin *beatus* 'blessed']

beating /ˈbiːtɪŋ/ *n.* **1** a physical punishment or assault. **2** a defeat. □ **take some** (or **a lot of**) **beating** be difficult to surpass.

beatitude /bɪˈatɪtjuːd/ *n.* **1** blessedness. **2** (also **Beatitude**) a declaration of blessedness, a blessing, esp. (in *pl.*) those made by Jesus (Matt. 5:3-11). **3** a title given to patriarchs in the Orthodox Church. [French *béatitude* or Latin *beatitudo*, from *beatus* 'blessed']

beatnik /ˈbiːtnɪk/ *n.* a member of the beat generation. [BEAT + *-nik* on the pattern of *sputnik*, perhaps influenced by US use of Yiddish *-nik* agent-suffix]

beat-up *adj. colloq.* dilapidated; in a state of disrepair.

beau /bəʊ/ *n.* (*pl.* **beaux** or **beaus** /bəʊz, bəʊ/) **1** esp. *US* an admirer; a boyfriend. **2** a fop; a dandy. [French, = handsome, from Latin *bellus*]

Beaufort scale /ˈbəʊfət skeɪl/ *n.* a scale of wind speed ranging from 0 (calm) to 12 (hurricane). See also Appendix XI. [Sir F. *Beaufort*, English admiral (d. 1857) who devised it]

beau geste /bəʊ ˈʒɛst, French bo ʒɛst/ *n.* (*pl.* ***beaux gestes*** *pronunc.* same) a generous or gracious act. [French, = splendid gesture]

beau idéal /bəʊ iːdeɪˈal/ *n.* the highest type of excellence or beauty. [French *beau idéal* = ideal beauty: see BEAU, IDEAL]

Beaujolais /ˈbəʊʒəleɪ/ *n.* a red or white burgundy wine from the Beaujolais district of France.

Beaujolais Nouveau /ˌbəʊʒəleɪ nuːˈvəʊ/ *n.* Beaujolais wine sold in the first year of a vintage. [BEAUJOLAIS + French *nouveau* 'new']

beau monde /bəʊ ˈmɒnd/ *n.* fashionable society. [French, = fine world]

beaut /bjuːt/ *n. & adj. Austral. & NZ slang* ● *n.* (also *US*) an excellent or beautiful person or thing. ● *adj.* excellent; beautiful. [abbreviation of BEAUTY]

beauteous /ˈbjuːtɪəs/ *adj. poet.* beautiful. [Middle English from BEAUTY + -OUS, on the pattern of *bounteous, plenteous*]

beautician /bjuːˈtɪʃ(ə)n/ *n.* **1** a person who gives beauty treatment. **2** a person who runs or owns a beauty salon.

beautiful /ˈbjuːtɪfʊl, -f(ə)l/ *adj.* **1** delighting the aesthetic senses (*a beautiful voice*). **2** pleasant, enjoyable (*had a beautiful time*). **3** excellent (*a beautiful specimen*). □ **beautifully** *adv.*

beautify /ˈbjuːtɪfʌɪ/ *v.tr.* (**-ies**, **-ied**) make beautiful; adorn. □ **beautification** /-fɪˈkeɪʃ(ə)n/ *n.* **beautifier** /-fʌɪə/ *n.*

beauty /ˈbjuːti/ *n.* (*pl.* **-ies**) **1 a** a combination of qualities such as shape, colour, etc., that pleases the aesthetic senses, esp. the sight. **b** a combination of qualities that pleases the intellect or moral sense (*the beauty of the argument*). **2** *colloq.* **a** an excellent specimen (*what a beauty!*). **b** an attractive feature; an advantage (*that's the beauty of it!*). **3** a beautiful woman. □ **beauty is only skin-deep** a pleasing appearance is not a guide to character. [Middle English from Anglo-French *beuté*, Old French *bealté, beauté*, ultimately from Latin (as BEAU)]

beauty parlour *n.* (also **beauty salon**) an establishment in which manicure, hairdressing, make-up, etc., are offered to women.

beauty queen *n.* the woman judged most beautiful in a competition.

beauty sleep *n.* sleep before midnight, supposed to be health-giving.

beauty spot *n.* **1** a place known for its beauty. **2** a small natural or artificial mark such as a mole on the face, considered to enhance another feature.

beauty treatment *n.* cosmetic treatment received in a beauty parlour.

beaux *pl.* of BEAU.

beaux arts /bəʊ'zɑː, French bozar/ *n.pl.* **1** fine arts. **2** (*attrib.*) relating to the rules and conventions of the École des Beaux-Arts in Paris (later called Académie des Beaux Arts). [French *beaux-arts*]

beaver[1] /'biːvə/ *n. & v.* ● *n.* (*pl.* same or **beavers**) **1 a** any large amphibious broad-tailed rodent of the genus *Castor*, native to N. America, Europe, and Asia, and able to gnaw through tree trunks and make dams. **b** its soft light brown fur. **c** a hat of this. **2** (in full **beaver cloth**) a heavy woollen cloth like beaver fur. **3** (**Beaver**) a boy aged six or seven who is an affiliate member of the Scout Association. ● *v.intr.* (usu. foll. by *away*) *colloq.* work hard. [Old English *be(o)for*, from Germanic]

beaver[2] /'biːvə/ *n. hist.* the lower face-guard of a helmet. [Old French *baviere* 'bib' via *baver* 'slaver' from *beve* 'saliva', from Romanic]

beaver[3] /'biːvə/ *n. Brit. slang* a bearded man. [20th c.: origin uncertain]

beaverboard /'biːvəbɔːd/ *n.* a kind of fibreboard. [BEAVER[1] + BOARD]

beaver lamb *n.* lambskin made to look like beaver fur.

bebop /'biːbɒp/ *n.* a type of jazz originating in the 1940s and characterized by complex harmony and rhythms. □ **bebopper** *n.* [imitative of the typical rhythm]

becalm /bɪ'kɑːm/ *v.tr.* (usu. in *passive*) deprive (a sailing ship) of wind.

became *past* of BECOME.

because /bɪ'kɒz/ *conj.* for the reason that; since. □ **because of** on account of; by reason of. [Middle English from BY *prep.* + CAUSE, influenced by Old French *par cause de* 'by reason of']

■ **Usage** See Usage Note at REASON.

béchamel /'beɪʃəmɛl/ *n.* a kind of thick white sauce. [invented by the Marquis de *Béchamel*, French courtier d. 1703]

bêche-de-mer /bɛʃdə'mɛː/ *n.* (*pl.* same or **bêches-de-mer** *pronunc.* same) **1** a kind of sea cucumber eaten in China usu. in long dried strips. **2** = BEACH-LA-MAR. [French, alteration of *biche de mer* from Portuguese *bicho do mar*, literally 'sea-worm']

beck[1] /bɛk/ *n. N.Engl.* a brook; a mountain stream. [Middle English via Old Norse *bekkr* from Germanic]

beck[2] /bɛk/ *n. poet.* a gesture requesting attention, e.g. a nod, wave, etc. □ **at a person's beck and call** having constantly to obey a person's orders. [*beck* (*v.*) from BECKON]

becket /'bɛkɪt/ *n. Naut.* a contrivance such as a hook, bracket, or rope-loop, for securing loose ropes, tackle, or spars. [18th c.: origin unknown]

beckon /'bɛk(ə)n/ *v.* **1** *tr.* **a** attract the attention of; summon by gesture. **b** entice. **2** *intr.* (usu. foll. by *to*) make a signal to attract a person's attention; summon a person by doing this. [Old English *bīecnan*, *bēcnan*, ultimately from West Germanic *baukna* BEACON]

becloud /bɪ'klaʊd/ *v.tr.* **1** obscure (*becloud the argument*). **2** cover with clouds.

become /bɪ'kʌm/ *v.* (*past* **became** /bɪ'keɪm/; *past part.* **become**) **1** *intr.* (foll. by compl.) begin to be (*became president*; *will become famous*). **2** *tr.* **a** look well on; suit (*blue becomes him*). **b** befit (*it ill becomes you to complain*). **3** *intr.* (as **becoming** *adj.*) **a** flattering the appearance. **b** suitable; decorous. □ **become of** happen to (*what will become of me?*). □ **becomingly** *adj.* **becomingness** *n.* [Old English *becuman* from Germanic (as BE-, COME)]

becquerel /'bɛkərɛl/ *n. Physics* the SI unit of radioactivity, corresponding to one disintegration per second. [A. H. *Becquerel*, French physicist d. 1908]

B.Ed. *abbr.* Bachelor of Education.

bed /bɛd/ *n. & v.* ● *n.* **1 a** a piece of furniture used for sleeping on, usu. a framework with a mattress and coverings. **b** a mattress, with or without coverings. **2** any place used by a person or animal for sleep or rest; a litter. **3 a** a garden plot, esp. one used for planting flowers. **b** a place where other things may be grown (*osier bed*). **4** the use of a bed: **a** on loan or hire; temporarily (*I need a bed for the night*). **b** *Brit. colloq.* for sexual intercourse (*only thinks of bed*). **c** *Brit.* for rest (*needs his bed*). **5** something flat, forming a support or base as in: **a** the bottom of the sea or a river. **b** the foundations of a road or railway. **c** the flat surface beneath the baize of a billiard table. **6** a stratum, such as a layer of oysters etc. ● *v.* (**bedded**, **bedding**) **1** *tr. & intr.* (usu. foll. by *down*) put or go to bed. **2** *tr.* (usu. foll. by *with*) *colloq.* have sexual intercourse with. **3** *tr.* (usu. foll. by *out*) plant in a garden bed. **4** *tr.* cover up or fix firmly in something. **5 a** *tr.* arrange as a layer. **b** *intr.* be or form a layer. □ **bed of roses** a life of ease. **brought to bed** (often foll. by *of*) *archaic* delivered of a child. **get out of bed on the wrong side** be bad-tempered all day long. **go to bed 1** retire for the night. **2** have sexual intercourse. **3** (of a newspaper) go to press. **keep one's bed** stay in bed because of illness. **make the bed** tidy and arrange the bed for use. **make one's bed and lie in it** accept the consequences of one's acts. **put to bed 1** cause to go to bed. **2** make (a newspaper) ready for press. **take to one's bed** stay in bed because of illness. [Old English *bed(d)* (*n.*), *beddian* (*v.*), from Germanic]

bedabble /bɪ'dab(ə)l/ *v.tr.* stain or splash with dirty liquid, blood, etc.

bedad /bɪ'dad/ *int. Ir.* by God! [corruption: cf. GAD[2]]

bed and board *n.* **1** lodging and food. **2** marital relations.

bed and breakfast *n. & v.* ● *n.* **1** one night's lodging and breakfast in a hotel etc. **2** an establishment that provides this. ● *v.tr.* (**bed-and-breakfast**) sell (shares) and buy back the next morning.

bedaub /bɪ'dɔːb/ *v.tr.* smear or daub with paint etc.; decorate gaudily.

bedazzle /bɪ'daz(ə)l/ *v.tr.* **1** dazzle. **2** confuse (a person). □ **bedazzlement** *n.*

bedbug /'bɛdbʌg/ *n.* either of two flat, wingless, evil-smelling insects of the genus *Cimex* infesting beds and unclean houses and sucking blood .

bedchamber /'bɛdtʃeɪmbə/ *n.* **1** *archaic* a bedroom. **2** (**Bedchamber**) part of the title of some of the sovereign's attendants (*Lady of the Bedchamber*).

bedclothes /'bɛdkləʊðz/ *n.pl.* coverings for a bed, such as sheets, blankets, etc.

bedcover /'bɛdkʌvə/ *n.* **1** a bedspread. **2** (in *pl.*) = BEDCLOTHES.

beddable /'bɛdəb(ə)l/ *adj. colloq.* considered seductive or sexually attractive. [BED + -ABLE]

bedder /'bɛdə/ *n.* **1** a plant suitable for a garden bed. **2** *Brit. colloq.* a college bedmaker.

bedding /'bɛdɪŋ/ *n.* **1** a mattress and bedclothes. **2** litter for cattle, horses, etc. **3** a bottom layer. **4** *Geol.* the stratification of rocks, esp. when clearly visible.

bedding plant *n.* a plant set into a garden bed or container when it is about to bloom, usu. an annual used for display and discarded at the end of the season.

beddy-byes /'bɛdɪbʌɪz/ *n.* (child's word for) bed, sleep. [BED + -Y[2] + BYE-BYE[2]]

bedeck /bɪ'dɛk/ *v.tr.* adorn.

bedeguar /'bɛdɪgɑː/ *n.* a mosslike growth on rose bushes produced by a gall wasp. [French *bédegar* from Persian *bād-āwar* 'wind-brought']

bedel /'biːd(ə)l, bɪ'dɛl/ *n.* (also **bedell**) *Brit.* a university official with chiefly processional duties. [archaic spelling of BEADLE]

bedevil /bɪˈdɛv(ə)l/ *v.tr.* (**bedevilled**, **bedevilling**; *US* **bedeviled**, **bedeviling**) **1** plague; afflict. **2** confound; confuse. **3** possess as if with a devil; bewitch. **4** treat with diabolical violence or abuse. □ **bedevilment** *n.*

bedew /bɪˈdjuː/ *v.tr.* **1** cover or sprinkle with dew or drops of water. **2** *poet.* sprinkle with tears.

bedfellow /ˈbɛdfɛləʊ/ *n.* **1** a person who shares a bed. **2** an associate.

Bedford cord /bɛdfəd ˈkɔːd/ *n.* a tough woven fabric having prominent ridges, similar to corduroy. [*Bedford* in S. England]

bedhead /ˈbɛdhɛd/ *n.* the upper end of a bed.

bed-hop *v.intr.* (**-hopped**, **-hopping**) *colloq.* engage in successive casual sexual affairs.

bedight /bɪˈdʌɪt/ *adj. archaic* arrayed; adorned. [Middle English past part. of *bedight* (*v.*) (as BE-, DIGHT)]

bedim /bɪˈdɪm/ *v.tr.* (**bedimmed**, **bedimming**) *poet.* make (the eyes, mind, etc.) dim.

bedizen /bɪˈdʌɪz(ə)n, -ˈdɪz-/ *v.tr. poet.* deck out gaudily. [BE- + obsolete *dizen* 'deck out']

bedjacket /ˈbɛddʒakɪt/ *n.* a jacket worn when sitting up in bed.

bedlam /ˈbɛdləm/ *n.* **1** a scene of uproar and confusion (*the traffic was bedlam*). **2** *archaic* a madhouse; an asylum. [hospital of St Mary of *Bethlehem* in London]

bedlinen /ˈbɛdlɪnɪn/ *n.* sheets, pillowcases, duvet covers, etc.

Bedlington terrier /ˈbɛdlɪŋt(ə)n/ *n.* **1** a terrier of a breed with a narrow head, long legs, and curly grey hair. **2** this breed. [*Bedlington* in N. England]

bedmaker /ˈbɛdmeɪkə/ *n. Brit.* a person employed to clean and tidy students' rooms in a college.

Bedouin /ˈbɛdʊɪn/ *n. & adj.* (also **Beduin**) ● *n.* (*pl.* same) **1** a nomadic Arab of the desert. **2** a wanderer; a nomad. ● *adj.* **1** of or relating to the Bedouin. **2** wandering; nomadic. [Middle English from Old French *beduin*, ultimately from Arabic *badawī*, *pl. badawīn* 'dwellers in the desert' from *badw* 'desert']

bedpan /ˈbɛdpan/ *n.* a receptacle used by a bedridden patient for urine and faeces.

bedplate /ˈbɛdpleɪt/ *n.* a metal plate forming the base of a machine.

bedpost /ˈbɛdpəʊst/ *n.* any of the four upright supports of a bedstead. □ **between you and me and the bedpost** *Brit. colloq.* in strict confidence.

bedraggle /bɪˈdrag(ə)l/ *v.tr.* **1** wet (a garment etc.) by trailing it, or so that it hangs limp. **2** (as **bedraggled** *adj.*) untidy; dishevelled. [BE- + DRAGGLE]

bedrest /ˈbɛdrɛst/ *n.* confinement of an invalid to bed.

bedridden /ˈbɛdrɪd(ə)n/ *adj.* **1** confined to bed by infirmity. **2** decrepit. [Old English *bedreda* from *ridan* 'ride']

bedrock /ˈbɛdrɒk/ *n.* **1** solid rock underlying alluvial deposits etc. **2** the underlying principles or facts of a theory, character, etc.

bedroll /ˈbɛdrəʊl/ *n.* esp. *N. Amer.* portable bedding rolled into a bundle, esp. a sleeping bag.

bedroom /ˈbɛdruːm, -rʊm/ *n.* **1** a room for sleeping in. **2** (*attrib.*) of or referring to sexual relations (*bedroom farce*).

Beds. *abbr.* Bedfordshire.

bedside /ˈbɛdsʌɪd/ *n.* **1** the space beside esp. a patient's bed. **2** (*attrib.*) of or relating to the side of a bed (*bedside lamp*). □ **bedside manner** (of a doctor) an approach or attitude to a patient.

bedsitter /bɛdˈsɪtə/ *n.* (also **bedsit**) *Brit. colloq.* = BED-SITTING ROOM. [contraction]

bed-sitting room /bɛdˈsɪtɪŋ/ *n. Brit.* a one-roomed unit of accommodation usu. consisting of combined bedroom and sitting room with cooking facilities.

bedskirt /ˈbɛdskəːt/ *n. N. Amer.* a valance for a bed.

bedsock /ˈbɛdsɒk/ *n.* esp. *Brit.* each of a pair of thick socks worn in bed.

bedsore /ˈbɛdsɔː/ *n.* a sore developed by an invalid because of pressure caused by lying in bed.

bedspread /ˈbɛdsprɛd/ *n.* an often decorative cloth used to cover a bed when not in use.

bedstead /ˈbɛdstɛd/ *n.* the framework of a bed.

bedstraw /ˈbɛdstrɔː/ *n.* **1** any herbaceous plant of the genus *Galium*, once used as straw for bedding. **2** (in full **lady's bedstraw**) a bedstraw, *G. verum*, with yellow flowers.

bedtable /ˈbɛdteɪb(ə)l/ *n. Brit.* a portable table or tray with legs used by a person sitting up in bed.

bedtime /ˈbɛdtʌɪm/ *n.* **1** the usual time for going to bed. **2** (*attrib.*) of or relating to bedtime (*bedtime drink*).

Beduin var. of BEDOUIN.

bed-wetting *n.* involuntary urination during the night. □ **bed-wetter** *n.*

bee /biː/ *n.* **1 a** (in full **honey bee**) a stinging hymenopterous insect of the genus *Apis* which collects nectar and pollen, produces wax and honey, and lives in large communities, esp. the domesticated *A. mellifera*. **b** a related insect of the superfamily Apoidea, either social or solitary. **2** (usu. **busy bee**) a busy person. **3** esp. *US* a meeting for communal work or amusement (*spelling bee*). □ **a bee in one's bonnet** an obsession. **the bee's knees** *slang* something outstandingly good (*thinks he's the bee's knees*). [Old English *bēo*, from Germanic]

Beeb /biːb/ *n.* (prec. by *the*) *Brit. colloq.* the BBC. [abbreviation]

bee-bread *n.* honey or pollen used as food by bees.

beech /biːtʃ/ *n.* **1** (also **beech tree**) any large forest tree of the genus *Fagus*, having smooth grey bark and glossy leaves. **2** (also **beechwood**) its wood. **3** *Austral.* any of various similar trees in Australia. [Old English *bēce*, from Germanic]

beech-fern *n.* any of several related ferns, esp. *Phegopteris connectilis*, found in damp woods.

beech marten *n.* the stone marten, *Martes foina*.

beechmast /ˈbiːtʃmɑːst/ *n.* (*pl.* same) the small rough-skinned fruit of the beech tree. [BEECH + MAST[2]]

beechwood see BEECH 2.

bee dance *n.* a dance performed by worker bees to inform the colony of the location of food.

bee-eater *n.* any bright-plumaged insect-eating bird of the family Meropidae with a long slender curved bill.

beef /biːf/ *n. & v.* ● *n.* **1** the flesh of the ox, bull, or esp. the cow, for eating. **2** *colloq.* well-developed male muscle. **3** (*pl.* **beeves** /biːvz/ a cow, bull, or ox fattened for beef; its carcass. **4** (*pl.* **beefs**) *slang* a complaint; a protest. ● *v.intr. slang* complain. □ **beef up** *slang* strengthen, reinforce, augment. [Middle English via Anglo-French, Old French *boef* from Latin *bos bovis* 'ox']

beefburger /ˈbiːfbəːgə/ *n.* a cake of minced beef usu. fried or grilled.

beefcake /ˈbiːfkeɪk/ *n. slang* well-developed male muscles, esp. when displayed for admiration.

beefeater /ˈbiːfiːtə/ *n.* a warder in the Tower of London; a Yeoman of the Guard. [from obsolete sense 'well-fed menial']

beefsteak /biːfˈsteɪk, ˈbiːf-/ *n.* a thick slice of lean beef, esp. from the rump, usu. for grilling or frying.

beefsteak fungus *n.* a red bracket fungus, *Fistulina hepatica*, resembling raw beef.

beefsteak tomato *n. N. Amer.* = BEEF TOMATO.

beef tea *n.* stewed extract of beef, given to invalids.

beef tomato *n. Brit.* an exceptionally large and firm variety of tomato.

beefwood /ˈbiːfwʊd/ *n.* **1** any of various Australian and W. Indian hardwood trees. **2** the close-grained red timber of these.

beefy /ˈbiːfi/ *adj.* (**beefier**, **beefiest**) **1** like beef. **2** solid; muscular. □ **beefily** *adv.* **beefiness** *n.*

beehive /ˈbiːhʌɪv/ *n.* **1** an artificial habitation for bees. **2** a busy place. **3** anything resembling a wicker beehive in being domed.

bee-keeping *n.* the occupation of keeping bees. □ **bee-keeper** *n.*

beeline /ˈbiːlʌm/ *n.* a straight line between two places. □ **make a beeline for** hurry directly to.

Beelzebub /bɪˈelzɪbʌb/ *n.* the Devil. [Old English via Latin from Greek *beelzeboul* & Hebrew *ba'al zᵉḇûḇ* 'lord of the flies', the name of a Philistine god]

bee-master *n.* a man who keeps bees.

been *past part.* of BE.

bee orchid *n.* a kind of European orchid, *Ophrys apifera*, with bee-shaped flowers.

beep /biːp/ *n.* & *v.* ● *n.* **1** the sound of a motor car horn. **2** any similar short high-pitched sound. ● *v.* **1** *intr.* emit a beep. **2** *tr.* cause to emit a beep. **3** *tr. N. Amer.* summon with a beeper. [imitative]

beeper /ˈbiːpə/ *n.* **1** a device that emits beeps. **2** *N. Amer.* = BLEEPER.

beer /bɪə/ *n.* **1 a** an alcoholic drink made from yeast-fermented malt etc., flavoured with hops. **b** a glass or can of this. **2** any of several other fermented drinks, e.g. ginger beer. □ **beer and skittles** *Brit.* amusement (*life is not all beer and skittles*). [Old English *bēor* via Late Latin *biber* 'drink' from Latin *bibere*]

beer belly *n.* a stomach which protrudes as a result of excessive consumption of beer.

beer cellar *n.* **1** an underground room for storing beer. **2** a basement or cellar for selling or drinking beer.

beer engine *n. Brit.* a machine that draws up beer from a barrel in a cellar.

beer garden *n.* a garden where beer is sold and drunk.

beer gut *n. slang* = BEER BELLY.

beer hall *n.* a large room where beer is sold and drunk.

beerhouse /ˈbɪəhaʊs/ *n. Brit.* a public house licensed to sell beer but not spirits.

beer mat *n. Brit.* a small table mat for a beer glass.

beer pump *n.* = BEER ENGINE.

beery /ˈbɪəri/ *adj.* (**beerier**, **beeriest**) **1** showing the influence of drink in one's appearance or behaviour. **2** smelling or tasting of beer. □ **beerily** *adv.* **beeriness** *n.*

beestings /ˈbiːstɪŋz/ *n.pl.* (also treated as *sing.*) the first milk (esp. of a cow) after giving birth. [Old English *bysting*, from West Germanic]

beeswax /ˈbiːzwaks/ *n.* & *v.* ● *n.* **1** the wax secreted by bees to make honeycombs. **2** this wax refined and used to polish wood. ● *v.tr.* polish (furniture etc.) with beeswax.

beeswing /ˈbiːzwɪŋ/ *n.* a filmy second crust on old port.

beet /biːt/ *n.* any plant of the genus *Beta* with an edible root (see BEETROOT, SUGAR BEET). [Old English *bēte* from Latin *beta*, perhaps of Celtic origin]

beetle[1] /ˈbiːt(ə)l/ *n.* & *v.* ● *n.* **1** any insect of the order Coleoptera, with modified front wings forming hard protective cases closing over the back wings. **2** *colloq.* any similar, usu. black, insect. **3** *Brit.* a dice game in which a beetle is drawn or assembled. ● *v.intr.* (foll. by *about, away, etc.*) *colloq.* hurry, scurry. [Old English *bitula* 'biter' from *bītan* BITE]

beetle[2] /ˈbiːt(ə)l/ *n.* & *v.* ● *n.* **1** a tool with a heavy head and a handle, used for ramming, crushing, driving wedges, etc. **2** a machine used for heightening the lustre of cloth by pressure from rollers. ● *v.tr.* **1** ram, crush, drive, etc., with a beetle. **2** finish (cloth) with a beetle. [Old English *bētel*, from Germanic]

beetle[3] /ˈbiːt(ə)l/ *adj.* & *v.* ● *adj.* (esp. of the eyebrows) projecting, shaggy, scowling. ● *v.intr.* (usu. as **beetling** *adj.*) (of brows, cliffs, etc.) project; overhang threateningly. [Middle English: origin unknown]

beetle-browed *adj.* with shaggy, projecting, or scowling eyebrows. [BEETLE[3]]

beetle-crusher *n. Brit. colloq.* a large boot or foot. [BEETLE[1]]

beetroot /ˈbiːtruːt/ *n. Brit.* **1** a beet, *Beta vulgaris*, with an edible spherical dark red root. **2** this root used as a vegetable.

beet sugar *n.* sugar obtained from sugar beet.

beeves *pl.* of BEEF.

BEF *abbr. hist.* British Expeditionary Force.

befall /bɪˈfɔːl/ *v.* (*past* **befell** /bɪˈfel/; *past part.* **befallen** /bɪˈfɔːlən/) *poet.* **1** *intr.* happen (*so it befell*). **2** *tr.* happen to (a person etc.) (*what has befallen her?*). [Old English *befeallan* (as BE-, *feallan* FALL)]

befit /bɪˈfɪt/ *v.tr.* (**befitted**, **befitting**) **1** be fitted or appropriate for; suit. **2** be incumbent on. □ **befitting** *adj.* **befittingly** *adv.*

befog /bɪˈfɒg/ *v.tr.* (**befogged**, **befogging**) **1** confuse; obscure. **2** envelop in fog.

befool /bɪˈfuːl/ *v.tr.* make a fool of; delude.

before /bɪˈfɔː/ *conj., prep.,* & *adv.* ● *conj.* **1** earlier than the time when (*crawled before he walked*). **2** rather than that (*would starve before he stole*). ● *prep.* **1 a** in front of (*before her in the queue*). **b** ahead of (*crossed the line before him*). **c** under the impulse of (*recoil before the attack*). **d** awaiting (*the future before them*). **2** earlier than; preceding (*Lent comes before Easter*). **3** rather than (*death before dishonour*). **4 a** in the presence of (*appear before the judge*). **b** for the attention of (*a plan put before the committee*). ● *adv.* **1 a** earlier than the time in question; already (*heard it before*). **b** in the past (*happened long before*). **2** ahead (*go before*). **3** on the front (*hit before and behind*). □ **before God** a solemn oath meaning 'as God sees me'. **before time** see TIME. [Old English *beforan*, from Germanic]

before Christ *adv.* (of a date) reckoned backwards from the birth of Christ.

beforehand /bɪˈfɔːhand/ *adv.* in anticipation; in advance; in readiness (*had prepared the meal beforehand*). □ **be beforehand with** anticipate; forestall. [Middle English from BEFORE + HAND: cf. Anglo-French *avant main*]

befoul /bɪˈfaʊl/ *v.tr. poet.* **1** make foul or dirty. **2** degrade; defile (*befouled her name*).

befriend /bɪˈfrend/ *v.tr.* act as a friend to; help.

befuddle /bɪˈfʌd(ə)l/ *v.tr.* **1** make drunk. **2** confuse. □ **befuddlement** *n.*

beg /beg/ *v.* (**begged**, **begging**) **1 a** *intr.* (usu. foll. by *for*) ask for (esp. food, money, etc.) (*begged for alms*). **b** *tr.* ask for (food, money, etc.) as a gift. **c** *intr.* live by begging. **2** *tr.* & *intr.* (usu. foll. by *for*, or *to* + infin.) ask earnestly or humbly (*begged for forgiveness; begged to be allowed out; please, I beg of you; beg your indulgence for a time*). **3** *tr.* ask formally for (*beg leave*). **4** *intr.* (of a dog etc.) sit up with the front paws raised expectantly. **5** *tr.* take or ask leave (to do something) (*I beg to differ; beg to enclose*). □ **beg one's bread** live by begging. **beg off 1** decline to take part or attend. **2** get (a person) excused a penalty etc. **beg pardon** apologize. **beg the question 1** assume the truth of an argument or proposition to be proved, without arguing it. **2** *disp.* pose the question. **3** *colloq.* evade a difficulty. **go begging** (or *Brit.* **a-begging**) (of a chance or a thing) not be taken; be unwanted. [Middle English, probably from Old English *bedecian* from Germanic: related to BID]

■ **Usage** Many people use the phrase *beg the question* in the disputed sense (sense 2 above). It originally meant, and still means, 'to assume the truth of the thing that is to be proved', e.g. *By devoting such a large part of the budget for the fight against drug addiction to education, we are begging the question of its significance in the battle against drugs*, i.e. we are assuming that through education we can radically reduce drug-taking. Over the years *beg the question* has been misunderstood and another meaning has arisen, 'to raise the question', or 'invite the obvious question', and this is now the more common use of the phrase, e.g. *Most people continue to live in cities, which begs the question as to whether city life or country life is more desirable.* This use has been extended even further in phrases such as *The question that still needs to be begged is ....*

begad /bɪ'gad/ *int. archaic colloq.* by God! [corruption: cf. GAD[2]]

began *past* of BEGIN.

begat *archaic past* of BEGET.

beget /bɪ'gɛt/ *v.tr.* (**begetting**; *past* **begot** /bɪ'gɒt/; *archaic* **begat** /bɪ'gat/; *past part.* **begotten** /bɪ'gɒt(ə)n/) *literary* **1** (usu. of a father, sometimes of a father and mother) procreate. **2** give rise to; cause (*beget strife*). □ **begetter** *n.* [Old English *begietan* (as BE- + GET = procreate)]

beggar /'bɛgə/ *n.* & *v.* ● *n.* **1** a person who begs, esp. one who lives by begging. **2** a poor person. **3** *colloq.* a person; a fellow (*poor beggar*). ● *v.tr.* **1** reduce to poverty. **2** outshine. **3** exhaust the resources of (*it beggars description*). □ **beggars cannot** (or **must not**) **be choosers** those without other resources must take what is offered. [Middle English from BEG + -AR[3]]

beggarly /'bɛgəli/ *adj.* **1** poverty-stricken; needy. **2** intellectually poor. **3** mean; sordid. **4** ungenerous. □ **beggarliness** *n.*

beggar-my-neighbour *n.* **1** a card game in which a player seeks to capture an opponent's cards. **2** (*attrib.*) (esp. of national policy) self-aggrandizing at the expense of competitors.

beggary /'bɛgəri/ *n.* extreme poverty.

begging bowl *n.* **1** a bowl etc. held out for food or alms. **2** an earnest appeal for help.

begging letter *n. Brit.* a letter asking for a charitable gift.

begin /bɪ'gɪn/ *v.* (**beginning**; *past* **began** /bɪ'gan/; *past part.* **begun** /bɪ'gʌn/) **1** *tr.* perform the first part of; start (*begin work*; *begin crying*; *begin to understand*). **2** *intr.* come into being; arise: **a** in time (*war began in 1939*). **b** in space (*Wales begins beyond the river*). **3** *tr.* (usu. foll. by *to* + infin.) start at a certain time (*then began to feel ill*). **4** *intr.* be begun (*the meeting will begin at 7*). **5 a** *tr.* & *intr.* start speaking (*'No,' he began*). **b** *intr.* take the first step; be the first to do something (*who wants to begin?*). **6** *intr.* (usu. with *neg.*) *colloq.* show any attempt or likelihood (*can't begin to compete*). □ **begin at** start from. **begin on** (or **upon**) set to work at. **begin school** attend school for the first time. **begin with** take (a subject, task, etc.) first or as a starting point. **to begin with** in the first place; as the first thing. [Old English *beginnan*, from Germanic]

beginner /bɪ'gɪnə/ *n.* a person just beginning to learn a skill etc. □ **beginner's luck** good luck supposed to attend a beginner at games etc.

beginning /bɪ'gɪnɪŋ/ *n.* **1** the time or place at which anything begins. **2** a source or origin. **3** the first part. □ **the beginning of the end** the first clear sign of a final result.

begone /bɪ'gɒn/ *int. poet.* go away at once!

begonia /bɪ'gəʊnɪə/ *n.* a plant of the genus *Begonia*, having flowers with brightly coloured sepals and no petals, and often glossy foliage. [M. *Bégon*, French patron of science, d. 1710]

begorra /bɪ'gɒrə/ *int. Ir.* by God! [corruption]

begot *past* of BEGET.

begotten *past part.* of BEGET.

begrime /bɪ'graɪm/ *v.tr.* make grimy.

begrudge /bɪ'grʌdʒ/ *v.tr.* **1** resent; be dissatisfied at. **2** envy (a person) the possession of. □ **begrudgingly** *adv.*

beguile /bɪ'gaɪl/ *v.tr.* **1** charm; amuse. **2** divert attention pleasantly from (toil etc.). **3** (often foll. by *of*, *out of*, or *into* + verbal noun) delude; cheat (*beguiled him into paying*). □ **beguilement** *n.* **beguiler** *n.* **beguiling** *adj.* **beguilingly** *adv.* [BE- + obsolete *guile* 'to deceive']

beguine /beɪ'gi:n/ *n.* **1** a popular dance of W. Indian origin. **2** its rhythm. [W. Indian French from French *béguin* 'infatuation']

begum /'beɪgəm/ *n.* (in the Indian subcontinent) **1** a Muslim lady of high rank. **2** (**Begum**) the title of a married Muslim woman, equivalent to Mrs. [Urdu *begam* from Eastern Turkish *bīgam* 'princess', fem. of *big* 'prince']

begun *past part.* of BEGIN.

behalf /bɪ'hɑ:f/ *n.* □ **on** (or esp. *US* **in**) **behalf of** (or **on a person's behalf**) **1** in the interests of (a person, principle, etc.). **2** as representative of (*acting on behalf of my client*). [mixture of earlier phrases *on his halve* and *bihalve him*, both = on his side: see BY, HALF]

■ **Usage** *On behalf of* should not be confused with *on the part of*, which means 'proceeding from, done or initiated by'. *Behalf* cannot replace *part* in *His death was largely due to panic on his part*. Note the different senses expressed by *a long struggle on behalf of the strikers* (the struggle being carried out by people other than the strikers), and *a long struggle on the part of the strikers* (the struggle being carried out by the strikers).

behave /bɪ'heɪv/ *v.* **1** *intr.* **a** act or react (in a specified way) (*behaved well*). **b** (esp. to or of a child) conduct oneself properly. **c** (of a machine etc.) work well (or in a specified way) (*the computer is not behaving today*). **2** *refl.* (esp. of or to a child) show good manners (*behaved herself*). □ **behave towards** treat (in a specified way). [BE- + HAVE]

behaviour /bɪ'heɪvjə/ *n.* (*US* **behavior**) **1 a** the way one conducts oneself; manners. **b** the treatment of others; moral conduct. **2** the way in which a ship, machine, chemical substance, etc., acts or works. **3** *Psychol.* the response (of a person, animal, etc.) to a stimulus. □ **be on one's good** (or **best**) **behaviour** behave well when being observed. [BEHAVE on the pattern of *demeanour* and influenced by obsolete *haviour* from *have*]

behavioural /bɪ'heɪvjər(ə)l/ *adj.* (*US* **behavioral**) of or relating to behaviour. □ **behaviouralist** *n.*

behavioural science *n.* the scientific study of human and animal behaviour.

behaviourism /bɪ'heɪvjərɪz(ə)m/ *n.* (*US* **behaviorism**) *Psychol.* **1** the theory that human behaviour is determined by conditioning rather than by thoughts or feelings, and that psychological disorders are best treated by altering behaviour patterns. **2** such study and treatment in practice. □ **behaviourist** *n.* **behaviouristic** /-'rɪstɪk/ *adj.*

behaviour therapy *n.* the treatment of neurotic symptoms by training the patient's reactions to stimuli (see BEHAVIOURISM).

behead /bɪ'hɛd/ *v.tr.* cut off the head of (a person), esp. as a form of execution; kill in this way. [Old English *behēafdian* (as BE-, *hēafod* HEAD)]

beheld *past* and *past part.* of BEHOLD.

behemoth /bɪ'hi:mɒθ, 'bi:hɪməʊθ/ *n.* an enormous creature or thing. [Middle English from Hebrew *b[e]hēmôṯ*, intensive pl. of *b[e]hēmāh* 'beast', perhaps from Egyptian *p-ehe-mau* 'water-ox']

behest /bɪ'hɛst/ *n. literary* a command; an entreaty (*went at his behest*). [Old English *behǣs*, from Germanic]

behind /bɪ'hʌɪnd/ *prep.*, *adv.*, & *n.* ● *prep.* **1 a** in, towards, or to the rear of. **b** on the further side of (*behind the bush*). **c** hidden by (*something behind that remark*). **2 a** in the past in relation to (*trouble is behind me now*). **b** late in relation to (*behind schedule*). **3** inferior to; weaker than (*rather behind the others in his maths*). **4 a** in support of (*she's right behind us*). **b** responsible for; giving rise to (*the man behind the project*; *the reasons behind his resignation*). **5** in the tracks of; following. ● *adv.* **1 a** in or to or towards the rear; further back (*the street behind*; *glance behind*). **b** on the further side (*a high wall with a field behind*). **2** remaining after departure (*leave behind*; *stay behind*). **3** (usu. foll. by *with*) **a** in arrears (*behind with the rent*). **b** late in accomplishing a task etc. (*working too slowly and getting behind*). **4** in a weak position; backward (*behind in Latin*). **5** following (*his dog running behind*). ● *n.* **1** *colloq.* the buttocks. **2** (in Australian Rules) a kick etc. sending the ball over the behind line, scoring one point. □ **behind a person's back** without a person's knowledge. **behind the scenes** see SCENE. **behind time** late. **behind the times** antiquated. **come from behind** win after lagging. **put behind one 1**

refuse to consider. **2** get over (an unhappy experience etc.). [Old English *behindan, bihindan* from *bi* BY + *hindan* 'from behind']

behindhand /bɪˈhʌɪndhand/ *adv. & predic.adj.* **1** (usu. foll. by *with, in*) late (in discharging a duty, paying a debt, etc.). **2** out of date; behind time. [BEHIND + HAND: cf. BEFOREHAND]

behind line *n.* (in Australian Rules) the line between an inner and outer goalpost.

behold /bɪˈhəʊld/ *v.tr.* (*past* and *past part.* **beheld** /bɪˈheld/) (esp. in *imper.*) *literary* see, observe. ▫ **beholder** *n.* [Old English *bihaldan* (as BE-, *haldan* 'hold')]

beholden /bɪˈhəʊld(ə)n/ *predic.adj.* (usu. foll. by *to*) under obligation. [past part. (obsolete except in this use) of BEHOLD, = bound]

behoof /bɪˈhuːf/ *n.* (prec. by *to, for, on*; foll. by *of*) *archaic* benefit; advantage. [Old English *behōf*]

behove /bɪˈhəʊv/ *v.tr.* (*US* **behoove** /-ˈhuːv/) (prec. by *it* as subject; foll. by *to* + infin.) *formal* **1** be incumbent on. **2** (usu. with *neg.*) befit (*ill behoves him to protest*). [Old English *behōfian* from *behōf*: see BEHOOF]

beige /beɪʒ, beɪdʒ/ *n. & adj.* ● *n.* a pale sandy fawn colour. ● *adj.* of this colour. [French: ultimate origin unknown]

being /ˈbiːɪŋ/ *n.* **1** existence. **2** the nature or essence (of a person etc.) (*his whole being revolted*). **3** a human being. **4** anything that exists or is imagined. ▫ **in being** existing.

bejabers /bɪˈdʒeɪbəz/ *int.* (also **bejabbers** /-ˈdʒabəz/) *Ir.* by Jesus! [corruption]

bejewelled /bɪˈdʒuːəld/ *adj.* (*US* **bejeweled**) adorned with jewels.

bel /bɛl/ *n.* a unit used in the comparison of power levels in electrical communication or intensities of sound, corresponding to an intensity ratio of 10 to 1 (cf. DECIBEL). [A. G. *Bell*, inventor of telephone d. 1922]

belabour /bɪˈleɪbə/ *v.tr.* (*US* **belabor**) **1 a** thrash; beat. **b** attack verbally. **2** argue or elaborate (a subject) in excessive detail. [BE- + LABOUR = exert one's strength]

belated /bɪˈleɪtɪd/ *adj.* **1** coming late or too late. **2** overtaken by darkness. ▫ **belatedly** *adv.* **belatedness** *n.* [past part. of obsolete *belate* 'delay' (as BE-, LATE)]

belay /bɪˈleɪ/ *v. & n.* ● *v.* **1** *tr.* fix (a running rope) round a cleat, pin, rock, etc., to secure it. **2** *tr. & intr.* (usu. in *imper.*) *Naut. slang* stop; enough! (esp. *belay there!*). ● *n.* **1** an act of belaying. **2** a spike of rock etc. used for belaying. [Dutch *beleggen*]

■ **Usage** In mountaineering contexts, this word is often stressed on the first syllable /ˈbiːleɪ/.

belaying-pin *n.* a fixed wooden or iron pin used to secure a rope which is fastened around it.

bel canto /bɛl ˈkantəʊ/ *n.* **1** a lyrical style of operatic singing using a full rich broad tone and smooth phrasing. **2** (*attrib.*) (of a type of aria or voice) characterized by this type of singing. [Italian, = fine song]

belch /bɛltʃ/ *v. & n.* ● *v.* **1** *intr.* emit wind noisily from the stomach through the mouth. **2** *tr.* **a** (of a chimney, volcano, gun, etc.) send (smoke etc.) out or up. **b** utter forcibly. ● *n.* an act of belching. [Old English *belcettan*]

beldam /ˈbɛldəm/ *n.* (also **beldame**) *archaic* **1** an old woman; a hag. **2** a virago. [Middle English & Old French *bel* 'beautiful' + DAM², DAME]

beleaguer /bɪˈliːgə/ *v.tr.* **1** besiege. **2** vex; harass. [Dutch *belegeren* 'camp round' (as BE-, *leger* 'a camp')]

belemnite /ˈbɛləmnʌɪt/ *n.* any extinct cephalopod of the order Belemnoidea, having a bullet-shaped internal shell often found in fossilized form. [modern Latin *belemnites* from Greek *belemnon* 'dart' + -ITE¹]

bel esprit /bɛl ɛˈspriː, French bɛl ɛspri/ *n.* (*pl.* ***beaux esprits*** /bəʊz ɛˈspriː, French boz ɛspri/) a witty person. [French, literally 'fine mind']

belfry /ˈbɛlfri/ *n.* (*pl.* **-ies**) **1** a bell tower or steeple housing bells, esp. forming part of a church. **2** a space for hanging bells in a church tower. ▫ **bats in the belfry** see BAT². [Middle English via Old French *berfrei* from Frankish: altered by association with *bell*]

Belgian /ˈbɛldʒ(ə)n/ *n. & adj.* ● *n.* **1** a native or national of Belgium in W. Europe. **2** a person of Belgian descent. ● *adj.* of or relating to Belgium.

Belgian hare *n.* a dark red long-eared breed of domestic rabbit.

Belgic /ˈbɛldʒɪk/ *adj.* **1** of the ancient Belgae of N. Gaul. **2** of the Low Countries. [Latin *Belgicus* from *Belgae*]

Belial /ˈbiːlɪəl/ *n.* the Devil. [Hebrew *bᵉliyya'al* 'worthless']

belie /bɪˈlʌɪ/ *v.tr.* (**belying**) **1** give a false notion of; fail to corroborate (*its appearance belies its age*). **2 a** fail to fulfil (a promise etc.). **b** fail to justify (a hope etc.). [Old English *belēogan* (as BE-, *lēogan* LIE²)]

belief /bɪˈliːf/ *n.* **1 a** a person's religion; religious conviction (*has no belief*). **b** a firm opinion (*my belief is that he did it*). **c** an acceptance (of a thing, fact, statement, etc.) (*belief in the afterlife*). **2** (usu. foll. by *in*) trust or confidence. ▫ **beyond belief** incredible. **to the best of my belief** in my genuine opinion. [Middle English from Old English *gelēafa* (as BELIEVE)]

believe /bɪˈliːv/ *v.* **1** *tr.* accept as true or as conveying the truth (*I believe it*; *don't believe him*; *believes what he is told*). **2** *tr.* think, suppose (*I believe it's raining*; *Mr Smith, I believe?*). **3** *intr.* (foll. by *in*) **a** have faith in the existence of (*believes in God*). **b** have confidence in (a remedy, a person, etc.) (*believes in alternative medicine*). **c** have trust in the advisability of (*believes in telling the truth*). **4** *intr.* have (esp. religious) faith. ▫ **believe one's ears** (or **eyes**) accept that what one apparently hears or sees etc. is true. **believe it or not** *colloq.* it is true though surprising. **would you believe it?** *colloq.* = *believe it or not.* ▫ **believable** *adj.* **believability** /-ˌliːvəˈbɪlɪti/ *n.* [Old English *belȳfan, belēfan*, with change of prefix from *gelēfan*, from Germanic: related to LIEF]

believer /bɪˈliːvə/ *n.* **1** an adherent of a specified religion. **2** a person who believes, esp. in the efficacy of something (*a great believer in exercise*).

Belisha beacon /bɪˈliːʃə/ *n. Brit.* a flashing orange ball surmounted on a striped post, marking some pedestrian crossings. [L. Hore-*Belisha* (d. 1957), Minister of Transport 1934]

belittle /bɪˈlɪt(ə)l/ *v.tr.* **1** make seem unimportant; depreciate; disparage. **2** make small; diminish in size. ▫ **belittlement** *n.* **belittler** *n.* **belittlingly** *adv.*

bell¹ /bɛl/ *n. & v.* ● *n.* **1** a hollow usu. metal object in the shape of a deep inverted cup usu. widening at the lip, made to sound a clear musical note when struck (either externally or by means of a clapper inside). **2 a** a sound or stroke of a bell, esp. as a signal. **b** (prec. by a numeral) *Naut.* the time as indicated every half-hour of a watch by the striking of the ship's bell one to eight times. **3** anything that sounds like or functions as a bell, esp. an electronic device that rings etc. as a signal. **4 a** a bell-shaped object or part, e.g. of a musical instrument. **b** the corolla of a flower when bell-shaped. **5** (in *pl.*) *Mus.* a set of cylindrical metal tubes of different lengths, suspended in a frame and played by being struck with a hammer. ● *v.tr.* **1** provide with a bell or bells; attach a bell to. **2** (foll. by *out*) form into the shape of the lip of a bell. ▫ **clear** (or **sound**) **as a bell** perfectly clear or sound. **give a person a bell** *Brit. colloq.* telephone a person. **ring a bell** *colloq.* revive a distant recollection; sound familiar. [Old English *belle*: perhaps related to BELL²]

bell² /bɛl/ *n. & v.* ● *n.* the cry of a stag or buck at rutting time. ● *v.intr.* make this cry. [Old English *bellan* 'bark, bellow']

belladonna /bɛləˈdɒnə/ *n.* **1** deadly nightshade. **2** *Med.* a drug prepared from this. [modern Latin from Italian *bella donna* 'fair lady', perhaps from the use of its juice to make the eyes brilliant by dilating the pupils]

belladonna lily *n.* = AMARYLLIS 1.

bellbird /ˈbɛlbəːd/ *n.* any of various birds with a bell-like song, esp. any Central or S. American bird of the genus *Procnias,* or a New Zealand honeyeater, *Anthornis melanura.*

bell-bottom *n.* **1** a marked flare below the knee (of a trouser leg). **2** (in *pl.*) trousers with bell-bottoms. □ **bell-bottomed** *adj.*

bellboy /ˈbɛlbɔɪ/ *n.* esp. *N. Amer.* a page in a hotel or club.

bell-buoy *n.* a buoy equipped with a warning bell rung by the motion of the sea.

belle /bɛl/ *n.* **1** a beautiful woman. **2** a woman recognized as the most beautiful (*the belle of the ball*). [French from Latin *bella,* fem. of *bellus* 'beautiful']

belle époque /bɛl eɪˈpɒk, French bɛl epɔk/ *n.* the period of settled and comfortable life preceding the First World War. [French, = fine period]

belle laide /bɛl ˈleɪd, French bɛl lɛd/ *n.* (*pl.* ***belles laides*** *pronunc.* same) a fascinatingly ugly woman. [French from *belle* 'beautiful' + *laide* 'ugly']

belles-lettres /bɛlˈlɛtrə/ *n.pl.* (also treated as *sing.*) writings or studies of a literary nature, esp. essays and criticisms. □ **belletrism** /bɛlˈlɛtrɪz(ə)m/ *n.* **belletrist** /bɛlˈlɛtrɪst/ *n.* **belletristic** /bɛləˈtrɪstɪk/ *adj.* [French, = fine letters]

bellflower /ˈbɛlflaʊə/ *n.* = CAMPANULA.

bell-founder *n.* a person who casts large bells in a foundry.

bell-glass *n.* a bell-shaped glass cover for plants.

bellicose /ˈbɛlɪkəʊs/ *adj.* eager to fight; warlike. □ **bellicosity** /-ˈkɒsɪti/ *n.* [Middle English from Latin *bellicosus,* from *bellum* 'war']

belligerence /bɪˈlɪdʒ(ə)r(ə)ns/ *n.* (also **belligerency** /-r(ə)nsi/) **1** aggressive or warlike behaviour. **2** the status of a belligerent.

belligerent /bɪˈlɪdʒ(ə)r(ə)nt/ *adj. & n.* ● *adj.* **1** engaged in war or conflict. **2** given to constant fighting; pugnacious. ● *n.* a nation or person engaged in war or conflict. □ **belligerently** *adv.* [Latin *belligerare* 'wage war', from *bellum* 'war' + *gerere* 'wage']

bell jar *n.* a bell-shaped glass cover or container for use in a laboratory.

bellman /ˈbɛlmən/ *n.* (*pl.* **-men**) *hist.* a town crier.

bell metal *n.* an alloy of copper and tin for making bells (the tin content being greater than in bronze).

bellow /ˈbɛləʊ/ *v. & n.* ● *v.* **1** *intr.* **a** emit a deep loud roar. **b** cry or shout with pain. **2** *tr.* utter loudly and usu. angrily. ● *n.* a bellowing sound. [Middle English: perhaps related to BELL²]

bellows /ˈbɛləʊz/ *n.pl.* (also treated as *sing.*) **1** a device with an air bag that emits a stream of air when squeezed, esp.: **a** (in full **pair of bellows**) a kind with two handles used for blowing air on to a fire. **b** a kind used in a harmonium or small organ. **2** an expandable component, e.g. joining the lens to the body of a camera. [Middle English, probably from Old English *belga,* pl. of *belig* 'BELLY']

bell pull *n.* a cord or handle which rings a bell when pulled.

bell push *n. Brit.* a button that operates an electric bell when pushed.

bell-ringer *n.* a person who rings church bells or handbells. □ **bell-ringing** *n.*

bells and whistles *n.pl.* esp. *Computing* attractive additional features or trimmings; gimmicks. [an allusion to the old fairground organs with their multiplicity of bells and whistles]

Bell's palsy /bɛlz/ *n.* paralysis of the facial nerve causing muscular weakness in one side of the face. [Sir Charles *Bell,* Scottish anatomist d. 1842]

bell tent *n.* a cone-shaped tent supported by a central pole.

bell-wether *n.* **1** the leading sheep of a flock, with a bell on its neck. **2** a ringleader.

belly /ˈbɛli/ *n. & v.* ● *n.* (*pl.* **-ies**) **1** the part of the human body below the chest, containing the stomach and bowels. **2** the stomach, esp. representing the body's need for food. **3** the front of the body from the waist to the groin. **4** the underside of a four-legged animal. **5** **a** a cavity or bulging part of anything. **b** the surface of an instrument of the violin family, across which the strings are placed. ● *v.tr. & intr.* (**-ies**, **-ied**) (often foll. by *out*) swell or cause to swell; bulge. □ **go belly up** esp. *N. Amer. colloq.* go bankrupt; die. [Old English *belig* (originally = bag), from Germanic]

bellyache /ˈbɛlɪeɪk/ *n. & v.* ● *n. colloq.* a stomach pain. ● *v.intr. slang* complain noisily or persistently. □ **bellyacher** *n.*

bellyband /ˈbɛlɪband/ *n.* a band placed round a horse's belly, holding the shafts of a cart etc.

belly button *n. colloq.* the navel.

belly dance *n.* an oriental dance performed by a woman, involving voluptuous movements of the belly. □ **belly dancer** *n.* **belly dancing** *n.*

bellyflop /ˈbɛlɪflɒp/ *n. & v. colloq.* ● *n.* a dive into water in which the body lands with the belly flat on the water. ● *v.intr.* (**-flopped**, **-flopping**) perform such a dive.

bellyful /ˈbɛlɪfʊl, -f(ə)l/ *n.* (*pl.* **-fuls**) **1** enough to eat. **2** *colloq.* enough or more than enough of anything (esp. unwelcome).

belly landing *n.* a crash landing of an aircraft on the underside of the fuselage, without lowering the undercarriage.

belly laugh *n.* a loud unrestrained laugh.

belong /bɪˈlɒŋ/ *v.intr.* **1** (foll. by *to*) **a** be the property of. **b** be rightly assigned to as a duty, right, part, member, characteristic, etc. **c** be a member of (a club, family, group, etc.). **2** have the right personal or social qualities to be a member of a particular group (*he's nice but just doesn't belong*). **3** (foll. by *in, under*): **a** be rightly placed or classified. **b** fit a particular environment. □ **belongingness** *n.* [Middle English from intensive BE- + *longen* 'belong' related to Old English *gelang* 'at hand, together with']

belongings /bɪˈlɒŋɪŋz/ *n.pl.* one's movable possessions or luggage.

Belorussian /bɛləʊˈrʌʃ(ə)n/ *n. & adj.* (also **Byelorussian** /bjɛləʊ-/) ● *n.* **1** a native of Belarus in eastern Europe. **2** the East Slavonic language of Belarus. ● *adj.* of or relating to Belarus, its people, or its language. [Russian *Belorussiya* from *belyĭ* 'white' + *Russiya* 'Russia']

beloved /bɪˈlʌvɪd, -ˈlʌvd/ *adj. & n.* ● *adj.* much loved. ● *n.* a much loved person. [obsolete *belove,* from intensive BE- + LOVE *v.*]

below /bɪˈləʊ/ *prep. & adv.* ● *prep.* **1** lower in position (vertically, down a slope or stream, etc.) than. **2** beneath the surface of; at or to a greater depth than (*head below water; below 500 feet*). **3** lower or less than in amount or degree (*below freezing point*). **4** lower in rank, position, or importance than. **5** unworthy of. ● *adv.* **1** at or to a lower point or level. **2** **a** downstairs (*lives below*). **b** downstream. **3** (of a text reference) further forward on a page or in a book (*as noted below*). **4** on the lower side (*looks similar above and below*). **5** *literary* on earth; in hell. □ **below stairs** *Brit.* in the basement of a house esp. as the part occupied by servants. [BE- + LOW¹]

Bel Paese /bɛl pɑːˈeɪzi/ *n. propr.* a rich white mild creamy cheese of a kind originally made in Italy. [Italian, = fair country]

belt /bɛlt/ *n. & v.* ● *n.* **1** a strip of leather or other material worn round the waist or across the chest, esp. to retain or support clothes or to carry weapons or as a safety belt. **2** a belt worn as a sign of rank or achievement. **3** **a** a circular band of material used as a driving medium in machinery. **b** a conveyor belt. **c** a flexible strip carrying machine-gun cartridges. **4** a strip of colour or texture etc. differing from that on each side. **5** a distinct region or extent (*cotton belt; commuter belt; a belt of rain*). **6** *slang* a heavy blow. ● *v.* **1** *tr.* put a belt round. **2** *tr.* (often foll. by *on*) fasten with a belt. **3**

tr. **a** beat with a belt. **b** *slang* hit hard. **4** *intr. slang* rush, hurry (usu. with compl.: *belted along*; *belted home*). □ **below the belt** unfair or unfairly; disregarding the rules. **belt and braces** *Brit.* (of a policy etc.) of twofold security. **belt out** *slang* sing or utter loudly and forcibly. **belt up 1** *slang* be quiet. **2** *colloq.* put on a seat belt. **tighten one's belt** live more frugally. **under one's belt 1** (of food) eaten. **2** securely acquired (*has a degree under her belt*). □ **belter** *n.* (esp. in sense of *belt out*). [Old English via Germanic from Latin *balteus*]

Beltane /ˈbɛlteɪn/ *n.* an ancient Celtic festival celebrated on May Day. [Gaelic *bealltainn*]

belt drive *n.* a driving mechanism powered by a continuous flexible belt.

belted galloway see GALLOWAY 1.

beltman /ˈbɛltman/ *n.* (*pl.* **-men**) *Austral.* a member of a life-saving team of surfers.

beltway /ˈbɛltweɪ/ *n. US* **1** a ring road. **2** (usu. **Beltway**) (often *attrib.*) Washington, DC, esp. as representing the perceived insularity of the US government.

beluga /bɪˈluːgə/ *n.* **1 a** a large kind of sturgeon, *Huso huso*. **b** caviar obtained from it. **2** a white whale. [Russian *beluga* from *belyĭ* 'white']

belvedere /ˈbɛlvɪdɪə/ *n.* a summer house or open-sided gallery usu. at rooftop level. [Italian from *bel* 'beautiful' + *vedere* 'see']

belying *pres. part.* of BELIE.

BEM *abbr.* British Empire Medal.

bemire /bɪˈmʌɪə/ *v.tr.* **1** cover or stain with mud. **2** (in *passive*) be stuck in mud. [BE- + MIRE]

bemoan /bɪˈməʊn/ *v.tr.* **1** express regret or sorrow over; lament. **2** complain about. [BE- + MOAN]

bemuse /bɪˈmjuːz/ *v.tr.* stupefy or bewilder (a person). □ **bemusedly** /-zɪdli/ *adv.* **bemusement** *n.* [BE- + MUSE[2]]

ben[1] /bɛn/ *n. Sc.* a high mountain or mountain peak, esp. in names (*Ben Nevis*). [Gaelic *beann*]

ben[2] /bɛn/ *n. Sc.* an inner room, esp. of a two-roomed cottage. [elliptical use of *ben* (*adv.*), = within (Old English *binnan*)]

bench /bɛn(t)ʃ/ *n.* & *v.* ● *n.* **1** a long seat of wood or stone for seating several people. **2** a working-table, e.g. for a carpenter, mechanic, or scientist. **3** (prec. by *the*) **a** the office of judge or magistrate. **b** a judge's seat in a law court. **c** a law court. **d** judges and magistrates collectively. **4** (often in *pl.*) *Sport* an area to the side of a pitch, with seating where coaches and players not taking part can watch the game. **5** *Brit. Parl.* a seat appropriated as specified (*front bench*). **6** a level ledge in masonry or an earthwork, on a hill-slope, etc. ● *v.tr.* **1** exhibit (a dog) at a show. **2** *N. Amer. Sport* withdraw (a player) from the pitch to the benches. □ **on the bench 1** appointed a judge or magistrate. **2** *Sport* acting as substitute or reserve. [Old English *benc* from Germanic: related to BANK[1]]

bencher /ˈbɛn(t)ʃə/ *n.* **1** *Brit. Law* a senior member of any of the Inns of Court. **2** (in *comb.*) *Parl.* an occupant of a specified bench (*backbencher*).

benchmark /ˈbɛn(t)ʃmɑːk/ *n.* & *v.* ● *n.* **1** a surveyor's mark cut in a wall, pillar, building, etc., used as a reference point in measuring altitudes. **2 a** a standard or point of reference. **b** a problem designed to evaluate the performance of a computer system. ● *v.tr.* evaluate or check by comparison with a benchmark.

benchmark test *n.* a test using a benchmark.

bench test *n.* & *v.* esp. *Computing* ● *n.* a test carried out on a machine, component, etc. before it is released for use. ● *v.tr.* run a bench test on.

bend[1] /bɛnd/ *v.* & *n.* ● *v.* (*past* **bent**; *past part.* **bent** except in *bended knee*) **1 a** *tr.* force or adapt (something straight) into a curve or angle. **b** *intr.* (of an object) be altered in this way. **2** *intr.* move or stretch in a curved course (*the road bends to the left*). **3** *intr.* & *tr.* (often foll. by *down*, *over*, etc.) incline or cause to incline from the vertical (*bent down to pick it up*). **4** *tr.* interpret or modify (a rule) to suit oneself. **5** *tr.* & *refl.* (foll. by *to*, *on*) direct or devote (oneself or one's attention, energies, etc.). **6** *tr.* turn (one's steps or eyes) in a new direction. **7** *tr.* (in *passive*; foll. by *on*) have firmly decided; be determined (*was bent on selling*; *on pleasure bent*). **8 a** *intr.* stoop or submit (*bent before his master*). **b** *tr.* force to submit. **9** *tr. Naut.* attach (a sail or cable) with a knot. ● *n.* **1** a curve in a road or other course. **2** a departure from a straight course. **3** a bent part of anything. **4** (**the bends**) *colloq.* decompression sickness, esp. in divers. □ **bend over backwards** see BACKWARDS. **round** (or *US* **around**) **the bend** *colloq.* crazy, insane. □ **bendable** *adj.* [Old English *bendan*, from Germanic]

bend[2] /bɛnd/ *n.* **1** *Naut.* any of various knots for tying ropes (*fisherman's bend*). **2** *Heraldry* **a** a diagonal stripe from top right to bottom left of a shield. **b** (**bend sinister**) a diagonal stripe from top left to bottom right, as a sign of bastardy. [Old English *bend* 'band, bond', from Germanic]

bender /ˈbɛndə/ *n. slang* **1** a wild drinking spree. **2** *offens.* a homosexual. [BEND[1] + -ER[1]]

bendy /ˈbɛndi/ *adj.* (**bendier**, **bendiest**) *colloq.* capable of bending; soft and flexible. □ **bendiness** *n.*

beneath /bɪˈniːθ/ *prep.* & *adv.* ● *prep.* **1** not worthy of; too demeaning for (*it was beneath him to reply*). **2** below, under. ● *adv.* below, under, underneath. □ **beneath contempt** see CONTEMPT. [Old English *binithan*, *bineothan*, from *bi* BY + *nithan* etc. 'below', from Germanic]

benedicite /bɛnɪˈdʌɪsɪti/ *n.* a blessing, esp. a grace said at table in religious communities. [Middle English from Latin, = bless ye: see BENEDICTION]

Benedictine *n.* & *adj.* ● *n.* /bɛnɪˈdɪktɪn/ **1** a monk or nun of an order following the rule of St Benedict established *c.*540. **2** /bɛnɪˈdɪktiːn/ *propr.* a liqueur based on brandy, originally made by Benedictines in France. ● *adj.* /bɛnɪˈdɪktɪn/ of St Benedict or the Benedictines. [French *bénédictine* or modern Latin *benedictinus*, from *Benedictus* Benedict]

benediction /bɛnɪˈdɪkʃ(ə)n/ *n.* **1** the utterance of a blessing, esp. at the end of a religious service or as a special Roman Catholic service. **2** the state of being blessed. [Middle English via Old French from Latin *benedictio -onis*, from *benedicere -dict-* 'bless']

benedictory /bɛnɪˈdɪkt(ə)ri/ *adj.* of or expressing benediction. [Latin *benedictorius* (as BENEDICTION)]

Benedictus /bɛnɪˈdɪktəs/ *n.* **1** the section of the Roman Catholic Mass beginning *Benedictus qui venit in nomine Domini* (Blessed is he who comes in the name of the Lord). **2** a canticle beginning *Benedictus Dominus Deus* (Blessed be the Lord God) from Luke 1:68–79. [Latin, = blessed: see BENEDICTION]

benefaction /bɛnɪˈfakʃ(ə)n/ *n.* **1** a donation or gift. **2** an act of giving or doing good. [Late Latin *benefactio* (as BENEFIT)]

benefactor /ˈbɛnɪfaktə/ *n.* (*fem.* **benefactress** /-trɪs/) a person who gives support (esp. financial) to a person or cause. [Middle English from Late Latin (as BENEFIT)]

benefice /ˈbɛnɪfɪs/ *n.* **1** a living from a Church office. **2** the property attached to a Church office, esp. that bestowed on a rector or vicar. □ **beneficed** *adj.* [Middle English via Old French from Latin *beneficium* 'favour', from *bene* 'well' + *facere* 'do']

beneficent /bɪˈnɛfɪs(ə)nt/ *adj.* doing good; generous, actively kind. □ **beneficence** *n.* **beneficently** *adv.* [Latin *beneficent-* (as BENEFICE)]

beneficial /bɛnɪˈfɪʃ(ə)l/ *adj.* **1** advantageous; having benefits. **2** improving the health. **3** *Law* relating to the use or benefit of property; having rights to this use or benefit. □ **beneficially** *adv.* [Middle English from French *bénéficial* or Late Latin *beneficialis* (as BENEFICE)]

beneficiary /bɛnɪˈfɪʃ(ə)ri/ *n.* (*pl.* **-ies**) **1** a person who receives benefits, esp. under a trust, will, or life insurance policy. **2** a holder of a Church living. [Latin *beneficiarius* (as BENEFICE)]

benefit /ˈbɛnɪfɪt/ *n. & v.* ● *n.* **1** a favourable or helpful factor or circumstance; advantage, profit. **2** (often in *pl.*) payment made under insurance, social security, welfare, etc. (*sickness benefit*). **3** a public performance or game of which the proceeds go to a particular player or company or charitable cause. ● *v.* (**benefited**, **benefiting**; *US* **benefitted**, **benefitting**) **1** *tr.* do good to; bring advantage to. **2** *intr.* (often foll. by *from*, *by*) receive an advantage or gain. □ **benefit of clergy 1** *hist.* exemption of the English tonsured clergy and nuns from the jurisdiction of the ordinary civil courts. **2** ecclesiastical sanction or approval (*marriage without benefit of clergy*). **the benefit of the doubt** a concession that a person is innocent, correct, etc., although doubt exists. [Middle English via Anglo-French *benfet*, Old French *bienfet* from Latin *benefactum*, from *bene facere* 'do well']

benefit society *n.* = FRIENDLY SOCIETY.

Benelux /ˈbɛnɪlʌks/ *n.* Belgium, the Netherlands, and Luxembourg in association as a regional economic group. [*Be*lgium + *Ne*therlands + *Lux*embourg]

benevolent /bɪˈnɛv(ə)l(ə)nt/ *adj.* **1** wishing to do good; actively friendly and helpful. **2** charitable (*benevolent fund*; *benevolent society*). □ **benevolence** *n.* **benevolently** *adv.* [Middle English via Old French *benivolent* from Latin *bene volens -entis* 'well wishing' from *bene* 'well' + *velle* 'wish']

B.Eng. *abbr.* Bachelor of Engineering.

Bengali /bɛŋˈgɔːli/ *n. & adj.* ● *n.* (*pl.* **Bengalis**) **1** a native of Bengal, a former Indian province now consisting of Bangladesh and the Indian state of W. Bengal. **2** the language of the Bengalis. ● *adj.* of or relating to Bengal or its people or language.

Bengal light /bɛŋˈgɔːl/ *n.* a kind of firework giving off a blue flame, used for signals.

benighted /bɪˈnʌɪtɪd/ *adj.* **1** intellectually or morally ignorant. **2** overtaken by darkness. □ **benightedness** *n.* [obsolete *benight* (*v.*) from BE- + NIGHT]

benign /bɪˈnʌɪn/ *adj.* **1** gentle, mild, kindly. **2** fortunate, salutary. **3** (of the climate, soil, etc.) mild, favourable. **4** *Med.* (of a disease, tumour, etc.) not malignant. □ **benignly** *adv.* [Middle English via Old French *benigne* from Latin *benignus*, from *bene* 'well' + *-genus* 'born']

benignant /bɪˈnɪgnənt/ *adj.* **1** kindly, esp. to inferiors. **2** salutary, beneficial. **3** *Med.* = BENIGN 4. □ **benignancy** *n.* **benignantly** *adv.* [BENIGN, or Latin *benignus*, on the pattern of *malignant*]

benignity /bɪˈnɪgnɪti/ *n.* (*pl.* **-ies**) **1** kindliness. **2** an act of kindness. [Middle English from Old French *benignité* or Latin *benignitas* (as BENIGN)]

benign neglect *n.* non-interference or neglect, intended to benefit the subject more than continual attention.

benison /ˈbɛnɪz(ə)n, -s-/ *n. archaic* a blessing. [Middle English via Old French *beneiçun* from Latin *benedictio -onis* BENEDICTION]

bent[1] /bɛnt/ *past* and *past part.* of BEND[1] *v.* ● *adj.* **1** curved or having an angle. **2** esp. *Brit. slang* dishonest, illicit. **3** *Brit. slang offens.* sexually deviant; homosexual. **4** (foll. by *on*) determined to do or have. ● *n.* **1** an inclination or bias. **2** (foll. by *for*) a talent for something specified (*a bent for mimicry*).

bent[2] /bɛnt/ *n.* **1 a** any stiff grass of the genus *Agrostis*. **b** any of various grasslike reeds, rushes, or sedges. **2** a stiff stalk of a grass usu. with a flexible base. **3** *Brit. archaic* or *dial.* a heath or unenclosed pasture. [Middle English representing Old English *beonet-* (in place names), from Germanic]

Benthamism /ˈbɛntəmɪz(ə)m, ˈbɛnθ-/ *n.* the utilitarian philosophy of Jeremy Bentham, English philosopher d. 1832. □ **Benthamite** *n. & adj.*

benthos /ˈbɛnθɒs/ *n.* the flora and fauna found at the bottom of a sea or lake. □ **benthic** *adj.* [Greek, = depth of the sea]

bentonite /ˈbɛntənʌɪt/ *n.* a kind of absorbent clay used esp. as a filler. [Fort *Benton* in Montana, US, where it is found]

ben trovato /bɛn trə(ʊ)ˈvɑːtəʊ, Italian ben troˈvɑːto/ *adj.* **1** well invented. **2** characteristic if not true. [Italian, = well found]

bentwood /ˈbɛntwʊd/ *n.* wood that is artificially shaped for use in making furniture.

benumb /bɪˈnʌm/ *v.tr.* **1** make numb; deaden. **2** paralyse (the mind or feelings). [originally = deprived, as past part. of Middle English *benimen* from Old English *beniman* (as BE-, *niman* 'take')]

Benzedrine /ˈbɛnzɪdriːn/ *n. propr.* amphetamine. [BENZOIC + EPHEDRINE]

benzene /ˈbɛnziːn/ *n.* a colourless carcinogenic volatile liquid found in coal tar, petroleum, etc., and used as a solvent and in the manufacture of plastics etc. Chem. formula: C_6H_6. □ **benzenoid** *adj.* [BENZOIC + -ENE]

benzene ring *n.* the hexagonal unsaturated ring of six carbon atoms in the benzene molecule.

benzine /ˈbɛnziːn/ *n.* (also **benzin** /-zɪn/) a mixture of liquid hydrocarbons obtained from petroleum. [BENZOIN + -INE[4]]

benzodiazepine /ˌbɛnzəʊdʌɪˈeɪzɪpiːn, -ˈazəpiːn/ *n. Pharm.* any class of heterocyclic organic compounds used as tranquillizers, including Librium and Valium. [chemical name formed as *benzo-* (from BENZENE) + DI-[1] + AZO- + EPI- + -INE[4]]

benzoic /bɛnˈzəʊɪk/ *adj.* containing or derived from benzoin or benzoic acid. [BENZOIN + -IC]

benzoic acid *n.* a white crystalline substance used as a food preservative. Chem. formula: $C_7H_6O_2$.

benzoin /ˈbɛnzəʊɪn/ *n.* **1** a fragrant gum resin obtained from various E. Asian trees of the genus *Styrax*, and used in the manufacture of perfumes and incense; also called *gum benjamin*. **2** *Chem.* a white crystalline aromatic ketone present in this. [earlier *benjoin*, ultimately from Arabic *lubān jāwī* 'incense of Java']

benzol /ˈbɛnzɒl/ *n.* (also **benzole** /-zəʊl/) benzene, esp. unrefined and used as a fuel.

benzoquinone /bɛnzəʊˈkwɪnəʊn/ *n. Chem.* a yellow crystalline compound related to benzene but having the hydrogen atoms on a pair of opposite carbon atoms replaced by oxygen. Chem. formula: $C_6H_4O_2$.

benzoyl /ˈbɛnzəʊɪl/ *n.* (usu. *attrib.*) *Chem.* the radical C_6H_5CO–.

benzyl /ˈbɛnzʌɪl, -zɪl/ *n.* (usu. *attrib.*) *Chem.* the radical $C_6H_5CH_2$–.

bequeath /bɪˈkwiːð/ *v.tr.* **1** leave (a personal estate) to a person by a will. **2** hand down to posterity. □ **bequeathal** *n.* **bequeather** *n.* [Old English *becwethan* (as BE-, *cwethan* 'say': cf. QUOTH)]

bequest /bɪˈkwɛst/ *n.* **1** the act or an instance of bequeathing. **2** a thing bequeathed. [Middle English, from BE- + obsolete *quiste* from Old English *-cwiss*, *cwide* 'saying, testament']

berate /bɪˈreɪt/ *v.tr.* scold, rebuke. [BE- + RATE[2]]

Berber /ˈbəːbə/ *n. & adj.* ● *n.* **1** a member of the indigenous mainly Muslim Caucasian peoples of N. Africa. **2** the language of these peoples. ● *adj.* of the Berbers or their language. [Arabic *barbar*]

berberis /ˈbəːbərɪs/ *n.* = BARBERRY. [medieval Latin & Old French, of unknown origin]

berceuse /bɛːˈsəːz, French bersøz/ *n.* (*pl.* ***berceuses*** *pronunc.* same) **1** a lullaby. **2** an instrumental piece in the style of a lullaby. [French, from *bercer* 'to rock']

bereave /bɪˈriːv/ *v.tr.* (foll. by *of*) deprive of a relation, friend, etc., esp. by death. □ **bereaved** *adj.* **bereavement** *n.* [Old English *berēafian* (as BE-, REAVE)]

bereft /bɪˈrɛft/ *adj.* (foll. by *of*) deprived (esp. of a non-material asset) (*bereft of hope*). [past part. of BEREAVE]

beret /ˈbɛreɪ, -ri/ *n.* a round flattish cap of felt or cloth. [French *béret* 'Basque cap' from Provençal *berret*]

berg[1] /bəːg/ *n.* = ICEBERG. [abbreviation]

berg[2] /bəːg/ *n. S.Afr.* a mountain or hill. [Afrikaans from Dutch]

bergamot[1] /'bɜ:gəmɒt/ *n.* **1** an aromatic herb, esp. *Mentha citrata*. **2** an oily perfume extracted from the rind of the fruit of the citrus tree *Citrus bergamia*, a dwarf variety of the Seville orange tree. **3** the tree itself. [*Bergamo* in N. Italy]

bergamot[2] /'bɜ:gəmɒt/ *n.* a variety of fine pear. [French *bergamotte* via Italian *bergamotta* from Turkish *begarmudu* 'prince's pear', from *beg* 'prince' + *armud* 'pear' + *-u* possessive suffix]

bergschrund /'bɜ:gʃrʊnd/ *n.* a crevasse or gap at the head of a glacier or névé. [German]

berg wind *n. S. Afr.* a hot dry northerly wind blowing from the interior to coastal districts.

beribboned /bɪ'rɪb(ə)nd/ *adj.* decorated with ribbons.

beriberi /bɛrɪ'bɛri/ *n.* a disease causing inflammation of the nerves and heart failure, due to a deficiency of vitamin B_1. [Sinhalese, from *beri* 'weakness']

berk /bɜ:k/ *n.* (also **burk**) *Brit. slang* a fool; a stupid person. [abbreviation of *Berkeley* or *Berkshire Hunt*, rhyming slang for *cunt*]

■ **Usage** Despite its etymology, this word is not usually considered to be obscene.

berkelium /bɜ:'ki:lɪəm, 'bɜ:klɪəm/ *n. Chem.* a transuranic radioactive metallic element produced by bombardment of americium (symbol **Bk**). [modern Latin from *Berkeley* in California (where it was first made) + -IUM]

Berks. /bɑ:ks/ *abbr.* Berkshire.

Berliner /bɜ:'lɪnə/ *n.* **1** a native or citizen of Berlin in Germany. **2** a lightly fried yeast bun with jam filling and vanilla icing. [German]

berm /bɜ:m/ *n.* **1** a narrow path or grass strip beside a road, canal, etc. **2** a narrow ledge, esp. in a fortification between a ditch and the base of a parapet. **3** an artificial ridge or embankment. [French *berme* from Dutch *berm*]

Bermuda shorts /bə'mju:də/ *n.pl.* (also **Bermudas**) close-fitting shorts reaching the knees. [*Bermuda* in the W. Atlantic]

Bermuda triangle /bə'mju:də/ *n.* an area of the western Atlantic where ships and aircraft are reported to have disappeared without trace.

berry /'bɛri/ *n. & v.* ● *n.* (*pl.* **-ies**) **1** any small roundish juicy fruit without a stone. **2** *Bot.* a fruit with its seeds enclosed in a pulp (e.g. a banana, tomato, etc.). **3** any of various kernels or seeds (e.g. coffee bean etc.). **4** a fish egg or roe of a lobster etc. ● *v.intr.* (**-ies, -ied**) **1** (usu. as **berrying** *n.*) go gathering berries. **2** form a berry; bear berries. □ **berried** *adj.* (also in *comb.*). [Old English *berie*, from Germanic]

berserk /bə'sɜ:k, -z-/ *adj. & n.* ● *adj.* (esp. in **go berserk**) wild, frenzied; in a violent rage. ● *n.* (also **berserker** /-kə/) an ancient Norse warrior who fought with a wild frenzy. [Icelandic *berserkr* (*n.*) probably from *bern-* BEAR[2] + *serkr* 'coat']

berth /bɜ:θ/ *n. & v.* ● *n.* **1** a fixed bunk on a ship, train, etc., for sleeping in. **2** a ship's place at a wharf. **3** room for a ship to swing at anchor. **4** adequate sea room. **5** *colloq.* a situation or appointment. **6** the proper place for anything. ● *v.* **1** *tr.* moor (a ship) in its berth. **2** *tr.* provide a sleeping place for. **3** *intr.* (of a ship) come to its mooring place. □ **give a wide berth to** stay away from. [probably from nautical use of BEAR[1] + -TH[2]]

bertha /'bɜ:θə/ *n.* **1** a deep falling collar often of lace. **2** a small cape on a dress. [French *berthe* from *Berthe* 'Bertha' (the name)]

beryl /'bɛrɪl/ *n.* **1** a kind of transparent precious stone, esp. pale green, blue, or yellow, consisting of beryllium aluminium silicate in a hexagonal form. **2** a mineral species which includes this, emerald, and aquamarine. [Middle English via Old French from Latin *beryllus*, from Greek *bērullos*]

beryllium /bə'rɪlɪəm/ *n. Chem.* a hard white metallic element used in the manufacture of light corrosion-resistant alloys (symbol **Be**). [BERYL + -IUM]

beseech /bɪ'si:tʃ/ *v.tr.* (*past* and *past part.* **besought** /-'sɔ:t/ or **beseeched**) **1** (foll. by *for*, or *to* + infin.) entreat. **2** ask earnestly for. □ **beseeching** *adj.* [Middle English from BE- + Old English *secan* SEEK]

beset /bɪ'sɛt/ *v.tr.* (**besetting**; *past* and *past part.* **beset**) **1** attack or harass persistently (*beset by worries*). **2** surround or hem in (a person etc.). **3** *archaic* cover round with (*beset with pearls*). □ **besetting sin** the sin that especially or most frequently tempts one. [Old English *besettan*, from Germanic]

beside /bɪ'sʌɪd/ *prep.* **1** at the side of; near. **2** compared with. **3** irrelevant to (*beside the point*). □ **beside oneself** overcome with worry, anger, etc. [Old English *be sīdan* (as BY, SIDE)]

besides /bɪ'sʌɪdz/ *prep. & adv.* ● *prep.* in addition to; apart from. ● *adv.* also; as well; moreover.

■ **Usage** Note the difference in meaning between the prepositions *beside* and *besides*. *Beside* was in the past used to mean 'in addition to, apart from', but this is now rare.

besiege /bɪ'si:dʒ/ *v.tr.* **1** lay siege to. **2** crowd round oppressively. **3** harass with requests. □ **besieger** *n.* [Middle English from *assiege* by substitution of BE-, via Old French *asegier* from Romanic]

besmear /bɪ'smɪə/ *v.tr.* **1** smear with a greasy or sticky substance. **2** sully (a reputation etc.). [Old English *bismierwan* (as BE-, SMEAR)]

besmirch /bɪ'smɜ:tʃ/ *v.tr.* **1** soil, discolour. **2** dishonour; sully the reputation or name of. [BE- + SMIRCH]

besom /'bi:z(ə)m, 'bɪz-/ *n.* **1** a broom made of twigs tied round a stick. **2** esp. *N.Engl. derog.* or *joc.* a woman. [Old English *besema*, from West Germanic]

besotted /bɪ'sɒtɪd/ *adj.* **1** infatuated. **2** foolish, confused. **3** intoxicated, stupefied. [*besot* (v.) (as BE-, SOT)]

besought *past* and *past part.* of BESEECH.

bespangle /bɪ'spaŋg(ə)l/ *v.tr.* adorn with spangles.

bespatter /bɪ'spatə/ *v.tr.* **1** spatter (an object) all over. **2** spatter (liquid etc.) about. **3** overwhelm with abuse etc.

bespeak /bɪ'spi:k/ *v.tr.* (*past* **bespoke** /-'spəʊk/; *past part.* **bespoken** /-'spəʊk(ə)n/ or as *adj.* **bespoke**) **1** engage in advance. **2** order (goods). **3** suggest; be evidence of (*his gift bespeaks a kind heart*). **4** *literary* speak to. [Old English *bisprecan* (as BE-, SPEAK)]

bespectacled /bɪ'spɛktək(ə)ld/ *adj.* wearing spectacles.

bespoke /bɪ'spəʊk/ *past* and *past part.* of BESPEAK. ● *adj. Brit.* **1** (of goods, esp. clothing) made to order. **2** (of a tradesman) making goods to order.

bespoken *past part.* of BESPEAK.

besprinkle /bɪ'sprɪŋk(ə)l/ *v.tr.* **1** sprinkle or strew all over with liquid etc. **2** sprinkle (liquid etc.) over. [Middle English (as BE-, SPRINKLE)]

Bessemer converter /'bɛsɪmə/ *n.* a special furnace used to purify pig-iron using the Bessemer process. [Sir H. *Bessemer*, English engineer d. 1898]

Bessemer process /'bɛsɪmə/ *n.* a process once widely used, in which air is blown through molten pig-iron to remove carbon, silicon, and other impurities in order to render it suitable for making steel.

best /bɛst/ *adj., adv., n., & v.* ● *adj.* (*superl.* of GOOD) of the most excellent or outstanding or desirable kind (*my best work*; *the best solution*; *the best thing to do would be to confess*). ● *adv.* (*superl.* of WELL[1]) **1** in the best manner (*does it best*). **2** to the greatest degree (*like it best*). **3** most usefully (*is best ignored*). ● *n.* **1** that which is best (*the best is yet to come*). **2** the chief merit or advantage (*brings out the best in him*). **3** (foll. by *of*) a winning majority of (a certain number of games etc. played) (*the best of five*). **4** = SUNDAY BEST. ● *v.tr. colloq.* defeat, outwit, outbid, etc. □ **all the best** an expression used to wish a person good fortune. **as best one can** (or **may**) as effectively as possible under the circumstances. **at best** on the most optimistic view. **at one's best** in peak condition etc. **at the best of times** even in the most favourable circumstances. **be for** (or

all for) the best be desirable in the end. **the best part of** most of. **do one's best** do all one can. **get the best of** defeat, outwit. **give a person** (or **thing**) **best** (also *absol.*) *Brit.* admit the superiority of; give way to. **had best** would find it wisest to. **make the best of** derive what limited advantage one can from (something unsatisfactory or unwelcome); put up with. **to the best of one's ability, knowledge**, etc. as far as one can do, know, etc. **with the best of them** as well as anyone. [Old English *betest (adj.)*, *bet(o)st (adv.)*, from Germanic]

best bower see BOWER[2].

best boy *n.* esp. *US* the assistant to the chief electrician of a film crew.

best buy *n.* the purchase giving the best value in proportion to its price; a bargain.

best end of neck *n. Brit.* the rib end of a neck of lamb etc. for cooking.

bestial /'bɛstɪəl/ *adj.* **1** brutish, cruel, savage. **2** sexually depraved; lustful. **3** of or like a beast. ▫ **bestialize** *v.tr.* (also **-ise**). **bestially** *adv.* [Middle English via Old French and Late Latin *bestialis* from Latin *bestia* 'beast']

bestiality /bɛstɪ'alɪti/ *n.* (*pl.* **-ies**) **1** bestial behaviour or an instance of this. **2** sexual intercourse between a person and an animal. [French *bestialité* (as BESTIAL)]

bestiary /'bɛstɪəri/ *n.* (*pl.* **-ies**) a moralizing medieval treatise on real and imaginary beasts. [medieval Latin *bestiarium* from Latin *bestia* 'beast']

bestir /bɪ'stəː/ *v.refl.* (**bestirred**, **bestirring**) exert or rouse (oneself).

best-known *attrib.adj.* most well-known; most famous (*his best-known novel*).

best man *n.* the bridegroom's chief attendant at a wedding.

bestow /bɪ'stəʊ/ *v.tr.* **1** (foll. by *on*, *upon*) confer (a gift, right, etc.). **2** deposit. ▫ **bestowal** *n.* [Middle English from BE- + Old English *stow* 'a place']

bestrew /bɪ'struː/ *v.tr.* (*past part.* **bestrewed** or **bestrewn** /-'struːn/) **1** (foll. by *with*) cover or partly cover (a surface). **2** scatter (things) about. **3** lie scattered over. [Old English *bestrēowian* (as BE-, STREW)]

bestride /bɪ'strʌɪd/ *v.tr.* (*past* **bestrode** /-'strəʊd/; *past part.* **bestridden** /-'strɪd(ə)n/) **1** sit astride on. **2** stand astride over. [Old English *bestrīdan*]

best-seller *n.* **1** a book or other item that has sold in large numbers. **2** *Brit.* the author of such a book. ▫ **best-selling** *adj.*

bet /bɛt/ *v.* & *n.* ● *v.* (**betting**; *past* and *past part.* **bet** or **betted**) **1** *intr.* (foll. by *on* or *against* with reference to the outcome) risk a sum of money etc. against another's on the basis of the outcome of an unpredictable event (esp. the result of a race, game, etc., or the outcome in a game of chance). **2** *tr.* risk (an amount) on such an outcome or result (*bet £10 on a horse*). **3** *tr.* risk a sum of money against (a person). **4** *tr. colloq.* feel sure (*bet they've forgotten it*). ● *n.* **1** the act of betting (*make a bet*). **2** the money etc. staked (*put a bet on*). **3** *colloq.* an opinion, esp. a quickly formed or spontaneous one (*my bet is that he won't come*). **4** *colloq.* a choice or course of action (*she's our best bet*). ▫ **you bet** *colloq.* you may be sure. [16th c.: perhaps a shortened form of ABET]

beta /'biːtə/ *n.* **1** the second letter of the Greek alphabet (Β, β). **2** *Brit.* a second-class mark given for a piece of work or in an examination. **3** (**Beta**) *Astron.* the second (usu. second-brightest) star in a constellation (foll. by Latin genitive: *Beta Tauri*). **4** the second member of a series. [Middle English via Latin from Greek]

beta blocker *n. Pharm.* a drug that prevents the stimulation of increased cardiac action, used to treat angina and reduce high blood pressure.

beta decay *n.* radioactive decay in which an electron is emitted.

betake /bɪ'teɪk/ *v.refl.* (*past* **betook** /bɪ'tʊk/; *past part.* **betaken** /bɪ'teɪk(ə)n/) (foll. by *to*) go to (a place or person).

beta particle *n.* (also **beta ray**) a fast-moving electron emitted by radioactive decay of substances (originally regarded as rays).

beta rhythm *n.* (also **beta waves** *pl.*) *Physiol.* the normal electrical activity of the brain when conscious and alert, with a frequency of approx. 18 to 25 hertz.

beta test *n.* & *v.* ● *n.* a test of machinery, software, etc., in the final stages of its development, carried out by a party unconnected with its development. ● *v.tr.* subject (a product) to a beta test.

betatron /'biːtətrɒn/ *n. Physics* an apparatus for accelerating electrons in a circular path by magnetic induction. [BETA + -TRON]

betel /'biːt(ə)l/ *n.* the leaf of the Asian evergreen climbing plant *Piper betle*, chewed in the East with parings of the areca nut. [Portuguese from Malayalam *veṭṭila*]

betel-nut *n.* the areca nut.

bête noire /beɪt 'nwɑː, French bɛt nwar/ *n.* (*pl.* ***bêtes noires*** *pronunc.* same) a person or thing one particularly dislikes or fears. [French, = black beast]

bethink /bɪ'θɪŋk/ *v.refl.* (*past* and *past part.* **bethought** /-'θɔːt/) (foll. by *of*, *how*, or *that* + clause) *formal* **1** reflect; stop to think. **2** be reminded by reflection. [Old English *bithencan* from Germanic (as BE-, THINK)]

betide /bɪ'tʌɪd/ *v.* (only in infin. and 3rd sing. subjunctive) esp. *poet.* **1** *tr.* happen to (*woe betide him*). **2** *intr.* happen (*whate'er may betide*). [Middle English from obsolete *tide* 'befall' from Old English *tīdan*]

betimes /bɪ'tʌɪmz/ *adv. literary* early; in good time. [Middle English from obsolete *betime* (as BY, TIME)]

bêtise /beɪ'tiːz, French betiz/ *n.* **1** a foolish or ill-timed remark or action. **2** a piece of folly. [French]

betoken /bɪ'təʊk(ə)n/ *v.tr.* **1** be a sign of; indicate. **2** augur. [Old English (as BE-, *tācnian* 'signify': see TOKEN)]

betony /'bɛtəni/ *n.* (*pl.* **-ies**) **1** a purple-flowered plant, *Stachys officinalis*. **2** any of various similar plants. [Middle English via Old French *betoine* from Latin *betonica*]

betook *past* of BETAKE.

betray /bɪ'treɪ/ *v.tr.* **1** place (a person, one's country, etc.) in the hands or power of an enemy. **2** be disloyal to (another person, a person's trust, etc.). **3** reveal involuntarily or treacherously; be evidence of (*his shaking hand betrayed his fear*). **4** lead astray or into error. ▫ **betrayal** *n.* **betrayer** *n.* [Middle English from obsolete *tray*, ultimately from Latin *tradere* 'hand over']

betroth /bɪ'trəʊð, -θ/ *v.tr.* (usu. as **betrothed** *adj.*) bind with a promise to marry. ▫ **betrothal** *n.* [Middle English from BE- + *trouthe*, *treuthe* TRUTH, later assimilated to TROTH]

better[1] /'bɛtə/ *adj.*, *adv.*, *n.*, & *v.* ● *adj.* **1** (*compar.* of GOOD) of a more excellent or outstanding or desirable kind (*a better product*; *it would be better to go home*). **2** (*compar.* of WELL[1]) partly or fully recovered from illness (*feeling better*). ● *adv.* (*compar.* of WELL[1]) **1** in a better manner (*she sings better*). **2** to a greater degree (*like it better*). **3** more usefully or advantageously (*is better forgotten*). ● *n.* **1** that which is better (*the better of the two*). **2** (usu. in *pl.*; prec. by *my* etc.) one's superior in ability or rank (*take notice of your betters*). ● *v.* **1** *tr.* improve on; surpass (*I can better his offer*). **2** *tr.* make better; improve. **3** *refl.* improve one's position etc. **4** *intr.* become better; improve. ▫ **the better part of** most of. **for better or for worse** on terms accepting all results; whatever the outcome. **get the better of** defeat, outwit; win an advantage over. **go one better 1** outbid etc. by one. **2** outdo another person. **had better** would find it wiser to. [Old English *betera*, from Germanic]

better[2] /'bɛtə/ *n.* (also **bettor**) a person who bets.

better feelings *n.pl.* one's conscience.

better half *n. colloq.* one's wife or husband.

betterment /'bɛtəm(ə)nt/ *n.* **1** making better; improvement. **2** *Econ.* enhanced value (of real property) arising from local improvements.

better off *adj.* in a better (esp. financial) position.

betting /ˈbɛtɪŋ/ *n.* **1** gambling by risking money on an unpredictable outcome. **2** the odds offered in this. □ **what's the betting?** *Brit. colloq.* it is likely or to be expected (*what's the betting he'll be late?*).

betting shop *n. Brit.* a bookmaker's shop or office.

bettor var. of BETTER².

between /bɪˈtwiːn/ *prep. & adv.* ● *prep.* **1 a** at or to a point in the area or interval bounded by two or more other points in space, time, etc. (*broke down between London and Dover*; *we must meet between now and Friday*). **b** along the extent of such an area or interval (*there are five shops between here and the main road*; *works best between five and six*; *the numbers between 10 and 20*). **2** separating, physically or conceptually (*the distance between here and Leeds*; *the difference between right and wrong*). **3 a** by combining the resources of (*great potential between them*; *between us we could afford it*). **b** shared by; as the joint resources of (*£5 between them*). **c** by joint or reciprocal action (*an agreement between us*; *sorted it out between themselves*). **4** to and from (*runs between London and Sheffield*). **5** taking one and rejecting the other of (*decide between eating here and going out*). ● *adv.* (also **in between**) at a point or in the area bounded by two or more other points in space, time, sequence, etc. (*not fat or thin but in between*). □ **between ourselves** (or **you and me**) in confidence. **between times** (or **whiles**) in the intervals between other actions; occasionally. [Old English *betwēonum*, from Germanic (as BY, TWO)]

■ **Usage** Use in sense 3 with reference to more than two people or things is established and acceptable (e.g. *relations between Britain, France, and Germany*).

betwixt /bɪˈtwɪkst/ *prep. & adv. archaic* between. □ **betwixt and between** *colloq.* neither one thing nor the other. [Old English *betwēox*, from Germanic]

BeV *abbr.* = GeV. [*b*illion (10⁹) *e*lectron*v*olts]

bevatron /ˈbɛvətrɒn/ *n.* a synchrotron used to accelerate protons to energies in the billion electronvolt range. [BeV + -TRON]

bevel /ˈbɛv(ə)l/ *n. & v.* ● *n.* **1** a slope from the horizontal or vertical in carpentry and stonework; a sloping surface or edge. **2** (in full **bevel square**) a tool for marking angles in carpentry and stonework. ● *v.* (**bevelled**, **bevelling**; *US* **beveled**, **beveling**) **1** *tr.* reduce (a square edge) to a sloping edge. **2** *intr.* slope at an angle; slant. [Old French diminutive of *baïf* 'open-mouthed' from *baer* 'gape']

bevel gear *n.* a gear working another gear at an angle to it by means of bevel wheels.

bevel wheel *n.* a toothed wheel whose working face is oblique to the axis.

beverage /ˈbɛv(ə)rɪdʒ/ *n.* esp. *formal* a drink (*hot beverage*; *alcoholic beverage*). [Middle English from Old French *be(u)vrage*, ultimately from Latin *bibere* 'drink']

bevvy /ˈbɛvi/ *n.* (*pl.* **-ies**) *slang* a drink, esp. an alcoholic one. [abbreviation of BEVERAGE]

bevy /ˈbɛvi/ *n.* (*pl.* **-ies**) **1** a flock of quails or larks. **2** a company or group (originally of women). [Middle English: origin unknown]

bewail /bɪˈweɪl/ *v.tr.* **1** greatly regret or lament. **2** wail over; mourn for. □ **bewailer** *n.*

beware /bɪˈwɛː/ *v.* (only in *imper.* or *infin.*) **1** *intr.* (often foll. by *of*, or *that*, *lest*, etc. + clause) be cautious, take heed (*beware of the dog*; *told us to beware*; *beware that you don't fall*). **2** *tr.* be cautious of (*beware the Ides of March*). [BE + WARE³]

bewhiskered /bɪˈwɪskəd/ *adj.* **1** having whiskers. **2** very old.

Bewick's swan /ˈbjuːɪks/ *n.* a swan of northern Eurasia, a race of *Cygnus columbianus*. [T. *Bewick* (d. 1828), English engraver and naturalist]

bewigged /bɪˈwɪgd/ *adj.* wearing a wig.

bewilder /bɪˈwɪldə/ *v.tr.* utterly perplex or confuse. □ **bewilderedly** *adv.* **bewildering** *adj.* **bewilderingly** *adv.* **bewilderment** *n.* [BE- + obsolete *wilder* 'lose one's way']

bewitch /bɪˈwɪtʃ/ *v.tr.* **1** enchant; greatly delight. **2** cast a spell on. □ **bewitching** *adj.* **bewitchingly** *adv.* [Middle English from BE- + Old English *wiccian* 'enchant', from *wicca* WITCH¹]

bey /beɪ/ *n. hist.* (in the Ottoman Empire) the title of a governor of a province. [Turkish, = prince, governor]

beyond /bɪˈjɒnd/ *prep., adv., & n.* ● *prep.* **1** at or to the further side of (*beyond the river*). **2** outside the scope, range, or understanding of (*beyond repair*; *beyond a joke*; *it is beyond me*). **3** more than. ● *adv.* **1** at or to the further side. **2** further on. ● *n.* (prec. by *the*) the unknown after death. □ **the back of beyond** see BACK. [Old English *beg(e)ondan* (as BY, YON, YONDER)]

bezant /ˈbɛz(ə)nt/ *n.* **1** *hist.* a gold or silver coin originally minted at Byzantium. **2** *Heraldry* a gold roundel. [Middle English via Old French *besanz -ant* from Latin *Byzantius* 'Byzantine']

bezel /ˈbɛz(ə)l/ *n.* **1** the sloped edge of a chisel. **2** the oblique faces of a cut gem. **3 a** a groove holding a watch-glass or gem. **b** a rim holding a glass etc. cover. [Old French source of modern French *béseau*, *bizeau*, of unknown origin]

bezique /bɪˈziːk/ *n.* **1** a card game for two with a double pack of 64 cards, including the seven to ace only in each suit. **2** a combination of the queen of spades and the jack of diamonds in this game. [French *bésigue*, perhaps from Persian *bāzīgar* 'juggler']

bezoar /ˈbiːzɔː, ˈbɛzəʊɑː/ *n.* a small stone which may form in the stomachs of certain animals, esp. ruminants, and which was once used as an antidote for various ailments. [French *bezoard*, ultimately from Persian *pādzahr* 'antidote', Arabic *bāzahr*]

b.f. *abbr.* **1** *Brit. colloq.* bloody fool. **2** brought forward. **3** *Printing* boldface.

B-film *n.* = B-MOVIE.

bhaji /ˈbɑːdʒi/ *n.* (*pl.* **bhajis**) **1** an Indian dish of fried vegetables. **2** a small flat cake or ball of this, fried in batter (*onion bhaji*). [Hindi *bhājī* 'fried vegetables']

bhang /baŋ/ *n.* the dried leaves of Indian hemp. [Portuguese *bangue*, Persian & Urdu *bang* later assimilated to Hindi *bhāṅ*, from Sanskrit *bhaṅgā*]

bhangra /ˈbɑːŋgrə/ *n.* a kind of pop music that combines Punjabi folk traditions with Western pop music. [Punjabi *bhāṅgṛā*, a traditional folk dance]

bharal /ˈbʌr(ə)l/ *n.* (also **burhel**) a Himalayan wild sheep, *Pseudois nayaur*, with blue-black coat and horns curved rearward. [Hindi]

b.h.p. *abbr.* brake horsepower.

Bi *symb. Chem.* the element bismuth.

bi /bʌɪ/ *adj. & n. slang* = BISEXUAL. [abbreviation]

bi- /bʌɪ/ *comb. form* (often **bin-** before a vowel) forming nouns and adjectives meaning: **1** having two; a thing having two (*bilateral*; *binaural*; *biplane*). **2 a** occurring twice in every one or once in every two (*biweekly*). **b** lasting for two (*biennial*). **3** doubly; in two ways (*biconcave*). **4** *Chem.* a substance having a double proportion of the acid etc. indicated by the simple word (*bicarbonate*). **5** *Bot.* & *Zool.* (of division and subdivision) twice over (*bipinnate*). [Latin]

biannual /bʌɪˈanjʊəl/ *adj.* occurring, appearing, etc., twice a year (cf. BIENNIAL). □ **biannually** *adv.*

bias /ˈbʌɪəs/ *n. & v.* ● *n.* **1** (often foll. by *towards*, *against*) a predisposition or prejudice. **2** *Statistics* a systematic distortion of a statistical result due to a factor not allowed for in its derivation. **3** an edge cut obliquely across the weave of a fabric. **4** *Bowls* **a** the irregular shape given to a bowl. **b** the oblique course this causes it to run. **5** *Electr.* a steady voltage, magnetic field, etc., applied to an electronic system or device. ● *v.tr.* (**biased**, **biasing**; **biassed**, **biassing**) **1** (esp. as **biased** *adj.*) influence (usu. unfairly); prejudice. **2** give a bias to. □ **on the bias** obliquely, diagonally. [French *biais*, of unknown origin]

bias binding *n.* a strip of fabric cut obliquely and used to bind edges.

bias-ply *adj. US* = CROSS-PLY.

biathlon /bʌɪˈaθlɒn, -lən/ *n. Sport* an athletic contest in skiing and shooting or in cycling and running. □ **biathlete** /-liːt/ *n.* [BI-, on the pattern of PENTATHLON]

biaxial /bʌɪˈaksɪəl/ *adj.* (esp. of crystals) having two axes along which polarized light travels with equal velocity.

bib[1] /bɪb/ *n.* **1** a piece of cloth or plastic fastened round a child's neck to keep the clothes clean while eating. **2** the top front part of an apron, dungarees, etc. **3** the edible marine fish *Trisopterus luscus* of the cod family; also called *pout.* □ **best bib and tucker** best clothes. **stick** (or **poke** etc.) **one's bib in** *Austral. slang* interfere. [perhaps from BIB[2]]

bib[2] /bɪb/ *v.intr.* (**bibbed, bibbing**) *archaic* drink much or often. □ **bibber** *n.* [Middle English, perhaps from Latin *bibere* 'drink']

bib-cock *n.* a tap with a bent nozzle fixed at the end of a pipe. [perhaps from BIB[1] + COCK[1]]

bibelot /ˈbɪbələʊ/ *n.* a small curio or artistic trinket. [French]

Bible /ˈbʌɪb(ə)l/ *n.* **1 a** the Christian scriptures consisting of the Old and New Testaments. **b** the Jewish scriptures. **c** (**bible**) any copy of these (*three bibles on the table*). **d** a particular edition of the Bible (*New English Bible*). **2** *colloq.* any authoritative book (*the Britannica is his Bible*). **3** the scriptures of any religion. [Middle English via Old French and ecclesiastical Latin from Greek *biblia* 'books', originally diminutive of *biblos, bublos* 'papyrus']

Bible-bashing *n.* (also **Bible-thumping**, **Bible-punching**) *slang* aggressive fundamentalist preaching. □ **Bible-basher** *n.* (also **Bible-thumper**, **Bible-puncher**).

Bible belt *n.* the areas of the southern and central US and western Canada where fundamentalist Protestant beliefs prevail.

Bible oath *n.* a solemn oath taken on the Bible.

Bible paper *n.* = INDIA PAPER.

Bible-punching (also **Bible-thumping**) var. of BIBLE-BASHING.

biblical /ˈbɪblɪk(ə)l/ *adj.* (also **Biblical**) **1** of, concerning, or contained in the Bible. **2** resembling the language of the Authorized Version of the Bible. □ **biblically** *adv.*

biblio- /ˈbɪblɪəʊ/ *comb. form* denoting a book or books. [Greek from *biblion* 'book']

bibliography /bɪblɪˈɒgrəfi/ *n.* (*pl.* **-ies**) **1 a** a list of the books referred to in a scholarly work, usu. printed as an appendix. **b** a list of the books of a specific author or publisher, or on a specific subject, etc. **2 a** the history or description of books, including authors, editions, etc. **b** any book containing such information. □ **bibliographer** *n.* **bibliographic** /-əˈgrafɪk/ *adj.* **bibliographical** /-əˈgrafɪk(ə)l/ *adj.* **bibliographically** /-əˈgrafɪk(ə)li/ *adv.* **bibliographize** *v.tr.* (also **-ise**). [French *bibliographie* from modern Latin *bibliographia*, from Greek (as BIBLE, -GRAPHY)]

bibliomancy /ˈbɪblɪə(ʊ)mansi/ *n.* foretelling the future by the analysis of a randomly chosen passage from a book, esp. the Bible.

bibliomania /ˌbɪblɪə(ʊ)ˈmeɪnɪə/ *n.* an extreme enthusiasm for collecting and possessing books. □ **bibliomaniac** /-nɪak/ *n. & adj.*

bibliophile /ˈbɪblɪəfʌɪl/ *n.* a person who collects or is fond of books. □ **bibliophilic** /-ˈfɪlɪk/ *adj.* **bibliophily** /-ˈɒfɪli/ *n.* [French *bibliophile* (as BIBLIO-, -PHILE)]

bibliopole /ˈbɪblɪəpəʊl/ *n.* a seller of (esp. rare) books. [Latin *bibliopola* from Greek *bibliopōlēs*, from *biblion* 'book' + *pōlēs* 'seller']

bibulous /ˈbɪbjʊləs/ *adj.* given to drinking alcoholic liquor. □ **bibulously** *adv.* **bibulousness** *n.* [Latin *bibulus* 'freely drinking' from *bibere* 'drink']

bicameral /bʌɪˈkam(ə)r(ə)l/ *adj.* (of a parliament or legislative body) having two chambers. □ **bicameralism** *n.* [BI- + Latin *camera* 'chamber']

bicarb /bʌɪˈkɑːb/ *n. colloq.* = BICARBONATE 2. [abbreviation]

bicarbonate /bʌɪˈkɑːbəneɪt/ *n.* **1** *Chem.* any acid salt of carbonic acid. **2** (in full **bicarbonate of soda**) sodium bicarbonate used as an antacid or in baking powder.

bice /bʌɪs/ *n.* **1** any of various pigments made from blue or green basic copper carbonate. **2** any similar pigment made from smalt. **3** a shade of blue or green given by these. [originally = brownish grey, from Old French *bis* 'dark grey', of unknown origin]

bicentenary /bʌɪsɛnˈtiːnəri, -ˈtɛn-, bʌɪˈsɛntɪn-/ *n. & adj.* ● *n.* (*pl.* **-ies**) **1** a two-hundredth anniversary. **2** a celebration of this. ● *adj.* of or concerning a bicentenary.

bicentennial /bʌɪsɛnˈtɛnɪəl/ *n. & adj.* ● *n.* a bicentenary. ● *adj.* **1** lasting two hundred years or occurring every two hundred years. **2** of or concerning a bicentenary.

bicephalous /bʌɪˈsɛf(ə)ləs, -ˈkɛf-/ *adj.* having two heads. [BI- + Greek *kephalē* 'head' + -OUS]

biceps /ˈbʌɪsɛps/ *n.* (*pl.* same) a muscle having two heads or attachments at one end, esp. the muscle which bends the elbow. [Latin, = two-headed (as BI- + *-ceps* from *caput* 'head')]

bicker /ˈbɪkə/ *v.intr.* **1** quarrel pettily; wrangle. **2** *poet.* **a** (of a stream, rain, etc.) patter (over stones etc.). **b** (of a flame, light, etc.) flash, flicker. □ **bickerer** *n.* [Middle English *biker, beker*, of unknown origin]

bicky /ˈbɪki/ *n.* (also **bikky**) (*pl.* **-ies**) *Brit. colloq.* a biscuit.

bicolour /ˈbʌɪkʌlə/ *adj. & n.* ● *adj.* having two colours. ● *n.* a bicolour blossom or animal.

biconcave /bʌɪˈkɒnkeɪv/ *adj.* (esp. of a lens) concave on both sides.

biconvex /bʌɪˈkɒnvɛks/ *adj.* (esp. of a lens) convex on both sides.

bicultural /bʌɪˈkʌltʃ(ə)r(ə)l/ *adj.* having or combining two cultures.

bicuspid /bʌɪˈkʌspɪd/ *adj. & n.* ● *adj.* having two cusps or points. ● *n.* a tooth with two cusps, esp. a human premolar tooth. □ **bicuspidate** *adj.* [BI- + Latin *cuspis -idis* 'sharp point']

bicycle /ˈbʌɪsɪk(ə)l/ *n. & v.* ● *n.* a vehicle of two wheels held in a frame one behind the other, propelled by pedals and steered with handlebars attached to the front wheel. ● *v.intr.* ride a bicycle. □ **bicycler** *n.* **bicyclist** /-klɪst/ *n.* [French from BI- + Greek *kuklos* 'wheel']

bicycle chain *n.* a chain transmitting power from the bicycle pedals to the wheels.

bicycle clip *n.* either of two metal clips used to confine a cyclist's trousers at the ankle.

bicycle pump *n.* a portable pump for inflating bicycle tyres.

bicyclic /bʌɪˈsʌɪklɪk, -ˈsɪk-/ *adj. Chem.* having two (usu. fused) rings of atoms in the molecular structure. [BI- + CYCLIC]

bid /bɪd/ *v. & n.* ● *v.* (**bidding**; *past* **bid**, *archaic* **bade** /beɪd, bad/; *past part.* **bid**, *archaic* **bidden** /ˈbɪd(ə)n/) **1** *tr. & intr.* (*past* and *past part.* **bid**) (often foll. by *for, against*) **a** (esp. at an auction) offer (a certain price) (*did not bid for the vase; bid against the dealer; bid £20*). **b** offer to do work etc. for a stated price. **2** *tr. archaic* or *literary* **a** command; order (*bid the soldiers shoot*). **b** invite (*bade her start*). **3** *tr. archaic* or *literary* **a** utter (greeting or farewell) to (*I bade him welcome*). **b** proclaim (defiance etc.). **4** (*past* and *past part.* **bid**) *Cards* **a** *intr.* state before play how many tricks one intends to make. **b** *tr.* state (one's intended number of tricks). ● *n.* **1 a** (esp. at an auction) an offer (of a price) (*a bid of £5*). **b** an offer (to do work, supply goods, etc.) at a stated price; a tender. **2** *Cards* a statement of the number of tricks a player proposes to make. **3** *colloq.* an attempt; an effort (*a bid for power*). □ **bid fair to** seem likely to. **make a bid for** try to gain (*made a bid for freedom*). □ **bidder** *n.* [Old English *biddan* 'ask' from Germanic, & Old English *bēodan* 'offer, command']

biddable /ˈbɪdəb(ə)l/ *adj.* **1** obedient. **2** *Cards* (of a hand or suit) suitable for being bid. □ **biddability** /-ˈbɪlɪti/ *n.*

bidden *archaic past part.* of BID.

bidding /ˈbɪdɪŋ/ *n.* **1** the offers at an auction. **2** *Cards* the act of making a bid or bids. **3** a command, request, or invitation.

bidding prayer *n.* a prayer inviting the congregation to join in.

biddy /ˈbɪdi/ *n.* (*pl.* **-ies**) *slang derog.* a woman (esp. *old biddy*). [pet form of the name *Bridget*]

bide /bʌɪd/ *v.intr. archaic* or *dial.* remain; stay. □ **bide one's time** await one's best opportunity. [Old English *bīdan*, from Germanic]

bidet /ˈbiːdeɪ/ *n.* a low oval basin used esp. for washing the genital area. [French, = pony]

bidirectional /bʌɪdɪˈrɛkʃ(ə)n(ə)l, -dʌɪ-/ *adj.* functioning in two directions.

Biedermeier /ˈbiːdəmʌɪə/ *attrib.adj.* **1** (of styles, furnishings, etc.) characteristic of the period 1815–48 in Germany. **2** *derog.* conventional; bourgeois. [*Biedermaier* a fictitious German poet created by L. Eichrodt (1854)]

biennial /bʌɪˈɛnɪəl/ *adj. & n.* ● *adj.* **1** lasting two years. **2** recurring every two years (cf. BIANNUAL). ● *n.* **1** *Bot.* a plant that takes two years to grow from seed to fruition and die (cf. ANNUAL, PERENNIAL). **2** an event celebrated or taking place every two years. □ **biennially** *adv.* [Latin *biennis* (as BI-, *annus* 'year')]

biennium /bʌɪˈɛnɪəm/ *n.* (*pl.* **bienniums** or **biennia** /-nɪə/) a period of two years. [Latin (as BIENNIAL)]

bier /bɪə/ *n.* a movable frame on which a coffin or a corpse is placed, or taken to a grave. [Old English *bēr*, from the Germanic base of BEAR[1]]

biff /bɪf/ *n. & v. slang* ● *n.* a sharp blow. ● *v.tr.* strike (a person). [imitative]

biffin /ˈbɪfɪn/ *n. Brit.* a dark red cooking apple. [= *beefing* from BEEF + -ING[1], with reference to the colour]

bifid /ˈbʌɪfɪd/ *adj.* divided by a deep cleft into two parts. [Latin *bifidus* (as BI-, *fidus* from stem of *findere* 'cleave')]

bifocal /bʌɪˈfəʊk(ə)l/ *adj. & n.* ● *adj.* having two focuses, esp. of a lens with a part for distant vision and a part for near vision. ● *n.* (in *pl.*) bifocal spectacles.

BIFU /ˈbɪfuː/ *abbr.* Banking, Insurance, and Finance Union. [acronym]

bifurcate *v. & adj.* ● *v.tr. & intr.* /ˈbʌɪfəkeɪt/ divide into two branches; fork. ● *adj.* /bʌɪˈfəːkət/ forked; branched. [medieval Latin *bifurcare* from Latin *bifurcus* 'two-forked' (as BI-, *furca* 'fork')]

bifurcation /bʌɪfəˈkeɪʃ(ə)n/ *n.* **1 a** a division into two branches. **b** either or both of such branches. **2** the point of such a division.

big /bɪg/ *adj. & adv.* ● *adj.* (**bigger**, **biggest**) **1 a** of considerable size, amount, intensity, etc. (*a big mistake*; *a big helping*). **b** of a large or the largest size (*big toe*; *big drum*). **2** important; significant; outstanding (*the big race*; *my big chance*). **3 a** grown-up (*a big boy now*). **b** elder (*big sister*). **4** *colloq.* **a** boastful (*big words*). **b** often *iron.* generous (*big of him*). **c** ambitious (*big ideas*). **5** (usu. foll. by *with*) advanced in pregnancy; fecund (*big with child*; *big with consequences*). ● *adv. colloq.* in a big manner, esp.: **1** effectively (*went over big*). **2** boastfully (*talk big*). **3** ambitiously (*think big*). □ **the Big Three, Four, etc.** the dominant group of three, four, etc. **the big time** *slang* success in a profession, esp. show business. **come** (or **go**) **over big** make a great effect. **in a big way 1** on a large scale. **2** *colloq.* with great enthusiasm, display, etc. **look** (or **talk**) **big** boast. **think big** be ambitious. **too big for one's boots** (or **breeches**) *slang* conceited. □ **biggish** *adj.* **bigness** *n.* [Middle English: origin unknown]

bigamy /ˈbɪgəmi/ *n.* (*pl.* **-ies**) the crime of marrying when already married to another person. □ **bigamist** *n.* **bigamous** *adj.* [Middle English via Old French *bigamie* from *bigame* bigamous, from Late Latin *bigamus* (as BI-, Greek *gamos* 'marriage')]

Big Apple *n. N. Amer. slang* New York City.

big band *n.* a large jazz or pop orchestra.

big bang *n.* (also **Big Bang**) **1** the explosion of dense matter, postulated as the origin of the universe. **2** *Stock Exch.* (in the UK) the introduction in 1986 of important changes in the regulations and procedures for trading, esp. the widening of membership, the relaxation of rules for brokers, and the introduction of computerized communications.

Big Ben *n.* the great clock tower of the Houses of Parliament and its bell.

Big Board *n. US colloq.* the New York Stock Exchange.

Big Brother *n.* an all-powerful supposedly benevolent dictator (as in Orwell's *Nineteen Eighty-four*).

big bud *n.* a plant disease caused by the gall-mite.

big bug *n. slang* = BIGWIG.

big business *n.* large-scale financial dealings, esp. when sinister or exploitative.

Big Chief *n.* (also **Big Daddy**) *slang* = BIGWIG.

big deal *int. slang iron.* I am not impressed.

big dipper *n.* **1** *Brit.* a fairground switchback. **2** *N. Amer.* (**Big Dipper**) = PLOUGH *n.* 4.

big end *n.* (in a motor vehicle) the end of the connecting rod that encircles the crankpin.

Bigfoot /ˈbɪgfʊt/ *n.* (*pl.* **Bigfeet**) a supposed yeti-like animal of NW America; also called *Sasquatch*. [from the size of its footprints]

big game *n.* large animals hunted for sport.

biggie /ˈbɪgi/ *n. colloq.* a big person or thing; an important event.

big gun *n. slang* = BIGWIG.

big-head *n. colloq.* a conceited person. □ **big-headed** *adj.* **big-headedness** *n.*

big-hearted *adj.* generous.

bighorn /ˈbɪghɔːn/ *n.* an American sheep, *Ovis canadensis*, esp. native to the Rocky Mountains.

big house *n.* **1** the principal house in a village etc. **2** *slang* a prison.

bight /bʌɪt/ *n.* **1** a curve or recess in a coastline, river, etc. **2** a loop of rope. [Old English *byht*, from Germanic]

big idea *n.* often *iron.* an important intention or scheme.

big league *n. & adj. N. Amer.* ● *n.* a top league in a professional sport, esp. baseball (often hyphenated when *attrib.*: *big-league teams*). ● *attrib.adj.* (**big-league**) *colloq.* major; top; outstanding.

big lie *n.* esp. *US* an intentional distortion of facts, esp. by a politician, official body, etc.

big money *n.* large amounts of money; high profit; high pay.

big name *n.* a famous person (hyphenated when *attrib.*: *big-name guests*).

big noise *n. Brit.* (also **big pot** *Brit.* or **big shot**) *colloq.* = BIGWIG.

bigot /ˈbɪgət/ *n.* an obstinate and intolerant believer in a religion, political theory, etc. □ **bigotry** *n.* [16th c. from French: origin unknown]

bigoted /ˈbɪgətɪd/ *adj.* unreasonably prejudiced and intolerant.

big smoke *n. slang* **1** *Brit.* London. **2** any large town.

big stick *n.* a display of force.

big-timer *n. slang* a person who achieves success.

big top *n.* the main tent in a circus.

big tree *n. US* the giant sequoia, *Sequoiadendron giganteum*.

big wheel *n.* **1** a Ferris wheel. **2** *N. Amer. slang* = BIGWIG.

bigwig /ˈbɪgwɪg/ *n. colloq.* an important person.

bijou /ˈbiːʒuː, French biʒu/ *n. & adj.* ● *n.* (*pl.* ***bijoux*** *pronunc.* same) a jewel; a trinket. ● *attrib.adj.* (***bijou***) small and elegant. [French]

bijouterie /biːˈʒuːt(ə)ri, French biʒutri/ *n.* jewellery; trinkets. [French (as BIJOU, -ERY)]

bike /bʌɪk/ *n. & v. colloq.* ● *n.* a bicycle or motorcycle. ● *v.intr.* ride a bicycle or motorcycle. [abbreviation]

biker /ˈbʌɪkə/ *n.* a cyclist, esp. a motorcyclist.

bikini /bɪˈkiːni/ *n.* a two-piece swimsuit for women. [*Bikini*, an atoll in the Marshall Islands in the Pacific where an atom bomb was exploded in 1946, from the supposed 'explosive' effect]

bikini briefs *n.pl.* women's scanty briefs.

bikini line *n.* the area of skin around the edge of the bottom half of a bikini, esp. with reference to the cosmetic removal of the pubic hair in this area.

bikky var. of BICKY.

bilabial /bʌɪˈleɪbɪəl/ *adj. Phonet.* (of a sound etc.) made with closed or nearly closed lips.

bilateral /bʌɪˈlat(ə)r(ə)l/ *adj.* **1** of, on, or with two sides. **2** affecting or between two parties, countries, etc. (*bilateral negotiations*). □ **bilaterally** *adv.*

bilateral symmetry *n.* the property of being divisible into symmetrical halves on either side of a unique plane.

bilberry /ˈbɪlb(ə)ri/ *n.* (*pl.* **-ies**) **1** a hardy dwarf shrub, *Vaccinium myrtillus*, of N. Europe, growing on heaths and mountains, and having red drooping flowers and dark blue berries. **2** the small blue edible berry of this species. **3** any of various shrubs of the genus *Vaccinium* having dark blue berries. [origin uncertain: perhaps from Scandinavian]

bilbo /ˈbɪlbəʊ/ *n.* (*pl.* **-os** or **-oes**) *hist.* a sword noted for the temper and elasticity of its blade. [*Bilboa* = Bilbao in Spain, noted for the manufacture of fine blades]

bilboes /ˈbɪlbəʊz/ *n.pl. hist.* an iron bar with sliding shackles for a prisoner's ankles. [16th c.: origin unknown]

Bildungsroman /ˈbɪldʊŋzrəʊˌmɑːn, German ˈbɪldʊŋzroˌmɑːn/ *n.* a novel dealing with one person's early life and development. [German, from *Bildung* 'education' + *Roman* 'novel']

bile /bʌɪl/ *n.* **1** a bitter greenish-brown alkaline fluid which aids digestion and is secreted by the liver and stored in the gall bladder. **2** bad temper; peevish anger. [French from Latin *bilis*]

bile duct *n.* the duct which conveys bile from the liver and the gall bladder to the duodenum.

bi-level /ˈbʌɪlɛv(ə)l/ *adj. & n.* ● *adj.* **1** having or functioning on two levels; arranged on two planes. **2** *N. Amer.* designating a style of two-storey house in which the lower storey is partially sunk below ground level, and the main entrance is between the two storeys. ● *n. N. Amer.* a bi-level house.

bilge /bɪldʒ/ *n. & v.* ● *n.* **1** the area on the outer surface of a ship's hull where the flat bottom meets the vertical sides. **2 a** (in *pl.*) the lowest internal portion of the hull. **b** (in full **bilge water**) filthy water that collects inside the bilge. **3** *slang* nonsense; rot (*don't talk bilge*). ● *v.* **1** *tr.* stave in the bilge of (a ship). **2** *intr.* spring a leak in the bilge. **3** *intr.* swell out; bulge. [probably variant of BULGE]

bilge keel *n.* a plate or timber fastened under the bilge of a ship to prevent rolling.

bilharzia /bɪlˈhɑːtsɪə/ *n.* **1** a chronic disease, endemic in parts of Africa and S. America, caused by infestation with blood flukes (schistosomes). Also called *bilharziasis, schistosomiasis*. **2** = SCHISTOSOME. [modern Latin former genus name, from T. *Bilharz*, German physician d. 1862]

bilharziasis /bɪlhɑːˈtsʌɪəsɪs/ *n.* = BILHARZIA 1.

biliary /ˈbɪlɪəri/ *adj.* of the bile. [French *biliaire*: see BILE, -ARY[2]]

bilingual /bʌɪˈlɪŋgw(ə)l/ *adj. & n.* ● *adj.* **1** able to speak two languages, esp. fluently. **2** spoken or written in two languages. ● *n.* a bilingual person. □ **bilingualism** *n.* [Latin *bilinguis* (as BI-, *lingua* 'tongue')]

bilious /ˈbɪlɪəs/ *adj.* **1** affected by a disorder of the bile. **2** bad-tempered. □ **biliously** *adv.* **biliousness** *n.* [Latin *biliosus* from *bilis* 'bile']

bilirubin /bɪlɪˈruːbɪn/ *n.* an orange-yellow pigment formed by breakdown of haemoglobin and occurring in bile. [German from Latin *bilis* BILE + *ruber* 'red']

bilk /bɪlk/ *v.tr. slang* **1** cheat. **2** give the slip to. **3** avoid paying (a creditor or debt). □ **bilker** *n.* [origin uncertain, perhaps = BAULK: earliest use (17th c.) in cribbage, = spoil one's opponent's score]

bill[1] /bɪl/ *n. & v.* ● *n.* **1 a** a printed or written statement of charges for goods supplied or services rendered. **b** the amount owed (*ran up a bill of £300*). **2** a draft of a proposed law. **3 a** a poster; a placard. **b** = HANDBILL. **4 a** a printed list, esp. a theatre programme. **b** the entertainment itself (*top of the bill*). **5** *N. Amer.* a banknote (*ten-dollar bill*). ● *v.tr.* **1** put in the programme; announce. **2** (foll. by *as*) advertise. **3** send a note of charges to (*billed him for the books*). □ **billable** *adj.* [Middle English from Anglo-French *bille*, Anglo-Latin *billa*, probably alteration of medieval Latin *bulla* 'seal, sealed documents, BULL[2]']

bill[2] /bɪl/ *n. & v.* ● *n.* **1** the beak of a bird, esp. when it is slender, flattened, or weak, or belongs to a web-footed bird or a bird of the pigeon family. **2** the muzzle of a platypus. **3** a narrow promontory. **4** *Naut.* the point of an anchor-fluke. ● *v.intr.* (of doves etc.) stroke a bill with a bill. □ **bill and coo** exchange caresses. □ **billed** *adj.* (usu. in *comb.*). [Old English *bile*, of unknown origin]

bill[3] /bɪl/ *n.* **1** *hist.* a weapon like a halberd with a hook instead of a blade. **2** = BILLHOOK. [Old English *bil*, from West Germanic]

billabong /ˈbɪləbɒŋ/ *n. Austral.* a branch of a river forming a backwater or a stagnant pool. [Wiradhuri *bilabang* (originally as the name of the Bell River, NSW)]

billboard /ˈbɪlbɔːd/ *n.* a large outdoor board for advertisements etc.

billet[1] /ˈbɪlɪt/ *n. & v.* ● *n.* **1 a** a place where troops etc. are lodged, usu. with civilians. **b** a written order requiring a householder to lodge the bearer, usu. a soldier. **2** *colloq.* a situation; a job. ● *v.tr.* (**billeted, billeting**) **1** (usu. foll. by *on, in, at*) quarter (soldiers etc.). **2** (of a householder) provide (a soldier etc.) with board and lodging. □ **billetee** /-ˈtiː/ *n.* **billeter** *n.* [Middle English from Anglo-French *billette*, Anglo-Latin *billetta*, diminutive of *billa* BILL[1]]

billet[2] /ˈbɪlɪt/ *n.* **1** a thick piece of firewood. **2** a small metal bar. **3** *Archit.* each of a series of short rolls inserted at intervals in Norman decorative mouldings. [Middle English from French *billette* 'small log', ultimately probably of Celtic origin]

billet-doux /bɪlɪˈduː/ *n.* (*pl.* **billets-doux** /-ˈduːz/) often *joc.* a love letter. [French, = sweet note]

billfold /ˈbɪlfəʊld/ *n. N. Amer.* a wallet for keeping banknotes.

billhead /ˈbɪlhɛd/ *n.* a printed account form.

billhook /ˈbɪlhʊk/ *n.* a sickle-shaped tool with a sharp inner edge, used for pruning, lopping, etc.

billiards /ˈbɪljədz/ *n.* **1** a game played on an oblong cloth-covered table, with three balls struck with cues into pockets round the edge of the table. **2** (**billiard**) (in *comb.*) used in billiards (*billiard ball*; *billiard table*). [originally pl., from French *billard* 'billiards, cue', diminutive of *bille* 'log': see BILLET[2]]

billion /ˈbɪljən/ *n. & adj.* ● *n.* (*pl.* same or (in sense 3 of *n.*) **billions**) (in *sing.* prec. by *a* or *one*) **1** a thousand million (1,000,000,000 or 10^9). **2** (now less often, esp. *Brit.*) a million million (1,000,000,000,000 or 10^{12}). **3** (in *pl.*) *colloq.* a very large number (*billions of years*). ● *adj.* that amount to a billion. □ **billionth** *adj. & n.* [French (as BI-, MILLION)]

billionaire /bɪljəˈnɛː/ *n.* a person possessing over a billion pounds, dollars, etc. [on the pattern of *millionaire*]

bill of exchange *n. Econ.* a written order to pay a sum of money on a given date to the drawer or to a named payee.

bill of fare *n.* **1** a menu. **2** a programme (for a theatrical event).

bill of goods *n. N. Amer.* a consignment of merchandise. □ **sell a person a bill of goods** deceive a person.

bill of health *n.* **1** *Naut.* a certificate regarding infectious disease on a ship or in a port at the time of sailing. **2** (in phr. **clean bill of health**) **a** such a certificate stating that there is no disease. **b** a declaration that a person or thing examined has been found to be free of illness or in good condition.

bill of indictment *n. hist.* or *US* a written accusation as presented to a grand jury.

bill of lading *n. Naut.* **1** a shipmaster's detailed list of the ship's cargo. **2** *US* = WAYBILL.

Bill of Rights *n.* **1** *Law* the English constitutional settlement of 1689. **2** *Law* (in the US) the original constitutional amendments of 1791. **3** a statement of the rights of a class of people.

bill of sale *n. Econ.* a certificate of transfer of personal property, esp. as a security against debt.

billon /ˈbɪlən/ *n.* an alloy of gold or silver with a predominating admixture of a base metal. [French from *bille* BILLET[2]]

billow /ˈbɪləʊ/ *n.* & *v.* ● *n.* **1** a wave. **2** a soft upward-curving flow. **3** any large soft mass. ● *v.intr.* move or build up in billows. □ **billowy** *adj.* [Old Norse *bylgja*, from Germanic]

billposter /ˈbɪlpəʊstə/ *n.* (also **billsticker** /-stɪkə/) a person who pastes up advertisements on hoardings. □ **billposting** *n.*

billy[1] /ˈbɪli/ *n.* (*pl.* **-ies**) (in full **billycan** /ˈbɪlɪkan/) orig. *Austral.* a tin or enamel cooking pot with a lid and wire handle, for use out of doors. [perhaps from Aboriginal *billa* 'water']

billy[2] /ˈbɪli/ *n.* (*pl.* **-ies**) = BILLY GOAT.

billycan see BILLY[1].

billy goat *n.* a male goat. [*Billy*, pet form of the name *William*]

billy-o /ˈbɪləʊ/ *n.* □ **like billy-o** *Brit. slang* very much, hard, strongly, etc. (*raining like billy-o*). [19th c.: origin unknown]

bilobate /bʌɪˈləʊbeɪt/ *adj.* (also **bilobed** /-ˈləʊbd/) having or consisting of two lobes.

biltong /ˈbɪltɒŋ/ *n. S.Afr.* boneless meat salted and dried in strips. [Afrikaans from Dutch *bil* 'buttock' and *tong* 'tongue']

BIM *abbr.* British Institute of Management.

bimanal /ˈbɪmən(ə)l/ *adj.* (also **bimanous** /-nəs/) having two hands. [BI- + Latin *manus* 'hand']

bimbo /ˈbɪmbəʊ/ *n.* (*pl.* **-os**) *slang* usu. *derog.* **1** a woman, esp. a young empty-headed one. **2** a person. [Italian, = little child]

bi-media /bʌɪˈmiːdɪə/ *attrib.adj. Brit.* involving or working in two of the mass communication media, esp. radio and television.

bimetallic /bʌɪmɪˈtalɪk/ *adj.* **1** made of two metals. **2** of or relating to bimetallism. [French *bimétallique* (as BI-, METALLIC)]

bimetallic strip *n.* a sensitive element in some thermostats made of two bands of different metals that expand at different rates when heated, causing the strip to bend and thus to break a circuit.

bimetallism /bʌɪˈmɛt(ə)lɪz(ə)m/ *n.* a system of allowing the unrestricted currency of two metals (e.g. gold and silver) at a fixed ratio to each other, as coined money. □ **bimetallist** *n.*

bimillenary /bʌɪmɪˈlɛnəri, -ˈliːn-; bʌɪˈmɪlənəri/ *adj.* & *n.* ● *adj.* of or relating to a two-thousandth anniversary. ● *n.* (*pl.* **-ies**) a bimillenary year or festival.

bimodal /bʌɪˈməʊd(ə)l/ *adj.* esp. *Statistics* having two modes.

bimonthly /bʌɪˈmʌnθli/ *adj., adv.,* & *n.* ● *adj.* occurring twice a month or every two months. ● *adv.* twice a month or every two months. ● *n.* (*pl.* **-ies**) a periodical produced bimonthly.

■ **Usage** *Bimonthly*, *biweekly*, and *biyearly* are often avoided, because of the ambiguity of meaning, in favour of *two-monthly* and *twice-monthly* etc. or *every two months* and *twice a month* etc.

bin /bɪn/ *n.* & *v.* ● *n.* a large receptacle for storage or for depositing rubbish. ● *v.tr.* (**binned**, **binning**) *colloq.* **1** store or put in a bin. **2** *Brit.* throw away. [Old English *bin(n)*, *binne*]

bin- /bɪn, bʌɪn/ *prefix* var. of BI- before a vowel.

binary /ˈbʌɪnəri/ *adj.* & *n.* ● *adj.* **1 a** dual. **b** of or involving pairs. **2** of the arithmetical system using 2 as a base. ● *n.* (*pl.* **-ies**) **1** something having two parts. **2** a binary number. **3** a binary star. [Late Latin *binarius* from *bini* 'two together']

binary code *n. Computing* a coding system using the binary digits 0 and 1 to represent a letter, digit, or other character in a computer (see BCD).

binary compound *n. Chem.* a compound having two elements or radicals.

binary fission *n.* the division of a cell or organism into two parts.

binary number *n.* (also **binary digit**) one of two digits (usu. 0 or 1) in a binary system of notation.

binary star *n.* a system of two stars orbiting each other.

binary system *n.* a system in which information can be expressed by combinations of the digits 0 and 1 (corresponding to 'off' and 'on' in computing).

binary tree *n.* a data structure in which a record is branched to the left when greater and to the right when less than the previous record.

binate /ˈbʌɪneɪt/ *adj. Bot.* **1** growing in pairs. **2** composed of two equal parts. [modern Latin *binatus* from Latin *bini* 'two together']

binaural /bɪˈnɔːr(ə)l, bʌɪ-/ *adj.* **1** of or used with both ears. **2** (of sound) recorded using two microphones and usu. transmitted separately to the two ears.

bind /bʌɪnd/ *v.* & *n.* ● *v.* (*past* and *past part.* **bound** /baʊnd/) (see also BOUNDEN). **1** *tr.* (often foll. by *to, on, together*) tie or fasten tightly. **2** *tr.* **a** restrain; put in bonds. **b** (as **-bound** *adj.*) constricted, obstructed (*snowbound*). **3** *tr.* esp. *Cookery* cause (ingredients) to cohere using another ingredient. **4** *tr.* fasten or hold together as a single mass. **5** *tr.* compel; impose an obligation or duty on. **6** *tr.* **a** edge (fabric etc.) with braid etc. **b** fix together and fasten (the pages of a book) in a cover. **7** *tr.* constipate. **8** *tr.* ratify (a bargain, agreement, etc.). **9** *tr.* (in *passive*) be required by an obligation or duty (*am bound to answer*). **10** *tr.* (often foll. by *up*) **a** put a bandage or other covering round. **b** fix together with something put round (*bound her hair*). **11** *tr.* indenture as an apprentice. **12** *intr.* (of snow etc.) cohere, stick. **13** *intr.* be prevented from moving freely. **14** *intr. Brit. slang* complain. ● *n.* **1** *colloq.* a nuisance; a restriction. **2** = BINE. □ **be bound up with** be closely associated with. **bind over** *Law* order (a person) to do something, esp. keep the peace. **bind up** bandage. **I'll be bound** a statement of assurance, or guaranteeing the truth of something. [Old English *bindan*]

binder /ˈbʌɪndə/ *n.* **1** a cover for sheets of paper, for a book, etc. **2** a substance that acts cohesively. **3** a reaping machine that binds grain into sheaves. **4** a bookbinder.

bindery /ˈbʌɪnd(ə)ri/ *n.* (*pl.* **-ies**) a workshop or factory for binding books.

bindi-eye /ˈbɪndɪʌɪ/ *n.* a small perennial Australian plant, *Calotis cuneifolia*, which has a burlike fruit. [20th c.: perhaps Aboriginal]

binding /ˈbʌɪndɪŋ/ *n.* & *adj.* ● *n.* something that binds, esp. the covers, glue, etc., of a book. ● *adj.* (often foll. by *on*) obligatory.

bindweed /ˈbʌɪndwiːd/ *n.* **1** convolvulus. **2** any of various climbing plants such as honeysuckle.

bine /bʌɪn/ *n.* **1** the twisting stem of a climbing plant, esp. the hop. **2** a flexible shoot. [originally a dialect form of BIND]

bin-end *n. Brit.* one of the last bottles from a bin of wine, usu. sold at a reduced price.

Binet–Simon test /ˈbiːneɪˌsiːmɒ̃/ *adj.* (also **Binet test**) *Psychol.* a test used to measure intelligence, esp. of children. [A. *Binet* d. 1911 and T. *Simon* d. 1961, French psychologists]

binge /bɪn(d)ʒ/ *n. & v. slang* ● *n.* a spree; a period of uncontrolled eating, drinking, etc. ● *v.intr.* (**bingeing** or **binging**) go on a spree; indulge in uncontrolled eating, drinking, etc. [probably originally dialect, = soak]

bingo /ˈbɪŋgəʊ/ *n. & int.* ● *n.* a game for any number of players, each having a card of squares with numbers, which are marked off as numbers are randomly drawn by a caller. ● *int.* expressing sudden surprise, satisfaction, etc., as in winning at bingo. [probably imitative: cf. dialect *bing* 'with a bang']

bin liner *n. Brit.* a bag (usu. of plastic) for lining a rubbish bin.

binman /ˈbɪnman/ *n.* (*pl.* **-men**) *Brit. colloq.* a dustman.

binnacle /ˈbɪnək(ə)l/ *n.* a built-in housing for a ship's compass. [earlier *bittacle*, ultimately from Latin *habitaculum* 'habitation' from *habitare* 'inhabit']

binocular /bɪˈnɒkjʊlə/ *adj.* adapted for or using both eyes. [BIN- + Latin *oculus* 'eye']

binoculars /bɪˈnɒkjʊləz/ *n.pl.* an optical instrument with a lens for each eye, for viewing distant objects.

binocular vision *n.* vision using two eyes with overlapping fields of view, allowing good perception of depth.

binomial /bʌɪˈnəʊmɪəl/ *n. & adj.* ● *n.* **1** an algebraic expression of the sum or the difference of two terms. **2** a two-part name, esp. in taxonomy. ● *adj.* consisting of two terms. □ **binomially** *adv.* [French *binôme* or modern Latin *binomium* (as BI-, Greek *nomos* 'part, portion')]

binomial distribution *n.* a frequency distribution of the possible number of successful outcomes in a given number of trials in each of which there is the same probability of success.

binomial nomenclature *n.* a system of classification using two terms, the first one indicating the genus and the second the species.

binomial theorem *n.* a formula for finding any power of a binomial without multiplying at length.

binominal /bʌɪˈnɒmɪn(ə)l/ *adj.* = BINOMIAL. [Latin *binominis* (as BI-, *nomen -inis* name)]

bint /bɪnt/ *n. Brit. slang* usu. *offens.* a girl or woman. [Arabic, = daughter, girl]

binturong /ˈbɪntjʊrɒŋ/ *n.* a civet, *Arctictis binturong*, of S. Asia, with a shaggy black coat and a prehensile tail. [Malay]

bio- /ˈbʌɪəʊ/ *comb. form* **1** life (*biography*). **2** biological (*biomathematics*). **3** of living beings (*biophysics*). [Greek *bios* '(course of) human life']

bioassay /ˌbʌɪəʊəˈseɪ/ *n.* measurement of the concentration or potency of a substance by its effect on living cells or tissues. [BIO- + ASSAY]

biochemistry /bʌɪə(ʊ)ˈkɛmɪstri/ *n.* the study of the chemical and physico-chemical processes of living organisms. □ **biochemical** *adj.* **biochemist** *n.*

biocide /ˈbʌɪəsʌɪd/ *n.* **1** a poisonous substance, esp. a pesticide. **2** the destruction of life. [BIO- + -CIDE]

biocoenosis /ˌbʌɪə(ʊ)sɪˈnəʊsɪs/ *n.* (*US* **biocenosis**) (*pl.* **-noses** /-siːz/) **1** an association of different organisms forming a community. **2** the relationship existing between such organisms. □ **biocoenology** /-ˈnɒlədʒi/ *n.* **biocoenotic** /-ˈnɒtɪk/ *adj.* [modern Latin from BIO- + Greek *koinōsis* 'sharing' from *koinos* 'common']

biodegradable /ˌbʌɪə(ʊ)dɪˈgreɪdəb(ə)l/ *adj.* capable of being decomposed by bacteria or other living organisms. □ **biodegradability** /-ˈbɪlɪti/ *n.* **biodegradation** /ˌbʌɪəʊdɛgrəˈdeɪʃ(ə)n/ *n.*

biodiversity /ˌbʌɪə(ʊ)dʌɪˈvəːsɪti/ *n.* diversity of plant and animal life.

bioenergetics /ˌbʌɪəʊɛnəˈdʒɛtɪks/ *n.* the study of the transformation of energy in living organisms.

bioengineering /ˌbʌɪəʊɛndʒɪˈnɪərɪŋ/ *n.* **1** the industrial use of biosynthetic processes. **2** the use of artificial tissues, organs, or organ components to replace damaged or absent parts of the body, e.g. artificial limbs, heart pacemakers, etc. □ **bioengineer** *n. & v.*

bioethics /bʌɪəʊˈɛθɪks/ *n.pl.* (treated as *sing.*) the ethics of medical and biological research. □ **bioethicist** /-sɪst/ *n.*

biofeedback /bʌɪəʊˈfiːdbak/ *n.* the technique of using the feedback of a normally automatic bodily response to a stimulus, in order to acquire voluntary control of that response.

bioflavonoid /bʌɪəʊˈfleɪvənɔɪd/ *n.* a group of substances occurring mainly in citrus fruits and blackcurrants, and formerly regarded as a vitamin. Also called *citrin, vitamin P*. [BIO- + *flavonoid* from FLAVINE + -OID]

biogas /ˈbʌɪə(ʊ)gas/ *n.* gaseous fuel, esp. methane, produced by fermentation of organic matter.

biogenesis /bʌɪə(ʊ)ˈdʒɛnɪsɪs/ *n.* **1** the synthesis of substances by living organisms. **2** the hypothesis that a living organism arises only from another similar living organism. □ **biogenetic** /-dʒɪˈnɛtɪk/ *adj.*

biogenic /bʌɪə(ʊ)ˈdʒɛnɪk/ *adj.* produced by living organisms.

biogeography /ˌbʌɪəʊdʒɪˈɒgrəfi, -ˈdʒɒg-/ *n.* the scientific study of the geographical distribution of plants and animals. □ **biogeographical** /-dʒɪəˈgrafɪk(ə)l/ *adj.*

biography /bʌɪˈɒgrəfi/ *n.* (*pl.* **-ies**) **1 a** a written account of a person's life, usu. by another. **b** such writing as a branch of literature. **2** the course of a living (usu. human) being's life. □ **biographer** *n.* **biographic** /bʌɪəˈgrafɪk/ *adj.* **biographical** /bʌɪəˈgrafɪk(ə)l/ *adj.* [French *biographie* or modern Latin *biographia*, from medieval Greek]

biohazard /ˈbʌɪəʊˌhazəd/ *n.* a risk to human health or the environment arising from biological work, esp. with micro-organisms.

biological /bʌɪə(ʊ)ˈlɒdʒɪk(ə)l/ *adj.* **1** of or relating to biology or living organisms. **2** *Brit.* (of a detergent etc.) containing enzymes to assist the process of cleaning. □ **biologically** *adv.*

biological clock *n.* an innate mechanism controlling the rhythmic physiological activities of an organism.

biological control *n.* the control of a pest by the introduction of a natural enemy.

biological warfare *n.* warfare involving the use of toxins or micro-organisms.

biology /bʌɪˈɒlədʒi/ *n.* **1** the study of living organisms. **2** the plants and animals of a particular area. □ **biologist** *n.* [French *biologie* from German *Biologie* (as BIO-, -LOGY)]

bioluminescence /ˌbʌɪəʊluːmɪˈnɛs(ə)ns/ *n.* the emission of light by living organisms such as the firefly and glow-worm. □ **bioluminescent** *adj.*

biomass /ˈbʌɪə(ʊ)mas/ *n.* the total quantity or weight of organisms in a given area or volume. [BIO- + MASS]

biomathematics /ˌbʌɪə(ʊ)maθ(ə)ˈmatɪks/ *n.* the science of the application of mathematics to biology.

biome /ˈbʌɪəʊm/ *n.* **1** a large naturally occurring community of flora and fauna adapted to the particular conditions in which they occur, e.g. tundra. **2** the geographical region containing such a community. [BIO- + -OME]

biomechanics /ˌbʌɪə(ʊ)mɪˈkanɪks/ *n.* the study of the mechanical laws relating to the movement or structure of living organisms.

biomedical /bʌɪə(ʊ)ˈmɛdɪk(ə)l/ *adj.* of or relating to both biology and medicine. □ **biomedicine** *n.*

biometry /bʌɪˈɒmɪtri/ *n.* (also **biometrics** /bʌɪə(ʊ)ˈmɛtrɪks/) the application of statistical analysis to biological data. □ **biometric** /bʌɪə(ʊ)ˈmɛtrɪk/ *adj.*

biometrical /bʌɪə(ʊ)'mɛtrɪk(ə)l/ *adj.* **biometrician** /bʌɪə(ʊ)mɪ'trɪʃ(ə)n/ *n.*

biomorph /'bʌɪəʊmɔ:f/ *n.* a decorative form based on a living organism. □ **biomorphic** /-'mɔ:fɪk/ *adj.* [BIO- + Greek *morphē* 'form']

bionic /bʌɪ'ɒnɪk/ *adj.* **1** having artificial body parts or the superhuman powers resulting from these. **2** relating to bionics. □ **bionically** *adv.* [BIO-, on the pattern of *electronic*]

bionics /bʌɪ'ɒnɪks/ *n.* the study of mechanical systems that function like living organisms or parts of living organisms.

bionomics /bʌɪə(ʊ)'nɒmɪks/ *n.pl.* (treated as *sing.*) the study of the mode of life of organisms in their natural habitat and their adaptations to their surroundings; ecology. □ **bionomic** *adj.* [BIO-, on the pattern of *economics*]

biophysics /bʌɪə(ʊ)'fɪzɪks/ *n.* the science of the application of the laws of physics to biological phenomena. □ **biophysical** *adj.* **biophysicist** /-sɪst/ *n.*

biopic /'bʌɪəʊpɪk/ *n. colloq.* a biographical film. [*bio*graphical + PIC]

biopsy /'bʌɪɒpsi/ *n.* (*pl.* **-ies**) the examination of tissue removed from a living body to discover the presence, cause, or extent of a disease. [French *biopsie* from Greek *bios* 'life' + *opsis* 'sight', on the pattern of *necropsy*]

biorhythm /'bʌɪə(ʊ)rɪð(ə)m/ *n.* **1** any of the recurring cycles of biological processes thought to affect a person's emotional, intellectual, and physical activity. **2** any periodic change in the behaviour or physiology of an organism. □ **biorhythmic** /-'rɪðmɪk/ *adj.* **biorhythmically** /-'rɪðmɪk(ə)li/ *adv.*

bioscope /'bʌɪəskəʊp/ *n. S.Afr. slang* a cinema. [in early use 'a view of life', from BIO- + -SCOPE]

biosphere /'bʌɪə(ʊ)sfɪə/ *n.* the regions of the earth's crust and atmosphere occupied by living organisms. [German *Biosphäre* (as BIO-, SPHERE)]

biosynthesis /bʌɪə(ʊ)'sɪnθɪsɪs/ *n.* the production of organic molecules by living organisms. □ **biosynthetic** /-'θɛtɪk/ *adj.*

biota /bʌɪ'əʊtə/ *n.* the animal and plant life of a region. [modern Latin from Greek *biotē* 'life']

biotechnology /,bʌɪə(ʊ)tɛk'nɒlədʒi/ *n.* the exploitation of biological processes for industrial and other purposes, esp. genetic manipulation of micro-organisms (for the production of antibiotics, hormones, etc.).

biotic /bʌɪ'ɒtɪk/ *adj.* **1** relating to life or to living things. **2** of biological origin. [French *biotique* or Late Latin *bioticus*, from Greek *biōtikos* from *bios* 'life']

biotin /'bʌɪətɪn/ *n.* a vitamin of the B complex, found in egg yolk, liver, and yeast, and involved in the metabolism of carbohydrates, fats, and proteins. Also (esp. *US*) called *vitamin H.* [German, from Greek *bios* 'life' + -IN]

biotite /'bʌɪətʌɪt/ *n.* a black, dark brown, or green micaceous mineral occurring as a constituent of metamorphic and igneous rocks. [J. B. *Biot*, French mineralogist d. 1862]

bipartisan /,bʌɪpɑ:tɪ'zan/ *adj.* of or involving two (esp. political) parties. □ **bipartisanship** *n.*

bipartite /bʌɪ'pɑ:tʌɪt/ *adj.* **1** consisting of two parts. **2** shared by or involving two parties. **3** *Law* (of a contract, treaty, etc.) drawn up in two corresponding parts or between two parties. [Latin *bipartitus* from *bipartire* (as BI-, *partire* PART)]

biped /'bʌɪpɛd/ *n. & adj.* ● *n.* a two-footed animal. ● *adj.* two-footed. □ **bipedal** /bʌɪ'pi:d(ə)l/ *adj.* **bipedalism** /bʌɪ'pi:d(ə)lɪz(ə)m/ *n.* **bipedality** /bʌɪpi:'dalɪti/ *n.* [Latin *bipes -edis* (as BI-, *pes pedis* 'foot')]

biphenyl /bʌɪ'fi:nʌɪl, bʌɪ'fɛnɪl/ *n. Chem.* an organic compound containing two phenyl groups. Cf. PCB.

bipinnate /bʌɪ'pɪneɪt/ *adj.* (of a pinnate leaf) having leaflets that are further subdivided in a pinnate arrangement.

biplane /'bʌɪpleɪn/ *n.* an early type of aeroplane having two sets of wings, one above the other (cf. MONOPLANE).

bipolar /bʌɪ'pəʊlə/ *adj.* having two poles or extremities. □ **bipolarity** /-'larɪti/ *n.*

birch /bə:tʃ/ *n. & v.* ● *n.* **1** (also **birch tree**) any tree of the genus *Betula*, having thin peeling bark, bearing catkins, and found predominantly in northern temperate regions. **2** (in full **birchwood**) the hard fine-grained pale wood of these trees. **3** *NZ* any of various similar trees. **4** (in full **birch-rod**) a bundle of birch twigs used for flogging. ● *v.tr.* beat with a birch (in sense 4 of *n.*). □ **birchen** *adj.* [Old English *bi(e)rce*, from Germanic]

birch-bark *n.* **1** the bark of *Betula papyrifera* used to make canoes. **2** *N. Amer.* such a canoe.

bird /bə:d/ *n.* **1** a feathered vertebrate of the class Aves with a beak, two wings, and two feet, egg-laying and usu. able to fly. **2** a game bird. **3** *Brit. slang* a young woman. **4** *colloq.* a person (*a wily old bird*). **5** *Brit. slang* **a** a prison. **b** *rhyming slang* a prison sentence (short for *birdlime* = time). □ **a bird in the hand** something secured or certain. **the bird is** (or **has**) **flown** the prisoner, quarry, etc., has escaped. **the birds and the bees** *euphem.* sexual activity and reproduction. **birds of a feather** people of like character. **for** (or **strictly for**) **the birds** *colloq.* trivial, uninteresting. **get the bird** *Brit. slang* **1** be dismissed. **2** be hissed at or booed. **like a bird** *Brit.* without difficulty or hesitation. **a little bird** an unnamed informant. [Old English *brid*, of unknown origin]

bird bath *n.* a basin in a garden etc. with water for birds to bathe in.

birdbrain /'bə:dbreɪn/ *n. colloq.* a stupid or flighty person. □ **birdbrained** *adj.*

birdcage /'bə:dkeɪdʒ/ *n.* **1** a cage for birds usu. made of wire or cane. **2** an object of a similar design.

bird call *n.* **1** a bird's natural call. **2** an instrument imitating this.

bird cherry *n.* a wild cherry, *Prunus padus.*

birder /'bə:də/ *n.* esp. *N. Amer.* a birdwatcher. □ **birding** *n.*

bird-fancier *n.* a person who knows about, collects, breeds, or deals in, birds.

birdie /'bə:di/ *n. & v.* ● *n.* **1** *colloq.* a little bird. **2** *Golf* a score of one stroke less than par at any hole. ● *v.tr.* (**birdies, birdied, birdying**) *Golf* play (a hole) in a birdie.

birdlime /'bə:dlʌɪm/ *n.* sticky material painted on to twigs to trap small birds.

bird-nesting *n.* (also **bird's-nesting**) hunting for birds' nests, usu. to get eggs.

bird of paradise *n.* any bird of the family Paradiseidae, found chiefly in New Guinea, the males having very beautiful brilliantly coloured plumage.

bird of passage *n.* **1** a migrant. **2** any transient visitor.

bird of prey *n.* a bird which hunts animals for food.

bird sanctuary *n.* an area where birds are protected and encouraged to breed.

birdseed /'bə:dsi:d/ *n.* a blend of seed for feeding birds, esp. ones which are caged.

bird's-eye *n. & adj.* ● *n.* **1** any of several plants having small bright round flowers, such as the germander speedwell. **2** a pattern with many small spots. ● *adj.* of or having small bright round flowers (*bird's-eye primrose*).

bird's-eye view *n.* a general view from above.

bird's-foot *n.* (*pl.* **bird's-foots**) any plant having a part like the foot of a bird, esp. a vetch of the genus *Ornithopus*, with claw-shaped pods.

bird's-foot trefoil *n.* a small leguminous plant, *Lotus corniculatus*, having yellow flowers streaked with red.

bird's-nesting var. of BIRD-NESTING.

bird's nest soup *n.* soup made (esp. in Chinese cookery) from the dried gelatinous coating of the nests of swifts and other birds.

birdsong /ˈbɜːdsɒŋ/ *n.* the musical cry of a bird or birds.

bird-strike *n.* a collision between a bird and an aircraft.

bird table *n. Brit.* a raised platform on which food for birds is placed.

birdwatcher /ˈbɜːdwɒtʃə/ *n.* a person who observes birds in their natural surroundings. □ **birdwatching** *n.*

birefringent /bʌɪrɪˈfrɪn(d)ʒ(ə)nt/ *adj. Physics* having two different refractive indices. □ **birefringence** *n.*

bireme /ˈbʌɪriːm/ *n. hist.* an ancient Greek warship, with two files of oarsmen on each side. [Latin *biremis* (as BI-, *remus* 'oar')]

biretta /bɪˈrɛtə/ *n.* a square usu. black cap with three flat projections on top, worn by (esp. Roman Catholic) clergymen. [Italian *berretta* or Spanish *birreta*, from Late Latin *birrus* 'hooded cape']

biriani /bɪrɪˈɑːni/ *n.* (also **biryani**) an originally Indian dish made with highly seasoned rice, and meat or fish etc. [Urdu]

biro /ˈbʌɪrəʊ/ *n.* (*pl.* **-os**) *Brit. propr.* a kind of ballpoint pen. [L. *Biró* (d. 1985), Hungarian inventor of the ballpoint]

birth /bɜːθ/ *n. & v.* ● *n.* **1** the emergence of a (usu. fully developed) infant or other young from the body of its mother. **2** *literary* the beginning or coming into existence of something (*the birth of civilization*; *the birth of socialism*). **3 a** origin, descent, ancestry (*of noble birth*). **b** high or noble birth; inherited position. ● *v.tr. N. Amer. colloq.* **1** (also *absol.*) give birth to. **2** assist (a woman) to give birth. □ **give birth** bear a child etc. **give birth to 1** produce (young) from the womb. **2** cause to begin, found. [Middle English, from Old Norse *byrth* from Germanic: see BEAR[1], -TH[2]]

birth certificate *n.* an official document identifying a person by name, place, and date of birth.

birth control *n.* the control of the number of children one conceives, esp. by contraception.

birth control pill *n.* the contraceptive pill.

birthday /ˈbɜːθdeɪ/ *n.* **1** the day on which a person etc. was born. **2** the anniversary of this. □ **in one's birthday suit** *joc.* naked.

birthday honours *n.pl. Brit.* titles etc. given on a sovereign's official birthday.

birthing /ˈbɜːθɪŋ/ *n.* the act or process of giving birth (also *attrib.*: *birthing position*).

birthing pool *n.* a large bath for giving birth in.

birthmark /ˈbɜːθmɑːk/ *n.* an unusual brown or red mark on one's body at or from birth.

birth mother *n.* = MOTHER *n.* 1a.

birth pill *n. Brit.* = BIRTH CONTROL PILL.

birthplace /ˈbɜːθpleɪs/ *n.* the place where a person was born.

birth rate *n.* the number of live births per thousand of population per year.

birthright /ˈbɜːθrʌɪt/ *n.* a right of possession or privilege one has from birth, esp. as the eldest son.

birthstone /ˈbɜːθstəʊn/ *n.* a gemstone popularly associated with the month of one's birth.

birthweight /ˈbɜːθweɪt/ *n.* the weight of a baby at birth.

biryani var. of BIRIANI.

biscuit /ˈbɪskɪt/ *n. & adj.* ● *n.* **1** *Brit.* a small unleavened cake, usu. flat and crisp and often sweet. **2** fired unglazed pottery. **3** a light brown colour. ● *adj.* light brown. □ **biscuity** *adj.* [Middle English from Old French *bescoit* etc., ultimately from Latin *bis* 'twice' + *coctus*, past part. of *coquere* 'cook']

bise /biːz/ *n.* a keen dry northerly wind in Switzerland, southern France, etc. [French]

bisect /bʌɪˈsɛkt/ *v.tr.* divide into two (strictly, equal) parts. □ **bisection** /-ˈsɛkʃ(ə)n/ *n.* **bisector** *n.* [BI- + Latin *secare sect-* 'cut']

bisexual /bʌɪˈsɛksjʊəl, -ʃʊəl/ *adj. & n.* ● *adj.* **1** sexually attracted by persons of both sexes. **2** *Biol.* having characteristics of both sexes. **3** of or concerning both sexes. ● *n.* a bisexual person. □ **bisexuality** /-ˈalɪti/ *n.*

bish /bɪʃ/ *n. Brit. slang* a mistake. [20th c.: origin uncertain]

bishop /ˈbɪʃəp/ *n.* **1** a senior member of the Christian clergy usu. in charge of a diocese, and empowered to confer holy orders. **2** a chess piece with the top sometimes shaped like a mitre. **3** mulled and spiced wine. [Old English *biscop*, ultimately from Greek *episkopos* 'overseer' (as EPI-, *-skopos* '-looking')]

bishopric /ˈbɪʃəprɪk/ *n.* **1** the office of a bishop. **2** a diocese. [Old English *bisceoprīce* (as BISHOP, *rīce* 'realm')]

bismuth /ˈbɪzməθ/ *n. Chem.* **1** a brittle reddish-white metallic element, occurring naturally and used in alloys (symbol **Bi**). **2** any compound of this element used medicinally. [modern Latin *bisemutum*, Latinization of German *Wismut*, of unknown origin]

bison /ˈbʌɪs(ə)n/ *n.* (*pl.* same) either of two wild humpbacked shaggy-haired oxen of the genus *Bison*, native to N. America (*B. bison*) or Europe (*B. bonasus*). [Middle English, via Latin from Germanic]

bisque[1] /bɪsk, biːsk/ *n.* a rich shellfish soup, made esp. from lobster. [French]

bisque[2] /bɪsk/ *n. Tennis, Croquet, & Golf* an advantage of scoring one free point, or taking an extra turn or stroke. [French]

bisque[3] /bɪsk/ *n.* = BISCUIT 2.

bistable /bʌɪˈsteɪb(ə)l/ *adj.* (of an electrical circuit etc.) having two stable states.

bister var. of BISTRE.

bistort /ˈbɪstɔːt/ *n.* a herbaceous plant, *Polygonum bistorta*, with a twisted root and a cylindrical spike of flesh-coloured flowers. [French *bistorte* or medieval Latin *bistorta*, from *bis* 'twice' + *torta*, fem. past part. of *torquēre* 'twist']

bistoury /ˈbɪstʊri/ *n.* (*pl.* **-ies**) a surgical scalpel. [French *bistouri*, *bistorie*, originally = dagger, of unknown origin]

bistre /ˈbɪstə/ *n. & adj.* (*US* **bister**) ● *n.* **1** a brownish pigment made from the soot of burnt wood. **2** the brownish colour of this. ● *adj.* of this colour. [French, of unknown origin]

bistro /ˈbiːstrəʊ, ˈbɪs-/ *n.* (*pl.* **-os**) a small restaurant. [French]

bisulphate /bʌɪˈsʌlfeɪt/ *n.* (*US* **bisulfate**) *Chem.* a salt or ester of sulphuric acid.

bit[1] /bɪt/ *n.* **1** a small piece or quantity (*a bit of cheese*; *give me another bit*; *that bit is too small*). **2** (prec. by *a*) **a** a fair amount (*sold quite a bit*; *needed a bit of persuading*). **b** *colloq.* somewhat (*am a bit tired*). **c** (foll. by *of*) *colloq.* rather (*a bit of an idiot*). **d** (foll. by *of*) *colloq.* only a little; a mere (*a bit of a boy*). **3** a short time or distance (*wait a bit*; *move up a bit*). **4** *US slang* a unit of 12½ cents (used only in even multiples). □ **bit by bit** gradually. **bit of all right** *Brit. slang* a pleasing person or thing, esp. a woman. **bit of fluff** (or **skirt** or **stuff**) see FLUFF, SKIRT *n.* 5, STUFF. **bit of rough** see ROUGH. **bit on the side** *slang* **1** a sexual relationship involving infidelity to one's partner. **2** the person with whom one is unfaithful. **bits and pieces** (or **bobs**) an assortment of small items. **do one's bit** *colloq.* make a useful contribution to an effort or cause. **every bit as** see EVERY. **not a bit** (or *Brit.* **not a bit of it**) not at all. **to bits 1** into pieces. **2** *colloq.* very much; to a great degree (*love them to bits*; *thrilled to bits*). [Old English *bita* from Germanic, related to BITE]

bit[2] *past* of BITE.

bit[3] /bɪt/ *n. & v.* ● *n.* **1** a metal mouthpiece on a bridle, used to control a horse. **2** a (usu. metal) tool or piece for boring or drilling. **3** the cutting or gripping part of a plane, pincers, etc. **4** the part of a key that engages with the lock-lever. **5** the copper head of a soldering iron. ● *v.tr.* **1** put a bit into the mouth of (a horse). **2** restrain. □ **take the bit between one's teeth 1** take decisive personal action. **2** escape from control. [Old English *bite* from Germanic, related to BITE]

bit[4] /bɪt/ *n. Computing* a unit of information expressed as a choice between two possibilities; a 0 or 1 in binary notation. [BINARY + DIGIT]

bitch /bɪtʃ/ *n. & v.* ● *n.* **1** a female dog or other canine animal. **2** *slang offens.* a malicious or spiteful woman. **3** *slang* a very unpleasant or difficult thing or situation. ● *v. colloq.* **1** *intr.* (often foll. by *about*) **a** speak scathingly. **b** complain. **2** *tr.* be spiteful or unfair to. [Old English *bicce*]

bitchy /ˈbɪtʃi/ *adj.* (**bitchier**, **bitchiest**) *slang* spiteful; bad-tempered. □ **bitchily** *adv.* **bitchiness** *n.*

bite /bʌɪt/ *v. & n.* ● *v.* (*past* **bit** /bɪt/; *past part.* **bitten** /ˈbɪt(ə)n/) **1** *tr.* cut or puncture using the teeth. **2** *tr.* (foll. by *off, away,* etc.) detach with the teeth. **3** *tr.* (of an insect, snake, etc.) wound with a sting, fangs, etc. **4** *intr.* (of a wheel, screw, etc.) grip, penetrate. **5** *intr.* accept bait or an inducement. **6** *intr.* have a (desired) adverse effect. **7** *tr.* (in *passive*) **a** take in; swindle. **b** (foll. by *by, with,* etc.) be infected by (enthusiasm etc.). **8** *tr.* (as **bitten** *adj.*) cause a glowing or smarting pain to (*frostbitten*). **9** *intr.* (foll. by *at*) snap at. **10** *tr. colloq.* worry, perturb (*what's biting you?*). ● *n.* **1** an act of biting. **2** a wound or sore made by biting. **3** **a** a mouthful of food. **b** a snack or light meal. **4** the taking of bait by a fish. **5** pungency (esp. of flavour). **6** incisiveness, sharpness. **7** = OCCLUSION 3. □ **bite back** restrain (one's speech etc.) by or as if by biting the lips. **bite** (or *Brit.* **bite on**) **the bullet** *slang* behave bravely or stoically. **bite the dust** *slang* **1** die. **2** fail; break down. **bite the hand that feeds one** hurt or offend a benefactor. **bite a person's head off** *colloq.* respond fiercely or angrily. **bite one's lip** see LIP. **bite off more than one can chew** take on a commitment one cannot fulfil. **once bitten twice shy** an unpleasant experience induces caution. **put the bite on** *US slang* borrow or extort money from. □ **biter** *n.* [Old English *bītan*, from Germanic]

bite-sized *adj.* (also **bite-size**) **1** small enough to be eaten in one mouthful. **2** very small or short.

biting /ˈbʌɪtɪŋ/ *adj.* **1** stinging; intensely cold (*a biting wind*). **2** sharp; effective (*biting wit; biting sarcasm*). □ **bitingly** *adv.*

bitmap /ˈbɪtmap/ *n. & v. Computing* ● *n.* a representation in which each item is shown by one or more bits of information, esp. a display of the contents of a memory store. ● *v.tr.* (**-mapped**, **-mapping**) provide with or represent by a bitmap.

bit part *n.* a minor part in a play or a film.

bitten *past part.* of BITE.

bitter /ˈbɪtə/ *adj. & n.* ● *adj.* **1** having a sharp pungent taste; not sweet. **2** **a** caused by or showing mental pain or resentment (*bitter memories; bitter rejoinder*). **b** painful or difficult to accept (*bitter disappointment*). **3** **a** harsh; virulent (*bitter animosity*). **b** piercingly cold. ● *n.* **1** *Brit.* beer strongly flavoured with hops and having a bitter taste. **2** (in *pl.*) liquor with a bitter flavour (esp. of wormwood) used as an additive in cocktails. □ **to the bitter end** to the very end in spite of difficulties. □ **bitterly** *adv.* **bitterness** *n.* [Old English *biter*, probably from Germanic: *to the bitter end* may be associated with a nautical word *bitter* = 'last part of a cable': see BITTS]

bitter aloes see ALOE 2.

bitter-apple *n.* = COLOCYNTH.

bitterling /ˈbɪtəlɪŋ/ *n.* a small brightly coloured freshwater fish, *Rhodeus amarus*, from central Europe. [German *Bitterling*, from BITTER *adj.* + -LING[1]]

bittern[1] /ˈbɪtən/ *n.* any of a group of wading birds of the heron family, esp. of the genus *Botaurus* with a distinctive booming call. [Middle English from Old French *butor*, ultimately from Latin *butio* 'bittern' + *taurus* 'bull' (from its call); *-n* perhaps from association with HERON]

bittern[2] /ˈbɪtən/ *n. Chem.* the liquid remaining after the crystallization of common salt from sea water. [probably from BITTER *adj.*]

bitter orange *n.* = SEVILLE ORANGE.

bitter pill *n.* something unpleasant that has to be accepted.

bitter-sweet *adj. & n.* ● *adj.* **1** sweet with a bitter aftertaste. **2** arousing pleasure tinged with pain or sorrow. ● *n.* **1** **a** sweetness with a bitter aftertaste. **b** pleasure tinged with pain or sorrow. **2** = *woody nightshade* (see NIGHTSHADE).

bitts /bɪts/ *n.pl. Naut.* a pair of posts on the deck of a ship, for fastening cables etc. [Middle English, probably from Low German]

bitty /ˈbɪti/ *adj.* (**bittier**, **bittiest**) **1** esp. *Brit.* made up of unrelated bits; scrappy. **2** (esp. in phrs. **little bitty**, **itty-bitty**) *N. Amer. colloq.* tiny. □ **bittily** *adv.* **bittiness** *n.*

bitumen /ˈbɪtjʊmən/ *n.* **1** any of various tarlike mixtures of hydrocarbons derived from petroleum naturally or by distillation and used for road surfacing and roofing. **2** *Austral. colloq.* a tarred road. [Latin *bitumen -minis*]

bituminize /bɪˈtjuːmɪnʌɪz/ *v.tr.* (also **-ise**) convert into, impregnate with, or cover with bitumen. □ **bituminization** /-ˈzeɪʃ(ə)n/ *n.*

bituminous /bɪˈtjuːmɪnəs/ *adj.* of, relating to, or containing bitumen.

bituminous coal *n.* a form of coal burning with a smoky flame.

bivalent *adj. & n.* ● *adj.* **1** /bʌɪˈveɪl(ə)nt/ *Chem.* = DIVALENT. **2** /ˈbɪv(ə)l(ə)nt/ *Biol.* (of homologous chromosomes) associated in pairs. ● *n.* /ˈbɪv(ə)l(ə)nt/ *Biol.* any pair of homologous chromosomes. □ **bivalency** *n.* [BI- + Latin *valent-* pres. part. stem of *valere*: see VALENCY]

bivalve /ˈbʌɪvalv/ *n. & adj.* ● *n.* any of a group of aquatic molluscs of the class Bivalvia, with laterally compressed bodies enclosed within two hinged shells, e.g. oysters, mussels, etc. ● *adj.* **1** with a hinged double shell. **2** *Biol.* having two valves, e.g. of a pea pod.

bivouac /ˈbɪvʊak, ˈbɪvwak/ *n. & v.* ● *n.* a temporary open encampment without tents, esp. of soldiers. ● *v.intr.* (**bivouacked**, **bivouacking**) camp in a bivouac, esp. overnight. [earlier, 'a night watch by a whole army': French, probably from Swiss German *Beiwacht* 'additional guard at night']

biweekly /bʌɪˈwiːkli/ *adv., adj., & n.* ● *adv.* **1** every two weeks. **2** twice a week. ● *adj.* produced or occurring biweekly. ● *n.* (*pl.* **-ies**) a biweekly periodical.

■ **Usage** See Usage Note at BIMONTHLY.

biyearly /bʌɪˈjɪəli, -ˈjəː-/ *adv. & adj.* ● *adv.* **1** every two years. **2** twice a year. ● *adj.* produced or occurring biyearly.

■ **Usage** See Usage Note at BIMONTHLY.

biz /bɪz/ *n. colloq.* business. [abbreviation]

bizarre /bɪˈzɑː/ *adj.* strange in appearance or effect; eccentric; grotesque. □ **bizarrely** *adv.* **bizarreness** *n.* [French, = handsome, brave, via Spanish & Portuguese *bizarro* from Basque *bizarra* 'beard']

bizarrerie /bɪˈzɑːrəri/ *n.* a bizarre quality; bizarreness. [French]

Bk *symb. Chem.* the element berkelium.

bk. *abbr.* book.

BL *abbr.* **1** *Sc. & Ir.* Bachelor of Law. **2** British Library. **3** *hist.* British Leyland. **4** bill of lading.

bl. *abbr.* **1** barrel. **2** black.

blab /blab/ *v. & n.* ● *v.* (**blabbed**, **blabbing**) **1** *intr.* **a** talk foolishly or indiscreetly. **b** reveal secrets. **2** *tr.* reveal (a secret etc.) by indiscreet talk. ● *n.* a person who blabs. [Middle English, probably from Germanic]

blabber /ˈblabə/ *n. & v.* ● *n.* (also **blabbermouth** /ˈblabəmaʊθ/) a person who blabs. ● *v.intr.* (often foll. by *on*) talk foolishly or inconsequentially, esp. at length.

black /blak/ *adj., n., & v.* ● *adj.* **1** very dark, having no colour from the absorption of all or nearly all incident light (like coal or soot). **2** completely dark from the absence of a source of light (*black night*). **3** (also **Black**) **a** of the human group having dark-coloured skin, esp. of African or Australian Aboriginal descent. **b** of or relating to black people (*black rights*). **4** (of the sky, a cloud, etc.) dusky; heavily overcast. **5** angry, threatening (*a black look*). **6** implying disgrace or condemnation (*in his black books*). **7** wicked, sinister, deadly (*black-hearted*). **8** gloomy, depressed, sullen (*a black mood*). **9** portending trouble or difficulty (*things looked black*). **10** (of hands, clothes, etc.) dirty, soiled. **11** (of humour or its representation) with sinister or macabre, as well as comic, import (*black comedy*). **12** (of tea or coffee) without milk. **13** *Brit.* **a** (of industrial labour or its products) boycotted, esp. by a trade union, in an industrial dispute. **b** (of a person) doing work or handling goods that have been boycotted. **14** dark in colour as distinguished from a lighter variety (*black bear*; *black pine*). ● *n.* **1** a black colour or pigment. **2** black clothes or material (*dressed in black*). **3 a** (in a game or sport) a black piece, ball, etc. **b** the player using such pieces. **4** the credit side of an account (*in the black*). **5** (also **Black**) a member of a dark-skinned race, esp. of African or Australian descent. ● *v.tr.* **1** make black (*blacked his face*). **2** polish with blacking. **3** *Brit.* declare (goods etc.) 'black'. □ **black in the face** livid with strangulation, exertion, or passion. **black out 1 a** effect a blackout on. **b** undergo a blackout. **2** obscure windows etc. or extinguish all lights for protection esp. against an air attack. □ **blackish** *adj.* **blackly** *adv.* **blackness** *n.* [Old English *blæc*]

■ **Usage** When referring to dark-skinned people, *black* (rather than *Negro* or *Coloured*) is now the preferred term. In Britain and the US it is generally used to designate people of African descent while in Australia it is used of Aboriginals. The term *African-American* is also common in the US for people of African descent.

In Britain, the term *black* is often found alongside *Asian* with reference to the two largest ethnic minorities, e.g. *The organization is open to blacks, Asians, and anyone who believes they suffer discrimination.* In the US, *black* is often found alongside *Hispanic* in similar contexts.

Although *black* has been the preferred term for a number of years now, older people still tend to use other previously acceptable terms (e.g. *Negro* or *Coloured*). In order to avoid offence, however, these terms should not be used.

black Africa *n.* the area of Africa, generally south of the Sahara, where black people predominate.

blackamoor /ˈblakəmʊə, -mɔː/ *n.* *archaic* a black African; a very dark-skinned person. [BLACK + MOOR]

black and blue *adj.* discoloured by bruises.

Black and Tans *n.pl.* an armed force recruited to fight Sinn Fein in Ireland in 1921, wearing a mixture of military and constabulary uniforms.

black and white *n.* & *adj.* ● *n.* writing or printing (*in black and white*). ● *adj.* **1** recorded in writing or print (*down in black and white*). **2** (of film etc.) not in colour. **3** consisting of extremes only, oversimplified (*interpreted the problem in black and white terms*).

black art *n.* (prec. by *the*) = BLACK MAGIC.

blackball /ˈblakbɔːl/ *v.tr.* reject (a candidate) in a ballot (originally by voting with a black ball).

black bass see BASS[2] 4.

black bean *n.* **1 a** any of various plants of the genus *Phaseolus*, with small black seeds. **b** the dried seed of this used as a vegetable. **2** a fermented soya bean, used as flavouring in oriental cookery. **3** a large Australian leguminous tree with heavy seed pods, *Castanospermum australe*.

black beetle *n.* *Brit.* the common cockroach, *Blatta orientalis*.

black belt *n.* **1** a black belt worn by an expert in judo, karate, etc. **2** a person qualified to wear this.

blackberry /ˈblakb(ə)ri/ *n.* & *v.* ● *n.* (*pl.* **-ies**) **1** a thorny climbing shrub, *Rubus fruticosus* (rose family), bearing white or pink flowers; also called BRAMBLE. **2** an edible fruit of this plant, consisting of a cluster of soft black drupels. ● *v.intr.* (**-ies**, **-ied**) gather blackberries.

black bile *n.* *hist.* one of the four bodily humours, characterized as cold and dry, and associated with a melancholy temperament (cf. HUMOUR *n.* 5). [translation of Greek *melagkholia*: cf. MELANCHOLY, ATRABILIOUS]

blackbird /ˈblakbəːd/ *n.* **1** a common thrush, *Turdus merula*, the male of which is black with an orange beak. **2** *US* any of various birds, esp. grackles, with black plumage. **3** *hist.* a black or Polynesian captive on a slave ship.

blackboard /ˈblakbɔːd/ *n.* a board with a smooth usu. dark surface for writing on with chalk.

black body *n.* *Physics* a hypothetical perfect absorber and radiator of energy, with no reflecting power.

black bottom *n.* a popular dance of the 1920s.

black box *n.* **1** a flight recorder in an aircraft. **2** any complex piece of equipment, usu. a unit in an electronic system, with contents which are mysterious to the user.

blackboy /ˈblakbɔɪ/ *n.* any tree of the genus *Xanthorrhoea*, native to Australia, with a thick dark trunk and a head of grasslike leaves. Also called *grass tree*.

black bread *n.* a coarse dark-coloured type of rye bread.

black bryony *n.* a climbing plant, *Tamus communis*, with dark tubers and poisonous red berries.

blackbuck /ˈblakbʌk/ *n.* a small Indian gazelle, *Antilope cervicapra*, the male of which has a black back and white underbelly. Also called *sasin*.

blackcap /ˈblakkap/ *n.* a small warbler, *Sylvia atricapilla*, the male of which has a black-topped head.

blackcock /ˈblakkɒk/ *n.* the male of the black grouse (cf. GREYHEN).

Black Country *n.* (usu. prec. by *the*) a district of the Midlands with heavy industry.

blackcurrant /blakˈkʌr(ə)nt/ *n.* **1** a widely cultivated shrub, *Ribes nigrum*, bearing flowers in racemes. **2** the small round dark edible berry of this plant.

Black Death *n.* (usu. prec. by *the*) the widespread epidemic of bubonic plague in Europe in the 14th c.

black disc *n.* *Brit.* a long-playing gramophone record, as distinct from a compact disc.

black earth *n.* = CHERNOZEM.

black economy *n.* unofficial economic activity.

blacken /ˈblak(ə)n/ *v.* **1** *tr.* & *intr.* make or become black or dark. **2** *tr.* speak ill of, defame (*blacken someone's character*).

black English *n.* the form of English spoken by many black people, esp. as an urban dialect of the US.

black eye *n.* bruised skin around the eye resulting from a blow.

black-eyed bean *n.* (also **black-eye bean**, *US* **black-eyed pea**) a variety of bean, *Vigna sinensis*, with seeds often dried and stored prior to eating (so called from its black hilum).

black-eyed Susan *n.* any of several flowers, esp. of the genus *Rudbeckia*, with yellow-coloured petals and a dark centre.

blackface /ˈblakfeɪs/ *n.* **1** a variety of sheep with a black face. **2** the make-up used by a non-black performer playing a black role.

blackfellow /ˈblakˌfeləʊ/ *n.* *hist.* an Australian Aborigine.

blackfish /ˈblakfɪʃ/ *n.* (*pl.* usu. same) **1** any of several species of dark-coloured fish. **2** a salmon at spawning.

black flag *n.* **1** a pirate's ensign. **2** *hist.* a flag hoisted outside a prison to announce an execution.

blackfly /ˈblakflʌɪ/ *n.* (*pl.* **-flies**) **1** any of various thrips or aphids infesting plants, esp. *Aphis fabae*. **2** a biting fly of the genus *Simulium* or family Simuliidae.

Black Forest gateau *n.* (*N. Amer.* **Black Forest cake**) a chocolate sponge with layers of morello cherries or cherry jam and whipped cream and topped with chocolate icing, originally from S. Germany.

Black Friar *n.* a Dominican friar. [from the colour of the order's habit]
black frost *n.* a frost without white dew.
black ginger *n.* unscraped ginger.
black grouse *n.* (also **black game**) a European grouse, *Tetrao tetrix.*
blackguard /ˈblagɑːd, -gəd/ *n.* & *v.* ● *n.* a villain; a scoundrel; an unscrupulous, unprincipled person. ● *v.tr.* abuse scurrilously. □ **blackguardly** *adj.* [BLACK + GUARD: originally applied collectively to menials etc.]
blackhead /ˈblakhɛd/ *n.* a dark plug of sebum in a hair follicle.
black hole *n.* **1** a region of space having a gravitational field so intense that no matter and radiation can escape. **2** a place of confinement for punishment, esp. in the armed services.
black ice *n.* thin hard transparent ice, esp. on a road surface.
blacking /ˈblakɪŋ/ *n.* any black paste or polish, esp. for shoes.
blackjack[1] /ˈblakdʒak/ *n.* **1** the card game pontoon. **2** *N. Amer.* a flexible leaded bludgeon. [BLACK + JACK[1]]
blackjack[2] /ˈblakdʒak/ *n. hist.* a pirates' black flag. [BLACK + JACK[1]]
blackjack[3] /ˈblakdʒak/ *n.* a tarred-leather vessel for alcoholic liquor. [BLACK + JACK[2]]
blacklead /ˈblaklɛd/ *n.* & *v.* ● *n.* graphite. ● *v.tr.* polish with graphite.
blackleg /ˈblaklɛg/ *n.* & *v. Brit.* ● *n.* (often *attrib.*) *derog.* a person who fails to take part in industrial action. ● *v.intr.* (**-legged**, **-legging**) act as a blackleg.
black leopard *n.* = PANTHER 1.
black letter *n.* an old heavy style of type.
black light *n.* ultraviolet or infra-red radiation, invisible to the eye.
blacklist /ˈblaklɪst/ *n.* & *v.* ● *n.* a list of persons under suspicion, in disfavour, etc. ● *v.tr.* put the name of (a person) on a blacklist.
black magic *n.* magic involving supposed invocation of evil spirits.
blackmail /ˈblakmeɪl/ *n.* & *v.* ● *n.* **1 a** an extortion of payment in return for not disclosing discreditable information, a secret, etc. **b** any payment extorted in this way. **2** the use of threats or moral pressure. ● *v.tr.* **1** extort or try to extort money etc. from (a person) by blackmail. **2** threaten, coerce. □ **blackmailer** *n.* [BLACK + obsolete *mail* 'rent': Old English *māl* from Old Norse *mál* 'agreement']
Black Maria *n. colloq.* a police vehicle for transporting prisoners. [orig. US, apparently named after a *black* woman, *Maria* Lee, who kept a boarding house in Boston and helped the police in escorting drunk and disorderly customers to jail]
black mark *n.* a mark of discredit.
black market *n.* an illicit traffic in officially controlled or scarce commodities. □ **black marketeer** *n.*
black mass *n.* a travesty of the Roman Catholic Mass in worship of Satan.
Black Monk *n.* a Benedictine monk. [from the colour of the order's habit]
black Muslim *n. US* a member of an exclusively black Islamic sect proposing a separate black community.
black nationalism *n.* advocacy of the national civil rights of esp. US black people.
black nightshade see NIGHTSHADE.
blackout /ˈblakaʊt/ *n.* **1** a temporary or complete loss of vision, consciousness, or memory. **2** a loss of power, radio reception, etc. **3** a compulsory period of darkness as a precaution against air raids. **4** a temporary suppression of the release of information, esp. from police or government sources. **5** a sudden darkening of a theatre stage.
Black Panther *n.* (in the US) a member of an extremist organization set up to fight for the rights of black people.
black pepper *n.* the unripe ground or whole berries of *Piper nigrum* as a condiment.
black power *n.* a movement in support of rights and political power for black people.
black pudding *n. Brit.* a black sausage containing pork, dried pig's blood, suet, etc.
Black Rod *n. Brit.* the principal usher of the Lord Chamberlain's department, House of Lords, etc. [from the symbol of office]
black salsify *n.* scorzonera.
black sheep *n. colloq.* an unsatisfactory or disreputable member of a family, group, etc.; a misfit.
blackshirt /ˈblakʃəːt/ *n.* a member of a Fascist organization. [from the colour of the Italian Fascist uniform]
blacksmith /ˈblaksmɪθ/ *n.* **1** a smith who works in iron. **2** *N. Amer.* = FARRIER 2.
black spot *n.* **1** *Brit.* a place of danger or difficulty, esp. on a road (*an accident black spot*). **2** any of various diseases of plants, esp. of roses, producing black spots on leaves.
black swan *n.* **1** an Australian swan, *Cygnus atratus*, with black plumage. **2** *Brit.* something extremely rare.
black tea *n.* tea that is fully fermented before drying.
blackthorn /ˈblakθɔːn/ *n.* **1** a thorny shrub, *Prunus spinosa* (rose family), bearing white-petalled flowers before the leaves appear, and blue-black fruits; also called SLOE. **2** a cudgel or walking stick made from its wood.
blackthorn winter *n. Brit.* a spell of cold weather at the time in early spring when the blackthorn flowers.
black tie *n.* **1** a black bow tie worn with a dinner jacket. **2** *colloq.* formal evening dress.
blacktop /ˈblaktɒp/ *n.* & *v.* esp. *N. Amer.* ● *n.* **1** a type of road-surfacing material. **2** a road surfaced with this. ● *v.tr.* surface (a road) with blacktop.
black tracker *n. Austral.* an Aborigine employed to help find persons lost or hiding in the bush.
black velvet *n.* a drink of stout and champagne.
Black Watch *n.* (usu. prec. by *the*) the Royal Highland Regiment (so called from its dark tartan uniform).
blackwater fever /ˈblakwɔːtə/ *n.* a severe form of malaria in which blood cells are rapidly destroyed, resulting in dark urine.
black widow *n.* a venomous N. American spider, *Latrodectus mactans*, the female of which devours its mate.
bladder /ˈbladə/ *n.* **1 a** any of various membranous sacs in some animals, containing urine (**urinary bladder**), bile (**gall bladder**), or air (**swim-bladder**). **b** this or part of it or a similar object prepared for various uses. **2** an inflated pericarp or vesicle in various plants. **3** anything inflated and hollow. [Old English *blǣdre*, from Germanic]
bladderwort /ˈbladəwəːt/ *n.* an aquatic plant of the genus *Utricularia*, with leaves having small bladders for trapping and digesting insects.
bladderwrack /ˈbladərak/ *n.* a common brown seaweed, *Fucus vesiculosus*, with fronds containing air bladders which give buoyancy.
blade /bleɪd/ *n.* **1 a** the flat part of a knife, chisel, etc., that forms the cutting edge. **b** = RAZOR BLADE. **2** the flattened functional part of an oar, spade, propeller, bat, skate, etc. **3 a** the flat, narrow, usu. pointed leaf of grass and cereals. **b** the whole of such plants before the ear is formed (*in the blade*). **c** *Bot.* the broad thin part of a leaf apart from the petiole. **4** (in full **blade-bone**) a flat bone, e.g. in the shoulder. **5** *Archaeol.* a long narrow flake (see FLAKE[1] 3). **6** *poet.* a sword. **7** *colloq.* (usu. *archaic*) a carefree young fellow. □ **bladed** *adj.* (also in *comb.*). [Old English *blæd*, from Germanic]
blaeberry /ˈbleɪb(ə)ri/ *n.* (*pl.* **-ies**) *Brit.* = BILBERRY. [Middle English from *blae* (Scots and northern English dialect, via Middle English *blo* from Old Norse *blár*, from Germanic: see BLUE[1]) + BERRY]
blag /blag/ *n.* & *v. Brit. slang* ● *n.* robbery, esp. with violence; theft. ● *v.tr.* & *intr.* (**blagged**, **blagging**) rob

(esp. with violence); steal. □ **blagger** *n.* [19th c.: origin unknown]

blague /blɑːg, French blag/ *n.* humbug, claptrap. [French]

blagueur /blɑːˈgəː, French blagœr/ *n.* a pretentious talker. [French]

blah /blɑː/ *n.* (also **blah-blah**) *colloq.* pretentious nonsense. [imitative]

blain /bleɪn/ *n.* an inflamed swelling or sore on the skin. [Old English *blegen*, from West Germanic]

blakey /ˈbleɪki/ *n.* (also **Blakey**) (*pl.* **-eys**) *Brit.* a metal cap on the heel or toe of a shoe or boot. [*Blakey*, name of the manufacturer]

blame /bleɪm/ *v.* & *n.* ● *v.tr.* **1** assign fault or responsibility to. **2** (foll. by *on*) assign the responsibility for (an error or wrong) to a person etc. (*blamed his death on a poor diet*). ● *n.* **1** responsibility for a bad result; culpability (*shared the blame equally*; *put the blame on the bad weather*). **2** the act of blaming or attributing responsibility; censure (*she got all the blame*). □ **be to blame** (often foll. by *for*) be responsible; deserve censure (*she is not to blame for the accident*). **have only oneself to blame** be solely responsible (for something one suffers). **I don't blame you** etc. I think your etc. action was justifiable. □ **blameable** *adj.* (*US* also **blamable**). [Middle English via Old French *bla(s)mer* (*v.*), *blame* (*n.*) and popular Latin *blastemare* from ecclesiastical Latin *blasphemare* 'reproach, revile, blaspheme', from Greek *blasphēmeō* 'blaspheme']

blameful /ˈbleɪmfʊl, -f(ə)l/ *adj.* deserving blame; guilty. □ **blamefully** *adv.*

blameless /ˈbleɪmlɪs/ *adj.* innocent; free from blame. □ **blamelessly** *adv.* **blamelessness** *n.*

blameworthy /ˈbleɪmwəːði/ *adj.* deserving blame. □ **blameworthiness** *n.*

blanch /blɑːn(t)ʃ/ *v.* **1** *tr.* make white or pale by extracting colour. **2** *intr.* & *tr.* grow or make pale from shock, fear, etc. **3** *tr.* **a** peel (almonds etc.) by scalding. **b** immerse (vegetables or meat) briefly in boiling water. **4** *tr.* whiten (a plant) by depriving it of light. □ **blanch over** give a deceptively good impression of (a fault etc.) by misrepresentation. [Middle English from Old French *blanchir*, from *blanc* 'white, BLANK']

blancmange /bləˈmɒnʒ, -ˈmɑːnʒ/ *n.* a sweet opaque gelatinous dessert made with flavoured cornflour and milk. [Middle English from Old French *blancmanger*, from *blanc* 'white, BLANK' + *manger* 'eat', from Latin *manducare* MANDUCATE]

blanco /ˈblaŋkəʊ/ *n.* & *v. Brit. Mil.* ● *n.* **1** a white substance for whitening belts etc. **2** a similar coloured substance for colouring equipment etc. ● *v.tr.* (**-oes, -oed**) treat with blanco. [French *blanc* 'white, BLANK']

bland /bland/ *adj.* **1 a** mild, not irritating. **b** tasteless, unstimulating, insipid. **2** gentle in manner; suave. □ **blandly** *adv.* **blandness** *n.* [Latin *blandus* 'soft, smooth']

blandish /ˈblandɪʃ/ *v.tr.* flatter; coax, cajole. [Middle English via Old French *blandir* (see -ISH²) from Latin *blandiri* from *blandus* 'soft, smooth']

blandishment /ˈblandɪʃm(ə)nt/ *n.* (usu. in *pl.*) flattery; cajolery.

blank /blaŋk/ *adj., n.,* & *v.* ● *adj.* **1 a** (of paper) not written or printed on. **b** (of a document) with spaces left for a signature or details. **2 a** not filled; empty (*a blank space*). **b** unrelieved; sheer; plain, undecorated (*a blank wall*). **3 a** having or showing no interest or expression (*a blank face*). **b** void of incident or result. **c** puzzled, nonplussed. **d** having (temporarily) no knowledge or understanding (*my mind went blank*). **4** (with neg. import) complete, downright (*a blank refusal*; *blank despair*). **5** *euphem.* used in place of an adjective regarded as coarse or abusive. ● *n.* **1 a** a space left to be filled in a document. **b** a document having blank spaces to be filled. **2** (in full **blank cartridge**) a cartridge containing gunpowder but no bullet, used for training etc. **3** an empty space or period of time. **4 a** a coin-disc before stamping. **b** a metal or wooden block before final shaping. **5 a** a dash written instead of a word or letter, esp. instead of an obscenity. **b** *euphem.* used in place of a noun regarded as coarse. **6** a domino with one or both halves blank. **7** a lottery ticket that gains no prize. **8** the white centre of the target in archery etc. ● *v.tr.* **1** (usu. foll. by *off, out*) screen, obscure (*clouds blanked out the sun*). **2** (usu. foll. by *out*) cut (a metal blank). **3** *N. Amer.* defeat without allowing to score. □ **draw a blank** elicit no response; fail. □ **blankly** *adv.* **blankness** *n.* [Middle English from Old French *blanc* 'white', ultimately from Germanic]

blank cheque *n.* **1** a cheque with the amount left for the payee to fill in. **2** *colloq.* unlimited freedom of action (cf. CARTE BLANCHE).

blanket /ˈblaŋkɪt/ *n., adj.,* & *v.* ● *n.* **1** a large piece of woollen or other material used esp. as a bed-covering or to wrap up a person or an animal for warmth. **2** (usu. foll. by *of*) a thick mass or layer that covers something (*blanket of fog*; *blanket of silence*). **3** *Printing* a rubber surface transferring an impression from a plate to paper etc. in offset printing. ● *attrib.adj.* covering all cases or classes; inclusive (*blanket condemnation*; *blanket agreement*). ● *v.tr.* (**blanketed, blanketing**) **1** cover with or as if with a blanket (*snow blanketed the land*). **2** stifle; keep quiet (*blanketed all discussion*). **3** *Naut.* take wind from the sails of (another craft) by passing to windward. □ **born on the wrong side of the blanket** illegitimate. [Middle English, in the sense 'undyed woollen cloth', from Old French *blancquet*, *blanchet*, from *blanc* 'white, BLANK']

blanket bath *n. Brit.* a body wash given to a bedridden patient.

blanket bog *n.* an extensive flat peat bog formed in cool regions of high rainfall or humidity.

blanket stitch *n.* a stitch used to neaten the edges of a blanket or other material.

blankety /ˈblaŋkəti/ *adj.* & *n.* (also **blanky** /ˈblaŋki/) *Brit. colloq.* = BLANK *adj.* 5.

blank verse *n.* unrhymed verse, esp. iambic pentameters.

blanky var. of BLANKETY.

blanquette /blɒ̃ˈkɛt/ *n.* a dish consisting of white meat, e.g. veal, in a white sauce. [French (as BLANKET)]

blare /blɛː/ *v.* & *n.* ● *v.* **1** *tr.* & *intr.* sound or utter loudly. **2** *intr.* make the sound of a trumpet. ● *n.* a loud sound resembling that of a trumpet. [Middle English from Middle Dutch *blaren*, *bleren*, imitative]

blarney /ˈblɑːni/ *n.* & *v.* ● *n.* **1** cajoling talk; flattery. **2** nonsense. ● *v.* (**-eys, -eyed**) **1** *tr.* flatter (a person) with blarney. **2** *intr.* talk flatteringly. [*Blarney*, an Irish castle near Cork with a stone said to confer a cajoling tongue on whoever kisses it]

blasé /ˈblɑːzeɪ/ *adj.* **1** unimpressed or indifferent because of overfamiliarity. **2** tired of pleasure; surfeited. [French]

blaspheme /blasˈfiːm/ *v.* **1** *intr.* use religious names, or treat a religious or sacred subject, irreverently. **2** *tr.* talk irreverently about; use blasphemy against. □ **blasphemer** *n.* [Middle English via Old French *blasfemer* and ecclesiastical Latin *blasphemare* 'reproach, revile, blaspheme', from Greek *blasphēmeō*: cf. BLAME]

blasphemy /ˈblasfəmi/ *n.* (*pl.* **-ies**) **1** irreverent talk or treatment of a religious or sacred thing. **2** an instance of this. □ **blasphemous** *adj.* **blasphemously** *adv.* [Middle English via Old French *blasfemie* and ecclesiastical Latin from Greek *blasphēmia* 'slander, blasphemy']

blast /blɑːst/ *n., v.,* & *int.* ● *n.* **1** a strong gust of air. **2 a** a destructive wave of highly compressed air spreading outwards from an explosion. **b** such an explosion. **3** the single loud note of a wind instrument, car horn, whistle, etc. **4** *colloq.* a severe reprimand. **5** a strong current of air used in smelting etc. ● *v.* **1** *tr.* blow up (rocks etc.) with explosives. **2** *tr.* **a** wither, shrivel, or blight (a plant, animal, limb, etc.) (*blasted oak*). **b** destroy, ruin (*blasted her hopes*). **c** strike with divine anger; curse. **3** *intr.* & *tr.* make or cause to make a loud or explosive noise (*blasted away on his trumpet*). **4** *tr. colloq.* reprimand severely. **5** *colloq.* **a** *tr.* shoot; shoot at. **b** *intr.* shoot. ● *int. Brit.* expressing annoyance. □ **at full blast** *colloq.* working at maximum speed etc. **blast from the past** a forcefully nostalgic event or thing. **blast off** (of a rocket etc.) take off from a launching site. [Old English *blǣst*, from Germanic]

-blast /blast/ *comb. form Biol.* **1** an embryonic cell (*erythroblast*) (cf. -CYTE). **2** a germ layer of an embryo (*epiblast*). [Greek *blastos* 'sprout']

blasted /ˈblɑːstɪd/ *adj. & adv.* ● *attrib.adj.* damned; annoying (*that blasted dog!*). ● *adv. Brit. colloq.* damned; extremely (*it's blasted cold*).

blaster /ˈblɑːstə/ *n.* **1** in senses of BLAST *v.* **2** *Brit.* a heavy lofted golf club for playing from a bunker.

blast freezing *n.* the freezing of foodstuffs etc. by means of a rapid current of chilled air. □ **blast freeze** *v.tr.*

blast furnace *n.* a smelting furnace into which compressed hot air is driven.

blast-hole *n.* a hole containing an explosive charge for blasting.

blast-off *n.* **1** the launching of a rocket etc. **2** the initial thrust for this.

blastula /ˈblastjʊlə/ *n.* (*pl.* **blastulae** /-liː/ or *US* **blastulas**) *Biol.* an animal embryo at an early stage of development when it is a hollow ball of cells. [modern Latin from Greek *blastos* 'sprout']

blatant /ˈbleɪt(ə)nt/ *adj.* **1** flagrant, unashamed (*blatant attempt to steal*). **2** offensively noisy or obtrusive. □ **blatancy** *n.* **blatantly** *adv.* [a word used by Spenser (1596), perhaps influenced by Scots *blatand* = bleating]

blather /ˈblaðə/ *n. & v.* (also **blether** /ˈblɛðə/) ● *n.* foolish chatter. ● *v.intr.* chatter foolishly. [Middle English *blather*, Scots *blether*, from Old Norse *blathra* 'talk nonsense' from *blathr* 'nonsense']

blatherskite /ˈblaðəskʌɪt/ *n.* (also **bletherskate** /ˈblɛðəskeɪt/) **1** a person who blathers. **2** = BLATHER *n.* [BLATHER + *skite*, corruption of derog. use of SKATE[2]]

blaxploitation /blaksplɔɪˈteɪʃ(ə)n/ *n.* (usu. *attrib.*) esp. *US colloq.* the exploitation of black people, esp. with regard to stereotyped roles in films.

blaze[1] /bleɪz/ *n. & v.* ● *n.* **1** a bright flame or fire. **2 a** a bright glaring light (*the sun set in a blaze of orange*). **b** a full light (*a blaze of publicity*). **3** a violent outburst (of passion etc.) (*a blaze of patriotic fervour*). **4 a** a glow of colour (*roses were a blaze of scarlet*). **b** a bright display (*a blaze of glory*). ● *v.intr.* **1** burn with a bright flame. **2** be brilliantly lit. **3** be consumed with anger, excitement, etc. **4 a** show bright colours (*blazing with jewels*). **b** emit light (*stars blazing*). □ **blaze away** (often foll. by *at*) **1** fire continuously with rifles etc. **2** work enthusiastically. **blaze up 1** burst into flame. **2** burst out in anger. **like blazes** *slang* **1** with great energy. **2** very fast. **what the blazes!** *slang* what the hell! □ **blazingly** *adv.* [Old English *blæse* 'torch', from Germanic: ultimately related to BLAZE[2]]

blaze[2] /bleɪz/ *n. & v.* ● *n.* **1** a white mark on an animal's face. **2** a mark made on a tree by slashing the bark esp. to mark a route. ● *v.tr.* mark (a tree or a path) by chipping bark. □ **blaze a trail 1** mark out a path or route. **2** be the first to do, invent, or study something; pioneer. [17th c.: ultimately from Germanic, related to BLAZE[1] and probably to BLEMISH]

blaze[3] /bleɪz/ *v.tr.* proclaim as with a trumpet. □ **blaze abroad** spread (news) about. [Middle English from Low German or Dutch *blāzen* 'blow', from Germanic *blǣsan*]

blazer /ˈbleɪzə/ *n.* **1** a coloured, often striped, summer jacket worn by schoolchildren, sportsmen, etc., esp. as part of a uniform. **2** a man's plain jacket, often dark blue, not forming part of a suit. [BLAZE[1] + -ER[1]]

blazon /ˈbleɪz(ə)n/ *v. & n.* ● *v.tr.* **1** proclaim (esp. *blazon abroad*). **2** *Heraldry* **a** describe or paint (arms). **b** inscribe or paint (an object) with arms, names, etc. ● *n.* **1** *Heraldry* a correct description of armorial bearings etc. **2** a record or description, esp. of virtues etc. □ **blazonment** *n.* [Middle English from Old French *blason* 'shield', of unknown origin; verb also from BLAZE[3]]

blazonry /ˈbleɪz(ə)nri/ *n. Heraldry* **1 a** the art of describing or painting heraldic devices or armorial bearings. **b** such devices or bearings. **2** brightly coloured display.

bleach /bliːtʃ/ *v. & n.* ● *v.tr. & intr.* whiten by exposure to sunlight or by a chemical process. ● *n.* **1** a bleaching substance. **2** the process of bleaching. [Old English *blǣcan*, from Germanic]

bleacher /ˈbliːtʃə/ *n.* **1 a** a person who bleaches (esp. textiles). **b** a vessel or chemical used in bleaching. **2** (usu. in *pl.*) esp. *N. Amer.* a cheap bench seat at a sports ground, usu. in an outdoor uncovered stand.

bleaching powder *n.* calcium hypochlorite used esp. to remove colour from materials.

bleak[1] /bliːk/ *adj.* **1** bare, exposed; windswept. **2** unpromising; dreary (*bleak prospects*). □ **bleakly** *adv.* **bleakness** *n.* [16th c.: related to obsolete adjs. *bleach*, *blake* (from Old Norse *bleikr*) 'pale', ultimately from Germanic: cf. BLEACH]

bleak[2] /bliːk/ *n.* any of various small river fishes, esp. *Alburnus alburnus*. [Middle English, probably via Old Norse *bleikja*, Old High German *bleicha* from Germanic]

blear /blɪə/ *adj. & v. archaic* ● *adj.* **1** (of the eyes or the mind) dim, dull, filmy. **2** indistinct. ● *v.tr.* make dim or obscure; blur. [Middle English, of uncertain origin]

bleary /ˈblɪəri/ *adj.* (**blearier**, **bleariest**) **1** (of the eyes) dim with sleep. **2** indistinct; blurred. □ **blearily** *adv.* **bleariness** *n.*

bleary-eyed *adj.* **1** having dim sight or wits. **2** half awake.

bleat /bliːt/ *v. & n.* ● *v.* **1** *intr.* (of a sheep, goat, or calf) make a weak, wavering cry. **2** *intr. & tr.* (often foll. by *out*) speak or say feebly, foolishly, or plaintively. ● *n.* **1** the sound made by a sheep, goat, etc. **2** a weak, plaintive, or foolish cry. □ **bleater** *n.* **bleatingly** *adv.* [Old English *blǣtan* (imitative)]

bleb /blɛb/ *n.* **1** esp. *Med.* a small blister on the skin. **2** a small bubble in glass or on water. [variant of BLOB]

bleed /bliːd/ *v. & n.* ● *v.* (*past* and *past part.* **bled** /bled/) **1** *intr.* emit blood. **2** *tr.* draw blood from surgically. **3** *colloq.* **a** *tr.* extort money from. **b** *intr.* part with money lavishly; suffer extortion. **4** *intr.* (often foll. by *for*) suffer wounds or violent death (*bled for the Revolution*). **5** *intr.* **a** (of a plant) emit sap. **b** (of dye) come out in water. **6** *tr.* **a** allow (fluid or gas) to escape from a closed system through a valve etc. **b** treat (such a system) in this way. **7** *Printing* **a** *intr.* (of a printed area) be cut into when pages are trimmed. **b** *tr.* cut into the printed area of when trimming. **c** *tr.* extend (an illustration) to the cut edge of a page. ● *n.* an act of bleeding (cf. NOSEBLEED). □ **one's heart bleeds** usu. *iron.* one is very sorrowful. [Old English *blēdan*, from Germanic]

bleeder /ˈbliːdə/ *n.* **1** *Brit. coarse slang* a person (esp. as a term of contempt or disrespect) (*lucky bleeder*). **2** *colloq.* a haemophiliac.

bleeding /ˈbliːdɪŋ/ *adj. & adv. Brit. coarse slang* expressing annoyance or antipathy (*a bleeding nuisance*).

bleeding heart *n.* **1** *colloq.* a person considered to be dangerously soft-hearted. **2** any of various plants, esp. *Dicentra spectabilis* which has heart-shaped crimson flowers hanging from an arched stem.

bleep /bliːp/ *n. & v.* ● *n.* an intermittent high-pitched sound made electronically. ● *v.* **1 a** *intr.* make such a sound, esp. as a signal. **b** *tr.* cause to make such a sound. **2** *tr. Brit.* summon with a bleeper. [imitative]

bleeper /ˈbliːpə/ *n. Brit.* a small portable electronic device which emits bleeps when the wearer is contacted.

blemish /ˈblɛmɪʃ/ *n. & v.* ● *n.* a physical or moral defect; a stain; a flaw (*not a blemish on his character*).

● *v.tr.* spoil the beauty or perfection of; stain (*spots blemished her complexion*). [Middle English from Old French *ble(s)mir* (-ISH[2]) 'make pale', probably of Germanic origin and related to BLAZE[2]]

blench /blɛn(t)ʃ/ *v.intr.* flinch; quail. [Middle English from Old English *blencan*, ultimately from Germanic]

blend /blɛnd/ *v.* & *n.* ● *v.* (*poet. past* and *past part.* **blent**) **1** *tr.* **a** mix (esp. sorts of tea, spirits, tobacco, etc.) together to produce a desired flavour etc. **b** produce by this method (*blended whisky*). **2** *intr.* form a harmonious compound; become one. **3 a** *tr.* & *intr.* (often foll. by *with*) mingle or be mingled (*truth blended with lies*; *blends well with the locals*). **b** *tr.* (often foll. by *in, with*) mix thoroughly. **4** *intr.* (esp. of colours): **a** pass imperceptibly into each other. **b** go well together; harmonize. ● *n.* **1 a** a mixture, esp. of various sorts of tea, spirits, tobacco, fibres, etc. **b** a combination (of different abstract or personal qualities). **2** a portmanteau word. [Middle English probably from Old Norse *blanda* 'mix']

blende /blɛnd/ *n.* any naturally occurring metal sulphide, esp. zinc blende. [German from *blenden* 'deceive', so called because, while often resembling galena, it yielded no lead]

blender /'blɛndə/ *n.* **1** a mixing machine used in food preparation for liquidizing, chopping, or purééing. **2 a** a thing that blends. **b** a person who blends.

Blenheim /'blɛnɪm/ *n.* **1** a small spaniel of a red and white breed. **2** this breed. [the Duke of Marlborough's seat at Woodstock in S. England, named after his victory at Blenheim in Bavaria (1704)]

Blenheim Orange *n.* a golden-coloured apple which ripens late in the season.

blenny /'blɛni/ *n.* (*pl.* **-ies**) any of a family of small spiny-finned marine fish, esp. of the genus *Blennius*, having scaleless skins. [Latin *blennius* from Greek *blennos* 'mucus', with reference to its mucous coating]

blent /blɛnt/ *poet. past* and *past part.* of BLEND.

blepharitis /blɛfə'rʌɪtɪs/ *n.* inflammation of the eyelids. [Greek *blepharon* 'eyelid' + -ITIS]

blepharo- /'blɛf(ə)rəʊ/ *comb. form* of or relating to the eyelids. [Greek *blepharon* 'eyelid']

blesbok /'blɛsbɒk/ *n.* (also **blesbuck** /-bʌk/) a subspecies of bontebok, native to southern Africa, having small lyre-shaped horns. [Afrikaans, from *bles* BLAZE[2] (from the white mark on its forehead) + *bok* 'goat']

bless /blɛs/ *v.tr.* (*past* and *past part.* **blessed**, *poet.* **blest** /blɛst/) **1** (of God, a priest etc.) confer or invoke divine favour upon (*bless this house*). **2 a** consecrate (esp. bread and wine). **b** sanctify by the sign of the cross. **3** call (God) holy; adore. **4** attribute one's good fortune to (an auspicious time, one's fate, etc.); thank (*bless the day I met her*; *bless my stars*). **5** (usu. in *passive*; often foll. by *with*) make happy or successful (*blessed with children*; *they were truly blessed*). **6** *euphem.* curse; damn (*bless the boy!*). □ **(God) bless me** (or **my soul**) an exclamation of surprise, pleasure, indignation, etc. **(God) bless you! 1** an exclamation of endearment, gratitude, etc. **2** an exclamation made to a person who has just sneezed. **I'm** (or **well, I'm**) **blessed** (or **blest**) an exclamation of surprise etc. **not have a penny to bless oneself with** be impoverished. [Old English *blœ̄dsian, blēdsian, blētsian*, from *blōd* 'blood' (hence 'mark with blood, consecrate'): meaning influenced by its use at the conversion of the English to translate Latin *benedicare* 'praise']

blessed /'blɛsɪd, blɛst/ *adj.* (also *poet.* **blest** /blɛst/) **1 a** consecrated (*Blessed Sacrament*). **b** revered. **2** /blest/ (usu. foll. by *with*) often *iron.* fortunate (in the possession of) (*blessed with good health*; *blessed with children*). **3** *euphem.* cursed; damned (*blessed nuisance!*). **4 a** in paradise. **b** *RC Ch.* a title given to a dead person, esp. one formally beatified, as an acknowledgement of his or her holy life. **5** bringing happiness; blissful (*blessed ignorance*). □ **blessedly** *adv.*

blessedness /'blɛsɪdnɪs/ *n.* **1** happiness. **2** the enjoyment of divine favour. □ **single blessedness** *joc.* the state of being unmarried (perversion of Shakespeare's *A Midsummer Night's Dream* I. i. 78).

blessing /'blɛsɪŋ/ *n.* **1** the act of declaring, seeking, or bestowing (esp. divine) favour (*sought God's blessing*; *mother gave them her blessing*). **2** grace said before or after a meal. **3** a gift of God, nature, etc.; a thing one is glad of (*what a blessing he brought it!*). □ **blessing in disguise** an apparent misfortune that eventually has good results.

blest *poet.* var. of BLESSED.

blether *Brit.* var. of BLATHER.

bletherskate var. of BLATHERSKITE.

blew *past* of BLOW[1], BLOW[3].

blewits /'blu:ɪts/ *n.* any fungus of the genus *Tricholoma*, with edible lilac-stemmed mushrooms. [probably from BLUE[1]]

blight /blʌɪt/ *n.* & *v.* ● *n.* **1** a plant disease caused by mildews, rusts, smuts, fungi, or insects. **2** an insect or parasite causing such a disease. **3** any obscure force which is harmful or destructive. **4** an unsightly or neglected urban area. ● *v.tr.* **1** affect with blight. **2** harm, destroy. **3** spoil. [17th c.: origin unknown]

blighter /'blʌɪtə/ *n. Brit. colloq.* a person (esp. as a term of contempt or disparagement). [BLIGHT + -ER[1]]

Blighty /'blʌɪti/ *n. Brit. slang* (used originally by soldiers during the First World War) **1** Britain or England; home. **2** a wound securing return home. [Anglo-Indian corruption of Urdu *bilāyatī, wilāyatī* 'foreign, European']

blimey /'blʌɪmi/ *int.* (also **cor blimey** /kɔ:/) *Brit. coarse slang* an expression of surprise, excitement, alarm, etc. [corruption of (*God*) *blind me!*]

blimp /blɪmp/ *n.* **1** (also **(Colonel) Blimp**) *Brit.* a proponent of reactionary Establishment opinions. **2 a** a small non-rigid airship. **b** a barrage balloon. **3** a soundproof cover for a cine-camera. □ **blimpish** *adj.* [20th. c., of uncertain origin: in sense 1, a pompous, obese, elderly character invented by cartoonist David Low (d. 1963), and used in anti-German or anti-Government drawings before and during the Second World War]

blind /blʌɪnd/ *adj., v., n.,* & *adv.* ● *adj.* **1** lacking the power of sight. **2 a** without foresight, discernment, intellectual perception, or adequate information (*blind effort*). **b** (often foll. by *to*) unwilling or unable to appreciate (a factor, circumstance, etc.) (*blind to argument*). **3** not governed by purpose or reason (*blind forces*). **4** reckless (*blind hitting*). **5 a** concealed (*blind ditch*). **b** (of a door, window, etc.) walled up. **c** closed at one end. **6** *Aeron.* (of flying) without direct observation, using instruments only. **7** *slang* drunk. ● *v.* **1** *tr.* deprive of sight, permanently or temporarily (*blinded by tears*). **2** *tr.* (often foll. by *to*) rob of judgement; deceive (*blinded them to the danger*). **3** *intr. Brit. slang* go very fast and dangerously, esp. in a motor vehicle. ● *n.* **1 a** a screen for a window, esp. on a roller, or with slats (*roller blind*; *venetian blind*). **b** *Brit.* an awning over a shop window. **2 a** something designed or used to hide the truth; a pretext. **b** *Brit.* a legitimate business concealing a criminal enterprise (*he's a spy, and his job is just a blind*). **3** any obstruction to sight or light. **4** *Brit. slang* a heavy drinking bout. **5** *Cards* a stake put up by a poker player before the cards dealt are seen. **6** *US* = HIDE[1] *n.* ● *adv.* blindly (*fly blind*). □ **bake blind** bake (a flan case etc.) without a filling. **blind as a bat** completely blind. **blind to** incapable of appreciating. **blind with science** *Brit.* overawe with a display of (often spurious) knowledge. **go it blind** act recklessly or without proper consideration. **not a blind bit of** (or **not a blind**) *Brit. slang* not the slightest; not a single (*took not a blind bit of notice*; *not a blind word out of him*). **turn a** (or **one's**) **blind eye to** pretend not to notice. □ **blindly** *adv.* **blindness** *n.* [Old English, from Germanic]

blind alley *n.* **1** a cul-de-sac. **2** a course of action leading nowhere.
blind coal *n.* coal burning without a flame.
blind corner *n.* a corner round which a motorist etc. cannot see.
blind date *n.* **1** a social engagement between a man and a woman who have not previously met. **2** either of the couple on a blind date.
blind drunk *adj. colloq.* extremely drunk.
blinder /ˈblʌɪndə/ *n. colloq.* **1** *Brit.* an excellent performance in a game, race, etc. **2** (in *pl.*) *N. Amer.* blinkers.
blindfold /ˈblʌɪn(d)fəʊld/ *v., n., adj., & adv.* ● *v.tr.* **1** deprive (a person) of sight by covering the eyes, esp. with a tied cloth. **2** deprive of understanding; hoodwink. ● *n.* **1** a bandage or cloth used to blindfold. **2** any obstruction to understanding. ● *adj. & adv.* **1** (also **blindfolded**) with eyes bandaged. **2** (also **blindfolded**) without care or circumspection (*went into it blindfold*). **3** *Chess* without sight of board and men. [replacing (by association with FOLD[1]) Middle English *blindfellen*, past part. *blindfelled*, from Old English *geblindfellian* 'strike blind' (as BLIND, FELL[1])]
blind gut *n.* the caecum.
blind hookey *n.* a gambling guessing game at cards.
blinding /ˈblʌɪndɪŋ/ *n. & adj.* ● *n.* **1** the process of covering a newly made road etc. with grit to fill cracks. **2** such grit. ● *adj.* **1** causing blindness; very bright (*a blinding light*). **2** robbing one of judgement; disconcerting; brilliant (*blinding surprise*; *blinding performance*). □ **blindingly** *adv.*
blind man's buff *n.* esp. *Brit.* a game in which a blindfold player tries to catch others while being pushed about by them. [*buff* 'a blow': see BUFFET[2]]
blind side *n.* a direction in which one cannot see the approach of danger etc.
blind spot *n.* **1** *Anat.* the point of entry of the optic nerve on the retina, insensitive to light. **2** an area in which a person lacks understanding or impartiality. **3** a point of unusually weak radio reception.
blind stamping *n.* (also **blind tooling**) embossing a book cover without the use of colour or gold leaf.
blind stitch *n. & v.* ● *n.* sewing visible on one side only. ● *v.tr. & intr.* (**blind-stitch**) sew with this stitch.
blind trust *n.* a trust independently administering the private business interests of a person in public office to prevent conflict of interest.
blindworm /ˈblʌɪndwəːm/ *n.* = SLOW-WORM.
blink /blɪŋk/ *v. & n.* ● *v.* **1** *intr.* shut and open the eyes quickly and usu. involuntarily. **2** *intr.* (often foll. by *at*) look with eyes opening and shutting. **3** *tr.* **a** (often foll. by *back*) prevent (tears) by blinking. **b** (often foll. by *away, from*) clear (dust etc.) from the eyes by blinking. **4** *tr.* & (foll. by *at*) *intr.* shirk consideration of; ignore; condone. **5** *intr.* **a** shine with an unsteady or intermittent light. **b** cast a momentary gleam. **6** *tr.* blink with (eyes). ● *n.* **1** an act of blinking. **2** a momentary gleam or glimpse. **3** = ICEBLINK. □ **on the blink** *slang* out of order, esp. intermittently. [partly variant of *blenk* = BLENCH, partly from Middle Dutch *blinken* 'shine']
blinker /ˈblɪŋkə/ *n. & v.* ● *n.* **1** (usu. in *pl.*) either of a pair of screens attached to a horse's bridle to prevent it from seeing sideways. **2** a device that blinks, esp. a vehicle's indicator. ● *v.tr.* **1** obscure with blinkers. **2** (as **blinkered** *adj.*) having narrow and prejudiced views.
blinking /ˈblɪŋkɪŋ/ *adj. & adv. Brit. slang* an intensive, esp. expressing disapproval (*a blinking idiot*; *a blinking awful time*). [BLINK + -ING[2] (euphemism for BLOODY)]
blip /blɪp/ *n. & v.* ● *n.* **1** a minor deviation or error. **2** a quick popping sound, as of dripping water or an electronic device. **3** a small image of an object on a radar screen. ● *v.* (**blipped**, **blipping**) **1** *intr.* make a blip. **2** *tr.* strike or press briskly (*blip the throttle*). [imitative]
bliss /blɪs/ *n.* **1 a** perfect joy or happiness. **b** enjoyment; gladness. **2 a** being in heaven. **b** a state of blessedness. [Old English *blīths, bliss* from the Germanic base of BLITHE: sense influenced by BLESS]
blissful /ˈblɪsfʊl, -f(ə)l/ *adj.* perfectly happy; joyful. □ **blissful ignorance** fortunate unawareness of something unpleasant. □ **blissfully** *adv.* **blissfulness** *n.*
blister /ˈblɪstə/ *n. & v.* ● *n.* **1** a small bubble on the skin filled with serum and caused by friction, burning, etc. **2** a similar swelling on any other surface. **3** *Med.* anything applied to raise a blister. **4** *Brit. slang* an annoying person. ● *v.* **1** *tr.* raise a blister on. **2** *intr.* come up in a blister or blisters. **3** *tr.* attack sharply (*blistered them with his criticisms*). [Middle English, perhaps from Old French *blestre, blo(u)stre* 'swelling, pimple']
blister copper *n.* partly purified copper with a blistered surface formed during smelting.
blister gas *n.* a poison gas causing blisters on the skin.
blister pack *n.* a bubble pack.
blithe /blʌɪð/ *adj.* **1** *poet.* gay, joyous. **2** careless, casual (*with blithe indifference*). □ **blithely** *adv.* **blitheness** *n.* **blithesome** /-s(ə)m/ *adj.* [Old English *blīthe*, from Germanic]
blithering /ˈblɪð(ə)rɪŋ/ *adj. colloq.* **1** senselessly talkative. **2** (*attrib.*) hopeless; contemptible (esp. in *blithering idiot*). [*blither*, variant of BLATHER + -ING[2]]
B.Litt. *abbr.* Bachelor of Letters. [Latin *Baccalaureus Litterarum*]
blitz /blɪts/ *n. & v. colloq.* ● *n.* **1 a** an intensive or sudden (esp. aerial) attack. **b** an energetic intensive attack, usu. on a specific task (*must have a blitz on this room*). **2** (**the Blitz**) the German air raids on London in 1940. ● *v.tr.* attack, damage, or destroy by a blitz. [abbreviation of BLITZKRIEG]
blitzkrieg /ˈblɪtskriːg/ *n.* an intense military campaign intended to bring about a swift victory. [German, = lightning war]
blizzard /ˈblɪzəd/ *n.* a severe snowstorm with high winds. [US 'violent blow' (1829), 'snowstorm' (1876), perhaps imitative]
bloat /bləʊt/ *v.* **1** *tr. & intr.* inflate, swell (*wind bloated the sheets*; *bloated with gas*). **2** *tr.* (as **bloated** *adj.*) **a** swollen, puffed. **b** puffed up with pride or excessive wealth (*bloated plutocrat*). **3** *tr.* cure (a herring) by salting and smoking lightly. [obsolete *bloat* 'swollen, soft and wet', perhaps from Old Norse *blautr* 'soaked, flabby']
bloater /ˈbləʊtə/ *n.* a herring cured by bloating.
blob /blɒb/ *n.* **1** a small roundish mass; a drop of matter. **2** a drop of liquid. **3** a spot of colour. **4** *Cricket slang* a score of 0. [imitative: cf. BLEB]
bloc /blɒk/ *n.* a combination of parties, governments groups, etc. sharing a common purpose. [French, = block]
block /blɒk/ *n., v., & adj.* ● *n.* **1** a solid hewn or unhewn piece of hard material, esp. of rock, stone, or wood (*block of ice*). **2** a flat-topped block used as a base for chopping, beheading, standing something on, hammering on, or for mounting a horse from. **3 a** esp. *Brit.* a large building, esp. when subdivided (*block of flats*). **b** a compact mass of buildings bounded by (usu. four) streets. **4** an obstruction; anything preventing progress or normal working (*a block in the pipe*). **5** a chock for stopping the motion of a wheel etc. **6** a pulley or system of pulleys mounted in a case. **7** (in *pl.*) any of a set of solid cubes etc., used as a child's toy. **8** *Printing* a piece of wood or metal engraved for printing on paper or fabric. **9** a head-shaped mould used for shaping hats or wigs. **10** *slang* the head (*knock his block off*). **11** *N. Amer.* **a** the area between streets in a town or suburb. **b** the length of such an area, esp. as a measure of distance (*lives three blocks away*). **12** a stolid, unimaginative, or hard-hearted person. **13** a large quantity or allocation of things treated as a unit, esp. shares, seats in a theatre, etc. **14** esp. *Brit.* a set of

sheets of paper used for writing, or esp. drawing, glued along one edge. **15** *Cricket* a spot on which a batsman blocks the ball before the wicket, and rests the bat before playing. **16** *Athletics* = STARTING BLOCK. **17** *Amer. Football* a blocking action. **18** *Austral.* **a** a tract of land offered to an individual settler by a government. **b** a large area of land. **c** an urban or suburban building plot. ● *v.tr.* **1 a** (often foll. by *up*) obstruct (a passage etc.) (*the road was blocked; you are blocking my view*). **b** put obstacles in the way of (progress etc.). **2** restrict the use or conversion of (currency or any other asset). **3** use a block for making (a hat, wig, etc.). **4** emboss or impress a design on (a book cover). **5** *Cricket* stop (a ball) with a bat defensively. **6** *Amer. Football* impede the progress of (an opponent) with one's body. ● *attrib.adj.* treating (many similar things) as one unit (*block booking*). □ **block in 1** sketch roughly; plan. **2** confine. **block out 1 a** shut out (light, noise, etc.). **b** exclude from memory, as being too painful. **2** sketch roughly; plan. **block up 1** confine; shut (a person etc.) in. **2** infill (a window, doorway, etc.) with bricks etc. **on the block** *N. Amer.* being auctioned. **put the blocks on** prevent from proceeding. □ **blocker** *n.* [Middle English via Old French *bloc* (*n.*), *bloquer* (*v.*) from Middle Dutch *blok*, of unknown origin]

blockade /blɒˈkeɪd/ *n.* & *v.* ● *n.* **1** the surrounding or blocking of a place, esp. a port, by an enemy to prevent entry and exit of supplies etc. **2** anything that prevents access or progress. **3** *N. Amer.* an obstruction by snow etc. ● *v.tr.* **1** subject to a blockade. **2** obstruct (a passage, a view, etc.). □ **run a blockade** enter or leave a blockaded port by evading the blockading force. □ **blockader** *n.* [BLOCK + -ADE[1], probably influenced by *ambuscade*]

blockade-runner *n.* **1** a vessel which runs or attempts to run into or out of a blockaded port. **2** the owner, master, or one of the crew of such a vessel.

blockage /ˈblɒkɪdʒ/ *n.* **1** an obstruction. **2** a blocked state.

block and tackle *n.* a system of pulleys and ropes, esp. for lifting.

blockboard /ˈblɒkbɔːd/ *n. Brit.* a plywood board with a core of wooden strips.

blockbuster /ˈblɒkbʌstə/ *n. slang* **1** something of great power or size, esp. an epic film or a best-selling book. **2** a huge aerial bomb capable of destroying a whole block of buildings. □ **blockbusting** *adj.*

block capitals *n.pl.* letters printed without serifs, or written with each letter separate and in capitals.

block diagram *n.* a diagram showing the general arrangement of parts of an apparatus.

blockhead /ˈblɒkhɛd/ *n.* a stupid person. □ **blockheaded** *adj.*

blockhouse /ˈblɒkhaʊs/ *n.* **1** a reinforced concrete shelter used as an observation point etc. **2** *hist.* a one-storeyed timber building with loopholes, used as a fort. **3** a house made of squared logs.

blockish /ˈblɒkɪʃ/ *adj.* **1** resembling a block. **2** excessively dull; stupid, obtuse. **3** clumsy, rude, roughly hewn.

block letters *n.pl.* = BLOCK CAPITALS.

block mountain *n. Geol.* a mountain formed by natural faults.

blockship /ˈblɒkʃɪp/ *n. Naut.* a ship used to block a channel.

block system *n.* a system by which no railway train may enter a section that is not clear.

block tin *n.* refined tin cast in ingots.

block vote *n.* (also **bloc vote**) a vote proportional in power to the number of people a delegate represents.

bloke /bləʊk/ *n. Brit. colloq.* a man, a fellow. [Shelta]

blond /blɒnd/ *adj.* & *n.* ● *adj.* **1** (of hair) light-coloured; fair. **2** (of the complexion, esp. as an indication of race) light-coloured. ● *n.* a person with fair hair and skin. □ **blondish** *adj.* **blondness** *n.* [Middle English via French from medieval Latin *blondus, blundus* 'yellow', perhaps of Germanic origin]

blonde /blɒnd/ *adj.* & *n.* ● *adj.* (of a woman or a woman's hair) blond. ● *n.* a blond-haired woman. [French fem. of *blond*; see BLOND]

blood /blʌd/ *n.* & *v.* ● *n.* **1** a liquid, usually red and circulating in the arteries and veins of vertebrates, that carries oxygen to and carbon dioxide from the tissues of the body. **2** a corresponding fluid in invertebrates. **3** bloodshed, esp. killing. **4** passion, temperament. **5** race, descent, parentage (*of the same blood*). **6** family ties; relations (*own flesh and blood; blood is thicker than water*). **7** esp. *Brit. slang* a leader of fashion. ● *v.tr.* **1** give (a hound) a first taste of blood. **2** initiate (a person) by experience. □ **bad blood** ill feeling. **blood-and-thunder** (*attrib.*) *colloq.* sensational, melodramatic. **one's blood is up** one is in a fighting mood. **first blood 1** the first shedding of blood, esp. in boxing. **2** the first point gained in a contest etc. **in one's blood** inherent in one's character. **make one's blood boil** infuriate one. **make one's blood run cold** horrify one. **new** (or **fresh**) **blood** new members admitted to a group, esp. as an invigorating force. **of the blood** royal. **out for a person's blood** set on getting revenge. **taste blood** be stimulated by an early success. **young blood 1** a younger member or members of a group. **2** a rake or fashionable young man. [Old English *blōd*, from Germanic]

blood bank *n.* a place where supplies of blood or plasma for transfusion are stored.

bloodbath /ˈblʌdbɑːθ/ *n.* a massacre.

blood-borne *adj.* carried by the blood.

blood brother *n.* a brother by birth or by the ceremonial mingling of blood.

blood cell *n.* any of the kinds of cell normally circulating in the blood.

blood count *n.* **1** the counting of the number of corpuscles in a specific volume of blood. **2** the number itself.

blood-curdling *adj.* horrifying.

blood donor *n.* a person who gives blood for transfusion.

blooded /ˈblʌdɪd/ *adj.* **1** (of horses etc.) of good pedigree. **2** (in *comb.*) having blood or a disposition of a specified kind (*cold-blooded; red-blooded*).

blood feud *n.* a feud between families involving killing or injury.

blood fluke *n.* a flatworm parasitic in the blood, esp. a schistosome.

blood group *n.* any of the various types of human blood whose antigen characteristics determine compatibility in transfusion.

blood-heat *n.* the normal body temperature of a healthy human being, about 37°C or 98.4°F.

blood horse *n.* a thoroughbred horse.

bloodhound /ˈblʌdhaʊnd/ *n.* **1** a large hound of a breed used in tracking and having a very keen sense of smell. **2** this breed.

bloodless /ˈblʌdlɪs/ *adj.* **1** without blood. **2** unemotional; cold. **3** pale. **4** without bloodshed (*a bloodless coup*). **5** feeble; lifeless. □ **bloodlessly** *adv.* **bloodlessness** *n.*

bloodletting /ˈblʌdlɛtɪŋ/ *n.* **1** the surgical removal of some of a patient's blood. **2** often *joc.* bloodshed.

bloodline /ˈblʌdlʌɪn/ *n.* descent, pedigree, esp. as transmitting characteristics in an animal.

bloodlust /ˈblʌdlʌst/ *n.* the desire for shedding blood.

blood money *n.* **1** money paid to the next of kin of a person who has been killed. **2** money paid to a hired murderer. **3** money paid for information about a murder or murderer.

blood orange *n.* an orange with red or red-streaked pulp.

blood poisoning *n.* a diseased state caused by the presence of micro-organisms or their toxins in the blood.

blood pressure *n.* the pressure of the blood in the circulatory system, often measured for diagnosis since it is closely related to the force and rate of the heartbeat and the diameter and elasticity of the arterial walls.

blood red *n.* & *adj.* ● *n.* the bright red colour of blood. ● *adj.* (hyphenated when *attrib.*) of this colour.

blood relation *n.* (also **blood relative**) a relative by blood, not by marriage.

blood royal *n.* the royal family.

blood serum see SERUM.

bloodshed /'blʌdʃɛd/ *n.* **1** the spilling of blood. **2** slaughter.

bloodshot /'blʌdʃɒt/ *adj.* (of an eyeball) inflamed, tinged with blood.

blood spavin *n.* a soft swelling of a horse's hock due to distension of the main vein.

blood sport *n.* a sport involving the wounding or killing of animals, esp. hunting.

bloodstain /'blʌdsteɪn/ *n.* a discoloration caused by blood.

bloodstained /'blʌdsteɪnd/ *adj.* **1** stained with blood. **2** guilty of bloodshed.

bloodstock /'blʌdstɒk/ *n.* thoroughbred horses.

bloodstone /'blʌdstəʊn/ *n.* a type of green chalcedony spotted or streaked with red, often used as a gemstone.

bloodstream /'blʌdstriːm/ *n.* the blood in circulation.

bloodsucker /'blʌdsʌkə/ *n.* **1** an animal or insect that sucks blood, esp. a leech. **2** an extortioner. ◻ **bloodsucking** *adj.*

blood sugar *n.* the amount of glucose in the blood.

blood test *n.* a scientific examination of blood, esp. for diagnosis.

bloodthirsty /'blʌdθəːsti/ *adj.* (**bloodthirstier**, **bloodthirstiest**) eager for bloodshed. ◻ **bloodthirstily** *adv.* **bloodthirstiness** *n.*

blood transfusion *n.* the injection of a volume of blood, previously taken from a healthy person, into a patient.

blood vessel *n.* a vein, artery, or capillary carrying blood.

bloodworm /'blʌdwəːm/ *n.* **1** a bright red aquatic larva of any of several non-biting midges. **2** = TUBIFEX.

blood-wort *n.* any of various plants having red roots or leaves, esp. the red-veined dock.

bloody /'blʌdi/ *adj.*, *adv.*, & *v.* ● *adj.* (**bloodier**, **bloodiest**) **1 a** of or like blood. **b** running or smeared with blood (*bloody bandage*). **2 a** involving, loving, or resulting from bloodshed (*bloody battle*). **b** sanguinary; cruel (*bloody butcher*). **3** esp. *Brit. coarse slang* expressing annoyance or antipathy, or as an intensive (*a bloody shame*; *a bloody sight better*; *not a bloody chocolate left*). **4** red. ● *adv.* esp. *Brit. coarse slang* as an intensive (*a bloody good job*; *I'll bloody thump him*). ● *v.tr.* (**-ies**, **-ied**) make bloody; stain with blood. ◻ **bloodily** *adv.* **bloodiness** *n.* [Old English *blōdig* (as BLOOD, -Y[1])]

bloody hand *n.* *Heraldry* the armorial device of a baronet.

Bloody Mary *n.* a drink composed of vodka and tomato juice.

bloody-minded *adj.* *Brit. colloq.* deliberately uncooperative. ◻ **bloody-mindedly** *adv.* **bloody-mindedness** *n.*

bloody murder *N. Amer.* var. of BLUE MURDER.

bloom[1] /bluːm/ *n.* & *v.* ● *n.* **1 a** a flower, esp. one cultivated for its beauty. **b** the state of flowering (*in bloom*). **2** a state of perfection or loveliness; the prime (*in full bloom*). **3 a** (of the complexion) a flush; a glow. **b** a delicate powdery surface deposit on plums, grapes, leaves, etc., indicating freshness. **c** a cloudiness on a shiny surface. **4** (in full **algal bloom** or **water-bloom**) a rapid growth of microscopic algae in water, or a coloured scum formed by this. ● *v.* **1** *intr.* bear flowers; be in flower. **2** *intr.* **a** come into, or remain in, full beauty. **b** flourish; be in a healthy, vigorous state. **3** *tr.* *Photog.* coat (a lens) so as to reduce reflection from its surface. ◻ **take the bloom off** make stale. [Middle English via Old Norse *blóm*, *blómi* 'flower, blossom', from the Germanic base of BLOSSOM]

bloom[2] /bluːm/ *n.* & *v.* ● *n.* a mass of puddled iron hammered or squeezed into a thick bar. ● *v.tr.* make into bloom. [Old English *blōma*]

bloomer[1] /'bluːmə/ *n.* *Brit. slang* a blunder. [= BLOOMING *error*]

bloomer[2] /'bluːmə/ *n.* *Brit.* an oblong loaf with a rounded diagonally slashed top. [20th c.: origin uncertain]

bloomer[3] /'bluːmə/ *n.* **1** a plant that blooms (in a specified way) (*early autumn bloomer*). **2** *N. Amer.* a person who develops or matures (in a specified way) (*she's a late bloomer*).

bloomers /'bluːməz/ *n.pl.* **1** women's loose-fitting almost knee-length knickers. **2** *colloq.* any women's knickers. **3** *hist.* women's and girls' loose-fitting trousers, gathered at the knee or (originally) the ankle. [Mrs A. *Bloomer*, American social reformer (d. 1894), who advocated a similar garment]

bloomery /'bluːməri/ *n.* (*pl.* **-ies**) a factory that makes puddled iron into blooms.

blooming /'bluːmɪŋ/ *adj.* & *adv.* ● *adj.* **1** flourishing; healthy. **2** *Brit. slang* an intensive (*a blooming miracle*). ● *adv.* *Brit. slang* an intensive (*was blooming difficult*). [BLOOM[1] + -ING[2]: euphemism for BLOODY]

Bloomsbury /'bluːmzb(ə)ri/ *n.* & *adj.* ● *n.* (in full **Bloomsbury Group**) a group of writers, artists, and philosophers living in or associated with Bloomsbury in London in the early 20th c. ● *adj.* **1** associated with or similar to the Bloomsbury Group. **2** intellectual; highbrow.

blooper /'bluːpə/ *n.* esp. *N. Amer. colloq.* an embarrassing error. [imitative *bloop* + -ER[1]]

blossom /'blɒs(ə)m/ *n.* & *v.* ● *n.* **1** a flower or a mass of flowers, esp. of a fruit tree. **2** the stage or time of flowering (*the cherry tree in blossom*). **3** a promising stage (*the blossom of youth*). ● *v.intr.* **1** open into flower. **2** reach a promising stage; mature, thrive. ◻ **blossomy** *adj.* [Old English *blōstm(a)*, from the Germanic base of BLOOM[1]]

blot /blɒt/ *n.* & *v.* ● *n.* **1** a spot or stain of ink etc. **2** a moral defect in an otherwise good character; a disgraceful act or quality. **3** any disfigurement or blemish. **4** *Biochem.* a procedure in which proteins etc. separated on a gel are transferred directly to an immobilizing medium for identification. ● *v.* (**blotted**, **blotting**) **1 a** *tr.* spot or stain with ink; smudge. **b** *intr.* (of a pen, ink, etc.) make blots. **2** *tr.* **a** use blotting paper or other absorbent material to absorb excess ink. **b** (of blotting paper etc.) soak up (esp. ink). **3** *tr.* disgrace (*blotted his reputation*). **4** *tr. Biochem.* transfer by means of a blot. ◻ **blot one's copybook** *Brit.* damage one's reputation. **blot on the escutcheon of** see ESCUTCHEON. **blot out 1 a** obliterate (writing). **b** obscure (a view, sound, etc.). **2** obliterate (from the memory) as too painful. **3** destroy. [Middle English, probably from Scandinavian: cf. Icelandic *blettr* 'spot, stain']

blotch /blɒtʃ/ *n.* & *v.* ● *n.* **1** a discoloured or inflamed patch on the skin. **2** an irregular patch of ink or colour. ● *v.tr.* cover with blotches. ◻ **blotchy** *adj.* (**blotchier**, **blotchiest**). [17th c.: from obsolete *plotch* and BLOT]

blotter /'blɒtə/ *n.* **1** a sheet or sheets of blotting paper, usu. inserted into a frame. **2** *N. Amer.* a temporary recording-book, esp. a police charge sheet.

blotting paper *n.* unglazed absorbent paper used for soaking up excess ink.

blotto /'blɒtəʊ/ *adj.* *slang* very drunk, esp. unconscious from drinking. [20th c.: perhaps from BLOT]

blouse /blaʊz/ *n.* & *v.* ● *n.* **1 a** a woman's loose, usu. lightweight, upper garment, usu. buttoned and collared. **b** the upper part of a soldier's or airman's battledress. **2** a workman's or peasant's loose linen or cotton garment usu. belted at the waist. ● *v.* **1** *tr.* make (a bodice etc.) loose like a blouse. **2** *intr.* swell or hang loosely like a blouse. [French, of unknown origin]

blouson /ˈbluːzɒn/ *n.* a short blouse-shaped jacket. [French]

blow[1] /bləʊ/ *v.* & *n.* ● *v.* (*past* **blew** /bluː/; *past part.* **blown** /bləʊn/) **1 a** *intr.* (of the wind or air, or impersonally) move along; act as an air current (*it was blowing hard*). **b** *intr.* be driven by an air current (*waste paper blew along the gutter*). **c** *tr.* drive with an air current (*blew the door open*). **2 a** *tr.* send out (esp. air) by breathing (*blew cigarette smoke*; *blew a bubble*). **b** *intr.* send a directed air current from the mouth. **3** *tr.* & *intr.* sound or be sounded by blowing (*the whistle blew*; *they blew the trumpets*). **4** *tr.* **a** direct an air current at (*blew the embers*). **b** (foll. by *off*, *away*, etc.) clear by means of an air current (*blew the dust off*). **5** *tr.* (*past part.* **blowed**) (esp. in *imper.*) *Brit. slang* curse, damn (*blow it!*; *I'll be blowed!*; *let's take a taxi and blow the expense*). **6** *tr.* **a** clear (the nose) of mucus by blowing. **b** remove contents from (an egg) by blowing through it. **7 a** *intr.* puff, pant. **b** *tr.* (esp. in *passive*) exhaust of breath. **8** *slang* **a** *tr.* depart suddenly from (*blew the town yesterday*). **b** *intr.* depart suddenly. **9** *tr.* shatter or send flying by an explosion (*the bomb blew the tiles off the roof*; *blew them to smithereens*). **10** *tr.* make or shape (glass or a bubble) by blowing air in. **11** *tr.* & *intr.* melt or cause to melt from overloading (*the fuse has blown*). **12** *intr.* (of a whale) eject air and water through a blowhole. **13** *tr.* break into (a safe etc.) with explosives. **14** *tr. slang* **a** squander, spend recklessly (*blew £20 on a meal*). **b** spoil, bungle (an opportunity etc.) (*he's blown his chances of winning*). **c** reveal (a secret etc.). **15** *intr.* (of a food-tin etc.) swell and eventually burst from internal gas pressure. **16** *tr.* work the bellows of (an organ). **17** *tr.* (of flies) deposit eggs in. ● *n.* **1 a** an act of blowing (e.g. one's nose, a wind instrument). **b** *colloq.* a turn or spell of playing jazz (on any instrument); a musical session. **2 a** a gust of wind or air. **b** exposure to fresh air. □ **be blowed if one will** *slang* be unwilling to. **blow away** *slang* **1** kill, destroy, defeat. **2** astound, amaze. **blow the gaff** *Brit.* reveal a secret inadvertently. **blow hot and cold** *colloq.* vacillate. **blow in 1** break inwards by an explosion. **2** *colloq.* arrive unexpectedly. **blow a kiss** kiss one's hand and wave it to a distant person. **blow a person's mind** *slang* cause a person to have drug-induced hallucinations or a similar experience. **blow off 1** escape or allow (steam etc.) to escape forcibly. **2** *slang* break wind noisily. **blow on** (or **upon**) *archaic* **1** expose. **2** discredit. **blow out 1 a** extinguish by blowing. **b** send outwards by an explosion. **2** (of a tyre) burst. **3** (of a fuse etc.) melt. **4** *N. Amer. slang* **a** defeat convincingly. **b** render useless, break (*he blew out his arm*). **blow over** (of trouble etc.) fade away without serious consequences. **blow one's own trumpet** praise oneself. **blow one's socks off** see SOCK[1]. **blow one's top** (*N. Amer.* also **stack**) *colloq.* explode in rage. **blow up 1 a** shatter or destroy by an explosion. **b** explode, erupt. **2** *Brit. colloq.* rebuke strongly. **3** inflate (a tyre etc.). **4** *colloq.* **a** enlarge (a photograph). **b** exaggerate. **5** *colloq.* come to notice; arise. **6** *colloq.* lose one's temper. **blow the whistle on** see WHISTLE. [Old English *blāwan*, from Germanic]

blow[2] /bləʊ/ *n.* **1** a hard stroke with a hand or weapon. **2** a sudden shock or misfortune. □ **at one blow** by a single stroke; in one operation. **come to blows** end up fighting. **strike a blow for** (or **against**) show support for (or opposition to). [15th c.: origin unknown]

blow[3] /bləʊ/ *v.* & *n. archaic* ● *v.intr.* (*past* **blew** /bluː/; *past part.* **blown** /bləʊn/) burst into or be in flower. ● *n.* blossoming, bloom (*in full blow*). [Old English *blōwan*, from Germanic]

blow-ball *n.* the globular seed-head of a dandelion etc.

blow-by-blow *attrib.adj.* (of a description etc.) giving all the details in sequence.

blow-dry *v.* & *n.* ● *v.tr.* arrange (the hair) while drying it with a hand-held dryer. ● *n.* an act of doing this. □ **blow-dryer** *n.* (also **-drier**).

blower /ˈbləʊə/ *n.* **1** in senses of BLOW[1] *v.* **2** a device for creating a current of air. **3** esp. *Brit. colloq.* a telephone.

blowfish /ˈbləʊfɪʃ/ *n.* (*pl.* usu. same) any of several kinds of fish able to inflate their bodies when frightened etc., e.g. a globe-fish.

blowfly /ˈbləʊflʌɪ/ *n.* (*pl.* **-flies**) a fly of the family Calliphoridae, laying its eggs on meat and carcasses, e.g. a bluebottle.

blowgun /ˈbləʊgʌn/ *n. US* = BLOWPIPE 1.

blowhard /ˈbləʊhɑːd/ *n.* & *adj. colloq.* ● *n.* a boastful person. ● *adj.* boastful; blustering.

blowhole /ˈbləʊhəʊl/ *n.* **1** the nostril of a whale, on the top of its head. **2** a hole (esp. in ice) for breathing or fishing through. **3** a vent for air, smoke, etc., in a tunnel etc.

blow job *n. coarse slang* an act of fellatio.

blowlamp /ˈbləʊlamp/ *n. Brit.* a portable device with a very hot flame used for burning off paint, soldering, etc.

blown *past part.* of BLOW[1], BLOW[3].

blow-out *n.* **1** *colloq.* a burst tyre. **2** *colloq.* a melted fuse. **3** *colloq.* **a** a huge meal. **b** *N. Amer.* a large social gathering or party. **4** an uncontrolled uprush of oil or gas from a well. **5** *N. Amer. slang* a resounding defeat; failure.

blowpipe /ˈbləʊpʌɪp/ *n.* **1** a tube used esp. by primitive peoples for propelling arrows or darts by blowing. **2** a tube used to intensify the heat of a flame by blowing air or other gas through it at high pressure. **3** a tube used in glass-blowing.

blowtorch /ˈbləʊtɔːtʃ/ *n.* = BLOWLAMP.

blow-up *n.* **1** *colloq.* an enlargement (of a photograph etc.). **2** an explosion.

blowy /ˈbləʊi/ *adj.* (**blowier**, **blowiest**) windy, windswept.

blowzy /ˈblaʊzi/ *adj.* (**blowzier**, **blowziest**) **1** coarse-looking; red-faced. **2** dishevelled, slovenly. □ **blowzily** *adv.* **blowziness** *n.* [obsolete *blowze* 'beggar's wench', of unknown origin]

blub /blʌb/ *v.intr.* (**blubbed**, **blubbing**) *Brit. slang* sob. [abbreviation of BLUBBER[1]]

blubber[1] /ˈblʌbə/ *n.* & *v.* ● *n.* **1** whale fat. **2** a spell of weeping. **3** *colloq.* excess body fat. ● *v.* **1** *intr.* sob loudly. **2** *tr.* sob out (words). □ **blubberer** *n.* **blubbery** *adj.* [Middle English, perhaps imitative]

blubber[2] /ˈblʌbə/ *adj.* (of the lips) swollen, protruding. [earlier *blabber*, *blobber*, imitative]

bluchers /ˈbluːkəz/ *n.pl. hist.* strong leather half-boots or high shoes. [G. L. von *Blücher*, Prussian general (d. 1819)]

bludge /blʌdʒ/ *v.* & *n. Austral.* & *NZ slang* ● *v.* **1** *intr.* shirk responsibility or hard work. **2** *tr.* cadge, scrounge. ● *n.* an easy job or assignment. □ **bludge on** impose on. [back-formation from BLUDGER]

bludgeon /ˈblʌdʒ(ə)n/ *n.* & *v.* ● *n.* a club with a heavy end. ● *v.tr.* **1** beat with a bludgeon. **2** coerce. [18th c.: origin unknown]

bludger /ˈblʌdʒə/ *n. Austral.* & *NZ slang* **1** a hanger-on, a scrounger. **2** a loafer. [originally British slang, = pimp, from obsolete *bludgeoner* from BLUDGEON]

blue[1] /bluː/ *adj.*, *n.*, & *v.* ● *adj.* (**bluer**, **bluest**) **1** having a colour like that of a clear sky. **2** sad, depressed; (of a state of affairs) gloomy, dismal (*feel blue*; *blue times*). **3** indecent, pornographic (*a blue film*). **4** with bluish skin through cold, fear, anger, etc. **5** *Brit.* politically conservative. **6** having blue as a distinguishing colour (*blue jay*). ● *n.* **1** a blue colour or pigment. **2** blue clothes or material (*dressed in blue*). **3** *Brit.* **a** a person who has represented a university (esp. Oxford or Cambridge) in a sport. **b** this distinction. Cf. HALF-BLUE. **4** *Brit.* a supporter of the Conservative Party. **5** any of various small blue-coloured butterflies of the family Lycaenidae. **6** blue powder used to whiten laundry. **7** *Austral. slang* **a** an argument or row. **b** (as a nickname) a red-headed person. **8** a blue ball, piece, etc. in a game or sport. **9** (prec. by *the*) the clear sky. ● *v.tr.* (**blues**,

blued, **bluing** or **blueing**) **1** make blue. **2** treat with laundering blue. ◻ **blue in the face** in a state of extreme anger or exasperation. **once in a blue moon** very rarely. **out of the blue** unexpectedly. ◻ **blueness** *n.* [Middle English from Old French *bleu*, from Germanic]

blue[2] /bluː/ *v.tr.* (**blues**, **blued**, **bluing** or **blueing**) *Brit. slang* squander (money). [perhaps variant of BLOW[1]]

blue baby *n.* a baby with a blue complexion from lack of oxygen in the blood due to a congenital defect of the heart or major blood vessels.

Bluebeard /ˈbluːbɪəd/ *n.* **1** a man who murders his wives. **2** a person with a horrible secret. [a character in a fairy tale told originally in French (*Barbe-Bleue*) by Perrault]

bluebell /ˈbluːbɛl/ *n.* **1** a woodland plant of the lily family, *Hyacinthoides nonscripta*, with clusters of bell-shaped blue flowers on a stem arising from a rhizome; also called *wild hyacinth*, *wood hyacinth*. **2** *Sc.* = HAREBELL. **3** any of several other plants with blue bell-shaped flowers.

blueberry /ˈbluːb(ə)ri/ *n.* (*pl.* **-ies**) **1** any of several plants of the genus *Vaccinium* with small blue-black edible fruit, sometimes cultivated. **2** the fruit of these plants.

blue bice *n.* a shade of blue between ultramarine and azure derived from smalt.

bluebird /ˈbluːbəːd/ *n.* any of various N. American songbirds of the thrush family, esp. of the genus *Sialia*, with distinctive blue plumage usu. on the back or head.

blue-black *n.* & *adj.* ● *n.* a black colour with a tinge of blue. ● *adj.* of this colour.

blue blood *n.* **1** noble birth. **2** a person of noble lineage. ◻ **blue-blooded** *adj.*

blue book *n.* an official or widely recognized book of rules, economic or commercial information, names of officials, etc., esp. (in the UK) a report issued by Parliament or the Privy Council, bound in blue.

bluebottle /ˈbluːbɒt(ə)l/ *n.* **1** a large buzzing fly, *Calliphora vomitoria*, with a metallic-blue body; also called BLOWFLY. **2** *Austral.* a Portuguese man-of-war. **3** a dark blue cornflower. **4** *Brit. colloq.* a police officer.

blue box *n.* **1** esp. *US* an electronic device used to access long-distance telephone lines illegally. **2** esp. *Canad.* a blue plastic box for the collection of recyclable household materials.

blue cheese *n.* cheese produced with veins of blue mould, e.g. Stilton and Danish Blue.

blue-chip *attrib.adj.* (of shares) of reliable investment, though less secure than gilt-edged stock. [from *blue chip*, a high-value counter in gambling games]

blue-collar *attrib.adj.* (of a worker or work) manual; industrial.

blue ensign *n.* the ensign of government departments and formerly of the naval reserve etc.

blue-eyed boy *n.* esp. *Brit. colloq.* usu. *derog.* a favoured person; a favourite.

bluefish /ˈbluːfɪʃ/ *n.* (*pl.* usu. same) a voracious marine fish, *Pomatomus saltatrix*, inhabiting tropical and temperate waters and popular as a game fish.

blue funk *n. slang* **1** esp. *Brit.* a state of great terror or panic. **2** esp. *N. Amer.* a state of mild depression.

bluegrass /ˈbluːgrɑːs/ *n.* **1** any of several bluish-green grasses, esp. of Kentucky. **2** a kind of instrumental country and western music characterized by virtuosic playing of banjos, guitars, etc.

blue-green alga *n.* = CYANOBACTERIUM.

blue ground *n.* = KIMBERLITE.

bluegum /ˈbluːgʌm/ *n.* any tree of the genus *Eucalyptus*, esp. *E. regnans* with blue-green aromatic leaves.

blueish var. of BLUISH.

bluejacket /ˈbluːdʒakɪt/ *n. slang* a seaman in the Navy.

Blue John *n.* a purple and white banded variety of fluorite found in Derbyshire, England.

blue line *n. Ice Hockey* either of the two lines midway between the centre of the rink and each goal.

Bluemantle /ˈbluːmant(ə)l/ *n.* one of four pursuivants of the English College of Arms.

blue metal *n. Brit.* broken blue stone used for road-making.

blue mould *n.* a bluish fungus growing on food and other organic matter.

blue murder *n.* (*N. Amer.* **bloody murder**) a great commotion; a loud or alarming noise (esp. as an intensive: *yelled blue murder*).

blue-pencil *v.tr.* (**-pencilled**, **-pencilling**; *US* **-penciled**, **-penciling**) censor or make cuts in (a manuscript, film, etc.).

Blue Peter *n.* a blue flag with a white square raised on board a ship leaving port.

blueprint /ˈbluːprɪnt/ *n.* & *v.* ● *n.* **1** a photographic print of the final stage of engineering or other plans in white on a blue background. **2** a detailed plan, esp. in the early stages of a project or idea. ● *v.tr. US* work out (a programme, plan, etc.).

blue ribbon *n.* **1** a high honour. **2** *Brit.* the ribbon of the Order of the Garter.

blue rinse *n.* a preparation for tinting grey hair.

blue roan *adj.* & *n.* ● *adj.* black mixed with white. ● *n.* a blue roan animal.

blue rock *n.* = ROCK-DOVE.

blues /bluːz/ *n.pl.* **1** (prec. by *the*) a bout of depression (*had a fit of the blues*). **2 a** (prec. by *the*; often treated as *sing.*) melancholic music of black American folk origin, often in a twelve-bar sequence. **b** (*pl.* same) (treated as *sing.*) a piece of such music (*the band played a blues*). ◻ **bluesy** *adj.* (in sense 2).

bluestocking /ˈbluːstɒkɪŋ/ *n.* usu. *derog.* an intellectual or literary woman. [originally a frequenter of the 'blue-stocking' literary assemblies held in London *c.*1750 (from the less formal blue stockings worn by some men): later applied only to women]

bluestone /ˈbluːstəʊn/ *n.* **1** any of various bluish or grey building stones. **2** any of the smaller stones in the inner part of Stonehenge, made of dolerite.

bluet /ˈbluːɪt/ *n. US* a blue-flowered plant of the genus *Hedyotis*.

blue tit *n.* a common tit, *Parus caeruleus*, with a distinct blue crest on a black and white head.

blue vitriol *n.* crystalline copper sulphate.

blue water *n.* open sea.

blue whale *n.* a rorqual, *Balaenoptera musculus*, the largest known living mammal.

bluey /ˈbluːi/ *n.* (*pl.* **-eys**) *Austral. colloq.* **1** a bundle carried by a bushman. **2** = BLUE[1] *n.* 7b.

bluff[1] /blʌf/ *v.* & *n.* ● *v.* **1** *intr.* make a pretence of strength or confidence to gain an advantage. **2** *tr.* mislead by bluffing. ● *n.* an act of bluffing; a show of confidence or assertiveness intended to deceive. ◻ **call a person's bluff** challenge a person thought to be bluffing. ◻ **bluffer** *n.* [19th c. (originally in poker) from Dutch *bluffen* 'brag']

bluff[2] /blʌf/ *adj.* & *n.* ● *adj.* **1** (of a cliff, or a ship's bows) having a vertical or steep broad front. **2** (of a person or manner) blunt, frank, hearty. ● *n.* a steep cliff or headland. ◻ **bluffly** *adv.* (in sense 2 of *adj.*). **bluffness** *n.* (in sense 2 of *adj.*). [17th-c. nautical word: origin unknown]

bluish /ˈbluːɪʃ/ *adj.* (also **blueish**) somewhat blue.

blunder /ˈblʌndə/ *n.* & *v.* ● *n.* a clumsy or foolish mistake, esp. an important one. ● *v.* **1** *intr.* make a blunder; act clumsily or ineptly. **2** *tr.* deal incompetently with; mismanage. **3** *intr.* move about blindly or clumsily; stumble. ◻ **blunderer** *n.* **blunderingly** *adv.* [Middle English probably from Scandinavian: cf. Middle Swedish *blundra* 'shut the eyes']

blunderbuss /ˈblʌndəbʌs/ *n. hist.* a short large-bored gun firing balls or slugs. [alteration of Dutch *donderbus* 'thunder gun', associated with BLUNDER]

blunge /blʌn(d)ʒ/ *v.tr.* (in ceramics etc.) mix (clay etc.) with water. [portmanteau word, from PLUNGE + BLEND]

blunt /blʌnt/ *adj. & v.* ● *adj.* **1** (of a knife, pencil, etc.) lacking a sharp edge or point; having a worn-down point or edge. **2** (of a person or manner) direct, uncompromising, outspoken. ● *v.tr.* make blunt or less sharp. □ **bluntly** *adv.* (in sense 2 of *adj.*). **bluntness** *n.* [Middle English, in the sense 'dull, insensitive' (of perceptions or intellect), perhaps from Scandinavian: cf. Old Norse *blunda* 'shut the eyes']

blur /blɜː/ *v. & n.* ● *v.* (**blurred**, **blurring**) **1** *tr. & intr.* make or become unclear or less distinct. **2** *tr.* smear; partially efface. **3** *tr.* make (one's memory, perception, etc.) dim or less clear. ● *n.* something that appears or sounds indistinct or unclear. □ **blurry** *adj.* (**blurrier**, **blurriest**). [16th c.: perhaps related to BLEAR]

blurb /blɜːb/ *n.* a (usu. eulogistic) description of a book, esp. printed on its jacket, as promotion by its publishers. [coined by G. Burgess, American humorist d. 1951]

blurt /blɜːt/ *v.tr.* (usu. foll. by *out*) utter abruptly, thoughtlessly, or tactlessly. [probably imitative]

blush /blʌʃ/ *v. & n.* ● *v.intr.* **1 a** develop a pink tinge in the face from embarrassment or shame. **b** (of the face) redden in this way. **2** feel embarrassed or ashamed. **3** be or become red or pink. ● *n.* **1** the act of blushing. **2** a pink tinge. □ **at first blush** on the first glimpse or impression. **spare a person's blushes** refrain from causing embarrassment esp. by praise. [Middle English, from Old English *blyscan*]

blusher /ˈblʌʃə/ *n.* a cosmetic used to give a warmth of colour to the face.

bluster /ˈblʌstə/ *v. & n.* ● *v.intr.* **1** behave pompously and boisterously; utter empty threats. **2** (of the wind etc.) blow fiercely. ● *n.* **1** noisily self-assertive talk. **2** empty threats. □ **blusterer** *n.* **blustery** *adj.* [16th c.: ultimately imitative]

B-lymphocyte /biːˈlɪmfəsʌɪt/ *n. Physiol.* a lymphocyte not processed by the thymus gland, and responsible for producing antibodies (cf. T-LYMPHOCYTE). Also called *B-cell*. [*B* for *bursa*, referring to an organ in birds where it was first identified]

BM *abbr.* **1** British Museum. **2** Bachelor of Medicine.

BMA *abbr.* British Medical Association.

B-movie *n.* a supporting film in a cinema programme; a low-budget film.

B.Mus. *abbr.* Bachelor of Music.

BMX *n.* **1** organized bicycle racing on a dirt track, esp. for youngsters. **2** a kind of bicycle used for this. **3** (*attrib.*) of or related to such racing or the equipment used (*BMX gloves*). [abbreviation of *b*icycle *moto-cross*]

Bn. *abbr.* Battalion.

bn. *abbr.* billion.

BO *abbr. colloq.* body odour.

bo /bəʊ/ *int.* = BOO. [imitative]

boa /ˈbəʊə/ *n.* **1** a constrictor snake of the family Boidae, esp. any of the larger ones from the New World. **2** any snake which is a constrictor, e.g. an Old World python. **3** a long thin stole made of feathers or fur. [Latin]

boa constrictor *n.* a large snake, *Boa constrictor*, native to tropical America and the West Indies, which crushes its prey.

boar /bɔː/ *n.* **1** (in full **wild boar**) the tusked wild pig, *Sus scrofa*, from which domestic pigs are descended. **2** an uncastrated male pig. **3** its flesh. **4** a male guinea pig etc. [Old English *bār*, from West Germanic]

board /bɔːd/ *n. & v.* ● *n.* **1 a** a flat thin piece of sawn timber, usu. long and narrow. **b** a piece of material resembling this, made from compressed fibres. **c** a thin slab of wood or a similar substance, often with a covering, used for any of various purposes (*chessboard*; *ironing board*; *noticeboard*). **d** thick stiff card used in bookbinding. **2** the provision of regular meals, usu. with accommodation, for payment. **3** *archaic* a table spread for a meal. **4** the directors of a company; any other specially constituted administrative body, e.g. a committee or group of councillors, examiners, etc. **5** (in *pl.*) the stage of a theatre (cf. *tread the boards*). **6** *Naut.* the side of a ship. ● *v.* **1** *tr.* **a** go on board (a ship, train, aircraft, etc.). **b** force one's way on board (a ship etc.) in attack. **2 a** *intr.* receive regular meals, or (esp. of a schoolchild) meals and lodging, for payment. **b** *tr.* (often foll. by *out*) arrange accommodation away from home for (esp. a child). **c** *tr.* provide (a lodger etc.) with regular meals. **3** *tr.* (usu. foll. by *up*) cover with boards; seal or close. □ **go by the board** be neglected, omitted, or discarded. **on board** on or on to a ship, aircraft, oil rig, etc. **take on board** consider (a new idea etc.). [Old English *bord*, from Germanic]

boarder /ˈbɔːdə/ *n.* **1** a person who boards, esp. a pupil at a boarding school (see BOARD *v.* 2a). **2** a person who boards a ship, esp. an enemy.

board game *n.* a game played on a board.

boarding house *n.* an establishment providing board and lodging, esp. *Brit.* to holidaymakers.

boarding kennel *n.* (often in *pl.*) a boarding establishment for dogs.

boarding school *n.* a school where pupils are resident in term-time.

Board of Green Cloth see GREEN CLOTH.

board of trade *n. N. Amer.* a chamber of commerce.

boardroom /ˈbɔːdruːm, -rʊm/ *n.* a room in which a board of directors etc. meets regularly.

boardsailing /ˈbɔːdseɪlɪŋ/ *n.* = WINDSURFING. □ **boardsailor** *n.* (also **boardsailer**).

boardwalk /ˈbɔːdwɔːk/ *n. N. Amer.* **1** a wooden walkway across sand, marsh, etc. **2** a promenade along a beach.

boart var. of BORT.

boast /bəʊst/ *v. & n.* ● *v.* **1** *intr.* declare one's achievements, possessions, or abilities with indulgent pride and satisfaction. **2** *tr.* own or have as something praiseworthy etc. (*the hotel boasts magnificent views*). ● *n.* **1** an act of boasting. **2** something one is proud of. □ **boaster** *n.* **boastingly** *adv.* [Middle English from Anglo-French *bost*, of unknown origin]

boastful /ˈbəʊstfʊl, -f(ə)l/ *adj.* **1** given to boasting. **2** characterized by boasting (*boastful talk*). □ **boastfully** *adv.* **boastfulness** *n.*

boat /bəʊt/ *n. & v.* ● *n.* **1** a small vessel propelled on water by an engine, oars, or sails. **2** (in general use) a ship of any size. **3** an elongated boat-shaped jug used for holding sauce etc. ● *v.intr.* travel or go in a boat, esp. for pleasure. □ **in the same boat** sharing the same adverse circumstances. **push the boat out** *Brit. colloq.* celebrate lavishly. □ **boatful** *n.* (*pl.* **-fuls**). [Old English *bāt*, from Germanic]

boat-building *n.* the occupation of building boats. □ **boatbuilder** *n.*

boatel var. of BOTEL.

boater /ˈbəʊtə/ *n.* a flat-topped hardened straw hat with a brim (originally worn while boating).

boat-hook *n.* a long pole with a hook and a spike at one end, for moving boats.

boathouse /ˈbəʊthaʊs/ *n.* a shed at the edge of a river, lake, etc., for housing boats.

boatie /ˈbəʊti/ *n.* esp. *Austral. & NZ colloq.* a person who sails a boat; a boating enthusiast.

boating /ˈbəʊtɪŋ/ *n.* rowing or sailing in boats as a sport or form of recreation.

boatload /ˈbəʊtləʊd/ *n.* **1** enough to fill a boat. **2** *colloq.* a large number of people.

boatman /ˈbəʊtmən/ *n.* (*pl.* **-men**) a person who hires out boats or provides transport by boat.

boat people *n.* refugees who have left a country by sea.

boat race *n.* a race between rowing crews, esp. (**the Boat Race**) the one between Oxford and Cambridge.

boatswain /ˈbəʊs(ə)n/ *n.* (also **bo'sun, bosun, bo's'n**) a ship's officer in charge of equipment and the crew. [Old English *bātswegen* (as BOAT, SWAIN)]

boatswain's chair *n.* a seat suspended from ropes for work on the side of a ship or building.

boat-train *n.* a train scheduled to meet or go on a boat.

bob[1] /bɒb/ *v. & n.* ● *v.intr.* (**bobbed**, **bobbing**) **1** move quickly up and down; dance. **2** (usu. foll. by *back, up*) **a** bounce buoyantly. **b** emerge suddenly; become active or conspicuous again after a defeat etc. **3** curtsy. **4** (foll. by *for*) try to catch with the mouth alone (fruit etc. floating or hanging). ● *n.* **1** a jerking or bouncing movement, esp. upward. **2** a curtsy. **3** one of several kinds of change in long peals in bell-ringing. [14th c.: probably imitative]

bob[2] /bɒb/ *n. & v.* ● *n.* **1** a short hairstyle for women and children. **2** a weight on a pendulum, plumb line, or kite tail. **3** = BOBSLEIGH. **4** a horse's docked tail. **5** a short line at or towards the end of a stanza. **6** a knot of hair; a tassel-shaped curl. ● *v.* (**bobbed**, **bobbing**) **1** *tr.* cut (a woman's or child's hair) so that it hangs clear of the shoulders. **2** *intr.* ride on a bobsleigh. [Middle English: origin unknown]

bob[3] /bɒb/ *n.* (*pl.* same) *Brit. slang hist.* a shilling (now = 5 decimal pence). [19th c.: origin unknown]

bob[4] /bɒb/ *n.* □ **bob's your uncle** *Brit. slang* an expression of completion or satisfaction. [pet form of the name *Robert*]

bobber /ˈbɒbə/ *n.* a person who rides on a bobsleigh.

bobbin /ˈbɒbɪn/ *n.* **1 a** a cylinder or cone holding thread, yarn, wire, etc., used esp. in weaving and machine sewing. **b** a spool or reel. **2** a small bar and string for raising a door latch. [French *bobine*, of unknown origin]

bobbinet /ˈbɒbɪnɛt/ *n.* machine-made cotton net (imitating lace made with bobbins on a pillow). [BOBBIN + NET[1]]

bobbin lace *n.* lace made by hand with thread wound on bobbins.

bobble /ˈbɒb(ə)l/ *n. & v.* ● *n.* **1** a small woolly or tufted ball as a decoration or trimming. **2** *US* esp. *Sport* a mistake or error; a bungle. ● *v.tr. & intr. US* esp. *Sport* bungle or fumble, esp. in taking a catch. □ **bobbly** *adj.* [diminutive of BOB[2]]

bobby[1] /ˈbɒbi/ *n.* (*pl.* **-ies**) *Brit. colloq.* a police officer. [Sir *Robert* Peel, English statesman d. 1850, founder of the metropolitan police force]

bobby[2] /ˈbɒbi/ *n.* (*pl.* **-ies**) (in full **bobby calf**) an unweaned calf slaughtered for veal. [English dialect]

bobby-dazzler *n. Brit. colloq.* a remarkable or excellent person or thing. [dialect, related to DAZZLE: the first element is unknown]

bobby pin *n. N. Amer., Austral., & NZ* a flat hairpin. [BOB[2] + -Y[2]]

bobby socks *n.pl.* esp. *N. Amer.* short socks reaching just above the ankle. □ **bobby-soxer** *n.* [BOB[2] + -Y[2]]

bobcat /ˈbɒbkat/ *n.* a small N. American lynx, *Felix rufus*, with a spotted reddish-brown coat and a short tail. [BOB[2] + CAT[1]]

bobolink /ˈbɒbəlɪŋk/ *n.* a N. American oriole, *Dolichonyx oryzivorus*. [originally *Bob (o') Lincoln*: imitative of its call]

bobsled /ˈbɒbslɛd/ *n. N. Amer.* = BOBSLEIGH. □ **bobsledding** *n.*

bobsleigh /ˈbɒbsleɪ/ *n.* a mechanically steered and braked sledge used for racing down a steep ice-covered run. □ **bobsleighing** *n.* [BOB[2] + SLEIGH]

bobstay /ˈbɒbsteɪ/ *n.* the chain or rope holding down a ship's bowsprit. [probably BOB[1] + STAY[2]]

bobtail /ˈbɒbteɪl/ *n.* **1** a docked tail. **2** a horse or a dog with a bobtail. [BOB[2] + TAIL[1]]

bocage /bəˈkɑːʒ/ *n.* the representation of silvan scenery in ceramics. [French from Old French *boscage*: see BOSCAGE]

Boche /bɒʃ/ *n. & adj. slang derog.* ● *n.* **1** a German, esp. a soldier. **2** (prec. by *the*) Germans, esp. German soldiers, collectively. ● *adj.* German. [French slang, originally = rascal: applied to Germans in the First World War]

bock /bɒk/ *n.* a strong dark German beer. [French, from the German abbreviation of *Eimbockbier* from *Einbeck* in Hanover]

BOD *abbr.* biochemical oxygen demand.

bod /bɒd/ *n. colloq.* **1** *Brit.* a person. **2** *N. Amer.* a body. [abbreviation of BODY]

bodacious /bəˈdeɪʃəs/ *adj. N. Amer. slang* **1** remarkable, excellent. **2** esp. *US* bold, audacious. [perhaps variant of archaic *boldacious*, from BOLD + AUDACIOUS]

bode /bəʊd/ *v.tr.* **1** portend, foreshow. **2** foresee, foretell (evil). □ **bode well** (or **ill**) show good (or bad) signs for the future. [Old English *bodian* from *boda* 'messenger']

bodega /bəˈdiːgə/ *n.* a cellar or shop selling wine and food, esp. in a Spanish-speaking country. [Spanish via Latin *apotheca* from Greek *apothēkē* 'storehouse']

Bode's law /ˈbəʊdz, ˈbəʊdəz/ *n. Astron.* a formula by which the distances of the first seven planets from the sun are roughly derived in terms of powers of two. [J.E. *Bode*, German astronomer d. 1826]

bodge *Brit.* var. of BOTCH.

Bodhisattva /bɒdɪˈsɑːtvə/ *n.* (in Mahayana Buddhism) a person who is able to reach nirvana but delays doing so through compassion for suffering beings. [Sanskrit, = a person whose essence is perfect knowledge]

bodice /ˈbɒdɪs/ *n.* **1** the part of a woman's dress (excluding sleeves) which is above the waist. **2** a woman's undergarment, like a vest, for the same part of the body. [originally *pair of bodies* = stays, corsets]

bodice-ripper *n. colloq.* a sexually explicit romantic (esp. historical) novel or film with seduction of the heroine. □ **bodice-ripping** *adj.*

bodiless /ˈbɒdɪlɪs/ *adj.* **1** lacking a body. **2** incorporeal, insubstantial.

bodily /ˈbɒdɪli/ *adj. & adv.* ● *adj.* of or concerning the body. ● *adv.* **1** with the whole bulk; as a whole (*threw them bodily*). **2** in the body; as a person.

bodkin /ˈbɒdkɪn/ *n.* **1** a blunt thick needle with a large eye used esp. for drawing tape etc. through a hem. **2** a long pin for fastening hair. **3** a small pointed instrument for piercing cloth, removing a piece of type for correction, etc. [Middle English, perhaps from Celtic]

body /ˈbɒdi/ *n. & v.* ● *n.* (*pl.* **-ies**) **1** the physical structure, including the bones, flesh, and organs, of a person or an animal, whether dead or alive. **2** the trunk apart from the head and the limbs. **3 a** the main or central part of a thing (*body of the car*; *body of the attack*). **b** the bulk or majority; the aggregate (*body of opinion*). **4 a** a group of persons regarded collectively, esp. as having a corporate function (*governing body*). **b** (usu. foll. by *of*) a collection (*body of facts*). **5** a quantity (*body of water*). **6** a material object (*celestial body*). **7** *colloq.* a person. **8** a full or substantial quality of flavour, tone, etc., e.g. in wine, musical sounds, etc. **9** *Brit.* a bodysuit. ● *v.tr.* (**-ies**, **-ied**) (usu. foll. by *forth*) give body or substance to. □ **in a body** all together. **keep body and soul together** keep alive, esp. barely. **over my dead body** *colloq.* entirely without my assent. □ **-bodied** *adj.* (in *comb.*: *able-bodied*). [Old English *bodig*, of unknown origin]

body bag *n.* a bag for carrying a corpse from the scene of warfare, an accident, etc.

body blow *n.* a severe setback.

body-building *n.* the practice of strengthening the body, esp. shaping and enlarging the muscles, by exercise. □ **bodybuilder** *n.*

body-check *n. & v.* ● *n.* a deliberate obstruction of one player by another. ● *v.tr.* obstruct in this way.

body colour *n.* an opaque pigment.

body double *n.* a stand-in for a film actor during stunt or nude scenes.

bodyguard /ˈbɒdɪgɑːd/ *n.* a person or group of persons escorting and protecting another person (esp. a dignitary).

body language *n.* the process of communicating through conscious or unconscious gestures and poses.

body odour *n.* the smell of the human body, esp. when unpleasant.

body piercing *n.* the piercing of holes in parts of the body other than the ear lobes.

body politic *n.* the nation or state as a corporate body.

body-popping *n.* orig. *US* a kind of dancing with jerky robotic movements of the joints.

body scanner *n. Brit.* a scanning X-ray machine for taking tomograms of the whole body.

body search *n.* a search, esp. one conducted by customs officials or the police, of a person's body for illicit weapons, drugs, etc.

body shop *n.* a workshop where repairs to the bodywork of vehicles are carried out.

body stocking *n.* a woman's undergarment which covers the torso.

bodysuit /'bɒdɪsu:t, -sju:t/ *n.* a close-fitting one-piece stretch garment for women.

body warmer *n.* a sleeveless quilted or padded jacket worn as an outdoor garment.

body wave *n.* a soft light permanent wave designed to give the hair fullness.

body weight *n.* the weight of a person's body.

bodywork /'bɒdɪwə:k/ *n.* the outer shell of a vehicle.

body wrap *n.* a type of beauty treatment involving the application of skin-cleansing ingredients to the body followed by wrapping it in hot bandages, intended to result in a reduction in body measurements.

Boer /bɔ:, 'bəʊə, bʊə/ *n. & adj.* ● *n.* a South African of Dutch descent. ● *adj.* of or relating to the Boers. [Dutch *boer* 'farmer']

boffin /'bɒfɪn/ *n.* esp. *Brit. colloq.* a person engaged in scientific (esp. military) research. [20th c.: origin unknown]

Bofors gun /'bəʊfəz/ *n.* a type of light anti-aircraft gun. [*Bofors* in Sweden, where it was made]

bog /bɒg/ *n. & v.* ● *n.* **1 a** wet spongy ground. **b** a stretch of such ground. **2** *Brit. slang* a lavatory. ● *v.tr.* (**bogged**, **bogging**) (foll. by *down*; usu. in *passive*) impede (*was bogged down by difficulties*). □ **bog off** (usu. in *imper.*) *Brit. slang* go away. **bog standard** *Brit. slang* basic, standard, unexceptional. □ **boggy** *adj.* (**boggier**, **boggiest**). **bogginess** *n.* [Irish or Gaelic *bogach* from *bog* 'soft']

bog asphodel *n.* a yellow-flowered European marsh plant, *Narthecium ossifragum*, of the lily family.

bogbean /'bɒgbi:n/ *n.* = BUCKBEAN.

bog cotton *n.* = COTTON GRASS.

bogey[1] /'bəʊgi/ *n. & v. Golf* ● *n.* (*pl.* **-eys**) **1** a score of one stroke more than par at any hole. **2** (formerly) the number of strokes by which a good player should complete a hole or course; par. ● *v.tr.* (**-eys**, **-eyed**) play (a hole) in one stroke more than par. [perhaps from *Bogey* as an imaginary player]

bogey[2] /'bəʊgi/ *n.* (also **bogy**) (*pl.* **-eys** or **-ies**) **1** an evil or mischievous spirit; a devil. **2** an awkward thing or circumstance. **3** *Brit. slang* a piece of nasal mucus. [19th c., originally as a proper name applied to the Devil: cf. BOGLE]

bogeyman /'bəʊgɪman/ *n.* (also **bogyman**) (*pl.* **-men**) a person (real or imaginary) causing fear or difficulty.

boggle /'bɒg(ə)l/ *v. colloq.* **1** *intr.* be startled or baffled (esp. *the mind boggles*). **2** *intr.* (usu. foll. by *about, at*) hesitate, demur. **3** *tr.* overwhelm (mentally). [probably from dialect, related to BOGLE, BOGEY[2]]

bogie /'bəʊgi/ *n.* esp. *Brit.* **1** a wheeled undercarriage pivoted below the end of a rail vehicle. **2** a small truck used for carrying coal, rubble, etc. [19th-c. northern dialect word: origin unknown]

bogle /'bəʊg(ə)l/ *n.* **1** = BOGEY[2] 1. **2** a phantom. **3** a scarecrow. [originally Scots (16th c.), probably related to BOGEY[2]]

bog moss *n. Brit.* sphagnum.

bog myrtle *n.* a deciduous shrub, *Myrica gale*, which grows in damp open places and has short upright catkins and aromatic grey-green leaves. Also called (*sweet*) *gale*.

bog oak *n.* an ancient oak which has been preserved in a black state in peat.

bog spavin *n.* = BLOOD SPAVIN.

bogtrotter /'bɒgtrɒtə/ *n. slang offens.* an Irishman.

bogus /'bəʊgəs/ *adj.* sham, fictitious, spurious. □ **bogusly** *adv.* **bogusness** *n.* [19th-c. US word: origin unknown]

bogy var. of BOGEY[2].

bogyman var. of BOGEYMAN.

bohea /bəʊ'hi:/ *n.* a black China tea, the last crop of the season and usu. regarded as of low quality. [*Bu-i* (Wuyi) Hills in China, whence black tea first came to Britain]

Bohemian /bəʊ'hi:mɪən/ *n. & adj.* ● *n.* **1** a native of Bohemia, a former kingdom in central Europe corresponding to part of the modern Czech Republic; a Czech. **2** (also **bohemian**) a socially unconventional person, esp. an artist or writer. ● *adj.* **1** of, relating to, or characteristic of Bohemia or its people. **2** socially unconventional. □ **bohemianism** *n.* (in sense 2 of *adj.*). [*Bohemia* + -AN: sense 2 from French *bohémien* 'gypsy']

boho /'bəʊhəʊ/ *n. & adj. colloq.* ● *n.* (*pl.* **-os**) = BOHEMIAN *n.* 2. ● *adj.* = BOHEMIAN *adj.* 2. [abbreviation of BOHEMIAN + -O]

boil[1] /bɔɪl/ *v. & n.* ● *v.* **1** *intr.* **a** (of a liquid) start to bubble up and turn into vapour; reach a temperature at which this happens. **b** (of a vessel) contain boiling liquid (*the kettle is boiling*). **2 a** *tr.* bring (a liquid or vessel) to a temperature at which it boils. **b** *tr.* cook (food) by boiling. **c** *intr.* (of food) be cooked by boiling. **d** *tr.* subject to the heat of boiling water, e.g. to clean. **3** *intr.* **a** (of the sea etc.) undulate or seethe like boiling water. **b** (of a person or feelings) be greatly agitated, esp. by anger. ● *n.* the act or process of boiling; boiling point (*on the boil*; *bring to the boil*). □ **boil down 1** reduce volume by boiling. **2** reduce to essentials. **3** (foll. by *to*) amount to; signify basically. **boil over 1** spill over in boiling. **2** lose one's temper; become overexcited. **make one's blood boil** see BLOOD. [Middle English via Anglo-French *boiller*, Old French *boillir*, from Latin *bullire* 'to bubble', from *bulla* 'bubble']

boil[2] /bɔɪl/ *n.* an inflamed pus-filled swelling caused by infection of a hair follicle etc. [Old English *bȳl(e)*, from West Germanic]

boiled shirt *n.* a dress shirt with a starched front.

boiled sweet *n. Brit.* a hard sweet made of boiled sugar.

boiler /'bɔɪlə/ *n.* **1** a fuel-burning apparatus for heating water, esp. to supply a central heating system. **2** a tank for heating water, esp. for turning it to steam under pressure. **3** a metal tub for boiling laundry etc. **4** *Brit.* a fowl, vegetable, etc., suitable for cooking only by boiling.

boilermaker /'bɔɪləmeɪkə/ *n.* **1** a person who makes boilers. **2** a metalworker in heavy industry.

boiler room *n.* a room with a boiler and other heating equipment, esp. in the basement of a large building.

boiler suit *n. Brit.* a one-piece suit worn as overalls for heavy manual work.

boiling /'bɔɪlɪŋ/ *adj.* (also **boiling hot**) *colloq.* very hot.

boiling point *n.* **1** the temperature at which a liquid starts to boil. **2** a state of high excitement (*feelings reached boiling point*).

boisterous /'bɔɪst(ə)rəs/ *adj.* **1** (of a person) rough; noisily exuberant. **2** (of the sea, weather, etc.) stormy, rough. □ **boisterously** *adv.* **boisterousness** *n.* [variant of Middle English *boist(u)ous*, of unknown origin]

bolas /'bəʊləs/ *n.* (treated as *sing.* or *pl.*) (esp. in S. America) a missile consisting of a number of balls connected by strong cord, which when thrown entangles the limbs of the quarry. [Spanish & Portuguese, pl. of *bola* 'ball']

bold /bəʊld/ *adj.* **1** confidently assertive; adventurous, courageous. **2** forthright, impudent. **3** vivid, distinct, well-marked (*bold colours*; *a bold imagination*). **4** (in full **boldface** or **boldfaced**) printed in a thick black typeface. □ **as bold as brass** excessively bold or self-assured. **make** (or **be**) **so bold as to** presume to; venture to. ▫ **boldly** *adv.* **boldness** *n.* [Old English *bald* 'dangerous', from Germanic]

bole[1] /bəʊl/ *n.* the stem or trunk of a tree. [Middle English from Old Norse *bolr*, perhaps related to BAULK]

bole[2] /bəʊl/ *n.* fine compact earthy clay. [Late Latin BOLUS]

bolero /bəˈlɛːrəʊ/ *n.* (*pl.* **-os**) **1 a** a Spanish dance in simple triple time. **b** music for or in the time of a bolero. **2** /also ˈbɒlərəʊ/ a woman's short open jacket. [Spanish]

boletus /bəˈliːtəs/ *n.* a mushroom or toadstool of the genus *Boletus*, with pores on the underside of the cap. [Latin, = mushroom]

bolivar /bɒlɪˈvɑː, bɒˈliːvɑː/ *n.* the chief monetary unit of Venezuela. [S. *Bolívar* (d. 1830), a S. American soldier and statesman]

boliviano /bəlɪvɪˈɑːnəʊ/ *n.* (*pl.* **-os**) the basic monetary unit of Bolivia (1863–1962 and since 1987), equal to 100 centavos or cents. [BOLIVAR]

boll /bəʊl/ *n.* a rounded capsule containing seeds, esp. flax or cotton. [Middle English from Middle Dutch *bolle* 'rounded object': related to BOWL[1]]

bollard /ˈbɒlɑːd, -ləd/ *n.* **1** *Brit.* a short metal, concrete, or plastic post in the road, esp. as part of a traffic island. **2** a short post on a quay or ship for securing a rope. [Middle English, perhaps from Old Norse *bolr* BOLE[1] + -ARD]

Bollinger /ˈbɒlɪndʒə/ *n. propr.* a type of champagne from the Champagne area of France. [name of the *Bollinger* family who produce it]

bollocking /ˈbɒləkɪŋ/ *n.* esp. *Brit. coarse slang* a severe reprimand.

bollocks /ˈbɒləks/ *n.* (also **ballocks**) esp. *Brit. coarse slang* **1** the testicles. **2** (usu. as an exclamation of contempt) nonsense, rubbish. [Old English *beallucc*, related to BALL[1]]

boll-weevil *n.* a small American or Mexican weevil, *Anthonomus grandis*, whose larvae destroy cotton bolls.

bologna /bəˈləʊnjə, bəˈlɒnjə/ *n.* = BOLOGNA SAUSAGE.

Bologna sausage *n.* a large smoked sausage made of bacon, veal, pork suet, and other meats, and sold ready for eating. [*Bologna* in Italy]

bolometer /bəˈlɒmɪtə/ *n.* a sensitive electrical instrument for measuring radiant energy. ▫ **bolometry** *n.* **bolometric** /bəʊləˈmɛtrɪk/ *adj.* [Greek *bolē* 'ray' + -METER]

boloney var. of BALONEY.

Bolshevik /ˈbɒlʃɪvɪk/ *n. & adj.* ● *n.* **1** *hist.* a member of the radical faction of the Russian Social Democratic party, which became the Communist party in 1918. **2** a Russian communist. **3** (in general use) any revolutionary socialist. ● *adj.* **1** of, relating to, or characteristic of the Bolsheviks. **2** communist. ▫ **Bolshevism** *n.* **Bolshevist** *n.* [Russian, = a member of the majority, from the fact that this faction formed the majority group of the Russian Social Democratic Party in 1903, from *bol'she* 'greater']

Bolshie /ˈbɒlʃi/ *adj. & n.* (also **Bolshy**) *slang* ● *adj.* (usu. **bolshie**) **1** *Brit.* uncooperative, rebellious, awkward; bad-tempered. **2** left-wing, socialist. ● *n.* (*pl.* **-ies**) a Bolshevik. ▫ **bolshiness** *n.* (in sense 1 of *adj.*). [abbreviation of BOLSHEVIK]

bolster[1] /ˈbəʊlstə/ *n. & v.* ● *n.* **1** a long thick pillow. **2** a pad or support, esp. in a machine. **3** *Building* a short timber cap over a post to increase the bearing of the beams it supports. ● *v.tr.* (usu. foll. by *up*) **1** encourage, reinforce (*bolstered our morale*). **2** support with a bolster; prop up. ▫ **bolsterer** *n.* [Old English = cushion, from Germanic]

bolster[2] /ˈbəʊlstə/ *n.* a chisel for cutting bricks. [20th c.: origin uncertain]

bolt[1] /bəʊlt/ *n., v., & adv.* ● *n.* **1** a sliding bar and socket used to fasten or lock a door, gate, etc. **2** a large usu. metal pin with a head, usu. riveted or used with a nut, to hold things together. **3** a discharge of lightning. **4** an act of bolting (cf. sense 4 of *v.*); a sudden escape or dash for freedom. **5** an arrow for shooting from a crossbow. **6** a roll of fabric (originally as a measure). ● *v.* **1** *tr.* fasten or lock with a bolt. **2** *tr.* (foll. by *in, out*) keep (a person etc.) from leaving or entering by bolting a door. **3** *tr.* fasten together with bolts. **4** *intr.* **a** dash suddenly away, esp. to escape. **b** (of a horse) suddenly gallop out of control. **5** *tr.* gulp down (food) unchewed; eat hurriedly. **6** *intr.* (of a plant) run to seed. ● *adv.* (usu. in **bolt upright**) rigidly, stiffly. ▫ **a bolt from the blue** a complete surprise. **bolt on 1** fasten by bolts. **2** add as required. **shoot one's bolt** do all that is in one's power. ▫ **bolter** *n.* (in sense 4 of *v.*). [Old English *bolt* 'arrow']

bolt[2] /bəʊlt/ *v.tr.* (also **boult**) sift (flour etc.). [Middle English from Old French *bulter*, *buleter*, of unknown origin]

bolt-hole *n.* esp. *Brit.* **1** a means of escape. **2** a secret refuge.

bolt-on *adj. & n.* ● *adj.* **1** able to be fastened or attached by bolts. **2** able to be added when required. ● *n.* a thing that can be bolted on.

bolus /ˈbəʊləs/ *n.* (*pl.* **boluses**) **1** a soft ball, esp. of chewed food. **2** a large pill. [Late Latin from Greek *bōlos* 'clod']

bomb /bɒm/ *n. & v.* ● *n.* **1 a** a container with explosive, incendiary material, smoke, or gas etc., designed to explode on impact or by means of a lit fuse, time mechanism, or remote-control device. **b** an ordinary object fitted with an explosive device (*letter bomb*). **2** (prec. by *the*) the atomic or hydrogen bomb considered as a weapon with supreme destructive power. **3** *Brit. slang* a large sum of money (*cost a bomb*). **4** a mass of solidified lava thrown from a volcano. **5** *N. Amer. colloq.* a bad failure (esp. a theatrical one). **6** *Brit. slang* a drugged cigarette. ● *v.* **1** *tr.* attack with bombs; drop bombs on. **2** *tr.* (foll. by *out*) drive (a person etc.) out of a building or refuge by using bombs. **3** *intr.* throw or drop bombs. **4** *intr.* esp. *US slang* fail badly. **5** *intr.* (usu. foll. by *along, off*) *colloq.* move or go very quickly. ▫ **go down a bomb** *Brit. colloq.*, often *iron.* be very well received. **like a bomb** *Brit. colloq.* **1** often *iron.* very successfully. **2** very fast. [French *bombe* via Italian *bomba* and Latin *bombus* from Greek *bombos* 'boom, hum']

bombard /bɒmˈbɑːd/ *v.tr.* **1** attack with a number of bombs, shells, etc. **2** (often foll. by *with*) subject to persistent questioning, abuse, etc. **3** *Physics* direct a stream of high-speed particles at (a substance). ▫ **bombardment** *n.* [French *bombarder* from *bombarde*, from medieval Latin *bombarda* 'a stone-throwing engine': see BOMB]

bombarde /ˈbɒmbɑːd/ *n. Mus.* a medieval alto-pitched shawm. [Old French *bombarde*, medieval Latin *bombarda* probably from Latin *bombus* (see BOMB)]

bombardier /bɒmbəˈdɪə/ *n.* **1** *Brit.* a non-commissioned officer in the artillery. **2** *N. Amer.* a member of a bomber crew responsible for sighting and releasing bombs. [French (as BOMBARD)]

bombardon /ˈbɒmbɑːd(ə)n/ *n. Mus.* **1** a type of valved bass tuba. **2** an organ stop imitating this. [Italian *bombardone* from *bombardo* 'bassoon' (as BOMBARD)]

bombasine var. of BOMBAZINE.

bombast /ˈbɒmbast/ *n.* pompous or extravagant language. ▫ **bombastic** /-ˈbastɪk/ *adj.* **bombastically** /-ˈbastɪk(ə)li/ *adv.* [earlier *bombace* 'cotton wool', via French from medieval Latin *bombax -acis*, alteration of *bombyx*: see BOMBAZINE]

Bombay duck /bɒmˈbeɪ/ *n.* a dried fish, esp. bummalo, usu. eaten with curried dishes. [corruption of BUMMALO; influenced by *Bombay*, city in India]

bombazine /ˈbɒmbəziːn/ *n.* (also **bombasine**) a twilled dress material of worsted with or without an admixture of silk or cotton, esp., when black, formerly used for mourning. [French *bombasin* via medieval Latin *bombacinum* and Late Latin *bombycinus* 'silken', from *bombyx -ycis* 'silk or silkworm', from Greek *bombux*]

bomb bay *n.* a compartment in an aircraft used to hold bombs.

bomb disposal *n.* the defusing or removal and detonation of an unexploded bomb.

bombe /bɒmb, French bɔ̃b/ *n.* a dome-shaped dish or confection, often frozen. [French, = BOMB]

bombed /bɒmd/ *adj.* **1** subjected to bombing. **2** *slang* intoxicated by drink or drugs.

bombed-out *adj.* **1** (of a person) driven out by bombing. **2** (of a building etc.) rendered uninhabitable by bombing. **3** *slang* = BOMBED 2.

bomber /ˈbɒmə/ *n.* **1** an aircraft equipped to carry and drop bombs. **2** a person using bombs, esp. illegally.

bomber jacket *n.* a short leather or cloth jacket tightly gathered at the waist and cuffs.

bombora /bɒmˈbɔːrə/ *n. Austral.* a dangerous sea area where waves break over a submerged reef. [Aboriginal, perhaps Dharuk *bumbora*]

bombproof /ˈbɒmpruːf/ *adj.* strong enough to resist the effects of blast from a bomb.

bombshell /ˈbɒmʃɛl/ *n.* **1** an overwhelming surprise or disappointment. **2** an artillery bomb. **3** *slang* a very attractive woman (*blonde bombshell*).

bombsight /ˈbɒmsʌɪt/ *n.* a device in an aircraft for aiming bombs.

bomb-site *n.* an area where buildings have been destroyed by bombs.

bomb squad *n.* a division of a police force investigating crimes involving bombs.

bona fide /ˌbəʊnə ˈfʌɪdi/ *adj. & adv.* ● *adj.* genuine; sincere. ● *adv.* genuinely; sincerely. [Latin, ablative sing. of BONA FIDES]

bona fides /ˌbəʊnə ˈfʌɪdiːz/ *n.* **1** *esp. Law.* an honest intention; sincerity. **2** (treated as *pl.*) *colloq.* documentary evidence of acceptability (*his bona fides are in order*). [Latin, = good faith]

bonanza /bəˈnanzə/ *n. & adj.* ● *n.* **1** a source of wealth or prosperity. **2** a large output (esp. of a mine). **3 a** prosperity; good luck. **b** a run of good luck. ● *adj.* greatly prospering or productive. [originally US from Spanish, = fair weather, from Latin *bonus* 'good']

bona vacantia /ˌbəʊnə vəˈkantɪə/ *n. Law* goods without an apparent owner and to which the Crown has right. [Latin, = ownerless goods]

bon-bon /ˈbɒnbɒn/ *n.* a piece of confectionery; a sweet. [French from *bon* 'good' from Latin *bonus*]

bonce /bɒns/ *n. Brit.* **1** *slang* the head. **2** a large marble. [19th c.: origin unknown]

bond /bɒnd/ *n. & v.* ● *n.* **1 a** a thing that ties another down or together. **b** (usu. in *pl.*) a thing restraining bodily freedom (*broke his bonds*). **2** (often in *pl.*) **a** a uniting force (*sisterly bond*). **b** a restraint; a responsibility (*bonds of duty*). **3** a binding engagement; an agreement (*his word is his bond*). **4** *Commerce* **a** a certificate issued by a government or a public company promising to repay borrowed money at a fixed rate of interest at a specified time; a debenture. **b** an insurance policy held by a travel agent, tour operator, airline, etc., which protects travellers' holidays and money from the company's bankruptcy. **5** adhesiveness. **6** *Law* a deed by which a person is bound to make payment to another. **7** *Chem.* a linkage between atoms in a chemical compound. **8** *Building* the laying of bricks in one of various patterns in a wall in order to ensure strength (*English bond*; *Flemish bond*). ● *v.* **1** *tr.* **a** lay (bricks) overlapping. **b** bind together (resin with fibres, etc.). **2** *intr.* adhere; hold together. **3** *tr.* connect with a bond. **4** *tr.* place (goods) in bond. **5 a** *intr.* become emotionally attached. **b** *tr.* link by an emotional or psychological bond. □ **in bond** (of goods) stored in a bonded warehouse until the importer pays the duty owing (see BONDED). [Middle English variant of BAND[1]]

bondage /ˈbɒndɪdʒ/ *n.* **1** serfdom; slavery. **2** subjection to constraint, influence, obligation, etc. **3** sadomasochistic practices, including the use of physical restraints or mental enslavement. [Middle English from Anglo-Latin *bondagium*: influenced by BOND]

bonded /ˈbɒndɪd/ *adj.* **1** (of goods) placed in bond. **2** (of material) reinforced by or cemented to another. **3 a** (of a debt) secured by bonds. **b** (of a travel company etc.) protected by a bond (see BOND *n.* 4b).

bonded warehouse *n.* a customs-controlled warehouse for the retention of imported goods until the duty owed is paid.

bondholder /ˈbɒndhəʊldə/ *n.* a person holding a bond or bonds granted by a private person or a public company.

bond paper *n.* high-quality writing paper.

bondsman /ˈbɒn(d)zmən/ *n.* (*pl.* **-men**) **1** a slave. **2** a person in thrall to another. [variant of *bondman* (from archaic *bond* in serfdom or slavery) as though from *bond's* genitive of BOND]

bond-washing *n. Brit.* dividend-stripping.

bone /bəʊn/ *n. & v.* ● *n.* **1** any of the pieces of hard tissue making up the skeleton in vertebrates. **2** (in *pl.*) **a** the skeleton, esp. as remains after death. **b** the body, esp. as a seat of intuitive feeling (*felt it in my bones*). **3 a** the calcified material of which bones consist. **b** a similar substance such as ivory, dentine, or whalebone. **4** a thing made of bone. **5** (in *pl.*) the essential part of a thing (*the bare bones*). **6** (in *pl.*) **a** dice. **b** castanets. **7** a strip of stiffening in a corset etc. ● *v.* **1** *tr.* take out the bones from (meat or fish). **2** *tr.* stiffen (a garment) with bone etc. **3** *tr. Brit. slang* steal. □ **bone up** (often foll. by *on*) *colloq.* study (a subject) intensively. **close to** (or **near**) **the bone 1 a** tactless to the point of offensiveness. **b** near the limit of decency. **2** destitute; hard up. **have a bone to pick** (usu. foll. by *with*) have a cause for dispute (with another person). **make no bones about 1** admit or allow without fuss. **2** not hesitate or scruple. **point the bone** (usu. foll. by *at*) *Austral.* **1** wish bad luck on. **2** cast a spell on in order to kill. **to the bone 1** to the bare minimum. **2** penetratingly. **work one's fingers to the bone** work very hard, esp. thanklessly. □ **boneless** *adj.* [Old English *bān*, from Germanic]

bone china *n.* fine china made of clay mixed with the ash from bones.

bone dry *adj.* completely dry.

bonefish /ˈbəʊnfɪʃ/ *n.* (*pl.* usu. same) *N. Amer.* any of several species of large game fish, esp. *Albula vulpes*, having many small bones.

bonehead /ˈbəʊnhɛd/ *n. slang* a stupid person. □ **boneheaded** *adj.*

bone idle *adj.* (also **bone lazy**) utterly idle or lazy.

bone marrow see MARROW 2.

bonemeal /ˈbəʊnmiːl/ *n.* crushed or ground bones used esp. as a fertilizer.

bone of contention *n.* a source or ground of dispute.

boner /ˈbəʊnə/ *n. slang* a stupid mistake. [BONE + -ER[1]]

bone-setter *n.* a person who sets broken or dislocated bones, esp. without being a qualified surgeon.

boneshaker /ˈbəʊnʃeɪkə/ *n.* **1** a decrepit or uncomfortable old vehicle. **2** an old type of bicycle with solid tyres.

bone spavin *n.* **1** osteoarthritis or osteitis of the hock in horses. **2** a swelling due to this.

bonfire /ˈbɒnfʌɪə/ *n.* a large open-air fire, for burning rubbish, as part of a celebration, or as a signal. □ **make a bonfire of** destroy by burning. [earlier *bonefire* from BONE (bones being the chief material formerly used) + FIRE]

Bonfire Night *n. Brit.* 5 Nov., on which fireworks are displayed and an effigy of Guy Fawkes burnt (see GUY[1]).

bongo[1] /ˈbɒŋgəʊ/ *n.* (*pl.* **-os** or **-oes**) either of a pair of small long-bodied drums usu. held between the knees and played with the fingers. [Latin American Spanish *bongó*]

bongo[2] /ˈbɒŋgəʊ/ *n.* (*pl.* same or **-os**) a rare antelope, *Tragelaphus euryceros*, native to the forests of central

Africa, having spiralled horns and a chestnut-red coat with narrow white vertical stripes. [Congolese]

bonhomie /ˈbɒnəmiː/ *n.* geniality; good-natured friendliness. [French from *bonhomme* 'good fellow']

bonhomous /ˈbɒnəməs/ *adj.* full of bonhomie.

bonito /bəˈniːtəʊ/ *n.* (*pl.* **-os**) any of various striped tuna of warm seas. [Spanish]

bonk /bɒŋk/ *v.* & *n.* ● *v.* **1** *tr.* hit resoundingly. **2** *intr.* bang; bump. **3** *Brit. coarse slang* **a** *intr.* have sexual intercourse. **b** *tr.* have sexual intercourse with. ● *n.* an instance of bonking (*a bonk on the head*). [imitative: cf. BANG, BUMP, CONK[2]]

bonkers /ˈbɒŋkəz/ *predic.adj. slang* crazy. [20th c.: origin unknown]

bon mot /bɒn ˈməʊ/ *n.* (*pl.* **bons mots** *pronunc.* same or /-məʊz/) a witty saying. [French, = good word]

bonne bouche /bɒn buːʃ, French bɔn buʃ/ *n.* (*pl.* ***bonne bouches*** or ***bonnes bouches*** *pronunc.* same) a titbit, esp. to end a meal with. [French from *bonne* fem. 'good' + *bouche* 'mouth']

bonnet /ˈbɒnɪt/ *n.* **1 a** a woman's or child's hat tied under the chin and usu. with a brim framing the face. **b** a soft round brimless hat like a beret worn by men and boys in Scotland (cf. TAM-O'-SHANTER). **c** *colloq.* any hat. **2** *Brit.* a hinged cover over the engine of a motor vehicle. **3** the ceremonial feathered headdress of an American Indian. **4** the cowl of a chimney etc. **5** a protective cap in various machines. **6** *Naut.* additional canvas laced to the foot of a sail. □ **bonneted** *adj.* [Middle English via Old French *bonet* from medieval Latin *abonnis* 'headgear']

bonnethead /ˈbɒnɪthɛd/ *n.* a hammerhead shark, *Sphyrna tiburo*, with a relatively narrow head. Also called *shovelhead*.

bonnet monkey *n.* an Indian macaque, *Macaca radiata*, with a bonnet-like tuft of hair.

bonny /ˈbɒni/ *adj.* (also **bonnie**) (**bonnier**, **bonniest**) esp. *Sc.* & *N.Engl.* **1 a** physically attractive. **b** healthy-looking. **2** good, fine, pleasant. □ **bonnily** *adv.* **bonniness** *n.* [15th c.: perhaps from Old French *bon* 'good']

bonsai /ˈbɒnsʌɪ/ *n.* (*pl.* same) **1** the art of cultivating ornamental artificially dwarfed varieties of trees and shrubs. **2** (also **bonsai tree**) a tree or shrub grown by this method. [Japanese, from *bon* 'tray' + *sai* 'planting']

bonspiel /ˈbɒnspiːl/ *n.* esp. *Sc.* a curling match. [16th c.: perhaps from Low German]

bontebok /ˈbɒntəbɒk/ *n.* (also **bontbok** /ˈbɒntbɒk/) (*pl.* same or **-boks**) a large chestnut antelope, *Damaliscus dorcas*, native to southern Africa, having a white tail and a white patch on its head and rump. [Afrikaans from *bont* 'spotted' + *bok* BUCK[1]]

bonus /ˈbəʊnəs/ *n.* **1** an unsought or unexpected extra benefit. **2 a** a usu. seasonal gratuity to employees beyond their normal pay. **b** *Brit.* an extra dividend or issue paid to the shareholders of a company. **c** *Brit.* a distribution of profits to holders of an insurance policy. [Latin *bonus*, *bonum* 'good (thing)']

■ **Usage** The phrase *added bonus*, although common, is regarded as tautologous by some people and is to be avoided in formal usage.

bon vivant /bɔ̃ viːˈvɔ̃/ *n.* (*pl.* **bon vivants** or **bons vivants** *pronunc.* same) a person indulging in good living; a gourmand. [French, literally 'good liver', from *vivre* 'to live']

bon viveur /bɔ̃ viːˈvəː/ *n.* (*pl.* **bon viveurs** or **bons viveurs** *pronunc.* same) = BON VIVANT. [pseudo-French, after *bon vivant*: *viveur* 'a living person']

bon voyage /bɒn vɔɪˈjɑːʒ, bɔ̃ vwaˈjɑːʒ/ *int.* & *n.* an expression of good wishes to a departing traveller. [French, literally 'good journey']

bony /ˈbəʊni/ *adj.* (**bonier**, **boniest**) **1** (of a person) thin with prominent bones. **2** having many bones. **3** of or like bone. **4** (of a fish) having bones rather than cartilage. □ **boniness** *n.*

bonze /bɒnz/ *n.* a Japanese or Chinese Buddhist priest. [French *bonze* or Portuguese *bonzo*, probably from Japanese *bonzō*, *bonsō* 'priest']

bonzer /ˈbɒnzə/ *adj. Austral. slang* excellent, first-rate. [perhaps from BONANZA]

boo /buː/ *int.*, *n.*, & *v.* ● *int.* **1** an expression of disapproval or contempt. **2** a sound, made esp. to a child, intended to surprise. ● *n.* an utterance of *boo*, esp. as an expression of disapproval or contempt made to a performer etc. ● *v.* (**boos**, **booed**) **1** *intr.* utter a boo or boos. **2** *tr.* jeer at (a performer etc.) by booing. □ **can't** (or **wouldn't) say boo to a goose** is very shy or timid. [imitative]

boob[1] /buːb/ *n.* & *v. slang* ● *n.* **1** *Brit.* an embarrassing mistake. **2** a simpleton. ● *v.intr. Brit.* make an embarrassing mistake. [abbreviation of BOOBY]

boob[2] /buːb/ *n. slang* a woman's breast. [earlier *bubby*, *booby*, of uncertain origin]

booboo /ˈbuːbuː/ *n. slang* a mistake. [BOOB[1]]

boobook /ˈbuːbʊk/ *n.* (in full **boobook owl**) a brown spotted owl, *Ninox novaeseelandiae*, native to Australia and New Zealand. [imitative of its call]

boob tube *n. slang* **1** *Brit.* a woman's low-cut close-fitting usu. strapless top. **2** (usu. prec. by *the*) *N. Amer.* television; one's television set.

booby /ˈbuːbi/ *n.* (*pl.* **-ies**) **1** a stupid or childish person. **2** a small gannet of the genus *Sula*. [probably from Spanish *bobo* (in both senses) from Latin *balbus* 'stammering']

booby-hatch *n.* esp. *US slang offens.* a psychiatric hospital.

booby prize *n.* a prize given to the least successful competitor in a contest.

booby trap *n.* & *v.* ● *n.* **1** a trap intended as a practical joke, e.g. an object placed on top of a door ajar ready to fall on the next person to pass through. **2** *Mil.* an apparently harmless explosive device intended to kill or injure anyone touching it. ● *v.tr.* (**booby-trap**) place a booby trap or traps in or on.

boodle /ˈbuːd(ə)l/ *n. slang* money, esp. when gained or used dishonestly, e.g. as a bribe. [Dutch *boedel* 'possessions']

boogie /ˈbuːgi/ *v.* & *n.* ● *v.intr.* (**boogies**, **boogied**, **boogieing**) *slang* dance to pop music. ● *n.* **1** = BOOGIE-WOOGIE. **2** *slang* a dance to pop music. [20th c.: origin unknown]

boogie-woogie /buːgɪˈwuːgi/ *n.* a style of playing blues or jazz on the piano, marked by a persistent bass rhythm. [probably from BOOGIE]

boohoo /buːˈhuː/ *int.* & *v.* ● *int.* expressing weeping. ● *v.intr.* (**boohoos**, **boohooed**) (esp. of a child) weep loudly. [imitative]

book /bʊk/ *n.* & *v.* ● *n.* **1 a** a written or printed work consisting of pages glued or sewn together along one side and bound in covers. **b** a literary composition intended for publication (*is working on her book*). **2** a bound set of blank sheets for writing or keeping records in. **3** a set of tickets, stamps, matches, cheques, samples of cloth, etc., bound up together. **4** (in *pl.*) a set of records or accounts. **5** a main division of a literary work, or of the Bible (*the Book of Deuteronomy*). **6** (in full **book of words**) a libretto, script of a play, etc. **7** *colloq.* a magazine. **8** a telephone directory (*his number's in the book*). **9** a record of bets made and money paid out at a race meeting by a bookmaker. **10** a set of six tricks collected together in a card game. **11** an imaginary record or list (*the book of life*). ● *v.* **1** *tr.* **a** engage (a seat etc.) in advance; make a reservation of. **b** engage (a guest, supporter, etc.) for some occasion. **2** *tr.* **a** take the personal details of (an offender or rule-breaker). **b** enter in a book or list. **3** *tr.* make a reservation for (a person). **4** *intr.* make a reservation (*no need to book*). □ **book in** esp. *Brit.* register one's arrival at a hotel etc. **book up 1** *Brit.* buy tickets in advance for a theatre, concert, holiday, etc. **2** (as **booked up** *adj.*) with all places reserved. **bring to book** call to account.

go by the book proceed according to the rules. **in a person's bad** (or **good**) **books** in disfavour (or favour) with a person. **in my book** in my opinion. **make a book** (or *US* **make book**) take bets and pay out winnings at a race meeting. **not in the book** disallowed. **on the books** contained in a list of members etc. **suits my book** *Brit.* is convenient to me. **take a leaf out of a person's book** imitate a person. **throw the book at** *colloq.* charge or punish to the utmost. □ **booker** *n.* [Old English *bōc* (*n.*), *bōcian* (*v.*), from Germanic, usu. taken to be related to BEECH (the bark of which was used for writing on)]

bookable /ˈbʊkəb(ə)l/ *adj.* **1** that may be reserved or engaged in advance. **2** *Football* (of an offence) serious enough to be entered in the referee's book.

bookbinder /ˈbʊkbʌɪndə/ *n.* a person who binds books professionally. □ **bookbinding** *n.*

bookcase /ˈbʊkkeɪs/ *n.* a set of shelves for books in the form of a cabinet.

book club *n.* a society which sells its members selected books on special terms.

bookend /ˈbʊkɛnd/ *n.* a usu. ornamental prop used to keep a row of books upright, esp. one of a pair.

bookie /ˈbʊki/ *n. colloq.* = BOOKMAKER.

booking /ˈbʊkɪŋ/ *n.* the act or an instance of booking or being booked (see BOOK *v.* 1, 2).

booking clerk *n. Brit.* an official selling tickets at a railway station etc.

booking hall *n. Brit.* a room or area at a railway station in which tickets are sold.

booking office *n.* a place where tickets are sold, esp. at a railway station or theatre.

bookish /ˈbʊkɪʃ/ *adj.* **1** studious; fond of reading. **2** acquiring knowledge from books rather than practical experience. **3** (of a word, language, etc.) literary; not colloquial. □ **bookishly** *adv.* **bookishness** *n.*

bookkeeper /ˈbʊkki:pə/ *n.* a person who keeps accounts for a trader, a public office, etc. □ **bookkeeping** *n.*

bookland /ˈbʊkland/ *n. Brit. hist.* an area of common land granted by charter to a private owner (from an earlier sense of *book* = charter).

book learning *n.* mere theory.

booklet /ˈbʊklɪt/ *n.* a small book consisting of a few sheets usu. with paper covers.

book-louse *n.* a minute insect of the order Psocoptera, often damaging to books.

bookmaker /ˈbʊkmeɪkə/ *n.* a person who takes bets, esp. on horse races, calculates odds, and pays out winnings. □ **bookmaking** *n.*

bookman /ˈbʊkmən/ *n.* (*pl.* **-men**) a literary man, esp. a reviewer.

bookmark /ˈbʊkmɑ:k/ *n.* a strip of leather, card, etc., used to mark one's place in a book.

bookmobile /ˈbʊkmə,bi:l/ *n. N. Amer.* a mobile library. [on the pattern of AUTOMOBILE]

book of words see BOOK *n.* 6.

bookplate /ˈbʊkpleɪt/ *n.* a decorative label stuck in the front of a book, bearing the owner's name.

book-rest *n.* an adjustable support for an open book on a table.

bookseller /ˈbʊksɛlə/ *n.* esp. *Brit.* a dealer in books.

bookshelf /ˈbʊkʃɛlf/ *n.* (*pl.* **-shelves**) a shelf on which books can be stored.

bookshop /ˈbʊkʃɒp/ *n.* a shop where books are sold.

bookstall /ˈbʊkstɔ:l/ *n.* a stand for selling books, newspapers, etc., esp. out of doors or at a station etc.

bookstore /ˈbʊkstɔ:/ *n. N. Amer.* = BOOKSHOP.

booksy /ˈbʊksi/ *adj. Brit. colloq.* having literary or bookish pretensions.

book token *n. Brit.* a voucher which can be exchanged for books to a specified value.

book value *n.* the value of a commodity as entered in a firm's books (opp. MARKET VALUE).

bookwork /ˈbʊkwə:k/ *n.* the study of books (as opposed to practical work).

bookworm /ˈbʊkwə:m/ *n.* **1** *colloq.* a person devoted to reading. **2** the larva of a moth or beetle which feeds on the paper and glue used in books.

Boolean /ˈbu:lɪən/ *adj.* denoting a system of algebraic notation to represent logical propositions. [G. *Boole*, English mathematician d. 1864]

Boolean logic *n.* the use of the logical operators 'and', 'or', and 'not' in retrieving information from a computer database.

boom[1] /bu:m/ *n.* & *v.* ● *n.* a deep resonant sound. ● *v.intr.* make or speak with a boom. [imitative]

boom[2] /bu:m/ *n.* & *v.* ● *n.* a period of prosperity or sudden activity in commerce. ● *v.intr.* (esp. of commercial ventures) be suddenly prosperous or successful. □ **boomlet** *n.* [19th-c. US word, perhaps from BOOM[1]]

boom[3] /bu:m/ *n.* **1** *Naut.* a pivoted spar to which the foot of a sail is attached, allowing the angle of the sail to be changed. **2** a long pole over a television or film set, carrying a microphone or other equipment. **3** a floating barrier across the mouth of a harbour or river. [Dutch, = BEAM *n.* 'tree, pole']

boom box *n. slang* = GHETTO BLASTER.

boomer /ˈbu:mə/ *n.* **1** a large male kangaroo. **2** a large wave.

boomerang /ˈbu:məraŋ/ *n.* & *v.* ● *n.* **1** a curved flat hardwood missile used by Australian Aboriginals to kill prey, and often of a kind able to return in flight to the thrower. **2** a plan or scheme that recoils on its originator. ● *v.intr.* **1** act as a boomerang. **2** (of a plan or action) backfire. [Dharuk *bumarin*ʸ]

boomslang /ˈbu:mslaŋ/ *n.* a venomous tree-snake, *Dispholidus typus*, native to southern Africa. [Afrikaans from *boom* 'tree' + *slang* 'snake']

boom town *n.* a town undergoing sudden growth due to a boom.

boon[1] /bu:n/ *n.* **1** an advantage; a blessing. **2** *archaic* **a** a thing asked for; a request. **b** a gift; a favour. [Middle English, originally = prayer, via Old Norse *bón* from Germanic]

boon[2] /bu:n/ *adj.* close, intimate, favourite (usu. *boon companion*). [Middle English (originally = jolly, congenial) via Old French *bon* from Latin *bonus* 'good']

boondock /ˈbu:ndɒk/ *n.* (usu. in *pl.*) *N. Amer. slang* rough or isolated country. [Tagalog *bundok* 'mountain']

boondoggle /ˈbu:ndɒg(ə)l/ *n.* & *v. N. Amer. colloq.* ● *n.* **1** a trivial or useless undertaking. **2** a dishonest undertaking; a fraud. ● *v.intr.* take part in a trivial, useless, or dishonest undertaking. [20th c.: origin uncertain]

boonies /ˈbu:nɪz/ *n.pl. N. Amer. slang* = BOONDOCK.

boor /bʊə/ *n.* **1** a rude, ill-mannered person. **2** a clumsy person. □ **boorish** *adj.* **boorishly** *adv.* **boorishness** *n.* [Low German *būr* or Dutch *boer* 'farmer': cf. BOWER[3]]

boost /bu:st/ *v.* & *n.* ● *v.tr.* **1 a** promote or increase the reputation of (a person, scheme, commodity, etc.) by praise or advertising; push; increase or assist (*boosted his spirits*; *boost sales*). **b** push from below; assist (*boosted me up the tree*). **2 a** raise the voltage in (an electric circuit etc.). **b** amplify (a radio signal). ● *n.* **1** an act, process, or result of boosting; a push (*asked for a boost up the hill*). **2 a** an advertisement campaign. **b** the resulting advance in value, reputation, etc. [19th-c. US word: origin unknown]

booster /ˈbu:stə/ *n.* **1** a device for increasing electrical power or voltage. **2** an auxiliary engine or rocket used to give initial acceleration. **3** *Med.* a dose of an immunizing agent increasing or renewing the effect of an earlier one. **4** a person who boosts by helping or encouraging.

boot[1] /bu:t/ *n.* & *v.* ● *n.* **1** an outer covering for the foot, esp. of leather, reaching above the ankle, often to the knee. **2** *Brit.* the luggage compartment of a motor car, usu. at the rear. **3** *colloq.* a firm kick. **4** (prec. by *the*) *colloq.* dismissal, esp. *Brit.* from employment (*gave them the boot*). **5** a covering to protect the lower part of a horse's leg. **6** *hist.* an instrument of torture encasing and crushing the foot. **7** *derog.* a person. ● *v.tr.* **1** kick, esp. hard. **2** (often foll. by *out*) dismiss (a person) forcefully. **3** (usu. foll. by *up*) put (a computer) in a state of readiness (cf. BOOTSTRAP 2). □ **the boot** (or *N. Amer.* **shoe) is on the other foot** (or **leg**) the truth or responsibility is the other way round. **die with one's boots on** (of a soldier etc.) die fighting. **put the boot in** *Brit.* **1** kick brutally. **2** act decisively against a person. **you bet your boots** *slang* it is quite certain. □ **booted** *adj.* [Middle English, from Old Norse *bóti* or Old French *bote*, of unknown origin]

boot[2] /buːt/ *n.* □ **to boot** as well; to the good; in addition. [originally = 'advantage': Old English *bōt*, from Germanic]

bootblack /ˈbuːtblak/ *n. N. Amer.* esp. *hist.* a person who polishes boots and shoes.

bootboy /ˈbuːtbɔɪ/ *n.* **1** a boy employed to clean shoes. **2** a hooligan typically wearing heavy boots.

bootee /buːˈtiː/ *n.* **1** a soft shoe, esp. a woollen one, worn by a baby. **2** a woman's short boot.

booth /buːð, buːθ/ *n.* **1** a small temporary roofed structure of canvas, wood, etc., used esp. as a market stall, for puppet shows, etc. **2** an enclosure or compartment for various purposes, e.g. telephoning or voting. **3** a set of a table and benches in a restaurant or bar. [Middle English, from Scandinavian]

bootjack /ˈbuːtdʒak/ *n.* a device for holding a boot by the heel to ease withdrawal of the leg.

bootlace /ˈbuːtleɪs/ *n.* a cord or leather thong for lacing boots.

bootleg /ˈbuːtlɛg/ *adj., v., & n.* ● *adj.* (esp. of liquor) smuggled; illicitly sold; pirated. ● *v.tr.* (**-legged, -legging**) make, distribute, or smuggle (illicit goods, esp. alcohol); pirate (a musical recording). ● *n.* a pirated musical recording. □ **bootlegger** *n.* [from the smugglers' practice of concealing bottles in their boots]

bootless /ˈbuːtlɪs/ *adj. archaic* unavailing, useless. [Old English *bōtlēas* (as BOOT[2], LESS)]

bootlicker /ˈbuːtlɪkə/ *n. colloq.* a person who behaves obsequiously or servilely; a toady.

bootmaker /ˈbuːtmeɪkə/ *n.* a maker or manufacturer of boots and shoes.

boots /buːts/ *n. Brit.* a hotel servant who cleans boots and shoes, carries luggage, etc.

bootstrap /ˈbuːtstrap/ *n.* **1** a loop at the back of a boot used to pull it on. **2** *Computing* a technique of loading a program into a computer by means of a few initial instructions which enable the introduction of the rest of the program from an input device. □ **pull oneself up by one's bootstraps** better oneself by one's own efforts.

booty /ˈbuːti/ *n.* **1** plunder gained esp. in war or by piracy. **2** *colloq.* something gained or won. [Middle English from Middle Low German *būte, buite* 'exchange', of uncertain origin]

booze /buːz/ *n. & v. colloq.* ● *n.* **1** alcoholic drink. **2** the drinking of this (*on the booze*). ● *v.intr.* drink alcoholic liquor, esp. excessively or habitually. [earlier *bouse, bowse*, from Middle Dutch *būsen* 'drink to excess']

boozer /ˈbuːzə/ *n. colloq.* **1** a person who drinks alcohol, esp. to excess. **2** *Brit.* a public house.

booze-up *n. slang* a drinking bout.

boozy /ˈbuːzi/ *adj.* (**boozier, booziest**) *colloq.* intoxicated; addicted to drink. □ **boozily** *adv.* **booziness** *n.*

bop[1] /bɒp/ *n. & v. colloq.* ● *n.* **1** = BEBOP. **2** esp. *Brit.* **a** a spell of dancing, esp. to pop music. **b** an organized social occasion for this. ● *v.intr.* (**bopped, bopping**) move or dance, esp. to pop music. □ **bopper** *n.* [abbreviation of BEBOP]

bop[2] /bɒp/ *v. & n. colloq.* ● *v.tr.* (**bopped, bopping**) hit, punch lightly. ● *n.* a light blow or hit. [imitative]

bora[1] /ˈbɔːrə/ *n.* a strong cold dry NE wind blowing in the upper Adriatic. [Italian dialect from Latin *boreas* 'north wind': see BOREAL]

bora[2] /ˈbɔːrə/ *n. Austral.* an Aboriginal rite in which boys are initiated into manhood. [Kamilaroi *buuru*]

boracic /bəˈrasɪk/ *adj.* of borax; containing boron. [medieval Latin *borax -acis*: see BORAX]

boracic acid *n.* = BORIC ACID.

borage /ˈbɒrɪdʒ/ *n.* a plant of the genus *Borago*, esp. *Borago officinalis* with bright blue flowers and hairy leaves both used as flavouring. [Old French *bourrache* via medieval Latin *borrago*, perhaps from Arabic *'abū hurāš* 'father of roughness' (referring to the leaves)]

borak /ˈbɔːrak/ *n. Austral. & NZ slang* banter, ridicule. [Australian pidgin, ultimately from Wathawurung *burag* 'no, not']

borane /ˈbɔːreɪn/ *n. Chem.* any of the hydrides of boron.

borate /ˈbɔːreɪt/ *n.* a salt or ester of boric acid.

borax /ˈbɔːraks/ *n.* **1** the mineral salt sodium borate, occurring in alkaline deposits as an efflorescence or as crystals. **2** the purified form of this salt, used in making glass and china, and as an antiseptic. [Middle English via Old French *boras* and medieval Latin *borax* from Arabic *būraḳ*, from Persian *būrah*]

Borazon /ˈbɔːrəzɒn/ *n. propr.* a hard form of boron nitride, used as an abrasive. [BORON + AZO- nitrogen + *-on*]

borborygmus /bɔːbəˈrɪgməs/ *n.* (*pl.* **borborygmi** /-mʌɪ/) a rumbling of gas in the intestines. □ **borborygmic** *adj.* [modern Latin from Greek]

Bordeaux /bɔːˈdəʊ/ *n.* (*pl.* same /-ˈdəʊz/) any of various red, white, or rosé wines from the district of Bordeaux in SW France.

Bordeaux mixture *n.* a fungicide for vines, fruit trees, etc., composed of equal quantities of copper sulphate and calcium oxide in water. [first used in the vineyards of *Bordeaux* in SW France]

bordello /bɔːˈdɛləʊ/ *n.* (*pl.* **-os**) esp. *N. Amer.* a brothel. [Middle English (from Italian *bordello*) from Old French *bordel* 'cabin', diminutive of *borde*, ultimately from Frankish]

border /ˈbɔːdə/ *n. & v.* ● *n.* **1** the edge or boundary of anything, or the part near it. **2 a** the line separating two political or geographical areas, esp. countries. **b** the district on each side of this. **c** (**the Border**) a particular boundary and its adjoining districts, esp. between Scotland and England (usu. **the Borders**), or Northern Ireland and the Republic of Ireland. **3** a distinct edging round anything, esp. for strength or decoration. **4** a long narrow bed of flowers or shrubs in a garden (*herbaceous border*). ● *v.* **1** *tr.* be a border to. **2** *tr.* provide with a border. **3** *intr.* (usu. foll. by *on, upon*) **a** adjoin; come close to being. **b** approximate, resemble. [Middle English from Old French *bordure*: ultimately related (via Germanic) to BOARD]

Border collie *n.* a common working sheepdog. [originating near the border between England and Scotland]

borderer /ˈbɔːd(ə)rə/ *n.* a person who lives near a border, esp. that between Scotland and England.

borderland /ˈbɔːdəland/ *n.* **1** the district near a border. **2** an intermediate condition between two extremes. **3** an area for debate.

borderline /ˈbɔːdəlʌɪn/ *n. & adj.* ● *n.* **1** the line dividing two (often extreme) conditions. **2** a line marking a boundary. ● *adj.* **1** on the borderline. **2** verging on an extreme condition; only just acceptable.

Border terrier *n.* **1** a small terrier of a breed with rough hair, originating in the Cheviot Hills. **2** this breed. [originating near the border between England and Scotland]

bordure /ˈbɔːdjʊə/ *n. Heraldry* a border round the edge of a shield. [Middle English form of BORDER]

bore[1] /bɔː/ *v. & n.* ● *v.* **1** *tr.* make a hole in, esp. with a revolving tool. **2** *tr.* hollow out (a tube etc.). **3** *tr.* **a** make (a hole) by boring or excavation. **b** make (one's way) through a crowd etc. **4** *intr.* (of an athlete, racehorse, etc.) push another competitor out of the way. **5** *intr.* drill a well (for oil etc.). ● *n.* **1** the hollow of a firearm barrel or of a cylinder in an internal-combustion engine. **2** the diameter of this; the calibre. **3** = BOREHOLE. [Old English *borian*, from Germanic]

bore[2] /bɔː/ *n.* & *v.* ● *n.* a tiresome or dull person or thing. ● *v.tr.* weary by tedious talk or dullness. □ **bore a person to tears** weary (a person) in the extreme. [18th c.: origin unknown]

bore[3] /bɔː/ *n.* a high tidal wave caused by the meeting of two tides, or by the constriction of a spring tide, rushing up a narrow estuary. Also called *eagre*. [Middle English, perhaps from Old Norse *bára* 'wave']

bore[4] *past* of BEAR[1].

boreal /ˈbɔːrɪəl/ *adj.* **1** of the North or northern regions. **2** of the north wind. [Middle English via French *boréal* or Late Latin *borealis* from Latin *Boreas*, from Greek *Boreas* 'god of the north wind']

boredom /ˈbɔːdəm/ *n.* the state of being bored; ennui.

borehole /ˈbɔːhəʊl/ *n.* a deep narrow hole, esp. one made in the earth to find water, oil, etc.

borer /ˈbɔːrə/ *n.* **1** a worm, mollusc, insect, or insect larva which bores into wood, other plant material, or rock. **2** a tool for boring.

boric /ˈbɔːrɪk/ *adj.* of or containing boron.

boric acid *n.* an acid derived from borax, used as a mild antiseptic and in the manufacture of heat-resistant glass and enamels.

boring /ˈbɔːrɪŋ/ *adj.* that makes one bored; uninteresting, tedious, dull. □ **boringly** *adv.* **boringness** *n.*

born /bɔːn/ *adj.* **1** existing as a result of birth. **2 a** being such or likely to become such by natural ability or quality (*a born leader*). **b** (usu. foll. by *to* + infin.) having a specified destiny or prospect (*born lucky*; *born to be king*; *born to lead men*). **3** (in *comb.*) of a certain status by birth (*French-born*; *well-born*). □ **born and bred** by birth and upbringing. **in all one's born days** *colloq.* in one's life so far. **not born yesterday** *colloq.* not stupid; shrewd. [past part. of BEAR[1]]

■ **Usage** See Usage Note at BEAR[1].

born-again *attrib.adj.* converted (esp. to fundamentalist Christianity).

borne /bɔːn/ *past part.* of BEAR[1]. ● *adj.* (in *comb.*) carried or transported by (*airborne*).

borné /ˈbɔːneɪ, French bɔrne/ *adj.* **1** narrow-minded; of limited ideas. **2** having limitations. [French, past part. of *borner* 'limit']

Bornholm disease /ˈbɔːnhəʊm dɪˌziːz/ *n.* a viral infection with fever and pain in the muscles of the ribs. [*Bornholm* in Denmark, where it was first described]

boro- /ˈbɔːrəʊ/ *comb. form* indicating salts containing boron.

boron /ˈbɔːrɒn/ *n. Chem.* a non-metallic brown amorphous or black crystalline element extracted from borax and boracic acid and mainly used for hardening steel (symbol **B**). [BORAX + *-on* from *carbon* (which it resembles in some respects)]

boronia /bəˈrəʊnɪə/ *n. Austral.* any sweet-scented shrub of the genus *Boronia*. [F. *Borone*, Italian botanist d. 1794]

borosilicate /bɔːrəʊˈsɪlɪkeɪt/ *n.* any of many substances containing boron, silicon, and oxygen generally used in glazes and enamels and in the production of glass.

borough /ˈbʌrə/ *n.* **1** *Brit.* **a** a town (as distinct from a city) with a corporation and privileges granted by a royal charter. **b** *hist.* a town sending representatives to Parliament. **2** an administrative division of London. **3** a municipal corporation in certain US states. **4** each of five divisions of New York City. **5** (in Alaska) a county. [Old English *burg*, *burh* from Germanic: cf. BURGH]

borrow /ˈbɒrəʊ/ *v.* **1 a** *tr.* acquire temporarily with the promise or intention of returning. **b** *intr.* obtain money in this way. **2** *tr.* use (an idea, invention, etc.) originated by another; plagiarize. **3** *intr. Golf* **a** play the ball uphill so that it rolls back towards the hole. **b** allow for the wind or a slope. □ **borrowed time** an unexpected extension, esp. of life. □ **borrower** *n.* **borrowing** *n.* [Old English *borgian* 'give a pledge']

borrow pit *n.* a pit resulting from the excavation of material for use in embanking etc.

borsch var. of BORTSCH.

Borstal /ˈbɔːst(ə)l/ *n. Brit. hist.* an institution for reforming and training young offenders. [*Borstal* in S. England, where the first of these was established]

■ **Usage** The term *Borstal* has now been replaced by *detention centre* and *youth custody centre*.

bort /bɔːt/ *n.* (also **boart**) **1** an inferior or malformed diamond, used for cutting. **2** fragments of diamonds produced in cutting. [Dutch *boort*]

bortsch /bɔːtʃ/ *n.* (also **borsch** /bɔːʃ/) a highly seasoned Russian or Polish soup with various ingredients including beetroot and cabbage and served with sour cream. [Russian *borshch*]

borzoi /ˈbɔːzɔɪ/ *n.* **1** a large Russian wolfhound of a breed with a narrow head and silky, usu. white, coat. **2** this breed. [Russian, from *borzyĭ* 'swift']

boscage /ˈbɒskɪdʒ/ *n.* (also **boskage**) **1** masses of trees or shrubs. **2** wooded scenery. [Middle English via Old French *boscage* (modern BOCAGE) ultimately from the Germanic base of BUSH[1]]

bosh /bɒʃ/ *n.* & *int. slang* nonsense; foolish talk. [Turkish *boş* 'empty']

bosky /ˈbɒski/ *adj. literary* wooded, bushy. [Middle English *bosk*, variant of BUSH[1]]

bo's'n var. of BOATSWAIN.

bosom /ˈbʊz(ə)m/ *n.* **1 a** a person's breast or chest, esp. a woman's. **b** *colloq.* each of a woman's breasts. **c** the enclosure formed by a person's breast and arms. **2** an emotional centre, esp. as the source of an enfolding relationship (*in the bosom of one's family*). **3** the part of a woman's dress covering the breast. [Old English *bōsm*, from Germanic]

bosom friend *n.* a very close or intimate friend.

bosomy /ˈbʊz(ə)mi/ *adj.* (of a woman) having large breasts.

boson /ˈbəʊzɒn/ *n. Physics* any of several subatomic particles obeying the relations stated by Bose and Einstein, with a zero or integral spin, e.g. photons (cf. FERMION). [S. N. *Bose*, Indian physicist d. 1974]

boss[1] /bɒs/ *n.* & *v. colloq.* ● *n.* **1** a person in charge; an employer, manager, or overseer. **2** *US* a person who controls or dominates a political organization. ● *v.tr.* **1** (usu. foll. by *about*, *around*) treat domineeringly; give constant peremptory orders to. **2** be the master or manager of. [originally US: from Dutch *baas* 'master']

boss[2] /bɒs/ *n.* **1** a round knob, stud, or other protuberance, esp. on the centre of a shield or in ornamental work. **2** *Archit.* a piece of ornamental carving etc. covering the point where the ribs in a vault or ceiling cross. **3** *Geol.* a large mass of igneous rock. **4** *Mech.* an enlarged part of a shaft. [Middle English via Old French *boce* from Romanic]

bossa nova /bɒsə ˈnəʊvə/ *n.* **1** a dance like the samba, originating in Brazil. **2** a piece of music for this or in its rhythm. [Portuguese, = new style]

boss-eyed /ˈbɒsʌɪd/ *adj. Brit. colloq.* **1** having only one good eye; cross-eyed. **2** crooked; out of true. [dialect *boss* 'miss, bungle']

boss-shot /ˈbɒsʃɒt/ *n. Brit. dial.* & *slang* **1** a bad shot or aim. **2** an unsuccessful attempt. [as BOSS-EYED]

bossy /ˈbɒsi/ *adj.* (**bossier**, **bossiest**) *colloq.* domineering; tending to boss. □ **bossily** *adv.* **bossiness** *n.*

bossy-boots *n. Brit. colloq.* a domineering person.

bosun /ˈbəʊs(ə)n/ (also **bo'sun**) var. of BOATSWAIN.

bot /bɒt/ *n.* (also **bott**) any of various parasitic larvae of flies of the family Oestridae, infesting horses, sheep, etc. [probably of Low Dutch origin]

bot. *abbr.* **1** bottle. **2** botanic; botanical; botany. **3** bought.

botanize /ˈbɒtənʌɪz/ *v.intr.* (also **-ise**) study plants, esp. in their habitat.

Botany /ˈbɒt(ə)ni/ *n.* (in full **Botany wool**) merino wool, esp. from Australia. [*Botany Bay*, New South Wales, where the wool originally came from, named from the variety of its flora]

botany /ˈbɒt(ə)ni/ *n.* **1** the study of the physiology, structure, genetics, ecology, distribution, classification, and economic importance of plants. **2** the plant life of a particular area or time. □ **botanic** /bəˈtanɪk/ *adj.* **botanical** /bəˈtanɪk(ə)l/ *adj.* **botanically** /bəˈtanɪk(ə)li/ *adv.* **botanist** *n.* [*botanic* via French *botanique* or Late Latin *botanicus* from Greek *botanikos*, from *botanē* 'plant': *botany* is from *botanic*]

botch /bɒtʃ/ *v.* & *n.* (also **bodge** /bɒdʒ/) ● *v.tr.* **1** bungle; do badly. **2** patch or repair clumsily. ● *n.* bungled or spoilt work (*made a botch of it*). □ **botcher** *n.* [Middle English: origin unknown]

botel /bəʊˈtɛl/ *n.* (also **boatel**) **1** a waterside hotel with facilities for mooring boats. **2** a ship with the facilities of a hotel. [blend of BOAT and HOTEL]

botfly /ˈbɒtflʌɪ/ *n.* (*pl.* **-flies**) a dipterous fly of the genus *Oestrus*, with a stout hairy body and parasitic larvae (see BOT).

both /bəʊθ/ *predet., pron., & adv.* ● *predet. & pron.* the two, not only one (*both boys*; *both the boys*; *both of the boys*; *the boys are both here*). ● *adv.* with equal truth in two cases (*he is both here and hungry*). □ **have it both ways** alternate between two incompatible points of view to suit the needs of the moment. [Middle English, from Old Norse *báthir*]

■ **Usage** *Both* is widely used with *of*, esp. when followed by a pronoun (e.g. *both of us*) or a noun implying separate rather than collective consideration, e.g. *both of the boys* suggests *each boy* rather than the two together.

bother /ˈbɒðə/ *v., n., & int.* ● *v.* **1** *tr.* **a** give trouble to; worry, disturb. **b** *refl.* (often foll. by *about*) be anxious or concerned. **2** *intr.* **a** (often foll. by *about*, or *to* + infin.) worry or trouble oneself (*don't bother about that*; *didn't bother to tell me*). **b** (foll. by *with*) be concerned. ● *n.* **1 a** a person or thing that bothers or causes worry. **b** a minor nuisance. **2** trouble, worry, fuss. ● *int.* esp. *Brit.* expressing annoyance or impatience. □ **cannot be bothered** will not make the effort needed. [earlier 'noise, chatter', probably related to Irish *bodhraim* 'deafen, annoy']

botheration /bɒðəˈreɪʃ(ə)n/ *n. & int. colloq.* = BOTHER *n., int.*

bothersome /ˈbɒðəsəm/ *adj.* causing bother; troublesome.

both ways *adj. & adv.* = EACH WAY.

bothy /ˈbɒθi/ *n.* (also **bothie**) (*pl.* **-ies**) *Sc.* a small hut or cottage, esp. one for housing labourers or for use as a mountain refuge. [18th c.: origin unknown: perhaps related to BOOTH]

bo tree /bəʊ/ *n.* the Indian fig tree, *Ficus religiosa*, regarded as sacred by Buddhists. Also called *peepul*, *pipal*. [representing Sinhalese *bogaha* 'tree of knowledge' (Buddha's enlightenment having occurred beneath such a tree)]

botryoidal /ˈbɒtrɪɔɪd(ə)l/ *adj. Mineral.* shaped like a cluster of grapes. [Greek *botruoeidēs* from *botrus* 'bunch of grapes']

botrytis /bəˈtrʌɪtɪs/ *n.* a fungus of the genus *Botrytis*, esp. the grey mould *B. cinerea*, deliberately cultivated on the grapes used for certain wines (also called NOBLE ROT). [modern Latin, from Greek *botrus* 'cluster of grapes']

bott var. of BOT.

bottle /ˈbɒt(ə)l/ *n. & v.* ● *n.* **1** a container, usu. of glass or plastic and with a narrow neck, for storing liquid. **2** the amount that will fill a bottle. **3** *Brit.* a baby's feeding bottle. **4** = HOT-WATER BOTTLE. **5** a metal cylinder for liquefied gas. **6** *Brit. slang* courage, confidence. ● *v.tr.* **1** put into bottles or jars. **2** *Brit.* preserve (fruit etc.) in jars. **3** (usu. foll. by *up*) **a** conceal or restrain for a time (esp. a feeling). **b** keep (an enemy force etc.) contained or entrapped. **4** (as **bottled** *adj.*) *Brit. slang* drunk. □ **bottle out** (often foll. by *of*) *Brit. slang* fail to carry out some activity through lack of nerve. **hit the bottle** *slang* drink heavily. **on the bottle** *slang* drinking (alcohol) heavily. [Middle English via Old French *botele*, *botaille* from medieval Latin *butticula*, diminutive of Late Latin *buttis* BUTT[4]]

bottle bank *n. Brit.* a place where used bottles may be deposited for recycling.

bottle-brush *n.* **1** a cylindrical brush for cleaning inside bottles. **2** any of various plants with a flower of this shape.

bottle-feed *v.tr.* (*past* and *past part.* **-fed**) feed (a baby) with milk by means of a bottle.

bottle green *n. & adj.* ● *n.* dark green. ● *adj.* (hyphenated when *attrib.*) of this colour.

bottleneck /ˈbɒt(ə)lnɛk/ *n.* **1** a narrow place where the flow of traffic, production, etc., is constricted. **2** an obstruction to the flow of something (*information bottleneck*). **3 a** a device worn on a guitarist's finger, used to produce sliding effects on the strings. **b** the style of playing that uses this. **c** (in full **bottleneck guitar**) a guitar so played.

bottlenose /ˈbɒt(ə)lnəʊz/ *n. Brit.* a swollen nose.

bottlenose dolphin *n.* (also **bottlenosed dolphin**) a dolphin, *Tursiops truncatus*, with a bottle-shaped snout.

bottle party *n. Brit.* a party to which guests bring bottles of drink.

bottler /ˈbɒtlə/ *n.* **1** a person who bottles drinks etc. **2** *Austral. & NZ slang* an excellent person or thing.

bottle tree *n.* any of various Australian trees of the genus *Brachychiton* with a swollen bottle-shaped trunk.

bottle-washer *n.* (esp. in phr. **chief cook and bottle-washer**) *colloq.* a menial, a factotum.

bottom /ˈbɒtəm/ *n., adj., & v.* ● *n.* **1 a** the lowest point or part (*bottom of the stairs*). **b** the part on which a thing rests (*bottom of a saucepan*). **c** the underneath part (*scraped the bottom of the car*). **d** the furthest or inmost part (*bottom of the garden*). **2** *colloq.* **a** the buttocks. **b** the seat of a chair etc. **3 a** the less honourable, important, or successful end of a table, a class, etc. (*at the bottom of the list of requirements*). **b** a person occupying this place (*he's always bottom of the class*). **4** the ground under the water of a lake, a river, etc. (*swam until he touched the bottom*). **5** the basis; the origin (*he's at the bottom of it*). **6** the essential character; reality. **7** *Naut.* **a** the keel or hull of a ship. **b** a ship, esp. as a cargo carrier. **8** *archaic* staying power; endurance. ● *adj.* **1** lowest; last (*bottom button*; *bottom score*). **2** lower (*bottom half*). ● *v.* **1** *tr.* put a bottom to (a chair, saucepan, etc.). **2** *intr.* (of a ship) reach or touch the bottom. **3** *tr.* find the extent or real nature of; work out. **4** *tr.* (usu. foll. by *on*) base (an argument etc.) (*reasoning bottomed on logic*). **5** *tr.* touch the bottom or lowest point of. □ **at bottom** basically, essentially. **be at the bottom of** have caused. **bet one's bottom dollar** *slang* **1** stake all. **2** be very sure. **bottom falls** (or **drops**) **out** collapse occurs. **bottom out** reach the lowest level. **bottoms up!** a call to drain one's glass. **bottom up** *Brit.* upside-down. **get to the bottom of** fully investigate and explain. **knock the bottom out of** *Brit.* make invalid or useless; prove (a thing) worthless. □ **bottommost** /ˈbɒtəmməʊst/ *adj.* [Old English *botm*, from Germanic]

bottom dog *n.* = UNDERDOG.

bottom drawer *n. Brit.* linen etc. stored by a woman in preparation for her marriage.

bottom gear *n. Brit.* = FIRST GEAR.

bottomless /ˈbɒtəmlɪs/ *adj.* **1** without a bottom. **2** (of a supply etc.) inexhaustible.

bottom line *n. colloq.* the underlying or ultimate truth; the ultimate, esp. financial, criterion.

bottomry /ˈbɒtəmri/ *n.* & *v.* *Naut.* ● *n.* a system of using a ship as security against a loan to finance a voyage, the lender losing his or her money if the ship sinks. ● *v.tr.* (**-ies**, **-ied**) pledge (a ship) in this way. [BOTTOM = ship + -RY, influenced by Dutch *bodemerij*]

bottom-up *attrib.adj.* **1** proceeding from detail to general theory, or from the bottom upwards. **2** non-hierarchical.

botulism /ˈbɒtjʊlɪz(ə)m/ *n.* poisoning caused by a toxin produced by the bacillus *Clostridium botulinum* growing in poorly preserved food. [German *Botulismus* 'sausage poisoning' from Latin *botulus* 'sausage']

bouclé /ˈbuːkleɪ/ *n.* **1** a looped or curled yarn (esp. wool). **2** a fabric, esp. knitted, made of this. [French, = buckled, curled]

boudoir /ˈbuːdwɑː/ *n.* a woman's small private room or bedroom. [French, literally 'sulking-place' from *bouder* 'sulk']

bouffant /ˈbuːfɒ̃/ *adj.* (of a dress, hair, etc.) puffed out. [French, from *bouffer* 'swell']

bougainvillea /buːg(ə)nˈvɪlɪə/ *n.* (also **bougainvillaea**) any tropical widely cultivated plant of the genus *Bougainvillea*, with large coloured bracts (usu. purple, red, or white) almost concealing the inconspicuous flowers. [L. A. de *Bougainville*, French navigator d. 1811]

bough /baʊ/ *n.* a branch of a tree, esp. a main one. [Old English *bōg*, *bōh* 'bough, shoulder' from Germanic: related to BOW[3]]

bought *past* and *past part.* of BUY.

boughten /ˈbɔːt(ə)n/ *adj. dial.* bought at a shop, not home-made. [variant of past part. of BUY]

bougie /ˈbuːʒi/ *n.* **1** *Med.* a thin flexible surgical instrument for exploring, dilating, etc. the passages of the body. **2** a wax candle. [French from Arabic *Bijāya*, an Algerian town with a wax trade]

bouillabaisse /buːjəˈbeɪs/ *n.* a rich, spicy fish-stew, originally from Provence. [French from modern Provençal *bouiabaisso* 'boil down']

bouilli /ˈbuːji, French buji/ *n.* stewed or boiled meat. [French, = boiled]

bouillon /ˈbuːjɒ̃/ *n.* thin soup; broth. [French, from *bouillir* 'to boil']

boulder /ˈbəʊldə/ *n.* a large stone worn smooth by erosion. ◻ **bouldery** *adj.* [short for *boulderstone*, Middle English from Scandinavian]

boulder clay *n.* a mixture of boulders etc. deposited by massive bodies of melting ice, giving distinctive glacial formations.

boule[1] /buːl/ *n.* (also **boules** *pronunc.* same) a French form of bowls, played on rough ground with usu. metal balls. [French, = BOWL[2]]

boule[2] /ˈbuːli/ *n.* a legislative body of ancient or modern Greece. [Greek *boulē* 'senate']

boule[3] var. of BUHL.

boules var. of BOULE[1].

boulevard /ˈbuːləvɑːd/ *n.* **1** a broad tree-lined avenue. **2** esp. *US* a broad main road. [French from German *Bollwerk* BULWARK, originally of a promenade on a demolished fortification]

boulle var. of BUHL.

boult var. of BOLT[2].

bounce /baʊns/ *v.* & *n.* ● *v.* **1 a** *intr.* (of a ball etc.) rebound. **b** *tr.* cause to rebound. **c** *tr.* & *intr.* bounce repeatedly. **2** *intr. colloq.* (of a cheque) be returned by a bank when there are insufficient funds to meet it. **3** *intr.* **a** (foll. by *about, up*) (of a person, dog, etc.) jump or spring energetically. **b** (foll. by *in, out*, etc.) rush noisily, angrily, enthusiastically, etc. (*bounced into the room; bounced out in a temper*). **4** *tr.* (usu. foll. by *into* + verbal noun) *Brit. colloq.* hustle, persuade (*bounced him into signing*). **5** *intr. Brit. colloq.* talk boastfully. **6** *tr. slang* eject forcibly (from a dance hall, club, etc.). ● *n.* **1 a** a rebound. **b** the power of rebounding (*this ball has a good bounce*). **2** *Brit. colloq.* **a** swagger, self-confidence (*has a lot of bounce*). **b** liveliness. ◻ **bounce back** regain one's good health, spirits, prosperity, etc. [Middle English *bunsen* 'beat, thump' (perhaps imitative), or from Low German *bunsen*, Dutch *bons* 'thump']

bouncer /ˈbaʊnsə/ *n.* **1** *colloq.* a person employed to eject troublemakers from a dance hall, club, etc. **2** *Cricket* a ball bowled fast and short so as to rise high after pitching.

bouncing /ˈbaʊnsɪŋ/ *adj.* **1** (esp. of a baby) big and healthy. **2** boisterous.

bouncy /ˈbaʊnsi/ *adj.* (**bouncier**, **bounciest**) **1** (of a ball etc.) that bounces well. **2** cheerful and lively. **3** resilient, springy (*a bouncy sofa*). ◻ **bouncily** *adv.* **bounciness** *n.*

bound[1] /baʊnd/ *v.* & *n.* ● *v.intr.* **1 a** spring, leap (*bounded out of bed*). **b** walk or run with leaping strides. **2** (of a ball etc.) recoil from a wall or the ground; bounce. ● *n.* **1** a springy movement upwards or outwards; a leap. **2** a bounce. ◻ **by leaps and bounds** see LEAP. [French *bond*, *bondir* (originally 'resound', later 'rebound'), via Late Latin *bombitare* from Latin *bombus* 'hum']

bound[2] /baʊnd/ *n.* & *v.* ● *n.* (usu. in *pl.*) **1** a limitation; a restriction (*beyond the bounds of possibility*). **2** a border of a territory; a boundary. ● *v.tr.* **1** (esp. in *passive*; foll. by *by*) set bounds to; limit (*views bounded by prejudice*). **2** be the boundary of. ◻ **out of bounds 1** outside the part of a school etc. in which one is allowed to be. **2** beyond what is acceptable; forbidden. [Middle English via Anglo-French *bounde*, Old French *bodne*, *bonde*, etc., from medieval Latin *bodina*, earlier *butina*, of unknown origin]

bound[3] /baʊnd/ *adj.* **1** (usu. foll. by *for*) ready to start or having started (*bound for stardom*). **2** (in *comb.*) moving in a specified direction (*northbound; outward bound*). [Middle English from Old Norse *búinn*, past part. of *búa* 'get ready': *-d* euphonic, or influenced by BIND]

bound[4] /baʊnd/ *past* and *past part.* of BIND. ◻ **bound to** certain to (*he's bound to come*).

boundary /ˈbaʊnd(ə)ri/ *n.* (*pl.* **-ies**) **1** a line marking the limits of an area, territory, etc. (*the fence is the boundary; boundary between liberty and licence*). **2** *Cricket* a hit crossing the limits of the field, scoring 4 or 6 runs. [dialect *bounder* from BOUND[2] + -ER[1], perhaps on the pattern of *limitary*]

boundary layer *n.* a layer of more or less stationary fluid (e.g. water or air) immediately surrounding an immersed moving object.

boundary rider *n. Austral.* & *NZ* a person employed to ride round the fences etc. of a cattle or sheep station and keep them in good order.

boundary umpire *n.* (in Australian Rules) an umpire on the sidelines who signals when the ball is out.

bounden /ˈbaʊnd(ə)n/ *adj. archaic* obligatory. [archaic past part. of BIND]

bounden duty *n.* solemn responsibility.

bounder /ˈbaʊndə/ *n. Brit. colloq.* or *joc.* an ill-bred or dishonourable person.

boundless /ˈbaʊndlɪs/ *adj.* unlimited; immense (*boundless enthusiasm*). ◻ **boundlessly** *adv.* **boundlessness** *n.*

bounteous /ˈbaʊntɪəs/ *adj. poet.* **1** generous, liberal. **2** freely given (*bounteous affection*). ◻ **bounteously** *adv.* **bounteousness** *n.* [Middle English from Old French *bontif*, from *bonté* BOUNTY, on the pattern of *plenteous*]

bountiful /ˈbaʊntɪfʊl, -f(ə)l/ *adj.* **1** = BOUNTEOUS. **2** ample. ◻ **bountifully** *adv.* [BOUNTY + -FUL]

bounty /ˈbaʊnti/ *n.* (*pl.* **-ies**) **1** liberality; generosity. **2** a gift or reward, made usu. by the State, esp.: **a** a sum paid for a valiant act. **b** a sum paid to encourage a trading enterprise etc. **c** a sum paid to army or navy recruits on enlistment. [Middle English via Old French *bonté* from Latin *bonitas -tatis* from *bonus* 'good']

bounty hunter *n.* a person who pursues a criminal or seeks an achievement for the sake of the reward.

bouquet /bʊ'keɪ, bəʊ'keɪ, 'bʊkeɪ/ *n.* **1** a bunch of flowers, esp. for carrying at a wedding or other ceremony. **2** the scent of wine etc. **3** a favourable comment; a compliment. [French (earlier = clump of trees) from dialect variant of Old French *bos, bois* 'wood']

bouquet garni /'gɑ:ni/ *n.* (*pl.* **bouquets garnis** /bu:keɪz 'gɑ:ni/) a bunch of herbs used for flavouring stews etc. [French, literally 'garnished bouquet']

Bourbon /'bʊəbən/ *n. US* **1** a reactionary. **2** *Brit.* a chocolate-flavoured biscuit with a chocolate-cream filling. [the Bourbon family, whose descendants founded dynasties in France and Spain]

bourbon /'bɜ:bən, 'bʊə-/ *n.* an American whiskey distilled from maize and rye. [*Bourbon* County, Kentucky, where first made]

bourdon /'bʊəd(ə)n/ *n. Mus.* **1** a low-pitched stop in an organ or harmonium. **2** the lowest bell in a peal of bells. **3** the drone pipe of a bagpipe. [French, = bagpipe-drone, from Romanic: imitative]

bourgeois /'bʊəʒwɑ:/ *adj. & n.* often *derog.* ● *adj.* **1 a** conventionally middle-class. **b** humdrum, unimaginative. **c** selfishly materialistic. **2** upholding the interests of the capitalist class; non-communist. ● *n.* (*pl.* same) a bourgeois person. [French, earlier *burgeis*: see BURGESS]

bourgeoisie /bʊəʒwɑ:'zi:/ *n.* **1** the capitalist class. **2** the middle class. [French]

bourn[1] /bɔ:n, bʊən/ *n.* a small stream. [Middle English: S. English variant of BURN[2]]

bourn[2] /bɔ:n, bʊən/ *n.* (also **bourne**) *archaic* **1** a goal; a destination. **2** a limit. [French *borne* from Old French *bodne* BOUND[2]]

bourrée /'bʊəreɪ/ *n.* **1** a lively French dance like a gavotte. **2** the music for this dance. [French]

bourse /bʊəs/ *n.* **1** (**Bourse**) the Paris equivalent of the Stock Exchange. **2** a money market. [French, = purse, from medieval Latin *bursa*: see PURSE]

boustrophedon /baʊstrə'fi:d(ə)n, bu:-/ *adj. & adv.* (of written words) from right to left and from left to right in alternate lines. [Greek (*adv.*) = as an ox turns in ploughing from *bous* 'ox' + *-strophos* 'turning']

bout /baʊt/ *n.* (often foll. by *of*) **1 a** a limited period (of intensive work or exercise). **b** a drinking session. **c** a period (of illness) (*a bout of flu*). **2 a** a wrestling or boxing match. **b** a trial of strength. [16th c.: apparently the same as obsolete *bought* 'bending'; hence a 'turn' of work etc.]

boutique /bu:'ti:k/ *n.* a small shop or department of a store, selling (esp. fashionable) clothes or accessories. [French, = small shop, from Latin *apotheca* (as BODEGA)]

boutonnière /bu:tɒn'jɛ:/ *n.* a spray of flowers worn in a buttonhole. [French, = buttonhole]

bouzouki /bʊ'zu:ki/ *n.* a Greek form of mandolin. [modern Greek]

bovate /'bəʊveɪt/ *n. hist.* a measure of land, as much as one ox could plough in a year, varying from 10 to 18 acres. [medieval Latin *bovata* from Latin *bos bovis* 'ox']

bovine /'bəʊvʌɪn/ *adj.* **1** of or relating to cattle. **2** stupid, dull. ▫ **bovinely** *adv.* [Late Latin *bovinus* from Latin *bos bovis* 'ox']

bovine spongiform encephalopathy see BSE.

Bovril /'bɒvrɪl/ *n. propr.* a concentrated essence of beef diluted with hot water to make a drink. [Latin *bos bovis* 'ox, cow']

bovver /'bɒvə/ *n. Brit. slang* deliberate trouble-making. [cockney pronunciation of BOTHER]

bovver boot *n. Brit. slang* a heavy laced boot worn typically by skinheads.

bovver boy *n. Brit. slang* a violent hooligan.

bow[1] /bəʊ/ *n. & v.* ● *n.* **1 a** a slip-knot with a double loop. **b** a ribbon, shoelace, etc., tied with this. **c** a decoration (on clothing, or painted etc.) in the form of a bow. **2** a device for shooting arrows with a taut string joining the ends of a curved piece of wood etc. **3 a** a rod with horsehair stretched along its length, used for playing the violin, cello, etc. **b** a single stroke of a bow over strings. **4 a** a shallow curve or bend. **b** a rainbow. **5** = SADDLE BOW. **6** a metal ring forming the handle of scissors, a key, etc. **7** *US* the side piece of a spectacle frame. **8** *Archery* = BOWMAN[1]. ● *v.tr.* (also *absol.*) use a bow on (a violin etc.) (*he bowed vigorously*). ▫ **have two** (or **many**) **strings to one's bow** *Brit.* have (many) more than one resource. [Old English *boga* 'bow, arch', from Germanic: related to BOW[2]]

bow[2] /baʊ/ *v. & n.* ● *v.* **1** *intr.* incline the head or trunk, esp. in greeting or assent or acknowledgement of applause. **2** *intr.* submit (*bowed to the inevitable*). **3** *tr.* cause to incline or submit (*bowed his head*; *bowed his will to hers*). **4** *tr.* express (thanks, assent, etc.) by bowing (*bowed agreement to the plan*). **5** *tr.* (foll. by *in, out*) usher or escort obsequiously (*bowed us out of the restaurant*). ● *n.* an inclining of the head or body in greeting, assent, or in the acknowledgement of applause etc. ▫ **bow down 1** bend or kneel in submission or reverence (*bowed down before the king*). **2** (usu. in *passive*) make stoop; crush (*was bowed down by care*). **bow out 1** make one's exit (esp. formally). **2** retreat, withdraw; retire gracefully. **make one's bow** make a formal exit or entrance. **take a bow** acknowledge applause. [Old English *būgan*, from Germanic: related to BOW[1]]

bow[3] /baʊ/ *n. Naut.* **1** (often in *pl.*) the fore-end of a boat or a ship. **2** = BOWMAN[2]. ▫ **on the bow** within 45° of the point directly ahead. **shot across the bows** a warning. [Low German *boog*, Dutch *boeg*, 'ship's bow', originally 'shoulder': related to BOUGH]

bow and scrape *v.intr.* be obsequious; fawn.

bow-compass *n.* (also **bow-compasses** *pl.*) compasses with jointed legs.

bowdlerize /'baʊdlərʌɪz/ *v.tr.* (also **-ise**) expurgate (a book etc.). ▫ **bowdlerism** *n.* **bowdlerization** /-'zeɪʃ(ə)n/ *n.* [T. *Bowdler* (d. 1825), expurgator of Shakespeare]

bowel /'baʊəl/ *n.* **1** (often in *pl.*) the part of the alimentary canal below the stomach; the intestine. **2** (in *pl.*) the depths; the innermost parts (*the bowels of the earth*). [Middle English via Old French *buel* from Latin *botellus* 'little sausage']

bowel movement *n.* **1** discharge from the bowels; defecation. **2** the faeces discharged from the body.

bower[1] /'baʊə/ *n. & v.* ● *n.* **1 a** a secluded place, esp. in a garden, enclosed by foliage; an arbour. **b** a summer house. **2** *poet.* an inner room; a boudoir. ● *v.tr. poet.* embower. [Old English *būr*, from Germanic]

bower[2] /'baʊə/ *n.* (in full **bower-anchor**) *Naut.* either of two anchors (**the best** (starboard) or **small** (port) **bower**) carried at a ship's bow. [BOW[3] + -ER[1]]

bower[3] /'baʊə/ *n.* either of two cards, the jack of trumps (**the right bower**) and the other jack of this colour (**the left bower**) at euchre and similar games. [German *Bauer* 'peasant, jack at cards', related to Dutch *boer*: see BOOR]

bowerbird /'baʊəbɜ:d/ *n.* **1** any of various birds of the family Ptilonorhynchidae, native to Australia and New Guinea, the males of which construct elaborate bowers of feathers, grasses, shells, etc. during courtship. **2** *Austral. slang* a person who collects trivia or odds and ends.

bower-cable *n.* the cable attached to a bower-anchor (see BOWER[2]).

bowery /'baʊəri/ *n.* (also **Bowery**) (*pl.* **-ies**) *US* a district known as a resort of drunks and down-and-outs. [originally *the Bowery*, a street in New York City, from Dutch *bouwerij* 'farm']

bowfin /'bəʊfɪn/ *n.* a voracious American freshwater fish, *Amia calva*. [BOW[1] + FIN]

bowhead /'bəʊhɛd/ *n.* an Arctic whale, *Balaena mysticetus*. [BOW[1] + HEAD]

bowie /'bəʊi/ *n.* (in full **bowie knife**) a long knife with a blade double-edged at the point, used as a weapon by American pioneers. [J. *Bowie*, American soldier (d. 1836) who popularized it]

bowl[1] /bəʊl/ *n.* **1 a** a usu. round deep basin used for food or liquid. **b** the quantity (of soup etc.) a bowl holds. **c** the contents of a bowl. **2 a** any deep-sided container shaped like a bowl (*lavatory bowl*). **b** the bowl-shaped part of a tobacco pipe, spoon, balance, etc. **3** *Geog.* a natural basin. **4 a** esp. *US* an amphitheatre or stadium, esp. in names (*Hollywood Bowl*). **b** (in full **bowl game**) *N. Amer.* an American football game played after the main season between leading college, professional, etc. teams. □ **bowlful** *n.* (*pl.* **-fuls**). [Old English *bolle, bolla*, from Germanic]

bowl[2] /bəʊl/ *n. & v.* ● *n.* **1 a** a wooden or hard rubber ball, slightly asymmetrical so that it runs on a curved course, used in the game of bowls. **b** a wooden ball or disc used in playing skittles. **c** a large ball with indents for gripping, used in tenpin bowling. **2** (in *pl.*; usu. treated as *sing.*) **a** a game played with bowls on grass (see sense 1a). **b** *Brit.* tenpin bowling. **c** *Brit.* skittles. **3** a spell or turn of bowling in cricket. ● *v.* **1 a** *tr.* roll (a ball, a hoop, etc.) along the ground. **b** *intr.* play bowls or skittles. **2** *tr.* (also *absol.*) *Cricket* etc. **a** deliver (a ball, an over, etc.) (*bowled six overs*; *bowled well*). **b** (often foll. by *out, for*) dismiss (a batsman or a side) by knocking down the wicket with a ball (*bowled him out*; *bowled for six*). **c** (often foll. by *down*) knock (a wicket) over. **3** *intr.* (often foll. by *along*) go along rapidly by revolving, esp. on wheels (*the cart bowled along the road*). □ **bowl out** *Cricket* etc. dismiss (a batsman or a side). **bowl over 1** knock down. **2** *colloq.* **a** impress greatly. **b** overwhelm (*bowled over by her energy*). [Middle English & French *boule* from Latin *bulla* 'bubble']

bow-legs *n.pl.* bandy legs. □ **bow-legged** *adj.*

bowler[1] /ˈbəʊlə/ *n.* **1** *Cricket* etc. a member of the fielding side who bowls or is bowling. **2** a player at bowls.

bowler[2] /ˈbəʊlə/ *n.* (in full **bowler hat**) a man's hard felt hat with a round dome-shaped crown. [*Bowler*, a hatter, who designed it in 1850]

bowler-hat *v.tr.* (**-hatted, -hatting**) *Brit. slang* retire (a person) from the army etc. (*he's been bowler-hatted*).

bowline /ˈbəʊlɪn/ *n. Naut.* **1** a rope attaching the weather side of a square sail to the bow. **2** a simple knot for forming a non-slipping loop at the end of a rope. [Middle English from Middle Low German *bōlīne* (as BOW[3], LINE[1])]

bowling /ˈbəʊlɪŋ/ *n.* **1** *Bowls* the game of bowls as a sport or recreation. **2** *Cricket* the delivery of the ball (also *attrib.*: *bowling technique*).

bowling alley *n.* **1** a long enclosure for skittles or tenpin bowling. **2** a building containing these.

bowling average *n. Cricket* a bowler's conceded runs per wicket taken.

bowling crease *n. Cricket* the line from behind which a bowler delivers the ball.

bowling green *n.* a smooth green used for playing bowls.

bowman[1] /ˈbəʊmən/ *n.* (*pl.* **-men**) an archer.

bowman[2] /ˈbaʊmən/ *n.* (*pl.* **-men**) the rower nearest the bow of esp. a racing boat.

bowsaw /ˈbəʊsɔː/ *n.* a narrow saw stretched like a bowstring on a light frame.

bowser /ˈbaʊzə/ *n.* **1** *Brit.* a tanker used for fuelling aircraft etc., or for supplying water. **2** *propr. a* petrol pump. [trade name]

bowshot /ˈbəʊʃɒt/ *n.* the distance to which a bow can send an arrow.

bowsprit /ˈbəʊsprɪt/ *n. Naut.* a spar running out from a ship's bow to which the forestays are fastened. [Middle English from Germanic (as BOW[3], SPRIT)]

Bow Street runner /bəʊ/ *n.* (also **Bow Street officer**) *hist.* a London policeman. [*Bow Street* in London, containing the chief metropolitan police court]

bowstring /ˈbəʊstrɪŋ/ *n. & v.* ● *n.* the string of an archer's bow. ● *v.tr.* strangle with a bowstring (a former Turkish method of execution).

bow tie *n.* a necktie in the form of a bow (see BOW[1] *n.* 1a).

bow wave *n.* a wave set up at the bows of a moving ship or in front of a body moving through a fluid.

bow window *n.* a curved bay window.

bow-wow *int. & n.* ● *int.* /baʊˈwaʊ/ an imitation of a dog's bark. ● *n.* /ˈbaʊwaʊ/ **1** *colloq.* a dog. **2** a dog's bark. [imitative]

bowyang /ˈbəʊjaŋ/ *n. Austral. & NZ* either of a pair of bands or straps worn round the trouser legs below the knee. [origin unknown]

bowyer /ˈbəʊjə/ *n.* a maker or seller of archers' bows.

box[1] /bɒks/ *n. & v.* ● *n.* **1** a container, usu. with flat sides and of firm material such as wood or card, esp. for holding solids. **2 a** the amount that will fill a box. **b** *Brit.* = CHRISTMAS BOX. **3** a separate compartment for any of various purposes, e.g. for a small group in a theatre, for witnesses in a law court, for horses in a stable or vehicle. **4** an enclosure or receptacle for a special purpose (often in *comb.*: *money box*; *telephone box*). **5** a facility at a newspaper office for receiving replies to an advertisement. **6** (prec. by *the*) *colloq.* television; one's television set (*what's on the box?*). **7** an enclosed area or space. **8** a space or area of print on a page, enclosed by a border. **9** *Brit.* a small country house for use when shooting or fishing, or for other sporting activity. **10** a protective casing for a piece of mechanism. **11** *Brit.* a light shield for protecting the genitals in sport, esp. in cricket. **12** (prec. by *the*) *Football colloq.* the penalty area. **13** *Baseball* the area occupied by the batter or the pitcher. **14** a coachman's seat. ● *v.tr.* **1** put in or provide with a box. **2** (foll. by *in, up*) confine; restrain from movement. **3** (foll. by *up*) *Austral. & NZ* mix up (different flocks of sheep). □ **box the compass** *Naut.* recite the points of the compass in the correct order. □ **boxful** *n.* (*pl.* **-fuls**). **boxlike** *adj.* [Old English via Late Latin *buxis* from Latin PYXIS: ultimately from Greek *puxos* BOX[3]]

box[2] /bɒks/ *v. & n.* ● *v.* **1 a** *tr.* fight (an opponent) at boxing. **b** *intr.* practise boxing. **2** *tr.* slap (esp. a person's ears). ● *n.* a slap with the hand, esp. on the ears. □ **box clever** *Brit. colloq.* act in a clever or effective way. [Middle English: origin unknown]

box[3] /bɒks/ *n.* **1** (also **box tree**) an evergreen shrub or small tree of the genus *Buxus*, esp. *B. sempervirens*, a slow-growing tree with glossy dark green leaves which is often used in hedging. **2** any of various trees in Australasia which have similar wood or foliage, esp. those of several species of *Eucalyptus*. **3** = BOXWOOD 1. [Old English from Latin *buxus*, Greek *puxos*]

Box and Cox /bɒks (ə)nd ˈkɒks/ *n. & v. Brit.* ● *n.* (often *attrib.*) two persons sharing accommodation etc., and using it at different times. ● *v.intr.* share accommodation, duties, etc. by a strictly timed arrangement. [the names of characters in a play (1847) by J. M. Morton]

box camera *n.* a simple box-shaped hand camera.

boxcar /ˈbɒkskɑː/ *n. N. Amer.* an enclosed railway goods wagon, usu. with sliding doors on the sides.

box elder *n.* the American ash-leaved maple, *Acer negundo.*

Boxer /ˈbɒksə/ *n. hist.* a member of a fiercely nationalistic Chinese secret society that flourished in the 19th c. [translation of Chinese *yì hé quán*, literally 'righteous harmony fists']

boxer /ˈbɒksə/ *n.* **1** a person who practises boxing, esp. for sport. **2 a** a medium-sized dog of a breed with a smooth brown coat and puglike face. **b** this breed.

boxer shorts *n.pl.* men's underpants similar to shorts.

box girder *n.* a hollow girder square in cross-section.

boxing /ˈbɒksɪŋ/ *n.* the practice of fighting with the fists, esp. in padded gloves as a sport.

Boxing Day /ˈbɒksɪŋ/ *n.* the first day (strictly, the first weekday) after Christmas. [from the custom of giving tradesmen a Christmas box on this day]

boxing glove *n.* each of a pair of heavily padded gloves used in boxing.

boxing weight *n.* each of a series of fixed weight ranges at which boxers are matched.

box junction *n. Brit.* a road area at a junction marked with a yellow grid, which a vehicle should enter only if its exit from it is clear.

box kite *n.* a kite in the form of a long box open at each end.

box number *n.* a number by which replies are made to a private advertisement in a newspaper.

box office *n.* **1** an office for booking seats and buying tickets at a theatre, cinema, etc. **2** the commercial aspect of the arts and entertainment (often *attrib.*: *a box-office failure*).

box pleat *n.* a pleat consisting of two parallel creases forming a raised band.

boxroom /ˈbɒksruːm, -rʊm/ *n. Brit.* a small room or large cupboard esp. for storing boxes, cases, etc.

box spanner *n. Brit.* a spanner with a box-shaped end fitting over the head of a nut.

box spring *n.* each of a set of vertical springs housed in a frame, e.g. in a mattress.

boxwood /ˈbɒkswʊd/ *n.* **1** the wood of the box tree, used esp. by engravers for the fineness of its grain and for its hardness. **2** = BOX³ 1.

boxy /ˈbɒksi/ *adj.* **(boxier, boxiest) 1** resembling a box; (of a room or space) very cramped. **2** (of recorded sound) restricted in tone.

boy /bɔɪ/ *n. & int.* ● *n.* **1** a male child or youth. **2** a young man, esp. regarded as not yet mature. **3** a male servant, attendant, etc. **4** (**the boys**) *colloq.* a group of men mixing socially. ● *int.* (also **oh boy**) expressing pleasure, surprise, etc. □ **boyhood** *n.* **boyish** *adj.* **boyishly** *adv.* **boyishness** *n.* [Middle English = servant, perhaps ultimately from Latin *boia* 'fetter']

boyar /bəʊˈjɑː/ *n. hist.* a member of the old aristocracy in Russia. [Russian *boyarin* 'grandee']

boycott /ˈbɔɪkɒt/ *v. & n.* ● *v.tr.* **1** combine in refusing social or commercial relations with (a person, group, country, etc.) usu. as punishment or coercion. **2** refuse to handle (goods) to this end. ● *n.* such a refusal. [Capt. C. C. *Boycott*, Irish land agent d. 1897, so treated from 1880]

boyfriend /ˈbɔɪfrɛnd/ *n.* a person's regular male companion or lover.

Boyle's law /ˈbɔɪlz/ *n.* the law that the pressure of a given mass of gas is inversely proportional to its volume at a constant temperature. [Robert *Boyle*, Irish scientist d. 1691]

boyo /ˈbɔɪəʊ/ *n.* (*pl.* **-os**) *Welsh & Ir. colloq.* boy, fellow (esp. as a form of address).

Boy Scout *n.* = SCOUT¹ *n.* 4.

boysenberry /ˈbɔɪz(ə)nbɛri, -s-/ *n.* (*pl.* **-ies**) **1** a hybrid of several species of bramble. **2** the large red edible fruit of this plant. [R. *Boysen* (d. 1950), American horticulturalist who developed it]

boys in blue *n.pl.* (often prec. by *the*) policemen; the police.

bozo /ˈbəʊzəʊ/ *n.* (*pl.* **-os**) esp. *N. Amer. slang* a stupid or insignificant person. [20th c.: origin unknown]

BP *abbr.* **1** boiling point. **2** blood pressure. **3** before the present (era). **4** British Petroleum. **5** British Pharmacopoeia.

Bp. *abbr.* Bishop.

BPC *abbr.* British Pharmaceutical Codex.

B.Phil. *abbr.* Bachelor of Philosophy.

bpi *abbr. Computing* bits per inch.

B-picture *n.* = B-MOVIE.

bps *abbr. Computing* bits per second.

Bq *abbr.* becquerel.

BR *abbr.* British Rail.

Br *symb. Chem.* the element bromine.

Br. *abbr.* **1** British. **2** Brother.

bra /brɑː/ *n.* (*pl.* **bras**) an undergarment worn by women to support the breasts. □ **braless** *adj.* [abbreviation of BRASSIERE]

brace /breɪs/ *n. & v.* ● *n.* **1 a** a device that clamps or fastens tightly. **b** a strengthening piece of iron or timber in building. **2** (in *pl.*) *Brit.* straps supporting trousers from the shoulders. **3** a wire device for straightening the teeth. **4** (*pl.* same) a pair (esp. of game). **5** a rope attached to the yard of a ship for trimming the sail. **6 a** a connecting mark { or } used in printing. **b** *Mus.* a similar mark connecting staves to be performed at the same time. ● *v.tr.* **1** fasten tightly, give firmness to. **2** make steady by supporting. **3** (esp. as **bracing** *adj.*) invigorate, refresh. **4** (often *refl.*) prepare for a difficulty, shock, etc. □ **bracingly** *adv.* **bracingness** *n.* [Middle English via Old French *brace* 'two arms', *bracier* 'embrace', from Latin *bra(c)chia* 'arms']

brace and bit *n.* a revolving tool with a D-shaped central handle for boring.

bracelet /ˈbreɪslɪt/ *n.* **1** an ornamental band, hoop, or chain worn on the wrist or arm. **2** *slang* a handcuff. [Middle English from Old French, diminutive of *bracel*, from Latin *bracchiale* from *bra(c)chium* 'arm']

bracer /ˈbreɪsə/ *n. colloq.* a tonic, esp. an alcoholic drink.

brachial /ˈbreɪkɪəl/ *adj.* **1** of or relating to the arm (*brachial artery*). **2** like an arm. [Latin *brachialis* from *bra(c)chium* 'arm']

brachiate *v. & adj.* ● *v.intr.* /ˈbrakɪeɪt/ (of certain apes and monkeys) move by using the arms to swing from branch to branch. ● *adj.* /ˈbrakɪət, ˈbreɪk-/ *Biol.* **1** having arms. **2** having paired branches on alternate sides. □ **brachiation** /-ˈeɪʃ(ə)n/ *n.* **brachiator** *n.* [Latin *bra(c)chium* 'arm']

brachiopod /ˈbrakɪəpɒd/ *n.* a marine invertebrate of the phylum Brachiopoda, having a ciliated feeding arm and a two-valved shell, often found fossilized. Also called *lamp shell.* [modern Latin from Greek *brakhiōn* 'arm' + *pous podos* 'foot']

brachiosaurus /brakɪəˈsɔːrəs/ *n.* any huge plant-eating dinosaur of the genus *Brachiosaurus* with forelegs longer than its hind legs. [modern Latin from Greek *brakhiōn* 'arm' + *sauros* 'lizard']

brachistochrone /brəˈkɪstəkrəʊn/ *n.* a curve between two points along which a body can move in a shorter time than for any other curve. [Greek *brakhistos* 'shortest' + *khronos* 'time']

brachy- /ˈbraki/ *comb. form* short. [Greek *brakhus* 'short']

brachycephalic /ˌbrakɪsɪˈfalɪk, -kɛˈfalɪk/ *adj. Anthropol.* having a broad short head. □ **brachycephalous** /brakɪˈsɛfələs, -kɛf-/ *adj.* [BRACHY- + Greek *kephalē* 'head']

brachylogy /brəˈkɪlədʒi/ *n.* (*pl.* **-ies**) **1** over-conciseness of expression. **2** an instance of this.

brack /brak/ *n. Ir.* cake or bread containing dried fruit etc. [abbreviation of BARMBRACK]

bracken /ˈbrak(ə)n/ *n.* **1** any large coarse fern, esp. *Pteridium aquilinum*, abundant on heaths and moorlands, and in woods; also called *brake.* **2** a mass of such ferns. [northern Middle English from Old Norse]

bracket /ˈbrakɪt/ *n. & v.* ● *n.* **1** a right-angled or other support attached to and projecting from a vertical surface. **2** a shelf fixed with such a support to a wall. **3** each of a pair of marks ( ) [ ] { } < > used to enclose words or figures. **4** a group classified as containing similar elements or falling between given limits (*income bracket*). **5** *Mil.* the distance between two artillery shots fired either side of the target to establish range. ● *v.tr.* (**bracketed**, **bracketing**) **1 a** couple (names etc.) with a bracket. **b** imply a connection or equality between. **2 a** enclose in brackets as parenthetic or spurious. **b** *Math.* enclose in brackets as having specific relations to what precedes or follows. **3** *Mil.* establish the range of (a target) by firing two preliminary shots one short of and the other beyond it. [French *braguette* or Spanish *bragueta* 'codpiece, bracket, corbel', diminutive of French *brague* 'mortice', pl. 'breeches' via Provençal *braga* from Latin *braca*, pl. *bracae* 'breeches']

bracket fungus *n.* a fungus forming shelf-like projections on tree trunks etc.

brackish /ˈbrakɪʃ/ *adj.* (of water etc.) slightly salty. □ **brackishness** *n.* [obsolete *brack* (adj.) from Middle Low German, Middle Dutch *brac*]

bract /brakt/ *n. Bot.* a modified and often brightly coloured leaf, with a flower or an inflorescence in its axil. □ **bracteal** *adj.* **bracteate** /-tɪət/ *adj.* [Latin *bractea* 'thin plate, gold leaf']

brad /brad/ *n.* a thin, flat, small-headed nail. [variant of Middle English *brod* 'goad, pointed instrument', from Old Norse *broddr* 'spike']

bradawl /ˈbradɔːl/ *n.* a small tool with a pointed end for boring holes by hand. [BRAD + AWL]

bradycardia /bradɪˈkɑːdɪə/ *n. Med.* abnormally slow heart action. [Greek *bradus* 'slow' + *kardia* 'heart']

brae /breɪ/ *n. Sc.* a steep bank or hillside. [Middle English from Old Norse *brá* 'eyelash': related to German *Braue* 'eyebrow': cf. BROW]

brag /brag/ *v. & n.* ● *v.* (**bragged**, **bragging**) **1** *intr.* talk boastfully. **2** *tr.* boast about. ● *n.* **1** a card game like poker. **2** a boastful statement; boastful talk. □ **bragger** *n.* **braggingly** *adv.* [Middle English, originally adj., = spirited, boastful: origin unknown]

braggadocio /bragəˈdəʊtʃɪəʊ/ *n.* empty boasting; a boastful manner of speech and behaviour. [*Braggadochio*, a braggart in Spenser's *Faerie Queene*, from BRAG or BRAGGART + Italian augmentative suffix *-occio*]

braggart /ˈbragət, -ɑːt/ *n. & adj.* ● *n.* a person given to bragging. ● *adj.* boastful. [French *bragard* from *braguer* BRAG]

Brahma /ˈbrɑːmə/ *n.* **1** the creator god in Hinduism. **2** = BRAHMAN 2. [Sanskrit, nominative of *brahman* 'priest']

Brahman /ˈbrɑːmən/ *n.* (also **brahman**) (*pl.* **-mans**) **1** a member of the highest Hindu caste, the priesthood caste. **2** the supreme being or ground of the universe in the Hindu scriptures. □ **Brahmanic** /-ˈmanɪk/ *adj.* **Brahmanical** /-ˈmanɪk(ə)l/ *adj.* **Brahmanism** *n.* [Sanskrit *brāhmana* from *brahman* 'priest']

brahmaputra /brɑːməˈpuːtrə/ *n.* (also **brahma**) **1** any bird of a large Asian breed of domestic fowl. **2** this breed. [river *Brahmaputra* in India, from where it was brought]

Brahmin /ˈbrɑːmɪn/ *n.* **1** = BRAHMAN 1. **2** a socially or culturally superior person, esp. from New England. [variant of BRAHMAN]

braid /breɪd/ *n. & v.* ● *n.* **1** a woven band of silk or thread used for edging or trimming. **2** a length of entwined hair. ● *v.tr.* **1** plait or intertwine (hair or thread). **2** trim or decorate with braid. [Old English *bregdan*, from Germanic]

braiding /ˈbreɪdɪŋ/ *n.* **1** various types of braid collectively. **2** braided work.

brail /breɪl/ *n. & v.* ● *n.* (in *pl.*) small ropes on the sides of fore-and-aft sails for trussing them before furling. ● *v.tr.* (foll. by *up*) haul up (sails) using brails. [Middle English via Old French *brai(el)* from medieval Latin *bracale* 'girdle']

Braille /breɪl/ *n. & v.* ● *n.* a system of writing and printing for the blind, in which characters are represented by patterns of raised dots. ● *v.tr.* print or transcribe in Braille. [L. *Braille*, French teacher (d. 1852), inventor of the system]

brain /breɪn/ *n. & v.* ● *n.* **1** an organ of soft nervous tissue contained in the skull of vertebrates, functioning as the coordinating centre of sensation, and of intellectual and nervous activity. **2** (in *pl.*) the substance of the brain, esp. as food. **3** **a** a person's intellectual capacity (*has a poor brain*). **b** (often in *pl.*) intelligence; high intellectual capacity (*has a brain*; *has brains*). **4** (usu. in *pl.*; prec. by *the*) *colloq.* **a** the cleverest person in a group. **b** a person who originates a complex plan or idea (*the brains behind the robbery*). **5** an electronic device with functions comparable to those of a brain. ● *v.tr.* **1** dash out the brains of. **2** strike hard on the head. □ **on the brain** *colloq.* obsessively in one's thoughts. [Old English *brægen*, from West Germanic]

brainbox /ˈbreɪnbɒks/ *n. Brit. colloq.* a clever person.

brainchild /ˈbreɪntʃʌɪld/ *n.* (*pl.* **-children**) *colloq.* an idea, plan, or invention regarded as the result of a person's mental effort.

brain coral *n.* a compact coral with a convoluted surface resembling that of the brain.

brain damage *n.* injury to the brain (permanently) impairing its functions. □ **brain-damaged** *adj.*

brain-dead *adj.* **1** having suffered brain death. **2** *colloq. derog.* feeble-minded; lacking any vitality.

brain death *n.* irreversible brain damage causing the end of independent respiration, regarded as indicative of death.

brain drain *n. colloq.* the loss of academics and skilled personnel by emigration.

brain fever *n.* inflammation of the brain.

brainless /ˈbreɪnlɪs/ *adj.* stupid, foolish.

brainpan /ˈbreɪnpan/ *n. colloq.* the skull.

brainpower /ˈbreɪnpaʊə/ *n.* mental ability or intelligence.

brainstem /ˈbreɪnstɛm/ *n.* the central trunk of the brain, upon which the cerebrum and cerebellum are set, and which continues downwards to form the spinal cord.

brainstorm /ˈbreɪnstɔːm/ *n. & v.* ● *n.* **1** a violent or excited outburst often as a result of a sudden mental disturbance. **2** *colloq.* mental confusion. **3** *N. Amer.* = BRAINWAVE 2. **4** (also **brainstorming session**) a concerted intellectual treatment of a problem by discussing spontaneous ideas about it. ● *v.intr.* engage in a brainstorming session. □ **brainstorming** *n.* (in sense 4).

brains trust *n. Brit.* a group of experts who give impromptu answers to questions, usu. publicly.

brain-teaser *n.* (also **brain-twister**) *colloq.* a puzzle or problem.

brain trust *n. US* a group of expert advisers.

brainwash /ˈbreɪnwɒʃ/ *v.tr.* subject (a person) to a prolonged process by which ideas other than and at variance with those already held are implanted in the mind. □ **brainwashing** *n.*

brainwave /ˈbreɪnweɪv/ *n.* **1** (usu. in *pl.*) an electrical impulse in the brain. **2** *colloq.* a sudden bright idea.

brainy /ˈbreɪni/ *adj.* (**brainier**, **brainiest**) intellectually clever or active. □ **brainily** *adv.* **braininess** *n.*

braise /breɪz/ *v.tr.* fry lightly and then stew slowly with a little liquid in a closed container. [French *braiser* from *braise* 'live coals', among which the container was formerly placed]

brake[1] /breɪk/ *n. & v.* ● *n.* **1** (often in *pl.*) a device for checking the motion of a mechanism, esp. a wheel or vehicle, or for keeping it at rest. **2** anything that has the effect of hindering or impeding (*shortage of money was a brake on their enthusiasm*). ● *v.* **1** *intr.* apply a brake. **2** *tr.* retard or stop with a brake. [probably obsolete *brake* in sense 'machine-handle, bridle']

brake[2] /breɪk/ *n. Brit.* a large estate car. [variant of BREAK[2]]

brake[3] /breɪk/ *n. & v.* ● *n.* **1** a toothed instrument used for crushing flax and hemp. **2** (in full **brake harrow**) a heavy kind of harrow for breaking up large lumps of earth. ● *v.tr.* crush (flax or hemp) by beating it. [Middle English, related to BREAK[1]]

brake[4] /breɪk/ *n.* **1** a thicket. **2** brushwood. [Old English *bracu*, related to Middle Low German *brake* 'branch, stump']

brake[5] /breɪk/ *n.* bracken. [Middle English, perhaps shortened from BRACKEN, *-en* being taken as a pl. ending]

brake[6] *archaic past* of BREAK[1].

brake block *n.* **1** a block (usu. of hardened rubber) which is applied to a bicycle wheel as a brake. **2** a block used to hold a brake shoe.

brake disc *n.* a disc attached to a wheel on which the brake pad presses to brake.

brake drum *n.* a cylinder attached to a wheel on which the brake shoe presses to brake.

brake fluid *n.* fluid used in a hydraulic brake system.

brake harrow see BRAKE[3] *n.* 2.

brake horsepower *n.* the power of an engine reckoned in terms of the force needed to brake it.

brake lining *n.* a strip of fabric attached to a brake shoe to increase its friction.

brakeman /ˈbreɪkmən/ *n.* (*pl.* **-men**) **1** *US* a railway worker responsible for maintenance of a train on a journey. **2** a person in charge of brakes. [BRAKE[1] + MAN]

brake pad *n.* a block which presses on the brake disc when brakes are applied.

brake shoe *n.* a long curved block which presses on the brake drum when brakes are applied.

brakesman /ˈbreɪksmən/ *n.* (*pl.* **-men**) *Brit.* = BRAKEMAN 2.

brakevan /ˈbreɪkvan/ *n. Brit.* a railway coach or vehicle from which the train's brakes can be controlled.

bramble /ˈbramb(ə)l/ *n.* & *v.* ● *n.* **1** any of various thorny shrubs of the rose family bearing fleshy red or black berries, esp. the blackberry bush, *Rubus fructicosus*. **2** *Brit.* the edible berry of these shrubs. **3** any of various other shrubs of the rose family with similar foliage, esp. the dog rose, *Rosa canina*. ● *v.intr.* gather blackberries (*go brambling*). □ **brambly** *adj.* [Old English *bræmbel* (earlier *brǣmel*), from the Germanic base of BROOM]

brambling /ˈbramblɪŋ/ *n.* a northern Eurasian finch, *Fringilla montifringilla*, which has brightly coloured plumage with a white rump. [origin uncertain, perhaps related to German *Brämling* from West Germanic]

Bramley /ˈbramli/ *n.* (*pl.* **-eys**) (in full **Bramley's seedling**) a large green variety of cooking apple. [M. *Bramley*, English butcher in whose garden it is said to have first grown *c.*1850]

bran /bran/ *n.* grain husks separated from the flour. [Middle English from Old French, of unknown origin]

branch /brɑːn(t)ʃ/ *n.* & *v.* ● *n.* **1** a limb extending from a tree or bough. **2** a lateral extension or subdivision, esp. of a river, road, or railway. **3** a conceptual extension or subdivision, as of a family, knowledge, a subject, etc. **4** a local division or office etc. of a large business, as of a bank, library, etc. ● *v.intr.* (often foll. by *off*) **1** diverge from the main part. **2** divide into branches. **3** (of a tree) bear or send out branches. □ **branch out** extend one's field of interest. □ **branched** *adj.* **branchlet** *n.* **branchlike** *adj.* **branchy** *adj.* [Middle English via Old French *branche* from Late Latin *branca* 'paw']

branchia /ˈbraŋkɪə/ *n.pl.* (also **branchiae** /-kɪiː/) gills. □ **branchial** *adj.* **branchiate** /-kɪət, -kɪeɪt/ *adj.* [Latin *branchia*, pl. *-ae*, from Greek *bragkhia* pl.]

brand /brand/ *n.* & *v.* ● *n.* **1 a** a particular make of goods. **b** (in full **brand name**) an identifying trade mark, label, etc. **2** (usu. foll. by *of*) a special or characteristic kind (*brand of humour*). **3** an identifying mark burned on livestock or (formerly) prisoners etc. with a hot iron. **4** an iron used for this. **5** a piece of burning, smouldering, or charred wood. **6** a stigma; a mark of disgrace. **7** *poet.* **a** a torch. **b** a sword. **8** a kind of blight, leaving leaves with a burnt appearance. ● *v.tr.* **1** mark with a hot iron. **2** stigmatize; mark with disgrace (*they branded him a liar*; *was branded for life*). **3** impress unforgettably on one's mind. **4** assign a trade mark or label to. □ **brander** *n.* [Old English, from Germanic]

brandish /ˈbrandɪʃ/ *v.tr.* wave or flourish as a threat or in display. □ **brandisher** *n.* [Old French *brandir*, ultimately from Germanic, related to BRAND]

brand leader *n.* the leading or best-selling product of its type.

brandling /ˈbrandlɪŋ/ *n.* a red earthworm, *Eisenia foetida*, with rings of a brighter colour, which is often found in manure and used as bait. [BRAND + -LING[1]]

brand name *n.* **1** see BRAND 1b. **2** a product with an identifying trade mark, label, etc.

brand new *adj.* completely or obviously new.

brandy /ˈbrandi/ *n.* (*pl.* **-ies**) a strong alcoholic spirit distilled from wine or fermented fruit juice. [earlier *brand(e)wine* from Dutch *brandewijn* 'burnt (distilled) wine']

brandy ball *n. Brit.* a kind of brandy-flavoured sweet.

brandy butter *n. Brit.* a rich sweet hard sauce made with brandy, butter, and sugar.

brandy snap *n.* a crisp rolled gingerbread wafer usu. filled with cream.

brank-ursine /braŋkˈəːsɪn/ *n.* = BEAR'S BREECH. [French *branche ursine*, medieval Latin *branca ursina* 'bear's claw': see BRANCH, URSINE]

brant *US* var. of BRENT.

bran tub *n. Brit.* a lucky dip with prizes concealed in bran.

brash[1] /braʃ/ *adj.* **1** vulgarly or ostentatiously self-assertive. **2** hasty, rash. **3** impudent. □ **brashly** *adv.* **brashness** *n.* [originally dialect, perhaps from RASH[1]]

brash[2] /braʃ/ *n.* **1** loose broken rock or ice. **2** clippings from hedges, shrubs, etc. [18th c.: origin unknown]

brass /brɑːs/ *n.* & *adj.* ● *n.* **1** a yellow alloy of copper and zinc. **2 a** an ornament or other decorated piece of brass. **b** brass objects collectively. **3** *Mus.* brass wind instruments (including trumpet, horn, trombone) forming a band or a section of an orchestra. **4** *Brit. slang* money. **5** (in full **horse brass**) a round flat brass ornament for the harness of a draught horse. **6** (in full **top brass**) *colloq.* persons in authority or of high (esp. military) rank. **7** *Brit.* an inscribed or engraved memorial tablet of brass. **8** *colloq.* effrontery (*then had the brass to demand money*). **9** a brass block or die used for making a design on a book binding. ● *adj.* made of brass. □ **brassed off** *Brit. slang* fed up. **not a brass farthing** *colloq.* no money or assets at all. [Old English *bræs*, of unknown origin]

brassard /ˈbrasɑːd/ *n.* a band worn on the sleeve, esp. with a uniform. [French *bras* 'arm' + -ARD]

brass band *n.* a group of musicians playing brass instruments, sometimes also with percussion.

brasserie /ˈbrasəri/ *n.* a restaurant, originally one serving beer with food. [French, = brewery]

brass hat *n. Brit. colloq.* an officer of high rank, usu. one with gold braid on the cap.

brassica /ˈbrasɪkə/ *n.* any cruciferous plant of the genus *Brassica*, having tap roots and erect branched stems, including cabbage, swede, Brussels sprout, mustard, rape, cauliflower, kohlrabi, calabrese, kale, and turnip. [Latin, = cabbage]

brassie /ˈbrasi, ˈbrɑːsi/ *n.* (also **brassy**) (*pl.* **-ies**) a wooden-headed golf club with a brass sole.

brassiere /ˈbrasɪə, -z-/ *n.* = BRA. [French, = child's vest]

brass monkey *n.* (in phr. **cold enough to freeze the balls off a brass monkey** and similar expressions) used to indicate extreme cold. [from a type of brass rack or 'monkey' in which cannon balls were stored and which contracted in very cold weather, ejecting the balls]

brass rubbing *n.* **1** the rubbing of heelball etc. over paper laid on an engraved brass to take an impression of its design. **2** an impression obtained by this.

brass tacks *n.pl. slang* actual details; real business (*get down to brass tacks*).

brassy[1] /ˈbrɑːsi/ *adj.* (**brassier**, **brassiest**) **1** like brass, esp. in colour. **2** impudent. **3** pretentious, showy. **4** loud and blaring. □ **brassily** *adv.* **brassiness** *n.*

brassy[2] var. of BRASSIE.

brat /brat/ *n.* usu. *derog.* a child, esp. a badly behaved one. ▫ **bratty** *adj.* [perhaps abbreviation of Scots *bratchet* 'infant', or from *brat* 'rough garment']

brat pack *n. slang* a rowdy and ostentatious group of young celebrities, esp. film stars. ▫ **brat packer** *n.*

brattice /'bratıs/ *n.* a wooden partition or shaft lining in a coal mine. [Middle English, ultimately from Old English *brittisc* BRITISH]

bratwurst /'bratvə:st/ *n.* a type of small German pork sausage. [German from *braten* 'fry, roast' + *Wurst* 'sausage']

bravado /brə'vɑ:dəʊ/ *n.* a bold manner or a show of boldness intended to impress. [Spanish *bravata* from *bravo*: cf. BRAVE, -ADO]

brave /breıv/ *adj., n., & v.* ● *adj.* **1** able or ready to face and endure danger or pain. **2** *formal* splendid, spectacular (*make a brave show*). ● *n.* an American Indian warrior. ● *v.tr.* defy; encounter bravely. ▫ **brave it out** behave defiantly under suspicion or blame. ▫ **bravely** *adv.* **braveness** *n.* [Middle English from French, via Italian or Spanish *bravo* 'courageous, untamed, savage', from Latin *barbarus* BARBAROUS]

bravery /'breıv(ə)ri/ *n.* **1** brave conduct. **2** a brave nature. [French *braverie* or Italian *braveria* (as BRAVE)]

bravo[1] /brɑ:'vəʊ, 'brɑ:vəʊ/ *int. & n.* ● *int.* expressing approval of a performer etc. ● *n.* (*pl.* **-os**) a cry of bravo. [French from Italian: see BRAVE]

bravo[2] /'brɑ:vəʊ/ *n.* (*pl.* **-oes** or **-os**) a hired ruffian or killer. [Italian: see BRAVE]

bravura /brə'v(j)ʊərə/ *n.* (often *attrib.*) **1** a brilliant or ambitious action or display. **2 a** a style of (esp. vocal) music requiring exceptional ability. **b** a passage of this kind. **3** bravado. [Italian, from *bravo* BRAVE]

braw /brɔ:/ *adj. Sc.* fine, good. [variant of *brawf* BRAVE]

brawl /brɔ:l/ *n. & v.* ● *n.* a noisy quarrel or fight. ● *v.intr.* **1** quarrel noisily or roughly. **2** (of a stream) run noisily. ▫ **brawler** *n.* [Middle English, probably ultimately related to BRAY[1]]

brawn /brɔ:n/ *n.* **1** muscular strength. **2** muscle; lean flesh. **3** *Brit.* a jellied preparation of the chopped meat from a boiled pig's head. [Middle English via Anglo-French *braun*, Old French *braon* from Germanic]

brawny /'brɔ:ni/ *adj.* (**brawnier**, **brawniest**) muscular, strong. ▫ **brawniness** *n.*

bray[1] /breı/ *n. & v.* ● *n.* **1** the cry of a donkey. **2** a sound like this cry, e.g. that of a harshly played brass instrument, a laugh, etc. ● *v.* **1** *intr.* make a braying sound. **2** *tr.* utter harshly. [Middle English from Old French *braire* 'to cry', perhaps ultimately from Celtic]

bray[2] /breı/ *v.tr. archaic* pound or crush to small pieces, esp. with a pestle and mortar. [Middle English from Anglo-French *braier*, Old French *breier* from the Germanic base of BREAK[1]]

braze[1] /breız/ *v. & n.* ● *v.tr.* solder with an alloy of copper and zinc at a high temperature. ● *n.* **1** a brazed joint. **2** the alloy used for brazing. [French *braser* 'solder' from *braise* 'live coals']

braze[2] /breız/ *v.tr.* **1 a** make of brass. **b** cover or ornament with brass. **2** make hard like brass. [Old English *bræsen* from *bræs* 'brass']

brazen /'breız(ə)n/ *adj. & v.* ● *adj.* **1** (also **brazen-faced**) flagrant and shameless; insolent. **2** of or like brass. **3** harsh in sound. ● *v.tr.* (foll. by *out*) face or undergo defiantly. ▫ **brazen it out** be defiantly unrepentant under censure. ▫ **brazenly** *adv.* **brazenness** /'breız(ə)nnıs/ *n.* [Old English *bræsen* from *bræs* brass]

brazier[1] /'breızjə, -ʒə/ *n.* **1** a portable heater consisting of a pan or stand for holding lighted coals. **2** *N. Amer.* a charcoal grill for cooking. [French *brasier* from *braise* 'hot coals']

brazier[2] /'breızjə, -ʒə/ *n.* a worker in brass. ▫ **braziery** *n.* [Middle English probably from BRASS + -IER, on the pattern of *glass, glazier*]

brazil /brə'zıl/ *n.* **1** (in full **Brazil nut**) a large three-sided nut with an edible kernel, obtained from the S. American forest tree *Bertholletia excelsa*. **2** (in full **Brazil wood**) a hard red wood from any tropical tree of the genus *Caesalpinia*, yielding dyes. [medieval Latin *brasilium*; the S. American country *Brazil* is named from the wood]

BRCS *abbr.* British Red Cross Society.

breach /bri:tʃ/ *n. & v.* ● *n.* **1** (often foll. by *of*) the breaking of or failure to observe a law, contract, etc. **2 a** a breaking of relations; an estrangement. **b** a quarrel. **3 a** a broken state. **b** a gap, esp. one made by artillery in fortifications. ● *v.tr.* **1** break through; make a gap in. **2** break (a law, contract, etc.). ▫ **stand in the breach** *archaic* bear the brunt of an attack. **step into the breach** give help in a crisis, esp. by replacing someone who has dropped out. [Middle English from Old French *breche*, ultimately from the Germanic base of BREAK[1]]

breach of promise *n.* the breaking of a promise, esp. a promise to marry.

breach of the peace *n.* an infringement or violation of the public peace by any disturbance or riot etc.

bread /brɛd/ *n. & v.* ● *n.* **1** baked dough made from flour usu. leavened with yeast and moistened, eaten as a staple food. **2 a** necessary food. **b** (also **daily bread**) one's livelihood. **3** *slang* money. ● *v.tr.* coat with breadcrumbs for cooking. ▫ **bread and circuses** the public provision of subsistence and entertainment. **bread and wine** the Eucharist. **cast one's bread upon the waters** do good without expecting gratitude or reward. **know which side one's bread is buttered** (or *US* **buttered on**) know where one's advantage lies. **take the bread out of a person's mouth** take away a person's living, esp. by competition etc. [Old English *brēad*, from Germanic]

bread and butter *n.* **1** bread spread with butter. **2 a** one's livelihood. **b** routine work to ensure an income (often, with hyphens, *attrib.*: *bread-and-butter sales*).

bread-and-butter letter *n.* a letter of thanks for hospitality.

breadbasket /'brɛdbɑ:skıt/ *n.* **1** a basket for bread or rolls. **2** *slang* the stomach. **3** a region etc. that supplies cereals to another.

bread bin *n. Brit.* a container for keeping bread in.

breadboard /'brɛdbɔ:d/ *n.* **1** a board for cutting bread on. **2** a board for making an experimental model of an electric circuit.

breadcrumb /'brɛdkrʌm/ *n.* **1** a small fragment of bread. **2** (in *pl.*) bread crumbled for use in cooking.

breadfruit /'brɛdfru:t/ *n.* **1** (also **breadfruit tree**) a tropical evergreen tree, *Artocarpus altilis*, bearing edible usu. seedless fruit. **2** the fruit of this tree, which when roasted becomes soft like new bread.

breadline /'brɛdlʌın/ *n.* **1** *Brit.* subsistence level (esp. *on the breadline*). **2** *N. Amer.* a queue of people waiting to receive free food.

bread sauce *n.* a white sauce thickened with breadcrumbs.

breadth /brɛdθ, -tθ/ *n.* **1** the distance or measurement from side to side of a thing; broadness. **2** a piece (of cloth etc.) of standard or full breadth. **3** extent, distance, room. **4** (usu. foll. by *of*) capacity to respect other opinions; freedom from prejudice or intolerance (esp. *breadth of mind* or *view*). **5** *Art* unity of the whole, achieved by the disregard of unnecessary details. ▫ **breadthways** *adv.* **breadthwise** *adv.* [obsolete *brede*, Old English *brǣdu*, from Germanic, related to BROAD]

breadwinner /'brɛdwınə/ *n.* a person who earns the money to support a family.

break[1] /breık/ *v. & n.* ● *v.* (*past* **broke** /brəʊk/ or *archaic* **brake** /breık/; *past part.* **broken** /'brəʊkən/ or *archaic* **broke**) **1** *tr. & intr.* **a** separate into pieces under a blow or strain; shatter. **b** make or become inoperative, esp. from damage (*the toaster has broken*). **c** break a bone in or dislocate (part of the body). **d** break the skin of (the head or crown). **2 a** *tr.* cause or effect an interruption in (*broke our journey*; *the spell was broken*; *broke the silence*). **b** *intr.* have an interval between spells of work (*let's break now; we broke for tea*). **3** *tr.* fail to observe or keep (a law, promise, etc.). **4 a** *tr. & intr.* make or become subdued or weakened; yield or cause to yield (*broke his spirit; he broke under the strain*). **b** *tr.* weaken the effect of (a fall, blow, etc.). **c** *tr.* = *break in* 3c. **d** *tr.* defeat, destroy (*broke the enemy's power*). **e** *tr.* defeat the object of (a strike, e.g. by engaging other personnel). **5** *tr.* surpass (a record). **6** *intr.* (foll. by *with*) quarrel or cease association with (another person etc.). **7** *tr.* **a** be no longer subject to (a habit). **b** (foll. by *of*) cause (a person) to be free of a habit (*broke them of their addiction*). **8** *tr. & intr.* reveal or be revealed; (cause to) become known (*broke the news; the story broke on Friday*). **9** *intr.* **a** (of the weather) change suddenly, esp. after a fine spell. **b** (of waves) curl over and dissolve into foam. **c** (of the day) dawn. **d** (of clouds) move apart; show a gap. **e** (of a storm) begin violently. **10** *tr. Electr.* disconnect (a circuit) (opp. MAKE *v.* 23). **11** *intr.* **a** (of the voice) change with emotion. **b** (of a boy's voice) change in register etc. at puberty. **12** *tr.* **a** (often foll. by *up*) divide (a set etc.) into parts, e.g. by selling to different buyers. **b** change (a banknote etc.) for coins. **13** *tr.* ruin (an individual or institution) financially (see also BROKE *predic.adj.*). **14** *tr.* penetrate (e.g. a safe) by force. **15** *tr.* decipher (a code). **16** *tr.* make (a way, path, etc.) by separating obstacles. **17** *intr.* burst forth (*the sun broke through the clouds*). **18** *Mil.* **a** *intr.* (of troops) disperse in confusion. **b** *tr.* make a rupture in (ranks). **19 a** *intr.* (usu. foll. by *free, loose, out,* etc.) escape from constraint by a sudden effort. **b** *tr.* escape or emerge from (prison, bounds, cover, etc.). **20** *tr. Tennis etc.* win a game against (an opponent's service). **21** *intr. Boxing* etc. (of two fighters, usu. at the referee's command) come out of a clinch. **22** *Mil. tr.* demote (an officer). **23** *intr.* esp. *Stock Exch.* (of prices) fall sharply. **24** *intr. Cricket* (of a bowled ball) change direction on bouncing. **25** *intr. Billiards* etc. make the first stroke at the beginning of a game. **26** *tr.* unfurl (a flag etc.). **27** *tr. Phonet.* subject (a vowel) to fracture. **28** *tr.* fail to rejoin (one's ship) after absence on leave. **29** *tr.* disprove (an alibi). ● *n.* **1 a** an act or instance of breaking. **b** a point where something is broken; a gap. **2** an interval, an interruption; a pause in work. **3** a sudden dash (esp. to escape). **4** *colloq.* **a** a piece of good luck; a fair chance. **b** (also **bad break**) an unfortunate remark or action, a blunder. **5** *Cricket* a change in direction of a bowled ball on bouncing. **6** *Billiards* etc. **a** a series of points scored during one turn. **b** the opening shot that disperses the balls. **7** *Mus.* (in jazz etc.) a short unaccompanied passage for a soloist, usu. improvised. **8** *Electr.* a discontinuity in a circuit. □ **break away** make or become free or separate (see also BREAKAWAY). **break the back of 1** do the hardest or greatest part of. **2** overburden (a person). **break bulk** see BULK. **break down 1 a** fail in mechanical action; cease to function. **b** (of human relationships etc.) fail, collapse. **c** fail in (esp. mental) health. **d** be overcome by emotion; collapse in tears. **2 a** demolish, destroy. **b** overcome (resistance). **c** force (a person) to yield under pressure. **3** analyse into components (see also BREAKDOWN). **break even** emerge from a transaction etc. with neither profit nor loss. **break a person's heart** see HEART. **break the ice 1** begin to overcome formality or shyness, esp. between strangers. **2** make a start. **break in 1** enter premises by force, esp. with criminal intent. **2** interrupt. **3 a** accustom to a habit etc. **b** wear etc. until comfortable. **c** esp. *Brit.* tame or discipline (an animal); accustom (a horse) to saddle and bridle etc. **4** *Austral. & NZ* bring (virgin land) into cultivation. **break in on** disturb; interrupt. **break into 1** enter forcibly or violently. **2 a** suddenly begin, burst forth with (a song, laughter, etc.). **b** suddenly change one's pace for (a faster one) (*broke into a gallop*). **3** interrupt. **break a leg** (as *int.*) *Theatr. slang* good luck. **break new** (or **fresh**) **ground** see GROUND[1]. **break of day** dawn. **break off 1** detach by breaking. **2** bring to an end. **3** cease talking etc. **break open** open forcibly. **break out 1** escape by force, esp. from prison. **2** begin suddenly; burst forth (*then violence broke out*). **3** (foll. by *in*) become covered in (a rash etc.). **4** exclaim. **5** release (a run-up flag). **6** *US* **a** open up (a receptacle) and remove its contents. **b** remove (articles) from a place of storage. **break step** get out of step. **break up 1** break into small pieces. **2** disperse; disband. **3** *Brit.* end the school term. **4 a** terminate a relationship; disband. **b** cause to do this. **5** *Brit.* (of the weather) change suddenly (esp. after a fine spell). **6** esp. *US* **a** upset or be upset. **b** excite or be excited. **c** convulse or be convulsed (see also BREAK-UP). **break wind** release gas from the anus. **break one's word** see WORD. [Old English *brecan*, from Germanic: related to BRAY[2], BREACH]

break[2] /breɪk/ *n.* **1** a carriage frame without a body, for breaking in young horses. **2** = BRAKE[2]. [perhaps = *brake* framework: 17th c., of unknown origin]

breakable /'breɪkəb(ə)l/ *adj. & n.* ● *adj.* that may or is apt to be broken easily. ● *n.* (esp. in *pl.*) a breakable thing.

breakage /'breɪkɪdʒ/ *n.* **1** an act or instance of breaking. **2 a** a broken thing. **b** damage caused by breaking.

breakaway /'breɪkəweɪ/ *n.* **1** the act or an instance of breaking away or seceding. **2** (*attrib.*) that breaks away or has broken away; separate. **3** *Austral.* a stampede, esp. at the sight or smell of water. **4** a false start in a race. **5** *Rugby* each of the two flank forwards on the outsides of the second row of a scrum formation.

break crop *n.* a crop grown to avoid the continual growing of cereals.

break-dancing *n.* an energetic and acrobatic style of street dancing, developed by US blacks.

breakdown /'breɪkdaʊn/ *n.* **1 a** a mechanical failure. **b** a loss of (esp. mental) health and strength. **2** a collapse or disintegration (*breakdown of communication*). **3** a detailed analysis (of statistics etc.).

breaker /'breɪkə/ *n.* **1** a person or thing that breaks something, esp. *Brit.* disused machinery. **2** a person who breaks in a horse. **3** a heavy wave that breaks.

breakfast /'brɛkfəst/ *n. & v.* ● *n.* the first meal of the day. ● *v.intr.* have breakfast. □ **have for breakfast** *slang* make mincemeat of (a person); defeat easily. □ **breakfaster** *n.* [BREAK[1] 'interrupt' + FAST[2]]

breakfast television *n.* early-morning television.

break-in *n.* an illegal forced entry into premises, esp. with criminal intent.

breaking and entering *n. Brit. hist. & US Law* the illegal entering of a building with intent to commit a felony.

breaking point *n.* the point of greatest strain, at which a thing breaks or a person gives way.

break-line *n. Printing* the last line of a paragraph (usu. not of full length).

breakneck /'breɪknɛk/ *attrib.adj.* (of speed) dangerously fast.

breakout /'breɪkaʊt/ *n.* a forcible escape.

break point *n.* **1** a place or time at which an interruption or change is made. **2** (usu. **breakpoint**) *Computing* a place in a computer program where the sequence of instructions is interrupted, esp. by another program. **3** *Tennis* **a** a point which would win the game for the player(s) receiving service (*three break points*). **b** the situation at which the receiver(s) may win such a point (*this is break point*). **4** = BREAKING POINT.

breakthrough /'breɪkθruː/ *n.* **1** a major advance or discovery. **2** an act of breaking through an obstacle etc.

break-up *n.* **1** the disintegration or collapse of a thing. **2** a dispersal.

breakwater /'breɪkwɔːtə/ *n.* a barrier built out into the sea to break the force of waves.

bream[1] /briːm/ *n.* (*pl.* same) **1** a yellowish deep-bodied freshwater fish, *Abramis brama*, of the carp family. **2** (in full **sea bream**) a similarly shaped marine fish of the family Sparidae, esp. of the genus *Pagellus* or *Spondyliosoma*, of the NE Atlantic. [Middle English via Old French *bre(s)me* from West Germanic]

bream[2] /bri:m/ *v.tr. Naut. hist.* clean (a ship's bottom) by burning and scraping. [probably from Low German and related to BROOM]

breast /brɛst/ *n. & v.* ● *n.* **1 a** either of two milk-secreting organs on the upper front of a woman's body. **b** the corresponding usu. rudimentary part of a man's body. **2 a** the upper front part of a human body; the chest. **b** the corresponding part of an animal. **3** the part of a garment that covers the breast. **4** the breast as a source of nourishment or emotion. ● *v.tr.* **1** face, meet in full opposition (*breast the wind*). **2** contend with (*breast it out against difficulties*). **3** reach the top of (a hill). □ **breast the tape** see TAPE. **make a clean breast of** (esp. in phr. **make a clean breast of it**) confess fully. □ **breasted** *adj.* (also in *comb.*). [Old English *brēost*, from Germanic]

breastbone /ˈbrɛs(t)bəʊn/ *n.* a thin flat vertical bone and cartilage in the chest connecting the ribs; the sternum.

breastfeed /ˈbrɛs(t)fi:d/ *v.* (*past* and *past part.* **-fed**) **1** *tr.* feed (a baby) from the breast. **2** *intr.* (of a baby) feed from the breast.

breast-high *adj. & adv.* as high as the breast; submerged to the breast.

breast-pin *n.* a brooch etc. worn on the breast.

breastplate /ˈbrɛs(t)pleɪt/ *n.* a piece of armour covering the breast.

breaststroke /brɛs(t)strəʊk/ *n.* a stroke made while swimming on the breast by extending arms forward and sweeping them back in unison.

breastsummer /ˈbrɛs(t)sʌmə/ *n. Archit.* a beam across a broad opening, sustaining a superstructure. [BREAST + SUMMER[2]]

breastwork /ˈbrɛs(t)wɜ:k/ *n.* a low temporary defence or parapet.

breath /brɛθ/ *n.* **1 a** the air taken into or expelled from the lungs. **b** one respiration of air. **c** an exhalation of air that can be seen, smelt, or heard (*breath steamed in the cold air*; *bad breath*). **2 a** a slight movement of air; a breeze. **b** a whiff of perfume etc. **3** a whisper, a murmur (esp. of a scandalous nature). **4** the power of breathing; life (*is there breath in him?*). □ **below** (or **under**) **one's breath** in a whisper. **breath of fresh air 1** a small amount of or a brief time in the fresh air. **2** a refreshing change. **breath of life** a necessity. **catch one's breath 1** cease breathing momentarily in surprise, suspense, etc. **2** rest after exercise to restore normal breathing. **draw breath** breathe; live. **hold one's breath** cease breathing temporarily. **in the same breath** (esp. of saying two contradictory things) within a short time. **out of breath** gasping for air, esp. after exercise. **take breath** pause for rest. **take one's breath away** astound; surprise; awe; delight. **waste one's breath** talk or give advice without effect. [Old English *brǣth*, from Germanic]

breathable /ˈbri:ðəb(ə)l/ *adj.* **1** (of the air etc.) fit or pleasant to breathe. **2** (of material) admitting air to the skin and allowing sweat to evaporate.

breathalyser /ˈbrɛθəlʌɪzə/ *n.* (*US & propr.* **breathalyzer**) an instrument for measuring the amount of alcohol in the breath (and hence in the blood) of a driver. □ **breathalyse** *v.tr.* (*US* **-lyze**). [BREATH + ANALYSE + -ER[1]]

breathe /bri:ð/ *v.* **1** *intr.* **a** take air into and expel it from the lungs. **b** take in oxygen. **2** *intr.* be or seem alive (*is she breathing?*). **3** *tr.* **a** utter; say (esp. quietly) (*breathed her forgiveness*). **b** express; display (*breathed defiance*). **4** *intr.* take breath, pause. **5** *tr.* send out or take in (as if) with breathed air; inhale (*breathed new life into them; breathed whisky*). **6** *intr.* **a** (of wine, the skin, etc.) be exposed to fresh air. **b** (of material) admit air or moisture. **7** *intr.* **a** sound, speak (esp. quietly). **b** (of wind) blow softly. **8** *tr.* allow (a horse etc.) to breathe; give rest after exertion. □ **breathe again** (or **freely**) recover from a shock, fear, etc., and be at ease. **breathe down a person's neck** follow or check up on a person, esp. menacingly. **breathe in** inhale. **breathe one's last** die. **breathe out** exhale. **breathe upon** *literary* tarnish, taint. **not breathe a word** keep silent. **not breathe a word of** keep quite secret. [Middle English, from BREATH]

breather /ˈbri:ðə/ *n.* **1** *colloq.* a brief pause for rest. **2** a safety-vent in the crankcase of a motor vehicle etc.

breathing /ˈbri:ðɪŋ/ *n.* **1** the process of taking air into and expelling it from the lungs. **2** a sign in Greek (ʻ or ʼ) indicating the presence of an aspirate (**rough breathing**) or the absence of an aspirate (**smooth breathing**).

breathing-space *n.* time to breathe; a pause.

breathless /ˈbrɛθlɪs/ *adj.* **1** panting, out of breath. **2** holding, or as if holding, the breath because of excitement, suspense, etc. (*a state of breathless expectancy*). **3** unstirred by wind; still. □ **breathlessly** *adv.* **breathlessness** *n.*

breathtaking /ˈbrɛθteɪkɪŋ/ *adj.* astounding; awe-inspiring. □ **breathtakingly** *adv.*

breath test *n. & v.* ● *n.* a test of a person's alcohol consumption, using a breathalyser. ● *v.tr.* (**breath-test**) administer a breath test to.

breathy /ˈbrɛθi/ *adj.* (**breathier**, **breathiest**) (of a singing voice etc.) containing the sound of breathing. □ **breathily** *adv.* **breathiness** *n.*

breccia /ˈbrɛtʃə, -tʃɪə/ *n. & v.* ● *n.* a rock of angular stones etc. cemented by finer material. ● *v.tr.* form into breccia. □ **brecciate** *v.tr.* **brecciation** /-ˈeɪʃ(ə)n/ *n.* [Italian, = gravel, from Germanic, related to BREAK[1]]

bred *past* and *past part.* of BREED.

breech /bri:tʃ/ *n. & v.* ● *n.* **1 a** the part of a cannon behind the bore. **b** the back part of a rifle or gun barrel. **2** *archaic* the buttocks. ● *v.tr. archaic* put (a boy) into breeches after being in petticoats since birth. [Old English *brōc*, pl. *brēc* (treated as sing. in Middle English), from Germanic]

breech birth *n.* (also **breech delivery**) the delivery of a baby which is so positioned in the womb that the buttocks or feet are delivered first.

breech-block *n.* a metal block which closes the breech aperture in a gun.

breeches /ˈbrɪtʃɪz/ *n.pl.* (also **pair of breeches** *sing.*) **1** short trousers, esp. fastened below the knee, now used esp. for riding or in court dress. **2** *colloq.* any trousers, knickerbockers, or underpants. [pl. of BREECH]

Breeches Bible *n.* the Geneva Bible of 1560 with *breeches* in Gen. 3:7 for the garments made by Adam and Eve.

breeches-buoy *n.* a lifebuoy suspended from a rope which has canvas breeches for the user's legs.

breech-loader *n.* a gun loaded at the breech, not through the muzzle. □ **breech-loading** *adj.*

breed /bri:d/ *v. & n.* ● *v.* (*past* and *past part.* **bred** /bred/) **1** *tr. & intr.* bear, generate (offspring). **2** *tr. & intr.* propagate or cause to propagate; raise (livestock). **3** *tr.* **a** yield, produce; result in (*war breeds famine*). **b** spread (*discontent bred by rumour*). **4** *intr.* arise; spread (*disease breeds in the Tropics*). **5** *tr.* bring up; train (*bred to the law*; *Hollywood breeds stars*). **6** *tr. Physics* create (fissile material) by nuclear reaction. ● *n.* **1** a stock of animals or plants within a species, having a similar appearance, and usu. developed by deliberate selection. **2** a race; a lineage. **3** a sort, a kind. □ **bred and born** = *born and bred* (see BORN). **bred in the bone** hereditary. **breed in** mate with or marry near relations. □ **breeder** *n.* [Old English *brēdan*: related to BROOD]

breeder reactor *n.* a nuclear reactor that can create more fissile material than it consumes.

breeding /ˈbri:dɪŋ/ *n.* **1** the process of developing or propagating (animals, plants, etc.). **2** generation; childbearing. **3** the result of training or education; behaviour. **4** good manners (as produced by an aristocratic heredity) (*has no breeding*).

breeks /bri:ks/ *n.pl. Sc.* breeches.

breeze[1] /bri:z/ *n. & v.* ● *n.* **1** a gentle wind. **2** *Meteorol.* a wind of force 2 to 6 on the Beaufort scale (4–31 m.p.h.). **3** a wind blowing from land at night or sea during the day. **4** esp. *Brit. colloq.* a quarrel or display of temper. **5** esp. *N. Amer. colloq.* an easy task. ● *v.intr.* (foll. by *in, out, along,* etc.) *colloq.* come or go in a casual or light-hearted manner. [probably from Old Spanish & Portuguese *briza* 'NE wind']

breeze[2] /bri:z/ *n.* small cinders. [French *braise* 'live coals']

breeze[3] /bri:z/ *n. Brit.* a gadfly or cleg. [Old English *briosa*, of unknown origin]

breeze-block *n. Brit.* a lightweight building block, esp. one made from breeze mixed with sand and cement.

breezy /'bri:zi/ *adj.* (**breezier**, **breeziest**) **1 a** windswept. **b** pleasantly windy. **2** *colloq.* lively; jovial. **3** *colloq.* careless (*with breezy indifference*). □ **breezily** *adv.* **breeziness** *n.*

bremsstrahlung /'brɛmzʃtrɑːlʊŋ/ *n.* (often *attrib.*) *Physics* electromagnetic radiation produced by the acceleration or esp. the deceleration of a charged particle after passing through the electric and magnetic fields of a nucleus. [German, = braking radiation]

Bren /brɛn/ *n.* (in full **Bren gun**) a lightweight quick-firing machine-gun. [*Br*no in the Czech Republic (where originally made) + *En*field in England (where later made)]

brent /brɛnt/ *n.* (*US* **brant** /brant/) (in full **brent-goose**) a small migratory Arctic-breeding goose, *Branta bernicla*, with black, grey, and white plumage. [16th c.: origin unknown]

brethren see BROTHER.

Breton /'brɛt(ə)n/ *n. & adj.* ● *n.* **1** a native of Brittany. **2** the Celtic language of Brittany. ● *adj.* of or relating to Brittany or its people or language. [Old French, = BRITON]

breve /bri:v/ *n.* **1** *Mus.* a note, now rarely used, having the time value of two semibreves. **2** a written or printed mark (˘) indicating a short or unstressed vowel. **3** *hist.* an authoritative letter from a sovereign or pope. [Middle English variant of BRIEF]

brevet /'brɛvɪt/ *n. & v.* ● *n.* (often *attrib.*) a document conferring a privilege from a sovereign or government, esp. a rank in the army, without the appropriate pay (*was promoted by brevet; brevet major*). ● *v.tr.* (**breveted**, **breveting** or **brevetted**, **brevetting**) confer brevet rank on. [Middle English, from Old French *brievet* 'little letter', diminutive of *bref* BRIEF]

breviary /'bri:vɪəri/ *n.* (*pl.* **-ies**) *RC Ch.* a book containing the service for each day, to be recited by those in orders. [earlier also, an abridged version of the psalms: Latin *breviarium* 'summary' from *breviare* 'abridge': see ABBREVIATE]

brevity /'brɛvɪti/ *n.* **1** economy of expression; conciseness. **2** shortness (of time etc.) (*the brevity of happiness*). [Anglo-French *breveté*, Old French *brieveté* from *bref* BRIEF]

brew /bru:/ *v. & n.* ● *v.* **1** *tr.* **a** make (beer etc.) by infusion, boiling, and fermentation. **b** make (tea etc.) by infusion or (punch etc.) by mixture. **2** *intr.* undergo either of these processes (*the tea is brewing*). **3** *intr.* (of trouble, a storm, etc.) gather force; threaten (*mischief was brewing*). **4** *tr.* bring about; set in train; concoct (*brewed their fiendish scheme*). ● *n.* **1** an amount (of beer etc.) brewed at one time (*this year's brew*). **2** what is brewed (esp. with regard to its quality) (*a good strong brew*). **3** the action or process of brewing. □ **brew up** *Brit.* make tea. □ **brewer** *n.* [Old English *brēowan*, from Germanic]

brewery /'brʊəri/ *n.* (*pl.* **-ies**) a place where beer etc. is brewed commercially.

brew-up *n. Brit. colloq.* an instance of making tea.

briar[1] var. of BRIER[1].

briar[2] var. of BRIER[2].

bribe /brʌɪb/ *v. & n.* ● *v.tr.* (often foll. by *to* + infin.) persuade (a person etc.) to act esp. illegally or dishonestly in one's favour by a gift of money, services, etc. (*bribed the guard to release the suspect*). ● *n.* money or services offered in the process of bribing. □ **bribable** *adj.* **briber** *n.* **bribery** *n.* [Middle English from Old French *briber*, *brimber* 'beg', of unknown origin]

bric-a-brac /'brɪkəbrak/ *n.* (also **bric-à-brac**, **bricabrac**) miscellaneous, often old, ornaments, trinkets, furniture, etc., of no great value. [French from obsolete *à bric et à brac* 'at random']

brick /brɪk/ *n., v., & adj.* ● *n.* **1 a** a small, usu. rectangular, block of fired or sun-dried clay, used in building. **b** the material used to make these. **c** a similar block of concrete etc. **2** *Brit.* a child's toy building block. **3** a brick-shaped solid object (*a brick of ice cream*). **4** *slang* a generous or loyal person. ● *v.tr.* (foll. by *in, up*) close or block with brickwork. ● *adj.* **1** built of brick (*brick wall*). **2** of a dull red colour. □ **bang** (or **knock** or **run**) **one's head against a brick wall** have one's efforts come to nothing; be continually rebuffed. **like a ton of bricks** *colloq.* with crushing weight, force, or authority. **see through a brick wall** have miraculous insight. □ **bricky** *adj.* [Middle English from Middle Low German, Middle Dutch *bri(c)ke*, of unknown origin]

brickbat /'brɪkbat/ *n.* **1** a piece of brick, esp. when used as a missile. **2** an uncomplimentary remark.

brick-built *adj.* (usu. *attrib.*) *Brit.* built of bricks.

brick-field *n.* a place at which bricks are made.

brickfielder /'brɪkfi:ldə/ *n. Austral.* a hot, dry north wind.

brickie /'brɪki/ *n. Brit. slang* a bricklayer.

bricklayer /'brɪkleɪə/ *n.* a worker who builds with bricks. □ **bricklaying** *n.*

brick red *n. & adj.* ● *n.* the dull red colour typical of bricks. ● *adj.* (hyphenated when *attrib.*) of this colour.

brickwork /'brɪkwə:k/ *n.* **1** work executed in brick. **2** building with bricks; bricklaying.

brickyard /'brɪkjɑ:d/ *n.* a place where bricks are made.

bridal /'brʌɪd(ə)l/ *adj.* of or concerning a bride or a wedding. □ **bridally** *adv.* [originally as noun, = wedding-feast, from Old English *brȳd-ealu* from *brȳd* BRIDE + *ealu* 'ale-drinking']

bride /brʌɪd/ *n.* a woman on her wedding day and for some time before and after it. [Old English *brȳd*, from Germanic]

bridegroom /'brʌɪdgru:m/ *n.* a man on his wedding day and for some time before and after it. [Old English *brȳdguma* (as BRIDE, *guma* 'man', assimilated to GROOM)]

bride price *n.* money or goods given to a bride's family by that of the bridegroom, esp. in tribal societies.

bridesmaid /'brʌɪdzmeɪd/ *n.* a girl or unmarried woman attending a bride on her wedding day. [earlier *bridemaid*, from BRIDE + MAID]

bridewell /'brʌɪdw(ə)l/ *n.* a prison; a reformatory. [St *Bride's Well* in London, near which such a building stood]

bridge[1] /brɪdʒ/ *n. & v.* ● *n.* (also *Sc. & N.Engl.* **brig** /brɪg/) **1 a** a structure carrying a road, path, railway, etc., across a stream, ravine, road, railway, etc. **b** anything providing a connection between different things (*English is a bridge between nations*). **2** the superstructure on a ship from which the captain and officers direct operations. **3** the upper bony part of the nose. **4** *Mus.* an upright piece of wood on a violin etc. over which the strings are stretched. **5** = BRIDGEWORK. **6** *Billiards* etc. **a** a long stick with a structure at the end which is used to support a cue for a difficult shot. **b** a support for a cue formed by a raised hand. **7** = LAND BRIDGE. ● *v.tr.* **1 a** be a bridge over (*a fallen tree bridges the stream*). **b** make a bridge over; span. **2** span as if with a bridge (*bridged their differences with understanding*). □ **cross a** (or **that**) **bridge when one comes to it** deal with a problem when and if it arises. □ **bridgeable** *adj.* [Old English *brycg*, from Germanic]

bridge[2] /brɪdʒ/ *n.* a card game derived from whist, in which one player's cards are exposed and are played by his or her partner (cf. AUCTION BRIDGE, CONTRACT BRIDGE). [19th c.: origin unknown]

bridge-building *n.* **1** the activity of building bridges. **2** the promotion of friendly relations, esp. between countries. □ **bridge-builder** *n.*

bridgehead /ˈbrɪdʒhɛd/ *n. Mil.* a fortified position held on the enemy's side of a river or other obstacle.

bridge of asses *n.* = PONS ASINORUM.

bridge of boats *n.* a bridge formed by mooring boats together abreast across a river etc.

bridge passage *n. Mus.* a transitional section between main themes.

bridge roll *n. Brit.* a small soft bread roll.

bridgework /ˈbrɪdʒwəːk/ *n.* a dental structure used to cover a gap, joined to and supported by the teeth on either side.

bridging loan *n.* esp. *Brit.* a loan from a bank etc. to cover the short interval between buying a house etc. and selling another.

bridle /ˈbrʌɪd(ə)l/ *n.* & *v.* ● *n.* **1 a** the headgear used to control a horse, consisting of buckled leather straps, a metal bit, and reins. **b** a restraining thing or influence (*put a bridle on your tongue*). **2** *Naut.* a mooring-cable. **3** *Anat.* a ligament checking the motion of a part. ● *v.* **1** *tr.* put a bridle on (a horse etc.). **2** *tr.* bring under control; curb. **3** *intr.* (often foll. by *at, up at*) express offence, resentment, etc., esp. by throwing up the head and drawing in the chin. [Old English *brīdel*, from Germanic]

bridle path *n.* (also **bridleway** /ˈbrʌɪd(ə)lweɪ/) a rough path or road fit only for riders or walkers, not vehicles.

bridoon /brɪˈduːn/ *n.* the snaffle and rein of a military bridle. [French *bridon* from *bride* 'bridle']

Brie /briː/ *n.* a kind of soft cheese. [*Brie* in N. France, where it was originally made]

brief /briːf/ *adj., n., & v.* ● *adj.* **1** of short duration. **2** concise in expression. **3** abrupt, brusque (*was rather brief with me*). **4** (of clothes) scanty (*wearing a brief skirt*). ● *n.* **1** (in *pl.*) close-fitting legless pants. **2** *Law* **a** *Brit.* a document instructing a barrister to appear as an advocate in court. **b** *US* a written summary of the facts and legal points supporting one side of a case, for presentation to a court. **3** esp. *Brit.* instructions given for a task, operation, etc. (originally a bombing plan given to an aircrew). **4** *RC Ch.* a letter from the Pope to a person or community on a matter of discipline. ● *v.tr.* **1** *Brit. Law* instruct (a barrister) by brief. **2** instruct (an employee, a participant, etc.) in preparation for a task; inform or instruct thoroughly in advance (*briefed him for the interview*) (cf. DEBRIEF). □ **be brief** use few words. **hold a brief for 1** argue in favour of. **2** *Brit.* be retained as counsel for. **in brief** in short. □ **briefly** *adv.* **briefness** *n.* [Middle English via Anglo-French *bref*, Old French *brief*, from Latin *brevis* 'short']

briefcase /ˈbriːfkeɪs/ *n.* a flat rectangular case for carrying documents etc.

briefing /ˈbriːfɪŋ/ *n.* **1** a meeting for giving information or instructions. **2** the information or instructions given; a brief. **3** the action of informing or instructing.

briefless /ˈbriːflɪs/ *adj. Brit. Law* (of a barrister) having no clients.

brier[1] /ˈbrʌɪə/ *n.* (also **briar**) any prickly bush esp. of a wild rose. □ **briery** *adj.* [Old English *brǣr, brēr*, of unknown origin]

brier[2] /ˈbrʌɪə/ *n.* (also **briar**) **1** a white heath, *Erica arborea*, native to S. Europe. **2** a tobacco pipe made from its root. [19th-c. *bruyer* from French *bruyère* 'heath']

brier rose *n.* dog rose.

Brig. *abbr.* Brigadier.

brig[1] /brɪg/ *n.* **1** a two-masted square-rigged ship, with an additional lower fore-and-aft sail on the gaff and a boom to the mainmast. **2** *slang* a prison, esp. on a warship. [abbreviation of BRIGANTINE]

brig[2] *Sc.* & *N.Engl.* var. of BRIDGE[1] *n.*

brigade /brɪˈgeɪd/ *n.* & *v.* ● *n.* **1** *Mil.* **a** a subdivision of an army. **b** a British infantry unit consisting usu. of three battalions and forming part of a division. **c** a corresponding armoured unit. **2** an organized or uniformed band of workers (*fire brigade*). **3** *colloq.* a group of people with a characteristic in common (*the couldn't-care-less brigade*). ● *v.tr.* form into a brigade. [French from Italian *brigata* 'company', from *brigare* 'be busy with', from *briga* 'strife']

brigadier /brɪgəˈdɪə/ *n. Brit. Mil.* **1** an officer commanding a brigade. **2 a** a staff officer of similar standing, above a colonel and below a major general. **b** the titular rank granted to such an officer. [French (as BRIGADE, -IER)]

brigadier general *n.* an officer ranking next above colonel in the US army, air force, and marine corps.

brigalow /ˈbrɪgələʊ/ *n. Austral.* any of various acacia trees, esp. *Acacia harpophylla*. [Aboriginal, perhaps Kamilaroi *burriigal*]

brigand /ˈbrɪg(ə)nd/ *n.* a member of a robber band living by pillage and ransom, usu. in wild terrain. □ **brigandage** *n.* **brigandry** *n.* [Middle English via Old French from Italian *brigante*, from *brigare*: see BRIGADE]

brigantine /ˈbrɪg(ə)ntiːn/ *n.* a two-masted sailing ship with a square-rigged foremast and a fore-and-aft-rigged mainmast. [in earlier use, a small vessel used by pirates: Old French *brigandine* or Italian *brigantino* from *brigante* BRIGAND]

bright /brʌɪt/ *adj., adv., & n.* ● *adj.* **1** emitting or reflecting much light; shining. **2** (of colour) intense, vivid. **3** clever, talented, quick-witted (*a bright idea; a bright child*). **4** cheerful, vivacious. ● *adv.* esp. *poet.* brightly (*the moon shone bright*). ● *n.* (in *pl.*) **1** bright colours. **2** *N. Amer.* headlights switched to full beam. □ **bright and early** very early in the morning. **bright-eyed and bushy-tailed** *colloq.* alert and sprightly. **look on the bright side** be optimistic. □ **brightish** *adj.* **brightly** *adv.* **brightness** *n.* [Old English *beorht*, (*adv.*) *beorhte*, from Germanic]

brighten /ˈbrʌɪt(ə)n/ *v.tr.* & *intr.* (often foll. by *up*) **1** make or become brighter. **2** make or become more cheerful.

bright lights *n.pl.* (prec. by *the*) the glamour and excitement of the city.

Bright's disease /ˈbrʌɪts dɪˌziːz/ *n.* nephritis. [R. *Bright*, English physician d. 1858]

bright spark *n. colloq.* a witty, lively, or intelligent person.

brill[1] /brɪl/ *n.* a European flatfish, *Scophthalmus rhombus*, resembling a turbot. [15th c.: origin unknown]

brill[2] /brɪl/ *adj. Brit. colloq.* = BRILLIANT *adj.* 4. [abbreviation]

brilliance /ˈbrɪlj(ə)ns/ *n.* (also **brilliancy** /-ənsi/) **1** great brightness; sparkling or radiant quality. **2** outstanding talent or intelligence.

brilliant /ˈbrɪlj(ə)nt/ *adj.* & *n.* ● *adj.* **1** very bright; sparkling. **2** outstandingly talented or intelligent. **3** showy; outwardly impressive. **4** *Brit. colloq.* excellent, superb. ● *n.* a diamond of the finest cut with many facets. □ **brilliantly** *adv.* [French *brillant*, part. of *briller* 'shine', from Italian *brillare*, probably from Latin *beryllus* BERYL]

brilliantine /ˈbrɪlj(ə)ntiːn/ *n.* **1** an oily liquid dressing for making the hair glossy. **2** *US* a lustrous dress fabric. [French *brillantine* (as BRILLIANT)]

brim /brɪm/ *n.* & *v.* ● *n.* **1** the edge or lip of a cup or other vessel, or of a hollow. **2** the projecting edge of a hat. ● *v.tr.* & *intr.* (**brimmed**, **brimming**) fill or be full to the brim. □ **brim over** overflow. □ **brimless** *adj.* **brimmed** *adj.* (usu. in *comb.*). [Middle English *brimme*, of unknown origin]

brim-full *adj.* (also **brimful**) (often foll. by *of*) filled to the brim.

brimstone /ˈbrɪmst(ə)n, -stəʊn/ *n.* **1** *archaic* the element sulphur. **2** a butterfly, *Gonepteryx rhamni*, or moth,

Opisthograptis luteolata, having yellow wings. [Middle English probably from Old English *bryne* 'burning' + STONE]

brindled /ˈbrɪnd(ə)ld/ *adj.* (also **brindle**) brownish or tawny with streaks of other colour (esp. of domestic animals). [earlier *brinded, brended* from *brend*, perhaps of Scandinavian origin]

brine /braɪn/ *n.* & *v.* ● *n.* **1** water saturated or strongly impregnated with salt. **2** sea water. ● *v.tr.* soak in or saturate with brine. [Old English *brīne*, of unknown origin]

brine shrimp *n.* a small crustacean of the genus *Artemia*, inhabiting salt lakes etc. and used as food for aquarium fish.

bring /brɪŋ/ *v.tr.* (*past* and *past part.* **brought** /brɔːt/) **1 a** come conveying esp. by carrying or leading. **b** come with. **2** cause to come or be present (*what brings you here?*). **3** cause or result in (*war brings misery*). **4** be sold for; produce as income. **5 a** prefer (a charge). **b** initiate (legal action). **6** cause to become or to reach a particular state (*brings me alive*). **7** adduce (evidence, an argument, etc.). □ **bring about 1** cause to happen. **2** turn (a ship) around. **bring back** call to mind. **bring down 1** cause to fall. **2** lower (a price). **3** *slang* make unhappy or less happy. **4** *colloq.* damage the reputation of; demean. **bring forth 1** produce, emit, cause. **2** give birth to. **bring forward 1** move to an earlier date or time. **2** transfer from the previous page or account. **3** draw attention to; adduce. **bring home to** cause to realize fully (*brought home to me that I was wrong*). **bring the house down** receive rapturous applause. **bring in 1** introduce (legislation, a custom, fashion, topic, etc.). **2** yield as income or profit. **bring into play** cause to operate; activate. **bring low 1** overcome; deject. **2** humiliate. **bring off** achieve successfully. **bring on 1** cause to happen or appear. **2** accelerate the progress of. **bring out 1** emphasize; make evident. **2** publish. **bring over** convert to one's own side. **bring round** (or *US* **around**) **1** restore to consciousness. **2** persuade. **bring through** aid (a person) through adversity, esp. illness. **bring to 1** restore to consciousness (*brought him to*). **2** check the motion of. **bring to bear** (usu. foll. by *on*) direct and concentrate (forces). **bring to light** see LIGHT[1]. **bring to mind** recall; cause one to remember. **bring to pass** cause to happen. **bring under** subdue. **bring up 1** rear (a child). **2** vomit, regurgitate. **3** call attention to. **4** (*absol.*) stop suddenly. **bring upon oneself** be responsible for (something one suffers). □ **bringer** *n.* [Old English *bringan*, from Germanic]

bring-and-buy sale *n. Brit.* a charity sale at which participants bring items for sale and buy what is brought by others.

brinjal /ˈbrɪndʒɔːl/ *n.* (in India and Africa) an aubergine. [ultimately from Portuguese *berinjela* from Arabic (as AUBERGINE)]

brink /brɪŋk/ *n.* **1** the extreme edge of land before a precipice, river, etc., esp. when a sudden drop follows. **2** the furthest point before something dangerous or exciting is discovered. □ **on the brink of** about to experience or suffer; in imminent danger of. [Middle English from Old Norse: origin unknown]

brinkmanship /ˈbrɪŋkmənʃɪp/ *n.* the art or policy of pursuing a dangerous course to the brink of catastrophe before desisting, esp in politics.

briny /ˈbraɪni/ *adj.* & *n.* ● *adj.* of brine or the sea; salty. ● *n.* (prec. by *the*) *Brit. slang* the sea. □ **brininess** *n.*

brio /ˈbriːəʊ/ *n.* dash, vigour, vivacity. [Italian]

brioche /briːˈɒʃ, ˈbriːɒʃ/ *n.* a small rounded sweet roll made with a light yeast dough. [French]

briquette /brɪˈkɛt/ *n.* (also **briquet**) a block of compressed coal dust used as fuel. [French *briquette*, diminutive of *brique* 'brick']

brisk /brɪsk/ *adj.* & *v.* ● *adj.* **1** quick, lively, keen (*a brisk pace; brisk trade*). **2** enlivening; fresh, keen (*a brisk wind*). ● *v.tr.* & *intr.* (often foll. by *up*) make or grow brisk. □ **brisken** *v.tr.* & *intr.* **briskly** *adv.* **briskness** *n.* [probably French *brusque* BRUSQUE]

brisket /ˈbrɪskɪt/ *n.* an animal's breast, esp. as a joint of meat. [Anglo-French from Old French *bruschet*, perhaps from Old Norse]

brisling /ˈbrɪslɪŋ, ˈbrɪz-/ *n.* (*pl.* same or **brislings**) a small herring or sprat. [Norwegian & Danish, = sprat]

bristle /ˈbrɪs(ə)l/ *n.* & *v.* ● *n.* **1** a short stiff hair, esp. one of those on an animal's back. **2** such hairs, or a man-made substitute, used in clumps to make a brush. ● *v.* **1 a** *intr.* (of the hair) stand upright, esp. in anger or pride. **b** *tr.* make (the hair) do this. **2** *intr.* show irritation or defensiveness. **3** *intr.* (usu. foll. by *with*) be covered or abundant (in) (*pages bristling with images*). [Middle English *bristel, brestel* from Old English *byrst*]

bristlecone pine /ˈbrɪs(ə)lkəʊn/ *n.* a very long-lived shrubby pine of western N. America, *Pinus aristata*, used in dendrochronology.

bristletail /ˈbrɪs(ə)lteɪl/ *n.* a small primitive wingless insect of the order Thysanura or Diplura, with three or two terminal bristles respectively, e.g. a silverfish.

bristly /ˈbrɪsli/ *adj.* full of bristles; rough, prickly.

Bristol board /ˈbrɪst(ə)l/ *n.* a kind of fine smooth pasteboard for drawing on. [*Bristol* in S. England]

Bristol fashion /ˈbrɪst(ə)l/ *n.* (functioning as *predic.adj.*) (in full **shipshape and Bristol fashion**) *Brit.* orig. *Naut.* with all in good order.

bristols /ˈbrɪst(ə)lz/ *n.pl. Brit. slang* a woman's breasts. [rhyming slang from *Bristol Cities* = *titties*]

Brit /brɪt/ *n. colloq.* a British person. [abbreviation]

Britannia /brɪˈtanjə/ *n.* the personification of Britain, esp. as a helmeted woman with shield and trident. [Latin from Greek *Brettania*, from *Brettanoi*, 'Britons']

Britannia metal *n.* a silvery alloy of tin, antimony, and copper.

Britannia silver *n.* silver that is at least 95.8 per cent pure.

Britannic /brɪˈtanɪk/ *adj.* (esp. in **His** (or **Her**) **Britannic Majesty**) of Britain. [Latin *Britannicus* (as BRITANNIA)]

Briticism /ˈbrɪtɪsɪz(ə)m/ *n.* (also **Britishism** /-ʃɪz(ə)m/) an idiom used only in Britain. [BRITISH, on the pattern of GALLICISM]

British /ˈbrɪtɪʃ/ *adj.* & *n.* ● *adj.* **1** of or relating to Great Britain or the United Kingdom, or to its people or language. **2** of the British Commonwealth or (formerly) the British Empire (*British subject*). ● *n.* (prec. by *the*; treated as *pl.*) the British people. □ **Britishness** *n.* [Old English *Brettisc* etc. from *Bret* 'Briton', from Latin *Britto* or its Celtic equivalent]

British English *n.* English as used in Great Britain, as distinct from that used elsewhere.

Britisher /ˈbrɪtɪʃə/ *n.* a British subject.

Britishism var. of BRITICISM.

British Legion *n.* = ROYAL BRITISH LEGION.

British Summer Time *n.* time as advanced one hour ahead of Greenwich Mean Time for daylight saving between March and October.

British thermal unit *n.* the amount of heat needed to raise 1 lb of water at maximum density through one degree Fahrenheit, equivalent to 1.055×10^3 joules.

Briton /ˈbrɪt(ə)n/ *n.* **1** one of the people of southern Britain before the Roman conquest. **2** a native or inhabitant of Great Britain or (formerly) of the British Empire. [Middle English & Old French *Breton*, from Latin *Britto -onis* or its Celtic equivalent]

brittle /ˈbrɪt(ə)l/ *adj.* & *n.* ● *adj.* hard and fragile; apt to break. ● *n.* a brittle sweet made from nuts and set melted sugar. □ **brittlely** *adv.* **brittleness** *n.* [Middle English, ultimately from a Germanic root related to Old English *brēotan* 'break up']

brittle-bone disease *n. Brit.* **1** = OSTEOPOROSIS. **2** a hereditary condition causing extreme fragility of the bones.

brittle-star *n.* an echinoderm of the class Ophiuroidea, with long flexible arms radiating from a small central body.

Brittonic /brɪ'tɒnɪk/ *adj. & n.* = BRYTHONIC. [Latin *Britto -onis* Briton]

bro. *abbr.* brother.

broach /brəʊtʃ/ *v. & n.* ● *v.* **1** *tr.* raise (a subject) for discussion. **2** *tr.* pierce (a cask) to draw liquor. **3** *tr.* open and start using the contents of (a box, bale, bottle, etc.). **4** *tr.* begin drawing (liquor). **5** *intr. & tr.* veer or cause (a ship) to veer and present a side to the wind and waves. ● *n.* **1** a bit for boring. **2** a roasting-spit. [Middle English from Old French *broche* (*n.*), *brocher* (*v.*), ultimately from Latin *brocc(h)us* 'projecting']

broach spire *n.* an octagonal church spire rising from a square tower without a parapet.

broad /brɔːd/ *adj. & n.* ● *adj.* **1** large in extent from one side to the other; wide. **2** (following a measurement) in breadth (*2 metres broad*). **3** spacious or extensive (*broad acres*; *a broad plain*). **4** full and clear (*broad daylight*). **5** explicit, unmistakable (*broad hint*). **6** general; not taking account of detail (*broad intentions*; *a broad inquiry*; *in the broadest sense of the word*). **7** (of speech) markedly regional (*broad Scots*). **8** chief or principal (*the broad facts*). **9** tolerant, liberal; widely inclusive (*take a broad view*). **10** somewhat coarse (*broad humour*). ● *n.* **1** the broad part of something (*broad of the back*). **2** *N. Amer. slang offens.* a woman. **3** (**the Broads**) *Brit.* large areas of fresh water in E. Anglia, formed where rivers widen. □ **broadness** *n.* **broadways** *adv.* **broadwise** *adv.* [Old English *brād*, from Germanic]

broad arrow *n.* a mark formerly used on British prison clothing and other Government stores.

broadband /'brɔːdband/ *attrib.adj.* relating to or using signals over a broad range of frequencies, esp. in high-capacity telecommunications.

broad bean *n.* **1** a kind of bean, *Vicia faba*, with pods containing large edible flat seeds. **2** one of these seeds.

broad-brush *attrib.adj.* as if painted with a broad brush; general; lacking in detail (*adopted a broad-brush approach*).

broadcast /'brɔːdkɑːst/ *v., n., adj., & adv.* ● *v.* (*past* **broadcast** and *past part.* **broadcast** or **broadcasted**) **1** *tr.* **a** transmit (programmes or information) by radio or television. **b** disseminate (information) widely. **2** *intr.* undertake or take part in a radio or television transmission. **3** *tr.* scatter (seed etc.) over a large area, esp. by hand. ● *n.* a radio or television programme or transmission. ● *adj.* **1** transmitted by radio or television. **2 a** scattered widely. **b** (of information etc.) widely disseminated. ● *adv.* over a large area. □ **broadcaster** *n.* **broadcasting** *n.* [BROAD + CAST *past part.*]

Broad Church *n.* **1** a group within the Anglican Church favouring a liberal interpretation of doctrine. **2** *Brit.* any group allowing its members a wide range of opinion.

broadcloth /'brɔːdklɒθ/ *n.* a fine cloth of wool, cotton, or silk. [originally with reference to width and quality]

broaden /'brɔːd(ə)n/ *v.tr. & intr.* make or become broader.

broad gauge *n.* a railway track with a gauge wider than the standard one.

broadleaved /brɔːd'liːvd/ *adj.* (of a tree) having relatively broad flat leaves rather than needles; non-coniferous. □ **broadleaf** *n. & attrib.adj.*

broadloom /'brɔːdluːm/ *adj.* (esp. of carpet) woven in broad widths.

broadly /'brɔːdli/ *adv.* in a broad manner; widely (*grinned broadly*). □ **broadly speaking** disregarding minor exceptions.

broad-minded /brɔːd'mʌɪndɪd/ *adj.* tolerant or liberal in one's views. □ **broad-mindedly** *adv.* **broad-mindedness** *n.*

broad pennant *n.* a short swallow-tailed pennant distinguishing the commodore's ship in a squadron.

broadsheet /'brɔːdʃiːt/ *n.* **1** a large sheet of paper printed on one side only, esp. with information. **2** a newspaper with a large format.

broadside /'brɔːdsʌɪd/ *n. & v.* ● *n.* **1** the firing of all guns from one side of a ship. **2** a vigorous verbal onslaught. **3** the side of a ship above the water between the bow and quarter. ● *v.tr. N. Amer.* collide with the side of (a vehicle etc.). □ **broadside on** sideways on.

broad spectrum *adj.* (of a medicinal substance) effective against a large variety of micro-organisms.

broadsword /'brɔːdsɔːd/ *n.* a sword with a broad blade, for cutting rather than thrusting.

broadtail /'brɔːdteɪl/ *n.* **1** the karakul sheep. **2** the fleece or wool from its lamb.

broadway /'brɔːdweɪ/ *n.* a large open or main road.

brocade /brə'keɪd/ *n. & v.* ● *n.* a rich fabric with a silky finish woven with a raised pattern, and often with gold or silver thread. ● *v.tr.* weave with this design. [Spanish & Portuguese *brocado* from Italian *broccato*, from *brocco* 'twisted thread']

broccoli /'brɒkəli/ *n.* **1** a variety of cabbage, similar to the cauliflower, with a loose cluster of greenish flower buds. **2** the flower stalk and head used as a vegetable. [Italian, pl. of *broccolo*, diminutive of *brocco* 'sprout']

broch /brɒk, brɒx/ *n.* (in Scotland) a prehistoric circular stone tower. [alteration of BURGH: cf. Old Norse *borg* 'castle']

brochette /brɒ'ʃɛt/ *n.* a skewer on which chunks of meat are cooked, esp. over an open fire. [French, diminutive of *broche* BROACH]

brochure /'brəʊʃə, brɒ'ʃʊə/ *n.* a pamphlet or leaflet, esp. one giving descriptive information. [French, literally 'a stitched work', from *brocher* 'stitch']

brock /brɒk/ *n. Brit.* (esp. in rural use) a badger. [Old English *broc(c)*, of Celtic origin: cf. Welsh *broch*, Irish, Gaelic *broc*]

Brocken spectre /'brɒk(ə)n/ *n.* a magnified shadow of the observer, often surrounded by rainbow-like bands, thrown on to a bank of cloud in high mountain areas when the sun is low. [*Brocken*, the highest of the Harz Mountains in Germany, where it was first reported]

brocket /'brɒkɪt/ *n.* any small deer of the genus *Mazama*, native to Central and S. America, having short straight antlers. [Middle English from Anglo-French *broque*, variant of *broche* BROACH]

broderie anglaise /ˌbrəʊd(ə)rɪ ɒŋ'gleɪz/ *n.* open embroidery on white linen or cambric, esp. in floral patterns. [French, = English embroidery]

brogue[1] /brəʊg/ *n.* **1** a strong outdoor shoe with ornamental perforated bands. **2** a rough shoe of untanned leather. [Gaelic & Irish *brōg* from Old Norse *brók*]

brogue[2] /brəʊg/ *n.* a marked accent, esp. Irish. [18th c.: origin unknown: perhaps allusively from BROGUE[1], referring to the rough footwear of Irish peasants]

broil[1] /brɔɪl/ *v.* esp. *N. Amer.* **1** *tr.* cook (meat) on a rack or a gridiron. **2** *tr. & intr.* make or become very hot, esp. from the sun. [Middle English from Old French *bruler* 'burn' from Romanic]

broil[2] /brɔɪl/ *n.* a row; a tumult. [obsolete *broil* 'to muddle': cf. EMBROIL]

broiler /'brɔɪlə/ *n.* **1** a young chicken raised for broiling or roasting. **2** *N. Amer.* a gridiron etc. for broiling. **3** *colloq.* a very hot day.

broiler house *n. Brit.* a building for rearing broiler chickens in close confinement.

broke /brəʊk/ *past* of BREAK[1]. ● *predic.adj. colloq.* having no money; financially ruined. □ **go for broke** *slang* risk everything in an all-out effort. [(*adj.*) archaic past part. of BREAK[1]]

broken /'brəʊk(ə)n/ *past part.* of BREAK[1]. ● *adj.* **1** that has been broken; out of order. **2** (of a person) reduced to despair; defeated. **3** (of a language or of speech) spoken falteringly and with many mistakes, as by a foreigner (*broken English*). **4** disturbed, interrupted (*broken time*). **5** uneven (*broken ground*). □ **brokenly** *adv.* **brokenness** /ˈbrəʊk(ə)nnɪs/ *n.*

broken chord *n. Mus.* a chord in which the notes are played successively.

broken-down *adj.* **1** worn out by age, use, or ill-treatment. **2** not functioning.

broken-hearted *adj.* overwhelmed with sorrow or grief. □ **broken-heartedness** *n.*

broken home *n.* a family in which the parents are divorced or separated.

broken reed *n.* a person who has become unreliable or ineffective.

broken wind *n.* a chronic disabling condition of a horse due to ruptured air-cells in the lungs. □ **broken-winded** *adj.*

broker /ˈbrəʊkə/ *n.* & *v.* ● *n.* **1** an agent who buys and sells for others; a middleman. **2** a member of the Stock Exchange dealing in stocks and shares. **3** *Brit.* an official appointed to sell or appraise distrained goods. ● *v.tr.* act as intermediary with respect to. [Middle English from Anglo-French *brocour*, of unknown origin]

■ **Usage** The term *broker* in sense 2 was officially replaced in the UK by *broker-dealer* in 1986, broker-dealers being entitled to act both as agents and principals in share dealings.

brokerage /ˈbrəʊk(ə)rɪdʒ/ *n.* **1** the action or service of a broker. **2** a company providing such a service. **3** a broker's fee or commission.

broker-dealer *n.* a person combining the former functions of a broker and jobber on the Stock Exchange.

broking /ˈbrəʊkɪŋ/ *n. Brit.* the business of a broker.

brolga /ˈbrɒlgə/ *n. Austral.* a large Australian crane, *Grus rubicunda*, with a booming call. [Kamilaroi (and other Aboriginal languages) *burralga*)]

brolly /ˈbrɒli/ *n.* (*pl.* **-ies**) *Brit.* **1** *colloq.* an umbrella. **2** *slang* a parachute. [abbreviation]

bromate /ˈbrəʊmeɪt/ *n. Chem.* a salt or ester of bromic acid.

brome /brəʊm/ *n.* any oatlike grass of the genus *Bromus*, having slender stems with flowering spikes. [modern Latin *Bromus* from Greek *bromos* 'oat']

bromelia /brəˈmiːlɪə/ *n.* (also **bromeliad** /-lɪad/) any plant of the family Bromeliaceae (esp. of the genus *Bromelia*), native to the New World, having short stems with rosettes of stiff usu. spiny leaves, e.g. pineapple. [O. *Bromel*, Swedish botanist d. 1705]

bromic /ˈbrəʊmɪk/ *adj. Chem.* of or containing bromine.

bromic acid *n.* a strong acid used as an oxidizing agent.

bromide /ˈbrəʊmʌɪd/ *n.* **1** *Chem.* any compound of bromine with another element or group. **2** *Pharm.* a preparation of usu. potassium bromide, used as a sedative. **3** a trite remark. **4** *Brit.* a reproduction or proof on bromide paper.

bromide paper *n.* a photographic printing paper coated with silver bromide emulsion.

bromine /ˈbrəʊmiːn/ *n. Chem.* a dark fuming liquid element with a choking irritating smell, extracted from bittern and used in the manufacture of chemicals for photography and medicine (symbol **Br**). □ **bromism** *n.* [French *brome* from Greek *brōmos* 'stink']

bromo- /ˈbrəʊməʊ/ *comb. form Chem.* bromine.

bronc /brɒŋk/ *n. N. Amer. colloq.* = BRONCO. [abbreviation]

bronchi *pl.* of BRONCHUS.

bronchial /ˈbrɒŋkɪəl/ *adj.* of or relating to the bronchi or bronchioles.

bronchial tree *n.* the branching system of bronchi and bronchioles conducting air from the windpipe into the lungs.

bronchiole /ˈbrɒŋkɪəʊl/ *n.* any of the minute divisions of a bronchus. □ **bronchiolar** /-ˈəʊlə/ *adj.*

bronchitis /brɒŋˈkʌɪtɪs/ *n.* inflammation of the mucous membrane in the bronchial tubes. □ **bronchitic** /-ˈkɪtɪk/ *adj.* & *n.*

broncho- /ˈbrɒŋkəʊ/ *comb. form* bronchi.

bronchodilator /ˌbrɒŋkəʊdʌɪˈleɪtə/ *n.* a substance which causes widening of the bronchi, used esp. to alleviate asthma.

bronchopneumonia /ˌbrɒŋkəʊnjuːˈməʊnɪə/ *n.* inflammation of the lungs, arising in the bronchi or bronchioles.

bronchoscope /ˈbrɒŋkəskəʊp/ *n.* a usu. fibre-optic instrument for inspecting the bronchi. □ **bronchoscopy** /-ˈkɒskəpi/ *n.*

bronchus /ˈbrɒŋkəs/ *n.* (*pl.* **bronchi** /-kʌɪ/) any of the major air passages of the lungs, esp. either of the two main divisions of the windpipe. [Late Latin from Greek *brogkhos*, 'windpipe']

bronco /ˈbrɒŋkəʊ/ *n.* (*pl.* **-os**) a wild or half-tamed horse of the western US. [Spanish, = rough]

broncobuster /ˈbrɒŋkəʊˌbʌstə/ *n. US slang* a person who breaks in horses.

brontosaurus /brɒntəˈsɔːrəs/ *n.* (also **brontosaur** /ˈbrɒntəsɔː/) = APATOSAURUS. [former genus name, from Greek *brontē* 'thunder' + *sauros* 'lizard']

bronze /brɒnz/ *n.*, *adj.*, & *v.* ● *n.* **1** an alloy of copper with up to one-third tin. **2** its brownish colour. **3** a thing made of bronze, esp. as a work of art. ● *adj.* made of or coloured like bronze. ● *v.* **1** *tr.* give a surface of bronze or resembling bronze to. **2** *tr.* & *intr.* make or become brown; tan. □ **bronzy** *adj.* [French from Italian *bronzo*, probably from Persian *birinj* 'copper']

Bronze Age *n.* the period preceding the Iron Age, when weapons and tools were usu. made of bronze.

bronze medal *n.* a bronze-coloured medal, usu. awarded as third prize.

brooch /brəʊtʃ/ *n.* an ornament fastened to clothing with a hinged pin. [Middle English *broche* = BROACH *n.*]

brood /bruːd/ *n.* & *v.* ● *n.* **1** the young of an animal (esp. a bird) produced at one hatching or birth. **2** *colloq.* the children in a family. **3** a group of related things. **4** bee or wasp larvae. **5** (*attrib.*) kept for breeding (*brood mare*). ● *v.* **1** *intr.* (often foll. by *on*, *over*, etc.) worry or ponder (esp. resentfully). **2 a** *intr.* sit as a hen on eggs to hatch them. **b** *tr.* sit on (eggs) to hatch them. **3** *intr.* (usu. foll. by *over*) (of silence, a storm, etc.) hang or hover closely. □ **broodingly** *adv.* [Old English *brōd* from Germanic: related to BREED]

brooder /ˈbruːdə/ *n.* **1** a heated house for chicks, piglets, etc. **2** a person who broods.

broody /ˈbruːdi/ *adj.* (**broodier**, **broodiest**) **1** (of a hen) wanting to brood. **2** sullenly thoughtful or depressed. **3** *Brit. colloq.* (of a woman) wanting to have a baby. □ **broodily** *adv.* **broodiness** *n.*

brook[1] /brʊk/ *n.* a small stream. □ **brooklet** /-lɪt/ *n.* [Old English *brōc*, of unknown origin]

brook[2] /brʊk/ *v.tr.* (usu. with *neg.*) *formal* tolerate, allow. [Old English *brūcan* from Germanic]

brooklime /ˈbrʊklʌɪm/ *n.* a kind of speedwell, *Veronica beccabunga*, growing in wet areas. [BROOK[1] + Old English *hleomoce*, name of the plant]

brookweed /ˈbrʊkwiːd/ *n.* a small white-flowered plant, *Samolus valerandi*, of the primrose family, growing in wet ground.

broom /bruːm/ *n.* **1** a long-handled brush of bristles, twigs, etc. for sweeping (originally one made of twigs of broom). **2** any of various shrubs, esp. *Cytisus scoparius*, bearing bright yellow flowers. [Old English *brōm*, from the Germanic base of BRAMBLE]

broomrape /ˈbruːmreɪp/ *n.* a parasitic plant of the genus *Orobanche*, with tubular flowers on a leafless brown stem, and living on the roots of broom and similar plants. [BROOM + Latin *rapum*, 'tuber']

broomstick /ˈbruːmstɪk/ *n.* the handle of a broom, esp. as allegedly ridden through the air by witches.

Bros. *abbr.* Brothers (esp. in the name of a firm).

brose /brəʊz/ *n.* esp. *Sc.* a dish of oatmeal with boiling water or milk poured on it. [Scots form of *brewis* 'broth': Middle English from Old French *bro(u)ez*, ultimately from Germanic]

broth /brɒθ/ *n.* **1 a** a thin soup of meat or fish stock. **b** unclarified meat or fish stock. **2** *Biol.* meat stock as a nutrient medium for bacteria. [Old English from Germanic: related to BREW]

brothel /ˈbrɒθ(ə)l/ *n.* a house etc. where prostitution takes place. [originally *brothel-house* from Middle English *brothel* 'worthless man, prostitute', from Old English *brēothan* 'go to ruin']

brothel creepers *n.pl. Brit. slang* soft-soled (usu. suede) shoes.

brother /ˈbrʌðə/ *n.* **1** a man or boy in relation to other sons and daughters of his parents. **2 a** (often as a form of address) a close male friend or associate. **b** a male fellow member of a trade union etc. **3** (*pl.* also **brethren** /ˈbrɛðrɪn/) **a** a member of a male religious order, esp. a monk. **b** a fellow member of the Christian Church, a religion, or (formerly) a guild etc. **4** a fellow human being. ◻ **brotherless** *adj.* **brotherly** *adj. & adv.* **brotherliness** *n.* [Old English *brōthor*, from Germanic]

brother german see GERMAN.

brotherhood /ˈbrʌðəhʊd/ *n.* **1 a** the relationship between brothers. **b** brotherly friendliness; companionship. **2 a** an association, society, or community of people linked by a common interest, religion, trade, etc. **b** its members collectively. **3** *N. Amer.* a trade union. **4** community of feeling between all human beings. [Middle English alteration of *brotherrede*, from Old English *brōthor-rǣden* (cf. KINDRED) influenced by words in -HOOD, -HEAD]

brother-in-law *n.* (*pl.* **brothers-in-law**) **1** the brother of one's wife or husband. **2** the husband of one's sister. **3** the husband of one's sister-in-law.

brother uterine see UTERINE 2.

brougham /ˈbruː(ə)m/ *n. hist.* **1** a horse-drawn closed carriage with a driver perched outside in front. **2** a motor car with an open driver's seat. [Lord *Brougham* (d. 1868), who designed the carriage]

brought *past* and *past part.* of BRING.

brouhaha /ˈbruːhɑːhɑː/ *n.* commotion, sensation; hubbub, uproar. [French: imitative]

brow /braʊ/ *n.* **1** the forehead. **2** (usu. in *pl.*) an eyebrow. **3** the summit of a hill or pass. **4** the edge of a cliff etc. **5** *colloq.* intellectual level. ◻ **-browed** *adj.* (in *comb.*). [Old English *brū*, from Germanic]

browbeat /ˈbraʊbiːt/ *v.tr.* (*past* **-beat**; *past part.* **-beaten**) intimidate with stern looks and words. ◻ **browbeater** *n.*

brown /braʊn/ *adj., n., & v.* ● *adj.* **1** having the colour produced by mixing red, yellow, and black, as of dark wood or rich soil. **2** dark-skinned or suntanned. **3** (of bread) made from a dark flour as wholemeal or wheatmeal. **4** (of species or varieties) distinguished by brown coloration. ● *n.* **1** a brown colour or pigment. **2** brown clothes or material (*dressed in brown*). **3** (in a game or sport) a brown ball, piece, etc. ● *v.tr. & intr.* make or become brown by cooking, sunburn, etc. ◻ **in a brown study** see STUDY. ◻ **brownish** *adj.* **brownness** /ˈbraʊnnɪs/ *n.* **browny** *adj.* [Old English *brūn*, from Germanic]

brown ale *n. Brit.* a dark, mild, bottled beer.

brown bag *n.* esp. *N. Amer.* a plain brown paper bag in which a lunch is packed and carried to work etc. ◻ **brown-bagger** *n.*

brown bear *n.* a large brown bear, *Ursus arctos*, found in parts of Eurasia and N. America.

brown coal *n.* = LIGNITE.

browned off *adj. Brit. slang* fed up, disheartened.

brown fat *n.* a dark-coloured adipose tissue with a rich supply of blood vessels.

brown goods *n.pl. Brit.* household goods such as television sets and audio equipment.

brown holland *n.* unbleached holland.

Brownian motion /ˈbraʊnɪən/ *n.* (also **Brownian movement**) *Physics* the erratic random movement of microscopic particles in a liquid, gas, etc., as a result of continuous bombardment from molecules of the surrounding medium. [R. *Brown*, Scots botanist d. 1858]

Brownie /ˈbraʊni/ *n.* **1** (*Brit.* in full **Brownie Guide**) a member of the junior branch of the Guides Association. **2** (**brownie**) **a** a small square of rich, usu. chocolate, cake with nuts. **b** *Austral. & NZ* a sweet currant-bread. **3** (**brownie**) a benevolent elf said to haunt houses and do household work secretly.

Brownie Guider *n.* the adult leader of a pack of Brownie Guides.

brownie point *n. colloq.* a notional credit for something done to please or win favour.

browning /ˈbraʊnɪŋ/ *n. Brit.* browned flour or any other additive to colour gravy.

brown-nose *n. & v.* esp. *N. Amer. slang* ● *n.* (also **brown-noser**) a sycophant. ● *v.intr. & tr.* curry favour (with).

brown owl *n.* **1** any of various owls, esp. the tawny owl. **2** (**Brown Owl**) *Brit. colloq.* the adult leader of a pack of Brownie Guides, officially termed *Brownie Guider* since 1968.

brown rice *n.* unpolished rice with only the husk of the grain removed.

Brownshirt /ˈbraʊnʃɜːt/ *n.* a Nazi; a member of a fascist organization.

brownstone /ˈbraʊnstəʊn/ *n. US* **1** a kind of reddish-brown sandstone used for building. **2** a building faced with this.

brown sugar *n.* unrefined or partially refined sugar.

brown trout *n.* a common European trout, *Salmo trutta*, esp. of a small dark non-migratory race found in small rivers and pools.

browse /braʊz/ *v. & n.* ● *v.* **1** *intr. & tr.* read or survey desultorily. **2** *intr.* (often foll. by *on*) feed (on leaves, twigs, or scanty vegetation). **3** *tr.* crop and eat. **4** *intr. & tr. Computing* read or survey (data files etc.), esp. via a network. ● *n.* **1** twigs, young shoots, etc., as fodder for cattle. **2** an act of browsing. ◻ **browser** *n.* [noun from earlier *brouse* from Old French *brost* 'young shoot', probably from Germanic; verb from French *broster*]

BRS *abbr.* British Road Services.

brucellosis /bruːsəˈləʊsɪs/ *n.* a disease caused by bacteria of the genus *Brucella*, affecting esp. cattle and causing undulant fever in humans. [*Brucella* (from Sir D. *Bruce*, Scots physician d. 1931) + -OSIS]

brucite /ˈbruːsʌɪt/ *n.* a white, grey, or greenish mineral form of magnesium hydroxide. [A. *Bruce*, US mineralogist d. 1818]

Bruin /ˈbruːɪn/ *n.* a personal name used for a bear. [Middle English from Dutch, = BROWN: used as a name in the fable *Reynard the Fox*]

bruise /bruːz/ *n. & v.* ● *n.* **1** an injury appearing as an area of discoloured skin on a human or animal body, caused by a blow or impact which ruptures underlying blood vessels. **2** an area of damage on a fruit etc. ● *v.* **1** *tr.* **a** inflict a bruise on. **b** hurt mentally. **2** *intr.* be susceptible to bruising. **3** *tr.* crush or pound (*bruised oats*). [Middle English from Old English *brȳsan* 'crush', reinforced by Anglo-French *bruser*, Old French *bruisier* 'break']

bruiser /ˈbruːzə/ *n. colloq.* **1** a large tough-looking person. **2** a professional boxer.

bruit /bruːt/ *v. & n.* ● *v.tr.* (often foll. by *abroad*, *about*) spread (a report or rumour). ● *n. archaic* a report or rumour. [French, = noise from *bruire* 'roar']

Brum /brʌm/ *n. Brit. colloq.* Birmingham (in England). [abbreviation of BRUMMAGEM]

brumby /ˈbrʌmbi/ *n.* (*pl.* **-ies**) *Austral.* a wild or unbroken horse. [19th c.: origin unknown]

brume /bruːm/ *n. literary* mist, fog. [French from Latin *bruma* 'winter']

Brummagem /ˈbrʌmədʒ(ə)m/ *adj.* **1** cheap and showy (*Brummagem goods*). **2** counterfeit. [dialect form of

Birmingham, England, with reference to counterfeit coins and plated goods once made there]

Brummie /ˈbrʌmi/ *n. & adj.* (also **Brummy**) *Brit. colloq.* ● *n.* (*pl.* **-ies**) a native of Birmingham. ● *adj.* of or characteristic of a Brummie (*a Brummie accent*). [BRUM]

brunch /brʌn(t)ʃ/ *n. & v.* ● *n.* a late-morning meal eaten as the first meal of the day. ● *v.intr.* eat brunch. [*br*eakfast + l*unch*]

brunette /bruːˈnɛt, brʊ-/ *n. & adj.* (*US* also **brunet**) ● *n.* a woman with dark brown hair. ● *adj.* (of a woman) having dark brown hair. [French, fem. of *brunet*, diminutive of *brun* BROWN]

brunt /brʌnt/ *n.* the chief or initial impact of an attack, task, etc. (esp. *bear the brunt of*). [Middle English: origin unknown]

brush /brʌʃ/ *n. & v.* ● *n.* **1** an implement with bristles, hair, wire, etc. varying in firmness set into a block or projecting from the end of a handle, for any of various purposes, esp. cleaning or scrubbing, painting, arranging the hair, etc. **2** the application of a brush; brushing. **3 a** (usu. foll. by *with*) a short esp. unpleasant encounter (*a brush with the law*). **b** a skirmish. **4 a** the bushy tail of a fox. **b** a brushlike tuft. **5** *Electr.* a piece of carbon or metal serving as an electrical contact esp. with a moving part. **6** esp. *N. Amer.* & *Austral.* **a** undergrowth, thicket; small trees and shrubs. **b** *US* such wood cut in faggots. **c** land covered with brush. **d** *Austral.* dense forest. **7** *Austral. & NZ slang* a girl or young woman. ● *v.* **1** *tr.* **a** sweep or scrub or put in order with a brush. **b** treat (a surface) with a brush so as to change its nature or appearance. **2** *tr.* **a** remove (dust etc.) with a brush. **b** apply (a liquid preparation) to a surface with a brush. **3** *tr. & intr.* graze or touch in passing. **4** *intr.* perform a brushing action or motion. □ **brush aside** dismiss or dispose of (a person, idea, etc.) curtly or lightly. **brush off** rebuff; dismiss abruptly. **brush over** paint lightly. **brush up 1** *Brit.* clean up or smarten. **2** (often foll. by *on*) revive one's former knowledge of (a subject). □ **brushlike** *adj.* **brushy** *adj.* [Middle English from Old French *brosse*]

brush discharge *n. Electr.* a broad electrical discharge occurring when the potential difference is not sufficient for a spark or arc.

brushed aluminium *n.* aluminium treated so that it has a lustreless surface.

brushed fabric *n.* fabric brushed so as to raise the nap.

brushless /ˈbrʌʃlɪs/ *adj.* not requiring the use of a brush.

brush-off *n.* a rebuff; an abrupt dismissal.

brush turkey *n. Austral.* a large mound-building bird, *Alectura lathami.*

brush-up *n. Brit.* the process or an instance of brushing up.

brushwood /ˈbrʌʃwʊd/ *n.* **1** cut or broken twigs etc. **2** undergrowth; thicket.

brushwork /ˈbrʌʃwəːk/ *n.* **1** manipulation of the brush in painting. **2** a painter's style in this.

brusque /brʊsk, bruːsk/ *adj.* abrupt or offhand in manner or speech. □ **brusquely** *adv.* **brusqueness** *n.* **brusquerie** /ˈbrʊsk(ə)riː, ˈbruː-/ *n.* [French from Italian *brusco* 'sour']

Brussels carpet /ˈbrʌs(ə)lz/ *n.* a carpet with a wool pile and a stout linen back. [*Brussels* in Belgium]

Brussels lace /ˈbrʌs(ə)lz/ *n.* an elaborate needlepoint or pillow lace.

Brussels sprout /ˈbrʌs(ə)lz/ *n.* **1** a variety of cabbage producing many small compact buds borne close together along a tall single stem. **2** one of these buds used as a vegetable.

brut /bruːt/ *adj.* (of wine) unsweetened. [French, = raw, rough]

brutal /ˈbruːt(ə)l/ *adj.* **1** savagely or coarsely cruel. **2** harsh, merciless. □ **brutality** /-ˈtalɪti/ *n.* (*pl.* **-ies**). **brutally** *adv.* [French *brutal* or medieval Latin *brutalis*, from *brutus* BRUTE]

brutalism /ˈbruːt(ə)lɪz(ə)m/ *n.* **1** brutality. **2** a heavy plain style of architecture etc. □ **brutalist** *n. & adj.*

brutalize /ˈbruːt(ə)lʌɪz/ *v.tr.* (also **-ise**) **1** make brutal. **2** treat brutally. □ **brutalization** /-ˈzeɪʃ(ə)n/ *n.*

brute /bruːt/ *n. & adj.* ● *n.* **1 a** a brutal or violent person or animal. **b** *colloq.* an unpleasant person. **2** an animal as opposed to a human being. ● *adj.* (usu. *attrib.*) **1** not possessing the capacity to reason. **2 a** animal-like, cruel. **b** stupid, sensual. **3** unthinking, merely material (*brute force*; *brute matter*). □ **brutehood** *n.* **brutish** *adj.* **brutishly** *adv.* **brutishness** *n.* [French from Latin *brutus* 'stupid']

bruxism /ˈbrʌksɪz(ə)m/ *n.* the involuntary or habitual grinding or clenching of the teeth. [Greek *brukhein* 'gnash the teeth']

Brylcreem /ˈbrɪlkriːm/ *n. propr.* a cream for working into the hair to give it a smooth shiny appearance. [corruption of BRILLIANT + CREAM]

bryology /brʌɪˈɒlədʒi/ *n.* the study of bryophytes. □ **bryological** /-əˈlɒdʒɪk(ə)l/ *adj.* **bryologist** *n.* [Greek *bruon* 'moss']

bryony /ˈbrʌɪəni/ *n.* (*pl.* **-ies**) any climbing plant of the genus *Bryonia*, esp. *B. dioica* bearing greenish-white flowers and red berries. [Latin *bryonia* from Greek *bruōnia*]

bryophyte /ˈbrʌɪə(ʊ)fʌɪt/ *n.* a cryptogamous plant of the division Bryophyta, comprising mosses and liverworts. □ **bryophytic** /-ˈfɪtɪk/ *adj.* [modern Latin *Bryophyta* from Greek *bruon* 'moss' + *phuton* 'plant']

bryozoan /brʌɪə(ʊ)ˈzəʊən/ *n. & adj.* ● *n.* any aquatic invertebrate animal of the phylum Bryozoa, forming colonies attached to rocks, seaweeds, etc. Also called *polyzoan.* ● *adj.* of or relating to the phylum Bryozoa. □ **bryozoology** /-zəʊˈɒlədʒi, -zuː-/ *n.* [Greek *bruon* 'moss' + *zōia* 'animals']

Brythonic /brɪˈθɒnɪk/ *n. & adj.* ● *n.* the southern group of the Celtic languages, comprising Welsh, Cornish, and Breton. Also called *Brittonic.* ● *adj.* of or relating to Brythonic. [Welsh *Brython* 'Britons' from Celtic]

BS *abbr.* **1** *US* Bachelor of Science. **2** Bachelor of Surgery. **3** Blessed Sacrament. **4** British Standard(s).

B.Sc. *abbr.* Bachelor of Science.

BSE *abbr.* bovine spongiform encephalopathy, a usu. fatal disease of cattle involving the central nervous system and causing extreme agitation. Also called *mad cow disease.*

BSI *abbr.* British Standards Institution.

B-side *n.* the side of a gramophone record regarded as less important.

BST *abbr.* **1** British Summer Time. **2** *hist.* British Standard Time (one hour ahead of GMT, in continuous use 1968–71). **3** bovine somatotrophin, a growth hormone produced naturally by cows and introduced into cattle feed to boost milk production.

BT *abbr.* British Telecom.

Bt. *abbr.* Baronet.

Btu *abbr.* (also **BTU**, **B.th.U.**) British thermal unit(s).

bu. *abbr.* bushel(s).

bub /bʌb/ *n. N. Amer. colloq.* a boy or a man, often used as a form of address. [earlier *bubby*, perhaps a childish form of BROTHER or from German *Bube* 'boy']

bubal /ˈbjuːb(ə)l/ *n.* = HARTEBEEST. [Latin *bubalus* from Greek *boubalos* 'oxlike antelope']

bubble /ˈbʌb(ə)l/ *n. & v.* ● *n.* **1 a** a thin sphere of liquid enclosing air etc. **b** an air-filled cavity in a liquid or a solidified liquid such as glass or amber. **2** the sound or appearance of bubbling; an agitated or bubbling motion. **3** a transparent domed cavity. **4** a visionary or unrealistic project or enterprise (*the South Sea Bubble*). ● *v.intr.* **1** rise in or send up bubbles. **2** make the sound of rising or bursting bubbles. □ **bubble over** (often foll. by *with*) be exuberant with laughter, excitement, anger, etc. [Middle English: probably imitative]

bubble and squeak *n. Brit.* cooked cabbage fried with cooked potatoes or meat. [from the sounds of it cooking]

bubble bath *n.* **1** a preparation for adding to bathwater to make it foam. **2** a bath with this added.

bubble car *n. Brit.* a small motor car with a transparent domed canopy.

bubble chamber *n. Physics* an apparatus designed to make the tracks of ionizing particles visible as a row of bubbles in a liquid.

bubblegum /ˈbʌb(ə)lgʌm/ *n.* chewing gum that can be blown into bubbles.

bubble memory *n. Computing* a type of memory which stores data as a pattern of magnetized regions in a thin layer of magnetic material.

bubble pack *n.* a small package enclosing goods in a transparent material on a backing.

bubble wrap *n.* plastic wrapping material in sheets containing numerous small air-filled bladders.

bubbly /ˈbʌbli/ *adj. & n.* ● *adj.* (**bubblier**, **bubbliest**) **1** having or resembling bubbles. **2** exuberant, vivacious. ● *n. colloq.* champagne.

bubbly-jock /ˈbʌblɪdʒɒk/ *n. Sc.* a turkeycock. [*bubbly* imitative of the bird's call + *Jock* male forename]

bubo /ˈbjuːbəʊ/ *n.* (*pl.* **-oes**) a swollen inflamed lymph node in the armpit or groin. ▫ **bubonic** /bjuːˈbɒnɪk/ *adj.* [medieval Latin *bubo -onis* 'swelling' from Greek *boubōn* 'groin']

bubonic plague *n.* a contagious bacterial disease characterized by fever, delirium, and the formation of buboes. Cf. PLAGUE *n.* 1a.

buccal /ˈbʌk(ə)l/ *adj.* **1** of or relating to the cheek. **2** of or in the mouth. [Latin *bucca* 'cheek']

buccaneer /bʌkəˈnɪə/ *n. & v.* ● *n.* **1** a pirate, originally off the Spanish-American coasts. **2** an unscrupulous adventurer. ● *v.intr.* be a buccaneer. ▫ **buccaneering** *n. & adj.* **buccaneerish** *adj.* [originally applied to European hunters in the Caribbean: French *boucanier* via *boucaner* 'cure meat on a barbecue' from *boucan* from Tupi *mukem*]

buccinator /ˈbʌksɪneɪtə/ *n.* a flat thin cheek muscle. [Latin from *buccinare* 'blow a trumpet', from *buccina* 'trumpet']

buck[1] /bʌk/ *n. & v.* ● *n.* **1** the male of various animals, esp. the deer, hare, or rabbit. **2** *archaic* a fashionable young man. **3** (*attrib.*) **a** *slang* male (*buck antelope*). **b** *US Mil. slang* of the lowest rank (*buck private*). ● *v.* **1** *intr.* (of a horse) jump upwards with back arched and feet drawn together. **2** *tr.* **a** (usu. foll. by *off*) throw (a rider or burden) in this way. **b** esp. *N. Amer.* oppose, resist (*tried to buck the trend*). **3** *tr. & intr.* (usu. foll. by *up*) *colloq.* **a** make or become more cheerful. **b** *Brit.* make or become more vigorous or lively; make an effort; hurry (*needs to buck up his ideas*). **4** *tr.* (as **bucked** *adj.*) *Brit. colloq.* encouraged, elated. [Old English *buc* 'male deer', *bucca* 'male goat', from Old Norse]

buck[2] /bʌk/ *n. N. Amer. & Austral. slang* a dollar. ▫ **a fast buck** easy money. [19th c.: origin unknown]

buck[3] /bʌk/ *n. slang* an article placed as a reminder before a player whose turn it is to deal at poker. ▫ **pass the buck** *colloq.* shift responsibility (to another). [19th c.: origin unknown]

buck[4] /bʌk/ *n.* **1** *N. Amer.* a sawhorse. **2** a vaulting horse. [Dutch (*zaag*)*boc*, as SAW[1], BUCK[1]]

buck[5] /bʌk/ *n.* the body of a cart. [perhaps from obsolete *bouk* 'belly, body' from Old English *būc*, from Germanic]

buckbean /ˈbʌkbiːn/ *n.* a bog plant, *Menyanthes trifoliata*, with white or pinkish hairy flowers. Also called *bogbean*. [Flemish *bocks boonen* 'goat's beans']

buckboard /ˈbʌkbɔːd/ *n. US* a horse-drawn vehicle with the body formed by a plank fixed to the axles. [BUCK[5] + BOARD]

bucket /ˈbʌkɪt/ *n. & v.* ● *n.* **1 a** a roughly cylindrical open container (usu. of metal or plastic) with a handle, used for carrying, drawing, or holding water etc. **b** the amount contained in this (*need three buckets to fill the bath*). **2** (in *pl.*) large quantities of liquid, esp. rain or tears (*wept buckets*). **3** a compartment on the outer edge of a waterwheel. **4** the scoop of a dredger or a grain-elevator. ● *v.* (**bucketed**, **bucketing**) **1** *intr.* (usu. foll. by *down*) (of liquid, esp. rain) pour heavily. **2** *intr. & tr.* (often foll. by *along*) move or drive jerkily or bumpily. ▫ **bucketful** *n.* (*pl.* **-fuls**). [Middle English & Anglo-French *buket*, *buquet*, perhaps from Old English *būc* 'pitcher']

bucket seat *n.* a seat with a rounded back to fit one person, esp. in a car.

bucket shop *n.* **1** an unauthorized office for gambling in stocks, speculating on markets, etc. **2** *Brit. colloq.* a travel agency specializing in cheap air tickets.

buckeye /ˈbʌkʌɪ/ *n.* **1** an American tree or shrub of the horse chestnut genus *Aesculus*, with large sticky buds and showy red or white flowers. **2** the shiny brown fruit of this plant.

buck fever *n. US* nervousness when called on to act.

buck-horn *n.* horn of buck as a material for knife handles etc.

buck-hound *n.* a small kind of staghound.

buckle /ˈbʌk(ə)l/ *n. & v.* ● *n.* **1** a flat often rectangular frame with a hinged pin, used for joining the ends of a belt, strap, etc. **2** a similarly shaped ornament, esp. on a shoe. ● *v.* **1** *tr.* (often foll. by *up*, *on*, etc.) fasten with a buckle. **2** *tr. & intr.* (often foll. by *up*) give way or cause to give way under longitudinal pressure; crumple up. ▫ **buckle down** make a determined effort. **buckle to** (or **down to**) prepare for, set about (work etc.). **buckle to** get to work, make a vigorous start. [Middle English via Old French *boucle* from Latin *buccula* 'cheek-strap of a helmet', from *bucca* 'cheek': sense 2 of *v.* from French *boucler* 'bulge']

buckler /ˈbʌklə/ *n.* **1** *hist.* a small round shield held by a handle. **2** *Bot.* any of several ferns of the genus *Dryopteris*, having buckler-shaped indusia; also called SHIELD FERN. [Middle English via Old French *bocler*, literally 'having a boss', from *boucle* BOSS[2]]

Buckley's /ˈbʌklɪz/ *n.* (in full **Buckley's chance**) *Austral. & NZ colloq.* little or no chance. [19th c.: origin uncertain]

buckling /ˈbʌklɪŋ/ *n. Brit.* a smoked herring. [German *Bückling* 'bloater']

buckminsterfullerene /ˌbʌkmɪnstəˈfʊləriːn/ *n. Chem.* a form of carbon with 60 atoms joined in a polyhedron of 20 hexagons and 12 pentagons. [R. *Buckminster Fuller* (d. 1983), US inventor of the geodesic dome]

bucko /ˈbʌkəʊ/ *n. & adj. Naut. slang* ● *n.* (*pl.* **-oes**) a swaggering or domineering person. ● *adj.* blustering, swaggering, bullying. [BUCK[1] + -O]

buck-passing *n.* the act of passing the buck or shifting responsibility to another person.

buckram /ˈbʌkrəm/ *n. & adj.* ● *n.* **1** a coarse linen or other cloth stiffened with gum or paste, and used as interfacing or in bookbinding. **2** *archaic* stiffness in manner. ● *adj. archaic* starchy; formal. ▫ **men in buckram** non-existent persons; figments (Shakespeare's *1 Henry IV* II. iv. 210–50). [Middle English from Anglo-French *bukeram*, Old French *boquerant*, perhaps from *Bokhara* (now *Bukhara*) in central Asia]

buck rarebit *n. Brit.* Welsh rarebit with a poached egg on top.

Bucks. /bʌks/ *abbr.* Buckinghamshire.

Buck's Fizz /bʌks/ *n. Brit.* a cocktail of champagne or sparkling white wine and orange juice. [*Buck's* Club in London + FIZZ]

buckshee /bʌkˈʃiː, ˈbʌkʃiː/ *adj. & adv. Brit. slang* free of charge. [corruption of BAKSHEESH]

buckshot /ˈbʌkʃɒt/ *n.* coarse lead shot.

buckskin /ˈbʌkskɪn/ *n.* **1 a** the skin of a male deer. **b** leather made from such skin. **2** a thick smooth cotton or woollen cloth.

buckthorn /ˈbʌkθɔːn/ *n.* any thorny shrub of the genus *Rhamnus*, esp. *R. cathartica* with berries formerly used as a cathartic.

buck-tooth *n.* an upper tooth that projects. □ **buck-toothed** *adj.*

buckwheat /ˈbʌkwiːt/ *n.* a cereal plant of the genus *Fagopyrum*, esp. *F. esculentum* with seeds used for fodder and for flour to make bread and pancakes. [Middle Dutch *boecweite* 'beech wheat', its grains being shaped like beechmast]

bucolic /bjuːˈkɒlɪk/ *adj. & n.* ● *adj.* of or concerning shepherds or the pastoral life; rural. ● *n.* **1** (usu. in *pl.*) a pastoral poem or poetry. **2** a peasant. □ **bucolically** *adv.* [Latin *bucolicus* from Greek *boukolikos*, from *boukolos* 'herdsman' from *bous* ox]

bud[1] /bʌd/ *n. & v.* ● *n.* **1 a** an immature knoblike shoot from which a stem, leaf, or flower develops. **b** a flower or leaf that is not fully open. **2** *Biol.* an asexual outgrowth from a parent organism that separates to form a new individual. **3** anything still undeveloped. ● *v.* (**budded**, **budding**) **1** *intr. Bot. & Zool.* form a bud or buds. **2** *intr.* begin to grow or develop (*a budding cricketer*). **3** *tr.* graft a bud (of a plant) on to another plant. □ **in bud** having newly formed buds. [Middle English: origin unknown]

bud[2] /bʌd/ *n. N. Amer. colloq.* (as a form of address) = BUDDY. [abbreviation]

Buddha /ˈbʊdə/ *n.* **1** a title given to successive teachers of Buddhism, esp. to its founder, Gautama. **2** a statue or picture of the Buddha. [Sanskrit, = enlightened, past part. of *budh* 'know']

Buddhism /ˈbʊdɪz(ə)m/ *n.* a widespread Asian religion or philosophy, founded by Gautama Buddha in India in the 5th c. BC, which teaches that elimination of the self and earthly desires is the highest goal (cf. NIRVANA). □ **Buddhist** *n. & adj.* **Buddhistic** /-ˈdɪstɪk/ *adj.* **Buddhistical** /-ˈdɪstɪk(ə)l/ *adj.*

buddleia /ˈbʌdlɪə/ *n.* any shrub of the genus *Buddleia*, with fragrant lilac, yellow, or white flowers attractive to butterflies. [A. *Buddle*, English botanist d. 1715]

buddy /ˈbʌdi/ *n. & v.* esp. *N. Amer. colloq.* ● *n.* (*pl.* **-ies**) **1** (often as a form of address) a close friend or mate. **2** a person who befriends and gives help to another with an incapacitating disease, esp. Aids. ● *v.intr.* (**-ies**, **-ied**) (often foll. by *up*) become friendly. [perhaps corruption of *brother*, or variant of BUTTY[1]]

buddy movie *n.* esp. *N. Amer. colloq.* a film featuring friendship between two individuals, esp. men.

budge /bʌdʒ/ *v.* (usu. with *neg.*) **1** *intr. Brit.* **a** make the slightest movement. **b** change one's opinion (*he's stubborn, he won't budge*). **2** *tr.* cause or compel to budge (*nothing will budge him*). □ **budge up** (or **over**) *Brit.* make room for another person by moving. [French *bouger* 'stir', ultimately from Latin *bullire* 'boil']

budgerigar /ˈbʌdʒ(ə)rɪɡɑː/ *n.* a small green parrot, *Melopsittacus undulatus*, native to Australia, and bred in coloured varieties which are often kept as cage birds. [Aboriginal, perhaps alteration of Kamilaroi (and related languages) *gijirrigaa*]

budget /ˈbʌdʒɪt/ *n. & v.* ● *n.* **1** the amount of money needed or available (for a specific item etc.) (*a budget of £200; mustn't exceed the budget*). **2 a** (**the Budget**) a usu. annual estimate of national revenue and expenditure. **b** a similar estimate of revenue or income and expenditure made by a company, family, private individual, etc. **3** (*attrib.*) inexpensive. **4** *archaic* a quantity of material etc., esp. written or printed. ● *v.tr. & intr.* (**budgeted**, **budgeting**) (often foll. by *for*) allow or arrange for in a budget (*have budgeted for a new car; can budget £60*). □ **on a budget** with a restricted amount of money. □ **budgetary** *adj.* [Middle English = pouch, via Old French *bougette*, diminutive of *bouge* 'leather bag', from Latin *bulga* (from Gaulish) 'knapsack': cf. BULGE]

budget account *n.* (also **budget plan**) *Brit.* a bank account, or account with a store or public utility, into which one makes regular, usu. monthly, payments to cover bills.

budgie /ˈbʌdʒi/ *n. colloq.* = BUDGERIGAR. [abbreviation]

buff /bʌf/ *adj., n., & v.* ● *adj.* yellowish beige (*buff envelope*). ● *n.* **1** a yellowish-beige colour. **2** *colloq.* an enthusiast, esp. for a particular hobby (*railway buff*). **3 a** a velvety dull yellow ox-leather. **b** (*attrib.*) (of a garment etc.) made of this (*buff gloves*). **4** (**the Buffs**) the former East Kent Regiment (from the colour of its uniform facings). ● *v.tr.* **1** polish (metal, fingernails, etc.). **2** make (leather) velvety like buff, by removing the surface. □ **in the buff** *colloq.* naked. [original sense 'buffalo', probably from French *buffle*; sense 2 of noun originally from buff uniforms formerly worn by New York volunteer firemen, applied to enthusiastic fire-watchers]

buffalo /ˈbʌfələʊ/ *n. & v.* ● *n.* (*pl.* same or **-oes**) **1 a** an Asiatic ox of the genus *Bubalus*, with heavy backswept horns, esp. (in full **water buffalo**) *B. arnee*, which is domesticated as a draught animal. **b** (in full **Cape buffalo**) a powerful wild ox, *Syncerus caffer*, of eastern and southern Africa. **2** a N. American bison, *Bison bison*. ● *v.tr.* (**-oes**, **-oed**) *N. Amer. slang* overawe, outwit. [probably from Portuguese *bufalo* via Late Latin *bufalus* and Latin *bubalus* from Greek *boubalos* 'antelope, wild ox']

buffalo grass *n.* **1** a grass, *Buchloe dactyloides*, of the N. American plains. **2** a grass, *Stenotaphrum secundatum*, of Australia and New Zealand.

buffer[1] /ˈbʌfə/ *n. & v.* ● *n.* **1 a** a device that protects against or reduces the effect of an impact. **b** *Brit.* such a device (usu. one of a pair) projecting from a cross-beam on the front and rear of a railway vehicle or at the end of a track. **2** *Chem.* a substance that acts to minimize the change in hydrogen ion concentration of a solution when an acid or alkali is added. **3** *Computing* a temporary memory area or queue for data to aid its transfer between devices or programs operating at different speeds etc. ● *v.tr.* **1** act as a buffer to. **2** *Chem.* treat with a buffer. [probably from obsolete *buff* (v.), imitative of the sound of a blow to a soft body]

buffer[2] /ˈbʌfə/ *n. Brit. slang* a silly or incompetent old man (esp. *old buffer*). [18th c.: probably formed as BUFFER[1] or with the sense 'stutterer']

buffer state *n.* a small state situated between two larger ones potentially hostile to one another and regarded as reducing the likelihood of open hostilities.

buffer stock *n. Brit.* a reserve of commodity to offset price fluctuations.

buffer zone *n.* a zone separating potential belligerents.

buffet[1] /ˈbʊfeɪ/ *n.* **1** a room or counter where light meals or snacks may be bought (*station buffet*). **2** a meal consisting of several dishes set out from which guests serve themselves (*buffet lunch*). **3** /also ˈbʌfɪt/ a sideboard or recessed cupboard for china etc. [French from Old French *buf(f)et* 'stool', of unknown origin]

buffet[2] /ˈbʌfɪt/ *v. & n.* ● *v.* (**buffeted**, **buffeting**) **1** *tr.* **a** strike or knock repeatedly (*wind buffeted the trees*). **b** strike, esp. repeatedly, with the hand or fist. **2** *tr.* (of fate etc.) treat badly; plague (*cheerful though buffeted by misfortune*). **3 a** *intr.* struggle; fight one's way (through difficulties etc.). **b** *tr.* contend with (waves etc.). ● *n.* **1** a blow, esp. of the hand or fist. **2** a shock. [Middle English from Old French, diminutive of *bufe* 'blow']

buffet[3] /ˈbʌfɪt/ *n. dial.* **1** a low stool; a footstool. **2** a hassock. [Old French *buf(f)et*, of unknown origin]

buffet car *n.* a railway coach serving light meals or snacks.

buffeting /ˈbʌfɪtɪŋ/ *n.* **1** a beating; repeated blows. **2** *Aeron.* an irregular oscillation, caused by air eddies, of part of an aircraft.

bufflehead /ˈbʌf(ə)lhɛd/ *n.* a large-headed black and white diving duck, *Bucephala albeola*, native to N. America. [obsolete *buffle* 'buffalo' + HEAD]

buffo /ˈbʊfəʊ/ *n. & adj.* ● *n.* (*pl.* **-os**) a comic actor, esp. in Italian opera. ● *adj.* comic, burlesque. [Italian, = puff of wind, buffoon]

buffoon /bəˈfu:n/ *n.* **1** a ludicrous person. **2** a jester; a mocker. □ **buffoonery** *n.* **buffoonish** *adj.* [French *bouffon* via Italian *buffone* and medieval Latin *buffo* 'clown' from Romanic]

bug /bʌg/ *n. & v.* ● *n.* **1 a** an insect of the order Hemiptera, with mouthparts modified for piercing and sucking. **b** any small insect. **2** *slang* a micro-organism, esp. a bacterium, or a disease caused by it. **3** a concealed microphone. **4** an error in a computer program or system etc. **5** *colloq.* an obsession, enthusiasm, etc. ● *v.* (**bugged**, **bugging**) **1** *tr.* conceal a microphone in (esp. a building or room). **2** *tr. slang* annoy, bother. **3** *intr.* esp. *N. Amer. slang* **a** (often foll. by *out*) leave quickly. **b** (foll. by *off*) go away. [17th c.: origin unknown]

bugaboo /ˈbʌgəbu:/ *n.* a bogey (see BOGEY[2]) or bugbear. [probably of dialect origin: cf. Welsh *bwcibo* 'the Devil', *bwci* 'hobgoblin']

bugbear /ˈbʌgbɛ:/ *n.* **1** a cause of annoyance or anger; a *bête noire*. **2** an object of baseless fear. **3** *archaic* a sort of hobgoblin or any other being invoked to intimidate children. [obsolete *bug* 'bogey' + BEAR[2]]

bug-eyed *adj.* with bulging eyes.

bugger /ˈbʌgə/ *n., v., & int. coarse slang* (except in sense 2 of *n.* and 3 of *v.*) ● *n.* **1** esp. *Brit.* **a** an unpleasant or awkward person or thing (*the bugger won't fit*). **b** a person of a specified kind (*he's a miserable bugger*; *you clever bugger!*). **2** a person who commits buggery. ● *v.tr.* **1** as an exclamation of annoyance (*bugger the thing!*). **2** (often foll. by *up*) **a** ruin; spoil (*really buggered it up*; *no good, it's buggered*). **b** (esp. as **buggered** *adj.*) *Brit.* exhaust, tire out. **3** commit buggery with. ● *int.* expressing annoyance. □ **bugger about** (or **around**) (often foll. by *with*) *Brit.* **1** mess about. **2** mislead; persecute. **bugger all** *Brit.* nothing. **bugger off** (often in *imper.*) *Brit.* go away. [Middle English via Middle Dutch from Old French *bougre*, originally 'heretic', from medieval Latin *Bulgarus* 'Bulgarian (member of the Greek Church)']

buggery /ˈbʌgəri/ *n.* **1** anal intercourse. **2** = BESTIALITY 2. [Middle English via Middle Dutch *buggerie* from Old French *bougerie*: see BUGGER]

buggy[1] /ˈbʌgi/ *n.* (*pl.* **-ies**) **1** a light, horse-drawn, esp. two-wheeled, vehicle for one or two people. **2** a small, sturdy, esp. open, motor vehicle (*beach buggy*; *dune buggy*). **3** = BABY BUGGY 1, 2. [18th c.: origin unknown]

buggy[2] /ˈbʌgi/ *adj.* (**buggier**, **buggiest**) infested with bugs.

bugle[1] /ˈbju:g(ə)l/ *n. & v.* ● *n.* (also **bugle-horn**) a brass instrument like a small trumpet, used esp. for military signals and in fox-hunting. ● *v.* **1** *intr.* sound a bugle. **2** *tr.* sound (a note, a call, etc.) on a bugle. □ **bugler** /ˈbju:glə/ *n.* [Middle English via Old French from Latin *buculus* diminutive of *bos* 'ox' (from the use of an ox's horn as a bugle]

bugle[2] /ˈbju:g(ə)l/ *n.* a creeping labiate plant, *Ajuga reptans*, with blue flowers. [Middle English, from Late Latin *bugula*]

bugle[3] /ˈbju:g(ə)l/ *n.* a tube-shaped bead sewn on a dress etc. for ornament. [16th c.: origin unknown]

bugloss /ˈbju:glɒs/ *n.* **1** any of various bristly plants related to borage, esp. of the genus *Anchusa* with bright blue tubular flowers. **2** = VIPER'S BUGLOSS. [French *buglosse* or Latin *buglossus*, from Greek *bouglōssos* 'ox-tongued']

buhl /bu:l/ *n.* (also **boule**, **boulle**) **1** pieces of brass, tortoiseshell, etc., cut to make a pattern and used as decorative inlays esp. on furniture. **2** work inlaid with buhl. **3** (*attrib.*) inlaid with buhl. [(*buhl* Germanized) from A. C. *Boulle*, French woodcarver d. 1732]

build /bɪld/ *v. & n.* ● *v.tr.* (*past* and *past. part.* **built** /bɪlt/) **1 a** construct (a house, vehicle, fire, road, model, etc.) by putting parts or material together. **b** commission, finance, and oversee the building of (*the council has built two new schools*). **2 a** (often foll. by *up*) establish, develop, make, or accumulate gradually (*built the business up from nothing*). **b** (often foll. by *on*) base (hopes, theories, etc.) (*ideas built on a false foundation*). **3** (as **built** *adj.*) having a specified build (*sturdily built*; *brick-built*). ● *n.* **1** the proportions of esp. the human body (*a slim build*). **2** a style of construction; a make (*build of his suit was pre-war*). □ **build in** incorporate as part of a structure. **build in** (or **round** or **up**) surround with houses etc.; block up. **build on** add (an extension etc.). **build up 1** increase in size or strength. **2** praise; boost. **3** gradually become established. **built on sand** unstable. [Old English *byldan* from *bold* 'dwelling', from Germanic]

builder /ˈbɪldə/ *n.* **1** a contractor for building houses etc.; a master builder. **2** a person engaged as a bricklayer etc. on a building site.

builders' merchant *n. Brit.* a supplier of materials to builders.

building /ˈbɪldɪŋ/ *n.* **1** a permanent fixed structure forming an enclosure and providing protection from the elements etc. (e.g. a house, school, factory, or stable). **2** the constructing of such structures.

building line *n.* a limit or boundary between a house and a street beyond which the owner may not build.

building site *n.* an area before or during the construction of a house etc.

building society *n. Brit.* a financial organization which accepts investments at interest and lends capital for mortgages on houses etc.

build-up *n.* **1** a favourable description in advance; publicity. **2** a gradual approach to a climax or maximum (*the build-up was slow but sure*). **3** an accumulation or increase.

built *past* and *past part.* of BUILD.

built-in *adj.* **1** forming an integral part of a structure. **2** inherent, integral, innate (*built-in obsolescence*; *built-in integrity*).

built-up *adj.* **1** (of a locality) densely covered by houses etc. **2** increased in height etc. by the addition of parts. **3** composed of separately prepared parts.

bulb /bʌlb/ *n.* **1 a** a fleshy-leaved storage organ of some plants (e.g. lily, onion) sending roots downwards and leaves upwards. **b** a plant grown from this, e.g. a daffodil. **2** = LIGHT BULB. **3** any object or part shaped like a bulb. [Latin *bulbus* from Greek *bolbos* 'onion']

bulbil /ˈbʌlbɪl/ *n. Bot.* **1** a small bulb which grows among the leaves or flowers of a plant. **2** a small bulb at the side of an ordinary bulb. [modern Latin *bulbillus*, diminutive of *bulbus* 'bulb']

bulbous /ˈbʌlbəs/ *adj.* **1** shaped like a bulb; fat or bulging. **2** having a bulb or bulbs. **3** (of a plant) growing from a bulb.

bulbul /ˈbʊlbʊl/ *n.* **1** an Asian or African songbird of the family Pycnonotidae, of dull plumage with contrasting bright patches. **2** a singer or poet. [Persian from Arabic, of imitative origin]

Bulgar /ˈbʌlgɑ:/ *n.* **1** a member of a tribe who settled in what is now Bulgaria in the 7th c. **2** a Bulgarian. [medieval Latin *Bulgarus* from Old Bulgarian *Blŭgarinŭ*]

bulgar /ˈbʌlgə/ *n.* (also **bulgur**) a cereal food of whole wheat partially boiled then dried, eaten esp. in Turkey. [Turkish]

Bulgarian /bʌlˈgɛ:rɪən/ *n. & adj.* ● *n.* **1 a** a native or national of Bulgaria. **b** a person of Bulgarian descent. **2** the language of Bulgaria. ● *adj.* of or relating to Bulgaria or its people or language. [medieval Latin *Bulgaria* from *Bulgarus*: see BULGAR]

bulge /bʌldʒ/ *n. & v.* ● *n.* **1 a** a convex part of an otherwise flat or flatter surface. **b** an irregular swelling; a lump. **2** *colloq.* a temporary increase in quantity or number (*baby bulge*). **3** *Naut.* the bilge of a ship. **4** *Mil.* a salient. ● *v.* **1** *intr.* swell outwards. **2** *intr.* be full or replete. **3** *tr.* swell (a bag, cheeks, etc.) by stuffing. □ **have** (or **get**) **the bulge on** *Brit. slang* have or get an advantage over. □ **bulgingly** *adv.* **bulgy** *adj.* [Middle English via Old French *boulge*, *bouge* from Latin *bulga*: see BUDGET]

bulgur var. of BULGAR.

bulimarexia /bjʊˌlɪməˈrɛksɪə, bʊ-/ *n.* esp. *US* = BULIMIA 2. ▫ **bulimarexic** *adj. & n.* [BULIMIA + ANOREXIA]

bulimia /bjʊˈlɪmɪə, bʊ-/ *n. Med.* **1** insatiable overeating. **2** (in full **bulimia nervosa**) an emotional disorder in which bouts of extreme overeating are followed by depression and self-induced vomiting, purging, or fasting. ▫ **bulimic** *adj. & n.* [modern Latin from Greek *boulimia* from *bous* 'ox' + *limos* 'hunger']

bulk /bʌlk/ *n. & v.* ● *n.* **1** (usu. prec. by *the* and foll. by *of*; the verb agrees with the complement) the greater part or number (*the bulk of the applicants are women*; *the bulk of the book is boring*). **2 a** size, magnitude, or volume (esp. large) (*its bulk is enormous*). **b** a large mass or shape. **c** great quantity or volume (often *attrib.*: *a bulk supplier*). **3** a bodily frame of large proportions (*jacket barely covered his bulk*). **4** roughage in food. **5** *Naut.* a ship's cargo, esp. unpackaged. ● *v.* **1** *intr.* seem in respect of size or importance (*bulks large in his reckoning*). **2** *tr.* make (a book, a textile yarn, etc.) seem thicker by suitable treatment (*bulked it with irrelevant stories*). **3** *tr.* combine (consignments etc.). ▫ **break bulk** begin unloading cargo. **in bulk 1** in large quantities, usu. at a lower price. **2** (of a cargo) loose, not packaged. [sense 'cargo' from Old Norse *búlki*; sense 'mass' etc. perhaps alteration of obsolete *bouk* (see BUCK[5])]

bulk buying *n.* **1** buying in large amounts at a discount. **2** the purchase by one buyer of all or most of a producer's output. ▫ **bulk-buy** *v.tr.*

bulkhead /ˈbʌlkhɛd/ *n.* an upright partition separating the compartments in a ship, aircraft, vehicle, etc. [*bulk* 'stall' from Old Norse *bálkr* + HEAD]

bulky /ˈbʌlki/ *adj.* (**bulkier**, **bulkiest**) **1** taking up much space, large. **2** awkwardly large, unwieldy. ▫ **bulkily** *adv.* **bulkiness** *n.*

bull[1] /bʊl/ *n., adj., & v.* ● *n.* **1 a** an uncastrated male bovine animal. **b** a male of the whale, elephant, and other large animals. **2** (**the Bull**) the zodiacal sign or constellation Taurus. **3** *Brit.* the bull's-eye of a target. **4** *Stock Exch.* a person who buys shares hoping to sell them at a higher price later (cf. BEAR[2]). ● *attrib.adj.* like that of a bull (*bull neck*). ● *v.* **1** *tr. & intr.* act or treat violently. **2** *Stock Exch.* **a** *intr.* speculate for a rise. **b** *tr.* raise price of (stocks, etc.). ▫ **bull at a gate** *Brit.* a hasty or rash person. **bull in a china shop** a reckless or clumsy person. **take the bull by the horns** face danger or challenge boldly. [Old English (in place names) from Old Norse *boli*: cf. BULLOCK]

bull[2] /bʊl/ *n.* a papal edict. [Middle English via Old French *bulle* from Latin *bulla* 'rounded object', in medieval Latin 'seal']

bull[3] /bʊl/ *n.* **1** (also **Irish bull**) an expression containing a contradiction in terms or implying ludicrous inconsistency. **2** *slang* (cf. BULLSHIT) **a** nonsense. **b** trivial or insincere talk or writing. **c** unnecessary routine tasks or discipline. **d** *US* a bad blunder. [17th c.: origin unknown]

bullace /ˈbʊlɪs/ *n.* a thorny shrub, *Prunus insititia*, of the rose family, bearing globular yellow or purple-black fruits, of which the damson is the cultivated form. [Middle English from Old French *buloce, beloce*]

bull ant *n. Austral.* = BULLDOG ANT.

bulldog /ˈbʊldɒg/ *n.* **1 a** a dog of a sturdy powerful breed with a large head and smooth hair. **b** this breed. **2** a tenacious and courageous person.

bulldog ant *n. Austral.* a large ant with a powerful sting.

bulldog clip *n. propr.* a strong sprung clip for papers.

bulldoze /ˈbʊldəʊz/ *v.tr.* **1** clear with a bulldozer. **2** *colloq.* **a** intimidate. **b** make (one's way) forcibly. [*bulldose* (or *-doze*) *US* = intimidate, from BULL[1]: second element uncertain]

bulldozer /ˈbʊldəʊzə/ *n.* **1** a powerful tractor with a broad curved upright blade at the front for clearing ground. **2** a forceful and domineering person.

bullet /ˈbʊlɪt/ *n.* **1** a projectile of lead etc. (orig. round but now usu. cylindrical and pointed) for firing from a rifle, revolver, etc. **2** *Printing* a small usu. solid circle used to introduce and emphasize a line, an item in a list, etc. [French *boulet*, *boulette*, diminutive of *boule* 'ball', from Latin *bulla* 'bubble']

bullet-headed *adj.* having a round head.

bulletin /ˈbʊlɪtɪn/ *n.* **1** a short official statement of news. **2** a regular list of information etc. issued by an organization or society. [French from Italian *bullettino*, diminutive of *bulletta* 'passport', diminutive of *bulla* 'seal, BULL[2]']

bulletin board *n.* **1** *N. Amer.* a noticeboard. **2** an information storage system for any authorized computer user to access and add to from a remote terminal.

bulletproof /ˈbʊlɪtpruːf/ *adj.* (of a material) designed to resist the penetration of bullets.

bullet train *n.* a high-speed passenger train, esp. in Japan.

bull-fiddle *n. US colloq.* a double bass.

bullfight /ˈbʊlfʌɪt/ *n.* a public spectacle, esp. in Spain, at which a bull is baited and, finally, usu. killed. ▫ **bullfighter** *n.* **bullfighting** *n.*

bullfinch /ˈbʊlfɪn(t)ʃ/ *n.* a stocky Eurasian finch of the genus *Pyrrhula* with a short stout bill, esp. *P. pyrrhula*, which is mainly grey with a pink breast.

bullfrog /ˈbʊlfrɒg/ *n.* a large frog, *Rana catesbiana*, native to N. America, with a deep croak.

bullhead /ˈbʊlhɛd/ *n.* any of various freshwater fishes with large flattened heads.

bull-headed *adj.* obstinate; impetuous; blundering. ▫ **bull-headedly** *adv.* **bull-headedness** *n.*

bullhorn /ˈbʊlhɔːn/ *n.* a megaphone.

bullion /ˈbʊlj(ə)n/ *n.* a metal (esp. gold or silver) in bulk before coining, or valued by weight. [Anglo-French = mint, variant of Old French *bouillon*, ultimately from Latin *bullire* 'boil']

bullish /ˈbʊlɪʃ/ *adj.* **1** like a bull, esp. in nature; impetuous, aggressive. **2 a** *Stock Exch.* causing or associated with a rise in prices. **b** aggressively optimistic. ▫ **bullishly** *adv.* **bullishness** *n.*

bull market *n.* a market with shares rising in price.

bull-nose *attrib.adj.* (also **bull-nosed**) with rounded end.

bullock /ˈbʊlək/ *n. & v.* ● *n.* a castrated male of domestic cattle, raised for beef. ● *v.intr.* (often foll. by *at*) *Austral. colloq.* work very hard. [Old English *bulluc*, diminutive of BULL[1]]

bullocky /ˈbʊləki/ *n. Austral. & NZ colloq.* a bullock driver.

bullring /ˈbʊlrɪŋ/ *n.* an arena for bullfights.

bull session *n. N. Amer.* an informal group discussion. [BULL[3]]

bull's-eye *n.* **1 a** the centre of a target. **b** a shot that hits this. **2** a large hard peppermint-flavoured sweet. **3** a hemisphere or thick disc of glass in a ship's deck or side to admit light. **4** a small circular window. **5 a** a hemispherical lens. **b** a lantern fitted with this. **6** a boss of glass at the centre of a blown glass sheet.

bullshit /ˈbʊlʃɪt/ *n. & v. coarse slang* ● *n.* **1** (often as *int.*) nonsense, rubbish. **2** trivial or insincere talk or writing. ● *v.intr. & tr.* (**-shitted**, **-shitting**) talk nonsense or as if one has specialist knowledge (to). ▫ **bullshitter** *n.* [BULL[3] + SHIT]

bull terrier *n.* **1** a short-haired dog of a breed that is a cross between a bulldog and a terrier. **2** this breed.

bulltrout /ˈbʊltraʊt/ *n. Brit.* a sea trout.

bully[1] /ˈbʊli/ *n. & v.* ● *n.* (*pl.* **-ies**) a person who uses strength or power to coerce others by fear. ● *v.tr.* (**-ies**, **-ied**) **1** persecute or oppress by force or threats. **2** (foll. by *into* + verbal noun) pressure or coerce (a person) to do something (*bullied him into agreeing*). [originally as a term of endearment, probably from Middle Dutch *boele* 'lover']

bully[2] /'bʊli/ *adj. & int. colloq.* ● *adj.* esp. *N. Amer.* very good; first-rate. ● *int.* (foll. by *for*) expressing admiration or approval (often *iron.*: *bully for them!*). [perhaps from BULLY[1]]

bully[3] /'bʊli/ *n. & v.* (in full **bully off**) ● *n.* (*pl.* **-ies**) the start of play in hockey in which two opponents strike each other's sticks three times and then go for the ball. ● *v.intr.* (**-ies, -ied**) start play in this way. [19th c.: perhaps from *bully*, a scrum in Eton football, of unknown origin]

bully[4] /'bʊli/ *n.* (in full **bully beef**) corned beef. [French *bouilli* 'boiled beef' from *bouillir* BOIL[1]]

bully boy *n.* a hired ruffian.

bullyrag var. of BALLYRAG.

bully tree /'bʊli/ *n.* = BALATA. [corruption]

bulrush /'bʊlrʌʃ/ *n.* **1** = REED MACE. **2** a rushlike water plant, *Scirpus lacustris*, used for weaving. **3** *Bibl.* a papyrus plant. [perhaps from BULL[1] = large, coarse, as in *bullfrog*, *bulltrout*, etc.]

bulwark /'bʊlwək/ *n.* **1** a defensive wall, esp. of earth; a rampart; a mole or breakwater. **2** a person, principle, etc., that acts as a defence. **3** (usu. in *pl.*) a ship's side above deck. [Middle English from Middle Low German, Middle Dutch *bolwerk*: see BOLE[1], WORK]

bum[1] /bʌm/ *n. Brit. slang* the buttocks. [Middle English *bom*, of unknown origin]

bum[2] /bʌm/ *n., v., & adj. slang* ● *n.* **1** *N. Amer.* a vagrant. **2** a habitual loafer; a lazy dissolute person (*beach bum*). ● *v.* (**bummed, bumming**) **1** *intr.* (often foll. by *about, around*) loaf or wander around; be a bum. **2** *tr.* get by begging; cadge. ● *attrib.adj.* of poor quality. □ **on the bum** vagrant, begging. [probably an abbreviation or back-formation from BUMMER]

bumbag /'bʌmbag/ *n. Brit. colloq.* a small pouch for money and other valuables, on a belt worn round the waist or hips.

bum-bailiff *n. hist.* a bailiff empowered to collect debts or arrest debtors for non-payment. [BUM[1], so called as approaching from behind]

bumble /'bʌmb(ə)l/ *v.intr.* **1** (foll. by *on*) speak in a rambling incoherent way. **2** (often as **bumbling** *adj.*) move or act ineptly; blunder. **3** make a buzz or hum. □ **bumbler** *n.* [BOOM[1] + -LE[4]: partly from *bumble* = blunderer]

bumble-bee /'bʌmb(ə)lbi:/ *n.* a large social bee of the genus *Bombus*, with a loud hum. Also called *humble-bee*. [as BUMBLE]

bumboat /'bʌmbəʊt/ *n.* a small boat plying with provisions etc. for ships. [BUM[1] (originally a scavenger's boat removing refuse etc. from ships)]

bumboy /'bʌmbɔɪ/ *n. slang* a young male homosexual, esp. a prostitute.

bumf /bʌmf/ *n.* (also **bumph**) *Brit. colloq.* **1** usu. *derog.* papers, documents. **2** lavatory paper. [abbreviation of *bum-fodder*]

bum fluff *n. slang* an adolescent's first beard growth.

bumiputra /bu:mɪ'pu:trə/ *n. & adj.* ● *n.* (*pl.* same or **-s**) a Malaysian of indigenous Malay origin. ● *adj.* of or relating to the bumiputra. [Malay from Sanskrit, = son of the soil]

bummalo /'bʌmələʊ/ *n.* (*pl.* same) a small fish, *Harpodon nehereus*, of S. Asian coasts, dried and used as food (see BOMBAY DUCK). [perhaps from Marathi *bombīl(a)*]

bummer /'bʌmə/ *n.* esp. *N. Amer. slang* **1** an idler; a loafer. **2** an unpleasant occurrence. [19th c.: perhaps from German *Bummler*]

bump /bʌmp/ *n., v., & adv.* ● *n.* **1** a dull-sounding blow or collision. **2** a swelling or dent caused by this. **3** an uneven patch on a road, field, etc. **4** *hist.* any prominence on the skull formerly thought to indicate a particular mental faculty. **5** (in narrow-river races where boats make a spaced start one behind another) the point at which a boat begins to overtake (and usu. touches) the boat ahead, thereby defeating it. **6** *Aeron.* **a** an irregularity in an aircraft's motion. **b** a rising air current causing this. **7** (**the bumps**) *Brit.* (on a person's birthday) the act of lifting a person by the arms and legs and letting him or her down on to the ground, once for each year of age. ● *v.* **1 a** *tr.* hit or come against with a bump. **b** *intr.* (of two objects) collide. **2** *intr.* (foll. by *against, into*) hit with a bump; collide with. **3** *tr.* (often foll. by *against, on*) hurt or damage by striking (*bumped my head on the ceiling*; *bumped the car while parking*). **4** *intr.* (usu. foll. by *along*) move or travel with much jolting (*we bumped along the road*). **5** *tr.* (in a boat race) gain a bump against. **6** *tr. N. Amer.* displace, esp. by seniority. ● *adv.* with a bump; suddenly; violently. □ **bump into** *colloq.* meet by chance. **bump off** *slang* murder. **bump up** *colloq.* increase (prices etc.). [16th c., imitative: perhaps from Scandinavian]

bumper /'bʌmpə/ *n.* **1** a horizontal bar or strip fixed across the front or back of a motor vehicle to reduce damage in a collision or as a trim. **2** (usu. *attrib.*) an unusually large or fine example (*a bumper crop*). **3** *Cricket* = BOUNCER 2. **4** a brim-full glass of wine etc.

bumper car *n.* = DODGEM.

bumph var. of BUMF.

bumpkin /'bʌm(p)kɪn/ *n.* a rustic or socially inept person. [perhaps Dutch *boomken* 'little tree' or Middle Dutch *bommekijn* 'little barrel']

bump-start *n. & v.tr. Brit.* = PUSH-START.

bumptious /'bʌm(p)ʃəs/ *adj.* offensively self-assertive or conceited. □ **bumptiously** *adv.* **bumptiousness** *n.* [BUMP, on the pattern of FRACTIOUS]

bumpy /'bʌmpi/ *adj.* (**bumpier, bumpiest**) **1** having many bumps (*a bumpy road*). **2** affected by bumps (*a bumpy ride*). □ **bumpily** *adv.* **bumpiness** *n.*

bum rap *n. N. Amer. slang* imprisonment on a false charge. [BUM[2]]

bum's rush *n.* (prec. by *the*) *N. Amer. slang* **1** forcible ejection. **2** abrupt dismissal. [BUM[2]]

bum steer *n. N. Amer. slang* false information. [BUM[2] + *steer* 'a piece of advice']

bum-sucker *n. Brit. coarse slang* a toady. □ **bum-sucking** *n.* [BUM[1]]

bun /bʌn/ *n.* **1** a small usu. sweetened bread roll or cake, often with dried fruit. **2** *Sc.* a rich fruit cake or currant bread. **3** hair worn drawn back into a tight coil at the back of the head. **4** (in *pl.*) *N. Amer. slang* the buttocks. □ **have a bun in the oven** *slang* be pregnant. [Middle English: origin unknown]

Buna /'bju:nə/ *n. propr.* a synthetic rubber made by polymerization of butadiene. [German (as BUTADIENE, *Na* chemical symbol for sodium)]

bunch /bʌn(t)ʃ/ *n. & v.* ● *n.* **1** a cluster of things growing or fastened together (*bunch of grapes*; *bunch of keys*). **2** a collection; a set or lot (*best of the bunch*). **3** *colloq.* a group; a gang. ● *v.* **1** *tr.* make into a bunch or bunches; gather into close folds. **2** *intr.* form into a group or crowd. □ **bunchy** *adj.* [Middle English: origin unknown]

bunch grass *n. N. Amer.* a grass that grows in clumps, esp. of the genus *Poa* or *Festuca*.

bunch of fives *n. Brit. slang* **1** a hand or fist. **2** a punch.

bunco /'bʌŋkəʊ/ *n. & v. N. Amer. slang* ● *n.* (*pl.* **-os**) a swindle, esp. by card-sharping or a confidence trick. ● *v.tr.* (**-oes, -oed**) swindle, cheat. [perhaps from Spanish *banca*, name of a card game]

buncombe var. of BUNKUM.

Bundesrat /'bʊndəzrɑ:t/ *n.* the Upper House of Parliament in Germany or in Austria. [German from *Bund* 'federation' + *Rat* 'council']

Bundestag /'bʊndəztɑ:g/ *n.* the Lower House of Parliament in Germany. [German from *Bund* 'federation' + *tagen* 'confer']

bundle /'bʌnd(ə)l/ *n. & v.* ● *n.* **1** a collection of things tied or fastened together. **2** a set of nerve fibres etc. banded together. **3** *slang* a large amount of money. ● *v.* **1** *tr.* (usu. foll. by *up*) tie in or make into a bundle (*bundled up my squash kit*). **2** *tr.* (usu. foll. by *into*) throw or push, esp. quickly or confusedly (*bundled the papers into the drawer*). **3** *tr.* (usu. foll. by *out, off, away,* etc.) send (esp. a person) away hurriedly or unceremoniously (*bundled them off the premises*). **4** *tr.* (foll. by *with*) (usu. as **bundled** *adj.*) *Computing* sell as a package with (*training is bundled with the software*). **5** *intr.* sleep clothed with another person, esp. a fiancé(e), as a local custom. □ **be a bundle of nerves** (or **prejudices etc.**) be extremely nervous (or prejudiced etc.). **bundle up** dress warmly or cumbersomely. **go a bundle on** *Brit. slang* be very fond of. □ **bundler** *n.* [Middle English, perhaps from Old English *byndelle* 'a binding', but also from Low German, Dutch *bundel*]

bun fight *n. Brit. slang* a tea party.

bung[1] /bʌŋ/ *n.* & *v.* ● *n.* a stopper for closing a hole in a container, esp. a cask. ● *v.tr.* **1** stop with a bung. **2** *Brit. slang* throw, toss. □ **bunged up** closed, blocked. [Middle Dutch *bonghe*]

bung[2] /bʌŋ/ *adj. Austral.* & *NZ slang* dead; ruined, useless. □ **go bung 1** die. **2** fail; go bankrupt. [Aboriginal, probably Yagara]

bungalow /ˈbʌŋɡələʊ/ *n.* a one-storeyed house. [Gujarati *bangalo* from Hindustani *baṅglā* 'belonging to Bengal']

bungee /ˈbʌndʒi/ *n.* (in full **bungee cord, rope**) an elasticated cord or rope, used for securing baggage and in bungee jumping. [origin unknown]

bungee jumping *n.* the sport of jumping from a height while secured by a bungee from the ankles, or by a harness. □ **bungee jumper** *n.*

bung-hole *n.* a hole for filling or emptying a cask etc.

bungle /ˈbʌŋɡ(ə)l/ *v.* & *n.* ● *v.* **1** *tr.* blunder over, mismanage, or fail at (a task). **2** *intr.* work badly or clumsily. ● *n.* a bungled attempt; bungled work. □ **bungler** *n.* [imitative: cf. BUMBLE]

bunion /ˈbʌnj(ə)n/ *n.* a swelling on the foot, esp. at the first joint of the big toe. [Old French *buignon* from *buigne* 'bump on the head']

bunk[1] /bʌŋk/ *n.* a sleeping berth, esp. a shelf-like bed against a wall, e.g. in a ship. [18th c.: origin unknown]

bunk[2] /bʌŋk/ *v.* & *n. Brit. slang* ● *v.tr.* (also *absol.*; often foll. by *off*) play truant from (school etc.). ● *n.* (in **do a bunk**) leave or abscond hurriedly. [19th c.: origin unknown]

bunk[3] /bʌŋk/ *n. slang* nonsense, humbug. [abbreviation of BUNKUM]

bunk bed *n.* each of two or more beds one above the other, forming a unit.

bunker /ˈbʌŋkə/ *n.* & *v.* ● *n.* **1** a large container or compartment for storing fuel. **2** a reinforced underground shelter, esp. for use in wartime. **3** a hollow filled with sand, used as an obstacle in a golf course. ● *v.tr.* **1** fill the fuel bunkers of (a ship etc.). **2** (usu. in *passive*) **a** trap in a bunker (in sense 3). **b** *Brit.* bring into difficulties. [19th c.: origin unknown]

bunkhouse /ˈbʌŋkhaʊs/ *n.* a house where workmen etc. are lodged.

bunkum /ˈbʌŋkəm/ *n.* (also **buncombe**) nonsense; humbug. [originally *buncombe* from *Buncombe* County in N. Carolina, mentioned in an inconsequential speech made by its Congressman solely to please his constituents, *c.*1820]

bunny /ˈbʌni/ *n.* (*pl.* **-ies**) **1** a child's name for a rabbit. **2** *Austral. slang* a victim or dupe. **3** (in full **bunny girl**) a club hostess, waitress, etc., wearing a skimpy costume with ears and a tail suggestive of a rabbit. [dialect *bun* 'rabbit']

Bunsen /ˈbʌns(ə)n/ *n.* (in full **Bunsen burner**) a small adjustable gas burner used in scientific work as a source of great heat. [R. W. *Bunsen*, German chemist d. 1899]

bunt[1] /bʌnt/ *n.* the baggy centre of a fishing net, sail, etc. [16th c.: origin unknown]

bunt[2] /bʌnt/ *n.* a disease of wheat caused by the fungus *Tilletia caries.* [17th c.: origin unknown]

bunt[3] /bʌnt/ *v.* & *n. US Baseball* ● *v.tr.* let (a ball) rebound from the bat without swinging. ● *n.* an instance of bunting. [19th c.: probably related to BUTT[1]]

buntal /ˈbʌnt(ə)l/ *n.* the straw from a talipot palm. [Tagalog]

bunting[1] /ˈbʌntɪŋ/ *n.* a seed-eating bird of the family Emberizidae, related to the finches, usu. with a streaked sparrow-like plumage. [Middle English: origin unknown]

bunting[2] /ˈbʌntɪŋ/ *n.* **1** flags and other decorations. **2** a loosely woven fabric used for these. [18th c.: origin unknown]

buntline /ˈbʌntlʌɪn/ *n.* a line for confining the bunt (see BUNT[1]) when furling a sail.

bunya /ˈbʌnjə/ *n.* (also **bunya bunya** /ˈbʌnjəbʌnjə/) *Austral.* a tall coniferous tree, *Araucaria bidwillii*, bearing large edible cones. [Aboriginal (Queensland)]

bunyip /ˈbʌnjɪp/ *n. Austral.* **1** a fabulous monster inhabiting swamps and lagoons. **2** an impostor. [Wemba-wemba *banib*]

buoy /bɔɪ/ *n.* & *v.* ● *n.* **1** an anchored float serving as a navigation mark or to show reefs etc. **2** a lifebuoy. ● *v.tr.* **1** (usu. foll. by *up*) **a** keep afloat. **b** sustain the courage or spirits of (a person etc.); uplift, encourage. **2** (often foll. by *out*) mark with a buoy or buoys. [Middle English probably from Middle Dutch *bo(e)ye*, from a Germanic base meaning 'signal']

buoyancy /ˈbɔɪənsi/ *n.* **1** the capacity to be or remain buoyant. **2** resilience; recuperative power. **3** cheerfulness.

buoyancy aid *n.* a sleeveless jacket lined with buoyant material, worn for water sports.

buoyant /ˈbɔɪənt/ *adj.* **1 a** able or apt to keep afloat or rise to the top of a liquid or gas. **b** (of a liquid or gas) able to keep something afloat. **2** light-hearted. □ **buoyantly** *adv.* [French *buoyant* or Spanish *boyante*, part. of *boyar* 'float' ultimately from the Germanic base of BUOY]

BUPA /ˈbuːpə/ *abbr.* British United Provident Association (a private health insurance organization).

bur /bəː/ *n.* (also **burr**) **1 a** a prickly clinging seed case or flower head. **b** any plant producing these. **2** a person hard to shake off. **3** = BURR *n.* 2. [Middle English: related to Danish *burre* 'bur, burdock', Swedish *kardborre* 'burdock']

burb /bəːb/ *n.* (usu. in *pl.*) *N. Amer. colloq.* a suburb. [abbreviation]

Burberry /ˈbəːb(ə)ri/ *n.* (*pl.* **-ies**) *propr.* a distinctive type of raincoat. [*Burberry's*, name of the manufacturer]

burble /ˈbəːb(ə)l/ *v.* & *n.* ● *v.intr.* **1** speak ramblingly; make a murmuring noise. **2** *Aeron.* (of an airflow) break up into turbulence. ● *n.* **1** a murmuring noise. **2** rambling speech. □ **burbler** *n.* [Middle English: imitative]

burbot /ˈbəːbət/ *n.* an eel-like flat-headed bearded freshwater fish, *Lota lota.* [Middle English, from Old French *borbete*, probably from *borbe* 'mud, slime']

burden /ˈbəːd(ə)n/ *n.* & *v.* (also *archaic* **burthen** /ˈbəːð(ə)n/) ● *n.* **1** a load, esp. a heavy one. **2** an oppressive duty, obligation, expense, emotion, etc. **3** the bearing of loads (*beast of burden*). **4** a ship's carrying capacity, tonnage. **5 a** the refrain or chorus of a song. **b** the chief theme or gist of a speech, book, poem, etc. ● *v.tr.* load with a burden; encumber, oppress. □ **burdensome** *adj.* [Old English *byrthen*: related to BIRTH]

burden of proof *n.* the obligation to prove one's case.

burdock /ˈbəːdɒk/ *n.* any plant of the genus *Arctium*, with prickly flowers and docklike leaves. [BUR + DOCK[3]]

bureau /ˈbjʊərəʊ/ *n.* (*pl.* **bureaux** or **bureaus** /-rəʊz/) **1 a** *Brit.* a writing desk with drawers and usu. an angled top opening downwards to form a writing surface. **b** *N. Amer.* a chest of drawers. **2 a** an office or department for transacting specific business. **b** a government department. [French, = desk, originally its baize covering, from Old French *burel* from *bure, buire* 'dark brown', ultimately from Greek *purros* 'red']

bureaucracy /bjʊ(ə)ˈrɒkrəsi/ *n.* (*pl.* **-ies**) **1 a** government by central administration. **b** a state or organization so governed. **2** the officials of such a government, esp. regarded as oppressive and inflexible. **3** conduct typical of such officials. [French *bureaucratie*: see BUREAU]

bureaucrat /ˈbjʊərəkrat/ *n.* **1** an official in a bureaucracy. **2** an inflexible or insensitive administrator. □ **bureaucratic** /-ˈkratɪk/ *adj.* **bureaucratically** /-ˈkratɪk(ə)li/ *adv.* [French *bureaucrate* (as BUREAUCRACY)]

bureaucratize /bjʊ(ə)ˈrɒkrətʌɪz/ *v.tr.* (also **-ise**) govern by or transform into a bureaucratic system. □ **bureaucratization** /-ˈzeɪʃ(ə)n/ *n.*

burette /bjʊˈrɛt/ *n.* (*US* **buret**) a graduated glass tube with a tap at one end, for measuring out small volumes of liquid in chemical analysis. [French]

burg /bəːg/ *n. N. Amer. colloq.* a town or city. [see BOROUGH]

burgage /ˈbəːgɪdʒ/ *n. hist.* (in England and Scotland) tenure of land in a town on a yearly rent. [Middle English, from medieval Latin *burgagium* from *burgus* BOROUGH]

burgee /bəːˈdʒiː/ *n.* a flag bearing the colours or emblem of a sailing club. [18th c.: perhaps = (ship)owner, ultimately French *bourgeois*: see BURGESS]

burgeon /ˈbəːdʒ(ə)n/ *v. & n. literary* ● *v.intr.* **1** begin to grow rapidly; flourish. **2** put forth young shoots; bud. ● *n.* a bud or young shoot. [Middle English from Old French *bor-*, *burjon*, ultimately from Late Latin *burra* 'wool']

burger /ˈbəːgə/ *n.* **1** *colloq.* a hamburger. **2** (in *comb.*) a certain kind of hamburger or variation of it (*beefburger*; *nutburger*). [abbreviation]

burgess /ˈbəːdʒɪs/ *n.* **1** *Brit.* an inhabitant of a town or borough, esp. of one with full municipal rights. **2** *Brit. hist.* a Member of Parliament for a borough, corporate town, or university. **3** *US* a borough magistrate or governor. [Middle English from Old French *burgeis*, ultimately from Late Latin *burgus* BOROUGH]

burgh /ˈbʌrə/ *n. hist.* a Scottish borough or chartered town. □ **burghal** /ˈbəːg(ə)l/ *adj.* [Scots form of BOROUGH]

burgher /ˈbəːgə/ *n.* **1** a citizen or freeman, esp. of a Continental town. **2** *S.Afr. hist.* a citizen of a Boer republic. **3** a descendant of a Dutch or Portuguese colonist in Sri Lanka. [German *Burger* or Dutch *burger*, from *Burg*, *burg* BOROUGH]

burglar /ˈbəːglə/ *n.* a person who commits burglary. □ **burglarious** /-ˈglɛːrɪəs/ *adj.* [legal Anglo-French *burgler*, related to Old French *burgier* 'pillage']

burglarize /ˈbəːglərʌɪz/ *v.tr. & intr.* (also **-ise**) *US* = BURGLE.

burglary /ˈbəːgləri/ *n.* (*pl.* **-ies**) **1** entry into a building illegally with intent to commit theft, do bodily harm, or do damage (before 1968, in English law, a crime under statute and in common law; after 1968 a statutory crime only). Cf. HOUSEBREAKING. **2** an instance of this. [legal Anglo-French *burglarie*: see BURGLAR]

burgle /ˈbəːg(ə)l/ *v.* **1** *tr.* commit burglary on (a building or person). **2** *intr.* commit burglary. [back-formation from BURGLAR]

burgomaster /ˈbəːgəmɑːstə/ *n.* the mayor of a Dutch or Flemish town. [Dutch *burgemeester* from *burg* BOROUGH: assimilated to MASTER]

burgrave /ˈbəːgreɪv/ *n. hist.* the ruler of a town or castle. [German *Burggraf* from *Burg* BOROUGH + *Graf* COUNT²]

burgundy /ˈbəːgəndi/ *n. & adj.* ● *n.* (*pl.* **-ies**) **1 a** wine (usu. red) from Burgundy in eastern France. **b** a similar wine from another place. **2** the red colour of burgundy wine. ● *adj.* of this colour.

burhel var. of BHARAL.

burial /ˈbɛrɪəl/ *n.* **1 a** the burying of a dead body. **b** a funeral. **2** *Archaeol.* a grave or its remains. [Middle English, erroneously formed as sing. of Old English *byrgels*, from Germanic: related to BURY]

burial ground *n.* a cemetery.

burin /ˈbjʊərɪn/ *n.* **1** a steel tool for engraving on copper or wood. **2** *Archaeol.* a flint tool with a chisel point. [French]

burk var. of BERK.

burka /ˈbʊəkə/ *n.* a long enveloping garment worn in public by Muslim women. [Urdu from Arabic *burḳa*']

Burkitt's lymphoma /ˈbəːkɪts/ *n. Med.* a malignant tumour of the lymphatic system, caused by the Epstein–Barr virus, esp. affecting children in central Africa. [D. P. *Burkitt*, British surgeon d. 1993]

burl /bəːl/ *n.* **1** a knot or lump in wool or cloth. **2** *N. Amer.* a rounded flat knotty growth on a tree. [Middle English from Old French *bourle* 'tuft of wool', diminutive of *bourre* 'coarse wool', from Late Latin *burra* 'wool']

burlap /ˈbəːlap/ *n.* **1** coarse canvas esp. of jute used for sacking etc. **2** a similar lighter material for use in dressmaking or furnishing. [17th c.: origin unknown]

burlesque /bəːˈlɛsk/ *n., adj., & v.* ● *n.* **1 a** comic imitation, esp. in parody of a dramatic or literary work. **b** a performance or work of this kind. **c** bombast, mock-seriousness. **2** *US* a variety show, often including striptease. ● *adj.* of or in the nature of burlesque. ● *v.tr.* (**burlesques**, **burlesqued**, **burlesquing**) make or give a burlesque of. □ **burlesquer** *n.* [French from Italian *burlesco*, from *burla* 'mockery']

burly /ˈbəːli/ *adj.* (**burlier**, **burliest**) of stout sturdy build; big and strong. □ **burliness** *n.* [Middle English *borli*, probably from an Old English form = 'stately, fit for the bower' (BOWER¹)]

Burman /ˈbəːmən/ *adj. & n.* (*pl.* **Burmans**) = BURMESE.

Burmese /bəːˈmiːz/ *n. & adj.* ● *n.* (*pl.* same) **1 a** a native or national of Burma (now Myanmar) in SE Asia. **b** a person of Burmese descent. **2** a member of the largest ethnic group of Burma. **3** the language of this group. **4** (in full **Burmese cat**) a breed of short-coated domestic cat. ● *adj.* of or relating to Burma or its people or language.

burn¹ /bəːn/ *v. & n.* ● *v.* (*past* and *past part.* **burnt** or **burned**) **1** *intr. & tr.* be or cause to be consumed or destroyed by fire. **2** *intr.* **a** blaze or glow with fire. **b** be in the state characteristic of fire. **3** *intr. & tr.* be or cause to be injured or damaged by fire or great heat or by radiation. **4** *tr. & intr.* use or be used as a source of heat, light, or other energy. **5** *tr. & intr.* char or scorch in cooking (*burned the vegetables*; *the vegetables are burning*). **6** *tr.* produce (a hole, a mark, etc.) by fire or heat. **7** *tr.* **a** subject (clay, chalk, etc.) to heat for a purpose. **b** harden (bricks) by fire. **c** make (lime or charcoal) by heat. **8** *tr.* colour, tan, or parch with heat or light (*we were burnt brown by the sun*). **9** *tr. & intr.* put or be put to death by fire. **10** *tr.* **a** cauterize, brand. **b** (foll. by *in*) imprint by burning. **11** *tr. & intr.* make or be hot, give or feel a sensation or pain of or like heat; smart or cause to smart. **12** *tr. & intr.* (often foll. by *with*) make or be passionate; feel or cause to feel great emotion (*burn with shame*). **13** *intr. slang* drive fast. **14** *tr. US slang* anger, infuriate. **15** *intr.* (foll. by *into*) (of acid etc.) gradually penetrate (into) causing disintegration. ● *n.* **1** a mark or injury caused by burning. **2** the ignition of a rocket engine in flight, giving extra thrust. **3** *N. Amer., Austral., & NZ* **a** the clearing of vegetation by burning. **b** an area so cleared. **4** *Brit. slang* a cigarette. **5** *Brit. slang* a car race. □ **burn one's boats** (or esp. *N. Amer.* **bridges**) commit oneself irrevocably. **burn the candle at both ends** exhaust one's strength or resources by undertaking too much. **burn down 1 a** destroy (a building) by burning. **b** (of a building) be destroyed by fire. **2** burn less vigorously as fuel fails. **burn one's fingers** suffer for meddling or rashness. **burn a hole in one's pocket** (of money) be quickly spent. **burn low** (of fire) be nearly out. **burn the midnight oil** read or work late into the night. **burn out 1** be reduced to nothing by burning. **2**

fail or cause to fail by burning. **3** (usu. *refl.*) suffer physical or emotional exhaustion. **4** consume the contents of by burning. **5** make (a person) homeless by burning his or her house. **burn up 1** get rid of by fire. **2** begin to blaze. **3** *N. Amer. slang* be or make furious. **4** *colloq.* traverse at high speed. **have money to burn** have more money than one needs. [Old English *birnan, bærnan*, from Germanic]

burn[2] /bɜːn/ *n. Sc. & N.Engl.* a small stream. [Old English *burna, burn(e)*, from Germanic]

burner /ˈbɜːnə/ *n.* the part of a gas cooker, lamp, etc. that emits and shapes the flame. ◻ **on the back** (or **front**) **burner** *colloq.* receiving little (or much) attention.

burnet /ˈbɜːnɪt/ *n.* **1** a plant of the genus *Sanguisorba* (rose family), with globular pinkish flower heads. **2** any of several diurnal moths of the family Zygaenidae, with crimson spots on greenish-black wings. [obsolete *burnet* (*adj.*) 'dark brown' from Old French *burnete*]

burning /ˈbɜːnɪŋ/ *adj.* **1** ardent, intense (*burning desire*). **2** hotly discussed, exciting; vital, urgent (*burning question*). **3** flagrant (*burning shame*). ◻ **burningly** *adv.*

burning bush *n.* **1** any of various shrubs with red fruits or red autumn leaves. **2** = FRAXINELLA. [with reference to Exod. 3:2]

burning-glass *n.* a lens for concentrating the sun's rays on an object to burn it.

burnish /ˈbɜːnɪʃ/ *v.tr.* polish by rubbing. ◻ **burnisher** *n.* [Middle English from Old French *burnir* = *brunir* 'make brown' from *brun* BROWN]

burnous /bɜːˈnuːs/ *n.* (*US* also **burnoose**) an Arab or Moorish hooded cloak. [French, via Arabic *burnus* from Greek *birros* 'cloak']

burn-out *n.* **1** physical or emotional exhaustion, esp. caused by stress. **2** depression, disillusionment.

burnt see BURN[1].

burnt ochre *n. & adj.* (also **burnt sienna** or **burnt umber**) ● *n.* a pigment darkened by burning. ● *adj.* of the colour of any of these pigments.

burnt offering *n.* **1** an offering burnt on an altar as a sacrifice. **2** *joc.* overcooked or charred food.

burnt-out *adj.* physically or emotionally exhausted.

bur oak *n.* a N. American oak, *Quercus macrocarpa* with large fringed acorn-cups.

burp /bɜːp/ *v. & n. colloq.* ● *v.* **1** *intr.* belch. **2** *tr.* make (a baby) belch, usu. by patting its back. ● *n.* a belch. [imitative]

burpee /ˈbɜːpiː/ *n.* a physical exercise consisting of a squat thrust made from and ending in a standing position. [Royal H. *Burpee*, US psychologist b. 1897]

burp gun *n. US slang* a lightweight sub-machine gun.

burr /bɜː/ *n. & v.* ● *n.* **1 a** a whirring sound. **b** a rough sounding of the letter *r*. **2** (also **bur**) **a** a rough edge left on cut or punched metal or paper. **b** a surgeon's or dentist's small drill. **3 a** a siliceous rock used for millstones. **b** a whetstone. **4** = BUR 1, 2. **5** the coronet of a deer's antler. ● *v.* **1** *tr.* pronounce with a burr. **2** *intr.* speak indistinctly. **3** *intr.* make a whirring sound. [variant of BUR]

burrawang /ˈbʌrəwaŋ/ *n. Austral.* **1** any palmlike tree of the genus *Macrozamia*. **2** the nut produced by this tree. [Mount *Budawang* in New South Wales]

burrito /bʌˈriːtəʊ/ *n.* (*pl.* **-os**) a tortilla rolled round a savoury filling. [Latin American Spanish, diminutive of *burro* BURRO]

burro /ˈbʌrəʊ/ *n.* (*pl.* **-os**) esp. *US* a small donkey used as a pack animal. [Spanish]

burrow /ˈbʌrəʊ/ *n. & v.* ● *n.* a hole or tunnel dug by a small animal, esp. a rabbit, as a dwelling. ● *v.* **1** *intr.* make or live in a burrow. **2** *tr.* (often foll. by *in, under*, etc.) make (a hole etc.) by digging. **3** *intr.* hide oneself. **4** *intr.* (foll. by *into*) investigate, search. ◻ **burrower** *n.* [Middle English, apparently variant of BOROUGH]

bursa /ˈbɜːsə/ *n.* (*pl.* **bursae** /-siː/ or **bursas**) *Anat.* a fluid-filled sac or saclike cavity, esp. one countering friction at a joint. ◻ **bursal** *adj.* [medieval Latin = bag: see PURSE]

bursar /ˈbɜːsə/ *n.* **1** a treasurer, esp. the person in charge of the funds and other property of a college. **2** *Brit.* the holder of a bursary. ◻ **bursarship** *n.* [French *boursier* or (in sense 1) medieval Latin *bursarius* from *bursa* 'bag': see PURSE]

bursary /ˈbɜːsəri/ *n.* (*pl.* **-ies**) **1** *Brit.* a grant, esp. a scholarship. **2** the post or room of a bursar. ◻ **bursarial** /-ˈsɛːrɪəl/ *adj.* [medieval Latin *bursaria* (as BURSAR)]

bursitis /bɜːˈsʌɪtɪs/ *n. Med.* inflammation of a bursa.

burst /bɜːst/ *v. & n.* ● *v.* (*past* and *past part.* **burst**) **1 a** *intr.* break suddenly and violently apart by expansion of contents or internal pressure. **b** *tr.* cause to do this. **c** *tr.* cause (a container etc.) to split apart or puncture. **2 a** *tr.* open forcibly. **b** *intr.* come open or be opened forcibly. **3 a** *intr.* (usu. foll. by *in, out*) make one's way suddenly, dramatically, or by force. **b** *tr.* break away from or through (*the river burst its banks*). **4** *tr. & intr.* fill or be full to overflowing. **5** *intr.* appear or come suddenly (*burst into flame*; *burst upon the view*; *sun burst out*). **6** *intr.* (foll. by *into*) suddenly begin to shed or utter (esp. *burst into tears* or *laughter* or *song*). **7** *intr.* be as if about to burst because of effort, excitement, etc. **8** *tr.* suffer bursting of (*burst a blood vessel*). **9** *tr.* separate (continuous stationery) into single sheets. ● *n.* **1** the act of or an instance of bursting; a split. **2** a sudden issuing forth (*burst of flame*). **3** a sudden outbreak (*burst of applause*). **4 a** a short sudden effort; a spurt. **b** a gallop. **5** an explosion. ◻ **burst out 1** suddenly begin (*burst out laughing*). **2** exclaim. ◻ **burster** *n.* (esp. in sense 9 of *v.*). [Old English *berstan*, from Germanic]

burstproof /ˈbɜːs(t)pruːf/ *adj.* (of a door lock) able to withstand a violent impact.

burthen *archaic* var. of BURDEN.

burton[1] /ˈbɜːt(ə)n/ *n.* ◻ **go for a burton** *Brit. slang* be lost or destroyed or killed. [20th c.: perhaps *Burton* ale from *Burton-on-Trent* in England]

burton[2] /ˈbɜːt(ə)n/ *n.* (in full **burton-tackle**) a light two-block tackle for hoisting. [Middle English *Breton tackles*: see BRETON]

bur walnut *n.* walnut wood containing knots, used as a veneer.

bury /ˈbɛri/ *v.tr.* (**-ies, -ied**) **1** place (a dead body) in the earth, in a tomb, or in the sea. **2** lose by death (*has buried three husbands*). **3 a** put under ground (*bury alive*). **b** hide (treasure, a bone, etc.) in the earth. **c** cover up; submerge. **4 a** put out of sight (*buried his face in his hands*). **b** consign to obscurity (*the idea was buried after brief discussion*). **c** put away; forget. **5** involve deeply (*buried himself in his work*; *was buried in a book*). ◻ **bury the hatchet** cease to quarrel. **bury one's head in the sand** ignore unpleasant realities, refuse to face facts. [Old English *byrgan*, from West Germanic: related to BURIAL]

burying beetle *n.* a sexton beetle.

burying ground *n.* (also **burying place**) a cemetery.

bus /bʌs/ *n. & v.* ● *n.* (*pl.* **buses** or *US* **busses**) **1** a large passenger vehicle, esp. one serving the public on a fixed route. **2** *colloq.* a motor car, aeroplane, etc. **3** *Computing* a defined set of conductors carrying data and control signals within a computer. ● *v.* (**buses** or **busses**, **bussed**, **bussing**) **1** *intr.* go by bus. **2** *tr.* esp. *N. Amer.* transport by bus, esp. to promote racial integration. **3** *tr. N. Amer.* **a** carry or clear away (dishes etc.) in a cafeteria. **b** clear (a cafeteria table) of dishes. [abbreviation of OMNIBUS]

busbar /ˈbʌsbɑː/ *n. Electr.* a system of conductors in a generating or receiving station on which power is concentrated for distribution.

busboy /ˈbʌsbɔɪ/ *n. N. Amer.* a person who clears tables etc. in a cafeteria.

busby /ˈbʌzbi/ *n.* (*pl.* **-ies**) (not in official use) a tall fur hat worn by hussars etc. [18th c.: origin unknown]

bush[1] /bʊʃ/ *n. & v.* ● *n.* **1** a shrub or clump of shrubs with stems of moderate length. **2** a thing resembling this, esp. a clump of hair or fur. **3** (esp. in Australia and Africa) a wild uncultivated district; woodland or forest. **4** *hist.* a bunch of ivy as a vintner's sign. ● *v.intr.* (usu. foll. by *out*) spread like a bush. □ **go bush** *Austral.* leave one's usual surroundings; run wild. [Middle English from Old English & Old Norse, ultimately from Germanic]

bush[2] /bʊʃ/ *n. & v.* ● *n. Brit.* **1** a metal lining for a round hole enclosing a revolving shaft etc. **2** a sleeve providing electrical insulation. ● *v.tr.* provide with a bush. [Middle Dutch *busse* BOX[1]]

bushbaby /ˈbʊʃbeɪbi/ *n.* (*pl.* **-ies**) a small nocturnal tree-dwelling African primate of the family Lorisidae, with very large eyes. Also called GALAGO.

bush basil *n.* a culinary herb, *Ocimum minimum*.

bushbuck /ˈbʊʃbʌk/ *n.* a small antelope, *Tragelaphus scriptus*, of southern Africa, having a chestnut coat with white stripes. [BUSH[1] + BUCK[1], influenced by Dutch *boschbok*]

bushed /bʊʃt/ *adj. colloq.* **1** *Austral.* & *NZ* **a** lost in the bush. **b** bewildered. **2** tired out.

bushel /ˈbʊʃ(ə)l/ *n.* **1** *Brit.* a measure of capacity equal to 8 gallons and equivalent to 36.4 litres, used for corn, fruit, liquids, etc. **2** *US* a measure of capacity equal to 64 US pints, used for dry goods. □ **hide one's light under a bushel** see HIDE[1]. □ **bushelful** *n.* (*pl.* **-fuls**). [Middle English from Old French *buissiel* etc., perhaps of Gaulish origin]

bushfire /ˈbʊʃfʌɪə/ *n.* a fire in a forest or in scrub, often spreading widely.

bushido /ˈbuːʃɪdəʊ, bʊˈʃiːdəʊ/ *n.* the code of honour and morals evolved by the Japanese samurai. [Japanese, from *bushi* 'samurai' + *dō* 'way']

bushing /ˈbʊʃɪŋ/ *n.* = BUSH[2] *n.*

bush jacket *n.* a light cotton jacket with a belt.

bush lawyer *n.* **1** *Austral.* & *NZ* a person claiming legal knowledge without qualifications for it. **2** *NZ* a bramble.

bush league *n. & adj. N. Amer.* ● *n.* a minor league of a professional sport. ● *attrib.adj.* (**bush-league**) *colloq.* inferior, minor, unsophisticated. □ **bush-leaguer** *n.*

bushman /ˈbʊʃmən/ *n.* (*pl.* **-men**) **1** a person who lives or travels in the Australian bush. **2** (**Bushman**) **a** a member of an aboriginal people in S. Africa. **b** the language of this people. [BUSH[1] + MAN: sense 2 influenced by Dutch *boschjesman*]

bushmaster /ˈbʊʃmɑːstə/ *n.* a venomous viper, *Lachesis muta*, of Central and S. America. [perhaps from Dutch *boschmeester*]

bushranger /ˈbʊʃreɪn(d)ʒə/ *n. hist.* an Australian outlaw living in the bush.

bush sickness *n.* a disease of animals due to a lack of cobalt in the soil.

bush telegraph *n.* a rapid informal spreading of information, a rumour, etc.; the network by which this takes place.

bushveld /ˈbʊʃfɛlt, -vɛlt/ *n.* open country consisting largely of bush. [BUSH[1] + VELD, influenced by Afrikaans *bosveld*]

bushwhack /ˈbʊʃwak/ *v.* **1** *intr. US, Austral.,* & *NZ* **a** clear woods and bush country. **b** live or travel in bush country. **2** *tr. US* ambush.

bushwhacker /ˈbʊʃwakə/ *n.* **1** *N. Amer., Austral.,* & *NZ* **a** a person who clears woods and bush country. **b** a person who lives or travels in bush country. **2** *US* a guerrilla fighter (originally in the American Civil War).

bushy[1] /ˈbʊʃi/ *adj.* (**bushier, bushiest**) **1** growing thickly like a bush. **2** having many bushes. **3** covered with bush. □ **bushily** *adv.* **bushiness** *n.*

bushy[2] /ˈbʊʃi/ *n.* (*pl.* **-ies**) *Austral.* & *NZ colloq.* a person who lives in the bush (as distinct from in a town).

busily see BUSY.

business /ˈbɪznɪs/ *n.* **1** one's regular occupation, profession, or trade. **2** a thing that is one's concern. **3 a** a task or duty. **b** a reason for coming (*what is your business?*). **4** serious work or activity (*get down to business*). **5** *derog.* **a** an affair, a matter (*sick of the whole business*). **b** *Brit.* a structure (*a lath-and-plaster business*). **6** a thing or series of things needing to be dealt with (*the business of the day*). **7** buying and selling; trade (*good stroke of business*). **8** a commercial house or firm. **9** *Theatr.* action on stage. **10** a difficult matter (*what a business it is!*; *made a great business of it*). **11** (**the business**) *Brit. colloq.* exactly what is required; an exemplary person or thing. □ **has no business to** has no right to. **in business 1** trading or dealing. **2** able to begin operations. **in the business of 1** engaged in. **2** intending to (*we are not in the business of surrendering*). **like nobody's business** *colloq.* extraordinarily. **make it one's business to** undertake to. **mind one's own business** not meddle. **on business** with a definite purpose, esp. one relating to one's regular occupation. **send a person about his or her business** dismiss a person; send a person away. [Old English *bisignis* (as BUSY, -NESS)]

business card *n.* a card printed with one's name and professional details.

business end *n.* (prec. by *the*) *colloq.* the functional part of a tool or device.

businesslike /ˈbɪznɪslʌɪk/ *adj.* efficient, systematic, practical.

businessman /ˈbɪznɪsmən/ *n.* (*pl.* **-men**; *fem.* **businesswoman**, *pl.* **-women**) a person engaged in trade or commerce, esp. at a senior level (see also BUSINESS PERSON).

business park *n.* an area designed to accommodate businesses and light industry.

business person *n.* a businessman or businesswoman.

business studies *n.pl.* training in economics, management, etc.

businesswoman see BUSINESSMAN.

busk /bʌsk/ *v.intr.* perform (esp. music) for voluntary donations, usu. in the street or in subways. □ **busker** *n.* **busking** *n.* [*busk* peddle etc. (perhaps from obsolete French *busquer* 'seek')]

buskin /ˈbʌskɪn/ *n.* **1** a thick-soled laced boot worn by an ancient Athenian tragic actor to gain height. **2** (usu. prec. by *the*) tragic drama; its style or spirit. **3** *hist.* a calf- or knee-high boot of cloth or leather worn in the Middle Ages. □ **buskined** *adj.* [probably from Old French *bouzequin*, variant of *bro(u)sequin*, of unknown origin]

bus lane *n.* a lane on a road marked off for use by buses.

busman /ˈbʌsmən/ *n.* (*pl.* **-men**) the driver of a bus.

busman's holiday *n.* leisure time spent in an activity similar to one's regular work.

buss /bʌs/ *n. & v. archaic* or *N. Amer. colloq.* ● *n.* a kiss. ● *v.tr.* kiss. [earlier *bass* (*n.* & *v.*): probably from French *baiser* from Latin *basiare*]

bus shelter *n.* a shelter from rain etc. beside a bus stop.

bus station *n.* a centre, esp. in a town, where (esp. long-distance) buses depart and arrive.

bus stop *n.* **1** a regular stopping place of a bus. **2** a sign marking this.

bust[1] /bʌst/ *n.* **1 a** the human chest, esp. that of a woman; the bosom. **b** the circumference of the body at bust level (*a 36-inch bust*). **c** the part of a woman's garment fitting over the bust. **2** a sculpture of a person's head, shoulders, and chest. [French *buste* from Italian *busto*, of unknown origin]

bust[2] /bʌst/ *v., n., & adj. colloq.* ● *v.* (*past* and *past part.* **busted** or **bust**) **1** *tr. & intr.* break, burst. **2** *tr.* esp. *US* reduce (a soldier etc.) to a lower rank; dismiss. **3** *tr.* esp. *N. Amer.* **a** raid, search. **b** arrest. ● *n.* **1** a sudden failure; a bankruptcy. **2** a police raid. **3** a drinking bout. **4** esp. *N. Amer.* a punch; a hit. **5** a worthless thing. **6** a bad hand at cards. ● *adj.* (also **busted**) **1** broken, burst, collapsed. **2** bankrupt. □ **bust up 1** bring or come to collapse; explode. **2** (of esp. a married couple) separate. **go bust** become bankrupt; fail. [originally a (dialect) pronunciation of BURST]

bustard /ˈbʌstəd/ *n.* any large terrestrial bird of the family Otididae, with long neck, long legs, and stout tapering body. [Middle English via Old French *bistarde* from Latin *avis tarda* 'slow bird' (? = slow on the ground; but possibly a perversion of a foreign word)]

bustee /ˈbʌstiː/ *n.* (in the Indian subcontinent) a shanty town; a slum. [Hindustani *bastī* 'dwelling']

buster /ˈbʌstə/ *n.* **1** *slang* mate; fellow (used esp. as a disrespectful form of address). **2** a violent gale.

bustier /ˈbʌstɪeɪ, ˈbʊst-/ *n.* a woman's strapless close-fitting bodice. [French]

bustle[1] /ˈbʌs(ə)l/ *v.* & *n.* ● *v.* **1** *intr.* (often foll. by *about*) **a** work etc. showily, energetically, and officiously. **b** scurry (*bustled about the kitchen banging saucepans*). **2** *tr.* make (a person) hurry or work hard (*bustled him into his overcoat*). **3** *intr.* (as **bustling** *adj.*) *colloq.* full of activity. ● *n.* excited activity; a fuss. [perhaps from *buskle* frequentative of *busk* 'prepare', from Old Norse]

bustle[2] /ˈbʌs(ə)l/ *n. hist.* a pad or frame worn under a skirt and puffing it out behind. [18th c.: origin unknown]

bust-up *n.* **1** a quarrel. **2** a collapse; an explosion.

busty /ˈbʌsti/ *adj.* (**bustier**, **bustiest**) (of a woman) having a prominent bosom. ▫ **bustiness** *n.*

busy /ˈbɪzi/ *adj., v.,* & *n.* ● *adj.* (**busier, busiest**) **1** (often foll. by *in, with, at,* or pres. part.) occupied or engaged in work etc. with the attention concentrated (*busy at their needlework; he was busy packing*). **2** full of activity or detail; fussy (*a busy evening; a picture busy with detail*). **3** employed continuously; unresting (*busy as a bee*). **4** meddlesome; prying. **5** esp. *N. Amer.* (of a telephone line) engaged. ● *v.tr.* (**-ies, -ied**) (often *refl.*) keep busy; occupy (*the work busied him for many hours; busied herself with the accounts*). ● *n.* (*pl.* **-ies**) *slang* a detective; a police officer. ▫ **busily** /ˈbɪzɪli/ *adv.* **busyness** /ˈbɪzɪnɪs/ *n.* (cf. BUSINESS). [Old English *bisig*]

busybody /ˈbɪzɪbɒdi/ *n.* (*pl.* **-ies**) **1** a meddlesome person. **2** a mischief-maker.

busy Lizzie /ˈlɪzi/ *n. Brit.* an E. African plant, *Impatiens walleriana*, with abundant red, pink, or white flowers, often grown as a bedding plant or house plant.

but[1] /bʌt, bət/ *conj., prep., adv., pron., n.,* & *v.* ● *conj.* **1 a** nevertheless, however (*tried hard but did not succeed; I am old, but I am not weak*). **b** on the other hand; on the contrary (*I am old but you are young*). **2** (prec. by *can* etc.; in *neg.* or *interrog.*) except, other than, otherwise than (*cannot choose but do it; what could we do but run?*). **3** without the result that (*it never rains but it pours*). **4** prefixing an interruption to the speaker's train of thought (*the weather is ideal — but is that a cloud on the horizon?*). ● *prep.* except; apart from; other than (*everyone went but me; nothing but trouble*). ● *adv.* **1** only; no more than; only just (*we can but try; is but a child; had but arrived; did it but once*). **2** introducing emphatic repetition; definitely (*wanted to see nobody, but nobody*). **3** *Austral., NZ,* & *Sc.* though, however (*didn't like it, but*). ● *rel.pron.* who not; that not (*there is not a man but feels pity*). ● *n.* an objection (*ifs and buts*). ● *v.tr.* (in phr. **but me no buts**) do not raise objections. ▫ **but for** without the help or hindrance etc. of (*but for you I'd be rich by now*). **but one** (or **two** etc.) excluding one (or two etc.) from the number (*next door but one; last but one*). **but that** (prec. by *neg.*) that (*I don't deny but that it's true*). **but that** (or *colloq.* **what**) other than that; except that (*who knows but that it is true?*). **but then** (or **yet**) however, on the other hand (*I won, but then the others were beginners*). [Old English *be-ūtan, būtan, būta* 'outside, without']

but[2] /bʌt/ *n. Sc.* an outer room, esp. of a two-roomed cottage. ▫ **but and ben** a two-roomed cottage; a humble home (see BEN[2]). [BUT[1] = outside]

butadiene /bjuːtəˈdʌɪiːn/ *n. Chem.* a colourless gaseous hydrocarbon used in the manufacture of synthetic rubbers. Chem. formula: C_4H_6. [BUTANE + DI-[1] + -ENE: cf. BUNA]

butane /ˈbjuːteɪn/ *n. Chem.* a gaseous hydrocarbon of the alkane series used in liquefied form as fuel. Chem. formula: C_4H_{10}. [BUTYL + -ANE[2]]

butch /bʊtʃ/ *adj.* & *n. slang* ● *adj.* masculine; tough-looking. ● *n.* **1** (often *attrib.*) **a** a mannish woman. **b** a mannish lesbian. **2** a tough, usu. muscular, youth or man. [perhaps abbreviation of BUTCHER]

butcher /ˈbʊtʃə/ *n.* & *v.* ● *n.* **1 a** a person whose trade is dealing in meat. **b** a person who slaughters animals for food. **2** a person who kills or has people killed indiscriminately or brutally. ● *v.tr.* **1** slaughter or cut up (an animal) for food. **2** kill (people) wantonly or cruelly. **3** ruin (esp. a job or a musical composition) through incompetence. ▫ **the butcher, the baker, the candlestick-maker** people of all kinds or trades. **butcher's** *Brit. rhyming slang* a look (short for *butcher's hook*). [Middle English from Old French *bo(u)chier* from *boc* BUCK[1]]

butcher-bird *n.* **1** a shrike (family Laniidae). **2** a similar bird of the Australasian family Cracticidae. [from its habit of impaling its prey on thorns]

butcher's broom *n.* a low evergreen shrub, *Ruscus aculeatus* (lily family), with stiff flat shoots resembling spine-tipped leaves.

butcher's meat *n. Brit.* (also **butcher meat**) slaughtered fresh meat excluding game, poultry, and bacon.

butchery /ˈbʊtʃəri/ *n.* (*pl.* **-ies**) **1** wanton or cruel slaughter (of people). **2** the butcher's trade. **3** *Brit.* a slaughterhouse. [Middle English from Old French *boucherie* (as BUTCHER)]

butle var. of BUTTLE.

butler /ˈbʌtlə/ *n.* the principal servant of a household, usu. a man, in charge of the wine cellar, pantry, etc. [Middle English, from Anglo-French *buteler*, Old French *bouteillier* 'cup-bearer', from *bouteille* BOTTLE]

butt[1] /bʌt/ *v.* & *n.* ● *v.* **1** *tr.* & *intr.* push with the head or horns. **2 a** *intr.* (usu. foll. by *against, upon*) touch with one end flat, meet end to end, abut. **b** *tr.* (usu. foll. by *against*) place (timber etc.) with the end flat against a wall etc. ● *n.* **1** a push with the head. **2** a join of two edges. ▫ **butt in** interrupt, meddle. **butt out** *slang* **1** esp. *N. Amer.* stop interfering. **2** *N. Amer.* stop doing something. [Middle English via Anglo-French *buter*, Old French *boter* from Germanic: influenced by BUTT[2] and ABUT]

butt[2] /bʌt/ *n.* **1** (often foll. by *of*) an object (of ridicule etc.) (*the butt of his jokes; made him their butt*). **2 a** a mound behind a target. **b** (in *pl.*) a shooting range. **c** a target. **3** a grouse-shooter's stand screened by low turf or a stone wall. [Middle English from Old French *but* 'goal', of unknown origin]

butt[3] /bʌt/ *n.* **1** (also **butt-end**) the thicker end, esp. of a tool or a weapon (*gun butt*). **2** (also **butt-end**) **a** the stub of a cigar or a cigarette. **b** the remaining part. **3** esp. *N. Amer. slang* the buttocks. **4** (also **butt-end**) the square end of a plank meeting a similar end. **5** the trunk of a tree, esp. the part just above the ground. [Dutch *bot* 'stumpy']

butt[4] /bʌt/ *n.* a cask, esp. as a measure of wine or ale. [Anglo-Latin *butta, bota*, Anglo-French *but*, from Old French *bo(u)t* from Late Latin *buttis*]

butt[5] /bʌt/ *n.* a flatfish (e.g. a sole, plaice, or turbot). [Middle Low German, Middle Dutch *but* 'flatfish']

butte /bjuːt/ *n. N. Amer.* a high isolated steep-sided hill. [French, = mound]

butter /ˈbʌtə/ *n.* & *v.* ● *n.* **1 a** a pale yellow edible fatty substance made by churning cream and used as a spread or in cooking. **b** a substance of a similar consistency or appearance (*peanut butter*). **2** excessive flattery. ● *v.tr.* spread, cook, or serve with butter (*butter the bread; buttered carrots*). ▫ **butter up** *colloq.* flatter excessively. **look as if butter wouldn't melt in one's mouth** seem demure or innocent, probably deceptively.

[Old English *butere* via Latin *butyrum* from Greek *bouturon*]

butter-and-eggs *n.* any of several plants having two shades of yellow in the flower, esp. yellow toadflax.

butterball /ˈbʌtəbɔːl/ *n.* **1** a piece of butter shaped into a ball. **2** *N. Amer.* = BUFFLEHEAD. **3** *N. Amer. slang* a plump person or animal.

butter-bean *n.* **1** a flat, dried, white lima bean. **2** a yellow-podded bean.

butterbur /ˈbʌtəbəː/ *n.* a waterside plant of the genus *Petasites* (daisy family) with pale purple flowers and large soft leaves formerly used to wrap butter.

butter-cream *n.* a mixture of butter, icing sugar, etc. used as a filling or a topping for a cake.

buttercup /ˈbʌtəkʌp/ *n.* a plant of the genus *Ranunculus* (family Ranunculaceae), having bright yellow cup-shaped flowers and common in grassland.

butterfat /ˈbʌtəfat/ *n.* the essential fats of pure butter.

butter-fingers *n. colloq.* a clumsy person prone to drop things.

butterfish /ˈbʌtəfɪʃ/ *n.* (*pl.* usu. same) = GUNNEL[1].

butterfly /ˈbʌtəflʌɪ/ *n.* (*pl.* **-flies**) **1** any insect of the order Lepidoptera which typically flies by day and has clubbed or dilated antennae and two pairs of usu. brightly coloured wings held erect when at rest. **2** a showy or frivolous person. **3** (in *pl.*) *colloq.* a nervous sensation felt in the stomach. **4** (in full **butterfly stroke**) a stroke in swimming, with both arms raised out of the water and lifted forwards together. [Old English *buttor-flēoge* (as BUTTER, FLY[2]): perhaps from the cream or yellow colour of common species, or from an old belief that the insects stole butter]

butterfly bush *n.* a buddleia, esp. *Buddleia davidii.*

butterfly fish *n.* a fish resembling a butterfly in shape or colour, esp. *Blennius ocellatus*, which has a broad dorsal fin with eye-spots, or any brightly coloured fish of the family Chaetodontidae.

butterfly net *n.* a fine net on a ring attached to a pole, used for catching butterflies.

butterfly nut *n.* a kind of wing nut.

butterfly stroke see BUTTERFLY 4.

butterfly valve *n.* a valve with hinged semicircular plates.

butter-icing *n.* = BUTTER-CREAM.

butter knife *n.* a blunt knife used for cutting butter at table.

buttermilk /ˈbʌtəmɪlk/ *n.* a slightly acid liquid left after churning butter.

butter muslin *n. Brit.* a thin, loosely woven cloth with a fine mesh, originally for wrapping butter.

butternut /ˈbʌtənʌt/ *n.* **1** a N. American tree, *Juglans cinerea*. **2** the oily nut of this tree.

butterscotch /ˈbʌtəskɒtʃ/ *n.* a brittle sweet made from butter, brown sugar, etc. [SCOTCH]

butterwort /ˈbʌtəwəːt/ *n.* a bog plant of the genus *Pinguicula*, esp. *P. vulgaris*, with violet-like flowers and sticky fleshy leaves that trap and digest small insects.

buttery[1] /ˈbʌt(ə)ri/ *n.* (*pl.* **-ies**) *Brit.* a room, esp. in a college, where provisions are kept and sold to students etc. [Middle English from Anglo-French *boterie* 'butt-store' (as BUTT[4])]

buttery[2] /ˈbʌt(ə)ri/ *adj.* like, containing, or spread with butter. □ **butteriness** *n.*

buttie var. of BUTTY[2].

buttle /ˈbʌt(ə)l/ *v.intr.* (also **butle**) *joc.* work as a butler. [back-formation from BUTLER]

buttock /ˈbʌtək/ *n.* (usu. in *pl.*) **1** either of the two fleshy protuberances on the lower rear part of the human body. **2** the corresponding part of an animal. [*butt* 'ridge' + -OCK]

button /ˈbʌt(ə)n/ *n.* & *v.* ● *n.* **1** a small disc or knob sewn on to a garment, either to fasten it by being pushed through a buttonhole, or as an ornament or badge. **2** a knob on a piece of electrical, electronic, etc., equipment which is pressed to operate it. **3 a** a small disc-shaped object (*chocolate buttons*). **b** (*attrib.*) anything resembling a button (*button nose*). **4 a** a bud. **b** a button mushroom. **5** *Fencing* a terminal knob on a foil making it harmless. ● *v.* **1** *tr.* & *intr.* = *button up* 1. **2** *tr.* supply with buttons. □ **buttoned up** *colloq.* **1** formal and inhibited in manner. **2** silent. **button one's lip** *slang* remain silent. **button up 1** fasten with buttons. **2** *colloq.* complete (a task etc.) satisfactorily. **3** *colloq.* become silent. **not worth a button** *Brit.* worthless. **on the button** esp. *N. Amer. slang* precisely. □ **buttoned** *adj.* **buttonless** *adj.* **buttony** *adj.* [Middle English from Old French *bouton*, ultimately from Germanic]

button-back *n.* (often *attrib.*) a chair or sofa with a quilted back, the stitching hidden by buttons.

buttonball tree /ˈbʌt(ə)nbɔːl/ *n.* the N. American plane tree, *Platanus occidentalis*.

button chrysanthemum *n.* a variety of chrysanthemum with small spherical flowers.

button-down *attrib.adj.* applied to a collar whose points are buttoned to the shirt.

buttonhole /ˈbʌt(ə)nhəʊl/ *n.* & *v.* ● *n.* **1** a slit made in a garment to receive a button for fastening. **2** *Brit.* a flower or spray worn in a lapel buttonhole. ● *v.tr.* **1** *colloq.* accost and detain (a reluctant listener). **2** make buttonholes in.

buttonhole stitch *n.* a looped stitch used for edging buttonholes.

buttonhook /ˈbʌt(ə)nhʊk/ *n.* a hook formerly used esp. for pulling the buttons on tight boots into place for fastening.

button mushroom *n.* a young unopened mushroom.

buttons /ˈbʌt(ə)nz/ *n. Brit. colloq.* a liveried page-boy. [from the rows of buttons on his jacket]

button-through *adj. Brit.* (of a dress) fastened with buttons from neck to hem like a coat.

buttonwood tree /ˈbʌt(ə)nwʊd/ *n.* = BUTTONBALL TREE.

buttress /ˈbʌtrɪs/ *n.* & *v.* ● *n.* **1 a** a projecting support of stone or brick etc. built against a wall. **b** a source of help or encouragement (*she was a buttress to him in his trouble*). **2** a projecting portion of a hill or mountain. ● *v.tr.* (often foll. by *up*) **1** support with a buttress. **2** support by argument etc. (*claim buttressed by facts*). [Middle English via Old French (*ars*) *bouterez* 'thrusting (arch)' from *bouteret*, from *bouter* BUTT[1]]

butt weld *n.* a weld in which the pieces are joined end to end.

butty[1] /ˈbʌti/ *n.* (*pl.* **-ies**) *Brit.* **1** *colloq.* or *dial.* a mate; a companion. **2** *hist.* a middleman negotiating between a mine owner and the miners. **3** a barge or other craft towed by another. [18th c.: perhaps from BOOTY in the phrase *play booty* 'join in sharing plunder']

butty[2] /ˈbʌti/ *n.* (also **buttie**) (*pl.* **-ies**) *N.Engl.* **1** a sandwich (*bacon butty*). **2** a slice of bread and butter. [BUTTER + -Y[2]]

butty-gang *n.* a gang of men contracted to work on a large job and sharing the profits equally.

butyl /ˈbjuːtʌɪl, -tɪl/ *n.* **1** *Chem.* the monovalent alkyl radical C_4H_9–. **2** *colloq.* butyl rubber. [BUTYRIC ACID + -YL]

butyl rubber *n.* a synthetic rubber used in the manufacture of tyre inner tubes and pond liners.

butyric acid /bjuːˈtɪrɪk/ *n. Chem.* either of two colourless syrupy liquid organic acids found in rancid butter and arnica oil. □ **butyrate** /ˈbjuːtɪreɪt/ *n.* [Latin *butyrum* BUTTER + -IC]

buxom /ˈbʌks(ə)m/ *adj.* (esp. of a woman) plump and healthy-looking; large and shapely; busty. □ **buxomness** *n.* [earlier sense *pliant*: Middle English, from stem of Old English *būgan* BOW[2] + -SOME[1]]

buy /bʌɪ/ *v.* & *n.* ● *v.* (**buys, buying**; *past* and *past part.* **bought** /bɔːt/) **1** *tr.* **a** obtain in exchange for money etc. **b** (often in *neg.*) serve to obtain (*money can't buy happiness*). **2** *tr.* **a** procure (the loyalty etc.) of a person by bribery, promises, etc. **b** win over (a person) in this way. **3** *tr.* get by sacrifice, great effort, etc. (*dearly bought*; *bought with our sweat*). **4** *tr. slang* accept, believe in, approve of (*it's a good scheme, I'll buy it; he bought it, he's so gullible*). **5** *absol.* be a buyer for a store etc. (*buys for Selfridges; are you buying or selling?*). ● *n. colloq.* a purchase (*that sofa was a good buy*). □ **buy in 1** buy a stock of. **2** withdraw (an item) at auction because of failure to reach the reserve price. **buy into** obtain a share in (an enterprise) by payment. **buy it** (usu. in *past*) *slang* be killed. **buy off** get rid of (a claim, a claimant, a blackmailer) by payment. **buy oneself out** obtain one's release (esp. from the armed services) by payment. **buy out** pay (a person) to give up an ownership, interest, etc. **buy over** bribe. **buy time** delay an event, conclusion, etc., temporarily. **buy up 1** buy as much as possible of. **2** absorb (another firm etc.) by purchase. [Old English *bycgan*, from Germanic]

buy-back *n.* the buying-back or repurchase of goods, shares, etc., often by contractual agreement (often *attrib.*: *buy-back scheme*).

buyer /'bʌɪə/ *n.* **1** a person employed to select and purchase stock for a large store etc. **2** a purchaser, a customer.

buyer's market *n.* (also **buyers' market**) an economic position in which goods are plentiful and cheap and buyers have the advantage.

buy-in *n.* esp. *US* **1** the purchase of shares on the Stock Exchange, esp. after the non-delivery of similar shares bought. **2** the buying-back of a company's own shares.

buyout /'bʌɪaʊt/ *n.* the purchase of a controlling share in a company etc.

buzz /bʌz/ *n.* & *v.* ● *n.* **1** the hum of a bee etc. **2** the sound of a buzzer. **3 a** a confused low sound as of people talking; a murmur. **b** a stir; hurried activity (*a buzz of excitement*). **c** *colloq.* a rumour. **4** *slang* a telephone call. **5** *slang* a thrill; a euphoric sensation. ● *v.* **1** *intr.* make a humming sound. **2 a** *tr.* & *intr.* signal or signal to with a buzzer. **b** *tr. slang* telephone. **3** *intr.* **a** (often foll. by *about*) move or hover busily. **b** (of a place) have an air of excitement or purposeful activity. **4** *tr. colloq.* throw hard. **5** *tr. Aeron. colloq.* fly fast and very close to (another aircraft, the ground, etc.). □ **buzz off** *slang* go or hurry away. [imitative]

buzzard /'bʌzəd/ *n.* **1** any of a group of predatory birds of the hawk family, esp. of the genus *Buteo*, with broad wings well adapted for soaring flight. **2** *N. Amer.* a vulture, esp. the turkey buzzard. [Middle English via Old French *busard*, *buson* from Latin *buteo -onis* 'falcon']

buzzer /'bʌzə/ *n.* **1** an electrical device, similar to a bell, that makes a buzzing noise. **2** a whistle or hooter.

buzz-saw *n. N. Amer.* a circular saw.

buzzword /'bʌzwəːd/ *n. slang* **1** a fashionable piece of esp. technical jargon. **2** a catchword; a slogan.

BVM *abbr.* Blessed Virgin Mary.

b/w *abbr.* black and white (as opposed to colour).

bwana /'bwɑːnə/ *n.* (in Africa) master, sir. [Swahili]

BWI *abbr. hist.* British West Indies.

BWR *abbr.* boiling water (nuclear) reactor.

by /bʌɪ/ *prep.*, *adv.*, & *n.* ● *prep.* **1** near, beside, in the region of (*stand by the door; sit by me; path by the river*). **2** through the agency, means, instrumentality, or causation of (*by proxy; bought by a millionaire; a poem by Donne; went by bus; succeeded by persisting; divide four by two*). **3** not later than; as soon as (*by next week; by now; by the time he arrives*). **4 a** past, beyond (*drove by the church; came by us*). **b** passing through; via (*went by Paris*). **5** in the circumstances of (*by day; by daylight*). **6** to the extent of (*missed by a foot; better by far*). **7** according to; using as a standard or unit (*judge by appearances; paid by the hour*). **8** with the succession of (*worse by the minute; day by day; one by one*). **9** concerning; in respect of (*did our duty by them; Smith by name; all right by me*). **10** used in mild oaths (originally = as surely as one believes in) (*by God; by gum; swear by all that is sacred*). **11** placed between specified lengths in two directions (*three feet by two*). **12** avoiding, ignoring (*pass by him; passed us by*). **13** (esp. in names of compass points) inclining to (*north by east* between north and north-north-east; *north-east by north* between north-east and north-north-east). ● *adv.* **1** near (*sat by, watching; lives close by*). **2** aside; in reserve (*put £5 by*). **3** past (*they marched by*). ● *n.* (*pl.* **byes**) = BYE[1]. □ **by and by** before long; eventually. **by and large** on the whole, everything considered. **by the by** (or **bye**) incidentally, parenthetically. **by oneself 1 a** unaided. **b** without prompting. **2** alone; without company. [Old English *bī*, *bi*, *be*, from Germanic]

by- /bʌɪ/ *prefix* (also **bye-**) subordinate, incidental, secondary (*by-product; byroad*).

by-blow /'bʌɪbləʊ/ *n. Brit.* **1** a side-blow not at the main target. **2** a man's illegitimate child.

bye[1] /bʌɪ/ *n.* **1** *Cricket* a run scored from a ball that passes the batsman without being hit. **2** the status of an unpaired competitor in a sport, who proceeds to the next round as if having won. **3** *Golf* one or more holes remaining unplayed after the match has been decided. □ **by the bye** = *by the by*. [BY used as noun]

bye[2] /bʌɪ/ *int. colloq.* = GOODBYE. [abbreviation]

bye- *prefix* var. of BY-.

bye-bye[1] /bʌɪ'bʌɪ/ *int. colloq.* = GOODBYE. [childish corruption]

bye-bye[2] /'bʌɪbʌɪ/ *n.* (also **bye-byes** /-bʌɪz/) (a child's word for) sleep. [Middle English, from the sound used in lullabies]

by-election /'bʌɪɪlɛkʃ(ə)n/ *n. Brit.* the election of an MP in a single constituency to fill a vacancy arising during a government's term of office.

Byelorussian var. of BELORUSSIAN.

by-form /'bʌɪfɔːm/ *n.* a collateral form of a word etc.

bygone /'bʌɪgɒn/ *adj.* & *n.* ● *adj.* past, antiquated (*bygone years*). ● *n.* (in *pl.*) past offences (*let bygones be bygones*).

by-law /'bʌɪlɔː/ *n.* (also **bye-law**) **1** *Brit.* a regulation made by a local authority or corporation. **2** a rule made by a company or society for its members. [Middle English probably from obsolete *byrlaw* local custom (Old Norse *býjar*, genitive sing. of *býr* 'town', but associated with BY)]

byline /'bʌɪlʌɪn/ *n.* **1** a line in a newspaper etc. naming the writer of an article. **2** a secondary line of work. **3** a goal line or touchline.

byname /'bʌɪneɪm/ *n.* a sobriquet; a nickname.

BYOB *abbr.* bring your own bottle.

bypass /'bʌɪpɑːs/ *n.* & *v.* ● *n.* **1** a road passing round a town or its centre to provide an alternative route for through traffic. **2 a** a secondary channel or pipe etc. to allow a flow when the main one is closed or blocked. **b** an alternative passage for the circulation of blood during a surgical operation on the heart. ● *v.tr.* **1** avoid; go round. **2** provide with a bypass.

bypath /'bʌɪpɑːθ/ *n.* **1** a secluded path. **2** a minor or obscure branch of a subject.

byplay /'bʌɪpleɪ/ *n.* a secondary action or sequence of events, esp. in a play.

by-product /'bʌɪprɒdʌkt/ *n.* **1** an incidental or secondary product made in the manufacture of something else. **2** a secondary result.

byre /'bʌɪə/ *n. Brit.* a cowshed. [Old English *bȳre*: perhaps related to BOWER[1]]

byroad /'bʌɪrəʊd/ *n.* a minor road.

Byronic /bʌɪ'rɒnɪk/ *adj.* **1** characteristic of Lord Byron, English poet d. 1824, or his romantic poetry. **2** (of a man) handsomely dark, mysterious, or moody.

byssinosis /bɪsɪ'nəʊsɪs/ *n. Med.* a lung disease caused by prolonged inhalation of textile fibre dust. [modern Latin from Greek *bussinos* 'made of byssus' + -OSIS]

byssus /'bɪsəs/ *n.* (*pl.* **byssuses** or **byssi** /-sʌɪ/) **1** *hist.* a fine textile fibre and fabric of flax. **2** a tuft of tough silky filaments by which some molluscs adhere to rocks etc. [Middle English via Latin from Greek *bussos*]

bystander /'bʌɪstandə/ *n.* a person who stands by but does not take part; a mere spectator.

byte /bʌɪt/ *n. Computing* a group of binary digits (usu. eight), operated on as a unit. [20th c.: based on BIT[4] and BITE]

byway /ˈbʌɪweɪ/ *n.* **1** a byroad or bypath. **2** a minor activity.

byword /ˈbʌɪwəːd/ *n.* **1** a person or thing cited as a notable example (*is a byword for luxury*). **2** a familiar saying; a proverb.

Byzantine /bɪˈzantʌɪn, bʌɪ-/ *adj. & n.* ● *adj.* **1** of Byzantium or the Eastern Roman Empire. **2** (of a political situation etc.): **a** extremely complicated. **b** inflexible. **c** carried on by underhand methods. **3** *Archit.* & *Art* of a highly decorated style developed in the Eastern Empire. ● *n.* a citizen of Byzantium or the Eastern Roman Empire. ▫ **Byzantinism** *n.* **Byzantinist** *n.* [French *byzantin* or Latin *Byzantinus* from *Byzantium*, the city later called Constantinople and now Istanbul]

Cc

C[1] /siː/ *n.* (also **c**) (*pl.* **Cs** or **C's**) **1** the third letter of the alphabet. **2** *Mus.* the first note of the diatonic scale of C major (the major scale having no sharps or flats). **3** the third hypothetical person or example. **4** the third highest class or category (of academic marks etc.). **5** (usu. ***c***) *Algebra* the third known quantity. **6** (as a Roman numeral) 100. **7** (**C**) the name of a computer programming language.

C[2] *abbr.* (also **C.**) **1** Cape. **2** Conservative. **3** *Brit.* Command Paper (second series, 1870–99). **4** Celsius, Centigrade.

C[3] *symb.* **1** *Chem.* the element carbon. **2** (also ©) copyright. **3** coulomb(s). **4** capacitance.

c[1] *abbr.* (also **c.**) **1** century; centuries. **2** chapter. **3** cent(s). **4** cold. **5** (usu. ***c.***) circa, about. **6** colt. **7** *Cricket* caught by.

c[2] *symb.* **1** (usu. ***c***) the speed of light in a vacuum. **2** centi-.

c/- *abbr. Austral. & NZ* care of.

CA *abbr.* **1** *US* California (in official postal use). **2** *Sc. & Canad.* chartered accountant.

Ca *symb. Chem.* the element calcium.

ca. *abbr.* circa, about.

CAA *abbr.* (in the UK) Civil Aviation Authority.

Caaba var. of KAABA.

CAB *abbr.* **1** Citizens' Advice Bureau. **2** *US* Civil Aeronautics Board.

cab /kab/ *n.* **1** a taxi. **2** the driver's compartment in a lorry, train, or crane. **3** *hist.* a hackney carriage. [abbreviation of CABRIOLET]

cabal /kəˈbal/ *n.* **1** a secret intrigue. **2** a political clique or faction. **3** *hist.* a committee of five ministers under Charles II, whose surnames happened to begin with C, A, B, A, and L. [French *cabale* from medieval Latin *cabala*, CABBALA]

cabala 1 var. of CABBALA. **2** (**Cabala**) var. of KABBALAH.

caballero /kabəˈljɛːrəʊ/ *n.* (*pl.* **-os**) a Spanish gentleman. [Spanish = gentleman, horseman, ultimately from Latin *caballus* 'horse': cf. CAVALIER, CHEVALIER]

cabana /kəˈbɑːnə/ *n. N. Amer.* a hut or shelter at a beach or swimming pool. [Spanish *cabaña* from Late Latin (as CABIN)]

cabaret /ˈkabəreɪ/ *n.* **1** an entertainment in a nightclub or restaurant while guests eat or drink at tables. **2** such a nightclub etc. [French, = wooden structure, tavern]

cabbage /ˈkabɪdʒ/ *n.* **1 a** any of several cultivated varieties of *Brassica oleracea*, with thick green or purple leaves forming a round heart or head. **b** these leaves usu. eaten as vegetable. **2** *Brit. colloq. derog.* a person who is inactive or lacks interest. □ **cabbagy** *adj.* [earlier *cabache*, *-oche* from Old French (Picard) *caboche* 'head', Old French *caboce*, of unknown origin]

cabbage palm *n.* any of various palm trees with cabbage-like buds (sometimes edible) or leaves.

cabbage rose *n.* a double rose with a large round compact flower.

cabbage tree *n.* **1** a palmlike tree, *Cordyline australis* (agave family), native to New Zealand and widely grown for its sugary sap or for ornament; also called *ti*. **2** = CABBAGE PALM.

cabbage white *n.* a butterfly, *Pieris brassicae*, whose caterpillars feed on cabbage leaves.

cabbala /kəˈbɑːlə, ˈkabələ/ *n.* **1** (also **cabala**, **kabbala**) mystic interpretation; any esoteric doctrine or occult lore. **2** (**Cabbala**) var. of KABBALAH. □ **cabbalism** *n.* **cabbalist** *n.* **cabbalistic** /-ˈlɪstɪk/ *adj.* [medieval Latin from Rabbinical Hebrew *ḳabbālâ* 'tradition']

cabby /ˈkabi/ *n.* (also **cabbie**) (*pl.* **-ies**) *colloq.* a taxi driver. [CAB + -Y[2]]

cab driver *n.* a taxi driver.

caber /ˈkeɪbə/ *n.* a roughly trimmed tree trunk used in the Scottish Highland sport of tossing the caber. [Gaelic *cabar* 'pole']

Cabernet /ˈkabəneɪ/ *n.* **1** a variety of black grape (esp. **Cabernet Franc** /frɒ̃/ or **Cabernet Sauvignon** /ˈsəʊvɪnjɒ̃/) used in wine-making. **2** a vine on which these grow. **3** a wine made from these grapes. [French]

cabin /ˈkabɪn/ *n. & v.* ● *n.* **1** a small shelter or house, esp. of wood. **2** a room or compartment in an aircraft or ship for passengers or crew. **3** a driver's cab. ● *v.tr.* (**cabined**, **cabining**) confine in a small place, cramp. [Middle English via Old French *cabane* and Provençal *cabana* from Late Latin *capanna*, *cavanna*]

cabin boy *n.* a boy who waits on a ship's officers or passengers.

cabin class *n.* the intermediate class of accommodation in a ship.

cabin crew *n.* the crew members on an aeroplane attending to passengers and cargo.

cabin cruiser *n.* a large motor boat with living accommodation.

cabinet /ˈkabɪnɪt/ *n.* **1 a** a cupboard or case with drawers, shelves, etc., for storing or displaying articles. **b** a piece of furniture housing a radio or television set etc. **2** (**Cabinet**) **a** the committee of senior ministers responsible for controlling government policy. **b** (in the US) a body of advisers to the President, composed of the heads of the executive departments of the government. **3** *archaic* a small private room. [CABIN + -ET[1], influenced by French *cabinet*]

cabinetmaker /ˈkabɪnɪtˌmeɪkə/ *n.* a skilled joiner. □ **cabinetmaking** *n.*

Cabinet minister *n. Brit.* a member of the Cabinet.

cabinet photograph *n.* a photograph of about 6 by 4 inches.

cabinet pudding *n.* a steamed pudding with dried fruit.

cabinetry /ˈkabɪnɪtri/ *n.* cabinets regarded collectively.

cable /ˈkeɪb(ə)l/ *n. & v.* ● *n.* **1** a thick rope of wire or hemp. **2 a** an encased group of insulated wires for transmitting electricity or electrical signals. **b** a cablegram. **c** = CABLE TELEVISION. **3 a** *Naut.* the chain of an anchor. **b** a measure of 200 yards or *US* 240 yards. **4** (in full **cable stitch**) a knitted stitch resembling twisted rope. **5** *Archit.* a rope-shaped ornament. ● *v.* **1 a** *tr.* transmit (a message) by cablegram. **b** *tr.* inform (a person) by cablegram. **c** *intr.* send a cablegram. **2** *tr.* furnish or fasten with a cable or cables. **3** *Archit. tr.* furnish with cables. [Middle English from Old French *chable*, ultimately from Late Latin *capulum* 'halter', from Arabic *ḥabl*]

cable car *n.* **1** a small cabin (often one of a series) suspended on an endless cable by which it is drawn up and down a mountainside etc., controlled from an engine room. **2** a carriage drawn along a cable railway.

cablegram /ˈkeɪb(ə)lgram/ *n.* a telegraph message sent by undersea cable etc.

cable-laid *adj.* (of rope) having three triple strands.

cable railway *n.* a railway along which carriages are drawn by an endless cable.

cable release *n. Photog.* a cable attached to a camera to allow the photographer to open the shutter without having to hold (and thus risk moving) the camera.

cable stitch see CABLE *n.* 4.

cable television *n.* a television broadcasting system with signals transmitted by cable to subscribers' sets.

cableway /ˈkeɪb(ə)lweɪ/ *n.* a transporting system with a usu. elevated cable.

cabman /ˈkabmən/ *n.* (*pl.* **-men**) *hist.* the driver of a hackney carriage.

cabochon /ˈkabəʃɒn/ *n.* (also *attrib.*) a gem polished but not faceted. □ ***en cabochon*** (of a gem) treated in this way. [French, diminutive of *caboche*: see CABBAGE]

caboodle /kəˈbuːd(ə)l/ *n.* □ **the whole caboodle** *slang* the whole lot (of persons or things). [19th c. US: perhaps from the phrase *kit and boodle*]

caboose /kəˈbuːs/ *n.* **1** *Brit.* a kitchen on a ship's deck. **2** *N. Amer.* a guard's van; a car on a freight train for workmen etc. [Dutch *cabūse*, of unknown origin]

cabotage /ˈkabətɑːʒ, -ɪdʒ/ *n.* **1** *Naut.* coastal navigation and trade. **2** esp. *Aeron.* the reservation to a country of (esp. air) traffic operation within its territory. [French from *caboter* 'to coast', perhaps from Spanish *cabo* CAPE[2]]

cabotin /kɑːbəˈtã, French kabɔtɛ̃/ *n.* (*fem.* ***cabotine*** /-ˈtiːn, French -tin/) a second-rate actor; a strolling player. [French, = strolling player, perhaps formed as CABOTAGE, from the resemblance to vessels travelling from port to port]

cabriole /kabrɪˈəʊl/ *n.* a kind of curved leg characteristic of Chippendale and Queen Anne furniture. [French from *cabrioler*, *caprioler* from Italian *capriolare* 'to leap in the air'; from the resemblance to a leaping animal's foreleg: see CAPRIOLE]

cabriolet /ˈkabrɪəleɪ/ *n.* **1** a light two-wheeled carriage with a hood, drawn by one horse. **2** a motor car with a folding top. [French from *cabriole* 'goat's leap' (cf. CAPRIOLE), applied to the carriage's motion]

ca'canny /kɑːˈkani/ *n. Brit.* **1** the practice of 'going slow' at work; a trade union policy of limiting output. **2** extreme caution. [Scots, = proceed warily: see CALL *v.* 16, CANNY]

cacao /kəˈkɑːəʊ, -ˈkeɪəʊ/ *n.* (*pl.* **-os**) **1** a seed pod from which cocoa and chocolate are made. **2** a small widely cultivated evergreen tree, *Theobroma cacao*, bearing these. [Spanish from Nahuatl *cacauatl* (*uatl* 'tree')]

cachalot /ˈkaʃəlɒt/ *n.* a sperm whale. [French from Spanish & Portuguese *cachalote*, from *cachola* 'big head']

cache /kaʃ/ *n.* & *v.* ● *n.* **1** a hiding place for treasure, provisions, ammunition, etc. **2** what is hidden in a cache. **3** (in full **cache memory**) *Computing* an auxiliary memory from which high-speed retrieval is possible. ● *v.tr.* put in a cache. [French from *cacher* 'to hide']

cachectic /kəˈkɛktɪk/ *adj. Med.* relating to or having the symptoms of cachexia.

cachet /ˈkaʃeɪ/ *n.* **1** a distinguishing mark or seal. **2** prestige. **3** *Med.* a flat capsule enclosing a dose of unpleasant-tasting medicine. [French from *cacher* 'press', ultimately from Latin *coactare* 'constrain']

cachexia /kəˈkɛksɪə/ *n.* (also **cachexy** /-ksi/) *Med.* a condition of weakness and wasting of the body associated with chronic disease. [French *cachexie* or Late Latin *cachexia* from Greek *kakhexia*, from *kakos* 'bad' + *hexis* 'habit']

cachinnate /ˈkakɪneɪt/ *v.intr. literary* laugh loudly. □ **cachinnation** /-ˈneɪʃ(ə)n/ *n.* **cachinnatory** /-ˈneɪt(ə)ri/ *adj.* [Latin *cachinnare cachinnat-* (imitative)]

cacholong /ˈkaʃəlɒŋ/ *n.* a kind of opal. [French, from Mongolian *kashchilon* 'beautiful stone']

cachou /ˈkaʃuː, kəˈʃuː/ *n.* **1** a lozenge to sweeten the breath. **2** var. of CATECHU. [French via Portuguese *cachu* from Malay *kāchu*: cf. CATECHU]

cachucha /kəˈtʃuːtʃə/ *n.* a Spanish solo dance. [Spanish]

cacique /kəˈsiːk/ *n.* **1** a W. Indian or American Indian native chief. **2** a political boss in Spain or Latin America. [Spanish or French, from Taino]

cack-handed /kakˈhandɪd/ *adj. Brit. colloq.* **1** awkward, clumsy. **2** left-handed. □ **cack-handedly** *adv.* **cack-handedness** *n.* [dialect *cack* 'excrement']

cackle /ˈkak(ə)l/ *n.* & *v.* ● *n.* **1** a clucking sound as of a hen or a goose. **2** a loud silly laugh. **3** noisy inconsequential talk. ● *v.* **1** *intr.* emit a cackle. **2** *intr.* talk noisily and inconsequentially. **3** *tr.* utter or express with a cackle. □ **cut the cackle** *colloq.* stop talking aimlessly and come to the point. [Middle English, probably from Middle Low German, Middle Dutch *kākelen* (imitative)]

cacodemon /kakəˈdiːmən/ *n.* (also **cacodaemon**) **1** an evil spirit. **2** a malignant person. [Greek *kakodaimōn*, from *kakos* 'bad' + *daimōn* 'spirit']

cacodyl /ˈkakədʌɪl, -dɪl/ *n.* **1** a malodorous, toxic, spontaneously flammable liquid, tetramethyldiarsine. **2** (often *attrib.*) a radical derived from this, $-As(CH_3)_2$. □ **cacodylic** /-ˈdʌɪlɪk, -ˈdɪlɪk/ *adj.* [Greek *kakōdēs* 'stinking' from *kakos* 'bad']

cacoethes /kakəʊˈiːθiːz/ *n.* an urge to do something inadvisable. [Latin from Greek *kakoēthes* neut. adj., from *kakos* 'bad' + *ēthos* 'disposition']

cacography /kəˈkɒgrəfi/ *n.* **1** bad handwriting. **2** bad spelling. □ **cacographer** *n.* **cacographic** /kakəˈgrafɪk/ *adj.* **cacographical** /kakəˈgrafɪk(ə)l/ *adj.* [Greek *kakos* 'bad', on the pattern of *orthography*]

cacology /kəˈkɒlədʒi/ *n.* **1** bad choice of words. **2** bad pronunciation. [Late Latin *cacologia* from Greek *kakologia* 'vituperation', from *kakos* 'bad']

cacomistle /ˈkakəmɪs(ə)l/ *n.* a raccoon-like American animal of the genus *Bassariscus*, with a dark-ringed tail, esp. *B. astutus* of N. America. [Latin American Spanish *cacomixtle* from Nahuatl *tlacomiztli*]

cacophony /kəˈkɒf(ə)ni/ *n.* (*pl.* **-ies**) **1** a harsh discordant mixture of sound. **2** dissonance; discord. □ **cacophonous** *adj.* [French *cacophonie* via Greek *kakophōnia* from *kakophōnos*, from *kakos* 'bad' + *phōnē* 'sound']

cactus /ˈkaktəs/ *n.* (*pl.* **cacti** /-tʌɪ/ or **cactuses**) any succulent plant of the family Cactaceae, native to arid parts of the New World, with a thick fleshy stem, usu. spines but no leaves, and often brilliantly coloured flowers. □ **cactaceous** /-ˈteɪʃəs/ *adj.* [Latin, from Greek *kaktos* 'cardoon' (an obsolete sense in English)]

cactus dahlia *n.* a dahlia with quilled petals resembling a cactus flower.

cacuminal /kəˈkjuːmɪn(ə)l/ *adj. Phonet.* = RETROFLEX 2. [Latin *cacuminare* 'make pointed' from *cacumen -minis* 'treetop']

CAD *abbr.* computer-aided design.

cad /kad/ *n.* a person (esp. a man) who behaves dishonourably. □ **caddish** *adj.* **caddishly** *adv.* **caddishness** *n.* [abbreviation of CADDIE in earlier sense 'odd-job man']

cadastral /kəˈdastr(ə)l/ *adj.* of or showing the extent, value, and ownership of land, esp. for taxation. [French from *cadastre* 'register of property' via Provençal *cadastro* from Italian *catast(r)o* (earlier *catastico*), from late Greek *katastikhon* 'list, register', from *kata stikhon* 'line by line']

cadaver /kəˈdɑːvə, -ˈdeɪ-/ *n.* esp. *Med.* a corpse. □ **cadaveric** /-ˈdav(ə)rɪk/ *adj.* [Middle English via Latin from *cadere* 'fall']

cadaverous /kəˈdav(ə)rəs/ *adj.* **1** corpselike. **2** deathly pale. [Latin *cadaverosus* (as CADAVER)]

caddie /ˈkadi/ *n.* & *v.* (also **caddy**) ● *n.* (*pl.* **-ies**) a person who assists a golfer during a match, by carrying clubs etc. ● *v.intr.* (**caddies**, **caddied**, **caddying**) act as caddie. [originally Scots from French CADET]

caddie car *n.* (also **caddie cart**) *Brit.* a light two-wheeled trolley for transporting golf clubs during a game.

caddis-fly /ˈkadɪs/ *n.* (*pl.* **-flies**) a small mothlike insect of the order Trichoptera, with aquatic larvae. [17th c.: origin unknown]

caddish see CAD.

caddis-worm /ˈkadɪs/ *n.* (also **caddis**) the aquatic larva of a caddis-fly, often making a protective cylindrical case of sticks, leaves, etc., and used as fishing bait. [as CADDIS-FLY]

caddy[1] /ˈkadi/ *n.* (*pl.* **-ies**) a small container, esp. a box for holding tea. [earlier *catty*, a unit of weight of 1⅓ lb (0.61kg), from Malay *kātī*]

caddy[2] var. of CADDIE.

cadence /ˈkeɪd(ə)ns/ *n.* **1** a fall in pitch of the voice, esp. at the end of a phrase or sentence. **2** intonation, tonal inflection. **3** *Mus.* the close of a musical phrase. **4** rhythm; the measure or beat of sound or movement. ◻ **cadenced** *adj.* [Middle English via Old French from Italian *cadenza*, ultimately from Latin *cadere* 'fall']

cadential /kəˈdɛnʃ(ə)l/ *adj.* of a cadence or cadenza.

cadenza /kəˈdɛnzə/ *n. Mus.* a virtuosic passage for a solo instrument or voice, usu. near the close of a movement of a concerto, sometimes improvised. [Italian: see CADENCE]

cadet /kəˈdɛt/ *n.* **1** a young trainee in the armed services or police force. **2** a boy or girl of 13–18 who undergoes voluntary army, navy, or air force training, together with adventure training, occasionally also undertaking public duties. **3** *NZ* an apprentice in sheep farming. **4** a younger son. ◻ **cadetship** *n.* [French from Gascon dialect *capdet*, ultimately from Latin *caput* 'head']

cadge /kadʒ/ *v.* **1** *tr.* get or seek by begging. **2** *intr.* beg. ◻ **cadger** *n.* [19th c.: origin unknown]

cadi /ˈkɑːdi, ˈkeɪdi/ *n.* (also **kadi**) (*pl.* **-is**) a judge in a Muslim country. [Arabic *ḳāḍī* from *ḳaḍā* 'to judge']

Cadmean /kadˈmiːən/ *adj.* = PYRRHIC[1]. [Latin *Cadmeus* from Greek *Kadmeios*, from *Kadmos* 'Cadmus': see CADMIUM]

cadmium /ˈkadmɪəm/ *n.* a soft bluish-white toxic metallic element occurring naturally with zinc ores, and used in the manufacture of solders and pigments and in electroplating (symbol **Cd**). [obsolete *cadmia* 'calamine' via Latin from Greek *kadm(e)ia (gē)* 'Cadmean (earth)', from *Kadmos* 'Cadmus', the name of the legendary founder of Thebes: see -IUM]

cadmium cell *n. Electr.* a standard primary cell.

cadmium yellow *n.* an intense yellow pigment containing cadmium sulphide and used in paints etc.

cadre /ˈkɑːdə, ˈkɑːdr(ə), ˈkadri/ *n.* **1** a basic unit, esp. of servicemen, forming a nucleus for expansion when necessary. **2** also /ˈkeɪdə/ **a** a group of activists in a communist or other revolutionary party. **b** a member of such a group. [in early use 'a framework, a plan': French via Italian *quadro* from Latin *quadrus* 'square']

caduceus /kəˈdjuːsɪəs/ *n.* (*pl.* **caducei** /-sɪʌɪ/) an ancient Greek or Roman herald's wand, esp. as carried by the messenger-god Hermes or Mercury. [Latin, from Doric Greek *karuk(e)ion* from *kērux* 'herald']

caducous /kəˈdjuːkəs/ *adj. Biol.* (of organs and parts) easily detached or shed at an early stage. ◻ **caducity** /-sɪti/ *n.* [Latin *caducus* 'falling' from *cadere* 'fall']

caecilian /sɪˈsɪlɪən/ *n.* (also **coecilian**) a burrowing wormlike amphibian of the order Gymnophiona, having poorly developed eyes and no limbs. [Latin *caecilia* 'slow-worm']

caecitis /sɪˈkʌɪtɪs/ *n.* (*US* **cecitis**) *Med.* inflammation of the caecum.

caecum /ˈsiːkəm/ *n.* (*US* **cecum**) (*pl.* **-ca** /-kə/) *Anat.* a blind-ended pouch at the junction of the small and large intestines. ◻ **caecal** *adj.* [Latin *(intestinum) caecum* 'blind (gut)', from *caecus* 'blind', translation of Greek *tuphlon enteron*]

Caerns. *abbr.* Caernarvonshire (a former county in Wales).

Caerphilly /kɛːˈfɪli, kɑː-, kə-/ *n.* a kind of mild white cheese originally made in Caerphilly in Wales.

Caesar /ˈsiːzə/ *n.* **1** the title of the Roman emperors, esp. from Augustus to Hadrian. **2** an autocrat. **3** *Brit. Med. slang* a Caesarean section; a case of this. [Latin, family name of Gaius Julius *Caesar*, Roman statesman d. 44 BC]

Caesarean /sɪˈzɛːrɪən/ *adj.* & *n.* (also **Caesarian**) ● *adj.* **1** of Caesar or the Caesars. **2** (*US* also **Ces-**) (of a birth) effected by Caesarean section. ● *n.* a Caesarean section. [Latin *Caesarianus*]

Caesarean section *n.* an operation for delivering a child by cutting through the wall of the mother's abdomen (Julius Caesar supposedly having been born this way).

Caesar salad *n.* a salad consisting of cos lettuce and croutons served with a dressing of olive oil, lemon juice, raw egg, Worcester sauce, and seasoning. [*Caesar* Cardini, Mexican restaurateur who invented it in 1924]

Caesar's wife *n.* a person required to be above suspicion.

caesious /ˈsiːzɪəs/ *adj. Bot.* bluish or greyish green. [Latin *caesius*]

caesium /ˈsiːzɪəm/ *n.* (*US* **cesium**) a rare soft silver-white element of the alkali metal group, occurring in certain minerals, and used in photoelectric cells and atomic clocks (symbol **Cs**). [as CAESIOUS (from its spectrum lines)]

caesura /sɪˈzjʊərə/ *n.* (*pl.* **caesuras**) *Prosody* **1** (in Greek and Latin verse) a break between words within a metrical foot. **2** (in modern verse) a pause near the middle of a line. ◻ **caesural** *adj.* [Latin from *caedere caes-* 'cut']

CAF *abbr. US* cost and freight.

cafard /kaˈfɑː/ *n.* melancholia. [French, = cockroach, hypocrite]

café /ˈkafeɪ, ˈkafi/ *n.* (also **cafe** /*pronunc.* same or *joc.* kaf, keɪf/) **1** a small coffee house or tea shop; a simple restaurant. **2** *N. Amer.* a bar or nightclub. [French, = coffee, coffee house]

café au lait /kafeɪ əʊ ˈleɪ, French kafe o lɛ/ *n.* **1** coffee with milk. **2** the colour of this.

café-bar *n.* (also **cafe-bar**) a café in which alcoholic drinks can be bought.

café noir /kafeɪ ˈnwɑː, French kafe nwar/ *n.* black coffee.

café society *n.* the regular patrons of fashionable restaurants and nightclubs.

cafeteria /kafɪˈtɪərɪə/ *n.* a restaurant in which customers collect their meals on trays at a counter and usu. pay before sitting down to eat. [Latin American Spanish *cafetería* 'coffee shop']

cafetière /kafˈtjɛː/ *n. Brit.* a coffee pot with a plunger that pushes the grounds to the bottom. [French]

caff /kaf/ *n. Brit. slang* = CAFÉ. [abbreviation]

caffeine /ˈkafiːn/ *n.* an alkaloid drug with stimulant action, found in tea leaves and coffee beans. [French *caféine* from *café* 'coffee']

Cafod /ˈkafɒd/ *abbr.* Catholic Fund for Overseas Development.

caftan var. of KAFTAN.

cage /keɪdʒ/ *n.* & *v.* ● *n.* **1** a structure of bars or wires, esp. for confining animals or birds. **2** any similar open framework, esp. an enclosed platform or lift in a mine or the compartment for passengers in a lift. **3** *colloq.* a camp for prisoners of war. ● *v.tr.* place or keep in a cage. [Middle English via Old French from Latin *cavea*]

cage bird *n.* a bird of the kind customarily kept in a cage.

cagey /ˈkeɪdʒi/ *adj.* (also **cagy**) (**cagier**, **cagiest**) *colloq.* cautious and uncommunicative; wary. ◻ **cagily** *adv.* **caginess** *n.* (also **cageyness**). [20th-c. US: origin unknown]

cagoule /kəˈguːl/ *n.* a thin hooded outer jacket (esp. one that is windproof and waterproof), worn in mountaineering etc. [French, literally 'cowl']

cahoots /kəˈhuːts/ *n.pl.* ◻ **in cahoots** (often foll. by *with*) *slang* in collusion. [19th c.: origin uncertain]

CAI *abbr.* computer-assisted (or -aided) instruction.

caiman var. of CAYMAN.

Cain /keɪn/ *n.* □ **raise Cain** *colloq.* make a disturbance; create trouble. [*Cain*, eldest son of Adam, who murdered his brother (Genesis 4)]

Cainozoic var. of CENOZOIC.

caique /kʌɪ'iːk, kɑː-/ *n.* **1** a light rowing boat on the Bosporus. **2** an eastern Mediterranean sailing ship. [French via Italian *caicco* from Turkish *kayik*]

cairn /kɛːn/ *n.* **1** a mound of rough stones built as a monument or landmark. **2** (in full **cairn terrier**) **a** a small terrier of a breed with short legs, a longish body, and a shaggy coat (perhaps so called from its being used to hunt among cairns). **b** this breed. [Gaelic *carn*]

cairngorm /'kɛːngɔːm/ *n.* a yellow or wine-coloured semi-precious form of quartz. [found on *Cairngorm*, a mountain in Scotland (Gaelic *carn gorm* 'blue cairn')]

caisson /'keɪs(ə)n, kə'suːn/ *n.* **1** a watertight chamber in which underwater construction work can be done. **2** a floating vessel used as a floodgate in docks. **3** an ammunition chest or wagon. [French (from Italian *cassone*) assimilated to *caisse* CASE[2]]

caisson disease *n.* = DECOMPRESSION SICKNESS.

caitiff /'keɪtɪf/ *n.* & *adj. poet.* or *archaic* ● *n.* a base or despicable person; a coward. ● *adj.* base, despicable, cowardly. [Middle English from Old French *caitif*, *chaitif*, ultimately from Latin *captivus* CAPTIVE]

cajole /kə'dʒəʊl/ *v.tr.* (often foll. by *into*, *out of*) persuade by flattery, deceit, etc. □ **cajolement** *n.* **cajolery** *n.* [French *cajoler*]

Cajun /'keɪdʒ(ə)n/ *n.* & *adj.* ● *n.* a French-speaking descendant of early settlers in Acadia, living esp. in the bayou areas of southern Louisiana. ● *adj.* of or relating to the Cajuns, esp. with reference to their music, cuisine, etc. [alteration of ACADIAN]

cake /keɪk/ *n.* & *v.* ● *n.* **1 a** a mixture of flour, butter, eggs, sugar, etc., baked in the oven. **b** a quantity of this baked in a flat round or ornamental shape and often iced and decorated. **2 a** other food in a flat round shape (*fish cake*). **b** = CATTLE CAKE. **3** a flattish compact mass (*a cake of soap*). **4** *Sc.* & *N.Engl.* thin oaten bread. ● *v.* **1** *tr.* & *intr.* form into a compact mass. **2** *tr.* (usu. foll. by *with*) cover (with a hard or sticky mass) (*boots caked with mud*). □ **cakes and ale** merrymaking. **have one's cake and eat it** *colloq.* enjoy both of two mutually exclusive alternatives. **a piece of cake** *colloq.* something easily achieved. **sell** (or **go**) **like hot cakes** be sold (or go) quickly; be popular. **a slice of the cake** *colloq.* participation in benefits. [Middle English, probably from Old Norse *kaka*]

cake-hole *n. Brit. slang* the mouth.

cakewalk /'keɪkwɔːk/ *n.* **1** a dance developed from an American black contest in graceful walking with a cake as a prize. **2** *colloq.* an easy task. **3** *Brit.* a form of fairground entertainment consisting of a promenade moved by machinery.

CAL *abbr.* computer-assisted learning.

Cal *abbr.* large calorie(s) or kilocalorie(s).

Cal. *abbr.* California.

cal *abbr.* small calorie(s).

Calabar bean /'kaləbɑː/ *n.* a poisonous seed of the tropical African climbing plant *Physostigma venosum*, containing alkaloids used in medicine. [*Calabar* in Nigeria]

calabash /'kaləbaʃ/ *n.* **1 a** an evergreen tree, *Crescentia cujete*, native to tropical America, bearing fruit in the form of large gourds. **b** a gourd from this tree. **2** the shell of this or a similar gourd used as a vessel for water, to make a tobacco pipe, etc. [French *calebasse* from Spanish *calabaza*, perhaps from Persian *karbuz* 'melon']

calaboose /kalə'buːs/ *n. US dial.* a prison. [black French *calabouse* from Spanish *calabozo* 'dungeon']

calabrese /'kaləbriːs, kalə'briːs, kalə'breɪsi/ *n. Brit.* a large succulent variety of sprouting broccoli. [Italian, = Calabrian]

calamanco /kalə'maŋkəʊ/ *n.* (*pl.* **-oes**) *hist.* a glossy woollen cloth chequered on one side. [16th c.: origin unknown]

calamander /'kaləmandə/ *n.* a fine-grained red-brown ebony streaked with black, from the Asian tree *Diospyros qualsita*, used in furniture. [19th c.: Sinhalese *kalu-madīriya*]

calamari /kalə'mɑːri/ *n.pl.* squid served as food. [Italian *calamari* (*pl.* of *calamaro*), or modern Greek *kalamari*: cf. CALAMARY]

calamary /'kaləməri/ *n.* (*pl.* **-ies**) *archaic* a squid, esp. one of the genus *Loligo*. [medieval Latin *calamarium* 'pen-case' from Latin *calamus* 'pen', with reference to its long tapering horny internal shell]

calamine /'kaləmʌɪn/ *n.* **1** a pink powder consisting of zinc carbonate and ferric oxide, used in lotions and ointments. **2** a zinc ore, esp. zinc carbonate as a mineral. [Middle English via French from medieval Latin *calamina*, alteration of Latin *cadmia*: *see* CADMIUM]

calamint /'kaləmɪnt/ *n.* an aromatic herb or shrub of the former genus *Calamintha* (now *Clinopodium*, mint family). [Middle English via Old French *calament*, medieval Latin *calamentum*, and Late Latin *calaminthe* from Greek *kalaminthē*]

calamity /kə'lamɪti/ *n.* (*pl.* **-ies**) **1** a disaster, a great misfortune. **2 a** adversity. **b** deep distress. □ **calamitous** *adj.* **calamitously** *adv.* [Middle English via French *calamité* from Latin *calamitas -tatis*]

Calamity Jane *n.* a prophet of disaster. [the nickname of Martha Jane Burke (d. 1903), American frontierswoman and markswoman]

calando /kə'landəʊ/ *adv. Mus.* gradually decreasing in speed and volume. [Italian, = slackening]

calash /kə'laʃ/ *n. hist.* **1 a** a light low-wheeled carriage with a removable folding hood. **b** the folding hood itself. **2** *Canad.* a two-wheeled horse-drawn vehicle. **3** a woman's hooped silk hood. [French *calèche* via German *Kalesche* from Polish *kolaska* or Czech *kolesa*, from *kolo* 'wheel']

calc- /kalk/ *comb. form* lime or calcium. [German *Kalk* from Latin CALX]

calcaneus /kal'keɪnɪəs/ *n.* (also **calcaneum** /-nɪəm/) (*pl.* **calcanei** /-nɪʌɪ/ or **calcanea** /-nɪə/) the bone forming the heel. [Latin]

calcareous /kal'kɛːrɪəs/ *adj.* (also **calcarious**) of or containing calcium carbonate; chalky. [Latin *calcarius* (as CALX)]

calceolaria /kalsɪə'lɛːrɪə/ *n.* a plant of the S. American genus *Calceolaria* (figwort family), with slipper-shaped flowers. [modern Latin, from Latin *calceolus*, diminutive of *calceus* 'shoe' + *-aria* fem. = -ARY[1]]

calceolate /'kalsɪəleɪt/ *adj. Bot.* slipper-shaped.

calces *pl.* of CALX.

calcicole /'kalsɪkəʊl/ *adj.* & *n.* ● *adj.* growing best in calcareous soil. ● *n.* a calcicole plant. [Latin CALX 'lime' + *colere* 'inhabit']

calciferol /kal'sɪfərɒl/ *n.* one of the D vitamins, routinely added to dairy products, essential for the deposition of calcium in bones. Also called *ergocalciferol*, *vitamin D_2*. [CALCIFEROUS + -OL[1]]

calciferous /kal'sɪf(ə)rəs/ *adj.* yielding calcium salts, esp. calcium carbonate. [Latin CALX 'lime' + -FEROUS]

calcifuge /'kalsɪfjuːdʒ/ *adj.* & *n.* ● *adj.* not suited to calcareous soil. ● *n.* a calcifuge plant. [Latin CALX 'lime' + -FUGE]

calcify /'kalsɪfʌɪ/ *v.tr.* & *intr.* (**-ies**, **-ied**) **1** harden or become hardened by deposition of calcium salts; petrify. **2** convert or be converted to calcium carbonate. □ **calcific** /-'sɪfɪk/ *adj.* **calcification** /-fɪ'keɪʃ(ə)n/ *n.*

calcine /'kalsʌɪn, -sɪn/ *v.* **1** *tr.* **a** reduce, oxidize, or desiccate by strong heat. **b** burn to ashes; consume by fire; roast. **c** reduce to calcium oxide by roasting or burning. **2** *tr.* consume or purify as if by fire. **3** *intr.* undergo any of these. □ **calcination** /-sɪ'neɪʃ(ə)n/ *n.* [Middle English via Old French *calciner* or medieval

Latin *calcinare* from Late Latin *calcina* 'lime', from Latin CALX]

calcite /'kalsʌɪt/ *n.* natural crystalline calcium carbonate. [German *Calcit* from Latin CALX 'lime']

calcium /'kalsɪəm/ *n.* a soft grey metallic element of the alkaline earth group occurring naturally in limestone, chalk, gypsum, etc., and whose ions and salts are essential to life (symbol **Ca**). [Latin CALX 'lime' + -IUM]

calcium carbonate *n.* a white insoluble solid occurring naturally as chalk, limestone, marble, and calcite, forming mollusc shells and stony corals, and used in the manufacture of lime and cement.

calcium hydroxide *n.* a white crystalline powder used in the manufacture of plaster and cement; slaked lime.

calcium oxide *n.* a white solid alkaline compound, commonly produced in the form of quicklime (see LIME[1] 1). Also called *calx*.

calcium phosphate *n.* the main constituent of animal bones, used as bone ash fertilizer.

calcium sulphate *n.* a white crystalline solid occurring as anhydrite and gypsum.

calcrete /'kalkriːt/ *n. Geol.* a conglomerate formed by the cementation of sand and gravel with calcium carbonate. [CALC- + con*crete*]

calcspar /'kalkspɑː/ *n.* = CALCITE. [CALC- + SPAR[3]]

calculable /'kalkjʊləb(ə)l/ *adj.* able to be calculated or estimated. □ **calculability** /-'bɪlɪti/ *n.* **calculably** *adv.*

calculate /'kalkjʊleɪt/ *v.* **1** *tr.* ascertain or determine beforehand, esp. by mathematics or by reckoning. **2** *tr.* plan deliberately. **3** *intr.* (foll. by *on, upon*) rely on; make an essential part of one's reckoning (*calculated on a quick response*). □ **calculative** /-lətɪv/ *adj.* [Late Latin *calculare* (as CALCULUS)]

calculated /'kalkjʊleɪtɪd/ *adj.* **1** (of an action) done with awareness of the likely consequences. **2** (foll. by *to* + infin.) designed or suitable; intended. □ **calculatedly** *adv.*

calculating /'kalkjʊleɪtɪŋ/ *adj.* (of a person) shrewd, scheming. □ **calculatingly** *adv.*

calculation /kalkjʊ'leɪʃ(ə)n/ *n.* **1** the act or process of calculating. **2** a result got by calculating. **3** a reckoning or forecast. [Middle English via Old French from Late Latin *calculatio* (as CALCULATE)]

calculator /'kalkjʊleɪtə/ *n.* **1** a device (esp. a small electronic one) used for making mathematical calculations. **2** a person or thing that calculates. **3** a set of tables used in calculation. [Middle English from Latin (as CALCULATE)]

calculus /'kalkjʊləs/ *n.* (*pl.* **calculuses** or **calculi** /-lʌɪ, -liː/) **1 a** a particular method of calculation or reasoning (*calculus of probabilities*). **b** *Math.* the infinitesimal calculuses of integration or differentiation (see INTEGRAL CALCULUS, DIFFERENTIAL CALCULUS). **2 a** *Med.* a stone or concretion of minerals formed within the body, esp. in the kidney or gall bladder. **b** = TARTAR 1. □ **calculous** *adj.* (in sense 2). [Latin, = small stone used in reckoning on an abacus]

caldera /kɒl'dɛːrə, -'dɪərə/ *n.* a large volcanic crater, esp. one whose breadth greatly exceeds that of the vent or vents within it. [Spanish from Late Latin *caldaria* 'boiling-pot']

caldron var. of CAULDRON.

Caledonian /kalɪ'dəʊnɪən/ *adj. & n.* ● *adj.* **1** of or relating to Scotland. **2** *Geol.* of a mountain-forming period in Europe in the Palaeozoic era. ● *n.* a Scotsman. [*Caledonia* the Latin name for northern Britain]

calefacient /kalɪ'feɪʃ(ə)nt/ *n. & adj. Med.* ● *n.* any substance producing or causing a sensation of warmth. ● *adj.* having this property. [Latin *calefacere*, from *calēre* 'be warm' + *facere* 'make']

calendar /'kalɪndə/ *n. & v.* ● *n.* **1** a system by which the beginning, length, and subdivisions of the year are fixed. **2** a chart or series of pages showing the days, weeks, and months of a particular year, or giving special seasonal information. **3** a timetable or programme of appointments, special events, etc. **4** a list or register, esp. of canonized saints, cases for trial, etc. ● *v.tr.* register or enter in a calendar or timetable etc. □ **calendric** /-'lɛndrɪk/ *adj.* **calendrical** /-'lɛndrɪk(ə)l/ *adj.* [Middle English via Anglo-French *calender*, Old French *calendier* from Latin *calendarium* 'account book' (as CALENDS)]

calendar month see MONTH 1.

calendar year see YEAR 2.

calender /'kalɪndə/ *n. & v.* ● *n.* a machine in which cloth, paper, etc., is pressed by rollers to glaze or smooth it. ● *v.tr.* press in a calender. [French *calendre(r)*, of unknown origin]

calends /'kalɪndz/ *n.pl.* (also **kalends**) the first of the month in the ancient Roman calendar. [Middle English via Old French *calendes* from Latin *kalendae*, the first day of the month, when the order of days was proclaimed, from the base of Latin *calare*, Greek *kalein* 'call, proclaim']

calendula /kə'lɛndjʊlə/ *n.* any plant of the genus *Calendula* (daisy family), with large yellow or orange flowers, e.g. marigold. [modern Latin diminutive of *calendae* (as CALENDS), perhaps = little clock]

calenture /'kal(ə)ntjʊə/ *n. hist.* a tropical delirium of sailors, who imagine the sea to be green fields. [French, from Spanish *calentura* 'fever' from *calentar* 'be hot', ultimately from Latin *calēre* 'be warm']

calf[1] /kɑːf/ *n.* (*pl.* **calves** /kɑːvz/) **1** (used esp. of domestic cattle) a young bovine animal. **2** the young of other animals, e.g. elephant, deer, and whale. **3** *Naut.* a floating piece of ice detached from an iceberg. □ **in** (or **with**) **calf** (of a cow) pregnant. □ **calflike** *adj.* [Old English *cælf*, from West Germanic]

calf[2] /kɑːf/ *n.* (*pl.* **calves** /kɑːvz/) the fleshy hind part of the human leg below the knee. □ **-calved** /kɑːvd/ *adj.* (in *comb.*). [Middle English from Old Norse *kálfi*, of unknown origin]

calf-length *adj.* (of a garment) reaching down to the calves.

calf love *n.* romantic attachment or affection between adolescents.

calfskin /'kɑːfskɪn/ *n.* calf leather, esp. in bookbinding and shoemaking.

calibrate /'kalɪbreɪt/ *v.tr.* **1** mark (a gauge) with a standard scale of readings. **2** correlate the readings of (an instrument) with a standard. **3** determine the calibre of. **4** determine the correct capacity or value of. □ **calibrator** *n.* [CALIBRE + -ATE[3]]

calibration /kalɪ'breɪʃ(ə)n/ *n.* **1** the act or process of calibrating something. **2** each of a set of graduations on an instrument etc.

calibre /'kalɪbə, kə'liːbə/ *n.* (*US* **caliber**) **1 a** the internal diameter of a gun or tube. **b** the diameter of a bullet or shell. **2** strength or quality of character; ability, importance (*we need someone of your calibre*). □ **calibred** *adj.* (also in *comb.*). [French *calibre* or Italian *calibro*, from Arabic *kālib* 'mould']

caliche /kə'liːtʃi/ *n.* **1** a mineral deposit of gravel, sand, and nitrates, esp. Chile saltpetre, found in dry areas of America. **2** = CALCRETE. [Latin American Spanish]

calico /'kalɪkəʊ/ *n. & adj.* ● *n.* (*pl.* **-oes** or *N. Amer.* **-os**) **1** *Brit.* a cotton cloth, esp. plain white or unbleached. **2** *N. Amer.* a printed cotton fabric. ● *adj.* **1** made of calico. **2** *N. Amer.* multicoloured, piebald. [earlier *calicut* from *Calicut* (now Kozhikode), a city and port in India from which the cloth was exported]

Calif. *abbr.* California.

California condor see CONDOR 2.

Californian /kalɪ'fɔːnɪən/ *adj. & n.* ● *adj.* of or relating to California, a state on the Pacific coast of N. America. ● *n.* a native or inhabitant of California.

Californian poppy *n.* a plant of the poppy family, *Eschscholtzia californica*, grown for its brilliant yellow or orange flowers.

californium /kalɪˈfɔːnɪəm/ *n. Chem.* a transuranic radioactive metallic element produced artificially from curium (symbol **Cf**). [*California* (where it was first made) + -IUM]

caliper var. of CALLIPER.

caliph /ˈkeɪlɪf, ˈka-/ *n.* esp. *hist.* the chief Muslim civil and religious ruler, regarded as the successor of Muhammad. □ **caliphate** *n.* [Middle English via Old French *caliphe* from Arabic *Ḵalīfa* 'successor']

calisthenics var. of CALLISTHENICS.

calk *US* var. of CAULK.

call /kɔːl/ *v. & n.* ● *v.* **1** *intr.* **a** (often foll. by *out*) cry, shout; speak loudly. **b** (of a bird or animal) emit its characteristic note or cry. **2** *tr.* communicate or converse with by telephone or radio. **3** *tr.* **a** bring to one's presence by calling; summon (*will you call the children?*). **b** arrange for (a person or thing) to come or be present (*called a taxi*). **4** *intr.* (often foll. by *at, in, on*) esp. *Brit.* pay a brief visit (*called at the house; called in to see you; come and call on me*). **5** *tr.* **a** order to take place; fix a time for (*called a meeting*). **b** direct to happen; announce (*call a halt*). **6 a** *intr.* require one's attention or consideration (*duty calls*). **b** *tr.* urge, invite, nominate (*call to the bar*). **7** *tr.* name; describe as (*call her Della*). **8** *tr.* consider; regard or estimate as (*I call that silly*). **9** *tr.* rouse from sleep (*call me at eight o'clock*). **10** *intr.* guess the outcome of tossing a coin etc. **11** *intr.* (foll. by *for*) order, require, demand (*called for silence*). **12** *tr.* (foll. by *over*) read out (a list of names to determine those present). **13** *intr.* (foll. by *on, upon*) invoke; appeal to; request or require (*called on us to be quiet*). **14** *tr. Cricket* (of an umpire) disallow a ball from (a bowler). **15** *tr. Cards* specify (a suit or contract) in bidding. **16** *tr. Sc.* drive (an animal, vehicle, etc.). **17** *tr.* (in country dancing etc.) announce (the next figure or set of steps) by shouting rhythmically. ● *n.* **1** a shout or cry; an act of calling. **2 a** the characteristic cry of a bird or animal. **b** an imitation of this. **c** an instrument for imitating it. **3** a brief visit (*paid them a call*). **4 a** an act of telephoning. **b** a telephone conversation. **5 a** an invitation or summons to appear or be present. **b** an appeal or invitation (from a specific source or discerned by a person's conscience etc.) to follow a certain profession, set of principles, etc. **6** (foll. by *for*, or *to* + infin.) a duty, need, or occasion (*no call to be rude; no call for violence*). **7** (foll. by *for, on*) a demand (*not much call for it these days; a call on one's time*). **8** a signal on a bugle etc.; a signalling whistle. **9** *Stock Exch.* an option of buying stock at a fixed price at a given date. **10** *Cards* **a** a player's right or turn to make a bid. **b** a bid made. **11** (in country dancing etc.) a direction called to the dancers. □ **at call** = *on call*. **call away** divert, distract. **call a person's bluff** see BLUFF[1]. **call down 1** invoke. **2** reprimand. **call forth** elicit. **call in** *tr.* **1** withdraw from circulation. **2** seek the advice or services of. **call in** (or **into**) **question** dispute; doubt the validity of. **call into play** give scope for; make use of. **call it a day** see DAY. **call a person names** abuse a person verbally. **call off 1** cancel (an arrangement etc.). **2** order (an attacker or pursuer) to desist. **call of nature** a need to urinate or defecate. **call out 1** summon (troops etc.) to action. **2** order (workers) to strike. **call the shots** (or **tune**) be in control; take the initiative. **call a spade a spade** see SPADE[1]. **call to account** see ACCOUNT. **call to mind** recollect; cause one to remember. **call to order 1** request to be orderly. **2** declare (a meeting) open. **call up 1** reach by telephone. **2** imagine, recollect. **3** summon, esp. to serve in the army. **on call 1** (of a doctor etc.) available if required but not formally on duty. **2** (of money lent) repayable on demand. **within call** near enough to be summoned by calling. [Old English *ceallian* from Old Norse *kalla*]

calla /ˈkalə/ *n.* **1** (in full **calla lily**) = ARUM LILY. **2** an aquatic plant, *Calla palustris*. [modern Latin]

call box *n.* esp. *Brit.* a public telephone box or kiosk.

call-boy *n.* **1** a theatre attendant who summons actors when needed on stage. **2** a male prostitute who accepts appointments by telephone.

caller /ˈkɔːlə/ *n.* **1** a person who pays a visit or makes a telephone call. **2** a person who calls out numbers in a game, directions in a dance, etc. **3** *Austral.* a racing commentator.

call-girl *n.* a prostitute who accepts appointments by telephone.

calligraphy /kəˈlɪgrəfi/ *n.* **1** handwriting, esp. when fine or pleasing. **2** the art of handwriting. □ **calligrapher** *n.* **calligraphic** /-ˈgrafɪk/ *adj.* **calligraphist** *n.* [Greek *kalligraphia* from *kallos* 'beauty' + *graphia* 'writing']

calling /ˈkɔːlɪŋ/ *n.* **1** a profession or occupation. **2** an inwardly felt call or summons; a vocation.

calling card *n. N. Amer.* = VISITING CARD.

calliope /kəˈlʌɪəpi/ *n.* an American keyboard instrument resembling an organ, with a set of steam whistles producing musical notes. [Greek *Kalliopē*, the name of the Muse of epic poetry (literally 'beautiful-voiced')]

calliper /ˈkalɪpə/ *n. & v.* (also **caliper**) ● *n.* **1** (in *pl.*) compasses with bowed legs for measuring the diameter of convex bodies, or with out-turned points for measuring internal dimensions. **2** (in full **calliper splint**) a metal splint to support the leg. ● *v.tr.* measure with callipers. [apparently variant of CALIBRE]

callisthenics /kalɪsˈθɛnɪks/ *n.pl.* (*US* **calisthenics**) gymnastic exercises to achieve bodily fitness and grace of movement. □ **callisthenic** *adj.* [Greek *kallos* 'beauty' + *sthenos* 'strength']

callop /ˈkaləp/ *n. Austral.* a gold-coloured freshwater fish, *Plectroplites ambiguus*, used as food. Also called GOLDEN PERCH. [perhaps Aboriginal (S. Australia)]

callosity /kəˈlɒsɪti/ *n.* (*pl.* **-ies**) a hard thick area of skin usu. occurring in parts of the body subject to pressure or friction. [French *callosité* or Latin *callositas*, from *callosus* (as CALLUS)]

callous /ˈkaləs/ *adj. & n.* ● *adj.* **1** unfeeling, insensitive. **2** (of skin) hardened or hard. ● *n.* = CALLUS 1. □ **calloused** *adj.* **callously** *adv.* (in sense 1 of *adj.*). **callousness** *n.* [Middle English from Latin *callosus* (as CALLUS) or French *calleux*]

call-out *n.* an instance of being called out, esp. in order to rescue, do repairs, etc. (often *attrib.*: *call-out charge*).

call-over *n. Brit.* **1** a roll-call. **2** reading aloud of a list of betting prices.

callow /ˈkaləʊ/ *adj.* inexperienced, immature. □ **callowly** *adv.* **callowness** *n.* [Old English *calu* 'bald' (the earliest sense, hence 'unfledged, immature')]

call sign *n.* (also **call signal**) a broadcast signal identifying the radio transmitter used.

calluna /kəˈluːnə/ *n.* the common heather, *Calluna vulgaris*, native to Europe and N. Africa. [modern Latin from Greek *kallunō* beautify from *kallos* 'beauty']

call-up *n.* the act or process of calling up (see *call up* 3).

callus /ˈkaləs/ *n.* **1** a hard thick area of skin or tissue. **2** a hard tissue formed round bone ends after a fracture. **3** *Bot.* a new protective tissue formed over a wound. [Latin *callum, callus* 'hardened skin']

calm /kɑːm/ *adj., n., & v.* ● *adj.* **1** tranquil, quiet, windless (*a calm sea; a calm night*). **2** (of a person or disposition) settled; not agitated (*remained calm throughout the ordeal*). **3** self-assured, confident (*his calm assumption that we would wait*). ● *n.* **1** a state of being calm; stillness, serenity. **2 a** a period without wind or storm. **b** *Meteorol.* absence of wind, force 0 on the Beaufort scale. **3** (in *pl.*) an area, esp. of the sea, with predominantly calm weather. ● *v.tr. & intr.* (often foll. by *down*) make or become calm. □ **calmly** *adv.* **calmness** *n.* [Middle English, ultimately via Late Latin *cauma* from Greek *kauma* 'heat' (of the day)]

calmative /ˈkɑːmətɪv, ˈkal-/ *adj. & n. Med.* ● *adj.* tending to calm or sedate. ● *n.* a calmative drug etc.

calomel /'kaləmɛl/ *n.* mercury chloride, Hg_2Cl_2, a white powder formerly used as a purgative. [modern Latin, perhaps from Greek *kalos* 'beautiful' + *melas* 'black', perhaps because originally obtained from a black mixture of mercury and mercuric chloride]

Calor gas /'kalə/ *n. Brit. propr.* liquefied butane gas stored under pressure in containers for domestic use and used as a substitute for mains gas. [Latin *calor* 'heat']

caloric /kə'lɒrɪk, 'kalərɪk/ *adj. & n.* ● *adj.* of heat or calories. ● *n. hist.* a supposed material form or cause of heat. [French *calorique* from Latin *calor* 'heat']

calorie /'kaləri/ *n.* (also **calory**) (*pl.* **-ies**) a unit of heat energy: **1** (in full **small calorie**) the energy needed to raise the temperature of 1 gram of water through 1°C (now usu. defined as 4.1868 joules) (abbr.: **cal**). **2** (in full **large calorie**) the energy needed to raise the temperature of 1 kilogram of water through 1°C, often used to measure the energy value of foods; (also called *kilocalorie*) (abbr.: **Cal**). [French, an arbitrary formation from Latin *calor* 'heat' + *-ie*]

calorific /kalə'rɪfɪk/ *adj.* producing heat. ▫ **calorifically** *adv.* [Latin *calorificus* from *calor* 'heat']

calorific value *n.* the amount of heat produced by a specified quantity of fuel, food, etc.

calorimeter /kalə'rɪmɪtə/ *n.* any of various instruments for measuring quantity of heat, esp. to find calorific values. ▫ **calorimetric** /-'mɛtrɪk/ *adj.* **calorimetry** *n.* [Latin *calor* 'heat' + -METER]

calory var. of CALORIE.

calque /kalk/ *n. Philol.* = LOAN-TRANSLATION. [French, = copy, tracing, from *calquer* 'trace', ultimately from Latin *calcare* 'tread']

caltrop /'kaltrəp/ *n.* (also **caltrap**) **1** *hist.* a four-spiked iron ball thrown on the ground to impede cavalry horses. **2** *Heraldry* a representation of this. **3** any creeping plant of the genus *Tribulus*, with woody carpels usu. having hard spines. [(sense 3) Old English *calcatrippe* from medieval Latin *calcatrippa*: (senses 1–2) Middle English from Old French *chauchetrape* from *chauchier* 'tread', *trappe* 'trap': ultimately the same word, perhaps from Latin *calx* 'heel' + a base meaning 'trap' (cf. TRAP[1])]

calumet /'kaljʊmɛt/ *n.* a N. American Indian peace pipe. [French, ultimately from Latin *calamus* 'reed' (referring to the pipe's reed stem)]

calumniate /kə'lʌmnɪeɪt/ *v.tr.* slander. ▫ **calumniation** /-'eɪʃ(ə)n/ *n.* **calumniator** *n.* **calumniatory** *adj.* [Latin *calumniari*]

calumny /'kaləmni/ *n. & v.* ● *n.* (*pl.* **-ies**) **1** slander; malicious representation. **2** an instance of this. ● *v.tr.* (**-ies, -ied**) slander. ▫ **calumnious** /kə'lʌmnɪəs/ *adj.* [Latin *calumnia*]

calvados /'kalvədɒs/ *n.* an apple brandy. [name of a department of Normandy, France, where it is made.]

Calvary /'kalv(ə)ri/ *n.* the place where Christ was crucified. [Middle English from Late Latin *calvaria* 'skull', translation of Greek *golgotha*, Aramaic *gûlgûltâ* (Matthew 27:33)]

calve /kɑːv/ *v.* **1 a** *intr.* give birth to a calf. **b** *tr.* (esp. in *passive*) give birth to (a calf). **2** *tr.* (also *absol.*) (of an iceberg) break off or shed (a mass of ice). [Old English *calfian*]

calves *pl.* of CALF[1], CALF[2].

Calvinism /'kalvɪnɪz(ə)m/ *n.* the theology of the French theologian J. Calvin (d. 1564) or his followers, in which predestination and justification by faith are important elements. ▫ **Calvinist** *n.* **Calvinistic** /-'nɪstɪk/ *adj.* **Calvinistical** /-'nɪstɪk(ə)l/ *adj.* [French *calvinisme* or modern Latin *calvinismus*]

calx /kalks/ *n.* (*pl.* **calces** /'kalsiːz/) **1** a powdery metallic oxide formed when an ore or mineral has been heated. **2** calcium oxide. [Latin *calx calcis* 'lime', probably from Greek *khalix* 'pebble, limestone']

calypso /kə'lɪpsəʊ/ *n.* (*pl.* **-os**) **1** a kind of West Indian music in syncopated African rhythm, usu. improvised on a topical theme. **2** a song in this style. [20th c.: origin unknown]

calyx /'kalɪks, 'keɪ-/ *n.* (also **calix**) (*pl.* **calyces** /-lɪsiːz/ or **calyxes**) **1** *Bot.* the sepals collectively, forming the protective layer of a flower in bud. **2** *Biol.* any cuplike cavity or structure. [Latin, from Greek *kalux* 'case of bud, husk', from the base of *kaluptein* 'to hide']

calzone /kal'tsəʊni, Italian kal'tsoːnɛ/ *n.* (*pl.* ***calzoni*** or ***calzones***) a type of pizza that is folded to contain a filling. [Italian dialect, probably related to *calzone* 'trouser leg']

cam /kam/ *n.* a projection on a rotating part in machinery, shaped to impart reciprocal or variable motion to the part in contact with it. [Dutch *kam* 'comb', as in *kamrad* 'cogwheel']

camaraderie /kamə'rɑːd(ə)ri, -riː/ *n.* mutual trust and sociability among friends. [French, from *camarade* COMRADE]

camarilla /kamə'rɪlə, -ljə/ *n.* a cabal or clique. [Spanish, diminutive of *camara* 'chamber']

camber /'kambə/ *n. & v.* ● *n.* **1** the slightly convex or arched shape of the surface of a road, ship's deck, aircraft wing, etc. **2** *Brit.* = BANK[1] *n.* 4a. **3** the slight sideways inclination of the front wheel of a motor vehicle. ● *v.* **1** *intr.* (of a surface) have a camber. **2** *tr.* give a camber to; build with a camber. [Old French *cambre* 'arched' from Latin *camurus* 'curved inwards']

Camberwell Beauty /'kambəwɛl 'bjuːti/ *n. Brit.* a butterfly, *Nymphalis antiopa*, with deep purple yellow-bordered wings. [named after *Camberwell* in London]

cambium /'kambɪəm/ *n.* (*pl.* **cambia** /-bɪə/ or **cambiums**) *Bot.* a cellular plant tissue responsible for the increase in girth of stems and roots. ▫ **cambial** *adj.* [medieval Latin, = change, exchange]

Cambodian /kam'bəʊdɪən/ *n. & adj.* ● *n.* **1 a** a native or national of Cambodia (Kampuchea) in SE Asia. **b** a person of Cambodian descent. **2** the language of Cambodia. ● *adj.* of or relating to Cambodia or its people or language. See also KAMPUCHEAN.

Cambrian /'kambrɪən/ *adj. & n.* ● *adj.* **1** Welsh. **2** *Geol.* of or relating to the first period in the Palaeozoic era, marked by the occurrence of many forms of invertebrate life (including trilobites and brachiopods). Cf. Appendix X. ● *n.* this period or system. [Latin *Cambria*, variant of *Cumbria*, from Welsh *Cymry* 'Welshman' or *Cymru* 'Wales']

cambric /'kambrɪk, 'keɪm-/ *n.* a fine white linen or cotton fabric. [*Kamerijk*, Flemish form of *Cambrai* in N. France, where it was originally made]

Cambridge blue /'keɪmbrɪdʒ/ *n. & adj. Brit.* ● *n.* **1** a pale blue. **2** = BLUE[1] *n.* 3a. ● *adj.* (hyphenated when *attrib.*) of this colour. [adopted by *Cambridge* University in S. England]

Cambs. *abbr.* Cambridgeshire.

camcorder /'kamkɔːdə/ *n.* a combined video camera and video recorder. [*camera* + *recorder*]

came *past* of COME.

camel /'kam(ə)l/ *n. & adj.* ● *n.* **1** a large cud-chewing mammal, domesticated in parts of Africa and Asia, with slender legs, broad cushioned feet, and either one or two fatty humps on the back. See also ARABIAN CAMEL, BACTRIAN CAMEL. **2** a yellowish-fawn colour. **3** an apparatus for providing additional buoyancy to ships etc. ● *adj.* yellowish fawn. [Old English via Latin *camelus* from Greek *kamēlos*, of Semitic origin]

cameleer /kamə'lɪə/ *n.* a camel driver.

camel-hair *n.* (also **camel's-hair**) **1 a** the hair of a camel. **b** a fabric made of this (often *attrib.*: *camel-hair coat.*) **2** a fine soft hair used in artists' brushes.

camellia /kə'miːlɪə, -'mɛlɪə/ *n.* any evergreen shrub of the genus *Camellia*, native to E. Asia, with shiny leaves and showy flowers. [named after J. *Camellus* or *Kamel*, 17th-c. Jesuit botanist]

camelopard /'kamɪlə(ʊ)pɑːd, kə'mɛləpɑːd/ *n. archaic* a giraffe. [Latin *camelopardus* from Greek *kamēlopardalis* (as CAMEL, PARD)]

camelry /'kam(ə)lri/ *n.* (*pl.* **-ies**) troops mounted on camels.

Camembert /'kamãbɛː, 'kaməmbɛː/ *n.* a kind of rich soft creamy cheese. [*Camembert* in N. France, where it was originally made]

cameo /'kamɪəʊ/ *n.* (*pl.* **-os**) **1 a** a small piece of onyx or other hard stone carved in relief with a background of a different colour. **b** a similar relief design using other materials. **2 a** a short descriptive literary sketch or acted scene. **b** a small character part in a play or film, usu. brief and played by a distinguished actor. [Middle English from Old French *camahieu* and medieval Latin *cammaeus*]

camera /'kam(ə)rə/ *n.* **1** an apparatus for taking photographs, consisting of a lightproof box to hold light-sensitive film, a lens, and a shutter mechanism, either for still photographs or for motion-picture film. **2** *Telev.* a piece of equipment which forms an optical image and converts it into electrical impulses for transmission or storage. □ **in camera 1** *Law* in a judge's private room. **2** privately; not in public. **on camera** (esp. of an actor) being filmed or televised at a particular moment. [originally = chamber: from Latin *camera* 'vault, arched chamber' from Greek *kamara*]

camera lucida /ˌkam(ə)rə 'luːsɪdə/ *n.* (*pl.* **camera lucidas**) an apparatus, now often attached to a microscope, by which an image is reflected on to a screen by a prism as an aid to drawing. [Latin, = bright chamber]

cameraman /'kamrəmən/ *n.* (*pl.* **-men**) a person who operates a camera professionally, esp. in film-making or television.

camera obscura /ˌkam(ə)rə ɒbs'kjʊərə/ *n.* (*pl.* **camera obscuras**) a darkened box or room with a lens or aperture for projecting the image of an external object on to a screen inside. [Latin, = dark chamber]

camera-ready *adj. Printing* (of copy) in a form suitable for immediate photographic reproduction.

camerawork /'kamrəwəːk/ *n.* the technique of using cameras in films or television.

camiknickers /'kamɪnɪkəz/ *n.pl. Brit.* a one-piece undergarment worn by women. [CAMISOLE + KNICKERS]

camisole /'kamɪsəʊl/ *n.* a woman's under-bodice, usu. embroidered. [French from Italian *camiciola* or Spanish *camisola*: see CHEMISE]

camomile /'kaməmʌɪl/ *n.* (also **chamomile**) any of several aromatic plants of the daisy family with white and yellow daisy-like flowers, esp. *Chamaemelum nobile*. [Middle English via Old French *camomille* and Late Latin *camomilla* or *chamomilla* from Greek *khamaimēlon* 'earth-apple' (from the apple-smell of its flowers)]

camomile tea *n.* an infusion of dried camomile flowers.

camouflage /'kaməflɑːʒ, -muf-/ *n.* & *v.* ● *n.* **1 a** the disguising of military vehicles, aircraft, ships, artillery, and installations by painting them or covering them to make them blend with their surroundings. **b** such a disguise. **2** the natural colouring of an animal which enables it to blend in with its surroundings. **3** a misleading or evasive precaution or expedient. ● *v.tr.* hide or disguise by means of camouflage. [French from *camoufler* 'disguise', from Italian *camuffare* 'disguise, deceive']

camp[1] /kamp/ *n.* & *v.* ● *n.* **1 a** a place where troops are lodged or trained. **b** the military life (*court and camp*). **2** temporary overnight lodging in tents etc. in the open. **3 a** temporary accommodation of various kinds, usu. consisting of huts or tents, for detainees, homeless persons, and other emergency use. **b** a complex of buildings for holiday accommodation, usu. with extensive recreational facilities. **4** an ancient fortified site or its remains. **5** the adherents of a particular party or doctrine regarded collectively (*the Labour camp was jubilant*). **6** *S.Afr.* a portion of veld fenced off for pasture on farms. **7** *Austral.* & *NZ* an assembly place of sheep or cattle. ● *v.intr.* **1** set up or spend time in a camp (in senses 1a and 2 of *n.*). **2** (often foll. by *out*) lodge in temporary quarters or in the open. **3** *Austral.* & *NZ* (of sheep or cattle) flock together esp. for rest. □ **camping** *n.* [French via Italian *campo* from Latin *campus* 'level ground']

camp[2] /kamp/ *adj.*, *n.*, & *v. colloq.* ● *adj.* **1** affected, effeminate. **2** homosexual. **3** done in an exaggerated way for effect. ● *n.* a camp manner or style. ● *v.intr.* & *tr.* behave or do in a camp way. □ **camp it up** overact; behave affectedly. □ **campy** *adj.* (**campier**, **campiest**). **campily** *adv.* **campiness** *n.* [20th c.: origin uncertain]

campaign /kam'peɪn/ *n.* & *v.* ● *n.* **1** an organized course of action for a particular purpose, esp. to arouse public interest (e.g. before a political election). **2 a** a series of military operations in a definite area or to achieve a particular objective. **b** military service in the field (*on campaign*). ● *v.intr.* conduct or take part in a campaign. □ **campaigner** *n.* [French *campagne* 'open country' via Italian *campagna* from Late Latin *campania*]

campanile /kampə'niːli/ *n.* a bell tower (usu. free-standing), esp. in Italy. [Italian from *campana* 'bell']

campanology /kampə'nɒlədʒi/ *n.* **1** the study of bells. **2** the art or practice of bell-ringing. □ **campanological** /-nə'lɒdʒɪk(ə)l/ *adj.* **campanologist** *n.* [modern Latin *campanologia* from Late Latin *campana* 'bell']

campanula /kam'panjʊlə/ *n.* any plant of the genus *Campanula*, with bell-shaped usu. blue, purple, or white flowers. Also called *bellflower*. [modern Latin, diminutive of Latin *campana* 'bell']

campanulate /kam'panjʊlət/ *adj. Bot.* bell-shaped.

camp bed *n. Brit.* a folding portable bed of a kind used in camping.

Campeachy wood /kam'piːtʃi/ *n.* = LOGWOOD. [*Campeche* in Mexico, from where it was first exported]

camper /'kampə/ *n.* **1** a person who camps out or lives temporarily in a tent, hut, etc., esp. on holiday. **2** a large motor vehicle with accommodation for camping out.

campfire /'kampfʌɪə/ *n.* an open-air fire in a camp etc.

camp follower *n.* **1** a civilian worker in a military camp. **2** a disciple or adherent.

campground /'kampgraʊnd/ *n.* = CAMPSITE.

camphor /'kamfə/ *n.* a white translucent crystalline volatile substance with aromatic smell and bitter taste, used to make celluloid and in medicine. □ **camphoric** /-'fɒrɪk/ *adj.* [Middle English via Old French *camphore* or medieval Latin *camphora* from Arabic *kāfūr*, from Sanskrit *karpūram*]

camphorate /'kamfəreɪt/ *v.tr.* impregnate or treat with camphor.

campion /'kampɪən/ *n.* **1** any plant of the genus *Silene* (pink family), with usu. pink or white notched flowers. **2** a similar cultivated plant of the genus *Lychnis*. [perhaps from obsolete *campion* from Old French, = CHAMPION: translation of Greek *lukhnis stephanōmatikē*, a plant used for (champions') garlands]

campsite /'kampsʌɪt/ *n.* a place for camping.

campus /'kampəs/ *n.* (*pl.* **campuses**) **1** the grounds and buildings of a university or college. **2** university or college life. [Latin, = field]

campylobacter /'kampɪləʊˌbaktə, ˌkampɪləʊ'baktə/ *n.* a curved or spiral bacterium of the genus *Campylobacter*, esp. as a cause of food poisoning. [modern Latin, from Greek *kampulos* 'bent' + BACTERIUM]

CAMRA /'kamrə/ *abbr. Brit.* Campaign for Real Ale.

camshaft /'kamʃɑːft/ *n.* a shaft with one or more cams attached to it.

camwood /'kamwʊd/ *n.* a red African wood, formerly that of the tree *Baphia nitida*, now usu. of the African padouk, *Pterocarpus soyauxii*. [perhaps from a West African word]

Can. *abbr.* Canada; Canadian.

can[1] /kan/ *v.aux.* (*3rd sing. present* **can**; *past* **could** /kʊd/) (foll. by infin. without *to*, or *absol.*; present and past only in use) **1 a** be able to; know how to (*I can run* *fast; can he?*; *can you speak German?*). **b** be potentially capable of (*you can do it if you try*). **c** (in past) *colloq.* feel inclined to (*I could murder him*). **2** be permitted to (*can we go to the party?*). [Old English *cunnan* 'know']

can² /kan/ *n. & v.* ● *n.* **1** a vessel for holding liquids. **2** a tin container in which food or drink is hermetically sealed to enable storage over long periods. **3** (in *pl.*) *Brit. slang* headphones. **4** (prec. by *the*) *slang* **a** prison (*sent to the can*). **b** *N. Amer.* lavatory. ● *v.tr.* (**canned, canning**) **1** put or preserve in a can. **2** record on film or tape for future use. **3** *N. Amer. colloq.* remove; dismiss (*he was canned from his job*). □ **in the can** *colloq.* completed, ready (originally of filmed or recorded material). □ **canner** *n.* [Old English *canne*]

Canaan /'keɪnən/ *n.* **1** a promised land (originally that west of the River Jordan, the Promised Land of the Israelites). **2** heaven. [ecclesiastical Latin via ecclesiastical Greek *Khanaan* from Hebrew *kᵉna'an*]

Canaanite /'keɪnənʌɪt/ *n. & adj. hist.* ● *n.* a native or inhabitant of Canaan. ● *adj.* of or relating to Canaan, its people, or its culture.

Canada balsam /'kanədə/ *n. Biol.* a yellow resin obtained from the balsam fir and used for mounting preparations on microscope slides (its refractive index being similar to that of glass).

Canada goose /'kanədə/ *n.* a wild goose, *Branta canadensis*, with brownish-grey plumage and white cheeks and breast, native to N. America.

Canadian /kə'neɪdɪən/ *n. & adj.* ● *n.* **1** a native or national of Canada. **2** a person of Canadian descent. ● *adj.* of or relating to Canada.

Canadian French *n.* the French language as used by French Canadians.

Canadian pondweed *n.* an invasive American aquatic plant of the frogbit family, *Elodea canadensis*, naturalized in Europe and grown in aquaria.

canaille /kə'nɑːi, French kanaj/ *n.* the rabble; the populace. [French, from Italian *canaglia* 'pack of dogs' from *cane* 'dog']

canal /kə'nal/ *n.* **1** an artificial waterway for inland navigation or irrigation. **2** any of various tubular ducts in a plant or animal, for carrying food, liquid, or air. **3** *Astron.* any of a number of spurious linear markings formerly reported as seen by telescope on the planet Mars but now thought to have arisen from eye or lens defects. [Middle English via Old French (earlier *chanel*) from Latin *canalis* or (in sense 3 directly) from Italian *canale* 'channel']

canal boat *n.* a long narrow boat for use on canals.

canalize /'kan(ə)lʌɪz/ *v.tr.* (also **-ise**) **1** make a canal through. **2** convert (a river) into a canal. **3** provide with canals. **4** give the desired direction or purpose to. □ **canalization** /-'zeɪʃ(ə)n/ *n.* [French *canaliser*: see CANAL]

canapé /'kanəpeɪ, -pi/ *n.* **1** a small piece of bread or pastry with a savoury on top, often served as an hors d'oeuvre. **2** a sofa. [French]

canard /kə'nɑːd, 'kanɑːd/ *n.* **1** an unfounded rumour or story. **2** an extra surface attached to an aeroplane forward of the main lifting surface, for extra stability or control. [French, = duck, hoax, from Old French *caner* 'to quack']

Canarese var. of KANARESE.

canary /kə'nɛːri/ *n.* (*pl.* **-ies**) **1** any of various small finches of the genus *Serinus*, esp. *S. canaria*, a songbird native to the Canary Islands, with mainly yellow plumage, often kept as a cage bird. **2** *hist.* a sweet wine from the Canary Islands. [Old Spanish *canario* 'of or from the *Canary* Islands' off the west coast of Africa]

canary-coloured *adj.* canary yellow in colour.

canary creeper *n.* a climbing plant, *Tropaeolium peregrinum*, having flowers with bright yellow deeply toothed petals which give the appearance of a small bird in flight.

canary grass *n.* a tall grass of the genus *Phalaris*, esp. *P. canariensis* of NW Africa and the Canary Islands, grown for birdseed.

canary yellow *n. & adj.* ● *n.* a bright yellow colour. ● *adj.* (hyphenated when *attrib.*) of this colour.

canasta /kə'nastə/ *n.* **1** a card game using two packs and resembling rummy, the aim being to collect sets (or melds) of cards. **2** a set of seven cards in this game. [Spanish, = basket]

canaster /kə'nastə/ *n.* tobacco made from coarsely broken dried leaves. [Spanish *canastro* 'basket' (used to pack tobacco) from medieval Latin: related to CANISTER]

cancan /'kankan/ *n.* a lively stage-dance with high kicking, performed by women in long skirts and petticoats. [French]

cancel /'kans(ə)l/ *v. & n.* ● *v.* (**cancelled, cancelling**; *US* also **canceled, canceling**) **1** *tr.* **a** withdraw or revoke (a previous arrangement). **b** discontinue (an arrangement in progress). **2** *tr.* obliterate or delete (writing etc.). **3** *tr.* mark or pierce (a ticket, stamp, etc.) to invalidate it. **4** *tr.* annul; make void; abolish. **5** (often foll. by *out*) **a** *tr.* (of one factor or circumstance) neutralize or counterbalance (another). **b** *intr.* (of two factors or circumstances) neutralize each other. **6** *tr. Math.* strike out (an equal factor) on each side of an equation or from the numerator and denominator of a fraction. ● *n.* **1** a countermand. **2** the cancellation of a postage stamp. **3** *Printing* a new page or section inserted in a book to replace the original text, usu. to correct an error. **4** *US Mus.* = NATURAL *n.* 3a. □ **canceller** *n.* [Middle English via French *canceller* from Latin *cancellare*, from *cancelli* 'lattice']

cancellate /'kans(ə)lət/ *adj.* (also **cancellated** /-leɪtɪd/) *Biol.* **1** marked with crossing lines. **2** = CANCELLOUS. [Latin *cancelli* 'lattice']

cancellation /kansə'leɪʃ(ə)n/ *n.* (*US* also **cancelation**) **1** the act or an instance of cancelling or being cancelled. **2** something that has been cancelled, esp. a booking or reservation. [Latin *cancellatio* (as CANCEL)]

cancellous /'kans(ə)ləs/ *adj.* (of a bone) having pores. [Latin *cancelli* 'lattice']

cancer /'kansə/ *n.* **1 a** any malignant growth or tumour from an abnormal and uncontrolled division of body cells. **b** a disease caused by this. **2** an evil influence or corruption spreading uncontrollably. **3** (**Cancer**) **a** *Astron.* a constellation (the Crab), said to represent a crab crushed under the foot of Hercules. **b** *Astrol.* the fourth sign of the zodiac, which the sun enters at the summer solstice (about 21 June). **c** *Astrol.* a person born when the sun is in this sign. □ **tropic of Cancer** see TROPIC *n.* 1. □ **Cancerian** /-'sɪərɪən, -'sɛːrɪən/ *n. & adj.* (in sense 3b, c). **cancerous** *adj.* [Middle English from Latin, = crab, cancer: related to Greek *karkinos*]

cancer stick *n. slang* a cigarette.

cancroid /'kaŋkrɔɪd/ *adj. & n.* ● *adj.* **1** crablike. **2** resembling cancer. ● *n.* a disease resembling cancer.

candela /kan'dɛlə, -'diːlə, 'kandɪlə/ *n.* the SI unit of luminous intensity (abbr.: **cd**). [Latin, = candle]

candelabrum /kandɪ'lɑːbrəm, -'leɪ-/ *n.* (also **candelabra** /-brə/) (*pl.* **candelabra, candelabras**; *US* also **candelabrums**) a large branched candlestick or lamp holder. [Latin from *candela* CANDLE]

■ **Usage** Strictly speaking, *candelabra* is the plural of *candelabrum* and is best kept so in written English. *Candelabra* (singular) and *candelabras* (plural) are often found in informal use, while in American English *candelabrums* (plural) is also used.

candelabrum tree *n.* a tropical E. African tree, *Euphorbia candelabrum*, with foliage shaped like a candelabrum.

candid /'kandɪd/ *adj.* **1** frank; not hiding one's thoughts. **2** (of a photograph) taken informally, usu. without the subject's knowledge. □ **candidly** *adv.* **candidness** *n.* [in earlier use 'white', hence 'pure, clear, ingenuous': French *candide* or Latin *candidus* 'white']

candida /ˈkandɪdə/ *n.* any yeastlike parasitic fungus of the genus *Candida*, esp. *C. albicans*, which causes thrush. [modern Latin, fem. of Latin *candidus*: see CANDID]

candidate /ˈkandɪdeɪt, -dət/ *n.* **1** a person who seeks or is nominated for an office, award, etc. **2** a person or thing likely to gain some distinction or position. **3** a person entered for an examination. □ **candidacy** *n.* **candidature** *n. Brit.* [French *candidat* or Latin *candidatus* 'white-robed' (Roman candidates wore white)]

candid camera *n.* a small camera for taking informal photographs of people, often without their knowledge.

candle /ˈkand(ə)l/ *n. & v.* ● *n.* **1** a cylinder or block of wax or tallow with a central wick, for giving light when burning. **2** = CANDLEPOWER. ● *v.tr.* test (an egg) for freshness or fertility by holding it to the light. □ **cannot hold a candle to** cannot be compared with; is much inferior to. **not worth the candle** not justifying the cost or trouble. □ **candler** *n.* [Old English *candel* from Latin *candela*, from *candēre* 'to shine']

candleholder /ˈkand(ə)lˌhəʊldə/ *n.* = CANDLESTICK.

candlelight /ˈkand(ə)llʌɪt/ *n.* **1** light provided by candles. **2** dusk. □ **candlelit** *adj.*

Candlemas /ˈkand(ə)lmas, -məs/ *n.* a Christian feast with blessing of candles (2 Feb.), commemorating the purification of the Virgin Mary and the presentation of Christ in the Temple. [Old English *Candelmæsse* (as CANDLE, MASS)]

candlepower /ˈkand(ə)lpaʊə/ *n.* a unit of luminous intensity.

candlestick /ˈkand(ə)lstɪk/ *n.* a holder for one or more candles.

candlewick /ˈkand(ə)lwɪk/ *n.* **1** a thick soft cotton yarn. **2** material made from this, usu. with a tufted pattern.

can-do *attrib.adj.* designating a determination or willingness to achieve something (*the American can-do philosophy*).

candour /ˈkandə/ *n.* (*US* **candor**) candid behaviour or action; frankness. [French *candeur* or Latin *candor* 'whiteness': for the development of meaning in English see CANDID]

C. & W. *abbr.* country and western.

candy /ˈkandi/ *n. & v.* ● *n.* (*pl.* **-ies**) **1** (in full **sugar-candy**) *Brit.* sugar crystallized by repeated boiling and slow evaporation. **2** *N. Amer.* sweets; a sweet. ● *v.tr.* (**-ies, -ied**) (usu. as **candied** *adj.*) preserve by coating and impregnating with a sugar syrup (*candied fruit*). [French *sucre candi* 'crystallized sugar' from Arabic *ḳand* 'sugar']

candy apple *n. N. Amer.* = TOFFEE APPLE.

candyfloss /ˈkandɪflɒs/ *n. Brit.* a fluffy mass of spun sugar wrapped round a stick.

candy stripe /ˈkandɪstrʌɪp/ *n.* a pattern consisting of alternate stripes of white and a colour (usu. pink). □ **candy-striped** *adj.*

candytuft /ˈkandɪtʌft/ *n.* any of various cruciferous plants of the genus *Iberis*, native to W. Europe, with white, pink, or purple flowers in tufts. [*Candy*, obsolete form of *Candia* 'Crete' + TUFT]

cane /keɪn/ *n. & v.* ● *n.* **1 a** the hollow jointed stem of giant reeds or grasses (*bamboo cane*). **b** the solid stem of slender palms (*malacca cane*). **2** = SUGAR CANE. **3** a raspberry cane. **4** material of cane used for wickerwork etc. **5 a** a cane used as a walking stick or a support for a plant or an instrument of punishment. **b** any slender walking stick. ● *v.tr.* **1** beat with a cane. **2** weave cane into (a chair etc.). □ **caner** *n.* (in sense 2 of *v.*). **caning** *n.* [Middle English via Old French and Latin *canna* from Greek *kanna*]

cane-brake *n. N. Amer.* a tract of land overgrown with canes.

cane chair *n.* a chair with a seat made of woven cane strips.

cane sugar *n.* sugar obtained from sugar cane.

cane toad *n.* a large brown toad, *Bufo marinus*, native to tropical America and introduced elsewhere originally for pest control.

cane-trash see TRASH *n.* 5.

canine /ˈkeɪnʌɪn, ˈka-/ *adj. & n.* ● *adj.* **1** of a dog or dogs. **2** of or belonging to the family Canidae, including dogs, wolves, foxes, etc. ● *n.* **1** a dog. **2** (in full **canine tooth**) a pointed tooth between the incisors and premolars. [Middle English from French *canin(e)* or from Latin *caninus*, from *canis* 'dog']

canister /ˈkanɪstə/ *n.* **1** a small container, usu. of metal and cylindrical, for storing tea etc. **2 a** a cylinder of shot, tear gas, etc., that explodes on impact. **b** such cylinders collectively. [Latin *canistrum* from Greek *kanastron* 'wicker basket', from *kanna* CANE]

canker /ˈkaŋkə/ *n. & v.* ● *n.* **1 a** a destructive fungal disease of trees and plants. **b** an open wound in the stem of a tree or plant. **2** *Zool.* an ulcerous ear disease of animals, esp. cats and dogs. **3** *Med.* an ulceration esp. of the lips. **4** a corrupting influence. ● *v.tr.* **1** consume with canker. **2** corrupt. **3** (as **cankered** *adj.*) soured, malignant, crabbed. □ **cankerous** *adj.* [Middle English via Old Northern French *cancre*, Old French *chancre* from Latin *cancer* 'crab']

cankerworm /ˈkaŋkəwəːm/ *n.* any caterpillar of various wingless moths which consume the buds and leaves of shade and fruit trees in N. America.

canna /ˈkanə/ *n.* any tropical plant of the genus *Canna* with bright flowers and ornamental leaves. [Latin: see CANE]

cannabinol /ˈkanəbɪnɒl, kəˈnab-/ *n. Chem.* a crystalline phenol whose derivatives, esp. THC, are the active principles of cannabis. [CANNABIS + -OL[1]]

cannabis /ˈkanəbɪs/ *n.* **1** a hemp plant of the genus *Cannabis*, esp. Indian hemp. **2** a preparation of parts of this used as an intoxicant or hallucinogen. [Latin from Greek]

cannabis resin *n.* a sticky product containing the active principles of cannabis, esp. from the flowering tops of the female cannabis plant.

canned /kand/ *adj.* **1** pre-recorded (*canned laughter*; *canned music*). **2** supplied in a can (*canned beer*). **3** *slang* drunk.

cannel /ˈkan(ə)l/ *n.* (in full **cannel coal**) a bituminous coal burning with a bright flame. [16th c.: originally northern English]

cannelloni /kanəˈləʊni/ *n.pl.* tubes or rolls of pasta stuffed with a meat or vegetable mixture. [Italian from *cannello* 'stalk']

cannelure /ˈkan(ə)ljʊə/ *n.* the groove round a bullet etc. [French from *canneler*, from *canne* 'reed, CANE']

cannery /ˈkanəri/ *n.* (*pl.* **-ies**) a factory where food is canned.

cannibal /ˈkanɪb(ə)l/ *n. & adj.* ● *n.* **1** a person who eats human flesh. **2** an animal that feeds on flesh of its own species. ● *adj.* of or like a cannibal. □ **cannibalism** *n.* **cannibalistic** /-bəˈlɪstɪk/ *adj.* **cannibalistically** /-bəˈlɪstɪk(ə)li/ *adv.* [originally pl. *Canibales* from Spanish: variant of *Caribes*, the name of a West Indian nation]

cannibalize /ˈkanɪb(ə)lʌɪz/ *v.tr.* (also **-ise**) use (a machine etc.) as a source of spare parts for others. □ **cannibalization** /-ˈzeɪʃ(ə)n/ *n.*

cannikin /ˈkanɪkɪn/ *n.* a small can. [Dutch *kanneken* (as CAN[2], -KIN)]

cannon /ˈkanən/ *n. & v.* ● *n.* **1** (*pl.* usu. same) *hist.* a large heavy gun installed on a carriage or mounting. **2** an automatic aircraft gun firing shells. **3** *Brit. Billiards* the hitting of two balls successively by the cue ball. **4** *Mech.* a hollow cylinder moving independently on a shaft. **5** (in full **cannon bit**) a smooth round bit for a horse. ● *v.intr. Brit.* **1** (usu. foll. by *against, into*) collide heavily or obliquely. **2** *Billiards* make a cannon shot. [French *canon* via Italian *cannone* 'large tube' from *canna* CANE: in Billiards sense from older CAROM]

cannonade /kanə'neɪd/ *n.* & *v.* ● *n.* a period of continuous heavy gunfire. ● *v.tr.* bombard with a cannonade. [French from Italian *cannonata*]

cannon ball *n. hist.* a large usu. metal ball fired by a cannon.

cannon-bone *n.* the tubular bone between the hock and fetlock of a horse.

cannon fodder *n.* soldiers regarded merely as material to be expended in war.

cannot /'kanɒt, ka'nɒt/ *v.aux.* can not.

cannula /'kanjʊlə/ *n.* (*pl.* **cannulae** /-liː, -lʌɪ/ or **cannulas**) *Surgery* a small tube for inserting into the body to allow fluid to enter or escape. [Latin, diminutive of *canna* 'cane']

cannulate /'kanjʊleɪt/ *v.tr. Surgery* introduce a cannula into.

canny /'kani/ *adj.* (**cannier**, **canniest**) **1 a** shrewd, worldly-wise. **b** thrifty. **c** circumspect. **2** sly, drily humorous. **3** *Sc.* & *N.Engl.* pleasant, agreeable. □ **cannily** *adv.* **canniness** *n.* [CAN[1] (in sense 'know') + -Y[1]]

canoe /kə'nuː/ *n.* & *v.* ● *n.* a small narrow boat with pointed ends usu. propelled by paddling. ● *v.intr.* (**canoes**, **canoed**, **canoeing**) travel in a canoe. □ **canoeist** *n.* [Spanish *canoa* via Arawak from Carib *canaoua*]

can of worms *n. colloq.* a complicated matter, likely to prove problematic or scandalous.

canon /'kanən/ *n.* **1 a** a general law, rule, principle, or criterion. **b** a Church decree or law. **2 a** a member of a cathedral chapter. **b** (*fem.* **canoness** /-nɪs/) a member of certain RC orders. **3 a** a collection or list of literary works, esp. of sacred books etc. accepted as genuine. **b** the recognized genuine works of a particular author; a list of these. **4** the part of the Roman Catholic Mass containing the words of consecration. **5** *Mus.* a piece with different parts taking up the same theme successively, either at the same or at a different pitch. [Old English via Latin from Greek *kanōn*, reinforced in Middle English by Anglo-French & Old French *canun*, *-on*; in sense 2 Middle English via Old French *canonie* from ecclesiastical Latin *canonicus*: cf. CANONICAL]

cañon var. of CANYON.

canonic /kə'nɒnɪk/ *adj.* = CANONICAL *adj.* [Old English via Old French *canonique* or Latin *canonicus* from Greek *kanonikos*, from *kanon* 'rule']

canonical /kə'nɒnɪk(ə)l/ *adj.* & *n.* ● *adj.* **1 a** according to or ordered by canon law. **b** included in the canon of Scripture. **2** authoritative, standard, accepted. **3** of a cathedral chapter or a member of it. **4** *Mus.* in canon form. ● *n.* (in *pl.*) the canonical dress of the clergy. □ **canonically** *adv.* [medieval Latin *canonicalis* (as CANONIC)]

canonical hours *n.pl. Eccl.* **1** the times of daily prayer appointed in the breviary, or the offices set for them. **2** (in the Church of England) the time during which a marriage may lawfully be celebrated (usu. between 8 a.m. and 6 p.m.).

canonicate /kə'nɒnɪkət/ *n.* = CANONRY.

canonicity /kanə'nɪsɪti/ *n.* the status of being canonical. [Latin *canonicus* 'canonical']

canonist /'kanənɪst/ *n.* an expert in canon law. [Middle English from French *canoniste* or from medieval Latin *canonista*: see CANON]

canonize /'kanənʌɪz/ *v.tr.* (also **-ise**) **1 a** declare officially to be a saint, usu. with a ceremony. **b** regard as a saint. **2** admit to the canon of Scripture. **3** sanction by Church authority. □ **canonization** /-'zeɪʃ(ə)n/ *n.* [Middle English from medieval Latin *canonizare*: see CANON]

canon law *n.* ecclesiastical law.

canon regular (also **regular canon**) see REGULAR *adj.* 9b.

canonry /'kanənri/ *n.* (*pl.* **-ies**) the office or benefice of a canon.

canoodle /kə'nuːd(ə)l/ *v.intr. colloq.* kiss and cuddle amorously. [19th-c. US: origin unknown]

can-opener *n.* a device for opening cans of food etc.

Canopic jar /kə'nəʊpɪk/ *n.* (also **Canopic vase**) an urn used for holding the entrails of an embalmed body in an ancient Egyptian burial. [Latin *Canopicus* from *Canopus*, a town in ancient Egypt]

canopy /'kanəpi/ *n.* & *v.* ● *n.* (*pl.* **-ies**) **1 a** a covering hung or held up over a throne, bed, person, etc. **b** the sky. **c** an overhanging shelter. **2** *Archit.* a rooflike projection over a niche etc. **3** the uppermost layers of foliage etc. in a forest. **4 a** the expanding part of a parachute. **b** the cover of an aircraft's cockpit. ● *v.tr.* (**-ies**, **-ied**) supply or be a canopy to. [Middle English via medieval Latin *canopeum* and Latin *conopeum* from Greek *kōnōpeion* 'couch with mosquito-curtains', from *kōnōps* 'gnat']

canorous /kə'nɔːrəs/ *adj.* melodious, resonant. [Latin *canorus* from *canere* 'sing']

canst /kanst/ *archaic 2nd person sing.* of CAN[1].

Cant. *abbr.* Canticles (Old Testament).

cant[1] /kant/ *n.* & *v.* ● *n.* **1** insincere pious or moral talk. **2** ephemeral or fashionable catchwords. **3** language peculiar to a class, profession, sect, etc.; jargon. ● *v.intr.* use cant. [earlier of musical sound, of intonation, and of beggars' whining; perhaps from the singing of religious mendicants: probably from Latin *canere* 'sing']

cant[2] /kant/ *n.* & *v.* ● *n.* **1 a** a slanting surface, e.g. of a bank. **b** a bevel of a crystal etc. **2** an oblique push or movement that upsets or partly upsets something. **3** a tilted or sloping position. ● *v.* **1** *tr.* push or pitch out of level; tilt. **2** *intr.* take or lie in a slanting position. **3** *tr.* impart a bevel to. **4** *intr. Naut.* swing round. [Middle English from Middle Low German *kant*, *kante*, Middle Dutch *cant*, 'point, side, edge', ultimately from Latin *cant(h)us* 'iron tire']

can't /kɑːnt/ *contr.* can not.

Cantab /'kantab/ *abbr.* of Cambridge University. [Latin *Cantabrigiensis*]

cantabile /kan'tɑːbɪli/ *adv.*, *adj.*, & *n. Mus.* ● *adv.* & *adj.* in a smooth singing style. ● *n.* a cantabile passage or movement. [Italian, = singable]

Cantabrigian /kantə'brɪdʒɪən/ *adj.* & *n.* ● *adj.* of Cambridge or Cambridge University. ● *n.* **1** a member of Cambridge University. **2** a native of Cambridge. [Latin *Cantabrigia* 'Cambridge']

cantal /'kantɑːl/ *n.* a type of hard strong French cheese. [*Cantal*, a department of Auvergne, France, where it is made]

cantaloupe /'kantəluːp/ *n.* (also **cantaloup**) a small round ribbed variety of melon with orange flesh. [French *cantaloup* from *Cantaluppi* near Rome, where it was first grown in Europe]

cantankerous /kan'taŋk(ə)rəs/ *adj.* bad-tempered, quarrelsome. □ **cantankerously** *adv.* **cantankerousness** *n.* [perhaps from Irish *cant* 'outbidding' + *rancorous*]

cantata /kan'tɑːtə/ *n. Mus.* a short narrative or descriptive composition with vocal solos and usu. chorus and orchestral accompaniment. [Italian *cantata* (*aria*) 'sung (air)' from *cantare* 'sing']

cant-dog *n.* an iron hook at the end of a long handle, used for rolling logs.

canteen /kan'tiːn/ *n.* **1 a** a restaurant for employees in an office or factory etc. **b** a shop selling provisions or liquor in a barracks or camp. **2** *Brit.* a case or box of cutlery. **3** a soldier's or camper's water-flask or set of eating or drinking utensils. [French *cantine* from Italian *cantina* 'cellar']

canter /'kantə/ *n.* & *v.* ● *n.* a gentle gallop. ● *v.* **1** *intr.* (of a horse or its rider) go at a canter. **2** *tr.* make (a horse) canter. □ **in a canter** *Brit.* easily (*win in a canter*). [short for *Canterbury pace*, from the supposed easy pace of medieval pilgrims to Canterbury in Kent]

canterbury /ˈkantəb(ə)ri/ *n.* (*pl.* **-ies**) a piece of furniture with partitions for holding music etc. [named after *Canterbury* in Kent]

Canterbury bell /ˈkantəb(ə)ri/ *n.* a cultivated campanula with large flowers. [after the bells on Canterbury pilgrims' horses: see CANTER]

cantharides /kanˈθarɪdiːz/ *n.pl.* = SPANISH FLY 2. [Latin, from Greek *kantharis* 'Spanish fly']

cant-hook *n.* = CANT-DOG.

canthus /kanθəs/ *n.* (*pl.* **canthi** /-θʌɪ/) the outer or inner corner of the eye, where the upper and lower lids meet. [Latin from Greek *kanthos*]

canticle /ˈkantɪk(ə)l/ *n.* **1** a hymn or chant usu. with a biblical text, forming a regular part of a church service. **2** (**Canticles**) (also **Canticle of Canticles**) the Song of Solomon. [Middle English from Old French *canticle* (variant of *cantique*) or Latin *canticulum*, diminutive of *canticum*, from *canere* 'sing']

cantilena /kantɪˈlemə, -ˈliːnə/ *n. Mus.* a simple or sustained melody. [Italian]

cantilever /ˈkantɪliːvə/ *n.* & *v.* ● *n.* **1** a long bracket or beam etc. projecting from a wall to support a balcony etc. **2** a beam or girder fixed at only one end. ● *v.* **1** *intr.* & *tr.* project as a cantilever. **2** *tr.* support by a cantilever or cantilevers. [17th c.: origin unknown]

cantilever bridge *n.* a bridge made of cantilevers projecting from the piers and connected by girders.

cantillate /ˈkantɪleɪt/ *v.tr.* & *intr.* chant or recite with musical tones. □ **cantillation** /-ˈleɪʃ(ə)n/ *n.* [Latin *cantillare* 'sing low': see CHANT]

cantina /kanˈtiːnə/ *n.* a bar room or wine shop. [Spanish & Italian]

canting arms *n.pl. Heraldry* arms containing an allusion to the name of the bearer. [CANT[1], in the obsolete dialect sense 'speak, say']

canto /ˈkantəʊ/ *n.* (*pl.* **-os**) a division of a long poem. [Italian, = song, from Latin *cantus*]

canton *n.* & *v.* ● *n.* **1** /ˈkantɒn/ **a** a subdivision of a country. **b** a state of the Swiss Confederation. **2** /ˈkant(ə)n/ *Heraldry* a square division, less than a quarter, in the upper (usu. dexter) corner of a shield. ● *v.tr.* **1** /kanˈtuːn/ *Brit.* put (troops) into quarters. **2** /kanˈtɒn/ divide into cantons. □ **cantonal** /ˈkantən(ə)l, kanˈtɒn(ə)l/ *adj.* [Old French, = corner, ultimately from Latin *cantus* (see CANT[2]): the verb also partly from French *cantonner*]

Cantonese /kantəˈniːz/ *adj.* & *n.* ● *adj.* of Canton or the Cantonese dialect of Chinese. ● *n.* (*pl.* same) **1** a native of Canton. **2** the dialect of Chinese spoken in SE China and Hong Kong. [*Canton*, the English name of the city of Guangzhou in China]

cantonment /kanˈtɒnm(ə)nt, -ˈtuːn-/ *n.* **1** a lodging assigned to troops. **2** *hist.* a permanent military station in India. [French *cantonnement*: see CANTON]

cantor /ˈkantɔː, -ə/ *n.* **1** the leader of the singing in church; a precentor. **2** the precentor in a synagogue. [Latin, = singer from *canere* 'sing']

cantorial /kanˈtɔːrɪəl/ *adj.* **1** of or relating to the cantor. **2** of the north side of the choir in a church, the side on which the cantor sits (cf. DECANAL 2).

cantoris /kanˈtɔːrɪs/ *adj. Mus.* to be sung by the cantorial side of the choir in antiphonal singing (cf. DECANI). [Latin, genitive of CANTOR]

cantrail /ˈkantreɪl/ *n. Brit.* a timber etc. support for the roof of a railway carriage. [CANT[2] + RAIL[1]]

cantrip /ˈkantrɪp/ *n. Sc.* **1** a witch's trick. **2** a piece of mischief; a playful act. [16th c.: origin unknown]

Canuck /kəˈnʌk/ *n.* & *adj.* esp. *Canad. colloq.* ● *n.* a Canadian. ● *adj.* Canadian. [apparently from *Canada*]

canvas /ˈkanvəs/ *n.* & *v.* ● *n.* **1 a** a strong coarse kind of cloth made from hemp or flax or other coarse yarn and used for sails and tents etc. and as a surface for oil painting. **b** a piece of this. **2** a painting on canvas, esp. in oils. **3** an open kind of canvas used as a basis for tapestry and embroidery. **4** *slang* the floor of a boxing or wrestling ring. **5** a racing boat's covered end. ● *v.tr.* (**canvassed**, **canvassing**; *US* **canvased**, **canvasing**) cover with canvas. □ **by a canvas** (in boat racing) by a small margin (*win by a canvas*). **under canvas 1** in a tent or tents. **2** with sails spread. [Middle English & Old Northern French *canevas*, ultimately from Latin *cannabis* 'hemp']

canvas-back *n.* a wild duck *Aythya valisineria*, of N. America, with back feathers the colour of unbleached canvas.

canvass /ˈkanvəs/ *v.* & *n.* ● *v.* **1 a** *intr.* solicit votes. **b** *tr.* solicit votes from (electors in a constituency). **2** *tr.* **a** ascertain opinions of. **b** seek custom from. **c** discuss thoroughly. **3** *tr. Brit.* propose (an idea or plan etc.). ● *n.* the process of or an instance of canvassing, esp. of electors. □ **canvasser** *n.* [originally = toss in a sheet, agitate, from CANVAS]

canyon /ˈkanjən/ *n.* (also **cañon**) a deep gorge, often with a stream or river. [Spanish *cañón* 'tube', ultimately from Latin *canna* CANE]

canzonetta /kanzəˈnɛtə, kantsəˈnɛtə/ *n.* (also **canzonet** /-ˈnɛt/) **1** a short light song. **2** a kind of madrigal. [Italian, diminutive of *canzone* 'song', from Latin *cantio -onis* from *canere* 'sing']

caoutchouc /ˈkaʊtʃʊk/ *n.* raw rubber. [French from Carib *cahuchu*]

CAP *abbr.* Common Agricultural Policy (of the EEC).

cap /kap/ *n.* & *v.* ● *n.* **1 a** a soft head covering, usu. with a peak but otherwise brimless. **b** a head covering worn in a particular profession (*nurse's cap*). **c** esp. *Brit.* a cap awarded as a sign of membership of a sports team. **d** an academic mortarboard or soft hat. **e** a special hat as part of Highland dress. **2 a** a cover like a cap in shape or position (*kneecap*; *toecap*). **b** a device to seal a bottle or protect the point of a pen, lens of a camera, etc. **3 a** = DUTCH CAP 1. **b** = PERCUSSION CAP. **4** = CROWN *n.* 9b. ● *v.tr.* (**capped**, **capping**) **1 a** put a cap on. **b** cover the top or end of. **c** set a limit to (*rate-capping*). **2 a** esp. *Brit.* award a sports cap to. **b** *Sc.* & *NZ* confer a university degree on. **3 a** lie on top of; form the cap of. **b** surpass, excel. **c** improve on (a story, quotation, etc.) esp. by producing a better or more apposite one. □ **cap in hand** humbly. **if the cap fits (wear it)** *Brit.* (said of a generalized comment) it seems to be true of the person in question. **set one's cap at** (or *US* **for**) try to attract as a suitor. □ **capful** *n.* (*pl.* **-fuls**). **capping** *n.* [Old English *cæppe* from Late Latin *cappa*, perhaps from Latin *caput* 'head']

cap. *abbr.* **1** capital. **2** capital letter. **3** chapter. [Latin *capitulum* or *caput*]

capability /keɪpəˈbɪlɪti/ *n.* (*pl.* **-ies**) **1** (often foll. by *of*, *for*, *to*) ability, power; the condition of being capable. **2** an undeveloped or unused faculty.

capable /ˈkeɪpəb(ə)l/ *adj.* **1** competent, able, gifted. **2** (foll. by *of*) **a** having the ability, fitness, or necessary quality for. **b** susceptible or admitting of (explanation or improvement etc.). □ **capably** *adv.* [in earlier use = able to take in or understand: French via Late Latin *capabilis* from Latin *capere* 'hold']

capacious /kəˈpeɪʃəs/ *adj.* roomy; able to hold much. □ **capaciously** *adv.* **capaciousness** *n.* [Latin *capax -acis* from *capere* 'hold']

capacitance /kəˈpasɪt(ə)ns/ *n. Electr.* **1** the ability of a system to store an electric charge. **2** the ratio of the change in an electric charge in a system to the corresponding change in its electric potential (symbol C). [CAPACITY + -ANCE]

capacitate /kəˈpasɪteɪt/ *v.tr.* **1** (usu. foll. by *for*, or *to* + infin.) render capable. **2** make legally competent.

capacitor /kəˈpasɪtə/ *n. Electr.* a device of one or more pairs of conductors separated by insulators used to store an electric charge.

capacity /kəˈpasɪti/ *n.* (*pl.* **-ies**) **1 a** the power of containing, receiving, experiencing, or producing (*capacity for heat, pain*, etc.). **b** the maximum amount that can be contained or produced etc. **c** the volume, e.g. of the cylinders in an internal-combustion engine. **d** (*attrib.*) fully occupying the available space, resources, etc. (*a capacity audience*). **2 a** mental power. **b** a faculty or talent. **3** a position or function (*in a civil capacity; in my capacity as a critic*). **4** legal competence. **5** *Electr.* capacitance. □ **to capacity** fully; using all resources (*working to capacity*). □ **capacitative** /-tətɪv/ *adj.* (also **capacitive**) (in sense 5). [Middle English via French from Latin *capacitas -tatis* (as CAPACIOUS)]

caparison /kəˈpærɪs(ə)n/ *n.* & *v.* ● *n.* **1** (usu. in *pl.*) a horse's trappings. **2** equipment, finery. ● *v.tr.* put caparisons on; adorn richly. [obsolete French *caparasson* from Spanish *caparazón* 'saddle-cloth', from *capa* CAPE[1]]

cape[1] /keɪp/ *n.* **1** a sleeveless cloak. **2** a short sleeveless cloak as a fixed or detachable part of a longer cloak or coat. □ **caped** *adj.* [French via Provençal *capa* from Late Latin *cappa* CAP]

cape[2] /keɪp/ *n.* **1** a headland or promontory. **2** (**the Cape**) **a** the Cape of Good Hope. **b** the S. African province containing it. [Middle English via Old French *cap* from Provençal *cap*, ultimately from Latin *caput* 'head']

Cape buffalo see BUFFALO *n.* 1b.

Cape Coloured *adj.* & *n.* *S.Afr.* ● *adj.* of the mixed white and non-white population of Cape Province. ● *n.* a member of this population.

Cape doctor *n.* *S.Afr. colloq.* a strong SE wind.

Cape Dutch *n.* *archaic* Afrikaans.

Cape gooseberry *n.* **1** an edible soft roundish yellow berry enclosed in a lantern-like husk. **2** the plant, *Physalis peruviana*, bearing these.

capelin /ˈkeɪplɪn, ˈkæp-/ *n.* (also **caplin**) a small smeltlike fish, *Mallotus villosus*, of the N. Atlantic, used as food and as bait for catching cod etc. [French from Provençal *capelan* 'chaplain']

caper[1] /ˈkeɪpə/ *v.* & *n.* ● *v.intr.* jump or run about playfully. ● *n.* **1** a playful jump or leap. **2 a** a fantastic proceeding; a prank. **b** *slang* any activity or occupation. □ **cut a caper** (or **capers**) act friskily. □ **caperer** *n.* [abbreviation of CAPRIOLE]

caper[2] /ˈkeɪpə/ *n.* **1** a bramble-like southern European shrub, *Capparis spinosa*. **2** (in *pl.*) its flower buds cooked and pickled for use as flavouring esp. for a savoury sauce. [Middle English *capres* & French *câpres* via Latin *capparis* from Greek *kapparis*, treated as pl.: cf. CHERRY, PEA]

capercaillie /kæpəˈkeɪli/ *n.* (also **capercailzie** /-lzi/) a large grouse, *Tetrao urogallus*, of coniferous forests in northern Europe. [Gaelic *capull coille* 'horse of the wood']

capeskin /ˈkeɪpskɪn/ *n.* a soft leather made from South African sheepskin.

capias /ˈkeɪpɪəs, ˈkæp-/ *n.* *Law* a writ ordering the arrest of the person named. [Latin, = you are to seize, from *capere* 'take']

capillarity /kæpɪˈlærɪti/ *n.* = CAPILLARY ACTION. [French *capillarité* (as CAPILLARY)]

capillary /kəˈpɪləri/ *adj.* & *n.* ● *adj.* **1** of or like a hair. **2** (of a tube) of hairlike internal diameter. **3** of one of the delicate ramified blood vessels intervening between arteries and veins. ● *n.* (*pl.* **-ies**) **1** a capillary tube. **2** a capillary blood vessel. [Latin *capillaris* from *capillus* 'hair']

capillary action *n.* the tendency of a liquid in a capillary tube or absorbent material to rise or fall as a result of surface tension. Also called *capillarity*.

capital[1] /ˈkæpɪt(ə)l/ *n.*, *adj.*, & *int.* ● *n.* **1** the most important town or city of a country or region, usu. its seat of government and administrative centre. **2 a** the money or other assets with which a company starts in business. **b** accumulated wealth, esp. as used in further production. **c** money invested or lent at interest. **3** capitalists generally. **4** a capital letter. ● *adj.* **1 a** principal; most important; leading. **b** *colloq.* excellent, first-rate. **2 a** involving or punishable by death (*capital punishment; a capital offence*). **b** (of an error etc.) vitally harmful; fatal. **3** (of letters of the alphabet) large in size and of the form used to begin sentences and names etc. ● *int.* expressing approval or satisfaction. □ **make capital out of** use to one's advantage. **with a capital** — emphatically such (*art with a capital A*). □ **capitally** *adv.* [Middle English via Old French from Latin *capitalis*, from *caput -itis* 'head']

capital[2] /ˈkæpɪt(ə)l/ *n.* *Archit.* the head or cornice of a pillar or column. [Middle English via Old French *capitel* from Late Latin *capitellum*, diminutive of Latin *caput* 'head']

capital gain *n.* a profit from the sale of investments or property.

capital gains tax *n.* a tax levied on the profit from the sale of investments or property.

capital goods *n.pl.* goods, esp. machinery, plant, etc., used or to be used in producing commodities (opp. CONSUMER GOODS).

capitalism /ˈkæpɪt(ə)lɪz(ə)m/ *n.* **1 a** an economic system in which the production and distribution of goods depend on invested private capital and profit-making. **b** the possession of capital or wealth. **2** *Polit.* the dominance of private owners of capital and production for profit.

capitalist /ˈkæpɪt(ə)lɪst/ *n.* & *adj.* ● *n.* **1** a person using or possessing capital; a rich person. **2** an advocate of capitalism. ● *adj.* of or favouring capitalism. □ **capitalistic** /-ˈlɪstɪk/ *adj.* **capitalistically** /-ˈlɪstɪk(ə)li/ *adv.*

capitalize /ˈkæpɪt(ə)lʌɪz/ *v.* (also **-ise**) **1** *tr.* **a** convert into or provide with capital. **b** calculate or realize the present value of an income. **c** reckon (the value of an asset) by setting future benefits against the cost of maintenance. **2** *tr.* **a** write (a letter of the alphabet) as a capital. **b** begin (a word) with a capital letter. **3** *intr.* (foll. by *on*) use to one's advantage; profit from. □ **capitalization** /-ˈzeɪʃ(ə)n/ *n.* [French *capitaliser* (as CAPITAL[1])]

capital levy *n.* **1** the appropriation by the State of a fixed proportion of the wealth in the country. **2** a wealth tax.

capital sum *n.* a lump sum of money, esp. payable to an insured person.

capital territory *n.* a territory containing the capital city of a country.

capital transfer tax *n.* *hist.* (in the UK) a tax levied on the transfer of capital by gift or bequest etc. (replaced in 1986 by INHERITANCE TAX).

capitation /kæpɪˈteɪʃ(ə)n/ *n.* **1** a tax or fee at a set rate per person. **2** the levying of such a tax or fee. [French *capitation* or Late Latin *capitatio* 'poll tax', from *caput* 'head']

capitation grant *n.* a grant of a sum calculated from the number of people to be catered for, esp. in education.

Capitol /ˈkæpɪt(ə)l/ *n.* (usu. prec. by *the*) (in the US) a building housing a legislature, esp. the seat of the US Congress in Washington, DC.

capitular /kəˈpɪtjʊlə/ *adj.* **1** of or relating to a cathedral chapter. **2** *Anat.* of or relating to a terminal protuberance of a bone. [Late Latin *capitularis* from Latin *capitulum* CHAPTER]

capitulary /kəˈpɪtjʊləri/ *n.* (*pl.* **-ies**) *hist.* a collection of ordinances, esp. of the Frankish kings. [Late Latin *capitularius* (as CAPITULAR)]

capitulate /kəˈpɪtjʊleɪt/ *v.intr.* surrender, esp. on stated conditions. □ **capitulator** *n.* **capitulatory** /-lət(ə)ri/ *adj.* [medieval Latin *capitulare* 'draw up under headings' from Latin *caput* 'head']

capitulation /kəpɪtjʊˈleɪʃ(ə)n/ *n.* **1** the act of capitulating; surrender. **2** a statement of the main divisions of a subject. **3** an agreement or set of conditions.

capitulum /kəˈpɪtjʊləm/ *n.* (*pl.* **capitula** /-lə/) *Bot.* a dense flat cluster of flowers or florets, as in the daisy family. [Latin, diminutive of *caput* 'head']

caplin var. of CAPELIN.

cap'n /ˈkapm/ *n. colloq.* captain. [contraction]

capo[1] /ˈkapəʊ/ *n.* (in full **capo tasto** /ˈtastəʊ/) (*pl.* **capos** or **capo tastos**) *Mus.* a device secured across the neck of a fretted instrument to raise equally the tuning of all strings by the required amount. [Italian *capo tasto* 'head stop']

capo[2] /ˈkapəʊ/ *n.* (*pl.* **-os**) esp. *US* the head of a crime syndicate or of one of its branches. [Italian, from Latin *caput* 'head']

cap of liberty *n. hist.* a conical cap given to Roman slaves on emanicipation, often used as a republican symbol.

cap of maintenance *n.* a cap or hat worn as a symbol of official dignity or carried before the sovereign etc.

capon /ˈkeɪp(ə)n/ *n.* a domestic cock castrated and fattened for eating. □ **caponize** *v.tr.* (also **-ise**). [Old English from Anglo-French *capun*, Old French *capon*, ultimately from Latin *capo -onis*]

caponier /kapəˈnɪə/ *n.* a covered passage across a ditch round a fort. [Spanish *caponera*, literally 'capon-pen']

capot /kəˈpɒt/ *n. & v.* ● *n.* (in piquet) the winning of all the tricks by one player. ● *v.tr.* (**capotted**, **capotting**) score a capot against (an opponent). [French, perhaps from a dialect variant of *chapoter* 'to castrate']

capo tasto see CAPO[1].

capote /kəˈpəʊt/ *n. hist.* a long cloak with a hood, formerly worn by soldiers and travellers etc. [French, diminutive of *cape* CAPE[1]]

cappuccino /kapʊˈtʃiːnəʊ/ *n.* (*pl.* **-os**) coffee with milk made frothy with pressurized steam, esp. made with espresso coffee. [Italian, = CAPUCHIN]

capriccio /kəˈprɪtʃɪəʊ/ *n.* (*pl.* **-os**) **1** a lively and usu. short musical composition. **2** a painting etc. representing a fantasy or a mixture of real and imaginary features. [Italian, = sudden start, originally 'horror']

capriccioso /kəprɪtʃɪˈəʊzəʊ/ *adv. & adj. Mus.* in a free and impulsive style. [Italian, = capricious]

caprice /kəˈpriːs/ *n.* **1 a** an unaccountable or whimsical change of mind or conduct. **b** a tendency to this. **2** a work of lively fancy in painting, drawing, or music; a capriccio. [French, from Italian CAPRICCIO]

capricious /kəˈprɪʃəs/ *adj.* **1** guided by or given to caprice. **2** irregular, unpredictable. □ **capriciously** *adv.* **capriciousness** *n.* [French *capricieux* from Italian CAPRICCIOSO]

Capricorn /ˈkaprɪkɔːn/ *n.* **1** (usu. **Capricornus** /-ˈkɔːnəs/) *Astron.* a constellation (the Goat), said to represent a goat with a fish's tail (or, in Hindu astrology, a crocodile). **2** *Astrol.* **a** the tenth sign of the zodiac, which the sun enters at the winter solstice (about 21 Dec.). **b** a person born when the sun is in this sign. □ **tropic of Capricorn** see TROPIC *n.* 1. □ **Capricornian** *n. & adj.* [Middle English via Old French *capricorne* from Latin *capricornus*, from *caper -pri* 'goat' + *cornu* 'horn']

caprine /ˈkaprʌɪn/ *adj.* of or like a goat. [Middle English from Latin *caprinus*, from *caper -pri* 'goat']

capriole /ˈkaprɪəʊl/ *n. & v.* ● *n.* **1** a leap or caper. **2** a trained horse's high leap and kick without advancing. ● *v.* **1** *intr.* (of a horse or its rider) perform a capriole. **2** *tr.* make (a horse) capriole. [French from Italian *capriola* 'leap', ultimately from *caper -pri* 'goat']

Capris /kəˈpriːz/ *n.pl.* (also **Capri pants**) women's close-fitting tapered trousers. [*Capri*, an island in the bay of Naples]

cap rock *n.* a hard rock or stratum overlying a deposit of oil, gas, coal, etc.

caps. *abbr.* capital letters.

Capsian /ˈkapsɪən/ *adj. & n.* ● *adj.* of or relating to a palaeolithic culture of N. Africa and S. Europe. ● *n.* this culture. [Latin *Capsa* = Gafsa in Tunisia]

capsicum /ˈkapsɪkəm/ *n.* **1** any plant of the genus *Capsicum* (nightshade family), having edible capsular fruits containing many seeds, esp. *C. annuum* yielding chilli and sweet peppers. **2** the fruit of any of these plants, which vary in size, colour, and pungency. [modern Latin, perhaps from Latin *capsa* 'box']

capsid[1] /ˈkapsɪd/ *n.* = MIRID. [modern Latin *Capsus*, genus name of a bug]

capsid[2] /ˈkapsɪd/ *n.* the protein coat or shell of a virus. [French *capside* from Latin *capsa* 'box']

capsize /kapˈsʌɪz/ *v.* **1** *tr.* upset or overturn (a boat). **2** *intr.* be capsized. □ **capsizal** *n.* [perhaps ultimately from Spanish *capuzar* ' sink (a ship) by the head', from *cabo* 'head' + *chapuzar* 'dive, duck']

cap sleeve *n.* a sleeve extending only a short distance from the shoulder.

capstan /ˈkapst(ə)n/ *n.* **1** a thick revolving cylinder with a vertical axis, for winding an anchor cable or a halyard etc. **2** a motor-driven revolving spindle on a tape recorder that guides the tape past the head at constant speed. [Provençal *cabestan*, ultimately from Latin *capistrum* 'halter', from *capere* 'seize']

capstan lathe *n.* a lathe with a revolving tool holder.

capstone /ˈkapstəʊn/ *n.* coping; a coping stone.

capsule /ˈkapsjuːl, -sjʊl/ *n.* **1** a small soluble case of gelatin enclosing a dose of medicine and swallowed with it. **2** a detachable compartment of a spacecraft or nose-cone of a rocket. **3** an enclosing membrane in the body. **4** a top or cover for a bottle, esp. the foil or plastic covering the cork of a wine bottle. **5 a** a dry fruit that releases its seeds when ripe. **b** the spore-producing part of mosses and liverworts. **6** *Biol.* an enveloping layer surrounding certain bacteria. **7** (*attrib.*) concise; highly condensed (*a capsule history of jazz*). □ **capsular** *adj.* **capsulate** *adj.* [French from Latin *capsula*, from *capsa* CASE[2]]

capsulize /ˈkapsjʊlʌɪz/ *v.tr.* (also **-ise**) put (information etc.) in compact form.

Capt. *abbr.* Captain.

captain /ˈkaptɪn/ *n. & v.* ● *n.* **1 a** a chief or leader. **b** the leader of a team, esp. in sports. **c** a powerful or influential person (*captain of industry*). **2 a** the person in command of a merchant or passenger ship. **b** the pilot of a civil aircraft. **3** (as a title **Captain**) **a** an army or (in the US and Canada) air force officer next above lieutenant. **b** a navy officer in command of a warship; one ranking below commodore or rear admiral and above commander. **c** (in the US) a police officer in charge of a precinct, ranking below a chief. **4 a** *Brit.* a foreman. **b** a head boy or girl in a school. **c** *colloq.* the adult leader of a company of Guides, officially termed *Guide Guider* since 1968. **d** *N. Amer.* a supervisor of waiters or bellboys. **5 a** a great soldier or strategist. **b** an experienced commander. ● *v.tr.* be captain of; lead. □ **captaincy** *n.* (*pl.* **-ies**). **captainship** *n.* [Middle English & Old French *capitain* via Late Latin *capitaneus* 'chief' from Latin *caput capit-* 'head']

Captain Cooker /ˌkaptɪn ˈkʊkə/ *n. NZ* a wild boar. [named after Capt. J. *Cook*, navigator and explorer d. 1779]

captain-general *n.* (in the UK) an honorary officer, esp. of artillery.

Captain of the Fleet *n.* (in the UK) a Navy staff officer in charge of maintenance.

caption /ˈkapʃ(ə)n/ *n. & v.* ● *n.* **1** a title or brief explanation appended to an illustration, cartoon, etc. **2** wording appearing on a cinema or television screen as part of a film or broadcast. **3** the heading of a chapter or article etc. **4** *Law* a certificate attached to or written on a document. ● *v.tr.* provide with a caption. [in earlier use = capture, seizure, hence a warrant for arrest: Middle English from Latin *captio*, from *capere capt-* 'take']

captious /ˈkapʃəs/ *adj.* given to finding fault or raising petty objections. □ **captiously** *adv.* **captiousness** *n.* [Middle English from Old French *captieux* or Latin *captiosus* (as CAPTION)]

captivate /ˈkaptɪveɪt/ *v.tr.* **1** overwhelm with charm or affection. **2** fascinate. □ **captivatingly** *adv.* **captivation**

/-ˈveɪʃ(ə)n/ *n.* [Late Latin *captivare* 'take captive' (as CAPTIVE)]

captive /ˈkaptɪv/ *n. & adj.* ● *n.* a person or animal that has been taken prisoner or confined. ● *adj.* **1 a** taken prisoner. **b** kept in confinement or under restraint. **2 a** unable to escape. **b** in a position of having to comply (*captive audience*; *captive market*). **3** of or like a prisoner (*captive state*). [Middle English from Latin *captivus*, from *capere capt-* 'take']

captive balloon *n.* a balloon held by a rope from the ground.

captivity /kapˈtɪvɪti/ *n.* (*pl.* **-ies**) **1 a** the condition or circumstances of being a captive. **b** a period of captivity. **2** (**the Captivity**) the captivity of the Jews in Babylon in the 6th c. BC.

captor /ˈkaptə/ *n.* a person who captures or holds captive (a person, group, etc.). [Latin (as CAPTIVE)]

capture /ˈkaptʃə/ *v. & n.* ● *v.tr.* **1 a** take prisoner; seize as a prize. **b** obtain by force or trickery. **2** portray in permanent form (*could not capture the likeness*). **3** *Physics* absorb (a subatomic particle). **4** (in board games) make a move that secures the removal of (an opposing piece) from the board. **5** (of a stream) divert the upper course of (another stream) by encroaching on its basin. **6** cause (data) to be stored in a computer. **7** *Astron.* (of a star, planet, etc.) bring (a less massive body) permanently within its gravitational influence. ● *n.* **1** the act of capturing. **2** a thing or person captured. □ **capturer** *n.* [French from Latin *captura*, from *capere capt-* 'take']

Capuchin /ˈkap(j)ʊtʃɪn/ *n.* **1** a Franciscan friar of the new rule of 1529. **2** a cloak and hood formerly worn by women. **3** (**capuchin**) **a** a monkey of the S. American genus *Cebus*, with cowl-like hair on the head. **b** a variety of pigeon with head and neck feathers resembling a cowl. [French from Italian *cappuccino*, via *cappuccio* 'cowl' from *cappa* CAPE[1]]

capybara /kapɪˈbɑːrə/ *n.* a very large semiaquatic rodent, *Hydrochoerus hydrochaeris*, native to S. America. [Tupi]

car /kɑː/ *n.* **1** (in full **motor car**) a usu. four-wheeled road vehicle, able to carry a small number of people and powered by an internal-combustion engine. **2** (in *comb.*) **a** a wheeled vehicle, esp. of a specified kind (*tramcar*). **b** a railway carriage of a specified type (*dining car*). **3** *N. Amer.* a railway carriage or van. **4** the passenger compartment of a lift, cableway, balloon, etc. **5** *poet.* a chariot. □ **carful** *n.* (*pl.* **-fuls**). [Middle English from Anglo-French & Old Northern French *carre*, ultimately from Latin *carrum*, *carrus*, of Old Celtic origin]

carabineer /karəbɪˈnɪə/ *n.* (also **carabinier**) *hist.* **1** a soldier whose principal weapon is a carbine. **2** (**the Carabineers**) the Royal Scots Dragoon Guards. [French *carabinier* from *carabine* CARBINE]

carabiniere /karəbɪnˈjɛːri, Italian karabiˈnjere/ *n.* (*pl.* ***carabinieri*** *pronunc.* same) an Italian gendarme. [Italian, literally 'carabineer']

caracal /ˈkarəkal/ *n.* a lynx, *Felis caracal*, native to N. Africa and SW Asia. [French or Spanish from Turkish *karakulak*, from *kara* 'black' + *kulak* 'ear' (from its black ear-tufts)]

caracara /karəˈkɑːrə/ *n.* any of several mainly tropical American birds of prey related to falcons but resembling vultures. [Spanish or Portuguese *caracará*, from Tupi-Guarani (imitative)]

caracole /ˈkarəkəʊl/ *n. & v.* ● *n.* a horse's half-turn to the right or left. ● *v.* **1** *intr.* (of a horse or its rider) perform a caracole. **2** *tr.* make (a horse) caracole. [French]

caracul var. of KARAKUL.

carafe /kəˈraf, -ˈrɑːf/ *n.* a glass container for water or wine, esp. at a table or bedside. [French from Italian *caraffa*, ultimately from Arabic *ġarrāfa* 'drinking vessel']

carambola /kar(ə)mˈbəʊlə/ *n.* **1** a small tree, *Averrhoa carambola*, native to SE Asia, bearing golden-yellow ribbed fruit. **2** this fruit; also called *star fruit*. [Portuguese, probably from Marathi *karambal*]

caramel /ˈkarəmɛl, -m(ə)l/ *n. & adj.* ● *n.* **1 a** sugar or syrup heated until it turns brown, then used as a flavouring or to colour spirits etc. **b** a kind of soft toffee made with sugar, butter, etc., melted and further heated. **2** the light brown colour of caramel. ● *adj.* of this colour. [French from Spanish *caramelo*]

caramelize /ˈkar(ə)məlʌɪz/ *v.* (also **-ise**) **1 a** *tr.* convert (sugar or syrup) into caramel. **b** *intr.* (of sugar or syrup) be converted into caramel. **2** *tr.* coat or cook (food) with caramelized sugar or syrup. □ **caramelization** /-ˈzeɪʃ(ə)n/ *n.*

carangid /kəˈrandʒɪd/ *adj. & n.* ● *adj.* of or relating to the large fish family Carangidae, including scads and pompanos. ● *n.* a fish of this family. [Latin *Caranx*, the genus name of a member + -ID[3]]

carapace /ˈkarəpeɪs/ *n.* the hard upper shell of a tortoise or a crustacean. [French from Spanish *carapacho*]

carat /ˈkarət/ *n.* **1** a unit of weight for precious stones, now equivalent to 200 milligrams. **2** (*US* **karat**) a measure of purity of gold, pure gold being 24 carats. [French via Italian *carato* from Arabic *ḳīrāṭ* 'weight of four grains', from Greek *keration* 'fruit of the carob' (diminutive of *keras* 'horn')]

caravan /ˈkarəvan, karəˈvan/ *n. & v.* ● *n.* **1 a** *Brit.* a vehicle equipped for living in and usu. towed by a motor vehicle or a horse. **b** *N. Amer.* a covered wagon or lorry. **2** a company of merchants or pilgrims etc. travelling together, esp. across a desert in Asia or N. Africa. **3** a covered cart or carriage. ● *v.intr.* (**caravanned**, **caravanning**) travel or live in a caravan. □ **caravanner** *n.* [French *caravane* from Persian *kārwān*]

caravanette /karəvaˈnɛt/ *n. Brit.* a motor vehicle with a caravan-like rear compartment for eating, sleeping, etc.

caravanserai /karəˈvansərʌɪ, -ri/ *n.* (*US* also **caravansary**) an Eastern inn with a central court where caravans (see CARAVAN 2) may rest. [Persian *kārwānsarāy* from *sarāy* 'palace']

caravan site *n.* (also **caravan park**) *Brit.* a place where caravans are parked as dwellings, often with special amenities.

caravel /ˈkarəvɛl/ *n.* (also **carvel** /ˈkɑːv(ə)l/) *hist.* a small light fast ship, chiefly Spanish and Portuguese of the 15th–17th c. [French *caravelle* via Portuguese *caravela* from Greek *karabos* 'horned beetle, light ship']

caraway /ˈkarəweɪ/ *n.* an umbelliferous plant, *Carum carvi*, bearing clusters of tiny white flowers. [medieval Latin *carui* from Arabic *alkarāwiyā*, perhaps from Greek *karon*, *kareon* 'cumin']

caraway seed *n.* the fruit of the caraway plant used as flavouring and as a source of oil.

carb /kɑːb/ *n. colloq.* a carburettor. [abbreviation]

carbamate /ˈkɑːbəmeɪt/ *n. Chem.* a salt or ester of an amide of carbonic acid. [CARBONIC + AMIDE]

carbide /ˈkɑːbʌɪd/ *n. Chem.* a binary compound of carbon.

carbine /ˈkɑːbʌɪn/ *n.* a short firearm, usu. a rifle, originally for cavalry use. [French *carabine* (this form also earlier in English), weapon of the *carabin* 'mounted musketeer']

carbo- /ˈkɑːbəʊ/ *comb. form* carbon (*carbohydrate*; *carbolic*; *carboxyl*).

carbohydrate /kɑːbəˈhʌɪdreɪt/ *n. Biochem.* any of a large group of energy-producing organic compounds containing carbon, hydrogen, and oxygen, e.g. starch, glucose, and other sugars.

carbolic /kɑːˈbɒlɪk/ *n.* (in full **carbolic acid**) phenol, esp. when used as a disinfectant. [CARBO- + -OL[1] + -IC]

carbolic soap *n.* soap containing carbolic.

car bomb *n.* a terrorist bomb concealed in or under a parked car.

carbon /'kɑ:b(ə)n/ *n.* **1** a non-metallic element occurring naturally as diamond, graphite, and charcoal, and in all organic compounds (symbol **C**). **2 a** = CARBON COPY 1. **b** = CARBON PAPER. **3** a rod of carbon in an arc lamp. [French *carbone*, from Latin *carbo -onis* 'charcoal']

carbon-12 *n.* the commonest natural carbon isotope, of mass 12, used in calculations of atomic mass units.

carbon-14 *n.* a long-lived naturally occurring radioactive carbon isotope of mass 14, used in radiocarbon dating, and as a tracer in biochemistry.

carbonaceous /kɑ:bə'neɪʃəs/ *adj.* **1** consisting of or containing carbon. **2** of or like coal or charcoal.

carbonado /kɑ:bə'neɪdəʊ/ *n.* (*pl.* **-os**) a dark opaque or impure kind of diamond used as an abrasive, for drills etc. [Portuguese]

carbonate /'kɑ:bəneɪt/ *n.* & *v.* ● *n. Chem.* a salt of carbonic acid. ● *v.tr.* **1** impregnate with carbon dioxide; aerate. **2** convert into a carbonate. □ **carbonation** /-'neɪʃ(ə)n/ *n.* [French *carbonat* from modern Latin *carbonatum* (as CARBON)]

carbon black *n.* a fine carbon powder made by burning hydrocarbons in insufficient air.

carbon copy *n.* **1** a copy made with carbon paper. **2** a person or thing identical or similar to another (*is a carbon copy of his father*).

carbon cycle *n. Biol.* the cycle in which carbon compounds are interconverted, usu. by living organisms.

carbon dating *n.* the determination of the age of an organic object from the ratio of isotopes which changes as carbon-14 decays.

carbon dioxide *n.* a colourless odourless gas occurring naturally in the atmosphere and formed by respiration. Chem. formula: CO_2.

carbon disulphide *n.* a colourless liquid used as a solvent. Chem. formula: CS_2.

carbon fibre *n.* a thin strong crystalline filament of carbon used as strengthening material in resins, ceramics, etc.

carbonic /kɑ:'bɒnɪk/ *adj. Chem.* containing carbon.

carbonic acid *n.* a very weak acid formed from carbon dioxide dissolved in water.

carbonic acid gas *n. archaic* carbon dioxide.

carboniferous /kɑ:bə'nɪf(ə)rəs/ *adj.* & *n.* ● *adj.* **1** producing coal. **2** (**Carboniferous**) *Geol.* of or relating to the fifth period in the Palaeozoic era, with evidence of the first reptiles and extensive coal-forming swamp forests. Cf. Appendix X. ● *n.* (**Carboniferous**) *Geol.* this period or system.

carbonize /'kɑ:bənʌɪz/ *v.tr.* (also **-ise**) **1** convert into carbon by heating. **2** reduce to charcoal or coke. **3** coat with carbon. □ **carbonization** /-'zeɪʃ(ə)n/ *n.*

carbon monoxide *n.* a colourless odourless toxic gas formed by the incomplete burning of carbon. Chem. formula: CO.

carbonnade /kɑ:bə'nɑ:d, -'neɪd/ *n.* a rich beef stew made with onions and beer. [French]

carbon paper *n.* a thin carbon-coated paper used for making (esp. typed) copies.

carbon steel *n.* a steel with properties dependent on the percentage of carbon present.

carbon tax *n.* a proposed tax on the carbon emissions that result from burning fossil fuels (e.g. in motor vehicles) because of their contribution to the greenhouse effect.

carbon tetrachloride *n.* a colourless volatile liquid used as a solvent. Chem. formula: CCl_4.

carbonyl /'kɑ:bənʌɪl, -nɪl/ *n.* (used *attrib.*) *Chem.* the divalent radical :C=O.

carbonyl chloride *n. Chem.* = PHOSGENE.

car boot sale *n. Brit.* a usu. outdoor sale at which participants sell unwanted possessions from the boots of their cars or from tables.

carborundum /kɑ:bə'rʌndəm/ *n.* a compound of carbon and silicon used esp. as an abrasive. [CARBON + CORUNDUM]

carboxyl /kɑ:'bɒksʌɪl, -sɪl/ *n. Chem.* the monovalent acid radical -COOH, present in most organic acids. [CARBON + OXYGEN + -YL]

carboxylic acid /kɑ:bɒk 'sɪlɪk/ *n. Chem.* an organic acid containing the carboxyl group. □ **carboxylate** /kɑ:'bɒksɪˌleɪt/ *n.*

carboy /'kɑ:bɔɪ/ *n.* a large globular glass bottle usu. protected by a frame, for containing esp. liquids. [Persian *karāba* 'large glass flagon']

carbuncle /'kɑ:bʌŋk(ə)l/ *n.* **1** a severe abscess in the skin. **2** a bright red gem. □ **carbuncular** /-'bʌŋkjʊlə/ *adj.* [Middle English via Old French *charbucle* etc. from Latin *carbunculus* 'small coal', from *carbo* 'coal']

carburation /kɑ:bjʊ'reɪʃ(ə)n/ *n.* the process of charging air with a spray of liquid hydrocarbon fuel, esp. in an internal-combustion engine. [as CARBURET]

carburet /kɑ:bjʊ'rɛt/ *v.tr.* (**carburetted**, **carburetting**; *US* **carbureted**, **carbureting**) combine (a gas etc.) with carbon. [earlier *carbure* via French from Latin *carbo* (as CARBON)]

carburettor /kɑ:bjʊ'rɛtə, -bə-/ *n.* (also **carburetter**, *US* **carburetor**) an apparatus for carburation of petrol and air in an internal-combustion engine. [as CARBURET + -OR[1]]

carburize /'kɑ:bjʊrʌɪz/ *v.tr.* (also **-ise**) add carbon to (iron). □ **carburization** /-'zeɪʃ(ə)n/ *n.* [*carburet* 'carbide' + -IZE]

carcajou /'kɑ:kədʒu:, -əʒu:/ *n. N. Amer.* = GLUTTON 3. [French, apparently of Algonquian origin (cf. KINKAJOU)]

carcass /'kɑ:kəs/ *n.* (also *Brit.* **carcase**) **1** the dead body of an animal, esp. a trunk for cutting up as meat. **2** the bones of a cooked bird. **3** *derog.* the human body, living or dead. **4** the skeleton or framework of a building, ship, etc. **5** worthless remains. [Middle English from Anglo-French *carcois* (Old French *charcois*) and from French *carcasse*: ultimate origin unknown]

carcass meat *n. Brit.* raw meat as distinct from corned or tinned meat.

carcinogen /kɑ:'sɪnədʒ(ə)n/ *n.* any substance that causes cancer. [as CARCINOMA + -GEN]

carcinogenesis /ˌkɑ:s(ɪ)nə'dʒɛnɪsɪs/ *n.* the production of cancer.

carcinogenic /ˌkɑ:s(ɪ)nə'dʒɛnɪk/ *adj.* tending to cause cancer. □ **carcinogenicity** /-'nɪsɪti/ *n.*

carcinoma /kɑ:sɪ'nəʊmə/ *n.* (*pl.* **carcinomata** /-tə/ or **carcinomas**) a cancer, esp. one arising in epithelial tissue. □ **carcinomatous** *adj.* [Latin from Greek *karkinōma*, from *karkinos* 'crab']

car coat *n.* a short coat designed esp. for car drivers.

Card. *abbr.* Cardinal.

card[1] /kɑ:d/ *n.* & *v.* ● *n.* **1** thick stiff paper or thin pasteboard. **2 a** a flat piece of this, esp. for writing or printing on. **b** = POSTCARD. **c** a card used to send greetings, issue an invitation, etc. (*birthday card*). **d** = VISITING CARD. **e** = BUSINESS CARD. **f** a ticket of admission or membership etc. **3 a** = PLAYING CARD. **b** a similar card in a set designed for particular games, e.g. happy families. **c** (in *pl.*) card-playing; a card game. **4** (in *pl.*) *Brit. colloq.* an employee's documents, esp. for tax and national insurance, held by the employer. **5 a** a programme of events at a race meeting etc. **b** *Cricket* a scorecard. **c** a list of holes on a golf course, on which a player's scores are entered. **6** *colloq.* a person, esp. an odd or amusing one (*what a card!*; *a knowing card*). **7** a plan or expedient (*sure card*). **8** a printed or written notice, set of rules, etc., for display. **9 a** a small rectangular piece of plastic issued by a bank, building society, etc., with personal (often machine-readable) data on it, used chiefly to obtain cash or credit (*cheque card*; *credit card*; *do you have a card?*). **b** a similar piece of plastic, e.g. a phonecard, sold or issued for various purposes. **10** a printed circuit board. ● *v.tr.* **1** fix to a card. **2** write on a card, esp. for indexing. □ **ask for** (or **get**) **one's cards** *Brit.* ask (or be told) to leave one's employment. **card up one's sleeve** *Brit.* a plan in reserve; a hidden advantage. **on** (*N. Amer.* **in**) **the cards** possible or likely. **put** (or **lay**) **one's cards on the table** reveal one's resources, intentions, etc. [Middle English via Old French *carte* and Latin *charta* from Greek *khartēs* 'papyrus leaf']

card² /kɑːd/ *n. & v.* ● *n.* a toothed instrument, wire brush, etc., for raising a nap on cloth or for disentangling fibres before spinning. ● *v.tr.* brush, comb, cleanse, or scratch with a card. □ **carder** *n.* [Middle English via Old French *carde* from Provençal *carda*, from *cardar* 'tease, comb', ultimately from Latin *carere* 'to card']

cardamom /ˈkɑːdəməm/ *n.* (also **cardamum**) **1** an aromatic SE Asian plant, *Elettaria cardamomum*. **2** the seed capsules of this used as a spice. [Latin *cardamomum* or French *cardamome* from Greek *kardamōmon*, from *kardamon* 'cress' + *amōmon* the name of a spice plant]

cardan joint /ˈkɑːd(ə)n/ *n. Engin.* a universal joint. [named after G. *Cardano*, Italian mathematician d. 1576]

cardan shaft /ˈkɑːd(ə)n/ *n. Brit. Engin.* a shaft with a universal joint at one or both ends.

cardboard /ˈkɑːdbɔːd/ *n. & adj.* ● *n.* pasteboard or stiff paper, esp. for making cards or boxes. ● *adj.* **1** made of cardboard. **2** flimsy, insubstantial.

cardboard city *n.* an urban area where homeless people make shelters at night from cardboard boxes etc.

card-carrying *attrib.adj.* registered as a member (esp. of a political party or trade union).

card game *n.* a game in which playing cards are used.

cardholder /ˈkɑːdhəʊldə/ *n.* the holder of a credit card.

cardiac /ˈkɑːdɪak/ *adj. & n.* ● *adj.* **1** of or relating to the heart. **2** of or relating to the part of the stomach nearest the oesophagus. ● *n. colloq.* a person with heart disease. [French *cardiaque* or Latin *cardiacus* from Greek *kardiakos*, from *kardia* 'heart']

cardiac tamponade see TAMPONADE.

cardie var. of CARDY.

cardigan /ˈkɑːdɪg(ə)n/ *n.* a knitted jacket fastening down the front, usu. with long sleeves. [named after the 7th Earl of *Cardigan* (d. 1868), whose troops first wore such garments during the Crimean war]

cardinal /ˈkɑːd(ɪ)n(ə)l/ *n. & adj.* ● *n.* **1** (as a title **Cardinal**) a leading dignitary of the Roman Catholic Church, one of the college electing the Pope. **2** any American songbird of the subfamily Cardinalinae, esp. the common *Cardinalis cardinalis*, the male of which has scarlet plumage. **3** *hist.* a woman's cloak, originally of scarlet cloth with a hood. ● *adj.* **1** chief, fundamental; on which something hinges. **2** of deep scarlet (like a cardinal's cassock). □ **cardinalate** /-leɪt/ *n.* (in sense 1 of *n.*). **cardinally** *adv.* **cardinalship** *n.* (in sense 1 of *n.*). [Middle English via Old French from Latin *cardinalis*, from *cardo -inis* 'hinge': in English first applied to the four virtues on which conduct 'hinges']

cardinal flower *n.* the scarlet lobelia.

cardinal humour see HUMOUR *n.* 5.

cardinal number *n.* a number denoting quantity (one, two, three, etc.), as opposed to an ordinal number (first, second, third, etc.).

cardinal point *n.* each of the four main points of the compass (N., S., E., W.).

cardinal virtue *n.* each of the chief moral attributes (originally of scholastic philosophy): justice, prudence, temperance, and fortitude.

card index *n. & v.* ● *n.* an index in which each item is entered on a separate card. ● *v.tr.* (**card-index**) make a card index of.

carding wool *n.* short-stapled wool.

cardio- /ˈkɑːdɪəʊ/ *comb. form* heart (*cardiogram*; *cardiology*). [Greek *kardia* 'heart']

cardiogram /ˈkɑːdɪə(ʊ)gram/ *n.* a record of muscle activity within the heart, made by a cardiograph.

cardiograph /ˈkɑːdɪə(ʊ)grɑːf/ *n.* an instrument for recording heart muscle activity, e.g an electrocardiograph. □ **cardiographer** /-ˈɒgrəfə/ *n.* **cardiography** /-ˈɒgrəfi/ *n.*

cardioid /ˈkɑːdɪɔɪd/ *n. & adj.* ● *n.* **1** *Math.* a heart-shaped curve traced by a point on the circumference of a circle as it rolls around another identical circle. **2** a directional microphone with a pattern of sensitivity of this shape. ● *adj.* **1** of the shape of a cardioid. **2** (of a microphone) having a cardioid pattern of sensitivity. [Greek *kardioeidēs* 'heart-shaped', from *kardia* 'heart' + -OID]

cardiology /kɑːdɪˈɒlədʒi/ *n.* the branch of medicine concerned with diseases and abnormalities of the heart. □ **cardiologist** *n.*

cardiomyopathy /ˌkɑːdɪəʊmʌɪˈɒpəθi/ *n. Med.* chronic disease of the heart muscle.

cardiopulmonary /ˌkɑːdɪəʊˈpʌlmən(ə)ri/ *adj. Med.* of or relating to the heart and the lungs.

cardiovascular /ˌkɑːdɪə(ʊ)ˈvaskjʊlə/ *adj.* of or relating to the heart and blood vessels.

cardoon /kɑːˈduːn/ *n.* a thistle-like plant, *Cynara cardunculus*, allied to the globe artichoke, with leaves used as a vegetable. [French *cardon*, ultimately from Latin *cardu(u)s* 'thistle']

cardphone /ˈkɑːdfəʊn/ *n. Brit.* a public telephone operated by the insertion of a prepaid plastic machine-readable card instead of money.

card-playing *n.* the playing of card games.

card-sharp *n.* (also **card-sharper**) a swindler at card games.

card table *n.* a table for card-playing, esp. a folding one.

card vote *n. Brit.* a block vote, esp. in trade-union meetings.

cardy /ˈkɑːdi/ *n.* (also **cardie**) (*pl.* **-ies**) *Brit. colloq.* a cardigan. [abbreviation]

care /kɛː/ *n. & v.* ● *n.* **1** worry, anxiety. **2** an occasion for this. **3** serious attention; heed, caution, pains (*assembled with care*; *handle with care*). **4 a** protection, charge. **b** *Brit.* = CHILDCARE. **5** a thing to be done or seen to. ● *v.intr.* **1** (usu. foll. by *about*, *for*, *whether*, *if*, etc.) feel concern, interest, or emotion. **2** (foll. by *for*, *about*, and with neg. expressed or implied) feel liking, regard, or deference (*don't care for jazz*; *don't care about what he thinks*). **3** (foll. by *for* or *to* + infin.) wish or be willing (*more times than I care to count*; *would you care for a cup of coffee?*). □ **care for** provide for; look after. **care of** at the address of (*sent it care of his sister*). **for all one cares** *colloq.* denoting uninterest or unconcern (*for all I care they can leave tomorrow*; *I could be dying for all you care*). **have a care** take care; be careful. **I** etc. **couldn't** (*US* also **could**) **care less** *colloq.* an expression of complete indifference. **in care** *Brit.* (of a child) taken into the care of a local authority. **take care 1** be careful. **2** (foll. by *to* + infin.) not fail or neglect. **take care of 1** look after; keep safe. **2** deal with. **3** dispose of. [Old English *caru*, *carian*, from Germanic]

careen /kəˈriːn/ *v.* **1** *tr.* turn (a ship) on one side for cleaning, caulking, or repair. **2 a** *intr.* tilt; lean over. **b** *tr.* cause to do this. **3** *intr. N. Amer.* swerve about; career. □ **careenage** *n.* [earlier as noun, = careened position of ship, from French *carène* from Italian *carena* from Latin *carina* 'keel']

■ **Usage** Sense 3 of *careen* is influenced by *career* (v.).

career /kəˈrɪə/ *n. & v.* ● *n.* **1 a** one's advancement through life, esp. in a profession. **b** the progress through history of a group or institution. **2** a profession or occupation, esp. as offering advancement. **3** (*attrib.*) **a** pursuing or wishing to pursue a career (*career woman*). **b** working permanently in a specified profession (*career diplomat*). **4** swift course; impetus (*in full career*). ● *v.intr.* **1** move or swerve about wildly. **2** go swiftly. [in earlier use, a racecourse or road: French *carrière* via Italian *carriera* from a Romanic word meaning 'carriage-road', ultimately from Latin *carrus* CAR]

careerist /kə'rɪərɪst/ *n. & adj.* ● *n.* a person predominantly concerned with personal advancement in a career, esp. by unscrupulous means. ● *adj.* intent on such advancement. □ **careerism** *n.*

career structure *n.* a recognized pattern of advancement within a job or profession.

carefree /'kɛːfriː/ *adj.* free from anxiety or responsibility; light-hearted. □ **carefreeness** *n.*

careful /'kɛːfʊl, -f(ə)l/ *adj.* **1** painstaking, thorough. **2** cautious. **3** done with care and attention. **4** (usu. foll. by *that* + clause, or *to* + infin.) taking care; not neglecting. **5** (foll. by *for, of*) concerned for; taking care of. □ **carefully** *adv.* **carefulness** *n.* [Old English *carful* (as CARE, -FUL)]

caregiver /'kɛːgɪvə/ *n.* a person who regularly cares for a child or for an elderly or disabled person (cf. CARER).

care label *n.* a label attached to clothing, with instructions for washing etc.

careless /'kɛːlɪs/ *adj.* **1** not taking care or paying attention. **2** unthinking, insensitive. **3** done without care; inaccurate. **4** light-hearted. **5** (foll. by *of*) not concerned about; taking no heed of. **6** effortless; casual. □ **carelessly** *adv.* **carelessness** *n.* [Old English *carlēas* (as CARE, -LESS)]

carer /'kɛːrə/ *n. Brit.* a person who cares for a sick or elderly person, esp. a relative at home.

caress /kə'rɛs/ *v. & n.* ● *v.tr.* **1** touch or stroke gently or lovingly; kiss. **2** treat fondly or kindly. ● *n.* a loving or gentle touch or kiss. □ **caressingly** *adv.* [French *caresse* (*n.*), *caresser* (*v.*), from Italian *carezza*, ultimately from Latin *carus* 'dear']

caret /'karət/ *n.* a mark (‸, ⋏) indicating a proposed insertion in printing or writing. [Latin, = is lacking]

caretaker /'kɛːteɪkə/ *n.* **1** a person employed to look after something, esp. a house in the owner's absence, or *Brit.* a public building. **2** (*attrib.*) exercising temporary authority (*caretaker government*).

careworn /'kɛːwɔːn/ *adj.* showing the effects of prolonged worry.

carfare /'kɑːfɛː/ *n. N. Amer.* a passenger's fare to travel by public transport.

cargo /'kɑːgəʊ/ *n.* (*pl.* **-oes** or **-os**) **1 a** goods carried on a ship or aircraft. **b** a load of such goods. **2** *US* **a** goods carried in a motor vehicle. **b** a load of such goods. [Spanish, = Old French *charge* from Late Latin *car(ri)care*: see CHARGE]

cargo cult *n.* (originally in the Pacific Islands) a belief in the forthcoming arrival of ancestral spirits bringing cargoes of food and other goods.

carhop /'kɑːhɒp/ *n. N. Amer. colloq.* a waiter at a drive-in restaurant.

cariama var. of SERIEMA.

Carib /'karɪb/ *n. & adj.* ● *n.* **1** an aboriginal inhabitant of the southern W. Indies or the adjacent coasts. **2** the language of the Caribs. ● *adj.* of or relating to the Caribs or their language. [Spanish *Caribe* from Haitian Creole]

Caribbean /karɪ'biːən, kə'rɪbɪən/ *n. & adj.* ● *n.* the part of the Atlantic between the southern W. Indies and Central America. ● *adj.* **1** of or relating to this region. **2** of the Caribs or their language or culture.

caribou /'karɪbuː/ *n.* (*pl.* same) a N. American reindeer. [Canadian French, from Micmac *γalipu* literally 'snow-shoveller']

caricature /'karɪkətjʊə/ *n. & v.* ● *n.* **1** a grotesque usu. comic representation of a person by exaggeration of characteristic traits, in a picture, writing, or mime. **2** a ridiculously poor or absurd imitation or version. ● *v.tr.* make or give a caricature of. □ **caricatural** *adj.* **caricaturist** *n.* [French from Italian *caricatura*, from *caricare* 'load, exaggerate' (as CHARGE)]

caries /'kɛːriːz/ *n.* (*pl.* same) decay and crumbling of a tooth or bone. [Latin]

carillon /'karɪljən, -lɒn, kə'rɪljən/ *n.* **1** a set of bells sounded either from a keyboard or mechanically. **2** a tune played on bells. **3** an organ stop imitating a peal of bells. [French from Old French *quarregnon* 'peal of four bells', alteration of Romanic *quaternio* from Latin *quattuor* 'four']

carina /kə'rʌɪnə, -'riː-/ *n. Biol.* a keel-shaped structure, esp. the ridge of a bird's breastbone. □ **carinal** *adj.* [Latin, = keel]

carinate /'karɪneɪt, -ət/ *adj.* (of a bird) having a keeled breastbone (opp. RATITE). [Latin *carinatus* 'keeled' from *carina* 'keel']

caring /'kɛːrɪŋ/ *adj.* **1** kind, humane. **2** (*attrib.*) concerned with looking after the sick, elderly, or disabled (*caring professions*).

carioca /karɪ'əʊkə/ *n.* **1 a** a Brazilian dance resembling the samba. **b** the music for this. **2** a native of Rio de Janeiro. [Portuguese]

cariogenic /kɛːrɪə'dʒɛnɪk, kar-/ *adj.* causing caries.

cariole var. of CARRIOLE.

carious /'kɛːrɪəs/ *adj.* (of bones or teeth) decayed. [Latin *cariosus*]

carjacking /'kɑːdʒakɪŋ/ *n.* the hijacking of a car. □ **carjack** *v.tr.* **carjacker** *n.*

carking /'kɑːkɪŋ/ *adj. archaic* burdensome (*carking care*). [part. of obsolete verb *cark* 'worry, burden', via Old Northern French *carkier* from Romanic, related to CHARGE]

carl /kɑːl/ *n. Sc.* a man; a fellow. [Old English from Old Norse *karl*, related to CHURL]

carline /'kɑːlɪn/ *n.* a thistle-like plant of the genus *Carlina*, esp. *C. vulgaris*. [French from medieval Latin *carlina*, perhaps for *cardina* (Latin *carduus* 'thistle'), associated with *Carolus Magnus* 'Charlemagne', to whom its medicinal properties were said to have been revealed]

carload /'kɑːləʊd/ *n.* **1** a quantity that can be carried in a car. **2** *US* the minimum quantity of goods for which a lower rate is charged for transport.

Carlovingian/kɑːlə'vɪndʒɪən/ var. of CAROLINGIAN.

Carmelite /'kɑːmɪlʌɪt/ *n. & adj.* ● *n.* a friar or nun of a contemplative order dedicated to Our Lady of Mount Carmel. ● *adj.* of or relating to the Carmelites. [French *Carmelite* or medieval Latin *carmelita*, from Mount *Carmel* in Palestine, where the order was founded in the 12th c.]

carminative /'kɑːmɪnətɪv, kɑː'mɪnətɪv/ *adj. & n.* ● *adj.* relieving flatulence. ● *n.* a carminative drug. [French *carminatif -ive*, or medieval Latin *carminare* 'heal (by incantation)': related to CHARM]

carmine /'kɑːmʌɪn, -mɪn/ *adj. & n.* ● *adj.* of a vivid crimson colour. ● *n.* **1** this colour. **2** a vivid crimson pigment made from cochineal. [French *carmin* or medieval Latin *carminium*, ultimately from Arabic *ķirmiz* KERMES]

carnage /'kɑːnɪdʒ/ *n.* great slaughter, esp. of human beings in battle. [French via Italian *carnaggio* and medieval Latin *carnaticum* from Latin *caro carnis* 'flesh']

carnal /'kɑːn(ə)l/ *adj.* **1** of the body or flesh; worldly. **2** sensual, sexual. □ **carnality** /-'nalɪti/ *n.* **carnalize** *v.tr.* (also **-ise**). **carnally** *adv.* [Middle English from Late Latin *carnalis*, from *caro carnis* 'flesh']

carnal knowledge *n.* esp. *Law* sexual intercourse.

carnassial /kɑː'nasɪəl/ *adj. & n.* ● *adj.* (of a carnivore's upper premolar and lower molar teeth) adapted for shearing flesh; sectorial. ● *n.* such a tooth. [French *carnassier* 'carnivorous']

carnation[1] /kɑː'neɪʃ(ə)n/ *n.* a cultivated variety of clove pink, with variously coloured showy flowers. [origin uncertain: in 16th c. varying with *coronation*; perhaps ultimately from a misreading of Arabic *ķaranful* 'clove, clove pink', from Greek *karyophyllon*]

carnation[2] /kɑː'neɪʃ(ə)n/ *n. & adj.* ● *n.* a rosy pink colour. ● *adj.* of this colour. [French from Italian *carnagione*, ultimately from Latin *caro carnis* 'flesh']

carnauba /kɑːˈnɔːbə, -ˈnaʊbə/ *n.* **1** a fan palm, *Copernicia cerifera*, native to NE Brazil; also called WAX PALM. **2** (in full **carnauba wax**) the yellowish wax exuded by the leaves of this tree and used as a polish etc. [Portuguese from Tupi]

carnelian var. of CORNELIAN.

carnet /ˈkɑːneɪ/ *n.* **1** a customs permit to take a motor vehicle across a frontier for a limited period. **2** *Brit.* a permit allowing use of a campsite. [French, = notebook]

carnival /ˈkɑːnɪv(ə)l/ *n.* **1 a** the festivities usual during the period before Lent in Roman Catholic countries. **b** a festival usu. occurring at a regular date and involving a procession. **2** merrymaking, revelry, or a period of such revelry. **3** *N. Amer.* a travelling funfair or circus. □ **carnivalesque** /-ˈlɛsk/ *adj.* [Italian *carne-*, *carnovale* via medieval Latin *carnelevarium* etc. 'Shrovetide' from Latin *caro carnis* 'flesh' + *levare* 'put away']

carnivore /ˈkɑːnɪvɔː/ *n.* **1 a** any mammal of the order Carnivora, with powerful jaws and teeth adapted for stabbing, tearing, and eating flesh, including cats, dogs, and bears. **b** any other flesh-eating animal. **2** a carnivorous plant. [French, from Latin *carnivorus* CARNIVOROUS]

carnivorous /kɑːˈnɪv(ə)rəs/ *adj.* **1** (of an animal) feeding on flesh. **2** (of a plant) digesting trapped insects or other animal substances. **3** of or relating to the order Carnivora. □ **carnivorously** *adv.* **carnivorousness** *n.* [Latin *carnivorus* from *caro carnis* 'flesh' + -VOROUS]

carob /ˈkarəb/ *n.* **1** (in full **carob tree**) an evergreen tree, *Ceratonia siliqua*, native to the Mediterranean, bearing edible pods. **2** its bean-shaped edible seed pod, sometimes used as a substitute for chocolate. [obsolete French *carobe* via medieval Latin *carrubia*, *-um* from Arabic *ḵarrūba*]

carol /ˈkar(ə)l/ *n.* & *v.* ● *n.* a joyous song, esp. a Christmas hymn. ● *v.* (**carolled**, **carolling**; *US* **caroled**, **caroling**) **1** *intr.* sing carols, esp. outdoors at Christmas. **2** *tr.* & *intr.* sing joyfully. □ **caroller** *n.* (*US* **caroler**). [Middle English from Old French *carole*, *caroler*, of unknown origin]

Carolina duck /karəˈlʌɪnə/ *n.* a duck of N. American woodland, *Aix sponsa*.

Caroline /ˈkarəlʌɪn/ *adj.* **1** (also **Carolean** /-ˈliːən/) of the time of Charles I or II of England. **2** = CAROLINGIAN *adj.* 2. [Latin *Carolus* 'Charles']

Carolingian /karəˈlɪndʒɪən/ *adj.* & *n.* (also **Carlovingian** /ˌkɑːləˈvɪndʒɪən/) ● *adj.* **1** of or relating to the second Frankish dynasty, founded by Charlemagne (d. 814). **2** of a style of script developed in France at the time of Charlemagne. ● *n.* **1** a member of the Carolingian dynasty. **2** the Carolingian style of script. [French *carlovingien* from *Karl* 'Charles', on the pattern of *mérovingien* (see MEROVINGIAN), influenced by Latin *Carolus*]

carol-singing *n.* the singing of carols, esp. by groups who go from door to door at Christmas with the object of raising money. □ **carol-singer** *n.*

carom /ˈkarəm/ *n.* & *v.* *N. Amer. Billiards* ● *n.* a cannon. ● *v.intr.* **1** make a carom. **2** (usu. foll. by *off*) strike and rebound. [abbreviation of *carambole* from Spanish *carambola*]

carotene /ˈkarətiːn/ *n.* an orange or red plant pigment found in carrots etc. and acting as a source of vitamin A. [German *Carotin*, from Latin *carota* CARROT]

carotenoid /kəˈrɒtɪnɔɪd/ *n.* any of a class of mainly yellow, orange, or red fat-soluble pigments, including carotene, giving colour to plant parts, e.g. ripe tomatoes, autumn leaves, etc.

carotid /kəˈrɒtɪd/ *n.* & *adj.* ● *n.* each of the two main arteries carrying blood to the head and neck. ● *adj.* of or relating to either of these arteries. [French *carotide* or modern Latin *carotides* from Greek *karōtides* (pl.), from *karoō* 'stupefy' (compression of these arteries being thought to cause stupor)]

carouse /kəˈraʊz/ *v.* & *n.* ● *v.intr.* **1** have a noisy or lively drinking party. **2** drink heavily. ● *n.* a noisy or lively drinking party. □ **carousal** *n.* **carouser** *n.* [originally as *adv.* = right out, in the phrase *drink carouse* from German *gar aus trinken*]

carousel /karəˈsɛl, -ˈzɛl/ *n.* **1** *N. Amer.* a merry-go-round or roundabout. **2** a rotating delivery or conveyor system, esp. for passengers' luggage at an airport. **3** *hist.* a kind of equestrian tournament. [French *carrousel* from Italian *carosello*]

carp[1] /kɑːp/ *n.* (*pl.* same) any freshwater fish of the family Cyprinidae, esp. *Cyprinus carpio*, often bred for use as food. [Middle English via Old French *carpe* from Provençal or from Late Latin *carpa*]

carp[2] /kɑːp/ *v.intr.* (usu. foll. by *at*) find fault; complain pettily. □ **carper** *n.* [obsolete Middle English senses 'talk, say, sing' from Old Norse *karpa* 'to brag': modern sense from or influenced by Latin *carpere* 'pluck at, slander']

carpaccio /kɑːˈpatʃɪəʊ/ *n.* an Italian delicacy based on thin slices of raw meat or fish. [Italian]

carpal /ˈkɑːp(ə)l/ *adj.* & *n.* ● *adj.* of or relating to the bones in the wrist. ● *n.* any of the bones forming the wrist. [CARPUS + -AL]

car park *n.* esp. *Brit.* an area for parking cars.

carpel /ˈkɑːp(ə)l/ *n. Bot.* the female reproductive organ of a flower, consisting of a stigma, style, and ovary. □ **carpellary** *adj.* [French *carpelle* or modern Latin *carpellum* from Greek *karpos* 'fruit']

carpenter /ˈkɑːp(ə)ntə/ *n.* & *v.* ● *n.* a person skilled in woodwork, esp. of a structural kind (cf. JOINER). ● *v.* **1** *intr.* do carpentry. **2** *tr.* make by means of carpentry. **3** *tr.* (often foll. by *together*) construct; fit together. [Middle English & Anglo-French *carpenter*, Old French *carpentier* from Late Latin *carpentarius* (*artifex*) 'carriage(-maker)', from *carpentum* 'wagon' from Gaulish]

carpenter ant *n.* any large ant of the genus *Camponotus*, which bores into wood to nest.

carpenter bee *n.* any of various solitary bees which bore into wood.

carpentry /ˈkɑːp(ə)ntri/ *n.* **1** the work or occupation of a carpenter. **2** woodwork made by a carpenter. [Middle English from Old French *carpenterie* from *carpentier* CARPENTER]

carpet /ˈkɑːpɪt/ *n.* & *v.* ● *n.* **1 a** thick fabric for covering a floor or stairs. **b** a usu. large rug. **2** an expanse or layer resembling a carpet in being smooth, soft, bright, or thick (*carpet of snow*). ● *v.tr.* (**carpeted**, **carpeting**) **1** cover with or as with a carpet. **2** *colloq.* reprimand, reprove. □ **on the carpet 1** *colloq.* being reprimanded. **2** under consideration. **sweep under the carpet** conceal (a problem or difficulty) in the hope that it will be forgotten. [Middle English via Old French *carpite* or medieval Latin *carpita*, from obsolete Italian *carpita* 'woollen counterpane', ultimately from Latin *carpere* 'pluck, pull to pieces']

carpet-bag *n.* a travelling bag of a kind originally made of carpet-like material.

carpet-bagger *n.* **1** esp. *N. Amer.* a political candidate in an area where the candidate has no local connections (originally a northerner in the southern US after the Civil War). **2** an unscrupulous opportunist.

carpet beetle *n.* a small beetle of the genus *Anthrenus*, whose larvae are destructive to carpets and other materials.

carpet bombing *n.* intensive bombing.

carpeting /ˈkɑːpɪtɪŋ/ *n.* **1** material for carpets. **2** carpets collectively.

carpet layer *n.* a person who lays carpets for a living.

carpet slipper *n.* a kind of slipper with the upper made originally of carpet-like material.

carpet sweeper *n.* a household implement with a revolving brush or brushes for sweeping carpets.

car phone *n.* a radio-telephone for use in a motor vehicle.

carpology /kɑːˈpɒlədʒi/ *n.* the study of the structure of fruit and seeds. [Greek *karpos* 'fruit']

carport /ˈkɑːpɔːt/ *n.* a shelter with a roof and open sides for a car, usu. beside a house.

carpus /ˈkɑːpəs/ *n.* (*pl.* **carpi** /-pʌɪ/) the small bones between the forelimb and metacarpus in terrestrial vertebrates, forming the wrist in humans. [modern Latin, from Greek *karpos* 'wrist']

carr /kɑː/ *n.* **1** a marsh or fen, esp. overgrown with shrubs or reclaimed as meadowland. **2** a marshy copse, esp. of alders. [Old Norse *kjarr* 'brushwood']

carrack /ˈkarək/ *n. hist.* a large armed merchant ship. [Middle English via French *caraque* and Spanish *carraca* from Arabic *karākir*]

carrageen /ˈkarəgiːn/ *n.* (also **carragheen**) an edible red seaweed, *Chondrus crispus*, of the northern hemisphere. Also called *Irish moss.* [origin uncertain: perhaps from Irish *cosáinín carraige* 'carrageen', literally 'little stem of the rock']

carrageenan /karəˈgiːnən/ *n.* a mixture of polysaccharides extracted from red and purple seaweeds and used as a thickening or emulsifying agent in food products. [CARRAGEEN + *-an* chemical suffix]

carrel /ˈkar(ə)l/ *n.* **1** a small cubicle for a reader in a library. **2** *hist.* a small enclosure or study in a cloister. [Old French *carole*, medieval Latin *carola*, of unknown origin]

carriage /ˈkarɪdʒ/ *n.* **1** *Brit.* a railway passenger vehicle. **2** a wheeled passenger vehicle, esp. one with four wheels and pulled by horses. **3** *Brit.* **a** the conveying of goods. **b** the cost of this (*carriage paid*). **4** the part of a machine (e.g. a typewriter) that carries other parts into the required position. **5** a gun carriage. **6** a manner of carrying oneself; one's bearing or deportment. [Middle English from Old Northern French *cariage*, from *carier* CARRY]

carriage and pair *n.* a carriage with two horses pulling it.

carriage clock *n.* a portable clock in a rectangular case with a handle on top.

carriage dog *n.* a dalmatian. [formerly trained to run behind a carriage as a guard dog]

carriage return key see RETURN *n.* 11a.

carriageway /ˈkarɪdʒweɪ/ *n. Brit.* the part of a road intended for vehicles.

carrick bend /ˈkarɪk bɛnd/ *n. Naut.* a kind of knot used to join ropes. [BEND²: *carrick* perhaps from CARRACK]

carrier /ˈkarɪə/ *n.* **1** a person or thing that carries. **2** a person or company undertaking to convey goods or passengers for payment. **3** *Brit.* = CARRIER BAG. **4** a part of a bicycle etc. for carrying luggage or a passenger. **5** a person or animal that may transmit a disease or a hereditary characteristic without suffering from or displaying it. **6** = AIRCRAFT CARRIER. **7** a substance used to support or convey a pigment, a catalyst, radioactive material, etc. **8** *Physics* a mobile electron or hole that carries a charge in a semiconductor. **9** *Biochem.* a molecule that transfers another molecule or ion, esp. across a cell membrane.

carrier bag *n. Brit.* a disposable plastic or paper bag with handles.

carrier pigeon *n.* a pigeon trained to carry messages tied to its neck or leg.

carrier wave *n.* a high-frequency electromagnetic wave modulated in amplitude or frequency to convey a signal.

carriole /ˈkarɪəʊl/ *n.* (also **cariole**) **1** a small open carriage for one. **2** a covered light cart. **3** a Canadian sledge. [French from Italian *carriuola*, diminutive of *carro* CAR]

carrion /ˈkarɪən/ *n.* & *adj.* ● *n.* **1** dead putrefying flesh. **2** something vile or filthy. ● *adj.* rotten, loathsome. [Middle English from Anglo-French & Old Northern French *caroine*, *-oigne*, Old French *charoigne*, ultimately from Latin *caro* 'flesh']

carrion crow *n.* a black crow, *Corvus corone*, native to Europe, feeding mainly on carrion.

carrion flower *n.* = STAPELIA.

carrot /ˈkarət/ *n.* **1 a** an umbelliferous plant, *Daucus carota*, with a tapering orange-coloured root. **b** this root as a vegetable. **2** a means of enticement or persuasion (frequently opposed to *stick*). **3** (in *pl.*) *slang* a red-haired person. □ **carroty** *adj.* [French *carotte* via Latin *carota* from Greek *karōton*]

carry /ˈkari/ *v.* & *n.* ● *v.* (**-ies**, **-ied**) **1** *tr.* support or hold up, esp. while moving. **2** *tr.* convey with one from one place to another. **3** *tr.* have on one's person (*carry a watch*). **4** *tr.* conduct or transmit (*pipe carries water*; *wire carries electric current*). **5** *tr.* take (a process etc.) to a specified point (*carry into effect*; *carry a joke too far*). **6** *tr.* (foll. by *to*) continue or prolong (*carry modesty to excess*). **7** *tr.* involve, imply; have as a feature or consequence (*carries a two-year guarantee*; *principles carry consequences*). **8** *tr.* (in reckoning) transfer (a figure) to a column of higher value. **9** *tr.* hold in a specified way (*carry oneself erect*). **10** *tr.* **a** (of a newspaper or magazine) publish; include in its contents, esp. regularly. **b** (of a radio or television station) broadcast, esp. regularly. **11** *tr.* (of a retailing outlet) keep a regular stock of (particular goods for sale) (*have stopped carrying that brand*). **12** *intr.* **a** (of sound, esp. a voice) be audible at a distance. **b** (of a missile) travel, penetrate. **13** *tr.* (of a gun etc.) propel to a specified distance. **14** *tr.* **a** win victory or acceptance for (a proposal etc.). **b** win acceptance from (*carried the audience with them*). **c** win, capture (a prize, a fortress, etc.). **d** *US* gain (a state or district) in an election. **e** *Golf* cause the ball to pass beyond (a bunker etc.). **15** *tr.* **a** endure the weight of; support (*columns carry the dome*). **b** be the chief cause of the effectiveness of; be the driving force in (*you carry the sales department*). **16** *tr.* be pregnant with (*is carrying twins*). **17** *tr.* **a** (of a motive, money, etc.) cause or enable (a person) to go to a specified place. **b** (of a journey) bring (a person) to a specified point. ● *n.* (*pl.* **-ies**) **1** an act of carrying. **2** *Golf* the distance a ball travels before reaching the ground. **3** a portage between rivers etc. **4** the range of a gun etc. □ **carry all before one** gain complete success; overcome all opposition. **carry away 1** remove. **2** inspire; affect emotionally or spiritually. **3** deprive of self-control (*got carried away*). **4** *Naut.* **a** lose (a mast etc.) by breakage. **b** break off or away. **carry back** take (a person) back in thought to a past time. **carry one's bat** *Cricket* be not out at the end of a side's completed innings. **carry the can** *Brit. colloq.* bear the responsibility or blame. **carry conviction** be convincing. **carry the day** be victorious or successful. **carry forward** transfer to a new page or account. **carry it off** (or **carry it off well**) do well under difficulties. **carry off 1** take away, esp. by force. **2** win (a prize). **3** (esp. of a disease) kill. **4** render acceptable or passable. **carry on 1** continue (*carry on eating*; *carry on, don't mind me*). **2** engage in (a conversation or a business). **3** *colloq.* behave strangely or excitedly. **4** (often foll. by *with*) *Brit. colloq.* flirt or have a love affair. **5** advance (a process) by a stage. **carry out** put (ideas, instructions, etc.) into practice. **carry over 1** = *carry forward*. **2** postpone (work etc.). **3** *Stock Exch.* keep over to the next settling day. **carry through 1** complete successfully. **2** bring safely out of difficulties. **carry weight** be influential or important. **carry with one** bear in mind. [Middle English from Anglo-French & Old Northern French *carier* (as CAR)]

carry-all *n.* **1** a light carriage (cf. CARRIOLE). **2** *US* a car with seats placed sideways. **3** *N. Amer.* a large bag or case.

carrycot /ˈkarɪkɒt/ *n. Brit.* a portable cot for a baby.

carrying capacity *n.* **1** the quantity of people, things, etc., which can be conveyed by a vehicle, container, etc. **2** *Ecol.* the number of people, animals, or crops which a region can support without environmental degradation.

carryings-on *n.pl.* (also **carrying-on**) = CARRY-ON.

carrying trade *n.* the conveying of goods from one country to another by water or air as a business.

carry-on *n. Brit. slang* **1** a state of excitement or fuss. **2** a questionable piece of behaviour. **3** a flirtation or love affair.

carry-out *attrib.adj. & n.* esp. *Sc. & US* = TAKEAWAY.

carry-over *n.* **1** something carried over. **2** *Stock Exch.* postponement to the next settling day.

carse /kɑːs/ *n. Sc.* fertile lowland beside a river. [Middle English, perhaps from *carrs* 'swamps']

carsick /ˈkɑːsɪk/ *adj.* affected with nausea caused by the motion of a car. □ **carsickness** *n.*

cart /kɑːt/ *n. & v.* ● *n.* **1** a strong vehicle with two or four wheels for carrying loads, usu. drawn by a horse. **2** a light vehicle for pulling by hand. **3** a light vehicle with two wheels for driving in, drawn by a single horse. **4** *US* (in full **shopping cart**) a supermarket trolley. ● *v.tr.* **1** convey in or as in a cart. **2** *colloq.* carry (esp. a cumbersome thing) with difficulty or over a long distance (*carted it all the way home*). □ **cart off** remove, esp. by force. **in the cart** *Brit. slang* in trouble or difficulty. **put the cart before the horse 1** reverse the proper order or procedure. **2** take an effect for a cause. □ **carter** *n.* **cartful** *n.* (*pl.* **-fuls**). [Middle English from Old Norse *kartr* cart (= Old English *cræt*), probably influenced by Anglo-French & Old Northern French *carete*, diminutive of *carre* CAR]

cartage /ˈkɑːtɪdʒ/ *n.* the price paid for carting.

carte var. of QUART 4.

carte blanche /kɑːt ˈblɑːnʃ/ *n.* full discretionary power given to a person. [French, = blank paper]

cartel /kɑːˈtɛl/ *n.* **1** an informal association of manufacturers or suppliers to maintain prices at a high level, and control production, marketing arrangements, etc. **2** a political combination between parties. □ **cartelize** /ˈkɑːt(ə)lʌɪz/ *v.tr. & intr.* (also **-ise**). [in earlier use = a written challenge or agreement: German *Kartell* via French *cartel* from Italian *cartello*, diminutive of *carta* CARD[1]]

Cartesian /kɑːˈtiːzjən, -ʒ(ə)n/ *adj. & n.* ● *adj.* of or relating to R. Descartes, 17th-c. French philosopher and mathematician. ● *n.* a follower of Descartes. □ **Cartesianism** *n.* [modern Latin *Cartesianus* from *Cartesius*, Latinized form of the name of *Descartes*]

Cartesian coordinates *n.pl.* a system for locating a point by reference to its distance from two or three axes intersecting at right angles.

carthorse /ˈkɑːthɔːs/ *n.* a thickset horse suitable for heavy work.

Carthusian /kɑːˈθjuːzɪən/ *n. & adj.* ● *n.* a monk or nun of an austere contemplative order founded by St Bruno in 1084. ● *adj.* of or relating to this order. [medieval Latin *Carthusianus* from Latin *Cart(h)usia* 'Chartreuse', near Grenoble, where the order was founded]

cartilage /ˈkɑːt(ɪ)lɪdʒ/ *n.* a firm flexible connective tissue forming the infant skeleton, which is mainly replaced by bone in adulthood; gristle. □ **cartilaginoid** /-ˈladʒɪnɔɪd/ *adj.* **cartilaginous** /-ˈladʒɪnəs/ *adj.* [French, from Latin *cartilago -ginis*]

cartilaginous fish *n.* a fish of the class Selachii, with a skeleton of cartilage rather than bone, e.g. a shark, a ray.

cartload /ˈkɑːtləʊd/ *n.* **1** an amount filling a cart. **2** a large quantity of anything.

cartogram /ˈkɑːtəgram/ *n.* a map with diagrammatic statistical information. [French *cartogramme* from *carte* 'map, card']

cartography /kɑːˈtɒgrəfi/ *n.* the science or practice of map-drawing. □ **cartographer** *n.* **cartographic** /-təˈgrafɪk/ *adj.* **cartographical** /-təˈgrafɪk(ə)l/ *adj.* [French *cartographie* from *carte* 'map, card']

cartomancy /ˈkɑːtəmansi/ *n.* fortune-telling by interpreting a random selection of playing cards. [French *cartomancie* from *carte* CARD[1]]

carton /ˈkɑːt(ə)n/ *n.* a light box or container, esp. one made of cardboard. [French (as CARTOON)]

cartoon /kɑːˈtuːn/ *n. & v.* ● *n.* **1** a humorous drawing in a newspaper, magazine, etc., esp. as a topical comment. **2** a sequence of drawings, often with speech indicated, telling a story. **3** a filmed sequence of drawings using the technique of animation. **4** a full-size drawing on stout paper as an artist's preliminary design for a painting, tapestry, mosaic, etc. ● *v.* **1** *tr.* draw a cartoon of. **2** *intr.* draw cartoons. □ **cartoonish** *adj.* **cartoonist** *n.* **cartoony** *adj.* [Italian *cartone* from *carta* CARD[1]]

cartoon strip *n.* = COMIC STRIP.

cartouche /kɑːˈtuːʃ/ *n.* **1 a** *Archit.* a scroll-like ornament, e.g. the volute of an Ionic capital. **b** a tablet imitating, or a drawing of, a scroll with rolled-up ends, used ornamentally or bearing an inscription. **c** an ornate frame. **2** *Archaeol.* an oval ring enclosing Egyptian hieroglyphs, usu. representing the name and title of a king. [French, = cartridge, from Italian *cartoccio*, from *carta* CARD[1]]

cartridge /ˈkɑːtrɪdʒ/ *n.* **1** a casing containing a charge of propelling explosive for firearms or blasting, with the addition of a bullet or shot if for small arms. **2** a spool of film, magnetic tape, etc., in a sealed container ready for insertion. **3** a component carrying the stylus on the pick-up head of a record player. **4** an ink-container for insertion in a pen or in a laser or ink-jet printer. [corruption of CARTOUCHE (but recorded earlier)]

cartridge belt *n.* a belt with pockets or loops for cartridges (see CARTRIDGE 1).

cartridge paper *n.* thick rough paper used for cartridges, for drawing, and for strong envelopes.

cart track *n.* a track or road too rough for ordinary vehicles.

cartwheel /ˈkɑːtwiːl/ *n.* **1** the (usu. spoked) wheel of a cart. **2** a circular sideways handspring with the arms and legs extended.

cartwright /ˈkɑːtrʌɪt/ *n.* a maker of carts.

caruncle /ˈkarəŋk(ə)l, kəˈrʌŋ-/ *n.* **1** *Zool.* a fleshy excrescence, e.g. a turkeycock's wattles or the red prominence at the inner angle of the eye. **2** *Bot.* an outgrowth from a seed near the micropyle. □ **caruncular** /-kjʊlə/ *adj.* [obsolete French from Latin *caruncula*, from *caro carnis* 'flesh']

carve /kɑːv/ *v.* **1** *tr.* produce or shape (a statue, representation in relief, etc.) by cutting into a hard material (*carved a figure out of rock*; *carved it in wood*). **2** *tr.* **a** cut patterns, designs, letters, etc. in (hard material). **b** (foll. by *into*) form a pattern, design, etc., from (*carved it into a bust*). **c** (foll. by *with*) cover or decorate (material) with figures or designs cut in it. **3** *tr.* (also *absol.*) cut (meat etc.) into slices for eating. □ **carve out 1** take from a larger whole. **2** establish (a career etc.) purposefully (*carved out a name for themselves*). **carve up 1** divide into several pieces; subdivide (territory etc.). **2** drive aggressively into the path of (another vehicle). [Old English *ceorfan* 'cut', from West Germanic]

carvel var. of CARAVEL.

carvel-built *adj.* (of a boat) made with planks flush, not overlapping (cf. CLINKER-BUILT).

carven /ˈkɑːv(ə)n/ *archaic past part.* of CARVE.

Carver /ˈkɑːvə/ *n. US* a chair with arms, a rush seat, and a back having horizontal and vertical spindles. [named after J. *Carver*, first governor of Plymouth Colony, d. 1621, for whom a prototype was allegedly made]

carver /ˈkɑːvə/ *n.* **1** a person who carves. **2 a** a carving knife. **b** (in *pl.*) a knife and fork for carving. **3** *Brit.* the principal chair, with arms, in a set of dining chairs, intended for the person who carves.

■ **Usage** Note the distinction between sense 3 of *carver* and *Carver*.

carvery /ˈkɑːvəri/ *n.* (*pl.* **-ies**) esp. *Brit.* a buffet or restaurant with cooked joints displayed, and carved as required, in front of customers.

carve-up *n. Brit. slang* a sharing-out, esp. of spoils.

carving /ˈkɑːvɪŋ/ *n.* a carved object, esp. as a work of art.

carving knife *n.* a knife with a long blade, for carving meat.

car wash *n.* **1** an establishment containing equipment for washing vehicles automatically. **2** the equipment itself.

caryatid /karɪ'atɪd/ *n.* (*pl.* **caryatides** /-diːz/ or **caryatids**) *Archit.* a pillar in the form of a draped female figure, supporting an entablature. [French *caryatide* from Italian *cariatide* or their Latin source, from Greek *karuatis -idos* 'priestess at Caryae' (*Karuai*) in Laconia]

caryopsis /karɪ'ɒpsɪs/ *n.* (*pl.* **caryopses** /-siːz/) *Bot.* a dry one-seeded indehiscent fruit, as in wheat and maize. [modern Latin, from Greek *karuon* 'nut' + *opsis* 'appearance']

Casanova /kasə'nəʊvə, -z-/ *n.* a man notorious for seducing women. [G. J. *Casanova* de Seingalt, Italian adventurer d. 1798]

casbah var. of KASBAH.

cascade /kas'keɪd/ *n.* & *v.* ● *n.* **1** a small waterfall, esp. forming one in a series or part of a large broken waterfall. **2** a mass or quantity (of material, hair, etc.) in descending waves. **3** (foll. by *of*) a succession (of notes, ideas, etc.). **4 a** a process consisting of a series of similar stages with a cumulative effect. **b** a succession of devices, events, etc., each of which triggers or initiates the next. ● *v.intr.* fall in or like a cascade. [French from Italian *cascata*, from *cascare* 'to fall', ultimately from Latin *casus*: see CASE[1]]

cascara /ka'skɑːrə/ *n.* (in full **cascara sagrada** /sə'grɑːdə/) the bark of a Californian buckthorn, *Rhamnus purshiana*, used as a purgative. [Spanish, = sacred bark]

case[1] /keɪs/ *n.* **1** an instance of something occurring. **2** a state of affairs, hypothetical or actual. **3 a** an instance of a person receiving professional guidance or treatment, e.g. from a doctor or social worker. **b** this person or the circumstances involved. **4** a matter under official investigation, esp. by the police. **5** *Law* **a** a cause or suit for trial. **b** a statement of the facts in a cause sub judice, drawn up for a higher court's consideration (*judge states a case*). **c** a cause that has been decided and may be cited (*leading case*). **6 a** the sum of the arguments on one side, esp. in a lawsuit (*that is our case*). **b** a set of arguments, esp. in relation to persuasiveness (*have a good case*; *have a weak case*). **c** a valid set of arguments (*have no case*). **7** *Gram.* **a** the relation of a word to other words in a sentence. **b** a form of a noun, adjective, or pronoun expressing this. **8** *colloq.* a comical person. **9** one's position or circumstances (*in our case*). □ **as the case may be** according to the situation. **in any case** whatever the truth is; whatever may happen; what's more. **in case 1** in the event that; if. **2** lest; in provision against a stated or implied possibility (*take an umbrella in case it rains*; *took it in case*). **in case of** in the event of. **in the case of** as regards. **in no case** under no circumstances. **in that case** if that is true; should that happen. **is** (or **is not**) **the case** is (or is not) so. [Middle English in the sense 'a thing that befalls': via Old French *cas* from Latin *casus* 'fall', from *cadere cas-* 'to fall']

case[2] /keɪs/ *n.* & *v.* ● *n.* **1** a container or covering serving to enclose or contain. **2** a container with its contents. **3** the outer protective covering of a watch, book, seed vessel, sausage, etc. **4** *Brit.* an item of luggage, esp. a suitcase. **5** *Printing* a partitioned receptacle for type. **6** a glass box for showing specimens, curiosities, etc. ● *v.tr.* **1** enclose in a case. **2** (foll. by *with*) surround. **3** (esp. in phr. **case the joint**) *slang* reconnoitre (a house etc.), esp. with a view to robbery. [Middle English via Old French *casse*, *chasse* from Latin *capsa*, from *capere* 'hold']

casebook /'keɪsbʊk/ *n.* a book containing a record of legal or medical cases.

case-bound *adj.* (of a book) in a hard cover.

case-harden *v.tr.* **1** harden the surface of, esp. give a steel surface to (iron) by carbonizing. **2** make callous.

case history *n.* information about a person for use in professional treatment, e.g. by a doctor.

casein /'keɪsiːn, -sɪɪn/ *n.* the main protein in milk, which occurs in coagulated form in cheese, and is used in plastics, adhesives, paint, etc. [Latin *caseus* 'cheese']

case knife *n.* a knife carried in a sheath.

case law *n.* the law as established by the outcome of former cases (cf. COMMON LAW, STATUTE LAW).

caseload /'keɪsləʊd/ *n.* the cases with which a doctor etc. is concerned at one time.

casemate /'keɪsmeɪt/ *n.* **1** a chamber in the thickness of the wall of a fortress, with embrasures. **2** an armoured enclosure for guns on a warship. [French *casemate* & Italian *casamatta* or Spanish *-mata*, from *camata*, perhaps from Greek *khasma -atos* 'gap']

casement /'keɪsm(ə)nt/ *n.* **1** a window or part of a window hinged vertically to open like a door. **2** *poet.* a window. [Middle English from Anglo-Latin *cassimentum*, from *cassa* CASE[2]]

case of conscience *n.* a matter in which one's conscience has to decide a conflict of principles.

case-shot *n.* **1** bullets in an iron case fired from a cannon. **2** shrapnel.

case study *n.* **1** an attempt to understand a person, institution, etc., from collected information. **2** a record of such an attempt. **3** the use of a particular instance as an exemplar of general principles.

casework /'keɪswəːk/ *n.* social work concerned with individuals, esp. involving understanding of the client's family and background. □ **caseworker** *n.*

cash[1] /kaʃ/ *n.* & *v.* ● *n.* **1** money in coins or notes, as distinct from cheques or orders. **2** (also **cash down**) money paid as full payment at the time of purchase, as distinct from credit. **3** *colloq.* wealth. ● *v.tr.* give or obtain cash for (a note, cheque, etc.). □ **cash in 1** obtain cash for. **2** (usu. foll. by *on*) *colloq.* profit (from); take advantage (of). **3** pay into a bank etc. **4** (in full **cash in one's checks**) *colloq.* die. **cash up** *Brit.* count and check cash takings at the end of a day's trading. □ **cashable** *adj.* **cashless** *adj.* [in earlier use = a box for money: obsolete French *casse* 'box' or Italian *cassa*, from Latin *capsa* CASE[2]]

cash[2] /kaʃ/ *n.* (*pl.* same) *hist.* any of various small coins of China or the E. Indies. [Portuguese *ca(i)xa* via Tamil *kāsu* from Sanskrit *karsha*, influenced by CASH[1]]

cash and carry *n.* **1** a system of wholesaling in which goods are paid for in cash and taken away by the purchaser. **2** a store where this system operates.

cash book *n.* a book in which receipts and payments of cash are recorded.

cash box *n.* a box for keeping cash in.

cash card *n.* *Brit.* a plastic card (see CARD[1] *n.* 9a) which enables the holder to draw money from a cash dispenser.

cash cow *n.* *colloq.* a business, or part of one, that provides a steady cash flow.

cash crop *n.* a crop produced for sale, not for use as food etc.

cash desk *n.* a counter or compartment in a shop where goods are paid for.

cash dispenser *n.* *Brit.* an automatic machine from which customers of a bank etc. may withdraw cash, esp. by using a cash card.

cashew /'kaʃuː, kə'ʃuː/ *n.* **1** (also **cashew tree**) a bushy evergreen tree, *Anacardium occidentale*, native to Central and S. America, bearing kidney-shaped nuts attached to fleshy fruits. **2** (in full **cashew nut**) the edible nut of this tree. [Portuguese from Tupi *(a)caju*]

cashew apple *n.* the edible fleshy fruit of the cashew tree.

cash flow *n.* the movement of money into and out of a business, as a measure of profitability, or as affecting liquidity.

cashier[1] /ka'ʃɪə/ *n.* a person dealing with cash transactions in a shop, bank, etc. [Dutch *cassier* or French *caissier* (as CASH[1])]

cashier[2] /kə'ʃɪə, ka-/ *v.tr.* dismiss from service, esp. from the armed forces with disgrace. [Flemish *kasseren* 'disband, revoke' via French *casser* from Latin *quassare* QUASH]

cashmere /kaʃ'mɪə, 'kaʃmɪə/ *n.* **1** a fine soft wool, esp. that of a breed of Himalayan goat. **2** a material made from this. [*Kashmir* in Asia]

cash on delivery *n.* a system of paying the carrier for goods when they are delivered.

cashpoint /'kaʃpɔɪnt/ *n. Brit.* = CASH DISPENSER.

cash register *n.* a machine in a shop etc. with a drawer for money, recording the amount of each sale, totalling receipts, etc.

casing /'keɪsɪŋ/ *n.* **1** a protective or enclosing cover or shell. **2** the material for this.

casino /kə'si:nəʊ/ *n.* (*pl.* **-os**) a public room or building for gambling. [Italian, diminutive of *casa* 'house', from Latin *casa* 'cottage']

cask /kɑ:sk/ *n.* **1** a large barrel-like container made of wood, metal, or plastic, esp. one for alcoholic liquor. **2** its contents. **3** its capacity. [French *casque* or Spanish *casco* 'helmet']

casket /'kɑ:skɪt/ *n.* **1** a small often ornamental box or chest for jewels, letters, etc. **2 a** *Brit.* a small wooden box for cremated ashes. **b** *N. Amer.* a coffin, esp. a rectangular one. [perhaps from Anglo-French form of Old French *cassette* from Italian *cassetta*, diminutive of *cassa*, from Latin *capsa* CASE[2]]

casque /kɑ:sk/ *n.* **1** *hist.* or *poet.* a helmet. **2** *Zool.* a helmet-like structure, e.g. the process on the bill of the cassowary. [French from Spanish *casco*]

Cassandra /kə'sandrə/ *n.* a prophet of disaster, esp. one who is disregarded. [Latin from Greek *Kassandra*, the name of a daughter of Priam King of Troy: she was condemned by Apollo to prophesy correctly but not be believed]

cassata /kə'sɑ:tə/ *n.* a type of ice cream containing candied or dried fruit and nuts. [Italian]

cassation /kə'seɪʃ(ə)n/ *n. Mus.* an informal instrumental composition of the 18th c., similar to a divertimento and originally often for outdoor performance. [German *Kassation* 'serenade' from Italian *cassazione*]

cassava /kə'sɑ:və/ *n.* **1 a** any plant of the genus *Manihot* (spurge family), esp. the cultivated varieties *M. esculenta* (**bitter cassava**) and *M. dulcis* (**sweet cassava**), having starchy tuberous roots. **b** the roots themselves. **2** a starch or flour obtained from these roots. Also called *manioc*. See also TAPIOCA. [Taino *casavi*, influenced by French *cassave*]

Cassegrain telescope /'kasɪgreɪn/ *n.* a reflecting telescope in which light reflected from a convex secondary mirror passes through a hole in the primary mirror. [named after N. *Cassegrain*, 17th-cent. French scientist, who devised it]

casserole /'kasərəʊl/ *n. & v.* ● *n.* **1** a covered dish, usu. of earthenware or glass, in which food is cooked, esp. slowly in the oven. **2** food cooked in a casserole. ● *v.tr.* cook in a casserole. [French from *cassole*, diminutive of *casse*, via Provençal *casa* and Late Latin *cattia* 'ladle, pan' from Greek *kuathion*, diminutive of *kuathos* 'cup']

cassette /kə'sɛt/ *n.* a sealed case containing a length of tape, ribbon, etc., ready for insertion in a machine, esp.: **1** a length of audiotape or videotape wound on to spools, ready for insertion in a tape recorder or video recorder. **2** a length of photographic film, ready for insertion in a camera. [French, diminutive of *casse* CASE[2]]

cassette deck *n.* a tape deck for playing and recording audio cassettes.

cassette player *n.* a tape recorder for playing back audio cassettes.

cassette recorder *n.* a tape recorder for recording and playing back audio cassettes.

cassette tape *n.* a cassette of esp. audiotape.

cassia /'kasɪə/ *n.* **1** (also **cassia tree**) any tree of the genus *Cassia*, bearing leaves from which senna is extracted. **2** the cinnamon-like bark of this tree used as a spice. [Latin via Greek *kasia* from Hebrew *ḳᵉṣī'āh* 'bark like cinnamon']

cassingle /ka'sɪŋg(ə)l/ *n. colloq.* an audio cassette containing a single piece of (usu. popular) music on each side. [portmanteau word from CASSETTE + SINGLE]

cassis /ka'si:s, 'kasɪs/ *n.* a syrupy usu. alcoholic blackcurrant flavouring for drinks etc. [French, = blackcurrant]

cassiterite /kə'sɪtərʌɪt/ *n.* a naturally occurring ore of tin dioxide, from which tin is extracted. Also called *tinstone*. [Greek *kassiteros* 'tin']

cassock /'kasək/ *n.* a full-length usu. black or red garment worn by clergy, members of choirs, etc. □ **cassocked** *adj.* [French *casaque* 'long coat' from Italian *casacca* 'horseman's coat', probably from Turkic *kazak*: see COSSACK]

cassoulet /'kasʊleɪ/ *n.* a ragout of meat and beans. [French, diminutive of dialect *cassolo* 'stew-pan']

cassowary /'kasəwəri, -wɛ:ri/ *n.* (*pl.* **-ies**) a large flightless Australasian bird of the genus *Casuarius*, with heavy body, stout legs, a wattled neck, and a bony crest on its forehead. [Malay *kasuārī, kasavārī*]

cast /kɑ:st/ *v. & n.* ● *v.* (*past* and *past part.* **cast**) **1** *tr.* throw, esp. deliberately or forcefully. **2** *tr.* (often foll. by *on, over*) **a** direct or cause to fall (one's eyes, a glance, light, a shadow, a spell, etc.). **b** express (doubts, aspersions, etc.). **3** *tr.* throw out (a net, fishing line, etc.) into the water. **4** *tr.* let down (an anchor or sounding line). **5** *tr.* **a** throw off, get rid of. **b** shed (skin etc.) esp. in the process of growth. **c** (of a horse) lose (a shoe). **6** *tr.* record, register, or give (a vote). **7** *tr.* **a** shape (molten metal or plastic material) in a mould. **b** make (a product) in this way. **8** *tr. Printing* make (type). **9** *tr.* **a** (usu. foll. by *as*) assign (an actor) to play a particular character. **b** allocate roles in (a play, film, etc.). **10** *tr.* (foll. by *in, into*) arrange or formulate (facts etc.) in a specified form. **11** *tr. & intr.* reckon, add up, calculate (accounts or figures). **12** *tr.* calculate and record details of (a horoscope). ● *n.* **1 a** the throwing of a missile etc. **b** the distance reached by this. **2** a throw or a number thrown at dice. **3** a throw of a net, sounding line, or fishing line. **4** *Fishing* **a** that which is cast, esp. the extremity of a line with hook and fly. **b** a place for casting. **5 a** an object of metal, clay, etc., made in a mould. **b** a moulded mass of solidified material, esp. plaster protecting a broken limb. **6** the actors taking part in a play, film, etc. **7** form, type, or quality (*cast of features*; *cast of mind*). **8** a tinge or shade of colour. **9 a** (in full **cast in the eye**) a slight squint. **b** a twist or inclination. **10 a** a mass of earth excreted by a worm. **b** a mass of indigestible food regurgitated by a hawk, owl, etc. **11** the form into which any work is thrown or arranged. **12 a** a wide area covered by a dog or pack to find a trail. **b** *Austral. & NZ* a wide sweep made by a sheepdog in mustering sheep. □ **cast about** (or **around** or **round**) make an extensive search (actually or mentally) (*cast about for a solution*). **cast adrift** leave to drift. **cast ashore** (of waves etc.) throw to the shore. **cast aside** give up using; abandon. **cast away 1** reject. **2** (in *passive*) be shipwrecked (cf. CASTAWAY). **cast one's bread upon the waters** see BREAD. **cast down** depress, deject (cf. DOWNCAST *adj.* 2). **cast loose** detach; detach oneself. **cast lots** see LOT. **cast off 1** abandon. **2** *Knitting* take the stitches off the needle by looping each over the next to finish the edge. **3** *Naut.* **a** set a ship free from a quay etc. **b** loosen and throw off (rope etc.). **4** *Printing* estimate the space that will be taken in print by manuscript copy. **cast on** *Knitting* make the first row of loops on the needle. **cast out** expel. **cast up 1** (of the sea) deposit on the shore. **2** add up (figures etc.). [Middle English from Old Norse *kasta*]

castanet /kastə'nɛt/ *n.* (usu. in *pl.*) a small concave piece of hardwood, ivory, etc., in pairs held in the hands and clicked together by the fingers as a rhythmic accompaniment, esp. by Spanish dancers. [Spanish *castañeta*, diminutive of *castaña*, from Latin *castanea* 'chestnut']

castaway /'kɑːstəweɪ/ *n. & adj.* ● *n.* a shipwrecked person. ● *adj.* **1** shipwrecked. **2** cast aside; rejected.

caste /kɑːst/ *n.* **1** any of the Hindu hereditary classes, distinguished by relative degrees of purity or pollution, whose members have no social contact with other classes but are socially equal with one another and often follow the same occupations. **2** a more or less exclusive social class. **3** a system of such classes. **4** the position it confers. **5** *Zool.* a form of social insect having a particular function. □ **lose caste** descend in the social order. [Spanish and Portuguese *casta* 'lineage, race, breed', fem. of *casto* 'pure, CHASTE']

casteism /'kɑːstɪz(ə)m/ *n.* often *derog.* the caste system.

castellan /'kastələn/ *n. hist.* the governor of a castle. [Middle English via Old Northern French *castelain* from medieval Latin *castellanus*: see CASTLE]

castellated /'kastəleɪtɪd/ *adj.* **1** having battlements. **2** castle-like. □ **castellation** /-'leɪʃ(ə)n/ *n.* [medieval Latin *castellatus*: see CASTLE]

caste mark *n.* a symbol on a person's forehead denoting his or her caste.

caster /'kɑːstə/ *n.* **1** var. of CASTOR[1]. **2** a person who casts. **3** a machine for casting type.

caster sugar *n.* (also **castor sugar**) *Brit.* finely granulated white sugar.

castigate /'kastɪgeɪt/ *v.tr.* rebuke or punish severely. □ **castigation** /-'geɪʃ(ə)n/ *n.* **castigator** *n.* **castigatory** *adj.* [Latin *castigare* 'reprove' from *castus* 'pure']

Castile soap /ka'stiːl/ *n.* a fine hard white or mottled soap made with olive oil and soda. [*Castile* in Spain]

Castilian /ka'stɪlɪən/ *n. & adj.* ● *n.* **1** a native of Castile in Spain. **2** the language of Castile, standard spoken and literary Spanish. ● *adj.* of or relating to Castile or Castilian.

casting /'kɑːstɪŋ/ *n.* an object made by casting, esp. of molten metal.

casting couch *n. slang* a couch in a director's office on which actresses are said to be seduced in return for being awarded parts.

casting vote *n.* a deciding vote usu. given by the chairperson when the votes on two sides are equal. [From an obsolete sense of *cast* = turn the scale]

cast iron *n. & adj.* ● *n.* a hard alloy of iron, carbon, and silicon cast in a mould. ● *adj.* (**cast-iron**) **1** made of cast iron. **2** hard, unchallengeable, unchangeable.

castle /'kɑːs(ə)l/ *n. & v.* ● *n.* **1 a** a large fortified building or group of buildings; a stronghold. **b** a formerly fortified mansion. **2** *Chess* = ROOK[2]. ● *v. Chess* **1** *intr.* make a special move (once only in a game on each side) in which the king is moved two squares along the back rank and the nearer rook is moved to the square passed over by the king. **2** *tr.* move (the king) by castling. □ **castled** *adj.* [Anglo-French & Old Northern French *castel*, *chastel* from Latin *castellum*, diminutive of *castrum* 'fort']

castle in the air *n.* (also **castle in Spain**) (usu. in *pl.*) a visionary unattainable scheme; a daydream.

cast net *n.* a net thrown out and immediately drawn in.

cast-off *adj. & n.* ● *adj.* abandoned, discarded. ● *n.* a cast-off thing, esp. a garment.

castor[1] /'kɑːstə/ *n.* (also **caster**) **1** a small swivelled wheel (often one of a set) fixed to a leg (or the underside) of a piece of furniture. **2** a small container with holes in the top for sprinkling the contents. [originally a variant of CASTER (in the general sense)]

castor[2] /'kɑːstə/ *n.* an oily substance secreted by beavers and used in medicine and perfumes. [French or Latin from Greek *kastōr* 'beaver']

castor action *n.* swivelling of vehicle wheels to ensure stability.

castor oil /'kɑːstə/ *n.* **1** an oil from the seeds of a plant, *Ricinus communis*, used as a purgative and lubricant. **2** (in full **castor oil plant**) this plant. [18th c.: origin uncertain: perhaps so called as having succeeded CASTOR[2] in medical use]

castor oil bean *n.* (also **castor bean**) the seed of the castor oil plant, containing the highly toxic substance ricin.

castor sugar var. of CASTER SUGAR.

castrate /ka'streɪt, 'kastreɪt/ *v.tr.* **1** remove the testicles of; geld. **2** deprive of vigour. □ **castration** /-'streɪʃ(ə)n/ *n.* **castrator** *n.* [Latin *castrare*]

castrato /ka'strɑːtəʊ/ *n.* (*pl.* **castrati** /-ti/) *hist.* a male singer castrated in boyhood so as to retain a soprano or alto voice. [Italian, past part. of *castrare*: see CASTRATE]

casual /'kaʒjʊəl, -zj-/ *adj. & n.* ● *adj.* **1** accidental; due to chance. **2** not regular or permanent; temporary, occasional (*casual work*; *a casual affair*). **3 a** unconcerned, uninterested (*was very casual about it*). **b** made or done without great care or thought (*a casual remark*). **c** acting carelessly or unmethodically. **4** (of clothes) informal. ● *n.* **1** a casual worker. **2** (usu. in *pl.*) casual clothes or shoes. □ **casually** *adv.* **casualness** *n.* [Middle English from Old French *casuel* and Latin *casualis*, from *casus* CASE[1]]

casualty /'kaʒjʊəlti, -zj-/ *n.* (*pl.* **-ies**) **1** a person killed or injured in a war or accident. **2** a thing lost or destroyed. **3** *Brit.* = CASUALTY DEPARTMENT. **4** an accident, mishap, or disaster. [Middle English from medieval Latin *casualitas* (as CASUAL), on the pattern of ROYALTY etc.]

casualty department *n.* (also **casualty ward**) the part of a hospital where casualties are treated.

casuarina /kasjʊə'riːnə/ *n.* any tree of the genus *Casuarina*, native to Australia and SE Asia, having tiny scale-leaves on slender jointed branches, resembling gigantic horsetails. [modern Latin *casuarius* 'cassowary' (from the resemblance between branches and feathers)]

casuist /'kazjʊɪst, -ʒj-/ *n.* **1** a person, esp. a theologian, who resolves problems of conscience, duty, etc., often with clever but false reasoning. **2** a sophist or quibbler. □ **casuistic** /-'ɪstɪk/ *adj.* **casuistical** /-'ɪstɪk(ə)l/ *adj.* **casuistically** /-'ɪstɪk(ə)li/ *adv.* **casuistry** *n.* [French *casuiste* via Spanish *casuista* from Latin *casus* CASE[1]]

casus belli /ˌkeɪsəs 'bɛlʌɪ, ˌkɑːsʊs 'bɛli/ *n.* an act or situation provoking or justifying war. [Latin]

CAT *abbr.* **1** computer-assisted (or -aided) testing. **2** *Med.* computerized axial tomography (*CAT scanner*).

cat[1] /kat/ *n. & v.* ● *n.* **1** a small soft-furred four-legged domesticated animal, *Felis catus*. **2** any wild animal of the family Felidae, e.g. a lion, tiger, or leopard. **3** a catlike animal of any other family (*civet cat*). **4** *colloq.* a malicious or spiteful woman. **5** *slang* a jazz enthusiast. **6** *Naut.* = CATHEAD. **7** = CAT-O'-NINE-TAILS. **8** a short tapered stick in the game of tipcat. ● *v.tr.* (also *absol.*) (**catted**, **catting**) *Naut.* raise (an anchor) from the surface of the water to the cathead. □ **let the cat out of the bag** reveal a secret, esp. involuntarily. **like a cat** *Brit.* **on hot bricks** (or **on a hot tin roof**) very agitated or agitatedly. **put** (or **set**) **the cat among the pigeons** *Brit.* cause trouble. **rain cats and dogs** rain very hard. [Old English *catt(e)* from Germanic, reinforced in Middle English by forms from Late Latin *cattus*]

cat[2] /kat/ *n.* a catalytic converter. [abbreviation]

cata- /'katə/ *prefix* (usu. **cat-** before a vowel or *h*) **1** down, downwards (*catadromous*). **2** wrongly, badly (*catachresis*). **3** completely (*catalogue*). **4** against, alongside (*catapult*). [Greek *kata* 'down']

catabolism /kə'tabəlɪz(ə)m/ *n.* (also **katabolism**) *Biochem.* the breakdown of complex molecules in living organisms to form simpler ones with the release of energy; destructive metabolism (opp. ANABOLISM). □ **catabolic** /katə'bɒlɪk/ *adj.* [Greek *katabolē* 'descent' (as CATA- + *bolē* from *ballō* 'throw')]

catachresis /katə'kriːsɪs/ *n.* (*pl.* **catachreses** /-siːz/) an incorrect use of words. □ **catachrestic** /-'kriːstɪk, -'krɛstɪk/ *adj.* [Latin from Greek *katakhrēsis* (as CATA-, *kresthai* 'use')]

cataclasis /katəˈkleɪsɪs/ *n.* (*pl.* **cataclases** /-siːz/) *Geol.* the natural process of fracture, shearing, or breaking up of rocks. □ **cataclastic** /-ˈklastɪk/ *adj.* [modern Latin from Greek *kataklasis* 'breaking down', (as CATA-, *klaō* 'to break')]

cataclasm /ˈkatəklaz(ə)m/ *n.* a violent break; a disruption. [Greek *kataklasma* (as CATA-, *klaō* 'to break')]

cataclysm /ˈkatəklɪz(ə)m/ *n.* **1 a** a violent, esp. social or political, upheaval or disaster. **b** a great change. **2** a great flood or deluge. □ **cataclysmal** /-ˈklɪzm(ə)l/ *adj.* **cataclysmic** /-ˈklɪzmɪk/ *adj.* **cataclysmically** /-ˈklɪzmɪk(ə)li/ *adv.* [French *cataclysme* via Latin *cataclysmus* from Greek *kataklusmos* (as CATA- + *klusmos* 'flood' from *kluzō* 'wash')]

catacomb /ˈkatəkuːm, -kəʊm/ *n.* (often in *pl.*) **1** an underground cemetery, esp. a Roman subterranean gallery with recesses for tombs. **2** a similar underground construction; a cellar. [French *catacombes* from Late Latin *catacumbas* (name given in the 5th c. to the cemetery of St Sebastian near Rome), of unknown origin]

catadromous /katəˈdrəʊməs/ *adj.* (of a fish, e.g. the eel) that swims down rivers to the sea to spawn (opp. ANADROMOUS). [Greek *katadromos* (as CATA- + *dromos* 'running')]

catafalque /ˈkatəfalk/ *n.* a decorated wooden framework for supporting the coffin of a distinguished person during a funeral or while lying in state. [French from Italian *catafalco*, of unknown origin: related to SCAFFOLD]

Catalan /ˈkatəlan/ *n.* & *adj.* ● *n.* **1** a native of Catalonia in Spain. **2** the language of Catalonia. ● *adj.* of or relating to Catalonia, its people, or its language. [French from Spanish]

catalase /ˈkatəleɪz/ *n. Biochem.* an enzyme that catalyses the reduction of hydrogen peroxide. [CATALYSIS]

catalectic /katəˈlɛktɪk/ *adj.* & *n. Prosody* ● *adj.* lacking one syllable in the last foot. ● *n.* a catalectic line or verse. [Late Latin *catalecticus* from Greek *katalēktikos* from *katalēgein* 'leave off' (as CATA-, *lēgein* 'cease')]

catalepsy /ˈkat(ə)lɛpsi/ *n.* a state of trance or seizure with loss of sensation and consciousness accompanied by rigidity of the body. □ **cataleptic** /-ˈlɛptɪk/ *adj.* & *n.* [French *catalepsie* or Late Latin *catalepsia* from Greek *katalēpsis* (as CATA-, *lēpsis* 'seizure')]

catalogue /ˈkat(ə)lɒg/ *n.* & *v.* (*US* also **catalog**) ● *n.* **1** a complete list of items (e.g. articles for sale, books held by a library), usu. in alphabetical or other systematic order and often with a description of each. **2** an extensive list (*a catalogue of crimes*). **3** *US* a university course-list etc. ● *v.tr.* (**catalogues**, **catalogued**, **cataloguing**; *US* **catalogs**, **cataloged**, **cataloging**) **1** make a catalogue of. **2** enter in a catalogue. □ **cataloguer** *n.* (*US* **cataloger**). [French via Late Latin *catalogus* from Greek *katalogos*, from *katalegō* 'enrol' (as CATA-, *legō* 'choose')]

catalogue raisonné /ˌkat(ə)lɒg reɪzɒˈneɪ/ *n.* (*pl.* **catalogues raisonnés** *pronunc.* same) a descriptive catalogue with explanations or comments. [French, = explained catalogue]

catalpa /kəˈtalpə/ *n.* any tree of the genus *Catalpa*, with heart-shaped leaves, trumpet-shaped flowers, and long pods. [American Indian (Creek)]

catalyse /ˈkat(ə)lʌɪz/ *v.tr.* (*US* **catalyze**) *Chem.* produce (a reaction) by catalysis. [as CATALYSIS, on the pattern of *analyse*]

catalyser /ˈkat(ə)lʌɪzə/ *n. Brit.* = CATALYTIC CONVERTER.

catalysis /kəˈtalɪsɪs/ *n.* (*pl.* **catalyses** /-siːz/) *Chem.* & *Biochem.* the acceleration of a chemical or biochemical reaction by a catalyst. [Greek *katalusis* 'dissolution' (as CATA-, *luō* 'set free')]

catalyst /ˈkat(ə)lɪst/ *n.* **1** *Chem.* a substance that, without itself undergoing any permanent chemical change, increases the rate of a reaction. **2** a person or thing that precipitates a change. [as CATALYSIS, on the pattern of *analyst*]

catalytic /katəˈlɪtɪk/ *adj. Chem.* relating to or involving catalysis.

catalytic converter *n.* a device incorporated in the exhaust system of a motor vehicle, with a catalyst for converting pollutant gases into less harmful ones.

catalytic cracker *n.* a device for cracking (see CRACK *v.* 9) petroleum oils by catalysis.

catalyze *US* var. of CATALYSE.

catamaran /katəməˈran/ *n.* **1** a boat with twin hulls in parallel. **2** a raft of yoked logs or boats. **3** *colloq.* a quarrelsome woman. [Tamil *kaṭṭumaram* 'tied wood']

catamite /ˈkatəmʌɪt/ *n.* **1** a boy kept for homosexual practices. **2** the passive partner in sodomy. [Latin *catamitus* via Etruscan from Greek *Ganumēdēs* 'Ganymede', the name of Zeus' cupbearer]

catamountain /katəˈmaʊntɪn/ *n.* (also **catamount**) **1** a lynx, leopard, puma, or similar cat. **2** *archaic* a wild quarrelsome person. [Middle English from *cat of the mountain*]

catananche /katəˈnaŋki/ *n.* a plant of the genus *Catananche* (daisy family), with blue or yellow flowers. [modern Latin via Latin *catanancē*, a plant used in love potions, from Greek *katanagkē* (as CATA-, *anagkē* 'compulsion')]

cat-and-dog *adj.* (of a relationship etc.) full of quarrels.

cataplexy /ˈkatəplɛksi/ *n.* sudden temporary paralysis due to fright etc. □ **cataplectic** /-ˈplɛktɪk/ *adj.* [Greek *kataplēxis* 'stupefaction' (as CATA-, *plēssein* 'to strike')]

catapult /ˈkatəpʌlt/ *n.* & *v.* ● *n.* **1** esp. *Brit.* a forked stick etc. with elastic for shooting stones. **2** *hist.* a military machine worked by a lever and ropes for hurling large stones etc. **3** a mechanical device for launching a glider, an aircraft from the deck of a ship, etc. ● *v.* **1** *tr.* **a** hurl from or launch with a catapult. **b** fling forcibly. **2** *intr.* leap or be hurled forcibly. [French *catapulte* or Latin *catapulta* from Greek *katapeltēs* (as CATA-, *pallō* 'hurl')]

cataract /ˈkatərakt/ *n.* **1 a** a large waterfall or cascade. **b** a downpour; a rush of water. **2** *Med.* a condition in which the eye lens becomes progressively opaque resulting in blurred vision. [Latin *cataracta* from Greek *katarrhaktēs* 'down-rushing'; in medical sense probably from obsolete sense 'grating on a window']

catarrh /kəˈtɑː/ *n.* **1** inflammation of the mucous membrane of the nose, air passages, etc. **2** a watery discharge in the nose or throat due to this. □ **catarrhal** *adj.* [French *catarrhe* via Late Latin *catarrhus* from Greek *katarrhousin* from *katarrhe* 'flow down' (as CATA-, *rhein* 'flow')]

catarrhine /ˈkatərʌɪn/ *adj.* & *n. Zool.* ● *adj.* (of primates) having nostrils close together and directed downwards, as in a baboon, chimpanzee, or human. ● *n.* such an animal (cf. PLATYRRHINE). [CATA- + *rhis rhinos* 'nose']

catastrophe /kəˈtastrəfi/ *n.* **1** a great and usu. sudden disaster. **2** the denouement of a drama. **3** a disastrous end; ruin. **4** an event producing a subversion of the order of things. □ **catastrophic** /-ˈstrɒfɪk/ *adj.* **catastrophically** /-ˈstrɒfɪk(ə)li/ *adv.* [Latin *catastropha* from Greek *katastrophē* (as CATA-, *strophē* 'turning' from *strephō* 'turn')]

catastrophe theory *n.* a branch of mathematics concerned with systems displaying abrupt discontinuous change.

catastrophism /kəˈtastrəfɪz(ə)m/ *n. Geol.* the theory that changes in the earth's crust have occurred in sudden violent and unusual events. □ **catastrophist** *n.*

catatonia /katəˈtəʊnɪə/ *n.* **1** schizophrenia with intervals of catalepsy and sometimes violence. **2** catalepsy. □ **catatonic** /-ˈtɒnɪk/ *adj.* & *n.* [German *Katatonie* (as CATA-, TONE)]

catawba /kəˈtɔːbə/ *n.* **1** a US variety of grape. **2** a white wine made from this. [River *Catawba* in S. Carolina]

catbird /ˈkatbəːd/ *n.* any of several birds with a mewing call like a cat, esp. a N. American mockingbird, *Dumetalla carolinensis*.

catboat /ˈkatbəʊt/ *n.* a sailing boat with a single mast placed well forward and carrying only one sail. [perhaps from *cat*, a former type of coaler in NE England, + BOAT]

cat burglar *n.* a burglar who enters by climbing to an upper storey.

catcall /ˈkatkɔːl/ *n.* & *v.* ● *n.* a shrill whistle of disapproval made at meetings etc. ● *v.* **1** *intr.* make a catcall. **2** *tr.* make a catcall at.

catch /katʃ/ *v.* & *n.* ● *v.* (*past* and *past part.* **caught** /kɔːt/) **1** *tr.* **a** lay hold of so as to restrain or prevent from escaping; capture in a trap, in one's hands, etc. **b** (also **catch hold of**) get into one's hands so as to retain, operate, etc. (*caught hold of the handle*). **2** *tr.* detect or surprise (a person, esp. in a wrongful or embarrassing act) (*caught me in the act*; *caught him smoking*). **3** *tr.* **a** intercept and hold (a moving thing) in the hands etc. (*failed to catch the ball*; *a bowl to catch the drips*). **b** *Cricket* dismiss (a batsman) by catching the ball before it reaches the ground. **4** *tr.* **a** contract (a disease) by infection or contagion. **b** acquire (a quality or feeling) from another's example (*caught her enthusiasm*). **5** *tr.* **a** reach in time and board (a train, bus, etc.). **b** be in time to see etc. (a person or thing about to leave or finish) (*if you hurry you'll catch them*; *caught the end of the performance*). **6** *tr.* **a** apprehend with the senses or the mind (esp. a thing occurring quickly or briefly) (*didn't catch what he said*). **b** (of an artist etc.) reproduce faithfully. **7 a** *intr.* become fixed or entangled; be checked (*the bolt began to catch*). **b** *tr.* cause to do this (*caught her tights on a nail*). **c** *tr.* (often foll. by *on*) hit, deal a blow to (*caught him on the nose*; *caught his elbow on the table*). **8** *tr.* draw the attention of; captivate (*caught his eye*; *caught her fancy*). **9** *intr.* begin to burn. **10** *tr.* (often foll. by *up*) reach or overtake (a person etc. ahead). **11** *tr.* check suddenly (*caught his breath*). **12** *tr.* (foll. by *at*) grasp or try to grasp. ● *n.* **1 a** an act of catching. **b** *Cricket* a chance or act of catching the ball. **2 a** an amount of a thing caught, esp. of fish. **b** a thing or person caught or worth catching, esp. in marriage. **3 a** a question, trick, etc., intended to deceive, incriminate, etc. **b** an unexpected or hidden difficulty or disadvantage. **4** a device for fastening a door or window etc. **5** *Mus.* a round, esp. with words arranged to produce a humorous effect. □ **catch at a straw** see STRAW. **catch one's death of cold** see DEATH. **catch fire** see FIRE. **catch it** *slang* be punished or in trouble. **catch on** *colloq.* **1** (of a practice, fashion, etc.) become popular. **2** (of a person) understand what is meant. **catch out** *Brit.* **1** detect in a mistake etc. **2** take unawares; cause to be bewildered or confused. **3** = sense 3b of *v.* **catch the sun 1** be in a sunny position. **2** *Brit.* become sunburnt. **catch up 1 a** (often foll. by *with*) reach a person etc. ahead (*he caught up in the end*; *he caught us up*; *he caught up with us*). **b** (often foll. by *with, on*) make up arrears (of work etc.) (*must catch up with my correspondence*). **2** snatch or pick up hurriedly. **3** (often in *passive*) **a** involve; entangle (*caught up in suspicious dealings*). **b** fasten up (*hair caught up in a ribbon*). **(you wouldn't) catch me!** etc. (often foll. by *pres. part.*) *colloq.* you may be sure I etc. shall not. □ **catchable** *adj.* [Middle English from Anglo-French & Old Northern French *cachier*, Old French *chacier*, ultimately from Latin *captare* 'try to catch']

catch-22 /ˌkatʃtwɛntɪˈtuː/ *n.* (often *attrib.*) *colloq.* a dilemma or circumstance from which there is no escape because of mutually conflicting or dependent conditions. [title of a novel by J. Heller (1961) featuring a dilemma of this kind]

catch-all *n.* (often *attrib.*) a thing designed to be all-inclusive.

catch-as-catch-can *n.* & *adj.* ● *n.* a style of wrestling with few holds barred. ● *adj.* using whatever is available (*a catch-as-catch-can repair*).

catch crop *n.* a crop grown between two staple crops (in position or time).

catcher /ˈkatʃə/ *n.* **1** a person or thing that catches. **2** *Baseball* a fielder positioned behind the home plate.

catchfly /ˈkatʃflʌɪ/ *n.* (*pl.* **-flies**) any plant of the genus *Silene* or *Lychnis* with a sticky stem.

catching /ˈkatʃɪŋ/ *adj.* **1 a** (of a disease) infectious. **b** (of a practice, habit, etc.) likely to be imitated. **2** attractive; captivating.

catchline /ˈkatʃlʌɪn/ *n. Printing* a short line of type esp. at the head of copy or as a running headline.

catchment /ˈkatʃm(ə)nt/ *n.* the collection of rainfall.

catchment area *n.* **1** the area from which rainfall flows into a river etc. **2** the area served by a school, hospital, etc.

catchpenny /ˈkatʃpɛni/ *adj.* intended merely to sell quickly; superficially attractive.

catchphrase /ˈkatʃfreɪz/ *n.* a phrase in frequent use.

catchup var. of KETCHUP.

catchweight /ˈkatʃweɪt/ *adj.* & *n.* ● *adj.* unrestricted as regards weight. ● *n.* unrestricted weight, as a weight category in sports.

catchword /ˈkatʃwəːd/ *n.* **1** a word or phrase in common (often temporary) use; a topical slogan. **2** a word so placed as to draw attention. **3** *Theatr.* an actor's cue. **4** *Printing* the first word of a page given at the foot of the previous one.

catchy /ˈkatʃi/ *adj.* (**catchier**, **catchiest**) **1** (of a tune) easy to remember; attractive. **2** that snares or entraps; deceptive. **3** (of the wind etc.) fitful, spasmodic. □ **catchily** *adv.* **catchiness** *n.* [CATCH + -Y[1]]

cate /keɪt/ *n.* (usu. in *pl.*) *archaic* choice food, delicacies. [obsolete *acate* 'purchase' from Anglo-French *acat*, Old French *achat*, from *acater*, *achater* 'buy': see CATER]

catechetical /katɪˈkɛtɪk(ə)l/ *adj.* (also **catechetic**) **1** of or by oral teaching. **2** according to the catechism of a Church. **3** consisting of or proceeding by question and answer. □ **catechetically** *adv.* **catechetics** *n.* [ecclesiastical Greek *katēkhētikos* from *katēkhētēs* 'oral teacher': see CATECHIZE]

catechism /ˈkatɪkɪz(ə)m/ *n.* **1 a** a summary of the principles of a religion in the form of questions and answers. **b** a book containing this. **2** a series of questions put to anyone. □ **catechismal** /-ˈkɪzm(ə)l/ *adj.* [ecclesiastical Latin *catechismus* (as CATECHIZE)]

catechist /ˈkatɪkɪst/ *n.* a religious teacher, esp. one using a catechism.

catechize /ˈkatɪkʌɪz/ *v.tr.* (also **-ise**) **1** instruct by means of question and answer, esp. from a catechism. **2** put questions to; examine. □ **catechizer** *n.* [Late Latin *catechizare* from ecclesiastical Greek *katēkhizō*, from *katēkheō* 'make hear' (as CATA-, *ēkheō* 'sound')]

catecholamine /katɪˈkəʊləmiːn/ *n. Biochem.* any of a class of aromatic amines, many of which are neurotransmitters (e.g. adrenalin, dopamine). [*catechol* the parent compound (originally extracted from CATECHU) + AMINE]

catechu /ˈkatɪtʃuː/ *n.* (also **cachou** /ˈkaʃuː/) gambier or similar vegetable extract, containing tannin. [modern Latin from Malay *kachu*]

catechumen /katɪˈkjuːmɛn/ *n.* a Christian convert under instruction before baptism. [Middle English via Old French *catechumene* or ecclesiastical Latin *catechumenus* from Greek *katēkheō*: see CATECHIZE]

categorical /katɪˈgɒrɪk(ə)l/ *adj.* (also **categoric**) unconditional, absolute; explicit, direct (*a categorical refusal*). □ **categorically** *adv.* [French *catégorique* or Late Latin *categoricus* from Greek *katēgorikos*: see CATEGORY]

categorical imperative *n. Ethics* an unconditional moral obligation derived from pure reason; the bidding of conscience as ultimate moral law.

categorize /ˈkatɪgərʌɪz/ *v.tr.* (also **-ise**) place in a category or categories. □ **categorization** /-ˈzeɪʃ(ə)n/ *n.*

category /ˈkatɪg(ə)ri/ *n.* (*pl.* **-ies**) **1** a class or division. **2** *Philos.* **a** one of a possibly exhaustive set of classes among which all things might be distributed. **b** one of the a priori conceptions applied by the mind to sense-impressions. **c** any relatively fundamental philosophical concept. □ **categorial** /-'gɔ:rɪəl/ *adj.* [French *catégorie* or Late Latin *categoria* from Greek *katēgoria* 'statement', from *katēgoros* 'accuser']

catena /kə'ti:nə/ *n.* (*pl.* **catenae** /-nɪ/ or **catenas**) **1** a connected series of patristic comments on Scripture. **2** a series or chain. [Latin, = chain: originally *catena patrum* 'chain of the Fathers' (of the Church)]

catenary /kə'ti:nəri/ *n. & adj.* ● *n.* (*pl.* **-ies**) a curve formed by a uniform chain hanging freely from two points not in the same vertical line. ● *adj.* of or resembling such a curve. [Latin *catenarius* from *catena* 'chain']

catenary bridge *n.* a suspension bridge hung from catenaries.

catenate /'katɪneɪt/ *v.tr.* connect like links of a chain. □ **catenation** /-'neɪʃ(ə)n/ *n.* [Latin *catenare catenat-* (as CATENARY)]

cater /'keɪtə/ *v.* **1 a** *intr.* (often foll. by *for*) provide food. **b** *tr.* (as **catered** *adj.*) esp. *N. Amer.* with food provided, esp. by a professional caterer (*catered party*). **2** *intr.* (foll. by *for, to*) provide what is desired or needed by. **3** *intr.* (foll. by *to*) pander to (esp. low tastes). [obsolete noun *cater* (now *caterer*), from Anglo-French *acatour* 'buyer' from *acater* 'buy', ultimately from Latin *captare* 'seize']

cateran /'kat(ə)r(ə)n/ *n. Sc. hist.* a Highland irregular fighting man; a marauder. [Middle English from medieval Latin *cateranus* & Gaelic *ceathairne* 'peasantry']

cater-cornered /'keɪtəkɔ:nəd/ *adj. & adv.* (also **cater-corner**, **catty-cornered** /'katɪ-/, **kitty-cornered** /'kɪtɪ-/) *N. Amer.* ● *adj.* placed or situated diagonally. ● *adv.* diagonally. [dialect adv. *cater* 'diagonally' (related to obsolete *cater* 'the four on dice', via French *quatre* from Latin *quattuor* 'four')]

caterer /'keɪt(ə)rə/ *n.* a person who supplies food for social events, esp. professionally.

catering /'keɪt(ə)rɪŋ/ *n.* the work of a caterer.

caterpillar /'katəpɪlə/ *n.* **1 a** the larva of a butterfly or moth. **b** (in general use) any similar larva of various insects. **2 a** (in full **caterpillar track** or **tread**) *propr.* an endless articulated steel band passing round the wheels of a tractor etc. for travel on rough ground. **b** a vehicle with these tracks, e.g. a tractor or tank. [perhaps Anglo-French variant of Old French *chatepelose*, literally 'hairy cat', influenced by obsolete *piller* 'ravager']

caterwaul /'katəwɔ:l/ *v. & n.* ● *v.intr.* make the shrill howl of a cat. ● *n.* a caterwauling noise. [Middle English from CAT[1] + *-waul* (imitative)]

catfish /'katfɪʃ/ *n.* (*pl.* usu. same) any of various esp. freshwater fish, usu. having whisker-like barbels round the mouth.

cat flap *n.* (also **cat door**) a small swinging flap in an outer door, for a cat to pass in and out.

catgut /'katgʌt/ *n.* a material used for the strings of musical instruments and surgical sutures, made of the dried twisted intestines of the sheep, horse, or ass (but not the cat).

Cath. *abbr.* **1** Cathedral. **2** Catholic.

Cathar /'kaθɑ:/ *n.* (*pl.* **Cathars** or **Cathari** /-ri/) a member of a medieval sect which sought to achieve great spiritual purity. □ **Catharism** *n.* **Catharist** *n.* [medieval Latin *Cathari* (pl.) from Greek *katharoi* 'pure']

catharsis /kə'θɑ:sɪs/ *n.* (*pl.* **catharses** /-si:z/) **1** an emotional release in drama or art. **2** *Psychol.* the process of freeing repressed emotion by association with the cause, and elimination by abreaction. **3** *Med.* purgation. [modern Latin from Greek *katharsis*, from *kathairō* 'cleanse': sense 1 from Aristotle's *Poetics*]

cathartic /kə'θɑ:tɪk/ *adj. & n.* ● *adj.* **1** effecting catharsis. **2** purgative. ● *n.* a cathartic drug. □ **cathartically** *adv.* [Late Latin *catharticus* from Greek *kathartikos* (as CATHARSIS)]

Cathay /ka'θeɪ/ *n. archaic* or *poet.* the country China. [medieval Latin *Cataya*]

cathead /'kathɛd/ *n. Naut.* a horizontal beam from each side of a ship's bow for raising and carrying the anchor.

cathectic see CATHEXIS.

cathedral /kə'θi:dr(ə)l/ *n.* the principal church of a diocese, containing the bishop's throne. [Middle English (as *adj.*) from Old French *cathedral* or from Late Latin *cathedralis*, via Latin from Greek *kathedra* 'seat']

cathedral city *n.* a city in which there is a cathedral.

Catherine wheel /'kaθrɪn/ *n.* **1** a firework in the form of a flat coil which spins when fixed and lit. **2** a circular window with radial divisions. [modern Latin *Catharina* from Greek *Aikaterina*, the name of a saint martyred on a spiked wheel]

catheter /'kaθɪtə/ *n. Med.* a tube for insertion into a body cavity for introducing or removing fluid. [Late Latin from Greek *kathetēr*, from *kathiēmi* 'send down']

catheterize /'kaθɪtərʌɪz/ *v.tr.* (also **-ise**) *Med.* insert a catheter into.

cathetometer /kaθɪ'tɒmɪtə/ *n.* a telescope mounted on a graduated scale along which it can slide, used for accurate measurement of small vertical distances. [Latin *cathetus* from Greek *kathetos* 'perpendicular line' (as CATHETER + -METER)]

cathexis /kə'θɛksɪs/ *n.* (*pl.* **cathexes** /-si:z/) *Psychol.* concentration of mental energy in one channel. □ **cathectic** *adj.* [Greek *kathexis* 'retention']

cathode /'kaθəʊd/ *n.* (also **kathode**) *Electr.* **1** the positive terminal of an electrical device (opp. ANODE). **2** the terminal or electrode by which electric current leaves a device. □ **cathodal** *adj.* **cathodic** /kə'θɒdɪk/ *adj.* [Greek *kathodos* 'descent' (as CATA- + *hodos* 'way')]

cathode ray *n.* a beam of electrons emitted from the cathode of a high-vacuum tube.

cathode ray tube *n.* a high-vacuum tube in which cathode rays produce a luminous image on a fluorescent screen (abbr.: **CRT**).

cathodic protection *n.* protection of a metal structure from corrosion underwater by making it act as an electrical cathode.

catholic /'kaθ(ə)lɪk/ *adj. & n.* ● *adj.* **1** of interest or use to all; universal. **2** all-embracing; of wide sympathies or interests (*has catholic tastes*). **3** (**Catholic**) **a** of the Roman Catholic religion. **b** including all Christians. **c** including all of the Western Church. ● *n.* (**Catholic**) a Roman Catholic. □ **catholically** *adv.* **Catholicism** /kə'θɒlɪsɪz(ə)m/ *n.* **catholicity** /kaθə'lɪsɪti/ *n.* **catholicly** *adv.* [Middle English via Old French *catholique* or Late Latin *catholicus* from Greek *katholikos* 'universal', from *kata* 'in respect of' + *holos* 'whole']

catholicize /kə'θɒlɪsʌɪz/ *v.tr. & intr.* (also **-ise**) **1** make or become catholic. **2** (**Catholicize**) make or become a Roman Catholic.

cat-ice *n.* thin ice unsupported by water.

cation /'katʌɪən/ *n.* a positively charged ion; an ion that is attracted to the cathode in electrolysis (opp. ANION). [CATA- + ION]

cationic /katʌɪ'ɒnɪk/ *adj.* **1** of a cation or cations. **2** having an active cation.

catkin /'katkɪn/ *n.* a spike of usu. downy or silky male or female flowers hanging from a willow, hazel, etc. [obsolete Dutch *katteken* 'kitten']

catlick /'katlɪk/ *n. Brit. colloq.* a perfunctory wash.

catlike /'katlʌɪk/ *adj.* **1** like a cat. **2** stealthy.

catmint /'katmɪnt/ *n.* esp. *Brit.* a plant, *Nepeta cataria* (mint family), with downy leaves, purple-spotted white flowers, and a mintlike smell attractive to cats. Also called *catnip*.

catnap /'katnap/ *n. & v.* ● *n.* a short sleep. ● *v.intr.* (**-napped**, **-napping**) have a catnap.

catnip /ˈkatnɪp/ *n.* = CATMINT. [CAT[1] + dialect *nip* 'catmint', variant of dialect *nep* from medieval Latin *nepta* from Latin *nepeta*]

cat-o'-nine-tails *n. hist.* a rope whip with nine knotted lashes for flogging sailors, soldiers, or criminals.

catoptric /kaˈtɒptrɪk/ *adj.* of or relating to a mirror, a reflector, or reflection. □ **catoptrics** *n.* [Greek *katoptrikos* from *katoptron* 'mirror']

cat's cradle *n.* a child's game in which a loop of string is held between the fingers and patterns are formed.

Catseye /ˈkatsʌɪ/ *n. Brit. propr.* one of a series of reflector studs set into a road.

cat's-eye /ˈkatsʌɪ/ *n.* a precious stone of Sri Lanka and the Malabar Coast.

cat's-foot *n.* a small plant of the genus *Antennaria* (daisy family), having soft woolly leaves and growing on the surface of the ground.

cat's-paw *n.* **1** a person used as a tool by another. **2** a slight breeze rippling the surface of water.

cat's-tail *n.* = REED MACE.

catsuit /ˈkatsuːt, -sjuːt/ *n. Brit.* a close-fitting garment with trouser legs, covering the body from neck to feet.

catsup *US* var. of KETCHUP.

cat's whisker *n.* a fine adjustable wire in a crystal radio receiver. □ **the cat's whiskers** (or **pyjamas**) *slang* an excellent person or thing.

cattery /ˈkatəri/ *n.* (*pl.* **-ies**) a place where cats are boarded or bred.

cattish /ˈkatɪʃ/ *adj.* = CATTY. □ **cattishly** *adv.* **cattishness** *n.*

cattle /ˈkat(ə)l/ *n.pl.* **1** large ruminant animals with horns and cloven hoofs, e.g. cows, bison, and buffalo, esp. of the genus *Bos.* **2** *archaic* livestock. [Middle English & Anglo-French *catel* from Old French *chatel* CHATTEL]

cattle cake *n. Brit.* a concentrated food for cattle, in cake form.

cattle grid *n. Brit.* a grid covering a ditch, allowing vehicles to pass over but not cattle, sheep, etc.

cattle guard *n. N. Amer.* = CATTLE GRID.

cattleman /ˈkat(ə)lmən/ *n.* (*pl.* **-men**) *N. Amer.* a person who tends or rears cattle.

cattle-plague *n.* rinderpest.

cattle stop *n. NZ* = CATTLE GRID.

cattleya /ˈkatlɪə/ *n.* any epiphytic orchid of the genus *Cattleya*, with violet, pink, or yellow flowers. [modern Latin, named after W. *Cattley*, English patron of botany d. 1832]

catty /ˈkati/ *adj.* (**cattier**, **cattiest**) **1** sly, spiteful; deliberately hurtful in speech. **2** catlike. □ **cattily** *adv.* **cattiness** *n.*

catty-cornered var. of CATER-CORNERED.

catwalk /ˈkatwɔːk/ *n.* **1** a narrow footway along a bridge, above a theatre stage, etc. **2** a narrow platform or gangway used in fashion shows etc.

Caucasian /kɔːˈkeɪzjən, -ʒ(ə)n/ *adj. & n.* ● *adj.* **1** of or relating to the white or light-skinned division of humankind. **2** of or relating to the Caucasus. ● *n.* a Caucasian person. [*Caucasus*, mountains between the Black Sea and Caspian Sea, the supposed place of origin of this people]

Caucasoid /ˈkɔːkəsɔɪd/ *adj.* = CAUCASIAN *adj.* 1.

caucus /ˈkɔːkəs/ *n. & v.* ● *n.* (*pl.* **caucuses**) **1** (in N. America and New Zealand) **a** a meeting of the members of a legislative body belonging to a particular political party, to decide policy. **b** a bloc of such members. **c** this system as a political force. **2** often *derog.* (esp. in the UK) **a** a usu. secret meeting of a group within a larger organization or party. **b** such a group. ● *v.intr.* (**caucused**, **caucusing**) hold or form a caucus. [18th-c. US, perhaps from Algonquian *cau'-cau-as'u* 'adviser']

caudal /ˈkɔːd(ə)l/ *adj.* **1** of or like a tail. **2** of the posterior part of the body. □ **caudally** *adv.* [modern Latin *caudalis* from Latin *cauda* 'tail']

caudate /ˈkɔːdeɪt/ *adj.* having a tail. [see CAUDAL]

caudillo /kaʊˈdiːljəʊ/ *n.* (*pl.* **-os**) (in Spanish-speaking countries) a military or political leader. [Spanish from Late Latin *capitellum*, diminutive of *caput* 'head']

caught *past* and *past part.* of CATCH.

caul /kɔːl/ *n.* **1 a** the inner membrane enclosing a foetus. **b** part of this occasionally found on a child's head at birth, thought to bring good luck. **2** *hist.* **a** a woman's close-fitting indoor headdress. **b** the plain back part of a woman's indoor headdress. **3** the omentum. [Middle English perhaps from Old French *cale* 'small cap']

cauldron /ˈkɔːldr(ə)n, ˈkɒl-/ *n.* (also **caldron**) a large deep bowl-shaped vessel for boiling over an open fire; an ornamental vessel resembling this. [Middle English from Anglo-French & Old Northern French *caudron*, ultimately from Latin *caldarium* 'hot bath' from *calidus* 'hot']

cauliflower /ˈkɒlɪflaʊə/ *n.* **1** a variety of cabbage with a large immature flower head of small usu. creamy-white flower buds. **2** the flower head eaten as a vegetable. [earlier *cole-florie* etc. from obsolete French *chou fleuri* 'flowered cabbage', assimilated to COLE and FLOWER]

cauliflower cheese *n. Brit.* a savoury dish of cauliflower in a cheese sauce.

cauliflower ear *n.* an ear thickened or deformed by repeated blows, esp. in boxing.

caulk /kɔːk/ *n. & v.* (*US* also **calk**) ● *n.* a waterproof filler and sealant, used in building (*bathroom caulk*). ● *v.tr.* **1** seal (a seam etc.) with caulk. **2 a** stop up (the seams of a boat etc.) with oakum etc. and waterproofing material, or by driving plate-junctions together. **b** make (esp. a boat) watertight by this method. □ **caulker** *n.* [Old French dialect *cauquer* 'tread, press with force', from Latin *calcare* 'tread' from *calx* 'heel']

causal /ˈkɔːz(ə)l/ *adj.* **1** of, forming, or expressing a cause or causes. **2** relating to, or of the nature of, cause and effect. □ **causally** *adv.* [Late Latin *causalis*: see CAUSE]

causality /kɔːˈzalɪti/ *n.* **1** the relation of cause and effect. **2** the principle that everything has a cause.

causation /kɔːˈzeɪʃ(ə)n/ *n.* **1** the act of causing or producing an effect. **2** = CAUSALITY 1. [French *causation* or Latin *causatio* 'pretext' etc., in medieval Latin 'the action of causing', from *causare* CAUSE]

causative /ˈkɔːzətɪv/ *adj.* **1** acting as cause. **2** (foll. by *of*) producing; having as effect. **3** *Gram.* expressing cause. □ **causatively** *adv.* [Middle English from Old French *causatif* or from Late Latin *causativus*: see CAUSATION]

cause /kɔːz/ *n. & v.* ● *n.* **1 a** that which produces an effect, or gives rise to an action, phenomenon, or condition. **b** a person or thing that occasions something. **c** a reason or motive; a ground that may be held to justify something (*no cause for complaint*). **2** a reason adjudged adequate (*show cause*). **3** a principle, belief, or purpose which is advocated or supported (*faithful to the cause*). **4 a** a matter to be settled at law. **b** an individual's case offered at law (*plead a cause*). **5** the side taken by any party in a dispute. ● *v.tr.* **1** be the cause of, produce, make happen (*caused a commotion*). **2** (foll. by *to* + infin.) induce (*caused me to smile*; *caused it to be done*). □ **cause and effect 1** a cause and the effect it produces; the doctrine of causation. **2** the operation or relation of a cause and its effect. **in the cause of** to maintain, defend, or support (*in the cause of justice*). **make common cause with** join the side of. □ **causable** *adj.* **causeless** *adj.* **causer** *n.* [Middle English via Old French from Latin *causa* (*n.*), *causare* (*v.*)]

'cause /kɒz, kəz/ *conj. & adv. colloq.* = BECAUSE. [abbreviation]

cause célèbre /kɔːz sɛˈlɛbr(ə)/ *n.* (*pl.* **causes célèbres** *pronunc.* same) **1** a lawsuit that attracts much attention. **2** an issue that gives rise to widespread public discussion. [French]

causerie /ˈkəʊzəri, French kozri/ *n.* (*pl.* ***causeries*** *pronunc.* same) an informal article or talk, esp. on a literary subject. [French from *causer* 'talk']

causeway /ˈkɔːzweɪ/ *n.* **1** a raised road or track across low or wet ground or a stretch of water. **2** a raised path by a road. [earlier *cauce, cauceway* from Old Northern French *caucié,* ultimately from Latin CALX 'lime, limestone']

causey /ˈkɔːzi, -si/ *n. archaic* or *dial.* = CAUSEWAY.

caustic /ˈkɔːstɪk, ˈkɒst-/ *adj. & n.* ● *adj.* **1** that burns or corrodes organic tissue. **2** sarcastic, biting. **3** *Chem.* strongly alkaline. **4** *Physics* formed by the intersection of reflected or refracted parallel rays from a curved surface. ● *n.* **1** a caustic substance. **2** *Physics* a caustic surface or curve. □ **caustically** *adv.* **causticity** /-ˈtɪsɪti/ *n.* [Latin *causticus* from Greek *kaustikos,* from *kaustos* 'burnt', from *kaiō* 'burn']

caustic potash *n.* potassium hydroxide.

caustic soda *n.* sodium hydroxide.

cauterize /ˈkɔːtərʌɪz/ *v.tr.* (also **-ise**) *Med.* burn or coagulate (tissue) with a heated instrument or caustic substance, esp. to stop bleeding. □ **cauterization** /-ˈzeɪʃ(ə)n/ *n.* [French *cautériser* via Late Latin *cauterizare* from Greek *kautēriazō,* from *kautērion* 'branding-iron', from *kaiō* 'burn']

cautery /ˈkɔːt(ə)ri/ *n.* (*pl.* **-ies**) *Med.* **1** an instrument or caustic for cauterizing. **2** the operation of cauterizing. [Latin *cauterium* from Greek *kautērion*: see CAUTERIZE]

caution /ˈkɔːʃ(ə)n/ *n. & v.* ● *n.* **1** attention to safety; prudence, carefulness. **2 a** esp. *Brit.* a warning, esp. a formal one in law. **b** a formal warning and reprimand. **3** *colloq.* an amusing or surprising person or thing. ● *v.tr.* **1** (often foll. by *against,* or *to* + infin.) warn or admonish. **2** esp. *Brit.* issue a caution to. [Middle English via Old French from Latin *cautio -onis,* from *cavēre caut-* 'take heed']

cautionary /ˈkɔːʃ(ə)n(ə)ri/ *adj.* that gives or serves as a warning (*a cautionary tale*).

caution money *n. Brit.* a sum deposited as security for good conduct.

cautious /ˈkɔːʃəs/ *adj.* careful, prudent; attentive to safety. □ **cautiously** *adv.* **cautiousness** *n.* [Middle English via Old French from Latin: see CAUTION]

cavalcade /kav(ə)lˈkeɪd, ˈkav(ə)lkeɪd/ *n.* a procession or formal company of riders, motor vehicles, etc. [French from Italian *cavalcata* from *cavalcare* 'ride', ultimately from Latin *caballus* 'packhorse']

cavalier /kavəˈlɪə/ *n. & adj.* ● *n.* **1** *hist.* (**Cavalier**) a supporter of Charles I in the Civil War. **2** a courtly gentleman, esp. as a lady's escort. **3** *archaic* a horseman. ● *adj.* offhand, supercilious, blasé. □ **cavalierly** *adv.* [French from Italian *cavaliere,* ultimately from Latin *caballus* 'horse': cf. CABALLERO, CHEVALIER]

cavalry /ˈkav(ə)lri/ *n.* (*pl.* **-ies**) (usu. treated as *pl.*) soldiers on horseback or in armoured vehicles. [French *cavallerie* via Italian *cavalleria* from *cavallo* 'horse', from Latin *caballus*]

cavalryman /ˈkav(ə)lrɪmən/ *n.* (*pl.* **-men**) a soldier of a cavalry regiment.

cavalry twill *n.* a strong fabric in a double twill.

cavatina /kavəˈtiːnə/ *n.* **1** a short simple song. **2** a similar piece of instrumental music, usu. slow and emotional. [Italian]

cave[1] /keɪv/ *n. & v.* ● *n.* **1** a large hollow in the side of a cliff, hill, etc., or underground. **2** *Brit. hist.* a dissident political group. ● *v.intr.* explore caves, esp. interconnecting or underground. □ **cave in 1 a** (of a wall, earth over a hollow, etc.) subside, collapse. **b** cause (a wall, earth, etc.) to do this. **2** yield or submit under pressure; give up. □ **cavelike** *adj.* **caver** *n.* [Middle English via Old French from Latin *cava,* from *cavus* 'hollow': *cave in* probably from E. Anglian dialect *calve in,* ultimately from Germanic]

cave[2] /keɪvi/ *int. Brit. school slang* look out! (as a warning cry). □ **keep cave** act as lookout. [Latin, = beware]

caveat /ˈkavɪat, ˈkeɪ-/ *n.* **1** a warning or proviso. **2** *Law* a process in court to suspend proceedings. [Latin, = let a person beware]

caveat emptor /kavɪat ˈɛmptɔː/ *n.* the principle that the buyer alone is responsible if dissatisfied. [Latin, = let the buyer beware]

cave bear *n.* an extinct kind of large bear, whose bones have been found in caves.

cave dweller *n.* = CAVEMAN.

cave-in *n.* **1** a collapse of a wall, earth over a hollow, etc. **2** an instance of yielding under pressure.

caveman /ˈkeɪvman/ *n.* (*pl.* **-men**; *fem.* **cavewoman**, *pl.* **-women**) **1** a prehistoric man living in a cave. **2** a primitive or crude man.

cave painting *n.* a prehistoric or primitive picture on the interior of a cave, esp. depicting animals.

cavern /ˈkav(ə)n/ *n.* **1** a cave, esp. a large or dark one. **2** a dark cavelike place, e.g. a room. □ **cavernous** *adj.* **cavernously** *adv.* [Middle English from Old French *caverne* or from Latin *caverna,* from *cavus* 'hollow']

caviar /ˈkavɪɑː, kavɪˈɑː/ *n.* (also **caviare**) the pickled roe of sturgeon or other large fish, eaten as a delicacy. [early forms representing Italian *caviale,* French *caviar,* probably from medieval Greek *khaviari*]

cavil /ˈkav(ə)l/ *v. & n.* ● *v.intr.* (**cavilled**, **cavilling**; *US* **caviled**, **caviling**) (usu. foll. by *at, about*) make petty objections; carp. ● *n.* a trivial objection. □ **caviller** *n.* [French *caviller* from Latin *cavillari,* from *cavilla* 'mockery']

caving /ˈkeɪvɪŋ/ *n.* exploring caves as a sport or pastime.

cavitation /kavɪˈteɪʃ(ə)n/ *n.* **1** the formation of a cavity in a structure. **2** the formation of bubbles or cavities in a liquid by the movement through it of a propeller etc.

cavity /ˈkavɪti/ *n.* (*pl.* **-ies**) **1** a hollow within a solid body. **2** a decayed part of a tooth. [French *cavité* or Late Latin *cavitas,* from Latin *cavus* 'hollow']

cavity wall *n.* a wall formed from two skins of brick or blockwork with a space between.

cavort /kəˈvɔːt/ *v.intr. colloq.* caper excitedly; gambol, prance. [US, perhaps from CURVET]

cavy /ˈkeɪvi/ *n.* (*pl.* **-ies**) any small rodent of the family Caviidae, native to S. America and having a sturdy body and vestigial tail, including guinea pigs. [modern Latin *cavia* from Galibi *cabiai*]

caw /kɔː/ *n. & v.* ● *n.* the harsh cry of a rook, crow, etc. ● *v.intr.* utter this cry. [imitative]

cay /keɪ, kiː/ *n.* a low insular bank or reef of coral, sand, etc. (cf. KEY[2]). [Spanish *cayo* 'shoal, reef' from French *quai*: see QUAY]

cayenne /keɪˈɛn/ *n.* (in full **cayenne pepper**) a pungent red pepper prepared from ground dried chillies. [Tupi *kyynha* assimilated to *Cayenne,* the capital of French Guiana]

cayman /ˈkeɪmən/ *n.* (also **caiman**) any of several reptiles related to alligators, esp. of the genus *Caiman* of Central and S. America. [Spanish & Portuguese *caiman,* from Carib *acayuman*]

CB *abbr.* **1** citizens' band. **2** (in the UK) Companion of the Order of the Bath.

CBC *abbr.* Canadian Broadcasting Corporation.

CBE *abbr.* Commander of the Order of the British Empire.

CBI *abbr.* (in the UK) Confederation of British Industry.

CBS *abbr.* (in the US) Columbia Broadcasting System.

CC *abbr.* **1** *Brit.* **a** City Council. **b** County Council. **c** County Councillor. **2** Cricket Club. **3** Companion of the Order of Canada.

cc *abbr.* (also **c.c.**) **1** cubic centimetre(s). **2** carbon copy.

CCD *abbr. Electronics* charge-coupled device, a high-speed semiconductor device used esp. in image detection.

CD *abbr.* **1** compact disc. **2** Civil Defence. **3** *Corps Diplomatique.*
Cd *symb. Chem.* the element cadmium.
Cd. *abbr. Brit.* Command Paper (third series, 1900–18).
cd *abbr.* candela.
CDC *abbr.* (in the US) Centers for Disease Control.
Cdr. *abbr. Mil.* Commander.
Cdre. *abbr.* Commodore.
CD-ROM /siːdiːˈrɒm/ *abbr.* compact disc read-only memory (for retrieval of text or data on a VDU screen).
CDT *abbr.* **1** Central Daylight Time (one hour ahead of Central Standard Time). **2** craft, design, and technology.
CD video *n.* a system of simultaneously reproducing high-quality sound and video pictures from a compact disc.
CE *abbr.* **1** Church of England. **2** civil engineer. **3** Common Era.
Ce *symb. Chem.* the element cerium.
ceanothus /siːəˈnəʊθəs/ *n.* any shrub of the genus *Ceanothus*, with small blue or white flowers. [modern Latin, from Greek *keanōthos*, a kind of thistle]
cease /siːs/ *v. & n.* ● *v.tr. & intr.* stop; bring or come to an end (*ceased breathing*). ● *n.* (in **without cease**) unendingly. □ **cease fire** *Mil.* stop firing. [Middle English from Old French *cesser*, Latin *cessare* frequentative of *cedere cess-* 'yield']
ceasefire /ˈsiːsfʌɪə/ *n. Mil.* **1** an order to stop firing. **2** a period of truce; a suspension of hostilities.
ceaseless /ˈsiːslɪs/ *adj.* without end; not ceasing. □ **ceaselessly** *adv.*
cecitis *US* var. of CAECITIS.
cecum *US* var. of CAECUM.
cedar /ˈsiːdə/ *n.* **1** any spreading evergreen conifer of the genus *Cedrus*, bearing tufts of small needles and cones of papery scales, esp. (more fully **cedar of Lebanon**) *Cedrus libani*, native to Asia Minor. **2** any of various similar conifers yielding timber. **3** = CEDARWOOD. □ **cedarn** *adj. poet.* [Middle English via Old French *cedre* and Latin *cedrus* from Greek *kedros*]
cedarwood /ˈsiːdəwʊd/ *n.* the fragrant durable wood of any cedar tree.
cede /siːd/ *v.tr.* give up one's rights to or possession of. [French *céder* or Latin *cedere* 'yield']
cedi /ˈsiːdi/ *n.* (*pl.* same or **cedis**) the chief monetary unit of Ghana. [Ghanaian, perhaps from alteration of SHILLING]
cedilla /sɪˈdɪlə/ *n.* **1** a mark written under the letter *c*, esp. in French, to show that it is sibilant (as in *façade*). **2** a similar mark under *s* in Turkish and other oriental languages. [Spanish *cedilla*, diminutive of *zeda*, from Greek *zēta*, the letter Z]
Ceefax /ˈsiːfaks/ *n. Brit. propr.* a teletext service provided by the BBC. [representing the pronunciation of *see*ing + *fac*simile]
CEGB *abbr.* (in the UK) Central Electricity Generating Board.
ceilidh /ˈkeɪli/ *n.* orig. *Ir. & Sc.* an informal gathering for conversation, music, dancing, songs, and stories. [Gaelic, from Old Irish *céilide* 'visit, visiting' from *céile* 'companion']
ceiling /ˈsiːlɪŋ/ *n.* **1 a** the upper interior surface of a room or other similar compartment. **b** the material forming this. **2** an upper limit on prices, wages, performance, etc. **3** *Aeron.* the maximum altitude a given aircraft can reach. **4** *Naut.* the inside planking of a ship's bottom and sides. [Middle English *celynge*, *siling*, perhaps ultimately from Latin *caelum* 'heaven' or *celare* 'hide']
celadon /ˈsɛlədɒn/ *n. & adj.* ● *n.* **1** a willow-green colour. **2** a grey-green glaze used on some pottery. **3** Chinese pottery glazed in this way. ● *adj.* of a grey-green colour. [French, from the name of the hero in d'Urfé's pastoral romance *L'Astrée* (1607–27)]
celandine /ˈsɛləndʌɪn/ *n.* either of two yellow-flowered plants, the greater celandine, *Chelidonium majus*, and the lesser celandine, *Ranunculus ficaria*. [Middle English and Old French *celidoine*, ultimately from Greek *khelidōn* 'swallow': the flowering of the plant was associated with the arrival of swallows]
-cele /siːl/ *comb. form* (also **-coele**) *Med.* swelling, hernia (*gastrocele*). [Greek *kēlē* 'tumour']
celeb /sɪˈlɛb/ *n. colloq.* = CELEBRITY 1. [abbreviation]
celebrant /ˈsɛlɪbr(ə)nt/ *n.* a person who performs a rite, esp. a priest at the Eucharist. [French *célébrant* or Latin *celebrare celebrant-*: see CELEBRATE]
celebrate /ˈsɛlɪbreɪt/ *v.* **1** *tr.* mark (a festival or special event) with festivities etc. **2** *tr.* perform publicly and duly (a religious ceremony etc.). **3 a** *tr.* officiate at (the Eucharist). **b** *intr.* officiate, esp. at the Eucharist. **4** *intr.* engage in festivities, usu. after a special event etc. **5** *tr.* (esp. as **celebrated** *adj.*) honour publicly, make widely known. □ **celebration** /-ˈbreɪʃ(ə)n/ *n.* **celebrator** *n.* **celebratory** *adj.* [Latin *celebrare* from *celeber -bris* 'frequented, honoured']
celebrity /sɪˈlɛbrɪti/ *n.* (*pl.* **-ies**) **1** a well-known person. **2** fame. [French *célébrité* or Latin *celebritas*, from *celeber*: see CELEBRATE]
celeriac /sɪˈlɛrɪak/ *n.* a variety of celery with a swollen turnip-like stem base used as a vegetable. [CELERY: *-ac* is unexplained]
celerity /sɪˈlɛrɪti/ *n. archaic* or *literary* swiftness (esp. of a living creature). [Middle English via French *célérité* from Latin *celeritas -tatis*, from *celer* 'swift']
celery /ˈsɛləri/ *n.* an umbelliferous plant, *Apium graveolens*, with closely packed succulent leaf-stalks used as a vegetable. [French *céleri* via Italian dialect *selleri* and Latin *selinum* from Greek *selinon* 'parsley']
celery pine *n.* an Australasian tree, *Phyllocladus trichomanoides*, with branchlets like celery leaves.
celesta /sɪˈlɛstə/ *n. Mus.* a small keyboard instrument resembling a glockenspiel, with hammers striking steel plates suspended over wooden resonators, giving an ethereal bell-like sound. [pseudo-Latin from French *céleste*: see CELESTE]
celeste /sɪˈlɛst/ *n. Mus.* **1** an organ and harmonium stop with a soft tremulous tone. **2** = CELESTA. [French *céleste* 'heavenly' from Latin *caelestis*, from *caelum* 'heaven']
celestial /sɪˈlɛstɪəl/ *adj.* **1** heavenly; divinely good or beautiful; sublime. **2** of the sky, or of outer space as observed in astronomy etc. □ **celestially** *adv.* [Middle English via Old French and medieval Latin from Latin *caelestis*: see CELESTE]
celestial equator *n.* the great circle of the sky in the plane perpendicular to the earth's axis.
celestial horizon see HORIZON 1c.
celestial navigation *n.* navigation by the stars etc.
celestial sphere *n.* an imaginary sphere of which the observer is the centre and in which celestial objects are represented as lying.
celiac *US* var. of COELIAC.
celibate /ˈsɛlɪbət/ *adj. & n.* ● *adj.* **1** committed to abstention from sexual relations and from marriage, esp. for religious reasons. **2** abstaining from sexual relations. ● *n.* a celibate person. □ **celibacy** *n.* [French *célibat* or Latin *caelibatus* 'unmarried state', from *caelebs -ibis* 'unmarried']
cell /sɛl/ *n.* **1** a small room, esp. in a prison or monastery. **2** a small compartment, e.g. in a honeycomb. **3** a small group as a nucleus of political activity, esp. of a subversive kind. **4** *hist.* a small monastery or nunnery dependent on a larger one. **5** *Biol.* **a** the structural and functional usu. microscopic unit of an organism, consisting of cytoplasm and a nucleus enclosed in a membrane. **b** an enclosed cavity in an organism etc. **6** *Electr.* a vessel for containing electrodes within an electrolyte for current-generation or electrolysis. □ **celled** *adj.* (also in *comb.*). **cell-like** *adj.* [Middle English from Old French *celle* or from Latin *cella* 'storeroom, chamber']
cellar /ˈsɛlə/ *n. & v.* ● *n.* **1** a room below ground level in a house, used for storage, esp. of wine or coal. **2** a stock of wine in a cellar (*has a good cellar*). ● *v.tr.* store or

put in a cellar. [Middle English via Anglo-French *celer*, Old French *celier* from Late Latin *cellarium* 'storehouse']

cellarage /ˈsɛlərɪdʒ/ *n.* **1** cellar accommodation. **2** the charge for the use of a cellar or storehouse.

cellarer /ˈsɛlərə/ *n. hist.* a monastic officer in charge of wine.

cellaret /sɛləˈrɛt/ *n.* (*US* also **cellarette**) a case or sideboard for holding wine bottles in a dining room.

cellarman /ˈsɛləmən/ *n.* a man in charge of a wine cellar.

cell block *n.* a block of prison cells.

Cellnet /ˈsɛlnɛt/ *n. propr.* a cellular telephone service.

cello /ˈtʃɛləʊ/ *n.* (*pl.* **-os**) a bass instrument of the violin family, held upright on the floor between the legs of the seated player. ◻ **cellist** *n.* [abbreviation of VIOLONCELLO]

cellophane /ˈsɛləfeɪn/ *n. propr.* a thin transparent wrapping material made from viscose. [CELLULOSE + *-phane* (suggested by DIAPHANOUS)]

cellphone /ˈsɛlfəʊn/ *n.* a small portable radio-telephone having access to a cellular radio system.

cellular /ˈsɛljʊlə/ *adj.* **1** of or having small compartments or cavities. **2** of open texture; porous. **3** *Physiol.* of or consisting of cells. **4** designating or relating to a mobile telephone system that uses a number of short-range radio stations to cover the area it serves, the signal being automatically switched from one station to another as the user travels about. ◻ **cellularity** /-ˈlarɪti/ *n.* **cellulate** *adj.* **cellulous** *adj.* [French *cellulaire* from modern Latin *cellularis*: see CELLULE]

cellular blanket *n.* a blanket of open texture.

cellular phone *n.* (also **cellular radio**) a system of mobile radio-telephone transmission with an area divided into 'cells' each served by its own small transmitter.

cellular plant *n.* a plant with no distinct stem, leaves, etc.

cellule /ˈsɛljuːl/ *n. Biol.* a small cell or cavity. [French *cellule* or Latin *cellula*, diminutive of *cella* CELL]

cellulite /ˈsɛljʊlʌɪt/ *n.* a lumpy form of fat, esp. on the hips and thighs of women, causing puckering of the skin. [French (as CELLULE)]

cellulitis /sɛljʊˈlʌɪtɪs/ *n.* inflammation of subcutaneous connective tissue.

celluloid /ˈsɛljʊlɔɪd/ *n.* **1** a transparent flammable plastic made from camphor and nitrocellulose. **2** cinema film. [CELLULOSE + -OID]

cellulose /ˈsɛljʊləʊz, -s/ *n.* **1** *Biochem.* a carbohydrate forming the main constituent of plant cell walls, used in the production of textile fibres. **2** (in general use) a paint or lacquer consisting of esp. cellulose acetate or nitrate in solution. ◻ **cellulosic** /-ˈləʊsɪk/ *adj.* [French (as CELLULE)]

cellulose acetate *n. Chem.* the cellulose ester of acetic acid, widely used as an artificial fibre or plastic.

cell wall *n. Biol.* the rigid layer that encloses a plant or bacterial cell.

celom *US* var. of COELOM.

Celsius /ˈsɛlsɪəs/ *adj.* of or denoting a temperature on the Celsius scale. [named after A. *Celsius*, Swedish astronomer d. 1744]

■ **Usage** See Usage Note at CENTIGRADE.

Celsius scale *n.* a scale of temperature on which water freezes at 0° and boils at 100° under standard conditions.

Celt /kɛlt, s-/ *n.* a member of a group of western European peoples, including the pre-Roman inhabitants of Britain and Gaul and their descendants, esp. in Ireland, Wales, Scotland, Cornwall, Brittany, and the Isle of Man. [Latin *Celtae* (pl.) from Greek *Keltoi*]

celt /sɛlt/ *n. Archaeol.* a stone or metal prehistoric implement with a chisel edge. [medieval Latin *celtes* 'chisel']

Celtic /ˈkɛltɪk, ˈs-/ *adj. & n.* ● *adj.* of or relating to the Celts. ● *n.* a group of languages spoken by Celtic peoples, including Gaelic, Welsh, Cornish, and Breton. ◻ **Celticism** /-sɪz(ə)m/ *n.* [Latin *celticus* (as CELT) or French *celtique*]

Celtic cross *n.* a Latin cross with a circle round the centre.

Celtic fringe *n.* **1** the Highland Scots, Irish, Welsh, and Cornish in relation to the rest of Britain. **2** the land inhabited by these peoples.

cembalo /ˈtʃɛmbələʊ/ *n.* (*pl.* **-os**) a harpsichord. ◻ **cembalist** *n.* [abbreviation of CLAVICEMBALO]

cement /sɪˈmɛnt/ *n. & v.* ● *n.* **1** a powdery substance made by calcining lime and clay, mixed with water to form mortar or used in concrete (see also PORTLAND CEMENT). **2** any similar substance that hardens and fastens on setting. **3** a uniting factor or principle. **4** a substance for filling cavities in teeth. **5** (also **cementum**) *Anat.* a thin layer of bony material that fixes teeth to the jaw. ● *v.tr.* **1 a** unite with or as with cement. **b** establish or strengthen (a friendship etc.). **2** apply cement to. **3** line or cover with cement. ◻ **cementer** *n.* [Middle English via Old French *ciment* from Latin *caementum* 'quarry stone', from *caedere* 'hew']

cementation /siːmɛnˈteɪʃ(ə)n/ *n.* **1** the act or process of cementing or being cemented. **2** the heating of iron with charcoal powder to form steel.

cement mixer *n.* a machine (usu. with a revolving drum) for mixing cement with water.

cemetery /ˈsɛmɪtri/ *n.* (*pl.* **-ies**) a burial ground, esp. one not in a churchyard. [Late Latin *coemeterium* from Greek *koimētērion* 'dormitory', from *koimaō* 'put to sleep']

C.Eng. *abbr. Brit.* chartered engineer.

cenobite *US* var. of COENOBITE.

cenotaph /ˈsɛnətɑːf, -taf/ *n.* a tomblike monument, esp. a war memorial, to a dead person whose body is elsewhere. [French *cénotaphe* from Late Latin *cenotaphium*, from Greek *kenos* 'empty' + *taphos* 'tomb']

Cenozoic /siːnəˈzəʊɪk/ *adj. & n.* (also **Cainozoic** /kʌɪnə-/) *Geol.* ● *adj.* of or relating to the most recent era of geological time, marked by the evolution and development of mammals, birds, and flowers. Cf. Appendix X. ● *n.* this era (cf. MESOZOIC, PALAEOZOIC). [Greek *kainos* 'new' + *zōion* 'animal']

censer /ˈsɛnsə/ *n.* a vessel in which incense is burnt, esp. during a religious procession or ceremony. [Middle English from Anglo-French *censer*, Old French *censier* from *encens* INCENSE[1]]

censor /ˈsɛnsə/ *n. & v.* ● *n.* **1** an official authorized to examine printed matter, films, news, etc., before public release, and to suppress any parts on the grounds of obscenity, a threat to security, etc. **2** *Rom.Hist.* either of two annual magistrates responsible for holding censuses and empowered to supervise public morals. **3** *Psychol.* an impulse which is said to prevent certain ideas and memories from emerging into consciousness. ● *v.tr.* **1** act as a censor of. **2** make deletions or changes in. ◻ **censorial** /-ˈsɔːrɪəl/ *adj.* **censorship** *n.* [Latin from *censēre* 'assess': in sense 3 mistranslation of German *Zensur* 'censorship']

■ **Usage** As a verb, *censor* is often confused with *censure* 'to criticize sharply'.

censorious /sɛnˈsɔːrɪəs/ *adj.* severely critical; fault-finding; quick or eager to criticize. ◻ **censoriously** *adv.* **censoriousness** *n.* [Latin *censorius*: see CENSOR]

censure /ˈsɛnʃə/ *v. & n.* ● *v.tr.* criticize harshly; reprove. ● *n.* harsh criticism; expression of disapproval. ◻ **censurable** *adj.* [Middle English via Old French from Latin *censura*, from *censēre* 'assess']

■ **Usage** See Usage Note at CENSOR.

census /ˈsɛnsəs/ *n.* (*pl.* **censuses**) the official count of a population or of a class of things, often with various statistics noted. [Latin from *censēre* 'assess']

cent /sɛnt/ *n.* **1 a** a monetary unit in various countries, equal to one-hundredth of a dollar or other decimal currency unit. **b** a coin of this value. **2** *colloq.* a very small sum of money. **3** see PER CENT. [French *cent*, Italian *cento*, or Latin *centum* 'hundred']

cent. *abbr.* century.

centaur /'sɛntɔː/ *n.* a creature in Greek mythology with the head, arms, and torso of a man and the body and legs of a horse. [Middle English via Latin *centaurus* from Greek *kentauros*, of unknown origin: the Greek name for a Thessalonian tribe of expert horsemen]

centaury /'sɛntɔːri/ *n.* (*pl.* **-ies**) any plant of the genus *Centaurium*, esp. *C. erythraea*, formerly used in medicine. [Late Latin *centaurea*, ultimately from Greek *kentauros* CENTAUR: from the legend that it was discovered by the centaur Chiron]

centavo /sɛn'tɑːvəʊ/ *n.* (*pl.* **-os**) a small coin of Spain, Portugal, and some Latin American countries, worth one-hundredth of the standard unit. [Spanish from Latin *centum* 'hundred']

centenarian /sɛntɪ'nɛːrɪən/ *n.* & *adj.* ● *n.* a person a hundred or more years old. ● *adj.* a hundred or more years old.

centenary /sɛn'tiːnəri, -'tɛn-; 'sɛntɪnəri/ *n.* & *adj.* ● *n.* (*pl.* **-ies**) **1** a hundredth anniversary. **2** a celebration of this. ● *adj.* **1** of or relating to a centenary. **2** occurring every hundred years. [Latin *centenarius* via *centeni* 'a hundred each' from *centum* 'a hundred']

centennial /sɛn'tɛnɪəl/ *adj.* & *n.* ● *adj.* **1** lasting for a hundred years. **2** occurring every hundred years. ● *n.* = CENTENARY *n.* [Latin *centum* 'a hundred', on the pattern of BIENNIAL]

center *US* var. of CENTRE.

centerboard *US* var. of CENTREBOARD.

centerfold *US* var. of CENTREFOLD.

centering *US* var. of CENTRING.

centesimal /sɛn'tɛsɪm(ə)l/ *adj.* reckoning or reckoned by hundredths. □ **centesimally** *adv.* [Latin *centesimus* 'hundredth' from *centum* 'a hundred']

centi- /'sɛnti/ *comb. form* **1** one-hundredth, esp. of a unit in the metric system (*centigram*; *centilitre*). **2** hundred (abbr.: **c**). [Latin *centum* 'a hundred']

centigrade /'sɛntɪgreɪd/ *adj.* **1** = CELSIUS. **2** having a scale of a hundred degrees. [French, from Latin *centum* 'a hundred' + *gradus* 'step']

■ **Usage** In sense 1, *Celsius* is usually preferred in technical contexts.

centigram /'sɛntɪgram/ *n.* (also **centigramme**) a metric unit of mass, equal to one-hundredth of a gram.

centilitre /'sɛntɪliːtə/ *n.* (*US* **centiliter**) a metric unit of capacity, equal to one-hundredth of a litre.

centime /'sɒntiːm/ *n.* **1** a monetary unit in various countries, equal to one-hundredth of a franc or other decimal currency unit. **2** a coin of this value. [French from Latin *centum* 'a hundred']

centimetre /'sɛntɪmiːtə/ *n.* (*US* **centimeter**) a metric unit of length, equal to one-hundredth of a metre.

centimetre-gram-second system *n.* the system of measurement using the centimetre, the gram, and the second as basic units of length, mass, and time respectively (abbr.: **cgs**).

centipede /'sɛntɪpiːd/ *n.* a predatory arthropod of the class Chilopoda, with a flattened elongated body of many segments, most bearing a pair of legs. [French *centipède* or Latin *centipeda*, from *centum* 'a hundred' + *pes pedis* 'foot']

cento /'sɛntəʊ/ *n.* (*pl.* **-os**) a composition made up of quotations from other authors. [Latin, = patchwork garment]

central /'sɛntr(ə)l/ *adj.* **1** of, at, or forming the centre. **2** from the centre. **3** chief, essential, most important. □ **centrality** /-'tralɪti/ *n.* **centrally** *adv.* [French *central* or Latin *centralis*, from *centrum* CENTRE]

Central America *n.* the isthmus joining North and South America. □ **Central American** *adj.*

central bank *n.* a national bank issuing currency etc.

central heating *n.* a method of warming a building by pipes, radiators, etc., fed from a central source of heat.

centralism /'sɛntr(ə)lɪz(ə)m/ *n.* a system that centralizes (esp. an administration) (see also DEMOCRATIC CENTRALISM). □ **centralist** *n.*

centralize /'sɛntrəlʌɪz/ *v.* (also **-ise**) **1** *tr.* & *intr.* bring or come to a centre. **2** *tr.* **a** concentrate (administration) at a single centre. **b** subject (a state) to this system. □ **centralization** /-'zeɪʃ(ə)n/ *n.*

central locking *n.* a locking system in motor vehicles whereby the locks of several doors can be operated from a single lock.

central nervous system *n. Anat.* the complex of nerve tissues that controls the activities of the body, in vertebrates the brain and spinal cord.

central processing unit *n.* (also **central processor**) the part of a computer in which the control and execution of operations occur (abbr.: **CPU**).

central reservation see RESERVATION 5.

Central Standard Time *n.* (also **Central Time**) the standard time in a zone including the central states of the US and provinces of Canada, six hours behind GMT.

centre /'sɛntə/ *n.* & *v.* (*US* **center**) ● *n.* **1** the middle point, esp. of a line, circle, or sphere, equidistant from the ends or from any point on the circumference or surface. **2** a pivot or axis of rotation. **3 a** a place or group of buildings forming a central point in a district, city, etc., or a main area for an activity (*shopping centre*; *town centre*). **b** (with preceding word) a piece or set of equipment for a number of connected functions (*music centre*). **4** a point of concentration or dispersion; a nucleus or source. **5** a political party or group holding moderate opinions. **6** the filling in a chocolate etc. **7** *Sport* **a** the middle player in a line or group in some field games. **b** a kick or hit from the side to the centre of the pitch. **8** (in a lathe etc.) a conical adjustable support for the workpiece. **9** (*attrib.*) of or at the centre. ● *v.* **1** *intr.* (foll. by *in, on*; *disp.* foll. by *round*) have as its main centre; focus on. **2** *tr.* place in the centre. **3** *tr.* mark with a centre. **4** *tr.* (foll. by *in, on,* etc.) concentrate or focus (a thing) in, around, etc. **5** *tr. Sport* kick or hit (the ball) from the side to the centre of the pitch. □ **centred** *adj.* (often in *comb.*). **centremost** *adj.* **centric** *adj.* **centrical** *adj.* **centricity** /-'trɪsɪti/ *n.* [Middle English via Old French *centre* or Latin *centrum* from Greek *kentron* 'sharp point, stationary point of a pair of compasses']

■ **Usage** The use of the verb *centre* in sense 1 'to focus on' with *round* is common and found among good writers, but it is still considered incorrect by some people because centre designates a specific point. In such cases it is better to use *centre on*, e.g. *The discussion centred on ways of raising money.*

centre-back *n. Sport* a middle player or position in a back line.

centre bit *n.* a boring tool with a centre point and side cutters.

centreboard /'sɛntəbɔːd/ *n.* (*US* **centerboard**) a board for lowering through a boat's keel to prevent leeway.

centrefold /'sɛntəfəʊld/ *n.* (*US* **centerfold**) **1** a printed and usu. illustrated sheet folded to form the centre spread of a magazine etc. **2** a model, usu. naked or scantily clad, pictured on such a spread.

centre forward *n. Sport* the middle player or position in a forward line.

centre half *n. Sport* the middle player or position in a defensive line.

centreing var. of CENTRING.

centre line *n.* a real or imaginary line through the centre of a thing.

centre of attention *n.* **1** a person or thing that draws general attention. **2** *Physics* the point to which bodies tend by gravity.

centre of flotation *n.* the centre of gravity in a floating body.

centre of gravity *n.* a point from which the weight of a body or system may be considered to act: in uniform gravity the same as the centre of mass.

centre of mass *n.* a point representing the mean position of the matter in a body or system.

centrepiece /ˈsɛntəpiːs/ *n.* **1** an ornament for the middle of a table. **2** a principal item.

centre spread *n.* the two facing middle pages of a newspaper etc.

centre stage *n. & adv.* ● *n.* **1** the centre of a stage. **2** the centre of attention. ● *adv.* in or into this position.

-centric /ˈsɛntrɪk/ *comb. form* forming adjectives with the sense 'having a (specified) centre' (*anthropocentric*; *eccentric*). [on the pattern of *concentric* etc. from Greek *kentrikos*: see CENTRE]

centrifugal /sɛnˈtrɪfjʊg(ə)l, ˈsɛntrɪfjuːg(ə)l, sɛntrɪˈfjuːg(ə)l/ *adj.* moving or tending to move from a centre (cf. CENTRIPETAL). ▫ **centrifugally** *adv.* [modern Latin *centrifugus*, from Latin *centrum* 'centre' + *fugere* 'flee']

centrifugal force *n.* an apparent force that acts outwards on a body moving about a centre, caused by the body's inertia.

centrifuge /ˈsɛntrɪfjuːdʒ/ *n. & v.* ● *n.* a machine with a rapidly rotating container designed to apply centrifugal force to its contents, usu. to separate liquids from solids, or fluids of different densities (e.g. cream from milk). ● *v.tr.* **1** subject to the action of a centrifuge. **2** separate by centrifuge. ▫ **centrifugation** /-fjʊˈgeɪʃ(ə)n/ *n.*

centring /ˈsɛntrɪŋ/ *n.* (also **centreing** /ˈsɛnt(ə)rɪŋ/, *US* **centering** /ˈsɛnt(ə)rɪŋ/) a temporary frame used to support an arch, dome, etc., while under construction.

centriole /ˈsɛntrɪəʊl/ *n. Biol.* a minute organelle, usu. within a centrosome, involved esp. in the development of spindles in cell division. [medieval Latin *centriolum*, diminutive of *centrum* 'centre']

centripetal /sɛnˈtrɪpɪt(ə)l, ˈsɛntrɪpiːt(ə)l, sɛntrɪˈpiːt(ə)l/ *adj.* moving or tending to move towards a centre (cf. CENTRIFUGAL). ▫ **centripetally** *adv.* [modern Latin *centripetus*, from Latin *centrum* 'centre' + *petere* 'seek']

centripetal force *n.* a force acting on a moving body in the direction of the centre about which it is moving.

centrist /ˈsɛntrɪst/ *n. Polit.* often *derog.* a person who holds moderate views. ▫ **centrism** *n.*

centromere /ˈsɛntrəmɪə/ *n. Biol.* the point on a chromosome by which it is attached to the spindle during cell division. [Latin *centrum* 'centre' + Greek *meros* 'part']

centrosome /ˈsɛntrəsəʊm/ *n. Biol.* a distinct part of the cytoplasm in a cell, usu. near the nucleus, that contains the centriole. [German *Centrosoma*, from Latin *centrum* 'centre' + Greek *sōma* 'body']

centuple /ˈsɛntjʊp(ə)l/ *n., adj., & v.* ● *n.* a hundredfold amount. ● *adj.* increased a hundredfold. ● *v.tr.* multiply by a hundred; increase a hundredfold. [French *centuple* or ecclesiastical Latin *centuplus*, *centuplex*, from Latin *centum* 'hundred']

centurion /sɛnˈtjʊərɪən/ *n.* the commander of a century in the ancient Roman army. [Middle English from Latin *centurio -onis* (as CENTURY)]

century /ˈsɛntʃʊri/ *n.* (*pl.* **-ies**) **1 a** a period of one hundred years. **b** any of the centuries reckoned from the birth of Christ (*twentieth century* = 1901–2000; *fifth century* BC = 500–401 BC). **2 a** a score etc. of a hundred in a sporting event, esp. a hundred runs by one batsman in cricket. **b** a group of a hundred things. **3 a** a company in the ancient Roman army, originally of 100 men. **b** an ancient Roman political division for voting. [Latin *centuria* from *centum* 'hundred']

▪ **Usage** Strictly speaking, since the first century ran from the year 1–100, the first year of a given century should be that ending in 01. However, in popular use this has been moved back a year, and so the twenty-first century will commonly be regarded as running from 2000–2099.

century plant *n.* the American aloe, *Agave americana* (see ALOE 3).

cep /sɛp/ *n.* an edible mushroom, *Boletus edulis*, with a stout stalk, a smooth brown cap, and pores rather than gills. [French *cèpe* via Gascon *cep* from Latin *cippus* 'stake']

cephalic /sɪˈfalɪk, kɛ-/ *adj.* of or in the head. [French *céphalique* via Latin *cephalicus* from Greek *kephalikos*, from *kephalē* 'head']

-cephalic /sɪˈfalɪk, kɛ-/ *comb. form* = -CEPHALOUS.

cephalic index *n. Anthropol.* a number expressing the ratio of a head's greatest breadth and length.

cephalopod /ˈsɛf(ə)ləpɒd, ˈkɛ-/ *n.* a marine mollusc of the class Cephalopoda, having a distinct head with large eyes and a ring of tentacles around a beaked mouth, including the octopus, squid, and cuttlefish. [Greek *kephalē* 'head' + *pous podos* 'foot']

cephalothorax /sɛf(ə)ləʊˈθɔːraks, kɛ-/ *n.* (*pl.* **-thoraces** /-rəsiːz/ or **-thoraxes**) *Anat.* the fused head and thorax of a spider, crab, or other arthropod.

-cephalous /ˈsɛf(ə)ləs, ˈkɛf-/ *comb. form* -headed (*brachycephalous*; *dolichocephalous*). [Greek *kephalē* 'head']

cepheid /ˈsiːfɪɪd, ˈsɛ-/ *n.* (in full **cepheid variable**) *Astron.* a variable star having a regular cycle of brightness with a frequency related to its luminosity, so allowing estimation of its distance. [from the name of the variable star *Delta Cephei*, which typifies this class of stars]

ceramic /sɪˈramɪk/ *adj. & n.* ● *adj.* **1** made of (esp.) clay and permanently hardened by heat (*a ceramic bowl*). **2** of or relating to ceramics (*the ceramic arts*). ● *n.* **1** a ceramic article or product. **2** a substance, esp. clay, used to make ceramic articles. [Greek *keramikos* from *keramos* 'pottery']

ceramicist /sɪˈramɪsɪst/ *n.* a person who makes ceramics.

ceramics /sɪˈramɪks/ *n.pl.* **1** ceramic products collectively (*exhibition of ceramics*). **2** (usu. treated as *sing.*) the art of making ceramic articles.

cerastes /sɪˈrastiːz/ *n.* a N. African viper of the genus *Cerastes*, esp. *C. cerastes*, which has a sharp upright spike over each eye. [Latin, from Greek *kerastēs* from *keras* 'horn']

cerastium /sɪˈrastɪəm/ *n.* any plant of the genus *Cerastium* (pink family), with white flowers and often horn-shaped capsules. [modern Latin, from Greek *kerastes* 'horned' from *keras* 'horn']

cercaria /səːˈkɛːrɪə/ *n.* (*pl.* **-iae** /-ɪiː/) *Zool. & Med.* a free-swimming larval stage in which a parasitic fluke passes from an intermediate host (often a snail) to another intermediate host or to the final vertebrate host. [modern Latin, formed irregularly from Greek *kerkos* 'tail']

cercus /ˈsəːkəs/ *n.* (*pl.* **cerci** /-kʌɪ/) *Zool.* either of a pair of small appendages at the end of the abdomen of some insects and other arthropods. [modern Latin, from Greek *kerkos* 'tail']

cere /sɪə/ *n.* a waxy fleshy covering at the base of the upper beak in some birds. [Latin *cera* 'wax']

cereal /ˈsɪərɪəl/ *n. & adj* ● *n.* **1** (usu. in *pl.*) **a** any kind of grain used for food. **b** any grass producing this, e.g. wheat, maize, rye, etc. **2** a breakfast food made from a cereal and requiring no cooking. ● *adj.* of or relating to edible grain or products of it. [Latin *cerealis* from *Ceres*, the name of the goddess of agriculture]

cerebellum /sɛrɪˈbɛləm/ *n.* (*pl.* **cerebellums** or **cerebella** /-lə/) the part of the brain at the back of the skull in vertebrates, which coordinates and regulates muscular activity. ▫ **cerebellar** *adj.* [Latin, diminutive of CEREBRUM]

cerebral /ˈsɛrɪbr(ə)l/ *adj.* **1** of the brain. **2** intellectual rather than emotional. **3** *Phonet.* = RETROFLEX 2. ▫ **cerebrally** *adv.* [Latin *cerebrum* 'brain']

cerebral hemisphere *n.* each of the two halves of the vertebrate cerebrum.

cerebral palsy *n.* a condition marked by weakness and impaired coordination of the limbs, esp. caused by damage to the brain before or at birth.

cerebration /sɛrɪ'breɪʃ(ə)n/ *n.* working of the brain. ▫ **cerebrate** /'sɛrɪbreɪt/ *v.intr.*

cerebro- /'sɛrɪbrəʊ/ *comb. form* brain (*cerebrospinal*). [Latin *cerebrum* 'brain']

cerebrospinal /ˌsɛrɪbrəʊ'spʌɪn(ə)l/ *adj.* of the brain and spine.

cerebrospinal fluid *n. Anat.* a clear watery fluid which fills the space between the arachnoid membrane and the pia mater.

cerebrovascular /ˌsɛrɪbrəʊ'vaskjʊlə/ *adj.* of the brain and its blood vessels.

cerebrum /'sɛrɪbrəm/ *n.* (*pl.* **cerebra** /-brə/) the principal part of the brain in vertebrates, located in the front area of the skull, which integrates complex sensory and neural functions. [Latin, = brain]

cerecloth /'sɪəklɒθ/ *n. hist.* waxed cloth used as a waterproof covering or (esp.) as a shroud. [earlier *cered cloth* from *cere* 'to wax', via Latin *cerare* from *cera* 'wax']

cerement /'sɪəm(ə)nt/ *n.* (usu. in *pl.*) *literary* **1** cerecloth for wrapping the dead. **2** burial clothes. [first used by Shakespeare in *Hamlet* (1602): apparently from CERECLOTH]

ceremonial /sɛrɪ'məʊnɪəl/ *adj. & n.* ● *adj.* **1** with or concerning ritual or ceremony. **2** formal (*a ceremonial bow*). ● *n.* **1** a system of rites etc. to be used esp. at a formal or religious occasion. **2** the formalities or behaviour proper to any occasion (*with all due ceremonial*). **3** *RC Ch.* a book containing an order of ritual. ▫ **ceremonialism** *n.* **ceremonialist** *n.* **ceremonially** *adv.* [Late Latin *caerimonialis* (as CEREMONY)]

ceremonious /sɛrɪ'məʊnɪəs/ *adj.* **1** = CEREMONIAL *adj.* **2** full of ceremony; accompanied by rites. **3** having or showing a fondness for ritualistic observance or formality; punctilious. ▫ **ceremoniously** *adv.* **ceremoniousness** *n.* [French *cérémonieux* or Late Latin *caerimoniosus* (as CEREMONY)]

ceremony /'sɛrɪməni/ *n.* (*pl.* **-ies**) **1** a formal religious or public occasion, esp. celebrating a particular event or anniversary. **2** formalities, esp. of an empty or ritualistic kind (*ceremony of exchanging compliments*). **3** excessively polite behaviour (*bowed low with great ceremony*). ▫ **stand on ceremony** insist on the observance of formalities. **without ceremony** informally. [Middle English from Old French *ceremonie* or Latin *caerimonia* 'religious worship']

Cerenkov radiation /tʃə'rɛŋkɒf reɪdɪ'eɪʃ(ə)n/ *n.* (also **Cherenkov**) the electromagnetic radiation emitted by particles moving in a medium at speeds faster than that of light in the same medium. [named after P. A. *Cherenkov*, Russian physicist d. 1990]

ceresin /'sɛrɪsɪn/ *n.* a hard whitish wax used with or instead of beeswax. [modern Latin *ceres*, from Latin *cera* 'wax' + -IN]

cerise /sɛ'riːz, -s/ *adj. & n.* ● *adj.* of a light clear red colour. ● *n.* this colour. [French, = CHERRY]

cerium /'sɪərɪəm/ *n. Chem.* a silvery metallic element of the lanthanide series occurring naturally in various minerals and used in the manufacture of lighter flints (symbol **Ce**). [named after the asteroid *Ceres*, discovered (1801) about the same time as this]

cermet /'səːmɛt/ *n.* a heat-resistant material made of ceramic and sintered metal. [*cer*amic + *met*al]

CERN /səːn/ *abbr.* European Organization for Nuclear Research. [French *Conseil Européen pour la Recherche Nucléaire*, its former title]

cero- /'sɪərəʊ/ *comb. form* wax (cf. CEROGRAPHY, CEROPLASTIC). [Latin *cera* or Greek *kēros* 'wax']

cerography /sɪə'rɒgrəfi/ *n.* the technique of engraving or designing on or with wax.

ceroplastic /sɪərəʊ'plastɪk/ *adj.* **1** modelled in wax. **2** of or concerning wax-modelling.

cert /səːt/ *n. Brit. slang* (esp. **dead cert**) **1** an event or result regarded as certain to happen. **2** a horse strongly tipped to win. [abbreviation of CERTAIN, CERTAINTY]

cert. *abbr.* **1** a certificate. **2** certified.

certain /'səːt(ə)n, -tɪn/ *adj. & pron.* ● *adj.* **1 a** (often foll. by *of*, or *that* + clause) confident, convinced (*certain that I put it here*). **b** (often foll. by *that* + clause) indisputable; known for sure (*it is certain that he is guilty*). **2** (often foll. by *to* + infin.) **a** that may be relied on to happen (*it is certain to rain*). **b** destined (*certain to become a star*). **3** definite, unfailing, reliable (*a certain indication of the coming storm*; *his touch is certain*). **4** (of a person, place, etc.) that might be specified, but is not (*a certain lady*; *of a certain age*). **5** some though not much (*a certain reluctance*). **6** (of a person, place, etc.) existing, though probably unknown to the reader or hearer (*a certain John Smith*). ● *pron.* (treated as *pl.*) some but not all (*certain of them were wounded*). ▫ **for certain** without doubt. **make certain** = *make sure* (see SURE). [Middle English from Old French, ultimately from Latin *certus* 'settled']

certainly /'səːt(ə)nli, -tɪn-/ *adv.* **1** undoubtedly, definitely. **2** confidently. **3** (in affirmative answer to a question or command) yes; by all means.

certainty /'səːt(ə)nti, -tɪn-/ *n.* (*pl.* **-ies**) **1 a** an undoubted fact. **b** a certain prospect (*his return is a certainty*). **2** (often foll. by *of*, or *that* + clause) an absolute conviction (*has a certainty of his own worth*). **3** (often foll. by *to* + infin.) a thing or person that may be relied on (*a certainty to win the Derby*). ▫ **for a certainty** beyond the possibility of doubt. [Middle English from Anglo-French *certainté*, Old French *certaineté* (as CERTAIN)]

Cert. Ed. *abbr.* (in the UK) Certificate in Education.

certifiable /'səːtɪfʌɪəb(ə)l/ *adj.* **1** able or needing to be certified. **2** *colloq.* insane.

certificate *n. & v.* ● *n.* /sə'tɪfɪkət/ a formal document attesting a fact, esp. birth, marriage, or death, a medical condition, a level of achievement, a fulfilment of requirements, ownership of shares, etc. ● *v.tr.* /sə'tɪfɪkeɪt/ (esp. as **certificated** *adj.*) provide with or license or attest by a certificate. ▫ **certification** /səːtɪfɪ'keɪʃ(ə)n/ *n.* [French *certificat* or medieval Latin *certificatum*, from *certificare*: see CERTIFY]

Certificate of Secondary Education *n. hist.* **1** an examination set for secondary-school pupils in England and Wales, replaced in 1988 by the General Certificate of Secondary Education (GCSE). **2** the certificate gained by passing it.

certified cheque *n.* a cheque the validity of which is guaranteed by a bank.

certified mail *n. N. Amer.* = RECORDED DELIVERY.

certified milk *n. hist.* milk guaranteed free from the tuberculosis bacillus.

certify /'səːtɪfʌɪ/ *v.tr.* (**-ies, -ied**) **1** make a formal statement of; attest; attest to (*certified that he had witnessed the crime*). **2** declare by certificate (that a person is qualified or competent) (*certified as a trained bookkeeper*). **3** officially declare insane (*he should be certified*). [Middle English via Old French *certifier* and medieval Latin *certificare* from Latin *certus* 'certain']

certiorari /səːtɪə'rɛːrʌɪ, -'rɑːri/ *n. Law* a writ from a higher court requesting the records of a case tried in a lower court. [Late Latin, passive of *certiorare* 'inform', from *certior*, comparative of *certus* 'certain']

certitude /'səːtɪtjuːd/ *n.* a feeling of absolute certainty or conviction. [Middle English from Late Latin *certitudo*, from *certus* 'certain']

cerulean /sɪ'ruːlɪən/ *adj. & n. literary* ● *adj.* deep blue like a clear sky. ● *n.* this colour. [Latin *caeruleus* 'sky blue' from *caelum* 'sky']

cerumen /sɪ'ruːmən/ *n.* the yellow waxy substance in the outer ear. ▫ **ceruminous** *adj.* [modern Latin, from Latin *cera* 'wax']

ceruse /ˈsɪəruːs, sɪˈruːs/ *n.* white lead, used in ointments and (formerly) cosmetics. [Middle English via Old French from Latin *cerussa*, perhaps from Greek *kēros* 'wax']
cervelat /ˈsəːvəlɑː, -lat/ *n.* a kind of smoked pork sausage. [obsolete French, from Italian *cervellata*]
cervical /ˈsəːvɪk(ə)l, səːˈvʌɪk(ə)l/ *adj. Anat.* **1** of or relating to the neck (*cervical vertebrae*). **2** of or relating to the cervix. [French *cervical* or modern Latin *cervicalis*, from Latin *cervix -icis* 'neck']
cervical screening *n.* examination of a large number of apparently healthy women for cervical cancer.
cervical smear *n.* esp. *Brit.* a specimen of cellular material from the neck of the womb spread on a microscope slide for examination for cancerous cells.
cervine /ˈsəːvʌɪn/ *adj.* of or like a deer. [Latin *cervinus* from *cervus* 'deer']
cervix /ˈsəːvɪks/ *n.* (*pl.* **cervices** /-siːz/) *Anat.* **1** the neck. **2** any necklike structure, esp. the neck of the womb. [Latin]
Cesarean (also **Cesarian**) *US Med.* var. of CAESAREAN.
Cesarewitch /sɪˈzarəwɪtʃ/ *n.* a horse race run annually at Newmarket, England. [Russian *tsesarevich* 'heir to the throne': named in honour of the Russian prince (later Alexander II) who attended the inaugural race (1839)]
cesium *US* var. of CAESIUM.
cess[1] /sɛs/ *n.* (also **sess**) (in Scotland, Ireland, and India) a tax; a levy. [properly *sess* for obsolete noun *assess*: see ASSESS]
cess[2] /sɛs/ *n. Ir.* □ **bad cess to** may evil befall (*bad cess to their clan*). [perhaps from CESS[1]]
cessation /sɛˈseɪʃ(ə)n/ *n.* **1** a ceasing (*cessation of the truce*). **2** a pause (*resumed fighting after the cessation*). [Middle English from Latin *cessatio*, from *cessare* CEASE]
cesser /ˈsɛsə/ *n. Law* a coming to an end; a cessation (of a term, a liability, etc.). [Anglo-French & Old French, = CEASE]
cession /ˈsɛʃ(ə)n/ *n.* **1** (often foll. by *of*) the ceding or giving up (of rights, property, and esp. of territory by a state). **2** the territory etc. so ceded. [Middle English via Old French *cession* or Latin *cessio* from *cedere cess-* 'go away']
cessionary /ˈsɛʃ(ə)n(ə)ri/ *n.* (*pl.* **-ies**) *Law* = ASSIGN *n.*
cesspit /ˈsɛspɪt/ *n.* **1** a pit for the disposal of refuse. **2** = CESSPOOL. [*cess* in CESSPOOL + PIT[1]]
cesspool /ˈsɛspuːl/ *n.* **1** an underground container for the temporary storage of liquid waste or sewage. **2** a centre of corruption, depravity, etc. [perhaps alteration, influenced by POOL[1], of earlier *cesperalle*, from *suspiral* 'vent, water pipe, settling tank', via Old French *souspirail* 'air-hole' from Latin *suspirare* 'breathe, sigh' (as SUB-, *spirare* 'breathe')]
cestode /ˈsɛstəʊd/ *n.* (also **cestoid** /ˈsɛstɔɪd/) a flatworm of the class Cestoda, which comprises tapeworms. [Latin *cestus* from Greek *kestos* 'girdle']
CET *abbr.* Central European Time.
cetacean /sɪˈteɪʃ(ə)n/ *n.* & *adj.* ● *n.* any marine mammal of the order Cetacea with streamlined hairless body and dorsal blowhole for breathing, including whales, dolphins, and porpoises. ● *adj.* of cetaceans. □ **cetaceous** *adj.* [modern Latin *Cetacea* via Latin *cetus* from Greek *kētos* 'whale']
cetane /ˈsiːteɪn/ *n. Chem.* a colourless liquid hydrocarbon of the alkane series used in standardizing ratings of diesel fuel. [from spermaceti (from which it was derived) on the pattern of *methane* etc.]
cetane number *n.* a measure of the ignition properties of diesel fuel.
ceteris paribus /ˌkeɪtərɪs ˈparɪbʊs, ˌsɛt-, ˌsiːt-/ *adv.* other things being equal. [Latin]
Ceylon moss /sɪˈlɒn/ *n.* a red seaweed, *Gracilaria lichenoides*, of the Indian subcontinent, the main source of agar. [*Ceylon*, a former name of Sri Lanka]
Ceylon satinwood see SATINWOOD 1a.
CF *abbr. Brit.* Chaplain to the Forces.
Cf *symb. Chem.* the element californium.
cf. *abbr.* compare. [Latin *confer*, imperative of *conferre* 'compare']
c.f. *abbr.* carried forward.
CFC *abbr. Chem.* chlorofluorocarbon, any of a class of usu. gaseous compounds of carbon, hydrogen, chlorine, and fluorine, used in refrigerants, aerosol propellants, etc., and harmful to the ozone layer in the earth's atmosphere owing to the release of chlorine on exposure to solar ultraviolet.
CFE *abbr. Brit.* College of Further Education.
cg *abbr.* centigram(s).
CGS *abbr. Brit.* Chief of General Staff.
cgs *abbr.* centimetre-gram-second.
CH *abbr.* (in the UK) Companion of Honour.
ch. *abbr.* **1** church. **2** chapter. **3** chestnut.
cha var. of CHAR[3].
Chablis /ˈʃabliː/ *n.* (*pl.* same /-lɪz/) a dry white burgundy wine. [*Chablis* in E. France, where it is produced]
cha-cha /ˈtʃɑːtʃɑː/ *n.* & *v.* (also **cha-cha-cha** /tʃɑːtʃɑːˈtʃɑː/) ● *n.* **1** a ballroom dance with a Latin American rhythm. **2** music for or in the rhythm of a cha-cha. ● *v.intr.* (**cha-chas**, **cha-chaed** /-tʃɑːd/ or **cha-cha'd**, **cha-chaing** /-tʃɑː(r)ɪŋ/) dance the cha-cha. [Latin American Spanish]
chaconne /ʃəˈkɒn/ *n. Mus.* **1 a** a musical form consisting of variations on a ground bass. **b** a musical composition in this style. **2** *hist.* a dance performed to this music. [French, from Spanish *chacona*]
chador /ˈtʃɑːdɔː, ˈtʃɑːdə, ˈtʃʌdə/ *n.* (also **chadar**, **chuddar**) a large piece of cloth worn in some countries by Muslim women, wrapped around the body to leave only the face exposed. [Urdu, from Persian *čādar* 'sheet, veil']
chaetognath /ˈkiːtənaθ/ *n.* any dart-shaped worm of the phylum Chaetognatha, usu. living among marine plankton, and having a head with external grasping spines. Also called *arrow worm*. [modern Latin *Chaetognatha*, from Greek *khaitē* 'long hair' + *gnathos* 'jaw']
chafe /tʃeɪf/ *v.* & *n.* ● *v.* **1** *tr.* & *intr.* make or become sore or damaged by rubbing. **2** *tr.* rub (esp. the skin to restore warmth or sensation). **3** *tr.* & *intr.* make or become annoyed; fret (*was chafed by the delay*). ● *n.* **1 a** an act of chafing. **b** a sore resulting from this. **2** a state of annoyance. [Middle English from Old French *chaufer* 'make hot', ultimately from Latin *calefacere* from *calēre* 'be hot' + *facere* 'make']
chafer /ˈtʃeɪfə/ *n.* any of various large slow-moving strong-flying beetles of the family Scarabaeidae, e.g. the cockchafer. [Old English *ceafor*, *cefer*, from Germanic]
chaff /tʃɑːf, tʃaf/ *n.* & *v.* ● *n.* **1** the husks of corn or other seed separated by winnowing or threshing. **2** chopped hay and straw used as fodder. **3** light-hearted joking; banter. **4** worthless things; rubbish. **5** strips of metal foil released in the atmosphere to obstruct radar detection. ● *v.tr.* **1** tease; banter. **2** chop (straw etc.). □ **separate the wheat from the chaff** distinguish good from bad. □ **chaffy** *adj.* [Old English *ceaf*, *cæf*, probably from Germanic: sense 3 of the noun & 1 of the verb perhaps from CHAFE]
chaff-cutter *n.* a machine for chopping fodder.
chaffer /ˈtʃafə/ *v.* & *n.* ● *v.intr.* haggle; bargain. ● *n.* bargaining; haggling. □ **chafferer** *n.* [Middle English, in the sense 'traffic, trade', from Old English *ceapfaru* from *ceap* 'bargain' + *faru* 'journey']
chaffinch /ˈtʃafɪn(t)ʃ/ *n.* a common European finch, *Fringilla coelebs*, the male of which has a blue-grey head with pinkish cheeks and breast. [Old English *ceaffinc* 'chaff finch': from its foraging around barns etc.]
chafing dish /ˈtʃeɪfɪŋ/ *n.* **1** a cooking pot with an outer pan of hot water, used for keeping food warm. **2** a dish with a spirit lamp etc. for cooking at table. [obsolete sense of CHAFE = warm]

Chagas' disease /ˈtʃɑːɡəs/ *n.* (also **Chagas's disease**) a disease caused by trypanosomes transmitted by bloodsucking bugs, endemic in S. America and causing damage to the heart and central nervous system. [named after C. *Chagas*, Brazilian physician d. 1934, who first described it]

chagrin /ˈʃaɡrɪn/ *n. & v.* ● *n.* acute vexation or mortification. ● *v.tr.* affect with chagrin. [French *chagrin(er)*, of uncertain origin]

chain /tʃeɪn/ *n. & v.* ● *n.* **1 a** a connected flexible series of esp. metal links as decoration or for a practical purpose. **b** something resembling this (*formed a human chain*). **2** (in *pl.*) **a** fetters used to confine prisoners. **b** any restraining force. **3** a sequence, series, or set (*chain of events*; *mountain chain*). **4** a group of associated hotels, shops, etc. **5** a badge of office in the form of a chain worn round the neck (*mayoral chain*). **6 a** a jointed measuring-line consisting of linked metal rods. **b** its length (66 ft). **7** *Chem.* a group of (esp. carbon) atoms bonded in sequence in a molecule. **8** a figure in a quadrille or similar dance. **9** (in *pl.*) *Naut.* channels (see CHANNEL²). **10** (also **chain-shot**) *hist.* two cannon balls or half balls joined by a chain and used in sea battles for bringing down a mast etc. ● *v.tr.* **1** (often foll. by *up*) secure or confine with a chain. **2** confine or restrict (a person) (*is chained to the office*). [Middle English via Old French *cha(e)ine* from Latin *catena*]

chain armour *n.* = CHAIN MAIL.

chain bridge *n.* a suspension bridge on chains.

chain drive *n.* a system of transmission by endless chains.

chain gang *n.* a team of convicts chained together and forced to work in the open air.

chain gear *n.* a gear transmitting motion by means of an endless chain.

chain letter *n.* one of a sequence of letters, each recipient in the sequence being requested to send copies to a specific number of other people.

chain link *adj.* made of wire in a diamond-shaped mesh (*chain link fencing*).

chain mail *n.* armour made of interlaced rings.

chain reaction *n.* **1** *Physics* a self-sustaining nuclear reaction, esp. one in which a neutron from a fission reaction initiates a series of these reactions. **2** *Chem.* a self-sustaining molecular reaction in which intermediate products initiate further reactions. **3** a series of events, each caused by the previous one.

chainsaw /ˈtʃeɪnsɔː/ *n.* a motor-driven saw with teeth on an endless chain.

chain-smoker *n.* a person who smokes continually, esp. one who lights a cigarette etc. from the stub of the last one smoked. □ **chain-smoke** *v.tr. & intr.*

chain stitch *n.* an ornamental embroidery or crochet stitch resembling chains.

chain store *n.* one of a series of shops owned by one firm and selling the same sort of goods.

chain-wale *n.* = CHANNEL².

chain wheel *n.* a wheel transmitting power by a chain fitted to its edges.

chair /tʃɛː/ *n. & v.* ● *n.* **1** a separate seat for one person, of various forms, usu. having a back and four legs. **2 a** a professorship (*offered the chair in physics*). **b** a seat of authority, esp. on a board of directors. **c** *Brit.* a mayoralty. **3 a** a chairperson. **b** the seat or office of a chairperson (*will you take the chair?*; *I'm in the chair*). **4** *US* = ELECTRIC CHAIR. **5** esp. *Brit.* an iron or steel socket holding a railway rail in place. **6** *hist.* = *sedan chair* (see SEDAN 1). ● *v.tr.* **1** act as chairperson of or preside over (a meeting). **2** *Brit.* carry (a person) aloft in a chair or in a sitting position, in triumph. **3** install in a chair, esp. as a position of authority. □ **take a chair** sit down. [Middle English via Anglo-French *chaere*, Old French *chaiere* from Latin *cathedra*, from Greek *kathedra* 'seat']

chair-bed *n.* a chair that unfolds into a bed.

chair-borne *adj. colloq.* (of an administrator) not active.

chair-car *n.* a railway carriage with chairs instead of long seats.

chairlady /ˈtʃɛːleɪdi/ *n.* (*pl.* **-ies**) = CHAIRWOMAN (see CHAIRMAN).

chairlift /ˈtʃɛːlɪft/ *n.* a series of chairs on an endless cable for carrying passengers up and down a mountain etc.

chairman /ˈtʃɛːmən/ *n.* (*pl.* **-men**; *fem.* also **chairwoman**, *pl.* **-women**) **1** a person chosen to preside over a meeting. **2 a** the permanent president of a committee, a board of directors, *Brit.* a firm, etc. **b** (**Chairman**) (since 1949) the leading figure in the Chinese Communist Party. **3** the master of ceremonies at an entertainment etc. **4** *hist.* either of two sedan-bearers. □ **chairmanship** *n.*

chairperson /ˈtʃɛːpəːs(ə)n/ *n.* a chairman or chairwoman (used as a neutral alternative).

chaise /ʃeɪz/ *n.* **1** esp. *hist.* a horse-drawn carriage for one or two persons, esp. one with an open top and two wheels. **2** = POST-CHAISE. **3** *US* = CHAISE LONGUE. [French, variant of *chaire*: see CHAIR]

chaise longue /ʃeɪz ˈlɒŋɡ/ *n.* (*pl.* **chaise longues** or **chaises longues** *pronunc.* same) **1** a sofa with a backrest at only one end. **2** a chair with a lengthened seat for reclining on; a sunbed. [French, literally 'long chair']

chaise lounge /ʃeɪz ˈlaʊndʒ/ *n. US* = CHAISE LONGUE. [*lounge* corruption of *longue*]

chakra /ˈtʃʌkrə/ *n.* each of the centres of spiritual power in the human body, recognized in yoga. [Sanskrit *cakra* (cognate with WHEEL *n.*)]

chalaza /kəˈleɪzə/ *n.* (*pl.* **chalazae** /-ziː/) each of two twisted membranous strips joining the yolk to the ends of an egg. [modern Latin from Greek, = small knot, hailstone]

chalcedony /kalˈsɛdəni/ *n.* (*pl.* **-ies**) a type of quartz occurring in several different forms, e.g. onyx, agate, tiger's eye, etc. □ **chalcedonic** /kalsɪˈdɒnɪk/ *adj.* [Middle English via Latin *c(h)alcedonius* from Greek *khalkēdōn*]

chalcolithic /kalkəˈlɪθɪk/ *adj. Archaeol.* of a prehistoric period in which both stone and copper implements were used. [Greek *khalkos* 'copper' + *lithos* 'stone']

chalcopyrite /kalkəˈpʌɪrʌɪt/ *n.* a yellow mineral, a double sulphide of copper and iron, which is the principal ore of copper. Also called *copper pyrites*. [Greek *khalkos* 'copper' + PYRITE]

Chaldean /kalˈdiːən/ *n. & adj.* ● *n.* **1 a** a native of ancient Chaldea or Babylonia. **b** the language of the Chaldeans. **2** an astrologer. **3** a member of a Syrian Uniate (formerly Nestorian) Church in Iran etc. ● *adj.* **1** of or relating to ancient Chaldea or its people or language. **2** of or relating to astrology. **3** of or relating to the East Syrian Uniat Church. [Latin *Chaldaeus* via Greek *Khaldaios* from Assyrian *Kaldu*]

Chaldee /kalˈdiː, ˈkaldiː/ *n.* **1** the language of the Chaldeans. **2** a native of ancient Chaldea. **3** the Aramaic language as used in Old Testament books. [Middle English, representing Latin *Chaldaei* (pl.) (as CHALDEAN)]

chalet /ˈʃaleɪ/ *n.* **1** a small suburban house or bungalow, esp. with an overhanging roof. **2** a small, usu. wooden, hut or house on a beach or in a holiday camp. **3** a Swiss cowherd's hut, or wooden cottage, with overhanging eaves. [Swiss French, ultimately from Latin *casa* 'hut, cottage']

chalice /ˈtʃalɪs/ *n.* **1** *literary* a goblet. **2** a wine cup used in the Communion service. [Middle English via Old French from Latin *calix -icis* 'cup']

chalk /tʃɔːk/ *n. & v.* ● *n.* **1** a white soft earthy limestone (calcium carbonate) formed from the skeletal remains of sea creatures. **2 a** a similar substance (calcium sulphate), sometimes coloured, used for writing or drawing. **b** a piece of this (*a box of chalks*). **3** a series of strata consisting mainly of chalk. **4** = FRENCH CHALK. ● *v.tr.* **1** rub, mark, draw, or write with chalk. **2** (foll. by *up*) **a** write or record with chalk. **b** register (a success etc.). **c** *Brit.* charge (to an account). □ **as different as chalk and** (or **from**) **cheese** *Brit.* fundamentally different. **by a long chalk** *Brit.* by far (from the use of chalk to mark the score in games). **chalk and talk** *Brit.* traditional teaching (employing blackboard and chalk in a presentation to a class). **chalk out** sketch or plan a thing to be accomplished. [Old English *cealc*, ultimately (via West Germanic) from Latin CALX]

chalkboard /ˈtʃɔːkbɔːd/ *n. N. Amer.* = BLACKBOARD.

chalk pit *n. Brit.* a quarry in which chalk is dug.

chalk-stone *n.* a concretion of urates like chalk in tissues and joints esp. of hands and feet.

chalk-stripe *n.* a pattern of thin white stripes on a dark background. □ **chalk-striped** *adj.*

chalky /ˈtʃɔːki/ *adj.* (**chalkier**, **chalkiest**) **1 a** abounding in chalk. **b** white as chalk. **2** like or containing chalk-stones. □ **chalkiness** *n.*

challah /ˈhɑːlə, xɑːˈlɑː/ *n.* (*pl.* **challahs** or **chalot(h)** /xɑːˈlɒt/) a usu. plaited loaf of white leavened bread, traditionally baked to celebrate the Jewish sabbath. [Hebrew *ḥalah*, perhaps from *ḥll* 'to pierce' or Akkadian *ellu* 'pure']

challenge /ˈtʃalɪn(d)ʒ/ *n. & v.* ● *n.* **1 a** a summons to take part in a contest or a trial of strength etc., esp. to a duel. **b** a summons to prove or justify something. **2** a demanding or difficult task (*rose to the challenge of the new job*). **3** *Law* an objection made to a jury member. **4** a call to respond, esp. a sentry's call for a password etc. **5** an invitation to a sporting contest, esp. one issued to a reigning champion. **6** *Med.* a test of immunity after immunization treatment. ● *v.tr.* **1** (often foll. by *to* + infin.) **a** invite to take part in a contest, game, debate, duel, etc. **b** invite to prove or justify something. **2** dispute, deny (*I challenge that remark*). **3 a** stretch, stimulate (*challenges him to produce his best*). **b** (as **challenging** *adj.*) demanding; stimulatingly difficult. **4** (of a sentry) call to respond. **5** claim (attention etc.). **6** *Law* object to (a jury member, evidence, etc.). **7** *Med.* test by a challenge. □ **challengeable** /-dʒəb(ə)l/ *adj.* **challenger** *n.* **challengingly** *adv.* [Middle English via Old French *c(h)alenge*, *c(h)alenger* from Latin *calumnia calumniari* 'calumny']

challenged /ˈtʃalɪndʒd/ *adj.* (in *comb.*) *euphem.* or *joc.* lacking a physical or mental attribute (*vertically challenged*; *intellectually challenged*).

challis /ˈʃalɪs, ˈʃali/ *n.* a lightweight soft clothing fabric. [perhaps from a surname]

chalybeate /kəˈlɪbɪət/ *adj.* (of mineral water etc.) impregnated with iron salts. [modern Latin *chalybeatus* via Latin *chalybs* from Greek *khalups -ubos* 'steel']

chamaephyte /ˈkamɪfʌɪt/ *n.* a plant whose buds are on or near the ground. [Greek *khamai* 'on the ground' + -PHYTE]

chamber /ˈtʃeɪmbə/ *n.* **1 a** a hall used by a legislative or judicial body. **b** the body that meets in it. **c** any of the houses of a parliament (*Chamber of Deputies*; *second chamber*). **2** (in *pl.*) *Law* **a** *Brit.* rooms used by a barrister or group of barristers, esp. in the Inns of Court. **b** a judge's room used for official proceedings not required to be held in open court. **3** *poet.* or *archaic* a room, esp. a bedroom. **4** a large underground cavity; a cave. **5** (*attrib.*) *Mus.* of or for a small group of instruments (*chamber orchestra*; *chamber music*). **6** an enclosed space in machinery etc. (esp. the part of a gun bore that contains the charge). **7 a** a cavity in a plant or in the body of an animal. **b** a compartment in a structure. **8** = CHAMBER POT. [Middle English via Old French *chambre* from Latin CAMERA]

chambered /ˈtʃeɪmbəd/ *adj.* (of a tomb) containing a burial chamber.

chamberlain /ˈtʃeɪmbəlɪn/ *n.* **1** an officer managing the household of a sovereign or a great noble. **2** *Brit.* the treasurer of a corporation etc. □ **chamberlainship** *n.* [Middle English, in the sense 'servant in a bedchamber', via Old French *chamberlain* etc. and Frankish from Latin *camera* CAMERA]

chambermaid /ˈtʃeɪmbəmeɪd/ *n.* **1** a housemaid at a hotel etc. **2** *N. Amer.* a housemaid.

Chamber of Commerce *n.* an association to promote local commercial interests.

Chamber of Deputies *n.* the lower legislative assembly in some parliaments.

Chamber of Horrors *n.* a place full of horrors (originally a room of criminals etc. in Madame Tussaud's waxworks).

chamber pot *n.* a receptacle for urine etc., used in a bedroom.

Chambertin /ˈʃɒ̃bətã/ *n.* a high-quality dry red burgundy wine. [*Gevrey Chambertin* region in E. France, where it is produced]

chambray /ˈʃambreɪ/ *n.* a linen-finished gingham cloth with a white weft and a coloured warp. [formed irregularly from *Cambrai*: see CAMBRIC]

chambré /ˈʃɒmbreɪ/ *adj.* (of red wine) brought to room temperature. [French, past part. of *chambrer*, from *chambre* 'room': see CHAMBER]

chameleon /kəˈmiːlɪən/ *n.* **1** any of a family of small lizards having grasping tails, long tongues, protruding eyes, and the power of changing colour. **2** a variable or inconstant person. □ **chameleonic** /-ˈɒnɪk/ *adj.* [Middle English via Latin from Greek *khamaileōn*, from *khamai* 'on the ground' + *leōn* 'lion']

chamfer /ˈtʃamfə/ *v. & n.* ● *v.tr.* bevel symmetrically (a right-angled edge or corner). ● *n.* a bevelled surface at an edge or corner. [back-formation from *chamfering*, from French *chamfrain*, from *chant* 'edge' (see CANT²) + *fraint* 'broken' via Old French *fraindre* 'break' from Latin *frangere*]

chamois *n.* **1** /ˈʃamwɑː/ (*pl.* same /-wɑːz/) an agile goat-antelope, *Rupicapra rupicapra*, native to the mountains of Europe and Asia. **2** /ˈʃami, ˈʃamwɑː/ (*pl.* same /-mɪz, -wɑːz/) (in full **chamois leather**) **a** soft pliable leather from sheep, goats, deer, etc. **b** a piece of this for polishing etc. [French: perhaps ultimately from Swiss Proto-Romance]

chamomile var. of CAMOMILE.

champ¹ /tʃamp/ *v. & n.* ● *v.* **1** *tr. & intr.* munch or chew noisily. **2** *tr.* (of a horse etc.) work (the bit) noisily between the teeth. **3** *intr.* fret with impatience (*is champing to be away*). ● *n.* a chewing noise or motion. □ **champ at the bit** be restlessly impatient. [probably imitative]

champ² /tʃamp/ *n. colloq.* a champion. [abbreviation]

champagne /ʃamˈpeɪn/ *n.* **1 a** a white sparkling wine from Champagne. **b** (loosely) a similar wine from elsewhere. **2** a pale cream or straw colour. [*Champagne*, former province in E. France, where it is produced]

■ **Usage** The use of *champagne* in sense 1b is, strictly speaking, incorrect.

champaign /ˈtʃampeɪn/ *n. literary* **1** open country. **2** an expanse of open country. [Middle English via Old French *champagne* from Late Latin *campania*: cf. CAMPAIGN]

champers /ˈʃampəz/ *n.* esp. *Brit. colloq.* champagne.

champerty /ˈtʃampəːti/ *n.* (*pl.* **-ies**) *Law* an illegal agreement in which a person not naturally interested in a lawsuit finances it with a view to sharing the disputed property. □ **champertous** *adj.* [Middle English via Anglo-French *champartie* from Old French *champart* 'feudal lord's share of produce', from Latin *campus* 'field' + *pars* 'part']

champion /ˈtʃampɪən/ *n., v., adj., & adv.* ● *n.* **1** (often *attrib.*) a person (esp. in a sport or game), an animal, plant, etc., that has defeated or surpassed all rivals in a competition etc. **2 a** a person who fights or argues for a cause or on behalf of another person. **b** *hist.* a knight etc. who fought in single combat on behalf of a king etc. ● *v.tr.* support the cause of, defend, argue in favour of.

● *adj. Brit. colloq.* or *dial.* first-class, splendid. ● *adv. Brit. colloq.* or *dial.* splendidly, well. [Middle English via Old French from medieval Latin *campio -onis* 'fighter', from Latin *campus* 'field, military exercise ground']

Champion of England *n.* (in the UK) a hereditary official at coronations.

championship /'tʃampɪənʃɪp/ *n.* **1** (often in *pl.*) a contest for the position of champion in a sport etc. **2** the position of champion over all rivals. **3** the advocacy or defence (of a cause etc.).

champlevé /'ʃampləveɪ, French ʃɑ̃ləve/ *n.* & *adj.* ● *n.* a type of enamelwork in which hollows made in a metal surface are filled with coloured enamels. ● *adj.* of or relating to *champlevé* (cf. CLOISONNÉ). [French, = raised field]

chance /tʃɑːns/ *n., adj., & v.* ● *n.* **1 a** a possibility (*just a chance we will catch the train*). **b** (often in *pl.*) probability (*the chances are against it*). **2** a risk (*have to take a chance*). **3 a** an accidental occurrence (*just a chance that they met*). **b** the absence of design or discoverable cause (*here merely because of chance*). **4** an opportunity (*didn't have a chance to speak to him*). **5** the way things happen; fortune; luck (*we'll just leave it to chance*). **6** (often **Chance**) the course of events regarded as a power; fate (*blind Chance rules the universe*). ● *adj.* fortuitous, accidental (*a chance meeting*). ● *v.* **1** *tr. colloq.* risk (*we'll chance it and go*). **2** *intr.* (often foll. by *that* + clause, or *to* + infin.) happen without intention (*it chanced that I found it; I chanced to find it*). □ **by any chance** as it happens; perhaps. **by chance** without design; unintentionally. **chance one's arm** *Brit. colloq.* make an attempt though unlikely to succeed. **chance on** (or **upon**) happen to find, meet, etc. **on the chance** (often foll. by *of*, or *that* + clause) in view of the possibility. **stand a chance** (usu. with *neg.* or *interrog.*) have a prospect of success etc. **take a chance** (or **chances**) behave riskily; risk failure. **take a** (or **one's**) **chance on** (or **with**) consent to take the consequences of; trust to luck. [Middle English from Anglo-French *ch(e)aunce*, Old French *chëance, chëoir* 'fall', ultimately from Latin *cadere*]

chancel /'tʃɑːns(ə)l/ *n.* the part of a church near the altar, reserved for the clergy, the choir, etc., usu. enclosed by a screen or separated from the nave by steps. [Middle English via Old French from Latin *cancelli* 'lattice']

chancellery /'tʃɑːns(ə)l(ə)ri, -sləri/ *n.* (*pl.* **-ies**) **1 a** the position, office, staff, department, etc., of a chancellor. **b** the official residence of a chancellor. **2** *US* an office attached to an embassy or consulate. [Middle English from Old French *chancellerie* (as CHANCELLOR)]

chancellor /'tʃɑːns(ə)lə/ *n.* **1** a state or legal official of various kinds. **2** (**Chancellor**) **a** the head of the government in some European countries, e.g. Germany. **b** = CHANCELLOR OF THE EXCHEQUER. **3** esp. *Brit.* the non-resident honorary head of a university. **4** a bishop's law officer. **5** *US* the president of a chancery court. **6** an officer of an order of knighthood who seals commissions etc. (*Chancellor of the Garter*). □ **chancellorship** *n.* [Old English via Anglo-French *c(h)anceler*, Old French *-ier* from Late Latin *cancellarius* 'porter, secretary' (originally a court official at the grating separating public from judges), from *cancelli* 'lattice']

Chancellor of the Duchy of Lancaster *n.* (in the UK) a member of the government legally representing the Crown as Duke of Lancaster, often a Cabinet minister employed on non-departmental work.

Chancellor of the Exchequer *n.* the finance minister of the United Kingdom.

chance-medley /tʃɑːns'mɛdli/ *n.* (*pl.* **-eys**) **1** *Law* a fight, esp. homicidal, beginning unintentionally. **2** inadvertency. [Anglo-French *chance medlee* (see MEDDLE) 'mixed chance']

chancery /'tʃɑːns(ə)ri/ *n.* (*pl.* **-ies**) **1** (**Chancery**) *Law* the Lord Chancellor's court, a division of the High Court of Justice. **2** *hist.* the records office of an order of knighthood. **3** *hist.* the court of a bishop's chancellor. **4** an office attached to an embassy or consulate. **5** a public record office. **6** *US* a court of equity. □ **in chancery** *slang* (of a boxer or wrestler) with his or her head held, contrary to the rules, between the opponent's arm and body and unable to avoid blows. [Middle English, contracted from CHANCELLERY]

chancre /'ʃaŋkə/ *n.* a painless ulcer developing in venereal disease etc. [French, from Latin CANCER]

chancroid /'ʃaŋkrɔɪd/ *n.* ulceration of lymph nodes in the groin, from venereal disease.

chancy /'tʃɑːnsi/ *adj.* (**chancier**, **chanciest**) subject to chance; uncertain; risky. □ **chancily** *adv.* **chanciness** *n.*

chandelier /ʃandə'lɪə/ *n.* an ornamental branched hanging support for several candles or electric light bulbs. [French, from *chandelle* CANDLE]

chandler /'tʃɑːndlə/ *n.* a dealer in candles, oil, soap, paint, groceries, etc. [Middle English from Anglo-French *chaundeler*, Old French *chandelier* 'candle-maker or -seller', from *chandelle* CANDLE]

chandlery /'tʃɑːndləri/ *n.* goods sold by a chandler.

change /tʃeɪn(d)ʒ/ *n.* & *v.* ● *n.* **1 a** the act or an instance of making or becoming different. **b** an alteration or modification (*the change in her expression*). **2 a** money given in exchange for money in larger units or a different currency. **b** money returned as the balance of that given in payment. **c** = SMALL CHANGE. **3** a new experience; variety (*fancied a change; for a change*). **4 a** the substitution of one thing for another; an exchange (*change of scene*). **b** a set of clothes etc. put on in place of another. **5** (in full **change of life**) *colloq.* the menopause. **6** (usu. in *pl.*) any of the different orders in which a peal of bells can be rung. **7** (**Change**) (also **'Change**) *hist.* a place where merchants etc. met to do business. **8** (of the moon) arrival at a fresh phase, esp. at the new moon. ● *v.* **1** *tr.* & *intr.* undergo, show, or subject to change; make or become different (*the wig changed his appearance; changed from an introvert into an extrovert*). **2** *tr.* **a** take or use another instead of; go from one to another (*change one's socks; changed his doctor; changed trains*). **b** (usu. foll. by *for*) give up or get rid of in exchange (*changed the car for a van*). **3** *tr.* **a** give or get change in smaller denominations for (*can you change a ten-pound note?*). **b** (foll. by *for*) exchange (a sum of money) for (*changed his dollars for pounds*). **4** *tr.* & *intr.* put fresh clothes or coverings on (*changed the baby as he was wet; changed into something loose*). **5** *tr.* (often foll. by *with*) give and receive, exchange (*changed places with him; we changed places*). **6** *intr.* change trains etc. (*changed at Crewe*). **7** *intr.* (of the moon) arrive at a fresh phase, esp. become new. □ **change colour** blanch or flush. **change down** *Brit.* engage a lower gear in a vehicle. **change gear** engage a different gear in a vehicle. **change hands 1** pass to a different owner. **2** substitute one hand for the other when performing an action etc. **change one's mind** adopt a different opinion or plan. **change of air** a different climate; variety. **change over** change from one system or situation to another. **change step** alter one's step so that the opposite leg is the one that marks time when marching etc. **change the subject** begin talking of something different, esp. to avoid embarrassment. **change one's tune 1** voice a different opinion from that expressed previously. **2** change one's style of language or manner, esp. from an insolent to a respectful tone. **change up** *Brit.* engage a higher gear in a vehicle. **get no change out of** *Brit. colloq.* **1** fail to get information from. **2** fail to get the better of (in business etc.). **ring the changes (on)** vary the ways of expressing, arranging, or doing something. □ **changeful** *adj.* **changer** *n.* [Middle English via Anglo-French *chaunge*, Old French *change, changer* from Late Latin *cambiare*, Latin *cambire* 'barter', probably of Celtic origin]

changeable /ˈtʃem(d)ʒəb(ə)l/ *adj.* **1** irregular, inconstant. **2** that can change or be changed. □ **changeability** /-ˈbɪlɪti/ *n.* **changeableness** *n.* **changeably** *adv.* [Middle English from Old French, formed as CHANGE]

changeless /ˈtʃem(d)ʒlɪs/ *adj.* unchanging. □ **changelessly** *adv.* **changelessness** *n.*

changeling /ˈtʃem(d)ʒlɪŋ/ *n.* a child believed to have been substituted for another by stealth, esp. by fairies.

change of heart *n.* a conversion to a different view.

change of life see CHANGE *n.* 5.

changeover /ˈtʃem(d)ʒəʊvə/ *n.* a change from one system or situation to another.

change-ringing *n.* the ringing of a set of bells in a constantly varying order. □ **change-ringer** *n.*

channel[1] /ˈtʃan(ə)l/ *n.* & *v.* ● *n.* **1 a** a length of water wider than a strait, joining two larger areas, esp. seas. **b** (**the Channel**) the English Channel between Britain and France. **2** a medium of communication; an agency for conveying information (*through the usual channels*). **3** *Broadcasting* **a** a band of frequencies used in radio and television transmission, esp. as used by a particular station. **b** a service or station using this. **4** the course in which anything moves; a direction. **5 a** a natural or artificial hollow bed of water. **b** the navigable part of a waterway. **6** a tubular passage for liquid. **7** *Electronics* a lengthwise strip on recording tape etc. **8** a groove or a flute, esp. in a column. ● *v.tr.* (**channelled**, **channelling**; *US* **channeled**, **channeling**) **1** guide, direct (*channelled them through customs*). **2** form channels in; groove. [Middle English via Old French *chanel* from Latin *canalis* CANAL]

channel[2] /ˈtʃan(ə)l/ *n.* *Naut.* any of the broad thick planks projecting horizontally from a ship's side abreast of the masts, used to widen the basis for the shrouds. [for *chain-wale*: cf. *gunnel* for *gunwale*]

channelize /ˈtʃan(ə)lʌɪz/ *v.tr.* (also **-ise**) convey in, or as if in, a channel; guide.

chanson /ˈʃɒsɒ̃, French ʃɑ̃sɔ̃/ *n.* a French song. [French]

chanson de geste /ˌʃɒsɒ̃ də ˈʒɛst, French ʃɑ̃sɔ̃ də ʒɛst/ *n.* (*pl.* ***chansons de geste*** *pronunc.* same) any of a group of medieval French epic poems. [French, = song of heroic deeds]

chant /tʃɑːnt/ *n.* & *v.* ● *n.* **1 a** a spoken sing-song phrase, esp. one performed in unison by a crowd etc. **b** a repetitious sing-song way of speaking. **2** *Mus.* **a** a short musical passage in two or more phrases used for singing unmetrical words, e.g. psalms, canticles. **b** the psalm or canticle so sung. **c** a song, esp. monotonous or repetitive. **3** a musical recitation, esp. of poetry. ● *v.tr.* & *intr.* **1** talk or repeat monotonously (*a crowd chanting slogans*). **2** sing or intone (a psalm etc.). [Middle English (originally as verb) via Old French *chanter* 'sing' from Latin *cantare*, frequentative of *canere cant-* 'sing']

chanter /ˈtʃɑːntə/ *n.* *Mus.* the melody-pipe, with finger-holes, of a bagpipe.

chanterelle /ˈtʃɑːntərɛl, tʃɑːntəˈrɛl/ *n.* an edible fungus, *Cantharellus cibarius*, with a yellow funnel-shaped cap and a smell of apricots. [French via modern Latin *cantharellus*, diminutive of *cantharus*, from Greek *kantharos*, a kind of drinking vessel]

chanteuse /ʃɑːnˈtəːz/ *n.* a female singer of popular songs. [French]

chanticleer /ˈtʃɑːntɪklɪə/ *n.* *literary* a name given to a domestic cock, esp. in fairy tales etc. [Middle English from Old French *chantecler* (as CHANT, CLEAR), a name in the fable *Reynard the Fox*]

Chantilly /ʃanˈtɪli/ *n.* **1** a delicate kind of bobbin lace. **2** sweetened or flavoured whipped cream. [named after *Chantilly*, a town near Paris]

chantry /ˈtʃɑːntri/ *n.* (*pl.* **-ies**) **1** an endowment for a priest or priests to celebrate masses for the founder's soul. **2** the priests, chapel, altar, etc., endowed for this purpose. [Middle English from Anglo-French *chaunterie*, Old French *chanterie* from *chanter* CHANT]

chanty var. of SHANTY[2].

Chanukkah var. of HANUKKAH.

chaos /ˈkeɪɒs/ *n.* **1 a** utter confusion. **b** *Sci.* behaviour so unpredictable as to appear random, owing to great sensitivity to small changes in conditions. **2** the formless matter supposed to have existed before the creation of the universe. □ **chaotic** /keɪˈɒtɪk/ *adj.* **chaotically** /-ˈɒtɪk(ə)li/ *adv.* [French or Latin from Greek *khaos*: *-otic* on the pattern of *erotic* etc.]

chaos theory *n.* the mathematical study of complex systems whose behaviour is highly sensitive to slight changes in conditions, so that small alterations can give rise to strikingly great consequences.

chap[1] /tʃap/ *v.* & *n.* ● *v.* (**chapped**, **chapping**) **1** *intr.* (esp. of the skin; also of dry ground etc.) crack in fissures, esp. because of exposure and dryness. **2** *tr.* (of the wind, cold, etc.) cause to chap. ● *n.* (usu. in *pl.*) **1** a crack in the skin. **2** an open seam in the ground. [Middle English, perhaps related to Middle Low German, Middle Dutch *kappen* 'chop off']

chap[2] /tʃap/ *n.* esp. *Brit. colloq.* a man; a boy; a fellow. [abbreviation of CHAPMAN]

chap[3] /tʃap/ *n.* the lower jaw or half of the cheek, esp. of a pig as food. [16th c.: variant of CHOP[2], of unknown origin]

chap. *abbr.* chapter.

chaparajos /ʃapəˈreɪhəʊs, tʃ-/ *n.pl.* *N. Amer.* a cowboy's leather protection for the front of the legs. [Mexican Spanish *chaparreras* from *chaparra* 'dwarf evergreen oak']

chaparral /ʃapəˈral, tʃ-/ *n.* *N. Amer.* dense tangled brushwood; undergrowth. [Spanish from *chaparra* 'dwarf evergreen oak']

chaparral cock *n.* = ROADRUNNER.

chapatti /tʃəˈpɑːti, -ˈpati/ *n.* (also **chapati**, **chupatty**) (*pl.* **-is** or **chupatties**) (in Indian cookery) a flat thin cake of unleavened wholemeal bread. [Hindi *capātī*]

chapbook /ˈtʃapbʊk/ *n.* **1** *hist.* a small pamphlet containing tales, ballads, tracts, etc., hawked by chapmen. **2** esp. *N. Amer.* a small paper-covered booklet of poems, fiction, etc. [19th c.: see CHAPMAN]

chape /tʃeɪp/ *n.* **1** the metal cap of a scabbard point. **2** the back-piece of a buckle attaching it to a strap etc. **3** a sliding loop on a belt or strap. [Middle English from Old French, = cope, hood, from Late Latin *cappa* CAP]

chapeau-bras /ʃapəʊˈbrɑː, French ʃapobra/ *n.* (*pl.* ***chapeaux-bras*** *pronunc.* same) a three-cornered flat silk hat often carried under the arm. [French from *chapeau* 'hat' + *bras* 'arm']

chapel /ˈtʃap(ə)l/ *n.* & *adj.* ● *n.* **1 a** a place for private Christian worship in a large church or esp. a cathedral, with its own altar and dedication (*Lady chapel*). **b** a place of Christian worship attached to a private house or institution. **2** *Brit.* **a** a place of worship for Nonconformist bodies. **b** a chapel service. **c** attendance at a chapel. **3** *Brit.* an Anglican church subordinate to a parish church. **4 a** a room or building for funeral services. **b** esp. *US* = CHAPEL OF REST. **5** *Brit. Printing* **a** the members or branch of a printers' trade union at a specific place of work. **b** a meeting of such a union branch. ● *predic.adj.* *Brit. colloq.* belonging to or regularly attending a Nonconformist chapel. [Middle English via Old French *chapele* from medieval Latin *cappella*, diminutive of *cappa* 'cloak': the first chapel was a sanctuary in which St Martin's sacred cloak (*cappella*) was preserved]

chapel of ease *n.* an Anglican chapel for the convenience of remote parishioners.

chapel of rest *n.* *Brit.* an undertaker's mortuary.

chapel royal *n.* a chapel in a royal palace.

chapelry /ˈtʃap(ə)lri/ *n.* (*pl.* **-ies**) a district served by an Anglican chapel.

chaperone /ˈʃapərəʊn/ *n.* & *v.* (also **chaperon**) ● *n.* **1** a person, esp. an older woman, who ensures propriety by accompanying a young unmarried woman on social occasions. **2** a person who takes charge of esp. young people in public. ● *v.tr.* act as a chaperone to. □ **chaperonage** /ˈʃap(ə)r(ə)nɪdʒ/ *n.* [French, fem. of *chaperon* 'hood' (regarded as giving protection), diminutive of *chape* 'cope': see CHAPE]

chap-fallen *adj.* dispirited, dejected (with the lower jaw hanging). [CHAP³]

chaplain /ˈtʃaplɪn/ *n.* a member of the clergy attached to a private chapel, institution, ship, regiment, etc. □ **chaplaincy** *n.* (*pl.* **-ies**). [Middle English via Anglo-French & Old French *c(h)apelain* from medieval Latin *cappellanus*, originally custodian of the cloak of St Martin: see CHAPEL]

chaplet /ˈtʃaplɪt/ *n.* **1** a garland or circlet for the head. **2** a string of 55 beads (one-third of the rosary number) for counting prayers, or as a necklace. **3** a bead-moulding. □ **chapleted** *adj.* [Middle English from Old French *chapelet*, ultimately from Late Latin *cappa* CAP]

chapman /ˈtʃapmən/ *n.* (*pl.* **-men**) *Brit. hist.* a pedlar. [Old English *cēapman* from *cēap* 'barter']

chappal /ˈtʃap(ə)l/ *n.* an Indian sandal, usu. of leather. [Hindi]

chappie /ˈtʃapi/ *n. Brit. colloq.* = CHAP².

chaps /ʃaps, tʃ-/ *n.* = CHAPARAJOS. [abbreviation]

chapter /ˈtʃaptə/ *n.* **1** a main division of a book. **2** a period of time (in a person's life, a nation's history, etc.). **3** a series or sequence (*a chapter of misfortunes*). **4 a** the canons of a cathedral or other religious community or knightly order. **b** a meeting of these. **5** an Act of Parliament numbered as part of a session's proceedings. **6 a** *N. Amer.* a local branch of a society. **b** a local group of Hell's Angels. □ **chapter and verse** an exact reference or authority. [Middle English via Old French *chapitre* from Latin *capitulum*, diminutive of *caput -itis* 'head']

chapter house *n.* **1** a building used for the meetings of a chapter. **2** *US* the place where a college fraternity or sorority meets.

char¹ /tʃɑː/ *v.tr. & intr.* (**charred**, **charring**) **1** make or become black by burning; scorch. **2** burn or be burnt to charcoal. [apparently back-formation from CHARCOAL]

char² /tʃɑː/ *n. & v. Brit. colloq.* ● *n.* = CHARWOMAN. ● *v.intr.* (**charred**, **charring**) work as a charwoman. [earlier *chare* from Old English *cerr* 'a turn', *cierran* 'to turn']

char³ /tʃɑː/ *n.* (also **cha** /tʃɑː/) *Brit. colloq.* tea. [Chinese *cha*]

char⁴ /tʃɑː/ *n.* (also **charr**) (*pl.* same) any small troutlike fish of the genus *Salvelinus*. [17th c.: origin unknown]

charabanc /ˈʃarəbaŋ/ *n. Brit. hist.* an early form of motor coach. [French *char à bancs* 'carriage with seats']

characin /ˈkarəsɪn/ *n.* a freshwater fish of the family Characidae, mainly of S. and Central America, including piranhas and tetras. [modern Latin *Characinus* genus name, from Greek *kharax*, a kind of fish]

character /ˈkarəktə/ *n. & v.* ● *n.* **1** the collective qualities or characteristics, esp. mental and moral, that distinguish a person or thing. **2 a** moral strength (*has a weak character*). **b** reputation, esp. good reputation. **3 a** a person in a novel, play, etc. **b** a part played by an actor; a role. **4** *colloq.* a person, esp. an eccentric or outstanding individual (*he's a real character*). **5 a** a printed or written letter, symbol, or distinctive mark (*Chinese characters*). **b** *Computing* any of a group of symbols representing a letter etc. **6** a written description of a person's qualities; a testimonial. **7** a characteristic (esp. of a biological species). ● *v.tr. archaic* inscribe; describe. □ **in** (or **out of**) **character** consistent (or inconsistent) with a person's character. □ **characterful** *adj.* **characterfully** *adv.* **characterless** *adj.* [Middle English via Old French *caractere* and Latin *character* from Greek *kharaktēr* 'stamp, impress']

character actor *n.* an actor who specializes in playing eccentric or unusual persons.

character assassination *n.* a malicious attempt to harm or destroy a person's good reputation.

characteristic /karəktəˈrɪstɪk/ *adj. & n.* ● *adj.* typical, distinctive (*with characteristic expertise*). ● *n.* **1** a characteristic feature or quality. **2** *Math.* the whole number or integral part of a logarithm. □ **characteristically** *adv.* [French *caractéristique* or medieval Latin *characterizare*, from Greek *kharaktērizō*]

characteristic curve *n.* a graph showing the relationship between two variable but interdependent quantities.

characteristic radiation *n.* radiation the wavelengths of which are peculiar to the element which emits them.

characterize /ˈkarəktərʌɪz/ *v.tr.* (also **-ise**) **1 a** describe the character of. **b** (foll. by *as*) describe as. **2** be characteristic of. **3** impart character to. □ **characterization** /-ˈzeɪʃ(ə)n/ *n.* [French *caractériser* or medieval Latin *characterizare*, from Greek *kharaktērizō*]

charade /ʃəˈrɑːd/ *n.* **1 a** (usu. in *pl.*, treated as *sing.*) a game of guessing a word from a written or acted clue given for each syllable and for the whole. **b** one such clue. **2** an absurd pretence. [French from modern Provençal *charrado* 'conversation', from *charra* 'chatter']

charas /ˈtʃɑːrəs/ *n.* a narcotic resin from the flower heads of hemp; cannabis resin. [Hindi]

charbroil /ˈtʃɑːbrɔɪl/ *v.tr.* grill (meat etc.) on a rack over charcoal. [CHARCOAL + BROIL¹]

charcoal /ˈtʃɑːkəʊl/ *n. & adj.* ● *n.* **1 a** an amorphous form of carbon consisting of a porous black residue from wood, bones, etc., heated in the absence of air. **b** (usu. in *pl.*) a piece of this used for drawing. **2** a drawing in charcoal. **3** (in full **charcoal grey**) a dark grey colour. ● *adj.* (in full **charcoal grey**; hyphenated when *attrib.*) dark grey. [Middle English COAL = charcoal: first element perhaps *chare* 'turn' (cf. CHAR¹, CHAR²)]

charcoal biscuit *n.* a biscuit containing wood charcoal to aid digestion.

charcuterie /ʃɑːˈkuːt(ə)riː/ *n.* **1** cold cooked meats. **2** a shop selling these. [French]

chard /tʃɑːd/ *n.* (in full **Swiss chard**) a kind of beet, *Beta vulgaris*, with edible broad white leaf-stalks and green blades. Also called *seakale beet*. [French *carde*, and *chardon* 'thistle': cf. CARDOON]

Chardonnay /ˈʃɑːdəneɪ/ *n.* **1** a variety of white grape used for making champagne and other wines. **2** the vine on which this grape grows. **3** a wine made from Chardonnay grapes. [French]

charge /tʃɑːdʒ/ *v. & n.* ● *v.* **1** *tr.* **a** ask (an amount) as a price (*charges £5 a ticket*). **b** ask (a person) for an amount as a price (*you forgot to charge me*). **2** *tr.* **a** (foll. by *to*, *up to*) debit the cost of to (a person or account) (*charge it to my account*; *charge it up to me*). **b** debit (a person or an account) (*bought a new car and charged the company*). **3** *tr.* **a** (often foll. by *with*) accuse (of an offence) (*charged him with theft*). **b** (foll. by *that* + clause) make an accusation that. **4** *tr.* (foll. by *to* + infin.) instruct or urge. **5** (foll. by *with*) **a** *tr.* entrust with. **b** *refl.* undertake. **6 a** *intr.* make a rushing attack; rush headlong. **b** *tr.* make a rushing attack on; throw oneself against. **7** (often foll. by *up*) **a** *tr.* give an electric charge to (a body); store energy in (a battery etc.). **b** *intr.* (of a battery etc.) receive and store energy. **8** *tr.* (often foll. by *with*) load or fill (a vessel, gun, etc.) to the full or proper extent. **9** *tr.* (usu. as **charged** *adj.*) **a** (foll. by *with*) saturated with (*air charged with vapour*). **b** (usu. foll. by *with*) pervaded (with strong feelings etc.) (*atmosphere charged with emotion*; *a charged atmosphere*). ● *n.* **1 a** a price asked for goods or services. **b** a financial liability or commitment. **2** an accusation, esp. against a prisoner brought to trial. **3 a** a task, duty, or commission. **b** care, custody, responsible possession. **c** a person or thing entrusted; a minister's congregation. **4 a** an impetuous rush or attack, esp. in a battle. **b** the signal for this. **5** the appropriate amount of material to be put into a receptacle, mechanism, etc. at one time, esp. of explosive for a gun. **6 a** a property of matter that is a consequence of the interaction between its constituent particles and exists in a positive or negative form, causing electrical phenomena. **b** the quantity of this carried by a body. **c** energy stored chemically for conversion into electricity. **d** the process of charging a battery. **7** an exhortation; directions, orders, esp. *Law* instructions given by a judge to a jury, or *Eccl.* by a bishop to his clergy. **8** a burden or load. **9** *Heraldry* a device; a bearing. □ **free of charge** free, without charge. **give a person in charge** *Brit.* hand a person over to the police. **in charge** having command. **lay to a person's charge** *Brit.* accuse a person of. **put a person on a charge** *Brit.* charge a person with a specified offence. **return to the charge** begin again, esp. in argument. **take charge** (often foll. by *of*) assume control or direction. □ **chargeable** *adj.* [Middle English via Old French *charger* and Late Latin *car(ri)care* 'to load' from Latin *carrus* CAR]

charge account *n. N. Amer.* a credit account at a shop etc.

charge card *n.* a credit card for which the account must be paid in full when a statement is issued.

charge-coupled device see CCD.

chargé d'affaires /ˌʃɑːʒeɪ daˈfɛː/ *n.* (also **chargé**) (*pl.* **chargés** *pronunc.* same) **1** an ambassador's deputy. **2** an envoy to a minor country. [French, = in charge of affairs]

chargehand /ˈtʃɑːdʒhand/ *n. Brit.* a worker, ranking below a foreman, in charge of others on a particular job.

charge nurse *n. Brit.* a nurse in charge of a ward.

charger[1] /ˈtʃɑːdʒə/ *n.* **1 a** a cavalry horse. **b** *poet.* any horse. **2** a device for charging a battery or battery-powered equipment. **3** a person or thing that charges.

charger[2] /ˈtʃɑːdʒə/ *n. archaic* a large flat dish. [Middle English from Anglo-French *chargeour*]

charge sheet *n. Brit.* a record of cases and charges made at a police station.

chariot /ˈtʃarɪət/ *n.* & *v.* ● *n.* **1** *hist.* **a** a two-wheeled vehicle drawn by horses, used in ancient warfare and racing. **b** a four-wheeled carriage with back seats only. **2** *poet.* a stately or triumphal vehicle. ● *v.tr. literary* convey in or as in a chariot. [Middle English from Old French, augmentative of *char* CAR]

charioteer /tʃarɪəˈtɪə/ *n.* a chariot driver.

charisma /kəˈrɪzmə/ *n.* (*pl.* **charismata** /kəˈrɪzmətə/) **1 a** the ability to inspire followers with devotion and enthusiasm. **b** an attractive aura; great charm. **2** a divinely conferred power or talent. [ecclesiastical Latin from Greek *kharisma*, from *kharis* 'favour, grace']

charismatic /karɪzˈmatɪk/ *adj.* & *n.* ● *adj.* **1** having charisma; inspiring enthusiasm. **2** (of Christian worship) characterized by spontaneity, ecstatic utterances, etc. ● *n.* a person who claims divine inspiration; an adherent of charismatic worship. □ **charismatically** *adv.*

charismatic movement *n.* a neo-pentecostal movement within Roman Catholic, Anglican, and other Christian Churches.

charitable /ˈtʃarɪtəb(ə)l/ *adj.* **1** generous in giving to those in need. **2** of, relating to, or connected with a charity or charities. **3** apt to judge favourably of persons, acts, and motives. □ **charitableness** *n.* **charitably** *adv.* [Middle English from Old French, from *charité* CHARITY]

charity /ˈtʃarɪti/ *n.* (*pl.* **-ies**) **1 a** giving voluntarily to those in need; alms-giving. **b** the help, esp. money, so given. **2** an institution or organization for helping those in need. **3 a** kindness, benevolence. **b** tolerance in judging others. **c** love of one's fellow human beings. [Old English via Old French *charité* from Latin *caritas -tatis*, from *carus* 'dear']

Charity Commission *n.* (in the UK) a board established to control charitable trusts.

charivari /ʃɑːrɪˈvɑːri/ *n.* (also esp. *US* **shivaree** /ʃɪvəˈriː/) **1** a serenade of banging saucepans etc. to a newly married couple. **2** a medley of sounds; a hubbub. [French, = a serenade with pans, trays, etc., to an unpopular person]

charlady /ˈtʃɑːleɪdi/ *n.* (*pl.* **-ies**) *Brit.* = CHARWOMAN.

charlatan /ˈʃɑːlət(ə)n/ *n.* a person falsely claiming a special knowledge or skill. □ **charlatanism** *n.* **charlatanry** *n.* [French from Italian *ciarlatano*, from *ciarlare* 'babble']

Charles' Law /ˈtʃɑːlz/ *n.* (also **Charles's Law** /ˈtʃɑːlzɪz/) *Chem.* the law stating that the volume of an ideal gas at constant pressure is directly proportional to the absolute temperature. [named after J. A. C. *Charles*, French scientist d. 1823, who first formulated it]

Charles's Wain /ˈtʃɑːlzɪz/ *n.* esp. *Brit.* = PLOUGH 4. [Old English *Carles wægn* 'the wain of Carl' (Charles the Great, Charlemagne), perhaps by association of the star Arcturus with legends of King Arthur and Charlemagne]

charleston /ˈtʃɑːlst(ə)n, -lz-/ *n.* & *v.* (also **Charleston**) ● *n.* a lively dance of the 1920s with side-kicks from the knee. ● *v.intr.* dance the charleston. [named after *Charleston*, a city in S. Carolina, US]

charley horse /ˈtʃɑːli/ *n. N. Amer. slang* stiffness or a cramp in an arm or leg. [19th c.: origin uncertain]

charlie /ˈtʃɑːli/ *n. Brit. slang* **1** a fool. **2** (in *pl.*) a woman's breasts. [diminutive of the name *Charles*]

charlock /ˈtʃɑːlɒk/ *n.* a wild mustard, *Sinapis arvensis*, with yellow flowers. Also called *field mustard*. [Old English *cerlic*, of unknown origin]

charlotte /ˈʃɑːlət/ *n.* a pudding made of stewed fruit with a casing or layers or covering of bread, sponge cake, biscuits, or breadcrumbs (*apple charlotte*). [French]

charlotte russe /ˈruːs/ *n.* custard etc. enclosed in sponge cake or a casing of sponge fingers. [French = Russian charlotte]

charm /tʃɑːm/ *n.* & *v.* ● *n.* **1 a** the power or quality of giving delight, arousing admiration, or influencing. **b** fascination, attractiveness. **c** (usu. in *pl.*) an attractive or enticing quality. **2** a trinket on a bracelet etc. **3 a** an object, act, or word(s) supposedly having occult or magic power; a spell. **b** a thing worn to avert evil etc.; an amulet. **4** *Physics* a property of matter manifested by certain quarks. ● *v.tr.* **1** delight, captivate (*charmed by the performance*). **2** influence or protect as if by magic (*leads a charmed life*). **3 a** gain by charm (*charmed agreement out of him*). **b** influence by charm (*charmed her into consenting*). **4** cast a spell on, bewitch. □ **like a charm** perfectly, wonderfully. □ **charmer** *n.* [Middle English via Old French *charme*, *charmer* from Latin *carmen* 'song']

charm bracelet *n.* a bracelet hung with small trinkets.

charmeuse /ʃɑːˈməːz/ *n.* a soft smooth silky dress fabric. [French, fem. of *charmeur* 'charmer' (as CHARM)]

charming /ˈtʃɑːmɪŋ/ *adj.* **1** delightful, attractive, pleasing. **2** (often as *int.*) *iron.* expressing displeasure or disapproval. □ **charmingly** *adv.*

charmless /ˈtʃɑːmlɪs/ *adj.* lacking charm; unattractive; ungracious. □ **charmlessly** *adv.* **charmlessness** *n.*

charm offensive *n.* the deliberate use of charm or cooperation in order to achieve a (usu. political) goal.

charnel house /ˈtʃɑːn(ə)l/ *n.* a house or vault in which dead bodies or bones are piled. [Middle English & Old French *charnel* 'burying place' via medieval Latin *carnale* from Late Latin *carnalis* CARNAL]

Charolais /ˈʃarə(ʊ)leɪ/ *n.* (also **Charollais**) (*pl.* same) **1** an animal of a breed of large white beef cattle. **2** this breed. [Monts du *Charollais* in E. France]

charpoy /ˈtʃɑːpɔɪ/ *n. Anglo-Ind.* a light bedstead. [Hindustani *chārpāi*]

charr var. of CHAR[4].

chart /tʃɑːt/ *n.* & *v.* ● *n.* **1** a geographical map or plan, esp. for navigation by sea or air. **2** a sheet of information in the form of a table, graph, or diagram. **3** (usu. in *pl.*) a listing of the currently most popular records, esp. pop singles. ● *v.tr.* make a chart of, map. [French *charte* from Latin *charta* CARD[1]]

chartbuster /ˈtʃɑːtbʌstə/ *n. colloq.* a best-selling popular song, record, etc.

charter /ˈtʃɑːtə/ *n.* & *v.* ● *n.* **1 a** a written grant of rights, by the sovereign or legislature, esp. the creation of a borough, company, university, etc. **b** a written constitution or description of an organization's functions etc. **2** a contract to hire an aircraft, ship, etc., for a special purpose. **3** = CHARTER PARTY. ● *v.tr.* **1** grant a charter to. **2** hire (an aircraft, ship, etc.). ▫ **charterer** *n.* [Middle English via Old French *chartre* from Latin *chartula*, diminutive of *charta* CARD[1]]

chartered /ˈtʃɑːtəd/ *adj. Brit.* (of an accountant, engineer, librarian, etc.) qualified as a member of a professional body that has a royal charter.

chartered libertine *n. Brit.* a person allowed to do as he or she pleases.

charter flight *n.* a flight by a chartered aircraft.

Charter Mark *n.* (in the UK) an award granted to institutions for exceptional public service under the terms of the Citizen's Charter.

charter member *n.* an original member of a society, corporation, etc.

charter party *n.* (*pl.* **-ies**) a deed between a shipowner and a merchant for the hire of a ship and the delivery of cargo. [French *charte partie* from medieval Latin *charta partita* 'divided charter, indenture']

Chartism /ˈtʃɑːtɪz(ə)m/ *n. hist.* the principles of the UK parliamentary reform movement of 1837–48. ▫ **Chartist** *n.* [Latin *charta* charter + -ISM: name taken from the manifesto 'People's Charter']

chartreuse /ʃɑːˈtrəːz/ *n.* & *adj.* ● *n.* **1** a pale green or yellow liqueur of brandy and aromatic herbs etc. **2** the pale yellow or pale green colour of this. **3** a dish of fruit enclosed in jelly etc. ● *adj.* pale green or pale yellow. [La Grande *Chartreuse* (Carthusian monastery near Grenoble), where the liqueur was first made]

chart-topping *attrib.adj.* occupying the first place in a chart of popular records etc. ▫ **chart-topper** *n.*

charwoman /ˈtʃɑːwʊmən/ *n.* (*pl.* **-women**) *Brit.* a woman employed as a cleaner in houses or offices.

chary /ˈtʃɛːri/ *adj.* (**charier**, **chariest**) **1** cautious, wary (*chary of employing such people*). **2** sparing; ungenerous (*chary of giving praise*). **3** shy. ▫ **charily** *adv.* [Old English *cearig*, related to CARE]

Charybdis see SCYLLA AND CHARYBDIS.

Chas. *abbr.* Charles.

chase[1] /tʃeɪs/ *v.* & *n.* ● *v.* **1** *tr.* pursue in order to catch. **2** *tr.* (foll. by *from*, *out of*, *to*, etc.) drive. **3** *intr.* **a** (foll. by *after*) hurry in pursuit of (a person). **b** (foll. by *round* etc.) *colloq.* act or move about hurriedly. **4** *tr.* (usu. foll. by *up*) *Brit. colloq.* pursue (overdue work, payment, etc. or the person responsible for it). **5** *tr. colloq.* **a** try to attain. **b** court persistently and openly. ● *n.* **1** pursuit. **2** *Brit.* unenclosed hunting land. **3** (prec. by *the*) hunting, esp. as a sport. **4** an animal etc. that is pursued. **5** = STEEPLECHASE. ▫ **go and chase oneself** (usu. in *imper.*) *Brit. colloq.* depart. [Middle English from Old French *chace chacier*, ultimately from Latin *capere* 'take']

chase[2] /tʃeɪs/ *v.tr.* emboss or engrave (metal). [apparently from earlier *enchase* from Old French *enchasser* (as EN-[1], CASE[2])]

chase[3] /tʃeɪs/ *n. Printing* a metal frame holding composed type. [French *châsse* from Latin *capsa* CASE[2]]

chase[4] /tʃeɪs/ *n.* **1** the part of a gun enclosing the bore. **2** a trench or groove cut to receive a pipe etc. [French *chas* 'enclosed space' via Provençal *ca(u)s* from medieval Latin *capsum* 'thorax, nave of a church']

chaser /ˈtʃeɪsə/ *n.* **1** a person or thing that chases. **2** a horse for steeplechasing. **3** *colloq.* a drink taken after another of a different kind, e.g. spirits after beer.

chasm /ˈkaz(ə)m/ *n.* **1** a deep fissure or opening in the earth, rock, etc. **2** a wide difference of feeling, interests, etc.; a gulf. **3** *archaic* a hiatus. ▫ **chasmic** *adj.* [Latin *chasma* from Greek *khasma* 'gaping hollow']

chassé /ˈʃaseɪ/ *n.* & *v.* ● *n.* a gliding step in dancing. ● *v.intr.* (**chasséd**; **chasséing**) make this step. [French, = chasing]

chasse /ʃɑːs, French ʃas/ *n.* a liqueur taken after coffee etc. [French from *chasser* CHASE[1]]

chasseur sauce /ʃaˈsəː/ *n.* a rich sauce with wine and mushrooms for serving esp. with poultry or game.

chassis /ˈʃasi, -iː/ *n.* (*pl.* same /-sɪz/) **1** the base frame of a motor vehicle, carriage, etc. **2** a frame to carry radio etc. components. [French *châssis*, ultimately from Latin *capsa* CASE[2]]

chaste /tʃeɪst/ *adj.* **1** abstaining from extramarital, or from all, sexual intercourse. **2** (of behaviour, speech, etc.) pure, virtuous, decent. **3** (of artistic etc. style) simple, unadorned. ▫ **chastely** *adv.* **chasteness** *n.* [Middle English via Old French from Latin *castus*]

chasten /ˈtʃeɪs(ə)n/ *v.tr.* **1** (esp. as **chastening, chastened** *adjs.*) subdue, restrain (*a chastening experience*; *chastened by his failure*). **2** discipline, punish. **3** moderate. ▫ **chastener** *n.* [obsolete verb *chaste* via Old French *chastier* from Latin *castigare* CASTIGATE]

chaste tree *n.* an ornamental shrub, *Vitex agnus-castus*, with blue or white flowers.

chastise /tʃaˈstʌɪz/ *v.tr.* **1** rebuke or reprimand severely. **2** punish, esp. by beating. ▫ **chastisement** /ˈtʃastɪzm(ə)nt, -ˈtʌɪzm(ə)nt/ *n.* **chastiser** *n.* [Middle English, apparently formed irregularly from obsolete verbs *chaste, chasty*: see CHASTEN]

chastity /ˈtʃastɪti/ *n.* **1** being chaste. **2** sexual abstinence; virginity. **3** simplicity of style or taste. [Middle English via Old French *chasteté* from Latin *castitas -tatis*, from *castus* CHASTE]

chastity belt *n. hist.* a woman's garment designed to prevent the wearer from having sexual intercourse.

chasuble /ˈtʃazjʊb(ə)l/ *n.* a loose sleeveless usu. ornate outer vestment worn by a priest celebrating Mass or the Eucharist. [Middle English from Old French *chesible*, later *-uble*, ultimately from Latin *casula* 'hooded cloak, little cottage', diminutive of *casa* 'cottage']

chat[1] /tʃat/ *v.* & *n.* ● *v.intr.* (**chatted**, **chatting**) talk in a light familiar way. ● *n.* **1** informal conversation or talk. **2** an instance of this. ▫ **chat up** *colloq.* chat to, esp. flirtatiously or with an ulterior motive. [Middle English: shortening of CHATTER]

chat[2] /tʃat/ *n.* any of various small birds with harsh calls, esp. a stonechat or whinchat or certain American or Australian warblers. [probably imitative]

chateau /ˈʃatəʊ/ *n.* (also **château**) (*pl.* **-teaux** *pronunc.* same or /-təʊz/) a large French country house or castle, often giving its name to wine made in its neighbourhood. [French from Old French *chastel* CASTLE]

chateaubriand /ˌʃatəʊbrɪˈjɒ̃/ *n.* a thick fillet of beef steak. [named after Vicomte de *Chateaubriand* (d. 1848), French writer and statesman]

chatelaine /ˈʃatəleɪn/ *n.* **1** the mistress of a large house. **2** *hist.* a set of short chains attached to a woman's belt, for carrying keys etc. [French *châtelaine*, fem. of *chatelain* 'lord of a castle', from medieval Latin *castellanus* CASTELLAN]

chatline /ˈtʃatlʌɪn/ *n.* a telephone service which sets up conference calls esp. among young people.

chat show *n. Brit.* a television or radio programme in which celebrities are interviewed informally.

chattel /ˈtʃat(ə)l/ *n.* (usu. in *pl.*) **1** *Law* any property other than freehold land, including tangible goods (**chattels personal**) and leasehold interests (**chattels real**). **2** (in general use) a personal possession. [Middle English from Old French *chatel*: see CATTLE]

chattel mortgage *n. N. Amer.* the conveyance of chattels by mortgage as security for a debt.

chatter /ˈtʃatə/ *v. & n.* ● *v.intr.* **1** talk quickly, incessantly, trivially, or indiscreetly. **2** (of a bird, monkey, etc.) emit short quick sounds. **3** (of the teeth) click repeatedly together (usu. from cold). **4** (of a tool) clatter from vibration. ● *n.* **1** chattering talk or sounds. **2** the vibration of a tool. □ **the chattering classes** *Brit. joc.* intellectuals as a social group. □ **chatterer** *n.* **chattery** *adj.* [Middle English: imitative]

chatterbox /ˈtʃatəbɒks/ *n.* a talkative person.

chatty /ˈtʃati/ *adj.* (**chattier**, **chattiest**) **1** fond of chatting; talkative. **2** resembling chat; informal and lively (*a chatty letter*). □ **chattily** *adv.* **chattiness** *n.*

chat-up *n. colloq.* an instance of chatting a person up (often *attrib.*: *chat-up lines*).

Chaucerian /tʃɔːˈsɪərɪən/ *adj. & n.* ● *adj.* of or relating to the English poet Chaucer (d. 1400) or his style. ● *n.* a student of Chaucer.

chaud-froid /ʃəʊˈfrwɑː/ *n.* a dish of cold cooked meat or fish in jelly or sauce. [French from *chaud* 'hot' + *froid* 'cold']

chauffeur /ˈʃəʊfə, ʃəʊˈfəː/ *n. & v.* ● *n.* (*fem.* **chauffeuse** /-ˈfəːz/) a person employed to drive a private or hired motor car. ● *v.tr.* drive (a car or a passenger) as a chauffeur. [French, = stoker]

chaulmoogra /tʃɔːlˈmuːgrə/ *n.* any of several tropical Asian trees of the family Flacourtiaceae, esp. *Hydnocarpus kurzii*, with seeds yielding an oil formerly used to treat skin diseases. [Bengali]

chautauqua /tʃɔːˈtɔːkwə, ʃ-/ *n. N. Amer. hist.* an institution that provided popular adult education courses and entertainment in the late 19th – early 20th c. [*Chautauqua* in New York State, where such courses were held]

chauvinism /ˈʃəʊv(ɪ)nɪz(ə)m/ *n.* **1** exaggerated or aggressive patriotism. **2** excessive or prejudiced support or loyalty for one's cause or group or sex (*male chauvinism*). [named after N. *Chauvin*, a Napoleonic veteran popularized as a character in the Cogniards' *Cocarde Tricolore* (1831)]

chauvinist /ˈʃəʊv(ɪ)nɪst/ *n.* **1** a person exhibiting chauvinism. **2** (in full **male chauvinist**) a man showing excessive loyalty to men and prejudice against women. □ **chauvinistic** /-ˈnɪstɪk/ *adj.* **chauvinistically** /-ˈnɪstɪk(ə)li/ *adv.*

Ch.B. *abbr.* Bachelor of Surgery. [Latin *Chirurgiae Baccalaureus*]

cheap /tʃiːp/ *adj. & adv.* ● *adj.* **1** low in price; worth more than its cost (*a cheap holiday*; *cheap labour*). **2** charging low prices; offering good value (*a cheap restaurant*). **3** of poor quality; inferior (*cheap housing*). **4 a** costing little effort or acquired by discreditable means and hence of little worth (*cheap popularity*; *a cheap joke*). **b** contemptible; despicable (*a cheap criminal*). **5** *N. Amer. colloq.* stingy. ● *adv.* cheaply (*got it cheap*). □ **cheap and cheerful** *Brit.* inexpensive but not unattractive. **cheap and nasty** *Brit.* of low cost and bad quality. **dirt cheap** very cheap. **feel cheap** feel ashamed or contemptible. **on the cheap** cheaply. □ **cheapish** *adj.* **cheaply** *adv.* **cheapness** *n.* [obsolete phrase *good cheap* 'a good bargain', from Old English *cēap* 'barter', ultimately from Latin *caupo* 'innkeeper']

cheapen /ˈtʃiːp(ə)n/ *v.tr. & intr.* make or become cheap or cheaper; depreciate, degrade.

cheapie /ˈθʃiːpi/ *n. & adj.* esp. *N. Amer. slang* ● *n.* a cheap product. ● *adj.* (usu. *attrib.*) cheap.

cheapjack /ˈtʃiːpdʒak/ *n. & adj.* ● *n.* a seller of inferior goods at low prices. ● *adj.* inferior, shoddy. [CHEAP + JACK[1]]

cheapo /ˈtʃiːpəʊ/ *adj.* (usu. *attrib.*) *slang* cheap.

cheapskate /ˈtʃiːpskeɪt/ *n. colloq.* a stingy or parsimonious person; a miser. [CHEAP + *skate* 'a worn-out horse; a mean, contemptible, or dishonest person' (19th c.: origin unknown)]

cheat /tʃiːt/ *v. & n.* ● *v.* **1** *tr.* **a** (often foll. by *into*, *out of*) deceive or trick (*cheated into parting with his savings*). **b** (foll. by *of*) deprive of (*cheated of a chance to reply*). **2** *intr.* gain unfair advantage by deception or breaking rules, esp. in a game or examination. **3** *tr.* avoid (something undesirable) by luck or skill (*cheated the bad weather*). **4** *tr. archaic* divert attention from, beguile (time, tedium, etc.). ● *n.* **1** a person who cheats. **2** a trick, fraud, or deception. **3** an act of cheating. □ **cheat on** *colloq.* be sexually unfaithful to. [Middle English *chete* from *achete*, variant of ESCHEAT]

cheater /ˈtʃiːtə/ *n.* **1** a person who cheats. **2** (in *pl.*) *N. Amer. slang* spectacles.

Chechen /ˈtʃɛtʃɛn/ *n. & adj.* ● *n.* (*pl.* **-s** or same) a member of a Muslim Caucasian people inhabiting Chechnya, an autonomous republic in SE Russia. ● *adj.* of or relating to this people. [from obsolete Russian *chechen* (modern Russian *chechenets*)]

check[1] /tʃɛk/ *v.*, *n.*, *& int.* ● *v.* **1** *tr.* (also *absol.*) **a** examine the accuracy, quality, or condition of. **b** (often foll. by *that* + clause) make sure; verify; establish to one's satisfaction (*checked that the doors were locked*; *checked the train times*). **2** *tr.* **a** stop or slow the motion of; curb, restrain (*progress was checked by bad weather*). **b** *colloq.* find fault with; rebuke. **3** *tr. Chess* move a piece into a position that directly threatens (the opposing king). **4** *intr. US* agree or correspond when compared. **5** *tr. US* mark with a tick etc. **6** *tr. N. Amer.* deposit (luggage etc.) for storage or dispatch. **7** *intr.* (of hounds) pause to ensure or regain scent. ● *n.* **1** a means or act of testing or ensuring accuracy, quality, satisfactory condition, etc. **2 a** a stopping or slowing of motion; a restraint on action. **b** a rebuff or rebuke. **c** a person or thing that restrains. **3** (also as *int.*) *Chess* **a** the exposure of a king to direct attack from an opposing piece. **b** an announcement of this by the attacking player. **4** *US* a bill in a restaurant. **5** (in full **baggage** or **luggage check**) esp. *N. Amer.* a token of identification for left luggage etc. **6** *US Cards* a counter used in various games. **7** a temporary loss of the scent in hunting. **8** a crack or flaw in timber. ● *int. N. Amer. colloq.* expressing assent or agreement. □ **check in 1** arrive or register at a hotel, airport, etc. **2** record the arrival of. **check into** register one's arrival at (a hotel etc.). **check off** mark on a list etc. as having been examined or dealt with. **check on** examine carefully or in detail; ascertain the truth about; keep a watch on (a person, work done, etc.). **check out 1** (often foll. by *of*) leave a hotel etc. with due formalities. **2** *colloq.* investigate; examine for authenticity or suitability. **3** *N. Amer. slang* die. **check over** examine for errors; verify. **check through** inspect or examine exhaustively; verify successive items of. **check up** ascertain, verify, make sure. **check up on** = *check on*. **in check** under control, restrained. □ **checkable** *adj.* [Middle English from Old French *eschequier* 'play chess, give check to', and Old French *eschec*, ultimately from Persian *šāh* 'king']

check[2] /tʃɛk/ *n.* **1** a pattern of small squares. **2** fabric having this pattern. **3** (*attrib.*) so patterned. [Middle English, probably from CHEQUER]

check[3] *US* var. of CHEQUE.

checked /tʃɛkt/ *adj.* having a check pattern.

checker[1] /ˈtʃɛkə/ *n.* **1** a person or thing that verifies or examines, esp. in a factory etc. **2** *US* a cashier in a supermarket etc.

checker[2] /ˈtʃɛkə/ *n.* **1** var. of CHEQUER. **2** *N. Amer.* **a** (in *pl.*, usu. treated as *sing.*) the game of draughts. **b** = CHECKERMAN.

checkerberry /ˈtʃɛkəbɛri/ *n.* (*pl.* **-ies**) **1** a N. American creeping evergreen shrub, *Gaultheria procumbens*, with spiny scented leaves and white flowers; also called *wintergreen*. **2** the edible red fruit of this plant. [*checkers* 'berries of the service tree' (from their colour)]

checkerboard *US* var. of CHEQUERBOARD.

checkerman /ˈtʃɛkəman/ *n.* (*pl.* **-men**) *N. Amer.* each of the pieces in a game of draughts.

check-in *n.* the act or place of checking in.

checking account /'tʃɛkɪŋ/ *n. US* a current account at a bank. [CHECK³]

checklist /'tʃɛklɪst/ *n.* a list for reference and verification.

checkmate /'tʃɛkmeɪt/ *n.* & *v.* ● *n.* **1** (also as *int.*) *Chess* **a** a check from which a king cannot escape. **b** an announcement of this. **2** a final defeat or deadlock. ● *v.tr.* **1** *Chess* put into checkmate. **2** defeat; frustrate. [Middle English via Old French *eschec mat* from Persian *šāh māt* 'the king is dead']

checkout /'tʃɛkaʊt/ *n.* **1** an act of checking out. **2** a point at which goods are paid for in a supermarket etc.

checkpoint /'tʃɛkpɔɪnt/ *n.* a place, esp. a barrier or manned entrance, where documents, vehicles, etc., are inspected.

check-rein *n.* a rein attaching one horse's rein to another's bit, or preventing a horse from lowering its head.

checkroom /'tʃɛkru:m, -rʊm/ *n. N. Amer.* **1** a cloakroom in a hotel or theatre. **2** an office for left luggage etc.

check sum *n.* a digit representing the sum of the digits in a digital signal and transmitted with it as a check against errors.

check-up *n.* a thorough (esp. medical) examination.

check valve *n.* a valve allowing flow in one direction only.

Cheddar /'tʃɛdə/ *n.* a kind of firm smooth yellow, white, or orange cheese originally made in Cheddar but now widely imitated. [*Cheddar*, a village in SW England]

cheek /tʃi:k/ *n.* & *v.* ● *n.* **1 a** the side of the face below the eye. **b** the side wall of the mouth. **2 a** impertinent speech. **b** impertinence; cool confidence (*had the cheek to ask for more*). **3** *slang* either buttock. **4 a** either of the side posts of a door etc. **b** either of the jaws of a vice. **c** either of the side pieces of various parts of machines arranged in lateral pairs. ● *v.tr.* speak impertinently to. □ **cheek by jowl** close together; intimate. **turn the other cheek** accept attack etc. meekly; refuse to retaliate. [Old English *cē(a)ce, cēoce*]

cheekbone /'tʃi:kbəʊn/ *n.* the bone below the eye; the zygomatic bone.

cheeky /'tʃi:ki/ *adj.* (**cheekier**, **cheekiest**) impertinent, impudent. □ **cheekily** *adv.* **cheekiness** *n.*

cheep /tʃi:p/ *n.* & *v.* ● *n.* the weak shrill cry of a young bird. ● *v.intr.* make such a cry. [imitative: cf. PEEP²]

cheer /tʃɪə/ *n.* & *v.* ● *n.* **1** a shout of encouragement or applause. **2** mood, disposition (*full of good cheer*). **3** (in *pl.*; as *int.*) *colloq.* **a** expressing good wishes before drinking or *Brit.* before parting. **b** esp. *Brit.* expressing gratitude. ● *v.* **1** *tr.* **a** applaud with shouts. **b** (usu. foll. by *on*) urge or encourage with shouts. **2** *intr.* shout for joy. **3** *tr.* gladden; comfort. □ **cheer up** make or become less depressed. **three cheers** three successive hurrahs for a person or thing honoured. [Middle English, in the sense 'face, expression, mood', via Anglo-French *chere*, Old French *chiere* and Late Latin *cara* 'face' from Greek *kara* 'head']

cheerful /'tʃɪəfʊl, -f(ə)l/ *adj.* **1** in good spirits, noticeably happy (*a cheerful disposition*). **2** bright, pleasant (*a cheerful room*). **3** willing, not reluctant. □ **cheerfully** *adv.* **cheerfulness** *n.*

cheerio /tʃɪərɪ'əʊ/ *int. Brit. colloq.* expressing good wishes on parting or *archaic* before drinking.

cheerleader /'tʃɪəli:də/ *n.* a person who leads cheers of applause etc.

cheerless /'tʃɪəlɪs/ *adj.* gloomy, dreary, miserable. □ **cheerlessly** *adv.* **cheerlessness** *n.*

cheerly /'tʃɪəli/ *adv.* & *adj.* ● *adv.* esp. *Naut.* heartily, with a will. ● *adj. archaic* cheerful.

cheery /'tʃɪəri/ *adj.* (**cheerier**, **cheeriest**) lively; in good spirits; genial, cheering. □ **cheerily** *adv.* **cheeriness** *n.*

cheese¹ /tʃi:z/ *n.* **1 a** a food made from the pressed curds of milk. **b** a complete cake of this with rind. **2** *Brit.* a conserve having the consistency of soft cheese (*lemon cheese*). **3** a round flat object, e.g. the heavy flat wooden disc used in skittles. □ **hard cheese** *Brit. slang* bad luck. [Old English *cēse*, ultimately from Latin *caseus*]

cheese² /tʃi:z/ *v.tr. slang* (usu. as **cheesed** *adj.*) (often foll. by *off*) exasperate. □ **cheese it 1** *Brit. archaic* stop it, leave off. **2** *US* look out; run away. [19th c.: origin unknown]

cheese³ /tʃi:z/ *n.* (also **big cheese**) *slang* an important person. [perhaps from Hindustani *chīz* thing]

cheeseboard /'tʃi:zbɔ:d/ *n.* **1** a board from which cheese is served. **2** a selection of cheeses.

cheeseburger /'tʃi:zbɜ:gə/ *n.* a beefburger with a slice of cheese on it, usu. served in a roll.

cheesecake /'tʃi:zkeɪk/ *n.* **1** a tart filled with sweetened curds etc. **2** *slang* the portrayal of women in a sexually attractive manner.

cheesecloth /'tʃi:zklɒθ/ *n.* thin loosely woven cloth, used originally for wrapping cheese.

cheese-cutter *n.* **1** a knife with a broad curved blade. **2** a device for cutting cheese by pulling a wire through it.

cheese-fly *n.* (*pl.* **-flies**) a small black fly, *Piophila casei*, breeding in cheese.

cheese-head *n. Brit.* a type of screw head shaped like a squat cylinder.

cheesemaker /'tʃi:zmeɪkə/ *n.* a maker of cheese. □ **cheesemaking** *n.*

cheese-mite *n.* any mite of the genus *Tyroglyphus* feeding on cheese.

cheesemonger /'tʃi:zmʌŋgə/ *n. Brit.* a dealer in cheese, butter, etc.

cheese-paring *adj.* & *n.* ● *adj.* stingy. ● *n.* stinginess. □ **cheese-pare** *v.tr.* & *intr.*

cheese plant *n.* = SWISS CHEESE PLANT.

cheese-skipper *n.* = CHEESE-FLY.

cheese straw *n.* a thin cheese-flavoured strip of pastry.

cheesewood /'tʃi:zwʊd/ *n.* **1** an Australian tree of the genus *Pittosporum*. **2** its hard yellowish wood.

cheesy /'tʃi:zi/ *adj.* (**cheesier**, **cheesiest**) **1** like cheese in taste, smell, appearance, etc. **2** *slang* corny, tacky. □ **cheesiness** *n.*

cheetah /'tʃi:tə/ *n.* a swift-running feline, *Acinonyx jubatus*, with a leopard-like spotted coat. [Hindi *cītā*, perhaps from Sanskrit *citraka* 'speckled']

chef /ʃɛf/ *n.* a cook, esp. the chief cook in a restaurant etc. [French, = head]

chef-d'œuvre /ʃeɪ'də:vr(ə), French ʃɛdœvr/ *n.* (*pl.* ***chefs-d'œuvre*** *pronunc.* same) a masterpiece. [French, = chief (piece of) work]

cheiro- *comb. form* var. of CHIRO-.

Chekhovian /tʃɛ'kəʊvɪən/ *adj.* of or characteristic of the work of Anton Chekhov (d. 1904), esp. in attaching dramatic and symbolic significance to detail.

chela¹ /'ki:lə/ *n.* (*pl.* **chelae** /-li:/) a prehensile claw of crabs, lobsters, scorpions, etc. [modern Latin from Latin *chele*, or Greek *khēlē* 'claw']

chela² /'tʃeɪlə/ *n.* (*pl.* **chelas**) (esp. in Hinduism) a disciple; a pupil. [Hindi, = servant]

chelate /'ki:leɪt/ *n.*, *adj.*, & *v.* ● *n. Chem.* a usu. organometallic compound containing a ligand which bonds to a central atom at two or more points. ● *adj.* **1** *Chem.* of, involving, or able to form a chelate. **2** *Zool.* & *Anat.* of or having chelae. ● *v.intr. Chem.* form a chelate. □ **chelation** /-'leɪʃ(ə)n/ *n.* [CHELA¹ + -ATE¹,²]

chelicerate /kə'lɪsəreɪt, -(ə)rət/ *adj.* & *n. Zool.* ● *adj.* of or relating to the subphylum Chelicerata of arthropods with a pair of appendages modified as pincer-like jaws. ● *n.* a chelicerate anthropod, e.g. an arachnid. [modern Latin *Chelicerata*, from Greek *khēlē* 'claw' + *keras* 'horn' + -ATE¹]

Chellean /'ʃɛlɪən/ *adj. Archaeol.* = ABBEVILLIAN. [French *chelléen* from *Chelles* near Paris]

chelonian /kɪ'ləʊnɪən/ *n.* & *adj.* ● *n.* any reptile of the order Chelonia, including turtles, terrapins, and tortoises, having a shell of bony plates covered with horny scales. ● *adj.* of or relating to this order. [modern Latin *Chelonia* from Greek *khelōnē* 'tortoise']

Chelsea bun /ˈtʃɛlsi/ *n. Brit.* a kind of currant bun in the form of a flat spiral. [*Chelsea* in London]

Chelsea pensioner /ˈtʃɛlsi/ *n.* (in the UK) an inmate of the Chelsea Royal Hospital for old or disabled soldiers.

Chelsea ware /ˈtʃɛlsi/ *n.* any of various soft-paste porcelains made at Chelsea in the 18th c.

chemi- /ˈkɛmi/ *comb. form* var. of CHEMO-.

chemical /ˈkɛmɪk(ə)l/ *adj. & n.* ● *adj.* of, made by, or employing chemistry or chemicals. ● *n.* a substance obtained or used in chemistry. □ **chemically** *adv.* [*chemic* 'alchemic', via French *chimique* or modern Latin *chimicus, chymicus* from medieval Latin *alchymicus*: see ALCHEMY]

chemical bond *n.* an interaction by which atoms are held together in a molecule or crystal.

chemical engineer *n.* an engineer specializing in the design and operation of industrial chemical plants. □ **chemical engineering** *n.*

chemical reaction *n.* a process that involves change in the structure of atoms, molecules, or ions.

chemical warfare *n.* warfare using poison gas and other chemicals.

chemical weapon *n.* a weapon depending for its effect on the release of a toxic or noxious substance.

chemico- /ˈkɛmɪkəʊ/ *comb. form* chemical; chemical and (*chemico-physical*).

chemiluminescence /ˌkɛmɪˌluːmɪˈnɛs(ə)ns, -ˌljuːmɪˈnɛs(ə)ns/ *n.* the emission of light during a chemical reaction. □ **chemiluminescent** *adj.* [German *Chemilumineszenz* (as CHEMI-, LUMINESCENCE)]

chemin de fer /ʃəˌmã də ˈfɛː/ *n.* a form of baccarat. [French, = railway, literally 'road of iron']

chemise /ʃəˈmiːz/ *n.* a woman's loose-fitting undergarment or dress hanging straight from the shoulders. [Middle English via Old French from Late Latin *camisia* 'shirt']

chemisorption /kɛmɪˈsɔːpʃ(ə)n/ *n.* adsorption by chemical bonding. [CHEMI- + ADSORPTION (see ADSORB)]

chemist /ˈkɛmɪst/ *n.* **1** *Brit.* **a** a dealer in medicinal drugs, usu. also selling other medical goods and toiletries. **b** an authorized dispenser of medicines. **2** a person practising or trained in chemistry. [earlier *chymist*, via French *chimiste* from modern Latin *chimista*, from *alchimista* ALCHEMIST (see ALCHEMY)]

chemistry /ˈkɛmɪstri/ *n.* (*pl.* **-ies**) **1** the study of the elements and the compounds they form and the reactions they undergo. **2** the chemical composition and properties of a substance. **3** any complex (esp. emotional) change or process (*the chemistry of fear*). **4** *colloq.* **a** a person's personality or temperament. **b** the attraction or interaction between people.

chemo- /ˈkiːməʊ, ˈkɛməʊ/ *comb. form* (also **chemi-** /ˈkɛmi/) chemical.

chemoreceptor /ˈkiːməʊrɪsɛptə/ *n. Biol.* a sensory organ responsive to chemical stimuli.

chemosynthesis /kiːmə(ʊ)ˈsɪnθɪsɪs/ *n.* the synthesis of organic compounds by energy derived from chemical reactions.

chemotherapy /kiːmə(ʊ)ˈθɛrəpi, kɛm-/ *n.* the treatment of disease, esp. cancer, by use of chemical substances. □ **chemotherapist** *n.*

chemurgy /ˈkɛməːdʒi/ *n. US* the chemical and industrial use of organic raw materials. □ **chemurgic** /-ˈməːdʒɪk/ *adj.* [CHEMO-, after *metallurgy*]

chenille /ʃəˈniːl/ *n.* **1** a tufty velvety cord or yarn, used in trimming furniture etc. **2** fabric made from this. [French, = hairy caterpillar, from Latin *canicula*, diminutive of *canis* 'dog']

cheongsam /tʃɪɒŋˈsam, tʃɒŋ-/ *n.* a woman's garment with a high neck and slit skirt, worn in China. [Chinese]

cheque /tʃɛk/ *n.* (*US* **check**) **1** a written order to a bank to pay the stated sum from the drawer's account. **2** the printed form on which such an order is written. [special use of CHECK[1] to mean 'device for checking the amount of an item']

chequebook /ˈtʃɛkbʊk/ *n.* a book of forms for writing cheques.

chequebook journalism *n.* the payment of large sums for exclusive rights to material for (esp. personal) newspaper stories.

cheque card *n. Brit.* a card issued by a bank to guarantee the honouring of cheques up to a stated amount.

chequer /ˈtʃɛkə/ *n. & v.* (also **checker**) ● *n.* **1** (often in *pl.*) a pattern of squares often alternately coloured. **2** (in *pl.*) (usu. as **checkers**) *US* the game of draughts. ● *v.tr.* **1** mark with chequers. **2** variegate; break the uniformity of. **3** (as **chequered** *adj.*) with varied fortunes (*a chequered career*). [Middle English from EXCHEQUER]

chequerboard /ˈtʃɛkəbɔːd/ *n.* (*US* **checkerboard**) **1** a chessboard. **2** a pattern resembling it.

chequered flag *n. Motor Racing* a flag with a black and white chequered pattern, displayed to drivers at the moment of finishing a race.

Cherenkov radiation var. of CERENKOV RADIATION.

cherish /ˈtʃɛrɪʃ/ *v.tr.* **1** protect or tend (a child, plant, etc.) lovingly. **2** hold dear, cling to (hopes, feelings, etc.). [Middle English from Old French *cherir*, from *cher*, from Latin *carus* 'dear']

chernozem /ˈtʃəːnəzɛm/ *n.* a fertile black soil rich in humus, found in temperate regions, esp. S. Russia. Also called *black earth*. [Russian, from *chernyĭ* 'black' + *zemlya* 'earth']

Cherokee /tʃɛrəˈkiː/ *n. & adj.* ● *n.* **1 a** an American Indian tribe formerly inhabiting much of the southern US. **b** a member of this tribe. **2** the language of this tribe. ● *adj.* of or relating to the Cherokees or their language. [Cherokee *tsaliki*]

Cherokee rose *n.* a fragrant white rose, *Rosa laevigata*, of the southern US.

cheroot /ʃəˈruːt/ *n.* a cigar with both ends open. [French *cheroute* from Tamil *shuruṭṭu* 'roll']

cherry /ˈtʃɛri/ *n. & adj.* ● *n.* (*pl.* **-ies**) **1 a** a small soft round stone fruit. **b** (also **cherry tree**) any of several trees of the genus *Prunus* bearing this or grown for their ornamental flowers. **2** = CHERRYWOOD. **3** *coarse slang* **a** virginity. **b** the hymen. **4** a bright deep red colour. ● *adj.* of a bright deep red colour. [Middle English via Old Northern French *cherise* (taken as pl.: cf. PEA) from medieval Latin *ceresia*, perhaps via Latin from Greek *kerasos*]

cherry brandy *n.* a dark red liqueur of brandy in which cherries have been steeped.

cherry laurel *n. Brit.* a small evergreen tree, *Prunus laurocerasus*, with white flowers and cherry-like fruits.

cherry-pick *v.tr.* (also *absol.*) pick (the best) from a group.

cherry picker *n. colloq.* a hydraulic crane with a railed platform at the end, for raising and lowering people working on overhead lighting, cables, high windows, etc.

cherry pie *n.* **1** a pie made with cherries. **2** a garden heliotrope.

cherry plum *n.* **1** a tree, *Prunus cerasifera*, native to SW Asia, with solitary white flowers and red fruits. **2** the fruit of this tree.

cherry red *n. & adj.* ● *n.* = CHERRY *n.* 4. ● *adj.* (hyphenated when *attrib.*) = CHERRY *adj.*

cherry tomato *n.* a miniature tomato with a strong flavour.

cherrywood /ˈtʃɛrɪwʊd/ *n.* the wood of the cherry.

chersonese /kəːsəˈniːs, -z/ *n.* a peninsula, esp. the Thracian peninsula west of the Hellespont. [Latin *chersonesus* from Greek *khersonēsos*, from *khersos* 'dry' + *nēsos* 'island']

chert /tʃəːt/ *n.* a flintlike form of quartz composed of chalcedony. □ **cherty** *adj.* [17th c.: origin unknown]

cherub /ˈtʃɛrəb/ *n.* **1** (*pl.* **cherubim** /-bɪm/) an angelic being of the second order of the celestial hierarchy. **2 a** a representation of a winged child or the head of a winged child. **b** a beautiful or innocent child. □ **cherubic** /tʃɪˈruːbɪk/ *adj.* **cherubically** /tʃɪˈruːbɪk(ə)li/ *adv.* [Old English *cherubin*, ultimately from Hebrew *kᵉrūḇ*, pl. *kᵉrūḇîm*]

chervil /ˈtʃəːvɪl/ *n.* an umbelliferous plant, *Anthriscus cerefolium*, with small white flowers, used as a herb for flavouring soup, salads, etc. [Old English *cerfille* via Latin *chaerephylla* from Greek *khairephullon*]

Ches. *abbr.* Cheshire.

Cheshire /ˈtʃɛʃə/ *n.* a kind of firm crumbly cheese, originally made in Cheshire. □ **like a Cheshire cat** with a broad fixed grin. [*Cheshire*, a county in England]

chess /tʃɛs/ *n.* a game for two with 16 men each, played on a chessboard. [Middle English from Old French *esches*, pl. of *eschec* CHECK[1]]

chessboard /ˈtʃɛsbɔːd/ *n.* a chequered board of 64 squares on which chess and draughts are played.

chessman /ˈtʃɛsman/ *n.* (*pl.* **-men**) any of the 32 pieces and pawns with which chess is played.

chess set *n.* a set of chessmen with a chessboard.

chest /tʃɛst/ *n.* **1** a large strong box, esp. for storage or transport. **2 a** the part of a human or animal body enclosed by the ribs. **b** the circumference of the body at chest level. **c** the front surface of the body from neck to waist. **3** a small cabinet for medicines etc. **4** *Brit.* **a** the treasury or financial resources of an institution. **b** the money available from it. □ **get a thing off one's chest** *colloq.* disclose a fact, secret, etc., to relieve one's anxiety about it. **play (one's cards, a thing**, etc.) **close to one's chest** *colloq.* be cautious or secretive about. □ **-chested** *adj.* (in *comb.*). [Old English *cest*, *cyst* via Germanic and Latin from Greek *kistē*]

chesterfield /ˈtʃɛstəfiːld/ *n.* **1** a sofa with arms and back of the same height and curved outwards at the top. **2** a man's plain overcoat usu. with a velvet collar. [named after 19th-c. Earl of *Chesterfield*]

chest freezer *n.* a freezer shaped like a chest (see CHEST 1), opening at the top.

chestnut /ˈtʃɛsnʌt/ *n.* & *adj.* ● *n.* **1** (also **chestnut tree**) **a** the tree *Castanea sativa*, bearing flowers in catkins and nuts enclosed in a spiny fruit; also called *Spanish chestnut* or *sweet chestnut*. **b** any other tree of the genus *Castanea*. **2** the glossy hard brown edible nut of *Castanea sativa*. **3** = HORSE CHESTNUT. **4** (in full **chestnut wood**) the heavy wood of any chestnut tree. **5** a horse of a reddish-brown or yellowish-brown colour. **6** *colloq.* a stale joke or anecdote. **7** a small hard patch on a horse's leg. **8** (in full **chestnut brown**) a reddish-brown colour. ● *adj.* (in full **chestnut brown**; hyphenated when *attrib.*) of the colour chestnut. [obsolete *chesten* via Old French *chastaine* and Latin *castanea* from Greek *kastanea*]

chest of drawers *n.* a piece of furniture consisting of a set of drawers in a frame.

chest voice *n.* the lowest register of the voice in singing or speaking.

chesty /ˈtʃɛsti/ *adj.* (**chestier**, **chestiest**) **1** *Brit. colloq.* inclined to or symptomatic of chest disease. **2** *colloq.* having a large chest or prominent breasts. **3** *N. Amer. slang* arrogant. □ **chestily** *adv.* **chestiness** *n.*

chetnik /ˈtʃɛtnɪk/ *n. hist.* a member of a guerrilla force in the Balkans, esp. during the First and Second World Wars. [Serbian *četnik* from *četa* 'band, troop']

cheval glass /ʃəˈval/ *n.* a tall mirror swung on an upright frame. [French *cheval* 'horse, frame']

chevalier /ʃɛvəˈlɪə/ *n.* **1 a** a member of certain orders of knighthood, and of modern French orders, as the Legion of Honour. **b** *archaic* or *hist.* a knight. **2** (**Chevalier**) *Brit. hist.* the title of the Old and Young Pretenders. **3** a chivalrous man; a cavalier. [Middle English via Anglo-French *chevaler*, Old French *chevalier* from medieval Latin *caballarius*, from Latin *caballus* 'horse': cf. CABALLERO, CAVALIER]

chevet /ʃəˈveɪ/ *n.* the apsidal end of a church, sometimes with an attached group of apses. [French, = pillow, from Latin *capitium*, from *caput* 'head']

Cheviot /ˈtʃɛvɪət/ *n.* **1 a** a large sheep of a breed with short thick wool. **b** this breed. **2** (**cheviot**) the wool or cloth obtained from this breed. [*Cheviot* Hills in N. England and Scotland where the sheep were bred]

chèvre /ʃɛːvr(ə)/ *n.* a variety of goat's-milk cheese. [French, = goat, she-goat]

chevron /ˈʃɛvrən/ *n.* **1** a badge in a V shape on the sleeve of a uniform indicating rank or length of service. **2** *Heraldry* & *Archit.* a bent bar of an inverted V shape. **3** any V-shaped line or stripe. [Middle English from Old French, ultimately from Latin *caper* 'goat': cf. Latin *capreoli* (diminutive of *caper*) used to mean 'pair of rafters']

chevrotain /ˈʃɛvrəteɪn/ *n.* (also **chevrotin** /-tɪn/) any small deerlike animal of the family Tragulidae, native to Africa and SE Asia, and having small tusks. Also called *mouse deer*. [French, diminutive of Old French *chevrot*, diminutive of *chèvre* 'goat']

chevy var. of CHIVVY.

chew /tʃuː/ *v.* & *n.* ● *v.tr.* (also *absol.*) work (food etc.) between the teeth; crush or indent with the teeth. ● *n.* **1** an act of chewing. **2** something for chewing, esp. a chewy sweet. □ **chew the cud** reflect, ruminate. **chew the fat** (or **rag**) *slang* **1** chat. **2** grumble. **chew on 1** work continuously between the teeth (*chewed on a piece of string*). **2** think about; meditate on. **chew out** *N. Amer. colloq.* reprimand. **chew over 1** discuss, talk over. **2** think about; meditate on. □ **chewable** *adj.* **chewer** *n.* [Old English *cēowan*]

chewing gum *n.* flavoured gum, esp. chicle, for chewing.

chewy /ˈtʃuːi/ *adj.* (**chewier**, **chewiest**) **1** needing much chewing. **2** suitable for chewing. □ **chewiness** *n.*

Cheyenne /ʃʌɪˈan/ *n.* & *adj.* ● *n.* **1 a** an American Indian tribe formerly living between the Missouri and Arkansas rivers. **b** a member of this tribe. **2** the language of this tribe. ● *adj.* of or relating to the Cheyennes or their language. [Canadian French from Sioux *Sahiyena*]

Cheyne-Stokes /tʃeɪnˈstəʊks/ *adj. Med.* designating a breathing cycle involving a gradual decrease of movement to a complete stop, followed by a gradual increase. [named after J. *Cheyne*, Scots physician d. 1836, and W. *Stokes*, Irish physician d. 1878]

chez /ʃeɪ/ *prep.* at the house or home of. [French from Old French *chiese* from Latin *casa* 'cottage']

chi /kʌɪ/ *n.* the twenty-second letter of the Greek alphabet (Χ, χ). [Middle English from Greek *khi*]

Chianti /kɪˈanti/ *n.* (*pl.* **Chiantis**) a dry red Italian wine. [*Chianti*, an area in Tuscany, Italy]

chiaroscuro /kɪˌɑːrəˈskʊərəʊ/ *n.* **1** the treatment of light and shade in drawing and painting. **2** the use of contrast in literature etc. **3** (*attrib.*) half-revealed. [Italian from *chiaro* 'CLEAR' + *oscuro* 'dark, OBSCURE']

chiasma /kʌɪˈazmə, kɪ-/ *n.* (*pl.* **chiasmata** /-tə/) *Biol.* the point at which paired chromosomes remain in contact after crossing over during meiosis. [modern Latin from Greek *chiasma* 'a cross-shaped mark']

chiasmus /kʌɪˈazməs, kɪ-/ *n.* inversion in the second of two parallel phrases of the order followed in the first (e.g. *to stop too fearful and too faint to go*). □ **chiastic** *adj.* [modern Latin from Greek *khiasmos* 'crosswise arrangement', from *khiazō* 'mark with letter CHI']

chibouk /tʃɪˈbuːk/ *n.* (also **chibouque**) a long Turkish tobacco pipe. [Turkish *çubuk* 'tube']

chic /ʃiːk/ *adj.* & *n.* ● *adj.* (**chic-er**, **chic-est**) stylish, elegant (in dress or appearance). ● *n.* stylishness, elegance. □ **chicly** *adv.* [French]

chicane /ʃɪˈkeɪn/ *n.* & *v.* ● *n.* **1** an artificial barrier or obstacle, esp. a sharp double bend, on a motor-racing track. **2** *Bridge* a hand without trumps, or without cards of one suit. **3** chicanery. ● *v. archaic* **1** *intr.* use chicanery. **2** *tr.* (usu. foll. by *into, out of*, etc.) cheat (a person). [French *chicane(r)* 'quibble']

chicanery /ʃɪ'keɪnəri/ *n.* (*pl.* **-ies**) **1** clever but misleading talk; a false argument. **2** trickery, deception. [French *chicanerie* (as CHICANE)]

Chicano /tʃɪ'kɑːnəʊ, ʃɪ-, -'keɪn-/ *n.* (*pl.* **-os**; *fem.* **Chicana** /-nə/) esp. *US* an American of Mexican origin. [Spanish *mejicano* 'Mexican']

chichi /'ʃiːʃiː/ *adj.* & *n.* ● *adj.* **1** (of a thing) frilly, showy. **2** (of a person or behaviour) fussy, affected. ● *n.* **1** over-refinement, pretentiousness, fussiness. **2** a frilly, showy, or pretentious object. [French]

chick[1] /tʃɪk/ *n.* **1** a young bird, esp. one newly hatched. **2** *slang* **a** a young woman. **b** a child. [Middle English: shortening of CHICKEN]

chick[2] /tʃɪk/ *n. Anglo-Ind.* a screen for a doorway etc., made from split bamboo and twine. [Hindi *chik*]

chickadee /'tʃɪkədiː/ *n. N. Amer.* any of various small birds of the tit family. [imitative]

chicken /'tʃɪkɪn/ *n., adj.,* & *v.* ● *n.* **1** a domestic fowl, esp. a young bird. **2 a** a domestic fowl prepared as food. **b** its flesh. **3** a youthful person; a young and inexperienced person (usu. with *neg.*: *is no chicken*). Cf. SPRING CHICKEN. **4** *colloq.* a children's pastime testing courage, usu. recklessly. ● *adj. colloq.* cowardly. ● *v.intr.* (foll. by *out*) *colloq.* withdraw from or fail in some activity through fear or lack of nerve. [Old English *cīcen, cȳcen*, from Germanic]

chicken-and-egg *attrib.adj.* designating an unresolved question as to which of two things caused the other (*it's a chicken-and-egg problem*).

chicken brick *n. Brit.* an earthenware container in two halves for roasting a chicken in its own juices.

chicken cholera *n.* an infectious disease of fowls.

chicken feed *n.* **1** food for poultry. **2** *colloq.* an unimportant amount, esp. of money.

chicken-hearted *adj.* (also **chicken-livered**) easily frightened; lacking nerve or courage.

chickenpox /'tʃɪkɪnpɒks/ *n.* an infectious disease, esp. of children, with a rash of small blisters. Also called *varicella*.

chicken wire *n.* a light wire netting with a hexagonal mesh.

chickpea /'tʃɪkpiː/ *n.* **1** a leguminous plant, *Cicer arietinum*, with short swollen pods containing yellow beaked seeds. **2** this seed used as a vegetable. [originally *ciche pease* from Latin *cicer* 'chickpea': see PEASE]

chickweed /'tʃɪkwiːd/ *n.* any of numerous small plants of the pink family, esp. *Stellaria media*, a garden weed with slender stems and tiny white flowers.

chicle /'tʃɪk(ə)l, -kli/ *n.* the milky juice of the sapodilla tree, used in the manufacture of chewing gum. [Latin American Spanish from Nahuatl *tzietli*]

chicory /'tʃɪk(ə)ri/ *n.* (*pl.* **-ies**) **1** a blue-flowered plant, *Cichorium intybus* (daisy family), cultivated for its salad leaves and its root. **2** its root, roasted and ground for use with or instead of coffee. **3** *N. Amer.* = ENDIVE. [Middle English via obsolete French *cicorée* 'endive', medieval Latin *cic(h)orea*, and Latin *cichorium* from Greek *kikhorion*]

chide /tʃʌɪd/ *v.tr.* & *intr.* (*past* **chided** or **chid** /tʃɪd/; *past part.* **chided** or **chidden** /'tʃɪd(ə)n/) esp. *archaic* or *literary* scold, rebuke. □ **chider** *n.* **chidingly** *adv.* [Old English *cīdan*, of unknown origin]

chief /tʃiːf/ *n.* & *adj.* ● *n.* **1 a** a leader or ruler. **b** the head of a tribe, clan, etc. **2** the head of a department; the highest official. **3** *Heraldry* the upper third of a shield. ● *adj.* (usu. *attrib.*) **1** first in position, importance, influence, etc. (*chief engineer*). **2** prominent, leading. □ **chiefdom** *n.* [Middle English from Old French *ch(i)ef*, ultimately from Latin *caput* 'head']

Chief Constable *n. Brit.* the head of the police force of a county or other region.

chiefly /'tʃiːfli/ *adv.* above all; mainly but not exclusively.

Chief of Staff *n.* the senior staff officer of a service or command.

Chief Rabbi *n.* the religious head of the Jewish communities in Britain.

chieftain /'tʃiːft(ə)n, -tɪn/ *n.* (*fem.* **chieftainess** /-nɪs/) the leader of a tribe, clan, etc. □ **chieftaincy** /-si/ *n.* (*pl.* **-ies**). **chieftainship** *n.* [Middle English via Old French *chevetaine* from Late Latin *capitaneus* CAPTAIN: assimilated to CHIEF]

chief technician *n.* a non-commissioned officer in the RAF ranking above sergeant.

chiffchaff /'tʃɪftʃaf/ *n.* a small European warbler, *Phylloscopus collybita*, with a distinctive repetitive song. [imitative]

chiffon /'ʃɪfɒn/ *n.* & *adj.* ● *n.* a light diaphanous fabric of silk, nylon, etc. ● *adj.* **1** made of chiffon. **2** (of a pie filling, dessert, etc.) light-textured. [French from *chiffe* 'rag']

chiffonier /ʃɪfə'nɪə/ *n.* **1** a movable low cupboard with a sideboard top. **2** *US* a tall chest of drawers. [French *chiffonnier, -ière* 'ragpicker, chest of drawers for odds and ends']

chigger /'tʃɪgə/ *n.* (also **jigger** /'dʒɪgə/) **1** a tropical flea, *Tunga penetrans*, the females of which burrow beneath the skin causing painful sores. Also called *chigoe, sand flea*. **2** *US* a harvest mite. [variant of CHIGOE]

chignon /'ʃiːnjɒ̃/ *n.* a coil or mass of hair at the back of a woman's head. [French, originally = nape of the neck]

chigoe /'tʃɪgəʊ/ *n.* = CHIGGER 1. [from a W. African language]

chihuahua /tʃɪ'wɑːwə/ *n.* **1** a very small dog of a smooth-haired large-eyed breed originating in Mexico. **2** this breed. [*Chihuahua*, state and city in Mexico]

chilblain /'tʃɪlbleɪn/ *n.* a painful itching swelling of the skin usu. on a hand, foot, etc., caused by exposure to cold and by poor circulation. □ **chilblained** *adj.* [CHILL + BLAIN]

child /tʃʌɪld/ *n.* (*pl.* **children** /'tʃɪldr(ə)n/) **1 a** a young human being below the age of puberty. **b** an unborn or newborn human being. **2** one's son or daughter (at any age). **3** (foll. by *of*) a descendant, follower, adherent, or product of (*children of Israel*; *child of God*; *child of nature*). **4** a childish person. □ **childless** *adj.* **childlessness** *n.* [Old English *cild*]

child abuse *n.* maltreatment of a child, esp. by physical violence or sexual molestation.

child allowance *n.* **1** = CHILD BENEFIT. **2** *hist.* (in the UK) a tax allowance granted to parents of dependent children.

childbearing /'tʃʌɪl(d)bɛːrɪŋ/ *n.* (often *attrib.*) giving birth to a child or children.

childbed /'tʃʌɪl(d)bɛd/ *n. archaic* = CHILDBIRTH.

child benefit *n.* (in the UK) regular payment by the state to the parents of a child up to a certain age.

childbirth /'tʃʌɪl(d)bəːθ/ *n.* the act of giving birth to a child.

childcare /'tʃʌɪl(d)kɛː/ *n.* the care of a child or children, esp. by a crèche or childminder while parents are working, or *Brit.* by a local authority when a normal home life is lacking.

child-centred *adj.* focusing on the interests, needs, etc. of the child.

Childe /tʃʌɪld/ *n. archaic* a youth of noble birth (*Childe Harold*). [variant of CHILD]

Childermas /'tʃɪldəmas/ *n. archaic* the feast of the Holy Innocents, 28 Dec. [Old English *cildramæsse*, from *cildra*, genitive pl. of *cild* CHILD + *mæsse* MASS]

childhood /'tʃʌɪldhʊd/ *n.* the state or period of being a child. [Old English *cildhād*]

childish /'tʃʌɪldɪʃ/ *adj.* **1** of, like, or proper to a child. **2** immature, silly. □ **childishly** *adv.* **childishness** *n.*

childlike /'tʃʌɪl(d)lʌɪk/ *adj.* having the good qualities of a child such as innocence, frankness, etc.

childminder /'tʃʌɪl(d)mʌɪndə/ *n. Brit.* a person who looks after children for payment, strictly speaking a person registered with the local authority to give paid daytime care in his or her own home for children under eight.

child molester *n.* a person who sexually abuses a child.

childproof /ˈtʃʌɪl(d)pruːf/ *adj.* that cannot be damaged or operated by a child.

children *pl.* of CHILD.

child's play *n.* an easy task.

chile var. of CHILLI.

Chilean /ˈtʃɪlɪən/ *n.* & *adj.* ● *n.* **1** a native or national of Chile in S. America. **2** a person of Chilean descent. ● *adj.* of or relating to Chile.

Chile pine /ˈtʃɪli/ *n.* a monkey-puzzle tree.

Chile saltpetre /ˈtʃɪli/ *n.* (also **Chile nitre**) naturally occurring sodium nitrate.

chili var. of CHILLI.

chiliad /ˈkɪlɪad/ *n.* **1** a thousand. **2** a thousand years. [Late Latin *chilias chiliad-* from Greek *khilias -ados*]

chiliast /ˈkɪlɪast/ *n.* = MILLENARIAN *n.* □ **chiliasm** *n.* [Late Latin *chiliastes* from Greek *khiliasmos*: see CHILIAD]

chiliastic /kɪlɪˈastɪk/ *adj.* relating to or believing in a future period of happiness, prosperity, and ideal or divine government (cf. MILLENARIAN).

chill /tʃɪl/ *n., v.,* & *adj.* ● *n.* **1 a** an unpleasant cold sensation; lowered body temperature. **b** a feverish cold (*catch a chill*). **2** unpleasant coldness (of air, water, etc.). **3 a** a depressing influence (*cast a chill over*). **b** a feeling of fear or dread accompanied by coldness. **4** coldness of manner. ● *v.* **1** *tr.* & *intr.* make or become cold. **2** *tr.* **a** depress, dispirit. **b** horrify, frighten. **3** *tr.* cool (food or drink); preserve by cooling. **4** *tr.* harden (molten metal) by contact with cold material. **5** *intr.* esp. *N. Amer. colloq.* (usu. foll. by *with*) pass time idly, hang around. ● *adj. literary* chilly. □ **chill out** esp. *N. Amer. colloq.* **1** relax; become less tense. **2** = sense 5 of *v.* **take the chill off** warm slightly. □ **chillingly** *adv.* **chillness** *n.* **chillsome** *adj. literary.* [Old English *cele, ciele* 'cold, coldness': in modern senses the verb is the oldest (Middle English)]

chiller /ˈtʃɪlə/ *n.* **1** = SPINE-CHILLER. **2** a cold cabinet or refrigerator, esp. in a shop, garage, etc.

chill factor *n.* the perceived lowering of the air temperature caused by the wind etc.

chilli /ˈtʃɪli/ *n.* (also **chile**, *US* **chili**) (*pl.* **chillies, chiles,** or *US* **chilies**) **1** (in full **chilli pepper**) a small hot-tasting (dried) pod, usu. red or green, of a capsicum, *Capsicum anuum*, used in sauces, relishes, etc. **2** = CHILLI POWDER. **3** esp. *N. Amer.* = CHILLI CON CARNE. [Spanish *chile, chili,* from Nahuatl *chilli*]

chilli con carne /kɒn ˈkɑːni/ *n.* a stew of chilli-flavoured minced beef and beans. [Spanish, literally 'chilli with meat']

chilli powder *n.* hot cayenne.

chilli sauce *n.* a hot sauce made with tomatoes, chillies, and spices.

chilly /ˈtʃɪli/ *adj.* (**chillier, chilliest**) **1** (of the weather or an object) somewhat cold. **2** (of a person or animal) feeling somewhat cold; sensitive to the cold. **3** unfriendly; unemotional. □ **chilliness** *n.*

Chiltern Hundreds /ˌtʃɪlt(ə)n ˈhʌndrədz/ *n.pl.* (in the UK) a Crown manor, whose administration is a nominal office for which an MP applies as a way of resigning from the House of Commons. [*Chiltern* Hills in S. England]

chimaera var. of CHIMERA.

chime[1] /tʃʌɪm/ *n.* & *v.* ● *n.* **1 a** a set of attuned bells. **b** the series of sounds given by this. **c** (usu. in *pl.*) a set of attuned bells as a doorbell. **2** agreement, correspondence, harmony. ● *v.* **1 a** *intr.* (of bells) ring. **b** *tr.* sound (a bell or chime) by striking. **2** *tr.* show (the hour) by chiming. **3** *intr.* (usu. foll. by *together, with*) be in agreement, harmonize. □ **chime in 1** interject a remark. **2** join in harmoniously. **3** (foll. by *with*) agree with. □ **chimer** *n.* [Middle English, probably from *chym(b)e* 'bell', via Old English *cimbal* and Latin *cymbalum* from Greek *kumbalon* CYMBAL]

chime[2] /tʃʌɪm/ *n.* (also **chimb**) the projecting rim at the end of a cask. [Middle English, probably from an Old English form: cf. Middle Dutch, Middle Low German *kimme*]

chimera /kʌɪˈmɪərə, kɪ-/ *n.* (also **chimaera**) **1** (in Greek mythology) a fire-breathing female monster with a lion's head, a goat's body, and a serpent's tail. **2** a fantastic or grotesque product of the imagination; a bogey. **3** any fabulous beast with parts taken from various animals. **4** *Biol.* **a** an organism containing genetically different tissues, formed by fusion of early embryos, grafting, mutation, etc. **b** a nucleic acid formed by laboratory manipulation. **5** any cartilaginous fish of the family Chimaeridae, usu. having erect pointed fins and a long tail. □ **chimeric** /-ˈmɛrɪk/ *adj.* **chimerical** /-ˈmɛrɪk(ə)l/ *adj.* **chimerically** /-ˈmɛrɪk(ə)li/ *adv.* [Latin, from Greek *khimaira* 'she-goat, chimera']

chimichanga /tʃɪmɪˈtʃɑːŋgə/ *n.* a tortilla rolled round a savoury filling and deep-fried. [Mexican Spanish, = 'trinket']

chimney /ˈtʃɪmni/ *n.* (*pl.* **-eys**) **1** a vertical channel conducting smoke or combustion gases etc. up and away from a fire, furnace, engine, etc. **2** the part of this which projects above a roof. **3** a glass tube protecting the flame of a lamp. **4** a narrow vertical crack in a rock face, often used by mountaineers to ascend. [Middle English via Old French *cheminée* and Late Latin *caminata* 'having a fireplace', via Latin *caminus* from Greek *kaminos* 'oven']

chimney breast *n.* a projecting interior wall surrounding a chimney.

chimney piece *n. Brit.* an ornamental structure around an open fireplace; a mantelpiece.

chimney pot *n.* an earthenware or metal pipe at the top of a chimney, narrowing the aperture and increasing the updraught.

chimney stack *n.* **1** a number of chimneys grouped in one structure. **2** = CHIMNEY 2.

chimney sweep *n.* a person whose job is removing soot from inside chimneys.

chimp /tʃɪmp/ *n. colloq.* = CHIMPANZEE. [abbreviation]

chimpanzee /tʃɪmpanˈziː/ *n.* either of two anthropoid apes of central and W. Africa, *Pan troglodytes* and (in full **pygmy chimpanzee**) *Pan paniscus*. [French *chimpanzé* from Kongo]

chin /tʃɪn/ *n.* the front of the lower jaw. □ **chin up** *colloq.* cheer up. **keep one's chin up** *colloq.* remain cheerful, esp. in adversity. **take on the chin 1** suffer a severe blow from (a misfortune etc.). **2** endure courageously. □ **-chinned** *adj.* (in *comb.*). [Old English *cin(n)*, from Germanic]

china /ˈtʃʌɪnə/ *n.* & *adj.* ● *n.* **1** a kind of fine white or translucent ceramic ware, porcelain, etc. **2** things made from ceramic, esp. household tableware. **3** *Brit. rhyming slang* one's 'mate', i.e. husband or wife (short for *china plate*). ● *adj.* made of china. [originally *China ware* (from China in Asia): the name is from Persian *chīnī*]

China aster *n.* a Chinese plant, *Callistephus chinensis*, related to the asters, cultivated for its bright and showy flowers.

china clay *n.* kaolin.

chinagraph /ˈtʃʌɪnəgrɑːf/ *n.* a waxy coloured pencil used to write on china, glass, etc.

Chinaman /ˈʃʌɪnəmən/ *n.* (*pl.* **-men**) **1** *archaic* or *derog.* (now usu. *offens.*) a native of China. **2** *Cricket* a ball bowled by a left-handed bowler that spins from off to leg.

China syndrome *n.* an imaginary sequence of events following the meltdown of a nuclear reactor, in which the core melts through its containment structure and deep into the earth. [*China*, as being on the opposite side of the earth from a reactor in the US]

China tea *n.* smoke-cured tea from a small-leaved tea plant grown in China.

Chinatown /ˈtʃʌmətaʊn/ *n.* a district of any non-Chinese town, esp. a city or seaport, in which the population is predominantly Chinese.

chinch /tʃɪn(t)ʃ/ *n.* (in full **chinch bug**) **1** a N. American plant bug, *Blissus leucopterus*, that destroys the shoots of grasses and grains. **2** *N. Amer.* a bedbug. [Spanish *chinche* from Latin *cimex -icis*]

chincherinchee /tʃɪntʃərɪnˈtʃiː/ *n.* a white-flowered bulbous plant, *Ornithogalum thyrsoides* (lily family), native to S. Africa. [imitative of the squeaky sound made by the rubbing of its stalks]

chinchilla /tʃɪnˈtʃɪlə/ *n.* **1 a** any small rodent of the genus *Chinchilla*, native to S. America, having soft silver-grey fur and a bushy tail. **b** its highly valued fur. **2** a breed of cat or rabbit. [Spanish, probably from S. American native name]

chin-chin /tʃɪnˈtʃɪn/ *int. Brit. colloq.* a toast; a greeting or farewell. [Chinese *qingqing* (pr. ch-)]

Chindit /ˈtʃɪndɪt/ *n. hist.* a member of the Allied forces behind the Japanese lines in Burma (now Myanmar) in 1943–5. [Burmese *chinthé*, a mythical creature]

chine[1] /tʃʌɪn/ *n. & v.* ● *n.* **1 a** a backbone, esp. of an animal. **b** a joint of meat containing all or part of this. **2** a ridge or arête. ● *v.tr.* cut (meat) across or along the backbone. [Middle English via Old French *eschine* from Latin *spina* SPINE]

chine[2] /tʃʌɪn/ *n.* a deep narrow ravine in the Isle of Wight or Dorset. [Old English *cinu* 'cleft, chink', from Germanic]

chine[3] /tʃʌɪn/ *n.* the join between the side and the bottom of a ship etc. [variant of CHIME[2]]

Chinese /tʃʌɪˈniːz/ *adj. & n.* ● *adj.* **1** of or relating to China. **2** of Chinese descent. ● *n.* (*pl.* same) **1** the Chinese language. **2 a** a native or national of China. **b** a person of Chinese descent.

Chinese burn *n. colloq.* an act of placing two hands on a person's arm and then twisting it with a wringing motion to produce a burning sensation.

Chinese cabbage *n.* = CHINESE LEAF.

Chinese chequers *n.pl.* (*US* **Chinese checkers**) (usu. treated as *sing.*) a board game for two to six players who attempt to move marbles etc. from one corner to the opposite one on a star-shaped board.

Chinese gooseberry *n.* = KIWI FRUIT.

Chinese lantern *n.* **1** a collapsible paper lantern. **2** a plant of the nightshade family, *Physalis alkekengi*, bearing white flowers and globular orange fruits enclosed in an orange-red papery calyx.

Chinese leaf *n.* a lettuce-like cabbage, *Brassica chinensis*.

Chinese puzzle *n.* a very intricate puzzle or problem.

Chinese water chestnut see WATER CHESTNUT 2.

Chinese white *n.* zinc oxide as a white pigment.

Chink /tʃɪŋk/ *n. slang offens.* a Chinese. [abbreviation]

chink[1] /tʃɪŋk/ *n.* **1** an unintended crack that admits light or allows an attack. **2** a narrow opening; a slit. [16th c.: related to CHINE[2]]

chink[2] /tʃɪŋk/ *v. & n.* ● *v.* **1** *intr.* make a slight ringing sound, as of glasses or coins striking together. **2** *tr.* cause to make this sound. ● *n.* this sound. [imitative]

Chinky /ˈtʃɪŋki/ *n.* (*pl.* **-ies**) *slang* **1** *offens.* a Chinese. **2** a Chinese restaurant.

chinless /ˈtʃɪnlɪs/ *adj. colloq.* weak or feeble in character.

chinless wonder *n. Brit. colloq.* an ineffectual esp. upper-class person.

Chino- /ˈtʃʌɪnəʊ/ *comb. form* = SINO-.

chino /ˈtʃiːnəʊ/ *n.* (*pl.* **-os**) **1** a cotton twill fabric, usu. khaki-coloured. **2** (in *pl.*) a garment, esp. trousers, made from this. [Latin American Spanish, = toasted]

chinoiserie /ʃɪnˈwɑːzəri/ *n.* **1** the imitation or evocation of Chinese motifs and techniques in Western art and architecture, esp. in the 18th c. **2** an object or objects in this style. [French]

chinook /tʃɪˈnʊk/ *n.* **1 a** a warm dry wind which blows east of the Rocky Mountains. **b** a warm wet southerly wind which blows west of the Rocky Mountains. **2** (**Chinook**) **a** (*pl.* same or **Chinooks**) a member of a N. American Indian people. **b** their language. [Salishan *tsinúk*, the name of the people]

Chinook jargon *n.* a pidgin composed of elements from Chinook, Nootka, English, French, and other languages, used formerly in the Pacific north-west of N. America.

chinook salmon *n.* a large salmon, *Oncorhynchus tshawytscha*, of the N. Pacific.

chinstrap /ˈtʃɪnstrap/ *n.* a strap for fastening a hat etc. under the chin.

chintz /tʃɪn(t)s/ *n. & adj.* ● *n.* a printed multicoloured cotton fabric with a glazed finish. ● *adj.* made from or upholstered with this fabric. [earlier *chints* (pl.) from Hindi *chīṇt* 'spattering, stain', from Sanskrit *citra* 'variegated']

chintzy /ˈtʃɪn(t)si/ *adj.* (**chintzier**, **chintziest**) **1** like chintz. **2** gaudy, cheap. **3** characteristic of the decor associated with chintz soft furnishings. □ **chintzily** *adv.* **chintziness** *n.*

chin-up *n.* esp. *N. Amer.* = PULL-UP 1.

chinwag /ˈtʃɪnwag/ *n. & v. Brit. slang* ● *n.* a talk or chat. ● *v.intr.* (**-wagged**, **-wagging**) have a gossip.

chionodoxa /kʌɪənəˈdɒksə/ *n.* a plant of the genus *Chionodoxa* (lily family), with early-blooming blue flowers. Also called *glory-of-the-snow*. [modern Latin, from Greek *khiōn* 'snow' + *doxa* 'glory']

chip /tʃɪp/ *n. & v.* ● *n.* **1** a small piece removed by or in the course of chopping, cutting, or breaking, esp. from hard material such as wood or stone. **2** the place where such a chip has been made. **3 a** (usu. in *pl.*) esp. *Brit.* a strip of potato, deep-fried. **b** (in full **potato chip**) (usu. in *pl.*) *N. Amer.* a potato crisp. **4** a counter used in some gambling games to represent money. **5** *Electronics* = MICROCHIP. **6** *Brit.* **a** a thin strip of wood, straw, etc., used for weaving hats, baskets, etc. **b** a basket made from these. **7** *Football* etc. & *Golf* a short shot, kick, or pass with the ball describing an arc. ● *v.* (**chipped**, **chipping**) **1** *tr.* (often foll. by *off*, *away*) cut or break (a piece) from a hard material. **2** *intr.* (foll. by *at*, *away at*) cut pieces off (a hard material) to alter its shape, break it up, etc. **3** *intr.* (of stone, china, etc.) be susceptible to being chipped; be apt to break at the edge (*will chip easily*). **4** *tr.* (also *absol.*) *Football* etc. & *Golf* strike or kick (the ball) with a chip (cf. sense 7 of *n.*). **5** *tr.* (usu. as **chipped** *adj.*) *Brit.* cut (potatoes) into chips. □ **chip in** *Brit. colloq.* **1** interrupt or contribute abruptly to a conversation (*chipped in with a reminiscence*). **2** contribute (money or resources). **a chip off the old block** a child who resembles a parent, esp. in character. **a chip on one's shoulder** *colloq.* a disposition or inclination to feel resentful or aggrieved. **have had one's chips** *Brit. colloq.* be unable to avoid defeat, punishment, etc. **when the chips are down** *colloq.* when it comes to the point. [Middle English from Old English *cipp*, *cyp* 'beam': the verb related to Old English *forcippian* 'cut off']

chipboard /ˈtʃɪpbɔːd/ *n.* a rigid sheet or panel made from compressed wood chips and resin.

chip heater *n. Austral.* & *NZ* a domestic water heater that burns wood chips.

chipmunk /ˈtʃɪpmʌŋk/ *n.* a N. American ground squirrel of the genus *Tamias*, having alternate light and dark stripes running down the body. [Algonquian]

chipolata /tʃɪpəˈlɑːtə/ *n. Brit.* a small thin sausage. [French, from Italian *cipollata* 'a dish of onions' from *cipolla* 'onion']

Chippendale /ˈtʃɪp(ə)ndeɪl/ *adj.* **1** (of furniture) designed or made by the English cabinetmaker Thomas Chippendale (d. 1779). **2** in the ornately elegant style of Chippendale's furniture.

chipper /ˈtʃɪpə/ *adj.* esp. *N. Amer. colloq.* **1** cheerful. **2** smartly dressed. [perhaps from northern English dialect *kipper* 'lively']

chippie var. of CHIPPY.

chipping /'tʃɪpɪŋ/ *n. Brit.* **1** a small fragment of stone, wood, etc. **2** (in *pl.*) these used as a surface for roads, roofs, etc.

chippy /'tʃɪpi/ *n. & adj.* ● *n.* (also **chippie**) (*pl.* **-ies**) *Brit. colloq.* **1** a fish-and-chip shop. **2** a carpenter. ● *adj.* **1** *colloq.* or *dial.* irritable. **2** *N. Amer. Ice Hockey* prone to fighting; belligerent.

Chips /tʃɪps/ *n. Naut. slang* a ship's carpenter.

chip shot *n.* = CHIP *n.* 7.

chiral /'kʌɪər(ə)l/ *adj. Chem.* (of an optically active compound) asymmetric and not superposable on its mirror image. ▫ **chirality** /-'ralɪti/ *n.* [Greek *kheir* 'hand']

chi-rho *n.* a monogram of chi (X) and rho (P) as the first two letters of Greek *Khristos* Christ.

chiro- /'kʌɪrəʊ/ *comb. form* (also **cheiro-**) of the hand. [Greek *kheir* 'hand']

chirography /kʌɪ'rɒgrəfi/ *n.* handwriting, calligraphy.

chiromancy /'kʌɪrəmansi/ *n.* palmistry.

chiropody /kɪ'rɒpədi/ *n.* the treatment of the feet (originally also the hands) and their ailments. ▫ **chiropodist** *n.* [CHIRO- + Greek *pous podos* 'foot']

chiropractic /kʌɪrə'praktɪk/ *n.* the diagnosis and manipulative treatment of mechanical disorders of the joints, esp. of the spinal column. ▫ **chiropractor** /'kʌɪrə(ʊ)-/ *n.* [CHIRO- + Greek *praktikos*: see PRACTICAL]

chiropteran /kʌɪ'rɒpt(ə)rən/ *n.* any mammal of the order Chiroptera, which comprises the bats. ▫ **chiropterous** *adj.* [CHIRO- + Greek *pteron* 'wing']

chirp /tʃə:p/ *v. & n.* ● *v.* **1** *intr.* (usu. of small birds, grasshoppers, etc.) utter a short sharp high-pitched note. **2** *tr. & intr.* (esp. of a child) speak or utter in a lively or jolly way. ● *n.* a chirping sound. ▫ **chirper** *n.* [Middle English, earlier *chirk*, *chirt*: imitative]

chirpy /'tʃə:pi/ *adj.* (**chirpier**, **chirpiest**) *colloq.* cheerful, lively. ▫ **chirpily** *adv.* **chirpiness** *n.*

chirr /tʃə:/ *v. & n.* (also **churr**) ● *v.intr.* (esp. of insects) make a prolonged low trilling sound. ● *n.* this sound. [imitative]

chirrup /'tʃɪrəp/ *v. & n.* ● *v.intr.* (**chirruped**, **chirruping**) (esp. of small birds) chirp, esp. repeatedly; twitter. ● *n.* a chirruping sound. ▫ **chirrupy** *adj.* [trilled form of CHIRP]

chisel /'tʃɪz(ə)l/ *n. & v.* ● *n.* a hand tool with a squared bevelled blade for shaping wood, stone, or metal. ● *v.* (**chiselled**, **chiselling**; *US* **chiseled**, **chiseling**) **1** *tr.* cut or shape with a chisel. **2** *tr.* (as **chiselled** *adj.*) (of facial features) clear-cut, fine. **3** *tr. & intr. slang* cheat, swindle. ▫ **chiseller** *n.* [Middle English from Old Northern French, ultimately from Late Latin *cisorium* from Latin *caedere caes-* 'cut']

chi-square test *n.* a method of comparing observed and theoretical values in statistics.

chit[1] /tʃɪt/ *n.* **1** *derog.* or *joc.* a young, small, or frail girl or woman (esp. *a chit of a girl*). **2** a young child. [Middle English, = whelp, cub, kitten, perhaps = dialect *chit* 'sprout']

chit[2] /tʃɪt/ *n.* **1** a note of requisition; a note of a sum owed, esp. for food or drink. **2** esp. *Brit.* a note or memorandum. [earlier *chitty*: Anglo-Indian from Hindi *ciṭṭhī* 'pass', from Sanskrit *citra* 'mark']

chital /'tʃi:t(ə)l/ *n.* = AXIS[2]. [Hindi *cītal*]

chit-chat /'tʃɪttʃat/ *n. & v. colloq.* ● *n.* light conversation; gossip. ● *v.intr.* (**-chatted**, **-chatting**) talk informally; gossip. [reduplication of CHAT[1]]

chitin /'kʌɪtɪn/ *n. Chem.* a polysaccharide forming the major constituent in the exoskeleton of arthropods and in the cell walls of fungi. ▫ **chitinous** *adj.* [French *chitine*, formed irregularly from Greek *khitōn*: see CHITON]

chiton /'kʌɪtɒn, -t(ə)n/ *n.* **1** a long woollen tunic worn by ancient Greeks. **2** any marine mollusc of the class Amphineura, having a shell of overlapping plates. [Greek *khitōn* 'tunic']

chitterling /'tʃɪtəlɪŋ/ *n.* (usu. in *pl.*) the smaller intestines of pigs etc., esp. as cooked for food. [Middle English: origin uncertain]

chitty /'tʃɪti/ *n.* (*pl.* **-ies**) = CHIT[2].

chivalrous /'ʃɪv(ə)lrəs/ *adj.* **1** (usu. of a male) gallant, honourable, courteous. **2** involving or showing chivalry. ▫ **chivalrously** *adv.* [Middle English from Old French *chevalerous*: see CHEVALIER]

chivalry /'ʃɪv(ə)lri/ *n.* **1** the medieval knightly system with its religious, moral, and social code. **2** the combination of qualities expected of an ideal knight, esp. courage, honour, courtesy, justice, and readiness to help the weak. **3** a man's courteous behaviour, esp. towards women. **4** *archaic* knights, noblemen, and horsemen collectively. ▫ **chivalric** *adj.* [Middle English via Old French *chevalerie* etc. from medieval Latin *caballerius*, for Late Latin *caballarius* 'horseman': see CAVALIER]

chive /tʃʌɪv/ *n.* a small allium, *Allium schoenoprasum*, having purple-pink flowers and dense tufts of long tubular leaves which are used as a herb. [Middle English via Old French *cive* from Latin *cepa* 'onion']

chivvy /'tʃɪvi/ *v.tr.* (also **chivy**, **chevy** /'tʃɛvi/) (**-ies**, **-ied**) hurry (a person) up; harass, nag; pursue. [*chevy* (*n.* & *v.*), probably from a skirmish described in the ballad of *Chevy Chase*, a place on the Scottish border]

chlamydia /klə'mɪdɪə/ *n.* (*pl.* **chlamydiae** /-dɪi:/) any small parasitic bacterium of the genus *Chlamydia*, e.g. those which cause diseases such as trachoma, psittacosis, and non-specific urethritis. [modern Latin, from Greek *khlamus -udos* 'cloak']

chlamydomonas /ˌklamɪdə'məʊnəs/ *n.* a motile unicellular green alga of the genus *Chlamydomonas*. [modern Latin (as CHLAMYDIA)]

chlor- /klɔ:/ var. of CHLORO-.

chloracne /klɔ:'rakni/ *n. Med.* a skin disease resembling severe acne, caused by exposure to chlorinated chemicals. [CHLORINE + ACNE]

chloral /'klɔ:ral/ *n.* **1** a colourless liquid aldehyde used in making DDT. **2** (in full **chloral hydrate**) *Pharm.* a colourless crystalline solid made from chloral and used as a sedative. [French from *chlore* 'chlorine' + *alcool* 'alcohol']

chloramphenicol /klɔ:ram'fɛnɪkɒl/ *n. Pharm.* an antibiotic prepared from *Streptomyces venezuelae* or produced synthetically and used esp. against typhoid fever. [CHLORO- + AMIDE + PHENO- + NITRO- + GLYCOL]

chlorate /'klɔ:reɪt/ *n. Chem.* any salt of chloric acid.

chlorella /klə'rɛlə/ *n.* a non-motile unicellular green alga of the genus *Chlorella*. [modern Latin, diminutive of Greek *khlōros* 'green']

chloric acid /'klɔ:rɪk/ *n. Chem.* a colourless liquid acid with strong oxidizing properties. [CHLORO- + -IC]

chloride /'klɔ:rʌɪd/ *n. Chem.* **1** any compound of chlorine with another element or group. **2** any bleaching agent containing chloride. [CHLORO- + -IDE]

chlorinate /'klɔ:rɪneɪt, 'klɒ-/ *v.tr.* **1** impregnate or treat with chlorine. **2** *Chem.* cause to react or combine with chlorine. ▫ **chlorinator** *n.*

chlorination /klɔ:rɪ'neɪʃ(ə)n/ *n.* **1** the treatment of water with chlorine to disinfect it. **2** *Chem.* a reaction in which chlorine is introduced into a compound.

chlorine /'klɔ:ri:n/ *n. Chem.* a poisonous greenish-yellow gaseous element of the halogen group occurring naturally esp. as sodium chloride in salt, sea water, rock salt, etc., and used in disinfectants and bleaches, and the manufacture of many organic chemicals (symbol Cl). [Greek *khlōros* 'green' + -INE[4]]

chlorite[1] /'klɔ:rʌɪt/ *n. Mineral.* a dark green mineral found in many rocks, consisting of a basic aluminosilicate of magnesium, iron, etc. ▫ **chloritic** /-'rɪtɪk/ *adj.*

chlorite[2] /'klɔ:rʌɪt/ *n. Chem.* any salt of chlorous acid.

chloro- /'klɔ:rəʊ, 'klɒrəʊ/ *comb. form* (also **chlor-** esp. before a vowel) **1** *Biol. & Mineral.* green. **2** *Chem.*

chlorine. [Greek *khlōros* 'green': in sense 2 from CHLORINE]

chlorofluorocarbon /ˌklɔːrəʊfluərəʊˈkɑːb(ə)n/ see CFC.

chloroform /ˈklɔːrəfɔːm, ˈklɒr-/ *n.* & *v.* ● *n.* a colourless volatile sweet-smelling liquid used as a solvent and formerly as a general anaesthetic. Chem. formula: $CHCl_3$. ● *v.tr.* render (a person) unconscious with this. [French *chloroforme*, formed as CHLORO- + *formyle* from FORMIC ACID]

Chloromycetin /klɔːrə(ʊ)ˈmʌɪsɪtɪn, klɒrə(ʊ)-, -mʌɪˈsiːtɪn/ *n. propr.* = CHLORAMPHENICOL. [CHLORO- + Greek *mukēs -ētos* 'fungus']

chlorophyll /ˈklɔːrəfɪl, ˈklɒr-/ *n.* the green pigment found in most plants, responsible for light absorption to provide energy by photosynthesis. □ **chlorophyllous** /-ˈfɪləs/ *adj.* [French *chlorophylle* from Greek *phullon* 'leaf': see CHLORO-]

chloroplast /ˈklɔːrəplast, -plɑːst, ˈklɒr-/ *n.* a plastid containing chlorophyll, found in plant cells undergoing photosynthesis. [German: (as CHLORO-, PLASTID)]

chloroquine /ˈklɒrəkwiːn, ˈklɔːr-/ *n. Pharm.* a drug related to quinoline and used esp. against malaria. [CHLORO- + QUININE]

chlorosis /klɒˈrəʊsɪs/ *n.* **1** *Med.* a severe form of anaemia from iron deficiency esp. in young women, causing a greenish complexion (cf. GREENSICK). **2** *Bot.* a reduction or loss of the normal green coloration of leaves. □ **chlorotic** *adj.* [CHLORO- + -OSIS]

chlorous acid /ˈklɔːrəs/ *n. Chem.* a pale yellow liquid acid with oxidizing properties. Chem. formula: $HClO_2$. [CHLORO- + -OUS]

chlorpromazine /klɔːˈprəʊməzɪn, -ziːn/ *n. Pharm.* a drug used as a sedative and to control nausea and vomiting. [French (as CHLORO-, PROMETHAZINE)]

Ch.M. *abbr.* Master of Surgery. [Latin *Chirurgiae Magister*]

choc /tʃɒk/ *n.* & *adj. Brit. colloq.* chocolate. [abbreviation]

chocaholic var. of CHOCOHOLIC.

chocho /ˈtʃəʊtʃəʊ/ *n.* (*pl.* **-os**) *W.Ind.* = CHOKO.

choc ice *n. Brit.* a bar of ice cream covered with a thin coating of chocolate.

chock /tʃɒk/ *n., v.,* & *adv.* ● *n.* a block or wedge of wood to check motion, esp. of a cask or a wheel. ● *v.tr.* **1** fit or make fast with chocks. **2** (usu. foll. by *up*) *Brit.* cram full. ● *adv.* as closely or tightly as possible. [probably from Old French *çouche, çoche* 'block, log', of unknown origin]

chocka /ˈtʃɒkə/ *adj.* & *adv. colloq.* = CHOCK-A-BLOCK. [abbreviation]

chock-a-block /tʃɒkəˈblɒk/ *adj.* & *adv.* crammed close together; crammed full (*a street chock-a-block with cars*). [originally nautical, with reference to tackle with the two blocks run close together]

chocker /ˈtʃɒkə/ *adj. Brit. slang* fed up, disgusted. [CHOCK-A-BLOCK]

chock-full /tʃɒkˈfʊl/ *adj.* & *adv.* crammed full (*chock-full of rubbish*). [CHOCK + FULL[1]: Middle English *chokkefulle* (related to CHOKE[1]) is doubtful]

chockstone /ˈtʃɒkstəʊn/ *n. Mountaineering* a stone wedged in a vertical cleft.

chocoholic /tʃɒkəˈhɒlɪk/ *n.* & *adj.* (also **chocaholic**) ● *n.* a person who is addicted to or very fond of chocolate. ● *adj.* of or relating to chocoholics. [blend of CHOCOLATE and ALCOHOLIC]

chocolate /ˈtʃɒk(ə)lət/ *n.* & *adj.* ● *n.* **1 a** a food preparation in the form of a paste or solid block made from roasted and ground cacao seeds, usually sweetened. **b** a sweet made of or coated with this. **c** a drink made with chocolate. **2** = CHOCOLATE BROWN *n.* ● *adj.* **1** made from or of chocolate. **2** = CHOCOLATE BROWN *adj.* □ **chocolatey** *adj.* (also **chocolaty**). [French *chocolat* or Spanish *chocolate*, from Nahuatl *chocolatl*]

chocolate box *n.* **1** a decorated box filled with chocolates. **2** (**chocolate-box** *attrib.*) stereotypically pretty or romantic.

chocolate brown *n.* & *adj.* ● *n.* a deep brown colour. ● *adj.* (hyphenated when *attrib.*) of this colour.

Choctaw /ˈtʃɒktɔː/ *n.* & *adj.* ● *n.* (*pl.* same or **Choctaws**) **1 a** a member of a N. American Indian people originally from Alabama. **b** the language of this people. **2** (in skating) a step from one edge of a skate to the other edge of the other skate in the opposite direction. ● *adj.* of or relating to the Choctaws or their language. [native name]

choice /tʃɔɪs/ *n.* & *adj.* ● *n.* **1 a** the act or an instance of choosing. **b** a thing or person chosen (*not a good choice*). **2** a range from which to choose. **3** (usu. foll. by *of*) the elite, the best. **4** the power or opportunity to choose (*what choice have I?*). ● *adj.* of superior quality; carefully chosen. □ **choicely** *adv.* **choiceness** *n.* [Middle English from Old French *chois*, from *choisir* CHOOSE]

choir /ˈkwʌɪə/ *n.* **1** a regular group of singers, esp. taking part in church services. **2** the part of a cathedral or large church between the altar and the nave, used by the choir and clergy. **3** a company of singers, birds, angels etc. (*a heavenly choir*). **4** *Mus.* a group of instruments of one family playing together. [Middle English via Old French *quer* from Latin *chorus*: see CHORUS]

choirboy /ˈkwʌɪəbɔɪ/ *n.* (*fem.* **choirgirl** /-gəːl/) a boy or girl who sings in a church or cathedral choir.

choirman /ˈkwʌɪəmən/ *n.* (*pl.* **choirmen**) a man who sings in a choir.

choir organ *n.* the softest of three parts making up a large organ having its row of keys the lowest of the three.

choir stall *n.* = STALL[1] *n.* 3a.

choke[1] /tʃəʊk/ *v.* & *n.* ● *v.* **1** *tr.* hinder or impede the breathing of (a person or animal) esp. by constricting the windpipe or (of gas, smoke, etc.) by being unbreathable. **2** *intr.* suffer a hindrance or stoppage of breath. **3** *tr.* & *intr.* make or become speechless from emotion. **4** *tr.* retard the growth of or kill (esp. plants) by the deprivation of light, air, nourishment, etc. **5** *tr.* (often foll. by *back*) suppress (feelings) with difficulty. **6** *tr.* block or clog (a passage, tube, etc.). **7** *tr.* (as **choked** *adj.*) *Brit. colloq.* disgusted, disappointed. **8** *tr.* enrich the fuel mixture in (an internal-combustion engine) by reducing the intake of air. ● *n.* **1** the valve in the carburettor of an internal-combustion engine that controls the intake of air, esp. to enrich the fuel mixture. **2** *Electr.* an inductance coil used to smooth the variations of an alternating current or to alter its phase. □ **choke down** swallow with difficulty. **choke up** block (a channel etc.). [Middle English from Old English *ācēocian*, from *cēoce, cē(a)ce* CHEEK]

choke[2] /tʃəʊk/ *n.* the centre part of an artichoke. [probably a confusion of the ending of *artichoke* with CHOKE[1]]

chokeberry /ˈtʃəʊkb(ə)ri/ *n.* (*pl.* **-ies**) **1** a shrub of the genus *Aronia* (rose family). **2** its scarlet berry-like fruit.

choke chain *n.* a chain looped round a dog's neck to exert control by pressure on its windpipe when the dog pulls.

choke cherry *n.* an astringent N. American cherry, *Prunus virginiana*.

choke-damp *n.* carbon dioxide in mines, wells, etc.

choker /ˈtʃəʊkə/ *n.* **1** a close-fitting necklace or ornamental neckband. **2** a clerical or other high collar.

choko /ˈtʃəʊkəʊ/ *n.* (*pl.* **-os**) *Austral.* & *NZ* a succulent green pear-shaped vegetable like a cucumber in flavour. [Brazilian Indian *chocho*]

choky[1] /ˈtʃəʊki/ *n.* (also **chokey**) (*pl.* **-ies** or **-eys**) *Brit. slang* prison. [originally Anglo-Indian, from Hindi *caukī* 'shed']

choky[2] /ˈtʃəʊki/ *adj.* (**chokier**, **chokiest**) tending to choke or to cause choking.

cholangiography /ˌkɒlandʒɪˈɒgrəfi/ *n. Med.* X-ray examination of the bile ducts, used to locate and identify an obstruction. [CHOLE- + Greek *aggeion* 'vessel' + -GRAPHY]

chole- /ˈkɒli/ *comb. form* (also **chol-** esp. before a vowel) *Med. & Chem.* bile. [Greek *kholē* 'gall, bile']

cholecalciferol /ˌkɒlɪkalˈsɪf(ə)rɒl/ *n.* one of the D vitamins, produced by the action of sunlight on a cholesterol derivative widely distributed in the skin, a deficiency of which results in rickets in children and osteomalacia in adults. Also called *vitamin* D_3. [CHOLE- + CALCIFEROL]

cholecystography /ˌkɒlɪsɪˈstɒgrəfi/ *n. Med.* X-ray examination of the gall bladder, esp. used to detect the presence of gallstones. [CHOLE- + CYSTO- + -GRAPHY]

choler /ˈkɒlə/ *n.* **1** *hist.* = YELLOW BILE. **2** *poet.* or *archaic* anger, irascibility. [Middle English via Old French *colere* 'bile, anger' and Latin *cholera* from Greek *kholera* 'diarrhoea', in Late Latin = bile, anger, from Greek *kholē* 'bile']

cholera /ˈkɒlərə/ *n. Med.* an infectious and often fatal disease of the small intestine caused by the mainly water-borne bacterium *Vibrio cholerae*, resulting in severe vomiting and diarrhoea. ◻ **choleraic** /-ˈreɪɪk/ *adj.* [Middle English from Latin from Greek *kholera*: see CHOLER]

choleric /ˈkɒlərɪk/ *adj.* irascible, angry. ◻ **cholerically** *adv.* [Middle English via Old French *cholerique* and Latin *cholericus* from Greek *kholerikos*: see CHOLER]

cholesterol /kəˈlɛstərɒl/ *n. Biochem.* a sterol found in most body tissues, including the blood, where high concentrations can promote arteriosclerosis. [earlier *cholesterin* from Greek *kholē* 'bile' + *stereos* 'stiff']

choli /ˈtʃəʊli/ *n.* (*pl.* **cholis**) a type of short-sleeved bodice worn by Indian women. [Hindi *colī*]

choliamb /ˈkəʊlɪam(b)/ *n. Prosody* = SCAZON. ◻ **choliambic** /kəʊlɪˈambɪk/ *adj.* [Late Latin *choliambus* from Greek *khōliambos*, from *khōlos* 'lame': see IAMBUS]

choline /ˈkəʊliːn, -ɪn/ *n. Biochem.* a basic nitrogenous organic compound occurring widely in living matter. [German *Cholin* from Greek *kholē* 'bile']

cholla /ˈtʃɔɪə/ *n.* any of several opuntias of Mexico and the south-west US. [Mexican Spanish, literally 'skull, head']

chomp /tʃɒmp/ *v.tr.* = CHAMP¹. [imitative]

Chomskian /ˈtʃɒmskɪən/ *adj.* of or relating to N.L. Chomsky, American linguist (b. 1928), or his work.

chondrite /ˈkɒndrʌɪt/ *n.* a stony meteorite containing small mineral granules. [German *Chondrit* from Greek *khondros* 'granule']

chondrocranium /kɒndrəʊˈkreɪmɪəm/ *n. Anat.* the embryonic skull composed of cartilage and later replaced by bone. [Greek *khondros* 'grain, cartilage']

choo-choo /ˈtʃuːtʃuː/ *n.* (also **choo-choo train**) *colloq.* (esp. as a child's word) a railway train or locomotive, esp. a steam engine. [imitative]

chook /tʃʊk/ *n.* (also **chookie** /ˈtʃʊki/) *Austral. & NZ* **1** *colloq.* a chicken or fowl. **2** *slang* an older woman. [English dialect *chuck* 'chicken']

choose /tʃuːz/ *v.* (*past* **chose** /tʃəʊz/; *past part.* **chosen** /ˈtʃəʊz(ə)n/) **1** *tr.* select out of a greater number. **2** *intr.* (usu. foll. by *between, from*) take or select one or another. **3** *tr.* (usu. foll. by *to* + infin.) decide, be determined (*chose to stay behind*). **4** *tr.* (foll. by complement) select as (*was chosen king*). **5** *tr. Theol.* (esp. as **chosen** *adj.*) destine to be saved (*God's chosen people*). ◻ **cannot choose but** *archaic* must. **nothing** (or **little**) **to choose between them** they are equivalent. ◻ **chooser** *n.* [Old English *cēosan*, from Germanic]

choosy /ˈtʃuːzi/ *adj.* (**choosier**, **choosiest**) *colloq.* fastidious. ◻ **choosily** *adv.* **choosiness** *n.*

chop¹ /tʃɒp/ *v. & n.* ● *v.tr.* (**chopped**, **chopping**) **1** (usu. foll. by *off, down*, etc.) cut or fell by a blow, usu. with an axe. **2** (often foll. by *up*) cut (esp. meat or vegetables) into small pieces. **3** strike (esp. a ball) with a short heavy edgewise blow. **4** cut as if by chopping; dispense with; reduce, shorten (*chopped £100 off the budget*; *chopped the penultimate scene from the play*; *chopped his sentence short*). ● *n.* **1** a cutting blow, esp. with an axe. **2** a thick slice of meat (esp. pork or lamb) usu. including a rib. **3** a short heavy edgewise stroke or blow in tennis, cricket, boxing, etc. **4** the broken motion of water, usu. owing to the action of the wind against the tide. **5** (prec. by *the*) *Brit. slang* **a** dismissal from employment. **b** the action of killing or being killed. **c** cancellation (of a project etc.). [Middle English, variant of CHAP¹]

chop² /tʃɒp/ *n.* (usu. in *pl.*) the jaw of an animal etc. [16th-c. variant (occurring earlier) of CHAP³, of unknown origin]

chop³ /tʃɒp/ *v.intr.* (**chopped**, **chopping**) ◻ **chop and change** *Brit.* vacillate; change direction frequently. **chop logic** argue pedantically. [Middle English, = barter, exchange, perhaps related to *chap* (as in CHAPMAN) from Old English *cēapian* (as CHEAP)]

chop⁴ /tʃɒp/ *n. Brit. archaic* a trade mark; a brand of goods. ◻ **not much chop** esp. *Austral. & NZ* no good. [originally in India & China, from Hindi *chāp* 'an official stamp']

chop-chop /tʃɒpˈtʃɒp/ *adv. & int.* (pidgin English) quickly, quick. [Chinese dialect *k'wâi-k'wâi*]

chopper /ˈtʃɒpə/ *n.* **1 a** *Brit.* a short axe with a large blade. **b** a butcher's cleaver. **2** *colloq.* a helicopter. **3** a device for regularly interrupting an electric current or light beam. **4** a type of bicycle (**Chopper** *propr.*), or motorcycle, with high handlebars. **5** (in *pl.*) *slang* teeth.

choppy /ˈtʃɒpi/ *adj.* (**choppier**, **choppiest**) (of the sea, the weather, etc.) fairly rough. ◻ **choppily** *adv.* **choppiness** *n.* [CHOP¹ + -Y¹]

chopstick /ˈtʃɒpstɪk/ *n.* each of a pair of small thin sticks of wood or ivory etc., held both in one hand as eating utensils by the Chinese, Japanese, etc. [pidgin English from *chop* = quick + STICK¹, equivalent of Cantonese *k'wâi-tsze* 'nimble ones']

chop suey /tʃɒpˈsuːi/ *n.* (*pl.* **-eys**) a Chinese-style dish of meat stewed and fried with bean sprouts, bamboo shoots, onions, and served with rice. [Cantonese *shap sui* 'mixed bits']

choral /ˈkɔːr(ə)l/ *adj.* of, for, or sung by a choir or chorus. ◻ **chorally** *adv.* [medieval Latin *choralis* from Latin *chorus*: see CHORUS]

chorale /kɒˈrɑːl/ *n.* (also **choral**) **1** a stately and simple hymn tune; a harmonized version of this. **2** esp. *US* a choir or choral society. [German *Choral(gesang)* from medieval Latin *cantus choralis*]

choral ode *n.* a song of the chorus in a Greek drama.

choral society *n.* a group which meets regularly to sing choral music.

chord¹ /kɔːd/ *n. Mus.* a group of (usu. three or more) notes sounded together, as a basis of harmony. ◻ **chordal** *adj.* [originally *cord* from ACCORD: later confused with CHORD²]

chord² /kɔːd/ *n.* **1** *Math. & Aeron.* etc. a straight line joining the ends of an arc, the wings of an aeroplane, etc. **2** *Anat.* = CORD 2. **3** *poet.* the string of a harp etc. **4** *Engin.* one of the two principal members, usu. horizontal, of a truss. ◻ **strike a chord 1** recall something to a person's memory. **2** elicit sympathy. **touch the right chord** appeal skilfully to the emotions. ◻ **chordal** *adj.* [16th-c. refashioning of CORD reflecting its source, Latin *chorda*]

chordate /ˈkɔːdeɪt/ *n. & adj.* ● *n.* any animal of the phylum Chordata, possessing a notochord at some stage during its development. ● *adj.* of or relating to the chordates. [modern Latin *chordata* from Latin *chorda* CHORD², on the pattern of *Vertebrata* etc.]

chording /ˈkɔːdɪŋ/ *n. Mus.* the playing, singing, or arrangement of chords. ◻ **chord** *v.intr.*

chore /tʃɔː/ *n.* a tedious or routine task, esp. a domestic one. [originally dialect and US form of CHAR²]

chorea /kɒˈrɪə/ *n. Med.* a disorder characterized by jerky involuntary movements affecting esp. the shoulders, hips, and face. [Latin from Greek *khoreia* 'dance' (as CHORUS)]

choreograph /ˈkɒrɪəgrɑːf/ *v.tr.* compose the choreography for (a ballet etc.). □ **choreographer** /-ɪˈɒgrəfə/ *n.* [back-formation from CHOREOGRAPHY]

choreography /kɒrɪˈɒgrəfi/ *n.* **1** the design or arrangement of a ballet or other staged dance. **2** the sequence of steps and movements in dance. **3** the written notation for this. □ **choreographic** /kɒrɪəˈgrafɪk/ *adj.* **choreographically** /kɒrɪəˈgrafɪk(ə)li/ *adv.* [Greek *khoreia* 'dance' + -GRAPHY]

choreology /kɒrɪˈɒlədʒi/ *n.* the study and description of the movements of dancing. □ **choreologist** *n.*

choriambus /kɒrɪˈambəs/ *n.* (*pl.* **choriambi** /-bʌɪ/) *Prosody* a metrical foot consisting of two short (unstressed) syllables between two long (stressed) ones. □ **choriambic** *adj.* [Late Latin from Greek *khoriambos*, from *khoreios* 'of the dance' + IAMBUS]

choric /ˈkɒrɪk, ˈkɔːrɪk/ *adj.* of, like, or for a chorus in drama or recitation. [Late Latin *choricus* from Greek *khorikos* (as CHORUS)]

chorine /ˈkɔːriːn/ *n.* a chorus girl. [CHORUS + -INE[3]]

chorion /ˈkɔːrɪən/ *n.* the outermost membrane surrounding an embryo of a reptile, bird, or mammal. □ **chorionic** /-ˈɒnɪk/ *adj.* [Greek *khorion*]

chorister /ˈkɒrɪstə/ *n.* **1** a member of a choir, esp. a choirboy or choirgirl. **2** *US* the leader of a church choir. [Middle English, ultimately from Old French *cueriste* from *quer* CHOIR]

chorography /kɔːˈrɒgrəfi/ *n.* the systematic description of regions or districts. □ **chorographer** *n.* **chorographic** /kɒrəˈgrafɪk/ *adj.* [French *chorographie* or Latin *chorographia* from Greek *khōrographia*, from *khōra* 'region']

choroid /ˈkɔːrɔɪd, ˈkɒr-/ *adj. & n.* ● *adj.* like a chorion in shape or vascularity. ● *n.* (in full **choroid coat** or **membrane**) a layer of the eyeball between the retina and the sclera. [Greek *khoroeidēs* for *khorioeidēs*: see CHORION]

chortle /ˈtʃɔːt(ə)l/ *v. & n.* ● *v.intr.* chuckle gleefully. ● *n.* a gleeful chuckle. [portmanteau word coined by Lewis Carroll, probably from CHUCKLE + SNORT]

chorus /ˈkɔːrəs/ *n. & v.* ● *n.* (*pl.* **choruses**) **1** a group (esp. a large one) of singers; a choir. **2** a piece of music composed for a choir. **3** the refrain or the main part of a popular song, in which a chorus participates. **4** any simultaneous utterance by many persons etc. (*a chorus of disapproval followed*). **5** a group of singers and dancers performing in concert in a musical comedy, opera, etc. **6** *Gk Antiq.* **a** in Greek tragedy, a group of performers who comment together in voice and movement on the main action. **b** an utterance of the chorus. **7** esp. in Elizabethan drama, a character who speaks the prologue and other linking parts of the play. **8** the part spoken by this character. ● *v.tr. & intr.* (**chorused**, **chorusing**) (of a group) speak or utter simultaneously. □ **in chorus** (uttered) together; in unison. [Latin, from Greek *khoros*]

chorus girl *n.* a young woman who sings or dances in the chorus of a musical comedy etc.

chose *past* of CHOOSE.

chosen *past part.* of CHOOSE.

chough /tʃʌf/ *n.* a bird of the genus *Pyrrhocorax* (crow family), with glossy blue-black plumage and red legs. [Middle English, probably originally imitative]

choux pastry /ʃuː/ *n.* very light pastry enriched with eggs. [French, pl. of *chou* 'cabbage, rosette': in English originally a round cream-filled pastry]

chow /tʃaʊ/ *n.* **1** *slang* food. **2** *offens.* a Chinese. **3 a** a dog of a Chinese breed with long hair and bluish-black tongue. **b** this breed. [shortened from CHOW-CHOW]

chow-chow /ˈtʃaʊtʃaʊ/ *n.* **1** = CHOW 1,2,3. **2** a Chinese preserve of ginger, orange peel, etc., in syrup. **3** a mixed vegetable pickle. [pidgin English]

chowder /ˈtʃaʊdə/ *n. N. Amer.* a rich soup usu. containing fresh fish, clams, or corn with potatoes, onions, etc. [perhaps French *chaudière* 'pot': see CAULDRON]

chowkidar /ˈtʃəʊkɪdɑː/ *n. Anglo-Ind.* a watchman or gatekeeper. [Urdu *chaukīdār*]

chow mein /tʃaʊ ˈmeɪn/ *n.* a Chinese-style dish of fried noodles with shredded meat or shrimps etc. and vegetables. [Chinese *chao mian* 'fried flour']

Chr. *abbr.* Chronicles (Old Testament).

chrestomathy /krɛˈstɒməθi/ *n.* (*pl.* **-ies**) a selection of passages used esp. to help in learning a language. [French *chrestomathie* or Greek *khrēstomatheia*, from *khrēstos* 'useful' + *-matheia* 'learning']

chrism /ˈkrɪz(ə)m/ *n.* a consecrated oil or unguent used esp. for anointing in Catholic and Greek Orthodox rites. [Old English *crisma* via ecclesiastical Latin from Greek *khrisma* 'anointing']

chrisom /ˈkrɪz(ə)m/ *n.* **1** = CHRISM. **2** (in full **chrisom-cloth**) *hist.* a white robe put on a child at baptism, and used as its shroud if it died within the month. [Middle English, as popular pronunciation of CHRISM]

Christ /krʌɪst/ *n. & int.* ● *n.* **1** the title, also now treated as a name, given to Jesus of Nazareth, believed by Christians to have fulfilled the Old Testament prophecies of a coming Messiah. **2** the Messiah as prophesied in the Old Testament. **3** an image or picture of Jesus. ● *int. slang* expressing surprise, anger, etc. □ **Christhood** *n.* **Christlike** *adj.* **Christly** *adj.* [Old English *Crīst* via Latin *Christus* from Greek *khristos* 'anointed one', from *khriō* 'anoint': translation of Hebrew *māšîaḥ* MESSIAH]

Christadelphian /krɪstəˈdɛlfɪən/ *n. & adj.* ● *n.* a member of a Christian sect rejecting the doctrine of the Trinity and expecting a second coming of Christ on earth. ● *adj.* of or adhering to this sect and its beliefs. [CHRIST + Greek *adelphos* 'brother']

christen /ˈkrɪs(ə)n/ *v.tr.* **1** give a Christian name to at baptism as a sign of admission to a Christian Church. **2** give a name to (a thing), esp. formally or with a ceremony. **3** *colloq.* use for the first time. □ **christener** *n.* **christening** *n.* [Old English *crīstnian* 'make Christian']

Christendom /ˈkrɪs(ə)ndəm/ *n.* Christians worldwide, regarded as a collective body. [Old English *cristendōm*, from *cristen* CHRISTIAN + -DOM]

Christian /ˈkrɪstʃ(ə)n, -tɪən/ *adj. & n.* ● *adj.* **1** of Christ's teaching or religion. **2** believing in or following the religion of Jesus Christ. **3** showing the qualities associated with Christ's teaching. **4** *colloq.* (of a person) kind, fair, decent. ● *n.* **1 a** a person who has received Christian baptism. **b** an adherent of Christ's teaching. **2** a person exhibiting Christian qualities. □ **Christianize** *v.tr. & intr.* (also **-ise**). **Christianization** /ˌkrɪstʃ(ə)nʌɪˈzeɪʃ(ə)n, -tɪən-/ *n.* **Christianly** *adv.* [Latin *Christianus* from *Christus* CHRIST]

Christian era *n.* the era reckoned from the traditional date of Christ's birth.

Christianity /krɪstɪˈanɪti/ *n.* **1** the Christian religion; its beliefs and practices. **2** being a Christian; Christian quality or character. **3** = CHRISTENDOM. [Middle English *cristianite* from Old French *crestienté*, from *crestien* CHRISTIAN]

Christian name *n.* a forename, esp. as given at baptism.

Christian Science *n.* the beliefs and practices of The Church of Christ Scientist, a Christian body founded by Mary Baker Eddy in 1879, and holding that only God and the mind have ultimate reality, sin and illness being illusions overcome by prayer and faith. □ **Christian Scientist** *n.*

Christie /ˈkrɪsti/ *n.* (also **Christy**) (*pl.* **-ies**) *Skiing* a sudden turn in which the skis are kept parallel, used for changing direction fast or stopping short. [abbreviation of *Christiania* (now Oslo) in Norway]

Christingle /ˈkrɪstɪŋg(ə)l/ *n.* a lighted candle symbolizing Christ as the light of the world, held by children esp. at Advent services. [perhaps from German *Christkindl*, diminutive of *Christkind* 'Christ child']

Christmas /'krɪsməs/ *n. & int.* ● *n.* (*pl.* **Christmases**) **1** (also **Christmas Day**) the annual festival of Christ's birth, celebrated on 25 Dec. **2** the season in which this occurs; the time immediately before and after 25 Dec. ● *int. slang* expressing surprise, dismay, etc. □ **Christmassy** *adj.* [Old English *Crīstes mœsse* (MASS)]

Christmas box *n. Brit.* a present or gratuity given at Christmas esp. to tradesmen and employees.

Christmas cake *n. Brit.* a rich fruit cake usu. covered with marzipan and icing and eaten at Christmas.

Christmas card *n.* a card sent with greetings at Christmas.

Christmas Eve *n.* the day or the evening before Christmas Day.

Christmas pudding *n. Brit.* a rich boiled pudding eaten at Christmas, made with flour, suet, dried fruit, etc.

Christmas rose *n.* a small white-flowered winter-blooming plant, *Helleborus niger*.

Christmas stocking *n.* a real or ornamental stocking hung up by children on Christmas Eve for Father Christmas to fill with presents.

Christmas tree *n.* an evergreen (usu. spruce) or artificial tree set up with decorations at Christmas.

Christo- /'krɪstəʊ/ *comb. form* Christ.

Christology /krɪ'stɒlədʒi/ *n.* the branch of theology relating to Christ. □ **Christological** /-tə'lɒdʒɪk(ə)l/ *adj.*

Christy var. of CHRISTIE.

chroma /'krəʊmə/ *n.* purity or intensity of colour. [Greek *khrōma* 'colour']

chromate /'krəʊmeɪt/ *n. Chem.* a salt in which the anion contains both chromium (esp. in a higher valency) and oxygen.

chromatic /krə(ʊ)'matɪk/ *adj.* **1** of or produced by colour; in (esp. bright) colours. **2** *Mus.* **a** of or having notes not belonging to a diatonic scale. **b** (of a scale) ascending or descending by semitones. □ **chromatically** *adv.* **chromaticism** /-tɪsɪz(ə)m/ *n.* [French *chromatique* or Latin *chromaticus* from Greek *khrōmatikos*, from *khrōma -atos* 'colour']

chromatic aberration *n. Optics* the failure of different wavelengths of electromagnetic radiation to come to the same focus after refraction.

chromaticity /krəʊmə'tɪsɪti/ *n.* the quality of colour regarded independently of brightness.

chromatic semitone *n. Mus.* an interval between a note and its flat or sharp.

chromatid /'krəʊmətɪd/ *n. Biol.* either of two threadlike strands into which a chromosome divides longitudinally during cell division. [Greek *khrōma -atos* 'colour' + -ID²]

chromatin /'krəʊmətɪn/ *n. Biochem.* the material in a cell nucleus that stains with basic dyes and consists of protein, RNA, and DNA, of which eukaryotic chromosomes are composed. [German: see CHROMATID]

chromato- /'krəʊmətəʊ/ *comb. form* (also **chromo-** /'krəʊməʊ/) colour (*chromatopsia*). [Greek *khrōma -atos* 'colour']

chromatography /krəʊmə'tɒgrəfi/ *n. Chem.* a technique for the separation of a mixture by passing it in solution or suspension through a medium in which the components move at different rates. □ **chromatograph** /-'matəgrɑːf/ *n.* **chromatographic** /-mətə(ʊ)'grafɪk/ *adj.* [German *Chromatographie* (as CHROMATO-, -GRAPHY)]

chromatopsia /krəʊmə'tɒpsɪə/ *n. Med.* abnormally coloured vision. [CHROMATO- + Greek *-opsia* 'seeing']

chrome /krəʊm/ *n.* **1** chromium, esp. as plating. **2** (in full **chrome yellow**) a yellow pigment obtained from lead chromate. [French, = chromium, from Greek *khrōma* 'colour']

chrome leather *n.* leather tanned with chromium salts.

chrome steel *n.* a hard fine-grained steel containing much chromium and used for tools etc.

chromic /'krəʊmɪk/ *adj. Chem.* of or containing trivalent chromium.

chromic acid *n.* an acid that exists only in solution or in the form of chromate salts.

chrominance /'krəʊmɪnəns/ *n. Telev.* the colorimetric difference between a given colour and a standard colour of equal luminance. [Greek *khrōma* 'colour' + LUMINANCE]

chromite /'krəʊmʌɪt/ *n.* **1** *Mineral.* a black mineral of chromium and iron oxides, which is the principal ore of chromium. **2** *Chem.* a salt of divalent chromium.

chromium /'krəʊmɪəm/ *n. Chem.* a hard white metallic transition element, occurring naturally as chromite and used as a shiny decorative electroplated coating (symbol **Cr**). [modern Latin from French CHROME]

chromium-plate *n. & v.* ● *n.* an electrolytically deposited protective coating of chromium. ● *v.tr.* **1** coat with this. **2** (as **chromium-plated** *adj.*) pretentiously decorative.

chromium steel *n.* = CHROME STEEL.

chromo-¹ /'krəʊməʊ/ *comb. form Chem.* chromium.

chromo-² var. of CHROMATO-.

chromodynamics see QUANTUM CHROMODYNAMICS.

chromolithograph /krəʊməʊ'lɪθəgrɑːf/ *n. & v.* ● *n.* a coloured picture printed by lithography. ● *v.tr.* print or produce by this process. □ **chromolithographer** /-'θɒgrəfə/ *n.* **chromolithographic** /-ˌlɪθə'grafɪk/ *adj.* **chromolithography** /-lɪ'θɒgrəfi/ *n.*

chromosome /'krəʊməsəʊm/ *n. Biol.* each of the rodlike or threadlike structures of DNA and protein found in the nuclei of cells that carry the genetic information in the form of genes. □ **chromosomal** *adj.* [German *Chromosom* (as CHROMO-², -SOME³)]

chromosome map *n.* a plan showing the relative positions of genes along the length of a chromosome.

chromosphere /'krəʊməsfɪə/ *n.* a gaseous layer of the sun's atmosphere between the photosphere and the corona. □ **chromospheric** /-'sfɛrɪk/ *adj.* [CHROMO-² + SPHERE]

Chron. *abbr.* Chronicles (Old Testament).

chronic /'krɒnɪk/ *adj.* **1** persisting for a long time (usu. of an illness or a personal or social problem). **2** having a chronic complaint. **3** *colloq.* habitual, inveterate (*a chronic liar*). **4** *Brit. colloq.* very bad; intense, severe. □ **chronically** *adv.* **chronicity** /krɒ'nɪsɪti/ *n.* [French *chronique* from Latin *chronicus* (in Late Latin of disease), from Greek *khronikos* from *khronos* 'time']

▪ **Usage** The use of *chronic* in sense 3 is very informal, and its use in sense 4 is considered incorrect by some people.

chronic fatigue syndrome *n.* = ME 2.

chronicle /'krɒnɪk(ə)l/ *n. & v.* ● *n.* **1** a register of events in order of their occurrence. **2** a narrative, a full account. **3** (**Chronicles**) the name of two of the historical books of the Old Testament or Hebrew Bible. ● *v.tr.* record (events) in the order of their occurrence. □ **chronicler** *n.* [Middle English from Anglo-French *cronicle*, ultimately via Latin *chronica* from Greek *khronika* 'annals': see CHRONIC]

chrono- /'krɒnəʊ/ *comb. form* time. [Greek *khronos* 'time']

chronograph /'krɒnəgrɑːf/ *n.* **1** an instrument for recording time with extreme accuracy. **2** a stopwatch. □ **chronographic** /-'grafɪk/ *adj.*

chronological /krɒnə'lɒdʒɪk(ə)l/ *adj.* **1** (of a number of events) arranged or regarded in the order of their occurrence. **2** of or relating to chronology. □ **chronologically** *adv.*

chronology /krə'nɒlədʒi/ *n.* (*pl.* **-ies**) **1** the study of historical records to establish the dates of past events. **2 a** the arrangement of events, dates, etc. in the order of their occurrence. **b** a table or document displaying this. ▫ **chronologist** *n.* **chronologize** *v.tr.* (also **-ise**). [modern Latin *chronologia* (as CHRONO-, -LOGY)]

chronometer /krə'nɒmɪtə/ *n.* a time-measuring instrument, esp. one keeping accurate time in spite of motion and variation in temperature, humidity, etc., and used in navigation.

chronometry /krə'nɒmɪtri/ *n.* the science of accurate time-measurement. ▫ **chronometric** /krɒnə'mɛtrɪk/ *adj.* **chronometrical** /krɒnə'mɛtrɪk(ə)l/ *adj.* **chronometrically** /krɒnə'mɛtrɪk(ə)li/ *adv.*

chrysalid /'krɪs(ə)lɪd/ *n.* = CHRYSALIS. [formed as CHRYSALIS]

chrysalis /'krɪs(ə)lɪs/ *n.* (*pl.* **chrysalises** or **chrysalides** /krɪ'salɪdiːz/) **1 a** a quiescent pupa of a butterfly or moth. **b** the hard outer case enclosing it. **2** a preparatory or transitional state. [Latin from Greek *khrusallis -idos*, from *khrusos* 'gold']

chrysanth /krɪ'sanθ, -z-/ *n. Brit. colloq.* a cultivated chrysanthemum. [abbreviation]

chrysanthemum /krɪ'sanθɪməm, -z-/ *n.* a plant of the genus *Chrysanthemum* or (if cultivated usu.) the genus *Dendranthema* (daisy family), having brightly coloured flowers. [Latin from Greek *khrusanthemon*, from *khrusos* 'gold' + *anthemon* 'flower']

chryselephantine /krɪsɛlɪ'fantʌɪn/ *adj.* (of ancient Greek sculpture) overlaid with gold and ivory. [Greek *khruselephantinos* from *khrusos* 'gold' + *elephas* 'ivory']

chrysoberyl /krɪsə'bɛrɪl/ *n.* a yellowish-green gem consisting of a beryllium salt. [Latin *chrysoberyllus*, from Greek *khrusos* 'gold' + *bērullos* 'beryl']

chrysolite /'krɪsəlʌɪt/ *n.* a precious stone, a yellowish-green or brownish variety of olivine. [Middle English via Old French *crisolite*, medieval Latin *crisolitus*, and Latin *chrysolithus* from Greek *khrusolithos*, from *khrusos* 'gold' + *lithos* 'stone']

chrysoprase /'krɪsəpreɪz/ *n.* **1** an apple-green variety of chalcedony containing nickel and used as a gem. **2** (in the New Testament) probably a golden-green variety of beryl. [Middle English via Old French *crisopace* from Latin *chrysopassus*, variant of Latin *chrysoprasus*, from Greek *khrusoprasos* from *khrusos* 'gold' + *prason* 'leek']

chrysotile /'krɪsətʌɪl/ *n.* a form of asbestos. [Greek *khrusos* 'gold' + *tilos* 'fibre']

chthonic /'kθɒnɪk, 'θɒnɪk/ *adj.* (also **chthonian** /'kθəʊnɪən, 'θəʊ-/) of, relating to, or inhabiting the underworld. [Greek *khthōn* 'earth']

chub /tʃʌb/ *n.* a thick-bodied coarse-fleshed river fish, *Leuciscus cephalus*. [15th c.: origin unknown]

Chubb /tʃʌb/ *n.* (in full **Chubb lock**) *propr.* a lock with a device for fixing the bolt immovably should someone try to pick it. [C. *Chubb*, London locksmith d. 1845]

chubby /'tʃʌbi/ *adj.* (**chubbier**, **chubbiest**) plump and rounded (esp. of a person or a part of the body). ▫ **chubbily** *adv.* **chubbiness** *n.* [CHUB]

chuck[1] /tʃʌk/ *v. & n.* ● *v.tr.* **1** *colloq.* fling or throw carelessly or with indifference. **2** (often (*Brit.*) foll. by *in*, *up*) *colloq.* give up; reject (*chucked in my job*). **3** touch playfully, esp. under the chin. ● *n.* **1** a playful touch under the chin. **2** a toss. **3** (prec. by *the*) *Brit. slang* dismissal (*he got the chuck*). ▫ **chuck it** *slang* stop, desist. **chuck out** *colloq.* **1** expel (a person) from a gathering etc. **2** get rid of, discard. [16th c., perhaps from French *chuquer*, *choquer* 'to knock']

chuck[2] /tʃʌk/ *n. & v.* ● *n.* **1** a cut of beef between the neck and the ribs. **2** a device for holding a workpiece in a lathe or a tool in a drill. ● *v.tr.* fix (wood, a tool, etc.) to a chuck. [variant of CHOCK]

chuck[3] /tʃʌk/ *n. N. Amer. dial.* food, provisions. [19th c.: perhaps from CHUCK[2]]

chuck[4] /tʃʌk/ *n. dial.* (as a form of address) dear, darling. [alteration of CHICK[1]]

chucker-out *n. Brit. colloq.* a person employed to expel troublesome people from a gathering etc.

chuckle /'tʃʌk(ə)l/ *v. & n.* ● *v.intr.* laugh quietly or inwardly. ● *n.* a quiet or suppressed laugh. ▫ **chuckler** *n.* [*chuck* 'cluck']

chucklehead /'tʃʌk(ə)lhɛd/ *n. colloq.* a stupid person. ▫ **chuckleheaded** *adj.* [*chuckle* 'clumsy', probably related to CHUCK[2]]

chuckwagon /'tʃʌkwag(ə)n/ *n. N. Amer.* **1** a provision cart on a ranch etc. **2** a roadside eating place. [CHUCK[3]]

chuddar var. of CHADOR.

chuff /tʃʌf/ *v.intr.* (of a steam engine etc.) work with a regular sharp puffing sound. [imitative]

chuffed /tʃʌft/ *adj. Brit. slang* delighted. [dialect *chuff* 'pleased']

chug /tʃʌg/ *v. & n.* ● *v.intr.* (**chugged**, **chugging**) **1** emit a regular muffled explosive sound, as of an engine running slowly. **2** move with this sound. ● *n.* a chugging sound. [imitative]

chukar /'tʃʊkɑː/ *n.* a red-legged partridge, *Alectoris chukar*, native to India. [Hindi *cakor*]

chukka /'tʃʌkə/ *n.* (*US* **chukker**) each of the periods of play (7–7½ minutes) into which a game of polo is divided. [Hindi *cakkar* from Sanskrit *cakra* 'wheel']

chum[1] /tʃʌm/ *n. & v.* ● *n. colloq.* (esp. among schoolchildren) a close friend. ● *v.intr.* (often foll. by *with*) share rooms. ▫ **chum up** (often foll. by *with*) become a close friend (of). ▫ **chummy** *adj.* (**chummier**, **chummiest**). **chummily** *adv.* **chumminess** *n.* [17th c.: probably short for *chamber-fellow*]

chum[2] /tʃʌm/ *n. & v. N. Amer.* ● *n.* **1** refuse from fish. **2** chopped fish used as bait. ● *v.* **1** *intr.* fish using chum. **2** *tr.* bait (a fishing place) using chum. [19th c.: origin unknown]

chump /tʃʌmp/ *n.* **1** *colloq.* a foolish person. **2** *Brit.* the thick end, esp. of a loin of lamb or mutton (*chump chop*). **3** a short thick block of wood. **4** *Brit. slang* the head. ▫ **off one's chump** *Brit. slang* crazy. [18th c.: probably a blend of CHUNK and LUMP[1]]

chunder /'tʃʌndə/ *v.intr. & n. Austral. slang* vomit. [20th c.: origin unknown]

chunk /tʃʌŋk/ *n.* **1** a thick solid slice or piece of something firm or hard. **2** a substantial amount or piece. [probably variant of CHUCK[2]]

chunky /'tʃʌŋki/ *adj.* (**chunkier**, **chunkiest**) **1** containing or consisting of chunks. **2** short and thick; small and sturdy. **3** (of clothes) made of a thick material. ▫ **chunkiness** *n.*

Chunnel /'tʃʌn(ə)l/ *n. colloq.* a tunnel under the English Channel linking England and France. [portmanteau word from *Channel tunnel*]

chunter /'tʃʌntə/ *v.intr. Brit. colloq.* mutter, grumble. [probably imitative]

chupatty var. of CHAPATTI.

church /tʃəːtʃ/ *n. & v.* ● *n.* **1** a building for public (usu. Christian) worship. **2** a meeting for public worship in such a building (*go to church*; *met after church*). **3** (usu. **Church**) (prec. by *the*) the body of all Christians. **4** (usu. **Church**) the clergy or clerical profession (*went into the Church*). **5** (usu. **Church**) an organized Christian group or society of any time, country, or distinct principles of worship (*the primitive Church*; *Church of Scotland*; *High Church*). **6** (usu. **Church**) institutionalized religion as a political or social force (*Church and State*). ● *v.tr. archaic* take (esp. a woman after childbirth) to church for a service of thanksgiving. [Old English *cirice*, *circe*, etc. via medieval Greek *kurikon* from Greek *kuriakon* (*dōma*) 'Lord's (house)', from *kurios* 'Lord': cf. KIRK]

Church Army *n.* (in the UK) an organization of the Church of England concerned with social welfare.

Church Commissioners *n.pl.* a body managing the finances of the Church of England.

churchgoer /'tʃəːtʃgəʊə/ *n.* a person who goes to church, esp. regularly. ▫ **churchgoing** *n. & adj.*

churchman /'tʃəːtʃmən/ *n.* (*pl.* **-men**) **1** a member of the clergy or of a Church. **2** a supporter of the Church.

Church Militant *n.* (prec. by *the*) the whole body of Christian believers as striving to combat evil on earth. [contrasted with 'the Church Triumphant' in heaven]

Church of England *n.* the English branch of the Western Christian Church, which combines Catholic and Protestant traditions, rejects the pope's authority, and has the monarch as its titular head.

church school *n.* **1** (in the UK) a school founded by or associated with the Church of England. **2** (in the US) a private school supported by a particular Church or parish.

churchwarden /'tʃə:tʃwɔ:d(ə)n/ *n.* **1 a** either of the two main elected lay representatives in an Anglican parish, formally responsible for movable church property and for keeping order in church. **b** *US* a church administrator. **2** *Brit.* a long-stemmed clay pipe.

churchwoman /'tʃə:tʃwʊmən/ *n.* (*pl.* **-women**) **1** a woman member of the clergy or of a Church. **2** a woman supporter of the Church.

churchy /'tʃə:tʃi/ *adj.* **1** obtrusively or intolerantly devoted to the Church or opposed to religious dissent. **2** like a church. ▫ **churchiness** *n.*

churchyard /'tʃə:tʃjɑ:d/ *n.* the enclosed ground around a church, esp. as used for burials.

churinga /tʃʌ'rɪŋgə/ *n.* (*pl.* same or **churingas**) a sacred object, esp. an amulet, among the Australian Aboriginals. [Aranda *j^werrenge* 'object from the dreaming']

churl /tʃə:l/ *n.* **1** an ill-bred person. **2** *archaic* a peasant; a person of low birth. **3** *archaic* a surly or mean person. [Old English *ceorl* from a West Germanic root, = man]

churlish /'tʃə:lɪʃ/ *adj.* surly; mean. ▫ **churlishly** *adv.* **churlishness** *n.* [Old English *cierlisc, ceorlisc* from *ceorl* CHURL]

churn /tʃə:n/ *n.* & *v.* ● *n.* **1** *Brit.* a large milk can. **2** a machine for making butter by agitating milk or cream. ● *v.* **1** *tr.* agitate (milk or cream) in a churn. **2** *tr.* produce (butter) in this way. **3** *tr.* (usu. foll. by *up*) cause distress to; upset, agitate. **4** *intr.* (of a liquid) seethe, foam violently (*the churning sea*). **5** *tr.* agitate or move (liquid) vigorously, causing it to foam. ▫ **churn out** produce routinely or mechanically, esp. in large quantities. [Old English *cyrin*, from Germanic]

churr var. of CHIRR.

churrascaria /tʃʊ,raskə'rɪə/ *n.* a restaurant specializing in churrasco. [Spanish]

churrasco /tʃʊ'raskəʊ/ *n.* a S. American dish consisting of steak barbecued over a wood or charcoal fire. [Spanish, probably from Spanish dialect *churrascar* 'burn']

chute[1] /ʃu:t/ *n.* **1** a sloping channel or slide, with or without water, for conveying things to a lower level. **2** a slide into a swimming pool. [French *chute* 'fall' (of water etc.), from Old French *cheoite*, fem. past part. of *cheoir* 'fall', from Latin *cadere*; in some senses = SHOOT]

chute[2] /ʃu:t/ *n. colloq.* parachute. ▫ **chutist** *n.* [abbreviation]

chutney /'tʃʌtni/ *n.* (*pl.* **-eys**) a pungent originally Indian condiment made of fruits or vegetables, vinegar, spices, sugar, etc. [Hindi *caṭnī*]

chutzpah /'xʊtspə, 'hʊ-/ *n. slang* shameless audacity; cheek. [Yiddish]

chyle /kʌɪl/ *n. Physiol.* lymph containing fats absorbed by the lacteals from the small intestine. ▫ **chylous** *adj.* [Late Latin *chylus* from Greek *khulos* 'juice']

chyme /kʌɪm/ *n. Physiol.* the acidic semi-solid and partly digested food produced in the stomach by gastric activity. ▫ **chymous** *adj.* [Late Latin *chymus* from Greek *khumos* 'juice']

chypre /ʃi:pr(ə)/ *n.* a heavy perfume made from sandalwood. [French, = Cyprus, perhaps where it was first made]

CI *abbr.* **1** Channel Islands. **2** *hist.* Order of the Crown of India.

Ci *abbr.* curie.

CIA *abbr.* (in the US) Central Intelligence Agency.

ciabatta /tʃə'bɑ:tə/ *n.* (*pl.* **ciabattas**) **1** a type of moist aerated Italian bread made with olive oil. **2** a loaf of this. [Italian dialect, literally 'slipper' (from its shape)]

ciao /tʃaʊ/ *int. colloq.* **1** goodbye. **2** hello. [Italian]

ciborium /sɪ'bɔ:rɪəm/ *n.* (*pl.* **ciboria** /-rɪə/) **1** a vessel with an arched cover used to hold the Eucharist. **2** *Archit.* **a** a canopy. **b** a shrine with a canopy. [medieval Latin from Greek *kibōrion* 'seed vessel of the water lily, a cup made from it']

cicada /sɪ'kɑ:də/ *n.* (also **cicala** /sɪ'kɑ:lə/) any transparent-winged large insect of the family Cicadidae, the males of which make a loud rhythmic chirping sound. [Latin *cicada, cicala*]

cicatrice /'sɪkətrɪs/ *n.* (also **cicatrix** /'sɪkətrɪks/) (*pl.* **cicatrices** /sɪkə'trʌɪsi:z/) **1** any mark left by a healed wound; a scar. **2** *Bot.* **a** a mark on a stem etc. left when a leaf or other part becomes detached. **b** a scar on the bark of a tree. ▫ **cicatricial** /sɪkə'trɪʃ(ə)l/ *adj.* [Middle English from Old French *cicatrice* or Latin *cicatrix -icis*]

cicatrize /'sɪkətrʌɪz/ *v.* (also **-ise**) **1** *tr.* heal (a wound) by scar formation. **2** *intr.* (of a wound) heal by scar formation. ▫ **cicatrization** /-'zeɪʃ(ə)n/ *n.* [French *cicatriser*: see CICATRICE]

cicely /'sɪsɪli/ *n.* (*pl.* **-ies**) any of various umbelliferous plants, esp. sweet cicely. [apparently from Latin *seselis* from Greek, assimilated to the woman's Christian name]

cicerone /tʃɪtʃə'rəʊni, sɪs-/ *n.* (*pl.* **ciceroni** *pronunc.* same) a guide who gives information about antiquities, places of interest, etc. to sightseers. [Italian, from Latin (see CICERONIAN) apparently alluding to the guides' eloquence and learning]

Ciceronian /sɪsə'rəʊnɪən/ *adj.* (of language) eloquent, classical, or rhythmical, in the style of Cicero. [Latin *Ciceronianus* from Marcus Tullius *Cicero*, Roman statesman and orator d. 43 BC]

cichlid /'sɪklɪd/ *n.* a tropical freshwater fish of the family Cichlidae, esp. of a kind kept in aquaria. [modern Latin *Cichlidae* from Greek *kikhlē*, a kind of fish]

CID *abbr.* (in the UK) Criminal Investigation Department.

-cide /sʌɪd/ *suffix* forming nouns meaning: **1** a person or substance that kills (*regicide*; *insecticide*). **2** the killing of (*infanticide*; *suicide*). [French from Latin *-cida* (sense 1), *-cidium* (sense 2), from *caedere* 'kill']

cider /'sʌɪdə/ *n.* (also *Brit.* **cyder**) **1** *Brit.* an alcoholic drink made from fermented apple juice. **2** (in full **apple cider**) *N. Amer.* a cloudy usu. unfermented drink made from crushing apples. [Middle English from Old French *sidre*, ultimately from Hebrew *šēkār* 'strong drink']

cider press *n.* a press for crushing apples to make cider.

ci-devant /si:də'vɒ̃, French sidvɑ̃/ *adj.* & *adv.* that has been (with person's earlier name or status); former or formerly. [French, = heretofore]

CIE *abbr. hist.* Companion (of the Order) of the Indian Empire.

c.i.f. *abbr.* cost, insurance, freight (as being included in a price).

cig /sɪg/ *n. colloq.* cigarette, cigar. [abbreviation]

cigala /sɪ'gɑ:lə/ *n.* = CICADA. [French *cigale*, Italian & Provençal *cigala* from Latin *cicada*]

cigar /sɪ'gɑ:/ *n.* a cylinder of tobacco rolled in tobacco leaves for smoking. [French *cigare* or Spanish *cigarro*]

cigarette /sɪgə'rɛt/ *n.* (*US* **cigaret**) **1** a thin cylinder of finely cut tobacco rolled in paper for smoking. **2** a similar cylinder containing a narcotic, herbs, or a medicated substance. [French, diminutive of *cigare* CIGAR]

cigarette card *n. Brit.* a small picture card of a kind formerly included in a packet of cigarettes.

cigarette end *n. Brit.* the unsmoked remainder of a cigarette.

cigarillo /sɪgə'rɪləʊ, -ljəʊ/ *n.* (*pl.* **-os**) a small cigar. [Spanish, diminutive of *cigarro* CIGAR]

ciggy /'sɪgi/ *n.* (*pl.* **-ies**) *colloq.* cigarette. [abbreviation]

CIGS *abbr. hist.* Chief of the Imperial General Staff.

ciliary /ˈsɪlɪəri/ *adj.* **1** *Biol.* of or relating to cilia. **2** *Anat.* **a** of or relating to the eyelids or eyelashes. **b** of or denoting the part of the eye (**ciliary body**) connecting the iris to the choroid, and the muscle in it which controls the shape of the lens.

ciliate /ˈsɪlɪeɪt/ *adj. & n.* ● *adj.* having cilia. ● *n.* a protozoan with cilia, of the phylum Ciliophora.

cilice /ˈsɪlɪs/ *n.* **1** haircloth. **2** a garment of this. [French via Latin *cilicium* from Greek *kilikion*, from *Kilikia*, the Greek name of Cilicia in Asia Minor]

cilium /ˈsɪlɪəm/ *n.* (*pl.* **cilia** /-lɪə/) **1** *Anat.* & *Biol.* a short minute hairlike vibrating structure occurring, usu. in large numbers, on the surface of some cells, causing currents in the surrounding fluid or, in some small organisms, providing propulsion. **2** an eyelash. □ **ciliated** *adj.* **ciliation** /-ˈeɪʃ(ə)n/ *n.* [Latin, = eyelash]

cill var. of SILL.

cimbalom /ˈsɪmb(ə)l(ə)m/ *n.* a dulcimer. [Hungarian from Italian *cembalo*]

C.-in-C. *abbr.* Commander-in-Chief.

cinch /sɪn(t)ʃ/ *n. & v.* ● *n.* **1** *colloq.* **a** a sure thing; a certainty. **b** an easy task. **2** a firm hold. **3** a girth for a saddle or pack, used in Mexico and the western US. ● *v.tr.* **1 a** tighten as with a cinch (*cinched at the waist with a belt*). **b** secure a grip on. **2** *slang* make certain of. **3** esp. *US* fix (a saddle etc.) securely by means of a girth; put a cinch on (a horse). [Spanish *cincha*]

cinchona /sɪŋˈkəʊnə/ *n.* **1 a** any evergreen tree or shrub of the S. American genus *Cinchona*, of the madder family, having fragrant flowers. **b** (in full **cinchona bark**) the bark of this tree, containing quinine. **2** any drug from this bark formerly used as a tonic and to stimulate the appetite. □ **cinchonic** /-ˈkɒnɪk/ *adj.* **cinchonine** /ˈsɪŋkəniːn/ *n.* [modern Latin, named after a Countess of *Chinchón* d. 1641, who introduced the drug into Spain]

cincture /ˈsɪŋktʃə/ *n.* **1** *literary* a girdle, belt, or border. **2** *Archit.* a ring at either end of a column shaft. [Latin *cinctura* from *cingere cinct-* 'gird']

cinder /ˈsɪndə/ *n.* **1** the residue of coal or wood etc. that has stopped giving off flames but still has combustible matter in it. **2** slag. **3** (in *pl.*) ashes. □ **burnt to a cinder** made useless by burning. □ **cindery** *adj.* [Old English *sinder* from Germanic, assimilated to the unconnected French *cendre* and Latin *cinis* 'ashes': cf. SINTER]

Cinderella /sɪndəˈrɛlə/ *n.* **1** a person or thing of unrecognized or disregarded merit or beauty. **2** a neglected or despised member of a group. [the name of a girl in a fairy tale]

cine- /ˈsɪni/ *comb. form* cinematographic (*cine-camera*; *cinephotography*). [abbreviation]

cineaste /ˈsɪnɪast/ *n.* (also **cineast**) a cinema enthusiast. [French *cinéaste* (as CINE-): cf. ENTHUSIAST]

cinema /ˈsɪnɪmə, -mɑː/ *n.* **1** *Brit.* a theatre where motion-picture films (see FILM *n.* 3) are shown. **2 a** films collectively. **b** the production of films as an art or industry; cinematography. [French *cinéma*: see CINEMATOGRAPH]

cinema organ *n. Mus.* a kind of organ with extra stops and special effects.

cinematheque /sɪnɪməˈtɛk/ *n.* **1** a film library or archive. **2** a small cinema. [French *cinémathèque* (as CINEMA), after *bibliothèque* 'library']

cinematic /sɪnɪˈmatɪk/ *adj.* **1** having the qualities characteristic of the cinema. **2** of or relating to the cinema. □ **cinematically** *adv.*

cinematograph /sɪnɪˈmatəgrɑːf/ *n.* (also **kinematograph** /kɪn-/) esp. *Brit. hist.* an apparatus for making or showing motion-picture films. [French *cinématographe* from Greek *kinēma -atos* 'movement', from *kineō* 'move']

cinematography /sɪnɪməˈtɒgrəfi/ *n.* the art of making motion-picture films. □ **cinematographer** *n.* **cinematographic** /-matəˈgrafɪk/ *adj.* **cinematographically** /-matəˈgrafɪk(ə)li/ *adv.*

cinéma-vérité /ˌsɪnɪməˈvɛrɪteɪ, French sinemaverite/ *n.* *Cinematog.* **1** the art or process of making realistic (esp. documentary) films which avoid artificiality and artistic effect. **2** such films collectively. [French, = cinema truth]

cinephile /ˈsɪnɪfʌɪl/ *n.* a person who is fond of the cinema.

cineraria /sɪnəˈrɛːrɪə/ *n.* a plant, *Pericallis cruenta* (daisy family), cultivated for its bright flowers. [modern Latin former genus name, fem. of Latin *cinerarius* 'of ashes' from *cinis -eris* 'ashes', from the ash-coloured down on the leaves]

cinerarium /sɪnəˈrɛːrɪəm/ *n.* (*pl.* **cinerariums**) a place where a cinerary urn is deposited. [Late Latin, neut. of *cinerarius*: see CINERARIA]

cinerary /ˈsɪnərəri/ *adj.* of ashes. [Latin *cinerarius*: see CINERARIA]

cinerary urn *n.* an urn for holding the ashes after cremation.

cinereous /sɪˈnɪərɪəs/ *adj.* (esp. of a bird or plumage) ash-grey. [Latin *cinereus* from *cinis -eris* 'ashes']

ciné-vérité /sɪnɪˌvɛrɪteɪ, French sineverite/ *n.* *Cinematog.* = CINÉMA-VÉRITÉ.

Cingalese /sɪŋgəˈliːz/ *adj. & n.* (*pl.* same) *archaic* Sinhalese. [French *cing(h)alais*: see SINHALESE]

cingulum /ˈsɪŋgjʊləm/ *n.* (*pl.* **cingula** /-lə/) *Anat.* a girdle, belt, or analogous structure, esp. a ridge surrounding the base of the crown of a tooth. [Latin, = belt]

cinnabar /ˈsɪnəbɑː/ *n. & adj.* ● *n.* **1** a bright red mineral form of mercuric sulphide from which mercury is obtained. **2** vermilion. **3** a moth, *Tyria jacobaeae*, with red wing markings. ● *adj.* bright red. [Middle English via Latin *cinnabaris* from Greek *kinnabari*, of oriental origin]

cinnamon /ˈsɪnəmən/ *n. & adj.* ● *n.* **1** an aromatic spice from the peeled, dried, and rolled bark of a SE Asian tree. **2** any tree of the genus *Cinnamomum*, esp. *C. zeylanicum*, yielding the spice. **3** yellowish brown. ● *adj.* of this colour. [Middle English via Old French *cinnamome* and Latin *cinnamomum* from Greek *kinnamōmon*, and Latin *cinnamon* from Greek *kinnamon*, from Semitic (cf. Hebrew *ḳinnāmôn*)]

cinque /sɪŋk/ *n.* (also **cinq**) the five on dice. [Middle English via Old French *cinc*, *cink* from Latin *quinque* 'five']

cinquecento /tʃɪŋkwɪˈtʃɛntəʊ/ *n.* the style of Italian art and literature of the 16th c., with a reversion to classical forms. □ **cinquecentist** *n.* [Italian, = 500 (shortened from *milcinquecento* '1500') used with reference to the years 1500–99]

cinquefoil /ˈsɪŋkfɔɪl/ *n.* **1** a herbaceous plant of the genus *Potentilla* (rose family), with compound leaves of five leaflets. **2** *Archit.* a five-cusped ornament in a circle or arch. [Middle English from Latin *quinquefolium*, from *quinque* 'five' + *folium* 'leaf']

Cinque Ports /sɪŋk ˈpɔːts/ *n.pl.* (in the UK) a group of ports (originally five only, Hastings, Sandwich, Dover, Romney, and Hythe, later also Rye and Winchelsea) on the SE coast of England with ancient privileges. [Middle English from Old French *cink porz*, Latin *quinque portus* 'five ports']

cion *US* var. of SCION 1.

cipher /ˈsʌɪfə/ *n. & v.* (also **cypher**) ● *n.* **1 a** a secret or disguised way of writing. **b** a thing written in this way. **c** the key to it. **2** the arithmetical symbol (0) denoting no amount but used to occupy a vacant place in decimal etc. numeration (as in 12.05). **3** a person or thing of no importance. **4** the interlaced initials of a person or company etc.; a monogram. **5** any Arabic numeral. **6** continuous sounding of an organ pipe, caused by a mechanical defect. ● *v.* **1** *tr.* put into secret writing, encipher. **2 a** *tr.* (usu. foll. by *out*) work out by arithmetic, calculate. **b** *intr. archaic* do arithmetic. [Middle English, from Old French *cif(f)re*, ultimately from Arabic *ṣifr* ZERO]

cipolin /'sɪpəlɪn/ *n.* an Italian white and green marble. [French *cipolin* or Italian *cipollino* from *cipolla* 'onion']

circa /'sə:kə/ *prep.* (often preceding a date) about; approximately. [Latin]

circadian /sə:'keɪdɪən/ *adj. Physiol.* occurring or recurring about once per day. [formed irregularly from Latin *circa* 'about' + *dies* 'day']

circinate /'sə:sɪnət, -eɪt/ *adj. Bot. & Zool.* rolled up with the apex in the centre, e.g. of young fronds of ferns. [Latin *circinatus*, past part. of *circinare* 'make round', from *circinus* 'pair of compasses']

circle /'sə:k(ə)l/ *n. & v.* ● *n.* **1 a** a round plane figure whose circumference is everywhere equidistant from its centre. **b** the line enclosing a circle. **2** a roundish enclosure or structure. **3** a ring. **4** a curved upper tier of seats in a theatre etc. (*dress circle*). **5** a circular route. **6** *US* = CIRCUS *n.* 3. **7** *Archaeol.* a group of (usu. large embedded) stones arranged in a circle. **8** *Hockey* = STRIKING-CIRCLE. **9** persons grouped round a centre of interest. **10** a set or class or restricted group (*literary circles*; *not done in the best circles*). **11** a period or cycle (*the circle of the year*). **12** (in full **vicious circle**) **a** an unbroken sequence of reciprocal cause and effect. **b** an action and reaction that intensify each other (cf. VIRTUOUS CIRCLE). **c** the fallacy of proving a proposition from another which depends on the first for its own proof. ● *v.* **1** *intr.* (often foll. by *round*, *about*) move in a circle. **2** *tr.* **a** revolve round. **b** form a circle round. □ **circle back** move in a wide loop towards the starting point. **come full circle** return to the starting point. **go round in circles** make no progress despite effort. **run round in circles** *colloq.* be fussily busy with little result. [Middle English via Old French *cercle* from Latin *circulus*, diminutive of *circus* 'ring']

circlet /'sə:klɪt/ *n.* **1** a small circle. **2** a circular band, esp. of gold or jewelled etc., as an ornament.

circlip /'sə:klɪp/ *n.* a metal ring sprung into a slot or groove in a bar etc. to hold a thing in place. [blend of CIRCLE, CIRCULAR, etc. and CLIP[1] *n.* 1]

circs /sə:ks/ *n.pl. colloq.* circumstances. [abbreviation]

circuit /'sə:kɪt/ *n.* **1 a** a line or course enclosing an area; the distance round. **b** the area enclosed. **2** *Electr.* **a** the path of a current. **b** the apparatus through which a current passes. **3 a** the journey of a judge in a particular district to hold courts. **b** this district. **c** the lawyers following a circuit. **4** a chain of theatres or cinemas etc. under a single management. **5** *Brit.* a motor racing track. **6 a** a sequence of sporting events (*the US tennis circuit*). **b** a sequence of athletic exercises. **7** a roundabout journey. **8 a** a group of local Methodist Churches forming a minor administrative unit. **b** the journey of an itinerant minister within this. **9** an itinerary or route followed by an entertainer, politician, etc.; a sphere of operation (*election circuit*; *cabaret circuit*). [Middle English via Old French from Latin *circuitus*, from CIRCUM- + *ire it-* 'go']

circuit board *n.* a thin rigid board containing an electric circuit, esp. = PRINTED CIRCUIT.

circuit-breaker *n.* an automatic device for stopping the flow of current in an electric circuit.

circuitous /sə:'kju:ɪtəs/ *adj.* **1** indirect (and usu. long). **2** going a long way round. □ **circuitously** *adv.* **circuitousness** *n.* [medieval Latin *circuitosus* from *circuitus* CIRCUIT]

circuitry /'sə:kɪtri/ *n.* (*pl.* **-ies**) **1** a system of electric circuits. **2** the equipment forming this.

circular /'sə:kjʊlə/ *adj. & n.* ● *adj.* **1 a** having the form of a circle. **b** moving or taking place along a circle (*circular tour*). **2** *Logic* (of reasoning) depending on a vicious circle. **3** (of a letter or advertisement etc.) for distribution to a large number of people. ● *n.* a circular letter, leaflet, etc. □ **circularity** /-'larɪti/ *n.* **circularly** *adv.* [Middle English from Anglo-French *circuler*, Old French *circulier*, *cerclier*, via Late Latin *circularis* from Latin *circulus* CIRCLE]

circularize /'sə:kjʊlərʌɪz/ *v.tr.* (also **-ise**) **1** distribute circulars to. **2** *US* seek opinions of (people) by means of a questionnaire. □ **circularization** /-'zeɪʃ(ə)n/ *n.*

circular saw *n.* a power saw with a rapidly rotating toothed disc.

circulate /'sə:kjʊleɪt/ *v.* **1** *intr.* go round from one place or person etc. to the next and so on; be in circulation. **2** *tr.* **a** cause to go round; put into circulation. **b** give currency to (a report etc.). **c** circularize. **3** *intr.* be actively sociable at a party, gathering, etc. □ **circulative** *adj.* **circulator** *n.* [Latin *circulare circulat-* from *circulus* CIRCLE]

circulating library *n. hist.* a small library with books lent for a small fee to subscribers.

circulating medium *n.* notes or gold etc. used in exchange.

circulation /sə:kjʊ'leɪʃ(ə)n/ *n.* **1 a** movement to and fro, or from and back to a starting point, esp. of a fluid in a confined area or circuit. **b** the movement of blood to and from the tissues of the body. **c** a similar movement of sap etc. **2 a** the transmission or distribution (of news or information or books etc.). **b** the number of copies sold, esp. of journals and newspapers. **3 a** currency, coin, etc. **b** the movement or exchange of this in a country etc. □ **in** (or **out of**) **circulation** participating (or not participating) in activities etc. [French *circulation* or Latin *circulatio*, from *circulare* CIRCULATE]

circulatory /'sə:kjʊlət(ə)ri, sə:kjʊ'leɪt(ə)ri/ *adj.* of or relating to the circulation of blood or sap.

circum- /'sə:kəm/ *prefix* round, about, around, used: **1** adverbially (*circumambient*; *circumfuse*). **2** prepositionally (*circumlunar*; *circumocular*). [from or suggested by Latin *circum* prep. = round, about]

circumambient /sə:kəm'ambɪənt/ *adj.* (esp. of air or another fluid) surrounding. □ **circumambience** *n.* **circumambiency** *n.*

circumambulate /sə:kəm'ambjʊleɪt/ *v.tr. & intr. formal* walk round or about. □ **circumambulation** /-'leɪʃ(ə)n/ *n.* **circumambulatory** *adj.* [CIRCUM- + *ambulate* from Latin *ambulare* 'walk']

circumcircle /'sə:kəmsə:k(ə)l/ *n. Geom.* a circle touching all the vertices of a triangle or polygon.

circumcise /'sə:kəmsʌɪz/ *v.tr.* **1** cut off the foreskin of, as a Jewish or Muslim rite or a surgical operation. **2** cut off the clitoris (and sometimes the labia) of, as a traditional practice among some peoples. **3** *Bibl.* purify (the heart etc.). [Middle English via Old French from Latin *circumcidere circumcis-* (as CIRCUM-, *caedere* 'cut')]

circumcision /sə:kəm'sɪʒ(ə)n/ *n.* **1** the act or rite of circumcising or being circumcised. **2** (**Circumcision**) *Eccl.* the feast of the Circumcision of Christ, 1 Jan. [Middle English via Old French *circoncision* from Late Latin *circumcisio -onis* (as CIRCUMCISE)]

circumference /sə'kʌmf(ə)r(ə)ns/ *n.* **1** the enclosing boundary, esp. of a circle or other figure enclosed by a curve. **2** the distance round. □ **circumferential** /-'rɛnʃ(ə)l/ *adj.* **circumferentially** /-'rɛnʃ(ə)li/ *adv.* [Middle English via Old French *circonference* from Latin *circumferentia* (as CIRCUM-, *ferre* 'bear')]

circumflex /'sə:kəmflɛks/ *n. & adj.* ● *n.* (in full **circumflex accent**) a mark (^ or ˜) placed over a vowel in some languages to indicate a contraction, length, or a special quality. ● *adj. Anat.* curved, bending round something else (*circumflex nerve*). [Latin *circumflexus* (as CIRCUM-, *flectere flex-* 'bend'), translation of Greek *perispōmenos* 'drawn around']

circumfluent /sə:'kʌmflʊənt/ *adj.* flowing round, surrounding. □ **circumfluence** *n.* [Latin *circumfluere* (as CIRCUM-, *fluere* 'flow')]

circumfuse /sə:kəm'fju:z/ *v.tr.* pour round or about. [CIRCUM- + Latin *fundere fus-* 'pour']

circumjacent /sə:kəm'dʒeɪs(ə)nt/ *adj.* situated around. [Latin *circumjacēre* (as CIRCUM-, *jacēo* 'lie')]

circumlocution /sə:kəmlə'kju:ʃ(ə)n/ *n.* **1 a** a roundabout expression. **b** evasive talk. **2** the use of many words where fewer would do; verbosity.

□ **circumlocutional** *adj.* **circumlocutionary** *adj.* **circumlocutionist** *n.* **circumlocutory** /-'lɒkjʊt(ə)ri/ *adj.* [Middle English from French *circumlocution* or Latin *circumlocutio* (as CIRCUM-, LOCUTION), translation of Greek PERIPHRASIS]

circumlunar /sə:kəm'lu:nə/ *adj.* moving or situated around the moon.

circumnavigate /sə:kəm'navɪgeɪt/ *v.tr.* sail round (esp. the world). □ **circumnavigation** /-'geɪʃ(ə)n/ *n.* **circumnavigator** *n.* [Latin *circumnavigare* (as CIRCUM-, NAVIGATE)]

circumpolar /sə:kəm'pəʊlə/ *adj.* **1** *Geog.* around or near one of the earth's poles. **2** *Astron.* (of a star or motion etc.) above the horizon at all times in a given latitude.

circumscribe /'sə:kəmskrʌɪb/ *v.tr.* **1** (of a line etc.) enclose or outline. **2** lay down the limits of; confine, restrict. **3** *Geom.* draw (a figure) round another, touching it at points but not cutting it (cf. INSCRIBE 4). □ **circumscribable** /-'skrʌɪbəb(ə)l/ *adj.* **circumscriber** *n.* **circumscription** /-'skrɪpʃ(ə)n/ *n.* [Latin *circumscribere* (as CIRCUM-, *scribere script-* 'write')]

circumsolar /sə:kəm'səʊlə/ *adj.* moving or situated around or near the sun.

circumspect /'sə:kəmspɛkt/ *adj.* wary, cautious; taking everything into account. □ **circumspection** /-'spɛkʃ(ə)n/ *n.* **circumspectly** *adv.* [Middle English from Latin *circumspicere circumspect-* (as CIRCUM-, *specere spect-* 'look')]

circumstance /'sə:kəmst(ə)ns/ *n.* **1 a** a fact, occurrence, or condition, esp. (in *pl.*) the time, place, manner, cause, occasion, etc., or surroundings of an act or event. **b** (in *pl.*, or *sing.* as non-count noun) the external conditions that affect or might affect an action (*a victim of circumstance(s)*). **2** (often foll. by *that* + clause) an incident, occurrence, or fact, as needing consideration (*the circumstance that he left early*). **3** (in *pl.*) one's state of financial or material welfare (*in reduced circumstances*). **4** ceremony, fuss (*pomp and circumstance*). **5** full detail in a narrative (*told it with much circumstance*). □ **in** (or **under**) **the** (or **these**) **circumstances** the state of affairs being what it is. **in** (or **under**) **no circumstances** not at all; never. □ **circumstanced** *adj.* [Middle English from Old French *circonstance* or Latin *circumstantia* (as CIRCUM-, *stantia* from *stare* 'stand': see -ANCE)]

circumstantial /sə:kəm'stanʃ(ə)l/ *adj.* **1** given in full detail (*a circumstantial account*). **2** (of evidence, a legal case, etc.) tending to establish a conclusion by inference from known facts hard to explain otherwise. **3 a** depending on circumstances. **b** adventitious, incidental. □ **circumstantiality** /-ʃɪ'alɪti/ *n.* **circumstantially** *adv.* [Latin *circumstantia*: see CIRCUMSTANCE]

circumterrestrial /sə:kəmtə'rɛstrɪəl/ *adj.* moving or situated around the earth.

circumvallate /sə:kəm'valeɪt/ *v.tr.* surround with or as with a rampart. [Latin *circumvallare circumvallat-* (as CIRCUM-, *vallare* from *vallum* 'rampart')]

circumvent /sə:kəm'vɛnt/ *v.tr.* **1 a** evade (a difficulty); find a way round. **b** baffle, outwit. **2** entrap (an enemy) by surrounding. □ **circumvention** *n.* [Latin *circumvenire circumvent-* (as CIRCUM-, *venire* 'come')]

circumvolution /sə:kəmvə'lu:ʃ(ə)n/ *n.* **1** rotation. **2** the winding of one thing round another. **3** a sinuous movement. [Middle English from Latin *circumvolvere circumvolut-* (as CIRCUM-, *volvere* 'roll')]

circus /'sə:kəs/ *n.* (*pl.* **circuses**) **1** a travelling show of performing animals, acrobats, clowns, etc. **2** *colloq.* **a** a scene of lively action; a disturbance. **b** a group of people in a common activity, esp. sport. **3** *Brit.* a rounded open space in a town, where several streets converge (*Piccadilly Circus*). **4** a circular hollow surrounded by hills. **5** *Rom. Antiq.* **a** a rounded or oval arena with tiers of seats, for equestrian and other sports and games. **b** a performance given there (*bread and circuses*). **6** (**the Circus**) *slang* the British secret service. [Latin, = ring]

ciré /'si:reɪ/ *n.* & *adj.* ● *n.* a fabric with a smooth shiny surface obtained esp. by waxing and heating. ● *adj.* having such a surface. [French, = waxed]

cire perdue /sɪə pə:'dju:, French sir pɛrdy/ *n.* a method of bronze-casting using a clay core and a wax coating placed in a mould: the wax is melted in the mould and bronze poured into the space left, producing a hollow bronze figure when the core is discarded. [French, = lost wax]

cirque /sə:k/ *n.* **1** *Geol.* a deep bowl-shaped hollow at the head of a valley or on a mountainside. **2** *poet.* **a** a ring. **b** an amphitheatre or arena. [French, from Latin CIRCUS]

cirrhosis /sɪ'rəʊsɪs/ *n.* *Med.* a chronic disease of the liver marked by the degeneration of cells, inflammation, and the fibrous thickening of tissue, as a result of alcoholism, hepatitis, etc. □ **cirrhotic** /sɪ'rɒtɪk/ *adj.* [modern Latin, from Greek *kirrhos* 'tawny']

cirriped /'sɪrɪpɛd/ *n.* (also **cirripede** /'sɪrɪpi:d/) any marine crustacean of the class Cirripedia, which comprises the barnacles. [modern Latin *Cirripedia*, from Latin *cirrus* 'curl' (from the form of the legs) + *pes pedis* 'foot']

cirro- /'sɪrəʊ/ *comb. form* denoting cloud types formed at high altitudes (above 6 km or 20,000 feet). [CIRRUS]

cirrocumulus /sɪrəʊ'kju:mjʊləs/ *n.* *Meteorol.* cloud forming a broken layer of small fleecy clouds at high altitude, as in a mackerel sky.

cirrostratus /sɪrəʊ'stra:təs/ *n.* *Meteorol.* cloud forming a thin, fairly uniform layer at high altitude.

cirrus /'sɪrəs/ *n.* (*pl.* **cirri** /-rʌɪ/) **1** *Meteorol.* **a** cloud formed at high altitude as delicate white wisps. **b** a cloud of this type. **2** *Bot.* a tendril. **3** *Zool.* a long slender appendage or filament. □ **cirrose** *adj.* **cirrous** *adj.* [Latin, = curl]

CIS *abbr.* Commonwealth of Independent States (consisting of countries of the former Soviet Union).

cis- /sɪs/ *prefix* (opp. TRANS- or ULTRA-). **1** on this side of; on the side nearer to the speaker or writer (*cisatlantic*). **2** *Rom. Antiq.* on the Roman side of (*cisalpine*). **3** (of time) closer to the present (*cis-Elizabethan*). **4** *Chem.* (of an isomer) having two atoms or groups on the same side of a given plane in the molecule. [Latin *cis* 'on this side of']

cisalpine /sɪs'alpʌɪn/ *adj.* on the southern side of the Alps.

cisatlantic /sɪsət'lantɪk/ *adj.* on this side of the Atlantic.

cisco /'sɪskəʊ/ *n.* (*pl.* **-oes**) any of various N. American freshwater whitefish of the genus *Coregonus*. [19th c.: origin unknown]

cislunar /sɪs'lu:nə/ *adj.* between the earth and the moon.

cispontine /sɪs'pɒntʌɪn/ *adj.* *archaic* on the north (originally the better-known) side of the Thames in London. [CIS- + Latin *pons pont-* 'bridge']

cissy var. of SISSY.

cist[1] /sɪst/ *n.* (also **kist** /kɪst/) *Archaeol.* a coffin or burial chamber made from stone or a hollowed tree. [Welsh, = CHEST]

cist[2] /sɪst/ *n.* *Gk Antiq.* a box used for sacred utensils. [Latin *cista* from Greek *kistē* 'box']

Cistercian /sɪ'stə:ʃ(ə)n/ *n.* & *adj.* ● *n.* a monk or nun of an order founded in 1098 as a stricter branch of the Benedictines. ● *adj.* of the Cistercians. [French *cistercien* from *Cistercium*, the Latin name of Cîteaux near Dijon in France, where the order was founded]

cistern /'sɪstən/ *n.* **1** a tank for storing water, esp. supplying taps or as part of a flushing lavatory. **2** an underground reservoir for rainwater. [Middle English via Old French *cisterne* from Latin *cisterna* (as CIST[2])]

cistus /'sɪstəs/ *n.* any shrub of the genus *Cistus*, with large white or red flowers. Also called ROCK ROSE. [modern Latin, from Greek *kistos*]

citadel /'sɪtəd(ə)l, -dɛl/ *n.* **1** a fortress, usu. on high ground protecting or dominating a city. **2** a meeting hall of the Salvation Army. [French *citadelle* or Italian *citadella*, ultimately from Latin *civitas -tatis* 'city']

citation /sʌɪˈteɪʃ(ə)n/ *n.* **1** the citing of a book or other source; a passage cited. **2** a mention in an official dispatch. **3** a note accompanying an award, describing the reasons for it.

cite /sʌɪt/ *v.tr.* **1** adduce as an instance. **2** quote (a passage, book, or author) in support of an argument etc. **3** mention in an official dispatch. **4** summon to appear in a law court. □ **citable** *adj.* [Middle English via French from Latin *citare*, from *ciēre* 'set moving']

CITES /ˈsʌɪtiːz/ *abbr.* Convention on International Trade in Endangered Species.

citified /ˈsɪtɪfʌɪd/ *adj.* (also **cityfied**) usu. *derog.* city-like or urban in appearance or behaviour.

citizen /ˈsɪtɪz(ə)n/ *n.* **1** a member of a state or commonwealth, either native or naturalized (*British citizen*). **2** (usu. foll. by *of*) **a** an inhabitant of a city. **b** a freeman of a city. **3** *US* a civilian. □ **citizenhood** *n.* **citizenry** *n.* **citizenship** *n.* [Middle English from Anglo-French *citesein*, Old French *citeain*, ultimately from Latin *civitas -tatis* 'city': cf. DENIZEN]

citizen of the world *n.* a person who is at home anywhere; a cosmopolitan.

Citizens' Advice Bureau *n.* (in the UK) an office at which the public can receive free advice and information on civil matters.

citizen's arrest *n.* an arrest by an ordinary person without a warrant, allowable in certain cases.

citizens' band *n.* a system of local intercommunication by individuals on special radio frequencies.

Citizen's Charter *n. Polit.* a document, esp. a British government document of 1991, guaranteeing citizens the right of redress where a public service fails to meet certain standards.

citole /sɪˈtəʊl/ *n. hist.* a musical instrument akin to the lute, a precursor of the cittern. [Middle English from Old French: related to CITTERN with diminutive suffix]

citrate /ˈsɪtreɪt/ *n. Chem.* a salt or ester of citric acid.

citric /ˈsɪtrɪk/ *adj.* derived from citrus fruit. □ **citrate** *n.* [French *citrique* from Latin *citrus* 'citron']

citric acid *n.* a sharp-tasting water-soluble organic acid found in the juice of lemons and other sour fruits and used as a flavouring and setting agent.

citrin /ˈsɪtrɪn/ *n.* = BIOFLAVONOID.

citrine /ˈsɪtrɪn/ *adj.* & *n.* ● *adj.* lemon-coloured. ● *n.* a transparent yellow variety of quartz; also called *false topaz*. [Middle English from Old French *citrin* (as CITRUS)]

citron /ˈsɪtr(ə)n/ *n.* **1** a shrubby tree, *Citrus medica*, bearing large lemon-like fruits with thick fragrant peel. **2** this fruit. [French from Latin CITRUS, on the pattern of *limon* 'lemon']

citronella /sɪtrəˈnɛlə/ *n.* **1** any fragrant grass of the genus *Cymbopogon*, native to S. Asia. **2** the scented oil from these, used in insect repellent, and perfume and soap manufacture. [modern Latin, formed as CITRON + diminutive suffix]

citrus /ˈsɪtrəs/ *n.* (*pl.* **citruses**) **1** any tree of the genus *Citrus* (rue family), including citron, lemon, lime, orange, and grapefruit. **2** (in full **citrus fruit**) a fruit from such a tree. □ **citrous** *adj.* [Latin, = citron tree or thuja]

cittern /ˈsɪt(ə)n/ *n. hist.* a wire-stringed lutelike instrument usu. played with a plectrum. [Latin *cithara*, Greek *kithara*, a kind of harp, assimilated to GITTERN]

city /ˈsɪti/ *n.* (*pl.* **-ies**) **1 a** a large town. **b** *Brit.* (strictly) a town created a city by charter and containing a cathedral. **c** *US* a municipal state-chartered corporation occupying a definite area. **2** (**the City**) *Brit.* **a** the part of London governed by the Lord Mayor and the Corporation. **b** the business part of this. **c** commercial circles; high finance. **3** (*attrib.*) of a city or the City. □ **cityward** *adj.* & *adv.* **citywards** *adv.* [Middle English via Old French *cité* from Latin *civitas -tatis*, from *civis* 'citizen']

City Company *n.* (in the UK) a corporation descended from an ancient trade guild.

city desk *n.* a department of a newspaper dealing *Brit.* with business news or *N. Amer.* with local news.

City editor *n.* **1** *Brit.* the editor dealing with financial news in a newspaper or magazine. **2** (**city editor**) *N. Amer.* the editor dealing with local news.

city father *n.* (usu. in *pl.*) a person concerned with or experienced in the administration of a city.

cityfied var. of CITIFIED.

city hall *n. N. Amer.* municipal offices or officers.

city manager *n. N. Amer.* (in some cities) an official directing the administration of a city.

city page *n. Brit.* the part of a newspaper or magazine dealing with the financial and business news.

cityscape /ˈsɪtɪskeɪp/ *n.* **1** a view of a city (actual or depicted). **2** city scenery.

city slicker *n.* usu. *derog.* **1** a smart and sophisticated city dweller. **2** a plausible rogue as usu. found in cities.

city state *n.* esp. *hist.* a city that with its surrounding territory forms an independent state.

City Technology College *n.* a type of secondary school, set up mainly in towns and cities through partnerships between the Government and business and concentrating on technology and science.

civet /ˈsɪvɪt/ *n.* **1** (in full **civet cat**) a slender catlike animal of the family Viverridae, esp. *Viverra civetta* of central Africa, having well-developed anal scent glands. **2** a strong musky perfume obtained from the secretions of these scent glands. [French *civette* via Italian *zibetto* and medieval Latin *zibethum* from Arabic *azzabād*, from *al* 'the' + *zabād* = sense 2]

civic /ˈsɪvɪk/ *adj.* **1** of a city; municipal. **2** of or proper to citizens (*civic virtues*). **3** of citizenship, civil. □ **civically** *adv.* [French *civique* or Latin *civicus*, from *civis* 'citizen']

civic centre *n.* the area in a town where municipal offices and other public buildings are situated; the buildings themselves.

civics /ˈsɪvɪks/ *n.pl.* (usu. treated as *sing.*) the study of the rights and duties of citizenship.

civil /ˈsɪv(ə)l, -ɪl/ *adj.* **1** of or belonging to citizens. **2** of ordinary citizens and their concerns, as distinct from military or naval or ecclesiastical matters. **3** polite, obliging, not rude. **4** *Law* relating to civil law, not criminal or political matters (*civil court; civil lawyer*). **5** (of the length of a day, year, etc.) fixed by custom or law, not natural or astronomical. □ **civilly** *adv.* [Middle English via Old French from Latin *civilis*, from *civis* 'citizen']

civil aviation *n.* non-military, esp. commercial, aviation.

civil commotion *n. Brit. Law* a riot or similar disturbance.

civil defence *n.* the organization and training of civilians for the protection of lives and property during and after attacks in wartime.

civil disobedience *n.* the refusal to comply with certain laws or to pay taxes etc. as a peaceful form of political protest.

civil engineer *n.* an engineer who designs or maintains roads, bridges, dams, etc. □ **civil engineering** *n.*

civilian /sɪˈvɪlj(ə)n/ *n.* & *adj.* ● *n.* a person not in the armed services or the police force. ● *adj.* of or for civilians.

civilianize /sɪˈvɪlj(ə)nʌɪz/ *v.tr.* (also **-ise**) make civilian in character or function. □ **civilianization** /-ˈzeɪʃ(ə)n/ *n.*

civility /sɪˈvɪlɪti/ *n.* (*pl.* **-ies**) **1** politeness. **2** an act of politeness. [Middle English via Old French *civilité* from Latin *civilitas -tatis* (as CIVIL)]

civilization /ˌsɪvɪlʌɪˈzeɪʃ(ə)n/ *n.* (also **-isation**) **1** an advanced stage or system of social development. **2** those peoples of the world regarded as having this. **3** a people or nation (esp. of the past) regarded as an element of social evolution (*ancient civilizations*; *the Inca civilization*). **4** making or becoming civilized.

civilize /ˈsɪvɪlʌɪz/ *v.tr.* (also **-ise**) **1** bring out of a barbarous or primitive stage of society. **2** enlighten; refine and educate. □ **civilizable** *adj.* **civilizer** *n.* [French *civiliser* (as CIVIL)]

civil law *n.* **1** law concerning private rights (opp. CRIMINAL LAW). **2** Roman or non-ecclesiastical law, as of Quebec (in Canada), France, or Germany (cf. COMMON LAW).

civil liberty *n.* (often in *pl.*) freedom of action and speech subject to the law. □ **civil libertarian** *n.*

Civil List *n.* (in the UK) an annual allowance voted by Parliament for the royal family's household expenses.

civil marriage *n.* a marriage solemnized as a civil contract without religious ceremony.

civil parish see PARISH 2.

civil rights *n.pl.* the rights of citizens to political and social freedom and equality.

civil servant *n.* a member of the civil service.

civil service *n.* the permanent professional branches of State administration, excluding military and judicial branches and elected politicians.

civil state *n. Brit.* marital status; being single, married, or divorced, etc.

civil war *n.* a war between citizens of the same country.

civil year see YEAR 2.

civvy /ˈsɪvi/ *n.* & *adj.* (*pl.* **-ies**) *slang* ● *n.* **1** (in *pl.*) civilian clothes. **2** a civilian. ● *adj.* civilian. [abbreviation]

Civvy Street /ˈsɪvi/ *n. Brit. slang* civilian life. [abbreviation]

CJ *abbr.* Chief Justice.

CJD *abbr.* Creutzfeldt–Jakob disease.

Cl *symb. Chem.* the element chlorine.

cl *abbr.* **1** centilitre(s). **2** class.

clack /klak/ *v.* & *n.* ● *v.intr.* **1** make a sharp sound as of boards struck together. **2** chatter, esp. loudly. ● *n.* **1** a clacking sound. **2** clacking talk. □ **clacker** *n.* [Middle English, = to chatter, probably from Old Norse *klaka*, of imitative origin]

clad[1] /klad/ *adj.* **1** clothed (often in *comb.*: *leather-clad*; *scantily clad*). **2** provided with cladding. [past part. of CLOTHE]

clad[2] /klad/ *v.tr.* (**cladding**; *past* and *past part.* **cladded** or **clad**) provide with cladding. [apparently from CLAD[1]]

cladding /ˈkladɪŋ/ *n.* a covering or coating on a structure or material etc.

clade /kleɪd/ *n. Biol.* a group of organisms evolved from a common ancestor. [Greek *klados* 'branch']

cladistics /kləˈdɪstɪks/ *n. Biol.* a method of classification of animals and plants on the basis of those shared characteristics which are assumed to indicate common ancestry. □ **cladism** /ˈkladɪz(ə)m/ *n.* **cladistic** *adj.* [as CLADE + -IST + -ICS]

cladode /ˈkleɪdəʊd/ *n. Bot.* a flattened leaflike stem. [Greek *kladōdēs* 'many-shooted', from *klados* 'shoot']

cladogram /ˈkleɪdə(ʊ)gram/ *n. Biol.* a branching diagram showing the cladistic relationship between a number of species.

claim /kleɪm/ *v.* & *n.* ● *v.tr.* **1 a** (often foll. by *that* + clause) demand as one's due or property. **b** (usu. *absol.*) submit a request for payment under an insurance policy. **2 a** represent oneself as having or achieving (*claim victory*; *claim accuracy*). **b** (foll. by *to* + infin.) profess (*claimed to be the owner*). **c** assert, contend (*claim that one knows*). **3** have as an achievement or a consequence (*could then claim five wins*; *the fire claimed many victims*). **4** (of a thing) deserve (one's attention etc.). ● *n.* **1 a** a demand or request for something considered one's due (*lay claim to*; *put in a claim*). **b** an application for compensation under the terms of an insurance policy. **2** (foll. by *to*, *on*) a right or title to a thing (*his only claim to fame*; *have many claims on my time*). **3** a contention or assertion. **4** a thing claimed. **5** a statement of the novel features in a patent. **6** *Mining* a piece of land allotted or taken. □ **claimable** *adj.* **claimer** *n.* [Middle English via Old French *claime* (from *clamer* 'call out') from Latin *clamare*]

claimant /ˈkleɪm(ə)nt/ *n.* a person making a claim, esp. in a lawsuit or for a state benefit.

clairaudience /klɛːrˈɔːdɪəns/ *n.* the supposed faculty of perceiving, as if by hearing, what is inaudible. □ **clairaudient** *adj.* & *n.* [French *clair* CLEAR, + AUDIENCE, on the pattern of CLAIRVOYANCE]

clairvoyance /klɛːˈvɔɪəns/ *n.* **1** the supposed faculty of perceiving things or events in the future or beyond normal sensory contact. **2** exceptional insight. [French *clairvoyance*, from *clair* CLEAR + *voir voy-* 'see']

clairvoyant /klɛːˈvɔɪənt/ *n.* & *adj.* ● *n.* (*fem.* **clairvoyante**) a person having clairvoyance. ● *adj.* having clairvoyance. □ **clairvoyantly** *adv.*

clam /klam/ *n.* & *v.* ● *n.* **1** any bivalve mollusc, esp. the edible N. American hard or round clam (*Venus mercenaria*) or the soft or long clam (*Mya arenaria*). **2** *colloq.* a shy or withdrawn person. ● *v.intr.* (**clammed**, **clamming**) **1** dig for clams. **2** (foll. by *up*) *colloq.* refuse to talk. [16th c.: apparently from *clam* 'a clamp']

clamant /ˈkleɪm(ə)nt, ˈklam-/ *adj. literary* noisy; insistent, urgent. □ **clamantly** *adv.* [Latin *clamare clamant-* 'cry out']

clamber /ˈklambə/ *v.* & *n.* ● *v.intr.* climb with hands and feet, esp. with difficulty or laboriously. ● *n.* a difficult climb. [Middle English, probably from *clamb*, obsolete past tense of CLIMB]

clammy /ˈklami/ *adj.* (**clammier**, **clammiest**) **1** unpleasantly damp and sticky or slimy. **2** (of weather) cold and damp. □ **clammily** *adv.* **clamminess** *n.* [Middle English from *clam* 'to daub']

clamour /ˈklamə/ *n.* & *v.* (*US* **clamor**) ● *n.* **1** loud or vehement shouting or noise. **2** a protest or complaint; an appeal or demand. ● *v.* **1** *intr.* make a clamour. **2** *tr.* utter with a clamour. □ **clamorous** *adj.* **clamorously** *adv.* **clamorousness** *n.* [Middle English via Old French from Latin *clamor -oris*, from *clamare* 'cry out']

clamp[1] /klamp/ *n.* & *v.* ● *n.* **1** a device, esp. a brace or band of iron etc., for strengthening other materials or holding things together. **2** *Brit.* a device for immobilizing an illegally parked car. ● *v.tr.* **1** strengthen or fasten with a clamp. **2** place or hold firmly. **3** immobilize (an illegally parked car) by fixing a clamp to one of its wheels. □ **clamp down 1** (often foll. by *on*) be rigid in enforcing a rule etc. **2** (foll. by *on*) try to suppress. [Middle English, probably from Middle Dutch, Middle Low German *klamp(e)*]

clamp[2] /klamp/ *n.* **1** *Brit.* a heap of potatoes or other root vegetables stored under straw or earth. **2** a pile of bricks for firing. **3** a pile of turf or peat or garden rubbish etc. [16th c.: probably from Dutch *klamp* 'heap', related to CLUMP]

clampdown /ˈklampdaʊn/ *n.* an act of clamping down or trying to suppress.

clamshell /ˈklamʃɛl/ *n.* **1** the shell of a clam, formed of two roughly equal valves with a hinge. **2** a thing with a lid or opening section resembling this, e.g. a kind of mechanical digger, a hatch in an aircraft, a portable computer, a box for takeaway food.

clan /klan/ *n.* **1** a group of people with a common ancestor, esp. in the Scottish Highlands. **2** a large family as a social group. **3** a group with a strong common interest. **4 a** a genus, species, or class. **b** a family or group of animals, e.g. elephants. [Middle English via Gaelic *clann* from Latin *planta* 'sprout']

clandestine /klanˈdɛstɪn, ˈklandɛstɪn/ *adj.* surreptitious, secret. □ **clandestinely** *adv.* **clandestinity** /-ˈtɪnɪti/ *n.* [French *clandestin* or Latin *clandestinus*, from *clam* 'secretly']

clang /klaŋ/ *n.* & *v.* ● *n.* a loud resonant metallic sound as of a bell or hammer etc. ● *v.* **1** *intr.* make a clang. **2** *tr.* cause to clang. [imitative: influenced by Latin *clangere* 'resound']

clanger /'klaŋə/ *n.* esp. *Brit. slang* a mistake or blunder. □ **drop a clanger** commit a conspicuous indiscretion.

clangour /'klaŋgə/ *n.* (*US* **clangor**) **1** a prolonged or repeated clanging noise. **2** an uproar or commotion. □ **clangorous** *adj.* **clangorously** *adv.* [Latin *clangor* 'noise of trumpets etc.']

clank /klaŋk/ *n.* & *v.* ● *n.* a sound as of heavy pieces of metal meeting or a chain rattling. ● *v.* **1** *intr.* make a clanking sound. **2** *tr.* cause to clank. □ **clankingly** *adv.* [imitative: cf. CLANG, CLINK[1], Dutch *klank*]

clannish /'klanɪʃ/ *adj.* usu. *derog.* **1** (of a family or group) tending to hold together. **2** of or like a clan. □ **clannishly** *adv.* **clannishness** *n.*

clanship /'klanʃɪp/ *n.* **1** a patriarchal system of clans. **2** loyalty to one's clan.

clansman /'klanzmən/ *n.* (*pl.* **-men**; *fem.* **clanswoman**, *pl.* **-women**) a member or fellow member of a clan.

clap[1] /klap/ *v.* & *n.* ● *v.* (**clapped**, **clapping**) **1 a** *intr.* strike the palms of one's hands together as a signal or repeatedly as applause. **b** *tr.* strike (the hands) together in this way. **2** *tr. Brit.* applaud or show one's approval of (esp. a person) in this way. **3** *tr.* (of a bird) flap (its wings) audibly. **4** *tr.* put or place quickly or with determination (*clapped him in prison*; *clap a tax on whisky*). **5** *tr.* (foll. by *on*) slap (a person) encouragingly on (the back, shoulder, etc.). ● *n.* **1** the act of clapping, esp. as applause. **2** an explosive sound, esp. of thunder. **3** a slap, a pat. □ **clap eyes on** *colloq.* see. **clap on the back** = *slap on the back*. [Old English *clappian* 'throb, beat', of imitative origin]

clap[2] /klap/ *n. coarse slang* venereal disease, esp. gonorrhoea. [Old French *clapoir* 'venereal bubo']

clapboard /'klapbɔːd, 'klabəd/ *n. US* = WEATHERBOARD. [Anglicized from Low German *klappholt* 'cask-stave']

clapped out *adj.* (hyphenated when *attrib.*) *Brit. slang* worn out (esp. of machinery etc.); exhausted.

clapper /'klapə/ *n.* the tongue or striker of a bell. □ **like the clappers** *Brit. slang* very fast or hard.

clapperboard /'klapəbɔːd/ *n. Cinematog.* a device of hinged boards struck together to synchronize the starting of picture and sound machinery in filming.

claptrap /'klaptrap/ *n.* **1** insincere or pretentious talk, nonsense. **2** language used or feelings expressed only to gain applause. [CLAP[1] + TRAP[1]]

claque /klak, klɑːk/ *n.* a group of people hired to applaud in a theatre etc. [French, from *claquer* 'to clap']

claqueur /klɑː'kəː/ *n.* a member of a claque. [French (as CLAQUE)]

clarabella /klarə'bɛlə/ *n.* an organ stop with the quality of a flute. [fem. forms of Latin *clarus* 'clear' and *bellus* 'pretty']

clarence /'klar(ə)ns/ *n. hist.* a four-wheeled closed carriage with seats for four inside and two on the box. [named after the Duke of *Clarence*, afterwards William IV]

Clarenceux /'klar(ə)nsuː/ *n. Heraldry* (in the UK) the title given to the second King of Arms, with jurisdiction south of the Trent (cf. NORROY, KING OF ARMS). [Middle English from Anglo-French, from the dukedom of *Clarence* (named after *Clare* in Suffolk): the Clarence herald was made King of Arms]

claret /'klarət/ *n.* & *adj.* ● *n.* **1** red wine, esp. from Bordeaux. **2** a deep purplish red. **3** *Brit. archaic slang* blood. ● *adj.* claret-coloured. [Middle English via Old French (*vin*) *claret* and medieval Latin *claratum* (*vinum*) from Latin *clarus* 'clear']

clarify /'klarɪfʌɪ/ *v.* (**-ies**, **-ied**) **1** *tr.* & *intr.* make or become clearer. **2** *tr.* **a** free (liquid, butter, etc.) from impurities. **b** make transparent. **c** purify. □ **clarification** /-fɪ'keɪʃ(ə)n/ *n.* **clarificatory** /-fɪ'keɪt(ə)ri/ *n.* **clarifier** *n.* [Middle English via Old French *clarifier* from Latin *clarus* 'clear']

clarinet /klarɪ'nɛt/ *n.* **1 a** a woodwind instrument with a single-reed mouthpiece, a cylindrical tube with a flared end, holes, and keys. **b** a clarinet-player. **2** an organ stop with a quality resembling that of a clarinet. □ **clarinettist** *n.* (*US* **clarinetist**). [French *clarinette*, diminutive of *clarine*, a kind of bell]

clarion /'klarɪən/ *n.* & *adj.* ● *n.* **1** a clear rousing sound. **2** *hist.* a shrill narrow-tubed war trumpet. **3** an organ stop with a quality resembling that of a clarion. ● *adj.* clear and loud. [Middle English via medieval Latin *clario -onis* from Latin *clarus* 'clear']

clarity /'klarɪti/ *n.* the state or quality of being clear, esp. of sound or expression. [Middle English from Latin *claritas*, from *clarus* 'clear']

clarkia /'klɑːkɪə/ *n.* any plant of the genus *Clarkia*, native to N. America, with showy white, pink, or purple flowers. [modern Latin, named after W. *Clark*, US explorer (d. 1838), who discovered it]

clary /'klɛːri/ *n.* (*pl.* **-ies**) any of various aromatic herbs of the genus *Salvia*. [Middle English from obsolete French *clarie*, representing medieval Latin *sclarea*]

clash /klaʃ/ *n.* & *v.* ● *n.* **1 a** a loud jarring sound as of metal objects being struck together. **b** a collision, esp. with force. **2 a** a conflict or disagreement. **b** a discord of colours etc. ● *v.* **1 a** *intr.* make a clashing sound. **b** *tr.* cause to clash. **2** *intr.* collide; coincide awkwardly. **3** *intr.* (often foll. by *with*) **a** come into conflict or be at variance. **b** (of colours) be discordant. □ **clasher** *n.* [imitative: cf. *clack*, *clang*, *crack*, *crash*]

clasp /klɑːsp/ *n.* & *v.* ● *n.* **1 a** a device with interlocking parts for fastening. **b** a buckle or brooch. **c** a metal fastening on a book cover. **2 a** an embrace; a person's reach. **b** a grasp or handshake. **3** a bar of silver on a medal-ribbon with the name of the battle etc. at which the wearer was present. ● *v.* **1** *tr.* fasten with or as with a clasp. **2** *tr.* **a** grasp, hold closely. **b** embrace, encircle. **3** *intr.* fasten a clasp. □ **clasp hands** shake hands with fervour or affection. **clasp one's hands** interlace one's fingers. □ **clasper** *n.* [Middle English: origin unknown]

clasper /'klɑːspə/ *n.* (in *pl.*) the appendages of some male fish and insects used to hold the female in copulation.

clasp-knife *n.* a folding knife, usu. with a catch holding the blade when open.

class /klɑːs/ *n.*, *v.*, & *adj.* ● *n.* **1** any set of persons or things grouped together, or graded or differentiated from others esp. by quality (*first class*; *economy class*). **2 a** a division or order of society (*upper class*; *professional classes*). **b** a caste system, a system of social classes. **c** (**the classes**) *archaic* the rich or educated. **3** *colloq.* distinction or high quality in appearance, behaviour, etc.; stylishness. **4 a** a group of students or pupils taught together. **b** the occasion when they meet. **c** their course of instruction. **5** *US* all the college or school students of the same standing or graduating in a given year (*the class of 1990*). **6** (in conscripted armies) all the recruits of a given year (*the 1950 class*). **7** *Brit.* a division of candidates according to merit in an examination. **8** *Biol.* a grouping of organisms, the next major rank below a division or phylum. ● *v.tr.* assign to a class or category. ● *attrib.adj. colloq.* classy, stylish. □ **in a class of** (or **on**) **its** (or **one's**) **own** unequalled. **no class** *colloq.* a lack of quality or distinction. [Latin *classis* 'assembly']

class-conscious *adj.* aware of and reacting to social divisions or one's place in a system of social class. □ **class-consciousness** *n.*

classic /'klasɪk/ *adj.* & *n.* ● *adj.* **1 a** of the first class; of acknowledged excellence. **b** remarkably typical; outstandingly important (*a classic case*). **2 a** of ancient Greek and Latin literature, art, or culture. **b** (of style in art, music, etc.) simple, harmonious, well-proportioned; in accordance with established forms (cf. ROMANTIC *adj.* 4a). **3** having literary or historic associations (*classic ground*). **4** (of clothes) made in a simple elegant style not much affected by changes in fashion. ● *n.* **1** a classic writer, artist, work, or example. **2 a** an ancient Greek or Latin writer. **b** (in *pl.*) ancient Greek and Latin literature and history. **c** *archaic* a scholar of ancient Greek and Latin. **3** a follower of classic models. **4** a garment in classic style. **5** (in *pl.*) *Brit.* the classic races. [French *classique* or Latin *classicus*, from *classis* 'class']

classical /ˈklasɪk(ə)l/ *adj.* **1 a** of ancient Greek or Latin literature, art, or culture. **b** (of language) having the form used by the ancient standard authors (*classical Latin*; *classical Hebrew*). **c** based on the study of ancient Greek and Latin (*a classical education*). **d** learned in classical studies. **2 a** (of music) serious or conventional; following traditional principles and intended to be of permanent rather than ephemeral value (cf. POPULAR MUSIC, LIGHT² *adj.* 5a). **b** of the period from *c.*1750–1800 (cf. ROMANTIC *adj.* 4b). **3 a** in or following the restrained style of classical antiquity (cf. ROMANTIC *adj.* 4a). **b** (of a form or period of art etc.) representing an exemplary standard; having a long-established worth. **4** *Physics* relating to the concepts which preceded relativity and quantum theory. □ **classicalism** *n.* **classicalist** *n.* **classicality** /-ˈkalɪti/ *n.* **classically** *adv.* [Latin *classicus* (as CLASSIC)]

classicism /ˈklasɪsɪz(ə)m/ *n.* **1** the following of a classic style. **2 a** classical scholarship. **b** the advocacy of a classical education. **3** an ancient Greek or Latin idiom. □ **classicist** *n.*

classicize /ˈklasɪsʌɪz/ *v.* (also **-ise**) **1** *tr.* make classic. **2** *intr.* imitate a classical style.

classic race *n. Brit.* each of the five main flat races of the horse racing season, namely the Two Thousand and the One Thousand Guineas, the Derby, the Oaks, and the St Leger.

classified /ˈklasɪfʌɪd/ *adj. & n.* ● *adj.* **1** arranged in classes or categories. **2** (of information etc.) designated as officially secret. **3** *Brit.* (of a road) assigned to a category according to its importance. **4** (of newspaper advertisements) arranged in columns according to various categories. ● *n.* (in *pl.*) classified advertisements.

classify /ˈklasɪfʌɪ/ *v.tr.* (**-ies**, **-ied**) **1 a** arrange in classes or categories. **b** assign (a thing) to a class or category. **2** designate as officially secret or not for general disclosure. □ **classifiable** *adj.* **classification** /-fɪˈkeɪʃ(ə)n/ *n.* **classificatory** /-ˈkeɪt(ə)ri/ *adj.* **classifier** *n.* [back-formation from *classification* (from French, as CLASS)]

classism /ˈklɑːsɪz(ə)m/ *n.* discrimination on the grounds of social class. □ **classist** *adj. & n.*

classless /ˈklɑːslɪs/ *adj.* making or showing no distinction of classes (*classless society*; *classless accent*). □ **classlessness** *n.*

class-list *n. Brit.* a list of candidates in an examination with the class achieved by each.

classmate /ˈklɑːsmeɪt/ *n.* a fellow member of a class, esp. at school.

classroom /ˈklɑːsruːm, -rʊm/ *n.* a room in which a class of students is taught, esp. in a school.

class war *n.* conflict between social classes.

classy /ˈklɑːsi/ *adj.* (**classier**, **classiest**) *colloq.* superior, stylish. □ **classily** *adv.* **classiness** *n.*

clastic /ˈklastɪk/ *adj. Geol.* designating a rock composed of broken pieces of older rocks. [French *clastique* from Greek *klastos* 'broken in pieces']

clathrate /ˈklaθreɪt/ *n. Chem.* a solid in which one component is enclosed in the structure of another. [Latin *clathratus* from *clathri* 'lattice-bars', from Greek *klēthra*]

clatter /ˈklatə/ *n. & v.* ● *n.* **1** a rattling sound as of many hard objects struck together. **2** noisy talk. ● *v.* **1** *intr.* **a** make a clatter. **b** fall or move etc. with a clatter. **2** *tr.* cause (plates etc.) to clatter. [Old English, of imitative origin]

claudication /klɔːdɪˈkeɪʃ(ə)n/ *n. Med.* a cramping pain, esp. in the leg, caused by arterial obstruction; limping. [Latin *claudicare* 'limp' from *claudus* 'lame']

clause /klɔːz/ *n.* **1** *Gram.* a distinct part of a sentence, including a subject and predicate. **2** a single statement in a treaty, law, bill, or contract. □ **clausal** *adj.* [Middle English via Old French from Latin *clausula* 'conclusion', from *claudere claus-* 'shut']

claustral /ˈklɔːstr(ə)l/ *adj.* **1** of or associated with the cloister; monastic. **2** narrow-minded. [Middle English via Late Latin *claustralis* from Latin *claustrum* CLOISTER]

claustrophobia /klɔːstrəˈfəʊbɪə/ *n.* an abnormal fear of confined places. [modern Latin, from Latin *claustrum*: see CLOISTER]

claustrophobic /klɔːstrəˈfəʊbɪk/ *adj. & n.* ● *adj.* **1** suffering from claustrophobia. **2** inducing claustrophobia. ● *n.* a person who suffers from claustrophobia. □ **claustrophobically** *adv.*

clavate /ˈkleɪveɪt/ *adj. Bot.* club-shaped. [modern Latin *clavatus* from Latin *clava* 'club']

clave¹ /kleɪv, klɑːv/ *n. Mus.* a hardwood stick used in pairs to make a hollow sound when struck together. [Latin American Spanish from Spanish, = keystone, from Latin *clavis* 'key']

clave² *archaic past* of CLEAVE².

clavicembalo /klavɪˈtʃɛmbələʊ/ *n.* (*pl.* **-os**) a harpsichord. [Italian]

clavichord /ˈklavɪkɔːd/ *n.* a small keyboard instrument with a very soft tone. [Middle English from medieval Latin *clavichordium*, from Latin *clavis* 'key', *chorda* 'string': see CHORD²]

clavicle /ˈklavɪk(ə)l/ *n.* the collarbone. □ **clavicular** /kləˈvɪkjʊlə/ *adj.* [Latin *clavicula*, diminutive of *clavis* 'key' (from its shape)]

clavier /ˈklavɪə, kləˈvɪə/ *n. Mus.* **1** any keyboard instrument. **2** its keyboard. [French *clavier* or German *Klavier* from medieval Latin *claviarius*, originally = key-bearer, from Latin *clavis* 'key']

claviform /ˈklavɪfɔːm/ *adj.* club-shaped. [Latin *clava* 'club']

claw /klɔː/ *n. & v.* ● *n.* **1 a** a pointed horny nail on an animal's or bird's foot. **b** a foot bearing these. **2** the pincer of a crab or other crustacean. **3** a device for grappling, holding, etc. ● *v.* **1** *tr. & intr.* scratch, maul, or pull (a person or thing) with claws. **2** *tr.* make (one's way) with difficulty by pulling oneself (as if) using claws. **3** *tr. & intr. Sc.* scratch gently. **4** *intr. Naut.* beat to windward. □ **claw back** *Brit.* **1** regain laboriously or gradually. **2** recover (money paid out) from another source (e.g. taxation). □ **clawed** *adj.* (also in *comb.*). **clawless** *adj.* [Old English *clawu*, *clawian*]

clawback /ˈklɔːbak/ *n. Brit.* **1** the act of clawing back. **2** money recovered in this way.

claw hammer *n.* a hammer with one side of the head forked for extracting nails.

clay /kleɪ/ *n.* **1** a stiff sticky earth, used for making bricks, pottery, ceramics, etc. **2** *poet.* the substance of the human body. **3** (in full **clay pipe**) a tobacco pipe made of clay. □ **clayey** *adj.* **clayish** *adj.* **claylike** *adj.* [Old English *clǣg*, from West Germanic]

claymore /ˈkleɪmɔː/ *n.* **1** *hist.* **a** a Scottish two-edged broadsword. **b** a broadsword, often with a single edge, having a hilt with a basketwork design. **2** a type of anti-personnel mine. [Gaelic *claidheamh mór* 'great sword']

clay-pan *n. Austral.* a natural hollow in clay soil, retaining water after rain.

clay pigeon *n.* a breakable disc thrown up from a trap as a target for shooting.

Clayton's /ˈkleɪt(ə)nz/ *attrib.adj. Austral.* sham, illusory; being a poor substitute. [from the proprietary name of a soft drink marketed as 'the drink you have when you're not having a drink']

-cle /k(ə)l, *after s* (ə)l/ *suffix* forming (originally diminutive) nouns (*article*; *particle*). [as -CULE]

clean /kliːn/ *adj., adv., v., & n.* ● *adj.* **1** (often foll. by *of*) free from dirt or contaminating matter, unsoiled. **2** clear; unused or unpolluted; preserving what is regarded as the original state (*clean air*; *clean page*). **3** free from obscenity or indecency. **4 a** attentive to personal hygiene and cleanliness. **b** (of children and animals) toilet-trained or house-trained. **5** complete, clear-cut, unobstructed, even. **6 a** (of a ship, aircraft, or car) streamlined, smooth. **b** well formed, slender and shapely (*clean-limbed; the car has clean lines*). **7** adroit, skilful (*clean fielding*). **8** (of a nuclear weapon) producing relatively little fallout. **9 a** free from ceremonial defilement or from disease. **b** (of food) not prohibited. **10 a** free from any record of a crime, offence, etc. (*a clean driving licence*). **b** *slang* free from suspicion; not carrying a weapon or incriminating material. **c** observing the rules of a sport or game; fair (*a clean fight*). **11** (of a taste, smell, etc.) sharp, fresh, distinctive. **12** (of timber) free from knots. ● *adv.* **1** completely, outright, simply (*clean bowled; cut clean through; clean forgot*). **2** in a clean manner. ● *v.* **1** *tr.* (also foll. by *of*) & *intr.* make or become clean. **2** *tr.* eat all the food on (one's plate). **3** *tr.* remove the innards of (fish or fowl). **4** *intr.* make oneself clean. ● *n.* esp. *Brit.* the act or process of cleaning or being cleaned (*give it a clean*). □ **clean down** esp. *Brit.* clean by brushing or wiping. **clean out 1** clean thoroughly. **2** *slang* empty or deprive (esp. of money). **clean up 1 a** clear (a mess) away. **b** (also *absol.*) put (things) tidy. **c** make (oneself) clean. **2** restore order or morality to. **3** *slang* **a** acquire as gain or profit. **b** make a gain or profit. **come clean** *colloq.* own up; confess everything. **make a clean breast of** see BREAST. **make a clean job of** *colloq.* do thoroughly. **make a clean sweep of** see SWEEP. □ **cleanable** *adj.* **cleanish** *adj.* **cleanness** /'kliːnnɪs/ *n.* [Old English *clǣne (adj. & adv.), clēne (adv.)*, from West Germanic]

clean bill of health see BILL OF HEALTH 2.

clean break *n.* a quick and final separation.

clean-cut *adj.* **1** sharply outlined. **2** (of a person) clean and neat.

cleaner /'kliːnə/ *n.* **1** a person employed to clean the interior of a building. **2** (usu. in *pl.*) a commercial establishment for cleaning clothes. **3** a device or substance for cleaning. □ **take to the cleaners** *slang* **1** defraud or rob (a person) of all his or her money. **2** criticize severely.

clean hands *n.pl.* freedom from guilt.

clean-living *adj.* of upright character.

cleanly[1] /'kliːnli/ *adv.* **1** in a clean way. **2** efficiently; without difficulty. [Old English *clǣnlīce*: see CLEAN, -LY[2]]

cleanly[2] /'klɛnli/ *adj.* (**cleanlier, cleanliest**) habitually clean; with clean habits. □ **cleanliness** *n.* [Old English *clǣnlic*: see CLEAN, -LY[1]]

cleanse /klɛnz/ *v.tr.* **1** usu. *formal* make clean. **2** (often foll. by *of*) purify from sin or guilt. **3** *archaic* cure (a leper etc.). □ **cleanser** *n.* [Old English *clǣnsian* (see CLEAN)]

clean-shaven *adj.* without beard, whiskers, or moustache.

clean sheet *n.* freedom from commitments or imputations; the removal of these from one's record.

cleansing cream *n.* cream for removing unwanted matter from the face, hands, etc.

cleansing department *n. Brit.* a local service of refuse collection etc.

cleanskin /'kliːnskɪn/ *n. Austral.* **1** an unbranded animal. **2** *slang* a person free from blame, without a police record, etc.

clean slate *n.* = CLEAN SHEET.

clean-up *n.* an act of cleaning up.

clear /klɪə/ *adj., adv., & v.* ● *adj.* **1** free from dirt or contamination. **2** (of weather, the sky, etc.) not dull or cloudy. **3 a** transparent. **b** lustrous, shining; free from obscurity. **4** (of soup) not containing solid ingredients. **5** (of a fire) burning with little smoke. **6 a** distinct, easily perceived by the senses. **b** unambiguous, easily understood (*make a thing clear; make oneself clear*). **c** manifest; not confused or doubtful (*clear evidence*). **7** that discerns or is able to discern readily and accurately (*clear thinking*). **8** (usu. foll. by *about, on,* or *that* + clause) confident, convinced, certain. **9** (of a conscience) free from guilt. **10** (of a road etc.) unobstructed, open. **11 a** net, without deduction (*a clear £1,000*). **b** complete (*three clear days*). **12** (often foll. by *of*) free, unhampered; unencumbered by debt, commitments, etc. **13** (foll. by *of*) not obstructed by. ● *adv.* **1** clearly (*speak loud and clear*). **2** completely (*he got clear away*). **3** apart, out of contact (*keep clear; stand clear of the doors*). **4** (foll. by *to*) *US* all the way. ● *v.* **1** *tr. & intr.* make or become clear. **2 a** *tr.* (often foll. by *of*) free from prohibition or obstruction. **b** *tr. & intr.* make or become empty or unobstructed. **c** *tr.* free (land) for cultivation or building by cutting down trees etc. **d** *tr.* cause people to leave (a room etc.). **3** *tr.* (often foll. by *of*) show or declare (a person) to be innocent (*cleared them of complicity*). **4** *tr.* approve (a person) for special duty, access to information, etc. **5** *tr.* pass over or by, safely or without touching, esp. by jumping. **6** *tr.* make (an amount of money) as a net gain or to balance expenses. **7** *tr.* pass (a cheque) through a clearing house. **8** *tr.* pass through (a customs office etc.). **9** *tr.* remove (an obstruction, an unwanted object, etc.) (*clear them out of the way*). **10** *tr.* (also *absol.*) *Football* send (the ball) out of one's defensive zone. **11** *intr.* (often foll. by *away, up*) (of physical phenomena) disappear, gradually diminish (*mist cleared by lunchtime; my cold has cleared up*). **12** *tr.* (often foll. by *off*) discharge (a debt). □ **clear the air 1** make the air less sultry. **2** disperse an atmosphere of suspicion, tension, etc. **clear away 1** remove completely. **2** remove the remains of a meal from the table. **clear the decks** prepare for action. **clear off 1** get rid of. **2** *colloq.* go away. **clear out 1** empty. **2** remove. **3** *colloq.* go away. **clear one's throat** cough slightly to make one's voice clear. **clear up 1** tidy up. **2** solve (a mystery etc.). **3** (of weather) become fine. **4** disappear (*my cold has cleared up*). **clear the way 1** remove obstacles. **2** stand aside. **clear a thing with** get approval or authorization for a thing from (a person). **in clear** not in cipher or code. **in the clear** free from suspicion or difficulty. **out of a clear sky** as a complete surprise. □ **clearable** *adj.* **clearly** *adv.* **clearness** *n.* [Middle English via Old French *cler* from Latin *clarus*]

clearance /'klɪər(ə)ns/ *n.* **1 a** the removal of obstructions etc., esp. removal of buildings, persons, etc., so as to clear land. **b** the removal of contents, esp. of a house. **c** = CLEARANCE SALE. **2** clear space allowed for the passing of two objects or two parts in machinery etc. **3** special authorization or permission (esp. for an aircraft to take off or land, or for access to information etc.). **4 a** the clearing of a person, ship, etc., by customs. **b** a certificate showing this. **5** the clearing of cheques. **6** *Football* a kick sending the ball out of a defensive zone. **7** making clear.

clearance order *n.* an order for the demolition of buildings.

clearance sale *n.* a sale to get rid of superfluous stock.

clearcole /'klɪəkəʊl/ *n. & v.* ● *n.* a mixture of size and whiting or white lead, used as a primer for distemper. ● *v.tr.* paint with clearcole. [French *claire colle* 'clear glue']

clear-cut *adj. & v.* ● *adj.* sharply defined; obvious. ● *v.tr.* (**-cutting**; *past* and *past part.* **-cut**) cut down and remove every tree from (an area).

clearer /'klɪərə/ *n.* **1** a clearing bank. **2** a person or thing that clears or clears away.

clear-headed *adj.* thinking clearly; sensible.

clearing /'klɪərɪŋ/ *n.* **1** in senses of CLEAR *v.* **2** an area in a forest cleared for cultivation.

clearing bank *n. Brit.* a bank which is a member of a clearing house.

clearing house *n.* **1** a bankers' establishment where cheques and bills from member banks are exchanged, so that only the balances need be paid in cash. **2** an agency for collecting and distributing information etc.

clear-out *n.* an act or period of clearing out; a removal of unwanted items.

clear-sighted *adj.* seeing, thinking, or understanding clearly.

clearstory *US* var. of CLERESTORY.

clear-up *n.* **1** an act or period of clearing up or tidying. **2** (usu. *attrib.*) the solving of crimes (*clear-up rates*).

clearway /ˈklɪəweɪ/ *n. Brit.* a main road (other than a motorway) on which vehicles are not normally permitted to stop.

clearwing /ˈklɪəwɪŋ/ *n.* a day-flying moth with largely transparent wings, of the family Sesiidae.

cleat /kliːt/ *n.* **1** a piece of metal, wood, etc., bolted on for fastening ropes to, or to strengthen woodwork etc. **2** a projecting piece on a spar, gangway, boot, etc., to give footing or prevent a rope from slipping. **3** a wedge. [Old English: probably related to CLOT]

cleavage /ˈkliːvɪdʒ/ *n.* **1** the hollow between a woman's breasts, esp. as exposed by a low-cut garment. **2 a** a division or splitting. **b** *Biol.* cell division, esp. of a fertilized egg cell. **3** the splitting of rocks, crystals, etc., in a preferred direction.

cleave[1] /kliːv/ *v.* (*past* **clove** /kləʊv/ or **cleft** /kleft/ or **cleaved**; *past part.* **cloven** /ˈkləʊv(ə)n/ or **cleft** or **cleaved**) *literary* **1 a** *tr.* chop or break apart, split, esp. along the grain or the line of cleavage. **b** *intr.* come apart in this way. **2** *tr.* make one's way through (air or water). □ **cleavable** *adj.* [Old English *clēofan*, from Germanic]

cleave[2] /kliːv/ *v.intr.* (*past* **cleaved** or *archaic* **clave** /kleɪv/) (foll. by *to*) *literary* stick fast; adhere. [Old English *cleofian*, *clifian*, from the West Germanic base also of CLAY]

cleaver /ˈkliːvə/ *n.* **1** a tool for cleaving, esp. a heavy chopping tool used by butchers. **2** a person who cleaves.

cleavers /ˈkliːvəz/ *n.* (also **clivers** /ˈklɪvəz/) (treated as *sing.* or *pl.*) a plant, *Galium aparine*, having hooked bristles on its stem that catch on clothes etc. Also called *goosegrass*. [Old English *clife*, formed as CLEAVE[2]]

clef /klɛf/ *n. Mus.* any of several symbols placed at the beginning of a staff, indicating the pitch of the notes written on it. [French, from Latin *clavis* 'key']

cleft[1] /klɛft/ *adj.* split, partly divided. □ **in a cleft stick** *Brit.* in a difficult position, esp. one allowing neither retreat nor advance. [past part. of CLEAVE[1]]

cleft[2] /klɛft/ *n.* a split or fissure; a space or division made by cleaving. [Old English (related to CLEAVE[1]): assimilated to CLEFT[1]]

cleft lip *n.* a congenital split in the upper lip.

cleft palate *n.* a congenital split in the roof of the mouth.

cleg /klɛg/ *n. Brit.* a horsefly. [Old Norse *kleggi*]

cleistogamic /klʌɪstəˈgamɪk/ *adj. Bot.* (of a flower) permanently closed and self-fertilizing. [Greek *kleistos* 'closed' + *gamos* 'marriage']

clematis /ˈklɛmətɪs, kləˈmeɪtɪs/ *n.* an erect or climbing plant of the genus *Clematis* (buttercup family), bearing white, pink, or purple flowers and feathery seeds. [Latin from Greek *klēmatis*, from *klēma* 'vine branch']

clement /ˈklɛm(ə)nt/ *adj.* **1** mild (*clement weather*). **2** merciful. □ **clemency** *n.* [Middle English from Latin *clemens -entis*]

clementine /ˈklɛm(ə)ntʌɪn/ *n.* a small citrus fruit, thought to be a hybrid between a tangerine and sweet orange. [French *clémentine*]

clench /klɛn(t)ʃ/ *v.* & *n.* ● *v.tr.* **1** close (the teeth or fingers) tightly. **2** grasp firmly. **3** = CLINCH *v.* 4. ● *n.* **1** a clenching action. **2** a clenched state. [Old English from Germanic: related to CLING]

clepsydra /ˈklɛpsɪdrə/ *n.* an ancient time-measuring device worked by a flow of water. [Latin from Greek *klepsudra*, from *kleptō* 'steal' + *hudōr* 'water']

clerestory /ˈklɪəstɔːri/ *n.* (*US* also **clearstory**) (*pl.* **-ies**) **1** an upper row of windows in a cathedral or large church, above the level of the aisle roofs. **2** *US* a raised section of the roof of a railway carriage, with windows or ventilators. [Middle English from CLEAR + STOREY]

clergy /ˈkləːdʒi/ *n.* (*pl.* **-ies**) (usu. treated as *pl.*) **1** (usu. prec. by *the*) the body of all persons ordained for religious duties in the Christian Churches. **2** a number of such persons (*ten clergy were present*). [Middle English from Old French, ultimately from ecclesiastical Latin *clericus* CLERIC]

clergyman /ˈkləːdʒɪmən/ *n.* (*pl.* **-men**) a member of the clergy, esp. *Brit.* of the Church of England.

clergywoman /ˈkləːdʒɪwʊmən/ *n.* (*pl.* **-women**) a female member of the clergy.

cleric /ˈklɛrɪk/ *n.* a member of the clergy. [(originally *adj.*): ecclesiastical Latin *clericus* from Greek *klērikos*, from *klēros* 'lot, heritage', as in Acts 1:26]

clerical /ˈklɛrɪk(ə)l/ *adj.* **1** of the clergy or clergymen. **2** of or done by a clerk or clerks. □ **clericalism** *n.* **clericalist** *n.* **clerically** *adv.* [ecclesiastical Latin *clericalis* (as CLERIC)]

clerical collar *n.* a stiff upright white collar fastening at the back, as worn by the clergy in some Churches.

clerical error *n.* an error made in copying or writing out.

clerihew /ˈklɛrɪhjuː/ *n.* a short comic or nonsensical verse, usu. in two rhyming couplets with lines of unequal length and referring to a famous person. [named after E. *Clerihew* Bentley, English writer (d. 1956), its inventor]

clerk /klɑːk/ *n.* & *v.* ● *n.* **1** a person employed in an office, bank, shop, etc., to keep records, accounts, etc. **2** a secretary, agent, or record-keeper of a local council (*town clerk*), court, etc. **3** a lay officer of a church (*parish clerk*), college chapel, etc. **4** a senior official in Parliament. **5** *N. Amer.* an assistant in a shop, hotel, or post office. **6** *archaic* a clergyman. ● *v.intr.* work as a clerk. □ **clerkdom** *n.* **clerkess** *n. Sc.* **clerkish** *adj.* **clerkly** *adj.* **clerkship** *n.* [Old English *cleric*, *clerc*, & Old French *clerc*, from ecclesiastical Latin *clericus* CLERIC]

clerk in holy orders *n. formal* a clergyman.

Clerk of the Closet *n.* (in the UK) the sovereign's principal chaplain.

clerk of the course *n.* the judges' secretary etc. in horse or motor racing.

clerk of the works *n.* (also **clerk of works**) *Brit.* an overseer of building works etc.

clever /ˈklɛvə/ *adj.* (**cleverer**, **cleverest**) **1 a** skilful, talented; quick to understand and learn. **b** *colloq.* sensible, wise. **2** adroit, dextrous. **3** (of the doer or the thing done) ingenious, cunning. □ **cleverly** *adv.* **cleverness** *n.* [Middle English, = adroit: perhaps related to CLEAVE[2], with the sense 'apt to seize']

clever-clever *adj.* seeking to appear clever.

clever clogs *n. colloq.* = CLEVER DICK.

clever Dick *n.* esp. *Brit. colloq.* a person who is or purports to be smart or knowing.

clevis /ˈklɛvɪs/ *n.* **1** a U-shaped piece of metal at the end of a beam for attaching tackle etc. **2** a connection in which a bolt holds one part that fits between the forked ends of another. [16th c.: perhaps related to CLEAVE[1]]

clew /kluː/ *n.* & *v.* ● *n.* **1** *Naut.* **a** a lower or after corner of a sail. **b** a set of small cords suspending a hammock. **2** *archaic* **a** a ball of thread or yarn, esp. with reference to the legend of Theseus and the labyrinth. **b** *Brit.* = CLUE. ● *v.tr. Naut.* **1** (foll. by *up*) draw the lower ends of (a sail) to the upper yard or the mast ready for furling. **2** (foll. by *down*) let down (a sail) by the clews in unfurling. [Old English *cliwen*, *cleowen*]

clianthus /klʌɪˈanθəs, klɪ-/ *n.* any leguminous plant of the genus *Clianthus*, native to Australia and New Zealand, bearing drooping clusters of red pealike flowers. [modern Latin, apparently from Greek *klei-*, *kleos* 'glory' + *anthos* 'flower']

cliché /ˈkliːʃeɪ/ *n.* (also **cliche**) **1** a hackneyed phrase or opinion. **2** *Brit.* a metal casting of a stereotype or electrotype. [French, from *clicher* 'to stereotype']

clichéd /ˈkliːʃeɪd/ *adj.* (also **cliché'd**, **cliched**) hackneyed; full of clichés.

click /klɪk/ *n.* & *v.* ● *n.* **1** a slight sharp sound as of a switch being operated. **2** a speech sound in some languages, produced as a type of plosive by sudden withdrawal of the tongue from the soft palate. **3** a catch in machinery acting with a slight sharp sound. **4** an action causing a horse's hind foot to touch the shoe of a fore foot. ● *v.* **1 a** *intr.* make a click. **b** *tr.* cause (one's tongue, heels, etc.) to click. **2** *intr. colloq.* **a** become clear or understandable (often prec. by *it* as subject: *when I saw them it all clicked*). **b** be successful, secure one's object. **c** (foll. by *with*) become friendly, esp. with a person of the opposite sex. **d** come to an agreement. **3** *intr. & tr.* (often foll. by *on*) *Computing* press (one of the buttons on a mouse); select (an item represented on the screen, a particular function, etc.) by so doing. □ **clicker** *n.* [imitative: cf. Dutch *klikken*, French *cliquer*]

click beetle *n.* a beetle of the family Elateridae, springing up with a click if turned on its back.

click-clack *n. & v.* ● *n.* a repeated clicking sound as of shoe heels on a hard surface. ● *v.intr.* make such a sound.

client /'klʌɪənt/ *n.* **1** a person using the services of a lawyer, architect, social worker, or other professional person. **2** a customer. **3** *Rom.Hist.* a plebeian under the protection of a patrician. **4** *archaic* a dependant or hanger-on. □ **clientship** *n.* [Middle English from Latin *cliens -entis*, from *cluere* 'hear, obey']

clientele /kliːɒn'tɛl/ *n.* **1** clients collectively. **2** customers, esp. of a shop. **3** the patrons of a theatre etc. [Latin *clientela* 'clientship' & French *clientèle*]

client-server *attrib.adj.* designating a computer system in which a central server provides data to a number of networked workstations.

cliff /klɪf/ *n.* a steep rock face, esp. *Brit.* at the edge of the sea. □ **clifflike** *adj.* **cliffy** *adj.* [Old English *clif*, from Germanic]

cliffhanger /'klɪfhaŋə/ *n.* a story etc. with a strong element of suspense; a suspenseful ending to an episode of a serial. □ **cliffhanging** *adj.*

climacteric /klʌɪ'makt(ə)rɪk, klʌɪmak'tɛrɪk/ *n. & adj.* ● *n.* **1** *Med.* the period of life when fertility and sexual activity are in decline. **2** a supposed critical period in life (esp. occurring at intervals of seven years). ● *adj.* **1** *Med.* occurring at the climacteric. **2** constituting a crisis; critical. [French *climatérique* or Latin *climactericus* from Greek *klimaktērikos*, from *klimaktēr* 'critical period', from *klimax -akos* 'ladder, climax']

climactic /klʌɪ'maktɪk/ *adj.* of or forming a climax. □ **climactically** *adv.* [CLIMAX + -IC, perhaps influenced by SYNTACTIC or CLIMACTERIC]

climate /'klʌɪmət/ *n.* **1** the prevailing weather conditions of an area. **2** a region with particular weather conditions. **3** the prevailing trend of opinion or public feeling. □ **climatic** /-'matɪk/ *adj.* **climatical** /-'matɪk(ə)l/ *adj.* **climatically** /-'matɪk(ə)li/ *adv.* [Middle English via Old French *climat* or Late Latin *clima climat-* from Greek *klima*, from *klinō* 'slope, zone']

climatology /klʌɪmə'tɒlədʒi/ *n.* the scientific study of climate. □ **climatological** /-tə'lɒdʒɪk(ə)l/ *adj.* **climatologist** *n.*

climax /'klʌɪmaks/ *n. & v.* ● *n.* **1** the event or point of greatest intensity or interest; a culmination or apex. **2** a sexual orgasm. **3** *Rhet.* **a** a series arranged in order of increasing importance etc. **b** the last term in such a series. **4** *Ecol.* a state of equilibrium reached by a plant community. ● *v.tr. & intr. colloq.* bring or come to a climax. [Late Latin from Greek *klimax -akos* 'ladder, climax']

climb /klʌɪm/ *v. & n.* ● *v.* **1** *tr. & intr.* (often foll. by *up*) ascend, mount, go or come up, esp. by using one's hands. **2** *intr.* (of a plant) grow up a wall, tree, trellis, etc. by clinging with tendrils or by twining. **3** *intr.* move along by grasping or clinging; go with effort; clamber (*climbed across the ditch*; *climbed into bed*). **4** *intr.* make progress in social rank, intellectual or moral strength, etc. **5** *intr.* (of an aircraft, the sun, etc.) go upwards. **6** *intr.* slope upwards. ● *n.* **1** an ascent by climbing. **2 a** a place, esp. a hill, climbed or to be climbed. **b** a recognized route up a mountain etc. □ **climb down 1** descend with the help of one's hands. **2** withdraw from a position taken up in argument, negotiation, etc. **climb into** put on (clothes). □ **climbable** *adj.* [Old English *climban* from West Germanic, related to CLEAVE[2]]

climbdown /'klʌɪmdaʊn/ *n.* a withdrawal from a position taken up in argument, negotiation, etc.

climber /'klʌɪmə/ *n.* **1** a mountaineer. **2** a climbing plant. **3** a person with strong social etc. aspirations.

climbing frame *n. Brit.* a structure of joined bars etc. for children to climb on.

climbing iron *n.* a set of spikes attachable to a boot for climbing trees or ice slopes.

climbing perch *n.* a S. Asian freshwater fish, *Anabas testudinens*, able to breathe air and move over land. Also called *anabas*.

clime /klʌɪm/ *n. literary* **1** a region. **2** a climate. [Late Latin *clima*: see CLIMATE]

clinch /klɪn(t)ʃ/ *v. & n.* ● *v.* **1** *tr.* confirm or settle (an argument, bargain, etc.) conclusively. **2** *intr. Boxing & Wrestling* (of participants) become too closely engaged. **3** *intr. colloq.* embrace. **4** *tr.* secure (a nail or rivet) by driving the point sideways when through. **5** *tr. Naut.* fasten (a rope) with a particular half hitch. ● *n.* **1 a** a clinching action. **b** a clinched state. **2** *colloq.* an (esp. amorous) embrace. **3** *Boxing & Wrestling* an action or state in which participants become too closely engaged. [16th-c. variant of CLENCH]

clincher /'klɪn(t)ʃə/ *n. colloq.* a remark or argument that settles a matter conclusively.

clincher-built var. of CLINKER-BUILT.

cline /klʌɪn/ *n.* **1** *Biol.* a graded sequence of differences within a species etc. **2** a continuum with an infinite number of gradations. □ **clinal** *adj.* [Greek *klinein* 'to slope']

cling /klɪŋ/ *v. & n.* ● *v.intr.* (*past* and *past part.* **clung** /klʌŋ/) **1** (foll. by *to*) adhere, stick, or hold on (by means of stickiness, suction, grasping, or embracing). **2** (foll. by *to*) remain persistently or stubbornly faithful (to a friend, habit, idea, etc.). **3** maintain one's grasp; keep hold; resist separation. ● *n.* = CLINGSTONE. □ **cling together** remain in one body or in contact. □ **clinger** *n.* **clingingly** *adv.* [Old English *clingan* from Germanic, related to CLENCH]

cling film *n. Brit.* a very thin clinging transparent plastic film, used as a covering esp. for food.

clingstone /'klɪŋstəʊn/ *n.* a variety of peach or nectarine in which the flesh adheres to the stone (cf. FREESTONE 2).

clingy /'klɪŋi/ *adj.* (**clingier**, **clingiest**) liable to cling. □ **clinginess** *n.*

clinic /'klɪnɪk/ *n.* **1** a private or specialized hospital. **2** a place or occasion for giving specialist medical treatment or advice (*eye clinic*; *fertility clinic*). **3** a gathering at a hospital bedside for the teaching of medicine or surgery. **4** *N. Amer.* a conference or short course on a particular subject (*golf clinic*). □ **clinician** /klɪ'nɪʃ(ə)n/ *n.* [French *clinique* from Greek *klinikē* (*tekhnē*) 'clinical', literally 'bedside (art)']

clinical /'klɪnɪk(ə)l/ *adj.* **1** *Med.* **a** of or for the treatment of patients. **b** taught or learnt at the hospital bedside. **2** dispassionate, coldly detached. **3** (of a room, building, etc.) bare, functional. □ **clinically** *adv.* [Latin *clinicus* from Greek *klinikos*, from *klinē* 'bed']

clinical death *n.* death judged by observation of a person's condition.

clinical medicine *n.* medicine dealing with the observation and treatment of patients.

clinical thermometer *n.* a thermometer with a small range, for taking a person's temperature.

clink[1] /klɪŋk/ *n. & v.* ● *n.* a sharp ringing sound. ● *v.* **1** *intr.* make a clink. **2** *tr.* cause (glasses etc.) to clink. [Middle English, probably from Middle Dutch *klinken*; cf. CLANG, CLANK]

clink[2] /klɪŋk/ *n.* (often prec. by *in*) *slang* prison. [16th c.: origin unknown]

clinker[1] /ˈklɪŋkə/ *n.* **1** a mass of slag or lava. **2** a stony residue from burnt coal. [earlier *clincard* etc. from obsolete Dutch *klinkaerd*, from *klinken* CLINK[1]]

clinker[2] /ˈklɪŋkə/ *n.* **1** *Brit. slang* something excellent or outstanding. **2** *N. Amer. colloq.* a mistake or blunder. [CLINK[1] + -ER[1]]

clinker-built /klɪŋkəˈbɪlt/ *adj.* (also **clincher-built** /klɪn(t)ʃəˈbɪlt/) (of a boat) having external planks overlapping downwards and secured with clinched copper nails (cf. CARVEL-BUILT). [*clink*, northern English variant of CLINCH + -ER[1]]

clinkstone /ˈklɪŋkstəʊn/ *n.* a kind of feldspar that rings like iron when struck.

clinometer /klʌɪˈnɒmɪtə, klɪ-/ *n. Surveying* an instrument for measuring slopes. [Greek *klinō* 'to slope' + -METER]

clint /klɪnt/ *n. Geol.* a block forming part of a natural limestone pavement. Cf. GRIKE. [Danish and Swedish *klint*]

cliometrics /klʌɪəˈmɛtrɪks/ *n.* a method of historical research making much use of statistical information and methods. [*Clio*, the name of the Muse of history + METRIC + -ICS]

clip[1] /klɪp/ *n. & v.* ● *n.* **1** a device for holding things together or for attachment to an object as a marker, esp. a paper clip or a device worked by a spring. **2** a piece of jewellery fastened by a clip. **3** a set of attached cartridges for a firearm. ● *v.tr.* (**clipped**, **clipping**) **1** fix with a clip. **2** grip tightly. **3** surround closely. [Old English *clyppan* 'embrace', from West Germanic]

clip[2] /klɪp/ *v. & n.* ● *v.tr.* (**clipped**, **clipping**) **1** cut with shears or scissors, esp. cut short or trim (hair, wool, etc.). **2** trim or remove the hair or wool of (a person or animal). **3** *colloq.* hit smartly. **4 a** curtail, diminish, cut short. **b** omit (a letter etc.) from a word; omit letters or syllables of (words pronounced). **5** *Brit.* remove a small piece of (a ticket) to show that it has been used. **6** cut (an extract) from a newspaper etc. **7** *slang* swindle, rob. **8** pare the edge of (a coin). ● *n.* **1** an act of clipping, esp. shearing or hair-cutting. **2** *colloq.* a smart blow, esp. with the hand. **3** a short sequence from a motion picture. **4** the quantity of wool clipped from a sheep, flock, etc. **5** *colloq.* speed, esp. rapid. □ **clip a person's wings** prevent a person from pursuing ambitions or acting effectively. □ **clippable** *adj.* [Middle English from Old Norse *klippa*, probably imitative]

clipboard /ˈklɪpbɔːd/ *n.* a small board with a spring clip for holding papers etc. and providing support for writing.

clip-clop /ˈklɪpklɒp/ *n. & v.* ● *n.* a sound such as the beat of a horse's hoofs. ● *v.intr.* (**-clopped**, **-clopping**) make such a sound. [imitative]

clip joint *n. slang* a nightclub etc. charging exorbitant prices.

clip-on *adj.* attached by a clip.

clipper /ˈklɪpə/ *n.* **1** (usu. in *pl.*) any of various instruments for clipping hair, fingernails, hedges, etc. **2** a fast sailing ship, esp. one with raking bows and masts. **3** a fast horse.

clippie /ˈklɪpi/ *n. Brit. colloq.* a bus conductress.

clipping /ˈklɪpɪŋ/ *n.* a piece clipped or cut from something, esp. from a newspaper, hedge, etc.

clique /kliːk/ *n.* a small exclusive group of people. □ **cliquey** *adj.* (**cliquier**, **cliquiest**). **cliquish** *adj.* **cliquishness** *n.* [French, from *cliquer* CLICK]

C.Lit. *abbr.* (in the UK) Companion of Literature.

clitic /ˈklɪtɪk/ *n.* (often *attrib.*) an enclitic or proclitic. □ **cliticization** /-tɪkʌɪˈzeɪʃ(ə)n/ *n.*

clitoridectomy /klɪt(ə)rɪˈdɛktəmi/ *n.* (*pl.* **-ies**) removal of the clitoris.

clitoris /ˈklɪt(ə)rɪs/ *n.* a small erectile part of the female genitals at the anterior end of the vulva. □ **clitoral** *adj.* [modern Latin from Greek *kleitoris*]

clivers var. of CLEAVERS.

Cllr. *abbr. Brit.* Councillor.

cloaca /kləʊˈeɪkə/ *n.* (*pl.* **cloacae** /-siː, -kiː/) **1** the genital and excretory cavity at the end of the intestinal canal in birds, reptiles, etc. **2** a sewer. □ **cloacal** *adj.* [Latin, = sewer]

cloak /kləʊk/ *n. & v.* ● *n.* **1** an outdoor overgarment, usu. sleeveless, hanging loosely from the shoulders. **2** a covering (*cloak of snow*). **3** (in *pl.*) *Brit.* = CLOAKROOM 2. ● *v.tr.* **1** cover with a cloak. **2** conceal, disguise. □ **under the cloak of** using as a pretext. [Middle English from Old French *cloke*, dialect variant of *cloche* 'bell, cloak' (from its bell shape) from medieval Latin *clocca* 'bell': see CLOCK[1]]

cloak-and-dagger *adj.* involving intrigue and espionage.

cloakroom /ˈkləʊkruːm, -rʊm/ *n.* **1** a room where outdoor clothes or luggage may be left by visitors, clients, etc. **2** *Brit. euphem.* a lavatory.

clobber[1] /ˈklɒbə/ *n. Brit. slang* clothing or personal belongings. [19th c.: origin unknown]

clobber[2] /ˈklɒbə/ *v.tr. slang* **1** hit; beat up. **2** defeat. **3** inflict a punishment or loss on. [20th c.: origin unknown]

cloche /klɒʃ, kləʊʃ/ *n.* **1** a small translucent cover for protecting or forcing outdoor plants. **2** (in full **cloche hat**) a woman's close-fitting bell-shaped hat. [French, = bell, from medieval Latin *clocca*: see CLOCK[1]]

clock[1] /klɒk/ *n. & v.* ● *n.* **1** an instrument for measuring time, driven mechanically or electrically and indicating hours, minutes, etc., by hands on a dial or by displayed figures. **2 a** any measuring device resembling a clock. **b** *colloq.* a speedometer, taximeter, or stopwatch. **3** time taken as an element in competitive sports etc. (*ran against the clock*). **4** *Brit. slang* a person's face. **5** *Brit.* a downy seed-head, esp. that of a dandelion. ● *v.tr.* **1** *colloq.* **a** (often foll. by *up*) attain or register (a stated time, distance, or speed, esp. in a race). **b** time (a race) with a stopwatch. **2** *slang* hit, esp. on the head. **3** *slang* **a** see or spot (a person or thing). **b** watch, stare at. □ **clock in** (or **on**) register one's arrival at work, esp. by means of an automatic recording clock. **clock off** (or **out**) register one's departure similarly. **round the clock** all day and (usu.) night. **watch the clock** = CLOCK-WATCH. [Middle English via Middle Dutch, Middle Low German *klocke* from medieval Latin *clocca* 'bell', perhaps from Celtic]

clock[2] /klɒk/ *n.* an ornamental pattern on the side of a stocking or sock near the ankle. [16th c.: origin unknown]

clock golf *n.* a game in which a golf ball is putted into a hole from successive points in a circle.

clockmaker /ˈklɒkmeɪkə/ *n.* a person who makes and repairs clocks and watches. □ **clockmaking** *n.*

clock radio *n.* a combined radio and alarm clock.

clock tower *n.* a tower, esp. forming part of a church or civic building, displaying a large clock.

clock-watch *v.intr.* work over-anxiously to time, esp. so as not to exceed minimum working hours. □ **clock-watcher** *n.* **clock-watching** *n.*

clockwise /ˈklɒkwʌɪz/ *adj. & adv.* in a curve corresponding in direction to the movement of the hands of a clock.

clockwork /ˈklɒkwəːk/ *n.* **1** a mechanism like that of a mechanical clock, with a spring and gears. **2** (*attrib.*) **a** driven by clockwork. **b** regular, mechanical. □ **like clockwork** smoothly, regularly, automatically.

clod /klɒd/ *n.* **1** a lump of earth, clay, etc. **2** *colloq.* a silly or foolish person. **3** meat cut from the neck of an ox. [Middle English: variant of CLOT]

cloddish /ˈklɒdɪʃ/ *adj.* loutish, foolish, clumsy. □ **cloddishly** *adv.* **cloddishness** *n.*

clodhopper /ˈklɒdhɒpə/ *n. colloq.* **1** (usu. in *pl.*) a large heavy shoe. **2** = CLOD 2.

clodhopping /ˈklɒdhɒpɪŋ/ *adj. colloq.* = CLODDISH.

clodpoll /ˈklɒdpɒl/ *n. slang* = CLOD 2.

clog /klɒg/ *n. & v.* ● *n.* **1** a shoe with a thick wooden sole. **2** *archaic* an encumbrance or impediment. **3** a block of wood to impede an animal's movement. ● *v.* (**clogged**, **clogging**) **1** (often foll. by *up*) **a** *tr.* obstruct, esp. by accumulation of glutinous matter. **b** *intr.* become obstructed. **2** *tr.* impede, hamper. **3** *tr. & intr.*

(often foll. by *up*) fill with glutinous or choking matter. [Middle English: origin unknown]

clog dance *n.* a dance performed in clogs.

cloggy /ˈklɒgi/ *adj.* (**cloggier**, **cloggiest**) **1** lumpy, knotty. **2** sticky.

cloisonné /ˈklwɑːzɒneɪ, -ˈzɒneɪ/ *n.* & *adj.* ● *n.* **1** an enamel finish produced by forming areas of different colours separated by strips of wire placed edgeways on a metal backing. **2** this process. ● *adj.* (of enamel) made by this process. [French, from *cloison* 'compartment']

cloister /ˈklɔɪstə/ *n.* & *v.* ● *n.* **1** a covered walk, often with a wall on one side and a colonnade open to a quadrangle on the other, esp. in a convent, monastery, college, or cathedral. **2** monastic life or seclusion. **3** a convent or monastery. ● *v.tr.* seclude or shut up, usu. in a convent or monastery. □ **cloistral** *adj.* [Middle English via Old French *cloistre* from Latin *claustrum*, *clostrum* 'lock, enclosed place', from *claudere claus-* CLOSE[2]]

cloistered /ˈklɔɪstəd/ *adj.* **1** secluded, sheltered. **2** monastic.

clomp /klɒmp/ var. of CLUMP *v.* 2.

clone /kləʊn/ *n.* & *v.* ● *n.* **1 a** a group of cells or organisms produced asexually from one stock or ancestor. **b** one such cell or organism. **2** a person or thing regarded as identical with another. ● *v.tr.* propagate as a clone. □ **clonal** *adj.* [Greek *klōn* 'twig, slip']

clonk /klɒŋk/ *n.* & *v.* ● *n.* an abrupt heavy sound of impact. ● *v.* **1** *intr.* make such a sound. **2** *tr. colloq.* hit. [imitative]

clonus /ˈkləʊnəs/ *n. Physiol.* a spasm with alternate muscular contractions and relaxations. □ **clonic** *adj.* [Greek *klonos* 'turmoil']

clop /klɒp/ *n.* & *v.* ● *n.* the sound made by a horse's hoofs. ● *v.intr.* (**clopped**, **clopping**) make this sound. [imitative]

cloqué /ˈkləʊkeɪ, French klɔke/ *n.* a fabric with an irregularly raised surface. [French, = blistered]

close[1] /kləʊs/ *adj.*, *adv.*, & *n.* ● *adj.* **1** (often foll. by *to*) situated at only a short distance or interval. **2 a** having a strong or immediate relation or connection (*close friend*; *close relative*). **b** in intimate friendship or association (*were very close*). **c** corresponding almost exactly (*close resemblance*). **d** fitting tightly (*close cap*). **e** (of hair etc.) short, near the surface. **3** in or almost in contact (*close combat*; *close proximity*). **4** dense, compact, with no or only slight intervals (*close texture*; *close writing*; *close formation*; *close thicket*). **5** in which competitors are almost equal (*close contest*; *close election*). **6** leaving no gaps or weaknesses, rigorous (*close reasoning*). **7** concentrated, searching (*close examination*; *close attention*). **8** (of air etc.) stuffy or humid. **9** closed, shut. **10** limited or restricted to certain persons etc. (*close corporation*; *close scholarship*). **11 a** hidden, secret, covered. **b** secretive. **12** (of a danger etc.) directly threatening, narrowly avoided (*that was close*). **13** niggardly. **14** (of a vowel) produced with a relatively narrow opening of the mouth and with the tongue close to the palate. **15** narrow, confined, contracted. **16** under prohibition. ● *adv.* **1** (often foll. by *by*, *to*) at only a short distance or interval (*they live close by*; *close to the church*). **2** closely, in a close manner (*shut close*). ● *n.* **1** an enclosed space. **2** *Brit.* a street closed at one end. **3** *Brit.* the precinct of a cathedral. **4** *Brit.* a school playing field or playground. **5** *Sc.* an entry from the street to a common stairway or to a court at the back. □ **close on** (or **upon**) *Brit.* nearly, very near to (*it took close on three hours*). **close to the wind** see WIND[1]. **go close** (of a racehorse) win or almost win. □ **closely** *adv.* **closeness** *n.* **closish** *adj.* [Middle English via Old French *clos* from Latin *clausum* 'enclosure' & *clausus*, past part. of *claudere* 'shut']

close[2] /kləʊz/ *v.* & *n.* ● *v.* **1 a** *tr.* shut (a lid, box, door, room, house, etc.). **b** *intr.* be shut (*the door closed slowly*). **c** *tr.* block up. **2 a** *tr.* & *intr.* bring or come to an end. **b** *intr.* finish speaking (*closed with an expression of thanks*). **c** *tr.* settle (a bargain etc.). **3 a** *intr.* end the day's business. **b** *tr.* end the day's business at (a shop, office, etc.). **4** *tr.* & *intr.* bring or come closer or into contact (*close ranks*). **5** *tr.* make (an electric circuit etc.) continuous. **6** *intr.* (foll. by *with*) express agreement (with an offer, terms, or the person offering them). **7** *intr.* (often foll. by *with*) come within striking distance; grapple. **8** *intr.* (foll. by *on*) (of a hand, box, etc.) grasp or entrap. ● *n.* **1** a conclusion, an end. **2** *Mus.* a cadence. □ **close down 1** discontinue (or cause to discontinue) business, esp. permanently. **2** *Brit.* (of a broadcasting station) end transmission, esp. until the next day. **close one's eyes 1** (foll. by *to*) pay no attention. **2** die. **close in 1** enclose. **2** come nearer. **3** (of days) get successively shorter with the approach of the winter solstice. **close out** *N. Amer.* discontinue, terminate, dispose of (a business). **close up 1** (often foll. by *to*) move closer. **2** shut, esp. temporarily. **3** block up. **4** (of an aperture) grow smaller. **5** coalesce. □ **closable** *adj.* **closer** *n.* [Middle English via Old French *clos-* stem of *clore* from Latin *claudere* 'shut']

close-coupled *adj.* **1** attached or fixed close together. **2** (of a lavatory unit) with the cistern and pan directly connected.

close-cropped *adj.* (esp. of hair or grass) cut very short.

closed /kləʊzd/ *adj.* **1** not giving access; shut. **2** (of a shop etc.) having ceased business temporarily. **3** (of a society, system, etc.) self-contained; not communicating with others. **4** (of a sport etc.) restricted to specified competitors etc.

closed book *n.* a subject about which one is ignorant.

closed-circuit *attrib.adj.* (of television) transmitted by wires to a restricted set of receivers.

closed-end *adj.* having a predetermined extent (cf. OPEN-ENDED).

closed-in *adj.* **1** enclosed. **2** lacking in space; restricted.

close-down *n.* **1** an act of closing down (a business etc.); a cessation of work or use. **2** *Brit.* the end of transmission of broadcasting until the next day.

closed season *N. Amer.* var. of CLOSE SEASON.

closed shop *n.* **1** a place of work etc. where all employees must belong to an agreed trade union. **2** this system.

closed syllable *n.* a syllable ending in a consonant.

close-fisted *adj.* niggardly.

close-fitting *adj.* (of a garment) fitting close to the body.

close-grained *adj.* without gaps between fibres etc.

close harmony *n.* harmony in which the notes of the chord are close together, esp. in vocal music.

close-hauled *adj.* (of a ship) with the sails hauled aft to sail close to the wind.

close-in *attrib.adj.* **1** close-range. **2** close to the centre.

close-knit *adj.* tightly bound or interlocked; closely united in friendship.

close-mouthed *adj.* reticent.

close quarters *n.pl.* (usu. in phr. **at** or **from close quarters**) a very short distance. □ **close-quarter** *attrib.adj.* (*a close-quarter glimpse*).

close-range *attrib.adj.* **1** at or from a short distance. **2** (of a weapon) designed to be fired over a short distance.

close-run *attrib.adj.* (of a race, election, etc.) closely contested; almost even in outcome.

close season *n.* (*N. Amer.* **closed season**) the season when something, esp. the killing of game etc., is illegal.

close-set *adj.* set close together; separated only by a small interval or intervals.

close shave *n. colloq.* a narrow escape.

closet /ˈklɒzɪt/ *n.* & *v.* ● *n.* **1** a small or private room. **2** a cupboard or recess. **3** *Brit.* = WATER CLOSET. **4** (*attrib.*) secret, covert (*closet homosexual*). ● *v.tr.* (**closeted**, **closeting**) shut away, esp. in private conference or study. [Middle English from Old French, diminutive of *clos*: see CLOSE[1]]

closet play *n.* (also **closet drama**) a play to be read rather than acted.

close-up *n. & adj.* ● *n.* **1** a photograph etc. taken at close range and showing the subject on a large scale. **2** an intimate description. ● *attrib.adj.*at close range.

closing time *n.* the time at which a public house, shop, etc., ends business.

clostridial /klɒˈstrɪdɪəl/ *adj.* of, relating to, or caused by rod-shaped bacteria of the genus *Clostridium*, many which cause disease (e.g. tetanus, botulism). [modern Latin genus name *Clostridium*, from Greek *klōstēr* 'spindle']

closure /ˈkləʊʒə/ *n. & v.* ● *n.* **1** the act or process of closing. **2** a closed condition. **3** something that closes or seals, e.g. a cap or tie. **4** esp. *Brit.* a procedure for ending a debate and taking a vote, esp. in a legislative assembly. ● *v.tr.* apply the closure to (a motion, speakers, etc.) in a legislative assembly. [Middle English via Old French from Late Latin *clausura*, from *claudere claus-* CLOSE[2]]

clot /klɒt/ *n. & v.* ● *n.* **1 a** a thick mass of coagulated liquid, esp. of blood. **b** a mass of material stuck together. **2** *Brit. colloq.* a silly or foolish person. ● *v.tr. & intr.* (**clotted**, **clotting**) form into clots. [Old English *clot(t)* from West Germanic: probably related to CLEAT]

cloth /klɒθ/ *n.* (*pl.* **cloths** /klɒθz, klɒðz/) **1** woven or felted material. **2** a piece of this. **3** a piece of cloth for a particular purpose; a tablecloth, dishcloth, etc. **4** woollen woven fabric as used for clothes. **5 a** profession or status, esp. of the clergy, as shown by clothes (*respect due to his cloth*). **b** (prec. by *the*) the clergy. [Old English *clāth*, of unknown origin]

cloth-cap *adj. Brit.* relating to or associated with the working class.

clothe /kləʊð/ *v.tr.* (*past* and *past part.* **clothed** or *archaic* or *literary* **clad** /klad/) **1** put clothes on; provide with clothes (see also CLAD[1]). **2** cover as with clothes or a cloth. **3** (foll. by *with*) endue (with qualities etc.). [Old English: related to CLOTH]

cloth-eared *adj. Brit. colloq.* somewhat deaf or insensitive to sound.

clothes /kləʊ(ð)z/ *n.pl.* **1** garments worn to cover the body and limbs. **2** bedclothes. [Old English *clāthas* pl. of *clāth* CLOTH]

clothes horse *n.* **1** a frame for airing washed clothes. **2** *colloq.* an affectedly fashionable person.

clothes line *n.* a rope or wire etc. on which washed clothes are hung to dry.

clothes-moth see MOTH 2.

clothes-peg *n. Brit.* a clip or forked device for securing clothes to a clothes line.

clothes-pin *n. N. Amer.* a clothes-peg.

clothier /ˈkləʊðɪə/ *n.* a seller of men's clothes. [Middle English *clother* from CLOTH]

clothing /ˈkləʊðɪŋ/ *n.* clothes collectively.

cloth of gold *n.* (also **cloth of silver**) tissue of gold (or silver) threads interwoven with silk or wool.

clotted cream *n.* esp. *Brit.* thick cream obtained by slow scalding.

cloture /ˈkləʊtjʊə/ *n. & v. US* ● *n.* = CLOSURE *n.* 4. ● *v.tr.* = CLOSURE *v.* [French *clôture* from Old French CLOSURE]

clou /kluː, French klu/ *n.* **1** the point of greatest interest; the chief attraction. **2** the central idea. [French, = nail]

cloud /klaʊd/ *n. & v.* ● *n.* **1** a visible mass of condensed watery vapour floating in the atmosphere high above the general level of the ground. **2** a mass of smoke or dust. **3** (foll. by *of*) a great number of insects, birds, etc., moving together. **4 a** a state of gloom, trouble, or suspicion. **b** a frowning or depressed look (*a cloud on his brow*). **5** a local dimness or a vague patch of colour in or on a liquid or a transparent body. **6** an unsubstantial or fleeting thing. **7** obscurity. ● *v.* **1** *tr.* cover or darken with clouds or gloom or trouble. **2** *intr.* (often foll. by *over*, *up*) become overcast or gloomy. **3** *tr.* make unclear. **4** *tr.* variegate with vague patches of colour. □ **in the clouds 1** unreal, imaginary, mystical. **2** (of a person) abstracted, inattentive. **on cloud nine** (or *archaic* **seven**) *colloq.* extremely happy. **under a cloud** out of favour, discredited, under suspicion. **with one's head in the clouds** daydreaming, unrealistic. □ **cloudless** *adj.* **cloudlessly** *adv.* **cloudlet** *n.* [Old English *clūd* 'mass of rock or earth', probably related to CLOD]

cloud base *n.* the mass of cloud that is lowest in altitude.

cloudberry /ˈklaʊdbɛri, -b(ə)ri/ *n.* (*pl.* **-ies**) a small mountain bramble, *Rubus chamaemorus*, with a white flower and an orange-coloured fruit.

cloudburst /ˈklaʊdbəːst/ *n.* a sudden violent rainstorm.

cloud-castle *n. Brit.* a daydream.

cloud chamber *n.* a device containing vapour for tracking the paths of charged particles, X-rays, and gamma rays.

cloud cover *n.* **1** a canopy of clouds. **2** the extent of this canopy.

cloud-cuckoo-land *n.* a fanciful or ideal place. [translation of Greek *Nephelokokkugia*, from *nephelē* 'cloud' + *kokkux* 'cuckoo' (in Aristophanes' *Birds*)]

clouded leopard *n.* a large spotted arboreal cat, *Neofelis nebulosa*, of SE Asia.

cloud-hopping *n.* movement of an aircraft from cloud to cloud, esp. for concealment.

cloud-land *n.* a utopia or fairyland.

cloudscape /ˈklaʊdskeɪp/ *n.* **1** a picturesque grouping of clouds. **2** a picture or view of clouds. [CLOUD *n.*, on the pattern of *landscape*]

cloudy /ˈklaʊdi/ *adj.* (**cloudier**, **cloudiest**) **1 a** (of the sky) covered with clouds, overcast. **b** (of weather) characterized by clouds. **2** not transparent; unclear. □ **cloudily** *adv.* **cloudiness** *n.*

clough /klʌf/ *n. dial.* a steep valley usu. with a torrent bed; a ravine. [Old English *clōh*, from Germanic]

clout /klaʊt/ *n. & v.* ● *n.* **1** a heavy blow. **2** *colloq.* influence, power of effective action, esp. in politics or business. **3** *dial.* a piece of cloth or clothing (*cast not a clout*). **4** *Archery hist.* a piece of canvas on a frame, used as a mark. **5** a nail with a large flat head. **6** a patch. ● *v.tr.* **1** hit hard. **2** mend with a patch. [Old English *clūt*, related to CLEAT, CLOT]

clove[1] /kləʊv/ *n.* **1 a** a dried flower bud of a tropical plant, *Eugenia aromatica*, used as a pungent aromatic spice. **b** this plant. **2** (in full **clove gillyflower** or **clove pink**) a clove-scented pink, *Dianthus caryophyllus*, the original of the carnation and other double pinks. [Middle English from Old French *clou* (*de girofle*) 'nail (of gillyflower)', from its shape, GILLYFLOWER being originally the name of the spice; later applied to the similarly scented pink]

clove[2] /kləʊv/ *n.* any of the small bulbs making up a compound bulb of garlic, shallot, etc. [Old English *clufu*, related to CLEAVE[1]]

clove[3] *past* of CLEAVE[1].

clove hitch *n.* a knot by which a rope is secured by passing it twice round a spar or rope that it crosses at right angles. [old past part. of CLEAVE[1], as showing parallel separate lines]

cloven /ˈkləʊv(ə)n/ *adj.* split, partly divided. [past part. of CLEAVE[1]]

cloven hoof *n.* (also **cloven foot**) the divided hoof of ruminant quadrupeds (e.g. oxen, sheep, goats); also ascribed to the god Pan, and so to the Devil. □ **show the cloven hoof** reveal one's evil nature. □ **cloven-footed** /-ˈfʊtɪd/ *adj.* **cloven-hoofed** /-ˈhuːft/ *adj.*

clove pink see CLOVE[1] 2.

clover /ˈkləʊvə/ *n.* any leguminous fodder plant of the genus *Trifolium*, having dense flower heads and leaves each consisting of usu. three leaflets. □ **in clover** in ease and luxury. [Old English *clāfre*, from Germanic]

cloverleaf /ˈkləʊvəliːf/ *n.* a junction of roads intersecting at different levels with connecting sections forming the pattern of a four-leaved clover.

clown /klaʊn/ *n. & v.* ● *n.* **1** a comic entertainer, esp. in a pantomime or circus, usu. with traditional costume and make-up. **2** a silly, foolish, or playful person. **3** *archaic* a rustic. ● *v.* **1** *intr.* (often foll. by *about*, *around*) behave like a clown; act foolishly or playfully. **2** *tr.* perform (a part, an action, etc.) like a clown. □ **clownery** *n.* **clownish** *adj.* **clownishly** *adv.* **clownishness** *n.* [16th c.: perhaps of Low German origin]

cloy /klɔɪ/ *v.tr.* (usu. foll. by *with*) satiate or sicken with an excess of sweetness, richness, etc. □ **cloyingly** *adv.* [Middle English from obsolete *accloy*, via Anglo-French *acloyer*, Old French *encloyer* from Romanic]

cloze /kləʊz/ *n.* the exercise of supplying a word that has been omitted from a passage as a test of readability or comprehension (usu. *attrib.*: *cloze test*). [CLOSURE]

club /klʌb/ *n. & v.* ● *n.* **1** a heavy stick with a thick end, used as a weapon etc. **2** a stick used in a game, esp. a stick with a head used in golf. **3 a** a playing card of a suit denoted by a black trefoil. **b** (in *pl.*) this suit. **4** an association of persons united by a common interest, usu. meeting periodically for a shared activity (*tennis club*; *yacht club*). **5** an organization or premises offering members social amenities, meals and temporary residence, etc. **6** a commercial organization offering subscribers special deals (*book club*). **7** a group of persons, nations, etc., having something in common. **8** = CLUBHOUSE. **9** a structure or organ, esp. in a plant, with a knob at the end. ● *v.* (**clubbed**, **clubbing**) **1** *tr.* beat with or as with a club. **2** *intr.* (foll. by *together*) combine with others for joint action, esp. making up a sum of money for a purpose. **3** *tr.* contribute (money etc.) to a common stock. **4** *intr. colloq.* go out to nightclubs (*went clubbing every weekend*). □ **in the club** *Brit. slang* pregnant. □ **clubber** *n.* [Middle English from Old Norse *klubba*, assimilated form of *klumba* 'club', related to CLUMP]

clubbable /ˈklʌbəb(ə)l/ *adj.* sociable; fit for membership of a club. □ **clubbability** /-ˈbɪlɪti/ *n.* **clubbableness** *n.*

clubby /ˈklʌbi/ *adj.* (**clubbier**, **clubbiest**) esp. *US* sociable; friendly.

club car *n. N. Amer.* a railway carriage equipped with a lounge and other amenities.

club class *n. Brit.* a class of fare on aircraft etc. designed for the business traveller.

club foot *n.* a congenitally deformed foot. □ **club-footed** *adj.*

clubhouse /ˈklʌbhaʊs/ *n.* the premises used by a club.

clubland /ˈklʌbland/ *n. Brit.* an area where many clubs are, esp. St James's in London.

clubman /ˈklʌbmən/ *n.* (*pl.* **-men**) a member of one or more clubs (see CLUB *n.* 5).

clubmate /ˈklʌbmeɪt/ *n.* a fellow member of a sports club.

clubmoss /ˈklʌbmɒs/ *n.* a usu. small creeping plant of the pteridophyte family Lycopodiaceae, bearing upright spikes of spore cases.

clubroot /ˈklʌbruːt/ *n.* a disease of cabbages etc. with swelling at the base of the stem.

club sandwich *n.* a sandwich of meat (esp. chicken and bacon), tomato, lettuce, and dressing, usu. with two layers of filling between three slices of toast or bread.

club soda *n. N. Amer.* = SODA 2.

cluck /klʌk/ *n. & v.* ● *n.* **1** a guttural cry like that of a hen. **2** *slang* a silly or foolish person (*dumb cluck*). ● *v.intr.* emit a cluck or clucks. [imitative]

clucky /ˈklʌki/ *adj.* (of a hen) sitting on eggs.

clue /kluː/ *n. & v.* ● *n.* **1** a fact or idea that serves as a guide, or suggests a line of enquiry, in a problem or investigation. **2** a piece of evidence etc. in the detection of a crime. **3** a verbal formula serving as a hint as to what is to be inserted in a crossword. **4 a** the thread of a story. **b** a train of thought. ● *v.tr.* (**clues**, **clued**, **cluing** or **clueing**) provide a clue to. □ **clue in** (or *Brit.* **up**) *slang* inform. **not have a clue** *colloq.* be ignorant or incompetent. [variant of CLEW]

clued-up *adj.* well informed, intelligent.

clueless /ˈkluːlɪs/ *adj. colloq.* ignorant, stupid. □ **cluelessly** *adv.* **cluelessness** *n.*

clump /klʌmp/ *n. & v.* ● *n.* **1** (foll. by *of*) a cluster of plants, esp. trees or shrubs. **2** an agglutinated mass of blood cells etc. **3** a thick extra sole on a boot or shoe. ● *v.* **1 a** *intr.* form a clump. **b** *tr.* heap or plant together. **2** *intr.* (also **clomp** /klɒmp/) walk with heavy tread. **3** *tr. colloq.* hit. □ **clumpy** *adj.* (**clumpier**, **clumpiest**). [Middle Low German *klumpe*, Middle Dutch *klompe*, related to CLUB]

clumsy /ˈklʌmzi/ *adj.* (**clumsier**, **clumsiest**) **1** awkward in movement or shape; ungainly. **2** difficult to handle or use. **3** tactless. □ **clumsily** *adv.* **clumsiness** *n.* [obsolete *clumse* 'be numb with cold' (probably from Scandinavian)]

clung *past* and *past part.* of CLING.

clunk /klʌŋk/ *n. & v.* ● *n.* a dull sound as of thick pieces of metal meeting. ● *v.intr.* make such a sound. [imitative]

clunker /ˈklʌŋkə/ *n. N. Amer. colloq.* **1** a dilapidated vehicle or machine. **2** a failure, a flop.

clunky /ˈklʌŋki/ *adj.* (**clunkier**, **clunkiest**) *colloq.* **1** making a clunking sound. **2** *N. Amer.* awkward, clumsy.

cluster /ˈklʌstə/ *n. & v.* ● *n.* **1** a close group or bunch of similar things growing together. **2** a close group or swarm of people, animals, faint stars, gems, etc. **3** a group of successive consonants or vowels. ● *v.* **1** *tr.* bring into a cluster or clusters. **2** *intr.* be or come into a cluster or clusters. **3** *intr.* (foll. by *round*, *around*) gather, congregate. [Old English *clyster*]

cluster bomb *n.* an anti-personnel bomb spraying pellets on impact.

clustered /ˈklʌstəd/ *adj.* **1** growing in or brought into a cluster. **2** *Archit.* (of pillars, columns, or shafts) several close together, or disposed round or half-detached from a pier.

cluster fly *n.* a dipterous fly, *Pollenia rudis*, with larvae parasitic on earthworms, which gathers around buildings in autumn.

cluster pine *n.* a Mediterranean pine, *Pinus pinaster*, with clustered cones. Also called *pinaster*.

clutch[1] /klʌtʃ/ *v. & n.* ● *v.* **1** *tr.* seize eagerly; grasp tightly. **2** *intr.* (foll. by *at*) try, esp. desperately, to seize or grasp. ● *n.* **1 a** a tight grasp. **b** (foll. by *at*) an act of grasping. **2** (in *pl.*) grasping hands, esp. as representing a cruel or relentless grasp or control. **3 a** (in a motor vehicle) a device for connecting and disconnecting the engine and the transmission. **b** the pedal operating this. **c** an arrangement for connecting or disconnecting working parts of a machine. [Middle English *clucche*, *clicche* via Old English *clyccan* 'crook, clench' from Germanic]

clutch[2] /klʌtʃ/ *n.* **1** a set of eggs for hatching. **2** a brood of chickens. [18th c.: probably southern English variant of *cletch*, from *cleck* 'to hatch' from Old Norse *klekja*, associated with CLUTCH[1]]

clutch bag *n.* a slim flat handbag without handles.

clutter /ˈklʌtə/ *n. & v.* ● *n.* **1** a crowded and untidy collection of things. **2** an untidy state. ● *v.tr.* (often foll. by *up*, *with*) crowd untidily, fill with clutter. [partly a variant of *clotter* 'coagulate', partly associated with CLUSTER, CLATTER]

Clydesdale /ˈklʌɪdzdeɪl/ *n.* **1 a** a horse of a heavy powerful breed, used as draught horses. **b** this breed. **2** a kind of small terrier. [originally bred near the river *Clyde* in Scotland: see DALE]

clypeus /ˈklɪpɪəs/ *n.* (*pl.* **clypei** /-pɪʌɪ/) a broad plate at the front of an insect's head. □ **clypeal** *adj.* **clypeate** *adj.* [Latin, = round shield]

clyster /ˈklɪstə/ *n. & v. archaic* ● *n.* an enema. ● *v.tr.* treat with an enema. [Middle English via Old French *clystere* or Latin *clyster* from Greek *klustēr* 'syringe', from *kluzō* 'wash out']

CM *abbr.* Member of the Order of Canada.

Cm *symb. Chem.* the element curium.
Cm. *abbr. Brit.* Command Paper (sixth series, 1986–).
cm *abbr.* centimetre(s).
Cmd. *abbr. Brit.* Command Paper (fourth series, 1918–56).
Cmdr. *abbr.* Commander.
Cmdre. *abbr.* Commodore.
CMG *abbr.* (in the UK) Companion (of the Order) of St Michael and St George.
Cmnd. *abbr. Brit.* Command Paper (fifth series, 1956–86).
CNAA *abbr.* (in the UK) Council for National Academic Awards.
CND *abbr.* (in the UK) Campaign for Nuclear Disarmament.
cnr. *abbr.* corner.
CNS *abbr.* central nervous system.
CO *abbr.* **1** Commanding Officer. **2** conscientious objector. **3** *US* Colorado (in official postal use).
Co *symb. Chem.* the element cobalt.
Co. *abbr.* **1** company. **2** county. □ **and Co.** /kəʊ/ *colloq.* and the rest of them; and similar things.
co- /kəʊ/ *prefix* **1** added to: **a** nouns, with the sense 'joint, mutual, common' (*co-author*; *co-equality*). **b** adjectives and adverbs, with the sense 'jointly, mutually' (*co-belligerent*; *co-equal*; *co-equally*). **c** verbs, with the sense 'together with another or others' (*cooperate*; *co-author*). **2** *Math.* **a** of the complement of an angle (*cosine*). **b** the complement of (*co-latitude*; *coset*). [originally a form of COM-]
c/o *abbr.* care of.
coach /kəʊtʃ/ *n.* & *v.* ● *n.* **1** esp. *Brit.* a single-decker bus, usu. comfortably equipped for longer journeys. **2** a railway carriage. **3** a horse-drawn carriage, usu. closed, esp. a State carriage or a stagecoach. **4 a** an instructor or trainer in sport. **b** a private tutor. **5** *N. Amer.* economy class seating in an aircraft. **6** *Austral.* a docile cow or bullock used as a decoy to attract wild cattle. ● *v.* **1** *tr.* **a** train or teach (a pupil, sports team, etc.) as a coach. **b** give hints to; prime with facts. **2** *intr.* travel by stagecoach (*in the old coaching days*). [French *coche* from Hungarian *kocsi* (*szeker*) '(wagon from) *Kocs*', a town in Hungary]
coach-built *adj. Brit.* (of motor car bodies) individually built by craftsmen. □ **coachbuilder** *n.*
coach house *n.* an outhouse for carriages.
coachload /ˈkəʊtʃləʊd/ *n.* a number of people, esp. holidaymakers, taken by coach.
coachman /ˈkəʊtʃmən/ *n.* (*pl.* **-men**) the driver of a horse-drawn carriage.
coach station *n.* a stopping place for a number of coaches, usu. with buildings and amenities.
coachwood /ˈkəʊtʃwʊd/ *n. Austral.* any tree, esp. *Ceratopetalum apetalum*, with close-grained wood suitable for cabinetmaking.
coachwork /ˈkəʊtʃwɜːk/ *n.* the bodywork of a road or rail vehicle.
coadjutor /kəʊˈadʒʊtə/ *n.* an assistant, esp. an assistant bishop. [Middle English via Old French *coadjuteur* from Late Latin *coadjutor* (as co-, *adjutor* from *adjuvare -jut-* 'help')]
coagulant /kəʊˈagjʊlənt/ *n.* a substance that produces coagulation.
coagulate /kəʊˈagjʊleɪt/ *v.tr.* & *intr.* **1** change from a fluid to a solid or semi-solid state. **2** clot, curdle. **3** set, solidify. □ **coagulable** *adj.* **coagulative** /-lətɪv/ *adj.* **coagulator** *n.* [Middle English from Latin *coagulare*, from *coagulum* 'rennet']
coagulation /kəʊagjʊˈleɪʃ(ə)n/ *n.* the process by which a liquid changes to a semi-solid mass. [as COAGULATE]
coagulum /kəʊˈagjʊləm/ *n.* (*pl.* **coagula** /-lə/) a mass of coagulated matter. [Latin: see COAGULATE]
coal /kəʊl/ *n.* & *v.* ● *n.* **1 a** a hard black or blackish rock, mainly carbonized plant matter, found in underground seams and used as a fuel and in the manufacture of gas, tar, etc. **b** *Brit.* a piece of this for burning. **2** a red-hot piece of coal, wood, etc. in a fire. ● *v.* **1** *intr.* take in a supply of coal. **2** *tr.* put coal into (an engine, fire, etc.). □ **coals to Newcastle** something brought or sent to a place where it is already plentiful. **haul** (or **call**) **over the coals** reprimand. □ **coaly** *adj.* [Old English *col*, from Germanic]
coal black *n.* & *adj.* ● *n.* a completely black colour. ● *adj.* (hyphenated when *attrib.*) of this colour.
coal dust *n.* powdered coal.
coaler /ˈkəʊlə/ *n.* a ship etc. transporting coal.
coalesce /kəʊəˈlɛs/ *v.intr.* **1** come together and form one whole. **2** combine in a coalition. □ **coalescence** *n.* **coalescent** *adj.* [Latin *coalescere* (as co-, *alescere alit-* 'grow' from *alere* 'nourish')]
coalface /ˈkəʊlfeɪs/ *n.* an exposed surface of coal in a mine.
coalfield /ˈkəʊlfiːld/ *n.* an extensive area with strata containing coal.
coal-fired *adj.* heated or driven by coal.
coalfish /ˈkəʊlfɪʃ/ *n.* (*pl.* usu. same) = SAITHE.
coal gas *n.* mixed gases extracted from coal and used for lighting and heating.
coal-hole *n. Brit.* a compartment or small cellar for storing coal.
coalhouse /ˈkəʊlhaʊs/ *n.* a building for storing coal.
coalition /kəʊəˈlɪʃ(ə)n/ *n.* **1** *Polit.* a temporary alliance for combined action, esp. of distinct parties forming a government, or of states. **2** fusion into one whole. □ **coalitionist** *n.* [medieval Latin *coalitio* (as COALESCE)]
coalman /ˈkəʊlmən/ *n.* (*pl.* **-men**) a man who carries or delivers coal.
coal measures *n.pl.* a series of rocks formed by seams of coal with intervening strata.
coal mine *n.* a mine in which coal is dug. □ **coal miner** *n.* **coal mining** *n.* (often *attrib.*).
coalmouse /ˈkəʊlmaʊs/ *n.* (also **colemouse**) (*pl.* **-mice**) = COAL TIT. [Old English *colmāse*, from *col* COAL + *māse* as TITMOUSE]
coal-sack *n.* **1** a sack for carrying coal. **2** a dark nebula in the Milky Way, esp. one near the Southern Cross.
coal scuttle *n.* a container for coal to supply a domestic fire.
coal-seam *n.* a stratum of coal suitable for mining.
coal tar *n.* a thick black oily liquid distilled from coal and used as a source of hydrocarbons.
coal tit *n.* (also **cole tit**) a small greyish bird, *Parus ater*, with a black head. Also called *coalmouse*.
coaming /ˈkəʊmɪŋ/ *n.* a raised border round the hatches etc. of a ship to keep out water. [17th c.: origin unknown]
coarctate /kəʊˈɑːkteɪt/ *adj.* **1** esp. *Anat.* & *Biol.* pressed close together, compressed. **2** *Zool.* (of an insect pupa) concealed by the larval cuticle. [Latin *coar(c)tatus* from *coar(c)tare* from co- + *artus* 'confined']
coarctation /kəʊɑːkˈteɪʃ(ə)n/ *n.* **1** compression. **2** *Med.* congenital narrowing of the aorta.
coarse /kɔːs/ *adj.* **1 a** rough or loose in texture or grain; made of large particles. **b** (of a person's features) rough or large. **2** lacking refinement or delicacy; crude, obscene (*coarse humour*). **3** rude, uncivil. **4** inferior, common. □ **coarsely** *adv.* **coarseness** *n.* **coarsish** *adj.* [Middle English: origin unknown]
coarse fish *n. Brit.* any freshwater fish other than salmon and trout. □ **coarse fishing** *n.*
coarsen /ˈkɔːs(ə)n/ *v.tr.* & *intr.* make or become coarse.
coast /kəʊst/ *n.* & *v.* ● *n.* **1 a** the border of the land near the sea; the seashore. **b** (**the Coast**) *N. Amer.* the Pacific coast of N. America. **2 a** a run, usu. downhill, on a bicycle without pedalling or in a motor vehicle without using the engine. **b** *N. Amer.* a toboggan slide or slope. ● *v.intr.* **1** ride or move, usu. downhill, without use of power, freewheel. **2** make progress without much effort. **3** *N. Amer.* slide down a hill on a toboggan. **4 a** sail along the coast. **b** trade between ports on the same coast. □ **the coast is clear** there is no danger of being observed or caught. □ **coastal** *adj.* [Middle English via

Old French *coste, costeier* from Latin *costa* 'rib, flank, side']

coaster /ˈkəʊstə/ *n.* **1** a ship that travels along the coast from port to port. **2** a small tray or mat for a bottle or glass. **3** *N. Amer.* **a** a toboggan for coasting. **b** a roller coaster.

coastguard /ˈkəʊs(t)ɡɑːd/ *n.* **1** an organization keeping watch on the coasts and on local shipping to save life, prevent smuggling, etc. **2** a member of this.

coastland /ˈkəʊs(t)lənd, -land/ *n.* (usu. in *pl.*) an expanse of land near the sea.

coastline /ˈkəʊs(t)lʌɪn/ *n.* the line of the seashore, esp. with regard to its shape (*a rugged coastline*).

coast to coast *adj. & adv.* (usu. hyphenated when *attrib.*) across an island or continent.

coastwise /ˈkəʊstwʌɪz/ *adj. & adv.* along, following, or connected with the coast.

coat /kəʊt/ *n. & v.* ● *n.* **1** an outer garment with sleeves and often extending below the hips; an overcoat or jacket. **2** **a** an animal's fur, hair, etc. **b** *Physiol.* a structure, esp. a membrane, enclosing or lining an organ. **c** a skin, rind, or husk. **d** a layer of a bulb etc. **3** **a** a layer or covering. **b** a covering of paint etc. laid on a surface at one time. ● *v.tr.* **1** (usu. foll. by *with, in*) **a** apply a coat of paint etc. to; provide with a layer or covering. **b** (as **coated** *adj.*) covered with. **2** (of paint etc.) form a covering to. □ **on a person's coat-tails** undeservedly benefiting from another's success. □ **coated** *adj.* (also in *comb.*). [Middle English via Old French *cote* and Romanic from Frankish, of unknown origin]

coat armour *n.* coats of arms.

coat check *n. N. Amer.* a cloakroom with an attendant.

coat checker *n. N. Amer.* a cloakroom attendant.

coat dress *n.* a woman's tailored dress resembling a coat.

coatee /kəʊˈtiː/ *n. Brit.* **1** a woman's or infant's short coat. **2** *archaic* a close-fitting short coat.

coat-hanger see HANGER[1] 2.

coati /kəʊˈɑːti/ *n.* (*pl.* **coatis**) a raccoon-like flesh-eating mammal of Central and S. America, of the genus *Nasua* or *Nasuella*, with a long flexible snout and a long usu. ringed tail. [Tupi, from *cua* 'belt' + *tim* 'nose']

coatimundi /kəʊˌɑːtɪˈmʌndi/ *n.* (*pl.* **coatimundis**) = COATI. [as COATI + Tupi *mondi* 'solitary']

coating /ˈkəʊtɪŋ/ *n.* **1** a thin layer or covering of paint etc. **2** material for making coats.

coat of arms *n.* the heraldic bearings or shield of a person, family, or corporation.

coat of mail *n. hist.* a jacket covered with mail or composed of mail.

coatroom /ˈkəʊtruːm, -rʊm/ *n. N. Amer.* = CLOAKROOM 1.

coat-stand *n.* a stand with hooks on which to hang coats, hats, etc.

coat-tail *n.* each of the flaps formed by the back of a tailcoat.

co-author /kəʊˈɔːθə/ *n. & v.* ● *n.* a joint author. ● *v.tr.* be a joint author of.

■ **Usage** See Usage Note at AUTHOR.

coax[1] /kəʊks/ *v.tr.* **1** (usu. foll. by *into*, or *to* + infin.) persuade (a person) gradually or by flattery. **2** (foll. by *out of*) obtain (a thing from a person) by coaxing. **3** manipulate (a thing) carefully or slowly. □ **coaxer** *n.* **coaxingly** *adv.* [16th c.: from 'make a *cokes* of' (obsolete *cokes* 'simpleton'), of unknown origin]

coax[2] /ˈkəʊaks/ *n. colloq.* coaxial cable. [abbreviation]

coaxial /kəʊˈaksɪəl/ *adj.* **1** having a common axis. **2** *Electr.* (of a cable or line) transmitting by means of two concentric conductors separated by an insulator. □ **coaxially** *adv.*

cob[1] /kɒb/ *n.* **1** a roundish lump of coal etc. **2** *Brit.* a domed loaf of bread. **3** = CORN COB. **4** (in full **cobnut**) a large hazelnut. **5** a sturdy short-legged horse for riding. **6** a male swan. [Middle English: origin unknown]

cob[2] /kɒb/ *n. Brit.* a material for walls, made from compressed earth, clay, or chalk reinforced with straw. [17th c.: origin unknown]

cobalt /ˈkəʊbɔːlt, -ɒlt/ *n. & adj.* ● *n. Chem.* a silvery-white magnetic metallic element occurring naturally as a mineral in copper and nickel ores and used in many alloys (symbol **Co**). ● *n. & adj.* = COBALT BLUE. □ **cobaltic** /kə(ʊ)ˈbɔːltɪk, -ˈbɒlt-/ *adj.* **cobaltous** /kə(ʊ)ˈbɔːltəs, -ˈbɒlt-/ *adj.* [German *Kobalt* = KOBOLD in mines from the belief that cobalt was harmful to the ores with which it occurred]

cobalt blue *n. & adj.* ● *n.* **1** a pigment containing a cobalt salt. **2** the deep blue colour of this. ● *adj.* (hyphenated when *attrib.*) of this colour.

cobber /ˈkɒbə/ *n. Austral. & NZ colloq.* a companion or friend. [19th c.: perhaps related to English dialect *cob* 'take a liking to']

cobble[1] /ˈkɒb(ə)l/ *n. & v.* ● *n.* **1** (in full **cobblestone**) a small rounded stone of a size used for paving. **2** (in *pl.*) *Brit.* coal in lumps of this size. ● *v.tr.* pave with cobbles. [Middle English *cobel(-ston)*, from COB[1]]

cobble[2] /ˈkɒb(ə)l/ *v.tr.* **1** mend or patch up (esp. shoes). **2** (often foll. by *together*) join or assemble roughly. [back-formation from COBBLER]

cobbler /ˈkɒblə/ *n.* **1** a person who mends shoes, esp. professionally. **2** an iced drink of wine etc., sugar, and lemon (*sherry cobbler*). **3** **a** a pie topped with scones. **b** esp. *US* a fruit pie with a rich thick crust. **4** (in *pl.*) *Brit. slang* nonsense. **5** *Austral. & NZ slang* the last sheep to be shorn. [Middle English, of unknown origin: sense 4 from rhyming slang *cobbler's awls* = *balls*: sense 5 with pun on LAST[3]]

cobblestone see COBBLE[1] *n.* 1.

co-belligerent /kəʊbɪˈlɪdʒ(ə)r(ə)nt/ *n. & adj.* ● *n.* any of two or more nations engaged in war as allies. ● *adj.* of or as a co-belligerent. □ **co-belligerence** *n.* **co-belligerency** *n.*

coble /ˈkəʊb(ə)l/ *n.* a flat-bottomed fishing boat in Scotland and NE England. [Old English, perhaps from Celtic]

cobnut see COB[1] 4.

COBOL /ˈkəʊbɒl/ *n. Computing* a programming language designed for use in commerce. [*co*mmon *b*usiness *o*riented *l*anguage]

cobra /ˈkəʊbrə, ˈkɒbrə/ *n.* any venomous snake of the genus *Naja*, native to Africa and Asia, able to dilate its neck like a hood when excited. [Portuguese, from Latin *colubra* 'snake']

cobweb /ˈkɒbwɛb/ *n.* **1** **a** a fine network of threads spun by a spider from a liquid extruded from its spinnerets, used to trap insects etc. **b** the thread of this. **2** anything compared with a cobweb, esp. in flimsiness of texture. **3** a trap or insidious entanglement. **4** (in *pl.*) (esp. in phr. **blow** or **clear away the cobwebs**) a state of lethargy; fustiness. □ **cobwebbed** *adj.* **cobwebby** *adj.* [Middle English *cop(pe)web* from obsolete *coppe* 'spider']

coca /ˈkəʊkə/ *n.* **1** a S. American shrub, *Erythroxylum coca*. **2** its dried leaves, chewed as a stimulant. [Spanish, from Aymara *kuka* or Quechua *koka*]

Coca-Cola /kəʊkəˈkəʊlə/ *n. propr.* a carbonated non-alcoholic drink. [COCA + COLA]

cocaine /kə(ʊ)ˈkeɪn/ *n.* a drug derived from coca or prepared synthetically, used as a local anaesthetic and as a stimulant. [COCA + -INE[4]]

coccidiosis /kɒkˌsɪdɪˈəʊsɪs/ *n.* a disease of birds and mammals caused by any of various parasitic protozoa, esp. of the genus *Eimeria*, affecting the intestine. [*coccidium* (modern Latin from Greek *kokkis*, diminutive of *kokkos* 'berry') + -OSIS]

coccus /ˈkɒkəs/ *n.* (*pl.* **cocci** /ˈkɒk(s)ʌɪ, ˈkɒk(s)iː/) any spherical or roughly spherical bacterium. □ **coccal** *adj.* **coccoid** *adj.* [modern Latin from Greek *kokkos* 'berry']

coccyx /ˈkɒksɪks/ *n.* (*pl.* **coccyges** /-ɪdʒiːz/ or **coccyxes**) the small triangular bone at the base of the spinal column in humans and some apes. □ **coccygeal** /kɒkˈsɪdʒɪəl/ *adj.* [Latin from Greek *kokkux -ugos* 'cuckoo' (from its shape, which resembles the cuckoo's bill)]

Cochin /'kɒtʃɪn/ *n.* (in full **Cochin China** /'tʃʌɪnə/) **1** a fowl of an Asian breed with feathery legs. **2** this breed. [*Cochin China* in Vietnam, where the breed originated]

cochineal /'kɒtʃɪniːl/ *n.* **1** a scarlet dye used esp. for colouring food. **2** the dried bodies of the female of the Mexican insect, *Dactylopius coccus*, yielding this. [French *cochenille* or Spanish *cochinilla* from Latin *coccinus* 'scarlet', from Greek *kokkos* 'berry']

cochlea /'kɒklɪə/ *n.* (*pl.* **cochleae** /-klɪiː/) the spiral cavity of the internal ear, in which sound vibrations are converted into nervous impulses. ▫ **cochlear** *adj.* [Latin, = snail shell, from Greek *kokhlias*]

cock[1] /kɒk/ *n.* & *v.* ● *n.* **1 a** a male bird, esp. of a domestic fowl. **b** *Brit.* a male lobster, crab, or salmon. **c** = WOODCOCK. **2** *Brit. slang* (usu. **old cock** as a form of address) a friend; a fellow. **3** *coarse slang* the penis. **4** *Brit. slang* nonsense. **5 a** a firing lever in a gun which can be raised to be released by the trigger. **b** the cocked position of this (*at full cock*). **6** a tap or valve controlling flow. ● *v.tr.* **1** raise or make upright or erect. **2** turn or move (the eye or ear) attentively or knowingly. **3** set aslant, or turn up the brim of (a hat). **4** raise the cock of (a gun). ▫ **at half cock** only partly ready. **cock a snook** see SNOOK[1]. **cock up** *Brit. slang* bungle; make a mess of. [Old English *cocc* and Old French *coq*, probably from medieval Latin *coccus*]

cock[2] /kɒk/ *n.* & *v.* ● *n.* a small pile of hay, straw, etc. with vertical sides and a rounded top. ● *v.tr.* pile into cocks. [Middle English, perhaps of Scandinavian origin]

cockabully /'kɒkəbʊli/ *n.* *NZ* any of various small blunt-nosed freshwater fishes, esp. of the genus *Gobiomorphus*. [Maori *kokopu*]

cockade /kɒ'keɪd/ *n.* a rosette etc. worn in a hat as a badge of office or party, or as part of a livery. ▫ **cockaded** *adj.* [French *cocarde* originally in *bonnet à la coquarde*, from fem. of obsolete *coquard* 'saucy' from *coq* COCK[1]]

cock-a-doodle-doo /ˌkɒkəduːd(ə)l'duː/ *n.* a cock's crow.

cock-a-hoop *adj.* & *adv.* ● *adj.* exultant; crowing boastfully. ● *adv.* exultantly. [16th c.: originally in the phrase *set cock a hoop* denoting some action preliminary to hard drinking]

cock-a-leekie /kɒkə'liːki/ *n.* (also **cocky-leeky** /kɒkɪ-/) a soup traditionally made in Scotland with boiling fowl and leeks. [COCK[1] + LEEK]

cockalorum /kɒkə'lɔːrəm/ *n.* *colloq.* a self-important little man. [18th c.: arbitrary formation from COCK[1]]

cock and bull story *n.* an absurd or incredible account.

cockatiel /kɒkə'tiːl/ *n.* (also **cockateel**) *Austral.* a small delicately coloured crested parrot, *Nymphicus hollandicus*. [Dutch *kaketielje*]

cockatoo /kɒkə'tuː/ *n.* **1** an Australasian parrot of the family Cacatuidae, with a powerful beak and an erectile crest. **2** *Austral.* & *NZ colloq.* a small farmer. [Dutch *kaketoe* from Malay *kakatua*, assimilated to COCK[1]]

cockatrice /'kɒkətrʌɪs, -trɪs/ *n.* **1** = BASILISK 1. **2** *Heraldry* a fabulous animal, a cock with a serpent's tail. [Middle English via Old French *cocatris* from Latin *calcare* 'tread, track', rendering Greek *ikhneumōn* 'tracker': see ICHNEUMON]

cockboat /'kɒkbəʊt/ *n.* a small ship's boat. [obsolete *cock* 'small boat' (from Old French *coque*) + BOAT]

cockchafer /'kɒktʃeɪfə/ *n.* a large nocturnal beetle, *Melolontha melolontha*, which feeds on leaves and whose larva feeds on roots of crops etc. Also called *May-bug*. [perhaps from COCK[1] (as expressing size or vigour) + CHAFER]

cockcrow /'kɒkkrəʊ/ *n.* dawn.

cocked hat *n.* **1** a brimless triangular hat pointed at the front, back, and top. **2** *hist.* a hat with a wide brim permanently turned up towards the crown (e.g. a tricorne). ▫ **knock into a cocked hat** defeat utterly.

cocker /'kɒkə/ *n.* (in full **cocker spaniel**) **1** a small spaniel of a breed with a silky coat. **2** this breed. [as COCK[1], from the breed's use in hunting woodcocks etc.]

cockerel /'kɒk(ə)r(ə)l/ *n.* a young cock. [Middle English: diminutive of COCK[1]]

cock-eyed /kɒ'kʌɪd/ *adj.* *colloq.* **1** crooked, askew, not level. **2** (of a scheme etc.) absurd, not practical. **3** drunk. **4** squinting. [19th c.: apparently from COCK[1] + EYE]

cockfight /'kɒkfʌɪt/ *n.* a fight between cocks as sport. ▫ **cockfighting** *n.*

cockle[1] /'kɒk(ə)l/ *n.* **1 a** any edible bivalve mollusc of the genus *Cardium*, having a chubby ribbed shell. **b** its shell. **2** (in full **cockleshell**) a small shallow boat. ▫ **warm the cockles of one's heart** make one contented; be satisfying. [Middle English from Old French *coquille* 'shell', ultimately from Greek *kogkhulion*, from *kogkhē* CONCH]

cockle[2] /'kɒk(ə)l/ *n.* **1** (in full **corncockle**) a pink-flowered plant, *Agrostemma githago* (pink family), formerly common in cornfields. **2** a disease of wheat that turns the grains black. [Old English *coccul*, perhaps ultimately from Late Latin *coccus*]

cockle[3] /'kɒk(ə)l/ *v.* & *n.* ● *v.* **1** *intr.* pucker, wrinkle. **2** *tr.* cause to cockle. ● *n.* a pucker or wrinkle in paper, glass, etc. [French *coquiller* 'blister (bread in cooking)' from *coquille*: see COCKLE[1]]

cocklebur /'kɒk(ə)lbəː/ *n.* a weed of the genus *Xanthium* (daisy family) with fruit covered in hooked bristles. [COCKLE[2] + BUR]

cockleshell see COCKLE[1] 2.

cockney /'kɒkni/ *n.* & *adj.* ● *n.* (*pl.* **-eys**) **1 a** a native of East London, esp. one born within hearing of Bow Bells. **b** the dialect or accent typical of this area. **2** *Austral.* a young snapper fish, *Chrysophrys auratus*. ● *adj.* of or characteristic of cockneys or their dialect or accent. ▫ **cockneyism** *n.* [Middle English *cokeney* 'cock's egg', later a derogatory term for a town-dweller]

cock-of-the-rock *n.* a S. American bird, a cotinga of the genus *Rupicola*, having bright orange or red plumage and a prominent crest.

cock-of-the-walk *n.* a dominant or arrogant person.

cock-of-the-wood *n.* **1** a capercaillie. **2** *N. Amer.* a red-crested woodpecker.

cockpit /'kɒkpɪt/ *n.* **1 a** a compartment for the pilot (or the pilot and crew) of an aircraft or spacecraft. **b** a similar compartment for the driver in a racing car. **c** a space for the helmsman in some small yachts. **2** an arena of war or other conflict. **3** a place where cockfights are held. [originally in sense 3, from COCK[1] + PIT[1]]

cockroach /'kɒkrəʊtʃ/ *n.* a stout-bodied beetle-like scavenging insect of the order Dictyoptera, esp. *Blatta orientalis* and *Periplaneta americana*, which infests kitchens, warehouses, etc. [Spanish *cucaracha*, assimilated to COCK[1], ROACH[1]]

cockscomb /'kɒkskəʊm/ *n.* **1** the crest or comb of a cock. **2** a garden plant, *Celosia cristata*, with a terminal plume of tiny white or red flowers.

cocksfoot /'kɒksfʊt/ *n.* *Brit.* any pasture grass of the genus *Dactylis*, with broad leaves and green or purplish spikes.

cockshy /'kɒkʃʌɪ/ *n.* (*pl.* **-shies**) *Brit.* **1 a** a target for throwing at with sticks, stones, etc. **b** a throw at this. **2** an object of ridicule or criticism.

cock sparrow *n.* **1** a male sparrow. **2** a lively quarrelsome person.

cocksure /kɒk'ʃʊə/ *adj.* **1** presumptuously or arrogantly confident. **2** (foll. by *of*, *about*) absolutely sure. ▫ **cocksurely** *adv.* **cocksureness** *n.* [*cock* = God + SURE, later associated with COCK[1]]

cocktail /'kɒkteɪl/ *n.* **1** a usu. alcoholic drink made by mixing various spirits, fruit juices, etc. **2** a dish of mixed ingredients (*fruit cocktail*; *prawn cocktail*). **3** any (esp. unpleasant or dangerous) mixture or concoction.

[origin unknown: cf. earlier sense 'docked horse' from COCK[1]: the connection is unclear]

cocktail dress *n.* a usu. short evening dress suitable for wearing at a drinks party.

cocktail stick *n. Brit.* a small pointed stick for serving an olive, cherry, small sausage, etc.

cock-up *n. Brit. slang* a muddle or mistake.

cocky[1] /'kɒki/ *adj.* (**cockier, cockiest**) **1** conceited, arrogant. **2** saucy, impudent. □ **cockily** *adv.* **cockiness** *n.* [COCK[1] + -Y[1]]

cocky[2] /'kɒki/ *n.* (*pl.* **-ies**) *Austral. & NZ colloq.* = COCKATOO 2. [abbreviation]

cocky-leeky var. of COCK-A-LEEKIE.

coco /'kəʊkəʊ/ *n.* (also **cocoa**) (*pl.* **cocos** or **cocoas**) the coconut palm. [abbreviation of COCONUT, though in earlier use as a separate word]

cocoa /'kəʊkəʊ/ *n.* **1** a powder made from crushed cacao seeds, often with other ingredients. **2** a drink made from this. [alteration of CACAO]

cocoa bean *n.* a cacao seed.

cocoa butter *n.* a fatty substance obtained from cocoa beans and used for confectionery, cosmetics, etc.

coco-de-mer /ˌkəʊkəʊdə'mɛː/ *n.* a tall palm tree, *Lodoicea maldivica*, of the Seychelles. [French, = coco from the sea: the tree was first known from nuts found floating in the sea]

coconut /'kəʊkənʌt/ *n.* (also **cocoanut**) **1 a** the large ovate brown seed of a tall tropical palm, *Cocos nucifera*, with a fibrous husk around a hard shell lined with edible white flesh enclosing a white liquid. **b** (in full **coconut palm** or **tree**) the palm itself. **c** the flesh of a coconut. **2** *slang* the human head. [from Spanish and Portuguese *coco* 'grimace' + NUT (the base of the shell resembling a face)]

coconut butter *n.* a solid fat obtained from the flesh of the coconut, and used in soap, candles, ointment, etc.

coconut ice *n. Brit.* a sweet of sugar and desiccated coconut.

coconut matting *n.* a matting made of fibre from coconut husks.

coconut milk *n.* the watery white liquid inside a coconut.

coconut palm see COCONUT 1b.

coconut shy *n. Brit.* a fairground sideshow where balls are thrown to dislodge coconuts. [SHY[2]]

cocoon /kə'kuːn/ *n. & v.* ● *n.* **1 a** a silky case spun by many insect larvae for protection as pupae. **b** a similar structure made by other animals. **2** a thing that encloses like a cocoon; a protective covering, esp. to prevent corrosion of metal equipment. ● *v.* **1** *tr.* (usu. as **cocooned** *adj.*) wrap (as) in a cocoon; protect, enclose. **2** *tr.* spray with a protective coating. **3** *intr.* form a cocoon. [French *cocon* from modern Provençal *coucoun*, diminutive of *coca* 'shell']

cocotte /kɒ'kɒt/ *n.* **1** a heatproof dish or small casserole in which food can be both cooked and served, often as an individual portion. **2** *archaic* a fashionable prostitute. [French]

COD *abbr.* **1 a** cash on delivery. **b** *N. Amer.* collect on delivery. **2** Concise Oxford Dictionary.

cod[1] /kɒd/ *n.* (*pl.* same) any large marine fish of the family Gadidae, esp. *Gadus morrhua*, an important food fish. [Middle English: origin unknown]

cod[2] /kɒd/ *n. & v. Brit.* ● *n. slang* **1** a parody. **2** a hoax. **3** (*attrib.*) = MOCK *adj.* ● *v.* (**codded, codding**) *slang* or *dial.* **1 a** *intr.* perform a hoax. **b** *tr.* play a trick on; fool. **2** *tr.* parody. [19th c.: origin unknown]

cod[3] /kɒd/ *n. Brit. slang* nonsense. [abbreviation of CODSWALLOP]

coda /'kəʊdə/ *n.* **1** *Mus.* the concluding passage of a piece or movement, usu. forming an addition to the basic structure. **2** *Ballet* the concluding section of a dance. **3** a concluding event or series of events. [Italian, from Latin *cauda* 'tail']

coddle /'kɒd(ə)l/ *v.tr.* **1 a** treat as an invalid; protect attentively. **b** (foll. by *up*) *Brit.* strengthen by feeding. **2** cook (an egg) in water below boiling point. □ **coddler** *n.* [probably dialect variant of *caudle* 'invalids' gruel']

code /kəʊd/ *n. & v.* ● *n.* **1** a system of words, letters, figures, or symbols, used to represent others for secrecy or brevity. **2** a system of pre-arranged signals, esp. used to ensure secrecy in transmitting messages. **3** *Computing* a piece of program text. **4 a** a systematic collection of statutes, a body of laws so arranged as to avoid inconsistency and overlapping. **b** a set of rules on any subject. **5 a** the prevailing morality of a society or class (*code of honour*). **b** a person's standard of moral behaviour. ● *v.* **1** *tr.* put (a message, program, etc.) into code. **2** *intr.* (foll. by *for*) *Biochem.* be the genetic code for (an amino acid etc.). □ **coder** *n.* [Middle English via Old French from Latin CODEX]

code book *n.* a list of symbols etc. used in a code.

code-breaker *n.* a person who solves or breaks a code or codes. □ **code-breaking** *n.*

codeine /'kəʊdiːn, -dɪiːn/ *n.* an alkaloid derived from morphine and used to relieve pain. [Greek *kōdeia* 'poppy-head' + -INE[4]]

code name *n.* (also **code number**) a word or symbol (or number) used for secrecy or convenience instead of the usual name. □ **code-named** *adj.*

codependency /kəʊdɪ'pɛnd(ə)nsi/ *n.* mutual emotional dependency on fulfilling a supportive role in a relationship. □ **codependent** *adj. & n.* [CO- + DEPENDENCY]

co-determination /ˌkəʊdɪtəːmɪ'neɪʃ(ə)n/ *n.* cooperation between management and workers in decision-taking. [CO- + DETERMINATION, translating German *Mitbestimmung*]

codex /'kəʊdɛks/ *n.* (*pl.* **codices** /'kəʊdɪsiːz, 'kɒd-/ or **codexes**) **1** an ancient manuscript text in book form. **2** a collection of pharmaceutical descriptions of drugs etc. [Latin, = block of wood, tablet, book]

codfish /'kɒdfɪʃ/ *n.* (*pl.* usu. same) = COD[1].

codger /'kɒdʒə/ *n.* (usu. in **old codger**) *colloq.* a person, esp. an old or strange one. [perhaps a variant of *cadger*: see CADGE]

codices *pl.* of CODEX.

codicil /'kɒdɪsɪl, 'kəʊ-/ *n.* an addition explaining, modifying, or revoking a will or part of one. □ **codicillary** /kɒdɪ'sɪləri/ *adj.* [Latin *codicillus*, diminutive of CODEX]

codicology /kəʊdɪ'kɒlədʒi/ *n.* the study of manuscripts. □ **codicological** /-kə'lɒdʒɪk(ə)l/ *adj.* **codicologically** /-kə'lɒdʒɪk(ə)li/ *adv.* [French *codicologie* from Latin *codex codicis*: see CODEX]

codify /'kəʊdɪfʌɪ/ *v.tr.* (**-ies, -ied**) arrange (laws etc.) systematically into a code. □ **codification** /-fɪ'keɪʃ(ə)n/ *n.* **codifier** *n.*

codling[1] /'kɒdlɪŋ/ *n.* (also **codlin**) **1** *Brit.* any of several varieties of cooking apple, having a long tapering shape. **2** (in full **codling moth**) a small moth, *Carpocapsa pomonella*, the larva of which feeds on apples. [Middle English from Anglo-French *quer de lion* 'lion-heart']

codling[2] /'kɒdlɪŋ/ *n.* a small codfish.

codlings-and-cream *n. Brit.* the great hairy willowherb, *Epilobium hirsutum*.

cod liver oil *n.* an oil pressed from the fresh liver of cod, which is rich in vitamins D and A.

codomain /'kəʊdə(ʊ)meɪn/ *n. Math.* a set that includes all the possible expressions of a given function. [CO- + DOMAIN]

codon /'kəʊdɒn/ *n. Biochem.* a sequence of three nucleotides, forming a unit of genetic code in a DNA or RNA molecule. [CODE + -ON]

codpiece /'kɒdpiːs/ *n. hist.* an appendage like a small bag or flap at the front of a man's breeches. [Middle English, from *cod* 'scrotum' + PIECE]

co-driver /'kəʊdrʌɪvə/ *n.* a person who shares the driving of a vehicle with another, esp. in a race, rally, etc.

codswallop /'kɒdzwɒləp/ *n.* esp. *Brit. slang* nonsense. [20th c.: origin unknown]

coecilian var. of CAECILIAN.

coed /'kəʊɛd, kəʊ'ɛd/ *n. & adj. colloq.* ● *n.* **1** *Brit.* a co-educational system or institution. **2** *N. Amer.* a female student at a co-educational institution. ● *adj.* co-educational. [abbreviation]

co-education /,kəʊɛdju:'keɪʃ(ə)n/ *n.* the education of pupils of both sexes together. ▫ **co-educational** *adj.*

coefficient /kəʊɪ'fɪʃ(ə)nt/ *n.* **1** *Math.* a quantity placed before and multiplying an algebraic expression (e.g. *4* in *4x^y*). **2** *Physics* a multiplier or factor that measures some property (*coefficient of expansion*). [modern Latin *coefficiens* (as CO-, EFFICIENT)]

coelacanth /'si:ləkanθ/ *n.* a large bony marine fish, *Latimeria chalumnae*, with a three-lobed tail-fin and fleshy pectoral fins, thought to be related to the ancestors of land vertebrates and known only from fossils until 1938. [modern Latin *Coelacanthus*, from Greek *koilos* 'hollow' + *akantha* 'spine']

-coele *comb. form* var. of -CELE.

coelenterate /si:'lɛnt(ə)rət/ *n.* an aquatic invertebrate animal of the phylum Coelenterata (now usu. called Cnidaria), typically having a simple tube-shaped or cup-shaped body, and including jellyfish, corals, and sea anemones. [modern Latin *Coelenterata*, from Greek *koilos* 'hollow' + *enteron* 'intestine']

coeliac /'si:lɪak/ *adj.* (*US* **celiac**) *Med.* relating to or suffering from coeliac disease. [Latin *coeliacus* from Greek *koiliakos*, from *koilia* 'belly']

coeliac disease *n.* a disease in which chronic failure to digest food is triggered by hypersensititivy of the small intestine to gluten.

coelom /'si:ləm/ *n.* (*US* **celom**) (*pl.* **-oms** or **-omata** /-'ləʊmətə/) *Zool.* the principal body cavity in animals, between the intestinal canal and the body wall. ▫ **coelomate** *adj. & n.* [Greek *koilōma* 'cavity']

coelostat /'si:lə(ʊ)stat/ *n. Astron.* an instrument with a rotating mirror that continuously reflects the light from the same area of sky allowing the path of a celestial object to be monitored. [Latin *caelum* 'sky' + -STAT]

coenobite /'si:nəbʌɪt/ *n.* (*US* **cenobite**) a member of a monastic community. ▫ **coenobitic** /-'bɪtɪk/ *adj.* **coenobitical** /-'bɪtɪk(ə)l/ *adj.* [Old French *cenobite* or ecclesiastical Latin *coenobita* via Late Latin *coenobium* from Greek *koinobion* 'convent', from *koinos* 'common' + *bios* 'life']

coenzyme /'kəʊɛnzʌɪm/ *n. Biochem.* a non-protein compound that is necessary for the functioning of an enzyme.

coenzyme A *n.* a coenzyme derived from pantothenic acid, important in many biochemical reactions esp. respiration.

co-equal /kəʊ'i:kw(ə)l/ *adj. & n. archaic* or *literary* ● *adj.* equal with one another. ● *n.* an equal. ▫ **co-equality** /kəʊɪ'kwɒlɪti/ *n.* **co-equally** *adv.* [Middle English from Latin or ecclesiastical Latin *coaequalis* (as CO-, EQUAL)]

coerce /kəʊ'ə:s/ *v.tr.* (often foll. by *into*) persuade or restrain (an unwilling person) by force (*coerced you into signing*). ▫ **coercible** *adj.* [Middle English from Latin *coercēre* 'restrain' (as co-, *arcēre* 'restrain')]

coercion /kəʊ'ə:ʃ(ə)n/ *n.* **1** the act or process of coercing. **2** government by force. ▫ **coercive** *adj.* **coercively** *adv.* **coerciveness** *n.* [Old French *cohercion*, *-tion* from Latin *coer(c)tio*, *coercitio -onis* (as COERCE)]

coercivity /kəʊə'sɪvɪti/ *n. Physics* the resistance of a magnetic material to changes in magnetization, esp. measured as the field intensity necessary to demagnetize it when fully magnetized.

coeval /kəʊ'i:v(ə)l/ *adj. & n.* ● *adj.* **1** having the same age or date of origin. **2** living or existing at the same epoch. **3** having the same duration. ● *n.* a coeval person, a contemporary. ▫ **coevality** /-'valɪti/ *n.* **coevally** *adv.* [Late Latin *coaevus* (as co-, Latin *aevum* 'age')]

coexist /kəʊɪg'zɪst/ *v.intr.* (often foll. by *with*) **1** exist together (in time or place). **2** (esp. of nations) exist in mutual tolerance though professing different ideologies etc. ▫ **coexistence** *n.* **coexistent** *adj.* [Late Latin *coexistere* (as CO-, EXIST)]

coextensive /kəʊɪk'stɛnsɪv/ *adj.* extending over the same space or time.

C. of E. *abbr. Brit.* Church of England.

coffee /'kɒfi/ *n. & adj.* ● *n.* **1 a** a drink made from the roasted and ground beanlike seeds of a tropical shrub of the genus *Coffea*. **b** a cup of this. **2 a** the shrub yielding these seeds, one or more of which are contained in each berry. **b** these seeds raw, or roasted and ground. **3** a pale brown colour, as of coffee mixed with milk. ● *adj.* pale brown. [ultimately from Turkish *kahveh* from Arabic *ḳahwa*]

coffee bar *n.* a bar or café serving coffee and light refreshments from a counter.

coffee bean *n.* the beanlike seed of the coffee shrub.

coffee cup *n.* a small cup for serving coffee.

coffee essence *n. Brit.* a concentrated extract of coffee usu. containing chicory.

coffee grinder *n.* a small machine for grinding roasted coffee beans.

coffee house *n.* a place serving coffee and other refreshments.

coffee-maker *n.* = PERCOLATOR.

coffee mill *n.* = COFFEE GRINDER.

coffee morning *n. Brit.* a morning gathering at which coffee is served, often in aid of charity.

coffee nibs *n. Brit.* coffee beans removed from their shells.

coffee shop *n.* a small informal restaurant, esp. in a hotel or department store.

coffee table *n.* a small low table.

coffee-table book *n.* a large lavishly illustrated book.

coffer /'kɒfə/ *n.* **1** a box, esp. a large strongbox for valuables. **2** (in *pl.*) a treasury or store of funds. **3** a sunken panel in a ceiling etc. ▫ **coffered** *adj.* [Middle English via Old French *coffre* and Latin *cophinus* from Greek *kophinos* 'basket']

coffer-dam *n.* a watertight enclosure pumped dry to permit work below the waterline on building bridges etc., or for repairing a ship.

coffin /'kɒfɪn/ *n. & v.* ● *n.* **1** a long narrow usu. wooden box in which a corpse is buried or cremated. **2** the part of a horse's hoof below the coronet. ● *v.tr.* (**coffined, coffining**) put in a coffin. [Middle English via Old French *cof(f)in* 'little basket' etc. from Latin *cophinus*: see COFFER]

coffin-bone *n.* a bone in a horse's hoof.

coffin corner *n. Amer. Football* the corner formed by the goal line and sideline.

coffin-joint *n.* the joint at the top of a horse's hoof.

coffin-nail *n. slang* a cigarette.

coffle /'kɒf(ə)l/ *n.* a line of animals, slaves, etc., fastened together. [Arabic *ḳāfila* 'caravan']

cog /kɒg/ *n.* **1** each of a series of projections on the edge of a wheel or bar transferring motion by engaging with another series. **2** an unimportant member of an organization etc. ▫ **cogged** *adj.* [Middle English: probably of Scandinavian origin]

cogent /'kəʊdʒ(ə)nt/ *adj.* (of arguments, reasons, etc.) convincing, compelling. ▫ **cogency** *n.* **cogently** *adv.* [Latin *cogere* 'compel' (as co-, *agere act-* 'drive')]

cogitable /'kɒdʒɪtəb(ə)l/ *adj.* able to be grasped by the mind; conceivable. [Latin *cogitabilis* (as COGITATE)]

cogitate /'kɒdʒɪteɪt/ *v.tr. & intr.* ponder, meditate. ▫ **cogitation** /-'teɪʃ(ə)n/ *n.* **cogitative** /-tətɪv/ *adj.* **cogitator** *n.* [Latin *cogitare* 'think' (as CO-, AGITATE)]

cogito /'kəʊgɪtəʊ, -dʒɪ-/ *n. Philos.* the principle establishing the existence of a being from the fact of its thinking or awareness. [Latin, = I think, in the French philosopher Descartes's formula (1641) *cogito, ergo sum* 'I think, therefore I am']

cognac /ˈkɒnjak/ *n.* a high-quality brandy, properly that distilled in Cognac in western France.

cognate /ˈkɒɡneɪt/ *adj. & n.* ● *adj.* **1** related to or descended from a common ancestor (cf. AGNATE *adj.* 1). **2** *Philol.* (of a word) having the same linguistic family or derivation (as another); representing the same original word or root (e.g. English *father*, German *Vater*, Latin *pater*). ● *n.* **1** a relative. **2** *Philol.* a cognate word. □ **cognately** *adv.* **cognateness** *n.* [Latin *cognatus* (as co-, *natus* 'born')]

cognate object *n. Gram.* an object that is related in origin and sense to the verb governing it (as in *live a good life*).

cognition /kɒɡˈnɪʃ(ə)n/ *n.* **1** *Philos.* knowing, perceiving, or conceiving as an act or faculty distinct from emotion and volition. **2** a result of this; a perception, sensation, notion, or intuition. □ **cognitional** *adj.* **cognitive** /ˈkɒɡnɪtɪv/ *adj.* **cognitively** /ˈkɒɡnɪtɪvli/ *adv.* [Latin *cognitio* (as co-, *gnoscere gnit-* 'apprehend')]

cognitivist /ˈkɒɡnɪtɪvɪst/ *adj.* tending to emphasize the similarities between linguistic and non-linguistic knowledge. □ **cognitivism** *n.* [COGNITIVE (see COGNITION) + -IST]

cognizable /ˈkɒ(ɡ)nɪzəb(ə)l/ *adj.* (also **-isable**) **1** perceptible, recognizable; clearly identifiable. **2** within the jurisdiction of a court. □ **cognizably** *adv.* [COGNIZANCE + -ABLE]

cognizance /ˈkɒ(ɡ)nɪz(ə)ns/ *n.* (also **cognisance** /-z(ə)ns/) **1** knowledge or awareness; perception, notice. **2** the sphere of one's observation or concern. **3** *Law* the right of a court to deal with a matter. **4** *Heraldry* a distinctive device or mark. □ **have cognizance of** know, esp. officially. **take cognizance of** attend to; take account of. [Middle English from Old French *conoisance*, ultimately from Latin *cognoscent-* from *cognitio*: see COGNITION]

cognizant /ˈkɒ(ɡ)nɪz(ə)nt/ *adj.* (also **cognisant** /-z(ə)nt/) (foll. by *of*) having knowledge or being aware of.

cognomen /kɒɡˈnəʊmən/ *n.* **1** a nickname. **2** an ancient Roman's personal name or epithet, as in Marcus Tullius *Cicero*, Publius Cornelius Scipio *Africanus*. [Latin (as co-, (*g*)*nomen* 'name')]

cognoscente /kɒnjəˈʃɛnti/ *n.* (*pl.* **cognoscenti** /-ti/) (usu. in *pl.*) a connoisseur. [Italian, literally 'a person who knows']

cogwheel /ˈkɒɡwiːl/ *n.* a wheel with cogs.

cohabit /kəʊˈhabɪt/ *v.intr.* (**cohabited**, **cohabiting**) live together, esp. as husband and wife without being married to one another. □ **cohabitant** *n.* **cohabitation** /-ˈteɪʃ(ə)n/ *n.* **cohabitee** /-ˈtiː/ *n.* **cohabiter** *n.* [Latin *cohabitare* (as co-, *habitare* 'dwell')]

cohere /kə(ʊ)ˈhɪə/ *v.intr.* **1** (of parts or a whole) stick together, remain united. **2** (of reasoning etc.) be logical or consistent. [Latin *cohaerēre cohaes-* (as co-, *haerēre* 'stick')]

coherent /kə(ʊ)ˈhɪər(ə)nt/ *adj.* **1** (of a person) able to speak intelligibly and articulately. **2** (of speech, an argument, etc.) logical and consistent; easily followed. **3** cohering; sticking together. **4** *Physics* (of waves) having a constant phase relationship. □ **coherence** *n.* **coherency** *n.* **coherently** *adv.* [Latin *cohaerēre cohaerent-* (as COHERE)]

cohesion /kə(ʊ)ˈhiːʒ(ə)n/ *n.* **1 a** the act or condition of sticking together. **b** a tendency to cohere. **2** *Physics* the sticking together of molecules of the same substance. □ **cohesive** /-sɪv/ *adj.* **cohesively** /-sɪvli/ *adv.* **cohesiveness** /-sɪvnɪs/ *n.* [Latin *cohaes-* (see COHERE), on the pattern of *adhesion*]

coho /ˈkəʊhəʊ/ *n.* (also **cohoe**) (*pl.* **-os** or **-oes**) a silver salmon, *Oncorhynchus kisutch*, of the N. Pacific. [19th c.: origin unknown]

cohort /ˈkəʊhɔːt/ *n.* **1** an ancient Roman military unit, equal to one-tenth of a legion. **2** a band of warriors. **3 a** persons banded or grouped together, esp. in a common cause. **b** a group of persons with a common statistical characteristic. **4** *N. Amer.* a companion or colleague. [Middle English from French *cohorte* or Latin *cohors cohort-* 'enclosure, company']

■ **Usage** Sense 4 of *cohort*, though quite common, especially in North American English, is criticized by many people and should be avoided.

COHSE /ˈkəʊzi/ *abbr. hist.* (in the UK) Confederation of Health Service Employees, merged with NALGO and NUPE in 1993 to form UNISON.

COI *abbr.* (in the UK) Central Office of Information.

coif /kɔɪf/ *n. & v.* ● *n.* **1** a close-fitting cap, now esp. as worn by nuns under a veil. **2** esp. *N. Amer.* a coiffure, esp. an elaborate one. **3** *hist.* a protective metal skullcap worn under armour. ● *v.tr.* (**coiffed**, **coiffing**; *US* also **coifed**, **coifing**) **1 a** dress or arrange (the hair). **b** arrange the hair of (a person). **2** cover with or as if with a coif. [Middle English via Old French *coife* from Late Latin *cofia* 'helmet']

coiffeur /kwɑːˈfəː, kwɒ-/ *n.* (*fem.* **coiffeuse** /-ˈfəːz/) a hairdresser. [French]

coiffure /kwɑːˈfjʊə, kwɒ-/ *n.* the way hair is arranged; a hairstyle. □ **coiffured** *adj.* [French]

coign /kɔɪn/ *n.* □ **coign of vantage** a favourable position for observation or action. [earlier spelling of COIN in the sense 'cornerstone']

coil[1] /kɔɪl/ *n. & v.* ● *n.* **1** anything arranged in a joined sequence of concentric circles. **2** a length of rope, a spring, etc., arranged in this way. **3** a single turn of something coiled, e.g. a snake. **4** a lock of hair twisted and coiled. **5** an intrauterine contraceptive device in the form of a coil. **6** *Electr.* a device consisting of a coiled wire for converting low voltage to high voltage, esp. for transmission to the sparking plugs of an internal-combustion engine. **7** a piece of wire, piping, etc., wound in circles or spirals. **8** a roll of postage stamps. ● *v.* **1** *tr.* arrange in a series of concentric loops or rings. **2** *tr. & intr.* twist or be twisted into a circular or spiral shape. **3** *intr.* move sinuously. [Old French *coillir* from Latin *colligere* COLLECT[1]]

coil[2] /kɔɪl/ *n.* □ **this mortal coil** the bustle or turmoil of earthly life (with reference to Shakespeare's *Hamlet* III. i. 67). [16th c.: origin unknown]

coin /kɔɪn/ *n. & v.* ● *n.* **1** a piece of flat usu. round metal stamped and issued by authority as money. **2** (*collect.*) metal money. ● *v.tr.* **1** make (coins) by stamping. **2** make (metal) into coins. **3** invent or devise (esp. a new word or phrase). □ **coin money** (or **coin it, coin it in**) make much money quickly. **to coin a phrase** *iron.* introducing a banal remark or cliché. [Middle English from Old French, = stamping-die, from Latin *cuneus* 'wedge']

coinage /ˈkɔɪnɪdʒ/ *n.* **1** the act or process of coining. **2 a** coins collectively. **b** a system or type of coins in use (*decimal coinage*; *bronze coinage*). **3** an invention, esp. of a new word or phrase. [Middle English from Old French *coigniage*]

coin box *n.* **1** *Brit.* a telephone operated by inserting coins. **2** the receptacle for these.

coincide /kəʊɪnˈsʌɪd/ *v.intr.* **1** occur at or during the same time. **2** occupy the same portion of space. **3** (often foll. by *with*) be in agreement; have the same view. [medieval Latin *coincidere* (as CO-, INCIDENT)]

coincidence /kəʊˈɪnsɪd(ə)ns/ *n.* **1 a** occurring or being together. **b** an instance of this. **2** a remarkable concurrence of events or circumstances without apparent causal connection. **3** *Physics* the presence of ionizing particles etc. in two or more detectors simultaneously, or of two or more signals simultaneously in a circuit. [medieval Latin *coincidentia* (as COINCIDE)]

coincident /kəʊˈɪnsɪd(ə)nt/ *adj.* **1** occurring together in space or time. **2** (foll. by *with*) in agreement; harmonious. □ **coincidently** *adv.*

coincidental /kəʊɪnsɪˈdɛnt(ə)l/ *adj.* **1** in the nature of or resulting from a coincidence. **2** happening or existing at the same time. □ **coincidentally** *adv.*

coiner /ˈkɔɪnə/ *n.* **1** a person who coins money, esp. *Brit.* the maker of counterfeit coin. **2** a person who invents or devises something (esp. a new word or phrase).

coin-op *n.* a launderette etc. with automatic machines operated by inserting coins.

Cointreau /ˈkwɑːntrəʊ/ *n. propr.* a colourless orange-flavoured liqueur. [French]

coir /ˈkɔɪə/ *n.* fibre from the outer husk of the coconut, used for ropes, matting, in potting compost, etc. [Malayalam *kāyar* 'cord' from *kāyaru* 'be twisted']

coition /kəʊˈɪʃ(ə)n/ *n. Med.* = COITUS. [Latin *coitio* from *coire coit-* 'go together']

coitus /ˈkəʊɪtəs/ *n. Med.* sexual intercourse. □ **coital** *adj.* [Latin (as COITION)]

coitus interruptus /ɪntəˈrʌptəs/ *n.* sexual intercourse in which the penis is withdrawn before ejaculation.

Coke /kəʊk/ *n. propr.* Coca-Cola. [abbreviation]

coke[1] /kəʊk/ *n.* & *v.* ● *n.* **1** a solid substance left after the gases have been extracted from coal. **2** a residue left after the incomplete combustion of petrol etc. ● *v.tr.* convert (coal) into coke. [probably from northern English dialect *colk* 'core', of unknown origin]

coke[2] /kəʊk/ *n. slang* cocaine. [abbreviation]

Col. *abbr.* **1** Colonel. **2** Colossians (New Testament).

col /kɒl/ *n.* **1** a depression in the summit-line of a chain of mountains, generally affording a pass from one slope to another. **2** *Meteorol.* a low-pressure region between anticyclones. [French, = neck, from Latin *collum*]

col. *abbr.* column.

col- /kɒl, kəl/ *prefix* assim. form of COM- before *l.*

cola /ˈkəʊlə/ *n.* (also **kola**) **1** any small tree of the genus *Cola*, native to W. Africa, bearing seeds containing caffeine. **2** a carbonated drink usu. flavoured with these seeds. [Temne (a language of Sierra Leone)]

colander /ˈkʌləndə/ *n.* a perforated vessel used to strain off liquid in cookery. [Middle English, ultimately from Latin *colare* 'strain']

cola nut *n.* a seed of the cola tree.

co-latitude /kəʊˈlatɪtjuːd/ *n. Astron.* the complement of the latitude, the difference between it and 90°.

colchicine /ˈkɒltʃɪsiːn, ˈkɒlk-/ *n.* a yellow alkaloid obtained from colchicum, used in the treatment of gout.

colchicum /ˈkɒltʃɪkəm, ˈkɒlk-/ *n.* **1** a plant of the genus *Colchicum* (lily family), esp. meadow saffron. **2** its dried corm or seed. [Latin from Greek *kolkhikon* 'of Kolkhis', a region east of the Black Sea]

cold /kəʊld/ *adj., n., & adv.* ● *adj.* **1** of or at a low or relatively low temperature, esp. when compared with the human body. **2** not heated; cooled after being heated. **3** (of a person) feeling cold. **4** lacking ardour, friendliness, or affection; undemonstrative, apathetic. **5** depressing, dispiriting, uninteresting (*cold facts*). **6 a** dead. **b** *colloq.* unconscious. **7** *colloq.* at one's mercy (*had me cold*). **8** sexually frigid. **9** (of soil) slow to absorb heat. **10** (of a scent in hunting) having become weak. **11** (in children's games) far from finding or guessing what is sought. **12** without preparation or rehearsal. ● *n.* **1 a** the prevalence of a low temperature, esp. in the atmosphere. **b** cold weather; a cold environment (*went out into the cold*). **2** an infection in which the mucous membrane of the nose and throat becomes inflamed, causing running at the nose, sneezing, sore throat, etc. ● *adv.* **1** unrehearsed, without preparation. **2** esp. *US slang* completely, entirely (*was stopped cold mid-sentence*). □ **catch a cold 1** become infected with a cold. **2** encounter trouble or difficulties. **cold call** sell goods or services by making unsolicited calls on prospective customers by telephone or in person. **in cold blood** without feeling or passion; deliberately, ruthlessly. **out in the cold** ignored, neglected. **throw** (or **pour**) **cold water on** be discouraging or depreciatory about. □ **coldish** *adj.* **coldly** *adv.* **coldness** *n.* [Old English *cald* from Germanic, related to Latin *gelu* 'frost']

cold-blooded *adj.* **1** having a body temperature varying with that of the environment (e.g. of fish); poikilothermic. **2** callous; deliberately cruel. □ **cold-bloodedly** *adv.* **cold-bloodedness** *n.*

cold cathode *n.* a cathode that emits electrons without being heated.

cold chisel *n.* a chisel suitable for cutting metal.

cold comfort *n.* poor or inadequate consolation.

cold cream *n.* ointment for cleansing and softening the skin.

cold cuts *n.pl.* slices of cold cooked meats.

cold feet *n.pl. colloq.* loss of nerve or confidence.

cold frame *n.* an unheated frame with a glass top for growing small plants.

cold front *n.* the forward edge of an advancing mass of cold air.

cold-hearted *adj.* lacking affection or warmth; unfriendly. □ **cold-heartedly** *adv.* **cold-heartedness** *n.*

cold-short *adj.* (of a metal) brittle in its cold state. [Swedish *kallskör*, from *kall* 'cold' + *skör* 'brittle': assimilated to SHORT]

cold shoulder *n.* & *v.* ● *n.* a show of intentional unfriendliness. ● *v.tr.* (**cold-shoulder**) be deliberately unfriendly to.

cold snap see SNAP *n.* 4.

cold sore *n.* inflammation and blisters in and around the mouth, caused by infection with herpes simplex virus.

cold start *n.* & *v.* ● *n.* **1** the starting of an engine or machine at the ambient temperature. **2** the starting of a process, enterprise, etc. without prior preparation. ● *v.tr.* (**cold-start**) start something at the ambient temperature or without prior preparation.

cold steel *n.* cutting or thrusting weapons.

cold storage *n.* **1** storage in a refrigerator or other cold place for preservation. **2** a state in which something (esp. an idea) is put aside temporarily.

cold store *n.* a large refrigerated room for preserving usu. commercial food stocks at very low temperatures.

cold sweat *n.* a state of sweating induced by fear or illness.

cold table *n. Brit.* a selection of dishes of cold food.

cold turkey *n. slang* **1** abrupt withdrawal from addictive drugs; the symptoms of this. **2** *US* blunt statements or blunt treatment.

cold war *n.* a state of hostility between nations without actual fighting.

cold wave *n.* **1** a temporary spell of cold weather over a wide area. **2** a kind of permanent wave for the hair using chemicals and without heat.

cole /kəʊl/ *n.* (usu. in *comb.*) **1** cabbage. **2** = RAPE[2]. [Middle English via Old Norse *kál* from Latin *caulis* 'stem, cabbage']

colemouse var. of COALMOUSE.

coleopteran /kɒlɪˈɒpt(ə)r(ə)n/ *n.* any insect of the order Coleoptera, comprising the beetles and weevils, which have the forewings modified into sheaths to protect the hindwings, and biting mouthparts. □ **coleopterist** *n.* **coleopterous** *adj.* [modern Latin *Coleoptera* from Greek *koleopteros*, from *koleon* 'sheath' + *pteron* 'wing']

coleoptile /kɒlɪˈɒptʌɪl/ *n. Bot.* a sheath protecting a young shoot tip in grasses. [Greek *koleon* 'sheath' + *ptilon* 'feather']

coleseed /ˈkəʊlsiːd/ *n.* = COLE 2.

coleslaw /ˈkəʊlslɔː/ *n.* a dressed salad of sliced raw cabbage, carrot, onion, etc. [Dutch *koolsla*: see COLE, SLAW]

cole tit var. of COAL TIT.

coleus /ˈkəʊlɪəs/ *n.* a plant of the genus *Solenostemon* (formerly *Coleus*), having variegated coloured leaves. [modern Latin from Greek *koleon* 'sheath': from the way the stamens are joined together]

coley /ˈkəʊli/ *n.* (*pl.* **-eys**) *Brit.* = SAITHE. [perhaps from COALFISH]

colic /ˈkɒlɪk/ *n.* a severe spasmodic abdominal pain. □ **colicky** *adj.* [Middle English via French *colique* from Late Latin *colicus*: see COLON[2]]

coliseum /kɒlɪˈsiːəm/ *n.* (also **colosseum** /kɒlə-/) a large stadium or amphitheatre. [medieval Latin, neut. of *colosseus* 'gigantic' (as COLOSSUS)]

■ **Usage** *Coliseum* most commonly occurs in titles of buildings etc., and therefore with a capital initial. The name of the amphitheatre in Rome is spelt *Colosseum* while the names of these buildings in other countries are usually spelt *Coliseum*.

colitis /kəˈlʌɪtɪs/ *n. Med.* inflammation of the lining of the colon.

Coll. *abbr.* College.

collaborate /kəˈlabəreɪt/ *v.intr.* (often foll. by *with*) **1** work jointly, esp. in a literary or artistic production. **2** cooperate traitorously with an enemy. □ **collaboration** /-ˈreɪʃ(ə)n/ *n.* **collaborationist** /-ˈreɪʃ(ə)nɪst/ *n.* & *adj.* **collaborative** /-rətɪv/ *adj.* **collaboratively** /-rətɪvli/ *adv.* **collaborator** *n.* [Latin *collaborare collaborat-* (as COM-, *laborare* 'work')]

collage /kɒˈlɑːʒ/ *n.* **1** a form of art in which various materials (e.g. photographs, pieces of paper, fabric, or wood) are arranged and glued to a backing. **2** a work of art done in this way. **3** a collection of unrelated things. □ **collagist** *n.* [French, = gluing]

collagen /ˈkɒlədʒ(ə)n/ *n. Biochem.* the main structural protein found in animal connective tissue, yielding gelatin on boiling. [French *collagène*, from Greek *kolla* 'glue' + *-gène* = -GEN]

collapsar /kəˈlapsɑː/ *n. Astron.* an old star that has collapsed under its own gravity to form a white dwarf, neutron star, or black hole.

collapse /kəˈlaps/ *n.* & *v.* ● *n.* **1** the tumbling down or falling in of a structure; folding up; giving way. **2** a sudden failure of a plan, undertaking, etc. **3** a physical or mental breakdown. ● *v.* **1 a** *intr.* undergo or experience a collapse. **b** *tr.* cause to collapse. **2** *intr. colloq.* lie or sit down and relax, esp. after prolonged effort (*collapsed into a chair*). **3 a** *intr.* (of furniture etc.) be foldable into a small space. **b** *tr.* fold (furniture) in this way. □ **collapsible** *adj.* **collapsibility** /-ˈbɪlɪti/ *n.* [Latin *collapsus*, past part. of *collabi* (as COM-, *labi* 'slip')]

collar /ˈkɒlə/ *n.* & *v.* ● *n.* **1** the part of a shirt, dress, coat, etc., that goes round the neck, either upright or turned over. **2** a band of linen, lace, etc., completing the upper part of a garment. **3** a band of leather or other material put round an animal's (esp. a dog's) neck. **4** a restraining or connecting band, ring, or pipe in machinery. **5** a coloured marking resembling a collar round the neck of a bird or animal. **6** *Brit.* a piece of meat rolled up and tied. ● *v.tr.* **1** seize (a person) by the collar or neck. **2** capture, apprehend. **3** *colloq.* accost. **4** *slang* take, esp. illicitly. □ **collared** *adj.* (also in *comb.*). **collarless** *adj.* [Middle English via Anglo-French *coler*, Old French *colier*, from Latin *collare*, from *collum* 'neck']

collar-beam *n.* a horizontal beam connecting two rafters and forming with them an A-shaped roof-truss.

collarbone /ˈkɒləbəʊn/ *n.* either of two bones joining the breastbone and the shoulder blades. Also called *clavicle*.

collard /ˈkɒləd/ *n.* (also **collards**, **collard greens**) *N. Amer.* & *Brit. dial.* a variety of cabbage without a distinct heart. [reduced form of *colewort*, from COLE + WORT]

collared dove *n.* a dove, *Streptopelia decaocto*, having distinct neck-markings.

collate /kɒˈleɪt/ *v.tr.* **1** analyse and compare (texts, statements, etc.) to identify points of agreement and difference. **2** verify the order of (sheets of a book) by their signatures. **3** assemble (information) from different sources. **4** (often foll. by *to*) *Eccl.* appoint (a clergyman) to a benefice. □ **collator** *n.* [Latin *collat-*, past part. stem of *conferre* 'compare']

collateral /kɒˈlat(ə)r(ə)l/ *n.* & *adj.* ● *n.* **1** security pledged as a guarantee for repayment of a loan. **2** a person having the same descent as another but by a different line. ● *adj.* **1** descended from the same stock but by a different line. **2** side by side; parallel. **3 a** additional but subordinate. **b** contributory. **c** connected but aside from the main subject, course, etc. □ **collaterality** /-ˈralɪti/ *n.* **collaterally** *adv.* [Middle English from medieval Latin *collateralis* (as COM-, LATERAL)]

collateral damage *n.* destruction or injury beyond that intended or expected, esp. in the vicinity of a military target.

collateralize /kɒˈlat(ə)r(ə)lʌɪz/ *v.tr.* (also **-ise**) (usu. in *passive*) secure (a loan, bonds, etc.) with collateral.

collation /kɒˈleɪʃ(ə)n/ *n.* **1** the act or an instance of collating. **2 a** *RC Ch.* a light meal allowed during a fast. **b** a light informal meal. [Middle English from Old French from Latin *collatio -onis* (see COLLATE): sense 2a from Cassian's *Collationes Patrum* (= *Lives of the Fathers*) read by Benedictines and followed by a light meal]

colleague /ˈkɒliːg/ *n.* a fellow official or worker, esp. in a profession or business. [French *collègue* from Latin *collega* (as COM-, *legare* 'depute')]

collect[1] /kəˈlɛkt/ *v.*, *adj.*, & *adv.* ● *v.* **1** *tr.* & *intr.* bring or come together; assemble, accumulate. **2** *tr.* systematically seek and acquire (books, stamps, etc.), esp. as a continuing hobby. **3 a** *tr.* obtain (taxes, contributions, etc.) from a number of people. **b** *intr. colloq.* receive money. **4** *tr.* call for; fetch (*went to collect the laundry*). **5 a** *refl.* regain control of oneself esp. after a shock. **b** *tr.* concentrate (one's energies, thoughts, etc.). **c** *tr.* (as **collected** *adj.*) calm and cool; not perturbed or distracted. **6** *tr.* infer, gather, conclude. ● *adj.* & *adv. N. Amer.* to be paid for by the receiver (of a telephone call, parcel, etc.). □ **collectedly** *adv.* [French *collecter* or medieval Latin *collectare* from Latin *collectus*, past part. of *colligere* (as COM-, *legere* 'pick')]

collect[2] /ˈkɒlɛkt, -lɪkt/ *n.* a short prayer of the Anglican and Roman Catholic Church, esp. one assigned to a particular day or season. [Middle English via Old French *collecte* from Latin *collecta* 'gathering', fem. past part. of *colligere*: see COLLECT[1]]

collectable /kəˈlɛktəb(ə)l/ *adj.* & *n.* (also **collectible**) ● *adj.* **1** worth collecting. **2** able to be collected. ● *n.* an item sought by collectors. □ **collectability** /-ˈbɪlɪti/ *n.*

collection /kəˈlɛkʃ(ə)n/ *n.* **1** the act or process of collecting or being collected. **2** a group of things collected together (e.g. works of art, literary items, or specimens), esp. systematically. **3** (foll. by *of*) an accumulation; a mass or pile (*a collection of dust*). **4 a** the collecting of money, esp. in church or for a charitable cause. **b** the amount collected. **5** the regular removal of mail for dispatch, refuse for disposal, etc. **6** (in *pl.*) *Brit.* college examinations held at the end of a term, esp. at Oxford University. [Middle English via Old French from Latin *collectio -onis* (as COLLECT[1])]

collective /kəˈlɛktɪv/ *adj.* & *n.* ● *adj.* **1** formed by or constituting a collection. **2** taken as a whole; aggregate (*our collective opinion*). **3** of or from several or many individuals; common. ● *n.* **1 a** = COLLECTIVE FARM. **b** any cooperative enterprise. **c** its members. **2** = COLLECTIVE NOUN. □ **collectively** *adv.* **collectiveness** *n.* **collectivity** /-ˈtɪvɪti/ *n.* [French *collectif* or Latin *collectivus* (as COLLECT[1])]

collective bargaining *n.* negotiation of wages etc. by an organized body of employees.

collective farm *n.* a jointly-operated esp. state-owned amalgamation of several smallholdings.

collective memory *n.* the memory of a group of people, often passed from one generation to the next.

collective noun *n. Gram.* a noun that is grammatically singular and denotes a collection or number of individuals (e.g. *assembly*, *family*, *troop*).

collective ownership *n.* ownership of land, means of production, etc., by all for the benefit of all.

b *b*ut d *d*og f *f*ew g *g*et h *h*e j *y*es k *c*at l *l*eg m *m*an n *n*o p *p*en r *r*ed s *s*it t *t*op v *v*oice

collective unconscious *n. Psychol.* (in Jungian theory) the part of the unconscious mind which is derived from ancestral memory and experience, and is common to all humankind, as distinct from the individual's unconscious.

collectivism /kə'lɛktɪvɪz(ə)m/ *n.* the theory and practice of the collective ownership of land and the means of production. □ **collectivist** *n.* **collectivistic** /-'vɪstɪk/ *adj.*

collectivize /kə'lɛktɪvʌɪz/ *v.tr.* (also **-ise**) organize on the basis of collective ownership. □ **collectivization** /-'zeɪʃ(ə)n/ *n.*

collector /kə'lɛktə/ *n.* **1** a person who collects, esp. things of interest as a hobby. **2** a person who collects money etc. due (*tax collector*; *rent collector*). **3** *Electronics* the region in a transistor that absorbs carriers of a charge. [Middle English via Anglo-French *collectour* from medieval Latin *collector* (as COLLECT[1])]

collector's item *n.* (also **collector's piece**) a valuable object, esp. one of interest to collectors.

colleen /kɒ'li:n, 'kɒli:n/ *n. Ir.* a girl. [Irish *cailín*, diminutive of *caile* 'countrywoman']

college /'kɒlɪdʒ/ *n.* **1** an establishment for further or higher education, sometimes part of a university. **2** an establishment for specialized professional education (*business college*; *college of music*; *naval college*). **3** *Brit.* the buildings or premises of a college (*lived in college*). **4** the students and teachers in a college. **5** *Brit.* a private secondary school. **6** an organized body of persons with shared functions and privileges (*College of Physicians*). [Middle English from Old French *college* or Latin *collegium*, from *collega* (as COLLEAGUE)]

College of Arms *n.* (in the UK) a corporation recording lineage and granting arms.

college of education *n.* a training college for schoolteachers.

college pudding *n. Brit.* a small baked or steamed suet pudding with dried fruit.

collegial /kə'li:dʒɪəl, -dʒ(ə)l/ *adj.* **1** = COLLEGIATE 1. **2** relating to or involving shared responsibility, as among a group of colleagues. □ **collegiality** /kəli:dʒɪ'alɪti/ *n.*

collegian /kə'li:dʒɪən, -dʒ(ə)n/ *n.* a member of a college. [medieval Latin *collegianus* (as COLLEGE)]

collegiate /kə'li:dʒ(ɪ)ət/ *adj.* **1** of the nature of, constituted as, or belonging to, a college; corporate. **2** (of a university) composed of different colleges. **3** designed for use by college students. □ **collegiately** *adv.* [Late Latin *collegiatus* (as COLLEGE)]

collegiate church *n.* **1** a church endowed for a chapter of canons but without a bishop's see. **2** *US & Sc.* a church or group of churches established under a joint pastorate.

collenchyma /kə'lɛŋkɪmə/ *n. Bot.* a tissue of cells with thick cellulose cell walls, strengthening young stems etc. [Greek *kolla* 'glue' + *egkhuma* 'infusion']

Colles' fracture /'kɒlɪs/ *n.* a fracture of the lower end of the radius with a backward displacement of the hand. [A. *Colles*, Irish surgeon d. 1843]

collet /'kɒlɪt/ *n.* **1** a flange or socket for setting a gem in jewellery. **2** *Engin.* a segmented band or sleeve put round a shaft or spindle and tightened to grip it. **3** a small collar in a clock etc. to which the inner end of a balance spring is attached. [French, diminutive of COL]

collide /kə'lʌɪd/ *v.intr.* (often foll. by *with*) **1** come into abrupt or violent impact. **2** be in conflict. [Latin *collidere collis-* (as COM-, *laedere* 'strike, damage')]

collider /kə'lʌɪdə/ *n. Physics* an accelerator in which two beams of particles are made to collide.

collie /'kɒli/ *n.* **1** a sheepdog originally of a Scottish breed, with a long pointed nose and usu. dense long hair. **2** this breed. [perhaps from *coll* COAL (the breed originally being black)]

collier /'kɒlɪə/ *n.* **1** a coal miner. **2 a** a coal-ship. **b** *Brit.* a member of its crew. [Middle English, from COAL + -IER]

colliery /'kɒlɪəri/ *n.* (*pl.* **-ies**) a coal mine and its associated buildings.

colligate /'kɒlɪgeɪt/ *v.tr.* bring into connection (esp. isolated facts by a generalization). □ **colligation** /-'geɪʃ(ə)n/ *n.* [Latin *colligare colligat-* (as COM-, *ligare* 'bind')]

collimate /'kɒlɪmeɪt/ *v.tr.* **1** adjust the line of sight of (a telescope etc.). **2** make (telescopes or rays) accurately parallel. □ **collimation** /-'meɪʃ(ə)n/ *n.* [Latin *collimare*, erroneous for *collineare* 'align' (as COM-, *linea* 'line')]

collimator /'kɒlɪmeɪtə/ *n.* **1** a device for producing a parallel beam of rays or radiation. **2** a small fixed telescope used for adjusting the line of sight of an astronomical telescope etc.

collinear /kɒ'lɪnɪə/ *adj. Geom.* (of points) lying in the same straight line. □ **collinearity** /-'arɪti/ *n.*

Collins /'kɒlɪnz/ *n.* (in full **Tom Collins**) an iced drink made of gin or whisky etc. with soda, lemon or lime juice, and sugar. [20th c.: origin unknown]

collision /kə'lɪʒ(ə)n/ *n.* **1** a violent impact of a moving body, esp. a vehicle or ship, with another or with a fixed object. **2** the clashing of opposed interests or considerations. **3** *Physics* the action of particles striking or coming together. □ **collisional** *adj.* [Middle English from Late Latin *collisio* (as COLLIDE)]

collision course *n.* a course or action that is bound to cause a collision or conflict.

collocate /'kɒləkeɪt/ *v.tr.* **1** place together or side by side. **2** arrange; set in a particular place. **3** (often foll. by *with*) *Linguistics* juxtapose (a word etc.) with another. [Latin *collocare collocat-* (as COM-, *locare* 'to place')]

collocation /kɒlə'keɪʃ(ə)n/ *n.* **1** *Linguistics* **a** the juxtaposition or association of a particular word with another particular word or words. **b** the words so juxtaposed or associated. **2** the action of collocating; the state of being collocated.

collocutor /'kɒləkju:tə, kə'lɒkjʊtə/ *n.* a person who takes part in a conversation. [Late Latin, from *colloqui* (as COM-, *loqui locut-* 'talk')]

collodion /kə'ləʊdɪən/ *n.* a syrupy solution of nitrocellulose in a mixture of alcohol and ether, used in photography and surgery. [Greek *kollōdēs* 'glue-like', from *kolla* 'glue']

collogue /kɒ'ləʊg/ *v.intr.* (**collogues**, **collogued**, **colloguing**) (foll. by *with*) talk confidentially. [probably alteration of obsolete *colleague* 'conspire', by association with Latin *colloqui* 'converse']

colloid /'kɒlɔɪd/ *n.* **1** *Chem.* a non-crystalline substance consisting of ultramicroscopic particles, esp. large single molecules, usu. dispersed through a second substance, as in gels, sols, and emulsions. **2** *Med.* a substance of a homogeneous gelatinous consistency. □ **colloidal** /kə'lɔɪd(ə)l/ *adj.* [Greek *kolla* 'glue' + -OID]

collop /'kɒləp/ *n.* a slice, esp. of meat or bacon; an escalope. [Middle English, = fried bacon and eggs, of Scandinavian origin]

colloquial /kə'ləʊkwɪəl/ *adj.* belonging to or proper to ordinary or familiar conversation, not formal or literary. □ **colloquially** *adv.* [Latin *colloquium* COLLOQUY]

colloquialism /kə'ləʊkwɪəlɪz(ə)m/ *n.* **1** a colloquial word or phrase. **2** the use of colloquialisms.

colloquium /kə'ləʊkwɪəm/ *n.* (*pl.* **colloquiums** or **colloquia** /-kwɪə/) an academic conference or seminar. [Latin: see COLLOQUY]

colloquy /'kɒləkwi/ *n.* (*pl.* **-quies**) **1** *formal* **a** the act of conversing. **b** a conversation. **2** *Eccl.* a gathering for discussion of theological questions. [Latin *colloquium* (as COM-, *loqui* speak)]

collotype /'kɒlətʌɪp/ *n. Printing* **1** a thin sheet of gelatin exposed to light, treated with reagents, and used to make high-quality prints by lithography. **2** a print made by this process. [Greek *kolla* 'glue' + TYPE]

collude /kə'l(j)u:d/ *v.intr.* come to an understanding or conspire together, esp. for a fraudulent purpose.

□ **colluder** *n.* [Latin *colludere collus-* (as COM-, *ludere lus-* 'play')]

collusion /kə'l(j)u:ʒ(ə)n/ *n.* **1** a secret understanding, esp. for a fraudulent purpose. **2** *Law* such an understanding between ostensible opponents in a lawsuit. □ **collusive** *adj.* **collusively** *adv.* [Middle English from Old French *collusion* or Latin *collusio* (as COLLUDE)]

collyrium /kə'lɪrɪəm/ *n.* (*pl.* **collyria** /-rɪə/) a medicated eye-lotion. [Latin from Greek *kollurion* 'poultice', from *kollura* 'coarse bread roll']

collywobbles /'kɒlɪwɒb(ə)lz/ *n.pl. colloq.* **1** a rumbling or pain in the stomach. **2** a feeling of strong apprehension. [fanciful, from COLIC + WOBBLE]

Colo. *abbr.* Colorado.

colobus /'kɒləbəs/ *n.* any leaf-eating monkey of the genus *Colobus*, native to Africa, having shortened thumbs. [modern Latin from Greek *kolobos* 'docked']

colocynth /'kɒləsɪnθ/ *n.* (also **coloquintida** /kɒlə'kwɪntɪdə/) **1 a** a plant of the gourd family, *Citrullus colocynthis*, bearing a pulpy fruit. **b** this fruit. **2** a bitter purgative drug obtained from the fruit. [Latin *colocynthis* from Greek *kolokunthis*]

cologne /kə'ləʊn/ *n.* (in full **cologne water**) eau de Cologne or a similar scented toilet water. [*Cologne* in Germany]

colon[1] /'kəʊlən/ *n.* a punctuation mark (:), used esp. to introduce a quotation or a list of items or to separate clauses when the second expands or illustrates the first; also between numbers in a statement of proportion (as in 10:1) and in biblical references (as in Exodus 3:2). [Latin from Greek *kōlon* 'limb, clause']

colon[2] /'kəʊlən, -lɒn/ *n. Anat.* the greater part of the large intestine, from the caecum to the rectum. □ **colonic** /kə'lɒnɪk/ *adj.* [Middle English, ultimately from Greek *kolon*]

colonel /'kə:n(ə)l/ *n.* **1** an army officer in command of a regiment, immediately below a brigadier in rank. **2** *US* an officer of corresponding rank in the Air Force. **3** = LIEUTENANT COLONEL. □ **colonelcy** *n.* (*pl.* **-ies**). [obsolete French *coronel* from Italian *colonnello* 'column of soldiers', from *colonna* COLUMN]

Colonel Blimp see BLIMP *n.* 1.

colonial /kə'ləʊnɪəl/ *adj.* & *n.* ● *adj.* **1 a** of, relating to, or characteristic of a colony or colonies, esp. of a British Crown Colony. **b** of colonialism. **2** (esp. of architecture or furniture) built or designed in, or in a style characteristic of, the period of the British colonies in America before independence. ● *n.* **1** a native or inhabitant of a colony. **2** a house built in colonial style. □ **colonially** *adv.*

colonial goose *n. Austral.* & *NZ* a boned and stuffed roast leg of mutton.

colonialism /kə'ləʊnɪəlɪz(ə)m/ *n.* **1** a policy of acquiring or maintaining colonies. **2** *derog.* this policy regarded as the esp. economic exploitation of weak or backward peoples by a larger power. □ **colonialist** *n.*

colonist /'kɒlənɪst/ *n.* a settler in or inhabitant of a colony.

colonize /'kɒlənʌɪz/ *v.* (also **-ise**) **1** *tr.* **a** establish a colony or colonies in (a country or area). **b** settle as colonists. **2** *intr.* establish or join a colony. **3** *tr. Biol.* (of plants and animals) become established in (an area). □ **colonization** /-'zeɪʃ(ə)n/ *n.* **colonizer** *n.*

colonnade /kɒlə'neɪd/ *n.* a row of columns, esp. supporting an entablature or roof. □ **colonnaded** *adj.* [French, from *colonne* COLUMN]

colonoscopy /kɒlə'nɒskəpi/ *n.* (*pl.* **-ies**) an examination of the colon by means of a flexible tube inserted through the anus. □ **colonoscope** /kə'lɒnəskəʊp/ *n.*

colony /'kɒləni/ *n.* (*pl.* **-ies**) **1 a** a group of settlers in a new country (whether or not already inhabited) fully or partly subject to the mother country. **b** the settlement or its territory. **2 a** people of one nationality or race or occupation in a city, esp. if living more or less in isolation or in a special quarter. **b** a separate or segregated group (*nudist colony*). **3** *Biol.* a community of animals or plants of one kind forming a physically connected structure or living close together. [Middle English from Latin *colonia*, via *colonus* 'farmer' from *colere* 'cultivate']

colophon /'kɒləf(ə)n/ *n.* **1** a publisher's device or imprint, esp. on the title-page. **2** a tailpiece in a manuscript or book, often ornamental, giving the writer's or printer's name, the date, etc. [Late Latin from Greek *kolophōn* 'summit, finishing touch']

colophony /kə'lɒfəni, 'kɒləfəʊni/ *n.* = ROSIN. [Latin *colophonia* '(resin) from Colophon' (in Asia Minor)]

coloquintida var. of COLOCYNTH.

color etc. *US* var. of COLOUR etc.

Colorado beetle /kɒlə,rɑ:dəʊ 'bi:t(ə)l/ *n.* a yellow and black striped beetle, *Leptinotarsa decemlineata*, the larva of which is highly destructive to the potato plant. [*Colorado* in the US]

coloration /kʌlə'reɪʃ(ə)n/ *n.* (also **colouration**) **1** colouring; a scheme or method of applying colour. **2** the natural (esp. variegated) colour of living things or animals. [French *coloration* or Late Latin *coloratio*, from *colorare* COLOUR]

coloratura /kɒlərə'tjʊərə, -'tʊ-/ *n.* **1** elaborate ornamentation of a vocal melody. **2** a singer (esp. a soprano) skilled in coloratura singing. [Italian, from Latin *colorare* COLOUR]

colorific /kʌlə'rɪfɪk, kɒl-/ *adj.* **1** producing colour. **2** highly coloured. [French *colorifique* or modern Latin *colorificus* (as COLOUR)]

colorimeter /kʌlə'rɪmɪtə, kɒl-/ *n.* an instrument for measuring the intensity of colour. □ **colorimetric** /-'mɛtrɪk/ *adj.* **colorimetry** *n.* [Latin *color* COLOUR + -METER]

colossal /kə'lɒs(ə)l/ *adj.* **1** of immense size; huge, gigantic. **2** *colloq.* remarkable, splendid. **3** *Archit.* (of an order) having more than one storey of columns. **4** *Sculpture* (of a statue) about twice life size. □ **colossally** *adv.* [French, from *colosse* COLOSSUS]

colosseum var. of COLISEUM.

colossus /kə'lɒsəs/ *n.* (*pl.* **colossi** /-sʌɪ/ or **colossuses**) **1** a statue much bigger than life size. **2** a gigantic person, animal, building, etc. **3** an imperial power personified. [Latin from Greek *kolossos*]

colostomy /kə'lɒstəmi/ *n.* (*pl.* **-ies**) *Surgery* an operation in which the colon is shortened to remove a damaged part and the cut end diverted to an opening in the abdominal wall. [as COLON[2] + Greek *stoma* 'mouth']

colostrum /kə'lɒstrəm/ *n.* the first secretion from the mammary glands occurring after giving birth, rich in antibodies. [Latin]

colotomy /kə'lɒtəmi/ *n.* (*pl.* **-ies**) *Surgery* an incision in the colon. [as COLON[2] + -TOMY]

colour /'kʌlə/ *n.* & *v.* ● *n.* (*US* **color**) **1 a** the sensation produced on the eye by rays of light when resolved as by a prism, selective reflection, etc., into different wavelengths. **b** perception of colour; a system of colours. **2** one, or any mixture, of the constituents into which light can be separated as in a spectrum or rainbow, sometimes including (loosely) black and white. **3** a colouring substance, esp. paint. **4** the use of all colours, not only black and white, as in photography and television. **5 a** pigmentation of the skin, esp. when dark. **b** this as a ground for prejudice or discrimination. **6** ruddiness of complexion (*a healthy colour*). **7** (in *pl.*) appearance or aspect (*see things in their true colours*). **8** (in *pl.*) **a** *Brit.* a coloured ribbon or uniform etc. worn to signify membership of a school, club, team, etc. **b** the flag of a regiment or ship. **c** a national flag. **9** quality, mood, or variety in music, literature, speech, etc.; distinctive character or timbre. **10** a show of reason; a pretext (*lend colour to*; *under colour of*). **11** *Physics* a quantum number assigned to quarks and gluons in the theory of quantum chromodynamics. ● *v.* **1** *tr.* apply colour to, esp. by painting or dyeing or with coloured pens or pencils. **2** *tr.* influence (*an attitude coloured by experience*). **3** *tr.* misrepresent, exaggerate, esp. with spurious detail (*a highly coloured account*). **4** *intr.* take on colour; blush.

□ **show one's true colours** reveal one's true character or intentions. **under false colours** falsely, deceitfully. **with flying colours** see FLYING. [Middle English via Old French *color, colorer* from Latin *color, colorare*]

colourable /ˈkʌlərəb(ə)l/ *adj.* (*US* **colorable**) **1** specious, plausible. **2** counterfeit. □ **colourably** *adv.*

colourant /ˈkʌlər(ə)nt/ *n.* (*US* **colorant**) a colouring substance.

colouration var. of COLORATION.

colour bar *n.* the denial of services and facilities to non-white people.

colour-blind *adj.* unable to distinguish certain colours. □ **colour-blindness** *n.*

colour code *n.* & *v.* ● *n.* the use of colours as a standard means of identification. ● *v.tr.* (**colour-code**) identify by means of a colour code.

coloured /ˈkʌləd/ *adj.* & *n.* (*US* **colored**) ● *adj.* **1** having colour. **2** (often **Coloured**) often *offens.* **a** wholly or partly of non-white descent. **b** *S.Afr.* of mixed white and non-white descent. **c** of or relating to coloured people (*a coloured audience*). ● *n.* **1** (often **Coloured**) often *offens.* **a** a coloured person. **b** *S.Afr.* a person of mixed descent speaking Afrikaans or English as the mother tongue. **2** (in *pl.*) coloured clothing etc. for washing.

■ **Usage** The use of *coloured* to refer to people of racial groups not considered white is regarded as offensive by many people and should be avoided by using black, Asian, etc., as appropriate.

colour fast *adj.* dyed in colours that will not fade or be washed out. □ **colour fastness** *n.*

colourful /ˈkʌləfʊl, -f(ə)l/ *adj.* (*US* **colorful**) **1** having much or varied colour; bright. **2** full of interest; vivid, lively. □ **colourfully** *adv.* **colourfulness** *n.*

colouring /ˈkʌlərɪŋ/ *n.* (*US* **coloring**) **1** the process of or skill in using colour. **2** the style in which a thing is coloured, or in which an artist uses colour. **3** facial complexion.

colourist /ˈkʌlərɪst/ *n.* (*US* **colorist**) a person who uses colour, esp. in art.

colourless /ˈkʌləlɪs/ *adj.* (*US* **colorless**) **1** without colour. **2** lacking character or interest. **3** dull or pale in hue. **4** neutral, impartial, indifferent. □ **colourlessly** *adv.*

colour scheme *n.* an arrangement or planned combination of colours esp. in interior design.

colour-sergeant *n.* the senior sergeant of an infantry company.

colour supplement *n. Brit.* a magazine with coloured illustrations, issued as a supplement to a newspaper.

colour temperature *n. Astron.* & *Physics* the temperature at which a black body would emit radiation of the same colour as a given object.

colour wash *n.* & *v.* ● *n.* coloured distemper. ● *v.tr.* (**colour-wash**) paint with coloured distemper.

colourway /ˈkʌləweɪ/ *n.* (*US* **colorway**) a coordinated combination of colours.

coloury /ˈkʌləri/ *adj.* (*US* **colory**) having a distinctive colour, esp. as indicating good quality.

colposcopy /kɒlˈpɒskəpi/ *n.* examination of the vagina and the neck of the womb. □ **colposcope** /ˈkɒlpəˌskəʊp/ *n.* [Greek *kolpos* 'womb' + -SCOPY]

colt /kəʊlt/ *n.* **1** a young uncastrated male horse, usu. less than four years old. **2** *Brit. Sport* a young or inexperienced player; a member of a junior team. □ **colthood** *n.* **coltish** *adj.* **coltishly** *adv.* **coltishness** *n.* [Old English, = young ass or camel]

colter *US* var. of COULTER.

coltsfoot /ˈkəʊltsfʊt/ *n.* (*pl.* **coltsfoots**) a plant of the daisy family, *Tussilago farfara*, with large leaves and yellow flowers.

colubrid /ˈkɒljʊbrɪd/ *adj.* & *n. Zool.* ● *adj.* of or relating to the large family Colubridae to which most non-venomous snakes belong. ● *n.* a snake of this family. [Latin *coluber* 'snake' + -ID[3]]

colubrine /ˈkɒljʊbrʌɪn/ *adj.* **1** of the subfamily Colubrinae of colubrid snakes with solid teeth. **2** snakelike. [Latin *colubrinus* from *coluber* 'snake']

colugo /kəˈluːgəʊ/ *n.* (*pl.* **-os**) a flying lemur. [18th c.: origin unknown]

columbarium /kɒl(ə)mˈbɛːrɪəm/ *n.* a room or building with niches and shelves for cinerary urns to be stored. [Latin, = pigeon house (from *columba* 'pigeon')]

Columbine /ˈkɒl(ə)mbʌɪn/ *n.* the partner of Harlequin in pantomime. [French *Colombine* from Italian *Colombina*, from *colombino* 'dovelike']

columbine /ˈkɒl(ə)mbʌɪn/ *n.* an aquilegia, esp. *Aquilegia vulgaris*, which has purple-blue flowers. [Middle English via Old French *colombine* and medieval Latin *colombina herba* 'dovelike plant' from Latin *columba* 'dove' (from the supposed resemblance of the flower to a cluster of 5 doves)]

columbite /kəˈlʌmbʌɪt/ *n. Chem.* an ore of niobium containing iron and magnesium. [modern Latin *Columbia*, a poetic name for America, + -ITE[1]]

columbium /kəˈlʌmbɪəm/ *n.* esp. *N. Amer. Metallurgy* = NIOBIUM.

column /ˈkɒləm/ *n.* **1** *Archit.* an upright cylindrical pillar often slightly tapering and usu. supporting an entablature or arch, or standing alone as a monument. **2** a structure or part shaped like a column. **3** a vertical cylindrical mass of liquid or vapour. **4 a** a vertical division of a page, chart, etc., containing a sequence of figures or words. **b** the figures or words themselves. **5** a part of a newspaper regularly devoted to a particular subject (*gossip column*). **6 a** *Mil.* an arrangement of troops in successive lines, deep from front to rear but of narrow width. **b** *Naut.* a similar arrangement of ships. □ **dodge the column** *Brit. colloq.* shirk one's duty; avoid work. □ **columnar** /kəˈlʌmnə/ *adj.* **columned** *adj.* [Middle English from Old French *columpne*, Latin *columna* 'pillar']

column-inch *n.* a quantity of print (esp. newsprint) occupying a one-inch length of a column.

columnist /ˈkɒl(ə)m(n)ɪst/ *n.* a journalist contributing regularly to a newspaper.

colure /kəˈljʊə/ *n. Astron.* either of two great circles intersecting at right angles at the celestial poles and passing through the ecliptic at either the equinoxes or the solstices. [Middle English via Late Latin *colurus* from Greek *kolouros* 'truncated', so called because the lower part is cut off from view]

colza /ˈkɒlzə/ *n.* = RAPE[2]. [French *kolza(t)* from Low German *kōlsāt* (as COLE, SEED)]

COM *abbr.* computer output on microfilm or microfiche.

com- /kɒm, kəm/ *prefix* (also **co-**, **col-**, **con-**, **cor-**) with, together, jointly, altogether. [Latin *com-*, *cum* 'with']

■ **Usage** *Com-* is used before *b*, *m*, *p*, and occasionally before vowels and *f*; *co-* esp. before vowels, *h*, and *gn*; *col-* before *l*, *cor-* before *r*, and *con-* before other consonants.

coma[1] /ˈkəʊmə/ *n.* (*pl.* **comas**) a prolonged deep unconsciousness, caused esp. by severe injury or excessive use of drugs. [medieval Latin from Greek *kōma* 'deep sleep']

coma[2] /ˈkəʊmə/ *n.* (*pl.* **comae** /-miː/) **1** *Astron.* a cloud of gas and dust surrounding the nucleus of a comet. **2** *Bot.* a tuft of silky hairs at the end of some seeds. [Latin from Greek *komē* 'hair of head']

comatose /ˈkəʊmətəʊs, -z/ *adj.* **1** in a coma. **2** drowsy, sleepy, lethargic.

comb /kəʊm/ *n.* & *v.* ● *n.* **1** a toothed strip of rigid material for tidying and arranging the hair, or for keeping it in place. **2** a part of a machine having a similar design or purpose. **3 a** the red fleshy crest of a fowl, esp. a cock. **b** an analogous growth in other birds. **4** a honeycomb. ● *v.tr.* **1** arrange or tidy (the hair) by drawing a comb through. **2** curry (a horse). **3** dress (wool or flax) with a comb. **4** search (a place) thoroughly. □ **comb out 1** tidy and arrange (the hair) loosely by combing. **2** remove with a comb. **3** search or attack systematically. **4** search out and get rid of (anything unwanted). □ **combed** *adj.* [Old English *camb*, from Germanic]

combat /ˈkɒmbat, ˈkʌ-, -ət/ *n.* & *v.* ● *n.* a fight, struggle, or contest. ● *v.* (**combated**, **combating**) **1** *intr.* engage in combat. **2** *tr.* engage in combat with. **3** *tr.* oppose; strive against. [French, from *combattre* from Late Latin (as COM-, Latin *batuere* 'fight')]

combatant /ˈkɒmbət(ə)nt, ˈkʌm-/ *n.* & *adj.* ● *n.* a person engaged in fighting. ● *adj.* **1** fighting. **2** for fighting.

combat dress *n.* a soldier's uniform worn for combat and field training, usu. of olive-green, camouflage, or khaki fabric.

combat fatigue *n.* **1** mental disorder caused by stress in wartime combat. **2** see FATIGUE *n.* 5.

combative /ˈkɒmbətɪv, ˈkʌm-/ *adj.* ready or eager to fight; pugnacious. □ **combatively** *adv.* **combativeness** *n.*

combe var. of COOMB.

comber[1] /ˈkəʊmə/ *n.* **1** a person or thing that combs, esp. a machine for combing cotton or wool very fine. **2** a long curling wave; a breaker.

comber[2] /ˈkɒmbə/ *n. Brit.* a fish of the perch family, *Serranus cabrilla*. [18th c.: origin unknown]

combi /ˈkɒmbi/ *n.* a machine, appliance, etc. with a combined function or mode of action (often *attrib.*: *combi oven*). [abbreviation of COMBINATION]

combination /kɒmbɪˈneɪʃ(ə)n/ *n.* **1** the act or an instance of combining; the process of being combined. **2** a combined state (*in combination with*). **3** a combined set of things or people. **4** a sequence of numbers or letters used to open a combination lock. **5** *Brit.* a motorcycle with sidecar attached. **6** (in *pl.*) a single undergarment for the body and legs. **7** a group of things chosen from a larger number without regard to their arrangement. **8 a** united action. **b** *Chess* a coordinated and effective sequence of moves. **9** *Chem.* a union of substances in a compound with new properties. □ **combinational** *adj.* **combinative** /ˈkɒmbɪnətɪv/ *adj.* **combinatory** /ˈkɒmbɪnət(ə)ri/ *adj.* [obsolete French *combination* or Late Latin *combinatio* (as COMBINE)]

combination lock *n.* a lock that can be opened only by a specific sequence of movements.

combination oven *n.* an oven operating by both conventional heating and microwaves.

combinatorial /ˌkɒmbɪnəˈtɔːrɪəl/ *adj. Math.* relating to combinations of items.

combine *v.* & *n.* ● *v.* /kəmˈbʌɪn/ **1** *tr.* & *intr.* join together; unite for a common purpose. **2** *tr.* possess (esp. disparate qualities) in combination (*combines charm and authority*). **3 a** *intr.* coalesce in one substance. **b** *tr.* cause to do this. **c** *intr.* form a chemical compound. **4** *intr.* cooperate. **5** /ˈkɒmbʌɪn/ *tr.* harvest (crops etc.) by means of a combine harvester. ● *n.* /ˈkɒmbʌɪn/ **1** a combination of esp. commercial interests to control prices etc. **2** = COMBINE HARVESTER. □ **combinable** /kəmˈbʌɪnəb(ə)l/ *adj.* [Middle English from Old French *combiner* or Late Latin *combinare* (as COM-, Latin *bini* 'two')]

combine harvester *n.* a mobile machine that reaps and threshes in one operation.

combing /ˈkəʊmɪŋ/ *n.* **1** in senses of COMB *v.* **2** (in *pl.*) hairs combed off.

combing wool *n.* long-stapled wool, suitable for combing and making into worsted.

combining form *n. Gram.* a form of a word used (only) in compounds in combination with another element to form a word (e.g. *Anglo-* = English in *Anglo-Irish*, *bio-* = life in *biology*, *-graphy* = writing in *biography*).

■ **Usage** In this dictionary, *combining form* is used of an element that contributes to the particular sense of words (as with both elements of *biography*), as distinct from a prefix or suffix that adjusts the sense of or determines the function of words (as with *un-*, *-able*, and *-ation*).

comb-jelly *n.* a ctenophore.

combo /ˈkɒmbəʊ/ *n.* (*pl.* **-os**) *slang* **1** a small jazz or dance band. **2** a combination; a combined unit. [abbreviation of COMBINATION + -o]

combs /kɒmz/ *n.pl. colloq.* combinations (see COMBINATION 6).

combust /kəmˈbʌst/ *v.tr.* subject to combustion. [obsolete *combust* (*adj.*) from Latin *combustus* past part. (as COMBUSTION)]

combustible /kəmˈbʌstɪb(ə)l/ *adj.* & *n.* ● *adj.* **1** capable of or used for burning. **2** excitable; easily irritated. ● *n.* a combustible substance. □ **combustibility** /-ˈbɪlɪti/ *n.* [French *combustible* or medieval Latin *combustibilis* (as COMBUSTION)]

combustion /kəmˈbʌstʃ(ə)n/ *n.* **1** burning; consumption by fire. **2** *Chem.* the development of light and heat from the chemical combination of a substance with oxygen. □ **combustive** *adj.* [Middle English via French *combustion* or Late Latin *combustio* from Latin *comburere combust-* 'burn up']

combustion chamber *n.* a space in which combustion takes place, e.g. of gases in a boiler-furnace or fuel in an internal-combustion engine.

come /kʌm/ *v.* & *n.* ● *v.intr.* (*past* **came** /keɪm/; *past part.* **come**) **1** move, be brought towards, or reach a place thought of as near or familiar to the speaker or hearer (*come and see me*; *shall we come to your house?*; *the books have come*). **2** reach or be brought to a specified situation or result (*you'll come to no harm*; *have come to believe it*; *has come to be used wrongly*; *came into prominence*). **3** reach or extend to a specified point (*the road comes within a mile of us*). **4** traverse or progress (with compl.: *have come a long way*). **5 a** get to be in a certain condition (*how did you come to break your leg?*). **b** (of time) arrive in due course (*the day soon came*). **6** take or occupy a specified position (*it comes on the third page*; *came second in the race*; *Nero came after Claudius*; *it does not come within the scope of the inquiry*). **7** become perceptible or known (*the church came into sight*; *the news comes as a surprise*; *it will come to me*). **8** be available (*the dress comes in three sizes*; *this model comes with optional features*). **9** become (with compl.: *the handle has come loose*; *won't come clean*). **10** (foll. by *of*, *from*) **a** be descended from (*comes of a rich family*). **b** be the result of (*that comes from complaining*). **11** (foll. by *from*) **a** originate in; have as its source. **b** have as one's home. **12** *colloq.* play the part of; behave like (with compl.: *don't come the bully with me*). **13** *slang* have a sexual orgasm. **14** (in *subjunctive*) *colloq.* when a specified time is reached (*come next month*). **15** (also **come, come!**) (as *int.*) expressing caution or reserve (*come, it cannot be that bad*). ● *n. slang* semen ejaculated at a sexual orgasm. □ **as ... as they come** typically or supremely so (*is as tough as they come*). **come about** happen; take place. **come across 1** meet or find by chance (*came across an old jacket*). **2** *colloq.* be effective or understood; give a specified impression. **3** (foll. by *with*) *slang* hand over what is wanted. **come again** *colloq.* **1** make a further effort. **2** (as *imper.*) what did you say? **come along 1** make progress; move forward. **2** (as *imper.*) hurry up. **come and go 1** pass to and fro; be transitory. **2** pay brief visits. **come apart** fall or break into pieces; disintegrate. **come at 1** reach, discover; get access to. **2** attack (*came at me with a knife*). **come away 1** become detached or broken off (*came away in my hands*). **2** (foll. by *with*) be left with (a feeling, impression, etc.) (*came away with many misgivings*). **come back 1** return. **2** recur to one's memory. **3** become fashionable or popular again. **4** *N. Amer.* reply, retort. **come before** be dealt with by (a judge etc.). **come between 1** interfere with the relationship of. **2** separate; prevent contact between. **come by 1** pass; go past. **2** call on a visit (*why not come by tomorrow?*). **3** acquire, obtain (*came by a new bicycle*). **come clean** see CLEAN. **come down 1**

come to a place or position regarded as lower. **2** lose position or wealth (*has come down in the world*). **3** be handed down by tradition or inheritance. **4** be reduced; show a downward trend (*prices are coming down*). **5** (foll. by *against, in favour of,* etc.) reach a decision or recommendation (*the report came down against change*). **6** (foll. by *to*) signify or betoken basically; be dependent on (a factor) (*it comes down to who is willing to go*). **7** (foll. by *on*) criticize harshly; rebuke, punish. **8** (foll. by *with*) begin to suffer from (a disease). **come for 1** come to collect or receive. **2** attack (*came for me with a hammer*). **come forward 1** advance. **2** offer oneself for a task, post, etc. **come in 1** enter a house or room. **2** take a specified position in a race etc. (*came in third*). **3** become fashionable or seasonable. **4 a** have a useful role or function. **b** (with compl.) prove to be (*came in very handy*). **c** have a part to play (*where do I come in?*). **5** be received (*more news has just come in*). **6** begin speaking, esp. in radio transmission. **7** be elected; come to power. **8** *Cricket* begin an innings. **9** (foll. by *for*) receive; be the object of (usu. something unwelcome) (*came in for much criticism*). **10** (foll. by *on*) join (an enterprise etc.). **11** (of a tide) turn to high tide. **12** (of a train, ship, or aircraft) approach its destination. **13** return to base (*come in, number 9*). **come into 1** see senses 2, 7 of *v.* **2** receive, esp. as heir. **come near** see NEAR. **come of age** see AGE. **come off 1** *colloq.* (of an action) succeed; be accomplished. **2** (with compl.) fare; turn out (*came off badly; came off the winner*). **3** *Brit. coarse slang* have a sexual orgasm. **4** be detached or detachable (from). **5** *Brit.* fall (from). **6** be reduced or subtracted from (*£5 came off the price*). **come off it** (as *imper.*) *colloq.* an expression of disbelief or refusal to accept another's opinion, behaviour, etc. **come on 1** continue to come. **2** advance, esp. to attack. **3** make progress; thrive (*is really coming on*). **4** (foll. by *to* + infin.) *Brit.* begin (*it came on to rain*). **5** appear on the stage, field of play, etc. **6** be heard or seen on television, on the telephone, etc. **7** arise to be discussed. **8** (as *imper.*) expressing encouragement. **9** = *come upon.* **come out 1** emerge; become known (*it came out that he had left*). **2** appear or be published (*comes out every Saturday*). **3 a** declare oneself as being for or against something; make a decision (*came out in favour of joining*). **b** openly declare something (esp. that one is a homosexual). **4** *Brit.* go on strike. **5 a** be satisfactorily visible in a photograph etc., or present in a specified way (*the dog didn't come out; he came out badly*). **b** (of a photograph) be produced satisfactorily or in a specified way (*only three have come out; they all came out well*). **6** attain a specified result in an examination etc. **7** (of a stain etc.) be removed. **8** make one's debut in society. **9** (foll. by *in*) be covered with (*came out in spots*). **10** (of a problem) be solved. **11** (foll. by *with*) declare openly; disclose. **come over 1** come from some distance or nearer to the speaker (*came over from Paris; come over here a moment*). **2** change sides or one's opinion. **3 a** (of a feeling etc.) overtake or affect (a person). **b** *Brit. colloq.* feel suddenly (*came over faint*). **4** appear or sound in a specified way (*you came over very well; the ideas came over clearly*). **come round** (or *US* also **around**) **1** pay an informal visit. **2** recover consciousness. **3** be converted to another person's opinion. **4** (of a date or regular occurrence) recur; be imminent again. **come through 1** be successful; survive. **2** be received by telephone. **3** survive or overcome (a difficulty) (*came through the ordeal*). **come to 1** (also *refl.*) recover consciousness. **2** *Naut.* bring a vessel to a stop. **3** reach in total; amount to. **4** *Brit. colloq.* stop being foolish. **5** have as a destiny; reach (*what is the world coming to?*). **come to hand** become available; be recovered. **come to light** see LIGHT[1]. **come to nothing** have no useful result in the end; fail. **come to pass** happen, occur. **come to rest** cease moving. **come to one's senses** see SENSE. **come to that** *colloq.* in fact; if that is the case. **come under 1** be classified as or among. **2** be subject to (influence or authority). **come up 1** come to a place or position regarded as higher. **2** attain wealth or position (*come up in the world*). **3 a** (of an issue, problem, etc.) arise; present itself; be mentioned or discussed. **b** (of an event etc.) occur, happen (*coming up next on BBC1*). **4** (often foll. by *to*) **a** approach a person, esp. to talk. **b** (*US* also often foll. by *on*) approach or draw near to a specified time, event, etc. (*is coming up to eight o'clock*). **5** (foll. by *to*) match (a standard etc.). **6** (foll. by *with*) produce (an idea etc.), esp. in response to a challenge. **7** (of a plant etc.) spring up out of the ground. **8** become brighter (e.g. with polishing); shine more brightly. **come up against** be faced with or opposed by. **come upon 1** meet or find by chance. **2** attack by surprise. **come what may** no matter what happens. **have it coming to one** *colloq.* be about to get one's deserts. **how come?** *colloq.* how did that happen? **if it comes to that** in that case. **to come** future; in the future (*the year to come; many problems were still to come*). [Old English *cuman* from Germanic]

come-at-able /kʌm'atəb(ə)l/ *adj.* reachable, accessible.

comeback /'kʌmbak/ *n.* **1** a return to a previous (esp. successful) state. **2** *slang* a retaliation or retort. **3** *Austral.* a sheep bred from cross-bred and pure-bred parents for both wool and meat.

Comecon /'kɒmɪkɒn/ *n. hist.* an economic association of East European countries. [abbreviation of *Council for Mutual Economic Assistance*]

comedian /kə'mi:dɪən/ *n.* **1** a humorous entertainer on stage, television, etc. **2** an actor in comedy. **3** *slang* a buffoon; a foolish person. [French *comédien* from *comédie* COMEDY]

comedienne /kəmi:dɪ'ɛn, -mɛ-/ *n.* a female comedian. [French fem. (as COMEDIAN)]

comedist /'kɒmədɪst/ *n.* a writer of comedies.

comedo /'kɒmɪdəʊ, kə'mi:dəʊ/ *n.* (*pl.* **comedones** /-'dəʊni:z/) *Med.* a blackhead. [Latin, = glutton, from *comedere* 'eat up' (a name formerly given to parasitic worms, with reference to the wormlike matter which can be squeezed from a blackhead)]

comedown /'kʌmdaʊn/ *n.* **1** a loss of status; decline or degradation. **2** a disappointment.

comedy /'kɒmɪdi/ *n.* (*pl.* **-ies**) **1 a** a play, film, etc., of an amusing or satirical character, usu. with a happy ending. **b** the dramatic genre consisting of works of this kind (*she excels in comedy*) (cf. TRAGEDY 3). **2** an amusing or farcical incident or series of incidents in everyday life. **3** humour, esp. in a work of art etc. □ **comedic** /kə'mi:dɪk, -'mɛ-/ *adj.* [Middle English via Old French *comedie* and Latin *comoedia* from Greek *kōmōidia, kōmōidos* 'comic poet', via *kōmos* 'revel']

comedy of manners *n.* satirical portrayal of social behaviour, esp. of the upper classes.

come-hither *attrib.adj. colloq.* (of a look or manner) enticing, flirtatious.

comely /'kʌmli/ *adj.* (**comelier**, **comeliest**) (usu. of a woman) pleasant to look at. □ **comeliness** /'kʌmlɪnɪs/ *n.* [Middle English *cumelich, cumli* probably from *becumelich*, from BECOME]

come-on *n. slang* a lure or enticement.

comer /'kʌmə/ *n.* **1** a person who comes, esp. as an applicant, participant, etc. (*offered the job to the first comer*). **2** *colloq.* a person likely to be a success.

comestible /kə'mɛstɪb(ə)l/ *n.* (usu. in *pl.*) *formal* or *joc.* food. [Middle English via French and medieval Latin *comestibilis* from Latin *comedere comest-* 'eat up']

comet /'kɒmɪt/ *n.* a small body of ice and dust moving around the solar system in an eccentric orbit, visible in the night sky with a tail of gas and dust when near the sun (and historically considered a supernatural omen). □ **cometary** *adj.* [Middle English via Old French *comete* and Latin *cometa* from Greek *komētēs* 'long-haired (star)']

come-uppance /kʌm'ʌp(ə)ns/ *n. colloq.* one's deserved fate or punishment (*got his come-uppance*). [COME + UP + -ANCE]

comfit /ˈkʌmfɪt/ *n. archaic* a sweet consisting of a nut, seed, etc. coated in sugar. [Middle English via Old French *confit* from Latin *confectum,* past part. of *conficere* 'prepare': see CONFECTION]

comfort /ˈkʌmfət/ *n. & v.* ● *n.* **1** consolation; relief in affliction. **2 a** a state of physical well-being; being comfortable (*live in comfort*). **b** (usu. in *pl.*) things that make life easy or pleasant (*has all the comforts*). **3** a cause of satisfaction (*a comfort to me that you are here*). **4** a person who consoles or helps one (*he's a comfort to her in her old age*). **5** *US dial.* a warm quilt. ● *v.tr.* **1** soothe in grief; console. **2** make comfortable (*comforted by the warmth of the fire*). □ **comforting** *adj.* **comfortingly** *adv.* [Middle English via Old French *confort(er)* from Late Latin *confortare* 'strengthen' (as COM-, Latin *fortis* 'strong')]

comfortable /ˈkʌmf(ə)təb(ə)l/ *adj. & n.* ● *adj.* **1** ministering to comfort; giving ease (*a comfortable pair of shoes*). **2** free from discomfort; at ease (*I'm quite comfortable thank you*). **3** *colloq.* having an adequate standard of living; free from financial worry. **4** having an easy conscience (*did not feel comfortable about refusing him*). **5** with a wide margin (*a comfortable win*). ● *n. US dial.* a warm quilt. □ **comfortableness** *n.* **comfortably** *adv.* [Middle English from Anglo-French *confortable* (as COMFORT)]

comforter /ˈkʌmfətə/ *n.* **1** a person who comforts. **2** *Brit.* a baby's dummy. **3** *archaic* a woollen scarf. **4** *N. Amer.* a warm quilt. [Middle English from Anglo-French *confortour,* Old French *comfortëor* (as COMFORT)]

comfortless /ˈkʌmfətlɪs/ *adj.* **1** dreary, cheerless. **2** without comfort.

comfort station *n. N. Amer. euphem.* a public lavatory.

comfrey /ˈkʌmfri/ *n.* (*pl.* **-eys**) a plant of the genus *Symphytum* (borage family), esp. *S. officinale,* which has large hairy leaves and clusters of usu. white or purple bell-shaped flowers. [Middle English from Anglo-French *cumfrie,* ultimately from Latin *conferva* (as COM-, *fervēre* 'boil together, heal', referring to the plant's medicinal use)]

comfy /ˈkʌmfi/ *adj.* (**comfier, comfiest**) *colloq.* comfortable. □ **comfily** *adv.* **comfiness** *n.* [abbreviation]

comic /ˈkɒmɪk/ *adj. & n.* ● *adj.* **1** (often *attrib.*) of, or in the style of, comedy (*a comic actor*; *comic opera*). **2** causing or meant to cause laughter; funny (*comic to see his struggles*). ● *n.* **1** a professional comedian. **2 a** a children's periodical, mainly in the form of comic strips. **b** a similar publication intended for adults. **c** (in *pl.*) *US* comic strips. [Latin *comicus* from Greek *kōmikos,* from *kōmos* 'revel']

comical /ˈkɒmɪk(ə)l/ *adj.* funny; causing laughter. □ **comicality** /-ˈkalɪti/ *n.* **comically** *adv.* [COMIC]

comic opera *n.* **1** an opera with much spoken dialogue, usu. with humorous treatment. **2** this genre of opera.

comic strip *n.* a horizontal series of drawings in a comic, newspaper, etc. telling a story.

coming /ˈkʌmɪŋ/ *adj. & n.* ● *attrib.adj.* **1** approaching, next (*in the coming week*; *this coming Sunday*). **2** of potential importance (*a coming man*). ● *n.* arrival; approach. □ **coming and going** (or **comings and goings**) activity, esp. intense. **not know if one is coming or going** be confused from being very busy.

Comintern /ˈkɒmɪntəːn/ *n.* the Third International (see INTERNATIONAL *n.* 2), a communist organization (1919–43). [Russian *Komintern* from the Russian forms of *communist, international*]

comitadji /kɒmɪˈtadʒi/ *n.* (also **komitadji, komitaji**) a member of an irregular band of soldiers in the Balkans. [Turkish *komitacı,* literally 'member of a (revolutionary) committee']

comity /ˈkɒmɪti/ *n.* (*pl.* **-ies**) **1** courtesy, civility; considerate behaviour towards others. **2 a** an association of nations etc. for mutual benefit. **b** (in full **comity of nations**) the mutual recognition by nations of the laws and customs of others. [Latin *comitas* from *comis* 'courteous']

comma /ˈkɒmə/ *n.* **1** a punctuation mark (,) indicating a pause between parts of a sentence, or dividing items in a list, string of figures, etc. **2** *Mus.* a definite minute interval or difference of pitch. **3** (in full **comma butterfly**) a butterfly, *Polygonia c-album,* with a white comma-shaped mark on the underside of the hindwing. [Latin from Greek *komma* 'clause']

comma bacillus *n.* a comma-shaped bacillus causing cholera.

command /kəˈmɑːnd/ *v. & n.* ● *v.tr.* **1** (often foll. by *to* + infin., or *that* + clause) give formal order or instructions to (*commands us to obey*; *commands that it be done*). **2** (also *absol.*) have authority or control over. **3** (often *refl.*) restrain, master. **4** gain the use of; have at one's disposal or within reach (skill, resources, etc.) (*commands an extensive knowledge of history*; *commands a salary of £40,000*). **5** deserve and get (sympathy, respect, etc.). **6** *Mil.* dominate (a strategic position) from a superior height; look down over. ● *n.* **1** an authoritative order; an instruction. **2** mastery, control, possession (*a good command of languages*; *has command of the resources*). **3** the exercise or tenure of authority, esp. naval or military (*has command of this ship*). **4** *Mil.* **a** a body of troops etc. (*Bomber Command*). **b** a district under a commander (*Western Command*). **5** *Computing* **a** an instruction causing a computer to perform one of its basic functions. **b** a signal initiating such an operation. □ **at command** ready to be used at will. **at** (or **by**) **a person's command** in pursuance of a person's bidding. **in command of** commanding; having under control. **under command of** commanded by. **word of command 1** *Mil.* an order for a movement in a drill etc. **2** a pre-arranged spoken signal for the start of an operation. [Middle English via Anglo-French *comaunder,* Old French *comander* from Late Latin *commandare* COMMEND]

commandant /kɒmənˈdant, ˈkɒməndant; -ɑːnt/ *n.* a commanding officer, esp. of a particular force, military academy, etc. □ **commandantship** *n.* [French *commandant,* or Italian or Spanish *commandante* (as COMMAND)]

Commandant-in-Chief *n. Brit.* the supreme commandant.

command economy *n.* = PLANNED ECONOMY.

commandeer /kɒmənˈdɪə/ *v.tr.* **1** seize (men or goods) for military purposes. **2** take possession of without authority. [South African Dutch *kommanderen* from French *commander* COMMAND]

commander /kəˈmɑːndə/ *n.* **1** a person who commands, esp.: **a** a naval officer next in rank below captain. **b** = WING COMMANDER. **c** an officer in charge of a London police district. **2** (in full **knight commander**) a member of a higher class in some orders of knighthood. **3** a large wooden mallet. □ **commandership** *n.* [Middle English via Old French *comandere, -eör* from Romanic (as COMMAND)]

commander-in-chief *n.* (*pl.* **commanders-in-chief**) the supreme commander, esp. of a nation's forces.

Commander of the Faithful *n.* a title of a caliph.

commanding /kəˈmɑːndɪŋ/ *adj.* **1** dignified, exalted, impressive. **2** (of a hill or other high point) giving a wide view. **3** (of an advantage, a position, etc.) controlling; superior (*has a commanding lead*). □ **commandingly** *adv.*

commandment /kəˈmɑːn(d)m(ə)nt/ *n.* a divine command. [Middle English from Old French *comandement* (as COMMAND)]

command module *n.* the control compartment in a spacecraft.

commando /kəˈmɑːndəʊ/ *n.* (*pl.* **-os**) *Mil.* **1** (often **Commando**) **a** a unit of British amphibious shock troops. **b** a member of such a unit. **c** a similar unit or member of such a unit elsewhere. **2 a** a party of men called out for military service. **b** a body of troops. **3** (*attrib.*) of or concerning a commando (*a commando operation*). [Portuguese, from *commandar* COMMAND]

Command Paper *n.* (in the UK) a paper laid before Parliament by command of the Crown (in practice, by the Government).

command performance *n.* (in the UK) a theatrical or film performance given by royal command.

command post *n.* the headquarters of a military unit.

comme ci, comme ça /kɒm,si: kɒm'sɑ:/ *adv. & adj.* so so; middling or middlingly. [French, = like this, like that]

commedia dell'arte /kɒ'meɪdɪə dɛl'ɑ:teɪ, Italian kɔm'me:dia dɛl'lartɛ/ *n.* an improvised kind of popular comedy in Italian theatres in the 16th–18th c., based on stock characters. [Italian, = comedy of art]

comme il faut /ˌkɒm i:l 'fəʊ, French kɔm il fo/ *adj. & adv.* ● *predic.adj.* (esp. of behaviour, etiquette, etc.) proper, correct. ● *adv.* properly, correctly. [French, = as is necessary]

commemorate /kə'mɛməreɪt/ *v.tr.* **1** celebrate in speech or writing. **2 a** preserve in memory by some celebration. **b** (of a stone, plaque, etc.) be a memorial of. □ **commemorative** /kə'mɛm(ə)rətɪv/ *adj.* **commemorator** *n.* [Latin *commemorare* (as COM-, *memorare* 'relate' from *memor* 'mindful')]

commemoration /kəmɛmə'reɪʃ(ə)n/ *n.* **1** an act of commemorating. **2** a service or part of a service in memory of a person, an event, etc. [Middle English from French *commemoration* or Latin *commemoratio* (as COMMEMORATE)]

commence /kə'mɛns/ *v.tr. & intr. formal* begin. [Middle English via Old French *com(m)encier* from Romanic (as COM-, Latin *initiare* INITIATE)]

commencement /kə'mɛnsm(ə)nt/ *n. formal* **1** a beginning. **2** esp. *N. Amer.* a ceremony of degree conferment. [Middle English from Old French (as COMMENCE)]

commend /kə'mɛnd/ *v.tr.* **1** (often foll. by *to*) entrust, commit (*commends his soul to God*). **2** praise (*commends her singing voice*). **3** (often *refl.*) recommend (*idea commends itself; has much to commend it*). □ **commend me to** *archaic* remember me kindly to. **highly commended** (of a competitor etc.) just missing the top places. [Middle English from Latin *commendare* (as COM-, *mendare* = *mandare* 'entrust': see MANDATE)]

commendable /kə'mɛndəb(ə)l/ *adj.* praiseworthy. □ **commendably** *adv.* [Middle English via Old French from Latin *commendabilis* (as COMMEND)]

commendation /kɒmɛn'deɪʃ(ə)n/ *n.* **1** an act of commending or recommending (esp. a person to another's favour). **2** praise. [Middle English via Old French from Latin *commendatio* (as COMMEND)]

commendatory /kɒ'mɛndət(ə)ri/ *adj.* commending, recommending. [Late Latin *commendatorius* (as COMMEND)]

commensal /kə'mɛns(ə)l/ *adj. & n.* ● *adj.* **1** *Biol.* of, relating to, or exhibiting commensalism. **2** (of a person) eating at the same table as another. ● *n.* **1** *Biol.* a commensal organism. **2** a person who eats at the same table as another. □ **commensality** /kɒmən'salɪti/ *n.* [Middle English from French *commensal* or medieval Latin *commensalis* (in sense 2) (as COM-, *mensa* 'table')]

commensalism /kə'mɛns(ə)lɪz(ə)m/ *n. Biol.* an association between two organisms in which one benefits and the other derives neither benefit nor harm.

commensurable /kə'mɛnʃ(ə)rəb(ə)l, -sjə-/ *adj.* **1** (often foll. by *with, to*) measurable by the same standard. **2** (foll. by *to*) proportionate to. **3** *Math.* (of numbers) in a ratio equal to the ratio of integers. □ **commensurability** /-'bɪlɪti/ *n.* **commensurably** *adv.* [Late Latin *commensurabilis* (as COM-, MEASURE)]

commensurate /kə'mɛnʃ(ə)rət, -sjə-/ *adj.* **1** (usu. foll. by *with*) having the same size, duration, etc.; coextensive. **2** (often foll. by *to, with*) proportionate. □ **commensurately** *adv.* [Late Latin *commensuratus* (as COM-, MEASURE)]

comment /'kɒmɛnt/ *n. & v.* ● *n.* **1 a** a remark, esp. critical; an opinion (*passed a comment on her hat*). **b** commenting; criticism (*his behaviour aroused much comment; an hour of news and comment*). **2 a** an explanatory note (e.g. on a written text). **b** written criticism or explanation (e.g. of a text). **3** (of a play, book, etc.) a critical illustration; a parable (*his art is a comment on society*). ● *v.intr.* **1** (often foll. by *on, upon,* or *that* + clause) make (esp. critical) remarks (*commented on her choice of friends*). **2** (often foll. by *on, upon*) write explanatory notes. □ **no comment** *colloq.* I decline to answer your question. □ **commenter** *n.* [Middle English from Latin *commentum* 'contrivance' (in Late Latin also = interpretation), neut. past part. of *comminisci* 'devise', or in later use from French *commenter* (*v.*)]

commentary /'kɒmənt(ə)ri/ *n.* (*pl.* **-ies**) **1** a set of explanatory or critical notes on a text etc. **2** a descriptive spoken account (esp. on radio or television) of an event or a performance as it happens. [Latin *commentarius, -ium* (*adj.* used as a noun) (as COMMENT)]

commentate /'kɒmənteɪt/ *v.intr.* (often foll. by *on*) act as a commentator. [back-formation from COMMENTATOR]

commentator /'kɒmənteɪtə/ *n.* **1** a person who provides a commentary on an event etc. **2** the writer of a commentary. **3** a person who writes or speaks on current events. [Latin from *commentari,* frequentative of *comminisci* 'devise']

commerce /'kɒmə:s/ *n.* **1** financial transactions, esp. the buying and selling of merchandise, on a large scale. **2** social intercourse (*the daily commerce of gossip and opinion*). **3** *archaic* sexual intercourse. [French *commerce* or Latin *commercium* (as COM-, *mercium* from *merx mercis* 'merchandise')]

commercial /kə'mə:ʃ(ə)l/ *adj. & n.* ● *adj.* **1** of, engaged in, or concerned with, commerce. **2** having profit as a primary aim rather than artistic etc. value; philistine. **3** (of chemicals) supplied in bulk more or less unpurified. ● *n.* **1** a television or radio advertisement. **2** *Brit. archaic* a commercial traveller. □ **commerciality** /-ʃɪ'alɪti/ *n.* **commercially** *adv.*

commercial art *n.* art used in advertising, selling, etc.

commercial broadcasting *n.* television or radio broadcasting in which programmes are financed by advertisements.

commercialism /kə'mə:ʃ(ə)lɪz(ə)m/ *n.* **1** the principles and practice of commerce. **2** (esp. excessive) emphasis on financial profit as a measure of worth.

commercialize /kə'mə:ʃ(ə)lʌɪz/ *v.tr.* (also **-ise**) **1** exploit or spoil for the purpose of gaining profit. **2** make commercial. □ **commercialization** /-'zeɪʃ(ə)n/ *n.*

commercial space see SPACE *n.* 6b.

commercial traveller *n. Brit.* a firm's travelling salesman or saleswoman who visits shops to get orders.

commercial vehicle *n.* a vehicle used for carrying goods or fare-paying passengers.

commère /'kɒmɛ:/ *n. Brit.* a female compère. [French, fem. of COMPÈRE]

Commie /'kɒmi/ *n. slang derog.* a Communist. [abbreviation]

commination /kɒmɪ'neɪʃ(ə)n/ *n.* **1** the threatening of divine vengeance. **2 a** the recital of divine threats against sinners in the Anglican Liturgy for Ash Wednesday. **b** the service that includes this. [Middle English from Latin *comminatio,* from *comminari* 'threaten']

comminatory /'kɒmmɪnət(ə)ri/ *adj.* threatening, denunciatory. [medieval Latin *comminatorius* (as COMMINATION)]

commingle /kɒ'mɪŋg(ə)l/ *v.tr. & intr. literary* mingle together.

comminute /'kɒmɪnju:t/ *v.tr.* **1** reduce to small fragments. **2** divide (property) into small portions. □ **comminution** /-'nju:ʃ(ə)n/ *n.* [Latin *comminuere comminut-* (as COM-, *minuere* 'lessen')]

comminuted fracture *n.* a fracture producing multiple bone splinters.

commis /ˈkɒmi/ *n.* (*pl.* same /ˈkɒmi, ˈkɒmɪz/) a junior chef or *Brit.* waiter. [originally = deputy, clerk, from French, past part. of *commettre* 'entrust' (as COMMIT)]

commiserate /kəˈmɪzəreɪt/ *v.* **1** *intr.* (usu. foll. by *with*) express or feel pity. **2** *tr. archaic* express or feel pity for (*commiserate you on your loss*). □ **commiseration** /-ˈreɪʃ(ə)n/ *n.* **commiserative** /-rətɪv/ *adj.* [Latin *commiserari* (as COM-, *miserari* 'pity' from *miser* 'wretched')]

commissar /kɒmɪˈsɑː/ *n. hist.* **1** an official of the Soviet Communist Party responsible for political education and organization. **2** the head of a government department in the USSR before 1946. [Russian *komissar* from French *commissaire* (as COMMISSARY)]

commissariat /kɒmɪˈsɛːrɪət/ *n.* **1** esp. *Mil.* **a** a department for the supply of food etc. **b** the food supplied. **2** *hist.* a government department of the USSR before 1946. [French *commissariat* and medieval Latin *commissariatus* (as COMMISSARY)]

commissary /ˈkɒmɪs(ə)ri/ *n.* (*pl.* **-ies**) **1** a deputy or delegate. **2** a representative or deputy of a bishop. **3** *Mil.* an officer responsible for the supply of food etc. to soldiers. **4** *N. Amer.* **a** a restaurant in a film studio etc. **b** the food supplied. **5** *N. Amer. Mil.* a store for the supply of food etc. to soldiers. □ **commissarial** /-ˈsɛːrɪəl/ *adj.* **commissaryship** *n.* [Middle English from medieval Latin *commissarius* 'person in charge' (as COMMIT)]

commission /kəˈmɪʃ(ə)n/ *n.* & *v.* ● *n.* **1 a** the authority to perform a task or certain duties. **b** a person or group entrusted esp. by a government with such authority (*set up a commission to look into it*). **c** an instruction, command, or duty given to such a group or person (*their commission was to simplify the procedure*; *my commission was to find him*). **2** an order for something, esp. a work of art, to be produced specially. **3** *Mil.* **a** a warrant conferring the rank of officer in an army, navy, or air force. **b** the rank so conferred. **4 a** the authority to act as agent for a company etc. in trade. **b** a percentage paid to the agent from the profits of goods etc. sold, or business obtained (*his salary is low, but he gets 20% commission*). **c** the pay of a commissioned agent. **5** the act of committing (a crime, sin, etc.). **6** the office or department of a commissioner. ● *v.tr.* **1** authorize or empower by a commission. **2 a** give (an artist etc.) a commission for a piece of work. **b** order (a work) to be written (*commissioned a new concerto*). **3** *Naut.* **a** give (an officer) the command of a ship. **b** prepare (a ship) for active service. **4** bring (a machine, equipment, etc.) into operation. □ **in commission** (of a warship etc.) manned, armed, and ready for service. **out of commission** (esp. of a ship) not in service; not in working order. [Middle English via Old French from Latin *commissio -onis* (as COMMIT)]

commission agent *n. Brit.* a bookmaker.

commissionaire /kəmɪʃəˈnɛː/ *n.* esp. *Brit.* a uniformed door attendant at a theatre, cinema, etc. [French (as COMMISSIONER)]

commissioner /kəˈmɪʃ(ə)nə/ *n.* **1** a person appointed by a commission to perform a specific task, e.g. the head of the London police, a delegate to the General Assembly of the Church of Scotland, etc. **2** (esp. in titles) a person appointed as a member of a government commission (*Charity Commissioner*; *Civil Service Commissioner*). **3** a representative of the supreme authority in a district, department, etc. [Middle English from medieval Latin *commissionarius* (as COMMISSION)]

Commissioner for Oaths *n. Brit.* a solicitor authorized to administer an oath to a person making an affidavit.

commission of the peace *n. Brit.* **1** Justices of the Peace. **2** the authority given to them.

commissure /ˈkɒmɪsjʊə/ *n.* **1** a junction, joint, or seam. **2** *Anat.* **a** the joint between two bones. **b** a band of nerve tissue connecting the hemispheres of the brain, the two sides of the spinal cord, etc. **c** the line where the upper and lower lips, or eyelids, meet. **3** *Bot.* a joint etc. between different parts of a plant. □ **commissural** /kɒmɪˈsjʊər(ə)l/ *adj.* [Middle English from Latin *commissura* 'junction' (as COMMIT)]

commit /kəˈmɪt/ *v.tr.* (**committed**, **committing**) **1** (usu. foll. by *to*) entrust or consign for: **a** safe keeping (*I commit him to your care*). **b** treatment, usu. destruction (*committed the book to the flames*). **2** perpetrate, do (esp. a crime, sin, or blunder). **3** pledge, involve, or bind (esp. oneself) to a certain course or policy (*does not like committing herself*; *committed by the vow he had made*). **4** (as **committed** *adj.*) (often foll. by *to*) **a** morally dedicated or politically aligned (*a committed Christian*; *committed to the cause*; *a committed socialist*). **b** obliged (to take certain action) (*felt committed to staying there*). **5** *Polit.* refer (a bill etc.) to a committee. □ **commit to memory** learn (a thing) so as to be able to recall it. **commit to prison** consign officially to custody, esp. on remand. □ **committable** *adj.* **committer** *n.* [Middle English from Latin *committere* 'join, entrust' (as COM-, *mittere miss-* 'send')]

commitment /kəˈmɪtm(ə)nt/ *n.* **1** an engagement or (esp. financial) obligation that restricts freedom of action. **2** the process or an instance of committing oneself; a pledge or undertaking.

committal /kəˈmɪt(ə)l/ *n.* **1** the act of committing a person to an institution, esp. prison or a psychiatric hospital. **2** the burial of a corpse.

committee /kəˈmɪti/ *n.* **1 a** a body of persons appointed for a specific function by, and usu. out of, a larger body. **b** such a body appointed by Parliament etc. to consider the details of proposed legislation. **c** (**Committee**) (in the UK) the whole House of Commons when sitting as a committee. **2** /kɒmɪˈtiː/ *Law* a person entrusted with the charge of another person or another person's property. [COMMIT + -EE]

committee man *n.* (*fem.* **committee woman**) a member of a committee, esp. a habitual member of committees.

committee stage *n. Brit.* the third of five stages of a bill's progress through Parliament when it may be considered in detail and amendments made.

commix /kɒˈmɪks/ *v.tr.* & *intr. archaic* or *poet.* mix. □ **commixture** *n.* [Middle English: back-formation from *commixt*, past part., from Latin *commixtus* (as COM-, MIXED)]

commode /kəˈməʊd/ *n.* **1** a chest of drawers. **2** (also **night-commode**) **a** a bedside table with a cupboard containing a chamber pot. **b** a chamber pot concealed in a chair with a hinged cover. **c** *US* = LAVATORY 1. **3** = CHIFFONIER 1. [French (*adj.* used as a noun), from Latin *commodus* 'convenient' (as COM-, *modus* 'measure')]

commodification /kəˌmɒdɪfɪˈkeɪʃ(ə)n/ *n.* the action of turning something into, or treating something as, a (mere) commodity. □ **commodify** /kəˈmɒdɪfʌɪ/ *v.tr.* (**-ies**, **-ied**). COMMODITY; see -FICATION]

commodious /kəˈməʊdɪəs/ *adj.* **1** roomy and comfortable. **2** *archaic* convenient. □ **commodiously** *adv.* **commodiousness** *n.* [French *commodieux* or from medieval Latin *commodiosus*, from Latin *commodus* (as COMMODE)]

commodity /kəˈmɒdɪti/ *n.* (*pl.* **-ies**) **1** an article or raw material that can be bought and sold, esp. a product as opposed to a service. **2** a useful thing. [Middle English from Old French *commodité* or from Latin *commoditas* (as COMMODE)]

commodore /ˈkɒmədɔː/ *n.* **1** a naval officer above a captain and below a rear admiral. **2** the commander of a squadron or other division of a fleet. **3** the president of a yacht club. **4** the senior captain of a shipping line. [probably via Dutch *komandeur* from French *commandeur* COMMANDER]

Commodore-in-Chief *n. Brit.* the supreme officer in the Royal Air Force.

common /ˈkɒmən/ *adj.* & *n.* ● *adj.* (**commoner**, **commonest**) **1 a** occurring often (*a common mistake*). **b** ordinary; of ordinary qualities; without special rank or position (*no common mind*; *common soldier*; *the common people*). **2 a** shared by, coming from, or done by, more than one (*common knowledge*; *by common consent*; *our common benefit*). **b** belonging to, open to, or affecting, the whole community or the public (*common land*). **3** *derog.* low-class; vulgar; inferior (*a common little man*). **4** of the most familiar type (*common cold*; *common nightshade*). **5** *Math.* belonging to two or more quantities (*common denominator*; *common factor*). **6** *Gram.* (of gender) referring to individuals of either sex (e.g. *teacher*). **7** *Prosody* (of a syllable) that may be either short or long. **8** *Mus.* having two or four beats, esp. four crotchets, in a bar. **9** *Law* (of a crime) of lesser importance (cf. GRAND *adj.* 8, PETTY 4). ● *n.* **1** a piece of open public land, esp. in a village or town. **2** *Brit. slang* = COMMON SENSE (*use your common*). **3** *Eccl.* a service used for each of a group of occasions. **4** (in full **right of common**) *Law* a person's right over another's land, e.g. for pasturage. □ **common ground** a point or argument accepted by both sides in a dispute. **common or garden** *Brit. colloq.* ordinary. **in common 1** in joint use; shared. **2** of joint interest (*have little in common*). **in common with** in the same way as. **out of the common** *Brit.* unusual. □ **commonly** *adv.* **commonness** /ˈkɒmənnɪs/ *n.* [Middle English via Old French *comun* from Latin *communis*]

commonable /ˈkɒmənəb(ə)l/ *adj.* **1** (of an animal) that may be pastured on common land. **2** (of land) that may be held in common. [obsolete *common* 'to exercise right of common' + -ABLE]

commonage /ˈkɒmənɪdʒ/ *n.* **1** = *right of common* (see COMMON *n.* 4). **2 a** land held in common. **b** the state of being held in common. **3** the common people; commonalty.

commonality /kɒməˈnalɪti/ *n.* (*pl.* **-ies**) **1** the sharing of an attribute. **2** a common occurrence. **3** = COMMONALTY. [variant of COMMONALTY]

commonalty /ˈkɒmən(ə)lti/ *n.* (*pl.* **-ies**) **1** the common people. **2** the general body (esp. of humankind). **3** a corporate body. [Middle English via Old French *comunalté* from medieval Latin *communalitas -tatis* (as COMMON)]

common carrier *n.* a person or firm undertaking to transport any goods or person in a specified category.

common chord *n. Mus.* any note with its major or minor third and perfect fifth.

common crier *n.* = TOWN CRIER.

common denominator *n.* **1** a common multiple of the denominators of several fractions. **2** a common feature of members of a group.

commoner /ˈkɒmənə/ *n.* **1** one of the common people, as opposed to the aristocracy. **2** a person who has the right of common. **3** a student at a British university who does not have a scholarship. [Middle English from medieval Latin *communarius*, from *communa* (as COMMUNE[1])]

Common Era *n.* the Christian era.

commonhold /ˈkɒmənhəʊld/ *n.* (often *attrib.*) *Brit.* the freehold tenure of a flat within a multi-occupancy building, but with shared responsibility for common services. □ **commonholder** *n.*

common jury *n.* a jury with members of no particular social standing (cf. SPECIAL JURY).

common law *n.* law derived from custom and judicial precedent rather than statutes (cf. CASE LAW, STATUTE LAW).

common-law husband *n.* (*fem.* **common-law wife**) **1** a partner in a marriage recognized in some jurisdictions as valid by common law, though not brought about by a civil or ecclesiastical ceremony. **2** *colloq.* a partner in a relationship in which a man and woman cohabit for a period long enough to suggest stability.

common logarithm *n.* a logarithm to the base 10.

Common Market *n.* the European Community.

common metre *n.* a hymn stanza of four lines with 8, 6, 8, and 6 syllables.

common noun *n.* (also **common name**) *Gram.* a name denoting a class of objects or a concept as opposed to a particular individual (e.g. *boy, chocolate, beauty*).

commonplace /ˈkɒmənpleɪs/ *adj.* & *n.* ● *adj.* lacking originality; trite. ● *n.* **1 a** an everyday saying; a platitude (*uttered a commonplace about the weather*). **b** an ordinary topic of conversation. **2** anything usual or trite. **3** a notable passage in a book etc. copied into a commonplace book. □ **commonplaceness** *n.* [translation of Latin *locus communis* = Greek *koinos topos* 'general theme']

commonplace book *n.* a book into which notable extracts from other works are copied for personal use.

Common Prayer *n.* the Church of England liturgy originally set forth in the *Book of Common Prayer* of Edward VI (1549), esp. as revised in 1662.

common property *n.* a thing known by most people.

common room *n.* esp. *Brit* **1** a room in some colleges, schools, etc., which members may use for relaxation or work. **2** the members who use this.

commons /ˈkɒmənz/ *n.pl.* **1** (**the Commons**) = HOUSE OF COMMONS. **2 a** the common people. **b** (prec. by *the*) the common people regarded as a part of a political, esp. British, system. **3** provisions shared in common; daily fare. [Middle English, pl. of COMMON]

common salt see SALT *n.* 1.

common seal[1] *n.* a seal, *Phoca vitulina*, of northern oceans, with a mottled grey coat. [SEAL[2]]

common seal[2] *n.* the official seal of a corporate body. [SEAL[1]]

common sense *n.* sound practical sense, esp. in everyday matters (often hyphenated when *attrib.*: *a common-sense approach*).

commonsensical /kɒmənˈsɛnsɪk(ə)l/ *adj.* possessing or marked by common sense. [*common sense* (see COMMON)]

Common Serjeant *n.* a circuit judge of the Central Criminal Court with duties in the City of London.

common soldier see SOLDIER *n.* 2.

common stock *n.pl. N. Amer.* = ORDINARY SHARE.

common valerian see VALERIAN 1a.

commonweal /ˈkɒmənwiːl/ *n. archaic* **1** = COMMON WEAL. **2** = COMMONWEALTH 1a.

common weal *n.* public welfare.

commonwealth /ˈkɒmənwɛlθ/ *n.* **1 a** an independent state or community, esp. a democratic republic. **b** such a community or organization of shared interests in a non-political field (*the commonwealth of learning*). **2** (**the Commonwealth**) **a** (in full **the Commonwealth of Nations**) an international association consisting of the UK together with states that were previously part of the British Empire, and dependencies. **b** the republican period of government in Britain 1649–60. **c** a part of the title of Puerto Rico and some of the states of the US. **d** the title of the federated Australian states. [COMMON + WEALTH]

Commonwealth Day *n.* a day each year commemorating the British Commonwealth (formerly called *Empire Day*).

common year see YEAR 2.

commotion /kəˈməʊʃ(ə)n/ *n.* **1 a** a confused and noisy disturbance or outburst. **b** loud and confusing noise. **2** a civil insurrection. [Middle English from Old French *commotion* or Latin *commotio* (as COM-, MOTION)]

communal /ˈkɒmjʊn(ə)l, kəˈmjuː-/ *adj.* **1** relating to or benefiting a community; for common use (*communal baths*). **2** (of conflicts etc.) between different esp. ethnic or religious communities (*communal violence*). **3** of a commune, esp. the Paris Commune. □ **communality** /-ˈnalɪti/ *n.* **communally** *adv.* [French from Late Latin *communalis* (as COMMUNE[1])]

communalism /ˈkɒmjʊn(ə)lɪz(ə)m/ *n.* **1** a principle of political organization based on federated communes. **2** the principle of communal ownership etc. □ **communalist** *n.* **communalistic** /-ˈlɪstɪk/ *adj.*

communalize /ˈkɒmjʊn(ə)lʌɪz, kəˈmjuːnəlʌɪz/ *v.tr.* (also **-ise**) make communal. ▫ **communalization** /-ˈzeɪʃ(ə)n/ *n.*

communard /ˈkɒmjʊnɑːd/ *n.* **1** a member of a commune. **2** (also **Communard**) *hist.* a supporter of the Paris Commune. [French (as COMMUNE[1])]

commune[1] /ˈkɒmjuːn/ *n.* **1 a** a group of people, not necessarily related, sharing living accommodation, goods, etc., esp. as a political act. **b** a communal settlement esp. for the pursuit of shared interests. **2 a** the smallest French territorial division for administrative purposes. **b** a similar division elsewhere. **3** (**the Commune**) the communalistic government in Paris in 1871. [French from medieval Latin *communia*, neut. pl. of Latin *communis* 'common']

commune[2] /kəˈmjuːn/ *v.intr.* **1** (usu. foll. by *with*) **a** speak confidentially and intimately (*communed together about their loss*; *communed with his heart*). **b** feel in close touch (with nature etc.) (*communed with the hills*). **2** *N. Amer.* receive Holy Communion. [Middle English from Old French *comuner* 'share', from *comun* COMMON]

communicable /kəˈmjuːnɪkəb(ə)l/ *adj.* **1** (esp. of a disease) able to be passed on. **2** *archaic* communicative. ▫ **communicability** /-ˈbɪlɪti/ *n.* **communicably** *adv.* [Middle English from Old French *communicable* or Late Latin *communicabilis* (as COMMUNICATE)]

communicant /kəˈmjuːnɪk(ə)nt/ *n.* **1** a person who receives Holy Communion, esp. regularly. **2** a person who imparts information. [Latin *communicare communicant-* (as COMMON)]

communicate /kəˈmjuːnɪkeɪt/ *v.* **1** *tr.* **a** transmit or pass on by speaking or writing (*communicated his ideas*). **b** transmit (heat, motion, etc.). **c** pass on (an infectious illness). **d** impart (feelings etc.) non-verbally (*communicated his affection*). **2** *intr.* be in communication; succeed in conveying information, evoking understanding, etc. (*he communicates well*). **3** *intr.* (often foll. by *with*) share a feeling or understanding; relate socially. **4** *intr.* (often foll. by *with*) (of a room etc.) have a common door (*my room communicates with yours*). **5 a** *tr.* administer Holy Communion to. **b** *intr.* receive Holy Communion. ▫ **communicator** *n.* **communicatory** *adj.* [Latin *communicare communicat-* (as COMMON)]

communication /kəmjuːnɪˈkeɪʃ(ə)n/ *n.* **1 a** the act of imparting, esp. news. **b** an instance of this. **c** the information etc. communicated. **2** a means of connecting different places, such as a door, passage, road, or railway. **3** social intercourse (*it was difficult to maintain communication in the uproar*). **4** (in *pl.*) the science and practice of transmitting information esp. by electronic or mechanical means. **5** (in *pl.*) *Mil.* the means of transport between a base and the front. **6** *Brit.* a paper read to a learned society. ▫ **communicational** *adj.* (in senses 1 and 3).

communication cord *n. Brit.* a cord or chain in a railway carriage that may be pulled to stop the train in an emergency.

communication satellite *n.* (also **communications satellite**) an artificial satellite used to relay telephone circuits or broadcast programmes.

communication theory *n.* the study of the principles and methods by which information is conveyed.

communicative /kəˈmjuːnɪkətɪv/ *adj.* **1** open, talkative, informative. **2** ready to communicate. ▫ **communicatively** *adv.* [Late Latin *communicativus* (as COMMUNICATE)]

communion /kəˈmjuːnjən/ *n.* **1** a sharing, esp. of thoughts etc.; fellowship (*their minds were in communion*). **2** participation; a sharing in common (*communion of interests*). **3** (**Communion, Holy Communion**) **a** the Eucharist. **b** participation in the Communion service. **c** (*attrib.*) of or used in the Communion service (*Communion table*; *Communion rail*). **4** mutual recognition among branches of the Church (*in communion with Rome*). **5** a body or group within the Christian faith (*the Anglican communion*). [Middle English from Old French *communion* or Latin *communio*, from *communis* 'common']

communion of saints *n.* fellowship between Christians living and dead.

communiqué /kəˈmjuːnɪkeɪ/ *n.* an official communication, esp. a news report. [French, = communicated]

communism /ˈkɒmjʊnɪz(ə)m/ *n.* **1** a political theory advocating a society in which all property is publicly owned and each person is paid and works according to his or her needs and abilities. **2** (usu. **Communism**) **a** the communistic form of society established in the former USSR and elsewhere. **b** any movement or political doctrine advocating communism, esp. Marxism. **3** = COMMUNALISM. [French *communisme* from *commun* COMMON]

communist /ˈkɒmjʊnɪst/ *n. & adj.* ● *n.* **1** a person advocating or practising communism. **2** (**Communist**) a member of a Communist Party. ● *adj.* of or relating to communism (*a communist play*). ▫ **communistic** /-ˈnɪstɪk/ *adj.* [COMMUNISM]

communitarian /kəmjuːnɪˈtɛːrɪən/ *n. & adj.* ● *n.* a member of a communistic community. ● *adj.* of or relating to such a community. [COMMUNITY + -ARIAN on the pattern of *unitarian* etc.]

community /kəˈmjuːnɪti/ *n.* (*pl.* **-ies**) **1 a** all the people living in a specific locality. **b** a specific locality, including its inhabitants. **2** a body of people having a religion, a profession, etc., in common (*the immigrant community*). **3** fellowship of interests etc.; similarity (*community of intellect*). **4** a monastic, socialistic, etc. body practising common ownership. **5** joint ownership or liability (*community of goods*). **6** (prec. by *the*) the public. **7** a body of nations unified by common interests. **8** *Ecol.* a group of animals or plants living or growing together in the same area. [Middle English via Old French *comuneté* from Latin *communitas -tatis* (as COMMON)]

community architect *n.* an architect working in consultation with the local community in designing housing and other amenities. ▫ **community architecture** *n.*

community centre *n.* a place providing social etc. facilities for a neighbourhood.

community charge *n. hist.* (in the UK) a short-lived tax levied locally on every adult in a community, replaced in 1993 by the council tax.

community chest *n.* a fund for charity and welfare work in a community.

community college *n.* esp. *N. Amer.* a college providing further and higher education for members of the local community.

community home *n. Brit.* a centre for housing young offenders and other juveniles in need of custodial care.

community policing *n.* policing by officers intended to have personal knowledge of the community which they police. ▫ **community policeman** *n.*

community service *n.* work, esp. voluntary and unpaid, or stipulated by a community service order, in the community.

community service order *n. Brit.* an order for a convicted offender to perform a period of unpaid work in the community.

community singing *n.* singing by a large crowd or group, esp. of old popular songs or hymns.

community spirit *n.* a feeling of belonging to a community, expressed in mutual support etc.

community worker *n.* a person who works in a community to promote its welfare.

communize /ˈkɒmjʊnʌɪz/ *v.tr.* (also **-ise**) **1** make (land etc.) common property. **2** make (a person etc.) communistic. ▫ **communization** /-ˈzeɪʃ(ə)n/ *n.* [Latin *communis* COMMON]

commutable /kəˈmjuːtəb(ə)l/ *adj.* **1** convertible into money; exchangeable. **2** *Law* (of a punishment) able to be commuted. **3** within commuting distance.

□ **commutability** /-'bɪlɪti/ *n.* [Latin *commutabilis* (as COMMUTE)]

commutate /'kɒmjʊteɪt/ *v.tr. Electr.* **1** regulate the direction of (an alternating current), esp. to make it a direct current. **2** reverse the direction (of an electric current). [Latin *commutare commutat-* (as COMMUTE)]

commutation /kɒmjʊ'teɪʃ(ə)n/ *n.* **1** the act or process of commuting or being commuted (in legal and exchange senses). **2** *Electr.* the act or process of commutating or being commutated. **3** *Math.* the reversal of the order of two quantities. [French *commutation* or Latin *commutatio* (as COMMUTE)]

commutative /kə'mju:tətɪv, 'kɒmjʊtətɪv/ *adj.* **1** relating to or involving substitution. **2** *Math.* unchanged in result by the interchange of the order of quantities. [French *commutatif* or medieval Latin *commutativus* (as COMMUTE)]

commutator /'kɒmjʊteɪtə/ *n.* **1** *Electr.* a device for reversing electric current. **2** an attachment connected with the armature of a dynamo which directs and makes continuous the current produced.

commute /kə'mju:t/ *v.* **1** *intr.* travel to and from one's daily work, usu. in a city, esp. by car or train. **2** *tr.* (usu. foll. by *to*) *Law* change (a judicial sentence etc.) to another less severe. **3** *tr.* (often foll. by *into, for*) **a** change (one kind of payment) for another. **b** make a payment etc. to change (an obligation etc.) for another. **4** *tr.* **a** exchange; interchange (two things). **b** change (to another thing). **5** *tr. Electr.* commutate. **6** *intr. Math.* have a commutative relation. [Latin *commutare commutat-* (as COM-, *mutare* 'change')]

commuter /kə'mju:tə/ *n.* a person who travels some distance to work, esp. in a city, usu. by car or train.

comose /'kəʊməʊs/ *adj. Bot.* (of seeds etc.) having hairs; downy. [Latin *comosus* (as COMA[2])]

comp /kɒmp/ *n.* & *v. colloq.* ● *n.* **1** *Brit.* a competition. **2** *Printing* a compositor. **3** *Mus.* an accompaniment. ● *v.* **1** *Mus.* **a** *tr.* accompany. **b** *intr.* play an accompaniment. **2** *Printing* **a** *intr.* work as a compositor. **b** *tr.* work as a compositor on. [abbreviation]

compact[1] *adj., v.,* & *n.* ● *adj.* /kəm'pakt/ **1** closely or neatly packed together. **2** (of a piece of equipment, a room, etc.) well fitted and practical though small. **3** (of style etc.) condensed; brief. **4** (esp. of the human body) small but well-proportioned. **5** (foll. by *of*) composed or made up of. ● *v.tr.* /kəm'pakt/ **1** join or press firmly together. **2** condense. **3** (usu. foll. by *of*) compose; make up. ● *n.* /'kɒmpakt/ **1** a small flat usu. decorated case for face powder and a mirror, etc. **2** an object formed by compacting powder. **3** *N. Amer.* a medium-sized motor car. □ **compaction** *n.* **compactly** *adv.* **compactness** *n.* **compactor** *n.* [Middle English from Latin *compingere compact-* (as COM-, *pangere* 'fasten')]

compact[2] /'kɒmpakt/ *n.* an agreement or contract between two or more parties. [Latin *compactum* from *compacisci compact-* (as COM-, *pacisci* 'covenant'): cf. PACT]

compact disc /'kɒmpakt/ *n.* a disc on which information or sound is recorded digitally and reproduced by reflection of laser light.

compadre /kɒm'pɑ:dri/ *n.* (*pl.* **compadres**) esp. *US colloq.* friend, companion. [Spanish, = godfather]

compages /kəm'peɪdʒi:z/ *n.* (*pl.* same) **1** a framework; a complex structure. **2** something resembling a compages in complexity etc. [Latin *compages* (as COM-, *pages* from *pangere* 'fasten')]

companion[1] /kəm'panjən/ *n.* & *v.* ● *n.* **1 a** (often foll. by *in, of*) a person who accompanies, associates with, or shares with, another (*a companion in adversity; they were close companions*). **b** a person, esp. an unmarried or widowed woman, employed to live with and assist another. **2** a handbook or reference book on a particular subject (*A Companion to North Wales*). **3** a thing that matches another (*the companion of this bookend is over there*). **4** (**Companion**) a member of the lowest grade of some orders of knighthood (*Companion of the Bath*). **5** *Astron.* a star etc. that accompanies another. **6** *Brit.* equipment or a piece of equipment that combines several uses. ● *v.* **1** *tr.* accompany. **2** *intr.* (often foll. by *with*) *literary* be a companion. [Middle English from Old French *compaignon*, ultimately from Latin, = 'one who breaks bread with another' (as COM- + *panis* 'bread')]

companion[2] /kəm'panjən/ *n. Naut.* **1** a raised frame with windows let into the quarterdeck of a ship to allow light into the cabins etc. below. **2** = COMPANIONWAY. [obsolete Dutch *kompanje* 'quarterdeck' from Old French *compagne* from Italian (*camera della*) *compagna* '(storeroom for) provisions', probably ultimately related to COMPANION[1]]

companionable /kəm'panjənəb(ə)l/ *adj.* agreeable as a companion; sociable. □ **companionableness** *n.* **companionably** *adv.*

companionate /kəm'panjənət/ *adj.* **1** well-suited; (of clothes) matching. **2** of or like a companion.

companion hatch *n.* a wooden covering over a companionway.

companion hatchway *n.* an opening in a deck leading to a cabin.

companion-in-arms *n.* a fellow soldier.

companion ladder *n.* a ladder from a deck to a cabin.

Companion of Honour *n.* (in the UK) a member of an order founded in 1917.

Companion of Literature *n.* (in the UK) a member of an order founded in 1961.

companion set *n. Brit.* a set of fireside implements on a stand.

companionship /kəm'panjənʃɪp/ *n.* good fellowship; friendship.

companionway /kəm'panjənweɪ/ *n.* a staircase to a cabin.

company /'kʌmp(ə)ni/ *n.* & *v.* ● *n.* (*pl.* **-ies**) **1 a** a number of people assembled; a crowd; an audience (*addressed the company*). **b** guests or a guest (*am expecting company*). **2** a state of being a companion or fellow; companionship, esp. of a specific kind (*enjoys low company; do not care for his company*). **3 a** a commercial business. **b** (usu. **Co.**) the partner or partners not named in the title of a firm (*Smith and Co.*). **4** a troupe of actors or entertainers. **5** *Mil.* a subdivision of an infantry battalion, usu. commanded by a major or a captain. **6** *Brit.* a group of Guides. ● *v.* (**-ies, -ied**) **1** *tr. archaic* accompany. **2** *intr.* (often foll. by *with*) *literary* be a companion. □ **err** (or **be**) **in good company** discover that a celebrity, one's companions, etc., have done the same as oneself. **in company** not alone. **in company with** together with. **keep company** (often foll. by *with*) associate habitually. **keep** (or *archaic* **bear**) **a person company** accompany a person; be sociable. **part company** (often foll. by *with*) cease to associate. [Middle English via Anglo-French *compainie*, Old French *compai(g)nie*, from Romanic (as COMPANION[1])]

company car *n.* a car provided by a company for the business and usu. private use of an employee.

company officer *n.* a captain or a lower commissioned officer.

company promoter see PROMOTER 3.

company sergeant major *n. Brit. Mil.* the highest non-commissioned officer of a company.

comparable /'kɒmp(ə)rəb(ə)l/ *adj.* **1** (often foll. by *with*) able to be compared. **2** (often foll. by *to*) fit to be compared; worth comparing. □ **comparability** /-'bɪlɪti/ *n.* **comparableness** *n.* **comparably** *adv.* [Middle English via Old French from Latin *comparabilis* (as COMPARE)]

■ **Usage** The use of *comparable* with *to* and *with* corresponds to the senses at *compare*; *to* is more common.

comparative /kəm'parətɪv/ *adj.* & *n.* ● *adj.* **1** perceptible by comparison; relative (*in comparative comfort*). **2** estimated by comparison (*the comparative merits of the two ideas*). **3** of or involving comparison (esp. across branches of a science or subject of study). **4** *Gram.* (of an adjective or adverb) expressing a higher degree of a quality, but not the highest possible (e.g. *braver*; *more fiercely*) (cf. POSITIVE *adj.* 3b, SUPERLATIVE *adj.* 2). ● *n. Gram.* **1** the comparative expression or form of an adjective or adverb. **2** a word in the comparative. □ **comparatively** *adv.* [Middle English from Latin *comparativus* (as COMPARE)]

comparator /kəm'parətə/ *n. Engin.* a device for comparing a product, an output, etc., with a standard, esp. an electronic circuit comparing two signals.

compare /kəm'pɛː/ *v.* & *n.* ● *v.* **1** *tr.* (usu. foll. by *to*) express similarities in; liken (*compared the landscape to a painting*). **2** *tr.* (often foll. by *to, with*) estimate the similarity or dissimilarity of; assess the relation between (*compared radio with television*; *that lacks quality compared to this*). **3** *intr.* (often foll. by *with*) bear comparison (*compares favourably with the rest*). **4** *intr.* (often foll. by *with*) be equal or equivalent to. **5** *tr. Gram.* form the comparative and superlative degrees of (an adjective or an adverb). ● *n. literary* comparison (*beyond compare*; *without compare*; *has no compare*). □ **compare notes** exchange ideas or opinions. [Middle English via Old French *comparer* from Latin *comparare* (as COM-, *parare* from *par* 'equal')]

■ **Usage** In sense 2 *to* and *with* are generally interchangeable, but *with* often implies a greater element of formal analysis, as in *compared my account with yours*.

comparison /kəm'parɪs(ə)n/ *n.* **1** the act or an instance of comparing. **2** a simile or semantic illustration. **3** capacity for being likened; similarity (*there's no comparison*). **4** (in full **degrees of comparison**) *Gram.* the positive, comparative, and superlative forms of adjectives and adverbs. □ **bear** (or **stand**) **comparison** (often foll. by *with*) be able to be compared favourably. **beyond comparison 1** totally different in quality. **2** greatly superior; excellent. **in** (or **by**) **comparison with** compared to. [Middle English via Old French *comparesoun* from Latin *comparatio -onis* (as COMPARE)]

compartment /kəm'pɑːtm(ə)nt/ *n.* & *v.* ● *n.* **1** a space within a larger space, separated from the rest by partitions, e.g. in a railway carriage, wallet, desk, etc. **2** *Naut.* a watertight division of a ship. **3** an area of activity etc. kept apart from others in a person's mind. ● *v.tr.* put into compartments. □ **compartmentation** /-'teɪʃ(ə)n/ *n.* [French *compartiment* via Italian *compartimento* from Late Latin *compartiri* (as COM-, *partiri* 'share')]

compartmental /kɒmpɑː'tmɛnt(ə)l/ *adj.* consisting of or relating to compartments or a compartment. □ **compartmentally** *adv.*

compartmentalize /kɒmpɑː'tmɛnt(ə)lʌɪz/ *v.tr.* (also **-ise**) divide into compartments or categories. □ **compartmentalization** /-'zeɪʃ(ə)n/ *n.*

compass /'kʌmpəs/ *n.* & *v.* ● *n.* **1** (in full **magnetic compass**) an instrument showing the direction of magnetic north and bearings from it (see also GYROCOMPASS). **2** (usu. in *pl.*) (also **pair of compasses** *sing.*) an instrument for taking measurements and describing circles, with two arms connected at one end by a movable joint. **3** a circumference or boundary. **4** area, extent; scope (e.g. of knowledge or experience) (*beyond my compass*). **5** the range of tones of a voice or a musical instrument. ● *v.tr. literary* **1** hem in. **2** grasp mentally. **3** contrive, accomplish. **4** go round. □ **compassable** *adj.* [Middle English from Old French *compas*, ultimately from Latin *passus* PACE[1]]

compass card *n.* a circular rotating card showing the 32 principal bearings, forming the indicator of a magnetic compass.

compassion /kəm'paʃ(ə)n/ *n.* pity inclining one to help or be merciful. [Middle English via Old French from ecclesiastical Latin *compassio -onis*, from *compati* (as COM-, *pati pass-* 'suffer')]

compassionate /kəm'paʃ(ə)nət/ *adj.* sympathetic, pitying. □ **compassionately** *adv.* [obsolete French *compassioné* from *compassioner* 'feel pity' (as COMPASSION)]

compassionate leave *n.* leave granted on grounds of bereavement etc.

compassion fatigue *n.* indifference to charitable appeals, reports of hardship, etc., resulting from their frequency.

compass rose *n.* a circle of the principal directions marked on a chart.

compass saw *n.* a saw with a narrow blade, for cutting curves.

compass window *n.* a bay window with a semicircular curve.

compatible /kəm'patɪb(ə)l/ *adj.* & *n.* ● *adj.* **1** (often foll. by *with*) **a** able to coexist; well-suited; mutually tolerant (*a compatible couple*). **b** consistent (*their views are not compatible with their actions*). **2** (of equipment etc.) capable of being used in combination. ● *n.* (usu. in *comb.*) *Computing* a piece of equipment that can use software etc. designed for another brand of the same equipment (*IBM compatibles*). □ **compatibility** /-'bɪlɪti/ *n.* **compatibly** *adv.* [French from medieval Latin *compatibilis* (as COMPASSION)]

compatriot /kəm'patrɪət, -'peɪt-/ *n.* a fellow countryman. □ **compatriotic** /-'ɒtɪk/ *adj.* [French *compatriote* from Late Latin *compatriota* (as COM-, *patriota* PATRIOT)]

compeer /kəm'pɪə/ *n.* **1** an equal; a peer. **2** a comrade. [Middle English from Old French *comper* (as COM-, PEER[2])]

compel /kəm'pɛl/ *v.tr.* (**compelled, compelling**) **1** (usu. foll. by *to* + infin.) force, constrain (*compelled them to admit it*). **2** bring about (an action) by force (*compel submission*). **3** (as **compelling** *adj.*) rousing strong interest, attention, conviction, or admiration. **4** *archaic* drive forcibly. □ **compellingly** *adv.* [Middle English from Latin *compellere compuls-* (as COM-, *pellere* 'drive')]

compellable /kəm'pɛləb(ə)l/ *adj. Law* (of a witness etc.) that may be made to attend court or give evidence.

compendious /kəm'pɛndɪəs/ *adj.* (esp. of a book etc.) comprehensive but fairly brief. □ **compendiously** *adv.* **compendiousness** *n.* [Middle English via Old French *compendieux* from Latin *compendiosus* 'brief' (as COMPENDIUM)]

compendium /kəm'pɛndɪəm/ *n.* (*pl.* **compendiums** or **compendia** /-dɪə/) **1** esp. *Brit.* a usu. one-volume handbook or encyclopedia. **2 a** a summary or abstract of a larger work. **b** an abridgement. **3 a** (in full **compendium of games**) a collection of games in a box. **b** any collection or mixture. **4** a package of writing paper, envelopes, etc. [Latin, = what is weighed together, from *compendere* (as COM-, *pendere* 'weigh')]

compensate /'kɒmpɛnseɪt/ *v.* **1** *tr.* (often foll. by *for*) recompense (a person) (*compensated him for his loss*). **2** *intr.* (usu. foll. by *for* a thing, *Brit. to* a person) make amends (*compensated for the insult*; *will compensate to her in full*). **3** *tr.* counterbalance; make up for; make amends for. **4** *tr. Mech.* provide (a pendulum etc.) with extra or less weight etc. to neutralize the effects of temperature etc. **5** *intr. Psychol.* offset a disability or frustration by development in another direction. □ **compensative** /-sətɪv/ *adj.* **compensator** *n.* **compensatory** /-'pɛnsət(ə)ri, -'seɪt(ə)ri/ *adj.* [Latin *compensare* (as COM-, *pensare*, frequentative of *pendere pens-* 'weigh')]

compensation /kɒmpɛn'seɪʃ(ə)n/ *n.* **1 a** the act of compensating. **b** the process of being compensated. **2** something, esp. money, given as a recompense. **3** *Psychol.* **a** an act of compensating. **b** the result of compensating. **4** *N. Amer.* a salary or wages. □ **compensational** *adj.* [Middle English via Old French from Latin *compensatio* (as COMPENSATE)]

compensation pendulum *n. Physics* a pendulum designed to neutralize the effects of temperature variation.

compère /ˈkɒmpɛː/ *n. & v. Brit.* ● *n.* a person who introduces and links the artistes in a variety show etc.; a master of ceremonies. ● *v.* **1** *tr.* act as a compère to. **2** *intr.* act as compère. [French, = godfather, from Romanic (as COM-, Latin *pater* 'father')]

compete /kəmˈpiːt/ *v.intr.* **1** (often foll. by *with, against* a person, *for* a thing) strive for superiority or supremacy (*competed with his brother*; *compete against each other*; *compete for the job*). **2** (often foll. by *in*) take part (in a contest etc.) (*competed in the hurdles*). [Latin *competere competit-*, in late sense 'strive after or contend for (something)' (as COM-, *petere* 'seek')]

competence /ˈkɒmpɪt(ə)ns/ *n.* (also **competency** /-ənsi/) **1 a** (often foll. by *for*, or *to* + infin.) ability; the state of being competent. **b** an area in which a person is competent; a skill. **2** an income large enough to live on, usu. unearned. **3** *Law* the legal capacity (of a court, a magistrate, etc.) to deal with a matter.

competent /ˈkɒmpɪt(ə)nt/ *adj.* **1 a** (usu. foll. by *to* + infin. or *for*) adequately qualified or capable (*not competent to drive*). **b** effective (*a competent batsman*). **2** *Law* (of a judge, court, or witness) legally qualified or qualifying. □ **competently** *adv.* [Middle English from Old French *competent* or Latin *competent-*, pres. part. of *competere* 'be fit or proper' (as COMPETE)]

competition /kɒmpɪˈtɪʃ(ə)n/ *n.* **1** (often foll. by *for*) competing, esp. in an examination, in trade, etc. **2** an event or contest in which people compete. **3 a** the people competing against a person. **b** the opposition they represent. **4** *Biol.* interaction between organisms etc. that share a limited environmental resource. [Late Latin *competitio* 'rivalry' (as COMPETITIVE)]

competitive /kəmˈpɛtɪtɪv/ *adj.* **1** involving, offered for, or by competition (*competitive game*). **2** (of prices etc.) low enough to compare well with those of rival traders. **3** (of a person) having a strong urge to win; keen to compete. □ **competitively** *adv.* **competitiveness** *n.* [*competit-*, past part. stem of Latin *competere* COMPETE]

competitor /kəmˈpɛtɪtə/ *n.* **1** a person who competes. **2** a rival, esp. in business or commerce. [French *compétiteur* or Latin *competitor* (as COMPETE)]

compilation /kɒmpɪˈleɪʃ(ə)n/ *n.* **1 a** the act of compiling. **b** the process of being compiled. **2** something compiled, esp. a book etc. composed of separate articles, stories, etc. [Middle English via Old French from Latin *compilatio -onis* (as COMPILE)]

compile /kəmˈpʌɪl/ *v.tr.* **1 a** collect (material) into a list, volume, etc. **b** make up (a volume etc.) from such material. **2** accumulate (a score, lead, etc.) (*compiled a break of 98*). **3** *Computing* produce (a machine-coded form of a high-level program). [Middle English from Old French *compiler* or its apparent source, Latin *compilare* 'plunder, plagiarize']

compiler /kəmˈpʌɪlə/ *n.* **1** *Computing* a program for translating a high-level programming language into machine code. **2** a person who compiles.

complacency /kəmˈpleɪs(ə)nsi/ *n.* (also **complacence**) self-satisfaction or tranquil pleasure, esp. when uncritical or unwarranted. [medieval Latin *complacentia* from Latin *complacēre* (as COM-, *placēre* 'please')]

complacent /kəmˈpleɪs(ə)nt/ *adj.* **1** smugly self-satisfied. **2** calmly content. □ **complacently** *adv.* [Latin *complacēre*: see COMPLACENCY]

■ **Usage** *Complacent* should not be confused with *complaisant.*

complain /kəmˈpleɪn/ *v.intr.* **1** (often foll. by *about, at,* or *that* + clause) express dissatisfaction (*complained at the state of the room*; *is always complaining*). **2** (foll. by *of*) **a** announce that one is suffering from (an ailment) (*complained of a headache*). **b** state a grievance concerning (*complained of the delay*). **3 a** make a mournful sound. **b** groan or creak under a strain. □ **complainer** *n.* **complainingly** *adv.* [Middle English via Old French *complaindre* (stem *complaign-*) from medieval Latin *complangere* 'bewail' (as COM-, *plangere planct-* 'lament')]

complainant /kəmˈpleɪnənt/ *n. Law* a plaintiff in certain lawsuits.

complaint /kəmˈpleɪnt/ *n.* **1 a** a grievance or cause for dissatisfaction (*I have no complaints*). **b** a statement of dissatisfaction (*make a complaint*). **2** an ailment or illness. **3** *Law* the plaintiff's initial pleading in a civil action. [Middle English via Old French *complainte* from *complaint*, past part. of *complaindre*: see COMPLAIN]

complaisant /kəmˈpleɪz(ə)nt/ *adj.* **1** politely deferential. **2** willing to please; acquiescent. □ **complaisance** *n.* [French from *complaire* (stem *complais-*) 'acquiesce to please', from Latin *complacēre*: see COMPLACENCY]

■ **Usage** *Complaisant* should not be confused with *complacent.*

compleat *archaic* var. of COMPLETE.

complement *n. & v.* ● *n.* /ˈkɒmplɪm(ə)nt/ **1 a** something that completes. **b** one of a pair, or one of two things that go together. **2** (often **full complement**) the full number needed to man a ship, fill a conveyance, etc. **3** *Gram.* a word or phrase added to a verb to complete the predicate of a sentence. **4** *Biochem.* a group of proteins in the blood which, in conjunction with antibodies, assist in the destruction of bacteria etc. **5** *Math.* any element not belonging to a specified set or class. **6** *Geom.* the amount by which an angle is less than 90° (cf. SUPPLEMENT *n.* 5). ● *v.tr.* /ˈkɒmplɪmɛnt/ **1** complete. **2** form a complement to (*the scarf complements her dress*). □ **complemental** /-ˈmɛnt(ə)l/ *adj.* [Middle English from Latin *complementum* (as COMPLETE)]

complementarity /ˌkɒmplɪmɛnˈtarɪti/ *n.* (*pl.* **-ies**) **1** a complementary relationship or situation. **2** *Physics* the concept that a single model may not be adequate to explain atomic systems in different experimental conditions.

complementary /kɒmplɪˈmɛnt(ə)ri/ *adj.* **1** completing; forming a complement. **2** (of two or more things) complementing each other. □ **complementarily** *adv.* **complementariness** *n.*

complementary angle *n.* either of two angles making up 90°.

complementary colour *n.* a colour that, combined with a given colour, makes white or black.

complementary medicine *n.* = ALTERNATIVE MEDICINE.

complete /kəmˈpliːt/ *adj. & v.* ● *adj.* **1** having all its parts; entire (*the set is complete*). **2** finished (*my task is complete*). **3** of the maximum extent or degree (*a complete surprise*; *a complete stranger*). **4** (also **compleat** after Walton's *Compleat Angler*) usu. *joc.* accomplished (*the complete horseman*). ● *v.tr.* **1** finish. **2 a** make whole or perfect. **b** make up the amount of (*completes the quota*). **3** fill in the answers to (a questionnaire etc.). **4** (usu. *absol.*) *Law* conclude (a sale of property). □ **complete with** having (as an important accessory) (*comes complete with instructions*). □ **completely** *adv.* **completeness** *n.* **completion** /-ˈpliːʃ(ə)n/ *n.* [Middle English from Old French *complet* or Latin *completus*, past part. of *complēre* 'fill up']

completist /kəmˈpliːtist/ *n. & adj.* ● *n.* an obsessive or indiscriminate collector. ● *adj.* intent on completeness.

complex /ˈkɒmplɛks/ *n. & adj.* ● *n.* **1** a building, a series of rooms, a network, etc. made up of related parts (*the arts complex*). **2** *Psychol.* a related group of usu. repressed feelings or thoughts which cause abnormal behaviour or mental states (*inferiority complex*; *Oedipus complex*). **3** (in general use) a preoccupation or obsession (*has a complex about punctuality*). **4** *Chem.* a compound in which molecules or ions form coordinate bonds to a metal atom or ion. ● *adj.* **1** consisting of related parts; composite. **2** complicated (*a complex problem*). **3** *Math.* containing real and imaginary parts (cf. IMAGINARY). □ **complexity** /kəmˈplɛksɪti/ *n.* (*pl.* **-ies**).

complexly *adv.* [French *complexe* or Latin *complexus*, past part. of *complectere* 'embrace', associated with *complexus* 'plaited']

complexion /kəm'plɛkʃ(ə)n/ *n.* **1** the natural colour, texture, and appearance of the skin, esp. of the face. **2** an aspect; a character (*puts a different complexion on the matter*). □ **complexioned** *adj.* (in *comb.*). [originally = combination of supposed qualities determining the nature of a body: Middle English via Old French from Latin *complexio -onis* (as COMPLEX)]

complex sentence *n.* a sentence containing a subordinate clause or clauses.

compliance /kəm'plʌɪəns/ *n.* **1** the act or an instance of complying; obedience to a request, command, etc. **2** *Mech.* **a** the capacity to yield under an applied force. **b** the degree of such yielding. **3** unworthy acquiescence. □ **in compliance with** according to (a wish, command, etc.).

compliant /kəm'plʌɪənt/ *adj.* disposed to comply; yielding, obedient. □ **compliantly** *adv.*

complicate /'kɒmplɪkeɪt/ *v.tr. & intr.* **1** (often foll. by *with*) make or become difficult, confused, intricate, or complex. **2** (as **complicated** *adj.*) complex; intricate. □ **complicatedly** *adv.* **complicatedness** *n.* [Latin *complicare complicat-* (as COM-, *plicare* 'fold')]

complication /kɒmplɪ'keɪʃ(ə)n/ *n.* **1 a** an involved or confused condition or state. **b** a complicating circumstance; a difficulty. **2** *Med.* a secondary disease or condition aggravating a previous one. [French *complication* or Late Latin *complicatio* (as COMPLICATE)]

complicity /kəm'plɪsɪti/ *n.* partnership in a crime or wrongdoing. □ **complicit** *adj.* [*complice* (see ACCOMPLICE) + -ITY]

compliment *n. & v.* ● *n.* /'kɒmplɪm(ə)nt/ **1 a** a spoken or written expression of praise. **b** an act or circumstance implying praise (*their success was a compliment to their efforts*). **2** (in *pl.*) **a** formal greetings, esp. as a written accompaniment to a gift etc. (*with the compliments of the management*). **b** praise (*my compliments to the cook*). ● *v.tr.* /'kɒmplɪmɛnt/ **1** (often foll. by *on*) congratulate; praise (*complimented him on his roses*). **2** (often foll. by *with*) present as a mark of courtesy (*complimented her with his attention*). □ **pay a compliment to** praise. **return the compliment 1** give a compliment in return for another. **2** retaliate or recompense in kind. [French *complimenter* from Italian *complimento*, ultimately from Latin *complēre* 'fill up, fulfil' (the requirements of courtesy)]

complimentary /kɒmplɪ'mɛnt(ə)ri/ *adj.* **1** expressing a compliment; praising. **2** (of a ticket for a play etc.) given free of charge, esp. as a mark of favour. □ **complimentarily** *adv.*

compliments of the season *n.pl.* greetings appropriate to the time of year, esp. Christmas.

compliments slip *n.* esp. *Brit.* a printed slip of paper sent with a gift etc., esp. from a business firm.

compline /'kɒmplɪn, -ʌɪn/ *n. Eccl.* the office of the seventh canonical hour of prayer, originally said at the end of the day. [Middle English from Old French *complie*, fem. past part. of obsolete *complir* 'complete', ultimately from Latin *complēre* 'fill up']

comply /kəm'plʌɪ/ *v.intr.* (**-ies**, **-ied**) (often foll. by *with*) act in accordance (with a wish, command, etc.) (*complied with her conditions; had no choice but to comply*). [Italian *complire* via Catalan *complir*, Spanish *cumplir* from Latin *complēre* 'fill up']

compo[1] /'kɒmpəʊ/ *n. & adj.* ● *n.* (*pl.* **-os**) a composition of plaster etc., e.g. stucco. ● *adj. Brit.* = COMPOSITE *adj.* 1, 2. [abbreviation]

compo[2] /'kɒmpəʊ/ *n. Austral. & NZ slang* compensation, esp. that paid for an industrial injury. [abbreviation]

component /kəm'pəʊnənt/ *n. & adj.* ● *n.* **1** a part of a larger whole, esp. part of a motor vehicle. **2** *Math.* one of two or more vectors equivalent to a given vector. ● *adj.* being part of a larger whole (*assembled the component parts*). □ **componential** /kɒmpə'nɛnʃ(ə)l/ *adj.* [Latin *componere component-* (as COM-, *ponere* 'put')]

compo rations *n.pl. Brit.* a large pack of food designed to last for several days. [COMPO[1]]

comport /kəm'pɔːt/ *v.refl.* usu. *literary* conduct oneself; behave. □ **comport with** suit, befit. □ **comportment** *n.* [Latin *comportare* (as COM-, *portare* 'carry')]

compos /'kɒmpɒs/ *adj.* = COMPOS MENTIS.

compose /kəm'pəʊz/ *v.* **1 a** *tr.* construct or create (a work of art, esp. literature or music). **b** *intr.* compose music (*gave up composing in 1917*). **2** *tr.* constitute; make up (*six tribes which composed the German nation*). **3** *tr.* put together to form a whole, esp. artistically; order, arrange (*composed the group for the photographer*). **4** *tr.* **a** (often *refl.*) calm; settle (*compose your expression; composed himself to wait*). **b** (as **composed** *adj.*) calm, settled. **5** *tr.* settle (a dispute etc.). **6** *tr. Printing* **a** set up (type) to form words and blocks of words. **b** set up (a manuscript etc.) in type. □ **composed of** made up of; consisting of (*a flock composed of sheep and goats*). □ **composedly** /-zɪdli/ *adv.* [French *composer* from Latin *componere* (as COM-, *ponere* 'put')]

■ **Usage** In sense 2, *compose* is preferable to *comprise* (see Usage Note at *comprise*).

composer /kəm'pəʊzə/ *n.* a person who composes (esp. music).

composite /'kɒmpəzɪt/ *adj., n., & v.* ● *adj.* **1** made up of various parts; blended. **2** (esp. of a synthetic building material) made up of recognizable constituents. **3** (**Composite**) *Archit.* of the fifth classical order of architecture, consisting of elements of the Ionic and Corinthian orders. **4** *Bot.* of the plant family Compositae. ● *n.* **1** a thing made up of several parts or elements. **2** a synthetic building material. **3** *Bot.* a plant of the family Compositae, having a head of many small flowers forming one bloom, e.g. the daisy, the dandelion. **4** /'kɒmpəzʌɪt/ *Polit.* a resolution composed of two or more related resolutions. ● *v.tr.* /'kɒmpəzʌɪt/ *Polit.* amalgamate (two or more related resolutions). □ **compositely** *adv.* **compositeness** *n.* [French from Latin *compositus*, past part. of *componere* (as COM-, *ponere posit-* 'put')]

composition /kɒmpə'zɪʃ(ə)n/ *n.* **1 a** the act of putting together; formation or construction. **b** something so composed; a mixture. **c** the constitution of such a mixture; the nature of its ingredients (*the composition is two parts oil to one part vinegar*). **2 a** a literary or musical work. **b** the act or art of producing such a work. **c** an essay, esp. written by a schoolchild or student. **d** an artistic arrangement (of parts of a picture, subjects for a photograph, etc.). **3** mental constitution; character (*jealousy is not in his composition*). **4** (often *attrib.*) a compound artificial substance, esp. one serving the purpose of a natural one. **5** *Printing* the setting-up of type. **6** *Gram.* the formation of words into a compound word. **7** *Law* **a** a compromise, esp. a legal agreement to pay a sum in lieu of a larger sum, or other obligation (*made a composition with his creditors*). **b** a sum paid in this way. **8** *Math.* the combination of functions in a series. □ **compositional** *adj.* **compositionally** *adv.* [Middle English from Old French, from Latin *compositio -onis* (as COMPOSITE)]

compositor /kəm'pɒzɪtə/ *n. Printing* a person who sets up type for printing. [Middle English via Anglo-French *compositour* from Latin *compositor* (as COMPOSITE)]

compos mentis /'mɛntɪs/ *adj.* having control of one's mind; sane. [Latin]

compossible /kəm'pɒsɪb(ə)l/ *adj.* (often foll. by *with*) *formal* able to coexist. [Old French from medieval Latin *compossibilis* (as COM-, POSSIBLE)]

compost /'kɒmpɒst/ *n. & v.* ● *n.* **1 a** mixed manure, esp. of organic origin. **b** a loam soil or other medium with added compost, used for growing plants. **2** a mixture of ingredients (*a rich compost of lies and innuendo*). ● *v.tr.* **1** treat (soil) with compost. **2** make (manure, vegetable matter, etc.) into compost. [Middle

English via Old French *composte* from Latin *compos(i)tum* (as COMPOSITE)]

compost heap *n.* (also **compost pile**) a layered structure of garden refuse, soil, etc., which decays to become compost.

composure /kəm'pəʊʒə/ *n.* a tranquil manner; calmness. [COMPOSE + -URE]

compote /'kɒmpəʊt, -ɒt/ *n.* fruit preserved or cooked in syrup. [French from Old French *composte* (as COMPOSITE)]

compound[1] *n., adj., & v.* ● *n.* /'kɒmpaʊnd/ **1** a mixture of two or more things, qualities, etc. **2** (also **compound word**) a word made up of two or more existing words. **3** *Chem.* a substance formed from two or more elements chemically united in fixed proportions. ● *adj.* /'kɒmpaʊnd/ **1 a** made up of several ingredients. **b** consisting of several parts. **2** combined; collective. **3** *Zool.* consisting of individual organisms. **4** *Biol.* consisting of several or many parts. ● *v.* /kəm'paʊnd/ **1** *tr.* mix or combine (ingredients, ideas, motives, etc.) (*grief compounded with fear*). **2** *tr.* increase or complicate (difficulties etc.) (*anxiety compounded by discomfort*). **3** *tr.* make up (a composite whole). **4** *tr.* (also *absol.*) settle (a debt, dispute, etc.) by concession or special arrangement. **5** *tr. Law* **a** condone (a liability or offence) in exchange for money etc. **b** forbear from prosecuting (a felony) from private motives. **6** *intr.* (usu. foll. by *with, for*) *Law* come to terms with a person, for forgoing a claim etc. for an offence. **7** *tr.* combine (words or elements) into a word. □ **compoundable** /kəm'paʊndəb(ə)l/ *adj.* [Middle English *compoun(e)* via Old French *compondre* from Latin *componere* (as COM-, *ponere* 'put': *-d* as in *expound*)]

compound[2] /'kɒmpaʊnd/ *n.* **1** a large open enclosure for housing workers etc., esp. miners in S. Africa. **2** an enclosure, esp. in India, China, etc., in which a factory or a house stands (cf. KAMPONG). **3** a large enclosed space in a prison or prison camp. **4** = POUND[3]. [Portuguese *campon* or Dutch *kampong*, from Malay]

compounder /kəm'paʊndə/ *n.* a person who makes a compound of ingredients, e.g. drugs, animal feed.

compound eye *n.* an eye consisting of numerous visual units, as found in insects and crustaceans (cf. SIMPLE EYE).

compound fracture *n.* a fracture in which a bone pierces the skin, causing a risk of infection.

compound fruit *n.* **1** = AGGREGATE FRUIT. **2** = MULTIPLE FRUIT.

compound interest *n.* interest payable on both capital and the accumulated interest (cf. SIMPLE INTEREST).

compound interval *n. Mus.* an interval exceeding one octave.

compound leaf *n.* a leaf consisting of several or many leaflets.

compound sentence *n.* a sentence with more than one subject or predicate.

compound time *n. Mus.* a tempo with more than one group of simple time units in each bar.

comprador /kɒmprə'dɔː/ *n.* (also **compradore**) **1** *hist.* a Chinese business agent of a foreign company. **2** an agent of a foreign power. [Portuguese *comprador* 'buyer', via Late Latin *comparator* from Latin *comparare* 'purchase']

comprehend /kɒmprɪ'hɛnd/ *v.tr.* **1** grasp mentally; understand (a person or a thing). **2** include; take in. [Middle English from Old French *comprehender* or Latin *comprehendere comprehens-* (as COM-, *prehendere* 'grasp')]

comprehensible /kɒmprɪ'hɛnsɪb(ə)l/ *adj.* **1** that can be understood; intelligible. **2** that can be included or contained. □ **comprehensibility** /-'bɪlɪti/ *n.* **comprehensibly** *adv.* [French *compréhensible* or Latin *comprehensibilis* (as COMPREHEND)]

comprehension /kɒmprɪ'hɛnʃ(ə)n/ *n.* **1 a** the act or capability of understanding, esp. writing or speech. **b** *Brit.* an extract from a text set as an examination, with questions designed to test understanding of it. **2** inclusion. **3** *Eccl. hist.* the inclusion of Nonconformists in the Anglican Church. [French *compréhension* or Latin *comprehensio* (as COMPREHENSIBLE)]

comprehensive /kɒmprɪ'hɛnsɪv/ *adj. & n.* ● *adj.* **1** complete; including all or nearly all elements, aspects, etc. (*a comprehensive grasp of the subject*). **2** of or relating to understanding (*the comprehensive faculty*). **3** (of motor vehicle insurance) providing complete protection. ● *n.* (in full **comprehensive school**) *Brit.* a secondary school catering for children of all abilities from a given area. □ **comprehensively** *adv.* **comprehensiveness** *n.* [French *compréhensif -ive* or Late Latin *comprehensivus* (as COMPREHENSIBLE)]

compress *v. & n.* ● *v.tr.* /kəm'prɛs/ **1** squeeze together. **2** bring into a smaller space or shorter extent. ● *n.* /'kɒmprɛs/ a pad of lint etc. pressed on to part of the body to relieve inflammation, stop bleeding, etc. □ **compressible** /kəm'prɛsɪb(ə)l/ *adj.* **compressibility** /-'bɪlɪti/ *n.* **compressive** /kəm'prɛsɪv/ *adj.* [Middle English from Old French *compresser* or Late Latin *compressare*, frequentative of Latin *comprimere compress-* (as COM-, *premere* 'press')]

compressed air *n.* air at more than atmospheric pressure.

compression /kəm'prɛʃ(ə)n/ *n.* **1** the act of compressing or being compressed. **2** the reduction in volume (causing an increase in pressure) of the fuel mixture in an internal-combustion engine before ignition. [French from Latin *compressio* (as COMPRESS)]

compression ratio *n.* the ratio of the maximum to minimum volume in the cylinder of an internal-combustion engine.

compressor /kəm'prɛsə/ *n.* an instrument or device for compressing, esp. a machine used for increasing the pressure of air or other gases.

comprise /kəm'prʌɪz/ *v.* **1** *tr.* consist of, be made up of; contain (*the book comprises 350 pages*). **2** *tr. disp.* make up, compose (*the essays comprise his total work*). **3** *tr.* (in *passive*, foll. by *of*) *disp.* consist of (*the army was comprised of volunteers*). **4** *intr.* (foll. by *of*) *disp.* consist of (*the region comprises of three separate districts*). □ **comprisable** *adj.* [Middle English from French, fem. past part. of *comprendre* COMPREHEND]

■ **Usage** The use of *comprise* in senses 2 and 3 is still regarded as non-standard by some people and its use in sense 4, formed on analogy with *consist of*, is especially frowned upon. More acceptable alternatives are *consist of*, *be composed of*, or simply *comprise* without *of* (as in sense 1).

compromise /'kɒmprəmʌɪz/ *n. & v.* ● *n.* **1** the settlement of a dispute by mutual concession (*reached a compromise by bargaining*). **2** (often foll. by *between*) an intermediate state between conflicting opinions, actions, etc., reached by mutual concession or modification (*a compromise between ideals and material necessity*). ● *v.* **1 a** *intr.* settle a dispute by mutual concession (*compromised over the terms*). **b** *tr. archaic* settle (a dispute) by mutual concession. **2** *tr.* bring into disrepute or danger esp. by indiscretion or folly. □ **compromiser** *n.* **compromisingly** *adv.* [Middle English via Old French *compromis* from Late Latin *compromissum*, neut. past part. of *compromittere* (as COM-, *promittere* PROMISE)]

compte rendu /ˌkɔ̃t rɑ̃'djuː, French kɔ̃t rɑ̃dy/ *n.* (*pl.* ***comptes rendus*** *pronunc.* same) a report; a review; a statement. [French, = account rendered]

Comptometer /kɒm(p)'tɒmɪtə/ *n. Brit. propr.* an early type of calculating machine. [apparently from French *compte* COUNT[1] + -METER]

comptroller /kən'trəʊlə/ *n.* a controller (used in the title of some financial officers) (*Comptroller and Auditor General*). [variant of CONTROLLER, by erroneous association with COUNT[1], Late Latin *computus*]

compulsion /kəm'pʌlʃ(ə)n/ *n.* **1** a constraint; an obligation. **2** *Psychol.* an irresistible urge to behave in a certain way, esp. against one's conscious wishes. □ **under compulsion** because one is compelled. [Middle English via French from Late Latin *compulsio -onis* (as COMPEL)]

compulsive /kəm'pʌlsɪv/ *adj.* **1** compelling. **2** resulting or acting from, or as if from, compulsion (*a compulsive gambler*). **3** *Psychol.* resulting or acting from compulsion against one's conscious wishes. **4** irresistible (*compulsive viewing*). □ **compulsively** *adv.* **compulsiveness** *n.* [medieval Latin *compulsivus* (as COMPEL)]

compulsory /kəm'pʌls(ə)ri/ *adj.* **1** required by law or a rule (*it is compulsory to keep dogs on leads*). **2** essential; necessary. □ **compulsorily** *adv.* **compulsoriness** *n.* [medieval Latin *compulsorius* (as COMPEL)]

compulsory purchase *n. Brit.* the enforced purchase of land or property by a local authority etc., for public use.

compunction /kəm'pʌŋkʃ(ə)n/ *n.* (usu. with *neg.*) **1** the pricking of the conscience; remorse. **2** slight regret; a scruple (*without compunction; have no compunction in refusing him*). □ **compunctious** /-ʃəs/ *adj.* **compunctiously** /-ʃəsli/ *adv.* [Middle English via Old French *componction* and ecclesiastical Latin *compunctio -onis* from Latin *compungere compunct-* (as COM-, *pungere* 'prick')]

compurgation /kɒmpə:'geɪʃ(ə)n/ *n. Law hist.* an acquittal from a charge or accusation obtained by the oaths of witnesses. □ **compurgatory** /kəm'pə:gət(ə)ri/ *adj.* [medieval Latin *compurgatio* from Latin *compurgare* (as COM-, *purgare* 'purify')]

compurgator /'kɒmpə:geɪtə/ *n. Law hist.* a witness who swore to the innocence or good character of an accused person.

computation /kɒmpjʊ'teɪʃ(ə)n/ *n.* **1** the act or an instance of reckoning; calculation. **2** the use of a computer. **3** a result obtained by calculation. □ **computational** *adj.* **computationally** *adv.*

compute /kəm'pju:t/ *v.* **1** *tr.* (often foll. by *that* + clause) reckon or calculate (a number, an amount, etc.). **2** *intr.* make a reckoning, esp. using a computer. □ **computable** /-'pju:təb(ə)l, 'kɒm-/ *adj.* **computability** /-tə'bɪlɪti/ *n.* [French *computer* or Latin *computare* (as COM-, *putare* 'reckon')]

computer /kəm'pju:tə/ *n.* **1** a usu. electronic device for storing and processing data (usu. in binary form), according to instructions given to it in a variable program. **2** a person who computes or makes calculations.

computerate /kəm'pju:tərət/ *adj.* = COMPUTER-LITERATE. [COMPUTER + -ATE³, on the pattern of LITERATE]

computerize /kəm'pju:tərʌɪz/ *v.tr.* (also **-ise**) **1** equip with a computer; install a computer in. **2** store, perform, or produce by computer. □ **computerization** /-'zeɪʃ(ə)n/ *n.*

computer-literate *adj.* able to use computers; familiar with the operation of computers.

computer programmer *n.* a person who writes computer programs.

computer science *n.* the study of the principles and use of computers.

computer virus *n.* a hidden code within a computer program intended to corrupt a system or destroy data stored in it.

comrade /'kɒmreɪd/ *n.* **1** (also **comrade-in-arms**) **a** (usu. of males) a workmate, friend, or companion. **b** a fellow soldier etc. **2** *Polit.* a fellow socialist or communist (often as a form of address). □ **comradely** *adj.* **comradeship** *n.* [earlier *cama- camerade*, via French *camerade, camarade* (originally fem.) and Spanish *camarada* 'room-mate', from Latin CAMERA]

Comsat /'kɒmsat/ *n. propr.* a communication satellite. [abbreviation]

con¹ /kɒn/ *n. & v. slang* ● *n.* a confidence trick. ● *v.tr.* (**conned**, **conning**) swindle; deceive (*conned him into thinking he had won*). [abbreviation]

con² /kɒn/ *n., prep., & adv.* ● *n.* (usu. in *pl.*) a reason against. ● *prep. & adv.* against (cf. PRO²). [Latin *contra* 'against']

con³ /kɒn/ *n. slang* a convict. [abbreviation]

con⁴ /kɒn/ *v.tr.* (*US* **conn**) (**conned**, **conning**) *Naut.* direct the steering of (a ship). [apparently weakened form of obsolete *cond, condie*, via French *conduire*, from Latin *conducere* CONDUCT]

con⁵ /kɒn/ *v.tr.* (**conned**, **conning**) (often foll. by *over*) *archaic* study, learn by heart (*conned his part well*). [Middle English *cunn-, con*, forms of CAN¹]

con- /kɒn, kən/ *prefix* assim. form of COM- before *c, d, f, g, j, n, q, s, t, v*, and sometimes before vowels.

conacre /'kɒneɪkə/ *n. Ir.* the letting by a tenant of small portions of land prepared for crops or grazing. [CORN¹ + ACRE]

con amore /ˌkɒn a'mɔ:reɪ, Italian kɔn a'mo:rɛ/ *adv.* **1** with devotion or zeal. **2** *Mus.* tenderly. [Italian, = with love]

conation /kə'neɪʃ(ə)n/ *n. Philos. & Psychol.* **1** the desire to perform an action. **2** voluntary action; volition. □ **conative** /'kɒnətɪv, 'kəʊ-/ *adj.* [Latin *conatio* from *conari* 'try']

con brio /kɒn 'bri:əʊ/ *adv. Mus.* with vigour. [Italian]

concatenate /kən'katɪneɪt/ *v. & adj.* ● *v.tr.* link together (a chain of events, things, etc.). ● *adj.* joined; linked. □ **concatenation** /-'neɪʃ(ə)n/ *n.* [Late Latin *concatenare* (as COM-, *catenare* from *catena* 'chain')]

concave /'kɒnkeɪv/ *adj.* having an outline or surface curved like the interior of a circle or sphere (cf. CONVEX). □ **concavely** *adv.* **concavity** /-'kavɪti/ *n.* [Latin *concavus* (as COM-, *cavus* 'hollow'), or through French *concave*]

conceal /kən'si:l/ *v.tr.* **1** (often foll. by *from*) keep secret (*concealed her motive from him*). **2** not allow to be seen; hide (*concealed the letter in her pocket*). □ **concealer** *n.* **concealment** *n.* [Middle English via Old French *conceler* from Latin *concelare* (as COM-, *celare* 'hide')]

concede /kən'si:d/ *v.tr.* **1 a** (often foll. by *that* + clause) admit (a defeat etc.) to be true (*conceded that his work was inadequate*). **b** admit defeat in. **2** (often foll. by *to*) grant, yield, or surrender (a right, a privilege, points or a start in a game, etc.). **3** *Sport* fail to prevent an opponent from scoring (a goal) or winning (a match), etc. □ **conceder** *n.* [French *concéder* or Latin *concedere concess-* (as COM-, *cedere* 'yield')]

conceit /kən'si:t/ *n.* **1** personal vanity; pride. **2** *literary* **a** a far-fetched comparison, esp. as a stylistic affectation; a convoluted or unlikely metaphor. **b** a fanciful notion. [Middle English from CONCEIVE, influenced by *deceit, deceive*, etc.]

conceited /kən'si:tɪd/ *adj.* vain, proud. □ **conceitedly** *adv.* **conceitedness** *n.*

conceivable /kən'si:vəb(ə)l/ *adj.* capable of being grasped or imagined; understandable. □ **conceivability** /-'bɪlɪti/ *n.* **conceivably** *adv.*

conceive /kən'si:v/ *v.* **1** *intr.* become pregnant. **2** *tr.* become pregnant with (a child). **3** *tr.* (often foll. by *that* + clause) **a** imagine, fancy, think (*can't conceive that he could be guilty*). **b** (usu. in *passive*) formulate, express (a belief, a plan, etc.). □ **conceive of** form in the mind; imagine. [Middle English via Old French *conceiv-*, stressed stem of *concevoir*, from Latin *concipere concept-* (as COM-, *capere* 'take')]

concelebrate /kɒn'sɛlɪbreɪt/ *v.intr.* **1** (of priests) celebrate the Mass together. **2** (esp. of a newly ordained priest) celebrate the Mass with the ordaining bishop. □ **concelebrant** /-br(ə)nt/ *n.* **concelebration** /-'breɪʃ(ə)n/ *n.* [Latin *concelebrare* (as COM-, *celebrare* CELEBRATE)]

concentrate /'kɒns(ə)ntreɪt/ *v. & n.* ● *v.* **1** *intr.* (often foll. by *on, upon*) focus all one's attention or mental ability. **2** *tr.* bring together (troops, power, attention, etc.) to one point; focus. **3** *tr.* increase the strength of (a solution etc.) by removing water or other diluting agent. **4** *tr.* (as **concentrated** *adj.*) (of hate etc.) intense, strong. ● *n.* **1** a concentrated substance. **2** a concentrated form of esp. food. □ **concentratedly** *adv.* **concentrative** *adj.* **concentrator** *n.* [from earlier *concentre* or its source, French *concentrer* (as CON- + CENTRE)]

concentration /kɒns(ə)n'treɪʃ(ə)n/ *n.* **1** the act or power of focusing one's attention or mental ability (*needs to develop concentration; broke my concentration*). **2** the act of gathering or bringing together. **3** something so gathered (*a concentration of resources*). **4** *Chem.* **a** the act of strengthening a solution by the removal of solvent. **b** the strength of a solution, esp. the amount of solute per unit volume of solution.

concentration camp *n.* a camp for the detention of political prisoners, internees, etc., esp. in Nazi Germany.

concentre /kɒn'sɛntə/ *v.tr. & intr.* (*US* **concenter**) bring or come to a common centre. [French *concentrer*: see CONCENTRATE]

concentric /kən'sɛntrɪk/ *adj.* (often foll. by *with*) (esp. of circles) having a common centre (cf. ECCENTRIC *adj.* 2a). □ **concentrically** *adv.* **concentricity** /kɒnsɛn'trɪsɪti/ *n.* [Middle English from Old French *concentrique* or medieval Latin *concentricus* (as COM-, CENTRE)]

concept /'kɒnsɛpt/ *n.* **1** a general notion; an abstract idea (*the concept of evolution*). **2** *colloq.* an idea or invention to help sell or publicize a commodity (*a new concept in swimwear*). **3** *Philos.* an idea or mental picture of a group or class of objects formed by combining all their aspects. [Late Latin *conceptus* from *concept-*: see CONCEIVE]

conception /kən'sɛpʃ(ə)n/ *n.* **1** the act or an instance of conceiving; the process of being conceived. **2** an idea or plan, esp. as being new or daring (*the whole conception showed originality*). **3** (usu. foll. by *of*) understanding; ability to imagine (*has no conception of what it entails*). □ **conceptional** *adj.* [Middle English via Old French from Latin *conceptio -onis* (as CONCEPT)]

conceptive /kən'sɛptɪv/ *adj.* **1** conceiving mentally. **2** of conception. [Latin *conceptivus* (as CONCEPTION)]

conceptual /kən'sɛptjʊəl/ *adj.* of mental conceptions or concepts. □ **conceptually** *adv.* [medieval Latin *conceptualis* from *conceptus* (as CONCEPT)]

conceptualism /kən'sɛptjʊəlɪz(ə)m/ *n.* *Philos.* the theory that universals exist, but only as concepts in the mind. □ **conceptualist** *n.*

conceptualize /kən'sɛptjʊəlʌɪz/ *v.tr.* (also **-ise**) form a concept or idea of. □ **conceptualization** /-'zeɪʃ(ə)n/ *n.*

conceptus /kən'sɛptəs/ *n.* the product of conception in the womb, esp. the embryo in the early stages of pregnancy. [Latin, = conception, embryo]

concern /kən'sə:n/ *v. & n.* ● *v.tr.* **1 a** be relevant or important to (*this concerns you*). **b** relate to; be about. **2** (usu. *refl.*; often foll. by *with, in, about,* or *to* + infin.) interest or involve oneself (*don't concern yourself with my problems*). **3** worry, affect (*it concerns me that he is always late*). ● *n.* **1** anxiety, worry (*felt a deep concern*). **2 a** a matter of interest or importance to one (*no concern of mine*). **b** (usu. in *pl.*) affairs; private business (*chatted about departmental concerns*). **3** a business; a firm (*quite a prosperous concern*). **4** *colloq.* a complicated or awkward thing (*have lost the whole concern*). □ **have a concern in** have an interest or share in. **have no concern with** have nothing to do with. **to whom it may concern** to those who have a proper interest in the matter (as an address to the reader of a testimonial, reference, etc.). [French *concerner* or Late Latin *concernere* (as COM-, *cernere* 'sift, discern')]

concerned /kən'sə:nd/ *adj.* **1** involved, interested (*the people concerned; concerned with proving his innocence*). **2** (often foll. by *that, about, at, for,* or *to* + infin.) troubled, anxious (*concerned about him; concerned to hear that*). □ **as** (or **so**) **far as I am concerned** as regards my interests. **be concerned** (often foll. by *in*) take part. **I am not concerned** it is not my business. □ **concernedly** /-'sə:nɪdli/ *adv.* **concernedness** /-'sə:nɪdnɪs/ *n.*

concerning /kən'sə:nɪŋ/ *prep.* about, regarding.

concernment /kən'sə:nm(ə)nt/ *n.* *formal* **1** an affair or business. **2** importance. **3** (often foll. by *with*) a state of being concerned; anxiety.

concert *n. & v.* ● *n.* /'kɒnsət/ **1** a musical performance of usu. several separate compositions. **2** agreement, accordance, harmony. **3** a combination of voices or sounds. ● *v.tr.* /kən'sə:t/ arrange (by mutual agreement or coordination). □ **in concert 1** (often foll. by *with*) acting jointly and accordantly. **2** (*predic.*) (of a musician) in a performance. [French *concert* (*n.*), *concerter* (*v.*) from Italian *concertare* 'harmonize']

concertante /kɒntʃə'tanti/ *n.* (*pl.* **concertanti** *pronunc.* same) (often *attrib.*) *Mus.* **1** a piece of music containing one or more solo parts (usu. of less prominence or weight than in a concerto). **2** *hist.* those instrumental parts that are present throughout a piece of music. [Italian]

concerted /kən'sə:tɪd/ *adj.* **1** combined together; jointly arranged or planned (*a concerted effort*). **2** *Mus.* arranged in parts for voices or instruments.

concert-goer *n.* a person who often goes to concerts.

concert grand *n.* the largest size of grand piano, used for concerts.

concert hall *n.* a hall for the public performance of concerts.

concertina /kɒnsə'ti:nə/ *n. & v.* ● *n.* a musical instrument, usu. polygonal in form, held in the hands and stretched and squeezed like bellows, having reeds and a set of buttons at each end to control the valves. ● *v.tr. & intr.* (**concertinas**, **concertinaed** /-nəd/ or **concertina'd**, **concertinaing** /-nə(r)ɪŋ/) compress or collapse in folds like those of a concertina (*the car concertinaed into the bridge*). [CONCERT + -INA]

concertino /kɒntʃə'ti:nəʊ/ *n.* (*pl.* **-os**) *Mus.* **1** a simple or short concerto. **2** a solo instrument or solo instruments playing in a concerto. [Italian, diminutive of CONCERTO]

concert master *n.* esp. *N. Amer.* the leading first-violin player in some orchestras.

concerto /kən'tʃə:təʊ, -'tʃɛ:təʊ/ *n.* (*pl.* **-os** or **concerti** /-ti/) *Mus.* a composition for a solo instrument or instruments accompanied by an orchestra. [Italian (see CONCERT)]

concerto grosso /'grɒsəʊ/ *n.* (*pl.* **concerti grossi** /-si/) a composition for a group of solo instruments accompanied by an orchestra. [CONCERTO + *grosso* 'big']

concert overture *n.* *Mus.* a piece like an overture but intended for independent performance.

concert performance *n.* *Brit.* a performance (of an opera etc.) without scenery, costumes, or action.

concert pianist *n.* a classical pianist who regularly works as a soloist in concert performances.

concert pitch *n.* **1** *Mus.* the standard pitch, internationally agreed in 1960, whereby the A above middle C = 440 Hz. **2** a state of unusual readiness, efficiency, and keenness (for action etc.).

concession /kən'sɛʃ(ə)n/ *n.* **1 a** the act or an instance of conceding something asked or required (*made the concession that we were right*). **b** a thing conceded. **2** a reduction in price for a certain category of person. **3 a** the right to use land or other property, granted esp. by a government or local authority, esp. for a specific use. **b** the right, given by a company, to sell goods, esp. in a particular territory. **c** the land or property used or given. □ **concessional** *adj.* **concessionary** *adj.* [French *concession* from Latin *concessio* (as CONCEDE)]

concessionaire /kənsɛʃə'nɛ:/ *n.* (also **concessionnaire**) the holder of a concession or grant, esp. for the use of land or trading rights. [French *concessionnaire* (as CONCESSION)]

concessive /kən'sɛsɪv/ *adj.* **1** of or tending to concession. **2** *Gram.* **a** (of a preposition or conjunction) introducing a phrase or clause which might be expected to preclude the action of the main clause, but does not (e.g. *in spite of*, *although*). **b** (of a phrase or clause) introduced by a concessive preposition or conjunction. [Late Latin *concessivus* (as CONCEDE)]

conch /kɒŋk, kɒn(t)ʃ/ *n.* (*pl.* **conchs** /kɒŋks/ or **conches** /ˈkɒntʃɪz/) **1 a** a thick heavy spiral shell, occasionally bearing long projections, of various marine gastropod molluscs of the family Strombidae. **b** any of these gastropods. **2** *Archit.* the domed roof of a semicircular apse. **3** = CONCHA. [Latin *concha* 'shell', from Greek *kogkhē*]

concha /ˈkɒŋkə/ *n.* (*pl.* **conchae** /-kiː/) *Anat.* a part resembling a shell, esp. the depression in the external ear leading to its central cavity. [Latin: see CONCH]

conchie /ˈkɒnʃi/ *n.* (also **conchy**) (*pl.* **-ies**) *Brit. slang derog.* a conscientious objector. [abbreviation]

conchoidal /kɒŋˈkɔɪd(ə)l/ *adj. Mineral.* (of a solid fracture etc.) resembling the surface of a bivalve shell.

conchology /kɒŋˈkɒlədʒi/ *n. Zool.* the scientific study of molluscs and their shells. □ **conchological** /-kəˈlɒdʒɪk(ə)l/ *adj.* **conchologist** *n.* [Greek *kogkhē* 'shell' + -LOGY]

conchy var. of CONCHIE.

concierge /ˈkɒnsɪɛːʒ/ *n.* **1** (esp. in France) a doorkeeper or porter of a block of flats etc. **2** a person in a hotel employed to assist guests by booking tours, making reservations, etc. [French, probably ultimately from Latin *conservus* 'fellow slave']

conciliar /kənˈsɪlɪə/ *adj.* of or concerning a council, esp. an ecclesiastical council. [medieval Latin *consiliarius* 'counsellor']

conciliate /kənˈsɪlɪeɪt/ *v.tr.* **1** make calm and amenable; pacify. **2** gain (esteem or goodwill). **3** *archaic* reconcile, make compatible. □ **conciliative** /-ˈsɪlɪətɪv/ *adj.* **conciliator** *n.* **conciliatory** /-ˈsɪlɪət(ə)ri/ *adj.* **conciliatoriness** /-ˈsɪlɪət(ə)rɪnɪs/ *n.* [Latin *conciliare* 'combine, gain' from *concilium*: see COUNCIL]

conciliation /kənsɪlɪˈeɪʃ(ə)n/ *n.* the use of conciliating measures; reconcilement. [Latin *conciliatio* (as CONCILIATE)]

concinnity /kənˈsɪnɪti/ *n.* elegance or neatness of literary style. [Latin *concinnitas* from *concinnus* 'well-adjusted']

concise /kənˈsʌɪs/ *adj.* (of speech, writing, style, or a person) brief but comprehensive in expression. □ **concisely** *adv.* **conciseness** *n.* [French *concis* or Latin *concisus*, past part. of *concidere* (as COM-, *caedere* 'cut')]

concision /kənˈsɪʒ(ə)n/ *n.* (esp. of literary style) the quality of state of being concise; conciseness. [Middle English from Latin *concisio* (as CONCISE)]

conclave /ˈkɒŋkleɪv/ *n.* **1** a private meeting. **2** *RC Ch.* **a** the assembly of cardinals for the election of a pope. **b** the meeting place for a conclave. [Middle English via Old French from Latin *conclave* 'lockable room' (as COM-, *clavis* 'key')]

conclude /kənˈkluːd/ *v.* **1** *tr. & intr.* bring or come to an end. **2** *tr.* (often foll. by *from*, or *that* + clause) infer (from given premisses) (*what did you conclude?*; *concluded from the evidence that he had been mistaken*). **3** *tr.* settle, arrange (a treaty etc.). **4** *intr.* (usu. foll. by *to* + infin.) esp. *US* decide. [Middle English from Latin *concludere* (as COM-, *claudere* 'shut')]

conclusion /kənˈkluːʒ(ə)n/ *n.* **1** a final result; a termination. **2** a judgement reached by reasoning. **3** the summing-up of an argument, article, book, etc. **4** a settling; an arrangement (*the conclusion of peace*). **5** *Logic* a proposition that is reached from given premisses, esp. the third and last part of a syllogism. □ **in conclusion** lastly, to conclude. **try conclusions with** engage in a trial of skill etc. with. [Middle English from Old French *conclusion* or Latin *conclusio* (as CONCLUDE)]

conclusive /kənˈkluːsɪv/ *adj.* decisive, convincing. □ **conclusively** *adv.* **conclusiveness** *n.* [Late Latin *conclusivus* (as CONCLUSION)]

concoct /kənˈkɒkt/ *v.tr.* **1** make by mixing ingredients (*concocted a stew*). **2** invent (a story, a lie, etc.). □ **concocter** *n.* **concoction** /-ˈkɒkʃ(ə)n/ *n.* **concoctor** *n.* [Latin *concoquere concoct-* (as COM-, *coquere* 'cook')]

concomitance /kənˈkɒmɪt(ə)ns/ *n.* (also **concomitancy** /-(ə)nsi/) **1** coexistence. **2** *Theol.* the doctrine of the coexistence of the body and blood of Christ both in the bread and in the wine of the Eucharist. [medieval Latin *concomitantia* (as CONCOMITANT)]

concomitant /kənˈkɒmɪt(ə)nt/ *adj. & n.* ● *adj.* going together; associated (*concomitant circumstances*). ● *n.* an accompanying thing. □ **concomitantly** *adv.* [Late Latin *concomitari* (as COM-, *comitari* from Latin *comes -mitis* 'companion')]

concord /ˈkɒŋkɔːd/ *n.* **1** agreement or harmony between people or things. **2** a treaty. **3** *Mus.* a chord that is pleasing or satisfactory in itself. **4** *Gram.* agreement between words in gender, number, etc. [Middle English via Old French *concorde* from Latin *concordia*, from *concors* 'of one mind' (as COM-, *cors* from *cor cordis* 'heart')]

concordance /kənˈkɔːd(ə)ns/ *n.* **1** agreement. **2** a book containing an alphabetical list of the important words used in a book or by an author, usu. with citations of the passages concerned. [Middle English via Old French from medieval Latin *concordantia* (as CONCORDANT)]

concordant /kənˈkɔːd(ə)nt/ *adj.* **1** (often foll. by *with*) agreeing, harmonious. **2** *Mus.* in harmony. □ **concordantly** *adv.* [Middle English via Old French from Latin *concordare*, from *concors* (as CONCORD)]

concordat /kənˈkɔːdat/ *n.* an agreement, esp. between the Roman Catholic Church and a state. [French *concordat* or Latin *concordatum*, neut. past part. of *concordare* (as CONCORDANCE)]

concourse /ˈkɒŋkɔːs/ *n.* **1** a crowd. **2** a coming together; a gathering (*a concourse of ideas*). **3** an open central area in a large public building, a railway station, etc. [Middle English via Old French *concours* from Latin *concursus* (as CONCUR)]

concrescence /kənˈkrɛs(ə)ns/ *n. Biol.* coalescence; growing together. □ **concrescent** *adj.* [CON-, on the pattern of *excrescence* etc.]

concrete *adj., n., & v.* ● *adj.* /ˈkɒŋkriːt/ **1 a** existing in a material form; real. **b** specific, definite (*concrete evidence*; *a concrete proposal*). **2** *Gram.* (of a noun) denoting a material object as opposed to an abstract quality, state, or action. ● *n.* /ˈkɒŋkriːt/ (often *attrib.*) a composition of gravel, sand, cement, and water, used for building. ● *v.* **1** *tr.* /ˈkɒŋkriːt/ **a** cover with concrete. **b** embed in concrete. **2** /kənˈkriːt/ **a** *tr. & intr.* form into a mass; solidify. **b** *tr.* make concrete instead of abstract. □ **in the concrete** in reality or in practice. □ **concretely** *adv.* **concreteness** *n.* [French *concret* or Latin *concretus*, past part. of *concrescere* (as COM-, *crescere cret-* 'grow')]

concrete mixer *n.* a machine, usu. with a revolving drum, used for mixing concrete.

concrete music *n.* = MUSIQUE CONCRÈTE.

concrete poetry *n.* poetry in which part of the meaning is conveyed visually, by means of patterns of words or letters and other typographical devices.

concretion /kənˈkriːʃ(ə)n/ *n.* **1 a** a hard solid concreted mass. **b** the forming of this by coalescence. **2** *Med.* a stony mass formed within the body. **3** *Geol.* a small round mass of rock particles embedded in limestone or clay. □ **concretionary** *adj.* [French, from Latin *concretio* (as CONCRETE)]

concretize /ˈkɒŋkrɪtʌɪz/ *v.tr.* (also **-ise**) make concrete instead of abstract. □ **concretization** /-ˈzeɪʃ(ə)n/ *n.*

concubinage /kɒnˈkjuːbɪnɪdʒ/ *n.* **1** the cohabitation of a man and woman not married to each other. **2** the state of being or having a concubine. [Middle English from French (as CONCUBINE)]

concubine /ˈkɒŋkjʊbʌɪn/ *n.* **1** a woman who cohabits with a man without being his wife. **2** (in polygamous societies) a secondary wife. □ **concubinary** /kənˈkjuːbɪn(ə)ri/ *adj.* [Middle English via Old French from Latin *concubina* (as COM-, *cubina* from *cubare* 'lie')]

concupiscence /kənˈkjuːpɪs(ə)ns/ *n. formal* sexual desire. □ **concupiscent** *adj.* [Middle English via Old French and Late Latin *concupiscentia* from Latin *concupiscere* 'begin to desire' (as COM-, inceptive of *cupere* 'desire')]

concur /kənˈkəː/ *v.intr.* (**concurred**, **concurring**) **1** happen together; coincide. **2** (often foll. by *with*) **a** agree in opinion. **b** express agreement. **3** combine together for a cause; act in combination. [Latin *concurrere* (as COM-, *currere* 'run')]

concurrent /kənˈkʌr(ə)nt/ *adj.* **1** (often foll. by *with*) **a** existing or in operation at the same time (*served two concurrent sentences*). **b** existing or acting together. **2** *Geom.* (of three or more lines) meeting at or tending towards one point. **3** agreeing, harmonious. □ **concurrence** *n.* **concurrently** *adv.*

concuss /kənˈkʌs/ *v.tr.* **1** subject to concussion. **2** shake violently. **3** *archaic* intimidate. □ **concussive** *adj.* [Latin *concutere concuss-* (as COM-, *cutere* = *quatere* 'shake')]

concussion /kənˈkʌʃ(ə)n/ *n.* **1** *Med.* temporary unconsciousness or incapacity due to a blow on the head. **2** violent shaking; shock. [Latin *concussio* (as CONCUSS)]

condemn /kənˈdɛm/ *v.tr.* **1** express utter disapproval of; censure (*was condemned for his irresponsible behaviour*). **2 a** find guilty; convict. **b** (usu. foll. by *to*) sentence to (a punishment, esp. death). **c** bring about the conviction of (*his looks condemn him*). **3** pronounce (a building etc.) unfit for use or habitation. **4** (usu. foll. by *to*) doom or assign (to something unwelcome or painful) (*condemned to spending hours at the kitchen sink*). **5** declare (smuggled goods, property, etc.) to be forfeited. □ **condemnable** /-ˈdɛmnəb(ə)l/ *adj.* **condemnation** /kɒndɛmˈneɪʃ(ə)n/ *n.* **condemnatory** /-ˈdɛmnət(ə)ri/ *adj.* [Middle English via Old French *condem(p)ner* from Latin *condemnare* (as COM-, *damnare* DAMN)]

condemned cell *n. Brit.* a cell for a prisoner condemned to death.

condensate /ˈkɒnd(ə)nseɪt/ *n.* a substance produced by condensation.

condensation /kɒndɛnˈseɪʃ(ə)n/ *n.* **1** the act of condensing. **2** any condensed material (esp. water on a cold surface). **3** an abridgement. **4** *Chem.* the combination of molecules with the elimination of water or other small molecules. [Late Latin *condensatio* (as CONDENSE)]

condensation trail *n.* = VAPOUR TRAIL.

condense /kənˈdɛns/ *v.* **1** *tr.* make denser or more concentrated. **2** *tr.* express in fewer words; make concise. **3** *tr. & intr.* reduce or be reduced from a gas or vapour to a liquid (or occasionally a solid). □ **condensable** *adj.* [French *condenser* or Latin *condensare* (as COM-, *densus* 'thick')]

condensed milk *n.* milk thickened by evaporation and sweetened.

condenser /kənˈdɛnsə/ *n.* **1** an apparatus or vessel for condensing vapour. **2** *Electr.* = CAPACITOR. **3** a lens or system of lenses for concentrating light. **4** a person or thing that condenses.

condescend /kɒndɪˈsɛnd/ *v.intr.* **1** (usu. foll. by *to* + infin.) often *iron.* be gracious enough (to do a thing that one regards as undignified or below one's level of importance) (*condescended to speak to me in the street*). **2** (foll. by *to*) *derog.* behave as if one is on equal terms with (a person), while maintaining an overt attitude of superiority (*condescends to the junior staff*). **3** (as **condescending** *adj.*) patronizing; superciliously kind. □ **condescendingly** *adv.* [Middle English via Old French *condescendre* from ecclesiastical Latin *condescendere* (as COM-, DESCEND)]

condescension /kɒndɪˈsɛnʃ(ə)n/ *n.* **1** a patronizing manner. **2** affability towards inferiors. [obsolete French from ecclesiastical Latin *condescensio* (as CONDESCEND)]

condign /kənˈdʌɪn/ *adj.* (of a punishment etc.) severe and well-deserved. □ **condignly** *adv.* [Middle English via Old French *condigne* from Latin *condignus* (as COM-, *dignus* 'worthy')]

condiment /ˈkɒndɪm(ə)nt/ *n.* a seasoning or relish for food. [Middle English from Latin *condimentum*, from *condire* 'pickle']

condition /kənˈdɪʃ(ə)n/ *n. & v.* ● *n.* **1** a stipulation; something upon the fulfilment of which something else depends. **2 a** the state of being or fitness of a person or thing (*arrived in bad condition*; *not in a condition to be used*). **b** an ailment or abnormality (*a heart condition*). **3** (in *pl.*) circumstances, esp. those affecting the functioning or existence of something (*working conditions are good*). **4** *archaic* social rank (*all sorts and conditions of men*). **5** *Gram.* a conditional clause. **6** *US* **a** a requirement that a student must pass an examination etc. within a stated time to receive credit for a course. **b** an unsatisfactory grade indicating this requirement. ● *v.tr.* **1 a** bring into a good or desired state or condition. **b** make fit (esp. dogs or horses). **2** teach or accustom to adopt certain habits etc. (*conditioned by society*). **3** govern, determine (*his behaviour was conditioned by his drunkenness*). **4 a** impose conditions on. **b** be essential to (*the two things condition each other*). **5** test the condition of (textiles etc.). **6** *US* subject (a student) to a condition. □ **in** (or **out of**) **condition** in good (or bad) condition. **in no condition to** certainly not fit to. **on condition that** with the stipulation that. [Middle English via Old French *condicion* (*n.*), *condicionner* (*v.*) or medieval Latin *condicionare* from Latin *condicio -onis*, from *condicere* 'agree upon' (as COM-, *dicere* 'say')]

conditional /kənˈdɪʃ(ə)n(ə)l/ *adj. & n.* ● *adj.* **1** (often foll. by *on*) dependent; not absolute; containing a condition or stipulation (*a conditional offer*). **2** *Gram.* (of a clause, mood, etc.) expressing a condition. ● *n. Gram.* **1** a conditional clause etc. **2** the conditional mood. □ **conditionality** /-ˈnalɪti/ *n.* **conditionally** *adv.* [Middle English from Old French *condicionel* or from Late Latin *conditionalis* (as CONDITION)]

conditional discharge *n.* an order made by a criminal court whereby an offender will not be sentenced for an offence unless a further offence is committed within a stated period.

conditioned reflex *n.* a reflex response to a non-natural stimulus, established by training.

conditioner /kənˈdɪʃ(ə)nə/ *n.* an agent that brings something into better condition, esp. a substance applied to the hair.

condo /ˈkɒndəʊ/ *n.* (*pl.* **-os**) *N. Amer. colloq.* a condominium. [abbreviation]

condolatory /kənˈdəʊlət(ə)ri/ *adj.* expressing condolence. [CONDOLE, on the pattern of *consolatory* etc.]

condole /kənˈdəʊl/ *v.intr.* (foll. by *with*) express sympathy with (a person) over a loss, grief, etc. [Late Latin *condolēre* (as COM-, *dolēre* 'suffer')]

■ **Usage** *Condole* is often confused with *console* (see CONSOLE[1]). *Condole* 'to express sympathy' is always followed by *with*, e.g. *They condoled with him over the death of his brother*. It is less common than *console* 'to comfort', which is followed by a direct object, e.g. *They consoled him after the death of his brother*.

condolence /kənˈdəʊl(ə)ns/ *n.* (often in *pl.*) an expression of sympathy (*sent my condolences*).

condom /ˈkɒndəm/ *n.* a rubber sheath worn on the penis or (usu. **female condom**) in the vagina during sexual intercourse as a contraceptive or to prevent infection. [18th c.: origin unknown]

condominium /kɒndəˈmɪnɪəm/ *n.* **1** the joint control of a state's affairs by other states. **2** *N. Amer.* **a** a building containing flats, or an area of land containing a complex of houses, which are individually owned. **b** such a flat or house. [modern Latin (as COM-, *dominium* DOMINION)]

condone /kən'dəʊn/ *v.tr.* **1** forgive or overlook (an offence or wrongdoing). **2** approve or sanction, usu. reluctantly. **3** (of an action) atone for (an offence); make up for. □ **condonation** /kɒndə'neɪʃ(ə)n/ *n.* **condoner** *n.* [Latin *condonare* 'permit a debt, refrain from punishing' (as COM-, *donare* 'give')]

condor /'kɒndɔː/ *n.* **1** (in full **Andean condor**) a large vulture, *Vultur gryphus*, of S. America, having black plumage with a white neck ruff and a fleshy wattle on the forehead. **2** (in full **California condor**) a rare vulture, *Gymnogyps californianus*, of California. [Spanish, from Quechua *cuntur*]

condottiere /ˌkɒndɒtɪ'ɛːri, Italian kondot'tjere/ *n.* (*pl.* ***condottieri*** *pronunc.* same) *hist.* a leader or a member of a troop of mercenaries in Italy etc. [Italian from *condotto* 'troop under contract', from *condotta* 'contract' (as CONDUCT)]

conduce /kən'djuːs/ *v.intr.* (foll. by *to*) (usu. of an event or attribute) lead or contribute to (a result). [Latin *conducere conduct-* (as COM-, *ducere duct-* 'lead')]

conducive /kən'djuːsɪv/ *adj.* (often foll. by *to*) contributing or helping (towards something) (*not a conducive atmosphere for negotiation*; *good health is conducive to happiness*).

conduct *n.* & *v.* ● *n.* /'kɒndʌkt/ **1** behaviour (esp. in its moral aspect). **2** the action or manner of directing or managing (business, war, etc.). **3** *Art* the mode of treatment; execution. **4** the action of leading; guidance. ● *v.* /kən'dʌkt/ **1** *tr.* lead or guide (a person or persons). **2** *tr.* direct or manage (business etc.). **3** *tr.* (also *absol.*) be the conductor of (an orchestra, choir, etc.). **4** *tr. Physics* transmit (heat, electricity, etc.) by conduction. **5** *refl.* behave (*conducted himself appropriately*). □ **conductible** /kən'dʌktɪb(ə)l/ *adj.* **conductibility** /kəndʌktɪ'bɪlɪti/ *n.* [Middle English from Latin *conductus* (as COM-, *ducere duct-* 'lead'): the verb via Old French *conduite*, past part. of *conduire*]

conductance /kən'dʌkt(ə)ns/ *n. Physics* the power of a specified material to conduct electricity.

conducted tour *n.* a tour led by a guide on a fixed itinerary.

conduction /kən'dʌkʃ(ə)n/ *n.* **1 a** the transmission of heat through a substance from a region of higher temperature to a region of lower temperature. **b** the transmission of electricity through a substance by the application of an electric field. **2** the transmission of impulses along nerves. **3** the conducting of liquid through a pipe etc. [French *conduction* or Latin *conductio* (as CONDUCT)]

conductive /kən'dʌktɪv/ *adj.* having the property of conducting (esp. heat, electricity, etc.). □ **conductively** *adv.*

conductive education *n. Brit.* a system of education for children and adults with motor disorders.

conductivity /kɒndʌk'tɪvɪti/ *n.* the conducting power of a specified material.

conductor /kən'dʌktə/ *n.* **1** a person who directs the performance of an orchestra or choir etc. **2** (*fem.* **conductress** /-trɪs/) **a** a person who collects fares in a bus etc. **b** *US* an official in charge of a train. **3** *Physics* **a** a thing that conducts or transmits heat or electricity, esp. regarded in terms of its capacity to do this (*a poor conductor*). **b** = LIGHTNING CONDUCTOR. **4** a guide or leader. **5** a manager or director. □ **conductorship** *n.* [Middle English via French *conducteur* from Latin *conductor* (as CONDUCT)]

conductor rail *n. Brit.* a rail transmitting current to an electric train etc.

conduct sheet *n.* a record of a person's offences and punishments.

conductus /kən'dʌktəs/ *n.* (*pl.* **conducti** /-tʌɪ/) a musical composition of the 12th–13th c., with Latin text. [medieval Latin: see CONDUIT]

conduit /'kɒndɪt, -djʊɪt/ *n.* **1** a channel or pipe for conveying liquids. **2 a** a tube or trough for protecting insulated electric wires. **b** a length or stretch of this. [Middle English via Old French *conduit* from medieval Latin *conductus* CONDUCT *n.*]

condyle /'kɒndɪl, -dʌɪl/ *n. Anat.* a rounded process at the end of some bones, forming an articulation with another bone. □ **condylar** *adj.* **condyloid** *adj.* [French via Latin *condylus* from Greek *kondulos* 'knuckle']

cone /kəʊn/ *n.* & *v.* ● *n.* **1** a solid figure with a circular (or other curved) plane base, tapering to a point. **2** a thing of a similar shape, solid or hollow, e.g. as used to mark off areas of roads. **3** the dry fruit of a conifer. **4** an ice-cream cornet. **5** any of the minute cone-shaped structures in the retina. **6** a conical mountain esp. of volcanic origin. **7** (in full **cone-shell**) any marine gastropod mollusc of the family Conidae. **8** a ceramic pyramid, melting at a known temperature, used to indicate the temperature of a kiln. ● *v.tr.* **1** shape like a cone. **2** (foll. by *off*) *Brit.* mark off (a road etc.) with cones. [French *cône* via Latin *conus* from Greek *kōnos*]

coney var. of CONY.

confab /'kɒnfab/ *n.* & *v. colloq.* ● *n.* a conversation; a chat. ● *v.intr.* (**confabbed**, **confabbing**) = CONFABULATE. [abbreviation]

confabulate /kən'fabjʊleɪt/ *v.intr.* **1** converse, chat. **2** *Psychol.* fabricate imaginary experiences as compensation for the loss of memory. □ **confabulation** /-'leɪʃ(ə)n/ *n.* **confabulatory** *adj.* [Latin *confabulari* (as COM-, *fabulari* from *fabula* 'tale')]

confect /kən'fɛkt/ *v.tr. literary* make by putting together ingredients. [Latin *conficere confect-* 'put together' (as COM-, *facere* 'make')]

confection /kən'fɛkʃ(ə)n/ *n.* **1** a dish or delicacy made with sweet ingredients. **2** mixing, compounding. **3** a fashionable or elaborate article of women's dress. [Middle English via Old French from Latin *confectio -onis* (as CONFECT)]

confectioner /kən'fɛkʃ(ə)nə/ *n.* a maker or retailer of confectionery.

confectioner's custard *n.* a thick sweet custard used as a filling for cakes and pastries.

confectioner's sugar *n. US* icing sugar.

confectionery /kən'fɛkʃ(ə)n(ə)ri/ *n.* sweets and other confections.

confederacy /kən'fɛd(ə)rəsi/ *n.* (*pl.* **-ies**) **1** a league or alliance, esp. of confederate states. **2** a league for an unlawful or evil purpose; a conspiracy. **3** the condition or fact of being confederate; alliance; conspiracy. **4** (**the Confederacy**) the Confederate States. [Middle English from Anglo-French, Old French *confederacie* (as CONFEDERATE)]

confederate *adj.*, *n.*, & *v.* ● *adj.* /kən'fɛd(ə)rət/ esp. *Polit.* allied; joined by an agreement or treaty. ● *n.* /kən'fɛd(ə)rət/ **1** an ally, esp. (pejoratively) an accomplice. **2** (**Confederate**) a supporter of the Confederate States. ● *v.* /kən'fɛdəreɪt/ (often foll. by *with*) **1** *tr.* bring (a person, state, or oneself) into alliance. **2** *intr.* come into alliance. [Late Latin *confoederatus* (as COM-, FEDERATE)]

Confederate States *n.pl.* the southern states which seceded from the US in 1860–1.

confederation /kənfɛdə'reɪʃ(ə)n/ *n.* **1** a union or alliance of states etc. **2** the act or an instance of confederating; the state of being confederated. [French *confédération* (as CONFEDERATE)]

confer /kən'fəː/ *v.* (**conferred**, **conferring**) **1** *tr.* (often foll. by *on*, *upon*) grant or bestow (a title, degree, favour, etc.). **2** *intr.* (often foll. by *with*) converse, consult. □ **conferrable** *adj.* [Latin *conferre* (as COM-, *ferre* 'bring')]

conferee /kɒnfə'riː/ *n.* **1** a person on whom something is conferred. **2** a participant in a conference.

conference /ˈkɒnf(ə)r(ə)ns/ *n. & v.* ● *n.* **1** consultation, discussion. **2** a meeting for discussion, esp. a regular one held by an association or organization. **3** an annual assembly of the Methodist Church. **4** an association in commerce, sport, etc. **5** the linking of several telephones, computer terminals, etc., so that each user may communicate with the others simultaneously (often *attrib.*: *conference call*). ● *v.intr.* (usu. as **conferencing** *n.*) take part in a conference or conference call. □ **in conference** engaged in discussion. [French *conférence* or medieval Latin *conferentia* (as CONFER)]

conferment /kənˈfəːm(ə)nt/ *n.* **1** the conferring of a degree, honour, etc. **2** an instance of this.

conferral /kənˈfəːr(ə)l/ *n.* esp. *US* = CONFERMENT.

confess /kənˈfɛs/ *v.* **1 a** *tr.* (also *absol.*) acknowledge or admit (a fault, wrongdoing, etc.). **b** *intr.* (foll. by *to*) admit to (*confessed to having lied*). **2** *tr.* admit reluctantly (*confessed it would be difficult*). **3 a** *tr.* (also *absol.*) declare (one's sins) to a priest. **b** *tr.* (of a priest) hear the confession of. **c** *refl.* declare one's sins to a priest. [Middle English via Old French *confesser* and Romanic from Latin *confessus*, past part. of *confitēri* (as COM-, *fatēri* 'declare, avow')]

confessant /kənˈfɛs(ə)nt/ *n.* a person who confesses to a priest.

confessedly /kənˈfɛsɪdli/ *adv.* by one's own or general admission.

confession /kənˈfɛʃ(ə)n/ *n.* **1 a** confessing or acknowledgement of a fault, wrongdoing, a sin to a priest, etc. **b** an instance of this. **c** a thing confessed. **2** (in full **confession of faith**) **a** a declaration of one's religious beliefs. **b** a statement of one's principles. □ **confessionary** *adj.* [Middle English via Old French from Latin *confessio -onis* (as CONFESS)]

confessional /kənˈfɛʃ(ə)n(ə)l/ *n. & adj.* ● *n.* an enclosed stall in a church in which a priest hears confessions. ● *adj.* **1** of or relating to confession. **2** denominational. [French via Italian *confessionale* from medieval Latin, neut. of *confessionalis* (as CONFESSION)]

confessor /kənˈfɛsə/ *n.* **1** a person who makes a confession. **2** /also ˈkɒn-/ a priest who hears confessions and gives spiritual counsel. **3** a person who avows a religion in the face of its suppression, but does not suffer martyrdom. [Middle English via Anglo-French *confessur*, Old French *-our*, from ecclesiastical Latin *confessor* (as CONFESS)]

confetti /kənˈfɛti/ *n.* small pieces of coloured paper thrown by esp. wedding guests at the bride and groom. [Italian, = sweetmeats, from Latin (as COMFIT): from the real or imitation sweets thrown during Italian carnivals]

confidant /kɒnfɪˈdant, ˈkɒnfɪdant/ *n.* (*fem.* **confidante** *pronunc.* same) a person trusted with knowledge of one's private affairs. [18th c. for earlier CONFIDENT (*n.*), probably to represent the pronunciation of French *confidente* (as CONFIDE)]

confide /kənˈfʌɪd/ *v.* **1** *tr.* (usu. foll. by *to*) tell (a secret etc.) in confidence. **2** *tr.* (foll. by *to*) entrust (an object of care, a task, etc.) to. **3** *intr.* (foll. by *in*) **a** have trust or confidence in. **b** talk confidentially to. □ **confidingly** *adv.* [Latin *confidere* (as COM-, *fidere* 'trust')]

confidence /ˈkɒnfɪd(ə)ns/ *n.* **1** firm trust (*have confidence in his ability*). **2 a** a feeling of reliance or certainty. **b** a sense of self-reliance; boldness. **3 a** something told confidentially. **b** the telling of private matters with mutual trust. □ **in confidence** as a secret. **in a person's confidence** trusted with a person's secrets. **take into one's confidence** confide in. [Middle English from Latin *confidentia* (as CONFIDE)]

confidence level *n. Statistics* the probability that the value of a parameter falls within a specified range of values.

confidence man *n.* a man who robs or swindles by means of a confidence trick.

confidence trick *n.* (*US* **confidence game**) a swindle in which the victim is persuaded to trust the swindler in some way. □ **confidence trickster** *n.*

confident /ˈkɒnfɪd(ə)nt/ *adj. & n.* ● *adj.* **1** feeling or showing confidence; self-assured, bold (*spoke with a confident air*). **2** (often foll. by *of*, or *that* + clause) assured, trusting (*confident of your support*; *confident that he will come*). ● *n. archaic* = CONFIDANT. □ **confidently** *adv.* [French from Italian *confidente* (as CONFIDE)]

confidential /kɒnfɪˈdɛnʃ(ə)l/ *adj.* **1** spoken or written in confidence. **2** entrusted with secrets (*a confidential secretary*). **3** confiding. □ **confidentiality** /-ʃɪˈalɪti/ *n.* **confidentially** *adv.*

configuration /kənfɪgəˈreɪʃ(ə)n, -gjʊ-/ *n.* **1 a** an arrangement of parts or elements in a particular form or figure. **b** the form, shape, or figure resulting from such an arrangement. **2** *Astron.* & *Astrol.* the relative position of planets etc. **3** *Psychol.* = GESTALT. **4** *Physics* the distribution of electrons among the energy levels of an atom, or of nucleons among the energy levels of a nucleus, as specified by quantum numbers. **5** *Chem.* the fixed three-dimensional relationship of the atoms in a molecule. **6** *Computing* **a** the interrelating or interconnecting of a computer system or elements of it so that it will accommodate a particular specification. **b** an instance of this. □ **configurational** *adj.* **configure** /kənˈfɪgə/ *v.tr.* (in senses 1, 2, 6). [Late Latin *configuratio* from Latin *configurare* (as COM-, *figurare* 'fashion')]

confine *v. & n.* ● *v.tr.* /kənˈfʌɪn/ (often foll. by *in*, *to*, *within*) **1** keep or restrict (within certain limits etc.). **2** hold captive; imprison. ● *n.* /ˈkɒnfʌɪn/ (usu. in *pl.*) a limit or boundary (*within the confines of the town*). □ **be confined** be in childbirth. [ultimately from Latin *confinia* (as COM-, *finia*, neut. pl. from *finis* 'end, limit'), the verb via French *confiner*, the noun via French *confins* (*pl.*)]

confinement /kənˈfʌɪnm(ə)nt/ *n.* **1** the act or an instance of confining; the state of being confined. **2** the time of a woman's giving birth.

confirm /kənˈfəːm/ *v.tr.* **1** provide support for the truth or correctness of; make definitely valid (*confirmed my suspicions*; *confirmed his arrival time*). **2** (foll. by *in*) encourage (a person) in (an opinion etc.). **3** ratify (a treaty, possession, title, etc.); make formally valid. **4** establish more firmly (power, possession, etc.). **5** administer the religious rite of confirmation to. □ **confirmative** *adj.* **confirmatory** *adj.* [Middle English via Old French *confermer* from Latin *confirmare* (as COM-, FIRM[1])]

confirmand /kɒnfəˈmand/ *n. Eccl.* a person who is to be or has just been confirmed.

confirmation /kɒnfəˈmeɪʃ(ə)n/ *n.* **1** the act or an instance of confirming; the state or an instance of being confirmed. **2 a** a religious rite confirming a baptized person, esp. at the age of discretion, as a member of the Christian Church. **b** *Judaism* the ceremony of bar mitzvah. [Middle English via Old French from Latin *confirmatio -onis* (as CONFIRM)]

confirmed /kənˈfəːmd/ *adj.* firmly settled in some habit or condition (*confirmed in his ways*; *a confirmed bachelor*).

confiscate /ˈkɒnfɪskeɪt/ *v.tr.* **1** take or seize by authority. **2** appropriate to the public treasury (by way of a penalty). □ **confiscable** /kənˈfɪskəb(ə)l/ *adj.* **confiscation** /-ˈskeɪʃ(ə)n/ *n.* **confiscator** *n.* **confiscatory** /kənˈfɪskət(ə)ri/ *adj.* [Latin *confiscare* (as COM-, *fiscare* from *fiscus* 'treasury')]

conflagration /kɒnfləˈgreɪʃ(ə)n/ *n.* a great and destructive fire. [Latin *conflagratio* from *conflagrare* (as COM-, *flagrare* 'blaze')]

conflate /kənˈfleɪt/ *v.tr.* blend or fuse together (esp. two variant texts into one). □ **conflation** /-ˈfleɪʃ(ə)n/ *n.* [Latin *conflare* 'kindle, achieve, fuse' (as COM-, *flare* 'blow')]

conflict *n. & v.* ● *n.* /ˈkɒnflɪkt/ **1 a** a state of opposition or hostilities. **b** a fight or struggle. **2** (often foll. by *of*) **a**

the clashing of opposed principles etc. **b** an instance of this. **3** *Psychol.* **a** the opposition of incompatible wishes or needs in a person. **b** an instance of this. **c** the distress resulting from this. ● *v.intr.* /kən'flɪkt/ often foll. by *with*) **1** clash; be incompatible. **2** struggle or contend. **3** (as **conflicting** *adj.*) contradictory. □ **in conflict** conflicting. □ **confliction** /kən'flɪkʃ(ə)n/ *n.* **conflictual** /kən'flɪktʃʊəl/ *adj.* [Middle English from Latin *confligere conflict-* (as COM-, *fligere* 'strike')]

confluence /'kɒnflʊəns/ *n.* **1** a place where two rivers meet. **2 a** a coming together. **b** a crowd of people. [Latin *confluere* (as COM-, *fluere* 'flow')]

confluent /'kɒnflʊənt/ *adj. & n.* ● *adj.* flowing together, uniting. ● *n.* a stream joining another.

conflux /'kɒnflʌks/ *n.* = CONFLUENCE. [Late Latin *confluxus* (as CONFLUENCE)]

conform /kən'fɔ:m/ *v.* **1** *intr.* comply with rules or general custom. **2** *intr. & tr.* (often foll. by *to*) be or make accordant or suitable. **3** *tr.* (often foll. by *to*) form according to a pattern; make similar. **4** *intr.* (foll. by *to*, *with*) comply with; be in accordance with. □ **conformer** *n.* [Middle English via Old French *conformer* from Latin *conformare* (as COM-, FORM)]

conformable /kən'fɔ:məb(ə)l/ *adj.* **1** (often foll. by *to*) similar. **2** (often foll. by *with*) consistent. **3** (often foll. by *to*) adapted. **4** tractable, submissive. **5** *Geol.* (of strata in contact) lying in the same direction. □ **conformability** /-'bɪlɪti/ *n.* **conformably** *adv.* [medieval Latin *conformabilis* (as CONFORM)]

conformal /kən'fɔ:m(ə)l/ *adj.* (of a map) showing any small area in its correct shape. □ **conformally** *adv.* [Late Latin *conformalis* (as CONFORM)]

conformance /kən'fɔ:m(ə)ns/ *n.* (often foll. by *to, with*) = CONFORMITY 1, 2.

conformation /kɒnfɔ:'meɪʃ(ə)n/ *n.* **1** the way in which a thing is formed; shape, structure. **2** (often foll. by *to*) adjustment in form or character; adaptation. **3** *Chem.* any of the spatial arrangements which the atoms in a molecule may freely convert between, esp. by rotation about individual single bonds. [Latin *conformatio* (as CONFORM)]

conformist /kən'fɔ:mɪst/ *n. & adj.* ● *n.* **1** a person who conforms to an established practice; a conventional person. **2** *Brit.* a person who conforms to the practices of the Church of England. ● *adj.* (of a person) conforming to established practices; conventional. □ **conformism** *n.*

conformity /kən'fɔ:mɪti/ *n.* **1** (often foll. by *to, with*) action or behaviour in accordance with established practice; compliance. **2** (often foll. by *to, with*) correspondence in form or manner; likeness, agreement. **3** *Brit.* compliance with the practices of the Church of England. [Middle English from Old French *conformité* or Late Latin *conformitas* (as CONFORM)]

confound /kən'faʊnd/ *v. & int.* ● *v.tr.* **1** throw into perplexity or confusion. **2** mix up; confuse (in one's mind). **3** *archaic* defeat, overthrow. ● *int.* expressing annoyance (*confound you!*). [Middle English via Anglo-French *conf(o)undre*, Old French *confondre* from Latin *confundere* 'mix up' (as COM-, *fundere fus-* 'pour')]

confounded /kən'faʊndɪd/ *adj. colloq.* damned (*a confounded nuisance!*). □ **confoundedly** *adv.*

confraternity /kɒnfrə'tə:nɪti/ *n.* (*pl.* **-ies**) a brotherhood, esp. religious or charitable. [Middle English via Old French *confraternité* from medieval Latin *confraternitas* (as COM-, FRATERNITY)]

confrère /'kɒnfrɛ:/ *n.* a fellow member of a profession, scientific body, etc. [Middle English via Old French from medieval Latin *confrater* (as COM-, *frater* 'brother')]

confront /kən'frʌnt/ *v.tr.* **1 a** face in hostility or defiance. **b** face up to and deal with (a problem, difficulty, etc.). **2** (of a difficulty etc.) present itself to (*countless obstacles confronted us*). **3** (foll. by *with*) **a** bring (a person) face to face with (a circumstance), esp. by way of accusation (*confronted them with the evidence*). **b** set (a thing) face to face with (another) for comparison. **4** meet or stand facing. □ **confrontation** /kɒnfrʌn'teɪʃ(ə)n/ *n.* **confrontational** /kɒnfrʌn'teɪʃ(ə)n(ə)l/ *adj.* [French *confronter* from medieval Latin *confrontare* (as COM-, *frontare* from *frons frontis* 'face')]

Confucian /kən'fju:ʃ(ə)n/ *adj. & n.* ● *adj.* of or relating to Confucius, Chinese philosopher d. 479 BC, or his philosophy. ● *n.* a follower of Confucius. □ **Confucianism** *n.* **Confucianist** *n. & adj.* [*Confucius*, Latinization of *Kongfuze* 'Kong the master']

confusable /kən'fju:zəb(ə)l/ *adj.* that is able or liable to be confused. □ **confusability** /-'bɪlɪti/ *n.*

confuse /kən'fju:z/ *v.tr.* **1 a** disconcert, perplex, bewilder. **b** embarrass. **2** mix up in the mind; mistake (one for another). **3** make indistinct (*that point confuses the issue*). **4** (as **confused** *adj.*) mentally decrepit or senile. **5** (often as **confused** *adj.*) make muddled or disorganized; throw into disorder (*a confused jumble of clothes*). □ **confusedly** /kən'fju:zɪdli/ *adv.* **confusing** *adj.* **confusingly** *adv.* [back-formation from *confused*, via Old French *confus* from Latin *confusus*: see CONFOUND]

confusion /kən'fju:ʒ(ə)n/ *n.* **1 a** the act of confusing (*the confusion of fact and fiction*). **b** an instance of this; a misunderstanding (*confusions arise from a lack of communication*). **2 a** the result of confusing; a confused state; embarrassment; disorder (*thrown into confusion by his words*; *trampled in the confusion of battle*). **b** (foll. by *of*) a disorderly jumble (*a confusion of ideas*). **3 a** civil commotion (*confusion broke out at the announcement*). **b** an instance of this. [Middle English from Old French *confusion* or Latin *confusio* (as CONFUSE)]

confute /kən'fju:t/ *v.tr.* **1** prove (a person) to be in error. **2** prove (an argument) to be false. □ **confutation** /kɒnfjʊ'teɪʃ(ə)n/ *n.* [Latin *confutare* 'restrain' (as COM- + base of *refutare* 'refute')]

conga /'kɒŋgə/ *n. & v.* ● *n.* **1** a Latin American dance of African origin, usu. with several persons in a single line, one behind the other. **2** (also **conga drum**) a tall, narrow, low-toned drum beaten with the hands. ● *v.intr.* (**congas**, **congaed** /-gəd/ or **conga'd**, **congaing** /-gə(r)ɪŋ/) perform the conga. [Latin American Spanish from Spanish fem. of *congo* 'of the Congo']

congé /'kɒnʒeɪ, French kɔ̃ʒe/ *n.* an unceremonious dismissal; leave-taking. [Middle English via Old French *congié* from Latin *commeatus* 'leave of absence' from *commeare* 'go and come' (as COM-, *meare* 'go'): now usu. treated as modern French]

congeal /kən'dʒi:l/ *v.tr. & intr.* **1** make or become semi-solid by cooling. **2** (of blood etc.) coagulate. □ **congealable** *adj.* **congealment** *n.* [Middle English via Old French *congeler* from Latin *congelare* (as COM-, *gelare* from *gelu* 'frost')]

congelation /kɒndʒɪ'leɪʃ(ə)n/ *n.* **1** the process of congealing. **2** a congealed state. **3** a congealed substance. [Middle English from Old French *congelation* or Latin *congelatio* (as CONGEAL)]

congener /'kɒndʒɪnə, kən'dʒi:nə/ *n.* **1** a thing or person of the same kind or category as another, esp. animals or plants of a specified genus (*the raspberry and blackberry are congeners*). **2** esp. *US* a by-product giving a distinctive character to a wine or spirit. [Latin (as CON-, GENUS)]

congeneric /kɒndʒɪ'nɛrɪk/ *adj.* **1** of the same genus, kind, or race. **2** allied in nature or origin; akin. □ **congenerous** /kən'dʒɛn(ə)rəs/ *adj.*

congenial /kən'dʒi:nɪəl/ *adj.* **1** pleasant, agreeable (*congenial environment*). **2** (often foll. by *with, to*) (of a person, character, etc.) pleasant because akin to oneself in temperament or interests. **3** (often foll. by *to*) suited to the nature of anything (*congenial to my mood*). □ **congeniality** /-nɪ'ælɪti/ *n.* **congenially** *adv.* [CON- + GENIAL[1]]

congenital /kən'dʒɛnɪt(ə)l/ *adj.* **1** (esp. of a disease, defect, etc.) existing from birth. **2** that is (or as if) such from birth (*a congenital liar*). □ **congenitally** *adv.*

[Latin *congenitus* (as COM-, *genitus*, past part. of *gigno* 'beget')]

conger /'kɒŋgə/ *n.* (in full **conger eel**) any large marine eel of the family Congridae. [Middle English via Old French *congre* and Latin *conger*, *congrus* from Greek *goggros*]

congeries /kɒn'dʒɪəri:z, -ɪz, -ɪi:z/ *n.* (*pl.* same) a disorderly collection; a mass or heap. [Latin, from *congerere* CONGEST]

■ **Usage** Although *congeries* looks like a plural form, it is a singular noun, e.g. *A congeries of problems was identified.* It is unchanged in the plural.

congest /kən'dʒɛst/ *v.tr.* (esp. as **congested** *adj.*) affect with congestion; obstruct, block (*congested streets*; *congested lungs*). □ **congestive** *adj.* [Latin *congerere congest-* (as COM-, *gerere* 'bring')]

congestion /kən'dʒɛstʃ(ə)n/ *n.* abnormal accumulation, crowding, or obstruction, esp. of traffic etc. or of blood or mucus in a part of the body. [French from Latin *congestio -onis* (as CONGEST)]

conglomerate *adj.*, *n.*, & *v.* ● *adj.* /kən'glɒm(ə)rət/ **1** gathered into a rounded mass. **2** *Geol.* (of rock) made up of small stones held together (cf. AGGLOMERATE). ● *n.* /kən'glɒm(ə)rət/ **1** a number of things or parts forming a heterogeneous mass. **2** a group or corporation formed by the merging of separate and diverse firms. **3** *Geol.* conglomerate rock. ● *v.tr. & intr.* /kən'glɒməreɪt/ collect into a coherent mass. □ **conglomeration** /kənglɒmə'reɪʃ(ə)n/ *n.* [Latin *conglomeratus*, past part. of *conglomerare* (as COM-, *glomerare* from *glomus -eris* 'ball')]

Congolese /kɒŋgə'li:z/ *adj.* & *n.* ● *adj.* of or relating to Zaire or Congo, countries in central Africa, or the region surrounding the Zaire (formerly Congo) river. ● *n.* (*pl.* same) **1** a native of any of these regions. **2** any of the Bantu languages spoken by the Congolese people. [French *congolais*]

congou /'kɒŋgu:, -gəʊ/ *n.* a variety of black China tea. [Cantonese *kungfüch'a*, Mandarin *gōngfu chá* 'tea made for refined tastes']

congrats /kən'grats/ *n.pl.* & *int. colloq.* congratulations. [abbreviation]

congratulate /kən'gratjʊleɪt/ *v.tr.* & *refl.* (often foll. by *on*, *upon*) **1** *tr.* express pleasure at the happiness or good fortune or excellence of (a person) (*congratulated them on their success*). **2** *refl.* think oneself fortunate or clever. □ **congratulant** *adj.* & *n.* **congratulator** *n.* **congratulatory** /-lət(ə)ri/ *adj.* [Latin *congratulari* (as COM-, *gratulari* 'show joy' from *gratus* 'pleasing')]

congratulation /kəngratjʊ'leɪʃ(ə)n/ *n.* **1** congratulating. **2** (also as *int.*; usu. in *pl.*) an expression of this (*congratulations on winning!*). [Latin *congratulatio* (as CONGRATULATE)]

congregant /'kɒŋgrɪg(ə)nt/ *n.* a member of a congregation, esp. *Brit.* of a Jewish congregation. [Latin *congregare* (as CONGREGATE)]

congregate /'kɒŋgrɪgeɪt/ *v.intr.* & *tr.* collect or gather into a crowd or mass. [Middle English from Latin *congregare* (as COM-, *gregare* from *grex gregis* 'flock')]

congregation /kɒŋgrɪ'geɪʃ(ə)n/ *n.* **1** the process of congregating; collection into a crowd or mass. **2** a crowd or mass gathered together. **3 a** a body assembled for religious worship. **b** a body of persons regularly attending a particular church etc. **c** *RC Ch.* a body of persons obeying a common religious rule. **d** *RC Ch.* any of several permanent committees of the Roman Catholic College of Cardinals. **4** (**Congregation**) *Brit.* (in some universities) a general assembly of resident senior members. [Middle English from Old French *congregation* or Latin *congregatio* (as CONGREGATE)]

congregational /kɒŋgrɪ'geɪʃ(ə)n(ə)l/ *adj.* **1** of a congregation. **2** (**Congregational**) of or adhering to Congregationalism.

Congregationalism /kɒŋgrɪ'geɪʃ(ə)n(ə)lɪz(ə)m/ *n.* a system of ecclesiastical organization whereby individual churches are largely self-governing (in England and Wales such churches largely merging in the United Reformed Church from 1972). □ **Congregationalist** *n.* **Congregationalize** *v.tr.* (also **-ise**).

congress /'kɒŋgrɛs/ *n.* **1** a formal meeting of delegates for discussion. **2** (**Congress**) a national legislative body, esp. that of the US. **3** a society or organization. **4** coming together, meeting. □ **congressional** /kən'grɛʃ(ə)n(ə)l/ *adj.* [Latin *congressus* from *congredi* (as COM-, *gradi* 'walk')]

congressman /'kɒŋgrɛsmən/ *n.* (*pl.* **-men**; *fem.* **congresswoman**, *pl.* **-women**) a member of the US Congress.

congruence /'kɒŋgrʊəns/ *n.* (also **congruency** /-ənsi/) **1** agreement, consistency. **2** *Geom.* the state of being congruent. [Middle English from Latin *congruentia* (as CONGRUENT)]

congruent /'kɒŋgrʊənt/ *adj.* **1** (often foll. by *with*) suitable, agreeing. **2** *Geom.* (of figures) coinciding exactly when superimposed. □ **congruently** *adv.* [Middle English from Latin *congruere* 'agree']

congruous /'kɒŋgrʊəs/ *adj.* (often foll. by *with*) suitable, agreeing; fitting. □ **congruity** /-'gru:ɪti/ *n.* **congruously** *adv.* [Latin *congruus* (as CONGRUENT)]

conic /'kɒnɪk/ *adj.* & *n.* ● *adj.* of a cone. ● *n.* **1** a conic section. **2** (in *pl.*) the study of conic sections. [modern Latin *conicus* from Greek *kōnikos* (as CONE)]

conical /'kɒnɪk(ə)l/ *adj.* cone-shaped. □ **conically** *adv.*

conical projection *n.* (also **conic projection**) a map projection in which a spherical surface is projected on to a cone, usually with its vertex above the pole.

conic section *n.* a figure formed by the intersection of a cone and a plane.

conidium /kəʊ'nɪdɪəm/ *n.* (*pl.* **conidia** /-dɪə/) a spore produced asexually by various fungi. [modern Latin, from Greek *konis* 'dust' + diminutive suffix *-idium*]

conifer /'kɒnɪfə, 'kəʊn-/ *n.* a tree of the order Coniferales, typically bearing cones and needle-like leaves (often evergreen), e.g. a pine, yew, cedar, or redwood. □ **coniferous** /kə'nɪf(ə)rəs/ *adj.* [Latin (as CONE, -FEROUS)]

coniform /'kəʊnɪfɔ:m/ *adj.* cone-shaped. [Latin *conus* 'cone' + -FORM]

coniine /'kəʊnɪi:n/ *n.* a poisonous alkaloid found in hemlock, that paralyses the nerves. [Latin *conium* from Greek *kōneion* 'hemlock']

conjectural /kən'dʒɛktʃ(ə)r(ə)l/ *adj.* based on, involving, or given to conjecture. □ **conjecturally** *adv.* [French from Latin *conjecturalis* (as CONJECTURE)]

conjecture /kən'dʒɛktʃə/ *n.* & *v.* ● *n.* **1 a** the formation of an opinion on incomplete information; guessing. **b** an opinion or conclusion reached in this way. **2 a** (in textual criticism) the guessing of a reading not in the text. **b** a proposed reading. ● *v.* **1** *tr. & intr.* guess. **2** *tr.* (in textual criticism) propose (a reading). □ **conjecturable** *adj.* [Middle English from Old French *conjecture* or Latin *conjectura*, from *conjicere* 'put together in thought' (as COM-, *jacere* 'throw')]

conjoin /kən'dʒɔɪn/ *v.tr.* & *intr.* join, combine. [Middle English from Old French *conjoign-*, pres. stem of *conjoindre*, from Latin *conjungere* (as COM-, *jungere junct-* 'join')]

conjoint /kən'dʒɔɪnt/ *adj.* associated, conjoined. □ **conjointly** *adv.* [Middle English from Old French, past part. of *conjoindre* (see CONJOIN)]

conjugal /'kɒndʒʊg(ə)l/ *adj.* of marriage or the relation between husband and wife. □ **conjugality** /-'galɪti/ *n.* **conjugally** *adv.* [Latin *conjugalis* from *conjux* 'consort' (as COM- + *jug-* root of *jungere* 'join')]

conjugal rights *n.pl.* those rights (esp. to sexual relations) regarded as exercisable in law by each partner in a marriage.

conjugate *v.*, *adj.*, & *n.* ● *v.* /'kɒndʒʊgeɪt/ **1** *tr. Gram.* give the different forms of (a verb). **2** *intr. Biol.* **a** unite sexually. **b** (of gametes) become fused. **3** *intr. Chem.* (of protein) combine with non-protein. ● *adj.* /'kɒndʒʊgət/

1 joined together, esp. as a pair. **2** *Gram.* derived from the same root. **3** *Biol.* fused. **4** *Chem.* (of an acid or base) related by loss or gain of a proton. **5** *Math.* joined in a reciprocal relation, esp. having the same real parts, and equal magnitudes but opposite signs of imaginary parts. ● *n.* /'kɒndʒʊgət/ a conjugate word or thing. [Latin *conjugare* 'yoke together' (as COM-, *jugare* from *jugum* 'yoke')]

conjugation /kɒndʒʊ'geɪʃ(ə)n/ *n.* **1** *Gram.* a system of verbal inflection. **2** the act or an instance of conjugating or being conjugated. **3** *Biol.* **a** the fusion of two gametes in reproduction. **b** the temporary union of two unicellular organisms for the exchange of genetic material. □ **conjugational** *adj.* [Latin *conjugatio* (as CONJUGATE)]

conjunct /kən'dʒʌŋ(k)t/ *adj.* joined together; combined; associated. [Middle English from Latin *conjunctus* (as CONJOIN)]

conjunction /kən'dʒʌŋ(k)ʃ(ə)n/ *n.* **1 a** the action of joining; the condition of being joined. **b** an instance of this. **2** *Gram.* a word used to connect clauses or sentences or words in the same clause (e.g. *and, but, if*). **3 a** a combination (of events or circumstances). **b** a number of associated persons or things. **4** *Astron.* & *Astrol.* the alignment of two bodies in the solar system so that they have the same longitude as seen from the earth. □ **in conjunction with** together with. □ **conjunctional** *adj.* [Middle English via Old French *conjonction* from Latin *conjunctio -onis* (as CONJUNCT)]

conjunctiva /kɒndʒʌŋ(k)'tʌɪvə, kən'dʒʌŋ(k)tɪvə/ *n.* (*pl.* **conjunctivas**) *Anat.* the mucous membrane that covers the front of the eye and lines the inside of the eyelids. □ **conjunctival** *adj.* [medieval Latin (*membrana*) *conjunctiva* 'conjunctive membrane' (as CONJUNCTIVE)]

conjunctive /kən'dʒʌŋ(k)tɪv/ *adj.* & *n.* ● *adj.* **1** serving to join; connective. **2** *Gram.* of the nature of a conjunction. ● *n.* *Gram.* a conjunctive word. □ **conjunctively** *adv.* [Late Latin *conjunctivus* (as CONJOIN)]

conjunctivitis /kəndʒʌŋ(k)tɪ'vʌɪtɪs/ *n.* inflammation of the conjunctiva.

conjuncture /kən'dʒʌŋ(k)tʃə/ *n.* a combination of events; a state of affairs. [obsolete French from Italian *congiuntura* (as CONJOIN)]

conjuration /kʌndʒə'reɪʃ(ə)n, kɒndʒʊ(ə)-/ *n.* an incantation; a magic spell. [Middle English via Old French from Latin *conjuratio -onis* (as CONJURE)]

conjure /'kʌndʒə/ *v.* **1** *intr.* perform tricks which are seemingly magical, esp. by rapid movements of the hands. **2** *tr.* (usu. foll. by *out of, away, to,* etc.) cause to appear or disappear as if by magic (*conjured a rabbit out of a hat*; *conjured them to a desert island*; *his pain was conjured away*). **3** *tr.* call upon (a spirit) to appear. **4** *intr.* perform marvels. **5** *tr.* /kən'dʒʊə/ (often foll. by *to* + infin.) appeal solemnly to (a person). □ **conjure up 1** bring into existence or cause to appear as if by magic. **2** cause to appear to the eye or mind; evoke. [earlier in the sense 'oblige by oath, invoke (a spirit etc.)', Middle English via Old French *conjurer* 'plot, exorcise' from Latin *conjurare* 'band together by oath, conspire' (as COM-, *jurare* 'swear')]

conjuror /'kʌndʒərə/ *n.* (also **conjurer**) a performer of conjuring tricks. [Anglo-French *conjurour* (Old French *-eor*), from medieval Latin *conjurator* (also CONJURE + -ER[1])]

conk[1] /kɒŋk/ *v.intr.* (usu. foll. by *out*) *colloq.* **1** (of a machine etc.) break down. **2** (of a person) become exhausted and give up; faint; die. [20th c.: origin unknown]

conk[2] /kɒŋk/ *n.* & *v.* *slang* ● *n.* **1 a** *Brit.* the nose. **b** the head. **2 a** a punch on the head or *Brit.* nose. **b** a blow. ● *v.tr.* punch on the head, *Brit.* nose etc. [19th c.: perhaps = CONCH]

conker /'kɒŋkə/ *n.* **1** the hard fruit of a horse chestnut. **2** (in *pl.*) *Brit.* a children's game played with conkers on strings, one hit against another to try to break it. [dialect *conker* 'snail shell' (originally used in the game), associated with CONQUER]

conman /'kɒnman/ *n.* (*pl.* **-men**) *slang* = CONFIDENCE MAN.

con moto /kɒn 'məʊtəʊ/ *adv.* *Mus.* with movement. [Italian, = with movement]

Conn. *abbr.* Connecticut.

conn *US* var. of CON[4].

connate /'kɒneɪt/ *adj.* **1** existing in a person or thing from birth; innate. **2** formed at the same time. **3** allied, congenial. **4** *Bot.* (of organs) congenitally united so as to form one part. **5** *Geol.* (of water) trapped in sedimentary rock during its deposition. [Late Latin *connatus*, past part. of *connasci* (as COM-, *nasci* 'be born')]

connatural /kə'natʃ(ə)r(ə)l/ *adj.* **1** (often foll. by *to*) innate; belonging naturally. **2** of like nature. □ **connaturally** *adv.* [Late Latin *connaturalis* (as COM-, NATURAL)]

connect /kə'nɛkt/ *v.* **1 a** *tr.* (often foll. by *to, with*) join (one thing with another) (*connected the hose to the tap*). **b** *tr.* join (two things) (*a track connected the two villages*). **c** *intr.* be joined or joinable (*the two parts do not connect*). **2** *tr.* (often foll. by *with*) associate mentally or practically (*did not connect the two ideas*; *never connected her with the theatre*). **3** *intr.* (foll. by *with*) (of a train etc.) be synchronized at its destination with another train etc., so that passengers can transfer (*the train connects with the boat*). **4** *tr.* put into communication by telephone. **5 a** *tr.* (usu. in *passive*; foll. by *with*) unite or associate with others in relationships etc. (*am connected with the royal family*). **b** *intr.* form a logical sequence; be meaningful. **6** *intr.* *colloq.* hit or strike effectively. □ **connectable** *adj.* **connector** *n.* [Latin *connectere connex-* (as COM-, *nectere* 'bind')]

connected /kə'nɛktɪd/ *adj.* **1** joined in sequence. **2** (of ideas etc.) coherent. **3** related or associated. □ **connectedly** *adv.* **connectedness** *n.*

connecting rod *n.* the rod between the piston and the crankpin etc. in an internal-combustion engine or between the wheels of a locomotive.

connection /kə'nɛkʃ(ə)n/ *n.* (also *Brit.* **connexion**) **1 a** the act of connecting; the state of being connected. **b** an instance of this. **2** the point at which two things are connected (*broke at the connection*). **3 a** a thing or person that connects; a link (*a radio formed the only connection with the outside world*; *cannot see the connection between the two ideas*). **b** a telephone link (*got a bad connection*). **4 a** an arrangement or opportunity for catching a connecting train etc. **b** the train etc. itself (*missed the connection*). **5** *Electr.* **a** the linking up of an electric current by contact. **b** a device for effecting this. **6** (often in *pl.*) a relative or associate, esp. one with influence (*has connections in the Home Office*; *heard it through a business connection*). **7** a relation of ideas; a context (*in this connection I have to disagree*). **8** *slang* a supplier of narcotics. **9** a religious body, esp. Methodist. □ **in connection with** with reference to. **in this** (or **that**) **connection** with reference to this (or that). □ **connectional** *adj.* [Latin *connexio* (as CONNECT): spelling *-ct-* from CONNECT]

connective /kə'nɛktɪv/ *adj.* & *n.* ● *adj.* serving or tending to connect. ● *n.* something that connects.

connective tissue *n.* *Anat.* a tissue with relatively few cells in a non-living matrix that connects, supports, binds, or separates other tissues or organs, esp. fibrous tissue rich in collagen.

connectivity /kɒnɛk'tɪvɪti/ *n.* **1** *Computing* capacity for interconnection of systems, applications, etc. **2** the property or degree of being connected or interconnected.

conning tower /'kɒnɪŋ/ *n.* **1** the superstructure of a submarine from which steering, firing, etc., are directed on or near the surface, and which contains the periscope. **2** the armoured pilot house of a warship. [CON[4] + -ING[1]]

connivance /kə'nʌɪv(ə)ns/ *n.* **1** (often foll. by *at, in*) conniving (*connivance in the crime*). **2** tacit permission (*done with his connivance*). [French *connivence* or Latin *conniventia* (as CONNIVE)]

connive /kə'nʌɪv/ *v.intr.* **1** (foll. by *at*) disregard or tacitly consent to (a wrongdoing). **2** (usu. foll. by *with*) conspire. □ **conniver** *n.* [French *conniver* or Latin *connivēre* 'shut the eyes (to)']

connoisseur /kɒnə'sə:/ *n.* (often foll. by *of, in*) an expert judge in matters of taste (*a connoisseur of fine wine*). □ **connoisseurship** *n.* [French, obsolete spelling of *connaisseur*, from pres. stem of *connaître* 'know' + *-eur* -OR[1]: cf. RECONNOITRE]

connotation /kɒnə'teɪʃ(ə)n/ *n.* **1** that which is implied by a word etc. in addition to its literal or primary meaning (*a letter with sinister connotations*). **2** the act of connoting or implying.

connote /kə'nəʊt/ *v.tr.* **1** (of a word etc.) imply in addition to the literal or primary meaning. **2** (of a fact) imply as a consequence or condition. **3** mean, signify. □ **connotative** /'kɒnəteɪtɪv, kə'nəʊtətɪv/ *adj.* [medieval Latin *connotare* 'mark in addition' (as COM-, *notare* from *nota* 'mark')]

■ **Usage** *Connote* and *denote* are sometimes confused. *Connote* means 'to imply in addition to the primary meaning', e.g. *The words were harmless but the ideas they connoted were dangerous.* In popular usage it is frequently used to mean 'convey to the mind' or 'mean' and hence verges on the sense of *denote*.

connubial /kə'nju:bɪəl/ *adj.* of or relating to marriage or the relationship of husband and wife. □ **connubiality** /-bɪ'alɪti/ *n.* **connubially** *adv.* [Latin *connubialis* from *connubium* 'marriage' (as COM-, *nubium* from *nubere* 'marry')]

conoid /'kəʊnɔɪd/ *adj.* & *n.* ● *adj.* (also **conoidal** /-'nɔɪd(ə)l/) cone-shaped. ● *n.* a cone-shaped object.

conquer /'kɒŋkə/ *v.tr.* **1** **a** overcome and control (an enemy or territory) by military force. **b** *absol.* be victorious. **2** overcome (a habit, emotion, disability, etc.) by effort (*conquered his fear*). **3** climb (a mountain) successfully. □ **conquerable** *adj.* [Middle English via Old French *conquerre* and Romanic from Latin *conquirere* (as COM-, *quaerere* 'seek, get')]

conqueror /'kɒŋk(ə)rə/ *n.* **1** a person who conquers. **2** *Brit.* = CONKER. [Middle English from Anglo-French *conquerour* (Old French *-eor*), from *conquerre* (as CONQUER)]

conquest /'kɒŋkwɛst/ *n.* **1** the act or an instance of conquering; the state of being conquered. **2** **a** conquered territory. **b** something won. **3** a person whose affection or favour has been won. **4** (**the Conquest, the Norman Conquest**) the conquest of England by William of Normandy in 1066. □ **make a conquest of** win the affections of. [Middle English via Old French *conquest(e)* from Romanic (as CONQUER)]

conquistador /kɒn'kwɪstədɔ:/ *n.* (*pl.* **conquistadores** /-'dɔ:reɪz/ or **conquistadors**) a conqueror, esp. one of the Spanish conquerors of Mexico and Peru in the 16th c. [Spanish]

con-rod /'kɒnrɒd/ *n. Brit. colloq.* connecting rod. [abbreviation]

Cons. *abbr.* Conservative.

consanguineous /kɒnsaŋ'gwɪnɪəs/ *adj.* descended from the same ancestor; akin. □ **consanguinity** *n.* [Latin *consanguineus* (as COM-, *sanguis -inis* 'blood')]

conscience /'kɒnʃ(ə)ns/ *n.* **1** a moral sense of right and wrong esp. as felt by a person and affecting behaviour (*my conscience won't allow me to do that*). **2** an inner feeling as to the goodness or otherwise of one's behaviour (*my conscience is clear; has a guilty conscience*). □ **for conscience** (or **conscience'**) **sake** to satisfy one's conscience. **in all conscience** *colloq.* by any reasonable standard; by all that is fair. **on one's conscience** causing one feelings of guilt. □ **conscienceless** *adj.* [earlier in the sense 'inner thoughts or knowledge', Middle English via Old French from Latin *conscientia*, from *conscire* 'be privy to' (as COM-, *scire* 'know')]

conscience clause *n.* a clause in a law, ensuring respect for the consciences of those affected.

conscience money *n.* a sum paid to relieve one's conscience, esp. about a payment previously evaded.

conscience-stricken *adj.* (also **conscience-struck**) made uneasy by a bad conscience.

conscientious /kɒnʃɪ'ɛnʃəs/ *adj.* (of a person or conduct) diligent and scrupulous. □ **conscientiously** *adv.* **conscientiousness** *n.* [French *consciencieux* from medieval Latin *conscientiosus* (as CONSCIENCE)]

conscientious objector *n.* a person who for reasons of conscience objects to conforming to a requirement, esp. that of military service.

conscious /'kɒnʃəs/ *adj.* & *n.* ● *adj.* **1** awake and aware of one's surroundings and identity. **2** (usu. foll. by *of*, or *that* + clause) aware, knowing (*conscious of his inferiority*). **3** (of actions, emotions, etc.) realized or recognized by the doer; intentional (*made a conscious effort not to laugh*). **4** (in *comb.*) aware of; concerned with (*fashion-conscious*). ● *n.* (prec. by *the*) the conscious mind. □ **consciously** *adv.* [Latin *conscius* 'knowing with others or in oneself' from *conscire* (as COM-, *scire* 'know')]

consciousness /'kɒnʃəsnɪs/ *n.* **1** the state of being conscious (*lost consciousness during the fight*). **2** **a** awareness, perception (*had no consciousness of being ridiculed*). **b** (in *comb.*) awareness of (*class-consciousness*). **3** the totality of a person's thoughts, feelings, and sensations, or of a class of these (*moral consciousness*).

consciousness-raising *n.* the activity of increasing esp. social or political sensitivity or awareness.

conscribe /kən'skrʌɪb/ *v.tr.* = CONSCRIPT *v.* [Latin *conscribere* (as CONSCRIPTION)]

conscript *v.* & *n.* ● *v.tr.* /kən'skrɪpt/ enlist by conscription. ● *n.* /'kɒnskrɪpt/ a person enlisted by conscription. [verb is a back-formation from CONSCRIPTION: noun via French *conscrit* from Latin *conscriptus* (as CONSCRIPTION)]

conscription /kən'skrɪpʃ(ə)n/ *n.* compulsory enlistment for state service, esp. military service. [French via Late Latin *conscriptio* 'levying of troops' from Latin *conscribere conscript-* 'enrol' (as COM-, *scribere* 'write')]

consecrate /'kɒnsɪkreɪt/ *v.tr.* **1** make or declare sacred; dedicate formally to a religious or divine purpose. **2** (in Christian belief) make (bread and wine) into the body and blood of Christ. **3** (foll. by *to*) devote (one's life etc.) to (a purpose). **4** ordain (esp. a bishop) to a sacred office. □ **consecration** /-'kreɪʃ(ə)n/ *n.* **consecrator** *n.* **consecratory** *adj.* [Middle English from Latin *consecrare* (as COM-, *secrare* = *sacrare* 'dedicate' from *sacer* 'sacred')]

consecution /kɒnsɪ'kju:ʃ(ə)n/ *n.* **1** logical sequence (in argument or reasoning). **2** sequence, succession (of events etc.). [Latin *consecutio* from *consequi consecut-* 'overtake' (as COM-, *sequi* 'pursue')]

consecutive /kən'sɛkjʊtɪv/ *adj.* **1** **a** following continuously. **b** in unbroken or logical order. **2** *Gram.* expressing consequence. □ **consecutively** *adv.* **consecutiveness** *n.* [French *consécutif -ive* from medieval Latin *consecutivus* (as CONSECUTION)]

consecutive intervals *n.pl.* intervals of the same kind (esp. fifths or octaves), occurring in succession between two voices or parts in harmony.

consensual /kən'sɛnsjʊəl, -ʃʊəl/ *adj.* of or by consent or consensus. □ **consensually** *adv.* [Latin *consensus* (see CONSENSUS) + -AL]

consensus /kən'sɛnsəs/ *n.* (often foll. by *of*) **1** **a** general agreement (of opinion, testimony, etc.). **b** an instance of this. **2** (*attrib.*) majority view; collective opinion (*consensus politics*). [Latin, = agreement (as CONSENT)]

consent /kən'sɛnt/ *v.* & *n.* ● *v.intr.* (often foll. by *to*) express willingness; give permission; agree. ● *n.* voluntary agreement; permission; compliance. [Middle

English via Old French *consentir* from Latin *consentire* (as COM-, *sentire sens-* 'feel')]

consentient /kən'sɛnʃ(ə)nt/ *adj.* **1** agreeing; united in opinion. **2** concurrent. **3** (often foll. by *to*) consenting. [Latin *consentient-* (as CONSENT)]

consenting adult *n.* an adult who consents to something, esp. *Brit.* a homosexual act.

consequence /'kɒnsɪkw(ə)ns/ *n.* **1** the result or effect of an action or condition. **2 a** importance (*it is of no consequence*). **b** social distinction (*persons of consequence*). **3** (in *pl.*, often treated as *sing.*) a game in which a narrative (usu. describing the meeting of a man and woman and its consequences) is made up by the players, each ignorant of what has already been contributed. □ **in consequence** as a result. **take the consequences** accept the results of one's choice or action. [Middle English via Old French from Latin *consequentia* (as CONSEQUENT)]

consequent /'kɒnsɪkw(ə)nt/ *adj.* & *n.* ● *adj.* **1** (often foll. by *on, upon*) following as a result or consequence. **2** logically consistent. ● *n.* **1** a thing that follows another. **2** *Logic* the second part of a conditional proposition, dependent on the antecedent. [Middle English via Old French from Latin *consequi* 'overtake' (as COM-, *sequi* 'pursue')]

consequential /kɒnsɪ'kwɛnʃ(ə)l/ *adj.* **1** following as a result or consequence. **2** resulting indirectly (*consequential damage*). **3** important; significant. □ **consequentiality** /-ʃɪ'alɪti/ *n.* **consequentially** *adv.* [Latin *consequentia*]

consequentialism /kɒnsɪ'kwɛnʃ(ə)lɪz(ə)m/ *n. Philos.* the doctrine that the morality of an action is to be judged solely by its consequences. □ **consequentialist** *adj.* & *n.*

consequently /'kɒnsɪkw(ə)ntli/ *adv.* & *conj.* as a result; therefore.

conservancy /kən'sə:v(ə)nsi/ *n.* (*pl.* **-ies**) **1** *Brit.* a commission etc. controlling a port, river, etc. (*Thames Conservancy*). **2** a body concerned with the preservation of natural resources (*Nature Conservancy*). **3** conservation; official preservation (of forests etc.). [18th-c. alteration of obsolete *conservacy*, from Anglo-French *conservacie* via Anglo-Latin *conservatia* from Latin *conservatio* (as CONSERVE)]

conservation /kɒnsə'veɪʃ(ə)n/ *n.* preservation, esp. of the natural environment. □ **conservation of energy** (or **mass** or **momentum** etc.) *Physics* the principle that the total quantity of energy (or mass, momentum, etc.) remains constant in a system not subject to external influence. □ **conservational** *adj.* [Middle English from Old French *conservation* or Latin *conservatio* (as CONSERVE)]

conservation area *n.* an area containing a noteworthy environment and specially protected by law against undesirable changes.

conservationist /kɒnsə'veɪʃ(ə)nɪst/ *n.* a supporter or advocate of environmental conservation.

conservative /kən'sə:vətɪv/ *adj.* & *n.* ● *adj.* **1 a** averse to rapid change. **b** (of views, taste, etc.) moderate; avoiding extremes (*conservative in his dress*). **2** (of an estimate etc.) purposely low; moderate, cautious. **3** (**Conservative**) of or characteristic of Conservatives or the Conservative Party. **4** tending to conserve. ● *n.* **1** a conservative person. **2** (**Conservative**) a supporter or member of the Conservative Party. □ **conservatism** *n.* **conservatively** *adv.* **conservativeness** *n.* [Middle English from Late Latin *conservativus* (as CONSERVE)]

Conservative Judaism *n.* Judaism allowing only minor changes in traditional ritual etc.

Conservative Party *n.* **1** a British political party promoting free enterprise and private ownership. **2** a similar party elsewhere.

conservative surgery *n.* surgery that seeks to preserve tissues as far as possible.

conservatoire /kən'sə:vətwɑ:/ *n.* a (usu. European) school of music or other arts. [French from Italian *conservatorio* (as CONSERVATORY)]

conservator /'kɒnsəveɪtə, kən'sə:vətə/ *n.* a person who preserves something; an official custodian (of a museum etc.). [Middle English via Anglo-French *conservatour*, Old French *-ateur* via Latin *conservator -oris* (as CONSERVE)]

conservatorium /kənsə:və'tɔ:rɪəm/ *n. Austral.* = CONSERVATOIRE.

conservatory /kən'sə:vət(ə)ri/ *n.* (*pl.* **-ies**) **1** a greenhouse for tender plants; a room, esp. one attached to and communicating with a house, designed for the growing or displaying of plants. **2** = SUN LOUNGE. **3** esp. *N. Amer.* = CONSERVATOIRE. [Late Latin *conservatorium* (as CONSERVE): sense 3 via Italian *conservatorio*]

conserve /kən'sə:v/ *v.* & *n.* ● *v.tr.* **1** store up; keep from harm or damage, esp. for later use. **2** *Physics* maintain a quantity of (heat etc.). **3** preserve (food, esp. fruit), usu. with sugar. ● *n.* /also 'kɒnsə:v/ **1** fruit etc. preserved in sugar. **2** fresh fruit jam. [Middle English via Old French *conserver* from Latin *conservare* (as COM-, *servare* 'keep')]

consider /kən'sɪdə/ *v.tr.* (often *absol.*) **1 a** contemplate mentally, esp. in order to reach a conclusion; give attention to. **b** examine the merits of (a course of action, a candidate, claim, etc.). **2** look attentively at. **3** take into account; show regard for. **4** (foll. by *that* + clause) have the opinion. **5** (foll. by compl.) believe; regard as (*consider it to be genuine*; *consider it settled*). **6** (as **considered** *adj.*) formed after careful thought (*a considered opinion*). □ **all things considered** taking everything into account. [Middle English via Old French *considerer* from Latin *considerare* 'examine']

considerable /kən'sɪd(ə)rəb(ə)l/ *adj.* **1** enough in amount or extent to merit consideration; much; a lot of (*considerable pain*). **2** notable, important (*considerable achievement*). □ **considerably** *adv.*

considerate /kən'sɪd(ə)rət/ *adj.* **1** thoughtful towards other people; careful not to cause hurt or inconvenience. **2** *archaic* careful. □ **considerately** *adv.*

consideration /kənsɪdə'reɪʃ(ə)n/ *n.* **1** the act of considering; careful thought. **2** thoughtfulness for others; being considerate. **3** a fact or a thing taken into account in deciding or judging something. **4** compensation; a payment or reward. **5** *Law* (in a contractual agreement) anything given or promised or forborne by one party in exchange for the promise or undertaking of another. **6** *archaic* importance or consequence. □ **in consideration of** in return for; on account of. **take into consideration** include as a factor, reason, etc.; make allowance for. **under consideration** being considered. [Middle English via Old French from Latin *consideratio -onis* (as CONSIDER)]

considering /kən'sɪd(ə)rɪŋ/ *prep., conj.,* & *adv.* ● *prep.* & *conj.* in view of; taking into consideration (*considering their youth*; *considering that it was snowing*). ● *adv. colloq.* all in all; taking everything into account (*not so bad, considering*).

consign /kən'sʌɪn/ *v.tr.* (often foll. by *to*) **1** hand over; deliver to a person's possession or trust. **2** assign; commit decisively or permanently (*consigned it to the dustbin*; *consigned to years of misery*). **3** transmit or send (goods), usu. by a public carrier. □ **consignee** /kɒnsʌɪ'ni:/ *n.* **consignor** *n.* [Middle English from French *consigner* or Latin *consignare* 'mark with a seal' (as COM-, *signare* 'sign')]

consignment /kən'sʌɪnm(ə)nt/ *n.* **1** the act or an instance of consigning; the process of being consigned. **2** a batch of goods consigned.

consist /kən'sɪst/ *v.intr.* **1** (foll. by *of*) be composed of; have ingredients or elements as specified (*the house consists of five rooms*). **2** (foll. by *in*) have its essential features as specified (*its beauty consists in the use of colour*). **3** (usu. foll. by *with*) harmonize; be consistent. [Latin *consistere* 'stand firm or still, exist' (as COM-, *sistere* 'stop')]

consistency /kən'sɪst(ə)nsi/ *n.* (also **consistence**) (*pl.* **-ies** or **-es**) **1 a** the degree of firmness with which a substance holds together. **b** the degree of density, esp. of thick liquids. **2** the state of being consistent; conformity with other or earlier attitudes, practice, etc. [French *consistence* or Late Latin *consistentia* (as CONSIST)]

consistent /kən'sɪst(ə)nt/ *adj.* (usu. foll. by *with*) **1** compatible or in harmony; not contradictory. **2** (of a person) constant to the same principles of thought or action. □ **consistently** *adv.* [Latin *consistere* (as CONSIST)]

consistory /kən'sɪst(ə)ri/ *n.* (*pl.* **-ies**) **1** *RC Ch.* the council of cardinals (with or without the Pope). **2** (in full **consistory court**) (in the Church of England) a court presided over by a bishop, for the administration of ecclesiastical law in a diocese. **3** (in other Churches) a local administrative body. □ **consistorial** /kɒnsɪ'stɔːrɪəl/ *adj.* [Middle English via Anglo-French *consistorie*, Old French *-oire* from Late Latin *consistorium* (as CONSIST)]

consociation /kɒnsəʊʃɪ'eɪʃ(ə)n, -səʊsɪ-/ *n.* **1** close association, esp. of Churches or religious communities. **2** *Ecol.* a closely related sub-group of plants having one dominant species. [Latin *consociatio*, *-onis* from *consociare* (as COM-, *socius* 'fellow')]

consolation /kɒnsə'leɪʃ(ə)n/ *n.* **1** the act or an instance of consoling; the state of being consoled. **2** a consoling thing, person, or circumstance. □ **consolatory** /kən'sɒlət(ə)ri, -'səʊl-/ *adj.* [Middle English via Old French from Latin *consolatio -onis* (as CONSOLE[1])]

consolation prize *n.* a prize given to a competitor who just fails to win a main prize.

console[1] /kən'səʊl/ *v.tr.* comfort, esp. in grief or disappointment. □ **consolable** *adj.* **consoler** *n.* **consolingly** *adv.* [French *consoler* from Latin *consolari* (as COM-, *solari* 'soothe')]

■ **Usage** See Usage Note at CONDOLE.

console[2] /'kɒnsəʊl/ *n.* **1** a panel or unit accommodating a set of switches, controls, etc. **2** a cabinet for television or radio equipment etc. **3** *Mus.* a cabinet with the keyboards, stops, pedals, etc., of an organ. **4** an ornamented bracket supporting a shelf etc. [French, perhaps from *consolider* (as CONSOLIDATE)]

console table *n.* a table supported by a bracket against a wall.

consolidate /kən'sɒlɪdeɪt/ *v.* **1** *tr.* & *intr.* make or become strong or solid. **2** *tr.* reinforce or strengthen (one's position, power, etc.). **3** *tr.* combine (territories, companies, debts, etc.) into one whole. □ **consolidation** /-'deɪʃ(ə)n/ *n.* **consolidator** *n.* **consolidatory** *adj.* [Latin *consolidare* (as COM-, *solidare* from *solidus* 'solid')]

consolidated fund *n.* (also **consolidated annuities**) *Brit.* a Bank of England fund into which tax revenue is paid and from which payments not dependent on annual votes in Parliament are made.

consols /'kɒns(ə)lz/ *n.pl.* British government securities without redemption date and with fixed annual interest. [abbreviation of *consolidated annuities*]

consommé /kən'sɒmeɪ/ *n.* a clear soup made with concentrated meat stock. [French, past part. of *consommer* from Latin *consummare* (as CONSUMMATE)]

consonance /'kɒns(ə)nəns/ *n.* **1** agreement, harmony. **2** *Prosody* a recurrence of similar-sounding consonants. **3** *Mus.* a harmonious combination of notes; a harmonious interval. [Middle English from Old French *consonance* or Latin *consonantia* (as CONSONANT)]

consonant /'kɒns(ə)nənt/ *n.* & *adj.* ● *n.* **1** a speech sound in which the breath is at least partly obstructed, and which to form a syllable must be combined with a vowel. **2** a letter or letters representing this. ● *adj.* (foll. by *with*, *to*) **1** consistent; in agreement or harmony. **2** similar in sound. **3** *Mus.* making a concord. □ **consonantal** /-'nant(ə)l/ *adj.* **consonantly** *adv.* [Middle English via French from Latin *consonare* (as COM-, *sonare* 'to sound' from *sonus*)]

con sordino /kɒn sɔː'diːnəʊ/ *adv. Mus.* with the use of a mute. [Italian]

consort[1] *n.* & *v.* ● *n.* /'kɒnsɔːt/ **1** a wife or husband, esp. of royalty (*prince consort*). **2** a companion; an associate. **3** a ship sailing with another. ● *v.* /kən'sɔːt/ **1** *intr.* (usu. foll. by *with*, *together*) **a** keep company; associate. **b** harmonize. **2** *tr.* class or bring together. [Middle English via French from Latin *consors* 'sharer, comrade' (as COM-, *sors sortis* 'lot, destiny')]

consort[2] /'kɒnsɔːt/ *n. Mus.* a group of musicians who regularly perform together, esp. playing early music (*recorder consort*). [earlier form of CONCERT]

consortium /kən'sɔːtɪəm/ *n.* (*pl.* **consortia** /-tɪə/ or **consortiums**) **1** an association, esp. of several business companies. **2** *Law* the right of association with a husband or wife (*loss of consortium*). [Latin, = partnership (as CONSORT[1])]

conspecific /kɒnspə'sɪfɪk/ *adj. Biol.* of the same species.

conspectus /kən'spɛktəs/ *n.* **1** a general or comprehensive survey. **2** a summary or synopsis. [Latin from *conspicere conspect-* (as COM-, *spicere* 'look at')]

conspicuous /kən'spɪkjʊəs/ *adj.* **1** clearly visible; striking to the eye (*a conspicuous hole in his shirt*). **2** remarkable; noteworthy (*a conspicuous success*). **3** (of expenditure etc.) lavish, with a view to enhancing one's prestige. □ **conspicuously** *adv.* **conspicuousness** *n.* [Latin *conspicuus* (as CONSPECTUS)]

conspiracy /kən'spɪrəsi/ *n.* (*pl.* **-ies**) **1** a secret plan to commit a crime or do harm, often for political ends; a plot. **2** the act of conspiring. [Middle English via Anglo-French *conspiracie*, alteration of Old French *conspiration*, from Latin *conspiratio -onis* (as CONSPIRE)]

conspiracy of silence *n.* an agreement to say nothing.

conspiracy theory *n.* a belief that some covert but influential agency or organization is responsible for an unexplained event.

conspirator /kən'spɪrətə/ *n.* a person who takes part in a conspiracy. □ **conspiratorial** /-'tɔːrɪəl/ *adj.* **conspiratorially** /-'tɔːrɪəli/ *adv.* [Middle English from Anglo-French *conspiratour*, Old French *-teur* (as CONSPIRE)]

conspire /kən'spʌɪə/ *v.intr.* **1** combine secretly to plan and prepare an unlawful or harmful act. **2** (often foll. by *against*, or *to* + infin.) (of events or circumstances) seem to be working together, esp. disadvantageously. [Middle English via Old French *conspirer* from Latin *conspirare* 'agree, plot' (as COM-, *spirare* 'breathe')]

constable /'kʌnstəb(ə)l, 'kɒn-/ *n.* **1** esp. *Brit.* **a** a policeman or policewoman. **b** (also **police constable**) a police officer of the lowest rank. **2** the governor of a royal castle. **3** *hist.* the principal officer in a royal household. [Middle English via Old French *conestable* from Late Latin *comes stabuli* 'count (head officer) of the stable']

constabulary /kən'stabjʊləri/ *n.* & *adj.* ● *n.* (*pl.* **-ies**) an organized body of police; a police force. ● *attrib.adj.* of or concerning the police force. [medieval Latin *constabularius* (as CONSTABLE)]

constancy /'kɒnst(ə)nsi/ *n.* **1** the quality of being unchanging and dependable; faithfulness. **2** firmness, endurance. [Latin *constantia* (as CONSTANT)]

constant /'kɒnst(ə)nt/ *adj.* & *n.* ● *adj.* **1** continuous (*needs constant attention*). **2** occurring frequently (*receive constant complaints*). **3** (often foll. by *to*) unchanging, faithful, dependable. ● *n.* **1** anything that does not vary. **2** *Math.* a component of a relationship between variables that does not change its value. **3** *Physics* **a** a number expressing a relation, property, etc., and remaining the same in all circumstances. **b** such a number that remains the same for a substance in the same conditions. □ **constantly** *adv.* [Middle English via Old French from Latin *constare* (as COM-, *stare* 'stand')]

constantan /ˈkɒnst(ə)ntan/ *n.* an alloy of copper and nickel used in electrical equipment. [CONSTANT + -AN]

constellate /ˈkɒnstəleɪt/ *v.tr.* **1** form into (or as if into) a constellation. **2** adorn as with stars.

constellation /kɒnstəˈleɪʃ(ə)n/ *n.* **1** a group of fixed stars whose outline is traditionally regarded as forming a particular figure. **2** a group of associated persons, ideas, etc. [Middle English via Old French from Late Latin *constellatio -onis* (as COM-, *stella* 'star')]

consternate /ˈkɒnstəneɪt/ *v.tr.* (usu. in *passive*) dismay; fill with anxiety. [Latin *consternare* (as COM-, *sternere* 'throw down')]

consternation /kɒnstəˈneɪʃ(ə)n/ *n.* anxiety or dismay causing mental confusion. [French *consternation* or Latin *consternatio* (as CONSTERNATE)]

constipate /ˈkɒnstɪpeɪt/ *v.tr.* (esp. as **constipated** *adj.*) affect with constipation. [Latin *constipare* (as COM-, *stipare* 'press')]

constipation /kɒnstɪˈpeɪʃ(ə)n/ *n.* **1** a condition with hardened faeces and difficulty in emptying the bowels. **2** a restricted state. [Middle English from Old French *constipation* or Late Latin *constipatio* (as CONSTIPATE)]

constituency /kənˈstɪtjʊənsi/ *n.* (*pl.* **-ies**) **1** a body of voters in a specified area who elect a representative member to a legislative body. **2** *Brit.* the area represented in this way. **3** a body of customers, supporters, etc.

constituent /kənˈstɪtjʊənt/ *adj. & n.* ● *adj.* **1** composing or helping to make up a whole. **2** able to make or change a (political etc.) constitution (*constituent assembly*). **3** appointing or electing. ● *n.* **1** a member of a constituency (esp. political). **2** a component part. **3** *Law* a person who appoints another as agent. [Latin *constituent-*, partly via French *constituant* (as CONSTITUTE)]

constitute /ˈkɒnstɪtjuːt/ *v.tr.* **1** be the components or essence of; make up, form. **2 a** be equivalent or tantamount to (*this constitutes an official warning*). **b** formally establish (*does not constitute a precedent*). **3** give legal or constitutional form to; establish by law. [Latin *constituere* (as COM-, *statuere* 'set up')]

constitution /kɒnstɪˈtjuːʃ(ə)n/ *n.* **1** the act or method of constituting; the composition (of something). **2 a** the body of fundamental principles or established precedents according to which a state or other organization is acknowledged to be governed. **b** a (usu. written) record of this. **3** a person's physical state as regards vitality, health, strength, etc. **4** a person's mental or psychological make-up. **5** *hist.* a decree or ordinance. [Middle English from Old French *constitution* or Latin *constitutio* (as CONSTITUTE)]

constitutional /kɒnstɪˈtjuːʃ(ə)n(ə)l/ *adj. & n.* ● *adj.* **1** of, consistent with, authorized by, or limited by a political constitution (*a constitutional monarchy*). **2** inherent in, stemming from, or affecting the physical or mental constitution. ● *n.* a walk taken regularly to maintain or restore good health. □ **constitutionality** /-ˈnalɪti/ *n.* **constitutionalize** *v.tr.* (also **-ise**). **constitutionally** *adv.*

constitutionalism /kɒnstɪˈtjuːʃ(ə)n(ə)lɪz(ə)m/ *n.* **1** a constitutional system of government. **2** the adherence to or advocacy of such a system. □ **constitutionalist** *n.*

constitutive /ˈkɒnstɪtjuːtɪv/ *adj.* **1** able to form or appoint. **2** component. **3** essential. □ **constitutively** *adv.* [Late Latin *constitutivus* (as CONSTITUTE)]

constrain /kənˈstreɪn/ *v.tr.* **1** compel; urge irresistibly or by necessity. **2 a** confine forcibly; imprison. **b** restrict severely as regards action, behaviour, etc. **3** bring about by compulsion. **4** (as **constrained** *adj.*) forced, embarrassed (*a constrained voice*; *a constrained manner*). □ **constrainedly** /kənˈstreɪnɪdli/ *adv.* [Middle English via Old French *constraindre* from Latin *constringere* (as COM-, *stringere strict-* 'tie')]

constraint /kənˈstreɪnt/ *n.* **1** the act or result of constraining or being constrained; restriction of liberty. **2** something that constrains; a limitation on motion or action. **3** the restraint of natural feelings or their expression; a constrained manner. [Middle English from Old French *constreinte*, fem. past part. of *constraindre* (as CONSTRAIN)]

constrict /kənˈstrɪkt/ *v.tr.* **1** make narrow or tight; compress. **2** *Biol.* cause (organic tissue) to contract. □ **constriction** *n.* **constrictive** *adj.* [Latin, past part. stem of *constringere* (as CONSTRAIN)]

constrictor /kənˈstrɪktə/ *n.* **1** any snake (esp. a boa) that kills by coiling round its prey and compressing it. **2** *Anat.* any muscle that compresses or contracts an organ or part of the body. [modern Latin (as CONSTRICT)]

construct *v. & n.* ● *v.tr.* /kənˈstrʌkt/ **1** make by fitting parts together; build, form (something physical or abstract). **2** *Geom.* draw or delineate, esp. accurately to given conditions (*construct a triangle*). ● *n.* /ˈkɒnstrʌkt/ **1** a thing constructed, esp. by the mind. **2** *Linguistics* a group of words forming a phrase. □ **constructor** *n.* [Latin *construere construct-* (as COM-, *struere* 'pile, build')]

construction /kənˈstrʌkʃ(ə)n/ *n.* **1** the act or a mode of constructing. **2** a thing constructed. **3** an interpretation or explanation (*they put a generous construction on his act*). **4** *Gram.* an arrangement of words according to syntactical rules. □ **constructional** *adj.* **constructionally** *adv.* [Middle English via Old French from Latin *constructio -onis* (as CONSTRUCT)]

constructionism /kənˈstrʌkʃ(ə)nɪz(ə)m/ *n.* **1** *Art* = CONSTRUCTIVISM. **2** *US Law* interpretation of a legal document in a specified way (*strict constructionism*). □ **constructionist** *n.* (also *attrib.*).

construction site *n.* = BUILDING SITE.

constructive /kənˈstrʌktɪv/ *adj.* **1** of construction; tending to construct. **2** tending to form a basis for ideas; helpful, positive (*constructive criticism*; *a constructive approach*) (opp. DESTRUCTIVE 2). **3** derived by inference; not expressed (*constructive permission*). **4** belonging to the structure of a building. □ **constructively** *adv.* **constructiveness** *n.* [Late Latin *constructivus* (as CONSTRUCT)]

constructive dismissal *n.* the changing of an employee's job or working conditions with the aim of forcing resignation.

constructivism /kənˈstrʌktɪvɪz(ə)m/ *n. Art* a Russian movement in which assorted (usu. mechanical or industrial) objects are combined into non-representational and mobile structural forms. □ **constructivist** *n.* [CONSTRUCTIVE + -ISM, transliterating Russian *konstruktivizm*]

construe /kənˈstruː/ *v.tr.* (**construes**, **construed**, **construing**) **1** interpret (words or actions) (*their decision can be construed in many ways*). **2** (often foll. by *with*) combine (words) grammatically (*'rely' is construed with 'on'*). **3** analyse the syntax of (a sentence). **4** translate word for word. □ **construable** *adj.* **construal** *n.* [Middle English from Latin *construere* CONSTRUCT]

consubstantial /kɒnsəbˈstanʃ(ə)l/ *adj. Theol.* of the same substance (esp. of the three persons of the Trinity). □ **consubstantiality** /-ʃɪˈalɪti/ *n.* [Middle English from ecclesiastical Latin *consubstantialis*, translation of Greek *homoousios* (as COM-, SUBSTANTIAL)]

consubstantiation /ˌkɒnsəbstanʃɪˈeɪʃ(ə)n, -sɪ-/ *n. Theol.* (the doctrine of) the real substantial presence of the body and blood of Christ together with the bread and wine in the Eucharist. [modern Latin *consubstantiatio*, suggested by *transubstantiatio* TRANSUBSTANTIATION]

consuetude /ˈkɒnswɪtjuːd/ *n.* a custom, esp. one having legal force in Scotland. □ **consuetudinary** /-ˈtjuːdɪn(ə)ri/ *adj.* [Middle English via Old French *consuetude* or Latin *consuetudo -dinis* from *consuetus* 'accustomed']

consul /ˈkɒns(ə)l/ *n.* **1** an official appointed by a state to live in a foreign city and protect the state's citizens and interests there. **2** *hist.* either of two annually elected chief magistrates in ancient Rome. **3** any of the three chief magistrates of the French republic (1799–1804).

□ **consular** /ˈkɒnsjʊlə/ *adj.* **consulship** *n.* [Middle English from Latin, related to *consulere* 'take counsel']

consulate /ˈkɒnsjʊlət/ *n.* **1** the building officially used by a consul. **2** the office, position, or period of office of consul. **3** *hist.* government by consuls. **4** *hist.* the period of office of a consul. **5** (**Consulate**) *hist.* the government of France by three consuls (1799–1804). [Middle English from Latin *consulatus* (as CONSUL)]

consult /kənˈsʌlt/ *v.* **1** *tr.* seek information or advice from (a person, book, watch, etc.). **2** *intr.* (often foll. by *with*) refer to a person for advice, an opinion, etc. **3** *tr.* seek permission or approval from (a person) for a proposed action. **4** *tr.* take into account; consider (feelings, interests, etc.). □ **consultative** /-tətɪv/ *adj.* [French *consulter* from Latin *consultare*, frequentative of *consulere consult-* 'take counsel']

consultancy /kənˈsʌlt(ə)nsi/ *n.* (*pl.* **-ies**) the professional practice or position of a consultant.

consultant /kənˈsʌlt(ə)nt/ *n.* **1** a person providing professional advice etc., esp. for a fee. **2** *Brit.* a senior specialist in a branch of medicine responsible for patients in a hospital. [probably French (as CONSULT)]

consultation /kɒnsəlˈteɪʃ(ə)n/ *n.* **1** a meeting arranged to consult (esp. with a consultant). **2** the act or an instance of consulting. **3** a conference. [Middle English via Old French *consultation* or Latin *consultatio* from *consultare* (as CONSULT)]

consultee /kɒnsʌlˈtiː/ *n.* a person who is consulted.

consulting /kənˈsʌltɪŋ/ *attrib.adj.* giving professional advice to others working in the same field or subject (*consulting physician*).

consumable /kənˈsjuːməb(ə)l/ *adj.* & *n.* ● *adj.* that can be consumed; intended for consumption. ● *n.* (usu. in *pl.*) a commodity that is eventually used up, worn out, or eaten.

consume /kənˈsjuːm/ *v.tr.* **1** eat or drink. **2** completely destroy; reduce to nothing or to tiny particles (*fire consumed the building*). **3** engage the full attention of; engross; dominate (often in *passive*, foll. by *with* or *by*: *consumed with rage*). **4** use up (time, energy, etc.). □ **consumingly** *adv.* [Middle English from Latin *consumere* (as COM-, *sumere sumpt-* 'take up'): partly through French *consumer*]

consumer /kənˈsjuːmə/ *n.* **1** a person who consumes, esp. one who uses a product. **2** a purchaser of goods or services.

consumer durable *n.* a household product with a relatively long useful life (e.g. a radio or washing machine).

consumer goods *n.pl.* goods put to use by consumers, not used in producing other goods (opp. CAPITAL GOODS).

consumerism /kənˈsjuːmərɪz(ə)m/ *n.* **1** the protection or promotion of consumers' interests in relation to the producer. **2** often *derog.* a preoccupation with consumer goods and their acquisition. □ **consumerist** *adj.* & *n.*

consumer research *n.* investigation of purchasers' needs and opinions.

consumer society *n.* a society in which the marketing of goods and services is an important social and economic activity.

consummate *v.* & *adj.* ● *v.tr.* /ˈkɒnsəmeɪt, -sjʊ-/ **1** complete; make perfect. **2** complete (a marriage) by sexual intercourse. ● *adj.* /kənˈsʌmət, ˈkɒnsʌmət/ complete, perfect; fully skilled (*a consummate general*). □ **consummately** *adv.* **consummator** /ˈkɒnsəmeɪtə/ *n.* [Latin *consummare* (as COM-, *summare* 'complete' from *summus* 'utmost')]

consummation /kɒnsəˈmeɪʃ(ə)n, -sjʊ-/ *n.* **1** completion, esp. of a marriage by sexual intercourse. **2** a desired end or goal; perfection. [Middle English from Old French *consommation* or Latin *consummatio* (as CONSUMMATE)]

consumption /kənˈsʌm(p)ʃ(ə)n/ *n.* **1** the act or an instance of consuming; the process of being consumed. **2** any disease causing wasting of tissues, esp. pulmonary tuberculosis. **3** an amount consumed. **4** the purchase and use of goods etc. **5** use by a particular person or group (*a film unfit for children's consumption*). [Middle English via Old French *consomption* from Latin *consumptio* (as CONSUME)]

consumptive /kənˈsʌm(p)tɪv/ *adj.* & *n.* ● *adj.* **1** of or tending to consumption. **2** tending to or affected with pulmonary tuberculosis. ● *n.* a consumptive patient. □ **consumptively** *adv.* [medieval Latin *consumptivus* (as CONSUMPTION)]

cont. *abbr.* **1** contents. **2** continued.

contact *n.* & *v.* ● *n.* /ˈkɒntakt/ **1** the state or condition of touching, meeting, or communicating. **2** a person who is or may be communicated with for information, supplies, assistance, etc. **3** *Electr.* **a** a connection for the passage of a current. **b** a device for providing this. **4** a person likely to carry a contagious disease through being associated with an infected person. **5** (usu. in *pl.*) *colloq.* a contact lens. ● *v.tr.* /ˈkɒntakt, kənˈtakt/ **1** get into communication with (a person). **2** begin correspondence or personal dealings with. □ **contactable** *adj.* [Latin *contactus* from *contingere* (as COM-, *tangere* 'touch')]

contact lens *n.* a small lens placed directly on the eyeball to correct the vision.

contact print *n.* a photographic print made by placing a negative directly on sensitized paper etc. and illuminating it.

contact sheet *n.* a contact print showing several or all of the photographs on a film.

contact sport *n.* a sport in which participants necessarily come into bodily contact with one another.

contagion /kənˈteɪdʒ(ə)n/ *n.* **1 a** the communication of disease from one person to another by bodily contact. **b** a contagious disease. **2** a contagious or harmful influence. **3** moral corruption, esp. when tending to be widespread. [Middle English from Latin *contagio* (as COM-, *tangere* 'touch')]

contagious /kənˈteɪdʒəs/ *adj.* **1 a** (of a person) likely to transmit disease by contact. **b** (of a disease) transmitted in this way. **2** (of emotions, reactions, etc.) likely to affect others (*contagious enthusiasm*). □ **contagiously** *adv.* **contagiousness** *n.* [Middle English from Late Latin *contagiosus* (as CONTAGION)]

contagious abortion *n.* brucellosis of cattle.

contain /kənˈteɪn/ *v.tr.* **1** hold or be capable of holding within itself; include, comprise. **2** (of measures) consist of or be equal to (*a gallon contains eight pints*). **3** prevent (an enemy, difficulty, etc.) from moving or extending. **4** control or restrain (oneself, one's feelings, etc.). **5** (of a number) be divisible by (a factor) without a remainder. □ **containable** *adj.* [Middle English via Old French *contenir* from Latin *continēre content-* (as COM-, *tenēre* 'hold')]

container /kənˈteɪnə/ *n.* **1** a vessel, box, etc., for holding particular things. **2** a large boxlike receptacle of standard design for the transport of goods, esp. one readily transferable from one form of transport to another.

container-grown *adj.* (of a plant) grown in a container rather than in the ground.

containerize /kənˈteɪnərʌɪz/ *v.tr.* (also **-ise**) **1** pack in or transport by container. **2** adapt to transport by container. □ **containerization** /-ˈzeɪʃ(ə)n/ *n.*

container port *n.* a port specializing in handling goods stored in containers.

container ship *n.* a ship designed to carry goods stored in containers.

containment /kənˈteɪnm(ə)nt/ *n.* the action or policy of preventing the expansion of a hostile country or influence.

contaminate /kənˈtamɪneɪt/ *v.tr.* **1** pollute, esp. with radioactivity. **2** infect; corrupt. □ **contaminant** *n.* **contamination** /-ˈneɪʃ(ə)n/ *n.* **contaminator** *n.* [Latin *contaminare* (as COM-, *tamen-* related to *tangere* 'touch')]

contango /kənˈtaŋgəʊ/ *n.* (*pl.* **-os**) *Brit. Stock Exch.* **1** the postponement of the transfer of stock from one account day to the next. **2** a percentage paid by the buyer for such a postponement. [19th c.: probably an arbitrary formation, perhaps with the idea 'I make contingent': see CONTINGENT]

contango day *n. Stock Exch.* the eighth day before settling day.

Conté /ˈkɒnteɪ/ *attrib.adj.* designating a kind of pencil, crayon, or chalk. [N.J. *Conté*, French inventor d. 1805]

conte /kɒnt, French kɔ̃t/ *n.* **1** a short story (as a form of literary composition). **2** a medieval narrative tale. [French]

contemn /kənˈtɛm/ *v.tr. literary* despise; treat with disregard. □ **contemner** /-ˈtɛmə, -ˈtɛmnə/ *n.* [Middle English from Old French *contemner* or Latin *contemnere* (as COM-, *temnere tempt-* 'despise')]

contemplate /ˈkɒntəmpleɪt, -təm-/ *v.* **1** *tr.* survey with the eyes or in the mind. **2** *tr.* regard (an event) as possible. **3** *tr.* intend; have as one's purpose (*we contemplate leaving tomorrow*). **4** *intr.* meditate. □ **contemplation** /-ˈpleɪʃ(ə)n/ *n.* **contemplator** *n.* [Latin *contemplari* (as COM-, *templum* 'place for observations')]

contemplative /kənˈtɛmplətɪv/ *adj. & n.* ● *adj.* of or given to (esp. religious) contemplation; meditative. ● *n.* a person whose life is devoted to religious contemplation. □ **contemplatively** *adv.* [Middle English from Old French *contemplatif -ive*, or Latin *contemplativus* (as CONTEMPLATE)]

contemporaneous /kəntɛmpəˈreɪnɪəs, kɒn-/ *adj.* (usu. foll. by *with*) **1** existing or occurring at the same time. **2** of the same period. □ **contemporaneity** /-ˈniːɪti, -ˈneɪɪti/ *n.* **contemporaneously** *adv.* **contemporaneousness** *n.* [Latin *contemporaneus* (as COM-, *temporaneus* from *tempus -oris* 'time')]

contemporary /kənˈtɛmp(ə)r(ər)i/ *adj. & n.* ● *adj.* **1** living or occurring at the same time. **2** approximately equal in age. **3** following modern ideas or fashion in style or design. ● *n.* (*pl.* **-ies**) **1** a person or thing living or existing at the same time as another. **2** a person of roughly the same age as another. □ **contemporarily** *adv.* **contemporariness** *n.* [medieval Latin *contemporarius* (as CONTEMPORANEOUS)]

contempt /kənˈtɛm(p)t/ *n.* **1** a feeling that a person or a thing is beneath consideration, worthless, or deserving scorn or extreme reproach. **2** the condition of being held in contempt. **3** (in full **contempt of court**) disobedience to or disrespect for a court of law and its officers. □ **beneath contempt** utterly despicable. **hold in contempt** despise. [Middle English from Latin *contemptus*, from *contemnere* CONTEMN]

contemptible /kənˈtɛm(p)tɪb(ə)l/ *adj.* deserving contempt; despicable. □ **contemptibility** /-ˈbɪlɪti/ *n.* **contemptibly** *adv.* [Middle English via Old French or Late Latin *contemptibilis* from Latin *contemnere* CONTEMN]

contemptuous /kənˈtɛm(p)tjʊəs/ *adj.* (often foll. by *of*) showing contempt, scornful; insolent. □ **contemptuously** *adv.* **contemptuousness** *n.* [medieval Latin *contemptuosus* from Latin *contemptus* from *contemnere* CONTEMN]

contend /kənˈtɛnd/ *v.* **1** *intr.* (usu. foll. by *with*) strive, fight. **2** *intr.* (usu. foll. by *for, with*) compete (*contending for the title*; *contending emotions*). **3** *tr.* (usu. foll. by *that* + clause) assert, maintain. □ **contender** *n.* (esp. in sense 2). [Old French *contendre* or Latin *contendere* (as COM-, *tendere tent-* 'stretch, strive')]

content[1] /kənˈtɛnt/ *adj., v., & n.* ● *predic.adj.* **1** satisfied; adequately happy; in agreement. **2** (foll. by *to* + infin.) willing. ● *v.tr.* make content; satisfy. ● *n.* a contented state; satisfaction. □ **to one's heart's content** to the full extent of one's desires. [Middle English via Old French from Latin *contentus* 'satisfied', past part. of *continēre* (as CONTAIN)]

content[2] /ˈkɒntɛnt/ *n.* **1** (usu. in *pl.*) what is contained in something, esp. in a vessel, book, or house. **2** the amount of a constituent contained (*low sodium content*). **3** the substance or material dealt with (in a speech, work of art, etc.) as distinct from its form or style. **4** the capacity or volume of a thing. **5** (in *pl.*; in full **table of contents**) a list of the titles of chapters etc. given at the front of a book, periodical, etc. [Middle English from medieval Latin *contentum* (as CONTAIN)]

contented /kənˈtɛntɪd/ *adj.* (often foll. by *with*, or *to* + infin.) **1** happy, satisfied. **2** (foll. by *with*) willing to be content (*was contented with the outcome*). □ **contentedly** *adv.* **contentedness** *n.*

contention /kənˈtɛnʃ(ə)n/ *n.* **1** a dispute or argument; rivalry. **2** a point contended for in an argument (*it is my contention that you are wrong*). □ **in contention** competing, esp. with a good chance of success. [Middle English from Old French *contention* or Latin *contentio* (as CONTEND)]

contentious /kənˈtɛnʃəs/ *adj.* **1** argumentative, quarrelsome. **2** likely to cause an argument; disputed, controversial. □ **contentiously** *adv.* **contentiousness** *n.* [Middle English via Old French *contentieux* from Latin *contentiosus* (as CONTENTION)]

contentment /kənˈtɛntm(ə)nt/ *n.* a satisfied state; tranquil happiness.

conterminous /kɒnˈtəːmɪnəs/ *adj.* (often foll. by *with*) **1** having a common boundary. **2** coextensive in space, time, or meaning. □ **conterminously** *adv.* [Latin *conterminus* (as COM-, *terminus* 'boundary')]

contessa /kɒnˈtɛsə/ *n.* an Italian countess. [Italian from Late Latin *comitissa*: see COUNTESS]

contest *n. & v.* ● *n.* /ˈkɒntɛst/ **1** a process of contending; a competition. **2** a dispute; a controversy. ● *v.tr.* /kənˈtɛst/ **1** challenge or dispute (a decision etc.). **2** debate (a point, statement, etc.). **3** contend or compete for (a prize, parliamentary seat, etc.); compete in (an election). □ **contestable** /kənˈtɛstəb(ə)l/ *adj.* **contester** /kənˈtɛstə/ *n.* [earlier = bear witness, from Latin *contestari* (as COM-, *testis* 'witness')]

contestant /kənˈtɛst(ə)nt/ *n.* a person who takes part in a contest or competition.

contestation /kɒntɛˈsteɪʃ(ə)n/ *n.* **1** a disputation. **2** an assertion contended for. [Latin *contestatio*, partly through French (as CONTEST)]

context /ˈkɒntɛkst/ *n.* **1** the parts of something written or spoken that immediately precede and follow a word or passage and clarify its meaning. **2** the circumstances relevant to something under consideration. □ **in context** with the surrounding words or circumstances (*must be seen in context*). **out of context** without the surrounding words or circumstances and so not fully understandable. □ **contextual** /kənˈtɛkstjʊəl/ *adj.* **contextually** /kənˈtɛkstjʊəli/ *adv.* [Middle English from Latin *contextus* (as COM-, *texere text-* 'weave')]

contextualism /kənˈtɛkstjʊəlɪz(ə)m/ *n. Philos.* any doctrine which emphasizes the importance of the context of enquiry in a particular question. □ **contextualist** *n.*

contextualize /kənˈtɛkstjʊəlʌɪz/ *v.tr.* (also **-ise**) place in a context; study in context. □ **contextualization** /-ˈzeɪʃ(ə)n/ *n.*

contiguity /kɒntɪˈgjuːɪti/ *n.* **1** being contiguous; proximity; contact. **2** *Psychol.* the proximity of ideas or impressions in place or time, as a principle of association.

contiguous /kənˈtɪgjʊəs/ *adj.* **1** (usu. foll. by *with, to*) touching, esp. along a line; in contact. **2** neighbouring; connected. □ **contiguously** *adv.* [Latin *contiguus* (as COM-, *tangere* 'touch')]

continent[1] /ˈkɒntɪnənt/ *n.* **1** any of the main continuous expanses of land (Europe, Asia, Africa, N. and S. America, Australia, Antarctica). **2** (**the Continent**) the mainland of Europe as distinct from the British Isles. **3** continuous land; a mainland. [Latin *terra continens* 'continuous land']

continent[2] /ˈkɒntɪnənt/ *adj.* **1** able to control movements of the bowels and bladder. **2** exercising self-restraint, esp. sexually. □ **continence** *n.* **continently** *adv.* [Middle English from Latin (as CONTAIN)]

continental /kɒntɪˈnɛnt(ə)l/ *adj. & n.* ● *adj.* **1** of or characteristic of a continent. **2** (**Continental**) of, relating to, or characteristic of mainland Europe. ● *n.* an inhabitant of mainland Europe. □ **continentally** *adv.*

continental breakfast *n.* a light breakfast of coffee, rolls, etc.

continental climate *n.* a climate having wide variations of temperature.

continental day *n. Brit.* a school day lasting from early morning to early afternoon.

continental drift *n.* the hypothesis that the continents are moving slowly over the surface of the earth on a deep-lying plastic substratum.

continental quilt *n. Brit.* a duvet.

continental shelf *n.* an area of relatively shallow seabed between the shore of a continent and the deeper ocean.

contingency /kənˈtɪndʒ(ə)nsi/ *n.* (*pl.* **-ies**) **1** a future event or circumstance regarded as likely to occur, or as influencing present action. **2** something dependent on another uncertain event or occurrence. **3** uncertainty of occurrence. **4 a** one thing incident to another. **b** an incidental expense etc. [earlier *contingence* from Late Latin *contingentia* (as CONTINGENT)]

contingency fund *n.* a fund to cover incidental or unforeseen expenses.

contingency plan *n.* a plan designed to take account of a possible future event or circumstance.

contingent /kənˈtɪndʒ(ə)nt/ *adj. & n.* ● *adj.* **1** (usu. foll. by *on*, *upon*) conditional, dependent (on an uncertain event or circumstance). **2** associated. **3** (usu. foll. by *to*) incidental. **4 a** that may or may not occur. **b** fortuitous; occurring by chance. **5** true only under existing or specified conditions. ● *n.* a body forming part of a larger group. □ **contingently** *adv.* [Latin *contingere* (as COM-, *tangere* 'touch')]

continual /kənˈtɪnjʊəl/ *adj.* constantly or frequently recurring; always happening (*subjected to continual interruptions*). □ **continually** *adv.* [Middle English from Old French *continuel*, from *continuer* (as CONTINUE)]

■ **Usage** Note the difference in meaning between *continual* and *continuous*. *Continual* means 'happening frequently (but with breaks in between each occurrence)', while *continuous* means 'uninterrupted, incessant'.

continuance /kənˈtɪnjʊəns/ *n.* **1** a state of continuing in existence or operation. **2** the duration of an event or action. **3** *US Law* a postponement or an adjournment. [Middle English from Old French (as CONTINUE)]

■ **Usage** Note the difference between *continuance* and *continuation*. *Continuance* relates mainly to the intransitive senses of *continue* 'to be still in existence', while *continuation* relates to its transitive senses 'to keep up, resume', e.g. *the Prime Minister's continuance in office; our continuation of the project*.

continuant /kənˈtɪnjʊənt/ *n. & adj. Phonet.* ● *n.* a speech sound in which the vocal tract is only partly closed, allowing the breath to pass through and the sound to be prolonged (as with *f*, *r*, *s*, *v*). ● *adj.* of or relating to such a sound. [French *continuant* and Latin *continuare* (as CONTINUE)]

continuation /kəntɪnjʊˈeɪʃ(ə)n/ *n.* **1** the act or an instance of continuing; the process of being continued. **2** a part that continues something else. **3** *Brit. Stock Exch.* the carrying over of an account to the next settling day. [Middle English via Old French from Latin *continuatio -onis* (as CONTINUE)]

■ **Usage** See Usage Note at CONTINUANCE.

continuation day *n.* = CONTANGO DAY.

continuative /kənˈtɪnjʊətɪv/ *adj.* tending or serving to continue. [Late Latin *continuativus* (as CONTINUATION)]

continue /kənˈtɪnjuː/ *v.* (**continues**, **continued**, **continuing**) **1** *tr.* (often foll. by verbal noun, or *to* + infin.) persist in, maintain, not stop (an action etc.). **2 a** *tr.* (also *absol.*) resume or prolong (a narrative, journey, etc.). **b** *intr.* recommence after a pause (*the concert will continue shortly*). **3** *tr.* be a sequel to. **4** *intr.* **a** remain in existence or unchanged. **b** (with compl.) remain in a specified state (*the weather continued fine*). **5** *tr. US Law* postpone or adjourn (proceedings). □ **continuable** *adj.* **continuer** *n.* [Middle English via Old French *continuer* from Latin *continuare* 'make or be CONTINUOUS']

continuing education *n.* education for adults consisting esp. of short or part-time courses.

continuity /kɒntɪˈnjuːɪti/ *n.* (*pl.* **-ies**) **1 a** the state of being continuous. **b** an unbroken succession. **c** a logical sequence. **2** the detailed and self-consistent scenario of a film or broadcast. **3** the linking of broadcast items. [French *continuité* from Latin *continuitas -tatis* (as CONTINUOUS)]

continuity girl *n.* (also **continuity man**) the person responsible for agreement of detail between different sessions of filming.

continuo /kənˈtɪnjʊəʊ/ *n.* (*pl.* **-os**) *Mus.* an accompaniment providing a bass line and harmonies which are indicated by figures, often played on a keyboard instrument. [shortened from *basso continuo* (Italian, = continuous bass)]

continuous /kənˈtɪnjʊəs/ *adj.* **1** unbroken, uninterrupted, connected throughout in space or time (*continuous rain*). **2** *Gram.* = PROGRESSIVE *adj.* 7. □ **continuously** *adv.* **continuousness** *n.* [Latin *continuus* 'uninterrupted' from *continēre* (as COM-, *tenēre* 'hold')]

■ **Usage** See Usage Note at CONTINUAL.

continuous assessment *n. Brit.* the evaluation of a pupil's progress throughout a course of study, as well as or instead of by examination.

continuous creation *n.* the creation of the universe or the matter in it regarded as a continuous process.

continuous stationery *n. Brit.* a continuous ream of paper, usu. perforated to form single sheets.

continuum /kənˈtɪnjʊəm/ *n.* (*pl.* **continua** /-jʊə/) anything seen as having a continuous, not discrete, structure (*space-time continuum*). [Latin, neut. of *continuus*: see CONTINUOUS]

contort /kənˈtɔːt/ *v.tr.* twist or force out of normal shape. [Latin *contorquēre contort-* (as COM-, *torquēre* 'twist')]

contortion /kənˈtɔːʃ(ə)n/ *n.* **1** the act or process of twisting. **2** a twisted state, esp. of the face or body. [Latin *contortio* (as CONTORT)]

contortionist /kənˈtɔːʃ(ə)nɪst/ *n.* an entertainer who adopts contorted postures.

contour /ˈkɒntʊə/ *n. & v.* ● *n.* **1** an outline, esp. representing or bounding the shape or form of something. **2** the outline of a natural feature, e.g. a coast or mountain mass. **3** a line separating differently coloured parts of a design. **4** = CONTOUR LINE. ● *v.tr.* **1** mark with contour lines. **2** carry (a road or railway) round the side of a hill. [French from Italian *contorno*, from *contornare* 'draw in outline' (as COM-, *tornare* 'turn')]

contour feather *n.* any of the feathers which form the outline of a bird's plumage.

contour line *n.* a line on a map joining points of equal altitude.

contour map *n.* a map marked with contour lines.

contour ploughing *n.* ploughing along lines of constant altitude to minimize soil erosion.

contra /ˈkɒntrə/ *n.* (*pl.* **contras**) a member of a counter-revolutionary guerrilla force in Nicaragua. [abbreviation of Spanish *contrarevolucionario* 'counter-revolutionary']

contra- /ˈkɒntrə/ *prefix* **1** against, opposite (*contradict*). **2** *Mus.* (of instruments, organ stops, etc.) pitched an octave below (*contrabassoon*). [Latin *contra* 'against']

contraband /ˈkɒntrəband/ *n. & adj.* ● *n.* **1** goods that have been smuggled, or imported or exported illegally. **2** prohibited trade; smuggling. **3** (in full **contraband of war**) goods forbidden to be supplied by neutrals to belligerents. ● *adj.* **1** forbidden to be imported or exported (at all or without payment of duty). **2** concerning traffic in contraband (*contraband trade*). □ **contrabandist** *n.* [Spanish *contrabanda* from Italian (as CONTRA-, *bando* 'proclamation')]

contrabass /ˈkɒntrəbeɪs/ *n. Mus.* = DOUBLE BASS. [Italian (*basso* BASS[1])]

contraception /kɒntrəˈsɛpʃ(ə)n/ *n.* the intentional prevention of pregnancy; the use of contraceptives. [CONTRA- + CONCEPTION]

contraceptive /kɒntrəˈsɛptɪv/ *adj. & n.* ● *adj.* preventing pregnancy. ● *n.* a contraceptive device or drug.

contract *n. & v.* ● *n.* /ˈkɒntrakt/ **1** a written or spoken agreement between two or more parties, intended to be enforceable by law. **2** a document recording this. **3** marriage regarded as a binding commitment. **4** *Bridge* etc. an undertaking to win the number of tricks bid. **5** *slang* an arrangement for someone to be killed, usu. by a hired assassin. ● *v.* /kənˈtrakt/ **1** *tr. & intr.* **a** make or become smaller. **b** draw together (muscles, the brow, etc.), or be drawn together. **2 a** *intr.* (usu. foll. by *with*) make a contract. **b** *intr.* (usu. foll. by *for*, or *to* + infin.) enter formally into a business or legal arrangement. **c** *tr.* (often foll. by *out*) arrange (work) to be done by contract. **d** *tr.* place under a contract. **3** *tr.* catch or develop (a disease). **4** *tr.* form or develop (a friendship, habit, etc.). **5** *tr.* enter into (marriage). **6** *tr.* incur (a debt etc.). **7** *tr.* shorten (a word) by combination or elision. □ **contract** /ˈkɒn-/ **in** (or **out**) (also *refl.*) *Brit.* choose to be involved in (or withdraw or remain out of) a scheme or commitment. □ **contractive** *adj.* [earlier as adj., = contracted: Old French, from Latin *contractus* (as COM-, *trahere tract-* 'draw')]

contractable /kənˈtraktəb(ə)l/ *adj.* (of a disease) that can be contracted.

contract bridge *n.* the most common form of bridge, in which only tricks bid and won count towards the game.

contractible /kənˈtraktɪb(ə)l/ *adj.* that can be shrunk or drawn together.

contractile /kənˈtraktʌɪl/ *adj.* capable of or producing contraction. □ **contractility** /kɒntrakˈtɪlɪti/ *n.*

contraction /kənˈtrakʃ(ə)n/ *n.* **1** the act of contracting. **2** (often in *pl.*) *Med.* a shortening of the uterine muscles occurring at intervals during childbirth. **3** shrinking, diminution. **4 a** a shortening of a word by combination or elision. **b** a contracted word or group of words. [French from Latin *contractio -onis* (as CONTRACT)]

contractor /kənˈtraktə/ *n.* a person who undertakes a contract, esp. to provide materials, conduct building operations, etc. [Late Latin (as CONTRACT)]

contractual /kənˈtraktʃʊəl/ *adj.* of or in the nature of a contract. □ **contractually** *adv.*

contradict /kɒntrəˈdɪkt/ *v.tr.* **1** deny or express the opposite of (a statement). **2** deny or express the opposite of a statement made by (a person). **3** be in opposition to or in conflict with (*new evidence contradicted our theory*). □ **contradictor** *n.* [Latin *contradicere contradict-* (as CONTRA-, *dicere* 'say')]

contradiction /kɒntrəˈdɪkʃ(ə)n/ *n.* **1 a** statement of the opposite; denial. **b** an instance of this. **2** inconsistency. □ **contradiction in terms** a self-contradictory statement or group of words. [Middle English via Old French from Latin *contradictio -onis* (as CONTRADICT)]

contradictory /kɒntrəˈdɪkt(ə)ri/ *adj.* **1** expressing a denial or opposite statement. **2** (of statements etc.) mutually opposed or inconsistent. **3** (of a person) inclined to contradict. **4** *Logic* (of two propositions) so related that one and only one must be true. □ **contradictorily** *adv.* **contradictoriness** *n.* [Middle English from Late Latin *contradictorius* (as CONTRADICT)]

contradistinction /kɒntrədɪˈstɪŋ(k)ʃ(ə)n/ *n.* a distinction made by contrasting.

contradistinguish /kɒntrədɪˈstɪŋgwɪʃ/ *v.tr.* (usu. foll. by *from*) distinguish two things by contrasting them.

contraflow /ˈkɒntrəfləʊ/ *n. Brit.* a flow (esp. of road traffic) alongside, and in a direction opposite to, an established or usual flow, esp. as a temporary or emergency arrangement.

contrail /ˈkɒntreɪl/ *n.* a condensation trail, esp. from an aircraft. [abbreviation]

contraindicate /kɒntrəˈɪndɪkeɪt/ *v.tr. Med.* act as an indication against (the use of a particular substance or treatment). □ **contraindication** /-ˈkeɪʃ(ə)n/ *n.*

contralto /kənˈtraltəʊ/ *n.* (*pl.* **-os**) **1 a** the lowest female singing voice. **b** a singer with this voice. **2** a part written for contralto. [Italian (as CONTRA-, ALTO)]

contraposition /kɒntrəpəˈzɪʃ(ə)n/ *n.* **1** opposition or contrast. **2** *Logic* conversion of a proposition from *all A is B* to *all not-B is not-A*. □ **contrapositive** /-ˈpɒzɪtɪv/ *adj. & n.* [Late Latin *contrapositio* (as CONTRA-, *ponere posit-* 'place')]

contraption /kənˈtrapʃ(ə)n/ *n.* often *derog.* or *joc.* a machine or device, esp. a strange or cumbersome one. [19th c.: perhaps from CONTRIVE, INVENTION: associated with TRAP[1]]

contrapuntal /kɒntrəˈpʌnt(ə)l/ *adj. Mus.* of or in counterpoint. □ **contrapuntally** *adv.* **contrapuntist** *n.* [Italian *contrappunto* 'counterpoint']

contrariety /kɒntrəˈrʌɪəti/ *n.* **1** opposition in nature, quality, or action. **2** disagreement, inconsistency. [Middle English via Old French *contrarieté* from Late Latin *contrarietas -tatis*, from *contrarius* (as CONTRARY)]

contrariwise /kənˈtrɛːrɪwʌɪz, ˈkɒntrərɪwʌɪz/ *adv.* **1** on the other hand. **2** in the opposite way. **3** perversely. [Middle English from CONTRARY + -WISE]

contrary /ˈkɒntrəri/ *adj., n., & adv.* ● *adj.* **1** (usu. foll. by *to*) opposed in nature or tendency. **2** /kənˈtrɛːri/ *colloq.* perverse, self-willed. **3** (of a wind) unfavourable, impeding. **4** mutually opposed. **5** opposite in position or direction. ● *n.* (*pl.* **-ies**) (prec. by *the*) the opposite. ● *adv.* (foll. by *to*) in opposition or contrast (*contrary to expectations it rained*). □ **on the contrary** intensifying a denial of what has just been implied or stated. **to the contrary** to the opposite effect (*can find no indication to the contrary*). □ **contrarily** /ˈkɒntrərɪli/ (/kənˈtrɛːrɪli/ in sense 2 of *adj.*) *adv.* **contrariness** /ˈkɒntrərɪnɪs/ (/kənˈtrɛːrɪnɪs/ in sense 2 of *adj.*) *n.* [Middle English via Anglo-French *contrarie*, Old French *contraire*, from Latin *contrarius*, from *contra* 'against']

contrast *n. & v.* ● *n.* /ˈkɒntrɑːst/ **1 a** a juxtaposition or comparison showing striking differences. **b** a difference so revealed. **2** (often foll. by *to*) a thing or person having qualities noticeably different from another. **3 a** the degree of difference between tones in a television picture or a photograph. **b** the change of apparent brightness or colour of an object caused by the juxtaposition of other objects. ● *v.* /kənˈtrɑːst/ (often foll. by *with*) **1** *tr.* distinguish or set together so as to reveal a contrast. **2** *intr.* have or show a contrast. □ **contrastingly** /kənˈtrɑːstɪŋli/ *adv.* **contrastive** /kənˈtrɑːstɪv/ *adj.* [French *contraste*, *contraster*, via Italian *contrasto* from medieval Latin *contrastare* (as CONTRA-, *stare* 'stand')]

contrasty /ˈkɒntrɑːsti/ *adj.* (of a photograph, television picture, etc.) showing a high degree of contrast.

contra-suggestible /kɒntrəsəˈdʒɛstɪb(ə)l/ *adj. Psychol.* tending to respond to a suggestion by believing or doing the contrary.

contrate wheel /ˈkɒntreɪt/ *n.* = CROWN WHEEL. [medieval Latin & Romanic *contrata* 'lying opposite', from Latin *contra* 'against']

contravene /kɒntrəˈviːn/ *v.tr.* **1** infringe (a law or code of conduct). **2** (of things) conflict with. □ **contravener** *n.* [Late Latin *contravenire* (as CONTRA-, *venire vent-* 'come')]

contravention /kɒntrəˈvɛnʃ(ə)n/ *n.* **1** infringement. **2** an instance of this. □ **in contravention of** infringing, violating (a law etc.). [French from medieval Latin *contraventio* (as CONTRAVENE)]

contretemps /ˈkɒntrətɒ̃/ *n.* (*pl.* same /-tɑ̃z/) **1** an awkward or unfortunate occurrence; an unexpected mishap. **2** *colloq.* a dispute or disagreement. [French, originally = 'motion out of time' (as CONTRA-, *temps* 'time')]

contribute /kənˈtrɪbjuːt, ˈkɒntrɪbjuːt/ *v.* (often foll. by *to*) **1** *tr.* give (money, an idea, help, etc.) towards a common purpose (*contributed £5 to the fund*). **2** *intr.* help to bring about a result etc. (*contributed to their downfall*). **3** *tr.* (also *absol.*) supply (an article etc.) for publication with others in a journal etc. □ **contributive** /kənˈtrɪb-/ *adj.* [Latin *contribuere contribut-* (as COM-, *tribuere* 'bestow')]

■ **Usage** The second pronunciation of *contribute* given, with the stress on the first syllable, is considered incorrect by some people.

contribution /kɒntrɪˈbjuːʃ(ə)n/ *n.* **1** the act of contributing. **2** something contributed, esp. money. **3** an article etc. contributed to a publication. [Middle English from Old French *contribution* or Late Latin *contributio* (as CONTRIBUTE)]

contributor /kənˈtrɪbjʊtə/ *n.* a person who contributes (esp. an article or literary work).

contributory /kənˈtrɪbjʊt(ə)ri/ *adj.* & *n.* ● *adj.* **1** that contributes. **2** operated by means of contributions (*contributory pension scheme*). ● *n. Brit. Law* a person liable to contribute towards the payment of a wound-up company's debts. [medieval Latin *contributorius* (as CONTRIBUTE)]

contributory negligence *n.* negligence on the part of the injured party through failure to take precautions against an accident.

con-trick *n. slang* = CONFIDENCE TRICK. [abbreviation]

contrite /ˈkɒntrʌɪt/ *adj.* **1** completely penitent. **2** feeling remorse or penitence; affected by guilt. **3** (of an action) showing a contrite spirit. □ **contritely** *adv.* **contriteness** *n.* [Middle English via Old French *contrit* from Latin *contritus* 'bruised' (as COM-, *terere trit-* 'rub')]

contrition /kənˈtrɪʃ(ə)n/ *n.* the state of being contrite; thorough penitence. [Middle English via Old French from Late Latin *contritio -onis* (as CONTRITE)]

contrivance /kənˈtrʌɪv(ə)ns/ *n.* **1** something contrived, esp. a mechanical device or a plan. **2** an act of contriving, esp. deceitfully. **3** inventive capacity.

contrive /kənˈtrʌɪv/ *v.tr.* **1** devise; plan or make resourcefully or with skill. **2** (often foll. by *to* + infin.) manage (*contrived to make matters worse*). □ **contrivable** *adj.* **contriver** *n.* [Middle English via Old French *controver* 'find, imagine' from medieval Latin *contropare* 'compare']

contrived /kənˈtrʌɪvd/ *adj.* planned so carefully as to seem unnatural; artificial, forced (*the plot seemed contrived*).

control /kənˈtrəʊl/ *n.* & *v.* ● *n.* **1** the power of directing, command (*under the control of*). **2** the power of restraining, esp. self-restraint. **3** a means of restraint; a check. **4** (usu. in *pl.*) a means of regulating prices etc. **5** (usu. in *pl.*) switches and other devices by which a machine, esp. an aircraft or vehicle, is controlled (also *attrib.*: *control panel*; *control room*). **6 a** a place where something is controlled or verified. **b** a person or group that controls something. **7** a standard of comparison for checking the results of a survey or experiment (also *attrib.*: *control sample*). **8** a member of an intelligence organization who personally directs the activities of a spy. ● *v.tr.* (**controlled**, **controlling**) **1** have control or command of; dominate. **2** exert control over; regulate. **3** hold in check; restrain (*told him to control himself*). **4** serve as control to. **5** check, verify. □ **in control** (often foll. by *of*) directing an activity. **out of control** no longer subject to proper direction or restraint. **under control** being controlled; in order. □ **controllable** *adj.* **controllability** /-ˈbɪlɪti/ *n.* **controllably** *adv.* [Middle English via Anglo-French *contreroller* 'keep a copy of a roll of accounts' from medieval Latin *contrarotulare* (as CONTRA-, *rotulus* ROLL *n.*): the noun perhaps from French *contrôle*]

control group *n.* a group forming the standard of comparison in an experiment.

controller /kənˈtrəʊlə/ *n.* **1** a person or thing that controls. **2** a person in charge of expenditure, esp. a steward or comptroller. □ **controllership** *n.* [Middle English *counterroller* from Anglo-French *contrerollour* (as CONTROL)]

controlling interest *n.* a means of determining the policy of a business etc., esp. by ownership of a majority of the stock.

control rod *n.* a rod of neutron-absorbing material used to vary the output power of a nuclear reactor.

control tower *n.* a tall building at an airport etc. from which air traffic is controlled.

controversial /kɒntrəˈvəːʃ(ə)l/ *adj.* **1** causing or subject to controversy; disputed, esp. publicly. **2** of or relating to controversy. **3** given to controversy; prone to argue. □ **controversialism** *n.* **controversialist** *n.* **controversially** *adv.* [Late Latin *controversialis* (as CONTROVERSY)]

controversy /ˈkɒntrəvəːsi, kənˈtrɒvəsi/ *n.* (*pl.* **-ies**) **1** disagreement on a matter of opinion. **2** a prolonged argument or dispute, esp. when conducted publicly. [Middle English from Latin *controversia* (as CONTROVERT)]

■ **Usage** The second pronunciation, stressed on the second syllable, is considered incorrect by some people.

controvert /ˈkɒntrəvəːt, kɒntrəˈvəːt/ *v.tr.* **1** dispute, deny. **2** argue about; discuss. □ **controvertible** *adj.* [French *controvers(e)* from Latin *controversus* (as CONTRA-, *vertere vers-* 'turn')]

contumacious /kɒntjʊˈmeɪʃəs/ *adj.* insubordinate; stubbornly or wilfully disobedient, esp. to a court order. □ **contumaciously** *adv.* [Latin *contumax*, perhaps related to *tumēre* 'swell']

contumacy /ˈkɒntjʊməsi/ *n.* stubborn refusal to obey or comply. [Latin *contumacia* from *contumax*: see CONTUMACIOUS]

contumelious /kɒntjʊˈmiːlɪəs/ *adj.* reproachful, insulting, or insolent. □ **contumeliously** *adv.* [Middle English via Old French *contumelieus* from Latin *contumeliosus* (as CONTUMELY)]

contumely /ˈkɒntjuːmɪli, -tjuːmli/ *n.* **1** insolent or reproachful language or treatment. **2** disgrace. [Middle English via Old French *contumelie* from Latin *contumelia* (as COM-, *tumēre* 'swell')]

contuse /kənˈtjuːz/ *v.tr.* injure without breaking the skin; bruise. □ **contusion** *n.* [Latin *contundere contus-* (as COM-, *tundere* 'thump')]

conundrum /kəˈnʌndrəm/ *n.* **1** a riddle, esp. one with a pun in its answer. **2** a hard or puzzling question. [16th c.: origin unknown]

conurbation /kɒnəːˈbeɪʃ(ə)n/ *n.* an extended urban area, esp. one consisting of several towns and merging suburbs. [CON- + Latin *urbs urbis* 'city' + -ATION]

conure /ˈkɒnjʊə/ *n.* any medium-sized parrot of the genus *Pyrrhura*, with mainly green plumage and a long gradated tail. [modern Latin *conurus*, from Greek *kōnos* 'cone' + *oura* 'tail']

convalesce /kɒnvəˈlɛs/ *v.intr.* recover one's health after illness or medical treatment. [Middle English from Latin *convalescere* (as COM-, *valēre* 'be well')]

convalescent /kɒnvəˈlɛs(ə)nt/ *adj.* & *n.* ● *adj.* recovering from an illness. ● *n.* a convalescent person. □ **convalescence** *n.*

convection /kənˈvɛkʃ(ə)n/ *n.* **1** transference of heat in a gas or liquid by upward movement of the heated and less dense medium. **2** *Meteorol.* the transfer of heat by the upward flow of hot air or downward flow of cold air. □ **convectional** *adj.* **convective** *adj.* [Late Latin *convectio* from Latin *convehere convect-* (as COM-, *vehere vect-* 'carry')]

convection current *n.* circulation that results from convection.

convector /kən'vɛktə/ *n.* a heating appliance that circulates warm air by convection.

convenance /'kɒnvənɑːns, French kɔ̃vnɑ̃s/ *n.* (usu. in *pl.*) conventional propriety. [French from *convenir* 'be fitting' (as CONVENE)]

convene /kən'viːn/ *v.* **1** *tr.* summon or arrange (a meeting etc.). **2** *intr.* assemble. **3** *tr.* summon (a person) before a tribunal. □ **convenable** *adj.* [Middle English from Latin *convenire convent-* 'assemble, agree, fit' (as COM-, *venire* 'come')]

convener /kən'viːnə/ *n.* (also **convenor**) **1** a person who convenes a meeting. **2** *Brit.* a senior trade union official at a workplace.

convenience /kən'viːnɪəns/ *n.* **1** the quality of being convenient; suitability. **2** freedom from difficulty or trouble; material advantage (*for convenience*). **3** an advantage (*a great convenience*). **4** a useful thing, esp. an installation or piece of equipment. **5** *Brit.* a lavatory, esp. a public one. □ **at one's convenience** at a time or place that suits one. **at one's earliest convenience** as soon as one can. **make a convenience of** take advantage of (a person) insensitively. [Middle English from Latin *convenientia* (as CONVENE)]

convenience food *n.* food, esp. complete meals, sold in convenient form and requiring very little preparation.

convenience store *n.* a shop with extended opening hours, stocking a wide range of goods.

convenient /kən'viːnɪənt/ *adj.* **1** (often foll. by *for, to*) **a** serving one's comfort or interests. **b** suitable. **c** free of trouble or difficulty. **2** available or occurring at a suitable time or place (*will try to find a convenient moment*). **3 a** easily accessible. **b** well situated for some purpose (*convenient for the shops*). □ **conveniently** *adv.* [Middle English (as CONVENE)]

convenor var. of CONVENER.

convent /'kɒnv(ə)nt/ *n.* **1** a religious (usu. Christian) community, esp. of nuns, under vows. **2** the premises occupied by this. **3** (in full **convent school**) a school attached to and run by a convent. [Middle English via Anglo-French *covent*, Old French *convent* from Latin *conventus* 'assembly' (as CONVENE)]

conventicle /kən'vɛntɪk(ə)l/ *n.* esp. *hist.* **1** a secret or unlawful religious meeting, esp. of dissenters. **2** a building used for this. [Middle English from Latin *conventiculum* '(place of) assembly', diminutive of *conventus* (as CONVENE)]

convention /kən'vɛnʃ(ə)n/ *n.* **1 a** general agreement, esp. agreement on social behaviour etc. by implicit consent of the majority. **b** a custom or customary practice, esp. an artificial or formal one. **2 a** a formal assembly or conference for a common purpose. **b** *US* an assembly of the delegates of a political party to select candidates for office. **c** *hist.* a meeting of Parliament without a summons from the sovereign. **3 a** a formal agreement. **b** an agreement between states, esp. one less formal than a treaty. **4** *Cards* an accepted method of play (in leading, bidding, etc.) used to convey information to a partner. **5** the act of convening. [Middle English via Old French from Latin *conventio -onis* (as CONVENE)]

conventional /kən'vɛnʃ(ə)n(ə)l/ *adj.* **1** depending on or according with convention. **2** (of a person) attentive to social conventions. **3** usual; of agreed significance. **4** not spontaneous or sincere or original. **5** (of weapons or power) non-nuclear. **6** *Art* following tradition rather than nature. □ **conventionalism** *n.* **conventionalist** *n.* **conventionality** /-'nalɪti/ *n.* (*pl.* **-ies**). **conventionalize** *v.tr.* (also **-ise**). **conventionally** *adv.* [French *conventionnel* or Late Latin *conventionalis* (as CONVENTION)]

conventioneer /kənvɛnʃə'nɪə/ *n. US* a person attending a convention.

conventual /kən'vɛntʃʊəl/ *adj.* & *n.* ● *adj.* **1** of or belonging to a convent. **2** of the less strict branch of the Franciscans, living in large convents. ● *n.* **1** a member or inmate of a convent. **2** a conventual Franciscan. [Middle English from medieval Latin *conventualis* (as CONVENT)]

converge /kən'vəːdʒ/ *v.intr.* **1** come together as if to meet or join. **2** (of lines) tend to meet at a point. **3** (foll. by *on, upon*) approach from different directions. **4** *Math.* (of a series) approximate in the sum of its terms towards a definite limit. [Late Latin *convergere* (as COM-, *vergere* 'incline')]

convergent /kən'vəːdʒ(ə)nt/ *adj.* **1** converging. **2** *Biol.* (of unrelated organisms) showing a tendency to become similar while evolving to fill a similar ecological niche. **3** *Psychol.* (of thought) tending to reach only the most rational result. □ **convergence** *n.* **convergency** *n.*

conversant /kən'vəːs(ə)nt/ *adj.* (foll. by *with*) well experienced or acquainted with a subject, person, etc. □ **conversance** *n.* **conversancy** *n.* [Middle English from Old French, pres. part. of *converser* CONVERSE[1]]

conversation /kɒnvə'seɪʃ(ə)n/ *n.* **1** the informal exchange of ideas, information, etc. by spoken words. **2** an instance of this. [Middle English via Old French from Latin *conversatio -onis* (as CONVERSE[1])]

conversational /kɒnvə'seɪʃ(ə)n(ə)l/ *adj.* **1** of or in conversation. **2** fond of or good at conversation. **3** colloquial. □ **conversationally** *adv.*

conversationalist /kɒnvə'seɪʃ(ə)n(ə)lɪst/ *n.* a person who is good at or fond of conversing.

conversation piece *n.* **1** a small genre painting of a group of figures. **2** a thing that serves as a topic of conversation because of its unusualness etc.

conversation stopper *n. colloq.* an unexpected remark, esp. one that cannot readily be answered.

conversazione /ˌkɒnvəsatsɪ'əʊni, Italian konversat'tsjoːne/ *n.* (*pl.* ***conversaziones*** or ***conversazioni*** *pronunc.* same) a social gathering held by a learned or art society. [Italian from Latin (as CONVERSATION)]

converse[1] *v.* & *n.* ● *v.intr.* /kən'vəːs/ (often foll. by *with*) engage in conversation (*conversed with him about various subjects*). ● *n.* /'kɒnvəːs/ *archaic* conversation. □ **converser** /kən'vəːsə/ *n.* [Middle English via Old French *converser* from Latin *conversari* 'keep company (with)', frequentative of *convertere* (CONVERT)]

converse[2] /'kɒnvəːs/ *adj.* & *n.* ● *adj.* opposite, contrary, reversed. ● *n.* **1** something that is opposite or contrary. **2** a statement formed from another statement by the transposition of certain words, e.g. *some philosophers are men* from *some men are philosophers*. **3** *Math.* a theorem whose hypothesis and conclusion are the conclusion and hypothesis of another. □ **conversely** /'kɒnvəːsli, kən'vəːsli/ *adv.* [Latin *conversus*, past part. of *convertere* (see CONVERT)]

conversion /kən'vəːʃ(ə)n/ *n.* **1** the act or an instance of converting or the process of being converted, esp. in belief or religion. **2 a** an adaptation of a building for new purposes. **b** *Brit.* a converted building. **3** transposition, inversion. **4** *Theol.* the turning of sinners to God. **5** the transformation of fertile into fissile material in a nuclear reactor. **6** *Rugby* & *Amer. Football* the scoring of points by a successful kick at goal after scoring a try. **7** *Psychol.* the change of an unconscious conflict into a physical disorder or disease. [Middle English via Old French from Latin *conversio -onis* (as CONVERT)]

convert *v.* & *n.* ● *v.* /kən'vəːt/ **1** *tr.* (usu. foll. by *into*) change in form, character, or function. **2** *tr.* cause (a person) to change beliefs, opinion, party, etc. **3** *tr.* change (moneys, stocks, units in which a quantity is expressed, etc.) into others of a different kind. **4** *tr.* make structural alterations in (a building) to serve a new purpose. **5 a** *tr.* (also *absol.*) *Rugby* score extra points from (a try) by a successful kick at goal. **b** *intr. Amer. Football* make a conversion after a touchdown by kicking a goal or crossing the goal line. **6** *intr.* be converted or convertible (*the sofa converts into a bed*). **7** *tr. Logic* interchange the terms of (a proposition). ● *n.* /ˈkɒnvəːt/ (often foll. by *to*) a person who has been converted to a different belief, opinion, etc. □ **convert to one's own use** wrongfully make use of (another's property). [Middle English from Old French *convertir*, ultimately from Latin *convertere convers-* 'turn about' (as COM-, *vertere* 'turn')]

converter /kənˈvəːtə/ *n.* (also **convertor**) **1** a person or thing that converts. **2** *Electr.* **a** an electrical apparatus for the interconversion of alternating current and direct current. **b** *Electronics* an apparatus for converting a signal from one frequency to another. **3** a reaction vessel used in making steel.

converter reactor *n.* a nuclear reactor that converts fertile material into fissile material.

convertible /kənˈvəːtɪb(ə)l/ *adj.* & *n.* ● *adj.* **1** that may be converted. **2** (of currency etc.) that may be converted into other forms, esp. into gold or US dollars. **3** (of a car) having a folding or detachable roof. **4** (of terms) synonymous. ● *n.* a car with a folding or detachable roof. □ **convertibility** /-ˈbɪlɪti/ *n.* **convertibly** *adv.* [Old French from Latin *convertibilis* (as CONVERT)]

convex /ˈkɒnvɛks/ *adj.* having an outline or surface curved like the exterior of a circle or sphere (cf. CONCAVE). □ **convexity** /-ˈvɛksɪti/ *n.* **convexly** *adv.* [Latin *convexus* 'vaulted, arched']

convey /kənˈveɪ/ *v.tr.* **1** transport or carry (goods, passengers, etc.). **2** communicate (an idea, meaning, etc.). **3** *Law* transfer the title to (property). **4** transmit (sound, smell, etc.). □ **conveyable** *adj.* [Middle English via Old French *conveier* from medieval Latin *conviare* (as COM-, Latin *via* 'way')]

conveyance /kənˈveɪəns/ *n.* **1 a** the act or process of carrying. **b** the communication (of ideas etc.). **c** transmission. **2** a means of transport; a vehicle. **3** *Law* **a** the transfer of property from one owner to another. **b** a document effecting this. □ **conveyancer** *n.* (in sense 3). **conveyancing** *n.* (in sense 3).

conveyor /kənˈveɪə/ *n.* (also **conveyer**) a person or thing that conveys.

conveyor belt *n.* an endless moving belt for conveying articles or materials, esp. in a factory.

convict *v.* & *n.* ● *v.tr.* /kənˈvɪkt/ **1** (often foll. by *of*) prove to be guilty (of a crime etc.). **2** declare guilty by the verdict of a jury or the decision of a judge. ● *n.* /ˈkɒnvɪkt/ **1** a person found guilty of a criminal offence. **2** a person serving a prison sentence, esp. *hist.* in a penal colony. [Middle English from Latin *convincere convict-* (as COM-, *vincere* 'conquer'): noun from obsolete *convict* 'convicted']

conviction /kənˈvɪkʃ(ə)n/ *n.* **1 a** the act or process of proving or finding guilty. **b** an instance of this (*has two previous convictions*). **2 a** the action or resulting state of being convinced. **b** a firm belief or opinion. **c** an act of convincing. [Latin *convictio* (as CONVICT)]

convince /kənˈvɪns/ *v.tr.* **1** (often foll. by *of*, or *that* + clause) persuade (a person) to believe or realize. **2** (as **convinced** *adj.*) firmly persuaded (*a convinced pacifist*). □ **convincer** *n.* **convincible** *adj.* [Latin (as CONVICT)]

convincing /kənˈvɪnsɪŋ/ *adj.* **1** able to or such as to convince. **2** leaving no margin of doubt; substantial (*a convincing victory*). □ **convincingly** *adv.*

convivial /kənˈvɪvɪəl/ *adj.* **1** fond of good company; sociable and lively. **2** festive (*a convivial atmosphere*). □ **conviviality** /-ˈalɪti/ *n.* **convivially** *adv.* [Latin *convivialis* from *convivium* 'feast' (as COM-, *vivere* 'live')]

convocation /kɒnvəˈkeɪʃ(ə)n/ *n.* **1** the act of calling together. **2** a large formal gathering of people, esp.: **a** *Brit.* a provincial synod of the Anglican clergy of Canterbury or York. **b** *Brit.* a legislative or deliberative assembly of a university. **3** *N. Amer.* a formal ceremony for the conferment of university awards. □ **convocational** *adj.* [Middle English from Latin *convocatio* (as CONVOKE)]

convoke /kənˈvəʊk/ *v.tr. formal* call (people) together to a meeting etc.; summon to assemble. [Latin *convocare convocat-* (as COM-, *vocare* 'call')]

convoluted /ˈkɒnvəl(j)uːtɪd/ *adj.* **1** coiled, twisted. **2** complex, intricate. □ **convolutedly** *adv.* [past part. of *convolute*, from Latin *convolutus*, (as COM-, *volvere volut-* 'roll')]

convolution /kɒnvəˈluːʃ(ə)n/ *n.* **1** coiling, twisting. **2** a coil or twist. **3** complexity. **4** a sinuous fold in the surface of the brain. □ **convolutional** *adj.* [medieval Latin *convolutio* (as CONVOLUTED)]

convolve /kənˈvɒlv/ *v.tr.* & *intr.* (esp. as **convolved** *adj.*) roll together; coil up. [Latin *convolvere* (as CONVOLUTED)]

convolvulus /kənˈvɒlvjʊləs/ *n.* (*pl.* **convolvuluses**) any twining plant of the genus *Convolvulus*, with trumpet-shaped flowers, e.g. bindweed. [Latin, = bindweed (as CON-, *volvulus* from *volvere* 'to roll')]

convoy /ˈkɒnvɔɪ/ *n.* & *v.* ● *n.* **1** a group of ships travelling together or under escort. **2** a supply of provisions etc. under escort. **3** a group of vehicles travelling on land together or under escort. **4** the act of travelling or moving in a group or under escort. ● *v.tr.* **1** (of a warship) escort (a merchant or passenger vessel). **2** escort, esp. with armed force. □ **in convoy** under escort with others; as a group. [Old French *convoyer*, variant of *conveier* CONVEY]

convulsant /kənˈvʌls(ə)nt/ *adj.* & *n. Pharm.* ● *adj.* producing convulsions. ● *n.* a drug that may produce convulsions. [French from *convulser* (as CONVULSE)]

convulse /kənˈvʌls/ *v.tr.* **1** (usu. in *passive*) affect with convulsions. **2** *colloq.* cause to laugh uncontrollably. **3** shake violently; agitate, disturb. [Latin *convellere convuls-* 'pull violently, wrench' (as COM-, *vellere* 'pull')]

convulsion /kənˈvʌlʃ(ə)n/ *n.* **1** (usu. in *pl.*) violent irregular motion of a limb or limbs or the body caused by involuntary contraction of muscles, esp. as a disorder of infants. **2** a violent natural disturbance, esp. an earthquake. **3** violent social or political agitation. **4** (in *pl.*) *colloq.* uncontrollable laughter. □ **convulsionary** *adj.* [French *convulsion* or Latin *convulsio* (as CONVULSE)]

convulsive /kənˈvʌlsɪv/ *adj.* **1** characterized by or affected with convulsions. **2** producing convulsions. □ **convulsively** *adv.*

cony /ˈkəʊni/ *n.* (also **coney**) (*pl.* **-ies** or **-eys**) **1 a** *Heraldry* or *dial.* a rabbit. **b** its fur. **2** *Bibl.* a hyrax. [Middle English *cunin(g)* via Anglo-French *coning*, Old French *conin*, from Latin *cuniculus*]

coo /kuː/ *n.*, *v.*, & *int.* ● *n.* a soft murmuring sound like that of a dove or pigeon. ● *v.* (**coos, cooed**) **1** *intr.* make the sound of a coo. **2** *intr.* & *tr.* talk or say in a soft or amorous voice. ● *int. Brit. slang* expressing surprise or incredulity. [imitative]

co-occur /kəʊəˈkəː/ *v.intr.* (often foll. by *with*) occur together or simultaneously. □ **co-occurrence** /-ˈkʌr(ə)ns/ *n.*

cooee /ˈkuːɪ, -iː/ *n.*, *int.*, & *v. Brit. colloq.* ● *n.* & *int.* a sound used to attract attention, esp. at a distance. ● *v.intr.* (**cooees, cooeed, cooeeing**) make this sound. □ **within cooee** (or **a cooee**) **of** *Austral.* & *NZ colloq.* very near to. [imitative of a signal used by Australian Aboriginals and copied by settlers]

cook /kʊk/ *v.* & *n.* ● *v.* **1** *tr.* prepare (food) by heating it. **2** *intr.* (of food) undergo cooking. **3** *tr. colloq.* falsify (accounts etc.); alter to produce a desired result (esp. in **cook the books**). **4** *tr. slang* ruin, spoil. **5** *tr.* & *intr. US colloq.* do or proceed successfully. **6** *intr.* (as **be cooking**) *colloq.* be happening or about to happen (*went to find out what was cooking*). ● *n.* a person who cooks, esp. professionally or in a specified way (*a good cook*). □ **cook a person's goose** ruin a person's chances. **cook up** *colloq.* invent or concoct (a story, excuse, etc.). □ **cookable** *adj.* & *n.* [Old English *cōc*, from popular Latin *cocus* for Latin *coquus*]

cookbook /ˈkʊkbʊk/ *n.* a cookery book.

cook-chill *attrib.adj. Brit.* designating food which has been cooked and refrigerated by the manufacturer ready for reheating by the consumer.

cooker /'kʊkə/ *n.* **1 a** *Brit.* a stove used for cooking food. **b** (usu. in *comb.*) a container in which food is cooked (*pressure cooker*). **2** *Brit. colloq.* a fruit etc. (esp. an apple) that is more suitable for cooking than for eating raw.

cookery /'kʊk(ə)ri/ *n.* (*pl.* **-ies**) **1** the art or practice of cooking. **2** *US* a place or establishment for cooking.

cookery book *n. Brit.* a book containing recipes and other information about cooking.

cookhouse /'kʊkhaʊs/ *n.* **1** a camp kitchen. **2** an outdoor kitchen in warm countries. **3** a ship's galley.

cookie /'kʊki/ *n.* **1** *N. Amer.* a small sweet biscuit. **2** *slang* a person of a specified kind (*tough cookie*). **3** *Sc.* a plain bun. □ **the way the cookie crumbles** esp. *N. Amer. colloq.* how things turn out; the unalterable state of affairs. [Dutch *koekje*, diminutive of *koek* 'cake']

cooking /'kʊkɪŋ/ *n.* **1** the art or process by which food is cooked. **2** (*attrib.*) suitable for or used in cooking (*cooking apple*; *cooking utensils*).

cookout /'kʊkaʊt/ *n. N. Amer.* a gathering with an open-air cooked meal; a barbecue.

cookware /'kʊkwɛː/ *n.* utensils for cooking, esp. dishes, pans, etc.

cool /kuːl/ *adj., n., & v.* ● *adj.* **1** of or at a fairly low temperature; fairly cold (*a cool day*; *a cool bath*). **2** suggesting or achieving coolness (*cool colours*; *cool clothes*). **3** calm, unexcited. **4** lacking zeal or enthusiasm. **5** unfriendly; lacking cordiality (*got a cool reception*). **6** (of jazz playing) restrained, relaxed. **7** calmly audacious (*a cool customer*). **8** (prec. by *a*) *colloq.* (usu. as an intensive; esp. of large sums of money) not less than; a full (*cost me a cool thousand*). **9** *slang* **a** excellent, marvellous. **b** fashionable; having street credibility. ● *n.* **1** coolness. **2** cool air; a cool place. **3** *slang* calmness, composure (*keep one's cool*; *lose one's cool*). ● *v.tr. & intr.* (often foll. by *down*, *off*) make or become cool. □ **cool one's heels** see HEEL[1]. **cool it** *slang* relax, calm down. □ **coolish** *adj.* **coolly** /'kuːlli/ *adv.* **coolness** *n.* [Old English *cōl*, *cōlian*, from the Germanic base of COLD]

coolabah /'kuːləbɑː/ *n.* (also **coolibah** /-lɪbɑː/) *Austral.* any of various gum trees, esp. *Eucalyptus microtheca.* [Kamilaroi (and related languages) *gulabaa*]

coolant /'kuːl(ə)nt/ *n.* **1** a cooling agent, esp. fluid, to remove heat from an engine, nuclear reactor, etc. **2** a fluid used to lessen the friction of a cutting tool. [COOL + -ANT, on the pattern of *lubricant*]

cool bag *n.* (also **cool box**) *Brit.* an insulated container for keeping food cool.

cooler /'kuːlə/ *n.* **1** a vessel in which a thing is cooled. **2** *N. Amer.* **a** a refrigerator. **b** = COOL BAG. **3** a long drink, esp. a spritzer. **4** *slang* prison or a prison cell.

cool-headed *adj.* not easily excited.

coolibah var. of COOLABAH.

coolie /'kuːli/ *n.* (also **cooly**) (*pl.* **-ies**) **1** an unskilled native labourer in India, China, and some other Eastern countries. **2** *offens.* a person from the Indian subcontinent; a person of Indian descent. [Hindi and Telugu *Kūlī* 'day-labourer', probably from Tamil Telugu *Kūli* 'hire']

coolie hat *n.* a broad conical hat as worn by coolies.

cooling-off period *n.* an interval to allow for a change of mind before commitment to action.

cooling tower *n.* a tall structure for cooling hot water before reuse, esp. in industry.

coolth /kuːlθ/ *n.* coolness.

coomb /kuːm/ *n.* (also **combe**) *Brit.* **1** a valley or hollow on the side of a hill. **2** a short valley running up from the coast. [Old English *cumb*, from Celtic: cf. CWM]

coon /kuːn/ *n.* **1** *N. Amer.* a raccoon. **2** *slang offens.* a black person. [abbreviation]

coon-can /'kuːnkan/ *n.* a simple card game like rummy (originally Mexican). [probably from Spanish *con quién* 'with whom?']

coonskin /'kuːnskɪn/ *n.* **1** the skin of a raccoon. **2** a cap etc. made of this.

coop /kuːp/ *n. & v.* ● *n.* **1** a cage or pen for confining poultry. **2** a small place of confinement, esp. a prison. **3** *Brit.* a basket used in catching fish. ● *v.tr.* **1** put or keep (a fowl) in a coop. **2** (often foll. by *up*, *in*) confine (a person) in a small space. [Middle English *cupe* 'basket', from Middle Dutch, Middle Low German *kūpe*, ultimately from Latin *cupa* 'cask']

co-op /'kəʊɒp/ *n. colloq.* **1** *Brit.* a cooperative society or shop. **2** a cooperative business or enterprise. [abbreviation]

cooper /'kuːpə/ *n. & v.* ● *n.* a maker or repairer of casks, barrels, etc. ● *v.tr.* make or repair (a cask). [Middle English from Middle Dutch, Middle Low German *kūper*, from *kūpe* COOP]

cooperage /'kuːp(ə)rɪdʒ/ *n.* **1** the work or establishment of a cooper. **2** money payable for a cooper's work.

cooperate /kəʊ'ɒpəreɪt/ *v.intr.* (also **co-operate**) **1** (often foll. by *with*) work or act together; help, assist. **2** (of things) concur in producing an effect. □ **cooperant** *adj.* **cooperator** *n.* [ecclesiastical Latin *cooperari* (as CO-, *operari* from *opus operis* 'work')]

cooperation /kəʊˌɒpə'reɪʃ(ə)n/ *n.* (also **co-operation**) **1** the process of working together to the same end; assistance. **2** *Econ.* the formation and operation of cooperatives. [Middle English from Latin *cooperatio* (as COOPERATE): partly through French *coopération*]

cooperative /kəʊ'ɒp(ə)rətɪv/ *adj. & n.* (also **co-operative**) ● *adj.* **1** of or affording cooperation. **2** willing to cooperate. **3** *Econ.* (of a farm, business, enterprise, etc.) owned and run jointly by its members, with profits or benefits shared among them. ● *n.* a cooperative farm or society or business. □ **cooperatively** *adv.* **cooperativeness** *n.* [Late Latin *cooperativus* (as COOPERATE)]

co-opt /kəʊ'ɒpt/ *v.tr.* **1** appoint to membership of a body by invitation of the existing members. **2** absorb into a larger (esp. political) group; take over, adopt (an idea etc.). □ **co-optation** /-'teɪʃ(ə)n/ *n.* **co-option** *n.* **co-optive** *adj.* [Latin *cooptare* (as CO-, *optare* 'choose')]

coordinate *v., adj., & n.* (also **co-ordinate**) ● *v.* /kəʊ'ɔːdɪneɪt/ **1** *tr.* bring (various parts, movements, etc.) into a proper or required relation to ensure harmony or effective operation etc. **2** *intr.* work or act together effectively. ● *adj.* /kəʊ'ɔːdɪnət/ **1** equal in rank or importance. **2** in which the parts are coordinated; involving coordination. **3** *Gram.* (of parts of a compound sentence) equal in status. **4** *Chem.* denoting a type of covalent bond in which one atom provides both the shared electrons. ● *n.* /kəʊ'ɔːdɪnət/ **1** *Math.* each of a system of magnitudes used to fix the position of a point, line, or plane. **2** a person or thing equal in rank or importance. **3** (in *pl.*) matching items of clothing. □ **coordinative** /-neɪtɪv/ *adj.* **coordinator** /-neɪtə/ *n.* [CO- + Latin *ordinare ordinat-* from *ordo -inis* 'order']

Coordinated Universal Time *n.* = GREENWICH MEAN TIME (abbr.: **UTC**).

coordination /kəʊˌɔːdɪ'neɪʃ(ə)n/ *n.* **1** the harmonious or effective working together of different parts. **2** the arrangement of parts etc. into an effective relation. **3** *Chem.* the formation of a coordinate bond.

coot /kuːt/ *n.* **1** any black aquatic bird of the genus *Fulica*, esp. *F. atra* with the upper mandible extended backwards to form a white plate on the forehead. **2** *colloq.* a stupid person. [Middle English, probably from Low German]

cootie /kuːti/ *n. slang* a body louse. [perhaps from Malay *kutu*, a biting parasite]

co-own /kəʊ'əʊn/ *v.tr.* own jointly with another person or persons. □ **co-owner** *n.* **co-ownership** *n.*

cop[1] /kɒp/ *n. & v. slang* ● *n.* **1** a police officer. **2** *Brit.* a capture or arrest (*it's a fair cop*). ● *v.tr.* (**copped,**

copping) **1** catch or arrest (an offender). **2** receive, suffer. **3** take, seize. □ **cop a plea** *US slang* = PLEA BARGAIN *v.* (see PLEA BARGAINING). **cop it** *Brit.* **1** get into trouble; be punished. **2** be killed. **cop out 1** withdraw; give up an attempt. **2** go back on a promise. **3** escape. **not much** (or **no**) **cop** *Brit.* of little or no value or use. [perhaps from obsolete *cap* 'arrest' via Old French *caper* 'seize' from Latin *capere*: cf. COPPER[2]]

cop[2] /kɒp/ *n.* (in spinning) a conical ball of thread wound on a spindle. [Old English *cop* 'summit']

copacetic /kəʊpə'sɛtɪk, -'si:t-/ *adj.* *N. Amer. slang* excellent; in good order. [20th c.: origin unknown]

copaiba /kəʊ'pʌɪbə/ *n.* an aromatic oil or resin from any plant of the genus *Copaifera*, used in medicine and perfumery. [Spanish & Portuguese from Guarani *cupauba*]

copal /'kəʊp(ə)l/ *n.* a resin from any of various tropical trees, used for varnish. [Spanish from Nahuatl *copalli* 'incense']

co-partner /kəʊ'pɑ:tnə/ *n.* a partner or associate, esp. when sharing equally. □ **co-partnership** *n.*

cope[1] /kəʊp/ *v.intr.* **1** (foll. by *with*) deal effectively or contend successfully with a person or task. **2** manage successfully; deal with a situation or problem (*found they could no longer cope*). [earlier in the sense 'meet in battle': Middle English via Old French *coper, colper* (from *cop, colp* 'blow') from medieval Latin *colpus*, via Latin *colaphus* from Greek *kolaphos* 'blow with the fist']

cope[2] /kəʊp/ *n.* & *v.* ● *n.* **1** *Eccl.* a long cloaklike vestment worn by a priest or bishop in ceremonies and processions. **2** esp. *poet.* anything likened to a cloak or canopy. ● *v.tr.* cover with a cope or coping. [Middle English, ultimately from Late Latin *cappa* CAP, CAPE[1]]

copeck /'kəʊpɛk, 'kɒpɛk/ *n.* (also **kopeck, kopek**) a monetary unit of Russia and some other countries of the former USSR, equal to one-hundredth of a rouble. [Russian *kopeĭka*, diminutive of *kop'ë* 'lance' (from the figure on the coin in 1535 of Ivan IV bearing a lance instead of a sword)]

copepod /'kəʊpɪpɒd/ *n.* any small aquatic crustacean of the class Copepoda, many of which occur in plankton. [Greek *kōpē* 'oar-handle' + *pous podos* 'foot']

coper /'kəʊpə/ *n.* a horse-dealer. [obsolete *cope* 'buy', from Middle Dutch, Middle Low German *kōpen*, German *kaufen*: related to CHEAP]

Copernican system /kə'pə:nɪk(ə)n/ *n.* (also **Copernican theory**) *Astron.* the theory that the planets (including the earth) move round the sun (cf. PTOLEMAIC SYSTEM). [*Copernicus* latinized from M. *Kopernik*, Polish astronomer d. 1543]

copestone /'kəʊpstəʊn/ *n.* **1** = COPING STONE. **2** a finishing touch. [COPE[2] + STONE]

copiable /'kɒpɪəb(ə)l/ *adj.* that can or may be copied.

copier /'kɒpɪə/ *n.* a machine or person that copies (esp. documents).

co-pilot /'kəʊpʌɪlət/ *n.* a second pilot in an aircraft.

coping /'kəʊpɪŋ/ *n.* the top (usu. sloping) course of masonry in a wall or parapet. [COPE[2]]

coping saw /'kəʊpɪŋ/ *n.* a D-shaped saw for cutting curves in wood. [*cope* 'cut wood' from Old French *coper*: see COPE[1]]

coping stone *n.* a stone used in a coping.

copious /'kəʊpɪəs/ *adj.* **1** abundant, plentiful. **2** producing much. **3** providing much information. **4** profuse in speech. □ **copiously** *adv.* **copiousness** *n.* [Middle English from Old French *copieux* or from Latin *copiosus*, from *copia* 'plenty']

copita /kəʊ'pi:tə/ *n.* **1** a tulip-shaped sherry glass. **2** a glass of sherry. [Spanish, diminutive of *copa* 'cup']

coplanar /kəʊ'pleɪnə/ *adj.* *Geom.* in the same plane. □ **coplanarity** /-plə'narɪti/ *n.*

copolymer /kəʊ'pɒlɪmə/ *n.* *Chem.* a polymer with units of more than one kind. □ **copolymerize** *v.tr.* & *intr.* (also **-ise**). **copolymerization** /-rʌɪ'zeɪʃ(ə)n/ *n.* (also **-isation**).

cop-out *n.* **1** a cowardly or feeble evasion. **2** an escape; a way of escape.

copper[1] /'kɒpə/ *n., adj.,* & *v.* ● *n.* **1** *Chem.* a malleable red-brown metallic element of the transition series occurring naturally esp. in cuprite and malachite, and used esp. for electrical wiring (symbol **Cu**). **2** (usu. in *pl.*) a bronze coin, esp. one of little value. **3** *Brit.* a large metal vessel for boiling esp. laundry. **4** any of various butterflies with copper-coloured wings. ● *adj.* made of or coloured like copper. ● *v.tr.* cover (a ship's bottom, a pan, etc.) with copper. [Old English *copor, coper*, ultimately from Latin *cyprium aes* 'Cyprus metal']

copper[2] /'kɒpə/ *n. slang* a police officer. [COP[1] + -ER[1]]

copperas /'kɒp(ə)rəs/ *n.* hydrated ferrous sulphate, forming green crystals. [Middle English *coperose* via Old French *couperose* from medieval Latin *cup(e)rosa*: perhaps originally *aqua cuprosa* 'copper water']

copper beech *n.* a variety of beech with copper-coloured leaves.

copper belt *n.* a copper-mining area of central Africa.

copper bit *n.* a soldering tool pointed with copper.

copper-bottomed *adj.* **1** (esp. of a ship or pan) having a bottom sheathed with copper. **2** *Brit.* genuine or reliable, esp. financially.

copperhead /'kɒpəhɛd/ *n.* **1** a venomous viper, *Agkistrodon contortrix*, native to N. America. **2** a venomous cobra, *Denisonia superba*, native to Australia.

copperplate /'kɒpəpleɪt/ *n.* & *adj.* ● *n.* **1 a** a polished copper plate for engraving or etching. **b** a print made from this. **2** an ornate style of handwriting resembling that originally used in engravings. ● *adj.* of or in copperplate writing.

copper pyrites *n.* = CHALCOPYRITE.

coppersmith /'kɒpəsmɪθ/ *n.* a person who works in copper.

copper sulphate *n.* a blue crystalline solid used in electroplating, textile dyeing, etc.

copper vitriol *n.* copper sulphate.

coppery /'kɒp(ə)ri/ *adj.* of or like copper, esp. in colour.

coppice /'kɒpɪs/ *n.* & *v.* ● *n.* an area of undergrowth and small trees, grown for periodic cutting. ● *v.* **1** *tr.* cut back (young trees) periodically to stimulate growth of shoots. **2** *intr.* (of a tree) produce new shoots from a stump. □ **coppiced** *adj.* [Old French *copeïz*, ultimately from medieval Latin *colpus* 'blow': see COPE[1]]

copra /'kɒprə/ *n.* the dried kernels of the coconut. [Portuguese, from Malayalam *koppara* 'coconut']

co-precipitation /ˌkəʊprɪsɪpɪ'teɪʃ(ə)n/ *n.* *Chem.* the simultaneous precipitation of more than one compound from a solution.

copro- /'kɒprəʊ/ *comb. form* dung, faeces. [Greek *kopros* 'dung']

coprocessor /kəʊ'prəʊsɛsə/ *n.* *Computing* a microprocessor providing additional functions to supplement a primary processor.

co-produce /kəʊprə'dju:s/ *v.tr.* produce (a play, broadcast, etc.) jointly. □ **co-producer** *n.* **co-production** /-'dʌkʃ(ə)n/ *n.*

coprolite /'kɒprəlʌɪt/ *n.* *Archaeol.* fossil dung or a piece of it.

coprophagous /kɒ'prɒfəgəs/ *adj.* *Zool.* dung-eating. [COPRO-]

coprophilia /kɒprə(ʊ)'fɪlɪə/ *n.* an abnormal interest in faeces and defecation.

coprosma /kə'prɒzmə/ *n.* any small evergreen plant of the genus *Coprosma*, native to Australasia. [modern Latin, from Greek *kopros* 'dung' + *osmē* 'smell']

copse /kɒps/ *n.* **1** = COPPICE. **2** (in general use) a small wood. [shortened from COPPICE]

copsewood /'kɒpswʊd/ *n.* undergrowth.

cop shop *n.* *Brit.* a police station.

Copt /kɒpt/ *n.* **1** a native Egyptian in the Hellenistic and Roman periods. **2** a native Christian of the independent Egyptian Church. [French *Copte* or modern Latin

Coptus via Arabic *al-kibt, al-kubt* 'Copts' and Coptic *Gyptios* from Greek *Aiguptios* 'Egyptian']

Coptic /ˈkɒptɪk/ *n. & adj.* ● *n.* the language of the Copts, now used only in the Coptic Church. ● *adj.* of or relating to the Copts or their language.

copula /ˈkɒpjʊlə/ *n.* (*pl.* **copulas**) *Logic & Gram.* a connecting word, esp. a part of the verb *be* connecting a subject and predicate. □ **copular** *adj.* [Latin (as co-, *apere* 'fasten')]

copulate /ˈkɒpjʊleɪt/ *v.intr.* (often foll. by *with*) have sexual intercourse. □ **copulatory** *adj.* [Latin *copulare* 'fasten together' (as COPULA)]

copulation /kɒpjʊˈleɪʃ(ə)n/ *n.* **1** sexual union. **2** a grammatical or logical connection. [Middle English via Old French from Latin *copulatio* (as COPULATE)]

copulative /ˈkɒpjʊlətɪv/ *adj.* **1** serving to connect. **2** *Gram.* **a** (of a word) that connects words or clauses linked in sense (cf. DISJUNCTIVE 2). **b** connecting a subject and predicate. **3** relating to sexual union. □ **copulatively** *adv.* [Middle English from Old French *copulatif -ive* or Late Latin *copulativus* (as COPULATE)]

copy /ˈkɒpi/ *n. & v.* ● *n.* (*pl.* **-ies**) **1** a thing made to imitate or be identical to another. **2** a single specimen of a publication or issue (*ordered twenty copies*). **3 a** matter to be printed. **b** material for a newspaper or magazine article (*scandals make good copy*). **c** the text of an advertisement. **4 a** a model to be copied. **b** a page written after a model (of penmanship). ● *v.* (**-ies**, **-ied**) **1** *tr.* **a** make a copy of. **b** (often foll. by *out*) transcribe. **2** *intr.* make a copy rather than produce something original. **3** *tr.* (foll. by *to*) send a copy of (a letter) to a third party. **4** *tr.* do the same as; imitate. [Middle English from Old French *copie, copier*, ultimately from Latin *copia* 'abundance', pl. 'ability, opportunity' (in medieval Latin = transcript, from such phrases as *copiam describendi facere* 'give permission to transcribe')]

copybook /ˈkɒpɪbʊk/ *n.* **1** a book containing models of handwriting for learners to imitate. **2** (*attrib.*) **a** tritely conventional. **b** accurate, exemplary.

copycat /ˈkɒpɪkat/ *n.* **1** *colloq.* (esp. as a child's word) a person who copies another, esp. slavishly. **2** (*attrib.*) in imitation of a person, act, event, etc. (*copycat crimes*).

copydesk /ˈkɒpɪdɛsk/ *n.* the desk at which copy is edited for printing.

copy-edit *v.tr.* (**-edited**, **-editing**) edit (copy) for printing. □ **copy editor** *n.*

copyhold /ˈkɒpɪhəʊld/ *n. Brit. hist.* **1** tenure of land based on manorial records. **2** land held in this way.

copyholder /ˈkɒpɪhəʊldə/ *n.* **1** *Brit. hist.* a person who held land in copyhold. **2** a clasp for holding copy while it is keyboarded, typed, etc.

copyist /ˈkɒpɪɪst/ *n.* **1** a person who makes (esp. written) copies. **2** an imitator. [earlier *copist*, from French *copiste* or medieval Latin *copista* (as COPY)]

copyreader /ˈkɒpɪriːdə/ *n.* a person who reads and edits copy for a newspaper or book. □ **copyread** *v.tr.* (*past* and *past part.* **copyread** /-rɛd/).

copyright /ˈkɒpɪrʌɪt/ *n., adj., & v.* ● *n.* the exclusive legal right, given to the originator or his or her assignee for a fixed number of years, to print, publish, perform, film, or record literary, artistic, or musical material, and to authorize others to do the same. ● *adj.* (of such material) protected by copyright. ● *v.tr.* secure copyright for (material).

copyright library *n. Brit.* a library entitled to a free copy of each book published in the UK.

copy-typist *n.* a person who makes typewritten transcripts of documents.

copywriter /ˈkɒpɪrʌɪtə/ *n.* a person who writes or prepares copy (esp. of advertising material) for publication. □ **copywriting** *n.*

coq au vin /kɒk əʊ ˈvã/ *n.* a casserole of chicken pieces cooked in wine. [French]

coquetry /ˈkɒkɪtri, ˈkəʊ-/ *n.* (*pl.* **-ies**) **1** coquettish behaviour. **2** a coquettish act. **3** trifling with serious matters. [French *coquetterie* from *coqueter* (as COQUETTE)]

coquette /kɒˈkɛt/ *n.* **1** a woman who flirts. **2** any crested hummingbird of the genus *Lophornis*. □ **coquettish** *adj.* **coquettishly** *adv.* **coquettishness** *n.* [French, fem. of *coquet* 'wanton', diminutive of *coq* 'cock']

coquina /kəʊˈkiːnə/ *n.* a soft limestone of broken shells, used in road-making in the W. Indies and Florida. [Spanish, = cockle]

coquito /kəʊˈkiːtəʊ/ *n.* (*pl.* **-os**) a palm tree, *Jubaea chilensis*, native to Chile, yielding honey from its sap, and fibre. [Spanish, diminutive of *coco* 'coconut']

Cor. *abbr.* **1** Corinthians (New Testament). **2** *US* coroner.

cor /kɔː/ *int. Brit. slang* expressing surprise, excitement, alarm, etc. □ **cor blimey** see BLIMEY. [corruption of *God*]

cor- /kɒ, kə/ *prefix* assim. form of COM- before *r*.

coracle /ˈkɒrək(ə)l/ *n. Brit.* a small boat of wickerwork covered with watertight material, used on Welsh and Irish lakes and rivers. [Welsh *corwgl* (= Irish *currach* 'small boat': cf. CURRACH)]

coracoid /ˈkɒrəkɔɪd/ *n.* (in full **coracoid process**) a short projection from the shoulder blade in vertebrates. [modern Latin *coracoides* from Greek *korakoeidēs* 'raven-like', from *korax -akos* 'raven']

coral /ˈkɒr(ə)l/ *n. & adj.* ● *n.* **1 a** a hard calcareous substance secreted by certain marine coelenterates as an external skeleton and often forming large reefs. **b** any similar substance secreted by other marine organisms, esp. (in full **red coral**) a tough red substance produced by gorgonians of the genus *Corallium* and used in jewellery. **2** a marine coelenterate of the class Anthozoa, with a calcareous, horny, or soft skeleton, and often colonial, esp. (**stony** or **true coral**) of the reef-forming order Madreporaria. **3** a pinkish-red colour. **4** the unfertilized roe of a lobster or scallop. ● *adj.* **1** of a pinkish-red colour. **2** made of coral. [Middle English via Old French and Latin *corallum* from Greek *korallion*, probably of Semitic origin]

coral island *n.* an island formed by the growth of coral.

coralline /ˈkɒrəlʌɪn/ *n. & adj.* ● *n.* **1** any seaweed of the genus *Corallina* having a calcareous jointed stem. **2** (in general use) the name of various plantlike compound organisms. ● *adj.* **1** = CORAL *adj.* 1. **2** of or like coral. [French *corallin* & Italian *corallina* from Late Latin *corallinus* (as CORAL)]

corallite /ˈkɒrəlʌɪt/ *n.* **1** the coral skeleton of a marine polyp. **2** fossil coral. [Latin *corallum* CORAL]

coralloid /ˈkɒrəlɔɪd/ *adj. & n.* ● *adj.* like or akin to coral. ● *n.* a coralloid organism.

coral rag *n.* limestone containing beds of petrified corals.

coral reef *n.* a reef formed by the growth of coral.

coral-root *n.* **1** a woodland plant, *Cardamine bulbifera* (family Cruciferae), with purple flowers and scaly rhizomes. **2** (in full **coral-root orchid**) a brown saprophytic orchid of the genus *Corallorhiza*.

coral snake *n.* any of various brightly coloured snakes of the cobra family, esp. a venomous one of the American genus *Micrurus*.

coram populo /ˌkɔːrəm ˈpɒpjʊləʊ/ *adv.* in public. [Latin, = in the presence of the people]

cor anglais /kɔːr ˈɑːŋgleɪ, ˈɒŋgleɪ/ *n.* (*pl.* **cors anglais** *pronunc.* same) *Mus.* **1** an alto woodwind instrument of the oboe family. **2** a player of this instrument. **3** an organ stop with the quality of a cor anglais. [French, = English horn]

corbel /ˈkɔːb(ə)l/ *n. & v. Archit.* ● *n.* **1** a projection of stone, timber, etc., jutting out from a wall to support a weight. **2** a short timber laid longitudinally under a beam to help support it. ● *v.tr. & intr.* (**corbelled**, **corbelling**; *US* **corbeled**, **corbeling**) (foll. by *out, off*) support or project on corbels. [Middle English from Old

French, diminutive of *corp* 'crow' (see CORBIE): perhaps from the shape of a corbel, resembling a crow's beak]

corbel-table *n.* a projecting course resting on corbels.

corbie /ˈkɔːbi/ *n. Sc.* **1** a raven. **2** a carrion crow. [Middle English via Old French *corb, corp* from Latin *corvus* 'crow']

corbie-step *n.* (usu. in *pl.*) each of several steplike projections on the sloping sides of a gable.

cord /kɔːd/ *n. & v.* ● *n.* **1 a** long thin flexible string or rope made from several twisted strands. **b** a piece of this. **2** *Anat.* a structure in the body resembling a cord (*spinal cord*). **3 a** ribbed fabric, esp. corduroy. **b** (in *pl.*) corduroy trousers. **c** a cordlike rib on fabric. **4** an electric flex. **5** a measure of cut wood (usu. 128 cu.ft, 3.62 cubic metres). **6** a moral or emotional tie (*cords of affection*). ● *v.tr.* **1** fasten or bind with cord. **2** (as **corded** *adj.*) **a** (of cloth) ribbed. **b** provided with cords. **c** (of muscles) standing out like taut cords. □ **cordlike** *adj.* [Middle English via Old French *corde* and Latin *chorda* from Greek *khordē* 'gut, string of musical instrument']

cordage /ˈkɔːdɪdʒ/ *n.* cords or ropes, esp. in the rigging of a ship. [Middle English from French (as CORD)]

cordate /ˈkɔːdeɪt/ *adj.* heart-shaped. [modern Latin *cordatus* from Latin *cor cordis* 'heart']

Cordelier /kɔːdɪˈlɪə/ *n.* a Franciscan Observant (wearing a knotted cord round the waist). [Middle English from Old French from *cordele*, diminutive of *corde* CORD]

cordial /ˈkɔːdɪəl/ *adj. & n.* ● *adj.* **1** heartfelt, sincere. **2** warm, friendly. ● *n.* **1** *Brit.* a fruit-flavoured drink. **2** a comforting or pleasant-tasting medicine. **3** = LIQUEUR. □ **cordiality** /-ˈalɪti/ *n.* **cordially** *adv.* [Middle English via medieval Latin *cordialis* from Latin *cor cordis* 'heart']

cordillera /kɔːdɪlˈjɛːrə/ *n.* a system or group of usu. parallel mountain ranges together with intervening plateaux etc., esp. of the Andes and in Central America and Mexico. [Spanish from *cordilla*, diminutive of *cuerda* CORD]

cordite /ˈkɔːdʌɪt/ *n.* a smokeless explosive made from nitrocellulose and nitroglycerine. [CORD (from its appearance) + -ITE[1]]

cordless /ˈkɔːdlɪs/ *adj.* (of an electrical appliance, telephone, etc.) working without connection to a mains supply or central unit.

cordon /ˈkɔːd(ə)n/ *n. & v.* ● *n.* **1** a line or circle of police, soldiers, guards, etc., esp. preventing access to or from an area. **2 a** an ornamental cord or braid. **b** the ribbon of a knightly order. **3** a fruit tree trained to grow as a single stem. **4** *Archit.* a string-course. ● *v.tr.* (often foll. by *off*) enclose or separate with a cordon of police etc. [Italian *cordone*, augmentative of *corda* CORD, & French *cordon* (as CORD)]

cordon bleu /ˌkɔːdɒ̃ ˈbləː/ *adj. & n. Cookery* ● *adj.* of the highest class. ● *n.* a cook of this class. [French, = blue ribbon]

cordon sanitaire /ˌkɔːdɒ̃ sanɪˈtɛː/ *n.* **1** a guarded line between infected and uninfected districts. **2** any measure designed to prevent communication or the spread of undesirable influences. [French]

cordovan /ˈkɔːdəv(ə)n/ *n.* a kind of soft leather. [Spanish *cordovan* 'of Córdova' (Córdoba, a city in southern Spain) where it was originally made]

corduroy /ˈkɔːdərɔɪ/ *n.* **1** a thick cotton fabric with velvety ribs. **2** (in *pl.*) corduroy trousers. [18th c.: probably from CORD 'ribbed fabric' + obsolete *duroy* 'coarse woollen fabric']

corduroy road *n.* a road made of tree trunks laid across a swamp.

cordwainer /ˈkɔːdweɪnə/ *n. Brit. archaic* a shoemaker (usu. in names of guilds etc.). [obsolete *cordwain* CORDOVAN]

cordwood /ˈkɔːdwʊd/ *n.* wood that is or can easily be measured in cords.

CORE *abbr.* (in the US) Congress of Racial Equality.

core /kɔː/ *n. & v.* ● *n.* **1** the horny central part of various fruits, containing the seeds. **2 a** the central or most important part of anything (also *attrib.*: *core curriculum*). **b** the central part, of different character from the surroundings. **3** the central region of the earth. **4** the central part of a nuclear reactor, containing the fissile material. **5** a magnetic structural unit in a computer, storing one bit of data (see BIT[4]). **6** the inner strand of an electric cable, rope, etc. **7** a piece of soft iron forming the centre of an electromagnet or an induction coil. **8** an internal mould filling a space to be left hollow in a casting. **9** an internal part cut out (esp. of rock etc. in boring). **10** *Archaeol.* a piece of flint from which flakes or blades have been removed. ● *v.tr.* remove the core from. □ **corer** *n.* (usu. in *comb.*). [Middle English: origin unknown]

corelation var. of CORRELATION.

co-religionist /kəʊrɪˈlɪdʒ(ə)nɪst/ *n.* (*US* **coreligionist**) an adherent of the same religion.

corella /kəˈrɛlə/ *n.* any of several small Australian cockatoos of the genus *Cacatua* with pink-tinged white plumage and blue skin around the eye. [Wiradhuri]

core memory *n.* the memory of a computer consisting of many cores.

coreopsis /kɒrɪˈɒpsɪs/ *n.* any plant of the genus *Coreopsis* (daisy family), having rayed usu. yellow flowers. [modern Latin, from Greek *koris* 'bug' + *opsis* 'appearance', with reference to the shape of the seed]

co-respondent /kəʊrɪˈspɒnd(ə)nt/ *n.* (*US* **corespondent**) a person cited in a divorce case as having committed adultery with the respondent.

core time *n. Brit.* (in a flexitime system) the central part of the working day, when all employees must be present.

corf /kɔːf/ *n.* (*pl.* **corves** /kɔːvz/) *Brit.* **1** a basket in which fish are kept alive in the water. **2** a small wagon, formerly a large basket, used in mining. [Middle Dutch, Middle Low German *korf*, Old High German *chorp*, *korb*, from Latin *corbis* 'basket']

corgi /ˈkɔːgi/ *n.* (in full **Welsh corgi**) (*pl.* **corgis**) **1** a dog of a short-legged breed with foxlike head. **2** this breed. [Welsh from *cor* 'dwarf' + *ci* 'dog']

coriaceous /kɒrɪˈeɪʃəs/ *adj.* like leather; leathery. [Late Latin *coriaceus* from *corium* 'leather']

coriander /kɒrɪˈandə/ *n.* **1** an umbelliferous plant, *Coriandrum sativum*, with leaves used for flavouring and small round aromatic fruits. **2** (also **coriander seed**) the dried fruit of this plant used for flavouring curries etc. [Middle English via Old French *coriandre* and Latin *coriandrum* from Greek *koriannon*]

Corinthian /kəˈrɪnθɪən/ *adj. & n.* ● *adj.* **1** of or relating to ancient Corinth in southern Greece. **2** *Archit.* of an order characterized by ornate decoration and flared capitals with rows of acanthus leaves, used esp. by the Romans. **3** amateur (in sport). **4** *archaic* profligate. ● *n.* **1** a native of Corinth. **2** a wealthy amateur of sport. [Latin *Corinthius* from Greek *Korinthios* + -AN]

Coriolis effect /kɒrɪˈəʊlɪs/ *n.* an effect whereby a mass moving in a rotating system is accelerated perpendicular to its motion and to the axis of rotation, which helps to explain why wind patterns are clockwise in the northern hemisphere and anticlockwise in the southern. [named after G. G. *Coriolis*, French engineer d. 1843]

corium /ˈkɔːrɪəm/ *n. Anat.* the dermis. [Latin, = skin]

cork /kɔːk/ *n. & v.* ● *n.* **1 a** the buoyant light brown material obtained from beneath the bark of the cork oak. **b** *Bot.* a protective layer of dead cells immediately below the bark of woody plants. **2** a bottle stopper of cork or other material. **3** a float of cork used in fishing etc. **4** (*attrib.*) made of cork. ● *v.tr.* (often foll. by *up*) **1** stop or confine. **2** restrain (feelings etc.). **3** blacken with burnt cork. □ **corklike** *adj.* [Middle English via Dutch and Low German *kork* from Spanish *alcorque* 'cork sole', perhaps from Arabic]

corkage /ˈkɔːkɪdʒ/ *n.* a charge made by a restaurant or hotel for serving wine etc. when brought in by customers.

corked /kɔːkt/ *adj.* **1** stopped with a cork. **2** (of wine) spoilt by a decayed cork. **3** blackened with burnt cork.

corker /ˈkɔːkə/ *n. slang* an excellent or astonishing person or thing.

corking /ˈkɔːkɪŋ/ *adj.* esp. *Brit. slang* strikingly large or splendid.

cork oak *n.* an evergreen Mediterranean oak, *Quercus suber*, yielding cork.

corkscrew /ˈkɔːkskruː/ *n. & v.* ● *n.* **1** a spirally twisted steel device for extracting corks from bottles. **2** (often *attrib.*) a thing with a spiral shape. ● *v.tr. & intr.* move spirally; twist.

cork-tipped *adj. Brit.* (of a cigarette) having a filter of corklike material.

corkwood /ˈkɔːkwʊd/ *n.* **1** a shrub or tree yielding a light porous wood, esp. *Leitneria floridana* of the US and *Eritelea arborescens* of New Zealand. **2** this wood.

corky /ˈkɔːki/ *adj.* (**corkier**, **corkiest**) **1** corklike. **2** (of wine) corked.

corm /kɔːm/ *n. Bot.* an underground swollen stem base of some plants, e.g. the crocus. [modern Latin *cormus* from Greek *kormos* 'trunk with boughs lopped off']

cormorant /ˈkɔːm(ə)r(ə)nt/ *n.* any diving seabird of the family Phalacrocoracidae, esp. *Phalacrocorax carbo*, which has lustrous black plumage. [Middle English via Old French *cormaran* from medieval Latin *corvus marinus* 'sea-raven': for ending *-ant* cf. *peasant, tyrant*]

corn[1] /kɔːn/ *n. & v.* ● *n.* **1 a** esp. *Brit.* any cereal before or after harvesting, esp. the chief crop of a region, e.g. wheat, oats, etc. **b** *US & Austral.* = MAIZE. **c** a grain or seed of a cereal plant. **2** *colloq.* something corny or trite. ● *v.tr.* (as **corned** *adj.*) sprinkled or preserved with salt or brine (*corned beef*). [Old English from Germanic: related to Latin *granum* 'grain']

corn[2] /kɔːn/ *n.* a small area of horny usu. tender skin esp. on the toes, extending into subcutaneous tissue. [Middle English via Anglo-French from Latin *cornu* 'horn']

cornbrash /ˈkɔːnbraʃ/ *n. Brit. Geol.* an earthy limestone layer of the Jurassic period. [CORN[1] + BRASH[2]]

cornbread /ˈkɔːnbrɛd/ *n.* bread made of the meal of maize.

corn chandler *n.* a dealer in corn.

corn circle *n.* = CROP CIRCLE.

corn cob *n.* the cylindrical centre of the maize ear to which rows of grains are attached.

corn-cob pipe *n.* a tobacco pipe made from a corn cob.

corncockle see COCKLE[2] 1.

corncrake /ˈkɔːnkreɪk/ *n.* a rail, *Crex crex*, with a rasping call, inhabiting grassland and nesting on the ground.

corn dolly *n. Brit.* a symbolic or decorative figure made of plaited straw.

cornea /ˈkɔːnɪə/ *n.* the transparent layer covering the front of the eye. □ **corneal** *adj.* [medieval Latin *cornea tela* 'horny tissue', from Latin *cornu* 'horn']

cornel /ˈkɔːn(ə)l/ *n.* a shrub or tree of the genus *Cornus*, which includes dogwoods, esp. a dwarf kind, *C. suecica*. [Middle English from Latin *cornus*]

cornelian /kɔːˈniːlɪən/ *n.* (also **carnelian** /kɑː-/) **1** a dull red or reddish-white variety of chalcedony. **2** this colour. [Middle English from Old French *corneline*; *car-* suggested by Latin *caro carnis* 'flesh']

corneous /ˈkɔːnɪəs/ *adj.* hornlike, horny. [Latin *corneus* from *cornu* 'horn']

corner /ˈkɔːnə/ *n. & v.* ● *n.* **1** a place where converging sides or edges meet. **2** a projecting angle, esp. where two streets meet. **3** the internal space or recess formed by the meeting of two sides, esp. of a room. **4** a difficult position, esp. one from which there is no escape (*driven into a corner*). **5** a secluded or remote place. **6** a region or quarter, esp. a remote one (*from the four corners of the earth*). **7** the action or result of buying or controlling the whole available stock of a commodity, thereby dominating the market. **8** *Boxing & Wrestling* **a** an angle of the ring, esp. one where a contestant rests between rounds. **b** a contestant's supporters offering assistance at the corner between rounds. **9** *Football & Hockey* a free-kick or hit from a corner of the pitch after the ball has been sent over the goal line by a defending player. **10** *Brit.* a triangular cut of gammon or ham. ● *v.* **1** *tr.* force (a person or animal) into a difficult or inescapable position. **2** *tr.* **a** establish a corner in (a commodity). **b** dominate (dealers or the market) in this way. **3** *intr.* (esp. of or in a vehicle) go round a corner. □ **just round** (or **around**) **the corner** *colloq.* very near; imminent. [Middle English from Anglo-French, ultimately from Latin *cornu* 'horn']

cornerback /ˈkɔːnəbak/ *n.* (in American football etc.) a defensive player or position on the wing.

corner shop *n.* a small local shop, esp. at a street corner.

cornerstone /ˈkɔːnəstəʊn/ *n.* **1 a** a stone in a projecting angle of a wall. **b** a foundation stone. **2** an indispensable part or basis of something.

cornerwise /ˈkɔːnəwʌɪz/ *adv.* diagonally.

cornet[1] /ˈkɔːnɪt/ *n.* **1** *Mus.* **a** a brass instrument resembling a trumpet but shorter and wider. **b** a player of this instrument. **c** an organ stop with the quality of a cornet. **d** a cornetto. **2** *Brit.* a conical wafer for holding ice cream. □ **cornetist** /kɔːˈnɛtɪst/ *n.* (also **cornettist**). [Middle English from Old French, ultimately from Latin *cornu* 'horn']

cornet[2] /ˈkɔːnɪt/ *n. Brit. hist.* the fifth commissioned officer in a cavalry troop, who carried the colours. □ **cornetcy** *n.* (*pl.* **-ies**). [earlier in the sense 'pennon, standard': from French *cornette*, diminutive of *corne*, ultimately from Latin *cornua* 'horns']

cornett /ˈkɔːnɪt/ *n. Mus.* = CORNETTO. [variant of CORNET[1]]

cornetto /kɔːˈnɛtəʊ/ *n.* (*pl.* **cornetti** /-ti/) *Mus.* an old woodwind instrument with finger-holes and a cup-shaped mouthpiece. [Italian, diminutive of *corno* 'horn' (as CORNET[1])]

corn exchange *n. Brit.* a place for trade in corn.

corn-factor *n. Brit.* a dealer in corn.

cornfield /ˈkɔːnfiːld/ *n.* a field in which corn is being grown.

cornflake /ˈkɔːnfleɪk/ *n.* **1** (in *pl.*) a breakfast cereal of toasted flakes made from maize flour. **2** a flake of this cereal.

cornflour /ˈkɔːnflaʊə/ *n. Brit.* **1** a fine-ground maize flour; also called *cornstarch*. **2** a flour of rice or other grain.

cornflower /ˈkɔːnflaʊə/ *n.* any plant of the genus *Centaurea* (composite family), often growing among corn, esp. *C. cyanus*, with deep blue flowers.

cornice /ˈkɔːnɪs/ *n.* **1** *Archit.* **a** an ornamental moulding round the wall of a room just below the ceiling. **b** a horizontal moulded projection crowning a building or structure, esp. the uppermost member of the entablature of an order, surmounting the frieze. **2** *Mountaineering* an overhanging mass of hardened snow at the edge of a precipice. □ **corniced** *adj.* **cornicing** *n.* [French *corniche* etc. from Italian *cornice*, perhaps from Latin *cornix -icis* 'crow': cf. CORBEL]

corniche /ˈkɔːnɪʃ, kɔːˈniːʃ/ *n.* (in full **corniche road**) **1** a road cut into the edge of a cliff etc. **2** a coastal road with wide views. [French: see CORNICE]

Cornish /ˈkɔːnɪʃ/ *adj. & n.* ● *adj.* of or relating to Cornwall in SW England, or its Brythonic language. ● *n.* the ancient Celtic language of Cornwall. □ **Cornishman** *n.* (*pl.* **-men**).

Cornish cream *n.* clotted cream.

Cornish pasty *n.* a pasty containing seasoned meat and vegetables.

corn marigold *n.* a daisy-like yellow-flowered plant, *Chrysanthemum segetum*, growing amongst corn.

corn on the cob *n.* maize cooked and eaten from the corn cob.

cornrows /ˈkɔːnrəʊz/ *n.pl.* a style of braiding the hair, esp. among blacks, in which the hair is parted into rows and plaited tightly in geometric ribbing.

corn salad *n.* = LAMB'S LETTUCE.

corn spurrey see SPURREY.

cornstarch /ˈkɔːnstɑːtʃ/ *n.* = CORNFLOUR 1.

cornstone /ˈkɔːnstəʊn/ *n. Brit. Geol.* a mottled red and green limestone usu. formed under arid conditions, esp. in the Devonian period.

cornucopia /kɔːnjʊˈkəʊpɪə/ *n.* **1 a** a symbol of plenty consisting of a goat's horn overflowing with flowers, fruit, and corn. **b** an ornamental vessel shaped like this. **2** an abundant supply. ▫ **cornucopian** *adj.* [Late Latin from Latin *cornu copiae* 'horn of plenty']

corn whiskey *n. US* whisky distilled from maize.

corny /ˈkɔːni/ *adj.* (**cornier**, **corniest**) **1** *colloq.* **a** trite. **b** feebly humorous. **c** sentimental. **d** old-fashioned; out of date. **2** of or abounding in corn. ▫ **cornily** *adv.* **corniness** *n.* [CORN¹ + -Y¹: sense 1 from the sense 'rustic']

corolla /kəˈrɒlə/ *n. Bot.* a whorl or whorls of petals forming the inner envelope of a flower. [Latin, diminutive of *corona* 'crown']

corollary /kəˈrɒləri/ *n. & adj.* ● *n.* (*pl.* **-ies**) **1 a** a proposition that follows from (and is often appended to) one already proved. **b** an immediate deduction. **2** (often foll. by *of*) a natural consequence or result. ● *adj.* **1** supplementary, associated. **2** (often foll. by *to*) forming a corollary. [Middle English from Latin *corollarium* 'money paid for a garland, gratuity', neut. adj. from COROLLA used as a noun]

corona¹ /kəˈrəʊnə/ *n.* (*pl.* **coronae** /-niː/) **1 a** a small circle of light round the sun or moon. **b** the rarefied gaseous envelope of the sun, seen as an irregularly shaped area of light around the moon's disc during a total solar eclipse. **2** a circular chandelier hung from a roof. **3** *Anat.* a crown or crownlike structure. **4** *Bot.* a crownlike outgrowth from the inner side of a corolla. **5** *Archit.* a broad vertical face of a cornice, usu. of considerable projection. **6** *Electr.* the glow around a conductor at high potential. [Latin, = crown]

corona² /kəˈrəʊnə/ *n.* a long cigar with straight sides. [Spanish *La Corona* 'the crown', originally a proprietary name]

coronach /ˈkɒrənək, -x/ *n. Sc. & Ir.* a funeral song or dirge. [Irish *coranach*, Gaelic *corranach*, from *comh-* 'together' + *rànach* 'outcry']

coronagraph /kəˈrəʊnəgrɑːf/ *n.* an instrument for observing the sun's corona, esp. other than during a solar eclipse.

coronal¹ /kəˈrəʊn(ə)l, ˈkɒr(ə)n(ə)l/ *adj.* **1** *Astron. & Bot.* of a corona. **2** *Anat.* of the crown of the head. [French *coronal* or Latin *coronalis* (as CORONA¹)]

coronal² /ˈkɒr(ə)n(ə)l/ *n.* **1** a circlet (esp. of gold or gems) for the head. **2** a wreath or garland. [Middle English, apparently from Anglo-French from *corone* CROWN]

coronal bone *n.* the frontal bone of the skull.

coronal plane *n.* an imaginary plane dividing the body into dorsal and ventral parts.

coronal suture *n.* a transverse suture of the skull separating the frontal bone from the parietal bones.

coronary /ˈkɒr(ə)n(ə)ri/ *adj. & n.* ● *adj. Anat.* resembling or encircling like a crown, esp. denoting or involving the arteries which supply blood to the heart. ● *n.* (*pl.* **-ies**) = CORONARY THROMBOSIS. [Latin *coronarius* from *corona* 'crown']

coronary thrombosis *n.* a blockage of the blood flow caused by a blood clot in a coronary artery.

coronation /kɒrəˈneɪʃ(ə)n/ *n.* the ceremony of crowning a sovereign or a sovereign's consort. [Middle English via Old French from medieval Latin *coronatio -onis*, from *coronare* 'to crown' from CORONA¹]

coroner /ˈkɒr(ə)nə/ *n.* **1** an officer of a county, district, or municipality, holding inquests on deaths thought to be violent or accidental, and *Brit.* inquiries in cases of treasure trove. **2** *hist.* an officer charged with maintaining the rights of the private property of the Crown. ▫ **coronership** *n.* [Middle English from Anglo-French *cor(o)uner*, from *coro(u)ne* CROWN]

coronet /ˈkɒr(ə)nɪt/ *n.* **1** a small crown (esp. as worn, or used as a heraldic device, by a peer or peeress). **2** a circlet of precious materials, esp. as a woman's headdress or part of one. **3** a garland for the head. **4** the lowest part of a horse's pastern. **5** a ring of bone at the base of a deer's antler. ▫ **coroneted** *adj.* [Old French *coronet(t)e*, diminutive of *corone* CROWN]

corozo /kəˈrəʊzəʊ/ *n.* (*pl.* **-os**) any of various palm trees native to S. America. [Spanish, variant of dialect *carozo* 'fruit-stone, core']

corozo-nut *n.* = IVORY-NUT.

Corp. *abbr.* **1** Corporal. **2** *US* Corporation.

corpora *pl.* of CORPUS.

corporal¹ /ˈkɔːp(ə)r(ə)l/ *n.* **1** a non-commissioned army or air force officer ranking next below sergeant. **2** (in full **ship's corporal**) *Brit.* an officer under the master-at-arms, attending to police matters. **3** *US* = FALLFISH. [obsolete French, variant of *caporal*, from Italian *caporale*, probably from Latin *corporalis* (as CORPORAL²), confused with Italian *capo* 'head']

corporal² /ˈkɔːp(ə)r(ə)l/ *adj.* of or relating to the human body (cf. CORPOREAL 1). ▫ **corporally** *adv.* [Middle English via Old French from Latin *corporalis*, from *corpus -oris* 'body']

corporal³ /ˈkɔːp(ə)r(ə)l/ *n.* a cloth on which the vessels containing the consecrated elements are placed during the celebration of the Eucharist. [Old English from Old French *corporal* or medieval Latin *corporale pallium* 'body cloth' (as CORPORAL²)]

corporality /kɔːpəˈralɪti/ *n.* (*pl.* **-ies**) **1** material existence. **2** a body. [Middle English from Late Latin *corporalitas* (as CORPORAL²)]

corporal punishment *n.* punishment inflicted on the body, esp. by beating.

corporate /ˈkɔːp(ə)rət/ *adj. & n.* ● *adj.* **1** forming a corporation (*corporate body*; *body corporate*). **2** forming one body of many individuals. **3** of or belonging to a corporation or group (*corporate responsibility*). **4** corporative. ● *n.* a large industrial corporation. ▫ **corporately** *adv.* **corporatism** *n.* **corporatist** *adj.* [Latin *corporare corporat-* 'form into a body' from *corpus -oris* 'body']

corporate raider *n.* esp. *US* a person who mounts an unwelcome takeover bid by buying up a company's shares on the stock market, esp. one who makes a practice of doing so.

corporation /kɔːpəˈreɪʃ(ə)n/ *n.* **1** a group of people authorized to act as an individual and recognized in law as a single entity, esp. in business. **2** *Brit.* the municipal authorities of a borough, town, or city. **3** *joc.* a protruding stomach. [Late Latin *corporatio* (as CORPORATE)]

corporative /ˈkɔːp(ə)rətɪv/ *adj.* **1** of a corporation. **2** governed by or organized in corporations, esp. of employers and employed. ▫ **corporativism** *n.*

corporeal /kɔːˈpɔːrɪəl/ *adj.* **1** bodily, physical, material, esp. as distinct from spiritual (cf. CORPORAL²). **2** *Law* consisting of material objects. ▫ **corporeality** /-ˈalɪti/ *n.* **corporeally** *adv.* [Late Latin *corporealis* from Latin *corporeus*, from *corpus -oris* 'body']

corporeity /kɔːpəˈriːɪti, -ˈreɪɪti/ *n.* **1** the quality of being or having a material body. **2** bodily substance. [French *corporéité* or medieval Latin *corporeitas*, from Latin *corporeus* (as CORPOREAL)]

corposant /ˈkɔːpəzant/ *n.* a luminous electrical discharge sometimes seen on a ship or aircraft during a storm (see ST ELMO'S FIRE). [Old Spanish, Portuguese, Italian *corpo santo* 'holy body']

corps /kɔː/ *n.* (*pl.* **corps** /kɔːz/) **1** *Mil.* **a** a body of troops with special duties (*intelligence corps; Royal Army Medical Corps*). **b** a main subdivision of an army in the field, consisting of two or more divisions. **2** a body of people engaged in a special activity (*diplomatic corps; press corps*). [French (as CORPSE)]

corps de ballet /ˌkɔː də 'baleɪ/ *n.* the company of ensemble dancers in a ballet. [French]

corps d'élite /kɔː deɪ'liːt, French kɔr delit/ *n.* a select group. [French]

corps diplomatique /kɔː dɪpləmə'tiːk, French kɔr diplɔmatik/ *n.* a diplomatic corps. [French]

corpse /kɔːps/ *n.* & *v.* ● *n.* a dead (usu. human) body. ● *v. Theatr. slang* **1** *intr.* spoil a piece of acting by forgetting one's lines, laughing, etc. **2** *tr.* **a** confuse (an actor) in the performance of his or her part. **b** spoil (a piece of acting) by some blunder. [Middle English *corps*, variant spelling of *cors* (CORSE), via Old French *cors* from Latin *corpus* 'body']

corpse-candle *n.* **1** a lambent flame seen in a churchyard or over a grave, regarded as an omen of death. **2** a lighted candle placed beside a corpse before burial.

corpulent /'kɔːpjʊl(ə)nt/ *adj.* bulky in body; fat. □ **corpulence** *n.* **corpulency** *n.* [Middle English from Latin *corpulentus*, from *corpus* 'body']

corpus /'kɔːpəs/ *n.* (*pl.* **corpora** /'kɔːpərə/ or **corpuses**) **1** a body or collection of writings, texts, spoken material, etc. **2** *Anat.* a distinctive structure of some kind in a human or animal body. [Middle English from Latin, = body]

corpus callosum /ˌkɔːpəs kə'ləʊsəm/ *n. Anat.* a broad band of nerve fibres joining the two hemispheres of the brain. [modern Latin from CORPUS + *callosus, -um* 'tough']

Corpus Christi /ˌkɔːpəs 'krɪsti/ *n.* a feast commemorating the Eucharist, observed on the Thursday after Trinity Sunday. [Middle English from Latin, = Body of Christ]

corpuscle /'kɔːpʌs(ə)l/ *n.* **1** a minute body or cell in an organism, esp. (in *pl.*) the red or white cells in the blood of vertebrates. **2** *hist.* a minute particle regarded as the basic constituent of matter, light, etc. □ **corpuscular** /kɔː'pʌskjʊlə/ *adj.* [Latin *corpusculum* (as CORPUS)]

corpus delicti /ˌkɔːpəs dɪ'lɪktʌɪ/ *n. Law* the facts and circumstances constituting a breach of a law. [Latin, = body of offence]

corpus luteum /ˌkɔːpəs 'luːtɪəm/ *n. Anat.* a hormone-secreting structure developed in the ovary after discharge of the ovum, degenerating after a few days unless pregnancy has begun. [modern Latin, from CORPUS + *luteus, -um* 'yellow']

corral /kə'rɑːl/ *n.* & *v.* ● *n.* **1** *N. Amer.* a pen for cattle, horses, etc. **2** an enclosure for capturing wild animals. **3** esp. *US hist.* a defensive enclosure of wagons in an encampment. ● *v.tr.* (**corralled**, **corralling**) **1** put or keep in a corral. **2** form (wagons) into a corral. **3** *N. Amer. colloq.* gather in; acquire. [Spanish & Old Portuguese (as KRAAL)]

corrasion /kə'reɪʒ(ə)n/ *n. Geol.* erosion of the earth's surface by rock material being carried over it by water, ice, etc. [Latin *corradere corras-* 'scrape together' (as COM-, *radere* 'scrape')]

correct /kə'rɛkt/ *adj.* & *v.* ● *adj.* **1** true, right, accurate. **2** (of conduct, manners, etc.) proper, right. **3** in accordance with good standards of taste etc. ● *v.tr.* **1** set right; amend (an error, omission, etc., or the person responsible for it). **2** mark the errors in (written or printed work etc.). **3** substitute the right thing for (the wrong one). **4 a** admonish or rebuke (a person). **b** punish (a person or fault). **5** counteract (a harmful quality). **6** adjust (an instrument etc.) to function accurately or accord with a standard. □ **correctable** *adj.* **correctly** *adv.* **correctness** *n.* [Middle English (the adj. via French) from Latin *corrigere correct-* (as COM-, *regere* 'guide')]

correction /kə'rɛkʃ(ə)n/ *n.* **1 a** the act or process of correcting. **b** an instance of this. **2** a thing substituted for what is wrong. **3** *archaic* punishment (*house of correction*). □ **correctional** *adj.* [Middle English via Old French from Latin *correctio -onis* (as CORRECT)]

correction fluid *n.* a usu. white liquid that is painted over a typed or written error leaving a blank space for typing or writing afresh.

correctitude /kə'rɛktɪtjuːd/ *n.* correctness, esp. conscious correctness of conduct. [19th c., from CORRECT + RECTITUDE]

corrective /kə'rɛktɪv/ *adj.* & *n.* ● *adj.* serving or tending to correct or counteract something undesired or harmful. ● *n.* a corrective measure or thing. □ **correctively** *adv.* [French *correctif -ive* or Late Latin *correctivus* (as CORRECT)]

corrector /kə'rɛktə/ *n.* a person who corrects or points out faults. [Middle English from Anglo-French *correctour* from Latin *corrector* (as CORRECT)]

correlate /'kɒrəleɪt, -rɪl-/ *v.* & *n.* ● *v.* **1** *intr.* (foll. by *with, to*) have a mutual relation. **2** *tr.* (usu. foll. by *with*) bring into a mutual relation. ● *n.* each of two related or complementary things (esp. so related that one implies the other). [back-formation from CORRELATION, CORRELATIVE]

correlation /kɒrə'leɪʃ(ə)n, -rɪ-/ *n.* (also **corelation** /kəʊrɪ-/) **1** a mutual relation between two or more things. **2 a** interdependence of variable quantities. **b** a quantity measuring the extent of this. **3** the act of correlating. □ **correlational** *adj.* [medieval Latin *correlatio* (as CORRELATIVE)]

correlative /kə'rɛlətɪv/ *adj.* & *n.* ● *adj.* **1** (often foll. by *with, to*) having a mutual relation. **2** *Gram.* (of words) corresponding to each other and regularly used together (as *neither* and *nor*). ● *n.* a correlative word or thing. □ **correlatively** *adv.* **correlativity** /-'tɪvɪti/ *n.* [medieval Latin *correlativus* (as COM-, RELATIVE)]

correspond /kɒrɪ'spɒnd/ *v.intr.* **1 a** (usu. foll. by *to*) be analogous or similar. **b** (usu. foll. by *to*) agree in amount, position, etc. **c** (usu. foll. by *with, to*) be in harmony or agreement. **2** (usu. foll. by *with*) communicate by interchange of letters. □ **correspondingly** *adv.* [French *correspondre* from medieval Latin *correspondere* (as COM-, RESPOND)]

correspondence /kɒrɪ'spɒnd(ə)ns/ *n.* **1** (usu. foll. by *with, to, between*) agreement, similarity, or harmony. **2 a** communication by letters. **b** letters sent or received. [Middle English via Old French from medieval Latin *correspondentia* (as CORRESPOND)]

correspondence college *n.* (also **correspondence school**) a college conducting correspondence courses.

correspondence column *n. Brit.* the part of a newspaper etc. that contains letters from readers.

correspondence course *n.* a course of study conducted by post.

correspondent /kɒrɪ'spɒnd(ə)nt/ *n.* & *adj.* ● *n.* **1** a person who writes letters to a person or a newspaper, esp. regularly. **2** a person employed to contribute material for publication in a periodical or for broadcasting (*our chess correspondent; the BBC's Moscow correspondent*). **3** a person or firm having regular business relations with another, esp. in another country. ● *adj.* (often foll. by *to, with*) *archaic* corresponding. [Middle English from Old French *correspondant* or medieval Latin (as CORRESPOND)]

corresponding member *n.* an honorary member of a learned society etc. with no voice in the society's affairs.

corrida /kɔː'riːdə/ *n.* **1** a bullfight. **2** bullfighting. [Spanish *corrida de toros* 'running of bulls']

corridor /'kɒrɪdɔː/ *n.* **1** a passage from which doors lead into rooms (originally an outside passage connecting parts of a building, now usu. a main passage in a large building). **2** *Brit.* a passage in a railway carriage from which doors lead into compartments. **3** a strip of the territory of one state passing through that of another, esp. securing access to the sea. **4** a route to which aircraft are restricted, esp. over a foreign country. **5** a major route on which traffic is concentrated (*the M4 corridor*). [French from Italian *corridore* 'corridor' (for *corridojo* 'running-place') from *correre* 'run', by confusion with *corridore* 'runner']

corridors of power *n.pl.* places where covert influence is said to be exerted in government.

corrie /ˈkɒri/ *n.* esp. *Sc.* a circular hollow on a mountainside; a cirque. [Gaelic *coire* 'cauldron']

corrigendum /kɒrɪˈdʒɛndəm/ *n.* (*pl.* **corrigenda** /-də/) a thing to be corrected, esp. an error in a printed book. [Latin, neut. gerundive of *corrigere*: see CORRECT]

corrigible /ˈkɒrɪdʒɪb(ə)l/ *adj.* **1** capable of being corrected. **2** (of a person) submissive; open to correction. ▫ **corrigibly** *adv.* [Middle English via French from medieval Latin *corrigibilis* (as CORRECT)]

corroborate /kəˈrɒbəreɪt/ *v.tr.* confirm or give support to (a statement or belief, or the person holding it), esp. in relation to witnesses in a law court. ▫ **corroboration** /-ˈreɪʃ(ə)n/ *n.* **corroborative** /-rətɪv/ *adj.* **corroborator** *n.* **corroboratory** /-rət(ə)ri/ *adj.* [Latin *corroborare* 'strengthen' (as COM-, *roborare* from *robur -oris* 'strength')]

corroboree /kəˈrɒbəri/ *n.* **1** a festive or warlike dance-drama with song of Australian Aboriginals. **2** a noisy party. [Dharuk *garabari*, a style of dancing]

corrode /kəˈrəʊd/ *v.* **1 a** *tr.* wear away, esp. by chemical action. **b** *intr.* be worn away; decay. **2** *tr.* destroy gradually (*optimism corroded by recent misfortunes*). ▫ **corrodible** *adj.* [Middle English from Latin *corrodere corros-* (as COM-, *rodere* 'gnaw')]

corrosion /kəˈrəʊʒ(ə)n/ *n.* **1** the process of corroding, esp. of a rusting metal. **2 a** damage caused by corroding. **b** a corroded area.

corrosive /kəˈrəʊsɪv/ *adj.* & *n.* ● *adj.* tending to corrode or consume. ● *n.* a corrosive substance. ▫ **corrosively** *adv.* **corrosiveness** *n.* [Middle English from Old French *corosif -ive* (as CORRODE)]

corrosive sublimate *n.* mercuric chloride, a poisonous acid substance, used as a fungicide, antiseptic, etc.

corrugate /ˈkɒrʊgeɪt/ *v.* **1** *tr.* (esp. as **corrugated** *adj.*) form into alternate ridges and grooves, esp. to strengthen (*corrugated iron*; *corrugated paper*). **2** *tr.* & *intr.* contract into wrinkles or folds. ▫ **corrugation** /-ˈgeɪʃ(ə)n/ *n.* [Latin *corrugare* (as COM-, *rugare* from *ruga* 'wrinkle')]

corrugator /ˈkɒrʊgeɪtə/ *n. Anat.* either of two muscles that contract the brow in frowning. [modern Latin (as CORRUGATE)]

corrupt /kəˈrʌpt/ *adj.* & *v.* ● *adj.* **1** morally depraved; wicked. **2** influenced by or using bribery or fraudulent activity. **3** (of a text, language, etc.) harmed (esp. made suspect or unreliable) by errors or alterations. **4** rotten. ● *v.* **1** *tr.* & *intr.* make or become corrupt or depraved. **2** *tr.* affect or harm by errors or alterations. **3** *tr.* infect, taint. ▫ **corrupter** *n.* **corruptible** *adj.* **corruptibility** /-ˈbɪlɪti/ *n.* **corruptive** *adj.* **corruptly** *adv.* [Middle English from Old French *corrupt* or Latin *corruptus*, past part. of *corrumpere corrupt-* (as COM-, *rumpere* 'break')]

corruption /kəˈrʌpʃ(ə)n/ *n.* **1** moral deterioration, esp. widespread. **2** use of corrupt practices, esp. bribery or fraud. **3 a** irregular alteration (of a text, language, etc.) from its original state. **b** an irregularly altered form of a word. **4** decomposition, esp. of a corpse or other organic matter. [Middle English from Old French *corruption* or Latin *corruptio* (as CORRUPT)]

corrupt practices *n.pl.* fraudulent activity, esp. at elections.

corsac /ˈkɔːsak/ *n.* (also **corsak**) a fox, *Vulpes corsac*, of central Asia. [Turkic]

corsage /kɔːˈsɑːʒ, ˈkɔːsɑːʒ/ *n.* **1** a small bouquet worn by a woman. **2** the bodice of a woman's dress. [Middle English from Old French, from *cors* 'body': see CORPSE]

corsair /ˈkɔːsɛː/ *n.* **1** a pirate ship. **2** a pirate. **3** *hist.* a privateer, esp. of the Barbary Coast. [French *corsaire* from medieval Latin *cursarius*, via *cursus* 'inroad' from *currere* 'run']

corsak var. of CORSAC.

corse /kɔːs/ *n. archaic* a corpse. [variant of CORPSE]

corselet var. of CORSLET, CORSELETTE.

corselette /kɔːs(ə)ˈlɛt, ˈkɔːs(ə)lɛt/ *n.* (also **corselet**) a woman's foundation garment combining corset and brassiere.

corset /ˈkɔːsɪt/ *n.* & *v.* ● *n.* **1** a close-fitting undergarment worn by women to support the abdomen. **2** a similar garment worn by men and women because of injury, weakness, or deformity. ● *v.tr.* (**corseted, corseting**) **1** provide with a corset. **2** control closely. ▫ **corseted** *adj.* **corsetry** *n.* [Middle English from Old French, diminutive of *cors* 'body': see CORPSE]

corsetière /ˈkɔːsɪtjɛː/ *n.* a woman who makes or fits corsets. [French, fem. of *corsetier* (as CORSET, -IER)]

Corsican /ˈkɔːsɪk(ə)n/ *adj.* & *n.* ● *adj.* of or relating to Corsica, an island in the Mediterranean under French rule. ● *n.* **1** a native of Corsica. **2** the Italian dialect of Corsica.

corslet /ˈkɔːslɪt/ *n.* (also **corselet**) **1** a garment (usu. tight-fitting) covering the trunk but not the limbs. **2** *hist.* a piece of armour covering the trunk. [Old French *corselet*, diminutive of *cors* 'body': see CORPSE]

cortège /kɔːˈteɪʒ/ *n.* **1** a procession, esp. for a funeral. **2** a train of attendants. [French from Italian *corteggio*, from *corteggiare* 'attend court']

Cortes /ˈkɔːtɛs, -z/ *n.* the legislative assembly of Spain and formerly of Portugal. [Spanish & Portuguese, pl. of *corte* COURT]

cortex /ˈkɔːtɛks/ *n.* (*pl.* **cortices** /-tɪˌsiːz/) **1** *Anat.* the outer part of an organ, esp. of the brain (**cerebral cortex**) or kidneys (**renal cortex**). **2** *Bot.* **a** an outer layer of tissue immediately below the epidermis. **b** bark. ▫ **cortical** /ˈkɔːtɪk(ə)l/ *adj.* [Latin *cortex, -icis* 'bark']

corticate /ˈkɔːtɪkeɪt/ *adj.* (also **corticated**) **1** having bark or rind. **2** barklike. [Latin *corticatus* (as CORTEX)]

corticosteroid /ˌkɔːtɪkəʊˈstɪərɔɪd, -ˈstɛrɔɪd/ *n.* **1** any of a group of steroid hormones produced in the adrenal cortex and concerned with regulation of salts and carbohydrates, inflammation, and sexual physiology. **2** an analogous synthetic steroid.

corticotrophic hormone /ˌkɔːtɪkəʊˈtrəʊfɪk, -ˈtrɒfɪk/ *adj.* (also **corticotropic hormone** /-ˈtrəʊpɪk, -ˈtrɒpɪk/) = ADRENOCORTICOTROPHIC HORMONE.

corticotrophin /ˌkɔːtɪkəʊˈtrəʊfɪn/ *n.* (also **corticotropin** /-pɪn/) = ADRENOCORTICOTROPHIN.

cortisol /ˈkɔːtɪsɒl/ *n.* = HYDROCORTISONE.

cortisone /ˈkɔːtɪzəʊn/ *n. Biochem.* a steroid hormone produced by the adrenal cortex or synthetically, used medicinally esp. against inflammation and allergy. [chemical name 17-hydroxy-11-dehydro*corticosterone*]

corundum /kəˈrʌndəm/ *n. Mineral.* extremely hard crystallized alumina, used esp. as an abrasive, and varieties of which, e.g. ruby and sapphire, are used for gemstones. [Tamil *kurundam* from Sanskrit *kuruvinda* 'ruby']

coruscate /ˈkɒrəskeɪt/ *v.intr.* **1** give off flashing light; sparkle. **2** be showy or brilliant. ▫ **coruscation** /-ˈskeɪʃ(ə)n/ *n.* [Latin *coruscare* 'glitter']

corvée /ˈkɔːveɪ/ *n.* **1** *hist.* a day's work of unpaid labour due to a lord from a vassal. **2** labour exacted in lieu of paying taxes. **3** an onerous task. [Middle English from Old French, ultimately from Latin *corrogare* 'ask for, collect' (as COM-, *rogare* 'ask')]

corves *pl.* of CORF.

corvette /kɔːˈvɛt/ *n. Naut.* **1** a small naval escort vessel. **2** *hist.* a flush-decked warship with one tier of guns. [French from Middle Dutch *korf* 'kind of ship' + diminutive -ETTE]

corvid /ˈkɔːvɪd/ *n.* & *adj. Zool.* ● *n.* a bird of the crow family, Corvidae. ● *adj.* of or relating to this family. [modern Latin *corvidae* from Latin *corvus* 'raven']

corvine /ˈkɔːvʌɪn/ *adj.* of or like a raven or crow. [Latin *corvinus* from *corvus* 'raven']

corybantic /kɒrɪˈbantɪk/ *adj.* wild, frenzied. [*Corybantes*, the priests of Cybele who performed wild dances (Latin from Greek *Korubantes*)]

corymb /ˈkɒrɪmb/ *n. Bot.* a flat-topped cluster of flowers with the flower stalks proportionally longer lower down the stem. □ **corymbose** *adj.* [French *corymbe* or Latin *corymbus* from Greek *korumbos* 'cluster']

coryphée /ˈkɒrɪfeɪ/ *n.* a leading dancer in a *corps de ballet*. [French from Greek *koruphaios* 'leader of a chorus', from *koruphē* 'head']

coryza /kəˈrʌɪzə/ *n.* a catarrhal inflammation of the mucous membrane in the nose, caused e.g. by a cold or hay fever; a cold in the head. [Latin from Greek *koruza* 'running at the nose']

cos[1] /kɒs/ *n.* a variety of lettuce with crisp narrow leaves forming a long upright head. [*Kōs* (formerly *Cos*), the name of an island in the Aegean, where it originated]

cos[2] /kɒz, kɒs/ *abbr.* cosine.

cos[3] /kɒz, kəz/ *conj.* & *adv.* (also **'cos**) *colloq.* because. [abbreviation]

Cosa Nostra /ˈkəʊzə ˈnɒstrə/ *n.* a US criminal organization resembling and related to the Mafia. [Italian, = our affair]

cosec /ˈkəʊsɛk/ *abbr.* cosecant.

cosecant /kəʊˈsiːk(ə)nt, -ˈsɛk-/ *n. Math.* the ratio of the hypotenuse (in a right-angled triangle) to the side opposite an acute angle; the reciprocal of sine. [modern Latin *cosecans* and French *cosécant* (as CO-, SECANT)]

coseismal /kəʊˈsʌɪzm(ə)l/ *adj.* & *n.* ● *adj.* of or relating to points of simultaneous arrival of an earthquake wave. ● *n.* a straight line or a curve connecting these points. [CO- + SEISMAL (see SEISMIC)]

coset /ˈkəʊsɛt/ *n. Math.* a set composed of all the products obtained by multiplying on the right or on the left each element of a subgroup in turn by one particular element of the group containing the subgroup. [CO- + SET[2]]

cosh[1] /kɒʃ/ *n.* & *v. Brit. colloq.* ● *n.* a heavy blunt weapon. ● *v.tr.* hit with a cosh. [19th c.: origin unknown]

cosh[2] /kɒʃ, kɒˈseɪtʃ/ *abbr. Math.* hyperbolic cosine. [cos[2] + *h* for *hyperbolic*]

co-signatory /kəʊˈsɪɡnət(ə)ri/ *n.* & *adj.* (*US* **cosignatory**) ● *n.* (*pl.* **-ies**) a person or state signing a treaty etc. jointly with others. ● *adj.* signing jointly.

cosine /ˈkəʊsʌɪn/ *n. Math.* the ratio of the side adjacent to an acute angle (in a right-angled triangle) to the hypotenuse. [modern Latin *cosinus* (as CO-, SINE)]

cosmetic /kɒzˈmɛtɪk/ *adj.* & *n.* ● *adj.* **1** intended to adorn or beautify the body, esp. the face. **2** intended to improve only appearances; superficially improving or beneficial (*a cosmetic change*). **3** (of surgery or a prosthetic device) imitating, restoring, or enhancing the normal appearance. ● *n.* a cosmetic preparation, esp. for the face. □ **cosmetically** *adv.* [French *cosmétique* from Greek *kosmētikos*, via *kosmeō* 'adorn' from *kosmos* 'order, adornment']

cosmic /ˈkɒzmɪk/ *adj.* **1** of the universe or cosmos, esp. as distinct from the earth. **2** of or for space travel. □ **cosmical** *adj.* **cosmically** *adv.*

cosmic dust *n.* small particles of matter distributed throughout space.

cosmic rays *n.pl.* (also **cosmic radiation**) radiation from space etc. that reaches the earth from all directions, usu. with high energy and penetrative power.

cosmogony /kɒzˈmɒɡəni/ *n.* (*pl.* **-ies**) **1** the origin of the universe. **2** a theory about this. □ **cosmogonic** /-məˈɡɒnɪk/ *adj.* **cosmogonical** /-məˈɡɒnɪk(ə)l/ *adj.* **cosmogonist** *n.* [Greek *kosmogonia*, from *kosmos* 'world' + *-gonia* '-begetting']

cosmography /kɒzˈmɒɡrəfi/ *n.* (*pl.* **-ies**) a description or mapping of general features of the universe. □ **cosmographer** *n.* **cosmographic** /-məˈɡrafɪk/ *adj.* **cosmographical** /-məˈɡrafɪk(ə)l/ *adj.* [Middle English from French *cosmographie*, or via Late Latin from Greek *kosmographia* (as COSMOS[1], -GRAPHY)]

cosmology /kɒzˈmɒlədʒi/ *n.* **1** the science of the origin and development of the universe. **2** an account or theory of the origin of the universe. □ **cosmological** /-məˈlɒdʒɪk(ə)l/ *adj.* **cosmologist** *n.* [French *cosmologie* or modern Latin *cosmologia* (as COSMOS[1], -LOGY)]

cosmonaut /ˈkɒzmənɔːt/ *n.* a Russian astronaut. [Russian *kosmonavt*, as COSMOS[1], on the pattern of *astronaut*]

cosmopolis /kɒzˈmɒp(ə)lɪs/ *n.* a cosmopolitan city. [Greek *kosmos* 'world' + *polis* 'city']

cosmopolitan /kɒzməˈpɒlɪt(ə)n/ *adj.* & *n.* ● *adj.* **1 a** of or from or knowing many parts of the world. **b** consisting of people from many or all parts. **2** free from national limitations or prejudices. **3** *Ecol.* (of a plant, animal, etc.) widely distributed. ● *n.* **1** a cosmopolitan person. **2** *Ecol.* a widely distributed animal or plant. □ **cosmopolitanism** *n.* **cosmopolitanize** *v.tr.* & *intr.* (also **-ise**). [COSMOPOLITE + -AN]

cosmopolite /kɒzˈmɒp(ə)lʌɪt/ *n.* & *adj.* ● *n.* **1** a cosmopolitan person. **2** *Ecol.* = COSMOPOLITAN *n.* 2. ● *adj.* free from national attachments or prejudices. [French from Greek *kosmopolitēs*, from *kosmos* 'world' + *politēs* 'citizen']

cosmos[1] /ˈkɒzmɒs/ *n.* **1** the universe, esp. as a well-ordered whole. **2 a** an ordered system of ideas etc. **b** a sum total of experience. [Greek *kosmos* 'order, ornament, world']

cosmos[2] /ˈkɒzmɒs/ *n.* any plant of the genus *Cosmos* (daisy family), bearing single dahlia-like blossoms of various colours. [modern Latin, from Greek *kosmos* in the sense 'ornament']

COSPAR *abbr.* Committee on Space Research.

Cossack /ˈkɒsak/ *n.* & *adj.* ● *n.* **1** a member of a people of southern Russia, Ukraine, and Siberia, noted from late medieval times for their horsemanship and military skill. **2** a member of a Cossack military unit. ● *adj.* of, relating to, or characteristic of the Cossacks. [French *cosaque* via Russian *kazak* from Turkic, = vagabond]

cosset /ˈkɒsɪt/ *v.tr.* (**cosseted**, **cosseting**) pamper. [dialect *cosset* = pet lamb, probably via Anglo-French *coscet*, *cozet* from Old English *cotsǣta* 'cottager' (as COT[2], SIT)]

cost /kɒst/ *v.* & *n.* ● *v.* (*past* and *past part.* **cost**) **1** *tr.* be obtainable for (a sum of money); have as a price (*what does it cost?*; *it cost me £50*). **2** *tr.* involve as a loss or sacrifice (*it cost them much effort*; *it cost him his life*). **3** *tr.* (*past* and *past part.* **costed**) fix or estimate the cost or price of. **4** *colloq.* **a** *tr.* be costly to (*it'll cost you*). **b** *intr.* be costly. ● *n.* **1** what a thing costs; the price paid or to be paid. **2** a loss or sacrifice; an expenditure of time, effort, etc. **3** (in *pl.*) legal expenses, esp. those allowed in favour of the winning party or against the losing party in a suit. □ **at all costs** (or **at any cost**) no matter what the cost or risk may be. **at cost** at the initial cost; at cost price. **at the cost of** at the expense of losing or sacrificing. **cost a person dear** (or **dearly**) involve a person in a high cost or a heavy penalty. **to a person's cost** at a person's expense; with loss or disadvantage to a person. [Middle English from Old French *coster*, *couster*, *coust*, ultimately from Latin *constare* 'stand firm, stand at a price' (as COM-, *stare* 'stand')]

cost accountant *n.* an accountant who records costs and (esp. overhead) expenses in a business concern. □ **cost accounting** *n.*

costal /ˈkɒst(ə)l/ *adj.* of the ribs. [French via modern Latin *costalis* from Latin *costa* 'rib']

co-star /ˈkəʊstɑː/ *n.* & *v.* ● *n.* a cinema or stage star appearing with another or others of equal importance. ● *v.* (**-starred**, **-starring**) **1** *intr.* take part as a co-star. **2** *tr.* (of a production) include as a co-star.

costard /ˈkɒstəd, ˈkʌst-/ *n. Brit.* **1** a large ribbed variety of apple. **2** *archaic joc.* the head. [Middle English via Anglo-French (from *coste* 'rib') from Latin *costa*]

costate /ˈkɒsteɪt/ *adj.* ribbed; having ribs or ridges. [Latin *costatus* from *costa* 'rib']

cost-benefit *attrib.adj.* designating or relating to a process that assesses the relation between the cost of an operation and the value of the resulting benefits (*cost-benefit analysis*).

cost clerk *n.* (also *Brit.* **costing clerk**) a clerk who records costs and expenses in a business concern.

cost-conscious *adj.* aware of cost or costs.

cost-cutting *n.* the cutting of costs (often *attrib.*: *cost-cutting measures*).

cost-effective *adj.* effective or productive in relation to its cost. □ **cost-effectively** *adv.* **cost-effectiveness** *n.*

cost-efficient *adj.* = COST-EFFECTIVE. □ **cost-efficiency** *n.*

coster /ˈkɒstə/ *n. Brit.* = COSTERMONGER. [abbreviation]

costermonger /ˈkɒstəmʌŋgə/ *n. Brit.* a person who sells fruit, vegetables, etc., in the street from a barrow. [COSTARD + MONGER]

costing /ˈkɒstɪŋ/ *n.* (often in *pl.*) **1** the determination of the cost of producing or undertaking something. **2** the cost so arrived at.

costing clerk var. of COST CLERK.

costive /ˈkɒstɪv/ *adj.* **1** constipated. **2** niggardly. □ **costively** *adv.* **costiveness** *n.* [Middle English via Old French *costivé* from Latin *constipatus*: see CONSTIPATE]

costly /ˈkɒs(t)li/ *adj.* (**costlier**, **costliest**) **1** costing much; expensive. **2** of great value. □ **costliness** *n.*

costmary /ˈkɒstmɛːri/ *n.* (*pl.* **-ies**) an aromatic plant of the daisy family, *Balsamita major*, formerly used in medicine and for flavouring ale. [Old English *cost* via Latin *costum* and Greek *kostos* from Arabic *ḳust*, an aromatic plant + (*St*) *Mary* (with whom it was associated in medieval times)]

cost of living *n.* the level of prices esp. of the basic necessities of life.

cost-plus *attrib.adj.* designating or relating to a pricing system in which a fixed profit factor is added to cost incurred.

cost price *n. Brit.* the price paid for a thing by a person etc. who later sells it.

cost push *n.* factors other than demand that cause inflation.

costume /ˈkɒstjuːm/ *n.* & *v.* ● *n.* **1** a style or fashion of dress, esp. that of a particular place, time, or class. **2** a set of clothes. **3** clothing for a particular activity (*swimming costume*). **4** an actor's clothes for a part. **5** *Brit.* a woman's matching jacket and skirt. ● *v.tr.* provide with a costume. [French via Italian from Latin *consuetudo* CUSTOM]

costume drama *n.* a drama, esp. produced for television or the cinema, for which historical costume is worn.

costume jewellery *n.* artificial jewellery worn to adorn clothes.

costume play *n.* (also **costume piece**) a play in which the actors wear historical costume.

costumier /kɒˈstjuːmɪə/ *n.* (also **costumer** /-mə/) a person who makes or deals in costumes, esp. for theatrical use. [French *costumier* (as COSTUME)]

cosy /ˈkəʊzi/ *adj.*, *n.*, & *v.* (*US* **cozy**) ● *adj.* (**cosier**, **cosiest**) **1** comfortable and warm; snug. **2** *derog.* complacent; expedient, self-serving. **3** warm and friendly. ● *n.* (*pl.* **-ies**) **1** a cover to keep something hot, esp. a teapot or a boiled egg. **2** *Brit.* a canopied corner seat for two. ● *v.tr.* (**-ies**, **-ied**) (often foll. by *along*) *colloq.* reassure, esp. deceptively. □ **cosy up to** *US colloq.* **1** ingratiate oneself with. **2** snuggle up to. □ **cosily** *adv.* **cosiness** *n.* [18th c. from Scots, of unknown origin]

cot[1] /kɒt/ *n.* **1** *Brit.* a small bed with high sides, esp. for a baby or very young child. **2** a hospital bed. **3** *US* a small folding bed. **4** *Anglo-Ind.* a light bedstead. **5** *Naut.* a kind of swinging bed hung from deck beams, formerly used by officers. [Anglo-Indian, from Hindi *khāṭ* 'bedstead, hammock']

cot[2] /kɒt/ *n.* & *v.* ● *n.* **1** a small shelter; a cote (*bell-cot*; *sheep-cot*). **2** *poet.* a cottage. ● *v.tr.* (**cotted**, **cotting**) put (sheep) in a cot. [Old English from Germanic, related to COTE]

cot[3] /kɒt/ *abbr. Math.* cotangent.

cotangent /kəʊˈtandʒ(ə)nt/ *n. Math.* the ratio of the side adjacent to an acute angle (in a right-angled triangle) to the opposite side.

cot-case *n.* a person too ill to leave his or her bed.

cot death *n. Brit.* the unexplained death of a baby while sleeping.

cote /kəʊt/ *n.* a shelter, esp. for animals or birds; a shed or stall (*sheep-cote*). [Old English from Germanic, related to COT[2]]

coterie /ˈkəʊt(ə)ri/ *n.* **1** an exclusive group of people sharing interests. **2** a select circle in society. [French, originally = association of tenants, ultimately from Middle Low German *kote* COTE]

coterminous /kəʊˈtəːmɪnəs/ *adj.* (often foll. by *with*) having the same boundaries or extent (in space, time, or meaning). [CO- + TERMINUS + -OUS]

coth /kɒθ, kɒtˈeɪtʃ/ *abbr. Math.* hyperbolic cotangent. [COT[3] + *h* for *hyperbolic*]

co-tidal line /kəʊˈtʌɪd(ə)l/ *n.* a line on a map connecting points at which tidal levels (as high tide or low tide) occur simultaneously.

cotillion /kəˈtɪljən/ *n.* **1** a French dance with elaborate steps, figures, and ceremonial. **2** *US* **a** a ballroom dance resembling a quadrille. **b** a formal ball. [French *cotillon* 'petticoat', diminutive of *cotte* from Old French *cote* COAT]

cotinga /kəˈtɪŋgə/ *n.* a tropical American bird of the passerine family Cotingidae, often with brilliant plumage. [French from Tupi *cutinga*]

cotoneaster /kətəʊnɪˈastə/ *n.* a shrub of the genus *Cotoneaster* (rose family), bearing usu. bright red berries. [modern Latin, from Latin *cotoneum* QUINCE + -ASTER]

cotta /ˈkɒtə/ *n. Eccl.* a surplice-like garment usu. reaching just above the waist. [Italian, from the Romanic base of COAT]

cottage /ˈkɒtɪdʒ/ *n.* & *v.* ● *n.* **1** a small simple house, esp. in the country. **2** a dwelling forming part of a farm establishment, used by a worker. **3** *slang* a public toilet. ● *v.intr. slang* perform homosexual acts in public toilets. □ **cottagey** *adj.* [Middle English via Anglo-French, *cotag*, Anglo-Latin *cotāgium*, from COT[2] or COTE]

cottage cheese *n.* soft white cheese made from curds of skimmed milk without pressing.

cottage garden *n.* an informal garden well-stocked with colourful traditional hardy plants.

cottage hospital *n. Brit.* a small hospital not having resident medical staff.

cottage industry *n.* a business activity partly or wholly carried on at home.

cottage loaf *n. Brit.* a loaf formed of two round masses, the smaller on top of the larger.

cottage pie *n. Brit.* a dish of minced meat topped with browned mashed potato.

cottager /ˈkɒtɪdʒə/ *n.* a person who lives in a cottage.

cottar /ˈkɒtə/ *n.* (also **cotter**) **1** *Sc.* & *hist.* a farm-labourer or tenant occupying a cottage in return for labour as required. **2** *Ir. hist.* = COTTIER 2. [COT[2] + -ER[1] (Scots *-ar*)]

cotter /ˈkɒtə/ *n.* **1** a bolt or wedge for securing parts of machinery etc. **2** (in full **cotter pin**) a split pin that opens after passing through a hole. [17th c. (related to earlier *cotterel*): origin unknown]

cottier /ˈkɒtɪə/ *n. Brit.* **1** a cottager. **2** *hist.* an Irish peasant under cottier tenure. [Middle English via Old French *cotier* from medieval Latin *cotarius*: related to COTERIE]

cottier tenure *n. Ir. hist.* the letting of land in small portions at a rent fixed by competition.

cotton /ˈkɒt(ə)n/ *n. & v.* ● *n.* **1** a soft white fibrous substance covering the seeds of certain plants. **2 a** (in full **cotton plant**) a tropical or subtropical plant of the genus *Gossypium* (mallow family), grown for this fibre or for its seeds. **b** this plant as a crop. **3** thread or cloth made from the fibre. **4** (*attrib.*) made of cotton. ● *v.intr.* (foll. by *to*) be attracted by (a person). □ **cotton on** (often foll. by *to*) *colloq.* begin to understand. **cotton to** *US colloq.* begin to like. □ **cottony** *adj.* [Middle English via Old French *coton* from Arabic *ḳuṭn*]

cotton cake *n.* compressed cotton seed used as food for cattle.

cotton candy *n. N. Amer.* candyfloss.

cotton gin *n.* a machine for separating cotton from its seeds.

cotton grass *n.* any grasslike plant of the genus *Eriophorum*, with long white silky hairs.

cotton-picking *adj. N. Amer. slang* unpleasant, wretched.

cottontail /ˈkɒt(ə)nteɪl/ *n.* any rabbit of the genus *Sylvilagus*, native to America, having a mainly white fluffy tail.

cotton waste *n.* refuse yarn used to clean machinery etc.

cottonwood /ˈkɒt(ə)nwʊd/ *n.* **1** any of several poplars, native to N. America, having seeds covered in white cottony hairs. **2** any of several trees native to Australia, esp. a downy-leaved tree, *Bedfordia salicina*.

cotton wool *n.* **1** esp. *Brit.* fluffy wadding of a kind originally made from raw cotton. **2** *US* raw cotton.

cotyledon /kɒtɪˈliːd(ə)n/ *n. Bot.* **1** an embryonic leaf in seed-bearing plants. **2** any succulent plant of the southern African genus *Cotyledon* or the European genus *Umbilicus*, esp. navelwort. □ **cotyledonary** *adj.* **cotyledonous** *adj.* [Latin, = pennywort, from Greek *kotulēdōn* 'cup-shaped cavity' from *kotulē* 'cup']

coucal /ˈkuːk(ə)l, ˈkʊkɑːl/ *n.* any ground-nesting bird of the genus *Centropus*, related to the cuckoos. [French, perhaps from *coucou* 'cuckoo' + *alouette* 'lark']

couch[1] /kaʊtʃ/ *n. & v.* ● *n.* **1** an upholstered piece of furniture for several people; a sofa. **2** a long padded seat with a headrest at one end, esp. one on which a psychoanalyst's subject or doctor's patient reclines during examination. ● *v.* **1** *tr.* (foll. by *in*) express in words of a specified kind (*couched in simple language*). **2** *tr.* lay on or as on a couch. **3** *intr.* **a** (of an animal) lie, esp. in its lair. **b** lie in ambush. **4** *tr.* lower (a spear etc.) to the position for attack. **5** *tr. Med.* treat (a cataract) by displacing the lens of the eye. [Middle English via Old French *couche, coucher* from Latin *collocare* (as COM-, *locare* 'place')]

couch[2] /kaʊtʃ, kuːtʃ/ *n.* (in full **couch grass**) any of several grasses of the genus *Agropyron*, esp. *A. repens*, having long creeping roots. [variant of QUITCH]

couchant /ˈkaʊtʃ(ə)nt/ *adj.* (placed after noun) *Heraldry* (of an animal) lying with the body resting on the legs and the head raised. [French, pres. part. of *coucher*: see COUCH[1]]

couchette /kuːˈʃɛt/ *n.* **1** a railway carriage with seats convertible into sleeping berths. **2** a berth in this. [French, = little bed, diminutive of *couche* COUCH[1]]

couch potato *n.* esp. *N. Amer. slang* a person who likes lazing at home, esp. watching television.

coudé /kuːˈdeɪ/ *adj. & n.* ● *adj.* of or relating to a telescope in which the rays are bent to a focus at a fixed point off the axis. ● *n.* such a telescope. [French, past part. of *couder* 'bend at right angles' from *coude* 'elbow', from Latin *cubitum*]

Couéism /ˈkuːeɪɪz(ə)m/ *n.* a system of psychotherapy using usu. optimistic auto-suggestion. [named after E. *Coué*, French psychologist d. 1926]

cougar /ˈkuːgə/ *n. N. Amer.* a puma. [French, representing Guarani *guaçu ara*]

cough /kɒf/ *v. & n.* ● *v.intr.* **1** expel air from the lungs with a sudden sharp sound produced by abrupt opening of the glottis, to remove an obstruction or congestion. **2** (of an engine, gun, etc.) make a similar sound. **3** *Brit. slang* confess. ● *n.* **1** an act of coughing. **2** a condition of the respiratory organs causing coughing. **3** a tendency to cough. □ **cough out 1** eject by coughing. **2** say with a cough. **cough up 1** = *cough out.* **2** *colloq.* bring out or give (money or information) reluctantly. [Middle English *coghe, cowhe*, related to Middle Dutch *kuchen*, Middle High German *kūchen*, of imitative origin]

cough drop *n.* (also **cough sweet**) a medicated lozenge for relieving a cough.

cough mixture *n.* a liquid medicine for relieving a cough.

could *past* of CAN[1].

couldn't /ˈkʊd(ə)nt/ *contr.* could not.

coulée /kuːˈleɪ, ˈkuːli/ *n.* **1** *Geol.* a stream of molten or solidified lava. **2** *N. Amer. dial.* a deep ravine. [French, fem. past part. of *couler* 'flow', from Latin *colare* 'strain, filter']

coulis /ˈkuːli/ *n.* (*pl.* same) a fruit purée thin enough to pour. [French from *couler* 'flow, run']

coulisse /kuːˈliːs/ *n.* **1** (usu. in *pl.*) *Theatr.* a piece of side scenery or a space between two of these; the wings. **2** a place of informal discussion or negotiation. [French from *coulis* 'sliding': see PORTCULLIS]

couloir /ˈkuːlwɑː/ *n.* a steep narrow gully on a mountainside. [French from *couler* 'glide': see COULÉE]

coulomb /ˈkuːlɒm/ *n. Electr.* the SI unit of electric charge, equal to the quantity of electricity conveyed in one second by a current of one ampere (symbol **C**). [named after C. A. de *Coulomb*, French physicist d. 1806]

coulometry /kuːˈlɒmɪtri/ *n. Chem.* a method of chemical analysis by measurement of the number of coulombs used in electrolysis. □ **coulometric** /kuːləˈmɛtrɪk/ *adj.*

coulter /ˈkəʊltə/ *n.* (*US* **colter**) a vertical cutting blade fixed in front of a ploughshare. [Old English from Latin *culter*]

coumarin /ˈkuːmərɪn/ *n. Chem.* an aromatic compound found in many plants and formerly used for flavouring food. [French *coumarine* ultimately from Tupi *cumarú* 'substance from tonka beans']

coumarone /ˈkuːmərəʊn/ *n. Chem.* an organic compound present in coal tar and used in paints and varnishes. [COUMARIN + -ONE]

coumarone resin *n.* a thermoplastic resin formed by polymerization of coumarone.

council /ˈkaʊns(ə)l, -sɪl/ *n.* **1 a** an advisory, deliberative, or administrative body of people formally constituted and meeting regularly. **b** a meeting of such a body. **2** *Brit.* **a** the elected local administrative body of a parish, district, town, city, or administrative county and its paid officers and workforce. **b** (*attrib.*) (esp. of housing) provided by a local council (*council flat*; *council estate*). **3** a body of persons chosen as advisers (*Privy Council*). **4** an ecclesiastical assembly (*ecumenical council*). [Middle English via Anglo-French *cuncile* from Latin *concilium* 'convocation, assembly' (as COM- + *calare* 'summon'): cf. COUNSEL]

council chamber *n. Brit.* a room in which a council meets.

council house *n. Brit.* **1** a house owned and let by a local council. **2** a building in which a council meets.

councillor /ˈkaʊns(ə)lə/ *n.* (*US* **councilor**) an elected member of a council, esp. *Brit.* a local council or *US* a deliberative council. □ **councillorship** *n.* [Middle

English, alteration of COUNSELLOR: assimilated to COUNCIL]

councilman /ˈkaʊns(ə)lmən, -sɪl-/ *n.* (*pl.* **-men**; *fem.* **councilwoman**, *pl.* **-women**) esp. *US* a member of a council; a councillor.

council of war *n.* **1** an assembly of officers called in a special emergency. **2** any meeting held to plan a response to an emergency.

council tax *n.* a tax levied by local authorities, based on the estimated value of a property and the number of people living in it, replacing the community charge from 1993.

counsel /ˈkaʊns(ə)l/ *n.* & *v.* ● *n.* **1** advice, esp. formally given. **2** consultation, esp. to seek or give advice. **3** (*pl.* same) a barrister or other legal adviser; a body of these advising in a case. **4** a plan of action. ● *v.tr.* (**counselled**, **counselling**; *US* **counseled**, **counseling**) **1** (often foll. by *to* + infin.) advise (a person). **2 a** give advice to (a person) on social, psychological, or personal problems, esp. professionally. **b** assist or guide (a person) in resolving personal difficulties. **3** (often foll. by *that*) recommend (a course of action). □ **keep one's own counsel** not confide in others. **take counsel** (usu. foll. by *with*) consult. [Middle English via Old French *c(o)unseil*, *conseiller* from Latin *consilium* 'consultation, advice']

counselling /ˈkaʊns(ə)lɪŋ/ *n.* (*US* **counseling**) **1** the act or process of giving counsel. **2** the process of assisting and guiding clients, esp. by a trained person on a professional basis, to resolve esp. personal, social, or psychological problems and difficulties (cf. COUNSEL *v.* 2a).

counsellor /ˈkaʊns(ə)lə/ *n.* (*US* **counselor**) **1** a person who gives counsel; an adviser. **2** a person trained to give guidance on personal, social, or psychological problems (*marriage guidance counsellor*). **3** a senior officer in the diplomatic service. **4 a** (also **counselor-at-law**) *US* a barrister. **b** (also **counsellor-at-law**) *Ir.* an advising barrister. [Middle English from Old French *conseiller* (from Latin *consiliarius*), *conseillour*, *-eur* (from Latin *consiliator*): see COUNSEL]

counsel of despair *n.* action to be taken when all else fails.

counsel of perfection *n.* **1** advice that is ideal but not feasible. **2** advice guiding towards moral perfection.

count[1] /kaʊnt/ *v.* & *n.* ● *v.* **1** *tr.* determine the total number or amount of, esp. by assigning successive numbers (*count the stations*). **2** *intr.* repeat numbers in ascending order; conduct a reckoning. **3 a** *tr.* (often foll. by *in*; often as **counting** *prep.*) include in one's reckoning or plan (*you can count me in*; *fifteen people, counting the guide*). **b** *intr.* be included in a reckoning or plan. **4** *tr.* consider (a thing or a person) to be (lucky etc.) (*count no man happy until he is dead*). **5** *intr.* (often foll. by *for*) have value; matter (*his opinion counts for a great deal*). ● *n.* **1 a** the act of counting; a reckoning (*after a count of fifty*). **b** the sum total of a reckoning (*blood count*; *pollen count*). **2** *Law* each charge in an indictment (*guilty on ten counts*). **3** a count of up to ten seconds by a referee when a boxer is knocked down. **4** *Polit.* the act of counting the votes after a general or local election. **5** one of several points under discussion. **6** the measure of the fineness of a yarn expressed as the weight of a given length or the length of a given weight. **7** *Physics* the number of ionizing particles detected by a counter. □ **count against** be reckoned to the disadvantage of. **count one's blessings** be grateful for what one has. **count one's chickens** (**before they are hatched**) be over-optimistic or hasty in anticipating good fortune. **count the cost** consider the risks before taking action; calculate the damage resulting from an action. **count the days** (or **hours** etc.) be impatient. **count down** recite numbers backwards to zero, esp. as part of a rocket-launching procedure. **count on** (or **upon**) depend on, rely on; expect confidently. **count out 1** count while taking from a stock. **2** complete a count of ten seconds over (a fallen boxer etc.), indicating defeat. **3** (in children's games) select (a player) for dismissal or a special role by use of a counting rhyme etc. **4** *colloq.* exclude from a plan or reckoning (*I'm too tired, count me out*). **5** *Brit. Polit.* procure the adjournment of (the House of Commons) when fewer than 40 members are present. **count up** find the sum of. **keep count** take note of how many there have been etc. **lose count** fail to take note of how many there have been etc.; forget the number noted in counting. **not counting** excluding from the reckoning (see sense 3a of the *v.*). **out for the count 1** *Boxing* defeated by being unable to rise within ten seconds. **2 a** defeated or demoralized. **b** soundly asleep; unconscious. **take the count** *Boxing* be defeated. [Middle English via Old French *co(u)nter*, *co(u)nte* from Late Latin *computus*, *computare* COMPUTE]

count[2] /kaʊnt/ *n.* a foreign noble corresponding to an earl. □ **countship** *n.* [Old French *conte* from Latin *comes comitis* 'member of the imperial retinue']

countable /ˈkaʊntəb(ə)l/ *adj.* that can be counted.

countable noun *n. Gram.* a noun that can form a plural or be used with the indefinite article (e.g. *book*, *kindness*, meaning 'a kind act'). Cf. UNCOUNTABLE NOUN, MASS NOUN.

countback /ˈkaʊntbak/ *n. Sport* a system of scoring in which the winner of a tied contest is the contestant with the better score in the later part.

countdown /ˈkaʊntdaʊn/ *n.* **1 a** the act of counting down, esp. at the launching of a rocket etc. **b** the procedures carried out during this time. **2** the final moments before any significant event.

countenance /ˈkaʊnt(ə)nəns, -tɪn-/ *n.* & *v.* ● *n.* **1 a** the face. **b** the facial expression. **2** composure. **3** moral support. ● *v.tr.* **1** give approval to (an act etc.) (*cannot countenance this breach of the rules*). **2** (often foll. by *in*) encourage (a person or a practice). □ **change countenance** alter one's expression as an effect of emotion. **keep one's countenance** maintain composure, esp. by refraining from laughter. **keep a person in countenance** support or encourage a person. **lose countenance** become embarrassed. **out of countenance** disconcerted. [Middle English from Anglo-French *c(o)untenance*, Old French *contenance* 'bearing', from *contenir*: see CONTAIN]

counter[1] /ˈkaʊntə/ *n.* **1 a** a long flat-topped fitment in a shop, bank, etc., across which business is conducted with customers. **b** a similar structure used for serving food etc. in a cafeteria or bar. **c** *N. Amer.* = WORKTOP. **2 a** a small disc used for keeping the score etc. esp. in table games. **b** a token representing a coin. **c** something used in bargaining; a pawn (*a counter in the struggle for power*). **3 a** an apparatus used for counting. **b** *Physics* an apparatus used for counting individual ionizing particles etc. **4** a person who counts something. □ **over the counter** by ordinary retail purchase (see also OVER-THE-COUNTER). **under the counter** (esp. of the sale of scarce goods) surreptitiously, esp. illegally (see also UNDER-THE-COUNTER). [Anglo-French *count(e)our*, Old French *conteo(i)r*, from medieval Latin *computatorium* (as COMPUTE)]

counter[2] /ˈkaʊntə/ *v.*, *adv.*, *adj.*, & *n.* ● *v.* **1** *tr.* **a** oppose, contradict (*countered our proposal with their own*). **b** meet by a countermove. **2** *intr.* **a** make a countermove. **b** make an opposing statement (*'I shall!' he countered*). **3** *intr. Boxing* give a return blow while parrying. ● *adv.* **1** in the opposite direction (*ran counter to the fox*). **2** contrary (*his action was counter to my wishes*). ● *adj.* **1** opposed; opposite. **2** duplicate; serving as a check. ● *n.* **1** a parry; a countermove. **2** something opposite or opposed. □ **act** (or **go**) **counter to** disobey (instructions etc.). **go** (or *Brit.* **hunt** or **run**) **counter** run or ride against the direction taken by a quarry. **run counter to** act contrary to. [Middle English via Old French *countre* from Latin *contra* 'against': see COUNTER-]

counter[3] /ˈkaʊntə/ *n.* **1** the part of a horse's breast between the shoulders and under the neck. **2** the curved part of the stern of a ship. **3** *Printing* a part of a printing type etc. that is completely enclosed by an outline (e.g. the loop of P). [17th c.: origin unknown]

counter[4] /ˈkaʊntə/ *n.* the back part of a shoe or a boot round the heel. [abbreviation of *counterfort* 'buttress']

counter- /ˈkaʊntə/ *prefix* denoting: **1** retaliation, opposition, or rivalry (*counter-demonstration*; *counter-inflationary*). **2** opposite direction (*counter-current*). **3** correspondence, duplication, or substitution (*counterpart*; *countersign*). [from or suggested by Anglo-French *countre-*, Old French *contre*, from Latin *contra* 'against']

counteract /kaʊntərˈakt/ *v.tr.* **1** hinder or oppose by contrary action. **2** neutralize. □ **counteraction** *n.* **counteractive** *adj.*

counter-attack /ˈkaʊnt(ə)rətak/ *n.* & *v.* ● *n.* an attack in reply to an attack by an enemy or opponent. ● *v.tr.* & *intr.* attack in reply.

counter-attraction /ˈkaʊnt(ə)rəˌtrakʃ(ə)n/ *n.* **1** a rival attraction. **2** the attraction of a contrary tendency.

counterbalance *n.* & *v.* ● *n.* /ˈkaʊntəbal(ə)ns/ **1** a weight balancing another. **2** an argument, force, etc., balancing another. ● *v.tr.* /kaʊntəˈbal(ə)ns/ act as a counterbalance to.

counterblast /ˈkaʊntəblɑːst/ *n.* (often foll. by *to*) an energetic or violent verbal or written reply to an argument etc.

counterchange /ˈkaʊntətʃem(d)ʒ/ *v.* **1** *tr.* change (places or parts); interchange. **2** *tr. literary* chequer, esp. with contrasting colours etc. **3** *intr.* change places or parts. [French *contrechanger* (as COUNTER-, CHANGE)]

countercharge /ˈkaʊntətʃɑːdʒ/ *n.* & *v.* ● *n.* a charge or accusation in return for one received. ● *v.tr.* make a countercharge against.

countercheck /ˈkaʊntətʃɛk/ *n.* & *v.* ● *n.* **1 a** a restraint that opposes something. **b** a restraint that operates against another. **2** a second check, esp. for security or accuracy. **3** *archaic* a retort. ● *v.tr.* make a countercheck on.

counter-claim /ˈkaʊntəklem/ *n.* & *v.* ● *n.* **1** a claim made against another claim. **2** *Law* a claim made by a defendant in a suit against the plaintiff. ● *v.tr.* & *intr.* make a counter-claim (for).

counter-clockwise /kaʊntəˈklɒkwʌɪz/ *adv.* & *adj. N. Amer.* = ANTICLOCKWISE.

counter-culture /ˈkaʊntəkʌltʃə/ *n.* a way of life etc. opposed to that usually considered normal.

counter-espionage /kaʊntərˈɛspɪənɑːʒ, -ɪdʒ/ *n.* action taken to frustrate enemy spying.

counterfeit /ˈkaʊntəfɪt, -fiːt/ *adj.*, *n.*, & *v.* ● *adj.* **1** (of a coin, writing, etc.) made in imitation; not genuine; forged. **2** (of a claimant etc.) pretended. ● *n.* a forgery; an imitation. ● *v.tr.* **1 a** imitate fraudulently (a coin, handwriting, etc.); forge. **b** make an imitation of. **2** simulate (feelings etc.) (*counterfeited interest*). **3** resemble closely. □ **counterfeiter** *n.* [Middle English via Old French *contrefet*, *-fait*, past part. of *contrefaire*, from Romanic (as CONTRA- + Latin *facere* 'make')]

counterfoil /ˈkaʊntəfɔɪl/ *n.* esp. *Brit.* the part of a cheque, receipt, etc., retained by the person issuing it and containing details of the transaction.

counter-insurgency /kaʊnt(ə)rɪnˈsəːdʒ(ə)nsi/ *n.* (usu. *attrib.*) action against insurrection (*counter-insurgency operations*).

counter-intelligence /kaʊnt(ə)rɪnˈtɛlɪdʒ(ə)ns/ *n.* = COUNTER-ESPIONAGE.

counter-intuitive /kaʊnt(ə)rɪnˈtjuːɪtɪv/ *adj.* contrary to intuition.

counterirritant /kaʊnt(ə)rˈɪrɪt(ə)nt/ *n.* **1** *Med.* something used to produce surface irritation of the skin, thereby counteracting more painful symptoms. **2** anything resembling a counterirritant in its effects. □ **counterirritation** /-ˈteɪʃ(ə)n/ *n.*

countermand /kaʊntəˈmɑːnd/ *v.* & *n.* ● *v.tr.* **1** *Mil.* **a** revoke (an order or command). **b** recall (forces etc.) by a contrary order. **2** cancel an order for (goods etc.). ● *n.* an order revoking a previous one. [Middle English via Old French *contremander* from medieval Latin *contramandare* (as CONTRA-, *mandare* 'order')]

countermarch /ˈkaʊntəmɑːtʃ/ *v.* & *n.* ● *v.intr.* & *tr.* esp. *Mil.* march or cause to march in the opposite direction, e.g. with the front marchers turning and marching back through the ranks. ● *n.* an act of countermarching.

countermeasure /ˈkaʊntəmɛʒə/ *n.* an action taken to counteract a danger, threat, etc.

countermine /ˈkaʊntəmʌɪn/ *n.* & *v.* ● *n.* **1** *Mil.* **a** a mine dug to intercept another dug by an enemy. **b** a submarine mine sunk to explode an enemy's mines. **2** a counterplot. ● *v.tr.* make a countermine against.

countermove /ˈkaʊntəmuːv/ *n.* & *v.* ● *n.* a move or action in opposition to another. ● *v.intr.* make a countermove. □ **countermovement** *n.*

counter-offensive /ˈkaʊnt(ə)rəfɛnsɪv/ *n.* **1** *Mil.* an attack made from a defensive position in order to effect an escape. **2** any attack made from a defensive position.

counterpane /ˈkaʊntəpeɪn/ *n.* a bedspread. [alteration (with assimilation to *pane* in obsolete sense 'cloth') from obsolete *counterpoint*, via Old French *contrepointe* (alteration of *cou(l)tepointe*) from medieval Latin *culcita puncta* 'quilted mattress']

counterpart /ˈkaʊntəpɑːt/ *n.* **1 a** a person or thing extremely like another. **b** a person or thing forming a natural complement or equivalent to another. **2** *Law* one of two copies of a legal document.

counterpart fund *n.* a sum of money in a local currency equivalent to goods or services received from abroad.

counterplot /ˈkaʊntəplɒt/ *n.* & *v.* ● *n.* a plot intended to defeat another plot. ● *v.* (**-plotted**, **-plotting**) **1** *intr.* make a counterplot. **2** *tr.* make a counterplot against.

counterpoint /ˈkaʊntəpɔɪnt/ *n.* & *v.* ● *n.* **1** *Mus.* **a** the art or technique of setting, writing, or playing a melody or melodies in conjunction with another, according to fixed rules. **b** a melody played in conjunction with another. **2** a contrasting argument, plot, idea, or literary theme, etc., used to set off the main element. ● *v.tr.* **1** *Mus.* add counterpoint to. **2** set (an argument, plot, etc.) in contrast to (a main element). [Old French *contrepoint* from medieval Latin *contrapunctum* 'pricked or marked opposite', i.e. to the original melody (as CONTRA-, *pungere punct-* 'prick')]

counterpoise /ˈkaʊntəpɔɪz/ *n.* & *v.* ● *n.* **1** a force etc. equivalent to another on the opposite side. **2** a state of equilibrium. **3** a counterbalancing weight. ● *v.tr.* **1** counterbalance. **2** compensate. **3** bring into or keep in equilibrium. [Middle English from Old French *contrepeis*, *-pois* (*n.*), *contrepeser* (*v.*) (as COUNTER-, *peis*, *pois* from Latin *pensum* 'weight': cf. POISE[1])]

counter-productive /ˌkaʊntəprəˈdʌktɪv/ *adj.* having the opposite of the desired effect.

counterpunch /ˈkaʊntəpʌn(t)ʃ/ *n.* & *v.* ● *n.* a punch or attack given in return; a boxer's counter. ● *v.intr.* make a counterpunch or counterpunches. □ **counterpuncher** *n.*

counter-reformation /ˌkaʊntərɛfəˈmeɪʃ(ə)n/ *n.* **1** (**Counter-Reformation**) *hist.* the reform of the Church of Rome in the 16th and 17th centuries which took place in response to the Protestant Reformation. **2** a reformation running counter to another.

counter-revolution /ˌkaʊntərɛvəˈluːʃ(ə)n/ *n.* a revolution opposing a former one or reversing its results. □ **counter-revolutionary** *adj.* & *n.* (*pl.* **-ies**).

counterscarp /ˈkaʊntəskɑːp/ *n. Mil.* the outer wall or slope of a ditch in a fortification. [French *contrescarpe* from Italian *contrascarpa* (as CONTRA-, SCARP)]

countershaft /ˈkaʊntəʃɑːft/ *n.* an intermediate shaft driven by a main shaft and transmitting motion to a particular machine etc.

countersign /ˈkaʊntəsʌɪn/ *v.* & *n.* ● *v.tr.* **1** add a signature to (a document already signed by another). **2** ratify. ● *n.* **1** a watchword or password spoken to a person on guard. **2** a mark used for identification etc.

□ **counter-signature** /-ˈsɪgnətʃə/ *n.* [French *contresigner* (*v.*), *contresigne* (*n.*), from Italian *contrasegno* (as COUNTER-, SIGN)]

countersink /ˈkaʊntəsɪŋk/ *v.tr.* (*past* and *past part.* **-sunk**) **1** enlarge and bevel the rim of (a hole) so that a screw or bolt can be inserted flush with the surface. **2** sink (a screw etc.) in such a hole.

counterstroke /ˈkaʊntəstrəʊk/ *n.* a blow given in return for another.

counter-tenor /kaʊntəˈtɛnə/ *n. Mus.* **1 a** a male alto singing voice. **b** a singer with this voice. **2** a part written for counter-tenor. [Middle English via French *contre-teneur* from obsolete Italian *contratenore* (as CONTRA-, TENOR)]

countertop /ˈkaʊntətɒp/ *n. N. Amer.* = WORKTOP.

counter-transference /kəʊntəˈtransf(ə)r(ə)ns, -ˈtrɑːns-, -nz-/ *n. Psychol.* **1** the redirection of childhood emotions felt by an analyst towards a patient. **2** any emotion felt by an analyst towards a patient.

countervail /kaʊntəˈveɪl/ *v.* **1** *tr.* counterbalance. **2** *tr. & intr.* (often foll. by *against*) oppose forcefully and usu. successfully. [Middle English via Anglo-French *contrevaloir* from Latin *contra valēre* 'be of worth against']

countervailing duty *n.* a tax put on imports to offset a subsidy in the exporting country or a tax on similar goods not from abroad.

countervalue /ˈkaʊntəvaljuː/ *n. Brit.* an equivalent value, esp. in military strategy.

counterweight /ˈkaʊntəweɪt/ *n.* a counterbalancing weight.

countess /ˈkaʊntɪs/ *n.* **1** the wife or widow of a count or an earl. **2** a woman holding the rank of count or earl. [Middle English via Old French *contesse*, *cuntesse* from Late Latin *comitissa*, fem. of *comes* COUNT[2]]

counting house /ˈkaʊntɪŋ/ *n.* a place where accounts are kept.

countless /ˈkaʊntlɪs/ *adj.* too many to be counted.

count noun *n. Gram.* = COUNTABLE NOUN.

Count Palatine *n. hist.* a high official of the Holy Roman Empire with royal authority within his domain.

countrified /ˈkʌntrɪfʌɪd/ *adj.* (also **countryfied**) often *derog.* rural or rustic, esp. of manners, appearance, etc. [past part. of *countrify*, from COUNTRY]

country /ˈkʌntri/ *n.* (*pl.* **-ies**) **1 a** the territory of a nation with its own government; a state. **b** a territory possessing its own language, people, culture, etc. **2** (often *attrib.*) rural districts as opposed to towns or the capital (*a cottage in the country*; *a country town*). **3** the land of a person's birth or citizenship; a fatherland or motherland. **4 a** a territory, esp. an area of interest or knowledge. **b** a region associated with a particular person, esp. a writer (*Hardy country*). **5** a national population, esp. as voters (*the country won't stand for it*). □ **across country** not keeping to roads. **go** (or **appeal) to the country** *Brit.* test public opinion by dissolving Parliament and holding a general election. **in the country** *Cricket slang* far from the wickets; in the deep field. **line of country** *Brit.* a subject about which a person is knowledgeable. **unknown country** an unfamiliar place or topic. [Middle English via Old French *cuntree* from medieval Latin *contrata* (*terra*) '(land) lying opposite' (as CONTRA)]

country and western *n.* rural or cowboy songs originating in the US, and usu. accompanied by a guitar etc.

country club *n.* a sporting and social club in a rural setting.

country cousin *n.* often *derog.* a person with a countrified appearance or manners.

country dance *n.* a traditional sort of dance, esp. English, with couples facing each other in long lines.

countryfied var. of COUNTRIFIED.

country gentleman *n.* a gentleman with landed property.

country house *n.* a usu. large house in the country, often the seat of a country gentleman.

countryman /ˈkʌntrɪmən/ *n.* (*pl.* **-men**; *fem.* **countrywoman**, *pl.* **-women**) **1** a person living in a rural area. **2 a** (also **fellow countryman**) a person of one's own country or district. **b** (often in *comb.*) a person from a specified country or district (*north-countryman*).

country music *n.* = COUNTRY AND WESTERN.

country party *n. Brit.* a political party supporting agricultural interests.

country rock *n.* **1** rock which encloses a mineral deposit or an igneous intrusion. **2** a blend of rock music with country and western.

country seat *n.* a large country house belonging to an aristocratic family.

countryside /ˈkʌntrɪsʌɪd/ *n.* **1 a** a rural area. **b** rural areas in general. **2** the inhabitants of a rural area.

countrywoman see COUNTRYMAN.

county /ˈkaʊnti/ *n. & adj.* ● *n.* (*pl.* **-ies**) **1 a** a territorial division of some countries, forming the chief unit of local administration. **b** *US* a political and administrative division of a state. **2** often *iron.* the people of a county, esp. the leading families. ● *adj. Brit.* having the social status or characteristics of county families. [Middle English via Anglo-French *counté*, Old French *conté*, *cunté*, from Latin *comitatus* (as COUNT[2])]

county borough *n. Brit. hist.* a large borough ranking as a county for administrative purposes.

county corporate *n. Brit. hist.* a city or town ranking as an administrative county.

county council *n.* the elected governing body of an administrative county. □ **county councillor** *n.*

county court *n.* a judicial court for civil cases (in the US for civil and criminal cases).

county cricket *n. Brit.* cricket matches between teams representing counties.

county family *n. Brit.* an aristocratic family with an ancestral seat in a county.

County Palatine *n. hist.* the territory of a Count or Earl Palatine.

county school *n.* (in the UK) a school that is established and funded by the local education authority.

county town *n.* (*US* **county seat**) the administrative capital of a county.

coup /kuː/ *n.* (*pl.* **coups** /kuːz/) **1** a notable or successful stroke or move. **2** = COUP D'ÉTAT. **3** *Billiards* a direct pocketing of the cue ball. [French from medieval Latin *colpus* 'blow': see COPE[1]]

coup de foudre /kuː də ˈfuːdr(ə), French ku də fudr/ *n.* (*pl.* ***coups de foudre*** *pronunc.* same) **1** a sudden unforeseen event. **2** love at first sight. [French, literally 'stroke of lightning']

coup de grâce /kuː də ˈgrɑːs, French ku də gras/ *n.* (*pl.* ***coups de grâce*** *pronunc.* same) a finishing stroke, esp. to kill a wounded animal or person. [French, literally 'stroke of grace']

coup de main /kuː də ˈmã, French ku də mɛ̃/ *n.* (*pl.* ***coups de main*** *pronunc.* same) a sudden vigorous attack. [French, literally 'stroke of hand']

coup d'état /kuː deɪˈtɑː, French ku deta/ *n.* (*pl.* ***coups d'état*** *pronunc.* same) a violent or illegal seizure of power. [French, literally 'blow of State']

coup d'œil /kuː ˈdɔɪ, French ku dœj/ *n.* (*pl.* ***coups d'œil*** *pronunc.* same) **1** a comprehensive glance. **2** a general view. [French, literally 'stroke of eye']

coupe /kuːp/ *n.* **1** a shallow glass or dish used for serving fruit, ice cream, etc. **2** fruit, ice cream, etc. served in this. [French, = goblet]

coupé /ˈkuːpeɪ/ *n.* (*US* **coupe** /kuːp/) **1** a car with a hard roof, esp. one with two seats and a sloping rear. **2** *hist.* a four-wheeled enclosed carriage for two passengers and a driver. [French, past part. of *couper* 'cut' (formed as COUP)]

couple /ˈkʌp(ə)l/ *n. & v.* ● *n.* **1** (usu. foll. by *of*; often treated as *sing.*) **a** two (*a couple of girls*). **b** about two (*a* *couple of hours*). **2** (often treated as *sing.*) **a** a married, engaged, or similar pair. **b** a pair of partners in a dance, a game, etc. **c** a pair of rafters. **3** (*pl.* **couple**) a pair of hunting dogs (*six couple of hounds*). **4** (in *pl.*) a pair of joined collars used for holding hounds together. **5** *Mech.* a pair of equal and parallel forces acting in opposite directions, and tending to cause rotation about an axis perpendicular to the plane containing them. ● *v.* **1** *tr.* fasten or link together; connect (esp. railway carriages). **2** *tr.* (often foll. by *together, with*) associate in thought or speech (*papers coupled their names*; *couple our congratulations with our best wishes*). **3** *tr.* & *intr.* (often foll. by *with, up* (*with*)) bring or come together as companions or partners. **4** *intr.* copulate. **5** *tr. Physics* connect (oscillators) with a coupling. [Middle English via Old French *cople, cuple, copler, cupler* from Latin *copulare*, Latin COPULA]

coupler /'kʌplə/ *n.* **1** *Mus.* **a** a device in an organ for connecting two manuals, or a manual with pedals, so that they both sound when only one is played. **b** (also **octave coupler**) a similar device for connecting notes with their octaves above or below. **2** anything that connects two things, esp. a transformer used for connecting electric circuits.

couplet /'kʌplɪt/ *n. Prosody* two successive lines of verse, usu. rhyming and of the same length. [French, diminutive of *couple* COUPLE]

coupling /'kʌplɪŋ/ *n.* **1 a** a link connecting railway carriages etc. **b** a device for connecting parts of machinery. **2** *Physics* a connection between two systems, causing one to oscillate when the other does so. **3** *Mus.* **a** the arrangement of items on a gramophone record. **b** each such item.

coupon /'ku:pɒn/ *n.* **1** a form in a newspaper, magazine, etc., which may be filled in and sent as an application for a purchase, information, etc. **2** *Brit.* an entry form for a football pool or other competition. **3** a voucher given with a retail purchase, a certain number of which entitle the holder to a discount etc. **4 a** a detachable ticket entitling the holder to a ration of food, clothes, etc., esp. in wartime. **b** a similar ticket entitling the holder to payment, goods, services, etc. [French, = piece cut off, from *couper* 'cut': see COUPÉ]

courage /'kʌrɪdʒ/ *n.* the ability to disregard fear; bravery. □ **have the courage of one's convictions** have the courage to act on one's beliefs. **lose courage** become less brave. **pluck up** (or **take**) **courage** muster one's courage. **take one's courage in both hands** nerve oneself to a venture. [Middle English via Old French *corage* from Latin *cor* 'heart']

courageous /kə'reɪdʒəs/ *adj.* brave, fearless. □ **courageously** *adv.* **courageousness** *n.* [Middle English from Anglo-French *corageous*, Old French *corageus* (as COURAGE)]

courante /kʊ'rɒ̃(n)t, -rɑ:nt/ *n.* **1** *hist.* a running or gliding dance. **2** *Mus.* the music used for this, esp. as a movement of a suite. [French, fem. pres. part. (used as a noun) of *courir* 'run', from Latin *currere*]

courgette /kʊə'ʒɛt/ *n. Brit.* a small green variety of vegetable marrow. Also called ZUCCHINI. [French, diminutive of *courge* 'gourd']

courier /'kʊrɪə/ *n.* **1** a person employed, usu. by a travel company, to guide and assist a group of tourists. **2** a special messenger. [Middle English via French from Italian *corriere*, and from Old French *coreor*, both from Latin *currere* 'run']

course /kɔ:s/ *n.* & *v.* ● *n.* **1** a continuous onward movement or progression. **2 a** a line along which a person or thing moves; a direction taken (*has changed course*; *the course of the winding river*). **b** a correct or intended direction or line of movement. **c** the direction taken by a ship or aircraft. **3 a** the ground on which a race (or other sport involving extensive linear movement) takes place. **b** a series of fences, hurdles, or other obstacles to be crossed in a race etc. **4 a** a series of lectures, lessons, etc., in a particular subject. **b** a book for such a course (*A Modern French Course*). **5** any of the successive parts of a meal. **6** *Med.* a sequence of medical treatment etc. (*prescribed a course of antibiotics*). **7** a line of conduct (*disappointed by the course he took*). **8** *Archit.* a continuous horizontal layer of brick, stone, etc., in a building. **9** a channel in which water flows. **10** the pursuit of game (esp. hares) with hounds, esp. greyhounds, by sight rather than scent. **11** *Naut.* a sail on a square-rigged ship (*fore course*; *main course*). ● *v.* **1** *intr.* (esp. of liquid) run, esp. fast (*blood coursed through his veins*). **2** *tr.* (also *absol.*) **a** use (hounds) to hunt. **b** pursue (hares etc.) in hunting. □ **the course of nature** ordinary events or procedure. **in course of** in the process of. **in the course of** during. **in the course of time** as time goes by; eventually. **of course** naturally; as is or was to be expected; admittedly. **on** (or **off**) **course** following (or deviating from) the desired direction or goal. **run** (or **take**) **its course** (esp. of an illness) complete its natural development. □ **courser** *n.* (in sense 2 of *v.*). [Middle English via Old French *cours* from Latin *cursus*, from *currere curs-* 'run']

coursebook /'kɔ:sbʊk/ *n.* a book designed for use on a particular course of study.

courser[1] /'kɔ:sə/ *n. poet.* a swift horse. [Middle English via Old French *corsier* from Romanic]

courser[2] /'kɔ:sə/ *n.* any fast-running plover-like bird of the genus *Cursorius*, native to Africa and Asia, having long legs and a slender bill. [Late Latin *cursorius* 'adapted for running']

coursework /'kɔ:swə:k/ *n.* the work done during a course of study, esp. when counting towards a student's final assessment.

court /kɔ:t/ *n.* & *v.* ● *n.* **1** (in full **court of law**) **a** a body of persons presided over by a judge, judges, or a magistrate, and acting as a tribunal in civil and criminal cases. **b** = COURTROOM. **2 a** an enclosed quadrangular area for games, which may be open or covered (*tennis court*; *squash court*). **b** an area marked out for tennis etc. (*hit the ball out of court*). **3 a** a small enclosed street in a town, having a yard surrounded by houses, and adjoining a larger street. **b** *Brit.* = COURTYARD. **c** (**Court**) the name of a large house, block of flats, street, etc. (*Grosvenor Court*). **d** (at Cambridge University) a college quadrangle. **e** a subdivision of a building, usu. a large hall extending to the ceiling with galleries and staircases. **4 a** the establishment, retinue, and courtiers of a sovereign. **b** a sovereign and his or her councillors, constituting a ruling power. **c** a sovereign's residence. **d** an assembly held by a sovereign; a state reception. **5** attention paid to a person whose favour, love, or interest is sought (*paid court to her*). **6 a** the qualified members of a company or a corporation. **b** *Brit.* (in some Friendly Societies) a local branch. **c** a meeting of a court. ● *v.tr.* **1 a** try to win the affection or favour of (a person). **b** pay amorous attention to (also *absol.*: *courting couples*). **2** seek to win (applause, fame, etc.). **3** invite (misfortune) by one's actions (*you are courting disaster*). □ **go to court** take legal action. **in court** appearing as a party or an advocate in a court of law. **out of court 1** (of a plaintiff) not entitled to be heard. **2** (of a settlement) arranged before a hearing or judgement can take place. **3** not worthy of consideration (*that suggestion is out of court*). [Middle English from Anglo-French *curt*, Old French *cort*, ultimately from Latin *cohors, -hortis* 'yard, retinue': the verb influenced by Old Italian *corteare*, Old French *courtoyer*]

court bouillon /kɔ:t 'bu:jɒn, French kur bujɔ̃/ *n.* stock usu. made from wine, vegetables, etc., often used in fish dishes. [French from *court* 'short' + BOUILLON]

court card *n. Brit.* a playing card that is a king, queen, or jack. [originally *coat card*, from the decorative dress of the figures depicted]

court circular *n. Brit.* a daily report of royal court affairs, published in some newspapers.

court dress *n.* formal dress worn at a royal court.

courteous /'kə:tjəs/ *adj.* polite, kind, or considerate in manner; well-mannered. □ **courteously** *adv.*

courteousness *n.* [Middle English via Old French *corteis, curteis* from Romanic (as COURT): assimilated to words ending in -OUS]

courtesan /kɔːtɪ'zan/ *n. literary* **1** a prostitute, esp. one with wealthy or upper-class clients. **2** the mistress of a wealthy man. [French *courtisane* from Italian *cortigiana*, fem. of *cortigiano* 'courtier', from *corte* COURT]

courtesy /'kəːtɪsi/ *n.* (*pl.* **-ies**) **1** courteous behaviour; good manners. **2** a courteous act. **3** *archaic* = CURTSY. □ **by courtesy** by favour, not by right. **by courtesy of** with the formal permission of (a person etc.). [Middle English from Old French *curtesie, co(u)rtesie*, from *curteis* etc. COURTEOUS]

courtesy light *n.* a light in a car that is switched on by opening a door.

courtesy title *n.* a title held by courtesy, usu. having no legal validity, e.g. a title given to the heir of a duke etc.

courthouse /'kɔːthaʊs/ *n.* **1** a building in which a judicial court is held. **2** *US* a building containing the administrative offices of a county.

courtier /'kɔːtɪə/ *n.* a person who attends or frequents a sovereign's court. [Middle English via Anglo-French *courte(i)our*, from Old French, from *cortoyer* 'be present at court']

Court leet see LEET[1] 1.

courtly /'kɔːtli/ *adj.* (**courtlier**, **courtliest**) **1** polished or refined in manners. **2** obsequious. **3** punctilious. □ **courtliness** *n.* [COURT]

courtly love *n.* the conventional medieval tradition of knightly love for a lady, and the etiquette used in its (esp. literary) expression.

court martial /kɔːt 'mɑːʃ(ə)l/ *n.* & *v.* ● *n.* (*pl.* **courts martial**) a judicial court for trying members of the armed services. ● *v.tr.* (**court-martial**) (**-martialled**, **-martialling**; *US* **-martialed**, **-martialing**) try by a court martial.

Court of Appeal *n.* (*US* **Court of appeals**) a court of law hearing appeals against judgements in the Crown Court, High Court, County Court, etc.

court of first instance *n.* a court of primary jurisdiction.

court of law see COURT *n.* 1.

Court of Protection *n.* (in the UK) the department of the Supreme Court attending to the affairs of the mentally unfit.

court of record *n.* a court whose proceedings are recorded and available as evidence of fact.

court of review *n.* a court before which sentences etc. come for revision.

Court of Session *n.* the supreme civil court in Scotland.

Court of St James's *n.* the British sovereign's court.

court of summary jurisdiction *n. Brit.* a court having the authority to use summary proceedings and arrive at a judgement or conviction.

court order *n.* a direction issued by a court or a judge, usu. requiring a person to do or not do something.

court plaster *n. Brit. hist.* sticking plaster for cuts etc. [formerly used by ladies at court for face-patches]

court roll *n. Brit. hist.* a manorial court register of holdings.

courtroom /'kɔːtruːm, -rʊm/ *n.* the place or room in which a court of law meets.

courtship /'kɔːtʃɪp/ *n.* **1 a** courting with a view to marriage. **b** the courting behaviour of male animals, birds, etc. **c** a period of courting. **2** an attempt, often protracted, to gain advantage by flattery, attention, etc.

court shoe *n. Brit.* a woman's light, usu. high-heeled, shoe with a low-cut upper.

court tennis *n. N. Amer.* real tennis.

courtyard /'kɔːtjɑːd/ *n.* an area enclosed by walls or buildings, often opening off a street.

couscous /'kʊskʊs, 'kuːskuːs/ *n.* **1** a type of N. African semolina in granules made from crushed durum wheat. **2** a spicy dish of this, usu. with meat or fruit added. [French from Arabic *kuskus*, from *kaskasa* 'to pound']

cousin /'kʌz(ə)n/ *n.* **1** (also **first cousin**, **cousin german** (*pl.* **cousins german**)) a child of one's uncle or aunt. **2** (usu. in *pl.*) applied to the people of kindred races or nations (*our American cousins*). **3** *hist.* a title formerly used by a sovereign in addressing another sovereign or a noble of his or her own country. □ **first cousin once removed 1** a child of one's first cousin. **2** one's parent's first cousin. **first cousin twice removed 1** a grandchild of one's first cousin. **2** one's grandparent's first cousin. **second cousin** a child of one's parent's first cousin. **second cousin once removed 1** a child of one's second cousin. **2** one's parent's second cousin. **third cousin** a child of one's parent's second cousin. □ **cousinhood** *n.* **cousinly** *adj.* **cousinship** *n.* [Middle English via Old French *cosin, cusin*, from Latin *consobrinus* 'mother's sister's child']

couth /kuːθ/ *adj. joc.* cultured; well-mannered. [back-formation as antonym of UNCOUTH]

couture /kuː'tjʊə/ *n.* the design and manufacture of fashionable clothes; = HAUTE COUTURE. [French, = sewing, dressmaking]

couturier /kuː'tjʊərɪeɪ/ *n.* (*fem.* **couturière** /-rɪ'ɛː/) a fashion designer or dressmaker. [French]

couvade /kuː'vɑːd/ *n.* a custom in some cultures by which a man takes to his bed and goes through certain rituals when his child is being born. [French, via *couver* 'hatch' from Latin *cubare* 'lie down']

couvert /kuː'vɛː/ *n.* = COVER *n.* 6. [French]

couverture /'kuːvətjʊə/ *n. Brit.* chocolate for covering sweets, cakes, etc. [French, = covering]

covalency /kəʊ'veɪl(ə)nsi/ *n. Chem.* **1** the linking of atoms by a covalent bond. **2** the number of pairs of electrons an atom can share with another.

covalent /kəʊ'veɪl(ə)nt/ *adj. Chem.* relating to, designating, or characterized by chemical bonds formed by the sharing of electrons, usu. in pairs, by two atoms in a molecule. □ **covalence** *n.* **covalently** *adv.* [co- + *valent*, on the pattern of *trivalent* etc.]

cove[1] /kəʊv/ *n.* & *v.* ● *n.* **1** a small, esp. sheltered, bay or creek. **2** a sheltered recess. **3** *Archit.* a concave arch or arched moulding, esp. one formed at the junction of a wall with a ceiling. ● *v.tr. Archit.* **1** provide (a room, ceiling, etc.) with a cove. **2** slope (the sides of a fireplace) inwards. [Old English *cofa* 'chamber', from Germanic]

cove[2] /kəʊv/ *n. Brit. slang* a fellow; a chap. [16th-c.: perhaps from Romany *kova* 'thing, person']

coven /'kʌv(ə)n/ *n.* a group of witches. [variant of *covent*; see CONVENT]

covenant /'kʌv(ə)nənt/ *n.* & *v.* ● *n.* **1** an agreement; a contract. **2** *Law* **a** a contract drawn up under a seal, esp. undertaking to make regular payments to a charity. **b** a clause of a covenant. **3** (**Covenant**) *Bibl.* the agreement between God and the Israelites (see ARK OF THE COVENANT). ● *v.tr.* & *intr.* agree, esp. by legal covenant. □ **covenantal** /-'nant(ə)l/ *adj.* **covenantor** *n.* (also **covenanter**). [Middle English from Old French, pres. part. of *co(n)venir*, formed as CONVENE]

covenanted /'kʌv(ə)nəntɪd/ *adj.* bound by a covenant.

covenanter /'kʌv(ə)nəntə/ *n.* **1** var. of COVENANTOR (see COVENANT). **2** /also kʌvə'nantə/ (**Covenanter**) *hist.* an adherent of the National Covenant of the Solemn League and Covenant in 17th-c. Scotland, in support of Presbyterianism.

Coventry /'kɒv(ə)ntri, 'kʌv-/ *n.* □ **send a person to Coventry** esp. *Brit.* refuse to associate with or speak to a person. [*Coventry*, a city in the W. Midlands: origin of the phrase uncertain]

cover /'kʌvə/ *v.* & *n.* ● *v.tr.* **1** (often foll. by *with*) protect or conceal by means of a cloth, lid, etc. **2 a** extend over; occupy the whole surface of (*covered in dirt*; *covered with writing*). **b** (often foll. by *with*) strew thickly or thoroughly (*covered the floor with straw*). **c** lie over; be a covering to (*the blanket scarcely covered him*). **3 a**

protect; clothe. **b** (as **covered** *adj.*) wearing a hat; having a roof. **4** include; comprise; deal with (*the talk covered recent discoveries*). **5** travel (a specified distance) (*covered sixty miles*). **6** *Journalism* **a** report (events, a meeting, etc.). **b** investigate as a reporter. **7** be enough to defray (expenses, a bill, etc.) (*£20 should cover it*). **8 a** *refl.* take precautionary measures so as to protect oneself (*had covered myself by saying I might be late*). **b** (*absol.*; foll. by *for*) deputize or stand in for (a colleague etc.) (*will you cover for me?*). **9** *Mil.* **a** aim a gun etc. at. **b** (of a fortress, guns, etc.) command (a territory). **c** stand behind (a person in the front rank). **d** protect (an exposed person etc.) by being able to return fire. **10 a** esp. *Cricket* stand behind (another player) to stop any missed balls. **b** (in team games) mark (a corresponding player of the other side). **11** (also *absol.*) (in some card games) play a card higher than (one already played to the same trick). **12** make a cover version of (a song etc.) **13** (of a stallion, a bull, etc.) copulate with. ● *n.* **1** something that covers or protects, esp.: **a** a lid. **b** the binding of a book. **c** either board of this. **d** an envelope or the wrapper of a parcel (*under separate cover*). **e** the outer case of a pneumatic tyre. **f** (in *pl.*) bedclothes. **2** a hiding place; a shelter. **3** woods or undergrowth sheltering game or covering the ground (cf. COVERT *n.* 1). **4 a** a pretence; a screen (*under cover of humility*). **b** a spy's pretended identity or activity, intended as concealment. **c** *Mil.* a supporting force protecting an advance party from attack. **5** *Brit.* **a** funds, esp. obtained by insurance, to meet a liability or secure against a contingent loss. **b** the state of being so protected (*third-party cover*). **6** a place setting at table, esp. in a restaurant. **7** *Cricket* = COVER POINT. **8** (in full **cover version**) a recording of a previously recorded song etc., made esp. to take advantage of the original's success. □ **break cover** (of an animal, esp. game, or a hunted person) leave a place of shelter, esp. vegetation. **cover in** provide with a roof etc. **cover one's tracks** conceal evidence of what one has done. **cover up 1** completely cover or conceal. **2** conceal (circumstances etc., esp. illicitly) (also *absol.*: *refused to cover up for them*). **from cover to cover** from beginning to end of a book etc. **take cover** use a natural or prepared shelter against an attack. □ **coverable** *adj.* [Middle English via Old French *covrir, cuvrir* from Latin *cooperire* (as co-, *operire opert-* 'cover')]

coverage /ˈkʌv(ə)rɪdʒ/ *n.* **1** an area or an amount covered. **2** *Journalism* the amount of media publicity received by a particular story, person, etc. **3** a risk covered by an insurance policy. **4** an area reached by a particular broadcasting station or advertising medium.

coverall /ˈkʌvərɔːl/ *n.* & *adj.* ● *n.* **1** something that covers entirely. **2** (usu. in *pl.*) a full-length protective outer garment often zipped up the front. ● *attrib.adj.* covering entirely (*a coverall term*).

cover charge *n.* an extra charge levied per head in a restaurant, nightclub, etc.

cover crop *n.* a crop grown for the protection and enrichment of the soil.

cover drive *n. Cricket* a drive past cover point.

cover girl *n.* a female model whose picture appears on magazine covers etc.

covering /ˈkʌv(ə)rɪŋ/ *n.* something that covers, esp. a bedspread, blanket, etc., or clothing.

covering letter *n.* (also **covering note**) an explanatory letter (or note) sent with an enclosure.

coverlet /ˈkʌvəlɪt/ *n.* a bedspread. [Middle English via Anglo-French *covrelet, -lit* from Old French *covrir* 'cover' + *lit* 'bed']

cover letter *n. N. Amer.* = COVERING LETTER.

cover note *n. Brit.* a temporary certificate of current insurance.

cover point *n. Cricket* **1** a fielding position on the off side and halfway to the boundary. **2** a fielder at this position.

cover slip *n.* a small thin piece of glass used to protect a microscope specimen.

cover story *n.* a news story in a magazine, that is illustrated or advertised on the front cover.

covert *adj.* & *n.* ● *adj.* /ˈkʌvət, ˈkəʊvəːt/ secret or disguised (*a covert glance*; *covert operations*). ● *n.* /ˈkʌvət, ˈkʌvə/ **1** a shelter, esp. a thicket hiding game. **2** a feather covering the base of a bird's flight feather. □ **covertly** *adv.* **covertness** *n.* [Middle English from Old French *covert*, past part. of *covrir* COVER]

covert coat /ˈkʌvət, ˈkʌvə/ *n. Brit.* a short light overcoat worn for shooting, riding, etc.

coverture /ˈkʌvətjʊə/ *n.* **1** covering; shelter. **2** *Law hist.* the position of a married woman, considered to be under her husband's protection. [Middle English from Old French (as COVERT)]

cover-up *n.* an act of concealing circumstances, esp. illicitly.

cover version see COVER *n.* 8.

covet /ˈkʌvɪt/ *v.tr.* (**coveted**, **coveting**) desire greatly (esp. something belonging to another person) (*coveted her friend's earrings*). □ **covetable** *adj.* [Middle English via Old French *cu-, coveitier* from Romanic: related to CUPIDITY]

covetous /ˈkʌvɪtəs/ *adj.* (usu. foll. by *of*) **1** greatly desirous (esp. of another person's property). **2** grasping, avaricious. □ **covetously** *adv.* **covetousness** *n.* [Middle English via Old French *coveitous* from Gallo-Roman]

covey /ˈkʌvi/ *n.* (*pl.* **-eys**) **1** a brood or flock of partridges. **2** a small party or group of people or things. [Middle English via Old French *covee* and Romanic from Latin *cubare* 'lie']

covin /ˈkʌvɪn/ *n.* **1** *Law* a conspiracy to commit a crime etc. against a third party. **2** *archaic* fraud, deception. [Middle English via Old French *covin(e)* from medieval Latin *convenium -ia*, from *convenire*: see CONVENE]

coving *n.* = COVE[1] *n.* 3.

cow[1] /kaʊ/ *n.* **1 a** a fully grown female of any bovine animal, esp. of the genus *Bos*, used as a source of milk and beef. **b** a domestic bovine animal (regardless of sex or age). **c** a female domestic bovine animal which has borne a calf (cf. HEIFER 1). **2** the female of other large animals, esp. the elephant, whale, and seal. **3** *colloq. derog.* **a** a woman, esp. a coarse or unpleasant one. **b** *Austral.* & *NZ* an unpleasant person, thing, situation, etc. □ **till the cows come home** *colloq.* for an indefinitely long time. [Old English *cū* from Germanic, related to Latin *bos*, Greek *bous*]

cow[2] /kaʊ/ *v.tr.* (usu. in *passive*) intimidate or dispirit (*cowed by ill-treatment*). [probably from Old Norse *kúga* 'oppress']

cowabunga /kaʊəˈbʌŋgə, kɑːwə-/ *int. slang* expressing delight or satisfaction, or as a call to action. [probably fanciful]

cowage /ˈkaʊɪdʒ/ *n.* (also **cowhage**) a leguminous climbing plant, *Mucuna pruriens*, having hairy pods which cause stinging and itching. [Hindi *kawānch*]

coward /ˈkaʊəd/ *n.* & *adj.* ● *n.* a person who is easily frightened or intimidated by danger or pain. ● *adj. poet.* easily frightened. [Middle English from Old French *cuard, couard*, ultimately from Latin *cauda* 'tail': perhaps suggested by a frightened animal with its tail between its legs]

cowardice /ˈkaʊədɪs/ *n.* a lack of bravery. [Middle English from Old French *couardise* (as COWARD)]

cowardly /ˈkaʊədli/ *adj.* & *adv.* ● *adj.* **1** of or like a coward; lacking courage. **2** (of an action) done against a person who cannot retaliate. ● *adv. archaic* like a coward; with cowardice. □ **cowardliness** *n.*

cowardy /ˈkaʊədi/ *adj. Brit. colloq.* cowardly (esp. in the children's taunt **cowardy custard**).

cowbane /ˈkaʊbeɪn/ *n.* = WATER HEMLOCK.

cowbell /ˈkaʊbɛl/ *n.* **1** a bell worn round a cow's neck for easy location of the animal. **2** a similar bell used as a percussion instrument.

cowberry /ˈkaʊb(ə)ri/ *n.* (*pl.* **-ies**) **1** an evergreen shrub, *Vaccinium vitis-idaea*, bearing dark red berries. **2** the berry of this plant.

cowbird /'kaʊbəːd/ *n.* any of several N. American orioles which often eat insects stirred up by grazing cattle, esp. the brown-plumaged *Molothrus ater*, which lays its eggs in other birds' nests.

cowboy /'kaʊbɔɪ/ *n.* **1** (*fem.* **cowgirl**) a (usu. mounted) person who herds and tends cattle, esp. in the western US. **2** (*fem.* **cowgirl**) this as a conventional figure in American folklore, esp. in films. **3** *colloq.* an unscrupulous or reckless person in business, esp. an unqualified one.

cowcatcher /'kaʊkatʃə/ *n. N. Amer.* a peaked metal frame at the front of a locomotive for pushing aside obstacles on the line.

cower /'kaʊə/ *v.intr.* **1** crouch or shrink back, esp. in fear; cringe. **2** stand or squat in a bent position. [Middle English from Middle Low German *kūren* 'lie in wait', of unknown origin]

cowfish /'kaʊfɪʃ/ *n.* (*pl.* usu. same) **1** a marine fish, *Lactoria diaphana*, covered in hard bony plates and having hornlike spines over the eyes and on other parts of the body. **2** a manatee or a small cetacean.

cowgirl see COWBOY 1, 2.

cowhage var. of COWAGE.

cow-heel *n.* the foot of a cow or an ox stewed to a jelly.

cowherd /'kaʊhəːd/ *n.* a person who tends cattle.

cowhide /'kaʊhʌɪd/ *n.* **1 a** a cow's hide. **b** leather made from this. **2** a leather whip made from cowhide.

cow-house *n. Brit.* a shed or shelter for cows.

cowl /kaʊl/ *n.* **1 a** the hood of a monk's habit. **b** a loose hood. **c** a monk's hooded habit. **d** a cloak with wide sleeves worn by members of Benedictine orders. **2** the hood-shaped covering of a chimney or ventilating shaft. **3** the removable cover of a vehicle or aircraft engine. ▫ **cowled** *adj.* (in sense 1). [Old English *cugele*, *cūle* via ecclesiastical Latin *cuculla* from Latin *cucullus* 'hood of a cloak']

cow-lick *n.* a projecting lock of hair.

cowling /'kaʊlɪŋ/ *n.* = COWL 3.

cowl neck *n.* a neck on a woman's garment that hangs in draped folds (hyphenated when *attrib.*: *cowl-neck sweater*).

cowman /'kaʊmən/ *n.* (*pl.* **-men**) **1** = COWHERD. **2** *US* = COWBOY 1.

co-worker /kəʊ'wəːkə/ *n.* a person who works in collaboration with another.

cow-parsley *n.* a hedgerow plant, *Anthriscus sylvestris*, having lacelike umbels of flowers. Also called *Queen Anne's lace*.

cow-pat *n.* a flat round piece of cow-dung.

cowpoke /'kaʊpəʊk/ *n. N. Amer. colloq.* = COWBOY 1.

cowpox /'kaʊpɒks/ *n.* a disease of cows, of which the virus was formerly used in vaccination against smallpox.

cowpuncher /'kaʊpʌntʃə/ *n. N. Amer. colloq.* = COWBOY 1.

cowrie /'kaʊ(ə)ri/ *n.* (also **cowry**) (*pl.* **-ies**) **1** any gastropod mollusc of the family Cypraeidae, having a smooth, glossy, and often brightly coloured shell. **2** its shell, formerly used as money in parts of Africa and S. Asia. [Urdu & Hindi *kauṛī*]

co-write /kəʊ'rʌɪt/ *v.tr.* (*past* **co-wrote**; *past part.* **co-written**) write (a book, song, etc.) together with another person. ▫ **co-writer** *n.*

cowshed /'kaʊʃɛd/ *n.* **1** a shed for cattle that are not at pasture. **2** a milking shed.

cowslip /'kaʊslɪp/ *n.* **1** a primula, *Primula veris*, with fragrant yellow flowers and growing in pastures. **2** *US* a marsh marigold. [Old English *cūslyppe*, from *cū* cow[1] + *slyppe* 'slimy substance', i.e. cow-dung]

cow-tree *n.* a tropical American tree yielding a juice which looks and tastes like cow's milk, esp. the Venezuelan tree *Brosimum utile*.

cow-wheat *n.* any plant of the genus *Melampyrum* (figwort family), esp. *M. pratense*, which grows on heathland.

Cox /kɒks/ *n.* (in full **Cox's orange pippin**) a variety of eating apple with a red-tinged green skin. [bred by R. *Cox*, English amateur fruit-grower d. 1845]

cox /kɒks/ *n.* & *v.* ● *n.* a coxswain, esp. of a racing boat. ● *v.* **1** *intr.* act as a cox (*coxed for Cambridge*). **2** *tr.* act as cox for (*coxed the winning boat*). [abbreviation]

coxa /'kɒksə/ *n.* (*pl.* **coxae** /-siː/) **1** *Anat.* the hip bone or hip joint. **2** *Zool.* the first or basal segment in the leg in insects etc. ▫ **coxal** *adj.* [Latin]

coxcomb /'kɒkskəʊm/ *n.* an ostentatiously conceited man; a dandy. ▫ **coxcombry** /-kəmri/ *n.* (*pl.* **-ies**). [variant of COCKSCOMB, originally (a cap worn by) a jester]

coxswain /'kɒks(ə)n, -sweɪn/ *n.* & *v.* ● *n.* **1** the steersman of a ship's boat, lifeboat, racing boat, etc. **2** *Brit.* the senior petty officer in a small ship. ● *v.* **1** *intr.* act as a coxswain. **2** *tr.* act as a coxswain of. ▫ **coxswainship** *n.* [Middle English, from *cock* (see COCKBOAT) + SWAIN: cf. BOATSWAIN]

Coy. *abbr.* esp. *Mil.* Company.

coy /kɔɪ/ *adj.* (**coyer**, **coyest**) **1** archly or affectedly shy. **2** irritatingly reticent (*always coy about her age*). **3** modest or shy, esp. in sexual matters. ▫ **coyly** *adv.* **coyness** *n.* [Middle English via Old French *coi*, *quei* from Latin *quietus* QUIET]

coyote /'kɔɪəʊt, kɔɪ'əʊti/ *n.* (*pl.* same or **coyotes**) a wolflike wild dog, *Canis latrans*, native to N. America. [Mexican Spanish from Nahuatl *coyotl*]

coypu /'kɔɪpuː/ *n.* (*pl.* **coypus**) an aquatic beaver-like rodent, *Myocastor coypus*, native to S. America, naturalized in parts of Europe and the US, and kept in captivity for its fur. [Araucanian (a Chilean language)]

coz /kʌz/ *n. archaic* except *N. Amer.* cousin. [abbreviation]

cozen /'kʌz(ə)n/ *v. literary* **1** *tr.* (often foll. by *of*, *out of*) cheat, defraud. **2** *tr.* (often foll. by *into*) beguile; persuade. **3** *intr.* act deceitfully. ▫ **cozenage** *n.* [16th-c.: perhaps via Italian from Latin *cocio* 'dealer']

cozy *US* var. of COSY.

CP *abbr.* **1** Communist Party. **2** (in South Africa) Conservative Party.

cp. *abbr.* compare.

c.p. *abbr.* candlepower.

Cpl *abbr.* Corporal.

CPO *abbr.* Chief Petty Officer.

CPR *abbr.* **1** Canadian Pacific Railway. **2** cardiopulmonary resuscitation.

CPRE *abbr.* Council for the Protection of Rural England.

CPS *abbr.* (in the UK) Crown Prosecution Service.

cps *abbr.* (also **c.p.s.**) **1** *Computing* characters per second. **2** cycles per second.

CPSA *abbr.* (in the UK) Civil and Public Services Association.

CPU *abbr. Computing* central processing unit.

CR *abbr.* Community of the Resurrection.

Cr *symb. Chem.* the element chromium.

Cr. *abbr.* **1** Councillor. **2** credit.

crab[1] /krab/ *n.* **1 a** any of numerous ten-footed crustaceans having the first pair of legs modified as pincers. **b** the flesh of a crab, esp. *Cancer pagurus*, as food. **2** (**the Crab**) the zodiacal sign or constellation Cancer. **3** (in full **crab louse**) (often in *pl.*) a parasitic louse, *Phthirus pubis*, infesting hairy parts of the body and causing extreme irritation. **4** a machine for hoisting heavy weights. ▫ **catch a crab** *Rowing* effect a faulty stroke in which the oar is jammed under water or misses the water altogether. ▫ **crablike** *adj.* [Old English *crabba*, related to Old Norse *krafla* 'scratch']

crab[2] /krab/ *n.* **1** (in full **crab apple**) a small sour apple-like fruit. **2** (in full **crab tree** or **crab-apple tree**) a tree that bears such fruit, esp. the European wild apple, *Malus sylvestris*. **3** a sour person. [Middle English, perhaps alteration (influenced by CRAB[1] or CRABBED) of earlier *scrab*, probably of Scandinavian origin]

crab[3] /krab/ *v.* (**crabbed**, **crabbing**) *colloq.* **1** *tr.* & *intr.* criticize adversely or captiously; grumble. **2** *tr.* act so as to spoil (*the mistake crabbed his chances*). [originally of hawks fighting, from Middle Low German *krabben*]

crabbed /ˈkrabɪd, krabd/ *adj.* **1** = CRABBY 1. **2** (of handwriting) ill-formed and hard to decipher. **3** perverse or cross-grained. **4** difficult to understand. □ **crabbedly** *adv.* **crabbedness** *n.* [Middle English from CRAB[1], associated with CRAB[2]]

crabby /ˈkrabi/ *adj.* (**crabbier**, **crabbiest**) **1** irritable; morose. **2** = CRABBED 3. □ **crabbily** *adv.* **crabbiness** *n.*

crabgrass /ˈkrabgrɑːs/ *n.* a creeping grass, esp. the weed *Digitaria sanguinalis*.

crab louse see CRAB[1] 3.

crabmeat /ˈkrabmiːt/ *n.* = CRAB[1] 1b.

crab pot *n.* a wicker trap for crabs.

crabwise /ˈkrabwʌɪz/ *adv.* & *attrib.adj.* (of movement) sideways or backwards like a crab.

crack /krak/ *n.*, *v.*, & *adj.* ● *n.* **1 a** a sudden sharp or explosive noise (*the crack of a whip*; *a rifle crack*). **b** (in a voice) a sudden harshness or change in pitch. **2** a sharp blow (*a crack on the head*). **3 a** a narrow opening formed by a break (*entered through a crack in the wall*). **b** a partial fracture, with the parts still joined (*the teacup has a crack in it*). **c** a chink (*looked through the crack formed by the door*; *a crack of light*). **4** *colloq.* a mischievous or malicious remark or aside (*a nasty crack about my age*). **5** *colloq.* an attempt (*I'll have a crack at it*). **6** the exact moment (*the crack of dawn*). **7** *Brit. colloq.* a first-rate player, horse, etc. **8** *Brit. dial. colloq.* conversation; good company; fun (*only went there for the crack*). **9** *slang* a potent hard crystalline form of cocaine broken into small pieces and inhaled or smoked for its stimulating effect. ● *v.* **1** *tr.* & *intr.* break without a complete separation of the parts (*cracked the window*; *the cup cracked on hitting the floor*). **2** *intr.* & *tr.* make or cause to make a sudden sharp or explosive sound. **3** *intr.* & *tr.* break or cause to break with a sudden sharp sound. **4** *intr.* & *tr.* give way or cause to give way (under torture etc.); yield. **5** *intr.* (of the voice, esp. of an adolescent boy or a person under strain) become dissonant; break. **6** *tr. colloq.* find a solution to (a problem, code, etc.). **7** *tr.* say (a joke etc.) in a jocular way. **8** *tr. colloq.* hit sharply or hard (*cracked her head on the ceiling*). **9** *tr. Chem.* decompose (heavy oils) by heat and pressure with or without a catalyst to produce lighter hydrocarbons (such as petrol). **10** *tr.* break (wheat) into coarse pieces. ● *attrib.adj.* excellent; first-rate (*a crack regiment*; *a crack shot*). □ **crack a bottle** open a bottle, esp. of wine, and drink it. **crack a crib** *Brit. slang* break into a house. **crack down on** *colloq.* take severe measures against. **cracked up to be** *colloq.* glowingly asserted to be. **crack of doom** a peal of thunder announcing the Day of Judgement. **crack up** *colloq.* **1** collapse under strain. **2** burst into laughter. **fair crack of the whip** *Brit. colloq.* a fair chance to participate etc. **get cracking** *colloq.* begin promptly and vigorously. **have a crack at** *colloq.* attempt. [Old English *cracian* 'resound']

crack-brained *adj. colloq.* crazy.

crackdown /ˈkrakdaʊn/ *n. colloq.* severe measures (esp. against law-breakers etc.).

cracked /krakt/ *adj.* **1** having cracks. **2** (*predic.*) *slang* crazy.

cracked wheat *n.* wheat that has been crushed into small pieces.

cracker /ˈkrakə/ *n.* **1** a paper cylinder both ends of which are pulled at Christmas etc. making a sharp noise and releasing a small toy etc. **2** a firework exploding with a sharp noise. **3** (usu. in *pl.*) an instrument for cracking (*nutcrackers*). **4 a** a thin dry biscuit often eaten with cheese. **b** a light crisp made of rice or tapioca flour. **5** *Brit. slang* **a** an attractive person, esp. a woman. **b** a fine example of something (*a cracker of a match*). **6** *US offens.* = POOR WHITE.

cracker-barrel *attrib.adj. N. Amer.* (of philosophy etc.) homespun; unsophisticated.

crackerjack /ˈkrakədʒak/ *adj.* & *n. US slang* ● *adj.* exceptionally fine or expert. ● *n.* an exceptionally fine thing or person.

crackers /ˈkrakəz/ *predic.adj. slang* crazy.

cracking /ˈkrakɪŋ/ *adj.* & *adv. Brit. slang* ● *adj.* **1** outstanding; very good (*a cracking performance*). **2** (*attrib.*) fast and exciting (*a cracking speed*). ● *adv.* outstandingly (*a cracking good time*).

crack-jaw *adj.* & *n. colloq.* ● *adj.* (of a word) difficult to pronounce. ● *n.* such a word.

crackle /ˈkrak(ə)l/ *v.* & *n.* ● *v.intr.* make a repeated slight cracking sound (*radio crackled*; *fire was crackling*). ● *n.* **1** such a sound. **2 a** paintwork, china, or glass decorated with a pattern of minute surface cracks. **b** the smooth surface of such paintwork etc. □ **crackly** *adj.* [CRACK + -LE[4]]

crackling /ˈkraklɪŋ/ *n.* **1** the crisp skin of roast pork. **2** *Brit. slang offens.* attractive women regarded collectively as objects of sexual desire. □ **bit of crackling** *Brit. slang offens.* an attractive woman.

cracknel /ˈkrakn(ə)l/ *n.* a light crisp biscuit. [Middle English via French *craquelin* from Middle Dutch *krākelinc*, from *krāken* CRACK]

crackpot /ˈkrakpɒt/ *n.* & *adj. slang* ● *n.* an eccentric or impractical person. ● *adj.* mad, unworkable (*a crackpot scheme*).

cracksman /ˈkraksmən/ *n.* (*pl.* **-men**) *slang* a burglar, esp. a safe-breaker.

crack-up *n. colloq.* **1** a mental breakdown. **2** a car crash.

crack willow *n.* a species of willow, *Salix fragilis*, with brittle branches.

cracky /ˈkraki/ *adj.* covered with cracks.

-cracy /krəsi/ *comb. form* denoting a particular form of government, rule, or influence (*aristocracy*; *bureaucracy*). [from or suggested by French *-cratie* via medieval Latin *-cratia* from Greek *-kratia*, from *kratos* 'strength, power']

cradle /ˈkreɪd(ə)l/ *n.* & *v.* ● *n.* **1 a** a child's bed or cot, esp. one mounted on rockers. **b** a place in which a thing begins, esp. a civilization etc., or is nurtured in its infancy (*cradle of choral singing*; *cradle of democracy*). **2** a framework resembling a cradle, esp.: **a** that on which a ship, a boat, etc., rests during construction or repairs. **b** that on which a worker is suspended to work on a ceiling, a ship, the vertical side of a building, etc. **c** the part of a telephone on which the receiver rests when not in use. ● *v.tr.* **1** contain or shelter as if in a cradle (*cradled his head in her arms*). **2** place in a cradle. □ **from the cradle** from infancy. **from the cradle to the grave** from infancy till death (esp. of state welfare). [Old English *cradol*, perhaps related to Old High German *kratto* 'basket']

cradle-snatcher *n. slang* a person amorously attached to a much younger person.

cradle song *n.* a lullaby.

cradling /ˈkreɪdlɪŋ/ *n. Archit.* a wooden or iron framework, esp. one used as a structural support in a ceiling.

craft /krɑːft/ *n.* & *v.* ● *n.* **1** skill, esp. in practical arts. **2 a** (esp. in *comb.*) a trade or an art (*statecraft*; *handicraft*; *priestcraft*; *the craft of pottery*). **b** the members of a craft. **3** (*pl.* **craft**) **a** a boat or vessel. **b** an aircraft or spacecraft. **4** cunning or deceit. **5** (**the Craft**) the brotherhood of Freemasons. ● *v.tr.* make in a skilful way (*crafted a poem*; *a well-crafted piece of work*). [Old English *cræft*]

craft-brother *n.* a fellow worker in the same trade.

craft guild *n. hist.* a guild of workers of the same trade.

craftsman /ˈkrɑːf(t)smən/ *n.* (*pl.* **-men**; *fem.* **craftswoman**, *pl.* **-women**) **1** a skilled and usu. time-served worker. **2** a person who practises a handicraft. **3** *Brit.* a qualified private soldier in the Royal Electrical and Mechanical Engineers. □ **craftsmanship** *n.* [Middle English, originally *craft's man*]

craftsperson /ˈkrɑːf(t)spəːs(ə)n/ *n.* (*pl.* **craftspeople**) a craftsman or craftswoman.

craftwork /ˈkrɑːftwəːk/ *n.* work produced by a craftsperson. □ **craftworker** *n.*

crafty /ˈkrɑːfti/ *adj.* (**craftier**, **craftiest**) cunning, artful, wily. □ **craftily** *adv.* **craftiness** *n.* [Old English *cræftig*]

crag[1] /krag/ *n.* a steep or rugged rock. [Middle English, of Celtic origin]

crag[2] /krag/ *n. Brit. Geol.* rock consisting of a shelly sand. [18th c.: perhaps from CRAG[1]]

craggy /ˈkragi/ *adj.* (**craggier**, **craggiest**) **1** (esp. of a person's face) rugged; rough-textured. **2** (of a landscape) having crags. □ **craggily** *adv.* **cragginess** *n.*

cragsman /ˈkragzmən/ *n.* (*pl.* **-men**) a skilled climber of crags.

crake /kreɪk/ *n.* **1** a bird of the rail family, esp. a corncrake, or one of the shorter-billed kinds of the genus *Porzana*. **2** the cry of a corncrake. [Middle English from Old Norse *kráka* (imitative): cf. CROAK]

cram /kram/ *v.* (**crammed**, **cramming**) **1** *tr.* **a** fill to bursting; stuff (*the room was crammed*). **b** (foll. by *in*, *into*) force (a thing) into (*cram the sandwiches into the bag*). **2** *tr.* & *intr.* prepare for an examination by intensive study. **3** *tr.* (often foll. by *with*) feed (poultry etc.) to excess. **4** *tr.* & *intr. colloq.* eat greedily. □ **cram in** push in to bursting point (*crammed in another five minutes' work*). [Old English *crammian*, from Germanic]

crambo /ˈkrambəʊ/ *n.* a game in which a player gives a word or verse-line to which each of the others must find a rhyme. [earlier *crambe*, apparently allusive from Latin *crambe repetita* 'cabbage served up again', hence 'distasteful rhyming or repetition']

cram-full *adj.* as full as possible.

crammer /ˈkramə/ *n. Brit.* a person or institution that crams pupils for examinations.

cramp /kramp/ *n.* & *v.* ● *n.* **1 a** a painful involuntary contraction of a muscle or muscles due to cold, exertion, etc. **b** = WRITER'S CRAMP. **2** (also **cramp-iron**) a metal bar with bent ends for holding masonry etc. together. **3** a portable tool for holding two planks etc. together; a clamp. **4** a restraint. ● *v.tr.* **1** affect with cramp. **2** confine narrowly. **3** restrict (energies etc.). **4** (as **cramped** *adj.*) (of handwriting) small and difficult to read. **5** fasten with a cramp. □ **cramp a person's style** prevent a person from acting freely or naturally. **cramp up** confine narrowly. [Middle English via Old French *crampe* from Middle Dutch, Middle Low German *krampe*, Old High German *krampfo*, from an *adj.* meaning 'bent': cf. CRIMP]

crampon /ˈkrampən/ *n.* (usu. in *pl.*) **1** an iron plate with spikes fixed to a boot for walking on ice, climbing, etc. **2** a metal hook for lifting timber, rock, etc.; a grappling iron. [Middle English from French (as CRAMP)]

cran /kran/ *n. Sc.* a measure for fresh herrings (37½ gallons). [Gaelic *crann*, of uncertain origin]

cranage /ˈkreɪnɪdʒ/ *n.* **1** the use of a crane or cranes. **2** the money paid for this.

cranberry /ˈkranb(ə)ri/ *n.* (*pl.* **-ies**) **1** any evergreen shrub of the genus *Vaccinium*, esp. *V. macrocarpon* of America and *V. oxycoccos* of Europe, yielding small red acid berries. **2** a berry from this used for a sauce and in cooking. Also called *fen-berry*. [17th c.: named by American colonists from German *Kranbeere*, Low German *kranebere* 'crane-berry']

crane /kreɪn/ *n.* & *v.* ● *n.* **1** a machine for moving heavy objects, usu. by suspending them from a projecting arm or beam. **2** a tall bird of the family Gruidae, with long legs, long neck, and straight bill, esp. the grey *Grus grus* of Europe. **3** a moving platform supporting a television camera or cine-camera. ● *v.tr.* **1** (also *absol.*) stretch out (one's neck) in order to see something. **2** *tr.* move (an object) by a crane. [Old English *cran*, related to Latin *grus*, Greek *geranos*]

crane-fly *n.* (*pl.* **-flies**) a large two-winged fly of the family Tipulidae, with very long legs. Also called *daddy-long-legs*.

cranesbill /ˈkreɪnzbɪl/ *n.* any of various plants of the genus *Geranium*, with usu. purple, violet, or pink five-petalled flowers. [named from the long spur on the fruit, likened to a bird's bill]

cranial /ˈkreɪnɪəl/ *adj.* of or relating to the skull. [CRANIUM + -AL]

cranial index *n.* the ratio of the width and length of a skull.

cranial nerve *n. Anat.* each of twelve pairs of nerves arising directly from the brain, not from the spinal cord.

craniate /ˈkreɪnɪət/ *adj.* & *n. Zool.* ● *adj.* having a skull. ● *n.* a craniate animal. [modern Latin *craniatus* from CRANIUM]

cranio- /ˈkreɪnɪəʊ/ *comb. form* cranium.

craniology /kreɪnɪˈɒlədʒi/ *n.* the scientific study of the shape and size of the human skull. □ **craniological** /kreɪnɪəˈlɒdʒɪk(ə)l/ *adj.* **craniologist** *n.*

craniometry /kreɪnɪˈɒmɪtri/ *n.* the scientific measurement of skulls. □ **craniometric** /-nɪəˈmetrɪk/ *adj.*

craniotomy /kreɪnɪˈɒtəmi/ *n.* (*pl.* **-ies**) **1** surgical removal of a portion of the skull. **2** surgical perforation of the skull of a dead foetus to ease delivery.

cranium /ˈkreɪnɪəm/ *n.* (*pl.* **craniums** or **crania** /-nɪə/) the skull, esp. the part that encloses the brain. [Middle English via medieval Latin from Greek *kranion* 'skull']

crank[1] /kraŋk/ *n.* & *v.* ● *n.* **1** part of an axle or shaft bent at right angles for interconverting reciprocal and circular motion. **2** an elbow-shaped connection in bell-hanging. ● *v.tr.* **1** cause to move by means of a crank. **2 a** bend into a crank-shape. **b** furnish or fasten with a crank. □ **crank up 1** start (a car engine) by turning a crank. **2** *colloq.* increase (speed etc.) by intensive effort. [Old English *cranc*, apparently from *crincan*, related to *cringan* 'fall in battle', originally 'curl up']

crank[2] /kraŋk/ *n.* **1 a** an eccentric person, esp. one obsessed by a particular theory (*health-food crank*). **b** *N. Amer.* a bad-tempered person. **2** *literary* a fanciful turn of speech (*quips and cranks*). [back-formation from CRANKY]

crank[3] /kraŋk/ *adj. Naut.* liable to capsize. [perhaps from *crank* 'weak, shaky', or CRANK[1]]

crankcase /ˈkraŋkkeɪs/ *n.* a case enclosing a crankshaft.

crankpin /ˈkraŋkpɪn/ *n.* a pin by which a connecting rod is attached to a crank.

crankshaft /ˈkraŋkʃɑːft/ *n.* a shaft driven by a crank (see CRANK[1] *n.* 1).

cranky /ˈkraŋki/ *adj.* (**crankier**, **crankiest**) **1** *colloq.* eccentric, esp. obsessed with a particular theory (*cranky ideas about women*). **2** (esp. of a machine) working badly; shaky. **3** esp. *N. Amer.* ill-tempered or crotchety. □ **crankily** *adv.* **crankiness** *n.* [perhaps from obsolete *crank* 'rogue feigning sickness']

crannog /ˈkranəg/ *n.* an ancient lake-dwelling in Scotland or Ireland. [Irish from *crann* 'tree, beam']

cranny /ˈkrani/ *n.* (*pl.* **-ies**) a chink, a crevice, a crack. □ **crannied** /-ɪd/ *adj.* [Middle English via Old French *crané*, past part. of *craner*, from *cran*, from popular Latin *crena* 'notch']

crap[1] /krap/ *n.*, *v.*, & *adj. coarse slang* ● *n.* **1** (often as *int.*) nonsense, rubbish (*he talks crap*). **2** faeces. ● *v.intr.* (**crapped**, **crapping**) defecate. ● *adj.* of bad quality; useless, inferior. □ **crap out** *US* **1** be unsuccessful. **2** withdraw from a game etc. [earlier senses 'chaff, refuse from fat-boiling': Middle English from Dutch *krappe*]

crap[2] /krap/ *n. N. Amer.* a losing throw of 2, 3, or 12 in craps. [see CRAPS]

crape /kreɪp/ *n.* **1** crêpe, usu. of black silk or imitation silk, formerly used for mourning clothes. **2** a band of this formerly worn round a person's hat etc. as a sign of mourning. □ **crapy** *adj.* [earlier *crispe, crespe*, from French *crespe* CRÊPE]

crape fern *n.* a New Zealand fern, *Leptopteris superba*, with tall dark green fronds.

crape hair *n. Brit.* artificial hair used in stage make-up.

crap game *n.* a game of craps.

crappy /ˈkrapi/ *adj.* (**crappier**, **crappiest**) *coarse slang* **1** rubbishy, cheap. **2** disgusting.

craps /kraps/ *n.pl. N. Amer.* a gambling game played with dice. □ **shoot craps** play craps. [19th c.: perhaps from *crab* 'lowest throw at dice']

crapulent /ˈkrapjʊl(ə)nt/ *adj. literary* **1** given to indulging in alcohol. **2** resulting from drunkenness. **3** drunk. □ **crapulence** *n.* **crapulous** *adj.* [Late Latin *crapulentus* 'very drunk' via Latin *crapula* 'inebriation' from Greek *kraipalē* 'drunken headache']

craquelure /ˈkrakljʊə/ *n.* a network of fine cracks in a painting or its varnish. [French, from *craqueler* 'to crackle']

crash[1] /kraʃ/ *v., n., & adv.* ● *v.* **1** *intr. & tr.* make or cause to make a loud smashing noise (*the cymbals crashed; crashed the plates together*). **2** *tr. & intr.* throw, drive, move, or fall with a loud smashing noise. **3** *intr. & tr.* **a** collide or cause (a vehicle) to collide violently with another vehicle, obstacle, etc.; overturn at high speed. **b** fall or cause (an aircraft) to fall violently on to the land or the sea (*crashed the plane; the airman crashed into the sea*). **4** *intr.* (usu. foll. by *into*) collide violently (*crashed into the window*). **5** *intr.* undergo financial ruin. **6** *tr. colloq.* enter without permission (*crashed the cocktail party*). **7** *intr. colloq.* be heavily defeated (*crashed to a 4-0 defeat*). **8** *intr. Computing* (of a machine or system) fail suddenly. **9** *tr. colloq.* pass (a red traffic light etc.). **10** *intr.* (often foll. by *out*) *slang* go to sleep, esp. in an improvised setting. ● *n.* **1 a** a loud and sudden smashing noise (*a thunder crash; the crash of crockery*). **b** a breakage (esp. of crockery, glass, etc.). **2 a** a violent collision, esp. of one vehicle with another or with an object. **b** the violent fall of an aircraft on to the land or sea. **3** ruin, esp. financial. **4** *Computing* a sudden failure which puts a system out of action. **5** (*attrib.*) done rapidly or urgently (*a crash course in first aid; a crash diet*). ● *adv.* with a crash (*the window went crash*). [Middle English: imitative]

crash[2] /kraʃ/ *n.* a coarse plain linen, cotton, etc., fabric. [Russian *krashenina* 'coloured linen']

crash barrier *n. Brit.* a barrier intended to prevent a vehicle from leaving the road etc.

crash-dive *v. & n.* ● *v.* **1** *intr.* **a** (of a submarine or its pilot) dive hastily and steeply in an emergency. **b** (of an aircraft or its pilot) dive and crash. **2** *tr.* cause to crash-dive. ● *n.* such a dive.

crash-halt *n. Brit.* a sudden stop by a vehicle.

crash helmet *n.* a helmet worn esp. by a motorcyclist to protect the head in case of a crash.

crashing /ˈkraʃɪŋ/ *adj. colloq.* overwhelming (*a crashing bore*).

crash-land *v.* **1** *intr.* (of an aircraft or its pilot) land hurriedly with a crash, usu. without lowering the undercarriage. **2** *tr.* cause (an aircraft) to crash-land. □ **crash landing** *n.*

crash pad *n. slang* a place to sleep, esp. in an emergency.

crash-stop *n.* = CRASH-HALT.

crash-tackle *n. Brit. Football* a vigorous tackle.

crasis /ˈkreɪsɪs/ *n.* (*pl.* **crases** /-siːz/) the contraction of two adjacent vowels in ancient Greek into one long vowel or diphthong. [Greek *krasis* 'mixture']

crass /kras/ *adj.* **1** grossly stupid (*a crass idea*). **2** gross (*crass stupidity*). **3** *literary* thick or gross. □ **crassitude** *n.* **crassly** *adv.* **crassness** *n.* [Latin *crassus* 'solid, thick']

-crat /krat/ *comb. form* a member or supporter of a particular form of government or rule (*autocrat; democrat*). [from or suggested by French *-crate*: see -CRACY]

cratch /kratʃ/ *n. Brit. dial.* a rack used for holding food for farm animals out of doors. [Middle English via Old French *creche* from Germanic: related to CRIB]

crate /kreɪt/ *n. & v.* ● *n.* **1** a large wickerwork basket or slatted wooden case etc. for packing esp. fragile goods for transportation. **2** *slang* an old aeroplane or other vehicle. ● *v.tr.* pack in a crate. □ **crateful** *n.* (*pl.* **-fuls**). [Middle English, perhaps from Dutch *krat* 'basket']

crater /ˈkreɪtə/ *n. & v.* ● *n.* **1** the mouth of a volcano. **2** a bowl-shaped cavity, esp. that made by the explosion of a shell or bomb. **3** *Astron.* a hollow with a raised rim on the surface of a planet or moon, caused by the impact of a meteorite. **4** *Antiq.* a large ancient Greek bowl, used for mixing wine. ● *v.tr.* form a crater in. □ **craterous** *adj.* [Latin from Greek *kratēr* 'mixing-bowl': see CRASIS]

-cratic /ˈkratɪk/ *comb. form* (also **-critical**) denoting a particular kind of government or rule (*autocratic; democratic*). □ **-cratically** *comb. form* (*adv.*). [from or suggested by French *-cratique*: see -CRACY]

craton /ˈkratɒn/ *n. Geol.* a large stable block of the earth's crust. [alteration of *kratogen* (= craton) from Greek *kratus* 'strength' + -GEN]

cravat /krəˈvat/ *n.* **1** a scarf worn by men inside an open-necked shirt. **2** *hist.* a necktie. □ **cravatted** *adj.* [French *cravate* via German *Krawat, Kroat* from Serbo-Croat *Hrvat* 'Croat' (from the scarf worn by Croatian mercenaries in France)]

crave /kreɪv/ *v.* **1** *tr.* **a** long for (*craved affection*). **b** beg for (*craves a blessing*). **2** *intr.* (foll. by *for*) long for; beg for (*craved for comfort*). □ **craver** *n.* [Old English *crafian*, related to Old Norse *krof* 'a request']

craven /ˈkreɪv(ə)n/ *adj. & n.* ● *adj.* (of a person, behaviour, etc.) cowardly; abject. ● *n.* a cowardly person. □ **cravenly** *adv.* **cravenness** /ˈkreɪv(ə)nnɪs/ *n.* [Middle English *cravand* etc. perhaps from Old French *cravanté* 'defeated', past part. of *cravanter*, ultimately from Latin *crepare* 'burst'; assimilated to -EN[3]]

craving /ˈkreɪvɪŋ/ *n.* (usu. foll. by *for*) a strong desire or longing.

craw /krɔː/ *n. Zool.* the crop of a bird or insect. □ **stick in one's craw** be unacceptable. [Middle English, related to Middle Dutch *crāghe*, Middle Low German *krage*, Middle High German *krage* 'neck, throat']

crawfish /ˈkrɔːfɪʃ/ *n. & v.* ● *n.* (*pl.* same) esp. *N. Amer.* = CRAYFISH. ● *v.intr.* (often foll. by *out*) *US colloq.* retreat; back out. [variant of CRAYFISH]

crawl /krɔːl/ *v. & n.* ● *v.intr.* **1** move slowly, esp. on hands and knees. **2** (of an insect, snake, etc.) move slowly with the body close to the ground etc. **3** walk or move slowly (*the train crawled into the station*). **4** (often foll. by *to*) *colloq.* behave obsequiously or ingratiatingly in the hope of advantage. **5** (often foll. by *with*) be covered or filled with crawling or moving things, or with people etc. compared to this. **6** (esp. of the skin) feel a creepy sensation. **7** swim with a crawl stroke. ● *n.* **1** an act of crawling. **2** a slow rate of movement. **3** a high-speed swimming stroke with alternate overarm movements and rapid straight-legged kicks. **4 a** (usu. in *comb.*) *Brit. colloq.* a leisurely journey between places of interest (*church crawl*). **b** = PUB CRAWL. □ **crawlingly** *adv.* **crawly** *adj.* (in senses 5, 6 of *v.*). [Middle English: origin unknown: cf. Swedish *kravla*, Danish *kravle*]

crawler /ˈkrɔːlə/ *n.* **1** *Brit. colloq.* a person who behaves obsequiously in the hope of advantage. **2** anything that crawls, such as an insect, a slow-moving vehicle, etc. **3** a tractor moving on an endless caterpillar track. **4** (usu. in *pl.*) esp. *US* a baby's overall for crawling in; rompers.

crawl space *n.* an underfloor space giving access to ducts.

cray /kreɪ/ *n. Austral. & NZ* = CRAYFISH.

crayfish /ˈkreɪfɪʃ/ *n.* (*pl.* same) **1** a small lobster-like freshwater crustacean, esp. of the genus *Astacus*. **2** = SPINY LOBSTER. [Middle English from Old French *crevice, crevis*, ultimately from Old High German *krebiz* CRAB[1]: assimilated to FISH[1]]

crayon /ˈkreɪən/ *n.* & *v.* ● *n.* **1** a stick or pencil of coloured chalk, wax, etc., used for drawing. **2** a drawing made with this. ● *v.tr.* draw with crayons. [French from *craie* from Latin *creta* 'chalk']

craze /kreɪz/ *v.* & *n.* ● *v.* **1** *tr.* (usu. as **crazed** *adj.*) make insane (*crazed with grief*). **2 a** *tr.* produce fine surface cracks on (pottery glaze etc.). **b** *intr.* develop such cracks. ● *n.* **1 a** a usu. temporary enthusiasm (*a craze for hula hoops*). **b** the object of this. **2** an insane fancy or condition. [Middle English, originally = break, shatter, perhaps from Old Norse]

crazy /ˈkreɪzi/ *adj.* & *n.* ● *adj.* (**crazier**, **craziest**) **1** *colloq.* (of a person, an action, etc.) insane or mad; foolish. **2** (usu. foll. by *about*) *colloq.* extremely enthusiastic. **3** *slang* **a** exciting, unrestrained. **b** excellent. **4** (*attrib.*) (of paving, a quilt, etc.) made of irregular pieces fitted together. **5** *archaic* (of a ship, building, etc.) unsound, shaky. ● *n.* (*pl.* **-ies**) *colloq.* a crazy person or thing. □ **like crazy** *colloq.* = *like mad* (see MAD). □ **crazily** *adv.* **craziness** *n.*

crazy bone *n. US* the funny bone.

crazy paving see CRAZY 4.

CRC *abbr. Printing* camera-ready copy.

creak /kriːk/ *n.* & *v.* ● *n.* a harsh scraping or squeaking sound. ● *v.intr.* **1** make a creak. **2 a** move with a creaking noise. **b** move stiffly and awkwardly. **c** show weakness or frailty under strain. □ **creakingly** *adv.* [Middle English, imitative: cf. CRAKE, CROAK]

creaky /ˈkriːki/ *adj.* (**creakier**, **creakiest**) **1** liable to creak. **2 a** stiff or frail (*creaky joints*). **b** (of a practice, institution, etc.) decrepit, dilapidated, outmoded. □ **creakily** *adv.* **creakiness** *n.*

cream /kriːm/ *n.*, *v.*, & *adj.* ● *n.* **1 a** the fatty content of milk which gathers at the top and can be made into butter by churning. **b** this eaten (often whipped) with a dessert, as a cake filling, etc. (*strawberries and cream*; *cream gateau*). **2** the part of a liquid that gathers at the top. **3** (usu. prec. by *the*) the best or choicest part of something, esp.: **a** the point of an anecdote. **b** an elite group of people (*the cream of the nation*). **4** a creamlike preparation, esp. a cosmetic (*hand cream*). **5** a very pale yellow or off-white colour. **6 a** a dish or sweet like or made with cream. **b** a soup or sauce containing milk or cream. **c** a full-bodied mellow sweet sherry. **d** a biscuit with a creamy sandwich filling. **e** a chocolate-covered usu. fruit-flavoured fondant. ● *v.* **1** *tr.* **a** take the cream from (milk). **b** take the best or a specified part from. **2** *tr.* work (butter etc.) to a creamy consistency. **3** *tr.* treat (the skin etc.) with cosmetic cream. **4** *tr.* add cream to (coffee etc.). **5** *intr.* (of milk or any other liquid) form a cream or scum. **6** *tr. US colloq.* defeat (esp. in a sporting contest). ● *adj.* pale yellow; off-white. □ **cream off 1** take (the best or a specified part) from a whole (*creamed off the brightest pupils*). **2** take the best or a specified part from (a whole). [Middle English via Old French *cre(s)me* from Late Latin *cramum* (perhaps from Gaulish) & ecclesiastical Latin *chrisma* CHRISM]

cream bun *n.* (also **cream cake**) *Brit.* a bun or cake filled or topped with cream.

cream cheese *n.* a soft rich cheese made from unskimmed milk and cream.

cream-coloured *adj.* pale yellowish white.

cream cracker *n. Brit.* a crisp dry unsweetened biscuit usu. eaten with cheese.

creamer /ˈkriːmə/ *n.* **1** a flat dish used for skimming the cream off milk. **2** a machine used for separating cream from milk. **3** a cream or milk substitute for adding to coffee or tea. **4** *N. Amer.* a jug for cream.

creamery /ˈkriːm(ə)ri/ *n.* (*pl.* **-ies**) **1** a factory producing butter and cheese. **2** a shop where milk, cream, etc., are sold; a dairy. [CREAM, suggested by French *crémerie*]

cream of tartar *n.* crystallized potassium hydrogen tartrate, used in medicine, baking powder, etc.

cream puff *n.* **1** a cake made of puff pastry filled with cream. **2** *colloq.* an ineffectual or effeminate person.

cream soda *n.* a carbonated vanilla-flavoured soft drink.

cream tea *n. Brit.* afternoon tea with scones, jam, and cream.

creamware /ˈkriːmwɛː/ *n.* earthenware of a rich cream colour.

creamy /ˈkriːmi/ *adj.* (**creamier**, **creamiest**) **1** like cream in consistency or colour. **2** rich in cream. □ **creamily** *adv.* **creaminess** *n.*

crease[1] /kriːs/ *n.* & *v.* ● *n.* **1 a** a line in paper etc. caused by folding. **b** a fold or wrinkle. **2** *Cricket* a line marking the position of the bowler or batsman (see POPPING CREASE, BOWLING CREASE). **3** an area near the goal in ice hockey or lacrosse into which the puck or the ball must precede the players. ● *v.* **1** *tr.* make creases in (material). **2** *intr.* become creased (*linen creases badly*). **3** *tr.* & *intr.* (often foll. by *up*) *Brit. colloq.* make or become incapable through laughter. **4** *tr.* esp. *US slang* graze with a bullet. [earlier *creast* = CREST 'ridge' (in material)]

crease[2] var. of KRIS.

create /kriːˈeɪt/ *v.* **1** *tr.* **a** (of natural or historical forces) bring into existence; cause (*poverty creates resentment*). **b** (of a person or persons) make or cause (*create a diversion*; *create a good impression*). **2** *tr.* originate (*an actor creates a part*). **3** *tr.* invest (a person) with a rank (*created him a lord*). **4** *intr. Brit. colloq.* make a fuss; grumble. □ **creatable** *adj.* [Middle English from Latin *creare*]

creatine /ˈkriːətiːn/ *n.* a product of protein metabolism found (esp. as the phosphate) in the muscles etc. of vertebrates. [Greek *kreas* 'meat' + -INE[4]]

creation /kriːˈeɪʃ(ə)n/ *n.* **1 a** the act of creating. **b** an instance of this. **2 a** (usu. **the Creation**) the creating of the universe regarded as an act of God. **b** (usu. **Creation**) everything so created; the universe. **3** a product of human intelligence, esp. of imaginative thought or artistic ability. **4 a** the act of investing with a title or rank. **b** an instance of this. [Middle English via Old French from Latin *creatio -onis* (as CREATE)]

creationism /kriːˈeɪʃ(ə)nɪz(ə)m/ *n.* the belief that the universe and living organisms originate from specific acts of divine creation, as in the biblical account, rather than by natural processes such as evolution. □ **creationist** *n.*

creation science *n.* the reinterpretation of scientific knowledge in accord with belief in the literal truth of the Bible, esp. regarding the origin of matter, life, and humankind.

creative /kriːˈeɪtɪv/ *adj.* **1** inventive and imaginative. **2** creating or able to create. □ **creatively** *adv.* **creativeness** *n.* **creativity** /-ˈtɪvɪti/ *n.*

creative accountancy *n.* (also **creative accounting**) *colloq.* the exploitation of loopholes in financial legislation in order to gain advantage or present figures in a misleadingly favourable light.

creator /kriːˈeɪtə/ *n.* **1** a person who creates. **2** (as **the Creator**) God. [Middle English via Old French *creat(o)ur* from Latin *creator -oris* (as CREATE)]

creature /ˈkriːtʃə/ *n.* **1 a** an animal, as distinct from a human being. **b** any living being (*we are all God's creatures*). **2** a person of a specified kind (*poor creature*). **3** a person owing status to and obsequiously subservient to another. **4** anything created; a creation. □ **creaturely** *adj.* [Middle English via Old French from Late Latin *creatura* (as CREATE)]

creature comforts *n.pl.* material comforts such as good food, warmth, etc.

creature of habit *n.* a person set in an unvarying routine.

crèche /krɛʃ, kreɪʃ/ *n.* **1** *Brit.* a day nursery for babies and young children. **2** *US* a representation of a Nativity scene. [French (as CRATCH)]

cred /krɛd/ *n. colloq.* credibility. [abbreviation]

credal see CREED.

credence /'kriːd(ə)ns/ *n.* **1** belief. **2** (in full **credence table**) a small side table, shelf, or niche which holds the elements of the Eucharist before they are consecrated. □ **give credence to** believe. [Middle English via Old French from medieval Latin *credentia*, from *credere* 'believe']

credential /krɪ'dɛnʃ(ə)l/ *n.* (usu. in *pl.*) **1** evidence of a person's achievements or trustworthiness, usu. in the form of certificates, references, etc. **2** a letter or letters of introduction. [medieval Latin *credentialis* (as CREDENCE)]

credenza /krɪ'dɛnzə/ *n.* a sideboard or cupboard. [Italian from medieval Latin (as CREDENCE)]

credibility /krɛdɪ'bɪlɪti/ *n.* **1** the condition of being credible or believable. **2** reputation, status. **3** = STREET CREDIBILITY.

credibility gap *n.* an apparent difference between what is said and what is true.

credible /'krɛdɪb(ə)l/ *adj.* **1** (of a person or statement) believable or worthy of belief. **2** (of a threat etc.) convincing. □ **credibly** *adv.* [Middle English from Latin *credibilis*, from *credere* 'believe']

■ **Usage** Do not confuse *credible* 'able to be believed' with *credulous* 'too ready to believe'. The difference is illustrated by *he was such a credible trickster that he completely took in his credulous collegues.*

credit /'krɛdɪt/ *n.* & *v.* ● *n.* **1** (usu. of a person) a source of honour, pride, etc. (*is a credit to the school*). **2** the acknowledgement of merit (*must give him credit for consistency*). **3** a good reputation (*his credit stands high*). **4 a** belief or trust (*I place credit in that*). **b** something believable or trustworthy (*that statement has credit*). **5 a** a person's financial standing; the sum of money at a person's disposal in a bank etc. **b** the power to obtain goods etc. before payment (based on the trust that payment will be made). **6** (usu. in *pl.*) an acknowledgement of a contributor's services to a film, television programme, etc. **7** *Brit.* a grade above a pass in an examination. **8** a reputation for solvency and honesty in business. **9** (in bookkeeping) **a** an entry on the right-hand side or column side of an account recording a payment received. **b** the sum entered. **c** the total of such sums. **d** the credit side of an account. **10 a** a certificate or other acknowledgement of a student's completion of a course. **b** a unit of study counting towards a degree etc. ● *v.tr.* (**credited**, **crediting**) **1** believe (*cannot credit it*). **2** (usu. foll. by *to*, *with*; often in *passive*) **a** enter on the credit side of an account (*credited £20 to him*; *credited him with £20*). **b** ascribe an achievement or good quality to (*he was credited with the goal*; *success was credited to his good sense*). **c** deem to be the originator or source of a thing (*now credited as its founder*). □ **do credit to** (or **do a person credit**) enhance the reputation of. **get credit for** be given credit for. **give a person credit for 1** enter (a sum) to a person's credit. **2** ascribe (a good quality) to a person. **give credit to** believe. **on credit** with an arrangement to pay later. **to one's credit** in one's praise, commendation, or defence (*to his credit, he refused the offer*). [French *crédit* from Italian *credito* or Latin *creditum*, from *credere credit-* 'believe, trust']

creditable /'krɛdɪtəb(ə)l/ *adj.* (often foll. by *to*) bringing credit or honour. □ **creditability** /-'bɪlɪti/ *n.* **creditably** *adv.*

credit account *n. Brit.* an account with a shop etc. for obtaining goods or services before payment.

credit card *n.* a card from a bank etc. authorizing the obtaining of goods on credit.

credit note *n. Brit.* a note given by a shop etc. in return for goods returned, stating the value of goods owed to the customer.

creditor /'krɛdɪtə/ *n.* **1** a person to whom a debt is owing. **2** a person or company that gives credit for money or goods (cf. DEBTOR). [Middle English via Anglo-French *creditour* (Old French *-eur*) from Latin *creditor -oris* (as CREDIT)]

credit rating *n.* an estimate of a person's suitability to receive commercial credit.

credit sale *n. Brit.* the sale of goods on credit.

credit title *n.* a credit (see CREDIT *n.* 6) at the beginning or end of a film or broadcast etc.

credit transfer *n.* a transfer of money from one person's bank account to another's.

creditworthy /'krɛdɪtwəːði/ *adj.* considered suitable to receive commercial credit. □ **creditworthiness** *n.*

credo /'kriːdəʊ, 'kreɪ-/ *n.* (*pl.* **-os**) **1** (**Credo**) a statement of belief; a creed, esp. the Apostles' or Nicene creed beginning in Latin with *credo*. **2** a musical setting of the Nicene Creed. [Middle English from Latin, = I believe]

credulous /'krɛdjʊləs/ *adj.* **1** too ready to believe; gullible. **2** (of behaviour) showing such gullibility. □ **credulity** /krɪ'djuːlɪti/ *n.* **credulously** *adv.* **credulousness** *n.* [Latin *credulus* from *credere* 'believe']

■ **Usage** See Usage Note at CREDIBLE.

Cree /kriː/ *n.* & *adj.* ● *n.* (*pl.* same or **Crees**) **1 a** an American Indian people living in central Canada and around Hudson Bay. **b** a member of this people. **2** the Algonquian language of this people. ● *adj.* of or relating to the Crees or their language. [Canadian French *Cris* (earlier *Cristinaux*) from Algonquian]

creed /kriːd/ *n.* **1** a set of principles or opinions, esp. as a philosophy of life (*his creed is moderation in everything*). **2** a brief formal summary of Christian belief, esp. (often **the Creed**): **a** = APOSTLES' CREED. **b** = NICENE CREED (cf. ATHANASIAN CREED). □ **credal** /'kriːd(ə)l/ *adj.* **creedal** *adj.* [Old English *crēda* from Latin CREDO]

creek /kriːk/ *n.* & *adj.* ● *n.* **1** *Brit.* **a** a small bay or harbour on a sea coast. **b** a narrow inlet on a sea coast or in a river bank. **2 a** esp. *US* a tributary of a river. **b** *Austral. & NZ* a stream or brook. **3** (**Creek**) **a** (*pl.* same) a member of a North American Indian people originally from Alabama and Georgia, or of a confederation of nations including this people. **b** the language of this people. ● *adj.* (**Creek**) of or relating to the Creek or their language. □ **up the creek** *slang* **1** in difficulties or trouble. **2** crazy. [Middle English *crike* from Old Norse *kriki* 'nook' (or partly via Old French *crique* from Old Norse), & Middle English *crēke* from Middle Dutch *krēke* (or from *crike* by lengthening): ultimate origin unknown]

creel /kriːl/ *n.* **1** a large wicker basket for fish. **2** an angler's basket. [Middle English, originally Scots: ultimate origin unknown]

creep /kriːp/ *v.* & *n.* ● *v.intr.* (*past* and *past part.* **crept** /krɛpt/) **1** move with the body prone and close to the ground; crawl. **2** (often foll. by *in*, *out*, *up*, etc.) come, go, or move slowly and stealthily or timidly (*crept out without being seen*). **3** enter slowly (into a person's affections, life, awareness, etc.) (*a feeling crept over her*; *crept into her heart*). **4** *colloq.* act abjectly or obsequiously in the hope of advancement. **5** (of a plant) grow along the ground or up a wall by means of tendrils etc. **6** (as **creeping** *adj.*) developing slowly and steadily (*creeping inflation*). **7** (of the flesh) feel as if insects etc. were creeping over it, as a result of fear, horror, etc. **8** (of materials) undergo creep (see sense 5 of *n.*). ● *n.* **1 a** the act of creeping. **b** an instance of this. **2** (in *pl.*; prec. by *the*) *colloq.* a nervous feeling of revulsion or fear (*gives me the creeps*). **3** *colloq.* an unpleasant person. **4** the gradual downward movement of disintegrated rock due to gravitational forces etc. **5** a gradual deformation of materials under stress. **6** a low arch under a railway embankment, road, etc. □ **creep up on** approach (a person) stealthily or unnoticed. [Old English *crēopan*, from Germanic]

creeper /'kriːpə/ *n.* **1** *Bot.* any climbing or creeping plant. **2** any bird that climbs, esp. a treecreeper. **3** *slang* a soft-soled shoe.

creeping barrage /'kriːpɪŋ/ *n.* an artillery barrage moving ahead of advancing troops.

creeping Jenny *n.* any of various creeping plants, esp. moneywort.

creeping Jesus *n. Brit. slang* an abject or hypocritical person.

creepy /ˈkriːpi/ *adj.* (**creepier**, **creepiest**) **1** *colloq.* having or producing a creeping of the flesh (*I feel creepy; a creepy film*). **2** given to creeping. □ **creepily** *adv.* **creepiness** *n.* [CREEP]

creepy-crawly /kriːpɪˈkrɔːli/ *n. & adj. colloq.* ● *n.* (*pl.* **-ies**) an insect, worm, or other small crawling creature. ● *adj.* creeping and crawling.

creese var. of KRIS.

cremate /krɪˈmeɪt/ *v.tr.* burn (a corpse etc.) to ashes. □ **cremation** /-ˈmeɪʃ(ə)n/ *n.* **cremator** *n.* [Latin *cremare* 'burn']

crematorium /krɛməˈtɔːrɪəm/ *n.* (*pl.* **crematoria** or **crematoriums**) a place for cremating corpses in a furnace. [modern Latin (as CREMATE, -ORY[1])]

crematory /ˈkrɛmət(ə)ri/ *adj. & n.* ● *adj.* of or relating to cremation. ● *n.* (*pl.* **-ies**) *N. Amer.* = CREMATORIUM.

crème brûlée /krɛm bruːˈleɪ/ *n.* (*pl.* **crèmes brûlées** *pronunc.* same or **crème brûlées** /-ˈleɪz/) a pudding of cream or custard topped with caramelized sugar. [French, = burnt cream]

crème caramel /krɛm karəˈmɛl, ˈkarəmɛl/ *n.* (*pl.* **crèmes caramel** *pronunc.* same or **crème caramels** /-ˈmɛlz, -mɛlz/) a set custard coated with caramel. [French]

crème de cassis /krɛm də kaˈsiːs/ *n.* a blackcurrant-flavoured liqueur. [French, literally 'cream of blackcurrant']

crème de la crème /krɛm də lɑː ˈkrɛm/ *n.* the best part; the elite. [French, literally 'cream of the cream']

crème de menthe /krɛm də ˈmɒnθ/ *n.* a peppermint-flavoured liqueur. [French, literally 'cream of mint']

crème fraiche /krɛm ˈfrɛʃ/ *n.* a type of thick cream made from double cream with the addition of buttermilk, sour cream, or yogurt. [French *crème fraîche*, literally 'fresh cream']

crenate /ˈkriːneɪt/ *adj. Bot. & Zool.* having a notched edge or rounded teeth. □ **crenated** *adj.* **crenation** /-ˈneɪʃ(ə)n/ *n.* **crenature** /ˈkrɛnətjʊə, ˈkriː-/ *n.* [modern Latin *crenatus* from popular Latin *crena* 'notch']

crenel /ˈkrɛn(ə)l/ *n.* (also **crenelle** /krɪˈnɛl/) an indentation or gap in the parapet of a tower, castle, etc., originally for shooting through etc. [Middle English from Old French *crenel*, ultimately from popular Latin *crena* 'notch']

crenellate /ˈkrɛn(ə)leɪt/ *v.tr.* (also **crenelate**) provide (a tower etc.) with battlements or loopholes. □ **crenellation** /-ˈleɪʃ(ə)n/ *n.* [French *créneler* (as CRENEL)]

Creole /ˈkriːəʊl/ *n. & adj.* ● *n.* **1 a** a descendant of European (esp. Spanish) settlers in the W. Indies or Central or S. America. **b** a white descendant of French settlers in the southern US, esp. Louisiana. **c** a person of mixed European and black descent. **2** a mother tongue formed from the contact of a European language (esp. English, French, or Portuguese) with another (esp. African) language. ● *adj.* **1** of or relating to a Creole or Creoles. **2** (usu. **creole**) of Creole origin or production (*creole cooking*). [French *créole, criole* from Spanish *criollo*, probably via Portuguese *crioulo* 'home-born slave' from *criar* 'breed', from Latin *creare* CREATE]

creolize /ˈkriːə(ʊ)lʌɪz, ˈkrɪ-/ *v.tr.* (also **-ise**) form a Creole from (another language). □ **creolization** /-ˈzeɪʃ(ə)n/ *n.*

creosote /ˈkriːəsəʊt/ *n. & v.* ● *n.* **1** (in full **creosote oil**) a dark brown oil distilled from coal tar, used as a wood preservative. **2** a colourless oily fluid distilled from wood, used as an antiseptic. ● *v.tr.* treat with creosote. [German *Kreosote*, from Greek *kreas* 'flesh' + *sōtēr* 'preserver', with reference to its antiseptic properties]

creosote bush *n.* a shrub of arid parts of Mexico and the western US, *Larrea tridentata*, with leaves smelling of creosote.

crêpe /kreɪp/ *n.* **1** a fine often gauzelike fabric with a wrinkled surface. **2** a thin pancake, usu. with a savoury or sweet filling. **3** (also **crêpe rubber**) a very hard-wearing wrinkled sheet rubber used for the soles of shoes etc. □ **crêpey** *adj.* **crêpy** *adj.* [French via Old French *crespe* 'curled' from Latin *crispus*]

crêpe de Chine /də ˈʃiːn/ *n.* a fine silk crêpe. [French, = China crêpe]

crêpe paper *n.* thin crinkled paper.

crêpe Suzette /suːˈzɛt/ *n.* (*pl.* **crêpes Suzette** *pronunc.* same) a small dessert pancake flamed in alcohol at the table.

crepitate /ˈkrɛpɪteɪt/ *v.intr.* **1** make a crackling sound. **2** *Zool.* (of a beetle) eject pungent fluid with a sharp report. □ **crepitant** *adj.* [Latin *crepitare*, frequentative of *crepare* 'creak']

crepitation /krɛpɪˈteɪʃ(ə)n/ *n.* **1** *Med.* = CREPITUS. **2** the action or sound of crackling or rattling.

crepitus /ˈkrɛpɪtəs/ *n. Med.* **1** a grating noise from the ends of a fractured bone rubbing together. **2** a similar sound heard from the chest in pneumonia etc. [Latin from *crepare* 'rattle']

crept *past* and *past part.* of CREEP.

crepuscular /krɪˈpʌskjʊlə, krɛ-/ *adj.* **1 a** of twilight. **b** dim. **2** *Zool.* appearing or active in twilight. [Latin *crepusculum* 'twilight']

Cres. *abbr.* Crescent.

cresc. *abbr.* (also **cres.**) *Mus.* = CRESCENDO.

crescendo /krɪˈʃɛndəʊ/ *n., adv., adj., & v.* ● *n.* (*pl.* **-os** or **crescendi** /-di/) **1** *Mus.* **a** a gradual increase in loudness. **b** a passage to be performed with such an increase. **2 a** progress towards a climax (*a crescendo of emotions*). **b** *disp.* a climax (*the storm reached a crescendo then died away*). ● *adv. & adj. Mus.* with a gradual increase in loudness. ● *v.intr.* (**-oes**, **-oed**) increase gradually in loudness or intensity. [Italian, part. of *crescere* 'grow' (as CRESCENT)]

■ **Usage** When used figuratively, *crescendo* should mean 'progress towards a climax', not the climax itself. In examples such as that given at 2b, use *climax* instead.

---

crescent /ˈkrɛz(ə)nt, ˈkrɛs-/ *n. & adj.* ● *n.* **1** the curved sickle shape of the waxing or waning moon. **2** anything of this shape, esp. *Brit.* a street forming an arc. **3 a** the crescent-shaped emblem of Islam or Turkey. **b** (**the Crescent**) the world or power of Islam. ● *adj.* **1** *poet.* increasing. **2** crescent-shaped. □ **crescentic** /-ˈsɛntɪk/ *adj.* [Middle English via Anglo-French *cressaunt*, Old French *creissant*, from Latin *crescere* 'grow']

cresol /ˈkriːsɒl/ *n. Chem.* any of three isomeric phenols present in creosote and used as disinfectants. Chem. formula: $CH_3C_6H_4OH$. □ **cresyl** *n.* [CREOSOTE + -OL[2]]

cress /krɛs/ *n.* any of various cruciferous plants usu. with pungent edible leaves, e.g. watercress. [Old English *cresse*, from West Germanic]

cresset /ˈkrɛsɪt/ *n. hist.* a metal container for oil, coal, etc., to be set alight for illumination, usu. mounted on a pole. [Middle English from Old French *cresset, craisset*, from *craisse* = *graisse* GREASE]

crest /krɛst/ *n. & v.* ● *n.* **1 a** a comb or tuft of feathers, fur, etc. on a bird's or animal's head. **b** something resembling this, esp. a plume of feathers on a helmet. **c** a helmet; the top of a helmet. **2** the top of something, esp. of a mountain, wave, roof, etc. **3** *Heraldry* **a** a device above the shield and helmet of a coat of arms. **b** such a device reproduced on writing paper or on a seal, signifying a family. **4 a** a line along the top of the neck of some animals. **b** the hair growing from this; a mane. **5** *Anat.* a ridge along the surface of a bone. ● *v.* **1** *tr.* reach the crest of (a hill, wave, etc.). **2** *tr.* **a** provide with a crest. **b** serve as a crest to. **3** *intr.* (of a wave) form into a crest. □ **on the crest of a wave** at the most favourable moment in one's progress. □ **crested** *adj.* (also in *comb.*). **crestless** *adj.* [Middle English via Old French *creste* from Latin *crista* 'tuft']

crestfallen /ˈkrɛstfɔːl(ə)n/ *adj.* **1** dejected, dispirited. **2** with a fallen or drooping crest.

cretaceous /krɪˈteɪʃəs/ *adj. & n.* ● *adj.* **1** of the nature of chalk. **2** (**Cretaceous**) *Geol.* of or relating to the last period of the Mesozoic era, with evidence of the first flowering plants, the extinction of dinosaurs, and extensive deposits of chalk. Cf. Appendix X. ● *n.* (**Cretaceous**) *Geol.* this era or system. [Latin *cretaceus* from *creta* 'chalk']

Cretan /ˈkriːt(ə)n/ *n. & adj.* ● *n.* a native of Crete, an island SE of the Greek mainland. ● *adj.* of or relating to Crete or the Cretans. [Latin *Cretanus* 'from *Creta*', from Greek *Krētē* 'Crete']

cretic /ˈkriːtɪk/ *n. Prosody* a foot containing one short or unstressed syllable between two long or stressed ones. [Latin *Creticus* from Greek *Krētikos* (as CRETAN)]

cretin /ˈkrɛtɪn/ *n.* **1** a person who is deformed and mentally retarded as the result of a thyroid deficiency. **2** *colloq.* a stupid person. □ **cretinism** *n.* **cretinize** *v.tr.* (also **-ise**). **cretinous** *adj.* [French *crétin* via Swiss French *creitin, crestin* from Latin *Christianus* CHRISTIAN]

cretonne /krɛˈtɒn, ˈkrɛtɒn/ *n.* (often *attrib.*) a heavy cotton fabric with a usu. floral pattern printed on one or both sides, used for upholstery. [French, of unknown origin]

Creutzfeldt–Jakob disease /krɔɪtsfɛltˈjakɒb/ *n.* a type of spongiform encephalopathy affecting human beings, characterized by progressive dementia. [named after H. G. *Creutzfeldt* (d. 1964) and A. *Jakob* (d. 1931), German physicians]

crevasse /krɪˈvas/ *n.* **1** a deep open crack, esp. in a glacier. **2** *US* a breach in a river levee. [French from Old French *crevace*: see CREVICE]

crevice /ˈkrɛvɪs/ *n.* a narrow opening or fissure, esp. in a rock or building etc. [Middle English via Old French *crevace*, from *crever* 'burst', from Latin *crepare*]

crew[1] /kruː/ *n. & v.* ● *n.* (often treated as *pl.*) **1 a** a body of people manning a ship, aircraft, train, etc. **b** such a body as distinguished from the captain or officers. **c** a body of people working together; a team. **2** *colloq.* a company of people; a gang (*a motley crew*). ● *v.* **1** *tr.* supply or act as a crew or member of a crew for. **2** *intr.* act as a crew or member of a crew. [Middle English via Old French *creüe* 'increase', fem. past part. of *croistre* 'grow', from Latin *crescere*]

crew[2] *past* of CROW[2].

crew-cut *n.* a very short haircut.

crewel /ˈkruːəl/ *n.* a thin worsted yarn used for tapestry and embroidery. [Middle English *crule* etc., of unknown origin]

crewel work *n.* a design worked in crewel on linen or cloth.

crewman /ˈkruːmən/ *n.* (*pl.* **-men**) a member of a crew.

crew neck *n.* a close-fitting round neckline, esp. on a sweater.

crib /krɪb/ *n. & v.* ● *n.* **1 a** a child's bed with barred or latticed sides; a cot. **b** *Brit.* a model of the Nativity of Christ, with a manger as a bed. **2** a barred container or rack for animal fodder. **3** *colloq.* **a** a translation of a text for the (esp. surreptitious) use of students. **b** plagiarized work etc. **4** a small house or cottage. **5** a framework lining the shaft of a mine. **6** *colloq.* **a** cribbage. **b** a set of cards given to the dealer at cribbage by all the players. **7** heavy crossed timbers used in foundations in loose soil etc. **8** *slang* a brothel. **9** *Austral.* & *NZ* a light meal; food. ● *v.tr.* (also *absol.*) (**cribbed**, **cribbing**) **1** *colloq.* copy (another person's work) unfairly or without acknowledgement. **2** confine in a small space. **3** *colloq.* pilfer, steal. **4** *Brit. colloq.* grumble. □ **cribber** *n.* [Old English *crib(b)*]

cribbage /ˈkrɪbɪdʒ/ *n.* a card game for two, three, or four players, in which the dealer may score from the cards in the crib (see CRIB 6b). [17th c.: origin unknown]

cribbage board *n.* a board with pegs and holes used for scoring at cribbage.

crib-biting *n.* a horse's habit of biting the manger while noisily breathing in and swallowing.

cribo /ˈkriːbəʊ, ˈkrʌɪbəʊ/ *n.* (*pl.* **-os**) = INDIGO SNAKE. [19th c.: origin unknown]

cribriform /ˈkrɪbrɪfɔːm/ *adj. Anat.* & *Bot.* having numerous small holes. [Latin *cribrum* 'sieve' + -FORM]

cribwork /ˈkrɪbwəːk/ *n.* = CRIB *n.* 7.

crick /krɪk/ *n. & v.* ● *n.* a sudden painful stiffness in the neck or the back etc. ● *v.tr.* produce a crick in (the neck etc.). [Middle English: origin unknown]

cricket[1] /ˈkrɪkɪt/ *n. & v.* ● *n.* a game played on a grass pitch with two teams of 11 players taking turns to bowl at a wicket defended by a batting player of the other team. ● *v.intr.* (**cricketed**, **cricketing**) play cricket. □ **not cricket** *Brit. colloq.* underhand or dishonourable behaviour contrary to traditional standards. □ **cricketer** *n.* [16th c.: origin uncertain]

cricket[2] /ˈkrɪkɪt/ *n.* any of various grasshopper-like insects of the order Orthoptera and esp. of the family Gryllidae, the males of which produce a characteristic chirping sound. [Middle English from Old French *criquet*, from *criquer* 'creak' (imitative)]

cricket bag *n.* a long bag used for carrying a cricketer's bat etc.

cricoid /ˈkrʌɪkɔɪd/ *adj. & n.* ● *adj.* ring-shaped. ● *n.* (in full **cricoid cartilage**) *Anat.* the ring-shaped cartilage of the larynx. [modern Latin *cricoides* from Greek *krikoeidēs*, from *krikos* 'ring']

cri de cœur /kriː də ˈkəː, French kri də kœr/ *n.* (*pl.* ***cris de cœur*** *pronunc.* same) a passionate appeal, complaint, or protest. [French, = cry from the heart]

cried *past* and *past part.* of CRY.

crier /ˈkrʌɪə/ *n.* (also **cryer**) **1** a person who cries. **2** an officer who makes public announcements in a court of justice. [Middle English from Anglo-French *criour*, Old French *criere*, from *crier* CRY]

crikey /ˈkrʌɪki/ *int. Brit. colloq.* an expression of astonishment. [euphemism for CHRIST]

crim /krɪm/ *n. & adj. Austral. slang* = CRIMINAL. [abbreviation]

crime /krʌɪm/ *n. & v.* ● *n.* **1 a** a serious offence punishable by law. **b** illegal acts as a whole (*resorted to crime*). **2** an evil act (*a crime against humanity*). **3** *colloq.* a shameful act (*a crime to tease them*). **4** *Brit.* a soldier's offence against military regulations. ● *v.tr. Brit. Mil.* etc. charge with or convict of an offence. [Middle English via Old French from Latin *crimen -minis* 'judgement, offence']

crime fighter *n.* a person who fights crime. □ **crime-fighting** *n.*

crime passionnel /ˌkriːm pasjəˈnɛl, French krim pɑsjɔnɛl/ *n.* (*pl.* ***crimes passionnels*** *pronunc.* same) a crime, esp. murder, committed in a fit of sexual jealousy. [French, = crime of passion]

crime sheet *n. Brit. Mil.* a record of a defendant's offences.

crime wave *n.* a sudden increase in crime.

crime writer *n.* a writer of detective fiction or thrillers.

criminal /ˈkrɪmɪn(ə)l/ *n. & adj.* ● *n.* a person who has committed a crime or crimes. ● *adj.* **1** of, involving, or concerning crime (*criminal records*; *criminal offence*). **2** having committed (and usu. been convicted of) a crime. **3** *Law* relating to or expert in criminal law rather than civil or political matters (*criminal code*; *criminal lawyer*). **4** *colloq.* scandalous, deplorable. □ **criminality** /-ˈnalɪti/ *n.* **criminally** *adv.* [Middle English from Late Latin *criminalis* (as CRIME)]

criminalistic /ˌkrɪmɪnəˈlɪstɪk/ *adj.* relating to criminals or their habits.

criminalistics /ˌkrɪmɪnəˈlɪstɪks/ *n.* esp. *US* forensic science.

criminalize /ˈkrɪmɪn(ə)lʌɪz/ *v.tr.* (also **-ise**) **1** turn (an activity) into a criminal offence by making it illegal. **2** turn (a person) into a criminal, esp. by making his or her activities illegal. □ **criminalization** /-ˈzeɪʃ(ə)n/ *n.*

criminal law *n.* law concerned with punishment of offenders (opp. CIVIL LAW 1).

criminal libel *n. Law* a deliberate defamatory statement in a permanent form.

criminal record see RECORD *n.* 6.

criminology /krɪmɪˈnɒlədʒi/ *n.* the scientific study of crime. □ **criminological** /-nəˈlɒdʒɪk(ə)l/ *adj.* **criminologist** *n.* [Latin *crimen -minis* CRIME + -OLOGY]

crimp /krɪmp/ *v. & n.* ● *v.tr.* **1** compress into small folds or ridges; frill. **2** make narrow wrinkles or flutings in; corrugate. **3** make waves in (the hair) with a hot iron. ● *n.* a crimped thing or form. □ **put a crimp in** *N. Amer. slang* thwart; interfere with. □ **crimper** *n.* **crimpy** *adj.* **crimpily** *adv.* **crimpiness** *n.* [Middle English, probably ultimately from Old High German *krimphan*]

crimplene /ˈkrɪmpliːn/ *n. propr.* a synthetic crease-resistant fibre and fabric.

crimson /ˈkrɪmz(ə)n/ *adj., n., & v.* ● *adj.* of a rich deep red inclining to purple. ● *n.* this colour. ● *v.tr. & intr.* make or become crimson. [Middle English *cremesin, crimesin*, ultimately from Arabic *ḳirmizī* KERMES]

cringe /krɪn(d)ʒ/ *v. & n.* ● *v.intr.* (**cringing**) **1** shrink back in fear or apprehension; cower. **2** (often foll. by *to*) behave obsequiously. ● *n.* the act or an instance of cringing. □ **cringer** *n.* [Middle English *crenge, crenche*, Old English *cringan, crincan*: see CRANK[1]]

cringle /ˈkrɪŋg(ə)l/ *n. Naut.* an eye of rope containing a thimble for another rope to pass through. [Low German *kringel*, diminutive of *kring* 'ring', from the root of CRANK[1]]

crinkle /ˈkrɪŋk(ə)l/ *n. & v.* ● *n.* a wrinkle or crease in paper, cloth, etc. ● *v.* **1** *intr.* form crinkles. **2** *tr.* form crinkles in. □ **crinkly** *adj.* [Middle English from Old English *crincan*: see CRANK[1]]

crinkle-cut *adj.* (of vegetables) cut with wavy edges.

crinoid /ˈkrʌɪnɔɪd/ *n. & adj. Zool.* ● *n.* any echinoderm of the class Crinoidea, usu. sedentary with feathery arms, e.g. sea lilies and feather stars. ● *adj.* of or relating to this class. □ **crinoidal** /-ˈnɔɪd(ə)l/ *adj.* [Greek *krinoeidēs* 'lily-like' from *krinon* 'lily']

crinoline /ˈkrɪn(ə)lɪn/ *n.* **1** a stiffened or hooped petticoat formerly worn to make a long skirt stand out. **2** a stiff fabric of horsehair etc. used for linings, hats, etc. [French, from Latin *crinis* 'hair' + *linum* 'thread']

cripple /ˈkrɪp(ə)l/ *n. & v.* ● *n. archaic* or *offens.* a person who is permanently lame. ● *v.tr.* **1** make a cripple of; lame. **2** disable, impair. **3** weaken or damage (an institution, enterprise, etc.) seriously (*crippled by the loss of funding*). □ **crippledom** *n.* **crippler** *n.* [Old English *crypel*, related to CREEP]

■ **Usage** The term *cripple* is no longer acceptable as a noun referring to a person. *Disabled* is usually used instead.

cris var. of KRIS.

crisis /ˈkrʌɪsɪs/ *n.* (*pl.* **crises** /-siːz/) **1 a** a decisive moment. **b** a time of danger or great difficulty. **2** the turning point, esp. of a disease. [Latin from Greek *krisis* 'decision', from *krinō* 'decide']

crisis management *n.* the practice of taking managerial action only when a crisis has developed.

crisp /krɪsp/ *adj., n., & v.* ● *adj.* **1** hard but brittle. **2 a** (of air) bracing. **b** (of a style or manner) lively, brisk and decisive. **c** (of features etc.) neat and clear-cut. **d** (of paper) stiff and crackling. **e** (of hair) closely curling. ● *n.* (in full **potato crisp**) *Brit.* a wafer-thin slice of potato fried until crisp and eaten as a snack or appetizer. ● *v.tr. & intr.* **1** make or become crisp. **2** curl in short stiff folds or waves. □ **burn to a crisp** make inedible or useless by burning. □ **crisply** *adv.* **crispness** *n.* [Old English from Latin *crispus* 'curled']

crispate /ˈkrɪspeɪt/ *adj.* **1** crisped. **2** *Bot. & Zool.* having a wavy margin. [Latin *crispare* 'curl']

crispbread /ˈkrɪspbrɛd/ *n.* **1** a thin crisp biscuit of crushed rye etc. **2** these collectively (*a packet of crispbread*).

crisper /ˈkrɪspə/ *n.* a compartment in a refrigerator for storing fruit and vegetables.

crispy /ˈkrɪspi/ *adj.* (**crispier**, **crispiest**) **1** crisp, brittle. **2** curly. **3** brisk. □ **crispiness** *n.*

criss-cross /ˈkrɪskrɒs/ *n., adj., adv., & v.* ● *n.* **1** a pattern of crossing lines. **2** the crossing of lines or currents etc. ● *adj.* crossing; in cross lines (*criss-cross marking*). ● *adv.* crosswise; at cross purposes. ● *v.* **1** *intr.* **a** intersect repeatedly. **b** move crosswise. **2** *tr.* mark or make with a criss-cross pattern. [17th c., from *Christ's cross*: later treated as reduplication of CROSS]

crista /ˈkrɪstə/ *n.* (*pl.* **cristae** /-tiː/) **1** *Anat. & Zool.* a ridge or crest. **2** *Anat.* an inward fold of the inner membrane of a mitochondrion. □ **cristate** *adj.* [Latin]

cristobalite /krɪˈstəʊbəlʌɪt/ *n. Mineral.* a principal form of silica, occurring as opal. [German *Cristobalit*, from Cerro San *Cristóbal* in Mexico, where it was discovered]

crit /krɪt/ *n. Brit. colloq.* **1** = CRITICISM 2. **2** = CRITIQUE. **3** *Physics* critical mass. [abbreviation]

criterion /krʌɪˈtɪərɪən/ *n.* (*pl.* **criteria** /-rɪə/) a principle or standard that a thing is judged by. □ **criterial** *adj.* [Greek *kritērion* 'means of judging' (cf. CRITIC)]

■ **Usage** The plural form of *criterion, criteria*, is often used incorrectly as the singular. In the singular, *criterion* should always be used.

critic /ˈkrɪtɪk/ *n.* **1** a person who censures. **2** a person who reviews or judges the merits of literary, artistic, or musical works etc., esp. regularly or professionally. **3** a person engaged in textual criticism. [Latin *criticus* from Greek *kritikos*, via *kritēs* 'judge' from *krinō* 'judge, decide']

critical /ˈkrɪtɪk(ə)l/ *adj.* **1 a** making or involving adverse or censorious comments or judgements. **b** expressing or involving criticism. **2** skilful at or engaged in criticism. **3** providing textual criticism (*a critical edition of Milton*). **4 a** of or at a crisis; involving risk or suspense (*in a critical condition; a critical operation*). **b** decisive, crucial (*of critical importance; at the critical moment*). **5 a** *Math. & Physics* marking a transition from one state etc. to another (*critical angle*). **b** *Physics* (of a nuclear reactor) maintaining a self-sustaining chain reaction. □ **criticality** /-ˈkalɪti/ *n.* (in sense 5). **critically** *adv.* **criticalness** *n.* [Latin *criticus*: see CRITIC]

critical apparatus *n.* = APPARATUS 4.

critical mass *n.* **1** the amount of fissile material needed to maintain a nuclear chain reaction. **2** the minimum size required to start a thing off or to keep a thing going.

critical path *n.* the sequence of stages determining the minimum time needed for an operation.

critical temperature *n.* the temperature above which a gas cannot be liquefied by pressure.

criticaster /krɪtɪˈkastə, ˈkrɪtɪkastə/ *n.* a minor or inferior critic.

criticism /ˈkrɪtɪsɪz(ə)m/ *n.* **1 a** finding fault; censure. **b** a statement or remark expressing this. **2 a** the work of a critic. **b** an article, essay, etc., expressing or containing an analytical evaluation of something. [CRITIC or Latin *criticus* + -ISM]

criticize /ˈkrɪtɪsʌɪz/ *v.tr.* (also **-ise**) (also *absol.*) **1** find fault with; censure. **2** discuss critically. □ **criticizable** *adj.* **criticizer** *n.*

critique /krɪˈtiːk/ *n. & v.* ● *n.* a critical essay or analysis; an instance or the process of formal criticism. ● *v.tr.* (**critiques**, **critiqued**, **critiquing**) discuss critically. [French, from Greek *kritikē tekhnē* 'critical art']

critter /ˈkrɪtə/ *n.* **1** *dial.* or *joc.* a creature. **2** *derog.* a person. [variant of CREATURE]

croak /krəʊk/ *n.* & *v.* ● *n.* **1** a deep hoarse sound as of a frog or a raven. **2** a sound resembling this. ● *v.* **1 a** *intr.* utter a croak. **b** *tr.* utter with a croak or in a dismal manner. **2** *slang* **a** *intr.* die. **b** *tr.* kill. [Middle English: imitative]

croaker /ˈkrəʊkə/ *n.* **1** an animal that croaks. **2** a prophet of evil.

croaky /ˈkrəʊki/ *adj.* (**croakier**, **croakiest**) (of a voice) croaking; hoarse. ▫ **croakily** *adv.*

Croat /ˈkrəʊat/ *n.* & *adj.* ● *n.* **1 a** a native of Croatia in the former Yugoslavia. **b** a person of Croatian descent. **2** the Slavonic dialect of the Croats (cf. SERBO-CROAT). ● *adj.* of or relating to the Croats or their dialect. [modern Latin *Croatae* from Serbo-Croatian *Hrvat*]

Croatian /krəʊˈeɪʃɪən, -ʃ(ə)n/ *n.* & *adj.* = CROAT.

croc /krɒk/ *n. colloq.* a crocodile. [abbreviation]

croceate /ˈkrəʊsɪeɪt/ *adj.* saffron-coloured. [Latin *croceus* from CROCUS]

crochet /ˈkrəʊʃeɪ, -ʃi/ *n.* & *v.* ● *n.* **1** a handicraft in which yarn is made up into a patterned fabric by means of a hooked needle. **2** work made in this way. ● *v.* (**crocheted** /-ʃeɪd/; **crocheting** /-ʃeɪɪŋ/) **1** *tr.* make by crocheting. **2** *intr.* do crochet. ▫ **crocheter** /ˈkrəʊʃeɪə/ *n.* [French, diminutive of *croc* 'hook']

croci *pl.* of CROCUS.

crocidolite /krə(ʊ)ˈsɪdəlʌɪt/ *n.* a fibrous blue or green silicate of iron and sodium; blue asbestos. [Greek *krokis -idos* 'nap of cloth']

crock[1] /krɒk/ *n.* & *v. Brit. colloq.* ● *n.* **1** an inefficient, broken-down, or worn-out person. **2** a worn-out vehicle, ship, etc. ● *v.* **1** *intr.* (foll. by *up*) break down, collapse. **2** *tr.* (often foll. by *up*) disable, cause to collapse. [originally Scots, perhaps from Flemish: probably related to CRACK]

crock[2] /krɒk/ *n.* **1** an earthenware pot or jar. **2** a broken piece of earthenware. [Old English *croc(ca)*]

crockery /ˈkrɒk(ə)ri/ *n.* earthenware or china dishes, plates, etc. [obsolete *crocker* 'potter': see CROCK[2]]

crocket /ˈkrɒkɪt/ *n. Archit.* a small carved ornament (usu. a bud or curled leaf) on the inclined side of a pinnacle etc. [Middle English from a variant of Old French *crochet*: see CROCHET]

crocodile /ˈkrɒkədʌɪl/ *n.* **1 a** a large tropical or subtropical amphibious reptile (crocodilian) of the family Crocodylidae, with long jaws (narrower than those of an alligator). **b** leather from its skin, used to make bags, shoes, etc. **2** *Brit. colloq.* a line of schoolchildren etc. walking in pairs. [Middle English via Old French *cocodrille*, medieval Latin *cocodrillus*, and Latin *crocodilus* from Greek *krokodilos* 'worm of the stones', from *krokē* 'pebble' + *drilos* 'worm']

crocodile clip *n.* a clip with teeth for gripping.

crocodile tears *n.* insincere grief (from the belief that crocodiles wept while devouring or alluring their prey).

crocodilian /krɒkəˈdɪlɪən/ *n.* & *adj.* ● *n.* any large predatory amphibious reptile of the order Crocodilia, with long jaws, short legs, and a powerful tail, including crocodiles, alligators, caymans, and gharials. ● *adj.* of or relating to the crocodilians.

crocus /ˈkrəʊkəs/ *n.* (*pl.* **crocuses** or **croci** /-kʌɪ, -kiː/) a small spring-flowering plant of the genus *Crocus* (iris family), growing from a corm and having bright yellow, purple, or white flowers. See also AUTUMN CROCUS. [Middle English, = saffron (obtained from a species of crocus), via Latin from Greek *krokos* 'crocus', of Semitic origin]

Croesus /ˈkriːsəs/ *n.* a person of great wealth. [name of a king of Lydia (6th c. BC)]

croft /krɒft/ *n.* & *v. Brit.* ● *n.* **1** an enclosed piece of (usu. arable) land. **2** a small rented farm in Scotland or northern England. ● *v.intr.* farm a croft; live as a crofter. [Old English: origin unknown]

crofter /ˈkrɒftə/ *n. Brit.* a person who rents a smallholding, esp. a joint tenant of a divided farm in parts of Scotland.

Crohn's disease /ˈkrəʊnz/ *n.* a chronic inflammatory disease of the intestines, esp. the colon and ileum, causing ulcers and fistulae. [named after B. B. *Crohn*, US pathologist d. 1983]

croissant /ˈkrwasɒŋ/ *n.* a crescent-shaped roll made of rich yeast pastry. [French, formed as CRESCENT]

Cro-Magnon /krəʊˈmanjɒ̃, -ˈmagnən/ *adj. Anthropol.* of a tall broad-faced European race of late palaeolithic times. [name of a hill in the Dordogne, France, where remains were found in 1868]

cromlech /ˈkrɒmlɛk/ *n.* **1** (in Wales) a megalithic tomb. **2** (in Brittany) a stone circle. [Welsh (from *crom*, fem. of *crwm* 'arched' + *llech* 'flat stone'); in sense 2 via French from Breton *krommlec'h*]

crone /krəʊn/ *n.* **1** a withered old woman. **2** an old ewe. [Middle English, ultimately from Old Northern French *carogne* CARRION]

cronk /krɒŋk/ *adj. Austral. colloq.* **1** unsound; liable to collapse. **2 a** fraudulent. **b** (of a racehorse) dishonestly run, unfit. [19th c.: cf. CRANK[3]]

crony /ˈkrəʊni/ *n.* (*pl.* **-ies**) often *derog.* a close friend or companion. [17th-c. *chrony*, Cambridge university slang, from Greek *khronios* 'long-standing' from *khronos* 'time']

crook /krʊk/ *n.*, *v.*, & *adj.* ● *n.* **1** the hooked staff of a shepherd or bishop. **2 a** a bend, curve, or hook. **b** anything hooked or curved. **3** *colloq.* **a** a rogue; a swindler. **b** a professional criminal. ● *v.tr.* & *intr.* bend, curve. ● *adj.* **1** *Brit.* crooked. **2** *Austral.* & *NZ colloq.* **a** unsatisfactory, out of order; (of a person) unwell, injured. **b** unpleasant. **c** dishonest, unscrupulous. **d** bad-tempered, irritable, angry. ▫ **go crook** (usu. foll. by *at, on*) *Austral.* & *NZ colloq.* lose one's temper; become angry. ▫ **crookery** *n.* [Middle English from Old Norse *krókr* 'hook']

crookback /ˈkrʊkbak/ *n.* a hunchback. ▫ **crookbacked** *adj.*

crooked /ˈkrʊkɪd/ *adj.* (**crookeder**, **crookedest**) **1 a** not straight or level; bent, curved, twisted. **b** deformed, bent with age. **2** *colloq.* not straightforward; dishonest. **3** /krʊkt/ *Austral.* & *NZ slang* = CROOK *adj.* 2. **4** (foll. by *on*) *Austral. slang* hostile to. ▫ **crookedly** *adv.* **crookedness** *n.* [Middle English from CROOK, probably modelled on Old Norse *krókóttr*]

croon /kruːn/ *v.* & *n.* ● *v.tr.* & *intr.* hum or sing in a low subdued voice, esp. in a sentimental manner. ● *n.* such singing. ▫ **crooner** *n.* [Middle English (originally Scots & northern English) from Middle Dutch & Middle Low German *krōnen* 'groan, lament']

crop /krɒp/ *n.* & *v.* ● *n.* **1 a** the produce of cultivated plants, esp. cereals. **b** the season's total yield of this (*a good crop*). **2** a group or an amount produced or appearing at one time (*this year's crop of students*). **3** (in full **hunting crop**) the stock or handle of a whip. **4 a** a style of hair cut very short. **b** the cropping of hair. **5** *Zool.* **a** the pouch in a bird's gullet where food is stored or prepared for digestion. **b** a similar organ in other animals. **6** the entire tanned hide of an animal. **7** a piece cut off or out of something. ● *v.* (**cropped**, **cropping**) **1** *tr.* **a** cut off. **b** (of animals) bite off and eat (the tops of plants). **2** *tr.* cut (hair, cloth, edges of a book, etc.) short. **3** *tr.* gather or reap (produce). **4** *tr.* (foll. by *with*) sow or plant (land) with a crop. **5** *intr.* (of land) bear a crop. ▫ **crop out** *Geol.* appear at the surface. **crop up 1** (of a subject, circumstance, etc.) appear or come to one's notice unexpectedly. **2** *Geol.* appear at the surface. [Old English *crop(p)*]

crop circle *n.* a circular depression in a standing crop, often only visible from the air.

crop dusting *n.* the spraying of powdered insecticide or fertilizer on crops, esp. from the air.

crop-eared *adj.* having the ears (esp. of animals) or hair cut short.

crop-full *adj.* having a full crop or stomach.

crop-over *n.* a W. Indian celebration marking the end of the sugar cane harvest.

cropper /ˈkrɒpə/ *n.* a crop-producing plant of specified quality (*a good cropper*; *a heavy cropper*). □ **come a cropper** *colloq.* **1** fall heavily. **2** fail badly.

croquet /ˈkrəʊkeɪ, -ki/ *n.* & *v.* ● *n.* **1** a game played on a lawn, with wooden balls which are driven through a series of hoops with mallets. **2** the act of croqueting a ball. ● *v.tr.* (**croqueted** /-keɪd/; **croqueting** /-keɪɪŋ/) drive away (one's opponent's ball in croquet) by placing one's own against it and striking one's own. [perhaps a dialect form of French CROCHET 'hook']

croquette /krɒˈkɛt/ *n.* a fried breaded roll or ball of mashed potato or minced meat etc. [French from *croquer* 'crunch']

crore /krɔː/ *n. Anglo-Ind.* **1** ten million. **2** one hundred lakhs (of rupees, units of measurement, persons, etc.). [Hindi *k(a)rōr*, ultimately from Sanskrit *koṭi* 'apex']

crosier /ˈkrəʊzɪə, -ʒə/ *n.* (also **crozier**) **1** a hooked staff carried by a bishop as a symbol of pastoral office. **2** a crook. [originally = bearer of a crook, via Old French *crocier* & Old French *croisier* from *crois* CROSS]

cross /krɒs/ *n.*, *v.*, & *adj.* ● *n.* **1** an upright post with a transverse bar, as used in antiquity for crucifixion. **2 a** (**the Cross**) in Christianity, the cross on which Christ was crucified. **b** a representation of this as an emblem of Christianity. **c** = SIGN OF THE CROSS. **3** a staff surmounted by a cross and borne before an archbishop or in a religious procession. **4 a** a thing or mark shaped like a cross, esp. a figure made by two short intersecting lines (+ or ×). **b** a monument in the form of a cross, esp. one in the centre of a town or on a tomb. **5** a cross-shaped decoration indicating rank in some orders of knighthood or awarded for personal valour. **6 a** an intermixture of animal breeds or plant varieties. **b** an animal or plant resulting from this. **7** (foll. by *between*) a mixture or compromise of two things. **8 a** a crosswise movement, e.g. of an actor on stage. **b** *Football* etc. a pass of the ball across the pitch esp. towards the centre. **c** *Boxing* a blow with a crosswise movement of the fist. **9** a trial or affliction; something to be endured (*bear one's crosses*). ● *v.* **1** *tr.* (often foll. by *over*; also *absol.*) go across or to the other side of (a road, river, sea, etc.). **2 a** *intr.* intersect or be across one another (*the roads cross near the bridge*). **b** *tr.* cause to do this; place crosswise (*cross one's legs*). **3** *tr.* **a** draw a line or lines across. **b** *Brit.* mark (a cheque) with two parallel lines, and often an annotation, to indicate that it must be paid into a named bank account. **4** *tr.* (foll. by *off*, *out*, *through*) cancel or obliterate or remove from a list with lines drawn across. **5** *tr.* (often *refl.*) make the sign of the cross on or over. **6** *intr.* **a** pass in opposite or different directions. **b** (of letters between two correspondents) each be dispatched before receipt of the other. **c** (of telephone lines) become wrongly interconnected so that intrusive calls can be heard. **7** *tr. Football* etc. pass (the ball) across the pitch, esp. towards the centre. **8** *tr.* **a** cause to interbreed. **b** cross-fertilize (plants). **9** *tr.* thwart or frustrate (*crossed in love*). **10** *tr. slang* cheat. ● *adj.* **1** (often foll. by *with*) peevish, angry. **2** (usu. *attrib.*) transverse; reaching from side to side. **3** (usu. *attrib.*) intersecting. **4** (usu. *attrib.*) contrary, opposed, reciprocal. □ **as cross as two sticks** *Brit.* extremely angry or peevish. **at cross purposes** misunderstanding or conflicting with one another. **cross one's fingers** (or **keep one's fingers crossed**) **1** put one finger across another as a sign of hoping for good luck. **2** trust in good luck. **cross the floor** *Brit.* join the opposing side in a debating assembly. **cross one's heart** make a solemn pledge, esp. by crossing one's front. **cross one's mind** (of a thought etc.) occur to one, esp. transiently. **cross a person's palm** (usu. foll. by *with*) pay a person for a favour. **cross the path of 1** meet with (a person). **2** thwart. **cross swords** (often foll. by *with*) encounter in opposition; have an argument or dispute. **cross wires** (or **get one's wires crossed**) **1** become wrongly connected by telephone. **2** have a misunderstanding. **on the cross** *Brit.* **1** diagonally. **2** *slang* fraudulently, dishonestly. □ **crossly** *adv.* **crossness** *n.* [Old English *cros* via Old Norse *kross* and Old Irish *cros* from Latin *crux cruc-*]

cross- /krɒs/ *comb. form* **1** denoting movement or position across something (*cross-channel*; *cross-country*). **2** denoting interaction (*cross-breed*; *cross-curricular*; *cross-fertilize*). **3 a** passing from side to side; transverse (*crossbar*; *cross-current*). **b** having a transverse part (*crossbow*). **4** describing the form or figure of a cross (*cross-keys*; *crossroads*).

crossbar /ˈkrɒsbɑː/ *n.* a horizontal bar, esp. held on a pivot or between two upright bars etc., e.g. of a bicycle or of a football goal.

cross-bedding /ˈkrɒsbɛdɪŋ/ *n. Geol.* lines of stratification crossing the main rock strata. Also called *false bedding*.

cross-bench /ˈkrɒsbɛntʃ/ *n. Brit.* a seat in Parliament (now only the House of Lords) occupied by a member not taking the whip from a political party. □ **cross-bencher** *n.*

crossbill /ˈkrɒsbɪl/ *n.* a finch of the genus *Loxia*, having a bill with crossed mandibles with which it opens pine cones.

crossbones /ˈkrɒsbəʊnz/ *n.* a representation of two crossed thigh bones.

cross-border *adj.* passing, occurring, or performed across a border between two countries.

crossbow /ˈkrɒsbəʊ/ *n.* esp. *hist.* a bow fixed across a wooden stock, with a groove for usu. a bolt and with a mechanism for drawing and releasing the string. □ **crossbowman** *n.* (*pl.* **-men**).

cross-breed /ˈkrɒsbriːd/ *n.* & *v.* ● *n.* **1** a breed of animals or plants produced by crossing. **2** an individual animal or plant of a cross-breed. ● *v.tr.* (*past* and *past part.* **-bred**) produce by crossing.

cross-check /ˈkrɒstʃɛk/ *v.* & *n.* ● *v.tr.* check by a second or alternative method, or by several methods. ● *n.* an instance of cross-checking.

cross-country /krɒsˈkʌntri/ *adj.*, *adv.*, & *n.* ● *adj.* & *adv.* **1** across fields or open country. **2** not keeping to main or direct roads. ● *n.* (*pl.* **-ies**) a cross-country race.

cross-cultural /krɒsˈkʌltʃ(ə)r(ə)l/ *adj.* of or relating to different cultures or comparison between them.

cross-cut /ˈkrɒskʌt/ *adj.* & *n.* ● *adj.* cut across the main grain or axis. ● *n.* a diagonal cut, path, etc.

cross-cut saw *n.* a saw for cutting across the grain of wood.

cross-dating /ˈkrɒsdeɪtɪŋ/ *n. Archaeol.* dating by correlation with another site or level.

cross-dressing /krɒsˈdrɛsɪŋ/ *n.* the practice of wearing the clothes of the opposite sex. □ **cross-dress** *v.intr.* **cross-dresser** *n.*

crosse /krɒs/ *n.* a stick with a triangular net at the end for conveying the ball in lacrosse. [French from Old French *croce*, *croc* 'hook']

cross-examine /krɒsɪgˈzamɪn/ *v.tr.* examine (esp. a witness in a law court) to check or extend testimony already given. □ **cross-examination** /-ˈneɪʃ(ə)n/ *n.* **cross-examiner** *n.*

cross-eyed /ˈkrɒsʌɪd/ *adj.* (as a disorder) having one or both eyes turned permanently inwards towards the nose.

cross-fade /ˈkrɒsfeɪd/ *v.* & *n. Radio* etc. ● *v.intr.* fade in one sound as another is faded out. ● *n.* an act of cross-fading.

cross-fertilize /krɒsˈfəːtɪlʌɪz/ *v.tr.* (also **-ise**) **1** fertilize (an animal or plant) from another usu. of the same species. **2** help by the interchange of ideas etc. □ **cross-fertilization** /-ˈzeɪʃ(ə)n/ *n.*

crossfire /ˈkrɒsfʌɪə/ *n.* **1** firing in two crossing directions simultaneously. **2 a** attack or criticism from several sources at once. **b** a lively or combative exchange of views etc.

cross-grain /ˈkrɒsgreɪn/ *n.* a grain in timber that runs across the regular grain (often *attrib.*: *cross-grain shrinkage*).

cross-grained /ˈkrɒsgreɪnd/ *adj.* **1** (of timber) having a cross-grain. **2** perverse, intractable.

cross-hair /ˈkrɒshɛː/ *n.* a fine wire at the focus of an optical instrument for use in measurement etc.

cross-hatch /ˈkrɒshatʃ/ *v.tr.* shade with intersecting sets of parallel lines.

cross-head /ˈkrɒshɛd/ *n.* **1** a bar between the piston rod and connecting rod in a steam engine. **2** = CROSS-HEADING.

cross-heading /ˈkrɒshɛdɪŋ/ *n.* a heading to a paragraph printed across a column in the body of an article in a newspaper etc.

crossing /ˈkrɒsɪŋ/ *n.* **1** a place where things (esp. roads) cross. **2** a place at which one may cross a street etc. (*pedestrian crossing*). **3** a journey across water (*had a smooth crossing*). **4** the intersection of a church nave and transepts. **5** *Biol.* mating.

crossing over *n.* an exchange of genes between homologous chromosomes (cf. RECOMBINATION).

cross-legged /krɒsˈlɛgd, -ˈlɛgɪd, ˈkrɒs-/ *adj.* with one leg crossed over the other.

cross-link /ˈkrɒslɪŋk/ *n.* (also **cross-linkage**) *Chem.* a bond between chains of atoms in a polymer etc.

crossmatch /krɒsˈmatʃ/ *v.tr.* *Med.* test the compatibility of (a donor's and a recipient's blood or tissue). ▫ **crossmatching** *n.*

crossover /ˈkrɒsəʊvə/ *n.* & *adj.* ● *n.* **1** a point or place of crossing from one side to the other. **2** the process of crossing over, esp. from one style or genre to another. ● *adj.* **1** having a part that crosses over. **2** that crosses over, esp. from one style or genre to another.

crosspatch /ˈkrɒspatʃ/ *n.* *colloq.* a bad-tempered person. [CROSS *adj.* 1 + obsolete *patch* 'fool, clown']

crosspiece /ˈkrɒspiːs/ *n.* a transverse beam or other component of a structure etc.

cross-ply /ˈkrɒsplʌɪ/ *adj.* *Brit.* (of a tyre) having fabric layers with cords lying crosswise.

cross-pollinate /krɒsˈpɒlɪneɪt/ *v.tr.* pollinate (a plant) with pollen from another plant. ▫ **cross-pollination** /-ˈneɪʃ(ə)n/ *n.*

cross-question /krɒsˈkwɛstʃ(ə)n/ *v.tr.* = CROSS-EXAMINE.

cross-refer /krɒsrɪˈfəː/ *v.intr.* (**-referred**, **-referring**) refer from one part of a book, article, etc., to another.

cross-reference /ˈkrɒsrɛf(ə)r(ə)ns/ *n.* & *v.* ● *n.* a reference from one part of a book, article, etc., to another. ● *v.tr.* provide with cross-references.

cross-rhythm /ˈkrɒsrɪð(ə)m/ *n.* **1** a rhythm used simultaneously with another rhythm or other rhythms. **2** an instance of using two or more rhythms simultaneously.

crossroad /ˈkrɒsrəʊd/ *n.* **1** (usu. in *pl.*) an intersection of two or more roads. **2** *US* a road that crosses a main road or joins two main roads. ▫ **at the crossroads** at a critical point in one's life.

cross-ruff /ˈkrɒsrʌf/ *n.* & *v.* *Bridge* etc. ● *n.* the alternate trumping of partners' leads. ● *v.intr.* play in this way.

cross-section /krɒsˈsɛkʃ(ə)n/ *n.* **1 a** a cutting of a solid at right angles to an axis. **b** a plane surface produced in this way. **c** a representation of this. **2** a representative sample, esp. of people. **3** *Physics* a quantity expressing the probability of interaction between subatomic particles. ▫ **cross-sectional** *adj.*

cross stitch *n.* & *v.* ● *n.* **1** a stitch formed of two stitches crossing each other. **2** needlework done using this stitch. ● *v.tr.* (**cross-stitch**) sew or embroider with cross stitches.

cross-subsidize /krɒsˈsʌbsɪdʌɪz/ *v.tr.* (also **-ise**) subsidize out of the profits of another business or activity. ▫ **cross-subsidy** *n.*

crosstalk /ˈkrɒstɔːk/ *n.* **1** unwanted transfer of signals between communication channels. **2** *Brit.* witty talk; repartee.

crosstrees /ˈkrɒstriːz/ *n.pl.* *Naut.* a pair of horizontal timbers at the top of a lower mast, supporting the topmast.

cross-voting /ˈkrɒsvəʊtɪŋ/ *n.* voting for a party not one's own, or for more than one party.

crosswalk /ˈkrɒswɔːk/ *n.* *N. Amer.* & *Austral.* a pedestrian crossing.

crossways /ˈkrɒsweɪz/ *adv.* = CROSSWISE.

crosswind /ˈkrɒswɪnd/ *n.* a wind blowing across one's direction of travel.

crosswise /ˈkrɒswʌɪz/ *adj.* & *adv.* **1** in the form of a cross; intersecting. **2** transverse or transversely.

crossword /ˈkrɒswəːd/ *n.* (also **crossword puzzle**) a puzzle of a grid of squares and blanks into which words crossing vertically and horizontally have to be filled from clues.

crostini /krɒˈstiːni/ *n.pl.* small pieces of toasted or fried bread served with a topping as a starter. [Italian, pl. of *crostino* 'little crust']

crotch /krɒtʃ/ *n.* a place where something forks, esp. the legs of the human body or a garment (cf. CRUTCH 3). [perhaps = Middle English & Old French *croc(he)* 'hook', formed as CROOK]

crotchet /ˈkrɒtʃɪt/ *n.* **1** *Brit.* *Mus.* a note having the time value of a quarter of a semibreve and usu. representing one beat, drawn as a large dot with a stem. **2** a whimsical fancy. **3** a hook. [Middle English from Old French *crochet*, diminutive of *croc* 'hook' (see CROTCH)]

crotchety /ˈkrɒtʃɪti/ *adj.* peevish, irritable. ▫ **crotchetiness** *n.* [CROTCHET 2 + -Y[1]]

croton /ˈkrəʊt(ə)n/ *n.* **1** any small tree or shrub of the genus *Croton*, producing a capsule-like fruit. **2** any small tree or shrub of the genus *Codiaeum*, esp. *C. variegatum*, with coloured ornamental leaves. [modern Latin from Greek *krotōn* 'sheep-tick, croton' (from the shape of its seeds)]

croton oil *n.* a powerful purgative obtained from the fruit of *Croton tiglium*.

crouch /kraʊtʃ/ *v.* & *n.* ● *v.intr.* (often foll. by *down*) lower the body with the limbs close to the chest, esp. for concealment, or (of an animal) before pouncing; be in this position. ● *n.* an act of crouching; a crouching position. [Middle English, perhaps via Old French *crochir* 'be bent' from *croc* 'hook': cf. CROOK]

croup[1] /kruːp/ *n.* an inflammation of the larynx and trachea in children, with a hard cough and difficulty in breathing. ▫ **croupy** *adj.* [dialect *croup* 'to croak' (imitative)]

croup[2] /kruːp/ *n.* the rump or hindquarters esp. of a horse. [Middle English from Old French *croupe*, related to CROP]

croupier /ˈkruːpɪə, -pɪeɪ/ *n.* **1** the person in charge of a gaming table, raking in and paying out money etc. **2** the assistant chairperson at a public dinner, seated at the foot of the table. [earlier in the sense 'advisor standing behind a gambler': French, originally = rider on the croup: see CROUP[2]]

crouton /ˈkruːtɒn/ *n.* a small piece of fried or toasted bread served with soup or used as a garnish. [French *croûton* from *croûte* CRUST]

crow[1] /krəʊ/ *n.* **1** any large bird of the genus *Corvus*, having a powerful black beak, a harsh call, and usu. glossy black plumage. **2** any bird of the family Corvidae. **3** *slang derog.* a woman, esp. an old or ugly one. ▫ **as the crow flies** in a straight line. **eat crow** *N. Amer.* submit to humiliation. [Old English *crāwe*, ultimately from West Germanic]

crow[2] /krəʊ/ *v.* & *n.* ● *v.intr.* (*past* **crowed** or **crew** /kruː/) **1** (of a cock) utter its characteristic loud cry. **2** (of a baby) utter happy cries. **3** (usu. foll. by *over*) express unrestrained gleeful satisfaction. ● *n.* **1** the cry of a cock. **2** a happy cry of a baby. [Old English *crāwan*, of imitative origin]

crowbar /ˈkrəʊbɑː/ *n.* an iron bar with a flattened end, used as a lever.

crowberry /ˈkrəʊb(ə)ri/ *n.* (*pl.* **-ies**) **1 a** a heathlike evergreen shrub, *Empetrum nigrum*, bearing black berries. **b** the flavourless edible berry of this plant. **2** *US* a cranberry.

crowd /kraʊd/ *n.* & *v.* ● *n.* **1** a large number of people gathered together, usu. without orderly arrangement. **2** a mass of spectators; an audience. **3** *colloq.* a particular company or set of people (*met the crowd from the sales department*). **4** (prec. by *the*) the mass or multitude of people (*go along with the crowd*). **5** a large number (of things). **6** actors representing a crowd. ● *v.* **1 a** *intr.* come together in a crowd. **b** *tr.* cause to do this. **c** *intr.* force one's way. **2** *tr.* **a** (foll. by *into*) force or compress into a confined space. **b** (often foll. by *with*; usu. in *passive*) fill or make abundant with (*was crowded with tourists*). **3** *tr.* **a** (of a number of people) come aggressively close to. **b** *colloq.* harass or pressure (a person). □ **crowd out** exclude by crowding. □ **crowdedness** *n.* [Old English *crūdan* 'press, drive']

crowd-puller *n. colloq.* an event, person, or thing that attracts a large audience.

crowfoot /ˈkrəʊfʊt/ *n.* any of various aquatic plants of the genus *Ranunculus*, with white buttercup-like flowers held above the water.

crown /kraʊn/ *n.* & *v.* ● *n.* **1** a monarch's ornamental and usu. jewelled headdress. **2** (**the Crown**) **a** the monarch, esp. as head of state. **b** the power or authority residing in the monarchy. **3 a** a wreath of leaves or flowers etc. worn on the head, esp. as an emblem of victory. **b** an award or distinction gained by a victory or achievement, esp. in sport. **4** a crown-shaped thing, esp. a device or ornament. **5** the top part of a thing, esp. of the head or a hat. **6 a** the highest or central part of an arched or curved thing (*crown of the road*). **b** a thing that completes or forms the summit. **7** the part of a plant just above and below the ground. **8** the upper part of a cut gem above the girdle. **9 a** the part of a tooth projecting from the gum. **b** an artificial replacement or covering for this. **10 a** a former British coin equal to five shillings (25p). **b** any of several foreign coins with a name meaning 'crown', esp. the krona or krone. **11** a former size of paper, 504 × 384 mm. ● *v.tr.* **1** put a crown on (a person or a person's head). **2** invest (a person) with a royal crown or authority. **3** be a crown to; encircle or rest on the top of. **4 a** (often as **crowning** *adj.*) be or cause to be the consummation, reward, or finishing touch to (*the crowning glory*). **b** bring (efforts) to a happy issue. **5** fit a crown to (a tooth). **6** *slang* hit on the head. **7** promote (a piece in draughts) to king. [Middle English via Anglo-French *corune*, Old French *corone* from Latin *corona*]

crown cap *n.* (also **crown cork**) a cork-lined metal cap for a bottle.

Crown Colony *n.* a British colony controlled by the Crown.

Crown Court *n.* a court of criminal jurisdiction in England and Wales.

Crown Derby *n.* a soft-paste porcelain made at Derby and often marked with a crown above the letter 'D'.

crown glass *n.* glass made without lead or iron and originally in a circular sheet; used formerly in windows, now as optical glass of low refractive index.

crown green *n. Brit.* a kind of bowling green rising towards the middle.

crown imperial *n.* a tall fritillary, *Fritillaria imperialis*, with a flower cluster at the top of the stalk.

crown jewels *n.pl.* the regalia and other jewellery worn by the sovereign on certain state occasions.

Crown Office *n.* (in the UK) an office of the Supreme Court transacting common-law business of Chancery.

crown of thorns *n.* any starfish of the genus *Acanthaster* feeding on coral.

Crown prince *n.* a male heir to a sovereign throne.

Crown princess *n.* **1** the wife of a Crown prince. **2** a female heir to a sovereign throne.

crown roast *n.* a roast of rib-pieces of pork or lamb arranged like a crown.

crown saw *n.* a cylinder with a toothed edge for making a circular hole.

crown wheel *n.* a wheel with teeth set at right angles to its plane, esp. in the gears of motor vehicles.

crow's-foot /ˈkrəʊzfʊt/ *n.* (*pl.* **-feet**) **1** (usu. in *pl.*) a wrinkle at the outer corner of a person's eye. **2** *Mil.* a caltrop.

crow's-nest *n.* a barrel or platform fixed at the masthead of a sailing vessel as a shelter for a lookout.

crow step *n.* (usu. in *pl.*) = CORBIE-STEP. □ **crow-stepped** *adj.*

crozier var. of CROSIER.

CRT *abbr.* cathode ray tube.

cru /kruː, French kry/ *n.* **1** a French vineyard or wine-producing region. **2** the grade of wine produced from it. [French from *crû* 'grown']

cruces *pl.* of CRUX.

crucial /ˈkruːʃ(ə)l/ *adj.* **1** decisive, critical. **2** *disp.* very important. **3** *slang* excellent. □ **cruciality** /-ʃɪˈælɪti/ *n.* (*pl.* **-ies**). **crucially** *adv.* [French, from Latin *crux crucis* 'cross']

■ **Usage** The use of *crucial* in sense 2 should be restricted to informal contexts.

crucian /ˈkruːʃ(ə)n/ *n.* (in full **crucian carp**) a yellow cyprinoid fish, *Carassius carassius*, allied to the goldfish. [Low German *karusse* etc.]

cruciate /ˈkruːʃɪət, -eɪt/ *adj.* esp. *Anat.* cross-shaped. [modern Latin *cruciatus* from Latin (as CRUCIBLE)]

cruciate ligament *n.* either of a pair of ligaments in the knee which cross each other and connect the femur and the tibia.

crucible /ˈkruːsɪb(ə)l/ *n.* **1** a melting pot for metals etc. **2** a severe test or trial. [Middle English via medieval Latin *crucibulum* 'night-lamp, crucible' (perhaps originally a lamp hanging in front of a crucifix), from Latin *crux crucis* 'cross']

crucifer /ˈkruːsɪfə/ *n.* **1** a cruciferous plant. **2** a person carrying a processional cross or crucifix.

cruciferous /kruːˈsɪf(ə)rəs/ *adj. Bot.* of the plant family Cruciferae, having flowers with four petals arranged in a cross. [Late Latin *crucifer* (as CRUCIAL, -FEROUS)]

crucifix /ˈkruːsɪfɪks/ *n.* a model or image of a cross with a figure of Christ on it. [Middle English via Old French and ecclesiastical Latin *crucifixus* from Latin *cruci fixus* 'fixed to a cross']

crucifixion /kruːsɪˈfɪkʃ(ə)n/ *n.* **1 a** crucifying or being crucified. **b** an instance of this. **2** (**Crucifixion**) **a** the crucifixion of Christ. **b** a representation of this. [ecclesiastical Latin *crucifixio* (as CRUCIFIX)]

cruciform /ˈkruːsɪfɔːm/ *adj.* cross-shaped (esp. of a church with transepts). [Latin *crux crucis* 'cross' + -FORM]

crucify /ˈkruːsɪfʌɪ/ *v.tr.* (**-ies**, **-ied**) **1** put to death by fastening to a cross. **2 a** cause extreme pain to. **b** persecute, torment. **c** *slang* defeat thoroughly in an argument, match, etc. □ **crucifier** *n.* [Middle English via Old French *crucifier* from Late Latin *crucifigere* (as CRUCIFIX)]

cruck /krʌk/ *n. Brit. hist.* either of a pair of curved timbers extending to the ground in the framework of a type of medieval house-roof. [variant of CROOK]

crud /krʌd/ *n. slang* **1** unwanted impurities; dirt. **2** an unpleasant person. **3** nonsense. □ **cruddy** *adj.* (**cruddier**, **cruddiest**). [variant of CURD]

crude /kruːd/ *adj.* & *n.* ● *adj.* **1 a** in the natural or raw state; not refined. **b** rough, unpolished; lacking finish. **2 a** (of an action or statement or manners) rude, blunt. **b** offensive, indecent (*a crude gesture*). **3 a** *Statistics* (of figures) not adjusted or corrected. **b** rough (*a crude estimate*). ● *n.* natural mineral oil. □ **crudely** *adv.* **crudeness** *n.* **crudity** *n.* [Middle English from Latin *crudus* 'raw, rough']

crudités /ˈkruːdɪteɪ/ *n.pl.* an hors d'oeuvre of mixed raw vegetables often served with a sauce into which they are dipped. [French]

cruel /krʊəl/ *adj. & v.* ● *adj.* (**crueller**, **cruellest** or **crueler**, **cruelest**) **1** indifferent to or gratified by another's suffering. **2** causing pain or suffering, esp. deliberately. ● *v.tr.* (**cruelled**, **cruelling**) *Austral. slang* thwart, spoil. □ **cruelly** *adv.* **cruelness** *n.* [Middle English via Old French from Latin *crudelis*, related to *crudus* (as CRUDE)]

cruelty /ˈkrʊəlti/ *n.* (*pl.* **-ies**) **1** a cruel act or attitude; indifference to another's suffering. **2** a succession of cruel acts; a continued cruel attitude (*suffered much cruelty*). **3** *Law* physical or mental harm inflicted (whether or not intentional), esp. as a ground for divorce. [Old French *crualté*, ultimately from Latin *crudelitas*]

cruelty-free *adj.* (of cosmetics etc.) produced without involving cruelty to animals in the development or manufacturing process.

cruet /ˈkruːɪt/ *n.* **1** *Brit.* a small container for salt, pepper, oil, or vinegar for use at table. **2** (in full **cruet-stand**) *Brit.* a stand holding cruets. **3** *Eccl.* a small container for the wine and water in the celebration of the Eucharist. [Middle English via Anglo-French and Old French *crue* 'pot' from Old Saxon *krūka*: related to CROCK²]

cruise /kruːz/ *v. & n.* ● *v.* **1** *intr.* make a journey by sea calling at a series of ports usu. according to a predetermined plan, esp. for pleasure. **2** *intr.* sail about without a precise destination. **3** *intr.* **a** (of a motor vehicle or aircraft) travel at a moderate or economical speed. **b** (of a vehicle or its driver) travel at random, esp. slowly. **4** *intr.* achieve an objective, win a race etc., with ease. **5** *intr. & tr. slang* walk or drive about (the streets etc.) in search of a sexual (esp. homosexual) partner. ● *n.* a cruising voyage, esp. as a holiday. [probably from Dutch *kruisen* 'to cross', from *kruis* CROSS]

cruise control *n.* a device which maintains a motor vehicle at a preset constant speed without the use of the accelerator pedal.

cruise missile *n.* a missile able to fly at a low altitude and guide itself by reference to the features of the region it traverses.

cruiser /ˈkruːzə/ *n.* **1** a warship of high speed and medium armament. **2** = CABIN CRUISER. **3** *N. Amer.* a police patrol car. [Dutch *kruiser* (as CRUISE)]

cruiserweight /ˈkruːzəweɪt/ *n.* esp. *Brit.* = LIGHT HEAVYWEIGHT.

cruising speed /ˈkruːzɪŋ/ *n.* a comfortable and economical speed for a motor vehicle, below its maximum speed.

cruller /ˈkrʌlə/ *n. N. Amer.* a small cake made of a rich dough twisted or curled and fried in fat. [probably from Dutch *krullen* 'curl']

crumb /krʌm/ *n. & v.* ● *n.* **1 a** a small fragment, esp. of bread. **b** a small particle (*a crumb of comfort*). **2** the soft inner part of a loaf of bread. **3** *slang* an objectionable person. ● *v.tr.* **1** cover with breadcrumbs. **2** break into crumbs. [Old English *cruma*]

crumble /ˈkrʌmb(ə)l/ *v. & n.* ● *v.* **1** *tr. & intr.* break or fall into crumbs or fragments. **2** *intr.* (of power, a reputation, etc.) gradually disintegrate. ● *n.* **1** *Brit.* **a** a mixture of flour and fat, rubbed to the texture of breadcrumbs and cooked as a topping for fruit etc. **b** a usu. specified dish having such a topping (*apple crumble*; *vegetable crumble*). **2** a crumbly or crumbled substance. [Middle English from Old English, formed as CRUMB]

crumbly /ˈkrʌmbli/ *adj. & n.* ● *adj.* (**crumblier**, **crumbliest**) consisting of, or apt to fall into, crumbs or fragments. ● *n.* (*pl.* **-ies**) *slang offens.* an old person. □ **crumbliness** *n.*

crumbs /krʌmz/ *int. Brit. slang* expressing dismay or surprise. [euphemism for *Christ*]

crumby /ˈkrʌmi/ *adj.* (**crumbier**, **crumbiest**) **1** like or covered in crumbs. **2** *colloq.* = CRUMMY.

crumhorn var. of KRUMMHORN.

crummy /ˈkrʌmi/ *adj.* (**crummier**, **crummiest**) *colloq.* dirty, squalid; inferior, worthless. □ **crummily** *adv.* **crumminess** *n.* [variant of CRUMBY]

crump /krʌmp/ *n. & v. Mil. slang* ● *n.* the sound of a bursting bomb or shell. ● *v.intr.* make this sound. [imitative]

crumpet /ˈkrʌmpɪt/ *n.* **1** a soft flat cake of a yeast mixture cooked on a griddle and eaten toasted and buttered. **2** *Brit. slang offens.* **a** a sexually attractive person, esp. a woman. **b** women regarded collectively, esp. as objects of sexual desire. **3** *Brit. archaic slang* the head. [17th c.: origin uncertain]

crumple /ˈkrʌmp(ə)l/ *v. & n.* ● *v.* **1** *tr. & intr.* (often foll. by *up*) **a** crush or become crushed into creases. **b** ruffle, wrinkle. **2** *intr.* (often foll. by *up*) collapse, give way. ● *n.* a crease or wrinkle. □ **crumply** *adj.* [obsolete *crump* (*v.* & *adj.*) '(make or become) curved']

crumple zone *n.* a part of a motor vehicle, esp. the extreme front and rear, designed to crumple easily in a crash and absorb impact.

crunch /krʌn(t)ʃ/ *v. & n.* ● *v.* **1** *tr.* **a** crush noisily with the teeth. **b** grind (gravel, dry snow, etc.) under foot, wheels, etc. **2** *intr.* (often foll. by *up*, *through*) make a crunching sound in walking, moving, etc. ● *n.* **1** crunching; a crunching sound. **2** *colloq.* a decisive event or moment. [earlier *cra(u)nch* (probably imitative), assimilated to *munch*]

crunchy /ˈkrʌntʃi/ *adj.* (**crunchier**, **crunchiest**) that can be or has been crunched or crushed into small pieces; hard and crispy. □ **crunchily** *adv.* **crunchiness** *n.*

crupper /ˈkrʌpə/ *n.* **1** a strap buckled to the back of a saddle and looped under the horse's tail to hold the harness back. **2** the hindquarters of a horse. [Middle English from Old French *cropiere* (cf. CROUP²)]

crural /ˈkrʊər(ə)l/ *adj. Anat.* of the leg. [French *crural* or Latin *cruralis*, from *crus cruris* 'leg']

crusade /kruːˈseɪd/ *n. & v.* ● *n.* **1 a** any of several medieval military expeditions made by Europeans to recover the Holy Land from the Muslims. **b** a war instigated by the Church for alleged religious ends. **2** a vigorous campaign in favour of a cause. ● *v.intr.* engage in a crusade. □ **crusader** *n.* [earlier *croisade* (French from *croix* 'cross') or *crusado* (Spanish from *cruz* 'cross')]

cruse /kruːz/ *n. archaic* an earthenware pot or jar. [Old English *crūse*, of unknown origin]

crush /krʌʃ/ *v. & n.* ● *v.tr.* **1** compress with force or violence, so as to break, bruise, etc. **2** reduce to powder by pressure. **3** crease or crumple by rough handling. **4** defeat or subdue completely (*crushed by my reply*). ● *n.* **1** an act of crushing. **2** a crowded mass of people. **3** a drink made from the juice of crushed fruit. **4** *colloq.* **a** (usu. foll. by *on*) a (usu. passing) infatuation. **b** the object of an infatuation (*who's the latest crush?*). □ **crushable** *adj.* **crusher** *n.* **crushing** *adj.* (esp. in sense 4 of *v.*). **crushingly** *adv.* [Middle English via Anglo-French *crussir*, *corussier*, Old French *croissir*, *cruissir*, 'gnash (teeth), crack', from Romanic]

crush bar *n. Brit.* a place in a theatre for audiences to buy drinks in the intervals.

crush barrier *n. Brit.* a barrier, esp. a temporary one, for restraining a crowd.

crust /krʌst/ *n. & v.* ● *n.* **1 a** the hard outer part of a loaf of bread. **b** a piece of this with some soft bread attached. **c** a hard dry scrap of bread. **d** esp. *Austral. slang* a livelihood (*what do you do for a crust?*). **2** the pastry covering of a pie. **3** a hard casing of a softer thing, e.g. a harder layer over soft snow. **4** *Geol.* the outer rocky portion of the earth, esp. the part overlying the mantle. **5 a** a coating or deposit on the surface of anything. **b** a hard dry formation on the skin, a scab. **6** a deposit of tartar formed in bottles of old wine. **7 a**

slang impudence (*you have a crust!*). **b** a superficial hardness of manner. ● *v.tr. & intr.* **1** cover or become covered with a crust. **2** form into a crust. □ **crustal** *adj.* (in sense 4 of *n.*). [Middle English via Old French *crouste* from Latin *crusta* 'rind, shell']

crustacean /krʌˈsteɪʃ(ə)n/ *n. & adj.* ● *n.* any arthropod of the subphylum Crustacea, having a hard shell and numerous legs, and usu. aquatic, e.g. the crab, lobster, and shrimp. ● *adj.* of or relating to crustaceans. □ **crustaceology** /-ʃɪˈɒlədʒi/ *n.* **crustaceous** /-ʃəs/ *adj.* [modern Latin *crustaceus* from *crusta*: see CRUST]

crusted /ˈkrʌstɪd/ *adj.* **1 a** having a crust. **b** (of wine) having deposited a crust. **2** antiquated, venerable.

crustose /krʌˈstəʊs/ *adj.* (esp. of a lichen) forming or resembling a crust. [Latin *crustosus* from *crusta* 'crust']

crusty /ˈkrʌsti/ *adj.* (**crustier**, **crustiest**) **1** having a crisp crust (*a crusty loaf*). **2** irritable, curt. **3** hard, crustlike. □ **crustily** *adv.* **crustiness** *n.*

crutch /krʌtʃ/ *n.* **1** a support for a lame person, usu. with a crosspiece at the top fitting under the armpit (*pair of crutches*). **2** any support or prop. **3** the crotch of the human body or garment. [Old English *cryc(c)*, from Germanic]

crux /krʌks/ *n.* (*pl.* **cruxes** or **cruces** /ˈkru:si:z/) **1** the decisive point at issue. **2** a difficult matter; a puzzle. [Latin, = cross]

cruzado /kru:ˈzɑ:dəʊ/ *n.* (*pl.* **-os**) the chief monetary unit of Brazil between 1988 and 1990. [Portuguese *cruzado*, *crusado*, = marked with the cross]

cruzeiro /kru:ˈzɛ:rəʊ/ *n.* (*pl.* **-os**) the chief monetary unit of Brazil 1990–93. [Portuguese, = large cross]

cry /krʌɪ/ *v. & n.* ● *v.* (**cries**, **cried**) **1** *intr.* (often foll. by *out*, *for*) make a loud or shrill sound, esp. to express pain, grief, etc., or to appeal for help. **2 a** *intr.* shed tears; weep. **b** *tr.* shed (tears). **3** *tr.* (often foll. by *out*) say or exclaim loudly or excitedly. **4** *intr.* (of an animal, esp. a bird) make a loud call. **5** *tr.* (of a hawker etc.) proclaim (wares etc.) in the street. ● *n.* (*pl.* **cries**) **1** a loud inarticulate utterance of grief, pain, fear, joy, etc. **2** a loud excited utterance of words. **3** an urgent appeal or entreaty. **4** a spell of weeping. **5 a** public demand; a strong movement of opinion. **b** a watchword or rallying call. **6** the natural utterance of an animal, esp. of hounds on the scent. **7** the street-call of a hawker etc. □ **cry down** disparage, belittle. **cry one's eyes** (or **heart**) **out** weep bitterly. **cry for the moon** *Brit.* ask for what is unattainable. **cry from the heart** a passionate appeal or protest. **cry off** *Brit. colloq.* withdraw from a promise or undertaking. **cry out for** demand as a self-evident requirement or solution. **cry over spilt** (or *US* **spilled**) **milk** see MILK. **cry stinking fish** disparage one's own efforts, products, etc. **cry up** praise, extol. **cry wolf** see WOLF. **a far cry from 1** a long way from. **2** a very different thing from. **for crying out loud** *colloq.* an exclamation of surprise or annoyance. **in full cry** (of hounds) in keen pursuit. [Middle English via Old French *crier*, *cri* from Latin *quiritare* 'wail']

cry-baby *n.* a person, esp. a child, who sheds tears frequently.

cryer var. of CRIER.

crying /ˈkrʌɪɪŋ/ *attrib.adj.* (of an injustice or other evil) flagrant, demanding redress (*a crying need*; *a crying shame*).

cryo- /ˈkrʌɪəʊ/ *comb. form* (extreme) cold. [Greek *kruos* 'frost']

cryobiology /ˌkrʌɪəʊbʌɪˈɒlədʒi/ *n.* the biology of organisms below their normal temperatures. □ **cryobiological** /-bʌɪəˈlɒdʒɪk(ə)l/ *adj.* **cryobiologist** *n.*

cryogen /ˈkrʌɪə(ʊ)dʒ(ə)n/ *n.* a freezing-mixture; a substance used to produce very low temperatures.

cryogenics /krʌɪə(ʊ)ˈdʒɛnɪks/ *n.* **1** the branch of physics dealing with the production and effects of very low temperatures. **2** = CRYONICS. □ **cryogenic** *adj.*

cryolite /ˈkrʌɪəlʌɪt/ *n. Mineral.* a lustrous sodium aluminium fluoride mineral, used in the smelting of aluminium.

cryonics /krʌɪˈɒnɪks/ *n.* the practice or technique of deep-freezing the bodies of those who have died of an incurable disease, in the hope of a future cure. □ **cryonic** *adj.* [contraction of CRYOGENICS]

cryoprotectant /ˌkrʌɪəʊprəˈtɛkt(ə)nt/ *n. Biochem.* a substance that prevents the freezing of tissues, or prevents damage to cells etc. during freezing.

cryopump /ˈkrʌɪəʊpʌmp/ *n.* a vacuum pump using liquefied gases.

cryostat /ˈkrʌɪə(ʊ)stat/ *n.* an apparatus for maintaining a very low temperature.

cryosurgery /krʌɪəʊˈsə:dʒ(ə)ri/ *n.* surgery using the local application of intense cold for anaesthesia or therapy.

crypt /krɪpt/ *n.* **1** an underground room or vault, esp. one beneath a church, used usu. as a burial place. **2** *Anat.* a small tubular gland, pit, or recess. [Middle English via Latin *crypta* from Greek *kruptē*, from *kruptos* 'hidden']

cryptanalysis /krɪptəˈnalɪsɪs/ *n.* the art or process of solving cryptograms by analysis; code-breaking. □ **cryptanalyst** /-ˈan(ə)lɪst/ *n.* **cryptanalytic** /-anəˈlɪtɪk/ *adj.* **cryptanalytical** /-anəˈlɪtɪk(ə)l/ *adj.* [CRYPTO- + ANALYSIS]

cryptic /ˈkrɪptɪk/ *adj.* **1 a** obscure in meaning. **b** (of a crossword clue etc.) indirect; indicating the solution in a way that is not obvious. **c** secret, mysterious, enigmatic. **2** *Zool.* (of coloration etc.) serving for concealment. □ **cryptically** *adv.* [Late Latin *crypticus* from Greek *kruptikos* (as CRYPTO-)]

crypto /ˈkrɪptəʊ/ *n.* (*pl.* **-os**) *colloq.* a person having a secret allegiance to a political creed etc., esp. communism. [as CRYPTO-]

crypto- /ˈkrɪptəʊ/ *comb. form* concealed, secret (*crypto-communist*). [Greek *kruptos* 'hidden']

cryptocrystalline /krɪptəʊˈkrɪst(ə)lʌɪn/ *adj.* having a crystalline structure visible only when magnified.

cryptogam /ˈkrɪptə(ʊ)gam/ *n. Bot.* a plant that has no true flowers or seeds, e.g. ferns, mosses, algae, and fungi. □ **cryptogamic** /-ˈgamɪk/ *adj.* **cryptogamous** /-ˈtɒgəməs/ *adj.* [French *cryptogame* from modern Latin *cryptogamae* (*plantae*), formed as CRYPTO- + Greek *gamos* 'marriage']

cryptogram /ˈkrɪptəgram/ *n.* a text written in cipher.

cryptography /krɪpˈtɒgrəfi/ *n.* the art of writing or solving codes. □ **cryptographer** *n.* **cryptographic** /-təˈgrafɪk/ *adj.* **cryptographically** /-təˈgrafɪk(ə)li/ *adv.*

cryptology /krɪpˈtɒlədʒi/ *n.* = CRYPTOGRAPHY. □ **cryptologist** *n.* **cryptological** /-təˈlɒdʒɪk(ə)l/ *adj.*

cryptomeria /krɪptə(ʊ)ˈmɪərɪə/ *n.* a tall evergreen tree, *Cryptomeria japonica*, native to China and Japan, with long curved spirally arranged leaves and short cones. Also called *Japanese cedar*. [CRYPTO- + Greek *meros* 'part' (because the seeds are enclosed by scales)]

crystal /ˈkrɪst(ə)l/ *n. & adj.* ● *n.* **1 a** a clear transparent mineral, esp. rock crystal. **b** a piece of this. **2** (in full **crystal glass**) **a** highly transparent glass; flint glass. **b** articles made of this. **3** the glass over a watch face. **4** *Electronics* a crystalline piece of semiconductor. **5** *Chem.* **a** an aggregation of atoms or molecules with a regular internal structure and the external form of a solid enclosed by symmetrically arranged plane faces. **b** a solid whose constituent particles are symmetrically arranged. ● *adj.* (usu. *attrib.*) made of, like, or clear as crystal. □ **crystal clear** (hyphenated when *attrib.*) **1** unclouded, transparent. **2** readily understood. [Old English via Old French *cristal* and Latin *crystallum* from Greek *krustallos* 'ice, crystal']

crystal ball *n.* a solid globe of glass or esp. rock crystal, used in crystal-gazing.

crystal class *n.* each of 32 categories of crystals classified according to their symmetry.

crystal-gazing *n.* the process of concentrating one's gaze on a crystal ball supposedly in order to obtain a picture of future events etc.

crystal lattice *n.* the regular repeating pattern of atoms, ions, or molecules in a crystalline substance.

crystalline /ˈkrɪst(ə)lʌɪn/ *adj.* **1** of, like, or clear as crystal. **2** *Chem. & Mineral.* having the structure and form of a crystal. □ **crystallinity** /-ˈlɪnɪti/ *n.* [Middle English via Old French *cristallin* and Latin *crystallinus* from Greek *krustallinos* (as CRYSTAL)]

crystalline lens *n.* a transparent lens enclosed in a membranous capsule behind the iris of the eye.

crystallite /ˈkrɪst(ə)lʌɪt/ *n.* **1** a small crystal. **2** an individual perfect crystal or grain in a metal etc. **3** *Bot.* a region of cellulose etc. with a crystal-like structure.

crystallize /ˈkrɪst(ə)lʌɪz/ *v.* (also **-ise**) **1** *tr. & intr.* form or cause to form crystals. **2** (often foll. by *out*) **a** *intr.* (of ideas or plans) become definite. **b** *tr.* make definite. **3** *tr. & intr.* coat or impregnate or become coated or impregnated with sugar (*crystallized fruit*). □ **crystallizable** *adj.* **crystallization** /-ˈzeɪʃ(ə)n/ *n.*

crystallography /krɪstəˈlɒgrəfi/ *n.* the science of crystal form and structure. □ **crystallographer** *n.* **crystallographic** /-ləˈgrafɪk/ *adj.*

crystalloid /ˈkrɪst(ə)lɔɪd/ *adj. & n.* ● *adj.* **1** crystal-like. **2** having a crystalline structure. ● *n.* a substance that in solution is able to pass through a semi-permeable membrane (cf. COLLOID).

crystal set *n.* a simple early form of radio receiving apparatus with a crystal touching a metal wire as the rectifier.

crystal system *n.* each of seven distinct symmetrical forms (cubic, tetragonal, orthorhombic, trigonal, hexagonal, monoclinic, and triclinic) into which crystals can be classified according to the relations of their axes..

CS *abbr.* **1** Civil Service. **2** *Brit.* chartered surveyor. **3** Court of Session.

Cs *symb. Chem.* the element caesium.

c/s *abbr.* cycles per second.

csardas /ˈtʃɑːdɑːʃ, ˈzɑːdəs/ *n.* (also **czardas**) (*pl.* same) a Hungarian dance with a slow start and a quick wild finish. [Hungarian *csárdás* from *csárda* 'inn']

CSC *abbr.* **1** Civil Service Commission. **2** *Brit.* Conspicuous Service Cross.

CSE *abbr. hist.* (in the UK) Certificate of Secondary Education (replaced in 1988 by GCSE).

CS gas *n.* a gas causing tears and choking, used to control riots etc. [named after B. B. Corson (b. 1896) & R. W. Stoughton (d. 1957), American chemists]

CSI *abbr.* Companion of the Order of the Star of India.

CSIRO *abbr.* Commonwealth Scientific and Industrial Research Organization.

CSM *abbr.* (in the UK) Company Sergeant Major.

CST *abbr.* Central Standard Time.

CSU *abbr.* (in the UK) Civil Service Union.

CT *abbr. US* Connecticut (in official postal use).

ct. *abbr.* **1** carat. **2** cent.

CTC *abbr.* **1** (in the UK) Cyclists' Touring Club. **2** (in the UK) City Technology College.

ctenoid /ˈtiːnɔɪd/ *adj. Zool.* (of fish scales) having projections on the edge like the teeth of a comb (cf. PLACOID *adj.* 1). [Greek *kteis ktenos* 'comb']

ctenophore /ˈtiːnəfɔː, ˈtɛn-/ *n.* any marine animal of the phylum Ctenophora, having a jellyfish-like body bearing rows of cilia, e.g. sea gooseberries. Also called *comb-jelly*. [modern Latin *ctenophorus* (as CTENOID)]

CU *abbr.* Cambridge University.

Cu *symb. Chem.* the element copper. [Late Latin *cuprum*]

cu. *abbr.* cubic.

cub /kʌb/ *n. & v.* ● *n.* **1** the young of a fox, bear, lion, etc. **2** an ill-mannered young man. **3** (**Cub**) (in full **Cub Scout**) a member of the junior branch of the Scout Association. **4** (in full **cub reporter**) *colloq.* a young or inexperienced newspaper reporter. **5** *US* an apprentice. ● *v.* (**cubbed**, **cubbing**) **1** *tr.* (also *absol.*) give birth to (cubs). **2** *intr.* hunt fox cubs. □ **cubhood** *n.* [16th c.: origin unknown]

Cuban /kjuːbən/ *adj. & n.* ● *adj.* of or relating to Cuba, an island republic in the Caribbean, or its people. ● *n.* a native or national of Cuba.

Cuban heel *n.* a moderately high straight heel of a man's or woman's shoe.

cubby /ˈkʌbi/ *n.* (*pl.* **-ies**) (in full **cubby hole**) **1** a very small room. **2** a snug or confined space. [dialect *cub* 'stall, pen', of Low German origin]

cube /kjuːb/ *n. & v.* ● *n.* **1** a solid contained by six equal squares. **2** a cube-shaped block. **3** *Math.* the product of a number multiplied by its square. ● *v.tr.* **1** find the cube of (a number). **2** cut (food for cooking etc.) into small cubes. [French *cube* or Latin *cubus*, from Greek *kubos*]

cubeb /ˈkjuːbɛb/ *n.* **1** a SE Asian shrub, *Piper cubeba* (pepper family), bearing pungent berries. **2** this berry crushed for use in medicated cigarettes. [Middle English from Old French *cubebe*, *quibibe*, ultimately from Arabic *kobāba*, *kubāba*]

cube root *n.* the number which produces a given number when cubed.

cubic /ˈkjuːbɪk/ *adj.* **1** cube-shaped. **2** of three dimensions. **3** involving the cube (and no higher power) of a number (*cubic equation*). **4** *Crystallog.* having three equal axes at right angles. **5** (*attrib.*) designating a unit of measure equal to the volume of a cube whose side is one of the linear unit specified (*cubic metre*). [French *cubique* or Latin *cubicus* from Greek *kubikos* (as CUBE)]

cubical /ˈkjuːbɪk(ə)l/ *adj.* cube-shaped. □ **cubically** *adv.*

cubic content *n.* the volume of a solid expressed in cubic metres.

cubicle /ˈkjuːbɪk(ə)l/ *n.* **1** a small partitioned space, screened for privacy. **2** a small separate sleeping compartment. [Latin *cubiculum* from *cubare* 'lie down']

cubiform /ˈkjuːbɪfɔːm/ *adj.* cube-shaped.

cubism /ˈkjuːbɪz(ə)m/ *n.* a style and movement in art, esp. painting, in which objects are represented as an assemblage of geometrical forms. □ **cubist** *n. & adj.* [French *cubisme* (as CUBE)]

cubit /ˈkjuːbɪt/ *n.* an ancient measure of length, approximately equal to the length of a forearm. [Middle English from Latin *cubitum* 'elbow, cubit']

cubital /ˈkjuːbɪt(ə)l/ *adj.* **1** *Anat.* of the forearm. **2** *Zool.* of the corresponding part in animals. [Middle English from Latin *cubitalis* (as CUBIT)]

cuboid /ˈkjuːbɔɪd/ *adj. & n.* ● *adj.* cube-shaped; like a cube. ● *n.* **1** *Geom.* a rectangular parallelepiped. **2** (in full **cuboid bone**) *Anat.* the outer bone of the tarsus. □ **cuboidal** /-ˈbɔɪd(ə)l/ *adj.* [modern Latin *cuboides* from Greek *kuboeidēs* (as CUBE)]

cub reporter see CUB *n.* 4.

Cub Scout see CUB *n.* 3.

cucking-stool /ˈkʌkɪŋstuːl/ *n. hist.* a chair on which disorderly women were ducked as a punishment. [Middle English from obsolete *cuck* 'defecate']

cuckold /ˈkʌk(ə)ld/ *n. & v.* ● *n.* the husband of an adulteress. ● *v.tr.* (of a man) have a sexual relationship with the wife of (another man). □ **cuckoldry** *n.* [Middle English *cukeweld*, *cokewold*, from Old French *cucu* 'cuckoo']

cuckoo /ˈkʊkuː/ *n. & adj.* ● *n.* a long-tailed songbird of the family Cuculidae, esp. the migratory European bird *Cuculus canorus*, which has a characteristic two-note call and deposits its eggs in the nests of small birds which rear the young as their own. ● *predic.adj. colloq.* crazy, foolish. □ **cuckoo in the nest** an unwelcome intruder. [Middle English from Old French *cucu*, imitative]

cuckoo bee *n.* (also **cuckoo wasp**) a bee (or wasp) which lays its eggs in the nest of another species.

cuckoo clock *n.* a clock that strikes the hour with a sound like a cuckoo's call, usu. with the emergence on each note of a mechanical cuckoo.

cuckoo flower *n.* **1** a meadow plant, *Cardamine pratensis*, with pale lilac flowers; also called *lady's smock*. **2** = RAGGED ROBIN.

cuckoo pint *n.* a wild arum, *Arum maculatum*, with arrow-shaped leaves and scarlet berries. Also called *lords and ladies*, JACK-IN-THE-PULPIT. [earlier *-pintle*, with reference to the shape of the spadix: see PINTLE]

cuckoo spit *n.* froth exuded by larvae of insects of the family Cercopidae on leaves, stems, etc.

cuckoo wasp see CUCKOO BEE.

cucumber /'kju:kʌmbə/ *n.* **1** a long green fleshy fruit, used in salads. **2** the climbing plant, *Cucumis sativus*, yielding this fruit. [Middle English via Old French *co(u)combre* from Latin *cucumer*]

cucurbit /kjʊ'kə:bɪt/ *n.* = GOURD 1b. □ **cucurbitaceous** /-'teɪʃəs/ *adj.* [Latin *cucurbita*]

cud /kʌd/ *n.* half-digested food returned from the first stomach of ruminants to the mouth for further chewing. [Old English *cwidu*, *cudu* 'what is chewed', corresponding to Old High German *kuti*, *quiti* 'glue']

cuddle /'kʌd(ə)l/ *v.* & *n.* ● *v.* **1** *tr.* hug, embrace, fondle. **2** *intr.* **a** (often foll. by *up*) nestle together; lie close and snug. **b** kiss and fondle each other amorously. ● *n.* a prolonged and fond hug. □ **cuddlesome** *adj.* [16th c.: perhaps from dialect *couth* 'snug']

cuddly /'kʌdli/ *adj.* (**cuddlier**, **cuddliest**) tempting to cuddle; given to cuddling.

cuddy /'kʌdi/ *n.* (*pl.* **-ies**) *Sc.* **1** a donkey. **2** a stupid person. [perhaps a pet form of the name *Cuthbert*]

cudgel /'kʌdʒ(ə)l/ *n.* & *v.* ● *n.* a short thick stick used as a weapon. ● *v.tr.* (**cudgelled**, **cudgelling**; *US* **cudgeled**, **cudgeling**) beat with a cudgel. □ **cudgel one's brains** think hard about a problem. **take up the cudgels** (often foll. by *for*) make a vigorous defence. [Old English *cycgel*, of unknown origin]

cudweed /'kʌdwi:d/ *n.* a plant of the genus *Gnaphalium* or *Filago* (daisy family), with hairy or downy leaves.

cue[1] /kju:/ *n.* & *v.* ● *n.* **1 a** the last words of an actor's speech serving as a signal to another actor to enter or speak. **b** a similar signal to a singer or player etc. **2 a** a stimulus to perception etc. **b** a signal for action. **c** a hint on how to behave in particular circumstances. **3** a facility for cueing audio equipment by allowing the tape to be played at high speed during fast forward wind and stopped when the desired place is reached. ● *v.tr.* (**cues**, **cued**, **cueing** or **cuing**) **1** give a cue to. **2** put (a piece of audio equipment, esp. a record player or tape recorder) in readiness to play a particular part of the recorded material. □ **cue in 1** insert a cue for. **2** give information to. **on cue** at the correct moment. **take one's cue from** follow the example or advice of. [16th c.: origin unknown]

cue[2] /kju:/ *n.* & *v.* *Billiards* etc. ● *n.* a long straight tapering rod for striking the ball. ● *v.* (**cues**, **cued**, **cueing** or **cuing**) **1** *tr.* strike (a ball) with a cue. **2** *intr.* use a cue. □ **cueist** *n.* [variant of QUEUE]

cue ball *n.* *Billiards* the ball that is to be struck with the cue.

cue-bid *n.* *Bridge* an artificial bid to show a particular card etc. in the bidder's hand.

cuesta /'kwɛstə/ *n.* *Geog.* a gentle slope, esp. one ending in a steep drop. [Spanish, = slope, from Latin *costa*: see COAST]

cuff[1] /kʌf/ *n.* **1 a** the end part of a sleeve. **b** a separate band of linen worn round the wrist so as to appear under the sleeve. **c** the part of a glove covering the wrist. **2** *N. Amer.* a trouser turn-up. **3** (in *pl.*) *colloq.* handcuffs. □ **off the cuff** *colloq.* without preparation, extempore. □ **cuffed** *adj.* (also in *comb.*). [Middle English: origin unknown]

cuff[2] /kʌf/ *v.* & *n.* ● *v.tr.* strike with an open hand. ● *n.* such a blow. [16th c.: perhaps imitative]

cuff link *n.* a device of two joined studs etc. to fasten the sides of a cuff together.

Cufic var. of KUFIC.

cui bono? /kwi: 'bɒnəʊ, 'bəʊ-/ who stands, or stood, to gain? (with the implication that this person is responsible). [Latin, = to whom (is it) a benefit?]

cuirass /kwɪ'ras/ *n.* **1** *hist.* a piece of armour consisting of breastplate and back-plate fastened together. **2** a device for artificial respiration. [Middle English from Old French *cuirace*, ultimately from Late Latin *coriaceus* from *corium* 'leather']

cuirassier /kwɪrə'si:ə/ *n.* *hist.* a cavalry soldier wearing a cuirass. [French (as CUIRASS)]

cuisine /kwɪ'zi:n/ *n.* a style or method of cooking, esp. of a particular country or establishment. [French from Latin *coquina*, from *coquere* 'to cook']

cuisse /kwɪs/ *n.* (also **cuish** /kwɪʃ/) (usu. in *pl.*) *hist.* thigh armour. [Middle English, via Old French *cuisseaux*, pl. of *cuissel*, from Late Latin *coxale*, from *coxa* 'hip']

culchie /'kʌl(t)ʃi/ *n.* & *adj.* (also **culshie**) *Ir. slang*, often *derog.* ● *n.* a country bumpkin. ● *adj.* provincial, rustic. [perhaps alteration of *Kilti*magh, a country town in County Mayo, Ireland]

cul-de-sac /'kʌldəsak, kʊldə'sak/ *n.* (*pl.* **culs-de-sac** *pronunc.* same) **1** a street or passage closed at one end. **2** a route or course leading nowhere; a position from which one cannot escape. **3** *Anat.* = DIVERTICULUM. [French, = sack-bottom]

-cule /kju:l/ *suffix* forming (originally diminutive) nouns (*molecule*). [French *-cule* or Latin *-culus*]

culinary /'kʌlɪn(ə)ri/ *adj.* of or for cooking or the kitchen. □ **culinarily** *adv.* [Latin *culinarius* from *culina* 'kitchen']

cull /kʌl/ *v.* & *n.* ● *v.tr.* **1** select, choose, or gather from a large quantity or amount (*knowledge culled from books*). **2** pick or gather (flowers, fruit, etc.). **3 a** select (animals) according to quality, esp. poor surplus specimens for killing. **b** reduce the population of (an animal) by selective slaughter. ● *n.* **1** an act of culling. **2** an animal or animals culled. □ **culler** *n.* [Middle English from Old French *coillier* etc., ultimately from Latin *colligere* COLLECT[1]]

cullet /'kʌlɪt/ *n.* recycled waste or broken glass used in glass-making. [variant of COLLET, in the obsolete sense 'glass left on the blowing-iron when the finished article is removed']

culm[1] /kʌlm/ *n.* **1** coal dust, esp. of anthracite. **2** *Geol.* strata under coal measures, esp. in SW England. [Middle English, probably related to COAL]

culm[2] /kʌlm/ *n.* *Bot.* the stem of a plant, esp. of grasses. □ **culmiferous** /-'mɪfərəs/ *adj.* [Latin *culmus* 'stalk']

culminant /'kʌlmɪnənt/ *adj.* **1** at or forming the top. **2** *Astron.* on the meridian. [as CULMINATE + -ANT]

culminate /'kʌlmɪneɪt/ *v.* **1** *intr.* (usu. foll. by *in*) reach its highest or final point (*the antagonism culminated in war*). **2** *tr.* bring to its highest or final point. **3** *intr.* *Astron.* be on the meridian. □ **culmination** /-'neɪʃ(ə)n/ *n.* [Late Latin *culminare culminat-* from *culmen* 'summit']

culottes /kju:'lɒts/ *n.pl.* women's (usu. short) trousers cut to resemble a skirt. [French, = knee-breeches]

culpa /'kʌlpə/ *n.* *Law* neglect resulting in damage; negligence. [Latin, = fault, blame]

culpable /'kʌlpəb(ə)l/ *adj.* deserving blame. □ **culpability** /-'bɪlɪti/ *n.* **culpably** *adv.* [Middle English via Old French *coupable* from Latin *culpabilis*, via *culpare* from *culpa* 'blame']

culprit /'kʌlprɪt/ *n.* a person accused of or guilty of an offence. [17th c.: originally in the formula *Culprit, how will you be tried?*, said by the Clerk of the Crown to a prisoner pleading Not Guilty: perhaps from an abbreviation of Anglo-French *Culpable*: *prest d'averrer notre bille* '(You are) guilty: (We are) ready to prove our indictment']

culshie var. of CULCHIE.

cult /kʌlt/ *n.* **1** a system of religious worship esp. as expressed in ritual. **2 a** devotion or homage to a person or thing (*the cult of aestheticism*). **b** a popular fashion esp. followed by a specific section of society. **3** (*attrib.*) denoting a person or thing popularized in this way (*cult film*; *cult figure*). □ **cultic** *adj.* **cultism** *n.* **cultist** *n.*

[French *culte* or Latin *cultus* 'worship', from *colere cult-* 'inhabit, till, worship']

cultivar /'kʌltɪvɑː/ *n. Bot.* a cultivated plant variety produced by selective breeding. [CULTIVATE + VARIETY]

cultivate /'kʌltɪveɪt/ *v.tr.* **1 a** prepare and use (soil etc.) for crops or gardening. **b** break up (the ground) with a cultivator. **2 a** raise or produce (crops). **b** culture (bacteria, cells, etc.). **3 a** (often as **cultivated** *adj.*) apply oneself to improving or developing (the mind, manners, etc.). **b** pay attention to or nurture (a person or a person's friendship); ingratiate oneself with (a person). □ **cultivable** *adj.* **cultivatable** *adj.* **cultivation** /-'veɪʃ(ə)n/ *n.* [medieval Latin *cultivare* from *cultiva (terra)* 'arable (land)' (as CULT)]

cultivator /'kʌltɪveɪtə/ *n.* **1** a mechanical implement for breaking up the ground and uprooting weeds. **2** a person or thing that cultivates.

cultural /'kʌltʃ(ə)r(ə)l/ *adj.* of or relating to the cultivation of the mind or manners, esp. through artistic or intellectual activity. □ **culturally** *adv.*

culture /'kʌltʃə/ *n. & v.* ● *n.* **1 a** the arts and other manifestations of human intellectual achievement regarded collectively (*a city lacking in culture*). **b** a refined understanding of this; intellectual development (*a person of culture*). **2** the customs, civilization, and achievements of a particular time or people (*studied Chinese culture*). **3** improvement by mental or physical training. **4 a** the cultivation of plants; the rearing of bees, silkworms, etc. **b** the cultivation of the soil. **5 a** the cultivation of bacteria, tissue cells, etc. in an artificial nutrient medium. **b** a growth of cells etc. so obtained. ● *v.tr.* maintain (cells etc.) in conditions suitable for growth. [Middle English from French *culture* or Latin *cultura* (as CULT): the verb from obsolete French *culturer* or medieval Latin *culturare*]

culture-bound *adj.* restricted in character or outlook by belonging to a particular culture.

cultured /'kʌltʃəd/ *adj.* having refined taste and manners and a good education.

cultured pearl *n.* a pearl formed by an oyster after the insertion of a foreign body into its shell.

culture shock *n.* the feeling of disorientation experienced by a person suddenly subjected to an unfamiliar culture or way of life.

culture vulture *n. colloq.* a person eager to acquire culture.

cultus /'kʌltəs/ *n.* a system of religious worship; a cult. [Latin: see CULT]

culverin /'kʌlv(ə)rɪn/ *n. hist.* **1** a long cannon. **2** a small firearm. [Middle English from Old French *coulevrine*, from *couleuvre* 'snake', ultimately from Latin *colubra*]

culvert /'kʌlvət/ *n.* **1** an underground channel carrying water across a road etc. **2** *Brit.* a channel for an electric cable. [18th c.: origin unknown]

cum[1] /kʌm/ *prep.* (usu. in *comb.*) with, combined with, also used as (*a bedroom-cum-study*). [Latin]

cum[2] /kʌm/ *n. slang* = COME *n.* [corruption]

cumber /'kʌmbə/ *v. & n.* ● *v.tr. literary* hamper, hinder, inconvenience. ● *n.* a hindrance, obstruction, or burden. [Middle English, probably from ENCUMBER]

Cumberland sausage /'kʌmbələnd/ *n. Brit.* a type of coarse-grained sausage traditionally made in a continuous strip from which the amount required is cut.

cumbersome /'kʌmbəs(ə)m/ *adj.* inconvenient in size, weight, or shape; unwieldy. □ **cumbersomely** *adv.* **cumbersomeness** *n.* [Middle English from CUMBER + -SOME[1]]

cumbia /'kʊmbɪə/ *n.* **1** a kind of dance music of Colombian origin, similar to salsa. **2** a dance performed to this music. [adapted from Colombian Spanish, perhaps from Spanish *cumbé*]

Cumbrian /'kʌmbrɪən/ *adj. & n.* ● *adj.* **1** of Cumberland in northern England. **2 a** of the ancient British kingdom of Cumbria. **b** of the modern county of Cumbria. ● *n.* a native of Cumberland or of ancient or modern Cumbria. [medieval Latin *Cumbria*, from Welsh *Cymry* 'Welshmen', + -AN]

cumbrous /'kʌmbrəs/ *adj.* = CUMBERSOME. □ **cumbrously** *adv.* **cumbrousness** *n.* [CUMBER + -OUS]

cum grano salis /kʌm ˌgrɑːnəʊ 'sɑːlɪs/ *adv.* with a grain of salt (cf. *take with a pinch of salt* (see SALT)). [Latin]

cumin /'kʌmɪn/ *n.* (also **cummin**) **1** an umbelliferous plant, *Cuminum cyminum*, bearing aromatic seeds. **2** these seeds used as flavouring, esp. ground and used in curry powder. [Middle English via Old French *cumin*, *comin* and Latin *cuminum* from Greek *kuminon*, probably of Semitic origin]

cummerbund /'kʌməbʌnd/ *n.* a waist sash. [Hindustani & Persian *kamar-band* 'loin-band']

cummin var. of CUMIN.

cumquat var. of KUMQUAT.

cumulate *v. & adj.* ● *v.tr. & intr.* /'kjuːmjʊleɪt/ accumulate, amass; combine. ● *adj.* /'kjuːmjʊlət/ heaped up, massed. □ **cumulation** /-'leɪʃ(ə)n/ *n.* [Latin *cumulare* from *cumulus* 'heap']

cumulative /'kjuːmjʊlətɪv/ *adj.* **1 a** increasing or increased in amount, force, etc., by successive additions (*cumulative evidence*). **b** formed by successive additions (*learning is a cumulative process*). **2** *Stock Exch.* (of shares) entitling holders to arrears of interest before any other distribution is made. □ **cumulatively** *adv.* **cumulativeness** *n.*

cumulative error *n. Statistics* an error that increases with the size of the sample revealing it.

cumulative voting *n.* a system in which each voter has as many votes as there are candidates and may give all to one candidate.

cumulo- /'kjuːmjʊləʊ/ *comb. form* cumulus (cloud).

cumulonimbus /ˌkjuːmjʊləʊ'nɪmbəs/ *n.* (*pl.* **cumulonimbuses** or **cumulonimbi** /-bʌɪ/) *Meteorol.* a cloud like cumulus but formed in towering masses, as in thunderstorms.

cumulus /'kjuːmjʊləs/ *n.* (*pl.* **cumuli** /-lʌɪ, -liː/) *Meteorol.* **1** clouds formed in rounded masses heaped on each other above a flat base at fairly low altitude. **2** a cloud of this type. □ **cumulous** *adj.* [Latin, = heap]

cuneate /'kjuːnɪət/ *adj.* wedge-shaped. [Latin *cuneus* 'wedge']

cuneiform /'kjuːnɪfɔːm, -nɪf-/ *adj. & n.* ● *adj.* **1** wedge-shaped. **2** of, relating to, or using the wedge-shaped writing impressed usu. in clay in ancient Babylonian etc. inscriptions. ● *n.* cuneiform writing. [French *cunéiforme* or modern Latin *cuneiformis*, from Latin *cuneus* 'wedge']

cunjevoi /'kʌndʒɪvɔɪ/ *n. Austral.* **1** a tall plant of the arum family, *Alocasia macrorrhiza*. **2** a sea squirt. [Aboriginal (NSW), senses 1 and 2 perhaps unconnected]

cunnilingus /kʌnɪ'lɪŋgəs/ *n.* (also **cunnilinctus** /-'lɪŋ(k)təs/) oral stimulation of the female genitals. [Latin, from *cunnus* 'vulva' + *lingere* 'lick']

cunning /'kʌnɪŋ/ *adj. & n.* ● *adj.* (**cunninger**, **cunningest**) **1 a** skilled in ingenuity or deceit. **b** selfishly clever or crafty. **2** ingenious (*a cunning device*). **3** *N. Amer.* attractive, quaint. ● *n.* **1** craftiness; skill in deceit. **2** skill, ingenuity. □ **cunningly** *adv.* **cunningness** *n.* [Middle English from Old Norse *kunnandi* 'knowing', from *kunna* 'know': cf. CAN[1]]

cunt /kʌnt/ *n. coarse slang* **1** the female genitals. **2** *offens.* an unpleasant or stupid person. [Middle English, from Germanic]

CUP *abbr.* Cambridge University Press.

cup /kʌp/ *n. & v.* ● *n.* **1** a small bowl-shaped container, usu. with a handle for drinking from. **2 a** its contents (*a cup of tea*). **b** = CUPFUL. **3** a cup-shaped thing, esp. the calyx of a flower or the socket of a bone. **4** flavoured wine, cider, etc., usu. chilled. **5** an ornamental cup-shaped trophy as a prize for victory or prowess, esp. in a sports contest. **6** one's fate or fortune (*a bitter cup*). **7** either of the two cup-shaped parts of a brassiere. **8** the chalice used or the wine taken at the

Eucharist. **9** *Golf* the hole on a putting green or the metal container in it. ● *v.tr.* (**cupped**, **cupping**) **1** form (esp. one's hands) into the shape of a cup. **2** take or hold as in a cup. **3** *hist.* bleed (a person) by using a glass in which a partial vacuum is formed by heating. □ **one's cup of tea** *colloq.* what interests or suits one. **in one's cups** *colloq.* while drunk; drunk. [Old English *cuppe* from medieval Latin *cuppa* probably from Latin *cupa* 'tub']

cupbearer /ˈkʌpbɛːrə/ *n.* a person who serves wine, esp. an officer of a royal or noble household.

cupboard /ˈkʌbəd/ *n.* a recess or piece of furniture with a door and (usu.) shelves, in which things are stored. [Middle English from CUP + BOARD]

cupboard love *n.* a display of affection meant to secure some gain.

cupcake /ˈkʌpkeɪk/ *n.* a small cake baked in a cup-shaped foil or paper container and often iced.

cupel /ˈkjuːp(ə)l/ *n.* & *v.* ● *n.* a small flat porous vessel used in assaying gold or silver in the presence of lead. ● *v.tr.* (**cupelled**, **cupelling**; *US* **cupeled**, **cupeling**) assay or refine in a cupel. □ **cupellation** /-ˈleɪʃ(ə)n/ *n.* [French *coupelle* from Late Latin *cupella*, diminutive of *cupa*: see CUP]

Cup Final *n. Brit.* the final match in a competition for a cup.

cupful /ˈkʌpfʊl/ *n.* (*pl.* **-fuls**) **1** the amount held by a cup, esp. *N. Amer.* a half-pint or 8-ounce measure in cookery. **2** the contents of a full cup (*drank a cupful of water*).

■ **Usage** A *cupful* is a measure, and so *three cupfuls* is a quantity regarded in terms of a cup; *three cups full* denotes the actual cups, as in *he brought us three cups full of water*.

Cupid /ˈkjuːpɪd/ *n.* **1** (in Roman mythology) the Roman god of love represented as a naked winged boy with a bow and arrows. **2** (also **cupid**) a representation of Cupid. [Middle English from Latin *Cupido*, from *cupere* 'desire']

cupidity /kjuːˈpɪdɪti/ *n.* greed for gain; avarice. [Middle English from Old French *cupidité* or Latin *cupiditas*, from *cupidus* 'desirous': related to COVET]

Cupid's bow *n.* the upper lip etc. shaped like the double-curved bow carried by Cupid.

cup lichen *n.* a lichen, *Cladonia pyxidata*, with cup-shaped processes arising from the thallus.

cupola /ˈkjuːpələ/ *n.* **1 a** a rounded dome forming a roof or ceiling. **b** a small rounded dome adorning a roof. **2** a revolving dome protecting mounted guns on a warship or in a fort. **3** (in full **cupola furnace**) a furnace for melting metals. □ **cupolaed** /-ləd/ *adj.* [Italian from Late Latin *cupula*, diminutive of *cupa* 'cask']

cuppa /ˈkʌpə/ *n.* (also **cupper**) *Brit. colloq.* **1** a cup of. **2** a cup of tea. [corruption]

cuprammonium /kjuːprəˈməʊnɪəm/ *n. Chem.* a complex ion of divalent copper and ammonia, solutions of which dissolve cellulose. [Late Latin *cuprum* 'copper' + AMMONIUM]

cupreous /ˈkjuːprɪəs/ *adj.* of or like copper. [Late Latin *cupreus* from *cuprum* 'copper']

cupric /ˈkjuːprɪk/ *adj. Chem.* of copper, esp. divalent copper. □ **cupriferous** /-ˈprɪf(ə)rəs/ *adj.* [Late Latin *cuprum* 'copper']

cuprite /ˈkjuːprʌɪt/ *n. Mineral.* native cuprous oxide, a red mineral and major copper ore.

cupro- /ˈkjuːprəʊ/ *comb. form* copper (*cupro-nickel*).

cupro-nickel /kjuːprəʊˈnɪk(ə)l/ *n.* an alloy of copper and nickel, esp. in the proportions 3:1 as used in 'silver' coins.

cuprous /ˈkjuːprəs/ *adj. Chem.* of copper, esp. monovalent copper. [Late Latin *cuprum* 'copper']

cup-tie *n. Brit.* a match in a competition for a cup.

cupule /ˈkjuːpjʊl/ *n. Bot.* & *Zool.* a cup-shaped organ, receptacle, etc. [Late Latin *cupula* CUPOLA]

cur /kəː/ *n.* **1** a worthless or snappy dog. **2** *colloq.* a contemptible man. [Middle English, probably originally in *cur-dog*, perhaps from Old Norse *kurr* 'grumbling']

curable /ˈkjʊərəb(ə)l/ *adj.* that can be cured. □ **curability** /-ˈbɪlɪti/ *n.* [CURE]

curaçao /kjʊərəˈsəʊ/ *n.* (also **curaçoa** /-ˈsəʊə/) (*pl.* **-os** or **curaçoas**) a liqueur of spirits flavoured with the peel of bitter oranges. [*Curaçao*, the name of the Caribbean island producing these oranges]

curacy /ˈkjʊərəsi/ *n.* (*pl.* **-ies**) a curate's office or the tenure of it.

curare /kjʊˈrɑːri/ *n.* a resinous bitter substance prepared from S. American plants of the genera *Strychnos* and *Chondodendron*, paralysing the motor nerves, used by American Indians to poison arrows and blowpipe darts, and formerly used as a muscle relaxant in surgery. [Carib]

curassow /ˈkjʊərəsəʊ/ *n.* any game bird of the family Cracidae, found in Central and S. America. [Anglicized from *Curaçao*, an island in the Caribbean]

curate[1] /ˈkjʊərət/ *n.* **1** a member of the clergy engaged as assistant to a parish priest. **2** *archaic* an ecclesiastical pastor. [Middle English from medieval Latin *curatus*, from Latin *cura* CURE]

curate[2] /kjʊ(ə)ˈreɪt/ *v.* **1** *tr.* act as curator of (a museum, exhibits, etc.); look after and preserve. **2** *intr.* perform the duties of a curator. □ **curation** *n.* [back-formation from CURATOR]

curate-in-charge *n.* = PRIEST-IN-CHARGE.

curate's egg *n.* esp. *Brit.* a thing that is partly good and partly bad. [CURATE[1], originating in a story of a meek curate who on being given a stale egg stated that 'parts of it' were 'excellent']

curative /ˈkjʊərətɪv/ *adj.* & *n.* ● *adj.* tending or able to cure (esp. disease). ● *n.* a curative medicine or agent. [French *curatif -ive* via medieval Latin *curativus* from Latin *curare* CURE]

curator /kjʊ(ə)ˈreɪtə/ *n.* a keeper or custodian of a museum or other collection. □ **curatorial** /kjʊərəˈtɔːrɪəl/ *adj.* **curatorship** *n.* [Middle English from Anglo-French *curatour* (Old French *-eur*) or Latin *curator* (as CURATIVE)]

curb /kəːb/ *n.* & *v.* ● *n.* **1** a check or restraint. **2** a strap etc. fastened to the bit and passing under a horse's lower jaw, used as a check. **3** an enclosing border or edging such as the frame round the top of a well or a fender round a hearth. **4** = KERB. ● *v.tr.* **1** restrain. **2** put a curb on (a horse). [Middle English via Old French *courber* from Latin *curvare* 'bend, CURVE']

curb roof *n.* a roof of which each face has two slopes, the lower one steeper.

curcuma /ˈkəːkjʊmə/ *n.* **1** the spice turmeric. **2** any tuberous plant of the genus *Curcuma*, yielding this and other commercial substances. [medieval Latin from Arabic *kurkum* 'saffron' from Sanskrit *kuṅkuma*[m]]

curd /kəːd/ *n.* **1** (often in *pl.*) a coagulated substance formed by the action of acids on milk, which may be made into cheese or eaten as food. **2** a fatty substance found between flakes of boiled salmon flesh. **3** the edible head of a cauliflower. □ **curdy** *adj.* [Middle English: origin unknown]

curd cheese *n.* a soft smooth cheese made from skimmed milk curds.

curdle /ˈkəːd(ə)l/ *v.tr.* & *intr.* make into or become curds; coagulate, congeal. □ **make one's blood curdle** fill one with horror. □ **curdler** *n.* [frequentative form of CURD (as verb)]

curd soap *n.* a white soap made of tallow and soda.

cure /kjʊə/ *v.* & *n.* ● *v.* **1** *tr.* (often foll. by *of*) restore (a person or animal) to health; relieve (*was cured of pleurisy*). **2** *tr.* eliminate (a disease, evil, etc.). **3** *tr.* preserve (meat, fruit, tobacco, or skins) by salting, drying, etc. **4** *tr.* **a** vulcanize (rubber). **b** harden (concrete or plastic). **5** *intr.* effect a cure. **6** *intr.* undergo a process of curing. ● *n.* **1** restoration to health. **2** a thing that effects a cure. **3** a course of medical or healing treatment. **4 a** the process of curing rubber or plastic. **b** (with qualifying adj.) the degree of this. **5 a** the office or function of a curate. **b** a parish or other sphere of spiritual ministration. □ **curer** *n.* [Middle English via Old French *curer* from Latin *curare* 'take care of', from *cura* 'care']

curé /'kjʊəreɪ/ *n.* a parish priest in France etc. [French from medieval Latin *curatus*: see CURATE[1]]

cure-all /'kjʊərɔːl/ *n.* a panacea; a universal remedy.

curettage /kjʊə'rɛtɪdʒ, kjʊərɪ'tɑːʒ/ *n.* the use of or an operation involving the use of a curette. [French (as CURETTE)]

curette /kjʊə'rɛt/ *n.* & *v.* ● *n.* a surgeon's small instrument for scraping. ● *v.tr.* & *intr.* clean or scrape with a curette. [French, from *curer* 'cleanse' (as CURE)]

curfew /'kəːfjuː/ *n.* **1 a** a regulation restricting or forbidding the public circulation of people, esp. requiring people to remain indoors between specified hours, usu. at night. **b** the hour designated as the beginning of such a restriction. **c** a daily signal indicating this. **2** *hist.* **a** a medieval regulation requiring people to extinguish fires at a fixed hour in the evening. **b** the hour for this. **c** the bell announcing it. **3** the ringing of a bell at a fixed evening hour. [Middle English from Anglo-French *coeverfu*, Old French *cuevrefeu*, from the stem of *couvrir* COVER + *feu* 'fire']

Curia /'kjʊərɪə/ *n.* (also **curia**) the papal court; the government departments of the Vatican. □ **Curial** *adj.* [Latin: originally a division of an ancient Roman tribe, the Senate house at Rome, a feudal court of justice]

curie /'kjʊəri/ *n.* **1** a unit of radioactivity, corresponding to 3.7×10^{10} disintegrations per second (abbr.: **Ci**). **2** a quantity of radioactive substance having this activity. [named after Pierre *Curie* (see CURIUM)]

curio /'kjʊərɪəʊ/ *n.* (*pl.* **-os**) a rare or unusual object or person. [19th-c. abbreviation of CURIOSITY]

curiosa /kjʊərɪ'əʊsə/ *n.pl.* **1** curiosities. **2** erotic or pornographic books. [neut. pl. of Latin *curiosus*: see CURIOUS]

curiosity /kjʊərɪ'ɒsɪti/ *n.* (*pl.* **-ies**) **1** an eager desire to know; inquisitiveness. **2** strangeness. **3** a strange, rare, or interesting object. [Middle English via Old French *curiouseté* from Latin *curiositas -tatis* (as CURIOUS)]

curious /'kjʊərɪəs/ *adj.* **1** eager to learn; inquisitive. **2** strange, surprising, odd. **3** *euphem.* (of books etc.) erotic, pornographic. □ **curiously** *adv.* **curiousness** *n.* [Middle English via Old French *curios* from Latin *curiosus* 'careful', from *cura* 'care']

curium /'kjʊərɪəm/ *n.* an artificially made transuranic radioactive metallic element, first produced by bombarding plutonium with helium ions (symbol **Cm**). [named after Marie *Curie* (d. 1934) and Pierre *Curie* (d. 1906), French scientists, discoverers of radium]

curl /kəːl/ *v.* & *n.* ● *v.* **1** *tr.* & *intr.* (often foll. by *up*) bend or coil into a spiral; form or cause to form curls. **2** *intr.* move in a spiral form (*smoke curling upwards*). **3 a** *intr.* (of the upper lip) be raised slightly on one side as an expression of contempt or disapproval. **b** *tr.* cause (the lip) to do this. **4** *intr.* play curling. ● *n.* **1** a lock of curled hair. **2** anything spiral or curved inwards. **3 a** a curling movement or act. **b** the state of being curled. **4** a disease of plants in which the leaves are curled up. □ **curl up 1** lie or sit with the knees drawn up. **2** *colloq.* writhe with embarrassment or horror. **make a person's hair curl** *colloq.* shock or horrify a person. **out of curl** *Brit.* lacking energy. [Middle English from obsolete adj. *crolle, crulle* 'curly', from Middle Dutch *krul*]

curler /'kəːlə/ *n.* **1** a pin or roller etc. for curling the hair. **2** a player in the game of curling.

curlew /'kəːl(j)uː/ *n.* (*pl.* same or **curlews**) a wading bird of the genus *Numenius*, with a long slender down-curved bill, esp. the European *N. arquatus*. [Middle English from Old French *courlieu, courlis*, originally imitative, but assimilated to *courliu* 'courier', from *courre* 'run' + *lieu* 'place']

curlicue /'kəːlɪkjuː/ *n.* a decorative curl or twist. [CURLY + CUE[2] (= pigtail) or Q[1]]

curling /'kəːlɪŋ/ *n.* **1** in senses of CURL *v.* **2** a game played on ice, esp. in Scotland, in which large round flat stones are slid across the surface towards a mark.

curling tongs *n.pl.* (also **curling iron** or **curling pins**) a heated device for twisting the hair into curls.

curly /'kəːli/ *adj.* (**curlier**, **curliest**) **1** having or arranged in curls. **2** moving in curves. □ **curliness** *n.*

curly endive see ENDIVE 1.

curly kale *n.* a form of kale with wrinkled leaves.

curmudgeon /kəː'mʌdʒ(ə)n/ *n.* a bad-tempered or miserly person. □ **curmudgeonly** *adj.* [16th c.: origin unknown]

currach /'kʌrə(x)/ *n.* (also **curragh**) *Ir.* a coracle. [Irish: cf. CORACLE]

currajong var. of KURRAJONG.

currant /'kʌr(ə)nt/ *n.* **1** a dried fruit of a small seedless variety of grape originally grown in the E. Mediterranean region and much used in cookery. **2 a** a shrub of the genus *Ribes* producing red, white, or black berries. **b** a berry of such a shrub. [Middle English *raysons of coraunce* from Anglo-French, = grapes of Corinth (the original source)]

currawong /'kʌrəwɒŋ/ *n. Austral.* a large Australian woodland songbird of the genus *Strepera*, resembling the magpie and having a resonant call. [Aboriginal, probably Yagara *garrawan*]

currency /'kʌr(ə)nsi/ *n.* (*pl.* **-ies**) **1 a** the money in general use in a country. **b** any other commodity used as a medium of exchange. **2** the condition of being current; prevalence (e.g. of words or ideas). **3** the time during which something is current.

current /'kʌr(ə)nt/ *adj.* & *n.* ● *adj.* **1** belonging to the present time; happening now (*current events*; *the current week*). **2** (of money, opinion, a rumour, a word, etc.) in general circulation or use. ● *n.* **1** a body of water, air, etc., moving in a definite direction, esp. through a stiller surrounding body. **2 a** a flow of electricity, i.e. an ordered movement of electrically charged particles. **b** a quantity representing the rate of this. **3** (usu. foll. by *of*) a general tendency or course (of events, opinions, etc.). □ **pass current** *Brit.* be generally accepted as true or genuine. [Middle English via Old French *corant* 'running' from Latin *currere* 'run']

current account *n. Brit.* a bank account from which money may be drawn without notice.

currently /'kʌrəntli/ *adv.* at the present time; now.

curricle /'kʌrɪk(ə)l/ *n. hist.* a light open two-wheeled carriage drawn by two horses abreast. [Latin *curriculum*: see CURRICULUM]

curriculum /kʌ'rɪkjʊləm/ *n.* (*pl.* **curricula** /-lə/) **1** the subjects that are studied or prescribed for study in a school (*not part of the school curriculum*). **2** any programme of activities. □ **curricular** *adj.* [Latin, = course, race-chariot, from *currere* 'run']

curriculum vitae /kʌˌrɪkjʊləm 'viːtʌɪ, 'vʌɪtiː/ *n.* (*pl.* **curricula vitae** or **vitarum**) a brief account of one's education, qualifications, and previous occupations. [Latin, = course of life]

currier /'kʌrɪə/ *n.* a person who dresses and colours tanned leather. [Middle English via Old French *corier* from Latin *coriarius*, from *corium* 'leather']

currish /'kəːrɪʃ/ *adj.* **1** like a cur; snappish. **2** ignoble. □ **currishly** *adv.* **currishness** *n.*

curry[1] /'kʌri/ *n.* & *v.* ● *n.* (*pl.* **-ies**) a dish of meat, vegetables, etc., cooked in a sauce of hot-tasting spices, usu. served with rice. ● *v.tr.* (**-ies**, **-ied**) prepare or flavour with a sauce of hot-tasting spices (*curried eggs*). [Tamil *kari*]

curry[2] /'kʌri/ *v.tr.* (**-ies**, **-ied**) **1** groom (a horse) with a curry-comb. **2** treat (tanned leather) to improve its properties. **3** thrash. □ **curry favour** ingratiate oneself. [Middle English from Old French *correier*, ultimately from Germanic]

curry-comb *n.* a hand-held serrated device used in grooming horses.

curry powder *n.* a preparation of turmeric and other spices for making curry.

curse /kəːs/ *n. & v.* ● *n.* **1** a solemn utterance intended to invoke a supernatural power to inflict destruction or punishment on a person or thing. **2** the evil supposedly resulting from a curse. **3** a violent exclamation of anger; a profane oath. **4** a thing that causes evil or harm. **5** (prec. by *the*) *colloq.* menstruation. **6** a sentence of excommunication. ● *v.* **1** *tr.* **a** utter a curse against. **b** (in *imper.*) may God curse. **2** *tr.* (usu. in *passive*; foll. by *with*) afflict with (*cursed with blindness*). **3** *intr.* utter expletive curses; swear. **4** *tr.* excommunicate. □ **curser** *n.* [Old English *curs, cursian*, of unknown origin]

cursed /'kəːsɪd, kəːst/ *adj.* (*archaic* **curst** /kəːst/) damnable, abominable. □ **cursedly** *adv.* **cursedness** *n.*

cursillo /kʊə'siːjəʊ, -'siːljəʊ/ *n.* (*pl.* **-os**) *RC Ch.* a short informal spiritual retreat by a group of devotees esp. in Latin America. [Spanish, = little course]

cursive /'kəːsɪv/ *adj. & n.* ● *adj.* (of writing) done with joined characters. ● *n.* cursive writing (cf. PRINT *v.* 4, UNCIAL). □ **cursively** *adv.* [medieval Latin (*scriptura*) *cursiva* from Latin *currere curs-* 'run']

cursor /'kəːsə/ *n.* **1** *Math.* etc. a transparent slide engraved with a hairline and forming part of a slide rule. **2** *Computing* a movable indicator on a VDU screen identifying a particular position in the display, esp. the position that the program will operate on with the next keystroke. [Latin, = runner (as CURSIVE)]

cursorial /kəː'sɔːrɪəl/ *adj. Zool.* having limbs adapted for running. [as CURSOR + -IAL]

cursory /'kəːs(ə)ri/ *adj.* hasty, hurried (*a cursory glance*). □ **cursorily** *adv.* **cursoriness** *n.* [Latin *cursorius* 'of a runner' (as CURSOR)]

curst *archaic* var. of CURSED.

curt /kəːt/ *adj.* noticeably or rudely brief. □ **curtly** *adv.* **curtness** *n.* [Latin *curtus* 'cut short, abridged']

curtail /kəː'teɪl/ *v.tr.* **1** cut short; reduce; terminate esp. prematurely (*curtailed his visit to America*). **2** (foll. by *of*) *archaic* deprive of. □ **curtailment** *n.* [obsolete *curtal* 'horse with docked tail', via French *courtault* from *court* 'short', from Latin *curtus*: assimilated to *tail*]

curtain /'kəːt(ə)n/ *n. & v.* ● *n.* **1** a piece of cloth etc. hung up as a screen, usu. movable sideways or upwards, esp. at a window or between the stage and auditorium of a theatre. **2** *Theatr.* **a** the rise or fall of the stage curtain at the beginning or end of an act or scene. **b** = CURTAIN CALL. **3** a partition or cover. **4** (in *pl.*) *slang* the end. ● *v.tr.* **1** furnish or cover with a curtain or curtains. **2** (foll. by *off*) shut off with a curtain or curtains. [Middle English via Old French *cortine* from Late Latin *cortina*, translation of Greek *aulaia* from *aulē* 'court']

curtain call *n.* an audience's summons to actor(s) to take a bow after the fall of the curtain.

curtain fire *n. Brit. Mil.* a concentration of rapid and continuous fire.

curtain lecture *n.* a wife's private reproof to her husband, originally behind bed-curtains.

curtain-raiser *n.* **1** *Theatr.* a piece prefaced to the main performance. **2** a preliminary event.

curtain wall *n.* **1** the plain wall of a fortified place, connecting two towers etc. **2** *Archit.* a piece of plain wall not supporting a roof.

curtana /kəː'tɑːnə, -'teɪnə/ *n. Brit.* an unpointed sword borne before English sovereigns at their coronation, as an emblem of mercy. [Middle English via Anglo-Latin *curtana* (*spatha* 'sword') from Anglo-French *curtain*, Old French *cortain*, the name of Roland's similar sword, from *cort* 'short' (as CURT)]

curtilage /'kəːt(ɪ)lɪdʒ/ *n.* an area attached to a dwelling house and forming one enclosure with it. [Middle English from Anglo-French *curtilage*, Old French *co(u)rtillage*, via *co(u)rtil* 'small court' from *cort* COURT]

curtsy /'kəːtsi/ *n. & v.* (also **curtsey**) ● *n.* (*pl.* **-ies** or **-eys**) a woman's or girl's formal greeting or salutation made by bending the knees and lowering the body. ● *v.intr.* (**-ies**, **-ied** or **-eys**, **-eyed**) make a curtsy. [variant of COURTESY]

curule /'kjʊəruːl/ *adj. Rom.Hist.* designating or relating to the authority exercised by the senior Roman magistrates, chiefly the consul and praetor, who were entitled to use the *sella curulis* ('curule seat' or seat of office). [Latin *curulis* from *currus* 'chariot' (in which the chief magistrate was conveyed to the seat of office)]

curvaceous /kəː'veɪʃəs/ *adj.* (esp. of a woman) having a shapely curved figure.

curvature /'kəːvətʃə/ *n.* **1** the act or state of curving. **2** a curved form. **3** *Geom.* **a** the deviation of a curve from a straight line, or of a curved surface from a plane. **b** the quantity expressing this. [Old French from Latin *curvatura* (as CURVE)]

curve /kəːv/ *n. & v.* ● *n.* **1** a line or surface having along its length a regular deviation from being straight or flat, as exemplified by the surface of a sphere or lens. **2** a curved form or thing. **3** a curved line on a graph. **4** *Baseball* a ball caused to deviate by the pitcher's spin. ● *v.tr. & intr.* bend or shape so as to form a curve. □ **curved** *adj.* [originally as *adj.* (in *curve line*) from Latin *curvus* 'bent': the verb from Latin *curvare*]

curvet /kəː'vɛt/ *n. & v.* ● *n.* a horse's leap with the forelegs raised together and the hind legs raised with a spring before the forelegs reach the ground. ● *v.intr.* (**curvetted**, **curvetting** or **curveted**, **curveting**) (of a horse or rider) make a curvet. [Italian *corvetta*, diminutive of *corva* CURVE]

curvi- /'kəːvi/ *comb. form* curved. [Latin *curvus* 'curved']

curvifoliate /kəːvɪ'fəʊlɪət/ *adj. Bot.* with the leaves bent back.

curviform /'kəːvɪfɔːm/ *adj.* having a curved shape.

curvilinear /kəːvɪ'lɪnɪə/ *adj.* contained by or consisting of curved lines. □ **curvilinearly** *adv.* [CURVI-, on the pattern of *rectilinear*]

curvirostral /kəːvɪ'rɒstr(ə)l/ *adj.* with a curved beak.

curvy /'kəːvi/ *adj.* (**curvier**, **curviest**) **1** having many curves. **2** (of a woman's figure) shapely. □ **curviness** *n.*

cuscus[1] var. of KHUS-KHUS.

cuscus[2] /'kʊskʊs/ *n.* any of several nocturnal arboreal marsupials of the genus *Phalanger*, native to New Guinea and northern Australia. [native name]

cusec /'kjuːsɛk/ *n.* a unit of flow (esp. of water) equal to one cubic foot per second. [abbreviation]

cush /kʊʃ/ *n.* esp. *Billiards colloq.* a cushion. [abbreviation]

cushat /'kʌʃət/ *n. Sc.* a wood pigeon. [Old English *cūscute*, of unknown origin]

cush-cush /'kʊʃkʊʃ/ *n.* a yam, *Dioscorea trifida*, native to S. America. [perhaps ultimately of African origin]

Cushing's disease /'kʊʃɪŋz/ *n. Med.* Cushing's syndrome as caused by a tumour of the pituitary gland.

Cushing's syndrome *n. Med.* a metabolic disorder caused by overactivity of the adrenal cortex and often involving obesity and hypertension. [named after H.W. *Cushing*, US surgeon (d. 1939), who identified it]

cushion /'kʊʃ(ə)n/ *n. & v.* ● *n.* **1** a bag of cloth etc. stuffed with a mass of soft material, used as a soft support for sitting or leaning on etc. **2** a means of protection against shock. **3** the elastic lining of the sides of a billiard table, from which the ball rebounds. **4** a body of air supporting a hovercraft etc. **5** the frog of a horse's hoof. ● *v.tr.* **1** provide or protect with a cushion or cushions. **2** provide with a defence; protect. **3** mitigate the adverse effects of (*cushioned the blow*). **4** quietly suppress. **5** place or bounce (the ball) against the cushion in billiards. □ **cushiony** *adj.* [Middle English via Old French *co(i)ssin*, *cu(i)ssin* and Gallo-Roman from Latin *culcita* 'mattress, cushion']

Cushitic /kʊ'ʃɪtɪk/ *n. & adj.* ● *n.* a group of E. African languages of the Hamitic type. ● *adj.* of this group.

[*Cush*, the name of an ancient country in the Nile valley + -ITE[1] + -IC]

cushy /ˈkʊʃi/ *adj.* (**cushier**, **cushiest**) *colloq.* **1** (of a job etc.) easy and pleasant. **2** *US* (of a seat, surroundings, etc.) soft, comfortable. ▫ **cushiness** *n.* [Anglo-Indian via Urdu *ḵushī* 'pleasure' from Persian *ḵuš*]

cusp /kʌsp/ *n.* **1** an apex or peak. **2** the horn of a crescent moon etc. **3** *Astrol.* the initial point of an astrological sign or house. **4** *Archit.* a projecting point between small arcs in Gothic tracery. **5** *Geom.* the point at which two arcs meet from the same direction terminating with a common tangent. **6** *Bot.* a pointed end, esp. of a leaf. **7** a cone-shaped prominence on the surface of a tooth, esp. of a molar or premolar. **8** *Anat.* a pocket or fold in a valve of the heart. ▫ **cuspate** /-speɪt/ *adj.* **cusped** *adj.* **cuspidal** *adj.* [Latin *cuspis, -idis* 'point, apex']

cuspidor /ˈkʌspɪdɔː/ *n. N. Amer.* a spittoon. [Portuguese, = spitter from *cuspir* 'spit', from Latin *conspuere*]

cuss /kʌs/ *n. & v. colloq.* ● *n.* **1** a curse. **2** usu. *derog.* a person; a creature. ● *v.tr. & intr.* curse. [variant of CURSE]

cussed /ˈkʌsɪd/ *adj. colloq.* awkward and stubborn. ▫ **cussedly** *adv.* **cussedness** *n.* [variant of CURSED]

cuss word *n. colloq.* a swear word.

custard /ˈkʌstəd/ *n.* **1** a sweet sauce made with milk and flavoured cornflour. **2** a dish made with milk and eggs, usu. sweetened. [originally an open pie containing meat or fruit in a sauce: Middle English, earlier *crusta(r)de* via Anglo-French from Old French *crouste* CRUST]

custard apple *n.* a W. Indian fruit, *Annona reticulata*, with a custard-like pulp.

custard pie *n.* **1** a pie containing custard or foam, commonly thrown in slapstick comedy. **2** (*attrib.*) denoting slapstick comedy.

custard powder *n.* a preparation of cornflour etc. for making custard.

custodian /kʌˈstəʊdɪən/ *n.* a guardian or keeper, esp. of a public building etc. ▫ **custodianship** *n.* [CUSTODY + -AN, on the pattern of *guardian*]

custody /ˈkʌstədi/ *n.* **1** guardianship; protective care. **2** imprisonment. ▫ **take into custody** arrest. ▫ **custodial** /kʌˈstəʊdɪəl/ *adj.* [Latin *custodia* from *custos -odis* 'guardian']

custom /ˈkʌstəm/ *n.* **1 a** the usual way of behaving or acting (*a slave to custom*). **b** a particular established way of behaving (*our customs seem strange to foreigners*). **2** *Law* established usage having the force of law. **3** esp. *Brit.* business patronage; regular dealings or customers (*lost a lot of custom*). **4** (in *pl.*; also treated as *sing.*) **a** a duty levied on certain imported and exported goods. **b** the official department that administers this. **c** the area at a port, frontier, etc., where customs officials deal with incoming goods, baggage, etc. [Middle English and Old French *custume*, ultimately from Latin *consuetudo -dinis*: see CONSUETUDE]

customary /ˈkʌstəm(ə)ri/ *adj. & n.* ● *adj.* **1** usual; in accordance with custom. **2** *Law* in accordance with custom. ● *n.* (*pl.* **-ies**) *Law* a book etc. listing the customs and established practices of a community. ▫ **customarily** *adv.* **customariness** *n.* [medieval Latin *custumarius* from *custuma*, from Anglo-French *custume* (as CUSTOM)]

custom-built *adj.* made to a customer's order.

customer /ˈkʌstəmə/ *n.* **1** a person who buys goods or services from a shop or business. **2** a person one has to deal with (*an awkward customer*). [Middle English from Anglo-French *custumer* (as CUSTOMARY), or from CUSTOM + -ER[1]]

custom house *n.* (also **customs house**) the office at a port or frontier etc. at which customs duties are levied.

customize /ˈkʌstəmʌɪz/ *v.tr.* (also **-ise**) make to order or modify according to individual requirements.

custom-made *adj.* = CUSTOM-BUILT.

customs union *n.* a group of states with an agreed common tariff, and usu. free trade with each other.

cut /kʌt/ *v. & n.* ● *v.* (**cutting**; *past* and *past part.* **cut**) **1** *tr.* (also *absol.*) penetrate or wound with a sharp-edged instrument (*cut his finger*; *the knife won't cut*). **2** *tr. & intr.* (often foll. by *into*) divide or be divided with a knife etc. (*cut the bread*; *cut the cloth into metre lengths*). **3** *tr.* **a** trim or reduce the length of (hair, a hedge, etc.) by cutting. **b** detach all or the significant part of (flowers, corn, etc.) by cutting. **4** *tr.* (foll. by *loose*, *open*, etc.) make loose, open, etc. by cutting. **5** *tr.* (esp. as **cutting** *adj.*) cause sharp physical or mental pain to (*a cutting remark*; *a cutting wind*; *was cut to the quick*). **6** *tr.* (often foll. by *down*) **a** reduce (wages, prices, time, etc.). **b** reduce or cease (services etc.). **7** *tr.* **a** shape or fashion (a coat, gem, key, record, etc.) by cutting. **b** make (a path, tunnel, etc.) by removing material. **8** *tr.* perform, execute, make (*cut a caper*; *cut a sorry figure*). **9** *tr.* (also *absol.*) cross, intersect (*the line cuts the circle at two points*; *the two lines cut*). **10** *intr.* (foll. by *across*, *through*, etc.) pass or traverse, esp. in a hurry or as a shorter way (*cut across the grass*). **11** *tr.* **a** ignore or refuse to recognize (a person). **b** renounce (a connection). **12** *tr.* esp. *N. Amer.* deliberately fail to attend (a class etc.). **13** *Cards* **a** *tr.* divide (a pack) into two parts. **b** *intr.* select a dealer etc. by dividing the pack. **14** *Cinematog.* **a** *tr.* edit (a film or tape). **b** *intr.* (often in *imper.*) stop filming or recording. **c** *intr.* (foll. by *to*) go quickly to (another shot). **15** *tr.* switch off (an engine etc.). **16** *tr.* **a** hit (a ball) with a chopping motion. **b** *Golf* slice (the ball). **17** *tr. N. Amer.* dilute, adulterate. **18** *tr.* (as **cut** *adj.*) *Brit. slang* drunk. **19** *intr. Cricket* (of the ball) turn sharply on pitching. **20** *intr. slang* run. **21** *tr.* castrate. ● *n.* **1** an act of cutting. **2** a division or wound made by cutting. **3** a stroke with a knife, sword, whip, etc. **4 a** a reduction (in prices, wages, etc.). **b** *Brit.* a cessation (of a power supply etc.). **5** an excision of part of a play, film, book, etc. **6** a wounding remark or act. **7** the way or style in which a garment, the hair, etc., is cut. **8** a piece of meat etc. cut from a carcass. **9** *colloq.* commission; a share of profits. **10** *Tennis & Cricket* etc. a stroke made by cutting. **11** ignoring of or refusal to recognize a person. **12 a** an engraved block for printing. **b** = WOODCUT 1, 2. **13** a railway cutting. **14** a new channel made for a river. ▫ **a cut above** *colloq.* noticeably superior to. **be cut out** (foll. by *for*, or *to* + infin.) be suited (*was not cut out to be a teacher*). **cut across 1** transcend or take no account of (normal limitations etc.) (*their concern cuts across normal rivalries*). **2** see sense 10 of *v.* **cut and dried 1** completely decided; pre-arranged; inflexible. **2** (of opinions etc.) ready-made, lacking freshness. **cut and run** *colloq.* run away. **cut and thrust 1** a lively interchange of argument etc. **2** the use of both the edge and the point of a sword. **cut back 1** reduce (expenditure etc.). **2** prune (a tree etc.). **3** *Cinematog.* repeat part of a previous scene for dramatic effect. **cut both ways 1** serve both sides of an argument etc. **2** (of an action) have both good and bad effects. **cut one's coat according to one's cloth 1** adapt expenditure to resources. **2** limit ambition to what is feasible. **cut a corner** go across and not round it. **cut corners** do a task etc. perfunctorily or incompletely, esp. to save time. **cut a dash** see DASH. **cut dead** completely refuse to recognize (a person). **cut down 1 a** bring or throw down by cutting. **b** kill by means of a sword or disease. **2** see sense 6 of *v.* **3** reduce the length of (*cut down the trousers to make shorts*). **4** (often foll. by *on*) reduce one's consumption (*tried to cut down on beer*). **cut a person down to size** *colloq.* ruthlessly expose the limitations of a person's importance, ability, etc. **cut one's eye-teeth** attain worldly wisdom. **cut in 1** interrupt. **2** pull in too closely in front of another vehicle (esp. having overtaken it). **3** give a share of profits etc. to (a person). **4** connect (a source of electricity). **5** join in a card game by taking the place of a player who cuts out. **6** interrupt a dancing couple to take over from one partner. **cut into 1** make a cut in (*they cut into the cake*). **2** interfere with and reduce (*travelling cuts into my free time*). **cut it fine** see FINE[1]. **cut it out** (usu. in *imper.*) *colloq.* stop doing that (esp. quarrelling). **cut the knot** solve a problem in an irregular but efficient way. **cut loose 1** begin to act freely. **2** see sense 4 of *v.* **cut one's losses** (or **a loss**) abandon an unprofitable enterprise before losses become too great. **cut the mustard** *N. Amer. slang* reach the required standard. **cut no ice** *colloq.* **1** have no influence or importance. **2** achieve little or nothing. **cut off 1** remove (an appendage) by cutting. **2 a** (often in *passive*) bring to an abrupt end or (esp. early) death. **b** intercept, interrupt; prevent from continuing (*cut off supplies*; *cut off the gas*). **c** disconnect (a person engaged in a telephone conversation) (*was suddenly cut off*). **3 a** prevent from travelling or venturing out (*was cut off by the snow*). **b** (as **cut off** *adj.*) isolated, remote (*felt cut off in the country*). **4** disinherit (*was cut off without a penny*). **cut out 1** remove from the inside by cutting. **2** make by cutting from a larger whole. **3** omit; leave out. **4** *colloq.* stop doing or using (something) (*managed to cut out chocolate*; *let's cut out the arguing*). **5** cease or cause to cease functioning (*the engine cut out*). **6** outdo or supplant (a rival). **7** *US* detach (an animal) from the herd. **8** *Cards* be excluded from a card game as a result of a decision taken by cutting the pack. **cut short 1** interrupt; terminate prematurely (*cut short his visit*). **2** make shorter or more concise. **cut one's teeth on** acquire initial practice or experience from (something). **cut a tooth** have it appear through the gum. **cut up 1** cut into pieces. **2** destroy utterly. **3** (usu. in *passive*) *Brit.* distress greatly (*was very cut up about it*). **4** criticize severely. **5** *N. Amer. derog.* behave in a comical or unruly manner. **cut up rough** *Brit. colloq.* show anger or resentment. **cut up well** *Brit. slang* bequeath a large fortune. **have one's work cut out** see WORK. [Middle English *cutte*, *kitte*, *kette*, probably from Old English]

cut-and-come-again *n. Brit.* the opportunity of helping oneself as often as one likes; abundance (usu. *attrib.*: *a cut-and-come-again fruit cake*).

cut-and-paste *n.* the process of assembling text by adding or combining sections from other texts (often *attrib.*: *cut-and-paste montage*).

cutaneous /kju:'teɪnɪəs/ *adj.* of the skin. [modern Latin *cutaneus* from Latin *cutis* 'skin']

cutaway /'kʌtəweɪ/ *adj.* **1** (of a diagram etc.) with some parts left out to reveal the interior. **2** (of a coat) with the front below the waist cut away.

cutback /'kʌtbak/ *n.* an instance or the act of cutting back, esp. a reduction in expenditure.

cut-down *adj.* that has been reduced, esp. in length (*a cut-down raincoat*; *a cut-down version of the play*).

cute /kju:t/ *adj. colloq.* **1 a** attractive, pretty; quaint. **b** affectedly attractive. **2** clever, ingenious. □ **cutely** *adv.* **cuteness** *n.* [shortening of ACUTE]

cutesy /'kju:tsi/ *adj. colloq.* dainty or quaint to an affected degree.

cut glass *n.* glass with patterns and designs cut on it.

cuticle /'kju:tɪk(ə)l/ *n.* **1** the dead skin at the base of a fingernail or toenail. **2** the outer cellular layer of a hair. **3** the epidermis. **4** *Bot.* & *Zool.* the outer layer of an organism, esp. a protective often waxy layer covering the epidermis of a plant or invertebrate. □ **cuticular** /-'tɪkjʊlə/ *adj.* [Latin *cuticula*, diminutive of *cutis* 'skin']

cutie /'kju:ti/ *n. slang* an attractive young woman.

cut-in *n.* something that is cut in, esp. an interposed scene in a film.

cutis /'kju:tɪs/ *n. Anat.* the true skin or dermis, underlying the epidermis. [Latin, = skin]

cutlass /'kʌtləs/ *n.* a short sword with a slightly curved blade, esp. of the type formerly used by sailors. [French *coutelas*, ultimately from Latin *cultellus*: see CUTLER]

cutler /'kʌtlə/ *n.* a person who makes or deals in cutlery. [Middle English via Anglo-French *cotillere*, Old French *coutelier*, from *coutel*, from Latin *cultellus*, diminutive of *culter* COULTER]

cutlery /'kʌtləri/ *n.* knives, forks, and spoons for use at table. [Old French & French *coutel(l)erie* (as CUTLER)]

cutlet /'kʌtlɪt/ *n.* **1** *Brit.* a neck-chop of mutton or lamb. **2** a small piece of veal etc. for frying. **3** a flat cake of minced meat or nuts and breadcrumbs etc. [French *côtelette*, Old French *costelet*, diminutive of *coste* 'rib', from Latin *costa*]

cut-line *n.* **1** a caption to an illustration. **2** the line in squash above which a served ball must strike the wall.

cut-off *n.* **1** the point at which something is cut off. **2** a device for stopping a flow. **3** *US* a short cut. **4** (in *pl.*) shorts, esp. made from cut-down jeans.

cut-out *n.* **1** a figure cut out of paper etc. **2** a device for automatic disconnection, the release of exhaust gases, etc.

cut-out box *n. US* = FUSE BOX.

cut-price *adj.* (also **cut-rate**) selling or sold at a reduced price.

cutpurse /'kʌtpə:s/ *n. archaic* a pickpocket; a thief.

cutter /'kʌtə/ *n.* **1** a person or thing that cuts. **2** a tailor etc. who takes measurements and cuts cloth. **3** *Naut.* **a** a small fast sailing ship. **b** a small boat carried by a large ship. **4** *Cricket* a ball turning sharply on pitching. **5** *N. Amer.* a light horse-drawn sleigh.

cut-throat *n.* & *adj.* ● *n.* **1** a murderer. **2** (in full **cut-throat razor**) *Brit.* a razor having a long blade set in a handle and usu. folding like a penknife. **3** a species of trout, *Salmo clarki*, with a red mark under the jaw. ● *adj.* **1** (of competition) ruthless and intense. **2** (of a card game) three-handed.

cutting /'kʌtɪŋ/ *n.* & *adj.* ● *n.* **1** *Brit.* a piece cut from a newspaper etc. **2** a piece cut from a plant for propagation. **3** an excavated channel through high ground for a railway or road. ● *adj.* in senses of CUT *v.* 5. □ **cuttingly** *adv.*

cutting edge *n.* & *adj.* ● *n.* **1** an edge that cuts. **2** the forefront of a movement etc. **3** the most significant factor. ● *attrib.adj.* (**cutting-edge**) pioneering, innovative.

cuttle /'kʌt(ə)l/ *n.* = CUTTLEFISH. [Old English *cudele*, Middle English *codel*, related to *cod* 'bag', with reference to its ink-bag]

cuttle-bone *n.* the internal shell of the cuttlefish crushed and used for polishing teeth etc. or as a supplement to the diet of a cage bird.

cuttlefish /'kʌt(ə)lfɪʃ/ *n.* (*pl.* usu. same) any marine cephalopod mollusc of the genera *Sepia* and *Sepiola*, having ten arms and ejecting a black fluid when threatened or pursued.

cutty /'kʌti/ *adj.* & *n. Sc.* & *N.Engl.* ● *adj.* cut short; abnormally short. ● *n.* (*pl.* **-ies**) a short tobacco pipe.

cutty-stool *n. hist.* a stool provided for an offender to be publicly rebuked during a church service.

cutwater /'kʌtwɔ:tə/ *n.* **1** the forward edge of a ship's prow. **2** a wedge-shaped projection from the pier of a bridge.

cutworm /'kʌtwə:m/ *n.* any of various caterpillars that eat through the stems of young plants level with the ground.

cuvée /kju:'veɪ/ *n.* a blend or batch of wine. [French, = vatful, from *cuve* 'cask', from Latin *cupa*]

cuvette /kju:'vɛt/ *n.* **1** a shallow vessel for liquid. **2** a straight-sided transparent container for holding a liquid sample in a spectrophotometer etc. [French, diminutive of *cuve* 'cask', from Latin *cupa*]

CV *abbr.* curriculum vitae.

CVO *abbr. Brit.* Commander of the Royal Victorian Order.

CVS *abbr.* chorionic villus sample, a test on a pregnant woman to detect any chromosomal abnormalities in the foetus.

Cwlth. *abbr.* Commonwealth.

cwm /kʊm/ *n.* **1** (in Wales) = COOMB. **2** *Geog.* a cirque. [Welsh]

c.w.o. *abbr.* cash with order.

cwt. *abbr.* hundredweight.

-cy /si/ *suffix* (see also -ACY, -ANCY, -CRACY, -ENCY, -MANCY). **1** denoting state or condition (*bankruptcy*; *idiocy*). **2** denoting rank or status (*captaincy*). [from or suggested by Latin *-cia*, *-tia*, Greek *-k(e)ia*, *-t(e)ia*]

cyan /'sʌɪən/ *n. & adj.* ● *n.* a greenish-blue colour. ● *adj.* of this colour. [Greek *kuan(e)os* 'dark blue']

cyanamide /sʌɪ'anəmʌɪd/ *n. Chem.* **1** a weakly acidic colourless crystalline amide of cyanogen. Chem. formula: CH_2N_2. **2** any salt of this, esp. a calcium salt used as a fertilizer. [CYANOGEN + AMIDE]

cyanic acid /sʌɪ'anɪk/ *n.* a highly unstable acid. Chem. formula: HOCN. [CYANOGEN]

cyanide /'sʌɪənʌɪd/ *n.* any of the highly poisonous salts or esters of hydrocyanic acid, esp. the potassium salt used in the extraction of gold and silver. [CYANOGEN + -IDE]

cyanobacterium /ˌsʌɪənəʊbak'tɪərɪəm/ *n.* any prokaryotic organism of the division Cyanobacteria, found in many environments and capable of photosynthesizing. Also called *blue-green alga*. [CYANOGEN + BACTERIUM]

cyanocobalamin /ˌsʌɪənəʊkə'baləmɪn/ *n.* a vitamin of the B complex, found in foods of animal origin such as liver, fish, and eggs, a deficiency of which can cause pernicious anaemia. Also called *vitamin B_{12}*. [CYANOGEN + *cobalamin* from COBALT + VITAMIN]

cyanogen /sʌɪ'anədʒ(ə)n/ *n. Chem.* a colourless highly poisonous gas intermediate in the preparation of many fertilizers. Chem. formula: C_2N_2. [French *cyanogène* from Greek *kuanos* 'dark blue mineral', as being a constituent of Prussian blue]

cyanogenic /sʌɪənə'dʒɛnɪk/ *adj.* capable of providing cyanide.

cyanosis /sʌɪə'nəʊsɪs/ *n. Med.* a bluish discoloration of the skin due to the presence of oxygen-deficient blood. ▫ **cyanotic** /-'nɒtɪk/ *adj.* [modern Latin from Greek *kuanōsis* 'blueness' (as CYANOGEN)]

cyber- /'sʌɪbə/ *prefix* forming words relating to electronic communication networks and virtual reality. [back-formation from CYBERNETICS]

cybernation /sʌɪbə'neɪʃ(ə)n/ *n.* control by machines. ▫ **cybernate** /'sʌɪ-/ *v.tr.* [CYBERNETICS + -ATION]

cybernetics /sʌɪbə'nɛtɪks/ *n.* the science of communications and automatic control systems in both machines and living things. ▫ **cybernetic** *adj.* **cybernetician** /-'tɪʃ(ə)n/ *n.* **cyberneticist** /-sɪst/ *n.* [Greek *kubernētēs* 'steersman']

cyberpunk /'sʌɪbəpʌŋk/ *n.* a style of science fiction featuring urban counter-culture in a world of high technology and virtual reality. [CYBER- + PUNK]

cyberspace /'sʌɪbəspeɪs/ *n.* the notional environment in which electronic communication occurs; virtual reality. [CYBER- + SPACE *n.*]

cyborg /'sʌɪbɔːg/ *n.* a person whose physical abilities are extended beyond normal human limitations by machine technology (as yet undeveloped). [CYBER- + ORGANISM]

cycad /'sʌɪkad/ *n.* a palmlike plant of the order Cycadales (including fossil forms) inhabiting tropical and subtropical regions and often growing to a great height. [modern Latin *cycas*, *cycad-* from supposed Greek *kukas*, scribal error for *koikas*, pl. of *koix* 'Egyptian palm']

Cycladic /sɪ'kladɪk, sʌɪ-/ *adj.* of the Cyclades, a group of islands east of the Greek mainland, esp. of the Bronze Age civilization that flourished there. [Latin *Cyclades*, from Greek *Kuklades*, from *kuklos* 'circle' (of islands)]

cyclamate /'sɪkləmeɪt, 'sʌɪk-/ *n.* any of various compounds related to sulphamic acid and formerly used as artificial sweetening agents. [contraction of chemical name *cyclohexylsulphamate*]

cyclamen /'sɪkləmən/ *n. & adj.* ● *n.* (*pl.* same or **cyclamens**) **1** any plant of the genus *Cyclamen*, originating in Europe, having pink, red, or white flowers with reflexed petals, often grown in pots. **2** the shade of colour of the red or pink cyclamen flower. ● *adj.* of this colour. [medieval Latin from Greek *kuklaminos*, perhaps from *kuklos* 'circle', with reference to its bulbous roots]

cycle /'sʌɪk(ə)l/ *n. & v.* ● *n.* **1 a** a recurrent round or period (of events, phenomena, etc.). **b** the time needed for one such round or period. **2 a** *Physics* etc. a recurrent series of operations or states. **b** *Electr.* = HERTZ. **3** a series of songs, poems, etc., usu. on a single theme. **4** a bicycle, tricycle, or similar machine. ● *v.intr.* **1** ride a bicycle etc. **2** move in cycles. [Middle English from Old French, or Late Latin *cyclus* from Greek *kuklos* 'circle']

cycle track *n.* (also **cycleway**) *Brit.* a path or road for bicycles.

cyclic /'sʌɪklɪk/ *adj.* **1 a** recurring in cycles. **b** belonging to a chronological cycle. **2** *Chem.* with constituent atoms forming a ring. **3** of a cycle of songs etc. **4** *Bot.* (of a flower) with its parts arranged in whorls. **5** *Math.* of a circle or cycle. [French *cyclique* or Latin *cyclicus* from Greek *kuklikos* (as CYCLE)]

cyclical /'sʌɪklɪk(ə)l/ *adj.* = CYCLIC 1. ▫ **cyclically** *adv.*

cyclist /'sʌɪklɪst/ *n.* a rider of a cycle, esp. of a bicycle.

cyclo- /'sʌɪkləʊ/ *comb. form* circle, cycle, or cyclic (*cyclometer*; *cyclorama*). [Greek *kuklos* circle]

cycloalkane /sʌɪkləʊ'alkeɪn/ *n. Chem.* a saturated cyclic hydrocarbon.

cyclo-cross /'sʌɪkləʊkrɒs/ *n.* cross-country racing on bicycles.

cyclograph /'sʌɪkləgrɑːf/ *n.* an instrument for tracing circular arcs.

cyclohexane /sʌɪkləʊ'hɛkseɪn/ *n. Chem.* a colourless liquid cycloalkane used as a solvent and paint remover. Chem. formula: C_6H_{12}.

cycloid /'sʌɪklɔɪd/ *n. Math.* a curve traced by a point on a circle when the circle is rolled along a straight line. ▫ **cycloidal** /-'klɔɪd(ə)l/ *adj.* [Greek *kukloeidēs* (as CYCLE, -OID)]

cyclometer /sʌɪ'klɒmɪtə/ *n.* **1** an instrument for measuring circular arcs. **2** an instrument for measuring the distance traversed by a bicycle etc.

cyclone /'sʌɪkləʊn/ *n.* **1** a system of winds rotating inwards to an area of low barometric pressure; a depression. **2** (in full **tropical cyclone**) a violent wind system of this kind, formed in localized areas over tropical oceans, with winds of hurricane force. ▫ **cyclonic** /-'klɒnɪk/ *adj.* **cyclonically** /-'klɒnɪk(ə)li/ *adv.* [probably from Greek *kuklōma* 'wheel, coil of a snake']

cycloparaffin /sʌɪkləʊ'parəfɪn/ *n. Chem.* = CYCLOALKANE.

Cyclopean /sʌɪklə'piːən, -'kləʊpɪən/ *adj.* (also **Cyclopian**) **1** (of ancient masonry) made with massive irregular blocks. **2** of or resembling a Cyclops.

cyclopedia /sʌɪklə(ʊ)'piːdɪə/ *n.* (also **cyclopaedia**) an encyclopedia. ▫ **cyclopedic** *adj.* [shortening of ENCYCLOPEDIA]

cyclopropane /sʌɪklə(ʊ)'prəʊpeɪn/ *n. Chem.* a colourless gaseous cycloalkane used as a general anaesthetic. Chem. formula: C_3H_6.

Cyclops /'sʌɪklɒps/ *n.* **1** (*pl.* **Cyclops** or **Cyclopses** or **Cyclopes** /sʌɪ'kləʊpiːz/) (in Greek mythology) a member of a race of one-eyed giants. **2** (**cyclops**) (*pl.* **cyclops** or **cyclopes**) *Zool.* a crustacean of the genus *Cyclops*, with a single central eye. [Latin from Greek *Kuklōps*, from *kuklos* 'circle' + *ōps* 'eye']

cyclorama /sʌɪklə'rɑːmə/ *n.* a circular panorama, curved wall, or cloth at the rear of a stage, esp. one used to represent the sky. ▫ **cycloramic** /-'ramɪk/ *adj.*

cyclosporin /sʌɪklə(ʊ)'spɔːrɪn/ *n. Med.* a peptide drug used to prevent the rejection of grafts and transplants. [CYCLO- + *-sporum* part of the name of a fungus which produces it + -IN]

cyclostome /'sʌɪkləstəʊm/ *n.* an eel-like jawless vertebrate of the subclass Cyclostomata, having a large sucking mouth, e.g. a lamprey. □ **cyclostomate** /-ˈklɒstəmət/ *adj.* [CYCLO- + Greek *stoma* 'mouth']

cyclostyle /ˈsʌɪkləstʌɪl/ *n. & v.* ● *n.* an apparatus for printing copies of writing from a stencil. ● *v.tr.* print or reproduce with this.

cyclothymia /sʌɪklə(ʊ)ˈθʌɪmɪə/ *n. Psychol.* a disorder characterized by the occurrence of marked swings of mood from cheerfulness to misery. □ **cyclothymic** *adj.* [CYCLO- + Greek *thumos* 'temper']

cyclotron /ˈsʌɪklətrɒn/ *n. Physics* an apparatus in which charged atomic and subatomic particles are accelerated by an alternating electric field while following an outward spiral or circular path in a magnetic field. [CYCLO- + -TRON]

cyder *Brit.* var. of CIDER.

cygnet /ˈsɪgnɪt/ *n.* a young swan. [Middle English from Anglo-French *cignet*, diminutive of Old French *cigne* 'swan', via medieval Latin *cycnus* from Greek *kuknos*]

cylinder /ˈsɪlɪndə/ *n.* **1 a** a uniform solid or hollow body with straight sides and a circular section. **b** a thing of this shape, e.g. a container for liquefied gas. **2** a cylinder-shaped part of various machines, esp. a piston-chamber in an engine. **3** *Printing* a metal roller. □ **cylindrical** /-ˈlɪndrɪk(ə)l/ *adj.* **cylindrically** /-ˈlɪndrɪk(ə)li/ *adv.* [Latin *cylindrus* from Greek *kulindros*, from *kulindō* 'roll']

cylinder saw *n.* = CROWN SAW.

cylinder seal *n. Antiq.* a small barrel-shaped object of stone or baked clay bearing a cuneiform inscription, esp. for use as a seal.

cyma /ˈsʌɪmə/ *n.* **1** *Archit.* an ogee moulding of a cornice. **2** = CYME. [modern Latin from Greek *kuma* 'wave, wavy moulding']

cymbal /ˈsɪmb(ə)l/ *n.* a musical instrument consisting of a concave brass or bronze plate, struck with another or with a stick etc. to make a ringing sound. □ **cymbalist** *n.* [Middle English via Latin *cymbalum* from Greek *kumbalon*, from *kumbē* 'cup']

cymbidium /sɪmˈbɪdɪəm/ *n.* any tropical orchid of the genus *Cymbidium*, with a recess in the flower-lip. [modern Latin from Greek *kumbē* 'cup']

cymbiform /ˈsɪmbɪfɔːm/ *adj. Anat. & Bot.* boat-shaped. [Latin *cymba* from Greek *kumbē* 'boat' + -FORM]

cyme /sʌɪm/ *n. Bot.* an inflorescence in which the primary axis bears a single terminal flower that develops first, the system being continued by the axes of secondary and higher orders each with a flower (cf. RACEME). □ **cymose** *adj.* [French, variant of *cime* 'summit', ultimately from Greek *kuma* 'wave']

Cymric /ˈkɪmrɪk/ *adj.* Welsh. [Welsh *Cymru* 'Wales']

cynic /ˈsɪnɪk/ *n. & adj.* ● *n.* **1** a person who has little faith in human sincerity and integrity. **2** (**Cynic**) one of a school of ancient Greek philosophers founded by Antisthenes, marked by ostentatious contempt for ease and pleasure. ● *adj.* **1** (**Cynic**) of the Cynics. **2** = CYNICAL. □ **cynicism** /-sɪz(ə)m/ *n.* [Latin *cynicus* from Greek *kunikos*, from *kuōn kunos* 'dog', nickname for a Cynic]

cynical /ˈsɪnɪk(ə)l/ *adj.* **1** of or characteristic of a cynic; incredulous of human sincerity or integrity. **2** disregarding accepted or appropriate standards (*a cynical attempt to secure votes*). **3** sneering, mocking. □ **cynically** *adv.*

cynocephalus /sʌɪnə(ʊ)ˈsɛf(ə)ləs, sɪn-/ *n.* **1** a fabled dog-headed man. **2** a flying lemur. [Greek *kunokephalos*, from *kuōn kunos* 'dog' + *kephalē* 'head']

cynosure /ˈsɪnəzjʊə, ˈsʌɪn-, -sjʊə/ *n.* **1** a centre of attraction or admiration. **2** a guiding star. [French *cynosure* or Latin *cynosura* from Greek *kunosoura* 'dog's tail, Ursa Minor', from *kuōn kunos* 'dog' + *oura* 'tail']

cypher var. of CIPHER.

cy pres /siː preɪ/ *adv. & adj. Law* as near as possible to the testator's or donor's intentions when these cannot be precisely followed. [Anglo-French, = *si près* 'so near']

cypress /ˈsʌɪprəs/ *n.* **1** (also **cypress tree**) any evergreen coniferous tree of the genus *Cupressus* or *Chamaecyparis*, having flattened shoots with scalelike leaves, esp. *Cupressus sempervirens*, with hard wood and dark foliage. **2** this tree, or branches from it, as a symbol of mourning. [Middle English via Old French *cipres* and Late Latin *cypressus* from Greek *kuparissos*]

Cyprian /ˈsɪprɪən/ *n. & adj.* = CYPRIOT. [Latin *Cyprius* 'of Cyprus']

cyprinoid /ˈsɪprɪnɔɪd/ *adj. & n.* ● *adj.* of or like a carp. ● *n.* a carp or related fish. [Latin *cyprinus* from Greek *kuprinos* 'carp']

Cypriot /ˈsɪprɪət/ *n. & adj.* (also **Cypriote** /-əʊt/) ● *n.* a native or national of Cyprus. ● *adj.* of Cyprus. [Greek *Kupriōtes* from *Kupros* 'Cyprus', an island in the E. Mediterranean]

cypripedium /sɪprɪˈpiːdɪəm/ *n.* any orchid of the genus *Cypripedium*, esp. the lady's slipper. [modern Latin, from Greek *Kupris* 'Aphrodite' + *pedilon* 'slipper']

cypsela /ˈsɪpsɪlə/ *n.* (*pl.* **cypselae** /-ˌliː/) *Bot.* a dry single-seeded fruit formed from a double ovary of which only one develops into a seed, characteristic of the daisy family Compositae. [modern Latin from Greek *kupselē* 'hollow vessel']

Cyrillic /sɪˈrɪlɪk/ *adj. & n.* ● *adj.* denoting the alphabet used by the Slavonic peoples of the Orthodox Church; now used esp. for Russian and Bulgarian. ● *n.* this alphabet. [named after St *Cyril* (d. 869), its reputed inventor]

cyst /sɪst/ *n.* **1** *Med.* **a** a sac or cavity of abnormal character containing fluid. **b** a structure containing a larval parasite. **2** *Biol.* **a** a hollow organ, bladder, etc., in an animal or plant, containing a liquid secretion. **b** a cell or cavity enclosing reproductive bodies, an embryo, etc. [Late Latin *cystis* from Greek *kustis* 'bladder']

cysteine /ˈsɪstɪiːn, -tɪɪn, -teɪn, -tiːn/ *n. Biochem.* a sulphur-containing amino acid, essential in the human diet and a constituent of many enzymes. [CYSTINE + *-eine* (variant of -INE[4])]

cystic /ˈsɪstɪk/ *adj.* **1** of the urinary bladder. **2** of the gall bladder. **3** of the nature of a cyst. [French *cystique* or modern Latin *cysticus* (as CYST)]

cystic fibrosis *n.* a hereditary disease affecting the exocrine glands and usu. resulting in respiratory infections.

cystine /ˈsɪstiːn, -tɪn/ *n. Biochem.* an organic base which is a naturally occurring dimer of cysteine. [Greek *kustis* 'bladder' (because first found in urinary calculi) + -INE[4]]

cystitis /sɪˈstʌɪtɪs/ *n.* inflammation of the urinary bladder, often caused by infection, and usu. accompanied by frequent painful urination.

cysto- /ˈsɪstəʊ/ *comb. form* the urinary bladder (*cystoscope*; *cystotomy*). [Greek *kustē*, *kustis* 'bladder']

cystoscope /ˈsɪstəskəʊp/ *n.* an instrument inserted in the urethra for examining the urinary bladder. □ **cystoscopic** /-ˈskɒpɪk/ *adj.* **cystoscopy** /sɪˈstɒskəpi/ *n.*

cystotomy /sɪˈstɒtəmi/ *n.* (*pl.* **-ies**) a surgical incision into the urinary bladder.

-cyte /sʌɪt/ *comb. form Biol.* a mature cell (*leucocyte*) (cf. -BLAST). [Greek *kutos* 'vessel']

cytidine /ˈsʌɪtɪdiːn/ *n.* a nucleoside obtained from RNA by hydrolysis. [German *Cytidin* (as -CYTE)]

cyto- /ˈsʌɪtəʊ/ *comb. form Biol.* cells or a cell. [as -CYTE]

cytochrome /ˈsʌɪtə(ʊ)krəʊm/ *n. Biochem.* a compound consisting of a protein linked to a haem, which is involved in electron transfer reactions.

cytogenetics /ˌsʌɪtəʊdʒəˈnɛtɪks/ *n.* the study of inheritance in relation to the structure and function of cells. □ **cytogenetic** *adj.* **cytogenetical** *adj.* **cytogenetically** *adv.* **cytogeneticist** /-sɪst/ *n.*

cytology /sʌɪˈtɒlədʒi/ *n.* the study of cells. □ **cytological** /sʌɪtəˈlɒdʒɪk(ə)l/ *adj.* **cytologically** /sʌɪtəˈlɒdʒɪk(ə)li/ *adv.* **cytologist** *n.*

cytomegalovirus /sʌɪtəʊˈmɛg(ə)lə(ʊ),vʌɪrəs/ *n. Med.* a kind of herpes virus which may cause nerve damage in babies or people with weakened immune systems (abbr.: CMV).

cytoplasm /'sʌɪtə(ʊ)plaz(ə)m/ *n.* the protoplasmic content of a cell excluding its nucleus. □ **cytoplasmic** /-'plazmɪk/ *adj.*

cytosine /'sʌɪtəsiːn/ *n. Biochem.* a pyrimidine derivative found in all living tissue as a component base of DNA and RNA.

cytoskeleton /'sʌɪtəʊˌskɛlɪt(ə)n/ *n. Biol.* a network of protein filaments and tubules giving shape and coherence to a living cell.

cytotoxic /sʌɪtə(ʊ)'tɒksɪk/ *adj.* toxic to cells.

czar etc. var. of TSAR etc.

czardas var. of CSARDAS.

Czech /tʃɛk/ *n. & adj.* ● *n.* **1** a native or national of the Czech Republic, Bohemia, or (*hist*) Czechoslovakia. **2** the West Slavonic language of the Czech people (cf. SLOVAK). ● *adj.* of or relating to the Czechs or their language. [Polish spelling of Bohemian *Čech*]

Czechoslovak /tʃɛkə(ʊ)'sləʊvak/ *n. & adj.* (also **Czechoslovakian** /-slə'vakɪən/) ● *n.* a native or national of Czechoslovakia, a former state in central Europe including Bohemia, Moravia, and Slovakia. ● *adj.* of or relating to Czechoslovaks or the former state of Czechoslovakia. [CZECH + SLOVAK]

Dd

D[1] /diː/ *n.* (also **d**) (*pl.* **Ds** or **D's**) **1 a** the fourth letter of the alphabet. **b** a thing shaped like this. **2** *Mus.* the second note of the diatonic scale of C major. **3** (as a Roman numeral) 500. **4** the fourth highest class or category (of academic marks etc.).

D[2] *abbr.* (also **D.**) **1** *US* Democrat. **2** dimension (*3-D*).

D[3] *symb.* **1** *Chem.* the isotope deuterium. **2** electric flux density. **3** dextrorotatory.

d[1] *abbr.* (also **d.**) **1** died. **2** departs. **3** delete. **4** daughter. **5** diameter. **6** depth.

d[2] *symb.* **1** deci-. **2** *Brit.* (pre-decimal) penny. [sense 2 from Latin *denarius* 'silver coin']

'd *abbr. colloq.* (usu. after pronouns) had, would (*I'd*; *he'd*).

DA *abbr.* **1** *US* district attorney. **2** *slang* = DUCK'S ARSE.

D/A *abbr. Computing* digital to analogue.

da *abbr.* deca-.

dab[1] /dab/ *v.* & *n.* ● *v.* (**dabbed, dabbing**) **1** *tr.* press (a surface) briefly with a cloth, sponge, etc., without rubbing, esp. in cleaning or to apply a substance. **2** *tr.* press (a sponge etc.) lightly on a surface. **3** *tr.* (foll. by *on*) apply (a substance) by dabbing a surface. **4** *intr.* (usu. foll. by *at*) aim a feeble blow; tap. **5** *tr.* strike lightly; tap. ● *n.* **1** a brief application of a cloth, sponge, etc., to a surface without rubbing. **2** a small amount of something applied in this way (*a dab of paint*). **3** a light blow or tap. **4** (in *pl.*) *Brit. slang* fingerprints. □ **dabber** *n.* [Middle English, imitative]

dab[2] /dab/ *n.* a small flatfish of the genus *Limanda*. [Middle English: origin unknown]

dabble /'dab(ə)l/ *v.* **1** *intr.* (usu. foll. by *in*, *at*) take a casual or superficial interest or part (in a subject or activity). **2** *intr.* move the feet, hands, etc. about in (usu. a small amount of) liquid. **3** *tr.* wet partly or intermittently; moisten, stain, splash. □ **dabbler** *n.* [16th c.: from Dutch *dabbelen* or DAB[1]]

dabbling duck /'dablɪŋ/ *n.* a duck that habitually feeds in shallow usu. fresh water by dabbling at or near the surface, esp. one of the tribe Anatini, including mallard, teal, etc.

dabchick /'dabtʃɪk/ *n.* = LITTLE GREBE. [16th c., in earlier forms *dap-*, *dop-*: perhaps related to the Old English source of DIP]

dab hand *n.* (usu. foll. by *at*) a person especially skilled (in) (*a dab hand at cooking*). [*dab* (*adj.*) 17th c.: origin unknown]

da capo /dɑː 'kɑːpəʊ/ *adv. Mus.* (a direction at the end of a piece of music to repeat) from the beginning. [Italian]

dace /deɪs/ *n.* (*pl.* same) any of several small freshwater fishes related to the carp, esp. *Leuciscus leuciscus*. [Old French *dars*: see DART]

dacha /'datʃə/ *n.* a country house or cottage in Russia. [Russian, originally = grant (of land)]

dachshund /'dakshʊnd, -s(ə)nd/ *n.* **1** a dog of a short-legged long-bodied breed. **2** this breed. [German, = badger-dog]

dacite /'deɪsʌɪt/ *n. Geol.* a volcanic rock similar to andesite. [from *Dacia*, a Roman province in central Europe + -ITE[1]]

dacoit /də'kɔɪt/ *n.* (in India or Myanmar) a member of a band of armed robbers. [Hindi *ḍakait* from *ḍākā* 'gang-robbery']

dactyl /'daktɪl/ *n.* a metrical foot (‒ ᴗ ᴗ) consisting of one long (or stressed) syllable followed by two short (or unstressed). [Middle English via Latin *dactylus* from Greek *daktulos* 'finger', the three bones corresponding to the three syllables]

dactylic /dak'tɪlɪk/ *adj.* & *n.* ● *adj.* of or using dactyls. ● *n.* (usu. in *pl.*) dactylic verse. [Latin *dactylicus* from Greek *daktulikos* (as DACTYL)]

dactylic hexameter *n.* a hexameter having five dactyls and a spondee or trochee, any of the first four feet, and sometimes the fifth, being replaceable by a spondee.

dad /dad/ *n. colloq.* father. [perhaps imitative of a child's *da, da* (cf. DADDY)]

Dada /'dɑːdɑː/ *n.* an early 20th-c. international movement in art, literature, music, and film, repudiating and mocking artistic and social conventions. □ **Dadaism** /-dəɪz(ə)m/ *n.* **Dadaist** /-dəɪst/ *n.* & *adj.* **Dadaistic** /-'ɪstɪk/ *adj.* [French (the title of an early 20th-c. review) from *dada* 'hobby horse']

daddy /'dadi/ *n.* (*pl.* **-ies**) *colloq.* **1** father. **2** (usu. foll. by *of*) the oldest or a supreme example (*had a daddy of a headache*). [DAD + -Y[3]]

daddy-long-legs *n.* **1** *Brit.* a crane-fly. **2** *US* a harvestman.

dado /'deɪdəʊ/ *n.* (*pl.* **-os**) **1** the lower part of the wall of a room when visually distinct from the upper part. **2** the plinth of a column. **3** the cube of a pedestal between the base and the cornice. [Italian, = DIE[2]]

daemon var. of DEMON 5.

daemonic var. of DEMONIC.

daff /daf/ *n. colloq.* = DAFFODIL 1. [abbreviation]

daffodil /'dafədɪl/ *n.* & *adj.* ● *n.* **1 a** a bulbous plant, *Narcissus pseudonarcissus*, with a yellow trumpet-shaped corona. **b** any of various other large-flowered plants of the genus *Narcissus*. **2** (in full **daffodil yellow**) a pale yellow colour. ● *adj.* (in full **daffodil yellow**; hyphenated when *attrib.*) pale yellow. [earlier *affodill*, as ASPHODEL]

daffy /'dafi/ *adj.* (**daffier, daffiest**) *colloq.* = DAFT. □ **daffily** *adv.* **daffiness** *n.* [*daff* 'simpleton' + -Y[2]]

daft /dɑːft/ *adj.* esp. *Brit.* **1** silly, foolish, crazy. **2** (foll. by *about*) fond of; infatuated with. [Old English *gedæfte* 'mild, meek', from Germanic]

dag /dag/ *n.* & *v. Austral.* & *NZ* ● *n.* **1** (usu. in *pl.*) a lock of wool clotted with dung on the hinder parts of a sheep. **2** *slang* an eccentric or noteworthy person; a character (*he's a bit of a dag*). ● *v.tr.* (**dagged, dagging**) remove dags from (a sheep). □ **rattle one's dags** *slang* hurry up. □ **dagger** *n.* [originally English dialect]

dagga /'dagə/ *n. S.Afr.* **1** hemp used as a narcotic. **2** any plant of the genus *Leonotis* used similarly. [Afrikaans from Nama *dachab*]

dagger /'dagə/ *n.* **1** a short stabbing weapon with a pointed and edged blade. **2** *Printing* = OBELUS. □ **at daggers drawn** in bitter enmity. **look daggers at** glare angrily or venomously at. [Middle English, perhaps from obsolete *dag* 'pierce', influenced by Old French *dague* 'long dagger']

daggerboard /'dagəbɔːd/ *n. Naut.* a sliding centreboard.

daggy /'dagi/ *adj.* (**daggier, daggiest**) *Austral.* & *NZ slang* **1** dowdy, scruffy. **2** unfashionable. [DAG *n.* + -Y[1]]

dago /ˈdeɪgəʊ/ *n.* (*pl.* **-os** or **-oes**) *slang offens.* a foreigner, esp. a Spaniard, Portuguese, or Italian. [Spanish *Diego* = James]

daguerreotype /dəˈgɛrə(ʊ)tʌɪp/ *n.* **1** a photograph taken by an early photographic process employing an iodine-sensitized silvered plate and mercury vapour. **2** this process. [named after L. *Daguerre*, French inventor d. 1851]

dah /dɑː/ *n.* (in the Morse system) = DASH (cf. DIT). [imitative]

dahlia /ˈdeɪlɪə/ *n.* any garden plant of the genus *Dahlia* (daisy family), of Mexican origin, cultivated for its many-coloured single or double flowers. [named after A. *Dahl*, Swedish botanist d. 1789]

Dáil /dɔɪl/ *n.* (in full **Dáil Éireann** /ˈɛːr(ə)n/) the lower House of Parliament in the Republic of Ireland. [Irish, = assembly (of Ireland)]

daily /ˈdeɪli/ *adj., adv., & n.* ● *adj.* **1** done, produced, or occurring every day or every weekday. **2** constant, regular. ● *adv.* **1** every day; from day to day. **2** constantly. ● *n.* (*pl.* **-ies**) *colloq.* **1** a daily newspaper. **2** *Brit.* a charwoman or domestic help working daily. [Middle English from DAY + -LY[1], -LY[2]]

daily bread *n.* necessary food; a livelihood.

daily dozen *n. colloq.* regular exercises, esp. on rising.

daimon /ˈdʌɪməʊn/ *n.* = DEMON 5a. □ **daimonic** /-ˈməʊnɪk, -ˈmɒnɪk/ *adj.* [Greek, = deity]

dainty /ˈdeɪnti/ *adj. & n.* ● *adj.* (**daintier**, **daintiest**) **1** delicately pretty. **2** delicate of build or in movement. **3** (of food) choice. **4** fastidious; having delicate taste and sensibility. ● *n.* (*pl.* **-ies**) a choice morsel; a delicacy. □ **daintily** *adv.* **daintiness** *n.* [Anglo-French *dainté*, Old French *daintié*, *deintié* from Latin *dignitas -tatis*, from *dignus* 'worthy']

daiquiri /ˈdʌɪkɪri, ˈdak-/ *n.* (*pl.* **daiquiris**) a cocktail of rum, lime juice, etc. [*Daiquiri*, a rum-producing district in Cuba]

dairy /ˈdɛːri/ *n.* (*pl.* **-ies**) **1** a building or room for the storage, processing, and distribution of milk and its products. **2** a shop where milk and milk products are sold. **3** (*attrib.*) **a** of, containing, or concerning milk and its products (and sometimes eggs). **b** used for dairy products (*dairy cow*). [Middle English *deierie* from *deie* 'maidservant', from Old English *dǣge* 'kneader of dough']

dairying /ˈdɛːrɪɪŋ/ *n.* the business of producing, storing, and distributing milk and its products.

dairymaid /ˈdɛːrɪmeɪd/ *n.* a woman employed in a dairy.

dairyman /ˈdɛːrɪmən/ *n.* (*pl.* **-men**) **1** a man dealing in dairy products. **2** a man employed in a dairy.

dais /ˈdeɪɪs, deɪs/ *n.* a low platform, usu. at the upper end of a hall and used to support a table, lectern, etc. [Middle English via Old French *deis* from Latin *discus* 'disc, dish', in medieval Latin = table]

daisy /ˈdeɪzi/ *n.* (*pl.* **-ies**) **1 a** a small plant, *Bellis perennis* (family Compositae), bearing flowers each with a yellow disc and white rays. **b** any other plant of this family with daisy-like flowers (*ox-eye daisy*; *Michaelmas daisy*; *Shasta daisy*). **2** *slang* a first-rate specimen of anything. □ **pushing up the daisies** *slang* dead and buried. [Old English *dæges ēage* 'day's eye', the flower opening in the morning]

daisy chain *n.* a string of daisies threaded together.

daisy-cutter *n. Cricket* a ball bowled so as to roll along the ground.

daisy wheel *n.* a disc of spokes extending radially from a central hub, each terminating in a printing character, used as a printer in word processors and typewriters.

Dak. *abbr.* Dakota.

dal var. of DHAL.

Dalai Lama /dalʌɪ ˈlɑːmə/ *n.* the spiritual head of Tibetan Buddhism, formerly also the chief ruler of Tibet (see LAMA). [Mongolian *dalai* 'ocean'; see LAMA]

dalasi /dɑːˈlɑːsiː/ *n.* (*pl.* same or **dalasis**) the chief monetary unit of the Gambia. [name of an earlier local coin]

dale /deɪl/ *n.* a valley, esp. in northern England. [Old English *dæl*, from Germanic]

dalesman /ˈdeɪlzmən/ *n.* (*pl.* **-men**) an inhabitant of the dales in northern England.

dalliance /ˈdalɪəns/ *n.* **1** a leisurely or frivolous passing of time. **2** an instance of light-hearted flirting; a casual love affair. [DALLY + -ANCE]

dally /ˈdali/ *v.intr.* (**-ies**, **-ied**) **1** delay; waste time, esp. frivolously. **2** (often foll. by *with*) play about; flirt, treat frivolously (*dallied with her affections*). □ **dally away** waste or fritter (one's time, life, etc.). [Middle English from Old French *dalier* 'chat']

Dalmatian /dalˈmeɪʃ(ə)n/ *n.* **1** a dog of a large white short-haired breed with dark spots. **2** this breed. [*Dalmatia*, a region in Croatia]

dalmatic /dalˈmatɪk/ *n.* a wide-sleeved long loose vestment open at the sides, worn by deacons and bishops, and by a monarch at his or her coronation. [Middle English from Old French *dalmatique* or Late Latin *dalmatica* (*vestis*) '(robe) of Dalmatia']

dal segno /dal ˈsemjəʊ/ *adv. Mus.* (a direction in a piece of music to repeat) from the point marked by a sign. [Italian, = from the sign]

dalton /ˈdɔːlt(ə)n/ *n. Chem.* = ATOMIC MASS UNIT. [named after J. *Dalton* (see DALTONISM)]

daltonism /ˈdɔːlt(ə)nɪz(ə)m/ *n.* colour-blindness, esp. a congenital inability to distinguish between red and green. [French *daltonisme* from the name of J. *Dalton*, English chemist (d. 1844) who suffered from it]

dam[1] /dam/ *n. & v.* ● *n.* **1** a barrier constructed to hold back water and raise its level, forming a reservoir or preventing flooding. **2** a barrier constructed in a stream by a beaver. **3** anything functioning as a dam does. **4** *Brit.* a causeway. ● *v.tr.* (**dammed**, **damming**) **1** provide or confine with a dam. **2** (often foll. by *up*) block up; hold back; obstruct. [Middle English from Middle Low German, Middle Dutch]

dam[2] /dam/ *n.* the female parent of an animal, esp. a mammal. [Middle English: variant of DAME]

damage /ˈdamɪdʒ/ *n. & v.* ● *n.* **1** harm or injury impairing the value or usefulness of something, or the health or normal function of a person. **2** (in *pl.*) *Law* a sum of money claimed or awarded in compensation for a loss or an injury. **3** the loss of what is desirable. **4** (prec. by *the*) *slang* cost (*what's the damage?*). ● *v.tr.* **1** inflict damage on. **2** (esp. as **damaging** *adj.*) detract from the reputation of (*a most damaging admission*). □ **damagingly** *adv.* [Middle English via Old French *damage* (*n.*), *damagier* (*v.*), from *dam*(*me*) 'loss', from Latin *damnum* 'loss, damage']

damascene /ˈdaməsiːn, daməˈsiːn/ *v., n., & adj.* ● *v.tr.* decorate (metal, esp. iron or steel) by etching or inlaying esp. with gold or silver, or with a watered pattern produced in welding. ● *n.* a design or article produced in this way. ● *adj.* of, relating to, or produced by this process. [*Damascene* 'of Damascus', via Latin *Damascenus* from Greek *Damaskēnos*]

damask /ˈdaməsk/ *n., adj., & v.* ● *n.* **1 a** a figured woven fabric (esp. silk or linen) with a pattern visible on both sides. **b** twilled table linen with woven designs shown by the reflection of light. **2** a tablecloth made of this material. **3** *hist.* steel with a watered pattern produced in welding. ● *adj.* **1** made of or resembling damask. **2** coloured like a damask rose, velvety pink or vivid red. ● *v.tr.* **1** weave with figured designs. **2** = DAMASCENE *v.* **3** ornament. [Middle English, ultimately from Latin *Damascus*]

damask rose *n.* an old sweet-scented variety of rose, with very soft velvety petals, used to make attar.

dame /deɪm/ *n.* **1** (**Dame**) **a** (in the UK) the title given to a woman with the rank of Knight Commander or holder of the Grand Cross in the Orders of Chivalry. **b** a woman holding this title. **2** *Brit.* a comic middle-aged female character in modern pantomime, usu. played by a man. **3** *archaic* a mature woman. **4** *N. Amer. slang* a woman. [Middle English via Old French from Latin *domina* 'mistress']

dame school *n. hist.* a primary school of a kind kept by elderly women.

damfool /ˈdamfuːl/ *adj. colloq.* foolish, stupid. [DAMN + FOOL[1]]

dammar /ˈdamə/ *n.* **1** an E. Asian or Australasian tree, esp. of the genus *Agathis* or *Shorea*, yielding a resin used in varnish-making. **2** this resin. [Malay *damar*]

dammit /ˈdamɪt/ *int.* damn it.

damn /dam/ *v., n., adj., & adv.* ● *v.tr.* **1** (often *absol.* or as *int.* of anger or annoyance, = *may God damn*) curse (a person or thing). **2** doom to hell; cause the damnation of. **3** condemn, censure (*a review damning the performance*). **4 a** (often as **damning** *adj.*) (of a circumstance, piece of evidence, etc.) show or prove to be guilty; bring condemnation upon (*evidence against them was damning*). **b** be the ruin of. ● *n.* **1** an uttered curse. **2** *colloq.* a negligible amount (*not worth a damn*). ● *adj. & adv. colloq.* = DAMNED. ◻ **damn all** *Brit. colloq.* nothing at all. **damn well** *colloq.* (as an emphatic) simply (*damn well do as I say*). **damn with faint praise** commend so unenthusiastically as to imply disapproval. **I'm** (or **I'll be**) **damned if** *colloq.* I certainly do not, will not, etc. **not give a damn** see GIVE. **well I'm** (or **I'll be**) **damned** *colloq.* exclamation of surprise, dismay, etc. ◻ **damningly** *adv.* [Middle English via Old French *damner* from Latin *damnare* 'inflict loss on', from *damnum* 'loss']

damnable /ˈdamnəb(ə)l/ *adj.* hateful, annoying. ◻ **damnably** *adv.* [Middle English from Old French (as DAMN)]

damnation /damˈneɪʃ(ə)n/ *n. & int.* ● *n.* condemnation to eternal punishment, esp. in hell. ● *int.* expressing anger or annoyance. [Middle English from Old French (as DAMN)]

damnatory /ˈdamnət(ə)ri/ *adj.* conveying or causing censure or damnation. [Latin *damnatorius* (as DAMN)]

damned /damd/ *adj. & adv. colloq.* ● *adj.* damnable, infernal, unwelcome. ● *adv.* extremely (*damned hot*; *damned lovely*). ◻ **damned well** (as an emphatic) simply (*you've damned well got to*). **do one's damnedest** do one's utmost.

damnify /ˈdamnɪfʌɪ/ *v.tr.* (**-ies, -ied**) *Law* cause injury to. ◻ **damnification** /-fɪˈkeɪʃ(ə)n/ *n.* [Old French *damnifier* etc. from Late Latin *damnificare* 'injure' (as DAMN)]

damp /damp/ *adj., n., & v.* ● *adj.* slightly wet; moist. ● *n.* **1** diffused moisture in the air, on a surface, or in a solid, esp. as a cause of inconvenience or danger. **2** dejection; discouragement. **3** = FIREDAMP. ● *v.tr.* **1** make damp; moisten. **2** (often foll. by *down*) **a** take the force or vigour out of (*damp one's enthusiasm*). **b** make flaccid or spiritless. **c** make (a fire) burn less strongly by reducing the flow of air to it. **3** reduce or stop the vibration of (esp. the strings of a musical instrument). **4** quieten. ◻ **damp off** (of a plant) die from a fungus attack in damp conditions. ◻ **dampish** *adj.* **damply** *adv.* **dampness** *n.* [Middle English from Middle Low German, = vapour etc., Old High German *dampf* 'steam', from West Germanic]

damp course *n.* a layer of waterproof material in the wall of a building near the ground, to prevent rising damp.

dampen /ˈdamp(ə)n/ *v.* **1** *tr. & intr.* make or become damp. **2** *tr.* make less forceful or vigorous; stifle, choke. ◻ **dampener** *n.*

damper /ˈdampə/ *n.* **1** a person or thing that discourages, or tempers enthusiasm. **2** a device that reduces shock or noise. **3** a metal plate in a flue to control the draught, and so the rate of combustion. **4** *Mus.* a pad silencing a piano string except when removed by a pedal or by the note's being struck. **5** esp. *Austral. & NZ* an unleavened loaf or cake of flour and water baked in wood ashes. ◻ **put a damper on** take the vigour or enjoyment out of.

damp-proof *adj. & v.* ● *adj.* impervious to damp. ● *v.tr.* make damp-proof.

damp-proof course *n.* = DAMP COURSE.

damp squib *n. Brit.* an unsuccessful attempt to impress etc.

damsel /ˈdamz(ə)l/ *n. archaic* or *literary* a young unmarried woman. [Middle English from Old French *dam(e)isele*, ultimately from Latin *domina* 'mistress']

damselfish /ˈdamz(ə)lfɪʃ/ *n.* (*pl.* usu. same) a small brightly coloured tropical marine fish of the family Pomacentridae, esp. *Chromis chromis*, found in or near coral reefs.

damselfly /ˈdamz(ə)lflʌɪ/ *n.* (*pl.* **-flies**) an insect of the order Odonata, like a slender dragonfly but with its wings folded over the body when resting.

damson /ˈdamz(ə)n/ *n. & adj.* ● *n.* **1 a** a small dark purple plumlike fruit. **b** (also **damson tree**) the small deciduous tree, *Prunus institia*, bearing this. **2** a dark purple colour. ● *adj.* damson-coloured. [Middle English *damacene, -scene, -sene* from Latin *damascenum* (*prunum*) '(plum) of *Damascus*': see DAMASCENE]

damson cheese *n.* a solid preserve of damsons and sugar.

Dan. *abbr.* Daniel (Old Testament).

dan[1] /dan/ *n.* **1** any of ten degrees of advanced proficiency in judo or karate. **2** a person who has achieved any of these. [Japanese]

dan[2] /dan/ *n.* (in full **dan buoy**) a small buoy used as a marker in deep-sea fishing, or to mark the limits of an area cleared by minesweepers. [17th c.: origin unknown]

dance /dɑːns/ *v. & n.* ● *v.* **1** *intr.* move about rhythmically alone or with a partner or in a set, usu. in fixed steps or sequences to music, for pleasure or as entertainment. **2** *intr.* move in a lively way; skip or jump about. **3** *tr.* **a** perform (a specified dance or form of dancing). **b** perform (a specified role) in a ballet etc. **4** *intr.* move up and down (on water, in the field of vision, etc.). **5** *tr.* move (esp. a child) up and down; dandle. ● *n.* **1 a** a piece of dancing; a sequence of steps in dancing. **b** a special form of this. **2** a single round or turn of a dance. **3** a social gathering for dancing, a ball. **4** a piece of music for dancing to or in a dance rhythm. **5** a dancing or lively motion. ◻ **dance attendance on** follow or wait on (a person) obsequiously. **dance to a person's tune** accede obsequiously to a person's demands and wishes. **lead a person a dance** (or **merry dance**) *Brit.* cause a person much trouble in following a course one has instigated. ◻ **danceable** *adj.* [Middle English via Old French *dance, danse* (*n.*), *dancer, danser* (*v.*), from Romanic, of unknown origin]

dance band *n.* a band that plays music for dancing to.

dance floor *n.* a usu. uncarpeted area of floor reserved for dancing.

dance hall *n.* a public hall for dancing.

dance of death *n.* a medieval allegorical representation in which a personified Death leads all to the grave.

dancer /ˈdɑːnsə/ *n.* **1** a person who performs a dance. **2** a person whose profession is dancing.

dancing dervish see WHIRLING DERVISH.

dancing girl *n.* a female professional dancer, esp. a member of a group.

d. and c. *n.* dilatation (of the cervix) and curettage (of the uterus), performed after a miscarriage or for the removal of cysts, tumours, etc.

dandelion /ˈdandɪlʌɪən/ *n.* a plant of the genus *Taraxacum* (daisy family), esp. the common *T. officinale*, with jagged leaves and a large bright yellow flower on a hollow stalk, followed by a globular head of seeds with downy tufts. [French *dent-de-lion*, translation of medieval Latin *dens leonis* 'lion's tooth' (from the shape of the leaves)]

dandelion clock *n.* the downy seed-head of a dandelion.

dandelion coffee *n.* dried and powdered dandelion roots; a drink made from this.

dander /ˈdandə/ *n. colloq.* temper, anger, indignation. □ **get one's dander up** lose one's temper; become angry. [19th c.: origin uncertain]

dandify /ˈdandɪfʌɪ/ *v.tr.* (**-ies**, **-ied**) (usu. as **dandified** *adj.*) cause to resemble a dandy in stylish appearance.

dandle /ˈdand(ə)l/ *v.tr.* **1** dance (a child) on one's knees or in one's arms. **2** pamper, pet. [16th c.: origin unknown]

dandruff /ˈdandrʌf/ *n.* dead skin in small scales among the hair. [16th c.: *-ruff* perhaps related to Middle English *rove* 'scurfiness', from Old Norse *hrufa* or Middle Low German, Middle Dutch *rōve*]

dandy /ˈdandi/ *n. & adj.* ● *n.* (*pl.* **-ies**) **1** a man unduly devoted to style, smartness, and fashion in dress and appearance. **2** *colloq.* an excellent thing. ● *adj.* (**dandier**, **dandiest**) esp. *N. Amer. colloq.* very good of its kind; splendid, first-rate. □ **dandyish** *adj.* **dandyism** *n.* [18th c.: perhaps an abbreviation of *Jack-a-dandy*: *dandy* may be a pet form of *Andrew*]

dandy brush *n.* a brush for grooming a horse.

dandy roll *n.* (also **dandy roller**) a device for solidifying, and impressing a watermark in, paper during manufacture.

Dane /deɪn/ *n.* **1** a native or national of Denmark. **2** *hist.* a Viking invader of England in the 9th–11th c. [Middle English from Old Norse *Danir* (pl.), Late Latin *Dani*]

Danegeld /ˈdeɪngɛld/ *n. hist.* **1** (in pre-Conquest England) an annual tax to raise funds for protection against Danish invaders. **2** appeasement by bribery. [Old English (as DANE + Old Norse *gjald* 'payment')]

Danelaw /ˈdeɪnlɔː/ *n. hist.* the part of N. & E. England occupied or administered by Danes in the 9th–11th c. [Old English *Dena lagu* 'Danes' law']

danger /ˈdeɪn(d)ʒə/ *n.* **1** liability or exposure to harm; an unwelcome possibility. **2** a thing that causes or is likely to cause harm. **3** *Brit.* the status of a railway signal directing a halt or caution. □ **in danger of** likely to incur or to suffer from. [earlier in the sense 'jurisdiction, power': Middle English from Old French *dangier*, ultimately from Latin *dominus* 'lord']

danger list *n. Brit.* a list of those dangerously ill, esp. in a hospital.

danger man *n.* a man perceived as posing a particular threat, esp. an outstanding sportsman.

danger money *n. Brit.* extra payment for dangerous work.

dangerous /ˈdeɪn(d)ʒ(ə)rəs/ *adj.* involving or causing danger. □ **dangerously** *adv.* **dangerousness** *n.* [Middle English from Anglo-French *dangerous*, *daungerous*, Old French *dangereus* (as DANGER)]

dangle /ˈdaŋg(ə)l/ *v.* **1** *intr.* be loosely suspended, so as to be able to sway to and fro. **2** *tr.* hold or carry loosely suspended. **3** *tr.* hold out (a hope, temptation, etc.) enticingly. **4** *intr. Gram.* (as **dangling** *adj.*) (of a participle in an absolute clause or phrase) with the subject omitted, e.g. of *having* in *having said that, the problem can be solved.* □ **dangler** *n.* **dangly** *adj.* [16th c. (imitative): cf. Swedish *dangla*, Danish *dangle*]

Daniell cell /ˈdanj(ə)l/ *n. Physics & Chem.* a primary voltaic cell with a copper anode and a zinc-amalgam cathode giving a standard electromotive force when either copper sulphate or sulphuric acid is used as the electrolyte. [named after John *Daniell*, British chemist (d. 1845), its inventor]

Danish /ˈdeɪnɪʃ/ *adj. & n.* ● *adj.* of or relating to Denmark or the Danes. ● *n.* **1** the Danish language. **2** (prec. by *the*; treated as *pl.*) the Danish people. **3** *colloq.* = DANISH PASTRY. [Middle English via Anglo-French *danes*, Old French *daneis* from medieval Latin *Danensis* (as DANE)]

Danish blue *n.* a soft salty white cheese with blue veins.

Danish pastry *n.* a cake of sweetened yeast pastry topped with icing, fruit, nuts, etc.

dank /daŋk/ *adj.* disagreeably damp and cold. □ **dankly** *adv.* **dankness** *n.* [Middle English probably from Scandinavian: cf. Swedish *dank* 'marshy spot']

danse macabre /dɑːns məˈkɑːbr(ə), French dɑ̃s makabr/ *n.* = DANCE OF DEATH. [French (as DANCE, MACABRE)]

danseur /dɑːnˈsəː/ *n.* (*fem.* **danseuse** /-ˈsəːz/) a ballet dancer. [French, = dancer]

Dantean /ˈdantɪən, danˈtiːən/ *adj. & n.* ● *adj.* **1** of Dante. **2** in the style of or reminiscent of Dante's writings. ● *n.* a student or imitator of Dante. □ **Dantesque** /-ˈtɛsk/ *adj.* [*Dante* Alighieri, Italian poet d. 1321]

danthonia /danˈθəʊnɪə/ *n. Austral. & NZ* any tufted pasture grass of the genus *Danthonia.* [modern Latin: named after E. *Danthoine* 19th-c. French botanist]

dap /dap/ *v.* (**dapped**, **dapping**) **1** *intr.* fish by letting the bait bob on the water. **2** *tr. & intr.* dip lightly. **3** *tr. & intr.* bounce on the ground. [cf. DAB[1]]

daphne /ˈdafni/ *n.* any flowering shrub of the genus *Daphne*, e.g. the spurge laurel or mezereon. [Middle English, = laurel, from Greek *daphnē*, *Daphnē*, the name of a nymph in Greek mythology who escaped Apollo's advances by being changed into a laurel]

daphnia /ˈdafnɪə/ *n.* a minute freshwater crustacean of the genus *Daphnia*, enclosed in a transparent carapace and with long antennae and prominent eyes. Also called *water flea.* [modern Latin from *Daphne*: see DAPHNE]

dapper /ˈdapə/ *adj.* **1** neat and precise, esp. in dress or movement. **2** sprightly. □ **dapperly** *adv.* **dapperness** *n.* [Middle English from Middle Low German, Middle Dutch *dapper* 'strong, stout']

dapple /ˈdap(ə)l/ *v. & n.* ● *v.* **1** *tr.* mark with spots or rounded patches of colour or shade. **2** *intr.* become marked in this way. ● *n.* **1** a dappled effect. **2** a dappled animal, esp. a horse. [Middle English *dappled*, *dappeld*, (*adj.*), of unknown origin]

dapple grey *adj. & n.* ● *adj.* (hyphenated when *attrib.*) (of an animal's coat) grey or white with darker spots. ● *n.* a dapple-grey horse.

dapsone /ˈdapsəʊn/ *n. Pharm.* a bacteriostatic sulphur compound used esp. to treat leprosy. [chemical name *di*(para-*a*mino*p*henyl) *s*ulph*one*]

darbies /ˈdɑːbɪz/ *n.pl. Brit. slang* handcuffs. [allusive use of *Father Darby's bands*, some rigid form of agreement for debtors (16th c.)]

Darby and Joan /ˌdɑːbɪ (ə)n ˈdʒəʊn/ *n.* esp. *Brit.* a devoted old married couple. [18th c.: perhaps from a poem of 1735 in the *Gentleman's Magazine*]

Darby and Joan club *n. Brit.* a club for people over 60.

dare /dɛː/ *v. & n.* ● *v.tr.* (*3rd sing. present* usu. **dare** before an expressed or implied infinitive without *to*; *past* **dared** or *archaic* or *dial.* **durst** /dəːst/) **1** (foll. by infin. with or without *to*) venture (to); have the courage or impudence (to) (*dare he do it?*; *if they dare to come*; *how dare you?*; *I dare not speak*; *I do not dare to jump*). **2** (usu. foll. by *to* + infin.) defy or challenge (a person) (*I dare you to own up*). **3** *literary* attempt; take the risk of (*dare all things*; *dared their anger*). ● *n.* **1** an act of daring. **2** a challenge, esp. to prove courage. □ **I dare say 1** (often foll. by *that* + clause) it is probable. **2** probably; I grant that much (*I dare say, but you are still wrong*). □ **darer** *n.* [Old English *durran*, with Germanic cognates: cf. Sanskrit *dhṛṣh*, Greek *tharseō* 'be bold']

daredevil /ˈdɛːdɛv(ə)l/ *n. & adj.* ● *n.* a recklessly daring person. ● *adj.* recklessly daring. □ **daredevilry** *n.*

darg /dɑːg/ *n. Sc., N.Engl., & Austral.* **1** a day's work. **2** a definite amount of work; a task. [Middle English from *daywerk* or *daywark* 'daywork']

daring /ˈdɛːrɪŋ/ *n. & adj.* ● *n.* adventurous courage. ● *adj.* adventurous, bold; prepared to take risks. □ **daringly** *adv.*

dariole /ˈdarɪəʊl/ *n.* a savoury or sweet dish cooked and served in a small mould usu. shaped like a flowerpot. [Middle English from Old French]

Darjeeling /dɑːˈdʒiːlɪŋ/ *n.* a high-quality tea from Darjeeling in NE India.

dark /dɑːk/ *adj. & n.* ● *adj.* **1** with little or no light. **2** of a deep or sombre colour. **3** (of a person) with deep brown or black hair, complexion, or skin. **4** gloomy, depressing, dismal (*dark thoughts*). **5** evil, sinister (*dark deeds*). **6** sullen, angry (*a dark mood*). **7** remote, secret, mysterious, little known (*the dark and distant past*; *keep it dark*). **8** ignorant, unenlightened (*dark ages*). ● *n.* **1** absence of light. **2** nightfall (*don't go out after dark*). **3** a lack of knowledge. **4** a dark area or colour, esp. in painting (*the skilled use of lights and darks*). □ **in the dark 1** with little or no light. **2** lacking information. □ **darkish** *adj.* **darkly** *adv.* **darkness** *n.* **darksome** *adj. poet.* [Old English *deorc*, probably from Germanic]

Dark Ages *n.pl.* (also **Dark Age**) (prec. by *the*) **1** the period of European history preceding the Middle Ages, esp. the 5th–10th c. **2** (often **dark ages**) any period of supposed unenlightenment.

Dark Continent *n.* (prec. by *the*) a name for Africa, esp. when little known to Europeans.

darken /ˈdɑːk(ə)n/ *v.* **1** *tr.* make dark or darker. **2** *intr.* become dark or darker. □ **never darken a person's door** keep away permanently. □ **darkener** *n.*

dark glasses *n.pl.* spectacles with dark-tinted lenses; sunglasses.

dark horse *n.* a little-known person who unexpectedly becomes successful or prominent.

darkie /ˈdɑːki/ *n.* (also **darky**) (*pl.* **-ies**) *slang offens.* a black person.

darkling /ˈdɑːklɪŋ/ *adj. & adv. poet.* in the dark; in the night.

dark matter *n. Astron.* hypothetical non-luminous material in space, not detected, but predicted by many cosmological theories.

darkroom /ˈdɑːkruːm, -rʊm/ *n.* a room for photographic work, with normal light excluded.

dark star *n.* a starlike object which emits little or no visibile light but is known to exist from other evidence (e.g. by its eclipsing of other stars).

darky var. of DARKIE.

darling /ˈdɑːlɪŋ/ *n. & adj.* ● *n.* **1** a beloved or lovable person or thing. **2** a favourite. **3** *colloq.* a pretty or endearing person or thing. ● *adj.* **1** beloved, lovable. **2** favourite. **3** *colloq.* charming or pretty. [Old English *dēorling* (as DEAR, -LING[1])]

darn[1] /dɑːn/ *v. & n.* ● *v.tr.* **1** mend (esp. knitted material, or a hole in it) by interweaving yarn across the hole with a needle. **2** embroider with a large running stitch. ● *n.* a darned area in material. [17th c.: perhaps from obsolete *dern* 'hide']

darn[2] /dɑːn/ *v.tr., int., adj., & adv.* (*US* also **durn** /dəːn/) *colloq.* = DAMN (in imprecatory senses). [corruption of DAMN]

darned /dɑːnd/ *adj. & adv.* (*US dial.* also **durned** /dəːnd/) *colloq.* = DAMNED.

darnel /ˈdɑːn(ə)l/ *n.* any of several grasses of the genus *Lolium*, esp. *L. temulentum*, a weed of cereal crops esp. in Mediterranean countries. [Middle English: cf. Walloon *darnelle*]

darner /ˈdɑːnə/ *n.* a person or thing that darns, esp. a darning needle.

darning /ˈdɑːnɪŋ/ *n.* **1** the action of a person who darns. **2** things to be darned.

darning needle *n.* a long needle with a large eye, used in darning.

dart /dɑːt/ *n. & v.* ● *n.* **1** a small pointed missile thrown or fired as a weapon. **2 a** a small pointed missile with a feather or plastic flight, used in the game of darts. **b** (in *pl.*; usu. treated as *sing.*) an indoor game in which such darts are thrown at a circular target to score points. **3** a sudden rapid movement. **4** *Zool.* a dartlike structure, such as an insect's sting or the calcareous projections of a snail (used during copulation). **5** a tapering tuck stitched in a garment. ● *v.* **1** *intr.* (often foll. by *out*, *in*, *past*, etc.) move or go suddenly or rapidly (*darted into the shop*). **2** *tr.* throw (a missile). **3** *tr.* direct suddenly (a glance etc.). [Middle English via Old French *darz*, *dars* from Frankish]

dartboard /ˈdɑːtbɔːd/ *n.* a circular board marked with numbered segments, used as a target in darts.

darter /ˈdɑːtə/ *n.* **1** a fish-eating diving bird of the genus *Anhinga*, with a long thin neck. **2** any of various small quick-moving freshwater fish of the family Percidae, native to N. America.

Dartmoor pony /ˈdɑːtmʊə, -mɔː/ *n.* **1** a pony of a small hardy breed with a long shaggy coat in winter. **2** this breed. [*Dartmoor* in SW England, where the breed originated]

Darwinian /dɑːˈwɪnɪən/ *adj. & n.* ● *adj.* of or relating to Darwin's theory of the evolution of species by the action of natural selection (cf. NEO-DARWINIAN). ● *n.* an adherent of this theory. □ **Darwinism** /ˈdɑː-/ *n.* **Darwinist** /ˈdɑː-/ *n. & adj.* [from C. *Darwin*, English naturalist d. 1882]

dash /daʃ/ *v. & n.* ● *v.* **1** *intr.* rush hastily or forcefully (*dashed up the stairs*). **2** *tr.* strike or fling with great force, esp. so as to shatter (*dashed it to the ground*; *the cup was dashed from my hand*). **3** *tr.* frustrate, daunt, dispirit (*dashed their hopes*). **4** *tr. Brit. colloq.* (**dash it** or **dash it all**) = DAMN *v.* 1. ● *n.* **1** a rush or onset; a sudden advance (*made a dash for shelter*). **2** a horizontal stroke in writing or printing to mark a pause or break in sense or to represent omitted letters or words. **3** impetuous vigour or the capacity for this. **4** showy appearance or behaviour; stylishness. **5** *N. Amer.* a sprinting race. **6** the longer signal of the two used in Morse code (cf. DOT[1] *n.* 3). **7** a slight admixture, esp. of a liquid. **8** = DASHBOARD. □ **cut a dash** make a brilliant show. **dash down** (or **off**) write or finish hurriedly. [Middle English, probably imitative]

dashboard /ˈdaʃbɔːd/ *n.* **1** the surface below the windscreen of a motor vehicle or aircraft, containing instruments and controls. **2** *hist.* a board of wood or leather in front of a carriage, to keep out mud.

dashiki /ˈdɑːʃɪki/ *n.* a loose brightly coloured shirt worn by American blacks. [West African, probably Yoruba from Hausa]

dashing /ˈdaʃɪŋ/ *adj.* **1** spirited, lively. **2** stylish. □ **dashingly** *adv.* **dashingness** *n.*

dashpot /ˈdaʃpɒt/ *n.* a device for damping shock or vibration.

dassie /ˈdasi/ *n. S.Afr.* **1** a rock hyrax of southern Africa, *Procavia capensis*; also called ROCK RABBIT. **2** a small coastal fish, *Diplodus sargus*, with a black spot on the tail. [Afrikaans from Dutch *dasje*, diminutive of *das* 'badger']

dastardly /ˈdastədli, ˈdɑː-/ *adj.* cowardly, despicable. □ **dastardliness** *n.* [*dastard* 'base coward', probably from *dazed* past part. + -ARD, or obsolete *dasart* 'dullard, DOTARD']

dasyure /ˈdasɪjʊə/ *n.* any small catlike flesh-eating marsupial of the genus *Dasyurus*. [French from modern Latin *dasyurus*, Greek *dasus* 'rough' + *oura* 'tail']

DAT *abbr.* digital audio tape.

data /ˈdeɪtə/ *n.pl.* (also treated as *sing.*, although the singular form is strictly *datum*) **1** known facts or things used as a basis for inference or reckoning. **2** quantities or characters operated on by a computer etc. [pl. of DATUM]

■ **Usage** (1) In scientific, philosophical, and general use, this word is usually considered to denote a number of items and is thus treated as plural with *datum* as the singular. (2) In computing and allied subjects (and sometimes in general use), it is treated as a mass (or collective) noun and used with words like *this*, *that*, and *much*, with singular verbs, e.g. *useful data has been collected*. Some people consider use (2) to be incorrect but it is more common than use (1). However, *data* is not a singular countable noun and cannot be preceded by *a*, *every*, *each*, *either*, or *neither*, or be given a plural form *datas*.

data bank *n.* **1** a store or source of data. **2** = DATABASE.

database /ˈdeɪtəbeɪs/ *n.* a structured set of data held in a computer, esp. one that is accessible in various ways.

datable /ˈdeɪtəb(ə)l/ *adj.* (often foll. by *to*) capable of being dated (to a particular time).

data capture *n.* the action or process of entering data into a computer.

data processing *n.* a series of operations on data, esp. by a computer, to retrieve or classify etc. information. □ **data processor** *n.*

data protection *n. Brit.* legal control over access to data stored in computers.

date[1] /deɪt/ *n.* & *v.* ● *n.* **1** a day of the month, esp. specified by a number. **2** a particular day or year, esp. when a given event occurred. **3** a statement (usu. giving the day, month, and year) in a document or inscription etc., of the time of composition or publication. **4** the period to which a work of art etc. belongs. **5** the time when an event happens or is to happen. **6** *colloq.* **a** an appointment or social engagement, esp. with a person of the opposite sex. **b** esp. *N. Amer.* a person with whom one has a social engagement. ● *v.* **1** *tr.* mark with a date. **2** *tr.* **a** assign a date to (an object, event, etc.). **b** (foll. by *to*) assign to a particular time, period, etc. **3** *intr.* (often foll. by *from*, *back to*, etc.) have its origins at a particular time. **4** *intr.* be recognizable as from a past or particular period; become evidently out of date (*a design that does not date*). **5** *tr.* indicate or expose as being out of date (*that hat really dates you*). **6** *colloq.* **a** *tr.* make an arrangement with (a person) to meet socially. **b** *intr.* meet socially by agreement (*they are now dating regularly*). □ **to date** until now. [Middle English via Old French from medieval Latin *data*, fem. past part. of *dare* 'give': from the Latin formula used in dating letters, *data* (*epistola*) '(letter) given or delivered' (at a particular time or place)]

date[2] /deɪt/ *n.* **1** a dark oval single-stoned fruit. **2** (in full **date palm**) the tall tree *Phoenix dactylifera*, native to W. Asia and N. Africa, bearing this fruit. [Middle English via Old French from Latin *dactylus*, from Greek *daktulos* 'finger', from the shape of its leaf]

datebook /ˈdeɪtbʊk/ *n. N. Amer.* an engagement diary.

dateless /ˈdeɪtlɪs/ *adj.* **1** having no date. **2** of immemorial age. **3** not likely to become out of date.

date line *n.* **1** (**Date Line**) (in full **International Date Line**) an imaginary north-south line through the Pacific Ocean, mainly along the meridian furthest from Greenwich, to the east of which the date is a day earlier than it is to the west. **2** a line at the head of a dispatch or special article in a newspaper showing the date and place of writing.

date rape *n.* the rape of a girl or woman by a person with whom she is on a date.

date stamp *n.* & *v.* ● *n.* **1** an adjustable rubber stamp etc. used to record a date. **2** the impression made by this. ● *v.tr.* (**date-stamp**) mark with a date stamp.

dative /ˈdeɪtɪv/ *n.* & *adj. Gram.* ● *n.* the case of nouns and pronouns (and words in grammatical agreement with them) indicating an indirect object or recipient. ● *adj.* of or in the dative. □ **datival** /dəˈtʌɪv(ə)l/ *adj.* [Middle English from Latin (*casus*) *dativus*, from *dare dat-* 'give']

datum /ˈdeɪtəm/ *n.* (*pl.* **data**: see DATA) **1** a piece of information. **2** a thing known or granted; an assumption or premiss from which inferences may be drawn (see SENSE DATUM). **3** a fixed starting point of a scale etc. (*datum line*). [Latin, = thing given, neut. past part. of *dare* 'give']

datura /dəˈtjʊərə/ *n.* any poisonous plant of the genus *Datura*, e.g. the thorn apple. [modern Latin from Hindi *dhatura*]

daub /dɔːb/ *v.* & *n.* ● *v.tr.* **1** spread (paint, plaster, or some other thick substance) crudely or roughly on a surface. **2** coat or smear (a surface) with paint etc. **3 a** (also *absol.*) paint crudely or unskilfully. **b** lay (colours) on crudely and clumsily. ● *n.* **1** paint or other substance daubed on a surface. **2** plaster, clay, etc., for coating a surface, esp. mixed with straw and applied to laths or wattles to form a wall. **3** a crude painting. [Middle English via Old French *dauber* from Latin *dealbare* 'whitewash', from *albus* 'white']

daube /dəʊb/ *n.* a stew of braised meat (usu. beef) with wine etc. [French]

dauber /ˈdɔːbə/ *n.* a person or implement that daubs, esp. in painting.

daughter /ˈdɔːtə/ *n.* **1** a girl or woman in relation to either or both of her parents. **2** a female descendant. **3** (foll. by *of*) a female member of a family, nation, etc. **4** (foll. by *of*) a woman who is regarded as the spiritual descendant of, or as spiritually attached to, a person or thing. **5** a product or attribute personified as a daughter in relation to its source (*Fortune and its daughter Confidence*). **6** *Physics* a nuclide formed by the radioactive decay of another. **7** *Biol.* a cell etc. formed by the division etc. of another. □ **daughterhood** *n.* **daughterly** *adj.* [Old English *dohtor*, from Germanic]

daughter-in-law *n.* (*pl.* **daughters-in-law**) the wife of one's son.

daunt /dɔːnt/ *v.tr.* discourage, intimidate. □ **daunting** *adj.* **dauntingly** *adv.* [Middle English via Anglo-French *daunter*, Old French *danter*, *donter* from Latin *domitare*, frequentative of *domare* 'tame']

dauntless /ˈdɔːntlɪs/ *adj.* intrepid, persevering. □ **dauntlessly** *adv.* **dauntlessness** *n.*

dauphin /ˈdɔːfɪn, ˈdəʊfã/ *n. hist.* the eldest son of the King of France. [Middle English from French, ultimately from Latin *delphinus* DOLPHIN, as a family name]

Davenport /ˈdav(ə)npɔːt/ *n.* **1** *Brit.* an ornamental writing desk with drawers and a sloping surface for writing. **2** *US* a large heavily upholstered sofa. [probably from Capt. *Davenport*, for whom early examples of this type of desk were made in the late 18th c.]

davit /ˈdavɪt, ˈdeɪv-/ *n.* a small crane on board a ship, esp. one of a pair for suspending or lowering a lifeboat. [Anglo-French & Old French *daviot*, diminutive of *Davi* 'David']

Davy /ˈdeɪvi/ *n.* (*pl.* **-ies**) (in full **Davy lamp**) a miner's safety lamp with the flame enclosed by wire gauze to reduce the risk of an explosion of gas. [named after Sir H. *Davy*, English chemist (d. 1829) who invented it]

Davy Jones /deɪvɪ ˈdʒəʊnz/ *n. slang* **1** (in full **Davy Jones's locker**) the bottom of the sea, esp. regarded as the grave of those drowned at sea. **2** the evil spirit of the sea. [18th c.: origin unknown]

daw /dɔː/ *n.* = JACKDAW. [Middle English: related to Old High German *tāha*]

dawdle /ˈdɔːd(ə)l/ *v.* & *n.* ● *v.* **1** *intr.* **a** walk slowly and idly. **b** delay; waste time. **2** *tr.* (foll. by *away*) waste (time). ● *n.* an act or instance of dawdling. □ **dawdler** *n.* [perhaps related to dialect *daddle*, *doddle* 'idle, dally']

dawn /dɔːn/ *n.* & *v.* ● *n.* **1** the first light of day; daybreak. **2** the beginning or incipient appearance of something. ● *v.intr.* **1** (of a day) begin; grow light. **2** (often foll. by *on*, *upon*) begin to become evident or understood (by a person). [originally as verb: back-formation from *dawning*, Middle English from earlier *dawing* influenced by similar Scandinavian words: related to DAY]

dawn chorus *n.* the singing of many birds at the break of day.

dawning /ˈdɔːnɪŋ/ *n.* **1** daybreak. **2** the first beginning of something.

dawn redwood *n.* a Chinese deciduous coniferous tree, *Metasequoia glyptostroboides*, of a genus first known only from fossils.

day /deɪ/ *n.* **1** the time between sunrise and sunset. **2 a** a period of 24 hours as a unit of time, esp. from midnight to midnight, corresponding to a complete revolution of the earth on its axis. **b** a corresponding period on other planets (*Martian day*). **3** daylight (*clear as day*). **4** the time in a day during which work is normally done (*an eight-hour day*). **5 a** (also *pl.*) a period of the past or present (*the modern day*; *the old days*). **b** (prec. by *the*) the present time (*the issues of the day*). **6** the lifetime of a person or thing, esp. regarded as useful or productive (*have had my day*; *in my day things were different*). **7** a point of time (*will do it one day*). **8** the date of a particular festival or event (*graduation day*; *pay day*; *Christmas Day*). **9** a particular date; a date agreed on. **10** a day's endeavour, or the period of an endeavour, esp. as bringing success (*win the day*). □ **all in a** (or **the**) **day's work** part of normal routine. **at the end of the day** esp. *Brit.* in the final reckoning, when all is said and done. **call it a day** end a period of activity, esp. resting content that enough has been done. **day after day** without respite. **day and night** all the time. **day by day** gradually. **day in, day out** routinely, constantly. **day of rest** the sabbath. **from day one** from the beginning. **not one's day** a day of successive misfortunes for a person. **one of these days** before very long. **one of those days** a day when things go badly. **that will be the day** *colloq.* that will never happen. **this day and age** the present time or period. □ **dayless** *adj.* [Old English *dæg*, from Germanic]

Dayak var. of DYAK.

daybed /ˈdeɪbɛd/ *n.* a bed for daytime rest.

daybook /ˈdeɪbʊk/ *n.* an account book in which a day's transactions are entered, for later transfer to a ledger.

day-boy *n.* (*fem.* **day-girl**) *Brit.* a boy or girl who goes daily from home to school, esp. a school that also has boarders.

daybreak /ˈdeɪbreɪk/ *n.* the first appearance of light in the morning.

day care *n.* (often hyphenated when *attrib.*) **1** the supervision of young children during the working day. **2** the care provided by a day centre.

day centre *n.* (also **day care centre**) a place providing care for the elderly or handicapped during the day.

daydream /ˈdeɪdriːm/ *n.* & *v.* ● *n.* pleasant fantasy or reverie. ● *v.intr.* indulge in this. □ **daydreamer** *n.*

Day-Glo /ˈdeɪgləʊ/ *n.* & *adj.* ● *n. propr.* a make of fluorescent paint or other colouring. ● *adj.* coloured with or like this. [DAY + GLOW]

day labourer *n.* an unskilled labourer hired by the day.

daylight /ˈdeɪlʌɪt/ *n.* **1** the light of day. **2** dawn (*before daylight*). **3 a** openness, publicity. **b** open knowledge. **4** a visible gap or interval, e.g. between boats in a race. **5** (in *pl.*) *colloq.* one's life or consciousness (originally the internal organs) esp. as representing vulnerability to fear, attack, etc. (*scared the daylights out of me*; *beat the living daylights out of them*). □ **see daylight** begin to understand what was previously obscure.

daylight robbery *n. Brit. colloq.* a blatantly excessive charge.

daylight saving *n.* the achieving of longer evening daylight, esp. in summer, by setting the time an hour ahead of the standard time.

daylight time *n.* esp. *N. Amer.* time as adjusted for daylight saving (cf. SUMMER TIME).

day lily *n.* any plant of the genus *Hemerocallis*, whose flowers last only a day.

day-long *adj.* lasting for a day.

day nursery *n.* a nursery where children are looked after during the working day.

Day of Atonement *n.* the most solemn religious fast of the Jewish year, ten days after the Jewish New Year.

day off *n.* a day's holiday from work.

Day of Judgement *n.* = JUDGEMENT DAY.

day of obligation *n. Eccl.* a day on which all are required to attend Mass or Communion.

day of reckoning *n.* the time when something must be atoned for or avenged.

day out *n. Brit.* a trip or excursion for a day.

day owl *n.* any owl hunting by day esp. the short-eared owl.

daypack /ˈdeɪpak/ *n. N. Amer.* = DAYSACK.

day release *n. Brit.* a system of allowing employees days off work for education.

day return *n. Brit.* a fare or ticket at a reduced rate for a journey out and back in one day.

day room *n.* a room, esp. a communal room in an institution, used during the day.

daysack /ˈdeɪsak/ *n. Brit.* a small rucksack for use on one-day hikes.

day school *n.* a school for pupils living at home.

dayside /ˈdeɪsʌɪd/ *n.* **1** *US* staff, esp. of a newspaper, who work during the day. **2** *Astron.* the side of a planet that faces the sun.

daytime /ˈdeɪtʌɪm/ *n.* the part of the day when there is natural light.

day-to-day *adj.* mundane, routine.

day trip *n.* a trip or excursion completed in one day. □ **day tripper** *n. Brit.*

daywork /ˈdeɪwəːk/ *n.* work paid for according to the time taken.

daze /deɪz/ *v.* & *n.* ● *v.tr.* stupefy, bewilder. ● *n.* a state of confusion or bewilderment (*in a daze*). □ **dazedly** /-zɪdli/ *adv.* [Middle English *dased* past part., from Old Norse *dasathr* 'weary']

dazzle /ˈdaz(ə)l/ *v.* & *n.* ● *v.* **1** *tr.* blind temporarily or confuse the sight of by an excess of light. **2** *tr.* impress or overpower (a person) with knowledge, ability, or any brilliant display or prospect. **3** *intr. archaic* (of eyes) be dazzled. ● *n.* bright confusing light. □ **dazzlement** *n.* **dazzler** *n.* **dazzling** *adj.* **dazzlingly** *adv.* [Middle English, from DAZE + -LE[4]]

dB *abbr.* decibel(s).

DBE *abbr.* (in the UK) Dame Commander of the Order of the British Empire.

DBS *abbr.* **1** direct-broadcast satellite. **2** direct broadcasting by satellite.

DC *abbr.* **1** (also **dc**) direct current. **2** District of Columbia. **3** da capo. **4** District Commissioner.

DCB *abbr.* (in the UK) Dame Commander of the Order of the Bath.

DCL *abbr.* Doctor of Civil Law.

DCM *abbr.* (in the UK) Distinguished Conduct Medal.

DCMG *abbr.* (in the UK) Dame Commander of the Order of St Michael and St George.

DCVO *abbr.* (in the UK) Dame Commander of the Royal Victorian Order.

DD *abbr.* Doctor of Divinity.

D-Day /ˈdiːdeɪ/ *n.* **1** the day (6 June 1944) on which Allied forces invaded northern France. **2** the day on which an important operation is to begin or a change to take effect. [*D* for *day* + DAY]

ddC *abbr.* dideoxycytidine, a drug intended for use in the treatment of Aids.

ddI *abbr.* dideoxyinosine, a drug intended for use in the treatment of Aids.

DDR *abbr. hist.* German Democratic Republic. [German *Deutsche Demokratische Republik*]

DDT *abbr.* dichlorodiphenyltrichloroethane, a synthetic organic compound used as an insecticide, but now widely banned for its damaging effects on wildlife.

DE *abbr. US* Delaware (in official postal use).

de- /diː, dɪ/ *prefix* **1** forming verbs and their derivatives: **a** down, away (*descend*; *deduct*). **b** completely (*declare*; *denude*; *deride*). **2** added to verbs and their derivatives to form verbs and nouns implying removal or reversal (*decentralize*; *de-ice*; *demoralization*). [from or suggested by Latin *de* (*adv.* & *prep.*) = off, from: sense 2 via Old French *des-* from Latin *dis-*]

deaccession /diːəkˈsɛʃ(ə)n/ *v.tr.* (of a museum, library, etc.) sell (a work).

deacon /ˈdiːk(ə)n/ *n. & v.* ● *n.* **1** (in episcopal Churches) a minister of the third order, below bishop and priest. **2** (in Nonconformist Churches) a lay officer attending to a congregation's secular affairs. **3** (in the early Church) an appointed minister of charity. ● *v.tr.* appoint or ordain as a deacon. □ **deaconate** *n.* **deaconship** *n.* [Old English *diacon* via ecclesiastical Latin *diaconus* from Greek *diakonos* 'servant']

deaconess /diːkəˈnɛs, ˈdiːk(ə)nɪs/ *n.* a woman in the early Church and in some modern Churches with functions analogous to a deacon's. [DEACON, suggested by Late Latin *diaconissa*]

deactivate /diːˈaktɪveɪt/ *v.tr.* make inactive or less reactive. □ **deactivation** /-ˈveɪʃ(ə)n/ *n.* **deactivator** *n.*

dead /dɛd/ *adj., adv., & n.* ● *adj.* **1** no longer alive. **2** *colloq.* extremely tired or unwell. **3** benumbed; affected by loss of sensation (*my fingers are dead*). **4** (foll. by *to*) unappreciative or unconscious of; insensitive to. **5** no longer effective or in use; obsolete, extinct. **6** (of a match, of coal, etc.) no longer burning; extinguished. **7** inanimate. **8 a** lacking force or vigour; dull, lustreless, muffled. **b** (of sound) not resonant. **c** (of sparkling wine etc.) no longer effervescent. **9 a** quiet; lacking activity (*the dead season*). **b** motionless, idle. **10 a** (of a microphone, telephone, etc.) not transmitting any sound, esp. because of a fault. **b** (of a circuit, conductor, etc.) carrying or transmitting no current; not connected to a source of electricity (*a dead battery*). **11** (of the ball in a game) out of play. **12** abrupt, complete, exact, unqualified, unrelieved (*come to a dead stop*; *a dead faint*; *a dead calm*; *in dead silence*; *a dead certainty*). **13** without spiritual life. ● *adv.* **1** absolutely, exactly, completely (*dead on target*; *dead level*; *dead tired*). **2** *Brit. colloq.* very, extremely (*dead good*; *dead easy*). ● *n.* (prec. by *the*) **1** (treated as *pl.*) those who have died. **2** a time of silence or inactivity (*the dead of night*). □ **dead as the** (or **a**) **dodo** see DODO. **dead as a doornail** see DOORNAIL. **dead from the neck up** *colloq.* stupid. **dead to the world** *colloq.* fast asleep; unconscious. **make a dead set at** see SET[2]. **wouldn't be seen dead in** (or **with** etc.) *colloq.* shall refuse to wear etc.; shall have nothing to do with. □ **deadness** *n.* [Old English *dēad* from Germanic, related to DIE[1]]

dead-and-alive *adj. Brit.* (of a place, person, activity, etc.) dull, monotonous; lacking interest.

dead-ball line *n. Rugby* a line behind the goal line beyond which the ball is considered out of play.

dead bat *n. Cricket* a bat held loosely so that it imparts no motion to the ball when struck.

deadbeat /ˈdɛdbiːt/ *adj. & n.* ● *adj.* (usu. **dead beat** /-ˈbiːt/ when *predic.*) **1** *colloq.* exhausted. **2** *Physics* (of an instrument or clock escapement) without recoil. ● *n.* **1** *colloq.* an idle, feckless, or disreputable person. **2** *US slang* a person constantly in debt.

deadbolt /ˈdɛdbəʊlt/ *n.* esp. *US* a bolt engaged by turning a knob or key, rather than by spring action.

dead centre *n.* **1** the exact centre. **2** the position of a crank etc. in line with the connecting rod and not exerting torque.

dead cert *Brit.* see CERT.

dead duck *n. colloq.* an unsuccessful or useless person or thing.

deaden /ˈdɛd(ə)n/ *v.* **1** *tr. & intr.* deprive of or lose vitality, force, brightness, sound, feeling, etc. **2** *tr.* (foll. by *to*) make insensitive. □ **deadener** *n.*

dead end *n.* **1** a closed end of a road, passage, etc. **2** (often, with hyphen, *attrib.*) a situation offering no prospects of progress or advancement.

deadeye /ˈdɛdʌɪ/ *n.* **1** *Naut.* a circular wooden block with a groove round the circumference to take a lanyard, used singly or in pairs to tighten a shroud. **2** *US colloq.* an expert marksman.

deadfall /ˈdɛdfɔːl/ *n. N. Amer.* a trap in which a raised weight is made to fall on and kill esp. large game.

dead hand *n.* an oppressive persisting influence, esp. posthumous control.

dead-head *n. & v.* ● *n.* **1** *Brit.* a faded flower head. **2** *colloq.* a passenger or member of an audience who has made use of a free ticket. **3** *colloq.* a useless or unenterprising person. ● *v.* **1** *tr.* remove dead-heads from (a plant). **2** *intr. US colloq.* (of a driver etc.) complete a journey with an empty train, bus, etc.

dead heat *n. & v.* ● *n.* **1** a race in which two or more competitors finish exactly level. **2** the result of such a race. ● *v.intr.* (**dead-heat**) run a dead heat.

dead language *n.* a language no longer spoken, e.g. Latin.

dead letter *n.* **1** a law or practice no longer observed or recognized. **2** an unclaimed or undelivered letter.

dead lift *n.* the exertion of one's utmost strength to lift something.

deadlight /ˈdɛdlʌɪt/ *n.* **1** *Naut.* a shutter inside a porthole. **2** *US* a skylight that cannot be opened.

deadline /ˈdɛdlʌɪn/ *n.* **1** a time limit for the completion of an activity etc. **2** *hist.* a line beyond which prisoners were not allowed to go.

deadlock /ˈdɛdlɒk/ *n. & v.* ● *n.* **1** a situation, esp. one involving opposing parties, in which no progress can be made. **2** a type of lock requiring a key to open or close it. ● *v.tr. & intr.* bring or come to a standstill.

dead loss *n.* **1** *colloq.* a useless person or thing. **2** a complete loss.

deadly /ˈdɛdli/ *adj. & adv.* ● *adj.* (**deadlier, deadliest**) **1 a** causing or able to cause fatal injury or serious damage. **b** poisonous (*deadly snake*). **2** intense, extreme (*deadly dullness*). **3** (of an aim etc.) extremely accurate or effective. **4** deathlike (*deadly pale*; *deadly faintness*; *deadly gloom*). **5** *colloq.* dreary, dull. **6** implacable. ● *adv.* **1** like death; as if dead (*deadly faint*). **2** extremely, intensely (*deadly serious*). □ **deadliness** *n.* [Old English *dēadlic*, *dēadlīce* (as DEAD, -LY[1])]

deadly nightshade *n.* a highly poisonous plant, *Atropa belladonna*, with drooping purple flowers and black cherry-like fruit. Also called BELLADONNA or *dwale*.

deadly sin *n.* a sin regarded as leading to damnation, esp. pride, covetousness, lust, gluttony, envy, anger, and sloth.

dead man's fingers *n.* **1** a kind of orchis, *Orchis mascula*. **2** any soft coral of the genus *Alcyonium*, with spiny lobes. **3** the finger-like divisions of a lobster's or crab's gills.

dead man's handle *n.* (also **dead man's pedal**) a controlling device esp. on an electric train, allowing power to be connected only as long as the operator presses on it.

dead march *n.* a funeral march.

dead men *n.pl. colloq.* bottles after the contents have been drunk.

dead nettle *n.* a plant of the genus *Lamium* or a related genus of the mint family, having nettle-like leaves but without stinging hairs.

dead on *adj.* exactly right.

deadpan /ˈdɛdpan/ *adj., adv., & v.* ● *adj. & adv.* with a face or manner totally lacking expression or emotion. ● *v.* (**deadpanned, deadpanning**) **1** *intr.* speak or behave in a deadpan manner. **2** *tr.* say or behave towards in a deadpan manner.

dead reckoning *n.* calculation of a ship's position from the log, compass, etc., when observations are impossible.

dead ringer see RINGER.

dead set *n.* a determined attack or attempt.

dead shot *n.* person who shoots extremely accurately.

deadstock /ˈdɛdstɒk/ *n.* farm machinery. [in contrast to *livestock*]

dead time *n. Physics* the period after the recording of a pulse etc. when the detector is unable to record another.

dead weight *n.* (also **dead-weight**) **1 a** an inert mass. **b** a heavy weight or burden. **2** a debt not covered by assets. **3** the total weight carried on a ship.

dead wood *n. colloq.* one or more useless people or things.

de-aerate /diːˈɛːreɪt/ *v.tr.* remove air from. □ **de-aeration** /-ˈreɪʃ(ə)n/ *n.*

deaf /dɛf/ *adj.* **1** wholly or partly without hearing (*deaf in one ear*). **2** (foll. by *to*) refusing to listen or comply. **3** insensitive to harmony, rhythm, etc. (*tone-deaf*). □ **deaf as a post** completely deaf. **fall on deaf ears** be ignored. **turn a deaf ear** (usu. foll. by *to*) be unresponsive. □ **deafness** *n.* [Old English *dēaf*, from Germanic]

deaf aid *n. Brit.* a hearing aid.

deaf-and-dumb alphabet *n.* (also **deaf-and-dumb language** etc.) finger alphabet; sign language.

■ **Usage** *Sign language* is the preferred term in official use.

deaf-blind *adj.* (of a person) both deaf and blind.

deafen /ˈdɛf(ə)n/ *v.tr.* **1** (often as **deafening** *adj.*) overpower with sound. **2** deprive of hearing by noise, esp. temporarily. □ **deafeningly** *adv.*

deaf mute *n.* a person who is both deaf and dumb.

■ **Usage** The term *deaf mute* is now generally avoided in favour of the term *profoundly deaf*. If complete unambiguity is needed, *deaf without speech* can be used.

deal[1] /diːl/ *v. & n.* ● *v.* (*past* and *past part.* **dealt** /dɛlt/) **1** *intr.* **a** (foll. by *with*) take measures concerning (a problem, person, etc.), esp. in order to put something right. **b** (foll. by *with*) do business with; associate with. **c** (foll. by *with*) discuss or treat (a subject). **d** (often foll. by *by*) behave in a specified way towards a person (*dealt honourably by them*). **2** *intr.* (foll. by *in*) sell or be concerned with commercially (*deals in insurance*). **3** *tr.* (often foll. by *out*, or *Brit. round*) distribute or apportion to several people etc. **4** *tr.* (also *absol.*) distribute (cards) to players for a game or round. **5** *tr.* cause to be received; administer (*deal a heavy blow*). **6** *tr.* assign as a share or deserts to a person (*Providence dealt them much happiness*). **7** *tr.* (foll. by *in*) *colloq.* include (a person) in an activity (*you can deal me in*). ● *n.* **1** (usu. **a good** or **great deal**) **a** a large amount (*a good deal of trouble*). **b** to a considerable extent (*is a great deal better*). **2** a business arrangement; a transaction. **3** a specified form of treatment given or received (*gave them a rough deal*; *got a fair deal*). **4 a** the distribution of cards by dealing. **b** a player's turn to do this (*it's my deal*). **c** the round of play following this. **d** a set of hands dealt to players. □ **it's a deal** *colloq.* expressing assent to an agreement. [Old English *dǣl*, *dǣlan*, from Germanic]

deal[2] /diːl/ *n.* **1** fir or pine timber, esp. sawn into boards of a standard size. **2 a** a board of this timber. **b** such boards collectively. [Middle English from Middle Low German, Middle Dutch *dele* 'plank', from Germanic]

dealer /ˈdiːlə/ *n.* **1** a person or business dealing in (esp. retail) goods (*contact your dealer*; *car-dealer*; *a dealer in tobacco*). **2** the player dealing at cards. **3** a jobber on the Stock Exchange. □ **dealership** *n.* (in sense 1).

■ **Usage** The term *dealer* in sense 3 was officially replaced by *broker-dealer* in 1986 (see Usage Note at BROKER).

dealings /ˈdiːlɪŋs/ *n.pl.* contacts or transactions, esp. in business. □ **have dealings with** associate with.

dealt *past* and *past part.* of DEAL[1].

dean[1] /diːn/ *n.* **1 a** the head of the chapter of a cathedral or collegiate church. **b** (usu. **rural dean**) *Brit.* a member of the clergy exercising supervision over a group of parochial clergy within a division of an archdeaconry. **2 a** a college or university official, esp. one of several fellows of a college, with disciplinary and advisory functions. **b** the head of a university faculty or department or of a medical school. **3** = DOYEN. [Middle English via Anglo-French *deen*, Old French *deien* from Late Latin *decanus*, from *decem* 'ten'; originally = chief of a group of ten]

dean[2] var. of DENE[1].

deanery /ˈdiːn(ə)ri/ *n.* (*pl.* **-ies**) **1** a dean's house or office. **2** *Brit.* the group of parishes presided over by a rural dean.

Dean of Faculty *n.* the president of the Faculty of Advocates in Scotland.

dear /dɪə/ *adj., n., adv., & int.* ● *adj.* **1 a** beloved or much esteemed. **b** as a merely polite or ironic form (*my dear man*). **2** used as a formula of address, esp. at the beginning of letters (*Dear Sir*). **3** (often foll. by *to*) precious; much cherished. **4** (usu. in *superl.*) earnest, deeply felt (*my dearest wish*). **5 a** high-priced relative to its value. **b** having high prices. **c** (of money) available as a loan only at a high rate of interest. ● *n.* (esp. as a form of address) dear person. ● *adv.* at a high price or great cost (*buy cheap and sell dear*; *will pay dear*). ● *int.* expressing surprise, dismay, pity, etc. (*dear me!*; *oh dear!*; *dear, dear!*). □ **for dear life** see LIFE. □ **dearness** *n.* [Old English *dēore*, from Germanic]

dearie /ˈdɪəri/ *n.* (esp. as a form of address) usu. *joc.* or *iron.* my dear. □ **dearie me!** *int.* expressing surprise, dismay, etc.

Dear John *n. colloq.* a letter terminating a personal relationship.

dearly /ˈdɪəli/ *adv.* **1** affectionately, fondly (*loved him dearly*). **2 a** earnestly; keenly. **b** very much, greatly (*would dearly love to go*). **3** at a high price or great cost.

dearth /dəːθ/ *n.* scarcity or lack. [Middle English, formed as DEAR]

deasil /ˈdɛs(ə)l, ˈdjɛʃ(ə)l/ *adv.* esp. *Sc.* in the direction of the sun's apparent course (considered as lucky); clockwise (opp. WIDDERSHINS). [Gaelic *deiseil*]

death /dɛθ/ *n.* **1** the final cessation of vital functions in an organism; the ending of life. **2** the event that terminates life. **3 a** the fact or process of being killed or killing (*stone to death*; *fight to the death*). **b** the fact or state of being dead (*eyes closed in death*; *their deaths caused rioting*). **4 a** the destruction or permanent cessation of something (*was the death of our hopes*). **b** *colloq.* something terrible or appalling. **5** (usu. **Death**) a personification of death, esp. as a destructive power, usu. represented by a skeleton. **6** a lack of religious faith or spiritual life. □ **as sure as death** quite certain. **at death's door** close to death. **be in at the death 1** be present when an animal is killed, esp. in hunting. **2** witness the (esp. sudden) ending of an enterprise etc. **be the death of 1** cause the death of. **2** be very harmful to. **catch one's death of cold** *colloq.* catch a serious chill etc. **do to death 1** overdo. **2** kill. **fate worse than death** *colloq.* a disastrous misfortune or experience. **like death warmed up** (or *US* **over**) *colloq.* very tired or ill. **put to death** kill; execute. **to death** to the utmost, extremely (*bored to death*; *worked to death*). □ **deathless** *adj.* **deathlessness** *n.* **deathlike** *adj.* [Old English *dēath* from Germanic: related to DIE[1]]

death adder *n.* any of various venomous snakes of the genus *Acanthophis*, esp. *A. antarcticus* of Australia.

deathbed /ˈdɛθbɛd/ *n.* a bed as the place where a person is dying or has died.

death blow *n.* **1** a blow or other action that causes death. **2** an event or circumstance that abruptly ends an activity, enterprise, etc.

death camp *n.* a prison camp in which many people die or are put to death.

death cap *n.* a poisonous toadstool, *Amanita phalloides*.

death cell *n.* a prison cell for a person condemned to death.

death certificate *n.* an official statement of the cause and date and place of a person's death.

death duty *n. Brit. hist.* a tax levied on property after the owner's death (replaced in 1975 by *capital transfer tax*, which was replaced in 1986 by *inheritance tax*).

death grant *n. Brit.* a state grant towards funeral expenses.

death knell *n.* **1** the tolling of a bell to mark a person's death. **2** an event that heralds the end or destruction of something.

deathly /ˈdɛθli/ *adj. & adv.* ● *adj.* (**deathlier**, **deathliest**) suggestive of death (*deathly silence*). ● *adv.* in a deathly way (*deathly pale*).

death mask *n.* a cast taken of a dead person's face.

death penalty *n.* punishment by being put to death.

death rate *n.* the number of deaths per thousand of population per year.

death rattle *n.* a gurgling sound sometimes heard in a dying person's throat.

death roll *n. Brit.* **1** those killed in an accident, battle, etc. **2** a list of these.

death row *n.* (esp. with reference to the US) a prison block or section for prisoners sentenced to death.

death's head *n.* a human skull as an emblem of mortality.

death's head moth *n.* a large dark hawkmoth, *Acherontia atropos*, with skull-like markings on the back of the thorax.

death squad *n.* an armed paramilitary group formed to kill political enemies etc.

death tax *n. US* a tax on property payable on the owner's death.

death toll *n.* the number of people killed in an accident, battle, etc.

death trap *n. colloq.* a dangerous or unhealthy building, vehicle, etc.

death warrant *n.* **1** an order for the execution of a condemned person. **2** anything that causes the end of an established practice etc.

death-watch *n.* (in full **death-watch beetle**) a small beetle, *Xestobium rufovillosum*, which makes a sound like a watch ticking, once supposed to portend death, and whose larva bores in old wood.

death wish *n.* a desire (usu. unconscious) for the death of oneself or another.

deattribute /diːəˈtrɪbjuːt/ *v.tr.* cease to attribute (a work of art) to a particular artist. □ **deattribution** /ˌdiːatrɪˈbjuːʃ(ə)n/ *n.*

deb /dɛb/ *n. colloq.* a debutante. [abbreviation]

debacle /deɪˈbɑːk(ə)l/ *n.* (also **débâcle**) **1 a** an utter defeat, failure, or disaster. **b** a sudden collapse or downfall. **2** a confused rush or rout; a stampede. **3 a** a break-up of ice in a river, with resultant flooding. **b** a sudden rush of water carrying along blocks of stone and other debris. [French, from *débâcler* 'unbar']

debag /diːˈbag/ *v.tr.* (**debagged**, **debagging**) *Brit. slang* remove the trousers of (a person), esp. as a joke.

debar /dɪˈbɑː/ *v.tr.* (**debarred**, **debarring**) (foll. by *from*) exclude from admission or from a right; prohibit from an action (*was debarred from entering*). □ **debarment** *n.* [Middle English from French *débarrer*, Old French *desbarrer* (as DE-, BAR[1])]

debark[1] /diːˈbɑːk/ *v.tr. & intr.* land from a ship. □ **debarkation** /-ˈkeɪʃ(ə)n/ *n.* [French *débarquer* (as DE-, BARK[3])]

debark[2] /diːˈbɑːk/ *v.tr.* remove the bark from (a tree).

debase /dɪˈbeɪs/ *v.tr.* **1** lower in quality, value, or character. **2** depreciate (coin) by alloying etc. □ **debasement** *n.* **debaser** *n.* [DE- + obsolete *base* for ABASE]

debatable /dɪˈbeɪtəb(ə)l/ *adj.* **1** questionable; subject to dispute. **2** capable of being debated. □ **debatably** *adv.* [Old French *debatable* or Anglo-Latin *debatabilis* (as DEBATE)]

debate /dɪˈbeɪt/ *v. & n.* ● *v.* **1** *tr.* (also *absol.*) discuss or dispute about (an issue, proposal, etc.), esp. formally in a legislative assembly, public meeting, etc. **2 a** *tr.* consider or ponder (a matter). **b** *intr.* consider different sides of a question. ● *n.* **1** a formal discussion on a particular matter, esp. in a legislative assembly etc. **2** debating, discussion (*open to debate*). □ **debater** *n.* [Middle English via Old French *debatre*, *debat* from Romanic (as DE-, BATTLE)]

debating point *n.* an inessential matter used to gain advantage in a debate.

debauch /dɪˈbɔːtʃ/ *v. & n.* ● *v.tr.* **1** corrupt morally. **2** make intemperate or sensually indulgent. **3** deprave or debase (taste or judgement). **4** (as **debauched** *adj.*) dissolute. **5** *archaic* seduce (a woman). ● *n.* **1** a bout of sensual indulgence. **2** debauchery. □ **debaucher** *n.* [French *débauche(r)*, Old French *desbaucher*, of unknown origin]

debauchee /dɪbɔːˈtʃiː, -ˈʃiː/ *n.* a person given to excessive sensual indulgence. [French *débauché* past part.: see DEBAUCH, -EE]

debauchery /dɪˈbɔːtʃ(ə)ri/ *n.* excessive sensual indulgence; licentiousness.

debenture /dɪˈbɛn(t)ʃə/ *n.* **1** *Brit.* an acknowledgement of indebtedness, esp. a bond of a company or corporation acknowledging a debt and providing for payment of interest at fixed intervals. **2** *US* (in full **debenture bond**) a fixed-interest bond of a company or corporation, backed by general credit rather than specified assets. [Middle English from Latin *debentur* 'are owing', from *debēre* 'owe': assimilated to -URE]

debenture stock *n. Brit.* stock comprising debentures, with only the interest secured.

debilitate /dɪˈbɪlɪteɪt/ *v.tr.* enfeeble, enervate. □ **debilitatingly** *adv.* **debilitation** /-ˈteɪʃ(ə)n/ *n.* **debilitative** /-tətɪv/ *adj.* [Latin *debilitare* (as DEBILITY)]

debility /dɪˈbɪlɪti/ *n.* feebleness, esp. of health. [Middle English via Old French *debilité* from Latin *debilitas -tatis*, from *debilis* 'weak']

debit /ˈdɛbɪt/ *n. & v.* ● *n.* **1** (in bookkeeping) **a** an entry in the left-hand side or column of an account recording a sum owed. **b** the sum recorded. **c** the total of such sums. **2** the debit side of an account. ● *v.tr.* (**debited**, **debiting**) **1** (foll. by *against*, *to*) enter (an amount) on the debit side of an account (*debited £500 against me*). **2** (foll. by *with*) enter (a person) on the debit side of an account (*debited me with £500*). [French *débit* from Latin *debitum* DEBT]

debit card *n.* a card allowing the holder to transfer money from one bank account to another via a computer terminal when making a purchase etc.

debonair /dɛbəˈnɛː/ *adj.* **1** carefree, cheerful, self-assured. **2** having pleasant manners; urbane. □ **debonairly** *adv.* [Middle English from Old French *debonaire* = *de bon aire* 'of good stock']

debouch /dɪˈbaʊtʃ, -ˈbuːʃ/ *v.intr.* **1** (of troops or a stream) issue from a ravine, wood, etc., into open ground. **2** (often foll. by *into*) (of a river, road, etc.) merge into a larger body or area. □ **debouchment** *n.* [French *déboucher* (as DE-, *bouche* 'mouth')]

debridement /deɪˈbriːdmɒ̃, dɪˈbriːdm(ə)nt/ *n. Med.* the removal of damaged tissue or foreign matter from a wound etc. [French, literally 'unbridling']

debrief /diːˈbriːf/ *v.tr. colloq.* interrogate (a person, e.g. a diplomat or pilot) about a completed mission or undertaking. □ **debriefing** *n.*

debris /ˈdɛbriː, ˈdeɪbriː/ *n.* **1** scattered fragments, esp. of something wrecked or destroyed. **2** *Geol.* an accumulation of loose material, e.g. from rocks or plants. [French *débris* from obsolete *débriser* 'break down' (as DE-, *briser* 'break')]

debt /dɛt/ *n.* **1** something that is owed, esp. money. **2** a state of obligation to pay something owed (*in debt*; *out of debt*; *get into debt*). □ **in a person's debt** under an obligation to a person. [Middle English *det(te)* from Old French *dette* (later *debte*), ultimately from Latin *debitum*, past part. of *debēre* 'owe']

debt collector *n.* a person who is employed to collect debts for creditors.

debt of honour *n.* a debt not legally recoverable, esp. a sum lost in gambling.

debtor /ˈdɛtə/ *n.* a person who owes a debt, esp. money (cf. CREDITOR). [Middle English via Old French *det(t)or*, *-our* from Latin *debitor* (as DEBT)]

debug /diːˈbʌg/ *v.tr.* (**debugged**, **debugging**) **1** trace and remove concealed listening devices from (a room etc.). **2** identify and remove defects from (a machine, computer program, etc.). **3** remove bugs from; delouse.

debugger /diːˈbʌgə/ *n. Computing* a program for debugging other programs.

debunk /diːˈbʌŋk/ *v.tr. colloq.* **1** show the good reputation or aspirations of (a person, institution, etc.) to be spurious. **2** expose the falseness of (a claim etc.). □ **debunker** *n.*

debus /diːˈbʌs/ *v.tr. & intr.* (**debussed**, **debussing**) esp. *Brit. Mil.* unload (personnel or stores) or alight from a motor vehicle.

debut /ˈdeɪbjuː, -buː/ *n.* (also **début**) **1** the first public appearance of a performer on stage etc.; the opening performance of a show etc. **2** the first appearance of a debutante in society. [French, from *débuter* 'lead off']

debutant /ˈdɛbjuːtɒ̃, ˈdeɪ-/ *n.* (also **débutant**) a male performer making his first public appearance.

debutante /ˈdɛbjʊtɑːnt, ˈdeɪ-/ *n.* (also **débutante**) **1** a (usu. wealthy) young woman making her social debut. **2** a female performer making her first public appearance. [French, fem. part. of *débuter*: see DEBUT]

Dec. *abbr.* December.

dec. *abbr.* **1** deceased. **2** declared.

deca- /ˈdɛkə/ *comb. form* (also **dec-** before a vowel) **1** having ten. **2** tenfold. **3** ten, esp. of a metric unit (*decagram*; *decalitre*). [Greek *deka* 'ten']

decade /ˈdɛkeɪd, dɪˈkeɪd/ *n.* **1** a period of ten years. **2** a set, series, or group of ten. [Middle English via French *décade* and Late Latin *decas -adis* from Greek, from *deka* 'ten']

■ **Usage** The second pronunciation given, with the stress on the second syllable, is considered incorrect by some people, even though it is much used in broadcasting.

decadence /ˈdɛkəd(ə)ns/ *n.* **1** moral or cultural deterioration, esp. after a peak or culmination of achievement. **2** decadent behaviour; a state of decadence. [French *décadence* from medieval Latin *decadentia*, from *decadere* DECAY]

decadent /ˈdɛkəd(ə)nt/ *adj. & n.* ● *adj.* **1 a** in a state of moral or cultural deterioration; showing or characterized by decadence. **b** of a period of decadence. **2** self-indulgent. ● *n.* a decadent person. □ **decadently** *adv.* [French *décadent* (as DECADENCE)]

decaf /ˈdiːkaf/ *n. & adj.* (also **decaff**) ● *n. propr.* decaffeinated coffee. ● *adj.* decaffeinated.

decaffeinate /diːˈkafɪneɪt/ *v.tr.* **1** remove the caffeine from. **2** reduce the quantity of caffeine in (usu. coffee).

decagon /ˈdɛkəg(ə)n/ *n.* a plane figure with ten sides and angles. □ **decagonal** /dɪˈkag(ə)n(ə)l/ *adj.* [medieval Latin *decagonum* from Greek *dekagōnon* (as DECA-, -GON)]

decagynous /dɪˈkadʒɪnəs/ *adj. Bot.* having ten pistils. [modern Latin *decagynus* (as DECA-, Greek *gūne* 'woman')]

decahedron /dɛkəˈhiːdr(ə)n, -ˈhɛd-/ *n.* (*pl.* **decahedra** /-drə/ or **decahedrons**) a solid figure with ten faces. □ **decahedral** *adj.* [DECA- + -HEDRON after POLYHEDRON]

decal /ˈdiːkal/ *n. colloq.* = DECALCOMANIA 2. [abbreviation]

decalcify /diːˈkalsɪfʌɪ/ *v.tr.* (**-ies**, **-ied**) remove lime or calcareous matter from (a bone, tooth, etc.). □ **decalcification** /-fɪˈkeɪʃ(ə)n/ *n.* **decalcifier** *n.*

decalcomania /dɪˌkalkəˈmeɪnɪə/ *n. US* **1** a process of transferring designs from specially prepared paper to the surface of glass, porcelain, etc. **2** a picture or design used in or made by this process. [French *décalcomanie* from *décalquer* 'transfer']

decalitre /ˈdɛkəliːtə/ *n.* (*US* **decaliter**) a metric unit of capacity, equal to 10 litres.

Decalogue /ˈdɛkəlɒg/ *n.* the Ten Commandments. [Middle English via French *décalogue* or ecclesiastical Latin *decalogus* from Greek *dekalogos* (after *hoi deka logoi* 'the Ten Commandments')]

decametre /ˈdɛkəmiːtə/ *n.* (*US* **decameter**) a metric unit of length, equal to 10 metres.

decamp /dɪˈkamp/ *v.intr.* **1** break up or leave a camp. **2** depart suddenly; abscond. □ **decampment** *n.* [French *décamper* (as DE-, CAMP[1])]

decanal /dɪˈkeɪn(ə)l, ˈdɛk(ə)n(ə)l/ *adj.* **1** of a dean or deanery. **2** of the south side of a choir, the side on which the dean sits (cf. CANTORIAL 2). [medieval Latin *decanalis* from Late Latin *decanus* DEAN[1]]

decandrous /dɪˈkandrəs/ *adj. Bot.* having ten stamens. [DECA- + Greek *andr-* 'man']

decani /dɪˈkeɪnʌɪ/ *adj. Mus.* to be sung by the decanal side in antiphonal singing (cf. CANTORIS). [Latin, genitive of *decanus* DEAN[1]]

decant /dɪˈkant/ *v.tr.* **1** gradually pour off (liquid, esp. wine or a solution) from one container to another, esp. without disturbing the sediment. **2** *colloq.* transfer as if by pouring. [medieval Latin *decanthare* (as DE-, CANTHUS, used for the lip of a beaker)]

decanter /dɪˈkantə/ *n.* a stoppered glass container into which wine or spirit is decanted.

decapitate /dɪˈkapɪteɪt/ *v.tr.* **1** behead (esp. as a form of capital punishment). **2** cut the head or end from. □ **decapitation** /-ˈteɪʃ(ə)n/ *n.* **decapitator** *n.* [Late Latin *decapitare* (as DE-, *caput -itis* 'head')]

decapod /ˈdɛkəpɒd/ *n.* **1** any crustacean of the chiefly marine order Decapoda, characterized by five pairs of walking legs, e.g. shrimps, crabs, and lobsters. **2** any of various cephalopod molluscs having ten tentacles, e.g. squids and cuttlefish. □ **decapodan** /dɪˈkapəd(ə)n/ *adj.* [French *décapode*, from Greek *deka* 'ten' + *pous podos* 'foot']

decarbonize /diːˈkɑːb(ə)nʌɪz/ *v.tr.* (also **-ise**) remove carbon or carbonaceous deposits from (an internal-combustion engine etc.). □ **decarbonization** /-ˈzeɪʃ(ə)n/ *n.*

decastyle /ˈdɛkəstʌɪl/ *n. & adj. Archit.* ● *n.* a ten-columned portico. ● *adj.* having ten columns. [Greek *dekastulos*, from *deka* 'ten' + *stulos* 'column']

decasyllable /ˈdɛkəˌsɪləb(ə)l/ *n.* a metrical line of ten syllables. □ **decasyllabic** /-sɪˈlabɪk/ *adj. & n.*

decathlon /dɪˈkaθlɒn, -lən/ *n.* an athletic contest in which each competitor takes part in ten different events. □ **decathlete** /-liːt/ *n.* [DECA- + Greek *athlon* 'contest']

decay /dɪˈkeɪ/ *v. & n.* ● *v.* **1 a** *intr.* rot, decompose. **b** *tr.* cause to rot or decompose. **2** *intr. & tr.* decline or cause to decline in quality, power, wealth, energy, beauty, etc. **3** *intr. Physics* **a** (usu. foll. by *to*) (of a substance etc.) undergo change by radioactivity. **b** undergo a gradual decrease in magnitude of a physical quantity. ● *n.* **1** a rotten or ruinous state; a process of wasting away. **2** a decline in health, quality, etc. **3** *Physics* **a** a change into another substance etc. by radioactivity. **b** a decrease in the magnitude of a physical quantity, esp. the intensity of radiation or amplitude of oscillation. **4** decayed tissue. [Middle English via Old French *decair* from Romanic (as DE-, Latin *cadere* 'fall')]

decease /dɪˈsiːs/ *n. & v. formal* esp. *Law* ● *n.* death. ● *v.intr.* die. [Middle English via Old French *deces* Latin *decessus*, from *decedere* (as DE-, *cedere cess-* 'go')]

deceased /dɪˈsiːst/ *adj. & n. formal* ● *adj.* dead. ● *n.* (usu. prec. by *the*) a person who has died, esp. recently.

decedent /dɪˈsiːd(ə)nt/ *n. N. Amer. Law* a deceased person. [Latin *decedere* 'die': see DECEASE]

deceit /dɪˈsiːt/ *n.* **1** the act or process of deceiving or misleading, esp. by concealing the truth. **2** a dishonest trick or stratagem. **3** a tendency to deceive or mislead. [Middle English via Old French, past part. of *deceveir*, used as a noun from Latin *decipere* 'deceive' (as DE-, *capere* 'take')]

deceitful /dɪˈsiːtfʊl, -f(ə)l/ *adj.* **1** (of a person) using deceit, esp. habitually. **2** (of an act, practice, etc.) intended to deceive. □ **deceitfully** *adv.* **deceitfulness** *n.*

deceive /dɪˈsiːv/ *v.* **1** *tr.* make (a person) believe what is false, mislead purposely. **2** *tr.* be unfaithful to, esp.

sexually. **3** *intr.* use deceit. **4** *tr. archaic* disappoint (esp. hopes). □ **be deceived** be mistaken or deluded. **deceive oneself** persist in a mistaken belief. □ **deceivable** *adj.* **deceiver** *n.* [Middle English from Old French *deceivre* or *deceiv-*, stressed stem of *deceveir* (as DECEIT)]

decelerate /diːˈsɛləreɪt/ *v.* **1** *intr. & tr.* begin or cause to begin to reduce speed. **2** *tr.* make slower (*decelerated motion*). □ **deceleration** /-ˈreɪʃ(ə)n/ *n.* **decelerator** *n.* **decelerometer** /-ˈrɒmɪtə/ *n.* [DE-, on the pattern of ACCELERATE]

December /dɪˈsɛmbə/ *n.* the twelfth month of the year. [Middle English via Old French *decembre* from Latin *December*, from *decem* 'ten': originally the tenth month of the Roman year]

decency /ˈdiːs(ə)nsi/ *n.* (*pl.* **-ies**) **1** generally accepted standards of behaviour or propriety. **2** avoidance of obscenity. **3** (in *pl.*) the requirements of correct behaviour. [Latin *decentia* from *decēre* 'be fitting']

decennial /dɪˈsɛnɪəl/ *adj.* **1** lasting ten years. **2** recurring every ten years. □ **decennially** *adv.* [Latin *decennis* 'of ten years', from *decem* 'ten' + *annus* 'year']

decent /ˈdiːs(ə)nt/ *adj.* **1 a** conforming with generally accepted standards of behaviour or propriety. **b** avoiding obscenity. **2** respectable. **3** acceptable, passable; good enough. **4** *Brit.* kind, obliging, generous (*was decent enough to apologize*). □ **decently** *adv.* [French *décent*, or from Latin *decēre* 'be fitting']

decentralize /diːˈsɛntrəlʌɪz/ *v.tr.* (also **-ise**) **1** transfer (powers etc.) from a central to a local authority. **2** reorganize (a centralized institution, organization, etc.) on the basis of greater local autonomy. □ **decentralist** /-lɪst/ *n. & adj.* **decentralization** /-ˈzeɪʃ(ə)n/ *n.*

decentre /diːˈsɛntə/ *v.tr.* (*US* **decenter**) remove the centre from.

deception /dɪˈsɛpʃ(ə)n/ *n.* **1** the act or an instance of deceiving; the process of being deceived. **2** a thing that deceives; a trick or sham. [Middle English from Old French or Late Latin *deceptio*, from *decipere* (as DECEIT)]

deceptive /dɪˈsɛptɪv/ *adj.* apt to deceive; easily mistaken for something else or as having a different quality. □ **deceptively** *adv.* **deceptiveness** *n.* [Old French *deceptif -ive* or Late Latin *deceptivus* (as DECEPTION)]

decerebrate /diːˈsɛrɪbrət/ *adj.* having had the cerebrum removed.

deci- /ˈdɛsi/ *comb. form* one-tenth, esp. of a unit in the metric system (*decilitre*; *decimetre*). [Latin *decimus* 'tenth']

decibel /ˈdɛsɪbɛl/ *n.* a unit (one-tenth of a bel) used in the comparison of two power levels relating to electrical signals or sound intensities, one of the pair usually being taken as a standard (abbr.: **dB**).

decide /dɪˈsʌɪd/ *v.* **1 a** *intr.* (often foll. by *on, about*) come to a resolution as a result of consideration. **b** *tr.* (usu. foll. by *to* + infin., or *that* + clause) have or reach as one's resolution about something (*decided to stay*; *decided that we should leave*). **2** *tr.* **a** cause (a person) to reach a resolution (*was unsure about going but the weather decided me*). **b** resolve or settle (a question, dispute, etc.). **3** *intr.* (usu. foll. by *between, for, against, in favour of,* or *that* + clause) give a judgement concerning a matter. □ **decidable** *adj.* [Middle English from French *décider* or from Latin *decidere* (as DE-, *caedere* 'cut')]

decided /dɪˈsʌɪdɪd/ *adj.* **1** (usu. *attrib.*) definite, unquestionable (*a decided difference*). **2** (of a person, esp. as a characteristic) having clear opinions, resolute, not vacillating. □ **decidedness** *n.*

decidedly /dɪˈsʌɪdɪdli/ *adv.* undoubtedly, undeniably.

decider /dɪˈsʌɪdə/ *n.* **1** a game, race, etc., to decide between competitors finishing equal in a previous contest. **2** any person or thing that decides.

deciduous /dɪˈsɪdjʊəs/ *adj.* **1** (of a tree) shedding its leaves annually (cf. EVERGREEN). **2** (of leaves, horns, teeth, etc.) shed periodically. **3** (of an ant etc.) shedding its wings after copulation. **4** fleeting, transitory. □ **deciduousness** *n.* [Latin *deciduus* from *decidere*, from *cadere* 'fall']

decigram /ˈdɛsɪgram/ *n.* (also **decigramme**) a metric unit of mass, equal to 0.1 gram.

decile /ˈdɛsʌɪl/ *n. Statistics* any of the nine values of a random variable which divide a frequency distribution into ten groups, each containing one-tenth of the total population. [French *décile*, ultimately from Latin *decem* 'ten']

decilitre /ˈdɛsɪliːtə/ *n.* (*US* **deciliter**) a metric unit of capacity, equal to 0.1 litre.

decimal /ˈdɛsɪm(ə)l/ *adj. & n.* ● *adj.* **1** (of a system of numbers, weights, measures, etc.) based on the number ten, in which the smaller units are related to the principal units as powers of ten (units, tens, hundreds, thousands, etc.). **2** of tenths or ten; reckoning or proceeding by tens. ● *n.* a decimal fraction. □ **decimally** *adv.* [modern Latin *decimalis* from Latin *decimus* 'tenth']

decimal fraction *n.* a fraction whose denominator is a power of ten, esp. when expressed positionally by units to the right of a decimal point.

decimalize /ˈdɛsɪm(ə)lʌɪz/ *v.tr.* (also **-ise**) **1** express as a decimal. **2** convert to a decimal system (esp. of coinage). □ **decimalization** /-ˈzeɪʃ(ə)n/ *n.*

decimal place *n.* the position of a digit to the right of a decimal point.

decimal point *n.* a full point or dot placed before the numerator in a decimal fraction.

decimal scale *n.* a scale with successive places denoting units, tens, hundreds, etc.

decimate /ˈdɛsɪmeɪt/ *v.tr.* **1** *disp.* kill or remove a large proportion of. **2** orig. *Mil.* kill or remove one in every ten of. □ **decimation** /-ˈmeɪʃ(ə)n/ *n.* **decimator** *n.* [Latin *decimare* 'take the tenth man', from *decimus* 'tenth']

■ **Usage** Sense 1 is now the usual sense of *decimate* although it is often deplored as an inappropriate use. This word should not be used to mean 'defeat utterly'.

decimetre /ˈdɛsɪmiːtə/ *n.* (*US* **decimeter**) a metric unit of length, equal to 0.1 metre.

decipher /dɪˈsʌɪfə/ *v.tr.* **1** convert (a text written in cipher) into an intelligible script or language. **2** determine the meaning of (anything obscure or unclear). □ **decipherable** *adj.* **decipherment** *n.*

decision /dɪˈsɪʒ(ə)n/ *n.* **1** the act or process of deciding. **2** a conclusion or resolution reached, esp. as to future action, after consideration (*have made my decision*). **3** (often foll. by *of*) **a** the settlement of a question. **b** a formal judgement. **4** a tendency to decide firmly; resoluteness. [Middle English from Old French *decision* or Latin *decisio* (as DECIDE)]

decisive /dɪˈsʌɪsɪv/ *adj.* **1** that decides an issue; conclusive. **2** (of a person, esp. as a characteristic) able to decide quickly and effectively. □ **decisively** *adv.* **decisiveness** *n.* [French *décisif -ive* from medieval Latin *decisivus* (as DECIDE)]

deck /dɛk/ *n. & v.* ● *n.* **1 a** a platform in a ship covering all or part of the hull's area at any level and serving as a floor. **b** the accommodation on a particular deck of a ship. **2** anything similar to a ship's deck, e.g. the floor or compartment of a bus. **3** a component or unit in sound-reproduction equipment that incorporates a playing or recording mechanism for discs, tapes, etc. **4 a** *N. Amer.* a pack of cards. **b** *US slang* a packet of narcotics. **5** *slang* the ground. **6** any floor or platform, esp. the floor of a pier or a platform for sunbathing. ● *v.tr.* **1** (often foll. by *out*) decorate, adorn. **2** furnish with or cover as a deck. **3** *slang* knock (a person) to the ground; floor. □ **below deck** (or **decks**) in or into the space below the main deck. **on deck 1** in the open air on a ship's main deck. **2** esp. *US* ready for action, work, etc. [Middle English, = covering, from Middle Dutch *dec* 'roof, cloak']

deckchair /ˈdɛktʃɛː/ *n.* a folding chair of wood and canvas, of a kind used on deck on passenger ships.

-decker /ˈdɛkə/ *comb. form* having a specified number of decks or layers (*double-decker*).

deckhand /ˈdɛkhand/ *n.* a person employed in cleaning and odd jobs on a ship's deck.

deckle /ˈdɛk(ə)l/ *n.* a device in a papermaking machine for limiting the size of the sheet. [German *Deckel*, diminutive of *Decke* 'cover']

deckle edge *n.* the rough uncut edge formed by a deckle. □ **deckled-edged** *adj.*

deck quoits *n.pl.* a game played, esp. on ships, in which rope quoits are aimed at a peg.

deck tennis *n.* a game played, esp. on ships, in which a quoit of rope, rubber, etc., is tossed to and fro over a net.

declaim /dɪˈkleɪm/ *v.* **1** *intr.* & *tr.* speak or utter rhetorically or affectedly. **2** *intr.* practise oratory or recitation. **3** *intr.* (foll. by *against*) protest forcefully. **4** *intr.* deliver an impassioned (rather than reasoned) speech. □ **declaimer** *n.* [Middle English from French *déclamer* or from Latin *declamare* (as DE-, CLAIM)]

declamation /dɛkləˈmeɪʃ(ə)n/ *n.* **1** the act or art of declaiming. **2** a rhetorical exercise or set speech. **3** an impassioned speech; a harangue. □ **declamatory** /dɪˈklamət(ə)ri/ *adj.* [French *déclamation* or Latin *declamatio* (as DECLAIM)]

declarant /dɪˈklɛːr(ə)nt/ *n.* a person who makes a legal declaration. [French *déclarant*, part. of *déclarer* (as DECLARE)]

declaration /dɛkləˈreɪʃ(ə)n/ *n.* **1** the act or process of declaring. **2 a** a formal, emphatic, or deliberate statement or announcement. **b** a statement asserting or protecting a legal right. **3** a written public announcement of intentions, terms of an agreement, etc. **4** *Cricket* an act of declaring an innings closed. **5** *Cards* **a** the naming of trumps. **b** an announcement of a combination held. **6** *Law* **a** a plaintiff's statement of claim. **b** an affirmation made instead of taking an oath. **7** (in full **declaration of the poll**) *Brit.* a public official announcement of the votes cast for candidates in an election. [Middle English from Latin *declaratio* (as DECLARE)]

Declaration of Independence *n.* a document declaring the US to be independent of the British Crown, signed in 1776.

Declaration of Indulgence *n.* the proclamation of religious liberties, esp. under Charles II in 1672 and James II in 1687.

declarative /dɪˈklarətɪv/ *adj.* & *n.* ● *adj.* **1 a** of the nature of, or making, a declaration. **b** *Gram.* (of a sentence) that takes the form of a simple statement. **2** *Computing* designating high-level programming languages which can be used to solve problems without requiring the programmer to specify an exact procedure to be followed. ● *n.* **1** a declaratory statement or act. **2** *Gram.* a declarative sentence. □ **declaratively** *adv.* [Old French *déclaratif -ive* or Latin *declarativus* (as DECLARE)]

declare /dɪˈklɛː/ *v.* **1** *tr.* announce openly or formally (*declare war*; *declare a dividend*). **2** *tr.* pronounce (a person or thing) to be something (*declared him to be an impostor*; *declared it invalid*). **3** *tr.* (usu. foll. by *that* + clause) assert emphatically; state explicitly. **4** *tr.* acknowledge possession of (dutiable goods, income, etc.). **5** *tr.* (as **declared** *adj.*) who admits to be such (*a declared atheist*). **6** *tr.* (also *absol.*) *Cricket* close (an innings) voluntarily before all the wickets have fallen. **7** *tr. Cards* **a** (also *absol.*) name (the trump suit). **b** announce that one holds (certain combinations of cards etc.). **8** *tr.* (of things) make evident, prove (*your actions declare your honesty*). **9** *intr.* (foll. by *for*, *against*) take the side of one party or another. □ **declare oneself** reveal one's intentions or identity. **well, I declare** (or **I do declare**) an exclamation of incredulity, surprise, or vexation. □ **declarable** *adj.* **declaratory** /-ˈklarət(ə)ri/ *adj.* **declaredly** /-rɪdli/ *adv.* **declarer** *n.* [Middle English from Latin *declarare* (as DE-, *clarare* from *clarus* 'clear')]

declass /diːˈklɑːs/ *v.tr.* remove from one's social class.

déclassé /deɪˈklaseɪ/ *adj.* (*fem.* **déclassée** *pronunc.* same) that has fallen in social status. [French]

declassify /diːˈklasɪfʌɪ/ *v.tr.* (**-ies**, **-ied**) declare (information etc.) to be no longer secret. □ **declassification** /-fɪˈkeɪʃ(ə)n/ *n.*

declension /dɪˈklɛnʃ(ə)n/ *n.* **1** *Gram.* **a** the variation of the form of a noun, pronoun, or adjective, by which its grammatical case, number, and gender are identified. **b** the class in which a noun etc. is put according to the exact form of this variation. **2** deterioration, declining. □ **declensional** *adj.* [Old French *declinaison*, from *decliner* DECLINE, suggested by Latin *declinatio*: assimilated to ASCENSION etc.]

declination /dɛklɪˈneɪʃ(ə)n/ *n.* **1** a downward bend or turn. **2** *Astron.* the angular distance of a star etc. north or south of the celestial equator. **3** the angular deviation of a compass needle from true north. **4** *US* a formal refusal. □ **declinational** *adj.* [Middle English from Latin *declinatio* (as DECLINE)]

decline /dɪˈklʌɪn/ *v.* & *n.* ● *v.* **1** *intr.* deteriorate; lose strength or vigour; decrease. **2 a** *tr.* reply with formal courtesy that one will not accept (an invitation, honour, etc.). **b** *tr.* refuse, esp. formally and courteously (*declined to be made use of*; *declined doing anything*). **c** *tr.* turn away from (a challenge, battle, discussion, etc.). **d** *intr.* give or send a refusal. **3** *intr.* slope downwards. **4** *intr.* bend down, droop. **5** *tr. Gram.* state the forms of (a noun, pronoun, or adjective) corresponding to cases, number, and gender. **6** *intr.* (of a day, life, etc.) draw to a close. **7** *intr.* decrease in price etc. **8** *tr.* bend down. ● *n.* **1** gradual loss of vigour or excellence (*on the decline*). **2** decay, deterioration. **3** the sun's gradual setting; the last part of the course (of the sun, of life, etc.). **4** a fall in price. **5** *archaic* tuberculosis or a similar wasting disease. □ **declinable** *adj.* **decliner** *n.* [Middle English via Old French *decliner* from Latin *declinare* (as DE-, *clinare* 'bend')]

declining years *n.pl.* old age.

declivity /dɪˈklɪvɪti/ *n.* (*pl.* **-ies**) a downward slope, esp. a piece of sloping ground. □ **declivitous** *adj.* [Latin *declivitas* from *declivis* (as DE-, *clivus* 'slope')]

declutch /diːˈklʌtʃ/ *v.intr.* disengage the clutch of a motor vehicle.

deco /ˈdɛkəʊ/ *n.* (also **Deco**) (usu. *attrib.*) = ART DECO. [French *décoratif* DECORATIVE]

decoct /dɪˈkɒkt/ *v.tr.* extract the essence from by decoction. [Middle English from Latin *decoquere* 'boil down']

decoction /dɪˈkɒkʃ(ə)n/ *n.* **1** concentration of, or extraction of the essence of, a substance by boiling in water etc. **2** the extracted liquor resulting from this. [Middle English from Old French *decoction* or Late Latin *decoctio* (as DE-, Latin *coquere coct-* 'boil')]

decode /diːˈkəʊd/ *v.tr.* convert (a coded message) into intelligible language. □ **decodable** *adj.*

decoder /diːˈkəʊdə/ *n.* **1** a person or thing that decodes. **2** an electronic device for analysing signals and feeding separate amplifier channels.

decoke *v.* & *n. Brit. colloq.* ● *v.tr.* /diːˈkəʊk/ remove carbon or carbonaceous material from (an internal-combustion engine). ● *n.* /ˈdiːkəʊk/ the process of decoking.

decollate /diːkəˈleɪt/ *v.tr. formal* **1** behead. **2** truncate. □ **decollation** /diːkəˈleɪʃ(ə)n/ *n.* [Latin *decollare decollat-* (as DE-, *collum* 'neck')]

décolletage /deɪkɒlˈtɑːʒ/ *n.* a low neckline of a woman's dress etc. [French (as DE-, *collet* 'collar of a dress')]

décolleté /deɪˈkɒl(ə)teɪ/ *adj.* & *n.* ● *adj.* (also **décolletée**) **1** (of a dress etc.) having a low neckline. **2** (of a woman) wearing a dress with a low neckline. ● *n.* a low neckline. [French (as DÉCOLLETAGE)]

decolonize /diːˈkɒlənʌɪz/ *v.tr.* (also **-ise**) (of a state) withdraw from (a colony), leaving it independent. □ **decolonization** /-ˈzeɪʃ(ə)n/ *n.*

decolorize /di:ˈkʌlərʌɪz/ *v.* (also **-ise**) **1** *tr.* remove the colour from. **2** *intr.* lose colour. ◻ **decolorization** /-ˈzeɪʃ(ə)n/ *n.*

decommission /di:kəˈmɪʃ(ə)n/ *v.tr.* **1** close down (a nuclear reactor etc.). **2** take (a ship) out of service.

decompose /di:kəmˈpəʊz/ *v.* **1** *intr.* decay, rot; disintegrate, break up. **2** *tr.* break down or separate into its elements or simpler constituents; cause to decay or rot. ◻ **decomposition** /ˌdi:kɒmpəˈzɪʃ(ə)n/ *n.* [French *décomposer* (as DE-, COMPOSE)]

decomposer /di:kəmˈpəʊzə/ *n.* a thing, esp. a living organism, that performs decomposition.

decompress /di:kəmˈprɛs/ *v.tr.* subject to decompression; relieve or reduce the compression on.

decompression /di:kəmˈprɛʃ(ə)n/ *n.* **1** release from compression. **2** a gradual reduction of air pressure on a person who has been subjected to high pressure (esp. underwater).

decompression chamber *n.* an enclosed space for subjecting a person to decompression.

decompression sickness *n.* a condition caused by too rapid decompression, resulting in the formation of nitrogen bubbles in the tissues, pain, nausea, paralysis, etc. Also called *caisson disease, the bends* (see BEND[1] *n.* 4).

decompressor /di:kəmˈprɛsə/ *n. Brit.* a device for reducing pressure in the engine of a motor vehicle.

decongestant /di:k(ə)nˈdʒɛst(ə)nt/ *adj. & n.* ● *adj.* that relieves (esp. nasal) congestion. ● *n.* a medicinal agent that relieves nasal congestion.

deconsecrate /di:ˈkɒnsɪkreɪt/ *v.tr.* transfer (esp. a building) from sacred to secular use. ◻ **deconsecration** /-ˈkreɪʃ(ə)n/ *n.*

deconstruct /di:k(ə)nˈstrʌkt/ *v.tr.* subject to deconstruction. ◻ **deconstructive** *adj.* [back-formation from DECONSTRUCTION]

deconstruction /di:k(ə)nˈstrʌkʃ(ə)n/ *n.* a method of critical analysis of philosophical and literary language. ◻ **deconstructionism** *n.* **deconstructionist** *adj. & n.* [French *déconstruction* (as DE-, CONSTRUCTION)]

decontaminate /di:k(ə)nˈtamɪneɪt/ *v.tr.* remove contamination from (an area, person, clothes, etc.). ◻ **decontamination** /-ˈneɪʃ(ə)n/ *n.*

decontextualize /di:k(ə)nˈtɛkstjʊəlʌɪz/ *v.tr.* (also **-ise**) study or treat in isolation from its context. ◻ **decontextualization** /-ˈzeɪʃ(ə)n/ *n.*

decontrol /di:k(ə)nˈtrəʊl/ *v. & n.* ● *v.tr.* (**decontrolled, decontrolling**) release (a commodity etc.) from controls or restrictions, esp. those imposed by the State. ● *n.* the act of decontrolling.

decor /ˈdeɪkɔ:, ˈdɛ-/ *n.* (also **décor**) **1** the furnishing and decoration of a room etc. **2** the decoration and scenery of a stage. [French from *décorer* (as DECORATE)]

decorate /ˈdɛkəreɪt/ *v.tr.* **1** provide with adornments. **2** esp. *Brit.* provide (a room or building) with new paint, wallpaper, etc. **3** serve as an adornment to. **4** confer an award or distinction on. [Latin *decorare decorat-* from *decus -oris* 'beauty']

Decorated style *n.* the second stage of English Gothic (14th c.), with increasing use of decoration and geometrical tracery.

decoration /dɛkəˈreɪʃ(ə)n/ *n.* **1** the process or art of decorating. **2** a thing that decorates or serves as an ornament. **3** a medal etc. conferred and worn as an honour. **4** (in *pl.*) flags etc. put up on an occasion of public celebration. [French *décoration* or Late Latin *decoratio* (as DECORATE)]

Decoration Day *n.* (in the US) Memorial Day.

decorative /ˈdɛk(ə)rətɪv/ *adj.* serving to decorate. ◻ **decoratively** *adv.* **decorativeness** *n.* [French *décoratif* (as DECORATE)]

decorator /ˈdɛkəreɪtə/ *n.* a person who decorates, esp. *Brit.* one who paints or papers houses professionally.

decorous /ˈdɛk(ə)rəs/ *adj.* respecting good taste or propriety; dignified. ◻ **decorously** *adv.* **decorousness** *n.* [Latin *decorus* 'seemly']

decorticate /di:ˈkɔ:tɪkeɪt/ *v.tr.* **1** remove the bark, rind, or husk from. **2** remove the outside layer from (the kidney, brain, etc.). [Latin *decorticare decorticat-* (as DE-, *cortex -icis* 'bark')]

decortication /dɪˌkɔ:tɪˈkeɪʃ(ə)n/ *n.* **1** the removal of the outside layer from an organ (e.g. the kidney) or structure. **2** *Brit.* an operation removing the blood clot and scar tissue formed after bleeding in the chest cavity.

decorum /dɪˈkɔ:rəm/ *n.* **1 a** seemliness, propriety. **b** behaviour required by politeness or decency. **2** a particular requirement of this kind. **3** etiquette. [Latin, neut. of *decorus* 'seemly']

découpage /deɪku:ˈpɑ:ʒ/ *n.* the decoration of surfaces with paper cut-outs. [French, = the action of cutting out]

decouple /di:ˈkʌp(ə)l/ *v.tr.* **1** *Electr.* make the interaction between (oscillators etc.) so weak that there is little transfer of energy between them. **2** separate, disengage, dissociate.

decoy *n. & v.* ● *n.* /ˈdi:kɔɪ, dɪˈkɔɪ/ **1 a** a person or thing used to lure an animal or person into a trap or danger. **b** a bait or enticement. **2** a pond from which narrow netted channels lead, into which wild duck may be enticed for capture. ● *v.tr.* /dɪˈkɔɪ, ˈdi:kɔɪ/ (often foll. by *into, out of*) allure or entice, esp. by means of a decoy. [17th c.: perhaps from Dutch *de kooi* 'the decoy', from *de* THE + *kooi* from Latin *cavea* 'cage']

decrease *v. & n.* ● *v.tr. & intr.* /dɪˈkri:s/ make or become smaller or fewer. ● *n.* /ˈdi:kri:s/ **1** the act or an instance of decreasing. **2** the amount by which a thing decreases. ◻ **decreasingly** *adv.* [Middle English from Old French *de(s)creiss-*, present stem of *de(s)creistre*, ultimately from Latin *decrescere* (as DE-, *crescere cret-* 'grow')]

decree /dɪˈkri:/ *n. & v.* ● *n.* **1** an official order issued by a legal authority. **2** a judgement or decision of certain law courts, esp. in matrimonial cases. ● *v.tr.* (**decrees, decreed, decreeing**) ordain by decree. [Middle English via Old French *decré* from Latin *decretum*, neut. past part. of *decernere* 'decide' (as DE-, *cernere* 'sift')]

decree absolute *n. Brit.* a final order for divorce, enabling either party to remarry.

decree nisi *n. Brit.* a provisional order for divorce, made absolute unless cause to the contrary is shown within a fixed period.

decrement /ˈdɛkrɪm(ə)nt/ *n.* **1** *Physics* the ratio of the amplitudes in successive cycles of a damped oscillation. **2** the amount lost by diminution or waste. **3** the act of decreasing. [Latin *decrementum* (as DECREASE)]

decrepit /dɪˈkrɛpɪt/ *adj.* **1** weakened or worn out by age and infirmity. **2** worn out by long use; dilapidated. ◻ **decrepitude** *n.* [Middle English from Latin *decrepitus* (as DE-, *crepitus*, past part. of *crepare* 'creak')]

decrepitate /dɪˈkrɛpɪteɪt/ *v.* **1** *tr.* roast or calcine (a mineral or salt) until it stops crackling. **2** *intr.* crackle under heat. ◻ **decrepitation** /-ˈteɪʃ(ə)n/ *n.* [probably modern Latin *decrepitare*, from DE- + Latin *crepitare* 'crackle']

decrescendo /di:krɪˈʃɛndəʊ/ *adv., adj., & n.* (*pl.* **-os**) = DIMINUENDO. [Italian, pres. part. of *decrescere* DECREASE]

decrescent /dɪˈkrɛs(ə)nt/ *adj.* (usu. of the moon) waning, decreasing. [Latin *decrescere*: see DECREASE]

decretal /dɪˈkri:t(ə)l/ *n.* **1** a papal decree. **2** (in *pl.*) a collection of these, forming part of canon law. [Middle English via medieval Latin *decretale* from Late Latin (*epistola*) *decretalis* '(letter) of decree', from Latin *decernere*: see DECREE]

decriminalize /di:ˈkrɪmɪn(ə)lʌɪz/ *v.tr.* (also **-ise**) cease to treat (an action etc.) as criminal. ◻ **decriminalization** /-ˈzeɪʃ(ə)n/ *n.*

decry /dɪˈkrʌɪ/ *v.tr.* (**-ies, -ied**) disparage, belittle. ◻ **decrier** *n.* [suggested by French *décrier*: cf. *cry down*]

decrypt /di:ˈkrɪpt/ *v.tr.* decipher (a cryptogram), with or without knowledge of its key. ◻ **decryption** *n.* [DE- + CRYPTOGRAM]

decumbent /dɪˈkʌmb(ə)nt/ *adj. Bot. & Zool.* (of a plant, shoot, or bristles) lying along the ground or a surface. [Latin *decumbere decumbent-* 'lie down']

decurve /diːˈkɜːv/ *v.tr. & intr. Zool. & Bot.* (esp. as **decurved** *adj.*) curve or bend down (*a decurved bill*). □ **decurvature** *n.*

decussate *adj. & v.* ● *adj.* /dɪˈkʌsət/ **1** X-shaped. **2** *Bot.* with pairs of opposite leaves etc. each at right angles to the pair below. ● *v.tr. & intr.* /dɪˈkʌseɪt, ˈdɛkəseɪt/ **1** arrange or be arranged in a decussate form. **2** intersect. □ **decussation** /-ˈseɪʃ(ə)n/ *n.* [Latin *decussatus*, past part. of *decussare* 'divide in a cross shape', via *decussis*, = the numeral ten or the shape X, from *decem* 'ten']

dedans /dəˈdɑ̃/ *n.* **1** (in real tennis) the open gallery at the end of the service side of a court. **2** the spectators watching from this gallery. [French, = inside]

dedicate /ˈdɛdɪkeɪt/ *v.tr.* **1** (foll. by *to*) devote (esp. oneself) to a special task or purpose. **2** (foll. by *to*) address (a book, piece of music, etc.) as a compliment to a friend, patron, etc. **3** (often foll. by *to*) devote (a building etc.) to a deity or a sacred person or purpose. **4** (as **dedicated** *adj.*) **a** (of a person) devoted to an aim or vocation; having single-minded loyalty or integrity. **b** (of equipment, esp. a computer) designed for a specific purpose. □ **dedicatedly** *adv.* **dedicatee** /-kəˈtiː/ *n.* **dedicative** *adj.* **dedicator** *n.* **dedicatory** *adj.* [Latin *dedicare* (DE-, *dicare* 'declare, dedicate')]

dedication /dɛdɪˈkeɪʃ(ə)n/ *n.* **1** the act or an instance of dedicating; the process or quality of being dedicated. **2** the words with which a book etc. is dedicated. **3** a dedicatory inscription. [Middle English from Old French *dedicacion* or Latin *dedicatio* (as DEDICATE)]

deduce /dɪˈdjuːs/ *v.tr.* **1** (often foll. by *from*) infer; draw as a logical conclusion. **2** *archaic* trace the course or derivation of. □ **deducible** *adj.* [Latin *deducere* (as DE-, *ducere duct-* 'lead')]

deduct /dɪˈdʌkt/ *v.tr.* (often foll. by *from*) subtract, take away, withhold (an amount, portion, etc.). [Latin (as DEDUCE)]

deductible /dɪˈdʌktɪb(ə)l/ *adj. & n.* ● *adj.* that may be deducted, esp. from tax to be paid or taxable income. ● *n. US* = EXCESS *n.* 6. □ **deductibility** /-ˈbɪlɪti/ *n.*

deduction /dɪˈdʌkʃ(ə)n/ *n.* **1 a** the act of deducting. **b** an amount deducted. **2 a** the inferring of particular instances from a general law (cf. INDUCTION). **b** a conclusion deduced. [Middle English from Old French *deduction* or Latin *deductio* (as DEDUCE)]

deductive /dɪˈdʌktɪv/ *adj.* of or reasoning by deduction. □ **deductively** *adv.* [medieval Latin *deductivus* (as DEDUCE)]

dee /diː/ *n.* **1** the letter D. **2 a** a thing shaped like this. **b** *Physics* either of two hollow semicircular electrodes in a cyclotron. [the name of the letter]

deed /diːd/ *n. & v.* ● *n.* **1** a thing done intentionally or consciously. **2** a brave, skilful, or conspicuous act. **3** actual fact or performance (*kind in word and deed*; *in deed and not in name*). **4** *Law* a written or printed document often used for a legal transfer of ownership and bearing the disposer's signature. ● *v.tr. US* convey or transfer by legal deed. [Old English *dǣd*, from Germanic: related to DO[1]]

deed-box *n.* a strongbox for keeping deeds and other documents.

deed of covenant *n. Brit.* an agreement to pay a specified amount regularly to a charity etc., enabling the recipient to recover the tax paid by the donor on an equivalent amount of income.

deed poll *n.* esp. *Brit.* a deed made and executed by one party only, esp. to change one's name (the paper being polled or cut even, not indented).

deejay /diːˈdʒeɪ, ˈdiːdʒeɪ/ *n. colloq.* a disc jockey. [representing the pronunciation of *DJ*]

deem /diːm/ *v.tr. formal* regard, consider, judge (*deem it my duty*; *was deemed sufficient*). [Old English *dēman*, from Germanic, related to DOOM]

de-emphasize /diːˈɛmfəsʌɪz/ *v.tr.* (also **-ise**) **1** remove emphasis from. **2** reduce emphasis on.

deemster /ˈdiːmstə/ *n.* a judge in the Isle of Man. [DEEM + -STER]

deep /diːp/ *adj., n., & adv.* ● *adj.* **1 a** extending far down from the top (*deep hole*; *deep water*). **b** extending far in from the surface or edge (*deep wound*; *deep plunge*; *deep shelf*; *deep border*). **2** (*predic.*) **a** extending to or lying at a specified depth (*water six feet deep*; *ankle-deep in mud*). **b** in a specified number of ranks one behind another (*soldiers drawn up six deep*). **3** situated far down or back or in (*hands deep in his pockets*). **4** coming or brought from far down or in (*deep breath*; *deep sigh*). **5** low-pitched, full-toned, not shrill (*deep voice*; *deep note*; *deep bell*). **6** intense, vivid, extreme (*deep disgrace*; *deep sleep*; *deep colour*; *deep secret*). **7** heartfelt, absorbing (*deep affection*; *deep feelings*; *deep interest*). **8** (*predic.*) fully absorbed or overwhelmed (*deep in a book*; *deep in debt*). **9** profound, penetrating, not superficial; difficult to understand (*deep thinker*; *deep thought*; *deep insight*; *deep learning*). **10** *Cricket* distant from the batsman (*deep mid-off*). **11** *Football* distant from the front line of one's team. **12** *colloq.* cunning or secretive (*a deep one*). ● *n.* **1** (prec. by *the*) *poet.* the sea. **2** a deep part of the sea. **3** an abyss, pit, or cavity. **4** (prec. by *the*) *Cricket* the position of a fielder distant from the batsman. **5** a deep state (*deep of the night*). **6** *poet.* a mysterious region of thought or feeling. ● *adv.* **1** deeply; far down or in (*dig deep*; *read deep into the night*). **2** *Sport* distant from the batsman or other focus of play. □ **go off** (or **go in off**) **the deep end** *colloq.* give way to anger or emotion. **in deep water** (or **waters**) in trouble or difficulty. **jump** (or **be thrown**) **in at the deep end** face a difficult problem, undertaking, etc., with little experience of it. □ **deeply** *adv.* **deepness** *n.* [Old English *dēop* (*adj.*), *dīope*, *dēope* (*adv.*), from Germanic: related to DIP]

deep breathing *n.* breathing with long breaths, esp. as a form of exercise.

deep-drawn *adj.* (of metal etc.) shaped by forcing through a die when cold.

deepen /ˈdiːp(ə)n/ *v.tr. & intr.* make or become deep or deeper.

deep-freeze *n. & v.* ● *n.* **1** a refrigerator in which food can be quickly frozen and kept for long periods at a very low temperature. **2** a suspension of activity. ● *v.tr.* (**-froze**, **-frozen**) freeze or store (food) in a deep-freeze.

deep-fry *v.tr.* (**-fries**, **-fried**) fry (food) in an amount of fat or oil sufficient to cover it.

deep kiss *n.* a kiss with contact between tongues.

deep-laid *adj.* (of a scheme) secret and elaborate.

deep mourning *n.* mourning expressed by wearing only black clothes.

deep-mouthed *adj.* (esp. of a dog) having a deep voice.

deep-rooted *adj.* (esp. of convictions) firmly established.

deep sea *n.* the deeper parts of the ocean (often hyphenated when *attrib.*: *deep-sea diving*).

deep-seated *adj.* (of emotion, disease, etc.) firmly established, profound.

Deep South *n.* the south-eastern region of the US regarded as embodying traditional southern culture and traditions.

deep space *n.* the regions beyond the solar system or the earth's atmosphere.

deep therapy *n.* curative treatment with short-wave X-rays of high penetrating power.

deer /dɪə/ *n.* (*pl.* same) any hoofed grazing or browsing animal of the family Cervidae, the males of which usu. have deciduous branching antlers. [Old English *dēor* 'animal, deer']

deer fly *n.* any bloodsucking fly of the genus *Chrysops*.

deer forest *n.* an extensive area of wild land reserved for the stalking of deer.

deerhound /ˈdɪəhaʊnd/ *n.* a large rough-haired greyhound.

deer-lick *n.* a spring or damp spot impregnated with salt etc. where deer come to lick.

deer mouse *n.* a mouse of the American genus *Peromyscus*, esp. *P. maniculatus.*

deerskin /ˈdɪəskɪn/ *n. & adj.* ● *n.* leather from a deer's skin. ● *adj.* made from a deer's skin.

deerstalker /ˈdɪəstɔːkə/ *n.* **1** a soft cloth cap with peaks in front and behind and ear-flaps often joined at the top. **2** *Brit.* a person who stalks deer.

de-escalate /diːˈɛskəleɪt/ *v.tr.* reduce the level or intensity of. □ **de-escalation** /-ˈleɪʃ(ə)n/ *n.*

def /dɛf/ *adj.* esp *US slang* excellent. [corruption of DEATH or shortened from DEFINITIVE]

deface /dɪˈfeɪs/ *v.tr.* **1** spoil the appearance of; disfigure. **2** make illegible. □ **defaceable** *adj.* **defacement** *n.* **defacer** *n.* [Middle English via French *défacer* from Old French *desfacier* (as DE-, FACE)]

de facto /deɪ ˈfaktəʊ, diː/ *adv. & adj.* ● *adv.* in fact, whether by right or not. ● *adj.* that exists or is such in fact (*a de facto ruler*). [Latin]

defalcate /ˈdiːfalkeɪt/ *v.intr. formal* misappropriate property in one's charge, esp. money. □ **defalcator** *n.* [medieval Latin *defalcare* 'lop' (as DE-, Latin *falx -cis* 'sickle')]

defalcation /diːfalˈkeɪʃ(ə)n/ *n. formal* **1** *Law* **a** a misappropriation of money. **b** an amount misappropriated. **2** a shortcoming. **3** defection. [Middle English from medieval Latin *defalcatio* (as DEFALCATE)]

defame /dɪˈfeɪm/ *v.tr.* attack the good reputation of; speak ill of. □ **defamation** /dɛfəˈmeɪʃ(ə)n, diːf-/ *n.* **defamatory** /dɪˈfamət(ə)ri/ *adj.* **defamer** *n.* [Middle English via Old French *diffamer* etc. from Latin *diffamare* 'spread evil report' (as DIS-, *fama* 'report')]

defat /diːˈfat/ *v.tr.* (**defatted, defatting**) remove fat or fats from.

default /dɪˈfɔːlt/ *n. & v.* ● *n.* **1** failure to fulfil an obligation, esp. to pay money, appear in a law court, etc. **2** lack, absence. **3** a pre-selected option adopted by a computer program when no alternative is specified by the user or programmer. ● *v.* **1** *intr.* fail to fulfil an obligation, esp. to pay money or to appear in a law court. **2** *tr.* declare (a party) in default and give judgement against that party. □ **by default 1** because of inaction. **2** because of a lack of opposition. **go by default** fail by default. **in default of** because of the absence of. [Middle English via Old French *defaut(e)*, from *defaillir* 'fail', from Romanic (as DE-, Latin *fallere* 'deceive'): cf. FAIL]

defaulter /dɪˈfɔːltə/ *n.* a person who defaults, esp. *Brit.* a soldier guilty of a military offence.

defeasance /dɪˈfiːz(ə)ns/ *n.* the act or process of rendering null and void. [Middle English from Old French *defesance*, from *de(s)faire* 'undo' (as DE-, *faire* 'make' from Latin *facere*)]

defeasible /dɪˈfiːzɪb(ə)l/ *adj.* **1** capable of annulment. **2** liable to forfeiture. □ **defeasibility** /-ˈbɪlɪti/ *n.* **defeasibly** *adv.* [Anglo-French (as DEFEASANCE)]

defeat /dɪˈfiːt/ *v. & n.* ● *v.tr.* **1** overcome in a battle or other contest. **2** frustrate, baffle. **3** reject (a motion etc.) by voting. **4** *Law* annul. ● *n.* the act or an instance of defeating or being defeated. [Middle English via Old French *deffait*, *desfait*, past part. of *desfaire*, from medieval Latin *disfacere* (as DIS-, Latin *facere* 'do')]

defeatism /dɪˈfiːtɪz(ə)m/ *n.* **1** an excessive readiness to accept defeat. **2** conduct conducive to this. □ **defeatist** *n. & adj.* [French *défaitisme* from *défaite* DEFEAT]

defecate /ˈdɛfɪkeɪt, ˈdiːf-/ *v.intr.* discharge faeces from the body. □ **defecation** /-ˈkeɪʃ(ə)n/ *n.* [earlier as *adj.*, = purified, from Latin *defaecare* (as DE-, *faex faecis* 'dregs')]

defect *n. & v.* ● *n.* /ˈdiːfɛkt, dɪˈfɛkt/ **1** lack of something essential or required; imperfection. **2** a shortcoming or failing. **3** a blemish. **4** the amount by which a thing falls short. ● *v.intr.* /dɪˈfɛkt/ abandon one's country, cause, etc. in favour of another. □ **defector** *n.* [Latin *defectus* from *deficere* 'desert, fail' (as DE-, *facere* 'do')]

defection /dɪˈfɛkʃ(ə)n/ *n.* the abandonment of one's country, cause, etc. for another. [Latin *defectio* (as DEFECT)]

defective /dɪˈfɛktɪv/ *adj. & n.* ● *adj.* **1** having a defect or defects; incomplete, imperfect, faulty. **2** *archaic* or *offens.* mentally handicapped. **3** (usu. foll. by *in*) lacking, deficient. **4** *Gram.* not having all the usual inflections. ● *n. archaic* or *offens.* a mentally handicapped person. □ **defectively** *adv.* **defectiveness** *n.* [Middle English from Old French *defectif -ive* or Late Latin *defectivus* (as DEFECT)]

defence /dɪˈfɛns/ *n.* (*US* **defense**) **1** the act of defending from or resisting attack. **2 a** a means of resisting attack. **b** a thing that protects. **c** the military resources of a country. **3** (in *pl.*) fortifications. **4 a** justification, vindication. **b** a speech or piece of writing used to this end. **5 a** the defendant's case in a lawsuit. **b** the counsel for the defendant. **6 a** the action or role of defending one's goal etc. against attack. **b** the players in a team who perform this role. □ **defenceless** *adj.* **defencelessly** *adv.* **defencelessness** *n.* [Middle English via Old French *defens(e)* from Late Latin *defensum, -a,* past part. of *defendere*: see DEFEND]

defenceman /dɪˈfɛnsmən/ *n.* (*US* **defenseman**) (*pl.* **-men**) (in ice hockey and lacrosse) a player in a defensive position.

defence mechanism *n.* **1** the body's reaction against disease organisms. **2** a usu. unconscious mental process to avoid conscious conflict or anxiety.

defend /dɪˈfɛnd/ *v.tr.* (also *absol.*) **1** (often foll. by *against, from*) resist an attack made on; protect (a person or thing) from harm or danger. **2** support or uphold by argument; speak or write in favour of. **3** conduct the case for (a defendant in a lawsuit). **4** compete to retain (a title) in a contest. **5** *absol.* (in various sports and games) try to prevent the opposition scoring goals, points, etc.; resist attacks. □ **defendable** *adj.* **defender** *n.* [Middle English via Old French *defendre* from Latin *defendere*: cf. OFFEND]

defendant /dɪˈfɛnd(ə)nt/ *n.* a person etc. sued or accused in a court of law. [Middle English from Old French, part. of *defendre*: see DEFEND]

defenestration /ˌdiːfɛnɪˈstreɪʃ(ə)n/ *n. formal* or *joc.* the action of throwing (esp. a person) out of a window. □ **defenestrate** /diːˈfɛnɪstreɪt/ *v.tr.* [modern Latin *defenestratio* (as DE-, Latin *fenestra* 'window')]

defense *US* var. of DEFENCE.

defenseman *US* var. of DEFENCEMAN.

defensible /dɪˈfɛnsɪb(ə)l/ *adj.* **1** justifiable; supportable by argument. **2** that can be easily defended militarily. □ **defensibility** /-ˈbɪlɪti/ *n.* **defensibly** *adv.* [Middle English from Late Latin *defensibilis* (as DEFEND)]

defensive /dɪˈfɛnsɪv/ *adj.* **1** done or intended for defence or to defend. **2** (of a person or attitude) concerned to challenge criticism. □ **on the defensive 1** expecting criticism. **2** in an attitude or position of defence. □ **defensively** *adv.* **defensiveness** *n.* [Middle English via French *défensif -ive* from medieval Latin *defensivus* (as DEFEND)]

defensive end *n. Amer. Football* either of the two defensive players who line up next to the nose tackle.

defer[1] /dɪˈfəː/ *v.tr.* (**deferred, deferring**) **1** put off to a later time; postpone. **2** *US* postpone the conscription of (a person). □ **deferment** *n.* **deferrable** *adj.* **deferral** *n.* [Middle English, originally the same as DIFFER]

defer[2] /dɪˈfəː/ *v.intr.* (**deferred, deferring**) (foll. by *to*) yield or make concessions in opinion or action. □ **deferrer** *n.* [Middle English via French *déférer* from Latin *deferre* (as DE-, *ferre* 'bring')]

deference /ˈdɛf(ə)r(ə)ns/ *n.* **1** courteous regard, respect. **2** compliance with the advice or wishes of another (*pay deference to*). □ **in deference to** out of respect for. [French *déférence* (as DEFER[2])]

deferential /dɛfəˈrɛnʃ(ə)l/ *adj.* showing deference; respectful. □ **deferentially** *adv.* [DEFERENCE, after PRUDENTIAL etc.]

deferred payment *n.* payment by instalments.

defiance /dɪˈfʌɪəns/ *n.* **1** open disobedience; bold resistance. **2** a challenge to fight or maintain a cause, assertion, etc. □ **in defiance of** disregarding; in conflict with. [Middle English from Old French (as DEFY)]

defiant /dɪˈfʌɪənt/ *adj.* **1** showing defiance. **2** openly disobedient. □ **defiantly** *adv.*

defibrillation /ˌdiːfɪbrɪˈleɪʃ(ə)n/ *n. Med.* the stopping of the fibrillation of the heart. □ **defibrillator** /diːˈfɪbrɪleɪtə/ *n.*

deficiency /dɪˈfɪʃ(ə)nsi/ *n.* (*pl.* **-ies**) **1** the state or condition of being deficient. **2** (usu. foll. by *of*) a lack or shortage. **3** a thing lacking. **4** the amount by which a thing, esp. revenue, falls short.

deficiency disease *n.* a disease caused by the lack of some essential or important element in the diet.

deficient /dɪˈfɪʃ(ə)nt/ *adj.* **1** (usu. foll. by *in*) incomplete; not having enough of a specified quality or ingredient. **2** insufficient in quantity, force, etc. **3** (in full **mentally deficient**) *archaic* or *offens.* having a mental handicap. □ **deficiently** *adv.* [Latin *deficiens*, part. of *deficere* (as DEFECT)]

deficit /ˈdɛfɪsɪt, ˈdiː-/ *n.* **1** the amount by which a thing (esp. a sum of money) is too small. **2** an excess of liabilities over assets in a given period, esp. a financial year (opp. SURPLUS *n.* 2a). [French *déficit* from Latin *deficit*, 3rd sing. present of *deficere* (as DEFECT)]

deficit financing *n.* financing of (esp. state) spending by borrowing.

deficit spending *n.* spending (esp. by the State), financed by borrowing.

defier /dɪˈfʌɪə/ *n.* a person who defies.

defilade /dɛfɪˈleɪd/ *v.* & *n.* ● *v.tr.* secure (a fortification) against enfilading fire. ● *n.* this precaution or arrangement. [DEFILE[2] + -ADE[1]]

defile[1] /dɪˈfʌɪl/ *v.tr.* **1** make dirty; pollute, befoul. **2** corrupt. **3** desecrate, profane. **4** *euphem.* deprive (esp. a woman) of virginity; rape. **5** make ceremonially unclean. □ **defilement** *n.* **defiler** *n.* [Middle English *defoul* from Old French *defouler* 'trample down, outrage' (as DE-, *fouler* 'tread, trample'), influenced by obsolete *befile* from Old English *befȳlan* (BE-, *fūl* FOUL)]

defile[2] /dɪˈfʌɪl/ *n.* & *v.* ● *n.* /also ˈdiːfʌɪl/ **1** a narrow way through which troops can march only in file. **2** a gorge. ● *v.intr.* march in file. [French *défiler* and *défilé*, past part. (as DE-, FILE[2])]

define /dɪˈfʌɪn/ *v.tr.* **1** give the exact meaning of (a word etc.). **2** describe or explain the scope of (*define one's position*). **3** make clear, esp. in outline (*well-defined image*). **4** mark out the boundary or limits of. **5** (of properties) make up the total character of. □ **definable** *adj.* **definer** *n.* [Middle English from Old French *definer*, ultimately from Latin *definire* (as DE-, *finire* 'finish', from *finis* 'end')]

definite /ˈdɛfɪnɪt/ *adj.* & *n.* ● *adj.* **1** having exact and discernible limits. **2** clear and distinct; not vague. **3** certain, sure (*a definite offer*; *are you definite he was there?*). ● *n.* a definite thing, esp. *Gram.* a noun denoting a definite thing or object. □ **definiteness** *n.* [Latin *definitus*, past part. of *definire* (as DEFINE)]

■ **Usage** See Usage Note at DEFINITIVE.

definite article *n. Gram.* the word (*the* in English) preceding a noun and implying a specific or known instance (as in *the book on the table*; *the art of government*; *the famous public school in Berkshire*).

definite integral *n. Math.* an integral expressed as the difference between the values of the integral at specified upper and lower limits of the independent variable.

definitely /ˈdɛfɪnɪtli/ *adv.* & *int.* ● *adv.* **1** in a definite manner. **2** certainly; without doubt (*they were definitely there*). ● *int. colloq.* yes, certainly.

definition /dɛfɪˈnɪʃ(ə)n/ *n.* **1 a** the act or process of defining. **b** a statement of the meaning of a word or the nature of a thing. **2 a** the degree of distinctness in outline of an object or image (esp. of an image produced by a lens or shown in a photograph or on a cinema or television screen). **b** making or being distinct in outline. □ **definitional** *adj.* **definitionally** *adv.* [Middle English via Old French from Latin *definitio* (as DEFINE)]

definitive /dɪˈfɪnɪtɪv/ *adj.* & *n.* ● *adj.* **1** (of an answer, treaty, verdict, etc.) decisive, unconditional, final. **2** (of an edition of a book etc.) most authoritative. **3** (of a postage stamp) for permanent use, not special or commemorative etc. ● *n.* a definitive postage stamp. □ **definitively** *adv.* [Middle English via Old French *definitif -ive* from Latin *definitivus* (as DEFINE)]

■ **Usage** In sense 1, *definitive* is often confused with *definite*, which does not have connotations of authority and conclusiveness: *a definite no* is a firm refusal, whereas *a definitive no* is an authoritative judgement or decision that something is not the case.

deflagrate /ˈdɛfləgreɪt/ *v.tr.* & *intr.* burn away with sudden flame. □ **deflagration** /-ˈreɪʃ(ə)n/ *n.* **deflagrator** *n.* [Latin *deflagrare* (as DE-, *flagrare* 'blaze')]

deflate /dɪˈfleɪt/ *v.* **1 a** *tr.* let air or gas out of (a tyre, balloon, etc.). **b** *intr.* be emptied of air or gas. **2 a** *tr.* cause to lose confidence or conceit. **b** *intr.* lose confidence. **3** *Econ.* **a** *tr.* subject (a currency or economy) to deflation. **b** *intr.* pursue a policy of deflation. **4** *tr.* reduce the importance of, depreciate. □ **deflator** *n.* [DE- + INFLATE]

deflation /dɪˈfleɪʃ(ə)n/ *n.* **1** the act or process of deflating or being deflated. **2** *Econ.* reduction of the amount of money in circulation to increase its value as a measure against inflation. **3** *Geol.* the removal of particles of rock etc. by the wind. □ **deflationary** *adj.* **deflationist** *n.* & *adj.*

deflect /dɪˈflɛkt/ *v.* **1** *tr.* & *intr.* bend or turn aside from a straight course or intended purpose. **2** (often foll. by *from*) **a** *tr.* cause to deviate. **b** *intr.* deviate. [Latin *deflectere* (as DE-, *flectere flex-* 'bend')]

deflection /dɪˈflɛkʃ(ə)n/ *n.* (also **deflexion**) **1** the act or process of deflecting or being deflected. **2** a lateral bend or turn; a deviation. **3** *Physics* the displacement of a pointer on an instrument from its zero position. [Late Latin *deflexio* (as DEFLECT)]

deflector /dɪˈflɛktə/ *n.* a thing that deflects, esp. a device for deflecting a flow of air etc.

defloration /diːflɔːˈreɪʃ(ə)n/ *n.* deflowering. [Middle English from Old French or from Late Latin *defloratio* (as DEFLOWER)]

deflower /diːˈflaʊə/ *v.tr.* **1** deprive (esp. a woman) of virginity. **2** ravage, spoil. **3** strip of flowers. [Middle English from Old French *deflourer*, *des-*, ultimately from Late Latin *deflorare* (as DE-, Latin *flos floris* 'flower')]

defocus /diːˈfəʊkəs/ *v.tr.* & *intr.* (**defocused**, **defocusing** or **defocussed**, **defocussing**) put or go out of focus.

defoliate /diːˈfəʊlɪeɪt/ *v.tr.* remove leaves from, esp. as a military tactic. □ **defoliant** *n.* & *adj.* **defoliation** /-ˈeɪʃ(ə)n/ *n.* **defoliator** *n.* [Late Latin *defoliare*, from *folium* 'leaf']

deforest /diːˈfɒrɪst/ *v.tr.* clear of forests or trees. □ **deforestation** /-ˈsteɪʃ(ə)n/ *n.*

deform /dɪˈfɔːm/ *v.* **1** *tr.* make ugly, deface. **2** *tr.* put out of shape, misshape. **3** *intr.* undergo deformation; be deformed. □ **deformable** *adj.* [Middle English via Old French *deformer* etc. from medieval Latin *difformare*, ultimately from Latin *deformare* (as DE-, *formare* from *forma* 'shape')]

deformation /diːfɔːˈmeɪʃ(ə)n/ *n.* **1** disfigurement. **2** *Physics* **a** (often foll. by *of*) change in shape. **b** a quantity representing the amount of this change. **3** an altered form of a word (e.g. *dang* for *damn*). □ **deformational** *adj.* [Middle English from Old French *deformation* or Latin *deformatio* (as DEFORM)]

deformed /dɪˈfɔːmd/ *adj.* (of a person or limb) misshapen.

deformity /dɪˈfɔːmɪti/ *n.* (*pl.* **-ies**) **1** the state of being deformed; ugliness, disfigurement. **2** a malformation, esp. of body or limb. **3** a moral defect; depravity. [Middle English via Old French *deformité* etc. from Latin *deformitas -tatis*, from *deformis* (as DE-, *forma* 'shape')]

defraud /dɪ'frɔːd/ *v.tr.* (often foll. by *of*) cheat by fraud. □ **defrauder** *n.* [Middle English from Old French *defrauder* or Latin *defraudare* (as DE-, FRAUD)]

defray /dɪ'freɪ/ *v.tr.* provide money to pay (a cost or expense). □ **defrayable** *adj.* **defrayal** *n.* **defrayment** *n.* [French *défrayer* (as DE-, obsolete *frai(t)* 'cost', from medieval Latin *fredum, -us* 'fine for breach of the peace')]

defrock /diː'frɒk/ *v.tr.* deprive (a person, esp. a priest) of ecclesiastical status. [French *défroquer* (as DE-, FROCK)]

defrost /diː'frɒst/ *v.* **1** *tr.* **a** free (the interior of a refrigerator) of excess frost, usu. by turning it off for a period. **b** remove frost or ice from (esp. the windscreen of a motor vehicle). **2** *tr.* unfreeze (frozen food). **3** *intr.* become unfrozen. □ **defroster** *n.*

deft /dɛft/ *adj.* neatly skilful or dexterous; adroit. □ **deftly** *adv.* **deftness** *n.* [Middle English, variant of DAFT in obsolete sense 'meek']

defunct /dɪ'fʌŋ(k)t/ *adj.* **1** no longer existing. **2** no longer used or in fashion. **3** dead or extinct. [Latin *defunctus* 'dead', past part. of *defungi* (as DE-, *fungi* 'perform')]

defuse /diː'fjuːz/ *v.tr.* **1** remove the fuse from (an explosive device). **2** reduce the tension or potential danger in (a crisis, difficulty, etc.).

defy /dɪ'fʌɪ/ *v.tr.* (**-ies**, **-ied**) **1** resist openly; refuse to obey. **2** (of a thing) present insuperable obstacles to (*defies solution*). **3** (foll. by *to* + infin.) challenge (a person) to do or prove something. **4** *archaic* challenge to combat. [Middle English via Old French *defier* from Romanic (as DIS-, Latin *fidus* 'faithful')]

deg. *abbr.* degree.

dégagé /deɪ'gɑːʒeɪ/ *adj.* (*fem.* **dégagée**) relaxed, unconcerned, unconstrained. [French, past part. of *dégager* 'set free']

degas /diː'gas/ *v.tr.* (**degassed**, **degassing**) remove unwanted gas from.

degauss /diː'gaʊs/ *v.tr.* neutralize the magnetism in (a thing) by encircling it with a current-carrying conductor. □ **degausser** *n.* [DE- + GAUSS]

degenerate *adj., n., & v.* ● *adj.* /dɪ'dʒɛn(ə)rət/ **1** having lost the qualities that are normal and desirable or proper to its kind; fallen from former excellence. **2** *Biol.* having a simplified structure. ● *n.* /dɪ'dʒɛn(ə)rət/ a degenerate person or animal. ● *v.intr.* /dɪ'dʒɛnəreɪt/ become degenerate. □ **degeneracy** *n.* **degenerately** *adv.* [Latin *degeneratus*, past part. of *degenerare* (as DE-, *genus -eris* 'race')]

degeneration /dɪˌdʒɛnə'reɪʃ(ə)n/ *n.* **1** **a** the process of becoming degenerate. **b** the state of being degenerate. **2** *Med.* morbid deterioration of tissue or change in its structure. [Middle English from French *dégéneration* or from Late Latin *degeneratio* (as DEGENERATE)]

degenerative /dɪ'dʒɛn(ə)rətɪv/ *adj.* **1** of or tending to degeneration. **2** (of disease) characterized by progressive often irreversible deterioration.

degrade /dɪ'greɪd/ *v.* **1** *tr.* reduce to a lower rank, esp. as a punishment. **2** *tr.* bring into dishonour or contempt. **3** *tr.* lower in character or quality; debase (*degraded water quality*). **4** *tr. Chem.* reduce to a simpler molecular structure. **5** *tr. Physics* reduce (energy) to a less convertible form. **6** *tr. Geol.* wear down (rocks etc.) by disintegration. **7** *intr.* degenerate. **8** *intr. Chem.* disintegrate. □ **degradable** *adj.* **degradability** /-ə'bɪlɪti/ *n.* **degradation** /dɛgrə'deɪʃ(ə)n/ *n.* **degradative** /-dətɪv/ *adj.* **degrader** *n.* [Middle English via Old French *degrader* from ecclesiastical Latin *degradare* (as DE-, Latin *gradus* 'step')]

degrading /dɪ'greɪdɪŋ/ *adj.* humiliating; causing a loss of self-respect. □ **degradingly** *adv.*

degrease /diː'griːs/ *v.tr.* remove unwanted grease or fat from. □ **degreaser** *n.*

degree /dɪ'griː/ *n.* **1** a stage in an ascending or descending scale, series, or process. **2** a stage in intensity or amount (*to a high degree; in some degree*). **3** relative condition (*each is good in its degree*). **4** *Math.* a unit of measurement of angles, one-ninetieth of a right angle or the angle subtended by one-three-hundred-and-sixtieth of the circumference of a circle (symbol° as in *45°*). **5** *Physics* a unit in a scale of temperature, hardness, etc. (abbr.: **deg.**) (or omitted in the Kelvin scale of temperature). **6** *Med.* each of a set of grades (usu. three) used to classify burns according to their severity (often *attrib.*: *third-degree burns*). **7** an academic rank conferred by a college or university after examination or after completion of a course, or conferred as an honour on a distinguished person. **8** a grade of crime or criminality (*murder in the first degree*). **9** a step in direct genealogical descent. **10** social or official rank. **11** *Math.* the highest power of unknowns or variables in an equation etc. (*equation of the third degree*). **12** a masonic rank. **13** a thing placed like a step in a series; a tier or row. **14** *Mus.* the classification of a note by its position in the scale. □ **by degrees** a little at a time; gradually. **to a degree** *colloq.* considerably. □ **degreeless** *adj.* [Middle English via Old French *degré* from Romanic (as DE-, Latin *gradus* 'step')]

degree of freedom *n.* **1** *Physics* the independent direction in which motion can occur. **2** *Chem.* the number of independent factors required to specify a system at equilibrium. **3** *Statistics* the number of independent values or quantities which can be assigned to a statistical distribution.

degrees of comparison see COMPARISON.

degressive /dɪ'grɛsɪv/ *adj.* **1** (of taxation) at successively lower rates on low amounts. **2** reducing in amount. [Latin *degredi* (as DE-, *gradi* 'walk')]

de haut en bas /də ˌəʊt ɒ̃ 'bɑː, French də ot ɑ̃ bɑ/ *adv.* in a condescending or superior manner. [French, = from above to below]

dehisce /dɪ'hɪs/ *v.intr.* gape or burst open (esp. of a pod or seed vessel or of a cut or wound). □ **dehiscence** *n.* **dehiscent** *adj.* [Latin *dehiscere* (as DE-, *hiscere* inceptive of *hiare* 'gape')]

dehorn /diː'hɔːn/ *v.tr.* remove the horns from (an animal).

dehumanize /diː'hjuːmənʌɪz/ *v.tr.* (also **-ise**) **1** deprive of human characteristics. **2** make impersonal or machine-like. □ **dehumanization** /-'zeɪʃ(ə)n/ *n.*

dehumidify /diːhjuː'mɪdɪfʌɪ/ *v.tr.* (**-ies**, **-ied**) reduce the degree of humidity of; remove moisture from (a gas, esp. air). □ **dehumidification** /-fɪ'keɪʃ(ə)n/ *n.* **dehumidifier** *n.*

dehydrate /diː'hʌɪdreɪt/ *v.* **1** *tr.* **a** remove water from (esp. foods for preservation and storage in bulk). **b** make dry, esp. make (the body) deficient in water. **c** render lifeless or uninteresting. **2** *intr.* lose water. □ **dehydration** /-'dreɪʃ(ə)n/ *n.* **dehydrator** *n.*

dehydrogenate /diːhʌɪ'drɒdʒəneɪt/ *v.tr. Chem.* remove a hydrogen atom or atoms from (a compound). □ **dehydrogenation** /-'neɪʃ(ə)n/ *n.*

de-ice /diː'ʌɪs/ *v.tr.* **1** remove ice from. **2** prevent the formation of ice on.

de-icer /diː'ʌɪsə/ *n.* a device or substance for de-icing, esp. a windscreen or ice on an aircraft.

deicide /'diːɪsʌɪd, 'deɪɪ-/ *n.* **1** the killer of a god. **2** the killing of a god. [ecclesiastical Latin *deicida*, from Latin *deus* 'god' + -CIDE]

deictic /'dʌɪktɪk/ *adj. & n. Philol. & Gram.* ● *adj.* pointing, demonstrative. ● *n.* a deictic word. [Greek *deiktikos* via *deiktos* 'capable of proof' from *deiknumi* 'show']

deify /'diːɪfʌɪ, 'deɪɪ-/ *v.tr.* (**-ies**, **-ied**) **1** make a god of. **2** regard or worship as a god. □ **deification** /-fɪ'keɪʃ(ə)n/

n. [Middle English via Old French *deifier* from ecclesiastical Latin *deificare*, from *deus* 'god']

deign /deɪn/ *v.* **1** *intr.* (foll. by *to* + infin.) think fit, condescend. **2** *tr.* (usu. with *neg.*) *archaic* condescend to give (an answer etc.). [Middle English via Old French *degnier*, *deigner*, *daigner* from Latin *dignare*, *-ari* 'deem worthy', from *dignus* 'worthy']

Dei gratia /ˌdeɪɪ ˈgrɑːtɪə, -ʃɪə/ *adv.* by the grace of God. [Latin]

de-industrialization /ˌdiːɪndʌstrɪəlʌɪˈzeɪʃ(ə)n/ *n.* (also **de-industrialisation**) the process of removing industry from a place.

deinothere /ˈdʌɪnə(ʊ)θɪə/ *n.* (also **dinothere**) an extinct elephant-like animal of the genus *Deinotherium*, having downward curving tusks. [modern Latin *dinotherium*, from Greek *deinos* 'terrible' + *thērion* 'wild beast']

deinstitutionalize /ˈdiːɪnstɪˈtjuːʃ(ə)n(ə)lʌɪz/ *v.tr.* (also **-ise**) (usu. as **deinstitutionalized** *adj.*) **1** remove from an institution or from the effects of institutional life. **2** make less institutional; reorganize on more individual lines. ▫ **deinstitutionalization** /-ˈzeɪʃ(ə)n/ *n.*

deionize /diːˈʌɪənʌɪz/ *v.tr.* (also **-ise**) remove the ions or ionic constituents from (water, air, etc.). ▫ **deionization** /-ˈzeɪʃ(ə)n/ *n.* **deionizer** *n.*

deism /ˈdiːɪz(ə)m, ˈdeɪɪ-/ *n.* belief in the existence of a supreme being arising from reason rather than revelation (cf. THEISM). ▫ **deist** *n.* **deistic** /-ˈɪstɪk/ *adj.* **deistical** /-ˈɪstɪk(ə)l/ *adj.* [Latin *deus* 'god' + -ISM]

deity /ˈdiːɪti, ˈdeɪɪ-/ *n.* (*pl.* **-ies**) **1** a god or goddess. **2** divine status, quality, or nature. **3** (**the Deity**) the Creator, God. [Middle English via Old French *deité* from ecclesiastical Latin *deitas -tatis*, translation of Greek *theotēs* from *theos* 'god']

déjà vu /deɪʒɑː ˈvuː/ *n.* (also **deja vu**) **1** *Psychol.* an illusory feeling of having already experienced a present situation. **2** tedious familiarity. [French, = already seen]

deject /dɪˈdʒɛkt/ *v.tr.* (usu. as **dejected** *adj.*) make sad or dispirited; depress. ▫ **dejectedly** *adv.* [Middle English from Latin *dejicere* (DE-, *jacĕre* 'throw')]

dejection /dɪˈdʒɛkʃ(ə)n/ *n.* a dejected state; low spirits. [Middle English from Latin *dejectio* (as DEJECT)]

de jure /diː ˈdʒʊəri, deɪ ˈjʊəreɪ/ *adj.* & *adv.* ● *adj.* rightful. ● *adv.* rightfully; by right. [Latin]

dekko /ˈdɛkəʊ/ *n.* (*pl.* **-os**) *Brit. slang* a look or glance (*took a quick dekko*). [Hindi *dekho*, imperative of *dekhnā* 'look']

Del. *abbr.* Delaware.

delate /dɪˈleɪt/ *v.tr. archaic* **1** inform against; impeach (a person). **2** report (an offence). ▫ **delation** /-ˈleɪʃ(ə)n/ *n.* **delator** *n.* [Latin *delat-* (as DE-, *lat-*, past part. stem of *ferre* 'carry')]

delay /dɪˈleɪ/ *v.* & *n.* ● *v.* **1** *tr.* postpone; defer. **2** *tr.* make late (*was delayed at the traffic lights*). **3** *intr.* loiter; be late (*don't delay!*). ● *n.* **1** the act or an instance of delaying; the process of being delayed. **2** time lost by inaction or the inability to proceed. **3** a hindrance. ▫ **delayer** *n.* [Middle English from Old French *delayer* (*v.*), *delai* (*n.*), probably from *des-* DIS- + *laier* 'leave': see RELAY[1]]

delayed action *n.* (hyphenated when *attrib.*) the operation of something, esp. a bomb or camera, some time after being primed or set.

delaying action *n.* **1** *Mil.* an action fought to delay the advance of an enemy. **2** any action taken to delay an unwelcome event or process.

delay line *n.* a device producing a desired delay in the transmission of a signal.

dele /ˈdiːli/ *v.* & *n. Printing* ● *v.tr.* (**deled**, **deleing**) delete or mark for deletion (a letter, word, etc., struck out of a text). ● *n.* a sign marking something to be deleted; a deletion. [Latin, imperative of *delēre*: see DELETE]

delectable /dɪˈlɛktəb(ə)l/ *adj.* **1** *literary* or *joc.* delightful, lovely. **2** (of food) delicious. ▫ **delectability** /-ˈbɪlɪti/ *n.* **delectably** *adv.* [Middle English via Old French from Latin *delectabilis*, from *delectare* DELIGHT]

delectation /diːlɛkˈteɪʃ(ə)n/ *n. literary* pleasure, enjoyment (*sang for his delectation*). [Middle English from Old French (as DELECTABLE)]

delegacy /ˈdɛlɪgəsi/ *n.* (*pl.* **-ies**) **1** a system of delegating. **2 a** an appointment as a delegate. **b** a body of delegates; a delegation.

delegate *n.* & *v.* ● *n.* /ˈdɛlɪgət/ **1** an elected representative sent to a conference. **2** a member of a committee. **3** a member of a deputation. ● *v.tr.* /ˈdɛlɪgeɪt/ **1** (often foll. by *to*) **a** commit (authority, power, etc.) to an agent or deputy. **b** entrust (a task) to another person. **2** send or authorize (a person) as a representative; depute. ▫ **delegable** /ˈdɛlɪgəb(ə)l/ *adj.* **delegator** *n.* [Middle English from Latin *delegatus* (as DE-, *legare* 'depute')]

delegation /dɛlɪˈgeɪʃ(ə)n/ *n.* **1** a body of delegates; a deputation. **2** the act or process of delegating or being delegated. [Latin *delegatio* (as DELEGATE)]

delete /dɪˈliːt/ *v.tr.* remove or obliterate (written or printed matter), esp. by striking out. ▫ **deletion** /-ˈliːʃ(ə)n/ *n.* [Latin *delēre delet-* 'efface']

deleterious /dɛlɪˈtɪərɪəs/ *adj.* harmful (to the mind or body). ▫ **deleteriously** *adv.* [medieval Latin *deleterius* from Greek *dēlētērios* 'noxious']

delft /dɛlft/ *n.* (also **delftware** /ˈdɛlftwɛː/) **1** glazed, usu. blue and white, earthenware, made in Delft in Holland. **2** similar earthenware made in England.

deli /ˈdɛli/ *n.* (*pl.* **delis**) *colloq.* = DELICATESSEN. [abbreviation]

deliberate *adj.* & *v.* ● *adj.* /dɪˈlɪb(ə)rət/ **1 a** intentional (*a deliberate foul*). **b** fully considered; not impulsive (*made a deliberate choice*). **2** slow in deciding; cautious (*a ponderous and deliberate mind*). **3** (of movement etc.) leisurely and unhurried. ● *v.* /dɪˈlɪbəreɪt/ **1** *intr.* think carefully; take counsel (*the jury deliberated for an hour*). **2** *tr.* consider, discuss carefully (*deliberated the question*). ▫ **deliberately** /dɪˈlɪb(ə)rətli/ *adv.* **deliberateness** /dɪˈlɪb(ə)rətnɪs/ *n.* **deliberator** /dɪˈlɪbəreɪtə/ *n.* [Latin *deliberatus*, past part. of *deliberare* (as DE-, *librare* 'weigh' from *libra* 'balance')]

deliberation /dɪˌlɪbəˈreɪʃ(ə)n/ *n.* **1** careful consideration. **2 a** the discussion of reasons for and against. **b** a debate or discussion. **3 a** caution and care. **b** (of movement) slowness or ponderousness. [Middle English via Old French from Latin *deliberatio -onis* (as DELIBERATE)]

deliberative /dɪˈlɪb(ə)rətɪv/ *adj.* of, or appointed for the purpose of, deliberation or debate (*a deliberative assembly*). ▫ **deliberatively** *adv.* **deliberativeness** *n.* [French *délibératif -ive* or Latin *deliberativus* (as DELIBERATE)]

delicacy /ˈdɛlɪkəsi/ *n.* (*pl.* **-ies**) **1** (esp. in craftsmanship or artistic or natural beauty) fineness or intricacy of structure or texture; gracefulness. **2** susceptibility to injury or disease; weakness. **3** the quality of requiring discretion or sensitivity (*a situation of some delicacy*). **4** a choice or expensive food. **5 a** consideration for the feelings of others. **b** avoidance of immodesty or vulgarity. **6** (esp. in a person, a sense, or an instrument) accuracy of perception; sensitiveness. [Middle English, from DELICATE + -ACY]

delicate /ˈdɛlɪkət/ *adj.* **1 a** fine in texture or structure; soft, slender, or slight. **b** of intricate or exquisite quality or workmanship. **c** (of colour) subtle or subdued; not bright. **d** subtle, hard to appreciate. **2** (of a person) easily injured; susceptible to illness. **3 a** requiring sensitive or careful handling; tricky (*a delicate situation*). **b** (of an instrument) highly sensitive. **4** deft (*a delicate touch*). **5** (of a person) avoiding the vulgar or offensive. **6** (esp. of actions) considerate. **7** (of food) dainty; suitable for an invalid. ▫ **in a delicate condition** *archaic* pregnant. ▫ **delicately** *adv.* **delicateness** *n.* [Middle English from Old French *delicat* or Latin *delicatus*, of unknown origin]

delicatessen /ˌdɛlɪkəˈtɛs(ə)n/ *n.* **1** a shop selling cooked meats, cheeses, and unusual or foreign prepared foods. **2** (often *attrib.*) such foods collectively (*a delicatessen counter*). [German *Delikatessen* or Dutch *delicatessen* from French *délicatesse*, from *délicat* (as DELICATE)]

delicious /dɪˈlɪʃəs/ *adj.* **1** highly delightful and enjoyable to the taste or sense of smell. **2** (of a joke etc.) very witty or much appreciated. □ **deliciously** *adv.* **deliciousness** *n.* [Middle English via Old French and Late Latin *deliciosus* from Latin *deliciae* 'delight']

delict /dɪˈlɪkt, ˈdiːlɪkt/ *n. archaic* a violation of the law; an offence. [Latin *delictum*, neut. past part. of *delinquere* 'offend' (as DE-, *linquere* 'leave')]

delight /dɪˈlʌɪt/ *v. & n.* ● *v.* **1** *tr.* (often foll. by *with*, or *that* + clause, or *to* + infin.) please greatly (*the gift delighted them; was delighted that you won; delighted with the result; am delighted to help*). **2** *intr.* (often foll. by *in*, or *to* + infin.) take great pleasure; be highly pleased (*delighted in her success; they delighted to help*). ● *n.* **1** great pleasure. **2** something giving pleasure (*her singing is a delight*). □ **delighted** *adj.* **delightedly** *adv.* [Middle English via Old French *delitier*, *delit*, from Latin *delectare*, frequentative of *delicere*: spelling with *-gh-* influenced by *light* etc.]

delightful /dɪˈlʌɪtfʊl, -f(ə)l/ *adj.* causing delight; very pleasant, charming. □ **delightfully** *adv.* **delightfulness** *n.*

Delilah /dɪˈlʌɪlə/ *n.* a seductive and wily temptress. [*Delilah*, betrayer of Samson (Judges 16)]

delimit /dɪˈlɪmɪt/ *v.tr.* (**delimited**, **delimiting**) **1** determine the limits of. **2** fix the territorial boundary of. □ **delimitation** /-ˈteɪʃ(ə)n/ *n.* **delimiter** *n.* [French *délimiter* from Latin *delimitare* (as DE-, *limitare* from *limes -itis* 'boundary')]

delimitate /dɪˈlɪmɪteɪt/ *v.tr.* = DELIMIT.

delineate /dɪˈlɪnɪeɪt/ *v.tr.* portray by drawing etc. or in words (*delineated her character*). □ **delineation** /-ˈeɪʃ(ə)n/ *n.* **delineator** *n.* [Latin *delineare delineat-* (as DE-, *lineare* from *linea* 'line')]

delinquency /dɪˈlɪŋkw(ə)nsi/ *n.* (*pl.* **-ies**) **1 a** minor crime in general, esp. that of young people (*juvenile delinquency*). **b** a crime, usu. not of a serious kind; a misdeed. **2** wickedness (*moral delinquency; an act of delinquency*). **3** neglect of one's duty. [ecclesiastical Latin *delinquentia* from Latin *delinquens*, part. of *delinquere* (as DELICT)]

delinquent /dɪˈlɪŋkw(ə)nt/ *n. & adj.* ● *n.* an offender (*juvenile delinquent*). ● *adj.* **1** guilty of a minor crime or a misdeed. **2** failing in one's duty. **3** *US* in arrears. □ **delinquently** *adv.*

deliquesce /dɛlɪˈkwɛs/ *v.intr.* **1** become liquid, melt. **2** *Chem.* dissolve in water absorbed from the air. □ **deliquescence** *n.* **deliquescent** *adj.* [Latin *deliquescere* (as DE-, *liquescere*, inceptive of *liquēre* 'be liquid')]

delirious /dɪˈlɪrɪəs/ *adj.* **1** affected with delirium; temporarily or apparently mad; raving. **2** wildly excited, ecstatic. **3** (of behaviour) betraying delirium or ecstasy. □ **deliriously** *adv.*

delirium /dɪˈlɪrɪəm/ *n.* **1** an acutely disordered state of mind involving incoherent speech, hallucinations, and frenzied excitement, occurring in metabolic disorders, intoxication, fever, etc. **2** great excitement, ecstasy. [Latin, from *delirare* 'be deranged' (as DE-, *lira* 'ridge between furrows')]

delirium tremens /ˈtriːmɛnz, ˈtrɛ-/ *n.* a psychosis of chronic alcoholism involving tremors and hallucinations. [Latin, = trembling delirium]

deliver /dɪˈlɪvə/ *v.tr.* **1 a** distribute (letters, parcels, ordered goods, etc.) to the addressee or the purchaser. **b** (often foll. by *to*) hand over (*delivered the boy safely to his teacher*). **2** (often foll. by *from*) save, rescue, or set free (*delivered him from his enemies*). **3 a** give birth to (*delivered a girl*). **b** (in *passive*; often foll. by *of*) give birth (*was delivered of a child*). **c** assist at the birth of (*delivered six babies that week*). **d** assist in giving birth (*delivered the patient successfully*). **4 a** (often *refl.*) utter or recite (an opinion, a speech, etc.) (*delivered himself of the observation; delivered the sermon well*). **b** (of a judge) pronounce (a judgement). **5** (often foll. by *up, over*) abandon; surrender; hand over (*delivered his soul up to God*). **6** present or render (an account). **7** launch or aim (a blow, a ball, or an attack). **8** *Law* hand over formally (esp. a sealed deed to a grantee). **9** (*absol.*) *colloq.* = *deliver the goods*. **10** *US* cause (voters etc.) to support a candidate. □ **deliver the goods** *colloq.* carry out one's part of an agreement. □ **deliverable** *adj. & n.* **deliverer** *n.* [Middle English via Old French *delivrer* from Gallo-Roman (as DE-, LIBERATE)]

deliverance /dɪˈlɪv(ə)r(ə)ns/ *n.* **1 a** the act or an instance of rescuing; the process of being rescued. **b** a rescue. **2** a formally expressed opinion. [Middle English from Old French *delivrance* (as DELIVER)]

delivery /dɪˈlɪv(ə)ri/ *n.* (*pl.* **-ies**) **1 a** the delivering of letters etc. **b** a regular distribution of letters etc. (*two deliveries a day*). **c** something delivered. **2 a** the process of childbirth. **b** an act of this. **3** deliverance. **4 a** an act of pitching, esp. of a cricket ball. **b** the style of such an act (*a good delivery*). **5** the act of giving or surrendering (*delivery of the town to the enemy*). **6 a** the uttering of a speech etc. **b** the manner or style of such a delivery (*a measured delivery*). **7** *Law* **a** the formal handing over of property. **b** the transfer of a deed to a grantee or a third party. □ **take delivery of** receive (something purchased). [Middle English from Anglo-French *delivree*, fem. past part. of *delivrer* (as DELIVER)]

dell /dɛl/ *n.* a small usu. wooded hollow or valley. [Old English from Germanic]

Della Cruscan /dɛlə ˈkrʌskən/ *adj. & n.* ● *adj.* **1** of or relating to the Academy della Crusca in Florence, concerned with the purity of the Italian language. **2** of or concerning a late 18th-c. school of English poets with an artificial style. ● *n.* a member of the Academy della Crusca or the late 18th-c. school of English poets. [Italian (*Accademia*) *della Crusca* '(Academy) of the bran' (with reference to sifting)]

delocalize /diːˈləʊk(ə)lʌɪz/ *v.tr.* (also **-ise**) **1 a** detach or remove (a thing) from its place. **b** not limit to a particular location. **2** (as **delocalized** *adj.*) *Chem.* (of electrons) shared among more than two atoms in a molecule. □ **delocalization** /-ˈzeɪʃ(ə)n/ *n.*

delouse /diːˈlaʊs/ *v.tr.* rid (a person or animal) of lice.

Delphic /ˈdɛlfɪk/ *adj.* (also **Delphian** /-fɪən/) **1** (of an utterance, prophecy, etc.) obscure, ambiguous, or enigmatic. **2** of or concerning the ancient Greek oracle at Delphi.

delphinium /dɛlˈfɪnɪəm/ *n.* (*pl.* **delphiniums**) any garden plant of the genus *Delphinium* (buttercup family), with tall spikes of usu. blue flowers. [modern Latin from Greek *delphinion* 'larkspur', from *delphin* 'dolphin' (from the shape of the spur)]

delphinoid /ˈdɛlfɪnɔɪd/ *adj. & n.* ● *adj.* **1** *Zool.* of or relating to the cetacean division Delphinoidea, which includes dolphins, porpoises, grampuses, etc. **2** dolphin-like. ● *n.* **1** *Zool.* a member of the division Delphinoidea. **2** a dolphin-like animal. [Greek *delphinoeidēs* from *delphin* 'dolphin']

delta /ˈdɛltə/ *n.* **1** a triangular tract of deposited earth, alluvium, etc., at the mouth of a river, formed by its diverging outlets. **2 a** the fourth letter of the Greek alphabet (Δ, δ). **b** *Brit.* a fourth-class mark given for a piece of work or in an examination. **3** (**Delta**) *Astron.* the fourth (usu. fourth-brightest) star in a constellation (foll. by Latin genitive: *Delta Cephei*). **4** *Math.* an increment of a variable. □ **deltaic** /dɛlˈteɪɪk/ *adj.* [Middle English via Greek from Phoenician *daleth*]

delta connection *n.* a triangular arrangement of three-phase windings with circuit wire from each angle.

delta rays *n.pl.* rays of low penetrative power consisting of slow electrons ejected from an atom by the impact of ionizing radiation.

delta rhythm *n.* (also **delta waves**) low-frequency electrical activity of the brain during sleep.

delta wing *n.* the triangular swept-back wing of an aircraft.

deltiology /dɛltɪˈɒlədʒi/ *n.* the collecting and study of postcards. ◻ **deltiologist** *n.* [Greek *deltion*, diminutive of *deltos* 'writing-tablet' + -LOGY]

deltoid /ˈdɛltɔɪd/ *adj. & n.* ● *adj.* triangular; like a river delta. ● *n.* (in full **deltoid muscle**) a thick triangular muscle covering the shoulder joint and used for raising the arm away from the body. [French *deltoïde* or modern Latin *deltoides* from Greek *deltoeidēs* (as DELTA, -OID)]

delude /dɪˈluːd, -ˈljuːd/ *v.tr.* deceive or mislead (*deluded by false optimism*). ◻ **deluder** *n.* [Middle English from Latin *deludere* 'mock' (as DE-, *ludere lus-* 'play')]

deluge /ˈdɛljuːdʒ/ *n. & v.* ● *n.* **1** a great flood. **2** (**the Deluge**) the biblical Flood (Gen. 6-8). **3** a great outpouring (of words, paper, etc.). **4** a heavy fall of rain. ● *v.tr.* **1** flood. **2** inundate with a great number or amount (*deluged with complaints*). [Middle English via Old French from Latin *diluvium*, related to *lavare* 'wash']

delusion /dɪˈluːʒ(ə)n, -ˈljuː-/ *n.* **1** a false belief or impression. **2** *Psychol.* this as a symptom or form of mental disorder. ◻ **delusional** *adj.* [Middle English from Late Latin *delusio* (as DELUDE)]

delusions of grandeur *n.pl.* a false idea of oneself as being important, noble, famous, etc.

delusive /dɪˈluːsɪv, -ˈljuː-/ *adj.* **1** deceptive or unreal. **2** disappointing. ◻ **delusively** *adv.* **delusiveness** *n.*

delusory /dɪˈluːs(ə)ri, -ˈljuː-; -z-/ *adj.* = DELUSIVE. [Late Latin *delusorius* (as DELUSION)]

delustre /diːˈlʌstə/ *v.tr.* (*US* **deluster**) remove the lustre from (a textile).

de luxe /dɪ ˈlʌks, ˈlʊks/ *adj.* **1** luxurious or sumptuous. **2** of a superior kind. [French, = of luxury]

delve /dɛlv/ *v.* **1** *intr.* (often foll. by *in, into*) **a** search energetically (*delved into his pocket*). **b** make a laborious search in documents etc.; research (*delved into his family history*). **2** *tr. & intr. poet.* dig. ◻ **delver** *n.* [Old English *delfan*, from West Germanic]

Dem. *abbr. US* Democrat.

demagnetize /diːˈmagnɪtʌɪz/ *v.tr.* (also **-ise**) remove the magnetic properties of. ◻ **demagnetization** /-ˈzeɪʃ(ə)n/ *n.* **demagnetizer** *n.*

demagogue /ˈdɛməgɒg/ *n.* (*US* **-gog**) **1** a political agitator appealing to the basest instincts of a mob. **2** a leader of the people, esp. in ancient times. ◻ **demagogic** /-ˈgɒgɪk/ *adj.* **demagoguery** /-ˈgɒg(ə)ri/ *n.* **demagogy** *n.* [Greek *dēmagōgos*, from *dēmos* 'the people' + *agōgos* 'leading']

demand /dɪˈmɑːnd/ *n. & v.* ● *n.* **1** an insistent and peremptory request, made as of right. **2** *Econ.* the desire of purchasers or consumers for a commodity (*no demand for solid tyres these days*). **3** an urgent claim (*care of her mother makes demands on her*). ● *v.tr.* **1** (often foll. by *of, from,* or *to* + infin., or *that* + clause) ask for (something) insistently and urgently, as of right (*demanded to know*; *demanded five pounds from him*; *demanded that his wife be present*). **2** require or need (*a task demanding skill*). **3** insist on being told (*demanded her business*). **4** (as **demanding** *adj.*) making demands; requiring skill, effort, etc. (*a demanding but worthwhile job*). ◻ **in demand** sought after. **on demand** as soon as a demand is made (*a cheque payable on demand*). ◻ **demander** *n.* **demandingly** *adv.* [Middle English via Old French *demande* (*n.*), *demander* (*v.*) from Latin *demandare* 'entrust' (as DE-, *mandare* 'order': see MANDATE)]

demand feeding *n.* the practice of feeding a baby when it cries for a feed rather than at set times.

demand-led *adj. Econ.* motivated or propelled by demand, esp. from consumers.

demand note *n.* **1** a written request for payment. **2** *N. Amer.* a bill payable at sight.

demand pull *n.* available money as a factor causing economic inflation.

demantoid /dɪˈmantɔɪd/ *n.* a lustrous green garnet. [German, from obsolete *Demant* 'diamond']

demarcation /diːmɑːˈkeɪʃ(ə)n/ *n.* **1** the act of marking a boundary or limits. **2** *Brit.* the trade-union practice of strictly assigning specific jobs to different unions. ◻ **demarcate** /ˈdiː-/ *v.tr.* **demarcator** /ˈdiː-/ *n.* [Spanish *demarcación* from *demarcar* 'mark the bounds of' (as DE-, MARK[1])]

demarcation dispute *n. Brit.* an inter-union dispute about who does a particular job.

démarche /deɪˈmɑːʃ/ *n.* a political step or initiative. [French from *démarcher* 'take steps' (as DE-, MARCH[1])]

dematerialize /diːməˈtɪərɪəlʌɪz/ *v.tr. & intr.* (also **-ise**) make or become non-material or spiritual (esp. of psychic phenomena etc.). ◻ **dematerialization** /-ˈzeɪʃ(ə)n/ *n.*

deme /diːm/ *n.* **1 a** a political division of Attica in ancient Greece. **b** an administrative division in modern Greece. **2** *Biol.* a local population of closely related plants or animals. [Greek *dēmos* 'the people']

demean[1] /dɪˈmiːn/ *v.tr.* (usu. *refl.*) lower the dignity or status of (*would not demean myself to take it*). [DE- + MEAN[2], on the pattern of *debase*]

demean[2] /dɪˈmiːn/ *v.refl.* (with *adv.*) behave (*demeaned himself well*). [Middle English via Old French *demener* from Romanic (as DE-, Latin *minare* 'drive animals' from *minari* 'threaten')]

demeanour /dɪˈmiːnə/ *n.* (*US* **demeanor**) outward behaviour or bearing. [DEMEAN[2], probably influenced by obsolete *havour* 'behaviour']

dement /dɪˈmɛnt/ *n. archaic* a demented person. [originally *adj.*, from French *dément* or Latin *demens* (as DEMENTED)]

demented /dɪˈmɛntɪd/ *adj.* mad; crazy. ◻ **dementedly** *adv.* **dementedness** *n.* [past part. of earlier verb *dement*: from Old French *dementer* or from Late Latin *dementare*, from *demens* 'out of one's mind' (as DE-, *mens mentis* 'mind')]

démenti /deɪˈmɒ̃ti, French demɑ̃ti/ *n.* an official denial of a rumour etc. [French from *démentir* 'accuse of lying']

dementia /dɪˈmɛnʃə/ *n. Med.* a chronic or persistent disorder of the mental processes marked by memory disorders, personality changes, impaired reasoning, etc., due to brain disease or injury. [Latin from *demens* (as DEMENTED)]

dementia praecox /ˈpriːkɒks/ *n.* schizophrenia.

demerara /dɛməˈrɛːrə, -ˈrɑːrə/ *n.* (in full **demerara sugar**) light brown cane sugar coming originally and chiefly from Demerara. [*Demerara*, region of Guyana]

demerge /diːˈməːdʒ/ *v.tr.* separate (a business) from another.

demerger /diːˈməːdʒə/ *n.* the act of demerging a business.

demerit /diːˈmɛrɪt/ *n.* **1** a quality or action deserving blame; a fault. **2** *N. Amer.* a mark awarded against an offender. ◻ **demeritorious** /-ˈtɔːrɪəs/ *adj.* [Middle English from Old French *de(s)merite* or Latin *demeritum*, neut. past part. of *demerēri* 'deserve']

demersal /dɪˈməːs(ə)l/ *adj.* (of a fish etc.) being or living near the sea bottom (cf. PELAGIC). [Latin *demersus*, past part. of *demergere* (as DE-, *mergere* 'plunge')]

demesne /dɪˈmeɪn, dɪˈmiːn/ *n.* **1 a** a sovereign's or state's territory; a domain. **b** land attached to a mansion etc. **c** landed property; an estate. **2** (usu. foll. by *of*) a region or sphere. **3** *Law hist.* possession (of real property) as one's own. ◻ **held in demesne** (of an estate) occupied by the owner, not by tenants. [Middle English via Anglo-French, Old French *demeine* (later Anglo-French *demesne*) 'belonging to a lord' from Latin *dominicus* (as DOMINICAL)]

demi- /ˈdɛmi/ *prefix* **1** half; half-size. **2** partially or imperfectly such (*demigod*). [Middle English via French from medieval Latin *dimedius* 'half', for Latin *dimidius*]

demigod /ˈdɛmɪgɒd/ *n.* (*fem.* **-goddess** /-gɒdɪs/) **1 a** a partly divine being. **b** the offspring of a god or goddess and a mortal. **2** *colloq.* a person of compelling beauty, powers, or personality.

demijohn /ˈdɛmɪdʒɒn/ *n.* a bulbous narrow-necked bottle holding from 3 to 10 gallons and usu. in a wicker cover. [probably corruption of French *dame-jeanne* 'Lady Jane', assimilated to DEMI- + the name *John*]

demilitarize /diːˈmɪlɪt(ə)rʌɪz/ *v.tr.* (also **-ise**) remove a military organization or forces from (a frontier, a zone, etc.). □ **demilitarization** /-ˈzeɪʃ(ə)n/ *n.*

demi-mondaine /ˈdɛmɪmɒnˌdeɪn, French dəmimɔ̃dɛn/ *n.* a woman of a *demi-monde.*

demi-monde /dɛmɪˈmɒnd, French dəmimɔ̃d/ *n.* **1 a** *hist.* a class of women in 19th-c. France considered to be of doubtful social standing and morality. **b** a similar class of women in any society. **2** any group considered to be on the fringes of respectable society. [French, = half-world]

demineralize /diːˈmɪn(ə)r(ə)lʌɪz/ *v.tr.* (also **-ise**) remove salts from (sea water etc.). □ **demineralization** /-ˈzeɪʃ(ə)n/ *n.*

demi-pension /dɛmɪˈpɒ̃sjɒ̃, French dəmipɑ̃sjɔ̃/ *n.* hotel accommodation with bed, breakfast, and one main meal per day. [French (as DEMI-, PENSION²)]

demirep /ˈdɛmɪrɛp/ *n. archaic* a woman of doubtful sexual reputation. [abbreviation of *demi-reputable*]

demise /dɪˈmʌɪz/ *n. & v.* ● *n.* **1** death (*left a will on her demise; the demise of the agreement*). **2** *Law* conveyance or transfer (of property, a title, etc.) by demising. ● *v.tr. Law* **1** convey or grant (an estate) by will or lease. **2** transmit (a title etc.) by death. [Anglo-French, past part. of Old French *de(s)mettre* DISMISS, in refl. 'abdicate', used as a noun]

demisemiquaver /ˈdɛmɪsɛmɪˌkweɪvə/ *n. Brit. Mus.* a note having the time value of half a semiquaver and represented by a large dot with a three-hooked stem.

demist /diːˈmɪst/ *v.tr.* clear mist from (a windscreen etc.). □ **demister** *n.*

demit /dɪˈmɪt/ *v.tr.* (**demitted, demitting**) (often *absol.*) resign or abdicate (an office etc.). □ **demission** /-ˈmɪʃ(ə)n/ *n.* [French *démettre* from Latin *demittere* (as DE-, *mittere miss-* 'send')]

demitasse /ˈdɛmɪtas/ *n.* **1** a small coffee cup. **2** its contents. [French, = half-cup]

demiurge /ˈdiːmɪəːdʒ, ˈdɛm-/ *n.* **1** (in the philosophy of Plato) the creator of the universe. **2** (in Gnosticism etc.) a heavenly being subordinate to the Supreme Being. □ **demiurgic** /-ˈəːdʒɪk/ *adj.* [ecclesiastical Latin from Greek *dēmiourgos* 'craftsman', from *dēmios* 'public' (from *dēmos* 'people') + *-ergos* 'working']

demo /ˈdɛməʊ/ *n.* (*pl.* **-os**) *colloq.* **1** = DEMONSTRATION 2, 3. **2** (*attrib.*) demonstrating the capabilities of computer software, a group of musicians, etc. (*demo software; demo tape*). [abbreviation]

demob /diːˈmɒb/ *v. & n. Brit. colloq.* ● *v.tr.* (**demobbed, demobbing**) demobilize. ● *n.* demobilization. [abbreviation]

demobilize /diːˈməʊbɪlʌɪz/ *v.tr.* (also **-ise**) disband (troops etc.). □ **demobilization** /-ˈzeɪʃ(ə)n/ *n.* [French *démobiliser* (as DE-, MOBILIZE)]

democracy /dɪˈmɒkrəsi/ *n.* (*pl.* **-ies**) **1 a** a system of government by the whole population, usu. through elected representatives. **b** a state so governed. **c** any organization governed on democratic principles. **2** an egalitarian and tolerant form of society. [French *démocratie* via Late Latin *democratia* from Greek *dēmokratia*, from *dēmos* 'the people' + -CRACY]

democrat /ˈdɛməkrat/ *n.* **1** an advocate of democracy. **2** (**Democrat**) (in the US) a member of the Democratic Party. [French *démocrate* (as DEMOCRACY), on the pattern of *aristocrate*]

democratic /dɛməˈkratɪk/ *adj.* **1** of, like, practising, advocating, or constituting democracy or a democracy. **2** favouring social equality. □ **democratically** *adv.* [French *démocratique* via medieval Latin *democraticus* from Greek *dēmokratikos*, from *dēmokratia* DEMOCRACY]

democratic centralism *n.* an organizational system in which policy is decided centrally and is binding on all members.

Democratic Party *n.* one of the two main US political parties, considered to favour social reform. (cf. REPUBLICAN PARTY).

democratize /dɪˈmɒkrətʌɪz/ *v.tr.* (also **-ise**) make (a state, institution, etc.) democratic. □ **democratization** /-ˈzeɪʃ(ə)n/ *n.*

démodé /deɪˈməʊdeɪ, French demɔde/ *adj.* out of fashion. [French, past part. of *démoder* (as DE-, *mode* 'fashion')]

demodulate /diːˈmɒdjʊleɪt/ *v.tr. Physics* **1** extract (a modulating signal) from its carrier. **2** separate a modulating signal from. □ **demodulation** /ˌdiːmɒdjʊˈleɪʃ(ə)n/ *n.* **demodulator** *n.*

demographics /dɛməˈgrafɪks/ *n.pl.* statistical data relating to the population and groups within it, used esp. in the identification of consumer markets.

demography /dɪˈmɒgrəfi/ *n.* the study of the statistics of births, deaths, disease, etc., as illustrating the conditions of life in communities. □ **demographer** *n.* **demographic** /dɛməˈgrafɪk/ *adj.* **demographical** /dɛməˈgrafɪk(ə)l/ *adj.* **demographically** /dɛməˈgrafɪk(ə)li/ *adv.* [Greek *dēmos* 'the people' + -GRAPHY]

demoiselle /dɛmwɑːˈzɛl/ *n.* **1** (in full **demoiselle crane**) a small crane, *Anthropoides virgo*, native to Asia and N. Africa. **2 a** a damselfly. **b** a damselfish. **3** *archaic* a young woman. [French, = DAMSEL]

demolish /dɪˈmɒlɪʃ/ *v.tr.* **1 a** pull down (a building). **b** completely destroy or break. **2** overthrow (an institution). **3** refute (an argument, theory, etc.). **4** *joc.* eat up completely and quickly. □ **demolisher** *n.* **demolition** /dɛməˈlɪʃ(ə)n/ *n.* **demolitionist** /dɛməˈlɪʃ(ə)nɪst/ *n.* [French *démolir* from Latin *demoliri* (as DE-, *moliri molit-* 'construct' from *moles* 'mass')]

demon /ˈdiːmən/ *n.* **1 a** an evil spirit or devil, esp. one thought to possess a person. **b** the personification of evil passion. **2** a malignant supernatural being; the Devil. **3** (often *attrib.*) a forceful, fierce, or skilful performer (*a demon on the tennis court; a demon player*). **4** a cruel or destructive person. **5** (also **daemon**) **a** an inner or attendant spirit; a genius (*the demon of creativity*). **b** a divinity or supernatural being in ancient Greece. □ **a demon for work** *colloq.* a person who works strenuously. [Middle English via medieval Latin *demon* and Latin *daemon* from Greek *daimōn* 'deity']

demon bowler *n. Cricket* a particularly successful bowler in a match or series.

demonetize /diːˈmʌnɪtʌɪz, -mɒn-/ *v.tr.* (also **-ise**) withdraw (a coin etc.) from use as money. □ **demonetization** /-ˈzeɪʃ(ə)n/ *n.* [French *démonétiser* (as DE-, Latin *moneta* MONEY)]

demoniac /dɪˈməʊnɪak/ *adj. & n.* ● *adj.* = DEMONIC. ● *n.* a person supposedly possessed by an evil spirit. □ **demoniacal** /diːməˈnʌɪək(ə)l/ *adj.* **demoniacally** /diːməˈnʌɪək(ə)li/ *adv.* [Middle English via Old French *demoniaque* from ecclesiastical Latin *daemoniacus*, from *daemonium*, from Greek *daimonion*, diminutive of *daimōn*: see DEMON)]

demonic /dɪˈmɒnɪk/ *adj.* (also **daemonic**) **1** fiercely energetic or frenzied. **2 a** supposedly possessed by an evil spirit. **b** of or concerning such possession. **3** of or like demons. **4** having or seeming to have supernatural genius or power. [Late Latin *daemonicus* from Greek *daimonikos* (as DEMON)]

demonism /ˈdiːmənɪz(ə)m/ *n.* belief in the power of demons.

demonize /ˈdiːmənʌɪz/ *v.tr.* (also **-ise**) **1** make into or like a demon. **2** represent as a demon. □ **demonization** /-ˈzeɪʃ(ə)n/ *n.*

demonolatry /diːməˈnɒlətri/ *n.* the worship of demons.

demonology /diːməˈnɒlədʒi/ *n.* the study of demons etc. □ **demonologist** *n.*

demonopolize /diːməˈnɒpəlʌɪz/ *v.tr.* (also **-ise**) make no longer a monopoly.

demonstrable /dɪˈmɒnstrəb(ə)l, ˈdɛmən-/ *adj.* capable of being shown or logically proved. □ **demonstrability** /-ˈbɪlɪti/ *n.* **demonstrably** *adv.* [Middle English from Latin *demonstrabilis* (as DEMONSTRATE)]

demonstrate /ˈdɛmənstreɪt/ *v.* **1** *tr.* show evidence of (feelings etc.). **2** *tr.* describe and explain (a scientific proposition, machine, etc.) by experiment, practical use, etc. **3** *tr.* **a** logically prove the truth of. **b** be proof of the existence of. **4** *intr.* take part in or organize a public demonstration. **5** *intr.* act as a demonstrator. [Latin *demonstrare* (as DE-, *monstrare* 'show')]

demonstration /dɛmənˈstreɪʃ(ə)n/ *n.* **1** (foll. by *of*) **a** the outward showing of feeling etc. **b** an instance of this. **2** a public meeting, march, etc., for a political or moral purpose. **3 a** a practical exhibition or explanation of something, designed to teach or inform. **b** a practical display of a piece of equipment to show its capabilities. **4** proof provided by logic, argument, etc. **5** *Mil.* a show of military force. □ **demonstrational** *adj.* [Middle English from Old French *demonstration* or Latin *demonstratio* (as DEMONSTRATE)]

demonstrative /dɪˈmɒnstrətɪv/ *adj. & n.* ● *adj.* **1** given to or marked by an open expression of feeling, esp. of affection (*a very demonstrative person*). **2** (usu. foll. by *of*) logically conclusive; giving proof (*the work is demonstrative of their skill*). **3 a** serving to point out or exhibit. **b** involving esp. scientific demonstration (*demonstrative technique*). **4** *Gram.* (of an adjective or pronoun) indicating the person or thing referred to (e.g. *this, that, those*). ● *n. Gram.* a demonstrative adjective or pronoun. □ **demonstratively** *adv.* **demonstrativeness** *n.* [Middle English via Old French *demonstratif -ive* from Latin *demonstrativus* (as DEMONSTRATION)]

demonstrator /ˈdɛmənstreɪtə/ *n.* **1** a person who takes part in a political demonstration etc. **2 a** a person who demonstrates, esp. machines, equipment, etc., to prospective customers. **b** a machine, etc., esp. a car, used for such demonstrations. **3** a person who teaches by demonstration, esp. in a laboratory etc. [Latin (as DEMONSTRATE)]

demoralize /dɪˈmɒrəlʌɪz/ *v.tr.* (also **-ise**) **1** destroy the morale of; make hopeless. **2** *archaic* corrupt the morals of. □ **demoralization** /-ˈzeɪʃ(ə)n/ *n.* **demoralizing** *adj.* **demoralizingly** *adv.* [French *démoraliser* (as DE-, MORAL)]

demote /diːˈməʊt/ *v.tr.* reduce to a lower rank or class. □ **demotion** /-ˈməʊʃ(ə)n/ *n.* [DE- + PROMOTE]

demotic /dɪˈmɒtɪk/ *n. & adj.* ● *n.* **1** the popular colloquial form of modern Greek. **2 a** a popular simplified form of ancient Egyptian writing (cf. HIERATIC 2). **b** a popular written or spoken form of modern Greek. ● *adj.* **1** (esp. of language) popular, colloquial, or vulgar. **2** of or concerning the ancient Egyptian or modern Greek demotic. [Greek *dēmotikos* via *dēmotēs* 'one of the people' from *dēmos* 'the people']

demotivate /diːˈməʊtɪveɪt/ *v.tr.* (also *absol.*) cause to lose motivation; discourage. □ **demotivation** /-ˈveɪʃ(ə)n/ *n.*

demount /diːˈmaʊnt/ *v.tr.* **1** take (apparatus, a gun, etc.) from its mounting. **2** dismantle for later reassembly. □ **demountable** *adj. & n.* [French *démonter*: cf. DISMOUNT]

demulcent /dɪˈmʌls(ə)nt/ *adj. & n.* ● *adj.* soothing. ● *n.* an agent that forms a protective film, soothing irritation or inflammation in the mouth. [Latin *demulcēre* (as DE-, *mulcēre* 'soothe')]

demur /dɪˈməː/ *v. & n.* ● *v.intr.* (**demurred**, **demurring**) **1** (often foll. by *to*, *at*) raise scruples or objections. **2** *Law* put in a demurrer. ● *n.* (also **demurral** /dɪˈmʌr(ə)l/) (usu. in *neg.*) **1** an objection (*agreed without demur*). **2** the act or process of objecting. [Middle English via Old French *demeure* (*n.*), *demeurer* (*v.*) from Romanic (as DE-, Latin *morari* 'delay')]

demure /dɪˈmjʊə/ *adj.* (**demurer**, **demurest**) **1** composed, quiet, and reserved; modest. **2** affectedly shy and quiet; coy. **3** decorous (*a demure high collar*). □ **demurely** *adv.* **demureness** *n.* [Middle English, perhaps via Anglo-French *demuré* from Old French *demoré*, past part. of *demorer* 'remain, stay' (as DEMUR): influenced by Old French *meür* from Latin *maturus* 'ripe']

demurrable /dɪˈməːrəb(ə)l/ *adj.* esp. *Law* open to objection.

demurrage /dɪˈmʌrɪdʒ/ *n.* **1 a** a rate or amount payable to a shipowner by a charterer for failure to load or discharge a ship within the time agreed. **b** a similar charge on railway trucks or goods. **2** a detention or delay in loading or discharging. [Old French *demo(u)rage* from *demorer* (as DEMUR)]

demurrer /dɪˈməːrə/ *n.* an objection, esp. *Law* a pleading that an opponent's point is irrelevant. [Anglo-French (infinitive used as a noun), = DEMUR]

demy /dɪˈmʌɪ/ *n. Printing* a size of paper, 564 × 444 mm. [Middle English, variant of DEMI-]

demystify /diːˈmɪstɪfʌɪ/ *v.tr.* (**-ies**, **-ied**) **1** clarify or remove the mystery from (obscure beliefs or subjects etc.). **2** reduce or remove the irrationality in (a person). □ **demystification** /-fɪˈkeɪʃ(ə)n/ *n.*

demythologize /diːmɪˈθɒlədʒʌɪz/ *v.tr.* (also **-ise**) **1** remove mythical elements from (a legend, famous person's life, etc.). **2** reinterpret what some consider to be the mythological elements in (the Bible).

den /dɛn/ *n. & v.* ● *n.* **1** a wild animal's lair. **2** a place of crime or vice (*den of iniquity*; *opium den*). **3 a** a small private room or place for pursuing a hobby etc. **b** a hideout or secret place for children. ● *v.intr.* (**denned**, **denning**) live in or retreat to a den. [Old English *denn* from Germanic, related to DENE[1]]

denarius /dɪˈnɛːrɪəs, dɪˈnɑːrɪəs/ *n.* (*pl.* **denarii** /-rɪʌɪ, -rɪiː/) an ancient Roman silver coin. [Latin, = '(coin) of ten asses' (as DENARY: see AS[2])]

denary /ˈdiːn(ə)ri/ *adj.* of ten; decimal. [Latin *denarius* 'containing ten' from *deni* 'by tens']

denary scale *n.* = DECIMAL SCALE.

denationalize /diːˈnaʃ(ə)n(ə)lʌɪz/ *v.tr.* (also **-ise**) **1** transfer (a nationalized industry or institution etc.) from public to private ownership. **2 a** deprive (a nation) of its status or characteristics as a nation. **b** deprive (a person) of nationality or national characteristics. □ **denationalization** /-ˈzeɪʃ(ə)n/ *n.* [French *dénationaliser* (as DE-, NATIONAL)]

denaturalize /diːˈnatʃ(ə)rəlʌɪz/ *v.tr.* (also **-ise**) **1** change the nature or properties of; make unnatural. **2** deprive of the rights of citizenship. **3** = DENATURE 2. □ **denaturalization** /-ˈzeɪʃ(ə)n/ *n.*

denature /diːˈneɪtʃə/ *v.tr.* **1** change the properties of (a protein etc.) by heat, acidity, etc. **2** make (alcohol) unfit for drinking, esp. by the addition of another substance. □ **denaturant** *n.* **denaturation** /diːˌnatʃəˈreɪʃ(ə)n/ *n.* [French *dénaturer* (as DE-, NATURE)]

dendrite /ˈdɛndrʌɪt/ *n.* **1 a** a stone or mineral with natural treelike or mosslike markings. **b** such marks on stones or minerals. **2** *Chem.* a crystal with branching treelike growth. **3** *Zool. & Anat.* a branching process of a nerve cell conducting signals to a cell body. [French, from Greek *dendritēs* (*adj.*) from *dendron* 'tree']

dendritic /dɛnˈdrɪtɪk/ *adj.* **1** of or like a dendrite. **2** treelike in shape or markings. □ **dendritically** *adv.*

dendrochronology /ˌdɛndrəʊkrəˈnɒlədʒi/ *n.* **1** a system of dating using the characteristic patterns of annual growth rings of trees to assign dates to timber. **2** the study of these growth rings. □ **dendrochronological** /-krɒnəˈlɒdʒɪk(ə)l/ *adj.* **dendrochronologist** *n.* [Greek *dendron* 'tree' + CHRONOLOGY]

dendrogram /ˈdɛndrəgram/ *n. Biol.* a branched diagram showing the relationship between kinds of organism. [Greek *dendron* 'tree' + -GRAM]

dendroid /ˈdɛndrɔɪd/ *adj.* tree-shaped. [Greek *dendrōdēs* 'treelike' + -OID]

dendrology /dɛn'drɒlədʒi/ *n.* the scientific study of trees. □ **dendrological** /-drə'lɒdʒɪk(ə)l/ *adj.* **dendrologist** *n.* [Greek *dendron* 'tree' + -LOGY]

dene[1] /diːn/ *n.* (also **dean**) *Brit.* **1** a narrow wooded valley. **2** a vale (esp. as the ending of place names). [Old English *denu*, related to DEN]

dene[2] /diːn/ *n. Brit.* a bare sandy tract, or a low sandhill, by the sea. [origin unknown: perhaps related to DUNE]

denest /diː'nɛst/ *v.tr.* remove (a word or phrase, esp. a compound noun) from a dictionary entry for another word and enter it as a main entry itself.

de-net /diː'nɛt/ *v.tr.* (**de-netted, de-netting**) (in the UK) sell (a book) at a price lower than that fixed under the terms of the Net Book Agreement.

dengue /'dɛŋgi/ *n.* an infectious viral disease of the tropics, transmitted by mosquitoes and causing a fever and acute pains in the joints. [West Indian Spanish, from Swahili *denga, dinga*, with assimilation to Spanish *dengue* 'fastidiousness', with reference to the stiffness of the patient's neck and shoulders]

deniable /dɪ'nʌɪəb(ə)l/ *adj.* that may be denied. □ **deniability** /-ə'bɪlɪti/ *n.*

denial /dɪ'nʌɪ(ə)l/ *n.* **1** the act or an instance of denying. **2** a refusal of a request or wish. **3** a statement that a thing is not true; a rejection (*denial of the accusation*). **4** a disavowal of a person as one's leader etc. **5** = SELF-DENIAL. **6** *Psychol.* the usu. subconscious suppression of an unacceptable truth or emotion.

denier /'dɛnɪə/ *n.* a unit of weight by which the fineness of silk, rayon, or nylon yarn is measured. [originally the name of a small coin: Middle English via Old French from Latin *denarius*]

denigrate /'dɛnɪgreɪt/ *v.tr.* defame or disparage the reputation of (a person); blacken. □ **denigration** /-'greɪʃ(ə)n/ *n.* **denigrator** *n.* **denigratory** /-'greɪt(ə)ri/ *adj.* [Latin *denigrare* (as DE-, *nigrare* from *niger* 'black')]

denim /'dɛnɪm/ *n.* **1** (often *attrib.*) a usu. blue hard-wearing cotton twill fabric used for jeans, overalls, etc. (*a denim skirt*). **2** (in *pl.*) *colloq.* jeans, overalls, etc. made of this. [for *serge de Nim* 'serge of *Nîmes*', a city in S. France]

denitrify /diː'nʌɪtrɪfʌɪ/ *v.tr.* (**-ies, -ied**) remove the nitrates or nitrites from (soil etc.). □ **denitrification** /-fɪ'keɪʃ(ə)n/ *n.*

denizen /'dɛnɪz(ə)n/ *n.* **1** (usu. foll. by *of*) an inhabitant or occupant. **2** *Brit.* a foreigner admitted to certain rights in his or her adopted country. **3** a naturalized foreign word, animal, or plant. □ **denizenship** *n.* [Middle English via Anglo-French *deinzein* from Old French *deinz* 'within', from Latin *de* 'from' + *intus* 'within' + *-ein* from Latin *-aneus*: see -ANEOUS]

denominate /dɪ'nɒmɪneɪt/ *v.tr.* **1** give a name to. **2** call or describe (a person or thing) as. **3** (in *passive*; usu. foll. by *in*) express in a specified monetary unit. [Latin *denominare* (as DE-, NOMINATE)]

denomination /dɪˌnɒmɪ'neɪʃ(ə)n/ *n.* **1** a Church or religious sect. **2** a class of units within a range or sequence of numbers, weights, money, etc. (*money of small denominations*). **3 a** a name or designation, esp. a characteristic or class name. **b** a class or kind having a specific name. **4** the rank of a playing card within a suit, or of a suit relative to others. [Middle English from Old French *denomination* or Latin *denominatio* (as DENOMINATE)]

denominational /dɪˌnɒmɪ'neɪʃ(ə)n(ə)l/ *adj.* **1** of or relating to a particular denomination. **2** (of education) according to the principles of a Church or sect. □ **denominationalism** *n.*

denominative /dɪ'nɒmɪnətɪv/ *adj.* serving as or giving a name. [Late Latin *denominativus* (as DENOMINATION)]

denominator /dɪ'nɒmɪneɪtə/ *n. Math.* the number below the line in a vulgar fraction; a divisor. [French *dénominateur* or medieval Latin *denominator* (as DE-, NOMINATE)]

de nos jours /də nəʊ 'ʒʊə, French də no ʒur/ *adj.* (placed after noun) of the present time. [French, = of our days]

denote /dɪ'nəʊt/ *v.tr.* **1** be a sign of; indicate (*the arrow denotes direction*). **2** (usu. foll. by *that* + clause) mean, convey. **3** stand as a name for; signify. □ **denotation** /diːnə(ʊ)'teɪʃ(ə)n/ *n.* **denotative** /-tətɪv/ *adj.* [French *dénoter* or from Latin *denotare* (as DE-, *notare* 'mark' from *nota* NOTE)]

■ **Usage** See Usage Note at CONNOTE.

denouement /deɪ'nuːmɒ̃, -mɒŋ/ *n.* (also **dénouement**) **1** the final unravelling of a plot or complicated situation. **2** the final scene in a play, novel, etc., in which the plot is resolved. [French *dénouement* from *dénouer* 'unknot' (as DE-, Latin *nodare* from *nodus* 'knot')]

denounce /dɪ'naʊns/ *v.tr.* **1** accuse publicly; condemn (*denounced him as a traitor*). **2** inform against (*denounced her to the police*). **3** give notice of the termination of (an armistice, treaty, etc.). □ **denouncement** *n.* **denouncer** *n.* [Middle English via Old French *denoncier* from Latin *denuntiare* (as DE-, *nuntiare* 'make known' from *nuntius* 'messenger')]

de nouveau /də nuː'vəʊ, French də nuvo/ *adv.* starting again; anew. [French]

de novo /deɪ 'nəʊvəʊ, diː/ *adv.* starting again; anew. [Latin]

dense /dɛns/ *adj.* **1** closely compacted in substance; thick (*dense fog*). **2** crowded together (*the population is less dense on the outskirts*). **3** *colloq.* stupid. □ **densely** *adv.* **denseness** *n.* [French *dense* or Latin *densus*]

densitometer /dɛnsɪ'tɒmɪtə/ *n.* an instrument for measuring the photographic density of an image on a film or photographic print.

density /'dɛnsɪti/ *n.* (*pl.* **-ies**) **1** the degree of compactness of a substance. **2** *Physics* degree of consistency measured by the quantity of mass per unit volume. **3** the opacity of a photographic image. **4** a crowded state. **5** *colloq.* stupidity. [French *densité* or Latin *densitas* (as DENSE)]

dent /dɛnt/ *n.* & *v.* ● *n.* **1** a slight mark or hollow in a surface made by, or as if by, a blow with a hammer etc. **2** a noticeable effect (*the lavish lunch made a dent in our funds*). ● *v.tr.* **1** mark with a dent. **2** have (esp. an adverse) effect on (*the news dented our hopes*). [Middle English, probably from INDENT[1]]

dental /'dɛnt(ə)l/ *adj.* **1** of the teeth; of or relating to dentistry. **2** *Phonet.* (of a consonant) produced with the tongue-tip against the upper front teeth (as *th*) or the ridge of the teeth (as *n, d, t*). □ **dentalize** *v.tr.* (also **-ise**). [Late Latin *dentalis* from Latin *dens dentis* 'tooth']

dental floss *n.* a thread of floss silk etc. used to clean between the teeth.

dentalium /dɛn'teɪlɪəm/ *n.* (*pl.* **dentalia** /-lɪə/) **1** a tusk shell, esp. of the genus *Dentalium*. **2** this shell used as an ornament or as a form of currency. [modern Latin from Late Latin *dentalis*: *see* DENTAL]

dental mechanic *n. Brit.* a person who makes and repairs artificial teeth.

dental surgeon *n.* a dentist.

dentate /'dɛnteɪt/ *adj. Bot.* & *Zool.* toothed; with toothlike notches; serrated. [Latin *dentatus* from *dens dentis* 'tooth']

denticle /'dɛntɪk(ə)l/ *n. Zool.* a small tooth or toothlike projection, scale, etc. □ **denticulate** /den'tɪkjʊlət/ *adj.* [Middle English from Latin *denticulus*, diminutive of *dens dentis* 'tooth']

dentifrice /'dɛntɪfrɪs/ *n.* a paste or powder for cleaning the teeth. [French from Latin *dentifricium*, from *dens dentis* 'tooth' + *fricare* 'rub']

dentil /'dɛntɪl/ *n. Archit.* each of a series of small rectangular blocks as a decoration under the moulding of a cornice in classical architecture. [obsolete French *dentille*, diminutive of *dent* 'tooth', from Latin *dens dentis*]

dentilingual /dɛntɪˈlɪŋgw(ə)l/ *adj. Phonet.* formed by the teeth and the tongue.

dentine /ˈdɛntiːn/ *n.* (*US* **dentin** /-tɪn/) a hard dense bony tissue forming the bulk of a tooth. ▫ **dentinal** /ˈdɛntɪn(ə)l/ *adj.* [Latin *dens dentis* 'tooth' + -INE[4]]

dentist /ˈdɛntɪst/ *n.* a person who is qualified to treat the diseases and conditions that affect the mouth, jaws, teeth, and their supporting tissues, esp. the repair and extraction of teeth and the insertion of artificial ones. ▫ **dentistry** *n.* [French *dentiste* from *dent* 'tooth']

dentition /dɛnˈtɪʃ(ə)n/ *n.* **1** the type, number, and arrangement of teeth in a species etc. **2** the cutting of teeth; teething. [Latin *dentitio* from *dentire* 'to teethe']

denture /ˈdɛntʃə/ *n.* (usu. in *pl.*) a removable artificial replacement for one or more teeth carried on a removable plate or frame. [French from *dent* 'tooth']

denturist /ˈdɛntʃərɪst/ *n.* a maker of dentures.

denuclearize /diːˈnjuːklɪərʌɪz/ *v.tr.* (also **-ise**) remove nuclear armaments from (a country etc.). ▫ **denuclearization** /-ˈzeɪʃ(ə)n/ *n.*

denude /dɪˈnjuːd/ *v.tr.* **1** make naked or bare. **2** (foll. by *of*) **a** strip of clothing, a covering, etc. **b** deprive of a possession or attribute. **3** *Geol.* lay (rock or a formation etc.) bare by removing what lies above. ▫ **denudation** /diːnjʊˈdeɪʃ(ə)n/ *n.* **denudative** /-dətɪv/ *adj.* [Latin *denudare* (as DE-, *nudus* 'naked')]

denumerable /dɪˈnjuːm(ə)rəb(ə)l/ *adj. Math.* countable by correspondence with the infinite set of integers. ▫ **denumerability** /-ˈbɪlɪti/ *n.* **denumerably** *adv.* [Late Latin *denumerare* (as DE-, *numerare* NUMBER)]

denunciation /dɪˌnʌnsɪˈeɪʃ(ə)n/ *n.* **1** the act of denouncing (a person, policy, etc.); public condemnation. **2** an instance of this. ▫ **denunciate** /-ˈnʌnsɪeɪt/ *v.tr.* **denunciative** /-ˈnʌnsɪətɪv/ *adj.* **denunciator** /-ˈnʌnsɪeɪtə, -ˈnʌnʃɪeɪtə/ *n.* **denunciatory** /dɪˈnʌnsɪət(ə)ri, -ˈnʌnʃɪət(ə)ri/ *adj.* [French *dénonciation* or Latin *denunciatio* (as DENOUNCE)]

deny /dɪˈnʌɪ/ *v.tr.* (**-ies**, **-ied**) **1** declare untrue or non-existent (*denied the charge*; *denied that it is so*; *denied having lied*). **2** repudiate or disclaim (*denied his faith*; *denied his signature*). **3** (often foll. by *to*) refuse (a person or thing, or something to a person) (*this was denied to me*; *denied him the satisfaction*). **4** refuse access to (a person sought) (*denied him his son*). ▫ **deny oneself** be abstinent. ▫ **denier** *n.* [Middle English via Old French *denier* from Latin *denegare* (as DE-, *negare* 'say no')]

deoch an doris /dɒx (ə)n ˈdɒrɪs, dɒk/ *n.* (also **doch an dorris**) *Sc. & Ir.* a drink taken at parting; a stirrup cup. [Gaelic *deoch an doruis* 'drink at the door']

deodar /ˈdiːə(ʊ)dɑː/ *n.* the Himalayan cedar *Cedrus deodara*, the tallest of the cedar family, with drooping branches bearing large barrel-shaped cones. [Hindi *dē̃odār* from Sanskrit *deva-dāru* 'divine tree']

deodorant /dɪˈəʊd(ə)r(ə)nt/ *n.* (often *attrib.*) a substance sprayed or rubbed on to the body or sprayed into the air to remove or conceal unwanted or unpleasant smells (*a roll-on deodorant*; *has a deodorant effect*). [as DEODORIZE + -ANT]

deodorize /dɪˈəʊdərʌɪz/ *v.tr.* (also **-ise**) remove or destroy the (usu. unpleasant) smell of. ▫ **deodorization** /-ˈzeɪʃ(ə)n/ *n.* **deodorizer** *n.* [DE- + Latin *odor* 'smell']

Deo gratias /deɪəʊ ˈgrɑːtɪəs, -ʃɪəs/ *int.* thanks be to God. [Latin, = (we give) thanks to God]

deontic /dɪˈɒntɪk/ *adj. Philos.* of or relating to duty and obligation as ethical concepts. [Greek *deont-*, part. stem of *dei* 'it is right']

deontology /diːɒnˈtɒlədʒi/ *n. Philos.* the study of duty. ▫ **deontological** /-təˈlɒdʒɪk(ə)l/ *adj.* **deontologist** *n.*

Deo volente /deɪəʊ vɒˈlɛnteɪ/ *adv.* God willing; if nothing prevents it. [Latin]

deoxygenate /diːˈɒksɪdʒəneɪt/ *v.tr.* remove oxygen, esp. free oxygen, from. ▫ **deoxygenation** /-ˈneɪʃ(ə)n/ *n.*

deoxyribonucleic acid /dɪˌɒksɪrʌɪbəʊnjuːˈkleɪɪk/ *n.* see DNA. [DE- + OXYGEN + RIBONUCLEIC ACID]

deoxyribose /dɪˌɒksɪˈrʌɪbəʊz, -s/ *n. Biochem.* a sugar related to ribose and found in the nucleosides of DNA. [DE- + OXY-[2] + RIBOSE]

dep. *abbr.* **1** departs. **2** deputy.

depart /dɪˈpɑːt/ *v.* **1** *intr.* **a** (usu. foll. by *from*) go away; leave (*the train departs from this platform*). **b** (usu. foll. by *for*) start; set out (*trains depart for Crewe every hour*). **2** *intr.* (usu. foll. by *from*) diverge; deviate (*departs from standard practice*). **3 a** *intr.* leave by death; die. **b** *tr. formal* or *literary* leave by death (*departed this life*). [Middle English from Old French *departir*, ultimately from Latin *dispertire* 'divide']

departed /dɪˈpɑːtɪd/ *adj.* & *n.* ● *adj.* bygone (*departed greatness*). ● *n.* (prec. by *the*) *euphem.* a particular dead person or dead people (*we are here to mourn the departed*).

department /dɪˈpɑːtm(ə)nt/ *n.* **1** a separate part of a complex whole, esp.: **a** a branch of municipal or State administration (*Housing Department*; *Department of Social Security*). **b** a branch of study and its administration at a university, school, etc. (*the physics department*). **c** a specialized section of a large store (*hardware department*). **2** *colloq.* an area of special expertise. **3** an administrative district in France and other countries. [French *département* (as DEPART)]

departmental /diːpɑːtˈmɛnt(ə)l/ *adj.* of or belonging to a department. ▫ **departmentalism** *n.* **departmentalize** *v.tr.* (also **-ise**). **departmentalization** /-ˈzeɪʃ(ə)n/ *n.* **departmentally** *adv.*

department store *n.* (also *Brit.* **departmental store**) a large shop stocking many varieties of goods in different departments.

departure /dɪˈpɑːtʃə/ *n.* **1** the act or an instance of departing. **2** (often foll. by *from*) a deviation (from the truth, a standard, etc.). **3** (often *attrib.*) the starting of a train, an aircraft, etc. (*the departure was late*; *departure lounge*). **4** a new course of action or thought (*driving a car is rather a departure for him*). **5** *Naut.* the amount of a ship's change of longitude. [Old French *departeüre* (as DEPART)]

depasture /diːˈpɑːstʃə/ *v. Brit.* **1 a** *tr.* (of cattle) graze upon. **b** *intr.* graze. **c** *tr.* put (cattle) to graze. **2** *tr.* (of land) provide pasturage for (cattle). ▫ **depasturage** /-ɪdʒ/ *n.*

dépaysé /deɪˈpeɪzeɪ, French depeize/ *adj.* (*fem.* ***dépaysée*** *pronunc.* same) removed from one's habitual surroundings. [French, = removed from one's own country]

depend /dɪˈpɛnd/ *v.intr.* **1** (often foll. by *on*, *upon*) be controlled or determined by (*success depends on hard work*; *it depends on whether they agree*; *it depends how you tackle the problem*). **2** (foll. by *on*, *upon*) **a** be unable to do without (*depends on her mother*). **b** rely on (*I'm depending on you to come*). **3** (foll. by *on*, *upon*) be grammatically dependent on. **4** (often foll. by *from*) *archaic* or *poet.* hang down. ▫ **depending on** according to; taking into account. **depend upon it!** you may be sure! **it** (or **it all** or **that**) **depends** expressing uncertainty or qualification in answering a question (*Will they come? It depends*). [Middle English from Old French *dependre*, ultimately from Latin *dependēre* (as DE-, *pendēre* 'hang')]

dependable /dɪˈpɛndəb(ə)l/ *adj.* reliable. ▫ **dependability** /-ˈbɪlɪti/ *n.* **dependably** *adv.*

dependant /dɪˈpɛnd(ə)nt/ *n.* (*US* **dependent**) **1** a person who relies on another esp. for financial support. **2** a servant or subordinate. [French *dépendant*, pres. part. of *dépendre* (as DEPEND)]

dependence /dɪˈpɛnd(ə)ns/ *n.* **1** the state of being dependent (see DEPENDENT 1, 2, 3). **2** reliance; trust; confidence (*shows great dependence on his judgement*). [French *dépendance* (as DEPEND)]

dependency /dɪˈpɛnd(ə)nsi/ *n.* (*pl.* **-ies**) **1** a country or province controlled by another. **2** anything subordinate or dependent. **3** = DEPENDENCE 1.

dependency culture *n.* a way of life characterized by dependency on state benefits.

dependent /dɪˈpɛnd(ə)nt/ *adj. & n.* ● *adj.* **1** (usu. foll. by *on*) depending, conditional, or subordinate. **2** unable to do without (esp. a drug). **3** maintained at another's cost. **4** *Math.* (of a variable) having a value determined by that of another variable. **5** *Gram.* (of a clause, phrase, or word) subordinate to a sentence or word. ● *n. US* var. of DEPENDANT. □ **dependently** *adv.* [Middle English, earlier *-ant* = DEPENDANT]

depersonalization /di:ˌpə:s(ə)n(ə)lʌɪˈzeɪʃ(ə)n/ *n.* (also **-isation**) esp. *Psychol.* **1** the act of depersonalizing or state of being depersonalized. **2** *Psychiatry* a loss of one's sense of identity; a feeling of unreality.

depersonalize /di:ˈpə:s(ə)n(ə)lʌɪz/ *v.tr.* (also **-ise**) **1** make impersonal. **2** deprive of personality.

depict /dɪˈpɪkt/ *v.tr.* **1** represent in a drawing or painting etc. **2** portray in words; describe (*the play depicts him as vain and petty*). □ **depicter** *n.* **depiction** /-ˈpɪkʃ(ə)n/ *n.* **depictive** *adj.* **depictor** *n.* [Latin *depingere depict-* (as DE-, *pingere* 'paint')]

depilate /ˈdɛpɪleɪt/ *v.tr.* remove the hair from. □ **depilation** /-ˈleɪʃ(ə)n/ *n.* [Latin *depilare* (as DE-, *pilare* from *pilus* 'hair')]

depilatory /dɪˈpɪlət(ə)ri/ *adj. & n.* ● *adj.* that removes unwanted hair. ● *n.* (*pl.* **-ies**) a depilatory substance.

deplane /di:ˈpleɪn/ *v.* esp. *US* **1** *intr.* disembark from an aeroplane. **2** *tr.* remove from an aeroplane.

deplete /dɪˈpli:t/ *v.tr.* (esp. in *passive*) **1** reduce in numbers or quantity (*depleted forces*). **2** empty out; exhaust (*their energies were depleted*). □ **depletion** /-ˈpli:ʃ(ə)n/ *n.* [Latin *deplēre* (as DE-, *plēre plet-* 'fill')]

deplorable /dɪˈplɔ:rəb(ə)l/ *adj.* **1** exceedingly bad (*a deplorable meal*). **2** that can be deplored. □ **deplorably** *adv.*

deplore /dɪˈplɔ:/ *v.tr.* feel or express strong disapproval of. □ **deploringly** *adv.* [French *déplorer* or Italian *deplorare* from Latin *deplorare* (as DE-, *plorare* 'bewail')]

deploy /dɪˈplɔɪ/ *v.* **1** *Mil.* **a** *tr.* cause (troops) to spread out from a column into a line. **b** *intr.* (of troops) spread out in this way. **2** *tr.* bring (arguments, forces, etc.) into effective action. □ **deployment** *n.* [French *déployer* from Latin *displicare* (as DIS-, *plicare* 'fold') & Late Latin *deplicare* 'explain']

deplume /dɪˈplu:m/ *v.tr.* **1** strip of feathers, pluck. **2** deprive of honours etc. [Middle English from French *déplumer* or from medieval Latin *deplumare* (as DE-, Latin *pluma* 'feather')]

depolarize /di:ˈpəʊlərʌɪz/ *v.tr.* (also **-ise**) *Physics* reduce or remove the polarization of. □ **depolarization** /-ˈzeɪʃ(ə)n/ *n.*

depoliticize /di:pəˈlɪtɪsʌɪz/ *v.tr.* (also **-ise**) **1** make (a person, an organization, etc.) non-political. **2** remove from political activity or influence. □ **depoliticization** /-ˈzeɪʃ(ə)n/ *n.*

depolymerize /di:ˈpɒlɪmərʌɪz/ *v.tr. & intr.* (also **-ise**) *Chem.* break down into monomers or other smaller units. □ **depolymerization** /-ˈzeɪʃ(ə)n/ *n.*

deponent /dɪˈpəʊnənt/ *adj. & n.* ● *adj. Gram.* (of a verb, esp. in Latin or Greek) passive or middle in form but active in meaning. ● *n.* **1** *Gram.* a deponent verb. **2** *Law* **a** a person making a deposition under oath. **b** a witness giving written testimony for use in court etc. [Latin *deponere* (as DE-, *ponere posit-* 'place'): the adj. from the notion that the verb had laid aside the passive sense]

depopulate /di:ˈpɒpjʊleɪt/ *v.* **1** *tr.* reduce the population of. **2** *intr.* decline in population. □ **depopulation** /-ˈleɪʃ(ə)n/ *n.* [Latin *depopulari* (as DE-, *populari* 'lay waste' from *populus* 'people')]

deport /dɪˈpɔ:t/ *v.tr.* **1 a** remove (an immigrant or foreigner) forcibly to another country; banish. **b** exile (a native) to another country. **2** *refl. literary* or *archaic* conduct (oneself) or behave (in a specified manner) (*deported himself well*). □ **deportable** *adj.* **deportation** /di:pɔ:ˈteɪʃ(ə)n/ *n.* [Old French *deporter* and (sense 1) French *déporter* (as DE-, Latin *portare* 'carry')]

deportee /di:pɔ:ˈti:/ *n.* a person who has been or is being deported.

deportment /dɪˈpɔ:tm(ə)nt/ *n.* bearing, demeanour, or manners, esp. of a cultivated kind. [French *déportement* (as DEPORT)]

depose /dɪˈpəʊz/ *v.* **1** *tr.* remove from office, esp. dethrone. **2** *intr.* (usu. foll. by *to*, or *that* + clause) *Law* bear witness, esp. on oath in court. [Middle English from Old French *deposer*, based on Latin *deponere deposit-*: see DEPONENT, POSE[1]]

deposit /dɪˈpɒzɪt/ *n. & v.* ● *n.* **1 a** a sum of money placed or kept in an account in a bank. **b** anything stored or entrusted for safe keeping, usu. in a bank. **2 a** a sum paid towards the price of a house etc. before starting a mortgage loan, or as first instalment for an item bought on hire purchase, or as a pledge for a contract. **b** a returnable sum payable on the short-term hire of a car, boat, etc. **3** *Brit. Polit.* a sum of money deposited by an election candidate and forfeited if he or she fails to receive a certain proportion of the votes. **4 a** a natural layer of sand, rock, coal, etc. **b** a layer of accumulated matter on a surface, e.g. fur on a kettle. ● *v.tr.* (**deposited**, **depositing**) **1 a** put or lay down in a (usu. specified) place (*deposited the book on the floor*). **b** (of water, wind, etc.) leave (matter etc.) lying in a displaced position. **2 a** store or entrust for keeping. **b** pay (a sum of money) into a bank account, esp. a deposit account. **3** pay (a sum) as a first instalment or as a pledge for a contract. □ **on deposit** (of money) placed in a deposit account. [Latin *depositum* (*n.*), medieval Latin *depositare* from Latin *deponere deposit-* (as DEPONENT)]

deposit account *n. Brit.* a bank account that pays interest but from which money cannot usu. be withdrawn without notice or loss of interest.

depositary /dɪˈpɒzɪt(ə)ri/ *n.* (*pl.* **-ies**) a person to whom something is entrusted; a trustee. [Late Latin *depositarius* (as DEPOSIT)]

deposition /dɛpəˈzɪʃ(ə)n, di:-/ *n.* **1** the act or an instance of deposing, esp. a monarch; dethronement. **2** *Law* **a** the process of giving sworn evidence; allegation. **b** an instance of this. **c** evidence given under oath; a testimony. **3** the act or an instance of depositing. **4** (**the Deposition**) **a** the taking down of the body of Christ from the Cross. **b** a representation of this. [Middle English via Old French from Latin *depositio -onis*, from *deponere*: see DEPOSIT]

depositor /dɪˈpɒzɪtə/ *n.* a person who deposits money, property, etc.

depository /dɪˈpɒzɪt(ə)ri/ *n.* (*pl.* **-ies**) **1 a** a storehouse or repository. **b** a store (of wisdom, knowledge, etc.) (*the book is a depository of wit*). **2** = DEPOSITARY. [Late Latin *depositorium* (as DEPOSIT)]

depot /ˈdɛpəʊ/ *n.* **1** a storehouse. **2** *Mil.* **a** a storehouse for equipment etc. **b** the headquarters of a regiment. **3 a** a building for the servicing, parking, etc. of esp. buses, trains, or goods vehicles. **b** *N. Amer.* a railway or bus station. [French *dépôt*, Old French *depost* from Latin (as DEPOSIT)]

deprave /dɪˈpreɪv/ *v.tr.* pervert or corrupt, esp. morally. □ **depravation** /dɛprəˈveɪʃ(ə)n/ *n.* [Middle English from Old French *depraver* or Latin *depravare* (as DE-, *pravare* from *pravus* 'crooked')]

depravity /dɪˈpravɪti/ *n.* (*pl.* **-ies**) **1 a** moral corruption; wickedness. **b** an instance of this; a wicked act. **2** *Theol.* the innate corruptness of human nature. [DE- + obsolete *pravity* from Latin *pravitas* (as DEPRAVE)]

deprecate /ˈdɛprɪkeɪt/ *v.tr.* **1** express disapproval of or a wish against (a plan, proceeding, purpose, etc.); deplore; plead earnestly against (*deprecate hasty action*). **2 a** express disapproval of (a person); reprove. **b** = DEPRECIATE 2. **3** *archaic* pray against. □ **deprecatingly** *adv.* **deprecation** /-ˈkeɪʃ(ə)n/ *n.* **deprecative** /ˈdɛprɪkətɪv/ *adj.* **deprecator** *n.* **deprecatory** /-ˈkeɪt(ə)ri/ *adj.* [Latin *deprecari* (as DE-, *precari* 'pray')]

■ **Usage** Although frequently encountered, the use of *deprecate* in sense 2b is widely regarded as incorrect. It is especially common, however, and no longer considered incorrect, in combination with *self-*, with *self-deprecation*, *self-deprecating*, and *self-deprecatory* being used far more often than *self-depreciation*, *self-depreciating*, and *self-depreciatory*.

depreciate /dɪˈpriːʃɪeɪt, -sɪ-/ *v.* **1** *tr. & intr.* diminish in value (*the pound is still depreciating*). **2** *tr.* disparage; belittle (*they are always depreciating his taste*). **3** *tr.* reduce the purchasing power of (money). □ **depreciatory** /dɪˈpriːʃ(ɪ)ət(ə)ri/ *adj.* [Late Latin *depretiare* (as DE-, *pretiare* from *pretium* 'price')]

■ **Usage** See Usage Note at DEPRECATE.

depreciation /dɪˌpriːʃɪˈeɪʃ(ə)n, -sɪˈeɪ-/ *n.* **1** the amount of wear and tear (of a property etc.) for which a reduction may be made in a valuation, an estimate, or a balance sheet. **2** *Econ.* **a** the decrease in the value of a currency. **b** an instance of this. **3** an instance of disparagement; belittlement.

depredation /dɛprɪˈdeɪʃ(ə)n/ *n.* (usu. in *pl.*) **1** despoiling, ravaging, or plundering. **2** an instance or instances of this. [French *déprédation* from Late Latin *depraedatio* (as DE-, *praedatio -onis* from Latin *praedari* 'plunder')]

depredator /ˈdɛprɪdeɪtə/ *n.* a despoiler or pillager. □ **depredatory** /ˈdɛprɪdeɪt(ə)ri, dɪˈprɛdət(ə)ri/ *adj.* [Late Latin *depraedator* (as DEPREDATION)]

depress /dɪˈprɛs/ *v.tr.* **1** push or pull down; lower (*depressed the lever*). **2** make dispirited or dejected. **3** *Econ.* reduce the activity of (esp. trade). **4** (as **depressed** *adj.*) **a** dispirited or miserable. **b** *Psychol.* suffering from depression. □ **depressible** *adj.* **depressing** *adj.* **depressingly** *adv.* [Middle English from Old French *depresser* from Late Latin *depressare* (as DE-, *pressare*, frequentative of *premere* 'press')]

depressant /dɪˈprɛs(ə)nt/ *adj. & n.* ● *adj.* **1** that depresses. **2** *Med.* sedative. ● *n.* **1** *Med.* an agent, esp. a drug, that sedates. **2** an influence that depresses.

depressed area *n.* an area suffering from economic depression.

depression /dɪˈprɛʃ(ə)n/ *n.* **1** **a** *Med.* a pathological state of extreme dejection or melancholy, characterized by a mood of hopelessness and feelings of inadequacy, often with physical symptoms. **b** a reduction in vitality, vigour, or spirits. **2** **a** a long period of financial and industrial decline; a slump. **b** (**the Depression**) (in the UK) the depression of 1929–34. **3** *Meteorol.* a lowering of atmospheric pressure, esp. the centre of a region of minimum pressure or the system of winds round it. **4** a sunken place or hollow on a surface. **5** **a** a lowering or sinking (often foll. by *of*: *depression of freezing point*). **b** pressing down. **6** *Astron.* & *Geog.* the angular distance of an object below the horizon or a horizontal plane. [Middle English from Old French or Latin *depressio* (as DE-, *premere press-* 'press')]

depressive /dɪˈprɛsɪv/ *adj. & n.* ● *adj.* **1** tending to depress. **2** *Psychol.* involving or characterized by depression. ● *n. Psychol.* a person suffering or with a tendency to suffer from depression. [French *dépressif -ive* or medieval Latin *depressivus* (as DEPRESSION)]

depressor /dɪˈprɛsə/ *n.* **1** *Anat.* **a** (in full **depressor muscle**) a muscle that causes the lowering of some part of the body. **b** a nerve that lowers blood pressure. **2** *Surgery* an instrument for pressing down an organ etc. [Latin (as DEPRESSION)]

depressurize /diːˈprɛʃərʌɪz/ *v.tr.* (also **-ise**) cause an appreciable drop in the pressure of the gas inside (a container), esp. to the ambient level. □ **depressurization** /-ˈzeɪʃ(ə)n/ *n.*

deprivation /dɛprɪˈveɪʃ(ə)n/ *n.* **1** (usu. foll. by *of*) the act or an instance of depriving; the state of being deprived (*deprivation of liberty*; *suffered many deprivations*). **2** **a** deposition from esp. an ecclesiastical office. **b** an instance of this. [medieval Latin *deprivatio* (as DEPRIVE)]

deprive /dɪˈprʌɪv/ *v.tr.* **1** (usu. foll. by *of*) strip, dispossess; debar from enjoying (*illness deprived him of success*). **2** (as **deprived** *adj.*) **a** (of a child etc.) suffering from the effects of a poor or loveless home. **b** (of an area) with inadequate housing, facilities, employment, etc. **3** *archaic* depose (esp. a clergyman) from office. □ **deprivable** *adj.* **deprival** *n.* [Middle English via Old French *depriver* from medieval Latin *deprivare* (as DE-, Latin *privare* 'deprive')]

de profundis /deɪ prəˈfʊndɪs/ *adv. & n.* ● *adv.* from the depths (of sorrow etc.). ● *n.* a cry from the depths. [opening Latin words of Psalm 130]

Dept. *abbr.* Department.

depth /dɛpθ/ *n.* **1** **a** deepness (*the depth is not great at the edge*). **b** the measurement from the top down, from the surface inwards, or from the front to the back (*depth of the drawer is 12 inches*). **2** difficulty; abstruseness. **3** **a** sagacity; wisdom. **b** intensity of emotion etc. (*the poem has little depth*). **4** an intensity of colour, darkness, etc. **5** (in *pl.*) **a** deep water, a deep place; an abyss. **b** a low, depressed state. **c** the lowest or inmost part (*the depths of the country*). **6** the middle (*in the depth of winter*). □ **in depth** comprehensively, thoroughly, or profoundly (cf. IN-DEPTH). **out of one's depth** **1** in water over one's head. **2** engaged in a task or on a subject too difficult for one. [Middle English (as DEEP, -TH[2])]

depth charge *n.* (also **depth bomb**) a bomb capable of exploding under water, esp. for dropping on a submerged submarine etc.

depthless /ˈdɛpθlɪs/ *adj.* **1** extremely deep; fathomless. **2** shallow, superficial.

depth psychology *n.* psychoanalysis to reveal hidden motives etc.

depurate /dɪˈpjʊəreɪt, ˈdɛpjʊreɪt/ *v.tr. & intr.* make or become free from impurities. □ **depuration** /-ˈreɪʃ(ə)n/ *n.* **depurative** /dɪˈpjʊərətɪv/ *adj. & n.* **depurator** *n.* [medieval Latin *depurare* (as DE-, *purus* 'pure')]

deputation /dɛpjʊˈteɪʃ(ə)n/ *n.* a group of people appointed to represent others, usu. for a specific purpose; a delegation. [Middle English from Late Latin *deputatio* (as DEPUTE)]

depute *v. & n.* ● *v.tr.* /dɪˈpjuːt/ (often foll. by *to*) **1** appoint as a deputy. **2** delegate (a task, authority, etc.) (*deputed the leadership to her*). ● *n.* /ˈdɛpjuːt/ *Sc.* a deputy. [Middle English via Old French *deputé*, past part. of *deputer*, from Latin *deputare* 'regard as, allot' (as DE-, *putare* 'think')]

deputize /ˈdɛpjʊtʌɪz/ *v.intr.* (also **-ise**) (usu. foll. by *for*) act as a deputy or understudy.

deputy /ˈdɛpjʊti/ *n.* (*pl.* **-ies**) **1** a person appointed or delegated to act for another or others (also *attrib.*: *deputy manager*). **2** *Polit.* a parliamentary representative in certain countries, e.g. France. **3** *Brit.* a coal mine official responsible for safety. □ **by deputy** by proxy. □ **deputyship** *n.* [Middle English variant of DEPUTE *n.*]

deputy lieutenant *n. Brit.* the deputy of the Lord Lieutenant of a county.

deracinate /dɪˈrasɪneɪt/ *v.tr. literary* **1** tear up by the roots. **2** obliterate, expunge. □ **deracination** /-ˈneɪʃ(ə)n/ *n.* [French *déraciner* (as DE-, *racine* from Late Latin *radicina*, diminutive of *radix* 'root')]

derail /dɪˈreɪl/ *v.tr.* (usu. in *passive*) cause (a train etc.) to leave the rails. □ **derailment** *n.* [French *dérailler* (as DE-, RAIL[1])]

derailleur /dɪˈreɪlə, -ljə/ *n.* a bicycle gear in which the ratio is changed by switching the line of the chain while pedalling so that it jumps to a different sprocket. [French *dérailleur* (as DERAIL)]

derange /dɪˈreɪn(d)ʒ/ *v.tr.* **1** throw into confusion; disorganize; cause to act irregularly. **2** (esp. as **deranged** *adj.*) make insane (*deranged by the tragic events*). **3** disturb; interrupt. □ **derangement** *n.* [French *déranger* (as DE-, *rang* RANK[1])]

derate /diːˈreɪt/ *v. Brit.* **1** *tr.* remove part or all of the burden of rates from. **2** *intr.* diminish or remove rates.

deration /diːˈraʃ(ə)n/ *v.tr.* free (food etc.) from rationing.

Derby /ˈdɑːbi/ *n.* (*pl.* **-ies**) **1 a** an annual horse race run on the flat at Epsom. **b** a similar race elsewhere (*Kentucky Derby*). **2** (also **derby**) **a** any important sporting contest. **b** = LOCAL DERBY. **3** (**derby**) *N. Amer.* a bowler hat. [named after the 12th Earl of *Derby*, d. 1834, founder of the horse race]

Derby Day *n.* the day on which the Derby is run.

derecognize /diːˈrɛkəgnʌɪz/ *v.tr.* (also **-ise**) cease to recognize the status of (esp. a trade union). □ **derecognition** /-ˈnɪʃ(ə)n/ *n.*

de règle /də ˈrɛgl(ə), French də rɛgl/ *predic.adj.* customary; proper. [French, = of rule]

deregulate /diːˈrɛgjʊleɪt/ *v.tr.* remove regulations or restrictions from. □ **deregulation** /-ˈleɪʃ(ə)n/ *n.*

derelict /ˈdɛrəlɪkt/ *adj.* & *n.* ● *adj.* **1** abandoned, ownerless (esp. of a ship at sea or an empty decrepit property). **2** (esp. of property) ruined; dilapidated. **3** *N. Amer.* negligent (of duty etc.). ● *n.* **1** a social outcast; a person without a home, a job, or property. **2** abandoned property, esp. a ship. [Latin *derelictus*, past part. of *derelinquere* (as DE-, *relinquere* 'leave')]

dereliction /dɛrəˈlɪkʃ(ə)n/ *n.* **1** (usu. foll. by *of*) **a** neglect; failure to carry out one's obligations (*dereliction of duty*). **b** an instance of this. **2** the act or an instance of abandoning; the fact or process of being abandoned. **3 a** the retreat of the sea exposing new land. **b** the land so exposed. [Latin *derelictio* (as DERELICT)]

derequisition /ˌdiːrɛkwɪˈzɪʃ(ə)n/ *v.tr.* return (requisitioned property) to its former owner.

derestrict /diːrɪˈstrɪkt/ *v.tr.* **1** remove restrictions from. **2** *Brit.* remove speed restrictions from (a road, area, etc.). □ **derestriction** *n.*

deride /dɪˈrʌɪd/ *v.tr.* laugh scornfully at; ridicule. □ **derider** *n.* **deridingly** *adv.* [Latin *deridēre* (as DE-, *ridēre ris-* 'laugh')]

de-rig /diːˈrɪg/ *v.tr.* (**de-rigged**, **de-rigging**) (also *absol.*) dismantle the rigging of (a ship or aircraft).

de rigueur /də rɪˈgəː/ *predic.adj.* required by custom or etiquette (*evening dress is de rigueur*). [French, = of strictness]

derision /dɪˈrɪʒ(ə)n/ *n.* ridicule; mockery (*bring into derision*). □ **hold** (or **have**) **in derision** *archaic* mock at. □ **derisible** /dɪˈrɪzɪb(ə)l/ *adj.* [Middle English via Old French from Late Latin *derisio -onis* (as DERIDE)]

derisive /dɪˈrʌɪsɪv, -z-/ *adj.* scoffing; ironical; scornful (*derisive cheers*). □ **derisively** *adv.* **derisiveness** *n.*

■ **Usage** See Usage Note at DERISORY.

derisory /dɪˈrʌɪs(ə)ri, -z-/ *adj.* **1** so small or unimportant as to be ridiculous (*derisory offer*; *derisory costs*). **2** = DERISIVE. [Late Latin *derisorius* (as DERISION)]

■ **Usage** Note the difference between *derisory* and *derisive*. Both words mean 'scoffing', but *derisory* also means 'ridiculously small', which is now its more usual sense.

derivation /dɛrɪˈveɪʃ(ə)n/ *n.* **1** the act or an instance of deriving or obtaining from a source; the fact or process of being derived. **2 a** the formation of a word from another word or from a root. **b** a derivative. **c** the tracing of the origin of a word. **d** a statement or account of this. **3** extraction, descent. **4** *Math.* a sequence of statements showing that a formula, theorem, etc., is a consequence of previously accepted statements. □ **derivational** *adj.* [French *dérivation* or Latin *derivatio* (as DERIVE)]

derivative /dɪˈrɪvətɪv/ *adj.* & *n.* ● *adj.* derived from another source; not original (*his music is derivative and uninteresting*). ● *n.* **1** something derived from another source, esp.: **a** a word derived from another or from a root (e.g. *quickly* from *quick*). **b** *Chem.* a chemical compound that is derived from another. **2** *Math.* a quantity measuring the rate of change of another. □ **derivatively** *adv.* [French *dérivatif -ive* from Latin *derivativus* (as DERIVE)]

derive /dɪˈrʌɪv/ *v.* **1** *tr.* **a** (usu. foll. by *from*) get, obtain, or form (*derived satisfaction from work*). **b** (in *passive*; foll. by *from*) (of a word etc.) originate, be formed from. **2** *intr.* (foll. by *from*) **a** arise from, originate in, be descended or obtained from (*happiness derives from many things*). **b** = sense 1b. **3** *tr.* gather or deduce (*derived the information from the clues*). **4** *tr.* **a** trace the descent of (a person). **b** show the origin of (a thing). **5** *tr.* (usu. foll. by *from*) show or state the origin or formation of (a word etc.) (*derived the word from Latin*). **6** *tr. Math.* obtain (a function) by differentiation. □ **derivable** *adj.* [Middle English from Old French *deriver* or from Latin *derivare* (as DE-, *rivus* 'stream')]

derm (also **derma**) var. of DERMIS.

dermatitis /dəːməˈtʌɪtɪs/ *n.* inflammation of the skin. [Greek *derma -atos* 'skin' + -ITIS]

dermatoglyphics /dəːmətəʊˈglɪfɪks/ *n.* the science or study of skin markings or patterns, esp. of the fingers, hands, and feet. □ **dermatoglyphic** *adj.* **dermatoglyphically** *adv.* [as DERMATITIS + Greek *gluphē* 'carving': see GLYPH]

dermatology /dəːməˈtɒlədʒi/ *n.* the study of the diagnosis and treatment of skin disorders. □ **dermatological** /-təˈlɒdʒɪk(ə)l/ *adj.* **dermatologist** *n.* [as DERMATITIS + -LOGY]

dermis /ˈdəːmɪs/ *n.* (also **derm** /dəːm/ or **derma** /ˈdəːmə/) **1** (in general use) the skin. **2** *Anat.* the true skin, the thick layer of living tissue below the epidermis. □ **dermal** *adj.* **dermic** *adj.* [modern Latin, suggested by EPIDERMIS]

dernier cri /dəːnjeɪ ˈkriː/ *n.* the very latest fashion. [French, = last cry]

derogate /ˈdɛrəgeɪt/ *v.intr.* (foll. by *from*) *formal* **1** take away a part from; detract from (a merit, a right, etc.). **2** deviate from (correct behaviour etc.). □ **derogative** /dɪˈrɒgətɪv/ *adj.* [Latin *derogare* (as DE-, *rogare* 'ask')]

derogation /dɛrəˈgeɪʃ(ə)n/ *n.* **1** (foll. by *of*) a lessening or impairment of (a law, authority, position, dignity, etc.). **2** deterioration; debasement. [Middle English from French *dérogation* or Latin *derogatio* (as DEROGATE)]

derogatory /dɪˈrɒgət(ə)ri/ *adj.* (often foll. by *to*) involving disparagement or discredit; insulting, depreciatory (*made a derogatory remark*; *derogatory to my position*). □ **derogatorily** *adv.* [Late Latin *derogatorius* (as DEROGATE)]

derrick /ˈdɛrɪk/ *n.* **1** a kind of crane for moving or lifting heavy weights, having a movable pivoted arm. **2** the framework over an oil well or similar excavation, holding the drilling machinery. [obsolete senses *hangman*, *gallows*, from the name of a London hangman *c.*1600]

derrière /dɛrɪˈɛː/ *n. colloq. euphem.* the buttocks. [French, = behind]

derring-do /dɛrɪŋˈduː/ *n. literary* or *joc.* heroic courage or action. [Middle English, = *daring to do*, misinterpreted by Spenser and by Scott]

derringer /ˈdɛrɪn(d)ʒə/ *n.* a small large-bore pistol. [named after H. *Deringer*, American inventor d. 1868]

derris /ˈdɛrɪs/ *n.* **1** any woody tropical climbing leguminous plant of the genus *Derris*, bearing leathery pods. **2** an insecticide made from the powdered root of some kinds of derris. [modern Latin from Greek, = leather covering (with reference to its pod)]

derry /ˈdɛri/ *n.* □ **have a derry on** *Austral.* & *NZ colloq.* be prejudiced against (a person). [apparently from the song-refrain *derry down*]

derv /dəːv/ *n. Brit.* diesel oil for road vehicles. [*d*iesel-*e*ngined *r*oad-*v*ehicle]

dervish /ˈdəːvɪʃ/ *n.* a member of any of several Muslim fraternities vowed to poverty and austerity. [Turkish *derviş* from Persian *darvēsh* 'poor, a mendicant']

DES *abbr. hist.* (in the UK) Department of Education and Science (replaced in 1992 by the DFE).

desalinate /diːˈsælɪneɪt/ *v.tr.* remove salt from (esp. sea water). □ **desalination** /-ˈneɪʃ(ə)n/ *n.*

desalinize /diːˈsælɪnʌɪz/ *v.tr.* *US* = DESALINATE. □ **desalinization** /-ˈzeɪʃ(ə)n/ *n.*

desalt /diːˈsɔːlt, -ˈsɒlt/ *v.tr.* = DESALINATE.

descale /diːˈskeɪl/ *v.tr.* remove the scale from.

descant *n.* & *v.* ● *n.* /ˈdɛskant/ **1** *Mus.* an independent treble melody usu. sung or played above a basic melody, esp. of a hymn tune. **2** *poet.* a melody; a song. ● *v.intr.* /dɪˈskant, dɛ-/ **1** (foll. by *on*, *upon*) talk lengthily and tediously, esp. in praise of. **2** *Mus.* sing or play a descant. [Middle English via Old French *deschant* from medieval Latin *discantus* (as DIS-, *cantus* 'song, CHANT')]

descant recorder *n.* *Brit.* the most common size of recorder, with a range of two octaves.

descend /dɪˈsɛnd/ *v.* **1** *tr.* & *intr.* go or come down (a hill, stairs, etc.). **2** *intr.* (of a thing) sink, fall (*rain descended heavily*). **3** *intr.* slope downwards, lie along a descending slope (*fields descended to the beach*). **4** *intr.* (usu. foll. by *on*) **a** make a sudden attack. **b** make an unexpected and usu. unwelcome visit (*hope they don't descend on us at the weekend*). **5** *intr.* (usu. foll. by *from*, *to*) (of property, qualities, rights, etc.) be passed by inheritance (*the house descends from my grandmother*; *the property descended to me*). **6** *intr.* **a** sink in rank, quality, etc. **b** (foll. by *to*) degrade oneself or stoop morally to (an unworthy act) (*descend to violence*). **7** *intr.* *Mus.* (of sound) become lower in pitch. **8** *intr.* (usu. foll. by *to*) proceed (in discourse or writing): **a** in time (to a subsequent event etc.). **b** from the general (to the particular) (*now let's descend to details*). **9** *tr.* go along (a river etc.) to the sea etc. **10** *intr.* *Printing* (of a letter) have its tail below the line. □ **be descended from** have as an ancestor. □ **descendent** *adj.* [Middle English via Old French *descendre* from Latin *descendere* (as DE-, *scandere* 'climb')]

descendant /dɪˈsɛnd(ə)nt/ *n.* (often foll. by *of*) a person or thing descended from another (*a descendant of Charles I*). [French, part. of *descendre* (as DESCEND)]

descender /dɪˈsɛndə/ *n.* *Printing* a part of a letter that extends below the line.

descendible /dɪˈsɛndɪb(ə)l/ *adj.* **1** (of a slope etc.) that may be descended. **2** *Law* capable of descending by inheritance. [Old French *descendable* (as DESCEND)]

descent /dɪˈsɛnt/ *n.* **1 a** the act of descending. **b** an instance of this. **c** a downward movement. **2 a** a way or path etc. by which one may descend. **b** a downward slope. **3 a** being descended; lineage, family origin (*traces his descent from William the Conqueror*). **b** the transmission of qualities, property, privileges, etc., by inheritance. **4 a** a decline; a fall. **b** a lowering (of pitch, temperature, etc.). **5** a sudden violent attack. [Middle English from Old French *descente*, from *descendre* DESCEND]

descramble /diːˈskramb(ə)l/ *v.tr.* **1** convert or restore (a signal) to intelligible form. **2** counteract the effects of (a scrambling device). **3** recover an original signal from (a scrambled signal). □ **descrambler** *n.*

describe /dɪˈskrʌɪb/ *v.tr.* **1 a** state the characteristics, appearance, etc. of, in spoken or written form (*described the landscape*). **b** (foll. by *as*) assert to be; call (*described him as a habitual liar*). **2 a** mark out or draw (esp. a geometrical figure) (*described a triangle*). **b** move in (a specified way, esp. a curve) (*described a parabola through the air*). □ **describable** *adj.* **describer** *n.* [Latin *describere* (as DE-, *scribere script-* 'write')]

description /dɪˈskrɪpʃ(ə)n/ *n.* **1 a** the act or an instance of describing; the process of being described. **b** a spoken or written representation (of a person, object, or event). **2** a sort, kind, or class (*no food of any description*). □ **answers** (or **fits**) **the description** has the qualities specified. [Middle English via Old French from Latin *descriptio -onis* (as DESCRIBE)]

descriptive /dɪˈskrɪptɪv/ *adj.* **1** serving or seeking to describe (*a descriptive writer*). **2** describing or classifying without expressing feelings or judging (*a purely descriptive account*). **3** *Linguistics* describing a language without comparing, endorsing, or condemning particular usage, vocabulary, etc. (opp. PRESCRIPTIVE). **4** *Gram.* (of an adjective) describing the noun, rather than its relation, position, etc., e.g. *blue* as distinct from *few*. □ **descriptively** *adv.* **descriptiveness** *n.* [Late Latin *descriptivus* (as DESCRIBE)]

descriptor /dɪˈskrɪptə/ *n.* *Linguistics* a word or expression etc. used to describe or identify. [Latin, = describer (as DESCRIBE)]

descry /dɪˈskrʌɪ/ *v.tr.* (**-ies**, **-ied**) *literary* catch sight of; discern (*descried him in the crowd*; *descries no glimmer of light in her situation*). [Middle English (earlier senses 'proclaim, DECRY') from Old French *descrier*: probably confused with variant of obsolete *descrive* from Old French *descrivre* DESCRIBE]

desecrate /ˈdɛsɪkreɪt/ *v.tr.* **1** violate (a sacred place or thing) with violence, profanity, etc. **2** deprive (a church, a sacred object, etc.) of sanctity; deconsecrate. □ **desecration** /-ˈkreɪʃ(ə)n/ *n.* **desecrator** *n.* [DE- + CONSECRATE]

deseed /diːˈsiːd/ *v.tr.* *Brit.* remove the seeds from (a plant, vegetable, etc.).

deseeder /diːˈsiːdə/ *n.* a machine for deseeding.

desegregate /diːˈsɛgrɪgeɪt/ *v.tr.* abolish racial segregation in (schools etc.) or of (people etc.). □ **desegregation** /-ˈgeɪʃ(ə)n/ *n.*

deselect /diːsɪˈlɛkt/ *v.tr.* *Brit.* *Polit.* decline to select or retain as a constituency candidate in an election. □ **deselection** *n.*

desensitize /diːˈsɛnsɪtʌɪz/ *v.tr.* (also **-ise**) reduce or destroy the sensitiveness of (photographic materials to light, a person to an allergen, etc.). □ **desensitization** /-ˈzeɪʃ(ə)n/ *n.* **desensitizer** *n.*

desert[1] /dɪˈzəːt/ *v.* **1** *tr.* abandon, give up, leave (*deserted the sinking ship*). **2** *tr.* forsake or abandon (a cause or a person, people, etc., having claims on one) (*deserted his wife and children*). **3** *tr.* fail (*his presence of mind deserted him*). **4** *intr.* *Mil.* run away (esp. from military service). **5** *tr.* (as **deserted** *adj.*) empty, abandoned (*a deserted house*). □ **deserter** *n.* (in sense 4). **desertion** /-ˈzəːʃ(ə)n/ *n.* [French *déserter* via Late Latin *desertare* from Latin *desertus* (as DESERT[2])]

desert[2] /ˈdɛzət/ *n.* & *adj.* ● *n.* **1** a dry barren often sand-covered area of land, characteristically desolate, waterless, and without vegetation. **2** an uninteresting or barren subject, period, etc. (*a cultural desert*). ● *adj.* **1** uninhabited, desolate. **2** uncultivated, barren. [Middle English via Old French from Latin *desertus*, ecclesiastical Latin *desertum* (*n.*), past part. of *deserere* 'leave, forsake']

desert[3] /dɪˈzəːt/ *n.* **1** (in *pl.*) **a** acts or qualities deserving reward or punishment. **b** such reward or punishment (esp. in phr. **get one's just deserts**). **2** the fact of being worthy of reward or punishment; deservingness. [Middle English via Old French from *deservir* DESERVE]

desert boot *n.* a suede etc. boot reaching to or extending just above the ankle.

desertification /dɛˌzəːtɪfɪˈkeɪʃ(ə)n/ *n.* the process of making or becoming a desert.

desert island *n.* a remote (usu. tropical) island presumed to be uninhabited.

desert rat *n.* *Brit.* *colloq.* a soldier of the 7th British armoured division (with the jerboa as a badge) in the N. African desert campaign of 1941–2.

deserve /dɪˈzəːv/ *v.tr.* (often foll. by *to* + infin.) show conduct or qualities worthy of (reward, punishment, etc.) (*deserves to be imprisoned*; *deserves a prize*). □ **deserve well** (or **ill**) **of** be worthy of good (or bad) treatment at the hands of (*deserves well of the electorate*). □ **deservedly** /-vɪdli/ *adv.* **deservedness** /-vɪdnɪs/ *n.* [Middle English via Old French *deservir* from Latin *deservire* (as DE-, *servire* 'serve')]

deserving /dɪˈzəːvɪŋ/ *adj.* meritorious. □ **deserving of** showing conduct or qualities worthy of (praise, blame, help, etc.). □ **deservingly** *adv.* **deservingness** *n.*

desex /diːˈsɛks/ *v.tr.* **1** castrate or spay (an animal). **2** deprive of sexual qualities or attraction.

desexualize /diːˈsɛksjʊəlʌɪz, -ˈsɛkʃʊəl-/ *v.tr.* (also **-ise**) deprive of sexual character or of the distinctive qualities of a sex.

déshabillé /dɛzaˈbiːeɪ, French dezabije/ *n.* (also ***déshabille*** /deɪzaˈbiːl, French dezabi/, **dishabille** /dɪsaˈbiːl/) a state of being only partly or carelessly clothed. [French, = undressed]

desiccant /ˈdɛsɪk(ə)nt/ *n. Chem.* a hygroscopic substance used as a drying agent.

desiccate /ˈdɛsɪkeɪt/ *v.tr.* remove the moisture from, dry (esp. food for preservation) (*desiccated coconut*). ▫ **desiccation** /-ˈkeɪʃ(ə)n/ *n.* **desiccative** /-kətɪv/ *adj.* [Latin *desiccare* (as DE-, *siccus* 'dry')]

desiccator /ˈdɛsɪkeɪtə/ *n.* **1** an apparatus for desiccating. **2** *Chem.* an apparatus containing a drying agent to remove the moisture from specimens.

desiderate /dɪˈzɪdəreɪt, -ˈsɪd-/ *v.tr. archaic* feel to be missing; regret the absence of; wish to have. [Latin *desiderare* (as DE-, *siderare* as in CONSIDER)]

desiderative /dɪˈzɪd(ə)rətɪv, -ˈsɪd-/ *adj. & n.* ● *adj.* **1** *Gram.* (of a verb, conjugation, etc.) formed from another verb etc. and denoting a desire to perform the action of that verb etc. **2** desiring. ● *n. Gram.* a desiderative verb, conjugation, etc. [Late Latin *desiderativus* (as DESIDERATE)]

desideratum /dɪˌzɪdəˈrɑːtəm, -ˈreɪtəm; -ˌsɪd-/ *n.* (*pl.* **desiderata** /-tə/) something that is needed or desirable. [Latin, neut. past part. of *desiderare* DESIDERATE]

design /dɪˈzʌɪn/ *n. & v.* ● *n.* **1 a** a preliminary plan, sketch, or concept, for the making or production of a building, machine, garment, etc. **b** the art of producing these. **2** a scheme of lines or shapes forming a pattern or decoration. **3** a plan, purpose, or intention. **4 a** an example or a completed version of a sketch, concept, or pattern. **b** an established version of a product (*one of our most popular designs*). ● *v.tr.* **1** produce a design for (a building, machine, picture, garment, etc.). **2** intend, plan, or purpose (*the remark was designed to offend*; *a course designed for beginners*; *designed an attack*). **3** (*absol.*) be a designer. ▫ **by design** on purpose. **have designs on** have one's sights set on; plan to attack or appropriate. [French *désigner* 'appoint' or obsolete French *desseing*, ultimately from Latin *designare* DESIGNATE]

designate *v. & adj.* ● *v.tr.* /ˈdɛzɪgneɪt/ **1** (often foll. by *as*) appoint to an office or function (*designated him as postmaster general*; *designated his own successor*). **2** specify or particularize (*receives guests at designated times*). **3** (often foll. by *as*) describe as; entitle, style. **4** serve as the name or distinctive mark of (*English uses French words to designate ballet steps*). ● *adj.* /ˈdɛzɪgnət/ (placed after noun) appointed to an office but not yet installed (*bishop designate*). ▫ **designator** /-neɪtə/ *n.* [Latin *designat-*, past part. stem of *designare* (as DE-, *signare* from *signum* 'mark')]

designation /dɛzɪgˈneɪʃ(ə)n/ *n.* **1** a name, description, or title. **2** the act or process of designating. [Middle English from Old French *designation* or Latin *designatio* (as DESIGNATE)]

designedly /dɪˈzʌɪnɪdli/ *adv.* by design; on purpose.

designer /dɪˈzʌɪnə/ *n.* **1** a person who makes artistic designs or plans for construction, e.g. for clothing, machines, theatre sets; a draughtsman. **2** (*attrib.*) (of clothing etc.) bearing the name or label of a famous designer; prestigious.

designer drug *n.* a synthetic analogue of an illegal drug, esp. one not itself illegal.

designing /dɪˈzʌɪnɪŋ/ *adj.* crafty, artful, or scheming. ▫ **designingly** *adv.*

desirable /dɪˈzʌɪərəb(ə)l/ *adj. & n.* ● *adj.* **1** worth having or wishing for (*it is desirable that nobody should smoke*). **2** arousing sexual desire; very attractive. ● *n.* a desirable person or thing. ▫ **desirability** /-ˈbɪlɪti/ *n.* **desirableness** *n.* **desirably** *adv.* [Middle English from Old French (as DESIRE)]

desire /dɪˈzʌɪə/ *n. & v.* ● *n.* **1 a** an unsatisfied longing or craving. **b** an expression of this; a request (*expressed a desire to rest*). **2** sexual appetite, lust. **3** something desired (*achieved his heart's desire*). ● *v.tr.* **1 a** (often foll. by *to* + infin., or *that* + clause) long for; crave. **b** feel sexual desire for. **2** request (*desires a cup of tea*). **3** *archaic* pray, entreat, or command (*desire him to wait*). [Middle English via Old French *desir*, from *desirer*, from Latin *desiderare* DESIDERATE]

desirous /dɪˈzʌɪərəs/ *predic.adj.* **1** (usu. foll. by *of*) ambitious, desiring (*desirous of stardom*; *desirous of doing well*). **2** (usu. foll. by *to* + infin., or *that* + clause) wishful; hoping (*desirous to do the right thing*). [Middle English via Anglo-French *desirous*, Old French *desireus* from Romanic (as DESIRE)]

desist /dɪˈzɪst, dɪˈsɪst/ *v.intr.* (often foll. by *from*) *literary* abstain; cease (*please desist from interrupting*; *when requested, he desisted*). [Old French *desister* from Latin *desistere* (as DE-, *sistere* 'stop', reduplication of *stare* 'stand')]

desk /dɛsk/ *n.* **1** a piece of furniture with a flat or sloped surface for writing on, and often drawers. **2** a counter in a hotel, bank, etc., which separates the customer from the assistant. **3** a section of a newspaper office, radio station, etc., dealing with a specified topic (*the sports desk*; *the features desk*). **4** *Mus.* a music stand in an orchestra regarded as a unit of two players. [Middle English via medieval Latin *desca* from Latin DISCUS 'disc']

desk-bound *adj.* obliged to remain working at a desk.

deskill /diːˈskɪl/ *v.tr.* **1** render (a skilled worker) unskilled. **2** remove the need for skill from (a job, production, etc.).

desktop /ˈdɛsktɒp/ *n.* **1** the working surface of a desk. **2** (*attrib.*) (esp. of a microcomputer) suitable for use at an ordinary desk.

desktop publishing *n.* the production of printed matter with a desktop computer and printer.

desman /ˈdɛsmən/ *n.* (*pl.* **desmans**) either of two aquatic flesh-eating shrewlike mammals, one originating in Russia (*Desmana moschata*) and one in the Pyrenees (*Galemys pyrenaicus*). [French & German from Swedish *desman-råtta* 'muskrat']

desmid /ˈdɛsmɪd/ *n.* a microscopic unicellular freshwater alga of the family Desmidiaceae. [modern Latin genus name *Desmidium*, from Greek *desmos* 'band, chain']

desolate *adj. & v.* ● *adj.* /ˈdɛs(ə)lət/ **1** left alone; solitary. **2** (of a building or place) uninhabited, ruined, neglected, barren, dreary, empty (*a desolate moor*). **3** forlorn; wretched; miserable (*was left desolate and weeping*). ● *v.tr.* /ˈdɛsəleɪt/ **1** depopulate or devastate; lay waste to. **2** (esp. as **desolated** *adj.*) make wretched or forlorn (*desolated by grief*; *inconsolable and desolated*). ▫ **desolately** /-lətli/ *adv.* **desolateness** /-lətnɪs/ *n.* **desolator** /-leɪtə/ *n.* [Middle English from Latin *desolatus*, past part. of *desolare* (as DE-, *solare* from *solus* 'alone')]

desolation /dɛsəˈleɪʃ(ə)n/ *n.* **1 a** the act of desolating. **b** the process of being desolated. **2** loneliness, grief, or wretchedness, esp. caused by desertion. **3** a neglected, ruined, barren, or empty state. [Middle English from Late Latin *desolatio* (as DESOLATE)]

desorb /diːˈsɔːb/ *v.* **1** *tr.* cause the release of (an adsorbed substance) from a surface. **2** *intr.* (of an adsorbed substance) become released. ▫ **desorbent** *adj. & n.* **desorption** *n.* [DE-, ADSORB]

despair /dɪˈspɛː/ *n. & v.* ● *n.* the complete loss or absence of hope. ● *v.intr.* **1** (often foll. by *of*) lose or be without hope (*despaired of ever seeing her again*). **2** (foll. by *of*) lose hope about (*his life is despaired of*). ▫ **be the despair of** be the cause of despair by badness or unapproachable excellence (*he's the despair of his parents*). ▫ **despairingly** *adv.* [Middle English via Old

French *desespeir*, *desperer* from Latin *desperare* (as DE-, *sperare* 'hope')]

despatch var. of DISPATCH.

desperado /dɛspəˈrɑːdəʊ/ *n.* (*pl.* **-oes** or *US* **-os**) a desperate or reckless person, esp. a criminal. [pseudo-Spanish from obsolete noun DESPERATE]

desperate /ˈdɛsp(ə)rət/ *adj.* **1** reckless from despair; violent and lawless. **2 a** extremely dangerous or serious (*a desperate situation*). **b** staking all on a small chance (*a desperate remedy*). **3** very bad (*a desperate night*; *desperate poverty*). **4** (usu. foll. by *for*) needing or desiring very much (*desperate for recognition*). □ **desperately** *adv.* **desperateness** *n.* **desperation** /-ˈreɪʃ(ə)n/ *n.* [Middle English from Latin *desperatus*, past part. of *desperare* (as DE-, *sperare* 'hope')]

despicable /dɪˈspɪkəb(ə)l, ˈdɛspɪk-/ *adj.* vile; contemptible, esp. morally. □ **despicably** *adv.* [Late Latin *despicabilis* from *despicari* (as DE-, *specere* 'look at')]

despise /dɪˈspʌɪz/ *v.tr.* look down on as inferior, worthless, or contemptible. □ **despiser** *n.* [Middle English from *despis-*, pres. stem of Old French *despire*, from Latin *despicere* (as DE-, *specere* 'look at')]

despite /dɪˈspʌɪt/ *prep.* & *n.* ● *prep.* in spite of. ● *n. archaic* or *literary* **1** outrage, injury. **2** malice, hatred (*died of mere despite*). □ **despite** (or **in despite**) **of** *archaic* in spite of. □ **despiteful** *adj.* [Middle English via Old French *despit* from Latin *despectus* 'looking down on', from *despicere* (as DESPISE)]

despoil /dɪˈspɔɪl/ *v.tr.* (often foll. by *of*) *literary* plunder; rob; deprive (*despoiled the roof of its lead*). □ **despoiler** *n.* **despoilment** *n.* **despoliation** /dɪˌspəʊlɪˈeɪʃ(ə)n/ *n.* [Middle English via Old French *despoill(i)er* from Latin *despoliare* (as DE-, *spoliare* SPOIL)]

despond /dɪˈspɒnd/ *v.* & *n.* ● *v.intr.* lose heart or hope; be dejected. ● *n. archaic* despondency. [Latin *despondēre* 'give up, abandon' (as DE-, *spondēre* 'promise')]

despondent /dɪˈspɒnd(ə)nt/ *adj.* in low spirits, dejected. □ **despondence** *n.* **despondency** *n.* **despondently** *adv.*

despot /ˈdɛspɒt/ *n.* **1** an absolute ruler. **2** a tyrant or oppressor. □ **despotic** /-ˈspɒtɪk/ *adj.* **despotically** /-ˈspɒtɪk(ə)li/ *adv.* [French *despote* via medieval Latin *despota* from Greek *despotēs* 'master, lord']

despotism /ˈdɛspətɪz(ə)m/ *n.* **1 a** rule by a despot. **b** a country ruled by a despot. **2** absolute power or control; tyranny.

desquamate /ˈdɛskwəmeɪt/ *v.intr. Med.* (esp. of the skin) come off in scales (as in some diseases). □ **desquamation** /-ˈmeɪʃ(ə)n/ *n.* **desquamative** /-ˈskwamətɪv/ *adj.* **desquamatory** /-ˈskwamət(ə)ri/ *adj.* [Latin *desquamare* (as DE-, *squama* 'scale')]

des res /dɛz ˈrɛz/ *n. Brit. colloq.* a desirable residence. [abbreviation]

dessert /dɪˈzəːt/ *n.* **1** the sweet course of a meal, served at or near the end. **2** *Brit.* a course of fruit, nuts, etc., served after a meal. [French, past part. of *desservir* 'clear the table' (as DIS-, *servir* SERVE)]

dessertspoon /dɪˈzəːtspuːn/ *n.* **1** a spoon used for dessert, smaller than a tablespoon and larger than a teaspoon. **2** the amount held by this. □ **dessertspoonful** *n.* (*pl.* **-fuls**).

dessert wine *n.* usu. sweet wine drunk with or following dessert.

destabilize /diːˈsteɪbɪlʌɪz, -b(ə)l-/ *v.tr.* (also **-ise**) **1** render unstable. **2** subvert (esp. a foreign government). □ **destabilization** /-ˈzeɪʃ(ə)n/ *n.*

destination /dɛstɪˈneɪʃ(ə)n/ *n.* a place to which a person or thing is going. [Old French *destination* or Latin *destinatio* (as DESTINE)]

destine /ˈdɛstɪn/ *v.tr.* (often foll. by *to*, *for*, or *to* + infin.) set apart; appoint; preordain; intend (*destined him for the navy*). □ **be destined to** be fated or preordained to (*was destined to become a great man*). [Middle English via French *destiner* from Latin *destinare* (ultimately from *stare* 'stand')]

destiny /ˈdɛstɪni/ *n.* (*pl.* **-ies**) **1 a** the predetermined course of events; fate. **b** this regarded as a power. **2** what is destined to happen to a particular person etc. (*it was their destiny to be rejected*). [Middle English via Old French *destinée* from Romanic, past part. of *destinare*: see DESTINE]

destitute /ˈdɛstɪtjuːt/ *adj.* **1** without food, shelter, etc.; completely impoverished. **2** (usu. foll. by *of*) lacking (*destitute of friends*). □ **destitution** /-ˈtjuːʃ(ə)n/ *n.* [Middle English from Latin *destitutus*, past part. of *destituere* 'forsake' (as DE-, *statuere* 'place')]

destock /diːˈstɒk/ *v.intr.* reduce the stock or quantity held.

destrier /ˈdɛstrɪə, dɛˈstriːə/ *n. hist.* a warhorse. [Middle English from Anglo-French *destrer*, Old French *destrier*, ultimately from Latin DEXTER[1] 'right' (as the knight's horse was led by the squire with the right hand)]

destroy /dɪˈstrɔɪ/ *v.tr.* **1** pull or break down; demolish (*destroyed the bridge*). **2** put an end to (*the accident destroyed her confidence*). **3** kill (esp. a sick or savage animal) by humane means. **4** make useless; spoil utterly. **5** ruin financially, professionally, or in reputation. **6** defeat utterly (*destroyed the enemy*). [Middle English from Old French *destruire*, ultimately from Latin *destruere* (as DE-, *struere struct-* 'build')]

destroyer /dɪˈstrɔɪə/ *n.* **1** a person or thing that destroys. **2** *Naut.* a fast warship with guns and torpedoes used to protect other ships.

destroying angel *n.* a poisonous white toadstool, *Amanita virosa*.

destruct /dɪˈstrʌkt/ *v.* & *n.* ● *v.* **1** *tr.* destroy (esp. one's own rocket) deliberately, esp. for safety reasons. **2** *intr.* be destroyed in this way. ● *n.* an act of destructing a rocket etc. [Latin *destruere* (as DESTROY) or as back-formation from DESTRUCTION]

destructible /dɪˈstrʌktɪb(ə)l/ *adj.* able to be destroyed. □ **destructibility** /-ˈbɪlɪti/ *n.* [French *destructible* or Late Latin *destructibilis* (as DESTROY)]

destruction /dɪˈstrʌkʃ(ə)n/ *n.* **1** the act or an instance of destroying; the process of being destroyed. **2** a cause of ruin; something that destroys (*greed was their destruction*). [Middle English via Old French from Latin *destructio -onis* (as DESTROY)]

destructive /dɪˈstrʌktɪv/ *adj.* **1** (often foll. by *to*, *of*) destroying or tending to destroy (*destructive of her peace of mind*; *is destructive to organisms*; *a destructive child*). **2** negative in attitude or criticism; refuting without suggesting, helping, amending, etc. (opp. CONSTRUCTIVE) (*has only destructive criticism to offer*). □ **destructively** *adv.* **destructiveness** *n.* [Middle English via Old French *destructif -ive* from Late Latin *destructivus* (as DESTROY)]

destructor /dɪˈstrʌktə/ *n. Brit.* a refuse-burning furnace.

desuetude /dɪˈsjuːɪtjuːd, ˈdɛswɪ-/ *n.* a state of disuse (*the custom fell into desuetude*). [French *désuétude* or Latin *desuetudo* (as DE-, *suescere suet-* 'be accustomed')]

desulphurize /diːˈsʌlfərʌɪz/ *v.tr.* (also **-ise**, *US* **desulfurize**) remove sulphur or sulphur compounds from. □ **desulphurization** /-ˈzeɪʃ(ə)n/ *n.*

desultory /ˈdɛs(ə)lt(ə)ri, -z-/ *adj.* **1** going constantly from one subject to another, esp. in a half-hearted way. **2** disconnected; unmethodical; superficial. □ **desultorily** *adv.* **desultoriness** *n.* [Latin *desultorius* 'superficial', from *desultor* 'vaulter' from *desult-* (as DE-, *salt-*, past part. stem of *salire* 'leap')]

detach /dɪˈtatʃ/ *v.tr.* **1** (often foll. by *from*) unfasten or disengage and remove (*detached the buttons*; *detached himself from the group*). **2** *Mil.* send (a ship, regiment, officer, messenger, etc.) on a separate mission. **3** (as **detached** *adj.*) **a** impartial; unemotional (*a detached viewpoint*). **b** esp. *Brit.* (esp. of a house) not joined to another or others; separate. □ **detachable** *adj.* **detachedly** /dɪˈtatʃɪdli/ *adv.* [French *détacher* (as DE-, ATTACH)]

detached retina *n.* a retina that has become detached from the underlying tissue, causing partial or total blindness.

detachment /dɪˈtatʃm(ə)nt/ *n.* **1 a** a state of aloofness from or indifference to other people, one's surroundings, public opinion, etc. **b** disinterested independence of judgement. **2 a** the act or process of detaching or being detached. **b** an instance of this. **3** *Mil.* a separate group or unit of an army etc. used for a specific purpose. [French *détachement* (as DETACH)]

detail /ˈdiːteɪl/ *n.* & *v.* ● *n.* **1 a** a small or subordinate particular; an item. **b** such a particular, considered (ironically) to be unimportant (*the truth of the statement is just a detail*). **2 a** small items or particulars (esp. in an artistic work) regarded collectively (*has an eye for detail*). **b** the treatment of them (*the detail was insufficient and unconvincing*). **3** (often in *pl.*) a number of particulars; an aggregate of small items (*filled in the details on the form*). **4 a** a minor decoration on a building, in a picture, etc. **b** a small part of a picture etc. shown alone. **5** *Mil.* **a** the distribution of orders for the day. **b** a small detachment of soldiers etc. for special duty. ● *v.tr.* **1** give particulars of (*detailed the plans*). **2** relate circumstantially (*detailed the anecdote*). **3** *Mil.* assign for special duty. **4** (as **detailed** *adj.*) **a** (of a picture, story, etc.) having many details. **b** itemized (*a detailed list*). □ **go into detail** give all the items or particulars. **in detail** item by item, minutely. [French *détail*, *détailler* (as DE-, *tailler* 'cut', formed as TAIL²)]

detain /dɪˈteɪn/ *v.tr.* **1** keep in confinement or under restraint. **2** keep waiting; delay. □ **detainment** *n.* [Middle English from Old French *detenir*, ultimately from Latin *detinēre detent-* (as DE-, *tenēre* 'hold')]

detainee /dɪteɪˈniː, diː-/ *n.* a person detained in custody, esp. for political reasons.

detainer /dɪˈteɪnə/ *n.* *Law* **1** the wrongful detaining of goods taken from the owner for distraint etc. **2** the detention of a person in prison etc. [Anglo-French *detener* from Old French *detenir* (as DETAIN)]

detect /dɪˈtɛkt/ *v.tr.* **1 a** (often foll. by *in*) reveal the guilt of; discover (*detected him in his crime*). **b** discover (a crime). **2** discover or perceive the existence or presence of (*detected a smell of burning*; *do I detect a note of sarcasm?*). **3** *Physics* use an instrument to observe (a signal, radiation, etc.). □ **detectable** *adj.* **detectably** *adv.* [Latin *detegere detect-* (as DE-, *tegere* 'cover')]

detection /dɪˈtɛkʃ(ə)n/ *n.* **1** the act or an instance of detecting; the process or an instance of being detected. **2** the work of a detective. **3** *Physics* the extraction of a desired signal; a demodulation. [Late Latin *detectio* (as DETECT)]

detective /dɪˈtɛktɪv/ *n.* & *adj.* ● *n.* (often *attrib.*) a person, esp. a member of a police force, employed to investigate crimes. ● *adj.* serving to detect. [DETECT]

detector /dɪˈtɛktə/ *n.* **1** a person or thing that detects. **2** *Physics* a device for the detection or demodulation of signals.

detent /dɪˈtɛnt/ *n.* **1** a catch by the release of which machinery is allowed to move. **2** (in a clock etc.) a catch that regulates striking. [French *détente* from Old French *destente*, from *destendre* 'slacken' (as DE-, Latin *tendere*)]

détente /deɪˈtɑːnt/ *n.* (also **detente**) an easing of strained relations esp. between states. [French, = relaxation]

detention /dɪˈtɛnʃ(ə)n/ *n.* **1** detaining or being detained. **2 a** being kept in school after hours as a punishment. **b** an instance of this. **3** custody; confinement. [French *détention* or Late Latin *detentio* (as DETAIN)]

detention centre *n.* an institution for the brief detention of esp. young offenders.

deter /dɪˈtəː/ *v.tr.* (**deterred**, **deterring**) **1** (often foll. by *from*) discourage or prevent (a person) through fear or dislike of the consequences. **2** discourage, check, or prevent (a thing, process, etc.). [Latin *deterrēre* (as DE-, *terrēre* 'frighten')]

detergent /dɪˈtəːdʒ(ə)nt/ *n.* & *adj.* ● *n.* **1** a water-soluble cleansing agent which combines with impurities and dirt to make them more soluble, and differs from soap in not forming a scum with the salts in hard water. **2** any additive with a similar action, e.g. holding dirt in suspension in lubricating oil. ● *adj.* cleansing, esp. in the manner of a detergent. [Latin *detergēre* (as DE-, *tergēre ters-* 'wipe')]

deteriorate /dɪˈtɪərɪəreɪt/ *v.tr.* & *intr.* make or become bad or worse (*food deteriorates in hot weather*; *his condition deteriorated after the operation*). □ **deterioration** /-ˈreɪʃ(ə)n/ *n.* **deteriorative** /-rətɪv/ *adj.* [Late Latin *deteriorare deteriorat-* from Latin *deterior* 'worse']

determinant /dɪˈtəːmɪnənt/ *adj.* & *n.* ● *adj.* serving to determine or define. ● *n.* **1** a determining factor, element, word, etc. **2** *Math.* a quantity obtained by the addition of products of the elements of a square matrix according to a given rule. [Latin *determinare* (as DETERMINE)]

determinate /dɪˈtəːmɪnət/ *adj.* **1** limited in time, space, or character. **2** of definite scope or nature. □ **determinacy** *n.* **determinately** *adv.* **determinateness** *n.* [Middle English from Latin *determinatus*, past part. of *determinare* DETERMINE]

determination /dɪˌtəːmɪˈneɪʃ(ə)n/ *n.* **1** firmness of purpose; resoluteness. **2** the process of deciding, determining, or calculating. **3 a** the conclusion of a dispute by the decision of an arbitrator. **b** the decision reached. **4** *Law* the cessation of an estate or interest. **5** *Law* a judicial decision or sentence. **6** *archaic* a tendency to move in a fixed direction. [Middle English via Old French from Latin *determinatio -onis* (as DETERMINE)]

determinative /dɪˈtəːmɪnətɪv/ *adj.* & *n.* ● *adj.* serving to define, qualify, or direct. ● *n.* a determinative thing or circumstance. □ **determinatively** *adv.* [French *déterminatif -ive* (as DETERMINE)]

determine /dɪˈtəːmɪn/ *v.* **1** *tr.* find out or establish precisely (*have to determine the extent of the problem*). **2** *tr.* decide or settle (*determined who should go*). **3** *tr.* be a decisive factor in regard to (*demand determines supply*). **4** *intr.* & *tr.* make or cause (a person) to make a decision (*we determined to go at once*; *what determined you to do it?*). **5** *tr.* & *intr.* esp. *Law* bring or come to an end. **6** *tr.* *Geom.* fix or define the position of. □ **be determined** be resolved (*was determined not to give up*). □ **determinable** *adj.* [Middle English via Old French *determiner* from Latin *determinare* (as DE-, *terminus* 'end')]

determined /dɪˈtəːmɪnd/ *adj.* showing determination; resolute, unflinching. □ **determinedly** *adv.* **determinedness** *n.*

determiner /dɪˈtəːmɪnə/ *n.* **1** a person or thing that determines. **2** *Gram.* any of a class of words (e.g. *a*, *the*, *every*) that determine the kind of reference a noun or noun group has.

determinism /dɪˈtəːmɪnɪz(ə)m/ *n.* *Philos.* the doctrine that all events, including human action, are determined by causes regarded as external to the will. □ **determinist** *n.* **deterministic** /-ˈnɪstɪk/ *adj.* **deterministically** /-ˈnɪstɪk(ə)li/ *adv.*

deterrent /dɪˈtɛr(ə)nt/ *adj.* & *n.* ● *adj.* that deters. ● *n.* a deterrent thing or factor, esp. a nuclear weapon regarded as deterring an enemy from attack. □ **deterrence** *n.*

detest /dɪˈtɛst/ *v.tr.* hate, loathe. □ **detester** *n.* [Latin *detestari* (as DE-, *testari* 'call to witness' from *testis* 'witness')]

detestable /dɪˈtɛstəb(ə)l/ *adj.* intensely disliked; very unpleasant; hateful. □ **detestably** *adv.*

detestation /diːtɛˈsteɪʃ(ə)n/ *n.* **1** intense dislike, hatred. **2** a detested person or thing. [Middle English via Old French from Latin *detestatio -onis* (as DETEST)]

dethrone /diːˈθrəʊn, dɪ-/ *v.tr.* **1** remove from the throne, depose. **2** remove from a position of authority or influence. □ **dethronement** *n.*

detonate /ˈdɛtəneɪt/ *v.* **1** *tr.* set off (an explosive charge). **2** *intr.* (of an explosive charge) be set off, explode, esp. loudly. □ **detonative** *adj.* [Latin *detonare detonat-* (as DE-, *tonare* 'thunder')]

detonation /dɛtəˈneɪʃ(ə)n/ *n.* **1 a** the act or process of detonating. **b** a loud explosion. **2** the premature combustion of fuel in an internal-combustion engine, causing it to pink. [French *détonation* from *détoner* (as DETONATE)]

detonator /ˈdɛtəneɪtə/ *n.* **1** a device or a small sensitive charge used to detonate an explosive. **2** a warning signal on a railway line which is set off when a train passes over it.

detour /ˈdiːtʊə/ *n.* & *v.* ● *n.* **1** a divergence from a direct or intended route; a roundabout course. **2** *US* = DIVERSION 4. ● *v.intr.* & *tr.* make or cause to make a detour. [French *détour* 'change of direction' from *détourner* 'turn away' (as DE-, TURN)]

detox *n.* & *v.* esp. *US colloq.* ● *n.* /ˈdiːtɒks/ = DETOXIFICATION. ● *v.* /diːˈtɒks/ **1** *tr.* subject (an alcoholic or drug addict) to detoxification. **2** *intr.* (of a person) subject oneself to detoxification; undergo treatment to come off drugs.

detoxicate /diːˈtɒksɪkeɪt/ *v.tr.* = DETOXIFY. □ **detoxication** /-ˈkeɪʃ(ə)n/ *n.* [DE- + Latin *toxicum* 'poison', on the pattern of *intoxicate*]

detoxification /diːˌtɒksɪfɪˈkeɪʃ(ə)n/ *n.* the process of detoxifying, esp. an alcoholic or drug addict.

detoxification centre *n.* a (usu. residential) centre for the treatment of alcoholism or drug addiction.

detoxify /diːˈtɒksɪfʌɪ/ *v.tr.* (**-ies, -ied**) remove the poison from. [DE- + Latin *toxicum* 'poison']

detract /dɪˈtrakt/ *v.* **1** *intr.* (foll. by *from*) **a** reduce. **b** diminish, belittle. **2** *tr.* (usu. foll. by *from*) take away (a part of something). □ **detraction** *n.* **detractive** *adj.* **detractor** *n.* [Latin *detrahere detract-* (as DE-, *trahere* 'draw')]

detrain /diːˈtreɪn/ *v.intr.* & *tr.* alight or cause to alight from a train. □ **detrainment** *n.*

detribalize /diːˈtrʌɪb(ə)lʌɪz/ *v.tr.* (also **-ise**) **1** make (a person) no longer a member of a tribe. **2** destroy the tribal habits of. □ **detribalization** /-ˈzeɪʃ(ə)n/ *n.*

detriment /ˈdɛtrɪm(ə)nt/ *n.* **1** harm, damage. **2** something causing this. [Middle English from Old French *detriment* or Latin *detrimentum* (as DE-, *terere trit-* 'rub, wear')]

detrimental /dɛtrɪˈmɛnt(ə)l/ *adj.* harmful; causing loss. □ **detrimentally** *adv.*

detrition /dɪˈtrɪʃ(ə)n/ *n.* wearing away by friction. [medieval Latin *detritio* (as DETRIMENT)]

detritus /dɪˈtrʌɪtəs/ *n.* **1** matter produced by erosion, such as gravel, sand, silt, rock-debris, etc. **2** debris of any kind; rubbish, waste. □ **detrital** /dɪˈtrʌɪt(ə)l/ *adj.* [French *détritus* from Latin *detritus* = wearing down (as DETRIMENT)]

de trop /də ˈtrəʊ/ *predic.adj.* not wanted, unwelcome, in the way. [French, = excessive]

Dettol /ˈdɛtɒl, -t(ə)l/ *n. propr.* a type of surgical or household disinfectant. [invented name]

detumescence /diːtjʊˈmɛs(ə)ns/ *n.* subsidence from a swollen state. [Latin *detumescere* (as DE-, *tumescere* 'swell')]

detune /diːˈtjuːn/ *v.tr.* adjust (a mechanism, musical instrument, etc.) so that it is no longer tuned.

deuce[1] /djuːs/ *n.* **1** the two on dice or playing cards. **2** *Tennis* the score of 40 all, at which two consecutive points are needed to win. [Old French *deus* from Latin *duo* (accusative *duos*) 'two']

deuce[2] /djuːs/ *n. colloq.* misfortune, the Devil, used esp. as an exclamation of surprise or annoyance (*who the deuce are you?*). □ **a** (or **the**) **deuce of a** a very bad or remarkable (*a deuce of a problem*; *a deuce of a fellow*). **the deuce to pay** trouble to be expected. [Low German *duus*, formed as DEUCE[1], two aces at dice being the worst throw]

deuced /ˈdjuːsɪd, djuːst/ *adj.* & *adv. archaic* damned, confounded (*a deuced liar*). □ **deucedly** /ˈdjuːsɪdli/ *adv.*

deus ex machina /ˌdeɪʊs ɛks ˈmakɪnə, ˌdiːəs ɛks məˈʃiːnə/ *n.* an unexpected power or event saving a seemingly hopeless situation, esp. in a play or novel. [modern Latin translation of Greek *theos ek mēkhanēs*, = god from the machinery (by which in the Greek theatre the gods were suspended above the stage)]

Deut. *abbr.* Deuteronomy (Old Testament).

deuteragonist /djuːtəˈragənɪst/ *n.* the person second in importance to the protagonist in a drama. [Greek *deuteragōnistēs* (as DEUTERO-, *agōnistēs* 'actor')]

deuterate /ˈdjuːtəreɪt/ *v.tr.* replace the usual isotope of hydrogen in (a substance) by deuterium. □ **deuteration** /-ˈreɪʃ(ə)n/ *n.*

deuterium /djuːˈtɪərɪəm/ *n. Chem.* a stable isotope of hydrogen with a mass about double that of the usual isotope. [modern Latin, formed as DEUTERO- + -IUM]

deutero- /ˈdjuːtərəʊ/ *comb. form* second. [Greek *deuteros* 'second']

deuterocanonical /ˌdjuːtərəʊkəˈnɒnɪk(ə)l/ *adj.* of or forming a secondary canon (of sacred writings).

■ **Usage** See Usage Note at APOCRYPHA.

Deutero-Isaiah /ˌdjuːtərəʊʌɪˈzʌɪə/ *n.* the supposed later author of Isaiah 40–55.

deuteron /ˈdjuːtərɒn/ *n. Physics* the nucleus of a deuterium atom, consisting of a proton and a neutron. [DEUTERIUM + -ON]

Deutschmark /ˈdɔɪtʃmɑːk/ *n.* (also **Deutsche Mark** /ˈdɔɪtʃə mɑːk/) the chief monetary unit of Germany. [German, = German mark (see MARK[2])]

deutzia /ˈdjuːtsɪə, ˈdɔɪt-/ *n.* any ornamental shrub of the genus *Deutzia*, with usu. white flowers. [named after J. *Deutz*, 18th-c. Dutch patron of botany]

devalue /diːˈvaljuː/ *v.tr.* (**devalues, devalued, devaluing**) **1** reduce the value of. **2** *Econ.* reduce the value of (a currency) in relation to other currencies or to gold (opp. REVALUE). □ **devaluation** /-ˈeɪʃ(ə)n/ *n.*

Devanagari /deɪvəˈnɑːg(ə)ri, dɛv-/ *n.* the alphabet used for Sanskrit, Hindi, and other Indian languages. [Sanskrit, = divine town script]

devastate /ˈdɛvəsteɪt/ *v.tr.* **1** lay waste; cause great destruction to. **2** (often in *passive*) overwhelm with shock or grief; upset deeply. □ **devastation** /-ˈsteɪʃ(ə)n/ *n.* **devastator** *n.* [Latin *devastare devastat-* (as DE-, *vastare* 'lay waste')]

devastating /ˈdɛvəsteɪtɪŋ/ *adj.* crushingly effective; overwhelming. □ **devastatingly** *adv.*

devein /diːˈveɪn/ *v.tr.* remove the main central vein from (a shrimp or prawn).

develop /dɪˈvɛləp/ *v.* (**developed, developing**) **1** *tr.* & *intr.* **a** make or become bigger or fuller or more elaborate or systematic (*the new town developed rapidly*). **b** bring or come to an active or visible state or to maturity (*developed a plan of action*). **c** bring or come into existence (*an argument developed*). **2** *tr.* begin to exhibit or suffer from (*developed a rattle*). **3** *tr.* **a** construct new buildings on (land). **b** convert (land) to a new purpose so as to use its resources more fully. **4** *tr.* treat (photographic film etc.) to make the latent image visible. **5** *tr. Mus.* elaborate (a theme) by modification of the melody, harmony, rhythm, etc. **6** *tr. Chess* bring (a piece) into position for effective use. □ **developer** *n.* [French *développer* from Romanic (as DIS-, origin of second element unknown)]

developable /dɪˈvɛləpəb(ə)l/ *adj.* that can be developed.

developable surface *n.* a surface that can be flattened into a plane without overlap or separation, e.g. a cylinder.

developing country *n.* a poor or undeveloped country that is becoming more advanced economically and socially.

development /dɪˈvɛləpm(ə)nt/ *n.* **1** the act or an instance of developing; the process of being developed. **2 a** a stage of growth or advancement. **b** a thing that has developed, esp. an event or circumstance (*the latest developments*). **3** a full-grown state. **4** the process of developing a photograph. **5** a developed area of land. **6** industrialization or economic advancement of a country or an area. **7** *Mus.* the elaboration of a theme or themes, esp. in the middle section of a sonata movement. **8** *Chess* the developing of pieces from their original position.

developmental /dɪˌvɛləp'mɛnt(ə)l/ *adj.* **1** incidental to growth (*developmental diseases*). **2** evolutionary. □ **developmentally** *adv.*

development area *n. Brit.* one where new industries are encouraged in order to counteract unemployment.

deviant /'di:vɪənt/ *adj. & n.* ● *adj.* that deviates from the normal, esp. in social or sexual behaviour. ● *n.* a deviant person or thing. □ **deviance** *n.* **deviancy** *n.* [Middle English (as DEVIATE)]

deviate *v., n., & adj.* ● *v.intr.* /'di:vɪeɪt/ (often foll. by *from*) turn aside or diverge (from a course of action, rule, truth, etc.); digress. ● *n.* /'di:vɪət/ a deviant, esp. a sexual pervert. ● *adj.* /'di:vɪət/ = DEVIANT *adj.* □ **deviator** *n.* **deviatory** /-vɪət(ə)ri/ *adj.* [Late Latin *deviare deviat-* (as DE-, *via* 'way')]

deviation /di:vɪ'eɪʃ(ə)n/ *n.* **1 a** deviating, digressing. **b** an instance of this. **2** *Polit.* a departure from accepted (esp. Communist) party doctrine. **3** *Statistics* the amount by which a single measurement differs from the mean. **4** *Naut.* the deflection of a ship's compass needle caused by iron in the ship etc. □ **deviational** *adj.* **deviationism** *n.* **deviationist** *n.* [French *déviation* from medieval Latin *deviatio -onis* (as DEVIATE)]

device /dɪ'vʌɪs/ *n.* **1 a** a thing made or adapted for a particular purpose, esp. a mechanical contrivance. **b** an explosive contrivance; a bomb. **2** a plan, scheme, or trick. **3 a** an emblematic or heraldic design. **b** a drawing or design. **4** *archaic* make, look (*things of rare device*). □ **leave a person to his or her own devices** leave a person to do as he or she wishes. [Middle English from Old French *devis*, ultimately from Latin (as DIVIDE)]

devil /'dɛv(ə)l/ *n. & v.* ● *n.* **1** (usu. **the Devil**) (in Christian and Jewish belief) the supreme spirit of evil; Satan. **2 a** an evil spirit; a demon; a superhuman malignant being. **b** a personified evil force or attribute. **3 a** a wicked or cruel person. **b** a mischievously energetic, clever, or self-willed person. **4** *colloq.* a person, a fellow (*lucky devil*). **5** fighting spirit, mischievousness (*the devil is in him tonight*). **6** *colloq.* something difficult or awkward (*this door is a devil to open*). **7** (**the devil** or **the Devil**) *colloq.* used as an exclamation of surprise or annoyance (*who the devil are you?*). **8** *Brit.* a literary hack exploited by an employer. **9** a junior legal counsel. **10** = TASMANIAN DEVIL. **11** an instrument or machine, esp. one fitted with sharp teeth or spikes, used for tearing or other destructive work. **12** *S.Afr.* = DUST DEVIL. ● *v.* (**devilled**, **devilling**; *US* **deviled**, **deviling**) **1** *tr.* cook (food) with hot seasoning. **2** *intr. Brit.* act as a devil for an author or barrister. **3** *tr. US* harass, worry. □ **between the devil and the deep blue sea** in a dilemma. **devil-may-care** cheerful and reckless. **a devil of** *colloq.* a considerable, difficult, or remarkable. **devil a one** not even one. **devil's own** *colloq.* very difficult or unusual (*the devil's own job*). **devil take the hindmost** a motto of selfish competition. **the devil to pay** trouble to be expected. **go to the devil** **1** be damned. **2** (in *imper.*) depart at once. **like the devil** with great energy. **play the devil with** cause severe damage to. **speak** (or **talk**) **of the devil** said when a person appears just after being mentioned. **the very devil** (*predic.*) *colloq.* a great difficulty or nuisance. [Old English *dēofol* via Late Latin *diabolus* from Greek *diabolos* 'accuser, slanderer', from *dia* 'across' + *ballō* 'to throw']

devilfish /'dɛv(ə)lfɪʃ/ *n.* (*pl.* usu. same) **1** = DEVIL RAY. **2** any of various fish, esp. the stonefish. **3** *hist.* an octopus.

devilish /'dɛv(ə)lɪʃ/ *adj. & adv.* ● *adj.* **1** of or like a devil; evil. **2** mischievous. ● *adv. colloq.* very, extremely. □ **devilishly** *adv.* **devilishness** *n.*

devilment /'dɛv(ə)lm(ə)nt/ *n.* mischief, wild spirits.

devil ray *n.* any cartilaginous fish of the family Mobulidae, esp. the manta.

devilry /'dɛv(ə)lri/ *n.* (also **deviltry**) (*pl.* **-ies**) **1 a** wickedness; reckless mischief. **b** an instance of this. **2 a** black magic. **b** the Devil and his works. [Old French *diablerie*: *-try* suggested by *harlotry* etc.]

devil's advocate *n.* **1** a person who argues against a proposition, to test it or provoke discussion. **2** *RC Ch. hist.* a person appointed to challenge a proposed beatification, canonization, etc.

devil's bit *n.* any of various plants whose roots look bitten off, esp. a kind of scabious (*Succisa pratensis*).

devil's coach-horse *n. Brit.* a large rove beetle, *Staphylinus olens.*

devil's darning needle *n.* a dragonfly or damselfly.

devil's dozen *n.* thirteen.

devils-on-horseback *n.pl. Brit.* a savoury of prunes or plums wrapped in slices of bacon.

devious /'di:vɪəs/ *adj.* **1** (of a person etc.) not straightforward, underhand. **2** winding, circuitous. **3** erring, straying. □ **deviously** *adv.* **deviousness** *n.* [Latin *devius* from DE- + *via* 'way']

devise /dɪ'vʌɪz/ *v. & n.* ● *v.tr.* **1** plan or invent by careful thought. **2** *Law* leave (real estate) by the terms of a will (cf. BEQUEATH). ● *n.* **1** the act or an instance of devising. **2** *Law* a devising clause in a will. □ **devisable** *adj.* **devisee** /-'zi:/ *n.* (in sense 2 of *v.*). **deviser** *n.* **devisor** *n.* (in sense 2 of *v.*). [Middle English from Old French *deviser*, ultimately from Latin *dividere divis-* DIVIDE: the noun via Old French *devise* from medieval Latin *divisa*, fem. past part. of *dividere*]

devitalize /di:'vʌɪt(ə)lʌɪz/ *v.tr.* (also **-ise**) take away strength and vigour from. □ **devitalization** /-'zeɪʃ(ə)n/ *n.*

devitrify /di:'vɪtrɪfʌɪ/ *v.tr.* (**-ies**, **-ied**) deprive of vitreous qualities; make (glass or vitreous rock) opaque and crystalline. □ **devitrification** /-fɪ'keɪʃ(ə)n/ *n.*

devoid /dɪ'vɔɪd/ *predic.adj.* (foll. by *of*) quite lacking or free from (*a book devoid of all interest*). [Middle English, past part. of obsolete *devoid* from Old French *devoidier* (as DE-, VOID)]

devoir /də'vwɑ:/ *n. archaic* **1** duty, one's best (*do one's devoir*). **2** (in *pl.*) courteous or formal attentions; respects (*pay one's devoirs to*). [Middle English from Anglo-French *dever* = Old French *deveir*, from Latin *debēre* 'owe']

devolute /'di:vəlu:t, 'dɛv-/ *v.tr.* transfer by devolution. [as DEVOLVE]

devolution /di:və'lu:ʃ(ə)n, dɛv-/ *n.* **1** the delegation of power, esp. by central government to local or regional administration. **2 a** descent or passing on through a series of stages. **b** descent by natural or due succession from one to another of property or qualities. **3** the lapse of an unexercised right to an ultimate owner. **4** *Biol.* degeneration. □ **devolutionary** *adj.* **devolutionist** *n.* [Late Latin *devolutio* (as DEVOLVE)]

devolve /dɪ'vɒlv/ *v.* **1** (foll. by *on*, *upon*, etc.) **a** *tr.* pass (work or duties) to (a deputy etc.). **b** *intr.* (of work or duties) pass to (a deputy etc.). **2** *intr.* (foll. by *on*, *to*, *upon*) *Law* (of property etc.) descend or fall by succession to. □ **devolvement** *n.* [Middle English from Latin *devolvere devolut-* (as DE-, *volvere* 'roll')]

Devonian /dɛ'vəʊnɪən, dɪ-/ *adj. & n.* ● *adj.* **1** of or relating to Devon in SW England. **2** *Geol.* of or relating to the fourth period of the Palaeozoic era with evidence of the first amphibians and tree forests. Cf. Appendix X. ● *n.* **1** this period or system. **2** a native of Devon. [medieval Latin *Devonia* 'Devonshire']

dévot /deɪ'vəʊ, French devo/ *n.* (*fem.* ***dévote*** /-'vɒt, French -vɔt/) a devotee. [French from Old French (as DEVOUT)]

devote /dɪˈvəʊt/ *v.tr. & refl.* **1** (foll. by *to*) apply or give over (resources etc. or oneself) to (a particular activity or purpose or person) (*devoted their time to reading*; *devoted himself to his guests*). **2** *archaic* doom to destruction. ▫ **devotement** *n.* [Latin *devovēre devot-* (as DE-, *vovēre* 'vow')]

devoted /dɪˈvəʊtɪd/ *adj.* very loving or loyal (*a devoted husband*). ▫ **devotedly** *adv.* **devotedness** *n.*

devotee /dɛvəʊˈtiː/ *n.* **1** (usu. foll. by *of*) a zealous enthusiast or supporter. **2** a zealously pious or fanatical person.

devotion /dɪˈvəʊʃ(ə)n/ *n.* **1** (usu. foll. by *to*) enthusiastic attachment or loyalty (to a person or cause); great love. **2 a** religious worship. **b** (in *pl.*) prayers. **c** devoutness, religious fervour. ▫ **devotional** *adj.* [Middle English from Old French *devotion* or Latin *devotio* (as DEVOTE)]

devour /dɪˈvaʊə/ *v.tr.* **1** eat hungrily or greedily. **2** (of fire etc.) engulf, destroy. **3** take in greedily with the eyes or ears (*devoured book after book*). **4** absorb the attention of (*devoured by anxiety*). ▫ **devourer** *n.* **devouringly** *adv.* [Middle English via Old French *devorer* from Latin *devorare* (as DE-, *vorare* 'swallow')]

devout /dɪˈvaʊt/ *adj.* **1** earnestly religious. **2** earnestly sincere (*devout hope*). ▫ **devoutly** *adv.* **devoutness** *n.* [Middle English via Old French *devot* from Latin *devotus*, past part. of *devovēre* DEVOTE]

DEW *abbr.* distant early warning.

dew /ˈdjuː/ *n. & v.* ● *n.* **1** atmospheric vapour condensing in small drops on cool surfaces at night. **2** beaded or glistening moisture resembling this, e.g. tears. **3** freshness, refreshing quality. ● *v.tr.* wet with or as with dew. [Old English *dēaw*, from Germanic]

dewan /dɪˈwɑːn/ *n.* the prime minister or finance minister of an Indian state. [Arabic & Persian *diwān* 'fiscal register']

dewar /ˈdjuːə/ *n.* a double-walled flask of steel or silvered glass with a vacuum between the walls to reduce the transfer of heat. [named after Sir James *Dewar*, British physicist d. 1923]

dewater /diːˈwɔːtə/ *v.tr.* remove water from.

dewberry /ˈdjuːb(ə)ri/ *n.* (*pl.* **-ies**) **1** a bluish fruit like the blackberry. **2** the shrub, *Rubus caesius*, bearing this.

dewclaw /ˈdjuːklɔː/ *n.* **1** a rudimentary inner toe found on some dogs. **2** a false hoof on a deer etc.

dewdrop /ˈdjuːdrɒp/ *n.* **1** a drop of dew. **2** something resembling this.

Dewey decimal classification /ˈdjuːi/ *n.* (also **Dewey system** *colloq.*) a decimal system of library classification. [named after M. *Dewey*, American librarian d. 1931, its deviser]

dewfall /ˈdjuːfɔːl/ *n.* **1** the time when dew begins to form. **2** evening.

dewlap /ˈdjuːlap/ *n.* **1** a loose fold of skin hanging from the throat of cattle, dogs, etc. **2** similar loose skin round the throat of an elderly person. [Middle English from DEW + LAP[1], perhaps suggested by an Old Norse word]

deworm /diːˈwəːm/ *v.tr.* rid (a dog, cat, etc.) of worms.

dew point *n.* the temperature at which dew forms.

dew-pond *n. Brit.* a shallow usu. artificial pond once supposed to have been fed by atmospheric condensation.

dewy /ˈdjuːi/ *adj.* (**dewier**, **dewiest**) **1 a** wet with dew. **b** moist as if with dew. **2** of or like dew. ▫ **dewily** *adv.* **dewiness** *n.* [Old English *dēawig* (as DEW, -Y[1])]

dewy-eyed *adj.* innocently trusting; naively sentimental.

Dexedrine /ˈdɛksədriːn, -drɪn/ *n. Pharm. propr.* the more active dextrorotatory isomer of amphetamine. [DEXTRO- + BENZEDRINE]

dexter[1] /ˈdɛkstə/ *adj.* esp. *Heraldry* on or of the right-hand side (the observer's left) of a shield etc. [Latin, = on the right]

dexter[2] /ˈdɛkstə/ *n.* **1** an animal of a small hardy breed of Irish cattle. **2** this breed. [19th c.: perhaps from the name of a breeder]

dexterity /dɛkˈstɛrɪti/ *n.* **1** skill in handling. **2** manual or mental adroitness. **3** right-handedness, using the right hand. [French *dextérité* from Latin *dexteritas* (as DEXTER[1])]

dexterous /ˈdɛkst(ə)rəs/ *adj.* (also **dextrous**) having or showing dexterity. ▫ **dexterously** *adv.* **dexterousness** *n.* [Latin DEXTER[1] + -OUS]

dextral /ˈdɛkstr(ə)l/ *adj. & n.* ● *adj.* **1** (of a person) right-handed. **2** of or on the right. **3** *Zool.* (of a spiral shell) with whorls rising to the right and coiling in an anticlockwise direction. **4** *Zool.* (of a flatfish) with the right side uppermost. ● *n.* a right-handed person. ▫ **dextrality** /-ˈstralɪti/ *n.* **dextrally** *adv.* [medieval Latin *dextralis* from Latin *dextra* 'right hand']

dextran /ˈdɛkstran/ *n. Chem. & Pharm.* **1** a polymer of glucose formed by the action of certain bacteria on sucrose etc. **2** a degraded form of this used as a substitute for blood plasma. [German (as DEXTRO- + *-an* chemical suffix)]

dextrin /ˈdɛkstrɪn/ *n. Chem.* a soluble gummy substance obtained by boiling starch and used as an adhesive. [French *dextrine* from Latin *dextra*: see DEXTRO-, -IN]

dextro- /ˈdɛkstrəʊ/ *comb. form* on or to the right (*dextrorotatory*; *dextrose*). [Latin *dexter*, *dextra* 'on or to the right']

dextrorotatory /dɛkstrəʊˈrəʊtət(ə)ri/ *adj. Chem.* having the property of rotating the plane of a polarized light ray to the right (cf. LAEVOROTATORY). ▫ **dextrorotation** *n.*

dextrorse /ˈdɛkstrɔːs/ *adj.* rising towards the right, esp. of a spiral stem. [Latin *dextrorsus* (as DEXTRO-)]

dextrose /ˈdɛkstrəʊz, -s/ *n. Chem.* the dextrorotatory form of glucose. [formed as DEXTRO- + -OSE[2]]

dextrous var. of DEXTEROUS.

DF *abbr.* **1** Defender of the Faith. **2** direction-finder. [in sense 1 from Latin *Defensor Fidei*]

DFC *abbr. Brit.* Distinguished Flying Cross.

DFE *abbr.* (in the UK) Department for Education (replacing the DES from 1992).

Dfl *abbr.* Dutch florins.

DFM *abbr. Brit.* Distinguished Flying Medal.

DG *abbr.* **1** *Dei gratia*. **2** *Deo gratias*. **3** director-general.

dhal /dɑːl/ *n.* (also **dal**) **1** split pulses, a common foodstuff in India. **2** a dish made with these. [Hindi]

dharma /ˈdɑːmə, ˈdəːmə/ *n.* **1** esp. *Hinduism* **a** the eternal law of the cosmos. **b** moral or social custom; right behaviour. **2** *Buddhism* universal truth. [Sanskrit, = decree, custom]

Dharuk /ˈdʌrʊk/ *n.* an Aboriginal language of the area around Sydney, Australia, now extinct.

dhobi /ˈdəʊbi/ *n.* (*pl.* **dhobis**) (in the Indian subcontinent) a washerman or washerwoman. [Hindi *dhobī* from *dhob* 'washing']

dhobi itch *n.* (also **dhobi's itch**) a tropical skin disease; an allergic dermatitis.

dhole /dəʊl/ *n.* the Asiatic wild dog, *Cuon alpinus*. [origin unknown]

dhoti /ˈdəʊti/ *n.* (*pl.* **dhotis**) the loincloth worn by male Hindus. [Hindi *dhotī*]

dhow /daʊ/ *n.* a lateen-rigged ship used on the Arabian sea. [Arabic *dāwa*, probably related to Marathi *dāw*]

DHSS *abbr. hist.* (in the UK) Department of Health and Social Security (cf. DoH, DSS).

dhurra var. of DURRA.

DI *abbr.* (in the UK) Defence Intelligence.

di-[1] /dʌɪ, dɪ/ *comb. form* **1** twice, two-, double. **2** *Chem.* containing two atoms, molecules, or groups of a specified kind (*dichromate*; *dioxide*). [Greek from *dis* 'twice']

di-[2] /dɪ, dʌɪ/ *prefix* form of DIS- occurring before *l*, *m*, *n*, *r*, *s* (foll. by a consonant), *v*, usu. *g*, and sometimes *j*. [Latin variant of *dis-*]

di-[3] /dʌɪ/ *prefix* form of DIA- before a vowel.

dia. *abbr.* diameter.

dia- /dʌɪə/ *prefix* (also **di-** before a vowel) **1** through (*diaphanous*). **2** apart (*diacritical*). **3** across (*diameter*). [Greek from *dia* 'through']

diabase /'dʌɪəbeɪs/ *n. Geol.* dolerite, esp. (in British use) altered dolerite. [French, as if from DI-[1] + BASE[1], but associated with Greek *diabasis* 'transition']

diabetes /dʌɪə'biːtiːz/ *n.* any disorder of the metabolism with excessive thirst and the production of large amounts of urine, esp. diabetes mellitus. [Latin from Greek, literally 'syphon', from *diabainō* 'go through']

diabetes insipidus /ɪn'sɪpɪdəs/ *n.* a rare form of diabetes caused by a deficiency of a pituitary hormone regulating kidney function.

diabetes mellitus /mɪ'lʌɪtəs/ *n.* the commonest form of diabetes, caused by a deficiency of insulin, in which sugar and starch are not properly metabolized and the blood and urine contain excessive amounts of sugars, causing a risk of convulsions and coma. [Latin *mellitus* 'sweet']

diabetic /dʌɪə'bɛtɪk/ *adj. & n.* ● *adj.* **1** of or relating to or having diabetes. **2** for use by diabetics. ● *n.* a person suffering from diabetes.

diablerie /dɪ'ɑːbləri/ *n.* **1** the Devil's work; sorcery. **2** wild recklessness. **3** the realm of devils; devil-lore. [French from *diable*, from Latin *diabolus* DEVIL]

diabolic /dʌɪə'bɒlɪk/ *adj.* **1** of the Devil. **2** devilish; inhumanly cruel or wicked. □ **diabolically** *adv.* [Middle English via Old French *diabolique* or Late Latin *diabolicus* from Latin *diabolus* (as DEVIL)]

diabolical /dʌɪə'bɒlɪk(ə)l/ *adj.* **1** = DIABOLIC 1. **2** = DIABOLIC 2. **3** *colloq.* outrageous; disgracefully bad.

diabolism /dʌɪ'abəlɪz(ə)m/ *n.* **1 a** belief in or worship of the Devil. **b** sorcery. **2** devilish conduct or character. □ **diabolist** *n.* [Greek *diabolos* DEVIL]

diabolize /dʌɪ'abəlʌɪz/ *v.tr.* (also **-ise**) make into or represent as a devil.

diabolo /dɪ'abələʊ, dʌɪ-/ *n.* (*pl.* **-os**) **1** a game in which a two-headed top is thrown up and caught with a string stretched between two sticks. **2** the top itself. [Italian, = DEVIL: formerly called *devil on two sticks*]

diachronic /dʌɪə'krɒnɪk/ *adj. Linguistics* etc. concerned with the historical development of a subject (esp. a language) (opp. SYNCHRONIC). □ **diachronically** *adv.* **diachronism** /dʌɪ'akrənɪz(ə)m/ *n.* **diachronistic** /dʌɪˌakrə'nɪstɪk/ *adj.* **diachronous** /dʌɪ'akrənəs/ *adj.* **diachrony** /dʌɪ'akrəni/ *n.* [French *diachronique* (as DIA-, CHRONIC)]

diaconal /dʌɪ'ak(ə)n(ə)l/ *adj.* of a deacon. [ecclesiastical Latin *diaconalis* from *diaconus* DEACON]

diaconate /dʌɪ'akəneɪt, -ət/ *n.* **1 a** the office of deacon. **b** a person's time as deacon. **2** a body of deacons. [ecclesiastical Latin *diaconatus* (as DIACONAL)]

diacritic /dʌɪə'krɪtɪk/ *n. & adj.* ● *n.* a sign (e.g. an accent, diaeresis, cedilla) used to indicate different sounds or values of a letter. ● *adj.* = DIACRITICAL *adj.* [Greek *diakritikos* (as DIA-, CRITIC)]

diacritical /dʌɪə'krɪtɪk(ə)l/ *adj. & n.* ● *adj.* distinguishing, distinctive. ● *n.* (in full **diacritical mark** or **sign**) = DIACRITIC *n.*

diadelphous /dʌɪə'dɛlfəs/ *adj. Bot.* with the stamens united in two bundles (cf. MONADELPHOUS, POLYADELPHOUS). [DI-[1] + Greek *adelphos* 'brother']

diadem /'dʌɪədɛm/ *n. & v.* ● *n.* **1** a crown or headband worn as a sign of sovereignty. **2** a wreath of leaves or flowers worn round the head. **3** sovereignty. **4** a crowning distinction or glory. ● *v.tr.* (esp. as **diademed** *adj.*) adorn with or as with a diadem. [Middle English via Old French *diademe* and Latin *diadema* from Greek *diadēma* (as DIA-, *deō* 'bind')]

diaeresis /dʌɪ'ɪərɪsɪs, -'ɛr-/ *n.* (*US* **dieresis**) (*pl.* **-ses** /-siːz/) **1** a mark (as in *naïve*) over a vowel to indicate that it is sounded separately. **2** *Prosody* a break where a foot ends at the end of a word. [Latin from Greek, = separation]

diagenesis /dʌɪə'dʒɛnɪsɪs/ *n. Geol.* the transformation occurring during the conversion of sedimentation to sedimentary rock.

diagnose /'dʌɪəgnəʊz, -'nəʊz/ *v.tr.* make a diagnosis of (a disease, a mechanical fault, etc.) from its symptoms. □ **diagnosable** *adj.*

diagnosis /dʌɪəg'nəʊsɪs/ *n.* (*pl.* **diagnoses** /-siːz/) **1 a** the identification of a disease by means of a patient's symptoms. **b** an instance or formal statement of this. **2 a** the identification of the cause of a mechanical fault etc. **b** an instance of this. **3 a** the distinctive characterization in precise terms of a genus, species, etc. **b** an instance of this. [modern Latin from Greek (as DIA-, *gignōskō* 'recognize')]

diagnostic /dʌɪəg'nɒstɪk/ *adj. & n.* ● *adj.* of or assisting diagnosis. ● *n.* a symptom. □ **diagnostically** *adv.* **diagnostician** /-nɒ'stɪʃ(ə)n/ *n.* [Greek *diagnōstikos* (as DIAGNOSIS)]

diagnostics /dʌɪəg'nɒstɪks/ *n.* **1** (treated as *pl.*) *Computing* programs and other mechanisms used to detect and identify faults in hardware or software. **2** (treated as *sing.*) the science or study of diagnosing disease.

diagonal /dʌɪ'ag(ə)n(ə)l/ *adj. & n.* ● *adj.* **1** crossing a straight-sided figure from corner to corner. **2** slanting, oblique. ● *n.* a straight line joining two non-adjacent corners. □ **diagonally** *adv.* [Latin *diagonalis* from Greek *diagōnios* (as DIA-, *gōnia* 'angle')]

diagram /'dʌɪəgram/ *n. & v.* ● *n.* **1** a drawing showing the general scheme or outline of an object and its parts. **2** a graphic representation of the course or results of an action or process. **3** *Geom.* a figure made of lines used in proving a theorem etc. ● *v.tr.* (**diagrammed**, **diagramming**; *US* **diagramed**, **diagraming**) represent by means of a diagram. □ **diagrammatic** /-grə'matɪk/ *adj.* **diagrammatically** /-grə'matɪk(ə)li/ *adv.* [Latin *diagramma* from Greek (as DIA-, -GRAM)]

diagrid /'dʌɪəgrɪd/ *n. Brit. Archit.* a supporting structure of diagonally intersecting ribs of metal etc. [DIAGONAL + GRID]

diakinesis /dʌɪəkʌɪ'niːsɪs/ *n.* (*pl.* **diakineses** /-siːz/) *Biol.* a stage during the prophase of meiosis when the separation of homologous chromosomes is complete and crossing over has occurred. [modern Latin from German *Diakinese* (as DIA-, Greek *kinēsis* 'motion')]

dial /dʌɪəl/ *n. & v.* ● *n.* **1** the face of a clock or watch, marked to show the hours etc. **2** a similar flat plate marked with a scale for measuring weight, volume, pressure, consumption, etc., indicated by a pointer. **3** a movable disc on a telephone, with finger-holes and numbers for making a connection. **4 a** a plate or disc etc. on a radio or television set for selecting wavelength or channel. **b** a similar selecting device on other equipment, e.g. a washing machine. **5** *Brit. slang* a person's face. ● *v.* (**dialled**, **dialling**; *US* **dialed**, **dialing**) **1** *tr.* (also *absol.*) select (a telephone number) by means of a dial or set of buttons (*dialled 999*). **2** *tr.* measure, indicate, or regulate by means of a dial. □ **dialler** *n.* [Middle English, = sundial, from medieval Latin *diale* 'clock-dial', ultimately from Latin *dies* 'day']

dialect /'dʌɪəlɛkt/ *n.* **1** a form of speech peculiar to a particular region. **2** a subordinate variety of a language with non-standard vocabulary, pronunciation, or grammar. □ **dialectal** /-'lɛkt(ə)l/ *adj.* **dialectology** /-'tɒlədʒi/ *n.* **dialectologist** /-'tɒlədʒɪst/ *n.* [French *dialecte* or Latin *dialectus* from Greek *dialektos* 'discourse', from *dialegomai* 'converse']

dialectic /dʌɪə'lɛktɪk/ *n. & adj. Philos.* ● *n.* **1** (often in *pl.*, usu. treated as *sing.*) **a** the art of investigating the truth of opinions. **b** logical disputation. **2 a** enquiry into metaphysical contradictions and their solutions, esp. in the thought of Kant and Hegel. **b** the existence or action of opposing social forces etc. ● *adj.* **1** of or relating to logical disputation. **2** fond of or skilled in logical disputation. [Middle English via Old French *dialectique* or Latin *dialectica* from Greek *dialektikē* (*tekhnē*) '(art) of debate' (as DIALECT)]

dialectical /dʌɪəˈlɛktɪk(ə)l/ *adj.* of dialectic or dialectics. □ **dialectically** *adv.*

dialectical materialism *n.* the Marxist theory that political and historical events are due to a conflict of social forces caused by man's material needs.

dialectician /dʌɪəlɛkˈtɪʃ(ə)n/ *n.* a person skilled in dialectic. [French *dialecticien* from Latin *dialecticus*]

dialectics /dʌɪəˈlɛktɪks/ *n.* (treated as *sing.* or *pl.*) = DIALECTIC *n.* 1.

dialling code *n. Brit.* a sequence of numbers dialled to connect a telephone with the exchange of the telephone being called.

dialling tone *n.* (*N. Amer.* **dial tone**) a sound indicating that a caller may start to dial.

dialogic /dʌɪəˈlɒdʒɪk/ *adj.* of or in dialogue. [Late Latin *dialogicus* from Greek *dialogikos* (as DIALOGUE)]

dialogist /dʌɪˈalədʒɪst/ *n.* a speaker in or writer of dialogue. [Late Latin *dialogista* from Greek *dialogistēs* (as DIALOGUE)]

dialogue /ˈdʌɪəlɒg/ *n.* (*US* **dialog**) **1 a** conversation. **b** conversation in written form; this as a form of composition. **2 a** a discussion, esp. one between representatives of two political groups. **b** a conversation, a talk (*long dialogues between the two main characters*). [Middle English via Old French *dialoge* and Latin *dialogus* from Greek *dialogos*, from *dialegomai* 'converse']

dialogue box *n.* (*US* **dialog box**) *Computing* a small area on-screen, usu. temporarily displayed, in which the user is prompted to provide information, select commands, etc.

dial tone *N. Amer.* var. of DIALLING TONE.

dialyse /ˈdʌɪəlʌɪz/ *v.tr.* (*US* **dialyze**) separate by means of dialysis.

dialysis /dʌɪˈalɪsɪs/ *n.* (*pl.* **dialyses** /-siːz/) **1** *Chem.* the separation of particles in a liquid by differences in their ability to pass through a membrane into another liquid. **2** *Med.* the clinical purification of blood by this technique, as a substitute for the normal function of the kidney. □ **dialytic** /dʌɪəˈlɪtɪk/ *adj.* [Latin from Greek *dialusis* (as DIA-, *luō* 'set free')]

diamagnetic /dʌɪəmagˈnɛtɪk/ *adj.* & *n.* ● *adj.* tending to become magnetized in a direction at right angles to the applied magnetic field. ● *n.* a diamagnetic body or substance. □ **diamagnetically** *adv.* **diamagnetism** /-ˈmagnɪtɪz(ə)m/ *n.*

diamanté /dɪəˈmɒnteɪ/ *adj.* & *n.* ● *adj.* decorated with powdered crystal or another sparkling substance. ● *n.* fabric or costume jewellery so decorated. [French, past part. of *diamanter* 'set with diamonds' from *diamant* DIAMOND]

diamantiferous /dʌɪəmənˈtɪf(ə)rəs/ *adj.* diamond-yielding. [French *diamantifère* from *diamant* DIAMOND]

diamantine /dʌɪəˈmantʌɪn, -iːn/ *adj.* of or like diamonds. [French *diamantin* (as DIAMANTIFEROUS)]

diameter /dʌɪˈamɪtə/ *n.* **1 a** a straight line passing from side to side through the centre of a body or figure, esp. a circle or sphere. **b** the length of this line. **2** a transverse measurement; width, thickness. **3** a unit of linear measurement of magnifying power (*a lens magnifying 2,000 diameters*). □ **diametral** *adj.* [Middle English via Old French *diametre* and Latin *diametrus* from Greek *diametros* (*grammē*) '(line) measuring across', from *metron* 'measure']

diametrical /dʌɪəˈmɛtrɪk(ə)l/ *adj.* (also **diametric**) **1** of or along a diameter. **2** (of opposition, difference, etc.) complete, like that between opposite ends of a diameter. □ **diametrically** *adv.* [Greek *diametrikos* (as DIAMETER)]

diamond /ˈdʌɪəmənd/ *n.*, *adj.*, & *v.* ● *n.* **1** a precious stone of pure carbon crystallized in octahedrons etc., the hardest naturally occurring substance. **2** a figure shaped like the cross-section of a diamond; a rhombus. **3 a** a playing card of a suit denoted by a red rhombus. **b** (in *pl.*) this suit. **4** a glittering particle or point (of frost etc.). **5** a tool with a small diamond for glass-cutting. **6** *Baseball* **a** the space delimited by the bases. **b** the entire field. ● *adj.* **1** made of or set with diamonds or a diamond. **2** rhombus-shaped. ● *v.tr.* adorn with or as with diamonds. □ **diamond cut diamond** *Brit.* wit or cunning meets its match. □ **diamondiferous** /-ˈdɪf(ə)rəs/ *adj.* [Middle English via Old French *diamant* from medieval Latin *diamas diamant-*, variant of Latin *adamas* ADAMANT, from Greek]

diamondback /ˈdʌɪəməndbak/ *n.* **1** an edible freshwater terrapin, *Malaclemys terrapin*, native to N. America, with lozenge-shaped markings on its shell. **2** any rattlesnake of the genus *Crotalus*, native to N. America, with diamond-shaped markings.

diamond-bird *n. Austral.* = PARDALOTE.

diamond in the rough *n. US* = ROUGH DIAMOND 2.

diamond jubilee *n.* the 60th (or 75th) anniversary of an event, esp. a sovereign's accession.

diamond wedding *n.* a 60th (or 75th) wedding anniversary.

diandrous /dʌɪˈandrəs/ *adj.* having two stamens. [DI-[1] + Greek *anēr andr-* 'man']

dianthus /dʌɪˈanθəs/ *n.* any flowering plant of the genus *Dianthus*, e.g. a carnation or pink. [Greek *Dios* 'of Zeus' + *anthos* 'flower']

diapason /dʌɪəˈpeɪs(ə)n, -z-/ *n.* **1** the compass of a voice or musical instrument. **2** a fixed standard of musical pitch. **3** (in full **open** or **stopped diapason**) either of two main organ stops extending through the organ's whole compass. **4 a** a combination of musical notes or parts in a harmonious whole. **b** a melodious succession of musical notes, esp. a grand swelling burst of harmony. **5** an entire compass, range, or scope. [Middle English, in the sense 'octave', via Latin *diapason* from Greek *dia pasōn* (*khordōn*) 'through all (notes)']

diapause /ˈdʌɪəpɔːz/ *n.* in some insects, a period of suspended development ended by an appropriate environmental stimulus.

diaper /ˈdʌɪəpə/ *n.* & *v.* ● *n.* **1** *N. Amer.* a baby's nappy. **2 a** a linen or cotton fabric with a small diamond pattern. **b** this pattern. **3** a similar ornamental design of diamonds etc. for panels, walls, etc. ● *v.tr.* **1** decorate with a diaper pattern. **2** *N. Amer.* change the nappy of (a baby). [Middle English via Old French *diapre* and medieval Latin *diasprum* from medieval Greek *diaspros* (*adj.*) (as DIA-, *aspros* 'white')]

diaphanous /dʌɪˈaf(ə)nəs/ *adj.* (of fabric etc.) light and delicate, and almost transparent. [medieval Latin *diaphanus* from Greek *diaphanes* (as DIA-, *phainō* 'show')]

diaphoresis /dʌɪəfəˈriːsɪs/ *n. Med.* sweating, esp. artificially induced. [Late Latin from Greek, from *diaphoreō* 'carry through']

diaphoretic /dʌɪəfəˈrɛtɪk/ *adj.* & *n. Med.* ● *adj.* inducing perspiration. ● *n.* an agent inducing perspiration. [Late Latin *diaphoreticus* from Greek *diaphorētikos* (formed as DIAPHORESIS)]

diaphragm /ˈdʌɪəfram/ *n.* **1** a muscular partition separating the thorax from the abdomen in mammals. **2** a partition in animal and plant tissues. **3** a disc pierced by one or more holes in optical and acoustic systems etc. **4** a device for varying the effective aperture of the lens in a camera etc. **5** a thin contraceptive cap fitting over the cervix. **6** a thin sheet of material used as a partition etc. □ **diaphragmatic** /-fragˈmatɪk/ *adj.* [Middle English via Late Latin *diaphragma* from Greek (as DIA-, *phragma -atos* from *phrassō* 'fence in')]

diaphragm pump *n.* a pump using a flexible diaphragm in place of a piston.

diapir /ˈdʌɪəpɪə/ *n. Geol.* an anticline in which the upper strata are pierced by a rock core from below. [Greek *diapeirainein* 'pierce through']

diapositive /dʌɪəˈpɒzɪtɪv/ *n.* a positive photographic slide or transparency.

diarchy /ˈdʌɪɑːki/ *n.* (also **dyarchy**) (*pl.* **-ies**) **1** government by two independent authorities (esp. in India 1919–35). **2** an instance of this. □ **diarchal**

/dʌɪ'ɑ:k(ə)l/ *adj.* **diarchic** /dʌɪ'ɑ:kɪk/ *adj.* [DI-[1] + Greek *-arkhia* 'rule', on the pattern of *monarchy*]

diarist /'dʌɪərɪst/ *n.* a person who keeps a diary. ◻ **diaristic** /-'rɪstɪk/ *adj.*

diarize /'dʌɪərʌɪz/ *v.* (also **-ise**) **1** *intr.* keep a diary. **2** *tr.* enter in a diary.

diarrhoea /dʌɪə'rɪə/ *n.* (*US* **diarrhea**) a condition of excessively frequent and loose bowel movements. ◻ **diarrhoeal** *adj.* **diarrhoeic** *adj.* [Middle English via Late Latin from Greek *diarrhoia* (as DIA-, *rheō* 'flow')]

diary /'dʌɪəri/ *n.* (*pl.* **-ies**) **1** a daily record of events or thoughts. **2** a book for this or for noting future engagements, usu. printed and with a calendar and other information. [Latin *diarium* from *dies* 'day']

diascope /'dʌɪəskəʊp/ *n.* an optical projector giving images of transparent objects.

Diaspora /dʌɪ'asp(ə)rə/ *n.* **1** (prec. by *the*) **a** the dispersion of the Jews among the Gentiles mainly in the 8th–6th c. BC. **b** Jews dispersed in this way. **2** (also **diaspora**) **a** any group of people similarly dispersed. **b** their dispersion. [Greek from *diaspeirō* (as DIA-, *speirō* 'scatter')]

diastase /'dʌɪəsteɪz/ *n.* *Biochem.* = AMYLASE. ◻ **diastasic** /-'steɪzɪk/ *adj.* **diastatic** /-'statɪk/ *adj.* [French from Greek *diastasis* 'separation' (as DIA-, *stasis* 'placing')]

diastema /dʌɪə'sti:mə/ *n.* a space between adjacent teeth, esp. in front of the premolars in rodents and ungulates. [Late Latin from Greek, = space between]

diastole /dʌɪ'astəli/ *n.* *Physiol.* the period between two contractions of the heart when the heart muscle relaxes and allows the chambers to fill with blood (cf. SYSTOLE). ◻ **diastolic** /dʌɪə'stɒlɪk/ *adj.* [Late Latin from Greek *diastellō* (as DIA-, *stellō* 'place')]

diathermancy /dʌɪə'θə:m(ə)nsi/ *n.* the quality of transmitting radiant heat. ◻ **diathermic** *adj.* **diathermous** *adj.* [French *diathermansie*, from Greek *dia* 'through' + *thermansis* 'heating': assimilated to -ANCY]

diathermy /'dʌɪəθə:mi/ *n.* the application of high-frequency electric currents to produce heat in the deeper tissues of the body. [German *Diathermie*, from Greek *dia* 'through' + *thermon* 'heat']

diathesis /dʌɪ'aθəsɪs/ *n.* *Med.* a constitutional predisposition to a certain state, esp. a diseased one. [modern Latin from Greek, from *diatithēmi* 'arrange']

diatom /'dʌɪətəm/ *n.* a microscopic unicellular alga with a siliceous cell wall, found as plankton and forming fossil deposits. ◻ **diatomaceous** /-'meɪʃəs/ *adj.* [modern Latin genus name *Diatoma*, from Greek *diatomos* (as DIA-, *temnō* 'cut')]

diatomaceous earth /dʌɪətə'meɪʃəs/ *n.* = KIESELGUHR. [DIATOM + -ACEOUS]

diatomic /dʌɪə'tɒmɪk/ *adj.* consisting of two atoms. [DI-[1] + ATOM]

diatomite /dʌɪ'atəmʌɪt/ *n.* *Geol.* a pale sedimentary deposit formed from the siliceous skeletons of diatoms. Cf. KIESELGUHR.

diatonic /dʌɪə'tɒnɪk/ *adj.* *Mus.* **1** (of a scale, interval, etc.) involving only notes proper to the prevailing key without chromatic alteration. **2** (of a melody or harmony) constructed from such a scale. [French *diatonique* or Late Latin *diatonicus* from Greek *diatonikos* 'at intervals of a tone' (as DIA-, TONIC)]

diatribe /'dʌɪətrʌɪb/ *n.* a forceful verbal attack; a piece of bitter criticism. [French via Latin *diatriba* from Greek *diatribē* 'spending of time, discourse', from *diatribō* (as DIA-, *tribō* 'rub')]

diazepam /dʌɪ'azɪpam, -'eɪz-/ *n.* a tranquillizing muscle-relaxant drug with anticonvulsant properties used to relieve anxiety, tension, etc., e.g. Valium. [benzo*diazep*ine + *am*]

diazo /dʌɪ'azəʊ, -'eɪzəʊ/ *n.* (in full **diazotype**) a copying or colouring process using a diazo compound decomposed by ultraviolet light. [DI-[1] + AZO-]

diazo compound *n.* a chemical compound containing two usu. multiply-bonded nitrogen atoms, often highly coloured and used as dyes.

dib /dɪb/ *v.intr.* (**dibbed**, **dibbing**) = DAP. [variant of DAB[1]]

dibasic /dʌɪ'beɪsɪk/ *adj.* *Chem.* having two replaceable protons. [DI-[1] + BASE[1] *n.* 6]

dibber /'dɪbə/ *n.* = DIBBLE.

dibble /'dɪb(ə)l/ *n.* & *v.* ● *n.* a hand tool for making holes in the ground for seeds or young plants. ● *v.* **1** *tr.* sow or plant with a dibble. **2** *tr.* prepare (soil) with a dibble. **3** *intr.* use a dibble. [Middle English: perhaps related to DIB]

dibs /dɪbz/ *n.pl.* *Brit.* *slang* money. [earlier sense 'pebbles for game', also *dib-stones*, perhaps from DIB]

dice /dʌɪs/ *n.* & *v.* ● *n.pl.* **1** **a** small cubes with faces bearing one to six spots used in games of chance. **b** (treated as *sing.*) one of these cubes (see DIE[2]). **2** a game played with one or more such cubes. **3** food cut into small cubes for cooking. ● *v.* **1** **a** *intr.* play dice. **b** *intr.* take great risks, gamble (*dicing with death*). **c** *tr.* (foll. by *away*) gamble away. **2** *tr.* cut (food) into small cubes. **3** *tr.* *Austral.* *slang* reject; leave alone. **4** *tr.* chequer, mark with squares. ◻ **no dice** *colloq.* (there is) no chance of success, cooperation, etc. ◻ **dicer** *n.* (in sense 1a of *v.*). [pl. of DIE[2]]

■ **Usage** See Usage Note at DIE[2].

dicey /'dʌɪsi/ *adj.* (**dicier**, **diciest**) *slang* risky, unreliable. [DICE + -Y[1]]

dichotomy /dʌɪ'kɒtəmi, dɪ-/ *n.* (*pl.* **-ies**) **1** **a** a division into two classes, parts, etc., esp. of things that are opposed or entirely different. **b** a sharp or paradoxical contrast. **2** *Bot.* & *Zool.* repeated bifurcation. ◻ **dichotomic** /-kə'tɒmɪk/ *adj.* **dichotomize** *v.* (also **-ise**). **dichotomous** *adj.* [modern Latin *dichotomia* from Greek *dikhotomia*, from *dikho-* 'apart' + -TOMY]

■ **Usage** The use of *dichotomy* to mean 'dilemma' or 'ambivalence', as in *I was faced with the dichotomy of wanting to pass the exam but not wanting to please my teacher*; *She alone in the book conveys the dichotomy of the white immigrants towards blacks*, is considered incorrect in standard English.

dichroic /dʌɪ'krəʊɪk/ *adj.* (esp. of doubly refracting crystals) showing two colours. ◻ **dichroism** *n.* [Greek *dikhroos* (as DI-[1], *khrōs* 'colour')]

dichromatic /dʌɪkrə(ʊ)'matɪk/ *adj.* **1** two-coloured. **2** **a** (of animal species) having individuals that show different colorations. **b** having vision sensitive to only two of the three primary colours. ◻ **dichromatism** /dʌɪ'krəʊmətɪz(ə)m/ *n.* [DI-[1] + Greek *khrōmatikos* from *khrōma -atos* 'colour']

dick[1] /dɪk/ *n.* **1** *Brit.* *colloq.* (in certain set phrases) fellow; person (*clever dick*). **2** *coarse slang* the penis. [pet form of the name *Richard*]

dick[2] /dɪk/ *n.* *slang* a detective. [perhaps abbreviation]

dick[3] /dɪk/ *n.* ◻ **take one's dick** (often foll. by *that* + clause) *Brit.* *slang* swear, affirm. [abbreviation of *declaration*]

dicken /'dɪk(ə)n/ *int.* *Austral.* *slang* an expression of disgust or disbelief. [usu. associated with DICKENS or the name *Dickens*]

dickens /'dɪkɪnz/ *n.* (usu. prec. by *how*, *what*, *why*, etc., *the*) *colloq.* (esp. in exclamations) deuce; the Devil (*what the dickens are you doing here?*). [16th c.: probably a use of the surname *Dickens*]

Dickensian /dɪ'kɛnzɪən/ *adj.* & *n.* ● *adj.* **1** of or relating to Charles Dickens, English novelist d. 1870, or his work. **2** resembling or reminiscent of the situations, poor social conditions, or comically repulsive characters described in Dickens's work. ● *n.* an admirer or student of Dickens or his work.

dicker /'dɪkə/ *v.* & *n.* esp. *US* ● *v.* **1** **a** *intr.* bargain, haggle. **b** *tr.* barter, exchange. **2** *intr.* dither, hesitate. ● *n.* a deal, a barter. ◻ **dickerer** *n.* [perhaps from *dicker* 'set of ten (hides)', as a unit of trade]

dickhead /ˈdɪkhɛd/ *n. coarse slang* a stupid or obnoxious person, esp. a man; an idiot. [DICK[1]]

dicky[1] /ˈdɪki/ *n.* (also **dickey**) (*pl.* **-ies** or **-eys**) *colloq.* **1** a false shirt-front. **2** (in full **dicky bird**) a child's word for a little bird. **3** *Brit.* a driver's seat in a carriage. **4** *Brit.* an extra folding seat at the back of a vehicle. **5** (in full **dicky bow**) *Brit.* a bow tie. [some senses from *Dicky* (as DICK[1])]

dicky[2] /ˈdɪki/ *adj.* (**dickier**, **dickiest**) *Brit. slang* unsound; likely to collapse or fail. [18th c.: perhaps from the saying 'as queer as Dick's hatband']

dicot /ˈdʌɪkɒt/ *n.* = DICOTYLEDON. [abbreviation]

dicotyledon /ˌdʌɪkɒtɪˈliːd(ə)n/ *n.* any flowering plant with an embryo which bears two cotyledons. □ **dicotyledonous** *adj.* [modern Latin *dicotyledones* (as DI-[1], COTYLEDON)]

dicrotic /dʌɪˈkrɒtɪk/ *adj.* (of the pulse) having a double beat. [Greek *dikrotos*]

dicta *pl.* of DICTUM.

Dictaphone /ˈdɪktəfəʊn/ *n. propr.* a machine for recording and playing back dictated letters etc. [DICTATE + -PHONE]

dictate *v.* & *n.* ● *v.* /dɪkˈteɪt/ **1** *tr.* say or read aloud (words to be written down or recorded). **2 a** *tr.* prescribe or lay down authoritatively (terms, things to be done). **b** *intr.* lay down the law; give orders. ● *n.* /ˈdɪkteɪt/ (usu. in *pl.*) an authoritative instruction (*dictates of conscience*). [Latin *dictare dictat-*, frequentative of *dicere dict-* 'say']

dictation /dɪkˈteɪʃ(ə)n/ *n.* **1 a** the saying of words to be written down or recorded. **b** an instance of this, esp. as a school exercise. **c** the material that is dictated. **2 a** authoritative prescription. **b** an instance of this. **c** a command.

dictation speed *n.* a slow rate of speech suitable for dictation.

dictator /dɪkˈteɪtə/ *n.* **1** a ruler with (often usurped) unrestricted authority. **2** a person with supreme authority in any sphere. **3** a domineering person. **4** a person who dictates for transcription. **5** *Rom.Hist.* a chief magistrate with absolute power, appointed in an emergency. [Middle English from Latin (as DICTATE)]

dictatorial /dɪktəˈtɔːrɪəl/ *adj.* **1** of or like a dictator. **2** imperious, overbearing. □ **dictatorially** *adv.* [Latin *dictatorius* (as DICTATOR)]

dictatorship /dɪkˈteɪtəʃɪp/ *n.* **1** a state ruled by a dictator. **2 a** the position, rule, or period of rule of a dictator. **b** rule by a dictator. **3** absolute authority in any sphere.

diction /ˈdɪkʃ(ə)n/ *n.* **1** the manner of enunciation in speaking or singing. **2** the choice of words or phrases in speech or writing. [French *diction* or Latin *dictio*, from *dicere dict-* 'say']

dictionary /ˈdɪkʃ(ə)n(ə)ri/ *n.* (*pl.* **-ies**) **1** a book that lists (usu. in alphabetical order) and explains the words of a language or gives equivalent words in another language. **2** a reference book on any subject, the items of which are arranged in alphabetical order (*dictionary of architecture*). [medieval Latin *dictionarium* (*manuale* 'manual') & *dictionarius* (*liber* 'book') from Latin *dictio* (as DICTION)]

dictum /ˈdɪktəm/ *n.* (*pl.* **dicta** /-tə/ or **dictums**) **1** a formal utterance or pronouncement. **2** a saying or maxim. **3** *Law* = OBITER DICTUM. [Latin, = neut. past part. of *dicere* 'say']

did *past* of DO[1].

didactic /dɪˈdaktɪk, dʌɪ-/ *adj.* **1** meant to instruct. **2** (of a person) tediously pedantic. □ **didactically** *adv.* **didacticism** /-tɪsɪz(ə)m/ *n.* [Greek *didaktikos* from *didaskō* 'teach']

didakai var. of DIDICOI.

diddicoy var. of DIDICOI.

diddle /ˈdɪd(ə)l/ *v. colloq.* **1** *tr.* cheat, swindle. **2** *intr. US* waste time. □ **diddler** *n.* [probably a back-formation from Jeremy *Diddler*, a character in Kenney's 'Raising the Wind' (1803), who constantly borrowed small sums of money which he did not repay]

diddly-squat /ˈdɪdlɪˌskwɒt/ *n.* (also **doodly-squat**) *N. Amer. slang* **1** (foll. by *neg.*) anything, the least bit (*doesn't mean diddly-squat to me*). **2** nothing at all. [variant of DOODLY-SQUAT, probably from US slang *doodle* 'excrement', *squat* 'to void excrement']

diddums /ˈdɪdəmz/ *int. Brit.* expressing commiseration esp. to a child. [from *did 'em*, i.e. 'did they (tease you etc.)?']

didgeridoo /dɪdʒ(ə)rɪˈduː/ *n.* (also **didjeridoo**) an Australian Aboriginal musical wind instrument of long tubular shape. [imitative]

didicoi /ˈdɪdɪkɔɪ/ *n.* (also **didakai**, **diddicoy**) *Brit. slang* a gypsy; an itinerant tinker. [Romany]

didn't /ˈdɪd(ə)nt/ *contr.* did not.

dido /ˈdʌɪdəʊ/ *n.* (*pl.* **-oes** or **-os**) *US colloq.* an antic, a caper, a prank. □ **cut** (or **cut up**) **didoes** play pranks. [19th c.: origin unknown]

didst /dɪdst/ *archaic 2nd sing. past* of DO[1].

didymium /dɪˈdɪmɪəm/ *n. Chem.* a mixture of praseodymium and neodymium, originally regarded as an element. [modern Latin from Greek *didumos* 'twin' (from being closely associated with lanthanum)]

die[1] /dʌɪ/ *v.* (**dies**, **died**, **dying** /ˈdʌɪɪŋ/) **1** *intr.* (often foll. by *of*) (of a person, animal, or plant) cease to live; expire, lose vital force (*died of hunger*). **2** *intr.* **a** come to an end, cease to exist, fade away (*the project died within six months*). **b** cease to function; break down (*the engine died*). **c** (of a flame) go out. **3** *intr.* (foll. by *on*) die or cease to function while in the presence or charge of (a person). **4** *intr.* (usu. foll. by *of*, *from*, *with*) be exhausted or tormented (*nearly died of boredom*; *was dying from the heat*). **5** *tr.* suffer (a specified death) (*died a natural death*). □ **be dying** (foll. by *for*, or *to* + infin.) wish for longingly or intently (*was dying for a drink*; *am dying to see you*). **die away** become weaker or fainter to the point of extinction. **die back** (of a plant) decay from the tip towards the root. **die down** become less loud or strong. **die hard** die reluctantly, not without a struggle (*old habits die hard*). **die off** die one after another until few or none are left. **die out** become extinct, cease to exist. **never say die** keep up one's courage, not give in. **to die for** (*predic.*) *colloq.* extremely good or desirable (*chocolate to die for*). [Middle English, probably from Old Norse *deyja*, from Germanic]

die[2] /dʌɪ/ *n.* **1** *sing.* of DICE *n.* 1a. **2** (*pl.* **dies**) **a** an engraved device for stamping a design on coins, medals, etc. **b** a device for stamping, cutting, or moulding material into a particular shape. **3** (*pl.* **dice** /dʌɪs/) *Archit.* the cubical part of a pedestal between the base and the cornice; a dado or plinth. □ **as straight** (or **true**) **as a die 1** quite straight. **2** entirely honest or loyal. **the die is cast** an irrevocable step has been taken. [Middle English via Old French *de* from Latin *datum*, neut. past part. of *dare* 'give, play']

■ **Usage** *Dice*, rather than *die*, is now the standard singular as well as plural form in the games sense (sense 1 above), e.g. *one dice, two dice.*

die-away *adj.* having a languishing or affectedly feeble manner.

die-back *n.* the progressive dying back of a shrub or tree shoot owing to disease or unfavourable conditions.

die-casting *n.* the process or product of casting from metal moulds. □ **die-cast** *v.tr.*

dieffenbachia /diːf(ə)nˈbakɪə/ *n.* any tropical American evergreen plant of the genus *Dieffenbachia* (arum family), often grown as a house plant and having acrid toxic sap. [modern Latin, named after E. *Dieffenbach*, German horticulturalist, d. 1855]

diehard /ˈdʌɪhɑːd/ *n.* a conservative or stubborn person.

dieldrin /ˈdiːldrɪn/ *n.* a toxic insecticide produced by the oxidation of aldrin, now little used because of its persistence in the environment. [from O. *Diels*, German chemist d. 1954 + ALDRIN]

dielectric /dʌɪɪ'lɛktrɪk/ *adj. & n. Electr.* ● *adj.* insulating. ● *n.* an insulating medium or substance. □ **dielectrically** *adv.* [DI-[3] + ELECTRIC = through which electricity is transmitted (without conduction)]

dielectric constant *n.* permittivity.

diene /'dʌɪi:n/ *n. Chem.* any organic compound possessing two double bonds between carbon atoms. [DI-[1] + -ENE]

dieresis *US* var. of DIAERESIS.

diesel /'di:z(ə)l/ *n.* **1** (in full **diesel engine**) an internal-combustion engine in which the heat produced by the compression of air in the cylinder ignites the fuel. **2** a vehicle driven by a diesel engine. **3** fuel for a diesel engine. □ **dieselize** *v.tr.* (also **-ise**). [named after R. *Diesel*, German engineer d. 1913, who invented the engine]

diesel-electric *n. & adj.* ● *n.* a vehicle driven by the electric current produced by a diesel-engined generator. ● *adj.* of or powered by this means.

diesel oil *n.* a heavy petroleum fraction used as fuel in diesel engines.

die-sinker *n.* an engraver of dies.

Dies irae /ˌdi:eɪz 'ɪərʌɪ, 'ɪəreɪ/ *n.* a Latin hymn sung in a Mass for the dead. [Latin (the opening words), = day of wrath]

dies non /ˌdʌɪi:z 'nɒn/ *n. Law* **1** a day on which no legal business can be done. **2** a day that does not count for legal purposes. [Latin, short for *dies non juridicus* 'non-judicial day']

die-stamping *n.* embossing paper etc. with a die.

diet[1] /'dʌɪət/ *n., v., & adj.* ● *n.* **1** the kinds of food that a person or animal habitually eats. **2** a special course of food to which a person is restricted, esp. for medical reasons or to control weight. **3** a regular occupation or series of activities to which one is restricted or which form one's main concern, usu. for a purpose (*a diet of light reading and fresh air*). ● *v.* (**dieted**, **dieting**) **1** *intr.* restrict oneself to small amounts or special kinds of food, esp. to control one's weight. **2** *tr.* restrict (a person or animal) to a special diet. ● *attrib. adj.* with reduced fat or sugar content. □ **dieter** *n.* [Middle English via Old French *diete* (*n.*), *dieter* (*v.*) and Latin *diaeta* from Greek *diaita* 'a way of life']

diet[2] /'dʌɪət/ *n.* **1** a legislative assembly in certain countries. **2** *hist.* a national or international conference, esp. of a federal state or confederation. **3** *Sc. Law* a meeting or session of a court. [Middle English from medieval Latin *dieta* 'day's work, wages, etc.']

dietary /'dʌɪət(ə)ri/ *adj. & n.* ● *adj.* of or relating to a diet. ● *n.* (*pl.* **-ies**) a regulated or restricted diet. [Middle English from medieval Latin *dietarium* (as DIET[1])]

dietetic /dʌɪə'tɛtɪk/ *adj.* of or relating to diet. □ **dietetically** *adv.* [Latin *dieteticus* from Greek *diaitētikos* (as DIET[1])]

dietetics /dʌɪə'tɛtɪks/ *n.pl.* (usu. treated as *sing.*) the scientific study of diet and nutrition.

diethyl ether /dʌɪ'i:θʌɪl/ *n. Chem.* = ETHER 1a.

dietitian /dʌɪə'tɪʃ(ə)n/ *n.* (also **dietician**) an expert in dietetics.

dif- /dɪf/ *prefix* assim. form of DIS- before *f.* [Latin variant of DIS-]

differ /'dɪfə/ *v.intr.* **1** (often foll. by *from*) be unlike or distinguishable. **2** (often foll. by *with*) disagree; be at variance (with a person). [Middle English via Old French *differer* from Latin *differre* 'differ, DEFER[1]' (as DIS-, *ferre* 'bear, tend')]

difference /'dɪf(ə)r(ə)ns/ *n. & v.* ● *n.* **1** the state or condition of being different or unlike. **2** a point in which things differ; a distinction. **3** a degree of unlikeness. **4 a** the quantity by which amounts differ; a deficit (*will have to make up the difference*). **b** the remainder left after subtraction. **5 a** a disagreement, quarrel, or dispute. **b** the grounds of disagreement (*put aside their differences*). **6** *Heraldry* an alteration in a coat of arms distinguishing members of a family. ● *v.tr. Heraldry* alter (a coat of arms) to distinguish members of a family. □ **make a** (or **all the** etc.) **difference** (often foll. by *to*) have a significant effect or influence (on a person, situation, etc.). **make no difference** (often foll. by *to*) have no effect (on a person, situation, etc.). **with a difference** having a new or unusual feature. [Middle English via Old French from Latin *differentia* (as DIFFERENT)]

different /'dɪf(ə)r(ə)nt/ *adj.* **1** (often foll. by *from*, *to*, *than*) unlike, distinguishable in nature, form, or quality (from another). **2** distinct, separate; not the same one (as another). **3** *colloq.* unusual (*wanted to do something different*). □ **differently** *adv.* **differentness** *n.* [Middle English via Old French from Latin *different-* (as DIFFER)]

■ **Usage** In sense 1 *different from* is generally regarded as the most acceptable collocation; *to* is common in less formal British use; *than* is established in US use and also found in British use, esp. when followed by a clause, e.g. *I am a different person than I was a year ago.*

differentia /dɪfə'rɛnʃɪə/ *n.* (*pl.* **differentiae** /-ʃɪi:/) a distinguishing mark, esp. between species within a genus. [Latin: see DIFFERENCE]

differential /dɪfə'rɛnʃ(ə)l/ *adj. & n.* ● *adj.* **1 a** of, exhibiting, or depending on a difference. **b** varying according to circumstances. **2** *Math.* relating to infinitesimal differences. **3** constituting a specific difference; distinctive; relating to specific differences (*differential diagnosis*). **4** *Physics & Mech.* concerning the difference of two or more motions, pressures, etc. ● *n.* **1** a difference between individuals or examples of the same kind. **2** a difference in wage or salary between industries or categories of employees in the same industry. **3** a difference between rates of interest etc. **4** *Math.* **a** an infinitesimal difference between successive values of a variable. **b** a function expressing this as a rate of change with respect to another variable. **5** (in full **differential gear**) a gear allowing a vehicle's driven wheels to revolve at different speeds in cornering. □ **differentially** *adv.* [medieval & modern Latin *differentialis* (as DIFFERENCE)]

differential calculus *n.* a method of calculating rates of change, maximum or minimum values, etc. (cf. INTEGRAL CALCULUS).

differential coefficient *n. Math.* = DERIVATIVE *n.* 2.

differential equation *n.* an equation involving differentials among its quantities.

differentiate /dɪfə'rɛnʃɪeɪt/ *v.* **1** *tr.* constitute a difference between or in. **2** *tr.* & (often foll. by *between*) *intr.* find differences (between); discriminate. **3** *tr.* & *intr.* make or become different in the process of growth or development (species, word-forms, etc.). **4** *tr. Math.* transform (a function) into its derivative. □ **differentiation** /-'eɪʃ(ə)n/ *n.* **differentiator** *n.* [medieval Latin *differentiare* *differentiat-* (as DIFFERENCE)]

differently abled *adj. euphem.* disabled.

difficult /'dɪfɪk(ə)lt/ *adj.* **1 a** needing much effort or skill. **b** troublesome, perplexing. **2** (of a person): **a** not easy to please or satisfy. **b** uncooperative, troublesome. **3** characterized by hardships or problems (*a difficult period in his life*). □ **difficultly** *adv.* **difficultness** *n.* [Middle English, back-formation from DIFFICULTY]

difficulty /'dɪfɪk(ə)lti/ *n.* (*pl.* **-ies**) **1** the state or condition of being difficult. **2 a** a difficult thing; a problem or hindrance. **b** (often in *pl.*) a cause of distress or hardship (*in financial difficulties*; *there was someone in difficulties in the water*). □ **with difficulty** not easily. [Middle English from Latin *difficultas* (as DIS-, *facultas* FACULTY)]

diffident /'dɪfɪd(ə)nt/ *adj.* **1** shy, lacking self-confidence. **2** excessively modest and reticent. □ **diffidence** *n.* **diffidently** *adv.* [Latin *diffidere* (as DIS-, *fidere* 'trust')]

diffract /dɪ'frakt/ *v.tr. Physics* (of the edge of an opaque body, a narrow slit, etc.) break up (a beam of light) into a series of dark or light bands or coloured spectra, or (a beam of radiation or particles) into a series of alternately high and low intensities. □ **diffraction** *n.*

diffractive *adj.* **diffractively** *adv.* [Latin *diffringere diffract-* (as DIS-, *frangere* 'break')]

diffraction grating *n.* a plate of glass or metal ruled with very close parallel lines, producing a spectrum by diffraction and interference of light.

diffractometer /dɪfrak'tɒmɪtə/ *n.* an instrument for measuring diffraction, esp. in crystallographic work.

diffuse *adj.* & *v.* ● *adj.* /dɪ'fju:s/ **1** (of light, inflammation, etc.) spread out, dispersed, not concentrated or localized. **2** (of prose, speech, etc.) not concise; long-winded, verbose. ● *v.tr.* & *intr.* /dɪ'fju:z/ **1** disperse or be dispersed from a centre. **2** spread or be spread widely; reach a large area. **3** *Physics* intermingle by diffusion. □ **diffusely** /dɪ'fju:sli/ *adv.* **diffuseness** /dɪ'fju:snɪs/ *n.* **diffusible** /dɪ'fju:zɪb(ə)l/ *adj.* **diffusive** /dɪ'fju:sɪv/ *adj.* [Middle English from French *diffus* or Latin *diffusus* 'extensive' (as DIS-, *fusus*, past part. of *fundere* 'pour')]

diffuser /dɪ'fju:zə/ *n.* (also **diffusor**) **1** a person or thing that diffuses, esp. a device for diffusing light. **2** *Engin.* a duct for broadening an airflow and reducing its speed.

diffusion /dɪ'fju:ʒ(ə)n/ *n.* **1** the act or an instance of diffusing; the process of being diffused. **2** *Physics* & *Chem.* the interpenetration of substances by the natural movement of their particles. **3** *Anthropol.* the spread of elements of culture etc. to another region or people. □ **diffusionist** *n.* [Middle English from Latin *diffusio* (as DIFFUSE)]

dig /dɪg/ *v.* & *n.* ● *v.* (**digging**; *past* and *past part.* **dug** /dʌg/) **1** *intr.* break up and remove or turn over soil, ground, etc., with a tool, one's hands, (of an animal) claws, etc. **2** *tr.* **a** break up and displace (the ground etc.) in this way. **b** (foll. by *up*) break up the soil of (fallow land). **3** *tr.* make (a hole, grave, tunnel, etc.) by digging. **4** *tr.* (often foll. by *up, out*) **a** obtain or remove by digging. **b** find or discover after searching. **5** *tr.* (also *absol.*) excavate (an archaeological site). **6** *tr. slang* like, appreciate, or understand. **7** *tr.* & *intr.* (foll. by *in, into*) thrust or poke into or down into. **8** *intr.* make one's way by digging (*dug through the mountainside*). ● *n.* **1** a piece of digging. **2** a thrust or poke (*a dig in the ribs*). **3** (often foll. by *at*) *colloq.* a pointed or critical remark. **4** an archaeological excavation. **5** (in *pl.*) esp. *Brit. colloq.* lodgings. □ **dig one's feet** (or **heels** or **toes**) **in** be obstinate. **dig in** *colloq.* begin eating. **dig oneself in 1** prepare a defensive trench or pit. **2** establish one's position. [Middle English *digge*, of uncertain origin: perhaps from Old English *dīc* 'ditch']

digamma /dʌɪ'gamə/ *n.* the sixth letter (Ϝ, ϝ) of the early Greek alphabet (probably pronounced w), later disused. [Latin from Greek (as DI-[1], GAMMA)]

digastric /dʌɪ'gastrɪk/ *adj.* & *n.* *Anat.* ● *adj.* (of a muscle) having two wide parts with a tendon between. ● *n.* the muscle that opens the jaw. [modern Latin *digastricus* (as DI-[1], Greek *gastēr* 'belly')]

digest *v.* & *n.* ● *v.tr.* /dʌɪ'dʒɛst, dɪ-/ **1** break down (food) in the stomach and bowels into simpler molecules that can be assimilated by the body. **2** understand and assimilate mentally. **3** *Chem.* treat (a substance) with heat, enzymes, or a solvent in order to decompose it, extract the essence, etc. **4 a** reduce to a systematic or convenient form; classify; summarize. **b** think over; arrange in the mind. ● *n.* /'dʌɪdʒɛst/ **1 a** a methodical summary esp. of a body of laws. **b** (**the Digest**) the compendium of Roman law compiled in the reign of Justinian (6th c. AD). **2** a regular or occasional synopsis of current literature or news. □ **digester** *n.* **digestible** *adj.* **digestibility** /-'bɪlɪti/ *n.* [Middle English from Latin *digerere digest-* 'distribute, dissolve, digest' (as DI-[2], *gerere* 'carry')]

digestion /dʌɪ'dʒɛstʃ(ə)n, dɪ-/ *n.* **1** the process of digesting. **2** the capacity to digest food (*has a weak digestion*). **3** digesting a substance by means of heat, enzymes, or a solvent. [Middle English via Old French from Latin *digestio -onis* (as DIGEST)]

digestive /dʌɪ'dʒɛstɪv, dɪ-/ *adj.* & *n.* ● *adj.* **1** of or relating to digestion. **2** aiding or promoting digestion. ● *n.* **1** a substance that aids digestion. **2** (in full **digestive biscuit**) *Brit.* a usu. round semi-sweet wholemeal biscuit. □ **digestively** *adv.* [Middle English from Old French *digestif -ive* or Latin *digestivus* (as DIGEST)]

digger /'dɪgə/ *n.* **1** a person or machine that digs, esp. a mechanical excavator. **2** a miner, esp. a gold-digger. **3** *colloq.* an Australian or New Zealander, esp. a private soldier. **4** *Austral.* & *NZ colloq.* (as a form of address) mate, fellow.

digger wasp *n.* any of various mainly solitary wasps which burrow in soil.

diggings /'dɪgɪŋz/ *n.pl.* **1 a** a mine or goldfield. **b** material dug out of a mine etc. **2** *Brit. colloq.* lodgings, accommodation.

dight /dʌɪt/ *adj. archaic* clothed, arrayed. [past part. of *dight* from Old English *dihtan*, from Latin *dictare* DICTATE]

digit /'dɪdʒɪt/ *n.* **1** any numeral from 0 to 9, esp. when forming part of a number. **2** *Anat.* & *Zool.* a finger, thumb, or toe. [Middle English from Latin *digitus*]

digital /'dɪdʒɪt(ə)l/ *adj.* **1** designating, relating to, operating with, or created using, signals or information represented by digits (*a digital recording*). **2** (of a clock, watch, etc.) giving a reading by means of displayed digits as opposed to hands (cf. ANALOGUE *adj.* 2). □ **digitalize** *v.tr.* (also **-ise**). **digitally** *adv.* [Latin *digitalis* (as DIGIT)]

digital audio tape *n.* magnetic tape on which sound is recorded digitally.

digitalin /dɪdʒɪ'teɪlɪn/ *n.* the pharmacologically active constituent(s) of the foxglove. [DIGITALIS + -IN]

digitalis /dɪdʒɪ'teɪlɪs/ *n.* a drug prepared from the dried leaves of foxgloves and containing substances that stimulate the heart muscle. [modern Latin, = relating to the finger, genus name of foxglove, influenced by German *Fingerhut* 'foxglove, thimble': see DIGITAL]

digital to analog converter *n.* a device for converting digital values to analog form.

digitate /'dɪdʒɪtət, -eɪt/ *adj.* **1** *Zool.* having separate fingers or toes. **2** *Bot.* having deep radiating divisions. □ **digitately** *adv.* **digitation** /-'teɪʃ(ə)n/ *n.* [Latin *digitatus* (as DIGIT)]

digitigrade /'dɪdʒɪtɪgreɪd/ *adj.* & *n.* *Zool.* ● *adj.* (of an animal) walking on its toes and not touching the ground with its heels, e.g. dogs, cats, and rodents. ● *n.* a digitigrade animal (cf. PLANTIGRADE). [French, from Latin *digitus* + *-gradus* '-walking']

digitize /'dɪdʒɪtʌɪz/ *v.tr.* (also **-ise**) convert (data etc.) into digital form, esp. for processing by a computer. □ **digitization** /-'zeɪʃ(ə)n/ *n.*

dignified /'dɪgnɪfʌɪd/ *adj.* having or expressing dignity; noble or stately in appearance or manner. □ **dignifiedly** *adv.*

dignify /'dɪgnɪfʌɪ/ *v.tr.* (**-ies, -ied**) **1** give dignity or distinction to. **2** ennoble; make worthy or illustrious. **3** give the form or appearance of dignity to (*dignified the house with the name of mansion*). [obsolete French *dignifier* via Old French *dignefier* from Late Latin *dignificare*, from *dignus* 'worthy']

dignitary /'dɪgnɪt(ə)ri/ *n.* (*pl.* **-ies**) a person holding high rank or office. [DIGNITY + -ARY[1], on the pattern of PROPRIETARY]

dignity /'dɪgnɪti/ *n.* (*pl.* **-ies**) **1** a composed and serious manner or style. **2** the state of being worthy of honour or respect. **3** worthiness, excellence (*the dignity of work*). **4** a high or honourable rank or position. **5** high regard or estimation. □ **beneath one's dignity** not considered worthy enough for one to do. **stand on one's dignity** insist (esp. by one's manner) on being treated with due respect. [Middle English via Old French *digneté, dignité* from Latin *dignitas -tatis*, from *dignus* 'worthy']

digraph /ˈdʌɪgrɑːf/ *n.* a group of two letters representing one sound, as in *ph* and *ey*. ▫ **digraphic** /-ˈgrafɪk/ *adj.*

■ **Usage** *Digraph* is sometimes confused with *ligature* which means 'two or more letters joined together'.

digress /dʌɪˈgrɛs/ *v.intr.* depart from the main subject temporarily in speech or writing. ▫ **digresser** *n.* **digression** /-ˈgrɛʃ(ə)n/ *n.* **digressive** *adj.* **digressively** *adv.* **digressiveness** *n.* [Latin *digredi digress-* (as DI-[2], *gradi* 'walk')]

digs see DIG *n.* 5.

dihedral /dʌɪˈhiːdr(ə)l/ *adj.* & *n.* ● *adj.* having or contained by two plane faces. ● *n.* = DIHEDRAL ANGLE. [*dihedron* from DI-[1] + -HEDRON]

dihedral angle *n.* an angle formed by two plane surfaces, esp. by an aircraft wing with the horizontal.

dihybrid /dʌɪˈhʌɪbrɪd/ *n.* & *adj.* ● *n.* a hybrid that is heterozygous for alleles of two different genes. ● *adj.* relating to the inheritance of alleles of two different genes.

dihydric /dʌɪˈhʌɪdrɪk/ *adj. Chem.* (of an alcohol) containing two hydroxyl groups. [DI-[1] + HYDROGEN + -IC]

dik-dik /ˈdɪkdɪk/ *n.* any dwarf antelope of the genus *Madoqua*, native to Africa. [name in E. Africa and in Afrikaans]

dike[1] var. of DYKE[1].

dike[2] var. of DYKE[2].

diktat /ˈdɪktat/ *n.* a categorical statement or decree, esp. terms imposed after a war by a victor. [German, = DICTATE]

dilapidate /dɪˈlapɪdeɪt/ *v.intr.* & *tr.* fall or cause to fall into disrepair or ruin. [Latin *dilapidare* 'demolish, squander' (as DI-[2], *lapis lapid-* 'stone')]

dilapidated /dɪˈlapɪdeɪtɪd/ *adj.* in a state of disrepair or ruin, esp. as a result of age or neglect.

dilapidation /dɪˌlapɪˈdeɪʃ(ə)n/ *n.* **1 a** the process of dilapidating. **b** a state of disrepair. **2** (in *pl.*) repairs required at the end of a tenancy or lease. **3** *Eccl.* a sum charged against an incumbent for wear and tear during a tenancy. [Middle English from Late Latin *dilapidatio* (as DILAPIDATE)]

dilatation /dʌɪleɪˈteɪʃ(ə)n, dɪ-, -lə-/ *n.* **1** the widening or expansion of a hollow organ or cavity. **2** the process of dilating.

dilatation and curettage see D. AND C.

dilate /dʌɪˈleɪt/ *v.* **1** *tr.* & *intr.* make or become wider or larger (esp. of an opening in the body). **2** *intr.* (often foll. by *on, upon*) speak or write at length. ▫ **dilatable** *adj.* **dilation** *n.* [Middle English via Old French *dilater* from Latin *dilatare* 'spread out' (as DI-[2], *latus* 'wide')]

dilator /dʌɪˈleɪtə, dɪ-/ *n.* **1** *Anat.* a muscle that dilates an organ or aperture. **2** *Surgery* an instrument for dilating a tube or cavity in the body.

dilatory /ˈdɪlət(ə)ri/ *adj.* given to or causing delay. ▫ **dilatorily** *adv.* **dilatoriness** *n.* [Late Latin *dilatorius* (as DI-[2], *dilat-*, past part. stem of *differre* DEFER[1])]

dildo /ˈdɪldəʊ/ *n.* (*pl.* **-os** or **-oes**) an object shaped like an erect penis and used, esp. by women, for sexual stimulation. [16th c.: origin unknown]

dilemma /dɪˈlɛmə, dʌɪ-/ *n.* **1** a situation in which a choice has to be made between two equally undesirable alternatives. **2** a state of indecision between two alternatives. **3** *disp.* a difficult situation; a problem. **4** an argument forcing an opponent to choose either of two unfavourable alternatives. [Latin from Greek (as DI-[1], *lēmma* 'premiss')]

■ **Usage** The use of *dilemma* in sense 3 is considered incorrect by some people.

dilettante /dɪlɪˈtanti/ *n.* & *adj.* ● *n.* (*pl.* **dilettanti** /-ti/ or **dilettantes**) **1** a person who studies a subject or area of knowledge superficially. **2** a person who enjoys the arts. ● *adj.* trifling, not thorough; amateurish. ▫ **dilettantish** *adj.* **dilettantism** *n.* [Italian from pres. part. of *dilettare* 'delight', from Latin *delectare*]

diligence[1] /ˈdɪlɪdʒ(ə)ns/ *n.* **1** careful and persistent application or effort. **2** (as a characteristic) industriousness. [Middle English via Old French from Latin *diligentia* (as DILIGENT)]

diligence[2] /ˈdɪlɪdʒ(ə)ns/ *n. hist.* a public stagecoach, esp. in France. [French, for *carrosse de diligence* 'coach of speed']

diligent /ˈdɪlɪdʒ(ə)nt/ *adj.* **1** careful and steady in application to one's work or duties. **2** showing care and effort. ▫ **diligently** *adv.* [Middle English via Old French from Latin *diligens* 'assiduous', part. of *diligere* 'love, take delight in' (as DI-[2], *legere* 'choose')]

dill[1] /dɪl/ *n.* **1** an umbelliferous herb, *Anethum graveolens*, with yellow flowers and aromatic seeds. **2** the leaves (in full **dill weed**) or seeds of this plant used for flavouring and medicinal purposes. [Old English *dile*]

dill[2] /dɪl/ *n. Austral.* & *NZ slang* **1** a fool or simpleton. **2** the victim of a trickster. [apparently back-formation from DILLY[2]]

dill pickle *n.* pickled cucumber etc. flavoured with dill.

dill-water *n.* a distillate of dill used as a carminative.

dilly[1] /ˈdɪli/ *n.* (*pl.* **-ies**) esp. *US slang* a remarkable or excellent person or thing. [*dilly* (*adj.*) from DELIGHTFUL or DELICIOUS]

dilly[2] /ˈdɪli/ *adj. Austral. slang* **1** odd or eccentric. **2** foolish, stupid, mad. [perhaps from DAFT, SILLY]

dillybag /ˈdɪlɪbag/ *n. Austral.* a small bag or basket. [Yagara *dilly* '(a bag made of) coarse grass or reeds']

dilly-dally /ˈdɪlɪdali/ *v.intr.* (**-ies, -ied**) *colloq.* **1** dawdle, loiter. **2** vacillate. [reduplication of DALLY]

diluent /ˈdɪljʊənt/ *adj.* & *n. Chem.* & *Biochem.* ● *adj.* that serves to dilute. ● *n.* a diluting agent. [Latin *diluere diluent-* DILUTE]

dilute /dʌɪˈl(j)uːt, dɪ-/ *v.* & *adj.* ● *v.tr.* **1** reduce the strength of (a fluid) by adding water or another solvent. **2** weaken or reduce the strength or forcefulness of, esp. by adding something. ● *adj.* /also ˈdʌɪ-/ **1** (esp. of a fluid) diluted, weakened. **2** (of a colour) washed out; low in saturation. **3** *Chem.* **a** (of a solution) having relatively low concentration of solute. **b** (of a substance) in solution (*dilute sulphuric acid*). ▫ **diluter** *n.* **dilution** *n.* [Latin *diluere dilut-* (as DI-[2], *luere* 'wash')]

diluvial /dʌɪˈl(j)uːvɪəl, dɪ-/ *adj.* **1** of a flood, esp. of the Flood in Genesis. **2** *Geol.* of or consisting of diluvium. [Late Latin *diluvialis* from *diluvium* DELUGE]

diluvium /dʌɪˈl(j)uːvɪəm, dɪ-/ *n.* (*pl.* **diluvia** /-vɪə/) *Geol.* = DRIFT *n.* 8. [Latin: see DILUVIAL]

dim /dɪm/ *adj.* & *v.* ● *adj.* (**dimmer, dimmest**) **1 a** only faintly luminous or visible; not bright. **b** obscure; ill-defined. **2** not clearly perceived or remembered. **3** *colloq.* stupid; slow to understand. **4** (of the eyes) not seeing clearly. ● *v.* (**dimmed, dimming**) **1** *tr.* & *intr.* make or become dim or less bright. **2** *tr. US* dip (headlights). ▫ **take a dim view of** *colloq.* **1** disapprove of. **2** feel gloomy about. ▫ **dimly** *adv.* **dimmish** *adj.* **dimness** *n.* [Old English *dim, dimm*, of unknown origin]

dim. *abbr.* diminuendo.

dime /dʌɪm/ *n. N. Amer.* **1** a ten-cent coin. **2** *colloq.* a small amount of money. ▫ **a dime a dozen** very cheap or commonplace. **on a dime** *N. Amer. colloq.* **1** within a small area or short distance. **2** quickly, instantly. [Middle English (originally = tithe) via Old French *disme* from Latin *decima pars* 'tenth part']

dime novel *n. N. Amer.* a cheap popular novel.

dimension /dɪˈmɛnʃ(ə)n, dʌɪ-/ *n.* & *v.* ● *n.* **1** a measurable extent of any kind, as length, breadth, depth. **2** (in *pl.*) size, scope, extent. **3** an aspect or facet of a situation, problem, etc. **4** *Algebra* one of a number of unknown or variable quantities contained as factors in a product (*x^3, x^2y, xyz, are all of three dimensions*). **5** *Physics* the product of mass, length, time, etc., raised to the appropriate power, in a derived physical quantity. ● *v.tr.* (usu. as **dimensioned** *adj.*) mark the dimensions on (a diagram etc.). ▫ **dimensional** *adj.* (also in *comb.*).

dimensionless *adj.* [Middle English via Old French from Latin *dimensio -onis* (as DI-², *metiri mensus* 'measure')]

dimer /'dʌɪmə/ *n. Chem.* a compound consisting of two identical molecules linked together (cf. MONOMER). □ **dimeric** /-'mɛrɪk/ *adj.* [DI-¹ + *-mer* on the pattern of POLYMER]

dimerize /'dʌɪmərʌɪz/ *v.tr. & intr.* (also **-ise**) *Chem.* convert or be converted to a dimer. □ **dimerization** /-'zeɪʃ(ə)n/ *n.*

dimerous /'dɪm(ə)rəs/ *adj.* (of a plant) having two parts in a whorl etc. [modern Latin *dimerus* from Greek *dimerēs* 'bipartite']

dimeter /'dɪmɪtə/ *n. Prosody* a line of verse consisting of two metrical feet. [Late Latin *dimetrus* from Greek *dimetros* (as DI-¹, *metron* 'measure')]

dimethylsulphoxide /dʌɪˌmiːθʌɪlsʌl'fɒksʌɪd/ *n.* (*US* **dimethylsulfoxide**) *Chem.* a colourless liquid used as a solvent and in medicine esp. to treat inflammation (abbr.: **DMSO**). Chem. formula: $(CH_3)_2SO$.

dimetrodon /dʌɪ'miːtrədɒn/ *n.* a large carnivorous quadrupedal reptile of the genus *Dimetrodon*, of the Permian period, with long spines on its back forming a sail-like crest. [modern Latin from DI-¹ + Greek *metron* 'measure' + *odous odont-* 'tooth' (taken in sense 'two long teeth')]

diminish /dɪ'mɪnɪʃ/ *v.* **1** *tr. & intr.* make or become smaller or less. **2** *tr.* lessen the reputation or influence of (a person). □ **diminishable** *adj.* [Middle English, blending of earlier *minish* from Old French *menusier* ultimately from Latin, and *diminue* from Old French *diminuer* MINUTIA, from Latin *diminuere diminut-* 'break up small']

diminished /dɪ'mɪnɪʃt/ *adj.* **1** reduced; made smaller or less. **2** *Mus.* (of an interval, usu. a seventh or fifth) less by a semitone than the corresponding minor or perfect interval.

diminished responsibility *n. Brit.* the limitation of criminal responsibility on the ground of mental weakness or abnormality.

diminuendo /dɪˌmɪnjʊ'ɛndəʊ/ *n., adv., adj., & v. Mus.* ● *n.* (*pl.* **-os** or **diminuendi** /-di/) **1** a gradual decrease in loudness. **2** a passage to be performed with such a decrease. ● *adv. & adj.* with a gradual decrease in loudness. ● *v.intr.* (**-oes**, **-oed**) decrease gradually in loudness or intensity. [Italian, part. of *diminuire* DIMINISH]

diminution /dɪmɪ'njuːʃ(ə)n/ *n.* **1** **a** the act or an instance of diminishing. **b** the amount by which something diminishes. **2** *Mus.* the repetition of a passage in notes shorter than those originally used. [Middle English via Old French from Latin *diminutio -onis* (as DIMINISH)]

diminutive /dɪ'mɪnjʊtɪv/ *adj. & n.* ● *adj.* **1** remarkably small; tiny. **2** *Gram.* (of a word or suffix) implying smallness, either actual or imputed in token of affection, scorn, etc. (e.g. *-let*, *-kins*). ● *n. Gram.* a diminutive word or suffix. □ **diminutival** /-'tʌɪv(ə)l/ *adj.* **diminutively** *adv.* **diminutiveness** *n.* [Middle English via Old French *diminutif, -ive* from Late Latin *diminutivus* (as DIMINISH)]

dimissory /'dɪmɪs(ə)ri/ *adj.* **1** ordering or permitting to depart. **2** *Eccl.* granting permission for a candidate to be ordained outside the bishop's own see (*dimissory letters*). [Middle English from Late Latin *dimissorius*, from *dimittere dimiss-* 'send away' (as DI-², *mittere* 'send')]

dimity /'dɪmɪti/ *n.* (*pl.* **-ies**) a cotton fabric woven with stripes or checks. [Middle English via Italian *dimito* or medieval Latin *dimitum* from Greek *dimitos* (as DI-¹, *mitos* 'warp-thread')]

dimmer /'dɪmə/ *n.* **1** (in full **dimmer switch**) a device for varying the brightness of an electric light. **2** *US* **a** (in *pl.*) small parking lights on a motor vehicle. **b** a headlight on low beam.

dimorphic /dʌɪ'mɔːfɪk/ *adj.* (also **dimorphous** /dʌɪ'mɔːfəs/) *Biol., Chem., & Mineral.* exhibiting, or occurring in, two distinct forms. □ **dimorphism** *n.* [Greek *dimorphos* (as DI-¹, *morphē* 'form')]

dimple /'dɪmp(ə)l/ *n. & v.* ● *n.* a small hollow or dent in the flesh, esp. in the cheeks or chin. ● *v.* **1** *intr.* produce or show dimples. **2** *tr.* produce dimples in (a cheek etc.). □ **dimply** *adj.* [Middle English probably from Old English, from a Germanic root *dump-*, perhaps a nasalized form related to DEEP]

dim sum /dɪm 'sʌm/ *n.* (also **dim sim** /'sɪm/) a Chinese dish of small steamed or fried savoury dumplings containing various fillings, served as a snack or course. [Cantonese *tím sam*, from *tím* 'dot' + *sam* 'heart']

dimwit /'dɪmwɪt/ *n. colloq.* a stupid person. □ **dim-witted** *adj.*

DIN /dɪn/ *n.* any of a series of technical standards originating in Germany and used internationally, esp. to designate electrical connections, film speeds, and paper sizes. [German, from *D*eutsche *I*ndustrie-*N*orm]

din /dɪn/ *n. & v.* ● *n.* a prolonged loud and distracting noise. ● *v.* (**dinned**, **dinning**) **1** *tr.* (foll. by *into*) instil (something to be learnt) by constant repetition. **2** *intr.* make a din. [Old English *dyne, dynn, dynian*, from Germanic]

dinar /'diːnɑː/ *n.* **1** the chief monetary unit of the states of the former Yugoslavia. **2** the chief monetary unit of certain countries of the Middle East and N. Africa. [Arabic & Persian *dīnār* via Greek *dēnarion* from Latin *denarius*: see DENIER]

din-din /'dɪndɪn/ *n.* (also **din-dins**) *colloq.* a jocular or child's word for dinner. [reduplication of first syllable of DINNER]

dine /dʌɪn/ *v.* **1** *intr.* **a** eat dinner. **b** (foll. by *on, upon*) eat for dinner. **2** *tr.* give dinner to. □ **dine out 1** dine away from home. **2** (foll. by *on*) be entertained to dinner etc. on account of (one's ability to relate an interesting event, story, etc.). [Middle English from Old French *diner, disner*, ultimately from DIS- + Late Latin *jejunare* from *jejunus* 'fasting']

diner /'dʌɪnə/ *n.* **1** a person who dines, esp. in a restaurant. **2** a railway dining car. **3** *N. Amer.* a small restaurant, esp. one resembling a dining car. **4** a small dining room.

dinero /dɪ'nɛːrəʊ/ *n. US slang* money, cash.

dinette /dʌɪ'nɛt/ *n.* **1** a small room or part of a room used for eating meals. **2** *N. Amer.* a set of table and chairs for this.

ding¹ /dɪŋ/ *v. & n.* ● *v.intr.* make a ringing sound. ● *n.* a ringing sound, as of a bell. [imitative: influenced by DIN]

ding² /dɪŋ/ *n. Austral. slang* a party or celebration, esp. a wild one. [perhaps from DING-DONG OR WINGDING]

ding-a-ling /'dɪŋəlɪŋ/ *n.* **1** the sound of a bell. **2** *N. Amer.* an eccentric or stupid person.

Ding an sich /ˌdɪŋ an 'zɪx, German 'zɪç/ *n. Philos.* a thing in itself. [German]

dingbat /'dɪŋbat/ *n. slang* **1** *N. Amer. & Austral.* a stupid or eccentric person. **2** (in *pl.*) *Austral. & NZ* **a** madness. **b** discomfort, unease (*gives me the dingbats*). [19th c., in early use applied to various vaguely specified objects: perhaps from *ding* 'to beat' + BAT¹, influenced by BAT², BATTY]

ding-dong /'dɪŋdɒŋ, dɪŋ'dɒŋ/ *n., adj., & adv.* ● *n.* **1** the sound of alternate chimes, as of two bells. **2** *Brit. colloq.* an intense argument or fight. **3** *Brit. colloq.* a riotous party. ● *adj.* (of a contest etc.) evenly matched and intensely waged; thoroughgoing. ● *adv. Brit.* with vigour and energy (*hammer away at it ding-dong*). [16th c.: imitative]

dinge /dɪn(d)ʒ/ *n. & v.* ● *n.* a dent or hollow caused by a blow. ● *v.tr.* make such a dent in. [17th c.: origin unknown]

dinghy /'dɪŋgi/ *n.* (*pl.* **-ies**) **1** a small boat carried by a ship. **2** a small pleasure boat. **3** a small inflatable rubber boat (esp. for emergency use). [originally a rowing boat used on Indian rivers, from Hindi *ḍīṅgī, ḍeṅgī*]

dingle /ˈdɪŋg(ə)l/ *n.* a deep wooded valley or dell. [Middle English: origin unknown]

dingo /ˈdɪŋgəʊ/ *n.* (*pl.* **-oes** or **-os**) **1** a wild or half-domesticated Australian dog, *Canis dingo*. **2** *Austral. slang* a coward or scoundrel. [Dharuk *din-gu* or *dayn-gu* 'domesticated dingo']

dingy /ˈdɪn(d)ʒi/ *adj.* (**dingier**, **dingiest**) dirty-looking, drab, dull-coloured. □ **dingily** *adv.* **dinginess** *n.* [perhaps ultimately from Old English *dynge* DUNG]

dining car *n.* a railway carriage equipped as a restaurant.

dining hall *n.* a hall in which meals are eaten.

dining room *n.* a room in which meals are eaten.

dining table *n.* a table on which meals are served in a dining room.

dink /dɪŋk/ *n.* = DINKY².

dinkum /ˈdɪŋkəm/ *adj. Austral.* & *NZ colloq.* genuine, right. □ **fair dinkum 1** fair play. **2** genuine(ly), honest(ly), true, truly. [19th c.: origin unknown]

dinkum oil *n. Austral.* & *NZ colloq.* the honest truth.

dinky¹ /ˈdɪŋki/ *adj.* (**dinkier**, **dinkiest**) *colloq.* **1** *Brit.* (esp. of a thing) neat and attractive; small, dainty. **2** *N. Amer.* trifling, insignificant. [Scots *dink* 'neat, trim', of unknown origin]

dinky² /ˈdɪŋki/ *n.* (*pl.* **-ies**) *colloq.* **1** a well-off young working couple with no children. **2** either partner of this. [contraction of *d*ouble *i*ncome *n*o *k*ids + -Y²]

dinner /ˈdɪnə/ *n.* **1** the main meal of the day, taken either at midday or in the evening. **2** a formal evening meal, often in honour of a person or event. [Middle English from Old French *diner, disner*: see DINE]

dinner dance *n.* a formal dinner followed by dancing.

dinner jacket *n.* a man's short usu. black formal jacket for evening wear.

dinner lady *n. Brit.* a woman who supervises children's lunch in a school.

dinner party *n.* a party to which guests are invited to eat dinner together.

dinner service *n.* a set of usu. matching crockery for serving a meal.

dinner time *n.* the time at which dinner is customarily eaten.

dinoflagellate /dʌɪnə(ʊ)ˈfladʒəleɪt/ *n.* a unicellular aquatic organism with two flagella, of a group variously classed as algae and protozoa. [modern Latin *Dinoflagellata*, from Greek *dinos* 'whirling' + Latin FLAGELLUM]

dinosaur /ˈdʌɪnəsɔː/ *n.* **1** an extinct reptile of the Mesozoic era, often of enormous size. **2** a large unwieldy system or organization, esp. one not adapting to new conditions. □ **dinosaurian** /-ˈsɔːrɪən/ *adj.* & *n.* [modern Latin *dinosaurus*, from Greek *deinos* 'terrible' + *sauros* 'lizard']

dinothere var. of DEINOTHERE.

dint /dɪnt/ *n.* & *v.* ● *n.* **1** a dent. **2** *archaic* a blow or stroke. ● *v.tr.* mark with dints. □ **by dint of** by force or means of. [Middle English from Old English *dynt*, and partly from cognate Old Norse *dyntr*: ultimate origin unknown]

diocesan /dʌɪˈɒsɪs(ə)n/ *adj.* & *n.* ● *adj.* of or concerning a diocese. ● *n.* the bishop of a diocese. [Middle English via French *diocésain* from Late Latin *diocesanus* (as DIOCESE)]

diocese /ˈdʌɪəsɪs/ *n.* a district under the pastoral care of a bishop. [Middle English via Old French *diocise*, Late Latin *diocesis*, and Latin *dioecesis* from Greek *dioikēsis* 'administration' (as DI-³, *oikeō* 'inhabit')]

diode /ˈdʌɪəʊd/ *n. Electronics* **1** a semiconductor allowing the flow of current in one direction only and having two terminals. **2** a thermionic valve having two electrodes. [DI-¹ + ELECTRODE]

dioecious /dʌɪˈiːʃəs/ *adj.* **1** *Bot.* having male and female organs on separate plants. **2** *Zool.* having the two sexes in separate individuals (cf. MONOECIOUS). [DI-¹ + Greek *-oikos* '-housed']

dioestrus /dʌɪˈiːstrəs/ *n.* (*US* **diestrus**) an interval between periods of oestrus.

diol /ˈdʌɪɒl/ *n. Chem.* any alcohol containing two hydroxyl groups in each molecule. [DI-¹ + -OL¹]

Dionysiac /dʌɪəˈnɪzɪak/ *adj.* (also **Dionysian** /-zɪən/) **1** wildly sensual; unrestrained. **2** (in Greek mythology) of or relating to Dionysus, the Greek god of wine, or his worship. [Late Latin *Dionysiacus* via Latin *Dionysus* from Greek *Dionusos*]

Diophantine equation /dʌɪə(ʊ)ˈfantɪn, -tʌɪn/ *n. Math.* an equation with integral coefficients for which integral solutions are required. [named after *Diophantus* of Alexandria, mathematician *c.* 3rd century]

dioptre /dʌɪˈɒptə/ *n.* (*US* **diopter**) *Optics* a unit of refractive power of a lens, equal to the reciprocal of its focal length in metres. [French *dioptre* via Latin *dioptra* from Greek: see DIOPTRIC]

dioptric /dʌɪˈɒptrɪk/ *adj. Optics* **1** serving as a medium for sight; assisting sight by refraction (*dioptric glass*; *dioptric lens*). **2** of refraction; refractive. [Greek *dioptrikos* from *dioptra*, a kind of theodolite]

dioptrics /dʌɪˈɒptrɪks/ *n.pl.* (treated as *sing.*) *Optics* the part of optics that deals with refraction.

diorama /dʌɪəˈrɑːmə/ *n.* **1** a scenic painting in which changes in colour and direction of illumination simulate a sunrise etc. **2** a small representation of a scene with three-dimensional figures, viewed through a window etc. **3** a small-scale model or film set. □ **dioramic** /-ˈramɪk/ *adj.* [DI-³ + Greek *horama -atos* from *horaō* 'see']

diorite /ˈdʌɪərʌɪt/ *n. Geol.* a coarse-grained plutonic igneous rock containing quartz. □ **dioritic** /-ˈrɪtɪk/ *adj.* [French, from Greek *diorizō* 'distinguish']

dioxan /dʌɪˈɒksan/ *n.* (also **dioxane** /-eɪn/) *Chem.* a colourless toxic liquid used as a solvent. Chem. formula: $C_4H_8O_2$.

dioxide /dʌɪˈɒksʌɪd/ *n. Chem.* an oxide containing two atoms of oxygen which are not linked together (*carbon dioxide*).

dioxin /dʌɪˈɒksɪn/ *n. Chem.* any of a class of cyclic compounds produced as chemical by-products, esp. the highly toxic tetrachlorodibenzoparadioxin (TCDD).

DIP /dɪp/ *n. Computing* a form of integrated circuit consisting of a small plastic or ceramic slab with two parallel rows of pins. [acronym from *d*ual *i*n-line *p*ackage]

Dip. *abbr.* Diploma.

dip /dɪp/ *v.* & *n.* ● *v.* (**dipped**, **dipping**) **1** *tr.* put or let down briefly into liquid etc.; immerse. **2** *intr.* **a** go below a surface or level (*the sun dipped below the horizon*). **b** (of a level of income, activity, etc.) decline slightly, esp. briefly (*profits dipped in May*). **3** *intr.* extend downwards; take or have a downward slope (*the road dips after the bend*). **4** *intr.* go under water and emerge quickly. **5** *intr.* (foll. by *into*) **a** read briefly from (a book etc.). **b** take a cursory interest in (a subject). **6** (foll. by *into*) **a** *intr.* put a hand, ladle, etc., into a container to take something out. **b** *tr.* put (a hand etc.) into a container to do this. **c** *intr.* spend from or make use of one's resources (*dipped into our savings*). **7** *tr.* & *intr.* lower or be lowered, esp. in salute. **8** *tr. Brit.* lower the beam of (a vehicle's headlights) to reduce dazzle. **9** *tr.* colour (a fabric) by immersing it in dye. **10** *tr.* wash (sheep) by immersion in a vermin-killing liquid. **11** *tr.* make (a candle) by immersing a wick briefly in hot tallow. **12** *tr.* baptize by immersion. **13** *tr.* (often foll. by *up, out of*) remove or scoop up (liquid, grain, etc., or something from liquid). ● *n.* **1** an act of dipping or being dipped. **2** a liquid into which something is dipped. **3** a brief bathe in the sea, river, etc. **4** a brief downward slope, followed by an upward one, in a road etc. **5** a sauce or dressing into which food is dipped before eating. **6** a depression in the skyline. **7** *Astron.* & *Surveying* the apparent depression of the horizon from the line of observation, due to the curvature of the earth. **8** *Physics* the angle made with the horizontal at any point by the earth's magnetic field. **9** *Geol.* the angle a stratum makes with the horizon. **10** *slang* a pickpocket. **11** *US slang* a foolish or bumbling person. **12** a quantity dipped up. **13** a candle made by dipping. □ **dip out** *Austral. slang* fail; miss an opportunity. [Old English *dyppan* from Germanic: related to DEEP]

Dip. A.D. *abbr. Brit.* Diploma in Art and Design.

Dip. Ed. /dɪp'ɛd/ *abbr. Brit.* Diploma in Education.

dipeptide /dʌɪ'pɛptʌɪd/ *n. Biochem.* a peptide formed by the combination of two amino acids.

Dip. H.E. *abbr. Brit.* Diploma of Higher Education.

diphosphate /dʌɪ'fɒsfeɪt/ *n. Chem.* a compound with two phosphate groups in the molecule, or a salt with two phosphate anions per cation.

diphtheria /dɪf'θɪərɪə, *disp.* dɪp-/ *n.* an acute infectious bacterial disease with inflammation of a mucous membrane esp. of the throat, resulting in the formation of a false membrane causing difficulty in breathing and swallowing. □ **diphtherial** *adj.* **diphtheric** /-'θɛrɪk/ *adj.* **diphtheritic** /-θə'rɪtɪk/ *adj.* **diphtheroid** /'dɪfθərɔɪd/ *adj.* [modern Latin via French *diphthérie*, earlier *diphthérite* from Greek *diphthera* 'skin, hide']

■ **Usage** The second pronunciation given is considered incorrect by some people.

diphthong /'dɪfθɒŋ/ *n.* **1** a speech sound in one syllable in which the articulation begins as for one vowel and moves towards another (as in *coin*, *loud*, and *side*). **2 a** a digraph representing the sound of a diphthong or single vowel (as in *feat*). **b** a compound vowel character; a ligature (as *æ*). □ **diphthongal** /-'θɒŋg(ə)l/ *adj.* [French *diphtongue* via Late Latin *diphthongus* from Greek *diphthoggos* (as DI-[1], *phthoggos* 'voice')]

diphthongize /'dɪfθɒŋʌɪz/ *v.tr.* (also **-ise**) pronounce as a diphthong. □ **diphthongization** /-'zeɪʃ(ə)n/ *n.*

diplo- /'dɪpləʊ/ *comb. form* double. [Greek *diplous* 'double']

diplococcus /dɪplə(ʊ)'kɒkəs/ *n.* (*pl.* **diplococci** /-k(s)ʌɪ, -k(s)iː/) *Biol.* any coccus that occurs mainly in pairs.

diplodocus /dɪ'plɒdəkəs/ *n.* a huge plant-eating dinosaur of the genus *Diplodocus*, of the Jurassic period, with a long neck and long slender tail. [DIPLO- + Greek *dokos* 'wooden beam']

diploid /'dɪplɔɪd/ *adj. & n. Biol.* ● *adj.* (of an organism or cell) having two complete sets of chromosomes per cell. ● *n.* a diploid cell or organism. [German (as DIPLO-, -OID)]

diploidy /'dɪplɔɪdi/ *n. Biol.* the condition of being diploid.

diploma /dɪ'pləʊmə/ *n.* **1** a certificate of qualification awarded by a college etc. **2** a document conferring an honour or privilege. **3** a state paper; an official document; a charter. □ **diplomaed** /-məd/ *adj.* (also **diploma'd**). [Latin from Greek *diplōma -atos* 'folded paper', via *diploō* 'to fold' from *diplous* 'double']

diplomacy /dɪ'pləʊməsi/ *n.* **1 a** the management of international relations. **b** expertise in this. **2** adroitness in personal relations; tact. [French *diplomatie*, from *diplomatique* DIPLOMATIC, on the pattern of *aristocratie* 'aristocracy']

diplomat /'dɪpləmat/ *n.* **1** an official representing a country abroad; a member of a diplomatic service. **2** a tactful person. [French *diplomate*, back-formation from *diplomatique*: see DIPLOMATIC]

diplomate /'dɪpləmeɪt/ *n.* esp. *US* a person who holds a diploma, esp. in medicine.

diplomatic /dɪplə'matɪk/ *adj.* **1 a** of or involved in diplomacy. **b** skilled in diplomacy. **2** tactful; adroit in personal relations. **3** (of an edition etc.) exactly reproducing the original. □ **diplomatically** *adv.* [modern Latin *diplomaticus* and French *diplomatique* from Latin DIPLOMA]

diplomatic bag *n. Brit.* a container in which official mail etc. is dispatched to or from an embassy, not usu. subject to customs inspection.

diplomatic corps *n.* the body of diplomats representing other countries at a seat of government.

diplomatic immunity *n.* the exemption of diplomatic staff abroad from arrest, taxation, etc.

diplomatic pouch *n. US* = DIPLOMATIC BAG.

diplomatic service *n. Brit.* the branch of public service concerned with the representation of a country abroad.

diplomatist /dɪ'pləʊmətɪst/ *n.* = DIPLOMAT.

diplont /'dɪplɒnt/ *n. Biol.* an animal or plant which has a diploid number of chromosomes in its cells (other than gametes). [DIPLO- + Greek *ont-*, stem of *ōn* 'being']

diplopia /dɪ'pləʊpɪə/ *n. Med.* double vision.

diplotene /'dɪplə(ʊ)tiːn/ *n. Biol.* a stage during the prophase of meiosis where paired chromosomes begin to separate. [DIPLO- + Greek *tainia* 'band']

dipolar /dʌɪ'pəʊlə/ *adj.* having two poles, as in a magnet.

dipole /'dʌɪpəʊl/ *n.* **1** *Physics* two equal and oppositely charged or magnetized poles separated by a distance. **2** *Chem.* a molecule in which a concentration of positive charges is separated from a concentration of negative charges. **3** an aerial consisting of a horizontal metal rod with a connecting wire at its centre.

dipole moment *n. Physics* the product of the separation of the charges etc. of a dipole and their magnitudes.

dipper /'dɪpə/ *n.* **1** a diving bird, *Cinclus cinclus*; also called *water ouzel*. **2** a ladle. **3** *Brit. colloq.* an Anabaptist or Baptist.

dippy /'dɪpi/ *adj.* (**dippier**, **dippiest**) *slang* crazy, silly. [20th c.: origin uncertain]

dipshit /'dɪpʃɪt/ *n.* esp. *N. Amer. slang* a contemptible or inept person. [perhaps from DIPPY + SHIT]

dipso /'dɪpsəʊ/ *n.* (*pl.* **-os**) *colloq.* a dipsomaniac. [abbreviation]

dipsomania /dɪpsə(ʊ)'meɪnɪə/ *n.* an abnormal craving for alcohol. □ **dipsomaniac** /-'meɪnɪak/ *n.* [Greek *dipso-* from *dipsa* 'thirst' + -MANIA]

dipstick /'dɪpstɪk/ *n.* **1** a graduated rod for measuring the depth of a liquid, esp. in a vehicle's engine. **2** *slang* a foolish or inept person; an idiot.

DIP switch *n.* an arrangement of switches on an electronic device for selecting an operating mode (cf. DIP).

dip switch *n. Brit.* a switch for dipping a vehicle's headlight beams.

dipteral /'dɪpt(ə)r(ə)l/ *adj. Archit.* having a double peristyle. [Latin *dipteros* from Greek (as DI-[1], *pteron* 'wing')]

dipteran /'dɪpt(ə)r(ə)n/ *n. & adj.* ● *n.* a dipterous insect. ● *adj.* = DIPTEROUS 1. [modern Latin *diptera* from Greek *diptera*, neut. pl. of *dipterous* 'two-winged' (as DI-[1], *pteron* 'wing')]

dipterous /'dɪpt(ə)rəs/ *adj.* **1** of or relating to the insect order Diptera, whose members (the 'true' flies) have two membranous wings, the hindwings being reduced to halteres or balancing organs, e.g. houseflies, mosquitoes, etc. **2** *Bot.* having two winglike appendages. [modern Latin *dipterus* from Greek *dipteros*: see DIPTERAN]

diptych /'dɪptɪk/ *n.* **1** a painting, esp. an altarpiece, on two hinged usu. wooden panels which may be closed like a book. **2** an ancient writing-tablet consisting of two hinged leaves with waxed inner sides. [Late Latin *diptycha* from Greek *diptukha* (as DI-[1], *ptukhē* 'fold')]

dire /'dʌɪə/ *adj.* **1 a** calamitous, dreadful (*in dire straits*). **b** ominous (*dire warnings*). **c** (*predic.*) *Brit. colloq.* very bad. **2** urgent (*in dire need*). □ **direly** *adv.* **direness** *n.* [Latin *dirus*]

direct /dɪ'rɛkt, dʌɪ-/ *adj., adv., & v.* ● *adj.* **1** extending or moving in a straight line or by the shortest route; not crooked or circuitous. **2 a** straightforward; going straight to the point. **b** frank; not ambiguous. **3** without intermediaries or the intervention of other factors (*direct rule*; *the direct result*; *made a direct approach*). **4**

(of descent) lineal, not collateral. **5** exact, complete, greatest possible (esp. where contrast is implied) (*the direct opposite*). **6** *Astron.* (of planetary etc. motion) proceeding from west to east; not retrograde. ● *adv.* **1** without an intermediary or intervening factor (*dealt with them direct*). **2** by a direct route (*send it direct to London*). ● *v.tr.* **1** control, guide; govern the movements of. **2** (foll. by *to* + infin., or *that* + clause) give a formal order or command to. **3** (foll. by *to*) **a** address or give indications for the delivery of (a letter etc.). **b** tell or show (a person) the way to a destination. **4** (foll. by *at*, *to*, *towards*) **a** point, aim, or cause (a blow or missile) to move in a certain direction. **b** point or address (one's attention, a remark, etc.). **5** guide as an adviser, as a principle, etc. (*I do as duty directs me*). **6 a** (also *absol.*) supervise the performing, staging, etc., of (a film, play, etc.). **b** supervise the performance of (an actor etc.). **7** (also *absol.*) guide the performance of (a group of musicians), esp. as a participant. □ **directness** *n.* [Middle English from Latin *directus*, past part. of *dirigere direct-* (as DI-[2], *regere* 'put straight')]

direct access *n.* the facility of retrieving data immediately from any part of a computer file.

direct action *n.* action such as a strike or sabotage directly affecting the public and meant to reinforce demands on a government, employer, etc.

direct address *n. Computing* an address (see ADDRESS *n.* 1c) which specifies the location of data to be used in an operation.

direct current *n.* an electric current flowing in one direction only (abbr.: **DC, dc**).

direct debit *n. Brit.* an arrangement for the prompt and regular debiting of a bank account at the request of the payee.

direct dialling *n.* the facility of dialling a telephone number without making use of the operator. □ **direct dial** *attrib.adj.*

direct-grant school *n. hist.* (in the UK) a school receiving funds from the Government and not from a local authority.

direction /dɪˈrɛkʃ(ə)n, dʌɪ-/ *n.* **1** the act or process of directing; supervision. **2** (usu. in *pl.*) an order or instruction, esp. each of a set guiding use of equipment etc. **3 a** the course or line along which a person or thing moves or looks, or which must be taken to reach a destination. **b** (in *pl.*) guidance on how to reach a destination. **c** the point to or from which a person or thing moves or looks. **4** the tendency or scope of a theme, subject, or inquiry. □ **directionless** *adj.* [Middle English from French *direction* or Latin *directio* (as DIRECT)]

directional /dɪˈrɛkʃ(ə)n(ə)l, dʌɪ-/ *adj.* **1** of or indicating direction. **2** *Electronics* **a** concerned with the transmission of radio or sound waves in a particular direction. **b** (of equipment) designed to receive radio or sound waves most effectively from a particular direction or directions and not others. □ **directionality** /-ˈnalɪti/ *n.* **directionally** *adv.*

direction-finder *n.* a device for determining the source of radio waves, esp. as an aid in navigation.

directive /dɪˈrɛktɪv, dʌɪ-/ *n.* & *adj.* ● *n.* a general instruction from one in authority. ● *adj.* serving to direct. [Middle English from medieval Latin *directivus* (as DIRECT)]

directly /dɪˈrɛktli, dʌɪ-/ *adv.* & *conj.* ● *adv.* **1 a** at once; without delay. **b** presently, shortly. **2** exactly, immediately (*directly opposite*; *directly after lunch*). **3** in a direct manner. ● *conj. Brit. colloq.* as soon as (*will tell you directly they come*).

direct mail *n.* advertising sent unsolicited through the post to prospective customers. □ **direct mailing** *n.*

direct method *n.* a system of teaching a foreign language using only that language and without the study of formal grammar.

direct object *n.* the primary object of the action of a transitive verb.

Directoire /dɪˈrɛktwɑː/ *adj. Needlework* & *Art* in imitation of styles prevalent during the French Directory. [French (as DIRECTORY)]

Directoire drawers *n.pl.* (also **Directoire knickers**) *Brit.* knickers which are straight, full, and knee-length.

director /dɪˈrɛktə, dʌɪ-/ *n.* **1** a person who directs or controls something. **2** a member of the managing board of a commercial company. **3** a person who directs a film etc., esp. professionally. **4** a spiritual adviser. **5** = MUSICAL DIRECTOR. □ **directorial** /-ˈtɔːrɪəl/ *adj.* **directorship** *n.* (esp. in sense 2). [Anglo-French *directour* from Late Latin *director* 'governor' (as DIRECT)]

directorate /dɪˈrɛkt(ə)rət, dʌɪ-/ *n.* **1** a board of directors. **2** the office of director.

director-general *n.* (*pl.* **director-generals**) esp. *Brit.* the chief executive of a large (esp. public) organization.

director of public prosecutions *n. Brit.* = PUBLIC PROSECUTOR.

directory /dɪˈrɛkt(ə)ri, dʌɪ-/ *n.* (*pl.* **-ies**) **1** a book listing alphabetically or thematically a particular group of individuals (e.g. telephone subscribers) or organizations with various details. **2** a computer file listing other files or programs etc. **3** (**Directory**) *hist.* the revolutionary executive of five persons in power in France 1795–9. **4** a book of rules, esp. for the order of private or public worship. [Late Latin *directorium* (as DIRECT)]

directory enquiries *n.pl.* (*N. Amer.* **directory assistance**) a telephone service providing a subscriber's number on request.

direct proportion *n.* a relation between quantities whose ratio is constant.

directress /dɪˈrɛktrɪs, dʌɪ-/ *n.* (also **directrice**) a woman director. [DIRECTOR, French *directrice* (as DIRECTRIX)]

directrix /dɪˈrɛktrɪks, dʌɪ-/ *n.* (*pl.* **directrices** /-trɪsiːz/) *Geom.* a fixed line used in describing a curve or surface. [medieval Latin from Late Latin *director*: see DIRECTOR, -TRIX]

direct speech *n.* words actually spoken, not reported in the third person (opp. REPORTED SPEECH).

direct tax *n.* a tax levied on the person who ultimately bears the burden of it, esp. on income.

direful /ˈdʌɪəfʊl, -f(ə)l/ *adj. literary* terrible, dreadful. □ **direfully** *adv.* [DIRE + -FUL]

dirge /dəːdʒ/ *n.* **1** a lament for the dead, esp. forming part of a funeral service. **2** any mournful song or lament. □ **dirgeful** *adj.* [Middle English from Latin *dirige* (imperative) 'direct', the first word of an antiphon (Psalm 5:8) used in the Latin Office for the Dead]

dirham /ˈdɪərhəm/ *n.* the chief monetary unit of Morocco and the United Arab Emirates. [Arabic, from Latin DRACHMA]

dirigible /ˈdɪrɪdʒɪb(ə)l/ *adj.* & *n.* ● *adj.* capable of being guided. ● *n.* a dirigible balloon or airship. [Latin *dirigere* 'arrange, direct': see DIRECT]

dirigisme /ˈdɪrɪʒɪz(ə)m/ *n.* state control of economic and social matters. □ **dirigiste** *adj.* [French from *diriger* DIRECT]

diriment /ˈdɪrɪm(ə)nt/ *adj. Law* nullifying. [Latin *dirimere*, from *dir-* = DIS- + *emere* 'take']

diriment impediment *n.* a factor (e.g. the existence of a prior marriage) rendering a marriage null and void from the beginning.

dirk /dəːk/ *n.* a short dagger, esp. as formerly worn by Scottish Highlanders. [16th-c. *durk*, of unknown origin]

dirndl /ˈdəːnd(ə)l/ *n.* **1** a woman's dress styled in imitation of Alpine peasant costume, with close-fitting bodice, tight waistband, and full skirt. **2** (in full **dirndl skirt**) a full skirt of this kind. [German dialect, diminutive of *Dirne* 'girl']

dirt /dəːt/ *n.* **1** unclean matter that soils. **2 a** earth, soil. **b** earth, cinders, etc., used to make a surface for a road etc. (usu. *attrib.*: *dirt track*). **3** foul or malicious words or talk. **4** excrement. **5** a dirty condition. **6** a person or thing considered worthless. □ **do a person dirt** *slang* harm or injure a person's reputation maliciously. **eat dirt 1** suffer insults etc. without retaliating. **2** *US* make a humiliating confession. **treat like dirt** treat (a person) contemptuously; abuse. [Middle English from Old Norse *drit* 'excrement']

dirt bike *n.* a motorcycle designed for use on unmade roads and tracks, esp. in scrambling.

dirt cheap *adj. & adv. colloq.* extremely cheap.

dirt track *n.* a course made of rolled cinders, soil, etc., for motorcycle racing or flat racing (often hyphenated when *attrib.*: *dirt-track race*). ◻ **dirt-tracker** *n.*

dirty /ˈdəːti/ *adj., adv., & v.* ● *adj.* (**dirtier, dirtiest**) **1** soiled, unclean. **2** causing one to become dirty (*a dirty job*). **3** sordid, lewd; morally illicit or questionable (*dirty joke*). **4** unpleasant, nasty. **5** dishonest, dishonourable, unfair (*dirty play*). **6** (of weather) rough, squally. **7** (of a colour) not pure or clear, dingy. **8** *colloq.* (of a nuclear weapon) producing considerable radioactive fallout. ● *adv. slang* **1** *Brit.* (with adjectives expressing magnitude) very (*a dirty great diamond*). **2** dirtily; unfairly (*play dirty*). ● *v.tr. & intr.* (**-ies, -ied**) make or become dirty. ◻ **the dirty end of the stick** esp. *Brit. colloq.* the difficult or unpleasant part of an undertaking, situation, etc. **do the dirty on** *Brit. colloq.* play a mean trick on. ◻ **dirtily** *adv.* **dirtiness** *n.*

dirty dog *n. colloq.* a scoundrel; a despicable person.

dirty linen *n. colloq.* intimate secrets, esp. of a scandalous nature.

dirty look *n. colloq.* a look of disapproval, anger, or disgust.

dirty money *n.* **1** money obtained unlawfully or immorally. **2** *Brit.* extra money paid to those who handle dirty materials.

dirty old man *n. colloq.* a lecherous man.

dirty trick *n.* **1** a dishonourable and deceitful act. **2** (in *pl.*) underhand political activity, esp. to discredit an opponent.

dirty weekend *n. Brit. colloq.* a weekend spent clandestinely with a lover.

dirty word *n.* **1** an offensive or indecent word. **2** a word for something which is disapproved of (*profit is a dirty word*).

dirty work *n.* dishonourable or illegal activity, esp. done clandestinely.

dis /dɪs/ *v. & n.* (also **diss**) *US slang* ● *v.tr.* (**dissed, dissing**) put a person down; bad-mouth. ● *n.* disrespect. [abbreviation of DISRESPECT]

dis- /dɪs/ *prefix* forming nouns, adjectives, and verbs: **1** expressing negation (*dishonest*). **2** indicating reversal or absence of an action or state (*disengage*; *disbelieve*). **3** indicating removal of a thing or quality (*dismember*; *disable*). **4** indicating separation (*distinguish*; *disperse*). **5** indicating completeness or intensification of the action (*disembowel*; *disgruntled*). **6** indicating expulsion from (*disbar*). [Latin *dis-*, sometimes via Old French *des-*]

disability /dɪsəˈbɪlɪti/ *n.* (*pl.* **-ies**) **1** a physical incapacity, either congenital or caused by injury, disease, etc., esp. when limiting a person's ability to work. **2** a lack of some asset, quality, or attribute, that prevents a person from doing something. **3** a legal disqualification.

disable /dɪsˈeɪb(ə)l/ *v.tr.* **1** render unable to function. **2** (often as **disabled** *adj.*) deprive of physical or mental ability, esp. through injury or disease. ◻ **disablement** *n.*

disablist /dɪsˈeɪblɪst/ *adj.* discriminating or prejudiced against disabled people.

disabuse /dɪsəˈbjuːz/ *v.tr.* **1** (foll. by *of*) free from a mistaken idea. **2** disillusion, undeceive.

disaccharide /dʌɪˈsakərʌɪd/ *n. Chem.* a sugar whose molecule contains two linked monosaccharides.

disaccord /dɪsəˈkɔːd/ *n. & v.* ● *n.* disagreement, disharmony. ● *v.intr.* (usu. foll. by *with*) disagree; be at odds. [Middle English from French *désaccorder* (as ACCORD)]

disadvantage /dɪsədˈvɑːntɪdʒ/ *n. & v.* ● *n.* **1** an unfavourable circumstance or condition. **2** damage to one's interest or reputation. ● *v.tr.* cause disadvantage to. ◻ **at a disadvantage** in an unfavourable position or aspect. [Middle English from (Old) French *désavantage*: see ADVANTAGE]

disadvantaged /dɪsədˈvɑːntɪdʒd/ *adj.* placed in unfavourable circumstances (esp. of a person lacking the normal social opportunities).

disadvantageous /ˌdɪsadv(ə)nˈteɪdʒəs/ *adj.* **1** involving disadvantage. **2** derogatory; discreditable. ◻ **disadvantageously** *adv.*

disaffected /dɪsəˈfɛktɪd/ *adj.* **1** disloyal, esp. to one's superiors. **2** estranged; no longer friendly; discontented. ◻ **disaffectedly** *adv.* [past part. of *disaffect*, originally = dislike, disorder (as DIS-, AFFECT²)]

disaffection /dɪsəˈfɛkʃ(ə)n/ *n.* **1** disloyalty. **2** political discontent.

disaffiliate /dɪsəˈfɪlɪˌeɪt/ *v.* **1** *tr.* end the affiliation of. **2** *intr.* end one's affiliation. **3** *tr.* & *intr.* detach. ◻ **disaffiliation** /-ˈeɪʃ(ə)n/ *n.*

disaffirm /dɪsəˈfəːm/ *v.tr. Law* **1** reverse (a previous decision). **2** repudiate (a settlement). ◻ **disaffirmation** /dɪsˌafəˈmeɪʃ(ə)n/ *n.*

disafforest /dɪsəˈfɒrɪst/ *v.tr. Brit.* **1** clear of forests or trees. **2** reduce from the legal status of forest to that of ordinary land. ◻ **disafforestation** /-ˈsteɪʃ(ə)n/ *n.* [Middle English from Anglo-Latin *disafforestare* (as DIS-, AFFOREST)]

disaggregate /dɪsˈagrɪgeɪt/ *v.tr.* separate into component parts; cease to treat as aggregated. ◻ **disaggregation** /-ˈgeɪʃ(ə)n/ *n.*

disagree /dɪsəˈgriː/ *v.intr.* (**disagrees, disagreed, disagreeing**) (often foll. by *with*) **1** hold a different opinion. **2** quarrel. **3** (of factors or circumstances) not correspond. **4** have an adverse effect upon (a person's health, digestion, etc.). ◻ **disagreement** *n.* [Middle English from Old French *desagreer* (as DIS-, AGREE)]

disagreeable /dɪsəˈgriːəb(ə)l/ *adj.* **1** unpleasant, not to one's liking. **2** quarrelsome; rude or bad-tempered. ◻ **disagreeableness** *n.* **disagreeably** *adv.* [Middle English from Old French *desagreable* (as DIS-, AGREEABLE)]

disallow /dɪsəˈlaʊ/ *v.tr.* refuse to allow or accept as valid; prohibit. ◻ **disallowance** *n.* [Middle English from Old French *desalouer* (as DIS-, ALLOW)]

disambiguate /dɪsamˈbɪgjʊeɪt/ *v.tr.* remove ambiguity from. ◻ **disambiguation** /-ˈeɪʃ(ə)n/ *n.*

disamenity /dɪsəˈmiːnɪti, -ˈmɛnɪti/ *n.* (*pl.* **-ies**) an unpleasant feature (of a place etc.); a disadvantage.

disappear /dɪsəˈpɪə/ *v.intr.* **1** cease to be visible; pass from sight. **2** cease to exist or be in circulation or use (*trams had all but disappeared*). **3** (of a person or thing) go missing. ◻ **disappearance** *n.*

disappearing act *n.* an instance of vanishing as if by magic, esp. to avoid unpleasantness.

disappoint /dɪsəˈpɔɪnt/ *v.tr.* **1** (also *absol.*) fail to fulfil a desire or expectation of (a person). **2** frustrate (hopes etc.); cause the failure of (a plan etc.). ◻ **be disappointed** (foll. by *with, at, in,* or *to* + infin., or *that* + clause) fail to have one's expectation etc. fulfilled in some regard (*was disappointed with you*; *disappointed at the result*; *am disappointed to be last*). ◻ **disappointedly** *adv.* **disappointing** *adj.* **disappointingly** *adv.* [Middle English from French *désappointer* (as DIS-, APPOINT)]

disappointment /dɪsəˈpɔɪntm(ə)nt/ *n.* **1** an event, thing, or person that disappoints. **2** a feeling of distress, vexation, etc., resulting from this (*I cannot hide my disappointment*).

disapprobation /dɪsˌaprəˈbeɪʃ(ə)n/ *n.* strong (esp. moral) disapproval.

disapprove /dɪsəˈpruːv/ *v.* **1** *intr.* (usu. foll. by *of*) have or express an unfavourable opinion. **2** *tr.* be displeased with. ◻ **disapproval** *n.* **disapprover** *n.* **disapproving** *adj.* **disapprovingly** *adv.*

disarm /dɪsˈɑːm/ *v.* **1** *tr.* **a** take weapons away from (a person, state, etc.) (often foll. by *of*: *were disarmed of their rifles*). **b** *Fencing* etc. deprive of a weapon. **2** *tr.* deprive (a ship etc.) of its means of defence. **3** *intr.* (of a state etc.) disband or reduce its armed forces. **4** *tr.* remove the fuse from (a bomb etc.). **5** *tr.* deprive of the power to injure. **6** *tr.* pacify or allay the hostility or suspicions of; mollify; placate. ▫ **disarmer** *n.* **disarming** *adj.* (esp. in sense 6). **disarmingly** *adv.* [Middle English from Old French *desarmer* (as DIS-, ARM²)]

disarmament /dɪsˈɑːməm(ə)nt/ *n.* the reduction by a state of its military forces and weapons.

disarrange /dɪsəˈreɪn(d)ʒ/ *v.tr.* bring into disorder. ▫ **disarrangement** *n.*

disarray /dɪsəˈreɪ/ *n.* & *v.* ● *n.* (often prec. by *in*, *into*) disorder, confusion (esp. among people). ● *v.tr.* throw into disorder.

disarticulate /dɪsɑːˈtɪkjʊleɪt/ *v.tr.* & *intr.* separate at the joints. ▫ **disarticulation** /-ˈleɪʃ(ə)n/ *n.*

disassemble /dɪsəˈsɛmb(ə)l/ *v.tr.* take (a machine etc.) to pieces. ▫ **disassembly** *n.*

disassembler /dɪsəˈsɛmblə/ *n.* *Computing* a program for converting machine code into assembly language.

disassociate /dɪsəˈsəʊʃɪeɪt, -sɪ-/ *v.tr.* & *intr.* = DISSOCIATE. ▫ **disassociation** /-ˈeɪʃ(ə)n/ *n.*

disaster /dɪˈzɑːstə/ *n.* **1** a great or sudden misfortune. **2** **a** a complete failure. **b** a person or enterprise ending in failure. ▫ **disastrous** *adj.* **disastrously** *adv.* [originally 'unfavourable aspect of a star': from French *désastre* or Italian *disastro* (as DIS-, *astro* from Latin *astrum* 'star')]

disavow /dɪsəˈvaʊ/ *v.tr.* disclaim knowledge of, responsibility for, or belief in. ▫ **disavowal** *n.* [Middle English from Old French *desavouer* (as DIS-, AVOW)]

disband /dɪsˈband/ *v.* **1** *intr.* (of an organized group etc.) cease to work or act together; disperse. **2** *tr.* cause (such a group) to disband. ▫ **disbandment** *n.* [obsolete French *desbander* (as DIS-, BAND²)]

disbar /dɪsˈbɑː/ *v.tr.* (**disbarred**, **disbarring**) deprive (a barrister) of the right to practise; expel from the Bar. ▫ **disbarment** *n.*

disbelieve /dɪsbɪˈliːv/ *v.* **1** *tr.* be unable or unwilling to believe (a person or statement). **2** *intr.* have no faith. ▫ **disbelief** *n.* **disbeliever** *n.* **disbelievingly** *adv.*

disbenefit /dɪsˈbɛnɪfɪt/ *n.* *Brit.* a drawback; an undesirable feature or consequence.

disbound /dɪsˈbaʊnd/ *adj.* (of a pamphlet etc.) removed from a bound volume.

disbud /dɪsˈbʌd/ *v.tr.* (**disbudded**, **disbudding**) remove (esp. superfluous) buds from.

disburden /dɪsˈbəːd(ə)n/ *v.tr.* **1** relieve (a person, one's mind, etc.) of a burden (often foll. by *of*: *was disburdened of all worries*). **2** get rid of, discharge (a duty, anxiety, etc.).

disburse /dɪsˈbəːs/ *v.* **1** *tr.* expend (money). **2** *tr.* defray (a cost). **3** *intr.* pay money. ▫ **disbursal** *n.* **disbursement** *n.* **disburser** *n.* [Old French *desbourser* (as DIS-, BOURSE)]

disc /dɪsk/ *n.* (also **disk** esp. *US* and in sense 4a) **1** **a** a flat thin circular object. **b** a round flat or apparently flat surface (*the sun's disc*). **c** a mark of this shape. **2** **a** a layer of cartilage between vertebrae. **b** the close-packed cluster of tubular florets in the centre of a composite flower. **3** a gramophone record. **4** **a** (usu. **disk**; in full **magnetic disk**) a computer storage device consisting of a rotatable disc or discs with a magnetic coating. **b** (in full **optical disc**) a smooth non-magnetic disc with large storage capacity for data recorded and read by laser, esp. a CD-ROM. **5** *Brit.* a device with a pointer or rotating disc indicating time of arrival or latest permitted time of departure, for display in a parked motor vehicle. ▫ **diskless** *adj.* *Computing.* [French *disque* or Latin *discus*: see DISCUS]

discalced /dɪsˈkalst/ *adj.* (of a friar or a nun) barefoot or wearing only sandals. [variant of *discalceated* (influenced by French *déchaux*) from Latin *discalceatus* (as DIS-, *calceatus* from *calceus* 'shoe')]

discard *v.* & *n.* ● *v.tr.* /dɪˈskɑːd/ **1** reject or get rid of as unwanted or superfluous. **2** (also *absol.*) *Cards* remove or put aside (a card) from one's hand. ● *n.* /ˈdɪskɑːd/ a discarded item, esp. a card in a card game. ▫ **discardable** /-ˈkɑːdəb(ə)l/ *adj.* [DIS- + CARD¹]

discarnate /dɪsˈkɑːnət/ *adj.* having no physical body; separated from the flesh. [DIS-, Latin *caro carnis* 'flesh']

disc brake *n.* a brake employing the friction of pads against a disc.

discern /dɪˈsəːn/ *v.tr.* **1** perceive clearly with the mind or the senses. **2** make out by thought or by gazing, listening, etc. ▫ **discerner** *n.* **discernible** *adj.* **discernibly** *adv.* [Middle English via Old French *discerner* from Latin (as DIS-, *cernere cret-* 'separate')]

discerning /dɪˈsəːnɪŋ/ *adj.* having or showing good judgement or insight. ▫ **discerningly** *adv.*

discernment /dɪˈsəːnm(ə)nt/ *n.* good judgement or insight.

discerptible /dɪˈsəːptɪb(ə)l/ *adj.* *literary* able to be plucked apart; divisible. ▫ **discerptibility** /-ˈbɪlɪti/ *n.* [Latin *discerpere discerpt-* (as DIS-, *carpere* 'pluck')]

discerption /dɪˈsəːpʃ(ə)n/ *n.* *archaic* **1** **a** pulling apart; severance. **b** an instance of this. **2** a severed piece. [Late Latin *discerptio* (as DISCERPTIBLE)]

discharge *v.* & *n.* ● *v.* /dɪsˈtʃɑːdʒ/ **1** *tr.* **a** let go, release, esp. from a duty, commitment, or period of confinement. **b** relieve (a bankrupt) of residual liability. **2** *tr.* dismiss from office, employment, army commission, etc. **3** *tr.* **a** fire (a gun etc.). **b** (of a gun etc.) fire (a bullet etc.). **4** **a** *tr.* (also *absol.*) pour out or cause to pour out (pus, liquid, etc.) (*the wound was discharging*). **b** *tr.* utter (abuse etc.). **c** *intr.* (foll. by *into*) (of a river etc.) flow into (esp. the sea). **5** *tr.* **a** carry out, perform (a duty or obligation). **b** relieve oneself of (a financial commitment) (*discharged his debt*). **6** *tr.* *Law* cancel (an order of court). **7** *tr.* *Physics* release an electrical charge from. **8** *tr.* **a** relieve (a ship etc.) of its cargo. **b** unload (a cargo) from a ship. ● *n.* /ˈdɪstʃɑːdʒ, dɪsˈtʃɑːdʒ/ **1** the act or an instance of discharging; the process of being discharged. **2** a dismissal, esp. from the armed services. **3** **a** a release, exemption, acquittal, etc. **b** a written certificate of release etc. **4** an act of firing a gun etc. **5** **a** an emission (of pus, liquid, etc.). **b** the liquid or matter so discharged. **6** (usu. foll. by *of*) **a** the payment (of a debt). **b** the performance (of a duty etc.). **7** *Physics* **a** the release of a quantity of electric charge from an object. **b** a flow of electricity through the air or other gas, esp. when accompanied by the emission of light. **c** the conversion of chemical energy in a cell into electrical energy. **8** the unloading (of a ship or a cargo). ▫ **dischargeable** *adj.* **discharger** *n.* (in sense 7 of *v.*). [Middle English from Old French *descharger* (as DIS-, CHARGE)]

disc harrow *n.* a harrow with cutting edges consisting of a row of concave discs set at an oblique angle.

disciple /dɪˈsʌɪp(ə)l/ *n.* **1** a follower or pupil of a leader, teacher, philosophy, etc. (*a disciple of Zen Buddhism*). **2** **a** a personal follower of Christ, esp. one of the twelve Apostles. **b** any early believer in Christ. ▫ **discipleship** *n.* **discipular** /dɪˈsɪpjʊlə/ *adj.* [Old English *discipul* from Latin *discipulus*, from *discere* 'learn']

disciplinarian /ˌdɪsɪplɪˈnɛːrɪən/ *n.* a person who upholds or practises firm discipline (*a strict disciplinarian*).

disciplinary /ˈdɪsɪplɪn(ə)ri, dɪsɪˈplɪn-/ *adj.* of, promoting, or enforcing discipline. [medieval Latin *disciplinarius* (as DISCIPLINE)]

discipline /ˈdɪsɪplɪn/ *n.* & *v.* ● *n.* **1** **a** control or order exercised over people or animals, esp. children, prisoners, military personnel, church members, etc. **b** the system of rules used to maintain this control. **c** the behaviour of groups subjected to such rules (*poor discipline in the ranks*). **2** **a** mental, moral, or physical training. **b** adversity as used to bring about such training (*left the course because he couldn't take the discipline*). **3** a branch of instruction or learning (*philosophy is a hard discipline*). **4** punishment. **5** *Eccl.* mortification by physical self-punishment, esp. scourging. ● *v.tr.* **1** punish, chastise. **2** bring under control by training in obedience; drill. ▫ **disciplinable** *adj.* **disciplinal** /dɪsɪ'plʌɪn(ə)l, 'dɪsɪplɪn(ə)l/ *adj.* [Middle English from Old French *discipliner* or Late Latin & medieval Latin *disciplinare* (*v.*), *disciplina* (*n.*), from *discipulus* DISCIPLE]

disc jockey *n.* the presenter of a selection of usu. recorded popular music, esp. in a broadcast.

disclaim /dɪs'kleɪm/ *v.tr.* **1** deny or disown (*disclaim all responsibility*). **2** (often *absol.*) *Law* renounce a legal claim to (property etc.). [Middle English from Anglo-French *desclaim-*, stressed stem of *desclamer* (as DIS-, CLAIM)]

disclaimer /dɪs'kleɪmə/ *n.* **1** a renunciation or disavowal, esp. of responsibility. **2** *Law* an act of repudiating another's claim or renouncing one's own. [Middle English from Anglo-French (= DISCLAIM, used as a noun)]

disclose /dɪs'kləʊz/ *v.tr.* **1** make known; reveal (*disclosed the truth*). **2** remove the cover from; expose to view. ▫ **discloser** *n.* [Middle English via Old French *desclos-*, stem of *desclore*, from Gallo-Roman (as DIS-, CLOSE[2])]

disclosure /dɪs'kləʊʒə/ *n.* **1** the act or an instance of disclosing; the process of being disclosed. **2** something disclosed; a revelation. [DISCLOSE + -URE, on the pattern of *closure*]

disco /'dɪskəʊ/ *n.* & *v. colloq.* ● *n.* (*pl.* **-os**) **1** = DISCOTHEQUE. **2** = DISCO MUSIC. ● *v.intr.* (**-oes**, **-oed**) **1** attend a discotheque. **2** dance to disco music (*discoed the night away*). [abbreviation]

discobolus /dɪ'skɒbələs/ *n.* (*pl.* **discoboli** /-lʌɪ/) **1** a discus-thrower in ancient Greece. **2** a statue of a discobolus. [Latin from Greek *diskobolos*, from *diskos* DISCUS + *-bolos* '-throwing' from *ballō* 'to throw']

discography /dɪ'skɒgrəfi/ *n.* (*pl.* **-ies**) **1** a descriptive catalogue of gramophone records, esp. of a particular performer or composer. **2** the study of gramophone records. ▫ **discographer** *n.* [DISC + -GRAPHY, on the pattern of *biography*]

discoid /'dɪskɔɪd/ *adj.* disc-shaped. [Greek *diskoeidēs* (as DISCUS, -OID)]

discolour /dɪs'kʌlə/ *v.tr.* & *intr.* (*US* **discolor**) spoil or cause to spoil the colour of; stain; tarnish. ▫ **discoloration** /-'reɪʃ(ə)n/ *n.* (also **discolouration**). [Middle English from Old French *descolorer* or medieval Latin *discolorare* (as DIS-, COLOUR)]

discombobulate /dɪskəm'bɒbjʊleɪt/ *v.tr. N. Amer. slang* disturb; disconcert. [probably based on *discompose* or *discomfit*]

discomfit /dɪs'kʌmfɪt/ *v.tr.* (**discomfited**, **discomfiting**) **1 a** disconcert or baffle. **b** thwart. **2** *archaic* defeat in battle. ▫ **discomfiture** *n.* [Middle English via Old French *disconfit*, past part. of *desconfire*, from Romanic (as DIS-, Latin *conficere* 'put together': see CONFECTION)]

■ **Usage** Care should be taken not to confuse *discomfit* with *discomfort*. Examples of each are: *We were discomfited by his request to walk through the pouring rain rather than take a taxi*, and *He was by nature a recluse, discomforted by every encounter*.

discomfort /dɪs'kʌmfət/ *n.* & *v.* ● *n.* **1 a** a lack of ease; slight pain (*tight collar caused discomfort*). **b** mental uneasiness (*his presence caused her discomfort*). **2** a lack of comfort. ● *v.tr.* make uneasy; distress. [Middle English from Old French *desconfort(er)* (as DIS-, COMFORT)]

■ **Usage** See Usage Note at DISCOMFIT.

discommode /dɪskə'məʊd/ *v.tr.* inconvenience (a person etc.). ▫ **discommodious** *adj.* [obsolete French *discommoder*, variant of *incommoder* (as DIS-, INCOMMODE)]

discompose /dɪskəm'pəʊz/ *v.tr.* disturb the composure of; agitate; disturb. ▫ **discomposure** /-'pəʊʒə/ *n.*

disco music *n.* popular dance music characterized by a heavy bass rhythm.

disconcert /dɪskən'səːt/ *v.tr.* **1** disturb the composure of; agitate; fluster (*disconcerted by his expression*). **2** spoil or upset (plans etc.). ▫ **disconcertedly** *adv.* **disconcerting** *adj.* **disconcertingly** *adv.* **disconcertion** /-'səːʃ(ə)n/ *n.* **disconcertment** *n.* [obsolete French *desconcerter* (as DIS-, CONCERT)]

disconfirm /dɪskən'fəːm/ *v.tr. formal* disprove or tend to disprove (a hypothesis etc.). ▫ **disconfirmation** /ˌdɪskɒnfə'meɪʃ(ə)n/ *n.*

disconformity /dɪskən'fɔːmɪti/ *n.* (*pl.* **-ies**) **1 a** lack of conformity. **b** an instance of this. **2** *Geol.* a difference of plane between two parallel, approximately horizontal sets of strata.

disconnect /dɪskə'nɛkt/ *v.tr.* **1** (often foll. by *from*) break the connection of (things, ideas, etc.). **2** put (an electrical device) out of action by disconnecting the parts, esp. by pulling out the plug.

disconnected /dɪskə'nɛktɪd/ *adj.* (of speech, writing, argument, etc.) incoherent and illogical. ▫ **disconnectedly** *adv.* **disconnectedness** *n.*

disconnection /dɪskə'nɛkʃ(ə)n/ *n.* (also **disconnexion**) the act or an instance of disconnecting; the state of being disconnected.

disconsolate /dɪs'kɒns(ə)lət/ *adj.* **1** forlorn or inconsolable. **2** unhappy or disappointed. ▫ **disconsolately** *adv.* **disconsolateness** *n.* **disconsolation** /-'leɪʃ(ə)n/ *n.* [Middle English from medieval Latin *disconsolatus* (as DIS-, *consolatus*, past part. of Latin *consolari* 'console')]

discontent /dɪskən'tɛnt/ *n.*, *adj.*, & *v.* ● *n.* lack of contentment; restlessness, dissatisfaction. ● *adj.* dissatisfied (*was discontent with his lot*). ● *v.tr.* (esp. as **discontented** *adj.*) make dissatisfied. ▫ **discontentedly** *adv.* **discontentedness** *n.* **discontentment** *n.*

discontinue /dɪskən'tɪnjuː/ *v.* (**discontinues**, **discontinued**, **discontinuing**) **1** *intr.* & *tr.* cease or cause to cease to exist or be made (*a discontinued line*). **2** *tr.* give up, cease from (*discontinued his visits*). **3** *tr.* cease taking or paying (a newspaper, a subscription, etc.). ▫ **discontinuance** *n.* **discontinuation** /-'eɪʃ(ə)n/ *n.* [Middle English via Old French *discontinuer* from medieval Latin *discontinuare* (as DIS-, CONTINUE)]

discontinuous /dɪskən'tɪnjʊəs/ *adj.* lacking continuity in space or time; intermittent. ▫ **discontinuity** /ˌdɪskɒntɪ'njuːɪti/ *n.* **discontinuously** *adv.* [medieval Latin *discontinuus* (as DIS-, CONTINUOUS)]

discord *n.* & *v.* ● *n.* /'dɪskɔːd/ **1** disagreement; strife. **2** harsh clashing noise; clangour. **3** *Mus.* **a** a lack of harmony between notes sounding together. **b** an unpleasing or unfinished chord needing to be completed by another. **c** any interval except unison, an octave, a perfect fifth and fourth, a major and minor third and sixth, and their octaves. **d** a single note dissonant with another. ● *v.intr.* /dɪ'skɔːd/ **1** (usu. foll. by *with*) **a** disagree or quarrel. **b** be different or inconsistent. **2** jar, clash, be dissonant. [Middle English via Old French *descord*, (*n.*), *descorder* (*v.*) from Latin *discordare*, from *discors* 'discordant' (as DIS-, *cor cord-* 'heart')]

discordant /dɪ'skɔːd(ə)nt/ *adj.* (usu. foll. by *to*, *from*, *with*) **1** disagreeing; at variance. **2** (of sounds) not in harmony; dissonant. ▫ **discordance** *n.* **discordancy** *n.* **discordantly** *adv.* [Middle English from Old French, part. of *discorder*: see DISCORD]

discotheque /'dɪskətɛk/ *n.* **1** a club etc. for dancing to recorded popular music. **2** *Brit.* **a** the professional lighting and sound equipment used at a discotheque. **b** a business that provides this. **3** *Brit.* a party with dancing to popular music, esp. using such equipment. [French, = record-library]

discount *n.* & *v.* ● *n.* /'dɪskaʊnt/ **1** a deduction from a bill or amount due, given esp. in consideration of prompt or advance payment or to a special class of buyers. **2** a deduction from the amount of a bill of exchange etc. by a person who gives value for it before it is due. **3** the act or an instance of discounting. ● *v.tr.* /dɪs'kaʊnt/ **1** disregard as being unreliable or unimportant (*discounted his story*). **2** reduce the effect of (an event etc.) by previous action. **3 a** deduct (esp. an amount from a bill etc.). **b** reduce in price. **4** give or get the present worth of (a bill not yet due). □ **at a discount 1** below the nominal or usual price (cf. PREMIUM). **2** not in demand; depreciated. □ **discountable** /-'kaʊntəb(ə)l/ *adj.* **discounter** /-'kaʊntə/ *n.* [obsolete French *descompte, -conte, descompter* or Italian (*di*)*scontare* (as DIS-, COUNT[1])]

discountenance /dɪs'kaʊntɪnəns/ *v.tr.* **1** (esp. in *passive*) disconcert (*was discountenanced by his abruptness*). **2** refuse to countenance; show disapproval of.

discount house *n.* **1** *Brit.* a firm that discounts bills. **2** *US* = DISCOUNT STORE.

discount rate *n. US* the minimum lending rate.

discount store *n.* a shop etc. that sells goods at less than the normal retail price.

discourage /dɪs'kʌrɪdʒ/ *v.tr.* **1** deprive of courage, confidence, or energy. **2** (usu. foll. by *from*) dissuade (*discouraged him from going*). **3** inhibit or seek to prevent (an action etc.) by showing disapproval; oppose (*smoking is discouraged*). □ **discouragement** *n.* **discouragingly** *adv.* [Middle English from Old French *descouragier* (as DIS-, COURAGE)]

discourse *n. & v.* ● *n.* /'dɪskɔːs, -'kɔːs/ **1** *literary* **a** conversation; talk. **b** a dissertation or treatise on an academic subject. **c** a lecture or sermon. **2** *Linguistics* a connected series of utterances; a text. ● *v.* /dɪs'kɔːs/ **1** *intr.* talk; converse. **2** *intr.* (usu. foll. by *of, on, upon*) speak or write learnedly or at length (on a subject). **3** *tr. archaic* give forth (music etc.). [Middle English from Latin *discursus* (as DIS-, COURSE): the verb influenced by French *discourir*]

discourteous /dɪs'kəːtjəs/ *adj.* impolite; rude. □ **discourteously** *adv.* **discourteousness** *n.*

discourtesy /dɪs'kəːtəsi/ *n.* (*pl.* **-ies**) **1** bad manners; rudeness. **2** an impolite act or remark.

discover /dɪ'skʌvə/ *v.tr.* **1** (often foll. by *that* + clause) **a** find out or become aware of, whether by research or searching or by chance (*discovered a new entrance; discovered that they had been overpaid*). **b** be the first to find or find out (*who discovered America?*). **2** *Chess* give (check) by removing one's own obstructing piece. **3** (in show business) find and promote as a new singer, actor, etc. **4** *archaic* **a** make known. **b** exhibit; manifest. **c** disclose; betray. □ **discoverable** *adj.* **discoverer** *n.* [Middle English via Old French *descovrir* from Late Latin *discooperire* (as DIS-, COVER)]

discovery /dɪ'skʌv(ə)ri/ *n.* (*pl.* **-ies**) **1 a** the act or process of discovering or being discovered. **b** an instance of this (*the discovery of a new planet*). **2** a person or thing discovered. **3** *Law* the compulsory disclosure, by a party to an action, of facts or documents on which the other party wishes to rely. [DISCOVER, on the pattern of *recover, recovery*]

discredit /dɪs'kredɪt/ *n. & v.* ● *n.* **1** harm to reputation (*brought discredit on the enterprise*). **2** a person or thing causing this (*he is a discredit to his family*). **3** lack of credibility; doubt; disbelief (*throws discredit on her story*). **4** the loss of commercial credit. ● *v.tr.* (**discredited, discrediting**) **1** harm the good reputation of. **2** cause to be disbelieved. **3** refuse to believe.

discreditable /dɪs'kredɪtəb(ə)l/ *adj.* bringing discredit; shameful. □ **discreditably** *adv.*

discreet /dɪ'skriːt/ *adj.* (**discreeter, discreetest**) **1 a** circumspect in speech or action, esp. to avoid social disgrace or embarrassment. **b** tactful; trustworthy. **2** unobtrusive (*a discreet touch of rouge*). □ **discreetly** *adv.* **discreetness** *n.* [Middle English via Old French *discret -ete* from Latin *discretus* 'separate' (as DIS-, *cretus*, past part. of *cernere* 'sift'), with Late Latin sense from its derivative *discretio* 'discernment']

discrepancy /dɪs'krep(ə)nsi/ *n.* (*pl.* **-ies**) **1** difference; failure to correspond; inconsistency. **2** an instance of this. □ **discrepant** *adj.* [Latin *discrepare* 'be discordant' (as DIS-, *crepare* 'creak')]

discrete /dɪ'skriːt/ *adj.* individually distinct; separate, discontinuous. □ **discretely** *adv.* **discreteness** *n.* [Middle English from Latin *discretus*: see DISCREET]

discretion /dɪ'skreʃ(ə)n/ *n.* **1** being discreet; discreet behaviour (*treats confidences with discretion*). **2** prudence; self-preservation. **3** the freedom to act and think as one wishes, usu. within legal limits (*it is within his discretion to leave*). **4** *Law* a court's freedom to decide a sentence etc. □ **age** (or **years**) **of discretion** the esp. legal age at which a person is able to manage his or her own affairs. **at discretion** as one pleases. **at the discretion of** to be settled or disposed of according to the judgement or choice of. **discretion is the better part of valour** reckless courage is often self-defeating. **use one's discretion** act according to one's own judgement. □ **discretionary** *adj.* [Middle English via Old French from Latin *discretio -onis* (as DISCREET)]

discriminate /dɪ'skrɪmɪneɪt/ *v.* **1** *intr.* (often foll. by *between*) make or see a distinction; differentiate (*cannot discriminate between right and wrong*). **2** *intr.* make a distinction, esp. unjustly and on the basis of race, age, sex, etc. **3** *intr.* (foll. by *against*) select for unfavourable treatment. **4** *tr.* (usu. foll. by *from*) make or see or constitute a difference in or between (*many things discriminate one person from another*). **5** *intr.* observe distinctions carefully; have good judgement. **6** *tr.* mark as distinctive; be a distinguishing feature of. □ **discriminately** /-nətli/ *adv.* **discriminative** /-nətɪv/ *adj.* **discriminator** *n.* **discriminatory** /-nət(ə)ri/ *adj.* [Latin *discriminare* from *discrimen -minis* 'distinction', from *discernere* DISCERN]

discriminating /dɪ'skrɪmɪneɪtɪŋ/ *adj.* **1** able to discern, esp. distinctions. **2** having good taste. □ **discriminatingly** *adv.*

discrimination /dɪˌskrɪmɪ'neɪʃ(ə)n/ *n.* **1** unfavourable treatment based on prejudice, esp. regarding race, age, or sex. **2** good taste or judgement in artistic matters etc. **3** the power of discriminating or observing differences. **4** a distinction made with the mind or in action.

discursive /dɪs'kəːsɪv/ *adj.* **1** rambling or digressive. **2** *Philos.* proceeding by argument or reasoning (opp. INTUITIVE). □ **discursively** *adv.* **discursiveness** *n.* [medieval Latin *discursivus* from Latin *discurrere discurs-* (as DIS-, *currere* 'run')]

discus /'dɪskəs/ *n.* (*pl.* **discuses**) **1** a heavy thick-centred disc thrown in ancient Greek games. **2** a similar disc thrown in modern field events. [Latin from Greek *diskos*]

discuss /dɪ'skʌs/ *v.tr.* **1** hold a conversation about. **2** examine by argument, esp. written; debate. □ **discussable** *adj.* **discussant** *n.* **discusser** *n.* [earlier in the sense 'dispel, disperse': Middle English from Latin *discutere discuss-* 'disperse' (as DIS-, *quatere* 'shake')]

discussion /dɪ'skʌʃ(ə)n/ *n.* **1** a conversation, esp. on specific subjects; a debate (*had a discussion about what they should do*). **2** an examination by argument, written or spoken. [Middle English via Old French from Late Latin *discussio -onis* (as DISCUSS)]

disdain /dɪs'deɪn, -z-/ *n. & v.* ● *n.* scorn; contempt. ● *v.tr.* **1** regard with disdain. **2** think oneself superior to; reject (*disdained his offer; disdained to enter; disdained answering*). [Middle English from Old French *desdeign(ier)*, ultimately from Latin *dedignari* (as DE-, *dignari* from *dignus* 'worthy')]

disdainful /dɪs'deɪnfʊl, -f(ə)l, -z-/ *adj.* showing disdain or contempt. □ **disdainfully** *adv.* **disdainfulness** *n.*

disease /dɪ'ziːz/ *n.* **1** an unhealthy condition of the body (or a part of it) or the mind; illness, sickness. **2** a corresponding physical condition of plants. **3** a particular kind of disease with special symptoms or location. [Middle English from Old French *desaise*]

diseased /dɪ'zi:zd/ *adj.* **1** affected with disease. **2** abnormal, disordered. [Middle English, past part. of *disease*, from Old French *desaisier* (as DISEASE)]

diseconomy /dɪsɪ'kɒnəmi/ *n. Econ.* the absence or reverse of economy, esp. the increase of costs in a large-scale operation.

disembark /dɪsɪm'bɑ:k, dɪsɛm-/ *v.tr. & intr.* put or go ashore or land from a ship; remove from or leave an aircraft, train, etc. □ **disembarkation** /-'keɪʃ(ə)n/ *n.* [French *désembarquer* (as DIS-, EMBARK)]

disembarrass /dɪsɪm'barəs, dɪsɛm-/ *v.tr.* **1** (usu. foll. by *of*) relieve (of a load etc.). **2** free from embarrassment. □ **disembarrassment** *n.*

disembody /dɪsɪm'bɒdi, dɪsɛm-/ *v.tr.* (**-ies, -ied**) **1** (esp. as **disembodied** *adj.*) separate or free (esp. the soul) from the body or a concrete form (*disembodied spirit; disembodied voice*). **2** *archaic* disband (troops). □ **disembodiment** *n.*

disembogue /dɪsɪm'bəʊg, dɪsɛm-/ *v.tr. & intr.* (**disembogues**, **disembogued**, **disemboguing**) (of a river etc.) discharge or flow into the sea etc. [Spanish *desembocar* (as DIS-, *en* 'in', *boca* 'mouth')]

disembowel /dɪsɪm'baʊəl, dɪsɛm-/ *v.tr.* (**disembowelled**, **disembowelling**; *US* **disemboweled**, **disemboweling**) remove the bowels or entrails of. □ **disembowelment** *n.*

disembroil /dɪsɪm'brɔɪl, dɪsɛm-/ *v.tr.* extricate from confusion or entanglement.

disempower /dɪsɪm'paʊə, dɪsɛm-/ *v.tr.* remove the power to act from (a person, group, etc). □ **disempowerment** *n.*

disenchant /dɪsɪn'tʃɑ:nt, dɪsɛn-/ *v.tr.* free from enchantment; disillusion. □ **disenchantingly** *adv.* **disenchantment** *n.* [French *désenchanter* (as DIS-, ENCHANT)]

disencumber /dɪsɪn'kʌmbə, dɪsɛn-/ *v.tr.* free from encumbrance.

disendow /dɪsɪn'daʊ, dɪsɛn-/ *v.tr.* strip (esp. the Church) of endowments. □ **disendowment** *n.*

disenfranchise /dɪsɪn'fran(t)ʃʌɪz, dɪsɛn-/ *v.tr.* (also **disfranchise** /dɪs'fran(t)ʃʌɪz/) **1 a** deprive (a person) of the right to vote. **b** deprive (a place) of the right to send a representative to Parliament. **2** deprive (a person) of rights as a citizen or of a franchise held. □ **disenfranchisement** *n.*

disengage /dɪsɪn'geɪdʒ, dɪsɛn-/ *v. & n.* ● *v.* **1** *tr.* detach, free, loosen, or separate (parts etc.) (*disengaged the clutch*). **2** *tr. Mil.* remove (troops) from a battle or a battle area. **3** *intr.* become detached. **4** *intr. Fencing* pass the point of one's sword to the other side of one's opponent's. **5** *intr.* (as **disengaged** *adj.*) **a** unoccupied; free; vacant. **b** uncommitted, esp. politically. ● *n. Fencing* a disengaging movement.

disengagement /dɪsɪn'geɪdʒm(ə)nt, dɪsɛn-/ *n.* **1 a** the act of disengaging. **b** an instance of this. **2** freedom from ties; detachment. **3** the dissolution of an engagement to marry. **4** ease of manner or behaviour. **5** *Fencing* = DISENGAGE.

disentail /dɪsɪn'teɪl, dɪsɛn-/ *v.tr. Law* free (property) from entail; break the entail of.

disentangle /dɪsɪn'taŋg(ə)l, dɪsɛn-/ *v.* **1** *tr.* **a** unravel, untwist. **b** free from complications; extricate (*disentangled her from the difficulty*). **2** *intr.* become disentangled. □ **disentanglement** *n.*

disenthral /dɪsɪn'θrɔ:l, dɪsɛn-/ *v.tr.* (*US* **disenthrall**) (**-enthralled**, **-enthralling**) *literary* free from enthralment. □ **disenthralment** *n.*

disentitle /dɪsɪn'tʌɪt(ə)l, dɪsɛn-/ *v.tr.* (usu. foll. by *to*) deprive of any rightful claim. □ **disentitlement** *n.*

disentomb /dɪsɪn'tu:m, dɪsɛn-/ *v.tr. literary* **1** remove from a tomb; disinter. **2** unearth. □ **disentombment** /-'tu:mm(ə)nt/ *n.*

disequilibrium /ˌdɪsi:kwɪ'lɪbrɪəm, dɪsɛ-/ *n.* a lack or loss of equilibrium; instability.

disestablish /dɪsɪ'stablɪʃ, dɪsɛ-/ *v.tr.* **1** deprive (a church) of state support. **2** depose from an official position. **3** terminate the establishment of. □ **disestablishment** *n.*

disesteem /dɪsɪ'sti:m, dɪsɛ-/ *v. & n.* ● *v.tr.* have a low opinion of; despise. ● *n.* low esteem or regard.

diseuse /di:'zə:z, French dizøz/ *n.* (*masc.* ***diseur*** /di:'zə:, French dizœr/) a female artiste entertaining with spoken monologues. [French, = talker, from *dire dis-* 'say']

disfavour /dɪs'feɪvə/ *n. & v.* (*US* **disfavor**) ● *n.* **1** disapproval or dislike. **2** the state of being disliked (*fell into disfavour*). ● *v.tr.* regard or treat with disfavour.

disfigure /dɪs'fɪgə/ *v.tr.* spoil the beauty of; deform; deface. □ **disfigurement** *n.* [Middle English via Old French *desfigurer* from Romanic (as DIS-, FIGURE)]

disforest /dɪs'fɒrɪst/ *v.tr. Brit.* = DISAFFOREST. □ **disforestation** /-'steɪʃ(ə)n/ *n.*

disfranchise /dɪs'fran(t)ʃʌɪz/ var. of DISENFRANCHISE.

disfrock /dɪs'frɒk/ *v.tr.* unfrock.

disgorge /dɪs'gɔ:dʒ/ *v.tr.* **1** eject from the throat or stomach. **2** pour forth, discharge (contents, ill-gotten gains, etc.). □ **disgorgement** *n.* [Middle English from Old French *desgorger* (as DIS-, GORGE)]

disgrace /dɪs'greɪs/ *n. & v.* ● *n.* **1** the loss of reputation; shame; ignominy (*brought disgrace on his family*). **2** a dishonourable, inefficient, or shameful person, thing, state of affairs, etc. (*the bus service is a disgrace*). ● *v.tr.* **1** bring shame or discredit on; be a disgrace to. **2** degrade from a position of honour; dismiss from favour. □ **in disgrace** having lost respect or reputation; out of favour. [French *disgrâce*, *disgracier* from Italian *disgrazia, disgraziare* (as DIS-, GRACE)]

disgraceful /dɪs'greɪsfʊl, -f(ə)l/ *adj.* shameful; dishonourable; degrading. □ **disgracefully** *adv.*

disgruntled /dɪs'grʌnt(ə)ld/ *adj.* discontented; moody; sulky. □ **disgruntlement** *n.* [DIS- + *gruntle*, obsolete frequentative of GRUNT]

disguise /dɪs'gʌɪz/ *v. & n.* ● *v.tr.* **1** (often foll. by *as*) alter the appearance, sound, smell, etc., of so as to conceal the identity; make unrecognizable (*disguised herself as a policewoman; disguised the taste by adding sugar*). **2** misrepresent or cover up (*disguised the truth; disguised their intentions*). ● *n.* **1 a** a costume, false beard, make-up, etc., used to alter the appearance so as to conceal or deceive. **b** any action, manner, etc., used for deception. **2 a** the act or practice of disguising; the concealment of reality. **b** an instance of this. □ **in disguise** **1** wearing a concealing costume etc. **2** appearing to be the opposite (*a blessing in disguise*). □ **disguisement** *n.* [Middle English from Old French *desguis(i)er* (as DIS-, GUISE)]

disgust /dɪs'gʌst/ *n. & v.* ● *n.* (usu. foll. by *at, for*) **1** strong aversion; repugnance; profound indignation. **2** a strong distaste for a food, drink, medicine, etc.; nausea. ● *v.tr.* cause disgust in (*their behaviour disgusts me; was disgusted to find a slug*). □ **in disgust** as a result of disgust (*left in disgust*). □ **disgustedly** *adv.* [Old French *degoust, desgouster*, or Italian *disgusto, disgustare* (as DIS-, GUSTO)]

disgustful /dɪs'gʌstfʊl, -f(ə)l/ *adj.* **1** disgusting; repulsive. **2** (of curiosity etc.) caused by disgust.

disgusting /dɪs'gʌstɪŋ/ *adj.* arousing aversion or indignation (*disgusting behaviour*). □ **disgustingly** *adv.* **disgustingness** *n.*

dish /dɪʃ/ *n. & v.* ● *n.* **1 a** a shallow, usu. flat-bottomed container for cooking or serving food, made of glass, ceramics, metal, etc. **b** the food served in a dish (*all the dishes were delicious*). **c** a particular kind of food (*a meat dish*). **2** (in *pl.*) dirty plates, cutlery, cooking pots, etc. after a meal. **3 a** a dish-shaped receptacle, object, or cavity. **b** = SATELLITE DISH. **4** *slang* a sexually attractive person. ● *v.tr.* **1** put (food) into a dish ready for serving. **2** *Brit. colloq.* **a** outmanoeuvre. **b** destroy (one's hopes, chances, etc.). **3** make concave or dish-shaped. □ **dish out** *slang* distribute, esp. carelessly or indiscriminately. **dish up** **1** serve or prepare to serve (food). **2** *colloq.* seek to present (facts, argument, etc.) attractively. **dish**

(up) the dirt (often foll. by *on*) *colloq.* spread scandal or gossip. □ **dishful** *n.* (*pl.* **-fuls**). [Old English *disc* 'plate, bowl' (with Germanic and Old Norse cognates) from Latin *discus* DISC]

dishabille var. of DÉSHABILLÉ.

disharmony /dɪsˈhɑːməni/ *n.* a lack of harmony; discord. □ **disharmonious** /-ˈməʊnɪəs/ *adj.* **disharmoniously** /-ˈməʊnɪəsli/ *adv.* **disharmonize** /-nʌɪz/ *v.tr.* (also **-ise**).

dishcloth /ˈdɪʃklɒθ/ *n.* a usu. open-weave cloth for washing dishes.

dishcloth gourd *n.* a loofah.

dishearten /dɪsˈhɑːt(ə)n/ *v.tr.* cause to lose courage or confidence; make despondent. □ **dishearteningly** *adv.* **disheartenment** *n.*

dishevelled /dɪˈʃɛv(ə)ld/ *adj.* (*US* **disheveled**) (of the hair, a person, etc.) untidy; ruffled; disordered. □ **dishevel** *v.tr.* (**dishevelled**, **dishevelling**; *US* **disheveled**, **disheveling**). **dishevelment** *n.* [Middle English *dischevelee* from Old French *deschevelé* past part. (as DIS-, *chevel* 'hair' from Latin *capillus*)]

dishonest /dɪsˈɒnɪst/ *adj.* (of a person, act, or statement) fraudulent or insincere. □ **dishonestly** *adv.* [Middle English from Old French *deshoneste* (as DIS-, HONEST)]

dishonesty /dɪsˈɒnɪsti/ *n.* (*pl.* **-ies**) **1 a** a lack of honesty. **b** deceitfulness, fraud. **2** a dishonest or fraudulent act. [Middle English from Old French *deshon(n)esté* (as DISHONEST)]

dishonour /dɪsˈɒnə/ *n.* & *v.* (*US* **dishonor**) ● *n.* **1** a state of shame or disgrace; discredit. **2** something that causes dishonour (*a dishonour to his profession*). ● *v.tr.* **1** treat without honour or respect. **2** disgrace (*dishonoured his name*). **3** refuse to accept or pay (a cheque or a bill of exchange). **4** *archaic* violate the chastity of; rape. [Middle English via Old French *deshonor* (*n.*), *deshonorer* (*v.*) from medieval Latin *dishonorare* (as DIS-, HONOUR)]

dishonourable /dɪsˈɒn(ə)rəb(ə)l/ *adj.* (*US* **dishonorable**) **1** causing disgrace; ignominious. **2** unprincipled. □ **dishonourableness** *n.* **dishonourably** *adv.*

dishrag /ˈdɪʃrag/ *n.* = DISHCLOTH.

dishwasher /ˈdɪʃwɒʃə/ *n.* **1** a machine for automatically washing dishes. **2** a person employed to wash dishes.

dishwater /ˈdɪʃwɔːtə/ *n.* water in which dishes have been washed.

dishy /ˈdɪʃi/ *adj.* (**dishier**, **dishiest**) *Brit. slang* sexually attractive. [DISH *n.* 4 + -Y[1]]

disillusion /dɪsɪˈluːʒ(ə)n, -ˈljuː-/ *n.* & *v.* ● *n.* freedom from illusions; disenchantment. ● *v.tr.* rid of illusions; disenchant. □ **disillusionize** *v.tr.* (also **-ise**). **disillusionment** *n.*

disincentive /dɪsɪnˈsɛntɪv/ *n.* & *adj.* ● *n.* **1** something that tends to discourage a particular action etc. **2** *Econ.* a source of discouragement to productivity or progress. ● *adj.* tending to discourage.

disinclination /ˌdɪsɪnklɪˈneɪʃ(ə)n/ *n.* (usu. foll. by *for*, or *to* + infin.) the absence of willingness; a reluctance (*a disinclination for work*; *disinclination to go*).

disincline /dɪsɪnˈklʌɪn/ *v.tr.* (usu. foll. by *to* + infin. or *for*) make unwilling or reluctant.

disincorporate /dɪsɪnˈkɔːpəreɪt/ *v.tr.* dissolve (a corporate body).

disinfect /dɪsɪnˈfɛkt/ *v.tr.* cleanse (a wound, a room, clothes, etc.) of infection, esp. with a disinfectant. □ **disinfection** *n.* [French *désinfecter* (as DIS-, INFECT)]

disinfectant /dɪsɪnˈfɛkt(ə)nt/ *n.* & *adj.* ● *n.* a usu. commercially produced chemical liquid that destroys germs etc. ● *adj.* causing disinfection.

disinfest /dɪsɪnˈfɛst/ *v.tr.* rid (a person, a building, etc.) of vermin, infesting insects, etc. □ **disinfestation** /-ˈsteɪʃ(ə)n/ *n.*

disinflation /dɪsɪnˈfleɪʃ(ə)n/ *n. Econ.* a policy designed to counteract inflation without causing deflation. □ **disinflationary** *adj.*

disinformation /ˌdɪsɪnfəˈmeɪʃ(ə)n/ *n.* false information, intended to mislead.

disingenuous /dɪsɪnˈdʒɛnjʊəs/ *adj.* having secret motives; dishonest; insincere. □ **disingenuously** *adv.* **disingenuousness** *n.*

disinherit /dɪsɪnˈhɛrɪt/ *v.tr.* (**disinherited**, **disinheriting**) reject as one's heir; deprive of the right of inheritance. □ **disinheritance** *n.* [Middle English from DIS- + INHERIT in obsolete sense 'make heir']

disintegrate /dɪsˈɪntɪɡreɪt/ *v.* **1** *tr.* & *intr.* **a** separate into component parts or fragments; crumble; decay. **b** lose or cause to lose cohesion. **2** *intr. colloq.* deteriorate mentally or physically. **3** *intr.* & *tr. Physics* undergo or cause to undergo disintegration. □ **disintegrative** /-ɡrətɪv/ *adj.* **disintegrator** *n.*

disintegration /dɪsˌɪntɪˈɡreɪʃ(ə)n/ *n.* **1** the act or an instance of disintegrating. **2** *Physics* any process in which a nucleus emits a particle or particles or divides into smaller nuclei.

disinter /dɪsɪnˈtəː/ *v.tr.* (**disinterred**, **disinterring**) **1** remove (esp. a corpse) from the ground; unearth; exhume. **2** find by delving (*disinterred the letter from the back of the drawer*). □ **disinterment** *n.* [French *désenterrer* (as DIS-, INTER)]

disinterest /dɪsˈɪnt(ə)rɪst/ *n.* **1** *disp.* lack of interest; unconcern. **2** impartiality.

■ **Usage** The use of *disinterest* in sense 1 to mean 'lack of interest' is sometimes objected to, but it is in this sense that is is most commonly found and the alternative *uninterest* is rare. The phrase *lack of interest* avoids both ambiguity and accusations of incorrect usage.

disinterested /dɪsˈɪnt(ə)rɪstɪd/ *adj.* **1** not influenced by one's own advantage; impartial. **2** *disp.* uninterested. □ **disinterestedly** *adv.* **disinterestedness** *n.* [past part. of *disinterest* 'divest of interest']

■ **Usage** *Disinterested* is commonly used informally to mean 'uninterested', but this is widely regarded as incorrect.

disinvest /dɪsɪnˈvɛst/ *v.intr.* (foll. by *from*, or *absol.*) reduce or dispose of one's investment (in a place, company, etc.). □ **disinvestment** *n.*

disjecta membra /dɪsˌdʒɛktə ˈmɛmbrə/ *n.pl.* scattered remains; fragments, esp. of written work. [Latin, alteration of *disjecti membra poetae* (Horace) 'limbs of a dismembered poet']

disjoin /dɪsˈdʒɔɪn/ *v.tr.* separate or disunite; part. [Middle English via Old French *desjoindre* from Latin *disjungere* (as DIS-, *jungere junct-* 'join')]

disjoint /dɪsˈdʒɔɪnt/ *v.* & *adj.* ● *v.tr.* **1** take apart at the joints. **2** (as **disjointed** *adj.*) (esp. of conversation) incoherent; desultory. **3** disturb the working or connection of; dislocate. ● *adj.* (of two or more sets) having no elements in common. □ **disjointedly** *adv.* **disjointedness** *n.* [Middle English from obsolete *disjoint* (*adj.*), from past part. of Old French *desjoindre* (as DISJOIN)]

disjunct /ˈdɪsdʒʌŋ(k)t/ *n.* **1** *Logic* each of the terms of a disjunctive proposition. **2** *Gram.* an adverb or adverbial phrase that expresses a writer's or speaker's attitude to the content of the sentence in which it occurs.

disjunction /dɪsˈdʒʌŋ(k)ʃ(ə)n/ *n.* **1 a** the process of disjoining; separation. **b** an instance of this. **2** *Logic* the relation of two mutually incompatible alternatives; a statement expressing this (esp. using the word 'or'). [Middle English from Old French *disjunction* or Latin *disjunctio* (as DISJOIN)]

disjunctive /dɪsˈdʒʌŋ(k)tɪv/ *adj.* & *n.* ● *adj.* **1** involving separation; disjoining. **2** *Gram.* (esp. of a conjunction) expressing a choice between two words etc., e.g. *or* in *asked if he was going or staying* (cf. COPULATIVE 2a). **3** *Logic* (of a proposition) expressing alternatives. ● *n.* **1**

Gram. a disjunctive conjunction or other word. **2** *Logic* a disjunctive proposition. ◻ **disjunctively** *adv.* [Middle English from Latin *disjunctivus* (as DISJOIN)]

disjuncture /dɪsˈdʒʌŋ(k)tʃə/ *n.* a disjointed state; a separation, a disconnection. [medieval Latin *disjunctura*, *disjunct-* (as DISJUNCTION)]

disk var. of DISC (esp. *US* & *Computing*).

disk drive *n.* a mechanism for rotating a disk and reading or writing data from or to it.

diskette /dɪˈskɛt/ *n. Computing* = FLOPPY *n.*

dislike /dɪsˈlʌɪk/ *v.* & *n.* ● *v.tr.* have an aversion or objection to; not like. ● *n.* **1** a feeling of repugnance or not liking. **2** an object of dislike. ◻ **dislikable** *adj.* (also **dislikeable**).

dislocate /ˈdɪslə(ʊ)keɪt/ *v.tr.* **1** disturb the normal connection of (esp. a joint in the body). **2** disrupt; put out of order. **3** displace. [probably back-formation from DISLOCATION]

dislocation /dɪslə(ʊ)ˈkeɪʃ(ə)n/ *n.* **1** the act or result of dislocating. **2** *Crystallog.* the displacement of part of a crystal lattice structure. [Middle English from Old French *dislocation* or medieval Latin *dislocatio*, from *dislocare* (as DIS-, *locare* 'place')]

dislodge /dɪsˈlɒdʒ/ *v.tr.* remove from an established or fixed position (*was dislodged from his directorship*). ◻ **dislodgement** *n.* (also **dislodgment**). [Middle English from Old French *dislog(i)er* (as DIS-, LODGE)]

disloyal /dɪsˈlɔɪ(ə)l/ *adj.* (often foll. by *to*) **1** not loyal; unfaithful. **2** untrue to one's allegiance; treacherous to one's government etc. ◻ **disloyalist** *n.* **disloyally** *adv.* **disloyalty** *n.* [Middle English from Old French *desloial* (as DIS-, LOYAL)]

dismal /ˈdɪzm(ə)l/ *adj.* **1** causing or showing gloom; miserable. **2** dreary or sombre (*dismal brown walls*). **3** *colloq.* feeble or inept (*a dismal performance*). ◻ **the dismals** *colloq.* melancholy. ◻ **dismally** *adv.* **dismalness** *n.* [originally noun = unlucky days: Middle English via Anglo-French *dis mal* from medieval Latin *dies mali*, two days in each month held to be unpropitious]

dismal science *n.* (prec. by *the*) *joc.* economics.

dismantle /dɪsˈmant(ə)l/ *v.tr.* **1** take to pieces; pull down. **2** deprive of defences or equipment. **3** (often foll. by *of*) strip of covering or protection. ◻ **dismantlement** *n.* **dismantler** *n.* [Old French *desmanteler* (as DIS-, MANTLE)]

dismast /dɪsˈmɑːst/ *v.tr.* deprive (a ship) of masts; break down the mast or masts of.

dismay /dɪsˈmeɪ/ *v.* & *n.* ● *v.tr.* fill with consternation or anxiety; discourage or depress; reduce to despair. ● *n.* **1** consternation or anxiety. **2** depression or despair. [Middle English from Old French, ultimately from a Germanic root = deprive of power (as DIS-, MAY)]

dismember /dɪsˈmɛmbə/ *v.tr.* **1** tear or cut the limbs from. **2** partition or divide up (an empire, country, etc.). ◻ **dismemberment** *n.* [Middle English via Old French *desmembrer* from Romanic (as DIS-, Latin *membrum* 'limb')]

dismiss /dɪsˈmɪs/ *v.* **1 a** *tr.* send away, cause to leave one's presence, disperse; disband (an assembly or army). **b** *intr.* (of an assembly etc.) disperse; break ranks. **2** *tr.* discharge from employment, office, etc., esp. dishonourably. **3** *tr.* put out of one's thoughts; cease to feel or discuss (*dismissed him from memory*). **4** *tr.* treat (a subject) summarily (*dismissed his application*). **5** *tr. Law* refuse further hearing to (a case); send out of court. **6** *tr. Cricket* put (a batsman or a side) out (*was dismissed for 75 runs*). **7** *intr.* (in *imper.*) *Mil.* a word of command at the end of drilling. ◻ **dismissal** *n.* **dismissible** *adj.* [Middle English, from medieval Latin *dismiss-* (as DIS-, Latin *mittere miss-* 'send')]

dismissive /dɪsˈmɪsɪv/ *adj.* tending to dismiss from consideration; disdainful. ◻ **dismissively** *adv.* **dismissiveness** *n.*

dismount /dɪsˈmaʊnt/ *v.* **1 a** *intr.* alight from a horse, bicycle, etc. **b** *tr.* (usu. in *passive*) throw from a horse, unseat. **2** *tr.* remove (a thing) from its mounting (esp. a gun from its carriage).

disobedient /dɪsəˈbiːdɪənt/ *adj.* disobeying; rebellious, rule-breaking. ◻ **disobedience** *n.* **disobediently** *adv.* [Middle English from Old French *desobedient* (as DIS-, OBEDIENT)]

disobey /dɪsəˈbeɪ/ *v.tr.* (also *absol.*) fail or refuse to obey; disregard (orders); break (rules) (*disobeyed his mother*; *how dare you disobey!*). ◻ **disobeyer** *n.* [Middle English via Old French *desobeir* from Romanic (as DIS-, OBEY)]

disoblige /dɪsəˈblʌɪdʒ/ *v.tr.* **1** refuse to consider the convenience or wishes of. **2** (as **disobliging** *adj.*) uncooperative. [French *désobliger* from Romanic (as DIS-, OBLIGE)]

disorder /dɪsˈɔːdə/ *n.* & *v.* ● *n.* **1** a lack of order; confusion. **2** a riot; a commotion. **3** *Med.* a usu. minor ailment or disease. ● *v.tr.* **1** throw into confusion; disarrange. **2** *Med.* put out of good health; upset. ◻ **disordered** *adj.* [Middle English, alteration influenced by ORDER *v.* of earlier *disordain* from Old French *desordener* (as DIS-, ORDAIN)]

disorderly /dɪsˈɔːdəli/ *adj.* **1** untidy; confused. **2** irregular; unruly; riotous. **3** *Law* contrary to public order or morality. ◻ **disorderliness** *n.*

disorderly house *n.* a brothel.

disorganize /dɪsˈɔːɡənʌɪz/ *v.tr.* (also **-ise**) **1** destroy the system or order of; throw into confusion. **2** (as **disorganized** *adj.*) lacking organization or system. ◻ **disorganization** /-ˈzeɪʃ(ə)n/ *n.* [French *désorganiser* (as DIS-, ORGANIZE)]

disorient /dɪsˈɔːrɪɛnt/ *v.tr.* = DISORIENTATE. [French *désorienter* (as DIS-, ORIENT *v.*)]

disorientate /dɪsˈɔːrɪɛnteɪt/ *v.tr.* **1** confuse (a person) as to his or her whereabouts or bearings. **2** confuse (a person) (*disorientated by his unexpected behaviour*). ◻ **disorientation** /-ˈteɪʃ(ə)n/ *n.*

disown /dɪsˈəʊn/ *v.tr.* **1** refuse to recognize; repudiate; disclaim. **2** renounce one's connection with or allegiance to. ◻ **disowner** *n.*

disparage /dɪˈsparɪdʒ/ *v.tr.* **1** speak slightingly of; depreciate. **2** bring discredit on. ◻ **disparagement** *n.* **disparagingly** *adv.* [Middle English from Old French *desparagier* 'marry unequally' (as DIS-, *parage* 'equality of rank', ultimately from Latin *par* 'equal')]

disparate /ˈdɪsp(ə)rət/ *adj.* & *n.* ● *adj.* essentially different in kind; without comparison or relation. ● *n.* (in *pl.*) things so unlike that there is no basis for their comparison. ◻ **disparately** *adv.* **disparateness** *n.* [Latin *disparatus* 'separated' (as DIS-, *paratus*, past part. of *parare* 'prepare'), influenced in sense by Latin *dispar* 'unequal']

disparity /dɪˈsparɪti/ *n.* (*pl.* **-ies**) **1** inequality; difference; incongruity. **2** an instance of this. [French *disparité* from Late Latin *disparitas -tatis* (as DIS-, PARITY[1])]

dispassionate /dɪsˈpaʃ(ə)nət/ *adj.* free from passion; calm; impartial. ◻ **dispassionately** *adv.* **dispassionateness** *n.*

dispatch /dɪˈspatʃ/ *v.* & *n.* (also **despatch**) ● *v.tr.* **1** send off to a destination or for a purpose (*dispatched him with the message*; *dispatched the letter yesterday*). **2** perform (business, a task, etc.) promptly; finish off. **3** kill, execute (*dispatched him with the revolver*). **4** *colloq.* eat (food, a meal, etc.) quickly. ● *n.* **1** the act or an instance of sending (a messenger, letter, etc.). **2** the act or an instance of killing; execution. **3 a** an official written message on state or esp. military affairs. **b** a report sent in by a newspaper's correspondent, usu. from a foreign country. **c** any written message requiring fast delivery. **4** promptness, efficiency (*done with dispatch*). ◻ **dispatcher** *n.* [Italian *dispacciare* or Spanish *despachar* 'expedite' (as DIS-, Italian *impacciare* and Spanish *empachar* 'hinder', of uncertain origin)]

dispatch box *n.* (also **dispatch case**) a container for esp. official state or military documents or dispatches.

dispatch rider *n.* a motorcyclist or rider on horseback carrying dispatches.

dispel /dɪ'spɛl/ *v.tr.* (**dispelled**, **dispelling**) dissipate; disperse; scatter (*the dawn dispelled their fears*). ▫ **dispeller** *n.* [Latin *dispellere* (as DIS-, *pellere* 'drive')]

dispensable /dɪ'spɛnsəb(ə)l/ *adj.* **1** able to be done without; unnecessary. **2** (of a law etc.) able to be relaxed in special cases. ▫ **dispensability** /-'bɪlɪti/ *n.* [medieval Latin *dispensabilis* (as DISPENSE)]

dispensary /dɪ'spɛns(ə)ri/ *n.* (*pl.* **-ies**) **1** a place where medicines etc. are dispensed. **2** a public or charitable institution for medical advice and the dispensing of medicines. [medieval Latin *dispensarius* (as DISPENSE)]

dispensation /dɪspɛn'seɪʃ(ə)n/ *n.* **1 a** the act or an instance of dispensing or distributing. **b** (foll. by *with*) the state of doing without (a thing). **c** something distributed. **2** (usu. foll. by *from*) **a** exemption from a penalty or duty; an instance of this. **b** permission to be exempted from a religious observance; an instance of this. **3** a religious or political system obtaining in a nation etc. (*the Christian dispensation*). **4 a** the ordering or management of the world by Providence. **b** a specific example of such ordering (of a community, a person, etc.). ▫ **dispensational** *adj.* [Middle English from Old French *dispensation* or Latin *dispensatio* (as DISPENSE)]

dispense /dɪ'spɛns/ *v.* **1** *tr.* distribute; deal out. **2** *tr.* administer (a sacrament, justice, etc.). **3** *tr.* make up and give out (medicine etc.) according to a doctor's prescription. **4** *tr.* (usu. foll. by *from*) grant a dispensation to (a person) from an obligation, esp. a religious observance. **5** *intr.* (foll. by *with*) **a** do without; render needless. **b** give exemption from (a rule). [Middle English via Old French *despenser* from Latin *dispensare*, frequentative of *dispendĕre* 'weigh or pay out' (as DIS-, *pendĕre pens-* 'weigh')]

dispenser /dɪ'spɛnsə/ *n.* **1** a person or thing that dispenses something, e.g. medicine, good advice. **2** an automatic machine that dispenses an item or a specific amount of something (e.g. cash).

dispensing chemist *n. Brit.* a chemist qualified to make up and give out medicine etc.

dispensing optician *n.* = OPTICIAN 2.

dispersant /dɪ'spəːs(ə)nt/ *n. Chem.* an agent used to disperse small particles in a medium.

disperse /dɪ'spəːs/ *v.* **1** *intr.* & *tr.* go, send, drive, or distribute in different directions or over a wide area. **2 a** *intr.* (of people at a meeting etc.) leave and go their various ways. **b** *tr.* cause to do this. **3** *tr.* send to or station at separate points. **4** *tr.* put in circulation; disseminate. **5** *tr. Chem.* distribute (small particles) uniformly in a medium. **6** *tr. Physics* divide (white light) into its coloured constituents. ▫ **dispersable** *adj.* **dispersal** *n.* **disperser** *n.* **dispersible** *adj.* **dispersive** *adj.* [Middle English from Latin *dispergere dispers-* (as DIS-, *spargere* 'scatter')]

dispersion /dɪ'spəːʃ(ə)n/ *n.* **1** the act or an instance of dispersing; the process of being dispersed. **2** *Chem.* a mixture of one substance dispersed in another. **3** *Physics* the separation of white light into colours or of any radiation according to wavelength. **4** *Statistics* the extent to which values of a variable differ from the mean. **5** *Ecol.* the pattern of distribution of individuals within the habitat. **6** (**the Dispersion**) = DIASPORA 1. [Middle English from Late Latin *dispersio* (as DISPERSE), translation of Greek *diaspora*: see DIASPORA]

dispirit /dɪ'spɪrɪt/ *v.tr.* **1** (esp. as **dispiriting** *adj.*) make despondent; discourage. **2** (as **dispirited** *adj.*) dejected; discouraged. ▫ **dispiritedly** *adv.* **dispiritedness** *n.* **dispiritingly** *adv.*

displace /dɪs'pleɪs/ *v.tr.* **1** shift from its accustomed place. **2** remove from office. **3** take the place of; oust.

displaced person *n.* a person who is forced to leave his or her home country because of war, persecution, etc.; a refugee.

displacement /dɪs'pleɪsm(ə)nt/ *n.* **1** the act or an instance of displacing; the process or an instance of being displaced. **2** *Physics* the amount of a fluid displaced by a solid floating or immersed in it (*a ship with a displacement of 11,000 tons*). **3** *Psychol.* **a** the substitution of one idea or impulse for another. **b** the unconscious transfer of strong unacceptable emotions from one object to another. **4** the amount by which a thing is moved from a position.

displacement activity *n. Psychol.* an animal or human activity which seems irrelevant to the situation (e.g. head-scratching when confused).

displacement ton see TON[1] 4.

display /dɪ'spleɪ/ *v.* & *n.* ● *v.tr.* **1** expose to view; exhibit; show. **2** show ostentatiously. **3** allow to appear; reveal; betray (*displayed his ignorance*). ● *n.* **1** the act or an instance of displaying. **2 a** an exhibition or show. **b** a thing or things intended to be looked at. **3** ostentation; flashiness. **4** the distinct behaviour of some birds and fish, esp. used to attract a mate. **5 a** the presentation of signals or data on a visual display unit etc. **b** the information so presented. **6** *Printing* the arrangement and choice of type in order to attract attention. ▫ **displayer** *n.* [Middle English via Old French *despleier* from Latin *displicare* (as DIS-, *plicare* 'fold'): cf. DEPLOY]

displease /dɪs'pliːz/ *v.tr.* make indignant or angry; offend; annoy. ▫ **be displeased** (often foll. by *at*, *with*) be indignant or dissatisfied; disapprove. ▫ **displeasing** *adj.* **displeasingly** *adv.* [Middle English from Old French *desplaisir* (as DIS-, Latin *placēre* 'please')]

displeasure /dɪs'plɛʒə/ *n.* & *v.* ● *n.* disapproval; anger; dissatisfaction. ● *v.tr. archaic* cause displeasure to; annoy. [Middle English from Old French (as DISPLEASE): assimilated to PLEASURE]

disport /dɪ'spɔːt/ *v.* & *n.* ● *v.intr.* & *refl.* frolic; gambol; enjoy oneself (*disported on the sand*; *disported themselves in the sea*). ● *n. archaic* **1** relaxation. **2** a pastime. [Middle English from Anglo-French & Old French *desporter* (as DIS-, *porter* 'carry' from Latin *portare*)]

disposable /dɪ'spəʊzəb(ə)l/ *adj.* & *n.* ● *adj.* **1** intended to be used once and then thrown away (*disposable nappies*). **2** that can be got rid of, made over, or used. **3** (esp. of financial assets) at the owner's disposal. ● *n.* a thing designed to be thrown away after one use. ▫ **disposability** /-'bɪlɪti/ *n.*

disposable income *n.* **1** income after tax and other necessary expenditure. **2** the total amount of money at the disposal of consumers in a country, community, etc.

disposal /dɪ'spəʊz(ə)l/ *n.* (usu. foll. by *of*) **1** the act or an instance of disposing of something. **2** the arrangement, disposition, or placing of something. **3** control or management (of a person, business, etc.). **4** (esp. as **waste disposal**) the disposing of rubbish. **5** *N. Amer. colloq.* a waste disposal unit. ▫ **at one's disposal 1** available for one's use. **2** subject to one's orders or decisions.

■ **Usage** *Disposal* is the noun corresponding to the verb *dispose of* 'get rid of, deal with, etc.'. *Disposition* is the noun corresponding to *dispose* 'arrange, incline'.

dispose /dɪ'spəʊz/ *v.* **1** *tr.* (usu. foll. by *to*, or *to* + infin.) **a** make willing; incline (*disposed him to the idea*; *was disposed to release them*). **b** have a tendency to (*the wheel was disposed to buckle*). **2** *tr.* place suitably or in order (*disposed the pictures in sequence*). **3** *tr.* (as **disposed** *adj.*) having a specified mental inclination (usu. in *comb.*: *ill-disposed*). **4** *intr.* determine the course of events (*man proposes, God disposes*). ▫ **dispose of 1 a** deal with. **b** get rid of. **c** finish. **d** kill. **2** sell. **3** prove (a claim, an argument, an opponent, etc.) to be incorrect. **4** consume (food). ▫ **disposer** *n.* [Middle English from Old French *disposer* (as DIS-, POSE[1]), based on Latin *disponere disposit-*]

disposition /dɪspə'zɪʃ(ə)n/ *n.* **1** (often foll. by *to*) a natural tendency; an inclination; a person's temperament (*a happy disposition*; *a disposition to overeat*). **2 a** setting in order; arranging. **b** the relative position of parts; an arrangement. **3** (usu. in *pl.*) **a** *Mil.*

the stationing of troops ready for attack or defence. **b** preparations; plans. **4 a** a bestowal by deed or will. **b** control; the power of disposing. **5** ordinance, dispensation. [Middle English via Old French from Latin *dispositio* (as DIS-, *ponere posit-* 'place')]

■ Usage See Usage Note at DISPOSAL.

dispossess /dɪspəˈzɛs/ *v.tr.* **1** dislodge; oust (a person). **2** (usu. foll. by *of*) deprive. □ **dispossession** /-ˈzɛʃ(ə)n/ *n.* [Old French *despossesser* (as DIS-, POSSESS)]

dispraise /dɪsˈpreɪz/ *v. & n.* ● *v.tr.* express disapproval or censure of. ● *n.* disapproval, censure. [Middle English from Old French *despreisier*, ultimately from Late Latin *depretiare* DEPRECIATE]

disproof /dɪsˈpruːf/ *n.* **1** something that disproves. **2 a** refutation. **b** an instance of this.

disproportion /dɪsprəˈpɔːʃ(ə)n/ *n.* **1** a lack of proportion. **2** an instance of this. □ **disproportional** *adj.* **disproportionally** *adv.*

disproportionate /dɪsprəˈpɔːʃ(ə)nət/ *adj.* **1** lacking proportion. **2** relatively too large or small, long or short, etc. □ **disproportionately** *adv.* **disproportionateness** *n.*

disprove /dɪsˈpruːv/ *v.tr.* prove false; refute. □ **disprovable** *adj.* [Middle English from Old French *desprover* (as DIS-, PROVE)]

disputable /dɪˈspjuːtəb(ə)l, ˈdɪspjʊtəb(ə)l/ *adj.* open to question; uncertain. □ **disputably** *adv.* [French or from Latin *disputabilis* (as DISPUTE)]

disputation /dɪspjuːˈteɪʃ(ə)n, -pjʊˈt-/ *n.* **1 a** disputing, debating. **b** an argument; a controversy. **2** a formal debate. [Middle English from French *disputation* or Latin *disputatio* (as DISPUTE)]

disputatious /dɪspjuːˈteɪʃəs, -pjʊˈt-/ *adj.* fond of or inclined to argument. □ **disputatiously** *adv.* **disputatiousness** *n.*

dispute *v. & n.* ● *v.* /dɪˈspjuːt/ **1** *intr.* (usu. foll. by *with*, *against*) **a** debate, argue (*was disputing with them about the meaning of life*). **b** quarrel. **2** *tr.* discuss, esp. heatedly (*disputed whether it was true*). **3** *tr.* question the truth or correctness or validity of (a statement, alleged fact, etc.) (*I dispute that number*). **4** *tr.* contend for; strive to win (*disputed the crown; disputed the field*). **5** *tr.* resist (a landing, advance, etc.). ● *n.* /dɪˈspjuːt, ˈdɪspjuːt/ **1** a controversy; a debate. **2** a quarrel. **3** a disagreement between management and employees, esp. one leading to industrial action. □ **beyond** (or **past** or **without**) **dispute** certainly; indisputably. **in dispute 1** being argued about. **2** *Brit.* (of a workforce) involved in industrial action. □ **disputant** /-ˈspjuːt(ə)nt/ *n.* **disputer** *n.* [Middle English via Old French *desputer* from Latin *disputare* 'estimate' (as DIS-, *putare* 'reckon')]

disqualification /dɪsˌkwɒlɪfɪˈkeɪʃ(ə)n/ *n.* **1** the act or an instance of disqualifying; the state of being disqualified. **2** something that disqualifies.

disqualify /dɪsˈkwɒlɪfʌɪ/ *v.tr.* (**-ies, -ied**) **1** (often foll. by *from*) debar from a competition or pronounce ineligible as a winner because of an infringement of the rules etc. (*disqualified from the race for taking drugs*). **2** (often foll. by *for, from*) make or pronounce ineligible or unsuitable (*his age disqualifies him for the job; a criminal record disqualified him from applying*). **3** (often foll. by *from*) incapacitate legally; pronounce unqualified (*disqualified from practising as a doctor*).

disquiet /dɪsˈkwʌɪət/ *v. & n.* ● *v.tr.* deprive of peace; worry. ● *n.* anxiety; unrest. □ **disquieting** *adj.* **disquietingly** *adv.*

disquietude /dɪsˈkwʌɪətjuːd/ *n.* a state of uneasiness; anxiety.

disquisition /dɪskwɪˈzɪʃ(ə)n/ *n.* a long or elaborate treatise or discourse on a subject. □ **disquisitional** *adj.* [French from Latin *disquisitio* (as DIS-, *quaerere quaesit-* 'seek')]

disrate /dɪsˈreɪt/ *v.tr. Naut.* reduce (a sailor) to a lower rating or rank.

disregard /dɪsrɪˈɡɑːd/ *v. & n.* ● *v.tr.* **1** pay no attention to; ignore. **2** treat as of no importance. ● *n.* (often foll. by *of, for*) indifference; neglect. □ **disregardful** *adj.* **disregardfully** *adv.*

disrelish /dɪsˈrɛlɪʃ/ *n. & v.* ● *n.* dislike; distaste. ● *v.tr.* regard with dislike or distaste.

disremember /dɪsrɪˈmɛmbə/ *v.tr. & intr.* esp. *US* or *dial.* fail to remember; forget.

disrepair /dɪsrɪˈpɛː/ *n.* poor condition due to neglect (*in disrepair; in a state of disrepair*).

disreputable /dɪsˈrɛpjʊtəb(ə)l/ *adj.* **1** of bad reputation; discreditable. **2** not respectable in appearance; dirty, untidy. □ **disreputableness** *n.* **disreputably** *adv.*

disrepute /dɪsrɪˈpjuːt/ *n.* a lack of good reputation or respectability; discredit (esp. *fall into disrepute*).

disrespect /dɪsrɪˈspɛkt/ *n.* a lack of respect; discourtesy. □ **disrespectful** *adj.* **disrespectfully** *adv.*

disrobe /dɪsˈrəʊb/ *v.tr. & refl.* (also *absol.*) **1** divest (oneself or another) of a robe or a garment; undress. **2** divest (oneself or another) of office, authority, etc.

disrupt /dɪsˈrʌpt/ *v.tr.* **1** interrupt the flow or continuity of (a meeting, speech, etc.); bring disorder to. **2** separate forcibly; shatter. □ **disrupter** *n.* (also **disruptor**). **disruption** *n.* **disruptive** *adj.* **disruptively** *adv.* **disruptiveness** *n.* [Latin *disrumpere disrupt-* (as DIS-, *rumpere* 'break')]

diss var. of DIS.

dissatisfy /dɪ(s)ˈsatɪsfʌɪ/ *v.tr.* (**-ies, -ied**) make discontented; fail to satisfy (*dissatisfied with the accommodation; dissatisfied to find him gone*). □ **dissatisfaction** /-ˈfakʃ(ə)n/ *n.* **dissatisfactory** /-ˈfakt(ə)ri/ *adj.* **dissatisfiedly** *adv.*

dissect /dɪˈsɛkt, *disp.* dʌɪ-/ *v.tr.* **1** cut into pieces. **2** cut up (a plant or animal) to examine its parts, structure, etc., or (a corpse) for a post-mortem. **3** analyse; criticize or examine in detail. □ **dissection** *n.* **dissector** *n.* [Latin *dissecare dissect-* (as DIS-, *secare* 'cut')]

dissemble /dɪˈsɛmb(ə)l/ *v.* **1** *intr.* conceal one's motives; talk or act hypocritically. **2** *tr.* **a** disguise or conceal (a feeling, intention, act, etc.). **b** (as **dissembled** *adj.*) simulated, pretended. □ **dissemblance** *n.* **dissembler** *n.* **dissemblingly** *adv.* [Middle English, alteration, suggested by *semblance*, of obsolete *dissimule*, via Old French *dissimuler* from Latin *dissimulare* (as DIS-, SIMULATE)]

disseminate /dɪˈsɛmɪneɪt/ *v.tr.* scatter about, spread (esp. ideas) widely. □ **dissemination** /-ˈneɪʃ(ə)n/ *n.* **disseminator** *n.* [Latin *disseminare* (as DIS-, *semen -inis* 'seed')]

disseminated sclerosis see SCLEROSIS 2.

dissension /dɪˈsɛnʃ(ə)n/ *n.* disagreement giving rise to discord. [Middle English via Old French from Latin *dissensio* (as DIS-, *sentire sens-* 'feel')]

dissent /dɪˈsɛnt/ *v. & n.* ● *v.intr.* (often foll. by *from*) **1** think differently, disagree; express disagreement. **2** differ in religious opinion, esp. from the doctrine of an established or orthodox Church. ● *n.* **1 a** a difference of opinion. **b** an expression of this. **2** the refusal to accept the doctrines of an established or orthodox Church; nonconformity. □ **dissenting** *adj.* [Middle English from Latin *dissentire* (as DIS-, *sentire* 'feel')]

dissenter /dɪˈsɛntə/ *n.* **1** a person who dissents. **2** (**Dissenter**) *Brit.* a member of a non-established Church; a Nonconformist.

dissentient /dɪˈsɛnʃɪənt, -ʃ(ə)nt/ *adj. & n.* ● *adj.* disagreeing with a majority or official view. ● *n.* a person who dissents. [Latin *dissentire* (as DIS-, *sentire* 'feel')]

dissertation /dɪsəˈteɪʃ(ə)n/ *n.* a detailed discourse on a subject, esp. one submitted in partial fulfilment of the requirements of a degree or diploma. □ **dissertational** *adj.* [Latin *dissertatio* from *dissertare* 'discuss', frequentative of *disserere dissert-* 'examine' (as DIS-, *serere* 'join')]

disservice /dɪ(s)ˈsəːvɪs/ *n.* an ill turn; an injury, esp. done when trying to help.

dissever /dɪ(s)ˈsɛvə/ *v.tr. & intr.* sever; divide into parts. □ **disseverance** *n.* **disseverment** *n.* [Middle

English via Anglo-French *dis(c)everer*, Old French *dessevrer* from Late Latin *disseparare* (as DIS-, SEPARATE)]

dissidence /ˈdɪsɪd(ə)ns/ *n.* disagreement; dissent. [French *dissidence* or Latin *dissidentia* (as DISSIDENT)]

dissident /ˈdɪsɪd(ə)nt/ *adj. & n.* ● *adj.* disagreeing, esp. with an established government, system, etc. ● *n.* a dissident person. [French, or from Latin *dissidēre* 'disagree' (as DIS-, *sedēre* 'sit')]

dissimilar /dɪˈsɪmɪlə/ *adj.* (often foll. by *to*) unlike, not similar. □ **dissimilarity** /-ˈlærɪti/ *n.* (*pl.* **-ies**). **dissimilarly** *adv.*

dissimilate /dɪˈsɪmɪleɪt/ *v.* (often foll. by *to*) *Phonet.* **1** *tr.* change (a sound or sounds in a word) to another when the word originally had identical sounds near each other, as in *cinnamon*, originally *cinnamom*. **2** *intr.* (of a sound) be changed in this way. □ **dissimilation** /-ˈleɪʃ(ə)n/ *n.* **dissimilatory** /-lət(ə)ri/ *adj.* [Latin *dissimilis* (as DIS-, *similis* 'like'), on the pattern of *assimilate*]

dissimilitude /dɪsɪˈmɪlɪtjuːd/ *n.* unlikeness, dissimilarity. [Latin *dissimilitudo* (as DISSIMILATE)]

dissimulate /dɪˈsɪmjʊleɪt/ *v.tr. & intr.* dissemble. □ **dissimulation** /-ˈleɪʃ(ə)n/ *n.* **dissimulator** *n.* [Latin *dissimulare* (as DIS-, SIMULATE)]

dissipate /ˈdɪsɪpeɪt/ *v.* **1 a** *tr.* cause (a cloud, vapour, fear, darkness, etc.) to disappear or disperse. **b** *intr.* disperse, scatter, disappear. **2** *intr. & tr.* break up; bring or come to nothing. **3** *tr.* squander or fritter away (money, energy, etc.). **4** *intr.* (as **dissipated** *adj.*) given to dissipation, dissolute. □ **dissipater** *n.* **dissipative** *adj.* **dissipator** *n.* [Latin *dissipare dissipat-* (as DIS-, *supare* 'throw')]

dissipation /dɪsɪˈpeɪʃ(ə)n/ *n.* **1** intemperate, dissolute, or debauched living. **2** (usu. foll. by *of*) wasteful expenditure (*dissipation of resources*). **3** scattering, dispersion, or disintegration. **4** a frivolous amusement. [French *dissipation* or Latin *dissipatio* (as DISSIPATE)]

dissociate /dɪˈsəʊʃɪeɪt, -sɪ-/ *v.* **1** *tr. & intr.* (usu. foll. by *from*) disconnect or become disconnected; separate (*dissociated her from their guilt*). **2** *tr. Chem.* decompose, esp. reversibly. **3** *tr. Psychol.* cause (a person's mind) to develop more than one centre of consciousness. □ **dissociate oneself from 1** declare oneself unconnected with. **2** decline to support or agree with (a proposal etc.). □ **dissociative** /-ətɪv/ *adj.* [Latin *dissociare* (as DIS-, *socius* 'companion')]

dissociated personality *n.* the pathological coexistence of two or more distinct personalities in the same person.

dissociation /dɪˌsəʊʃɪˈeɪʃ(ə)n, -sɪ-/ *n.* **1** the act or an instance of dissociating. **2** *Psychol.* the state of suffering from dissociated personality.

dissoluble /dɪˈsɒljʊb(ə)l/ *adj.* able to be disintegrated, loosened, or disconnected; soluble. □ **dissolubility** /-ˈbɪlɪti/ *n.* **dissolubly** *adv.* [French *dissoluble* or Latin *dissolubilis* (as DIS-, SOLUBLE)]

dissolute /ˈdɪsəluːt/ *adj.* lax in morals; licentious. □ **dissolutely** *adv.* **dissoluteness** *n.* [Middle English from Latin *dissolutus*, past part. of *dissolvere* DISSOLVE]

dissolution /dɪsəˈluːʃ(ə)n/ *n.* **1** disintegration; decomposition. **2** (usu. foll. by *of*) the undoing or relaxing of a bond, esp. a marriage, a partnership, or an alliance. **3** the dismissal or dispersal of an assembly, esp. of a parliament at the end of its term. **4** death. **5** bringing or coming to an end; fading away; disappearance. **6** dissipation; debauchery. [Middle English from Old French *dissolution* or Latin *dissolutio* (as DISSOLVE)]

dissolve /dɪˈzɒlv/ *v. & n.* ● *v.* **1** *tr. & intr.* incorporate or become incorporated into a liquid so as to form a solution. **2** *intr. & tr.* disappear or cause to disappear gradually. **3 a** *tr.* dismiss or disperse (an assembly, esp. Parliament). **b** *intr.* (of an assembly) be dissolved (cf. DISSOLUTION 3). **4** *tr.* annul or put an end to (a partnership, marriage, etc.). **5** *intr.* (of a person) become enfeebled or emotionally overcome (*completely dissolved when he saw her*; *dissolved into tears*). **6** *intr.* (often foll. by *into*) *Cinematog.* change gradually (from one picture into another). ● *n. Cinematog.* the act or process of dissolving a picture. □ **dissolvable** *adj.* [Middle English from Latin *dissolvere dissolut-* (as DIS-, *solvere* 'loosen')]

dissolvent /dɪˈzɒlv(ə)nt/ *adj. & n.* ● *adj.* tending to dissolve or dissipate. ● *n.* a dissolvent substance. [Latin *dissolvere* (as DISSOLVE)]

dissonant /ˈdɪs(ə)nənt/ *adj.* **1** *Mus.* harsh-toned; inharmonious. **2** incongruous; clashing. □ **dissonance** *n.* **dissonantly** *adv.* [Middle English from Old French *dissonant* or Latin *dissonare* (as DIS-, *sonare* 'sound')]

dissuade /dɪˈsweɪd/ *v.tr.* (often foll. by *from*) discourage (a person); persuade against (*dissuaded him from continuing*; *was dissuaded from his belief*). □ **dissuader** *n.* **dissuasion** /-ˈsweɪʒ(ə)n/ *n.* **dissuasive** /-ˈsweɪsɪv/ *adj.* [Latin *dissuadēre* (as DIS-, *suadēre suas-* 'persuade')]

dissyllable var. of DISYLLABLE.

dissymmetry /dɪˈsɪmɪtri/ *n.* (*pl.* **-ies**) **1 a** lack of symmetry. **b** an instance of this. **2** symmetry as of mirror images or the left and right hands (esp. of crystals with two corresponding forms). □ **dissymmetrical** /-ˈmɛtrɪk(ə)l/ *adj.*

distaff /ˈdɪstɑːf/ *n.* **1 a** a cleft stick holding wool or flax wound for spinning by hand. **b** the corresponding part of a spinning wheel. **2** women's work. [Old English *distæf* (as STAFF[1]), the first element being apparently related to Low German *diesse*, Middle Low German *dise(ne)* 'bunch of flax']

distaff side *n.* the female side or members of a family etc. (opp. SPEAR SIDE).

distal /ˈdɪst(ə)l/ *adj. Anat.* situated away from the centre of the body or point of attachment (opp. PROXIMAL). □ **distally** *adv.* [DISTANT + -AL]

distance /ˈdɪst(ə)ns/ *n. & v.* ● *n.* **1** the condition of being far off; remoteness. **2 a** a space or interval between two things. **b** the length of this (*a distance of twenty miles*). **3** a distant point or place (*came from a distance*). **4** the avoidance of familiarity; aloofness; reserve (*there was a certain distance between them*). **5** a remoter field of vision (*saw him in the distance*). **6** an interval of time (*can't remember what happened at this distance*). **7 a** the full length of a race etc. **b** *Brit. Racing* a length of 240 yards from the winning post on a racecourse. **c** *Boxing* the scheduled length of a fight. ● *v.tr.* (often *refl.*) **1** place far off (*distanced herself from them*; *distanced the painful memory*). **2** leave far behind in a race or competition. □ **at a distance** far off. **go the distance 1** *Boxing* complete a fight without being knocked out. **2** complete, esp. a hard task; endure an ordeal. **keep one's distance** maintain one's reserve. **within hailing** (or **walking**) **distance** near enough to reach by hailing or walking. [Middle English via Old French *distance*, *destance* from Latin *distantia*, from *distare* 'stand apart' (as DI-[2], *stare* 'stand')]

distance learning *n.* education by correspondence course or from broadcasts, telephone tutorials, etc.

distance post *n.* a post at the distance on a racecourse, used to disqualify runners who have not reached it by the end of the race.

distance runner *n.* an athlete who competes in long- or middle-distance races.

distant /ˈdɪst(ə)nt/ *adj.* **1 a** far away in space or time. **b** (usu. *predic.*; often foll. by *from*) at a specified distance (*three miles distant from them*). **2** remote or far apart in position, time, resemblance, etc. (*a distant prospect*; *a distant relation*; *a distant likeness*). **3** not intimate; reserved; cool (*a distant nod*). **4** remote; abstracted (*a distant stare*). **5** faint, vague (*he was a distant memory to her*). □ **distantly** *adv.* [Middle English from Old French *distant* or Latin *distant-*, part. stem of *distare*: see DISTANCE]

distant early warning *n.* a radar system in North America for the early detection of a missile attack.

distant signal *n. Brit.* a railway signal preceding a home signal to give warning.

distaste /dɪsˈteɪst/ *n.* (usu. foll. by *for*) dislike; repugnance; aversion, esp. slight (*a distaste for prunes*; *a distaste for polite company*). ▫ **distasteful** *adj.* **distastefully** *adv.* **distastefulness** *n.*

distemper[1] /dɪˈstɛmpə/ *n. & v.* ● *n.* **1** *Brit.* a kind of paint using glue or size instead of an oil-base, for use on walls or for scene-painting. **2** a method of mural and poster painting using this. ● *v.tr. Brit.* paint (walls etc.) with distemper. [earlier as verb, in the sense 'dilute, steep': from Old French *destremper* or Late Latin *distemperare* 'soak, macerate': see DISTEMPER[2]]

distemper[2] /dɪˈstɛmpə/ *n.* **1** a viral disease of some animals, esp. dogs, causing fever, coughing, and catarrh. **2** *archaic* political disorder. [earlier as verb, in the sense 'upset, derange': Middle English from Late Latin *distemperare* (as DIS-, *temperare* 'mingle correctly')]

distend /dɪˈstɛnd/ *v.tr. & intr.* swell out by pressure from within (*distended stomach*). ▫ **distensible** /-ˈstɛnsɪb(ə)l/ *adj.* **distensibility** /-ˈbɪlɪti/ *n.* **distension** /-ˈstɛnʃ(ə)n/ *n.* [Middle English from Latin *distendere* (as DIS-, *tendere tens-* 'stretch')]

distich /ˈdɪstɪk/ *n. Prosody* a pair of verse lines; a couplet. [Latin *distichon* from Greek *distikhon* (as DI-[1], *stikhos* 'line')]

distichous /ˈdɪstɪkəs/ *adj. Bot.* arranged in two opposite vertical rows. [Latin *distichus* (as DISTICH)]

distil /dɪˈstɪl/ *v.* (*US* **distill**) (**distilled**, **distilling**) **1** *tr. Chem.* purify (a liquid) by vaporizing it with heat, then condensing it with cold and collecting the resulting liquid. **2** *tr.* **a** *Chem.* extract the essence of (a plant etc.) usu. by heating it in a solvent. **b** extract the essential meaning or implications of (an idea etc.). **3** *tr.* make (whisky, essence, etc.) by distilling raw materials. **4** *tr.* (foll. by *off*, *out*) *Chem.* drive (a volatile constituent) off or out by heat. **5** *tr. & intr.* come as or give forth in drops; exude. **6** *intr.* undergo distillation. ▫ **distillatory** *adj.* [Middle English from Latin *distillare*, from *destillare* (as DE-, *stilla* 'drop')]

distillate /ˈdɪstɪleɪt/ *n.* a product of distillation.

distillation /dɪstɪˈleɪʃ(ə)n/ *n.* **1** the process of distilling or being distilled (in various senses). **2** something distilled.

distiller /dɪˈstɪlə/ *n.* a person who distils, esp. a manufacturer of alcoholic liquor.

distillery /dɪˈstɪləri/ *n.* (*pl.* **-ies**) a place where alcoholic liquor is distilled.

distinct /dɪˈstɪŋ(k)t/ *adj.* **1** (often foll. by *from*) **a** not identical; separate; individual. **b** different in kind or quality; unlike. **2 a** clearly perceptible; plain. **b** clearly understandable; definite. **3** unmistakable, decided (*had a distinct impression of being watched*). ▫ **distinctly** *adv.* **distinctness** *n.* [Middle English from Latin *distinctus*, past part. of *distinguere* DISTINGUISH]

▪ **Usage** *Distinct* is sometimes confused with *distinctive*. Note the difference in sense between *There was a distinct smell of soap in the bathroom* (an unmistakable, clearly perceptible smell), and *The hall had its own distinctive smell of polish* (a characteristic smell).

distinction /dɪˈstɪŋ(k)ʃ(ə)n/ *n.* **1 a** the act or an instance of discriminating or distinguishing. **b** the difference made by distinguishing. **2 a** something that differentiates, e.g. a mark, name, or title. **b** the fact of being different. **3** special consideration or honour. **4** distinguished character; excellence; eminence (*a film of distinction*; *shows distinction in his bearing*). **5** a grade in an examination denoting great excellence (*passed with distinction*). ▫ **distinction without a difference** a merely nominal or artificial distinction. [Middle English via Old French from Latin *distinctio -onis* (as DISTINGUISH)]

distinctive /dɪˈstɪŋ(k)tɪv/ *adj.* distinguishing, characteristic. ▫ **distinctively** *adv.* **distinctiveness** *n.*

▪ **Usage** See Usage Note at DISTINCT.

distingué /dɪˈstaŋgeɪ, French distɛ̃ge/ *adj.* (*fem.* ***distinguée*** *pronunc.* same) having a distinguished air, features, manner, etc. [French, past part. of *distinguer*: see DISTINGUISH]

distinguish /dɪˈstɪŋgwɪʃ/ *v.* **1** *tr.* (often foll. by *from*) **a** see or point out the difference of; draw distinctions between (*cannot distinguish one from the other*). **b** constitute such a difference (*the mole distinguishes him from his twin*). **c** treat as different; differentiate (*do not distinguish the mind from the body*). **2** *tr.* be a mark or property of; characterize (*distinguished by his greed*). **3** *tr.* discover by listening, looking, etc. (*could distinguish two voices*). **4** *tr.* (usu. *refl.*; often foll. by *by*) make prominent or noteworthy (*distinguished himself by winning first prize*). **5** *tr.* (often foll. by *into*) divide; classify. **6** *intr.* (foll. by *between*) make or point out a difference between. ▫ **distinguishable** *adj.* [French *distinguer* or Latin *distinguere* (as DIS-, *stinguere stinct-* 'extinguish'): cf. EXTINGUISH]

distinguished /dɪˈstɪŋgwɪʃt/ *adj.* **1** (often foll. by *for*, *by*) of high standing; eminent; famous. **2** = DISTINGUÉ.

distort /dɪˈstɔːt/ *v.tr.* **1 a** put out of shape; make crooked or unshapely. **b** distort the appearance of, esp. by curved mirrors etc. **2** misrepresent (motives, facts, statements, etc.). **3** change the form of (an electrical signal) during transmission, amplification, etc. ▫ **distortedly** *adv.* **distortedness** *n.* [Latin *distorquēre distort-* (as DIS-, *torquēre* 'twist')]

distortion /dɪˈstɔːʃ(ə)n/ *n.* **1** the act or an instance of distorting; the process of being distorted. **2** *Electronics* a change in the form of a signal during transmission etc. usu. with some impairment of quality. ▫ **distortional** *adj.* **distortionless** *adj.* [Latin *distortio* (as DISTORT)]

distract /dɪˈstrakt/ *v.tr.* **1** (often foll. by *from*) draw away the attention of (a person, the mind, etc.). **2** bewilder, perplex. **3** (as **distracted** *adj.*) troubled or distraught (*distracted by grief*; *distracted with worry*). **4** amuse, esp. in order to take the attention from pain or worry. ▫ **distractedly** *adv.* **distractor** *n.* [Middle English from Latin *distrahere distract-* (as DIS-, *trahere* 'draw')]

distraction /dɪˈstrakʃ(ə)n/ *n.* **1 a** the act of distracting, esp. the mind. **b** something that distracts; an interruption. **2** a relaxation from work; an amusement. **3** a lack of concentration. **4** confusion; perplexity. **5** frenzy; madness. ▫ **to distraction** almost to a state of madness. [Middle English from Old French *distraction* or Latin *distractio* (as DISTRACT)]

distrain /dɪˈstreɪn/ *v.intr.* (usu. foll. by *upon*) *Law* impose distraint (on a person, goods, etc.). ▫ **distrainer** *n.* **distrainment** *n.* **distrainor** *n.* [Middle English via Old French *destreindre* from Latin *distringere* (as DIS-, *stringere strict-* 'draw tight')]

distraint /dɪˈstreɪnt/ *n. Law* the seizure of chattels to make a person pay rent etc. or meet an obligation, or to obtain satisfaction by their sale. [DISTRAIN, on the pattern of *constraint*]

distrait /dɪˈstreɪ, ˈdɪstreɪ/ *adj.* (*fem.* **distraite** /-ˈstreɪt/) not paying attention; absent-minded; distraught. [Middle English from Old French *destrait*, past part. of *destraire* (as DISTRACT)]

distraught /dɪˈstrɔːt/ *adj.* distracted with worry, fear, etc.; extremely agitated. [Middle English, alteration of obsolete *distract* (*adj.*) (as DISTRACT), influenced by *straught*, obsolete past part. of STRETCH]

distress /dɪˈstrɛs/ *n. & v.* ● *n.* **1** severe pain, sorrow, anguish, etc. **2** the lack of money or comforts. **3** *Law* = DISTRAINT. **4** breathlessness; exhaustion. ● *v.tr.* **1** subject to distress; exhaust, afflict. **2** cause anxiety to; make unhappy; vex. ▫ **in distress 1** suffering or in danger. **2** (of a ship, aircraft, etc.) in danger or damaged. ▫ **distressful** *adj.* **distressingly** *adv.* [Middle English via Old French *destresse* etc., Anglo-French *destresser*, Old French *-ecier* from Gallo-Roman (as DISTRAIN)]

distressed /dɪˈstrɛst/ *adj.* **1** suffering from distress. **2** impoverished (*distressed gentlefolk*; *in distressed* *circumstances*). **3** (of furniture, leather, etc.) having simulated marks of age and wear.

distressed area *n.* a region of high unemployment and poverty.

distress signal *n.* a signal from a ship in danger.

distress warrant *n.* a warrant authorizing distraint.

distributary /dɪ'strɪbjʊt(ə)ri/ *n.* (*pl.* **-ies**) a branch of a river or glacier that does not return to the main stream after leaving it (as in a delta).

distribute /dɪ'strɪbju:t, *disp.* 'dɪstrɪbju:t/ *v.tr.* **1** give shares of; deal out. **2** spread about; scatter (*distributed the seeds evenly over the garden*). **3** divide into parts; arrange; classify. **4** *Printing* separate (type that has been set up) and return the characters to their separate boxes. **5** *Logic* use (a term) to include every individual of the class to which it refers. ▫ **distributable** *adj.* [Middle English from Latin *distribuere distribut-* (as DIS-, *tribuere* 'assign')]

■ **Usage** The second pronunciation given, with the stress on the first syllable, is considered incorrect by some people.

distributed system *n.* a number of independent computers linked by a network.

distribution /dɪstrɪ'bju:ʃ(ə)n/ *n.* **1** the act or an instance of distributing; the process of being distributed. **2** *Econ.* **a** the dispersal of goods etc. among consumers, brought about by commerce. **b** the extent to which different groups, classes, or individuals share in the total production or wealth of a community. **3** *Statistics* the way in which a characteristic is spread over members of a class. ▫ **distributional** *adj.* [Middle English from Old French *distribution* or Latin *distributio* (as DISTRIBUTE)]

distributive /dɪ'strɪbjʊtɪv/ *adj.* & *n.* ● *adj.* **1** of, concerned with, or produced by distribution. **2** *Logic* & *Gram.* (of a pronoun etc.) referring to each individual of a class, not to the class collectively (e.g. *each*, *either*). ● *n. Gram.* a distributive word. ▫ **distributively** *adv.* [Middle English from French *distributif -ive* or Late Latin *distributivus* (as DISTRIBUTE)]

distributor /dɪ'strɪbjʊtə/ *n.* **1** a person or thing that distributes. **2** an agent who supplies goods. **3** *Electr.* a device in an internal-combustion engine for passing current to each spark plug in turn.

district /'dɪstrɪkt/ *n.* & *v.* ● *n.* **1 a** (often *attrib.*) a territory marked off for special administrative etc. purposes. **b** *Brit.* a division of a county or region electing its own councillors. **2** an area which has common characteristics; a region (*the wine-growing district*). ● *v.tr. US* divide into districts. [French from medieval Latin *districtus* '(territory of) jurisdiction' (as DISTRAIN)]

district attorney *n.* (in the US) the prosecuting officer of a district.

district court *n.* (in the US) the federal or state court of first instance.

district heating *n.* a supply of heat or hot water from one source to a district or a group of buildings.

district nurse *n. Brit.* a peripatetic nurse serving a rural or urban area.

district visitor *n. Brit.* a person working for a member of the clergy in a section of a parish.

distrust /dɪs'trʌst/ *n.* & *v.* ● *n.* a lack of trust; doubt; suspicion. ● *v.tr.* have no trust or confidence in; doubt. ▫ **distruster** *n.* **distrustful** *adj.* **distrustfully** *adv.*

disturb /dɪ'stə:b/ *v.tr.* **1** break the rest, calm, or quiet of; interrupt. **2** agitate; worry (*your story disturbs me*). **3** move from a settled position, disarrange (*the papers had been disturbed*). **4** (as **disturbed** *adj.*) *Psychol.* emotionally or mentally unstable or abnormal. ▫ **disturber** *n.* **disturbing** *adj.* **disturbingly** *adv.* [Middle English via Old French *desto(u)rber* from Latin *disturbare* (as DIS-, *turbare* from *turba* 'tumult')]

disturbance /dɪ'stə:b(ə)ns/ *n.* **1** the act or an instance of disturbing; the process of being disturbed. **2** a tumult; an uproar. **3** agitation; worry. **4** an interruption. **5** *Law* interference with rights or property; molestation. [Middle English from Old French *desto(u)rbance* (as DISTURB)]

disulphide /dʌɪ'sʌlfʌɪd/ *n.* (*US* **disulfide**) *Chem.* a binary chemical containing two atoms of sulphur in each molecule.

disunion /dɪs'ju:njən, -ɪən/ *n.* a lack of union; separation; dissension. ▫ **disunite** /-'nʌɪt/ *v.tr.* & *intr.* **disunity** *n.*

disuse *n.* & *v.* ● *n.* /dɪs'ju:s/ **1** lack of use or practice; discontinuance. **2** a disused state. ● *v.tr.* /dɪs'ju:z/ cease to use. ▫ **fall into disuse** cease to be used. [Middle English from Old French *desuser* (as DIS-, USE)]

disutility /dɪsju:'tɪlɪti/ *n.* (*pl.* **-ies**) **1** harmfulness, injuriousness. **2** a factor tending to nullify the utility of something; a drawback.

disyllable /dʌɪ'sɪləb(ə)l, dɪ-, 'dʌɪsɪl-/ *n.* (also **dissyllable** /dɪ'sɪl-/) *Prosody* a word or metrical foot of two syllables. ▫ **disyllabic** /-'labɪk/ *adj.* [French *disyllabe* via Latin *disyllabus* from Greek *disullabos* (as DI-[1], SYLLABLE)]

dit /dɪt/ *n.* (in the Morse system) = DOT[1] *n.* 3 (cf. DAH). [imitative]

ditch /dɪtʃ/ *n.* & *v.* ● *n.* **1** a long narrow excavated channel esp. for drainage or to mark a boundary. **2** a watercourse, stream, etc. ● *v.* **1** *intr.* make or repair ditches (*hedging and ditching*). **2** *tr.* provide with ditches; drain. **3** *tr. colloq.* leave in the lurch; abandon. **4** *tr. colloq.* **a** bring (an aircraft) down on the sea in an emergency. **b** drive (a vehicle) into a ditch. **5** *intr. colloq.* (of an aircraft) make a forced landing on the sea. **6** *tr. US* derail (a train). ▫ **ditcher** *n.* [Old English *dīc*, of unknown origin: cf. DYKE[1]]

ditchwater /'dɪtʃwɔ:tə/ *n.* stagnant water in a ditch. ▫ **dull as ditchwater** extremely dull.

ditheism /'dʌɪθi:ɪz(ə)m/ *n. Theol.* **1** a belief in two gods; dualism. **2** a belief in equal independent ruling principles of good and evil. ▫ **ditheist** *n.*

dither /'dɪðə/ *v.* & *n.* ● *v.intr.* **1** hesitate; be indecisive. **2** *dial.* tremble; quiver. ● *n. colloq.* **1** a state of agitation or apprehension. **2** a state of hesitation; indecisiveness. ▫ **all of a dither** *colloq.* in a state of extreme agitation or vacillation. ▫ **ditherer** *n.* **dithery** *adj.* [variant of dialect *didder* related to DODDER[1]]

dithyramb /'dɪθɪram(b)/ *n.* **1 a** a wild choral hymn in ancient Greece, esp. to Dionysus. **b** a Bacchanalian song. **2** a passionate or inflated poem, speech, etc. ▫ **dithyrambic** /-'rambɪk/ *adj.* [Latin *dithyrambus* from Greek *dithurambos*, of unknown origin]

ditsy var. of DITZY.

dittany /'dɪtəni/ *n.* (*pl.* **-ies**) **1 a** (in full **dittany of Crete**) a dwarf shrub, *Origanum dictamnus* (mint family), with woolly leaves. **b** *US* a similar herb, *Cunila origanoides*. **2** = FRAXINELLA. [Middle English via Old French *dita(i)n*, medieval Latin *dictamus*, and Latin *dictamnus* from Greek *diktamnon*, perhaps from *Diktē*, the name of a mountain in Crete]

ditto /'dɪtəʊ/ *n.* & *v.* ● *n.* (*pl.* **-os**) **1** (in accounts, inventories, lists, etc.) the aforesaid, the same. **2** *colloq.* (replacing a word or phrase to avoid repetition) the same (*came in late last night and ditto the night before*). **3** a similar thing; a duplicate. ● *v.tr.* (**-oes, -oed**) repeat (another's action or words). ▫ **say ditto to** *colloq.* agree with; endorse. [Italian dialect from Latin *dictus*, past part. of *dicere* 'say']

■ **Usage** In sense 1, the word *ditto* is often replaced by ditto marks under the word or sum to be repeated.

dittography /dɪ'tɒgrəfi/ *n.* (*pl.* **-ies**) **1** a copyist's mistaken repetition of a letter, word, or phrase. **2** an example of this. ▫ **dittographic** /-'grafɪk/ *adj.* [Greek *dittos* 'double' + -GRAPHY]

ditto marks *n.pl.* two commas („) etc. representing 'ditto'.

ditty /'dɪti/ *n.* (*pl.* **-ies**) a short simple song. [Middle English via Old French *dité* 'composition' from Latin *dictatum*, neut. past part. of *dictare* DICTATE]

ditty bag /'dɪti/ *n.* (also **ditty box**) a sailor's or fisherman's receptacle for odds and ends. [19th c.: origin unknown]

ditzy /'dɪtsi/ *adj.* (also **ditsy**) *N. Amer. slang* **1 a** silly or foolish. **b** conceited. **2** cute. **3** (of a thing) fussy, intricate. [20th c.: origin unknown]

diuresis /dʌɪjʊ(ə)'ri:sɪs/ *n. Med.* increased excretion of urine, esp. in excess. [modern Latin from Greek (as DI-[3], *ourēsis* 'urination')]

diuretic /dʌɪjʊ(ə)'rɛtɪk/ *adj.* & *n.* ● *adj.* causing increased output of urine. ● *n.* a diuretic drug. [Middle English via Old French *diuretique* or Late Latin *diureticus* from Greek *diourētikos*, from *dioureō* 'urinate']

diurnal /dʌɪ'ə:n(ə)l/ *adj.* **1** of or during the day; not nocturnal. **2** daily; of each day. **3** *Astron.* occupying one day. **4** *Zool.* (of animals) active in the daytime. **5** *Bot.* (of plants) open only during the day. ▫ **diurnally** *adv.* [Middle English via Late Latin *diurnalis* from Latin *diurnus*, from *dies* 'day']

Div. *abbr.* Division.

diva /'di:və/ *n.* (*pl.* **divas**) a great or famous woman singer; a prima donna. [Italian from Latin, = goddess]

divagate /'dʌɪvəgeɪt/ *v.intr. literary* stray; digress. ▫ **divagation** /-'geɪʃ(ə)n/ *n.* [Latin *divagari* (as DI-[2], *vagari* 'wander')]

divalent /dʌɪ'veɪl(ə)nt/ *adj. Chem.* having a valency of two.

divan /dɪ'van, dʌɪ'van, 'dʌɪvan/ *n.* **1 a** a long, low, backless sofa. **b** a bed consisting of a base and mattress, usu. without a board at either end. **2** an oriental State legislative body, council chamber, or court of justice. **3** *archaic* **a** a cigar shop. **b** a smoking room attached to such a shop. [French *divan* or Italian *divano* via Turkish *dīvān* and Arabic *dīwān* from Persian *dīvān* 'anthology, register, court, bench']

divaricate /dʌɪ'varɪkeɪt, dɪ-/ *v.intr.* diverge, branch; separate widely. ▫ **divaricate** /-kət/ *adj.* **divarication** /-'keɪʃ(ə)n/ *n.* [Latin *divaricare* (as DI-[2], *varicus* 'straddling')]

dive /dʌɪv/ *v.* & *n.* ● *v.* (*past* and *past part.* **dived** or *US* also **dove** /dəʊv/) **1** *intr.* plunge head first into water, esp. as a sport. **2** *intr.* **a** *Aeron.* (of an aircraft) plunge steeply downwards at speed. **b** *Naut.* (of a submarine) submerge. **c** (of a person) plunge downwards. **3** *intr.* (foll. by *into*) *colloq.* **a** put one's hand into (a pocket, handbag, container, etc.) quickly and deeply. **b** occupy oneself suddenly and enthusiastically with (a subject, meal, etc.). **4** *tr.* (foll. by *into*) plunge (a hand etc.) into. ● *n.* **1** an act of diving; a plunge. **2 a** the submerging of a submarine. **b** the steep descent of an aircraft. **3** a sudden darting movement. **4** *colloq.* a disreputable nightclub etc.; a drinking den (*found themselves in a low dive*). **5** *Boxing slang* a pretended knockout (*took a dive in the second round*). ▫ **dive in** *colloq.* help oneself (to food). [Old English *dūfan* (*v.intr.*) 'dive, sink', and *dȳfan* (*v.tr.*) 'immerse', from Germanic: related to DEEP, DIP]

dive-bomb *v.tr.* bomb (a target) while diving in an aircraft. ▫ **dive-bomber** *n.*

diver /'dʌɪvə/ *n.* **1** a person who dives. **2 a** a person who wears a diving suit to work under water for long periods. **b** a pearl-diver etc. **3** any large waterbird of the family Gaviidae, with a straight, sharply pointed bill; also called LOON.

diverge /dʌɪ'və:dʒ, dɪ-/ *v.* **1** *intr.* **a** proceed in a different direction or in different directions from a point (*diverging rays*; *the path diverges here*). **b** take a different course or different courses (*their interests diverged*). **2** *intr.* **a** (often foll. by *from*) depart from a set course (*diverged from the track*; *diverged from his parents' wishes*). **b** differ markedly (*they diverged as to the best course*). **3** *tr.* cause to diverge; deflect. **4** *intr. Math.* (of a series) increase indefinitely as more of its terms are added. [medieval Latin *divergere* (as DI-[2], Latin *vergere* 'incline')]

divergent /dʌɪ'və:dʒ(ə)nt, dɪ-/ *adj.* **1** diverging. **2** *Psychol.* (of thought) tending to reach a variety of possible solutions when analysing a problem. **3** *Math.* (of a series) increasing indefinitely as more of its terms are added; not convergent. ▫ **divergence** *n.* **divergency** *n.* **divergently** *adv.*

divers /'dʌɪvəz/ *adj. archaic* or *literary* more than one; sundry; several. [Middle English via Old French from Latin *diversus* DIVERSE (as DI-[2], *versus*, past part. of *vertere* 'turn')]

diverse /dʌɪ'və:s, 'dʌɪvə:s/ *adj.* unlike in nature or qualities; varied. ▫ **diversely** *adv.* [Middle English (as DIVERS)]

diversify /dʌɪ'və:sɪfʌɪ, dɪ-/ *v.* (**-ies**, **-ied**) **1** *tr.* make diverse; vary; modify. **2** *tr. Commerce* **a** spread (investment) over several enterprises or products, esp. to reduce the risk of loss. **b** introduce a spread of investment in (an enterprise etc.). **3** *intr.* (often foll. by *into*) esp. *Commerce* (of a firm etc.) expand the range of products handled. ▫ **diversification** /-fɪ'keɪʃ(ə)n/ *n.* [Middle English via Old French *diversifier* from medieval Latin *diversificare* (as DIVERS)]

diversion /dʌɪ'və:ʃ(ə)n, dɪ-/ *n.* **1 a** the act of diverting; deviation. **b** an instance of this. **2 a** the diverting of attention deliberately. **b** a stratagem for this purpose (*created a diversion to secure their escape*). **3** a recreation or pastime. **4** *Brit.* an alternative route when a road is temporarily closed to traffic. ▫ **diversional** *adj.* **diversionary** *adj.* [Late Latin *diversio* (as DIVERT)]

diversionist /dʌɪ'və:ʃ(ə)nɪst, dɪ-/ *n.* **1** a person who engages in disruptive or subversive activities. **2** *Polit.* (esp. used by communists) a conspirator against the State; a saboteur.

diversity /dʌɪ'və:sɪti, dɪ-/ *n.* (*pl.* **-ies**) **1** being diverse; variety. **2** a different kind; a variety. [Middle English via Old French *diversité* from Latin *diversitas -tatis* (as DIVERS)]

divert /dʌɪ'və:t, dɪ-/ *v.tr.* **1** (often foll. by *from*, *to*) **a** turn aside; deflect. **b** draw the attention of; distract. **2** (often as **diverting** *adj.*) entertain; amuse. ▫ **divertingly** *adv.* [Middle English via French *divertir* from Latin *divertere* (as DI-[2], *vertere* 'turn')]

diverticular /dʌɪvə'tɪkjʊlə/ *adj. Med.* of or relating to a diverticulum.

diverticular disease *n.* a condition with abdominal pain as a result of muscle spasms in the presence of diverticula.

diverticulitis /ˌdʌɪvətɪkjʊ'lʌɪtɪs/ *n. Med.* inflammation of a diverticulum.

diverticulum /dʌɪvə'tɪkjʊləm/ *n.* (*pl.* **diverticula** /-lə/) *Anat.* a blind tube formed in a cavity or passage, esp. an abnormal one in the alimentary tract. ▫ **diverticulosis** /-'ləʊsɪs/ *n.* [medieval Latin, variant of Latin *deverticulum* 'byway' from *devertere* (as DE-, *vertere* 'turn')]

divertimento /dɪˌvə:tɪ'mɛntəʊ, -ˌvɛ:t-/ *n.* (*pl.* **divertimenti** /-ti/ or **-os**) *Mus.* a light and entertaining composition, often in the form of a suite for chamber orchestra. [Italian, = diversion]

divertissement /dɪv'ə:tɪsmənt, di:vɛ:'ti:smɒ̃/ *n.* **1** a diversion; an entertainment. **2** a short ballet etc. between acts or longer pieces. [French, from *divertiss-*, stem of *divertir* DIVERT]

Dives /'dʌɪvi:z/ *n.* a rich man. [Latin, in Vulgate translation of the Bible, Luke 16]

divest /dʌɪ'vɛst, dɪ-/ *v.tr.* (usu. foll. by *of*; often *refl.*) **1** unclothe; strip (*divested himself of his jacket*). **2** deprive, dispossess; free, rid (*cannot divest himself of the idea*). ▫ **divestment** *n.* **divesture** *n.* [earlier *devest* from Old French *desvestir* etc. (as DIS-, Latin *vestire* from *vestis* 'garment')]

divi var. of DIVVY[1].

divide /dɪ'vʌɪd/ *v.* & *n.* ● *v.* **1** *tr.* & *intr.* (often foll. by *in*, *into*) separate or be separated into parts; break up; split (*the river divides into two*; *the road divides*; *divided them into three groups*). **2** *tr.* & *intr.* (often foll. by *out*) distribute; deal; share (*divided it out between them*). **3** *tr.* **a** cut off; separate; part (*divide the sheep from the goats*). **b** mark out into parts (*a ruler divided into inches*). **c** specify different kinds of, classify (*people can be divided into two types*). **4** *tr.* cause to disagree; set at variance (*religion divided them*). **5** *Math.* **a** *tr.* find how many times (a number) contains another (*divide 20 by 4*). **b** *intr.* (of a number) be contained in (a number) without a remainder (*4 divides into 20*). **c** *intr.* be susceptible of division (*10 divides by 2 and 5*). **d** *tr.* find how many times (a number) is contained in another (*divide 4 into 20*). **6** *intr. Math.* do division (*can divide well*). **7** *Parl.* **a** *intr.* (of a legislative assembly etc.) part into two groups for voting (*the House divided*). **b** *tr.* so part (a Parliament etc.) for voting. ● *n.* **1** a dividing or boundary line (*the divide between rich and poor*). **2** *Geog.* a watershed. □ **divided against itself** formed into factions. **divide and rule** maintain supremacy by preventing opponents from joining forces. [Middle English from Latin *dividere divis-* (as DI-², *vid-* 'separate')]

divided highway *n. N. Amer.* a dual carriageway.

divided skirt *n.* culottes.

dividend /ˈdɪvɪdɛnd/ *n.* **1 a** a sum of money to be divided among a number of persons, esp. that paid by a company to shareholders. **b** a similar sum payable to winners in a football pool, to members of a cooperative, or to creditors of an insolvent estate. **c** an individual's share of a dividend. **2** *Math.* a number to be divided by a divisor. **3** a benefit from any action (*their long training paid dividends*). [Anglo-French *dividende* from Latin *dividendum* (as DIVIDE)]

dividend-stripping *n. Brit.* the evasion of tax on dividends by arrangement between the company liable to pay tax and another able to claim repayment of tax.

dividend warrant *n. Brit.* the documentary authority for a shareholder to receive a dividend.

dividend yield *n.* a dividend expressed as a percentage of a current share price.

divider /dɪˈvʌɪdə/ *n.* **1** a screen, piece of furniture, etc., dividing a room into two parts. **2** (in *pl.*) a measuring compass, esp. with a screw for setting small intervals.

divi-divi /ˈdɪvɪˌdɪvi/ *n.* (*pl.* **divi-divis**) **1** a small tree, *Caesalpinia coriaria*, native to tropical America, bearing curved pods. **2** this pod used as a source of tannin. [Carib]

divination /dɪvɪˈneɪʃ(ə)n/ *n.* **1** supposed insight into the future or the unknown gained by supernatural means. **2 a** a skilful and accurate forecast. **b** a good guess. □ **divinatory** *adj.* [Middle English from Old French *divination* or Latin *divinatio* (as DIVINE)]

divine /dɪˈvʌɪn/ *adj., v., & n.* ● *adj.* (**diviner, divinest**) **1 a** of, from, or like God or a god. **b** devoted to God; sacred (*divine service*). **2 a** more than humanly excellent, gifted, or beautiful. **b** *colloq.* excellent; delightful. ● *v.* **1** *tr.* discover by guessing, intuition, inspiration, or magic. **2** *tr.* foresee, predict, conjecture. **3** *intr.* practise divination. ● *n.* **1** a cleric, usu. an expert in theology. **2** (**the Divine**) providence or God. □ **divinely** *adv.* **divineness** *n.* **diviner** *n.* **divinize** /ˈdɪvɪ-/ *v.tr.* (also **-ise**). [Middle English via Old French *devin -ine* from Latin *divinus*, from *divus* 'godlike']

divine office see OFFICE 10b.

divine right of kings *n.* the doctrine that kings derive their sovereignty and authority from God, not from their subjects.

diving beetle *n.* a predatory water beetle of the family Dytiscidae which stores air under the elytra while diving.

diving bell *n.* an open-bottomed box or bell, supplied with air, in which a person can descend into deep water.

diving board *n.* an elevated board used for diving from.

diving duck *n.* a duck that habitually dives for food, esp. one of the tribe Aythyini, which includes the pochard, scaup, etc.

diving suit *n.* a watertight suit usu. with a helmet and an air supply, worn for working under water.

divining rod *n.* = DOWSING ROD.

divinity /dɪˈvɪnɪti/ *n.* (*pl.* **-ies**) **1** the state or quality of being divine. **2 a** a god; a divine being. **b** (as **the Divinity**) God. **3** the study of religion; theology. [Middle English via Old French *divinité* from Latin *divinitas -tatis* (as DIVINE)]

divisible /dɪˈvɪzɪb(ə)l/ *adj.* **1** capable of being divided, physically or mentally. **2** (foll. by *by*) *Math.* containing (a number) a number of times without a remainder (*15 is divisible by 3 and 5*). □ **divisibility** /-ˈbɪlɪti/ *n.* [French *divisible* or Late Latin *divisibilis* (as DIVIDE)]

division /dɪˈvɪʒ(ə)n/ *n.* **1** the act or an instance of dividing; the process of being divided. **2** *Math.* the process of dividing one number by another (see also LONG DIVISION, SHORT DIVISION). **3** disagreement or discord (*division of opinion*). **4** *Parl.* the separation of members of a legislative body into two sets for counting votes for and against. **5** one of two or more parts into which a thing is divided. **6** a major unit of administration or organization, esp.: **a** a group of army brigades or regiments. **b** *Sport* a grouping of teams within a league, *Brit.* usu. by ability. **7 a** a district defined for administrative purposes. **b** *Brit.* a part of a county or borough returning a Member of Parliament. **8 a** *Bot.* a major taxonomic grouping. **b** *Zool.* a subsidiary category between major levels of classification. **9** *Logic* a classification of kinds, parts, or senses. □ **division of labour** the improvement of efficiency by giving different parts of a manufacturing process etc. to different people. □ **divisional** *adj.* **divisionally** *adv.* **divisionary** *adj.* [Middle English via Old French *divisiun* from Latin *divisio -onis* (as DIVIDE)]

divisionalize /dɪˈvɪʒ(ə)n(ə)lʌɪz/ *v.tr.* (also **-ise**) (also *absol.*) organize (a company etc.) into separate divisions. □ **divisionalization** /-ˈzeɪʃ(ə)n/ *n.*

division sign *n.* the sign (÷) indicating that one quantity is to be divided by another.

divisive /dɪˈvʌɪsɪv/ *adj.* tending to divide, esp. in opinion; causing disagreement. □ **divisively** *adv.* **divisiveness** *n.* [Late Latin *divisivus* (as DIVIDE)]

divisor /dɪˈvʌɪzə/ *n. Math.* **1** a number by which another is to be divided. **2** a number that divides another without a remainder. [Middle English from French *diviseur* or Latin *divisor* (as DIVIDE)]

divorce /dɪˈvɔːs/ *n. & v.* ● *n.* **1 a** the legal dissolution of a marriage. **b** a legal decree of this. **2** a severance or separation (*a divorce between thought and feeling*). ● *v.* **1 a** *tr.* (usu. as **divorced** *adj.*) (often foll. by *from*) legally dissolve the marriage of (*a divorced couple*; *he wants to get divorced from her*). **b** *intr.* separate by divorce (*they divorced last year*). **c** *tr.* end one's marriage with (*divorced him for neglect*). **2** *tr.* (often foll. by *from*) detach, separate (*divorced from reality*). **3** *tr. archaic* dissolve (a union). □ **divorcement** *n.* [Middle English via Old French *divorce* (*n.*), *divorcer* (*v.*) and Late Latin *divortiare* from Latin *divortium*, from *divortere* (as DI-², *vertere* 'turn')]

divorcee /dɪvɔːˈsiː/ *n.* (*US masc.* **divorcé**, *fem.* **divorcée** /-ˈseɪ/) a divorced person.

divot /ˈdɪvət/ *n.* **1** a piece of turf cut out by a golf club in making a stroke. **2** esp. *Sc.* a piece of turf; a sod. [16th c.: origin unknown]

divulge /dʌɪˈvʌldʒ, dɪ-/ *v.tr.* disclose; reveal (a secret etc.). □ **divulgation** /-ˈgeɪʃ(ə)n/ *n.* **divulgement** *n.* **divulgence** *n.* [Latin *divulgare* (as DI-², *vulgare* 'publish' from *vulgus* 'common people')]

divvy¹ /ˈdɪvi/ *n. & v.* (also **divi**) *colloq.* ● *n.* (*pl.* **-ies**) **1** *Brit.* a dividend; a share, esp. of profits earned by a cooperative. **2** a distribution. ● *v.tr.* (**-ies, -ied**) (often foll. by *up*) share out; divide. [abbreviation of DIVIDEND]

divvy[2] /ˈdɪvi/ *adj. & n. Brit. slang* or *dial.* ● *adj.* foolish, idiotic. ● *n.* (*pl.* **-ies**) a foolish person, an idiot. [20th c.: origin uncertain]

Diwali /dɪˈwɑːliː/ *n.* a Hindu festival with lights, held in the period October to November. [Hindustani *dīwālī* from Sanskrit *dīpāvalī* 'row of lights', from *dīpa* 'lamp']

Dixie /ˈdɪksi/ *n.* the southern states of the US. [19th c.: origin uncertain]

dixie /ˈdɪksi/ *n.* a large iron cooking pot used by campers etc. [Hindustani *degchī* 'cooking pot' from Persian *degcha*, diminutive of *deg* 'pot']

Dixieland /ˈdɪksɪland/ *n.* **1** = DIXIE. **2** a kind of jazz with a strong two-beat rhythm and collective improvisation. [DIXIE]

DIY *abbr.* esp. *Brit.* do-it-yourself.

dizzy /ˈdɪzi/ *adj. & v.* ● *adj.* (**dizzier**, **dizziest**) **1 a** giddy, unsteady. **b** lacking mental stability; confused. **c** *colloq.* scatterbrained. **2** causing giddiness (*dizzy heights*; *dizzy speed*). ● *v.tr.* (**-ies**, **-ied**) **1** make dizzy. **2** bewilder. □ **dizzily** *adv.* **dizziness** *n.* [Old English *dysig*, from West Germanic]

DJ *abbr.* **1** *Brit.* dinner jacket. **2** disc jockey.

djellaba /ˈdʒɛləbə/ *n.* (also **djellabah**, **jellaba**) a loose hooded woollen cloak worn or as worn by Arab men. [Arabic *jallaba*, *jallābīya*]

djibba (also **djibbah**) var. of JIBBA.

djinn var. of JINNEE.

DL *abbr.* Deputy Lieutenant.

dl *abbr.* decilitre(s).

D-layer /ˈdiːleɪə/ *n.* the lowest layer of the ionosphere able to reflect low-frequency radio waves. [*D* (arbitrary)]

D.Litt. *abbr.* Doctor of Letters. [Latin *Doctor Litterarum*]

DM *abbr.* (also **D-mark**) Deutschmark.

dm *abbr.* decimetre(s).

D-mark *n.* = DEUTSCHMARK. [abbreviation]

DMs *abbr.* Dr Martens.

DMSO *abbr.* dimethylsulphoxide.

D.Mus. *abbr.* Doctor of Music.

DMZ *abbr. US* demilitarized zone.

DNA *abbr.* deoxyribonucleic acid, a self-replicating material which is present in nearly all living organisms, esp. as a constituent of chromosomes, and is the carrier of genetic information.

DNA fingerprinting *n.* = GENETIC FINGERPRINTING.

DNase /diːɛnˈeɪz/ *n. Biochem.* an enzyme which breaks DNA into smaller molecules. [DNA + -ASE]

DNB *abbr.* Dictionary of National Biography.

D-notice /ˈdiːnəʊtɪs/ *n. Brit.* a government notice to news editors not to publish items on specified subjects, for reasons of security. [*defence* + NOTICE]

do[1] /duː/ *v., v.aux., & n.* ● *v.* (*3rd sing. present* **does** /dʌz/; *past* **did** /dɪd/; *past part.* **done** /dʌn/) **1** *tr.* perform, carry out, achieve, complete (work etc.) (*did his homework*; *there's a lot to do*; *he can do anything*). **2** *tr.* **a** produce, make (*she was doing a painting*; *I did a translation*; *decided to do a casserole*). **b** provide (*do you do lunches?*). **3** *tr.* bestow, grant; have a specified effect on (*a walk would do you good*; *do me a favour*). **4** *intr.* act, behave, proceed (*do as I do*; *she would do well to accept the offer*). **5** *tr.* **a** work at for a living, be occupied with (*what does your father do?*). **b** work at, study; take as one's subject (*he did chemistry at university*; *we're doing Chaucer next term*). **6 a** *intr.* be suitable or acceptable; suffice (*this dress won't do for a wedding*; *a sandwich will do until we get home*; *that will never do*). **b** *tr.* satisfy; be suitable for (*that hotel will do me nicely*). **7** *tr.* deal with; put in order (*the garden needs doing*; *the barber will do you next*; *I must do my hair before we go*). **8** *intr.* **a** fare; get on (*the patients were doing excellently*; *he did badly in the test*). **b** perform, work (*could do better*). **9** *tr.* **a** solve; work out (*we did the puzzle*). **b** (prec. by *can* or *be able to*) be competent at (*can you do cartwheels?*; *I never could do maths*). **10** *tr.* **a** traverse (a certain distance) (*we did fifty miles today*). **b** travel at a specified speed (*he overtook us doing about eighty*). **11** *tr. colloq.* **a** act or behave like (*did a Houdini*). **b** play the part of (*she was asked to do hostess*). **12** *intr.* **a** *colloq.* finish (*have you done annoying me?*; *I've done in the bathroom*). **b** (as **done** *adj.*) be over (*the day is done*). **13** *tr.* produce or give a performance of (*the school does many plays and concerts*; *we've never done 'Pygmalion'*). **14** *tr.* cook, esp. to the right degree (*do it in the oven*; *the potatoes aren't done yet*). **15** *intr.* be in progress (*what's doing?*). **16** *tr. colloq.* visit; see the sights of (*we did all the art galleries*). **17** *tr. colloq.* **a** (often as **done** *adj.*) exhaust; tire out (*the climb has completely done me*). **b** beat up, defeat, kill. **c** ruin (*now you've done it*). **18** *tr.* (foll. by *into*) translate or transform (*the book was done into French*). **19** *tr.* (with qualifying adverb) *Brit. colloq.* provide food etc. for in a specified way (*they do one very well here*). **20** *tr. slang* **a** rob (*they did a shop in Soho*). **b** swindle (*I was done at the market*). **21** *tr. Brit. slang* prosecute, convict (*they were done for shoplifting*). **22** *tr. slang* undergo (a specified term of imprisonment) (*he did two years for fraud*). **23** *tr. coarse slang* have sexual intercourse with. **24** *tr. slang* take (a drug). ● *v.aux.* **1 a** (except with *be, can, may, ought, shall, will*) in questions and negative statements (*do you understand?*; *I don't smoke*). **b** (except with *can, may, ought, shall, will*) in negative commands (*don't be silly*; *do not come tomorrow*). **2** *ellipt.* or in place of verb or verb and object (*you know her better than I do*; *I wanted to go and I did so*; *tell me, do!*). **3** forming emphatic present and past tenses (*I do want to*; *do tell me*; *they did go but she was out*). **4** in inversion for emphasis (*rarely does it happen*; *did he but know it*). ● *n.* (*pl.* **dos** or **do's**) **1** *colloq.* an elaborate social event, party, or operation. **2** *Brit. slang* a swindle or hoax. □ **be done with** see DONE. **be nothing to do with 1** be no business or concern of (*his financial situation is nothing to do with me*). **2** be unconnected with (*his depression is nothing to do with his father's death*). **be to do with** be concerned or connected with (*the argument was to do with money*). **do about** see ABOUT *prep.* 1d. **do away with** *colloq.* **1** abolish. **2** kill. **do battle** enter into combat. **do one's best** see BEST. **do one's bit** see BIT[1]. **do by** treat or deal with in a specified way (*do as you would be done by*). **do credit to** see CREDIT. **do down** *Brit. colloq.* **1** cheat, swindle. **2** get the better of; overcome. **do for 1** be satisfactory or sufficient for. **2** *colloq.* (esp. as **done for** *adj.*) destroy, ruin, kill (*he knew he was done for*). **3** *Brit. colloq.* act as housekeeper for. **do one's head** (or **nut**) *Brit. slang* be extremely angry or agitated. **do the honours** see HONOUR. **do in 1** *slang* **a** kill. **b** ruin, do injury to. **2** *colloq.* exhaust, tire out. **do justice to** see JUSTICE. **do nothing for** (or **to**) *colloq.* detract from the appearance or quality of (*such behaviour does nothing for our reputation*). **do or die** persist regardless of danger. **do out** *Brit. colloq.* clean or redecorate (a room). **do a person out of** *colloq.* unjustly deprive a person of; swindle out of (*he was done out of his holiday*). **do over 1** *slang* attack; beat up. **2** *colloq.* redecorate, refurbish. **3** *N. Amer. colloq.* do again. **do proud** see PROUD. **dos and don'ts** rules of behaviour. **do something for** (or **to**) *colloq.* enhance the appearance or quality of (*that carpet does something for the room*). **do one's stuff** see STUFF. **do to** (*archaic* **unto**) = *do by*. **do to death** see DEATH. **do the trick** see TRICK. **do up 1** fasten, secure. **2** *colloq.* **a** refurbish, renovate. **b** adorn, dress up. **3** *Brit. slang* **a** ruin, get the better of. **b** beat up. **do well for oneself** prosper. **do well out of** profit by. **do with** (prec. by *could*) would be glad to have; would profit by (*I could do with a rest*; *you could do with a wash*). **do without** manage without; forgo (also *absol.*: *we shall just have to do without*). **have nothing to do with 1** have no connection or dealings with (*our problem has nothing to do with the latest news*; *after the disagreement he had nothing to do with his father*). **2** be no business or concern of (*the decision has nothing to do with him*). **have to do** (or **something to do**) **with** be connected with (*his limp has to do with a car accident*). [Old English *dōn* from

Germanic: related to Sanskrit *dādhāmi* 'put', Greek *tithemi* 'place', Latin *facere* 'do']

do[2] var. of DOH.

do. *abbr.* ditto.

DOA *abbr.* dead on arrival (at hospital etc.).

doable /ˈduːəb(ə)l/ *adj.* that can be done.

dob /dɒb/ *v.tr.* (**dobbed**, **dobbing**) (foll. by *in*) *Austral. slang* inform against; implicate; betray. [variant of DAB[1]]

dobbin /ˈdɒbɪn/ *n.* a draught horse; a farm horse. [pet form of the name *Robert*]

dobe /ˈdəʊbi/ *n. US colloq.* adobe. [abbreviation]

Dobermann /ˈdəʊbəmən/ *n.* (in full **Dobermann pinscher** /ˈpɪnʃə/) **1** a large dog of a German breed with a smooth coat. **2** this breed. [named after L. *Dobermann*, 19th-c. German dog breeder, + German *Pinscher* 'terrier']

dobsonfly /ˈdɒbs(ə)nflʌɪ/ *n.* (*pl.* **-flies**) a large neuropterous insect of the family Corydalidae, esp. *Corydalis cornutus* of N. America, whose predatory aquatic larva are used as bait. [origin unknown]

doc /dɒk/ *n. colloq.* **1** doctor. **2** documentary (*video-doc*). **3** *Computing* document. [abbreviation]

doch an dorris var. of DEOCH AN DORIS.

docile /ˈdəʊsʌɪl/ *adj.* **1** submissive, easily managed. **2** *archaic* teachable. □ **docilely** /ˈdəʊsʌɪlli/ *adv.* **docility** /-ˈsɪlɪti/ *n.* [Middle English from Latin *docilis*, from *docēre* 'teach']

dock[1] /dɒk/ *n.* & *v.* ● *n.* **1** an artificially enclosed body of water for the loading, unloading, and repair of ships. **2** (in *pl.*) a range of docks with wharves and offices; a dockyard. **3** *US* a ship's berth, a wharf. **4** = DRY DOCK. **5** *Theatr.* = SCENE-DOCK. ● *v.* **1** *tr.* & *intr.* bring or come into a dock. **2 a** *tr.* join (spacecraft) together in space. **b** *intr.* (of spacecraft) be joined. **3** *tr.* provide with a dock or docks. □ **in dock** *Brit. colloq.* in hospital or (of a vehicle) laid up for repairs. [Middle Dutch *docke*, of unknown origin]

dock[2] /dɒk/ *n.* the enclosure in a criminal court for the accused. □ **in the dock** *Brit.* on trial. [16th c.: probably originally slang and related to Flemish *dok* 'cage', of unknown origin]

dock[3] /dɒk/ *n.* any coarse, broadleaved weed of the genus *Rumex*. [Old English *docce*]

dock[4] /dɒk/ *v.* & *n.* ● *v.tr.* **1 a** cut short (an animal's tail). **b** cut short the tail of (an animal). **2 a** (often foll. by *from*) deduct (a part) from wages, supplies, etc. **b** reduce (wages etc.) in this way. ● *n.* **1** the solid bony part of an animal's tail. **2** *Brit.* the crupper of a saddle or harness. [Middle English, of uncertain origin]

dockage /ˈdɒkɪdʒ/ *n.* **1** the charge made for using docks. **2** dock accommodation. **3** the berthing of ships in docks.

dock brief *n.* a brief handed direct to a barrister selected by a prisoner in the dock.

docker /ˈdɒkə/ *n.* a person employed to load and unload ships.

docket /ˈdɒkɪt/ *n.* & *v.* ● *n.* **1** *Brit.* **a** a document or label listing goods delivered or the contents of a package, or recording payment of customs dues etc. **b** a voucher; an order form. **2** *US* a list of causes for trial or persons having causes pending. **3** *US* a list of things to be done. ● *v.tr.* (**docketed**, **docketing**) label with a docket. [15th c.: origin unknown]

dock-glass *n.* a large glass for wine tasting.

dockland /ˈdɒklənd/ *n.* a district near docks.

dockside /ˈdɒksʌɪd/ *n.* (often *attrib.*) the area immediately adjacent to a dock.

dock-tailed *adj.* having a docked tail.

dockyard /ˈdɒkjɑːd/ *n.* an area with docks and equipment for building and repairing ships, esp. *Brit.* for naval use.

Doc Martens var. of DR MARTENS.

doctor /ˈdɒktə/ *n.* & *v.* ● *n.* **1 a** a qualified practitioner of medicine; a physician. **b** *N. Amer.* a qualified dentist or veterinary surgeon. **2** a person who holds a doctorate (*Doctor of Civil Law*). **3** *colloq.* a person who carries out repairs. **4** *archaic* a teacher or learned person. **5** *slang* a cook on board a ship or in a camp. **6** (in full **doctor-blade**) *Brit. Printing* a blade for removing surplus ink etc. **7** an artificial fishing-fly. ● *v. colloq.* **1 a** *tr.* treat medically. **b** *intr.* (esp. as **doctoring** *n.*) practise as a physician. **2** *tr. Brit.* castrate or spay. **3** *tr.* patch up (machinery etc.); mend. **4** *tr.* adulterate. **5** *tr.* tamper with, falsify. **6** *tr.* confer a degree of doctor on. □ **go for the doctor** *Austral. slang* **1** make an all-out effort. **2** bet all one has. **what the doctor ordered** *colloq.* something beneficial or desirable. □ **doctorial** /-ˈtɔːrɪəl/ *adj.* **doctorly** *adj.* **doctorship** *n.* [Middle English via Old French *doctour* from Latin *doctor*, from *docēre doct-* 'teach']

doctoral /ˈdɒkt(ə)r(ə)l/ *adj.* of or for a degree of doctor.

doctorate /ˈdɒkt(ə)rət/ *n.* the highest university degree in any faculty, often honorary.

Doctor Martens var. of DR MARTENS.

Doctor of Philosophy *n.* **1** a doctorate in any faculty except law, medicine, or sometimes theology. **2** a person holding such a degree.

Doctor of the Church *n.* any of several early Christian and later Catholic theologians.

doctrinaire /dɒktrɪˈnɛː/ *adj.* & *n.* ● *adj.* seeking to apply a theory or doctrine in all circumstances without regard to practical considerations; theoretical and impractical. ● *n.* a doctrinaire person; a pedantic theorist. □ **doctrinairism** *n.* **doctrinarian** *n.* [French, from *doctrine* DOCTRINE + *-aire* -ARY[1]]

doctrinal /dɒkˈtrʌɪn(ə)l, ˈdɒktrɪn-/ *adj.* of or inculcating a doctrine or doctrines. □ **doctrinally** *adv.* [Late Latin *doctrinalis* (as DOCTRINE)]

doctrine /ˈdɒktrɪn/ *n.* **1** what is taught; a body of instruction. **2 a** a principle of religious or political etc. belief. **b** a set of such principles; dogma. □ **doctrinism** *n.* **doctrinist** *n.* [Middle English via Old French from Latin *doctrina* 'teaching' (as DOCTOR)]

docudrama /ˈdɒkjʊdrɑːmə/ *n.* a dramatized television film based on real events. [DOCUMENTARY + DRAMA]

document *n.* & *v.* ● *n.* /ˈdɒkjʊm(ə)nt/ a piece of written or printed matter that provides a record or evidence of events, an agreement, ownership, identification, etc. ● *v.tr.* /ˈdɒkjʊmɛnt/ **1** prove by or provide with documents or evidence. **2** record in a document. □ **documental** /-ˈmɛnt(ə)l/ *adj.* [Middle English via Old French from Latin *documentum* 'proof', from *docēre* 'teach']

documentalist /dɒkjʊˈmɛnt(ə)lɪst/ *n.* a person engaged in documentation.

documentarian /ˌdɒkjʊmɛnˈtɛːrɪən/ *n.* **1 a** a photographer specializing in producing a factual record. **b** a director or producer of documentaries. **2** an expert analyst of historical documents.

documentarist /dɒkjʊˈmɛnt(ə)rɪst/ *n.* = DOCUMENTARIAN 1b.

documentary /dɒkjʊˈmɛnt(ə)ri/ *adj.* & *n.* ● *adj.* **1** consisting of documents (*documentary evidence*). **2** providing a factual record or report. ● *n.* (*pl.* **-ies**) a documentary film etc. □ **documentarily** *adv.*

documentation /ˌdɒkjʊmɛnˈteɪʃ(ə)n/ *n.* **1** the accumulation, classification, and dissemination of information. **2** the material collected or disseminated. **3** the collection of documents relating to a process or event, esp. the written specification and instructions accompanying a computer program.

DOD *abbr. US* Department of Defense.

dodder[1] /ˈdɒdə/ *v.intr.* tremble or totter, esp. from age. □ **dodderer** *n.* [17th c.: variant of obsolete dialect *dadder*: cf. DITHER]

dodder[2] /ˈdɒdə/ *n.* any climbing parasitic plant of the genus *Cuscuta*, with slender leafless threadlike stems. [Middle English from Germanic]

doddered /ˈdɒdəd/ *adj.* (of a tree, esp. an oak) having lost its top or branches. [probably from obsolete *dod* 'poll, lop']

dodder-grass *n.* quaking-grass.

doddery /ˈdɒd(ə)ri/ *adj.* tending to tremble or totter, esp. from age. □ **dodderiness** *n.* [DODDER[1] + -Y[1]]

doddle /ˈdɒd(ə)l/ *n. Brit. colloq.* an easy task. [perhaps from *doddle* = TODDLE]

dodeca- /ˈdəʊdɛkə/ *comb. form* twelve. [Greek *dōdeka* 'twelve']

dodecagon /dəʊˈdɛkəg(ə)n/ *n.* a plane figure with twelve sides.

dodecahedron /ˌdəʊdɛkəˈhiːdr(ə)n, -ˈhɛd-/ *n.* (*pl.* **dodecahedra** /-drə/ or **dedecahedrons**) a solid figure with twelve faces. □ **dodecahedral** *adj.*

dodecaphonic /ˌdəʊdɛkəˈfɒnɪk/ *adj. Mus.* = TWELVE-NOTE.

dodge /dɒdʒ/ *v. & n.* ● *v.* **1** *intr.* (often foll. by *about, behind, round*) move quickly to one side or quickly change position, to elude a pursuer, blow, etc. (*dodged behind the chair*). **2** *tr.* **a** evade by cunning or trickery (*dodged paying the fare*). **b** elude (a pursuer, opponent, blow, etc.) by a sideward movement etc. **3** *tr. Austral. slang* acquire dishonestly. **4** *intr.* (of a bell in change-ringing) move one place contrary to the normal sequence. ● *n.* **1** a quick movement to avoid or evade something. **2** a clever trick or expedient. **3** the dodging of a bell in change-ringing. □ **dodge the column** *Brit.* see COLUMN. [16th c.: origin unknown]

dodgem /ˈdɒdʒ(ə)m/ *n.* (in full **dodgem car**) a small electrically powered car with rubber bumpers all round, driven in an enclosure at a funfair with the aim of bumping or avoiding other such cars. [US proprietary name, DODGE + 'EM]

dodger /ˈdɒdʒə/ *n.* **1** a person who dodges, esp. an artful or elusive person. **2** a screen on a ship's bridge etc. as protection from spray etc. **3** *US* a small handbill. **4** *slang* a sandwich; bread; food.

dodging /ˈdɒdʒɪŋ/ *n.* **1** in senses of the verb. **2** *Photog.* the deliberate modification of the intensity of a particular part of a photograph during processing or enlarging.

dodgy /ˈdɒdʒi/ *adj.* (**dodgier**, **dodgiest**) **1** *colloq.* awkward, unreliable, tricky. **2** *Brit.* cunning, artful.

dodo /ˈdəʊdəʊ/ *n.* (*pl.* **-os** or **-oes**) **1** a large extinct flightless bird, *Raphus cucullatus*, formerly native to Mauritius. **2** an old-fashioned, stupid, or inactive person. □ **as dead as the** (or **a**) **dodo 1** completely or unmistakably dead. **2** entirely obsolete. [Portuguese *doudo* 'simpleton']

DoE *abbr.* (in the UK) Department of the Environment.

doe /dəʊ/ *n.* a female fallow deer, reindeer, hare, rabbit, etc. [Old English *dā*]

doe-eyed *adj.* (esp. of a woman) having large gentle dark eyes.

doek /dʊk/ *n. S.Afr.* a cloth, esp. a head-cloth. [Afrikaans]

doer /ˈduːə/ *n.* **1** a person who does something. **2** a person who acts rather than merely talking or thinking. **3** (in full **hard doer**) *Austral.* an eccentric or amusing person.

does *3rd sing. present* of DO[1].

doeskin /ˈdəʊskɪn/ *n.* **1 a** the skin of a doe fallow deer. **b** leather made from this. **2** a fine cloth resembling it.

doesn't /ˈdʌz(ə)nt/ *contr.* does not.

doest /ˈduːɪst/ *archaic 2nd sing. present* of DO[1].

doeth /ˈduːɪθ/ *archaic* = DOTH.

doff /dɒf/ *v.tr.* esp. *literary* take off (one's hat, clothing). [Middle English, = *do off*]

dog /dɒg/ *n. & v.* ● *n.* **1 a** a domesticated carnivorous mammal, *Canis familiaris*, usu. having a long snout and non-retractile claws, and occurring in many different breeds kept as pets or for work or sport. **b** a wild animal of the genus *Canis*, including wolves, jackals, and coyotes, or of the family Canidae, including foxes. **2** the male of the dog, or of the fox (also **dog-fox**) or wolf (also **dog-wolf**). **3** *colloq.* **a** a despicable person. **b** a person of a specified kind (*a lucky dog*). **c** *US & Austral. slang* an informer; a traitor. **d** *slang* a horse that is difficult to handle. **4** a mechanical device for gripping. **5** *N. Amer. slang* something poor; a failure. **6** = FIREDOG. **7** (in *pl.*; prec. by *the*) *Brit. colloq.* greyhound racing. ● *v.tr.* (**dogged**, **dogging**) **1** follow closely and persistently; pursue, track. **2** *Mech.* grip with a dog. □ **die like a dog** die miserably or shamefully. **dog it** esp. *US colloq.* act lazily; idle, shirk. **dog's breakfast** *colloq.* a mess. **dog's dinner** *Brit. colloq.* **1** = *dog's breakfast*. **2** (in phr. **dressed** etc. **like a dog's dinner**) dressed over-elaborately or vulgarly (*she was got up like a dog's dinner*). **go to the dogs** *slang* deteriorate, be ruined. **not a dog's chance** no chance at all. **put on the dog** *N. Amer. colloq.* behave pretentiously. □ **doglike** *adj.* [Old English *docga*, of unknown origin]

dogberry /ˈdɒgb(ə)ri, -bɛri/ *n.* (*pl.* **-ies**) the fruit of the dogwood.

dog biscuit *n.* a hard thick biscuit for feeding dogs.

dog box *n. Austral. slang* a compartment in a railway carriage without a corridor.

dog cart *n.* a two-wheeled cart for driving in, with cross seats back to back.

dog-clutch *n.* a device for coupling two shafts in the transmission of power, one member having teeth which engage with slots in another.

dog collar *n.* **1** a collar for a dog. **2 a** *colloq.* a clerical collar. **b** a straight high collar.

dog days *n.pl.* the hottest period of the year (reckoned in antiquity from the heliacal rising of the dog-star).

doge /dəʊdʒ/ *n. hist.* the chief magistrate of Venice or Genoa. [French via Italian and Venetian *doze* from Latin *dux ducis* 'leader']

dog-eared *adj.* (of a book etc.) with the corners worn or battered with use.

dog-eat-dog *adj. colloq.* ruthlessly competitive.

dog-end *n. slang* a cigarette end.

dogface /ˈdɒgfeɪs/ *n. US slang* a US soldier, esp. an infantryman.

dog-fall *n.* a fall in which wrestlers touch the ground together.

dogfight /ˈdɒgfʌɪt/ *n.* **1** a close combat between fighter aircraft. **2** uproar; a fight like that between dogs. □ **dogfighter** *n.* **dogfighting** *n.*

dogfish /ˈdɒgfɪʃ/ *n.* (*pl.* usu. same) any of various small sharks, esp. of the families Scyliorhinidae and Squalidae.

dogged /ˈdɒgɪd/ *adj.* tenacious; grimly persistent. □ **it's dogged as does it** *colloq.* persistence succeeds. □ **doggedly** *adv.* **doggedness** *n.* [Middle English from DOG + -ED[1]]

dogger[1] /ˈdɒgə/ *n.* a two-masted bluff-bowed Dutch fishing boat. [Middle English from Middle Dutch, = fishing boat]

dogger[2] /ˈdɒgə/ *n. Geol.* a large spherical concretion occurring in sedimentary rock. [dialect, = kind of ironstone, perhaps from DOG]

doggerel /ˈdɒg(ə)r(ə)l/ *n.* poor or trivial verse. [Middle English, apparently from DOG: cf. -REL]

doggie var. of DOGGY *n.*

doggish /ˈdɒgɪʃ/ *adj.* **1** of or like a dog. **2** currish, malicious, snappish.

doggo /ˈdɒgəʊ/ *adv.* □ **lie doggo** *Brit. slang* lie motionless or hidden, making no sign. [probably from DOG: cf. -O]

doggone /ˈdɒgɒn/ *adj., adv., & int.* esp. *N. Amer. slang* ● *adj. & adv.* damned. ● *int.* expressing annoyance. [probably from *dog on it* = *God damn it*]

doggy /ˈdɒgi/ *adj. & n.* ● *adj.* **1** of or like a dog. **2** devoted to dogs. ● *n.* (also **doggie**) (*pl.* **-ies**) a little dog; a pet name for a dog. □ **dogginess** *n.*

doggy bag *n.* a bag given to a customer in a restaurant or to a guest at a party etc. for putting leftovers in to take home.

doggy-paddle var. of DOG-PADDLE.

dog handler *n.* a person, esp. a police officer, in charge of a dog or dogs. □ **dog-handling** *n.*

doghouse /ˈdɒghaʊs/ *n. N. Amer.* a dog's kennel. □ **in the doghouse** *slang* in disgrace or disfavour.

dogie /ˈdəʊgi/ *n. N. Amer.* a motherless or neglected calf. [19th c.: origin unknown]

dog in the manger *n.* a person who prevents others from using something, although that person has no use for it.

dog-leg *n., adj., & v.* ● *n.* a sharp bend like that in a dog's hind leg. ● *adj.* (also **dog-legged**) bent sharply. ● *v.intr.* (**-legged**, **-legging**) bend sharply.

dog-leg hole *n.* a hole at which a golf player cannot aim directly at the green from the tee.

dogma /ˈdɒgmə/ *n.* **1 a** a principle, tenet, or system of these, esp. as laid down by the authority of a Church. **b** such principles collectively. **2** an arrogant declaration of opinion. [Latin from Greek *dogma -matos* 'opinion', from *dokeō* 'seem']

dogman /ˈdɒgmən/ *n.* (*pl.* **-men**) *Austral.* a person giving directional signals to the operator of a crane, often while sitting on the crane's load.

dogmatic /dɒgˈmatɪk/ *adj.* **1 a** (of a person) given to asserting or imposing personal opinions; arrogant. **b** intolerantly authoritative. **2 a** of or in the nature of dogma; doctrinal. **b** based on a priori principles, not on induction. □ **dogmatically** *adv.* [Late Latin *dogmaticus* from Greek *dogmatikos* (as DOGMA)]

dogmatics /dɒgˈmatɪks/ *n.* **1** the study of religious dogmas; dogmatic theology. **2** a system of dogma. [DOGMATIC]

dogmatism /ˈdɒgmətɪz(ə)m/ *n.* a tendency to be dogmatic. □ **dogmatist** *n.* [French *dogmatisme* from medieval Latin *dogmatismus* (as DOGMA)]

dogmatize /ˈdɒgmətʌɪz/ *v.* (also **-ise**) **1** *intr.* make positive unsupported assertions; speak dogmatically. **2** *tr.* express (a principle etc.) as a dogma. [French *dogmatiser* or via Late Latin *dogmatizare* from Greek (as DOGMA)]

do-gooder /du:ˈgʊdə/ *n.* a well-meaning but unrealistic philanthropist or reformer. □ **do-good** /ˈdu:gʊd/ *adj. & n.* **do-goodery** *n.* **do-goodism** *n.*

dog-paddle *n. & v.* (also **doggy-paddle**) ● *n.* an elementary swimming stroke like that of a dog. ● *v.intr.* swim using this stroke.

dog rose *n.* a wild hedge-rose, *Rosa canina.* Also called *brier rose.*

dogsbody /ˈdɒgzbɒdi/ *n.* (*pl.* **-ies**) *Brit.* **1** *colloq.* a drudge. **2** *Naut. slang* a junior officer.

dog's disease *n. Austral. slang* influenza.

dogshore /ˈdɒgʃɔ:/ *n.* a temporary wooden support for a ship just before launching.

dogskin /ˈdɒgskɪn/ *n.* leather made of or imitating dog's skin, used for gloves.

dog sled *n.* a sled designed to be pulled by dogs.

dog's life *n.* a life of misery or harassment.

dog's meat *n.* horse's or other flesh as food for dogs; carrion.

dog's mercury *n.* a woodland plant of the spurge family, *Mercurialis perennis*, with small green flowers.

dogs of war *n.pl. poet.* the havoc accompanying war.

dog's-tail *n.* (also **dog-tail**) any grass of the genus *Cynosurus*, esp. *C. cristatus*, a common pasture grass.

dog-star *n.* Sirius, the brightest star in the sky. [so called as it appears to follow at the heels of Orion the hunter]

dog's tooth *n.* **1** (in full **dog's tooth violet**) any plant of the genus *Erythronium* (lily family), esp. *E. dens-canis* with speckled leaves, purple flowers, and a toothed perianth. **2** = DOG-TOOTH 2.

dog tag *n.* **1** a tag attached to a dog's collar, giving its owner's address etc. **2** *N. Amer. slang* a soldier's metal identity tag.

dog-tail var. of DOG'S-TAIL.

dog-tired *adj.* tired out.

dog-tooth *n.* **1** a small pointed ornament or moulding, esp. in Norman and Early English architecture. **2** a broken check pattern used esp. in cloth for suits.

dog trials *n.pl. Austral. & NZ* a public competitive display of the skills of sheepdogs.

dogtrot /ˈdɒgtrɒt/ *n.* a gentle easy trot.

dog-violet *n.* any of various scentless wild violets, esp. *Viola riviniana.*

dogwatch /ˈdɒgwɒtʃ/ *n. Naut.* either of two short watches (4–6 or 6–8 p.m.).

dogwood /ˈdɒgwʊd/ *n.* **1** any of various shrubs of the genus *Cornus*, esp. the wild cornel, *C. sanguinea*, with dark red branches, greenish-white flowers, and purple berries, found in woods and hedgerows. **2** any of various similar trees. **3** the wood of the dogwood.

DoH *abbr.* (in the UK) Department of Health.

doh /dəʊ/ *n.* (also **do**) *Mus.* **1** (in tonic sol-fa) the first and eighth note of a major scale. **2** the note C in the fixed-doh system. [18th c.: from Italian *do*, an arbitrarily chosen syllable replacing *ut*: see GAMUT]

doily /ˈdɔɪli/ *n.* (also **doyley**) (*pl.* **-ies** or **-eys**) a small ornamental mat of paper, lace, etc., on a plate for cakes etc. [originally the name of a fabric: from *Doiley*, the name of a 17th-c. London draper]

doing /ˈdu:ɪŋ/ *n.* **1 a** an action; the performance of a deed (*famous for his doings*; *it was my doing*). **b** activity, effort (*it takes a lot of doing*). **2** *colloq.* a scolding; a beating. **3** (in *pl.*) esp. *Brit. slang* things needed; adjuncts; things whose names are not known (*have we got all the doings?*).

doit /dɔɪt/ *n. archaic* a very small amount of money. [Middle Low German *doyt*, Middle Dutch *duit*, of unknown origin]

do-it-yourself *adj. & n.* ● *adj.* (of work, esp. building, painting, decorating, etc.) done or to be done by an amateur at home. ● *n.* such work.

dojo /ˈdəʊdʒəʊ/ *n.* (*pl.* **-os**) **1** a room or hall in which judo and other martial arts are practised. **2** a mat on which judo etc. is practised. [Japanese, from *dō* 'way, pursuit' + *jō* 'a place']

dol. *abbr.* dollar(s).

Dolby /ˈdɒlbi, ˈdəʊl-/ *n. propr.* an electronic noise-reduction system used esp. in tape-recording to reduce hiss. [named after R. M. *Dolby*, US inventor]

dolce /ˈdɒltʃeɪ/ *adv. & adj. Mus.* ● *adv.* sweetly and softly. ● *adj.* performed in this manner. [Italian, = sweet]

dolce far niente /ˌdɒltʃeɪ fɑ: nɪˈɛnti, Italian ˌdoltʃe far niˈɛnte/ *n.* pleasant idleness. [Italian, = sweet doing nothing]

Dolcelatte /dɒltʃeɪˈlati/ *n.* a kind of soft creamy blue-veined cheese from Italy. [Italian, = sweet milk]

dolce vita /dɒltʃeɪ ˈvi:tə, Italian doltʃe ˈvi:ta/ *n.* a life of pleasure and luxury. [Italian, = sweet life]

doldrums /ˈdɒldrəmz/ *n.pl.* (usu. prec. by *the*) **1** low spirits; a feeling of boredom or depression. **2** a period of inactivity or state of stagnation. **3** an equatorial ocean region of calms, sudden storms, and light unpredictable winds. [probably from *dull* and *tantrum*]

dole[1] /dəʊl/ *n. & v.* ● *n.* **1** (usu. prec. by *the*) *Brit. colloq.* benefit claimable by the unemployed from the State. **2 a** charitable distribution. **b** a charitable (esp. sparing, niggardly) gift of food, clothes, or money. **3** *archaic* one's lot or destiny. ● *v.tr.* (usu. foll. by *out*) deal out sparingly. □ **on the dole** *colloq.* receiving state benefit for the unemployed. [Old English *dāl*, from Germanic]

dole[2] /dəʊl/ *n. poet.* grief, woe; lamentation. [Middle English via Old French *do(e)l* etc. and popular Latin *dolus* from Latin *dolēre* 'grieve']

dole-bludger *n. Austral. slang* a person who allegedly prefers the dole to work.

doleful /ˈdəʊlfʊl, -f(ə)l/ *adj.* **1** mournful, sad. **2** dreary, dismal. □ **dolefully** *adv.* **dolefulness** *n.* [Middle English from DOLE[2] + -FUL]

dolerite /ˈdɒlərʌɪt/ *n.* a coarse basaltic rock. [French *dolérite* from Greek *doleros* 'deceptive' (because it is difficult to distinguish from diorite)]

dolichocephalic /ˌdɒlɪkəʊsɪˈfalɪk, -keˈfalɪk/ *adj.* (also **dolichocephalous** /-ˈsɛf(ə)ləs, -ˈkɛf-/) having a long or narrow head. [Greek *dolikhos* 'long' + -CEPHALIC, -CEPHALOUS]

dolina /dɒ'li:nə/ *n.* (also **doline** /dɒ'li:n/) *Geol.* an extensive depression or basin. [Russian *dolina* 'valley']

doll /dɒl/ *n. & v.* ● *n.* **1** a small model of a human figure, esp. a baby or a child, as a child's toy. **2 a** *colloq.* a pretty but silly young woman. **b** *slang* a young woman (or also *US* a young man), esp. an attractive one. **3** a ventriloquist's dummy. ● *v.tr. & intr.* (foll. by *up*; often *refl.*) dress up smartly. [pet form of the name *Dorothy*]

dollar /'dɒlə/ *n.* **1** the chief monetary unit of the US, Canada, and Australia. **2** the chief monetary unit of certain countries in the Pacific, West Indies, SE Asia, Africa, and S. America. [Low German *daler* from German *Taler*, short for *Joachimstaler*, a coin from the silver mine of *Joachimstal*, now *Jáchymov* in the Czech Republic]

dollar area *n.* the area in which currency is linked to the US dollar.

dollar diplomacy *n.* diplomatic activity aimed at advancing a country's international influence by furthering its financial and commercial interests abroad.

dollar gap *n.* the excess of a country's import trade with the dollar area over the corresponding export trade.

dollarization /dɒlərʌɪ'zeɪʃ(ə)n/ *n.* (also **-sation**) a dominating effect of the US on the economy of a country, esp. the linkage of a currency to the US dollar.

dollar mark *n.* (also **dollar sign**) the sign $, representing a dollar.

dollar spot *n.* **1** a fungal disease of lawns etc. **2** a discoloured patch caused by this.

dollop /'dɒləp/ *n. & v.* ● *n.* a shapeless lump of food etc. ● *v.tr.* (**dolloped**, **dolloping**) (usu. foll. by *out*) serve out in large shapeless quantities. [perhaps from Scandinavian]

doll's house *n.* (*N. Amer.* **dollhouse**) **1** a miniature toy house for dolls. **2** a very small house.

dolly /'dɒli/ *n., v., & adj.* ● *n.* (*pl.* **-ies**) **1** a child's name for a doll. **2** a movable platform for a cine-camera. **3** *Cricket colloq.* an easy catch or hit. **4** a stick for stirring clothes in a washtub. **5** = CORN DOLLY. **6** *colloq.* = DOLLY-BIRD. ● *v.* (**-ies**, **-ied**) **1** *tr.* (foll. by *up*) dress up smartly. **2** *intr.* (foll. by *in*, *up*) move a cine-camera in or up to a subject, or out from it. ● *adj.* (**dollier**, **dolliest**) **1** *Brit. colloq.* (esp. of a girl) attractive, stylish. **2** *Cricket colloq.* easily hit or caught.

dolly-bird *n. Brit. colloq.* an attractive and stylish young woman.

dolly mixture *n. Brit.* any of a mixture of small variously shaped and coloured sweets.

Dolly Varden /dɒlɪ 'vɑ:d(ə)n/ *n.* **1** a woman's large hat with one side drooping and with a floral trimming. **2** a brightly spotted char, *Salvelinus malma*, of western N. America. [a character in Dickens's *Barnaby Rudge*]

dolma /'dɒlmə/ *n.* (*pl.* **dolmas** or **dolmades** /-'mɑ:ðez/) a Greek and Turkish delicacy of spiced rice or meat etc. wrapped in vine or cabbage leaves. [Turkish from *dolmak* 'fill, be filled': *dolmades* from modern Greek]

dolman /'dɒlmən/ *n.* **1** a long Turkish robe open in front. **2** a hussar's jacket worn with the sleeves hanging loose. **3** a woman's mantle with capelike or dolman sleeves. [ultimately from Turkish *dolama*]

dolman sleeve *n.* a loose sleeve cut in one piece with the body of a garment.

dolmen /'dɒlmɛn/ *n.* a megalithic tomb with a large flat stone laid on upright ones. [French, perhaps from Cornish *tolmēn* 'hole of stone']

dolomite /'dɒləmʌɪt/ *n.* a mineral or rock of calcium magnesium carbonate. □ **dolomitic** /dɒlə'mɪtɪk/ *adj.* [French, named after D. de *Dolomieu*, French geologist d. 1801]

dolorous /'dɒl(ə)rəs/ *adj. literary* or *joc.* **1** distressing, painful; doleful, dismal. **2** distressed, sad. □ **dolorously** *adv.* [Middle English via Old French *doleros* from Late Latin *dolorosus* (as DOLOUR)]

dolour /'dɒlə/ *n.* (*US* **dolor**) *literary* sorrow, distress. [Middle English via Old French from Latin *dolor -oris* 'pain, grief']

dolphin /'dɒlfɪn/ *n.* **1** any of various porpoise-like sea mammals of the family Delphinidae having a slender beaklike snout. **2** = DORADO 1. **3** a bollard, pile, or buoy for mooring. **4** a structure for protecting the pier of a bridge. **5** *Brit.* a curved fish in heraldry, sculpture, etc. [Middle English, also *delphin*, via Latin *delphinus* from Greek *delphis -inos*]

dolphinarium /dɒlfɪ'nɛ:rɪəm/ *n.* (*pl.* **dolphinariums**) *Brit.* an aquarium for dolphins, esp. one open to the public.

dolt /dəʊlt/ *n.* a stupid person. □ **doltish** *adj.* **doltishly** *adv.* **doltishness** *n.* [apparently related to *dol*, *dold*, obsolete variant of DULL]

Dom /dɒm/ *n.* **1** a title prefixed to the names of some Roman Catholic dignitaries, and Benedictine and Carthusian monks. **2** the Portuguese equivalent of *Don* (see DON[1] 2a, b). [Latin *dominus* 'master': sense 2 via Portuguese]

-dom /dəm/ *suffix* forming nouns denoting: **1** state or condition (*freedom*). **2** rank or status (*earldom*). **3** domain (*kingdom*). **4** a class of people (or the attitudes etc. associated with them) regarded collectively (*officialdom*). [Old English *-dōm*, originally = DOOM]

domain /də(ʊ)'meɪn/ *n.* **1** an area under one rule; a realm. **2** an estate or lands under one control. **3** a sphere of control or influence. **4** *Math.* the set of possible values of an independent variable. **5** *Physics* a discrete region of magnetism in ferromagnetic material. □ **domanial** /də'meɪnɪəl/ *adj.* [Middle English from French *domaine*, Old French *demeine* DEMESNE, associated with Latin *dominus* 'lord']

domaine /də'meɪn/ *n.* a vineyard. [French: see DOMAIN]

dome /dəʊm/ *n. & v.* ● *n.* **1 a** a rounded vault as a roof, with a circular, elliptical, or polygonal base; a large cupola. **b** the revolving openable hemispherical roof of an observatory. **2 a** a natural vault or canopy (of the sky, trees, etc.). **b** the rounded summit of a hill etc. **3** *Geol.* a dome-shaped structure. **4** *slang* the head. **5** *poet.* a stately building. ● *v.tr.* (usu. as **domed** *adj.*) cover with or shape as a dome. □ **domelike** *adj.* [French *dôme* via Italian *duomo* 'cathedral, dome' from Latin *domus* 'house']

Domesday /'du:mzdeɪ/ *n.* (in full **Domesday Book**) a record of the lands of England made in 1086 by order of William I. [Middle English variant of DOOMSDAY, as being a book of final authority]

domestic /də'mɛstɪk/ *adj. & n.* ● *adj.* **1** of the home, household, or family affairs. **2 a** of one's own country, not foreign or international. **b** home-grown or home-made. **3** (of an animal) kept by or living with humans. **4** fond of home life. ● *n.* a household servant. □ **domestically** *adv.* [French *domestique* from Latin *domesticus*, from *domus* 'home']

domesticate /də'mɛstɪkeɪt/ *v.tr.* **1** tame (an animal) to live with humans. **2** accustom to home life and management. **3** naturalize (a plant or animal). □ **domesticable** /-kəb(ə)l/ *adj.* **domestication** /-'keɪʃ(ə)n/ *n.* [medieval Latin *domesticare* (as DOMESTIC)]

domesticity /dɒmɛ'stɪsɪti, dəʊm-/ *n.* **1** the state of being domestic. **2** domestic or home life.

domestic science *n.* the study of household management.

domicile /'dɒmɪsʌɪl, -sɪl/ *n. & v.* (also **domicil** /-sɪl/) ● *n.* **1** a dwelling place; one's home. **2** *Law* **a** a place of permanent residence. **b** the fact of residing. **3** the place at which a bill of exchange is made payable. ● *v.tr.* **1** (usu. as **domiciled** *adj.*) (usu. foll. by *at*, *in*) establish or settle in a place. **2** (usu. foll. by *at*) make (a bill of exchange) payable at a certain place. [Middle English via Old French from Latin *domicilium*, from *domus* 'home']

domiciliary /dɒmɪˈsɪlɪəri/ *adj.* of a dwelling place (esp. *Brit.* of a doctor's, official's, etc., visit to a person's home). [French *domiciliaire* from medieval Latin *domiciliarius* (as DOMICILE)]

dominance /ˈdɒmɪnəns/ *n.* **1** the state of being dominant. **2** control, authority.

dominant /ˈdɒmɪnənt/ *adj. & n.* ● *adj.* **1** dominating, prevailing, most influential. **2** (of a high place) prominent, overlooking others. **3 a** (of an allele) expressed even when inherited from only one parent. **b** (of an inherited characteristic) appearing in an individual even when its allelic counterpart is also inherited (cf. RECESSIVE). ● *n. Mus.* the fifth note of the diatonic scale of any key. □ **dominantly** *adv.* [French from Latin *dominari* (as DOMINATE)]

dominate /ˈdɒmɪneɪt/ *v.* **1** *tr.* & (foll. by *over*) *intr.* have a commanding influence on; exercise control over (*fear dominated them for years*; *dominates over his friends*). **2** *intr.* (of a person, sound, feature of a scene, etc.) be the most influential or conspicuous. **3** *tr.* & (foll. by *over*) *intr.* (of a building etc.) have a commanding position over; overlook. □ **dominator** *n.* [Latin *dominari dominat-* from *dominus* 'lord']

domination /dɒmɪˈneɪʃ(ə)n/ *n.* **1** command, control. **2** the act or an instance of dominating; the process of being dominated. **3** (in *pl.*) angelic beings of the fourth order of the celestial hierarchy (see ORDER *n.* 19). [Middle English via Old French from Latin *dominatio -onis* (as DOMINATE)]

dominatrix /dɒmɪˈneɪtrɪks/ *n.* (*pl.* **dominatrices** /-trɪsiːz/) a female dominator or ruler, esp. in sadomasochistic practices. [Latin]

domineer /dɒmɪˈnɪə/ *v.intr.* (often as **domineering** *adj.*) behave in an arrogant and overbearing way. □ **domineeringly** *adv.* [Dutch *domineren* from French *dominer*]

dominical /dəˈmɪnɪk(ə)l/ *adj.* **1** of the Lord's day, of Sunday. **2** of the Lord (Jesus Christ). [French *dominical* or Latin *dominicalis* from Latin *dominicus*, from *dominus* 'lord']

dominical letter *n.* (in the Christian Church) one of the seven letters A–G used to indicate the dates of Sundays in a year.

■ **Usage** The seven letters A–G are used in succession to denote the first seven days of the year (Jan. 1–7), then in rotation for the rest of the days, so that if, for example, Jan. 3 be a Sunday, the dominical letter for the year is C.

Dominican /dəˈmɪnɪk(ə)n/ *adj. & n.* ● *adj.* **1** of or relating to St Dominic or the order of preaching friars which he founded in 1215–16. **2** of or relating to either of the two orders of female religious orders founded on Dominican principles. ● *n.* a Dominican friar, nun, or sister (see also BLACK FRIAR). [medieval Latin *Dominicanus* from *Dominicus*, the Latin name of *Domingo* de Guzmán (St Dominic)]

dominie /ˈdɒmɪni/ *n. Sc.* a schoolmaster. [later spelling of *domine* 'sir', vocative of Latin *dominus* 'lord']

dominion /dəˈmɪnjən/ *n.* **1** sovereignty, control. **2** the territory of a sovereign or government; a domain. **3** *hist.* the title of each of the self-governing territories of the British Commonwealth. [Middle English via Old French and medieval Latin *dominio -onis* from Latin *dominium*, from *dominus* 'lord']

domino /ˈdɒmɪnəʊ/ *n.* (*pl.* **-oes**) **1 a** any of 28 small oblong pieces marked with 0–6 pips in each half. **b** (in *pl.*, usu. treated as *sing.*) a game played with these. **2** a loose cloak with a mask for the upper part of the face, worn at masquerades. [French, probably from Latin *dominus* 'lord', but unexplained]

domino effect *n.* (also **domino theory**) the effect whereby (or the theory that) one event will cause a sequence of similar events, like a row of falling dominoes.

don[1] /dɒn/ *n.* **1** a university teacher, esp. a senior member of a college at Oxford or Cambridge. **2** (**Don**) **a** a Spanish title prefixed to a male forename. **b** a Spanish gentleman; a Spaniard. **c** *N. Amer. slang* a high-ranking member of the Mafia. [Spanish from Latin *dominus* 'lord']

don[2] /dɒn/ *v.tr.* (**donned**, **donning**) put on (clothing). [= *do on*]

dona /ˈdəʊnə/ *n.* (also **donah**) *Brit. slang* a woman; a sweetheart. [Spanish *doña* or Portuguese *dona* from Latin (as DONNA)]

donate /də(ʊ)ˈneɪt/ *v.tr.* give or contribute (money etc.), esp. voluntarily to a fund or institution. □ **donator** *n.* [back-formation from DONATION]

donation /də(ʊ)ˈneɪʃ(ə)n/ *n.* **1** the act or an instance of donating. **2** something, esp. an amount of money, donated. [Middle English via Old French from Latin *donatio -onis*, from *donare* 'give' from *donum* 'gift']

donative /ˈdəʊnətɪv/ *n. & adj.* ● *n.* a gift or donation, esp. one given formally or officially as a largess. ● *adj.* **1** given as a donation or bounty. **2** *hist.* (of a benefice) given directly, not presentative. [Middle English from Latin *donativum* 'gift, largess', from *donare*: see DONATION]

done /dʌn/ *past part.* of DO[1]. ● *adj.* **1** *colloq.* socially acceptable (*the done thing*; *it isn't done*). **2** (often with *in*, *up*) *colloq.* tired out. **3** (esp. as *int.* in reply to an offer etc.) accepted. □ **be done with** have finished with, be finished with. **done for** *colloq.* in serious trouble. **have done** have ceased or finished. **have done with** be rid of; have finished dealing with.

donee /dəʊˈniː/ *n.* the recipient of a gift. [DONOR + -EE]

doner kebab /ˈdɒnə, ˈdəʊnə/ *n.* spiced lamb cooked on a spit and served in slices, often with pitta bread. [Turkish *döner* 'rotating' + KEBAB]

dong[1] /dɒŋ/ *v. & n.* ● *v.* **1** *intr.* make the deep sound of a large bell. **2** *tr. Austral. & NZ colloq.* hit, punch. ● *n.* **1** the deep sound of a large bell. **2** *Austral. & NZ colloq.* a heavy blow. **3** *coarse slang* the penis. [imitative]

dong[2] /dɒŋ/ *n.* the chief monetary unit of Vietnam. [Vietnamese]

donga /ˈdɒŋgə/ *n. S.Afr. & Austral.* **1** a dry watercourse. **2** a ravine caused by erosion. [Nguni]

dongle /ˈdɒŋg(ə)l/ *n. Computing* a security attachment which is needed for the use of protected computer software. [arbitrary formation]

donjon /ˈdɒndʒ(ə)n, ˈdʌn-/ *n.* the great tower or innermost keep of a castle. [archaic spelling of DUNGEON]

Don Juan /dɒn ˈdʒʊən, ˈwɑːn, ˈxwɑːn/ *n.* a seducer of women; a libertine. [name of a legendary Spanish nobleman celebrated in fiction, e.g. by Byron]

donkey /ˈdɒŋki/ *n.* (*pl.* **-eys**) **1** a domestic ass. **2** *colloq.* a stupid or foolish person. [earlier with pronunciation as *monkey*: perhaps from DUN[1], or the name *Duncan*]

donkey derby *n.* a race between competitors riding donkeys.

donkey engine *n.* a small auxiliary engine.

donkey jacket *n. Brit.* a thick weatherproof jacket worn by workers and as a fashion garment.

donkey's years *n.pl. colloq.* a very long time.

donkey work *n.* the laborious part of a job; drudgery.

donna /ˈdɒnə/ *n.* **1** an Italian, Spanish, or Portuguese lady. **2** (**Donna**) a title prefixed to the forename of such a lady. [Italian from Latin *domina* 'mistress', fem. of *dominus*: cf. DON[1]]

donnée /ˈdɒneɪ, French dɔne/ *n.* (also ***donné***) **1** the subject or theme of a story etc. **2** a basic fact or assumption. [French, fem. or masc. past part. of *donner* 'give']

donnish /ˈdɒnɪʃ/ *adj.* like or resembling a college don, esp. in supposed pedantry. □ **donnishly** *adv.* **donnishness** *n.*

donor /ˈdəʊnə, -nɔː/ *n.* **1** a person who gives or donates something (e.g. to a charity). **2** a person who provides blood for a transfusion, semen for insemination, or an organ or tissue for transplantation. **3** *Chem.* an atom or molecule that provides a pair of electrons in forming a coordinate bond. **4** *Physics* an impurity atom in a semiconductor which contributes a conducting electron to the material. [Middle English via Anglo-French *donour*, Old French *doneur* from Latin *donator -oris*, from *donare* 'give']

donor card *n.* an official card authorizing use of organs for transplant, carried by the donor.

don't /dəʊnt/ *contr.* do not. ● *n.* a prohibition (*dos and don'ts*).

donut *US* var. of DOUGHNUT.

doodad /'du:dad/ *n. N. Amer.* = DOODAH. [20th c.: origin unknown]

doodah /'du:dɑ:/ *n. colloq.* **1** a fancy article; a trivial ornament. **2** a gadget or 'thingummy'. □ **all of a doodah** excited, dithering. [from the refrain of the song *Camptown Races*]

doodle /'du:d(ə)l/ *v. & n.* ● *v.intr.* scribble or draw, esp. absent-mindedly. ● *n.* a scrawl or drawing so made. □ **doodler** *n.* [originally = foolish person: from Low German *dudelkopf*]

doodlebug /'du:d(ə)lbʌg/ *n.* **1** *US* any of various insects, esp. the larva of an ant-lion. **2** *US* an unscientific device for locating minerals. **3** *Brit. colloq.* a flying bomb.

doodly-squat var. of DIDDLY-SQUAT.

doohickey /'du:hɪki/ *n.* (*pl.* **-eys**) *N. Amer. colloq.* a small object, esp. mechanical. [DOODAD + HICKEY]

doojigger /'du:dʒɪgə/ *n. US colloq.* = DOOHICKEY. [DOODAD + JIGGER[1]]

doom /du:m/ *n. & v.* ● *n.* **1 a** a grim fate or destiny. **b** death or ruin. **2 a** a condemnation; a judgement or sentence. **b** the Last Judgement (*the crack of doom*). **3** *hist.* a statute, law, or decree. ● *v.tr.* **1** (usu. foll. by *to*) condemn or destine (*a city doomed to destruction*). **2** (esp. as **doomed** *adj.*) consign to misfortune or destruction. [Old English *dōm* 'statute, judgement', from Germanic: related to DO[1]]

doom-laden *adj.* portending, suggesting, or predicting doom.

doomsayer /'du:mseɪə/ *n.* a person who predicts disaster, esp. in politics or economics. □ **doomsaying** *n.*

doomsday /'du:mzdeɪ/ *n.* the day of the Last Judgement. □ **till doomsday** for ever (cf. DOMESDAY). [Old English *dōmes dæg*: see DOOM]

doomster /'du:mstə/ *n.* = DOOMSAYER. [variant of DEEMSTER on the pattern of DOOM *v.*]

doomwatch /'du:mwɒtʃ/ *n.* organized vigilance or observation to avert danger, esp. from environmental pollution. □ **doomwatcher** *n.*

Doona /'du:nə/ *n. Austral. propr.* a quilted eiderdown or duvet. [20th c.: origin unknown]

door /dɔ:/ *n.* **1 a** a hinged, sliding, or revolving barrier for closing and opening an entrance to a building, room, cupboard, etc. **b** this as representing a house etc. (*lives two doors away*). **2 a** an entrance or exit; a doorway. **b** a means of access or approach. □ **close the door to** exclude the opportunity for. **lay** (or **lie**) **at the door of** impute (or be imputable) to. **leave the door open** ensure that an option remains available. **open the door to** create an opportunity for. □ **doored** *adj.* (also in *comb.*). [Old English *duru*, *dor*, from Germanic]

doorbell /'dɔ:bɛl/ *n.* a bell in a house etc. rung by visitors outside to signal their arrival.

doorcase /'dɔ:keɪs/ *n.* (also **door frame**) the structure into which a door is fitted.

do-or-die *attrib.adj.* denoting a determination not to be deterred by any danger or difficulty.

door head *n.* the upper part of a doorcase.

doorkeeper /'dɔ:ki:pə/ *n.* = DOORMAN.

doorknob /'dɔ:nɒb/ *n.* a knob for turning to release the latch of a door.

doorknock /'dɔ:nɒk/ *n. Austral.* a campaign of house visits to collect for charity, promote a cause, etc.

door knocker *n.* **1** a handle of metal or wood fixed to a door by a hinge to allow visitors to signal their arrival by knocking. **2** a person who visits a number of houses to sell products, canvass votes, etc.

doorman /'dɔ:mən/ *n.* (*pl.* **-men**) a person on duty at the door to a large building; a janitor or porter.

doormat /'dɔ:mat/ *n.* **1** a mat at an entrance for wiping mud etc. from the shoes. **2** a feebly submissive person.

doornail /'dɔ:neɪl/ *n.* a nail with which doors were studded for strength or ornament. □ **dead as a doornail** completely or unmistakably dead.

door plate *n.* a plate on the door of a house or room bearing the name of the occupant.

doorpost /'dɔ:pəʊst/ *n.* each of the uprights of a door frame.

doorstep /'dɔ:stɛp/ *n. & v.* ● *n.* **1** a step leading up to the outer door of a house etc. **2** *Brit. slang* a thick slice of bread. ● *v.* (**-stepped**, **-stepping**) *Brit.* **1** *intr.* go from door to door selling, canvassing, etc. **2** *tr.* (of a reporter) wait on the doorstep for (a person), to obtain an interview, photograph, etc. **3** *tr.* leave (a child) to the care of someone else. □ **on one's** (or **the**) **doorstep** very close.

doorstop /'dɔ:stɒp/ *n.* a device for keeping a door open or to prevent it from striking a wall etc. when opened.

door-to-door *adj.* (of selling etc.) done at each house in turn.

doorway /'dɔ:weɪ/ *n.* an opening filled by a door.

dooryard /'dɔ:jɑ:d/ *n. N. Amer.* a yard or garden near a house door.

doozy /'du:zi/ *n.* (also **doozie**) (*pl.* **-ies**) *N. Amer. slang* something amazing, remarkable, or incredible. [20th c.: origin uncertain]

dop /dɒp/ *n. S.Afr.* **1** a cheap kind of brandy. **2** a tot of liquor. [Afrikaans]

dopa /'dəʊpə/ *n. Biochem.* an amino acid derivative which is a precursor of dopamine. See also L-DOPA. [German from *D*ioxy*p*henyl*a*lanine, former name of the compound]

dopamine /'dəʊpəmi:n/ *n. Biochem.* an amine present in the body as a neurotransmitter and a precursor of other substances including adrenalin. [DOPA + AMINE]

dopant /'dəʊp(ə)nt/ *n. Electronics* a substance used in doping a semiconductor.

dope /dəʊp/ *n. & v.* ● *n.* **1** a varnish applied to the cloth surface of aeroplane parts to strengthen them, keep them airtight, etc. **2** a thick liquid used as a lubricant etc. **3** a substance added to petrol etc. to increase its effectiveness. **4 a** *slang* a narcotic; a stupefying drug. **b** a drug etc. given to a horse or greyhound, or taken by an athlete, to affect performance. **5** *slang* a stupid person. **6** *slang* **a** information about a subject, esp. if not generally known. **b** misleading information. ● *v.* **1** *tr.* administer dope to, drug. **2** *tr. Electronics* add an impurity to (a semiconductor) to produce a desired electrical characteristic. **3** *tr.* smear, daub; apply dope to. **4** *intr.* take addictive drugs. □ **dope out** *slang* discover. □ **doper** *n.* [Dutch *doop* 'sauce' from *doopen* 'to dip']

dopey /'dəʊpi/ *adj.* (also **dopy**) (**dopier**, **dopiest**) *colloq.* **1 a** half asleep. **b** stupefied by or as if by a drug. **2** stupid, silly. □ **dopily** *adv.* **dopiness** *n.*

doppelgänger /'dɒp(ə)lgɛŋə, -gaŋə/ *n.* an apparition or double of a living person. [German, literally 'double-goer']

Dopper /'dɒpə/ *n. S.Afr.* a member of the Gereformeerde Kerk, a strictly orthodox Calvinistic denomination, usu. regarded as old-fashioned in ideas etc. [Afrikaans: origin unknown]

Doppler effect /'dɒplə/ *n.* (also **Doppler shift**) *Physics* an increase (or decrease) in the frequency of sound, light, or other waves as the source and observer move towards (or away) from each other. [named after C. J. *Doppler*, Austrian physicist d. 1853]

dopy var. of DOPEY.

dor /dɔ:/ *n.* (in full **dor-beetle**) a beetle that makes a buzzing sound in flight, esp. a dung-beetle of the genus *Geotrupes*. [Old English *dora*]

dorado /dəˈrɑːdəʊ/ *n.* (*pl.* **-os**) **1** a blue and silver marine fish, *Coryphaena hippurus*, showing brilliant colours when alive; also called *dolphin*. **2** a gold-coloured freshwater fish, *Salminus maxillosus*, native to S. America. [Spanish from Late Latin *deauratus* 'gilt', from *aurum* 'gold']

Dorian /ˈdɔːrɪən/ *n.* & *adj.* ● *n.* (in *pl.*) a Greek-speaking people thought to have entered Greece from the north *c.*1100 BC and settled in parts of Central and S. Greece. ● *adj.* of or relating to the Dorians or to Doris in Central Greece. [Latin *Dorius* from Greek *Dōrios*, from *Dōros*, the name of their mythical ancestor]

Dorian mode *n.* the mode represented by the natural diatonic scale D–D.

Doric /ˈdɒrɪk/ *adj.* & *n.* ● *adj.* **1** (of a dialect) broad, rustic. **2** *Archit.* of the oldest, sturdiest, and simplest of the Greek orders. **3** of or relating to the ancient Greek dialect of the Dorians. ● *n.* **1** rustic English or esp. Scots. **2** *Archit.* the Doric order. **3** the dialect of the Dorians in ancient Greece. [Latin *Doricus* from Greek *Dōrikos* (as DORIAN)]

dork /dɔːk/ *n. slang* **1** the penis. **2** a stupid or contemptible person. [20th *c.*: origin unknown]

dorm /dɔːm/ *n. colloq.* dormitory. [abbreviation]

dormant /ˈdɔːm(ə)nt/ *adj.* **1** lying inactive as in sleep; sleeping. **2 a** (of a volcano etc.) temporarily inactive. **b** (of potential faculties etc.) in abeyance. **3** (of plants) alive but not actively growing. **4** *Heraldry* (of a beast) lying with its head on its paws. ▫ **dormancy** *n.* [Middle English from Old French, pres. part. of *dormir*, from Latin *dormire* 'sleep']

dormer /ˈdɔːmə/ *n.* (in full **dormer window**) a projecting upright window in a sloping roof. [formerly = the window of a dormitory or bedroom: Old French *dormëor* (as DORMANT)]

dormer bungalow *n.* a two-storeyed house with dormer windows in the upper storey.

dormitory /ˈdɔːmɪt(ə)ri/ *n.* (*pl.* **-ies**) **1** a sleeping room with several beds, esp. in a school or institution. **2** (in full **dormitory town** etc.) a small town or suburb from which people travel to work in a city etc. **3** *US* a university or college hall of residence or hostel. [Middle English from Latin *dormitorium*, from *dormire dormit-* 'sleep']

Dormobile /ˈdɔːmə(ʊ)biːl/ *n. Brit. propr.* a type of motor caravan with a rear compartment convertible for sleeping and eating in. [blend of DORMITORY, AUTOMOBILE]

dormouse /ˈdɔːmaʊs/ *n.* (*pl.* **dormice**) any mouselike rodent of the family Gliridae, often having a bushy tail, esp. *Muscardinus avellanarius*, noted for its long hibernation. [Middle English: origin unknown, but associated with French *dormir*, Latin *dormire*: see DORMANT]

dormy /ˈdɔːmi/ *adj. Golf* (of a player or side) ahead by as many holes as there are holes left to play (*dormy five*). [19th c.: origin unknown]

doronicum /dəˈrɒnɪkəm/ *n.* = LEOPARD'S BANE. [modern Latin (Linnaeus), ultimately from Arabic *darānaj*]

dorp /dɔːp/ *n. S.Afr.* a village or small township. [Dutch (as THORP)]

dorsal /ˈdɔːs(ə)l/ *adj. Anat., Zool., & Bot.* **1** of, on, or near the back (cf. VENTRAL). **2** ridge-shaped. ▫ **dorsally** *adv.* [French *dorsal* or Late Latin *dorsalis* from Latin *dorsum* 'back']

dorsum /ˈdɔːsəm/ *n. Anat. & Zool.* the dorsal part of an organism or structure. [Latin, = back]

dory[1] /ˈdɔːri/ *n.* (*pl.* **-ies**) a marine fish of the family Zeidae, with a thin deep body, esp. the John Dory. [Middle English from French *dorée*, fem. past part. of *dorer* 'gild' (as DORADO)]

dory[2] /ˈdɔːri/ *n.* (*pl.* **-ies**) *N. Amer.* & *W.Ind.* a flat-bottomed fishing boat with high sides. [Miskito *dóri* 'dugout']

doryphore /ˈdɒrɪfɔː/ *n.* a self-righteously pedantic critic. [French, = Colorado beetle, from Greek *doruphoros* 'spear-carrier']

DOS /dɒs/ *n. Computing* a program for manipulating information on a disk. [abbreviation of *d*isk *o*perating *s*ystem]

dos-à-dos /dəʊzəˈdəʊ, French dozado/ *adj.* & *n.* ● *adj.* (of two books) bound together with a shared central board and facing in opposite directions. ● *n.* (*pl.* same) a seat, carriage, etc., in which the occupants sit back to back (cf. DO-SE-DO). [French, = back to back]

dosage /ˈdəʊsɪdʒ/ *n.* **1** the size of a dose of medicine, radiation, etc. **2** the giving of medicine in doses.

dose /dəʊs/ *n.* & *v.* ● *n.* **1** an amount of a medicine or drug taken or recommended to be taken at one time. **2** a quantity of something administered or allocated (e.g. work, praise, punishment, etc.). **3** the amount of ionizing radiation received by a person or thing. **4** *slang* a venereal infection. ● *v.tr.* **1** treat (a person or animal) with doses of medicine. **2** give a dose or doses to. **3** adulterate or blend (esp. wine with spirit). ▫ **like a dose of salts** *Brit. colloq.* very fast and efficiently. [French via Late Latin *dosis* from Greek *dosis* 'gift', from *didōmi* 'give']

do-se-do /dəʊzɪˈdəʊ, -sɪ-/ *n.* (also **do-si-do**) (*pl.* **-os**) a figure in which two dancers pass round each other back to back and return to their original positions. [corruption of DOS-À-DOS]

dosh /dɒʃ/ *n. Brit. slang* money. [20th c.: origin unknown]

dosimeter /dəʊˈsɪmɪtə/ *n.* (also **dosemeter** /ˈdəʊsmiːtə/) a device used to measure an absorbed dose of ionizing radiation. ▫ **dosimetric** /-ˈmɛtrɪk/ *adj.* **dosimetry** *n.*

doss /dɒs/ *v.* & *n. Brit. slang* ● *v.intr.* **1** (often foll. by *down*) sleep, esp. roughly or in cheap lodgings. **2** (often foll. by *about*, *around*) spend time idly. ● *n.* **1** a bed, esp. in cheap lodgings. **2** an easy task; an opportunity for, or spell of, idling. [18th c.: origin uncertain, perhaps ultimately from Latin *dorsum* 'back']

dossal /ˈdɒs(ə)l/ *n.* a hanging cloth behind an altar or round a chancel. [medieval Latin *dossale* from Late Latin *dorsalis* DORSAL]

dosser /ˈdɒsə/ *n. Brit. slang* **1** a person who dosses. **2** = DOSS-HOUSE.

doss-house *n. Brit.* a cheap lodging house, esp. for vagrants.

dossier /ˈdɒsɪə, -ɪeɪ, -jeɪ/ *n.* a set of documents, esp. a collection of information about a person, event, or subject. [French, so called from the label on the back, from *dos* 'back' from Latin *dorsum*]

dost /dʌst/ *archaic 2nd sing. present* of DO[1].

DoT *abbr.* (in the UK) Department of Transport.

dot[1] /dɒt/ *n.* & *v.* ● *n.* **1 a** a small spot, speck, or mark. **b** such a mark written or printed as part of an *i* or *j*, as a diacritical mark, as one of a series of marks to signify omission, or as a full stop. **c** a decimal point. **2** *Mus.* a dot used to denote the lengthening of a note or rest, or to indicate staccato. **3** the shorter signal of the two used in Morse code (cf. DASH *n.* 6). **4** a tiny or apparently tiny object (*a dot on the horizon*). ● *v.tr.* (**dotted**, **dotting**) **1 a** mark with a dot or dots. **b** place a dot over (a letter). **2** *Mus.* mark (a note or rest) to show that the time value is increased by half. **3** (often foll. by *about*) scatter like dots. **4** partly cover as with dots (*a sea dotted with ships*). **5** *Brit. slang* hit (*dotted him one in the eye*). ▫ **dot the i's and cross the t's** *colloq.* **1** be minutely accurate, emphasize details. **2** add the final touches to a task, exercise, etc. **on the dot** exactly on time. **the year dot** *Brit. colloq.* a time far in the past. ▫ **dotter** *n.* [Old English *dott* 'head of a boil', perhaps influenced by Dutch *dot* 'knot']

dot[2] /dɒt, French dɔt/ *n.* a woman's dowry. [French, from Latin *dos dotis*, related to *dare* 'give']

dotage /ˈdəʊtɪdʒ/ *n.* feeble-minded senility (*in his dotage*). [from DOTE + -AGE, cf. French *radotage*, from *radoter* 'ramble on']

dotard /ˈdəʊtəd/ *n.* a person who is feeble-minded, esp. from senility. [Middle English from DOTE + -ARD]

dote /dəʊt/ *v.intr.* **1** (foll. by *on, upon*) be foolishly or excessively fond of. **2** be silly or feeble-minded, esp. from old age. □ **doter** *n.* **dotingly** *adv.* [Middle English, corresponding to Middle Dutch *doten* 'be silly']

doth /dʌθ/ *archaic 3rd sing. present* of DO[1].

dot matrix *n.* a regular array of positions that are filled selectively to create a character (on a screen or on paper).

dot matrix printer *n.* a printer with characters formed from dots printed by configurations of the tips of small wires.

dotted line *n.* a line of dots on a document, esp. to show a place left for a signature.

dotterel /ˈdɒt(ə)r(ə)l/ *n.* a small migratory plover, *Eudromias morinellus*. [Middle English from DOTE + -REL, named from the ease with which it is caught, taken to indicate stupidity]

dottle /ˈdɒt(ə)l/ *n.* a remnant of unburnt tobacco in a pipe. [DOT[1] + -LE[1]]

dotty /ˈdɒti/ *adj.* (**dottier**, **dottiest**) esp. *Brit. colloq.* **1** feeble-minded, silly. **2** eccentric. **3** absurd. **4** (foll. by *about, on*) infatuated with; obsessed by. □ **dottily** *adv.* **dottiness** *n.* [19th c.: origin uncertain]

douane /duːˈɑːn/ *n.* a foreign custom house. [French via Italian *do(g)ana* from Turkish *duwan*, Arabic *dīwān*: cf. DIVAN]

Douay Bible /ˈduːeɪ, ˈdaʊeɪ/ *n.* (also **Douay version**) an English translation of the Bible formerly used in the Roman Catholic Church, completed at Douai in France early in the seventeenth century.

double /ˈdʌb(ə)l/ *adj., adv., n., & v.* ● *adj.* **1 a** consisting of two usu. equal parts or things; twofold. **b** consisting of two identical parts. **2** twice as much or many (*double the amount*; *double the number*; *double thickness*). **3** having twice the usual size, quantity, strength, etc. (*double whisky*). **4** designed for two people (*double bed*). **5 a** having some part double. **b** (of a flower) having more than one circle of petals. **c** (of a domino) having the same number of pips on each half. **6** having two different roles or interpretations, esp. implying confusion or deceit (*double meaning*; *leads a double life*). **7** *Mus.* lower in pitch by an octave (*double bassoon*). ● *adv.* **1** at or to twice the amount etc. (*counts double*). **2** two together (*sleep double*). ● *n.* **1 a** a double quantity or thing; twice as much or many. **b** *colloq.* a double measure of spirits. **2 a** a counterpart of a person or thing; a person who looks exactly like another. **b** an understudy. **c** a wraith. **3** (in *pl.*) *Sport* (in tennis, badminton, etc.) a game between two pairs of players. **4** *Sport* a pair of victories over the same team, a pair of championships at the same game, etc. **5** a system of betting in which the winnings and stake from the first bet are transferred to a second. **6** *Bridge* the doubling of an opponent's bid. **7** *Darts* a hit on the narrow ring enclosed by the two outer circles of a dartboard, scoring double. **8** a sharp turn, esp. of the tracks of a hunted animal, or the course of a river. ● *v.* **1** *tr. & intr.* make or become twice as much or many; increase twofold; multiply by two. **2** *tr.* amount to twice as much as. **3 a** *tr.* fold or bend (paper, cloth, etc.) over on itself. **b** *intr.* become folded. **4 a** *tr.* (of an actor) play (two parts) in the same piece. **b** *intr.* (often foll. by *for*) be understudy etc. **5** *intr.* (usu. foll. by *as*) play a twofold role. **6** *intr.* turn sharply in flight or pursuit; take a tortuous course. **7** *tr. Naut.* sail round (a headland). **8** *tr. Bridge* make a call increasing the value of the points to be won or lost on (an opponent's bid). **9** *Mus.* **a** *intr.* (often foll. by *on*) play two or more musical instruments (*the clarinettist doubles on tenor sax*). **b** *tr.* add the same note in a higher or lower octave to (a note). **10** *tr.* clench (a fist). **11** *intr.* move at twice the usual speed; run. **12** *Billiards* **a** *intr.* rebound. **b** *tr.* cause to rebound. □ **at** (or *US* **on**) **the double** running, hurrying. **bent double** folded, stooping. **double back** take a new direction opposite to the previous one. **double or nothing** (or *Brit.* **quits**) a gamble to decide whether a player's loss or debt be doubled or cancelled. **double up 1 a** bend or curl up. **b** cause to do this, esp. by a blow. **2** be overcome with pain or laughter. **3** share or assign to a room, quarters, etc., with another or others. **4** fold or become folded. **5** use winnings from a bet as stake for another. □ **doubler** *n.* **doubly** *adv.* [Middle English via Old French *doble, duble* (*n.*), *dobler, dubler* (*v.*) from Latin *duplus* DUPLE]

double acrostic *n.* an acrostic using the first and last letters of each line.

double act *n.* an act involving two people.

double agent *n.* an agent who purports to spy for one country while working for another.

double axe *n.* an axe with two blades.

double-banking *n.* **1** *Brit.* double-parking. **2** *Austral. & NZ* riding two on a horse etc.

double-barrelled *adj.* **1** (of a gun) having two barrels. **2** *Brit.* (of a surname) having two parts joined by a hyphen. **3** twofold.

double bass *n.* **1** the largest and lowest-pitched instrument of the violin family. **2** its player.

double bill *n.* a programme with two principal items.

double bind *n.* a dilemma.

double-blind *adj. & n.* ● *adj.* (of a test or experiment) in which neither the tester nor the subject has knowledge of identities etc. that might lead to bias. ● *n.* such a test or experiment.

double bluff *n.* an action or statement intended to appear as a bluff, but in fact genuine.

double boiler *n.* a saucepan with a detachable upper compartment heated by boiling water in the lower one.

double bond *n.* a pair of bonds between two atoms in a molecule.

double-book *v.tr.* accept two reservations simultaneously for (the same seat, room, etc.).

double-breasted *adj.* (of a coat etc.) having two fronts overlapping across the body.

double-check *v.tr.* verify twice or in two ways.

double chin *n.* a chin with a fold of loose flesh below it. □ **double-chinned** *adj.*

double coconut *n.* a very large nut of the coco-de-mer.

double concerto *n.* a concerto for two solo instruments.

double cream *n. Brit.* thick cream with a high fat content.

double-cross *v. & n.* ● *v.tr.* deceive or betray (a person one is supposedly helping). ● *n.* an act of doing this. □ **double-crosser** *n.*

double dagger *n.* = DOUBLE OBELUS.

double-dealing *n. & adj.* ● *n.* deceit, esp. in business. ● *adj.* deceitful; practising deceit. □ **double-dealer** *n.*

double-decker *n.* **1** a bus having an upper and lower deck. **2** *colloq.* anything consisting of two layers.

double-declutch *v.intr. Brit.* release and re-engage the clutch twice when changing gear.

double decomposition *n. Chem.* a reaction in which two compounds exchange radicals or ions. Also called *metathesis*.

double density *adj. Computing* designating a storage device, esp. a disk, having twice the basic capacity.

double dummy *n. Bridge* play with two hands exposed, allowing every card to be located.

double Dutch *n.* **1** *Brit. colloq.* incomprehensible talk. **2** *US* a jumping game, played with two skipping ropes swung in opposite directions so that they rhythmically cross.

double-dyed *adj.* deeply affected with guilt.

double eagle *n.* **1** a figure of a two-headed eagle. **2** *US Golf* = ALBATROSS 2. **3** a former US coin worth twenty dollars.

double-edged *adj.* **1** having two functions or (often contradictory) applications. **2** (of a knife etc.) having two cutting edges.

double entendre /ˌdu:b(ə)l ɒ̃'tɒ̃dr(ə)/ *n.* **1** a word or phrase open to two interpretations, one usu. risqué or indecent. **2** humour using such words or phrases. [obsolete French, = double understanding]

double entry *n.* a system of bookkeeping in which each transaction is entered as a debit in one account and a credit in another.

double exposure *n.* the accidental or deliberate repeated exposure of a plate, film, etc.

double-faced *adj.* **1** insincere. **2** (of a fabric or material) finished on both sides so that either may be used as the right side.

double fault *n. & v. Tennis* ● *n.* two consecutive faults in serving. ● *v.intr.* (**double-fault**) serve a double fault.

double feature *n.* a cinema programme with two full-length films.

double figures *n.pl.* the numbers from 10 to 99.

double first *n. Brit.* **1** first-class honours in two subjects or examinations at a university. **2** a person achieving this.

double-fronted *adj.* (of a house) with principal windows on either side of the front door.

double-ganger /'dʌb(ə)lgaŋə/ *n.* = DOPPELGÄNGER.

double glazing *n.* **1** glazing consisting of two layers of glass with a space between them, designed to reduce loss of heat and exclude noise. **2** the provision of this. ▫ **double-glazed** *adj.*

double Gloucester *n.* a kind of hard cheese originally made in Gloucestershire.

double-headed *adj.* **1** having a double head or two heads. **2** (of a train) pulled by two locomotives.

double header *n.* **1** a train pulled by two locomotives coupled together. **2** *N. Amer.* two games etc. in succession between the same opponents. **3** *Austral. colloq.* a coin with a head on both sides.

double helix *n.* a pair of parallel helices with a common axis, esp. in the structure of the DNA molecule.

double-jointed *adj.* having joints that allow unusual bending of the fingers, limbs, etc.

double knitting *n.* a grade of yarn that is double the usual thickness.

double-lock *v.tr.* lock by a double turn of the key.

double napoleon *n. hist.* a forty-franc piece.

double negative *n.* a negative statement containing two negative elements (e.g. *didn't say nothing*).

▪ **Usage** The use of the double negative as illustrated is considered ungrammatical in standard English.

double obelus *n.* (also **double obelisk**) a sign (‡) used to introduce a reference.

double-park *v.tr. & intr.* park (a vehicle) alongside one that is already parked at the roadside.

double play *n. Baseball* putting out two runners.

double pneumonia *n.* pneumonia affecting both lungs.

double quick *adj. & adv.* very quick or quickly.

double refraction *n.* refraction forming two separate rays from a single incident ray.

double rhyme *n.* a rhyme including two syllables.

double salt *n.* a salt composed of two simple salts and having different crystal properties from either.

double saucepan *n. Brit.* = DOUBLE BOILER.

double shuffle *n.* a shuffle executed twice with one foot and then twice with the other.

double-sided *adj.* that can be used on both sides.

doublespeak /'dʌb(ə)lspi:k/ *n.* language or talk that is (usu. deliberately) ambiguous or obscure.

double standard *n.* **1** a rule or principle applied more strictly to some people than to others (or to oneself). **2** bimetallism.

double star *n.* two stars actually or apparently very close together.

double-stopping *n. Mus.* the sounding of two strings at once on a violin etc. ▫ **double stop** *n.*

doublet /'dʌblɪt/ *n.* **1** either of a pair of similar things, esp. either of two words of the same derivation but different sense (e.g. *fashion* and *faction*, *cloak* and *clock*). **2** *hist.* a man's short close-fitting jacket, with or without sleeves. **3** a historical or biblical account occurring twice in differing contexts, usu. traceable to different sources. **4** (in *pl.*) the same number on two dice thrown at once. **5** a pair of associated lines close together in a spectrum. **6** a combination of two simple lenses. [Middle English from Old French, from *double*: see DOUBLE]

double take *n.* a delayed reaction to a situation etc. immediately after one's first reaction.

double-talk *n.* = DOUBLESPEAK.

doublethink /'dʌb(ə)lθɪŋk/ *n.* the mental capacity to accept contrary opinions or beliefs at the same time esp. as a result of political indoctrination. [coined by George Orwell in *Nineteen Eighty-Four* (1949)]

double time *n.* **1** payment of an employee at twice the normal rate. **2** *Mil.* the regulation running pace.

double-tonguing *n. Mus.* a method of tonguing using two alternate tongue movements, usu. made by sounding *t* and *k* alternately, in order to facilitate rapid playing of a wind instrument.

double top *n. Darts* a score of double twenty.

double whammy *n. colloq.* a twofold blow or setback.

doubloon /dʌ'blu:n/ *n.* **1** *hist.* a Spanish gold coin. **2** (in *pl.*) *slang* money. [French *doublon* or Spanish *doblón* (as DOUBLE)]

doublure /du:b'ljʊə, French dublyr/ *n.* an ornamental lining, usu. leather, inside a book cover. [French, = lining, from *doubler* 'to line']

doubt /daʊt/ *n. & v.* ● *n.* **1** a feeling of uncertainty; an undecided state of mind (*be in no doubt about*; *have no doubt that*). **2** (often foll. by *of*, *about*) an inclination to disbelieve (*have one's doubts about*). **3** an uncertain state of things. **4** a lack of full proof or clear indication (*benefit of the doubt*). ● *v.* **1** *tr.* (often foll. by *whether*, *if*, *that* + clause; also foll. (after *neg.* or *interrog.*) by *but*, *but that*) feel uncertain or undecided about (*I doubt that you are right*; *I do not doubt but that you are wrong*). **2** *tr.* hesitate to believe or trust. **3** *intr.* (often foll. by *of*) feel uncertain or undecided; have doubts (*never doubted of success*). **4** *tr.* call in question. **5** *tr. Brit. archaic* or *dial.* rather think that; suspect or fear that (*I doubt we are late*). ▫ **beyond doubt** certainly. **in doubt** uncertain; open to question. **no doubt** certainly; probably; admittedly. **without doubt** (or **a doubt**) certainly. ▫ **doubtable** *adj.* **doubter** *n.* **doubtingly** *adv.* [Middle English via Old French *doute* (*n.*), *douter* (*v.*) from Latin *dubitare* 'hesitate']

doubtful /'daʊtfʊl, -f(ə)l/ *adj.* **1** feeling doubt or misgivings; unsure or guarded in one's opinion. **2** causing doubt; ambiguous; uncertain in meaning etc. **3** unreliable (*a doubtful ally*). ▫ **doubtfully** *adv.* **doubtfulness** *n.*

doubting Thomas *n.* an incredulous or sceptical person (after John 20:24–29).

doubtless /'daʊtlɪs/ *adv.* (often qualifying a sentence) **1** certainly; no doubt. **2** probably. ▫ **doubtlessly** *adv.*

douce /du:s/ *adj. Sc.* sober, gentle, sedate. [Middle English via Old French *dous douce* from Latin *dulcis* 'sweet']

douche /du:ʃ/ *n. & v.* ● *n.* **1** a jet of liquid applied to part of the body for cleansing or medicinal purposes. **2** a device for producing such a jet. ● *v.* **1** *tr.* treat with a douche. **2** *intr.* use a douche. [French from Italian *doccia* 'pipe', from *docciare* 'pour by drops', ultimately from Latin *ductus*: see DUCT]

dough /dəʊ/ *n.* **1** a thick mixture of flour etc. and liquid (usu. water), for baking into bread, pastry, etc. **2** *slang* money. [Old English *dāg*, from Germanic]

doughboy /'dəʊbɔɪ/ *n.* **1** a boiled or *US* deep-fried dumpling. **2** *US colloq.* a United States infantryman, esp. in the First World War.

doughnut /'dəʊnʌt/ *n.* (*US* **donut**) **1** a small fried cake of sweetened dough, usu. in the shape of a ball or ring. **2** a ring-shaped object, esp. *Physics* a vacuum chamber for acceleration of particles in a betatron or synchrotron.

doughnutting /'dəʊnʌtɪŋ/ *n.* the clustering of politicans round a speaker during a televised debate to make him or her appear well supported.

doughty /'daʊti/ *adj.* (**doughtier**, **doughtiest**) *archaic* or *joc.* valiant, stout-hearted. ◻ **doughtily** *adv.* **doughtiness** *n.* [Old English *dohtig*, variant of *dyhtig*, from Germanic]

doughy /'dəʊi/ *adj.* (**doughier**, **doughiest**) **1** having the form or consistency of dough. **2** pale and sickly in colour. ◻ **doughiness** *n.*

Douglas fir /'dʌgləs/ *n.* (also **Douglas pine** or **Douglas spruce**) any large conifer of the genus *Pseudotsuga*, of western N. America. [named after D. *Douglas*, Scots botanist d. 1834]

doum /du:m/ *n.* (in full **doum-palm**) a palm tree, *Hyphaene thebaica*, with edible fruit. [Arabic *dawm*, *dūm*]

dour /'dʊə/ *adj.* severe, stern, or sullenly obstinate in manner or appearance. ◻ **dourly** *adv.* **dourness** *n.* [Middle English (originally Scots), probably from Gaelic *dúr* 'dull, obstinate', perhaps from Latin *durus* 'hard']

douroucouli /dʊərʊ'ku:li/ *n.* (*pl.* **douroucoulis**) any nocturnal monkey of the genus *Aotus*, native to S. America, having large staring eyes. Also called *night monkey*, *owl monkey*. [native name]

douse /daʊs/ *v.tr.* (also **dowse**) **1 a** throw water over. **b** plunge into water. **2** extinguish (a light). **3** *Naut.* **a** lower (a sail). **b** close (a porthole). [16th c.: perhaps related to Middle Dutch, Low German *dossen* 'strike']

dove[1] /dʌv/ *n.* **1** any bird of the family Columbidae, with short legs, small head, and large breast. **2** a gentle or innocent person. **3** *Polit.* an advocate of peace or peaceful policies (cf. HAWK[1]). **4** (**Dove**) *Relig.* a representation of the Holy Spirit (John 1:32). **5** a soft grey colour. ◻ **dovelike** *adj.* [Middle English from Old Norse *dúfa*, from Germanic]

dove[2] /dəʊv/ *US past* and *past part.* of DIVE.

dovecote /'dʌvkɒt/ *n.* (also **dovecot**) a shelter with nesting-holes for domesticated pigeons.

dove grey *n.* & *adj.* ● *n.* a grey colour. ● *adj.* (hyphenated when *attrib.*) of this colour.

dovekie /'dʌvki/ *n. N. Amer. & Sc.* = LITTLE AUK. [Scots, diminutive of DOVE[1]]

dove's-foot *n.* a cranesbill, *Geranium molle.*

dovetail /'dʌvteɪl/ *n.* & *v.* ● *n.* **1** a joint formed by a mortise with a tenon shaped like a dove's spread tail or a reversed wedge. **2** such a tenon. ● *v.* **1** *tr.* join together by means of a dovetail. **2** *tr. & intr.* (often foll. by *into*, *with*) fit readily together; combine neatly or compactly.

dove tree *n.* a tree, *Davidia involucrata*, native to China, whose flowers bear large white bracts like doves' wings.

dowager /'daʊədʒə/ *n.* **1** a widow with a title or property derived from her late husband (*Queen dowager*; *dowager duchess*). **2** *colloq.* a dignified elderly woman. [Old French *douag(i)ere* from *douage* (as DOWER)]

dowdy /'daʊdi/ *adj.* & *n.* ● *adj.* (**dowdier**, **dowdiest**) **1** (of clothes) unattractively dull; unfashionable. **2** (of a person, esp. a woman) dressed in dowdy clothes. ● *n.* (*pl.* **-ies**) a dowdy woman. ◻ **dowdily** *adv.* **dowdiness** *n.* [Middle English *dowd* 'slut', of unknown origin]

dowel /'daʊəl/ *n.* & *v.* ● *n.* a headless peg of wood, metal, or plastic for holding together components of a structure. ● *v.tr.* (**dowelled**, **dowelling**; *US* **doweled**, **doweling**) fasten with a dowel or dowels. [Middle English from Middle Low German *dovel*: perhaps related to THOLE[1]]

dowelling /'daʊəlɪŋ/ *n.* (*US* **doweling**) cylindrical rods for cutting into dowels.

dower /'daʊə/ *n.* & *v.* ● *n.* **1** a widow's share for life of her husband's estate. **2** *archaic* a dowry. **3** a natural gift or talent. ● *v.tr.* **1** *archaic* give a dowry to. **2** (foll. by *with*) endow with talent etc. ◻ **dowerless** *adj.* [Middle English via Old French *douaire* and medieval Latin *dotarium* from Latin *dos dotis*; related to *dare* 'give']

dower house *n. Brit.* a smaller house near a big one, forming part of a widow's dower.

dowitcher /'daʊɪtʃə/ *n.* a wading bird of the genus *Limnodromus*, breeding in northern N. America and related to sandpipers. [Iroquoian]

Dow-Jones index /daʊ'dʒəʊnz/ *n.* (also **Dow-Jones average**) a figure based on the average price of selected stocks, indicating the relative price of shares on the New York Stock Exchange. [named after C. H. *Dow* d. 1902 & E. D. *Jones* d. 1920, American economists]

down[1] /daʊn/ *adv., prep., adj., v.,* & *n.* ● *adv.* (*superl.* **downmost**) **1** into or towards a lower place, esp. to the ground (*fall down*; *knelt down*). **2** in a lower place or position (*blinds were down*). **3** to or in a place regarded as lower, esp.: **a** southwards. **b** *Brit.* away from a major city or a university. **4 a** in or into a low or weaker position, mood, or condition (*hit a man when he's down*; *many down with colds*). **b** in a position of lagging behind or losing (*our team was three goals down*; *£5 down on the transaction*). **c** (of a computer system) out of action or unavailable for use (esp. temporarily). **5** from an earlier to a later time (*customs handed down*; *down to 1600*). **6** to a finer or thinner consistency or a smaller amount or size (*grind down*; *water down*; *boil down*). **7** cheaper; lower in price or value (*bread is down*; *shares are down*). **8** into a more settled state (*calm down*). **9** in writing; in or into recorded or listed form (*copy it down*; *I got it down on tape*; *you are down to speak next*). **10** (of part of a larger whole) paid, dealt with (*£5 down, £20 to pay*; *three down, six to go*). **11** *Naut.* **a** with the current or wind. **b** (of a ship's helm) with the rudder to windward. **12** inclusively of the lower limit in a series (*read down to the third paragraph*). **13** (as *int.*) lie down, put (something) down, etc. **14** (of a crossword clue or answer) read vertically (*cannot do five down*). **15** downstairs, esp. after rising (*is not down yet*). **16** swallowed (*could not get the pill down*). **17** *Amer. Football* (of the ball) out of play. ● *prep.* **1** downwards along, through, or into. **2** from top to bottom of. **3** along (*walk down the road*; *cut down the middle*). **4** at or in a lower part of (*situated down the river*). ● *adj.* (*superl.* **downmost**) **1** directed downwards. **2** *Brit.* of travel away from a capital or centre (*the down train*; *the down platform*). ● *v.tr. colloq.* **1** knock or bring down. **2** swallow (a drink). ● *n.* **1 a** *Sport* an act of putting down. **b** *Amer. Football* any of a series of chances to advance the ball for a score. **2** a reverse of fortune (*ups and downs*). **3** *colloq.* a period of depression. **4** the play of the first piece in dominoes. ◻ **be** (or **have a**) **down on** *colloq.* disapprove of; show animosity towards. **be down to 1** be attributable to. **2** be the responsibility of. **3** have used up everything except (*down to their last tin of rations*). **down on one's luck** *colloq.* **1** temporarily unfortunate. **2** dispirited by misfortune. **down to the ground** *colloq.* completely. **down tools** *Brit. colloq.* cease work, esp. to go on strike. **down with** *int.* expressing strong disapproval or rejection of a specified person or thing. [Old English *dūn(e)* aphetic form of *adūne* 'downward']

down[2] /daʊn/ *n.* **1 a** the first covering of young birds. **b** a bird's under-plumage, used in cushions etc. **c** a layer of fine soft feathers. **2** fine soft hair esp. on the face. **3** short soft hairs on some leaves, fruit, seeds, etc. **4** a fluffy substance, e.g. thistledown. [Middle English from Old Norse *dúnn*]

down[3] /daʊn/ *n.* **1** an area of open rolling land. **2** (in *pl.*; usu. prec. by *the*) **a** undulating chalk and limestone uplands esp. in southern England, with few trees and used mainly for pasture. **b** (**Downs**) a part of the sea (opposite the North Downs) off E. Kent. □ **downy** *adj.* [Old English *dūn*, perhaps from Celtic]

down and out *adj.* & *n.* ● *adj.* (hyphenated when *attrib.*) **1** penniless, destitute. **2** *Boxing* unable to resume the fight. ● *n.* (**down-and-out**) a destitute person.

down at heel *adj.* esp. *Brit.* **1** (of a shoe) with the heel worn down. **2** (of a person) impoverished; shabby, slovenly.

downbeat /'daʊnbiːt/ *n.* & *adj.* ● *n. Mus.* an accented beat, usu. the first of the bar. ● *adj.* **1** pessimistic, gloomy. **2** relaxed.

downcast /'daʊnkɑːst/ *adj.* & *n.* ● *adj.* **1** (of eyes) looking downwards. **2** (of a person) dejected. ● *n.* a shaft dug in a mine for extra ventilation.

downcomer /'daʊnkʌmə/ *n.* a pipe for the downward transport of water or gas.

down draught *n.* a downward draught, esp. one down a chimney into a room.

downer /'daʊnə/ *n. slang* **1** a depressant or tranquillizing drug, esp. a barbiturate. **2** a depressing person or experience; a failure. **3** = DOWNTURN.

downfall /'daʊnfɔːl/ *n.* **1 a** a fall from prosperity or power. **b** the cause of this. **2** a sudden heavy fall of rain etc.

downfield /daʊn'fiːld/ *adv.* esp. *N. Amer.* = UPFIELD.

downfold /'daʊnfəʊld/ *n. Geol.* a syncline.

downgrade *v.* & *n.* ● *v.tr.* /'daʊngreɪd, daʊn'greɪd/ **1** make lower in rank or status. **2** speak disparagingly of. ● *n.* /'daʊngreɪd/ esp. *US* **1** a downward gradient, esp. on a railway or road; a downward course. **2** a deterioration or decline. **3** an instance of downgrading or being downgraded (in sense 1 of *v.*). □ **on the downgrade** *US* in decline.

downhearted /daʊn'hɑːtɪd/ *adj.* dejected; in low spirits. □ **downheartedly** *adv.* **downheartedness** *n.*

downhill *adv.*, *adj.*, & *n.* ● *adv.* /daʊn'hɪl/ in a descending direction, esp. towards the bottom of an incline. ● *adj.* /'daʊnhɪl/ **1** sloping down, descending. **2** declining; deteriorating. ● *n.* /'daʊnhɪl/ **1** *Skiing* a downhill race. **2** a downward slope. **3** a decline. □ **go downhill** *colloq.* decline, deteriorate (in health, state of repair, moral state, etc.). □ **downhiller** *n. Skiing.*

down-home *attrib.adj.* esp. *US* reminiscent of one's home; unpretentious.

down in the mouth *adj. colloq.* looking unhappy.

downland /'daʊnlənd/ *n.* = DOWN³.

download *v.* & *n. Computing* ● *v.tr.* /daʊn'ləʊd/ transfer (data) from one storage device or system to another (esp. a smaller remote one). ● *n.* /'daʊnləʊd/ (often *attrib.*) a transfer of this type (*download utilities*).

downmarket /daʊn'mɑːkɪt, 'daʊn-/ *adj.* & *adv.* esp. *Brit. colloq.* towards or relating to the cheaper or less affluent sector of the market.

downmost /'daʊnməʊst/ *adj.* & *adv.* esp. *Brit.* the furthest down.

down payment *n.* a partial payment made at the time of purchase.

downpipe /'daʊnpʌɪp/ *n. Brit.* a pipe to carry rainwater from a roof to a drain or to ground level.

downplay /daʊn'pleɪ/ *v.tr.* play down; minimize the importance of.

downpour /'daʊnpɔː/ *n.* a heavy fall of rain.

downrate /daʊn'reɪt/ *v.tr.* make lower in value, standard, importance, etc.; downgrade.

downright /'daʊnrʌɪt/ *adj.* & *adv.* ● *adj.* **1** plain, definite, straightforward, blunt. **2** utter, complete (*a downright lie*; *downright nonsense*). ● *adv.* thoroughly, completely, positively (*downright inconsiderate*). □ **downrightness** *n.*

downriver *adv.* & *adj.* ● *adv.* /daʊn'rɪvə/ at or towards a point nearer the mouth of a river. ● *adj.* /'daʊnrɪvə/ situated or occurring downriver.

downscale /'daʊnskeɪl/ *v.* & *adj. US* ● *v.tr.* reduce or restrict in size, scale, or extent. ● *adj.* at the lower end of a scale, esp. a social scale; inferior.

downshift /'daʊnʃɪft/ *n.* & *v.* ● *n.* a movement downwards, esp. a change to a lower gear in a motor vehicle. ● *v.intr.* make a downshift.

downside /'daʊnsʌɪd/ *n.* **1** the negative aspect of something; a disadvantage or drawback. **2** a downward movement of share prices etc.

downsize /'daʊnsʌɪz/ *v.tr.* & *intr.* esp. *US* reduce in size.

downspout /'daʊnspaʊt/ *n. US* = DOWNPIPE.

Down's syndrome /daʊnz/ *n. Med.* a congenital disorder due to a chromosome defect, characterized by diminished intelligence and physical abnormalities including short stature and a broad facial profile (cf. MONGOLISM, TRISOMY). [named after J. L. H. *Down*, English physician d. 1896]

downstage /'daʊnsteɪdʒ, -'steɪdʒ/ *adj.* & *adv.* at or to the front of the stage.

downstairs *adv.*, *adj.*, & *n.* ● *adv.* /daʊn'stɛːz/ **1** down a flight of stairs. **2** to or on a lower floor. ● *adj.* /'daʊnstɛːz/ (also **downstair**) situated downstairs. ● *n.* /'daʊnstɛːz/ the lower floor.

downstate /'daʊnsteɪt/ *adj.*, *n.*, & *adv. US* ● *adj.* of or in a part of a state remote from large cities, esp. the southern part. ● *n.* a downstate area. ● *adv.* in a downstate area.

downstream *adv.* & *adj.* ● *adv.* /daʊn'striːm/ in the direction of the flow of a stream etc. ● *adj.* /'daʊnstriːm/ moving downstream.

downstroke /'daʊnstrəʊk/ *n.* a stroke made or written downwards.

downswing /'daʊnswɪŋ/ *n.* **1** a downward trend, esp. in economic conditions. **2** *Golf* the downward movement of the club when the player is about to hit the ball.

downthrow /'daʊnθrəʊ/ *n. Geol.* a downward dislocation of strata.

down time *n.* time during which a machine, esp. a computer, is out of action or unavailable for use.

down-to-earth *adj.* practical, realistic.

downtown *adj.*, *n.*, & *adv.* esp. *N. Amer.* ● *adj.* /'daʊntaʊn/ of or in the more central or lower part, or the business part, of a town or city. ● *n.* /'daʊntaʊn/ a downtown area. ● *adv.* /daʊn'taʊn/ in or into a downtown area.

down town *adv.* **1** into a town from a higher or outlying part. **2** esp. *N. Amer.* to or in the business part of a city (see also DOWNTOWN).

downtrodden /'daʊntrɒd(ə)n/ *adj.* oppressed; badly treated; kept under.

downturn /'daʊntəːn/ *n.* a decline, esp. in economic or business activity.

down under *adv.* & *n. colloq.* ● *adv.* in or to the antipodes, i.e. to Australia or New Zealand. ● *n.* the antipodes; Australia or New Zealand.

downward /'daʊnwəd/ *adv.* & *adj.* ● *adv.* (also **downwards**) towards what is lower, inferior, less important, or later. ● *adj.* moving, extending, pointing, or leading downward. □ **downwardly** *adv.*

downwarp /'daʊnwɔːp/ *n. Geol.* a broad surface depression; a syncline.

downwind /daʊn'wɪnd/ *adj.* & *adv.* in the direction in which the wind is blowing.

downy /'daʊni/ *adj.* (**downier**, **downiest**) **1 a** of, like, or covered with down. **b** soft and fluffy. **2** *Brit. slang* aware, knowing. □ **downily** *adv.* **downiness** *n.*

dowry /'daʊ(ə)ri/ *n.* (*pl.* **-ies**) **1** property or money brought by a bride to her husband. **2** a talent, a natural gift. [Middle English from Anglo-French *dowarie*, Old French *douaire* DOWER]

dowse¹ /daʊz/ *v.intr.* search for underground water or minerals by holding a Y-shaped stick or rod which dips abruptly when over the right spot. □ **dowser** *n.* [17th c.: origin unknown]

dowse² var. of DOUSE.

dowsing rod *n.* a stick or rod used in dowsing.

doxology /dɒk'sɒlədʒi/ *n.* (*pl.* **-ies**) a liturgical formula of praise to God. □ **doxological** /-sə'lɒdʒɪk(ə)l/ *adj.*

[medieval Latin *doxologia* from Greek *doxologia*, from *doxa* 'glory' + -LOGY]

doxy /'dɒksi/ *n.* (*pl.* **-ies**) *literary* **1** a lover or mistress. **2** a prostitute. [16th-c. cant: origin unknown]

doyen /'dɔɪən, 'dwɑːjã/ *n.* (*fem.* **doyenne** /'dɔɪɛn, dɔɪ'ɛn, dwɑː'jɛn/) the most senior or most prominent of a particular category or body of people. [French (as DEAN[1])]

doyley var. of DOILY.

doz. *abbr.* dozen.

doze /dəʊz/ *v.* & *n.* ● *v.intr.* sleep lightly; be half asleep. ● *n.* a short light sleep. □ **doze off** fall lightly asleep. [17th c.: origin unknown, perhaps related to Danish *døse* 'make drowsy']

dozen /'dʌz(ə)n/ *n.* **1** (prec. by *a* or a number) (*pl.* **dozen**) twelve, regarded collectively (*a dozen eggs*; *two dozen packets*; *ordered three dozen*). **2** a set or group of twelve (*packed in dozens*). **3** *colloq.* about twelve, a fairly large indefinite number. **4** (in *pl.*; usu. foll. by *of*) *colloq.* very many (*made dozens of mistakes*). **5** (**the dozens**) a black American game or ritualized exchange of verbal insults. □ **by the dozen** in large quantities. **talk nineteen to the dozen** *Brit.* talk incessantly. □ **dozenth** *adj.* [Middle English from Old French *dozeine*, ultimately from Latin *duodecim* 'twelve']

dozer /'dəʊzə/ *n. colloq.* = BULLDOZER 1. [abbreviation]

dozy /'dəʊzi/ *adj.* (**dozier, doziest**) **1** drowsy; tending to doze. **2** *Brit. colloq.* stupid or lazy. □ **dozily** *adv.* **doziness** *n.*

DP *abbr.* **1** data processing. **2** displaced person.

D.Phil. *abbr.* Doctor of Philosophy.

DPP *abbr.* (in the UK) Director of Public Prosecutions.

Dr *abbr.* **1** Doctor. **2** Drive. **3** debtor; debit.

dr. *abbr.* **1** drachm(s). **2** drachma(s). **3** dram(s).

drab[1] /drab/ *adj.* & *n.* ● *adj.* (**drabber, drabbest**) **1** dull, uninteresting. **2** of a dull brownish colour. ● *n.* **1** drab colour. **2** monotony. □ **drably** *adv.* **drabness** *n.* [probably from obsolete *drap* 'cloth' via Old French from Late Latin *drappus*, perhaps of Celtic origin]

drab[2] see DRIBS AND DRABS.

drab[3] /drab/ *n.* **1** a slut; a slattern. **2** a prostitute. [perhaps related to Low German *drabbe* 'mire', Dutch *drab* 'dregs']

drabble /'drab(ə)l/ *v.intr.* & *tr.* become or make dirty and wet with water or mud. [Middle English from Low German *drabbelen* 'paddle in water or mire': cf. DRAB[3]]

dracaena /drə'siːnə/ *n.* any of various shrubs and trees of the genera *Dracaena* and *Cordyline* (agave family) grown for their foliage. [modern Latin from Greek *drakaina*, fem. of *drakōn* 'dragon']

drachm /dram/ *n.* a weight or measure formerly used by apothecaries, equivalent to 60 grains or one-eighth of an ounce, or (in full **fluid drachm**) 60 minims, one-eighth of a fluid ounce. [Middle English *dragme* via Old French *dragme* or Late Latin *dragma* from Latin *drachma*, from Greek *drakhmē*, an Attic weight and coin]

drachma /'drakmə/ *n.* (*pl.* **drachmas** or **drachmae** /-miː/) **1** the chief monetary unit of Greece. **2** a silver coin of ancient Greece. [Latin from Greek *drakhmē*]

drack /drak/ *adj. Austral. slang* **1** (esp. of a woman) unattractive. **2** dismal, dull. [20th c.: origin unknown]

dracone /'drakəʊn/ *n. Brit.* a large flexible container for liquids, towed on the surface of the sea. [Latin *draco -onis* from Greek *drakōn* 'serpent': from its shape]

draconian /drə'kəʊnɪən, dreɪ-/ *adj.* (also **draconic** /-'kɒnɪk/) very harsh or severe (esp. of laws and their application). [*Drakōn*, the name of a 7th-c. BC Athenian legislator]

draff /draf/ *n.* **1** dregs, lees. **2** refuse. [Middle English, perhaps from Old English]

draft /drɑːft/ *n.* & *v.* ● *n.* **1 a** a preliminary written version of a speech, document, etc. **b** a rough preliminary outline of a scheme. **c** a sketch of work to be carried out. **2 a** a written order for payment of money by a bank. **b** the drawing of money by means of this. **3** (foll. by *on*) a demand made on a person's confidence, friendship, etc. **4 a** a party detached from a larger group for a special duty or purpose. **b** the selection of this. **5** *US* compulsory military service. **6** a reinforcement. **7** *US* = DRAUGHT. ● *v.tr.* **1** prepare a draft of (a document, scheme, etc.). **2** select for a special duty or purpose. **3** *US* conscript for military service. □ **draftee** /-'tiː/ *n.* **drafter** *n.* [phonetic spelling of DRAUGHT]

draft dodger *n. US* a person who tries to avoid compulsory military service. □ **draft dodging** *n.*

draftsman /'drɑːf(t)smən/ *n.* (*pl.* **-men**) **1** a person who drafts documents. **2** = DRAUGHTSMAN 1. [phonetic spelling of DRAUGHTSMAN]

drafty *US* var. of DRAUGHTY.

drag /drag/ *v.* & *n.* ● *v.* (**dragged, dragging**) **1** *tr.* pull along with effort or difficulty. **2 a** *tr.* allow (one's feet, tail, etc.) to trail along the ground. **b** *intr.* trail along the ground. **c** *intr.* (of time etc.) go or pass heavily or slowly or tediously. **3 a** *intr.* (usu. foll. by *for*) use a grapnel or drag (to find a drowned person or lost object). **b** *tr.* search the bottom of (a river etc.) with grapnels, nets, or drags. **4** *tr.* (often foll. by *to*) *colloq.* take (a person to a place etc., esp. against his or her will). **5** *intr.* (foll. by *on, at*) *colloq.* draw on (a cigarette etc.). **6** *intr.* (often foll. by *on*) continue at tedious length. ● *n.* **1 a** an obstruction to progress. **b** *Aeron.* the longitudinal retarding force exerted by air. **c** slow motion; impeded progress. **d** an iron shoe for retarding a horse-drawn vehicle downhill. **2** *colloq.* a boring or dreary person, duty, performance, etc. **3 a** a strong-smelling lure drawn before hounds as a substitute for a fox. **b** a hunt using this. **4** an apparatus for dredging or recovering drowned persons etc. from under water. **5** = DRAGNET 1. **6** *slang* a draw on a cigarette etc. **7** *slang* **a** women's clothes worn by men. **b** a party at which these are worn. **c** clothes in general. **8** an act of dragging. **9 a** *Brit. slang* a motor car. **b** (in full **drag race**) an acceleration race between cars usu. for a quarter of a mile. **10** *US slang* influence, pull. **11** *slang* a street or road (*the main drag*). **12** *hist.* a private vehicle like a stagecoach, drawn by four horses. □ **drag one's feet** (or **heels**) be deliberately slow or reluctant to act. **drag in** introduce (a subject) irrelevantly. **drag out** protract. **drag up** *colloq.* **1** deliberately mention (an unwelcome subject). **2** *Brit.* rear (a child) roughly and without proper training. [Middle English from Old English *dragan* or Old Norse *draga* DRAW]

drag-anchor *n.* & *v.* ● *n.* = SEA ANCHOR. ● *v.intr.* (**drag anchor**) (of a ship) move from a moored position when the anchor fails to hold.

dragée /'drɑːʒeɪ/ *n.* **1** a sugar-coated almond etc. **2** a small silver ball for decorating a cake. **3** a chocolate-coated sweet. [French: see DREDGE[2]]

draggle /'drag(ə)l/ *v.* **1** *tr.* make dirty or wet or limp by trailing. **2** *intr.* hang trailing. **3** *intr.* lag; straggle in the rear. [DRAG + -LE[4]]

draggle-tailed *adj.* (of a woman) with untidily trailing skirts.

draggy /'dragi/ *adj.* (**draggier, draggiest**) *colloq.* **1** tedious. **2** unpleasant.

drag-hound *n.* a hound used to hunt with a drag.

dragline /'draglʌɪn/ *n.* an excavator with a bucket pulled in by a wire rope.

dragnet /'dragnɛt/ *n.* **1** a net drawn through a river or across ground to trap fish or game. **2** a systematic hunt for criminals etc.

dragoman /'dragə(ʊ)mən/ *n.* (*pl.* **dragomans** or **dragomen**) an interpreter or guide, esp. in countries speaking Arabic, Turkish, or Persian. [French via Italian *dragomano*, medieval Greek *dragomanos*, Arabic *tarjumān* (from *tarjama* 'interpret'), and Aramaic *targēm* from Assyrian *targumânu* 'interpreter']

dragon /'drag(ə)n/ *n.* **1** a mythical monster like a reptile, usu. with wings and claws and able to breathe out fire. **2** a fierce person, esp. a woman. **3** (in full **flying dragon**) = FLYING LIZARD. [Middle English via

Old French and Latin *draco -onis* from Greek *drakōn* 'serpent']

dragonet /'drag(ə)nɪt/ *n.* any spiny marine fish of the family Callionymidae, the males of which are brightly coloured. [Middle English from French, diminutive of DRAGON]

dragonfish /'drag(ə)nfɪʃ/ *n.* (*pl.* usu. same) any deep-water marine fish of the order Stomiiformes, having a long slender body and a barbel on the chin with luminous tissue, serving to attract prey.

dragonfly /'drag(ə)nflʌɪ/ *n.* (*pl.* **-flies**) any of various predatory insects of the order Odonata, having a long slender body with two pairs of large transparent wings usu. spread while resting, and aquatic larvae.

dragonnade /dragə'neɪd/ *n.* & *v.* ● *n.* a persecution by use of troops, esp. (in *pl.*) of French Protestants under Louis XIV by quartering dragoons on them. ● *v.tr.* subject to a dragonnade. [French from *dragon*: see DRAGOON]

dragon's blood *n.* a red gum that exudes from the fruit of some palms and the dragon tree.

dragon's teeth *n.pl. Brit. colloq.* obstacles resembling teeth pointed upwards, used esp. against tanks.

dragon tree *n.* a palmlike tree, *Dracaena draco* of the agave family, native to the Canary Islands.

dragoon /drə'gu:n/ *n.* & *v.* ● *n.* **1** a cavalryman (originally a mounted infantryman armed with a carbine). **2** a rough fierce man. **3** a variety of pigeon. ● *v.tr.* **1** (foll. by *into*) coerce into doing something, esp. by use of forceful methods. **2** persecute, esp. with troops. [originally = carbine (thought of as breathing fire) from French *dragon* DRAGON]

drag queen *n. slang* a male homosexual transvestite.

drag race see DRAG *n.* 9b.

dragster /'dragstə/ *n.* a car built or modified to take part in drag races.

drail /dreɪl/ *n.* a fish-hook and line weighted with lead for dragging below the surface of the water. [apparently variant of TRAIL]

drain /dreɪn/ *v.* & *n.* ● *v.* **1** *tr.* draw off liquid from, esp.: **a** make (land etc.) dry by providing an outflow for moisture. **b** (of a river) carry off the superfluous water of (a district). **c** remove purulent matter from (an abscess). **2** *tr.* (foll. by *off, away*) draw off (liquid) esp. by a pipe. **3** *intr.* (foll. by *away, off, through*) flow or trickle away. **4** *intr.* (of a wet cloth, piece of crockery, etc.) become dry as liquid flows away (*put it there to drain*). **5** *tr.* (often foll. by *of*) exhaust or deprive (a person or thing) of strength, resources, property, etc. **6** *tr.* **a** drink (liquid) to the dregs. **b** empty (a container) by drinking the contents. ● *n.* **1 a** a channel, conduit, or pipe carrying off liquid, esp. an artificial conduit for water or sewage. **b** a tube for drawing off the discharge from an abscess etc. **2** a constant outflow, withdrawal, or expenditure (*a great drain on my resources*). □ **down the drain** *colloq.* lost, wasted. **laugh like a drain** *Brit.* laugh copiously; guffaw. [Old English *drē(a)hnian*, from Germanic]

drainage /'dreɪnɪdʒ/ *n.* **1** the process or means of draining (*the land has poor drainage*). **2** a system of drains, artificial or natural. **3** what is drained off, esp. sewage.

drainboard /'dreɪnbɔ:d/ *n. N. Amer.* = DRAINING BOARD.

draincock /'dreɪnkɒk/ *n.* a cock for draining the water out of a boiler etc.

drainer /'dreɪnə/ *n.* **1** a device for draining; anything on which things are put to drain, e.g. a draining board. **2** a person who drains.

draining board *n.* a sloping usu. grooved surface beside a sink, on which washed dishes etc. are left to drain.

drainpipe /'dreɪnpʌɪp/ *n.* **1** a pipe for carrying off water, sewage, etc., from a building. **2** (*attrib.*) (of trousers etc.) very narrow. **3** (in *pl.*) very narrow trousers.

drake /dreɪk/ *n.* a male duck. [Middle English, probably from West Germanic]

Dralon /'dreɪlɒn/ *n. Brit. propr.* **1** a synthetic acrylic fibre used in textiles. **2** a fabric made from this. [suggested by NYLON]

dram /dram/ *n.* **1** a small drink of spirits. **2** = DRACHM. [Middle English from Old French *drame* or medieval Latin *drama, dragma*: cf. DRACHM]

drama /'drɑ:mə/ *n.* **1** a play for acting on stage or for broadcasting. **2 a** the art of writing and presenting plays. **b** the art of acting. **3** an exciting or emotional event, set of circumstances, etc. **4** dramatic quality (*the drama of the situation*). [Late Latin from Greek *drama -atos*, from *draō* 'do']

drama-documentary *n.* (also **drama-doc** *slang*) a film (esp. for television) based on or dramatizing real events.

dramatic /drə'matɪk/ *adj.* **1** of drama or the study of drama. **2** (of an event, circumstance, etc.) sudden and exciting or unexpected. **3** vividly striking. **4** (of a gesture etc.) theatrical, overdone, absurd. □ **dramatically** *adv.* [Late Latin *dramaticus* from Greek *dramatikos* (as DRAMA)]

dramatic irony *n.* = TRAGIC IRONY.

dramatics /drə'matɪks/ *n.pl.* **1** (often treated as *sing.*) the production and performance of plays. **2** exaggerated or showy behaviour.

dramatis personae /ˌdramətɪs pə:'səʊnʌɪ, -ni:/ *n.pl.* (often treated as *sing.*) **1** the characters in a play. **2** a list of these. [Latin, = persons of the drama]

dramatist /'dramətɪst/ *n.* a writer of dramas.

dramatize /'dramətʌɪz/ *v.* (also **-ise**) **1 a** *tr.* adapt (a novel etc.) to form a stage play. **b** *intr.* admit of such adaptation. **2** *tr.* make a drama or dramatic scene of. **3** *tr.* (also *absol.*) express or react to in a dramatic way. □ **dramatization** /-'zeɪʃ(ə)n/ *n.*

dramaturge /'dramətə:dʒ/ *n.* **1** a specialist in theatrical production. **2** a dramatist. [French from Greek *dramatourgos* (as DRAMA, *-ergos* 'worker')]

dramaturgy /'dramətə:dʒi/ *n.* **1** the art of theatrical production; the theory of dramatics. **2** the application of this. □ **dramaturgic** /-'tə:dʒɪk/ *adj.* **dramaturgical** /-'tə:dʒɪk(ə)l/ *adj.*

Drambuie /dram'bu:i, -'bjʊi/ *n. propr.* a Scotch whisky liqueur. [Gaelic *dram buidheach* 'satisfying drink']

drank *past* of DRINK.

drape /dreɪp/ *v.* & *n.* ● *v.tr.* **1** hang, cover loosely, or adorn with cloth etc. **2** arrange (clothes or hangings) carefully in folds. ● *n.* **1** (often in *pl.*) a curtain or drapery. **2** a piece of drapery. **3** the way in which a garment or fabric hangs. [Middle English via Old French *draper*, from *drap*, from Late Latin *drappus* 'cloth']

draper /'dreɪpə/ *n. Brit.* a retailer of textile fabrics. [Middle English from Anglo-French, Old French *drapier* (as DRAPE)]

drapery /'dreɪp(ə)ri/ *n.* (*pl.* **-ies**) **1** clothing or hangings arranged in folds. **2** (often in *pl.*) a curtain or hanging. **3** *Brit.* cloth; textile fabrics. **4** *Brit.* the trade of a draper. **5** the arrangement of clothing in sculpture or painting. [Middle English from Old French *draperie*, from *drap* 'cloth']

drastic /'drastɪk, 'drɑ:-/ *adj.* having a strong or far-reaching effect; severe. □ **drastically** *adv.* [Greek *drastikos* from *draō* 'do']

drat /drat/ *v.* & *int. colloq.* ● *v.tr.* (**dratted**, **dratting**) (usu. as an exclamation) curse, confound (*drat the thing!*). ● *int.* expressing anger or annoyance. □ **dratted** *adj.* [for *'od* (= God) *rot*]

draught /drɑ:ft/ *n.* & *v.* (*US* **draft**) ● *n.* **1** a current of air in a confined space (e.g. a room or chimney). **2** pulling, traction. **3** *Naut.* the depth of water needed to float a ship. **4** the drawing of liquor from a cask etc. **5 a** a single act of drinking. **b** the amount drunk in this. **c** a dose of liquid medicine. **6** (in *pl.*; usu. treated as *sing.*) *Brit.* a game for two played with twelve pieces each on a draughtboard. **7 a** the drawing in of a fishing net. **b** the fish taken at one drawing. ● *v.tr.* = DRAFT. □ **feel the draught** *colloq.* suffer from adverse (usu. financial) conditions. [Middle English *draht* from Old Norse *drahtr*, *dráttr*, from Germanic, related to DRAW]

draught beer *n.* beer drawn from a cask, not bottled.

draughtboard /ˈdrɑːf(t)bɔːd/ *n. Brit.* a chequered board, identical to a chessboard, used in draughts.

draught horse *n.* a horse used for pulling heavy loads, esp. a cart or plough.

draught-proof *adj.* & *v.* ● *adj.* proof against draughts. ● *v.tr.* make draught-proof.

draughtsman /ˈdrɑːf(t)smən/ *n.* (*pl.* **-men**) **1** a person who makes drawings, plans, or sketches. **2** a piece in the game of draughts. **3** = DRAFTSMAN 1. □ **draughtsmanship** *n.* [*draught's* + MAN]

draughty /ˈdrɑːfti/ *adj.* (*US* **drafty**) (**-ier**, **-iest**) (of a room etc.) letting in sharp currents of air. □ **draughtily** *adv.* **draughtiness** *n.*

Dravidian /drəˈvɪdɪən/ *n.* & *adj.* ● *n.* **1** a member of a dark-skinned aboriginal people of S. India and Sri Lanka (including the Tamils and Kanarese). **2** any of the group of languages spoken by this people. ● *adj.* of or relating to this people or group of languages. [Sanskrit *Dravida*, a province of S. India]

draw /drɔː/ *v.* & *n.* ● *v.* (*past* **drew** /druː/; *past part.* **drawn** /drɔːn/) **1** *tr.* pull or cause to move towards or after one. **2** *tr.* pull (a thing) up, over, or across. **3** *tr.* pull (curtains etc.) open or shut. **4** *tr.* take (a person) aside, esp. to talk to. **5** *tr.* attract; bring to oneself or to something; take in (*drew a deep breath*; *I felt drawn to her*; *drew my attention to the matter*; *draw him into conversation*; *the match drew large crowds*). **6** *intr.* (foll. by *at*, *on*) suck smoke from (a cigarette, pipe, etc.). **7** *tr.* (also *absol.*) take out; remove (e.g. a tooth, a gun from a holster, etc.). **8** *tr.* obtain or take from a source (*draw a salary*; *draw inspiration*; *drew £100 from my account*). **9** *tr.* trace (a line, mark, furrow, or figure). **10 a** *tr.* produce (a picture) by tracing lines and marks. **b** *tr.* represent (a thing) by this means. **c** *absol.* make a drawing. **11** *tr.* (also *absol.*) finish (a contest or game) with neither side winning. **12** *intr.* make one's or its way, proceed, move, come (*drew near the bridge*; *draw to a close*; *the second horse drew level*; *drew ahead of the field*; *the time draws near*). **13** *tr.* infer, deduce (a conclusion). **14** *tr.* **a** elicit, evoke (*draw criticism*; *draw ruin upon oneself*). **b** bring about, entail. **c** induce (a person) to reveal facts, feelings, or talent (*refused to be drawn*). **d** (foll. by *to* + infin.) induce (a person) to do something. **e** *Cards* cause to be played (*drew all the trumps*). **15** *tr.* haul up (water) from a well. **16** *tr.* bring out (liquid from a container or blood from a wound). **17** *tr.* extract a liquid essence from. **18** *intr.* (of a chimney or pipe) promote or allow a draught. **19** *intr.* (of tea) infuse. **20 a** *tr.* obtain by lot (*drew the winner*). **b** *absol.* draw lots. **21** *intr.* (foll. by *on*) make a demand on a person, a person's skill, memory, imagination, etc. **22** *tr.* write out (a bill, cheque, or draft) (*drew a cheque on the bank*). **23** *tr.* frame (a document) in due form, compose. **24** *tr.* formulate or perceive (a comparison or distinction). **25** *tr.* (of a ship) require (a specified depth of water) to float in. **26** *tr.* disembowel (*hang, draw, and quarter*; *draw the fowl before cooking it*). **27** *tr. Hunting* search (cover) for game. **28** *tr.* drag (a badger or fox) from a hole. **29** *tr.* **a** protract, stretch, elongate (*long-drawn agony*). **b** make (wire) by pulling a piece of metal through successively smaller holes. **30** *tr.* **a** *Golf* drive (the ball) to the left (or, of a left-handed player, the right) esp. purposely. **b** *Bowls* cause (a bowl) to travel in a curve to the desired point. **31** *intr.* (of a sail) swell tightly in the wind. ● *n.* **1** an act of drawing. **2 a** a person or thing that draws custom, attention, etc. **b** the power to attract attention. **3** the drawing of lots, esp. a raffle. **4** a drawn game. **5** a suck on a cigarette etc. **6** the act of removing a gun from its holster in order to shoot (*quick on the draw*). **7** strain, pull. **8** *US* the movable part of a drawbridge. □ **draw back** withdraw from an undertaking. **draw a bead on** see BEAD. **draw bit** *Brit.* = *draw rein* (see REIN). **draw a blank** see BLANK. **draw bridle** *Brit.* = *draw rein* (see REIN). **draw a person's fire** attract hostility, criticism, etc., away from a more important target. **draw in 1 a** (of successive days) become shorter because of the changing seasons. **b** (of a day) approach its end. **c** (of successive evenings or nights) start earlier because of the changing seasons. **2** persuade to join, entice. **3** (of a train etc.) arrive at a station. **draw in one's horns** become less assertive or ambitious; draw back. **draw the line at** set a limit (of tolerance etc.) at. **draw lots** see LOT. **draw off** withdraw (troops). **draw on 1** approach, come near. **2** lead to, bring about. **3** allure. **4** put (gloves, boots, etc.) on. **draw out 1** prolong. **2** elicit. **3** induce to talk. **4** (of successive days) become longer because of the changing seasons. **5** (of a train etc.) leave a station etc. **6** write out in proper form. **7** lead out, detach, or array (troops). **draw rein** see REIN. **draw the short straw** see STRAW. **draw stumps** *Cricket* take the stumps out of the ground at the close of play. **draw one's sword against** attack. **draw up 1** compose or draft (a document etc.). **2** bring or come into regular order. **3** come to a halt. **4** make (oneself) stiffly erect. **5** (foll. by *with*, *to*) gain on or overtake. **quick on the draw** quick to act or react. [Old English *dragan*, from Germanic]

drawback /ˈdrɔːbak/ *n.* **1** a thing that impairs satisfaction; a disadvantage. **2** (foll. by *from*) a deduction. **3** an amount of excise or import duty paid back or remitted on goods exported.

drawback lock *n.* a lock with a spring bolt that can be drawn back by an inside knob.

drawbridge /ˈdrɔːbrɪdʒ/ *n.* a bridge, esp. over water, hinged at one end so that it may be raised to prevent passage or to allow ships etc. to pass.

drawcord /ˈdrɔːkɔːd/ *n.* a cord on clothing etc. that can be drawn up tight.

drawdown /ˈdrɔːdaʊn/ *n.* an act of raising money through loans; borrowing.

drawee /drɔː(r)ˈiː/ *n.* the person on whom a draft or bill is drawn.

drawer *n.* **1** /ˈdrɔː(r)ə/a person or thing that draws, esp. a person who draws a cheque etc. **2** /drɔː/ a boxlike storage compartment without a lid, sliding in and out of a frame, table, etc. (*chest of drawers*). **3** (in *pl.*: /drɔːz/) *archaic* or *joc.* knickers or underpants. □ **drawerful** *n.* (*pl.* **-fuls**).

drawing /ˈdrɔː(r)ɪŋ/ *n.* **1 a** the art of representing by line. **b** delineation without colour or with a single colour. **c** the art of representing with pencils, pens, crayons, etc., rather than paint. **2** a picture produced in this way. □ **out of drawing** incorrectly depicted.

drawing board *n.* a board for spreading drawing paper on. □ **back to the drawing board** back to begin afresh (after the failure of an enterprise).

drawing paper *n.* usu. thick paper for drawing pictures etc. on.

drawing pin *n. Brit.* a flat-headed pin for fastening paper etc. (originally drawing paper) to a surface.

drawing room *n.* (hyphenated when *attrib.*) **1** a room for comfortable sitting or entertaining in a private house. **2** (*attrib.*) restrained; observing social proprieties (*drawing-room conversation*). **3** *US* a private compartment in a train. **4** *hist.* a levee, a formal reception esp. at court. [earlier *withdrawing room*, because originally used for women to withdraw to after dinner]

drawl /drɔːl/ *v.* & *n.* ● *v.* **1** *intr.* speak with drawn-out vowel sounds. **2** *tr.* utter in this way. ● *n.* a drawling utterance or way of speaking. □ **drawler** *n.* [16th c.: probably originally slang, from Low German, Dutch *dralen* 'delay, linger']

drawn /drɔːn/ *past part.* of DRAW. ● *adj.* **1** looking strained from fear, anxiety, or pain. **2** (of butter) melted. **3** (of a position in chess etc.) that will result in a draw if both players make the best moves available.

drawn-out *adj.* = LONG-DRAWN.

drawn work *n.* (also **drawn-thread-work**) ornamental work on linen etc., done by drawing out threads, usu. with additional needlework.

draw-sheet *n.* a sheet that can be taken from under a patient without remaking the bed.

drawstring /ˈdrɔːstrɪŋ/ *n.* a string that can be pulled to tighten the mouth of a bag, the waist of a garment, etc.

draw-well *n.* a deep well with a rope and a bucket.

dray[1] /dreɪ/ *n.* **1** a low cart without sides for heavy loads, esp. beer barrels. **2** *Austral.* & *NZ* a two-wheeled cart. [Middle English from Old English *dræge* 'dragnet', related to *dragan* DRAW]

dray[2] var. of DREY.

dray horse *n.* a large, powerful horse.

drayman /ˈdreɪmən/ *n.* (*pl.* **-men**) a brewer's driver.

dread /drɛd/ *v., n., & adj.* ● *v.tr.* **1** (foll. by *that*, or *to* + infin.) fear greatly. **2** shrink from; look forward to with great apprehension. **3** be in great fear of. ● *n.* **1** great fear, apprehension, awe. **2** an object of fear or awe. ● *adj.* **1** dreaded. **2** *archaic* awe-inspiring, revered. [Old English *ādrǣdan, ondrǣdan*]

dreaded /ˈdrɛdɪd/ *adj.* **1** regarded with fear, apprehension, or awe. **2** *colloq.* regarded with mock fear.

dreadful /ˈdrɛdfʊl, -f(ə)l/ *adj.* **1** terrible; inspiring fear or awe. **2** *colloq.* troublesome, disagreeable; very bad. □ **dreadfully** *adv.* **dreadfulness** *n.*

dreadlocks /ˈdrɛdlɒks/ *n.pl.* **1** a Rastafarian hairstyle in which the hair is twisted into tight braids or ringlets hanging down on all sides. **2** hair dressed in this way. □ **dreadlocked** *adj.*

dreadnought /ˈdrɛdnɔːt/ *n.* **1** (usu. **Dreadnought**) *hist.* a type of battleship greatly superior in armament to all its predecessors (from the name of the first, launched in 1906). **2** *archaic* a fearless person. **3** *archaic* **a** a thick coat for stormy weather. **b** the cloth used for such coats.

dream /driːm/ *n. & v.* ● *n.* **1 a** a series of pictures or events in the mind of a sleeping person. **b** the act or time of seeing this. **c** (in full **waking dream**) a similar experience of one awake. **2** a daydream or fantasy. **3** an ideal, aspiration, or ambition, esp. of a nation. **4** a beautiful or ideal person or thing. **5** a state of mind without proper perception of reality (*goes about in a dream*). ● *v.* (*past* and *past part.* **dreamed** /drɛmt, driːmd/ or **dreamt** /drɛmt/) **1** *intr.* experience a dream. **2** *tr.* imagine in or as if in a dream. **3** (usu. with *neg.*) **a** *intr.* (foll. by *of*) contemplate the possibility of, have any conception or intention of (*would not dream of upsetting them*). **b** *tr.* (often foll. by *that* + clause) think of as a possibility (*never dreamt that he would come*). **4** *tr.* (foll. by *away*) spend (time) unprofitably. **5** *intr.* be inactive or unpractical. **6** *intr.* fall into a reverie. □ **dream up** imagine, invent. **like a dream** *colloq.* easily, effortlessly. □ **dreamful** *adj.* **dreamless** *adj.* **dreamlike** *adj.* [Middle English from Old English *drēam* 'joy, music']

dreamboat /ˈdriːmbəʊt/ *n. colloq.* **1** a very attractive or ideal person, esp. of the opposite sex. **2** a very desirable or ideal thing.

dreamer /ˈdriːmə/ *n.* **1** a person who dreams. **2** a romantic or unpractical person.

dreamland /ˈdriːmland/ *n.* an ideal or imaginary land.

dreamscape /ˈdriːmskeɪp/ *n.* a dreamed or dreamlike landscape or scene. [DREAM + -SCAPE]

dream ticket *n.* an ideal pair of candidates standing together for esp. political office.

dreamtime /ˈdriːmtʌɪm/ *n. Austral.* the alcheringa.

dream-world *n.* a state of mind distanced from reality.

dreamy /ˈdriːmi/ *adj.* (**dreamier**, **dreamiest**) **1** given to daydreaming; fanciful; unpractical. **2** dreamlike; vague; misty. **3** *colloq.* delightful; marvellous. **4** *poet.* full of dreams. □ **dreamily** *adv.* **dreaminess** *n.*

drear /drɪə/ *adj. poet.* = DREARY. [abbreviation]

dreary /ˈdrɪəri/ *adj.* (**drearier**, **dreariest**) dismal, dull, gloomy. □ **drearily** *adv.* **dreariness** *n.* [Old English *drēorig* from *drēor* 'gore': related to *drēosan* 'to drop', from Germanic]

dredge[1] /drɛdʒ/ *v. & n.* ● *v.* **1** *tr.* **a** (often foll. by *up*) bring up (lost or hidden material) as if with a dredge (*don't dredge all that up again*). **b** (often foll. by *away*, *up*, *out*) bring up or clear (mud etc.) from a river, harbour, etc. with a dredge. **2** *tr.* clean (a harbour, river, etc.) with a dredge. **3** *intr.* use a dredge. ● *n.* an apparatus used to scoop up objects or to clear mud etc. from a river or seabed. [15th-c. Scots *dreg*, perhaps related to Middle Dutch *dregghe*]

dredge[2] /drɛdʒ/ *v.tr.* **1** sprinkle with flour, sugar, etc. **2** (often foll. by *over*) sprinkle (flour, sugar, etc.) on. [obsolete *dredge* 'sweetmeat' from Old French *dragie*, *dragee*, perhaps via Latin *tragemata* from Greek *tragēmata* 'spices']

dredger[1] /ˈdrɛdʒə/ *n.* **1** a machine used for dredging rivers etc.; a dredge. **2** a boat containing this.

dredger[2] /ˈdrɛdʒə/ *n.* a container with a perforated lid used for sprinkling flour, sugar, etc.

dree /driː/ *v.tr.* (**drees**, **dreed**, **dreeing**) *Sc.* or *archaic* endure. □ **dree one's weird** submit to one's destiny. [Old English *drēogan*, from Germanic]

dreg /drɛg/ *n.* **1** (usu. in *pl.*) **a** a sediment; grounds, lees, etc. **b** a worthless part; refuse (*the dregs of humanity*). **2** a small remnant (*not a dreg*). □ **drain** (or **drink**) **to the dregs** consume leaving nothing (*drained life to the dregs*). □ **dreggy** *adj. colloq.* [Middle English, probably from Old Norse *dreggjar*]

drench /drɛn(t)ʃ/ *v. & n.* ● *v.tr.* **1 a** wet thoroughly (*was drenched by the rain*). **b** saturate; soak (in liquid). **2** force (an animal) to take medicine. **3** *archaic* cause to drink. ● *n.* **1** a soaking; a downpour. **2** medicine administered to an animal. **3** *archaic* a medicinal or poisonous draught. [Old English *drencan*, *drenc* from Germanic: related to DRINK]

Dresden china /ˈdrɛzd(ə)n/ *n.* (also **Dresden porcelain**) **1** delicate and elaborate chinaware originally made at Dresden in Germany, now made at nearby Meissen. **2** (*attrib.*) delicately pretty.

dress /drɛs/ *v. & n.* ● *v.* **1 a** *tr.* clothe; array (*dressed in rags*; *dressed her quickly*). **b** *intr.* wear clothes of a specified kind or in a specified way (*dresses well*). **2** *intr.* **a** put on clothes. **b** put on formal or evening clothes, esp. for dinner. **3** *tr.* decorate or adorn. **4** *tr. Med.* **a** treat (a wound) with ointment etc. **b** apply a dressing to (a wound). **5** *tr.* trim, comb, brush, or smooth (the hair). **6** *tr.* **a** clean and prepare (poultry, a crab, etc.) for cooking or eating. **b** add a dressing to (a salad etc.). **7** *tr.* apply manure etc. to a field, garden, etc. **8** *tr.* finish the surface of (fabric, building stone, etc.). **9** *tr.* groom (a horse). **10** *tr.* curry (leather etc.). **11** *Mil.* **a** *tr.* correct the alignment of (troops etc.). **b** *intr.* (of troops) come into alignment. **12** *tr.* make (an artificial fly) for use in fishing. ● *n.* **1** a one-piece woman's garment consisting of a bodice and skirt. **2** clothing, esp. a whole outfit etc. (*fussy about his dress*; *wore the dress of a highlander*). **3** formal or ceremonial attire (*evening dress*; *morning dress*). **4** an external covering; the outward form (*birds in their winter dress*). □ **dress down** *colloq.* **1** reprimand or scold. **2** dress informally. **dress out** attire conspicuously. **dress up 1** dress (oneself or another) elaborately for a special occasion. **2** dress in fancy dress. **3** disguise (unwelcome facts) by embellishment. [Middle English from Old French *dresser*, ultimately from Latin *directus* DIRECT]

dressage /ˈdrɛsɑːʒ, -ɑːdʒ/ *n.* the training of a horse in obedience and deportment, esp. for competition. [French from *dresser* 'to train']

dress circle *n.* the first gallery in a theatre, in which evening dress was formerly required.

dress coat *n.* a man's swallow-tailed evening coat.

dresser[1] /ˈdrɛsə/ *n.* **1** a kitchen sideboard with shelves above for displaying plates etc. **2** *N. Amer.* a dressing table or chest of drawers. [Middle English from Old French *dresseur*, from *dresser* 'prepare']

dresser[2] /ˈdrɛsə/ *n.* **1** a person who assists actors to dress, takes care of their costumes, etc. **2** *Brit. Med.* a surgeon's assistant in operations. **3** a person who dresses elegantly or in a specified way (*a snappy dresser*).

dressing /ˈdrɛsɪŋ/ *n.* **1** in senses of DRESS *v.* **2 a** a sauce for salads, esp. a mixture of oil, vinegar, etc. (*French dressing*). **b** *N. Amer.* stuffing. **3 a** a bandage for a wound. **b** ointment etc. used to dress a wound. **4** size or stiffening used to finish fabrics. **5** compost etc. spread over land (*a top dressing of peat*).

dressing case *n.* a case containing toiletries etc.

dressing down *n. colloq.* a scolding; a severe reprimand.

dressing gown *n.* a loose usu. belted robe worn over nightwear or while resting.

dressing room *n.* **1** a room for changing the clothes etc. in a theatre, sports ground, etc. **2** a small room attached to a bedroom, containing clothes.

dressing station *n.* a place for giving emergency treatment to wounded people.

dressing table *n.* a table with a mirror, drawers, etc., used while applying make-up etc.

dress length *n.* a piece of material sufficient to make a dress.

dressmaker /ˈdrɛsmeɪkə/ *n. Brit.* a person, esp. a woman, who makes clothes professionally. □ **dressmaking** *n.*

dress parade *n.* **1** *Mil.* a military parade in full dress uniform. **2** a display of clothes worn by models.

dress rehearsal *n.* the final rehearsal of a play etc., wearing costume.

dress shield *n.* (also **dress preserver**) a piece of waterproof material fastened in the armpit of a dress to protect it from sweat.

dress shirt *n.* **1** a man's usu. starched white shirt worn with evening dress. **2** *US* any man's long-sleeved shirt, usu. worn with a tie.

dressy /ˈdrɛsi/ *adj.* (**dressier**, **dressiest**) **1 a** fond of smart clothes. **b** overdressed. **c** (of clothes) stylish or elaborate. **2** over-elaborate (*the design is rather dressy*). □ **dressiness** *n.*

drew *past* of DRAW.

drey /dreɪ/ *n.* (also **dray**) a squirrel's nest. [17th c.: origin unknown]

dribble /ˈdrɪb(ə)l/ *v. & n.* ● *v.* **1** *intr.* allow saliva to flow from the mouth. **2** *intr. & tr.* flow or allow to flow in drops or a trickling stream. **3** *tr.* (also *absol.*) (esp. in football and hockey) move (the ball) forward with slight touches of the feet, the stick, etc., or (in basketball etc.) by continuous bouncing. ● *n.* **1** the act or an instance of dribbling. **2** a small trickling stream. □ **dribbler** *n.* **dribbly** *adj.* [frequentative of obsolete *drib*, variant of DRIP]

driblet /ˈdrɪblɪt/ *n.* **1 a** a small quantity. **b** a petty sum. **2** a thin stream; a dribble. [*drib* (see DRIBBLE) + -LET]

dribs and drabs /drɪbz (ə)n ˈdrabz/ *n.pl. colloq.* small scattered amounts (*did the work in dribs and drabs*). [as DRIBBLE + *drab* 'reduplication']

dried *past* and *past part.* of DRY.

drier[1] *compar.* of DRY.

drier[2] var. of DRYER.

driest *superl.* of DRY.

drift /drɪft/ *n. & v.* ● *n.* **1 a** slow movement or variation. **b** such movement caused by a slow current. **2** the intention, meaning, scope, etc. of what is said etc. (*didn't understand his drift*). **3** a large mass of snow, sand, etc., accumulated by the wind. **4** esp. *derog.* a state of inaction. **5 a** *Naut.* a ship's deviation from its course, due to currents. **b** *Aeron.* an aircraft's deviation due to side winds. **c** a projectile's deviation due to its rotation. **d** a controlled slide of a racing car etc. **6** *Mining* a horizontal passage following a mineral vein. **7** a large mass of esp. flowering plants (*a drift of bluebells*). **8** *Geol.* **a** material deposited by the wind, a current of water, etc. **b** (**Drift**) Pleistocene ice detritus, e.g. boulder clay. **9** *Brit. hist.* the movement of cattle, esp. a gathering in a forest on an appointed day to determine ownership etc. **10** a tool for enlarging or shaping a hole in metal. **11** *S.Afr.* a ford. ● *v.* **1** *intr.* be carried by or as if by a current of air or water. **2** *intr.* move or progress passively, casually, or aimlessly (*drifted into teaching*). **3 a** *tr. & intr.* pile or be piled by the wind into drifts. **b** *tr.* cover (a field, a road, etc.) with drifts. **4** *tr.* form or enlarge (a hole) with a drift. **5** *tr.* (of a current) carry. □ **driftage** *n.* [Middle English from Old Norse & Middle Dutch, Middle High German *trift* 'movement of cattle': related to DRIVE]

drifter /ˈdrɪftə/ *n.* **1** an aimless or rootless person. **2** a boat used for drift-net fishing.

drift-ice *n.* ice driven or deposited by water.

drift-net *n.* a large net for herrings etc., allowed to drift with the tide. □ **drift-netter** *n.* **drift-netting** *n.*

driftwood /ˈdrɪftwʊd/ *n.* wood etc. driven or deposited by water or wind.

drill[1] /drɪl/ *n. & v.* ● *n.* **1 a** a pointed, esp. revolving, steel tool or machine used for boring cylindrical holes, sinking wells, etc. **b** a dentist's rotary tool for cutting away part of a tooth etc. **2 a** esp. *Mil.* instruction or training in military exercises. **b** rigorous discipline or methodical instruction, esp. when learning or performing tasks. **c** routine procedure to be followed in an emergency (*fire drill*). **d** a routine or exercise (*drills in irregular verb patterns*). **3** *colloq.* a recognized procedure (*I expect you know the drill*). **4** any of various molluscs, esp. *Urosalpinx cinerea*, that bore into the shells of young oysters. ● *v.* **1** *tr.* (also *absol.*) **a** (of a person or a tool) make a hole with a drill through or into (wood, metal, etc.). **b** make (a hole) with a drill. **2** *tr. & intr.* esp. *Mil.* subject to or undergo discipline by drill. **3** *tr.* impart (knowledge etc.) by a strict method. **4** *tr. slang* shoot with a gun (*drilled him full of holes*). □ **driller** *n.* [earlier as verb, from Middle Dutch *drillen* 'bore', of unknown origin]

drill[2] /drɪl/ *n. & v.* ● *n.* **1** a machine used for making furrows, sowing, and covering seed. **2** a small furrow for sowing seed in. **3** a ridge with such furrows on top. **4** a row of plants so sown. ● *v.tr.* **1** sow (seed) with a drill. **2** plant (the ground) in drills. [18th c., of unknown origin: perhaps from DRILL[1]]

drill[3] /drɪl/ *n.* a W. African baboon, *Mandrillus leucophaeus*, related to the mandrill. [probably of African origin: cf. MANDRILL]

drill[4] /drɪl/ *n.* a coarse twilled cotton or linen fabric. [earlier *drilling* via German *Drillich* from Latin *trilix -licis*, from *tri-* 'three' + *licium* 'thread']

drilling rig *n.* a structure with equipment for drilling an oil well etc.

drill stem see STEM[1] *n.* 7.

drily /ˈdrʌɪli/ *adv.* (also **dryly**) **1** (said) in a dry manner; humorously. **2** in a dry way or condition.

drink /drɪŋk/ *v. & n.* ● *v.* (*past* **drank** /draŋk/; *past part.* **drunk** /drʌŋk/) **1 a** *tr.* swallow (a liquid). **b** *tr.* swallow the liquid contents of (a container). **c** *intr.* swallow liquid, take draughts (*drank from the stream*). **2** *intr.* take alcohol, esp. to excess (*I have heard that he drinks*). **3** *tr.* (of a plant, porous material, etc.) absorb (moisture). **4** *refl.* bring (oneself etc.) to a specified condition by drinking (*drank himself into a stupor*). **5** *tr.* (usu. foll. by *away*) spend (wages etc.) on drink (*drank away the money*). **6** *tr.* wish (a person's good health, luck, etc.) by drinking (*drank his health*). ● *n.* **1 a** a liquid for drinking (*milk is a sustaining drink*). **b** a draught or specified amount of this (*had a drink of milk*). **2 a** alcoholic liquor (*got the drink in for Christmas*). **b** a portion, glass, etc. of this (*have a drink*). **c** excessive indulgence in alcohol (*drink is his vice*). **3** (as **the drink**) *colloq.* the sea. □ **drink deep** take a large draught or draughts. **drink in** listen to closely or eagerly (*drank in his every word*). **drink off** drink the whole (contents) of at once. **drink to** toast; wish success to. **drink a person under the table** remain sober longer than one's drinking companion. **drink up** drink the whole of; empty. **in drink** drunk. □ **drinkable** *adj.* [Old English *drincan* (*v.*), *drinc(a)* (*n.*), from Germanic]

drink-driving *n. Brit.* the act of driving a vehicle with an excess of alcohol in the blood. □ **drink-driver** *n.*

drinker /'drɪŋkə/ *n.* **1 a** a person who drinks (something). **b** a person who takes alcohol, esp. to excess. **2** (in full **drinker moth**) a large brownish moth, *Euthrix potatoria*, whose caterpillar is noted for drinking dew.

drinking song *n.* a song sung while drinking, usu. concerning drink.

drinking-up time *n. Brit.* a short period legally allowed for finishing drinks bought before closing time in a public house.

drinking water *n.* water pure enough for drinking.

drip /drɪp/ *v.* & *n.* ● *v.* (**dripped**, **dripping**) **1** *intr.* & *tr.* fall or let fall in drops. **2** *intr.* (often foll. by *with*) be so wet as to shed drops (*dripped with blood*). ● *n.* **1 a** the act or an instance of dripping (*the steady drip of rain*). **b** a drop of liquid (*a drip of paint*). **c** a sound of dripping. **2** *colloq.* a stupid, dull, or ineffective person. **3** *Med.* = DRIP-FEED *n.* **4** *Archit.* a projection, esp. from a window sill, keeping the rain off the walls. □ **be dripping with** be full of or covered with (*a duchess dripping with pearls*). **dripping wet** very wet. [Middle Danish *drippe*, from Germanic (cf. DROP)]

drip-dry *v.* & *adj.* ● *v.* (**-dries**, **-dried**) **1** *intr.* (of fabric etc.) dry crease-free when hung up to drip. **2** *tr.* leave (a garment etc.) hanging up to dry. ● *adj.* able to be drip-dried.

drip-feed *v.* & *n.* ● *v.tr.* feed intravenously in drops. ● *n.* **1** the continuous intravenous introduction of fluid into the body. **2** the fluid so introduced. **3** the apparatus used to do this.

drip-mat *n. Brit.* a small mat under a glass.

drip-moulding *n.* a stone or other projection that deflects rain etc. from walls.

dripping /'drɪpɪŋ/ *n.* **1** fat melted from roasted meat and used esp. for cooking. **2** (in *pl.*) water, grease, etc., dripping from anything.

drippy /'drɪpi/ *adj.* (**drippier**, **drippiest**) **1** tending to drip. **2** *colloq.* ineffectual; sloppily sentimental. □ **drippily** *adv.* **drippiness** *n.*

dripstone /'drɪpstəʊn/ *n.* **1** = DRIP-MOULDING. **2** a stone formation made by dripping water, e.g. a stalactite.

drive /drʌɪv/ *v.* & *n.* ● *v.* (*past* **drove** /drəʊv/; *past part.* **driven** /'drɪv(ə)n/) **1** *tr.* (usu. foll. by *away*, *back*, *in*, *out*, *to*, etc.) urge in some direction, esp. forcibly (*drove back the wolves*). **2** *tr.* **a** (usu. foll. by *to* + infin., or *to* + verbal noun) compel or constrain forcibly (*was driven to complain*; *drove her to stealing*). **b** (often foll. by *to*) force into a specified state (*drove him mad*; *driven to despair*). **c** (often *refl.*) urge to overwork (*drives himself too hard*). **3 a** *tr.* (also *absol.*) operate and direct the course of (a vehicle, a locomotive, etc.) (*drove a sports car*; *drives well*). **b** *tr.* & *intr.* convey or be conveyed in a vehicle, esp. a private car (*drove them to the station*; *he drives to work*) (cf. RIDE). **c** *tr.* (also *absol.*) be licensed or competent to drive (a vehicle) (*does he drive?*). **d** *tr.* (also *absol.*) urge and direct the course of (an animal drawing a vehicle or plough). **e** *tr. colloq.* operate (an electronic device etc.) (*bought a new computer but hasn't learnt to drive it yet*). **4** *tr.* (of wind, water, etc.) carry along, propel, send, or cause to go in some direction (*pure as the driven snow*). **5** *tr.* **a** (often foll. by *into*) force (a stake, nail, etc.) into place by blows (*drove the nail home*). **b** *Mining* bore (a tunnel, horizontal cavity, etc.). **6** *tr.* effect or conclude forcibly (*drove a hard bargain*; *drove his point home*). **7** *tr.* (of steam or other power) set or keep (machinery) going. **8** *intr.* (usu. foll. by *at*) work hard; dash, rush, or hasten. **9** *tr.* hit (a ball) hard from a freely swung bat or racket. **10** *tr.* (often *absol.*) *Golf* strike (a ball) with a driver from the tee. **11** *tr.* chase or frighten (game, wild beasts, an enemy in warfare, etc.) from a large area to a smaller, to kill or capture; corner. **12** *tr. Brit. hist.* hold a drift in (a forest etc.) (see DRIFT *n.* 9). ● *n.* **1** an act of driving in a motor vehicle; a journey or excursion in such a vehicle (*went for a pleasant drive*; *lives an hour's drive from us*). **2 a** the capacity for achievement; motivation and energy (*lacks the drive needed to succeed*). **b** *Psychol.* an inner urge to attain a goal or satisfy a need (*unconscious emotional drives*). **3 a** a usu. landscaped street or road. **b** a usu. private road through a garden or park to a house. **4** *Cricket*, *Golf*, & *Tennis* a driving stroke of the bat etc. **5** an organized effort to achieve a usu. charitable purpose (*a famine-relief drive*). **6 a** the transmission of power to machinery, the wheels of a motor vehicle, etc. (*belt drive*; *front-wheel drive*). **b** the position of a steering wheel in a motor vehicle (*left-hand drive*). **c** *Computing* = DISK DRIVE. **7** *Brit.* an organized competition, for many players, of whist, bingo, etc. **8** an act of driving game or an enemy. **9** *Austral.* & *NZ* a line of partly cut trees on a hillside felled when the top one topples on the others. □ **drive at** seek, intend, or mean (*what is he driving at?*). **drive out** take the place of; oust; exorcize, cast out (evil spirits etc.). **driving rain** an excessive windblown downpour. **let drive** aim a blow or missile. □ **drivable** *adj.* (also **driveable**). [Old English *drīfan*, from Germanic]

drive-by *attrib.adj.* (of a crime etc.) carried out from a moving vehicle.

drive-in *adj.* & *n.* ● *attrib.adj.* (of a bank, cinema, etc.) able to be used while sitting in one's car. ● *n.* such a bank, cinema, etc.

drivel /'drɪv(ə)l/ *n.* & *v.* ● *n.* silly nonsense; twaddle. ● *v.* (**drivelled**, **drivelling**; *US* **driveled**, **driveling**) **1** *intr.* run at the mouth or nose; dribble. **2** *intr.* talk childishly or idiotically. **3** *tr.* (foll. by *away*) fritter; squander away. □ **driveller** *n.* (*US* **driveler**). [Old English *dreflian* (*v.*)]

driven *past part.* of DRIVE.

drive-on *attrib.adj.* (also **drive-on/drive-off**) (of a ship) on to and from which motor vehicles may be driven.

driver /'drʌɪvə/ *n.* **1** (often in *comb.*) a person who drives a vehicle (*bus driver*; *train driver*). **2** *Golf* a club with a flat face and wooden head, used for driving from the tee. **3** *Electr.* a device or part of a circuit providing power for output. **4** *Mech.* a wheel etc. receiving power directly and transmitting motion to other parts. **5** *Computing* a program that controls the operation of a device. □ **in the driver's seat** in charge. □ **driverless** *adj.*

driver's license *N. Amer.* var. of DRIVING LICENCE.

driver's test *N. Amer.* var. of DRIVING TEST.

driveshaft /'drʌɪvʃɑːft/ *n.* a shaft transmitting torque.

drive-through *attrib.adj.* esp. *N. Amer.* **1** designating a shop, restaurant, etc. which has a window at which customers are served without leaving their cars. **2** suitable for driving through (*a drive-through tunnel*).

drive-time *n.* (often *attrib.*) the parts of the day when many people commute by car (*a drive-time radio show*).

driveway /'drʌɪvweɪ/ *n.* = DRIVE *n.* 3b.

driving licence *n.* (*N. Amer.* **driver's license**) a licence permitting a person to drive a motor vehicle.

driving range *n. Golf* an area for practising drives.

driving test *n.* (*N. Amer.* **driver's test**) an official test of a motorist's competence which must be passed to obtain a driving licence.

driving wheel *n.* **1** the large wheel of a locomotive. **2** a wheel transmitting motive power in machinery.

drizzle /'drɪz(ə)l/ *n.* & *v.* ● *n.* **1** very fine rain. **2** esp. *Cookery* fine drops; a fine trickle. ● **1** *v.intr.* (esp. of rain) fall in very fine drops (*it's drizzling again*). **2** *v.tr.* esp. *Cookery* sprinkle in fine drops or a thin trickle. □ **drizzly** *adj.* [probably from Middle English *drēse*, Old English *drēosan* 'fall']

Dr Martens /dɒktə 'mɑːtɪnz/ *n.pl.* (also **Doc Martens**, **Doctor Martens**) *propr.* a type of heavy usu. laced boot or shoe with a cushioned sole. [from *Dr* K. *Maertens*, the name of the German inventor of the sole]

drogue /drəʊg/ *n.* **1** *Naut.* **a** a buoy at the end of a harpoon line. **b** a sea anchor. **2** *Aeron.* a truncated cone of fabric used as a brake, a target for gunnery, a windsock, etc. [18th c.: origin unknown]

droit /drɔɪt/ *n. Law* a right or due. [Middle English via Old French from Latin *directum* (*n.*), from *directus* DIRECT]

droit de seigneur /drwɑː də sɛn'jəː/ *n. hist.* the alleged right of a feudal lord to have sexual intercourse with a vassal's bride on her wedding night. [French, = lord's right]

droll /drəʊl/ *adj. & n.* ● *adj.* **1** quaintly amusing. **2** strange; odd; surprising. ● *n. archaic* **1** a jester; an entertainer. **2** a quaintly amusing person. ▫ **drollery** *n.* (*pl.* **-ies**). **drolly** /'drəʊlli/ *adv.* **drollness** *n.* [French *drôle*, perhaps from Middle Dutch *drolle* 'little man']

drome /drəʊm/ *n. colloq. archaic* aerodrome. [abbreviation]

-drome /drəʊm/ *comb. form* forming nouns denoting: **1** a place for running, racing, or other forms of movement (*aerodrome*; *hippodrome*). **2** a thing that runs or proceeds in a certain way (*palindrome*; *syndrome*). [Greek *dromos* 'course, running']

dromedary /'drɒmɪd(ə)ri, 'drʌm-/ *n.* (*pl.* **-ies**) = ARABIAN CAMEL. [Middle English from Old French *dromedaire* or Late Latin *dromedarius*, ultimately from Greek *dromas -ados* 'runner']

dromond /'drɒmənd, 'drʌm-/ *n. hist.* a large medieval ship used for war or commerce. [Middle English via Old French *dromon(t)* and Late Latin *dromo -onis* from late Greek *dromōn* 'light vessel']

drone /drəʊn/ *n. & v.* ● *n.* **1** a non-working male of the honey bee, whose sole social function is to mate with fertile females. **2** an idler. **3** a deep humming sound. **4** a monotonous speech or speaker. **5 a** a pipe, esp. of a bagpipe, sounding a continuous note of fixed low pitch. **b** the note emitted by this. **c** (on a stringed instrument) a string used to produce a continuous droning sound. **6** a remote-controlled pilotless aircraft or missile. ● *v.* **1** *intr.* make a deep humming sound. **2** *intr. & tr.* speak or utter monotonously. **3 a** *intr.* be idle. **b** *tr.* (often foll. by *away*) idle away (one's time etc.). [Old English *drān*, *drǣn*, probably from West Germanic]

drongo /'drɒŋgəʊ/ *n.* (*pl.* **-os** or **-oes**) **1** any black bird of the family Dicruridae, native to Asia, Africa, and Australia, having a long forked tail. **2** *Austral. & NZ slang derog.* a simpleton. [Malagasy]

droob /druːb/ *n. Austral. slang* a hopeless-looking ineffectual person. [perhaps from DROOP]

drool /druːl/ *v. & n.* ● *v.intr.* **1** drivel; slobber. **2** (often foll. by *over*) show much pleasure or infatuation. ● *n.* slobbering; drivelling. [contraction of *drivel*]

droop /druːp/ *v. & n.* ● *v.* **1** *intr. & tr.* hang or allow to hang down; languish, decline, or sag, esp. from weariness. **2** *intr.* **a** (of the eyes) look downwards. **b** *poet.* (of the sun) sink. **3** *intr.* lose heart; be dejected; flag. ● *n.* **1** a drooping attitude. **2** a loss of spirit or enthusiasm. [Middle English from Old Norse *drúpa* 'hang the head', from Germanic: cf. DROP]

droop-snoot *adj. & n. colloq.* ● *attrib.adj.* (of an aircraft) having an adjustable nose or leading-edge flap. ● *n.* **1** such an aircraft. **2** the nose or leading-edge flap of such an aircraft.

droopy /'druːpi/ *adj.* (**droopier**, **droopiest**) **1** drooping. **2** dejected, gloomy. ▫ **droopily** *adv.* **droopiness** *n.*

drop /drɒp/ *n. & v.* ● *n.* **1 a** a small round or pear-shaped portion of liquid that hangs or falls or adheres to a surface (*drops of dew*; *tears fell in large drops*). **b** a very small amount of usu. drinkable liquid (*just a drop left in the glass*). **c** a glass etc. of alcoholic liquor (*take a drop with us*). **2 a** an abrupt fall or slope. **b** the amount of this (*a drop of fifteen feet*). **c** an act of falling or dropping (*had a nasty drop*). **d** a reduction in prices, temperature, etc. **e** a deterioration or worsening (*a drop in status*). **3** something resembling a drop of liquid, esp.: **a** a pendant or earring. **b** a crystal ornament on a chandelier etc. **c** (often in *comb.*) a sweet or lozenge (*pear drop*; *cough drop*). **4** something that drops or is dropped, esp.: **a** *Theatr.* a painted curtain or scenery let down on to the stage. **b** a platform or trapdoor on a gallows, the opening of which causes the victim to fall. **c** (in *comb.*) = sense 11 of *v.* (*drop handlebars*). **5** *Med.* **a** the smallest separable quantity of a liquid. **b** (in *pl.*) liquid medicine to be measured in drops (*eye drops*). **6** a minute quantity (*not a drop of pity*). **7** *colloq.* a delivery. **8** *slang* **a** a hiding place for stolen or illicit goods. **b** a secret place where documents etc. may be left or passed on in espionage. **9** *slang* a bribe. **10** *US* a letter box. ● *v.* (**dropped**, **dropping**) **1** *intr. & tr.* fall or let fall in drops (*tears dropped on to the book*; *dropped the soup down his shirt*). **2** *intr. & tr.* fall or allow to fall; relinquish; let go (*dropped the box*; *the egg dropped from my hand*). **3 a** *intr. & tr.* sink or cause to sink or fall to the ground from exhaustion, a blow, a wound, etc. **b** *intr.* die. **4 a** *intr. & tr.* cease or cause to cease; lapse or let lapse; abandon (*the connection dropped*; *dropped the friendship*; *drop everything and come at once*). **b** *tr. colloq.* cease to associate with. **5** *tr.* set down (a passenger etc.) (*drop me at the station*). **6** *tr. & intr.* utter or be uttered casually (*dropped a hint*; *the remark dropped into the conversation*). **7** *tr.* send casually (*drop me a postcard*). **8 a** *intr. & tr.* fall or allow to fall in direction, amount, condition, degree, pitch, etc. (*his voice dropped*; *the wind dropped*; *we dropped the price by £20*; *the road dropped southwards*). **b** *intr.* (of a person) jump down lightly; let oneself fall. **c** *tr.* remove (clothes, esp. trousers) rapidly, allowing them to fall to the ground. **9** *tr. colloq.* lose (money, esp. in gambling). **10** *tr.* omit (a letter, esp. aitch, a syllable etc.) in speech. **11** *tr.* (as **dropped** *adj.*) in a lower position than usual (*dropped handlebars*; *dropped waist*). **12** *tr.* give birth to (esp. a lamb, a kitten, etc.). **13 a** *intr.* (of a card) be played in the same trick as a higher card. **b** *tr.* play or cause (a card) to be played in this way. **14** *tr. Sport* lose (a game, a point, a contest, a match, etc.). **15** *tr. Aeron.* deliver (supplies etc.) by parachute. **16** *tr. Rugby* **a** send (a ball) by a drop kick. **b** score (a goal) by a drop kick. **17** *tr. colloq.* dismiss or omit (*was dropped from the team*). ▫ **at the drop of a hat** given the slightest excuse. **drop anchor** anchor ship. **drop asleep** fall gently asleep. **drop away** decrease or depart gradually. **drop back** (or **behind** or **to the rear**) fall back; get left behind. **drop back into** return to (a habit etc.). **drop a brick** esp. *Brit. colloq.* make an indiscreet or embarrassing remark. **drop a curtsy** *Brit.* make a curtsy. **drop dead!** *slang* an exclamation of intense scorn. **drop down** descend a hill etc. **drop in** (or **by**) *colloq.* call casually as a visitor. **a drop in the ocean** (or **a bucket**) a very small amount, esp. compared with what is needed or expected. **drop into** *colloq.* **1** call casually at (a place). **2** fall into (a habit etc.). **drop it!** *slang* stop that! **drop off 1** decline gradually. **2** *colloq.* fall asleep. **3** = sense 5 of *v.* **drop on** *Brit.* reprimand or punish. **drop out** *colloq.* cease to participate, esp. in a race, a course of study, or in conventional society. **drop a stitch** let a stitch fall off the end of a knitting needle. **drop to** *Brit. slang* become aware of. **fit** (or **ready**) **to drop** extremely tired. **have the drop on** *colloq.* have the advantage over. **have had a drop too much** *colloq.* be slightly drunk. ▫ **droplet** *n.* [Old English *dropa* (*n.*), *drop(p)ian* (*v.*), ultimately from Germanic: cf. DRIP, DROOP]

drop curtain *n.* = DROP *n.* 4a.

drop-dead *attrib.adj. slang* stunningly beautiful; brilliant, excellent.

drop-forging *n.* a method of forcing white-hot metal through an open-ended die by a heavy weight. ▫ **drop-forge** *v.tr.*

drop goal *n. Rugby* a goal scored from a drop kick during play.

drop hammer *n.* a heavy weight raised mechanically and allowed to drop, as used in drop-forging and piledriving.

drophead /'drɒphɛd/ *n. Brit.* the adjustable fabric roof of a car.

drop-in centre *n.* a meeting place where people may call casually for advice, conversation, etc.

drop kick *n. Rugby* a kick made by dropping the ball and kicking it on the bounce.

drop-leaf *attrib.adj.* (of a table etc.) having a hinged flap.

drop-off *n.* **1** an act of dropping off or delivering something or someone. **2** a decline, a decrease (*a drop-off in sales*). **3** *N. Amer.* a sheer downward slope, a cliff.

drop-out *n.* **1** *colloq.* a person who has dropped out. **2** *Rugby* the restarting of a game by a drop kick.

dropper /ˈdrɒpə/ *n.* **1** a device for administering liquid, esp. medicine, in drops. **2** *Austral., NZ, & S.Afr.* a light vertical stave in a fence.

droppings /ˈdrɒpɪŋz/ *n.pl.* **1** the dung of animals or birds. **2** something that falls or has fallen in drops, e.g. wax from candles.

drop scene *n.* = DROP *n.* 4a.

drop scone *n. Brit.* a small thick pancake made by dropping batter into a frying pan etc.

drop shot *n.* (in tennis, badminton, etc.) a shot dropping abruptly over the net.

dropsy /ˈdrɒpsi/ *n.* (*pl.* **-ies**) **1** = OEDEMA. **2** *Brit. slang* a tip or bribe. ▫ **dropsical** *adj.* (in sense 1). [Middle English, shortened form of *idrop(e)sie* from Old French *idropesie*, ultimately via Latin *hydropisis* from Greek *hudrōps* 'dropsy' (as HYDRO-)]

drop test *n. & v. Engin.* ● *n.* a test done by dropping under standard conditions. ● *v.tr.* (**drop-test**) carry out a drop test on.

dropwort /ˈdrɒpwəːt/ *n.* a plant, *Filipendula vulgaris*, with tuberous root fibres.

drop zone *n.* a zone designated for parachutists to land in.

droshky /ˈdrɒʃki/ *n.* (*pl.* **-ies**) a Russian low four-wheeled open carriage. [Russian *drozhki*, diminutive of *drogi* 'wagon', from *droga* 'shaft']

drosophila /drɒˈsɒfɪlə/ *n.* a small fruit fly of the genus *Drosophila*, used extensively in genetic research because of its large chromosomes, numerous varieties, and rapid rate of reproduction. [modern Latin, from Greek *drosos* 'dew, moisture' + *philos* 'loving']

dross /drɒs/ *n.* **1** rubbish, refuse. **2 a** the scum separated from metals in melting. **b** foreign matter mixed with anything; impurities. ▫ **drossy** *adj.* [Old English *drōs*: related to Middle Low German *drōsem*, Old High German *truosana*]

drought /draʊt/ *n.* **1** the continuous absence of rain; dry weather. **2** the prolonged lack of something. **3** *archaic* a lack of moisture; thirst; dryness. ▫ **droughty** *adj.* [Old English *drūgath* from *drȳge* DRY]

drouth /draʊθ/ *n. Sc., Ir., US, & poet.* var. of DROUGHT.

drove[1] *past* of DRIVE.

drove[2] /drəʊv/ *n.* **1 a** a large number (of people etc.) moving together; a crowd; a multitude; a shoal. **b** (in *pl.*) *colloq.* a great number (*people arrived in droves*). **2** a herd or flock being driven or moving together. [Old English *drāf* from *drīfan* DRIVE]

drover /ˈdrəʊvə/ *n.* a person who drives herds to market; a cattle-dealer. ▫ **drove** *v.tr.* **droving** *n.*

drove road *n.* esp. *Sc.* an ancient cattle track.

drown /draʊn/ *v.* **1** *tr. & intr.* kill or be killed by submersion in liquid. **2** *tr.* submerge; flood; drench (*drowned the fields in six feet of water*). **3** *tr.* (often foll. by *in*) deaden (grief etc.) with drink (*drowned his sorrows in whisky*). **4** *tr.* (often foll. by *out*) make (a sound) inaudible by means of a louder sound. ▫ **drown out** drive out by flood. **like a drowned rat** *colloq.* extremely wet and bedraggled. [Middle English (originally northern) *drun(e)*, *droun(e)*, related to Old Norse *drukkna* 'be drowned', from the Germanic base of DRINK]

drowned valley *n.* a valley partly or wholly submerged by a change in land levels.

drowse /draʊz/ *v. & n.* ● *v.* **1** *intr.* be dull and sleepy or half asleep. **2** *tr.* **a** (often foll. by *away*) pass (the time) in drowsing. **b** make drowsy. **3** *intr. archaic* be sluggish. ● *n.* a condition of sleepiness. [back-formation from DROWSY]

drowsy /ˈdraʊzi/ *adj.* (**drowsier**, **drowsiest**) **1** half asleep; dozing. **2** soporific; lulling. **3** sluggish. ▫ **drowsily** *adv.* **drowsiness** *n.* [probably related to Old English *drūsian* 'be languid or slow', *drēosan* 'fall': cf. DREARY]

drub /drʌb/ *v.tr.* (**drubbed**, **drubbing**) **1** thump; belabour. **2** beat in a fight. **3** (usu. foll. by *into*, *out of*) beat (an idea, attitude, etc.) into or out of a person. ▫ **drubbing** *n.* [ultimately from Arabic *ḍaraba* 'beat']

drudge /drʌdʒ/ *n. & v.* ● *n.* a servile worker, esp. at menial tasks; a hack. ● *v.intr.* (often foll. by *at*) work slavishly (at menial, hard, or dull work). ▫ **drudgery** /ˈdrʌdʒ(ə)ri/ *n.* [Middle English: perhaps related to DRAG, DREE]

drug /drʌg/ *n. & v.* ● *n.* **1** a medicinal substance. **2** a narcotic, hallucinogen, or stimulant, esp. one causing addiction. ● *v.* (**drugged**, **drugging**) **1** *tr.* add a drug to (food or drink). **2** *tr.* **a** administer a drug to. **b** stupefy with a drug. **3** *intr. Brit.* take drugs as an addict. [Middle English *drogges*, *drouges* from Old French *drogue*, of unknown origin]

drug addict *n.* a person who is addicted to a narcotic drug.

drugget /ˈdrʌgɪt/ *n.* **1** a coarse woven fabric used as a floor or table covering. **2** such a covering. [French *droguet*, of unknown origin]

druggist /ˈdrʌgɪst/ *n.* esp. *N. Amer.* a pharmacist. [French *droguiste* (as DRUG)]

druggy /ˈdrʌgi/ *n. & adj. colloq.* ● *n.* (also **druggie**) (*pl.* **-ies**) a drug addict. ● *adj.* of or associated with narcotic drugs.

drug peddler *n.* (also *colloq.* **drug pusher**) a person who sells esp. addictive drugs illegally.

drug squad *n. Brit.* a division of a police force investigating crimes involving illegal drugs.

drugstore /ˈdrʌgstɔː/ *n. N. Amer.* a chemist's shop also selling light refreshments and other articles.

Druid /ˈdruːɪd/ *n.* (*fem.* **Druidess** /-dɪs/) **1** an ancient Celtic priest, magician, or soothsayer of Gaul, Britain, or Ireland. **2** a member of a Welsh etc. Druidic order, esp. the Gorsedd. ▫ **Druidic** /-ˈɪdɪk/ *adj.* **Druidical** /-ˈɪdɪk(ə)l/ *adj.* **Druidism** *n.* [French *druide* or Latin pl. *druidae*, *-des*, Greek *druidai* from Gaulish *druides*]

drum[1] /drʌm/ *n. & v.* ● *n.* **1 a** a percussion instrument or toy made of a hollow cylinder or hemisphere covered at one or both ends with stretched skin or parchment and sounded by striking (*bass drum*; *kettledrum*). **b** (often in *pl.*) a drummer or a percussion section (*the drums are playing too loud*). **c** a sound made by or resembling that of a drum. **2** something resembling a drum in shape, esp.: **a** a cylindrical container or receptacle for oil, dried fruit, etc. **b** a cylinder or barrel in machinery on which something is wound etc. **c** *Archit.* the solid part of a Corinthian or composite capital. **d** *Archit.* a stone block forming a section of a shaft. **e** *Austral. & NZ* swag, a bundle. **3** *Zool. & Anat.* the membrane of the middle ear; the eardrum. **4** *Brit. slang* **a** a house. **b** a nightclub. **c** a brothel. **5** (in full **drum fish**) any marine fish of the family Sciaenidae, having a swim-bladder that produces a drumming sound. **6** *hist.* an evening or afternoon tea party. **7** *Austral. slang* a piece of reliable information, esp. a racing tip. ● *v.* (**drummed**, **drumming**) **1** *intr. & tr.* play on a drum. **2** *tr. & intr.* beat, tap, or thump (knuckles, feet, etc.) continuously (on something) (*drummed on the table*; *drummed his feet*; *drumming at the window*). **3** *intr.* (of a bird or an insect) make a loud, hollow noise with quivering wings. **4** *tr. Austral. slang* provide with reliable information. ▫ **drum into** drive (a lesson) into (a person) by persistence. **drum out** *Mil.* cashier (a soldier) by the beat of a drum; dismiss with ignominy. **drum up** summon, gather, or call up (*needs to drum up more support*). [obsolete *drombslade*, *drombyllsclad*, from Low German *trommelslag* 'drumbeat', from *trommel* 'drum' + *slag* 'beat']

drum[2] /drʌm/ *n.* (also **drumlin** /'drʌmlɪn/) *Geol.* a long oval mound of boulder clay moulded by glacial action. ◻ **drumlinoid** *n.* [Gaelic & Irish *druim* 'ridge': *-lin* perhaps for -LING[1]]

drumbeat /'drʌmbi:t/ *n.* a stroke or the sound of a stroke on a drum.

drum brake *n.* a brake in which shoes on a vehicle press against the drum on a wheel.

drumfire /'drʌmfʌɪə/ *n.* **1** *Mil.* heavy continuous rapid artillery fire, usu. heralding an infantry attack. **2** a barrage of criticism etc.

drum fish see DRUM[1] *n.* 5.

drumhead /'drʌmhɛd/ *n.* **1** the skin or membrane of a drum. **2** an eardrum. **3** the circular top of a capstan. **4** (*attrib.*) improvised (*drumhead court martial*).

drum kit *n.* a set of drums, cymbals, etc.

drumlin var. of DRUM[2].

drum machine *n.* an electronic device that imitates the sound of percussion instruments.

drum major *n.* **1** the leader of a marching band. **2** *archaic* an NCO commanding the drummers of a regiment.

drum majorette *n.* esp. *US* a member of a female baton-twirling parading group.

drummer /'drʌmə/ *n.* **1** a person who plays a drum or drums. **2** esp. *US colloq.* a commercial traveller. **3** *Brit. slang* a thief.

drumstick /'drʌmstɪk/ *n.* **1** a stick used for beating a drum. **2** the lower joint of the leg of a cooked chicken, turkey, etc.

drunk /drʌŋk/ *adj.* & *n.* ● *adj.* **1** rendered incapable by alcohol (*blind drunk*; *dead drunk*; *drunk as a lord*). **2** (often foll. by *with*) overcome or elated with joy, success, power, etc. ● *n.* **1** a habitually drunk person. **2** *slang* a drinking bout; a period of drunkenness. [past part. of DRINK]

drunkard /'drʌŋkəd/ *n.* a person who is drunk, esp. habitually.

drunken /'drʌŋk(ə)n/ *adj.* (usu. *attrib.*) **1** caused by or exhibiting drunkenness (*a drunken brawl*). **2** fond of drinking; often drunk. ◻ **drunkenly** *adv.* **drunkenness** /'drʌŋk(ə)nnɪs/ *n.*

drunken driving *n.* = DRINK-DRIVING.

drupe /dru:p/ *n.* any fleshy or pulpy fruit enclosing a stone containing one or a few seeds, e.g. an olive, plum, or peach. ◻ **drupaceous** /-'peɪʃəs/ *adj.* [Latin *drupa* from Greek *druppa* 'olive']

drupel /'dru:p(ə)l/ *n.* (also **drupelet** /'dru:plɪt/) a small drupe usu. in an aggregate fruit, e.g. a blackberry or raspberry.

druse /dru:z/ *n.* **1** a crust of crystals lining a rock cavity. **2** a cavity lined with this. [French from German, = weathered ore]

druther /'drʌðə/ *adv.* & *n.* *N. Amer. colloq.* ● *adv.* rather, by preference (*I'd druther not go*). ● *n.* (in *pl.*) preference, choice; one's way (*if I had my druthers*). [from a US dialect pronunciation of *would rather*]

Druze /dru:z/ *n.* (also **Druse**) (often *attrib.*) a member of a political or religious sect linked with Islam and living near Mount Lebanon (*Druze militia*). [French from Arabic *durūz* (pl.), probably from the name of their founder, Muhammad ibn Ismail *al-Darazī* (d. 1019)]

dry /drʌɪ/ *adj.*, *v.*, & *n.* ● *adj.* (**drier** /'drʌɪə/; **driest** /'drʌɪɪst/) **1** free from moisture, not wet, esp.: **a** with any moisture having evaporated, drained, or been wiped away (*the clothes are not dry yet*). **b** (of the eyes) free from tears. **c** (of a climate etc.) with insufficient rainfall; not rainy (*a dry spell*). **d** (of a river, well, etc.) dried up; not yielding water. **e** (of a liquid) having disappeared by evaporation etc. **f** not connected with or for use without moisture (*dry shampoo*). **g** (of a shave) with an electric razor. **2** (of wine etc.) not sweet (*dry sherry*). **3 a** meagre, plain, or bare (*dry facts*). **b** uninteresting; dull (*dry as dust*). **4** (of a sense of humour, a joke, etc.) subtle, ironic, and quietly expressed; not obvious. **5 a** (of a country, of legislation, etc.) prohibiting the sale of alcoholic drink. **b** (of a person) abstaining from alcohol or drugs. **6** (of toast, bread, etc.) without butter, margarine, etc. **7** *Brit.* (of provisions, groceries, etc.) solid, not liquid. **8** impassive, unsympathetic; hard; cold. **9** (of a cow etc.) not yielding milk. **10** *colloq.* thirsty or thirst-making (*feel dry*; *this is dry work*). **11** *Brit. Polit. colloq.* of or being a political 'dry' (see sense 3 of *n.*). ● *v.* (**dries, dried**) **1** *tr.* & *intr.* make or become dry by wiping, evaporation, draining, etc. **2** *tr.* (usu. as **dried** *adj.*) preserve (food etc.) by removing the moisture (*dried egg*; *dried fruit*; *dried flowers*). **3** *intr.* (often foll. by *up*) *Theatr. colloq.* forget one's lines. **4** *tr.* & *intr.* (often foll. by *off*, *up*) cease or cause (a cow etc.) to cease yielding milk. ● *n.* (*pl.* **dries**) **1** the process or an instance of drying. **2** (prec. by *the*) a dry place (*come into the dry*). **3** *Brit. colloq.* a politician, esp. a Conservative, who advocates individual responsibility, free trade, and economic stringency, and opposes high government spending. **4 a** (prec. by *the*) esp. *Austral. colloq.* the dry season. **b** *Austral.* a desert area, waterless country. **5 a** dry ginger ale. **b** dry wine, sherry, etc. ◻ **dry out 1** become fully dry. **2** (of a drug addict, alcoholic, etc.) undergo treatment to cure addiction. **dry up 1** make utterly dry. **2** *Brit.* dry dishes. **3** (of moisture) disappear utterly. **4** (of a well etc.) cease to yield water. **5** (esp. in *imper.*) *colloq.* cease talking. **go dry** enact legislation for the prohibition of alcohol. ◻ **dryish** *adj.* **dryness** *n.* [Old English *drȳge*, *drygan*, related to Middle Low German *dröge*, Middle Dutch *drōghe*, from Germanic]

dryad /'drʌɪəd, -ad/ *n.* *Mythol.* a nymph inhabiting a tree; a wood nymph. [Middle English via Old French *dryade* and Latin from Greek *druas -ados*, from *drus* 'tree']

dry battery *n.* an electric battery consisting of dry cells.

dry cell *n.* a cell in which the electrolyte is absorbed in a solid and cannot be spilled.

dry-clean *v.tr.* & *intr.* clean (clothes etc.), or be cleanable, with organic solvents without using water. ◻ **dry-cleaner** *n.*

dry cough *n.* a cough not producing phlegm.

dry cure *v.tr.* cure (meat etc.) without pickling in liquid.

dry dock *n.* an enclosure for the building or repairing of ships, from which water can be pumped out.

dryer /'drʌɪə/ *n.* (also **drier**) **1 a** a machine or appliance for drying the hair, laundry, the hands, etc. **b** = CLOTHES HORSE 1. **2** a substance mixed with oil paint or ink to promote drying.

dry-eyed *adj.* not weeping.

dry fly *n.* & *v.* ● *n.* an artificial fly which floats on the water (often hyphenated when *attrib.*: *dry-fly anglers*). ● *v.intr.* (**dry-fly**) (**-flies, -flied**) fish using a dry fly.

dry goods *n.pl.* **1** *Brit.* solid as opposed to liquid foodstuffs. **2** *US* fabrics, clothing, etc.

dry ice *n.* solid carbon dioxide.

dry land *n.* **1** land as opposed to the sea, a river, etc. **2** (**dryland** /'drʌɪlənd/) (usu. in *pl.*) esp. *N. Amer.* an area or land where rainfall is low (also *attrib.*: *dryland farming*).

dryly var. of DRILY.

dry measure *n.* a measure of capacity for dry goods.

dry milk *n.* *US* dried milk.

dry-nurse *n.* a nurse for young children, not required to breastfeed.

dry plate *n.* a photographic plate with sensitized film hard and dry for convenience of keeping, developing at leisure, etc.

dry-point *n.* **1** a needle for engraving on a bare copper plate without acid. **2** an engraving produced with this.

dry rot *n.* **1** a type of decay affecting wood in poorly ventilated conditions, caused by certain fungi. **2** these fungi.

dry run *n.* *colloq.* a rehearsal.

dry-salt *v.tr.* = DRY CURE.

dry-salter *n. Brit. hist.* a dealer in dyes, gums, drugs, oils, pickles, tinned meats, etc.

dry-shod *adj. & adv.* without wetting the shoes.

dry slope *n.* an artificial ski slope used esp. for practice.

drystone /ˈdrʌɪstəʊn/ *attrib.adj. Brit.* (of a wall etc.) built without mortar.

drywall /ˈdrʌɪwɔːl/ *n.* esp. *N. Amer.* = PLASTERBOARD.

DS *abbr.* **1** dal segno. **2** *Brit.* disseminated sclerosis.

DSC *abbr.* Distinguished Service Cross.

D.Sc. *abbr.* Doctor of Science.

DSM *abbr.* Distinguished Service Medal.

DSO *abbr.* (in the UK) Distinguished Service Order.

DSS *abbr.* (in the UK) Department of Social Security (formerly DHSS).

DT *abbr.* (also **DT's** /diːˈtiːz/) delirium tremens.

DTI *abbr.* (in the UK) Department of Trade and Industry.

DTP *abbr.* desktop publishing.

dual /ˈdjuːəl/ *adj., n., & v.* ● *adj.* **1** of two; twofold. **2** divided in two; double (*dual ownership*). **3** *Gram.* (in some languages) denoting two persons or things (additional to singular and plural). ● *n.* (also **dual number**) *Gram.* a dual form of a noun, verb, etc. ● *v.tr.* (**dualled**, **dualling**) *Brit.* convert (a road) into a dual carriageway. □ **duality** /-ˈalɪti/ *n.* **dualize** *v.tr.* (also **-ise**). **dually** *adv.* [Latin *dualis* from *duo* 'two']

dual carriageway *n. Brit.* a road with a dividing strip between the traffic in opposite directions.

dual control *adj.* (of a vehicle or an aircraft) having two sets of controls, one of which is used by the instructor.

dual in-line package see DIP.

dualism /ˈdjuːəlɪz(ə)m/ *n.* **1** being twofold; duality. **2** *Philos.* the theory that in any domain of reality there are two independent underlying principles, e.g. mind and matter, form and content (cf. IDEALISM, MATERIALISM, MONISM). **3** *Theol.* **a** the theory that the forces of good and evil are equally balanced in the universe. **b** the theory of the dual (human and divine) personality of Christ. □ **dualist** *n.* **dualistic** /-ˈlɪstɪk/ *adj.* **dualistically** /-ˈlɪstɪk(ə)li/ *adv.*

dual-purpose *adj.* (of a vehicle) usable for passengers or goods.

dub[1] /dʌb/ *v.tr.* (**dubbed**, **dubbing**) **1** make (a person) a knight by the ritual touching of the shoulder with a sword. **2** give (a person) a name, nickname, or title (*dubbed him a crank*). **3** *Brit.* dress (an artificial fishing-fly). **4** smear (leather) with grease. [Old English from Anglo-French *duber*, *aduber*, Old French *adober* 'equip with armour, repair', of unknown origin]

dub[2] /dʌb/ *v.tr.* (**dubbed**, **dubbing**) **1** provide (a film etc.) with an alternative soundtrack, esp. in a different language. **2** add (sound effects or music) to a film or a broadcast. **3** combine (soundtracks) into one. **4** transfer or make a copy of (recorded sound or images). [abbreviation of DOUBLE]

dub[3] /dʌb/ *n. & v.* ● *n.* esp. *US slang* an inexperienced or unskilful person. ● *v.tr.* (**dubbed**, **dubbing**) *Golf* misplay (a shot). [perhaps from DUB[1] in sense 'beat flat']

dub[4] /dʌb/ *v.intr.* (**dubbed**, **dubbing**) (foll. by *in*, *up*) *slang* pay up; contribute money. [19th c.: origin uncertain]

dubbin /ˈdʌbɪn/ *n. & v.* ● *n.* (also **dubbing** /ˈdʌbɪŋ/) prepared grease for softening and waterproofing leather. ● *v.tr.* (**dubbined**, **dubbining**) apply dubbin to (boots etc.). [see DUB[1] 4]

dubbing /ˈdʌbɪŋ/ *n.* an alternative soundtrack to a film etc.

dubiety /djuːˈbʌɪɪti/ *n.* (*pl.* **-ies**) *literary* **1** a feeling of doubt. **2** a doubtful matter. [Late Latin *dubietas* from *dubium* 'doubt']

dubious /ˈdjuːbɪəs/ *adj.* **1** hesitating or doubting (*dubious about going*). **2** of questionable value or truth (*a dubious claim*). **3** unreliable; suspicious (*dubious company*). **4** of doubtful result (*a dubious undertaking*). □ **dubiously** *adv.* **dubiousness** *n.* [Latin *dubiosus* from *dubium* 'doubt']

dubitation /djuːbɪˈteɪʃ(ə)n/ *n. literary* doubt, hesitation. [Middle English from Old French *dubitation* or Latin *dubitatio*, from *dubitare* DOUBT]

dubitative /ˈdjuːbɪtətɪv/ *adj. literary* of, expressing, or inclined to doubt or hesitation. [French *dubitatif -ive* or Late Latin *dubitativus* (as DUBITATION)]

Dublin Bay prawn /ˈdʌblɪn/ *n.* **1** NORWAY LOBSTER. **2** (in *pl.*) scampi. [*Dublin*, a city in Ireland]

Dubonnet /duːˈbɒneɪ, djuː-/ *n. propr.* **1** a sweet French aperitif. **2** a glass of this. [name of a family of French wine-merchants]

ducal /ˈdjuːk(ə)l/ *adj.* of, like, or bearing the title of a duke. [French, from *duc* DUKE]

ducat /ˈdʌkət/ *n.* **1** *hist.* a gold coin, formerly current in most European countries. **2** **a** a coin. **b** (in *pl.*) money. [Middle English from Italian *ducato* or medieval Latin *ducatus* DUCHY]

Duce /ˈduːtʃeɪ/ *n.* a leader, esp. (**Il Duce**) the title assumed by Mussolini (d. 1945). [Italian, = leader]

Duchenne muscular dystrophy /duːˈʃɛn/ *n.* a severe form of muscular dystrophy caused by a genetic defect and usually affecting boys. [named after G.B.A. *Duchenne*, French neurologist d. 1875]

duchess /ˈdʌtʃɪs, -ɛs/ *n.* (as a title usu. **Duchess**) **1** a duke's wife or widow. **2** a woman holding the rank of duke in her own right. **3** *Brit. slang* a girl or woman, esp. a man's wife or mother. [Middle English via Old French *duchesse* from medieval Latin *ducissa* (as DUKE)]

duchesse /duːˈʃɛs, ˈdʌtʃɪs, -ɛs/ *n.* **1** a soft heavy kind of satin. **2** a dressing table with a pivoting mirror. [French, = DUCHESS]

duchesse lace *n.* a kind of Brussels pillow lace.

duchesse potatoes *n.pl.* mashed potatoes mixed with egg, formed into small shapes, and baked.

duchesse set *n.* a cover or a set of covers for a dressing table.

duchy /ˈdʌtʃi/ *n.* (*pl.* **-ies**) **1** the territory of a duke or duchess; a dukedom. **2** (often as **the Duchy**) the royal dukedom of Cornwall or Lancaster, each with certain estates, revenues, and jurisdiction of its own. [Middle English via Old French *duché(e)* and medieval Latin *ducatus* from Latin *dux ducis* 'leader']

duck[1] /dʌk/ *n.* (*pl.* same or **ducks**) **1** **a** any waterbird of the family Anatidae, with a broad flat bill and large webbed feet, esp. the domesticated form of the mallard. **b** the female of this (opp. DRAKE). **c** the flesh of a duck as food. **2** (in full **duck's-egg**) *Cricket* the score of a batsman dismissed for nought. **3** (also **ducks**) *Brit. colloq.* (esp. as a form of address) dear, darling. □ **like a duck to water** adapting very readily. **like water off a duck's back** *colloq.* (of remonstrances etc.) producing no effect. **play ducks and drakes with** *colloq.* squander. [Old English *duce*, *dūce*: related to DUCK[2]]

duck[2] /dʌk/ *v. & n.* ● *v.* **1** *intr. & tr.* plunge, dive, or dip under water and emerge (*ducked him in the pond*). **2** *intr. & tr.* bend (the head or the body) quickly to avoid a blow or being seen, or as a bow or curtsy; bob (*ducked out of sight*; *ducked his head under the beam*). **3** *tr. & intr. colloq.* avoid or dodge; withdraw (from) (*ducked out of the engagement*; *ducked the meeting*). **4** *intr. Bridge* lose a trick deliberately by playing a low card. ● *n.* **1** a quick dip or swim. **2** a quick lowering of the head etc. □ **ducker** *n.* [Middle English from Germanic]

duck[3] /dʌk/ *n.* **1** a strong untwilled linen or cotton fabric used for small sails and the outer clothing of sailors. **2** (in *pl.*) trousers made of this (*white ducks*). [Middle Dutch *doek*, of unknown origin]

duck[4] /dʌk/ *n. colloq.* an amphibious landing craft. [*DUKW*, its official designation]

duckbill /ˈdʌkbɪl/ *n.* a duck-billed platypus (see PLATYPUS).

duckboard /ˈdʌkbɔːd/ *n.* (usu. in *pl.*) a path of wooden slats placed over muddy ground or in a trench.

duck-hawk *n.* **1** *dial.* a marsh harrier. **2** *N. Amer.* a peregrine.

ducking-stool *n. hist.* a chair fastened to the end of a pole, which could be plunged into a pond, used formerly for ducking scolds etc.

duckling /ˈdʌklɪŋ/ *n.* **1** a young duck. **2** its flesh as food.

ducks and drakes *n.* a game of making a flat stone skim along the surface of water.

duck's arse *n.* (*US* **duck's ass**) *slang* a haircut with the hair on the back of the head shaped like a duck's tail.

duck soup *n. US slang* an easy task.

duckweed /ˈdʌkwiːd/ *n.* a tiny aquatic plant of the family Lemnaceae, esp. of the genus *Lemna*, growing on the surface of still water.

ducky /ˈdʌki/ *n. & adj. Brit. colloq.* ● *n.* (*pl.* **-ies**) darling, dear. ● *adj.* sweet, pretty; splendid.

duct /dʌkt/ *n. & v.* ● *n.* **1** a channel or tube for conveying fluid, cable, etc. **2 a** a tube in the body conveying lymph or glandular secretions such as tears, bile, etc. **b** *Bot.* a tube formed by cells that have lost their intervening end walls, holding air, water, etc. ● *v.tr.* convey through a duct. [Latin *ductus* 'leading, aqueduct' from *ducere duct-* 'lead']

ductile /ˈdʌktʌɪl/ *adj.* **1** (of a metal) capable of being drawn into wire; pliable, not brittle. **2** (of a substance) easily moulded. **3** (of a person) docile, gullible. ▫ **ductility** /-ˈtɪlɪti/ *n.* [Middle English from Old French *ductile* or Latin *ductilis*, from *ducere duct-* 'lead']

ducting /ˈdʌktɪŋ/ *n.* **1** a system of ducts. **2** material in the form of a duct or ducts.

ductless /ˈdʌktlɪs/ *adj.* lacking or not using a duct or ducts.

ductless gland *n.* a gland secreting directly into the bloodstream; an endocrine gland.

dud /dʌd/ *n. & adj. slang* ● *n.* **1** a futile or ineffectual person or thing (*a dud at the job*). **2** a counterfeit article. **3** a shell etc. that fails to explode. **4** (in *pl.*) clothes. ● *adj.* **1** useless, worthless, unsatisfactory or futile. **2** counterfeit. [Middle English: origin unknown]

dude /duːd, djuːd/ *n. slang* **1** a fastidious aesthetic person, usu. male; a dandy. **2** a holidaymaker on a ranch in the western US. **3** a fellow; a guy. ▫ **dudish** *adj.* [19th c.: probably from German dialect *dude* 'fool']

dude ranch *n.* (in the western US) a cattle ranch converted to a holiday centre for tourists etc.

dudgeon /ˈdʌdʒ(ə)n/ *n.* a feeling of offence; resentment. ▫ **in high dudgeon** very angry or angrily. [16th c.: origin unknown]

due /djuː/ *adj., n., & adv.* ● *adj.* **1** (*predic.*) owing or payable as a debt or an obligation (*our thanks are due to him*; *£500 was due on the 15th*). **2** (often foll. by *to*) merited; appropriate; fitting (*his due reward*; *received the applause due to a hero*). **3** (*attrib.*) rightful; proper; adequate (*after due consideration*). **4** (*predic.*; foll. by *to*) to be ascribed to (a cause, an agent, etc.) (*the discovery was due to Newton*). **5** (*predic.*) intended to arrive at a certain time (*a train is due at 7.30*). **6** (foll. by *to* + infin.) under an obligation or agreement to do something (*due to speak tonight*). ● *n.* **1** a person's right; what is owed to a person (*a fair hearing is my due*). **2** (in *pl.*) **a** what one owes (*pays his dues*). **b** *Brit.* an obligatory payment; a fee; a legal charge (*harbour dues*; *university dues*). ● *adv.* (of a point of the compass) exactly, directly (*went due east*; *a due north wind*). ▫ **due to** *disp.* because of, owing to (*he was late due to an accident*) (cf. sense 4 of *adj.*). **fall** (or **become**) **due** (of a bill etc.) be immediately payable. **in due course 1** at about the appropriate time. **2** in the natural order. [Middle English from Old French *deü*, ultimately from Latin *debitus*, past part. of *debēre* 'owe']

■ **Usage** The use of *due to* to mean 'because of' as in the example *He was late due to an accident* is regarded as unacceptable by some people. It can be avoided by substituting *His lateness was due to an accident*, *It was due to an accident that he was late*, or *He was late owing to/because of an accident*.

due date *n.* the date on which payment of a bill etc., falls due.

duel /ˈdjuːəl/ *n. & v.* ● *n.* **1** *hist.* a contest with deadly weapons between two people, in the presence of two seconds, to settle a point of honour. **2** any contest between two people, parties, causes, animals, etc. (*a duel of wits*). ● *v.intr.* (**duelled**, **duelling**; *US* **dueled**, **dueling**) fight a duel or duels. ▫ **dueller** *n.* (*US* **dueler**). **duellist** *n.* (*US* **duelist**). [Italian *duello* or Latin *duellum* (archaic form of *bellum* 'war'), in medieval Latin = single combat]

duende /duːˈɛndeɪ/ *n.* **1** an evil spirit. **2** inspiration. [Spanish]

duenna /djuːˈɛnə/ *n.* an older woman acting as a governess and companion in charge of girls, esp. in a Spanish family; a chaperone. [Spanish *dueña* from Latin *domina* 'mistress']

duet /djuːˈɛt/ *n. & v.* ● *n.* **1** *Mus.* **a** a performance by two voices, instrumentalists, etc. **b** a composition for two performers. **2** a dialogue. ● *v.intr.* (**duetted**, **duetting**) perform a duet. ▫ **duettist** *n.* [German *Duett* or Italian *duetto*, diminutive of *duo* 'duet', from Latin *duo* 'two']

duff[1] /dʌf/ *n.* a boiled pudding. [northern English form of DOUGH]

duff[2] /dʌf/ *adj. Brit. slang* **1** worthless, counterfeit. **2** useless, broken. [perhaps = DUFF[1]]

duff[3] /dʌf/ *v.tr. slang* **1** *Brit. Golf* mishit (a shot, a ball); bungle. **2** *Austral.* steal and alter brands on (cattle). ▫ **duff up** *Brit. slang* beat; thrash. [perhaps back-formation from DUFFER]

duffel /ˈdʌf(ə)l/ *n.* (also **duffle**) **1** a coarse woollen cloth with a thick nap. **2** *US* a sportsman's or camper's equipment. [*Duffel*, a town in Belgium]

duffel bag *n.* a cylindrical canvas bag closed by a drawstring and carried over the shoulder.

duffel coat *n.* a hooded overcoat made of duffel and usu. fastened with toggles.

duffer /ˈdʌfə/ *n. slang* **1** an inefficient, useless, or stupid person. **2** *Austral.* a person who duffs cattle. **3** *Austral.* an unproductive mine. [perhaps from Scots *dowfart* 'stupid person' from *douf* 'spiritless']

dug[1] *past* and *past part.* of DIG.

dug[2] /dʌg/ *n.* **1** the udder, breast, teat, or nipple of a female animal. **2** *derog.* the breast of a woman. [16th c.: origin unknown]

dugong /ˈduːgɒŋ, ˈdjuː-/ *n.* (*pl.* same or **dugongs**) a marine mammal (sirenian), *Dugong dugon*, of Asian seas and coasts. [ultimately from Malay *dūyong*]

dugout /ˈdʌgaʊt/ *n.* **1 a** a roofed shelter esp. for troops in trenches. **b** an underground air-raid or nuclear shelter. **c** *N. Amer. Sport* = BENCH *n.* 4. **2** a canoe made from a hollowed tree trunk. **3** *Brit. slang* a retired officer etc. recalled to service.

duiker /ˈdʌɪkə/ *n.* **1** (also **duyker**) any African antelope of the genus *Cephalophus*, usu. having a crest of long hair between its horns. **2** *S.Afr.* the long-tailed cormorant, *Phalacrocorax africanus*. [Dutch *duiker* 'diver': in sense 1, from its habit of plunging through bushes when pursued]

duke /djuːk/ *n.* **1** (as a title usu. **Duke**) **a** a person holding the highest hereditary title of the nobility. **b** a sovereign prince ruling a duchy or small state. **2** (usu. in *pl.*) *slang* the hand; the fist (*put up your dukes!*). **3** (in full **duke cherry**) a hybrid between the sweet cherry, *Prunus avium*, and the sour cherry, *P. cerasus*. [Middle English via Old French *duc* from Latin *dux ducis* 'leader']

dukedom /ˈdjuːkdəm/ *n.* **1** a territory ruled by a duke. **2** the rank of duke.

dulcet /ˈdʌlsɪt/ *adj.* (esp. of sound) sweet and soothing. [Middle English, earlier *doucet* from the Old French diminutive of *doux*, from Latin *dulcis* 'sweet']

dulcify /ˈdʌlsɪfʌɪ/ *v.tr.* (**-ies**, **-ied**) *literary* **1** make gentle. **2** sweeten. □ **dulcification** /-fɪˈkeɪʃ(ə)n/ *n.* [Latin *dulcificare* from *dulcis* 'sweet']

dulcimer /ˈdʌlsɪmə/ *n.* a musical instrument with strings of graduated length stretched over a sounding board or box, played by being struck with hammers. [Old French *doulcemer*, said to represent Latin *dulce* 'sweet', *melos* 'song']

dulcitone /ˈdʌlsɪtəʊn/ *n.* a keyboard musical instrument with steel tuning forks which are struck by hammers. [Latin *dulcis* 'sweet' + TONE]

dulia /djʊˈlʌɪə/ *n. RC Ch.* the reverence accorded to saints and angels. [medieval Latin from Greek *douleia* 'servitude', from *doulos* 'slave']

dull /dʌl/ *adj. & v.* ● *adj.* **1** slow to understand; stupid. **2** tedious; boring. **3** (of the weather) overcast; gloomy. **4 a** (esp. of a knife-edge etc.) blunt. **b** (of colour, light, sound, or taste) not bright, shining, vivid, or keen. **5** (of a pain etc.) usu. prolonged and indistinct; not acute (*a dull ache*). **6 a** sluggish, slow-moving (*dull trading*). **b** (of a person) listless; lacking vitality (*dull and apathetic*). **7** (of the ears, eyes, etc.) without keen perception. ● *v.tr. & intr.* make or become dull. □ **dull the edge of** make less sensitive, interesting, effective, amusing, etc.; blunt. □ **dullish** *adj.* **dullness** *n.* (also **dulness**). **dully** /ˈdʌlli/ *adv.* [Middle English from Middle Low German, Middle Dutch *dul*, corresponding to Old English *dol* 'stupid']

dullard /ˈdʌləd/ *n.* a stupid person.

dulse /dʌls/ *n.* an edible seaweed, *Rhodymenia palmata*, with red wedge-shaped fronds. [Irish & Gaelic *duileasg*]

duly /ˈdjuːli/ *adv.* **1** in due time or manner. **2** rightly, properly, fitly.

Duma /ˈduːmə/ *n.* **1** a legislative body in the ruling assembly of Russia and of some other republics of the former USSR. **2** *hist.* **a** any of four elected legislative bodies existing in Russia between 1906 and 1917. **b** any similar pre-19th c. advisory municipal council in Russia. [Russian]

dumb /dʌm/ *adj. & v.* ● *adj.* **1 a** (of a person) unable to speak, usu. because of a congenital defect or deafness. **b** (of an animal) naturally unable to speak (*our dumb friends*). **2** silenced by surprise, shyness, etc. (*struck dumb by this revelation*). **3** taciturn or reticent, esp. insultingly (*dumb insolence*). **4** (of an action etc.) performed without speech. **5** (often in *comb.*) giving no sound; without voice or some other property normally belonging to things of the name (*a dumb piano*). **6** esp. *US colloq.* stupid; ignorant. **7** (usu. of a class, population, etc.) having no voice in government; inarticulate (*the dumb masses*). **8** (of a computer terminal etc.) able only to transmit data to or receive data from a computer; not programmable (opp. INTELLIGENT). ● *v.tr.* make dumb or unheard; silence. □ **dumb down** *N. Amer. slang* reduce or adapt to a lower level of understanding. □ **dumbly** /ˈdʌmli/ *adv.* **dumbness** /ˈdʌmnɪs/ *n.* [Old English: origin unknown: sense 6 from German *dumm*]

dumb animals *n.pl.* animals, esp. as objects of pity.

dumb-bell *n.* **1** a short bar with a weight at each end, used for exercise, muscle-building, etc. **2** *slang* a stupid person, esp. *Brit.* a woman. [from an 18th-c. apparatus like that for ringing a church bell, but without the bell, used for exercise]

dumb blonde *n.* a pretty but stupid blonde woman.

dumb cluck *n. slang* a stupid person.

dumbfound /dʌmˈfaʊnd/ *v.tr.* (also **dumfound**) strike dumb; confound; nonplus. [DUMB, CONFOUND]

dumbhead /ˈdʌmhɛd/ *n.* esp. *US slang* a stupid person.

dumb-iron *n.* the curved side piece of a motor vehicle chassis, joining it to the front springs.

dumbo /ˈdʌmbəʊ/ *n.* (*pl.* **-os**) *slang* a stupid person; a fool. [DUMB + -O]

dumb piano *n.* a silent or dummy piano keyboard for exercising the fingers.

dumbshow /ˈdʌmʃəʊ/ *n.* **1** significant gestures or mime, used when words are inappropriate. **2** a part of a play in early drama, acted in mime.

dumbstruck /ˈdʌmstrʌk/ *adj.* greatly shocked or surprised and so lost for words.

dumb waiter *n.* **1** a small lift for carrying food, plates, etc., between floors. **2** *Brit.* a movable table, esp. with revolving shelves, used in a dining room.

dumdum /ˈdʌmdʌm/ *n.* (in full **dumdum bullet**) a kind of soft-nosed bullet that expands on impact and inflicts laceration. [*Dum-Dum*, a town and arsenal in India, where it was first produced]

dumfound var. of DUMBFOUND.

dummy /ˈdʌmi/ *n., adj., & v.* ● *n.* (*pl.* **-ies**) **1** a model of a human being, esp.: **a** a ventriloquist's doll. **b** a figure used to model clothes in a shop window etc. **c** a target used for firearms practice. **2** (often *attrib.*) **a** a counterfeit object used to replace or resemble a real or normal one. **b** a prototype, esp. in publishing. **3** *Rugby & Football* a pretended pass. **4** *colloq.* a stupid person. **5** a person taking no significant part; a figurehead. **6** *Brit.* a rubber or plastic teat for a baby to suck on. **7** an imaginary fourth player at whist, whose hand is turned up and played by a partner. **8** *Bridge* **a** the partner of the declarer, whose cards are exposed after the first lead. **b** this player's hand. **9** *Mil.* a blank round of ammunition. ● *adj.* sham; counterfeit. ● *v.tr.* (**-ies**, **-ied**) (usu. *absol.*) *Rugby & Football* pretend to pass (the ball). □ **dummy up** *US slang* keep quiet; give no information. **sell the** (or **a**) **dummy** *Rugby colloq.* deceive (an opponent) by pretending to pass the ball. [DUMB + -Y[2]]

dummy run *n.* **1** a practice attack, etc.; a trial run. **2** a rehearsal.

dump /dʌmp/ *n. & v.* ● *n.* **1 a** a place for depositing rubbish. **b** a heap of rubbish. **2** *colloq.* an unpleasant or dreary place. **3** *Mil.* a temporary store of ammunition, provisions, etc. **4** an accumulated pile of ore, earth, etc. **5** *Computing* **a** a printout of stored data. **b** the process or result of dumping data. ● *v.tr.* **1** put down firmly or clumsily (*dumped the shopping on the table*). **2** deposit or dispose of (rubbish etc.). **3** *colloq.* abandon, desert. **4** *Mil.* leave (ammunition etc.) in a dump. **5** *Econ.* send (goods unsaleable at a high price in the home market) to a foreign market for sale at a low price, to keep up the price at home, and to capture a new market. **6** *Computing* **a** copy (stored data) to a different location. **b** reproduce the contents of (a store) externally. □ **dump on** esp. *US* criticize or abuse; get the better of. [Middle English perhaps from Norse; cf. Danish *dumpe*, Norwegian *dumpa* 'fall suddenly']

dumper /ˈdʌmpə/ *n.* **1 a** a person or thing that dumps. **b** (in full **dumper truck**) a truck with a body that tilts or opens at the back for unloading. **2** *Austral. & NZ* a large wave that breaks and hurls the swimmer or surfer on to the beach.

dumpling /ˈdʌmplɪŋ/ *n.* **1 a** a small savoury ball of usu. suet, flour, and water, boiled in stew or water. **b** a pudding consisting of apple or other fruit enclosed in dough and baked. **2** a small fat person. [apparently diminutive of *dump* 'small round object', but recorded much earlier]

dumps /dʌm(p)s/ *n.pl. colloq.* depression; melancholy (*down in the dumps*). [probably from Low German or Dutch, figurative use of Middle Dutch *domp* 'exhalation, haze, mist': related to DAMP]

dump truck *n. N. Amer.* = DUMPER 1b.

dumpy /ˈdʌmpi/ *adj.* (**dumpier**, **dumpiest**) short and stout. □ **dumpily** *adv.* **dumpiness** *n.* [*dump* (cf. DUMPLING) + -Y[1]]

dun[1] /dʌn/ *adj. & n.* ● *adj.* **1** of a dull greyish-brown colour. **2** *poet.* dark, dusky. ● *n.* **1** a dun colour. **2** a dun horse. **3** a dark fishing-fly. [Old English *dun*, *dunn*]

dun[2] /dʌn/ *n. & v.* ● *n.* **1** a debt collector; an importunate creditor. **2** a demand for payment. ● *v.tr.* (**dunned**, **dunning**) importune for payment of a debt; pester. [abbreviation of obsolete *dunkirk* privateer, from *Dunkirk*, a sea port in France]

dun-bird *n.* a pochard.

dunce /dʌns/ *n.* a person slow at learning; a dullard. [John *Duns* Scotus, scholastic theologian d. 1308, whose followers were ridiculed by 16th-c. humanists and reformers as enemies of learning]

dunce's cap *n.* a paper cone formerly put on the head of a dunce at school as a mark of disgrace.

Dundee cake /dʌn'di:/ *n.* esp. *Brit.* a rich fruit cake usu. decorated with almonds. [*Dundee*, a city in Scotland]

dunderhead /'dʌndəhɛd/ *n.* a stupid person. ▫ **dunderheaded** *adj.* [17th c.: perhaps related to dialect *dunner* 'resounding noise']

dun-diver *n.* a female or young male goosander.

dune /dju:n/ *n.* a mound or ridge of loose sand etc. formed by the wind, esp. beside the sea or in a desert. [French from Middle Dutch *dūne*: cf. DOWN[3]]

dune buggy *n.* = BEACH BUGGY.

dung /dʌŋ/ *n.* & *v.* ● *n.* the excrement of animals; manure. ● *v.tr.* apply dung to; manure (land). [Old English, related to Old High German *tunga*, Icelandic *dyngja*, of unknown origin]

dungaree /dʌŋgə'ri:/ *n.* **1** a coarse Indian calico. **2** (in *pl.*) **a** overalls etc. made of dungaree or similar material, worn as workwear. **b** *Brit.* trousers with a bib worn by children or as a fashion garment. [Hindi *dungrī*]

dung-beetle *n.* a beetle whose larvae develop in dung, esp. one of the family Scarabaeidae.

dungeon /'dʌn(d)ʒ(ə)n/ *n.* & *v.* ● *n.* **1** a strong underground cell for prisoners. **2** *archaic* a donjon. ● *v.tr.* (usu. foll. by *up*) *archaic* imprison in a dungeon. [originally = *donjon*: Middle English from Old French *donjon*, ultimately from Latin *dominus* 'lord']

dung-fly *n.* a fly which lays its eggs in dung, esp. one of the family Scatophagidae.

dunghill /'dʌŋhɪl/ *n.* a heap of dung or refuse, esp. in a farmyard.

dung-worm *n.* any of various earthworms found in cow-dung and used as bait.

dunk /dʌŋk/ *v.tr.* **1** dip (bread, a biscuit, etc.) into soup, coffee, etc. while eating. **2** immerse, dip (*was dunked in the river*). [Pennsylvanian German *dunke* 'to dip', from German *tunken*]

dunlin /'dʌnlɪn/ *n.* a long-billed sandpiper, *Calidris alpina*. [probably from DUN[1] + -LING[1]]

dunnage /'dʌnɪdʒ/ *n.* *Naut.* **1** mats, brushwood, etc., stowed under or among cargo to prevent wetting or chafing. **2** *Brit. colloq.* miscellaneous baggage. [Anglo-Latin *dennagium*, of unknown origin]

dunno /'dʌnəʊ, də'nəʊ/ *colloq.* (I) do not know. [corruption]

dunnock /'dʌnək/ *n.* a small European songbird, *Prunella modularis*. Also called *hedge sparrow*. [apparently from DUN[1] + -OCK, from its brown and grey plumage]

dunny /'dʌni/ *n.* (*pl.* **-ies**) **1** *Sc.* an underground passage or cellar, esp. in a tenement. **2** esp. *Austral.* & *NZ slang* an earth closet; an outdoor privy. [19th c. in the sense 'faeces': origin uncertain, perhaps related to DUNG]

duo /'dju:əʊ/ *n.* (*pl.* **-os**) **1** a pair of actors, entertainers, singers, etc. (*a comedy duo*). **2** *Mus.* a duet. [Italian from Latin, = two]

duodecimal /dju:ə(ʊ)'dɛsɪm(ə)l/ *adj.* & *n.* ● *adj.* relating to or using a system of numerical notation that has twelve as a base. ● *n.* **1** the duodecimal system. **2** duodecimal notation. ▫ **duodecimally** *adv.* [Latin *duodecimus* 'twelfth' from *duodecim* 'twelve']

duodecimo /dju:əʊ'dɛsɪməʊ/ *n.* (*pl.* **-os**) *Printing* **1** a size of book in which each leaf is one-twelfth of the size of the printing-sheet. **2** a book of this size. [Latin (*in*) *duodecimo* 'in a twelfth' (as DUODECIMAL)]

duodenary /dju:ə'di:nəri/ *adj.* proceeding by twelves or in sets of twelve. [Latin *duodenarius* from *duodeni*, distributive of *duodecim* 'twelve']

duodenum /dju:ə'di:nəm/ *n.* the first part of the small intestine immediately beyond the stomach. ▫ **duodenal** *adj.* **duodenitis** /-'nʌɪtɪs/ *n.* [Middle English from medieval Latin, from *duodeni* (see DUODENARY), from its length of about 12 fingers' breadth]

duologue /'djʊəlɒg/ *n.* **1** a conversation between two people. **2** a play or part of a play for two actors. [formed irregularly from Latin or Greek *duo* 'two', on the pattern of *monologue*]

duomo /'dwəʊməʊ/ *n.* (*pl.* **-os**) an Italian cathedral. [Italian, = DOME]

duopoly /djʊ'ɒpəli/ *n.* (*pl.* **-ies**) *Econ.* the possession of trade in a commodity etc. by only two sellers. [Greek *duo* 'two' + *pōleō* 'sell', on the pattern of *monopoly*]

duotone /'dju:ətəʊn/ *n.* & *adj.* *Printing* ● *n.* **1** a half-tone illustration in two colours from the same original with different screen angles. **2** the process of making a duotone. ● *adj.* in two colours. [Latin *duo* 'two' + TONE]

dupe /dju:p/ *n.* & *v.* ● *n.* a victim of deception. ● *v.tr.* make a fool of; cheat; gull. ▫ **dupable** *adj.* **duper** *n.* **dupery** *n.* [French from dialect French *dupe* 'hoopoe', from the bird's supposedly stupid appearance]

dupion /'dju:pɪən/ *n.* **1** a rough silk fabric woven from the threads of double cocoons. **2** an imitation of this with other fibres. [French *doupion* from Italian *doppione*, from *doppio* 'double']

duple /'dju:p(ə)l/ *adj.* of two parts. [Latin *duplus* from *duo* 'two']

duple ratio *n.* a ratio of 2 to 1.

duplet /'dju:plɪt/ *n.* a set of two things, esp. of two equal musical notes played in the time of three. [Latin *duplus* DUPLE, on the pattern of DOUBLET]

duple time *n.* rhythm consisting of two beats to the bar.

duplex /'dju:plɛks/ *n.* & *adj.* ● *n.* esp. *N. Amer.* **1** a flat or maisonette on two levels. **2** a house subdivided for two families. ● *adj.* **1** having two elements; twofold. **2** esp. *US* **a** (of a flat) two-storeyed. **b** (of a house) for two families. **3** (of a communications system, computer circuit, etc.) allowing the transmission of signals in both directions simultaneously (opp. SIMPLEX). [Latin *duplex duplicis*, from *duo* 'two' + *plic-* 'fold']

duplicate *adj.*, *n.*, & *v.* ● *adj.* /'dju:plɪkət/ **1** exactly like something already existing; copied (esp. in large numbers). **2 a** having two corresponding parts. **b** existing in two examples; paired. **c** twice as large or many; doubled. ● *n.* /'dju:plɪkət/ **1 a** one of two identical things, esp. a copy of an original. **b** one of two or more specimens of a thing exactly or almost identical. **2** *Law* a second copy of a letter or document. **3** (in full **duplicate bridge** or **whist**) a form of bridge or whist in which the same hands are played successively by different players. **4** *archaic* a pawnbroker's ticket. ● *v.tr.* /'dju:plɪkeɪt/ **1** multiply by two; double. **2 a** make or be an exact copy of. **b** make or supply copies of (*duplicated the leaflet for distribution*). **3** repeat (an action etc.), esp. unnecessarily. ▫ **in duplicate** consisting of two exact copies. ▫ **duplicable** /-kəb(ə)l/ *adj.* **duplication** /-'keɪʃ(ə)n/ *n.* [Latin *duplicatus*, past part. of *duplicare* (as DUPLEX)]

duplicate ratio *n.* the proportion of the squares of two numbers.

duplicator /'dju:plɪkeɪtə/ *n.* **1** a machine for making copies of a document, leaflet, etc. **2** a person or thing that duplicates.

duplicity /dju:'plɪsɪti, djʊ-/ *n.* **1** double-dealing; deceitfulness. **2** *archaic* doubleness. ▫ **duplicitous** *adj.* [Middle English from Old French *duplicité* or Late Latin *duplicitas* (as DUPLEX)]

duppy /'dʌpi/ *n.* (*pl.* **-ies**) *W.Ind.* a malevolent spirit or ghost. [perhaps of African origin]

dura var. of DURRA.

durable /'djʊərəb(ə)l/ *adj.* & *n.* ● *adj.* **1** capable of lasting; hard-wearing. **2** (of goods) not for immediate consumption; able to be kept. ● *n.* (in *pl.*) durable goods. ▫ **durability** /-'bɪlɪti/ *n.* **durableness** *n.* **durably**

adv. [Middle English via Old French from Latin *durabilis*, via *durare* 'endure' from *durus* 'hard']

Duralumin /djʊˈraljʊmɪn/ *n. propr.* a light hard alloy of aluminium with copper etc. [perhaps from *Düren*, a town in the Rhineland or from Latin *durus* 'hard' + ALUMINIUM]

dura mater /djʊərə ˈmeɪtə/ *n. Anat.* the tough outermost membrane enveloping the brain and spinal cord (see MENINX). [medieval Latin = hard mother, translation of Arabic *al-'umm al-jāfiya* ('mother' in Arabic indicating the relationship of things)]

duramen /djʊˈreɪmɛn/ *n.* = HEARTWOOD. [Latin from *durare* 'harden']

durance /ˈdjʊər(ə)ns/ *n. archaic* imprisonment (*in durance vile*). [Middle English via French, from *durer* 'last', from Latin *durare*: see DURABLE]

duration /djʊˈreɪʃ(ə)n/ *n.* **1** the length of time for which something continues. **2** a specified length of time (*after the duration of a minute*). ◻ **for the duration 1** for a very long time. **2** until the end of the war. ◻ **durational** *adj.* [Middle English via Old French from medieval Latin *duratio -onis* (as DURANCE)]

durative /ˈdjʊərətɪv/ *adj. Gram.* denoting continuing action.

durbar /ˈdəːbɑː/ *n. hist.* **1** the court of an Indian ruler. **2** a public levee of an Indian prince or an Anglo-Indian governor or viceroy. [Urdu from Persian *darbār* 'court']

durchkomponiert /ˈdʊəx,kɒmpɒnɪət, German ˈdʊrç kɔmponiːrt/ *adj. Mus.* (of a song) having different music for each verse. [German, from *durch* 'through' + *komponiert* 'composed']

duress /djʊ(ə)ˈrɛs, ˈdjʊərɛs/ *n.* **1** compulsion, esp. imprisonment, threats, or violence, illegally used to force a person to act against his or her will (*under duress*). **2** forcible restraint or imprisonment. [Middle English via Old French *duresse* from Latin *duritia*, from *durus* 'hard']

Durex /ˈdjʊərɛks/ *n. Brit. propr.* a contraceptive sheath; a condom. [20th c.: invented word]

durian /ˈdʊərɪən/ *n.* **1** a large tree, *Durio zibethinus*, native to SE Asia, bearing oval spiny fruits containing a creamy pulp with a fetid smell and an agreeable taste. **2** this fruit. [Malay *durīan* from *dūrī* 'thorn']

duricrust /ˈdjʊərɪkrʌst/ *n. Geol.* a hard mineral crust formed near the surface of soil in semi-arid regions by evaporation of groundwater. [Latin *durus* 'hard' + CRUST]

during /ˈdjʊərɪŋ/ *prep.* **1** throughout the course or duration of (*read during the meal*). **2** at some point in the duration of (*came in during the evening*). [Middle English from Old French *durant*, ultimately from Latin *durare* 'last, continue']

durmast /ˈdəːmɑːst/ *n.* an oak tree, *Quercus petraea*, having sessile acorns, and growing esp. on acid soils. [*dur-* (perhaps erroneous for DUN¹) + MAST²]

durn *US* var. of DARN².

durned *US dial.* var. of DARNED.

durra /ˈdʊrə, ˈdʊərə/ *n.* (also **dura**, **dhurra**) a variety of the sorghum *Sorghum bicolor*, native to Asia, Africa, and the US. [Arabic *ḏura*, *ḏurra*]

durst *archaic* or *dial. past* of DARE.

durum /ˈdjʊərəm/ *n.* a kind of wheat, *Triticum durum*, having hard seeds and yielding a flour used in the manufacture of spaghetti etc. [Latin, neut. of *durus* 'hard']

durzi /ˈdəːzi/ *n.* (*pl.* **durzis**) an Indian tailor. [Urdu from Persian *darzī*, from *darz* 'sewing']

dusk /dʌsk/ *n., adj., & v.* ● *n.* **1** the darker stage of twilight. **2** shade; gloom. ● *adj. poet.* shadowy; dim; dark-coloured. ● *v.tr. & intr. poet.* make or become shadowy or dim. [Old English *dox* 'dark, swarthy', *doxian* 'darken in colour']

dusky /ˈdʌski/ *adj.* (**duskier**, **duskiest**) **1** shadowy; dim. **2** dark-coloured, darkish. ◻ **duskily** *adv.* **duskiness** *n.*

dust /dʌst/ *n. & v.* ● *n.* **1 a** finely powdered earth, dirt, etc., lying on the ground or on surfaces, and blown about by the wind. **b** fine powder of any material (*pollen dust; gold dust*). **c** a cloud of dust. **2** a dead person's remains (*honoured dust*). **3** confusion or turmoil (*raised quite a dust*). **4** *archaic* or *poet.* the mortal human body (*we are all dust*). **5** the ground; the earth (*kissed the dust*). **6** an act of dusting (*give the table a dust*). ● *v.* **1** *tr.* (also *absol.*) clear (furniture etc.) of dust etc. by wiping, brushing, etc. **2** *tr.* **a** sprinkle (esp. a cake) with powder, dust, sugar, etc. **b** sprinkle or strew (sugar, powder, etc.). **3** *tr.* make dusty. **4** *intr. archaic* (of a bird) take a dust-bath. ◻ **dust and ashes** something very disappointing. **dust down** *Brit.* **1** wipe or brush the dust from. **2** *colloq.* reprimand. **3** = *dust off*. **dust off 1** remove the dust from (an object on which it has long been allowed to settle). **2** use and enjoy again after a long period of neglect. **in the dust 1** humiliated. **2** dead. **not see a person for dust** find that a person has made a hasty departure. **when the dust settles** when things quieten down. ◻ **dustless** *adj.* [Old English *dūst*: cf. Low German *dunst* 'vapour']

dust-bath *n.* a bird's rolling in dust to freshen its feathers.

dustbin /ˈdʌs(t)bɪn/ *n. Brit.* a container for household refuse, esp. one kept outside.

dust bowl *n.* an area denuded of vegetation by drought or erosion and reduced to desert.

dustcart /ˈdʌs(t)kɑːt/ *n. Brit.* a vehicle used for collecting household refuse.

dust cover *n.* **1** = DUST SHEET. **2** = DUST JACKET.

dust devil *n. S.Afr.* a whirlwind visible as a column of dust.

duster /ˈdʌstə/ *n.* **1 a** *Brit.* a cloth for dusting furniture etc. **b** a person or contrivance that dusts. **2** a woman's light, loose, full-length coat.

dusting powder *n.* **1** talcum powder. **2** any dusting or drying powder.

dust jacket *n.* a usu. decorated paper cover used to protect a book from dirt etc.

dustman /ˈdʌs(t)mən/ *n.* (*pl.* **-men**) *Brit.* **1** a man employed to clear household refuse. **2** = SANDMAN.

dustpan /ˈdʌs(t)pan/ *n.* a small pan into which dust etc. is brushed from the floor.

dust sheet *n. Brit.* a cloth put over furniture to protect it from dust.

dust-shot *n.* the smallest size of shot.

dust storm *n.* a storm with clouds of dust carried in the air.

dust-trap *n.* something on, in, or under which dust gathers.

dust-up *n. colloq.* a fight.

dust-wrapper *n.* = DUST JACKET.

dusty /ˈdʌsti/ *adj.* (**dustier**, **dustiest**) **1** full of, covered with, or resembling dust. **2** uninteresting; dry (*dusty legal paragraphs*). **3** (of a colour) dull or muted. ◻ **not so dusty** *Brit. slang* fairly good. ◻ **dustily** *adv.* **dustiness** *n.* [Old English *dūstig* (as DUST)]

dusty answer *n. Brit.* a curt rejection of a request.

dusty miller *n.* **1** any of various plants, esp. *Artemisia stelleriana*, having white dust on the leaves and flowers. **2** a kind of artificial fishing-fly.

Dutch /dʌtʃ/ *adj. & n.* ● *adj.* **1** of, relating to, or associated with the Netherlands. **2** *US archaic slang* German. **3** *S.Afr.* of Dutch descent. **4** *archaic* of Germany including the Netherlands. ● *n.* **1 a** the language of the Netherlands. **b** *S.Afr.* usu. *derog.* Afrikaans. **2** (prec. by *the*; treated as *pl.*) **a** the people of the Netherlands. **b** *S.Afr.* Afrikaans-speakers. **3** *archaic* the language of Germany including the Netherlands. ◻ **go Dutch** share expenses equally. [Middle Dutch *dutsch* etc., Hollandish, Netherlandish, German, Old High German *diutisc* 'national']

dutch /dʌtʃ/ *n. Brit. slang* = DUCHESS 3. [abbreviation]

Dutch auction *n.* a sale, usu. public, of goods in which the price is reduced by the auctioneer until a buyer is found.

Dutch bargain *n.* a bargain concluded by drinking together.

Dutch barn *n. Brit.* a barn roof over hay etc., set on poles and having no walls.

Dutch cap *n.* **1** *Brit.* a contraceptive diaphragm. **2** a woman's lace cap with triangular flaps on each side.

Dutch courage *n.* false courage gained from alcohol.

Dutch doll *n. Brit.* a jointed wooden doll.

Dutch door *n.* = STABLE DOOR 2.

Dutch elm disease *n.* a disease of elms, often fatal, caused by the fungus *Ceratocystis ulmi* and spread by bark beetles.

Dutch hoe *n.* a hoe used with a pushing action.

Dutch interior *n.* a painting of Dutch domestic life, esp. by P. de Hooch (d. 1683).

Dutchman /ˈdʌtʃmən/ *n.* (*pl.* **-men**; *fem.* **Dutchwoman**, *pl.* **-women**) **1 a** a native or national of the Netherlands. **b** a person of Dutch descent. **2** a Dutch ship. **3** *US archaic slang* a German. □ **I'm a Dutchman** *Brit.* expression of disbelief or refusal.

Dutchman's breeches *n. US* a plant of eastern N. America, *Dicentra cucullaria*, with white flowers and finely divided leaves.

Dutchman's pipe *n.* a climbing vine of eastern N. America, *Aristolochia durior*, with hooked tubular flowers.

Dutch metal *n.* a copper-zinc alloy imitating gold leaf.

Dutch oven *n.* **1** a metal box the open side of which is turned towards a fire. **2** a covered cooking pot for braising etc.

Dutch treat *n.* a party, outing, etc. to which each person makes a contribution.

Dutch uncle *n.* a person giving advice with benevolent firmness.

Dutch wife *n.* a framework of cane etc., or a bolster, used for resting the legs in bed.

Dutchwoman see DUTCHMAN.

duteous /ˈdjuːtɪəs/ *adj. literary* (of a person or conduct) dutiful; obedient. □ **duteously** *adv.* **duteousness** *n.* [DUTY + -OUS: cf. *beauteous*]

dutiable /ˈdjuːtɪəb(ə)l/ *adj.* liable to customs or other duties.

dutiful /ˈdjuːtɪfʊl, -f(ə)l/ *adj.* doing or observant of one's duty; obedient. □ **dutifully** *adv.* **dutifulness** *n.*

duty /ˈdjuːti/ *n.* (*pl.* **-ies**) **1 a** a moral or legal obligation; a responsibility (*his duty to report it*). **b** the binding force of what is right (*strong sense of duty*). **c** what is required of one (*do one's duty*). **2** payment to the public revenue, esp.: **a** that levied on the import, export, manufacture, or sale of goods (*customs duty*). **b** *Brit.* that levied on the transfer of property, licences, the legal recognition of documents, etc. (*death duty*; *probate duty*). **3** (often in *pl.*) a job or function (*his duties as caretaker*). **4** the behaviour due to a superior; deference, respect. **5** the measure of an engine's effectiveness in units of work done per unit of fuel. **6** *Eccl.* the performance of church services. □ **do duty for** serve as or pass for (something else). **on** (or **off**) **duty** engaged (or not engaged) in one's work. [Anglo-French *deweté*, *dueté* (as DUE)]

duty-bound *adj.* obliged by duty.

duty-free *adj.* (of goods) on which duty is not leviable.

duty-free shop *n.* a shop at an airport etc. at which duty-free goods can be bought.

duty officer *n.* the officer currently on duty.

duty-paid *adj.* (of goods) on which duty has been paid.

duty visit *n.* a visit paid from obligation, not from pleasure.

duumvir /djuːˈʌmvə/ *n. Rom.Hist.* one of two co-equal magistrates or officials. □ **duumvirate** /-vɪrət/ *n.* [Latin from *duum virum* 'of the two men']

duvet /ˈdjuːveɪ, ˈduː-/ *n.* esp. *Brit.* a thick soft quilt with a detachable cover, used instead of an upper sheet and blankets. [French, = DOWN[2]]

dux /dʌks/ *n. Sc., Austral., NZ, & S.Afr.* etc. the top pupil in a class or in a school. [Latin, = leader]

duyker var. of DUIKER 1.

DV *abbr. Deo volente.*

Dvr. *abbr. Brit.* Driver.

dwale /dweɪl/ *n.* deadly nightshade. [probably from Scandinavian]

dwarf /dwɔːf/ *n. & v.* ● *n.* (*pl.* **dwarfs** or **dwarves** /dwɔːvz/) **1 a** a person of abnormally small stature, esp. one with a normal-sized head and body but short limbs. **b** an animal or plant much below the ordinary size for the species. **2** a small mythological being with supernatural powers. **3** (in full **dwarf star**) a small usu. dense star. **4** (*attrib.*) **a** of a kind very small in size (*dwarf bean*). **b** puny, stunted. ● *v.tr.* **1** stunt in growth. **2** cause (something similar or comparable) to seem small or insignificant (*efforts dwarfed by their rivals' achievements*). □ **dwarfish** *adj.* [Old English *dweorg*, from Germanic]

■ **Usage** In sense 1, alternative terms such as *person of restricted growth* are now sometimes preferred.

dwarfism /ˈdwɔːfɪz(ə)m/ *n.* esp. *Med.* the condition of being a dwarf.

dweeb /dwiːb/ *n. US slang* a studious or boring person; a nerd. [20th c.: origin unknown]

dwell /dwɛl/ *v. & n.* ● *v.intr.* (*past* and *past part.* **dwelt** or **dwelled**) **1** (usu. foll. by *in*, *at*, *near*, *on*, etc.) *literary* live, reside (*dwelt in the forest*). **2** (of a horse) be slow in raising its feet; pause before taking a fence. ● *n.* a slight, regular pause in the motion of a machine. □ **dwell on** (or **upon**) **1** spend time on, linger over; write, brood, or speak at length on (a specified subject) (*always dwells on his grievances*). **2** prolong (a note, a syllable, etc.). □ **dweller** *n.* [Old English *dwellan* 'lead astray, hinder, delay', later 'continue in a place', from Germanic]

dwelling /ˈdwɛlɪŋ/ *n.* (also **dwelling place**) *formal* a house; a residence; an abode.

dwelling house *n.* a house used as a residence, not as an office etc.

dwindle /ˈdwɪnd(ə)l/ *v.intr.* **1** become gradually smaller; shrink; waste away. **2** lose importance; decline; degenerate. [*dwine* 'fade away' from Old English *dwīnan*, Old Norse *dvína*]

dwt. *abbr. hist.* pennyweight.

d.w.t. *abbr.* dead-weight tonnage.

Dy *symb. Chem.* the element dysprosium.

dyad /ˈdʌɪad/ *n. Math.* an operator which is a combination of two vectors. □ **dyadic** /-ˈadɪk/ *adj.* [Late Latin *dyas dyad-* from Greek *duas duados*, from *duo* 'two']

Dyak /ˈdʌɪak/ *n.* (also **Dayak**) an aboriginal of Borneo or Sarawak. [Malay *dayak* 'up-country']

dyarchy var. of DIARCHY.

dybbuk /ˈdɪbʊk/ *n.* (*pl.* **dybbukim** /-kɪm/ or **dybbuks**) a malevolent spirit in Jewish folklore. [Hebrew *dibbūk* from *dāḇak* 'cling']

dye /dʌɪ/ *n. & v.* ● *n.* **1 a** a substance used to change the colour of hair, fabric, wood, etc. **b** a colour produced by this. **2** (in full **dyestuff** /ˈdʌɪstʌf/) a substance yielding a dye, esp. when in solution. ● *v.* (**dyeing**) **1** *tr.* impregnate with dye. **2** *tr.* make (a thing) a specified colour with dye (*dyed it yellow*). **3** *intr.* take colour in the process of dyeing. □ **dyed in the wool** (or *Brit.* **grain**) **1** out and out; unchangeable, inveterate. **2** (of a fabric) made of yarn dyed in its raw state. □ **dyeable** *adj.* [Old English *deag*, *deagian*]

dye-line *n.* a print made by the diazo process.

dyer /ˈdʌɪə/ *n.* a person who dyes cloth etc.

dyer's greenweed *n.* (also **dyer's broom**) a bushy yellow-flowered leguminous plant, *Genista tinctoria*, formerly used to make a green dye.

dyer's oak *n.* an E. Mediterranean oak, *Quercus infectoria*, bearing galls formerly used to make a yellow dye.

dyestuff see DYE *n.* 2.

dying /'dʌɪɪŋ/ *attrib.adj.* connected with, or at the time of, death (*his dying words*). □ **to one's dying day** for the rest of one's life. [pres. part. of DIE[1]]

dying oath *n.* an oath made at, or with the solemnity proper to, death.

dyke[1] /dʌɪk/ *n.* & *v.* (also **dike**) ● *n.* **1** a long wall or embankment built to prevent flooding, esp. from the sea. **2 a** a ditch or artificial watercourse. **b** *Brit.* a natural watercourse. **3 a** a low wall, esp. of turf. **b** a causeway. **4** a barrier or obstacle; a defence. **5** *Geol.* an intrusion of igneous rock across sedimentary strata. **6** esp. *Austral. slang* a lavatory. ● *v.tr.* provide or defend with a dyke or dykes. [Middle English from Old Norse *dík* or Middle Low German *dīk* 'dam', Middle Dutch *dijc* 'ditch, dam': cf. DITCH]

dyke[2] /dʌɪk/ *n.* (also **dike**) *slang* a lesbian. [20th c.: origin unknown]

dyn /dʌɪn/ *abbr.* dyne.

dynamic /dʌɪ'namɪk/ *adj.* & *n.* ● *adj.* (also **dynamical**) **1** energetic; active; potent. **2** *Physics* **a** concerning motive force (opp. STATIC). **b** concerning force in actual operation. **3** of or concerning dynamics. **4** *Mus.* relating to the volume of sound. **5** *Philos.* relating to dynamism. **6** (as **dynamical**) *Theol.* (of inspiration) endowing with divine power, not impelling mechanically. ● *n.* **1** an energizing or motive force. **2** *Mus.* = DYNAMICS 3. □ **dynamically** *adv.* [French *dynamique* from Greek *dunamikos*, from *dunamis* 'power']

dynamic equilibrium *n.* a state of balance between continuing processes.

dynamics /dʌɪ'namɪks/ *n.pl.* **1** (usu. treated as *sing.*) **a** the branch of mechanics concerned with the motion of bodies under the action of forces (cf. STATICS). **b** the branch of any science in which forces or changes are considered (*aerodynamics*; *population dynamics*). **2** the motive forces, physical or moral, affecting behaviour and change in any sphere (*group dynamics*). **3** *Mus.* the varying degree of volume of sound in musical performance. □ **dynamicist** /-sɪst/ *n.* (in sense 1a).

dynamic viscosity *n.* a quantity measuring the force needed to overcome internal friction.

dynamism /'dʌɪnəmɪz(ə)m/ *n.* **1** energizing or dynamic action or power. **2** *Philos.* the theory that phenomena of matter or mind are due to the action of forces (rather than to motion or matter). □ **dynamist** *n.* [Greek *dunamis* 'power' + -ISM]

dynamite /'dʌɪnəmʌɪt/ *n.* & *v.* ● *n.* **1** a high explosive consisting of nitroglycerine mixed with an absorbent. **2** a potentially dangerous person, thing, or situation. **3** *Brit. slang* a narcotic, esp. heroin. **4** (often *attrib.*) *slang* a powerful or impressive person or thing. ● *v.tr.* charge or shatter with dynamite. □ **dynamiter** *n.* [formed as DYNAMISM + -ITE[1]]

dynamo /'dʌɪnəməʊ/ *n.* (*pl.* **-os**) **1** esp. *Brit.* a machine converting mechanical energy into electrical energy, esp. by rotating coils of copper wire in a magnetic field. **2** *colloq.* an energetic person. [abbreviation of *dynamo-electric machine*, from Greek *dunamis* 'power']

dynamometer /dʌɪnə'mɒmɪtə/ *n.* an instrument measuring energy expended by a mechanism, vehicle, etc. [French *dynamomètre* (as Greek *dunamis* 'power, force' + -METER)]

dynast /'dɪnəst, 'dʌɪnəst, -ast/ *n.* **1** a ruler. **2** a member of a dynasty. [Latin from Greek *dunastēs*, from *dunamai* 'be able']

dynasty /'dɪnəsti/ *n.* (*pl.* **-ies**) **1** a line of hereditary rulers. **2** a succession of leaders in any field. □ **dynastic** /-'nastɪk/ *adj.* **dynastically** /-'nastɪk(ə)li/ *adv.* [French *dynastie* or Late Latin *dynastia* from Greek *dunasteia* 'lordship' (as DYNAST)]

dynatron /'dʌɪnətrɒn/ *n.* *Electronics* a thermionic valve, used to generate continuous oscillations. [Greek *dunamis* 'power' + -TRON]

dyne /dʌɪn/ *n.* *Physics* a unit of force that, acting on a mass of one gram, increases its velocity by one centimetre per second every second along the direction that it acts (abbr.: **dyn**). [French from Greek *dunamis* 'force, power']

dys- /dɪs/ *comb. form* esp. *Med.* bad, difficult. [Greek *dus-* 'bad']

dysentery /'dɪs(ə)nt(ə)ri/ *n.* a disease with inflammation of the intestines, causing severe diarrhoea with blood and mucus. □ **dysenteric** /-'tɛrɪk/ *adj.* [Old French *dissenterie* or Latin *dysenteria* from Greek *dusenteria* (as DYS-, *enteria* from *entera* 'bowels')]

dysfunction /dɪs'fʌŋ(k)ʃ(ə)n/ *n.* an abnormality or impairment of function. □ **dysfunctional** *adj.*

dysgraphia /dɪs'grafɪə/ *n.* an inability to write coherently. □ **dysgraphic** *adj.* [DYS- + Greek *graphia* 'writing']

dyslexia /dɪs'lɛksɪə/ *n.* a disorder marked esp. by severe difficulty in reading and spelling. □ **dyslectic** /-'lɛktɪk/ *adj.* & *n.* **dyslexic** *adj.* & *n.* [German *Dyslexie* (as DYS-, Greek *lexis* 'speech', apparently by confusion of Greek *legein* 'to speak' and Latin *legere* 'to read')]

dysmenorrhoea /ˌdɪsmɛnə'ri:ə/ *n.* painful or difficult menstruation. [DYS- + MENORRHOEA]

dyspepsia /dɪs'pɛpsɪə/ *n.* indigestion. [Latin *dyspepsia* from Greek *duspepsia* (as DYS-, *peptos* 'cooked, digested')]

dyspeptic /dɪs'pɛptɪk/ *adj.* & *n.* ● *adj.* of or relating to dyspepsia or the resulting depression. ● *n.* a person suffering from dyspepsia.

dysphasia /dɪs'feɪzɪə/ *n.* *Med.* lack of coordination in speech, owing to brain damage. □ **dysphasic** *adj.* [Greek *dusphatos* 'hard to utter' (as DYS-, PHATIC)]

dysphoria /dɪs'fɔ:rɪə/ *n.* a state of unease or mental discomfort. □ **dysphoric** /-'fɒrɪk/ *adj.* [Greek *dusphoria* from *dusphoros* 'hard to bear' (as DYS-, *pherō* 'bear')]

dysplasia /dɪs'pleɪzɪə/ *n.* *Med.* abnormal growth of tissues etc. □ **dysplastic** /-'plastɪk/ *adj.* [modern Latin, formed as DYS- + Greek *plasis* 'formation']

dyspnoea /dɪsp'ni:ə/ *n.* (*US* **dyspnea**) *Med.* difficult or laboured breathing. □ **dyspnoeic** *adj.* [Latin from Greek *duspnoia* (as DYS-, *pneō* 'breathe')]

dysprosium /dɪs'prəʊzɪəm/ *n.* *Chem.* a naturally occurring soft metallic element of the lanthanide series, used as a component in certain magnetic alloys (symbol **Dy**). [modern Latin, from Greek *dusprositos* 'hard to get at' + -IUM]

dystocia /dɪs'təʊʃə/ *n.* *Med.* difficult or prolonged childbirth. [DYS- + Greek *tokos* 'childbirth']

dystopia /dɪs'təʊpɪə/ *n.* a nightmare vision of society, often as one dominated by a totalitarian state (opp. UTOPIA). □ **dystopian** *adj.* & *n.* [DYS- + UTOPIA]

dystrophic /dɪs'trɒfɪk, -'trəʊf-/ *adj.* **1** *Med.* relating to or affected by dystrophy. **2** *Ecol.* (of a lake etc.) containing much dissolved organic matter and little oxygen. [formed as DYSTROPHY + -IC]

dystrophy /'dɪstrəfi/ *n.* impaired nourishment of an organ or part of the body. See also MUSCULAR DYSTROPHY. [modern Latin *dystrophia*, formed as DYS- + Greek *-trophia* 'nourishment']

dysuria /dɪs'jʊərɪə/ *n.* painful or difficult urination. [Late Latin from Greek *dusouria* (as DYS-, *ouron* 'urine')]

dzo /ʒəʊ, zəʊ/ *n.* (also **dzho**, **zho**) (*pl.* same or **-os**) a hybrid of a cow and a yak. [Tibetan *mdso*]

Ee

E[1] /iː/ *n.* (also **e**) (*pl.* **Es** or **E's**) **1** the fifth letter of the alphabet. **2** *Mus.* the third note of the diatonic scale of C major.

E[2] *abbr.* (also **E.**) **1** East; Eastern. **2** Egyptian (*£E*). **3** *slang* **a** the drug ecstasy. **b** a tablet of this. **4** see E-NUMBER.

E[3] *symb. Physics* energy ($E = mc^2$).

e *symb.* **1** *Math.* the base of natural logarithms, equal to approx. 2.71828. **2** used on packaging (in conjunction with specification of weight, size, etc.) to indicate compliance with EEC regulations.

e- /ɪ, ɛ/ *prefix* form of EX-[1] 1 before some consonants.

ea. *abbr.* each.

each /iːtʃ/ *det. & pron.* ● *det.* every one of two or more persons or things, regarded and identified separately (*each person*; *five in each class*). ● *pron.* each person or thing (*each of us*; *have two books each*; *cost a penny each*). □ **each and every** every single. [Old English *ǣlc* from West Germanic phrase = ever alike, formed as AYE[2] + ALIKE]

each other *pron.* one another (*they hate each other*; *they wore each other's hats*).

each way *adj. & adv. Brit.* (of a bet) backing a horse etc. for either a win or a place.

eager /ˈiːɡə/ *adj.* **1 a** full of keen desire, enthusiastic. **b** (of passions etc.) keen, impatient. **2** (often foll. by *for*, or *to* + infin.) keen, impatient, strongly desirous (*eager to learn*; *eager for news*). □ **eagerly** *adv.* **eagerness** *n.* [Middle English from Anglo-French *egre*, Old French *aigre* 'keen', ultimately from Latin *acer acris*]

eager beaver *n. colloq.* an overzealous or extremely diligent person.

eagle /ˈiːɡ(ə)l/ *n. & v.* ● *n.* **1 a** any of various large birds of prey of the family Accipitridae, with keen vision and powerful flight. **b** a figure of an eagle, esp. as a symbol of the US, or formerly as a Roman or French ensign. **2** *Golf* a score of two strokes under par at any hole. **3** *US* a former gold coin worth ten dollars. ● *v.tr. Golf* play (a hole) in two strokes less than par. [Middle English via Anglo-French *egle*, Old French *aigle* from Latin *aquila*]

eagle eye *n.* keen sight, watchfulness. □ **eagle-eyed** *adj.*

eagle owl *n.* any large owl of the genus *Bubo*, with long ear-tufts.

eagle ray *n.* a large ray (fish) of the family Myliobatidae, with long pointed pectoral fins.

eaglet /ˈiːɡlɪt/ *n.* a young eagle.

eagre /ˈeɪɡə, ˈiː-/ *n.* = BORE[3]. [17th c.: origin unknown]

-ean /ˈiːən, ɪən/ *suffix* var. of -AN.

E. & O. E. *abbr.* errors and omissions excepted.

ear[1] /ɪə/ *n.* **1 a** the organ of hearing and balance in humans and vertebrates, esp. the external part of this. **b** an organ sensitive to sound in other animals. **2** the faculty for discriminating sounds (*an ear for music*). **3** an ear-shaped thing, esp. the handle of a jug. **4** listening, attention. □ **all ears** listening attentively. **bring about one's ears** bring down upon oneself. **give ear to** listen to. **have a person's ear** receive a favourable hearing. **have** (or **keep**) **an ear to the ground** be alert to rumours or the trend of opinion. **in one ear and out the other** heard but disregarded or quickly forgotten. **out on one's ear** dismissed ignominiously. **up to one's ears** (often foll. by *in*) *colloq.* deeply involved or occupied. □ **eared** *adj.* (also in *comb.*). **earless** *adj.* [Old English *ēare* from Germanic: related to Latin *auris*, Greek *ous*]

ear[2] /ɪə/ *n.* the seed-bearing head of a cereal plant. [Old English *ēar* from Germanic, related to Latin *acus*, *acer* 'husk']

earache /ˈɪəreɪk/ *n.* a (usu. prolonged) pain in the ear.

earbash /ˈɪəbaʃ/ *v.tr.* esp. *Austral. slang* talk inordinately to; harangue. □ **earbasher** *n.* **earbashing** *n.*

ear drops *n.pl.* **1** medicinal drops for the ear. **2** hanging earrings.

eardrum /ˈɪədrʌm/ *n.* the membrane of the middle ear (= TYMPANIC MEMBRANE).

earful /ˈɪəfʊl/ *n.* (*pl.* **-fuls**) *colloq.* **1** a copious or prolonged amount of talking. **2** a strong reprimand.

earhole /ˈɪəhəʊl/ *n.* the orifice of the ear.

earl /əːl/ *n.* a British nobleman ranking between a marquess and a viscount (cf. COUNT[2]). □ **earldom** *n.* [Old English *eorl*, of unknown origin]

Earl Grey *n.* a superior type of tea flavoured with bergamot.

Earl Marshal *n.* (in the UK) the officer presiding over the College of Heralds, with ceremonial duties on various royal occasions.

ear lobe *n.* the lower soft pendulous external part of the ear.

Earl Palatine *n. hist.* an earl having royal authority within his country or domain.

early /ˈəːli/ *adj., adv., & n.* ● *adj. & adv.* (**earlier**, **earliest**) **1** before the due, usual, or expected time (*was early for my appointment*; *the train arrived early*). **2 a** not far on in the day or night, or in time (*early evening*; *at the earliest opportunity*). **b** prompt; promptly (*early payment appreciated*; *reply early for a reduction*). **3 a** not far on in a period, development, or process of evolution; being the first stage (*Early English architecture*; *the early Christians*; *early Spring*). **b** of the distant past (*early man*). **c** not far on in a sequence or serial order (*the early chapters*; *appears early in the list*). **4 a** of childhood, esp. the pre-school years (*early learning*). **b** (of a piece of writing, music, etc.) immature, youthful (*an early work*). **5** flowering, ripening, etc., before other varieties (*early peaches*). ● *n.* (*pl.* **-ies**) (usu. in *pl.*) an early fruit or vegetable, esp. potatoes. □ **at the earliest** (often placed after a specified time) not before (*will arrive on Monday at the earliest*). **early** (or **earlier**) **on** at an early (or earlier) stage. □ **earliness** *n.* [originally as *adv.*, Old English *ǣrlīce*, *ārlīce*, from *ǣr* ERE]

early bird *n. colloq.* a person who arrives, gets up, etc. early.

early closing *n. Brit.* the shutting of business premises on the afternoon of one particular day of the week.

early days *n.pl. Brit.* early in time for something to happen etc.

early grave *n.* an untimely or premature death.

early hours *n.pl.* the very early morning, usu. before dawn.

early music *n.* medieval, Renaissance, and baroque music, esp. as revived and played on period instruments. □ **early musician** *n.*

early night *n.* an occasion on which a person goes to bed early.

early retirement *n.* retirement from one's occupation before the statutory retirement age, esp. on advantageous financial terms.

early warning *n.* advance warning of a problem or of an imminent (esp. nuclear) attack (often *attrib.*: *early warning system*).

earmark /ˈɪəmɑːk/ *n.* & *v.* ● *n.* **1** an identifying mark. **2** an owner's mark on the ear of an animal. ● *v.tr.* **1** (usu. foll. by *for*) set aside (money etc.) for a special purpose. **2** mark (sheep etc.) with an identifying mark.

earmuff /ˈɪəmʌf/ *n.* a wrap or cover for the ears, protecting them from cold, noise, etc.

earn /əːn/ *v.tr.* **1** (also *absol.*) **a** (of a person) obtain (income) in the form of money in return for labour or services (*earn a weekly wage*; *happy to be earning at last*). **b** (of capital invested) bring in as interest or profit. **2 a** deserve; be entitled to; obtain as the reward for hard work or merit (*have earned a holiday*; *earned our admiration*; *earn one's keep*). **b** incur (a reproach, reputation, etc.). [Old English *earnian* from West Germanic, related to Germanic roots associated with reaping]

earned income *n.* income derived from wages etc. (opp. UNEARNED INCOME).

earner /ˈəːnə/ *n.* **1** a person or thing that earns (often in *comb.*: *wage earner*). **2** *Brit. colloq.* a lucrative job or enterprise.

earnest[1] /ˈəːnɪst/ *adj.* & *n.* ● *adj.* ardently or intensely serious; zealous; not trifling or joking. ● *n.* seriousness. □ **in** (or **in real**) **earnest** serious(ly), not joking(ly); with determination. □ **earnestly** *adv.* **earnestness** *n.* [Old English *eornust, eornost*]

earnest[2] /ˈəːnɪst/ *n.* **1** money paid as an instalment, esp. to confirm a contract etc. **2** a token or foretaste (*in earnest of what is to come*). [Middle English *ernes*, probably via Old French and medieval Latin from Latin *arr(h)a* 'pledge']

earnings /ˈəːnɪŋz/ *n.pl.* money earned.

earnings-related *adj.* (of benefit, a pension, etc.) calculated on the basis of past or present income.

EAROM /ˈɪərɒm/ *n. Computing* electrically alterable read-only memory. [acronym]

earphone /ˈɪəfəʊn/ *n.* a device applied to the ear to aid hearing or receive radio or telephone communications.

earpiece /ˈɪəpiːs/ *n.* the part of a telephone etc. applied to the ear during use.

ear-piercing *adj.* & *n.* ● *adj.* loud and shrill. ● *n.* the piercing of the ears to allow the wearing of earrings.

earplug /ˈɪəplʌg/ *n.* a piece of wax etc. placed in the ear to protect against cold air, water, or noise.

earring /ˈɪərɪŋ/ *n.* a piece of jewellery worn in or on (esp. the lobe of) the ear.

earshot /ˈɪəʃɒt/ *n.* the distance over which something can be heard (esp. *within* or *out of earshot*).

ear-splitting *adj.* excessively loud.

ear-stopple see STOPPLE *n.* 2.

earth /əːθ/ *n.* & *v.* ● *n.* **1 a** (also **Earth**; often prec. by *the*) one of the planets of the solar system, orbiting about the sun between Venus and Mars; the planet on which we live. **b** (prec. by *the*) land and sea, as distinct from sky. **2 a** dry land; the ground (*fell to earth*). **b** soil, clay, mould. **c** bodily matter (*earth to earth*). **3** *Relig.* the present abode of humankind, as distinct from heaven or hell; the world. **4** *Brit. Electr.* the connection to the earth as an arbitrary reference voltage in an electrical circuit. **5** the hole of a badger, fox, etc. **6** (prec. by *the*) *colloq.* a huge amount; everything (*cost the earth*; *want the earth*). ● *v.* **1** *tr.* (foll. by *up*) *Brit.* cover (the roots and lower stems of plants) with heaped-up earth. **2 a** *tr.* drive (a fox) to its earth. **b** *intr.* (of a fox etc.) run to its earth. **3** *tr. Brit. Electr.* connect to the earth. □ **come back** (or **down**) **to earth** return to realities. **gone to earth** in hiding. **on earth** *colloq.* **1** existing anywhere (*the happiest man on earth*; *looked like nothing on earth*). **2** as an intensifier (*what on earth?*). □ **earthward** *adj.* & *adv.* **earthwards** *adv.* [Old English *eorthe*, from Germanic]

earthbound /ˈəːθbaʊnd/ *adj.* **1** attached to the earth or earthly things. **2** moving towards the earth.

earth closet *n. Brit.* a lavatory with dry earth used to cover excreta.

earthen /ˈəːθ(ə)n/ *adj.* **1** made of earth. **2** made of baked clay.

earthenware /ˈəːθ(ə)nwɛː/ *n.* & *adj.* ● *n.* pottery, vessels, etc., made of clay fired to a porous state which can be made impervious to liquids by the use of a glaze (cf. PORCELAIN, STONEWARE). ● *adj.* made of fired clay. [EARTHEN + WARE[1]]

earthling /ˈəːθlɪŋ/ *n.* an inhabitant of the earth, esp. as regarded in science fiction by aliens.

earthly /ˈəːθli/ *adj.* **1** of the earth or human life on earth; terrestrial. **2** (usu. with *neg.*) *colloq.* remotely possible or conceivable (*is no earthly use*; *there wasn't an earthly reason*). □ **not an earthly** *Brit. colloq.* no chance whatever. □ **earthliness** *n.*

earthly paradise see PARADISE 3.

earth mother *n.* **1** *Mythol.* a female spirit or deity symbolizing the earth. **2** a sensual and maternal woman.

earth mover *n.* a vehicle or machine for moving earth. □ **earth-moving** *n.*

earth-nut *n.* **1 a** any of various plants with an edible roundish tuber, esp. an umbelliferous woodland plant, *Conopodium majus*. **b** the tuber of such a plant. **2** the peanut.

earth-pig *n.* = AARDVARK.

earthquake /ˈəːθkweɪk/ *n.* **1** a convulsion of the earth's crust due to the release of accumulated stress as a result of faults in strata or volcanic action. **2** a social etc. disturbance.

earth sciences *n.pl.* the sciences concerned with the earth or part of it, or its atmosphere (e.g. geology, oceanography, meteorology).

earth-shattering *adj.* (also **earth-shaking**) *colloq.* having a traumatic or devastating effect. □ **earth-shatteringly** *adv.*

earthshine /ˈəːθʃʌɪn/ *n. Astron.* the glow caused by sunlight reflected by the earth, esp. on the darker portion of a crescent moon.

earthstar /ˈəːθstɑː/ *n.* any woodland fungus of the genus *Geastrum*, esp. *G. triplex*, with a spherical spore-containing fruit body surrounded by a fleshy star-shaped structure.

earth tremor see TREMOR *n.* 3.

earthwork /ˈəːθwəːk/ *n.* **1** an embankment, fortification, etc., made of earth. **2** the process of excavating soil in civil engineering work.

earthworm /ˈəːθwəːm/ *n.* any of various annelid worms, esp. of the genus *Lumbricus* or *Allolobophora*, living and burrowing in the ground.

earthy /ˈəːθi/ *adj.* (**earthier, earthiest**) **1** of or like earth or soil. **2** somewhat coarse or crude; unrefined (*earthy humour*). □ **earthily** *adv.* **earthiness** *n.*

ear-trumpet *n.* a trumpet-shaped device formerly used as a hearing aid.

earwax /ˈɪəwaks/ *n.* a yellow waxy secretion produced by the ear. Also called *cerumen*.

earwig /ˈɪəwɪg/ *n.* & *v.* ● *n.* **1** any small elongate insect of the order Dermaptera, with a pair of terminal appendages in the shape of forceps. **2** *US* a small centipede. ● *v.tr.* (**earwigged, earwigging**) *archaic* influence (a person) by secret communication. [Old English *ēarwicga*, from *ēare* EAR[1] + *wicga* 'earwig', probably related to *wiggle*: the earwig was once thought to crawl into the human ear]

ease /iːz/ *n.* & *v.* ● *n.* **1** absence of difficulty; facility, effortlessness (*did it with ease*). **2 a** freedom or relief from pain, anxiety, or trouble. **b** freedom from embarrassment or awkwardness. **c** freedom or relief from constraint or formality. ● *v.* **1** *tr.* relieve from pain or anxiety etc. (often foll. by *of*: *eased my mind*; *eased me of the burden*). **2** *intr.* (often foll. by *off, up*) **a** become less painful or burdensome. **b** relax; begin to take it easy. **c** slow down; moderate one's behaviour, habits, etc. **3** *tr. joc.* rob or extract money etc. from (*let* me ease you of your loose change). **4** *intr. Meteorol.* become less severe (*the wind will ease tonight*). **5 a** *tr.* relax; slacken; make a less tight fit. **b** *tr. & intr.* (foll. by *through, into,* etc.) move or be moved carefully into place (*eased it into the hole*). **6** *intr.* (often foll. by *off*) *Stock Exch.* (of shares etc.) descend in price or value. □ **at ease 1** free from anxiety or constraint. **2** *Mil.* **a** in a relaxed attitude while on parade, with the feet apart. **b** the order to stand in this way. **at one's ease** free from embarrassment, awkwardness, or undue formality. **ease away** (or **down** or **off**) *Naut.* slacken (a rope, sail, etc.). □ **easer** *n.* [Middle English from Anglo-French *ese*, Old French *eise*, ultimately from Latin *adjacens* ADJACENT]

easeful /ˈiːzfʊl, -f(ə)l/ *adj.* that gives ease, comfort, or relief; soothing.

easel /ˈiːz(ə)l/ *n.* **1** a standing frame, usu. of wood, for supporting an artist's work, a blackboard, etc. **2** an artist's work collectively. [Dutch *ezel* = German *Esel* ASS[1]: cf. HORSE *n.*]

easement /ˈiːzm(ə)nt/ *n. Law* a right of way or a similar right over another's land. [Middle English from Old French *aisement*]

easily /ˈiːzɪli/ *adv.* **1** without difficulty. **2** by far (*easily the best*). **3** very probably (*it could easily snow*).

east /iːst/ *n., adj., & adv.* ● *n.* **1 a** the point of the horizon where the sun rises at the equinoxes (cardinal point 90° to the right of north). **b** the compass point corresponding to this. **c** the direction in which this lies. **2** (usu. **the East**) **a** *Brit.* the regions or countries lying to the east of Europe. **b** *hist.* the former Communist states of eastern Europe. **3** the eastern part of a country, town, etc. **4** (**East**) *Bridge* a player occupying the position designated 'east'. ● *adj.* **1** towards, at, near, or facing east. **2** coming from the east (*east wind*). ● *adv.* **1** towards, at, or near the east. **2** (foll. by *of*) further east than. □ **to the east** (often foll. by *of*) in an easterly direction. [Old English *ēast-* from Germanic, related to Latin *aurora* 'dawn']

eastbound /ˈiːstbaʊnd/ *adj.* travelling or leading eastwards.

East End *n.* the part of London east of the City as far as the River Lea. □ **East Ender** *n.*

Easter /ˈiːstə/ *n.* **1** (also **Easter Day** or **Easter Sunday**) the festival (held on a variable Sunday in March or April) commemorating Christ's resurrection. **2** the season in which this occurs, esp. the weekend from Good Friday to Easter Monday. [Old English *ēastre*, apparently from *Ēostre*, the name of a goddess associated with spring, from Germanic]

Easter egg *n.* an artificial usu. chocolate egg given at Easter, esp. to children.

easterly /ˈiːstəli/ *adj., adv., & n.* ● *adj. & adv.* **1** in an eastern position or direction. **2** (of a wind) blowing from the east. ● *n.* (*pl.* **-ies**) a wind blowing from the east.

eastern /ˈiːst(ə)n/ *adj.* **1** of or in the east; inhabiting the east. **2** lying or directed towards the east. **3** (**Eastern**) of or in the Far, Middle, or Near East. □ **easternmost** *adj.* [Old English *ēasterne* (as EAST, -ERN)]

Eastern Church *n.* any of the Christian Churches originating in eastern Europe and the Middle East, esp. (in full **Eastern Orthodox Church**) the Orthodox Church.

easterner /ˈiːstənə/ *n.* a native or inhabitant of the east.

eastern hemisphere *n.* the half of the earth containing Europe, Asia, and Africa.

Eastern Standard Time *n.* (also **Eastern Time**) **1** the standard time in a zone including the eastern US and parts of Canada, five hours behind GMT. **2** the standard time in a zone including eastern Australia, ten hours ahead of GMT.

Eastertide /ˈiːstətʌɪd/ *n.* the period including Easter.

Easter week *n.* the week beginning on Easter Sunday.

East Germanic *n. & adj.* ● *n.* the extinct eastern group of Germanic languages, including Gothic. ● *adj.* of or relating to this group.

East Indiaman *n. hist.* a large ship engaged in trade with the East Indies.

East Indies *n.pl.* the islands etc. east of India, esp. the Malay archipelago.

easting /ˈiːstɪŋ/ *n. Naut.* etc. the distance travelled or the angle of longitude measured eastward from either a defined north–south grid line or a meridian.

east-north-east *n.* the direction or compass point midway between east and north-east.

east-south-east *n.* the direction or compass point midway between east and south-east.

eastward /ˈiːstwəd/ *adj., adv., & n.* ● *adj. & adv.* (also **eastwards**) towards the east. ● *n.* an eastward direction or region. □ **eastwardly** *adj. & adv.*

East–West *attrib.adj.* of or relating to countries of the East and the West (*East–West relations*).

easy /ˈiːzi/ *adj., adv., & int.* (**easier, easiest**) ● *adj.* **1** not difficult; achieved without great effort. **2 a** free from pain, discomfort, anxiety, etc. **b** comfortably off, affluent (*easy circumstances*). **3** free from embarrassment, awkwardness, constraint, etc.; relaxed and pleasant (*an easy manner*). **4** compliant, obliging; easily persuaded (*an easy touch*). **5** *Stock Exch.* (of goods, money on loan, etc.) not much in demand. ● *adv.* with ease; in an effortless or relaxed manner. ● *int.* go carefully; move gently. □ **easy as pie** see PIE[1]. **easy come easy go** *colloq.* what is easily got is soon lost or spent. **easy does it** *colloq.* go carefully. **easy of access** easily entered or approached. **easy on the eye** (or **ear** etc.) *colloq.* pleasant to look at (or listen to etc.). **go easy** (usu. foll. by *with, on*) be sparing or cautious. **I'm easy** *colloq.* I have no preference. **of easy virtue** (of a woman) sexually promiscuous. **stand easy!** *Brit. Mil.* permission to a squad standing at ease to relax their attitude further. **take it easy 1** proceed gently or carefully. **2** relax; avoid overwork. □ **easiness** *n.* [Middle English from Anglo-French *aisé*, Old French *aisié*, past part. of *aisier* EASE]

easy chair *n.* a large comfortable chair, usu. an armchair.

easygoing /iːzɪˈgəʊɪŋ/ *adj.* **1** placid and tolerant; relaxed in manner; accepting things as they are. **2** (of a horse) having an easy gait.

easy money *n.* money got without effort (esp. of dubious legality).

easy-peasy /iːzɪˈpiːzi/ *adj. Brit. slang* very simple. [reduplication of EASY]

Easy Street *n. colloq.* affluence.

easy terms *n.pl.* payment by instalments.

easy touch *n. slang* a gullible person, esp. one easily induced to part with money.

eat /iːt/ *v.* (*past* **ate** /ɛt, eɪt/; *past part.* **eaten** /ˈiːt(ə)n/) **1 a** *tr.* take into the mouth, chew, and swallow (food). **b** *intr.* consume food; take a meal. **c** *tr.* devour (*eaten by a lion*). **2** *intr.* (foll. by (*away*) *at, into*) **a** destroy gradually, esp. by corrosion, erosion, disease, etc. **b** begin to consume or diminish (resources etc.). **3** *tr. colloq.* trouble, vex (*what's eating you?*). □ **eat dirt** see DIRT. **eat one's hat** *colloq.* admit one's surprise in being wrong (only as a proposition unlikely to be fulfilled: *said he would eat his hat*). **eat one's heart out** suffer from excessive longing or envy. **eat humble pie** see HUMBLE. **eat out** have a meal away from home, esp. in a restaurant. **eat out of a person's hand** be entirely submissive to a person. **eat salt with** see SALT. **eat up 1** (also *absol.*) eat or consume completely. **2** use or deal with rapidly or wastefully (*eats up petrol; eats up the miles*). **3** encroach upon or annex (*eating up the neighbouring states*). **4** absorb, preoccupy (*eaten up with pride*). **eat one's words** admit that one was wrong. [Old English *etan*, from Germanic]

eatable /ˈiːtəb(ə)l/ *adj. & n.* ● *adj.* that is in a condition to be eaten (cf. EDIBLE). ● *n.* (usu. in *pl.*) food.

eater /ˈiːtə/ *n.* **1** a person who eats (*a big eater*). **2** *Brit.* an eating apple etc.

eatery /ˈiːtəri/ *n.* esp. *N. Amer.* (*pl.* **-ies**) *colloq.* a restaurant or eating place.

eating /ˈiːtɪŋ/ *adj.* **1** suitable for eating (*eating apple*). **2** used for eating (*eating house*). **3** of or relating to the process of eating (*eating habits*; *eating disorders*).

eats /iːts/ *n.pl. colloq.* food.

eau de Cologne /əʊ də kəˈləʊn/ *n.* an alcohol-based perfume of a kind made originally at Cologne. [French, literally 'water of Cologne']

eau-de-Nil /əʊdəˈniːl/ *n.* & *adj.* ● *n.* a pale greenish colour. ● *adj.* of this colour. [French, literally 'water of the Nile' (from the supposed resemblance)]

eau-de-vie /əʊdəˈviː/ *n.* spirits, esp. brandy. [French, literally 'water of life']

eaves /iːvz/ *n.pl.* the underside of a projecting roof. [originally sing., from Old English *efes*: probably related to OVER]

eavesdrop /ˈiːvzdrɒp/ *v.intr.* (**-dropped**, **-dropping**) listen secretly to a private conversation. □ **eavesdropper** *n.* [from an earlier noun *eavesdrop* 'the ground on to which water drips from the eaves', probably from Old Norse *upsardropi*; *eavesdropper* originally 'a person who listens by the wall (in the eavesdrop)': the modern verb by back-formation from eavesdropper]

ebb /ɛb/ *n.* & *v.* ● *n.* **1** the movement of the tide out to sea (also *attrib.*: *ebb tide*). **2** the process of draining away of flood-water etc. ● *v.intr.* (often foll. by *away*) **1** (of tidewater) flow out to sea; recede; drain away. **2** decline; run low (*his life was ebbing away*). □ **at a low ebb** in a poor condition or state of decline. **ebb and flow** a continuing process of decline and upturn in circumstances. **on the ebb** in decline. [Old English *ebba*, *ebbian*]

ebonite /ˈɛbənʌɪt/ *n.* = VULCANITE. [EBONY + -ITE[1]]

ebony /ˈɛb(ə)ni/ *n.* & *adj.* ● *n.* (*pl.* **-ies**) **1** a heavy hard dark wood used for furniture. **2** any of various tropical trees of the genus *Diospyros* producing this. ● *adj.* **1** made of ebony. **2** black like ebony. [ultimately from Latin *ebenus*, Greek *ebenos* 'ebony tree', perhaps on the pattern of *ivory*]

ebullient /ɪˈbʌljənt, -ˈbʊl-/ *adj.* **1** exuberant, high-spirited. **2** *Chem.* boiling. □ **ebullience** *n.* **ebulliency** *n.* **ebulliently** *adv.* [Latin *ebullire ebullient-* 'bubble out' (as E-, *bullire* 'boil')]

EC *abbr.* **1** East Central (London postal district). **2** executive committee. **3 a** European Community. **b** European Commission.

■ **Usage** The term *EC* meaning 'European Community' was replaced by *EU* 'European Union' in November 1993.

ecad /ˈiːkad/ *n. Ecol.* an organism modified by its environment. [Greek *oikos* 'house' + -AD[1]]

écarté /eɪˈkɑːteɪ/ *n.* **1** a card game for two persons in which cards from a player's hand may be exchanged for others from the pack. **2** a position in classical ballet with one arm and leg extended. [French, past part. of *écarter* 'discard']

Ecce Homo /ɛkeɪ ˈhɒməʊ, ˈhəʊməʊ/ *n. Art* (in Renaissance painting) a depiction of Christ wearing the crown of thorns. [Latin, = 'behold the man', the words of Pilate to the Jews after the crowning with thorns (John 19:5)]

eccentric /ɪkˈsɛntrɪk, ɛk-/ *adj.* & *n.* ● *adj.* **1** odd or capricious in behaviour or appearance; whimsical. **2** (also **excentric**) **a** not placed, or not having its axis etc. placed, centrally (cf. CONCENTRIC). **b** (often foll. by *to*) (of a circle) not concentric (with another). **c** (of an orbit) not circular. ● *n.* **1** an eccentric person. **2** (also **excentric**) *Mech.* an eccentric contrivance for changing rotatory into backward-and-forward motion, e.g. the cam used in an internal-combustion engine. □ **eccentrically** *adv.* **eccentricity** /-ˈtrɪsɪti/ *n.* (*pl.* **-ies**). [Late Latin *eccentricus* from Greek *ekkentros*, from *ek* 'out of' + *kentros* CENTRE]

ecchymosis /ɛkɪˈməʊsɪs/ *n.* (*pl.* **ecchymoses** /-siːz/) *Med.* an area of discoloration due to bleeding under the skin. [modern Latin from Greek *ekkhumōsis* 'escape of blood']

Eccles. *abbr.* Ecclesiastes (Old Testament).

Eccles cake /ˈɛk(ə)lz/ *n. Brit.* a round flat cake made of pastry filled with currants etc. [*Eccles*, a town in N. England]

ecclesial /ɪˈkliːzj(ə)l/ *adj.* = ECCLESIASTICAL. [Greek *ekklesia* 'assembly, church' via *ekklētos* 'summoned out' from *ek* 'out' + *kaleō* 'call']

ecclesiastic /ɪˌkliːzɪˈastɪk/ *n.* & *adj.* ● *n.* a priest or clergyman. ● *adj.* = ECCLESIASTICAL. □ **ecclesiasticism** /-sɪz(ə)m/ *n.* [French *ecclésiastique* or Late Latin *ecclesiasticus* from Greek *ekklēsiastikos*, from *ekklēsia* 'assembly, church': see ECCLESIAL]

ecclesiastical /ɪˌkliːzɪˈastɪk(ə)l/ *adj.* of or relating to the Church or the clergy. □ **ecclesiastically** *adv.*

ecclesiology /ɪˌkliːzɪˈɒlədʒi/ *n.* **1** the study of churches, esp. church building and decoration. **2** theology as applied to the nature and structure of the Christian Church. □ **ecclesiological** /-zɪəˈlɒdʒɪk(ə)l/ *adj.* **ecclesiologist** *n.* [Greek *ekklēsia* 'assembly, church' (see ECCLESIAL) + -LOGY]

Ecclus. *abbr.* Ecclesiasticus (Apocrypha).

eccrine /ˈɛkrʌɪn, -krɪn/ *adj.* (of a gland, e.g. a sweat gland) secreting without loss of cell material. [Greek *ek* 'out of' + *krinō* 'sift']

ecdysis /ˈɛkdɪsɪs, ɛkˈdʌɪsɪs/ *n.* the action of casting off skin or shedding an exoskeleton etc. [modern Latin from Greek *ekdusis*, from *ekduō* 'put off']

ECG *abbr.* electrocardiogram.

echelon /ˈɛʃəlɒn, ˈeɪʃ-/ *n.* & *v.* ● *n.* **1** a level or rank in an organization, in society, etc.; those occupying it (often in *pl.*: *the upper echelons*). **2** *Mil.* a formation of troops, ships, aircraft, etc., in parallel rows with the end of each row projecting further than the one in front (*in echelon*). ● *v.tr.* arrange in an echelon. [French *échelon* from *échelle* 'ladder', from Latin *scala*]

echeveria /ɛtʃɪˈvɪərɪə/ *n.* any succulent plant of the genus *Echeveria*, native to Central and S. America. [named after M. *Echeveri*, 19th-c. Mexican botanical illustrator]

echidna /ɪˈkɪdnə/ *n.* an egg-laying insectivorous mammal of the genus *Tachyglossus* or *Zaglossus*, native to Australia and New Guinea, with a covering of spines, a long snout, and long claws. Also called *spiny anteater*. [modern Latin, from Greek *ekhidna* 'viper']

echinoderm /ɪˈkʌɪnə(ʊ)dəːm, ˈɛkɪn-/ *n.* any marine invertebrate of the phylum Echinodermata, which includes starfishes, sea urchins, brittle-stars, crinoids, and sea cucumbers, typically having five-fold symmetry, a calcareous skeleton, and tube feet operated by water pressure. [ECHINUS + Greek *derma -atos* 'skin']

echinoid /ˈɛkɪnɔɪd/ *n.* a sea urchin.

echinus /ɪˈkʌɪnəs/ *n.* **1** any sea urchin of the genus *Echinus*, including the common European edible urchin, *E. esculentus*. **2** *Archit.* a rounded moulding below an abacus on a Doric or Ionic capital. [Middle English via Latin from Greek *ekhinos* 'hedgehog, sea urchin']

echo /ˈɛkəʊ/ *n.* & *v.* ● *n.* (*pl.* **-oes**) **1 a** the repetition of a sound by the reflection of sound waves. **b** the secondary sound produced. **2** a reflected radio or radar beam. **3** a close imitation or repetition of something already done. **4** a person who slavishly repeats the words or opinions of another. **5** (often in *pl.*) circumstances or events reminiscent of or remotely connected with earlier ones. **6** *Bridge* etc. a conventional mode of play to show the number of cards held in the suit led etc. ● *v.* (**-oes**, **-oed**) **1** *intr.* **a** (of a place) resound with an echo. **b** (of a sound) be repeated; resound. **2** *tr.* repeat (a sound) by an echo. **3** *tr.* **a** repeat (another's words). **b** imitate the words, opinions, or actions of (a person). □ **echoer** *n.*

echoless *adj.* [Middle English via Old French or Latin from Greek *ēkhō*, related to *ēkhē* 'a sound']
echocardiogram /ɛkəʊ'kɑːdɪəgram/ *n. Med.* a record produced by echocardiography.
echocardiography /ˌɛkəʊkɑːdɪ'ɒgrəfi/ *n. Med.* the use of ultrasound waves to investigate the action of the heart. □ **echocardiograph** /ɛkəʊ'kɑːdɪəgrɑːf/ *n.* **echocardiographer** *n.*
echo chamber *n.* an enclosure with sound-reflecting walls.
echoencephalogram /ˌɛkəʊɛn'sɛf(ə)lə(ʊ)gram/ *n. Med.* a record produced by echoencephalography.
echoencephalography /ˌɛkəʊɛnsɛfə'lɒgrəfi/ *n. Med.* the use of ultrasound waves to investigate intracranial structures.
echoey /'ɛkəʊi/ *adj.* of or like an echo; resounding with echoes.
echogram /'ɛkəʊgram/ *n.* a record made by an echo sounder.
echograph /'ɛkəʊgrɑːf/ *n.* a device for automatically recording echograms.
echoic /ɛ'kəʊɪk/ *adj.* (of a word) imitating the sound it represents; onomatopoeic. □ **echoically** *adv.*
echoism /'ɛkəʊɪz(ə)m/ *n.* = ONOMATOPOEIA.
echolalia /ɛkəʊ'leɪlɪə/ *n.* **1** the meaningless repetition of another person's spoken words. **2** the repetition of speech by a child learning to talk. [modern Latin, from Greek *ēkhō* 'echo' + *lalia* 'talk']
echolocation /'ɛkə(ʊ)lə(ʊ)ˌkeɪʃ(ə)n/ *n.* the location of objects by reflected sound, esp. ultrasound.
echo sounder *n.* a sounding apparatus for determining the depth of the sea beneath a ship by measuring the time taken for an echo to be received. □ **echo-sounding** *n.* (often *attrib.*).
echo verse *n.* a verse form in which a line repeats the last syllables of the previous line.
echovirus /'ɛkəʊvʌɪrəs/ *n.* (also **ECHO virus**) any of a group of enteroviruses sometimes causing mild meningitis, encephalitis, etc. [from *e*nteric *c*ytopathogenic *h*uman *o*rphan (because not originally assignable to any known disease) + VIRUS]
echt /ɛxt, German ɛçt/ *adj.* authentic, genuine, typical. [German]
éclair /eɪ'klɛː, ɪ-/ *n.* a small elongated cake of choux pastry filled with cream and iced with chocolate or coffee icing. [French, literally 'lightning']
éclaircissement /eɪklɛː'siːsmɒ̃, French eklɛrsismɑ̃/ *n. archaic* an enlightening explanation of something hitherto inexplicable (e.g. conduct etc.). [French from *éclaircir* 'clear up']
eclampsia /ɪ'klam(p)sɪə/ *n.* a condition involving convulsions leading to coma, occurring esp. in pregnant women. □ **eclamptic** *adj.* [modern Latin via French *eclampsie* from Greek *eklampsis* 'sudden development', from *eklampō* 'shine forth']
éclat /ɛ'klɑː, 'eɪklɑː/ *n.* **1** brilliant display; dazzling effect. **2** social distinction; conspicuous success; universal approbation (*with great éclat*). [French from *éclater* 'burst out']
eclectic /ɪ'klɛktɪk/ *adj.* & *n.* ● *adj.* **1** deriving ideas, tastes, style, etc., from various sources. **2** *Philos.* & *Art* selecting one's beliefs etc. from various sources; attached to no particular school of philosophy. ● *n.* **1** an eclectic person. **2** a person who subscribes to an eclectic school of thought. □ **eclectically** *adv.* **eclecticism** /-sɪz(ə)m/ *n.* [Greek *eklektikos* from *eklegō* 'pick out']
eclipse /ɪ'klɪps/ *n.* & *v.* ● *n.* **1** the obscuring of the light from one celestial body by the passage of another between it and the observer or between it and its source of illumination. **2** a deprivation of light or the period of this. **3** a rapid or sudden loss of importance or prominence, esp. in relation to another or a newly arrived person or thing. **4** *Zool.* a phase during which a bird's distinctive markings are obscured by moulting of the breeding plumage. ● *v.tr.* **1** (of a celestial body) obscure the light from or to (another). **2** intercept (light, esp. of a lighthouse). **3** deprive of prominence or importance; outshine, surpass. □ **in eclipse 1** surpassed; in decline. **2** (of a bird) having lost its breeding plumage. [Middle English via Old French and Latin from Greek *ekleipsis*, from *ekleipō* 'fail to appear, be eclipsed', from *leipō* 'leave']
eclipsing binary *n.* a binary star whose brightness varies periodically as the two components pass one in front of the other.
ecliptic /ɪ'klɪptɪk/ *n.* & *adj.* ● *n.* the sun's apparent path among the stars during the year. ● *adj.* of an eclipse or the ecliptic. [Middle English via Latin from Greek *ekleiptikos* (as ECLIPSE)]
eclogue /'ɛklɒg/ *n.* a short poem, esp. a pastoral dialogue. [Latin *ecloga* from Greek *eklogē* 'selection', from *eklegō* 'pick out']
eclosion /ɪ'kləʊʒ(ə)n/ *n.* the emergence of an insect from a pupa-case or of a larva from an egg. [French *éclosion* from *éclore* 'hatch' (as EX-[1], Latin *claudere* 'to close')]
eco- /'iːkəʊ, 'ɛkəʊ/ *comb. form* ecology, ecological.
ecocide /'iːkə(ʊ)sʌɪd/ *n.* destruction of the natural environment. [ECO- + -CIDE]
ecoclimate /'iːkəʊklʌɪmət/ *n.* climate considered as an ecological factor.
eco-friendly /iːkəʊ'frɛn(d)li/ *adj.* not harmful to the environment.
eco-label /'iːkəʊleɪb(ə)l/ *n.* a label identifying manufactured products that satisfy certain environmental conditions. □ **eco-labelling** *n.*
ecology /ɪ'kɒlədʒi, ɛ-/ *n.* **1** the branch of biology dealing with the relations of organisms to one another and to their physical surroundings. **2** (in full **human ecology**) the study of the interaction of people with their environment. □ **ecological** /iːkə'lɒdʒɪk(ə)l, ɛk-/ *adj.* **ecologically** /iːkə'lɒdʒɪk(ə)li, ɛk-/ *adv.* **ecologist** *n.* [German *Ökologie*, from Greek *oikos* 'house']
Econ. *abbr.* Economics.
econometrics /ɪˌkɒnə'mɛtrɪks/ *n.pl.* (usu. treated as *sing.*) a branch of economics concerned with the application of mathematical economics to economic data by the use of statistics. □ **econometric** *adj.* **econometrical** *adj.* **econometrician** /-mə'trɪʃ(ə)n/ *n.* **econometrist** *n.* [ECONOMY + -METRIC]
economic /iːkə'nɒmɪk, ɛk-/ *adj.* **1** of or relating to economics. **2** maintained for profit; on a business footing. **3** adequate to repay or recoup expenditure with some profit (*not economic to run buses on Sunday*; *an economic rent*). **4** practical; considered or studied with regard to human needs (*economic geography*). □ **economically** *adv.* [Middle English via Old French *economique* or Latin *oeconomicus* from Greek *oikonomikos* (as ECONOMY)]
economical /iːkə'nɒmɪk(ə)l, ɛk-/ *adj.* sparing in the use of resources; avoiding waste. □ **economically** *adv.*
economics /iːkə'nɒmɪks, ɛk-/ *n.pl.* (often treated as *sing.*) **1 a** the science of the production and distribution of wealth. **b** the application of this to a particular subject (*the economics of publishing*). **2** the condition of a country etc. as regards material prosperity.
economies of scale *n.pl.* proportionate savings gained by using larger quantities.
economist /ɪ'kɒnəmɪst/ *n.* **1** an expert in or student of economics. **2** a person who manages financial or economic matters. [Greek *oikonomos* (as ECONOMY) + -IST]
economize /ɪ'kɒnəmʌɪz/ *v.intr.* (also **-ise**) **1** be economical; make economies; reduce expenditure. **2** (foll. by *on*) use sparingly; spend less on. □ **economization** /-'zeɪʃ(ə)n/ *n.* **economizer** *n.*
economy /ɪ'kɒnəmi/ *n.* (*pl.* **-ies**) **1 a** the wealth and resources of a community, esp. in terms of the production and consumption of goods and services. **b** a particular kind of this (*a capitalist economy*). **c** the administration or condition of an economy. **2 a** the

careful management of (esp. financial) resources; frugality. **b** (often in *pl.*) an instance of this (*made many economies*). **3** sparing or careful use (*economy of language*). **4** (also **economy class**) the cheapest class of air travel. **5** (also **economy-size**) (*attrib.*) (of goods) consisting of a large quantity for a proportionally lower cost. [French *économie* or Latin *oeconomia* from Greek *oikonomia* 'household management', from *oikos* 'house' + *nemō* 'manage']

ecosphere /'i:kəʊsfɪə/ *n.* **1** the region of space including planets where conditions are such that living things can exist. **2** = BIOSPHERE.

écossaise /ɛkɒ'seɪz/ *n.* **1** an energetic dance in duple time. **2** the music for this. [French, fem. of *écossais* 'Scottish']

ecosystem /'i:kəʊsɪstəm/ *n.* a biological community of interacting organisms and their physical environment.

eco-terrorism /i:kəʊ'tɛrərɪz(ə)m/ *n.* violence carried out to further environmentalist ends. ▫ **eco-terrorist** *n.*

ecotourism /i:kəʊ'tʊərɪz(ə)m/ *n.* tourism directed towards exotic, often threatened, natural environments, esp. intended to support conservation efforts. ▫ **ecotourist** *n.*

ecotype /'i:kəʊtʌɪp/ *n. Biol.* a distinct form of a species occupying a particular habitat.

ecru /'eɪkru:, ɛ'kru:/ *n.* & *adj.* ● *n.* the colour of unbleached linen; light fawn. ● *adj.* of this colour. [French *écru* 'unbleached']

ecstasize /'ɛkstəsʌɪz/ *v.tr.* & *intr.* (also **-ise**) throw or go into ecstasies.

ecstasy /'ɛkstəsi/ *n.* (*pl.* **-ies**) **1** an overwhelming feeling of joy or rapture. **2** *Psychol.* an emotional or religious frenzy or trance-like state. **3** (usu. **Ecstasy**) *slang* methylenedioxymethamphetamine, a powerful stimulant and hallucinatory drug (see MDMA). [Middle English via Old French *extasie* and Late Latin *extasis* from Greek *ekstasis* 'standing outside oneself', from *ek* 'out' + *histēmi* 'to place']

ecstatic /ɪk'statɪk, ɛk-/ *adj.* & *n.* ● *adj.* **1** in a state of ecstasy. **2** very enthusiastic or excited (*was ecstatic about his new job*). **3** producing ecstasy; sublime (*an ecstatic embrace*). ● *n.* a person subject to (usu. religious) ecstasy. ▫ **ecstatically** *adv.* [French *extatique* from Greek *ekstatikos* (as ECSTASY)]

ECT *abbr.* electroconvulsive therapy.

ecto- /'ɛktəʊ/ *prefix* outside. [Greek *ekto-*, stem of *ektos* 'outside']

ectoderm /'ɛktə(ʊ)də:m/ *n. Zool.* the outermost layer of an embryo in early development. ▫ **ectodermal** /-'də:m(ə)l/ *adj.*

ectogenesis /ɛktə(ʊ)'dʒɛnɪsɪs/ *n. Biol.* the production of structures outside the organism. ▫ **ectogenetic** /-dʒɪ'nɛtɪk/ *adj.* **ectogenic** /-'dʒɛnɪk/ *adj.* **ectogenous** /ɛk'tɒdʒɪnəs/ *adj.* [modern Latin (as ECTO-, GENESIS)]

ectomorph /'ɛktə(ʊ)mɔ:f/ *n.* a person with a lean and delicate build of body and large skin surface in comparison with weight (cf. ENDOMORPH, MESOMORPH). ▫ **ectomorphic** /-'mɔ:fɪk/ *adj.* **ectomorphy** *n.* [ECTO- + Greek *morphē* 'form']

-ectomy /'ɛktəmi/ *comb. form* denoting a surgical operation in which a part of the body is removed (*appendectomy*). [Greek *ektomē* 'excision', from *ek* 'out' + *temnō* 'cut']

ectoparasite /ɛktəʊ'parəsʌɪt/ *n. Biol.* a parasite that lives on the outside of its host.

ectopic /ɛk'tɒpɪk/ *adj. Med.* in an abnormal place or position. [modern Latin *ectopia* from Greek *ektopos* 'out of place']

ectopic pregnancy *n.* a pregnancy occurring outside the womb.

ectoplasm /'ɛktə(ʊ)plaz(ə)m/ *n.* **1** the dense outer layer of the cytoplasm (cf. ENDOPLASM). **2** a supposed viscous substance exuding from the body of a medium during a spiritualistic trance. ▫ **ectoplasmic** /-'plazmɪk/ *adj.*

ecu /'ɛkju:, 'i:-, 'eɪ-; -ku:/ *n.* (*pl.* same or **ecus**) (also **Ecu, ECU**) European Currency Unit. [acronym]

ecumenical /i:kjʊ'mɛnɪk(ə)l, ɛ-/ *adj.* of or representing the whole Christian world, esp. seeking or promoting worldwide Christian unity. ▫ **ecumenically** *adv.* [Late Latin *oecumenicus* from Greek *oikoumenikos* 'of the inhabited earth' (*oikoumenē*)]

ecumenism /ɪ'kju:mənɪz(ə)m/ *n.* the principle or aim of the unity of Christians worldwide, transcending differences of doctrine.

eczema /'ɛksɪmə, 'ɛkzɪmə/ *n.* inflammation of the skin, with itching and discharge from blisters. ▫ **eczematous** /ɛk'zi:mətəs, ɛk'zɛm-/ *adj.* [modern Latin from Greek *ekzema -atos*, from *ek* 'out' + *zeō* 'boil']

ed. *abbr.* **1** edited by. **2** edition. **3** editor. **4** educated; education.

-ed[1] /d, ɪd, t/ *suffix* forming adjectives: **1** from nouns, meaning 'having, wearing, affected by, etc.' (*talented*; *trousered*; *diseased*). **2** from phrases of adjective and noun (*good-humoured*; *three-cornered*). [Old English *-ede*]

-ed[2] /d, ɪd, t/ *suffix* forming: **1** the past tense and past participle of weak verbs (*needed*; *risked*). **2** participial adjectives (*escaped prisoner*; *a pained look*). [Old English *-ed, -ad, -od*]

Edam /'i:dam/ *n.* a round Dutch cheese, usu. pale yellow with a red wax coating. [*Edam*, a town in the Netherlands, where it is made]

edaphic /ɪ'dafɪk/ *adj.* **1** *Bot.* of or relating to the soil. **2** *Ecol.* produced or influenced by the soil. [German *edaphisch*, from Greek *edaphos* 'floor']

Edda /'ɛdə/ *n.* **1** (also **Elder Edda, Poetic Edda**) a collection of medieval Icelandic poems on Norse legends. **2** (also **Younger Edda, Prose Edda**) a 13th-c. miscellaneous handbook to Icelandic poetry. [perhaps a name in a Norse poem or from Old Norse *óthr* 'poetry']

eddo /'ɛdəʊ/ *n.* (*pl.* **-oes**) = TARO. [West African word]

eddy /'ɛdi/ *n.* & *v.* ● *n.* (*pl.* **-ies**) **1** a circular movement of water causing a small whirlpool. **2** a movement of wind, fog, or smoke resembling this. ● *v.tr.* & *intr.* (**-ies, -ied**) whirl round in eddies. [probably Old English prefix *ed-* 'again, back', perhaps of Scandinavian origin]

eddy current *n. Electr.* a localized current induced in a conductor by a varying magnetic field.

edelweiss /'eɪd(ə)lvʌɪs/ *n.* an Alpine plant, *Leontopodium alpinum*, with woolly white bracts around the flower heads, growing in rocky places. [German from *edel* 'noble' + *weiss* 'white']

edema *US* var. of OEDEMA.

Eden /'i:d(ə)n/ *n.* (also **Garden of Eden**) a place or state of great happiness; paradise (with reference to the abode of Adam and Eve in the biblical account of the Creation). [Middle English via Late Latin and Greek *Ēdēn* from Hebrew *'ēden*, originally = delight]

edentate /ɪ'dɛnteɪt/ *adj.* & *n.* ● *adj.* **1** having no or few teeth. **2** *Zool.* of or belonging to the order Edentata (or Xenarthra) of mammals lacking incisor and canine teeth, including anteaters, sloths, and armadillos. ● *n.* *Zool.* an edentate mammal. [Latin *edentatus* (as E-, *dens dentis* 'tooth')]

edge /ɛdʒ/ *n.* & *v.* ● *n.* **1** a boundary line or margin of an area or surface. **2** a narrow surface of a thin object. **3** the meeting-line of two surfaces of a solid. **4 a** the sharpened side of the blade of a cutting instrument or weapon. **b** the sharpness of this (*the knife has lost its edge*). **5** the area close to a steep drop (*along the edge of the cliff*). **6** anything compared to an edge, esp. the crest of a ridge. **7 a** (as a personal attribute) incisiveness, excitement. **b** keenness, excitement (esp. as an element in an otherwise routine situation). ● *v.* **1** *tr.* & *intr.* (often foll. by *in, into, out*, etc.) move gradually or furtively towards an objective (*edged it into the corner*; *they edged towards the door*). **2** *tr.* **a** provide with an edge or border. **b** form a border to. **c** trim the edge of. **3** *tr.* sharpen (a knife, tool, etc.). **4** *tr.* *Cricket* strike (the ball) with the edge of the bat. ▫ **have the edge on** (or **over**) have a slight advantage over. **on edge 1** tense and restless or irritable. **2** eager, excited. **on the edge of** almost involved in or affected by. **set a person's**

teeth on edge (of a taste or sound) cause an unpleasant nervous sensation. **take the edge off** dull, weaken; make less effective or intense. □ **edgeless** *adj.* **edger** *n.* [Old English *ecg*, from Germanic]

edge-tool *n.* **1** a hand-worked or machine-operated cutting tool. **2** any implement with a sharp cutting edge.

edgeways /ˈɛdʒweɪz/ *adv.* (also **edgewise** /-wʌɪz/) **1** with the edge uppermost or towards the viewer. **2** edge to edge. □ **get a word in edgeways** contribute to a conversation when the dominant speaker pauses briefly.

edging /ˈɛdʒɪŋ/ *n.* **1** something forming an edge or border, e.g. a fringe or strip of lace. **2** the process of making an edge.

edging shears *n.pl.* shears for trimming the edges of a lawn.

edgy /ˈɛdʒi/ *adj.* (**edgier**, **edgiest**) **1** irritable; nervously anxious. **2** sharp-edged, not smooth (*edgy rhythms*). □ **edgily** *adv.* **edginess** *n.*

edh var. of ETH.

edible /ˈɛdɪb(ə)l/ *adj.* & *n.* ● *adj.* fit or suitable to be eaten (cf. EATABLE). ● *n.* (in *pl.*) food. □ **edibility** /-ˈbɪlɪti/ *n.* [Late Latin *edibilis* from *edere* 'eat']

edict /ˈiːdɪkt/ *n.* an order proclaimed by authority. □ **edictal** /ɪˈdɪkt(ə)l/ *adj.* [Middle English from Latin *edictum*, from *edicere* 'proclaim']

edifice /ˈɛdɪfɪs/ *n.* **1** a building, esp. a large imposing one. **2** a complex organizational or conceptual structure. [Middle English via Old French from Latin *aedificium*, from *aedis* 'dwelling' + *-ficium* from *facere* 'make']

edify /ˈɛdɪfʌɪ/ *v.tr.* (**-ies**, **-ied**) (of a circumstance, experience, etc.) instruct and improve morally or intellectually. □ **edification** /-fɪˈkeɪʃ(ə)n/ *n.* **edifying** *adj.* **edifyingly** *adv.* [Middle English via Old French *edifier* from Latin *aedificare* (as EDIFICE)]

edit /ˈɛdɪt/ *v.* & *n.* ● *v.tr.* (**edited**, **editing**) **1 a** assemble, prepare, modify, or condense (written material, esp. the work of another or others) for publication. **b** prepare an edition of (an author's work). **2** be in overall charge of the content and arrangement of (a newspaper etc.). **3** take extracts from and collate (films, tape recordings, etc.) to form a unified sequence. **4 a** prepare (data) for processing by a computer. **b** alter (a text entered in a word processor etc.). **5 a** reword to correct, or to alter the emphasis. **b** (foll. by *out*) remove (part) from a text etc. ● *n.* **1 a** a piece of editing. **b** an edited item. **2** a facility for editing. [French *éditer* (as EDITION): partly a back-formation from EDITOR]

edition /ɪˈdɪʃ(ə)n/ *n.* **1 a** one of the particular forms in which a text is published (*paperback edition*; *pocket edition*). **b** a copy of a book in a particular form (*a first edition*). **2** a whole number of copies of a book, newspaper, etc., issued at one time. **3** a particular version or instance of a broadcast, esp. of a regular programme or feature. **4** a person or thing similar to or resembling another (*a miniature edition of her mother*). [French *édition* from Latin *editio -onis*, from *edere edit-* 'put out' (as E-, *dare* 'give')]

editio princeps /ɪˌdɪʃɪəʊ ˈprɪnsɛps/ *n.* (*pl.* ***editiones principes*** /-ˌəʊniːz -sɪpiːz/) the first printed edition of a book, text, etc. [Latin]

editor /ˈɛdɪtə/ *n.* **1** a person who edits material for publication or broadcasting. **2** a person who directs the preparation of a newspaper or periodical, or a particular section of one (*sports editor*). **3** a person who selects or commissions material for publication. **4** a person who edits film, soundtrack, etc. **5** a program enabling the user to alter or rearrange text held in a computer. □ **editorship** *n.* [Late Latin, = producer (of games), publisher (as EDIT)]

editorial /ɛdɪˈtɔːrɪəl/ *adj.* & *n.* ● *adj.* **1** of or concerned with editing or editors. **2** written or approved by an editor. ● *n.* a newspaper article written by or on behalf of an editor, esp. one giving an opinion on a topical issue. □ **editorialist** *n.* **editorialize** *v.intr.* (also **-ise**). **editorially** *adv.*

-edly /ɪdli/ *suffix* forming adverbs from verbs, meaning 'in a manner characterized by performance of or undergoing of the verbal action' (*allegedly*; *disgustedly*; *hurriedly*).

EDP *abbr.* electronic data processing.

EDT *abbr.* Eastern Daylight Time (one hour ahead of Eastern Standard Time).

EDTA *abbr. Chem.* ethylenediamine tetra-acetic acid, a common chelating agent.

educate /ˈɛdjʊkeɪt/ *v.tr.* (also *absol.*) **1** give intellectual, moral, and social instruction to (a pupil, esp. a child), esp. as a formal and prolonged process. **2** provide education for. **3** (often foll. by *in*, or *to* + infin.) train or instruct for a particular purpose. **4** advise; give information to. □ **educable** /-kəb(ə)l/ *adj.* **educability** /-kəˈbɪlɪti/ *n.* **educatable** *adj.* **educative** /-kətɪv/ *adj.* **educator** *n.* [Latin *educare educat-*, related to *educere* EDUCE]

educated /ˈɛdjʊkeɪtɪd/ *adj.* **1** having had an education, esp. to a higher level than average. **2** resulting from a (good) education (*an educated accent*). **3** based on experience or study (*an educated guess*).

education /ɛdjʊˈkeɪʃ(ə)n/ *n.* **1** the act or process of educating or being educated; systematic instruction. **2** a particular kind of or stage in education (*further education*; *a classical education*). **3 a** development of character or mental powers. **b** a stage in or aspect of this (*travel will be an education for you*). □ **educational** *adj.* **educationalist** *n.* **educationally** *adv.* **educationist** *n.* [French *éducation* or Latin *educatio* (as EDUCATE)]

educe /ɪˈdjuːs/ *v.tr.* **1** bring out or develop from latent or potential existence; elicit. **2** infer; elicit a principle, number, etc., from data. □ **educible** *adj.* **eduction** /ɪˈdʌkʃ(ə)n/ *n.* **eductive** /ɪˈdʌktɪv/ *adj.* [Middle English from Latin *educere educt-* 'lead out' (as E-, *ducere* 'lead')]

edutainment /ɛdjʊˈteɪnm(ə)nt/ *n.* entertainment with an educational aspect; infotainment. [EDUCATION + ENTERTAINMENT]

Edw. *abbr.* Edward.

Edwardian /ɛdˈwɔːdɪən/ *adj.* & *n.* ● *adj.* of, characteristic of, or associated with the reign of King Edward VII (1901–10). ● *n.* a person belonging to this period.

-ee /iː/ *suffix* forming nouns denoting: **1** the person affected by the verbal action (*addressee*; *employee*; *lessee*). **2** a person concerned with or described as (*absentee*; *bargee*; *refugee*). **3** an object of smaller size (*bootee*). [from or suggested by Anglo-French past part. ending *-é*, from Latin *-atus*]

EEC *abbr.* European Economic Community.

■ **Usage** See Usage Note at EUROPEAN COMMUNITY.

EEG *abbr.* electroencephalogram.

eejit /ˈiːdʒɪt/ *n.* esp. *Ir.* & *Sc. dial.* an idiot. [representing dialect pronunciation of IDIOT]

eel /iːl/ *n.* **1** any of various snakelike fish, with slender body and poorly developed fins, esp. one of the genus *Anguilla* living in fresh water and breeding in the sea. **2** a slippery or evasive person or thing. □ **eel-like** *adj.* **eely** *adj.* [Old English *ǣl*, from Germanic]

eelgrass /ˈiːlgrɑːs/ *n.* **1** any marine plant of the genus *Zostera*, with long ribbon-like leaves. **2** any submerged freshwater plant of the genus *Vallisneria*.

eelpout /ˈiːlpaʊt/ *n.* a fish of the family Zoarcidae, with a slender body and dorsal and anal fins meeting to fuse with the tail. Also called *pout*. [Old English *ǣleputa* (as EEL, POUT[2])]

eelworm /ˈiːlwəːm/ *n.* any of various small nematode worms infesting plant roots.

e'en[1] /iːn/ *archaic* or *poet.* var. of EVEN[1].

e'en[2] /iːn/ *Sc.* var. of EVEN[2].

-een /iːn/ *suffix Ir.* forming diminutive nouns (*colleen*). [Irish diminutive suffix *-ín*]

e'er /ɛː/ *poet.* var. of EVER.

-eer /ɪə/ *suffix* forming: **1** nouns meaning 'person concerned with or engaged in' (*auctioneer*; *mountaineer*; *profiteer*). **2** verbs meaning 'be concerned with' (*electioneer*). [from or suggested by French *-ier*, from Latin *-arius*: cf. -IER, -ARY[1]]

eerie /ˈɪəri/ *adj.* (**eerier**, **eeriest**) gloomy and strange; weird, frightening (*an eerie silence*). □ **eerily** *adv.* **eeriness** *n.* [originally northern English and Scots *eri*, of obscure origin: cf. Old English *earg* 'cowardly']

EETPU *abbr.* (in the UK) Electrical, Electronic, Telecommunications, and Plumbing Union.

ef- /ɪf, ɛf/ *prefix* assim. form of EX-[1] 1 before *f*.

eff /ɛf/ *v. Brit. slang euphem.* **1** *tr. & intr.* (often foll. by *off*) = FUCK (in expletive use). **2** *intr.* say *fuck* or similar coarse slang words. □ **effing and blinding** using coarse slang. [name of the letter *F*, as a euphemistic abbreviation]

efface /ɪˈfeɪs/ *v.* **1** *tr.* rub or wipe out (a mark etc.). **2** *tr.* (in abstract senses) obliterate; wipe out (*effaced it from his memory*). **3** *tr.* utterly surpass; eclipse (*success has effaced all previous attempts*). **4** *refl.* make oneself insignificant or inconspicuous. □ **effacement** *n.* [French *effacer* (as EX-[1], FACE)]

effect /ɪˈfɛkt/ *n. & v.* ● *n.* **1** the result or consequence of an action etc. **2** efficacy (*had little effect*). **3** an impression produced on a spectator, hearer, etc. (*lights had a pretty effect*; *my words had no effect*). **4** (in *pl.*) property, luggage. **5** (in *pl.*) the lighting, sound, etc. used to accompany a play, film, broadcast, etc. **6** *Physics* a physical phenomenon, usually named after its discoverer (*Doppler effect*). **7** the state of being operative. ● *v.tr.* bring about; accomplish. □ **bring** (or **carry**) **into effect** accomplish. **for effect** to create an impression. **give effect to** make operative. **in effect** for practical purposes; in reality. **take effect** become operative. **to the effect that** the general substance or gist being. **to that effect** having that result or implication. **with effect from** coming into operation at or on (a stated time or day). [Middle English from Old French *effect* or Latin *effectus* (as EX-[1], *facere* 'make')]

■ **Usage** See Usage Note at AFFECT[1].

effective /ɪˈfɛktɪv/ *adj. & n.* ● *adj.* **1 a** having a definite or desired effect. **b** efficient. **2** powerful in visual, emotive, etc. effect; impressive. **3 a** actual; existing in fact rather than officially or theoretically (*took effective control in their absence*). **b** actually usable; realizable; equivalent in its effect (*effective money*; *effective demand*). **4** coming into operation (*effective as from 1 May*). **5** (of manpower) fit for work or service. ● *n.* a soldier available for service. □ **effectively** *adv.* **effectiveness** *n.* **effectivity** /-ˈtɪvɪti/ *n.* [Middle English from Latin *effectivus* (as EFFECT)]

effector /ɪˈfɛktə/ *adj. & n. Biol.* ● *adj.* acting in response to a stimulus. ● *n.* an effector organ.

effectual /ɪˈfɛktʃʊəl/ *adj.* **1** capable of producing the required result or effect; answering its purpose. **2** valid. □ **effectuality** /-ˈalɪti/ *n.* **effectually** *adv.* **effectualness** *n.* [Middle English from medieval Latin *effectualis* (as EFFECT)]

effectuate /ɪˈfɛktʃʊeɪt/ *v.tr.* cause to happen; accomplish. □ **effectuation** /-ˈeɪʃ(ə)n/ *n.* [medieval Latin *effectuare* (as EFFECT)]

effeminate /ɪˈfɛmɪnət/ *adj.* (of a man) feminine in appearance or manner; unmasculine. □ **effeminacy** *n.* **effeminately** *adv.* [Middle English from Latin *effeminatus*, past part. of *effeminare* (as EX-[1], *femina* 'woman')]

effendi /ɛˈfɛndi/ *n.* (*pl.* **effendis**) **1** a man of education or standing in eastern Mediterranean or Arab countries. **2** a former title of respect or courtesy in Turkey. [Turkish *efendi* via modern Greek *afentēs* from Greek *authentēs* 'lord, master': see AUTHENTIC]

efferent /ˈɛf(ə)r(ə)nt/ *adj. Physiol.* conducting outwards (*efferent nerves*; *efferent vessels*) (opp. AFFERENT). [Latin *efferre* (as EX-[1], *ferre* 'carry')]

effervesce /ɛfəˈvɛs/ *v.intr.* **1** give off bubbles of gas; bubble. **2** (of a person) be lively or energetic. □ **effervescence** *n.* **effervescency** *n.* **effervescent** *adj.* [Latin *effervescere* (as EX-[1], *fervēre* 'be hot')]

effete /ɪˈfiːt/ *adj.* **1** feeble and incapable, ineffectual. **2** worn out; exhausted of its essential quality or vitality, decadent. □ **effeteness** *n.* [Latin *effetus* 'worn out by bearing young' (as EX-[1], FOETUS)]

efficacious /ɛfɪˈkeɪʃəs/ *adj.* (of a thing) producing or sure to produce the desired effect. □ **efficaciously** *adv.* **efficaciousness** *n.* **efficacy** /ˈɛfɪkəsi/ *n.* [Latin *efficax* (as EFFICIENT)]

efficiency /ɪˈfɪʃ(ə)nsi/ *n.* (*pl.* **-ies**) **1** the state or quality of being efficient. **2** *Mech. & Physics* the ratio of useful work performed to the total energy expended or heat taken in. [Latin *efficientia* (as EFFICIENT)]

efficiency bar *n.* a point on a salary scale requiring evidence of efficiency for further promotion.

efficient /ɪˈfɪʃ(ə)nt/ *adj.* **1** productive with minimum waste or effort. **2** (of a person) capable; acting effectively. □ **efficiently** *adv.* [Middle English from Latin *efficere* (as EX-[1], *facere* 'make, accomplish')]

efficient cause *n. Philos.* an agent that brings a thing into being or initiates a change.

effigy /ˈɛfɪdʒi/ *n.* (*pl.* **-ies**) a sculpture or model of a person. □ **in effigy** in the form of a (usu. crude) representation of a person. [Latin *effigies* from *effingere* 'to fashion']

effleurage /ɛfləːˈrɑːʒ/ *n. & v.* ● *n.* a form of massage involving a circular inward stroking movement made with the palm of the hand, used esp. during childbirth. ● *v.tr.* massage with a circular stroking movement. [French, from *effleurer* 'to skim']

effloresce /ɛfləˈrɛs/ *v.intr.* **1** burst out into flower. **2** *Chem.* **a** (of a substance) turn to a fine powder on exposure to air. **b** (of salts) come to the surface and crystallize on it. **c** (of a surface) become covered with salt particles. □ **efflorescence** *n.* **efflorescent** *adj.* [Latin *efflorescere* (as EX-[1], *florēre* 'to bloom' from *flos floris* 'flower')]

effluence /ˈɛflʊəns/ *n.* **1** a flowing out (of light, electricity, etc.). **2** that which flows out. [French *effluence* or medieval Latin *effluentia* from Latin *effluere efflux-* 'flow out' (as EX-[1], *fluere* 'flow')]

effluent /ˈɛflʊənt/ *adj. & n.* ● *adj.* flowing forth or out. ● *n.* **1** sewage or industrial waste discharged into a river, the sea, etc. **2** a stream or lake flowing from a larger body of water. [Latin *effluere effluent-*: see EFFLUENCE]

effluvium /ɪˈfluːvɪəm/ *n.* (*pl.* **effluvia** /-vɪə/) an unpleasant or noxious odour or exhaled substance affecting the lungs or the sense of smell etc. [Latin from *effluere*: see EFFLUENCE]

efflux /ˈɛflʌks/ *n.* = EFFLUENCE. □ **effluxion** /ɪˈflʌkʃ(ə)n/ *n.* [medieval Latin *effluxus*: see EFFLUENCE]

effort /ˈɛfət/ *n.* **1** strenuous physical or mental exertion. **2** a vigorous or determined attempt. **3** *Mech.* a force exerted. **4** *colloq.* the result of an attempt; something accomplished (*not bad for a first effort*). □ **effortful** *adj.* **effortfully** *adv.* [French from Old French *esforcier*, ultimately from Latin *fortis* 'strong']

effortless /ˈɛfətlɪs/ *adj.* **1** requiring no effort (*effortless methods of cookery*). **2** natural, easy (*effortless grace*). □ **effortlessly** *adv.* **effortlessness** *n.*

effrontery /ɪˈfrʌnt(ə)ri/ *n.* (*pl.* **-ies**) **1** shameless insolence; impudent audacity (esp. *have the effrontery to*). **2** an instance of this. [French *effronterie* from *effronté*, ultimately from Late Latin *effrons -ontis* 'shameless' (as EX-[1], *frons* 'forehead')]

effulgent /ɪˈfʌldʒ(ə)nt/ *adj. literary* radiant; shining brilliantly. □ **effulgence** *n.* **effulgently** *adv.* [Latin *effulgēre* 'shine forth' (as EX-[1], *fulgēre* 'shine')]

effuse *adj. & v.* ● *adj.* /ɪˈfjuːs/ *Bot.* (of an inflorescence etc.) spreading loosely. ● *v.tr.* /ɪˈfjuːz/ **1** pour forth (liquid, light, etc.). **2** give out (ideas etc.). [Middle

English from Latin *effusus*, past part. of *effundere effus-* 'pour out' (as EX-[1], *fundere* 'pour')]

effusion /ɪ'fju:ʒ(ə)n/ *n.* **1** a copious outpouring. **2** usu. *derog.* an unrestrained flow of speech or writing. [Middle English from Old French *effusion* or Latin *effusio* (as EFFUSE)]

effusive /ɪ'fju:sɪv/ *adj.* **1** gushing, demonstrative, exuberant (*effusive praise*). **2** *Geol.* (of igneous rock) poured out when molten and later solidified, volcanic. □ **effusively** *adv.* **effusiveness** *n.*

EFL *abbr.* English as a foreign language.

eft /ɛft/ *n.* a newt. [Old English *efeta*, of unknown origin]

Efta /'ɛftə/ *abbr.* (also **EFTA**) European Free Trade Association. [abbreviation]

EFTPOS /'ɛftpɒz/ *abbr.* electronic funds transfer at point of sale.

e.g. *abbr.* for example. [Latin *exempli gratia*]

egad /ɪ'gad/ *int. archaic* or *joc.* by God. [probably originally *a* 'ah' + GOD]

egalitarian /ɪˌgalɪ'tɛ:rɪən/ *adj. & n.* ● *adj.* **1** of or relating to the principle of equal rights and opportunities for all (*an egalitarian society*). **2** advocating this principle. ● *n.* a person who advocates or supports egalitarian principles. □ **egalitarianism** *n.* [French *égalitaire* from *égal* EQUAL]

egg[1] /ɛg/ *n.* **1 a** the spheroidal reproductive body produced by females of animals such as birds, reptiles, fish, etc., enclosed in a protective layer and capable of developing into a new individual. **b** the egg of the domestic hen, used for food. **2** *Biol.* the female reproductive cell in animals and plants. **3** *colloq.* a person or thing qualified in some way (*a tough egg*). **4** anything resembling or imitating an egg, esp. in shape or appearance. □ **as sure as eggs is** (or **are**) **eggs** *colloq.* without any doubt. **have** (or **put**) **all one's eggs in one basket** *colloq.* risk everything on a single venture. **with egg on one's face** *colloq.* made to look foolish. □ **eggless** *adj.* **eggy** *adj.* (**eggier**, **eggiest**). [Middle English from Old Norse, related to Old English *ǣg*]

egg[2] /ɛg/ *v.tr.* (foll. by *on*) urge (*egged them on to do it*). [Middle English from Old Norse *eggja* = EDGE]

eggar /'ɛgə/ *n.* (also **egger**) any of various large moths of the family Lasiocampidae, esp. *Lasiocampa quercus*, with an egg-shaped cocoon. [probably from EGG[1] + -ER[1]]

egg-beater *n.* **1** a device for beating eggs. **2** *US slang* a helicopter.

eggcup /'ɛgkʌp/ *n.* a cup for holding a boiled egg.

egg custard *n.* = CUSTARD 1.

egghead /'ɛghɛd/ *n. colloq.* an intellectual; an expert.

egg-nog *n.* (also *Brit.* **egg-flip**) a drink of alcoholic spirit with beaten egg, milk, etc.

eggplant /'ɛgplɑ:nt/ *n.* esp. *N. Amer.* = AUBERGINE *n.* 1, 2.

eggs and bacon *n.* (also **egg and bacon**) any of various plants with orange-marked yellow flowers, esp. bird's-foot trefoil and yellow toadflax.

eggshell /'ɛgʃɛl/ *n. & adj.* ● *n.* **1** the shell of an egg. **2** anything very fragile. ● *adj.* **1** (of china) thin and fragile. **2** (of paint) with a slight gloss finish.

egg-spoon *n.* a small spoon for eating a boiled egg.

egg-timer *n.* a device for timing the cooking of an egg.

egg-tooth *n.* a projection of an embryo bird or reptile used for breaking out of the shell.

egg white *n.* the white of an egg.

eglantine /'ɛgləntʌɪn/ *n.* sweet-brier. [Middle English via French *églantine* from Old French *aiglent*, ultimately from Latin *acus* 'needle']

ego /'i:gəʊ, 'ɛ-/ *n.* (*pl.* **-os**) **1** *Metaphysics* a conscious thinking subject. **2** *Psychol.* the part of the mind that reacts to reality and has a sense of individuality. **3** a sense of self-esteem. [Latin, = I]

egocentric /ɛgə(ʊ)'sɛntrɪk, i:-/ *adj.* **1** centred in the ego. **2** self-centred, egoistic. □ **egocentrically** *adv.* **egocentricity** /-'trɪsɪti/ *n.* **egocentrism** *n.* [EGO + -CENTRIC, on the pattern of *geocentric* etc.]

ego-ideal *n.* **1** *Psychol.* the part of the mind developed from the ego by an awareness of social standards. **2** (in general use) idealization of oneself.

egoism /'ɛgəʊɪz(ə)m, 'i:-/ *n.* **1** an ethical theory that treats self-interest as the foundation of morality. **2** = EGOTISM. □ **egoist** *n.* **egoistic** /-'ɪstɪk/ *adj.* **egoistical** /-'ɪstɪk(ə)l/ *adj.* **egoistically** /-'ɪstɪk(ə)li/ *adv.* [French *égoïsme*, ultimately from modern Latin *egoismus* (as EGO)]

■ **Usage** The senses of *egoism* and *egotism* overlap, but *egoism* alone is a term used in philosophy and psychology to mean 'self-interest' (often contrasted with *altruism*).

egomania /ɛgə(ʊ)'meɪnɪə, i:-/ *n.* morbid egotism. □ **egomaniac** /-'meɪnɪak/ *n.* **egomaniacal** /-mə'nʌɪək(ə)l/ *adj.*

egotism /'ɛgətɪz(ə)m, 'i:-/ *n.* **1** the practice of continually talking about oneself; self-centredness. **2** an exaggerated opinion of oneself; conceit. **3** selfishness. □ **egotist** *n.* **egotistic** /-'tɪstɪk/ *adj.* **egotistical** /-'tɪstɪk(ə)l/ *adj.* **egotistically** /-'tɪstɪk(ə)li/ *adv.* **egotize** *v.intr.* (also **-ise**). [EGO + -ISM, with intrusive *-t-*]

■ **Usage** See Usage Note at EGOISM.

ego trip *n. colloq.* activity etc. devoted entirely to one's own interests or feelings.

egregious /ɪ'gri:dʒəs/ *adj.* **1** outstandingly bad; shocking (*egregious folly; an egregious ass*). **2** *archaic* or *joc.* remarkable. □ **egregiously** *adv.* **egregiousness** *n.* [Latin *egregius* 'illustrious', literally 'standing out from the flock', from *grex gregis* 'flock']

egress /'i:grɛs/ *n.* **1 a** going out. **b** the right of going out. **2** an exit; a way out. **3** *Astron.* the end of an eclipse or transit. [Latin *egressus* from *egredi egress-* (as E-, *gradi* 'to step')]

egret /'i:grɪt, 'ɛ-/ *n.* any of various herons of the genus *Egretta* or *Bulbulcus*, usu. having long white feathers in the breeding season. [Middle English, via Anglo-French *egrette*, Old French *aigrette* from Provençal *aigreta*, from *aigron* 'heron']

Egyptian /ɪ'dʒɪpʃ(ə)n/ *adj. & n.* ● *adj.* **1** of or relating to Egypt in NE Africa. **2** of or for Egyptian antiquities (e.g. in a museum) (*Egyptian room*). ● *n.* **1** a native of ancient or modern Egypt; a national of the Arab Republic of Egypt. **2** the Hamitic language used in ancient Egypt until the 3rd c. AD. □ **Egyptianize** *v.tr.* (also **-ise**). **Egyptianization** /-'zeɪʃ(ə)n/ *n.*

Egyptology /i:dʒɪp'tɒlədʒi/ *n.* the study of the language, history, and culture of ancient Egypt. □ **Egyptologist** *n.*

eh /eɪ/ *int. colloq.* **1** expressing enquiry or surprise. **2** inviting assent. **3** asking for something to be repeated or explained. [Middle English *ey*, instinctive exclamation]

-eian /ɪən/ *suffix* corresponding to *-ey* (or *-y*) + *-an* (*Bodleian; Rugbeian*).

Eid /i:d/ *n.* (also **Id**) a Muslim festival, esp.: **1** (in full **Eid ul-Fitr** /i:dʊl'fɪtrə/) that marking the end of the fast of Ramadan. **2** (in full **Eid ul-Adha** /i:dʊl'ɑ:də/) that marking the culmination of the annual pilgrimage to Mecca. [Arabic *'īd* 'feast']

eider /'ʌɪdə/ *n.* **1** (in full **eider duck**) any of several large northern ducks, esp. *Somateria mollissima*. **2** (in full **eider-down**) small soft feathers from the breast of the eider duck. [Icelandic *aethr*]

eiderdown /'ʌɪdədaʊn/ *n. Brit.* a quilt stuffed with down (originally from the eider) or some other soft material, esp. as the upper layer of bedclothes.

eidetic /ʌɪ'dɛtɪk/ *adj. & n.* ● *adj. Psychol.* (of a mental image) having unusual vividness and detail, as if actually visible. ● *n.* a person able to see eidetic images. □ **eidetically** *adv.* [German *eidetisch* from Greek *eidētikos*, from *eidos* 'form']

eidolon /ʌɪ'dəʊlɒn/ *n.* (*pl.* **eidolons** or **eidola** /-lə/) **1** a spectre; a phantom. **2** an idealized figure. [Greek *eidōlon*: see IDOL]

eigen- /ˈʌɪɡən/ *comb. form Math. & Physics* proper, characteristic. [German *eigen* OWN]

eigenfrequency /ˈʌɪɡən,friːkw(ə)nsi/ *n.* (*pl.* **-ies**) *Math. & Physics* one of the natural resonant frequencies of a system.

eigenfunction /ˈʌɪɡən,fʌn(k)ʃ(ə)n/ *n. Math. & Physics* that function which under a given operation generates some multiple of itself.

eigenvalue /ˈʌɪɡən,valjuː/ *n. Math. & Physics* that value by which an eigenfunction of an operation is multiplied after the eigenfunction has been subjected to that operation.

eight /eɪt/ *n. & adj.* ● *n.* **1** one more than seven, or two less than ten; the product of two units and four units. **2** a symbol for this (8, viii, VIII). **3** (in full **figure of eight**) (in ice-skating, country dancing, etc.) a figure resembling the form of 8. **4** a size etc. denoted by eight. **5** an eight-oared rowing boat or its crew. **6** eight o'clock. **7** a card with eight pips. ● *adj.* that amount to eight. □ **have one over the eight** *Brit. slang* have one drink too many. [Old English *ehta, eahta*]

eighteen /eɪˈtiːn, ˈeɪtiːn/ *n. & adj.* ● *n.* **1** one more than seventeen, or eight more than ten; the product of two units and nine units. **2** a symbol for this (18, xviii, XVIII). **3** a size etc. denoted by eighteen. **4** a set or team of eighteen individuals. **5** (**18**) *Brit.* (of films) classified as suitable for persons of 18 years and over. ● *adj.* that amount to eighteen. □ **eighteenth** *adj. & n.* [Old English *ehtatēne*]

eighteenmo /eɪˈtiːnməʊ/ *n.* (*pl.* **-os**) = OCTODECIMO.

eightfold /ˈeɪtfəʊld/ *adj. & adv.* **1** eight times as much or as many. **2** consisting of eight parts. **3** amounting to eight.

eighth /eɪtθ/ *n. & adj.* ● *n.* **1** the position in a sequence corresponding to the number 8 in the sequence 1–8. **2** something occupying this position. **3** one of eight equal parts of a thing. ● *adj.* that is the eighth. □ **eighthly** *adv.*

eighth note *n.* esp. *N. Amer. Mus.* = QUAVER.

eightsome /ˈeɪts(ə)m/ *n.* **1** (in full **eightsome reel**) a lively Scottish reel for eight dancers. **2** the music for this.

8vo *abbr.* octavo.

eighty /ˈeɪti/ *n. & adj.* ● *n.* (*pl.* **-ies**) **1** the product of eight and ten. **2** a symbol for this (80, lxxx, LXXX). **3** (in *pl.*) the numbers from 80 to 89, esp. the years of a century or of a person's life. ● *adj.* that amount to eighty. □ **eighty-first, -second**, etc. the ordinal numbers between eightieth and ninetieth. **eighty-one, -two**, etc. the cardinal numbers between eighty and ninety. □ **eightieth** *adj. & n.* **eightyfold** *adj. & adv.* [Old English *-eahtatig* (as EIGHT, -TY²)]

einkorn /ˈʌɪnkɔːn/ *n.* a kind of wheat (*Triticum monococcum*). [German, from *ein* 'one' + *Korn* 'seed']

einsteinium /ʌɪnˈstʌɪnɪəm/ *n. Chem.* a transuranic radioactive metallic element produced artificially from plutonium (symbol **Es**). [named after A. *Einstein*, German-American physicist d. 1955]

eirenic var. of IRENIC.

eirenicon /ʌɪˈriːnɪkɒn/ *n.* (also **irenicon**) a proposal made as a means of achieving peace. [Greek, neut. of *eirēnikos* (*adj.*) from *eirēnē* 'peace']

eisteddfod /ʌɪˈstɛðvɒd, ʌɪˈstɛdvəd/ *n.* (*pl.* **eisteddfods** or **eisteddfodau** /-ˈvɒdʌɪ/) a congress of Welsh bards; a national or local festival for musical competitions etc. □ **eisteddfodic** /-ˈvɒdɪk/ *adj.* [Welsh, literally 'session', from *eistedd* 'sit']

either /ˈʌɪðə, ˈiː-/ *conj., adv., pron., & det.* ● *conj.* (introducing a word, phrase, or clause that is paired with another word, phrase, or clause introduced by *or*) as one of two mutually exclusive possibilities (*either come in or go out; is either black or white*). ● *adv.* (after a neg. sentence) **1** any more than the person or thing just mentioned (*Tim didn't like it and Patrick didn't either*). **2** moreover, indeed (*there is no time to lose, either*). ● *pron.* one or the other of two (*either of you can go; I like both twins but Jeremy doesn't like either*). ● *det.* **1** one or the other of two (*you may have either book*). **2** each of two (*either side of the road*). □ **either way** in either case or event. [Old English *ǣgther*, from Germanic]

either/or *n. & adj.* ● *n.* an unavoidable choice between alternatives. ● *adj.* involving such a choice.

eiusdem generis /eɪ,(j)ʊsdɛm ˈdʒɛnɛrɪs/ *adj. Law* of the same kind. [Latin]

ejaculate *v. & n.* ● *v.tr.* /ɪˈdʒakjʊleɪt/ (also *absol.*) **1** utter suddenly (words esp. of prayer or other emotion). **2** eject (fluid etc., esp. semen) from the body. ● *n.* /ɪˈdʒakjʊlət/ semen that has been ejaculated from the body. □ **ejaculation** /-ˈleɪʃ(ə)n/ *n.* **ejaculator** /ɪˈdʒakjʊleɪtə/ *n.* **ejaculatory** /ɪˈdʒakjʊlət(ə)ri/ *adj.* [Latin *ejaculari* 'to dart' (as E-, *jaculum* 'javelin')]

eject /ɪˈdʒɛkt/ *v.tr.* **1** send or drive out precipitately or by force, esp. from a building or other property; compel to leave. **2 a** cause (the pilot etc.) to be propelled from an aircraft or spacecraft in an emergency. **b** (*absol.*) (of the pilot etc.) be ejected in this way (*they both ejected at 1,000 feet*). **3** cause to be removed or drop out (e.g. a spent cartridge from a gun). **4** dispossess (a tenant etc.) by legal process. **5** dart forth; emit. □ **ejective** *adj.* **ejectment** *n.* [Latin *ejicere eject-* (as E-, *jacere* 'throw')]

ejecta /ɪˈdʒɛktə/ *n.pl.* (also treated as *sing.*) material that is thrown out, esp. from a volcano or a star. [Latin, from *ejicere eject-* EJECT]

ejection /ɪˈdʒɛkʃ(ə)n/ *n.* the act or an instance of ejecting; the process of being ejected.

ejection seat *n.* = EJECTOR SEAT.

ejector /ɪˈdʒɛktə/ *n.* a device for ejecting.

ejector seat *n.* a device for the automatic ejection of the pilot etc. of an aircraft or spacecraft in an emergency.

eke /iːk/ *v.tr.* □ **eke out 1** (foll. by *with, by*) supplement; make the best use of (defective means etc.). **2** contrive to make (a livelihood) or support (an existence). [Old English *ēacan*, related to Latin *augēre* 'increase']

ekka /ˈɛkə/ *n. Anglo-Ind.* a small one-horse vehicle. [Hindi *ekkā* 'unit']

-el var. of -LE².

elaborate *adj. & v.* ● *adj.* /ɪˈlab(ə)rət/ **1** carefully or minutely worked out. **2** highly developed or complicated. ● *v.* /ɪˈlabəreɪt/ **1** *tr.* **a** work out or explain in detail. **b** (*absol.*) go into details (*I need not elaborate*). **2** *tr.* produce by labour. **3** *tr.* (of a natural agency) produce (a substance etc.) from its elements or sources. **4** *intr.* (foll. by *on*) explain in detail. □ **elaborately** /-rətli/ *adv.* **elaborateness** /-rətnɪs/ *n.* **elaboration** /-ˈreɪʃ(ə)n/ *n.* **elaborative** /-rətɪv/ *adj.* **elaborator** /-reɪtə/ *n.* [Latin *elaboratus*, past part. of *elaborare* (as E-, *labor* 'work')]

élan /eɪˈlɒ̃, eɪˈlan/ *n.* (also **elan**) vivacity, dash. [French, from *élancer* 'launch']

eland /ˈiːlənd/ *n.* any antelope of the genus *Tragelaphus*, native to Africa, having spirally twisted horns, esp. the largest of living antelopes, *T. derbianus*. [Dutch = elk]

elapse /ɪˈlaps/ *v.intr.* (of time) pass by. [Latin *elabor elaps-* 'slip away']

elasmobranch /ɪˈlazməbraŋk/ *n. Zool.* a cartilaginous fish of the subclass Elasmobranchii (or Chondrichthyes), including sharks, skates, rays. [modern Latin *elasmobranchii*, from Greek *elasmos* 'beaten metal' + *bragkhia* 'gills']

elasmosaurus /ɪ,lazməˈsɔːrəs/ *n.* a large extinct marine reptile with paddle-like limbs and tough crocodile-like skin. [modern Latin, from Greek *elasmos* 'beaten metal' + *sauros* 'lizard']

elastane /ɪˈlasteɪn/ *n.* an elastic polyurethane, used esp. for hosiery, underwear, and other close-fitting clothing. [ELASTIC + -ANE²]

elastic /ɪˈlastɪk/ *adj. & n.* ● *adj.* **1** able to resume its normal bulk or shape spontaneously after contraction, dilatation, or distortion. **2** springy. **3** (of a person or feelings) buoyant. **4** flexible, adaptable (*elastic* *conscience*). **5** *Econ.* (of demand) variable according to price. **6** *Physics* (of a collision) involving no decrease of kinetic energy. ● *n.* elastic cord or fabric, usu. woven with strips of rubber. □ **elastically** *adv.* **elasticity** /ɛlaˈstɪsɪti, iː-, ɪ-/ *n.* **elasticize** /ɪˈlastɪsʌɪz/ *v.tr.* (also **-ise**). [modern Latin *elasticus* from Greek *elastikos* 'propulsive', from *elaunō* 'drive']

elasticated /ɪˈlastɪkeɪtɪd/ *adj. Brit.* (of a fabric) made elastic by weaving with rubber thread.

elastic band *n.* = RUBBER BAND.

elastin /ɪˈlastɪn/ *n.* an elastic fibrous glycoprotein found in connective tissue. [ELASTIC + -IN]

elastomer /ɪˈlastəmə/ *n.* a natural or synthetic rubber or rubber-like plastic. □ **elastomeric** /-ˈmɛrɪk/ *adj.* [ELASTIC, on the pattern of *isomer*]

Elastoplast /ɪˈlastəplɑːst/ *n. propr.* a type of sticking plaster. [ELASTIC + -O- + PLASTER]

elate /ɪˈleɪt/ *v. & adj.* ● *v.tr.* **1** (esp. as **elated** *adj.*) inspirit, stimulate. **2** make proud. ● *adj. archaic* in high spirits; exultant, proud. □ **elatedly** *adv.* **elatedness** *n.* **elation** *n.* [Middle English from Latin *efferre elat-* 'raise']

elater /ˈɛlətə/ *n.* a click beetle. [modern Latin from Greek *elatēr* 'driver', from *elaunō* 'drive']

E-layer *n.* a layer of the ionosphere able to reflect medium-frequency radio waves. [*E* (arbitrary) + LAYER]

elbow /ˈɛlbəʊ/ *n. & v.* ● *n.* **1 a** the joint between the forearm and the upper arm. **b** the part of the sleeve of a garment covering the elbow. **2** an elbow-shaped bend or corner; a short piece of piping bent through a right angle. ● *v.tr.* (foll. by *in*, *out*, *aside*, etc.) **1** thrust or jostle (a person or oneself). **2** make (one's way) by thrusting or jostling. □ **at one's elbow** close at hand. **give a person the elbow** *colloq.* send a person away; dismiss or reject a person. **out at** (or **at the**) **elbows 1** (of a coat) worn out. **2** (of a person) ragged, poor. [Old English *elboga*, *elnboga*, from Germanic (as ELL, BOW[1])]

elbow grease *n. colloq.* vigorous polishing; hard work.

elbow room *n. colloq.* adequate space to move or work in.

eld /ɛld/ *n. archaic* or *poet.* **1** old age. **2** olden time. [Old English *(i)eldu*, from Germanic: cf. OLD]

elder[1] /ˈɛldə/ *adj. & n.* ● *attrib.adj.* (of two indicated persons, esp. when related) senior; of a greater age (*my elder brother*). ● *n.* (often prec. by *the*) **1 a** the older or more senior of two indicated (esp. related) persons (*which is the elder?*; *is my elder by ten years*). **b** (**Elder**) a title to distinguish between related persons of renown (*Pitt the Elder*). **2** (in *pl.*) **a** persons of greater age or seniority (*respect your elders*). **b** persons venerable because of age. **3** a person advanced in life. **4** *hist.* a member of a senate or governing body. **5** an official in the early Christian, Presbyterian, or Mormon Churches. □ **eldership** *n.* [Old English *eldra*, related to OLD]

elder[2] /ˈɛldə/ *n.* any shrub or tree of the genus *Sambucus*, with white flowers and usu. blue-black or red berries. [Old English *ellærn*]

elderberry /ˈɛldəbɛri, -b(ə)ri/ *n.* (*pl.* **-ies**) the berry of the elder, esp. the common elder (*Sambucus nigra*) used for making jelly, wine, etc.

elder brother *n.* (*pl.* **elder brethren**) *Brit.* each of thirteen senior members of Trinity House.

elderflower /ˈɛldəflaʊə/ *n.* the flower of the elder.

elder hand *n. Cards* the first player.

elderly /ˈɛldəli/ *adj.* **1** somewhat old. **2** (of a person) past middle age. □ **elderliness** *n.*

elder statesman *n.* an influential experienced person, esp. a politician, of advanced age.

eldest /ˈɛldɪst/ *adj. & n.* ● *adj.* first-born or oldest surviving (member of a family, son, daughter, etc.). ● *n.* (often prec. by *the*) the eldest of three or more indicated (*who is the eldest?*). [Old English (as ELDER[1])]

eldest hand *n. Cards* the first player.

eldorado /ɛldəˈrɑːdəʊ/ *n.* (*pl.* **-os**) **1** any imaginary country or city abounding in gold. **2** a place of great abundance. [Spanish *el dorado* 'the gilded']

eldritch /ˈɛl(d)rɪtʃ/ *adj. Sc. & N.Amer.* **1** weird. **2** hideous. [16th c.: perhaps related to ELF]

elecampane /ˌɛlɪkamˈpeɪn/ *n.* a sunflower-like plant, *Inula helenium*, with bitter aromatic leaves and roots, used in herbal medicine and cookery. [medieval Latin *enula campana* (*enula* from Greek *helenion* 'elecampane', *campana* probably 'of the fields' from *campus* 'field')]

elect /ɪˈlɛkt/ *v. & adj.* ● *v.tr.* (usu. foll. by *to* + infin.) **1** choose (*the principles they elected to follow*). **2** choose (a person) by vote (*elected a new chairman*). **3** *Theol.* (of God) choose (persons) in preference to others for salvation. ● *adj.* **1** chosen. **2** select, choice. **3** *Theol.* chosen by God. **4** (in *comb.*, after a noun designating office) chosen but not yet in office (*president-elect*). □ **electable** *adj.* [Middle English from Latin *electus*, past part. of *eligere elect-* (as E-, *legere* 'pick')]

election /ɪˈlɛkʃ(ə)n/ *n.* **1** the process of electing or being elected, esp. of members of a political body. **2** the act or an instance of electing. [Middle English via Old French from Latin *electio -onis* (as ELECT)]

electioneer /ɪˌlɛkʃəˈnɪə/ *v. & n.* ● *v.intr.* **1** take part in an election campaign. **2** *derog.* seek election by currying favour with voters. ● *n.* a person who electioneers.

elective /ɪˈlɛktɪv/ *adj. & n.* ● *adj.* **1 a** (of an office or its holder) filled or appointed by election. **b** (of authority) derived from election. **2** (of a body) having the power to elect. **3** having a tendency to act on or be concerned with some things rather than others (*elective affinity*). **4** (of a course of study) chosen by the student; optional. **5** (of a surgical operation etc.) optional; not urgently necessary. ● *n. US* an elective course of study. □ **electively** *adv.* [French *électif -ive* from Late Latin *electivus* (as ELECT)]

elector /ɪˈlɛktə/ *n.* **1** a person who has the right of voting to elect an MP etc. **2** (**Elector**) *hist.* a German prince entitled to take part in the election of the Emperor. **3** *US* a member of an electoral college. □ **electorship** *n.* [Middle English via French *électeur* from Latin *elector* (as ELECT)]

electoral /ɪˈlɛkt(ə)r(ə)l/ *adj.* relating to or ranking as electors. □ **electorally** *adv.*

electoral college *n.* **1** a body of persons representing the states of the US, who cast votes for the election of the President. **2** a body of electors.

electoral roll *n.* (also **electoral register**) an official list of those in a district, parish, etc., entitled to vote.

electorate /ɪˈlɛkt(ə)rət/ *n.* **1** a body of electors. **2** *Austral. & NZ* an area represented by one Member of Parliament. **3** *hist.* the office or territories of a German Elector.

Electra complex /ɪˈlɛktrə/ *n. Psychol.* a daughter's subconscious sexual attraction to her father and hostility towards her mother, corresponding to the Oedipus complex in a son. [from the name of *Electra* in Greek tragedy, who caused her mother to be murdered for having murdered Electra's father]

Electress /ɪˈlɛktrɪs/ *n. hist.* the wife of a German Elector.

electret /ɪˈlɛktrɪt/ *n. Physics* a permanently polarized piece of dielectric material, analogous to a permanent magnet. [ELECTRICITY + MAGNET]

electric /ɪˈlɛktrɪk/ *adj. & n.* ● *adj.* **1** of, worked by, or charged with electricity; producing or capable of generating electricity. **2** causing or charged with sudden and dramatic excitement (*the news had an electric effect*; *the atmosphere was electric*). ● *n.* **1** an electric light, vehicle, etc. **2** (in *pl.*) electrical equipment. □ **electrically** *adv.* [modern Latin *electricus* via Latin *electrum* from Greek *ēlektron* 'amber', the rubbing of which causes electrostatic phenomena]

electrical /ɪ'lɛktrɪk(ə)l/ *adj.* **1** of or concerned with or of the nature of electricity. **2** operating by electricity. **3** = ELECTRIC *adj.* 2.

electricals /ɪ'lɛktrɪk(ə)lz/ *n.pl.* **1** shares in companies manufacturing electrical goods. **2** electrical equipment or circuitry.

electric blanket *n.* an electrically wired blanket used for heating a bed.

electric blue *n. & adj.* ● *n.* a steely or brilliant light blue. ● *adj.* (hyphenated when *attrib.*) of this colour.

electric chair *n.* a chair used for capital punishment by electrocution in certain judicial systems.

electric eel *n.* an eel-like freshwater fish, *Electrophorus electricus*, native to S. America, that kills its prey by electric shock.

electric eye *n. colloq.* a photoelectric cell operating a relay when the beam of light illuminating it is obscured.

electric fence *n.* a fence charged with electricity, often consisting of one strand.

electric field *n.* a region of electrical influence.

electric fire *n. Brit.* an electrically operated incandescent or convector heater, usu. portable and for domestic use.

electric guitar *n.* a guitar with built-in electrical sound pick-up or pick-ups rather than a soundbox.

electric hare see HARE *n.* 2.

electrician /ɪlɛk'trɪʃ(ə)n, ɛl-/ *n.* a person who installs or maintains electrical equipment, esp. professionally.

electricity /ɪlɛk'trɪsɪti, ɛl-, iːl-/ *n.* **1** a form of energy resulting from the existence of charged particles (electrons, protons, etc.), either statically as an accumulation of charge or dynamically as a current. **2** the branch of physics dealing with electricity. **3** a supply of electric current for heating, lighting, etc. **4** a state of heightened emotion; excitement, tension.

electric organ *n.* **1** *Biol.* an organ in certain fishes able to produce an electrical discharge for stunning prey or sensing the surroundings, or as a defence. **2** *Mus.* an electrically operated organ.

electric ray *n.* any of several fish of the ray family Torpedinidae which can give an electric shock (see RAY^2).

electric shaver *n.* (also **electric razor**) an electrical device for shaving, with oscillating or rotating blades behind a metal guard.

electric shock *n.* the effect of a sudden discharge of electricity on a person or animal, usually with stimulation of the nerves and contraction of the muscles.

electric storm *n.* a violent disturbance of the electrical condition of the atmosphere.

electrify /ɪ'lɛktrɪfʌɪ/ *v.tr.* (**-ies, -ied**) **1** charge (a body) with electricity. **2** convert (machinery or the place or system employing it) to the use of electric power. **3** cause dramatic or sudden excitement in. □ **electrification** /-fɪ'keɪʃ(ə)n/ *n.* **electrifier** *n.*

electro /ɪ'lɛktrəʊ/ *n. & v.* ● *n.* (*pl.* **-os**) **1** = ELECTROTYPE *n.* **2** = ELECTROPLATE *n.* ● *v.tr.* (**-oes, -oed**) *colloq.* **1** = ELECTROTYPE *v.* **2** = ELECTROPLATE *v.* [abbreviation]

electro- /ɪ'lɛktrəʊ/ *comb. form* of, relating to, or caused by electricity (*electrocute*; *electromagnet*). [Greek *ēlektron* 'amber': see ELECTRIC]

electro-acoustic /ɪˌlɛktrəʊə'kuːstɪk/ *adj.* **1** involving the direct conversion of electrical into acoustic energy or vice versa. **2** (of music) performed or composed with the creative use of electronic equipment.

electrobiology /ɪˌlɛktrəʊbʌɪ'ɒlədʒi/ *n.* the study of the electrical phenomena of living things.

electrocardiogram /ɪˌlɛktrəʊ'kɑːdɪəgram/ *n.* a record of the heartbeat traced by an electrocardiograph. [German *Elektrocardiogramm* (as ELECTRO-, CARDIO-, -GRAM)]

electrocardiograph /ɪˌlɛktrəʊ'kɑːdɪəgrɑːf/ *n.* an instrument recording the electric currents generated by a person's heartbeat. □ **electrocardiographic** /-'grafɪk/ *adj.* **electrocardiography** /-'ɒgrəfi/ *n.*

electrochemistry /ɪˌlɛktrəʊ'kɛmɪstri/ *n.* the branch of science that deals with the relations between electrical and chemical phenomena. □ **electrochemical** *adj.* **electrochemically** *adv.* **electrochemist** *n.*

electroconvulsive /ɪˌlɛktrəʊkən'vʌlsɪv/ *adj.* (of a therapy) employing the application of electric shocks to the brain, which induces a convulsion, as in some treatments for mental illness.

electrocute /ɪ'lɛktrəkjuːt/ *v.tr.* **1** kill by electricity (as a form of capital punishment). **2** cause the death of by electric shock. □ **electrocution** /-'kjuːʃ(ə)n/ *n.* [ELECTRO-, after EXECUTE]

electrode /ɪ'lɛktrəʊd/ *n.* a conductor through which electricity enters or leaves an electrolyte, gas, vacuum, etc. [ELECTRIC + Greek *hodos* 'way']

electrodialysis /ɪˌlɛktrəʊdʌɪ'alɪsɪs/ *n.* dialysis in which the movement of ions is aided by an electric field applied across the semi-permeable membrane.

electrodynamics /ɪˌlɛktrəʊdʌɪ'namɪks/ *n.pl.* (usu. treated as *sing.*) the branch of mechanics concerned with electric current applied to motive forces. □ **electrodynamic** *adj.*

electroencephalogram /ɪˌlɛktrəʊɪn'sɛf(ə)ləgram, -'kɛf-/ *n.* a record of the brain's activity traced by an electroencephalograph. [German *Elektrenkephalogramm* (as ELECTRO-, ENCEPHALO-, -GRAM)]

electroencephalograph /ɪˌlɛktrəʊɪn'sɛf(ə)ləgrɑːf, -'kɛf-/ *n.* an instrument recording the electrical activity of the brain. □ **electroencephalography** /-'lɒgrəfi/ *n.*

electroluminescence /ɪˌlɛktrəʊluːmɪ'nɛs(ə)ns/ *n. Chem.* luminescence produced electrically, esp. by the application of a voltage. □ **electroluminescent** *adj.*

electrolyse /ɪ'lɛktrəlʌɪz/ *v.tr.* (*US* **-yze**) subject to or treat by electrolysis. □ **electrolyser** *n.* [ELECTROLYSIS, on the pattern of *analyse*]

electrolysis /ɪˌlɛk'trɒlɪsɪs, ˌɛlɛk'trɒlɪsɪs/ *n.* **1** *Chem.* the decomposition of a substance by the application of an electric current. **2** *Surgery* this process applied to the destruction of tumours, hair-roots, etc. □ **electrolytic** /ɪˌlɛktrə(ʊ)'lɪtɪk/ *adj.* **electrolytical** /-'lɪtɪk(ə)l/ *adj.* **electrolytically** /-'lɪtɪk(ə)li/ *adv.* [ELECTRO- + -LYSIS]

electrolyte /ɪ'lɛktrəlʌɪt/ *n.* **1** a liquid which contains ions and can be decomposed by electrolysis, esp. that present in a battery. **2** (usu. in *pl.*) *Physiol.* the ionized or ionizable constituents of a living cell, blood, etc. [ELECTRO- + Greek *lutos* 'released' from *luō* 'loosen']

electromagnet /ɪˌlɛktrə(ʊ)'magnɪt/ *n.* a soft metal core made into a magnet by the passage of electric current through a coil surrounding it.

electromagnetic /ɪˌlɛktrə(ʊ)mag'nɛtɪk/ *adj.* having both an electrical and a magnetic character or properties. □ **electromagnetically** /-'nɛtɪk(ə)li/ *adv.*

electromagnetic radiation *n.* a kind of radiation including visible light, radio waves, gamma rays, X-rays, etc., in which electric and magnetic fields vary simultaneously.

electromagnetic spectrum *n.* the range of wavelengths over which electromagnetic radiation extends.

electromagnetic units *n.pl.* a largely disused system of units derived primarily from the magnetic properties of electric currents.

electromagnetism /ɪˌlɛktrəʊ'magnɪtɪz(ə)m/ *n.* **1** the magnetic forces produced by electricity. **2** the study of this.

electromechanical /ɪˌlɛktrəʊmɪ'kanɪk(ə)l/ *adj.* relating to the application of electricity to mechanical processes, devices, etc.

electrometer /ɪlɛk'trɒmɪtə, ɛl-/ *n.* an instrument for measuring electrical potential without drawing any current from the circuit. □ **electrometric** /-'mɛtrɪk/ *adj.* **electrometry** *n.*

electromotive /ɪˌlɛktrə'məʊtɪv/ *adj.* producing or tending to produce an electric current.

electromotive force *n.* a difference in potential that tends to give rise to an electric current (abbr.: **emf**, **EMF**).

electron /ɪˈlɛktrɒn/ *n.* a stable subatomic particle with a charge of negative electricity, found in all atoms and acting as the primary carrier of electricity in solids. [ELECTRIC + -ON]

electron beam *n.* a stream of electrons in a gas or vacuum.

electron diffraction *n.* the diffraction of a beam of electrons by atoms or molecules, used for determining crystal structures etc.

electronegative /ɪˌlɛktrə(ʊ)ˈnɛgətɪv/ *adj.* **1** electrically negative. **2** *Chem.* (of an element) tending to acquire electrons in chemical reactions.

electron gun *n.* a device for producing a narrow stream of electrons from a heated cathode.

electronic /ɪlɛkˈtrɒnɪk, ɛl-/ *adj.* **1 a** produced by or involving the flow of electrons. **b** of or relating to electrons or electronics. **2** (of a device) using electronic components. **3 a** (of music) produced by electronic means and usu. recorded on tape. **b** (of a musical instrument) producing sounds by electronic means. ▫ **electronically** *adv.*

electronic flash *n.* a flash from a gas-discharge tube, used in high-speed photography.

electronic mail *n.* **1** messages distributed by electronic means esp. from one computer system to one or more recipients. **2** the electronic mail system. Also called *e-mail.*

electronic publishing *n.* the publishing of books etc. in machine-readable form rather than on paper.

electronics /ɪlɛkˈtrɒnɪks, ɛl-/ *n.pl.* **1** (treated as *sing.*) the branch of physics and technology concerned with the behaviour and movement of electrons in a vacuum, gas, semiconductor, etc. **2** (treated as *pl.*) the circuits used in this.

electronic tagging *n.* the attaching of electronic markers to people, goods, etc., enabling them to be traced.

electron lens *n.* a device for focusing a stream of electrons by means of electric or magnetic fields.

electron microscope *n.* a microscope with high magnification and resolution, employing electron beams in place of light and using electron lenses.

electron pair *n.* **1** *Chem.* two electrons in the same orbital in an atom or molecule. **2** *Physics* an electron and a positron produced in a high-energy reaction.

electron spin resonance *n.* a spectroscopic method of locating electrons within the molecules of a paramagnetic substance (abbr.: **ESR**).

electronvolt /ɪˈlɛktrɒnvəʊlt, -vɒlt/ *n.* a unit of energy equal to the work done on an electron in accelerating it through a potential difference of one volt (abbr.: **eV**).

electrophilic /ɪˌlɛktrə(ʊ)ˈfɪlɪk/ *adj. Chem.* having an affinity for electrons. ▫ **electrophile** /ɪˈlɛktrə(ʊ)fʌɪl/ *n.*

electrophoresis /ɪˌlɛktrə(ʊ)fəˈriːsɪs/ *n. Physics & Chem.* the movement of charged particles in a fluid or gel under the influence of an electric field. ▫ **electrophoretic** /-fəˈrɛtɪk/ *adj.* [ELECTRO- + Greek *phorēsis* 'being carried']

electrophorus /ɪlɛkˈtrɒf(ə)rəs, ɛl-/ *n.* a device for repeatedly generating static electricity by induction. [modern Latin, from ELECTRO- + Greek *-phoros* 'bearing']

electrophysiology /ɪˌlɛktrəʊfɪzɪˈɒlədʒi/ *n.* the branch of physiology that deals with the electrical phenomena associated with nervous and other bodily activity. ▫ **electrophysiological** /-ˈlɒdʒɪk(ə)l/ *adj.*

electroplate /ɪˈlɛktrə(ʊ)pleɪt, ɪˌlɛktrə(ʊ)ˈpleɪt/ *v.* & *n.* ● *v.tr.* coat (a utensil etc.) by electrolytic deposition with chromium, silver, etc. ● *n.* electroplated articles. ▫ **electroplater** *n.*

electroplexy /ɪˈlɛktrəplɛksi/ *n. Brit.* electroconvulsive therapy. [ELECTRO- + APOPLEXY]

electroporation /ɪˌlɛktrəʊpəˈreɪʃ(ə)n/ *n. Biol.* the action or process of introducing DNA or chromosomes into the cells of bacteria etc. using a pulse of electricity to open the pores in the cell membranes briefly. [ELECTRO- + PORE¹ -ATION]

electropositive /ɪˌlɛktrə(ʊ)ˈpɒsɪtɪv/ *adj.* **1** electrically positive. **2** *Chem.* (of an element) tending to lose electrons in chemical reactions.

electroscope /ɪˈlɛktrəskəʊp/ *n.* an instrument for detecting and measuring electricity, esp. as an indication of the ionization of air by radioactivity. ▫ **electroscopic** /-ˈskɒpɪk/ *adj.*

electro-shock /ɪˈlɛktrə(ʊ)ʃɒk/ *attrib.adj.* (of medical treatment) by means of electric shocks; electroconvulsive.

electrostatic /ɪˌlɛktrə(ʊ)ˈstatɪk/ *adj.* of or relating to stationary electric charges or electrostatics. [ELECTRO- + STATIC on the pattern of *hydrostatic*]

electrostatics /ɪˌlɛktrə(ʊ)ˈstatɪks/ *n.* the study of stationary electric charges or fields as opposed to electric currents.

electrostatic units *n.pl.* a system of units based primarily on the forces between electric charges.

electrotechnology /ɪˌlɛktrəʊtɛkˈnɒlədʒi/ *n.* the science of the application of electricity in technology. ▫ **electrotechnic** /-ˈtɛknɪk/ *adj.* **electrotechnical** /-ˈtɛknɪk(ə)l/ *adj.* **electrotechnics** /-ˈtɛknɪks/ *n.*

electrotherapy /ɪˌlɛktrə(ʊ)ˈθɛrəpi/ *n.* the treatment of diseases by the use of electricity. ▫ **electrotherapeutic** /-ˈpjuːtɪk/ *adj.* **electrotherapeutical** /-ˈpjuːtɪk(ə)l/ *adj.* **electrotherapist** *n.*

electrothermal /ɪˌlɛktrə(ʊ)ˈθəːm(ə)l/ *adj.* relating to heat electrically derived.

electrotype /ɪˈlɛktrə(ʊ)tʌɪp/ *v.* & *n.* ● *v.tr.* copy by the electrolytic deposition of copper on a mould, esp. for printing. ● *n.* a copy so formed. ▫ **electrotyper** *n.*

electrovalent /ɪˌlɛktrə(ʊ)ˈveɪl(ə)nt/ *adj. Chem.* (of bonding) resulting from electrostatic attraction between ions. ▫ **electrovalence** *n.* **electrovalency** *n.* [ELECTRO- + *-valent*, on the pattern of *trivalent* etc.]

electroweak /ɪˌlɛktrəʊˈwiːk/ *adj. Physics* relating to or denoting electromagnetic and weak interactions regarded as manifestations of the same interaction.

electrum /ɪˈlɛktrəm/ *n.* **1** an alloy of silver and gold used in ancient times. **2** native argentiferous gold ore. [Middle English via Latin from Greek *ēlektron* 'amber, electrum']

electuary /ɪˈlɛktjʊ(ə)ri/ *n.* (*pl.* **-ies**) medicinal powder etc. mixed with honey or other sweet substance. [Middle English from Late Latin *electuarium*, probably via Greek *ekleikton* from *ekleikhō* 'lick up']

eleemosynary /ˌɛliːˈmɒsɪnəri, -ˈmɒz-/ *adj.* **1** of or dependent on alms. **2** charitable. **3** gratuitous. [medieval Latin *eleemosynarius* from Late Latin *eleemosyna*: see ALMS]

elegant /ˈɛlɪg(ə)nt/ *adj.* **1** graceful in appearance or manner. **2** tasteful, refined. **3** (of a mode of life etc.) of refined luxury. **4** ingeniously simple and pleasing. **5** *US* excellent. ▫ **elegance** *n.* **elegantly** *adv.* [French *élégant* or Latin *elegant-*, related to *eligere*: see ELECT]

elegiac /ɛlɪˈdʒʌɪək/ *adj.* & *n.* ● *adj.* **1** (of a metre) used for elegies. **2** mournful. ● *n.* (in *pl.*) verses in an elegiac metre. ▫ **elegiacally** *adv.* [French *élégiaque* or from Late Latin *elegiacus* from Greek *elegeiakos*: see ELEGY]

elegiac couplet *n.* a pair of lines consisting of a dactylic hexameter and a pentameter, esp. in Greek and Latin verse.

elegize /ˈɛlɪdʒʌɪz/ *v.* (also **-ise**) **1** *intr.* (often foll. by *upon*) write an elegy. **2** *intr.* write in a mournful strain. **3** *tr.* write an elegy upon. ▫ **elegist** *n.*

elegy /ˈɛlɪdʒi/ *n.* (*pl.* **-ies**) **1** a song of lament, esp. for the dead (sometimes vaguely used of other poems). **2** a poem in elegiac metre. [French *élégie* or Latin *elegia* from Greek *elegeia*, from *elegos* 'mournful poem']

element /ˈɛlɪm(ə)nt/ *n.* **1** a component part or group; a contributing factor or thing. **2** *Chem.* & *Physics* any of the hundred or so substances that cannot be resolved by chemical means into simpler substances, each consisting of atoms with the same atomic number. **3 a** any of the four substances (earth, water, air, and fire) in ancient and medieval philosophy. **b** any of these as a being's natural abode or environment. **4** a resistance wire that heats up in an electric heater, cooker, etc.; an electrode. **5** (in *pl.*) atmospheric agencies, esp. wind and storm. **6** (in *pl.*) the rudiments of learning or of a branch of knowledge. **7** (in *pl.*) the bread and wine of the Eucharist. **8** *Math.* & *Logic* an entity that is a single member of a set. □ **in** (or **out of**) **one's element** in (or out of) one's accustomed or preferred surroundings. [Middle English via Old French from Latin *elementum*]

elemental /ɛlɪˈmɛnt(ə)l/ *adj. & n.* ● *adj.* **1** of the four elements. **2** of the powers of nature (*elemental worship*). **3** comparable to a force of nature (*elemental grandeur*; *elemental tumult*). **4** uncompounded (*elemental oxygen*). **5** essential. ● *n.* an entity or force thought to be physically manifested by occult means. □ **elementalism** *n.* (in senses 1, 2). [medieval Latin *elementalis* (as ELEMENT)]

elementary /ɛlɪˈmɛnt(ə)ri/ *adj.* **1 a** dealing with or arising from the simplest facts of a subject; rudimentary, introductory. **b** simple. **2** *Chem.* not decomposable. □ **elementarily** *adv.* **elementariness** *n.* [Middle English from Latin *elementarius* (as ELEMENT)]

elementary particle *n.* a subatomic particle, esp. one not known to be decomposable into simpler particles.

elementary school *n.* **1** *Brit. hist.* a school in which primary instruction is given. **2** *N. Amer.* a primary school for usu. the first six or eight grades.

elenchus /ɪˈlɛŋkəs/ *n.* (*pl.* **elenchi** /-kʌɪ/) *Logic* logical refutation. □ **elenctic** *adj.* [Latin from Greek *elegkhos*]

elephant /ˈɛlɪf(ə)nt/ *n.* (*pl.* same or **elephants**) **1** the largest living land animal, of which two species survive, the larger African (*Loxodonta africana*) and the smaller Indian (*Elephas maximus*), both with a trunk and long curved ivory tusks. **2** *Brit.* a size of paper (711 × 584 mm). □ **elephantoid** /-ˈfantɔɪd/ *adj.* [Middle English *olifaunt* etc. from Old French *oli-*, *elefant*, ultimately via Latin *elephantus*, *elephans* from Greek *elephas -antos* 'ivory, elephant']

elephant-bird *n.* an extinct giant flightless bird of Madagascar, of the genus *Aepyornis*.

elephant grass *n.* any of various tall African grasses, esp. *Pennisetum purpureum*.

elephantiasis /ˌɛlɪf(ə)nˈtʌɪəsɪs/ *n.* gross enlargement of the body, esp. the limbs, due to lymphatic obstruction by a nematode parasite transmitted by mosquitoes. [Latin from Greek (as ELEPHANT)]

elephantine /ɛlɪˈfantʌɪn/ *adj.* **1** of elephants. **2 a** huge. **b** clumsy, unwieldy (*elephantine movements*; *elephantine humour*). [Latin *elephantinus* from Greek *elephantinos* (as ELEPHANT)]

elephant seal *n.* a very large seal of the genus *Mirounga*, the male of which has an inflatable snout. Also called *sea elephant*.

elephant shrew *n.* any small insect-eating mammal of the family Macroscelididae, native to Africa, having a long snout and long hind limbs.

Eleusinian /ɛljʊˈsɪnɪən/ *adj.* of or relating to Eleusis near Athens. [Latin *Eleusinius* from Greek *Eleusinios*]

Eleusinian mysteries *n.pl. Gk Hist.* the annual celebrations held at ancient Eleusis in honour of Demeter.

elevate /ˈɛlɪveɪt/ *v.tr.* **1** bring to a higher position. **2** *Eccl.* hold up (the Host or the chalice) for adoration. **3** raise, lift (one's eyes etc.). **4** raise the axis of (a gun). **5** raise (a railway etc.) above ground level. **6** exalt in rank etc. **7** (usu. as **elevated** *adj.*) raise morally or intellectually (*elevated style*). **8** (as **elevated** *adj.*) *Brit. colloq.* slightly drunk. □ **elevatory** *adj.* [Latin *elevare* 'raise' (as E-, *levis* 'light')]

elevation /ɛlɪˈveɪʃ(ə)n/ *n.* **1 a** the process of elevating or being elevated. **b** the angle with the horizontal, esp. of a gun or of the direction of a celestial object. **c** the height above a given level, esp. sea level. **d** a high place or position. **2 a** a drawing or diagram made by projection on a vertical plane (cf. PLAN *n.* 2). **b** a flat drawing of the front, side, or back of a house etc. **3** *Ballet* **a** the capacity of a dancer to attain height in springing movements. **b** the action of tightening the muscles and uplifting the body. □ **elevational** *adj.* (in sense 2). [Middle English from Old French *elevation* or Latin *elevatio*: see ELEVATE]

elevator /ˈɛlɪveɪtə/ *n.* **1** a hoisting machine. **2** *Aeron.* the movable part of a tailplane for changing the pitch of an aircraft. **3** *N. Amer.* **a** = LIFT *n.* 3. **b** a place for lifting and storing quantities of grain. **4** that which elevates, esp. a muscle that raises a limb. [modern Latin (as ELEVATE)]

eleven /ɪˈlɛv(ə)n/ *n. & adj.* ● *n.* **1** one more than ten; the sum of six units and five units. **2** a symbol for this (11, xi, XI). **3** a size etc. denoted by eleven. **4** eleven o'clock. **5** a set or team of eleven individuals. ● *adj.* that amount to eleven. [Old English *endleofon*, from Germanic]

elevenfold /ɪˈlɛv(ə)nfəʊld/ *adj. & adv.* **1** eleven times as much or as many. **2** consisting of eleven parts.

eleven-plus *n.* esp. *hist.* (in the UK) an examination taken at the age of 11–12 to determine the type of secondary school a child should enter.

elevenses /ɪˈlɛv(ə)nzɪz/ *n.* (usu. in *pl.*) *Brit. colloq.* light refreshment, usu. with tea or coffee, taken about 11 a.m.

eleventh /ɪˈlɛv(ə)nθ/ *n. & adj.* ● *n.* **1** the position in a sequence corresponding to the number 11 in the sequence 1–11. **2** something occupying this position. **3** one of eleven equal parts of a thing. **4** *Mus.* **a** an interval or chord spanning an octave and a fourth in the diatonic scale. **b** a note separated from another by this interval. ● *adj.* that is the eleventh. □ **the eleventh hour** the last possible moment.

elevon /ˈɛlɪvɒn/ *n. Aeron.* the movable part of the trailing edge of a delta wing. [ELEVATOR + AILERON]

elf /ɛlf/ *n.* (*pl.* **elves** /ɛlvz/) **1** a mythological being, esp. one that is small and mischievous. **2** a sprite or little creature. □ **elfish** *adj.* **elvish** *adj.* [Old English, from Germanic]

elfin /ˈɛlfɪn/ *adj. & n.* ● *adj.* of elves; elflike. ● *n. archaic* a dwarf; a child. [ELF, perhaps influenced by Middle English *elvene*, genitive pl. of *elf*, and by *Elphin*, the name of a character in Arthurian romance]

elf-lock *n.* a tangled mass of hair.

elicit /ɪˈlɪsɪt/ *v.tr.* (**elicited**, **eliciting**) **1** draw out, evoke (an admission, response, etc.). **2** draw forth (what is latent). □ **elicitation** /-ˈteɪʃ(ə)n/ *n.* **elicitor** *n.* [Latin *elicere elicit-* (as E-, *lacere* 'entice')]

elide /ɪˈlʌɪd/ *v.tr.* omit (a vowel or syllable) by elision. [Latin *elidere elis-* 'crush out' (as E-, *laedere* 'knock')]

eligible /ˈɛlɪdʒɪb(ə)l/ *adj.* **1** (often foll. by *for*) fit or entitled to be chosen (*eligible for a rebate*). **2** desirable or suitable, esp. as a partner in marriage. □ **eligibility** /-ˈbɪlɪti/ *n.* **eligibly** *adv.* [French *éligible* from Late Latin *eligibilis* (as ELECT)]

eliminate /ɪˈlɪmɪneɪt/ *v.tr.* **1** remove, get rid of. **2** exclude from consideration; ignore as irrelevant. **3** exclude from further participation in a competition etc. on defeat. **4** *Physiol.* discharge (waste matter). **5** *Chem.* remove (a simpler substance) from a compound. **6** *Algebra* remove (a quantity) by combining equations. □ **eliminable** /-nəb(ə)l/ *adj.* **elimination** /-ˈneɪʃ(ə)n/ *n.* **eliminator** *n.* **eliminatory** /-nət(ə)ri/ *adj.* [Latin *eliminare* (as E-, *limen liminis* 'threshold')]

ELINT /ɪˈlɪnt/ *n.* (also **Elint**) covert intelligence-gathering by electronic means. [*el*ectronic *int*elligence]

elision /ɪˈlɪʒ(ə)n/ *n.* **1** the omission of a vowel or syllable in pronouncing (as in *I'm*, *let's*, *e'en*). **2** the omission of a passage in a book etc. [Late Latin *elisio* (as ELIDE)]

elite /eɪˈliːt, ɪ-/ *n.* (also **élite**) **1** (prec. by *the*) the best or choice part of a larger body or group. **2** a select group or class. **3** a size of letter in typewriting (12 per inch).

[French from obsolete past part. of *élire* 'elect', from Romanic]

elitism /eɪ'li:tɪz(ə)m, ɪ-/ *n.* (also **élitism**) **1** advocacy of or reliance on leadership or dominance by a select group. **2** a sense of belonging to an elite. □ **elitist** *n. & adj.* (also **élitist**).

elixir /ɪ'lɪksə, -sɪə/ *n.* **1 a** a preparation supposedly able to change metals into gold. **b** (in full **elixir of life**) a preparation supposedly able to prolong life indefinitely. **c** a supposed remedy for all ills. **2** *Pharm.* an aromatic solution used as a medicine or flavouring. [Middle English via medieval Latin from Arabic *al-iksīr*, from *al* 'the' + *iksīr*, probably from Greek *xērion* 'powder for drying wounds' from *xēros* 'dry']

Elizabethan /ɪ,lɪzə'bi:θ(ə)n/ *adj. & n.* ● *adj.* of the time of Queen Elizabeth I (1558–1603) or of Queen Elizabeth II (1952–). ● *n.* a person, esp. a writer, of the time of Queen Elizabeth I or II.

elk /ɛlk/ *n.* (*pl.* same or **elks**) **1** a large deer, *Alces alces*, of northern Eurasia and N. America, with palmate antlers and a growth of skin hanging from the neck; also called *moose*. **2** *N. Amer.* a wapiti. [Middle English, probably representing Old English *elh, eolh*]

elk-hound *n.* **1** a large hunting dog of a Scandinavian breed with a shaggy coat. **2** this breed.

ell /ɛl/ *n. hist.* a former measure of length, about 45 inches. [Old English *eln*, related to Latin *ulna*: see ULNA]

ellipse /ɪ'lɪps/ *n.* a regular oval, traced by a point moving in a plane so that the sum of its distances from two other points is constant, or resulting when a cone is cut by an oblique plane which does not intersect the base (cf. HYPERBOLA). [French via Latin *ellipsus* from Greek *elleipsis*, from *elleipō* 'come short' from *en* 'in' + *leipō* 'leave']

ellipsis /ɪ'lɪpsɪs/ *n.* (also **ellipse**) (*pl.* **ellipses** /-si:z/) **1** the omission from a sentence of words needed to complete the construction or sense. **2** the omission of a sentence at the end of a paragraph. **3** a set of three dots etc. indicating an omission.

ellipsoid /ɪ'lɪpsɔɪd/ *n.* a solid of which all the plane sections normal to one axis are circles and all the other plane sections are ellipses. □ **ellipsoidal** /ɛlɪp'sɔɪd(ə)l/ *adj.*

elliptic /ɪ'lɪptɪk/ *adj.* (also **elliptical**) of, relating to, or having the form of an ellipse or ellipsis. □ **elliptically** *adv.* **ellipticity** /ɛlɪp'tɪsɪti/ *n.* [Greek *elleiptikos* 'defective', from *elleipō* (as ELLIPSE)]

elm /ɛlm/ *n.* **1** (also **elm tree**) any tree of the genus *Ulmus*, with rough serrated leaves, esp. (in full **English elm**) *U. procera*. **2** (in full **elmwood** /'ɛlmwʊd/) the wood of the elm. □ **elmy** *adj.* [Old English, related to Latin *ulmus*]

elocution /ɛlə'kju:ʃ(ə)n/ *n.* **1** the art of clear and expressive speech, esp. of distinct pronunciation and articulation. **2** a particular style of speaking. □ **elocutionary** *adj.* **elocutionist** *n.* [Latin *elocutio* from *eloqui elocut-* 'speak out' (as E-, *loqui* 'speak')]

elongate /'i:lɒŋgeɪt/ *v. & adj.* ● *v.* **1** *tr.* lengthen, prolong. **2** *intr.* esp. *Biol.* grow longer. ● *adj. Bot. & Zool.* = ELONGATED 1. [Late Latin *elongare* (as E-, Latin *longus* 'long')]

elongated /'i:lɒŋgeɪtɪd/ *adj.* **1** long in relation to its width. **2** that has been made longer.

elongation /i:lɒŋ'geɪʃ(ə)n/ *n.* **1** the act or an instance of lengthening; the process of being lengthened. **2** a part of a line etc. formed by lengthening. **3** *Mech.* the amount of extension under stress. **4** *Astron.* the angular separation of a planet from the sun or of a satellite from a planet. [Middle English from Late Latin *elongatio* (as ELONGATE)]

elope /ɪ'ləʊp/ *v.intr.* **1** run away to marry secretly, esp. without parental consent. **2** run away with a lover. □ **elopement** *n.* **eloper** *n.* [Anglo-French *aloper*, perhaps from a Middle English form *alope*, related to LEAP]

eloquence /'ɛləkwəns/ *n.* **1** fluent and effective use of language. **2** rhetoric. [Middle English via Old French from Latin *eloquentia*, from *eloqui* 'speak out' (as E-, *loqui* 'speak')]

eloquent /'ɛləkwənt/ *adj.* **1** possessing or showing eloquence. **2** (often foll. by *of*) clearly expressive or indicative. □ **eloquently** *adv.* [Middle English via Old French from Latin *eloqui* (as ELOQUENCE)]

Elsan /'ɛlsan/ *n. Brit. propr.* a type of transportable chemical lavatory. [apparently from *E. L.* Jackson (its manufacturer) + SANITATION]

else /ɛls/ *adv.* **1** besides; in addition (*someone else; nowhere else; who else*). **2** instead; other, different (*what else could I say?; he did not love her, but someone else*). **3** otherwise; if not (*run, (or) else you will be late*). [Old English *elles*, related to Latin *alius*, Greek *allos*]

elsewhere /ɛls'wɛ:, 'ɛlswɛ:/ *adv.* in or to some other place. [Old English *elles hwǣr* (as ELSE, WHERE)]

eluant var. of ELUENT.

eluate /'ɛlju:ət, -eɪt/ *n. Chem.* a solution or gas stream obtained by elution. [formed as ELUENT]

elucidate /ɪ'lu:sɪdeɪt, ɪ'lju:-/ *v.tr.* throw light on; explain. □ **elucidation** /-'deɪʃ(ə)n/ *n.* **elucidative** *adj.* **elucidator** *n.* **elucidatory** *adj.* [Late Latin *elucidare* (as E-, LUCID)]

elude /ɪ'lu:d, ɪ'lju:d/ *v.tr.* **1** escape adroitly from (a danger, difficulty, pursuer, etc.); dodge. **2** avoid compliance with (a law, request, etc.) or fulfilment of (an obligation). **3** (of a fact, solution, etc.) escape from or baffle (a person's memory or understanding). □ **elusion** /-ʒ(ə)n/ *n.* [Latin *eludere elus-* (as E-, *ludere* 'play')]

eluent /'ɛljʊənt/ *n.* (also **eluant**) *Chem.* a fluid used for elution. [Latin *eluere* 'wash out' (as E-, *luere lut-* 'wash')]

elusive /ɪ'lu:sɪv, ɪ'lju:-/ *adj.* **1** difficult to find or catch; tending to elude. **2** difficult to remember or recall. **3** (of an answer etc.) avoiding the point raised; seeking to elude. □ **elusively** *adv.* **elusiveness** *n.*

elute /ɪ'lu:t, ɪ'lju:t/ *v.tr. Chem.* remove (an adsorbed substance) by washing with a solvent. □ **elution** *n.* [German *eluieren* (as ELUENT)]

elutriate /ɪ'lu:trɪeɪt, ɪ'lju:-/ *v.tr. Chem.* separate (lighter and heavier particles in a mixture) by suspension in an upward flow of liquid or gas. □ **elutriation** /-'eɪʃ(ə)n/ *n.* [Latin *elutriare elutriat-* (as E-, *lutriare* 'wash')]

elver /'ɛlvə/ *n.* a young eel. [variant of *eel-fare* (from obsolete *fare* 'journey') = a brood of young eels]

elves *pl.* of ELF.

elvish see ELF.

Elysium /ɪ'lɪzɪəm/ *n.* **1** (also **Elysian Fields**) (in Greek mythology) the abode of the blessed after death. **2** a place or state of ideal happiness. □ **Elysian** *adj.* [Latin from Greek *Elusion* (*pedion* 'plain')]

elytron /'ɛlɪtrɒn/ *n.* (*pl.* **elytra** /-trə/) each of the two wing-cases of a beetle. [Greek *elutron* 'sheath']

em /ɛm/ *n. Printing* **1** a unit for measuring the amount of printed matter in a line, usually equal to the nominal width of capital M. **2** a unit of measurement equal to 12 points. [name of the letter *M*]

em- /ɪm, ɛm/ *prefix* assim. form of EN-[1], EN-[2] before *b, p.*

'em /əm/ *pron. colloq.* them (*let 'em all come*). [originally a form of Middle English *hem*, dative and accusative 3rd person pl. pronoun: now regarded as an abbreviation of THEM]

emaciate /ɪ'meɪsɪeɪt, ɪ'meɪʃ-/ *v.tr.* (esp. as **emaciated** *adj.*) make abnormally thin or feeble. □ **emaciation** /-'eɪʃ(ə)n/ *n.* [Latin *emaciare emaciat-* (as E-, *macies* 'leanness')]

e-mail /'i:meɪl/ *n. & v.* (also **email**) ● *n.* = ELECTRONIC MAIL. ● *v.tr.* **1** send e-mail to (a person). **2** send by e-mail.

emanate /'ɛməneɪt/ *v.* **1** *intr.* (usu. foll. by *from*) (of an idea, rumour, etc.) issue, originate (from a source). **2** *intr.* (usu. foll. by *from*) (of gas, light, etc.) proceed, issue. **3** *tr.* emit; send forth. [Latin *emanare* 'flow out']

emanation /ɛmə'neɪʃ(ə)n/ *n.* **1** the act or process of emanating. **2** something that emanates from a source (esp. of virtues, qualities, etc.). **3** *Chem.* a radioactive gas formed by radioactive decay. □ **emanative** *adj.* [Late Latin *emanatio* (as EMANATE)]

emancipate /ɪ'mansɪpeɪt/ *v.tr.* **1** free from restraint, esp. legal, social, or political. **2** (usu. as **emancipated** *adj.*) cause to be less inhibited by moral or social convention. **3** free from slavery. □ **emancipation** /-'peɪʃ(ə)n/ *n.* **emancipator** *n.* **emancipatory** *adj.* [Latin *emancipare* 'transfer property' (as E-, *manus* 'hand' + *capere* 'take')]

emasculate *v.* & *adj.* ● *v.tr.* /ɪ'maskjʊleɪt/ **1** deprive of force or vigour; make feeble or ineffective. **2** castrate. ● *adj.* /ɪ'maskjʊlət/ **1** deprived of force or vigour. **2** castrated. **3** effeminate. □ **emasculation** /-'leɪʃ(ə)n/ *n.* **emasculator** *n.* **emasculatory** /-lət(ə)ri/ *adj.* [Latin *emasculatus*, past part. of *emasculare* (as E-, *masculus*, diminutive of *mas* 'male')]

embalm /ɪm'bɑːm, ɛm-/ *v.tr.* **1** preserve (a corpse) from decay, originally with spices, now by means of arterial injection. **2** preserve from oblivion. **3** give balmy fragrance to. □ **embalmer** *n.* **embalmment** *n.* [Middle English from Old French *embaumer* (as EN-[1], BALM)]

embank /ɪm'baŋk, ɛm-/ *v.tr.* shut in or confine (a river etc.) with an artificial bank.

embankment /ɪm'baŋkm(ə)nt, ɛm-/ *n.* an earth or stone bank for keeping back water, or for carrying a road or railway.

embargo /ɛm'bɑːgəʊ, ɪm-/ *n.* & *v.* ● *n.* (*pl.* **-oes**) **1** an order of a state forbidding foreign ships to enter, or any ships to leave, its ports. **2** an official suspension of commerce or other activity (*be under an embargo*). **3** an impediment. ● *v.tr.* (**-oes, -oed**) **1** place (ships, trade, etc.) under embargo. **2** seize (a ship, goods) for state service. [Spanish from *embargar* 'arrest', from Romanic (as IN-[2], BAR[1])]

embark /ɪm'bɑːk, ɛm-/ *v.* **1** *tr.* & *intr.* (often foll. by *for*) put or go on board a ship or aircraft (to a destination). **2** *intr.* (foll. by *on, upon*) engage in an activity or undertaking. □ **embarkation** /ɛmbɑː'keɪʃ(ə)n/ *n.* (in sense 1). [French *embarquer* (as IN-[2], BARK[3])]

embarras de choix /ɒm,baraː də 'ʃwɑː, French ɑ̃bara də ʃwa/ *n.* (also ***embarras de richesse(s)*** /riː'ʃɛs, French riʃɛs/) more choices than one needs or can deal with. [French, = embarrassment of choice, riches]

embarrass /ɪm'barəs, ɛm-/ *v.tr.* **1** cause (a person) to feel awkward or self-conscious or ashamed. **2** (as **embarrassed** *adj.*) encumbered with debts. **3** hamper, impede. **4** complicate (a question etc.). **5** perplex. □ **embarrassedly** *adv.* **embarrassingly** *adv.* **embarrassment** *n.* [French *embarrasser* via Spanish *embarazar* from Italian *imbarrare* 'bar in' (as IN-[2], BAR[1])]

embassy /'ɛmbəsi/ *n.* (*pl.* **-ies**) **1 a** the residence or offices of an ambassador. **b** the ambassador and staff attached to an embassy. **2** a deputation or mission to a foreign country. [earlier *ambassy* via Old French *ambassée* etc. and medieval Latin *ambasciata* from Romanic (as AMBASSADOR)]

embattle /ɪm'bat(ə)l, ɛm-/ *v.tr.* **1 a** set (an army etc.) in battle array. **b** fortify against attack. **2** provide (a building or wall) with battlements. **3** (as **embattled** *adj.*) **a** prepared or arrayed for battle. **b** involved in a conflict or difficult undertaking. **c** *Heraldry* like battlements in form. [Middle English from Old French *embataillier* (as EN-[1], BATTLE): see BATTLEMENT]

embay /ɪm'beɪ, ɛm-/ *v.tr.* (often in *passive*) **1** enclose in or as in a bay; shut in. **2** form (a coast) into bays. □ **embayment** *n.*

embed /ɪm'bɛd, ɛm-/ *v.tr.* (also **imbed**) (**-bedded, -bedding**) **1** (esp. as **embedded** *adj.*) fix firmly in a surrounding mass (*embedded in concrete*). **2** (of a mass) surround so as to fix firmly. **3** place in or as in a bed. □ **embedment** *n.*

embellish /ɪm'bɛlɪʃ, ɛm-/ *v.tr.* **1** beautify, adorn. **2** add interest to (a narrative) with fictitious additions. □ **embellisher** *n.* **embellishment** *n.* [Middle English from Old French *embellir* (as EN-[1], *bel* 'handsome' from Latin *bellus*)]

ember[1] /'ɛmbə/ *n.* **1** (usu. in *pl.*) a small piece of glowing coal or wood in a dying fire. **2** an almost extinct residue of a past activity, feeling, etc. [Old English *ǣmyrge*, from Germanic]

ember[2] /'ɛmbə/ *n.* (in full **ember-goose**) = GREAT NORTHERN DIVER. [Norwegian *immer, imbre*]

Ember days /'ɛmbə/ *n.pl.* any of the days traditionally reserved for fasting and prayer in the Christian Church, now associated with ordinations. [Old English *ymbren*, perhaps from *ymbryne* 'period', from *ymb* 'about' + *ryne* 'course']

embezzle /ɪm'bɛz(ə)l, ɛm-/ *v.tr.* (also *absol.*) divert (usu. company or public funds) fraudulently to one's own use. □ **embezzlement** *n.* **embezzler** *n.* [Anglo-French *embesiler* (as EN-[1], Old French *besillier* 'maltreat, ravage', of unknown origin)]

embitter /ɪm'bɪtə, ɛm-/ *v.tr.* **1** arouse bitter feelings in (a person). **2** make more bitter or painful. **3** render (a person or feelings) hostile. □ **embitterment** *n.*

emblazon /ɪm'bleɪz(ə)n, ɛm-/ *v.tr.* **1 a** portray conspicuously, as on a heraldic shield. **b** adorn (a shield) with heraldic devices. **2** adorn brightly and conspicuously. **3** celebrate, extol. □ **emblazonment** *n.*

emblem /'ɛmbləm/ *n.* **1** a symbol or representation typifying or identifying an institution, quality, etc. **2** (foll. by *of*) (of a person) the type (*the very emblem of courage*). **3** a heraldic device or symbolic object as a distinctive badge. □ **emblematic** /-'matɪk/ *adj.* **emblematical** /-'matɪk(ə)l/ *adj.* **emblematically** /-'matɪk(ə)li/ *adv.* [Middle English via Latin *emblema* from Greek *emblēma -matos* 'insertion', from *emballō* 'throw in' (as EN-[1], *ballō* 'throw')]

emblematize /ɛm'blɛmətʌɪz/ *v.tr.* (also **-ise**) **1** serve as an emblem of. **2** represent by an emblem.

emblements /'ɛmblɪm(ə)nts/ *n.pl. Law* crops normally harvested annually, regarded as personal property. [Middle English from Old French *emblaement*, from *emblaier* (as EN-[1], *blé* 'corn')]

embody /ɪm'bɒdi, ɛm-/ *v.tr.* (**-ies, -ied**) **1** give a concrete or discernible form to (an idea, concept, etc.). **2** (of a thing or person) be an expression of (an idea etc.). **3** express tangibly (*courage embodied in heroic actions*). **4** form into a body. **5** include, comprise. **6** provide (a spirit) with bodily form. □ **embodiment** *n.*

embolden /ɪm'bəʊld(ə)n, ɛm-/ *v.tr.* (often foll. by *to* + infin.) make bold; encourage.

embolism /'ɛmbəlɪz(ə)m/ *n. Med.* an obstruction of an artery by a clot of blood, air bubble, etc. [Middle English, = intercalation, via Late Latin *embolismus* from Greek *embolismos*, from *emballō* (as EMBLEM)]

embolus /'ɛmbələs/ *n.* (*pl.* **emboli** /-lʌɪ, iː/) an object causing an embolism. [Latin, = piston, from Greek *embolos* 'peg, stopper']

embonpoint /ɒmbɒn'pwɑ̃/ *n.* plumpness (of a person). [French *en bon point* 'in good condition']

embosom /ɪm'bʊz(ə)m, ɛm-/ *v.tr. literary* **1** embrace. **2** enclose, surround.

emboss /ɪm'bɒs, ɛm-/ *v.tr.* **1** carve or mould in relief. **2** form figures etc. so that they stand out on (a surface). **3** make protuberant. □ **embosser** *n.* **embossment** *n.* [Middle English, from Old French (as EN-[1], BOSS[2])]

embouchure /ɒmbʊ'ʃʊə/ *n.* **1** *Mus.* **a** the mode of applying the mouth to the mouthpiece of a brass or wind instrument. **b** the mouthpiece of some instruments. **2** the mouth of a river. **3** the opening of a valley. [French from *s'emboucher* 'discharge itself by the mouth' (as EN-[1], *bouche* 'mouth')]

embowel /ɪm'baʊ(ə)l, ɛm-/ *v.tr.* (**embowelled, embowelling**; *US* **emboweled, emboweling**) *archaic* = DISEMBOWEL. [Old French *emboweler* from *esboueler* (as EX-[1], BOWEL)]

embower /ɪm'baʊə, ɛm-/ *v.tr. literary* enclose as in a bower.

embrace /ɪm'breɪs, ɛm-/ *v.* & *n.* ● *v.tr.* **1 a** hold (a person) closely in the arms, esp. as a sign of affection. **b** (*absol.*, of two people) hold each other closely. **2** clasp, enclose. **3** accept eagerly (an offer, opportunity, etc.). **4** adopt (a course of action, doctrine, cause, etc.). **5** include, comprise. **6** take in with the eye or mind. ● *n.* an act of embracing; holding in the arms. □ **embraceable** *adj.* **embracement** *n.* **embracer** *n.* [Middle English from Old French *embracer*, ultimately from Latin *in-* IN-[1] + *bracchium* 'arm']

embranchment /ɪm'brɑːn(t)ʃm(ə)nt, ɛm-/ *n.* a branching-out (of the arm of a river etc.). [French *embranchement* BRANCH (as EN-[1], BRANCH)]

embrasure /ɪm'breɪʒə, ɛm-/ *n.* **1** the bevelling of a wall at the sides of a door or window; splaying. **2** a small opening in a parapet of a fortified building, splayed on the inside. □ **embrasured** *adj.* [French from *embraser* 'splay', of unknown origin]

embrittle /ɪm'brɪt(ə)l, ɛm-/ *v.tr.* make brittle. □ **embrittlement** *n.*

embrocation /ɛmbrə'keɪʃ(ə)n/ *n.* a liquid used for rubbing on the body to relieve muscular pain etc. [French *embrocation* or medieval Latin *embrocatio*, ultimately from Greek *embrokhē* 'lotion']

embroider /ɪm'brɔɪdə, ɛm-/ *v.tr.* **1** (also *absol.*) **a** decorate (cloth etc.) with needlework. **b** create (a design) in this way. **2** add interest to (a narrative) with fictitious additions. □ **embroiderer** *n.* [Middle English from Anglo-French *enbrouder* (as EN-[1], Old French *brouder*, *broisder* from Germanic)]

embroidery /ɪm'brɔɪd(ə)ri, ɛm-/ *n.* (*pl.* **-ies**) **1** the art of embroidering. **2** embroidered work; a piece of this. **3** unnecessary or extravagant ornament. **4** fictitious additions to (a story etc.). [Middle English from Anglo-French *enbrouderie* (as EMBROIDER)]

embroil /ɪm'brɔɪl, ɛm-/ *v.tr.* **1** (often foll. by *with*) involve (a person) in conflict or difficulties. **2** bring (affairs) into a state of confusion. □ **embroilment** *n.* [French *embrouiller* (as EN-[1], BROIL[2])]

embryo /'ɛmbrɪəʊ/ *n.* (*pl.* **-os**) **1 a** an unborn or unhatched offspring. **b** a human offspring in the first eight weeks from conception. **2** a rudimentary plant contained in a seed. **3** a thing in a rudimentary stage. **4** (*attrib.*) undeveloped, immature. □ **in embryo** undeveloped. □ **embryoid** *adj.* **embryonal** /'ɛmbrɪən(ə)l/ *adj.* **embryonic** /ɛmbrɪ'ɒnɪk/ *adj.* **embryonically** /-'ɒnɪk(ə)li/ *adv.* [Late Latin *embryo -onis* from Greek *embruon* 'foetus' (as EN-[2], *bruō* 'swell, grow')]

embryo- /'ɛmbrɪəʊ/ *comb. form* embryo.

embryogenesis /ˌɛmbrɪəʊ'dʒɛnɪsɪs/ *n.* the formation of an embryo.

embryology /ɛmbrɪ'ɒlədʒi/ *n.* the study of embryos. □ **embryologic** /-brɪə'lɒdʒɪk/ *adj.* **embryological** /-brɪə'lɒdʒɪk(ə)l/ *adj.* **embryologically** /-brɪə'lɒdʒɪk(ə)li/ *adv.* **embryologist** *n.*

embus /ɪm'bʌs, ɛm-/ *v.* (**embused**, **embusing** or **embussed**, **embussing**) *Mil.* **1** *tr.* put (troops, equipment, etc.) into a motor vehicle. **2** *intr.* board a motor vehicle.

emcee /ɛm'siː/ *n.* & *v. colloq.* ● *n.* a master of ceremonies or compère. ● *v.tr.* & *intr.* (**emcees**, **emceed**) compère. [the letters *MC*]

em dash *n.* = EM RULE.

-eme /iːm/ *suffix Linguistics* forming nouns denoting units of structure etc. (*grapheme*; *morpheme*). [French *-ème* 'unit' from Greek *-ēma*]

emend /ɪ'mɛnd/ *v.tr.* edit (a text etc.) to remove errors and corruptions. □ **emendation** /iːmɛn'deɪʃ(ə)n/ *n.* **emendator** /'iːmɛndeɪtə/ *n.* **emendatory** *adj.* [Middle English from Latin *emendare* (as E-, *menda* 'fault')]

emerald /'ɛm(ə)r(ə)ld/ *n.* & *adj.* ● *n.* **1** a bright green precious stone, a variety of beryl. **2** (in full **emerald green**) the colour of this. **3** (in full **emerald moth**) any of several green geometrid moths. ● *adj.* (in full **emerald green**; hyphenated when *attrib.*) bright green. □ **emeraldine** /-dʌɪn, -dɪn/ *adj.* [Middle English from Old French *emeraude*, *esm-*, ultimately from Greek *smaragdos*]

Emerald Isle *n. literary* Ireland.

emerge /ɪ'məːdʒ/ *v.intr.* (often foll. by *from*) **1** come up or out into view, esp. when formerly concealed. **2** come up out of a liquid. **3** (of facts, circumstances, etc.) come to light, become known, esp. as a result of enquiry etc. **4** become recognized or prominent (*emerged as a leading contender*). **5** (of a question, difficulty, etc.) become apparent. **6** survive (an ordeal etc.) with a specified result (*emerged unscathed*). □ **emergence** *n.* [Latin *emergere emers-* (as E-, *mergere* 'dip')]

emergency /ɪ'məːdʒ(ə)nsi/ *n.* (*pl.* **-ies**) **1** a sudden state of danger, conflict, etc., requiring immediate action. **2 a** a medical condition requiring immediate treatment. **b** a patient with such a condition. **3** (*attrib.*) characterized by or for use in an emergency (*emergency exit*). **4** *Austral. Sport* a reserve player. [medieval Latin *emergentia* (as EMERGE)]

emergent /ɪ'məːdʒ(ə)nt/ *adj.* **1** becoming apparent; emerging. **2** (of a nation) newly formed or made independent.

emeritus /ɪ'mɛrɪtəs, iː-/ *adj.* **1** retired and retaining one's title as an honour (*emeritus professor*; *professor emeritus*). **2** honourably discharged from service. [Latin, past part. of *emerēri* (as E-, *merēri* 'earn')]

emerse /ɪ'məːs/ *adj. Bot.* (of part of an aquatic plant) reaching above the surface of the water (opp. SUBMERSE). □ **emersed** *adj.*

emersion /ɪ'məːʃ(ə)n, iː-/ *n.* **1** the act or an instance of emerging, esp. from water. **2** *Astron.* the reappearance of a celestial body after its eclipse or occultation. [Late Latin *emersio* (as EMERGE)]

emery /'ɛm(ə)ri/ *n.* **1** a coarse rock of corundum and magnetite or haematite used for polishing metal or other hard materials. **2** (*attrib.*) covered with emery. [French *émeri(l)* from Italian *smeriglio*, ultimately from Greek *smuris*, *smēris* 'polishing powder']

emery board *n.* a strip of thin wood or board coated with emery or another abrasive, used as a nail file.

emery paper *n.* (also **emery cloth**) paper or cloth covered with emery, used for polishing or cleaning metals etc.

emetic /ɪ'mɛtɪk/ *adj.* & *n.* ● *adj.* that causes vomiting. ● *n.* an emetic medicine. [Greek *emetikos* from *emeō* 'vomit']

EMF *abbr.* **1** (usu. **emf**) electromotive force. **2** electromagnetic field(s). **3** European Monetary Fund.

-emia *US* var. of -AEMIA.

emigrant /'ɛmɪgr(ə)nt/ *n.* & *adj.* ● *n.* a person who emigrates. ● *adj.* emigrating.

emigrate /'ɛmɪgreɪt/ *v.* **1** *intr.* leave one's own country to settle in another. **2** *tr.* assist (a person) to emigrate. □ **emigration** /-'greɪʃ(ə)n/ *n.* **emigratory** *adj.* [Latin *emigrare emigrat-* (as E-, *migrare* 'depart')]

émigré /'ɛmɪgreɪ/ *n.* (also **emigre**) an emigrant, esp. a political exile. [French, past part. of *émigrer* EMIGRATE]

eminence /'ɛmɪnəns/ *n.* **1** distinction; recognized superiority. **2** a piece of rising ground. **3** (**Eminence**) a title used in addressing or referring to a cardinal (*Your Eminence*; *His Eminence*). **4** an important person. [Latin *eminentia* (as EMINENT)]

éminence grise /ˌɛmɪnɒ̃s 'griːz, French ɛminɑ̃s griz/ *n.* (*pl.* ***éminences grises*** *pronunc.* same) **1** a person who exercises power or influence without holding office. **2** a confidential agent. [French, = grey eminence (see EMINENCE): originally applied to Cardinal Richelieu's grey-cloaked private secretary, Père Joseph (d. 1638)]

eminent /'ɛmɪnənt/ *adj.* **1** distinguished, notable. **2** (of qualities) remarkable in degree. □ **eminently** *adv.* [Middle English from Latin *eminēre eminent-* 'jut']

eminent domain *n.* sovereign control over all property in a state, with the right of expropriation.

emir /ɛ'mɪə/ *n.* **1** a title of various Muslim rulers. **2** *archaic* a male descendant of Muhammad. [French *émir* from Arabic *'amīr*: cf. AMIR]

emirate /'ɛmɪərət/ *n.* the rank, domain, or reign of an emir.

emissary /'ɛmɪs(ə)ri/ *n.* (*pl.* **-ies**) a person sent on a special mission (usu. diplomatic, formerly usu. odious or underhand). [Latin *emissarius* 'scout, spy' (as EMIT)]

emission /ɪ'mɪʃ(ə)n/ *n.* **1** (often foll. by *of*) the process or an act of emitting. **2** a thing emitted. [Latin *emissio* (as EMIT)]

emission spectrum *n.* a spectrum of the electromagnetic radiation emitted by a source.

emissive /ɪ'mɪsɪv/ *adj.* having the power to radiate light, heat, etc. ▫ **emissivity** /iːmɪ'sɪvɪti/ *n.*

emit /ɪ'mɪt/ *v.tr.* (**emitted**, **emitting**) **1 a** send out (heat, light, vapour, etc.). **b** discharge from the body. **2** utter (a cry etc.). [Latin *emittere emiss-* (as E-, *mittere* 'send')]

emitter /ɪ'mɪtə/ *n.* **1** a thing which emits something. **2** *Electronics* a region in a transistor producing carriers of current.

Emmental /'ɛməntɑːl/ *n.* (also **Emmenthal**) a kind of hard Swiss cheese with many holes in it, similar to Gruyère. [German *Emmentaler* from *Emmental*, a valley in Switzerland, where it is made]

emmer /'ɛmə/ *n.* a kind of wheat, *Triticum dicoccum*, grown mainly for fodder. [German from old High German *amer* 'spelt']

emmet /'ɛmɪt/ *n. archaic* or *dial.* an ant. [Old English *ǣmete*: see ANT]

Emmy /'ɛmi/ *n.* (*pl.* **Emmys**) (in the US) a statuette awarded annually to an outstanding television programme or performer. [perhaps from *Immy* = *image orthicon* (a kind of television camera tube)]

emollient /ɪ'mɒlɪənt/ *adj.* & *n.* ● *adj.* that softens or soothes the skin. ● *n.* an emollient agent. ▫ **emollience** *n.* [Latin *emollire* (as E-, *mollis* 'soft')]

emolument /ɪ'mɒljʊm(ə)nt, ɛ-/ *n.* a salary, fee, or profit from employment or office. [Middle English from Old French *emolument* or Latin *emolumentum*, originally probably 'payment for corn-grinding', from *emolere* (as E-, *molere* 'grind')]

emote /ɪ'məʊt/ *v.intr. colloq.* show excessive emotion. ▫ **emoter** *n.* [back-formation from EMOTION]

emotion /ɪ'məʊʃ(ə)n/ *n.* **1** a strong mental or instinctive feeling such as love or fear. **2** emotional intensity or sensibility (*he spoke with emotion*). ▫ **emotionless** *adj.* [earlier = agitation, disturbance of the mind, from French *émotion*, from *émouvoir* 'excite']

emotional /ɪ'məʊʃ(ə)n(ə)l/ *adj.* **1** of or relating to the emotions. **2** (of a person) easily affected by or readily displaying emotion. **3** expressing or based on emotion (*an emotional appeal*). **4** arousing emotion (*an emotional issue*). ▫ **emotionalism** *n.* **emotionalist** *n.* **emotionality** /-'nalɪti/ *n.* **emotionalize** *v.tr.* (also **-ise**). **emotionally** *adv.*

■ **Usage** See Usage Note at EMOTIVE.

emotive /ɪ'məʊtɪv/ *adj.* **1** of or characterized by emotion. **2** arousing emotion. **3** arousing feeling; not purely descriptive. ▫ **emotively** *adv.* **emotiveness** *n.* **emotivity** /iːməʊ'tɪvɪti/ *n.* [Latin *emovēre emot-* (as E-, *movēre* 'move')]

■ **Usage** Although the senses of *emotive* and *emotional* overlap, e.g. both *an emotive issue* and *an emotional issue* are common, *emotive* should not be used of people to mean 'emotional'. It is wrong to say *He is an emotive person* unless what is meant is that he arouses emotion in others, and it is similarly incorrect to say *They reacted emotively*.

empanel /ɪm'pan(ə)l, ɛm-/ *v.tr.* (also **impanel**) (**-panelled**, **-panelling**; *US* **-paneled**, **-paneling**) enrol or enter on a panel (those eligible for jury service). ▫ **empanelment** *n.* [Anglo-French *empaneller* (as EN-[1], PANEL)]

empathize /'ɛmpəθʌɪz/ *v.* (also **-ise**) *Psychol.* **1** *intr.* (usu. foll. by *with*) exercise empathy. **2** *tr.* treat with empathy.

empathy /'ɛmpəθi/ *n. Psychol.* the power of identifying oneself mentally with (and so fully comprehending) a person or object of contemplation. ▫ **empathetic** /-'θɛtɪk/ *adj.* **empathetically** /-'θɛtɪk(ə)li/ *adv.* **empathic** /ɛm'paθɪk/ *adj.* **empathically** /ɛm'paθ-/ *adv.* **empathist** *n.* [translation of German *Einfühlung* (from *ein* 'in' + *Fühlung* 'feeling'), on the pattern of Greek *empatheia*: see SYMPATHY]

empennage /ɛm'pɛnɪdʒ/ *n. Aeron.* an arrangement of stabilizing surfaces at the tail of an aircraft. [French, from *empenner* 'to feather' (an arrow)]

emperor /'ɛmp(ə)rə/ *n.* **1** the sovereign of an empire. **2** a sovereign of higher rank than a king. ▫ **emperorship** *n.* [Middle English via Old French *emperere, empereor* from Latin *imperator -oris*, from *imperare* 'command']

emperor moth *n.* a large moth, *Saturnia pavonia*, related to the silk moths, with eye-spots on all four wings.

emperor penguin *n.* the largest kind of penguin, *Aptenodytes forsteri*, of the Antarctic.

emphasis /'ɛmfəsɪs/ *n.* (*pl.* **emphases** /-siːz/) **1** special importance or prominence attached to a thing, fact, idea, etc. (*emphasis on economy*). **2** stress laid on a word or words to indicate special meaning or importance. **3** vigour or intensity of expression, feeling, action, etc. **4** prominence, sharpness of contour. [Latin from Greek, from *emphainō* 'exhibit' (as EN-[2], *phainō* 'show')]

emphasize /'ɛmfəsʌɪz/ *v.tr.* (also **-ise**) **1** bring (a thing, fact, etc.) into special prominence. **2** lay stress on (a word in speaking).

emphatic /ɪm'fatɪk, ɛm-/ *adj.* **1** (of language, tone, or gesture) forcibly expressive. **2** (of words): **a** bearing the stress. **b** used to give emphasis. **3** expressing oneself with emphasis. **4** (of an action or process) forcible, significant. ▫ **emphatically** *adv.* [Late Latin *emphaticus* from Greek *emphatikos* (as EMPHASIS)]

emphysema /ɛmfɪ'siːmə/ *n.* **1** enlargement of the air sacs of the lungs causing breathlessness. **2** a swelling caused by the presence of air in the connective tissues of the body. [Late Latin from Greek *emphusēma*, from *emphusaō* 'puff up']

empire /'ɛmpʌɪə/ *n.* **1** an extensive group of states or countries under a single supreme authority, esp. an emperor or empress. **2 a** supreme dominion. **b** (often foll. by *over*) *archaic* absolute control. **3** a large commercial organization etc. owned or directed by one person or group. **4** (**the Empire**) *hist.* **a** the British Empire. **b** the Holy Roman Empire. **5** a type or period of government in which the sovereign is called emperor or empress. **6** (**Empire**) (*attrib.*) **a** denoting a style of furniture or dress fashionable during the first (1804–14) or second (1852–70) French Empire. **b** *Brit.* denoting produce from the Commonwealth. [Middle English via Old French from Latin *imperium*, related to *imperare*: see EMPEROR]

empire builder *n.* a person who deliberately acquires extra territory, authority, etc., seeking power for its own sake. ▫ **empire building** *n.*

Empire Day *n. hist.* the former name of Commonwealth Day, originally 24 May.

empiric /ɛm'pɪrɪk, ɪm-/ *adj.* & *n.* ● *adj.* = EMPIRICAL. ● *n. archaic* **1** a person relying solely on experiment. **2** a quack doctor. [Latin *empiricus* from Greek *empeirikos*, from *empeiria* 'experience' from *empeiros* 'skilled']

empirical /ɛm'pɪrɪk(ə)l, ɪm-/ *adj.* **1** based or acting on observation or experiment, not on theory. **2** *Philos.* regarding sense data as valid information. **3** deriving knowledge from experience alone. ▫ **empirically** *adv.*

empirical formula *n.* a formula giving the proportions of the elements present in a compound but not the actual numbers or arrangement of atoms.

empiricism /ɛm'pɪrɪsɪz(ə)m/ *n. Philos.* the theory that all knowledge is derived from sense-experience. □ **empiricist** *n. & adj.*

emplacement /ɪm'pleɪsm(ə)nt, ɛm-/ *n.* **1** the act or an instance of putting in position. **2** a platform or defended position where a gun is placed for firing. **3** situation, position. [French (as EN-[1], PLACE)]

emplane /ɪm'pleɪn, ɛm-/ *v.intr. & tr.* (also **enplane** /ɪn-, ɛn-/) go or put on board an aeroplane.

employ /ɪm'plɔɪ, ɛm-/ *v. & n.* ● *v.tr.* **1** use the services of (a person) in return for payment; keep (a person) in one's service. **2** (often foll. by *for, in, on*) use (a thing, time, energy, etc.) esp. to good effect. **3** (often foll. by *in*) keep (a person) occupied. ● *n.* the state of being employed, esp. for wages. □ **in the employ of** employed by. □ **employable** *adj.* **employability** /-'bɪlɪti/ *n.* **employer** *n.* [Middle English from Old French *employer*, ultimately from Latin *implicari* 'be involved' from *implicare* 'enfold': see IMPLICATE]

employee /ɛmplɔɪ'iː, ɛm'plɔɪiː, ɪm-/ *n.* (*US* also **employe**) a person employed for wages or salary, esp. at non-executive level.

employment /ɪm'plɔɪm(ə)nt, ɛm-/ *n.* **1** the act of employing or the state of being employed. **2** a person's regular trade or profession.

employment agency *n.* a business that finds employers or employees for those seeking them.

employment office *n.* (formerly **employment exchange**) esp. *Brit.* any of a number of government offices concerned with advising and finding work for the unemployed.

empolder var. of IMPOLDER.

emporium /ɛm'pɔːrɪəm, ɪm-/ *n.* (*pl.* **emporia** /-rɪə/ or **-ums**) **1** a large retail store selling a wide variety of goods. **2** a centre of commerce, a market. [Latin from Greek *emporion*, from *emporos* 'merchant']

empower /ɪm'paʊə, ɛm-/ *v.tr.* (foll. by *to* + infin.) **1** authorize, license. **2** give power to; make able. □ **empowerment** *n.*

empress /'ɛmprɪs/ *n.* **1** the wife or widow of an emperor. **2** a woman emperor. [Middle English from Old French *emperesse*, fem. of *emperere* EMPEROR]

empty /'ɛm(p)ti/ *adj., v., & n.* ● *adj.* (**emptier, emptiest**) **1** containing nothing. **2** (of a house etc.) unoccupied or unfurnished. **3** (of a transport vehicle etc.) without a load, passengers, etc. **4 a** meaningless, hollow, insincere (*empty threats; an empty gesture*). **b** without substance or purpose (*an empty existence*). **5** *colloq.* hungry. **6** (foll. by *of*) devoid, lacking. ● *v.* (**-ies, -ied**) **1** *tr.* **a** make empty; remove the contents of. **b** (foll. by *of*) deprive of certain contents (*emptied the room of its chairs*). **2** *tr.* (often foll. by *into*) transfer (the contents of a container). **3** *intr.* become empty. **4** *intr.* (usu. foll. by *into*) (of a river) discharge itself (into the sea etc.). ● *n.* (*pl.* **-ies**) *colloq.* a container (esp. a bottle) left empty of its contents. □ **on an empty stomach** see STOMACH. □ **emptily** *adv.* **emptiness** *n.* [Old English *ǣmtig, ǣmetig*, from *ǣmetta* 'leisure']

empty-handed *adj.* (usu. *predic.*) **1** bringing or taking nothing. **2** having achieved or obtained nothing.

empty-headed *adj.* foolish; lacking common sense.

empty-nester *n.* esp. *N. Amer.* either of a couple whose children have grown up and left home.

empurple /ɪm'pəːp(ə)l, ɛm-/ *v.tr.* **1** make purple or red. **2** make angry.

empyema /ɛmpʌɪ'iːmə/ *n. Med.* a collection of pus in a cavity, esp. in the pleura. [Late Latin from Greek *empuēma*, from *empueō* 'suppurate' (as EN-[2], *puon* 'pus')]

empyrean /ɛmpʌɪ'riːən, -pɪ-, ɛm'pɪrɪən/ *n. & adj.* ● *n.* **1** the highest heaven, as the sphere of fire in ancient cosmology or as the abode of God in early Christianity. **2** *poet.* the visible heavens. ● *adj.* of the empyrean. □ **empyreal** /ɛmpʌɪ'riːəl, -pɪ-, ɛm'pɪrɪəl/ *adj.* [medieval Latin *empyreus* from Greek *empurios* (as EN-[2], *pur* 'fire')]

em rule *n. Brit.* a long dash used in punctuation.

EMS *abbr.* European Monetary System.

EMU /iːɛm'juː, 'iːmjuː/ *abbr.* economic and monetary union (of the EC); European monetary union.

emu /'iːmjuː/ *n.* a large flightless bird, *Dromaius novaehollandiae*, native to Australia, and capable of running at high speed. [earlier *emia, eme*, from Portuguese *ema*]

e.m.u. *abbr.* electromagnetic unit(s).

emulate /'ɛmjʊleɪt/ *v.tr.* **1** try to equal or excel. **2** imitate zealously. **3** rival. **4** *Computing* reproduce the function or action of (a different computer or software system). □ **emulation** /-'leɪʃ(ə)n/ *n.* **emulative** /-lətɪv/ *adj.* **emulator** *n.* [Latin *aemulari* (as EMULOUS)]

emulous /'ɛmjʊləs/ *adj.* **1** (usu. foll. by *of*) seeking to emulate. **2** actuated by a spirit of rivalry. □ **emulously** *adv.* [Middle English from Latin *aemulus* 'rival']

emulsifier /ɪ'mʌlsɪfʌɪə/ *n.* **1** any substance that stabilizes an emulsion, esp. a food additive used to stabilize processed foods. **2** an apparatus used for producing an emulsion.

emulsify /ɪ'mʌlsɪfʌɪ/ *v.tr.* (**-ies, -ied**) convert into an emulsion. □ **emulsifiable** *adj.* **emulsification** /-fɪ'keɪʃ(ə)n/ *n.*

emulsion /ɪ'mʌlʃ(ə)n/ *n. & v.* ● *n.* **1** a fine dispersion of one liquid in another, esp. as paint, medicine, etc. **2** a mixture of a silver compound suspended in gelatin etc. for coating photographic plates or films. **3** *Brit.* = EMULSION PAINT. ● *v.tr. Brit.* paint with emulsion paint. □ **emulsionize** *v.tr.* (also **-ise**). **emulsive** *adj.* [French *émulsion* or modern Latin *emulsio*, from *emulgēre* (as E-, *mulgēre muls-* 'to milk')]

emulsion paint *n.* a paint consisting of pigment bound in a synthetic resin which forms an emulsion with water.

en /ɛn/ *n. Printing* a unit of measurement equal to half an em. [name of the letter *N*]

en-[1] /ɪn, ɛn/ *prefix* (also **em-** before *b, p*) forming verbs, = IN-[1]: **1** from nouns, meaning 'put into or on' (*engulf; entrust; embed*). **2** from nouns or adjectives, meaning 'bring into the condition of' (*enslave*); often with the suffix *-en* (*enlighten*). **3** from verbs: **a** in the sense 'in, into, on' (*enfold*). **b** as an intensive (*entangle*). [from or suggested by French *en-* from Latin *in-*]

en-[2] /ɪn, ɛn/ *prefix* (also **em-** before *b, p*) in, inside (*energy; enthusiasm*). [Greek]

-en[1] /(ə)n/ *suffix* forming verbs: **1** from adjectives, usu. meaning 'make or become so or more so' (*deepen; fasten; moisten*). **2** from nouns (*happen; strengthen*). [Old English *-nian*, from Germanic]

-en[2] /(ə)n/ *suffix* (also **-n**) forming adjectives from nouns, meaning: **1** made or consisting of (often with extended and figurative senses) (*wooden*). **2** resembling; of the nature of (*golden; silvern*). [Old English from Germanic]

-en[3] /(ə)n/ *suffix* (also **-n**) forming past participles of strong verbs: **1** as a regular inflection (*spoken; sworn*). **2** with restricted sense (*drunken*). [Old English from Germanic]

-en[4] /(ə)n/ *suffix* forming the plural of a few nouns (*children; brethren; oxen*). [Middle English reduction of Old English *-an*]

-en[5] /ɪn, (ə)n/ *suffix* forming diminutives of nouns (*chicken; maiden*). [Old English from Germanic]

-en[6] /(ə)n/ *suffix* **1** forming feminine nouns (*vixen*). **2** forming abstract nouns (*burden*). [Old English from Germanic]

enable /ɪn'eɪb(ə)l, ɛn-/ *v.tr.* **1** (foll. by *to* + infin.) give (a person etc.) the means or authority to do something. **2** make possible. **3** esp. *Computing* make (a device) operational; switch on. □ **enablement** *n.* **enabler** *n.*

enabling act *n.* a statute empowering a person or body to take certain action.

enact /ɪ'nakt, ɛ-/ *v.tr.* **1 a** (often foll. by *that* + clause) ordain, decree. **b** make (a bill etc.) law. **2** play (a part or scene on stage or in life). □ **enactable** *adj.* **enaction** *n.* **enactive** *adj.* **enactor** *n.*

enactment /ɪ'naktm(ə)nt, ɛ-/ *n.* **1** a law enacted. **2** the process of enacting.

enamel /ɪ'nam(ə)l/ *n. & v.* ● *n.* **1** a glasslike opaque or semi-transparent coating on metallic or other hard surfaces for ornament or as a preservative lining. **2 a** a smooth hard coating. **b** = ENAMEL PAINT. **c** a cosmetic simulating this. **3** the hard glossy natural coating over the crown of a tooth. **4** a work of art done in enamel. **5** *poet.* a smooth bright surface colouring, verdure, etc. ● *v.tr.* (**enamelled**, **enamelling**; *US* **enameled**, **enameling**) **1** inlay or encrust (a metal etc.) with enamel. **2** portray (figures etc.) with enamel. **3** *archaic* adorn with varied colours. □ **enameller** *n.* **enamelwork** *n.* [Middle English from Anglo-French *enameler, enamailler* (as EN-[1], Old French *esmail*, from Germanic)]

enamel paint *n.* a paint that dries to give a smooth hard coat.

enamelware /ɪ'nam(ə)lwɛː/ *n.* enamelled kitchenware.

enamour /ɪ'namə, ɛ-/ *v.tr.* (*US* **enamor**) (usu. in *passive*; foll. by *of*) **1** inspire with love or liking. **2** charm, delight. [Middle English from Old French *enamourer*, from *amourer* (as EN-[1], AMOUR)]

enanthema /ɛnən'θiːmə/ *n. Med.* an ulcer etc. occurring on a mucus-secreting surface such as the inside of the mouth. [modern Latin from Greek *enanthēma* 'eruption' (as EN-[1], EXANTHEMA)]

enantiomer /ɪ'nantɪə(ʊ)mə, ɛ-/ *n. Chem.* a molecule that is the mirror image of another; an optical isomer. □ **enantiomeric** /-'mɛrɪk/ *adj.* [Greek *enantios* 'opposite' + -MER]

enantiomorph /ɪ'nantɪə(ʊ)mɔːf, ɛ-/ *n.* a mirror image; a form (esp. of a crystal structure etc.) related to another as an object is to its mirror image. □ **enantiomorphic** /-'mɔːfɪk/ *adj.* **enantiomorphism** /-'mɔːfɪz(ə)m/ *n.* **enantiomorphous** /-'mɔːfəs/ *adj.* [German, from Greek *enantios* 'opposite' + *morphē* 'form']

enarthrosis /ɛnɑː'θrəʊsɪs/ *n.* (*pl.* **enarthroses** /-siːz/) *Anat.* a ball-and-socket joint. [Greek, from *enarthros* 'jointed' (as EN-[2], *arthron* 'joint')]

en bloc /ɒ̃ 'blɒk/ *adv.* in a block; all at the same time; wholesale. [French]

en brosse /ɒ̃ 'brɒs, French ɑ̃ brɔs/ *adj.* (of hair) cut short and bristly. [French]

enc. var. of ENCL.

encaenia /ɛn'siːnɪə/ *n.* **1** (at Oxford University) an annual celebration in memory of founders and benefactors. **2** a dedication festival. [Latin from Greek *egkainia* (as EN-[2], *kainos* 'new')]

encage /ɪn'keɪdʒ, ɛn-/ *v.tr.* confine in or as in a cage.

encamp /ɪn'kamp, ɛn-/ *v.tr. & intr.* **1** settle in a military camp. **2** lodge in the open in tents.

encampment /ɪn'kampm(ə)nt, ɛn-/ *n.* **1** a place where troops etc. are encamped. **2** the process of setting up a camp.

encapsulate /ɪn'kapsjʊleɪt, ɛn-/ *v.tr.* **1** enclose in or as in a capsule. **2** summarize; express the essential features of. **3** isolate. □ **encapsulation** /-'leɪʃ(ə)n/ *n.* [EN-[1] + Latin *capsula* CAPSULE]

encase /ɪn'keɪs, ɛn-/ *v.tr.* (also **incase**) **1** put into a case. **2** surround as with a case. □ **encasement** *n.*

encash /ɪn'kaʃ, ɛn-/ *v.tr. Brit.* **1** convert (bills etc.) into cash. **2** receive in the form of cash; realize. □ **encashable** *adj.* **encashment** *n.*

encaustic /ɛn'kɔːstɪk/ *adj. & n.* ● *adj.* **1** (in painting, ceramics, etc.) using pigments mixed with hot wax, which are burned in as an inlay. **2** (of bricks and tiles) inlaid with differently coloured clays burnt in. ● *n.* **1** the art of encaustic painting. **2** a painting done with this technique. [Latin *encausticus* from Greek *egkaustikos* (as EN-[2], CAUSTIC)]

-ence /(ə)ns/ *suffix* forming nouns expressing: **1** a quality or state or an instance of one (*patience*; *an impertinence*). **2** an action (*reference*; *reminiscence*). [from or suggested by French *-ence*, from Latin *-entia*, *-antia* (cf. -ANCE) from pres. part. stem *-ent-*, *-ant-*]

enceinte /ɒ̃'sãt/ *n. & adj.* ● *n.* an enclosure, esp. in fortification. ● *adj. archaic* pregnant. [French, ultimately from Latin *cingere cinct-* 'gird': see CINCTURE]

encephalic /ɛnsɪ'falɪk, ɛn'kɛf(ə)lɪk/ *adj.* of or relating to the brain. [Greek *egkephalos* 'brain' (as ENCEPHALO-)]

encephalin var. of ENKEPHALIN.

encephalitis /ɛn,sɛfə'lʌɪtɪs, -,kɛf-/ *n.* inflammation of the brain. □ **encephalitic** /-'lɪtɪk/ *adj.*

encephalitis lethargica /lɪ'θɑːdʒɪkə/ *n.* an infectious encephalitis caused by a virus, with headache and drowsiness leading to coma; sleepy sickness.

encephalo- /ɛn'sɛf(ə)ləʊ, ɛn'kɛf-/ *comb. form* brain. [Greek *egkephalos* 'brain' (as EN-[2], *kephalē* 'head')]

encephalogram /ɛn'sɛf(ə)lə(ʊ)gram, ɛn'kɛf-/ *n.* an X-ray photograph of the brain.

encephalograph /ɛn'sɛf(ə)lə(ʊ)grɑːf, ɛn'kɛf-/ *n.* an instrument for recording the electrical activity of the brain.

encephalomyelitis /ɛn,sɛf(ə)ləʊmʌɪə'lʌɪtɪs, ɛn,kɛf-/ *n.* inflammation of the brain and spinal cord, esp. due to viral infection.

encephalon /ɛn'sɛfəlɒn, -'kɛf-/ *n. Anat.* the brain.

encephalopathy /ɛn,sɛfə'lɒpəθi, ɛn,kɛf-/ *n.* (*pl.* **-ies**) a disease of the brain.

enchain /ɪn'tʃeɪn, ɛn-/ *v.tr.* **1** chain up, fetter. **2** hold fast (the attention, emotions, etc.). □ **enchainment** *n.* [Middle English from French *enchaîner*, ultimately from Latin *catena* 'chain']

enchant /ɪn'tʃɑːnt, ɛn-/ *v.tr.* **1** charm, delight. **2** bewitch. □ **enchantedly** *adv.* **enchanting** *adj.* **enchantingly** *adv.* **enchantment** *n.* [Middle English via French *enchanter* from Latin *incantare* (as IN-[2], *canere cant-* 'sing')]

enchanter /ɪn'tʃɑːntə, ɛn-/ *n.* (*fem.* **enchantress**/-trɪs/) a person who enchants, esp. by supposed use of magic.

enchanter's nightshade *n.* a small plant, *Circaea lutetiana*, with white flowers.

enchase /ɪn'tʃeɪs, ɛn-/ *v.tr.* **1** (foll. by *in*) place (a jewel) in a setting. **2** (foll. by *with*) set (gold etc.) with gems. **3** inlay with gold etc. **4** adorn with figures in relief. **5** engrave. [Middle English from French *enchâsser* (as EN-[1], CHASE[2])]

enchilada /ɛntʃɪ'lɑːdə/ *n.* a tortilla with chilli sauce and usu. a filling, esp. meat. [Latin American Spanish, fem. past part. of *enchilar* 'season with chilli']

enchiridion /ɛnkʌɪ'rɪdɪən/ *n.* (*pl.* **enchiridions** or **enchiridia** /-dɪə/) *formal* a handbook. [Late Latin from Greek *egkheiridion* (as EN-[2], *kheir* 'hand', diminutive suffix *-idion*)]

encipher /ɪn'sʌɪfə, ɛn-/ *v.tr.* **1** write (a message etc.) in cipher. **2** convert into coded form using a cipher. □ **encipherment** *n.*

encircle /ɪn'səːk(ə)l, ɛn-/ *v.tr.* **1** (usu. foll. by *with*) surround, encompass. **2** form a circle round. □ **encirclement** *n.*

encl. *abbr.* (also **enc.**) **1** enclosed. **2** enclosure.

en clair /ɒ̃ 'klɛː, French ɑ̃ klɛr/ *adj. & adv.* (of a telegram, official message, etc.) in ordinary language (not in code or cipher). [French, literally 'in clear']

enclasp /ɪn'klɑːsp, ɛn-/ *v.tr.* hold in a clasp or embrace.

enclave /'ɛnkleɪv/ *n.* **1** a portion of territory of one state surrounded by territory of another or others, as viewed by the surrounding territory (cf. EXCLAVE). **2** a group of people who are culturally, intellectually, or socially distinct from those surrounding them. [French from *enclaver* 'enclose, dovetail', ultimately from Latin *clavis* 'key']

enclitic /ɪn'klɪtɪk, ɛn-/ *adj. & n. Gram.* ● *adj.* (of a word) pronounced with so little emphasis that it forms part of the preceding word. ● *n.* such a word, e.g. *not* in *cannot*. □ **enclitically** *adv.* [Late Latin *encliticus* from Greek *egklitikos* (as EN-[2], *klinō* 'lean')]

enclose /ɪn'kləʊz, ɛn-/ *v.tr.* (also **inclose**) **1** (often foll. by *with, in*) **a** surround with a wall, fence, etc. **b** shut in on all sides. **2** fence in (common land) so as to make it private property. **3** put in a receptacle (esp. in an envelope together with a letter). **4** (usu. as **enclosed** *adj.*) seclude (a religious community) from the outside world. **5** esp. *Math.* bound on all sides; contain. **6** hem in on all sides. [Middle English from Old French *enclos*, past part. of *enclore*, ultimately from Latin *includere* (as INCLUDE)]

enclosure /ɪn'kləʊʒə, ɛn-/ *n.* (also **inclosure**) **1** the act of enclosing, esp. of common land. **2** *Brit.* an enclosed space or area, esp. for a special class of persons at a sporting event. **3** a thing enclosed with a letter. **4** an enclosing fence etc. [Anglo-French & Old French (as ENCLOSE)]

encode /ɪn'kəʊd, ɛn-/ *v.tr.* put (a message etc.) into code or cipher. □ **encoder** *n.*

encomiast /ɛn'kəʊmɪast/ *n.* **1** the composer of an encomium. **2** a flatterer. □ **encomiastic** /-'astɪk/ *adj.* [Greek *egkōmiastēs* (as ENCOMIUM)]

encomium /ɛn'kəʊmɪəm/ *n.* (*pl.* **encomiums** or **encomia** /-mɪə/) a formal or high-flown expression of praise. [Latin from Greek *egkōmion* (as EN-², *kōmos* 'revelry')]

encompass /ɪn'kʌmpəs, ɛn-/ *v.tr.* **1** surround or form a circle about, esp. to protect or attack. **2** contain. □ **encompassment** *n.*

encore /'ɒŋkɔː/ *n.*, *v.*, & *int.* ● *n.* **1** a call by an audience or spectators for the repetition of an item, or for a further item. **2** such an item. ● *v.tr.* **1** call for the repetition of (an item). **2** call back (a performer) for this. ● *int.* /also -'kɔː/ again, once more. [French, = again]

encounter /ɪn'kaʊntə, ɛn-/ *v.* & *n.* ● *v.tr.* **1** meet by chance or unexpectedly. **2** meet as an adversary. ● *n.* **1** a meeting by chance. **2** a meeting in conflict. **3** participation in an encounter group. [Middle English from Old French *encontrer*, *encontre*, ultimately from Latin *contra* 'against']

encounter group *n.* a group of persons seeking psychological benefit through close contact with one another.

encourage /ɪn'kʌrɪdʒ, ɛn-/ *v.tr.* **1** give courage, confidence, or hope to. **2** (foll. by *to* + infin.) urge, advise. **3** stimulate by help, reward, etc. **4** promote or assist (an enterprise, opinion, etc.). □ **encouragement** *n.* **encourager** *n.* **encouraging** *adj.* **encouragingly** *adv.* [Middle English from French *encourager* (as EN-¹, COURAGE)]

encroach /ɪn'krəʊtʃ, ɛn-/ *v.intr.* **1** (foll. by *on*, *upon*) intrude, esp. on another's territory or rights. **2** advance gradually beyond due limits. □ **encroacher** *n.* **encroachment** *n.* [Middle English from Old French *encrochier* 'seize, fasten upon' (as EN-¹, *crochier* from *croc* 'hook': see CROOK)]

encrust /ɪn'krʌst, ɛn-/ *v.* (also **incrust**) **1** *tr.* cover with a crust. **2** *tr.* overlay with an ornamental crust of precious material. **3** *intr.* form a crust. □ **encrustment** *n.* [French *incruster* from Latin *incrustare* (as IN-², *crustare* from *crusta* CRUST)]

encrustation var. of INCRUSTATION.

encrypt /ɛn'krɪpt/ *v.tr.* **1** convert (data) into code, esp. to prevent unauthorized access. **2** conceal by this means. □ **encryption** *n.* [EN-¹ + Greek *kruptos* 'hidden']

encumber /ɪn'kʌmbə, ɛn-/ *v.tr.* **1** be a burden to; hamper, impede. **2** burden (a person or estate) with debts, esp. mortgages. **3** fill or block (a place) esp. with lumber. [Middle English via Old French *encombrer* 'block up' from Romanic]

encumbrance /ɪn'kʌmbr(ə)ns, ɛn-/ *n.* **1** a burden; an impediment; an annoyance. **2** *Law* a mortgage or other charge on property. □ **without encumbrance** *archaic* having no children. [Middle English from Old French *encombrance* (as ENCUMBER)]

-ency /(ə)nsi/ *suffix* forming nouns denoting a quality (*efficiency*; *fluency*) or state (*presidency*) but not action (cf. -ENCE). [Latin *-entia* (cf. -ANCY)]

encyclical /ɛn'sɪklɪk(ə)l, ɪn-, -'sʌɪk-/ *n.* & *adj.* ● *n.* a papal letter sent to all bishops of the Roman Catholic Church. ● *adj.* (of a letter) for wide circulation. [Late Latin *encyclicus* from Greek *egkuklios* (as EN-², *kuklos* 'circle')]

encyclopedia /ɛn,sʌɪklə(ʊ)'piːdɪə, ɪn-/ *n.* (also **encyclopaedia**) a book, often in several volumes, giving information on many subjects, or on many aspects of one subject, usu. arranged alphabetically. [modern Latin, from spurious Greek *egkuklopaideia* for *egkuklios paideia* 'all-round education': cf. ENCYCLICAL]

encyclopedic /ɛn,sʌɪklə(ʊ)'piːdɪk, ɪn-/ *adj.* (also **encyclopaedic**) (of knowledge or information) comprehensive.

encyclopedism /ɛn,sʌɪklə(ʊ)'piːdɪz(ə)m, ɪn-/ *n.* (also **encyclopaedism**) encyclopedic learning.

encyclopedist /ɛn,sʌɪklə(ʊ)'piːdɪst, ɪn-/ *n.* (also **encyclopaedist**) a person who writes, edits, or contributes to an encyclopedia.

encyst /ɪn'sɪst, ɛn-/ *v.tr.* & *intr.* *Biol.* enclose or become enclosed in a cyst. □ **encystation** /-'teɪʃ(ə)n/ *n.* **encystment** *n.*

end /ɛnd/ *n.* & *v.* ● *n.* **1 a** the extreme limit; the point beyond which a thing does not continue. **b** an extremity of a line, or of the greatest dimension of an object. **c** the furthest point (*to the ends of the earth*). **2** the surface bounding a thing at either extremity; an extreme part (*a strip of wood with a nail in one end*). **3 a** conclusion, finish (*no end to his misery*). **b** the latter or final part. **c** death, destruction, downfall (*met an untimely end*). **d** result, outcome. **e** an ultimate state or condition. **4 a** a thing one seeks to attain; a purpose (*will do anything to achieve his ends*; *to what end?*). **b** the object for which a thing exists. **5** a remnant; a piece left over (*cigarette end*). **6** (prec. by *the*) *colloq.* the limit of endurability. **7** the half of a sports pitch or court occupied by one team or player. **8** the part or share with which a person is concerned (*no problem at my end*). **9** *Bowls* a unit of play in which play is from one side of the green towards the other. **10** *Amer. Football* a player positioned nearest the sideline along the line of scrimmage. ● *v.* **1** *tr.* & *intr.* bring or come to an end. **2** *tr.* put an end to; destroy. **3** *intr.* (foll. by *in*) have as its result (*will end in tears*). **4** *intr.* (foll. by *by*) do or achieve eventually (*ended by marrying an heiress*). □ **all ends up** completely. **at an end** exhausted or completed. **at the end of one's tether** see TETHER. **come to a bad** (or **sticky**) **end** meet with ruin or disgrace. **come to an end 1** be completed or finished. **2** become exhausted. **end it all** (or **end it**) *colloq.* commit suicide. **end of the road** the point at which a hope or endeavour has to be abandoned. **end of the world** the cessation of mortal life. **end on** with the end facing one, or with the end adjoining the end of the next object. **end to end** with the end of each of a series adjoining the end of the next. **end up** reach a specified state, action, or place eventually (*ended up a drunkard*; *ended up making a fortune*). **in the end** finally; after all. **keep one's end up** do one's part despite difficulties. **make an end of** put a stop to. **make ends** (or **both ends**) **meet** live within one's income. **no end** *colloq.* to a great extent, very much. **no end of** *colloq.* much or many of. **on end 1** upright (*hair stood on end*). **2** continuously (*for three weeks on end*). **put an end to 1** stop (an activity etc.). **2** abolish, destroy. [Old English *ende*, *endian*, from Germanic]

-end /ɛnd/ *suffix* forming nouns in the sense 'person or thing to be treated in a specified way' (*dividend*; *reverend*). [Latin gerundive ending *-endus*]

endanger /ɪn'deɪn(d)ʒə, ɛn-/ *v.tr.* place in danger. □ **endangerment** *n.*

endangered species *n.* a species in danger of extinction.

end-around *n.* & *adj.* ● *n.* *Amer. Football* an offensive play in which an end carries the ball round the opposite end. ● *adj.* *Computing* involving the transfer of a digit from one end of a register to the other.

en dash *n.* = EN RULE.

endear /ɪn'dɪə, ɛn-/ *v.tr.* (usu. foll. by *to*) make dear to or beloved by.

endearing /ɪn'dɪərɪŋ, ɛn-/ *adj.* inspiring affection. □ **endearingly** *adv.*

endearment /ɪn'dɪəm(ə)nt, ɛn-/ *n.* **1** an expression of affection. **2** liking, affection.

endeavour /ɪn'dɛvə, ɛn-/ *v. & n.* (*US* **endeavor**) ● *v.intr.* **1** (foll. by *to* + infin.) try earnestly. **2** (foll. by *after*) *archaic* strive. ● *n.* (often foll. by *at*, or *to* + infin.) effort directed towards a goal; an earnest attempt. [Middle English from *put oneself in devoir* 'do one's utmost': see DEVOIR]

endemic /ɛn'dɛmɪk/ *adj. & n.* ● *adj.* (often foll. by *to*) regularly or only found among a particular people or in a certain region. ● *n.* an endemic disease or plant. □ **endemically** *adv.* **endemicity** /ɛndɪ'mɪsɪti/ *n.* **endemism** /'ɛndɪmɪz(ə)m/ *n.* [French *endémique* or modern Latin *endemicus* from Greek *endēmos* 'native' (as EN-[2], *dēmos* 'the people')]

endermic /ɛn'də:mɪk/ *adj.* acting on or through the skin. □ **endermically** *adv.* [EN-[2] + Greek *derma* 'skin']

endgame /'ɛn(d)geɪm/ *n.* the final stage of a game (esp. chess), when few pieces remain.

ending /'ɛndɪŋ/ *n.* **1** an end or final part, esp. of a story. **2** an inflected final part of a word. [Old English (as END, -ING[1])]

endive /'ɛndʌɪv, -dɪv/ *n.* **1** (in full **curly endive**) a curly-leaved plant, *Cichorium endivia*, used in salads. **2** *N. Amer.* a chicory crown. [Middle English via Old French from Late Latin *endivia*, ultimately from Greek *entubon*]

endless /'ɛndlɪs/ *adj.* **1** infinite; without end; eternal. **2** continual, incessant (*tired of their endless complaints*). **3** *colloq.* innumerable. **4** (of a belt, chain, etc.) having the ends joined for continuous action over wheels etc. □ **endlessly** *adv.* **endlessness** *n.* [Old English *endelēas* (as END, -LESS)]

endless screw *n.* = WORM *n.* 7b.

endmost /'ɛn(d)məʊst/ *adj.* nearest the end.

endnote /'ɛn(d)nəʊt/ *n.* a note printed at the end of a book or section of a book.

endo- /'ɛndəʊ/ *prefix* internal. [Greek *endon* 'within']

endocarditis /,ɛndəʊkɑ:'dʌɪtɪs/ *n.* inflammation of the endocardium. □ **endocarditic** /-'dɪtɪk/ *adj.*

endocardium /ɛndəʊ'kɑ:dɪəm/ *n.* the lining membrane of the heart. [ENDO- + Greek *kardia* 'heart']

endocarp /'ɛndə(ʊ)kɑ:p/ *n.* the innermost layer of the pericarp. □ **endocarpic** /-'kɑ:pɪk/ *adj.* [ENDO- + PERICARP]

endocrine /'ɛndə(ʊ)krʌɪn, -krɪn/ *adj.* (of a gland) secreting directly into the blood; ductless. [ENDO- + Greek *krinō* 'sift']

endocrinology /,ɛndəʊkrɪ'nɒlədʒi/ *n.* the study of the structure and physiology of endocrine glands. □ **endocrinological** /-nə'lɒdʒɪk(ə)l/ *adj.* **endocrinologist** *n.*

endoderm /'ɛndə(ʊ)də:m/ *n.* the innermost layer of cells or tissue of an embryo in early development. □ **endodermal** /-'də:m(ə)l/ *adj.* [ENDO- + Greek *derma* 'skin']

endogamy /ɛn'dɒgəmi/ *n.* **1** *Anthropol.* marrying within the same tribe. **2** *Bot.* pollination from the same plant. □ **endogamous** *adj.* [ENDO- + Greek *gamos* 'marriage']

endogenous /ɛn'dɒdʒɪnəs, ɪn-/ *adj.* growing or originating from within. □ **endogenesis** /ɛndə(ʊ)'dʒɛnɪsɪs/ *n.* **endogeny** /ɛn'dɒdʒɪmi/ *n.*

endolymph /'ɛndəʊlɪmf/ *n.* the fluid in the membranous labyrinth of the ear.

endometriosis /,ɛndə(ʊ)mi:trɪ'əʊsɪs/ *n.* the appearance of endometrial tissue outside the womb.

endometrium /ɛndə(ʊ)'mi:trɪəm/ *n.* *Anat.* the membrane lining the womb. □ **endometrial** /ɛndə(ʊ)'mi:trɪəl/ *adj.* [ENDO- + Greek *mētra* 'womb']

endomorph /'ɛndə(ʊ)mɔ:f/ *n.* **1** a person with a soft round build of body and a high proportion of fat tissue (cf. ECTOMORPH, MESOMORPH). **2** *Mineral.* a mineral enclosed within another. □ **endomorphic** /-'mɔ:fɪk/ *adj.* **endomorphy** *n.* [ENDO- + Greek *morphē* 'form']

endoparasite /ɛndəʊ'parəsʌɪt/ *n.* a parasite that lives on the inside of its host. Also called *entoparasite.*

endoplasm /'ɛndə(ʊ)plaz(ə)m/ *n.* the more fluid granular inner layer of the cytoplasm in some protozoans (cf. ECTOPLASM 1).

endoplasmic reticulum /ɛndəʊ'plazmɪk/ *n.* *Biol.* a network of membranous tubules within the cytoplasm of a eukaryotic cell, continuous with the nuclear membrane and usu. having ribosomes attached.

endorphin /ɛn'dɔ:fɪn/ *n.* *Biochem.* any of a group of peptide neurotransmitters occurring naturally in the brain and having pain-relieving properties. [French *endorphine*, from *endogène* 'endogenous' + MORPHINE]

endorse /ɪn'dɔ:s, ɛn-/ *v.tr.* (also **indorse**) **1 a** confirm (a statement or opinion). **b** declare one's approval of. **2** sign or write on the back of (a document), esp. the back of (a bill, cheque, etc.) as the payee or to specify another as payee. **3** write (an explanation or comment) on the back of a document. **4** *Brit.* enter details of a conviction for a motoring offence on (a driving licence). □ **endorsable** *adj.* **endorsee** /ɛndɔ:'si:/ *n.* **endorser** *n.* [medieval Latin *indorsare* (as IN-[2], Latin *dorsum* 'back')]

endorsement /ɪn'dɔ:sm(ə)nt, ɛn-/ *n.* (also **indorsement**) **1** the act or an instance of endorsing. **2** something with which a document etc. is endorsed, esp. a signature. **3** a record in a driving licence of a conviction for a motoring offence. **4** a recommendation of a product which can be cited in advertising material.

endoscope /'ɛndəskəʊp/ *n.* *Surgery* an instrument for viewing the internal parts of the body. □ **endoscopic** /-'skɒpɪk/ *adj.* **endoscopically** /-'skɒpɪk(ə)li/ *adv.* **endoscopist** /ɛn'dɒskəpɪst/ *n.* **endoscopy** /ɛn'dɒskəpi/ *n.*

endoskeleton /'ɛndəʊ,skɛlɪt(ə)n/ *n.* an internal skeleton, as found in vertebrates, echinoderms, etc.

endosperm /'ɛndə(ʊ)spə:m/ *n.* albumen enclosed with the germ in seeds.

endospore /'ɛndə(ʊ)spɔ:/ *n.* **1** a spore formed by certain bacteria. **2** the inner coat of a spore.

endothelium /ɛndə(ʊ)'θi:lɪəm/ *n.* *Anat.* a layer of cells lining the blood vessels, heart, and lymphatic vessels. □ **endothelial** *adj.* [ENDO- + Greek *thēlē* 'teat']

endothermic /ɛndəʊ'θə:mɪk/ *adj.* **1** *Chem.* occurring or formed with the absorption of heat. **2** *Zool.* dependent on or capable of internal generation of heat. □ **endothermy** *n.* (in sense 2).

endotoxin /'ɛndəʊ,tɒksɪn/ *n.* a toxin present inside a bacterial cell and released when it disintegrates.

endow /ɪn'daʊ, ɛn-/ *v.tr.* **1** bequeath or give a permanent income to (a person, institution, etc.). **2** (esp. as **endowed** *adj.*) (usu. foll. by *with*) invest or provide (a person or thing) with a talent, ability, quality, etc. □ **endower** *n.* [Middle English from Anglo-French *endouer* (as EN-[1], Old French *douer* ultimately from Latin *dos dotis* DOWER)]

endowment /ɪn'daʊm(ə)nt, ɛn-/ *n.* **1** the act or an instance of endowing. **2** assets, esp. property or income with which a person or body is endowed. **3** (usu. in *pl.*) skill, talent, etc., with which a person is endowed. **4** (*attrib.*) denoting forms of insurance involving payment by the insurer of a sum on a specified date, or on the death of the insured person if earlier.

endowment mortgage *n.* *Brit.* a mortgage linked to endowment insurance of the mortgagor's life, the capital being repaid from the sum insured.

endpaper /'ɛn(d)peɪpə/ *n.* a usu. blank leaf of paper at the beginning and end of a book, fixed to the inside of the cover.

end-play *n.* *Bridge* a method of play in the last few tricks to force an opponent to make a disadvantageous lead.

end point *n.* the final stage of a process, esp. the point at which an effect is observed in titration, dilution, etc.

end product *n.* the final product of manufacture, radioactive decay, etc.

end result *n.* final outcome.

end run *n.* **1** *Amer. Football* an attempt by the ball-carrier to run round his or her own end. **2** *US* an evasive tactic esp. in war or politics.

end standard *n.* a standard of length in the form of a metal bar or block with the end faces the standard distance apart.

end-stopped *adj.* (of verse) having a pause at the end of each line.

endue /ɪn'dju:, ɛn-/ *v.tr.* (also **indue**) (**-dues**, **-dued**, **-duing**) (foll. by *with*) *literary* invest or provide (a person or thing) with qualities, powers, etc. [earlier = induct, put on clothes: Middle English via Old French *enduire* from Latin *inducere* 'lead in', associated in meaning with Latin *induere* 'put on (clothes)']

endurance /ɪn'djʊər(ə)ns, ɛn-/ *n.* **1** the power or habit of enduring (*beyond endurance*). **2** the ability to withstand prolonged strain (*endurance test*). **3** the act of enduring. [Old French from *endurer*: see ENDURE]

endure /ɪn'djʊə, ɛn-/ *v.* **1** *tr.* undergo (a difficulty, hardship, etc.). **2** *tr.* **a** tolerate (a person) (*cannot endure him*). **b** (esp. with *neg.*; foll. by *to* + infin.) bear. **3** *intr.* remain in existence; last. **4** *tr.* submit to. □ **endurable** *adj.* **endurability** /-'bɪlɪti/ *n.* **enduringly** *adv.* [Middle English via Old French *endurer* from Latin *indurare* 'harden' (as IN-[2], *durus* 'hard')]

enduro /ɪn'djʊərəʊ, ɛn-/ *n.* (*pl.* **-os**) a long-distance race for motor vehicles, designed to test endurance.

end-user *n.* the person, customer, etc., who is the ultimate user of a product.

endways /'ɛndweɪz/ *adv.* **1** with its end uppermost or foremost or turned towards the viewer. **2** end to end.

endwise /'ɛndwʌɪz/ *adv.* = ENDWAYS.

end zone *n.* *Amer. Football* the rectangular area at the end of the field into which the ball must be carried or passed to score a touchdown.

ENE *abbr.* east-north-east.

-ene /i:n/ *suffix* **1** forming names of inhabitants of places (*Nazarene*). **2** *Chem.* forming names of unsaturated hydrocarbons containing a double bond (*benzene*; *ethylene*). [from or suggested by Greek *-ēnos*]

enema /'ɛnɪmə/ *n.* (*pl.* **enemas** or **enemata** /ɪ'nɛmətə/) **1** the injection of liquid or gas into the rectum, esp. to expel its contents. **2** a fluid or syringe used for this. [Late Latin from Greek *enema*, from *eniēmi* 'inject' (as EN-[2], *hiēmi* 'send')]

enemy /'ɛnəmi/ *n.* (*pl.* **-ies**) **1** a person or group actively opposing or hostile to another, or to a cause etc. **2 a** a hostile nation or army, esp. in war. **b** a member of this. **c** a hostile ship or aircraft. **3** (usu. foll. by *of*, *to*) an adversary or opponent. **4** a thing that harms or injures. **5** (*attrib.*) of or belonging to an enemy (*destroyed by enemy action*). [Middle English via Old French *enemi* from Latin *inimicus* (as IN-[1], *amicus* 'friend')]

energetic /ɛnə'dʒɛtɪk/ *adj.* **1** strenuously active. **2** forcible, vigorous. **3** powerfully operative. □ **energetically** *adv.* [Greek *energētikos* from *energeō* (as EN-[2], *ergon* 'work')]

energetics /ɛnə'dʒɛtɪks/ *n.pl.* (usu. treated as *sing.*) the science of energy.

energize /'ɛnədʒʌɪz/ *v.tr.* (also **-ise**) **1** infuse energy into (a person or work). **2** provide energy for the operation of (a device). □ **energizer** *n.*

energumen /ɛnə'gju:mən/ *n.* an enthusiast or fanatic. [Late Latin *energumenus* from Greek *energoumenos*, passive part. of *energeō*: see ENERGETIC]

energy /'ɛnədʒi/ *n.* (*pl.* **-ies**) **1** force, vigour; capacity for activity. **2** (in *pl.*) individual powers in use (*devote your energies to this*). **3** *Physics* the capacity of matter or radiation to do work. **4** the means of doing work as provided by the utilization of physical or chemical resources (*nuclear energy*). [French *énergie* or Late Latin *energia* from Greek *energeia*, from *ergon* 'work']

enervate *v.* & *adj.* ● *v.tr.* /'ɛnəveɪt/ deprive of vigour or vitality. ● *adj.* /ɪ'nə:vət/ enervated. □ **enervation** /ɛnə'veɪʃ(ə)n/ *n.* [Latin *enervatus*, past part. of *enervare* (as E-, *nervus* 'sinew')]

en famille /ɒ̃ fa'mi:, French ɑ̃ famij/ *adv.* **1** in or with one's family. **2** at home. [French, = in family]

enfant gâté /ˌɒ̃fɒ̃ ga'teɪ, French ɑ̃fɑ̃ gɑte/ *n.* a person given undue flattery or indulgence. [French, = spoilt child]

enfant terrible /ˌɒ̃fɒ̃ tɛ'ri:bl(ə), French ɑ̃fɑ̃ teribl/ *n.* (*pl.* ***enfants terribles*** *pronunc.* same) a person who causes embarrassment by indiscreet or unruly behaviour. [French, = terrible child]

enfeeble /ɪn'fi:b(ə)l, ɛn-/ *v.tr.* make feeble. □ **enfeeblement** *n.* [Middle English from Old French *enfeblir* (as EN-[1], FEEBLE)]

en fête /ɒ̃ 'feɪt, French ɑ̃ fɛt/ *adv.* & *predic.adj.* holding or ready for a holiday or celebration. [French, = in festival]

enfetter /ɪn'fɛtə, ɛn-/ *v.tr.* *literary* **1** bind in or as in fetters. **2** (foll. by *to*) enslave.

enfilade /ɛnfɪ'leɪd/ *n.* & *v.* ● *n.* gunfire directed along a line from end to end. ● *v.tr.* direct an enfilade at (troops, a road, etc.). [French from *enfiler* (as EN-[1], *fil* 'thread')]

enfold /ɪn'fəʊld, ɛn-/ *v.tr.* **1** (usu. foll. by *in*, *with*) wrap up; envelop. **2** clasp, embrace.

enforce /ɪn'fɔ:s, ɛn-/ *v.tr.* **1** compel observance of (a law etc.). **2** (foll. by *on*, *upon*) impose (an action, conduct, one's will). **3** persist in (a demand or argument). □ **enforceable** *adj.* **enforceability** /-sə'bɪlɪti/ *n.* **enforcedly** /-sɪdli/ *adv.* **enforcer** *n.* [Middle English from Old French *enforcir*, *-ier*, ultimately from Latin *fortis* 'strong']

enforcement /ɪn'fɔ:sm(ə)nt, ɛn-/ *n.* the act or an instance of enforcing. [Middle English from Old French, as ENFORCE + -MENT]

enforcement notice *n.* *Brit.* an official notification to remedy a breach of planning legislation.

enfranchise /ɪn'fran(t)ʃʌɪz, ɛn-/ *v.tr.* **1** give (a person) the right to vote. **2** give (a town) municipal rights, esp. that of representation in Parliament. **3** *hist.* free (a slave, villein, etc.). □ **enfranchisement** /-ɪzm(ə)nt/ *n.* [Old French *enfranchir* (as EN-[1], *franc franche* 'free': see FRANK)]

ENG *abbr.* electronic news-gathering.

engage /ɪn'geɪdʒ, ɛn-/ *v.* **1** *tr.* esp. *Brit.* employ or hire (a person). **2** *tr.* **a** (usu. in *passive*) employ busily; occupy (*are you engaged tomorrow?*). **b** hold fast (a person's attention). **3** *tr.* (usu. in *passive*) bind by a promise, esp. of marriage. **4** *tr.* (usu. foll. by *to* + infin.) bind by a contract. **5** *tr.* arrange beforehand to occupy (a room, seat, etc.). **6** (usu. foll. by *with*) *Mech.* **a** *tr.* interlock (parts of a gear etc.); cause (a part) to interlock. **b** *intr.* (of a part, gear, etc.) interlock. **7 a** *intr.* (usu. foll. by *with*) (of troops etc.) come into battle. **b** *tr.* bring (troops) into battle. **c** *tr.* come into battle with (an enemy etc.). **8** *intr.* take part (*engage in politics*). **9** *intr.* (foll. by *that* + clause or *to* + infin.) pledge oneself. **10** *tr.* (usu. as **engaged** *adj.*) *Archit.* attach (a column) to a wall. **11** *tr.* (of fencers etc.) interlock (weapons). [French *engager*, related to GAGE[1]]

engagé /ɒŋga'ʒeɪ, French ɑ̃gaʒe/ *adj.* (of a writer etc.) morally committed. [French, past part. of *engager*: see ENGAGE]

engaged /ɪn'geɪdʒd, ɛn-/ *adj.* **1** under a promise to marry. **2 a** occupied, busy. **b** reserved, booked. **3** *Brit.* (of a telephone line) unavailable because already in use.

engaged signal *n.* (also **engaged tone**) *Brit.* a sound indicating that a telephone line is engaged.

engagement /ɪn'geɪdʒm(ə)nt, ɛn-/ *n.* **1** the act or state of engaging or being engaged. **2** an appointment with another person. **3** a betrothal. **4** an encounter between hostile forces. **5** a moral commitment. [French, from *engager*: see ENGAGE]

engagement ring *n.* a finger ring given by a man to a woman when they promise to marry.

engaging /ɪnˈgeɪdʒɪŋ, ɛn-/ *adj.* attractive, charming. □ **engagingly** *adv.* **engagingness** *n.*

engender /ɪnˈdʒɛndə, ɛn-/ *v.tr.* **1** give rise to; bring about (a feeling etc.). **2** *archaic* beget. [Middle English via Old French *engendrer* from Latin *ingenerare* (as IN-², *generare* GENERATE)]

engine /ˈɛndʒɪn/ *n.* **1** a mechanical contrivance consisting of several parts working together, esp. as a source of power. **2 a** a railway locomotive. **b** = FIRE ENGINE. **c** = STEAM ENGINE. **3** *archaic* a machine or instrument, esp. a contrivance used in warfare. □ **engined** *adj.* (also in *comb.*). **engineless** *adj.* [Old French *engin* from Latin *ingenium* 'talent, device': cf. INGENIOUS]

engine driver *n. Brit.* the driver of an engine, esp. a railway locomotive.

engineer /ɛndʒɪˈnɪə/ *n. & v.* ● *n.* **1** a person qualified in a branch of engineering, esp. as a professional. **2** = CIVIL ENGINEER. **3 a** a person who makes or is in charge of engines. **b** a person who maintains machines; a mechanic; a technician. **4** *N. Amer.* an engine driver. **5** a person who designs and constructs military works; a soldier trained for this purpose. **6** (foll. by *of*) a skilful or artful contriver. ● *v.* **1** *tr.* arrange, contrive, or bring about, esp. artfully. **2** *intr.* act as an engineer. **3** *tr.* construct or manage as an engineer. [Middle English via Old French *engigneor* from medieval Latin *ingeniator -oris*, from *ingeniare* (as ENGINE)]

engineering /ɛndʒɪˈnɪərɪŋ/ *n.* the application of science to the design, building, and use of machines, constructions, etc.

engineering science *n.* engineering as a field of study.

engine house *n.* a building where an engine is housed.

engine room *n.* a room containing engines (esp. in a ship).

enginery /ˈɛndʒɪn(ə)ri/ *n.* engines and machinery generally.

engird /ɪnˈgəːd, ɛn-/ *v.tr.* surround with or as with a girdle.

engirdle /ɪnˈgəːd(ə)l, ɛn-/ *v.tr.* engird.

English /ˈɪŋglɪʃ/ *adj. & n.* ● *adj.* of or relating to England or its people or language. ● *n.* **1** the language of England, now used in many varieties in the British Isles, the United States, and most Commonwealth or ex-Commonwealth countries, and often internationally. **2** (prec. by *the*; treated as *pl.*) the people of England. **3** *US Billiards* = SIDE *n.* 10. □ **Englishness** *n.* [Old English *englisc*, *ænglisc* (as ANGLE, -ISH¹)]

English bond *n.* a bond of brickwork arranged in alternate courses of stretchers and headers.

English elm see ELM 1.

English galingale see GALINGALE 2.

English horn *n.* = COR ANGLAIS.

Englishman /ˈɪŋglɪʃmən/ *n.* (*pl.* **-men**) a man who is English by birth or descent.

Englishwoman /ˈɪŋglɪʃwʊmən/ *n.* (*pl.* **-women**) a woman who is English by birth or descent.

engorge /ɪnˈgɔːdʒ, ɛn-/ *v.tr.* **1** (in *passive*) **a** be crammed. **b** *Med.* be congested with blood. **2** devour greedily. □ **engorgement** *n.* [French *engorger* (as EN-¹, GORGE)]

engraft /ɪnˈgrɑːft, ɛn-/ *v.tr.* (also **ingraft**) **1** (usu. foll. by *into*, *upon*) *Bot.* insert (a scion of one tree) into another tree. **2** (usu. foll. by *in*) implant (principles etc.) in a person's mind. **3** (usu. foll. by *into*) incorporate permanently. □ **engraftment** *n.*

engrail /ɪnˈgreɪl, ɛn-/ *v.tr.* (usu. as **engrailed** *adj.*) esp. *Heraldry* make semicircular indentations along the edge of. [Middle English from Old French *engresler* (as EN-¹, *gresle* 'hail')]

engrain var. of INGRAIN.

engram /ˈɛngram/ *n.* a supposed permanent change in the brain accounting for the existence of memory, a memory trace. □ **engrammatic** /-grəˈmatɪk/ *adj.* [German *Engramm*, from Greek *en* 'in' + *gramma* 'letter of the alphabet']

engrave /ɪnˈgreɪv, ɛn-/ *v.tr.* **1** (often foll. by *on*) inscribe, cut, or carve (a text or design) on a hard surface. **2** (often foll. by *with*) inscribe or ornament (a surface) in this way. **3** cut (a design) as lines on a metal plate for printing. **4** (often foll. by *on*) impress deeply on a person's memory etc. □ **engraver** *n.* [EN-¹ + GRAVE³]

engraving /ɪnˈgreɪvɪŋ, ɛn-/ *n.* **1** a print made from an engraved plate, block, or other surface. **2** the process or art of cutting a design etc. on a hard surface.

engross /ɪnˈgrəʊs, ɛn-/ *v.tr.* **1** absorb the attention of; occupy fully (*engrossed in studying*). **2** make a fair copy of (a legal document). **3** reproduce (a document etc.) in larger letters or larger format. **4** *archaic* monopolize (a conversation etc.). □ **engrossing** *adj.* (in sense 1). **engrossment** *n.* [Middle English from Anglo-French *engrosser*: senses 2 and 3 from *en* 'in' + *grosse* 'large writing': senses 1 and 4 from *en gros* 'wholesale']

engulf /ɪnˈgʌlf, ɛn-/ *v.tr.* (also **ingulf**) **1** flow over and swamp; overwhelm. **2** swallow or plunge into a gulf. □ **engulfment** *n.*

enhance /ɪnˈhɑːns, -hans, ɛn-/ *v.tr.* heighten or intensify (qualities, powers, value, etc.); improve (something already of good quality). □ **enhancement** *n.* **enhancer** *n.* [Middle English from Anglo-French *enhauncer*, probably alteration of Old French *enhaucier*, ultimately from Latin *altus* 'high']

enharmonic /ɛnhɑːˈmɒnɪk/ *adj. Mus.* of or having intervals smaller than a semitone (esp. such intervals as that between G sharp and A flat, these notes being made the same in a scale of equal temperament). □ **enharmonically** *adv.* [Late Latin *enharmonicus* from Greek *enarmonikos* (as EN-², *harmonia* HARMONY)]

enigma /ɪˈnɪgmə/ *n.* **1** a puzzling thing or person. **2** a riddle or paradox. □ **enigmatic** /ɛnɪgˈmatɪk/ *adj.* **enigmatical** /ɛnɪgˈmatɪk(ə)l/ *adj.* **enigmatically** /ɛnɪgˈmatɪk(ə)li/ *adv.* **enigmatize** *v.tr.* (also **-ise**). [Latin *aenigma* from Greek *ainigma -matos*, from *ainissomai* 'speak allusively' from *ainos* 'fable']

enjambment /ɪnˈdʒam(b)m(ə)nt, ɛn-/ *n.* (also **enjambement**) *Prosody* the continuation of a sentence without a pause beyond the end of a line, couplet, or stanza. [French *enjambement* from *enjamber* (as EN-¹, *jambe* 'leg')]

enjoin /ɪnˈdʒɔɪn, ɛn-/ *v.tr.* **1 a** (foll. by *to* + infin.) command or order (a person). **b** (foll. by *that* + clause) issue instructions. **2** (often foll. by *on*) impose or prescribe (an action or conduct). **3** (usu. foll. by *from*) *Law* prohibit (a person) by order. □ **enjoinment** *n.* [Middle English via Old French *enjoindre* from Latin *injungere* (as IN-², *jungere* 'join')]

enjoy /ɪnˈdʒɔɪ, ɛn-/ *v.tr.* **1** take delight or pleasure in. **2** have the use or benefit of. **3** *Brit.* experience (*enjoy poor health*). □ **enjoy oneself** experience pleasure. □ **enjoyer** *n.* **enjoyment** *n.* [Middle English from Old French *enjoier* 'give joy to' or *enjoïr* 'enjoy', ultimately from Latin *gaudēre* 'rejoice']

enjoyable /ɪnˈdʒɔɪəb(ə)l, ɛʌ-/ *adj.* pleasant; giving enjoyment. □ **enjoyability** /-ˈbɪlɪti/ *n.* **enjoyableness** *n.* **enjoyably** *adv.*

enkephalin /ɛnˈkɛf(ə)lɪn/ *n.* (also **encephalin** /ɛnˈsɛf-/) *Biochem.* either of two morphine-like peptides (endorphins) occurring naturally in the brain and thought to control levels of pain. [Greek *egkephalos* 'brain' as ENCEPHALO-]

enkindle /ɪnˈkɪnd(ə)l, ɛn-/ *v.tr. literary* **1 a** cause (flames) to flare up. **b** stimulate (feeling, passion, etc.). **2** inflame with passion.

enlace /ɪnˈleɪs, ɛn-/ *v.tr.* **1** encircle tightly. **2** entwine. **3** enfold. □ **enlacement** *n.* [Middle English from Old French *enlacier*, ultimately from Latin *laqueus* 'noose']

enlarge /ɪnˈlɑːdʒ, ɛn-/ *v.* **1** *tr. & intr.* make or become larger or wider. **2** *intr.* (usu. foll. by *upon*) expatiate. **3** *tr. Photog.* produce an enlargement of (a negative). [Middle English from Old French *enlarger* (as EN-¹, LARGE)]

enlargement /ɪnˈlɑːdʒm(ə)nt, ɛn-/ *n.* **1** the act or an instance of enlarging; the state of being enlarged. **2** *Photog.* a print that is larger than the negative from which it is produced, or larger than an enprint or than a print already made.

enlarger /ɪnˈlɑːdʒə/ *n. Photog.* an apparatus for enlarging or reducing negatives or positives.

enlighten /ɪnˈlʌɪt(ə)n, ɛn-/ *v.tr.* **1** (often foll. by *on*) instruct or inform (about a subject). **2** (esp. as **enlightened** *adj.*) free from prejudice or superstition. **3** *literary* or *poet.* **a** shed light on (an object). **b** give spiritual insight to (a person). □ **enlightener** *n.*

enlightenment /ɪnˈlʌɪt(ə)nm(ə)nt, ɛn-/ *n.* **1** the act or an instance of enlightening; the state of being enlightened. **2** (**the Enlightenment**) the 18th-c. philosophy emphasizing reason and individualism rather than tradition.

enlist /ɪnˈlɪst, ɛn-/ *v.* **1** *intr.* & *tr.* enrol in the armed services. **2** *tr.* secure as a means of help or support. □ **enlister** *n.* **enlistment** *n.*

enlisted man *n. US* a soldier or sailor below the rank of officer.

enliven /ɪnˈlʌɪv(ə)n, ɛn-/ *v.tr.* **1** give life or spirit to. **2** make cheerful, brighten (a picture or scene). □ **enlivener** *n.* **enlivenment** *n.*

en masse /ɒ̃ ˈmas/ *adv.* **1** all together. **2** in a mass. [French]

enmesh /ɪnˈmɛʃ, ɛn-/ *v.tr.* entangle in or as in a net. □ **enmeshment** *n.*

enmity /ˈɛnmɪti/ *n.* (*pl.* **-ies**) **1** the state of being an enemy. **2** a feeling of hostility. [Middle English via Old French *enemitié* from Romanic (as ENEMY)]

ennead /ˈɛnɪad/ *n.* a group of nine. [Greek *enneas enneados* from *ennea* 'nine']

ennoble /ɪˈnəʊb(ə)l, ɛn-/ *v.tr.* **1** make (a person) a noble. **2** make noble; elevate. □ **ennoblement** *n.* [French *ennoblir* (as EN-[1], NOBLE)]

ennui /ɒnˈwiː/ *n.* mental weariness from lack of occupation or interest; boredom. [French from Latin *in odio*: cf. ODIUM]

enology *US* var. of OENOLOGY.

enormity /ɪˈnɔːmɪti/ *n.* (*pl.* **-ies**) **1** extreme wickedness. **2** an act of extreme wickedness. **3** a serious error. **4** *disp.* great size; enormousness. [Middle English via French *énormité* from Latin *enormitas -tatis*, from *enormis* ENORMOUS]

■ **Usage** The use of *enormity* in sense 4 is often found, e.g. *the enormity of the problem*, but is regarded as incorrect by many people.

enormous /ɪˈnɔːməs/ *adj.* very large; huge (*enormous animals; an enormous difference*). □ **enormously** *adv.* **enormousness** *n.* [Latin *enormis* (as E-, *norma* 'pattern, standard')]

enosis /ɪˈnəʊsɪs, ˈɛnəsɪs/ *n.* the political union of Cyprus and Greece, as an ideal or proposal. [modern Greek *enōsis*, from *ena* 'one']

enough /ɪˈnʌf/ *det., adj., pron., adv., & int.* ● *det. & predic.adj.* as much or as many as required (*we have enough apples; we do not have enough sugar; earned enough money to buy a house; one book was enough to put her off*). ● *pron.* an amount or quantity that is enough (*we have enough of everything now; enough is as good as a feast*). ● *adv.* (after an adj. or adv.) **1** to the required degree, adequately (*are you warm enough?*). **2** fairly (*she sings well enough*). **3** very, quite (*you know well enough what I mean; oddly enough*). ● *int.* that is enough (in various senses, esp. to put an end to an action, thing said, etc.). □ **have had enough of** want no more of; be satiated with or tired of. [Old English *genog*, from Germanic]

en passant /ɒ̃ paˈsɑːnt, pasɒ̃/ *adv.* **1** by the way. **2** *Chess* used with reference to the permitted capture of an opponent's pawn that has just advanced two squares in its first move with a pawn that could have taken it if it had advanced only one square. [French, = in passing]

en pension /ɒ̃ pɒ̃ˈsjɒ̃, French ɑ̃ pɑ̃sjɔ̃/ *adv.* as a boarder or resident. [French: see PENSION[2]]

enplane /ɪnˈpleɪn, ɛn-/ var. of EMPLANE.

enprint /ˈɛnprɪnt/ *n. Brit.* a standard-sized photographic print. [*en*larged *print*]

enquire /ɪnˈkwʌɪə/ *v.* **1** *intr.* (often foll. by *of*) seek information; ask a question (of a person). **2** *intr.* (foll. by *after*, *for*) ask about a person, a person's health, etc. **3** *intr.* (foll. by *for*) ask about the availability of. **4** *tr.* ask for information as to (*enquired my name; enquired whether we were coming*). **5** *intr.* = INQUIRE 1. □ **enquirer** *n.* **enquiring** *adj.* **enquiringly** *adv.* [Middle English *enquere* from Old French *enquerre*, ultimately from Latin *inquirere* (as IN-[2], *quaerere quaesit-* 'seek')]

■ **Usage** A useful distinction exists between *enquire* and *inquire*, although some people use these two words interchangeably. *Enquire* is best used to mean 'to ask' in general contexts, while *inquire* is best reserved to mean 'to make a formal investigation'. In cases of academic investigation, *enquire* tends to be preferred e.g. *enquire into the nature of happiness*. The same distinction exists between *enquiry* and *inquiry*.

enquiry /ɪnˈkwʌɪri/ *n.* (*pl.* **-ies**) **1** the act or an instance of asking or seeking information. **2** = INQUIRY.

■ **Usage** See Usage Note at ENQUIRE.

enrage /ɪnˈreɪdʒ, ɛn-/ *v.tr.* (esp. as **enraged** *adj.*) (often foll. by *at*, *by*, *with*) make furious. □ **enragement** *n.* [French *enrager* (as EN-[1], RAGE)]

en rapport /ɒn raˈpɔː, French ɑ̃ rapɔr/ *adv.* (usu. foll. by *with*) in harmony or rapport. [French: see RAPPORT]

enrapture /ɪnˈraptʃə, ɛn-/ *v.tr.* give intense delight to.

enrich /ɪnˈrɪtʃ, ɛn-/ *v.tr.* **1** make rich or richer. **2** make richer in quality, flavour, nutritive value, etc. **3** add to the contents of (a collection, museum, or book). **4** increase the content of an isotope in (material), esp. enrich (uranium) with isotope U-235. □ **enrichment** *n.* [Middle English from Old French *enrichir* (as EN-[1], RICH)]

enrobe /ɪnˈrəʊb, ɛn-/ *v.tr.* cover with a robe or a coating.

enrol /ɪnˈrəʊl, ɛn-/ *v.* (*US* **enroll**) (**enrolled**, **enrolling**) **1** *intr.* enter one's name on a list, esp. as a commitment to membership. **2** *tr.* **a** write the name of (a person) on a list. **b** (usu. foll. by *in*) incorporate (a person) as a member of a society etc. **3** *tr. hist.* enter (a deed etc.) among the rolls of a court of justice. **4** *tr.* record. □ **enrollee** /-ˈliː/ *n.* [Middle English from Old French *enroller* (as EN-[1], *rolle* ROLL *n.*)]

enrolment /ɪnˈrəʊlm(ə)nt/ *n.* (*US* **enrollment**) **1** the act or an instance of enrolling; the state of being enrolled. **2** *US* the number of persons enrolled, esp. at a school or college.

en route /ɒn ˈruːt/ *adv.* (often foll. by *to*, *for*) on the way. [French]

en rule *n. Brit.* a short dash used in punctuation.

ensconce /ɪnˈskɒns, ɛn-/ *v.tr.* (usu. *refl.* or in *passive*) establish or settle comfortably, safely, or secretly.

ensemble /ɒ̃ˈsɒ̃ːb(ə)l, ɒnˈsɒmb(ə)l/ *n.* **1 a** a thing viewed as the sum of its parts. **b** the general effect of this. **2** a set of clothes worn together; an outfit. **3** a group of actors, dancers, musicians, etc., performing together, esp. subsidiary dancers in ballet etc. **4** *Mus.* **a** a concerted passage for an ensemble. **b** the manner in which this is performed (*good ensemble*). **5** *Math.* a group of systems with the same constitution but possibly in different states. [French, ultimately from Latin *insimul* (as IN-[2], *simul* 'at the same time')]

enshrine /ɪnˈʃrʌɪn, ɛn-/ *v.tr.* **1** enclose in or as in a shrine. **2** serve as a shrine for. **3** preserve or cherish. □ **enshrinement** *n.*

enshroud /ɪnˈʃraʊd, ɛn-/ *v.tr. literary* **1** cover with or as with a shroud. **2** cover completely; hide from view.

ensign /ˈɛnsʌɪn/ *n.* **1 a** a banner or flag, esp. the military or naval flag of a nation. **b** *Brit.* each of three flags, the blue, red, and white ensigns, with the union flag in the corner. **2** a standard-bearer. **3 a** *hist.* the lowest commissioned infantry officer. **b** *US* the lowest commissioned officer in the navy. □ **ensigncy** *n.* [Middle English via Old French *enseigne* from Latin *insignia*: see INSIGNIA]

ensilage /ˈɛnsɪlɪdʒ, ɛnˈsʌɪlɪdʒ/ *n. & v.* ● *n.* **1** the process of making silage. **2** = SILAGE *n.* 2. ● *v.tr.* treat (fodder) by ensilage. [French (as ENSILE)]

ensile /ɛnˈsʌɪl/ *v.tr.* **1** put (fodder) into a silo. **2** preserve (fodder) in a silo. [French *ensiler* from Spanish *ensilar* (as EN-[1], SILO)]

enslave /ɪnˈsleɪv, ɛn-/ *v.tr.* make (a person) a slave. □ **enslavement** *n.* **enslaver** *n.*

ensnare /ɪnˈsnɛː, ɛn-/ *v.tr.* catch in or as in a snare; entrap. □ **ensnarement** *n.*

ensue /ɪnˈsjuː, ɛn-/ *v.intr.* (**ensues**, **ensued**, **ensuing**) **1** happen afterwards. **2** (often foll. by *from, on*) occur as a result. [Middle English from Old French *ensuivre*, ultimately from Latin *sequi* 'follow']

en suite /ɒ̃ ˈswiːt/ *adv. & adj.* ● *adv.* forming a single unit (*bedroom with bathroom en suite*). ● *adj.* **1** forming a single unit (*en suite bathroom*). **2** with a bathroom attached (*seven en suite bedrooms*). [French, = in sequence]

ensure /ɪnˈʃʊə, ɛn-/ *v.tr.* **1** (often foll. by *that* + clause) make certain. **2** (usu. foll. by *to, for*) secure (a thing for a person etc.). **3** (usu. foll. by *against*) make safe. [Middle English via Anglo-French *enseürer* from Old French *aseürer* ASSURE]

enswathe /ɪnˈsweɪð, ɛn-/ *v.tr.* bind or wrap in or as in a bandage. □ **enswathement** *n.*

ENT *abbr.* ear, nose, and throat.

-ent /(ə)nt/ *suffix* **1** forming adjectives denoting attribution of an action (*consequent*) or state (*existent*). **2** forming nouns denoting an agent (*coefficient*; *president*). [from or suggested by French *-ent* or Latin *-ent-*, pres. part. stem of verbs (cf. -ANT)]

entablature /ɛnˈtablətʃə, ɪn-/ *n. Archit.* the upper part of a classical building supported by columns or a colonnade, comprising architrave, frieze, and cornice. [Italian *intavolatura* from *intavolare* 'board up' (as IN-[2], *tavola* 'table')]

entablement /ɛnˈteɪb(ə)lm(ə)nt, ɪn-/ *n.* a platform supporting a statue, above the dado and base. [French, from *entabler* (as EN-[1], TABLE)]

entail /ɪnˈteɪl, ɛn-/ *v. & n.* ● *v.tr.* **1** necessitate or involve unavoidably (*the work entails much effort*). **2** *Law* bequeath (property etc.) so that it remains within a family. **3** (usu. foll. by *on*) bestow (a thing) inalienably. ● *n. Law* **1** an entailed estate. **2** the succession to such an estate. □ **entailment** *n.* [Middle English, from EN-[1] + Anglo-French *taile* TAIL[2]]

entangle /ɪnˈtaŋg(ə)l, ɛn-/ *v.tr.* **1** cause to get caught in a snare or among obstacles. **2** cause to become tangled. **3** involve in difficulties or illicit activities. **4** make (a thing) tangled or intricate; complicate.

entanglement /ɪnˈtaŋg(ə)lm(ə)nt, ɛn-/ *n.* **1** the act or condition of entangling or being entangled. **2 a** a thing that entangles. **b** *Mil.* an extensive barrier erected to obstruct an enemy's movements (esp. one made of stakes and interlaced barbed wire). **3** a compromising (esp. amorous) relationship.

entasis /ˈɛntəsɪs/ *n.* (*pl.* **entases**) *Archit.* a slight convex curve in a column shaft to correct the visual illusion that straight sides give of curving inwards. [modern Latin from Greek, from *enteinō* 'to stretch']

entelechy /ɛnˈtɛləki, ɪn-/ *n. Philos.* **1** the realization of potential. **2** the supposed essential nature or guiding principle of a living thing. [Late Latin *entelechia* from Greek *entelekheia*, from *telos* 'end, perfection' + *ekhein* 'be in a state']

entellus /ɪnˈtɛləs, ɛn-/ *n.* = HANUMAN 1. [name of an aged Trojan in Virgil's *Aeneid*]

entente /ɒnˈtɒnt/ *n.* **1** = ENTENTE CORDIALE. **2** a group of states in such a relation. [French, = understanding (as INTENT)]

entente cordiale /ɒ̃ˈtɒ̃t kɔːdɪˈɑːl, French ɑ̃tɑ̃t kɔrdjal/ *n.* a friendly understanding between states, esp. (often **Entente Cordiale**) that reached in 1904 between Britain and France. [French, = cordial understanding: see ENTENTE]

enter /ˈɛntə/ *v.* **1 a** *intr.* (often foll. by *into*) go or come in. **b** *tr.* go or come into. **c** *intr.* come on stage (as a direction: *enter Macbeth*). **2** *tr.* penetrate; go through (*a bullet entered his chest*). **3** *tr.* (often foll. by *up*) write (a name, details, etc.) in a list, book, etc. **4 a** *intr.* register or announce oneself as a competitor (*entered for the long jump*). **b** *tr.* become a competitor in (an event). **c** *tr.* record the name of (a person etc.) as a competitor (*entered two horses for the Derby*). **5** *tr.* **a** become a member of (a society etc.). **b** enrol as a member or prospective member of a society, school, etc.; admit or obtain admission for. **6** *tr.* make known; present for consideration (*entered a protest*). **7** *tr.* put into an official record. **8** *intr.* (foll. by *into*) **a** engage in (conversation, relations, an undertaking, etc.). **b** subscribe to; bind oneself by (an agreement etc.). **c** form part of (one's calculations, plans, etc.). **d** sympathize with (feelings etc.). **9** *intr.* (foll. by *on, upon*) **a** begin, undertake; begin to deal with (a subject). **b** assume the functions of (an office). **c** assume possession of (property). **10** *intr.* (foll. by *up*) complete a series of entries in (account books etc.). [Middle English via Old French *entrer* from Latin *intrare*]

enteric /ɛnˈtɛrɪk/ *adj. & n.* ● *adj.* of the intestines. ● *n.* (in full **enteric fever**) typhoid. [Greek *enterikos* (as ENTERO-)]

enteritis /ɛntəˈrʌɪtɪs/ *n.* inflammation of the (small) intestine, often causing diarrhoea.

entero- /ˈɛntərəʊ/ *comb. form* intestine. [Greek *enteron* 'intestine']

enterostomy /ɛntəˈrɒstəmi/ *n.* (*pl.* **-ies**) *Surgery* a surgical operation in which the small intestine is brought through the abdominal wall and opened, in order to bypass the stomach or the colon.

enterotomy /ɛntəˈrɒtəmi/ *n.* (*pl.* **-ies**) the surgical cutting open of the intestine.

enterovirus /ˈɛnt(ə)rəʊˌvʌɪrəs/ *n.* a virus infecting the intestines and sometimes spreading to other parts of the body, esp. the central nervous system.

enterprise /ˈɛntəprʌɪz/ *n.* **1** an undertaking, esp. a bold or difficult one. **2** (as a personal attribute) readiness to engage in such undertakings (*has no enterprise*). **3** a business firm. □ **enterpriser** *n.* [Middle English from Old French *entreprise*, fem. past part. of *entreprendre* (variant of *emprendre*), ultimately from Latin *prendere*, *prehendere* 'take']

enterprise zone *n.* a depressed (usu. urban) area where State incentives such as tax concessions are designed to encourage investment.

enterprising /ˈɛntəprʌɪzɪŋ/ *adj.* **1** ready to engage in enterprises. **2** resourceful, imaginative, energetic. □ **enterprisingly** *adv.*

entertain /ɛntəˈteɪn/ *v.tr.* **1** amuse; occupy agreeably. **2 a** receive or treat as a guest. **b** (*absol.*) receive guests (*they entertain a great deal*). **3** give attention or consideration to (an idea, feeling, or proposal). [in earlier use = keep up, maintain: Middle English from French *entretenir*, ultimately from Latin *tenēre* 'hold']

entertainer /ɛntəˈteɪnə/ *n.* a person who entertains, esp. professionally on stage etc.

entertaining /ɛntəˈteɪnɪŋ/ *adj.* amusing, diverting. □ **entertainingly** *adv.*

entertainment /ɛntəˈteɪnm(ə)nt/ *n.* **1** the act or an instance of entertaining; the process of being entertained. **2** a public performance or show. **3** diversions or amusements for guests etc. **4** amusement (*much to my entertainment*). **5** hospitality.

enthalpy /ˈɛnθ(ə)lpi, ɛnˈθalpi/ *n. Physics* the total thermodynamic heat content of a system. [Greek *enthalpō* 'warm in' (as EN-[1], *thalpō* 'to heat')]

enthral /ɪn'θrɔ:l, ɛn-/ *v.tr.* (*US* **enthrall, inthrall**) (**-thralled, -thralling**) **1** captivate, please greatly. **2** enslave. □ **enthralment** *n.* (*US* **enthrallment**). [EN-[1] + THRALL]

enthrone /ɪn'θrəʊn, ɛn-/ *v.tr.* **1** install (a king, bishop, etc.) on a throne, esp. ceremonially. **2** exalt. □ **enthronement** *n.*

enthuse /ɪn'θju:z, ɛn-/ *v.intr. & tr. colloq.* be or make enthusiastic. [back-formation from ENTHUSIASM]

enthusiasm /ɪn'θju:zɪaz(ə)m, ɛn-/ *n.* **1** (often foll. by *for, about*) **a** strong interest or admiration. **b** great eagerness. **2** an object of enthusiasm. **3** *archaic* extravagant religious emotion. [French *enthousiasme* or Late Latin *enthusiasmus* from Greek *enthousiasmos*, from *entheos* 'possessed by a god, inspired' (as EN-[2], *theos* 'god')]

enthusiast /ɪn'θju:zɪast, ɛn-/ *n.* **1** (often foll. by *for*) a person who is full of enthusiasm. **2** a visionary; a self-deluded person. [French *enthousiaste* or ecclesiastical Latin *enthusiastes* from Greek (as ENTHUSIASM)]

enthusiastic /ɪn,θju:zɪ'astɪk, ɛn-/ *adj.* having or showing enthusiasm. □ **enthusiastically** *adv.* [Greek *enthousiastikos* (as ENTHUSIASM)]

enthymeme /'ɛnθɪmi:m/ *n. Logic* a syllogism in which one premiss is not explicitly stated. [Latin *enthymema* from Greek *enthumēma*, from *enthumeomai* 'consider' (as EN-[2], *thumos* 'mind')]

entice /ɪn'tʌɪs, ɛn-/ *v.tr.* (often foll. by *from, into*, or *to* + infin.) persuade by the offer of pleasure or reward. □ **enticement** *n.* **enticer** *n.* **enticing** *adj.* **enticingly** *adv.* [Middle English from Old French *enticier*, probably from Romanic]

entire /ɪn'tʌɪə, ɛn-/ *adj. & n.* ● *adj.* **1** whole, complete. **2** not broken or decayed. **3** unqualified, absolute (*an entire success*). **4** in one piece; continuous. **5** not castrated. **6** *Bot.* without indentation. ● *n.* an uncastrated animal. [Middle English via Anglo-French *enter*, Old French *entier* from Latin *integer* 'untouched, whole' (as IN-[2], *tangere* 'touch')]

entirely /ɪn'tʌɪəli, ɛn-/ *adv.* **1** wholly, completely (*the stock is entirely exhausted*). **2** solely, exclusively (*did it entirely for my benefit*).

entirety /ɪn'tʌɪərəti, -'tʌɪəti, ɛn-/ *n.* (*pl.* **-ies**) **1** completeness. **2** (usu. foll. by *of*) the sum total. □ **in its entirety** in its complete form; completely. [Middle English via Old French *entiereté*, from Latin *integritas -tatis*, from *integer*: see ENTIRE]

entitle /ɪn'tʌɪt(ə)l, ɛn-/ *v.tr.* **1 a** (usu. foll. by *to*) give (a person etc.) a just claim. **b** (foll. by *to* + infin.) give (a person etc.) a right. **2 a** give (a book etc.) the title of. **b** *archaic* give (a person) the title of (*entitled him Sultan*). □ **entitlement** *n.* [Middle English via Anglo-French *entitler*, Old French *entiteler* from Late Latin *intitulare* (as IN-[2], TITLE)]

entity /'ɛntɪti/ *n.* (*pl.* **-ies**) **1** a thing with distinct existence, as opposed to a quality or relation. **2** a thing's existence regarded distinctly; a thing's essential nature. □ **entitative** /-tətɪv/ *adj.* [French *entité* or medieval Latin *entitas* from Late Latin *ens* 'being']

ento- /'ɛntəʊ/ *prefix* within. [Greek *entos* 'within']

entomb /ɪn'tu:m, ɛn-/ *v.tr.* **1** place in or as in a tomb. **2** serve as a tomb for. □ **entombment** *n.* [Old French *entomber* (as EN-[1], TOMB)]

entomo- /'ɛntəməʊ/ *comb. form* insect. [Greek *entomos* 'cut up' (in neut. = INSECT, from its segmented body) from EN-[2] + *temnō* 'cut']

entomology /ɛntə'mɒlədʒi/ *n.* the study of the forms and behaviour of insects. □ **entomological** /-mə'lɒdʒɪk(ə)l/ *adj.* **entomologist** *n.* [French *entomologie* or modern Latin *entomologia* (as ENTOMO-, -LOGY)]

entomophagous /ɛntə'mɒfəgəs/ *adj. Zool.* insect-eating.

entomophilous /ɛntə'mɒfɪləs/ *adj. Biol.* pollinated by insects.

entoparasite /ɛntəʊ'parəsʌɪt/ *n. Biol.* = ENDOPARASITE.

entophyte /'ɛntə(ʊ)fʌɪt/ *n. Bot.* a plant growing inside a plant or animal.

entourage /'ɒntʊrɑ:ʒ, ɒntʊ(ə)'rɑ:ʒ/ *n.* **1** a group of people attending or surrounding an important person. **2** surroundings. [French, from *entourer* 'surround']

entr'acte /'ɒntrakt/ *n.* **1** an interval between two acts of a play. **2** a piece of music or a dance performed during this. [French, from *entre* 'between' + *acte* 'act']

entrails /'ɛntreɪlz/ *n.pl.* **1** the intestines of a person or animal. **2** the innermost parts (*entrails of the earth*). [Middle English via Old French *entrailles* and medieval Latin *intralia* alteration of Latin *interaneus* 'internal', from *inter* 'among']

entrain[1] /ɪn'treɪn, ɛn-/ *v.intr. & tr.* go or put on board a train.

entrain[2] /ɪn'treɪn, ɛn-/ *v.tr.* **1** (of a fluid) carry (particles etc.) along in its flow. **2** drag along. □ **entrainment** *n.* [French *entraîner* (as EN-[1], *traîner* 'drag', formed as TRAIN)]

entrain[3] /ɒ̃'trɒ̃, French ɑ̃trɛ̃/ *n.* enthusiasm, animation. [French]

entrammel /ɪn'tram(ə)l, ɛn-/ *v.tr.* (**entrammelled, entrammelling**; *US* **entrammeled, entrammeling**) entangle, hamper.

entrance[1] /'ɛntr(ə)ns/ *n.* **1** the act or an instance of going or coming in. **2** a door, passage, etc., by which one enters. **3** right of admission. **4** the coming of an actor on stage. **5** *Mus.* = ENTRY 8. **6** (foll. by *into, upon*) entering into office etc. **7** (in full **entrance fee**) esp. *Brit.* a fee paid for admission to a society, club, exhibition, etc. [Old French (as ENTER, -ANCE)]

entrance[2] /ɪn'trɑ:ns, ɛn-/ *v.tr.* **1** enchant, delight. **2** put into a trance. **3** (often foll. by *with*) overwhelm with strong feeling. □ **entrancement** *n.* **entrancing** *adj.* **entrancingly** *adv.*

entrant /'ɛntr(ə)nt/ *n.* a person who enters (esp. an examination, profession, etc.). [French, pres. part. of *entrer*: see ENTER]

entrap /ɪn'trap, ɛn-/ *v.tr.* (**entrapped, entrapping**) **1** catch in or as in a trap. **2** (often foll. by *into* + verbal noun) beguile or trick (a person). [Old French *entraper* (as EN-[1], TRAP[1])]

entrapment /ɪn'trapm(ə)nt, ɛn-/ *n.* **1** the act or an instance of entrapping; the process of being entrapped. **2** *Law* inducement to commit a crime, esp. by the authorities to secure a prosecution.

entreat /ɪn'tri:t, ɛn-/ *v.tr.* **1 a** (foll. by *to* + infin. or *that* + clause) ask (a person) earnestly. **b** ask earnestly for (a thing). **2** *archaic* treat; act towards (a person). □ **entreatingly** *adv.* [Middle English from Old French *entraiter* (as EN-[1], *traiter* TREAT)]

entreaty /ɪn'tri:ti, ɛn-/ *n.* (*pl.* **-ies**) an earnest request; a supplication. [ENTREAT, after TREATY]

entrechat /'ɑ:ntrəʃɑ:/ *n.* a leap in ballet, with one or more crossings of the legs while in the air. [French, from Italian (*capriola*) *intrecciata* 'complicated (caper)']

entrecôte /'ɒntrəkəʊt/ *n.* a boned steak cut off the sirloin. [French, from *entre* 'between' + *côte* 'rib']

entrée /'ɒntreɪ/ *n.* **1 a** *Brit.* a dish served between the fish and meat courses. **b** esp. *N. Amer.* the main dish of a meal. **2** the right or privilege of admission, esp. at Court. [French, = ENTRY]

entremets /ɒntrə'meɪ, French ɑ̃trəmɛ/ *n.* **1** a sweet dish. **2** a light dish served between two courses. [French, from *entre* 'between' + *mets* 'dish']

entrench /ɪn'trɛn(t)ʃ, ɛn-/ *v.* (also **intrench**) **1** *tr.* **a** establish firmly (in a defensible position, in office, etc.). **b** (as **entrenched** *adj.*) (of an attitude etc.) not easily modified. **2** *tr.* surround (a post, army, town, etc.) with a trench as a fortification. **3** *tr.* apply extra safeguards to (rights etc. guaranteed by legislation). **4** *intr.* entrench oneself. **5** *intr.* (foll. by *upon*) encroach, trespass. □ **entrench oneself** adopt a well-defended position. □ **entrenchment** *n.*

entre nous /ɒntrə 'nu:, French ɑ̃trə nu/ *adv.* **1** between you and me. **2** in private. [French, = between ourselves]

entrepôt /'ɒntrəpəʊ/ *n.* **1** a warehouse for temporary storage of goods in transit. **2** a commercial centre for import and export, and for collection and distribution. [French from *entreposer* 'to store', from *entre-* INTER- + *poser* 'place']

entrepreneur /ˌɒntrəprə'nə:/ *n.* **1** a person who undertakes an enterprise or business, with the chance of profit or loss. **2** a contractor acting as an intermediary. **3** the person in effective control of a commercial undertaking. **4** a person who organizes entertainments, esp. musical shows. ▫ **entrepreneurial** /-'n(j)ə:rɪəl, -'njʊərɪəl/ *adj.* **entrepreneurialism** /-'n(j)ə:rɪəlɪz(ə)m, -'njʊərɪəlɪz(ə)m/ *n.* (also **entrepreneurism**). **entrepreneurially** /-'n(j)ə:rɪəli, -'njʊərɪəli/ *adv.* **entrepreneurship** *n.* [French, from *entreprendre* undertake: see ENTERPRISE]

entresol /'ɒntrəsɒl/ *n.* a low storey between the first and the ground floor; a mezzanine floor. [French, from *entre* 'between' + *sol* 'ground']

entrism var. of ENTRYISM.

entropy /'ɛntrəpi/ *n.* **1** *Physics* a measure of the unavailability of a system's thermal energy for conversion into mechanical work, in some contexts interpreted as a measure of the degree of disorder or randomness in the system. **2** a measure of the rate of transfer of information in a message etc. ▫ **entropic** /-'trɒpɪk/ *adj.* **entropically** /-'trɒpɪk(ə)li/ *adv.* [German *Entropie* (as EN-[2], Greek *tropē* 'transformation')]

entrust /ɪn'trʌst, ɛn-/ *v.tr.* (also **intrust**) **1** (foll. by *to*) give responsibility for (a person or a thing) to a person in whom one has confidence. **2** (foll. by *with*) assign responsibility for a thing to (a person). ▫ **entrustment** *n.*

entry /'ɛntri/ *n.* (*pl.* **-ies**) **1 a** the act or an instance of going or coming in. **b** the coming of an actor on stage. **c** ceremonial entrance. **2** liberty to go or come in. **3 a** a place of entrance; a door, gate, etc. **b** *Brit.* a lobby. **4** *Brit.* a passage between buildings. **5** the mouth of a river. **6 a** an item entered in a diary, list, account book, etc. **b** the recording of this. **7 a** a person or thing competing in a race, contest, etc. **b** a list of competitors. **8** the start or resumption of music for a particular instrument in an ensemble. **9** *Law* the act of taking possession. **10** *Bridge* **a** an opportunity to transfer the lead to one's partner's hand. **b** a card providing this. [Middle English from Old French *entree*, ultimately from Latin *intrare* ENTER]

entry form *n.* an application form for a competition.

entryism /'ɛntrɪɪz(ə)m/ *n.* (also **entrism**) infiltration into a political organization to change or subvert its policies or objectives. ▫ **entrist** *n.* **entryist** *n.*

entry permit *n.* an authorization to enter a particular country etc.

entryphone /'ɛntrɪfəʊn/ *n. Brit. propr.* an intercom device at an entrance to a building by which callers may identify themselves to gain admission.

entwine /ɪn'twʌɪn, ɛn-/ *v.tr.* (also **intwine**) **1** (foll. by *with, about, round*) twine together (a thing with or round another). **2** interweave. ▫ **entwinement** *n.*

enucleate /ɪ'nju:klɪeɪt/ *v.tr. Surgery* extract (a tumour etc.). ▫ **enucleation** /-'eɪʃ(ə)n/ *n.* [Latin *enucleare* (as E-, NUCLEUS)]

E-number /'i:ˌnʌmbə/ *n. Brit.* **1** a code number preceded by the letter E, denoting food additives according to EC directives. **2** *colloq.* a food additive.

enumerate /ɪ'nju:məreɪt/ *v.tr.* **1** specify (items); mention one by one. **2** count; establish the number of. ▫ **enumerable** *adj.* **enumeration** /-'reɪʃ(ə)n/ *n.* **enumerative** /-rətɪv/ *adj.* [Latin *enumerare* (as E-, NUMBER)]

enumerator /ɪ'nju:məreɪtə/ *n.* **1** a person who enumerates. **2** a person employed in census-taking.

enunciate /ɪ'nʌnsɪeɪt/ *v.tr.* **1** pronounce (words) clearly. **2** express (a proposition or theory) in definite terms. **3** proclaim. ▫ **enunciation** /-'eɪʃ(ə)n/ *n.* **enunciative** /-sɪətɪv/ *adj.* **enunciator** *n.* [Latin *enuntiare* (as E-, *nuntiare* 'announce' from *nuntius* 'messenger')]

enure /ɪ'njʊə/ *v.intr. Law* = INURE 2. [variant of INURE]

enuresis /ɛnjʊə'ri:sɪs/ *n. Med.* involuntary urination. ▫ **enuretic** /-'rɛtɪk/ *adj. & n.* [modern Latin, from Greek *enoureō* 'urinate in' (as EN-[2], *ouron* 'urine')]

envelop /ɪn'vɛləp, ɛn-/ *v.tr.* (**enveloped, enveloping**) **1** (often foll. by *in*) **a** wrap up or cover completely. **b** make obscure; conceal (*was enveloped in mystery*). **2** *Mil.* completely surround (an enemy). ▫ **envelopment** *n.* [Middle English from Old French *envoluper* (as EN-[1], origin of second element unknown: cf. DEVELOP)]

envelope /'ɛnvələʊp, 'ɒn-/ *n.* **1** a folded paper container, usu. with a sealable flap, for a letter etc. **2** a wrapper or covering. **3** the structure within a balloon or airship containing the gas. **4** the outer metal or glass housing of a vacuum tube, electric light, etc. **5** *Electr.* a curve joining the successive peaks of a modulated wave. **6** *Bot.* an enveloping structure, esp. the calyx or corolla (or both). **7** *Math.* a line or curve tangent to each line or curve of a given family. [French *enveloppe* (as ENVELOP)]

envenom /ɪn'vɛnəm, ɛn-/ *v.tr.* **1** put poison on or into; make poisonous. **2** infuse venom or bitterness into (feelings, words, or actions). [Middle English from Old French *envenimer* (as EN-[1], *venim* VENOM)]

enviable /'ɛnvɪəb(ə)l/ *adj.* (of a person or thing) exciting or likely to excite envy. ▫ **enviably** *adv.*

envious /'ɛnvɪəs/ *adj.* (often foll. by *of*) feeling or showing envy. ▫ **enviously** *adv.* [Middle English from Anglo-French *envious*, Old French *envieus*, from *envie* ENVY]

environ /ɪn'vʌɪrən, ɛn-/ *v.tr.* encircle, surround (esp. hostilely or protectively). [Middle English via Old French *environer* from *environ* 'surroundings', from *en* 'in' + *viron* 'circuit' from *virer* 'turn, VEER[1]']

environment /ɪn'vʌɪrənm(ə)nt, ɛn-/ *n.* **1** the physical surroundings, conditions, circumstances, etc., in which a person lives (*poor home environment*). **2** the area surrounding a place. **3 a** external conditions as affecting plant and animal life. **b** (**the environment**) the totality of the physical conditions on the earth or a part of it, esp. as affected by human activity. **4** *Computing* the overall structure within which a user, computer, or program operates. **5** a structure designed to be experienced from inside as a work of art. ▫ **environmental** /-'mɛnt(ə)l/ *adj.* **environmentally** /-'mɛnt(ə)li/ *adv.*

environmentalist /ɪnˌvʌɪrən'mɛnt(ə)lɪst, ɛn-/ *n.* **1** a person who is concerned with or advocates the protection of the environment. **2** a person who considers that environment has the primary influence on the development of a person or group. ▫ **environmentalism** *n.*

environment-friendly *adj.* not harmful to the environment.

environs /ɪn'vʌɪrənz, ɛn-, 'ɛnvɪrənz/ *n.pl.* a surrounding district, esp. round an urban area.

envisage /ɪn'vɪzɪdʒ, ɛn-/ *v.tr.* **1** have a mental picture of (a thing or conditions not yet existing). **2** contemplate or conceive, esp. as a possibility or desirable future event. **3** *archaic* **a** face (danger, facts, etc.). **b** look in the face of. ▫ **envisagement** *n.* [French *envisager* (as EN-[1], VISAGE)]

envision /ɛn'vɪʒ(ə)n/ *v.tr.* envisage, visualize.

envoi /'ɛnvɔɪ/ *n.* (also **envoy**) **1** a short stanza concluding a ballade etc. **2** *archaic* an author's concluding words. [Middle English from Old French *envoi*, from *envoyer* (as ENVOY[1])]

envoy[1] /'ɛnvɔɪ/ *n.* **1** a messenger or representative, esp. on a diplomatic mission. **2** (in full **envoy extraordinary**) a minister plenipotentiary, ranking below ambassador and above chargé d'affaires.

□ **envoyship** *n.* [French *envoyé*, past part. of *envoyer* 'send', from *en voie* 'on the way', from Latin *via*]

envoy[2] var. of ENVOI.

envy /ˈɛnvi/ *n.* & *v.* ● *n.* (*pl.* **-ies**) **1** a feeling of discontented or resentful longing aroused by another's better fortune etc. **2** the object or ground of this feeling (*their house is the envy of the neighbourhood*). ● *v.tr.* (**-ies, -ied**) feel envy of (a person, circumstances, etc.) (*I envy you your position*). □ **envier** *n.* [Middle English via Old French *envie* from Latin *invidia*, from *invidēre* 'envy' (as IN-[1], *vidēre* 'see')]

enweave var. of INWEAVE.

enwrap /ɪnˈrap, ɛn-/ *v.tr.* (also **inwrap**) (**-wrapped, -wrapping**) (often foll. by *in*) *literary* wrap or enfold.

enwreathe /ɪnˈriːð, ɛn-/ *v.tr.* (also **inwreathe**) *literary* surround with or as with a wreath.

Enzed /ɛnˈzɛd/ *n.* *Austral.* & *NZ colloq.* a popular written form of: **1** New Zealand. **2** a New Zealander. □ **Enzedder** *n.* [pronunciation of *NZ*]

enzootic /ɛnzəʊˈɒtɪk/ *adj.* & *n.* ● *adj.* (of a disease) regularly affecting animals in a particular district or at a particular season (cf. ENDEMIC, EPIZOOTIC). ● *n.* an enzootic disease. [Greek *en* 'in' + *zōion* 'animal']

enzyme /ˈɛnzʌɪm/ *n.* *Biochem.* a protein acting as a catalyst in a specific biochemical reaction. □ **enzymatic** /-ˈmatɪk/ *adj.* **enzymic** /-ˈzʌɪmɪk/ *adj.* **enzymology** /-ˈmɒlədʒi/ *n.* [German *Enzym* from medieval Greek *enzumos* 'leavened', from Greek *en* 'in' + *zumē* 'leaven']

EOC *abbr.* Equal Opportunities Commission.

Eocene /ˈiːə(ʊ)siːn/ *adj.* & *n.* *Geol.* ● *adj.* of or relating to the second epoch of the Tertiary period with evidence of an abundance of mammals including horses, bats, and whales. Cf. Appendix X. ● *n.* this epoch or system. [Greek *ēōs* 'dawn' + *kainos* 'new']

eolian *US* var. of AEOLIAN.

eolith /ˈiːə(ʊ)lɪθ/ *n.* *Archaeol.* any of various roughly chipped flints found in Tertiary strata and originally thought to be early artefacts. [Greek *ēōs* 'dawn' + *lithos* 'stone']

eolithic /iːə(ʊ)ˈlɪθɪk/ *adj.* *Archaeol.* of the period preceding the palaeolithic age, thought to include the earliest use of flint tools. [French *éolithique* (as EOLITH)]

eon var. of AEON.

eosin /ˈiːə(ʊ)sɪn/ *n.* a red fluorescent dye used esp. as a stain in optical microscopy. [Greek *ēōs* 'dawn' + -IN]

eosinophil /iːə(ʊ)ˈsɪnəfɪl/ *n.* a white blood cell containing granules readily stained by eosin.

-eous /ɪəs/ *suffix* forming adjectives meaning 'of the nature of' (*erroneous*; *gaseous*).

EP *abbr.* **1** electroplate. **2** (esp. of a gramophone record) extended-play. **3** extreme pressure (used in grading lubricants).

Ep. *abbr.* Epistle.

ep- /ɛp, ɪp, iːp/ *prefix* form of EPI- before a vowel or *h*.

e.p. *abbr.* *Chess* en passant.

EPA *abbr.* (in the US) Environmental Protection Agency.

epact /ˈiːpakt/ *n.* the number of days by which the solar year exceeds the lunar year. [French *épacte* via Late Latin *epactae* from Greek *epaktai* (*hēmerai*) 'intercalated (days)', from *epagō* 'intercalate' (as EPI-, *agō* 'bring')]

eparch /ˈɛpɑːk/ *n.* the chief bishop of an eparchy. [Greek *eparkhos* (as EPI-, *arkhos* 'ruler')]

eparchy /ˈɛpɑːki/ *n.* (*pl.* **-ies**) a province of the Orthodox Church. [Greek *eparkhia* (as EPARCH)]

epaulette /ˈɛpəlɛt, -pɔːl-, ɛpəˈlɛt/ *n.* (*US* **epaulet**) an ornamental shoulder-piece on a coat, dress, etc., esp. on a uniform. [French *épaulette*, diminutive of *épaule* 'shoulder', from Latin *spatula*: see SPATULA]

épée /ˈeɪpeɪ, ˈɛp-/ *n.* a sharp-pointed duelling-sword, used (with the end blunted) in fencing. □ **épéeist** *n.* [French, = sword, from Old French *espee*: see SPAY]

epeirogenesis /ɪˌpʌɪrə(ʊ)ˈdʒɛnɪsɪs/ *n.* (also **epeirogeny** /-ˈrɒdʒəni/) *Geol.* the regional uplift of extensive areas of the earth's crust. □ **epeirogenic** /-ˈdʒɛnɪk/ *adj.* [Greek *ēpeiros* 'mainland' + GENESIS, -GENY]

epenthesis /ɛˈpɛnθɪsɪs/ *n.* (*pl.* **epentheses** /-siːz/) the insertion of a letter or sound within a word, e.g. *b* in *thimble*. □ **epenthetic** /ɛpɛnˈθɛtɪk/ *adj.* [Late Latin from Greek, from *epentithēmi* 'insert' (as EPI- + EN-[2] + *tithēmi* 'place')]

epergne /ɪˈpəːn/ *n.* an ornament (esp. in branched form) for the centre of a dinner-table, holding flowers or fruit. [18th c.: perhaps a corruption of French *épargne* 'saving, economy', in the phrase *taille* or *gravure d'épargne*, metal or etching in which parts are 'spared', i.e. left in relief]

epexegesis /ɛˌpɛksɪˈdʒiːsɪs/ *n.* (*pl.* **epexegeses** /-siːz/) **1** the addition of words to clarify meaning (e.g. *to do* in *difficult to do*). **2** the words added. □ **epexegetic** /-ˈdʒɛtɪk/ *adj.* **epexegetical** /-ˈdʒɛtɪk(ə)l/ *adj.* **epexegetically** /-ˈdʒɛtɪk(ə)li/ *adv.* [Greek *epexēgēsis* (as EPI-, EXEGESIS)]

Eph. *abbr.* Ephesians (New Testament).

ephebe /ɛˈfiːb, ɪ-, ˈɛfiːb/ *n.* *Gk Hist.* a young man of 18–20 undergoing military training. □ **ephebic** /ɛˈfiːbɪk, ɪ-/ *adj.* [Latin *ephebus* from Greek *ephēbos* (as EPI-, *hēbē* 'early manhood')]

ephedra /ɛˈfɛdrə/ *n.* any evergreen shrub of the genus *Ephedra*, with trailing stems and scalelike leaves. [modern Latin from Greek *ephedra* 'sitting upon']

ephedrine /ˈɛfədriːn/ *n.* an alkaloid drug found in some ephedras, causing constriction of the blood vessels and widening of the bronchial passages, and used to relieve asthma etc. [EPHEDRA + -INE[4]]

ephemera[1] /ɪˈfɛm(ə)rə, -ˈfiːm-, ɛ-/ *n.* (*pl.* **ephemeras** or **ephemerae** /-riː/) **1 a** an insect living only a day or a few days. **b** any insect of the order Ephemeroptera, e.g. the mayfly. **2** = EPHEMERON 1. [modern Latin from Greek *ephēmeros* 'lasting only a day' (as EPI-, *hēmera* 'day')]

ephemera[2] *pl.* of EPHEMERON 1.

ephemeral /ɪˈfɛm(ə)r(ə)l, -ˈfiːm-/ *adj.* **1** lasting or of use for only a short time; transitory. **2** lasting only a day. **3** (of an insect, flower, etc.) lasting a day or a few days. □ **ephemerality** /-ˈralɪti/ *n.* **ephemerally** *adv.* **ephemeralness** *n.* [Greek *ephēmeros*: see EPHEMERA[1]]

ephemeris /ɪˈfɛm(ə)rɪs, -ˈfiːm-/ *n.* (*pl.* **ephemerides** /ɛfɪˈmɛrɪdiːz/) *Astron.* **1** a table of the predicted positions of a celestial body. **2** a book of such tables, an almanac. [Latin from Greek *ephēmeris* 'diary' (as EPHEMERAL)]

ephemerist /ɪˈfɛm(ə)rɪst, -ˈfiːm-, ɛ-/ *n.* a collector of ephemera.

ephemeris time *n.* time on a scale defined by the orbital period rather than the axial rotation of the earth.

ephemeron /ɪˈfɛm(ə)rɒn, -ˈfiːm-/ *n.* **1** (*pl.* **ephemera** /-rə/) (usu. in *pl.*) **a** a thing (esp. a printed item) of short-lived interest or usefulness. **b** a short-lived thing. **2** (*pl.* **ephemerons**) = EPHEMERA[1] 1. [as EPHEMERA[1]]

ephod /ˈiːfɒd, ˈɛfɒd/ *n.* a Jewish priestly vestment. [Middle English from Hebrew *'ēpôḏ*]

ephor /ˈɛfɔː/ *n.* *Gk Hist.* each of five senior magistrates in ancient Sparta. □ **ephorate** *n.* [Greek *ephoros* 'overseer' (as EPI-, *horaō* 'see')]

epi- /ˈɛpi/ *prefix* (usu. **ep-** before a vowel or *h*) **1** upon (*epicycle*). **2** above (*epicotyl*). **3** in addition (*epiphenomenon*). [Greek *epi* (*prep.*)]

epiblast /ˈɛpɪblast/ *n.* *Biol.* the outermost layer of a gastrula etc.; the ectoderm. [EPI- + -BLAST]

epic /ˈɛpɪk/ *n.* & *adj.* ● *n.* **1** a long poem narrating the adventures or deeds of one or more heroic or legendary figures, e.g. the *Iliad*, *Paradise Lost*. **2** an imaginative work of any form, embodying a nation's conception of its past history. **3** a book or film based on an epic narrative or heroic in type or scale. **4** a subject fit for recital in an epic. ● *adj.* **1** of or like an epic. **2** grand, heroic. □ **epical** *adj.* **epically** *adv.* [Latin *epicus* from Greek *epikos*, from *epos* 'word, song']

epicarp /ˈɛpɪkɑːp/ *n.* *Bot.* the outermost layer of the pericarp. [EPI- + Greek *karpos* 'fruit']

epicedium /ɛpɪˈsiːdɪəm/ *n.* (*pl.* **epicedia** /-dɪə/) a funeral ode. □ **epicedian** *adj.* [Latin from Greek *epikēdeion* (as EPI-, *kēdos* 'care')]

epicene /ˈɛpɪsiːn/ *adj.* & *n.* ● *adj.* **1** *Gram.* denoting either sex without change of gender. **2** of, for, or used by both sexes. **3** having characteristics of both sexes. **4** having no characteristics of either sex. **5** effete, effeminate. ● *n.* an epicene person. [Middle English via Late Latin *epicoenus* from Greek *epikoinos* (as EPI-, *koinos* 'common')]

epicentre /ˈɛpɪsɛntə/ *n.* (*US* **epicenter**) **1** *Geol.* the point at which an earthquake reaches the earth's surface. **2** the central point of a difficulty. □ **epicentral** /-ˈsɛntr(ə)l/ *adj.* [Greek *epikentros* (*adj.*) (as EPI-, CENTRE)]

epicontinental /ˌɛpɪkɒntɪˈnɛnt(ə)l/ *adj.* (of the sea) over the continental shelf.

epicotyl /ɛpɪˈkɒtɪl/ *n.* *Bot.* the region of an embryo or seedling stem above the cotyledon(s).

epicure /ˈɛpɪkjʊə/ *n.* a person with refined tastes, esp. in food and drink. □ **epicurism** *n.* [medieval Latin *epicurus* 'one preferring sensual enjoyment': see EPICUREAN]

Epicurean /ˌɛpɪkjʊ(ə)ˈriːən/ *n.* & *adj.* ● *n.* **1** a disciple or student of the Greek philosopher Epicurus (d. 270 BC), who taught that the highest good is personal happiness. **2** (**epicurean**) a person devoted to (esp. sensual) enjoyment. ● *adj.* **1** of or concerning Epicurus or his ideas. **2** (**epicurean**) characteristic of an epicurean. □ **Epicureanism** *n.* [French *épicurien* or Latin *epicureus* from Greek *epikoureios*, from *Epikouros* 'Epicurus']

epicycle /ˈɛpɪsʌɪk(ə)l/ *n.* **1** *Geom.* a small circle whose centre moves round the circumference of a larger one. **2** *hist.* any such circle used to describe planetary orbits in the Ptolemaic system. □ **epicyclic** /-ˈsʌɪklɪk, -ˈsɪklɪk/ *adj.* [Middle English via Old French or Late Latin *epicyclus* from Greek *epikuklos* (as EPI-, *kuklos* 'circle')]

epicycloid /ɛpɪˈsʌɪklɔɪd/ *n.* *Math.* a curve traced by a point on the circumference of a circle rolling on the exterior of another circle. □ **epicycloidal** /-ˈklɔɪd(ə)l/ *adj.*

epideictic /ɛpɪˈdʌɪktɪk/ *adj.* meant for effect or display, esp. in speaking. [Greek *epideiktikos* (as EPI-, *deiknumi* 'show')]

epidemic /ɛpɪˈdɛmɪk/ *n.* & *adj.* ● *n.* **1** a widespread occurrence of a disease in a community at a particular time. **2** such a disease. **3** (foll. by *of*) a wide prevalence of something usu. undesirable. ● *adj.* in the nature of an epidemic (cf. ENDEMIC). □ **epidemically** *adv.* [French *épidémique* from *épidémie*, via Late Latin *epidemia* from Greek *epidēmia* 'prevalence of disease', from *epidēmios* (*adj.*) (as EPI-, *dēmos* 'the people')]

epidemiology /ˌɛpɪdiːmɪˈɒlədʒi/ *n.* the study of the incidence and distribution of diseases and of other factors relating to health. □ **epidemiological** /-mɪəˈlɒdʒɪk(ə)l/ *adj.* **epidemiologist** *n.*

epidermis /ɛpɪˈdəːmɪs/ *n.* **1** the outer cellular layer of the skin. **2** *Bot.* the outer layer of cells of leaves, stems, roots, etc. □ **epidermal** *adj.* **epidermic** *adj.* **epidermoid** *adj.* [Late Latin from Greek, formed as EPI- + *derma* 'skin']

epidiascope /ɛpɪˈdʌɪəskəʊp/ *n.* an optical projector capable of giving images of both opaque and transparent objects. [EPI- + DIA- + -SCOPE]

epididymis /ɛpɪˈdɪdɪmɪs/ *n.* (*pl.* **epididymides** /-dɪˈdɪmɪdiːz/) *Anat.* a convoluted duct behind the testis, along which sperm passes to the vas deferens. [Greek *epididumis* (as EPI-, *didumoi* 'testicles')]

epidural /ɛpɪˈdjʊər(ə)l/ *adj.* & *n.* ● *adj.* **1** *Anat.* on or around the dura mater. **2** (of an anaesthetic) introduced into the space around the dura mater of the spinal cord. ● *n.* an epidural anaesthetic, used esp. in childbirth to produce loss of sensation below the waist. [EPI- + DURA MATER]

epifauna /ˈɛpɪfɔːnə/ *n.* *Zool.* the animal life which lives on the surface of the seabed, a river bed, etc., or attached to submerged objects or to aquatic animals or plants (cf. INFAUNA). □ **epifaunal** *adj.* [Danish (as EPI-, FAUNA)]

epigastrium /ɛpɪˈgastrɪəm/ *n.* (*pl.* **epigastria** /-rɪə/) *Anat.* the part of the abdomen immediately over the stomach. □ **epigastric** *adj.* [Late Latin from Greek *epigastrion* (neut. *adj.*) (as EPI-, *gastēr* 'belly')]

epigeal /ɛpɪˈdʒiːəl/ *adj.* *Bot.* **1** having one or more cotyledons above the ground. **2** growing above the ground. [Greek *epigeios* (as EPI-, *gē* 'earth')]

epigene /ˈɛpɪdʒiːn/ *adj.* *Geol.* produced on the surface of the earth. [French *épigène* from Greek *epigenēs* (as EPI-, *genēs* 'born')]

epigenesis /ɛpɪˈdʒɛnɪsɪs/ *n.* *Biol.* the theory (now generally held) that the embryo develops from an undifferentiated egg cell. [EPI- + GENESIS]

epigenetic /ˌɛpɪdʒɪˈnɛtɪk/ *adj.* **1** *Biol.* **a** relating to epigenesis. **b** due to external not genetic influences. **2** *Geol.* formed later than the surrounding rock.

epiglottis /ɛpɪˈglɒtɪs/ *n.* *Anat.* a flap of cartilage at the root of the tongue, which is depressed during swallowing to cover the windpipe. □ **epiglottal** *adj.* **epiglottic** *adj.* [Greek *epiglōttis* (as EPI-, *glōtta* 'tongue')]

epigone /ˈɛpɪgəʊn/ *n.* (*pl.* **epigones** or **epigoni** /ɪˈpɪgənʌɪ, ɛ-/) a member of a later (and less distinguished) generation. [pl. from French *épigones* via Latin *epigoni* from Greek *epigonoi* 'those born afterwards' (as EPI-, root of *gignomai* 'be born')]

epigram /ˈɛpɪgram/ *n.* **1** a short witty poem. **2** **a** a saying or maxim, esp. a proverbial one. **b** a pointed remark or expression, esp. a witty one. **3** the use of concise witty remarks. □ **epigrammatic** /-grəˈmatɪk/ *adj.* **epigrammatically** /-grəˈmatɪk(ə)li/ *adv.* **epigrammatist** /-ˈgramətɪst/ *n.* **epigrammatize** /-ˈgramətʌɪz/ *v.tr.* & *intr.* (also **-ise**). [French *épigramme* or Latin *epigramma* from Greek *epigramma -atos* (as EPI-, -GRAM)]

epigraph /ˈɛpɪgrɑːf/ *n.* an inscription on a statue or coin, at the head of a chapter, etc. [Greek *epigraphē* from *epigraphō* (as EPI-, *graphō* 'write')]

epigraphy /ɪˈpɪgrəfi, ɛ-/ *n.* the study of (esp. ancient) inscriptions. □ **epigraphic** /-ˈgrafɪk/ *adj.* **epigraphical** /-ˈgrafɪk(ə)l/ *adj.* **epigraphically** /-ˈgrafɪk(ə)li/ *adv.* **epigraphist** *n.*

epilate /ˈɛpɪleɪt/ *v.tr.* *Med.* remove hair by the roots from. □ **epilation** /-ˈleɪʃ(ə)n/ *n.* [French *épiler* (as EX-[1], Latin *pilus* 'hair') cf. DEPILATE]

epilepsy /ˈɛpɪlɛpsi/ *n.* a neurological disorder marked by episodes of sensory disturbance, loss of consciousness, or convulsions. [French *épilepsie* or Late Latin *epilepsia* from Greek *epilēpsia*, from *epilambanō* 'attack' (as EPI-, *lambanō* 'take')]

epileptic /ɛpɪˈlɛptɪk/ *adj.* & *n.* ● *adj.* of or relating to epilepsy. ● *n.* a person with epilepsy. [French *épileptique* via Late Latin *epilepticus* from Greek *epilēptikos* (as EPILEPSY)]

epilimnion /ɛpɪˈlɪmnɪən/ *n.* (*pl.* **epilimnia** /-nɪə/) the upper layer of water in a stratified lake. [EPI- + Greek *limnion*, diminutive of *limnē* 'lake']

epilogist /ɪˈpɪlədʒɪst, ɛ-/ *n.* the writer or speaker of an epilogue.

epilogue /ˈɛpɪlɒg/ *n.* (also *US* **epilog**) **1** **a** the concluding part of a literary work. **b** an appendix. **2** a speech or short poem addressed to the audience by an actor at the end of a play. **3** *Brit.* a short piece at the end of a day's broadcasting (cf. PROLOGUE *n.* 1a). [Middle English via French *épilogue* and Latin *epilogus* from Greek *epilogos* (as EPI-, *logos* 'speech')]

epimer /ˈɛpɪmə/ *n.* *Chem.* either of two isomers with different configurations of atoms about one of several asymmetric carbon atoms present. □ **epimeric** /-ˈmɛrɪk/ *adj.* **epimerism** /ɪˈpɪm-, ɛ-/ *n.* [German (as EPI-, -MER)]

epimerize /ɪˈpɪmərʌɪz, ɛ-/ *v.tr.* (also **-ise**) *Chem.* convert from one epimeric form into the other.

epinasty /ˈɛpɪnasti/ *n. Bot.* a tendency in plant organs to grow more rapidly on the upper side. [EPI- + Greek *nastos* 'pressed']

epinephrine /ɛpɪˈnɛfrɪn, -riːn/ *n. Biochem.* = ADRENALIN. [Greek *epi* 'upon' + *nephros* 'kidney']

epiphany /ɪˈpɪf(ə)ni, ɛ-/ *n.* (*pl.* **-ies**) **1** (**Epiphany**) **a** the manifestation of Christ to the Magi according to the biblical account. **b** the festival commemorating this on 6 January. **2** any manifestation of a god or demigod. ▫ **epiphanic** /ɛpɪˈfanɪk/ *adj.* [Middle English from Greek *epiphaneia* 'manifestation', from *epiphainō* 'reveal' (as EPI-, *phainō* 'show'): sense 1 via Old French *epiphanie* and ecclesiastical Latin *epiphania*]

epiphenomenon /ˌɛpɪfəˈnɒmɪnən/ *n.* (*pl.* **epiphenomena** /-nə/) a secondary effect or by-product which arises from but does not causally influence a process, esp.: **1** *Med.* a secondary symptom, occurring simultaneously with a disease etc. but not directly related to it. **2** consciousness regarded as a by-product of brain activity. ▫ **epiphenomenal** *adj.*

epiphysis /ɪˈpɪfɪsɪs, ɛ-/ *n.* (*pl.* **epiphyses** /-siːz/) *Anat.* **1** the end part of a long bone, initially growing separately from the shaft. **2** = PINEAL BODY. [modern Latin from Greek *epiphusis* (as EPI-, *phusis* 'growth')]

epiphyte /ˈɛpɪfʌɪt/ *n.* a plant growing on another but not parasitic, e.g. a moss on a tree trunk. ▫ **epiphytal** /-ˈfʌɪt(ə)l/ *adj.* **epiphytic** /ɛpɪˈfɪtɪk/ *adj.* [EPI- + Greek *phuton* 'plant']

episcopacy /ɪˈpɪskəpəsi, ɛ-/ *n.* (*pl.* **-ies**) **1** government of a Church by bishops. **2** (prec. by *the*) the bishops.

episcopal /ɪˈpɪskəp(ə)l, ɛ-/ *adj.* **1** of a bishop or bishops. **2** (of a Church) constituted on the principle of government by bishops. ▫ **episcopalism** *n.* **episcopally** *adv.* [Middle English from French *épiscopal* or ecclesiastical Latin *episcopalis*, from *episcopus* BISHOP]

Episcopal Church *n.* the Anglican Church in Scotland and the US, with elected bishops.

episcopalian /ɪˌpɪskəˈpeɪlɪən, ɛ-/ *adj. & n.* ● *adj.* **1** of or advocating government of a Church by bishops. **2** of or belonging to an episcopal Church or (**Episcopalian**) the Episcopal Church. ● *n.* **1** an adherent of episcopacy. **2** (**Episcopalian**) a member of the Episcopal Church. ▫ **episcopalianism** *n.*

episcopate /ɪˈpɪskəpət, ɛ-/ *n.* **1** the office or tenure of a bishop. **2** (prec. by *the*) the bishops collectively. [ecclesiastical Latin *episcopatus* from *episcopus* BISHOP]

episcope /ˈɛpɪskəʊp/ *n.* an optical projector giving images of opaque objects.

episematic /ˌɛpɪsɪˈmatɪk/ *adj. Zool.* (of coloration, markings, etc.) serving to help recognition by animals of the same species. [EPI- + Greek *sēma sēmatos* 'sign']

episiotomy /ɪˌpɪsɪˈɒtəmi, ɛ-/ *n.* (*pl.* **-ies**) a surgical cut made at the opening of the vagina during childbirth, to aid delivery. [Greek *epision* 'pubic region']

episode /ˈɛpɪsəʊd/ *n.* **1** one event or a group of events as part of a sequence. **2** each of the parts of a serial story or broadcast. **3** an incident or set of incidents in a narrative. **4** an incident that is distinct but contributes to a whole (*a romantic episode in her life*). **5** *Mus.* a passage containing distinct material or introducing a new subject. **6** the part between two choric songs in Greek tragedy. [Greek *epeisodion* (as EPI- + *eisodos* 'entry', from *eis* 'into' + *hodos* 'way')]

episodic /ɛpɪˈsɒdɪk/ *adj.* (also **episodical** /-ˈsɒdɪk(ə)l/) **1** occurring as separate episodes. **2** sporadic; occurring at irregular intervals. ▫ **episodically** *adv.*

epistaxis /ɛpɪˈstaksɪs/ *n. Med.* bleeding from the nose. [modern Latin from Greek (as EPI-, *stazō* 'drip')]

epistemic /ɛpɪˈstiːmɪk, -ˈstɛm-/ *adj. Philos.* relating to knowledge or to the degree of its validation. ▫ **epistemically** *adv.* [Greek *epistēmē* 'knowledge']

epistemology /ɪˌpɪstɪˈmɒlədʒi, ɛ-/ *n.* the theory of knowledge, esp. with regard to its methods and validation. ▫ **epistemological** /-məˈlɒdʒɪk(ə)l/ *adj.* **epistemologically** /-məˈlɒdʒɪk(ə)li/ *adv.* **epistemologist** *n.*

epistle /ɪˈpɪs(ə)l/ *n.* **1** *formal* or *joc.* a letter, esp. a long one on a serious subject. **2** (also **Epistle**) **a** any of the letters of the Apostles in the New Testament. **b** an extract from an Epistle read in a church service. **3** a poem or other literary work in the form of a letter or series of letters. [Middle English via Old French and Latin *epistola* from Greek *epistolē*, from *epistellō* 'send news' (as EPI-, *stellō* 'send')]

epistolary /ɪˈpɪst(ə)l(ə)ri/ *adj.* **1** in the style or form of a letter or letters. **2** of, carried by, or suited to letters. [French *épistolaire* or Latin *epistolaris* (as EPISTLE)]

epistrophe /ɪˈpɪstrəfi, ɛ-/ *n.* the repetition of a word at the end of successive clauses. [Greek (as EPI-, *strophē* 'turning')]

epistyle /ˈɛpɪstʌɪl/ *n. Archit.* = ARCHITRAVE. [French *épistyle* or Latin *epistylium* from Greek *epistulion* (as EPI-, *stulos* 'pillar')]

epitaph /ˈɛpɪtɑːf, -taf/ *n.* words written in memory of a person who has died, esp. as a tomb inscription. [Middle English via Old French *epitaphe* and Latin *epitaphium* from Greek *epitaphion* 'funeral oration' (as EPI-, *taphos* 'tomb')]

epitaxy /ˈɛpɪtaksi/ *n. Crystallog.* the growth of crystals on a crystalline substrate that determines their orientation. ▫ **epitaxial** /-ˈtaksɪəl/ *adj.* [French *épitaxie* (as EPI-, Greek *taxis* 'arrangement')]

epithalamium /ˌɛpɪθəˈleɪmɪəm/ *n.* (*pl.* **epithalamiums** or **epithalamia** /-mɪə/) a song or poem celebrating a marriage. ▫ **epithalamial** *adj.* **epithalamic** /-ˈlamɪk/ *adj.* [Latin from Greek *epithalamion* (as EPI-, *thalamos* 'bridal chamber')]

epithelium /ɛpɪˈθiːlɪəm/ *n.* (*pl.* **epitheliums** or **epithelia** /-lɪə/) *Anat.* the tissue forming the outer layer of the body surface and lining the alimentary canal and other hollow structures. ▫ **epithelial** *adj.* [modern Latin, from EPI- + Greek *thēlē* 'teat']

epithet /ˈɛpɪθɛt/ *n.* **1** an adjective or other descriptive word expressing a quality or attribute, esp. used with or as a name. **2** such a word as a term of abuse. ▫ **epithetic** /-ˈθɛtɪk/ *adj.* **epithetical** /-ˈθɛtɪk(ə)l/ *adj.* **epithetically** /-ˈθɛtɪk(ə)li/ *adv.* [French *épithète* or Latin *epitheton* from Greek *epitheton*, from *epitithēmi* 'add' (as EPI-, *tithēmi* 'place')]

epitome /ɪˈpɪtəmi, ɛ-/ *n.* **1** a person or thing embodying a quality, class, etc. **2** a thing representing another in miniature. **3** a summary of a written work; an abstract. ▫ **epitomist** *n.* [Latin from Greek *epitomē*, from *epitemnō* 'abridge' (as EPI-, *temnō* 'cut')]

epitomize /ɪˈpɪtəmʌɪz, ɛ-/ *v.tr.* (also **-ise**) **1** be a perfect example of (a quality etc.); typify. **2** make an epitome of (a work). ▫ **epitomization** /-ˈzeɪʃ(ə)n/ *n.*

epizoon /ɛpɪˈzəʊɒn/ *n.* (*pl.* **epizoa** /-ˈzəʊə/) an animal living on another animal. [modern Latin (as EPI-, Greek *zōion* 'animal')]

epizootic /ˌɛpɪzəʊˈɒtɪk/ *adj. & n.* ● *adj.* (of a disease) temporarily prevalent and widespread in an animal population (cf. ENZOOTIC). ● *n.* an outbreak of such a disease. [French *épizootique* from *épizootie* (as EPIZOON)]

EPNS *abbr.* electroplated nickel silver.

epoch /ˈiːpɒk/ *n.* **1** a period of history or of a person's life marked by notable events. **2** the beginning of an era. **3** *Geol.* a division of a period, corresponding to a set of strata. ▫ **epochal** /ˈɛpɒk(ə)l, iːˈpɒk-/ *adj.* [modern Latin *epocha* from Greek *epokhē* 'stoppage, fixed point of time']

epoch-making *adj.* remarkable, historic; of major importance.

epode /ˈɛpəʊd/ *n.* **1** a form of lyric poem written in couplets each of a long line followed by a shorter one. **2** the third section of an ancient Greek choral ode or of one division of it. [French *épode* or Latin *epodos* from Greek *epōidos* (as EPI-, ODE)]

eponym /ˈɛpənɪm/ *n.* **1** a person (real or imaginary) after whom a discovery, invention, place, institution, etc., is named or thought to be named. **2** the name given. ▫ **eponymous** /ɪˈpɒnɪməs, ɛ-/ *adj.* [Greek *epōnumos* (as EPI-, *-ōnumos* from *onoma* 'name')]

EPOS /ˈiːpɒs/ *abbr.* electronic point-of-sale (of retail outlets recording information electronically).

epoxide /ɪˈpɒksʌɪd/ *n. Chem.* a compound containing an oxygen atom bonded in a triangular arrangement to two carbon atoms. [EPI- + OXIDE]

epoxy /ɪˈpɒksi, ɛ-/ *adj. Chem.* relating to or derived from an epoxide. [EPI- + OXY-[2]]

epoxy resin *n.* a synthetic thermosetting resin containing epoxy groups.

EPROM /ˈiːprɒm/ *n. Computing* a read-only memory whose contents can be erased and replaced by a special process. [*e*rasable *p*rogrammable *ROM*]

eps *abbr.* earnings per share.

epsilon /ˈɛpsɪlɒn, ɛpˈsʌɪlɒn/ *n.* the fifth letter of the Greek alphabet (Ε, ϵ). [Middle English from Greek, = bare or simple E, from *psilos* 'bare']

Epsom salts /ˈɛpsəm/ *n.pl.* a preparation of magnesium sulphate used as a purgative etc. [*Epsom*, a town in Surrey, where it was first found occurring naturally]

EPSRC *abbr.* (in the UK) Engineering and Physical Sciences Research Council.

Epstein–Barr virus /ɛpstʌɪnˈbɑː/ *n.* a herpes virus causing glandular fever and associated with certain cancers, e.g. Burkitt's lymphoma. [named after M.A. *Epstein*, British virologist b. 1921, and Y.M. *Barr*, Irish-born virologist b. 1932]

epyllion /ɪˈpɪlɪən, ɛ-/ *n.* (*pl.* **epyllia** /-lɪə/) a miniature epic poem. [Greek *epullion*, diminutive of *epos* 'word, song']

equable /ˈɛkwəb(ə)l/ *adj.* **1** even; not varying. **2** uniform and moderate (*an equable climate*). **3** (of a person) not easily disturbed or angered. ▫ **equability** /-ˈbɪlɪti/ *n.* **equably** *adv.* [Latin *aequabilis* (as EQUATE)]

equal /ˈiːkw(ə)l/ *adj., n., & v.* ● *adj.* **1** (often foll. by *to, with*) the same in quantity, quality, size, degree, rank, level, etc. **2** evenly balanced (*an equal contest*). **3** having the same rights or status (*human beings are essentially equal*). **4** uniform in application or effect. ● *n.* a person or thing equal to another, esp. in rank, status, or characteristic quality (*their treatment of the subject has no equal*; *is the equal of any man*). ● *v.tr.* (**equalled, equalling**; *US* **equaled, equaling**) **1** be equal to in number, quality, etc. **2** achieve something that is equal to (an achievement) or to the achievement of (a person). ▫ **be equal to** have the ability or resources for. [Middle English from Latin *aequalis*, from *aequus* 'even']

equalitarian /ɪˌkwɒlɪˈtɛːrɪən, iː-/ *n.* = EGALITARIAN. ▫ **equalitarianism** *n.* [EQUALITY, on the pattern of *humanitarian* etc.]

equality /ɪˈkwɒlɪti, iː-/ *n.* the state of being equal. [Middle English via Old French *equalité* from Latin *aequalitas -tatis* (as EQUAL)]

equalize /ˈiːkwəlʌɪz/ *v.* (also **-ise**) **1** *tr. & intr.* make or become equal. **2** *intr.* level the score in a match by scoring a goal etc. ▫ **equalization** /-ˈzeɪʃ(ə)n/ *n.*

equalizer /ˈiːkwəlʌɪzə/ *n.* (also **-iser**) **1** an equalizing score or goal etc. in a game. **2** *slang* a weapon, esp. a gun. **3** *Electr.* a connection in a system which compensates for any undesirable frequency or phase response with the system.

equally /ˈiːkw(ə)li/ *adv.* **1** in an equal manner (*treated them all equally*). **2** to an equal degree (*is equally important*).

■ **Usage** In sense 2, construction with *as* (e.g. *equally as important*) is often found, but is considered incorrect by some people.

equal opportunity *n.* (often in *pl.*) the opportunity or right to be employed, paid, etc., without discrimination on grounds of sex, race, etc. (often *attrib.*: *equal opportunity* (or *opportunities*) *employer*).

equal sign *n.* (also **equals sign**) the symbol =.

equal temperament see TEMPERAMENT 3.

equanimity /ɛkwəˈnɪmɪti, iː-/ *n.* mental composure, evenness of temper, esp. in misfortune. ▫ **equanimous** /ɪˈkwanɪməs, iː-/ *adj.* [Latin *aequanimitas* from *aequanimis*, from *aequus* 'even' + *animus* 'mind']

equate /ɪˈkweɪt/ *v.* **1** *tr.* (usu. foll. by *to, with*) regard as equal or equivalent. **2** *intr.* (foll. by *with*) **a** be equal or equivalent to. **b** agree or correspond. ▫ **equatable** *adj.* [Middle English from Latin *aequare aequat-*, from *aequus* 'equal']

equation /ɪˈkweɪʒ(ə)n/ *n.* **1** the process of equating or making equal; the state of being equal. **2** *Math.* a statement that two mathematical expressions are equal (indicated by the sign =). **3** *Chem.* a formula representing a chemical reaction expressed in terms of the molecules etc. taking part. ▫ **equation of the first order, second order**, etc. an equation involving only the first derivative, second derivative, etc. ▫ **equational** *adj.* [Middle English from Old French *equation* or Latin *aequatio* (as EQUATE)]

equator /ɪˈkweɪtə/ *n.* **1** an imaginary line around the earth or other body, equidistant from the poles. **2** *Astron.* = CELESTIAL EQUATOR. [Middle English from Old French *equateur* or medieval Latin *aequator* (as EQUATION)]

equatorial /ɛkwəˈtɔːrɪəl/ *adj.* of or near the equator. ▫ **equatorially** *adv.*

equatorial mount *n.* (also **equatorial mounting**) *Astron.* a mount for an astronomical telescope that rotates about two perpendicular axes aligned with the celestial poles.

equatorial telescope *n.* an astronomical telescope on an equatorial mount.

equerry /ɪˈkwɛri, ˈɛkwəri/ *n.* (*pl.* **-ies**) **1** an officer of the British royal household attending members of the royal family. **2** *hist.* an officer of a prince's or noble's household having charge over the horses. [earlier *esquiry* via Old French *esquierie* 'company of squires, prince's stables', from Old French *esquier* ESQUIRE: perhaps associated with Latin *equus* 'horse']

equestrian /ɪˈkwɛstrɪən, ɛ-/ *adj. & n.* ● *adj.* **1** of or relating to horses and horse-riding. **2** on horseback. ● *n.* (*fem.* **equestrienne** /-trɪˈɛn/) a rider or performer on horseback. ▫ **equestrianism** *n.* [Latin *equestris* from *eques* 'horseman, knight', from *equus* 'horse']

equi- /ˈiːkwi, ɛ-/ *comb. form* equal. [Latin *aequi-* from *aequus* 'equal']

equiangular /iːkwɪˈaŋgjʊlə, ɛ-/ *adj.* having equal angles.

equidistant /iːkwɪˈdɪst(ə)nt, ɛ-/ *adj.* at equal distances. ▫ **equidistantly** *adv.*

equilateral /iːkwɪˈlat(ə)r(ə)l, ɛ-/ *adj.* having all its sides equal in length.

equilibrate /iːkwɪˈlʌɪbreɪt, ɪˈkwɪlɪ-, iː-/ *v.* **1** *tr.* cause (two things) to balance. **2** *intr.* be in equilibrium; balance. ▫ **equilibration** /-ˈbreɪʃ(ə)n/ *n.* **equilibrator** /ɪˈkwɪlɪbreɪtə, iː-/ *n.* [Late Latin *aequilibrare aequilibrat-* (as EQUI-, *libra* 'balance')]

equilibrist /ɪˈkwɪlɪbrɪst, iː-; iːkwɪˈlɪb-, ɛ-/ *n.* an acrobat, esp. on a high rope.

equilibrium /iːkwɪˈlɪbrɪəm, ɛ-/ *n.* (*pl.* **equilibria** /-rɪə/ or **equilibriums**) **1** a state of physical balance. **2** a state of mental or emotional equanimity. **3** a state in which the energy in a system is evenly distributed and forces, influences, etc., balance each other. [Latin (as EQUI-, *libra* 'balance')]

equine /ˈiːkwʌɪn, ˈɛk-/ *adj.* of or like a horse. [Latin *equinus* from *equus* 'horse']

equinoctial /iːkwɪˈnɒkʃ(ə)l, ɛ-/ *adj. & n.* ● *adj.* **1** happening at or near the time of an equinox (*equinoctial gales*). **2** of or relating to equal day and night. **3** at or near the (terrestrial) equator. ● *n.* (in full **equinoctial line**) = CELESTIAL EQUATOR. [Middle English from Old French *equinoctial* or Latin *aequinoctialis* (as EQUINOX)]

equinoctial point *n.* the point at which the ecliptic cuts the celestial equator (twice each year at an equinox).

equinoctial year see YEAR 1.

equinox /ˈi:kwɪnɒks, ɛ-/ *n.* **1** the time or date (twice each year) at which the sun crosses the celestial equator, when day and night are of equal length (about 22 Sept. and 20 Mar.). **2** = EQUINOCTIAL POINT. [Middle English from Old French *equinoxe* or medieval Latin *equinoxium* for Latin *aequinoctium* (as EQUI-, *nox noctis* 'night')]

equip /ɪˈkwɪp/ *v.tr.* (**equipped**, **equipping**) supply with what is needed. □ **equipper** *n.* [French *équiper*, probably from Old Norse *skipa* 'to man (a ship)', from *skip* SHIP]

equipage /ˈɛkwɪpɪdʒ/ *n.* **1 a** requisites for an undertaking. **b** an outfit for a special purpose. **2** a carriage and horses with attendants. [French *équipage* (as EQUIP)]

equipment /ɪˈkwɪpm(ə)nt/ *n.* **1** the necessary articles, clothing, etc., for a purpose. **2** the process of equipping or being equipped. [French *équipement* (as EQUIP)]

equipoise /ˈɛkwɪpɔɪz, i:-/ *n. & v.* ● *n.* **1** equilibrium; a balanced state. **2** a counterbalancing thing. ● *v.tr.* counterbalance.

equipollent /i:kwɪˈpɒl(ə)nt, ɛ-/ *adj. & n.* ● *adj.* **1** equal in power, force, etc. **2** practically equivalent. ● *n.* an equipollent thing. □ **equipollence** *n.* **equipollency** *n.* [Middle English via Old French *equipolent* from Latin *aequipollens -entis* 'of equal value' (as EQUI-, *pollēre* 'be strong')]

equipotential /ˌi:kwɪpəˈtɛnʃ(ə)l, ˌɛ-/ *adj. & n. Physics* ● *adj.* (of a surface or line) having the potential of a force the same or constant at all its points. ● *n.* an equipotential line or surface.

equiprobable /i:kwɪˈprɒbəb(ə)l, ɛ-/ *adj. Logic* equally probable. □ **equiprobability** /-ˈbɪlɪti/ *n.*

equisetum /ɛkwɪˈsi:təm/ *n.* (*pl.* **equiseta** /-tə/, **-tums**) a horsetail (plant). [modern Latin, from Latin *equus* 'horse' + *saeta* 'bristle']

equitable /ˈɛkwɪtəb(ə)l/ *adj.* **1** fair, just. **2** *Law* valid in equity as distinct from law. □ **equitableness** *n.* **equitably** *adv.* [French *équitable* (as EQUITY)]

equitation /ɛkwɪˈteɪʃ(ə)n/ *n.* the art and practice of horsemanship and horse-riding. [French *équitation* or Latin *equitatio*, from *equitare* 'ride a horse' via *eques equitis* 'horseman' from *equus* 'horse']

equity /ˈɛkwɪti/ *n.* (*pl.* **-ies**) **1** fairness. **2** the application of general principles of justice to correct or supplement the law. **3 a** the value of the shares issued by a company. **b** (in *pl.*) stocks and shares not bearing fixed interest. **4** the net value of a mortgaged property after the deduction of charges. **5** (**Equity**) the actors' trade union. [Middle English via Old French *equité* from Latin *aequitas -tatis*, from *aequus* 'fair']

equivalent /ɪˈkwɪv(ə)l(ə)nt/ *adj. & n.* ● *adj.* **1** (often foll. by *to*) equal in value, amount, importance, etc. **2** corresponding. **3** (of words) having the same meaning. **4** having the same result. **5** *Chem.* (of a substance) equal in combining or displacing capacity. ● *n.* **1** an equivalent thing, amount, word, etc. **2** (in full **equivalent weight**) *Chem.* the weight of a substance that can combine with or displace one gram of hydrogen or eight grams of oxygen. □ **equivalence** *n.* **equivalency** *n.* **equivalently** *adv.* [Middle English via Old French from Late Latin *aequivalēre* (as EQUI-, *valēre* 'be worth')]

equivocal /ɪˈkwɪvək(ə)l/ *adj.* **1** of double or doubtful meaning; ambiguous. **2** of uncertain nature. **3** (of a person, character, etc.) questionable, suspect. □ **equivocality** /-ˈkalɪti/ *n.* **equivocally** *adv.* **equivocalness** *n.* [Late Latin *aequivocus* (as EQUI-, *vocare* 'call')]

equivocate /ɪˈkwɪvəkeɪt/ *v.intr.* use ambiguity to conceal the truth. □ **equivocation** /-ˈkeɪʃ(ə)n/ *n.* **equivocator** *n.* **equivocatory** *adj.* [Middle English from Late Latin *aequivocare* (as EQUIVOCAL)]

equivoque /ˈi:kwɪvəʊk, ˈɛ-/ *n.* (also **equivoke**) **1** a pun; wordplay. **2** ambiguity. [Middle English, in the sense 'equivocal', from Old French *equivoque* or Late Latin *aequivocus* EQUIVOCAL]

ER *abbr.* **1** Queen Elizabeth. **2** King Edward. [Latin *Elizabetha Regina*, *Edwardus Rex*]

Er *symb. Chem.* the element erbium.

er /ə:, ə/ *int.* expressing hesitation or a pause in speech. [imitative]

-er[1] /ə/ *suffix* forming nouns from nouns, adjectives, and many verbs, denoting: **1** a person, animal, or thing that performs a specified action or activity (*cobbler*; *lover*; *executioner*; *poker*; *computer*; *eye-opener*). **2** a person or thing that has a specified attribute or form (*foreigner*; *four-wheeler*; *second-rater*). **3** a person concerned with a specified thing or subject (*hatter*; *geographer*). **4** a person belonging to a specified place or group (*villager*; *New Zealander*; *sixth-former*). [originally 'a person who has to do with': Old English *-ere*, from Germanic]

-er[2] /ə/ *suffix* forming the comparative of adjectives (*wider*; *hotter*) and adverbs (*faster*). [Old English *-ra* (*adj.*), *-or* (*adv.*), from Germanic]

-er[3] /ə/ *suffix* used in slang formations usu. distorting the root word (*rugger*; *soccer*). [probably an extension of -ER[1]]

-er[4] /ə/ *suffix* forming frequentative verbs (*blunder*; *glimmer*; *twitter*). [Old English *-erian, -rian*, from Germanic]

-er[5] /ə/ *suffix* **1** forming nouns and adjectives through Old French or Anglo-French, corresponding to: **a** Latin *-aris* (*sampler*) (cf. -AR[1]). **b** Latin *-arius, -arium* (*butler*; *carpenter*; *danger*). **c** (through Old French *-eüre*) Latin *-atura* or (through Old French *-eör*) Latin *-atorium* (see COUNTER[1], FRITTER[2]). **2** = -OR[1].

-er[6] /ə/ *suffix* esp. *Law* forming nouns denoting verbal action or a document effecting this (*cesser*; *disclaimer*; *misnomer*). [Anglo-French infinitive ending of verbs]

era /ˈɪərə/ *n.* **1** a system of chronology reckoning from a noteworthy event (*the Christian era*). **2** a large distinct period of time, esp. regarded historically (*the pre-Roman era*). **3** a date at which an era begins. **4** *Geol.* a major division of time. [Late Latin *aera* 'number expressed in figures' (pl. of *aes aeris* 'money', treated as fem. sing.)]

eradicate /ɪˈradɪkeɪt/ *v.tr.* root out; destroy completely; get rid of. □ **eradicable** *adj.* **eradication** /-ˈkeɪʃ(ə)n/ *n.* **eradicator** *n.* [Middle English from Latin *eradicare* 'tear up by the roots' (as E-, *radix -icis* 'root')]

erase /ɪˈreɪz/ *v.tr.* **1** rub out; obliterate. **2** remove all traces of (*erased it from my memory*). **3** remove recorded material from (a magnetic tape or medium). □ **erasable** *adj.* **erasure** *n.* [Latin *eradere eras-* (as E-, *radere* 'scrape')]

eraser /ɪˈreɪzə/ *n.* a thing that erases, esp. a piece of rubber or plastic used for removing pencil and ink marks.

Erastian /ɪˈrastɪən/ *n. & adj.* ● *n.* a person who supports the doctrine that the state should have supremacy over the Church in ecclesiastical matters. ● *adj.* of or relating to this doctrine. □ **Erastianism** *n.* [*Erastus*, Swiss physician and theologian (d. 1583), to whom the doctrine was wrongly attributed, + -IAN]

erbium /ˈə:bɪəm/ *n. Chem.* a soft silvery metallic element of the lanthanide series, occurring naturally in apatite and xenotine (symbol **Er**). [modern Latin, from *Ytterby* in Sweden, where it was first found]

ere /ɛ:/ *prep. & conj. poet.* or *archaic* before (of time) (*ere noon*; *ere they come*). [Old English *ǣr*, from Germanic]

erect /ɪˈrɛkt/ *adj. & v.* ● *adj.* **1** upright, vertical. **2** (of the penis, clitoris, or nipples) enlarged and rigid, esp. in sexual excitement. **3** (of hair) bristling, standing up from the skin. ● *v.tr.* **1** raise; set upright. **2** build. **3** establish (*erect a theory*). □ **erectable** *adj.* **erectly** *adv.*

erectness *n.* **erector** *n.* [Middle English from Latin *erigere erect-* 'set up' (as E-, *regere* 'direct')]

erectile /ɪ'rɛktʌɪl/ *adj.* that can be erected or become erect. [French *érectile* (as ERECT)]

erection /ɪ'rɛkʃ(ə)n/ *n.* **1** the act or an instance of erecting; the state of being erected. **2** a building or structure. **3 a** *Physiol.* an enlarged and erect state of erectile tissue, esp. of the penis. **b** an occurrence of this. [French *érection* or Latin *erectio* (as ERECTILE)]

E-region var. of E-LAYER.

eremite /'ɛrɪmʌɪt/ *n.* a hermit or recluse (esp. Christian). □ **eremitic** /-'mɪtɪk/ *adj.* **eremitical** /-'mɪtɪk(ə)l/ *adj.* [Middle English from Old French, variant of *hermite, ermite* HERMIT]

erethism /'ɛrɪθɪz(ə)m/ *n.* **1** an excessive sensitivity to stimulation of any part of the body, esp. the sexual organs. **2** a state of abnormal mental excitement or irritation. [French *éréthisme* from Greek *erethismos*, from *erethizō* 'irritate']

erg[1] /ə:g/ *n.* *Physics* a unit of work or energy, equal to the work done by a force of one dyne when its point of application moves one centimetre in the direction of action of the force. [Greek *ergon* 'work']

erg[2] /ə:g/ *n.* (*pl.* **ergs** or **areg** /'ɑ:rɛg/) an area of shifting sand dunes in the Sahara. [French from Arabic *'irj*]

ergative /'ə:gətɪv/ *n. & adj. Gram.* ● *n.* (in some languages) a case of nouns that identifies the doer of an action as the object rather than the subject of a verb. ● *adj.* **1** of or in this case. **2** denoting a language in which the object of a verb is typically the doer of an action and the subject is typically the recipient of the action. [Greek *ergates* 'worker' + -IVE]

ergo /'ə:gəʊ/ *adv.* therefore. [Latin]

ergocalciferol /,ə:gə(ʊ)kal'sɪfərɒl/ *n.* = CALCIFEROL. [ERGOT + CALCIFEROL]

ergonomics /ə:gə'nɒmɪks/ *n.* the study of the efficiency of persons in their working environment. □ **ergonomic** *adj.* **ergonomist** /ə:'gɒnəmɪst/ *n.* [Greek *ergon* 'work': cf. ECONOMICS]

ergosterol /ə:'gɒstərɒl/ *n. Biochem.* a plant sterol that is converted to vitamin D_2 when irradiated with ultraviolet light. [ERGOT, on the pattern of CHOLESTEROL]

ergot /'ə:gɒt/ *n.* **1** a disease of rye and other cereals caused by the fungus *Claviceps purpurea*, the presence of which can cause food poisoning. **2 a** this fungus. **b** the dried spore-containing structures of this, used as a source of medicine to aid childbirth. **3** a small horny protuberance on the back of a horse's fetlock. [French from Old French *argot* 'cock's spur', from the appearance produced by the disease]

ergotism /'ə:gətɪz(ə)m/ *n.* poisoning produced by eating food affected by ergot.

erica /'ɛrɪkə/ *n.* any shrub of the genus *Erica*, with small leathery leaves and bell-like flowers; a heath or heather. [Latin from Greek *ereikē* 'heath']

ericaceous /ɛrɪ'keɪʃəs/ *adj.* **1** of or relating to the plant family Ericaceae, which includes heathers, azaleas, and rhododendrons. **2** (of compost) suitable for ericaceous and other lime-hating plants. [modern Latin *Ericaceae* from ERICA]

erigeron /ɪ'rɪdʒərɒn, ɛ-/ *n.* any hardy herbaceous plant of the genus *Erigeron* (daisy family), with daisy-like flowers. [Greek *ērigerōn*, from *ēri* 'early' + *gerōn* 'old man', because it flowers early in the year and some species bear grey down]

Erinys /ɛ'rɪnɪs/ *n.* (*pl.* **Erinyes** /ɛ'rɪnɪi:z/) *Mythol.* a Fury. [Greek]

eristic /ɛ'rɪstɪk/ *adj. & n.* ● *adj.* **1** of or characterized by disputation. **2** (of an argument or arguer) aiming at winning rather than at reaching the truth. ● *n.* **1** the practice of disputation. **2** an exponent of disputation. □ **eristically** *adv.* [Greek *eristikos* via *erizō* 'wrangle' from *eris* 'strife']

Eritrean /ɛrɪ'treɪən/ *adj. & n.* ● *adj.* of or relating to Eritrea in NE Africa. ● *n.* a native or inhabitant of Eritrea. [Italian *Eritrea*, from Latin *Mare Erythraeum* 'the Red Sea']

erk /ə:k/ *n. Brit. slang* **1** a naval rating. **2** *archaic* an aircraftman. **3** a disliked person. [20th c.: origin unknown]

erl-king /'ə:lkɪŋ/ *n.* (in Germanic mythology) a bearded giant or goblin who lures little children to the land of death. [German *Erlkönig* 'alder-king', a mistranslation of Danish *ellerkonge* 'king of the elves']

ERM *abbr.* exchange-rate mechanism.

ermine /'ə:mɪn/ *n.* (*pl.* same or **ermines**) **1** the stoat, esp. when in its white winter fur. **2** its white fur, used as trimming for the robes of judges, peers, etc. **3** *Heraldry* a white fur marked with black spots. □ **ermined** *adj.* [Middle English from Old French *(h)ermine*, probably from medieval Latin (*mus*) *Armenius* 'Armenian (mouse)']

ern *US* var. of ERNE.

-ern /ən/ *suffix* forming adjectives (*northern*). [Old English *-erne*, from Germanic]

erne /ə:n/ *n.* (*US* **ern**) *poet.* a sea eagle. [Old English *earn*, from Germanic]

Ernie /'ə:ni/ *n.* (in the UK) a device for drawing prizewinning numbers of Premium Bonds. [acronym from *e*lectronic *r*andom *n*umber *i*ndicator *e*quipment]

erode /ɪ'rəʊd/ *v.* **1** *tr. & intr.* wear away, destroy or be destroyed gradually. **2** *tr. Med.* (of ulcers etc.) destroy (tissue) little by little. □ **erodible** *adj.* [French *éroder* or Latin *erodere eros-* (as E-, *rodere ros-* 'gnaw')]

erogenous /ɪ'rɒdʒɪnəs, ɛ-/ *adj.* **1** (esp. of a part of the body) sensitive to sexual stimulation. **2** giving rise to sexual desire or excitement. [as EROTIC + -GENOUS]

erosion /ɪ'rəʊʒ(ə)n/ *n.* **1** *Geol.* the wearing away of the earth's surface by the action of water, wind, etc. **2** the act or an instance of eroding; the process of being eroded. □ **erosional** *adj.* **erosive** *adj.* [French *érosion* from Latin *erosio* (as ERODE)]

erotic /ɪ'rɒtɪk/ *adj.* of or causing sexual love, esp. tending to arouse sexual desire or excitement. □ **erotically** *adv.* [French *érotique* from Greek *erōtikos*, from *erōs erōtos* 'sexual love']

erotica /ɪ'rɒtɪkə/ *n.pl.* erotic literature or art.

eroticism /ɪ'rɒtɪsɪz(ə)m/ *n.* **1** erotic nature or character. **2** the use of or response to erotic images or stimulation.

eroticize /ɪ'rɒtɪsʌɪz/ *v.tr.* (also **-ise**) make erotic; stimulate sexually.

erotism /'ɛrətɪz(ə)m/ *n.* sexual desire or excitement; eroticism.

eroto- /ɪ'rɒtəʊ/ *comb. form* erotic, eroticism. [Greek *erōs erōtos* 'sexual love']

erotogenic /ɪ,rɒtə'dʒɛnɪk/ *adj.* (also **erotogenous** /ɛrə'tɒdʒɪnəs/) = EROGENOUS.

erotology /ɛrə'tɒlədʒi/ *n.* the study of sexual love.

erotomania /ɪ,rɒtə(ʊ)'meɪnɪə/ *n.* **1** excessive or abnormal erotic desire. **2** a preoccupation with sexual passion. □ **erotomaniac** /-nɪak/ *n.*

err /ə:/ *v.intr.* **1** be mistaken or incorrect. **2** do wrong; sin. □ **err on the right side** act so that the least harmful of possible errors is the most likely to occur. **err on the side of** act with a specified bias (*errs on the side of generosity*). [Middle English via Old French *errer* from Latin *errare* 'stray': related to Gothic *airzei* 'error', *airzjan* 'lead astray']

errand /'ɛr(ə)nd/ *n.* **1** a short journey, esp. on another's behalf, to take a message, collect goods, etc. **2** the object of such a journey. [Old English *ǣrende*, from Germanic]

errand of mercy *n.* a journey or mission to relieve suffering etc.

errant /'ɛr(ə)nt/ *adj.* **1** erring; deviating from an accepted standard. **2** *literary* or *archaic* travelling in search of adventure (*knight errant*). □ **errancy** *n.* (in sense 1). **errantry** *n.* (in sense 2). [Middle English: sense 1 formed as ERR: sense 2 from Old French *errer*, ultimately via Late Latin *itinerare* from *iter* 'journey']

erratic /ɪ'ratɪk/ *adj. & n.* ● *adj.* **1** inconsistently variable in conduct, opinions, etc., unpredictable, eccentric. **2** uncertain in movement. ● *n.* = ERRATIC BLOCK. □ **erratically** *adv.* **erraticism** *n.* [Middle English via Old French *erratique* from Latin *erraticus* (as ERR)]

erratic block *n.* a large rock carried from a distance by glacial action.

erratum /ɛ'rɑːtəm, -reɪt-/ *n.* (*pl.* **errata** /-tə/) an error in printing or writing, esp. (in *pl.*) a list of corrected errors attached to a book etc. [Latin, neut. past part. of *errare* (as ERR), used as a noun]

erroneous /ɪ'rəʊnɪəs, ɛ-/ *adj.* incorrect; arising from error. □ **erroneously** *adv.* **erroneousness** *n.* [Middle English from Old French *erroneus* or Latin *erroneus*, from *erro -onis* 'vagabond' (as ERR)]

error /'ɛrə/ *n.* **1** a mistake. **2** the condition of being wrong in conduct or judgement (*led into error*). **3** a wrong opinion or judgement. **4** the amount by which something is incorrect or inaccurate in a calculation or measurement. □ **errorless** *adj.* [Middle English via Old French *errour* from Latin *error -oris* (as ERR)]

ersatz /'əːsats, 'ɛː-/ *adj. & n.* ● *adj.* substitute, imitation (esp. of inferior quality). ● *n.* an ersatz thing. [German, = replacement]

Erse /əːs/ *adj. & n. archaic* or *derog.* ● *adj.* of or relating to Highland or esp. Irish Gaelic. ● *n.* the Gaelic language, esp. Irish Gaelic. [early Scots form of IRISH]

erst /əːst/ *adv. archaic* formerly; of old. [Old English *ǣrest*, superlative of *ǣr*: see ERE]

erstwhile /'əːstwʌɪl/ *adj. & adv.* ● *adj.* former, previous. ● *adv. archaic* = ERST.

erubescent /ɛrʊ'bɛs(ə)nt/ *adj.* reddening, blushing. [Latin *erubescere* (as E-, *rubescere* from *rubēre* 'be red')]

eructation /iːrʌk'teɪʃ(ə)n, ɪ-/ *n.* the act or an instance of belching. [Latin *eructatio* from *eructare* (as E-, *ructare* 'belch')]

erudite /'ɛrʊdʌɪt/ *adj.* **1** (of a person) learned. **2** (of writing etc.) showing great learning. □ **eruditely** *adv.* **erudition** /-'dɪʃ(ə)n/ *n.* [Middle English from Latin *eruditus*, past part. of *erudire* 'instruct, train' (as E-, *rudis* 'untrained')]

erupt /ɪ'rʌpt/ *v.intr.* **1** break out suddenly or dramatically. **2** (of a volcano) become active and eject lava etc. **3 a** (of a rash, boil, etc.) appear on the skin. **b** (of the skin) produce a rash etc. **4** (of the teeth) break through the gums in normal development. □ **eruption** *n.* **eruptive** *adj.* [Latin *erumpere erupt-* (as E-, *rumpere* 'break')]

-ery /əri/ *suffix* (also **-ry** /-ri/) forming nouns denoting: **1** a class or kind (*greenery*; *machinery*; *citizenry*). **2** an occupation or employment; a state, condition, or behaviour (*archery*; *slavery*; *bravery*). **3** a place set aside for an activity or characterized by a gathering together of things, animals, etc. (*brewery*; *orangery*). **4** often *derog.* all that has to do with (*knavery*; *popery*; *tomfoolery*). [Middle English, from or suggested by French *-erie*, *-ere*, ultimately from Latin *-ario-*, *-ator*]

erysipelas /ɛrɪ'sɪpɪləs/ *n. Med.* a streptococcal infection producing inflammation and a deep red colour on the skin, esp. of the face and scalp. [Middle English via Latin from Greek *erusipelas*, perhaps related to *eruthros* 'red' + a root *pel-* 'skin']

erythema /ɛrɪ'θiːmə/ *n.* a superficial reddening of the skin, usu. in patches. □ **erythemal** *adj.* **erythematic** /ˌɛrɪθɪ'matɪk/ *adj.* [modern Latin from Greek *eruthēma*, via *eruthainō* 'be red' from *eruthros* 'red']

erythrism /'ɛrɪθrɪz(ə)m/ *n.* abnormal red coloration esp. in a bird or animal. [ERYTHRO- + -ISM]

erythro- /ɪ'rɪθrəʊ/ *comb. form* red. [Greek *eruthros* 'red']

erythroblast /ɪ'rɪθrə(ʊ)blast/ *n.* an immature erythrocyte. [German]

erythrocyte /ɪ'rɪθrəsʌɪt/ *n.* a red blood cell, which contains the pigment haemoglobin and transports oxygen and carbon dioxide to and from the tissues. □ **erythrocytic** /-'sɪtɪk/ *adj.*

erythroid /'ɛrɪθrɔɪd/ *adj.* of or relating to erythrocytes.

Es *symb. Chem.* the element einsteinium.

-es[1] /ɪz, z/ *suffix* forming plurals of nouns ending in sibilant sounds (such words in *-e* dropping the *e*) (*kisses*; *cases*; *boxes*; *churches*) and of a few ending in *-o* (*potatoes*; *heroes*). [variant of -s[1]]

-es[2] /ɪz, z/ *suffix* forming the 3rd person sing. present of verbs ending in sibilant sounds (such words in *-e* dropping the *e*) and ending in *-o* (but not *-oo*) (*goes*; *places*; *pushes*). [variant of -s[2]]

ESA *abbr.* European Space Agency.

escadrille /ɛskə'drɪl/ *n.* a French squadron of aeroplanes. [French]

escalade /ɛskə'leɪd/ *n.* the scaling of fortified walls with ladders, as a military attack. [French via Spanish *escalada*, *-ado* from medieval Latin *scalare*, from *scala* 'ladder']

escalate /'ɛskəleɪt/ *v.* **1** *intr. & tr.* increase or develop (usu. rapidly) by stages. **2** *tr.* cause (an action, activity, or process) to become more intense. □ **escalation** /-'leɪʃ(ə)n/ *n.* [back-formation from ESCALATOR]

escalator /'ɛskəleɪtə/ *n.* a moving staircase consisting of a circulating belt forming steps. [from the stem of *escalade* 'climb a wall by ladder' + -ATOR]

escallonia /ɛskə'ləʊnɪə/ *n.* an evergreen shrub of the S. American genus *Escallonia*, bearing pink or white flowers. [named after *Escallon*, 18th-c. Spanish traveller]

escallop /ɪ'skaləp, ɛ-, -'skɒl-/ *n.* **1** = SCALLOP *n.* 1, 2. **2** = ESCALOPE. **3** (in *pl.*) = SCALLOP *n.* 3. **4** *Heraldry* a scallop shell as a device. [formed as ESCALOPE]

escalope /ɪ'skaləp, ɛ-, -'skɒl-, 'ɛskələʊp/ *n.* a thin slice of meat without any bone, esp. from a leg of veal. [French (in Old French = shell): see SCALLOP]

escapade /'ɛskəpeɪd, ɛskə'peɪd/ *n.* a piece of daring or reckless behaviour. [French from Provençal or Spanish *escapada* (as ESCAPE)]

escape /ɪ'skeɪp, ɛ-/ *v. & n.* ● *v.* **1** *intr.* (often foll. by *from*) get free of the restriction or control of a place, person, etc. **2** *intr.* (of a gas, liquid, etc.) leak from a container or pipe etc. **3** *intr.* succeed in avoiding danger, punishment, etc.; get off safely. **4** *tr.* get completely free of (a person, grasp, etc.). **5** *tr.* avoid or elude (a commitment, danger, etc.). **6** *tr.* elude the notice or memory of (*nothing escapes you*; *the name escaped me*). **7** *tr.* (of words etc.) issue unawares from (a person, a person's lips). ● *n.* **1** the act or an instance of escaping; avoidance of danger, injury, etc. **2** the state of having escaped (*was a narrow escape*). **3** a means of escaping (often *attrib.*: *escape hatch*). **4** a leakage of gas etc. **5** a temporary relief from reality or worry. **6** a garden plant running wild. **7** (in full **escape key**) *Computing* a key which either ends the current operation, or converts subsequent characters to a control sequence (*escape routine*; *escape sequence*). □ **escapable** *adj.* **escaper** *n.* [Middle English from Anglo-French, Old Northern French *escaper*, ultimately from medieval Latin (as EX-[1], *cappa* 'cloak')]

escape clause *n.* a clause specifying the conditions under which a contracting party is free from an obligation.

escapee /ɛskeɪ'piː, ɪ'skeɪpiː/ *n.* a person, esp. a prisoner, who has escaped.

escapement /ɪ'skeɪpm(ə)nt, ɛ-/ *n.* **1** the part of a clock or watch that connects and regulates the motive power. **2** the part of the mechanism in a piano that enables the hammer to fall back as soon as it has struck the string. **3** the mechanism in a typewriter that controls the leftward motion of the carriage. **4** *archaic* a means of escape. [French *échappement* from *échapper* ESCAPE]

escape road *n.* esp. *Brit.* a road for a vehicle to turn into if unable to negotiate a bend, descent, etc., safely (esp. on a racetrack).

escape velocity *n.* the minimum velocity needed to escape from the gravitational field of a body.

escape wheel *n.* a toothed wheel in the escapement of a watch or clock.

escapism /ɪ'skeɪpɪz(ə)m, ɛ-/ *n.* the tendency to seek distraction and relief from reality, esp. in the arts or through fantasy. □ **escapist** *n. & adj.*

escapology /ɛskə'pɒlədʒi/ *n.* the methods and techniques of escaping from confinement, esp. as a form of entertainment. □ **escapologist** *n.*

escargot /ɛ'skɑːgəʊ, ɪ-/ *n.* an edible snail. [French]

escarpment /ɪ'skɑːpm(ə)nt, ɛ-/ *n.* (also **escarp**) *Geol.* a long steep slope at the edge of a plateau etc. [French *escarpement* from *escarpe* SCARP]

-esce /ɛs/ *suffix* forming verbs, usu. initiating action (*effervesce*; *fluoresce*). [from or suggested by Latin *-escere*]

-escent /'ɛs(ə)nt/ *suffix* forming adjectives denoting the beginning of a state or action (*effervescent*; *fluorescent*). □ **-escence** *suffix* forming nouns. [from or suggested by French *-escent* or Latin *-escent-*, pres. part. stem of verbs ending in *-escere*]

eschatology /ɛskə'tɒlədʒi/ *n.* **1** the part of theology concerned with death and final destiny. **2** a belief or beliefs about the destiny of mankind and the world. □ **eschatological** /-tə'lɒdʒɪk(ə)l/ *adj.* **eschatologist** *n.* [Greek *eskhatos* 'last' + -LOGY]

escheat /ɪs'tʃiːt, ɛ-/ *n. & v. N. Amer.* ● *n.* **1** the reversion of property to the state, or (in feudal law) to a lord, on the owner's dying without legal heirs. **2** property affected by this. ● *v.* **1** *tr.* hand over (property) as an escheat. **2** *tr.* confiscate. **3** *intr.* revert by escheat. [Middle English from Old French *eschete*, ultimately from Latin *excidere* (as EX-[1], *cadere* 'fall')]

eschew /ɪs'tʃuː, ɛ-/ *v.tr. literary* avoid; abstain from. □ **eschewal** *n.* [Middle English from Old French *eschiver*, ultimately from Germanic: related to SHY[1]]

eschscholtzia /ɪ'ʃɒltsɪə, ɪs'kɒlʃə, ɛ-/ *n.* a yellow- or orange-flowered plant of the genus *Eschscholtzia*, esp. the Californian poppy. [named after J. F. von *Eschscholtz*, German botanist d. 1831]

escort *n. & v.* ● *n.* /'ɛskɔːt/ **1** one or more persons, vehicles, ships, etc., accompanying a person, vehicle, etc., esp. for protection or security or as a mark of rank or status. **2** a person accompanying a person of the opposite sex socially. ● *v.tr.* /ɪ'skɔːt, ɛ-/ act as an escort to. [French *escorte*, *escorter* from Italian *scorta*, fem. past part. of *scorgere* 'conduct']

escritoire /ɛskriː'twɑː/ *n.* a writing desk with drawers etc. [French from Latin *scriptorium* 'writing-room': see SCRIPTORIUM]

escrow /ɪ'skrəʊ, ɛ-/ *n. & v. Law* ● *n.* **1** money, property, or a written bond, kept in the custody of a third party until a specified condition has been fulfilled. **2** the status of this (*in escrow*). ● *v.tr.* place in escrow. [Anglo-French *escrowe*, Old French *escroe* 'scrap, scroll', via medieval Latin *scroda* from Germanic]

escudo /ɛ'skuːdəʊ/ *n.* (*pl.* **-os**) the chief monetary unit of Portugal and Cape Verde. [Spanish & Portuguese, from Latin *scutum* 'shield']

esculent /'ɛskjʊlənt/ *adj. & n.* ● *adj.* fit to eat; edible. ● *n.* an edible substance. [Latin *esculentus* from *esca* 'food']

escutcheon /ɪ'skʌtʃ(ə)n, ɛ-/ *n.* **1** a shield or emblem bearing a coat of arms. **2** the middle part of a ship's stern where the name is placed. **3** the protective plate around a keyhole or door handle. □ **blot on the escutcheon of** a stain on the character or name of. □ **escutcheoned** *adj.* [Anglo-French & Old Northern French *escuchon*, ultimately from Latin *scutum* 'shield']

Esd. *abbr.* Esdras (Apocrypha).

ESE *abbr.* east-south-east.

-ese /iːz/ *suffix* forming adjectives and nouns denoting: **1** an inhabitant or language of a country or city (*Japanese*; *Milanese*; *Viennese*). **2** often *derog.* character or style, esp. of language (*officialese*). [Old French *-eis*, ultimately from Latin *-ensis*]

esker /'ɛskə/ *n.* (also **eskar**) *Geol.* a long ridge of post-glacial gravel in river valleys. [Irish *eiscir*]

Eskimo /'ɛskɪməʊ/ *n. & adj.* (also **Esquimau**) often *offens.* ● *n.* (*pl.* same or **-os** or **Esquimaux**) **1** a member of a people inhabiting northern Canada, Alaska, Greenland, and eastern Siberia. **2** any of the languages of this people. ● *adj.* of or relating to the Eskimos or their language. [Danish from French *Esquimaux* (pl.), from Algonquian, literally 'eaters of raw flesh']

■ **Usage** In Canada and, increasingly, elsewhere the term *Inuit* is used to refer to Canadian Eskimos and also to Eskimos generally. The term *Eskimo* may offend some people.

Esky /'ɛski/ *n.* (*pl.* **-ies**) *Austral. propr.* a portable insulated container for keeping food or drink cool. [probably from ESKIMO, with reference to their cold climate]

ESL *abbr.* English as a second language.

ESN *abbr. hist.* educationally subnormal.

esophagus *US* var. of OESOPHAGUS.

esoteric /ɛsə'tɛrɪk, iːs-/ *adj.* (of a doctrine, mode of speech, etc.) intended only for, or intelligible only to, the initiated. □ **esoterically** *adv.* **esotericism** /-sɪz(ə)m/ *n.* **esotericist** /-sɪst/ *n.* [Greek *esōterikos* from *esōterō*, comparative of *esō* 'within': cf. EXOTERIC]

ESP *abbr.* extrasensory perception.

esp. *abbr.* especially.

espadrille /ɛspə'drɪl, 'ɛspədrɪl/ *n.* a light canvas shoe with a plaited fibre sole. [French from Provençal *espardillo*, from *espart* ESPARTO]

espalier /ɪ'spaljə, ɛ-/ *n. & v.* ● *n.* **1** a lattice or frame along which the branches of a tree or shrub are trained to grow flat against a wall etc. **2** a tree or shrub trained in this way. ● *v.tr.* train in this way. [French from Italian *spalliera*, from *spalla* 'shoulder']

esparto /ɛ'spɑːtəʊ, ɪ-/ *n.* (*pl.* **-os**) (in full **esparto grass**) a coarse grass, *Stipa tenacissima*, native to Spain and N. Africa, with tough narrow leaves, used to make ropes, wickerwork, and good-quality paper. [Spanish via Latin *spartum* from Greek *sparton* 'rope']

especial /ɪ'spɛʃ(ə)l, ɛ-/ *adj.* **1** notable, exceptional. **2** attributed or belonging chiefly to one person or thing (*your especial charm*). [Middle English via Old French from Latin *specialis* 'special']

especially /ɪ'spɛʃ(ə)li, ɛ-/ *adv.* chiefly; much more than in other cases.

Esperanto /ɛspə'rantəʊ/ *n.* an artificial universal language devised in 1887, based on roots from the chief European languages. □ **Esperantist** *n.* [the pen-name (from Latin *sperare* 'hope') of its inventor, L. L. Zamenhof, Polish physician d. 1917]

espial /ɪ'spʌɪ(ə)l, ɛ-/ *n.* **1** the act or an instance of catching sight of or of being seen. **2** *archaic* spying. [Middle English from Old French *espiaille*, from *espier*: see ESPY]

espionage /'ɛspɪənɑːʒ, -ɪdʒ/ *n.* the practice of spying or of using spies, esp. by governments. [French *espionnage* via *espionner* from *espion* SPY]

esplanade /ɛsplə'neɪd, -'nɑːd/ *n.* **1** a long open level area for walking on, esp. beside the sea. **2** a level space separating a fortress from a town. [French via Spanish *esplanada*, from *esplanar* 'make level', from Latin *explanare* (as EX-[1], *planus* 'level')]

espousal /ɪ'spaʊz(ə)l, ɛ-/ *n.* **1** (foll. by *of*) the espousing of a cause etc. **2** *archaic* a marriage or betrothal. [Middle English via Old French *espousailles* from Latin *sponsalia*, neut. pl. of *sponsalis* (as ESPOUSE)]

espouse /ɪ'spaʊz, ɛ-/ *v.tr.* **1** adopt or support (a cause, doctrine, etc.). **2** *archaic* **a** (usu. of a man) marry. **b** (usu. foll. by *to*) give (a woman) in marriage. □ **espouser** *n.* [Middle English via Old French *espouser* from Latin *sponsare*, from *sponsus*, past part. of *spondēre* 'betroth']

espresso /ɛ'sprɛsəʊ/ *n.* (also **expresso** /ɛk'spresəʊ/) (*pl.* **-os**) **1** strong concentrated black coffee made under steam pressure. **2** a machine for making this. [Italian, = pressed out]

esprit /ɛ'spri:, 'ɛspri:, French ɛspri/ *n.* **1** wit. **2** spirit, liveliness. [French, from Latin *spiritus* SPIRIT]

esprit de corps /də 'kɔ:, French də kɔr/ *n.* a feeling of devotion to and pride in the group one belongs to. [French, literally 'spirit of the body']

esprit de l'escalier /də lɛ'skaljeɪ, French də lɛskalje/ *n.* an apt retort or clever remark that comes to mind after the chance to make it is gone. [French, literally 'wit of the stairs']

espy /ɪ'spʌɪ, ɛ-/ *v.tr.* (**-ies**, **-ied**) *literary* catch sight of; perceive. [Middle English from Old French *espier*: see SPY]

Esq. *abbr.* Esquire.

-esque /ɛsk/ *suffix* forming adjectives meaning 'in the style of' or 'resembling' (*romanesque*; *Schumannesque*; *statuesque*). [French via Italian *-esco* from medieval Latin *-iscus*]

Esquimau var. of ESKIMO.

esquire /ɪ'skwʌɪə, ɛ-/ *n.* **1** (usu. as abbr. **Esq.**) **a** *Brit.* a title appended to a man's surname when no other form of address is used, esp. as a form of address for letters. **b** *US* a title appended to a lawyer's surname. **2** *archaic* = SQUIRE *n.* 2. [Middle English via Old French *esquier* from Latin *scutarius* 'shield-bearer', from *scutum* 'shield']

ESR *abbr. Physics* electron spin resonance .

ESRC *abbr.* (in the UK) Economic and Social Research Council.

-ess[1] /ɛs/ *suffix* forming nouns denoting females (*actress*; *lioness*; *mayoress*). [from or suggested by French *-esse* via Late Latin *-issa* from Greek *-issa*]

-ess[2] /ɛs/ *suffix* forming abstract nouns from adjectives (*duress*). [Middle English via French *-esse* from Latin *-itia*; cf. -ICE, -ISE[2]]

essay *n. & v.* ● *n.* /'ɛseɪ/ **1** a composition, usu. short and in prose, on any subject. **2** (often foll. by *at, in*) *formal* an attempt. ● *v.tr.* /ɛ'seɪ/ *formal* attempt, try. ▫ **essayist** *n.* [Middle English from ASSAY, assimilated to French *essayer*, ultimately via Late Latin *exagium* 'weighing' from *exigere* 'weigh': see EXACT]

essence /'ɛs(ə)ns/ *n.* **1** the indispensable quality or element identifying a thing or determining its character; fundamental nature or inherent characteristics. **2 a** an extract obtained by distillation etc., esp. a volatile oil. **b** a perfume or scent, esp. made from a plant or animal substance. **3** the constituent of a plant that determines its chemical properties. **4** an abstract entity; the reality underlying a phenomenon or all phenomena. ▫ **in essence** fundamentally. **of the essence** indispensable, vital. [Middle English via Old French from Latin *essentia*, from *esse* 'be']

Essene /'ɛsi:n/ *n.* a member of an ancient Jewish ascetic sect living communally and widely regarded as the authors of the Dead Sea Scrolls. [Latin pl. *Esseni* from Greek pl. *Essēnoi*]

essential /ɪ'sɛnʃ(ə)l/ *adj. & n.* ● *adj.* **1** absolutely necessary; indispensable. **2** fundamental, basic. **3** of or constituting the essence of a person or thing. **4** (of a disease) with no known external stimulus or cause; idiopathic. ● *n.* (esp. in *pl.*) a basic or indispensable element or thing. ▫ **essentiality** /-ʃɪ'alɪti/ *n.* **essentially** *adv.* **essentialness** *n.* [Middle English from Late Latin *essentialis* (as ESSENCE)]

essential element *n.* any of various elements required by living organisms for normal growth.

essentialism /ɪ'sɛnʃ(ə)lɪz(ə)m/ *n. Philos.* the belief that things have a set of characteristics which make them what they are. ▫ **essentialist** *n. & adj.*

essential oil *n.* a volatile oil derived from a plant etc. with its characteristic odour.

EST *abbr.* **1** Eastern Standard Time. **2** electro-shock treatment.

est /ɛst/ *n.* a group technique for raising self-awareness, including motivational theories from the business world. [acronym from *E*rhard *S*eminars *T*raining, from the name of W. *Erhard*, American businessman (b. 1935), who devised the technique]

est. *abbr.* established.

-est[1] /ɪst/ *suffix* forming the superlative of adjectives (*widest*; *nicest*; *happiest*) and adverbs (*soonest*). [Old English *-ost-*, *-ust-*, *-ast-*]

-est[2] /ɪst/ *suffix* (also **-st**) *archaic* forming the 2nd person sing. of verbs (*canst*; *findest*; *gavest*). [Old English *-est*, *-ast*, *-st*]

establish /ɪ'stablɪʃ, ɛ-/ *v.tr.* **1** set up or consolidate (a business, system, etc.) on a permanent basis. **2** (foll. by *in*) settle (a person or oneself) in some capacity. **3** (esp. as **established** *adj.*) achieve permanent acceptance for (a custom, belief, practice, institution, etc.). **4 a** validate; place beyond dispute (a fact etc.). **b** find out, ascertain. ▫ **establisher** *n.* [Middle English via Old French *establir* (stem *establiss-*) from Latin *stabilire*, from *stabilis* STABLE[1]]

established Church *n.* a Church recognized by the state as the national Church.

establishment /ɪ'stablɪʃm(ə)nt, ɛ-/ *n.* **1** the act or an instance of establishing; the process of being established. **2 a** a business organization or public institution. **b** a place of business. **c** a residence. **3 a** the staff or equipment of an organization. **b** a household. **4** any organized body permanently maintained for a purpose. **5** a Church system organized by law. **6 a** (**the Establishment**) the group in a society exercising authority or influence, and seen as resisting change. **b** any influential or controlling group (*the literary establishment*).

establishmentarian /ɪˌstablɪʃm(ə)n'tɛ:rɪən/ *adj. & n.* ● *adj.* adhering to or advocating the principle of an established Church. ● *n.* a person adhering to or advocating this. ▫ **establishmentarianism** *n.*

estaminet /ɛ'stammeɪ, French ɛstaminɛ/ *n.* a small French café etc. selling alcoholic drinks. [French, via Walloon *staminê* 'byre' from *stamo* 'a pole for tethering a cow', probably from German *Stamm* 'stem']

estate /ɪ'steɪt, ɛ-/ *n.* **1** a property consisting of an extensive area of land usu. with a large house. **2** *Brit.* a modern residential or industrial area with integrated design or purpose. **3** all of a person's assets and liabilities, esp. at death. **4** a property where rubber, tea, grapes, etc., are cultivated. **5** (in full **estate of the realm**) esp. *hist.* an order or class forming (or regarded as) a part of the body politic. **6** *archaic* or *literary* a state or position in life (*the estate of holy matrimony*; *poor man's estate*). **7** *Brit. colloq.* = ESTATE CAR. ▫ **the Three Estates** Lords Spiritual (the heads of the Church), Lords Temporal (the peerage), and the Commons. [Middle English from Old French *estat* (as STATUS)]

estate agent *n. Brit.* **1** a person whose business is the sale or lease of buildings and land on behalf of others. **2** the steward of an estate.

estate car *n. Brit.* a car with the passenger area extended and combined with space for luggage, usu. with an extra door at the rear.

estate duty *n. Brit. hist.* death duty levied on property (replaced in 1975 by *capital transfer tax* and in 1986 by *inheritance tax*).

estate of the realm see ESTATE 5.

esteem /ɪ'sti:m, ɛ-/ *v. & n.* ● *v.tr.* **1** (usu. in *passive*) have a high regard for; greatly respect; think favourably of. **2** *formal* consider, deem (*esteemed it an honour*). ● *n.* high regard; respect; favour (*held them in esteem*). [Middle English via Old French *estimer* from Latin *aestimare* 'fix the price of']

ester /'ɛstə/ *n. Chem.* any of a class of organic compounds produced by replacing the hydrogen of an acid by an alkyl, aryl, etc. radical, many of which occur naturally as oils and fats. ▫ **esterify** /ɛ'stɛrɪfʌɪ/ *v.tr.* (**-ies**, **-ied**). [German, probably from *Essig* 'vinegar' + *Äther* 'ether']

Esth. *abbr.* Esther (Old Testament & Apocrypha).

esthete *US* var. of AESTHETE.

esthetic *US* var. of AESTHETIC.

estimable /ˈɛstɪməb(ə)l/ *adj.* worthy of esteem. □ **estimably** *adv.* [French from Latin *aestimabilis* (as ESTEEM)]

estimate *n.* & *v.* ● *n.* /ˈɛstɪmət/ **1** an approximate judgement, esp. of cost, value, size, etc. **2** a price specified as that likely to be charged for work to be undertaken. ● *v.tr.* (also *absol.*) /ˈɛstɪmeɪt/ **1** form an estimate or opinion of. **2** (foll. by *that* + clause) make a rough calculation. **3** (often foll. by *at*) value or measure by estimation; adjudge. □ **estimative** /-mətɪv/ *adj.* **estimator** /-meɪtə/ *n.* [Latin *aestimare aestimat-* 'fix the price of']

estimation /ɛstɪˈmeɪʃ(ə)n/ *n.* **1** the process or result of estimating. **2** judgement or opinion of worth (*in my estimation*). **3** *archaic* esteem (*hold in estimation*). [Middle English from Old French *estimation* or Latin *aestimatio* (as ESTIMATE)]

estival *US* var. of AESTIVAL.

estivate *US* var. of AESTIVATE.

Estonian /ɪˈstəʊnɪən, ɛ-/ *n.* & *adj.* ● *n.* **1 a** a native of Estonia, a Baltic republic. **b** a person of Estonian descent. **2** the Finno-Ugric language of Estonia. ● *adj.* of or relating to Estonia or its people or language.

estop /ɪˈstɒp/ *v.tr.* (**estopped**, **estopping**) (foll. by *from*) *Law* bar or preclude, esp. by estoppel. □ **estoppage** *n.* [Middle English via Anglo-French, Old French *estoper* and Late Latin *stuppare* 'stop up' from Latin *stuppa* 'tow, oakum': cf. STOP, STUFF]

estoppel /ɪˈstɒp(ə)l/ *n.* *Law* the principle which precludes a person from asserting something contrary to what is implied by a previous action or statement of that person or by a previous pertinent judicial determination. [Old French *estouppail* 'bung' from *estoper* (as ESTOP)]

estovers /ɪˈstəʊvəz, ɛ-/ *n.pl.* *hist.* necessaries allowed by law to a tenant (esp. fuel, or wood for repairs). [Anglo-French *estover*, Old French *estoveir* 'be necessary', from Latin *est opus*]

estrange /ɪˈstreɪn(d)ʒ, ɛ-/ *v.tr.* **1** (usu. in *passive*; often foll. by *from*) cause (a person or group) to turn away in feeling or affection; alienate. **2** (as **estranged** *adj.*) (of a husband or wife) no longer living with his or her spouse. □ **estrangement** *n.* [Middle English via Anglo-French *estraunger*, Old French *estranger* from Latin *extraneare* 'treat as a stranger', from *extraneus* 'stranger']

estreat /ɪˈstriːt, ɛ-/ *n.* & *v.* *Law* ● *n.* **1** a copy of a court record of a fine etc. for use in prosecution. **2** the enforcement of a fine or forfeiture of a recognizance. ● *v.tr.* enforce the forfeit of (a fine etc., esp. surety for bail). [Middle English via Anglo-French *estrete*, Old French *estraite*, from *estraire*, from Latin *extrahere* EXTRACT]

estrogen *US* var. of OESTROGEN.

estrus etc. *US* var. of OESTRUS etc.

estuary /ˈɛstjʊ(ə)ri/ *n.* (*pl.* **-ies**) a wide tidal mouth of a river. □ **estuarine** /-rʌɪn/ *adj.* [Latin *aestuarium* 'tidal channel' from *aestus* 'tide']

e.s.u. *abbr.* electrostatic unit(s).

esurient /ɪˈsjʊərɪənt, ɛ-/ *adj.* *archaic* or *joc.* **1** hungry. **2** impecunious and greedy. □ **esuriently** *adv.* [Latin *esurire* 'to hunger' from *edere es-* 'eat']

ET *abbr.* extraterrestrial.

-et[1] /ɪt/ *suffix* forming nouns (originally diminutives) (*baronet*; *bullet*; *sonnet*). [Old French *-et -ete*]

-et[2] /ɪt/ *suffix* (also **-ete** /iːt/) forming nouns usu. denoting persons (*comet*; *poet*; *athlete*). [Greek *-ētēs*]

ETA[1] *abbr.* estimated time of arrival.

ETA[2] /ˈɛtə/ *n.* a Basque separatist movement in Spain. [Basque abbreviation, from *Euzkadi ta Azkatasuna* 'Basque homeland and liberty']

eta /ˈiːtə/ *n.* the seventh letter of the Greek alphabet (Η, η). [Greek]

et al. /ɛt ˈal/ *abbr.* and others. [Latin *et alii, et alia*, etc.]

etalon /ˈɛtəlɒn/ *n.* *Physics* a device consisting of two reflecting plates, for producing interfering light beams. [French *étalon*, literally 'standard of measurement']

etc. *abbr.* = ET CETERA.

et cetera /ɛtˈsɛt(ə)rə, ɪt-/ *adv.* & *n.* (also **etcetera**) ● *adv.* **1 a** and the rest; and similar things or people. **b** or similar things or people. **2** and so on. ● *n.* (in *pl.*) the usual sundries or extras. [Middle English from Latin]

etch /ɛtʃ/ *v.* & *n.* ● *v.* **1 a** *tr.* reproduce (a picture etc.) by engraving a design on a metal plate with acid (esp. to print copies). **b** *tr.* engrave (a plate) in this way. **2** *intr.* practise this craft. **3** *tr.* (foll. by *on*, *upon*) impress deeply (esp. on the mind). ● *n.* the action or process of etching. □ **etcher** *n.* [Dutch *etsen* via German *ätzen* 'etch' from Old High German *azzen* 'cause to eat or to be eaten', from Germanic]

etchant /ˈɛtʃ(ə)nt/ *n.* a corrosive used in etching.

etching /ˈɛtʃɪŋ/ *n.* **1** a print made from an etched plate. **2** the art of producing these plates.

-ete *suffix* var. of -ET[2].

eternal /ɪˈtəːn(ə)l, iː-/ *adj.* **1** existing always; without an end or (usu.) beginning in time. **2** essentially unchanging (*eternal truths*). **3** *colloq.* constant; seeming not to cease (*your eternal nagging*). □ **the Eternal** God. □ **eternality** /-ˈnalɪti/ *n.* **eternalize** *v.tr.* (also **-ise**). **eternally** *adv.* **eternalness** *n.* **eternize** *v.tr.* (also **-ise**). [Middle English via Old French and Late Latin *aeternalis* from Latin *aeternus*, from *aevum* 'age']

Eternal City *n.* (prec. by *the*) Rome.

eternal triangle *n.* a relationship between three people, usu. two of one sex and one of the other, involving sexual rivalry.

eternity /ɪˈtəːnɪti, iː-/ *n.* (*pl.* **-ies**) **1** infinite or unending (esp. future) time. **2** *Theol.* endless life after death. **3** the state of being eternal. **4** (often prec. by *an*) *colloq.* a very long time. **5** (in *pl.*) eternal truths. [Middle English via Old French *eternité* from Latin *aeternitas -tatis*, from *aeternus*: see ETERNAL]

eternity ring *n.* a finger ring set with gems all round, usu. given as a token of lasting affection.

Etesian /ɪˈtiːʒɪən, ɪˈtiːz-, ɪˈtiːʒ(ə)n/ *adj.* designating a dry NW wind blowing each summer in the eastern Mediterranean. [Latin *etesius* from Greek *etēsios* 'annual', from *etos* 'year']

eth /ɛð/ *n.* (also **edh** /ɛð/) the name of an Old English and Icelandic letter, = th. [Icelandic]

-eth[1] var. of -TH[1].

-eth[2] /ɪθ/ *suffix* (also **-th**) *archaic* forming the 3rd person sing. present of verbs (*doeth*; *saith*). [Old English *-eth, -ath, -th*]

ethanal /ˈɛθ(ə)nal/ *n.* = ACETALDEHYDE. [ETHANE + ALDEHYDE]

ethane /ˈiːθeɪn, ˈɛθ-/ *n.* *Chem.* a gaseous hydrocarbon of the alkane series, occurring in natural gas. Chem. formula: C_2H_6. [ETHER + -ANE[2]]

ethanediol /ˈiːθeɪn,dʌɪɒl, ˈɛθ-/ *n.* *Chem.* = ETHYLENE GLYCOL. [ETHANE + DIOL]

ethanoate /ɪˈθanəʊeɪt/ *n.* *Chem.* a salt or ester of ethanoic acid; also called *acetate*.

ethanoic acid /ɛθəˈnəʊɪk/ *n.* *Chem.* = ACETIC ACID. [ETHANE + *-oic*, suffix denoting carboxylic acids]

ethanol /ˈɛθənɒl/ *n.* *Chem.* = ALCOHOL 1. [ETHANE + ALCOHOL]

ethene /ˈɛθiːn/ *n.* *Chem.* = ETHYLENE. [ETHER + -ENE]

ether /ˈiːθə/ *n.* **1** *Chem.* **a** a colourless volatile organic liquid used as an anaesthetic or solvent (also called *diethyl ether*, *ethoxyethane*). Chem. formula: $C_2H_5OC_2H_5$. **b** any of a class of organic compounds with a similar structure to this, having an oxygen joined to two alkyl etc. groups. **2** (also **aether**) the clear sky; the upper regions of air beyond the clouds. **3** (also **aether**) *hist.* **a** a medium formerly assumed to permeate space and fill the interstices between particles of matter. **b** a medium through which electromagnetic waves were formerly thought to be transmitted. □ **etheric** /iːˈθɛrɪk, ˈiːθ(ə)rɪk/ *adj.* [Middle English via Old French *ether* or Latin *aether* from Greek *aithēr*, from the root of *aithō* 'burn, shine']

ethereal /ɪˈθɪərɪəl/ *adj.* (also **etherial**) **1** light, airy. **2** highly delicate, esp. in appearance. **3** heavenly, celestial. **4** *Chem.* of or relating to ether. □ **ethereality** /-ˈalɪti/ *n.* **ethereally** *adv.* [Latin *aethereus, -ius* from Greek *aitherios* (as ETHER)]

etherize /ˈiːθ(ə)rʌɪz/ *v.tr.* (also **-ise**) *hist.* treat or anaesthetize with ether. □ **etherization** /-ˈzeɪʃ(ə)n/ *n.*

Ethernet /ˈiːθənɛt/ *n.* *Computing* a system of communication for local area networks by coaxial cable that prevents simultaneous transmission by more than one station. [ETHER + NETWORK]

ethic /ˈɛθɪk/ *n. & adj.* ● *n.* a set of moral principles (*the Quaker ethic*). ● *adj.* = ETHICAL. [Middle English via Old French *éthique* or Latin *ethicus* from Greek *ēthikos* (as ETHOS)]

ethical /ˈɛθɪk(ə)l/ *adj.* **1** relating to morals, esp. as concerning human conduct. **2** morally correct; honourable. **3** (of a medicine or drug) not advertised to the general public, and usu. available only on a doctor's prescription. □ **ethicality** /-ˈkalɪti/ *n.* **ethically** *adv.*

ethical investment *n.* investment in companies that meet ethical and moral criteria specified by the investor.

ethics /ˈɛθɪks/ *n.pl.* **1** (usu. treated as *sing.*) the science of morals in human conduct; moral philosophy. **2 a** (treated as *pl.*) moral principles; rules of conduct. **b** (often treated as *pl.*) a set of these (*medical ethics*). □ **ethicist** /-sɪst/ *n.*

Ethiopian /iːθɪˈəʊpɪən/ *n. & adj.* ● *n.* **1 a** a native or national of Ethiopia in NE Africa. **b** a person of Ethiopian descent. **2** *archaic* a black person. ● *adj.* **1** of or relating to Ethiopia. **2** *Biol.* of or designating a biogeographical region comprising Africa south of the Sahara. [*Ethiopia* via Latin *Aethiops* from Greek *Aithiops*, from *aithō* 'burn' + *ōps* 'face']

Ethiopic /iːθɪˈɒpɪk/ *n. & adj.* ● *n.* the Christian liturgical language of Ethiopia. ● *adj.* of or in this language. [Latin *aethiopicus* from Greek *aithiopikos*: see ETHIOPIAN]

ethmoid /ˈɛθmɔɪd/ *adj.* sievelike. □ **ethmoidal** /-ˈmɔɪd(ə)l/ *adj.* [Greek *ēthmoeidēs* from *ēthmos* 'sieve']

ethmoid bone *n.* a square bone at the root of the nose, with many perforations through which the olfactory nerves pass to the nose.

ethnic /ˈɛθnɪk/ *adj. & n.* ● *adj.* **1 a** (of a social group) having a common national or cultural tradition. **b** (of clothes, music, etc.) characteristic of or influenced by the traditions of a particular people or culture, esp. one regarded as exotic. **2** denoting origin by birth or descent rather than nationality (*ethnic Turks*). **3** relating to race or culture (*ethnic group*; *ethnic origins*). **4** *archaic* pagan, heathen. ● *n.* **1** *N. Amer. & Austral.* a member of an (esp. minority) ethnic group. **2** (in *pl.*, usu. treated as *sing.*) = ETHNOLOGY. □ **ethnically** *adv.* **ethnicity** /-ˈnɪsɪti/ *n.* [Middle English via ecclesiastical Latin *ethnicus* from Greek *ethnikos* 'heathen', from *ethnos* 'nation']

ethnical /ˈɛθnɪk(ə)l/ *adj.* relating to ethnology.

ethnic cleansing *n. euphem.* the mass expulsion or extermination of people from opposing ethnic or religious groups within a certain area.

ethnic minority *n.* a (usu. identifiable) group differentiated from the main population of a community by racial origin or cultural background.

ethno- /ˈɛθnəʊ/ *comb. form* ethnic, ethnological. [Greek *ethnos* 'nation']

ethnoarchaeology /ˌɛθnəʊɑːkɪˈɒlədʒi/ *n.* the study of a society's institutions based on examination of its material attributes. □ **ethnoarchaeological** /-kɪəˈlɒdʒɪk(ə)l/ *adj.* **ethnoarchaeologist** *n.*

ethnobotany /ɛθnəʊˈbɒt(ə)ni/ *n.* **1** the traditional knowledge of a people concerning plants and their uses. **2** the study of such knowledge.

ethnocentric /ɛθnə(ʊ)ˈsɛntrɪk/ *adj.* evaluating other races and cultures by criteria specific to one's own. □ **ethnocentrically** *adv.* **ethnocentricity** /-ˈtrɪsɪti/ *n.* **ethnocentrism** *n.*

ethnography /ɛθˈnɒgrəfi/ *n.* the scientific description of races and cultures of humankind. □ **ethnographer** *n.* **ethnographic** /-nəˈgrafɪk/ *adj.* **ethnographical** /-nəˈgrafɪk(ə)l/ *adj.*

ethnology /ɛθˈnɒlədʒi/ *n.* the comparative scientific study of human peoples. □ **ethnologic** /-nəˈlɒdʒɪk/ *adj.* **ethnological** /-nəˈlɒdʒɪk(ə)l/ *adj.* **ethnologist** *n.*

ethnomethodology /ˌɛθnəʊmɛθəˈdɒlədʒi/ *n.* a method of sociological analysis that examines how individuals in everyday situations construct and maintain the social order of those situations. □ **ethnomethodological** /-dəˈlɒdʒɪk(ə)l/ *adj.* **ethnomethodologist** *n.*

ethnomusicology /ˌɛθnəʊmjuːzɪˈkɒlədʒi/ *n.* the study of the music of one or more (esp. non-European) cultures. □ **ethnomusicological** /-kəˈlɒdʒɪk(ə)l/ *adj.* **ethnomusicologist** *n.*

ethogram /ˈiːθəgram/ *n.* *Zool.* a list of the kinds of behaviour or activity observed in an animal. [Greek *ēthо-* (see ETHOS) + -GRAM]

ethology /iːˈθɒlədʒi/ *n.* **1** the science of animal behaviour. **2** the science of character-formation in human behaviour. □ **ethological** /iːθəˈlɒdʒɪk(ə)l/ *adj.* **ethologist** *n.* [Latin *ethologia* from Greek *ēthologia* (as ETHOS)]

ethos /ˈiːθɒs/ *n.* the characteristic spirit or attitudes of a community, people, or system, or of a literary work etc. [modern Latin from Greek *ēthos* 'nature, disposition']

ethoxyethane /iːˌθɒksɪˈiːθeɪn/ *n.* *Chem.* = ETHER 1a. [ETHER + OXY-[2] + ETHANE]

ethyl /ˈɛθʌɪl, -θɪl, ˈiː-/ *n.* (*attrib.*) *Chem.* the monovalent radical C_2H_5– derived from ethane by removal of a hydrogen atom (*ethyl alcohol*). [German (as ETHER, -YL)]

ethylene /ˈɛθɪliːn, -θ(ə)l-/ *n.* *Chem.* a gaseous hydrocarbon of the alkene series, occurring in natural gas and used in the manufacture of polythene (also called *ethene*). Chem. formula: C_2H_4. □ **ethylenic** /-ˈliːnɪk/ *adj.*

ethylene glycol *n.* a colourless viscous hygroscopic liquid used as an antifreeze and in the manufacture of polyesters (also called *ethanediol*). Chem. formula: $C_2H_6O_2$.

ethyne /ˈiːθʌɪn, ˈɛθ-/ *n.* *Chem.* = ACETYLENE.

-etic /ˈɛtɪk/ *suffix* forming adjectives and nouns (*ascetic*; *emetic*; *genetic*; *synthetic*). [Greek *-ētikos* or *-ētikos*: cf. -IC]

etiolate /ˈiːtɪə(ʊ)leɪt/ *v.tr.* **1** make (a plant) pale by excluding light. **2** give a sickly hue to (a person). □ **etiolation** /-ˈleɪʃ(ə)n/ *n.* [French *étioler* from Norman French *étieuler* 'make into haulm', from *éteule*, ultimately from Latin *stipula* 'straw']

etiology *US* var. of AETIOLOGY.

etiquette /ˈɛtɪkɛt, ɛtɪˈkɛt/ *n.* **1** the conventional rules of social behaviour. **2 a** the customary behaviour of members of a profession towards each other. **b** the unwritten code governing this (*medical etiquette*). [French *étiquette* 'label, etiquette']

Eton collar /ˈiːt(ə)n/ *n.* a broad stiff collar worn outside the coat-collar, esp. of an Eton jacket.

Etonian /iːˈtəʊnɪən/ *n. & adj.* ● *n.* a past or present member of Eton College in southern England. ● *adj.* of or relating to Eton College.

Eton jacket /ˈiːt(ə)n/ *n.* a short jacket reaching only to the waist, as formerly worn by pupils of Eton College.

étrier /ˈeɪtrɪeɪ/ *n.* *Mountaineering* a short rope ladder with a few rungs of wood or metal. [French, = stirrup]

Etruscan /ɪˈtrʌsk(ə)n/ *adj. & n.* ● *adj.* of or relating to ancient Etruria in Italy, esp. its pre-Roman civilization and physical remains. ● *n.* **1** a native of Etruria. **2** the language of Etruria. [Latin *Etruscus*]

et seq. *abbr.* (also **et seqq.**) and the following (pages etc.). [Latin *et sequentia*]

-ette /ɛt/ *suffix* forming nouns meaning: **1** small (*kitchenette*; *cigarette*). **2** imitation or substitute (*leatherette*; *flannelette*). **3** female (*usherette*; *suffragette*). [from or suggested by Old French *-ette*, fem. of -ET[1]]

étude /ˈeɪtjuːd, eɪˈtjuːd/ *n.* a short musical composition or exercise, usu. for one instrument, designed to improve the technique of the player. [French, = study]

étui /ɛˈtwiː/ *n.* a small case for needles etc. [French *étui* from Old French *estui* 'prison', from *estuier* 'shut up, keep']

-etum /ˈiːtəm/ *suffix* forming nouns denoting a collection of trees or other plants (*arboretum*; *pinetum*). [Latin]

etymologize /ɛtɪˈmɒlədʒʌɪz/ *v.* (also **-ise**) **1** *tr.* give or trace the etymology of. **2** *intr.* study etymology. [medieval Latin *etymologizare* from Latin *etymologia* (as ETYMOLOGY)]

etymology /ɛtɪˈmɒlədʒi/ *n.* (*pl.* **-ies**) **1 a** the historically verifiable sources of the formation of a word and the development of its meaning. **b** an account of these. **2** the branch of linguistics concerned with etymologies. □ **etymological** /-məˈlɒdʒɪk(ə)l/ *adj.* **etymologically** /-məˈlɒdʒɪk(ə)li/ *adv.* **etymologist** *n.* [Old French *ethimologie* via Latin *etymologia* from Greek *etumologia* (as ETYMON, -LOGY)]

etymon /ˈɛtɪmɒn/ *n.* (*pl.* **etyma** /-mə/) the word that gives rise to a derivative or a borrowed or later form. [earlier in the sense 'the literal sense or original form of a word': Latin from Greek *etumon*, neut. of *etumos* 'true']

EU *abbr.* European Union.

■ **Usage** See Usage Note at EUROPEAN COMMUNITY.

Eu *symb. Chem.* the element europium.

eu- /juː/ *comb. form* well, easily. [Greek]

eucalyptus /juːkəˈlɪptəs/ *n.* (also **eucalypt**) (*pl.* **eucalyptuses**, **eucalypti** /-tʌɪ/, or **eucalypts**) **1** any tree of the genus *Eucalyptus*, native to Australasia, many being cultivated for their timber, for the oil from their leaves, for gums and resins, or as ornamental trees. **2** (in full **eucalyptus oil**) the oil from eucalyptus leaves used as an antiseptic etc. [modern Latin, from EU- + Greek *kaluptos* 'covered' from *kaluptō* 'to cover', the unopened flower being protected by a cap]

eucaryote var. of EUKARYOTE.

eucharis /ˈjuːkərɪs/ *n.* any evergreen bulbous plant of the genus *Eucharis*, native to S. America, with white bell-shaped flowers. [Greek *eukharis* 'pleasing' (as EU-, *kharis* 'grace')]

Eucharist /ˈjuːk(ə)rɪst/ *n.* **1** the Christian sacrament commemorating the Last Supper, in which bread and wine are consecrated and consumed; also called (*Holy*) *Communion, the Lord's Supper, the Mass.* **2** the consecrated elements, esp. the bread (*receive the Eucharist*). □ **Eucharistic** /-ˈrɪstɪk/ *adj.* **Eucharistical** /-ˈrɪstɪk(ə)l/ *adj.* [Middle English from Old French *eucariste*, ultimately via ecclesiastical Greek *eukharistia* 'thanksgiving' from Greek *eukharistos* 'grateful' (as EU-, *kharizomai* 'offer willingly')]

euchre /ˈjuːkə/ *n.* & *v.* ● *n.* an American card game for two, three, or four players. ● *v.tr.* **1** (in euchre) gain the advantage over (another player) when that player fails to take three tricks. **2** deceive, outwit. **3** *Austral.* exhaust, ruin. [19th c.: German dialect *Jucker(spiel)*]

Euclidean /juːˈklɪdɪən/ *adj.* of or relating to Euclid, 3rd-c. BC Alexandrian geometrician. [Latin *Euclideus* from Greek *Eukleideios*]

Euclidean geometry *n.* the geometry of ordinary experience, in which the postulates of Euclid are valid. Cf. NON-EUCLIDEAN.

Euclidean space *n.* space for which Euclidean geometry is valid.

eudemonic /juːdiːˈmɒnɪk/ *adj.* (also **eudaemonic**) conducive to happiness. [Greek *eudaimonikos* (as EUDEMONISM)]

eudemonism /juːˈdiːmənɪz(ə)m/ *n.* (also **eudaemonism**) a system of ethics that bases moral obligation on the likelihood of actions producing happiness. □ **eudemonist** *n.* **eudemonistic** /-ˈnɪstɪk/ *adj.* [Greek *eudaimonismos* 'system of happiness' from *eudaimōn* 'happy' (as EU-, *daimōn* 'guardian spirit')]

eudiometer /juːdɪˈɒmɪtə/ *n. Chem.* a graduated glass tube in which gases may be chemically combined by an electric spark, used to measure changes in volume of gases during chemical reactions. □ **eudiometric** /-dɪəˈmɛtrɪk/ *adj.* **eudiometrical** /-dɪəˈmɛtrɪk(ə)l/ *adj.* **eudiometry** *n.* [Greek *eudios* 'clear (weather)': originally used to measure the amount of oxygen, thought to be greater in clear air]

eugenics /juːˈdʒɛnɪks/ *n.* the science of improving the (esp. human) population by controlled breeding for desirable inherited characteristics. □ **eugenic** *adj.* **eugenically** *adv.* **eugenicist** /juːˈdʒɛnɪsɪst/ *n.* **eugenist** /ˈjuːdʒɪnɪst/ *n.* [EU- + -GEN + -ICS]

euglena /juːˈgliːnə/ *n. Biol.* a single-celled freshwater flagellate of the genus *Euglena*, which can form a green scum on stagnant water. [modern Latin genus name, from EU- + Greek *glēnē* 'eyeball, socket of joint']

eukaryote /juːˈkarɪəʊt/ *n.* (also **eucaryote**) *Biol.* an organism consisting of a cell or cells in which the genetic material is DNA in the form of chromosomes contained within a distinct nucleus (cf. PROKARYOTE). □ **eukaryotic** /-ˈɒtɪk/ *adj.* [EU- + KARYO- + *-ote* as in ZYGOTE]

eulogium /juːˈləʊdʒɪəm/ *n.* (*pl.* **eulogia** /-dʒɪə/ or **-ums**) = EULOGY. [medieval Latin: see EULOGY]

eulogize /ˈjuːlədʒʌɪz/ *v.tr.* (also **-ise**) praise in speech or writing. □ **eulogist** *n.* **eulogistic** /-ˈdʒɪstɪk/ *adj.* **eulogistically** /-ˈdʒɪstɪk(ə)li/ *adv.*

eulogy /ˈjuːlədʒi/ *n.* (*pl.* **-ies**) **1 a** speech or writing in praise of a person. **b** an expression of praise. **2** *US* a funeral oration in praise of a person. [medieval Latin *eulogium* from Late Latin *eulogia* 'praise' (apparently by confusion with Latin *elogium* 'epitaph'), from Greek]

eunuch /ˈjuːnək/ *n.* **1** a castrated man, esp. one formerly employed at an oriental harem or court. **2** a person lacking effectiveness (*political eunuch*). [Middle English via Latin *eunuchus* from Greek *eunoukhos*, literally 'bedchamber attendant' from *eunē* 'bed' + second element related to *ekhō* 'hold']

euonymus /juːˈɒnɪməs/ *n.* any tree or shrub of the genus *Euonymus*, e.g. the spindle tree. [Latin from Greek *euōnumos* 'of lucky name' (as EU-, *onoma* 'name')]

eupeptic /juːˈpɛptɪk/ *adj.* of or having good digestion. [Greek *eupeptos* (as EU-, *peptō* 'digest')]

euphemism /ˈjuːfɪmɪz(ə)m/ *n.* **1** a mild or vague expression substituted for one thought to be too harsh or direct (e.g. *pass over* for *die*). **2** the use of such expressions. □ **euphemist** *n.* **euphemistic** /-ˈmɪstɪk/ *adj.* **euphemistically** /-ˈmɪstɪk(ə)li/ *adv.* **euphemize** *v.tr.* & *intr.* (also **-ise**). [Greek *euphēmismos* from *euphēmos* (as EU-, *phēmē* 'speaking')]

euphonious /juːˈfəʊnɪəs/ *adj.* **1** sounding pleasant, harmonious. **2** concerning euphony. □ **euphoniously** *adv.*

euphonium /juːˈfəʊnɪəm/ *n.* a brass wind instrument of the tuba family. [modern Latin, from Greek *euphōnos* (as EUPHONY)]

euphony /ˈjuːf(ə)ni/ *n.* (*pl.* **-ies**) **1 a** pleasantness of sound, esp. of a word or phrase; harmony. **b** a pleasant sound. **2** the tendency to make a phonetic change for ease of pronunciation. □ **euphonic** /-ˈfɒnɪk/ *adj.* **euphonize** *v.tr.* (also **-ise**). [French *euphonie* via Late Latin *euphonia* from Greek *euphōnia* (as EU-, *phōnē* 'sound')]

euphorbia /juːˈfɔːbɪə/ *n.* any plant of the genus *Euphorbia*, including spurges. [Middle English from Latin *euphorbea* from *Euphorbus*, the name of a 1st-c. Greek physician]

euphoria /juːˈfɔːrɪə/ *n.* a feeling of well-being, esp. one based on overconfidence or over-optimism. □ **euphoric**

/-ˈfɒrɪk/ *adj.* **euphorically** /-ˈfɒrɪk(ə)li/ *adv.* [Greek from *euphoros* 'borne well, healthy' (as EU-, *pherō* 'bear')]

euphoriant /juːˈfɔːrɪənt/ *adj.* & *n.* ● *adj.* inducing euphoria. ● *n.* a euphoriant drug.

euphuism /ˈjuːfjʊɪz(ə)m/ *n.* an affected or high-flown style of writing or speaking. □ **euphuist** *n.* **euphuistic** /-ˈɪstɪk/ *adj.* **euphuistically** /-ˈɪstɪk(ə)li/ *adv.* [Greek *euphuēs* 'well endowed by nature': originally of writing imitating Lyly's *Euphues* (1578–80)]

Eurasian /jʊ(ə)rˈeɪʃ(ə)n, -ʒ(ə)n/ *adj.* & *n.* ● *adj.* **1** of mixed European and Asian (formerly esp. Indian) parentage. **2** of Europe and Asia. ● *n.* a Eurasian person.

Euratom /jʊ(ə)rˈatəm/ *n.* European Atomic Energy Community. [abbreviation]

eureka /jʊ(ə)ˈriːkə/ *int.* & *n.* ● *int.* I have found it! (expressing joy at a discovery etc.). ● *n.* an exultant cry of 'eureka'. [Greek *heurēka*, 1st person sing. perfect of *heuriskō* 'find': attributed to Archimedes]

eurhythmic /jʊ(ə)ˈrɪðmɪk/ *adj.* of or in harmonious proportion (esp. of architecture). [*eurhythmy* 'harmony of proportions' via Latin *eur(h)ythmia* from Greek *eurhuthmia* (as EU-, *rhuthmos* 'proportion, rhythm')]

eurhythmics /jʊ(ə)ˈrɪðmɪks/ *n.pl.* (usu. treated as *sing.*) (*US* **eurythmics**) harmony of bodily movement, esp. as developed with music and dance into a system of education.

eurhythmy /jʊ(ə)ˈrɪðmi/ *n.* (*US* **eurythmy**) = EURHYTHMICS.

Euro /ˈjʊərəʊ/ *adj.* & *n.* ● *adj.* European. ● *n.* **1** a European. **2** a Eurodollar. [abbreviation]

Euro- /ˈjʊərəʊ/ *comb. form* Europe, European. [abbreviation]

euro /ˈjʊərəʊ/ *n.* (*pl.* **-os**) a large reddish wallaby, *Macropus robustus*. [Adnyamathanha *yuru*]

Eurobond /ˈjʊərəʊbɒnd/ *n.* an international bond issued outside the country in whose currency its value is stated.

Eurocentric /jʊərəʊˈsɛntrɪk/ *adj.* having or regarding Europe as its centre; presupposing the supremacy of Europe and Europeans. □ **Eurocentrism** *n.* [EURO- + -CENTRIC]

Eurocheque /ˈjʊərəʊtʃɛk/ *n.* **1** a cheque issued under a banking arrangement enabling account-holders from one European country to use their cheques in another. **2** this arrangement.

Eurocommunism /jʊərəʊˈkɒmjʊnɪz(ə)m/ *n.* a form of Communism in western European countries. □ **Eurocommunist** *adj.* & *n.*

Eurocrat /ˈjʊərə(ʊ)krat/ *n.* usu. *derog.* a bureaucrat in the administration of the European Union.

Euro-currency /ˈjʊərə(ʊ),kʌr(ə)nsi/ *n.* money held outside the country (usu. the US or Japan) in whose currency its value is stated.

Eurodollar /ˈjʊərəʊ,dɒlə/ *n.* a dollar held outside the US (not necessarily in Europe).

Euro-election /ˈjʊərəʊɪ,lɛkʃ(ə)n/ *n.* an election held for the European Parliament.

Euromarket /ˈjʊərəʊ,maːkɪt/ *n.* **1** the European money market. **2** the market of a particular Euro-currency.

Euro-MP *n.* a member of the European Parliament.

Europe /ˈjʊərəp/ *n.* **1** a continent of the northern hemisphere. **2** the European Union. [Greek *Eurōpē*]

European /jʊərəˈpiːən/ *adj.* & *n.* ● *adj.* **1** of or in Europe. **2 a** descended from natives of Europe. **b** originating in or characteristic of Europe. **3 a** happening in or extending over Europe. **b** concerning Europe as a whole rather than its individual countries. **4** of or relating to the European Union. ● *n.* **1 a** a native or inhabitant of Europe. **b** a person descended from natives of Europe. **c** a white person. **2** a person concerned with European matters. □ **Europeanism** *n.* **Europeanize** *v.tr.* & *intr.* (also **-ise**). **Europeanization** /-ˈzeɪʃ(ə)n/ *n.* [French *européen* via Latin *europaeus*, from *Europa*, from Greek *Eurōpē* 'Europe']

European Community *n.* an economic and political association of certain European countries as a unit with internal free trade and common external tariffs.

■ **Usage** The European Community (EC) was formed in 1967 from the European Coal and Steel Community (ECSC), the European Economic Community (EEC), and the European Atomic Energy Community (Euratom). The name 'European Communities' is used in legal contexts where the three distinct organizations are recognized. The name 'European Economic Community' (EEC) is sometimes used loosely for the merged organization. In November 1993 the EC became known as the European Union (EU).

European Economic Community see note at EUROPEAN COMMUNITY.

European plan *n. N. Amer.* a system of charging for a hotel room only without meals.

europium /jʊ(ə)rˈəʊpɪəm/ *n. Chem.* a soft silvery metallic element of the lanthanide series, occurring naturally in small quantities (symbol **Eu**). [modern Latin, from *Europe*]

Euro-rebel /ˈjʊərəʊ,rɛb(ə)l/ *n.* a person who does not share his or her political party's enthusiasm for the European Union.

Euro-sceptic /ˈjʊərəʊ,skɛptɪk/ *n.* a person who is not enthusiastic about increasing the powers of the European Union.

Eurovision /ˈjʊərəvɪʒ(ə)n/ *n.* a network of European television production administered by the European Broadcasting Union.

eurythmics *US* var. of EURHYTHMICS.

eurythmy *US* var. of EURHYTHMY.

Eustachian tube /juːˈsteɪʃ(ə)n/ *n. Anat.* a tube leading from the pharynx to the cavity of the middle ear and equalizing the pressure on each side of the eardrum. [Latin *Eustachius* = B. *Eustachio*, Italian anatomist d. 1574]

eustasy /ˈjuːstəsi/ *n.* a change in sea level throughout the world caused by tectonic movements, melting of glaciers, etc. □ **eustatic** /-ˈstatɪk/ *adj.* [back-formation from German *eustatisch* (*adj.*) (as EU-, STATIC)]

eutectic /juːˈtɛktɪk/ *adj.* & *n. Chem.* ● *adj.* (of a mixture, alloy, etc.) having the lowest freezing point of any possible proportions of its constituents. ● *n.* a eutectic mixture. [Greek *eutēktos* (as EU-, *tēkō* 'melt')]

eutectic point *n.* (also **eutectic temperature**) the minimum freezing point for a eutectic mixture.

euthanasia /juːθəˈneɪzɪə/ *n.* **1** the painless killing of a patient suffering from an incurable and painful disease. **2** such a death. [Greek (as EU-, *thanatos* 'death')]

eutherian /juːˈθɪərɪən/ *n.* & *adj. Zool.* ● *n.* a mammal of the infraclass Eutheria, giving nourishment to its unborn young through a placenta (as in humans). ● *adj.* of or relating to this infraclass, which includes all mammals except marsupials and monotremes. [EU- + Greek *thēr* 'wild beast']

eutrophic /juːˈtrəʊfɪk, -ˈtrɒf-/ *adj.* (of a lake etc.) rich in nutrients and so supporting a dense plant population, the decomposition of which kills animal life by depriving it of oxygen. □ **eutrophicate** *v.tr.* **eutrophication** /-ˈkeɪʃ(ə)n/ *n.* **eutrophy** /ˈjuːtrəfɪ/ *n.* [*eutrophy* from Greek *eutrophia* (as EU-, *trephō* 'nourish')]

eV *abbr.* electronvolt.

EVA *abbr.* (in astronautics) extravehicular activity.

evacuate /ɪˈvakjʊeɪt/ *v.tr.* **1 a** remove (people) from a place of danger to stay elsewhere for the duration of the danger. **b** empty (a place) in this way. **2** make empty (a vessel of air etc.). **3** (of troops) withdraw from (a place). **4 a** empty (the bowels or other bodily organ). **b** discharge (faeces etc.). □ **evacuant** *n.* & *adj.* **evacuation** /-ˈeɪʃ(ə)n/ *n.* **evacuative** /-kjʊətɪv/ *adj.* & *n.* **evacuator** *n.* [Latin *evacuare* (as E-, *vacuus* 'empty')]

evacuee /ɪ,vakjuːˈiː/ *n.* a person evacuated from a place of danger.

evade /ɪ'veɪd/ *v.tr.* **1 a** escape from, avoid, esp. by guile or trickery. **b** avoid doing (one's duty etc.). **c** avoid answering (a question) or yielding to (an argument). **2 a** avoid paying (tax) by illegitimate presentation of one's finances. **b** defeat the intention of (a law etc.), esp. while complying with its letter. **3** (of a thing) elude or baffle (a person). □ **evadable** *adj.* **evader** *n.* [French *évader* from Latin *evadere* (as E-, *vadere vas-* 'go')]

evaginate /ɪ'vadʒmeɪt/ *v.tr. Med. & Physiol.* turn (a tubular organ) inside out. □ **evagination** /-'neɪʃ(ə)n/ *n.* [Latin *evaginare* (as E-, *vaginare* as VAGINA)]

evaluate /ɪ'valjʊeɪt/ *v.tr.* **1** assess, appraise. **2 a** find or state the number or amount of. **b** find a numerical expression for. □ **evaluation** /-'eɪʃ(ə)n/ *n.* **evaluative** /-ətɪv/ *adj.* **evaluator** *n.* [back-formation from *evaluation*, from French *évaluation* from *évaluer* (as E-, VALUE)]

evanesce /i:və'nɛs, ɛv-/ *v.intr.* **1** fade from sight; disappear. **2** become effaced. [Latin *evanescere* (as E-, *vanus* 'empty')]

evanescent /i:və'nɛs(ə)nt, ɛv-/ *adj.* (of an impression or appearance etc.) quickly fading. □ **evanescence** *n.* **evanescently** *adv.*

evangel /ɪ'van(d)ʒɛl, -(d)ʒ(ə)l/ *n.* **1** *archaic* **a** the gospel. **b** any of the four Gospels. **2** a basic doctrine or set of principles. **3** *N. Amer.* = EVANGELIST. [Middle English via Old French *evangile* and ecclesiastical Latin *evangelium* from Greek *euaggelion* 'good news' (as EU-, ANGEL)]

evangelic /i:van'dʒɛlɪk, ɛv-/ *adj.* = EVANGELICAL.

evangelical /i:van'dʒɛlɪk(ə)l, ɛv-/ *adj. & n.* ● *adj.* **1** of or according to the teaching of the gospel or the Christian religion. **2** of a branch of Protestant Christianity emphasizing the authority of Scripture, personal conversion, and the doctrine of salvation by faith in the Atonement. **3** zealously advocating a cause. ● *n.* a member of the evangelical tradition. □ **evangelicalism** *n.* **evangelically** *adv.* [ecclesiastical Latin *evangelicus* from ecclesiastical Greek *euaggelikos* (as EVANGEL)]

evangelism /ɪ'van(d)ʒ(ə)lɪz(ə)m/ *n.* **1** the preaching or promulgation of the gospel. **2** zealous advocacy of a cause or doctrine.

evangelist /ɪ'van(d)ʒ(ə)lɪst/ *n.* **1** any of the writers of the four Gospels (Matthew, Mark, Luke, John). **2** a preacher of the gospel. **3** a lay person doing missionary work.

evangelistic /ɪ,van(d)ʒə'lɪstɪk/ *adj.* **1** of or relating to evangelism. **2** of the four evangelists.

evangelize /ɪ'van(d)ʒ(ə)lʌɪz/ *v.tr.* (also **-ise**) **1** (also *absol.*) preach the gospel to. **2** convert (a person) to Christianity. □ **evangelization** /-'zeɪʃ(ə)n/ *n.* **evangelizer** *n.* [Middle English via ecclesiastical Latin *evangelizare* from Greek *euaggelizomai* (as EVANGEL)]

evaporate /ɪ'vapəreɪt/ *v.* **1** *intr.* turn from solid or liquid into vapour. **2** *intr. & tr.* lose or cause to lose moisture as vapour. **3** *intr. & tr.* disappear or cause to disappear (*our courage evaporated*). □ **evaporable** *adj.* **evaporation** /-'reɪʃ(ə)n/ *n.* **evaporative** /-rətɪv/ *adj.* **evaporator** *n.* [Latin *evaporare* (as E-, *vaporare* as VAPOUR)]

evaporated milk *n.* milk concentrated by partial evaporation.

evaporite /ɪ'vapərʌɪt/ *n. Geol.* a natural salt or mineral deposit formed by evaporation of water. [EVAPORATE + -ITE[1]]

evasion /ɪ'veɪʒ(ə)n/ *n.* **1** the act of evading. **2 a** a subterfuge or prevaricating excuse. **b** an evasive answer. [Middle English via Old French from Latin *evasio -onis* (as EVADE)]

evasive /ɪ'veɪsɪv/ *adj.* **1** seeking to evade something. **2** not direct in one's answers etc. **3** enabling or effecting evasion (*evasive action*). **4** (of a person) tending to evasion; habitually practising evasion. □ **evasively** *adv.* **evasiveness** *n.*

eve /i:v/ *n.* **1** the evening or day before a church festival or any date or event (*Christmas Eve*; *the eve of the funeral*). **2** the time just before anything (*the eve of the election*). **3** *archaic* evening. [Middle English, = EVEN[2]]

evection /ɪ'vɛkʃ(ə)n/ *n. Astron.* a perturbation of the moon's motion caused by the sun's attraction. [Latin *evectio* (as E-, *vehere vect-* 'carry')]

even[1] /'i:v(ə)n/ *adj., adv., & v.* ● *adj.* (**evener, evenest**) **1** level; flat and smooth. **2 a** uniform in quality; constant. **b** equal in number, amount, value, score, etc. **c** equally balanced. **3** (usu. foll. by *with*) in the same plane or line. **4** (of a person's temper etc.) equable, calm. **5 a** (of a number such as 4, 6) divisible by two without a remainder. **b** bearing such a number (*no parking on even dates*). **c** not involving fractions; exact (*in even dozens*). ● *adv.* **1** used to invite comparison of the stated assertion, negation, etc., with an implied one that is less strong or remarkable (*never even opened* [let alone read] *the letter*; *does he even suspect* [not to say realize] *the danger?*; *ran even faster* [not just as fast as before]; *even if my watch is right we shall be late* [later if it is slow]). **2** used to introduce an extreme case (*even you must realize it*; *it might even cost £100*). ● *v.* **1** *tr. & intr.* (often foll. by *up* or *out*) make or become even. **2** *tr.* (often foll. by *to*) *archaic* treat as equal or comparable. □ **even as** at the very moment that. **even now 1** now as well as before. **2** at this very moment. **even so 1** notwithstanding that; nevertheless. **2** quite so. **3** in that case as well as in others. **even though** despite the fact that. **get** (or **be**) **even with** have one's revenge on. **of even date** *Law & Commerce* of the same date. **on an even keel 1** (of a ship or aircraft) not listing. **2** (of a plan or person) untroubled. □ **evenly** *adv.* **evenness** /'i:v(ə)nnɪs/ *n.* [Old English *efen, efne*]

even[2] /'i:v(ə)n/ *n. poet.* evening. [Old English *ǣfen*]

even break *n. colloq.* an equal chance.

even chance *n.* an equal chance of success or failure.

even-handed *adj.* impartial, fair. □ **even-handedly** *adv.* **even-handedness** *n.*

evening /'i:v(ə)nɪŋ/ *n. & int.* ● *n.* **1** the end part of the day, esp. from about 6 p.m., or sunset if earlier, to bedtime (*this evening*; *during the evening*; *evening meal*). **2** this time spent in a particular way (*had a lively evening*). **3** a time compared with this, esp. the last part of a person's life. ● *int. colloq.* = *good evening* (see GOOD *adj.* 14). [Old English *ǣfnung*, related to EVEN[2]]

evening dress *n.* formal dress for evening wear.

evening primrose *n.* any plant of the genus *Oenothera* with pale yellow flowers that open in the evening, and from whose seeds an oil is extracted for medicinal use.

evening star *n.* a planet, esp. Venus, when visible in the west after sunset.

even money *n. & adj.* ● *n.* betting odds offering the gambler the chance of winning the amount he or she staked. ● *adj.* equally likely to happen or not (*it's even money he'll fail to arrive*).

evens /'i:v(ə)nz/ *n.pl. Brit.* = EVEN MONEY.

evensong /'i:v(ə)nsɒŋ/ *n.* a service of evening prayer, esp. that of Anglican churches. [EVEN[2] + SONG]

event /ɪ'vɛnt/ *n.* **1** a thing that happens or takes place, esp. one of importance. **2 a** the fact of a thing's occurring. **b** a result or outcome. **3** an item in a sports programme, or the programme as a whole. **4** *Physics* a single occurrence of a process, e.g. the ionization of one atom. **5** something on the result of which money is staked. □ **at all events** (or **in any event**) whatever happens. **in the event** as it turns (or turned) out. **in the event of** if (a specified thing) happens (*in the event of his death*; *in the event of our losing*). **in the event that** *disp.* if it happens that. [Latin *eventus* from *evenire event-* 'happen' (as E-, *venire* 'come')]

■ **Usage** *In the event that* is considered awkward by some people. It can usually be avoided by rephrasing, e.g. *in the event that it rains* can be replaced by *in the event of rain*.

even-tempered *adj.* not easily annoyed or angered; equable.

eventer /ɪˈvɛntə/ *n. Brit.* a horse or rider who takes part in horse trials. [EVENT 3 as in *three day event*]

eventful /ɪˈvɛntfʊl, -f(ə)l/ *adj.* marked by noteworthy events. □ **eventfully** *adv.* **eventfulness** *n.*

event horizon *n.* the gravitational boundary enclosing a black hole, from which no light escapes.

eventide /iːv(ə)ntʌɪd/ *n. archaic* or *poet.* = EVENING. [Old English *ǣfentīd* (as EVEN², TIDE)]

eventide home *n.* esp. *Brit.* a home for the elderly, originally one run by the Salvation Army.

eventing /ɪˈvɛntɪŋ/ *n. Brit.* participation in horse trials, esp. cross-country, dressage, and showjumping. [EVENT 3 as in *three-day event*]

eventless /ɪˈvɛntlɪs/ *adj.* without noteworthy or remarkable events.

eventual /ɪˈvɛn(t)ʃʊəl/ *adj.* occurring or existing in due course or at last; ultimate. □ **eventually** *adv.* [as EVENT, on the pattern of *actual*]

eventuality /ɪˌvɛn(t)ʃʊˈalɪti/ *n.* (*pl.* **-ies**) a possible event or outcome.

eventuate /ɪˈvɛn(t)ʃʊeɪt/ *v.intr. formal* **1** turn out in a specified way as the result. **2** (often foll. by *in*) result. □ **eventuation** /-ˈeɪʃ(ə)n/ *n.* [as EVENT, on the pattern of *actuate*]

ever /ˈɛvə/ *adv.* **1** at all times; always (*ever hopeful*; *ever after*). **2** at any time (*have you ever been to Paris?*; *nothing ever happens*; *as good as ever*). **3** as an emphatic word: **a** in any way; at all (*how ever did you do it?*; *when will they ever learn?*). **b** (prec. by *as*) in any manner possible (*be as quick as ever you can*). **4** (often in *comb.*) constantly (*ever-present*; *ever-recurring*). **5** (foll. by *so*, *such*) *Brit. colloq.* very; very much (*is ever so easy*; *was ever such a nice man*; *thanks ever so*). **6** (foll. by *compar.*) constantly, continually; increasingly (*grew ever larger*; *ever more sophisticated*). □ **did you ever?** *colloq.* did you ever hear or see the like? **ever since** throughout the period since. **for ever 1** for all future time. **2** *colloq.* for a long time (cf. FOREVER). [Old English *ǣfre*]

■ **Usage** When *ever* is used with a question word for emphasis it is written separately (see sense 3). When used with a relative pronoun or adverb to give it indefinite or general force, *ever* is written as one word with the relative pronoun or adverb, e.g. *However it's done, it's difficult.*

evergreen /ˈɛvəgriːn/ *adj.* & *n.* ● *adj.* **1** always green or fresh. **2** (of a plant) retaining green leaves throughout the year. ● *n.* an evergreen plant (cf. DECIDUOUS).

everlasting /ɛvəˈlɑːstɪŋ/ *adj.* & *n.* ● *adj.* **1** lasting for ever. **2** lasting for a long time, esp. so as to become unwelcome. **3** (of flowers) keeping their shape and colour when dried. ● *n.* **1** eternity. **2** = IMMORTELLE. □ **everlastingly** *adv.* **everlastingness** *n.*

evermore /ɛvəˈmɔː/ *adv.* for ever; always.

evert /ɪˈvəːt/ *v.tr. Physiol.* turn (an organ etc.) outwards or inside out. □ **eversion** *n.* [Latin *evertere* (as E-, *vertere vers-* 'turn')]

every /ˈɛvri/ *det.* **1** each without exception in a group or collection of things or people (*heard every word*; *watched her every movement*). **2** each at a specified interval in a series (*take every third one*; *comes every four days*). **3** all possible; the utmost degree of (*there is every prospect of success*). □ **every bit as** *colloq.* (in comparisons) quite as (*every bit as good*). **every now and again** (or **now and then**) from time to time. **every other** each second in a series (*every other day*). **every so often** at intervals; occasionally. **every time** *colloq.* **1** without exception. **2** certainly. **every which way** *N. Amer. colloq.* **1** in all directions. **2** in a disorderly manner. [Old English *ǣfre ǣlc* 'ever each']

everybody /ˈɛvrɪbɒdi/ *pron.* every person.

everyday /ˈɛvrɪdeɪ, -ˈdeɪ/ *adj.* **1** occurring every day. **2** suitable for or used on ordinary days. **3** commonplace, usual.

Everyman /ˈɛvrɪman/ *n.* the ordinary or typical human being. [the name of the principal character in a 15th-c. morality play]

everyone /ˈɛvrɪwʌn/ *pron.* every person; everybody.

every one *n.* each one (see also EVERYONE).

everything /ˈɛvrɪθɪŋ/ *pron.* **1** all things; all the things of a group or class. **2** *colloq.* **a** a great deal (*he owes her everything*). **b** the essential consideration (*speed is everything*). □ **have everything** *colloq.* possess every attraction, advantage, etc.

everywhere /ˈɛvrɪwɛː/ *adv.* **1** in every place. **2** *colloq.* in many places.

evict /ɪˈvɪkt/ *v.tr.* expel (a tenant) from a property by legal process. □ **eviction** *n.* **evictor** *n.* [Latin *evincere evict-* (as E-, *vincere* 'conquer')]

evidence /ˈɛvɪd(ə)ns/ *n.* & *v.* ● *n.* **1** (often foll. by *for*, *of*) the available facts, circumstances, etc. supporting or otherwise a belief, proposition, etc., or indicating whether or not a thing is true or valid. **2** *Law* **a** information given personally or drawn from a document etc. and tending to prove a fact or proposition. **b** statements or proofs admissible as testimony in a law court. **3** clearness, obviousness. ● *v.tr.* be evidence of; attest. □ **call in evidence** *Law* summon (a person) as a witness. **in evidence** noticeable, conspicuous. [Middle English via Old French from Latin *evidentia* (as EVIDENT)]

evident /ˈɛvɪd(ə)nt/ *adj.* plain or obvious (visually or intellectually); manifest. [Middle English from Old French *evident* or Latin *evidēre evident-* (as E-, *vidēre* 'see')]

evidential /ɛvɪˈdɛnʃ(ə)l/ *adj.* of or providing evidence. □ **evidentially** *adv.*

evidentiary /ɛvɪˈdɛnʃ(ə)ri/ *adj.* = EVIDENTIAL.

evidently /ˈɛvɪd(ə)ntli/ *adv.* **1** plainly, obviously. **2** (qualifying a whole sentence) it is plain that; it would seem that (*evidently, we're too late*). **3** (said in reply) so it appears.

evil /ˈiːv(ə)l, -vɪl/ *adj.* & *n.* ● *adj.* **1** morally bad; wicked. **2** harmful or tending to harm, esp. intentionally or characteristically. **3** disagreeable or unpleasant (*has an evil temper*). **4** unlucky; causing misfortune (*evil days*). ● *n.* **1** an evil thing; an instance of something evil. **2** evil quality; wickedness, harm. □ **speak evil of** slander. □ **evilly** *adv.* **evilness** *n.* [Old English *yfel*, from Germanic]

evildoer /ˈiːv(ə)lduːə/ *n.* a person who does evil. □ **evildoing** *n.*

evil eye *n.* a gaze or stare superstitiously believed to be able to cause material harm.

evince /ɪˈvɪns/ *v.tr.* **1** indicate or make evident. **2** show that one has (a quality). □ **evincible** *adj.* **evincive** *adj.* [Latin *evincere*: see EVICT]

eviscerate /ɪˈvɪsəreɪt/ *v.tr. formal* **1** disembowel. **2** empty or deprive of essential contents. □ **evisceration** /-ˈreɪʃ(ə)n/ *n.* [Latin *eviscerare eviscerat-* (as E-, VISCERA)]

evocative /ɪˈvɒkətɪv/ *adj.* tending to evoke (esp. feelings or memories). □ **evocatively** *adv.* **evocativeness** *n.*

evoke /ɪˈvəʊk/ *v.tr.* **1** inspire or draw forth (memories, feelings, a response, etc.). **2** = INVOKE 3. □ **evocation** /ɛvəˈkeɪʃ(ə)n/ *n.* **evoker** *n.* [Latin *evocare* (as E-, *vocare* 'call')]

evolute /ˈiːvəluːt, -ljuːt, ˈɛv-/ *n.* (in full **evolute curve**) *Math.* a curve which is the locus of the centres of curvature of another curve that is its involute. [Latin *evolutus*, past part. of *evolvere* (as EVOLVE)]

evolution /iːvəˈluːʃ(ə)n, -ˈljuː-, ˈɛv-/ *n.* **1** gradual development, esp. from a simple to a more complex form. **2** a process by which species develop from earlier forms, as an explanation of their origins. **3** the appearance or presentation of events etc. in due succession (*the evolution of the plot*). **4** a change in the disposition of troops or ships. **5** the giving off or evolving of gas, heat, etc. **6** an opening out. **7** the unfolding of a curve. **8** *Math.* the extraction of a root from any given power (cf. INVOLUTION 6). □ **evolutional** *adj.* **evolutionally** *adv.* **evolutionary** *adj.* **evolutionarily** *adv.* [Latin *evolutio* 'unrolling' (as EVOLVE)]

evolutionist /iːvəˈluːʃ(ə)nɪst, -ˈljuː-, ɛ-/ *n.* a person who believes in evolution as explaining the origin of species. □ **evolutionism** *n.* **evolutionistic** /-ˈnɪstɪk/ *adj.*

evolve /ɪˈvɒlv/ *v.* **1** *intr. & tr.* develop gradually by a natural process. **2** *tr.* work out or devise (a theory, plan, etc.). **3** *intr. & tr.* unfold; open out. **4** *tr.* give off (gas, heat, etc.). □ **evolvable** *adj.* **evolvement** *n.* [Latin *evolvere evolut-* (as E-, *volvere* 'roll')]

evzone /ˈɛvzəʊn/ *n.* a member of a select Greek infantry regiment. [modern Greek *euzōnos* from Greek, = dressed for exercise (as EU-, *zōnē* 'belt')]

ewe /juː/ *n.* a female sheep. [Old English *ēowu*, from Germanic]

ewe lamb *n.* a person's most cherished possession (2 Sam. 12).

ewe-necked *adj.* (of a horse) having a thin concave neck.

ewer /ˈjuːə/ *n.* a large pitcher or water jug with a wide mouth. [Middle English from Old Northern French *eviere*, Old French *aiguiere*, ultimately via Latin *aquarius* 'of water' from *aqua* 'water']

ex[1] /ɛks/ *prep.* **1** (of goods) sold from (*ex-works*). **2** (of stocks or shares) without, excluding. [Latin, = out of]

ex[2] /ɛks/ *n. colloq.* a former husband or wife. [absol. use of EX-[1] 2]

ex-[1] /ɛks/ *prefix* (also **e-** before some consonants, **ef-** before *f*) **1** forming verbs meaning: **a** out, forth (*exclude*; *exit*). **b** upward (*extol*). **c** thoroughly (*excruciate*). **d** bring into a state (*exasperate*). **e** remove or free from (*expatriate*; *exonerate*). **2** forming nouns from titles of office, status, etc., meaning 'formerly' (*ex-convict*; *ex-president*; *ex-wife*). [Latin, from *ex* 'out of']

ex-[2] /ɛks/ *prefix* out (*exodus*). [Greek, from *ex* 'out of']

exa- /ˈɛksə/ *comb. form* denoting a factor of 10^{18}. [perhaps from HEXA-]

exacerbate /ɪɡˈzasəbeɪt, ɛkˈsas-/ *v.tr.* **1** make (pain, anger, etc.) worse. **2** irritate (a person). □ **exacerbation** /-ˈbeɪʃ(ə)n/ *n.* [Latin *exacerbare* (as EX-[1], *acerbus* 'bitter')]

exact /ɪɡˈzakt, ɛɡ-/ *adj. & v.* ● *adj.* **1** accurate; correct in all details (*an exact description*). **2 a** precise. **b** (of a person) tending to precision. ● *v.tr.* (often foll. by *from*, *of*) **1** demand and enforce payment of (money, fees, etc.) from a person. **2 a** demand; insist on. **b** (of circumstances) require urgently. □ **exactable** *adj.* **exactitude** *n.* **exactness** *n.* **exactor** *n.* [Latin *exigere exact-* (as EX-[1], *agere* 'drive')]

exacting /ɪɡˈzaktɪŋ, ɛɡ-/ *adj.* **1** making great demands. **2** calling for much effort. □ **exactingly** *adv.* **exactingness** *n.*

exaction /ɪɡˈzakʃ(ə)n, ɛɡ-/ *n.* **1** the act or an instance of exacting; the process of being exacted. **2 a** an illegal or exorbitant demand; an extortion. **b** a sum or thing exacted. [Middle English from Latin *exactio* (as EXACT)]

exactly /ɪɡˈzak(t)li, ɛɡ-/ *adv.* **1** accurately, precisely; in an exact manner (*worked it out exactly*). **2** in exact terms (*exactly when did it happen?*). **3** (said in reply) quite so; I quite agree. □ **not exactly** *colloq.* **1** by no means. **2** not precisely.

exact science *n.* a science admitting of absolute or quantitative precision.

exaggerate /ɪɡˈzadʒəreɪt, ɛɡ-/ *v.tr.* **1** (also *absol.*) give an impression of (a thing), esp. in speech or writing, that makes it seem larger or greater etc. than it really is. **2** enlarge or alter beyond normal or due proportions (*spoke with exaggerated politeness*). □ **exaggeratedly** *adv.* **exaggeratingly** *adv.* **exaggeration** /-ˈreɪʃ(ə)n/ *n.* **exaggerative** /-rətɪv/ *adj.* **exaggerator** *n.* [Latin *exaggerare* (as EX-[1], *aggerare* 'heap up' from *agger* 'heap')]

exalt /ɪɡˈzɔːlt, ɛɡ-/ *v.tr.* **1** raise in rank or power etc. **2** praise highly. **3** (usu. as **exalted** *adj.*) make lofty or noble (*exalted aims*; *an exalted style*). □ **exaltedly** *adv.* **exaltedness** *n.* [Middle English from Latin *exaltare* (as EX-[1], *altus* 'high')]

exaltation /ɛɡzɔːlˈteɪʃ(ə)n, ɛks-/ *n.* **1** the act or an instance of exalting; the state of being exalted. **2** elation; rapturous emotion. [Middle English from Old French *exaltation* or Late Latin *exaltatio* (as EXALT)]

exam /ɪɡˈzam, ɛɡ-/ *n. colloq.* = EXAMINATION 3b.

examination /ɪɡˌzamɪˈneɪʃ(ə)n, ɛɡ-/ *n.* **1** the act or an instance of examining; the state of being examined. **2** a detailed inspection. **3 a** the testing of the proficiency or knowledge of students or other candidates for a qualification by oral or written questions. **b** a test of this kind. **4** an instance of examining or being examined medically. **5** *Law* the formal questioning of the accused or of a witness in court. □ **examinational** *adj.* [Middle English via Old French from Latin *examinatio -onis* (as EXAMINE)]

examination paper *n.* **1** the printed questions in an examination. **2** a candidate's set of answers.

examine /ɪɡˈzamɪn, ɛɡ-/ *v.* **1** *tr.* enquire into the nature or condition etc. of. **2** *tr.* look closely or analytically at. **3** *tr.* test the proficiency of, esp. by examination (see EXAMINATION 3a). **4** *tr.* check the health of (a patient) by inspection or experiment. **5** *tr. Law* formally question (the accused or a witness) in court. **6** *intr.* (foll. by *into*) inquire. □ **examinable** *adj.* **examinee** /-ˈniː/ *n.* **examiner** *n.* [Middle English via Old French *examiner* from Latin *examinare* 'weigh, test', from *examen* 'tongue of a balance', ultimately from *exigere* 'examine, weigh': see EXACT]

example /ɪɡˈzɑːmp(ə)l, ɛɡ-/ *n. & v.* ● *n.* **1** a thing characteristic of its kind or illustrating a general rule. **2** a person, thing, or piece of conduct, regarded in terms of its fitness to be imitated or likelihood of being imitated (*must set him an example*; *you are a bad example*). **3** a circumstance or treatment seen as a warning to others; a person so treated (*shall make an example of you*). **4** a problem or exercise designed to illustrate a rule. ● *v.tr.* (usu. in *passive*) serve as an example of. □ **for example** by way of illustration. [Middle English via Old French from Latin *exemplum* (as EXEMPT)]

ex ante /ɛks ˈanti/ *adj. Econ.* based on expected results, forecast (cf. EX POST). [modern Latin, = 'from before']

exanthema /ɪkˈsanθɪmə, ɛksanˈθiːmə/ *n. Med.* a skin rash accompanying any eruptive disease or fever. [Late Latin from Greek *exanthēma* 'eruption', from *exantheō* (as EX-[2], *anthos* 'blossom')]

exarch /ˈɛksɑːk/ *n.* in the Orthodox Church, a bishop lower in rank than a patriarch and having jurisdiction wider than the metropolitan of a diocese. □ **exarchate** *n.* [ecclesiastical Latin from Greek *exarkhos* (as EX-[2], *arkhos* 'ruler')]

exasperate /ɪɡˈzasp(ə)reɪt, ɛɡ-/ *v.tr.* **1** (often as **exasperated** *adj.* or **exasperating** *adj.*) irritate intensely; infuriate. **2** make (a pain, ill feeling, etc.) worse. □ **exasperatedly** *adv.* **exasperatingly** *adv.* **exasperation** /-ˈreɪʃ(ə)n/ *n.* [Latin *exasperare exasperat-* (as EX-[1], *asper* 'rough')]

ex cathedra /ɛks kəˈθiːdrə/ *adj. & adv.* with full authority (esp. of a papal pronouncement, implying infallibility as doctrinally defined). [Latin, = from the (teacher's) chair]

excavate /ˈɛkskəveɪt/ *v.tr.* **1 a** make (a hole or channel) by digging. **b** dig out material from (the ground). **2** reveal or extract by digging. **3** (also *absol.*) *Archaeol.* dig systematically into the ground to explore (a site). □ **excavation** /-ˈveɪʃ(ə)n/ *n.* **excavator** *n.* [Latin *excavare* (as EX-[1], *cavus* 'hollow')]

exceed /ɪkˈsiːd, ɛk-/ *v.tr.* **1** (often foll. by *by* an amount) be more or greater than (in number, extent, etc.). **2** go beyond or do more than is warranted by (a set limit, esp. of one's instructions or rights). **3** surpass, excel (a person or achievement). [Middle English via Old

French *exceder* from Latin *excedere* (as EX-[1], *cedere cess-* 'go')]

exceeding /ɪk'si:dɪŋ, ɛk-/ *adj. & adv.* ● *adj.* **1** surpassing in amount or degree. **2** pre-eminent. ● *adv. archaic* = EXCEEDINGLY 2.

exceedingly /ɪk'si:dɪŋli, ɛk-/ *adv.* **1** very; to a great extent. **2** surpassingly, pre-eminently.

excel /ɪk'sɛl, ɛk-/ *v.* (**excelled**, **excelling**) (often foll. by *in*, *at*) **1** *tr.* be superior to. **2** *intr.* be pre-eminent or the most outstanding (*excels at games*). □ **excel oneself** surpass one's previous performance. [Middle English from Latin *excellere* (as EX-[1], *celsus* 'lofty')]

excellence /'ɛks(ə)l(ə)ns/ *n.* **1** the state of excelling; surpassing merit or quality. **2** the activity etc. in which a person excels. [Middle English from Old French *excellence* or Latin *excellentia* (as EXCEL)]

Excellency /'ɛks(ə)l(ə)nsi/ *n.* (*pl.* **-ies**) (usu. prec. by *Your*, *His*, *Her*, *Their*) a title used in addressing or referring to certain high officials, e.g. ambassadors and governors, and (in some countries) senior Church dignitaries. [Middle English from Latin *excellentia* (as EXCEL)]

excellent /'ɛks(ə)l(ə)nt/ *adj.* extremely good; pre-eminent. □ **excellently** *adv.* [Middle English from Old French (as EXCEL)]

excelsior /ɛk'sɛlsɪɔ:/ *int. & n.* ● *int.* higher, outstanding (esp. as a motto or trade mark). ● *n.* softwood shavings used for stuffing, packing, etc. [Latin, comparative of *excelsus* 'lofty']

excentric var. of ECCENTRIC (in technical senses).

except /ɪk'sɛpt, ɛk-/ *v., prep., & conj.* ● *v.tr.* (often as **excepted** *adj.* placed after object) exclude from a general statement, condition, etc. (*excepted him from the amnesty*; *present company excepted*). ● *prep.* (often foll. by *for*, or *that* + clause) not including; other than (*all failed except him*; *all here except for John*; *is all right except that it is too long*). ● *conj. archaic* unless (*except he be born again*). [Middle English from Latin *excipere except-* (as EX-[1], *capere* 'take')]

excepting /ɪk'sɛptɪŋ, ɛk-/ *prep. & conj.* ● *prep.* = EXCEPT *prep.* ● *conj. archaic* = EXCEPT *conj.*

■ **Usage** *Excepting* should be used only after *not* and *always*; otherwise, *except* should be used.

exception /ɪk'sɛpʃ(ə)n, ɛk-/ *n.* **1** the act or an instance of excepting; the state of being excepted (*made an exception in my case*). **2** a thing that has been or will be excepted. **3** an instance that does not follow a rule. □ **take exception** (often foll. by *to*) object; be resentful (about). **with the exception of** except; not including. [Middle English via Old French from Latin *exceptio -onis* (as EXCEPT)]

exceptionable /ɪk'sɛpʃənəb(ə)l, ɛk-/ *adj.* open to objection; to which exception may be taken. □ **exceptionably** *adv.*

■ **Usage** *Exceptionable* should not be confused with *exceptional*. Note the difference in meaning between *Her new book was unexceptionable* (i.e. it contained nothing that would cause objections) and *Her new book was unexceptional* (i.e. it was mediocre).

exceptional /ɪk'sɛpʃ(ə)n(ə)l, ɛk-/ *adj.* **1** forming an exception. **2** unusual; not typical (*exceptional circumstances*). **3** unusually good; outstanding. □ **exceptionality** /-'nalɪti/ *n.* **exceptionally** *adv.*

■ **Usage** See Usage Note at EXCEPTIONABLE.

excerpt *n. & v.* ● *n.* /'ɛksə:pt/ a short extract from a book, film, piece of music, etc. ● *v.tr.* /ɪk'sə:pt, ɛk-/ (also *absol.*) **1** take an excerpt or excerpts from (a book etc.). **2** take (an extract) from a book etc. □ **excerptible** /-'sə:ptɪb(ə)l/ *adj.* **excerption** /-'sə:pʃ(ə)n/ *n.* [Latin *excerpere excerpt-* (as EX-[1], *carpere* 'pluck')]

excess /ɪk'sɛs, ɛk-, 'ɛksɛs/ *n. & adj.* ● *n.* **1** the state or an instance of exceeding. **2** the amount by which one quantity or number exceeds another. **3** exceeding of a proper or permitted limit. **4 a** the overstepping of the accepted limits of moderation, esp. intemperance in eating or drinking. **b** (in *pl.*) outrageous or immoderate behaviour. **5** an extreme or improper degree or extent (*an excess of cruelty*). **6** *Brit.* part of an insurance claim to be paid by the insured, esp. by prior agreement. ● *attrib.adj.* /usu. 'ɛksɛs/ **1** that exceeds a limited or prescribed amount (*excess weight*). **2** *Brit.* required as extra payment (*excess postage*). □ **in** (or **to**) **excess** exceeding the proper amount or degree. **in excess of** more than; exceeding. [Middle English via Old French *exces* from Latin *excessus* (as EXCEED)]

excess baggage *n.* (also **excess luggage**) baggage exceeding a weight allowance and liable to an extra charge.

excessive /ɪk'sɛsɪv, ɛk-/ *adj.* **1** too much or too great. **2** more than what is normal or necessary. □ **excessively** *adv.* **excessiveness** *n.*

exchange /ɪks'tʃeɪndʒ, ɛks-/ *n. & v.* ● *n.* **1** the act or an instance of giving one thing and receiving another in its place. **2 a** the giving of money for its equivalent in the money of the same or esp. another country. **b** the fee or percentage charged for this. **3** a place or installation containing the apparatus for connecting telephone calls. **4** a place where merchants, bankers, etc. gather to transact business. **5 a** an office where certain information is given or a service provided, usu. involving two parties. **b** an employment office. **6** a system of settling debts between persons (esp. in different countries) without the use of money, by bills of exchange (see BILL OF EXCHANGE). **7 a** a short conversation, esp. a disagreement or quarrel. **b** a sequence of letters between correspondents. **8** *Chess* the capture of one piece by each player in immediate succession. **9** (*attrib.*) forming part of an exchange, e.g. of personnel between institutions (*an exchange student*). ● *v.* **1** *tr.* (often foll. by *for*) give or receive (one thing) in place of another. **2** *tr.* give and receive as equivalents (e.g. things or people, blows, information, etc.); give one and receive another of. **3** *intr.* (often foll. by *with*) make an exchange. □ **in exchange** (often foll. by *for*) as a thing exchanged (for). □ **exchangeable** *adj.* **exchangeability** /-'bɪlɪti/ *n.* **exchanger** *n.* [Middle English via Old French *eschangier* from Romanic (as EX-[1], CHANGE)]

exchange rate *n.* the value of one currency in terms of another.

exchequer /ɪks'tʃɛkə, ɛks-/ *n.* **1** *Brit.* the former government department in charge of national revenue. **2** a royal or national treasury. **3** the money of a private individual or group. [Middle English via Anglo-French *escheker*, Old French *eschequier* from medieval Latin *scaccarium* 'chessboard' (its original sense, with reference to keeping accounts on a chequered cloth)]

■ **Usage** With reference to sense 1, the functions of this department now belong to the Treasury, although the name formally survives, esp. in the title *Chancellor of the Exchequer*.

excimer /'ɛksɪmə/ *n. Chem. & Physics* a dimer existing only in an excited state, used in some lasers. [*excited* + DIMER]

excise[1] /'ɛksʌɪz/ *n. & v.* ● *n.* **1 a** a duty or tax levied on goods and commodities produced or sold within the country of origin. **b** a tax levied on certain licences. **2** *Brit.* a former government office collecting excise (now the *Board of Customs and Excise*). ● *v.tr.* **1** charge excise on (goods). **2** force (a person) to pay excise. [Middle Dutch *excijs*, *accijs*, perhaps from Romanic: related to CENSUS]

excise[2] /ɪk'sʌɪz, ɛk-/ *v.tr.* **1** remove (a passage of a book etc.). **2** cut out (an organ etc.) by surgery. □ **excision** /ɪk'sɪʒ(ə)n/ *n.* [Latin *excidere excis-* (as EX-[1], *caedere* 'cut')]

exciseman /'ɛksʌɪzmən/ *n.* (*pl.* **-men**) *Brit. hist.* an officer responsible for collecting excise duty.

excitable /ɪk'sʌɪtəb(ə)l, ɛk-/ *adj.* **1** (esp. of a person) easily excited. **2** (of an organism, tissue, etc.)

responding to a stimulus, or susceptible to stimulation. □ **excitability** /-'bɪlɪti/ *n.* **excitably** *adv.* [EXCITE + -ABLE]

excitation /ɛksɪ'teɪʃ(ə)n/ *n.* **1 a** the act or an instance of exciting. **b** the state of being excited; excitement. **2** the action of an organism, tissue, etc., resulting from stimulation. **3** *Electr.* **a** the process of applying current to the winding of an electromagnet to produce a magnetic field. **b** the process of applying a signal voltage to the control electrode of an electron tube or the base of a transistor. **4** *Physics* the process in which an atom etc. acquires a higher energy state.

excite /ɪk'sʌɪt, ɛk-/ *v.tr.* **1 a** rouse the feelings or emotions of (a person). **b** bring into play; rouse up (feelings, faculties, etc.). **c** arouse sexually. **2** provoke; bring about (an action or active condition). **3** promote the activity of (an organism, tissue, etc.) by stimulus. **4** *Electr.* **a** cause (a current) to flow in the winding of an electromagnet. **b** supply a signal. **5** *Physics* **a** cause the emission of (a spectrum). **b** cause (a substance) to emit radiation. **c** put (an atom etc.) into a state of higher energy. □ **excitant** /'ɛksɪt(ə)nt, ɪk'sʌɪt(ə)nt, ɛk-/ *adj. & n.* **excitative** /-tətɪv/ *adj.* **excitatory** /-tət(ə)ri/ *adj.* **excitedly** *adv.* **excitedness** *n.* **excitement** *n.* **exciter** *n.* (esp. in senses 4, 5). [Middle English from Old French *exciter* or Latin *excitare*, frequentative of *ciēre* (as EX-[1], *ciēre* 'set in motion')]

exciting /ɪk'sʌɪtɪŋ, ɛk-/ *adj.* arousing great interest or enthusiasm; stirring. □ **excitingly** *adv.* **excitingness** *n.*

exciton /'ɛksɪtɒn, ɪk'sʌɪ-, ɛk-/ *n. Physics* a mobile concentration of energy in a crystal formed by an excited electron and an associated hole. [EXCITATION + -ON]

exclaim /ɪk'skleɪm, ɛk-/ *v.* **1** *intr.* cry out suddenly, esp. in anger, surprise, pain, etc. **2** *tr.* (foll. by *that*) utter by exclaiming. [French *exclamer* or Latin *exclamare* (as EX-[1]: cf. CLAIM)]

exclamation /ɛksklə'meɪʃ(ə)n/ *n.* **1** the act or an instance of exclaiming. **2** words exclaimed; a strong sudden cry. [Middle English from Old French *exclamation* or Latin *exclamatio* (as EXCLAIM)]

exclamation mark *n.* (*US* also **exclamation point**) a punctuation mark (!) indicating an exclamation.

exclamatory /ɪk'sklamət(ə)ri, ɛk-/ *adj.* of or serving as an exclamation.

exclave /'ɛkskleɪv/ *n.* a portion of territory of one state completely surrounded by territory of another or others, as viewed by the home territory (cf. ENCLAVE 1). [EX-[1] + ENCLAVE]

exclosure /ɪk'skləʊʒə, ɛk-/ *n. Forestry* etc. an area from which unwanted animals are excluded. [EX-[1] + ENCLOSURE]

exclude /ɪk'sklu:d, ɛk-/ *v.tr.* **1** shut or keep out (a person or thing) from a place, group, privilege, etc. **2** expel and shut out. **3** remove from consideration (*no theory can be excluded*). **4** prevent the occurrence of; make impossible (*excluded all doubt*). □ **excludable** *adj.* **excluder** *n.* [Middle English from Latin *excludere exclus-* (as EX-[1], *claudere* 'shut')]

excluded middle *n. Logic* the principle that of two contradictory propositions one must be true.

exclusion /ɪk'sklu:ʒ(ə)n, ɛk-/ *n.* the act or an instance of excluding; the state of being excluded. □ **to the exclusion of** so as to exclude. □ **exclusionary** *adj.* [Latin *exclusio* (as EXCLUDE)]

exclusionist /ɪk'sklu:ʒ(ə)nɪst, ɛk-/ *adj. & n.* ● *adj.* favouring exclusion, esp. from rights or privileges. ● *n.* a person favouring exclusion.

exclusion order *n. Brit.* an official order preventing a person (esp. a suspected terrorist) from entering the UK.

exclusion principle see PAULI EXCLUSION PRINCIPLE.

exclusive /ɪk'sklu:sɪv, ɛk-/ *adj. & n.* ● *adj.* **1** excluding other things. **2** (*predic.*; foll. by *of*) not including; except for. **3** tending to exclude others, esp. socially; select. **4** catering for few or select customers; high-class. **5 a** (of a commodity) not obtainable elsewhere. **b** (of a newspaper article) not published elsewhere. **6** (*predic.*; foll. by *to*) restricted or limited to; existing or available only in. **7** (of terms etc.) excluding all but what is specified. **8** employed or followed or held to the exclusion of all else (*my exclusive occupation*; *exclusive rights*). ● *n.* an article or story published by only one newspaper or periodical. □ **exclusively** *adv.* **exclusiveness** *n.* **exclusivity** /ɛksklu:'sɪvɪti/ *n.* [medieval Latin *exclusivus* (as EXCLUDE)]

Exclusive Brethren *n.pl.* a more exclusive section of the Plymouth Brethren.

exclusivism /ɪk'sklu:sɪvɪz(ə)m, ɛk-/ *n.* a policy or doctrine of (esp. national, racial, or religious) exclusiveness. □ **exclusivist** *adj & n.*

excogitate /ɪks'kɒdʒɪteɪt, ɛks-/ *v.tr.* think out; contrive. □ **excogitation** /-'teɪʃ(ə)n/ *n.* [Latin *excogitare excogitat-* (as EX-[1], *cogitare* COGITATE)]

excommunicate *v., adj., & n. Eccl.* ● *v.tr.* /ɛkskə'mju:nɪkeɪt/ officially exclude (a person) from participation in the sacraments, or from formal communion with the Church. ● *adj.* /ɛkskə'mju:nɪkət/ excommunicated. ● *n.* /ɛkskə'mju:nɪkət/ an excommunicated person. □ **excommunication** /-'keɪʃ(ə)n/ *n.* **excommunicative** /-kətɪv/ *adj.* **excommunicator** *n.* **excommunicatory** /-'keɪt(ə)ri/ *adj.* [Latin *excommunicare -atus* (as EX-[1], *communis* COMMON)]

ex-con /ɛks'kɒn/ *n. colloq.* an ex-convict; a former inmate of a prison. [abbreviation]

excoriate /ɪk'skɔ:rɪeɪt, ɛks-/ *v.tr.* **1 a** remove part of the skin of (a person etc.) by abrasion. **b** strip or peel off (skin). **2** censure severely. □ **excoriation** /-'eɪʃ(ə)n/ *n.* [Latin *excoriare excoriat-* (as EX-[1], *corium* 'hide')]

excrement /'ɛkskrɪm(ə)nt/ *n.* (in *sing.* or *pl.*) faeces. □ **excremental** /-'mɛnt(ə)l/ *adj.* [French *excrément* or Latin *excrementum* (as EXCRETE)]

excrescence /ɪk'skrɛs(ə)ns, ɛks-/ *n.* **1** an abnormal or morbid outgrowth on the body or a plant. **2** an ugly addition. □ **excrescent** *adj.* **excrescential** /ɛkskrɪ'sɛnʃ(ə)l/ *adj.* [Latin *excrescentia* (as EX-[1], *crescere* 'grow')]

excreta /ɪk'skri:tə, ɛk-/ *n.pl.* waste discharged from the body, esp. faeces and urine. [Latin, neut. pl. of *excernere*: see EXCRETE]

excrete /ɪk'skri:t, ɛk-/ *v.tr.* (also *absol.*) (of an animal or plant) separate and expel (waste matter) as a result of metabolism. □ **excreter** *n.* **excretion** *n.* **excretive** *adj.* **excretory** *adj.* [Latin *excernere excret-* (as EX-[1], *cernere* 'sift')]

excruciate /ɪk'skru:ʃɪeɪt, ɛk-/ *v.tr.* (esp. as **excruciating** *adj.*) torment acutely (a person's senses); torture mentally. □ **excruciatingly** *adv.* **excruciation** /-'eɪʃ(ə)n/ *n.* [Latin *excruciare excruciat-* (as EX-[1], *cruciare* 'torment' from *crux crucis* 'cross')]

exculpate /'ɛkskʌlpeɪt/ *v.tr. formal* **1** free from blame. **2** (foll. by *from*) clear (a person) of a charge. □ **exculpation** /-'peɪʃ(ə)n/ *n.* **exculpatory** /ɪks'kʌlpət(ə)ri/ *adj.* [medieval Latin *exculpare exculpat-* (as EX-[1], *culpa* 'blame')]

excursion /ɪk'skə:ʃ(ə)n, ɛk-/ *n.* **1** a short journey for pleasure, with return to the starting point. **2** a digression. **3** *Astron.* a deviation from a regular path. **4** *archaic* a sortie (see ALARUM). □ **excursional** *adj.* **excursionary** *adj.* **excursionist** *n.* [Latin *excursio* from *excurrere excurs-* (as EX-[1], *currere* 'run')]

excursive /ɪk'skə:sɪv, ɛk-/ *adj.* digressive; diverse. □ **excursively** *adv.* **excursiveness** *n.*

excursus /ɪk'skə:səs, ɛk-/ *n.* (*pl.* **excursuses** or same) **1** a detailed discussion of a special point in a book, usu. in an appendix. **2** a digression in a narrative. [Latin, verbal noun, formed as EXCURSION]

excuse *v. & n.* ● *v.tr.* /ɪk'skju:z, ɛk-/ **1** attempt to lessen the blame attaching to (a person, act, or fault). **2** (of a fact or circumstance) serve in mitigation of (a person or act). **3** obtain exemption for (a person or oneself). **4**

(foll. by *from*, or with double object) release (a person) from a duty etc. (*excused from supervision duties*; *excused him the fee*). **5** overlook or forgive (a fault or offence). **6** (foll. by *for*) forgive (a person) for a fault. **7** not insist upon (what is due). **8** *refl.* apologize for leaving. ● *n.* /ɪk'skjuːs, ɛk-/ **1** a reason put forward to mitigate or justify an offence, fault, etc. **2** an apology (*made my excuses*). **3** (foll. by *for*) *colloq.* a poor or inadequate example of. □ **be excused** be allowed to leave a room etc., e.g. to go to the lavatory. **excuse me** a polite apology for lack of ceremony, for an interruption etc., or for disagreeing. □ **excusable** /-'skjuːzəb(ə)l/ *adj.* **excusably** /-'skjuːzəbli/ *adv.* **excusatory** /-'skjuːzət(ə)ri/ *adj.* [Middle English via Old French *escuser* from Latin *excusare* (as EX-[1], *causa* 'CAUSE, accusation')]

excuse-me *n. Brit.* a dance in which dancers may interrupt other pairs to change partners.

ex-directory /ɛksdɪ'rɛkt(ə)ri, -dʌɪ-/ *adj. Brit.* not listed in a telephone directory, at the wish of the subscriber; unlisted.

ex div. *abbr.* ex dividend.

ex dividend /ɛks 'dɪvɪdɛnd/ *adj. & adv.* (of stocks or shares) not including the next dividend.

exeat /'ɛksɪat/ *n. Brit.* **1** a permission from a college or other institution for temporary absence. **2** a permission granted to a priest by a bishop to move to another diocese. [Latin, 3rd sing. present subjunctive of *exire* 'go out' (as EX-[1], *ire* 'go')]

exec /ɪɡ'zɛk, ɛɡ-/ *n. colloq.* an executive. [abbreviation]

execrable /'ɛksɪkrəb(ə)l/ *adj.* abominable, detestable. □ **execrably** *adv.* [Middle English via Old French from Latin *execrabilis* (as EXECRATE)]

execrate /'ɛksɪkreɪt/ *v.* **1** *tr.* express or feel abhorrence for. **2** *tr.* curse (a person or thing). **3** *intr.* utter curses. □ **execration** /-'kreɪʃ(ə)n/ *n.* **execrative** *adj.* **execratory** *adj.* [Latin *exsecrare* (as EX-[1], *sacrare* 'devote' from *sacer* 'sacred, accursed')]

executant /ɪɡ'zɛkjʊt(ə)nt, ɛɡ-/ *n. formal* **1** a performer, esp. of music. **2** a person who carries something into effect. [French *exécutant*, pres. part. of *executer* (as EXECUTE)]

execute /'ɛksɪkjuːt/ *v.tr.* **1 a** carry out a sentence of death on (a condemned person). **b** *euphem.* kill as a political act. **2** carry into effect, perform (a plan, duty, command, operation, etc.). **3 a** carry out a design for (a product of art or skill). **b** perform (a musical composition, dance, etc.). **4** make (a legal instrument) valid by signing, sealing, etc. **5** put into effect (a judicial sentence, the terms of a will, etc.). □ **executable** *adj.* [Middle English via Old French *executer* and medieval Latin *executare* from Latin *exsequi exsecut-* (as EX-[1], *sequi* 'follow')]

execution /ɛksɪ'kjuːʃ(ə)n/ *n.* **1** the carrying out of a sentence of death. **2** the act or an instance of carrying out or performing something. **3** technique or style of performance in the arts, esp. music. **4 a** seizure of the property or person of a debtor in default of payment. **b** a judicial writ enforcing a judgement. □ **executionary** *adj.* [Middle English via Old French from Latin *executio -onis* (as EXECUTE)]

executioner /ɛksɪ'kjuːʃ(ə)nə/ *n.* an official who carries out a sentence of death.

executive /ɪɡ'zɛkjʊtɪv, ɛɡ-/ *n. & adj.* ● *n.* **1** a person or body with managerial or administrative responsibility in a business organization etc.; a senior businessman or businesswoman. **2** a branch of a government or organization concerned with executing laws, agreements, etc., or with other administration or management. ● *adj.* **1** concerned with executing laws, agreements, etc., or with other administration or management. **2** relating to or having the function of executing. □ **executively** *adv.* [medieval Latin *executivus* (as EXECUTE)]

executive session *n. US* a usu. private meeting of a legislative body for executive business.

executor /ɪɡ'zɛkjʊtə, ɛɡ-/ *n.* (*fem.* **executrix** /-trɪks/) a person appointed by a testator to carry out the terms of his or her will. □ **executorial** /-'tɔːrɪəl/ *adj.* **executorship** *n.* **executory** *adj.* [Middle English via Anglo-French *executor*, *-our* from Latin *executor -oris* (as EXECUTE)]

exegesis /ɛksɪ'dʒiːsɪs/ *n.* (*pl.* **exegeses** /-siːz/) critical explanation of a text, esp. of Scripture. □ **exegete** /'ɛksɪdʒiːt/ *n.* **exegetic** /-'dʒɛtɪk/ *adj.* **exegetical** /-'dʒɛtɪk(ə)l/ *adj.* **exegetist** /-'dʒiːtɪst/ *n.* [Greek *exēgēsis* from *exēgeomai* 'interpret' (as EX-[2], *hēgeomai* 'lead')]

exemplar /ɪɡ'zɛmplə, ɛɡ-/ *n.* **1** a model or pattern. **2** a typical instance of a class of things. **3** a parallel instance. [Middle English via Old French *exemplaire* from Late Latin *exemplarium* (as EXAMPLE)]

exemplary /ɪɡ'zɛmpləri, ɛɡ-/ *adj.* **1** fit to be imitated; outstandingly good. **2 a** serving as a warning. **b** *Law* (of damages) exceeding the amount needed for simple compensation. **3** illustrative, representative. □ **exemplarily** *adv.* **exemplariness** *n.* [Late Latin *exemplaris* (as EXAMPLE)]

exemplify /ɪɡ'zɛmplɪfʌɪ, ɛɡ-/ *v.tr.* (**-ies, -ied**) **1** illustrate by example. **2** be an example of. **3** *Law* make an attested copy of (a document) under an official seal. □ **exemplification** /-fɪ'keɪʃ(ə)n/ *n.* [Middle English from medieval Latin *exemplificare* (as EXAMPLE)]

exemplum /ɪɡ'zɛmpləm, ɛɡ-/ *n.* (*pl.* **exempla** /-plə/) an example or model, esp. a moralizing or illustrative story. [Latin, from *eximere*: see EXEMPT]

exempt /ɪɡ'zɛm(p)t, ɛɡ-/ *adj., n., & v.* ● *adj.* **1** free from an obligation or liability etc. imposed on others. **2** (foll. by *from*) not liable to. ● *n.* **1** a person who is exempt, esp. from payment of tax. **2** *Brit.* = EXON. ● *v.tr.* (usu. foll. by *from*) free from an obligation, esp. one imposed on others. □ **exemption** *n.* [Middle English from Latin *exemptus*, past part. of *eximere exempt-* (as EX-[1], *emere* 'take'): in sense 2 of the noun, from an earlier sense of an officer exempt from normal duties]

exequies /'ɛksɪkwɪz/ *n.pl. formal* funeral rites. [Middle English via Old French from Latin *exsequiae* (as EX-[1], *sequi* 'follow')]

exercise /'ɛksəsʌɪz/ *n. & v.* ● *n.* **1** activity requiring physical effort, done esp. as training or to sustain or improve health. **2** mental or spiritual activity, esp. as practice to develop a faculty. **3** (often in *pl.*) a particular task or set of tasks devised as exercise, practice in a technique, etc. **4 a** the use or application of a mental faculty, right, etc. **b** practice of an ability, quality, etc. **5** (often in *pl.*) military drill or manoeuvres. **6** (foll. by *in*) a process directed at or concerned with something specified (*was an exercise in public relations*). ● *v.* **1** *tr.* use or apply (a faculty, right, influence, restraint, etc.). **2** *tr.* perform (a function). **3 a** *intr.* take (esp. physical) exercise; do exercises. **b** *tr.* provide (an animal) with exercise. **c** *tr.* train (a person). **4** *tr.* **a** tax the powers of. **b** perplex, worry. □ **exercisable** *adj.* **exerciser** *n.* [Middle English via Old French *exercice* from Latin *exercitium*, from *exercere exercit-* 'keep at work' (as EX-[1], *arcēre* 'restrain')]

exercise book *n.* **1** a book containing exercises. **2** *Brit.* a book for writing school work, notes, etc., in.

exergue /ɪk'səːɡ, ɛk'səːɡ, 'ɛksəːɡ/ *n.* **1** a small space usu. on the reverse of a coin or medal, below the principal device. **2** an inscription on this space. [French from medieval Latin *exergum*, from Greek *ex-* (as EX-[2]) + *ergon* 'work']

exert /ɪɡ'zəːt, ɛɡ-/ *v.tr.* **1** exercise, bring to bear (a quality, force, influence, etc.). **2** *refl.* (often foll. by *for*, or *to* + infin.) use one's efforts or endeavours; strive. □ **exertion** *n.* [Latin *exserere exsert-* 'put forth' (as EX-[1], *serere* 'bind')]

exeunt /'ɛksɪʌnt/ *v.intr.* (as a stage direction) (actors) leave the stage. □ ***exeunt omnes*** all leave the stage. [Latin, = they go out: 3rd pl. pres. of *exire* 'go out': see EXIT]

exfiltrate /ˈɛksfɪltreɪt/ *v.tr.* (also *absol.*) withdraw (troops, spies, etc.) surreptitiously, esp. from danger. ▫ **exfiltration** /-ˈtreɪʃ(ə)n/ *n.*

exfoliate /ɪksˈfəʊlɪeɪt, ɛks-/ *v.* **1** *intr.* (of bone, the skin, a mineral, etc.) come off in scales or layers. **2** *tr.* **a** shed (material) in scales or layers. **b** (also *absol.*) cause (the skin etc.) to shed flakes or scales. **3** *intr.* (of a tree) throw off layers of bark. ▫ **exfoliation** /-ˈeɪʃ(ə)n/ *n.* **exfoliative** /-lɪətɪv/ *adj.* [Late Latin *exfoliare exfoliat-* (as EX-[1], *folium* 'leaf')]

ex gratia /ɛks ˈgreɪʃə/ *adv. & adj.* ● *adv.* as a favour rather than from an (esp. legal) obligation. ● *adj.* granted on this basis. [Latin, = from favour]

exhalation /ɛksəˈleɪʃ(ə)n/ *n.* **1 a** an expiration of air. **b** a puff of breath. **2** a mist, vapour. **3** an emanation or effluvium. [Middle English from Latin *exhalatio* (as EXHALE)]

exhale /ɪksˈheɪl, ɛks-/ *v.* **1** *tr.* (also *absol.*) breathe out (esp. air or smoke) from the lungs. **2** *tr. & intr.* give off or be given off in vapour. ▫ **exhalable** *adj.* [Middle English via Old French *exhaler* from Latin *exhalare* (as EX-[1], *halare* 'breathe')]

exhaust /ɪgˈzɔːst, ɛg-/ *v. & n.* ● *v.tr.* **1** consume or use up the whole of. **2** (often as **exhausted** *adj.* or **exhausting** *adj.*) use up the strength or resources of (a person); tire out. **3** study or expound on (a subject) completely. **4** (often foll. by *of*) empty (a container etc.) of its contents. ● *n.* **1 a** waste gases etc. expelled from an engine after combustion. **b** (also **exhaust pipe**) the pipe or system by which these are expelled. **c** the process of expulsion of these gases. **2 a** the production of an outward current of air by the creation of a partial vacuum. **b** an apparatus for this. ▫ **exhauster** *n.* **exhaustible** *adj.* **exhaustibility** /-ˈbɪlɪti/ *n.* [Latin *exhaurire exhaust-* (as EX-[1], *haurire* 'draw (water), drain')]

exhaustion /ɪgˈzɔːstʃ(ə)n, ɛg-/ *n.* **1** the act or an instance of draining a thing of a resource or emptying it of contents; the state of being depleted or emptied. **2** a total loss of strength or vitality. **3** the process of establishing a conclusion by eliminating alternatives. [Late Latin *exhaustio* (as EXHAUST)]

exhaustive /ɪgˈzɔːstɪv, ɛg-/ *adj.* **1** thorough, comprehensive. **2** tending to exhaust a subject. ▫ **exhaustively** *adv.* **exhaustiveness** *n.*

exhibit /ɪgˈzɪbɪt, ɛg-/ *v. & n.* ● *v.tr.* (**exhibited, exhibiting**) **1** show or reveal publicly (for interest or amusement, in competition, etc.). **2 a** show, display. **b** manifest (a quality). **3** submit for consideration. ● *n.* **1** a thing or collection of things forming part or all of an exhibition. **2** a document or other item or object produced in a law court as evidence. ▫ **exhibitory** *adj.* [Latin *exhibēre exhibit-* (as EX-[1], *habēre* 'hold')]

exhibition /ɛksɪˈbɪʃ(ə)n/ *n.* **1** a display (esp. public) of works of art, industrial products, etc. **2** the act or an instance of exhibiting; the state of being exhibited. **3** *Brit.* a scholarship, esp. from the funds of a school, college, etc. ▫ **make an exhibition of oneself** behave so as to appear ridiculous or foolish. [Middle English via Old French from Late Latin *exhibitio -onis* (as EXHIBIT)]

exhibitioner /ɛksɪˈbɪʃ(ə)nə/ *n. Brit.* a student who has been awarded an exhibition.

exhibitionism /ɛksɪˈbɪʃ(ə)nɪz(ə)m/ *n.* **1** a tendency towards display or extravagant behaviour. **2** *Psychol.* a mental condition characterized by the compulsion to display one's genitals in public. ▫ **exhibitionist** *n.* **exhibitionistic** /-ˈnɪstɪk/ *adj.* **exhibitionistically** /-ˈnɪstɪk(ə)li/ *adv.*

exhibitor /ɪgˈzɪbɪtə, ɛg-/ *n.* a person who provides an item or items for an exhibition.

exhilarate /ɪgˈzɪləreɪt, ɛg-/ *v.tr.* (often as **exhilarating** *adj.* or **exhilarated** *adj.*) affect with great liveliness or joy; raise the spirits of. ▫ **exhilarant** *adj. & n.* **exhilaratingly** *adv.* **exhilaration** /-ˈreɪʃ(ə)n/ *n.* **exhilarative** /-rətɪv/ *adj.* [Latin *exhilarare* (as EX-[1], *hilaris* 'cheerful')]

exhort /ɪgˈzɔːt, ɛg-/ *v.tr.* (often foll. by *to* + infin.) urge or advise strongly or earnestly. ▫ **exhortative** /-tətɪv/ *adj.* **exhortatory** /-tət(ə)ri/ *adj.* **exhorter** *n.* [Middle English from Old French *exhorter* or Latin *exhortari* (as EX-[1], *hortari* 'exhort')]

exhortation /ɛgzɔːˈteɪʃ(ə)n/ *n.* **1** the act or an instance of exhorting; the state of being exhorted. **2** a formal or liturgical address. [Middle English from Old French *exhortation* or Latin *exhortatio* (as EXHORT)]

exhume /ɛksˈ(h)juːm, ɪgˈzjuːm/ *v.tr.* dig out, unearth (esp. a buried corpse). ▫ **exhumation** /-ˈmeɪʃ(ə)n/ *n.* [French *exhumer* from medieval Latin *exhumare* (as EX-[1], *humus* 'ground')]

ex hypothesi /ɛks hʌɪˈpɒθəsʌɪ/ *adv.* according to the hypothesis proposed. [modern Latin]

exigency /ˈɛksɪdʒ(ə)nsi, ˈɛgzɪ-; ɪgˈzɪdʒ(ə)nsi, ɛg-/ *n.* (*pl.* **-ies**) (also **exigence** /ˈɛksɪdʒ(ə)ns, ˈɛgzɪ-/) **1** an urgent need or demand. **2** an emergency. [French *exigence* & Late Latin *exigentia* (as EXIGENT)]

exigent /ˈɛksɪdʒ(ə)nt, ˈɛgzɪ-/ *adj.* **1** requiring much; exacting. **2** urgent, pressing. [Middle English from Latin *exigere* 'enforce payment of': see EXACT]

exiguous /ɪgˈzɪgjʊəs, ɛg-/ *adj.* scanty, small. ▫ **exiguity** /-ˈgjuːɪti/ *n.* **exiguously** *adv.* **exiguousness** *n.* [Latin *exiguus* 'scanty' from *exigere* 'weigh exactly': see EXACT]

exile /ˈɛksʌɪl, ˈɛgz-/ *n. & v.* ● *n.* **1** expulsion, or the state of being expelled, from one's native land or (**internal exile**) native town etc. **2** long absence abroad, esp. enforced. **3** a person expelled or long absent from his or her native country. **4** (**the Exile**) the captivity of the Jews in Babylon in the 6th c. BC. ● *v.tr.* (foll. by *from*) officially expel (a person) from his or her native country or town etc. ▫ **exilic** /-ˈsɪlɪk, -ˈzɪlɪk/ *adj.* (esp. in sense 4 of *n.*). [Middle English via Old French *exil*, *exiler* from Latin *exilium* 'banishment']

exist /ɪgˈzɪst, ɛg-/ *v.intr.* **1** have a place as part of objective reality. **2 a** have being under specified conditions. **b** (foll. by *as*) exist in the form of. **3** (of circumstances etc.) occur; be found. **4** live with no pleasure under adverse conditions (*felt he was merely existing*). **5** continue in being; maintain life (*can hardly exist on this salary*). **6** be alive, live. [probably a back-formation from EXISTENCE; cf. Late Latin *existere*]

existence /ɪgˈzɪst(ə)ns, ɛg-/ *n.* **1** the fact or condition of being or existing. **2** continued being, esp. the manner of one's existing or living under adverse conditions (*a wretched existence*). **3** an existing thing. **4** all that exists. [Middle English via Old French *existence* or Late Latin *existentia* from Latin *exsistere* (as EX-[1], *stare* 'stand')]

existent /ɪgˈzɪst(ə)nt, ɛg-/ *adj.* existing, actual, current.

existential /ɛgzɪˈstɛnʃ(ə)l/ *adj.* **1** of or relating to existence. **2** *Logic* (of a proposition etc.) affirming or implying the existence of a thing. **3** *Philos.* concerned with existence, esp. with human existence as viewed by existentialism. ▫ **existentially** *adv.* [Late Latin *existentialis* (as EXISTENCE)]

existentialism /ɛgzɪˈstɛnʃ(ə)lɪz(ə)m/ *n.* a philosophical theory emphasizing the existence of the individual person as a free and responsible agent determining his or her own development. ▫ **existentialist** *n.* [German *Existentialismus* (as EXISTENTIAL)]

exit /ˈɛksɪt, ˈɛgzɪt/ *n. & v.* ● *n.* **1** a passage or door by which to leave a room, building, etc. **2 a** the act of going out. **b** the right or freedom to go out. **3** a place where vehicles can leave a motorway or major road. **4** the departure of an actor from the stage. **5** *literary* death. ● *v.* (**exited, exiting**) **1** *intr.* go out of a room, building, etc. **2** *intr.* (as a stage direction) (an actor) leaves the stage (*exit Macbeth*). **3** *intr. literary* die. **4** *tr.* go out of, leave (a place etc.). **5** *Computing* **a** *intr.* terminate a process etc.; return to an earlier or more general level of interaction. **b** *tr.* terminate (a process, program, etc.) in this way. [Latin, 3rd sing. present of *exire* 'go out' (as EX-[1], *ire* 'go'): cf. Latin *exitus* 'going out']

exit permit *n.* (also **exit visa** etc.) authorization to leave a particular country.

exit poll *n.* a poll of people leaving a polling station, asking how they voted.

ex-libris /ɛks'lɪbrɪs, -'li:b-, -'lʌɪb-, -'li:bri:s/ *n.* (*pl.* same) a usu. decorated bookplate or label bearing the owner's name, pasted into the front of a book. [Latin *ex libris* 'among the books of']

ex nihilo /ɛks 'nʌɪhɪləʊ/ *adv.* out of nothing (*creation ex nihilo*). [Latin]

exo- /'ɛksəʊ/ *prefix* external. [Greek *exō* 'outside']

exobiology /,ɛksəʊbʌɪ'ɒlədʒi/ *n.* the branch of science that deals with the possibility of life outside the earth. ▫ **exobiologist** *n.*

Exocet /'ɛksəsɛt/ *n. propr.* a French-made short-range guided missile used esp. in sea warfare. [French *exocet* 'flying fish']

exocrine /'ɛksə(ʊ)krʌɪn, -krɪn/ *adj.* (of a gland) secreting through a duct (cf. ENDOCRINE). [EXO- + Greek *krinō* 'sift']

Exod. *abbr.* Exodus (Old Testament).

exoderm /'ɛksə(ʊ)də:m/ *n. Biol.* = ECTODERM.

exodus /'ɛksədəs/ *n.* **1** a mass departure of people (esp. emigrants). **2** (**Exodus**) *Bibl.* **a** the departure of the Israelites from Egypt. **b** the book of the Old Testament relating this. [ecclesiastical Latin from Greek *exodos* (as EX-[2], *hodos* 'way')]

ex officio /ɛks ə'fɪʃɪəʊ/ *adv. & adj.* by virtue of one's office or status. [Latin]

exogamy /ɪk'sɒgəmi, ɛk-/ *n.* **1** *Anthropol.* marriage of a man outside his own tribe. **2** *Biol.* the fusion of reproductive cells from distantly related or unrelated individuals. ▫ **exogamous** *adj.*

exogenous /ɪk'sɒdʒɪnəs, ɛk-/ *adj.* growing or originating from outside. ▫ **exogenously** *adv.*

exon /'ɛksɒn/ *n. Brit.* each of the four officers acting as commanders of the Yeomen of the Guard. [representing French pronunciation of EXEMPT: see sense 2 of the noun]

exonerate /ɪg'zɒnəreɪt, ɛg-/ *v.tr.* (often foll. by *from*) **1** free or declare free from blame etc. **2** release from a duty etc. ▫ **exoneration** /-'reɪʃ(ə)n/ *n.* **exonerative** /-rətɪv/ *adj.* [Latin *exonerare exonerat-* (as EX-[1], *onus, oneris* 'burden')]

exophthalmic /ɛksɒf'θalmɪk/ *adj. Med.* characterized by protruding eyes.

exophthalmic goitre *n.* = GRAVES' DISEASE.

exophthalmos /ɛksɒf'θalmɒs/ *n.* (also **exophthalmus, exophthalmia** /-mɪə/) *Med.* abnormal protrusion of the eyeball. [modern Latin from Greek *exophthalmos* 'having prominent eyes' (as EX-[2], *ophthalmos* 'eye')]

exoplasm /'ɛksə(ʊ)plaz(ə)m/ *n. Biol.* = ECTOPLASM.

exor. *abbr.* executor.

exorbitant /ɪg'zɔ:bɪt(ə)nt/ *adj.* (of a price, demand, etc.) grossly excessive. ▫ **exorbitance** *n.* **exorbitantly** *adv.* [Late Latin *exorbitare* (as EX-[1], *orbita* ORBIT)]

exorcize /'ɛksɔ:sʌɪz/ *v.tr.* (also **-ise**) **1** expel (a supposed evil spirit) by invocation or by use of a holy name. **2** (often foll. by *of*) free (a person or place) of a supposed evil spirit. ▫ **exorcism** *n.* **exorcist** *n.* **exorcization** /-'zeɪʃ(ə)n/ *n.* [French *exorciser* or ecclesiastical Latin *exorcizare* from Greek *exorkizō* (as EX-[2], *horkos* 'oath')]

exordium /ɪg'zɔ:dɪəm, ɛg-/ *n.* (*pl.* **exordiums** or **exordia** /-dɪə/) the beginning or introductory part, esp. of a discourse or treatise. ▫ **exordial** *adj.* [Latin, from *exordiri* (as EX-[1], *ordiri* 'begin')]

exoskeleton /'ɛksəʊ,skɛlɪt(ə)n/ *n.* a rigid external covering for the body in certain animals, esp. arthropods, providing support and protection. ▫ **exoskeletal** *adj.*

exosphere /'ɛksə(ʊ)sfɪə/ *n.* the layer of atmosphere furthest from the earth.

exoteric /ɛksə(ʊ)'tɛrɪk/ *adj.* **1** (of a doctrine, mode of speech, etc.) intended for, or intelligible to, outsiders. **2** current among the general public; popular, ordinary. [Greek *exōterikos* from *exōterō*, comparative of *exō* 'outside': cf. ESOTERIC]

exothermic /ɛksə(ʊ)'θə:mɪk/ *adj.* (also **exothermal** /-m(ə)l/) esp. *Chem.* occurring or formed with the evolution of heat. ▫ **exothermally** *adv.* **exothermically** *adv.*

exotic /ɪg'zɒtɪk, ɛg-/ *adj. & n.* ● *adj.* **1** introduced from or originating in a foreign (esp. tropical) country (*exotic fruits*). **2** attractively or remarkably strange or unusual; bizarre. **3** (of a fuel, metal, etc.) of a kind newly brought into use. ● *n.* an exotic person or thing. ▫ **exotically** *adv.* **exoticism** /-tɪsɪz(ə)m/ *n.* [Latin *exoticus* from Greek *exōtikos*, from *exō* 'outside']

exotica /ɪg'zɒtɪkə, ɛg-/ *n.pl.* remarkably strange or rare objects. [Latin, neut. pl. of *exoticus*: see EXOTIC]

exotic dancer *n.* a striptease dancer.

exotoxin /'ɛksəʊtɒksɪn/ *n.* a toxin released by a living bacterial cell into its surroundings.

expand /ɪk'spand, ɛk-/ *v.* **1** *tr. & intr.* increase in size or bulk or importance. **2** *intr.* (often foll. by *on*) give a fuller description or account. **3** *intr.* become more genial or effusive; discard one's reserve. **4** *tr.* set or write out in full (something condensed or abbreviated). **5** *tr. & intr.* spread out flat. ▫ **expandable** *adj.* **expander** *n.* **expansible** *adj.* **expansibility** /-'bɪlɪti/ *n.* [Middle English from Latin *expandere expans-* 'spread out' (as EX-[1], *pandere* 'spread')]

expanded metal *n.* sheet metal slit and stretched into a mesh, used to reinforce concrete and other brittle materials.

expanse /ɪk'spans, ɛk-/ *n.* **1** a wide continuous area or extent of land, space, etc. **2** an amount of expansion. [modern Latin *expansum*, neut. past part. of *expandere* (as EXPAND)]

expansile /ɪk'spansʌɪl, ɛk-/ *adj.* **1** of expansion. **2** capable of expansion.

expansion /ɪk'spanʃ(ə)n, ɛk-/ *n.* **1** the act or an instance of expanding; the state of being expanded. **2** enlargement of the scale or scope of (esp. commercial) operations. **3** increase in the amount of a state's territory or area of control. **4** an increase in the volume of fuel etc. on combustion in the cylinder of an engine. ▫ **expansionary** *adj.* **expansionism** *n.* **expansionist** *n.* **expansionistic** /-'nɪstɪk/ *adj.* (all in senses 2, 3). [Late Latin *expansio* (as EXPAND)]

expansion card *n.* (also **expansion board**) *Computing* a circuit board that can be inserted in a computer to give extra facilities.

expansion joint *n.* a joint that allows for the thermal expansion of the parts joined.

expansion slot *n. Computing* a place in a computer where an expansion card can be added.

expansive /ɪk'spansɪv, ɛk-/ *adj.* **1** able or tending to expand. **2** extensive, wide-ranging. **3** (of a person, feelings, or speech) effusive, open. ▫ **expansively** *adv.* **expansiveness** *n.* **expansivity** /-'sɪvɪti/ *n.*

ex parte /ɛks 'pɑ:ti/ *adj. & adv. Law* in the interests of one side only or of an interested outside party. [Latin]

expat /ɛks'pat/ *n. & adj. colloq.* = EXPATRIATE. [abbreviation]

expatiate /ɪk'speɪʃɪeɪt, ɛk-/ *v.intr.* (usu. foll. by *on, upon*) speak or write at length or in detail. ▫ **expatiation** /-'eɪʃ(ə)n/ *n.* **expatiatory** /-ʃɪət(ə)ri/ *adj.* [Latin *exspatiari* 'digress' (as EX-[1], *spatium* SPACE)]

expatriate *adj., n., & v.* ● *adj.* /ɪks'patrɪət, -'peɪtrɪət, ɛks-/ **1** living abroad, esp. for a long period. **2** expelled from one's country; exiled. ● *n.* /ɪks'patrɪət, -'peɪtrɪət, ɛks-/ an expatriate person. ● *v.tr.* /ɪks'patrɪeɪt, -'peɪtrɪeɪt, ɛks-/ **1** expel or remove (a person) from his or her native country. **2** *refl.* withdraw (oneself) from one's citizenship or allegiance. ▫ **expatriation** /-'eɪʃ(ə)n/ *n.* [medieval Latin *expatriare* (as EX-[1], *patria* 'native country')]

expect /ɪk'spɛkt, ɛk-/ *v.tr.* **1** (often foll. by *to* + infin., or *that* + clause) **a** regard as likely; assume as a future event or occurrence. **b** (often foll. by *of*) look for as appropriate or one's due (from a person) (*I expect cooperation; expect you to be here; expected better of you*).

2 (often foll. by *that* + clause) *colloq.* think, suppose (*I expect we'll be on time*). 3 be shortly to have (a baby) (*is expecting twins*). □ **be expecting** *colloq.* be pregnant (with). □ **expectable** *adj.* [Latin *exspectare* (as EX-[1], *spectare* 'look', frequentative of *specere* 'see')]

expectancy /ɪk'spɛkt(ə)nsi, ɛk-/ *n.* (*pl.* **-ies**) **1** a state of expectation. **2** a prospect, esp. of future possession. **3** (foll. by *of*) a prospective chance. [Latin *exspectantia*, *exp-* (as EXPECT)]

expectant /ɪk'spɛkt(ə)nt, ɛk-/ *adj.* & *n.* ● *adj.* **1** (often foll. by *of*) expecting. **2** having the expectation of possession, status, etc. **3** (*attrib.*) expecting a baby (said of the mother or father). ● *n.* **1** a person who expects. **2** a candidate for office etc. □ **expectantly** *adv.*

expectation /ɛkspɛk'teɪʃ(ə)n/ *n.* **1** the act or an instance of expecting or looking forward. **2** something expected or hoped for. **3** (foll. by *of*) the probability of an event. **4** (in *pl.*) one's prospects of inheritance. [Latin *expectatio* (as EXPECT)]

expectorant /ɪk'spɛkt(ə)r(ə)nt, ɛk-/ *adj.* & *n.* ● *adj.* causing the coughing out of phlegm etc. ● *n.* an expectorant medicine.

expectorate /ɪk'spɛktəreɪt, ɛk-/ *v.tr.* (also *absol.*) cough or spit out (phlegm etc.) from the throat or lungs. □ **expectoration** /-'reɪʃ(ə)n/ *n.* **expectorator** *n.* [Latin *expectorare expectorat-* (as EX-[1], *pectus -oris* 'breast')]

expedient /ɪk'spi:dɪənt, ɛk-/ *adj.* & *n.* ● *adj.* **1** advantageous; advisable on practical rather than moral grounds. **2** suitable, appropriate. ● *n.* a means of attaining an end; a resource. □ **expedience** *n.* **expediency** *n.* **expediently** *adv.* [Middle English from Latin *expedire*: see EXPEDITE]

expedite /'ɛkspɪdʌɪt/ *v.tr.* **1** assist the progress of; hasten (an action, process, etc.). **2** accomplish (business) quickly. □ **expediter** *n.* [Latin *expedire expedit-* 'extricate (originally 'free the feet'), put in order' (as EX-[1], *pes pedis* 'foot')]

expedition /ɛkspɪ'dɪʃ(ə)n/ *n.* **1** a journey or voyage for a particular purpose, esp. exploration, scientific research, or war. **2** the personnel or ships etc. undertaking this. **3** promptness, speed. □ **expeditionist** *n.* [Middle English via Old French from Latin *expeditio -onis* (as EXPEDITE)]

expeditionary /ɛkspɪ'dɪʃ(ə)n(ə)ri/ *adj.* of or used in an expedition, esp. military.

expeditious /ɛkspɪ'dɪʃəs/ *adj.* **1** acting or done with speed and efficiency. **2** suited for speedy performance. □ **expeditiously** *adv.* **expeditiousness** *n.* [EXPEDITION + -OUS]

expel /ɪk'spɛl, ɛk-/ *v.tr.* (**expelled, expelling**) (often foll. by *from*) **1** deprive (a person) of the membership of or involvement in (a school, society, etc.). **2** force out or eject (a thing from its container etc.). **3** order or force to leave a building etc. □ **expellable** *adj.* **expellee** /-'li:/ *n.* **expellent** *adj.* **expeller** *n.* [Middle English from Latin *expellere expuls-* (as EX-[1], *pellere* 'drive')]

expend /ɪk'spɛnd, ɛk-/ *v.tr.* spend or use up (money, time, etc.). [Middle English from Latin *expendere expens-* (as EX-[1], *pendere* 'weigh')]

expendable /ɪk'spɛndəb(ə)l, ɛk-/ *adj.* **1** that may be sacrificed or dispensed with, esp. to achieve a purpose. **2 a** not regarded as worth preserving or saving. **b** unimportant, insignificant. **3** not normally reused. □ **expendability** /-'bɪlɪti/ *n.* **expendably** *adv.*

expenditure /ɪk'spɛndɪtʃə, ɛk-/ *n.* **1** the process or an instance of spending or using up. **2** a thing (esp. a sum of money) expended. [EXPEND, suggested by obsolete *expenditor* 'officer in charge of expenditure', via medieval Latin from *expenditus*, irregular past part. of Latin *expendere*]

expense /ɪk'spɛns, ɛk-/ *n.* **1** cost incurred; payment of money. **2** (usu. in *pl.*) **a** the cost incurred in doing a particular job etc. (*will pay your expenses*). **b** an amount paid to reimburse this (*offered me £40 per day expenses*). **3** a thing that is a cause of much expense (*the house is a real expense to run*). □ **at the expense of 1** so as to cause loss, deprivation, or harm to. **2** so as to incur the cost of. [Middle English via Anglo-French, alteration of Old French *espense*, from Late Latin *expensa* '(money) spent', past part. of Latin *expendere* EXPEND]

expense account *n.* a list of an employee's expenses to be reimbursed by the employer.

expensive /ɪk'spɛnsɪv, ɛk-/ *adj.* **1** costing much. **2** making a high charge. **3** causing much expense (*has expensive tastes*). □ **expensively** *adv.* **expensiveness** *n.*

experience /ɪk'spɪərɪəns, ɛk-/ *n.* & *v.* ● *n.* **1** actual observation of or practical acquaintance with facts or events. **2** knowledge or skill resulting from this. **3 a** an event regarded as affecting one (*an unpleasant experience*). **b** the fact or process of being so affected (*learnt by experience*). ● *v.tr.* **1** have experience of; undergo. **2** feel or be affected by (an emotion etc.). □ **experienceable** *adj.* [Middle English via Old French from Latin *experientia*, from *experiri expert-* 'try']

experienced /ɪk'spɪərɪənst, ɛk-/ *adj.* **1** having had much experience. **2** skilled from experience (*an experienced driver*).

experiential /ɪk,spɪərɪ'ɛntʃ(ə)l, ɛk-/ *adj.* involving or based on experience. □ **experientialism** *n.* **experientialist** *n.* **experientially** *adv.*

experiential philosophy *n.* a philosophy that treats all knowledge as based on experience.

experiment /ɪk'spɛrɪm(ə)nt, ɛk-/ *n.* & *v.* ● *n.* **1** a procedure undertaken to make a discovery, test a hypothesis, or demonstrate a known fact. **2** (foll. by *of*) a test or trial of. ● *v.intr.* /also -mɛnt/ (often foll. by *on*, *with*) make an experiment. □ **experimentation** /-mɛn'teɪʃ(ə)n/ *n.* **experimenter** *n.* [Middle English from Old French *experiment* or Latin *experimentum* (as EXPERIENCE)]

experimental /ɪk,spɛrɪ'mɛnt(ə)l, ɛk-/ *adj.* **1** based on or making use of experiment (*experimental psychology*). **2 a** used in experiments. **b** serving or resulting from (esp. incomplete) experiment; tentative, provisional. **3** based on experience, not on authority or conjecture. □ **experimentalism** *n.* **experimentalist** *n.* **experimentalize** *v.intr.* (also **-ise**). **experimentally** *adv.* [Middle English from medieval Latin *experimentalis* (as EXPERIMENT)]

expert /'ɛkspə:t/ *adj.* & *n.* ● *adj.* **1** (often foll. by *at*, *in*) having special skill at a task or knowledge in a subject. **2** (*attrib.*) involving or resulting from this (*expert evidence*; *an expert piece of work*). ● *n.* (often foll. by *at*, *in*) a person having special knowledge or skill. □ **expertly** *adv.* **expertness** *n.* [Middle English via Old French from Latin *expertus*, past part. of *experiri*: see EXPERIENCE]

expertise /ɛkspə:'ti:z/ *n.* expert skill, knowledge, or judgement. [French (as EXPERT)]

expertize /'ɛkspətʌɪz/ *v.* (also **-ise**) **1** *intr.* give an expert opinion. **2** *tr.* give an expert opinion concerning.

expert system *n.* *Computing* a system which can provide intelligent advice or decisions based on expert knowledge incorporated in the software.

expiate /'ɛkspɪeɪt/ *v.tr.* **1** pay the penalty for (wrongdoing). **2** make amends for. □ **expiable** /'ɛkspɪəb(ə)l/ *adj.* **expiation** /-'eɪʃ(ə)n/ *n.* **expiator** *n.* **expiatory** /-pɪət(ə)ri, -pɪ'eɪt(ə)ri/ *adj.* [Latin *expiare expiat-* (as EX-[1], *pius* 'devout')]

expiration /ɛkspɪ'reɪʃ(ə)n/ *n.* **1** breathing out. **2** expiry. [Latin *expiratio* (as EXPIRE)]

expire /ɪk'spʌɪə, ɛk-/ *v.* **1** *intr.* (of a period of time, validity, etc.) come to an end. **2** *intr.* (of a document, authorization, etc.) cease to be valid; become void. **3** *intr.* (of a person) die. **4** *tr.* (usu. foll. by *from*; also *absol.*) exhale (air etc.) from the lungs. □ **expiratory** *adj.* (in sense 4). [Middle English via Old French *expirer* from Latin *exspirare* (as EX-[1], *spirare* 'breathe')]

expiry /ɪk'spʌɪri, ɛk-/ *n.* **1** the end of the validity or duration of something. **2** death.

explain /ɪk'spleɪn, ɛk-/ *v.tr.* **1 a** make clear or intelligible (also *absol.*: *let me explain*). **b** make known in detail. **2** (foll. by *that* + clause) say by way of explanation. **3** account for (one's conduct etc.). □ **explain away** minimize the significance of (a difficulty or mistake) by explanation. **explain oneself 1** make one's meaning clear. **2** give an account of one's motives or conduct. □ **explainable** *adj.* **explainer** *n.* [Latin *explanare* (as EX-[1], *planus* 'flat', assimilated to PLAIN[1])]

explanation /ɛkspləˈneɪʃ(ə)n/ *n.* **1** the act or an instance of explaining. **2** a statement or circumstance that explains something. **3** a declaration made with a view to mutual understanding or reconciliation. [Middle English from Latin *explanatio* (as EXPLAIN)]

explanatory /ɪkˈsplanət(ə)ri, ɛk-/ *adj.* serving or intended to serve to explain. □ **explanatorily** *adv.* [Late Latin *explanatorius* (as EXPLAIN)]

explant *v.* & *n.* *Biol.* ● *v.tr.* /ɪksˈplɑːnt, ɛks-/ transfer (living cells, tissues, or organs) from animals or plants to a nutrient medium. ● *n.* /ˈɛksplɑːnt/ a piece of explanted tissue etc. □ **explantation** /-ˈteɪʃ(ə)n/ *n.* [modern Latin *explantare* (as EX-[1], *plantare* PLANT)]

expletive /ɪkˈspliːtɪv, ɛk-/ *n.* & *adj.* ● *n.* **1** an oath, swear word, or other expression, used in an exclamation. **2** a word used to fill out a sentence etc., esp. in verse. ● *adj.* serving to fill out (esp. a sentence, line of verse, etc.). [Late Latin *expletivus* (as EX-[1], *plēre plet-* 'fill')]

explicable /ɪkˈsplɪkəb(ə)l, ɛk-, ˈɛksplɪkəb(ə)l/ *adj.* that can be explained.

explicate /ˈɛksplɪkeɪt/ *v.tr.* **1** develop the meaning or implication of (an idea, principle, etc.). **2** make clear, explain (esp. a literary text). □ **explication** /-ˈkeɪʃ(ə)n/ *n.* **explicative** /ɛkˈsplɪkətɪv, ˈɛksplɪkeɪtɪv/ *adj.* **explicator** *n.* **explicatory** /ɛkˈsplɪkət(ə)ri, ˈɛksplɪkeɪt(ə)ri/ *adj.* [Latin *explicare explicat-* 'unfold' (as EX-[1], *plicare plicat-* or *plicit-* 'fold')]

explicit /ɪkˈsplɪsɪt, ɛk-/ *adj.* **1 a** expressly stated, leaving nothing merely implied; stated in detail. **b** describing or representing nudity or intimate sexual activity. **2** (of knowledge, a notion, etc.) definite, clear. **3** (of a person, book, etc.) expressing views unreservedly; outspoken. □ **explicitly** *adv.* **explicitness** *n.* [French *explicite* or Latin *explicitus* (as EXPLICATE)]

explode /ɪkˈspləʊd, ɛk-/ *v.* **1 a** *intr.* (of gas, gunpowder, a bomb, a boiler, etc.) expand suddenly with a loud noise owing to a release of internal energy. **b** *tr.* cause (a bomb etc.) to explode. **2** *intr.* give vent suddenly to emotion, esp. anger. **3** *intr.* (of a population etc.) increase suddenly or rapidly. **4** *tr.* show (a theory etc.) to be false or baseless. **5** *tr.* (as **exploded** *adj.*) (of a drawing etc.) showing the components of a mechanism as if separated by an explosion but in the normal relative positions. □ **exploder** *n.* [earliest in sense 4: Latin *explodere* 'hiss off the stage' (as EX-[1], *plodere plos-* = *plaudere* 'clap')]

exploit *n.* & *v.* ● *n.* /ˈɛksplɔɪt/ a bold or daring feat. ● *v.tr.* /ɪkˈsplɔɪt, ɛk-/ **1** make use of (a resource etc.); derive benefit from. **2** usu. *derog.* utilize or take advantage of (esp. a person) for one's own ends. □ **exploitable** /ɪkˈsplɔɪtəb(ə)l, ɛk-/ *adj.* **exploitation** /ɛksplɔɪˈteɪʃ(ə)n/ *n.* **exploitative** /ɪkˈsplɔɪtətɪv, ɛk-/ *adj.* **exploiter** *n.* **exploitive** /ɪkˈsplɔɪtɪv, ɛk-/ *adj.* [Middle English from Old French *esploit*, *exploiter*, ultimately from Latin *explicare*: see EXPLICATE]

exploration /ɛkspləˈreɪʃ(ə)n/ *n.* **1** an act or instance of exploring. **2** the process of exploring. □ **explorational** *adj.*

exploratory /ɪkˈsplɒrət(ə)ri, ɛk-/ *adj.* **1** (of discussion etc.) preliminary, serving to establish procedure etc. **2** involving exploration or investigation (*exploratory surgery*).

explore /ɪkˈsplɔː, ɛk-/ *v.tr.* **1** travel extensively through (a country etc.) in order to learn or discover about it. **2** inquire into; investigate thoroughly. **3** *Surgery* examine (a part of the body) in detail. □ **explorative** /ɪkˈsplɒrətɪv, ɛk-/ *adj.* [French *explorer* from Latin *explorare*]

explorer /ɪkˈsplɔːrə, ɛk-/ *n.* a traveller into undiscovered or uninvestigated territory, esp. to get scientific information.

explosion /ɪkˈspləʊʒ(ə)n, ɛk-/ *n.* **1** the act or an instance of exploding. **2** a loud noise caused by something exploding. **3 a** a sudden outburst of noise. **b** a sudden outbreak of feeling, esp. anger. **4** a rapid or sudden increase, esp. of population. [Latin *explosio* 'scornful rejection' (as EXPLODE)]

explosive /ɪkˈspləʊsɪv, ɛk-/ *adj.* & *n.* ● *adj.* **1** able or tending or likely to explode. **2** likely to cause a violent outburst etc.; (of a situation etc.) dangerously tense. ● *n.* an explosive substance. □ **explosively** *adv.* **explosiveness** *n.*

Expo /ˈɛkspəʊ/ *n.* (also **expo**) (*pl.* **-os**) a large international exhibition. [abbreviation of EXPOSITION 4]

exponent /ɪkˈspəʊnənt, ɛk-/ *n.* & *adj.* ● *n.* **1** a person who favours or promotes an idea etc. **2** a representative or practitioner of an activity, profession, etc. **3** a person who explains or interprets something. **4** a type or representative. **5** *Math.* a raised symbol or expression beside a numeral indicating how many times it is to be multiplied by itself (e.g. $2^3 = 2\times2\times2$). ● *adj.* that sets forth or interprets. [Latin *exponere* (as EX-[1], *ponere posit-* 'put')]

exponential /ɛkspə(ʊ)ˈnɛnʃ(ə)l/ *adj.* **1** *Math.* of or indicated by a mathematical exponent. **2** (of an increase etc.) more and more rapid. □ **exponentially** *adv.* [French *exponentiel* (as EXPONENT)]

exponential function *n.* *Math.* a function which increases as a quantity raised to a power determined by the variable on which the function depends.

exponential growth *n.* growth whose rate becomes ever more rapid in proportion to the growing total number or size.

export *v.* & *n.* ● *v.tr.* /ɪkˈspɔːt, ɛk-, ˈɛk-/ send out (goods or services) esp. for sale in another country. ● *n.* /ˈɛkspɔːt/ **1** the process of exporting. **2 a** an exported article or service. **b** (in *pl.*) the amount or value of goods exported (*exports exceeded £50m.*). **3** (*attrib.*) suitable for export, esp. of better quality. □ **exportable** *adj.* **exportability** /-ˈbɪlɪti/ *n.* **exportation** /-ˈteɪʃ(ə)n/ *n.* **exporter** /-ˈspɔːtə/ *n.* [Latin *exportare* (as EX-[1], *portare* 'carry')]

export reject *n.* an article sold in its country of manufacture, as being below the standard for export.

expose /ɪkˈspəʊz, ɛk-/ *v.tr.* **1** leave uncovered or unprotected, esp. from the weather. **2** (foll. by *to*) **a** put at risk of (*was exposed to great danger*). **b** lay open, subject, or introduce to (an influence etc.). **3** (as **exposed** *adj.*) **a** (foll. by *to*) open to; unprotected from (*exposed to the east*). **b** vulnerable, risky. **4** *Photog.* subject (a film) to light, esp. by operation of a camera. **5** reveal the identity or fact of (esp. a person or thing disapproved of or guilty of crime etc.). **6** disclose; make public. **7** exhibit, display. **8** leave (a child) in the open to die. □ **expose oneself** display one's body, esp. the genitals, publicly and indecently. □ **exposer** *n.* [Middle English from Old French *exposer*, based on Latin *exponere*: see EXPONENT, POSE[1]]

exposé /ɪkˈspəʊzeɪ, ɛk-/ *n.* **1** an orderly statement of facts. **2** the act or an instance of revealing something discreditable. [French, past part. of *exposer* (as EXPOSE)]

exposition /ɛkspəˈzɪʃ(ə)n/ *n.* **1** an explanatory statement or account. **2** an explanation or commentary; an interpretative article or treatise. **3** *Mus.* the part of a movement, esp. in sonata form, in which the principal themes are first presented. **4** a large public exhibition. **5** *archaic* exposure. □ **expositional** *adj.* **expositive** /-ˈspɒzɪtɪv/ *adj.* [Middle English from Old French *exposition*, or Latin *expositio* (as EXPONENT)]

expositor /ɪkˈspɒzɪtə, ɛk-/ *n.* an expounder or interpreter. □ **expository** *adj.*

ex post /ɛks ˈpəʊst/ *adj.* *Econ.* based on actual results (cf. EX ANTE). [modern Latin, = 'from after']

ex post facto /ˌɛks pəʊst 'faktəʊ/ *adj. & adv.* with retrospective action or force. [Latin *ex postfacto* 'in the light of subsequent events']

expostulate /ɪk'spɒstjʊleɪt, ɛk-/ *v.intr.* (often foll. by *with* a person) make a protest; remonstrate earnestly. □ **expostulation** /-'leɪʃ(ə)n/ *n.* **expostulatory** /-lət(ə)ri/ *adj.* [Latin *expostulare expostulat-* (as EX-[1], *postulare* 'demand')]

exposure /ɪk'spəʊʒə, ɛk-/ *n.* (foll. by *to*) **1** the act or condition of exposing or being exposed (to air, cold, danger, etc.). **2** a physical condition resulting from being exposed to the elements, esp. in severe conditions (*died from exposure*). **3** the revelation of an identity or fact, esp. when concealed or likely to find disapproval. **4** *Photog.* **a** the action of exposing a film etc. to the light. **b** the duration of this action. **c** the area of film etc. affected by it. **5** an aspect or outlook (*has a fine southern exposure*). [EXPOSE, on the pattern of *enclosure* etc.]

exposure meter *n. Photog.* a device for measuring the strength of the light to determine the correct duration of exposure.

expound /ɪk'spaʊnd, ɛk-/ *v.tr.* **1** set out in detail (a doctrine etc.). **2** explain or interpret (esp. Scripture). □ **expounder** *n.* [Middle English from Old French *espondre* (as EXPONENT)]

express[1] /ɪk'sprɛs, ɛk-/ *v.tr.* **1** represent or make known (thought, feelings, etc.) in words or by gestures, conduct, etc. **2** *refl.* say what one thinks or means. **3** esp. *Math.* represent by symbols. **4** squeeze out (liquid or air). □ **expresser** *n.* **expressible** *adj.* [Middle English via Old French *expresser* from Romanic (as EX-[1], PRESS[1])]

express[2] /ɪk'sprɛs, ɛk-/ *adj., adv., n., & v.* ● *adj.* **1** operating at high speed. **2** /also 'ɛksprɛs/ **a** definitely stated, not merely implied. **b** *archaic* (of a likeness) exact. **3 a** done, made, or sent for a special purpose. **b** (of messages or goods) delivered by a special messenger or service. ● *adv.* **1** at high speed. **2** by express train or delivery service. ● *n.* **1 a** an express train or delivery service. **b** an express rifle. **2** *US* a company undertaking the transport of parcels etc. ● *v.tr.* send by express messenger or delivery. □ **expressly** *adv.* (in senses 2 and 3a of *adj.*). [Middle English via Old French *expres* from Latin *expressus* 'distinctly shown', past part. of *exprimere* (as EX-[1], *premere* 'press')]

expression /ɪk'sprɛʃ(ə)n, ɛk-/ *n.* **1** the act or an instance of expressing. **2** a word or phrase expressed. **3** *Math.* a collection of symbols expressing a quantity. **4** a person's facial appearance or intonation of voice, esp. as indicating feeling. **5** the depiction of feeling, movement, etc., in art. **6** the conveying of feeling in the performance of a piece of music. □ **expressional** *adj.* **expressionless** *adj.* **expressionlessly** *adv.* **expressionlessness** *n.* [Middle English from Old French *expression* or Latin *expressio*, from *exprimere*: see EXPRESS[1]]

expressionism /ɪk'sprɛʃ(ə)nɪz(ə)m, ɛk-/ *n.* a style of painting, music, drama, etc., in which an artist or writer seeks to express emotional experience rather than impressions of the external world. □ **expressionist** *n. & adj.* **expressionistic** /-'nɪstɪk/ *adj.* **expressionistically** /-'nɪstɪk(ə)li/ *adv.*

expressive /ɪk'sprɛsɪv, ɛk-/ *adj.* **1** full of expression (*an expressive look*). **2** (foll. by *of*) serving to express (*words expressive of contempt*). □ **expressively** *adv.* **expressiveness** *n.* **expressivity** /-'sɪvɪti/ *n.* [Middle English from French *expressif -ive* or medieval Latin *expressivus* (as EXPRESSION)]

expresso var. of ESPRESSO.

express rifle *n.* a rifle that discharges a bullet at high speed.

express train *n.* a fast train, stopping at few intermediate stations.

expressway /ɪk'sprɛsweɪ, ɛk-/ *n. N. Amer. & Austral.* an urban motorway.

expropriate /ɪks'prəʊprɪeɪt, ɛks-/ *v.tr.* **1** (esp. of the state) take away (property) from its owner. **2** (foll. by *from*) dispossess. □ **expropriation** /-'eɪʃ(ə)n/ *n.* **expropriator** *n.* [medieval Latin *expropriare expropriat-* (as EX-[1], *proprium* 'property': see PROPER)]

expulsion /ɪk'spʌlʃ(ə)n, ɛk-/ *n.* the act or an instance of expelling; the process of being expelled. □ **expulsive** /-sɪv/ *adj.* [Middle English from Latin *expulsio* (as EXPEL)]

expunge /ɪk'spʌn(d)ʒ, ɛk-/ *v.tr.* (often foll. by *from*) erase, remove (esp. a passage from a book or a name from a list). □ **expunction** /ɪk'spʌŋ(k)ʃ(ə)n, ɛk-/ *n.* **expunger** *n.* [Latin *expungere expunct-* 'mark for deletion by means of points' (as EX-[1], *pungere* 'prick')]

expurgate /'ɛkspəːgeɪt/ *v.tr.* **1** remove matter thought to be objectionable from (a book etc.). **2** remove (such matter). □ **expurgation** /-'geɪʃ(ə)n/ *n.* **expurgator** *n.* **expurgatorial** /ˌɛkspəːgə'tɔːrɪəl/ *adj.* **expurgatory** /ɛk'spəːgət(ə)ri/ *adj.* [Latin *expurgare expurgat-* (as EX-[1], *purgare* 'cleanse')]

exquisite /'ɛkskwɪzɪt, ɪk'skwɪzɪt, ɛk-/ *adj. & n.* ● *adj.* **1** extremely beautiful or delicate. **2** acute; keenly felt (*exquisite pleasure*). **3** keen; highly sensitive or discriminating (*exquisite taste*). ● *n.* a person of refined (esp. affected) tastes. □ **exquisitely** *adv.* **exquisiteness** *n.* [Middle English, in the sense 'carefully ascertained, precise', from Latin *exquirere exquisit-* (as EX-[1], *quaerere* 'seek')]

exsanguinate /ɪk'saŋgwɪneɪt, ɛk-/ *v.tr. Med.* drain of blood. □ **exsanguination** /-'neɪʃ(ə)n/ *n.* [Latin *exsanguinatus* (as EX-[1], *sanguis -inis* 'blood')]

exsert /ɪk'səːt, ɛk-/ *v.tr. Biol.* put forth. [Latin *exserere*: see EXERT]

ex-service /ɛk(s)'səːvɪs/ *adj. Brit.* **1** having formerly been a member of the armed forces. **2** relating to former servicemen and -women.

ex-serviceman /ɛk(s)'səːvɪsmən/ *n.* (*pl.* **-men**) esp. *Brit.* a former member of the armed forces.

ex-servicewoman /ɛk(s)'səːvɪswʊmən/ *n.* (*pl.* **-women**) esp. *Brit.* a former woman member of the armed forces.

ex silentio /ɛks sɪ'lɛnʃɪəʊ/ *adv.* by the absence of contrary evidence. [Latin, = from silence]

ext. *abbr.* **1** exterior. **2** external.

extant /ɪk'stant, ɛk-, 'ɛkst(ə)nt/ *adj.* (esp. of a document etc.) still existing, surviving. [Latin *exstare exstant-* (as EX-[1], *stare* 'stand')]

extemporaneous /ɪkˌstɛmpə'reɪmɪəs, ɛk-/ *adj.* spoken or done without preparation. □ **extemporaneously** *adv.* **extemporaneousness** *n.*

extemporary /ɪk'stɛmp(ə)(rə)ri, ɛk-/ *adj.* = EXTEMPORANEOUS. □ **extemporarily** *adv.* **extemporariness** *n.*

extempore /ɪk'stɛmp(ə)ri, ɛk-/ *adj. & adv.* without preparation. [Latin *ex tempore* 'on the spur of the moment', (literally 'out of the time') from *tempus* 'time']

extemporize /ɪk'stɛmpərʌɪz, ɛk-/ *v.tr.* (also **-ise**) (also *absol.*) compose or produce (music, a speech, etc.) without preparation; improvise. □ **extemporization** /-'zeɪʃ(ə)n/ *n.*

extend /ɪk'stɛnd, ɛk-/ *v.* **1** *tr. & intr.* lengthen or make larger in space or time. **2** *tr.* stretch or lay out at full length. **3** *intr. & tr.* (foll. by *to, over*) reach or be or make continuous over a certain area. **4** *intr.* (foll. by *to*) have a certain scope (*the permit does not extend to camping*). **5** *tr.* offer or accord (an invitation, hospitality, kindness, etc.). **6** *tr.* (usu. *refl.* or in *passive*) tax the powers of (an athlete, horse, etc.) to the utmost. □ **extendable** *adj.* **extendability** /-də'bɪlɪti/ *n.* **extendible** *adj.* **extendibility** /-dɪ'bɪlɪti/ *n.* **extensible** /-sɪb(ə)l/ *adj.* **extensibility** /-sɪ'bɪlɪti/ *n.* [Middle English from Latin *extendere extens-* or *extent-* 'stretch out' (as EX-[1], *tendere* 'stretch')]

extended family *n.* a family including relatives living near.

extended-play *attrib.adj.* (of a gramophone record) playing for longer than most singles, usu. at 45 r.p.m.

extender /ɪk'stɛndə, ɛk-/ *n.* **1** a person or thing that extends. **2** a substance added to paint, ink, glue, etc., to dilute its colour or increase its bulk.

extensile /ɪk'stɛnsʌɪl, ɛk-/ *adj.* capable of being stretched out or protruded.

extension /ɪk'stɛnʃ(ə)n, ɛk-/ *n.* **1** the act or an instance of extending; the process of being extended. **2** prolongation; enlargement. **3** a part enlarging or added on to a main structure or building. **4** an additional part of anything. **5 a** a subsidiary telephone on the same line as the main one. **b** its number. **6 a** an additional period of time, esp. extending allowance for a project etc. **b** permission for the sale of alcoholic drinks until later than usual, granted to licensed premises on special occasions. **7** extramural instruction by a university or college (*extension course*). **8** extent, range. **9** *Logic* a group of things denoted by a term. ▫ **extensional** *adj.* [Middle English from Late Latin *extensio* (as EXTEND)]

extensive /ɪk'stɛnsɪv, ɛk-/ *adj.* **1** covering a large area in space or time. **2** having a wide scope; far-reaching (*an extensive knowledge of music*). **3** involving cultivation from a large area, with a minimum of special resources (cf. INTENSIVE *adj.* 3). ▫ **extensively** *adv.* **extensiveness** *n.* [French *extensif -ive* or Late Latin *extensivus* (as EXTENSION)]

extensometer /ɛkstɛn'sɒmɪtə/ *n.* **1** an instrument for measuring deformation of metal under stress. **2** an instrument using such deformation to record elastic strains in other materials. [Latin *extensus* (as EXTEND) + -METER]

extensor /ɪk'stɛnsə, ɛk-/ *n.* (in full **extensor muscle**) *Anat.* a muscle that extends or straightens out part of the body (cf. FLEXOR). [modern Latin (as EXTEND)]

extent /ɪk'stɛnt, ɛk-/ *n.* **1** the space over which a thing extends. **2** the width or limits of application; scope (*to a great extent; to the full extent of their power*). [Middle English via Anglo-French *extente* from medieval Latin *extenta*, past part. of Latin *extendere*: see EXTEND]

extenuate /ɪk'stɛnjʊeɪt, ɛk-/ *v.tr.* (often as **extenuating** *adj.*) lessen the seeming seriousness of (guilt or an offence) by reference to some mitigating factor. ▫ **extenuatingly** *adv.* **extenuation** /-'eɪʃ(ə)n/ *n.* **extenuatory** /-jʊət(ə)ri/ *adj.* [Latin *extenuare extenuat-* (as EX-[1], *tenuis* 'thin')]

exterior /ɪk'stɪərɪə, ɛk-/ *adj.* & *n.* ● *adj.* **1 a** of or on the outer side. **b** (foll. by *to*) situated on the outside of (a building etc.). **c** coming from outside. **2** *Cinematog.* outdoor. ● *n.* **1** the outward aspect or surface of a building etc. **2** the outward or apparent behaviour or demeanour of a person. **3** *Cinematog.* an outdoor scene. ▫ **exteriority** /-'ɒrɪti/ *n.* **exteriorize** *v.tr.* (also **-ise**). **exteriorly** *adv.* [Latin, comparative of *exterus* 'outside']

exterior angle *n.* the angle between the side of a rectilinear figure and the adjacent side extended outward.

exterminate /ɪk'stəːmɪneɪt, ɛk-/ *v.tr.* **1** destroy utterly (esp. something living). **2** get rid of; eliminate (a pest, disease, etc.). ▫ **extermination** /-'neɪʃ(ə)n/ *n.* **exterminator** *n.* **exterminatory** /-nət(ə)ri/ *adj.* [Latin *exterminare exterminat-* (as EX-[1], *terminus* 'boundary')]

external /ɪk'stəːn(ə)l, ɛk-/ *adj.* & *n.* ● *adj.* **1 a** of or situated on the outside or visible part. **b** coming or derived from the outside or an outside source. **2** relating to a country's foreign affairs. **3** outside the conscious subject (*the external world*). **4** (of medicine etc.) for use on the outside of the body. **5** for or concerning students taking the examinations of a university without attending it. ● *n.* (in *pl.*) **1** the outward features or aspect. **2** external circumstances. **3** inessentials. ▫ **externality** /ɛkstəː'nalɪti/ *n.* (*pl.* **-ies**). **externally** *adv.* [medieval Latin from Latin *externus*, from *exterus* 'outside']

external evidence *n.* evidence derived from a source independent of the thing discussed.

externalize /ɪk'stəːn(ə)lʌɪz, ɛk-/ *v.tr.* (also **-ise**) give or attribute external existence to. ▫ **externalization** /-'zeɪʃ(ə)n/ *n.*

exteroceptive /ˌɛkstərəʊ'sɛptɪv/ *adj.* *Biol.* relating to stimuli produced outside an organism. [formed irregularly from Latin *externus* 'exterior' + RECEPTIVE]

exterritorial /ˌɛkstɛrɪ'tɔːrɪəl/ *adj.* = EXTRATERRITORIAL. ▫ **exterritoriality** /-'alɪti/ *n.*

extinct /ɪk'stɪŋkt, ɛk-/ *adj.* **1** (of a family, class, or species) that has died out. **2 a** (of fire etc.) no longer burning. **b** (of a volcano) that no longer erupts. **3** (of life, hope, etc.) terminated, quenched. **4** (of an office etc.) obsolete. **5** (of a title of nobility) having no qualified claimant. [Middle English from Latin *exstinguere exstinct-* (as EX-[1], *stinguere* 'quench')]

extinction /ɪk'stɪŋ(k)ʃ(ə)n, ɛk-/ *n.* **1** the act of making extinct; the state of being or process of becoming extinct. **2** the act of extinguishing; the state of being extinguished. **3** total destruction or annihilation. **4** the wiping out of a debt. **5** *Physics* a reduction in the intensity of radiation by absorption, scattering, etc. ▫ **extinctive** *adj.* [Latin *extinctio* (as EXTINCT)]

extinguish /ɪk'stɪŋgwɪʃ, ɛk-/ *v.tr.* **1** cause (a flame, light, etc.) to die out; put out. **2** make extinct; annihilate, destroy (*a programme to extinguish disease*). **3** put an end to; terminate; obscure utterly (a feeling, quality, etc.). **4 a** abolish; wipe out (a debt). **b** *Law* render void. ▫ **extinguishable** *adj.* **extinguishment** *n.* [formed irregularly from Latin *extinguere* (as EXTINCT): cf. *distinguish*]

extinguisher /ɪk'stɪŋgwɪʃə, ɛk-/ *n.* a person or thing that extinguishes, esp. = FIRE EXTINGUISHER.

extirpate /'ɛkstəpeɪt/ *v.tr.* root out; destroy completely. ▫ **extirpation** /-'peɪʃ(ə)n/ *n.* **extirpator** *n.* [Latin *exstirpare exstirpat-* (as EX-[1], *stirps* 'stem')]

extol /ɪk'stəʊl, ɛk-/ *v.tr.* (**extolled**, **extolling**) praise enthusiastically. ▫ **extoller** *n.* **extolment** *n.* [Latin *extollere* (as EX-[1], *tollere* 'raise')]

extort /ɪk'stɔːt, ɛk-/ *v.tr.* obtain by force, threats, persistent demands, etc. ▫ **extorter** *n.* **extortive** *adj.* [Latin *extorquēre extort-* (as EX-[1], *torquēre* 'twist')]

extortion /ɪk'stɔːʃ(ə)n, ɛk-/ *n.* **1** the act or an instance of extorting, esp. money. **2** illegal exaction. ▫ **extortioner** *n.* **extortionist** *n.* [Middle English from Late Latin *extortio* (as EXTORT)]

extortionate /ɪk'stɔːʃ(ə)nət, ɛk-/ *adj.* **1** (of a price etc.) exorbitant. **2** using or given to extortion (*extortionate methods*). ▫ **extortionately** *adv.*

extra /'ɛkstrə/ *adj., adv.,* & *n.* ● *adj.* additional; more than is usual or necessary or expected. ● *adv.* **1** more than usually. **2** additionally (*was charged extra*). ● *n.* **1** an extra thing. **2** a thing for which an extra charge is made. **3** a person engaged temporarily to fill out a scene in a film or play, esp. as one of a crowd. **4** a special issue of a newspaper etc. **5** *Cricket* a run scored other than from a hit with the bat, and credited to the batting side but not to an individual batsman. [probably a shortening of EXTRAORDINARY]

extra- /'ɛkstrə/ *prefix* **1** outside, beyond (*extragalactic*). **2** beyond the scope of (*extra-curricular*). [medieval Latin from Latin *extra* 'outside']

extracellular /ɛkstrə'sɛljʊlə/ *adj.* situated or taking place outside a cell or cells.

extra cover *n.* *Cricket* **1** a fielding position on a line between cover point and mid-off, but beyond these. **2** a fielder at this position.

extract *v.* & *n.* ● *v.tr.* /ɪk'strakt, ɛk-/ **1** remove or take out, esp. by effort or force (anything firmly rooted). **2** obtain (money, an admission, etc.) with difficulty or against a person's will. **3** obtain (a natural resource) from the earth. **4** select or reproduce for quotation or performance (a passage of writing, music, etc.). **5** obtain (juice etc.) by suction, pressure, distillation, etc. **6** derive (pleasure etc.). **7** *Math.* find (the root of a number). **8** *archaic* deduce (a principle etc.). ● *n.* /'ɛkstrakt/ **1** a short passage taken from a book, piece of music, etc.; an excerpt. **2** a preparation containing the active principle of a substance in concentrated form (*malt extract*). □ **extractable** *adj.* **extractability** /-'bɪlɪti/ *n.* [Latin *extrahere extract-* (as EX-[1], *trahere* 'draw')]

extraction /ɪk'strakʃ(ə)n, ɛk-/ *n.* **1** the act or an instance of extracting; the process of being extracted. **2** the removal of a tooth. **3** origin, lineage, descent (*of Indian extraction*). [Middle English via French from Late Latin *extractio -onis* (as EXTRACT)]

extractive /ɪk'straktɪv, ɛk-/ *adj.* of or involving extraction, esp. extensive extracting of natural resources without provision for their renewal.

extractor /ɪk'straktə, ɛk-/ *n.* **1** a person or machine that extracts. **2** (*attrib.*) *Brit.* (of a device) that extracts stale air etc. or ventilates a room (*extractor fan*; *extractor hood*).

extra-curricular /ɛkstrəkə'rɪkjʊlə/ *adj.* (of an activity at school, college, etc.) not included in the normal curriculum.

extraditable /'ɛkstrədʌɪtəb(ə)l/ *adj.* **1** liable to extradition. **2** (of a crime) warranting extradition.

extradite /'ɛkstrədʌɪt/ *v.tr.* hand over (a person accused or convicted of a crime) to the foreign state etc. in which the crime was committed. [back-formation from EXTRADITION]

extradition /ɛkstrə'dɪʃ(ə)n/ *n.* **1** the extraditing of a person accused or convicted of a crime. **2** *Psychol.* the localizing of a sensation at a distance from the centre of sensation. [French (as EX-[1], TRADITION]

extrados /ɪk'streɪdɒs, ɛk-/ *n. Archit.* the upper or outer curve of an arch (opp. INTRADOS). [as EXTRA- + French *dos* 'back' from Latin *dorsum*]

extragalactic /ɛkstrəgə'laktɪk/ *adj.* occurring or existing outside the Galaxy.

extrajudicial /ɛkstrədʒuː'dɪʃ(ə)l/ *adj.* **1** not legally authorized. **2** (of a confession etc.) not made in court. □ **extrajudicially** *adv.*

extralinguistic /ɛkstrəlɪŋ'gwɪstɪk/ *adj.* outside the field of linguistics or the bounds of language.

extramarital /ɛkstrə'marɪt(ə)l/ *adj.* (esp. of sexual relations) occurring outside marriage. □ **extramaritally** *adv.*

extramundane /ɛkstrə'mʌndeɪn/ *adj.* outside or beyond the physical world.

extramural /ɛkstrə'mjʊər(ə)l/ *adj.* **1** taught or conducted off the premises of a university, college, or school. **2** *Brit.* additional to normal teaching or studies, esp. for non-resident students. **3** outside the walls or boundaries of a town or city. □ **extramurally** *adv.* [Latin *extra muros* 'outside the walls']

extraneous /ɪk'streɪnɪəs, ɛk-/ *adj.* **1** of external origin. **2** (often foll. by *to*) **a** separate from the object to which it is attached etc. **b** external to; irrelevant or unrelated to. □ **extraneously** *adv.* **extraneousness** *n.* [Latin *extraneus*]

extraordinary /ɪk'strɔːd(ə)n(ə)ri, ɛk-, ɛkstrə'ɔːdɪn(ə)ri/ *adj.* **1** unusual or remarkable; out of the usual course. **2** unusually great (*an extraordinary talent*). **3 a** (of an official etc.) additional; specially employed (*envoy extraordinary*). **b** (of a meeting) specially convened. □ **extraordinarily** *adv.* **extraordinariness** *n.* [Latin *extraordinarius* from *extra ordinem* 'outside the usual order']

extrapolate /ɪk'strapəleɪt, ɛk-/ *v.tr.* (also *absol.*) **1** *Math.* **a** extend (a range of values or a curve) by inferring unknown values from trends in the known data. **b** calculate (unknown values etc.) by extension of trends in a known range of values etc. **2** infer more widely from a limited range of known facts. □ **extrapolation** /-'leɪʃ(ə)n/ *n.* **extrapolative** /-lətɪv/ *adj.* **extrapolator** *n.* [EXTRA- + INTERPOLATE]

extrasensory /ɛkstrə'sɛns(ə)ri/ *adj.* derived by means other than the known senses, e.g. by telepathy, clairvoyance, etc. (*extrasensory perception*).

extraterrestrial /ɛkstrətɪ'rɛstrɪəl/ *adj.* & *n.* ● *adj.* **1** outside the earth or its atmosphere. **2** (in science fiction) from outer space. ● *n.* (in science fiction) a being from outer space.

extraterritorial /ˌɛkstrətɛrɪ'tɔːrɪəl/ *adj.* **1** situated or (of laws etc.) valid outside a country's territory. **2** (of an ambassador etc.) free from the jurisdiction of the territory of residence. □ **extraterritoriality** /-'alɪti/ *n.* [Latin *extra territorium* 'outside the territory']

extra time *n.* esp. *Brit.* a further period of play at the end of a match when the scores are equal.

extravagance /ɪk'stravəg(ə)ns, ɛk-/ *n.* **1** excessive spending or use of resources; being extravagant. **2** an instance or item of this. □ **extravagancy** *n.* (*pl.* **-ies**). [French (as EXTRAVAGANT)]

extravagant /ɪk'stravəg(ə)nt, ɛk-/ *adj.* **1** spending (esp. money) excessively; immoderate or wasteful in use of resources. **2** exorbitant; costing much. **3** exceeding normal restraint or sense; unreasonable, absurd (*extravagant claims*). □ **extravagantly** *adv.* [Middle English from medieval Latin *extravagari* (as EXTRA-, *vagari* 'wander')]

extravaganza /ɪkˌstravə'ganzə, ɛk-/ *n.* **1** a fanciful literary, musical, or dramatic composition. **2** a spectacular theatrical or television production, esp. of light entertainment. [Italian *estravaganza* 'extravagance']

extravasate /ɪk'stravəseɪt, ɛk-/ *v.* esp. *Med.* **1** *tr.* force out (a fluid, esp. blood) from its proper vessel. **2** *intr.* (of blood, lava, etc.) flow out. □ **extravasation** /-'seɪʃ(ə)n/ *n.* [Latin *extra* 'outside' + *vas* 'vessel']

extravehicular /ɛkstrəviː'hɪkjʊlə/ *adj.* outside a vehicle, esp. a spacecraft.

extravert var. of EXTROVERT.

extrema *pl.* of EXTREMUM.

extreme /ɪk'striːm, ɛk-/ *adj.* & *n.* ● *adj.* **1** reaching a high or the highest degree; exceedingly great or intense; exceptional (*extreme old age*; *in extreme danger*). **2 a** severe, stringent; lacking restraint or moderation (*take extreme measures*; *an extreme reaction*). **b** (of a person, opinion, etc.) going to great lengths; advocating immoderate measures. **3** outermost; furthest from the centre; situated at either end (*the extreme edge*). **4** *Polit.* on the far left or right of a party. **5** utmost; last. ● *n.* **1** (often in *pl.*) one or other of two things as remote or as different as possible. **2** a thing at either end of anything. **3** the highest or most extreme degree of anything. **4** *Math.* the first or the last term of a ratio or series. **5** *Logic* the subject or predicate in a proposition; the major or the minor term in a syllogism. □ **go to extremes** take an extreme course of action. **go to the other extreme** take a diametrically opposite course of action. **in the extreme** to an extreme degree. □ **extremely** *adv.* **extremeness** *n.* [Middle English via Old French from Latin *extremus*, superlative of *exterus* 'outward']

extreme unction *n. RC Ch.* (former name for) the sacrament of Anointing of the Sick, esp. when administered to the dying.

extremist /ɪk'striːmɪst, ɛk-/ *n.* (also *attrib.*) a person who holds extreme or fanatical political or religious views and esp. resorts to or advocates extreme action. □ **extremism** *n.*

extremity /ɪk'strɛmɪti, ɛk-/ *n.* (*pl.* **-ies**) **1** the extreme point; the very end. **2** (in *pl.*) the hands and feet. **3** a condition of extreme adversity or difficulty. [Middle English from Old French *extremité* or Latin *extremitas* (as EXTREME)]

extremum /ɪk'striːməm, ɛk-/ *n.* (*pl.* **extremums** or **extrema** /-mə/) *Math.* the maximum or minimum value of a function. □ **extremal** *adj.* [Latin, neut. of *extremus* EXTREME]

extricate /'ɛkstrɪkeɪt/ *v.tr.* (often foll. by *from*) free or disentangle from a constraint or difficulty. □ **extricable** *adj.* **extrication** /-'keɪʃ(ə)n/ *n.* [Latin *extricare extricat-* (as EX-[1], *tricae* 'perplexities')]

extrinsic /ɪk'strɪnsɪk, ɛk-/ *adj.* **1** not inherent or intrinsic; not essential (opp. INTRINSIC). **2** (often foll. by *to*) extraneous; lying outside; not belonging (to). **3** originating or operating from without. ▫ **extrinsically** *adv.* [Late Latin *extrinsicus* 'outward' from Latin *extrinsecus* (*adv.*) from *exter* 'outside' + *secus* 'beside']

extrovert /ˈɛkstrəvəːt/ *n. & adj.* (also **extravert**) ● *n.* **1** an outgoing or sociable person. **2** *Psychol.* a person predominantly concerned with external things or objective considerations. ● *adj.* typical or characteristic of an extrovert. ▫ **extroversion** /-ˈvəːʃ(ə)n/ *n.* **extroverted** *adj.* [*extro-* = EXTRA- (on the pattern of *intro-*) + Latin *vertere* 'turn']

■ **Usage** The original spelling, *extravert*, is often preferred in technical use.

extrude /ɪkˈstruːd, ɛk-/ *v.tr.* **1** (foll. by *from*) thrust or force out. **2** shape metal, plastic, etc., by forcing it through a die. ▫ **extrusion** /-ʒ(ə)n/ *n.* **extrusile** /-sʌɪl/ *adj.* **extrusive** /-sɪv/ *adj.* [Latin *extrudere extrus-* (as EX-¹, *trudere* 'thrust')]

exuberant /ɪgˈzjuːb(ə)r(ə)nt, ɛg-/ *adj.* **1** lively, high-spirited. **2** (of a plant etc.) prolific; growing copiously. **3** (of feelings etc.) abounding, lavish, effusive. ▫ **exuberance** *n.* **exuberantly** *adv.* [French *exubérant* from Latin *exuberare* (as EX-¹, *uberare* 'be fruitful' from *uber* 'fertile')]

exuberate /ɪgˈzjuːbəreɪt, ɛg-/ *v.intr.* be exuberant.

exude /ɪgˈzjuːd, ɛg-/ *v.* **1** *tr. & intr.* (of a liquid, moisture, etc.) escape or cause to escape gradually; ooze out; give off. **2** *tr.* emit (a smell). **3** *tr.* display (an emotion etc.) freely or abundantly (*exuded displeasure*). ▫ **exudate** /ˈɛgzjʊdeɪt/ *n.* **exudation** /-ˈdeɪʃ(ə)n/ *n.* **exudative** /ɪgˈzjuːdətɪv, ɛg-/ *adj.* [Latin *exsudare* (as EX-¹, *sudare* 'sweat')]

exult /ɪgˈzʌlt, ɛg-/ *v.intr.* (often foll. by *at, in, over,* or *to* + infin.) **1** be greatly joyful. **2** (often foll. by *over*) have a feeling of triumph (over a person). ▫ **exultancy** *n.* **exultant** *adj.* **exultantly** *adv.* **exultation** /-ˈteɪʃ(ə)n/ *n.* **exultingly** *adv.* [Latin *exsultare* (as EX-¹, *saltare*, frequentative of *salire salt-* 'leap')]

exurb /ˈɛksəːb/ *n.* a district outside a city or town, esp. a prosperous area beyond the suburbs. ▫ **exurban** /ɛkˈsəːb(ə)n/ *adj.* **exurbanite** /ɛkˈsəːb(ə)nʌɪt/ *n.* [Latin *ex* 'out of' + *urbs* 'city', or back-formation from *exurban* (as EX-¹ + URBAN, on the pattern of *suburban*)]

exurbia /ɛkˈsəːbɪə/ *n.* the exurbs collectively; the region beyond the suburbs. [EX-¹, on the pattern of *suburbia*]

exuviae /ɪgˈzjuːvɪiː, ɛg-/ *n.pl.* (also treated as *sing.*) an animal's cast skin or covering. ▫ **exuvial** *adj.* [Latin, = animal's skins, spoils of the enemy, from *exuere* 'divest oneself of']

exuviate /ɪgˈzjuːvɪeɪt, ɛg-/ *v.tr.* shed (a skin etc.). ▫ **exuviation** /-ˈeɪʃ(ə)n/ *n.*

ex-voto /ɛks ˈvəʊtəʊ/ *n.* (*pl.* **-os**) an offering made in pursuance of a vow. [Latin, = out of a vow]

-ey /i/ *suffix* var. of -Y².

eyas /ˈʌɪəs/ *n.* a young hawk, esp. one taken from the nest for training in falconry. [originally *nyas* from French *niais*, ultimately from Latin *nidus* 'nest': for loss of *n-* cf. ADDER]

eye /ʌɪ/ *n. & v.* ● *n.* **1 a** the organ of sight in humans and other animals. **b** the light-detecting organ in some invertebrates. **2** the eye characterized by the colour of the iris (*has blue eyes*). **3** the region round the eye (*eyes red from weeping*). **4** (in *sing.* or *pl.*) sight; the faculty of sight (*demonstrate to the eye*; *need perfect eyes to be a pilot*). **5** a particular visual faculty or talent; visual appreciation (*a straight eye*; *cast an expert eye over*). **6** (in *sing.* or *pl.*) a look, gaze, or glance, esp. as indicating the disposition of the viewer (*a friendly eye*). **7** mental awareness; consciousness. **8** a person or animal etc. that sees on behalf of another. **9** = ELECTRIC EYE. **10** *slang* = PRIVATE EYE. **11** a thing like an eye, esp.: **a** a spot on a peacock's tail (cf. EYELET *n.* 3). **b** the leaf bud of a potato. **12** the centre of something circular, e.g. a flower or target. **13** the relatively calm region at the centre of a storm or hurricane. **14** an aperture in an implement, esp. a needle, for the insertion of something, e.g. thread. **15** a ring or loop for a bolt or hook etc. to pass through. ● *v.tr.* (**eyes**, **eyed**, **eyeing** or **eying**) (often foll. by *up*) watch or observe closely, esp. admiringly or with curiosity or suspicion. ▫ **all eyes 1** watching intently. **2** general attention (*all eyes were on us*). **before one's** (or **one's very**) **eyes** right in front of one. **do a person in the eye** *Brit. colloq.* defraud or thwart a person. **an eye for an eye** retaliation in kind (Exod. 21:24). **eye of a needle** see NEEDLE'S EYE. **eyes front** (or **left** or **right**) *Mil.* a command to turn the head in the direction stated. **get** (or **keep**) **one's eye in** *Brit. Sport* accustom oneself (or keep oneself accustomed) to the conditions of play so as to judge speed, distance, etc. **have an eye for** be capable of perceiving or appreciating. **have one's eye on** wish or plan to procure. **have eyes for** be interested in; wish to acquire. **have an eye to** have as one's objective; prudently consider. **hit a person in the eye** (or **between the eyes**) *colloq.* be very obvious or impressive. **keep an eye on 1** pay attention to. **2** look after; take care of. **keep an eye open** (or **out**) (often foll. by *for*) watch out carefully. **keep one's eyes open** (or **peeled** or *Brit.* **skinned**) watch out; be on the alert. **lower one's eyes** look modestly or sheepishly down or away. **make eyes** (or **sheep's eyes**) (foll. by *at*) look amorously or flirtatiously at. **my** (or **all my**) **eye** *slang* nonsense. **one in the eye** (foll. by *for*) a disappointment or setback. **open a person's eyes** be enlightening or revealing to a person. **raise one's eyes** look upwards. **see eye to eye** (often foll. by *with*) be in full agreement. **set eyes on** catch sight of. **take one's eyes off** (usu. in *neg.*) stop watching; stop paying attention to. **under the eye of** under the supervision or observation of. **up to the** (or **one's**) **eyes in 1** deeply engaged or involved in; inundated with (*up to the eyes in work*). **2** to the utmost limit (*mortgaged up to the eyes*). **with one's eyes open** deliberately; with full awareness. **with one's eyes shut** (or **closed**) **1** easily; with little effort. **2** without awareness; unobservantly (*goes around with his eyes shut*). **with an eye to** with a view to; prudently considering. **with a friendly** (or **jealous** etc.) **eye** with a feeling of friendship, jealousy, etc. **with one eye on** directing one's attention partly to. **with one eye shut** easily; with little effort (*could do this with one eye shut*). ▫ **eyed** *adj.* (also in *comb.*). **eyeless** *adj.* [Old English *ēage*, from Germanic]

eyeball /ˈʌɪbɔːl/ *n. & v.* ● *n.* the ball of the eye within the lids and socket. ● *v. N. Amer. slang* **1** *tr.* look or stare at. **2** *intr.* look or stare. ▫ **eyeball to eyeball** confronting closely. **to** (or **up to**) **the eyeballs** *colloq.* completely (permeated, soaked, etc.).

eyebath /ˈʌɪbɑːθ/ *n.* a small glass or vessel for applying lotion etc. to the eye.

eyeblack /ˈʌɪblak/ *n. archaic* = MASCARA.

eye bolt *n.* a bolt or bar with an eye at the end for a hook etc.

eyebright /ˈʌɪbrʌɪt/ *n.* any plant of the genus *Euphrasia*, traditionally used as a remedy for weak eyes.

eyebrow /ˈʌɪbraʊ/ *n.* the line of hair growing on the ridge above the eye socket. ▫ **raise one's eyebrows** (or **an eyebrow**) show surprise, disbelief, or mild disapproval.

eye-catching *adj.* striking, attractive.

eye contact *n.* looking directly into another person's eyes.

eyecup /ˈʌɪkʌp/ *n.* = EYEBATH.

eyeful /ˈʌɪfʊl, -f(ə)l/ *n.* (*pl.* **-fuls**) *colloq.* **1** a long steady look. **2** a visually striking person or thing. **3** anything thrown or blown into the eye.

eyeglass /ˈʌɪglɑːs/ *n.* **1 a** a lens for correcting or assisting defective sight. **b** (in *pl.*) a pair of these held in the hand or kept in position on the nose by means of a frame or a spring. **c** (in *pl.*) esp. *N. Amer.* = SPECTACLES. **2** a small glass vessel for applying lotion etc. to the eye.

eyehole /ˈʌɪhəʊl/ *n.* a hole to look through.

eye language *n.* the process of communication by the expression of the eyes.

eyelash /ˈʌɪlaʃ/ *n.* each of the hairs growing on the edges of the eyelids. □ **by an eyelash** by a very small margin.

eyelet /ˈʌɪlɪt/ *n.* & *v.* ● *n.* **1** a small hole in paper, leather, cloth, etc., for string or rope etc. to pass through. **2** a metal ring reinforcement for this. **3** a small eye, esp. the ocellus on a butterfly's wing (cf. EYE *n.* 11a). **4** a form of decoration in embroidery. **5** a small hole for observation, shooting through, etc. ● *v.tr.* (**eyeleted**, **eyeleting**) provide with eyelets. [Middle English via Old French *oillet*, diminutive of *oil* 'eye' from Latin *oculus*]

eye level *n.* the level seen by the eyes looking horizontally (hyphenated when *attrib.*: *eye-level grill*).

eyelid /ˈʌɪlɪd/ *n.* the upper or lower fold of skin closing to cover the eye.

eyeliner /ˈʌɪlʌɪnə/ *n.* a cosmetic applied as a line round the eye.

eye mask *n.* **1** a covering of soft material saturated with a lotion for refreshing the eyes. **2** a covering for the eyes.

eye-opener *n. colloq.* **1** an enlightening experience; an unexpected revelation. **2** *US* an alcoholic drink taken on waking up. □ **eye-opening** *adj.*

eyepatch /ˈʌɪpatʃ/ *n.* a patch worn to protect an injured eye.

eyepiece /ˈʌɪpiːs/ *n.* the lens or lenses to which the eye is applied at the end of a microscope, telescope, etc.

eye-rhyme *n.* a correspondence of words in spelling but not in pronunciation (e.g. *love* and *move*).

eye-shade *n.* a device to protect the eyes, esp. from strong light.

eyeshadow /ˈʌɪʃadəʊ/ *n.* a coloured cosmetic applied to the skin round the eyes.

eyeshot /ˈʌɪʃɒt/ *n.* seeing-distance (*out of eyeshot*).

eyesight /ˈʌɪsʌɪt/ *n.* the faculty or power of seeing.

eyesore /ˈʌɪsɔː/ *n.* a visually offensive or ugly thing, esp. a building.

eye-spot *n.* **1 a** a light-sensitive area on the bodies of some invertebrate animals, e.g. flatworms, starfish, etc.; also called *ocellus*. **b** *Bot.* an area of light-sensitive pigment found in some algae etc. **2** a fungal disease of plants characterized by yellowish oval spots on the leaves and stems.

eye-stalk *n.* a movable stalk carrying the eye, esp. in crabs, shrimps, etc.

eye strain *n.* fatigue of the (internal or external) muscles of the eye.

Eyetie /ˈʌɪtʌɪ/ *n.* & *adj. Brit. slang offens.* Italian. [jocular pronunciation (abbreviation) of *Italian*]

eye-tooth *n.* a canine tooth just under or next to the eye, esp. one in the upper jaw.

eyewash /ˈʌɪwɒʃ/ *n.* **1** lotion for the eye. **2** *slang* nonsense, bunkum; pretentious or insincere talk.

eyewitness /ˈʌɪwɪtnɪs/ *n.* a person who has personally seen a thing done or happen and can give evidence of it.

eye-worm *n.* a nematode worm, *Loa loa*, parasitic on humans and other primates in Central and West Africa. [because it infects the eyes]

eyot var. of AIT.

eyra /ˈeɪrə/ *n. Zool.* a red form of jaguarundi. [Tupi *(e)irara*]

eyrie /ˈɪəri, ˈʌɪri, ˈɛːri/ *n.* (also **aerie**) **1** a nest of a bird of prey, esp. an eagle, built high up. **2** a house etc. perched high up. [medieval Latin *aeria, aerea*, etc., probably from Old French *aire* 'lair', ultimately from Latin *agrum* 'piece of ground']

Ezek. *abbr.* Ezekiel (Old Testament).

Ff

F[1] /ɛf/ *n.* (also **f**) (*pl.* **Fs** or **F's**) **1** the sixth letter of the alphabet. **2** *Mus.* the fourth note of the diatonic scale of C major.

F[2] *abbr.* (also **F.**) **1** Fahrenheit. **2** female. **3** *Brit.* fine (pencil lead). **4** *Biol.* filial generation (as F_1 for the first filial generation, F_2 for the second, etc.).

F[3] *symb.* **1** *Chem.* the element fluorine. **2** farad(s). **3** force. **4** (*F*) *Electr.* faraday.

f[1] *abbr.* (also **f.**) **1** female. **2** feminine. **3** following page etc. **4** (*f*) *Mus.* forte. **5** folio. **6** filly. **7** foreign.

f[2] *symb.* **1** focal length (cf. F-NUMBER). **2** femto-. **3** frequency.

FA *abbr.* **1** (in the UK) Football Association. **2** = FANNY ADAMS 1.

fa var. of FAH.

FAA *abbr.* **1** (in the UK) Fleet Air Arm. **2** (in the US) Federal Aviation Administration.

fab /fab/ *adj. colloq.* fabulous, marvellous. [abbreviation]

Fabian /'feɪbɪən/ *n.* & *adj.* ● *n.* a member or supporter of the Fabian Society, an organization of socialists aiming at a gradual rather than revolutionary achievement of socialism. ● *adj.* **1** relating to or characteristic of the Fabians. **2** employing a cautiously persistent and dilatory strategy to wear out an enemy (*Fabian tactics*). □ **Fabianism** *n.* **Fabianist** *n.* [Latin *Fabianus*, from the name of Q. *Fabius* Maximus Cunctator (= delayer), Roman general of the 3rd c. BC, noted for cautious strategies]

fable /'feɪb(ə)l/ *n.* & *v.* ● *n.* **1 a** a story, esp. a supernatural one, not based on fact. **b** a tale, esp. with animals as characters, conveying a moral. **2** (*collect.*) myths and legendary tales (*in fable*). **3 a** a false statement; a lie. **b** a thing only supposed to exist. ● *v.* **1** *intr.* tell fictitious tales. **2** *tr.* describe fictitiously. **3** *tr.* (as **fabled** *adj.*) celebrated in fable; famous, legendary. □ **fabler** /'feɪblə/ *n.* [Middle English via Old French *fabler* from Latin *fabulari*, from *fabula* 'discourse' from *fari* 'speak']

fabliau /'fablɪəʊ/ *n.* (*pl.* **fabliaux** /-əʊz/) a metrical tale in early French poetry, often coarsely humorous. [French from Old French dialect *fabliaux*, *-ax*, pl. of *fablel* diminutive of *fable*, from Latin *fabula* (see FABLE)]

Fablon /'fablɒn/ *n. propr.* flexible self-adhesive plastic sheeting used for covering furniture, table mats, etc.

fabric /'fabrɪk/ *n.* **1 a** a woven material; a textile. **b** other material resembling woven cloth. **2** a structure or framework, esp. the walls, floor, and roof of a building. **3** (in abstract senses) the essential structure or essence of a thing (*the fabric of society*). [Middle English via French *fabrique* from Latin *fabrica*, from *faber* 'worker in metal, stone, etc.']

fabricate /'fabrɪkeɪt/ *v.tr.* **1** construct or manufacture, esp. from prepared components. **2** invent or concoct (a story, evidence, etc.). **3** forge (a document). □ **fabrication** /-'keɪʃ(ə)n/ *n.* **fabricator** *n.* [Latin *fabricare fabricat-* (as FABRIC)]

fabric conditioner *n.* a liquid added as a conditioner when washing clothes etc.

fabulist /'fabjʊlɪst/ *n.* **1** a composer of fables. **2** a liar. [French *fabuliste* from Latin *fabula*: see FABLE]

fabulous /'fabjʊləs/ *adj.* **1** incredible, exaggerated, absurd (*fabulous wealth*). **2** *colloq.* excellent, marvellous (*looking fabulous*). **3 a** celebrated in fable. **b** legendary, mythical. □ **fabulosity** /-'lɒsɪti/ *n.* **fabulously** *adv.* **fabulousness** *n.* [French *fabuleux* or Latin *fabulosus* (as FABLE)]

façade /fə'sɑːd/ *n.* (also **facade**) **1** the face of a building, esp. its principal front. **2** an outward appearance or front, esp. a deceptive one. [French (as FACE)]

face /feɪs/ *n.* & *v.* ● *n.* **1** the front of the head from the forehead to the chin. **2** the expression of the facial features (*had a happy face*). **3** composure, coolness, effrontery. **4** the surface of a thing, esp. as regarded or approached, esp.: **a** the visible part of a celestial body. **b** a side of a mountain etc. (*the north face*). **c** the (usu. vertical) surface of a coal-seam. **d** *Geom.* each surface of a solid. **e** the façade of a building. **f** the plate of a clock or watch bearing the digits, hands, etc. **5 a** the functional or working side of a tool etc. **b** the distinctive side of a playing card. **c** the obverse of a coin. **6** = TYPEFACE. **7** the outward appearance or aspect (*the unacceptable face of capitalism*). **8** a person, esp. conveying some quality or association (*a face from the past*; *some young faces for a change*). **9** esteem, respectable reputation (*defeat would entail a loss of face*). ● *v.* **1** *tr.* & *intr.* look or be positioned towards or in a certain direction (*face towards the window*; *facing the window*; *the room faces north*). **2** *tr.* be opposite (*facing page 20*). **3** *tr.* **a** (often foll. by *down, out*) meet resolutely or defiantly; confront (*face one's critics*). **b** not shrink from (*face the facts*). **4** *tr.* present itself to; confront (*the problem that faces us*; *faces us with a problem*). **5** *tr.* **a** cover the surface of (a thing) with a coating, extra layer, etc. **b** put a facing on (a garment). **6** *intr.* & *tr.* turn or cause to turn in a certain direction. □ **face down** (or **downwards**) with the face or surface turned towards the ground, floor, etc. (see also sense 3a of *v.*). **face facts** (or **the facts**) recognize the truth. **face off** take up an attitude of confrontation, esp. at the start of a fight, game, etc. **face the music** put up with or stand up to unpleasant consequences, esp. criticism. **face to face** (often foll. by *with*) facing; confronting each other. **face up** (or **upwards**) with the face or surface turned upwards to view. **face up to** accept bravely; confront; stand up to. **have the face** be shameless enough. **in one's** (or **the**) **face 1** straight against one; as one approaches. **2** confronting. **in face** (or **the face**) **of 1** despite. **2** confronted by. **in your face** see IN-YOUR-FACE. **let's face it** *colloq.* we must be honest or realistic about it. **on the face of it** as it would appear. **put a bold** (or **brave**) **face on it** accept difficulty etc. cheerfully or with courage. **put one's face on** *colloq.* apply make-up to one's face. **put a good face on** make (a matter) look well. **put a new face on** alter the aspect of. **save face** preserve esteem; avoid humiliation. **save a person's face** enable a person to save face; forbear from humiliating a person. **set one's face against** oppose or resist with determination. **show one's face** see SHOW. **to a person's face** openly in a person's presence. □ **faced** *adj.* (also in *comb.*). **facing** *adj.* (also in *comb.*). [Middle English from Old French, ultimately from Latin *facies*]

face-ache *n. Brit.* **1** neuralgia. **2** *slang* a mournful-looking or ugly person.

face card *n.* = COURT CARD.

facecloth /'feɪsklɒθ/ *n.* **1** a cloth for washing one's face. **2** a smooth-surfaced woollen cloth.

face cream *n.* a cosmetic cream applied to the face to improve the complexion.

face flannel *n. Brit.* = FACECLOTH 1.

faceless /ˈfeɪslɪs/ *adj.* **1** without identity; purposely not identifiable. **2** lacking character. **3** without a face. □ **facelessness** *n.*

facelift /ˈfeɪslɪft/*n.* **1** cosmetic surgery to remove wrinkles etc. by tightening the skin of the face. **2** a procedure to improve the appearance of a thing.

face mask *n.* **1** a mask covering the nose and mouth or nose and eyes. **2** = FACE PACK.

face-off *n.* a direct confrontation.

face pack *n. Brit.* a preparation beneficial to the complexion, spread over the face and removed when dry.

face paint *n.* paint for applying to the face. □ **face-painter** *n.* **face-painting** *n.*

faceplate /ˈfeɪspleɪt/ *n.* **1** an enlarged end or attachment on the end of a mandrel of a lathe, on which work can be mounted. **2** a plate protecting a piece of machinery etc. **3** the glass window of a diver's helmet.

face powder *n.* a cosmetic powder for reducing the shine on the face.

facer /ˈfeɪsə/ *n. colloq.* **1** *Brit.* a sudden difficulty or obstacle. **2** a blow in the face.

face-saving *n.* (usu. *attrib.*) the preserving of one's reputation, credibility, etc. □ **face-saver** *n.*

facet /ˈfasɪt, -ɛt/ *n.* **1** a particular aspect of a thing. **2** one side of a many-sided body, esp. of a cut gem. **3** one segment of a compound eye. □ **faceted** *adj.* (also in *comb.*). [French *facette*, diminutive (as FACE, -ETTE)]

facetiae /fəˈsiːʃɪiː/ *n.pl.* **1** pleasantries, witticisms. **2** (in bookselling) pornography. [Latin, pl. of *facetia* 'jest' from *facetus* 'witty']

facetious /fəˈsiːʃəs/ *adj.* **1** characterized by flippant or inopportune humour. **2** (of a person) intending to be amusing, esp. inopportunely. □ **facetiously** *adv.* **facetiousness** *n.* [French *facétieux* from *facétie*, from Latin *facetia* 'jest']

face-to-face *attrib.adj.* with the people involved facing each other or in each other's presence (*face-to-face discussions*).

face value *n.* **1** the nominal value as printed or stamped on money. **2** the superficial appearance or implication of a thing.

faceworker /ˈfeɪswəːkə/ *n.* a miner who works at the coalface.

facia/ˈfeɪʃə/ *n.* (also **fascia**) **1** *Brit.* **a** the instrument panel of a motor vehicle. **b** any similar panel or plate for operating machinery. **2** the upper part of a shopfront with the proprietor's name etc.

facial /ˈfeɪʃ(ə)l/ *adj. & n.* ● *adj.* of or for the face. ● *n.* a beauty treatment for the face. □ **facially** *adv.* [medieval Latin *facialis* (as FACE)]

-facient /ˈfeɪʃ(ə)nt/ *comb. form* forming adjectives and nouns indicating an action or state produced (*abortifacient*). [from or after Latin *-faciens -entis*, part. of *facere* 'make']

facies /ˈfeɪʃɪiːz/ *n.* (*pl.* same) **1** *Med.* the appearance or facial expression of an individual. **2** *Geol.* the character of rock etc. expressed by its composition, fossil content, etc. [Latin, = FACE]

facile /ˈfasʌɪl, -sɪl/ *adj.* usu. *derog.* **1** easily achieved but of little value. **2** (of speech, writing, etc.) fluent, ready, glib. □ **facilely** *adv.* **facileness** *n.* [French *facile* or Latin *facilis*, from *facere* 'do']

facilitate /fəˈsɪlɪteɪt/ *v.tr.* make easy or less difficult or more easily achieved. □ **facilitation** /-ˈteɪʃ(ə)n/ *n.* **facilitative** /-tətɪv/ *adj.* **facilitator** *n.* [French *faciliter* via Italian *facilitare*, from *facile* 'easy', from Latin *facilis*]

facility /fəˈsɪlɪti/ *n.* (*pl.* **-ies**) **1** ease; absence of difficulty. **2** fluency, dexterity, aptitude (*facility of expression*). **3** (esp. in *pl.*) an opportunity, the equipment, or the resources for doing something. **4** *US* a plant, installation, or establishment. [French *facilité* or Latin *facilitas* (as FACILE)]

facing /ˈfeɪsɪŋ/ *n.* **1 a** a layer of material covering part of a garment etc. for contrast or strength. **b** (in *pl.*) the cuffs, collar, etc., of a military jacket. **2** an outer layer covering the surface of a wall etc.

facsimile /fakˈsɪmɪli/ *n. & v.* ● *n.* **1** an exact copy, esp. of writing, printing, a picture, etc. (often *attrib.*: *facsimile edition*). **2 a** production of an exact copy of a document etc. by electronic scanning and transmission of the resulting data (see also FAX). **b** a copy produced in this way. ● *v.tr.* (**facsimiled**, **facsimileing**) make a facsimile of. □ **in facsimile** as an exact copy. [modern Latin from Latin *fac*, imperative of *facere* 'make' + *simile*, neut. of *similis* 'like']

fact /fakt/ *n.* **1** a thing that is known to have occurred, to exist, or to be true. **2** a datum of experience (often foll. by an explanatory clause or phrase: *the fact that fire burns*; *the fact of my having seen them*). **3** (usu. in *pl.*) an item of verified information; a piece of evidence. **4** truth, reality. **5** a thing assumed as the basis for argument or inference. □ **before** (or **after**) **the fact** before (or after) the committing of a crime. **a fact of life** something that must be accepted. **facts and figures** precise details. **in** (or **in point of**) **fact 1** in reality; as a matter of fact. **2** (in summarizing) in short. [Latin *factum*, from *facere* 'do']

factice /ˈfaktɪs/ *n. Chem.* a rubber-like substance obtained by vulcanizing unsaturated vegetable oils. [German *Faktis* from Latin *facticius* 'artificial, FACTITIOUS']

faction[1] /ˈfakʃ(ə)n/ *n.* **1** a small organized dissentient group within a larger one, esp. in politics. **2** a state of dissension within an organization. [French from Latin *factio -onis*, from *facere fact-* 'do, make']

faction[2] /ˈfakʃ(ə)n/ *n.* a book, film, etc., using real events as a basis for a fictional narrative or dramatization. [blend of FACT and FICTION]

-faction /ˈfakʃ(ə)n/ *comb. form* forming nouns of action from verbs in *-fy* (*petrifaction*; *satisfaction*). [from or suggested by Latin *-factio -factionis* from *-facere* 'do, make']

factional /ˈfakʃ(ə)n(ə)l/ *adj.* **1** of or characterized by faction. **2** belonging to a faction. □ **factionalism** *n.* **factionalize** *v.tr. & intr.* (also **-ise**). **factionally** *adv.* [FACTION[1]]

factious /ˈfakʃəs/ *adj.* of, characterized by, or inclined to faction. □ **factiously** *adv.* **factiousness** *n.* [FACTION[1]]

■ **Usage** The similarity in sense between *faction* (see FACTION[1] 1) and *fraction* (see FRACTION 4) may lead to confusion between the adjectives *factious* and *fractious*. *Fractious*, however is now only used to mean 'unruly' or 'peevish'.

factitious /fakˈtɪʃəs/ *adj.* **1** specially contrived, not genuine (*factitious value*). **2** artificial, not natural (*factitious joy*). □ **factitiously** *adv.* **factitiousness** *n.* [Latin *facticius* from *facere fact-* 'do, make']

factitive /ˈfaktɪtɪv/ *adj. Gram.* (of a verb) having a sense of regarding or designating, and taking a complement as well as an object (e.g. *appointed me captain*). [modern Latin *factitivus*, formed irregularly from Latin *factitare*, frequentative of *facere fact-* 'do, make']

factoid /ˈfaktɔɪd/ *n. & adj.* ● *n.* **1** an assumption or speculation that is reported and repeated so often that it becomes accepted as fact; a simulated or imagined fact. **2** *US* a brief or trivial item of news or information. ● *adj.* being or having the character of a factoid; containing factoids.

factor /ˈfaktə/ *n. & v.* ● *n.* **1** a circumstance, fact, or influence contributing to a result. **2** *Math.* a whole number etc. that when multiplied with another produces a given number or expression. **3** *Biol.* a gene etc. determining hereditary character. **4** (foll. by identifying number) *Med.* any of a group of substances in the blood contributing to coagulation (*factor VIII*). **5 a** a business agent; a merchant buying and selling on commission. **b** *Sc.* a land agent or steward. **c** an agent or deputy. **6** a company that buys a manufacturer's invoices and takes responsibility for collecting the payments due on them. ● *v.tr.* **1** *Math.* resolve into factors or components. **2** *tr.* sell (one's receivable debts) to a factor. □ **factorable** *adj.* [French *facteur* or Latin *factor*, from *facere fact-* 'do, make']

factor VIII *n.* (also **factor eight**) *Med.* a blood protein involved in clotting, whose deficiency causes haemophilia.

factorage /'fakt(ə)rɪdʒ/ *n.* commission or charges payable to a factor.

factor analysis *n.* a process by which the relative importance of variables in the study of a sample is assessed by mathematical techniques.

factorial /fak'tɔːrɪəl/ *n.* & *adj. Math.* ● *n.* **1** the product of a number and all the whole numbers below it (*factorial four* = *4×3×2×1*) (symbol ! as in 4!). **2** the product of a series of factors in an arithmetical progression. ● *adj.* of a factor or factorial. □ **factorially** *adv.*

factorize /'faktərʌɪz/ *v.* (also **-ise**) *Math.* **1** *tr.* resolve into factors. **2** *intr.* be capable of resolution into factors. □ **factorization** /-'zeɪʃ(ə)n/ *n.*

factory /'fakt(ə)ri/ *n.* (*pl.* **-ies**) **1** a building or buildings containing plant or equipment, where manufacturing processes are carried out. **2** *hist.* a merchant company's foreign trading station. [Late Latin *factorium* and Portuguese *feitoria* ultimately from Latin (as FACTOR)]

factory farming *n.* a system of rearing livestock using industrial or intensive methods. □ **factory farm** *n.*

factory floor *n.* workers in industry as distinct from management.

factory ship *n.* a fishing ship with facilities for immediate processing of the catch.

factory shop *n.* (also **factory outlet**) a shop in which goods, often surplus stock, are sold directly by the manufacturers at a discount.

factotum /fak'təʊtəm/ *n.* (*pl.* **factotums**) an employee who does all kinds of work. [medieval Latin from Latin *fac*, imperative of *facere* 'do, make' + *totum*, neut. of *totus* 'whole']

fact sheet *n.* a paper setting out relevant information.

facts of life *n.pl.* (prec. by *the*) information about sexual functions and practices, esp. as given to children or teenagers.

factual /'faktʃʊəl/ *adj.* **1** based on or concerned with fact or facts. **2** actual, true. □ **factuality** /-'alɪti/ *n.* **factually** *adv.* **factualness** *n.* [FACT, on the pattern of *actual*]

factum /'faktəm/ *n.* (*pl.* **factums** or **facta** /-tə/) *Law* **1** an act or deed. **2** a statement of facts. [French from Latin: see FACT]

facture /'faktʃə/ *n.* the quality of execution, esp. of the surface of a painting. [Middle English via Old French from Latin *factura*, from *facere fact-* 'do, make']

facula /'fakjʊlə/ *n.* (*pl.* **faculae** /-liː/) *Astron.* a bright spot or streak on the sun. □ **facular** *adj.* **faculous** *adj.* [Latin, diminutive of *fax facis* 'torch']

facultative /'fak(ə)ltətɪv/ *adj.* **1** *Law* enabling an act to take place. **2** that may occur. **3** *Biol.* not restricted to a particular function, mode of life, etc. **4** of a faculty. □ **facultatively** *adv.* [French *facultatif -ive* (as FACULTY)]

faculty /'fak(ə)lti/ *n.* (*pl.* **-ies**) **1** an aptitude or ability for a particular activity. **2** an inherent mental or physical power. **3 a** *Brit.* a group of university departments concerned with a major division of knowledge (*faculty of modern languages*). **b** *N. Amer.* the teaching staff of a university or college. **c** *Brit.* a branch of art or science; those qualified to teach it. **4** the members of a particular profession, esp. medicine. **5** authorization, esp. by a Church authority. [Middle English via Old French *faculté* from Latin *facultas -tatis*, from *facilis* 'easy']

Faculty of Advocates *n.* the society constituting the Scottish Bar.

FAD *abbr.* flavin adenine dinucleotide.

fad /fad/ *n.* **1** a craze. **2** a peculiar notion or idiosyncrasy. □ **faddish** *adj.* **faddishly** *adv.* **faddishness** *n.* **faddism** *n.* **faddist** *n.* [19th c. (originally dialect): probably via *fidfad* from FIDDLE-FADDLE]

faddy /'fadi/ *adj.* (**faddier**, **faddiest**) *Brit.* having arbitrary likes and dislikes, esp. about food. □ **faddily** *adv.* **faddiness** *n.*

fade /feɪd/ *v.* & *n.* ● *v.* **1** *intr.* & *tr.* lose or cause to lose colour. **2** *intr.* lose freshness or strength; (of flowers etc.) droop, wither. **3** *intr.* **a** (of colour, light, etc.) disappear gradually; grow pale or dim. **b** (of sound) grow faint. **4** *intr.* (of a feeling etc.) diminish. **5** *intr.* (foll. by *away*, *out*) (of a person etc.) disappear or depart gradually. **6** *tr.* (foll. by *in*, *out*) *Cinematog.* & *Broadcasting* **a** cause (a picture) to come gradually in or out of view on a screen, or to merge into another shot. **b** make (the sound) more or less audible. **7** *intr.* (of a radio signal) vary irregularly in intensity. **8** *intr.* (of a brake) temporarily lose effectiveness. **9** *Golf* **a** *intr.* (of a ball) deviate from a straight course, esp. in a deliberate slice. **b** *tr.* cause (a ball) to fade. ● *n.* the action or an instance of fading. □ **do a fade** *slang* depart. **fade away** languish, grow thin. □ **fadeless** *adj.* **fader** *n.* (in sense 6 of *v.*). [Middle English from Old French *fader*, from *fade* 'dull, insipid', probably ultimately from Latin *fatuus* 'silly' + *vapidus* VAPID]

fade-in *n. Cinematog.* & *Broadcasting* the action or an instance of fading in a picture or sound.

fade-out *n.* **1** *colloq.* disappearance, death. **2** *Cinematog.* & *Broadcasting* the action or an instance of fading out a picture or sound.

fadge /fadʒ/ *n. Austral.* & *NZ* **1** a limp package of wool. **2** a loosely packed wool bale. [16th-c. English dialect: origin uncertain]

fado /'fɑːdəʊ/ *n.* (*pl.* **-os**) a type of (esp. plaintive) popular Portuguese song. [Portuguese, literally 'fate']

faeces /'fiːsiːz/ *n.pl.* (*US* **feces**) waste matter discharged from the bowels. □ **faecal** /'fiːk(ə)l/ *adj.* [Latin, pl. of *faex* 'dregs']

faerie /'feɪəri, 'fɛːri/ *n.* (also **faery**) *archaic* **1** fairyland; the fairies, esp. as represented by Spenser (*Faerie Queene*). **2** (*attrib.*) visionary, fancied. [variant of FAIRY]

Faeroese /fɛːrəʊ'iːz/ *adj.* & *n.* (also **Faroese**) ● *adj.* of or relating to the Faeroes, an island group in the N. Atlantic between Norway and Iceland. ● *n.* (*pl.* same) **1** a native of the Faeroes; a person of Faeroese descent. **2** the Norse language of the Faeroese.

faff /faf/ *v.* & *n. Brit. colloq.* ● *v.intr.* (often foll. by *about*, *around*) fuss, dither. ● *n.* a fuss. [imitative]

fag[1] /fag/ *n.* & *v.* ● *n.* **1** esp. *Brit. colloq.* a piece of drudgery; a wearisome or unwelcome task. **2** esp. *Brit. colloq.* a cigarette. **3** *Brit.* (at public schools) a junior pupil who runs errands for a senior. ● *v.* (**fagged**, **fagging**) **1** *colloq.* **a** *tr.* (often foll. by *out*) tire out; exhaust. **b** *intr. Brit.* toil. **2** *intr. Brit.* (at public schools) act as a fag. **3** *tr.* (often foll. by *out*) *Naut.* fray (the end of a rope etc.). [16th c., origin unknown: cf. FLAG[1]]

fag[2] /fag/ *n. N. Amer. slang offens.* a male homosexual. [abbreviation of FAGGOT]

fag end *n. colloq.* **1** *Brit.* a cigarette end. **2** an inferior or useless remnant.

faggot /'fagət/ *n.* & *v.* ● *n.* **1** (usu. in *pl.*) *Brit.* a ball or roll of seasoned chopped liver etc., baked or fried. **2** (*US* **fagot**) **a** a bundle of sticks or twigs bound together as fuel. **b** a bundle of iron rods for heat treatment. **c** a bunch of herbs. **3** *slang* **a** *Brit. derog.* an unpleasant woman. **b** *N. Amer. offens.* a male homosexual. ● *v.tr.* (**faggoted**, **faggoting**; *US* **fagoted**, **fagoting**) **1** bind in or make into faggots. **2** join by faggoting (see FAGGOTING). □ **faggoty** *adj.* [Middle English from Old French *fagot*, of uncertain origin]

faggoting /'fagətɪŋ/ *n.* (*US* **fagoting**) **1** embroidery in which threads are fastened together like a faggot. **2** the joining of materials in a similar manner.

fah /fɑː/ *n.* (also **fa**) *Mus.* **1** (in tonic sol-fa) the fourth note of a major scale. **2** the note F in the fixed-doh system. [Middle English *fa* from Latin *famuli*: see GAMUT]

Fahr. *abbr.* Fahrenheit.

Fahrenheit /ˈfar(ə)nhʌɪt, ˈfɑːr-/ *adj.* of or measured on a scale of temperature on which water freezes at 32° and boils at 212° under standard conditions. [named after G. *Fahrenheit*, German physicist d. 1736]

faience /fʌɪˈɒ̃s, feɪ-, -ˈɑːns/ *n.* decorated and glazed earthenware and porcelain, e.g. delft or majolica. [French *faïence* from *Faenza*, a city in Italy (originally denoting pottery made there)]

fail /feɪl/ *v.* & *n.* ● *v.* **1** *intr.* not succeed (*failed in persuading; failed to qualify; tried but failed*). **2 a** *tr.* & *intr.* be unsuccessful in (an examination, test, interview, etc.); be rejected as a candidate. **b** *tr.* (of a commodity etc.) not pass (a test of quality). **c** *tr.* reject (a candidate etc.); adjudge unsuccessful. **3** *intr.* be unable to; neglect to; choose not to (*I fail to see the reason; he failed to appear*). **4** *tr.* disappoint; let down; not serve when needed. **5** *intr.* (of supplies, crops, etc.) be or become lacking or insufficient. **6** *intr.* become weaker; cease functioning; break down (*her health is failing; the engine has failed*). **7** *intr.* **a** (of an enterprise) collapse; come to nothing. **b** become bankrupt. ● *n.* a failure in an examination or test. □ **without fail** for certain, whatever happens. [Middle English from Old French *faillir* (*v.*), *fail(l)e* (*n.*), ultimately from Latin *fallere* 'deceive']

failed /feɪld/ *adj.* **1** unsuccessful; not good enough (*a failed actor*). **2** weak, deficient; broken-down (*a failed crop; a failed battery*).

failing /ˈfeɪlɪŋ/ *n.* & *prep.* ● *n.* a fault or shortcoming; a weakness, esp. in character. ● *prep.* in default of; if not.

fail-safe *adj.* reverting to a safe condition in the event of a breakdown etc.

failure /ˈfeɪljə/ *n.* **1** lack of success; failing. **2** an unsuccessful person, thing, or attempt. **3** non-performance, non-occurrence. **4** breaking down or ceasing to function (*heart failure; engine failure*). **5** running short of supply etc. **6** bankruptcy, collapse. [earlier *failer* from Anglo-French, = Old French *faillir* FAIL]

fain /feɪn/ *adj.* & *adv.* *archaic* ● *predic.adj.* (foll. by *to* + infin.) **1** willing under the circumstances to. **2** left with no alternative but to. ● *adv.* gladly (esp. *would fain*). [Old English *fægen*, from Germanic]

fainéant /ˈfeɪneɪɒ̃/ *n.* & *adj.* ● *n.* an idle or ineffective person. ● *adj.* idle, inactive. [French, from *fait* 'does' + *néant* 'nothing']

faint /feɪnt/ *adj.*, *v.*, & *n.* ● *adj.* **1** indistinct, pale, dim; quiet; not clearly perceived. **2** (of a person) weak or giddy; inclined to faint. **3** slight, remote, inadequate (*a faint chance*). **4** feeble, half-hearted (*faint praise*). **5** = FEINT[2]. ● *v.intr.* **1** lose consciousness from a drop in blood pressure. **2** become faint. ● *n.* a sudden loss of consciousness; fainting. □ **not have the faintest** *colloq.* have no idea. □ **faintness** *n.* [Middle English from Old French, past part. of *faindre* FEIGN]

faint heart *n.* a cowardly nature.

faint-hearted *adj.* cowardly, timid. □ **faint-heartedly** *adv.* **faint-heartedness** *n.*

faintly /ˈfeɪntli/ *adv.* **1** very slightly (*faintly amused*). **2** indistinctly, feebly.

fair[1] /fɛː/ *adj.*, *adv.*, *n.*, & *v.* ● *adj.* **1** just, unbiased, equitable; in accordance with the rules. **2** blond; light or pale in colour or complexion. **3 a** of (only) moderate quality or amount; average. **b** considerable, satisfactory (*a fair chance of success*). **4** (of weather) fine and dry; (of the wind) favourable. **5** clean, clear, unblemished (*fair copy*). **6** beautiful, attractive. **7** *archaic* kind, gentle. **8 a** specious (*fair speeches*). **b** complimentary (*fair words*). **9** *Austral.* & *NZ* complete, unquestionable. ● *adv.* **1** in a fair manner (*play fair*). **2** *Brit.* exactly, completely (*was hit fair on the jaw*). ● *n.* **1** a fair thing. **2** *archaic* a beautiful woman. ● *v.* **1** *tr.* make (the surface of a ship, aircraft, etc.) smooth and streamlined. **2** *intr. dial.* (of the weather) become fair. □ **fair and square** *adv.* & *adj.* **1** exactly. **2** straightforward, honest, above board. **fair crack of the whip** see CRACK. **a fair deal** equitable treatment. **fair dinkum** see DINKUM. **fair dos** /duːz/ *Brit. colloq.* fair shares. **fair enough** *colloq.* that is reasonable or acceptable. **fair name** a good reputation. **fair's fair** *colloq.* all involved should act fairly. **a fair treat** *colloq.* a very enjoyable or attractive thing or person. **for fair** *US slang* completely. **in a fair way to** likely to. □ **fairish** *adj.* **fairness** *n.* [Old English *fæger*, from Germanic]

fair[2] /fɛː/ *n.* (also *pseudo-archaic* **fayre**) **1** a gathering of stalls, amusements, etc., for public (usu. outdoor) entertainment. **2** a periodical gathering for the sale of goods, often with entertainments. **3** an exhibition, esp. to promote particular products. [Middle English via Old French *feire* from Late Latin *feria*, sing. from Latin *feriae* 'holiday']

fair game *n.* a thing or person one may legitimately pursue, exploit, etc.

fairground /ˈfɛːgraʊnd/ *n.* an outdoor area where a fair is held.

fairing[1] /ˈfɛːrɪŋ/ *n.* **1** a streamlining structure added to a ship, aircraft, vehicle, etc. **2** the process of streamlining. [FAIR[1] *v.* 1 + -ING[1]]

fairing[2] /ˈfɛːrɪŋ/ *n. Brit. archaic* a present bought at a fair.

Fair Isle *n.* (also *attrib.*) a piece of knitwear knitted in a characteristic particoloured design. [*Fair Isle* in the Shetlands, where the design was first devised]

fairlead /ˈfɛːliːd/ *n. Naut.* a device to guide rope etc., e.g. to prevent cutting or chafing.

fairly /ˈfɛːli/ *adv.* **1** in a fair manner; justly. **2** moderately, acceptably (*fairly good*). **3** to a noticeable degree (*fairly narrow*). **4** utterly, completely (*fairly beside himself*). **5** actually (*fairly jumped for joy*). □ **fairly and squarely** = *fair and square* (see FAIR[1]).

fair-minded *adj.* just, impartial. □ **fair-mindedly** *adv.* **fair-mindedness** *n.*

fair play *n.* reasonable treatment or behaviour.

fair rent *n.* the amount of rent which a tenant may reasonably be expected to pay according to established guidelines.

fair sex *n.* (prec. by *the*) women.

fair-spoken *adj.* courteous.

fairwater /ˈfɛːwɔːtə/ *n.* a structure on a ship etc. assisting its passage through water.

fairway /ˈfɛːweɪ/ *n.* **1** a navigable channel; a regular course or track of a ship. **2** the part of a golf course between a tee and its green, kept free of rough grass.

fair-weather friend *n.* a friend or ally who is unreliable in times of difficulty.

fairy /ˈfɛːri/ *n.* & *adj.* ● *n.* (*pl.* **-ies**) **1** a small imaginary being of human form, believed to possess magical powers. **2** *slang offens.* a male homosexual. ● *adj.* of fairies, fairy-like, delicate, small. □ **fairy-like** *adj.* [Middle English from Old French *faerie*, from *fae* FAY]

fairy armadillo *n.* a very small furry burrowing armadillo of the genus *Chlamyphorus*.

fairy cake *n. Brit.* a small individual usu. iced sponge cake.

fairy cycle *n. Brit.* a small bicycle for a child.

fairy godmother *n.* a benefactress.

fairyland /ˈfɛːrɪland/ *n.* **1** the imaginary home of fairies. **2** an enchanted region.

fairy lights *n.pl.* esp. *Brit.* small coloured lights, esp. for outdoor decoration.

fairy ring *n.* a ring of darker grass caused by fungi.

fairy story *n.* (also **fairy tale**) **1** a children's tale about fairies. **2** an incredible story; a fabrication.

fait accompli /feɪt əˈkɒ̃pli, əˈkɒmpli/ *n.* (*pl.* **faits accomplis** *pronunc.* same) a thing that has been done and is past arguing against or altering. [French, = accomplished fact]

faith /feɪθ/ *n.* **1** complete trust or confidence. **2** firm belief, esp. without logical proof. **3 a** a system of religious belief (*the Christian faith*). **b** belief in religious doctrines. **c** spiritual apprehension of divine truth apart from proof. **d** things believed or to be believed. **4** duty or commitment to fulfil a trust, promise, etc.; obligation, allegiance (*keep faith*). **5** (*attrib.*) concerned with a supposed ability to cure by faith rather than treatment (*faith healing*). [Middle English via Anglo-French *fed* and Old French *feid* from Latin *fides*]

faithful /ˈfeɪθfʊl, -f(ə)l/ *adj.* **1** showing faith. **2** (often foll. by *to*) loyal, trustworthy, constant. **3** accurate; true to fact (*a faithful account*). **4 a** (**the Faithful**) the believers in a religion, esp. Muslims or Christians. **b** (**the faithful**) the loyal adherents of a political party. ◻ **faithfulness** *n.*

faithfully /ˈfeɪθfʊli, -f(ə)li/ *adv.* in a faithful manner. ◻ **yours faithfully** esp. *Brit.* a formula for ending a business or formal letter.

faith healing *n.* healing achieved by faith and prayer as opposed to conventional medicine. ◻ **faith healer** *n.*

faithless /ˈfeɪθlɪs/ *adj.* **1** false, unreliable, disloyal. **2** without religious faith. ◻ **faithlessly** *adv.* **faithlessness** *n.*

fajita /fəˈhiːtə, fəˈdʒiːtə/ *n.* a kind of soft tortilla wrapped around spiced meats, cheese, salad, etc. [Mexican Spanish]

fake[1] /feɪk/ *n., adj., & v.* ● *n.* **1** a thing or person that is not genuine. **2** a trick. ● *adj.* counterfeit; not genuine. ● *v.tr.* **1** make (a false thing) appear genuine; forge, counterfeit. **2** make a pretence of having (a feeling, illness, etc.). ◻ **faker** *n.* **fakery** *n.* [obsolete *feak, feague* 'thrash' from German *fegen* 'sweep, thrash']

fake[2] /feɪk/ *n. & v. Naut.* ● *n.* one round of a coil of rope. ● *v.tr.* coil (rope). [17th c.: perhaps related to Scottish *faik* 'fold']

fakir /ˈfeɪkɪə, ˈfa-/ *n.* (also **faquir**) a Muslim or (rarely) Hindu religious mendicant or ascetic. [Arabic *fakīr* 'needy man']

falafel var. of FELAFEL.

Falange /fəˈlan(d)ʒ, fəˈlɑːn(d)ʒ/ *n.* the Fascist movement in Spain, founded in 1933. ◻ **Falangism** *n.* **Falangist** *n.* [Spanish, = PHALANX]

Falasha /fəˈlɑːʃə/ *n.* (*pl.* same or **Falashas**) an Ethiopian holding the Jewish faith. [Amharic, = exile, immigrant]

falcate /ˈfalkeɪt/ *adj. Anat.* curved like a sickle. [Latin *falcatus* from *falx falcis* 'sickle']

falchion /ˈfɔːl(t)ʃ(ə)n/ *n. hist.* a broad curved sword with a convex edge. [Middle English *fauchoun* from Old French *fauchon*, ultimately from Latin *falx falcis* 'sickle']

falciform /ˈfalsɪfɔːm/ *adj. Anat.* curved like a sickle. [Latin *falx falcis* 'sickle']

falcon /ˈfɔː(l)k(ə)n, ˈfɒlk(ə)n/ *n.* **1** any diurnal bird of prey of the family Falconidae, having long pointed wings, and sometimes trained to hunt small game for sport. **2** (in falconry) a female falcon (cf. TERCEL). [Middle English via Old French *faucon* from Late Latin *falco -onis*, perhaps from Latin *falx* 'scythe', or from Germanic]

falconer /ˈfɔː(l)k(ə)nə, ˈfɒlk(ə)nə/ *n.* **1** a keeper and trainer of hawks. **2** a person who hunts with hawks. [Middle English from Anglo-French *fauconer*, Old French *fauconier* (as FALCON)]

falconet /ˈfɔː(l)k(ə)nɪt/ *n.* **1** *hist.* a light cannon. **2** *Zool.* a small falcon. [sense 1 from Italian *falconetto*, diminutive of *falcone* FALCON: sense 2 from FALCON + -ET[1]]

falconry /ˈfɔː(l)k(ə)nri, ˈfɒlk(ə)nri/ *n.* the breeding and training of hawks; the sport of hawking. [French *fauconnerie* (as FALCON)]

falderal /ˈfaldəral/ *n.* (also **folderol** /ˈfɒldərɒl/) **1** a gewgaw or trifle. **2** a nonsensical refrain in a song. **3** esp. *N. Amer.* nonsense; trivial display. [perhaps from *falbala* 'trimming on a dress': cf. FURBELOW]

faldstool /ˈfɔːldstuːl/ *n.* **1** a bishop's backless folding chair. **2** a small movable desk for kneeling at prayer. [Old English *fældestōl* from medieval Latin *faldistolium*, from West Germanic (as FOLD[1], STOOL)]

fall /fɔːl/ *v. & n.* ● *v.intr.* (*past* **fell** /fɛl/; *past part.* **fallen** /ˈfɔːl(ə)n/) **1 a** go or come down freely; descend rapidly from a higher to a lower level (*fell from the top floor*; *rain was falling*). **b** drop or be dropped (*supplies fell by parachute*; *the curtain fell*). **2 a** (often foll. by *over*) cease to stand upright (*fell into my arms*; *fell over the chair*). **b** come suddenly to the ground. **c** prostrate oneself in order to worship or implore. **3** (foll. by *into*) stumble or be drawn into (a trap, an error, etc.). **4** become detached and descend or disappear. **5** take a downward direction: **a** (of hair, clothing, etc.) hang down. **b** (of ground etc.) slope. **c** (foll. by *into*) (of a river etc.) discharge into. **6 a** find a lower level; sink lower. **b** subside, abate. **7** (of a barometer, thermometer, etc.) show a lower reading. **8** occur; become apparent or present (*darkness fell*). **9** decline, diminish (*demand is falling*; *standards have fallen*). **10 a** (of the face) show dismay or disappointment. **b** (of the eyes or a glance) look downwards. **11 a** lose power or status (*the government will fall*). **b** lose esteem, moral integrity, etc. **12** commit sin; yield to temptation. **13** take or have a particular direction or place (*his eye fell on me*; *the accent falls on the first syllable*). **14 a** find a place; be naturally divisible (*the subject falls into three parts*). **b** (foll. by *under, within*) be classed among. **15** occur at a specified time (*Easter falls early this year*). **16** come by chance or duty (*it fell to me to answer*). **17 a** pass into a specified condition (*fall into decay*; *fell ill*). **b** become (*fall asleep*). **18 a** (of a position etc.) be overthrown or captured; succumb to attack. **b** be defeated; fail. **19** die (*fall in battle*). **20** (foll. by *on, upon*) **a** attack. **b** meet with. **c** embrace or embark on avidly. **21** (foll. by *to* + verbal noun) begin (*fell to wondering*). **22** (foll. by *to*) lapse, revert (*revenues fall to the Crown*). ● *n.* **1** the act or an instance of falling; a sudden rapid descent. **2** that which falls or has fallen, e.g. snow, rocks, etc. **3** the recorded amount of rainfall etc. **4** a decline or diminution. **5** overthrow, downfall (*the fall of Rome*). **6 a** succumbing to temptation. **b** (**the Fall**) the sin of Adam and its consequences, as described in Genesis. **7 a** (of material, land, light, etc.) a downward direction; a slope. **b** a downward difference in height (*a fall of 3 inches from back to front*). **8** (also **Fall**) *N. Amer.* autumn. **9 a** (esp. in *pl.*) a waterfall, cataract, or cascade. **b** a long hairpiece. **10** *Mus.* a cadence. **11 a** a wrestling bout; a throw in wrestling which keeps the opponent on the ground for a specified time. **b** a controlled act of falling, esp. as a stunt or in judo etc. **12 a** the birth of young of certain animals. **b** the number of young born. **13** a rope of a hoisting-tackle. ◻ **fall about** *Brit. colloq.* be helpless, esp. with laughter. **fall apart** (or **to pieces**) **1** break into pieces. **2** (of a situation etc.) disintegrate; be reduced to chaos. **3** lose one's capacity to cope. **fall away 1** (of a surface) incline abruptly. **2** become few or thin; gradually vanish. **3** desert, revolt; abandon one's principles. **fall back** retreat. **fall back on** have recourse to in difficulty. **fall behind 1** be outstripped by one's competitors etc.; lag. **2** be in arrears. **fall down** (often foll. by *on*) fail; perform poorly; fail to deliver (payment etc.). **fall for** *colloq.* **1** be captivated or deceived by. **2** yield to the charms or merits of. **fall foul** (*N. Amer.* also **afoul**) **of** come into conflict with; quarrel with. **fall in 1 a** take one's place in military formation. **b** (as *int.*) the order to do this. **2** collapse inwards. **fall in love** see LOVE. **fall into line 1** take one's place in the ranks. **2** conform or collaborate with others. **fall into place** begin to make sense or cohere. **fall in with 1** meet by chance. **2** agree with; accede to; humour. **3** coincide with. **fall off 1** (of demand etc.) decrease, deteriorate. **2** withdraw. **fall out 1** quarrel. **2** (of the hair, teeth, etc.) become detached. **3** *Mil.* come out of formation. **4** result; come to pass; occur. **fall out of** gradually discontinue (a habit etc.). **fall over oneself** *colloq.* **1** be eager or competitive. **2** be awkward, stumble through haste, confusion, etc. **fall short 1** be or become deficient or inadequate. **2** (of a missile etc.) not reach its target. **fall short of** fail to reach or obtain. **fall through** fail; come to nothing; miscarry. **fall to** begin an activity, e.g. eating or working. [Old English *fallan*, *feallan*, from Germanic]

fallacy /'faləsi/ *n.* (*pl.* **-ies**) **1** a mistaken belief, esp. based on unsound argument. **2** faulty reasoning; misleading or unsound argument. **3** *Logic* a flaw that vitiates an argument. □ **fallacious** /fə'leɪʃəs/ *adj.* **fallaciously** /fə'leɪʃəsli/ *adv.* **fallaciousness** /fə'leɪʃəsnɪs/ *n.* [Latin *fallacia* via *fallax -acis* 'deceiving' from *fallere* 'deceive']

fall-back *n. & adj.* ● *n.* **1** a reserve; something that may be used in an emergency, esp. *Brit.* a fall-back wage. **2** a falling back or reduction. ● *attrib.adj.* **1** reserve, emergency. **2** *Brit.* (of a wage) comprising a minimum amount, paid when no work is available.

fallen /'fɔːl(ə)n/ *past part.* of FALL *v.* ● *adj.* **1** (*attrib.*) having lost one's honour or reputation. **2** killed in war. □ **fallenness** /'fɔːl(ə)nnɪs/ *n.*

faller /'fɔːlə/ *n.* a person, animal, or thing that falls, esp. a person or animal in a race, or the value of shares on the stock market.

fallfish /'fɔːlfɪʃ/ *n.* (*pl.* usu. same) a N. American freshwater fish, *Semotilus corporalis*, resembling the chub.

fall guy *n. slang* **1** an easy victim. **2** a scapegoat.

fallible /'falɪb(ə)l/ *adj.* **1** capable of making mistakes. **2** liable to be erroneous. □ **fallibility** /-'bɪlɪti/ *n.* **fallibly** *adv.* [medieval Latin *fallibilis* from Latin *fallere* 'deceive']

falling-out *n.* a quarrel.

falling star *n.* a meteor.

fall-off *n.* a decrease, deterioration, withdrawal, etc.

Fallopian tube /fə'ləʊpɪən/ *n. Anat.* either of two tubes in female mammals along which ova travel from the ovaries to the uterus. [*Fallopius*, Latinized name of G. *Fallopio*, Italian anatomist d. 1562]

fallout /'fɔːlaʊt/ *n.* **1** radioactive debris caused by a nuclear explosion or accident. **2** the adverse side effects of a situation etc.

fallow[1] /'faləʊ/ *adj., n., & v.* ● *adj.* **1 a** (of land) ploughed and harrowed but left unsown for a year. **b** uncultivated. **2** (of an idea etc.) potentially useful but not yet in use. **3** inactive. **4** (of a sow) not pregnant. ● *n.* fallow or uncultivated land. ● *v.tr.* break up (land) for sowing or to destroy weeds. □ **fallowness** *n.* [Middle English from Old English *fealh* (*n.*), *fealgian* (*v.*)]

fallow[2] /'faləʊ/ *adj.* of a pale brownish or reddish yellow. [Old English *falu*, *fealu*, from Germanic]

fallow deer *n.* a small deer, *Cervus dama*, having a white-spotted reddish-brown coat in the summer.

fall-pipe *n.* a downpipe.

false /fɔːls, fɒls/ *adj. & adv.* ● *adj.* **1** not according with fact; wrong, incorrect (*a false idea*). **2 a** spurious, sham, artificial (*false gods*; *false teeth*; *false modesty*). **b** acting as such; appearing to be such, esp. deceptively (*a false lining*). **3** illusory; not actually so (*a false economy*). **4** improperly so called (*false acacia*). **5** deceptive. **6** (foll. by *to*) deceitful, treacherous, or unfaithful. **7** fictitious or assumed (*gave a false name*). **8** illegal (*false imprisonment*). ● *adv.* in a false manner (esp. *play false*). □ **falsely** *adv.* **falseness** *n.* **falsity** *n.* (*pl.* **-ies**). [Old English *fals* and Old French *fals*, *faus* from Latin *falsus*, past part. of *fallere* 'deceive']

false acacia see ACACIA 2.

false alarm *n.* an alarm given needlessly.

false bedding *n. Geol.* = CROSS-BEDDING.

false colour *n.* colour introduced during the production of an image to aid interpretation and not present in the object.

false colours *n.pl. Brit.* deceitful pretence.

false dawn *n.* **1** a transient light in the east before dawn. **2** a promising sign which comes to nothing.

false gharial *n.* a crocodile, *Tomistoma schlegelii*, of Indonesia and Malaysia, similar to the gharial.

falsehood /'fɔːlshʊd, 'fɒls-/ *n.* **1** the state of being false, esp. untrue. **2** a false or untrue thing. **3 a** the act of lying. **b** a lie or lies.

false move *n.* an imprudent or careless act.

false pretences *n.pl.* misrepresentations made with intent to deceive (esp. *under false pretences*).

false rib *n.* = FLOATING RIB.

false scent *n.* **1** a scent trail laid to deceive. **2** false clues etc. intended to deflect pursuers.

false scorpion see SCORPION 2.

false start *n.* **1** an invalid or disallowed start in a race. **2** an unsuccessful attempt to begin something.

false step *n.* a slip; a mistake.

false topaz *n.* = CITRINE.

falsetto /fɔːl'setəʊ, fɒl-/ *n.* (*pl.* **-os**) **1** a method of voice production used by male singers, esp. tenors, to sing notes higher than their normal range. **2** a singer using this method. [Italian, diminutive of *falso* FALSE]

falsework /'fɔːlswəːk, 'fɒls-/ *n.* a temporary framework or support used during building to form arches etc.

falsies /'fɔːlsɪz, 'fɒls-/ *n.pl. colloq.* pads of material used to increase the apparent size of the breasts.

falsify /'fɔːlsɪfʌɪ, 'fɒls-/ *v.tr.* (**-ies**, **-ied**) **1** fraudulently alter or make false (a document, evidence, etc.). **2** misrepresent. **3** make wrong; pervert. **4** show to be false. **5** disappoint (a hope, fear, etc.). □ **falsifiable** *adj.* **falsifiability** /-fʌɪə'bɪlɪti/ *n.* **falsification** /-fɪ'keɪʃ(ə)n/ *n.* [Middle English via French *falsifier* or medieval Latin *falsificare* from Latin *falsificus* 'making false', from *falsus* 'false']

Falstaffian /fɔːl'stɑːfɪən, fɒl-/ *adj.* fat, jolly, or dissipated like Shakespeare's character Sir John Falstaff.

falter /'fɔːltə, 'fɒl-/ *v.* **1** *intr.* stumble, stagger; go unsteadily. **2** *intr.* waver; lose courage. **3** *tr. & intr.* stammer; speak hesitatingly. □ **falterer** *n.* **falteringly** *adv.* [Middle English: origin uncertain]

fame /feɪm/ *n.* **1** renown; the state of being famous. **2** *archaic* reputation. **3** *archaic* public report; rumour. [Middle English via Old French from Latin *fama*]

famed /feɪmd/ *adj.* **1** (foll. by *for*) famous; much spoken of (*famed for its good food*). **2** *archaic* currently reported.

familial /fə'mɪljəl/ *adj.* of, occurring in, or characteristic of a family or its members. [French from Latin *familia* FAMILY]

familiar /fə'mɪlɪə/ *adj. & n.* ● *adj.* **1 a** (often foll. by *to*) well known; no longer novel. **b** common, usual; often encountered or experienced. **2** (foll. by *with*) knowing a thing well or in detail (*am familiar with all the problems*). **3** (often foll. by *with*) **a** well acquainted (with a person); in close friendship; intimate. **b** sexually intimate. **4** excessively informal; impertinent. **5** unceremonious, informal. ● *n.* **1** a close friend or associate. **2** *RC Ch.* a person rendering certain services in a pope's or bishop's household. **3** (in full **familiar spirit**) a demon supposedly attending and obeying a witch etc. □ **familiarly** *adv.* [Middle English via Old French *familier* from Latin *familiaris* (as FAMILY)]

familiarity /fəmɪlɪ'arɪti/ *n.* (*pl.* **-ies**) **1** the state of being well known (*the familiarity of the scene*). **2** (foll. by *with*) close acquaintance. **3** a close relationship. **4 a** sexual intimacy. **b** (in *pl.*) acts of physical intimacy. **5** behaviour that is familiar or informal, esp. excessively so. [Middle English via Old French *familiarité* from Latin *familiaritas -tatis* (as FAMILIAR)]

familiarize /fə'mɪlɪərʌɪz/ *v.tr.* (also **-ise**) **1** (foll. by *with*) make (a person) conversant or well acquainted. **2** make (a thing) well known. □ **familiarization** /-'zeɪʃ(ə)n/ *n.* [French *familiariser* from *familiaire* (as FAMILIAR)]

famille /fa'miː, French famij/ *n.* a Chinese enamelled porcelain with a predominant colour: (***famille jaune*** /ʒəʊn, French ʒon/) yellow, (***famille noire*** /nwɑː, French nwar/) black, (***famille rose*** /rəʊz, French roz/) red, (*famille verte* /vɛːt, French vɛrt/) green. [French, = family]

family /ˈfamɪli, -m(ə)l-/ *n.* (*pl.* **-ies**) **1** a set of parents and children, or of relations, living together or not. **2 a** the members of a household, esp. parents and their children. **b** a person's children. **c** (*attrib.*) serving the needs of families (*family butcher*). **3 a** all the descendants of a common ancestor; a house, a lineage. **b** a race or group of peoples from a common stock. **4** all the languages ultimately derived from a particular early language, regarded as a group. **5** a group of persons or nations united by political or religious ties. **6** a group of objects distinguished by common features. **7** *Math.* a group of curves etc. obtained by varying one quantity. **8** *Biol.* a group of related genera of organisms within an order in taxonomic classification. □ **in the family way** *colloq.* pregnant. [Middle English from Latin *familia* 'household', from *famulus* 'servant']

family allowance *n. Brit.* a former name for CHILD BENEFIT.

family credit *n.* (in the UK) a regular payment by the state to a family with an income below a certain level.

Family Division *n.* (in the UK) a division of the High Court dealing with adoption, divorce, etc.

family man *n.* a man having a wife and children, esp. one fond of family life.

family name *n.* a surname.

family planning *n.* birth control.

family tree *n.* a chart showing relationships and lines of descent.

famine /ˈfamɪn/ *n.* **1 a** extreme scarcity of food. **b** a shortage of something specified (*a labour famine*). **2** *archaic* hunger, starvation. [Middle English from Old French, from *faim*, from Latin *fames* 'hunger']

famish /ˈfamɪʃ/ *v.* **1** *v.tr. & intr.* (usu. in *passive*) reduce or be reduced to extreme hunger. **2** *intr. colloq.* feel very hungry. [Middle English from obsolete *fame*, from Old French *afamer*, ultimately from Latin *fames* 'hunger']

famous /ˈfeɪməs/ *adj.* **1** (often foll. by *for*) celebrated; well known. **2** *colloq.* excellent. □ **famousness** *n.* [Middle English via Anglo-French, Old French *fameus* from Latin *famosus*, from *fama* 'fame']

famously /ˈfeɪməsli/ *adv.* **1** *colloq.* excellently (*got on famously*). **2** notably.

famulus /ˈfamjʊləs/ *n.* (*pl.* **famuli** /-lʌɪ, -liː/) *hist.* an attendant on a magician or scholar. [Latin, = servant]

fan[1] /fan/ *n. & v.* ● *n.* **1** an apparatus, usu. with rotating blades, giving a current of air for ventilation etc. **2** a device, usu. folding and forming a semicircle when spread out, for agitating the air to cool oneself. **3** anything spread out like a fan, e.g. a bird's tail or kind of ornamental vaulting (*fan tracery*). **4** a device for winnowing grain. **5** a fan-shaped deposit of alluvium, esp. where a stream begins to descend a gentler slope. **6** a small sail for keeping the head of a windmill towards the wind. ● *v.* (**fanned**, **fanning**) **1** *tr.* **a** blow a current of air on, with or as with a fan. **b** agitate (the air) with a fan. **2** *tr.* (of a breeze) blow gently on; cool. **3** *tr.* **a** winnow (grain). **b** winnow away (chaff). **4** *tr.* sweep away by or as by the wind from a fan. **5** *intr. & tr.* (usu. foll. by *out*) spread out in the shape of a fan. □ **fanlike** *adj.* **fanner** *n.* [Old English *fann* (in sense 4 of *n.*) from Latin *vannus* 'winnowing-fan']

fan[2] /fan/ *n.* a devotee of a particular activity, performer, etc. (*film fan*; *football fan*). [abbreviation of FANATIC]

fanatic /fəˈnatɪk/ *n. & adj.* ● *n.* a person filled with excessive and often misguided enthusiasm for something. ● *adj.* excessively enthusiastic. □ **fanatical** *adj.* **fanatically** *adv.* **fanaticism** /-tɪsɪz(ə)m/ *n.* **fanaticize** /-tɪsʌɪz/ *v.intr. & tr.* (also **-ise**). [originally in religious sense: French *fanatique* or Latin *fanaticus*, from *fanum* 'temple']

fan belt *n.* a belt that drives a fan to cool the radiator in a motor vehicle.

fancier /ˈfansɪə/ *n.* a connoisseur or follower of some activity or thing (*pigeon fancier*).

fanciful /ˈfansɪfʊl, -f(ə)l/ *adj.* **1** existing only in the imagination or fancy. **2** indulging in fancies; whimsical, capricious. **3** fantastically designed, ornamented, etc.; odd-looking. □ **fancifully** *adv.* **fancifulness** *n.*

fan club *n.* an organized group of devotees.

fancy /ˈfansi/ *n., adj., & v.* ● *n.* (*pl.* **-ies**) **1** an individual taste or inclination. **2** a caprice or whim. **3** a thing favoured, e.g. a horse to win a race. **4** an arbitrary supposition. **5 a** the faculty of using imagination or of inventing imagery. **b** a mental image. **6** delusion; unfounded belief. **7** (prec. by *the*) those who have a certain hobby; fanciers, esp. patrons of boxing. ● *adj.* (usu. *attrib.*) (**fancier**, **fanciest**) **1** ornamental; not plain. **2** capricious, whimsical, extravagant (*at a fancy price*). **3** based on imagination, not fact. **4** (of foods etc.) of fine quality. **5** (of flowers etc.) particoloured. **6** (of an animal) bred for particular points of beauty etc. ● *v.tr.* (**-ies**, **-ied**) **1** (foll. by *that* + clause) be inclined to suppose; rather think. **2** *Brit. colloq.* feel a desire for (*do you fancy a drink?*). **3** *Brit. colloq.* find sexually attractive. **4** *colloq.* have an unduly high opinion of (oneself, one's ability, etc.). **5** select (a horse, team, etc.) as the likely winner. **6** (in *imper.*) expressing surprise (*fancy their doing that!*). **7** picture to oneself; conceive, imagine. □ **catch** (or **take**) **a person's fancy** please or appeal to a person. **take a fancy to** become (esp. inexplicably) fond of. □ **fanciable** *adj.* (in sense 3 of *v.*). **fancily** *adv.* **fanciness** *n.* [contraction of FANTASY]

fancy dress *n.* fanciful costume, esp. for masquerading as a different person or as an animal etc. at a party.

fancy-free *adj.* (often in phr. **footloose and fancy-free**) without (esp. emotional) commitments.

fancy goods *n. pl.* ornamental novelties etc.

fancy man *n. slang derog.* **1** a woman's lover. **2** a pimp.

fancy woman *n. slang derog.* a mistress.

fancy-work *n.* ornamental sewing etc.

fan dance *n.* a dance in which the dancer is (apparently) nude and partly concealed by fans.

fandangle /fanˈdaŋg(ə)l/ *n.* **1** a fantastic ornament. **2** nonsense, tomfoolery. [perhaps from FANDANGO influenced by *newfangle*]

fandango /fanˈdaŋgəʊ/ *n.* (*pl.* **-oes** or **-os**) **1 a** a lively Spanish dance for two. **b** the music for this. **2** nonsense, tomfoolery. [Spanish: origin unknown]

fandom /ˈfandəm/ *n.* the world of fans and enthusiasts, esp. of fans of science fiction magazines and conventions.

fane /feɪn/ *n. poet.* = TEMPLE[1] *n.* 1. [Middle English from Latin *fanum*]

fanfare /ˈfanfɛː/ *n.* **1** a short showy or ceremonious sounding of trumpets, bugles, etc. **2** an elaborate welcome. [French, imitative]

fanfaronade /ˌfanfarəˈneɪd, -ˈnɑːd/ *n.* **1** arrogant talk; brag. **2** a fanfare. [French *fanfaronnade* from *fanfaron* 'braggart' (as FANFARE)]

fang /faŋ/ *n.* **1** a large sharp tooth, esp. a canine tooth of a dog or wolf. **2** (usu. in *pl.*) **a** the tooth of a venomous snake, by which poison is injected. **b** the biting mouthpart of a spider. **3** the root of a tooth or its prong. **4** *Brit. colloq.* a person's tooth. □ **fanged** *adj.* (also in *comb.*). **fangless** *adj.* [Old English via Old Norse *fang* from a Germanic root = to catch]

fan heater *n.* an electric heater in which a fan drives air over an element.

fan-jet *n.* = TURBOFAN.

fanlight /ˈfanlʌɪt/ *n.* a small originally semicircular window over a door or another window.

fan mail *n.* letters from fans.

fanny /ˈfani/ *n.* (*pl.* **-ies**) **1** *Brit. coarse slang* the female genitals. **2** *N. Amer. slang* the buttocks. [20th c.: origin unknown]

Fanny Adams /fanɪ 'adəmz/ *n. Brit. slang* **1** (also **sweet Fanny Adams**) nothing at all. **2** *Naut.* **a** tinned meat. **b** stew. [name of a murder victim *c.*1870]

■ **Usage** In sense 1, *Fanny Adams*, or its abbreviated form *FA*, is sometimes understood as a euphemism for *fuck all*.

fanny pack *n. N. Amer.* = BUMBAG.

fan palm *n.* a palm tree with fan-shaped leaves.

fantail /'fanteɪl/ *n.* **1** a pigeon with a broad tail. **2** any flycatcher of the genus *Rhipidura*, with a fan-shaped tail. **3** a fan-shaped tail or end. **4** the fan of a windmill. **5** the projecting part of a boat's stern. □ **fantailed** *adj.*

fan-tan /'fantan/ *n.* **1** a Chinese gambling game in which players try to guess the remainder after the banker has divided a number of hidden objects into four groups. **2** a card game in which players build on sequences of sevens. [Chinese, = repeated divisions]

fantasia /fan'teɪzɪə, fantə'ziːə/ *n.* a musical or other composition free in form and often in improvisatory style; a composition which is based on several familiar tunes. [Italian, = FANTASY]

fantasize /'fantəsʌɪz/ *v.* (also **phantasize**, **-ise**) **1** *intr.* have a fantasy or fanciful vision. **2** *tr.* imagine; create a fantasy about. □ **fantasist** *n.*

fantast /'fantast/ *n.* (also **phantast**) a visionary; a dreamer. [medieval Latin from Greek *phantastēs* 'boaster' via *phantazomai* 'make a show' from *phainō* 'show']

fantastic /fan'tastɪk/ *adj.* (also **fantastical**) **1** *colloq.* excellent, extraordinary. **2** extravagantly fanciful; capricious, eccentric. **3** grotesque or quaint in design etc. □ **fantasticality** /-'kalɪti/ *n.* **fantastically** *adv.* [Middle English via Old French *fantastique*, medieval Latin *fantasticus*, and Late Latin *phantasticus* from Greek *phantastikos* (as FANTAST)]

fantasticate /fan'tastɪkeɪt/ *v.tr.* make fantastic. □ **fantastication** /-'keɪʃ(ə)n/ *n.*

fantasy /'fantəsi, -zi/ *n.* & *v.* (also **phantasy**) ● *n.* (*pl.* **-ies**) **1** the faculty of inventing images, esp. extravagant or visionary ones. **2** a fanciful mental image; a daydream. **3** a whimsical speculation. **4** a fantastic invention or composition; a fantasia. **5** a genre of imaginative fiction involving fantastic stories, often in a magical pseudo-historical setting. ● *v.tr.* (**-ies**, **-ied**) imagine, fancy. [Middle English via Old French *fantasie* and Latin *phantasia* 'appearance' from Greek (as FANTAST)]

fantasy football *n.* (also **fantasy cricket** etc.) a competition in which participants select imaginary teams from among the players in a league etc. and score points according to the actual performance of their players.

Fanti /'fanti/ *n.* (also **Fante**) (*pl.* same or **Fantis**) **1** a member of a black people inhabiting southern Ghana. **2** the language of this people. [native name]

fanzine /'fanziːn/ *n.* a magazine for fans, esp. those of science fiction, sport, or popular music. [FAN[2] + MAGAZINE]

FAO *abbr.* Food and Agriculture Organization (of the United Nations).

far /fɑː/ *adv.* & *adj.* (**further**, **furthest** or **farther**, **farthest**) ● *adv.* **1** at or to or by a great distance (*far away*; *far off*; *far out*). **2** a long way (off) in space or time (*are you travelling far?*; *we talked far into the night*). **3** to a great extent or degree; by much (*far better*; *far too early*). ● *adj.* **1** situated at or extending over a great distance in space or time; remote (*a far country*). **2** more distant (*the far end of the hall*). **3** extreme (*far left*). □ **as far as 1** to the distance of (a place). **2** to the extent that (*travel as far as you like*). **by far** by a great amount. **far and away** by a very large amount. **far and near** everywhere. **far and wide** over a large area. **far be it from me** (foll. by *to* + infin.) I am reluctant to (esp. express criticism etc.). **far from** very different from being; tending to the opposite of (*the problem is far from being solved*). **go far 1** achieve much. **2** contribute greatly. **3** be adequate. **go too far** go beyond the limits of what is reasonable, polite, etc. **how far** to what extent. **so far 1** to such an extent or distance; to this point. **2** until now. **so** (or **in so**) **far as** (or **that**) to the extent that. **so far so good** progress has been satisfactory up to now. [Old English *feorr*]

farad /'farad/ *n. Electr.* the SI unit of capacitance, such that one coulomb of charge causes a potential difference of one volt (abbr.: **F**). [shortening of FARADAY]

faradaic /farə'deɪɪk/ *adj.* (also **faradic** /fə'radɪk/) *Electr.* inductive, induced. [see FARADAY]

faraday /'farədeɪ/ *n. Chem.* a unit of electric charge equal to Faraday's constant (abbr.: *F*). [named after M. *Faraday*, English physicist d. 1867]

Faraday cage *n. Electr.* an earthed metal screen used for excluding electrostatic influences.

Faraday effect *n. Physics* the rotation of the plane of polarization of electromagnetic waves in certain substances in a magnetic field.

Faraday's constant *n.* the quantity of electric charge carried by one mole of electrons (equal to 96.49 coulombs).

farandole /far(ə)n'dəʊl, 'far(ə)ndəʊl/ *n.* **1** a lively Provençal dance. **2** the music for this. [French from modern Provençal *farandoulo*]

faraway /'fɑːrəweɪ, fɑːrə'weɪ/ *attrib.adj.* **1** remote; long-past. **2** (of a look) dreamy. **3** (of a voice) sounding as if from a distance.

farce /fɑːs/ *n.* **1 a** a low comic dramatic work based on ludicrously improbable events. **b** this branch of drama. **2** absurdly futile proceedings; pretence, mockery; an instance of this. [French, originally = stuffing, from Old French *farsir* from Latin *farcire* 'to stuff', used metaphorically of interludes etc.]

farceur /fɑː'səː/ *n.* **1** a joker or wag. **2** an actor or writer of farces. [French from *farcer* 'act farces']

farcical /'fɑːsɪk(ə)l/ *adj.* **1** extremely ludicrous or futile. **2** of or like farce. □ **farcicality** /-'kalɪti/ *n.* **farcically** *adv.*

far cry *n.* (usu. foll. by *from*) a long way; a very different experience.

farcy /'fɑːsi/ *n.* glanders with inflammation of the lymph vessels. [Middle English via Old French *farcin* from Late Latin *farciminum*, from *farcire* 'to stuff']

farcy bud *n.* (also **farcy button**) a small lymphatic tumour as a result of farcy.

farded /'fɑːdɪd/ *adj. archaic* (of a face etc.) painted with cosmetics. [past part. of obsolete *fard*, from Old French *farder*]

fare /fɛː/ *n.* & *v.* ● *n.* **1 a** the price a passenger has to pay to be conveyed by bus, train, etc. **b** a passenger paying to travel in a public vehicle. **2** a range of food, esp. one provided by a restaurant etc. ● *v.intr. literary* **1** progress; get on (*how did you fare?*). **2** happen; turn out. **3** journey, go, travel. [Old English *fær*, *faru* 'journeying', *faran* (*v.*), from Germanic]

Far East *n.* (prec. by *the*) China, Japan, and other countries of E. Asia. □ **Far Eastern** *adj.*

fare stage *n. Brit.* **1** a section of a bus etc. route for which a fixed fare is charged. **2** a stop marking this.

farewell /fɛː'wɛl/ *int.* & *n.* ● *int.* goodbye, adieu. ● *n.* **1** leave-taking; departure (also *attrib.*: *a farewell kiss*). **2** parting good wishes. [Middle English, from imperative of FARE + WELL[1]]

far-fetched *adj.* (of an explanation etc.) strained, unconvincing.

far-flung *adj.* extending far; widely distributed.

far gone *adj.* **1** advanced in time. **2** *colloq.* in an advanced state of illness, drunkenness, etc.

farina /fə'rʌɪnə, -iːnə/ *n.* **1** the flour or meal of cereal, nuts, or starchy roots. **2** a powdery substance. **3** *Brit.* starch. □ **farinaceous** /farɪ'neɪʃəs/ *adj.* [Latin from *far* 'corn']

farl /fɑːl/ *n. Sc.* a thin cake, originally quadrant-shaped, of oatmeal or flour. [obsolete *fardel* 'quarter' (as FOURTH, DEAL[1])]

farm /fɑːm/ *n. & v.* ● *n.* **1** an area of land and its buildings used under one management for growing crops, rearing animals, etc. **2** a place or establishment for breeding a particular type of animal, growing fruit, etc. (*trout-farm*; *mink-farm*). **3** = FARMHOUSE. **4** a place for the storage of oil or oil products. **5** = SEWAGE FARM. ● *v.* **1 a** *tr.* use (land) for growing crops, rearing animals, etc. **b** *intr.* be a farmer; work on a farm. **2** *tr.* breed (fish etc.) commercially. **3** *tr.* (often foll. by *out*) **a** delegate or subcontract (work) to others. **b** contract (the collection of taxes) to another for a fee. **c** arrange for (a person, esp. a child) to be looked after by another, with payment. **4** *tr.* let the labour of (a person) for hire. **5** *tr.* contract to maintain and care for (a person, esp. a child) for a fixed sum. □ **farmable** *adj.* **farming** *n.* [originally applied only to leased land: Middle English via Old French *ferme* and medieval Latin *firma* 'fixed payment' from Latin *firmus* FIRM[1]]

farmer /ˈfɑːmə/ *n.* **1** a person who runs or cultivates a farm. **2** a person to whom the collection of taxes is contracted for a fee. [Middle English via Anglo-French *fermer*, Old French *fermier* from medieval Latin *firmarius*, *firmator*, from *firma* FIRM[2]]

farmhand /ˈfɑːmhand/ *n.* a worker on a farm.

farmhouse /ˈfɑːmhaʊs/ *n.* a dwelling place (esp. the main one) attached to a farm.

farmhouse loaf *n.* an oval or rectangular white loaf with a rounded top.

farmstead /ˈfɑːmstɛd/ *n.* a farm and its buildings regarded as a unit.

farmyard /ˈfɑːmjɑːd/ *n. & adj.* ● *n.* a yard or enclosure attached to a farmhouse. ● *attrib.adj.* disgusting or uncouth.

faro /ˈfɛːrəʊ/ *n.* a gambling card game in which bets are placed on the order of appearance of the cards. [French *pharaon* PHARAOH (said to have been the name of the king of hearts)]

Faroese var. of FAEROESE.

far-off *attrib.adj.* remote.

farouche /fəˈruːʃ/ *adj.* sullen, shy. [French via Old French *faroche*, *forache* and medieval Latin *forasticus* from Latin *foras* 'out of doors']

far out *adj.* (hyphenated when *attrib.*) *slang* **1** avant-garde, unconventional. **2** excellent.

farrago /fəˈrɑːgəʊ, fəˈreɪgəʊ/ *n.* (*pl.* **-os** or *US* **-oes**) a medley or hotchpotch; a confused mixture. □ **farraginous** /-ˈrɑːdʒɪnəs, -ˈreɪdʒ-/ *adj.* [Latin *farrago farraginis* 'mixed fodder' from *far* 'corn']

far-reaching *adj.* **1** widely applicable. **2** having important consequences or implications.

farrier /ˈfarɪə/ *n.* **1** a smith who shoes horses. **2** a person who treats the disease and injuries of horses. □ **farriery** *n.* [Old French *ferrier* from Latin *ferrarius*, from *ferrum* 'iron, horseshoe']

farrow /ˈfarəʊ/ *n. & v.* ● *n.* **1** a litter of pigs. **2** the birth of a litter. ● *v.tr.* (also *absol.*) (of a sow) produce (pigs). [Old English *fearh*, *færh* 'pig', from West Germanic]

farruca /fəˈruːkə/ *n.* a type of flamenco dance. [Spanish]

far-seeing *adj.* shrewd in judgement; prescient.

Farsi /ˈfɑːsiː/ *n.* the modern Persian language, the official language of Iran. [Persian: cf. PARSEE]

far-sighted *adj.* **1** having foresight, prudent. **2** esp. *N. Amer.* = LONG-SIGHTED. □ **far-sightedly** *adv.* **far-sightedness** *n.*

fart /fɑːt/ *v. & n. coarse slang* ● *v.intr.* **1** emit wind from the anus. **2** (foll. by *about*, *around*) behave foolishly; waste time. ● *n.* **1** an emission of wind from the anus. **2** an unpleasant person. [Old English (recorded in the verbal noun *feorting*) from Germanic]

farther var. of FURTHER *adv. & adj.*

farthest var. of FURTHEST.

farthing /ˈfɑːðɪŋ/ *n.* **1** *hist.*(in the UK) a former coin and monetary unit equal to a quarter of an old penny (withdrawn in 1961). **2** the least possible amount (*it doesn't matter a farthing*). [Old English *fēorthing* from *fēortha* 'fourth']

farthingale /ˈfɑːðɪŋgeɪl/ *n. hist.* a hooped petticoat or a stiff curved roll to extend a woman's skirt. [earlier *vardingale*, *verd-*, via French *verdugale* from Spanish *verdugado*, from *verdugo* 'rod']

fartlek /ˈfɑːtlɛk/ *n. Athletics* a method of training for middle- and long-distance running, mixing fast with slow work. [Swedish, from *fart* 'speed' + *lek* 'play']

Far West *n.* **1** the regions of N. America in the Rocky Mountains and along the Pacific coast. **2** *hist.* = MIDWEST.

fasces /ˈfasiːz/ *n.pl.* **1** *Rom.Hist.* a bundle of rods with a projecting axe-blade, carried by a lictor as a symbol of a magistrate's power. **2** *hist.* (in Fascist Italy) emblems of authority. [Latin, pl. of *fascis* 'bundle']

fascia /ˈfaʃɪə, ˈfeɪ-, -ʃə/ *n.* (*pl.* **fasciae** /-ʃɪiː/ or **fascias**) **1** *Archit.* **a** a long flat surface between mouldings on the architrave in classical architecture. **b** a flat board, usu. of wood, covering the ends of rafters. **2** a stripe or band. **3** /ˈfaʃə/ *Anat.* a thin sheath of fibrous tissue, esp. that enclosing a muscle or other organ. **4** = FACIA 1. **5** *Brit.* = FACIA 2. □ **fascial** *adj.* [Latin, = band, door frame, etc.]

fasciate /ˈfaʃɪeɪt, -ɪət/ *adj.* (also **fasciated**) **1** *Bot.* (of contiguous parts) compressed or growing into one. **2** striped or banded. □ **fasciation** /-ˈeɪʃ(ə)n/ *n.* [Latin *fasciatus*, past part. of *fasciare* 'swathe' (as FASCIA)]

fascicle /ˈfasɪk(ə)l/ *n.* **1** (also **fascicule** /-kjuːl/) a separately published instalment of a book, usu. not complete in itself. **2** a bunch or bundle. **3** (also **fasciculus** /faˈsɪkjʊləs/) *Anat.* a bundle of fibres. □ **fascicled** *adj.* **fascicular** /-ˈsɪkjʊlə/ *adj.* **fasciculate** /-ˈsɪkjʊlət/ *adj.* **fasciculation** /-ˈleɪʃ(ə)n/ *n.* [Latin *fasciculus* 'bundle', diminutive of *fascis*: see FASCES]

fasciitis /fasɪˈʌɪtɪs, faʃɪ-/ *n. Med.* inflammation of the fascia of a muscle etc.

fascinate /ˈfasɪneɪt/ *v.tr.* **1** capture the interest of; attract irresistibly. **2** (esp. of a snake) paralyse (a victim) with fear. □ **fascinated** *adj.* **fascinating** *adj.* **fascinatingly** *adv.* **fascination** /-ˈneɪʃ(ə)n/ *n.* **fascinator** *n.* [Latin *fascinare* from *fascinum* 'spell']

fascine /faˈsiːn/ *n.* a long faggot used for engineering purposes and (esp. in war) for lining trenches, filling ditches, etc. [French from Latin *fascina*, from *fascis* 'bundle': see FASCES]

Fascism /ˈfaʃɪz(ə)m, -sɪz(ə)m/ *n.* **1** the totalitarian principles and organization of the extreme right-wing nationalist movement in Italy (1922–43). **2** (also **fascism**) **a** any similar nationalist and authoritarian movement. **b** (loosely) any system of extreme right-wing or authoritarian views. □ **Fascist** *n. & adj.* (also **fascist**). **Fascistic** /-ˈʃɪstɪk/ *adj.* (also **fascistic**). [Italian *fascismo*, from *fascio* 'political group', from Latin *fascis* 'bundle': see FASCES]

■ **Usage** Some people find the use of *Fascism* in sense 2b unacceptable.

fashion /ˈfaʃ(ə)n/ *n. & v.* ● *n.* **1** the current popular custom or style, esp. in dress or social conduct. **2** a manner or style of doing something (*in a peculiar fashion*). **3** (in *comb.*) in a specified manner (*walk crab-fashion*). **4** fashionable society (*a woman of fashion*). ● *v.tr.* (often foll. by *into*) make into a particular or the required form. □ **after** (or **in**) **a fashion** as well as is practicable, though not satisfactorily. **in** (or **out of**) **fashion** fashionable (or not fashionable) at the time in question. □ **fashioner** *n.* [Middle English via Anglo-French *fasun*, Old French *façon* from Latin *factio -onis*, from *facere fact-* 'do, make']

fashionable /ˈfaʃ(ə)nəb(ə)l/ *adj.* **1** following, suited to, or influenced by the current fashion. **2** characteristic of or favoured by those who are leaders of social fashion. □ **fashionability** /-ˈbɪlɪti/ *n.* **fashionableness** *n.* **fashionably** *adv.*

fashion victim *n.* a slavish follower of trends in fashion.

fast[1] /fɑːst/ *adj. & adv.* ● *adj.* **1** rapid, quick-moving. **2** capable of high speed (*a fast car*). **3** enabling or causing or intended for high speed (*a fast road; fast bowler*). **4** (of a clock etc.) showing a time ahead of the correct time. **5** (of a pitch or ground etc. in a sport) likely to make the ball bounce or run quickly. **6 a** (of a photographic film) needing only a short exposure. **b** (of a lens) having a large aperture. **7 a** firmly fixed or attached. **b** secure; firmly established (*a fast friendship*). **8** (of a colour) not fading in light or when washed. **9** (of a person) immoral, dissipated. ● *adv.* **1** quickly; in quick succession. **2** firmly, fixedly, tightly, securely (*stand fast; eyes fast shut*). **3** soundly, completely (*fast asleep*). **4** close, immediately (*fast on their heels*). □ **pull a fast one** (often foll. by *on*) *colloq.* try to deceive or gain an unfair advantage. [Old English *fæst*, from Germanic]

fast[2] /fɑːst/ *v. & n.* ● *v.intr.* abstain from all or some kinds of food or drink, esp. as a religious observance. ● *n.* an act or period of fasting. [Old Norse *fasta*, from Germanic]

fast and furious *adv. & adj.* ● *adv.* **1** rapidly. **2** eagerly, uproariously. ● *adj.* (of mirth etc.) eager, uproarious.

fastback /ˈfɑːs(t)bak/ *n.* **1** a motor car with the rear sloping continuously down to the bumper. **2** such a rear.

fast breeder *n.* (also **fast breeder reactor**) a reactor using fast neutrons to produce the same fissile material as it uses.

fast buck see BUCK².

fasten /ˈfɑːs(ə)n/ *v.* **1** *tr.* make or become fixed or secure. **2** *tr.* (foll. by *in, up*) lock securely; shut in. **3** *tr.* **a** (foll. by *on, upon*) direct (a look, thoughts, etc.) fixedly or intently. **b** focus or direct the attention fixedly upon (*fastened him with her eyes*). **4** *tr.* (foll. by *on, upon*) fix (a designation or imputation etc.). **5** *intr.* (foll. by *on, upon*) **a** take hold of. **b** single out. **6** *tr.* (foll. by *off*) fix with stitches or a knot. □ **fastener** *n.* [Old English *fæstnian*, from Germanic]

fastening /ˈfɑːs(ə)nɪŋ/ *n.* a device that fastens something; a fastener.

fast food *n.* food that can be prepared and served quickly and easily, esp. in a snack bar or restaurant.

fast forward *n., adj., & v.* ● *n.* **1** a control on a tape or video player for advancing the tape rapidly. **2** = CUE¹ *n.* 3. ● *adj.* (**fast-forward**) designating such a control. ● *v.tr.* (**fast-forward**) advance (a tape) rapidly, sometimes while simultaneously playing it at high speed.

fastidious /faˈstɪdɪəs/ *adj.* **1** very careful in matters of choice or taste; fussy. **2** easily disgusted; squeamish. □ **fastidiously** *adv.* **fastidiousness** *n.* [Middle English from Latin *fastidiosus*, from *fastidium* 'loathing']

fastigiate /faˈstɪdʒɪət, -ɪeɪt/ *adj. Bot.* **1** having a conical or tapering outline. **2** having parallel upright branches. [Latin *fastigium* 'gable-top']

fast lane *n.* **1** a lane on a motorway etc. intended for overtaking. **2** (usu. hyphenated when *attrib.*) a hectic lifestyle.

fastness /ˈfɑːs(t)nɪs/ *n.* **1** a stronghold or fortress. **2** the state of being secure. [Old English *fæstnes* (as FAST¹)]

fast neutron *n.* a neutron with high kinetic energy, esp. not slowed by a moderator etc. (cf. SLOW NEUTRON).

fast reactor *n.* a nuclear reactor using mainly fast neutrons.

fast-talk *v.tr. N. Amer. colloq.* persuade by rapid or deceitful talk.

fast track *n.* (usu. hyphenated when *attrib.*) a route, course, method, etc., which provides for more rapid results than usual (*on the fast track for promotion*).

fast-wind *v.tr.* wind (magnetic tape) rapidly backwards or forwards.

fast worker *n. colloq.* a person who achieves quick results, esp. in love affairs.

fat /fat/ *n., adj., & v.* ● *n.* **1** a natural oily or greasy substance occurring esp. in animal bodies. **2** the part of anything containing this. **3** excessive presence of fat in a person or animal; corpulence. **4** *Chem.* any of a group of natural esters of glycerol and various fatty acids existing as solids at room temperature. ● *adj.* (**fatter, fattest**) **1** (of a person or animal) having excessive fat; corpulent. **2** (of an animal) made plump for slaughter; fatted. **3** containing much fat. **4** greasy, oily, unctuous. **5** (of land or resources) fertile, rich; yielding abundantly. **6 a** thick, substantial in content (*a fat book*). **b** substantial as an asset or opportunity (*a fat cheque; was given a fat part in the play*). **7 a** (of coal) bituminous. **b** (of clay etc.) sticky. **8** *colloq. iron.* very little; not much (*a fat chance; a fat lot*). ● *v.tr. & intr.* (**fatted, fatting**) make or become fat. □ **the fat is in the fire** trouble is imminent. **kill the fatted calf** celebrate, esp. at a prodigal's return (Luke 15). **live off** (or **on**) **the fat of the land** have the best of everything. □ **fatless** *adj.* **fatly** *adv.* **fatness** *n.* **fattish** *adj.* [Old English *fæt* (*adj.*), *fǣttian* (*v.*), from Germanic]

fatal /ˈfeɪt(ə)l/ *adj.* **1** causing or ending in death (*a fatal accident*). **2** (often foll. by *to*) destructive; ruinous; ending in disaster (*was fatal to their chances; made a fatal mistake*). **3** fateful, decisive. □ **fatally** *adv.* [Middle English from Old French *fatal* or Latin *fatalis* (as FATE)]

fatalism /ˈfeɪt(ə)lɪz(ə)m/ *n.* **1** the belief that all events are predetermined and therefore inevitable. **2** a submissive attitude to events as being inevitable. □ **fatalist** *n.* **fatalistic** /-ˈlɪstɪk/ *adj.* **fatalistically** /-ˈlɪstɪk(ə)li/ *adv.*

fatality /fəˈtalɪti, feɪ-/ *n.* (*pl.* **-ies**) **1 a** an occurrence of death by accident or in war etc. **b** a person killed in this way. **2** a fatal influence. **3** a predestined liability to disaster. **4** subjection to or the supremacy of fate. [French *fatalité* or Late Latin *fatalitas* from Latin *fatalis* FATAL]

fat cat *n. slang derog.* a wealthy person, esp. a wealthy businessman, politician, or civil servant.

fate /feɪt/ *n. & v.* ● *n.* **1** a power regarded as predetermining events unalterably. **2 a** the future regarded as determined by such a power. **b** an individual's appointed lot. **c** the ultimate condition or end of a person or thing (*that sealed our fate*). **3** death, destruction. **4** (usu. **Fate**) a goddess of destiny, esp. one of three Greek or Scandinavian goddesses. ● *v.tr.* **1** (usu. in *passive*) preordain (*was fated to win*). **2** (as **fated** *adj.*) doomed to destruction. □ **fate worse than death** see DEATH. [Middle English from Italian *fato* and Latin *fatum* 'that which is spoken', from *fari* 'speak']

fateful /ˈfeɪtfʊl, -f(ə)l/ *adj.* **1** important, decisive; having far-reaching consequences. **2** controlled as if by fate. **3** causing or likely to cause disaster. **4** prophetic. □ **fatefully** *adv.* **fatefulness** *n.*

fat farm *n. colloq.* esp. *N. Amer.* a health farm for overweight people.

fat-head *n. colloq.* a stupid person. □ **fat-headed** *adj.* **fat-headedness** *n.*

fat hen *n.* the white goosefoot, *Chenopodium album.*

father /ˈfɑːðə/ *n. & v.* ● *n.* **1 a** a man in relation to a child or children born from his fertilization of an ovum. **b** (in full **adoptive father**) a man who has continuous care of a child, esp. by adoption. **2** any male animal in relation to its offspring. **3** (usu. in *pl.*) a progenitor or forefather. **4** an originator, designer, or early leader. **5** a person who deserves special respect (*the father of his country*). **6** (**Fathers** or **Fathers of the Church**) early Christian theologians whose writings are regarded as especially authoritative. **7** (also **Father**) **a** (often as a title or form of address) a priest, esp. of a religious order. **b** a religious leader. **8** (**the Father**) (in Christian belief) the first person of the Trinity. **9** (**Father**) a venerable person, esp. as a title in personifications (*Father Time*). **10** the oldest member or doyen (*Father of the House*). **11** (usu. in *pl.*) the leading men or elders in a city or state (*city fathers*). ● *v.tr.* **1** beget; be the father of. **2** behave as a father towards. **3** originate (a scheme etc.). **4** appear as or admit that one is the father or originator of. **5** (foll. by *on*) assign the paternity of (a child, book) to a person. □ **fatherhood** *n.* **fatherless**

adj. **fatherlessness** n. **fatherlike** adj. & adv. [Old English *fæder* with many Germanic cognates: related to Latin *pater*, Greek *patēr*]

Father Christmas n. = SANTA CLAUS.

father figure n. an older man who is respected like a father; a trusted leader.

father-in-law n. (*pl.* **fathers-in-law**) the father of one's husband or wife.

fatherland /ˈfɑːðəland/ n. one's native country, now esp. Germany.

fatherly /ˈfɑːðəli/ adj. **1** like or characteristic of a father in affection, care, etc. (*fatherly concern*). **2** of or proper to a father. □ **fatherliness** n.

father of chapel n. (also **father of the chapel**) *Brit.* the shop steward of a printers' chapel.

Father's Day n. a day (usu. the third Sunday in June) established for a special tribute to fathers.

Father Time see TIME n. 2b.

fathom /ˈfað(ə)m/ n. & v. ● n. (*pl.* often **fathom** when prec. by a number) **1** a measure of six feet, esp. used in taking depth soundings. **2** *Brit.* a quantity of wood six feet square in cross-section. ● v.tr. **1** grasp or comprehend (a problem or difficulty). **2** measure the depth of (water) with a sounding line. □ **fathomable** adj. **fathomless** adj. [Old English *fæthm* 'outstretched arms', from Germanic]

fathometer /faˈðɒmɪtə/ n. a type of echo sounder.

fatigue /fəˈtiːg/ n. & v. ● n. **1** extreme tiredness after exertion. **2** weakness in materials, esp. metal, caused by repeated variations of stress. **3** a reduction in the efficiency of a muscle, organ, etc., after prolonged activity. **4** an activity that causes fatigue. **5** (in *pl.*) esp. *N. Amer.* clothing of various types worn by military personnel (*camouflage fatigues*; *combat fatigues*). **6** *archaic* **a** a non-military duty in the army, often as a punishment. **b** (in full **fatigue-party**) a group of soldiers ordered to do such a duty. **c** (in *pl.*) clothing worn for such a duty ● v.tr. (**fatigues**, **fatigued**, **fatiguing**) cause fatigue in; tire, exhaust. □ **fatiguable** adj. (also **fatigable**). **fatiguability** /-gəˈbɪlɪti/ n. (also **fatigability**). **fatigueless** adj. [French *fatigue*, *fatiguer* from Latin *fatigare* 'tire out']

Fatiha /ˈfɑːtɪə, ˈfat-/ n. (also **Fatihah**) the short first sura of the Koran, used by Muslims as a prayer. [Arabic *fātiḥa* 'opening' from *fataḥa* 'to open']

Fatimid /ˈfatɪmɪd/ n. & adj. (also **Fatimite** /-mʌɪt/) ● n. **1** a descendant of Fatima, the daughter of Muhammad. **2** a member of a dynasty ruling in N. Africa in the 10th–12th c. ● adj. of or relating to the Fatimids.

fatism var. of FATTISM.

fatist var. of FATTIST (see FATTISM).

fatling /ˈfatlɪŋ/ n. a young fatted animal.

fatso /ˈfatsəʊ/ n. (*pl.* **-oes**) *slang offens.* a fat person. [probably from FAT or the designation *Fats*]

fatstock /ˈfatstɒk/ n. *Brit.* livestock fattened for slaughter.

fatten /ˈfat(ə)n/ v. **1** *tr.* & *intr.* (esp. with reference to meat-producing animals) make or become fat. **2** *tr.* enrich (soil).

fattening /ˈfat(ə)nɪŋ/ adj. (of foods) easily causing an increase in weight.

fattism /ˈfatɪz(ə)m/ n. (also **fatism**) prejudice or discrimination against fat people. □ **fattist** n. & adj. (also **fatist**).

fatty /ˈfati/ adj. & n. ● adj. (**fattier**, **fattiest**) **1** like fat; oily, greasy. **2** consisting of or containing fat; adipose. **3** marked by abnormal deposition of fat, esp. in fatty degeneration. ● n. (*pl.* **-ies**) *colloq.* a fat person (esp. as a nickname). □ **fattiness** n.

fatty acid n. any of a class of organic compounds consisting of a hydrocarbon chain and a terminal carboxyl group, esp. those occurring as constituents of lipids.

fatty oil n. = FIXED OIL.

fatuous /ˈfatjʊəs/ adj. vacantly silly; purposeless, idiotic. □ **fatuity** /fəˈtjuːɪti/ n. (*pl.* **-ies**). **fatuously** adv. **fatuousness** n. [Latin *fatuus* 'foolish']

fatwa /ˈfatwɑː/ n. (in Islamic countries) an authoritative ruling on a religious matter. [Arabic *fatwā*]

faubourg /ˈfəʊbʊəg, French fobur/ n. a suburb, esp. of Paris. [French: cf. medieval Latin *falsus burgus* 'not the city proper']

fauces /ˈfɔːsiːz/ n.pl. *Anat.* a cavity at the back of the mouth. □ **faucial** /ˈfɔːʃ(ə)l/ adj. [Latin, = throat]

faucet /ˈfɔːsɪt/ n. esp. *US* a tap. [Middle English via Old French *fausset* 'vent-peg' from Provençal *falset*, from *falsar* 'to bore']

fault /fɔːlt, fɒlt/ n. & v. ● n. **1** a defect or imperfection of character or of structure, appearance, etc. **2** a break or other defect in an electric circuit. **3** a transgression, offence, or thing wrongly done. **4 a** *Tennis* etc. a service of the ball not in accordance with the rules. **b** (in showjumping) a penalty for an error. **5** responsibility for wrongdoing, error, etc. (*it will be your own fault*). **6** a defect regarded as the cause of something wrong (*the fault lies in the teaching methods*). **7** *Geol.* an extended break in the continuity of strata or a vein. ● v. **1** *tr.* find fault with; blame. **2** *tr.* declare to be faulty. **3** *tr.* *Geol.* break the continuity of (strata or a vein). **4** *intr.* commit a fault. **5** *intr.* *Geol.* show a fault. □ **at fault** guilty; to blame. **find fault** (often foll. by *with*) make an adverse criticism; complain. **to a fault** (usu. of a commendable quality etc.) excessively (*generous to a fault*). [Middle English *faut(e)* from Old French, ultimately from Latin *fallere* FAIL]

fault-finding n. continual criticism. □ **fault-finder** n.

faultless /ˈfɔːltlɪs, ˈfɒlt-/ adj. without fault; free from defect or error. □ **faultlessly** adv. **faultlessness** n.

faulty /ˈfɔːlti, ˈfɒlti/ adj. (**faultier**, **faultiest**) having faults; imperfect, defective. □ **faultily** adv. **faultiness** n.

faun /fɔːn/ n. one of a class of Latin rural deities with a human face and torso and a goat's horns, legs, and tail, identified with the Greek satyrs. [Middle English via Old French *faune* or Latin *Faunus*, the name of a Latin god identified with Greek Pan]

fauna /ˈfɔːnə/ n. (*pl.* **faunas**) **1** the animal life of a region or geological period (cf. FLORA). **2** a treatise on or list of this. □ **faunal** adj. **faunist** n. **faunistic** /-ˈnɪstɪk/ adj. [modern Latin, from the name of a rural goddess, sister of Faunus: see FAUN]

faute de mieux /fəʊt də ˈmjəː, French fot də mjø/ adv. for want of a better alternative. [French]

fauteuil /fəʊˈtəːi, French fotœj/ n. a kind of wooden seat in the form of an armchair with open sides and upholstered arms. [French, from Old French *faudestuel*, *faldestoel* FALDSTOOL]

fauve /fəʊv/ n. a person who practises or favours fauvism.

fauvism /ˈfəʊvɪz(ə)m/ n. a style of painting with vivid use of colour. □ **fauvist** n. [French *fauve* 'wild beast', applied to painters of the school of Matisse]

faux /fəʊ/ adj. false, imitation (*a faux fur hood*). [French, = false]

faux pas n. (*pl.* same /ˈpɑːz/) **1** a tactless mistake; a blunder. **2** a social indiscretion. [French, = false step]

fave /feɪv/ n. & adj. *slang* = FAVOURITE (esp. in show business). [abbreviation]

favela /faˈvɛlə/ n. a Brazilian shack, slum, or shanty town. [Portuguese]

favour /ˈfeɪvə/ n. & v. (*US* **favor**) ● n. **1** an act of kindness beyond what is due or usual (*did it as a favour*). **2** esteem, liking, approval, goodwill; friendly regard (*gained their favour*; *look with favour on*). **3** partiality; too lenient or generous treatment. **4** aid, support (*under favour of night*). **5** a thing given or worn as a mark of favour or support, e.g. a badge or a knot of ribbons. **6** *archaic* leave, pardon (*by your favour*). **7** *Commerce archaic* a letter (*your favour of yesterday*). ● v.tr. **1** regard or treat with favour or partiality. **2** give support or approval to; promote, prefer. **3 a** be to the advantage of (a person). **b** facilitate (a process etc.). **4** tend to confirm (an idea or theory). **5** (foll. by *with*) oblige (*favour me with a reply*). **6** (as **favoured** *adj.*) having special advantages. **7** *colloq.* resemble in features. □ **in favour 1** meeting with approval. **2** (foll. by *of*) **a** in support of. **b** to the advantage of. **out of favour** lacking approval. □ **favourer** *n.* [Middle English via Old French from Latin *favor -oris*, from *favēre* 'show kindness to']

favourable /ˈfeɪv(ə)rəb(ə)l/ *adj.* (*US* **favorable**) **1 a** well disposed; propitious. **b** commendatory, approving. **2** giving consent (*a favourable answer*). **3** promising, auspicious, satisfactory (*a favourable aspect*). **4** (often foll. by *to*) helpful, suitable. □ **favourableness** *n.* **favourably** *adv.* [Middle English via Old French *favorable* from Latin *favorabilis* (as FAVOUR)]

favourite /ˈfeɪv(ə)rɪt/ *adj.* & *n.* (*US* **favorite**) ● *adj.* preferred to all others (*my favourite book*). ● *n.* **1** a specially favoured or preferred person or thing. **2** *Sport* a competitor thought most likely to win. [obsolete French *favorit* from Italian *favorito*, past part. of *favorire* 'favour']

favourite son *n.* *US* a person supported as a presidential candidate by delegates from the candidate's home state.

favouritism /ˈfeɪv(ə)rɪtɪz(ə)m/ *n.* (*US* **favoritism**) the unfair favouring of one person or group at the expense of another.

fawn[1] /fɔːn/ *n.*, *adj.*, & *v.* ● *n.* **1** a young deer in its first year. **2** a light yellowish brown. ● *adj.* of a light yellowish-brown colour. ● *v.tr.* (also *absol.*) (of a deer) bring forth (young). □ **in fawn** (of a deer) pregnant. [Middle English from Old French *faon* etc., ultimately from Latin *fetus* 'offspring': cf. FOETUS]

fawn[2] /fɔːn/ *v.intr.* **1** (often foll. by *on*, *upon*) (of a person) behave servilely, show cringing affection. **2** (of an animal, esp. a dog) show extreme affection. □ **fawning** *adj.* **fawningly** *adv.* [Old English *fagnian*, *fægnian* (variant of FAIN)]

fax /faks/ *n.* & *v.* ● *n.* **1** facsimile transmission (see FACSIMILE *n.* 2). **2 a** a copy produced or message sent by this. **b** a machine for transmitting and receiving these. ● *v.tr.* transmit (a document) in this way. [abbreviation of FACSIMILE]

fay /feɪ/ *n.* *literary* a fairy. [Middle English via Old French *fae*, *faie* from Latin *fata* (pl.) 'the Fates']

fayre see FAIR[2].

faze /feɪz/ *v.tr.* (often as **fazed** *adj.*) *colloq.* disconcert, perturb, disorientate. [variant of *feeze* 'drive off', from Old English *fēsian*, of unknown origin]

FBA *abbr.* Fellow of the British Academy.

FBI *abbr.* (in the US) Federal Bureau of Investigation.

FC *abbr.* (in British names) Football Club.

FCC *abbr.* (in the US) Federal Communications Commission.

FCO *abbr.* (in the UK) Foreign and Commonwealth Office.

fcp. *abbr.* foolscap.

FD *abbr.* Defender of the Faith. [Latin *Fidei Defensor*]

FDA *abbr.* **1** (in the US) Food and Drug Administration. **2** (in the UK) First Division (Civil Servants) Association (cf. AFDCS).

FE *abbr.* further education.

Fe *symb.* *Chem.* the element iron. [Latin *ferrum*]

fealty /ˈfiːəlti/ *n.* (*pl.* **-ies**) **1** *hist.* **a** a feudal tenant's or vassal's fidelity to a lord. **b** an acknowledgement of this. **2** allegiance. [Middle English via Old French *feaulté* from Latin *fidelitas -tatis*, from *fidelis* 'faithful' from *fides* 'faith']

fear /fɪə/ *n.* & *v.* ● *n.* **1 a** an unpleasant emotion caused by exposure to danger, expectation of pain, etc. **b** a state of alarm (*be in fear*). **2** a cause of fear (*all fears removed*). **3** (often foll. by *of*) dread or fearful respect (towards) (*fear of heights*; *fear of one's elders*). **4** anxiety for the safety of (*in fear of their lives*). **5** danger; likelihood (of something unwelcome) (*there is little fear of failure*). ● *v.* **1 a** *tr.* feel fear about or towards (a person or thing). **b** *intr.* feel fear. **2** *intr.* (foll. by *for*) feel anxiety or apprehension about (*feared for my life*). **3** *tr.* apprehend; have uneasy expectation of (*fear the worst*). **4** *tr.* (usu. foll. by *that* + clause) apprehend with fear or regret (*I fear that you are wrong*). **5** *tr.* **a** (foll. by *to* + infin.) hesitate. **b** (foll. by verbal noun) shrink from; be apprehensive about (*he feared meeting his ex-wife*). **6** *tr.* show reverence towards. □ **for fear of** (or **that**) to avoid the risk of (or that). **never fear** there is no danger of that. **no fear** *Brit.* *colloq.* expressing strong denial or refusal. **without fear or favour** impartially. [Old English from Germanic]

fearful /ˈfɪəfʊl, -f(ə)l/ *adj.* **1** (usu. foll. by *of*, or *that* + clause) afraid. **2** terrible, awful. **3** *colloq.* extremely unwelcome or unpleasant (*a fearful row*). □ **fearfully** *adv.* **fearfulness** *n.*

fearless /ˈfɪəlɪs/ *adj.* **1** courageous, brave. **2** (foll. by *of*) without fear. □ **fearlessly** *adv.* **fearlessness** *n.*

fearsome /ˈfɪəs(ə)m/ *adj.* appalling or frightening, esp. in appearance. □ **fearsomely** *adv.* **fearsomeness** *n.*

feasibility /fiːzɪˈbɪlɪti/ *n.* the state or degree of being feasible.

feasibility study *n.* a study of the practicability of a proposed project.

feasible /ˈfiːzɪb(ə)l/ *adj.* **1** practicable, possible; easily or conveniently done. **2** *disp.* likely, probable (*it is feasible that it will rain*). □ **feasibly** *adv.* [Middle English via Old French *faisable*, *-ible*, from *fais-*, stem of *faire*, from Latin *facere* 'do, make']

■ **Usage** The use of *feasible* in sense 2 to mean 'possible' or 'probable' in the sense 'likely' is considered incorrect by many people. *Possible* or *probable* should be used instead.

---

feast /fiːst/ *n.* & *v.* ● *n.* **1** a large or sumptuous meal. **2** a gratification to the senses or mind. **3 a** an annual religious celebration. **b** a day dedicated to a particular saint. **4** *Brit.* an annual village festival. ● *v.* **1** *intr.* partake of a feast; eat and drink sumptuously. **2** *tr.* **a** regale. **b** pass (time) in feasting. □ **feast one's eyes on** take pleasure in beholding. **feast of reason** intellectual talk. □ **feaster** *n.* [Middle English via Old French *feste*, *fester* from Latin *festus* 'joyous']

feast day *n.* a day on which a feast (esp. a religious one) is held.

feast of Tabernacles *n.* = SUCCOTH.

feat /fiːt/ *n.* a noteworthy act or achievement. [Middle English from Old French *fait*, *fet* (as FACT)]

feather /ˈfeðə/ *n.* & *v.* ● *n.* **1** any of the appendages growing from a bird's skin, with a horny hollow stem and fine strands. **2** one or more of these as decoration etc. **3** (*collect.*) **a** plumage. **b** game birds. ● *v.* **1** *tr.* cover or line with feathers. **2** *tr.* *Rowing* turn (an oar) so that it passes through the air edgeways. **3** *tr.* *Aeron.* & *Naut.* **a** cause (the propeller blades) to rotate in such a way as to lessen the air or water resistance. **b** vary the angle of attack of (helicopter blades). **4** *intr.* float, move, or wave like feathers. □ **a feather in one's cap** an achievement to one's credit. **feather one's nest** enrich oneself. **in fine** (or **high**) **feather** in good spirits. □ **feathered** *adj.* (also in *comb.*). **featherless** *adj.* **feathery** *adj.* **featheriness** *n.* [Old English *fether*, *gefithrian*, from Germanic]

feather bed *n.* & *v.* ● *n.* a bed with a mattress stuffed with feathers. ● *v.tr.* (**feather-bed**) (**-bedded**, **-bedding**) provide with (esp. financial) advantages.

feather-bedding *n.* making or being made comfortable by favourable economic treatment, esp. the employment of excess staff.

feather-brain *n.* (also **feather-head**) a silly or absent-minded person. □ **feather-brained** *adj.* (also **feather-headed**).

feather edge *n.* the fine edge of a wedge-shaped board.

feathering /ˈfeð(ə)rɪŋ/ *n.* **1** bird's plumage. **2** the feathers of an arrow. **3** a feather-like structure in an animal's coat. **4** *Archit.* cusps in tracery.

feather-light *adj.* extremely light.

feather stitch *n. & v.* ● *n.* ornamental zigzag sewing. ● *v.tr.* (**feather-stitch**) sew with this stitch.

featherweight /ˈfɛðəweɪt/ *n.* **1 a** a weight in certain sports intermediate between bantamweight and lightweight, in the amateur boxing scale 54–7 kg but differing for professionals, wrestlers, and weightlifters. **b** a boxer etc. of this weight. **2** a very light person or thing. **3** (usu. *attrib.*) a trifling or unimportant thing.

feature /ˈfiːtʃə/ *n. & v.* ● *n.* **1** a distinctive or characteristic part of a thing. **2** (usu. in *pl.*) a distinctive part of the face, esp. with regard to shape and visual effect. **3** a distinctive or regular article in a newspaper or magazine. **4 a** (in full **feature film**) a full-length film intended as the main item in a cinema programme. **b** (in full **feature programme**) a broadcast devoted to a particular topic. ● *v.* **1** *tr.* make a special display or attraction of; give special prominence to. **2** *tr. & intr.* have as or be an important actor, participant, or topic in a film, broadcast, etc. **3** *intr.* be a feature. □ **featured** *adj.* (also in *comb.*). **featureless** *adj.* [Middle English via Old French *feture, faiture* 'form' from Latin *factura* 'formation': see FACTURE]

Feb. *abbr.* February.

febrifuge /ˈfɛbrɪfjuːdʒ/ *n.* a medicine or treatment that reduces fever; a cooling drink. □ **febrifugal** /fɪˈbrɪfjʊg(ə)l, fɛbrɪˈfjuːg(ə)l/ *adj.* [French *fébrifuge*, from Latin *febris* 'fever' + -FUGE]

febrile /ˈfiːbrʌɪl/ *adj.* of or relating to fever; feverish. □ **febrility** /fɪˈbrɪlɪti/ *n.* [French *fébrile* or medieval Latin *febrilis* from Latin *febris* 'fever']

February /ˈfɛbrʊəri, ˈfɛbjʊəri/ *n.* (*pl.* **-ies**) the second month of the year. [Middle English from Old French *feverier*, ultimately via Latin *februarius* from *februa*, the name of a purification feast held in this month]

feces *US* var. of FAECES.

feckless /ˈfɛklɪs/ *adj.* **1** feeble, ineffective. **2** unthinking, irresponsible (*feckless gaiety*). □ **fecklessly** *adv.* **fecklessness** *n.* [Scots *feck* from *effeck*, variant of EFFECT]

feculent /ˈfɛkjʊl(ə)nt/ *adj.* **1** murky; filthy. **2** containing sediments or dregs. □ **feculence** *n.* [French *féculent* or Latin *faeculentus* (as FAECES)]

fecund /ˈfɛk(ə)nd, ˈfiːk-/ *adj.* **1** prolific, fertile. **2** fertilizing. □ **fecundability** /fɪˌkʌndəˈbɪlɪti/ *n.* **fecundity** /fɪˈkʌndɪti/ *n.* [Middle English from French *fécond* or Latin *fecundus*]

fecundate /ˈfɛk(ə)ndeɪt, ˈfiːk-/ *v.tr.* **1** make fruitful. **2** = FERTILIZE 2. □ **fecundation** /-ˈdeɪʃ(ə)n/ *n.* [Latin *fecundare* from *fecundus* 'fruitful']

fed[1] *past* and *past part.* of FEED.

fed[2] /fɛd/ *n. US slang* **1** a federal agent or official, esp. a member of the FBI. **2** (**Fed**) (prec. by *the*) = FEDERAL RESERVE. [abbreviation of FEDERAL]

fedayeen /fɛdəˈjiːn/ *n.pl.* Arab guerrillas operating esp. against Israel. [colloq. Arabic *fidā'iyīn* (pl.) from Arabic *fidā'ī* 'adventurer']

federal /ˈfɛd(ə)r(ə)l/ *adj.* **1** of a system of government in which several states form a unity but remain independent in internal affairs. **2** relating to or affecting such a federation. **3** of or relating to the central government as distinguished from the separate units constituting a federation (*federal laws*). **4** (also **Federal**) favouring centralized government. **5** comprising an association of largely independent units. **6** (**Federal**) *US* of the Northern States in the Civil War. □ **federalism** *n.* **federalist** *n.* **federalize** *v.tr.* (also **-ise**). **federalization** /-ˈzeɪʃ(ə)n/ *n.* **federally** *adv.* [Latin *foedus -eris* 'league, covenant']

Federal Reserve *n.* (in the US) a national system of reserve cash available to banks.

federate *v. & adj.* ● *v.tr. & intr.* /ˈfɛdəreɪt/ organize or be organized on a federal basis. ● *adj.* /ˈfɛd(ə)rət/ having a federal organization. □ **federative** /ˈfɛd(ə)rətɪv/ *adj.* [Late Latin *foederare foederat-* (as FEDERAL)]

federation /fɛdəˈreɪʃ(ə)n/ *n.* **1** a federal group of states. **2** a federated society or group. **3** the act or an instance of federating. □ **federationist** *n.* [French *fédération* from Late Latin *foederatio* (as FEDERAL)]

fedora /fɪˈdɔːrə/ *n.* a low soft felt hat with a crown creased lengthways. [*Fédora*, the title of a drama by V. Sardou (1882)]

fed up *adj.* (also **fed to death**) (often foll. by *with*; hyphenated when *attrib.*) discontented or bored, esp. from a surfeit of something (*am fed up with the rain*; *fed-up commuters*).

fee /fiː/ *n. & v.* ● *n.* **1** a payment made to a professional person or to a professional or public body in exchange for advice or services. **2** money paid as part of a special transaction, for a privilege, admission to a society, etc. (*enrolment fee*). **3** (in *pl.*) money regularly paid (esp. to a school) for continuing services. **4** *Law* an inherited estate, unlimited (**fee simple**) or limited (**fee tail**) as to the category of heir. **5** *hist.* a fief; a feudal benefice. ● *v.tr.* (**fee'd** or **feed**) **1** pay a fee to. **2** engage for a fee. [Middle English via Anglo-French, = Old French *feu, fieu*, etc. from medieval Latin *feodum, feudum*, perhaps from Frankish: cf. FEUD[2], FIEF]

feeble /ˈfiːb(ə)l/ *adj.* (**feebler**, **feeblest**) **1** weak, infirm. **2** lacking energy, force, or effectiveness. **3** dim, indistinct. **4** deficient in character or intelligence. □ **feebleness** *n.* **feeblish** *adj.* **feebly** *adv.* [Middle English via Anglo-French and Old French *feble, fieble, fleible* from Latin *flebilis* 'lamentable', from *flēre* 'weep']

feeble-minded *adj.* **1** unintelligent. **2** mentally deficient. □ **feeble-mindedly** *adv.* **feeble-mindedness** *n.*

feed /fiːd/ *v. & n.* ● *v.* (*past* and *past part.* **fed** /fɛd/) **1** *tr.* **a** supply with food. **b** put food into the mouth of. **2** *tr.* **a** give as food, esp. to animals. **b** graze (cattle). **3** *tr.* serve as food for. **4** *intr.* (usu. foll. by *on*) (esp. of animals, or *colloq.* of people) take food; eat. **5** *tr.* nourish; make grow. **6 a** *tr.* maintain supply of raw material, fuel, etc., to (a fire, machine, etc.). **b** *tr.* (foll. by *into*) supply (material) to a machine etc. **c** *intr.* (often foll. by *into*) (of a river etc.) flow into another body of water. **d** *tr.* insert further coins into (a meter) to continue its function, validity, etc. **7** *intr.* (foll. by *on*) **a** be nourished by. **b** derive benefit from. **8** *tr.* use (land) as pasture. **9** *tr. Theatr. slang* supply (an actor etc.) with cues. **10** *tr. Sport* send passes to (a player) in a ball game. **11** *tr.* gratify (vanity etc.). **12** *tr.* provide (advice, information, etc.) to. ● *n.* **1** an amount of food, esp. for animals or *Brit.* infants. **2** the act or an instance of feeding; the giving of food. **3** *colloq.* a meal. **4** pasturage; green crops. **5 a** a supply of raw material to a machine etc. **b** the provision of this or a device for it. **6** the charge of a gun. **7** *Theatr. slang* an actor who supplies another with cues. □ **feed back** produce feedback. **feed up 1** fatten. **2** satiate (cf. FED UP). [Old English *fēdan*, from Germanic]

feedback /ˈfiːdbak/ *n.* **1** information about the result of an experiment etc.; response. **2** *Electronics* **a** the return of a fraction of the output signal from one stage of a circuit, amplifier, etc., to the input of the same or a preceding stage. **b** a signal so returned. **3** *Biol.* etc. the modification or control of a process or system by its results or effects, esp. in a biochemical pathway or behavioural response.

feeder /ˈfiːdə/ *n.* **1** a person or thing that feeds. **2** a person who eats in a specified manner. **3** *Brit.* a child's feeding bottle. **4** *Brit.* a bib for an infant. **5** a tributary stream. **6** a branch road, railway line, etc., linking outlying districts with a main communication system. **7** *Electr.* a main carrying electricity to a distribution point. **8** a hopper or feeding apparatus in a machine.

feeding bottle *n. Brit.* a bottle with a teat for feeding infants.

feedstock /ˈfiːdstɒk/ *n.* raw material to supply a machine or industrial process.

feedstuff /ˈfiːdstʌf/ *n.* fodder.

feel /fiːl/ *v. & n.* ● *v.* (*past* and *past part.* **felt** /fɛlt/) **1** *tr.* **a** examine or search by touch. **b** (*absol.*) have the sensation of touch (*was unable to feel*). **2** *tr.* perceive or ascertain by touch; have a sensation of (*could feel the warmth; felt that it was cold*). **3** *tr.* **a** undergo, experience (*shall feel my anger*). **b** exhibit or be conscious of (an emotion, sensation, conviction, etc.). **4** **a** *intr.* have a specified feeling or reaction (*felt strongly about it*). **b** *tr.* be emotionally affected by (*felt the rebuke deeply*). **5** *tr.* (foll. by *that* + clause) have a vague or unreasoned impression (*I feel that I am right*). **6** *tr.* consider, think (*I feel it useful to go*). **7** *intr.* seem; give an impression of being; be perceived as (*the air feels chilly*). **8** *intr.* be consciously; consider oneself (*I feel happy; do not feel well*). **9** *intr.* **a** (foll. by *with*) have sympathy with. **b** (foll. by *for*) have pity or compassion for. **10** *tr.* (often foll. by *up*) *slang* fondle clumsily for sexual gratification. ● *n.* **1** the act or an instance of feeling; testing by touch. **2** the sensation characterizing a material, situation, etc. **3** the sense of touch. ◻ **feel free** (often foll. by *to* + infin.) not be reluctant or hesitant (*do feel free to criticize*). **feel like** have a wish for; be inclined towards. **feel one's oats** see OAT. **feel oneself** be fit or confident etc. **feel out** investigate cautiously. **feel strange** see STRANGE. **feel up to** be ready to face or deal with. **feel one's way** proceed carefully; act cautiously. **get the feel of** become accustomed to using. **make one's influence** (or **presence etc.**) **felt** assert one's influence; make others aware of one's presence etc. [Old English *fēlan*, from West Germanic]

feeler /ˈfiːlə/ *n.* **1** an organ in certain animals for testing things by touch or for searching for food. **2** a tentative proposal or suggestion, esp. to elicit a response (*put out feelers*). **3** a person or thing that feels.

feeler gauge *n.* a gauge equipped with blades for measuring narrow gaps etc.

feel-good *attrib.adj.* that creates a feeling of well-being in people (*a feel-good film*).

feeling /ˈfiːlɪŋ/ *n. & adj.* ● *n.* **1** **a** the capacity to feel; a sense of touch (*lost all feeling in his arm*). **b** a physical sensation. **2** **a** (often foll. by *of*) a particular emotional reaction (*a feeling of despair*). **b** (in *pl.*) emotional susceptibilities or sympathies (*hurt my feelings; had strong feelings about it*). **3** a particular sensitivity (*had a feeling for literature*). **4** **a** an opinion or notion, esp. a vague or irrational one (*my feelings on the subject; had a feeling she would be there*). **b** vague awareness (*had a feeling of safety*). **c** sentiment (*the general feeling was against it*). **5** readiness to feel sympathy or compassion. **6** **a** the general emotional response produced by a work of art, piece of music, etc. **b** emotional commitment or sensibility in artistic execution (*played with feeling*). ● *adj.* **1** sensitive, sympathetic. **2** showing emotion or sensitivity. ◻ **feelingless** *adj.* **feelingly** *adv.*

feet *pl.* of FOOT.

feign /feɪn/ *v.* **1** *tr.* simulate; pretend to be affected by (*feign madness*). **2** *tr. archaic* invent (an excuse etc.). **3** *intr.* indulge in pretence. [Middle English from *feign-*, stem of Old French *feindre*, from Latin *fingere* 'mould, contrive']

feijoa /feɪˈ(d)ʒəʊə; fɛ-, fiː-, -ˈjəʊə/ *n.* **1** any evergreen shrub or tree of the genus *Feijoa*, bearing edible guava-like fruit. **2** this fruit. [modern Latin, named after J. da Silva *Feijo*, Brazilian naturalist d. 1824]

feint[1] /feɪnt/ *n. & v.* ● *n.* **1** a sham attack or blow etc. to divert attention or fool an opponent or enemy. **2** pretence. ● *v.intr.* make a feint. [French *feinte*, fem. past part. of *feindre* FEIGN]

feint[2] /feɪnt/ *adj.* esp. *Printing* designating the faint lines ruled on paper as a guide for handwriting. [Middle English from Old French (as FEINT[1]): see FAINT]

feisty /ˈfʌɪsti/ *adj.* (**feistier**, **feistiest**) *N. Amer. colloq.* **1** aggressive, spirited, exuberant. **2** touchy. ◻ **feistily** *adv.* **feistiness** *n.* [*feist* 'small dog']

felafel /fɛˈlɑːf(ə)l/ *n.* (also **falafel**) a spicy Middle Eastern dish of fried rissoles made from mashed chickpeas or beans. [Arabic *falāfil*]

feldspar /ˈfɛldspɑː/ *n.* (also **felspar** /ˈfɛlspɑː/) *Mineral.* any of a group of aluminosilicates of potassium, sodium, or calcium, which are the most abundant rock-forming minerals in the earth's crust, often occurring as large pale crystals. ◻ **feldspathic** /-ˈspaθɪk/ *adj.* **feldspathoid** /ˈfɛldspəθɔɪd/ *n.* [German *Feldspat*, *-spath*, from *Feld* FIELD + *Spat*, *Spath* SPAR[3]: *felspar* by false association with German *Fels* 'rock']

felicitate /fɪˈlɪsɪteɪt/ *v.tr.* (usu. foll. by *on*) congratulate. ◻ **felicitation** /-ˈteɪʃ(ə)n/ *n.* (usu. in *pl.*). [Late Latin *felicitare* 'make happy' from Latin *felix -icis* 'happy']

felicitous /fɪˈlɪsɪtəs/ *adj.* (of an expression, quotation, civilities, or a person making them) strikingly apt; pleasantly ingenious. ◻ **felicitously** *adv.* **felicitousness** *n.*

felicity /fɪˈlɪsɪti/ *n.* (*pl.* **-ies**) **1** intense happiness; being happy. **2** a cause of happiness. **3** **a** a capacity for apt expression; appropriateness. **b** an appropriate or well-chosen phrase. **4** a fortunate trait. [Middle English via Old French *felicité* from Latin *felicitas -tatis*, from *felix -icis* 'happy']

feline /ˈfiːlʌɪn/ *adj. & n.* ● *adj.* **1** of or relating to the cat family. **2** catlike, esp. in beauty or slyness. ● *n.* an animal of the cat family Felidae. ◻ **felinity** /fɪˈlɪnɪti/ *n.* [Latin *felinus* from *feles* 'cat']

fell[1] *past* of FALL *v.*

fell[2] /fɛl/ *v. & n.* ● *v.tr.* **1** cut down (esp. a tree). **2** strike or knock down (a person or animal). **3** stitch down (the edge of a seam) to lie flat. ● *n.* an amount of timber cut. ◻ **feller** *n.* [Old English *fellan* from Germanic, related to FALL]

fell[3] /fɛl/ *n. N.Engl.* **1** a hill. **2** a stretch of hills or moorland. [Middle English from Old Norse *fjall*, *fell* 'hill']

fell[4] /fɛl/ *adj. poet.* or *literary* **1** fierce, ruthless. **2** terrible, destructive. ◻ **at** (or **in**) **one fell swoop** in a single (originally deadly) action, in one go. [Middle English via Old French *fel* from Romanic FELON[1]]

fell[5] /fɛl/ *n.* an animal's hide or skin with its hair. [Old English *fel*, *fell*, from Germanic]

fellah /ˈfɛlə/ *n.* (*pl.* **fellahin** /-əˈhiːn/) an Egyptian peasant. [Arabic *fallāh* 'husbandman' from *falaha* 'till the soil']

fellatio /fɛˈleɪʃɪəʊ, -ˈlɑːt-/ *n.* oral stimulation of the penis. ◻ **fellate** /fɪˈleɪt/ *v.tr.* **fellator** /fɪˈleɪtə/ *n.* [modern Latin, from Latin *fellare* 'suck']

feller /ˈfɛlə/ *n.* = FELLOW 1, 2 (see also FELL[2]). [representing an affected or slang pronunciation]

felloe /ˈfɛləʊ/ *n.* (also **felly** /ˈfɛli/) (*pl.* **-oes** or **-ies**) the outer circle (or a section of it) of a wheel, to which the spokes are fixed. [Old English *felg*, of unknown origin]

fellow /ˈfɛləʊ/ *n.* **1** *colloq.* a man or boy (*poor fellow!; my dear fellow*). **2** *derog.* a person regarded with contempt. **3** (usu. in *pl.*) a person associated with another; a comrade (*were separated from their fellows*). **4** a counterpart or match; the other of a pair. **5** an equal; one of the same class. **6** a contemporary. **7** **a** *Brit.* an incorporated senior member of a college. **b** an elected graduate receiving a stipend for a period of research. **c** a member of the governing body in some universities. **8** a member of a learned society. **9** (*attrib.*) belonging to the same class or activity (*fellow soldier; fellow countryman*). [originally one who laid out money in a partnership: Old English *fēolaga* from Old Norse *félagi*, from *fé* 'cattle, property, money' + the Germanic base of LAY[1]]

fellow feeling *n.* sympathy from common experience.

fellowship /ˈfɛlə(ʊ)ʃɪp/ *n.* **1** companionship, friendliness. **2** participation; sharing; community of interest. **3** a body of associates; a company. **4** a brotherhood or fraternity. **5** a guild or corporation. **6** the status or emoluments of a fellow of a college or society.

fellow-traveller *n.* **1** a person who travels with another. **2** a sympathizer with, or a secret member of, the Communist Party.

fell walking *n.* the activity of walking on the fells. □ **fell walker** *n.*

felly var. of FELLOE.

felon[1] /ˈfɛlən/ *n. & adj.* ● *n.* a person who has committed a felony. ● *adj. archaic* cruel, wicked. □ **felonry** *n.* [Middle English via Old French from medieval Latin *felo -onis*, of unknown origin]

felon[2] /ˈfɛlən/ *n.* an inflammatory sore on the finger near the nail. [Middle English, perhaps as FELON[1]: cf. medieval Latin *felo, fello* in the same sense]

felonious /fɛˈləʊnɪəs, fɪ-/ *adj.* **1** criminal. **2** *Law* **a** of or involving felony. **b** who has committed felony. □ **feloniously** *adv.*

felony /ˈfɛləni/ *n.* (*pl.* **-ies**) a usu. violent crime, (in the UK formerly) regarded as graver than a misdemeanour. [Middle English from Old French *felonie* (as FELON[1])]

felspar var. of FELDSPAR.

felt[1] /fɛlt/ *n. & v.* ● *n.* **1** a kind of cloth made by rolling and pressing wool etc., or by weaving and shrinking it. **2** a similar material made from other fibres. ● *v.* **1** *tr.* make into felt; mat together. **2** *tr.* cover with felt. **3** *intr.* become matted. □ **felty** *adj.* [Old English from West Germanic]

felt[2] *past* and *past part.* of FEEL.

felt-tip pen *n.* (also **felt-tipped pen, felt tip**) a pen with a writing point made of felt or fibre.

felucca /fɛˈlʌkə/ *n.* a small Mediterranean coasting vessel with oars or lateen sails or both. [Italian *felucca* via obsolete Spanish *faluca* from Arabic *fulk*, perhaps from Greek *epholkion* 'sloop']

felwort /ˈfɛlwəːt/ *n.* a purple-flowered gentian, *Gentianella amarella.* [Old English *feldwyrt* (as FIELD, WORT)]

female /ˈfiːmeɪl/ *adj. & n.* ● *adj.* **1** of the sex that can bear offspring or produce eggs. **2** (of plants or their parts) fruit-bearing; having a pistil and no stamens. **3** of or consisting of women or female animals or female plants. **4** (of a screw, socket, etc.) manufactured hollow to receive a corresponding inserted part. ● *n.* a female person, animal, or plant. □ **femaleness** *n.* [Middle English via Old French *femelle* from Latin *femella*, diminutive of *femina* 'a woman', assimilated to *male*]

female condom see CONDOM.

female impersonator *n.* a male performer impersonating a woman.

feme /fiːm, fɛm/ *n. Law* a woman or wife. [Middle English via Anglo-French and Old French from Latin *femina* 'woman']

feme covert *n. Law* a married woman. [literally a woman covered (protected) by marriage]

feme sole *n. Law* a woman without a husband (esp. if divorced).

feminal /ˈfɛmɪn(ə)l/ *adj. archaic* womanly. □ **feminality** /-ˈnalɪti/ *n.* [medieval Latin *feminalis* from Latin *femina* 'woman']

femineity /fɛmɪˈniːɪti/ *n. archaic* womanliness; womanishness. [Latin *femineus* 'womanish' from *femina* 'woman']

feminine /ˈfɛmɪnɪn/ *adj. & n.* ● *adj.* **1** of or characteristic of women. **2** having qualities associated with women. **3** womanly, effeminate. **4** *Gram.* of or denoting the gender proper to words or grammatical forms classified as female. ● *n. Gram.* a feminine gender or word. □ **femininely** *adv.* **feminineness** *n.* **femininity** /-ˈnɪnɪti/ *n.* [Middle English from Old French *feminin -ine* or Latin *femininus*, from *femina* 'woman']

feminine rhyme *n. Prosody* a rhyme between stressed syllables followed by one or more unstressed syllables (e.g. *stocking/shocking, glamorous/amorous*) (cf. MASCULINE RHYME).

feminism /ˈfɛmɪnɪz(ə)m/ *n.* **1** the advocacy of women's rights on the ground of the equality of the sexes. **2** *Med.* the development of female characteristics in a male person. □ **feminist** *n. & adj.* (in sense 1). [Latin *femina* 'woman' (in sense 1 via French *féminisme*)]

feminity /fɪˈmɪnɪti/ *n.* = FEMININITY (see FEMININE). [Middle English via Old French *feminité* and medieval Latin *feminitas -tatis* from Latin *femina* 'woman']

feminize /ˈfɛmɪnʌɪz/ *v.tr. & intr.* (also **-ise**) make or become feminine or female. □ **feminization** /-ˈzeɪʃ(ə)n/ *n.*

femme fatale /fam fəˈtɑːl/ *n.* (*pl.* **femmes fatales** *pronunc.* same) a seductively attractive woman. [French]

femto- /ˈfɛmtəʊ/ *comb. form* denoting a factor of 10^{-15} (*femtometre*). [Danish or Norwegian *femten* 'fifteen']

femur /ˈfiːmə/ *n.* (*pl.* **femurs** or **femora** /ˈfɛm(ə)rə/) **1** *Anat.* the thigh bone, the thick bone between the hip and the knee. **2** *Zool.* the third segment of the leg of an insect, usu. the longest and thickest. □ **femoral** /ˈfɛm(ə)r(ə)l/ *adj.* [Latin *femur femoris* 'thigh']

fen[1] /fɛn/ *n.* **1** a low marshy or flooded area of land. **2** (**the Fens**) flat low-lying areas in and around Cambridgeshire. □ **fenny** *adj.* [Old English *fenn*, from Germanic]

fen[2] /fʌn/ *n.* (*pl.* same) a Chinese coin and monetary unit worth one-hundredth of a yuan. [Chinese *fēn* 'a hundredth part']

fen-berry *n.* (*pl.* **-berries**) = CRANBERRY.

fence /fɛns/ *n. & v.* ● *n.* **1** a barrier or railing or other upright structure enclosing an area of ground, esp. to prevent or control access. **2** a large upright obstacle in steeplechasing or showjumping. **3** *slang* a receiver of stolen goods. **4** a guard or guide in machinery. ● *v.* **1** *tr.* surround with or as with a fence. **2** *tr.* **a** (foll. by *in, off*) enclose or separate with or as with a fence. **b** (foll. by *up*) seal with or as with a fence. **3** *tr.* (foll. by *from, against*) screen, shield, protect. **4** *tr.* (foll. by *out*) exclude with or as with a fence; keep out. **5** *tr.* (also *absol.*) *slang* deal in (stolen goods). **6** *intr.* practise the sport of fencing; use a sword. **7** *intr.* (foll. by *with*) evade answering (a person or question). **8** *intr.* (of a horse etc.) leap fences. □ **sit on the fence** remain neutral or undecided in a dispute etc. □ **fenceless** *adj.* **fencer** *n.* [Middle English from DEFENCE]

fence post *n.* a post that supports a fence.

fencible /ˈfɛnsɪb(ə)l/ *n. hist.* a soldier liable only for home service. [Middle English from DEFENSIBLE]

fencing /ˈfɛnsɪŋ/ *n.* **1** a set or extent of fences. **2** material for making fences. **3** the art or sport of swordplay.

fend /fɛnd/ *v.* **1** *intr.* (foll. by *for*) look after (esp. oneself). **2** *tr.* (usu. foll. by *off*) keep away; ward off (an attack etc.). [Middle English from DEFEND]

fender /ˈfɛndə/ *n.* **1** a low frame bordering a fireplace to keep in falling coals etc. **2** *Naut.* a piece of old cable, matting, etc., hung over a vessel's side to protect it against impact. **3** a thing used to keep something off, prevent a collision, etc. **4** *N. Amer.* **a** the mudguard or area around the wheel well of a bicycle or motor vehicle. **b** *disp.* the bumper of a motor vehicle.

fender bender *n. N. Amer. slang* a (usu. minor) collision between vehicles.

fenestella /fɛnɪˈstɛlə/ *n. Archit.* a niche in a wall south of an altar, holding the piscina and often the credence. [Latin, diminutive of *fenestra* 'window']

fenestra /fɪˈnɛstrə/ *n.* (*pl.* **fenestrae** /-triː/) **1** *Anat.* a small hole or opening in a bone etc., esp. one of two (**fenestra ovalis, fenestra rotunda**) in the inner ear. **2** a perforation in a surgical instrument. **3** a hole made by surgical fenestration. [Latin, = window]

fenestrate /fɪˈnɛstrət, ˈfɛnəstrət/ *adj. Bot. & Zool.* having small window-like perforations or transparent areas. [Latin *fenestratus*, past part. of *fenestrare*, from *fenestra* 'window']

fenestrated /fɪˈnɛstreɪtɪd, ˈfɛnəstreɪtɪd/ *adj.* **1** *Archit.* having windows. **2** perforated. **3** = FENESTRATE. **4** *Surgery* having fenestrae.

fenestration /fɛnɪ'streɪʃ(ə)n/ *n.* **1** *Archit.* the arrangement of windows in a building. **2** *Bot.* & *Zool.* being fenestrate. **3** *Surgery* an operation in which a new opening is formed, esp. in the bony labyrinth of the inner ear, as a form of treatment in some cases of deafness.

fen-fire *n.* a will-o'-the-wisp.

feng shui /'fɛŋ ʃu:i, 'fʌŋ/ *n.* (in Chinese thought) a system of good and evil influences in the natural surroundings, considered when siting and designing buildings etc. [Chinese, from *feng* 'wind' + *shui* 'water']

Fenian /'fi:nɪən/ *n.* & *adj.* ● *n. hist.* a member of a 19th-c. league among the Irish in the US & Ireland for promoting revolution and overthrowing British government in Ireland. ● *adj.* of or relating to the Fenians. □ **Fenianism** *n.* [Old Irish *féne*, the name of an ancient Irish people, confused with *fiann*, the guard of legendary kings]

fenland /'fɛnlənd/ *n.* (often *attrib.*) an area of fens. [FEN[1]]

fennec /'fɛnɛk/ *n.* a small fox, *Vulpes zerda*, native to N. Africa and Arabia, having large pointed ears. [Arabic *fanak*]

fennel /'fɛn(ə)l/ *n.* **1** a yellow-flowered umbelliferous plant, *Foeniculum vulgare*, with fragrant seeds and fine leaves used as flavourings. **2** the seeds of this. **3** (in full **Florence** or **sweet fennel**) a variety of this with swollen leaf-bases eaten as a vegetable. [Old English *finugl* etc. and Old French *fenoil* from Latin *feniculum*, from *fenum* 'hay']

fenugreek /'fɛnjʊgri:k/ *n.* **1** a leguminous plant, *Trigonella foenum-graecum*, with aromatic seeds. **2** these seeds used as flavouring, esp. ground and used in curry powder. [Old English *fenogrecum*, superseded in Middle English from Old French *fenugrec* from Latin *faenugraecum* (*fenum graecum* 'Greek hay'), used by the Romans as fodder]

feoffment /'fi:fm(ə)nt, 'fɛf-/ *n. hist.* a mode of conveying a freehold estate by a formal transfer of possession. □ **feoffee** /fɛ'fi:/ *n.* **feoffor** *n.* [Middle English from Anglo-French *feoffement*, related to FEE]

feral /'fɪər(ə)l, 'fɛr-/ *adj.* **1** (esp. of an animal or animal population) in a wild state after escape from captivity or domestication. **2** resembling a wild animal; savage, brutal. **3** untamed, uncultivated. [Latin *ferus* 'wild']

fer de lance /fɛ: də 'lɑ:ns/ *n.* (*pl.* **fers de lance** *pronunc.* same or **fer de lances**) a large highly venomous snake, *Bothrops atrox*, native to Central and S. America. [French, = iron (head) of a lance]

feretory /'fɛrət(ə)ri/ *n.* (*pl.* **-ies**) **1** a shrine for a saint's relics. **2** a chapel containing such a shrine. [Middle English via Old French *fiertre* and Latin *feretrum* from Greek *pheretron* from *pherō* 'bear']

ferial /'fɪərɪəl, 'fɛr-/ *adj. Eccl.* **1** (of a day) ordinary; not appointed for a festival or fast. **2** (of a service etc.) for use on a ferial day. [Middle English via Old French *ferial* or medieval Latin *ferialis* from Latin *feriae*: see FAIR[2]]

fermata /fə:'mɑ:tə/ *n.* (*pl.* **fermatas**) *Mus.* **1** an unspecified prolongation of a note or rest. **2** a sign indicating this. [Italian from *fermare* 'to stop']

ferment *n.* & *v.* ● *n.* /'fə:mɛnt/ **1** agitation, excitement, tumult. **2 a** fermenting, fermentation. **b** a fermenting agent or leaven. ● *v.* /fə'mɛnt/ **1** *intr.* & *tr.* undergo or subject to fermentation. **2** *intr.* & *tr.* effervesce or cause to effervesce. **3** *tr.* excite; stir up; foment. □ **fermentable** /-'mɛntəb(ə)l/ *adj.* **fermenter** /-'mɛntə/ *n.* [Middle English via Old French *ferment* or Latin *fermentum* from Latin *fervēre* 'boil']

fermentation /fə:mɛn'teɪʃ(ə)n/ *n.* **1** the breakdown of a substance by micro-organisms, such as yeasts and bacteria, usu. in the absence of oxygen, esp. of sugar to ethyl alcohol in making beers, wines, and spirits. **2** agitation, excitement. □ **fermentative** /-'mɛntətɪv/ *adj.* [Middle English from Late Latin *fermentatio* (as FERMENT)]

fermi /'fə:mi/ *n.* (*pl.* **fermis**) a unit of length equal to 10^{-15} metre, formerly used in nuclear physics. [named after E. *Fermi*, Italian-American physicist d. 1954]

fermion /'fə:mɪɒn/ *n. Physics* any of several subatomic particles with half-integral spin, e.g. nucleons (cf. BOSON). [as FERMI + -ON]

fermium /'fə:mɪəm/ *n. Chem.* a transuranic radioactive metallic element produced artificially (symbol **Fm**). [as FERMI + -IUM]

fern /fə:n/ *n.* (*pl.* same or **ferns**) any flowerless plant of the order Filicopsida, reproducing by spores and usu. having feathery fronds. □ **fernery** *n.* (*pl.* **-ies**). **ferny** *adj.* [Old English *fearn*, from West Germanic]

ferocious /fə'rəʊʃəs/ *adj.* **1** fierce, savage; wildly cruel. **2** esp. *US colloq.* (as an intensifier) very great, extreme. □ **ferociously** *adv.* **ferociousness** *n.* [Latin *ferox -ocis*]

ferocity /fə'rɒsɪti/ *n.* (*pl.* **-ies**) **1** ferocious nature; the state of being ferocious. **2** a ferocious act. [French *férocité* or Latin *ferocitas* (as FEROCIOUS)]

-ferous /f(ə)rəs/ *comb. form* (usu. **-iferous**) forming adjectives with the sense 'bearing', 'having' (*auriferous*; *odoriferous*). □ **-ferously** *suffix.* **-ferousness** *suffix.* [from or suggested by French *-fère* or Latin *-fer* 'producing' from *ferre* 'bear']

ferrate /'fɛreɪt/ *n. Chem.* a salt in which the anion contains both iron (esp. in the trivalent form) and oxygen. [Latin *ferrum* 'iron']

ferrel var. of FERRULE.

ferret /'fɛrɪt/ *n.* & *v.* ● *n.* **1** a small half-tamed domesticated polecat, *Mustela putorius furo*, used in catching rabbits, rats, etc. **2** a person who searches assiduously. ● *v.* (**ferreted, ferreting**) **1** *intr.* hunt with ferrets. **2** *intr.* rummage; search about. **3** *tr.* (often foll. by *about, away, out,* etc.) **a** clear out (holes or an area of ground) with ferrets. **b** take or drive away (rabbits etc.) with ferrets. **4** *tr.* (foll. by *out*) search out (secrets, criminals, etc.). □ **ferreter** *n.* **ferrety** *adj.* [Middle English via Old French *fu(i)ret*, alteration of *fu(i)ron*, and Late Latin *furo -onis* from Latin *fur* 'thief']

ferri- /'fɛri/ *comb. form Chem.* containing iron, esp. in ferric compounds. [Latin *ferrum* 'iron']

ferriage /'fɛrɪɪdʒ/ *n.* **1** conveyance by ferry. **2** a charge for using a ferry.

ferric /'fɛrɪk/ *adj.* **1** of iron. **2** *Chem.* containing iron in a trivalent form (cf. FERROUS *adj.* 2).

ferrimagnetism /fɛrɪ'magnɪtɪz(ə)m/ *n. Physics* a form of ferromagnetism with parallel but opposite alignment of neighbouring atoms or ions. □ **ferrimagnetic** /-mag'nɛtɪk/ *adj.* [French *ferrimagnétisme* (as FERRI-, MAGNETISM)]

Ferris wheel /'fɛrɪs/ *n.* a fairground ride consisting of a giant revolving vertical wheel with passenger cars suspended on its outer edge. [named after G. W. G. *Ferris*, American engineer d. 1896]

ferrite /'fɛrʌɪt/ *n. Chem.* **1** a salt in which the anion contains both divalent iron and oxygen, often with magnetic properties. **2** an allotrope of pure iron occurring in low-carbon steel. □ **ferritic** /fɛ'rɪtɪk/ *adj.* [Latin *ferrum* 'iron']

ferro- /'fɛrəʊ/ *comb. form Chem.* **1** iron, esp. in ferrous compounds (*ferrocyanide*). **2** (of alloys) containing iron (*ferromanganese*). [Latin *ferrum* 'iron']

ferroconcrete /fɛrəʊ'kɒŋkri:t/ *n.* & *adj.* ● *n.* concrete reinforced with steel. ● *adj.* made of reinforced concrete.

ferroelectric /ˌfɛrəʊɪ'lɛktrɪk/ *adj.* & *n. Physics* ● *adj.* exhibiting permanent electric polarization which varies in strength with the applied electric field. ● *n.* a ferroelectric substance. □ **ferroelectricity** /-'trɪsɪti/ *n.* [ELECTRIC on the pattern of *ferromagnetic*]

ferromagnetism /fɛrə(ʊ)'magnɪtɪz(ə)m/ *n. Physics* a phenomenon in which a material has a high susceptibility to magnetization, the strength of which varies with the applied magnetizing field, and which may persist after removal of the applied field. □ **ferromagnetic** /-mag'nɛtɪk/ *adj.*

ferrous /'fɛrəs/ *adj.* **1** containing iron (*ferrous and non-ferrous metals*). **2** *Chem.* containing iron in a divalent form (cf. FERRIC *adj.* 2). [Latin *ferrum* 'iron']

ferruginous /fɛ'ru:dʒɪnəs/ *adj.* **1** of or containing iron rust, or iron as a chemical constituent. **2** rust-coloured; reddish brown. [Latin *ferrugo -ginis* 'rust' from *ferrum* 'iron']

ferruginous duck *n.* a European diving duck, *Aythya nyroca*, with mainly red-brown plumage.

ferrule /'fɛru:l, 'fɛr(ə)l/ *n.* (also **ferrel** /'fɛr(ə)l/) **1** a ring or cap strengthening the end of a stick or tube. **2** a band strengthening or forming a joint. [earlier *verrel* etc. via Old French *virelle, virol(e)*, from Latin *viriola*, diminutive of *viriae* 'bracelet': assimilated to Latin *ferrum* 'iron']

ferry /'fɛri/ *n. & v.* ● *n.* (*pl.* **-ies**) **1** a boat or aircraft etc. for conveying passengers and goods, esp. across water and as a regular service. **2** the service itself or the place where it operates. ● *v.* (**-ies, -ied**) **1** *tr. & intr.* convey or go in a boat etc. across water. **2** *intr.* (of a boat etc.) pass to and fro across water. **3** *tr.* transport from one place to another, esp. as a regular service. □ **ferryman** *n.* (*pl.* **-men**). [Middle English from Old Norse *ferja*, from Germanic]

fertile /'fə:tʌɪl/ *adj.* **1 a** (of soil) producing abundant vegetation or crops. **b** fruitful. **2 a** (of a seed, egg, etc.) capable of becoming a new individual. **b** (of animals and plants) able to conceive young or produce fruit. **3** (of the mind) inventive. **4** (of nuclear material) able to become fissile by the capture of neutrons. □ **fertility** /-'tɪlɪti/ *n.* [Middle English via French from Latin *fertilis*]

Fertile Crescent *n.* the fertile region extending in a crescent shape from the E. Mediterranean to the Persian Gulf.

fertilization /ˌfə:tɪlʌɪ'zeɪʃ(ə)n/ *n.* (also **-isation**) **1** *Biol.* the fusion of male and female gametes during sexual reproduction to form a zygote. **2 a** the act or an instance of fertilizing. **b** the process of being fertilized.

fertilize /'fə:tɪlʌɪz/ *v.tr.* (also **-ise**) **1** make (soil etc.) fertile or productive. **2** cause (an egg, female animal, or plant) to develop a new individual by introducing male reproductive material. □ **fertilizable** *adj.*

fertilizer /'fə:tɪlʌɪzə/ *n.* a chemical or natural substance added to soil to make it more fertile.

ferula /'fɛrjʊlə/ *n.* **1** any plant of the genus *Ferula*, esp. the giant fennel (*F. communis*), having a tall sticklike stem and thick roots. **2** = FERULE. [Middle English from Latin, = giant fennel, rod]

ferule /'fɛru:l/ *n. & v.* ● *n.* a flat ruler with a widened end formerly used for beating children. ● *v.tr.* beat with a ferule. [Middle English (as FERULA)]

fervent /'fə:v(ə)nt/ *adj.* **1** ardent, impassioned, intense (*fervent admirer; fervent hatred*). **2** hot, glowing. □ **fervency** *n.* **fervently** *adv.* [Middle English via Old French from Latin *fervēre* 'boil']

fervid /'fə:vɪd/ *adj.* **1** ardent, intense. **2** *poet.* hot, glowing. □ **fervidly** *adv.* [Latin *fervidus* (as FERVENT)]

fervour /'fə:və/ *n.* (*US* **fervor**) **1** vehemence, passion, zeal. **2** a glowing condition; intense heat. [Middle English via Old French from Latin *fervor -oris* (as FERVENT)]

fescue /'fɛskju:/ *n.* any fine-leaved grass of the genus *Festuca*, valuable for pasture and fodder. [Middle English *festu(e)* from Old French *festu*, ultimately from Latin *festuca* 'stalk, straw']

fess[1] /fɛs/ *n.* (also **fesse**) *Heraldry* a horizontal stripe across the middle of a shield. □ **in fess** arranged horizontally. [Middle English via Old French from Latin *fascia* 'band']

fess[2] /fɛs/ *v.intr.* (usu. foll. by *up*) *colloq.* confess. [contraction of CONFESS]

fess point *n. Heraldry* a point at the centre of a shield.

festal /'fɛst(ə)l/ *adj.* **1** joyous, merry. **2** engaging in holiday activities. **3** of a feast. □ **festally** *adv.* [Old French from Late Latin *festalis* (as FEAST)]

fester /'fɛstə/ *v.* **1** *tr. & intr.* make or become septic. **2** *intr.* cause continuing annoyance. **3** *intr.* rot, stagnate. [Middle English from obsolete *fester* (*n.*) or Old French *festrir*, via Old French *festre* from Latin *fistula*: see FISTULA]

festival /'fɛstɪv(ə)l/ *n. & adj.* ● *n.* **1** a day or period of celebration, religious or secular. **2** a concentrated series of concerts, plays, etc., held regularly in a town etc. (*Bath Festival*). ● *attrib.adj.* of or concerning a festival. [earlier as adj.: Middle English via Old French from medieval Latin *festivalis* (as FESTIVE)]

festival of lights *n.* **1** = HANUKKAH. **2** = DIWALI.

festive /'fɛstɪv/ *adj.* **1** of or characteristic of a festival. **2** cheerful, joyous, celebratory. **3** (of a person) fond of feasting; jovial. □ **festively** *adv.* **festiveness** *n.* [Latin *festivus* from *festum* (as FEAST)]

festivity /fɛ'stɪvɪti/ *n.* (*pl.* **-ies**) **1** gaiety, rejoicing. **2 a** a festive celebration. **b** (in *pl.*) festive proceedings. [Middle English from Old French *festivité* or Latin *festivitas* (as FESTIVE)]

festoon /fɛ'stu:n/ *n. & v.* ● *n.* **1** a chain of flowers, leaves, ribbons, etc., hung in a curve as a decoration. **2** a carved or moulded ornament representing this. ● *v.tr.* (often foll. by *with*) adorn with or form into festoons; decorate elaborately. □ **festoonery** *n.* [French *feston* from Italian *festone* 'festal ornament', from *festa* FEAST]

Festschrift /'fɛs(t)ʃrɪft/ *n.* (also **festschrift**) (*pl.* **-schriften** or **-schrifts**) a collection of writings published in honour of a scholar. [German, from *Fest* 'celebration' + *Schrift* 'writing']

feta /'fɛtə/ *n.* (also **fetta**) a white ewe's-milk or goat's-milk cheese made esp. in Greece. [modern Greek *pheta*]

fetch[1] /fɛtʃ/ *v. & n.* ● *v.tr.* **1** go for and bring back (a person or thing) (*fetch a doctor*). **2** cause to come (*the thought of food fetched him*). **3** cause (blood, tears, a sigh) to come out. **4** draw (breath). **5** *colloq.* give (a blow, slap, etc.) (usu. with recipient stated: *fetched him a slap on the face*). **6** be sold for; realize (a price) (*fetched £10*). **7** *Brit. colloq.* move to interest or delight (*that song always fetches the audience*). ● *n.* **1** an act of fetching. **2** a dodge or trick. **3** *Naut.* **a** the distance travelled by wind or waves across open water. **b** the distance a vessel must sail to reach open water. □ **fetch and carry** run backwards and forwards with things, be a mere servant. **fetch up 1** arrive, come to rest. **2** *Brit.* vomit. □ **fetcher** *n.* [Old English *fecc(e)an*, variant of *fetian*, probably related to a Germanic root = grasp]

fetch[2] /fɛtʃ/ *n. Brit.* a person's wraith or double. [17th c.: origin unknown]

fetching /'fɛtʃɪŋ/ *adj.* attractive. □ **fetchingly** *adv.*

fête /feɪt/ *n. & v.* ● *n.* **1** *Brit.* an outdoor function with the sale of goods, amusements, etc., esp. to raise funds for a charity or cause. **2** a great entertainment; a festival. **3** a saint's day. ● *v.tr.* honour or entertain lavishly. [French *fête* (as FEAST)]

fête champêtre /feɪt ʃɒ̃'peɪtr(ə), French fɛt ʃɑ̃pɛtr/ *n.* (*pl.* ***fêtes champêtres*** *pronunc.* same) an outdoor entertainment; a rural festival. [French (as FÊTE, *champêtre* 'rural')]

fête galante /feɪt ga'lɒ̃t, French fɛt galɑ̃t/ *n.* (*pl.* ***fêtes galantes*** *pronunc.* same) **1** an outdoor entertainment or rural festival, esp. as depicted in 18th-c. French painting. **2** a painting in this genre. [French (as FÊTE, *galante*, fem. of *galant* GALLANT)]

fetid /'fɛtɪd, 'fi:t-/ *adj.* (also **foetid**) stinking. □ **fetidly** *adv.* **fetidness** *n.* [Latin *fetidus* from *fetēre* 'stink']

fetish /'fɛtɪʃ/ *n.* **1** *Psychol.* a thing abnormally stimulating or attracting sexual desire. **2 a** an inanimate object worshipped by primitive peoples for its supposed inherent magical powers or as being inhabited by a spirit. **b** a thing evoking irrational devotion or respect. □ **fetishism** *n.* **fetishist** *n.* **fetishistic** /-'ʃɪstɪk/ *adj.* [French *fétiche* from Portuguese *feitiço* 'charm': originally an adj. = made by art, from Latin *factitius* FACTITIOUS]

fetishize /ˈfɛtɪʃʌɪz/ *v.tr.* (also **-ise**) make a fetish of; pay undue respect to. □ **fetishization** /-ˈzeɪʃ(ə)n/ *n.*

fetlock /ˈfɛtlɒk/ *n.* the part of a horse's leg between the cannon-bone and the pastern, forming a projection above and behind the hoof where a tuft of hair often grows. [Middle English, related to German *Fessel* 'fetlock', from the Germanic base of FOOT]

fetor /ˈfiːtə/ *n.* a stench. [Latin (as FETID)]

fetta var. of FETA.

fetter /ˈfɛtə/ *n.* & *v.* ● *n.* **1 a** a shackle for holding a prisoner by the ankles. **b** any shackle or bond. **2** (in *pl.*) captivity. **3** a restraint or check. ● *v.tr.* **1** put into fetters. **2** restrict, restrain, impede. [Old English *feter*, from Germanic]

fetterlock /ˈfɛtəlɒk/ *n.* **1** a D-shaped fetter for tethering a horse by the leg. **2** a heraldic representation of this.

fettle /ˈfɛt(ə)l/ *n.* & *v.* ● *n.* condition or trim (*in fine fettle*). ● *v.tr.* trim or clean (the rough edge of a metal casting, pottery before firing, etc.). [earlier as verb, from dialect *fettle* (*n.*) = girdle, from Old English *fetel*, from Germanic]

fettler /ˈfɛtlə/ *n.* **1** *Brit.* & *Austral.* a railway maintenance worker. **2** a person who fettles.

fettuccine /fɛtʊˈtʃiːni/ *n.* (also **fettucini**) pasta made in ribbons. [Italian, pl. of diminutive of *fetta* 'slice, ribbon']

fetus *US* var. of FOETUS.

feu /fjuː/ *n.* & *v. Sc.* ● *n.* **1** a perpetual lease at a fixed rent. **2** a piece of land so held. ● *v.tr.* (**feus, feued, feuing**) grant (land) on feu. [Old French: see FEE]

feud[1] /fjuːd/ *n.* & *v.* ● *n.* **1** a state of prolonged mutual hostility, esp. between two families, tribes, etc., with murderous assaults in revenge for a previous injury (*a family feud; be at feud with*). **2** a prolonged or bitter quarrel or dispute. ● *v.intr.* conduct a feud. [Middle English *fede* via Old French *feide, fede* and Middle Dutch, Middle Low German *vēde* from Germanic, related to FOE]

feud[2] /fjuːd/ *n.* a piece of land held under the feudal system or in fee; a fief. [medieval Latin *feudum*: see FEE]

feudal /ˈfjuːd(ə)l/ *adj.* **1** of, according to, or resembling the feudal system. **2** of a feud or fief. **3** outdated (*had a feudal attitude*). □ **feudalism** *n.* **feudalist** *n.* **feudalistic** /-ˈlɪstɪk/ *adj.* **feudalize** *v.tr.* (also **-ise**). **feudalization** /-ˈzeɪʃ(ə)n/ *n.* **feudally** *adv.* [medieval Latin *feudalis, feodalis* from *feudum, feodum* FEE, perhaps from Germanic]

feudality /fjuːˈdalɪti/ *n.* (*pl.* **-ies**) **1** the feudal system or its principles. **2** a feudal holding, a fief. [French *féodalité* from *féodal* (as FEUDAL)]

feudal system *n. hist.* the social system in medieval Europe whereby a vassal held land from a superior in exchange for allegiance and service.

feudatory /ˈfjuːdət(ə)ri/ *adj.* & *n.* ● *adj.* (often foll. by *to*) feudally subject; under overlordship. ● *n.* (*pl.* **-ies**) a feudal vassal. [medieval Latin *feudatorius* from *feudare* 'enfeoff' (as FEUD[2])]

feu de joie /fəː də ˈʒwɑː, French fø də ʒwa/ *n.* (*pl.* ***feux*** *pronunc.* same) a salute by firing rifles etc. on a ceremonial occasion. [French, = fire of joy]

feudist /ˈfjuːdɪst/ *n. US* a person who is conducting a feud.

feuilleton /ˈfəːɪtɒ̃/ *n.* **1** a part of a newspaper etc. devoted to fiction, criticism, light literature, etc. **2** an item printed in this. [French, = leaflet]

fever /ˈfiːvə/ *n.* & *v.* ● *n.* **1 a** an abnormally high body temperature, often with delirium etc. **b** a disease characterized by this (*scarlet fever; typhoid fever*). **2** nervous excitement; agitation. ● *v.tr.* (esp. as **fevered** *adj.*) affect with fever or excitement. [Old English *fēfor* and Anglo-French *fevre*, Old French *fievre*, from Latin *febris*]

feverfew /ˈfiːvəfjuː/ *n.* an aromatic bushy plant, *Tanacetum parthenium* (daisy family), with feathery leaves and white daisy-like flowers, used to treat migraine and, formerly, to reduce fever. [Old English *feferfuge* from Latin *febrifuga* (as FEBRIFUGE)]

feverish /ˈfiːv(ə)rɪʃ/ *adj.* **1** having the symptoms of a fever. **2** excited, fitful, restless. **3** (of a place) infested by fever; feverous. □ **feverishly** *adv.* **feverishness** *n.*

feverous /ˈfiːv(ə)rəs/ *adj.* **1** infested with or apt to cause fever. **2** *archaic* feverish.

fever pitch *n.* a state of extreme excitement.

fever tree *n.* **1** a yellow-flowered southern African tree, *Acacia xanthophloea*. **2** a tree yielding a febrifuge, esp. *Pickneya pubens* of the south-east US.

few /fjuː/ *adj., det.,* & *pron.* ● *adj.* & *det.* **1** not many (*very few people came; visitors are few; few doctors smoke*). **2** (prec. by *a*) a small number of (*everything depended on a few people; a few good restaurants*). ● *pron.* (treated as *pl.*) **1** (prec. by *a*) some but not many (*he only kept a few; a few of his friends were there*). **2** a small number, not many (*many are called but few are chosen*). **3** (prec. by *the*) **a** the minority. **b** the elect. **4** (**the Few**) *Brit.* the RAF pilots who took part in the Battle of Britain. □ **every few** once in every small group of (*every few days*). **few and far between** scarce. **a good few** *Brit. colloq.* a fairly large number. **have a few** *colloq.* take several alcoholic drinks. **no fewer than** as many as (a specified number). **not a few** a considerable number. **some few** some but not at all many. [Old English *fēawe, fēawa*, from Germanic]

■ **Usage** See Usage Note at LESS.

fey /feɪ/ *adj.* **1 a** strange, other-worldly; elfin; whimsical. **b** clairvoyant. **2** *Sc.* **a** fated to die soon. **b** overexcited or elated, as formerly associated with the state of mind of a person about to die. □ **feyly** *adv.* **feyness** *n.* [Old English *fǣge*, from Germanic]

Feynman diagram /ˈfʌɪnmən/ *n. Physics* a diagram of interactions between subatomic particles. [named after R. *Feynman*, US physicist d. 1988]

fez /fɛz/ *n.* (*pl.* **fezzes**) a flat-topped conical red cap with a tassel, worn by men in some Muslim countries. □ **fezzed** *adj.* [Turkish, perhaps from *Fez* in Morocco]

ff *abbr. Mus.* fortissimo.

ff. *abbr.* **1** following pages etc. **2** folios.

Fg. Off. *abbr.* (in the UK) Flying Officer.

fiacre /fɪˈɑːkrə/ *n. hist.* a small four-wheeled cab. [named after the Hôtel de St *Fiacre*, Paris, where such vehicles were first hired out]

fiancé /fɪˈɒnseɪ, -ˈɑːns-, -ˈɒ̃s-/ *n.* (*fem.* **fiancée** *pronunc.* same) a person to whom another is engaged to be married. [French, past part. of *fiancer* 'betroth' from Old French *fiance* 'a promise', ultimately from Latin *fidere* 'to trust']

fianchetto /fɪənˈtʃɛtəʊ, -ˈkɛtəʊ/ *n.* & *v. Chess* ● *n.* (*pl.* **-oes**) the development of a bishop to a long diagonal of the board. ● *v.tr.* (**-oes, -oed**) develop (a bishop) in this way. [Italian, diminutive of *fianco* FLANK]

Fianna Fáil /fɪˌanə ˈfɔɪl/ *n.* one of the two main political parties of the Republic of Ireland. [Irish, from *fianna* 'band of warriors' + *Fáil*, genitive of *Fál*, an ancient name for Ireland]

fiasco /fɪˈaskəʊ/ *n.* (*pl.* **-os**) a ludicrous or humiliating failure or breakdown (originally in a dramatic or musical performance); an ignominious result. [Italian, = bottle (with unexplained allusion): see FLASK]

fiat /ˈfʌɪat/ *n.* **1** an authorization. **2** a decree or order. [Latin, = let it be done]

fiat money *n. US* inconvertible paper money made legal tender by a Government decree.

fib /fɪb/ *n.* & *v.* ● *n.* a trivial or venial lie. ● *v.intr.* (**fibbed, fibbing**) tell a fib. □ **fibber** *n.* **fibster** *n.* [perhaps from obsolete *fible-fable* 'nonsense', reduplication of FABLE]

fiber *US* var. of FIBRE.

fiberboard *US* var. of FIBREBOARD.

fiberglass *US* var. of FIBREGLASS.

Fibonacci series /fɪbəˈnɑːtʃi/ *n. Math.* a series of numbers in which each number (**Fibonacci number**) is the sum of the two preceding numbers, esp. 1, 1, 2, 3, 5,

8, etc. [named after L. *Fibonacci*, Italian mathematician fl. 1200]

fibre /ˈfʌɪbə/ *n.* (*US* **fiber**) **1** any of the threads or filaments forming animal or vegetable tissue and textile substances. **2** a piece of glass in the form of a thread. **3 a** a substance formed of fibres. **b** a substance that can be spun, woven, or felted. **4** the structure, grain, or character of something (*lacks moral fibre*). **5** dietary material that is resistant to the action of digestive enzymes; roughage. □ **fibred** *adj.* (also in *comb.*). **fibreless** *adj.* **fibriform** /ˈfʌɪbrɪfɔːm/ *adj.* [Middle English via French from Latin *fibra*]

fibreboard /ˈfʌɪbəbɔːd/ *n.* (*US* **fiberboard**) a building material made of wood or other plant fibres compressed into boards.

fibrefill /ˈfʌɪbəfɪl/ *n.* a synthetic material used for padding garments, cushions, etc.

fibreglass /ˈfʌɪbəglɑːs/ *n.* (*US* **fiberglass**) **1** a textile fabric made from woven glass fibres. **2** a plastic reinforced by glass fibres.

fibre optics *n.* **1** (treated as *sing.*) the use of thin flexible fibres of glass or other transparent solids to transmit light signals, e.g. for telecommunications or internal inspection of the body. **2** (treated as *pl.*) the fibres etc. so used.

fibril /ˈfʌɪbrɪl/ *n.* **1** a small fibre. **2** a subdivision of a fibre. □ **fibrillar** *adj.* **fibrillary** *adj.* [modern Latin *fibrilla*, diminutive of Latin *fibra* 'fibre']

fibrillate /ˈfʌɪbrɪleɪt, ˈfɪ-/ *v.* **1** *intr.* **a** (of a fibre) split up into fibrils. **b** (of a muscle, esp. in the heart) undergo a quivering movement due to uncoordinated contraction of the individual fibrils. **2** *tr.* break (a fibre) into fibrils. □ **fibrillation** /-ˈleɪʃ(ə)n/ *n.*

fibrin /ˈfʌɪbrɪn, ˈfɪ-/ *n.* an insoluble protein formed during blood-clotting from fibrinogen. □ **fibrinoid** *adj.* [FIBRE + -IN]

fibrinogen /fʌɪˈbrɪnədʒ(ə)n, fɪ-/ *n.* a soluble blood plasma protein which produces fibrin when acted upon by the enzyme thrombin.

fibro /ˈfʌɪbrəʊ/ *n.* (*pl.* **-os**) *Austral.* **1** a mixture of asbestos and cement, used in sheets for building etc. **2** a house constructed mainly of this. [abbreviation of *fibrocement*]

fibro- /ˈfʌɪbrəʊ/ *comb. form* fibre.

fibroblast /ˈfʌɪbrə(ʊ)blɑːst/ *n.* *Anat.* a cell producing collagen fibres in connective tissue. [FIBRO- + -BLAST]

fibroid /ˈfʌɪbrɔɪd/ *adj.* & *n.* ● *adj.* **1** of or characterized by fibrous tissue. **2** resembling or containing fibres. ● *n.* a benign tumour of muscular and fibrous tissues, one or more of which may develop in the wall of the womb.

fibroin /ˈfʌɪbrəʊɪn/ *n.* a protein which is the chief constituent of silk. [FIBRO- + -IN]

fibroma /fʌɪˈbrəʊmə/ *n.* (*pl.* **fibromas** or **fibromata** /-mətə/) a fibrous tumour. [modern Latin, from Latin *fibra* 'fibre' + -OMA]

fibrosis /fʌɪˈbrəʊsɪs/ *n.* *Med.* a thickening and scarring of connective tissue, usu. as a result of injury. □ **fibrotic** /-ˈbrɒtɪk/ *adj.* [modern Latin, from Latin *fibra* 'fibre' + -OSIS]

fibrositis /fʌɪbrəˈsʌɪtɪs/ *n.* inflammation of fibrous connective tissue, usu. rheumatic and painful. □ **fibrositic** /-ˈsɪtɪk/ *adj.* [modern Latin, from Latin *fibrosus* 'fibrous' + -ITIS]

fibrous /ˈfʌɪbrəs/ *adj.* consisting of or like fibres. □ **fibrously** *adv.* **fibrousness** *n.*

fibula /ˈfɪbjʊlə/ *n.* (*pl.* **fibulae** /-liː/ or **fibulas**) **1** *Anat.* the smaller and outer of the two bones between the knee and the ankle in terrestrial vertebrates. **2** *Antiq.* a brooch or clasp. □ **fibular** *adj.* [Latin, perhaps related to *figere* 'fix']

-fic /fɪk/ *suffix* (usu. as **-ific**) forming adjectives meaning 'producing', 'making' (*prolific*; *pacific*). □ **-fically** *suffix* forming adverbs. [from or suggested by French *-fique* or Latin *-ficus* from *facere* 'do, make']

-fication /fɪˈkeɪʃ(ə)n/ *suffix* (usu. as **-ification**) forming nouns of action from verbs in *-fy* (*acidification*; *purification*; *simplification*). [from or suggested by French *-fication* or Latin *-ficatio -onis* from *-ficare*: see -FY]

fiche /fiːʃ/ *n.* (*pl.* same or **fiches**) a microfiche. [French, = slip of paper]

fichu /ˈfiːʃuː/ *n.* a woman's small triangular shawl of lace etc. for the shoulders and neck. [French]

fickle /ˈfɪk(ə)l/ *adj.* inconstant, changeable, esp. in loyalty. □ **fickleness** *n.* **fickly** *adv.* [Old English *ficol*: related to *befician* 'deceive', *fǣcne* 'deceitful']

fictile /ˈfɪktʌɪl, -tɪl/ *adj.* **1** made of earth or clay by a potter. **2** of pottery. [Latin *fictilis* from *fingere fict-* 'fashion']

fiction /ˈfɪkʃ(ə)n/ *n.* **1** an invented idea or statement or narrative; an imaginary thing. **2** literature, esp. novels, describing imaginary events and people; the genre comprising novels and stories. **3** a conventionally accepted falsehood (*legal fiction*; *polite fiction*). **4** the act or process of inventing imaginary things. □ **fictional** *adj.* **fictionality** /-ˈnalɪti/ *n.* **fictionalize** *v.tr.* (also **-ise**). **fictionalization** /-ˈzeɪʃ(ə)n/ *n.* **fictionally** *adv.* **fictionist** *n.* [Middle English via Old French from Latin *fictio -onis* (as FICTILE)]

fictitious /fɪkˈtɪʃəs/ *adj.* **1** imaginary, unreal. **2** counterfeit; not genuine. **3** (of a name or character) assumed. **4** of or in novels. **5** regarded as or called such by a legal or conventional fiction (*his fictitious son*). □ **fictitiously** *adv.* **fictitiousness** *n.* [Latin *ficticius* (as FICTILE)]

fictive /ˈfɪktɪv/ *adj.* **1** creating or created by imagination. **2** not genuine. □ **fictiveness** *n.* [French *fictif -ive* or medieval Latin *fictivus* (as FICTILE)]

ficus /ˈfiːkəs, ˈfʌɪkəs/ *n.* a tree or shrub of the large genus *Ficus* (mulberry family), including the fig and the rubber plant. [Latin, = fig, fig tree]

fid /fɪd/ *n.* **1** *Brit.* a small thick piece or wedge or heap of anything. **2** *Naut.* **a** a square wooden or iron bar to support the topmast. **b** a conical wooden pin used in splicing. [17th c.: origin unknown]

Fid. Def. *abbr.* *Brit.* Defender of the Faith. [Latin *Fidei Defensor*]

fiddle /ˈfɪd(ə)l/ *n.* & *v.* ● *n.* **1** *colloq.* or *derog.* a stringed instrument played with a bow, esp. a violin. **2** *Brit. colloq.* an instance of cheating or fraud. **3** a fiddly task. **4** *Naut.* a contrivance for stopping things from rolling or sliding off a table in bad weather. ● *v.* **1** *intr.* **a** (often foll. by *with*, *at*) play restlessly. **b** (often foll. by *about*) move aimlessly. **c** act idly or frivolously. **d** (usu. foll. by *with*) make minor adjustments; tinker (esp. in an attempt to make improvements). **2** *tr.* *Brit. slang* **a** cheat, swindle. **b** falsify. **c** get by cheating. **3 a** *intr.* play the fiddle. **b** *tr.* play (a tune etc.) on the fiddle. □ **as fit as a fiddle** in very good health. **face as long as a fiddle** a dismal face. **on the fiddle** engaged in cheating or swindling. **play second** (or **first**) **fiddle** take a subordinate (or leading) role. [Old English *fithele* via Germanic from a Romanic root related to VIOL, ultimately from Latin *vitulāri* 'celebrate a festival, be joyful']

fiddle-back *n.* a fiddle-shaped back of a chair or front of a chasuble.

fiddle-de-dee /fɪd(ə)lɪdɪˈdiː/ *int.* & *n.* nonsense.

fiddle-faddle /ˈfɪd(ə)lfad(ə)l/ *n.*, *v.*, *int.*, & *adj.* ● *n.* trivial matters. ● *v.intr.* fuss, trifle. ● *int.* nonsense! ● *adj.* (of a person or thing) petty, fussy. [reduplication of FIDDLE]

fiddle-head *n.* a scroll-like carving at a ship's bows.

fiddle pattern *n.* the pattern of spoons and forks with fiddle-shaped handles.

fiddler /ˈfɪdlə/ *n.* **1** a fiddle-player. **2** *Brit. slang* a swindler, a cheat. **3** any small crab of the genus *Uca*, the male having one of its claws held in a position like a violinist's arm. [Old English *fithelere* (as FIDDLE)]

fiddlestick /ˈfɪd(ə)lstɪk/ *n.* **1** (in *pl.*; as *int.*) nonsense! **2** *colloq.* a bow for a fiddle.

fiddling /ˈfɪdlɪŋ/ *adj.* **1 a** petty, trivial. **b** contemptible, futile. **2** *Brit.* = FIDDLY. **3** that fiddles.

fiddly /ˈfɪdli/ *adj.* (**fiddlier**, **fiddliest**) *Brit.* intricate, awkward, or tiresome to do or use.

fideism /ˈfʌɪdiɪz(ə)m/ *n.* the doctrine that all or some knowledge depends on faith or revelation. □ **fideist** *n.* **fideistic** /-ˈɪstɪk/ *adj.* [Latin *fides* 'faith' + -ISM]

fidelity /fɪˈdɛlɪti/ *n.* **1** (often foll. by *to*) faithfulness, loyalty. **2** strict conformity to truth or fact. **3** exact correspondence to the original. **4** precision in reproduction of sound (*high fidelity*). [French *fidélité* or Latin *fidelitas* (as FEALTY)]

fidelity insurance *n.* insurance taken out by an employer against losses incurred through an employee's dishonesty etc.

fidget /ˈfɪdʒɪt/ *v.* & *n.* ● *v.* (**fidgeted**, **fidgeting**) **1** *intr.* move or act restlessly or nervously, usu. while maintaining basically the same posture. **2** *intr.* be uneasy, worry. **3** *tr.* make (a person) uneasy or uncomfortable. ● *n.* **1** a person who fidgets. **2** (usu. in *pl.*) **a** bodily uneasiness seeking relief in spasmodic movements; such movements. **b** a restless mood. □ **fidgety** *adj.* **fidgetiness** *n.* [obsolete or dialect *fidge* 'to twitch']

Fido /ˈfʌɪdəʊ/ *n.* a device enabling aircraft to land by dispersing fog by means of petrol-burners on the ground. [acronym from *F*og *I*ntensive *D*ispersal *O*peration]

fiducial /fɪˈdjuːʃ(ə)l/ *adj.* *Surveying, Astron.*, etc. (of a line, point, etc.) assumed as a fixed basis of comparison. [Late Latin *fiducialis* via *fiducia* 'trust' from *fidere* 'to trust']

fiduciary /fɪˈdjuːʃ(ə)ri/ *adj.* & *n.* ● *adj.* **1 a** of a trust, trustee, or trusteeship. **b** held or given in trust. **2** (of a paper currency) depending for its value on public confidence or securities. ● *n.* (*pl.* **-ies**) a trustee. [Latin *fiduciarius* (as FIDUCIAL)]

fidus Achates /fʌɪdəs əˈkeɪtiːz/ *n.* a faithful friend; a devoted follower. [Latin, = faithful Achates (a companion of Aeneas in Virgil's *Aeneid*)]

fie /fʌɪ/ *int.* *archaic* expressing disgust, shame, or a pretence of outraged propriety. [Middle English via Old French from Latin *fi* an exclamation of disgust at a stench]

fief /fiːf/ *n.* **1** a piece of land held under the feudal system or in fee. **2** a person's sphere of operation or control. [French (as FEE)]

fiefdom /ˈfiːfdəm/ *n.* a fief.

field /fiːld/ *n.* & *v.* ● *n.* **1** an area of open land, esp. one used for pasture or crops, often bounded by hedges, fences, etc. **2** an area rich in some natural product (*gas field*; *diamond field*). **3** a piece of land for a specified purpose, esp. an area marked out for games (*football field*). **4 a** the participants in a contest or sport. **b** all the competitors in a race or all except those specified. **5** *Cricket* **a** the side fielding. **b** a fielder. **6** an expanse of ice, snow, sea, sky, etc. **7 a** the ground on which a battle is fought; a battlefield (*left his rival in possession of the field*). **b** the scene of a campaign. **c** (*attrib.*) (of artillery etc.) light and mobile for use on campaign. **d** *archaic* a battle. **8** an area of operation or activity; a subject of study (*each supreme in his own field*). **9 a** the region in which a force is effective (*gravitational field*; *magnetic field*). **b** the force exerted in such an area. **10** a range of perception (*field of view*; *wide field of vision*; *filled the field of the telescope*). **11** *Math.* a system subject to two operations analogous to those for the multiplication and addition of real numbers. **12** (*attrib.*) **a** (of an animal or plant) found in the countryside, wild (*field mouse*). **b** carried out or working in the natural environment, not in a laboratory etc. (*field test*). **13 a** the background of a picture, coin, flag, etc. **b** *Heraldry* the surface of an escutcheon or of one of its divisions. **14** *Computing* a part of a record, representing an item of data. ● *v.* **1** *Cricket, Baseball* etc. **a** *intr.* act as a fielder. **b** *tr.* stop (and return) (the ball). **2** *tr.* **a** select (a team or individual) to play in a game. **b** deploy (an army). **c** propose (a candidate). **3** *tr.* deal with (a succession of questions etc.). □ **hold the field** *Brit.* not be superseded. **in the field 1** campaigning. **2** working etc. away from one's laboratory, headquarters, etc. **keep the field** *Brit.* continue a campaign. **play the field** *colloq.* avoid exclusive attachment to one person or activity etc. **take the field 1** begin a campaign. **2** (of a sports team) go on to a pitch to begin a game. [Old English *feld*, from West Germanic]

field-book *n.* a book used in the field by a surveyor for technical notes.

field-cornet *n.* *S.Afr. hist.* a minor magistrate.

field day *n.* **1** wide scope for action or success; a time occupied with exciting events (*when crowds form, pickpockets have a field day*). **2** *Mil.* an exercise, esp. in manoeuvring; a review. **3** a day spent in exploration, scientific investigation, etc., in the natural environment.

field-effect transistor *n.* a semiconductor device with current flowing through a channel controlled by a transverse electric field.

fielder /ˈfiːldə/ *n.* *Cricket, Baseball*, etc. a member (other than the bowler or pitcher) of the side that is fielding.

field events *n.pl.* athletic sports other than races (e.g. shot-putting, jumping, discus-throwing).

fieldfare /ˈfiːldfɛː/ *n.* a thrush, *Turdus pilaris*, having grey plumage with a speckled breast. [Middle English *feldefare*, perhaps as FIELD + FARE]

field glasses *n.pl.* binoculars for outdoor use.

field goal *n.* **1** *Amer. Football* a goal scored by a drop kick or place kick from the field. **2** *Basketball* a goal scored when the ball is in normal play.

field hockey *n.* *N. Amer.* = HOCKEY[1].

field hospital *n.* a temporary hospital near a battlefield.

field marshal *n.* (in the British army) an officer of the highest rank.

field mouse *n.* a Eurasian mouse, *Apodemus sylvaticus*, with large eyes and ears and a long tail. Also called *wood mouse*.

field mushroom *n.* the common edible mushroom, *Agaricus campestris*.

field mustard *n.* = CHARLOCK.

field notes *n.pl.* notes made by a person while engaged in fieldwork.

field officer *n.* an army officer of field rank.

field of honour *n.* the place where a duel or battle is fought.

field of vision *n.* all that comes into view when the eyes are turned in some direction.

field rank *n.* esp. *Brit.* any rank in an army above captain and below general.

fieldsman /ˈfiːldzmən/ *n.* (*pl.* **-men**) *Cricket* = FIELDER.

field sports *n.pl.* outdoor sports, esp. hunting, shooting, and fishing.

fieldstone /ˈfiːldstəʊn/ *n.* stone used in its natural form.

field telegraph *n.* a movable telegraph for use on campaign.

fieldwork /ˈfiːldwəːk/ *n.* **1** the practical work of a surveyor, collector of scientific data, sociologist, etc., conducted in the natural environment rather than a laboratory, office, etc. **2** a temporary fortification. □ **fieldworker** *n.*

fiend /fiːnd/ *n.* **1 a** an evil spirit, a demon. **b** (prec. by *the*) the Devil. **2 a** a very wicked or cruel person. **b** a person causing mischief or annoyance. **3** (with a qualifying word) *colloq.* a devotee or addict (*a fitness fiend*). **4** something difficult or unpleasant. □ **fiendlike** *adj.* [Old English *fēond*, from Germanic]

fiendish /ˈfiːndɪʃ/ *adj.* **1** like a fiend; extremely cruel or unpleasant. **2** extremely difficult. □ **fiendishly** *adv.* **fiendishness** *n.*

fierce /fɪəs/ *adj.* (**fiercer**, **fiercest**) **1** vehemently aggressive or frightening in temper or action, violent. **2**

eager, intense, ardent. **3** unpleasantly strong or intense; uncontrolled (*fierce heat*). **4** (of a mechanism) not smooth or easy in action. □ **fiercely** *adv.* **fierceness** *n.* [Middle English via Anglo-French *fers*, Old French *fiers fier* 'proud' from Latin *ferus* 'savage']

fieri facias /ˌfʌɪərʌɪ ˈfeɪʃɪas/ *n. Law* a writ to a sheriff for executing a judgement. [Latin, = cause to be made or done]

fiery /ˈfʌɪəri/ *adj.* (**fierier**, **fieriest**) **1 a** consisting of or flaming with fire. **b** (of an arrow etc.) fire-bearing. **2** like fire in appearance, bright red. **3 a** hot as fire. **b** acting like fire; producing a burning sensation. **4 a** flashing, ardent (*fiery eyes*). **b** eager, pugnacious, spirited, irritable (*fiery temper*). **c** (of a horse) mettlesome. **5** (of gas, a mine, etc.) inflammable; liable to explosions. **6** *Cricket* (of a pitch) making the ball rise dangerously. □ **fierily** *adv.* **fieriness** *n.*

fiery cross *n.* a wooden cross charred or set on fire as a symbol.

fiesta /fɪˈɛstə/ *n.* **1** a holiday or festivity. **2** a religious festival in Spanish-speaking countries. [Spanish, = feast]

FIFA /ˈfiːfə/ *abbr.* International Football Federation. [French *Fédération Internationale de Football Association*]

fi. fa. *abbr.* fieri facias.

fife /fʌɪf/ *n.* & *v.* ● *n.* **1** a kind of small shrill flute used with the drum in military music. **2** its player. ● *v.* **1** *intr.* play the fife. **2** *tr.* play (an air etc.) on the fife. □ **fifer** *n.* [German *Pfeife* PIPE, or French *fifre* from Swiss German *Pfifre* 'piper']

fife-rail /ˈfʌɪfreɪl/ *n. Naut.* a rail round the mainmast with belaying-pins. [18th c.: origin unknown]

fifteen /fɪfˈtiːn, ˈfɪftiːn/ *n.* & *adj.* ● *n.* **1** one more than fourteen, or five more than ten; the product of three units and five units. **2** a symbol for this (15, xv, XV). **3** a size etc. denoted by fifteen. **4** a team of fifteen players, esp. in rugby. **5** (**the Fifteen**) *hist.* the Jacobite rebellion of 1715. **6** (**15**) *Brit.* (of films) classified as suitable for persons of 15 years and over. ● *adj.* that amount to fifteen. □ **fifteenth** *adj.* & *n.* [Old English *fīftēne* (as FIVE, -TEEN)]

fifth /fɪfθ/ *n.* & *adj.* ● *n.* **1** the position in a sequence corresponding to that of the number 5 in the sequence 1–5. **2** something occupying this position. **3** the fifth person etc. in a race or competition. **4** any of five equal parts of a thing. **5** *Mus.* **a** an interval or chord spanning five consecutive notes in the diatonic scale (e.g. C to G). **b** a note separated from another by this interval. **6** *US colloq.* **a** a fifth of a gallon of liquor. **b** a bottle containing this. ● *adj.* that is the fifth. □ **take the fifth** (in the US) exercise the right guaranteed by the Fifth Amendment to the Constitution of refusing to answer questions in order to avoid incriminating oneself. □ **fifthly** *adv.* [earlier and dialect *fift* from Old English *fīfta*, from Germanic, assimilated to FOURTH]

fifth column *n.* a group working for an enemy within a country at war etc. (from General Mola's reference to such support in besieged Madrid in 1936). □ **fifth columnist** *n.*

fifth-generation *adj.* denoting a proposed new class of computer employing artificial intelligence.

Fifth Monarchy *n.* the last of the five great kingdoms predicted in Daniel 2:44.

Fifth-monarchy-man *n. hist.* a 17th-c. zealot expecting the immediate second coming of Christ and repudiating all other government.

fifth wheel *n.* **1** an extra wheel of a coach. **2** a superfluous person or thing. **3** a horizontal turntable over the front axle of a carriage as an extra support to prevent its tipping.

fifty /ˈfɪfti/ *n.* & *adj.* ● *n.* (*pl.* **-ies**) **1** the product of five and ten. **2** a symbol for this (50, l, L). **3** (in *pl.*) the numbers from 50 to 59, esp. the years of a century or of a person's life. **4** a set of fifty persons or things. **5** a large indefinite number (*have fifty things to tell you*). ● *adj.* that amount to fifty. □ **fifty-first, -second**, etc. the ordinal numbers between fiftieth and sixtieth. **fifty-one, -two**, etc. the cardinal numbers between fifty and sixty. □ **fiftieth** *adj.* & *n.* **fiftyfold** *adj.* & *adv.* [Old English *fīftig* (as FIVE, -TY[2])]

fifty-fifty *adj.* & *adv.* ● *adj.* equal, with equal shares or chances (*on a fifty-fifty basis*). ● *adv.* equally, half-and-half (*go fifty-fifty*).

fig[1] /fɪg/ *n.* **1** a soft pear-shaped fruit with many seeds, eaten fresh or dried. **2** (in full **fig tree**) any deciduous tree or shrub of the genus *Ficus*, esp. *F. carica*, which has broad leaves and bears figs. □ **not care** (or **give**) **a fig** not care at all. [Middle English via Old French *figue* from Provençal *fig(u)a*, ultimately from Latin *ficus*]

fig[2] /fɪg/ *n.* & *v.* ● *n.* **1** dress or equipment (*in full fig*). **2** condition or form (*in good fig*). ● *v.tr.* (**figged**, **figging**) **1** (foll. by *out*) dress up (a person). **2** (foll. by *out, up*) make (a horse) lively. [variant of obsolete verb *feague* from German *fegen*: see FAKE[1]]

fig. *abbr.* figure.

fight /fʌɪt/ *v.* & *n.* ● *v.* (*past* and *past part.* **fought** /fɔːt/) **1** *intr.* (often foll. by *against, with*) contend or struggle in war, battle, single combat, etc. **2** *tr.* contend with (an opponent) in this way. **3** *tr.* take part or engage in (a battle, war, duel, etc.). **4** *tr.* contend about (an issue, an election); maintain (a lawsuit, cause, etc.) against an opponent. **5** *intr.* campaign or strive determinedly to achieve something. **6** *tr.* strive to overcome (disease, fire, fear, etc.). **7** *tr.* make (one's way) by fighting. **8** *tr.* cause (cocks or dogs) to fight. **9** *tr.* handle (troops, a ship, etc.) in battle. ● *n.* **1 a** a combat, esp. unpremeditated, between two or more persons, animals, or parties. **b** a boxing match. **c** a battle. **2** a conflict or struggle; a vigorous effort in the face of difficulty. **3** power or inclination to fight (*has no fight left*; *showed fight*). □ **fight back 1** counter-attack. **2** suppress (one's feelings, tears, etc.). **fight down** suppress (one's feelings, tears, etc.). **fight for 1** fight on behalf of. **2** fight to secure (a thing). **fight off** repel with effort. **fight out** (usu. **fight it out**) settle (a dispute etc.) by fighting. **fight shy of** avoid; be unwilling to approach (a person, task, etc.). **make a fight of it** (or **put up a fight**) offer resistance. [Old English *feohtan*, *feoht(e)*, from West Germanic]

fightback /ˈfʌɪtbak/ *n. Brit.* an act of retaliation; a rally or recovery.

fighter /ˈfʌɪtə/ *n.* **1** a person or animal that fights. **2** a fast military aircraft designed for attacking other aircraft.

fighter-bomber *n.* an aircraft serving as both fighter and bomber.

fighting chair *n. US* a fixed chair on a boat for use when catching large fish.

fighting chance *n.* an opportunity of succeeding by great effort.

fighting fish *n.* (in full **Siamese fighting fish**) a freshwater fish, *Betta splendens*, native to Thailand, the males of which fight vigorously.

fighting fit *adj.* fit enough to fight; at the peak of fitness.

fighting fund *n. Brit.* money raised to support a campaign.

fighting-top *n.* a circular gun platform high on a warship's mast.

fighting words *n.pl. colloq.* words indicating a willingness to fight.

fig leaf *n.* **1** a leaf of a fig tree. **2** a device for concealing something, esp. the genitals (Gen. 3:7).

figment /ˈfɪgm(ə)nt/ *n.* a thing invented or existing only in the imagination. [Middle English from Latin *figmentum*, related to *fingere* 'fashion']

figura /fɪˈgjʊərə/ *n. Literary Criticism* etc. a person or thing representing or symbolizing a fact etc. [modern Latin from Latin, = FIGURE]

figural /ˈfɪgjʊr(ə)l/ *adj.* **1** figurative. **2** relating to figures or shapes. **3** *Mus.* florid in style. [Old French *figural* or Late Latin *figuralis* from *figura* FIGURE]

figurant /ˈfɪgjʊr(ə)nt, French figyrɑ̃/ *n.* (*fem.* ***figurante*** /ˈfɪgjʊr(ə)nt, French figyrɑ̃t/) a ballet dancer appearing only in a group. [French, pres. part. of *figurer* FIGURE]

figuration /fɪgəˈreɪʃ(ə)n, -gjʊ-/ *n.* **1 a** the act of formation. **b** a mode of formation; a form. **c** a shape or outline. **2 a** ornamentation by designs. **b** *Mus.* ornamental patterns of scales, arpeggios, etc., often derived from an earlier motif. **3** allegorical representation. [Middle English from French or from Latin *figuratio* (as FIGURE)]

figurative /ˈfɪg(ə)rətɪv, -gjʊ-/ *adj.* **1 a** metaphorical, not literal. **b** metaphorically so called. **2** characterized by or addicted to figures of speech. **3** of pictorial or sculptural representation. **4** emblematic, serving as a type. □ **figuratively** *adv.* **figurativeness** *n.* [Middle English from Late Latin *figurativus* (as FIGURE)]

figure /ˈfɪgə/ *n.* & *v.* ● *n.* **1 a** the external form or shape of a thing. **b** bodily shape (*has a well-developed figure*). **2 a** a person as seen in outline but not identified (*saw a figure leaning against the door*). **b** a person as contemplated mentally (*a public figure*). **3** appearance as giving a certain impression (*cut a poor figure*). **4 a** a representation of the human form in drawing, sculpture, etc. **b** an image or likeness. **c** an emblem or type. **5** *Geom.* a two-dimensional space enclosed by a line or lines, or a three-dimensional space enclosed by a surface or surfaces; any of the classes of these, e.g. the triangle, the sphere. **6 a** a numerical symbol, esp. any of the ten in Arabic notation. **b** a number so expressed. **c** an amount of money, a value (*cannot put a figure on it*). **d** (in *pl.*) arithmetical calculations. **7** a diagram or illustrative drawing. **8** a decorative pattern. **9 a** a division of a set dance, an evolution. **b** (in skating) a prescribed pattern of movements from a stationary position. **10** *Mus.* a short succession of notes producing a single impression, a brief melodic or rhythmic formula out of which longer passages are developed. **11** (in full **figure of speech**) a recognized form of rhetorical expression giving variety, force, etc., esp. metaphor or hyperbole. **12** *Gram.* a permitted deviation from the usual rules of construction, e.g. ellipsis. **13** *Logic* the form of a syllogism, classified according to the position of the middle term. **14** a horoscope. ● *v.* **1** *intr.* appear or be mentioned, esp. prominently. **2** *tr.* represent in a diagram or picture. **3** *tr.* imagine; picture mentally. **4** *tr.* **a** embellish with a pattern (*figured satin*). **b** *Mus.* embellish with figures. **5** *tr.* mark with numbers (*figured bass*) or prices. **6 a** *tr.* calculate. **b** *intr.* do arithmetic. **7** *tr.* be a symbol of, represent typically. **8** esp. *N. Amer.* **a** *tr.* understand, ascertain, consider. **b** *intr. colloq.* be likely or understandable (*that figures*). □ **figure on** *US* count on, expect. **figure out 1** work out by arithmetic or logic. **2** estimate. **3** understand. □ **figureless** *adj.* [Middle English via Old French *figure* (n.), *figurer* (v.) from Latin *figura*, *figurare*, related to *fingere* 'fashion']

figured bass *n.* = CONTINUO.

figurehead /ˈfɪgəhɛd/ *n.* **1** a nominal leader or head without real power. **2** a carving, usu. a bust or a full-length figure, at a ship's prow.

figure of eight *n.* (usu. hyphenated when *attrib.*) **1** the shape of the number eight. **2** something that has this shape.

figure of fun *n.* a ridiculous person.

figure of speech see FIGURE *n.* 11.

figure skating *n.* skating in prescribed patterns from a stationary position. □ **figure skater** *n.*

figurine /ˈfɪgəriːn, -gjʊ-/ *n.* a statuette. [French from Italian *figurina*, diminutive of *figura* FIGURE]

figwort /ˈfɪgwəːt/ *n.* any plant of the genus *Scrophularia* (family Scrophulariaceae), with dull purplish-brown flowers, once believed to be useful against scrofula.

Fijian /fiːˈdʒiːən/ *adj.* & *n.* ● *adj.* of or relating to Fiji, its people, or language. ● *n.* **1** a native or national of Fiji. **2** the Austronesian language of this people.

filagree var. of FILIGREE.

filament /ˈfɪləm(ə)nt/ *n.* **1** a slender threadlike body or fibre (esp. in animal or vegetable structures). **2** a conducting wire or thread with a high melting point in an electric bulb or thermionic valve, heated or made incandescent by an electric current. **3** *Bot.* the part of the stamen that supports the anther. **4** *archaic* (of air, light, etc.) a notional train of particles following each other. □ **filamentary** /-ˈmɛnt(ə)ri/ *adj.* **filamented** *adj.* **filamentous** /-ˈmɛntəs/ *adj.* [French *filament* or modern Latin *filamentum* via Late Latin *filare* 'spin' from Latin *filum* 'thread']

filaria /fɪˈlɛːrɪə/ *n.* (*pl.* **filariae** /-rɪiː/) any threadlike parasitic nematode worm of the family Filariidae, introduced into the blood by certain biting flies and mosquitoes. □ **filarial** *adj.* [modern Latin, from Latin *filum* 'thread']

filariasis /fɪˌlɛːrɪˈeɪsɪs, fɪləˈrʌɪəsɪs/ *n. pl.* **filariases** /-rɪˈeɪsiːz, -ˈrʌɪəsiːz/) a tropical disease caused by the presence of filarial worms esp. in the lymph vessels.

filature /ˈfɪlətʃə, -tjə/ *n.* an establishment for or the action of reeling silk from cocoons. [French from Italian *filatura*, from *filare* 'spin']

filbert /ˈfɪlbət/ *n.* **1** a cultivated hazel, esp. *Corylus maxima*, bearing longish edible nuts. **2** this nut. **3** (in full **filbert brush**) an oval brush used in oil painting. [Middle English *philliberd* etc. from Anglo-French *philbert*, dialect French *noix de filbert*, a nut ripe about St Philibert's day (20 Aug.)]

filch /fɪltʃ/ *v.tr.* pilfer, steal. □ **filcher** *n.* [Middle English: origin unknown]

file[1] /fʌɪl/ *n.* & *v.* ● *n.* **1** a folder, box, etc., for holding loose papers, esp. arranged for reference. **2** a set of papers kept in this. **3** *Computing* a collection of (usu. related) data stored under one name. **4** a series of issues of a newspaper etc. in order. **5** a stiff pointed wire on which documents etc. are impaled for keeping. ● *v.tr.* **1** place (papers) in a file or among (esp. public) records. **2** submit (a petition for divorce, an application for a patent, etc.) to the appropriate authority. **3** (of a reporter) send (a story, information, etc.) to a newspaper. □ **file away** place in a file, or make a mental note of, for future reference. **on file** in a file or filing system. □ **filer** *n.* [French *fil* from Latin *filum* 'thread']

file[2] /fʌɪl/ *n.* & *v.* ● *n.* **1** a line of persons or things one behind another. **2** (foll. by *of*) *Mil.* a small detachment of men (now usu. two). **3** *Chess* a line of squares from player to player (cf. RANK[1] *n.* 6). ● *v.intr.* walk in a file. □ **file off** (or **away**) *Mil.* go off by files. [French *file* from Late Latin *filare* 'spin' or Latin *filum* 'thread']

file[3] /fʌɪl/ *n.* & *v.* ● *n.* a tool with a roughened surface or surfaces, usu. of steel, for smoothing or shaping wood, fingernails, etc. ● *v.tr.* **1** smooth or shape with a file. **2** elaborate or improve (a thing, esp. a literary work). □ **file away** remove (roughness etc.) with a file. □ **filer** *n.* [Old English *fīl*, from West Germanic]

filefish /ˈfʌɪlfɪʃ/ *n.* (*pl.* usu. same) any fish of the family Balistidae, with a spiny dorsal fin and rough skin. [FILE[3], from their rough skin, suggesting the surface of a file]

file server *n. Computing* a device which controls access to one or more separately stored files.

filet /ˈfiːleɪ, ˈfɪlɪt/ *n.* **1** a kind of net or lace with a square mesh. **2** a fillet of meat. [French, = thread]

filet mignon /ˌfiːleɪ ˈmiːnjɒ̃/ *n.* a small tender piece of beef from the end of the undercut. [French, literally 'dainty fillet']

filial /ˈfɪlɪəl/ *adj.* **1** of or due from a son or daughter. **2** *Biol.* bearing the relation of offspring (cf. F^2 4). □ **filially** *adv.* [Middle English via Old French *filial* or Late Latin *filialis* from *filius* 'son', *filia* 'daughter']

filiation /fɪlɪ'eɪʃ(ə)n/ *n.* **1** being the child of one or two specified parents. **2** (often foll. by *from*) descent or transmission. **3** the formation of offshoots. **4** a branch of a society or language. **5** a genealogical relation or arrangement. [French via Late Latin *filiatio -onis* from Latin *filius* 'son']

filibeg /'fɪlɪbɛg/ *n.* (also **philabeg** /'fɪlə-/) *Sc.* a kilt. [Gaelic *feileadh-beag* 'little fold']

filibuster /'fɪlɪbʌstə/ *n. & v.* ● *n.* **1 a** the obstruction of progress in a legislative assembly, esp. by prolonged speaking. **b** esp. *N. Amer.* a person who engages in a filibuster. **2** esp. *hist.* a person engaging in unauthorized warfare against a foreign state. ● *v.* **1** *intr.* act as a filibuster. **2** *tr.* act in this way against (a motion etc.). [ultimately from Dutch *vrijbuiter* FREEBOOTER, influenced by French *flibustier*, Spanish *filibustero*]

filigree /'fɪlɪgriː/ *n.* (also **filagree** /'fɪləgriː/) **1** ornamental work of fine (usu. gold or silver) wire formed into delicate tracery; fine metal openwork. **2** anything delicate resembling this. □ **filigreed** *adj.* [earlier *filigreen*, *filigrane* via French *filigrane* from Italian *filigrana*, from Latin *filum* 'thread' + *granum* 'seed']

filing /'fʌɪlɪŋ/ *n.* (usu. in *pl.*) a particle rubbed off by a file.

filing cabinet *n.* a case with drawers for storing documents.

Filipino /fɪlɪ'piːnəʊ/ *n. & adj.* ● *n.* (*pl.* **-os**; *fem.* **Filipina** /-nə/) a native or national of the Philippines, a group of islands in the SW Pacific. ● *adj.* of or relating to the Philippines or the Filipinos. [Spanish, = Philippine]

fill /fɪl/ *v. & n.* ● *v.* **1** *tr. & intr.* (often foll. by *with*) make or become full. **2** *tr.* occupy completely; spread over or through; pervade. **3** *tr.* block up (a cavity or hole in a tooth) with cement, amalgam, gold, etc.; drill and put a filling into (a decayed tooth). **4** *tr.* appoint a person to hold (a vacant post). **5** *tr.* hold (a position); discharge the duties of (an office). **6** *tr.* carry out or supply (an order, commission, etc.). **7** *tr.* occupy (vacant time). **8** *intr.* (of a sail) be distended by wind. **9** *tr.* (usu. as **filling** *adj.*) (esp. of food) satisfy, satiate. **10** *tr. Poker* etc. complete (a holding) by drawing the necessary cards. **11** *tr.* stock abundantly. ● *n.* **1** (prec. by possessive) as much as one wants or can bear (*eat your fill*). **2** enough to fill something (*a fill of tobacco*). **3** material used for filling. □ **fill the bill** be suitable or adequate. **fill in 1** *Brit.* add information to complete (a form, document, blank cheque, etc.). **2 a** complete (a drawing etc.) within an outline. **b** fill (an outline) in this way. **3** fill (a hole etc.) completely. **4** (often foll. by *for*) act as a substitute. **5** occupy oneself during (time between other activities). **6** *colloq.* inform (a person) more fully. **7** *Brit. slang* thrash, beat. **fill out 1** enlarge to the required size. **2** become enlarged or plump. **3** *US* fill in (a document etc.). **fill up 1** make or become completely full. **2** *Brit.* fill in (a document etc.). **3** fill the petrol tank of (a car etc.). **4** provide what is needed to occupy vacant parts or places or deal with deficiencies in. **5** do away with (a pond etc.) by filling. [Old English *fyllan* from Germanic, related to FULL[1]]

fille de joie /fiː də 'ʒwɑː, French fij də ʒwa/ *n.* a prostitute. [French, literally 'daughter of joy']

filler /'fɪlə/ *n.* **1** material or an object used to fill a cavity or increase bulk. **2** an item filling space in a newspaper etc. **3** a person or thing that fills.

filler cap *n.* a cap closing the pipe leading to the petrol tank of a motor vehicle.

fillet /'fɪlɪt/ *n. & v.* ● *n.* **1 a** a fleshy piece of meat from near the loins or the ribs. **b** (in full **fillet steak**) the undercut of a sirloin. **c** a boned longitudinal section of a fish. **2 a** a headband, ribbon, string, or narrow band, for binding the hair or worn round the head. **b** a band or bandage. **3 a** a thin narrow strip of anything. **b** a raised rim or ridge on any surface. **4** *Archit.* **a** a narrow flat band separating two mouldings. **b** a small band between the flutes of a column. **5** *Carpentry* an added triangular piece of wood to round off an interior angle. **6 a** a plain line impressed on the cover of a book. **b** a roller used to impress this. **7** *Heraldry* a horizontal division of a shield, a quarter of the depth of a chief. ● *v.tr.* (**filleted**, **filleting**) **1 a** remove bones from (fish). **b** divide (fish or meat) into fillets. **2** bind or provide with a fillet or fillets. **3** encircle with an ornamental band. □ **filleter** *n.* [Middle English via Old French *filet* from a Romanic diminutive of Latin *filum* 'thread']

filling /'fɪlɪŋ/ *n.* **1** material that fills or is used to fill, esp.: **a** a piece of material used to fill a cavity in a tooth. **b** the edible substance between the bread in a sandwich or between the pastry in a pie. **2** *US* weft.

filling station *n.* an establishment selling petrol etc. to motorists.

fillip /'fɪlɪp/ *n. & v.* ● *n.* **1** a stimulus or incentive. **2 a** a sudden release of a finger or thumb when it has been bent and checked by a thumb or finger. **b** a slight smart stroke given in this way. ● *v.* (**filliped**, **filliping**) **1** *tr.* stimulate (*fillip one's memory*). **2** *tr.* strike slightly and smartly. **3** *tr.* propel (a coin, marble, etc.) with a fillip. **4** *intr.* make a fillip. [imitative]

fillis /'fɪlɪs/ *n. Brit.* loosely twisted string used for tying up plants etc. [French *filasse* 'tow']

fillister /'fɪlɪstə/ *n.* a rabbet or rabbet plane for window sashes etc. [19th c.: perhaps from French *feuilleret*]

fill-up *n.* **1** a thing that fills something up. **2** an act of filling up a petrol tank etc.

filly /'fɪli/ *n.* (*pl.* **-ies**) **1** a young female horse, usu. before it is four years old. **2** *colloq.* a girl or young woman. [Middle English, probably from Old Norse *fylja*, from Germanic (as FOAL)]

film /fɪlm/ *n. & v.* ● *n.* **1** a thin coating or covering layer. **2** *Photog.* a strip or sheet of plastic or other flexible base coated with light-sensitive emulsion for exposure in a camera, either as individual visual representations or as a sequence of images which form the illusion of movement when shown in rapid succession. **3 a** a representation of a story, episode, etc., on film or videotape, with the illusion of movement. **b** a story represented in this way. **c** (in *pl.*) the cinema industry. **4** a slight veil or haze etc. **5** a dimness or abnormal opacity affecting the eyes. **6** a fine thread or filament. ● *v.* **1 a** *tr.* make a photographic or videotape film of (a scene, person, etc.). **b** *tr.* (also *absol.*) make a cinema or television film of (a book etc.). **c** *intr.* be (well or ill) suited for reproduction on film. **2** *tr. & intr.* cover or become covered with or as with a film. [Old English *filmen* 'membrane' from West Germanic, related to FELL[5]]

film clip *n.* = CLIP[2] *n.* 3.

film-goer *n.* a person who frequents the cinema. □ **film-going** *n.*

filmic /'fɪlmɪk/ *adj.* of or relating to films or cinematography.

film-maker *n.* a person who makes films. □ **film-making** *n.*

filmography /fɪl'mɒgrəfi/ *n.* (*pl.* **-ies**) a list of films by one director etc. or on one subject. [FILM + -GRAPHY after *bibliography*]

filmset /'fɪlmsɛt/ *v.tr.* (**-setting**; *past* and *past part.* **-set**) *Printing* set (material for printing) by filmsetting. □ **filmsetter** *n.*

filmsetting /'fɪlmsɛtɪŋ/ *n. Printing* typesetting using characters on photographic film.

film star *n.* a celebrated actor or actress in films.

filmstrip /'fɪlmstrɪp/ *n.* a series of transparencies in a strip for projection.

filmy /'fɪlmi/ *adj.* (**filmier**, **filmiest**) **1** thin and translucent. **2** covered with or as with a film. □ **filmily** *adv.* **filminess** *n.*

filo /'fiːləʊ/ *n.* (also **phyllo**) (usu. *attrib.*) a kind of dough usually layered in thin leaves to make sweet and savoury pastries (*filo dough*; *filo pastry*; *filo pie*). [modern Greek *phullo* 'leaf']

Filofax /ˈfʌɪlə(ʊ)faks/ *n. propr.* a portable loose-leaf filing system for personal or office use. [FILE[1] + *facts*, pl. of FACT]

filoselle /ˈfɪləsɛl/ *n.* floss silk. [French]

fils[1] /fɪls/ *n.* a monetary unit of Iraq, Bahrain, Jordan, Kuwait, and Yemen. [colloq. pronunciation of Arabic *fals*, a small copper coin]

fils[2] /fiːs, French fis/ *n.* (added to a surname to distinguish a son from a father of the same name) the son, junior (cf. PÈRE). [French, = son]

filter /ˈfɪltə/ *n. & v.* ● *n.* **1** a porous device for removing impurities or solid particles from a liquid or gas passed through it. **2** = FILTER TIP. **3** a screen or attachment for absorbing or modifying light, X-rays, etc. **4** a device for suppressing electrical or sound waves of frequencies not required. **5** *Brit.* **a** an arrangement for filtering traffic. **b** a traffic light signalling this. ● *v.intr. & tr.* **1** pass or cause to pass through a filter. **2** (foll. by *through, into,* etc.) make way gradually. **3** (foll. by *out*) leak or cause to leak. **4** *Brit.* allow (traffic) or (of traffic) be allowed to pass to the left or right at a junction while traffic going straight ahead is halted (esp. at traffic lights). □ **filter out** remove (impurities etc.) by means of a filter. [French *filtre* from medieval Latin *filtrum* 'felt used as a filter', from West Germanic]

filterable /ˈfɪlt(ə)rəb(ə)l/ *adj.* (also **filtrable** /ˈfɪltrəb(ə)l/) **1** *Med.* (of a virus) able to pass through a filter that retains bacteria. **2** that can be filtered.

filter-bed *n.* a tank or pond containing a layer of sand etc. for filtering large quantities of liquid.

filter-feeding *n. Zool.* feeding by filtering out plankton or nutrients suspended in water. □ **filter-feeder** *n.*

filter-paper *n.* porous paper for filtering.

filter tip *n.* **1** a filter attached to a cigarette for removing impurities from the inhaled smoke. **2** a cigarette with this. □ **filter-tipped** *adj.*

filth /fɪlθ/ *n.* **1** repugnant or extreme dirt. **2** vileness, corruption, obscenity. **3** foul or obscene language. **4** (prec. by *the*) *Brit. slang offens.* the police. [Old English *fȳlth* (as FOUL, -TH[2])]

filthy /ˈfɪlθi/ *adj. & adv.* ● *adj.* (**filthier**, **filthiest**) **1** extremely or disgustingly dirty. **2** obscene. **3** *Brit. colloq.* (of weather) very unpleasant. **4** vile; disgraceful. ● *adv.* **1** filthily (*filthy dirty*). **2** *colloq.* extremely (*filthy rich*). □ **filthily** *adv.* **filthiness** *n.*

filthy lucre *n.* **1** dishonourable gain (Tit. 1:11). **2** *joc.* money.

filtrable var. of FILTERABLE.

filtrate /ˈfɪltreɪt/ *v. & n.* ● *v.tr.* filter. ● *n.* filtered liquid. □ **filtration** /-ˈtreɪʃ(ə)n/ *n.* [modern Latin *filtrare* (as FILTER)]

fimbriate /ˈfɪmbrɪeɪt/ *adj.* (also **fimbriated**) **1** *Bot. & Zool.* fringed or bordered with hairs etc. **2** *Heraldry* having a narrow border. [Latin *fimbriatus* from *fimbriae* 'fringe']

fin /fɪn/ *n. & v.* ● *n.* **1** a flattened appendage on various parts of the body of many aquatic vertebrates and some invertebrates, including fish and cetaceans, for propelling, steering, and balancing (*dorsal fin*; *anal fin*). **2** a small projecting surface or attachment on an aircraft, rocket, or motor car for ensuring aerodynamic stability. **3** an underwater swimmer's flipper. **4** a sharp lateral projection on the share or coulter of a plough. **5** a finlike projection on any device, for improving heat transfer etc. ● *v.* (**finned**, **finning**) **1** *tr.* provide with fins. **2** *intr.* swim under water. □ **finless** *adj.* **finned** *adj.* (also in *comb.*). [Old English *fin(n)*]

finable see FINE[2].

finagle /fɪˈneɪɡ(ə)l/ *v.intr. & tr. colloq.* act or obtain dishonestly. □ **finagler** *n.* [dialect *fainaigue* 'cheat']

final /ˈfʌɪn(ə)l/ *adj. & n.* ● *adj.* **1** situated at the end, coming last. **2** conclusive, decisive, unalterable, putting an end to doubt. **3** concerned with the purpose or end aimed at. ● *n.* **1** the last or deciding heat or game in sports or in a competition (*Cup Final*). **2** the edition of a newspaper published latest in the day. **3 a** (usu. in *pl.*) *Brit.* the series of examinations at the end of a degree course. **b** *N. Amer.* an examination at the end of a term. **4** *Mus.* the principal note in any mode. □ **finally** *adv.* [Middle English from Old French or from Latin *finalis* from *finis* 'end']

final cause *n. Philos.* the end towards which a thing naturally develops or at which an action aims.

final clause *n. Gram.* a clause expressing purpose, introduced by *in order that, lest,* etc.

final drive *n.* the last part of the transmission system in a motor vehicle.

finale /fɪˈnɑːli/ *n.* **1 a** the last movement of an instrumental composition. **b** a piece of music closing an act in an opera. **2** the close of a drama etc. **3** a conclusion. [Italian (as FINAL)]

finalism /ˈfʌɪn(ə)lɪz(ə)m/ *n.* the doctrine that natural processes (e.g. evolution) are directed towards some goal. □ **finalistic** /-ˈlɪstɪk/ *adj.*

finalist /ˈfʌɪn(ə)lɪst/ *n.* a competitor in the final of a competition etc.

finality /fʌɪˈnalɪti/ *n.* (*pl.* **-ies**) **1** the quality or fact of being final. **2** the belief that something is final. **3** a final act, state, or utterance. **4** the principle of final cause viewed as operative in the universe. [French *finalité* from Late Latin *finalitas -tatis* (as FINAL)]

finalize /ˈfʌɪn(ə)lʌɪz/ *v.tr.* (also **-ise**) **1** put into final form. **2** complete; bring to an end. **3** approve the final form or details of. □ **finalization** /-ˈzeɪʃ(ə)n/ *n.*

final solution *n.* the Nazi policy (1941–5) of exterminating European Jews. [translation of German *Endlösung*]

finance /fʌɪˈnans, fɪ-; ˈfʌɪnans/ *n. & v.* ● *n.* **1** the management of (esp. public) money. **2** monetary support for an enterprise. **3** (in *pl.*) the money resources of a state, company, or person. ● *v.tr.* provide capital for (a person or enterprise). [Middle English from Old French, from *finer* 'settle a debt' from *fin* 'end': see FINE[2]]

finance company *n.* (also **finance house**) a company concerned mainly with providing money for hire purchase transactions.

financial /fʌɪˈnanʃ(ə)l, fɪ-/ *adj.* **1** of finance. **2** *Austral. & NZ slang* possessing money. □ **financially** *adv.*

financial year *n. Brit.* a year as reckoned for taxing or accounting (e.g. the British tax year, reckoned from 6 April).

financier *n. & v.* ● *n.* /fʌɪˈnansɪə, fɪ-/ a person engaged in large-scale finance. ● *v.intr.* /fʌɪnanˈsɪə, fɪ-/ usu. *derog.* conduct financial operations. [French (as FINANCE)]

fin-back *n.* = FIN WHALE.

finch /fɪn(t)ʃ/ *n.* any small seed-eating songbird esp. of the family Fringillidae, including crossbills, canaries, and chaffinches. [Old English *finc*, from West Germanic]

find /fʌɪnd/ *v. & n.* ● *v.tr.* (*past* and *past part.* **found** /faʊnd/) **1 a** discover by chance or effort (*found a key*). **b** become aware of. **c** (*absol.*) discover game, esp. a fox. **2 a** get possession of by chance (*found a treasure*). **b** obtain, receive (*idea found acceptance*). **c** succeed in obtaining (*cannot find the money*; *can't find time to read*). **d** summon up (*found courage to protest*). **e** *Brit. slang* steal. **3 a** seek out and provide (*will find you a book*). **b** supply, furnish (*each finds his own equipment*). **4** ascertain by study or calculation or inquiry (*could not find the answer*). **5 a** perceive or experience (*find no sense in it*; *find difficulty in breathing*). **b** (often in *passive*) recognize or discover to be present (*the word is not found in Shakespeare*). **c** regard or discover from experience (*finds England too cold*; *you'll find it pays*; *find it impossible to reply*). **6** *Law* (of a jury, judge, etc.) decide and declare (*found him guilty*; *found that he had done it*; *found it murder*). **7** reach by a natural or normal process (*water finds its own level*). **8 a** (of a letter) reach (a person). **b** (of an address) be adequate to enable a letter etc. to reach (a person). **9** *archaic* reach the conscience of. ● *n.* **1 a** a discovery of treasure, minerals, etc. **b** *Hunting* the finding of a fox. **2** a thing or person discovered, esp. when of value. □ **all found** *Brit.* (of an employee's wages) with board and lodging provided free. **find against** *Law* decide against (a person), judge to be guilty. **find fault** see FAULT. **find favour** prove acceptable. **find one's feet 1** become able to walk. **2** develop one's independent ability. **find for** *Law* decide in favour of (a person), judge to be innocent. **find it in one's heart** (esp. with *neg.*; foll. by *to* + infin.) prevail upon oneself, be willing. **find oneself 1** discover that one is (*woke to find myself in hospital*; *found herself agreeing*). **2** discover one's vocation. **3** provide for one's own needs. **find out 1** discover or detect (a wrongdoer etc.). **2** (often foll. by *about*) get information (*find out about holidays abroad*). **3** discover (*find out where we are*). **4** (often foll. by *about*) discover the truth, a fact, etc. (*he never found out*). **5** devise. **6** solve. **find one's way 1** (often foll. by *to*) manage to reach a place. **2** (often foll. by *into*) be brought or get. □ **findable** *adj.* [Old English *findan*, from Germanic]

finder /ˈfʌɪndə/ *n.* **1** a person who finds. **2** a small telescope attached to a large one to locate an object for observation. **3** the viewfinder of a camera. □ **finders keepers** *colloq.* whoever finds a thing is entitled to keep it.

fin de siècle /fã də ˈsjɛkl(ə), French fɛ̃ də sjɛkl/ *adj.* & *n.* ● *adj.* **1** characteristic of the end of the nineteenth century. **2** decadent. ● *n.* the end of a century, esp. the nineteenth century. [French, = end of century]

finding /ˈfʌɪndɪŋ/ *n.* **1** (often in *pl.*) a conclusion reached by an inquiry. **2** (in *pl.*) *US* small parts or tools used by workmen.

find-spot *n. Archaeol.* the place where an object is found.

fine[1] /fʌɪn/ *adj.*, *n.*, *adv.*, & *v.* ● *adj.* **1** of high quality (*fine fabrics*). **2 a** excellent; of notable merit (*a fine painting*). **b** good, satisfactory (*that will be fine*). **c** fortunate (*has been a fine thing for him*). **d** well conceived or expressed (*a fine saying*). **3 a** pure, refined. **b** (of gold or silver) containing a specified proportion of pure metal. **4** of handsome appearance or size; imposing, dignified (*fine buildings*; *a person of fine presence*). **5** in good health (*I'm fine, thank you*). **6** (of weather etc.) bright and clear with sunshine; free from rain. **7 a** thin; sharp. **b** in small particles. **c** worked in slender thread. **d** (esp. of print) small. **e** (of a pen) narrow-pointed. **8** *Cricket* behind the wicket and near the line of flight of the ball. **9** tritely complimentary; euphemistic (*say fine things about a person*; *call things by fine names*). **10** ornate, showy, smart. **11** fastidious, dainty, pretending refinement; (of speech or writing) affectedly ornate. **12 a** capable of delicate perception or discrimination. **b** perceptible only with difficulty (*a fine distinction*). **13 a** delicate, subtle, exquisitely fashioned. **b** (of feelings) refined, elevated. **14** (of wine or other goods) of a high standard; conforming to a specified grade. ● *n.* **1** fine weather (*in rain or fine*). **2** (in *pl.*) very small particles in mining, milling, etc. ● *adv.* **1** finely. **2** *colloq.* very well (*suits me fine*). ● *v.* **1** (often foll. by *down*) **a** *tr.* make (beer or wine) clear. **b** *intr.* (of liquid) become clear. **2** *tr.* & *intr.* (often foll. by *away*, *down*, *off*) make or become finer, thinner, or less coarse; dwindle or taper, or cause to do so. □ **cut** (or **run**) **it fine** allow very little margin of time etc. **fine up** *Austral. colloq.* (of the weather) become fine. **not to put too fine a point on it** (as a parenthetic remark) to speak bluntly. □ **finely** *adv.* **fineness** *n.* [Middle English from Old French *fin*, ultimately from Latin *finire* 'finish']

fine[2] /fʌɪn/ *n.* & *v.* ● *n.* **1** a sum of money exacted as a penalty. **2** *hist.* a sum of money paid by an incoming tenant in return for the rent's being small. ● *v.tr.* punish by a fine (*fined him £5*). □ **in fine** to sum up; in short. □ **finable** /ˈfʌɪnəb(ə)l/ *adj.* [Middle English via Old French *fin* and medieval Latin *finis* 'sum paid on settling a lawsuit' from Latin *finis* 'end']

fine[3] /fiːn/ *n.* = FINE CHAMPAGNE. [abbreviation]

fine arts *n.pl.* those appealing to the mind or to the sense of beauty, as poetry, music, and esp. painting, sculpture, and architecture.

fine champagne /fiːn ʃɒ̃ˈpɑːnj(ə), French fin ʃɑ̃paɲ/ *n.* old liqueur brandy. [French, = fine (brandy from) Champagne (vineyards in Charente)]

fine chemicals *n.pl.* chemicals of high purity usu. used in small amounts.

fine-draw *v.tr.* sew together (two pieces of cloth, edges of a tear, parts of a garment) so that the join is imperceptible.

fine-drawn *adj.* **1** extremely thin. **2** subtle.

Fine Gael /fiːnə ˈgeɪl/ *n.* one of the two major political parties of the Republic of Ireland. [Irish, literally 'tribe of Gaels']

fine-grained *adj.* having a fine grain; consisting of small particles.

fine print *n.* detailed printed information, esp. in legal documents, instructions, etc.

finery[1] /ˈfʌɪn(ə)ri/ *n.* showy dress or decoration. [FINE[1] + -ERY, on the pattern of BRAVERY]

finery[2] /ˈfʌɪnəri/ *n.* (*pl.* **-ies**) *hist.* a hearth where pig-iron was converted into wrought iron. [French *finerie* from *finer* 'refine']

fines herbes /fiːnz ˈɛːb, French finz ɛrb/ *n.pl.* mixed herbs used in cooking, esp. chopped as omelette-flavouring. [French, = fine herbs]

fine-spun *adj.* **1** delicate. **2** (of a theory etc.) too subtle, unpractical.

finesse /fɪˈnɛs/ *n.* & *v.* ● *n.* **1** refinement. **2** subtle or delicate manipulation. **3** artfulness, esp. in handling a difficulty tactfully. **4** *Cards* an attempt to win a trick with a card that is not the highest held. ● *v.* **1** *intr.* & *tr.* use or achieve by finesse. **2** *Cards* **a** *intr.* make a finesse. **b** *tr.* play (a card) by way of finesse. **3** *tr.* evade or trick by finesse. [French, related to FINE[1]]

fine-tooth comb *n.* a comb with narrow close-set teeth. □ **go over with a fine-tooth comb** check or search thoroughly.

fine-tune *v.tr.* make small adjustments to (a mechanism etc.) in order to obtain the best possible results. □ **fine tuning** *n.*

finger /ˈfɪŋgə/ *n.* & *v.* ● *n.* **1** any of the terminal projections of the hand (including or excluding the thumb). **2** the part of a glove etc. intended to cover a finger. **3 a** a finger-like object (*fish finger*). **b** a long narrow structure. **4** *colloq.* a measure of liquor in a glass, based on the breadth of a finger. **5** *slang* **a** an informer. **b** *Brit.* a pickpocket. **c** *Brit.* a police officer. ● *v.tr.* **1** touch, feel, or turn about with the fingers. **2** *Mus.* **a** play (a passage) with fingers used in a particular way. **b** mark (music) with signs showing which fingers are to be used. **c** play upon (an instrument) with the fingers. **3** *N. Amer. slang* indicate (a victim, or a criminal to the police). □ **all fingers and thumbs** *Brit.* clumsy. **get** (or **pull**) **one's finger out** *Brit. slang* cease procrastinating and start to act. **give a person the finger** *slang* make a gesture with the middle finger raised as an obscene sign of contempt. **have a finger in the pie** be (esp. officiously) concerned in the matter. **lay a finger on** touch however slightly. **put one's finger on** locate or identify exactly. **put the finger on** *slang* **1** inform against. **2** identify (an intended victim). **twist** (or **wind**) **round** (or *US* **around**) **one's finger** (or **little finger**) persuade (a person) without difficulty, dominate (a person) completely. **work one's fingers to the bone** see BONE. □ **fingered** *adj.* (also in *comb.*). **fingerless** *adj.* [Old English from Germanic]

finger alphabet *n.* a form of sign language using the fingers to spell out words.

fingerboard /ˈfɪŋgəbɔːd/ *n.* a flat strip on the neck of a stringed instrument, against which the strings are pressed to create different tones.

finger bowl *n.* (also **finger glass**) a small bowl for rinsing the fingers during a meal.

finger-dry *v.tr.* dry and style (the hair) by repeatedly running one's fingers through it.

fingering[1] /ˈfɪŋɡ(ə)rɪŋ/ *n.* **1** a manner or technique of using the fingers, esp. to play an instrument. **2** an indication of this in a musical score.

fingering[2] /ˈfɪŋɡ(ə)rɪŋ/ *n.* fine wool for knitting. [earlier *fingram*, perhaps from French *fin grain*, as GROGRAM from *gros grain*]

finger language *n.* language expressed by means of the finger alphabet.

fingerling /ˈfɪŋɡəlɪŋ/ *n.* a parr.

fingermark /ˈfɪŋɡəmɑːk/ *n.* a mark left on a surface by a finger.

fingernail /ˈfɪŋɡəneɪl/ *n.* the nail at the tip of each finger.

finger-paint *n.* & *v.* ● *n.* paint that can be applied with the fingers. ● *v.intr.* apply paint with the fingers.

fingerpick /ˈfɪŋɡəpɪk/ *n.* & *v.* ● *n.* a plectrum worn on a finger. ● *v.intr.* & *tr.* play (a guitar etc., music) using a fingerpick.

finger-plate *n.* a plate fixed to a door above the handle to prevent fingermarks.

finger-post *n. Brit.* a signpost at a road junction.

fingerprint /ˈfɪŋɡəprɪnt/ *n.* & *v.* ● *n.* **1** an impression made on a surface by the fingertips, esp. as used for identifying individuals. **2** a distinctive characteristic. ● *v.tr.* record the fingerprints of (a person).

finger-stall *n.* a cover to protect a finger, esp. when injured.

fingertip /ˈfɪŋɡətɪp/ *n.* the tip of a finger. □ **have at one's fingertips** be thoroughly familiar with (a subject etc.).

finial /ˈfɪnɪəl, ˈfʌɪn-/ *n. Archit.* **1** an ornament finishing off the apex of a roof, pediment, gable, tower-corner, canopy, etc. **2** the topmost part of a pinnacle. [Middle English via Old French *fin* from Latin *finis* 'end']

finical /ˈfɪnɪk(ə)l/ *adj.* = FINICKY. □ **finicality** /-ˈkalɪti/ *n.* **finically** *adv.* **finicalness** *n.* [16th c.: probably originally university slang from FINE[1] + -ICAL]

finicking /ˈfɪnɪkɪŋ/ *adj.* = FINICKY. [FINICAL + -ING[2]]

finicky /ˈfɪnɪki/ *adj.* **1** over-particular, fastidious. **2** needing much attention to detail; fiddly. □ **finickiness** *n.*

finis /ˈfiːnɪs, ˈfɪnɪs, ˈfʌɪnɪs/ *n.* **1** (at the end of a book) the end. **2** the end of anything, esp. of life. [Latin]

finish /ˈfɪnɪʃ/ *v.* & *n.* ● *v.* **1** *tr.* **a** (often foll. by *off*) bring to an end; come to the end of; complete. **b** (usu. foll. by *off*) *colloq.* kill; overcome completely. **c** (often foll. by *off, up*) consume or get through the whole or the remainder of (food or drink) (*finish up your dinner*). **2** *intr.* **a** come to an end, cease. **b** reach the end, esp. of a race. **c** = *finish up*. **3** *tr.* **a** complete the manufacture of (cloth, woodwork, etc.) by surface treatment. **b** put the final touches to; make perfect or highly accomplished (*finished manners*). **c** prepare (a girl) for entry into fashionable society. ● *n.* **1 a** the end, the last stage. **b** the point at which a race etc. ends. **c** the death of a fox in a hunt (*be in at the finish*). **2** a method, material, or texture used for surface treatment of wood, cloth, etc. (*mahogany finish*). **3** what serves to give completeness. **4** an accomplished or completed state. □ **fight to the finish** fight till one party is completely beaten. **finish off** provide with an ending. **finish up** (often foll. by *in, by*) esp. *Brit.* end in something, end by doing something (*he finished up last in the race; the plan finished up in the waste-paper basket; finished up by apologizing*). **finish with** have no more to do with, complete one's use of or association with. [Middle English via Old French *fenir* from Latin *finire*, from *finis* 'end']

finisher /ˈfɪnɪʃə/ *n.* **1** a person who finishes something. **2** a worker or machine doing the last operation in manufacture. **3** *colloq.* a discomfiting thing, a crushing blow, etc.

finishing school *n.* a private college where girls are prepared for entry into fashionable society.

finishing stroke *n.* a *coup de grâce*; a final and fatal stroke.

finishing touch *n.* (also **finishing touches** *pl.*) the final details completing and enhancing a piece of work etc.

finite /ˈfʌɪnʌɪt/ *adj.* **1** limited, bounded; not infinite. **2** *Gram.* (of a part of a verb) having a specific number and person. **3** not infinitely small. □ **finitely** *adv.* **finiteness** *n.* **finitude** /ˈfɪnɪtjuːd/ *n.* [Latin *finitus*, past part. of *finire* FINISH]

finitism /ˈfʌɪnʌɪtɪz(ə)m/ *n.* belief in the finiteness of the world, God, etc. □ **finitist** *n.*

fink /fɪŋk/ *n.* & *v. N. Amer. slang* ● *n.* **1** an unpleasant person. **2** an informer. **3** a strike-breaker; a blackleg. ● *v.intr.* **1** (foll. by *on*) inform on. **2 a** (foll. by *out*) back out of something. **b** (foll. by *out on*) back out of (a thing); let (a person) down. [20th c.: origin unknown]

Finlandization /fɪnləndʌɪˈzeɪʃ(ə)n/ *n.* (also **-isation**) *hist.* the economic policy of favouring (or at least not opposing) the interests of the former Soviet Union (as allegedly pursued by Finland from 1944). □ **Finlandize** *v.tr.* (also **-ise**). [translation of German *Finnlandisierung*]

Finn /fɪn/ *n.* a native or national of Finland; a person of Finnish descent. [Old English *Finnas* pl.]

finnan /ˈfɪnən/ *n.* (in full **finnan haddock**) a haddock cured with the smoke of green wood, turf, or peat. [*Findhorn* or *Findon* in Scotland]

finnesko /ˈfɪnəskəʊ/ *n.* (*pl.* same) a boot of tanned reindeer skin with the hair on the outside. [Norwegian *finn(e)sko* (as FINN, *sko* SHOE)]

Finnic /ˈfɪnɪk/ *adj.* **1** of the group of peoples related to the Finns. **2** of the group of languages including Finnish and Estonian.

Finnish /ˈfɪnɪʃ/ *adj.* & *n.* ● *adj.* of the Finns or their language. ● *n.* the language of the Finns.

Finno-Ugric /fɪnəʊˈuːɡrɪk, -ˈjuːɡrɪk/ *adj.* & *n.* (also **Finno-Ugrian** /-ˈuːɡrɪən, -ˈjuːɡrɪən/) ● *adj.* belonging to the group of Ural-Altaic languages including Finnish, Estonian, Lapp, and Magyar. ● *n.* this group.

finny /ˈfɪni/ *adj.* **1** having fins; like a fin. **2** *poet.* of or teeming with fish.

fino /ˈfiːnəʊ/ *n.* (*pl.* **-os**) a light-coloured dry sherry. [Spanish, = fine]

fin whale *n.* a large rorqual, *Balaenoptera physalus*, with a prominent dorsal fin.

fiord var. of FJORD.

fioritura /fɪˌɔːrɪˈtʊərə/ *n.* (*pl.* **fioriture** *pronunc.* same) *Mus.* the usu. improvised decoration of a melody. [Italian, = flowering, from *fiorire* 'to flower']

fipple /ˈfɪp(ə)l/ *n.* a plug at the mouth-end of a wind instrument. [17th c.: origin unknown]

fipple flute *n.* a flute played by blowing endwise, e.g. a recorder.

fir /fəː/ *n.* **1** (in full **fir tree**) any evergreen coniferous tree, esp. of the genus *Abies*, with needles borne singly on the stems (cf. PINE 1). **2** the wood of the fir. □ **firry** *adj.* [Middle English, probably from Old Norse *fyri-*, from Germanic]

fir cone *n. Brit.* the fruit of the fir.

fire /ˈfʌɪə/ *n.* & *v.* ● *n.* **1 a** the state or process of combustion, in which substances combine chemically with oxygen from the air and usu. give out bright light and heat. **b** the active principle operative in this. **c** flame or incandescence. **2** a conflagration, a destructive burning (*forest fire*). **3 a** burning fuel in a grate, furnace, etc. **b** *Brit.* = ELECTRIC FIRE. **c** = GAS FIRE. **4** firing of guns. **5 a** fervour, spirit, vivacity. **b** poetic inspiration, lively imagination. **c** vehement emotion. **6** burning heat, fever. **7** luminosity, glow (*St Elmo's fire*). ● *v.* **1 a** *tr.* discharge (a gun etc.). **b** *tr.* propel (a missile) from a gun etc. **c** *intr.* (often foll. by *at, into, on*) fire a gun or missile. **d** *tr.* produce (a broadside, salute, etc.) by discharge of guns. **e** *intr.* (of a gun etc.)

be discharged. **2** *tr.* cause (explosive) to explode. **3** *tr.* deliver or utter in rapid succession (*fired insults at us*). **4** *tr. slang* dismiss (an employee) from a job. **5** *tr.* **a** set fire to with the intention of destroying. **b** kindle (explosives). **6** *intr.* catch fire. **7** *intr.* (of an internal-combustion engine, or a cylinder in one) undergo ignition of its fuel. **8** *tr.* supply (a furnace, engine, boiler, or power station) with fuel. **9** *tr.* **a** stimulate (the imagination or an emotion). **b** fill (a person) with enthusiasm. **10** *tr.* **a** bake or dry (pottery, bricks, etc.). **b** cure (tea or tobacco) by artificial heat. **11** *intr.* become heated or excited. **12** *tr.* cause to glow or redden. □ **catch fire** begin to burn. **fire and brimstone** the supposed torments of hell. **fire away** *colloq.* begin; go ahead. **fire up 1** *colloq.* **a** stimulate, fill with enthusiasm, excite. **b** start up (an engine etc.). **2** show sudden anger. **go on fire** *Sc.* & *Ir.* catch fire. **go through fire and water** face all perils. **on fire 1** burning. **2** excited. **set fire to** (or **set on fire**) ignite, kindle, cause to burn. **set the world** (or *Brit.* **Thames) on fire** do something remarkable or sensational. **take fire** catch fire. **under fire** (often prec. by *come*) **1** being shot at. **2** being rigorously criticized or questioned. □ **fireless** *adj.* **firer** *n.* [Old English *fȳr*, *fȳrian*, from West Germanic]

fire alarm *n.* a device for giving warning of fire.

firearm /ˈfʌɪərɑːm/ *n.* (usu. in *pl.*) a gun, esp. a pistol or rifle.

fireback /ˈfʌɪəbak/ *n.* **1 a** the back wall of a fireplace. **b** an iron sheet for this. **2** a SE Asian pheasant of the genus *Lophura*.

fireball /ˈfʌɪəbɔːl/ *n.* **1** a large meteor. **2** a ball of flame, esp. from a nuclear explosion. **3** an energetic person. **4** ball lightning. **5** *Mil. hist.* a ball filled with combustibles.

fire-balloon *n.* a balloon made buoyant by the heat of a fire burning at its mouth.

fire blight *n.* a disease of plants, esp. hops and fruit trees, causing a scorched appearance.

firebomb /ˈfʌɪəbɒm/ *n.* & *v.* ● *n.* an incendiary bomb. ● *v.tr.* attack or destroy with a firebomb.

firebox /ˈfʌɪəbɒks/ *n.* the fuel-chamber of a steam engine or boiler.

firebrand /ˈfʌɪəbrand/ *n.* **1** a piece of burning wood. **2** a cause of trouble, esp. a person causing unrest.

firebreak /ˈfʌɪəbreɪk/ *n.* an obstacle to the spread of fire in a forest etc., esp. an open space.

firebrick /ˈfʌɪəbrɪk/ *n.* a fireproof brick used in a grate.

fire brigade *n.* esp. *Brit.* an organized body of firemen trained and employed to extinguish fires.

firebug /ˈfʌɪəbʌg/ *n. colloq.* a pyromaniac.

fireclay /ˈfʌɪəkleɪ/ *n.* clay capable of withstanding high temperatures, often used to make firebricks.

fire company *n.* **1** = FIRE BRIGADE. **2** *Brit.* a fire-insurance company.

fire-control *n.* a system of regulating the fire of a ship's or a fort's guns.

firecracker /ˈfʌɪəkrakə/ *n.* esp. *N. Amer.* an explosive firework; a banger.

firecrest /ˈfʌɪəkrɛst/ *n.* a warbler, *Regulus ignicapillus*, of European woodland, with a red and orange crest.

firedamp /ˈfʌɪədamp/ *n.* a miners' name for methane, which is explosive when mixed in certain proportions with air.

fire department *n. US* = FIRE BRIGADE.

firedog /ˈfʌɪədɒg/ *n.* a metal support for burning wood or for a grate or fire-irons.

fire door *n.* a fire-resistant door to prevent the spread of fire.

fire-drake /ˈfʌɪədreɪk/ *n.* (in Germanic mythology) a fiery dragon. [FIRE + *drake* from Old English *draca*, via West Germanic from Latin *draco* DRAGON]

fire drill *n.* **1** a rehearsal of the procedures to be used in case of fire. **2** a primitive device for kindling fire with a stick and wood.

fire-eater *n.* **1** a conjuror who appears to swallow fire. **2** a person fond of quarrelling or fighting.

fire engine *n.* a vehicle carrying equipment for fighting large fires.

fire escape *n.* an emergency staircase or apparatus for escape from a building on fire.

fire extinguisher *n.* an apparatus with a jet for discharging liquid chemicals, water, or foam to extinguish a fire.

firefight /ˈfʌɪəfʌɪt/ *n.* a fight using firearms, a gun battle.

firefighter /ˈfʌɪəfʌɪtə/ *n.* a person whose task is to extinguish fires. □ **fire-fighting** *n.* & *attrib.adj.*

firefly /ˈfʌɪəflʌɪ/ *n.* (*pl.* **-flies**) any soft-bodied beetle of the glow-worm family Lampyridae, emitting phosphorescent light, usu. in flashes.

fireguard /ˈfʌɪəgɑːd/ *n.* **1** a protective screen or grid placed in front of a fireplace. **2** *N. Amer.* a fire-watcher. **3** *N. Amer.* a firebreak.

fire hose *n.* a hosepipe used in extinguishing fires.

firehouse /ˈfʌɪəhaʊs/ *n. US* a fire station.

fire-irons *n.pl.* tongs, poker, and shovel, for tending a domestic fire.

firelight /ˈfʌɪəlʌɪt/ *n.* light from a fire in a fireplace. [Old English *fyr-leoht* (as FIRE, LIGHT[1])]

firelighter /ˈfʌɪəlʌɪtə/ *n. Brit.* a piece of inflammable material to help start a fire in a grate.

firelock /ˈfʌɪəlɒk/ *n. hist.* a musket in which the priming was ignited by sparks.

fireman /ˈfʌɪəmən/ *n.* (*pl.* **-men**) **1** a member of a fire brigade; a person employed to extinguish fires. **2** a person who tends a furnace or the fire of a steam engine or steamship.

fire-office *n. Brit.* a fire-insurance company.

fire-opal *n.* girasol.

fireplace /ˈfʌɪəpleɪs/ *n. Archit.* **1** a place for a domestic fire, esp. a grate or hearth at the base of a chimney. **2** a structure surrounding this. **3** the area in front of this.

fireplug /ˈfʌɪəplʌg/ *n.* esp. *US* a hydrant for a fire hose.

firepower /ˈfʌɪəpaʊə/ *n.* **1** the destructive capacity of guns etc. **2** financial, intellectual, or emotional strength.

fire practice *n. Brit.* a fire drill.

fireproof /ˈfʌɪəpruːf/ *adj.* & *v.* ● *adj.* able to resist fire or great heat. ● *v.tr.* make fireproof.

fire-raiser *n. Brit.* an arsonist. □ **fire-raising** *n.*

fire screen *n.* **1** a screen to keep off the direct heat of a fire. **2** a fireguard. **3** an ornamental screen for a fireplace.

fireship /ˈfʌɪəʃɪp/ *n. hist.* a ship loaded with combustibles and set adrift to ignite an enemy's ships etc.

fireside /ˈfʌɪəsʌɪd/ *n.* **1** the area round a fireplace. **2** a person's home or home life.

fireside chat *n.* an informal talk.

fire station *n.* the headquarters of a fire brigade.

fire-step *n.* = FIRING-STEP.

fire-stone *n.* stone that resists fire, used for furnaces etc.

firestorm /ˈfʌɪəstɔːm/ *n.* a very intense and destructive fire (usu. one caused by bombing) in which strong currents of air are drawn into the blaze from the surrounding area.

firethorn /ˈfʌɪəθɔːn/ *n.* = PYRACANTHA.

fire-tongs *n.pl.* tongs for picking up pieces of coal etc. in tending a fire.

fire trap *n.* a building without proper provision for escape in case of fire.

fire-walker *n.* a person who takes part in fire-walking.

fire-walking *n.* the (often ceremonial) practice of walking barefoot over hot stones, wood ashes, etc.

fire warden *n. N. Amer.* a person employed to prevent or extinguish fires.

fire-watcher *n.* a person keeping watch for fires, esp. those caused by bombs. □ **fire-watching** *n.*

firewater /ˈfʌɪəwɔːtə/ *n. colloq.* strong alcoholic liquor.

fireweed /'fʌɪəwi:d/ *n.* any of several plants that spring up on burnt land, esp. the rosebay willowherb.

firewood /'fʌɪəwʊd/ *n.* wood for use as fuel.

firework /'fʌɪəwə:k/ *n.* **1** a device containing combustible chemicals that cause explosions or spectacular effects. **2** (in *pl.*) **a** an outburst of passion, esp. anger. **b** a display of wit or brilliance.

firing /'fʌɪərɪŋ/ *n.* **1** the discharging of guns. **2** material for a fire, fuel. **3** the heating process which hardens clay into pottery etc.

firing line *n.* **1** the front line in a battle. **2** the leading part in an activity etc.

firing party *n.* a group detailed to fire the salute at a military funeral.

firing squad *n.* **1** a group detailed to shoot a condemned person. **2** a firing-party.

firing-step *n.* a step on which soldiers in a trench stand to fire.

firkin /'fə:kɪn/ *n.* **1** a small cask for liquids, butter, fish, etc. **2** *Brit.* (as a measure of beer etc.) half a kilderkin (usu. 9 imperial gallons or about 41 litres). [Middle English *ferdekyn*, probably from the Middle Dutch diminutive of *vierde* 'fourth']

firm[1] /fə:m/ *adj., adv., & v.* ● *adj.* **1 a** of solid or compact structure. **b** fixed, stable. **c** steady; not shaking. **2 a** resolute, determined. **b** not easily shaken (*firm belief*). **c** steadfast, constant (*a firm friend*). **3 a** (of an offer etc.) not liable to cancellation after acceptance. **b** (of a decree, law, etc.) established, immutable. **4** *Commerce* (of prices or goods) maintaining their level or value. ● *adv.* firmly (*stand firm*; *hold firm to*). ● *v.* **1** *tr. & intr.* (often foll. by *up*) make or become firm, secure, compact, or solid. **2** *tr.* (often foll. by *in*) fix (plants) firmly in the soil. □ **firmly** *adv.* **firmness** *n.* [Middle English via Old French *ferme* from Latin *firmus*]

firm[2] /fə:m/ *n.* **1 a** a business concern. **b** the partners in such a concern. **2** a group of persons working together, esp. of hospital doctors and assistants. [earlier = signature, business name: Spanish and Italian *firma* via medieval Latin from Latin *firmare* 'confirm by signature', from *firmus* FIRM[1]]

firmament /'fə:məm(ə)nt/ *n. literary* the sky regarded as a vault or arch. □ **firmamental** /-'ment(ə)l/ *adj.* [Middle English via Old French from Latin *firmamentum*, from *firmare* 'confirm' (as FIRM[2])]

firman /'fə:mən, fə:'mɑ:n/ *n.* **1** an oriental sovereign's edict. **2** a grant or permit. [Persian *fermān*, Sanskrit *pramāṇam* 'right measure, standard, authority']

firmware /'fə:mwɛ:/ *n. Computing* a permanent kind of software programmed into a read-only memory.

firry see FIR.

first /fə:st/ *adj., n., & adv.* ● *adj.* **1 a** earliest in time or order. **b** coming next after a specified or implied time (*shall take the first train*; *the first cuckoo*). **2** foremost in position, rank, or importance (*First Lord of the Treasury*; *first mate*). **3** *Mus.* performing the highest or chief of two or more parts for the same instrument or voice. **4** most willing or likely (*should be the first to admit the difficulty*). **5** basic or evident (*first principles*). ● *n.* **1** (prec. by *the*) the person or thing first mentioned or occurring. **2** the first occurrence of something notable. **3** *Brit.* **a** a place in the first class in an examination. **b** a person having this. **4** the first day of a month. **5** first gear. **6 a** first place in a race. **b** the winner of this. **7** (in *pl.*) goods of the best quality. ● *adv.* **1** before any other person or thing (*first of all*; *first and foremost*; *first come first served*). **2** before someone or something else (*must get this done first*). **3** for the first time (*when did you first see her?*). **4** in preference; rather (*will see him damned first*). **5** *Brit.* first-class (*I usually travel first*). □ **at first** at the beginning. **at first hand** directly from the original source. **first and last** taking one thing with another, on the whole. **first off** esp. *US colloq.* at first, first of all. **first or last** sooner or later. **first things first** the most important things before any others (*we must do first things first*). **first up 1** first of all. **2** *Austral.* at the first attempt. **from the first** from the beginning. **from first to last** throughout. **get to first base** *US* achieve the first step towards an objective. **in the first place** as the first consideration. **of the first water** see WATER. [Old English *fyrst*, from Germanic]

first aid *n.* (hyphenated when *attrib.*) help given to an injured person until proper medical treatment is available. □ **first aider** *n.*

first blood see BLOOD.

first-born *adj. & n.* ● *adj.* eldest. ● *n.* the eldest child of a person.

First Cause *n.* the Creator of the universe.

first-class *adj. & adv.* ● *adj.* **1** belonging to or travelling by the first class. **2** of the best quality; very good. ● *adv.* by first class (*travels first-class*).

first class *n.* **1** a set of persons or things grouped together as the best. **2** the best accommodation in a train, ship, etc. **3** the class of mail given priority in handling. **4** *Brit.* **a** the highest division in an examination list. **b** a place in this.

first cousin see COUSIN *n.* 1.

first-day cover *n.* an envelope with stamps postmarked on their first day of issue.

first-degree *adj. Med.* denoting burns that affect only the surface of the skin, causing reddening.

first finger *n.* the finger next to the thumb.

first floor *n.* (*N. Amer.* **second floor**) the floor above the ground floor.

first-foot *n. & v. Sc.* ● *n.* the first person to cross a threshold in the New Year. ● *v.intr.* be a first-foot.

first-fruit *n.* (usu. in *pl.*) **1** the first agricultural produce of a season, esp. as offered to God. **2** the first results of work etc. **3** *hist.* a payment to a superior by the new holder of an office.

first gear *n.* the lowest in a set of gears.

first-hand *adj. & adv.* from the original source; direct.

first intention *n. Med.* the healing of a wound by natural contact of the parts.

first intentions *n.pl. Logic* a person's primary conceptions of things (e.g. a tree, an oak).

First Lady *n.* (in the US) the wife of the President.

first lieutenant *n. US* an army or air force officer next below captain.

first light *n.* the time when light first appears in the morning.

firstling /'fə:s(t)lɪŋ/ *n.* (usu. in *pl.*) **1** the first result of anything, first-fruits. **2** the first offspring; the first born in a season.

firstly /'fə:s(t)li/ *adv.* (in enumerating topics, arguments, etc.) in the first place, first (cf. FIRST *adv.*).

first mate *n.* (on a merchant ship) the officer second in command to the master.

first name *n.* a personal or Christian name.

first night *n.* the first public performance of a play etc. □ **first-nighter** *n.*

first offender *n.* a criminal against whom no previous conviction is recorded.

first officer *n.* the mate on a merchant ship.

first past the post *adj.* **1** winning a race etc. by being the first to reach the finishing line. **2** *Brit.* (of an electoral system) selecting a candidate or party by simple majority (see also PROPORTIONAL REPRESENTATION, TRANSFERABLE VOTE).

first person see PERSON 3.

first post *n. Brit.* the first of several bugle calls giving notice of the hour of retiring at night.

first-rate *adj.* **1** of the highest class, excellent. **2** *colloq.* very well (*feeling first-rate*).

first reading *n.* the occasion when a Bill is presented to a legislature to permit its introduction.

first refusal see REFUSAL 2.

First Reich *n.* the Holy Roman Empire, 962–1806.

first school *n. Brit.* a school for children from 5 to 9 years old.

first sergeant *n. US* the highest-ranking non-commissioned officer in a company.

first strike *adj.* an aggressive attack with nuclear weapons before their use by the enemy (hyphenated when *attrib.*: *first-strike strategy*).

first thing *adv. & n. colloq.* ● *adv.* before anything else; very early in the morning (*shall do it first thing*). ● *n.* (prec. by *the*) even the most elementary fact or principle (*does not know the first thing about it*).

firth /fəːθ/ *n.* (also **frith** /frɪθ/) **1** a narrow inlet of the sea. **2** an estuary. [Middle English (originally Scots) from Old Norse *fjörthr* FJORD]

fir tree see FIR 1.

fisc /fɪsk/ *n. Rom.Hist.* the public treasury; the emperor's privy purse. [French *fisc* or Latin *fiscus* 'rush-basket, purse, treasury']

fiscal /'fɪsk(ə)l/ *adj. & n.* ● *adj.* of public revenue. ● *n.* **1** a legal official in some countries. **2** *Sc.* = PROCURATOR FISCAL. □ **fiscally** *adv.* [French *fiscal* or Latin *fiscalis* (as FISC)]

fiscality /fɪ'skalɪti/ *n.* (*pl.* **-ies**) **1** (in *pl.*) fiscal matters. **2** excessive regard for these.

fiscal year *n.* = FINANCIAL YEAR.

fish[1] /fɪʃ/ *n. & v.* ● *n.* (*pl.* same or **fishes**) **1** a vertebrate cold-blooded animal with gills and fins living wholly in water. **2** an invertebrate animal living wholly in water, e.g. cuttlefish, shellfish, jellyfish. **3** the flesh of fish as food. **4** *colloq.* a person remarkable in some way (usu. unfavourable) (*an odd fish*). **5** (**the Fish** or **Fishes**) the zodiacal sign or constellation Pisces. **6** *Naut. slang* a torpedo; a submarine. ● *v.* **1** *intr.* try to catch fish, esp. with a line or net. **2** *tr.* fish for (a certain kind of fish) or in (a certain stretch of water). **3** *intr.* (foll. by *for*) **a** search for in water or a concealed place. **b** seek by indirect means (*fishing for compliments*). **4** *tr.* (foll. by *up*, *out*, etc.) retrieve with careful or awkward searching. □ **drink like a fish** drink excessively. **fish out of water** a person in an unsuitable or unwelcome environment or situation. **other fish to fry** other matters to attend to. □ **fishlike** *adj.* [Old English *fisc*, *fiscian*, from Germanic]

■ **Usage** The collective plural *fish* is now usual, but the older form *fishes* is still used, especially in technical writing, when referring to different kinds of fish (e.g. *the freshwater fishes of Europe*), and in biblical allusions etc. (e.g. *five loaves and two small fishes*).

fish[2] /fɪʃ/ *n. & v.* ● *n.* **1** a flat plate of iron, wood, etc., to strengthen a beam or joint. **2** *Naut.* a piece of wood, convex and concave, used to strengthen a mast etc. ● *v.tr.* **1** mend or strengthen (a spar etc.) with a fish. **2** join (rails) with a fish-plate. [originally as verb: from French *ficher* 'fix', ultimately from Latin *figere*]

fish[3] /fɪʃ/ *n.* a piece of ivory etc. used as a counter in games. [French *fiche* (*ficher*; see FISH[2])]

fish-bolt *n.* a bolt used to fasten fish-plates and rails together.

fishbowl /'fɪʃbəʊl/ *n.* a usu. round glass bowl for keeping pet fish in.

fish cake *n.* a cake of shredded fish and mashed potato, usu. eaten fried.

fish eagle *n.* any eagle, esp. of the genus *Haliaeetus*, that catches and feeds on fish.

fisher /'fɪʃə/ *n.* **1** an animal that catches fish, esp. the pekan, a tree-living N. American marten, *Martes pennanti*, valued for its fur. **2** *archaic* a fisherman. [Old English *fiscere* from Germanic (as FISH[1])]

fisherfolk /'fɪʃəfəʊk/ *n.* (treated as *pl.*) people whose livelihood is fishing.

fisherman /'fɪʃəmən/ *n.* (*pl.* **-men**) **1** a person who catches fish as a livelihood or for sport. **2** a fishing boat.

fishery /'fɪʃ(ə)ri/ *n.* (*pl.* **-ies**) **1** a place where fish are caught or reared. **2** the occupation or industry of catching or rearing fish.

fish-eye lens *n.* a very wide-angle lens with a field of vision covering up to 180°, the scale being reduced towards the edges.

fish farm *n.* a place where fish are bred for food.

fish finger *n. Brit.* a small oblong piece of fish in batter or breadcrumbs.

fish-glue *n.* isinglass.

fish-hawk *n.* = OSPREY 1.

fish-hook see HOOK *n.* 1b.

fishing /'fɪʃɪŋ/ *n.* the activity of catching fish, esp. for food or as a sport.

fishing-fly *n.* = FLY[2] 4.

fishing line *n.* a long thread of silk etc. with a baited hook, sinker, float, etc., used for catching fish.

fishing rod *n.* a long tapering usu. jointed rod to which a fishing line is attached.

fish kettle *n.* an oval pan for boiling fish.

fish-knife *n.* a knife for eating or serving fish.

fishmeal /'fɪʃmiːl/ *n.* ground dried fish used as fertilizer or animal feed.

fishmonger /'fɪʃmʌŋgə/ *n.* esp. *Brit.* a dealer in fish for food.

fishnet /'fɪʃnɛt/ *n.* (often *attrib.*) an open-meshed fabric (*fishnet stockings*).

fish-plate *n.* **1** a flat piece of iron etc. connecting railway rails. **2** a flat piece of metal with ends like a fish's tail, used to position masonry.

fish pond *n.* a pond or pool in which fish are kept.

fishpot /'fɪʃpɒt/ *n.* a wicker trap for eels, lobsters, etc.

fish slice *n. Brit.* a flat utensil for lifting fish and fried foods during and after cooking.

fishtail /'fɪʃteɪl/ *n. & v.* ● *n.* anything resembling a fish's tail in shape or movement. ● *v.intr.* move the tail of a vehicle from side to side.

fishtail burner *n.* a kind of gas burner producing a broadening jet of flame.

fishwife /'fɪʃwʌɪf/ *n.* (*pl.* **-wives**) **1** a coarse-mannered or noisy woman. **2** a woman who sells fish.

fishy /'fɪʃi/ *adj.* (**fishier**, **fishiest**) **1 a** of or like (a) fish. **b** *joc.* or *poet.* abounding in fish. **2** *slang* arousing suspicion, questionable, mysterious (*something fishy going on*). □ **fishily** *adv.* **fishiness** *n.*

fisk /fɪsk/ *n. Sc.* the state treasury, the exchequer. [variant of FISC]

fissile /'fɪsʌɪl/ *adj.* **1** capable of undergoing nuclear fission. **2** cleavable; tending to split. □ **fissility** /-'sɪlɪti/ *n.* [Latin *fissilis* (as FISSURE)]

fission /'fɪʃ(ə)n/ *n. & v.* ● *n.* **1** the action of dividing or splitting into two or more parts. **2** *Physics* = NUCLEAR FISSION. **3** *Biol.* the division of a cell etc. into new cells etc. as a mode of reproduction. ● *v.intr. & tr.* undergo or cause to undergo fission. □ **fissionable** *adj.* [Latin *fissio* (as FISSURE)]

fission bomb *n.* an atom bomb.

fissiparous /fɪ'sɪp(ə)rəs/ *adj.* **1** *Biol.* reproducing by fission. **2** tending to split. □ **fissiparity** /-'parɪti/ *n.* **fissiparously** *adv.* **fissiparousness** *n.* [Latin *fissus*, past part. of *findere* (as FISSURE), on the pattern of *viviparous*]

fissure /'fɪʃə/ *n. & v.* ● *n.* **1** an opening, usu. long and narrow, made esp. by cracking, splitting, or separation of parts. **2** *Bot. & Anat.* a narrow opening in an organ etc., esp. a depression between convolutions of the brain. **3** a cleavage. ● *v.tr. & intr.* split or crack. [Middle English from Old French *fissure* or Latin *fissura*, from *findere fiss-* 'cleave']

fist /fɪst/ *n. & v.* ● *n.* **1** a tightly closed hand. **2** *slang* handwriting (*writes a good fist*; *I know his fist*). **3** *slang* a hand (*give us your fist*). ● *v.tr.* **1** strike with the fist. **2** *Naut.* handle (a sail, an oar, etc.). □ **make a good** (or **poor** etc.) **fist** (foll. by *at*, *of*) *colloq.* make a good (or poor etc.) attempt at. □ **fisted** *adj.* (also in *comb.*). **fistful** *n.* (*pl.* **-fuls**). [Old English *fȳst*, from West Germanic]

fist fight *n.* a fight with bare fists.

fistic /'fɪstɪk/ *adj.* (also **fistical**) *joc.* pugilistic.

fisticuffs /'fɪstɪkʌfs/ *n.pl.* fighting with the fists. [probably obsolete *fisty* adj. = FISTIC, + CUFF[2]]

fistula /ˈfɪstjʊlə/ *n.* (*pl.* **fistulas** or **fistulae** /-liː/) **1** *Med.* an abnormal or surgically made passage between a hollow organ and the body surface or between two hollow organs. **2** *Zool.* a natural pipe or spout in whales, insects, etc. □ **fistular** *adj.* **fistulous** *adj.* [Latin, = pipe, flute]

fit[1] /fɪt/ *adj., v., n., & adv.* ● *adj.* (**fitter, fittest**) **1 a** (usu. foll. by *for*, or *to* + infin.) well adapted or suited. **b** (foll. by *to* + infin.) qualified, competent, worthy. **c** (foll. by *for*, or *to* + infin.) in a suitable condition, ready. **d** (foll. by *for*) good enough (*a dinner fit for a king*). **e** (foll. by *to* + infin.) sufficiently exhausted, troubled, or angry (*fit to drop*). **2** in good health or athletic condition. **3** proper, becoming, right (*it is fit that*). ● *v.* (**fitted, fitting**) **1 a** *tr.* (also *absol.*) be of the right shape and size for (*the dress fits her; the key doesn't fit the lock; these shoes don't fit*). **b** *tr.* make, fix, or insert (a thing) so that it is of the right size or shape (*fitted shelves in the alcoves*). **c** *intr.* (often foll. by *in, into*) (of a component) be correctly positioned (*that bit fits here*). **d** *tr.* find room for (*can't fit another person on the bench*). **2** *tr.* (foll. by *for*, or *to* + infin.) **a** make suitable; adapt. **b** make competent (*fitted him to be a priest*). **3** *tr.* (usu. foll. by *with*) supply, furnish (*fitted the boat with a new rudder*). **4** *tr.* fix in place (*fit a lock on the door*). **5** *tr.* = *fit on*. **6** *tr.* be in harmony with, befit, become (*it fits the occasion; the punishment fits the crime*). **7** *tr.* (often foll. by *up*) esp. *Austral.* secure enough (genuine or false) evidence to convict; frame. ● *n.* the way in which a garment, component, etc., fits (*a bad fit; a tight fit*). ● *adv.* (foll. by *to* + infin.) *colloq.* in a suitable manner, appropriately (*was laughing fit to bust*). □ **fit the bill** = *fill the bill*. **fit in 1** (often foll. by *with*) be (esp. socially) compatible or accommodating (*doesn't fit in with the rest of the group; tried to fit in with their plans*). **2** find space or time for (an object, engagement, etc.) (*the dentist fitted me in at the last minute*). **fit on** *Brit.* try on (a garment). **fit out** (or **up**) (often foll. by *with*) equip. **see** (or **think**) **fit** (often foll. by *to* + infin.) decide or choose (a specified course of action). □ **fitly** *adv.* **fitness** *n.* [Middle English: origin unknown]

fit[2] /fɪt/ *n.* **1** a sudden seizure of epilepsy, hysteria, apoplexy, fainting, or paralysis, with unconsciousness or convulsions. **2** a sudden brief attack of an illness or of symptoms (*fit of coughing*). **3** a sudden short bout or burst (*fit of energy; fit of giggles*). **4** *colloq.* an attack of strong feeling (*fit of rage*). **5** a capricious impulse; a mood (*when the fit was on him*). □ **by** (or **in**) **fits and starts** spasmodically. **give a person a fit** *colloq.* surprise or outrage him or her. **have a fit** *colloq.* be greatly surprised or outraged. **in fits** laughing uncontrollably. [Old English *fitt* 'conflict', in Middle English = position of danger or excitement]

fit[3] /fɪt/ *n.* (also **fytte**) *archaic* a section of a poem. [Old English *fitt*, perhaps as FIT[2], or related to German *fitze* in the obsolete sense 'thread with which weavers mark off a day's work']

fitch /fɪtʃ/ *n.* **1** a polecat. **2 a** the hair of a polecat. **b** a brush made from this or similar hair. [Middle Dutch *fisse* etc.: cf. FITCHEW]

fitchew /ˈfɪtʃuː/ *n.* a polecat. [Middle English from Old French *ficheau, fissel*, diminutive of Middle Dutch *fisse*]

fitful /ˈfɪtfʊl, -f(ə)l/ *adj.* active or occurring spasmodically or intermittently. □ **fitfully** *adv.* **fitfulness** *n.*

fitment /ˈfɪtm(ə)nt/ *n.* (usu. in *pl.*) esp. *Brit.* a fixed item of furniture.

fitted /ˈfɪtɪd/ *adj.* esp. *Brit.* **1** made or shaped to fill a space or cover something closely or exactly (*a fitted carpet*). **2** provided with appropriate equipment, fittings, etc. (*a fitted kitchen*). **3** built-in; filling an alcove etc. (*fitted cupboards*).

fitter /ˈfɪtə/ *n.* **1** a person who supervises the cutting, fitting, altering, etc. of garments. **2** a mechanic who fits together and adjusts machinery.

fitting /ˈfɪtɪŋ/ *n. & adj.* ● *n.* **1** the process or an instance of having a garment etc. fitted (*needed several fittings*). **2 a** (in *pl.*) *Brit.* the fixtures and fitments of a building. **b** a piece of apparatus or furniture. ● *adj.* proper, becoming, right. □ **fittingly** *adv.* **fittingness** *n.*

fitting shop *n.* a place where machine parts are put together.

fit-up *n. Brit. Theatr. slang* **1** a temporary stage etc. **2** a travelling company.

FitzGerald contraction /fɪtsˈdʒɛr(ə)ld/ *n.* (also **FitzGerald–Lorentz contraction**) *Physics* the shortening of a moving body in the direction of its motion esp. at speeds close to that of light. [named after G. F. *FitzGerald*, Irish physicist d. 1901 and H. A. *Lorentz*, Dutch physicist d. 1928]

five /fʌɪv/ *n. & adj.* ● *n.* **1** one more than four or one half of ten; the sum of three units and two units. **2** a symbol for this (5, v, V). **3** a size etc. denoted by five. **4** a set or team of five individuals. **5** five o'clock. **6** a card with five pips. **7** *Cricket* a hit scoring five runs. ● *adj.* that amount to five. [Old English *fīf*, from Germanic]

five-a-side *adj. & n.* ● *adj.* designating football played with five players in each team. ● *n.* a game of five-a-side football.

five-corner *n.* (also **five-corners**) *Austral.* **1** a shrub of the genus *Styphelia*. **2** the pentagonal fruit of this.

five-eighth *n. Austral. & NZ Rugby* either of two players between the scrum-half and the centre three-quarter.

five-finger exercise *n.* **1** an exercise on the piano involving all the fingers. **2** an easy task.

fivefold /ˈfʌɪvfəʊld/ *adj. & adv.* **1** five times as much or as many. **2** consisting of five parts. **3** amounting to five.

five hundred *n.* a form of euchre in which 500 points make a game.

five o'clock shadow *n.* beard-growth visible on a man's face in the latter part of the day.

fiver /ˈfʌɪvə/ *n. colloq.* **1** *Brit.* a five-pound note. **2** *N. Amer.* a five-dollar bill.

fives /fʌɪvz/ *n.* a game played esp. in the UK, in which a ball is hit with a gloved hand or a bat against the walls of a court with three walls (**Eton fives**) or four walls (**Rugby fives**). [pl. of FIVE used as sing.: significance unknown]

five senses *n.pl.* (prec. by *the*) sight, hearing, smell, taste, and touch.

five-star *adj.* of the highest class. [from the system used to grade hotels]

fivestones /ˈfʌɪvstəʊnz/ *n. Brit.* jacks played with five pieces of metal etc. and usu. without a ball.

five-year plan *n.* **1** (in the former USSR) a government plan for economic development over five years, inaugurated in 1928. **2** a similar plan in another country.

fix /fɪks/ *v. & n.* ● *v.* **1** *tr.* make firm or stable; fasten, secure (*fixed a picture to the wall*). **2** *tr.* decide, settle, specify (a price, date, etc.). **3** *tr.* mend, repair. **4** *tr.* implant (an idea or memory) in the mind (*couldn't get the rules fixed in his head*). **5** *tr.* **a** (foll. by *on, upon*) direct steadily, set (one's eyes, gaze, attention, or affection). **b** attract and hold (a person's attention, eyes, etc.). **c** (foll. by *with*) single out with one's eyes etc. **6** *tr.* place definitely or permanently, establish, station. **7** *tr.* determine the exact nature, position, etc., of; refer (a thing or person) to a definite place or time; identify, locate. **8 a** *tr.* make (eyes, features, etc.) rigid. **b** *intr.* (of eyes, features, etc.) become rigid. **9** *tr.* esp. *N. Amer. colloq.* prepare (food or drink) (*fixed me a drink*). **10 a** *tr.* deprive of fluidity or volatility; congeal. **b** *intr.* lose fluidity or volatility, become congealed. **11** *tr. colloq.* punish, kill, silence, deal with (a person). **12** *tr. colloq.* **a** secure the support of (a person) fraudulently, esp. by bribery. **b** arrange the result of (a race, match, etc.) fraudulently (*the competition was fixed*). **13** *slang* **a** *tr.* inject (a person, esp. oneself) with a narcotic. **b** *intr.* take an injection of a narcotic. **14** *tr.* **a** make (a pigment, photographic image, etc.) fast or permanent. **b** *Biol.* preserve or stabilize (a specimen) prior to treatment or microscopic examination. **15** *tr.* (of a plant or micro-organism) assimilate (nitrogen or carbon dioxide) by forming a non-gaseous compound. **16** *tr.* castrate or spay (an animal). **17** *tr.* arrest changes or development in (a language or literature). **18** *tr.* determine the incidence of (liability etc.). **19** *intr. archaic* take up one's position. ● *n.* **1** *colloq.* a position hard to escape from; a dilemma or predicament. **2 a** the act of finding one's position by bearings or astronomical observations. **b** a position found in this way. **3** *slang* a dose of a narcotic drug to which one is addicted. **4** *slang* bribery; an illicit arrangement. □ **be fixed** (usu. foll. by *for*) be disposed or affected (regarding) (*how is he fixed for money?*; *how are you fixed for Friday?*). **fix on** (or **upon**) choose, decide on. **fix up 1** arrange, organize, prepare. **2** accommodate. **3** (often foll. by *with*) provide (a person) (*fixed me up with a job*). □ **fixable** *adj.* **fixedly** /ˈfɪksɪdli/ *adv.* **fixedness** /ˈfɪksɪdnɪs/ *n.* [Middle English, ultimately from Latin *fixus*, past part. of *figere* 'fix, fasten', partly via Old French *fix*, partly via medieval Latin *fixare*]

fixate /fɪkˈseɪt/ *v.tr.* **1** direct one's gaze on. **2** *Psychol.* **a** (usu. in *passive*; often foll. by *on*, *upon*) cause (a person) to acquire an abnormal attachment to persons or things (*was fixated on his son*). **b** arrest (part of the libido) at an immature stage, causing such attachment. [Latin *fixus* (see FIX) + -ATE[3]]

fixation /fɪkˈseɪʃ(ə)n/ *n.* **1** the act or an instance of being fixated. **2** an obsession, concentration on a single idea. **3** fixing or being fixed. **4** the process of rendering solid; coagulation. **5** the process of assimilating a gas to form a solid compound. [Middle English from medieval Latin *fixatio*, from *fixare*: see FIX]

fixative /ˈfɪksətɪv/ *adj.* & *n.* ● *adj.* tending to fix or secure. ● *n.* a substance used to fix colours, hair, biological specimens, etc.

fixed capital *n.* machinery etc. that remains in the owner's use.

fixed-doh *attrib.adj.* (also **fixed-do**) applied to a system of sight-singing in which C is called 'doh', D is called 'ray', etc., irrespective of the key in which they occur (cf. MOVABLE-DOH).

fixed focus *n.* a camera focus that cannot be adjusted, typically used with a small aperture lens having a large depth of field.

fixed idea *n.* = IDÉE FIXE.

fixed income *n.* income deriving from a pension, investment at fixed interest, etc.

fixed odds *n.pl.* predetermined odds in racing etc. (opp. STARTING PRICE).

fixed oil *n.* a non-volatile oil of animal or plant origin, used in varnishes, lubricants, illuminants, soaps, etc.

fixed point *n. Physics* a well-defined reproducible temperature.

fixed star see STAR *n.* 2.

fixer /ˈfɪksə/ *n.* **1** a person or thing that fixes. **2** *Photog.* a substance used for fixing a photographic image etc. **3** *colloq.* a person who makes arrangements, esp. of an illicit kind.

fixing /ˈfɪksɪŋ/ *n.* **1** a method or means of fixing. **2** (in *pl.*) *US* **a** apparatus or equipment. **b** the trimmings for a dish. **c** the trimmings of a dress etc.

fixity /ˈfɪksɪti/ *n.* **1** a fixed state. **2** stability; permanence. [obsolete *fix* fixed: see FIX]

fixture /ˈfɪkstʃə, -tjə/ *n.* **1 a** something fixed or fastened in position. **b** (usu. *predic.*) *colloq.* a person or thing confined to or established in one place (*he seems to be a fixture*). **2** *Brit.* **a** a sporting event, esp. a match, race, etc. **b** the date agreed for this. **3** (in *pl.*) *Law* articles attached to a house or land and regarded as legally part of it. [alteration of obsolete *fixure*, via Late Latin *fixura* from Latin *figere fix-* 'fix']

fizgig /ˈfɪzgɪg/ *n.* & *adj.* ● *n.* **1** *archaic* a silly or flirtatious young woman. **2** *archaic* a kind of small firework; a cracker. **3** *Austral. slang* a police informer. ● *adj. archaic* flighty. [probably from FIZZ + obsolete *gig* 'flighty girl']

fizz /fɪz/ *v.* & *n.* ● *v.intr.* **1** make a hissing or spluttering sound. **2** (of a drink) make bubbles; effervesce. ● *n.* **1** effervescence. **2** *colloq.* an effervescent drink, esp. champagne. [imitative]

fizzle /ˈfɪz(ə)l/ *v.* & *n.* ● *v.intr.* make a feeble hissing or spluttering sound. ● *n.* such a sound. □ **fizzle out** end feebly (*the party fizzled out at 10 o'clock*). [formed as FIZZ + -LE[4]]

fizzy /ˈfɪzi/ *adj.* (**fizzier**, **fizziest**) effervescent. □ **fizzily** *adv.* **fizziness** *n.*

FJI *abbr.* (in the UK) Fellow of the Institute of Journalists.

fjord /fjɔːd/ *n.* (also **fiord**) a long narrow inlet of sea between high cliffs, as in Norway. [Norwegian, via Old Norse *fjörthr* from Germanic: cf. FIRTH, FORD]

FL *abbr. US* Florida (in official postal use).

fl. *abbr.* **1** floor. **2** floruit. **3** fluid.

Fla. *abbr.* Florida.

flab /flab/ *n. colloq.* fat; flabbiness. [imitative, or back-formation from FLABBY]

flabbergast /ˈflabəgɑːst/ *v.tr.* (esp. as **flabbergasted** *adj.*) *colloq.* overwhelm with astonishment; dumbfound. [18th c.: perhaps from FLABBY + AGHAST]

flabby /ˈflabi/ *adj.* (**flabbier**, **flabbiest**) **1** (of flesh etc.) hanging down; limp; flaccid. **2** (of language or character) feeble. □ **flabbily** *adv.* **flabbiness** *n.* [alteration of earlier *flappy* from FLAP]

flaccid /ˈflaksɪd, ˈflasɪd/ *adj.* **1 a** (of flesh etc.) hanging loose or wrinkled; limp, flabby. **b** (of plant tissue) soft; less rigid. **2** relaxed, drooping. **3** lacking vigour; feeble. □ **flaccidity** /fləkˈsɪdɪti, fləˈsɪd-/ *n.* **flaccidly** *adv.* [French *flaccide* or Latin *flaccidus*, from *flaccus* 'flabby']

flack[1] /flak/ *n. US slang* a publicity agent. [20th c.: origin unknown]

flack[2] var. of FLAK.

flag[1] /flag/ *n.* & *v.* ● *n.* **1 a** a piece of cloth, usu. oblong or square, attachable by one edge to a pole or rope and used as a country's emblem or as a standard, signal, etc. **b** a small toy, device, etc., resembling a flag. **2** a device that is raised to indicate that a taxi is for hire. **3** *Naut.* a flag carried by a flagship as an emblem of an admiral's rank afloat. ● *v.* (**flagged**, **flagging**) **1** *intr.* **a** grow tired; lose vigour; lag (*his energy flagged after the first lap*). **b** hang down; droop; become limp. **2** *tr.* **a** place a flag on or over. **b** mark out with or as if with a flag or flags. **3** *tr.* (often foll. by *that*) **a** inform (a person) by flag signals. **b** communicate (information) by flagging. □ **flag down** signal to (a vehicle or driver) to stop. **keep the flag flying** continue the fight. **put the flag out** celebrate victory, success, etc. **show the flag 1** make an official visit to a foreign port etc. **2** ensure that notice is taken of one's country, oneself, etc.; make a patriotic display. □ **flagger** *n.* [16th c.: perhaps from obsolete *flag* 'drooping']

flag[2] /flag/ *n.* & *v.* ● *n.* **1** a flat usu. rectangular stone slab used for paving. **2** (in *pl.*) a pavement made of these. ● *v.tr.* (**flagged**, **flagging**) pave with flags. [Middle English, = sod: cf. Icelandic *flag* 'spot from which a sod has been cut out', Old Norse *flaga* 'slab of stone', and FLAKE[1]]

flag[3] /flag/ *n.* **1** any of various plants with sword-shaped leaves, esp. the yellow flag *Iris pseudacorus*; see also SWEET FLAG, YELLOW FLAG. **2** the long slender leaf of such a plant. [Middle English: related to Middle Dutch *flag*, Danish *flæg*]

flag[4] /flag/ *n.* (in full **flag-feather**) a quill-feather of a bird's wing. [perhaps related to obsolete *fag* 'loose flap': cf. FLAG[1] *v.*]

flag-boat *n.* a boat serving as a mark in sailing matches.

flag-captain *n.* the captain of a flagship.

Flag Day *n. US* 14 June, the anniversary of the adoption of the Stars and Stripes in 1777.

flag day *n. Brit.* a day on which money is raised for a charity by the sale of small paper flags etc. in the street.

flagellant /ˈfladʒ(ə)l(ə)nt, fləˈdʒɛl(ə)nt/ *n. & adj.* ● *n.* **1** a person who scourges himself or herself or others as a religious discipline. **2** a person who engages in flogging as a sexual stimulus. ● *adj.* of or concerning flagellation. [Latin *flagellare* 'to whip' from FLAGELLUM]

flagellate[1] /ˈfladʒ(ə)leɪt/ *v.tr.* scourge, flog (cf. FLAGELLANT). □ **flagellator** *n.* **flagellatory** /-lət(ə)ri/ *adj.*

flagellate[2] /ˈfladʒ(ə)lət, -eɪt/ *adj. & n.* ● *adj.* having flagella. ● *n.* a protozoan having one or more flagella.

flagellation /fladʒəˈleɪʃ(ə)n/ *n.* the act or practice of flagellating others or (esp.) oneself, as a sexual stimulus or religious discipline.

flagellum /fləˈdʒɛləm/ *n.* (*pl.* **flagella** /-lə/) **1** *Biol.* a long lashlike appendage found esp. on microscopic organisms. **2** *Bot.* a runner; a creeping shoot. □ **flagellar** *adj.* **flagelliform** *adj.* [Latin, = whip, diminutive of *flagrum* 'scourge']

flageolet[1] /fladʒəˈlɛt, ˈfladʒəlɪt, ˈflaʒə(ʊ)leɪ/ *n.* **1** a small flute blown at the end, like a recorder but with two thumb holes. **2** an organ stop having a similar sound. [French, diminutive of Old French *flag(e)ol* from Provençal *flajol*, of unknown origin]

flageolet[2] /fladʒəˈlɛt/ *n.* a kind of French kidney bean. [French, ultimately from Latin *phaseolus* 'bean']

flag-feather see FLAG[4].

flagitious /fləˈdʒɪʃəs/ *adj.* deeply criminal; utterly villainous. □ **flagitiously** *adv.* **flagitiousness** *n.* [Middle English from Latin *flagitiosus*, from *flagitium* 'shameful crime']

flag-lieutenant *n.* an admiral's ADC.

flag-list *n.* a roll of flag-officers.

flagman /ˈflagmən/ *n.* (*pl.* **-men**) a person who signals with or as with a flag, e.g. at races.

flag of convenience *n.* a foreign flag under which a ship is registered, usu. to avoid financial charges etc.

flag-officer *n.* an admiral, vice admiral, or rear admiral, or the commodore of a yacht club.

flag of truce *n.* a white flag indicating a desire for a truce.

flagon /ˈflag(ə)n/ *n.* **1** a large bottle in which wine, cider, etc., is sold, usu. holding 1.13 litres (about 2 pints). **2 a** a large vessel usu. with a handle, spout, and lid, to hold wine etc. **b** a similar vessel used for the Eucharist. [Middle English *flakon* from Old French *flacon*, ultimately from Late Latin *flasco -onis* FLASK]

flagpole /ˈflagpəʊl/ *n.* = FLAGSTAFF.

flag-rank *n.* the rank attained by flag-officers.

flagrant /ˈfleɪgr(ə)nt/ *adj.* (of an offence or an offender) glaring; notorious; scandalous. □ **flagrancy** /-gr(ə)nsi/ *n.* **flagrantly** *adv.* [French *flagrant* or Latin *flagrant-*, part. stem of *flagrare* 'blaze']

flagship /ˈflagʃɪp/ *n.* **1** a ship having an admiral on board. **2** something that is held to be the best or most important of its kind; a leader.

flagstaff /ˈflagstɑːf/ *n.* a pole on which a flag may be hoisted.

flag-station *n.* a station at which trains stop only if signalled.

flagstone /ˈflagstəʊn/ *n.* = FLAG[2] *n.* □ **flagstoned** *adj.*

flag-wagging *n. Brit. slang* **1** signalling with hand-held flags. **2** = FLAG-WAVING.

flag-waving *n.* populist agitation, chauvinism. □ **flag-waver** *n.*

flail /fleɪl/ *n. & v.* ● *n.* a threshing tool consisting of a wooden staff with a short heavy stick swinging from it. ● *v.* **1** *tr.* beat or strike with or as if with a flail. **2** *intr.* wave or swing wildly or erratically (*went into the fight with arms flailing*). [Old English, probably from Latin FLAGELLUM]

flair /flɛː/ *n.* **1** an instinct for selecting or performing what is excellent, useful, etc.; a talent (*has a flair for knowing what the public wants*; *has a flair for languages*). **2** talent or ability, esp. artistic or stylistic. [French *flairer* to smell, ultimately from Latin *fragrare*: see FRAGRANT]

flak /flak/ *n.* (also **flack**) **1** anti-aircraft fire. **2** adverse criticism; abuse. [German, abbreviation of *Flug(zeug)abwehrkanone* 'anti-aircraft gun']

flake[1] /fleɪk/ *n. & v.* ● *n.* **1 a** a small thin light piece of snow. **b** a similar piece of another material. **2** a thin broad piece of material peeled or split off. **3** *Archaeol.* a piece of hard stone chipped off and used as a tool. **4** a natural division of the flesh of some fish. **5** the dogfish or other shark as food. **6** *N. Amer. slang* a crazy, eccentric, or dim person. ● *v.tr. & intr.* (often foll. by *away, off*) **1** take off or come away in flakes. **2** sprinkle with or fall in snowlike flakes. □ **flake out** *colloq.* fall asleep or drop from exhaustion; faint. [Middle English, origin unknown: perhaps related to Old Norse *flakna* 'flake off']

flake[2] /fleɪk/ *n.* **1** a stage for drying fish etc. **2** a rack for storing oatcakes etc. [in earlier use, 'wicker hurdle': Middle English, perhaps from Old Norse *flaki*, *fleki* 'wicker shield']

flak jacket *n.* a protective jacket of heavy camouflage fabric reinforced with metal, worn by soldiers etc.

flaky /ˈfleɪki/ *adj.* (**flakier**, **flakiest**) **1** of or like flakes; separating easily into flakes. **2** esp. *N. Amer. slang* crazy, eccentric, dim. □ **flakily** *adv.* **flakiness** *n.*

flaky pastry *n.* pastry consisting of thin light layers.

flambé /ˈflɒmbeɪ/ *adj. & v.* ● *adj.* (of food) covered with spirits and set alight briefly. ● *v.tr.* (**flambés**, **flambéed**, **flambéing**) cover (food) with spirits and set alight briefly. [French, past part. of *flamber* 'singe' (as FLAMBEAU)]

flambeau /ˈflambəʊ/ *n.* (*pl.* **flambeaus** or **flambeaux** /-əʊz/) **1** a flaming torch, esp. composed of several thick waxed wicks. **2** a branched candlestick. [French from *flambe*, from Latin *flammula*, diminutive of *flamma* 'flame']

flamboyant /flamˈbɔɪənt/ *adj.* **1** ostentatious; showy. **2** floridly decorated. **3** gorgeously coloured. **4** *Archit.* (of decoration) marked by wavy flamelike lines. □ **flamboyance** *n.* **flamboyancy** *n.* **flamboyantly** *adv.* [French (in *Archit.* sense), pres. part. of *flamboyer* from *flambe*: see FLAMBEAU]

flame /fleɪm/ *n. & v.* ● *n.* **1 a** ignited gas (*the fire burnt with a steady flame*). **b** one portion of this (*the flame flickered and died*). **c** (usu. in *pl.*) visible combustion (*burst into flames*). **2 a** a bright light; brilliant colouring. **b** a brilliant orange-red colour. **3 a** strong passion, esp. love (*fan the flame*). **b** *colloq.* a boyfriend or girlfriend. ● *v.* **1** *intr. & tr.* (often foll. by *away, forth, out, up*) emit or cause to emit flames. **2** *intr.* (often foll. by *out, up*) **a** (of passion) break out. **b** (of a person) become angry. **3** *intr.* shine or glow like flame (*leaves flamed in the autumn sun*). **4** *intr. poet.* move like flame. **5** *tr.* send (a signal) by means of flame. **6** *tr.* subject to the action of flame. □ **flame out 1** (of a jet engine) lose power through the extinction of the flame in the combustion chamber. **2** esp. *N. Amer.* fail, esp. conspicuously. **go up in flames** be consumed by fire. □ **flameless** *adj.* **flamelike** *adj.* **flamy** *adj.* [Middle English via Old French *flame*, *flam(m)er* from Latin *flamma*]

flame gun *n.* a device for throwing flames to destroy weeds etc.

flamen /ˈfleɪmɛn, ˈflɑː-/ *n. Rom.Hist.* a priest serving a particular deity. [Middle English from Latin]

flamenco /fləˈmɛŋkəʊ/ *n.* (*pl.* **-os**) **1** a style of music played (esp. on the guitar) and sung by Spanish gypsies. **2** a dance performed to this music. [Spanish, = Flemish]

flameout /ˈfleɪmaʊt/ *n.* **1** *Aeron.* extinction of the flame in a jet engine causing loss of power. **2** esp. *N. Amer.* a complete or conspicuous failure.

flameproof /ˈfleɪmpruːf/ *adj. & v.* ● *adj.* (esp. of a fabric) treated so as to be non-flammable. ● *v.tr.* make flameproof.

flame-thrower *n.* (also **flame-projector**) a weapon for throwing a spray of flame.

flame tree *n.* any of various trees with brilliant red flowers, esp. a Madagascan poinciana, *Delonix regia*, or an Australian bottle tree, *Brachychiton australis*.

flaming /ˈfleɪmɪŋ/ *attrib.adj.* **1** emitting flames. **2** very hot (*flaming June*). **3** *colloq.* **a** passionate; intense (*a flaming row*). **b** expressing annoyance, or as an intensifier (*that flaming dog*). **4** brightly coloured (*flaming red hair*).

flamingo /fləˈmɪŋɡəʊ/ *n.* (*pl.* **-os** or **-oes**) any tall long-necked web-footed wading bird of the family Phoenicopteridae, with crooked bill and pink, scarlet, and black plumage. [Portuguese *flamengo* from Provençal *flamenc*, from *flama* 'flame' + *-enc* = -ING[3]]

flammable /ˈflaməb(ə)l/ *adj.* inflammable. □ **flammability** /-ˈbɪlɪti/ *n.* [Latin *flammare* from *flamma* 'flame']

■ **Usage** *Flammable* is used because *inflammable* can be mistaken for a negative (the true negative being *non-flammable*).

flan /flan/ *n.* **1 a** a pastry case with a savoury or sweet filling. **b** a sponge base with a sweet topping. **2** a disc of metal from which a coin etc. is made. [French (originally = round cake) via Old French *flaon* and medieval Latin *flado -onis* from Frankish]

flanch /flɑːn(t)ʃ/ *v.intr. & tr.* (also **flaunch** /flɔːn(t)ʃ/) (esp. with reference to a chimney) slope inwards or cause to slope inwards towards the top. □ **flanching** *n.* [perhaps from Old French *flanchir* from *flanche*, *flanc* FLANK]

flânerie /flanˈriː, French flanri/ *n.* idling, idleness. [French from *flâner* 'lounge']

flâneur /flaˈnəː, French flanœr/ *n.* an idler; a lounger. [French (as FLÂNERIE)]

flange /flan(d)ʒ/ *n. & v. Engin.* ● *n.* a projecting flat rim, collar, or rib, used for strengthening or attachment. ● *v.tr.* provide with a flange. □ **flangeless** *n.* [17th c.: perhaps from *flange* 'widen out', from Old French *flangir* (as FLANCH)]

flank /flaŋk/ *n. & v.* ● *n.* **1 a** the side of the body between the ribs and the hip. **b** the side of an animal carved as meat (*flank of beef*). **2** the side of a mountain, building, etc. **3** the right or left side of an army or other body of persons. ● *v.tr.* **1** (often in *passive*) be situated at both sides of (*a road flanked by mountains*). **2** *Mil.* **a** guard or strengthen on the flank. **b** menace the flank of. **c** rake with sweeping gunfire; enfilade. □ **in flank** at the side. [Middle English via Old French *flanc* from Frankish]

flanker /ˈflaŋkə/ *n.* **1** *Mil.* a fortification guarding or menacing the flank. **2** anything that flanks another thing. **3 a** (in rugby) a wing forward. **b** (in American football) an offensive player who lines up to the outside of an end. **4** *Brit. slang* a trick; a swindle (*pulled a flanker*).

flank forward *n. Rugby* a wing forward.

flannel /ˈflan(ə)l/ *n. & v.* ● *n.* **1 a** a kind of woven woollen fabric, usu. without a nap. **b** (in *pl.*) flannel garments, esp. trousers. **2** *Brit.* a small usu. towelling cloth, used for washing oneself. **3** *Brit. slang* nonsense; flattery. ● *v.* (**flannelled**, **flannelling**; *US* **flanneled**, **flanneling**) **1** *Brit. slang* **a** *tr.* flatter. **b** *intr.* use flattery. **2** *tr.* wash or clean with a flannel. [perhaps from Welsh *gwlanen*, from *gwlān* 'wool']

flannelboard /ˈflan(ə)lbɔːd/ *n.* a piece of flannel as a base for paper or cloth cut-outs, used as a toy or a teaching aid.

flannelette /flanəˈlɛt/ *n.* a napped cotton fabric imitating flannel. [FLANNEL]

flannelgraph /ˈflan(ə)lgrɑːf/ *n.* = FLANNELBOARD.

flannelled /ˈflan(ə)ld/ *adj.* (*US* also **flanneled**) wearing flannel trousers.

flannel-mouth *n. US slang* a flatterer; a braggart.

flap /flap/ *v. & n.* ● *v.* (**flapped**, **flapping**) **1 a** *tr.* move (wings, the arms, etc.) up and down when flying, or as if flying. **b** *intr.* (of wings, the arms, etc.) move up and down; beat. **2** *intr. colloq.* be agitated or panicky. **3** *intr.* (esp. of curtains, loose cloth, etc.) swing or sway about; flutter. **4** *tr.* (usu. foll. by *away*, *off*) strike (flies etc.) with something broad; drive. **5** *intr. colloq.* (of ears) listen intently. ● *n.* **1** a piece of cloth, wood, paper, etc. hinged or attached by one side only and often used to cover a gap, e.g. a pocket-cover, the folded part of an envelope, a table leaf. **2** one up-and-down motion of a wing, an arm, etc. **3** *colloq.* a state of agitation; panic (*don't get into a flap*). **4** a hinged or sliding section of a wing used to control lift. **5** a light blow with something broad. **6** an open mushroom-top. □ **flappy** *adj.* [Middle English, probably imitative]

flapdoodle /ˈflapduːd(ə)l/ *n. colloq.* nonsense. [19th c.: origin unknown]

flapjack /ˈflapdʒak/ *n.* **1** a cake made from oats and golden syrup etc. **2** *N. Amer.* a pancake. [FLAP + JACK[1]]

flapper /ˈflapə/ *n.* **1** a person or thing that flaps. **2** an instrument that is flapped to kill flies, scare birds, etc. **3** a person who panics easily or is easily agitated. **4** *slang* (in the 1920s) a young unconventional or lively woman. **5** *Brit.* a young mallard or partridge.

flare /flɛː/ *v. & n.* ● *v.* **1** *intr. & tr.* widen or cause to widen gradually outwards or towards the top or bottom (*flared trousers*). **2** *intr. & tr.* burn or cause to burn suddenly with a bright unsteady flame. **3** *intr.* burst into anger; burst forth. ● *n.* **1 a** a dazzling irregular flame or light, esp. in the open air. **b** a sudden outburst of flame. **2 a** a signal light used at sea. **b** a bright light used as a signal. **c** a flame dropped from an aircraft to illuminate a target etc. **3** *Astron.* a sudden burst of radiation from a star. **4 a** a gradual widening, esp. of a skirt or trousers. **b** (in *pl.*) wide-bottomed trousers. **5** an upward and outward curve of a ship's bows, designed to throw the water outwards when in motion. **6** *Photog.* extraneous illumination on film caused by internal reflection in the lens etc. □ **flare up 1** burst into a sudden blaze. **2** become suddenly angry or active. [16th c.: origin unknown]

flare-path *n.* an area illuminated to enable an aircraft to land or take off.

flare-up *n.* an outburst of flame, anger, activity, etc.

flash /flaʃ/ *v., n., & adj.* ● *v.* **1** *intr. & tr.* emit or reflect or cause to emit or reflect light briefly, suddenly, or intermittently; gleam or cause to gleam. **2** *intr.* break suddenly into flame; give out flame or sparks. **3** *tr.* send or reflect like a sudden flame or blaze (*his eyes flashed fire*). **4** *intr.* **a** burst suddenly into view or perception (*the explanation flashed upon me*). **b** move swiftly (*the train flashed through the station*). **5** *tr.* **a** send (news etc.) by radio, telegraph, etc. (*flashed a message to her*). **b** signal to (a person) by shining lights or headlights briefly. **6** *tr. colloq.* show ostentatiously (*flashed her engagement ring*). **7** *intr.* (of water) rush along; rise and flow. **8** *intr. slang* indecently expose oneself. ● *n.* **1** a sudden bright light or flame, e.g. of lightning. **2** a very brief time; an instant (*all over in a flash*). **3 a** a brief, sudden burst of feeling (*a flash of hope*). **b** a sudden display (of wit, understanding, etc.). **4** = NEWSFLASH. **5** *Photog.* = FLASHGUN. **6 a** a rush of water, esp. down a weir to take a boat over shallows. **b** a contrivance for producing this. **7** *Brit. Mil.* a coloured patch of cloth on a uniform etc. as a distinguishing emblem. **8** vulgar display, ostentation. **9** a bright patch of colour. **10** *Cinematog.* the momentary exposure of a scene. **11** excess plastic or metal oozing from a mould during moulding. ● *adj. Brit. colloq.* **1** gaudy; showy; vulgar (*a flash car*). **2** counterfeit (*flash notes*). **3** connected with thieves, the underworld, etc. □ **flash in the pan** a promising start followed by failure (from the priming of old guns). **flash out** (or **up**) show sudden passion. **flash over** *Electr.* make an electric circuit by sparking across a gap. [Middle English, originally with reference to the rushing of water: cf. SPLASH]

flashback /ˈflaʃbak/ *n.* a scene in a film, novel, etc. set in a time earlier than the main action.

flash-board *n.* a board used for sending more water from a mill-dam into a mill-race.

flashbulb /ˈflaʃbʌlb/ *n. Photog.* a bulb for a flashgun.

flash burn *n.* a burn caused by sudden intense heat, esp. from a nuclear explosion.

flashcard /ˈflaʃkɑːd/ *n.* a card containing a small amount of information, held up for pupils to see, as an aid to learning.

flash-cube *n.* a set of four flashbulbs arranged as a cube and operated in turn.

flasher /ˈflaʃə/ *n.* **1** *slang* a man who indecently exposes himself. **2 a** an automatic device for switching lights rapidly on and off. **b** a sign or signal using this. **3** a person or thing that flashes.

flash flood *n.* a sudden local flood due to heavy rain etc.

flashgun /ˈflaʃgʌn/ *n.* a device producing a flash of intense light, used for photographing by night, indoors, etc.

flashing /ˈflaʃɪŋ/ *n.* a usu. metallic strip used to prevent water penetration at the junction of a roof with a wall etc. [dialect *flash* 'seal with lead sheets' or obsolete *flash* 'flashing']

flashing point *n.* = FLASHPOINT.

flash lamp *n.* a portable flashing electric lamp, esp. an electric torch.

flashlight /ˈflaʃlʌɪt/ *n.* **1** an electric torch. **2** a flashing light used for signals and in lighthouses.

flash memory *n. Computing* a type of memory device that retains data in the absence of a power supply.

flash-over *n. Electr.* an instance of flashing over (see FLASH).

flashpoint /ˈflaʃpɔɪnt/ *n.* **1** the temperature at which vapour from oil etc. will ignite in air. **2** the point at which anger, indignation, etc. becomes uncontrollable.

flash unit *n.* = FLASHGUN.

flashy /ˈflaʃi/ *adj.* (**flashier**, **flashiest**) showy; gaudy; cheaply attractive. □ **flashily** *adv.* **flashiness** *n.*

flask /flɑːsk/ *n.* **1** a narrow-necked bulbous bottle for wine etc. or as used in chemistry. **2** = HIP FLASK. **3** *Brit.* = VACUUM FLASK. **4** *hist.* = POWDER FLASK. [French *flasque* and (probably) Italian *fiasco* from medieval Latin *flasca, flasco*: cf. FLAGON]

flat[1] /flat/ *adj., adv., n., & v.* ● *adj.* (**flatter**, **flattest**) **1 a** horizontally level (*a flat roof*). **b** even; smooth; unbroken; without projection or indentation (*a flat stomach*). **c** with a level surface and little depth; shallow (*a flat cap; a flat heel*). **2** unqualified; plain; downright (*a flat refusal; a flat denial*). **3 a** dull; lifeless; monotonous (*spoke in a flat tone*). **b** without energy; dejected. **4** (of a fizzy drink) having lost its effervescence. **5** *Brit.* (of an accumulator, a battery, etc.) having exhausted its charge. **6** *Mus.* **a** below true or normal pitch (*the violins are flat*). **b** (of a key) having a flat or flats in the signature. **c** (as **B flat**, **E flat**, etc.), a semitone lower than B, E, etc. **7** *Photog.* lacking contrast. **8 a** (of paint etc.) not glossy; matt. **b** (of a tint) uniform. **9** (of a tyre) punctured; deflated. **10** (of a market, prices, etc.) inactive; sluggish. **11** of or relating to flat racing. ● *adv.* **1** lying at full length; spread out, esp. on another surface (*lay flat on the floor; the ladder was flat against the wall*). **2** *colloq.* **a** completely, absolutely (*turned it down flat; flat broke*). **b** exactly (*in five minutes flat*). **3** *Mus.* below the true or normal pitch (*always sings flat*). ● *n.* **1** the flat part of anything; something flat (*the flat of the hand*). **2** level ground, esp. a plain or swamp. **3** *Mus.* **a** a note lowered a semitone below natural pitch. **b** the sign (♭) indicating this. **4** (as **the flat**) *Brit.* **a** flat racing. **b** the flat racing season. **5** *Theatr.* a flat section of scenery mounted on a frame. **6** *colloq.* a flat tyre, a puncture. **7** *Brit. slang* a foolish person. ● *v.tr.* (**flatted**, **flatting**) **1** make flat, flatten (esp. in technical use). **2** *US Mus.* make (a note) flat. □ **fall flat** fail to live up to expectations; not win applause. **flat out 1** at top speed. **2** using all one's strength, energy, or resources. **that's flat** *colloq.* let there be no doubt about it. □ **flatly** *adv.* **flatness** *n.* **flattish** *adj.* [Middle English via Old Norse *flatr* from Germanic]

flat[2] /flat/ *n. & v.* ● *n.* a set of rooms, usu. on one floor, used as a residence. ● *v.intr.* (**flatted**, **flatting**) (often foll. by *with*) *Austral.* share a flat. □ **flatlet** *n.* [alteration of obsolete *flet* 'floor, dwelling', from Germanic (as FLAT[1])]

flat arch *n. Archit.* an arch with a flat lower or inner curve.

flat boat *n.* (also **flat-bottomed boat**) a boat with a flat bottom for transport in shallow water.

flatcar /ˈflatkɑː/ *n.* a railway wagon without raised sides or ends.

flat-chested *adj.* (of a woman) having small breasts.

flatfish /ˈflatfɪʃ/ *n.* (*pl.* usu. same) any marine fish of various families having an asymmetric appearance with both eyes on one side of a flattened body, including sole, turbot, plaice, flounders, etc.

flatfoot /ˈflatfʊt/ *n.* (*pl.* **-foots** or **-feet**) *slang* a police officer.

flat foot *n.* a foot with an arch that is lower than usual.

flat-footed /flatˈfʊtɪd/ *adj.* **1** having flat feet. **2** *colloq.* downright, positive. **3** *colloq.* unprepared; off guard (*was caught flat-footed*). □ **flat-footedly** *adv.* **flat-footedness** *n.*

flat-four *adj. & n.* ● *adj.* (of an engine) having four cylinders all horizontal, two on each side of the crankshaft. ● *n.* such an engine.

flat-head *n.* **1** any marine fish of the family Platycephalidae, having a flattened body with both eyes on the top side. **2** *slang* a foolish person.

flat iron *n. hist.* an iron heated externally and used for pressing clothes etc.

flatmate /ˈflatmeɪt/ *n. Brit.* a person in relation to one or more others living in the same flat.

flat-pack *n. & v.* ● *n.* a piece of furniture etc. for self-assembly, packed flat in a box for easy transportation (often *attrib.*: *a flat-pack fitted kitchen*). ● *v.tr.* (usu. as **flat-packed** *adj.*) pack flat in a box.

flat race *n.* a horse race over level ground, as opposed to a steeplechase or hurdles. □ **flat racing** *n.*

flat rate *n.* a rate that is the same in all cases, not proportional.

flat spin *n.* **1** *Aeron.* a nearly horizontal spin. **2** *Brit. colloq.* a state of agitation or panic.

flatten /ˈflat(ə)n/ *v.* **1** *tr. & intr.* make or become flat. **2** *tr. colloq.* **a** humiliate. **b** knock down. □ **flatten out** bring an aircraft parallel to the ground. □ **flattener** *n.*

flatter /ˈflatə/ *v.tr.* **1** compliment unduly; overpraise, esp. for gain or advantage. **2** (usu. *refl.*; usu. foll. by *that* + clause) please, congratulate, or delude (oneself etc.) (*I flatter myself that I can sing*). **3 a** (of a colour, a style, etc.) make (a person) appear to the best advantage (*that blouse flatters you*). **b** (esp. of a portrait, a painter, etc.) represent too favourably. **4** gratify the vanity of; make (a person) feel honoured. **5** inspire (a person) with hope, esp. unduly (*was flattered into thinking himself invulnerable*). **6** please or gratify (the ear, the eye, etc.). □ **flatterer** *n.* **flattering** *adj.* **flatteringly** *adv.* [Middle English, perhaps related to Old French *flater* 'to smooth']

flattering unction *n.* a salve that one administers to one's own conscience or self-esteem (Shakespeare esp. *Hamlet* III. iv. 136).

flattery /ˈflat(ə)ri/ *n.* (*pl.* **-ies**) **1** exaggerated or insincere praise. **2** the act or an instance of flattering.

flattie /ˈflati/ *n.* (also **flatty**) (*pl.* **-ies**) *colloq.* **1** a flat-heeled shoe. **2** a flat-bottomed boat. **3** a police officer.

flat-top *n.* **1** *US slang* an aircraft carrier. **2** *slang* a man's short flat haircut.

flatulent /ˈflatjʊl(ə)nt/ *adj.* **1 a** causing formation of gas in the alimentary canal. **b** caused by or suffering from this. **2** (of speech etc.) inflated, pretentious.

□ **flatulence** *n.* **flatulency** *n.* **flatulently** *adv.* [French from modern Latin *flatulentus* (as FLATUS)]

flatus /ˈfleɪtəs/ *n.* wind in or from the stomach or bowels. [Latin, = blowing, from *flare* 'blow']

flatware /ˈflatwɛː/ *n.* **1** esp. *Brit.* plates, saucers, etc. (opp. HOLLOWWARE). **2** *N. Amer.* domestic cutlery.

flatworm /ˈflatwəːm/ *n.* any worm of the phylum Platyhelminthes, having a flattened body and no body cavity or blood vessels, including turbellarians, flukes, etc.

flaunch var. of FLANCH.

flaunt /flɔːnt/ *v.* & *n.* ● *v.tr.* & *intr.* **1** (often *refl.*) display ostentatiously (oneself or one's finery); show off; parade (*liked to flaunt his gold cuff-links*; *flaunted themselves before the crowd*). **2** wave or cause to wave proudly (*flaunted the banner*). ● *n.* an act or instance of flaunting. □ **flaunter** *n.* **flaunty** *adj.* [16th c.: origin unknown]

■ **Usage** *Flaunt* should not be confused with *flout*, which means 'to disobey contemptuously'.

flautist /ˈflɔːtɪst/ *n.* a flute-player. [Italian *flautista* from *flauto* FLUTE]

flavescent /fləˈvɛs(ə)nt/ *adj.* turning yellow; yellowish. [Latin *flavescere* from *flavus* 'yellow']

flavin /ˈfleɪvɪn/ *n.* (also **flavine** /-viːn/) **1** any of a group of cyclic compounds forming the nucleus of various natural yellow pigments. **2** a yellow dye formerly obtained from dyer's oak. [Latin *flavus* 'yellow' + -IN]

flavin adenine dinucleotide *n.* a coenzyme derived from riboflavin, important in various biochemical reactions (abbr.: **FAD**).

flavine /ˈfleɪviːn, -ɪn/ *n.* **1** *Pharm.* an antiseptic derived from acridine. **2** var. of FLAVIN. [as FLAVIN + -INE[4]]

flavone /ˈfleɪvəʊn/ *n.* *Biochem.* any of a class of naturally occurring white or yellow pigments found in plants. [as FLAVINE + -ONE]

flavoprotein /fleɪvə(ʊ)ˈprəʊtiːn/ *n.* *Biochem.* any of a class of conjugated proteins containing flavin that are involved in oxidation reactions in cells. [FLAVINE + PROTEIN]

flavorous /ˈfleɪv(ə)rəs/ *adj.* having a pleasant or pungent flavour.

flavour /ˈfleɪvə/ *n.* & *v.* (*US* **flavor**) ● *n.* **1** a distinctive mingled sensation of smell and taste (*has a cheesy flavour*). **2** an indefinable characteristic quality (*music with a romantic flavour*). **3** (usu. foll. by *of*) a slight admixture of a usu. undesirable quality (*the flavour of failure hangs over the enterprise*). **4** esp. *US* = FLAVOURING. ● *v.tr.* give flavour to; season. □ **flavour of the month** (or **week**) a temporary trend or fashion. □ **flavourful** *adj.* **flavourless** *adj.* **flavoursome** *adj.* [Middle English from Old French *flaor*, perhaps from Latin *flatus* 'blowing' and *foetor* 'stench': assimilated to *savour*]

flavouring /ˈfleɪv(ə)rɪŋ/ *n.* (*US* **flavoring**) a substance used to flavour food or drink.

flaw[1] /flɔː/ *n.* & *v.* ● *n.* **1** an imperfection; a blemish (*has a character without a flaw*). **2** a crack or similar fault (*the cup has a flaw*). **3** *Law* an invalidating defect in a legal matter. ● *v.tr.* & *intr.* crack; damage; spoil. □ **flawless** *adj.* **flawlessly** *adv.* **flawlessness** *n.* [Middle English, perhaps via Old Norse *flaga* 'slab' from Germanic: related to FLAKE[1], FLAG[2]]

flaw[2] /flɔː/ *n.* a squall of wind; a short storm. [probably from Middle Dutch *vlāghe*, Middle Low German *vlāge*, perhaps = stroke]

flax /flaks/ *n.* **1 a** a blue-flowered plant, *Linum usitatissimum*, cultivated for its textile fibre and its seeds (see LINSEED). **b** a plant resembling this. **2 a** dressed or undressed flax fibres. **b** *archaic* linen, cloth of flax. [Old English *flæx*, from West Germanic]

flaxen /ˈflaks(ə)n/ *adj.* **1** of flax. **2** (of hair) coloured like dressed flax; pale yellow.

flax-lily *n.* (*pl.* **-ies**) *NZ* a New Zealand plant, *Phormium tenax* (agave family), yielding valuable fibre.

flaxseed /ˈflakssiːd/ *n.* linseed.

flay /fleɪ/ *v.tr.* **1** strip the skin or hide off, esp. by beating. **2** criticize severely (*the play was flayed by the critics*). **3** peel off (skin, bark, peel, etc.). **4** strip (a person) of wealth by extortion or exaction. □ **flayer** *n.* [Old English *flēan*, from Germanic]

F-layer *n.* the highest and most strongly ionized region of the ionosphere. [*F* (arbitrary) + LAYER]

flea /fliː/ *n.* **1** a small wingless jumping insect of the order Siphonaptera, feeding on human and other blood. **2 a** (in full **flea beetle**) a small jumping beetle infesting hops, cabbages, etc. **b** (in full **water flea**) daphnia. □ **a flea in one's ear** a sharp reproof. [Old English *flēa*, *flēah*, from Germanic]

fleabag /ˈfliːbag/ *n.* *slang* a shabby or unattractive person or thing.

fleabane /ˈfliːbeɪn/ *n.* any of various plants of the genus *Inula* or *Pulicaria* (daisy family), formerly thought to drive away fleas.

flea bite *n.* **1** the bite of a flea. **2** a trivial injury or inconvenience.

flea-bitten *adj.* **1** bitten by or infested with fleas. **2** shabby.

flea-bug *n.* *US* = FLEA 2a.

flea-circus *n.* a show of performing fleas.

flea collar *n.* an insecticidal collar for pets.

flea market *n.* a street market selling second-hand goods etc.

fleapit /ˈfliːpɪt/ *n.* *Brit.* a dingy dirty place, esp. a run-down cinema.

fleawort /ˈfliːwəːt/ *n.* a plant of the genus *Tephroseris* (daisy family), related to ragwort, formerly thought to drive away fleas.

flèche /fleɪʃ, French flɛʃ/ *n.* a slender spire, often perforated with windows, esp. at the intersection of the nave and the transept of a church. [French, originally = arrow]

fleck /flɛk/ *n.* & *v.* ● *n.* **1** a small patch of colour or light (*eyes with green flecks*). **2** a small particle or speck, esp. of dust. **3** a spot on the skin; a freckle. ● *v.tr.* mark with flecks; dapple; variegate. [perhaps from Old Norse *flekkr* (*n.*), *flekka* (*v.*), or Middle Low German, Middle Dutch *vlecke*, Old High German *flec*, *fleccho*]

flection var. of FLEXION.

fled *past* and *past part.* of FLEE.

fledge /flɛdʒ/ *v.* **1** *intr.* (of a bird) grow feathers. **2** *tr.* provide (an arrow) with feathers. **3** *tr.* bring up (a young bird) until it can fly. **4** *tr.* (as **fledged** *adj.*) **a** able to fly. **b** independent; mature. **5** *tr.* deck or provide with feathers or down. [obsolete *fledge* (*adj.*) 'fit to fly', from Old English, from a Germanic root related to FLY[1]]

fledgling /ˈflɛdʒlɪŋ/ *n.* (also **fledgeling**) **1** a young bird. **2** an inexperienced person. [FLEDGE + -LING[1]]

flee /fliː/ *v.* (*past* and *past part.* **fled** /flɛd/) **1** *intr.* (often foll. by *from*, *before*) **a** run away. **b** seek safety by fleeing. **2** *tr.* run away from; leave abruptly; shun (*fled the room*; *fled his attentions*). **3** *intr.* vanish; cease; pass away. [Old English *flēon*, from Germanic]

fleece /fliːs/ *n.* & *v.* ● *n.* **1 a** the woolly covering of a sheep or a similar animal. **b** the amount of wool sheared from a sheep at one time. **2** something resembling a fleece, esp.: **a** a woolly or rough head of hair. **b** a soft warm fabric with a pile, used esp. as a lining. **c** a white cloud, a blanket of snow, etc. **3** *Heraldry* a representation of a fleece suspended from a ring. ● *v.tr.* **1** (often foll. by *of*) strip (a person) of money, valuables, etc.; swindle. **2** remove the fleece from (a sheep etc.); shear. **3** cover as if with a fleece (*a sky fleeced with clouds*). □ **fleeceable** *adj.* **fleeced** *adj.* (also in *comb.*). [Old English *flēos*, *flēs*, from West Germanic]

fleece-picker *n.* *Austral.* & *NZ* = FLEECY *n.*

fleecy /ˈfliːsi/ *adj.* & *n.* ● *adj.* (**fleecier**, **fleeciest**) **1** of or like a fleece. **2** covered with a fleece. ● *n.* (also **fleecie**) (*pl.* **-ies**) *Austral.* & *NZ* a person whose job is to pick up fleeces in a shearing shed. □ **fleecily** *adv.* **fleeciness** *n.*

fleer /fliːə/ *v. & n.* ● *v.intr.* laugh impudently or mockingly; sneer; jeer. ● *n.* a mocking look or speech. [Middle English, probably from Scandinavian: cf. Norwegian & Swedish dialect *flira* 'to grin']

fleet[1] /fliːt/ *n.* **1 a** a number of warships under one commander-in-chief. **b** (prec. by *the*) all the warships and merchant ships of a nation. **2** a number of ships, aircraft, buses, lorries, taxis, etc. operating together or owned by one proprietor. [Old English *flēot* 'ship, shipping' from *flēotan* 'float', FLEET[5]]

fleet[2] /fliːt/ *adj. poet.* or *literary* swift; nimble. □ **fleetly** *adv.* **fleetness** *n.* [probably from Old Norse *fljótr*, from Germanic: cf. FLEET[5]]

fleet[3] /fliːt/ *n. Brit. dial.* **1** a creek; an inlet. **2** (**the Fleet**) **a** an underground stream running into the Thames east of Fleet St. **b** *hist.* a prison that stood near it. [Old English *flēot*, from Germanic: cf. FLEET[5]]

fleet[4] /fliːt/ *adj. & adv. Brit. dial.* ● *adj.* (of water) shallow. ● *adv.* at or to a small depth (*plough fleet*). [origin uncertain: perhaps from Old English, related to FLEET[5]]

fleet[5] /fliːt/ *v.intr. archaic* **1** glide away; vanish; be transitory. **2** (usu. foll. by *away*) (of time) pass rapidly; slip away. **3** move swiftly; fly. [Old English *flēotan* 'float, swim', from Germanic]

Fleet Admiral *n. US* = ADMIRAL OF THE FLEET.

Fleet Air Arm *n. hist.* the aviation service of the Royal Navy.

fleet-footed *adj.* nimble; fast on one's feet. [FLEET[2]]

fleeting /ˈfliːtɪŋ/ *adj.* transitory; brief. □ **fleetingly** *adv.* [FLEET[5] + -ING[2]]

Fleet Street *n.* **1** the London press. **2** British journalism or journalists.

Fleming /ˈflɛmɪŋ/ *n.* **1** a native of medieval Flanders in the Low Countries. **2** a member of a Flemish-speaking people inhabiting N. and W. Belgium (cf. WALLOON). [Old English via Old Norse *Flæmingi* & Middle Dutch *Vlāming* from the root of *Vlaanderen* 'Flanders']

Flemish /ˈflɛmɪʃ/ *adj. & n.* ● *adj.* of or relating to Flanders. ● *n.* **1** the language of the Flemings. **2** (**the Flemish**) (*pl.*) Flemings. [Middle Dutch *Vlāmisch* (as FLEMING)]

Flemish bond *n. Building* a bond in which each course consists of alternate headers and stretchers.

flense /flɛns/ *v.tr.* (also **flench** /flɛn(t)ʃ/, **flinch** /flɪn(t)ʃ/) **1** cut up (a whale or seal). **2** flay (a seal). [Danish *flense*: cf. Norwegian *flinsa*, *flunsa* 'flay']

flesh /flɛʃ/ *n. & v.* ● *n.* **1 a** the soft, esp. muscular, substance between the skin and bones of an animal or a human. **b** plumpness; fat (*has put on flesh*). **c** *archaic* meat, esp. excluding poultry, game, and offal. **2** the body as opposed to the mind or the soul, esp. considered as sinful. **3** the pulpy substance of a fruit or a plant. **4 a** the visible surface of the human body with reference to its colour or appearance. **b** = FLESH COLOUR. **5** animal or human life. ● *v.tr.* **1** embody in flesh. **2** incite (a hound etc.) by the taste of blood. **3** *literary* initiate, esp. by aggressive or violent means, esp.: **a** use (a sword etc.) for the first time on flesh. **b** use (wit, the pen, etc.) for the first time. □ **flesh out** make or become substantial. **in the flesh** in bodily form, in person. **lose** (or **put on**) **flesh** grow thinner or fatter. **make a person's flesh creep** frighten or horrify a person, esp. with tales of the supernatural etc. **sins of the flesh** unchastity. **the way of all flesh** experience common to all humankind. □ **fleshless** *adj.* [Old English *flǣsc*, from Germanic]

flesh and blood *n. & adj.* ● *n.* **1** the body or its substance. **2** humankind. **3** human nature, esp. as being fallible. ● *adj.* actually living, not imaginary or supernatural. □ **one's own flesh and blood** near relatives; descendants.

flesh colour *n.* a light brownish pink. □ **flesh-coloured** *adj.*

flesher /ˈflɛʃə/ *n. Sc.* a butcher.

flesh-fly *n.* (*pl.* **-flies**) any fly of the family Sarcophagidae that deposits eggs or larvae in dead flesh.

fleshings /ˈflɛʃɪŋz/ *n.pl.* an actor's flesh-coloured tights.

fleshly /ˈflɛʃli/ *adj.* (**fleshlier**, **fleshliest**) **1** (of desire etc.) bodily; lascivious; sensual. **2** mortal, not divine. **3** worldly. [Old English *flæsclic* (as FLESH)]

fleshpots /ˈflɛʃpɒts/ *n.pl.* luxurious living (Exod. 16:3).

flesh side *n.* the side of a hide that adjoined the flesh.

flesh tints *n.pl.* flesh colours as rendered by a painter.

flesh wound *n.* a wound not reaching a bone or a vital organ.

fleshy /ˈflɛʃi/ *adj.* (**fleshier**, **fleshiest**) **1** plump, fat. **2** of flesh, without bone. **3** (of plant or fruit tissue) pulpy. **4** like flesh. □ **fleshiness** *n.*

fletcher /ˈflɛtʃə/ *n. archaic* a maker or seller of arrows. [Middle English from Old French *flech(i)er*, from *fleche* 'arrow']

fleur-de-lis /fləːdəˈliː/ *n.* (also **fleur-de-lys**) (*pl.* **fleurs-** *pronunc.* same) **1** the iris flower. **2** *Heraldry* **a** a lily composed of three petals bound together near their bases. **b** the former royal arms of France. [Middle English from Old French *flour de lys* 'flower of the lily']

■ **Usage** The usual French pronunciation of *fleur-de-lis* is /flœrdəlis/ with the final *-s* sounded.

fleuret /flʊəˈrɛt, fləː-/ *n.* an ornament like a small flower. [French *fleurette* from *fleur* 'flower']

fleuron /ˈflʊərɒn, ˈfləː-/ *n.* a flower-shaped ornament on a building, a coin, a book, etc. [Middle English via Old French *floron* from *flour* FLOWER]

fleury /ˈflʊəri/ *adj.* (also **flory** /ˈflɔːri/) *Heraldry* decorated with fleurs-de-lis. [Middle English from Old French *flo(u)ré* (as FLEURON)]

flew *past* of FLY[1].

flews /fluːz/ *n.pl.* the hanging lips of a bloodhound etc. [16th c.: origin unknown]

flex[1] /flɛks/ *v.* **1** *tr. & intr.* bend (a joint, limb, etc.) or be bent. **2** *tr. & intr.* move (a muscle) or (of a muscle) be moved to bend a joint. **3** *tr. Geol.* bend (strata). **4** *tr. Archaeol.* place (a corpse) with the legs drawn up under the chin. [Latin *flectere flex-* 'bend']

flex[2] /flɛks/ *n. Brit.* a flexible insulated cable used for carrying electric current to an appliance. [abbreviation of FLEXIBLE]

flexible /ˈflɛksɪb(ə)l/ *adj.* **1** able to bend without breaking; pliable; pliant. **2** easily led; manageable; docile. **3** adaptable; versatile; variable (*works flexible hours*). □ **flexibility** /-ˈbɪlɪti/ *n.* **flexibly** *adv.* [Middle English from Old French *flexible* or Latin *flexibilis* (as FLEX[1])]

flexile /ˈflɛksʌɪl/ *adj. archaic* **1** supple; mobile. **2** tractable; manageable. **3** versatile. □ **flexility** /-ˈsɪlɪti/ *n.* [Latin *flexilis* (as FLEX[1])]

flexion /ˈflɛkʃ(ə)n/ *n.* (also **flection**) **1 a** the act of bending or the condition of being bent, esp. of a limb or joint. **b** a bent part; a curve. **2** *Gram.* inflection. **3** *Math.* = FLEXURE 2. □ **flexional** *adj.* (in sense 2). **flexionless** *adj.* (in sense 2). [Latin *flexio* (as FLEX[1])]

flexitime /ˈflɛksɪtʌɪm/ *n.* (*N. Amer.* also **flextime** /ˈflɛkstʌɪm/) **1** a system of working a set number of hours with the starting and finishing times chosen within agreed limits by the employee. **2** the hours worked in this way. [FLEXIBLE + TIME]

flexography /flɛkˈsɒgrəfi/ *n. Printing* a rotary letterpress technique using rubber or plastic plates and synthetic inks or dyes for printing on fabrics, plastics, etc., as well as on paper. □ **flexographic** /-səˈgrafɪk/ *adj.* [Latin *flexus* 'a bending' from *flectere* 'bend' + -GRAPHY]

flexor /ˈflɛksə/ *n.* (in full **flexor muscle**) a muscle that bends part of the body (cf. EXTENSOR). [modern Latin (as FLEX[1])]

flexuous /ˈflɛksjʊəs/ *adj.* full of bends; winding. □ **flexuosity** /-ˈɒsɪti/ *n.* **flexuously** *adv.* [Latin *flexuosus* from *flexus* 'bending', formed as FLEX[1]]

flexure /ˈflɛkʃə/ *n.* **1 a** the act of bending or the condition of being bent. **b** a bend, curve, or turn. **2** *Math.* the curving of a line, surface, or solid, esp. from a straight line, plane, etc. **3** *Geol.* the bending of strata under pressure. □ **flexural** *adj.* [Latin *flexura* (as FLEX[1])]

flibbertigibbet /flɪbətɪˈdʒɪbɪt/ *n.* a gossiping, frivolous, or restless person. [imitative of chatter]

flick /flɪk/ *n.* & *v.* ● *n.* **1 a** a light, sharp, quickly retracted blow with a whip etc. **b** the sudden release of a bent finger or thumb, esp. to propel a small object. **2** a sudden movement or jerk. **3** a quick turn of the wrist in playing games, esp. in throwing or striking a ball. **4** a slight, sharp sound. **5** *colloq.* **a** a cinema film. **b** (in *pl.*; prec. by *the*) *Brit.* the cinema. ● *v.* **1** *tr.* (often foll. by *away, off*) strike or move with a flick (*flicked the ash off his cigar; flicked away the dust*). **2** *tr.* give a flick with (a whip, towel, etc.). **3** *intr.* make a flicking movement or sound. □ **flick through 1** turn over (cards, pages, etc.). **2 a** turn over the pages etc. of, by a rapid movement of the fingers. **b** look cursorily through (a book etc.). [Middle English, imitative]

flicker[1] /ˈflɪkə/ *v.* & *n.* ● *v.intr.* **1** (of light) shine unsteadily or fitfully. **2** (of a flame) burn unsteadily, alternately flaring and dying down. **3 a** (of a flag, a reptile's tongue, an eyelid, etc.) move or wave to and fro; quiver; vibrate. **b** (of the wind) blow lightly and unsteadily. **4** (of hope etc.) increase and decrease unsteadily and intermittently. ● *n.* **1** a flickering movement or light. **2** a brief spell of hope, recognition, etc. □ **flicker out** die away after a final flicker. [Old English *flicorian, flycerian*]

flicker[2] /ˈflɪkə/ *n.* any woodpecker of the genus *Colaptes*, native to N. America. [imitative of its call]

flick knife *n. Brit.* a weapon with a blade that springs out from the handle when a button is pressed.

flier var. of FLYER.

flight[1] /flʌɪt/ *n.* & *v.* ● *n.* **1 a** the act or manner of flying through the air (*studied swallows' flight*). **b** the swift movement or passage of a projectile etc. through the air (*the flight of an arrow*). **2 a** a journey made through the air or in space. **b** a timetabled journey made by an airline. **c** an RAF or USAF unit of about six aircraft. **3 a** a flock or large body of birds, insects, etc., esp. when migrating. **b** a migration. **4** (usu. foll. by *of*) a series, esp. of stairs between floors, or of hurdles across a racetrack (*lives up six flights*). **5** an extravagant soaring, a mental or verbal excursion or sally (of wit etc.) (*a flight of fancy; a flight of ambition*). **6** the trajectory and pace of a ball in games. **7** the distance that a bird, aircraft, or missile can fly. **8** (usu. foll. by *of*) a volley (*a flight of arrows*). **9** the tail of a dart. **10** the pursuit of game by a hawk. **11** swift passage (of time). ● *v.tr.* **1** *Brit.* vary the trajectory and pace of (a cricket ball etc.). **2** provide (an arrow) with feathers. **3** shoot (wildfowl etc.) in flight. □ **in the first** (or **top**) **flight** taking a leading place. **take** (or **wing**) **one's flight** fly. [Old English *flyht* from West Germanic: related to FLY[1]]

flight[2] /flʌɪt/ *n.* **1 a** the act or manner of fleeing. **b** a hasty retreat. **2** *Econ.* the selling of currency, investments, etc. in anticipation of a fall in value (*flight from sterling*). □ **put to flight** cause to flee. **take** (or **take to**) **flight** flee. [Old English from Germanic: related to FLEE]

flight attendant *n.* a steward or stewardess on an aeroplane.

flight bag *n.* a small zipped shoulder bag carried by air travellers.

flight control *n.* an internal or external system directing the movement of aircraft.

flight deck *n.* **1** the deck of an aircraft carrier used for take-off and landing. **2** the accommodation for the pilot, navigator, etc. in an aircraft.

flight feather *n.* any of the large primary or secondary feathers in a bird's wing, supporting it in flight.

flightless /ˈflʌɪtlɪs/ *adj.* (of a bird etc.) naturally unable to fly.

flight lieutenant *n.* an RAF officer next in rank below squadron leader.

flight officer *n. hist.* a rank in the WRAF, corresponding to flight lieutenant.

flight path *n.* the planned course of an aircraft or spacecraft.

flight plan *n. Aeron.* the pre-arranged plan for a particular flight.

flight recorder *n.* a device in an aircraft to record technical details during a flight, that may be used in the event of an accident to discover its cause.

flight sergeant *n.* a non-commissioned officer in the RAF ranking above chief technician.

flight-test *v.tr.* test (an aircraft, rocket, etc.) during flight.

flighty /ˈflʌɪti/ *adj.* (**flightier, flightiest**) **1** (usu. of a girl) frivolous, fickle, changeable. **2** crazy. □ **flightily** *adv.* **flightiness** *n.* [FLIGHT[1] + -Y[1]]

flimflam /ˈflɪmflam/ *n.* & *v.* ● *n.* **1** a trifle; nonsense; idle talk. **2** humbug; deception. ● *v.tr.* (**flimflammed, flimflamming**) cheat; deceive. □ **flimflammer** *n.* **flimflammery** *n.* (*pl.* **-ies**). [imitative reduplication]

flimsy /ˈflɪmzi/ *adj.* & *n.* ● *adj.* (**flimsier, flimsiest**) **1** lightly or carelessly assembled; insubstantial, easily damaged (*a flimsy structure*). **2** (of an excuse etc.) unconvincing (*a flimsy pretext*). **3** paltry; trivial; superficial (*a flimsy play*). **4** (of clothing) thin (*a flimsy blouse*). ● *n.* (*pl.* **-ies**) *Brit.* **1** a very thin paper. **b** a document, esp. a copy, made on this. **2** a flimsy thing, esp. women's underwear. □ **flimsily** *adv.* **flimsiness** *n.* [18th c.: probably from FLIMFLAM]

flinch[1] /ˈflɪn(t)ʃ/ *v.* & *n.* ● *v.intr.* **1** draw back in pain or expectation of a blow etc.; wince. **2** (often foll. by *from*) give way; shrink, turn aside (*flinched from his duty*). ● *n.* an act or instance of flinching. □ **flincher** *n.* **flinchingly** *adv.* [Old French *flenchir, flainchir*, from West Germanic]

flinch[2] var. of FLENSE.

flinders /ˈflɪndəz/ *n.pl.* fragments; splinters. [Middle English, probably from Scandinavian]

fling /flɪŋ/ *v.* & *n.* ● *v.* (*past* and *past part.* **flung** /flʌŋ/) **1** *tr.* throw or hurl (an object) forcefully. **2** *refl.* **a** (usu. foll. by *into*) rush headlong (into a person's arms, a train, etc.). **b** (usu. foll. by *into*) embark wholeheartedly (on an enterprise). **c** (usu. foll. by *on*) throw (oneself) on a person's mercy etc. **3** *tr.* utter (words) forcefully. **4** *tr.* (usu. foll. by *out*) suddenly spread (the arms). **5** *tr.* (foll. by *on, off*) put on or take off (clothes) carelessly or rapidly. **6** *intr.* go angrily or violently; rush (*flung out of the room*). **7** *tr.* put or send suddenly or violently (*was flung into jail*). **8** *tr.* (foll. by *away*) discard or put aside thoughtlessly or rashly (*flung away their reputation*). **9** *intr.* (usu. foll. by *out*) (of a horse etc.) kick and plunge. **10** *tr. archaic* send, emit (sound, light, smell). ● *n.* **1** an act or instance of flinging; a throw; a plunge. **2** a spell of indulgence or wild behaviour (*he's had his fling*). **3** an impetuous, whirling Scottish dance, esp. the Highland fling. □ **have a fling at 1** make an attempt at. **2** jeer at. □ **flinger** *n.* [Middle English, perhaps from Old Norse]

flint /flɪnt/ *n.* **1 a** a hard grey stone of nearly pure silica occurring naturally as nodules or bands in chalk. **b** a piece of this esp. as flaked or ground to form a primitive tool or weapon. **2** a piece of hard alloy of rare-earth metals used to give an igniting spark in a cigarette lighter etc. **3** a piece of flint used with steel to produce fire, esp. in a flintlock gun. **4** anything hard and unyielding. □ **flinty** *adj.* (**flintier, flintiest**). **flintily** *adv.* **flintiness** *n.* [Old English]

flint corn *n.* a variety of maize having hard translucent grains.

flint glass *n.* a pure lustrous kind of glass originally made with flint.

flintlock /ˈflɪntlɒk/ *n. hist.* **1** an old type of gun fired by a spark from a flint. **2** the lock producing such a spark.

flip[1] /flɪp/ *v., n., & adj.* ● *v.* (**flipped**, **flipping**) **1** *tr.* **a** flick or toss (a coin, pellet, etc.) with a quick movement so that it spins in the air. **b** remove (a small object) from a surface with a flick of the fingers. **2** *tr.* **a** strike or flick (a person's ear, cheek, etc.) lightly or smartly. **b** move (a fan, whip, etc.) with a sudden jerk. **3** *tr.* turn (a small object) over. **4** *intr.* **a** make a fillip or flicking noise with the fingers. **b** (foll. by *at*) strike smartly at. **5** *intr.* move about with sudden jerks. **6** *intr. slang* become suddenly angry, excited, or enthusiastic; go mad. ● *n.* **1** a smart light blow; a flick. **2** *Brit. colloq.* **a** a short pleasure flight in an aircraft. **b** a quick tour etc. **3** an act of flipping over (*gave the stone a flip*). ● *adj. colloq.* glib; flippant. □ **flip one's lid** *slang* **1** lose self-control. **2** go mad. **flip through** = *flick through*. [probably from FILLIP]

flip[2] /flɪp/ *n.* **1** a drink of heated beer and spirit. **2** = EGG-NOG. [perhaps from FLIP[1] in the sense 'whip up']

flip chart *n.* a large pad erected on a stand and bound so that one page can be turned over at the top to reveal the next.

flip-flop /ˈflɪpflɒp/ *n. & v.* ● *n.* **1** a usu. plastic or rubber sandal with a thong between the big and second toe. **2** *N. Amer.* a backward somersault. **3** an electronic switching circuit changed from one stable state to another, or through an unstable state back to its stable state, by a triggering pulse. **4** esp. *US* an abrupt reversal of policy. ● *v.intr.* (**-flopped**, **-flopping**) move with a sound or motion suggested by 'flip-flop'. [imitative]

flippant /ˈflɪp(ə)nt/ *adj.* lacking in seriousness; treating serious things lightly; disrespectful. □ **flippancy** *n.* **flippantly** *adv.* [FLIP[1] + -ANT]

flipper /ˈflɪpə/ *n.* **1** a broadened limb of a turtle, penguin, etc., used in swimming. **2** a flat rubber etc. attachment worn on the foot for underwater swimming. **3** *slang* a hand.

flipping /ˈflɪpɪŋ/ *adj. & adv. Brit. slang* expressing annoyance, or as an intensifier (*where's the flipping towel?; he flipping beat me*). [FLIP[1] + -ING[2]]

flip side *n. colloq.* **1** the less important side of a gramophone record. **2** the reverse or a concomitant of a thing.

flirt /flɜːt/ *v. & n.* ● *v.* **1** *intr.* (usu. foll. by *with*) behave in a frivolously amorous or sexually enticing manner. **2** *intr.* (usu. foll. by *with*) **a** superficially interest oneself (with an idea etc.). **b** trifle (with danger etc.) (*flirted with disgrace*). **3** *tr.* wave or move (a fan, a bird's tail, etc.) briskly. **4** *intr. & tr.* move or cause to move with a jerk. ● *n.* **1** a person who indulges in flirting. **2** a quick movement; a sudden jerk. □ **flirtation** /-ˈteɪʃ(ə)n/ *n.* **flirtatious** /-ˈteɪʃəs/ *adj.* **flirtatiously** /-ˈteɪʃəsli/ *adv.* **flirtatiousness** /-ˈteɪʃəsnɪs/ *n.* **flirty** *adj.* (**flirtier**, **flirtiest**). [imitative]

flit /flɪt/ *v. & n.* ● *v.intr.* (**flitted**, **flitting**) **1** move lightly, softly, or rapidly (*flitted from one room to another*). **2** fly lightly; make short flights (*flitted from branch to branch*). **3** *Brit. colloq.* leave one's house etc. secretly to escape creditors or obligations. **4** esp. *Sc. & N.Engl.* change one's home; move. ● *n.* **1** an act of flitting. **2** (also **moonlight flit**) a secret change of abode in order to escape creditors etc. □ **flitter** *n.* [Middle English from Old Norse *flytja*: related to FLEET[5]]

flitch /flɪtʃ/ *n.* **1** a side of bacon. **2** a slab of timber from a tree trunk, usu. from the outside. **3** (in full **flitch-plate**) a strengthening plate in a beam etc. [Old English *flicce*, from Germanic]

flitch beam *n.* a compound beam, esp. of an iron plate between two slabs of wood.

flitter /ˈflɪtə/ *v.intr.* flit about; flutter. [FLIT + -ER[4]]

flitter-mouse *n.* = BAT[2].

flivver /ˈflɪvə/ *n. US slang* **1** a cheap car or aircraft. **2** a failure. [20th c.: origin uncertain]

flixweed /ˈflɪkswiːd/ *n.* a cruciferous plant, *Descurainia sophia*, formerly thought to cure dysentery. [earlier *fluxweed*]

float /fləʊt/ *v. & n.* ● *v.* **1** *intr. & tr.* **a** rest or move or cause (a buoyant object) to rest or move on the surface of a liquid without sinking. **b** get afloat or set (a stranded ship) afloat. **2** *intr.* move with a liquid or current of air; drift (*the clouds floated high up*). **3** *intr. colloq.* **a** move in a leisurely or casual way (*floated about humming quietly*). **b** (often foll. by *before*) hover before the eye or mind (*the prospect of lunch floated before them*). **4** *intr.* (often foll. by *in*) move or be suspended freely in a liquid or a gas. **5** *tr.* **a** bring (a company, scheme, etc.) into being; launch. **b** offer (stock, shares, etc.) on the stock market. **6** *Commerce* **a** *intr.* (of currency) be allowed to have a fluctuating exchange rate. **b** *tr.* cause (currency) to float. **c** *intr.* (of an acceptance) be in circulation. **7** *tr.* (of water etc.) support; bear along (a buoyant object). **8** *intr. & tr.* circulate or cause (a rumour or idea) to circulate. **9** *tr.* waft (a buoyant object) through the air. **10** *tr. archaic* cover with liquid; inundate. ● *n.* **1** a thing that floats, esp.: **a** a raft. **b** a cork or quill on a fishing line as an indicator of a fish biting. **c** a cork supporting the edge of a fishing net. **d** a hollow or inflated part or organ supporting an organism in the water; an air bladder. **e** a hollow structure fixed underneath an aircraft enabling it to float on water. **f** a floating device on the surface of water, petrol, etc., controlling the flow. **2** *Brit.* a small vehicle or cart, esp. one powered by electricity (*milk float*). **3** a platform mounted on a lorry and carrying a display in a procession etc. **4** **a** *Brit.* a sum of money used at the beginning of a period of selling in a shop, a fête, etc. to provide change. **b** a small sum of money for minor expenditure; petty cash. **5** (in *sing.* or *pl.*) *Brit. Theatr.* footlights. **6** a tool used for smoothing plaster. **7** a soft drink with a scoop of ice cream floating in it. □ **floatable** *adj.* **floatability** /-ˈbɪlɪti/ *n.* [Old English *flot*, *flotian* 'float', *flota* 'ship', and Old Norse *flota*, *floti* related to FLEET[5]: in Middle English influenced by Old French *floter*]

floatage /ˈfləʊtɪdʒ/ *n.* **1** the act or state of floating. **2** *Brit.* **a** floating objects or masses; flotsam. **b** the right of appropriating flotsam. **3** **a** ships etc. afloat on a river. **b** the part of a ship above the waterline. **4** buoyancy; floating power.

floatation var. of FLOTATION.

float-board *n.* one of the boards of a waterwheel or paddle wheel.

floatel /fləʊˈtɛl/ *n.* a floating hotel. [blend of FLOAT and HOTEL]

floater /ˈfləʊtə/ *n.* **1** a person or thing that floats. **2** a floating voter. **3** *Brit. slang* a mistake; a gaffe. **4** a person who frequently changes occupation. **5** *Stock Exch.* a government stock certificate etc. recognized as a security.

float glass *n.* a kind of glass made by drawing the molten glass continuously on to a surface of molten metal for hardening.

floating /ˈfləʊtɪŋ/ *adj.* not settled in a definite place; fluctuating; variable (*the floating population*). □ **floatingly** *adv.*

floating anchor *n.* a sea anchor.

floating bridge *n.* **1** a bridge on pontoons etc. **2** a ferry working on chains.

floating debt *n.* a debt repayable on demand, or at a stated time.

floating dock *n.* a floating structure usable as a dry dock.

floating kidney *n.* **1** an abnormal condition in which the kidneys are unusually movable. **2** such a kidney.

floating light *n.* **1** a lightship. **2** a lifebuoy with a lantern.

floating point *n. Computing* a decimal point that does not occupy a fixed position in the numbers processed (hyphenated when *attrib.*: *floating-point operations*).

floating rib *n.* any of the lower ribs, which are not attached to the breastbone.

floating voter *n.* a voter without allegiance to any political party.

float process *n.* the process used to make float glass.

float-stone *n.* a light, porous stone that floats.

floaty /ˈfləʊti/ *adj.* esp. *Brit.* (esp. of a woman's garment or a fabric) light and airy. [FLOAT]

floc /flɒk/ *n.* a flocculent mass of fine particles. [abbreviation of FLOCCULUS]

flocculate /ˈflɒkjʊleɪt/ *v.tr. & intr.* form into flocculent masses. ▫ **flocculation** /-ˈleɪʃ(ə)n/ *n.*

floccule /ˈflɒkjuːl/ *n.* a small portion of matter resembling a tuft of wool.

flocculent /ˈflɒkjʊl(ə)nt/ *adj.* **1** like tufts of wool. **2** consisting of or showing tufts, downy. **3** *Chem.* (of precipitates) loosely massed. ▫ **flocculence** *n.* [Latin *floccus* FLOCK²]

flocculus /ˈflɒkjʊləs/ *n.* (*pl.* **flocculi** /-lʌɪ, -liː/) **1** a floccule. **2** *Anat.* a small ovoid lobe in the undersurface of the cerebellum. **3** *Astron.* a small cloudy wisp on the sun's surface. [modern Latin, diminutive of FLOCCUS]

floccus /ˈflɒkəs/ *n.* (*pl.* **flocci** /ˈflɒksʌɪ/) a tuft of woolly hairs or filaments. [Latin, = FLOCK²]

flock¹ /flɒk/ *n. & v.* ● *n.* **1 a** a number of animals of one kind, esp. birds, feeding, resting, or travelling together. **b** a number of domestic animals, esp. sheep, goats, or geese, kept together. **2** a large crowd of people. **3 a** a Christian congregation or body of believers, esp. in relation to one minister. **b** a family of children, a number of pupils, etc. ● *v.intr.* **1** congregate; mass. **2** (usu. foll. by *to, in, out, together*) go together in a crowd; troop (*thousands flocked to Wembley*). [Old English *flocc*]

flock² /flɒk/ *n.* **1** a lock or tuft of wool, cotton, etc. **2 a** (also in *pl.*; often *attrib.*) material for quilting and stuffing made of wool refuse or torn-up cloth (*a flock pillow*). **b** powdered wool or cloth. ▫ **flocky** *adj.* [Middle English via Old French *floc* from Latin *floccus*]

flock paper *n.* (also **flock wallpaper**) wallpaper sized and sprinkled with powdered wool to make a raised pattern.

floe /fləʊ/ *n.* a sheet of floating ice. [probably from Norwegian *flo*, from Old Norse *fló* 'layer']

flog /flɒg/ *v.* (**flogged, flogging**) **1** *tr.* **a** beat with a whip, stick, etc. (as a punishment or to urge on). **b** make work through violent effort (*flogged the engine*). **2** *tr. slang* **a** (often foll. by *off*) *Brit.* sell. **b** offer for sale. **3** *tr.* (usu. foll. by *into, out of*) drive (a quality, knowledge, etc.) into or out of a person, esp. by physical punishment. **4** *intr. & refl. Brit. slang* proceed by violent or painful effort. ▫ **flog a dead horse** waste energy on something unalterable. **flog to death** *colloq.* talk about or promote at tedious length. ▫ **flogger** *n.* [17th-c.: probably imitative or from Latin *flagellare* 'to whip']

flong /flɒŋ/ *n. Printing* prepared paper for making stereotype moulds. [French *flan* FLAN]

flood /flʌd/ *n. & v.* ● *n.* **1 a** an overflowing or influx of water beyond its normal confines, esp. over land; an inundation. **b** the water that overflows. **2 a** an outpouring of water; a torrent (*a flood of rain*). **b** something resembling a torrent (*a flood of tears*; *a flood of relief*). **3** the inflow of the tide (also in *comb.*: *flood tide*). **4** *colloq.* a floodlight. **5** (**the Flood**) the flood described in Genesis. **6** *poet.* a river; a stream; a sea. ● *v.* **1** *tr.* **a** cover with or overflow in a flood (*rain flooded the cellar*). **b** overflow as if with a flood (*the market was flooded with foreign goods*). **2** *tr.* irrigate (*flooded the paddy fields*). **3** *tr.* deluge (a burning house, a mine, etc.) with water. **4** *intr.* (often foll. by *in, through*) arrive in great quantities (*complaints flooded in*; *fear flooded through them*). **5** *intr.* become inundated (*the bathroom flooded*). **6** *tr.* overfill (a carburettor) with petrol. **7** *intr.* experience a uterine haemorrhage. **8** *tr.* (of rain etc.) fill (a river) to overflowing. ▫ **flood out** drive out (of one's home etc.) with a flood. [Old English *flōd*, from Germanic]

flood and field *n.* sea and land.

floodgate /ˈflʌdgeɪt/ *n.* **1** a gate opened or closed to admit or exclude water, esp. the lower gate of a lock. **2** (usu. in *pl.*) a last restraint holding back tears, rain, anger, etc.

floodlight /ˈflʌdlʌɪt/ *n. & v.* ● *n.* **1** a large powerful light (usu. one of several) to illuminate a building, sports ground, stage, etc. **2** the illumination so provided. ● *v.tr.* (*past* and *past part.* **floodlit**) illuminate with floodlights.

flood tide *n.* the periodical exceptional rise of the tide because of lunar or solar attraction.

flood water *n.* the water left by flooding.

floor /flɔː/ *n. & v.* ● *n.* **1 a** the lower surface of a room. **b** the boards etc. of which it is made. **2 a** the bottom of the sea, a cave, a cavity, etc. **b** any level area. **3** all the rooms etc. on the same level of a building; a storey (*lives on the ground floor*; *walked up to the sixth floor*). **4 a** (in a legislative assembly) the part of the house in which members sit and from which they speak. **b** the right to speak next in debate (*gave him the floor*). **5** *Stock Exch.* the large central hall where trading takes place. **6** the minimum of prices, wages, etc. **7** *colloq.* the ground. ● *v.tr.* **1** furnish with a floor; pave. **2** bring to the ground; knock (a person) down. **3** *colloq.* confound, baffle (*was floored by the puzzle*). **4** *colloq.* get the better of; overcome. **5** serve as the floor of (*leopard skins floored the hall*). ▫ **from the floor** (of a speech etc.) given by a member of the audience, not by those on the platform etc. **take the floor 1** begin to dance on a dance floor etc. **2** speak in a debate. ▫ **floorless** *adj.* [Old English *flōr*, from Germanic]

floorboard /ˈflɔːbɔːd/ *n.* a long wooden board used for flooring.

floorcloth /ˈflɔːklɒθ/ *n. Brit.* a cloth for washing the floor.

floor exercises *n.pl.* (in gymnastics) a routine of exercises without equipment.

flooring /ˈflɔːrɪŋ/ *n.* the boards etc. of which a floor is made.

floor lamp *n. N. Amer.* a standard lamp.

floor leader *n. US* the leader of a party in a legislative assembly.

floor-length *adj.* (esp. of clothing) reaching to the floor.

floor manager *n.* **1** the stage manager of a television production. **2** a shopwalker.

floor plan *n.* a diagram of the rooms etc. on one storey of a building.

floor polish *n.* a manufactured substance used for polishing floors.

floor show *n.* an entertainment presented on the floor (as opposed to the stage) of a nightclub etc.

floorwalker /ˈflɔːwɔːkə/ *n. US* a shopwalker.

floozie /ˈfluːzi/ *n.* (also **floozy**) (*pl.* **-ies**) *colloq.* a girl or a woman, esp. a disreputable one. [20th c.: perhaps related to FLOSSY and dialect *floosy* 'fluffy']

flop /flɒp/ *v., n., & adv.* ● *v.intr.* (**flopped, flopping**) **1** sway about heavily or loosely (*hair flopped over his face*). **2** move in an ungainly way (*flopped along the beach in flippers*). **3** (often foll. by *down, on, into*) sit, kneel, lie, or fall awkwardly or suddenly (*flopped down on to the bench*). **4** *slang* (esp. of a play, film, book, etc.) fail; collapse (*flopped on Broadway*). **5** *slang* sleep. **6** make a dull sound as of a soft body landing, or of a flat thing slapping water. ● *n.* **1 a** a flopping movement. **b** the sound made by it. **2** *slang* a failure. **3** esp. *US slang* a place to sleep, esp. cheaply. ● *adv.* with a flop. [variant of FLAP]

-flop /flɒp/ *comb. form Computing* floating-point operations per second (*megaflop*). [acronym, originally as *-flops*, but *s* for 'second' was taken as indicating a plural]

flophouse /ˈflɒphaʊs/ *n. slang* esp. *US* a doss-house.

floppy /ˈflɒpi/ *adj.* & *n.* ● *adj.* (**floppier**, **floppiest**) tending to flop; not firm or rigid. ● *n.* (*pl.* **-ies**) (in full **floppy disk**) *Computing* a flexible removable magnetic disc for the storage of data. ▫ **floppily** *adv.* **floppiness** *n.*

floptical /ˈflɒptɪk(ə)l/ *adj. Computing propr.* of, involving, or designed for a type of floppy disk drive using a laser to position the read-write head. [blend of FLOPPY and OPTICAL]

flor. *abbr.* floruit.

flora /ˈflɔːrə/ *n.* (*pl.* **floras** or **florae** /-riː/) **1** the plants of a particular region, geological period, or environment. **2** a treatise on or list of these. [modern Latin from the name of the goddess of flowers, from Latin *flos floris* 'flower']

floral /ˈflɔːr(ə)l/ *adj.* **1** of flowers. **2** decorated with or depicting flowers. **3** of flora or floras. ▫ **florally** *adv.* [Latin *floralis* or *flos floris* 'flower']

floreat /ˈflɒrɪat/ *v.intr.* may (he, she, or it) flourish. [Latin, 3rd sing. present subjunctive of *florēre* 'flourish']

Florence fennel see FENNEL 3.

Florentine /ˈflɒr(ə)ntʌɪn/ *adj.* & *n.* ● *adj.* **1** of or relating to Florence in Italy. **2** (**florentine** /-tiːn/) (of a dish) served on a bed of spinach. ● *n.* **1** a native or citizen of Florence. **2** a kind of biscuit consisting mainly of nuts and preserved fruit, coated on one side with chocolate. [French *Florentin -ine* or Latin *Florentinus* from *Florentia* 'Florence']

florescence /flɔːˈrɛs(ə)ns/ *n.* the process, state, or time of flowering. [modern Latin *florescentia* from Latin *florescere*, from *florēre* 'bloom']

floret /ˈflɒrɪt, ˈflɔː-/ *n.* **1** *Bot.* each of the small flowers making up a composite flower head. **2** each of the flowering stems making up a head of cauliflower, broccoli, etc. **3** a small flower. [Latin *flos floris* 'flower']

floriate /ˈflɔːrɪeɪt/ *v.tr.* decorate with flower-designs etc.

floribunda /flɒrɪˈbʌndə, flɔː-/ *n.* a plant, esp. a rose, bearing dense clusters of flowers. [modern Latin from *floribundus* 'freely flowering', from Latin *flos floris* 'flower', influenced by Latin *abundus* 'copious']

floriculture /ˈflɒrɪkʌltʃə, ˈflɔː-/ *n.* the cultivation of flowers. ▫ **floricultural** /-ˈkʌltʃ(ə)r(ə)l/ *adj.* **floriculturist** /-ˈkʌltʃ(ə)rɪst/ *n.* [Latin *flos floris* 'flower' + CULTURE, on the pattern of *horticulture*]

florid /ˈflɒrɪd/ *adj.* **1** ruddy; flushed; high-coloured (*a florid complexion*). **2** (of a book, a picture, music, architecture, etc.) elaborately ornate; ostentatious; showy. **3** adorned with or as with flowers; flowery. ▫ **floridity** /-ˈrɪdɪti/ *n.* **floridly** *adv.* **floridness** *n.* [French *floride* or Latin *floridus* from *flos floris* 'flower']

floriferous /flɒˈrɪf(ə)rəs, flɔː-/ *adj.* (of a seed or plant) producing many flowers. [Latin *florifer* from *flos floris* 'flower']

florilegium /flɒrɪˈliːdʒɪəm, flɔː-/ *n.* (*pl.* **florilegia** /-ˈliːdʒɪə/ or **florilegiums**) an anthology. [modern Latin, from Latin *flos floris* 'flower' + *legere* 'gather', translation of Greek *anthologion* ANTHOLOGY]

florin /ˈflɒrɪn/ *n. hist.* **1 a** a former British coin and monetary unit worth two shillings. **b** an English gold coin of the 14th c., worth 6s. 8d. **2** a foreign coin of gold or silver, esp. a Dutch guilder. [Middle English via Old French and Italian *fiorino*, diminutive of *fiore* 'flower', from Latin *flos floris*, the original coin bearing a fleur-de-lis]

florist /ˈflɒrɪst/ *n.* a person who deals in or grows flowers. ▫ **floristry** *n.* [Latin *flos floris* 'flower' + -IST]

floristic /fləˈrɪstɪk/ *adj.* relating to the study of the distribution of plants. ▫ **floristically** *adv.* **floristics** *n.*

floruit /ˈflɒrʊɪt, ˈflɔːr-/ *v.* & *n.* ● *v.intr.* (he or she) was alive and working; flourished (used of a person, esp. a painter, a writer, etc., whose exact dates are unknown). ● *n.* the period or date at which a person lived or worked. [Latin, = he or she flourished]

flory var. of FLEURY.

floscular /ˈflɒskjʊlə/ *adj.* (also **flosculous** /-kjʊləs/) *Bot.* having florets or composite flowers. [Latin *flosculus*, diminutive of *flos* 'flower']

floss /flɒs/ *n.* & *v.* ● *n.* **1** the rough silk enveloping a silkworm's cocoon. **2** untwisted silk thread used in embroidery. **3** = DENTAL FLOSS. ● *v.tr.* (also *absol.*) clean (the teeth) with dental floss. [French (*soie*) *floche* 'floss (silk)' from Old French *flosche* 'down, nap of velvet']

floss silk *n.* a rough silk used in cheap goods.

flossy /ˈflɒsi/ *adj.* (**flossier**, **flossiest**) **1** of or like floss. **2** *colloq.* fancy, showy.

flotation /fləʊˈteɪʃ(ə)n/ *n.* (also **floatation**) **1** the process of launching or financing a commercial enterprise. **2** the separation of the components of crushed ore etc. by their different capacities to float. **3** the capacity to float. [alteration of *floatation* from FLOAT, on the pattern of *rotation* etc.]

flotilla /fləˈtɪlə/ *n.* **1** a small fleet. **2** a fleet of boats or small ships. [Spanish, diminutive of *flota* 'fleet', related to Old French *flote* 'multitude', *floter* FLOAT]

flotsam /ˈflɒts(ə)m/ *n.* wreckage found floating (cf. JETSAM). [Anglo-French *floteson* from *floter* FLOAT]

flotsam and jetsam *n.* **1** odds and ends; rubbish. **2** vagrants etc.

flounce[1] /flaʊns/ *v.* & *n.* ● *v.intr.* (often foll. by *away*, *about*, *off*, *out*) go or move with an agitated, violent, or impatient motion (*flounced out in a huff*). ● *n.* a flouncing movement. [16th c.: origin unknown: perhaps imitative, as *bounce*, *pounce*]

flounce[2] /flaʊns/ *n.* & *v.* ● *n.* a wide ornamental strip of material gathered and sewn to a skirt, dress, etc.; a frill. ● *v.tr.* trim with a flounce or flounces. [alteration of earlier *frounce* 'fold, pleat', from Old French *fronce* from *froncir* 'wrinkle']

flounder[1] /ˈflaʊndə/ *v.* & *n.* ● *v.intr.* **1** struggle in mud, or as if in mud, or when wading. **2** perform a task badly or without knowledge; be out of one's depth. ● *n.* an act of floundering. ▫ **flounderer** *n.* [imitative: perhaps associated with *founder*, *blunder*]

flounder[2] /ˈflaʊndə/ *n.* **1** a small edible flatfish, *Pleuronectes flesus*, of European coastal waters. **2** any small flatfish of the family Pleuronectidae or Bothidae. [Middle English from Anglo-French *floundre*, Old French *flondre*, probably of Scandinavian origin]

flour /ˈflaʊə/ *n.* & *v.* ● *n.* **1** a meal or powder obtained by grinding and usu. sifting cereals, esp. wheat. **2** any fine powder. ● *v.tr.* **1** sprinkle or coat with flour. **2** *US* grind into flour. ▫ **floury** *adj.* (**flourier**, **flouriest**). **flouriness** *n.* [Middle English, differentiated spelling of FLOWER in the sense 'finest part']

flourish /ˈflʌrɪʃ/ *v.* & *n.* ● *v.* **1** *intr.* **a** grow vigorously; thrive. **b** prosper; be successful. **c** be in one's prime. **d** be in good health. **2** *intr.* (usu. foll. by *in*, *at*, *about*) spend one's life; be active (at a specified time) (*flourished in the Middle Ages*) (cf. FLORUIT). **3** *tr.* show ostentatiously (*flourished his chequebook*). **4** *tr.* wave (a weapon, one's limbs, etc.) vigorously. ● *n.* **1** an ostentatious gesture with a weapon, a hand, etc. (*removed his hat with a flourish*). **2** an ornamental curving decoration of handwriting. **3** a florid verbal expression; a rhetorical embellishment. **4** *Mus.* **a** a fanfare played by brass instruments. **b** an ornate musical passage. **c** an extemporized addition played esp. at the beginning or end of a composition. **5** *archaic* an instance of prosperity; a flourishing. ▫ **flourisher** *n.* [Middle English from Old French *florir*, ultimately via Latin *florēre* from *flos floris* 'flower']

flout /flaʊt/ *v.* & *n.* ● *v.* **1** *tr.* express contempt for (the law, rules, etc.) by word or action; mock; insult (*flouted convention by shaving her head*). **2** *intr.* (often foll. by *at*) mock or scoff. ● *n.* a flouting speech or act. [perhaps from Dutch *fluiten* 'whistle, hiss']

■ **Usage** *Flout* should not be confused with *flaunt*, which means 'to display proudly, show off'.

flow /fləʊ/ *v.* & *n.* ● *v.intr.* **1** glide along as a stream (*the Thames flows under London Bridge*). **2 a** (of a liquid, esp. water) gush out; spring. **b** (of blood, liquid, etc.) be spilt. **3** (of blood, money, electric current, etc.) circulate. **4** (of people or things) come or go in large numbers or smoothly (*traffic flowed down the hill*). **5** (of talk, literary style, etc.) proceed easily and smoothly. **6** (of a garment, hair, etc.) hang easily or gracefully; undulate. **7** (often foll. by *from*) result from; be caused by (*his failure flows from his diffidence*). **8** (esp. of the tide) be in flood; run full. **9** (of wine) be poured out copiously. **10** (of a rock or metal) undergo a permanent change of shape under stress. **11** (foll. by *with*) *archaic* be plentifully supplied with (*land flowing with milk and honey*). ● *n.* **1 a** a flowing movement in a stream. **b** the manner in which a thing flows (*a sluggish flow*). **c** a flowing liquid (*couldn't stop the flow*). **d** a copious outpouring; a stream (*a continuous flow of complaints*). **2** the rise of a tide or a river (*ebb and flow*). **3** the gradual deformation of a rock or metal under stress. **4** *Sc.* a bog or morass. □ **go with the flow** be relaxed and not resist the tide of events. [Old English *flōwan* from Germanic, related to FLOOD]

flow chart *n.* **1** a diagram of the movement or action of things or persons engaged in a complex activity. **2** a graphical representation of a computer program in relation to its sequence of functions (as distinct from the data it processes).

flow diagram *n.* = FLOW CHART.

flower /ˈflaʊə/ *n.* & *v.* ● *n.* **1** *Bot.* **a** the reproductive organ in a plant containing one or more pistils or stamens or both, and usu. a corolla and calyx, and from which the fruit or seed develops. **b** such an organ when brightly coloured and conspicuous; a blossom, a bloom. **c** a blossom on a cut stem, used in bunches for decoration. **2** a plant cultivated or noted for its flowers. **3** (in *pl.*) ornamental phrases (*flowers of speech*). ● *v.* **1** *intr.* (of a plant) produce flowers; bloom or blossom. **2** *intr.* reach a peak. **3** *tr.* cause or allow (a plant) to flower. **4** *tr.* decorate with worked flowers or a floral design. □ **the flower of** the best or best part of. **in flower** with the flowers out. □ **flowered** *adj.* (also in *comb.*). **flowerless** *adj.* **flower-like** *adj.* [Middle English via Anglo-French *flur*, Old French *flour*, *flor*, from Latin *flos floris*]

flower bed *n.* a garden bed in which flowers are grown.

flowerer /ˈflaʊərə/ *n.* a plant that flowers at a specified time (*a late flowerer*).

floweret /ˈflaʊərɪt/ *n.* a small flower.

flower girl *n. Brit.* a woman or girl who sells flowers, esp. in the street.

flower head *n.* = HEAD *n.* 4d.

flowering /ˈflaʊərɪŋ/ *adj.* **1** (of a plant) in bloom. **2** capable of producing flowers, esp. in contrast to a similar plant with the flowers inconspicuous or absent.

flowering plant *n. Bot.* an angiosperm.

flower people *n.pl. hist.* hippies carrying or wearing flowers as symbols of peace and love.

flowerpot /ˈflaʊəpɒt/ *n.* a pot in which a plant may be grown.

flower power *n. hist.* the ideas of the flower people regarded as an instrument in changing the world.

flowers of sulphur *n.pl. Chem.* a fine powder produced when sulphur evaporates and condenses.

flowers of zinc *n.pl.* = ZINC OXIDE.

flowery /ˈflaʊəri/ *adj.* **1** decorated with flowers or floral designs. **2** (of literary style, manner of speech, etc.) high-flown; ornate. **3** full of flowers (*a flowery meadow*). □ **floweriness** *n.*

flowing /ˈfləʊɪŋ/ *adj.* **1** (of literary style etc.) fluent; easy. **2** (of a line, a curve, or a contour) smoothly continuous, not abrupt. **3** (of hair, a garment, a sail, etc.) unconfined. □ **flowingly** *adv.*

flowing sheet *n. Naut.* a sheet eased for free movement in the wind.

flowmeter /ˈfləʊmiːtə/ *n.* an instrument for measuring the rate of flow of water, gas, fuel, etc., esp. in a pipe.

flown *past part.* of FLY[1].

flow-on *n. Austral.* a wage or salary adjustment made as a consequence of one already made in a similar or related occupation.

flowsheet /ˈfləʊʃiːt/ *n.* = FLOW CHART.

flowstone /ˈfləʊstəʊn/ *n.* rock deposited in a thin sheet by a flow of water.

FLQ *abbr.* (in Canada) Front de Libération du Québec.

Flt. Lt. *abbr.* (in the UK) Flight Lieutenant.

Flt. Off. *abbr. hist.* (in the UK) Flight Officer.

flu /fluː/ *n. colloq.* influenza. [abbreviation]

flub /flʌb/ *v.* & *n. N. Amer. colloq.* ● *v.tr.* & *intr.* (**flubbed**, **flubbing**) botch; bungle. ● *n.* something badly or clumsily done. [20th c.: origin unknown]

fluctuate /ˈflʌktʃʊeɪt, -tjʊ-/ *v.intr.* vary irregularly; be unstable, vacillate; rise and fall, move to and fro. □ **fluctuation** /-ˈeɪʃ(ə)n/ *n.* [Latin *fluctuare*, via *fluctus* 'flow, wave' from *fluere fluct-* 'flow']

flue /fluː/ *n.* **1** a smoke-duct in a chimney. **2** a channel for conveying heat, esp. a hot-air passage in a wall; a tube for heating water in some kinds of boiler. [Middle English: origin unknown]

flue-cure *v.tr.* cure (tobacco) by artificial heat from flues.

fluence /ˈfluːəns/ *n. Brit. colloq.* influence. □ **put the fluence on** apply hypnotic etc. power to (a person). [shortening of INFLUENCE]

fluency /ˈfluːənsi/ *n.* **1** a smooth, easy flow, esp. in speech or writing. **2** a ready command of words or of a specified foreign language.

fluent /ˈfluːənt/ *adj.* **1 a** (of speech or literary style) flowing naturally and readily. **b** having command of a foreign language (*is fluent in German*). **c** able to speak quickly and easily. **2** flowing easily or gracefully (*the fluent line of her arabesque*). **3** *archaic* liable to change; unsettled. □ **fluently** *adv.* [Latin *fluere* 'flow']

flue pipe *n.* an organ pipe into which the air enters directly, not striking a reed.

fluff /flʌf/ *n.* & *v.* ● *n.* **1** soft, light, feathery material coming off blankets etc. **2** soft fur or feathers. **3** *slang* **a** a mistake in delivering theatrical lines, in playing music, etc. **b** a mistake in playing a game. **4** something insubstantial or trifling, esp. sentimental writing. ● *v.* **1** *tr.* & *intr.* (often foll. by *up*) shake into or become a soft mass. **2** *tr.* & *intr. colloq.* make a mistake in (a theatrical part, a game, playing music, a speech, etc.); blunder (*fluffed his opening line*). **3** *tr.* make into fluff. **4** *tr.* put a soft surface on (the flesh side of leather). □ **bit of fluff** *slang offens.* a woman regarded as an object of sexual desire. [probably dialect alteration of *flue* 'fluff']

fluffy /ˈflʌfi/ *adj.* (**fluffier**, **fluffiest**) **1** of or like fluff. **2** covered in fluff; downy. □ **fluffily** *adv.* **fluffiness** *n.*

flugelhorn /ˈfluːg(ə)lhɔːn/ *n.* a valved brass wind instrument like a cornet but with a broader tone. [German *Flügelhorn*, from *Flügel* 'wing' + *Horn* 'horn']

fluid /ˈfluːɪd/ *n.* & *adj.* ● *n.* **1** a substance, esp. a gas or liquid, lacking definite shape and capable of flowing and yielding to the slightest pressure. **2** a fluid part or secretion. ● *adj.* **1** able to flow and alter shape freely. **2** constantly changing or fluctuating (*the situation is fluid*). **3** (of a clutch, coupling, etc.) in which liquid is used to transmit power. □ **fluidify** /-ˈɪdɪfʌɪ/ *v.tr.* (**-ies**, **-ied**). **fluidity** /-ˈɪdɪti/ *n.* **fluidly** *adv.* **fluidness** *n.* [French *fluide* or Latin *fluidus* from *fluere* 'flow']

fluid drachm see DRACHM.

fluidics /fluːˈɪdɪks/ *n.pl.* (usu. treated as *sing.*) the study and technique of using small interacting flows and fluid jets for functions usu. performed by electronic devices. □ **fluidic** *adj.*

fluidize /ˈfluːɪdʌɪz/ *v.tr.* (also **-ise**) cause (a finely divided solid) to acquire the characteristics of a fluid by the upward passage of a gas etc. □ **fluidization** /-ˈzeɪʃ(ə)n/ *n.*

fluidized bed *n.* a layer of a fluidized solid, used in chemical processes and in the efficient burning of coal for power generation.

fluid mechanics *n.* the study of forces and flow within fluids.

fluid ounce *n.* **1** *Brit.* a unit of capacity equal to one-twentieth of a pint (approx. 0.028 litre). **2** (also **fluidounce**) *US* a unit of capacity equal to one-sixteenth of a US pint (approx. 0.03 litre).

fluidram /ˈfluːɪdram/ *n.* *US* a fluid drachm (see DRACHM).

fluke[1] /fluːk/ *n.* & *v.* ● *n.* **1** a lucky accident (*won by a fluke*). **2** a chance breeze. ● *v.tr.* achieve by a fluke (*fluked that shot*). [19th c.: perhaps from dialect *fluke* 'guess']

fluke[2] /fluːk/ *n.* **1** any parasitic flatworm of the class Trematoda, esp. of the subclass Digenea, including liver flukes and blood flukes. **2** a flatfish, esp. a flounder. [Old English *flōc*]

fluke[3] /fluːk/ *n.* **1** *Naut.* a broad triangular plate on the arm of an anchor. **2** the barbed head of a lance, harpoon, etc. **3** either of the lobes of a whale's tail. [16th c.: perhaps from FLUKE[2]]

fluky /ˈfluːki/ *adj.* (**flukier**, **flukiest**) of the nature of a fluke; obtained more by chance than skill. □ **flukily** *adv.* **flukiness** *n.*

flume /fluːm/ *n.* & *v.* ● *n.* **1** an artificial channel conveying water etc. for industrial use. **2** a ravine with a stream. **3** a water chute or water slide at an amusement park or swimming pool. ● *v.* **1** *intr.* build flumes. **2** *tr.* convey down a flume. [Middle English via Old French *flum*, *flun* from Latin *flumen* 'river', from *fluere* 'flow']

flummery /ˈflʌm(ə)ri/ *n.* (*pl.* **-ies**) **1** empty compliments; trifles; nonsense. **2** a sweet dish made with beaten eggs, sugar, etc. [Welsh *llymru*, of unknown origin]

flummox /ˈflʌməks/ *v.tr. colloq.* bewilder, confound, disconcert. [19th c.: probably dialect, imitative]

flump /flʌmp/ *v.* & *n.* ● *v.* (often foll. by *down*) **1** *intr.* fall or move heavily. **2** *tr.* set or throw down with a heavy thud. ● *n.* the action or sound of flumping. [imitative]

flung *past* and *past part.* of FLING.

flunk /flʌŋk/ *v.* & *n. colloq.* ● *v.* **1** *tr.* **a** fail (an examination etc.). **b** fail (an examination candidate). **2** *intr.* (often foll. by *out*) fail utterly; give up. ● *n.* an instance of flunking. □ **flunk out** be dismissed from school etc. after failing an examination. [cf. FUNK[1] and obsolete *flink* 'be a coward']

flunkey /ˈflʌŋki/ *n.* (also **flunky**) (*pl.* **-eys** or **-ies**) usu. *derog.* **1** a liveried servant; a footman. **2** a toady; a snob. **3** *US* a person who does menial work. □ **flunkeyism** *n.* [18th c. (originally Scots): perhaps from FLANK with the sense 'sidesman, flanker']

fluoresce /flʊəˈrɛs, flɔː-/ *v.intr.* be or become fluorescent.

fluorescein /ˈflʊərəsiːn, -sɪn, ˈflɔː-/ *n. Chem.* an orange dye with a yellowish-green fluorescence, used in solution as an indicator in biochemistry and medicine. [FLUORESCENCE + -IN]

fluorescence /flʊəˈrɛs(ə)ns, flɔː-/ *n.* **1** the visible or invisible radiation produced from certain substances as a result of incident radiation of a shorter wavelength as X-rays, ultraviolet light, etc. **2** the property of absorbing light of short (invisible) wavelength and emitting light of longer (visible) wavelength. [FLUORSPAR (which fluoresces), on the pattern of *opalescence*]

fluorescent /flʊəˈrɛs(ə)nt, flɔː-/ *adj.* (of a substance) having or showing fluorescence.

fluorescent lamp *n.* (also **fluorescent bulb**) a lamp or bulb radiating largely by fluorescence, esp. a tubular lamp in which phosphor on the inside surface of the tube is made to fluoresce by ultraviolet radiation from mercury vapour.

fluorescent screen *n.* a screen coated with fluorescent material to show images from X-rays etc.

fluoridate /ˈflʊərɪdeɪt, ˈflɔː-/ *v.tr.* add traces of fluoride to (drinking water etc.).

fluoridation /flʊərɪˈdeɪʃ(ə)n, flɔː-/ *n.* (also **fluoridization** /-dʌɪˈzeɪʃ(ə)n/) the addition of traces of fluoride to drinking water in order to prevent or reduce tooth decay.

fluoride /ˈflʊərʌɪd, flɔː-/ *n.* any binary compound of fluorine.

fluorinate /ˈflʊərɪneɪt, ˈflɔː-/ *v.tr.* **1** = FLUORIDATE. **2** introduce fluorine into (a compound) (*fluorinated hydrocarbons*). □ **fluorination** /-ˈneɪʃ(ə)n/ *n.*

fluorine /ˈflʊəriːn, ˈflɔː-/ *n.* a poisonous pale yellow gaseous element of the halogen group occurring naturally in fluorite and cryolite, and the most reactive of all elements (symbol **F**). [French (as FLUORSPAR)]

fluorite /ˈflʊərʌɪt, ˈflɔː-/ *n.* a mineral form of calcium fluoride. [Italian (as FLUORSPAR)]

fluoro- /ˈflʊərəʊ, ˈflɔː-/ *comb. form* **1** fluorine (*fluorocarbon*). **2** fluorescence (*fluoroscope*). [FLUORINE, FLUORESCENCE]

fluorocarbon /flʊərə(ʊ)ˈkɑːb(ə)n, flɔː-/ *n.* a compound formed by replacing one or more of the hydrogen atoms in a hydrocarbon with fluorine atoms.

fluoroscope /ˈflʊərəskəʊp, ˈflɔː-/ *n.* an instrument with a fluorescent screen on which X-ray images may be viewed without taking and developing X-ray photographs.

fluorosis /flʊəˈrəʊsɪs, flɔː-/ *n.* poisoning by fluorine or its compounds. [French *fluorose* (as FLUORO- 1)]

fluorspar /ˈflʊəspɑː, ˈflɔː-/ *n.* = FLUORITE. [*fluor* 'a flow, a mineral used as a flux, fluorspar', from Latin *fluor*, from *fluere* 'flow' + SPAR[3]]

flurry /ˈflʌri/ *n.* & *v.* ● *n.* (*pl.* **-ies**) **1** a gust or squall (of snow or *Brit.* rain etc.). **2** a sudden burst of activity. **3** a commotion; excitement; nervous agitation (*a flurry of speculation; the flurry of the city*). ● *v.tr.* (**-ies**, **-ied**) confuse by haste or noise; agitate. [imitative: cf. obsolete *flurr* 'ruffle', *hurry*]

flush[1] /flʌʃ/ *v.* & *n.* ● *v.* **1** *intr.* **a** blush, redden (*he flushed with embarrassment*). **b** glow with a warm colour (*sky flushed pink*). **2** *tr.* (usu. as **flushed** *adj.*) cause to glow or blush (often foll. by *with*: *flushed with pride*). **3** *tr.* **a** cleanse (a drain, lavatory, etc.) by a rushing flow of water. **b** (often foll. by *away*, *down*) dispose of (an object) in this way (*flushed away the cigarette*). **4** *intr.* rush out, spurt. **5** *tr.* flood (*the river flushed the meadow*). **6** *intr.* (of a plant) throw out fresh shoots. ● *n.* **1 a** a blush. **b** a glow of light or colour. **2 a** a rush of water. **b** the cleansing of a drain, lavatory, etc. by flushing. **3 a** a rush of emotion. **b** the elation produced by a victory etc. (*the flush of triumph*). **4** sudden abundance. **5** freshness; vigour (*in the first flush of womanhood*). **6 a** (in full **hot flush**) a sudden feeling of heat during the menopause. **b** a feverish temperature. **c** facial redness, esp. caused by fever, alcohol, etc. **7** a fresh growth of grass etc. □ **flusher** *n.* [Middle English, perhaps = FLUSH[4], influenced by *flash* and *blush*]

flush[2] /flʌʃ/ *adj.* & *v.* ● *adj.* **1** (often foll. by *with*) in the same plane; level; even (*the sink is flush with the cooker; fitted it flush with the wall*). **2** (usu. *predic.*) *colloq.* **a** having plenty of money. **b** (of money) abundant, plentiful. **3** full to overflowing; in flood. ● *v.tr.* **1** make (surfaces) level. **2** fill in (a joint) level with a surface. □ **flushness** *n.* [probably from FLUSH[1]]

flush[3] /flʌʃ/ *n.* a hand of cards all of one suit, esp. in poker. [Old French *flus*, *flux* from Latin *fluxus* FLUX]

flush[4] /flʌʃ/ *v.* **1** *tr.* cause (esp. a game bird) to fly up from cover. **2** *intr.* (of a bird) fly up and away. □ **flush out 1** reveal. **2** drive out. [Middle English, imitative: cf. *fly*, *rush*]

fluster /ˈflʌstə/ *v.* & *n.* ● *v.* **1** *tr.* & *intr.* make or become nervous or confused; flurry (*was flustered by the noise; he flusters easily*). **2** *tr.* confuse with drink; half-intoxicate. **3** *intr.* bustle. ● *n.* a confused or agitated state. [17th c.: origin unknown: perhaps related to Icelandic *flaustr(a)* 'hurry, bustle']

flute /fluːt/ *n. & v.* ● *n.* **1 a** a high-pitched wind instrument of metal or wood in which the air is directed against a fixed edge, and having holes along it stopped by the fingers or keys, esp. (in full **transverse flute**) the modern orchestral instrument, with a mouthpiece on the side near one end. **b** an organ stop having a similar sound. **c** a flute-player. **2 a** *Archit.* an ornamental vertical groove in a column. **b** a trumpet-shaped frill on a dress etc. **c** any similar cylindrical groove. **3** a tall narrow wine glass. ● *v.* **1** *intr.* play the flute. **2** *intr.* speak, sing, or whistle in a fluting way. **3** *tr.* make flutes or grooves in. **4** *tr.* play (a tune etc.) on a flute. □ **flutelike** *adj.* **fluting** *n.* **flutist** *n. US* (cf. FLAUTIST). **fluty** *adj.* (in sense 1a of *n.*). [Middle English from Old French *flëute, flaüte, flahute*, probably from Provençal *flaüt*]

flutter /ˈflʌtə/ *v. & n.* ● *v.* **1 a** *intr.* flap the wings in flying or trying to fly (*butterflies fluttered in the sunshine*). **b** *tr.* flap (the wings). **2** *intr.* fall with a quivering motion (*leaves fluttered to the ground*). **3** *intr. & tr.* move or cause to move irregularly or tremblingly (*the wind fluttered the flag*). **4** *intr.* go about restlessly; flit; hover. **5** *tr.* agitate, confuse. **6** *intr.* (of a pulse or heartbeat) beat feebly or irregularly. **7** *intr.* tremble with excitement or agitation. ● *n.* **1 a** the act of fluttering. **b** an instance of this. **2** a state of tremulous excitement; a sensation (*was in a flutter*; *caused a flutter with his behaviour*). **3** *Brit. colloq.* a small bet, esp. on a horse. **4** an abnormally rapid but regular heartbeat. **5** *Aeron.* an undesired oscillation in a part of an aircraft etc. under stress. **6** *Mus.* a rapid movement of the tongue (as when rolling one's *r*s) in playing a wind instrument. **7** *Electronics* a rapid variation of pitch, esp. of recorded sound (cf. WOW[2]). **8** a vibration. □ **flutter the dovecots** cause alarm among normally imperturbable people. □ **flutterer** *n.* **fluttery** *adj.* [Old English *floterian, flotorian*, frequentative form related to FLEET[5]]

fluvial /ˈfluːvɪəl/ *adj.* of or found in a river or rivers. [Middle English from Latin *fluvialis*, via *fluvius* 'river' from *fluere* 'flow']

fluviatile /ˈfluːvɪətʌɪl/ *adj.* of, found in, or produced by a river or rivers. [French from Latin *fluviatilis*, via *fluviatus* 'moistened' from *fluvius* 'river']

fluvio- /ˈfluːvɪəʊ/ *comb. form* river (*fluviometer*). [Latin *fluvius* 'river' from *fluere* 'flow']

fluvioglacial /fluːvɪəʊˈgleɪʃ(ə)l, -sɪəl/ *adj. Geol.* of or caused by streams from glacial ice, or the combined action of rivers and glaciers.

fluviometer /fluːvɪˈɒmɪtə/ *n.* an instrument for measuring the rise and fall of rivers.

flux /flʌks/ *n. & v.* ● *n.* **1** a process of flowing or flowing out. **2** an issue or discharge. **3** continuous change (*in a state of flux*). **4** *Metallurgy* a substance mixed with a metal etc. to promote fusion. **5** *Physics* **a** the rate of flow of any fluid across a given area. **b** the amount of fluid crossing an area in a given time. **6** *Physics* the amount of radiation or particles incident on an area in a given time. **7** *Electr.* the total electric or magnetic field passing through a surface. **8** *Med.* an abnormal discharge of blood or excrement from the body. ● *v.* **1** *tr. & intr.* make or become fluid. **2** *tr.* **a** fuse. **b** treat with a fusing flux. [Middle English from Old French *flux* or Latin *fluxus* from *fluere flux-* 'flow']

fluxion /ˈflʌkʃ(ə)n/ *n. Math.* the rate at which a variable quantity changes; a derivative. [French *fluxion* or Latin *fluxio* (as FLUX)]

fly[1] /flʌɪ/ *v. & n.* ● *v.* (**flies**; *past* **flew** /fluː/; *past part.* **flown** /fləʊn/) **1** *intr.* move through the air under control, esp. with wings. **2** (of an aircraft or its occupants): **a** *intr.* travel through the air or through space. **b** *tr.* traverse (a region or distance) (*flew the Channel*). **3** *tr.* **a** control the flight of (esp. an aircraft). **b** transport in an aircraft. **4 a** *tr.* cause to fly or remain aloft. **b** *intr.* (of a flag, hair, etc.) wave or flutter. **5** *intr.* pass or rise quickly through the air or over an obstacle. **6** *intr.* go or move quickly; pass swiftly (*time flies*). **7** *intr.* **a** flee. **b** *colloq.* depart hastily. **8** *intr.* be driven or scattered; be forced off suddenly (*sent me flying*; *the door flew open*). **9** *intr.* (foll. by *at, upon*) **a** hasten or spring violently. **b** attack or criticize fiercely. **10** *tr.* flee from; escape in haste. ● *n.* (*pl.* **-ies**) **1** (*Brit.* usu. in *pl.*) **a** a flap on a garment, esp. trousers, to contain or cover a fastening. **b** this fastening. **2** a flap at the entrance of a tent. **3** (in *pl.*) the space over the proscenium in a theatre. **4** the act or an instance of flying. **5** (*pl.* usu. **flys**) *Brit. hist.* a one-horse hackney carriage. **6** a speed-regulating device in clockwork and machinery. □ **fly high 1** pursue a high ambition. **2** excel, prosper. **fly in the face of** openly disregard or disobey; conflict roundly with (probability, the evidence, etc.). **fly into a rage** (or **temper** etc.) become suddenly or violently angry. **fly a kite 1** try something out; test public opinion. **2** raise money by an accommodation bill. **fly off the handle** *colloq.* lose one's temper suddenly and unexpectedly. □ **flyable** *adj.* [Old English *flēogan*, from Germanic]

fly[2] /flʌɪ/ *n.* (*pl.* **flies**) **1** any insect of the order Diptera, with one pair of usu. transparent wings. **2** any other winged insect, e.g. a firefly or mayfly. **3** a disease of plants or animals caused by flies (usu. with a qualifying word: *potato-fly*). **4** a natural or artificial fly used as bait in fishing. □ **fly in the ointment** a minor irritation that spoils enjoyment. **fly on the wall** an unnoticed observer. **like flies** in large numbers (usu. of people dying in an epidemic etc.). **no flies on** *colloq.* nothing to diminish (a person's) astuteness. [Old English *flȳge, flēoge*, from West Germanic]

fly[3] /flʌɪ/ *adj.* (**flyer**, **flyest**) **1** *Brit. slang* knowing, clever, alert. **2** *N. Amer. slang* stylish; good-looking. □ **flyness** *n.* [19th c.: origin unknown]

fly agaric *n.* a poisonous fungus, *Amanita muscaria*, forming bright red mushrooms with white flecks.

flyaway /ˈflʌɪəweɪ/ *adj.* (of hair etc.) tending to fly out or up; streaming.

flyblown /ˈflʌɪbləʊn/ *adj.* tainted, esp. by flies.

fly boy *n. N. Amer. slang* a pilot, esp. one in the Air Force.

fly-by *n.* (*pl.* **-bys**) a flight past a position, esp. the approach of a spacecraft to a planet for observation.

fly-by-night *adj. & n.* ● *adj.* unreliable. ● *n.* an unreliable person.

fly-by-wire *n.* (often *attrib.*) a semi-automatic and usu. computer-regulated system for controlling the flight of an aircraft, spacecraft, etc.

flycatcher /ˈflʌɪkatʃə/ *n.* any of various passerine birds catching flying insects esp. in short flights from a perch, esp. of the family Muscicapidae, Tyrannidae (**tyrant flycatcher**), and Monarchidae (**monarch flycatcher**).

fly-drive *adj., n., & v.* ● *attrib.adj.* designating a holiday which combines the cost of the flight and of car rental. ● *n.* such a holiday. ● *v.intr.* take such a holiday.

flyer /ˈflʌɪə/ *n.* (also **flier**) **1** an airman or airwoman. **2** a thing that flies in a specified way (*a poor flyer*). **3** *colloq.* a fast-moving animal or vehicle. **4** an ambitious or outstanding person; an outstanding thing. **5** a small handbill. **6** *US* a speculative investment. **7** a flying jump.

fly-fish *v.intr.* fish with a fly.

fly-half *n. Rugby* a stand-off half.

flying /ˈflʌɪɪŋ/ *adj. & n.* ● *adj.* **1** fluttering or waving in the air; hanging loose. **2** hasty, brief (*a flying visit*). **3** designed for rapid movement. **4** (of an animal) able to make very long leaps by using winglike membranes etc. ● *n.* flight, esp. in an aircraft. □ **with flying colours** with distinction.

flying boat *n.* a large seaplane with a fuselage that resembles a boat.

flying bomb *n.* a pilotless aircraft with an explosive warhead.

flying buttress *n. Archit.* a buttress slanting from a separate column, usu. forming an arch with the wall it supports.

flying doctor *n.* a doctor (esp. in a large sparsely populated area) who visits distant patients by aircraft.

flying dragon see DRAGON 3.

Flying Dutchman *n.* **1** a ghostly ship supposedly doomed to sail the seas for ever. **2** its captain.

flying fish *n.* any tropical fish of the family Exocoetidae, with winglike pectoral fins for gliding through the air.

flying fox *n.* a large fruitbat, esp. of the genus *Pteropus*, with a foxlike head.

flying lemur *n.* either of two lemur-like mammals of the genus *Cynocephalus* of SE Asia, having a membrane between the fore and hind limbs for gliding from tree to tree. Also called *colugo*.

flying lizard *n.* a long-tailed lizard of the SE Asian genus *Draco*, with elongated ribs supporting membranes for gliding.

flying officer *n.* the RAF rank next below flight lieutenant.

flying phalanger *n.* any of various Australian marsupials of the genus *Petaurus* or *Petauroides* having a membrane between the fore and hind limbs for gliding.

flying picket *n. Brit.* an industrial picket that can be moved rapidly from one site to another, esp. to reinforce local pickets.

flying saucer *n.* any unidentified, esp. circular, flying object, popularly supposed to have come from outer space.

flying squad *n. Brit.* a police detachment or other body organized for rapid movement.

flying squirrel *n.* any squirrel of the subfamily Pteromyinae, with skin joining the fore and hind limbs for gliding from tree to tree.

flying start *n.* **1** a start (of a race etc.) in which the starting point is passed at full speed. **2** a vigorous start giving an initial advantage.

flying suit *n.* a one-piece garment worn by aircrew.

flying wing *n.* an aircraft with little or no fuselage and no tailplane.

flyleaf /ˈflʌɪliːf/ *n.* (*pl.* **-leaves**) a blank leaf at the beginning or end of a book.

flyover /ˈflʌɪəʊvə/ *n.* **1** *Brit.* a bridge carrying one road or railway over another. **2** *US* = FLY-PAST.

fly-paper *n.* sticky treated paper for catching flies.

fly-past *n. Brit.* a ceremonial flight of aircraft past a person or a place.

fly-pitcher *n. Brit. slang* a street trader. ▫ **fly-pitching** *n.*

fly-post *v.tr. Brit.* display (posters etc.) rapidly in unauthorized places.

flysheet /ˈflʌɪʃiːt/ *n.* **1** a tract or circular of two or four pages. **2** *Brit.* a fabric cover pitched outside and over a tent to give extra protection against bad weather.

fly-tip *v.tr. Brit.* illegally dump (waste). ▫ **fly-tipper** *n.* **fly-tipping** *n.*

flytrap /ˈflʌɪtrap/ *n.* any of various plants that catch flies, esp. the Venus flytrap.

flyweight /ˈflʌɪweɪt/ *n.* **1** a weight in certain sports intermediate between light flyweight and bantamweight, in the amateur boxing scale 48–51 kg but differing for professionals, wrestlers, and weightlifters. **2** a boxer etc. of this weight.

flywheel /ˈflʌɪwiːl/ *n.* a heavy wheel on a revolving shaft used to regulate machinery or accumulate power.

FM *abbr.* **1** Field Marshal. **2** frequency modulation.

Fm *symb. Chem.* the element fermium.

fm. *abbr.* (also **fm**) fathom(s).

f-number *n. Photog.* the ratio of the focal length to the effective diameter of a lens (e.g. *f5*, indicating that the focal length is five times the diameter). [*f* (denoting focal length) + NUMBER]

fo. *abbr.* folio.

foal /fəʊl/ *n.* & *v.* ● *n.* the young of a horse or related animal. ● *v.tr.* (of a mare etc.) give birth to (a foal). ▫ **in** (or **with**) **foal** (of a mare etc.) pregnant. [Old English *fola* from Germanic: cf. FILLY]

foam /fəʊm/ *n.* & *v.* ● *n.* **1** a mass of small bubbles formed on or in liquid by agitation, fermentation, etc. **2** a froth of saliva or sweat. **3** a substance resembling these, e.g. rubber (in full **foam rubber**) or plastic (in full **foam plastic**) in a cellular mass. ● *v.intr.* **1** emit foam; froth. **2** run with foam. **3** (of a vessel) be filled and overflow with foam. ▫ **foam at the mouth** be very angry. ▫ **foamless** *adj.* **foamy** *adj.* (**foamier**, **foamiest**). [Old English *fām*, from West Germanic]

fob[1] /fɒb/ *n.* & *v.* ● *n.* **1** (in full **fob-chain**) a chain attached to a watch for carrying in a waistcoat or waistband pocket. **2** a small pocket for carrying a watch. **3** a tab on a keyring. ● *v.tr.* (**fobbed**, **fobbing**) put in one's fob; pocket. [originally slang, probably from German]

fob[2] /fɒb/ *v.tr.* (**fobbed**, **fobbing**) ▫ **fob off 1** (often foll. by *with* a thing) deceive into accepting something inferior. **2** (often foll. by *on to* a person) palm or pass off (an inferior thing). [Middle English: cf. obsolete *fop* 'to dupe', German *foppen* 'deceive, cheat, banter']

f.o.b. *abbr.* free on board (see FREE).

focaccia /fəˈkatʃə/ *n.* (*pl.* **focaccias**) **1** a type of flat Italian bread made with yeast and olive oil and often flavoured with herbs etc. **2** a loaf of this. [Italian]

focal /ˈfəʊk(ə)l/ *adj.* of, at, or in terms of a focus. [modern Latin *focalis* (as FOCUS)]

focalize /ˈfəʊk(ə)lʌɪz/ *v.tr.* (also **-ise**) = FOCUS *v.* ▫ **focalization** /-ˈzeɪʃ(ə)n/ *n.*

focal length *n.* (also **focal distance**) **1** the distance between the centre of a lens or curved mirror and its focus. **2** the equivalent distance in a compound lens or telescope.

focal plane *n.* the plane through the focus perpendicular to the axis of a mirror or lens.

focal point *n.* **1** = FOCUS *n.* 1. **2** = FOCUS *n.* 3.

fo'c'sle var. of FORECASTLE.

focus /ˈfəʊkəs/ *n.* & *v.* ● *n.* (*pl.* **focuses** or **foci** /ˈfəʊsʌɪ/) **1** *Physics* **a** the point at which rays or waves meet after reflection or refraction. **b** the point from which diverging rays or waves appear to proceed. Also called *focal point*. **2 a** *Optics* the point at which an object must be situated for an image of it given by a lens or mirror to be well defined (*bring into focus*). **b** the adjustment of the eye or a lens necessary to produce a clear image (*the binoculars were not in focus*). **c** a state of clear definition (*the photograph was out of focus*). **3** the centre of interest or activity (*focus of attention*). **4** *Geom.* one of the points from which the distances to any point of a given curve are connected by a linear relation. **5** *Med.* the principal site of an infection or other disease. **6** *Geol.* the place of origin of an earthquake. ● *v.* (**focused**, **focusing** or **focussed**, **focussing**) **1** *tr.* bring into focus. **2** *tr.* adjust the focus of (a lens, the eye, etc.). **3** *tr.* & *intr.* (often foll. by *on*) concentrate or be concentrated on. **4** *intr.* & *tr.* converge or make converge to a focus. ▫ **focuser** *n.* [Latin, = hearth]

fodder /ˈfɒdə/ *n.* & *v.* ● *n.* dried hay or straw etc. for cattle, horses, etc. ● *v.tr.* give fodder to. [Old English *fōdor* from Germanic, related to FOOD]

FOE *abbr.* Friends of the Earth.

foe /fəʊ/ *n.* esp. *poet.* or *formal* an enemy or opponent. [Old English *fāh* hostile, related to FEUD[1]]

foehn var. of FÖHN.

foetid var. of FETID.

foetus /ˈfiːtəs/ *n.* (*US* **fetus**) (*pl.* **-tuses**) an unborn or unhatched offspring of a mammal, esp. an unborn human more than eight weeks after conception. ▫ **foetal** *adj.* **foeticide** /-tɪsʌɪd/ *n.* [Middle English from Latin *fetus* 'offspring']

fog[1] /fɒg/ *n.* & *v.* ● *n.* **1 a** a thick cloud of water droplets or smoke suspended in the atmosphere at or near the earth's surface restricting or obscuring visibility. **b** obscurity in the atmosphere caused by this. **2** *Photog.* cloudiness on a developed negative etc. obscuring the image. **3** an uncertain or confused position or state. ● *v.* (**fogged**, **fogging**) **1** *tr.* **a** (often foll. by *up*) cover with fog or condensed vapour. **b** bewilder or confuse as if with a fog. **2** *intr.* (often foll. by *up*) become covered with fog or condensed vapour. **3** *tr. Photog.* make (a negative etc.) obscure or cloudy. □ **in a fog** puzzled; at a loss. [perhaps back-formation from FOGGY]

fog[2] /fɒg/ *n.* & *v.* esp. *Brit.* ● *n.* **1** a second growth of grass after cutting; aftermath. **2** long grass left standing in winter. ● *v.tr.* (**fogged**, **fogging**) **1** leave (land) under fog. **2** feed (cattle) on fog. [Middle English: origin unknown]

fog bank *n.* a mass of fog at sea.

fogbound /'fɒgbaʊnd/ *adj.* unable to proceed because of fog.

fog-bow *n.* a manifestation like a rainbow, produced by light on fog.

fogey /'fəʊgi/ *n.* (also **fogy**) (*pl.* **-eys** or **-ies**) a dull old-fashioned person (esp. *old fogey*) (cf. YOUNG FOGEY). □ **fogeydom** *n.* **fogeyish** *adj.* [18th c.: related to slang *fogram*, of unknown origin]

foggy /'fɒgi/ *adj.* (**foggier**, **foggiest**) **1** (of the atmosphere) thick or obscure with fog. **2** of or like fog. **3** vague, confused, unclear. □ **not have the foggiest** esp. *Brit. colloq.* have no idea at all. □ **fogginess** *n.* [perhaps from FOG[2]]

foghorn /'fɒghɔːn/ *n.* **1** a deep-sounding instrument for warning ships in fog. **2** *colloq.* a loud penetrating voice.

fog lamp *n.* a lamp, esp. on a motor vehicle, used to improve visibility in fog.

foglight /'fɒglʌɪt/ *n.* = FOG LAMP.

fog signal *n.* a detonator placed on a railway line in fog to warn train drivers.

fogy var. of FOGEY.

föhn /fəːn/ *n.* (also **foehn**) **1** a hot southerly wind on the northern slopes of the Alps. **2** a warm dry wind on the lee side of mountains. [German, ultimately from Latin *Favonius* 'mild west wind']

foible /'fɔɪb(ə)l/ *n.* **1** a minor weakness or idiosyncrasy. **2** *Fencing* the part of a sword blade from the middle to the point. [French, obsolete form of *faible* (as FEEBLE)]

foie gras /fwɑː 'grɑː/ *n.* = PÂTÉ DE FOIE GRAS.

foil[1] /fɔɪl/ *v.* & *n.* ● *v.tr.* **1** frustrate, baffle, defeat. **2** *Hunting* **a** run over or cross (ground or a scent) to confuse the hounds. **b** (*absol.*) (of an animal) spoil the scent in this way. ● *n.* **1** *Hunting* the track of a hunted animal. **2** *archaic* a repulse or defeat. [Middle English, = trample down, perhaps from Old French *fouler* 'to full cloth, trample', ultimately from Latin *fullo* FULLER[1]]

foil[2] /fɔɪl/ *n.* **1 a** metal hammered or rolled into a thin sheet (*aluminium foil*). **b** a sheet of this, or of tin amalgam, attached to mirror glass as a reflector. **c** a leaf of foil placed under a precious stone etc. to brighten or colour it. **2** a person or thing that enhances the qualities of another by contrast. **3** *Archit.* a leaf-shaped curve formed by the cusping of an arch or circle. [Middle English via Old French from Latin *folium* 'leaf', and via Old French *foille* from Latin *folia* (pl.)]

foil[3] /fɔɪl/ *n.* a light blunt-edged sword with a button on its point used in fencing. □ **foilist** *n.* [16th c.: origin unknown]

foil[4] /fɔɪl/ *n.* = HYDROFOIL. [abbreviation]

foist /fɔɪst/ *v.tr.* **1** (foll. by *on*, *upon*) impose (an unwelcome person or thing) on. **2** (foll. by *on*, *upon*) falsely fix the authorship of (a composition) on. **3** (foll. by *in*, *into*) introduce surreptitiously or unwarrantably. [originally of palming a false die, from Dutch dialect *vuisten* 'take in the hand' from *vuist* FIST]

fol. *abbr.* folio.

folacin /'fəʊləsɪn/ *n.* = FOLIC ACID. [*fol*ic *ac*id + -IN]

fold[1] /fəʊld/ *v.* & *n.* ● *v.* **1** *tr.* **a** bend or close (a flexible thing) over upon itself. **b** (foll. by *back*, *over*, *down*) bend a part of (a flexible thing) in the manner specified (*fold down the flap*). **2** *intr.* become or be able to be folded. **3** *tr.* (foll. by *away*, *up*) make compact by folding. **4** *intr.* (often foll. by *up*) *colloq.* **a** collapse, disintegrate. **b** (of an enterprise) fail; go bankrupt. **5** *tr. poet.* embrace (esp. *fold in the arms* or *to the breast*). **6** *tr.* (foll. by *about*, *round*) clasp (the arms); wrap, envelop. **7** *tr.* (foll. by *in*) mix (an ingredient with others) using a gentle cutting and turning motion. ● *n.* **1** the act or an instance of folding. **2** a line made by or for folding. **3** a folded part. **4** *Brit.* a hollow among hills. **5** *Geol.* a curvature of strata. □ **fold one's arms** place one's arms across the chest, side by side or entwined. **fold one's hands** clasp them. □ **foldable** *adj.* [Old English *falden*, *fealden*, from Germanic]

fold[2] /fəʊld/ *n.* & *v.* ● *n.* **1** = SHEEPFOLD. **2** a body of believers or members of a Church. ● *v.tr.* enclose (sheep) in a fold. [Old English *fald*]

-fold /fəʊld/ *suffix* forming adjectives and adverbs from cardinal numbers, meaning: **1** in an amount multiplied by (*repaid tenfold*). **2** consisting of so many parts (*threefold blessing*). [originally in the sense 'folded in so many layers': Old English *-fald*, *-feald*, related to FOLD[1]]

foldaway /'fəʊldəweɪ/ *adj.* adapted or designed to be folded away.

folder /'fəʊldə/ *n.* **1** a folding cover or holder for loose papers. **2** a folded leaflet.

folderol var. of FALDERAL.

folding door *n.* a door with jointed sections, folding on itself when opened.

folding money *n.* esp. *US colloq.* banknotes.

fold-out *n.* an oversize page in a book etc. to be unfolded by the reader.

foliaceous /fəʊlɪ'eɪʃəs/ *adj.* **1** of or resembling a leaf or leaves. **2** esp. *Geol.* laminated. [Latin *foliaceus* 'leafy' from *folium* 'leaf']

foliage /'fəʊlɪɪdʒ/ *n.* **1** leaves, leafage. **2** a design in art resembling leaves. [Middle English via French *feuillage*, from *feuille* 'leaf', from Old French *foille*: see FOIL[2]]

foliage leaf *n.* a leaf excluding petals and other modified leaves.

foliar /'fəʊlɪə/ *adj.* of or relating to leaves. [modern Latin *foliaris* from Latin *folium* 'leaf']

foliar feed *n.* feed supplied to leaves of plants.

foliate *adj.* & *v.* ● *adj.* /'fəʊlɪət, -eɪt/ **1** leaflike. **2** having leaves. **3** (in *comb.*) having a specified number of leaflets (*trifoliate*). ● *v.* /'fəʊlɪeɪt/ **1** *intr.* split into laminae. **2** *tr.Archit.* decorate (an arch or door head) with foils. **3** *tr.* number leaves (not pages) of (a volume) consecutively. □ **foliation** /-'eɪʃ(ə)n/ *n.* [Latin *foliatus* 'leaved' from *folium* 'leaf']

folic acid /'fəʊlɪk, 'fɒl-/ *n.* a vitamin of the B complex, found in leafy green vegetables, liver, and kidney, a deficiency of which causes pernicious anaemia. Also called *folacin*, *pteroylglutamic acid*, *vitamin M.* [Latin *folium* 'leaf' (because it is found esp. in green leaves) + -IC]

folio /'fəʊlɪəʊ/ *n.* & *adj.* ● *n.* (*pl.* **-os**) **1** a leaf of paper etc., esp. one numbered only on the front. **2** a leaf-number of a book. **3** a sheet of paper folded once making two leaves of a book. **4** a book made of such sheets. ● *adj.* (of a book) made of folios, of the largest size. □ **in folio** made of folios. [Latin, ablative of *folium* 'leaf', = *on leaf* (as specified)]

foliole /'fəʊlɪəʊl/ *n.* a division of a compound leaf; a leaflet. [French from Late Latin *foliolum*, diminutive of Latin *folium* 'leaf']

foliose /'fəʊlɪəʊz/ *adj.* (of a lichen) having a lobed, leaf-like shape. [Latin *foliosus*, from *folium* 'leaf' + -OSE[1]]

folk /fəʊk/ *n.* (*pl.* **folk** or **folks**) **1** (treated as *pl.*) people in general or of a specified class (*few folk about*; *townsfolk*). **2** (in *pl.*) (usu. **folks**) one's parents or relatives. **3** (treated as *sing.*) a people. **4** (treated as *sing.*) *colloq.* = FOLK MUSIC. **5** (*attrib.*) of popular origin;

traditional (*folk art, folk hero*). [Old English *folc*, from Germanic]

folk dance *n.* **1** a dance of popular origin. **2** the music for such a dance. □ **folk dancer** *n.* **folk dancing** *n.*

folk etymology *n.* a popular modifying of the form of a word or phrase to make it seem to be derived from a more familiar word (e.g. *sparrowgrass* for *asparagus*).

folkie /ˈfəʊki/ *n. & adj. colloq.* ● *n.* a devotee of folk music; a folk singer. ● *attrib.adj.* of or relating to folk music (*folkie bands*).

folkish /ˈfəʊkɪʃ/ *adj.* of the common people; traditional, unsophisticated.

folklore /ˈfəʊklɔː/ *n.* the traditional beliefs and stories of a people; the study of these. □ **folkloric** *adj.* **folklorist** *n.* **folkloristic** /-ˈrɪstɪk/ *adj.*

folk memory *n.* recollection of the past persisting among a people.

folk music *n.* traditional music or modern music in this style.

folk rock *n.* folk music incorporating the stronger beat of rock music and using electric instruments.

folk singer *n.* a singer of folk songs.

folk song *n.* a song of popular or traditional origin or style.

folksy /ˈfəʊksi/ *adj.* (**folksier**, **folksiest**) **1** friendly, sociable, informal. **2 a** having the characteristics of folk art, culture, etc. **b** ostensibly or artificially folkish. □ **folksiness** *n.*

folk tale *n.* a popular or traditional story.

folkways /ˈfəʊkweɪz/ *n.pl.* the traditional behaviour of a people.

folkweave /ˈfəʊkwiːv/ *n. Brit.* a rough loosely woven fabric.

folky /ˈfəʊki/ *adj.* (**folkier**, **folkiest**) **1** = FOLKSY 2. **2** = FOLKISH. □ **folkiness** *n.*

follicle /ˈfɒlɪk(ə)l/ *n.* **1** *Anat.* a small secretory cavity, sac, or gland, esp.: **a** (in full **hair follicle**) the gland or cavity at the root of a hair. **b** = GRAAFIAN FOLLICLE. **2** *Bot.* a single-carpelled dry fruit opening on one side only to release its seeds. □ **follicular** /fɒˈlɪkjʊlə/ *adj.* **folliculate** /fɒˈlɪkjʊlət/ *adj.* **folliculated** /fɒˈlɪkjʊleɪtɪd/ *adj.* [Latin *folliculus*, diminutive of *follis* 'bellows']

follicle-stimulating hormone *n. Physiol.* a pituitary hormone which promotes the formation of ova or sperm (abbr.: **FSH**).

follow /ˈfɒləʊ/ *v.* **1** *tr.* or (foll. by *after*) *intr.* go or come after (a person or thing proceeding ahead). **2** *tr.* go along (a route, path, etc.). **3** *tr. & intr.* come after in order or time (*Nero followed Claudius*; *dessert followed*; *my reasons are as follows*). **4** *tr.* take as a guide or leader. **5** *tr.* conform to (*follow your example*). **6** *tr.* practise (a trade or profession). **7** *tr.* undertake (a course of study etc.). **8** *tr.* understand the meaning or tendency of (a speaker or argument). **9** *tr.* maintain awareness of the current state or progress of (events etc. in a particular sphere). **10** *tr.* (foll. by *with*) provide with a sequel or successor. **11** *intr.* happen after something else; ensue. **12** *intr.* **a** be necessarily true as a result of something else. **b** (foll. by *from*) be a result of. **13** *tr.* strive after; aim at; pursue (*followed fame and fortune*). □ **follow one's nose** trust to instinct. **follow on 1** continue. **2** (of a cricket team) have to bat again immediately after the first innings. **follow out** carry out; adhere precisely to (instructions etc.). **follow suit 1** *Cards* play a card of the suit led. **2** conform to another person's actions. **follow through 1** continue (an action etc.) to its conclusion. **2** *Sport* continue the movement of a stroke after the ball has been struck. **follow up 1** (foll. by *with*) pursue, develop, supplement. **2** make further investigation of. [Old English *folgian*, from Germanic]

follower /ˈfɒləʊə/ *n.* **1** an adherent or devotee. **2** a person or thing that follows.

following /ˈfɒləʊɪŋ/ *prep., n., & adj.* ● *prep.* coming after in time; as a sequel to. ● *n.* **1** a body of adherents or devotees. **2** (**the following**) (treated as *sing.* or *pl.*) the person(s) or thing(s) now to be mentioned. ● *adj.* that follows or comes after.

follow-on *n.* **1** *Cricket* a second innings immediately after the first. **2** the act or an instance of following on (often *attrib.*: *follow-on treatment*).

follow-the-leader *n.* (also *Brit.* **follow-my-leader**) a game in which players must do as the leader does.

follow-through *n.* the act or an instance of following through.

follow-up *n.* a subsequent or continued action, measure, experience, etc.

folly /ˈfɒli/ *n.* (*pl.* **-ies**) **1** foolishness; lack of good sense. **2** a foolish act, behaviour, idea, etc. **3** a costly ornamental building, usu. a tower or mock Gothic ruin. **4** (in *pl.*) *Theatr.* **a** a revue with glamorous female performers, esp. scantily-clad. **b** the performers in such a revue. [Middle English from Old French *folie*, from *fol* 'mad, FOOL[1]']

foment /fə(ʊ)ˈmɛnt/ *v.tr.* **1** instigate or stir up (trouble, sedition, etc.). **2 a** bathe with warm or medicated liquid. **b** apply warmth to. □ **fomenter** *n.* [Middle English via French *fomenter* and Late Latin *fomentare* from Latin *fomentum* 'poultice, lotion', from *fovēre* 'heat, cherish']

fomentation /fəʊmɛnˈteɪʃ(ə)n/ *n.* **1** the act or an instance of fomenting. **2** materials prepared for application to a wound etc. [Middle English from Old French or Late Latin *fomentatio* (as FOMENT)]

fond *adj.* **1** (*predic.*; foll. by *of*) having affection or a liking for. **2** (*attrib.*) affectionate, loving, doting. **3** (*attrib.*) (of beliefs etc.) foolishly optimistic or credulous; naive. □ **fondly** *adv.* **fondness** *n.* [Middle English from obsolete *fon* 'fool, be foolish']

fondant /ˈfɒnd(ə)nt/ *n.* a soft sweet of flavoured sugar. [French, pres. part. of *fondre* 'melt', from Latin *fundere* 'pour']

fondant icing *n.* icing made of a soft paste of flavoured sugar.

fondle /ˈfɒnd(ə)l/ *v. & n.* ● *v.tr.* touch or stroke lovingly; caress. ● *n.* an act of fondling. □ **fondler** *n.* [back-formation from *fondling* 'fondled person' (as FOND, -LING[1])]

fondue /ˈfɒnd(j)uː/ *n.* **1** a dish of flavoured melted cheese into which pieces of bread are dipped. **2** any other dish in which small pieces of food are dipped into hot oil or sauce. [French, fem. past part. of *fondre* 'melt', from Latin *fundere* 'pour']

font[1] /fɒnt/ *n.* **1** a receptacle in a church for baptismal water. **2** the reservoir for oil in a lamp. □ **fontal** *adj.* (in sense 1). [Old English *font, fant* via Old Irish *fant, font* from Latin *fons fontis* 'fountain, baptismal water']

font[2] /fɒnt/ *n.* (also *Brit.* **fount** /faʊnt/) *Printing* a set of type of one face or size. [French *fonte* from *fondre* FOUND[3]]

fontanelle /fɒntəˈnɛl/ *n.* (*US* **fontanel**) a membranous space in an infant's skull at the angles of the parietal bones. [in earlier use 'an outlet for bodily secretions': French *fontanelle* via modern Latin *fontanella* from Old French *fontenelle*, diminutive of *fontaine* 'fountain']

food /fuːd/ *n.* **1** a nutritious substance, esp. solid in form, that can be taken into an animal or a plant to maintain life and growth. **2** ideas as a resource for or stimulus to mental work (*food for thought*). [Old English *fōda* from Germanic: cf. FEED]

food additive *n.* a substance added to food to enhance its colour, flavour, or presentation, or for any other non-nutritional purpose.

food chain *n.* a series of organisms each dependent on the next as a source of food.

foodie /ˈfuːdi/ *n.* (also **foody**) (*pl.* **-ies**) *colloq.* a person with a particular interest in food; a gourmet.

food poisoning *n.* illness due to bacteria or toxins in food.

food processor *n.* a machine for chopping and mixing food materials.

foodstuff /ˈfuːdstʌf/ *n.* any substance suitable as food.

food value *n.* the relative nourishing power of a food.

fool[1] /fu:l/ *n., v., & adj.* ● *n.* **1** a person who acts unwisely or imprudently; a stupid person. **2** *hist.* a jester; a clown. **3** a dupe. ● *v.* **1** *tr.* deceive so as to cause to appear foolish. **2** *tr.* (foll. by *into* + verbal noun, or *out of*) trick; cause to do something foolish. **3** *tr.* play tricks on; dupe. **4** *intr.* act in a joking, frivolous, or teasing way. **5** *intr.* (foll. by *about, around*) **a** behave in a playful or silly way. **b** engage in sexual (esp. adulterous) activity. ● *adj. N. Amer. colloq.* foolish, silly. □ **act** (or **play**) **the fool** behave in a silly way. **make a fool of** make (a person or oneself) look foolish; trick or deceive. **no** (or **nobody's**) **fool** a shrewd or prudent person. [Middle English via Old French *fol* from Latin *follis* 'bellows, empty-headed person']

fool[2] /fu:l/ *n.* esp. *Brit.* a dessert of usu. stewed fruit crushed and mixed with cream, custard, etc. [16th c.: perhaps from FOOL[1]]

foolery /'fu:ləri/ *n.* (*pl.* **-ies**) **1** foolish behaviour. **2** a foolish act.

foolhardy /'fu:lhɑ:di/ *adj.* (**foolhardier, foolhardiest**) rashly or foolishly bold; reckless. □ **foolhardily** *adv.* **foolhardiness** *n.* [Middle English from Old French *folhardi*, from *fol* 'foolish' + *hardi* 'bold']

foolish /'fu:lɪʃ/ *adj.* (of a person, action, etc.) lacking good sense or judgement; unwise. □ **foolishly** *adv.* **foolishness** *n.*

foolproof /'fu:lpru:f/ *adj.* (of a procedure, mechanism, etc.) so straightforward or simple as to be incapable of misuse or mistake.

foolscap /'fu:lzkap, -lsk-/ *n. Brit.* **1** a size of paper, about 330 × 200 (or 400) mm. **2** foolscap paper. [named from the former watermark representing a fool's cap]

fool's errand *n.* a fruitless venture.

fool's gold *n.* iron pyrites.

fool's mate see MATE[2].

fool's paradise *n.* happiness founded on an illusion.

fool's parsley *n.* an umbelliferous plant resembling parsley.

foot /fʊt/ *n. & v.* ● *n.* (*pl.* **feet** /fi:t/) **1 a** the lower extremity of the leg below the ankle. **b** the part of a sock etc. covering the foot. **2 a** the lower or lowest part of anything, e.g. a mountain, a page, stairs, etc. **b** the lower end of a table. **c** the end of a bed where the user's feet normally rest. **d** a part of a chair, appliance, etc. on which it rests. **3** the base, often projecting, of anything extending vertically. **4** a step, pace, or tread; a manner of walking (*fleet of foot*). **5** (*pl.* **feet** or **foot**) a unit of linear measure equal to 12 inches (30.48 cm). **6** *Prosody* **a** a group of syllables (one usu. stressed) constituting a metrical unit. **b** a similar unit of speech etc. **7** *Brit. hist.* infantry (*a regiment of foot*). **8** *Zool.* the locomotive or adhesive organ of invertebrates. **9** *Bot.* the part by which a petal is attached. **10** a device on a sewing machine for holding the material steady as it is sewn. **11** (*pl.* **foots**) **a** dregs; oil refuse. **b** coarse sugar. ● *v.tr.* **1** (usu. as **foot it**) **a** traverse (esp. a long distance) by foot. **b** dance. **2** pay (a bill, esp. one considered large). □ **at a person's feet** as a person's disciple or subject. **feet of clay** a fundamental weakness in a person otherwise revered. **get one's feet wet** begin to participate. **have one's** (or **both**) **feet on the ground** be practical. **have a foot in the door** have a prospect of success. **have one foot in the grave** be near death or very old. **my foot!** *int. colloq.* expressing strong contradiction. **not put a foot wrong** make no mistakes. **off one's feet** so as to be unable to stand, or in a state compared with this (*was rushed off my feet*). **on one's feet 1** standing, esp. to make a speech. **2** well enough to walk about. **on foot** walking, not riding etc. **put one's best foot forward** make every effort; proceed with determination. **put one's feet up** *colloq.* take a rest. **put one's foot down** *colloq.* **1** be firmly insistent or repressive. **2** *Brit.* accelerate a motor vehicle. **put one's foot in it** *colloq.* commit a blunder or indiscretion. **set foot on** (or **in**) enter; go into. **set on foot** put (an action, process, etc.) in motion. **under one's feet** in the way. **under foot** on the ground. □ **footed** *adj.* (also in *comb.*). **footless** *adj.* [Old English *fōt*, from Germanic]

footage /'fʊtɪdʒ/ *n.* **1** length or distance in feet. **2** an amount of film made for showing, broadcasting, etc.

foot-and-mouth disease *n.* a contagious viral disease of cattle etc.

football /'fʊtbɔ:l/ *n. & v.* ● *n.* **1** any of several esp. outdoor games between two teams played with a ball on a pitch with goals at each end, esp. *Brit.* = ASSOCIATION FOOTBALL. **2** a large inflated ball of a kind used in these games. **3** a topical issue or problem that is the subject of continued argument or controversy. ● *v.intr.* play football. □ **footballer** *n.*

football hooligan *n.* a hooligan at a football match or travelling to or from one.

football pool *n.* (also **football pools** *pl.*) a form of gambling on the results of football matches, the winners receiving sums accumulated from entry money.

footbath /'fʊtbɑ:θ/ *n.* **1** an act of washing the feet. **2** a small shallow bath used for this.

footbed /'fʊtbɛd/ *n.* an insole in a boot or shoe, used for cushioning or to provide a better fit.

footboard /'fʊtbɔ:d/ *n.* **1** a board to support the feet or a foot. **2** an upright board at the foot of a bed.

footbrake /'fʊtbreɪk/ *n.* a brake operated by the foot in a motor vehicle.

footbridge /'fʊtbrɪdʒ/ *n.* a bridge for use by pedestrians.

footer[1] /'fʊtə/ *n.* **1** (in *comb.*) **a** a person or thing of so many feet in length or height (*six-footer*). **b** a specified kick of esp. a football (*a fine right-footer into the goal*). **2** a line or block of text appearing at the foot of each page of a document etc. (cf. HEADER 5).

footer[2] var. of FOOTY.

footfall /'fʊtfɔ:l/ *n.* the sound of a footstep.

foot-fault *n. & v.* ● *n.* (in tennis etc.) incorrect placement of the feet while serving. ● *v.* **1** *intr.* make a foot-fault. **2** *tr.* award a foot-fault against (a player).

foothill /'fʊthɪl/ *n.* (often in *pl.*) any of the low hills around the base of a mountain.

foothold /'fʊthəʊld/ *n.* **1** a place, esp. in climbing, where a foot can be supported securely. **2** a secure initial position or advantage.

footie var. of FOOTY.

footing /'fʊtɪŋ/ *n.* **1** a foothold; a secure position (*lost his footing*). **2** the basis on which an enterprise is established or operates; the position or status of a person in relation to others (*on an equal footing*). **3** (usu. in *pl.*) the foundations of a wall, usu. with a course of brickwork wider than the base of the wall.

footle /'fu:t(ə)l/ *v.intr.* (usu. foll. by *about*) esp. *Brit. colloq.* behave foolishly or trivially. [19th c.: perhaps from dialect *footer* 'idle']

footlights /'fʊtlʌɪts/ *n.pl.* a row of lights along the front of a stage at the level of the actors' feet.

footling /'fu:tlɪŋ/ *adj. colloq.* trivial, silly.

footloose /'fʊtlu:s/ *adj.* (often in phr. **footloose and fancy-free**) free to go where or act as one pleases.

footman /'fʊtmən/ *n.* (*pl.* **-men**) **1** a liveried servant attending at the door, at table, or on a carriage. **2** *hist.* an infantryman.

footmark /'fʊtmɑ:k/ *n.* a footprint.

footnote /'fʊtnəʊt/ *n. & v.* ● *n.* a note printed at the foot of a page. ● *v.tr.* supply with a footnote or footnotes.

footpad /'fʊtpad/ *n. hist.* an unmounted highwayman.

foot passenger *n.* a pedestrian, esp. as opposed to a passenger travelling with a car by ferry.

footpath /'fʊtpɑ:θ/ *n.* **1** *Brit.* a path for pedestrians, esp. an alley between buildings or a pavement at the side of a road. **2** a path for walking along through woods, fields, etc.

footplate /'fʊtpleɪt/ *n.* esp. *Brit.* the platform in the cab of a locomotive for the crew.

foot-pound *n.* (*pl.* **foot-pounds**) the amount of energy required to raise 1 lb a distance of 1 foot.

foot-pound-second system *n.* a system of measurement with the foot, pound, and second as basic units.

footprint /'fʊtprɪnt/ *n.* **1** the impression left by a foot or shoe. **2** the area over which an aircraft is audible, a broadcast can be received, etc. **3** *Computing* the area of desk space etc. occupied by a microcomputer or other piece of hardware.

footrest /'fʊtrɛst/ *n.* a support for the feet or a foot.

foot-rot *n.* a bacterial disease of the feet in sheep and cattle.

foot-rule *n.* a ruler 1 foot long.

Footsie /'fʊtsi/ *n. colloq.* the Financial Times-Stock Exchange 100 share index (based on the share values of Britain's hundred largest public companies). [fanciful acronym, influenced by FOOTSIE]

footsie /'fʊtsi/ *n. colloq.* amorous play with the feet. [jocular diminutive of FOOT]

footslog /'fʊtslɒg/ *v. & n. Brit.* ● *v.intr.* (**-slogged**, **-slogging**) walk or march, esp. laboriously for a long distance. ● *n.* a laborious walk or march. □ **footslogger** *n.*

foot soldier *n.* a soldier who fights on foot.

footsore /'fʊtsɔ:/ *adj.* having sore feet, esp. from walking.

footstalk /'fʊtstɔ:k/ *n.* **1** *Bot.* a stalk of a leaf or peduncle of a flower. **2** *Zool.* an attachment of a stalked barnacle etc.

footstep /'fʊtstɛp/ *n.* **1** a step taken in walking. **2** the sound of this. □ **follow** (or **tread**) **in a person's footsteps** do as another person did before.

footstool /'fʊtstu:l/ *n.* a low stool for resting the feet on when sitting.

footway /'fʊtweɪ/ *n. Brit.* a path or way for pedestrians.

footwear /'fʊtwɛ:/ *n.* shoes, socks, etc.

footwell /'fʊtwɛl/ *n.* a space for the feet in front of a seat in a car etc. [FOOT + WELL[2] (in the sense 'a depression in the floor')]

footwork /'fʊtwə:k/ *n.* the use of the feet, esp. skilfully, in sports, dancing, etc.

footy /'fʊti/ *n.* (also **footie**, **footer** /-tə/) *colloq.* = FOOTBALL 1.

foo yong /fu: 'jɒŋ/ *n.* a Chinese dish or sauce made with eggs and other ingredients. [Cantonese *foo yung*, literally 'hibiscus']

fop /fɒp/ *n.* an affectedly elegant or fashionable man; a dandy. □ **foppery** *n.* **foppish** *adj.* **foppishly** *adv.* **foppishness** *n.* [17th c.: perhaps from earlier *fop* 'fool']

for /fɔ:, fə/ *prep. & conj.* ● *prep.* **1** in the interest or to the benefit of; intended to go to (*these flowers are for you*; *wish to see it for myself*; *did it all for my country*; *silly for you to go*). **2** in defence, support, or favour of (*fight for one's rights*). **3** suitable or appropriate to (*a dance for beginners*; *not for me to say*). **4** in respect of or with reference to; regarding; so far as concerns (*usual for ties to be worn*; *don't care for him at all*; *ready for bed*; *MP for Lincoln*). **5** representing or in place of (*here for my uncle*). **6** in exchange against (*swopped it for a bigger one*). **7 a** as the price of (*give me £5 for it*). **b** at the price of (*bought it for £5*). **c** to the amount of (*a bill for £100*; *all out for 45*). **8** as the penalty of (*fined them heavily for it*). **9** in requital of (*that's for upsetting my sister*). **10** as a reward for (*here's £5 for your trouble*). **11** with a view to; in the hope or quest of; in order to get (*go for a walk*; *run for a doctor*; *did it for the money*). **12** corresponding to (*word for word*). **13** to reach; in the direction of; towards (*left for Rome*; *ran for the end of the road*). **14** conducive or conducively to; in order to achieve (*take the pills for a sound night's sleep*). **15** so as to start promptly at (*the meeting is at seven-thirty for eight*). **16** through or over (a distance or period); during (*walked for miles*; *sang for two hours*). **17** in the character of; as being (*for the last time*; *know it for a lie*; *I for one refuse*). **18** because of; on account of (*could not see for tears*). **19** in spite of; notwithstanding (*for all we know*; *for all your fine words*). **20** considering or making due allowance in respect of (*good for a beginner*). ● *conj.* because, since, seeing that. □ **be for it** *Brit. colloq.* be in imminent danger of punishment or other trouble. **for ever** see EVER (cf. FOREVER). **o** (or **oh**) **for** (as *int.*) expressing longing for a thing. [Old English, probably a reduction of a Germanic preposition meaning 'before' (of place and time)]

for- /fɔ:, unstressed fə/ *prefix* forming verbs and their derivatives meaning: **1** away, off, apart (*forget*; *forgive*). **2** prohibition (*forbid*). **3** abstention or neglect (*forgo*; *forsake*). **4** excess or intensity (*forlorn*). [Old English *for-*, *fœr-*]

f.o.r. *abbr.* free on rail (see FREE).

forage /'fɒrɪdʒ/ *n. & v.* ● *n.* **1** food for horses and cattle. **2** the act or an instance of searching for food. ● *v.* **1** *intr.* (often foll. by *for*) go searching; rummage (esp. for food). **2** *tr.* get by foraging. **3** *tr.* supply with food. □ **forager** *n.* [Middle English from Old French *fourrage*, *fourrager*, related to FODDER]

forage cap *n.* an infantry undress cap.

foramen /fə'reɪmɛn/ *n.* (*pl.* **foramina** /-'ramɪnə/) *Anat.* an opening, hole, or passage, esp. in a bone. [Latin *foramen -minis* from *forare* 'bore a hole']

foramen magnum /'magnəm/ *n. Anat.* the hole in the base of the skull through which the spinal cord passes. [Latin, = large opening]

foraminifer /fɒrə'mɪnɪfə/ *n.* (also **foraminiferan** /-'nɪf(ə)r(ə)n/) any protozoan of the mainly marine order Foraminifera, having a perforated shell through which amoeba-like pseudopodia emerge. □ **foraminiferous** /-'nɪf(ə)rəs/ *adj.*

forasmuch as /fərəz'mʌtʃ/ *conj. archaic* because, since. [= for as much]

foray /'fɒreɪ/ *n. & v.* ● *n.* a sudden attack; a raid or incursion. ● *v.intr.* make or go on a foray. [Middle English: back-formation from *forayer* from Old French *forrier* 'forager', related to FODDER]

forbade (also **forbad**) *past* of FORBID.

forbear[1] /fɔ:'bɛ:/ *v.intr. & tr.* (*past* **forbore** /-'bɔ:/; *past part.* **forborne** /-'bɔ:n/) (often foll. by *from*, or *to* + infin.) *literary* abstain or desist (from) (*could not forbear (from) speaking out*; *forbore to mention it*). [Old English *forberan* (as FOR-, BEAR[1])]

forbear[2] var. of FOREBEAR.

forbearance /fɔ:'bɛ:r(ə)ns/ *n.* patient self-control; tolerance.

forbid /fə'bɪd/ *v.tr.* (**forbidding**; *past* **forbade** /-'bad, -'beɪd/ or **forbad** /-'bad/; *past part.* **forbidden** /-'bɪd(ə)n/) **1** (foll. by *to* + infin.) order not (*I forbid you to go*). **2** refuse to allow (a thing, or a person to have a thing) (*I forbid it*; *was forbidden any wine*). **3** refuse a person entry to (*the gardens are forbidden to children*). [Old English *forbēodan* (as FOR-, BID)]

forbidden degrees *n.pl.* a number of degrees of consanguinity within which marriage between two related persons is forbidden.

forbidden fruit *n.* something desired or enjoyed all the more because not allowed.

forbidding /fə'bɪdɪŋ/ *adj.* uninviting, repellent, stern. □ **forbiddingly** *adv.*

forbore *past* of FORBEAR[1].

forborne *past part.* of FORBEAR[1].

forbye /fə'bʌɪ, fɔ:-/ *prep. & adv. archaic* or *Sc.* ● *prep.* besides. ● *adv.* in addition.

force[1] /fɔ:s/ *n. & v.* ● *n.* **1** power; exerted strength or impetus; intense effort. **2** coercion or compulsion, esp. with the use or threat of violence. **3 a** military strength. **b** (in *pl.*) troops; fighting resources. **c** an organized body of people, esp. soldiers, police, or workers. **4** binding power; validity. **5** effect; precise significance (*the force of their words*). **6 a** mental or moral strength; influence, efficacy (*force of habit*). **b** vividness of effect (*described with much force*). **7** *Physics* **a** an influence tending to change the motion of a body or produce motion or stress in a stationary body. **b** the intensity of this (calculated e.g. by multiplying the mass of the body and its acceleration). **8** a person or thing regarded as exerting influence (*is a force for good*). ● *v.* **1** *tr.* constrain (a person) by force or against his or her will. **2** *tr.* make a way through or into by force; break open by force. **3** *tr.* (usu. with prep. or adv.) drive or propel violently or against resistance (*forced it into the hole; the wind forced them back*). **4** *tr.* (foll. by *on, upon*) impose or press (on a person) (*forced their views on us*). **5** *tr.* **a** cause or produce by effort (*forced a smile*). **b** attain by strength or effort (*forced an entry; must force a decision*). **c** make (a way) by force. **6** *tr.* strain or increase to the utmost; overstrain. **7** *tr.* artificially hasten the development or maturity of (a plant). **8** *tr.* seek or demand quick results from; accelerate the process of (*force the pace*). **9** *intr. Cards* make a play that compels another particular play. □ **by force of** by means of. **force the bidding** (at an auction) make bids to raise the price rapidly. **force a person's hand** make a person act prematurely or unwillingly. **force the issue** render an immediate decision necessary. **in force 1** valid, effective. **2** in great strength or numbers. **join forces** combine efforts. □ **forceable** *adj.* **forcer** *n.* [Middle English from Old French *force, forcer*, ultimately from Latin *fortis* 'strong']

force[2] /fɔːs/ *n. N.Engl.* a waterfall. [Old Norse *fors*]

forced labour *n.* compulsory labour, esp. under harsh conditions.

forced landing *n.* the unavoidable landing of an aircraft in an emergency. □ **force-land** *v.tr. & intr.*

forced march *n.* a long and vigorous march esp. by troops.

force-feed *n.* force (esp. a prisoner) to take food.

force field *n.* (in science fiction) an invisible barrier of force.

forceful /ˈfɔːsfʊl, -f(ə)l/ *adj.* **1** vigorous, powerful. **2** (of speech) compelling, impressive. □ **forcefully** *adv.* **forcefulness** *n.*

force majeure /fɔːs maˈʒəː, French fɔrs maʒœr/ *n.* **1** irresistible compulsion or coercion. **2** an unforeseeable course of events excusing a person from the fulfilment of a contract. [French, = superior strength]

forcemeat /ˈfɔːsmiːt/ *n.* meat or vegetables etc. chopped and seasoned for use as a stuffing or a garnish. [obsolete *force, farce* 'stuff' from Old French *farsir*: see FARCE]

forceps /ˈfɔːsɛps, -sɪps/ *n.* (*pl.* same) **1** surgical pincers, used for grasping and holding. **2** *Bot. & Zool.* an organ or structure resembling forceps. [Latin *forceps forcipis*]

force-pump *n.* a pump that forces water under pressure.

forcible /ˈfɔːsɪb(ə)l/ *adj.* done by or involving force; forceful. □ **forcibly** *adv.* [Middle English from Anglo-French & Old French (as FORCE[1])]

ford /fɔːd/ *n. & v.* ● *n.* a shallow place where a river or stream may be crossed by wading or in a vehicle. ● *v.tr.* cross (water) at a ford. □ **fordable** *adj.* **fordless** *adj.* [Old English from West Germanic]

fore /fɔː/ *adj., n., int., & prep.* ● *adj.* situated in front. (cf. HIND *adj.*). ● *n.* the front part, esp. of a ship; the bow. ● *int. Golf* a warning to a person in the path of a ball. ● *prep. archaic* (in oaths) in the presence of (*fore God*). □ **come to the fore** take a leading part. **to the fore** in front; conspicuous. [Old English from Germanic: the adjective and noun from Middle English, from compounds with FORE-]

fore- /fɔː/ *prefix* forming: **1** verbs meaning: **a** in front (*foreshorten*). **b** beforehand; in advance (*foreordain; forewarn*). **2** nouns meaning: **a** situated in front of (*forecourt*). **b** the front part of (*forehead*). **c** of or near the bow of a ship (*forecastle*). **d** preceding (*forerunner*). [Old English, as FORE]

fore and aft *adv. & adj.* ● *adv.* at bow and stern; all over the ship. ● *adj.* (**fore-and-aft**) (of a sail or rigging) set lengthwise, not on yards.

fore-and-aft rigged *adj.* (of a vessel) having fore-and-aft rigging (opp. SQUARE-RIGGED).

forearm[1] /ˈfɔːrɑːm/ *n.* **1** the part of the arm from the elbow to the wrist or the fingertips. **2** the corresponding part in a foreleg or wing.

forearm[2] /fɔːrˈɑːm/ *v.tr.* prepare or arm beforehand.

forebear /ˈfɔːbɛː/ *n.* (also **forbear**) (usu. in *pl.*) an ancestor. [FORE + obsolete *bear, beer* (as BE, -ER[1])]

forebode /fɔːˈbəʊd/ *v.tr.* **1** betoken; be an advance warning of (an evil or unwelcome event). **2** have a presentiment of (usu. evil).

foreboding /fɔːˈbəʊdɪŋ/ *n.* an expectation of trouble or evil; a presage or omen. □ **forebodingly** *adv.*

forebrain /ˈfɔːbreɪn/ *n. Anat.* the anterior part of the brain, including the cerebrum, thalamus, and hypothalamus. Also called *prosencephalon*.

forecast /ˈfɔːkɑːst/ *v. & n.* ● *v.tr.* (*past* and *past part.* **-cast** or **-casted**) predict; estimate or calculate beforehand. ● *n.* a calculation or estimate of something future, esp. coming weather. □ **forecaster** *n.*

forecastle /ˈfəʊks(ə)l/ *n.* (also **fo'c'sle**) *Naut.* **1** the forward part of a ship where the crew has quarters. **2** *hist.* a short raised deck at the bow.

foreclose /fɔːˈkləʊz/ *v.tr.* **1** (also *absol.*; foll. by *on*) stop (a mortgage) from being redeemable or (a mortgager) from redeeming, esp. as a result of defaults in payment. **2** exclude, prevent. **3** shut out; bar. □ **foreclosure** *n.* [Middle English via Old French *forclos*, past part. of *forclore*, from *for-* 'out' from Latin *foras* + CLOSE[2]]

forecourt /ˈfɔːkɔːt/ *n.* **1** an enclosed space in front of a building. **2** *Brit.* the part of a filling station where petrol is supplied. **3** *Tennis* the part of the court between the service line and the net.

foredeck /ˈfɔːdɛk/ *n.* **1** the deck at the forward part of a ship. **2** the forward part of the deck.

foredoom /fɔːˈduːm/ *v.tr.* (often foll. by *to*) doom or condemn beforehand.

fore-edge /ˈfɔːrɛdʒ/ *n.* (also **foredge**) the front or outer edge (esp. of the pages of a book).

forefather /ˈfɔːfɑːðə/ *n.* (usu. in *pl.*) **1** an ancestor. **2** a member of a past generation of a family or people.

forefinger /ˈfɔːfɪŋgə/ *n.* the finger next to the thumb.

forefoot /ˈfɔːfʊt/ *n.* (*pl.* **-feet**) **1** either of the front feet of a four-footed animal. **2** *Naut.* the foremost section of a ship's keel.

forefront /ˈfɔːfrʌnt/ *n.* **1** the foremost part. **2** the leading position.

foregather /fɔːˈgaðə/ *v.intr.* (also **forgather**) assemble; meet together; associate. [15th-c. Scots from Dutch *vergaderen*, assimilated to FOR-, GATHER]

forego[1] /fɔːˈgəʊ/ *v.tr. & intr.* (**-goes**; *past* **-went** /-ˈwɛnt/; *past part.* **-gone** /-ˈgɒn/) precede in place or time. □ **foregoer** *n.* [Old English *foregān*]

forego[2] var. of FORGO.

foregoing /ˈfɔːgəʊɪŋ/ *adj.* preceding; previously mentioned.

foregone /fɔːˈgɒn/ *past part.* of FOREGO[1]. ● *attrib.adj.* /ˈfɔːgɒn/ previous, preceding, completed.

foregone conclusion *n.* an easily foreseen or predictable result.

foreground /ˈfɔːgraʊnd/ *n. & v.* ● *n.* **1** the part of a view, esp. in a picture, that is nearest the observer. **2** the most conspicuous position. ● *v.tr.* place in the foreground; make prominent. [Dutch *voorgrond* (as FORE-, GROUND[1])]

forehand /ˈfɔːhand/ *n.* **1** *Tennis* etc. **a** a stroke played with the palm of the hand facing the opponent. **b** (*attrib.*) (also **forehanded**) of or made with a forehand. **2** the part of a horse in front of the seated rider.

forehead /ˈfɒrɪd, ˈfɔːhɛd/ *n.* the part of the face above the eyebrows. [Old English *forhēafod* (as FORE-, HEAD)]

forehock /ˈfɔːhɒk/ *n. Brit.* a foreleg cut of pork or bacon.

foreign /ˈfɒr(ə)n/ *adj.* **1** of or from or situated in or characteristic of a country or a language other than one's own. **2** dealing with other countries (*foreign* *service*). **3** of another district, society, etc. **4** (often foll. by *to*) unfamiliar, strange, uncharacteristic (*his behaviour is foreign to me*). **5** coming or introduced from outside (*foreign matter in the mechanism*). □ **foreignness** /'fɒr(ə)nnɪs/ *n.* [Middle English from Old French *forein, forain*, ultimately from Latin *foras, -is* 'outside': for *-g-* cf. *sovereign*]

foreign aid *n.* money, food, etc. given or lent by one country to another.

Foreign and Commonwealth Office *n.* the British government department dealing with foreign affairs.

foreign body *n.* an extraneous material object, esp. one ingested, introduced, etc., into the body.

foreigner /'fɒr(ə)nə/ *n.* **1** a person born in or coming from a foreign country. **2** esp. *dial.* a person not belonging to a particular place or group. **3 a** a foreign ship. **b** an imported animal or article.

foreign exchange *n.* **1** the currency of other countries. **2** dealings in these.

foreign legion *n.* a body of foreign volunteers in a modern, esp. the French, army.

foreign minister *n.* (also **foreign secretary**) *Brit.* a government minister in charge of his or her country's relations with other countries.

Foreign Office *n. Brit. hist.* or *colloq.* = FOREIGN AND COMMONWEALTH OFFICE.

foreign service *n. N. Amer.* = DIPLOMATIC SERVICE.

foreign trade *n.* international trade.

forejudge /fɔː'dʒʌdʒ/ *v.tr.* judge or determine before knowing the evidence.

foreknow /fɔː'nəʊ/ *v.tr.* (*past* **-knew** /-'njuː/; *past part.* **-known** /-'nəʊn/) know beforehand; have prescience of. □ **foreknowledge** /fɔː'nɒlɪdʒ/ *n.*

forelady /'fɔːleɪdi/ *n.* (*pl.* **-ies**) *US* = FOREWOMAN.

foreland /'fɔːlənd/ *n.* **1** a cape or promontory. **2** a piece of land in front of something.

foreleg /'fɔːlɛg/ *n.* either of the front legs of a quadruped.

forelimb /'fɔːlɪm/ *n.* either of the front limbs of an animal.

forelock /'fɔːlɒk/ *n.* a lock of hair growing just above the forehead. □ **take time by the forelock** seize an opportunity. **touch** (or **tug**) **one's forelock** defer to a person of higher social rank.

foreman /'fɔːmən/ *n.* (*pl.* **-men**) **1** a worker with supervisory responsibilities. **2** the member of a jury who presides over its deliberations and speaks on its behalf.

foremast /'fɔːmɑːst/ *n.* the forward (lower) mast of a ship.

foremost /'fɔːməʊst/ *adj.* & *adv.* ● *adj.* **1** the chief or most notable. **2** the most advanced in position; the front. ● *adv.* before anything else in position; in the first place (*first and foremost*). [earlier *formost, formest*, superlative of Old English *forma* 'first', assimilated to FORE, MOST]

foremother /'fɔːmʌðə/ *n.* a female ancestor or predecessor.

forename /'fɔːneɪm/ *n.* a first or Christian name.

forenoon /'fɔːnuːn/ *n. archaic* except *Law* & *Naut.* the part of the day before noon.

forensic /fə'rɛnsɪk/ *adj.* & *n.* ● *adj.* **1** of or used in connection with courts of law, esp. in relation to crime detection (*forensic evidence*). **2** of or employing forensic science. ● *n.* (usu. in *pl.*) *colloq.* forensic science. □ **forensically** *adv.* [Latin *forensis* from FORUM]

■ **Usage** The use of *forensic* in sense 2 is common, but it is considered an illogical extension of sense 1 by some people.

forensic medicine *n.* the application of medical knowledge to legal problems.

forensic science *n.* the application of biochemical and other scientific techniques to the investigation of crime.

foreordain /fɔːrɔː'deɪn/ *v.tr.* predestinate; ordain beforehand. □ **foreordination** /-dɪ'neɪʃ(ə)n/ *n.*

forepaw /'fɔːpɔː/ *n.* either of the front paws of a quadruped.

forepeak /'fɔːpiːk/ *n. Naut.* the end of the forehold in the angle of the bows.

foreplay /'fɔːpleɪ/ *n.* stimulation preceding sexual intercourse.

forequarters /'fɔːkwɔːtəz/ *n.pl.* the front legs and adjoining parts of a quadruped.

forerun /fɔː'rʌn/ *v.tr.* (**-running**; *past* **-ran** /-'ran/; *past part.* **-run**) **1** go before. **2** indicate the coming of; foreshadow.

forerunner /'fɔːrʌnə/ *n.* **1** a predecessor. **2** an advance messenger.

foresail /'fɔːseɪl, -s(ə)l/ *n. Naut.* the principal sail on a foremast (the lowest square sail, or the fore-and-aft bent on the mast, or the triangular before the mast).

foresee /fɔː'siː/ *v.tr.* (*past* **-saw** /-'sɔː/; *past part.* **-seen** /-'siːn/) (often foll. by *that* + clause) see or be aware of beforehand. □ **foreseeable** *adj.* **foreseeability** /-'bɪlɪti/ *n.* **foreseeably** *adv.* **foreseer** /-'siːə/ *n.* [Old English *foresēon* (as FORE- + SEE[1])]

foreshadow /fɔː'ʃadəʊ/ *v.tr.* be a warning or indication of (a future event).

foresheets /'fɔːʃiːts/ *n.pl. Naut.* the inner part of the bows of a boat with gratings for the bowman to stand on.

foreshock /'fɔːʃɒk/ *n.* a lesser shock preceding the main shock of an earthquake.

foreshore /'fɔːʃɔː/ *n.* the part of the shore between high and low water marks, or between the water and cultivated or developed land.

foreshorten /fɔː'ʃɔːt(ə)n/ *v.tr.* show or portray (an object) with the apparent shortening due to visual perspective.

foreshow /fɔː'ʃəʊ/ *v.tr.* (*past part.* **-shown** /-ʃəʊn/) **1** foretell. **2** foreshadow, portend, prefigure.

foresight /'fɔːsʌɪt/ *n.* **1** regard or provision for the future. **2** the process of foreseeing. **3** the front sight of a gun. **4** *Surveying* a sight taken forwards. □ **foresighted** /-'sʌɪtɪd/ *adj.* **foresightedly** /-'sʌɪtɪdli/ *adv.* **foresightedness** /-'sʌɪtɪdnɪs/ *n.* [Middle English, probably suggested by Old Norse *forsjá, forsjó* (as FORE-, SIGHT)]

foreskin /'fɔːskɪn/ *n.* the fold of skin covering the end of the penis. Also called PREPUCE.

forest /'fɒrɪst/ *n.* & *v.* ● *n.* **1 a** (often *attrib.*) a large area covered chiefly with trees and undergrowth. **b** the trees growing in it. **c** a large number or dense mass of vertical objects (*a forest of masts*). **2** a district formerly a forest but now cultivated (*Sherwood Forest*). **3** *Brit. hist.* a woodland area usu. owned by the sovereign, kept for hunting, and having its own laws. ● *v.tr.* **1** plant with trees. **2** convert into a forest. [Middle English via Old French and Late Latin *forestis silva* 'wood outside the walls of a park' from Latin *foris* 'outside']

forestall /fɔː'stɔːl/ *v.tr.* **1** act in advance of in order to prevent. **2** anticipate (the action of another, or an event). **3** anticipate the action of. **4** deal with beforehand. **5** *hist.* buy up (goods) in order to profit by an enhanced price. □ **forestaller** *n.* **forestalment** *n.* [Middle English in sense 5: cf. Anglo-Latin *forestallare* from Old English *foresteall* 'an ambush' (as FORE-, STALL[1])]

forestation /fɒrɪ'steɪʃ(ə)n/ *n.* the planting or establishing of a forest.

forestay /'fɔːsteɪ/ *n. Naut.* a stay from the head of the foremast to the ship's deck to support the foremast.

forester /'fɒrɪstə/ *n.* **1** a person in charge of a forest or skilled in forestry. **2** a person or animal living in a forest. **3** (**Forester**) *Brit.* a member of the Ancient Order of Foresters (a friendly society). [Middle English from Old French *forestier* (as FOREST)]

forestry /'fɒrɪstri/ *n.* **1** the science or management of forests. **2** wooded country; forests.

forest tree *n.* a large tree suitable for a forest.

foretaste *n.* & *v.* ● *n.* /ˈfɔːteɪst/ partial enjoyment or suffering in advance; anticipation. ● *v.tr.* /fɔːˈteɪst/ taste beforehand; anticipate the experience of.

foretell /fɔːˈtɛl/ *v.tr.* (*past* and *past part.* **-told** /-ˈtəʊld/) tell of or presage (an event etc.) before it takes place; predict, prophesy. □ **foreteller** *n.*

forethought /ˈfɔːθɔːt/ *n.* **1** care or provision for the future. **2** previous thinking or devising. **3** deliberate intention.

foretoken *n.* & *v.* ● *n.* /ˈfɔːtəʊk(ə)n/ a sign of something to come. ● *v.tr.* /fɔːˈtəʊk(ə)n/ portend; indicate beforehand. [Old English *foretācn* (as FORE-, TOKEN)]

foretold *past* and *past part.* of FORETELL.

foretop /ˈfɔːtɒp, -təp/ *n. Naut.* a platform at the top of a foremast (see TOP[1] *n.* 10).

fore-topgallant-mast *n. Naut.* the mast above the fore-topmast.

fore-topgallant-sail *n. Naut.* the sail above the fore-topsail.

fore-topmast /fɔːˈtɒpmɑːst, -məst/ *n. Naut.* the mast above the foremast.

fore-topsail /fɔːˈtɒps(ə)l, -seɪl/ *n. Naut.* the sail above the foresail.

forever /fəˈrɛvə/ *adv.* continually, persistently (*is forever complaining*) (cf. *for ever*).

forevermore /fərɛvəˈmɔː/ *adv. US* (*Brit.* **for evermore**) an emphatic form of FOREVER or *for ever* (see EVER).

forewarn /fɔːˈwɔːn/ *v.tr.* warn beforehand. □ **forewarner** *n.*

forewent *past* of FOREGO[1], FOREGO[2].

forewing /ˈfɔːwɪŋ/ *n.* either of the two front wings of a four-winged insect.

forewoman /ˈfɔːwʊmən/ *n.* (*pl.* **-women**) **1** a female worker with supervisory responsibilities. **2** a woman who presides over a jury's deliberations and speaks on its behalf.

foreword /ˈfɔːwəːd/ *n.* introductory remarks at the beginning of a book, often by a person other than the author. [FORE- + WORD, translating German *Vorwort*]

foreyard /ˈfɔːjɑːd/ *n. Naut.* the lowest yard on a foremast.

forfeit /ˈfɔːfɪt/ *n., adj.,* & *v.* ● *n.* **1** a penalty for a breach of contract or neglect; a fine. **2 a** a trivial fine for a breach of rules in clubs etc. or in games. **b** (in *pl.*) a game in which forfeits are exacted. **3** something surrendered as a penalty. **4** the process of forfeiting. **5** *Law* property or a right or privilege lost as a legal penalty. ● *adj.* lost or surrendered as a penalty. ● *v.tr.* (**forfeited**, **forfeiting**) lose the right to, be deprived of, or have to pay as a penalty. □ **forfeitable** *adj.* **forfeiter** *n.* **forfeiture** *n.* [Middle English (= crime) from Old French *forfet, forfait*, past part. of *forfaire* 'transgress' from Latin *foris* 'outside' + *faire* from Latin *facere* 'do']

forfend /fɔːˈfɛnd/ *v.tr.* **1** *US* protect by precautions. **2** *archaic* avert; keep off.

forgather var. of FOREGATHER.

forgave *past* of FORGIVE.

forge[1] /fɔːdʒ/ *v.* & *n.* ● *v.tr.* **1 a** *Brit.* make (money etc.) in fraudulent imitation. **b** write (a document or signature) in order to pass it off as written by another. **2** fabricate, invent. **3** shape (esp. metal) by heating in a fire and hammering. ● *n.* **1** a blacksmith's workshop; a smithy. **2 a** a furnace or hearth for melting or refining metal. **b** a workshop containing this. □ **forgeable** *adj.* **forger** *n.* [Middle English via Old French *forge* (*n.*), *forger* (*v.*) from Latin *fabricare* FABRICATE]

forge[2] /fɔːdʒ/ *v.intr.* move forward gradually or steadily. □ **forge ahead 1** take the lead in a race. **2** move forward or make progress rapidly. [18th c.: perhaps an aberrant pronunciation of FORCE[1]]

forgery /ˈfɔːdʒ(ə)ri/ *n.* (*pl.* **-ies**) **1** the act or an instance of forging, counterfeiting, or falsifying a document etc. **2** a forged or spurious thing, esp. a document or signature.

forget /fəˈgɛt/ *v.* (**forgetting**; *past* **forgot** /-ˈgɒt/; *past part.* **forgotten** /-ˈgɒt(ə)n/ or esp. *US* **forgot**) **1** *tr.* & (often foll. by *about*) *intr.* lose the remembrance of; not remember (a person or thing). **2** *tr.* (foll. by clause or *to* + infin.) not remember; neglect (*forgot to come*; *forgot how to do it*). **3** *tr.* inadvertently omit to bring or mention or attend to. **4** *tr.* (also *absol.*) put out of mind; cease to think of (*forgive and forget*). □ **forget oneself 1** neglect one's own interests. **2** act unbecomingly or unworthily. □ **forgettable** *adj.* **forgetter** *n.* [Old English *forgietan* from West Germanic (as FOR-, GET)]

forgetful /fəˈgɛtfʊl, -f(ə)l/ *adj.* **1** apt to forget, absent-minded. **2** (often foll. by *of*) forgetting, neglectful. □ **forgetfully** *adj.* **forgetfulness** *n.*

forget-me-not *n.* any plant of the genus *Myosotis*, esp. *M. scorpioides* with small yellow-eyed bright blue flowers.

forgive /fəˈgɪv/ *v.tr.* (also *absol.* or with double object) (*past* **forgave**; *past part.* **forgiven**) **1** cease to feel angry or resentful towards; pardon (an offender or offence) (*forgive us our mistakes*). **2** remit or let off (a debt or debtor). □ **forgivable** *adj.* **forgivably** *adv.* **forgiver** *n.* [Old English *forgiefan* (as FOR-, GIVE)]

forgiveness /fəˈgɪvnɪs/ *n.* the act of forgiving; the state of being forgiven. [Old English *forgiefenes* (as FORGIVE)]

forgiving /fəˈgɪvɪŋ/ *adj.* inclined readily to forgive. □ **forgivingly** *adv.*

forgo /fɔːˈgəʊ, fə-/ *v.tr.* (also **forego**) (**-goes** /-ˈgəʊz/; *past* **-went** /-ˈwɛnt/; *past part.* **-gone** /-ˈgɒn/) **1** abstain from; go without; relinquish. **2** omit or decline to take or use (a pleasure, advantage, etc.). [Old English *forgān* (as FOR-, GO[1])]

forgot *past* of FORGET.

forgotten *past part.* of FORGET.

forint /ˈfɒrɪnt/ *n.* the chief monetary unit of Hungary. [Hungarian from Italian *fiorino*: see FLORIN]

fork /fɔːk/ *n.* & *v.* ● *n.* **1** an instrument with two or more prongs used in eating or cooking. **2** a similar much larger instrument used for digging, lifting, etc. **3** any pronged device or component (*tuning fork*). **4** a forked support for a bicycle wheel. **5 a** a divergence of anything, e.g. a stick or road, or *N. Amer.* a river, into two parts. **b** the place where this occurs. **c** either of the two parts (*take the left fork*). **6** a flash of forked lightning. **7** *Chess* a simultaneous attack on two pieces by one. ● *v.* **1** *intr.* form a fork or branch by separating into two parts. **2** *intr.* take one or other road etc. at a fork (*fork left for Banbury*). **3** *tr.* dig or lift etc. with a fork. **4** *tr. Chess* attack (two pieces) simultaneously with one. □ **fork out** (or **up**) *colloq.* hand over or pay, usu. reluctantly. **fork over 1** turn over (soil etc.) with a fork. **2** *colloq.* = *fork out.* [Old English *forca, force* from Latin *furca*]

forked /fɔːkt/ *adj.* **1** having a fork or forklike end or branches. **2** divergent, cleft. **3** (in *comb.*) having so many prongs (*three-forked*).

forked lightning *n.* a lightning flash in the form of a zigzag or branching line.

fork-lift truck *n.* a vehicle with a horizontal fork in front for lifting and carrying loads.

fork lunch *n.* (also **fork supper** etc.) *Brit.* a light meal eaten with a fork at a buffet etc.

forlorn /fəˈlɔːn/ *adj.* **1** sad and abandoned or lonely. **2** in a pitiful state; of wretched appearance. **3** desperate, hopeless, forsaken. □ **forlornly** *adv.* **forlornness** /fəˈlɔːnnɪs/ *n.* [past part. of obsolete *forlese* from Old English *forlēosan* (as FOR-, LOSE)]

forlorn hope *n.* **1** a faint remaining hope or chance. **2** a desperate enterprise. [Dutch *verloren hoop* 'lost troop', originally of a storming-party etc.]

form /fɔːm/ *n.* & *v.* ● *n.* **1 a** a shape; an arrangement of parts. **b** the outward aspect (esp. apart from colour) or shape of a body. **2** a person or animal as visible or tangible (*the familiar form of the postman*). **3** the mode in which a thing exists or manifests itself (*took the form of a book*). **4** a species, kind, or variety. **5 a** a printed document with blank spaces for information to be inserted. **b** a regularly drawn document. **6** esp. *Brit.* a class in a school. **7** a customary method; what is usually done (*common form*). **8** a set order of words; a formula. **9** behaviour according to a rule or custom. **10** (prec. by *the*) correct procedure (*knows the form*). **11 a** (of an athlete, horse, etc.) condition of health and training (*is in top form*). **b** *Racing* details of previous performances. **12** general state or disposition (*was in great form*). **13** *Brit. slang* a criminal record. **14** formality or mere ceremony. **15** *Gram.* **a** one of the ways in which a word may be spelt or pronounced or inflected. **b** the external characteristics of words apart from meaning. **16** arrangement and style in literary or musical composition. **17** *Philos.* the essential nature of a species or thing. **18** *Brit.* a long bench without a back. **19** esp. *US Printing* = FORME. **20** *Brit.* a hare's lair. **21** = SUTTERING 1. ● *v.* **1** *tr.* make or fashion into a certain shape or form. **2** *intr.* take a certain shape; be formed. **3** *tr.* be the material of; make up or constitute (*together form a unit*; *forms part of the structure*). **4** *tr.* train or instruct. **5** *tr.* develop or establish as a concept, institution, or practice (*form an idea*; *formed an alliance*; *form a habit*). **6** *tr.* (foll. by *into*) embody, organize. **7** *tr.* articulate (a word). **8** *tr.* & *intr.* (often foll. by *up*) esp. *Mil.* bring or be brought into a certain arrangement or formation. **9** *tr.* construct (a new word) by derivation, inflection, etc. □ **in form** fit for racing etc. **off form** esp. *Brit.* not playing or performing well. **on form** esp. *Brit.* playing or performing well. **out of form** not fit for racing etc. [Middle English via Old French *forme* from Latin *forma* 'mould, form']

-form /fɔːm/ *comb. form* (usu. as **-iform**) forming adjectives meaning: **1** having the form of (*cruciform*; *cuneiform*). **2** having such a number of (*uniform*; *multiform*). [from or suggested by French *-forme* from Latin *-formis*, from *forma* FORM]

formal /ˈfɔːm(ə)l/ *adj.* & *n.* ● *adj.* **1** used or done or held in accordance with rules, convention, or ceremony (*formal dress*; *a formal occasion*). **2** ceremonial; required by convention (*a formal call*). **3** precise or symmetrical (*a formal garden*). **4** prim or stiff in manner. **5** perfunctory, having the form without the spirit. **6** valid or correctly so called because of its form; explicit and definite (*a formal agreement*). **7** in accordance with recognized forms or rules. **8** of or concerned with (outward) form or appearance, esp. as distinct from content or matter. **9** *Logic* concerned with the form and not the matter of reasoning. **10** *Philos.* of the essence of a thing; essential not material. ● *n. N. Amer.* **1** an evening dress. **2** an occasion on which evening dress is worn. □ **formally** *adv.* [Middle English from Latin *formalis* (as FORM)]

formaldehyde /fɔːˈmaldɪhʌɪd/ *n.* a colourless pungent gas used as a disinfectant and preservative and in the manufacture of synthetic resins (also called *methanal*). Chem. formula: CH_2O. [FORMIC ACID + ALDEHYDE]

formalin /ˈfɔːm(ə)lɪn/ *n.* a colourless solution of formaldehyde in water used as a preservative for biological specimens etc.

formalism /ˈfɔːm(ə)lɪz(ə)m/ *n.* **1 a** excessive adherence to prescribed forms. **b** the use of forms without regard to inner significance. **2** *derog.* an artist's concentration on form at the expense of content. **3** the treatment of mathematics as a manipulation of meaningless symbols. **4** *Theatr.* a symbolic and stylized manner of production. **5** *Physics* & *Math.* the mathematical description of a physical situation etc. □ **formalist** *n.* **formalistic** /-ˈlɪstɪk/ *adj.*

formality /fɔːˈmalɪti/ *n.* (*pl.* **-ies**) **1 a** a formal or ceremonial act, requirement of etiquette, regulation, or custom (often with an implied lack of real significance). **b** a thing done simply to comply with a rule. **2** the rigid observance of rules or convention. **3** ceremony; elaborate procedure. **4** being formal; precision of manners. **5** stiffness of design. [French *formalité* or medieval Latin *formalitas* (as FORMAL)]

formalize /ˈfɔːm(ə)lʌɪz/ *v.tr.* (also **-ise**) **1** give definite shape or legal formality to. **2** make ceremonious, precise, or rigid; imbue with formalism. □ **formalization** /-ˈzeɪʃ(ə)n/ *n.*

formant /ˈfɔːm(ə)nt/ *n.* **1** *Phonet.* the characteristic pitch-constituent of a vowel. **2** *Linguistics* a morpheme occurring only in combination in a word or word-stem. [German, from Latin *formare formant-* 'to form']

format /ˈfɔːmat/ *n.* & *v.* ● *n.* **1** the shape and size of a book, periodical, etc. **2** the style or manner of an arrangement or procedure. **3** *Computing* a defined structure for holding data etc. in a record for processing or storage. ● *v.tr.* (**formatted**, **formatting**) **1** arrange or put into a format. **2** *Computing* prepare (a storage medium) to receive data. [French via German from Latin *formatus* (*liber*) 'shaped (book)', past part. of *formare* FORM]

formate /ˈfɔːmeɪt/ *n. Chem.* a salt or ester of formic acid.

formation /fɔːˈmeɪʃ(ə)n/ *n.* **1** the act or an instance of forming; the process of being formed. **2** a thing formed. **3** a structure or arrangement of parts. **4** a particular arrangement, e.g. of troops, aircraft in flight, etc. (also *attrib.*: *formation dancing*; *formation flying*). **5** *Geol.* an assemblage of rocks or series of strata having some common characteristic. □ **formational** *adj.* [Middle English from Old French *formation* or Latin *formatio* (as FORM)]

formative /ˈfɔːmətɪv/ *adj.* & *n.* ● *adj.* **1** serving to form or fashion; of formation. **2** *Gram.* (of a flexional or derivative suffix or prefix) used in forming words. ● *n. Gram.* a formative element. □ **formatively** *adv.* [Middle English from Old French *formatif -ive* or medieval Latin *formativus* (as FORM)]

form class *n.* a class of linguistic forms with grammatical or syntactical features in common.

form criticism *n.* textual analysis of the Bible etc. by tracing the history of its content by forms (e.g. proverbs, myths).

forme /fɔːm/ *n.* (*US* **form**) *Printing* **1** a body of type secured in a chase for printing. **2** a quantity of film arranged for making a plate etc. [variant of FORM]

former[1] /ˈfɔːmə/ *attrib.adj.* **1** of or occurring in the past or an earlier period (*in former times*). **2** having been previously (*her former husband*). **3** (prec. by *the*; often *absol.*) the first or first mentioned of two (opp. LATTER 1). [Middle English from *forme* 'first', influenced by FOREMOST]

former[2] /ˈfɔːmə/ *n.* **1** a person or thing that forms. **2** *Electr.* a frame or core for winding a coil on. **3** *Aeron.* a transverse strengthening member in a wing or fuselage. **4** (in *comb.*) *Brit.* a pupil of a specified form in a school (*fourth-former*).

formerly /ˈfɔːməli/ *adv.* in the past; in former times.

Formica /fɔːˈmʌɪkə/ *n. propr.* a hard durable plastic laminate used for working surfaces, cupboard doors, etc. [20th c.: origin uncertain]

formic acid /ˈfɔːmɪk/ *n.* a colourless irritant volatile acid contained in the fluid emitted by some ants (also called *methanoic acid*). Chem. formula: HCOOH. [Latin *formica* 'ant']

formication /fɔːmɪˈkeɪʃ(ə)n/ *n.* a sensation as of ants crawling over the skin. [Latin *formicatio* from *formica* 'ant']

formidable /ˈfɔːmɪdəb(ə)l, *disp.* fɔːˈmɪd-/ *adj.* **1** inspiring fear or dread. **2** inspiring respect or awe. **3** likely to be hard to overcome, resist, or deal with. □ **formidableness** *n.* **formidably** *adv.* [French *formidable* or Latin *formidabilis* from *formidare* 'fear']

■ **Usage** The second pronunciation given, with the stress on the second syllable, is common but considered incorrect by some people.

formless /ˈfɔːmlɪs/ *adj.* shapeless; without determinate or regular form. □ **formlessly** *adv.* **formlessness** *n.*

form letter *n.* a standardized letter to deal with frequently occurring matters.

formula /ˈfɔːmjʊlə/ *n.* (*pl.* **formulas** or (esp. in senses 1, 2) **formulae** /-liː/) **1** *Chem.* a set of chemical symbols showing the constituents of a substance and their relative proportions. **2** *Math.* a mathematical rule expressed in symbols. **3 a** a fixed form of words, esp. one used on social or ceremonial occasions. **b** a rule unintelligently or slavishly followed; an established or conventional usage. **c** a form of words embodying or enabling agreement, resolution of a dispute, etc. **4 a** a list of ingredients; a recipe. **b** esp. *N. Amer.* an infant's liquid food preparation, given as a substitute for breast milk. **5** a classification of racing car, esp. by the engine capacity. ▫ **formulaic** /-ˈleɪɪk/ *adj.* **formularize** *v.tr.* (also **-ise**). **formulize** *v.tr.* (also **-ise**). [Latin, diminutive of *forma* FORM]

formulary /ˈfɔːmjʊləri/ *n.* & *adj.* ● *n.* (*pl.* **-ies**) **1** a collection of formulas or set forms, esp. for religious use. **2** *Pharm.* a compendium of formulae used in the preparation of medicinal drugs. ● *adj.* **1** using formulae. **2** in or of formulae. [noun from French *formulaire* or medieval Latin *formularius* (*liber* 'book') from Latin (as FORMULA): the adjective from FORMULA]

formulate /ˈfɔːmjʊleɪt/ *v.tr.* **1** express in a formula. **2** express clearly and precisely. ▫ **formulation** /-ˈleɪʃ(ə)n/ *n.* **formulator** *n.*

formulism /ˈfɔːmjʊlɪz(ə)m/ *n.* adherence to or dependence on conventional formulas. ▫ **formulistic** /-ˈlɪstɪk/ *adj.*

formwork /ˈfɔːmwəːk/ *n.* = SHUTTERING 1.

fornicate /ˈfɔːnɪkeɪt/ *v.intr. archaic* or *joc.* (of people not married or not married to each other) have sexual intercourse voluntarily. ▫ **fornication** /-ˈkeɪʃ(ə)n/ *n.* **fornicator** *n.* [ecclesiastical Latin *fornicari* from Latin *fornix -icis* 'brothel']

forrader /ˈfɒrədə/ *colloq. compar.* of FORWARD.

forsake /fəˈseɪk/ *v.tr.* (*past* **forsook** /-ˈsʊk/; *past part.* **forsaken** /-ˈseɪk(ə)n/) **1** give up; break off from; renounce. **2** withdraw one's help, friendship, or companionship from; desert, abandon. ▫ **forsakenness** /fəˈseɪk(ə)nnɪs/ *n.* **forsaker** *n.* [Old English *forsacan* 'deny, renounce, refuse', from West Germanic, from the base of FOR- + Old English *sacan* 'quarrel']

forsooth /fəˈsuːθ/ *adv. archaic* or *joc.* truly; in truth; no doubt. [Old English *forsōth* (as FOR, SOOTH)]

forswear /fɔːˈswɛː, fə-/ *v.tr.* (*past* **forswore** /-ˈswɔː/; *past part.* **forsworn** /-ˈswɔːn/) **1** abjure; renounce on oath. **2** (*refl.* or in *passive*) swear falsely; commit perjury. [Old English *forswerian* (as FOR-, SWEAR)]

forsythia /fɔːˈsʌɪθɪə, fə-/ *n.* any ornamental shrub of the genus *Forsythia* bearing bright yellow flowers in early spring. [modern Latin, named after W. *Forsyth*, English botanist d. 1804]

fort /fɔːt/ *n.* **1** a fortified building or position. **2** *hist.* a trading station, originally fortified. [French *fort* or Italian *forte* from Latin *fortis* 'strong']

forte[1] /ˈfɔːteɪ, ˈfɔːti, fɔːt/ *n.* **1** a person's strong point; a thing in which a person excels. **2** *Fencing* the part of a sword blade from the hilt to the middle (cf. FOIBLE 2). [French *fort* 'strong' from Latin *fortis*]

forte[2] /ˈfɔːti/ *adj., adv.,* & *n. Mus.* ● *adj.* performed loudly. ● *adv.* loudly. ● *n.* a passage to be performed loudly. [Italian, = strong, loud]

fortepiano /ˌfɔːtɪpɪˈanəʊ/ *n.* (*pl.* **-os**) *Mus.* = PIANOFORTE (esp. with reference to an instrument of the 18th to early 19th centuries). [FORTE[2] + PIANO[2]]

forte piano *adj.* & *adv. Mus.* loud and then immediately soft.

forth /fɔːθ/ *adv. archaic* except in set phrases and after certain verbs, esp. *bring, come, go,* and *set.* **1** forward; into view. **2** onwards in time (*from this time forth*; *henceforth*). **3** forwards. **4** out from a starting point (*set forth*). ▫ **and so forth** and so on; and the like. [Old English from Germanic]

forthcoming /fɔːθˈkʌmɪŋ/ *adj.* **1 a** about or likely to appear or become available. **b** approaching. **2** produced when wanted (*no reply was forthcoming*). **3** (of a person) informative, responsive. ▫ **forthcomingness** *n.*

forthright /ˈfɔːθrʌɪt, fɔːθˈrʌɪt/ *adj.* & *adv.* ● *adj.* **1** direct and outspoken; straightforward. **2** decisive, unhesitating. ● *adv.* in a direct manner; bluntly. ▫ **forthrightly** *adv.* **forthrightness** *n.* [Old English *forthriht* (as FORTH, RIGHT)]

forthwith /fɔːθˈwɪθ, -ð/ *adv.* immediately; without delay. [earlier *forthwithal* (as FORTH, WITH, ALL)]

fortification /ˌfɔːtɪfɪˈkeɪʃ(ə)n/ *n.* **1** the act or an instance of fortifying; the process of being fortified. **2** *Mil.* **a** the art or science of fortifying. **b** (usu. in *pl.*) defensive works fortifying a position. [Middle English via French from Late Latin *fortificatio -onis* 'act of strengthening' (as FORTIFY)]

fortify /ˈfɔːtɪfʌɪ/ *v.tr.* (**-ies**, **-ied**) **1** provide or equip with defensive works so as to strengthen against attack. **2** strengthen or invigorate mentally or morally; encourage. **3** strengthen the structure of. **4** strengthen (wine) with alcohol. **5** increase the nutritive value of (food, esp. with vitamins). ▫ **fortifiable** *adj.* **fortifier** *n.* [Middle English via Old French *fortifier* and Late Latin *fortificare* from Latin *fortis* 'strong']

fortissimo /fɔːˈtɪsɪməʊ/ *adj., adv.,* & *n. Mus.* ● *adj.* performed very loudly. ● *adv.* very loudly. ● *n.* (*pl.* **-os** or **fortissimi** /-mi/) a passage to be performed very loudly. [Italian, superlative of FORTE[2]]

fortitude /ˈfɔːtɪtjuːd/ *n.* courage in pain or adversity. [Middle English via French from Latin *fortitudo -dinis*, from *fortis* 'strong']

fortnight /ˈfɔːtnʌɪt/ *n.* **1** a period of two weeks. **2** (prec. by a specified day) *Brit.* two weeks from (that day) (*Tuesday fortnight*). [Old English *fēowertīene niht* 'fourteen nights']

fortnightly /ˈfɔːtnʌɪtli/ *adj., adv.,* & *n.* esp. *Brit.* ● *adj.* done, produced, or occurring once a fortnight. ● *adv.* every fortnight. ● *n.* (*pl.* **-ies**) a magazine etc. issued every fortnight.

Fortran /ˈfɔːtran/ *n.* (also **FORTRAN**) *Computing* a high-level programming language used esp. for scientific calculations. [*for*mula *tran*slation]

fortress /ˈfɔːtrɪs/ *n.* a military stronghold, esp. a strongly fortified town fit for a large garrison. [Middle English from Old French *forteresse*, ultimately from Latin *fortis* 'strong']

fortuitous /fɔːˈtjuːɪtəs/ *adj.* due to or characterized by chance; accidental, casual. ▫ **fortuitously** *adv.* **fortuitousness** *n.* [Latin *fortuitus* from *forte* 'by chance']

fortuity /fɔːˈtjuːɪti/ *n.* (*pl.* **-ies**) **1** a chance occurrence. **2** accident or chance; fortuitousness.

fortunate /ˈfɔːtʃ(ə)nət/ *adj.* **1** favoured by fortune; lucky, prosperous. **2** auspicious, favourable. [Middle English from Latin *fortunatus* (as FORTUNE)]

fortunately /ˈfɔːtʃ(ə)nətli/ *adv.* **1** luckily, successfully. **2** (qualifying a whole sentence) it is fortunate that.

fortune /ˈfɔːtʃuːn, -tʃ(ə)n/ *n.* **1 a** chance or luck as a force in human affairs. **b** a person's destiny. **2** (**Fortune**) this force personified, often as a deity. **3** (in *sing.* or *pl.*) the good or bad luck that befalls a person or an enterprise. **4** good luck. **5** prosperity; a prosperous condition. **6** (also *colloq.* **small fortune**) great wealth; a huge sum of money. ▫ **make a** (or **one's**) **fortune** acquire wealth or prosperity. **tell a person's fortune** make predictions about a person's future. [Middle English via Old French from Latin *fortuna* 'luck, chance']

Fortune 500 *attrib.adj. US* designating the five hundred most profitable US industrial corporations.

fortune cookie *n. N. Amer.* a small biscuit containing a prediction etc. on a slip of paper.

fortune hunter *n. colloq.* a person seeking wealth by marriage.

fortune-teller *n.* a person who claims to predict future events in a person's life. ▫ **fortune-telling** *n.*

forty /ˈfɔːti/ *n. & adj.* ● *n.* (*pl.* **-ies**) **1** the product of four and ten. **2** a symbol for this (40, xl, XL). **3** (in *pl.*) the numbers from 40 to 49, esp. the years of a century or of a person's life. **4** (**the Forties**) *Brit.* the sea area between the NE coast of Scotland and the SW coast of Norway (so called from its depth of forty fathoms or more). ● *adj.* that amount to forty. □ **forty-first, -second**, etc. the ordinal numbers between fortieth and fiftieth. **the Forty-five** the Jacobite rebellion of 1745. **forty-one, -two**, etc. the cardinal numbers between forty and fifty. □ **fortieth** *adj. & n.* **fortyfold** *adj. & adv.* [Old English *fēowertig* (as FOUR, -TY[2])]

forty-five *n.* a gramophone record played at 45 r.p.m.

forty-niner *n.* a seeker for gold etc. in the Californian gold rush of 1849.

forty winks *n.pl. colloq.* a short sleep.

forum /ˈfɔːrəm/ *n.* **1** a place of or meeting for public discussion. **2** a periodical etc. giving an opportunity for discussion. **3** a court or tribunal. **4** *hist.* a public square or market place in an ancient Roman city used for judicial and other business. [Latin, in sense 4]

forward /ˈfɔːwəd/ *adj., n., adv., & v.* ● *adj.* **1** lying in one's line of motion. **2 a** onward or towards the front. **b** *Naut.* belonging to the forepart of a ship. **3** precocious; bold in manner; presumptuous. **4 a** *Commerce* relating to future produce, delivery, etc. (*forward contract*). **b** prospective; advanced; with a view to the future (*forward planning*). **5 a** advanced; progressing towards or approaching maturity or completion. **b** (of a plant etc.) well advanced or early. ● *n.* an attacking player positioned near the front of a team in football, hockey, etc. ● *adv.* **1** to the front; into prominence (*come forward*; *move forward*). **2** in advance; ahead (*sent them forward*). **3** onward so as to make progress (*not getting any further forward*). **4** towards the future; continuously onwards (*from this time forward*). **5** (also **forwards**) **a** towards the front in the direction one is facing. **b** in the normal direction of motion or of traversal. **c** with continuous forward motion (*backwards and forwards*; *rushing forward*). **6** *Naut.* & *Aeron.* in, near, or towards the bow or nose. ● *v.tr.* **1 a** send (a letter etc.) on to a further destination. **b** esp. *Brit.* dispatch (goods etc.) (*forwarding agent*). **2** help to advance; promote. □ **forwarder** *n.* **forwardly** *adv.* **forwardness** *n.* (esp. in sense 3 of *adj.*). [Old English *forweard*, variant of *forthweard* (as FORTH, -WARD)]

forward-looking *adj.* progressive; favouring change.

forwards var. of FORWARD *adv.* 5.

forwent *past* of FORGO.

fossa /ˈfɒsə/ *n.* (*pl.* **fossae** /-siː/) *Anat.* a shallow depression or cavity. [Latin, = 'ditch', fem. past part. of *fodere* 'dig']

fosse /fɒs/ *n.* **1** a long narrow trench or excavation, esp. in a fortification. **2** *Anat.* = FOSSA. [Middle English via Old French from Latin *fossa*: see FOSSA]

fossick /ˈfɒsɪk/ *v.intr. Austral. & NZ colloq.* **1** (foll. by *about, around*) rummage, search. **2** search for gold etc. in abandoned workings. □ **fossicker** *n.* [19th c.: cf. dialect *fossick* 'bustle about']

fossil /ˈfɒs(ə)l, -sɪl/ *n. & adj.* ● *n.* **1** the remains or impression of a prehistoric plant or animal, usu. petrified while embedded in rock, amber, etc. (often *attrib.*: *fossil bones*; *fossil shells*). **2** *colloq.* an antiquated or unchanging person or thing. **3** a word that has become obsolete except in set phrases or forms, e.g. *hue* in *hue and cry*. ● *adj.* **1** of or like a fossil. **2** antiquated; out of date. □ **fossiliferous** /fɒsɪˈlɪf(ə)rəs/ *adj.* **fossilize** *v.tr. & intr.* (also **-ise**). **fossilization** /-ˈzeɪʃ(ə)n/ *n.* [French *fossile* from Latin *fossilis*, from *fodere foss-* 'dig']

fossil fuel *n.* a natural fuel such as coal or gas formed in the geological past from the remains of living organisms.

fossil ivory *n.* ivory from the tusks of a mammoth.

fossorial /fɒˈsɔːrɪəl/ *adj.* **1** (of animals) burrowing. **2** (of limbs etc.) used in burrowing. [medieval Latin *fossorius* from *fossor* 'digger' (as FOSSIL)]

foster /ˈfɒstə/ *v. & adj.* ● *v.tr.* **1 a** promote the growth or development of. **b** encourage or harbour (a feeling). **2** (of circumstances) be favourable to. **3 a** bring up (a child that is not one's own by birth). **b** (often foll. by *out*) *Brit.* (of a local authority etc.) assign (a child) to be fostered. **4** cherish; have affectionate regard for (an idea, scheme, etc.). ● *adj.* **1** having a family connection by fostering and not by birth (*foster brother*; *foster child*; *foster parent*). **2** involving or concerned with fostering a child (*foster care*; *foster home*). □ **fosterage** *n.* (esp. in sense 3 of *v.*). **fosterer** *n.* [Old English *fōstrian*, *fōster*, related to FOOD]

fosterling /ˈfɒstəlɪŋ/ *n.* a foster child; a nursling or protégé. [Old English *fōsterling* (as FOSTER)]

fouetté /ˈfwɛteɪ/ *n. Ballet* a quick whipping movement of the raised leg. [French, past part. of *fouetter* 'whip']

fought *past* and *past part.* of FIGHT.

foul /faʊl/ *adj., n., adv., & v.* ● *adj.* **1** offensive to the senses; loathsome, stinking. **2** dirty, soiled, filthy. **3** *colloq.* revolting, disgusting. **4 a** containing or charged with noxious matter (*foul air*). **b** clogged, choked. **5** morally polluted; disgustingly abusive or offensive (*foul language*; *foul deeds*). **6** unfair; against the rules of a game etc. (*by fair means or foul*). **7** (of the weather) wet, rough, stormy. **8** (of a rope etc.) entangled. **9** (of a ship's bottom) overgrown with weeds, barnacles, etc. ● *n.* **1** *Sport* an unfair or invalid stroke or piece of play. **2** a collision or entanglement, esp. in riding, rowing, or running. **3** a foul thing. ● *adv.* unfairly; contrary to the rules. ● *v.* **1** *tr. & intr.* make or become foul or dirty. **2** *tr.* (of an animal) make dirty with excrement. **3** *Sport* **a** *tr.* commit a foul against (a player). **b** *intr.* commit a foul. **4 a** *tr.* (often foll. by *up*) cause (an anchor, cable, etc.) to become entangled or muddled. **b** *intr.* become entangled. **5** *tr.* jam or block (a crossing, railway line, or traffic). **6** *tr.* (usu. foll. by *up*) *colloq.* spoil or bungle. **7** *tr.* run foul of; collide with. **8** *tr.* pollute with guilt; dishonour. □ **foully** *adv.* **foulness** *n.* [Old English *fūl*, from Germanic]

foulard /ˈfuːlɑː, -ɑːd/ *n.* **1** a thin soft material of silk or silk and cotton. **2** an article made of this. [French]

foul brood *n.* a fatal disease of larval bees caused by bacteria.

foul mouth *n.* a person who uses foul language. □ **foul-mouthed** *adj.*

foul play *n.* **1** unfair play in games. **2** treacherous or violent activity, esp. murder.

foul-up *n.* a muddled or bungled situation.

foumart /ˈfuːmət, -mɑːt/ *n.* a polecat. [Middle English *fulmert* etc. (as FOUL, *mart* MARTEN)]

found[1] *past* and *past part.* of FIND.

found[2] /faʊnd/ *v.* **1** *tr.* **a** establish (esp. with an endowment). **b** originate or initiate (an institution). **2** *tr.* be the original builder or begin the building of (a town etc.). **3** *tr.* lay the base of (a building etc.). **4** (foll. by *on, upon*) **a** *tr.* construct or base (a story, theory, rule, etc.) according to a specified principle or ground. **b** *intr.* have a basis in. [Middle English via Old French *fonder* from Latin *fundare*, from *fundus* 'bottom']

found[3] /faʊnd/ *v.tr.* **1 a** melt and mould (metal). **b** fuse (materials for glass). **2** make by founding. □ **founder** *n.* [Middle English via Old French *fondre* from Latin *fundere fus-* 'pour']

foundation /faʊnˈdeɪʃ(ə)n/ *n.* **1 a** the solid ground or base, natural or artificial, on which a building rests. **b** (usu. in *pl.*) the lowest load-bearing part of a building, usu. below ground level. **2** a body or ground on which other parts are overlaid. **3** a basis or underlying principle; groundwork (*the report has no foundation*). **4 a** the act or an instance of establishing or constituting (esp. an endowed institution) on a permanent basis. **b** such an institution, e.g. a monastery, college, or hospital. **5** (in full **foundation garment**) a woman's supporting undergarment, e.g. a corset. □ **foundational** *adj.* [Middle English via Old French *fondation* from Latin *fundatio -onis* (as FOUND[2])]

foundation course *n.* a preliminary basic course of study.

foundation cream *n.* a cream used as a base for applying cosmetics.

foundation stone *n.* **1** a stone laid with ceremony to celebrate the founding of a building. **2** the main ground or basis of something.

founder[1] /ˈfaʊndə/ *n.* a person who founds an institution.

founder[2] /ˈfaʊndə/ *v. & n.* ● *v.* **1 a** *intr.* (of a ship) fill with water and sink. **b** *tr.* cause (a ship) to founder. **2** *intr.* (of a plan etc.) fail. **3** *intr.* (of earth, a building, etc.) fall down or in, give way. **4 a** *intr.* (of a horse or its rider) fall to the ground, fall from lameness, stick fast in mud etc. **b** *tr.* cause (a horse) to break down, esp. with founder. ● *n.* **1** inflammation of a horse's foot from overwork. **2** rheumatism of the chest muscles in horses. [Middle English from Old French *fondrer*, *esfondrer* 'submerge, collapse', ultimately from Latin *fundus* 'bottom']

founding father /ˈfaʊndɪŋ/ *n.* a person associated with a founding, esp. an American statesman at the time of the Revolution.

foundling /ˈfaʊndlɪŋ/ *n.* an abandoned infant of unknown parentage. [Middle English, perhaps from obsolete *funding* (as FIND, -ING[3]), assimilated to -LING[1]]

foundry /ˈfaʊndri/ *n.* (*pl.* **-ies**) a workshop for or a business of casting metal.

fount[1] /faʊnt/ *n. poet.* a spring or fountain; a source. [back-formation from FOUNTAIN, suggested by MOUNT[2]]

fount[2] *Brit.* var. of FONT[2].

fountain /ˈfaʊntɪn/ *n.* **1 a** a jet or jets of water made to spout for ornamental purposes or for drinking. **b** a structure provided for this. **2** a structure for the constant public supply of drinking water. **3** a natural spring of water. **4** a source (in physical or abstract senses). **5** = SODA FOUNTAIN. **6** a reservoir for oil, ink, etc. □ **fountained** *adj.* (also in *comb.*). [Middle English via Old French *fontaine* from Late Latin *fontana*, fem. of Latin *fontanus* (*adj.*), from *fons fontis* 'a spring']

fountainhead /ˈfaʊntɪnhɛd/ *n.* an original source.

fountain pen *n.* a pen with a reservoir or cartridge holding ink.

four /fɔː/ *n. & adj.* ● *n.* **1** one more than three, or six less than ten; the product of two units and two units. **2** a symbol for this (4, iv, IV, rarely iiii, IIII). **3** a size etc. denoted by four. **4** a four-oared rowing boat or its crew. **5** four o'clock. **6** a card with four pips. **7** a hit at cricket scoring four runs. ● *adj.* that amount to four. □ **on all fours** on hands and knees. [Old English *fēower*, from Germanic]

fourchette /fʊəˈʃɛt/ *n. Anat.* a thin fold of skin at the back of the vulva. [French, diminutive of *fourche* (as FORK)]

four-eyes *n. slang* a person wearing glasses.

four-flush *n. US* a poker hand of little value, having four cards of the same suit and one of another.

four-flusher *n. US* a bluffer or humbug.

fourfold /ˈfɔːfəʊld/ *adj. & adv.* **1** four times as much or as many. **2** consisting of four parts. **3** amounting to four.

four freedoms *n.pl.* (prec. by *the*) freedom of speech and religion, and freedom from fear and want.

four hundred *n. US* the social elite of a community.

Fourier analysis /ˈfʊrɪə, -rɪeɪ/ *n. Math.* the resolution of periodic data into harmonic functions using a Fourier series. [named after J. B. J. *Fourier*, French mathematician d. 1830]

Fourier series /ˈfʊrɪə, -rɪeɪ/ *n. Math.* an expansion of a periodic function as a series of trigonometric functions.

four-in-hand *n.* **1** a vehicle with four horses driven by one person. **2** *US* a necktie worn with a knot and two hanging ends superposed.

four-leaf clover *n.* (also **four-leaved clover**) a cloverleaf with four leaflets thought to bring good luck.

four-letter word *n.* any of several short words referring to sexual or excretory functions, regarded as coarse or offensive.

four o'clock *n.* = MARVEL OF PERU.

fourpence /ˈfɔːp(ə)ns/ *n. Brit.* the sum of four pence, esp. before decimalization.

fourpenny /ˈfɔːp(ə)ni/ *adj. Brit.* costing four pence, esp. before decimalization.

fourpenny one *n. Brit. colloq.* a hit or blow.

four-poster *n.* a bed with a post at each corner supporting a canopy.

fourscore /fɔːˈskɔː/ *n. archaic* eighty.

foursome /ˈfɔːs(ə)m/ *n.* **1** a group of four persons. **2** *Brit.* a golf match between two pairs with partners playing the same ball.

four-square *adj. & adv.* ● *adj.* **1** solidly based. **2** steady, resolute; forthright. **3** square-shaped. ● *adv.* steadily, resolutely.

four-stroke *adj. & n.* ● *attrib.adj.* **1** (of an internal-combustion engine) having a cycle of four strokes (intake, compression, combustion, and exhaust). **2** (of a vehicle) having a four-stroke engine. ● *n.* a four-stroke engine or vehicle.

fourteen /fɔːˈtiːn, ˈfɔːtiːn/ *n. & adj.* ● *n.* **1** one more than thirteen, or four more than ten; the product of two units and seven units. **2** a symbol for this (14, xiv, XIV). **3** a size etc. denoted by fourteen. ● *adj.* that amount to fourteen. □ **fourteenth** *adj. & n.* [Old English *fēowertīene* (as FOUR, -TEEN)]

fourth /fɔːθ/ *n. & adj.* ● *n.* **1** the position in a sequence corresponding to that of the number 4 in the sequence 1–4. **2** something occupying this position. **3** the fourth person etc. in a race or competition. **4** each of four equal parts of a thing; a quarter. **5** the fourth (and often highest) in a sequence of gears. **6** *Mus.* **a** an interval or chord spanning four consecutive notes in the diatonic scale (e.g. C to F). **b** a note separated from another by this interval. ● *adj.* that is the fourth. □ **fourthly** *adv.* [Old English *fēortha*, *fēowertha*, from Germanic]

fourth dimension *n.* **1** a postulated dimension additional to those determining area and volume. **2** time regarded as equivalent to linear dimensions.

fourth estate *n. joc.* the press; journalism.

4to *abbr.* quarto.

four-wheel drive *n.* drive acting on all four wheels of a vehicle (see DRIVE *n.* 6a).

fovea /ˈfəʊvɪə/ *n.* (*pl.* **foveae** /-vɪiː/) *Anat.* a small depression or pit, esp. the pit in the retina of the eye for focusing images. □ **foveal** *adj.* **foveate** /-vɪeɪt/ *adj.* [Latin]

fowl /faʊl/ *n. & v.* (*pl.* same or **fowls**) ● *n.* **1 a** (in full **domestic fowl**) a domestic cock or hen, a gallinaceous bird kept chiefly for its eggs and flesh. **b** any other domesticated bird kept for its eggs or flesh, e.g. the turkey, duck, goose, and guinea fowl. **2** the flesh of birds, esp. of the domestic cock or hen, as food. **3** (*archaic* except as *collect.* or in *comb.*) a bird (*guinea fowl*; *wildfowl*). ● *v.intr.* catch or hunt wildfowl. □ **fowler** *n.* **fowling** *n.* [Old English *fugol*, from Germanic]

fowl cholera *n.* = CHICKEN CHOLERA.

fowl pest *n.* an infectious virus disease of fowls.

fox /fɒks/ *n. & v.* ● *n.* **1 a** any of various doglike mammals of the genus *Vulpes* or a related genus, with a sharp snout and bushy tail, esp. the reddish *V. vulpes*. **b** the fur of a fox. **2** a cunning or sly person. **3** *N. Amer. slang* an attractive woman. ● *v.* **1 a** *intr.* act craftily. **b** *tr.* deceive, baffle, trick. **2** *tr.* (usu. as **foxed** *adj.*) discolour (the leaves of a book, engraving, etc.) with brownish marks. □ **foxing** *n.* (in sense 2 of *v.*). **foxlike** *adj.* [Old English from West Germanic]

foxglove /ˈfɒksglʌv/ *n.* any tall plant of the genus *Digitalis*, esp. *D. purpurea*, with erect spikes of purple or white bell-shaped flowers.

foxhole /ˈfɒkshəʊl/ *n.* **1** *Mil.* a hole in the ground used as a shelter against enemy fire or as a firing point. **2** a place of refuge or concealment.

foxhound /ˈfɒkshaʊnd/ *n.* a kind of hound bred and trained to hunt foxes.

fox-hunt /ˈfɒkshʌnt/ *n.* & *v.* ● *n.* **1** a hunt for a fox with hounds. **2** a particular group of people engaged in this. ● *v.intr.* engage in a fox-hunt. □ **fox-hunter** *n.* **fox-hunting** *n.* & *adj.*

foxtail /ˈfɒksteɪl/ *n.* any of several grasses of the genus *Alopecurus*, with brushlike spikes.

fox terrier *n.* **1** a terrier of a short-haired breed originally used for unearthing foxes. **2** this breed.

foxtrot /ˈfɒkstrɒt/ *n.* & *v.* ● *n.* **1** a ballroom dance with slow and quick steps. **2** the music for this. ● *v.intr.* (**foxtrotted**, **foxtrotting**) perform this dance.

foxy /ˈfɒksi/ *adj.* (**foxier**, **foxiest**) **1** of or like a fox. **2** sly or cunning. **3** reddish brown. **4** (of paper) damaged, esp. by mildew. **5** *N. Amer. slang* (of a woman) sexually attractive. □ **foxily** *adv.* **foxiness** *n.*

foyer /ˈfɔɪeɪ/ *n.* the entrance hall or other large area in a hotel, theatre, etc. [French, = hearth, home, ultimately from Latin *focus* 'fire']

FP *abbr.* freezing point.

fp *abbr.* forte piano.

FPA *abbr.* (in the UK) Family Planning Association.

FPS *abbr.* Fellow of the Pharmaceutical Society of Great Britain.

fps *abbr.* (also **f.p.s.**) **1** feet per second. **2** foot-pound-second.

Fr *symb. Chem.* the element francium.

Fr. *abbr.* (also **Fr**) Father.

fr. *abbr.* franc(s).

Fra /frɑː/ *n.* a prefixed title given to an Italian monk or friar. [Italian, abbreviation of *frate* 'brother']

frabjous /ˈfrabdʒəs/ *adj.* delightful, joyous. □ **frabjously** *adv.* [devised by Lewis Carroll, apparently to suggest *fair* and *joyous*]

fracas /ˈfrakɑː/ *n.* (*pl.* same /-kɑːz/) a noisy disturbance or quarrel. [French from *fracasser*, from Italian *fracassare* 'make an uproar']

fractal /ˈfrakt(ə)l/ *n.* & *adj. Math.* ● *n.* a curve or geometrical figure, each part of which has the same statistical character as the whole. ● *adj.* of or relating to a fractal. [FRACTION + -AL]

fraction /ˈfrakʃ(ə)n/ *n.* **1** a numerical quantity that is not a whole number (e.g. ½, 0.5). **2** a small, esp. very small, part, piece, or amount. **3** a portion of a mixture separated by distillation etc. **4** *Polit.* any organized dissentient group, esp. a group of communists in a non-communist organization. **5** *Eccl.* the division of the Eucharistic bread. □ **fractionary** *adj.* **fractionize** *v.tr.* (also **-ise**). [Middle English via Old French and Late Latin *fractio -onis* from Latin *frangere fract-* 'break']

fractional /ˈfrakʃ(ə)n(ə)l/ *adj.* **1** of or relating to or being a fraction. **2** very slight; incomplete. **3** *Chem.* relating to the separation of parts of a mixture by making use of their different physical properties (*fractional crystallization*; *fractional distillation*). □ **fractionalize** *v.tr.* (also **-ise**). **fractionally** *adv.* (esp. in sense 2).

fractionate /ˈfrakʃəneɪt/ *v.tr.* **1** break up into parts. **2** separate (a mixture) by fractional distillation etc. □ **fractionation** /-ˈneɪʃ(ə)n/ *n.*

fractious /ˈfrakʃəs/ *adj.* **1** irritable, peevish. **2** unruly. □ **fractiously** *adv.* **fractiousness** *n.* [FRACTION in obsolete sense 'discord, breach of the peace', probably suggested by *factious* etc.]

■ **Usage** See Usage Note at FACTIOUS.

fracto- /ˈfraktəʊ/ *comb. form Meteorol.* (of a cloud form) broken or fragmentary (*fracto-cumulus*; *fracto-nimbus*). [Latin *fractus* 'broken': see FRACTION]

fracture /ˈfraktʃə/ *n.* & *v.* ● *n.* **1 a** breakage or breaking, esp. of a bone or cartilage. **b** the result of breaking; a crack or split. **2** the surface appearance of a freshly broken rock or mineral. **3** *Linguistics* **a** the substitution of a diphthong for a simple vowel owing to an influence esp. of a following consonant. **b** a diphthong substituted in this way. ● *v.intr.* & *tr.* **1** *Med.* undergo or cause to undergo a fracture. **2** break or cause to break. [Middle English from French *fracture* or from Latin *fractura* (as FRACTION)]

fraenulum /ˈfriːnjʊləm/ *n.* (also **frenulum**) (*pl.* **-la** /-lə/) *Anat.* a small fraenum. [modern Latin, diminutive of FRAENUM]

fraenum /ˈfriːnəm/ *n.* (also **frenum**) (*pl.* **-na** /-nə/) *Anat.* a fold of mucous membrane or skin which checks the motion of the part to which it is attached, esp. one under the tongue. [Latin, = bridle]

fragile /ˈfradʒʌɪl/ *adj.* **1** easily broken; weak. **2** of delicate frame or constitution; not strong. □ **fragilely** *adv.* **fragility** /frəˈdʒɪlɪti/ *n.* [French *fragile* or Latin *fragilis* from *frangere* 'break']

fragment *n.* & *v.* ● *n.* /ˈfragm(ə)nt/ **1** a part broken off; a detached piece. **2** an isolated or incomplete part. **3** the remains of an otherwise lost or destroyed whole, esp. the extant remains or unfinished portion of a book or work of art. ● *v.tr.* & *intr.* /fragˈmɛnt/ break or separate into fragments. □ **fragmental** /-ˈmɛnt(ə)l/ *adj.* **fragmentize** /ˈfragm(ə)ntʌɪz/ *v.tr.* (also **-ise**). [Middle English from French *fragment* or Latin *fragmentum* (as FRAGILE)]

fragmentary /ˈfragm(ə)nt(ə)ri/ *adj.* **1** consisting of fragments. **2** disconnected. **3** *Geol.* composed of fragments of previously existing rocks. □ **fragmentarily** *adv.*

fragmentation /fragmɛnˈteɪʃ(ə)n/ *n.* the process or an instance of breaking into fragments.

fragmentation bomb *n.* a bomb designed to break up into small rapidly-moving fragments when exploded.

fragrance /ˈfreɪgr(ə)ns/ *n.* **1** sweetness of smell. **2** a sweet scent. □ **fragranced** *adj.* [French *fragrance* or Latin *fragrantia* (as FRAGRANT)]

fragrancy /ˈfreɪgr(ə)nsi/ *n.* (*pl.* **-ies**) = FRAGRANCE.

fragrant /ˈfreɪgr(ə)nt/ *adj.* sweet-smelling. □ **fragrantly** *adv.* [Middle English from French *fragrant* or Latin *fragrare* 'smell sweet']

frail /freɪl/ *adj.* & *n.* ● *adj.* **1** fragile, delicate. **2** in weak health. **3** morally weak; unable to resist temptation. **4** transient, insubstantial. ● *n.* *US slang* a woman. □ **frailly** *adv.* **frailness** *n.* [Middle English via Old French *fraile*, *frele* from Latin *fragilis* FRAGILE]

frailty /ˈfreɪlti/ *n.* (*pl.* **-ies**) **1** the condition of being frail. **2** liability to err or yield to temptation. **3** a fault, weakness, or foible. [Middle English via Old French *fraileté* from Latin *fragilitas -tatis* (as FRAGILE)]

Fraktur /ˈfraktʊə/ *n.* a German style of black-letter type. [German]

framboesia /framˈbiːzɪə/ *n.* (*US* **frambesia**) *Med.* = YAWS. [modern Latin via French *framboise* 'raspberry' from Latin *fraga ambrosia* 'ambrosial strawberry']

frame /freɪm/ *n.* & *v.* ● *n.* **1** a case or border enclosing a picture, window, door, etc. **2** the basic rigid supporting structure of anything, e.g. of a building, motor vehicle, or aircraft. **3** (in *pl.*) the structure of spectacles holding the lenses. **4** a human or animal body, esp. with reference to its size or structure (*his frame shook with laughter*). **5** a framed work or structure (*the frame of heaven*). **6 a** an established order, plan, or system (*the frame of society*). **b** construction, constitution, build. **7** a temporary state (esp. in **frame of mind**). **8** a single complete image or picture on a cinema film or transmitted in a series of lines by television. **9 a** a triangular structure for positioning the balls in snooker etc. **b** the balls positioned in this way. **c** a round of play in snooker etc. **10** a boxlike structure of glass etc. for protecting plants. **11** a removable box of slats for the building of a honeycomb in a beehive. **12** *N. Amer. slang* = FRAME-UP. ● *v.tr.* **1 a** set in or provide with a frame. **b** serve as a frame for. **2** construct by a combination of parts or in accordance with a design or plan. **3** formulate or devise the essentials of (a complex thing, idea, theory, etc.). **4** (foll. by *to*, *into*) adapt or fit. **5** *colloq.* concoct a false charge or evidence against; devise a plot with regard to. **6** articulate (words). □ **framable** *adj.* **frameless** *adj.* **framer** *n.* [Old English *framian* 'be of service' from *fram* 'forward': see FROM]

frame house *n.* a house constructed of a wooden skeleton covered with boards etc.

frame of reference *n.* **1** a set of standards or principles governing behaviour, thought, etc. **2** *Geom.* a system of geometrical axes for defining position.

frame-saw *n.* a saw stretched in a frame to make it rigid.

frame-up *n. colloq.* a conspiracy, esp. to make an innocent person appear guilty.

framework /'freɪmwə:k/ *n.* **1** an essential supporting structure. **2** a basic system.

framing /'freɪmɪŋ/ *n.* a framework; a system of frames.

franc /fraŋk/ *n.* the chief monetary unit of France, Belgium, Switzerland, Luxembourg, and several other countries. [Middle English from Old French, from *Francorum Rex* 'king of the Franks', the legend on the earliest gold coins so called (14th c.): see FRANK]

franchise /'fran(t)ʃʌɪz/ *n. & v.* ● *n.* **1 a** the right to vote at state (esp. parliamentary) elections. **b** the principle of qualification for this. **2** full membership of a corporation or state; citizenship. **3** authorization granted to an individual or group by a company to sell its goods or services in a particular way. **4** *hist.* legal immunity or exemption from a burden or jurisdiction. **5** a right or privilege granted to a person or corporation. ● *v.tr.* grant a franchise to. □ **franchisee** /-'zi:/ *n.* **franchiser** *n.* (also **franchisor**). [Middle English from Old French, from *franc, franche* 'free': see FRANK]

Franciscan /fran'sɪsk(ə)n/ *n. & adj.* ● *n.* a friar, sister, or lay member of an order founded in 1209 by St Francis of Assisi (see also GREY FRIAR). ● *adj.* of St Francis or his order. [French *franciscain* from modern Latin *Franciscanus*, from *Franciscus* 'Francis']

francium /'fransɪəm/ *n. Chem.* a radioactive metallic element occurring naturally in uranium and thorium ores (symbol **Fr**). [modern Latin from *France* (the discoverer's country)]

Franco- /'fraŋkəʊ/ *comb. form* (also **franco-**) **1** French; French and (*Franco-German*). **2** regarding France or the French (*Francophile*). [medieval Latin *Francus* FRANK]

francolin /'fraŋkəlɪn/ *n.* any medium-sized partridge of the genus *Francolinus*. [French from Italian *francolino*]

Francophile /'fraŋkə(ʊ)fʌɪl/ *n.* a person who is fond of France or the French.

francophone /'fraŋkə(ʊ)fəʊn/ *n. & adj.* ● *n.* a French-speaking person. ● *adj.* French-speaking. [FRANCO- + Greek *phōnē* 'voice']

frangible /'fran(d)ʒɪb(ə)l/ *adj.* breakable, fragile. [Old French *frangible* or medieval Latin *frangibilis* from Latin *frangere* 'to break']

frangipane /'fran(d)ʒɪpeɪn/ *n.* **1 a** an almond-flavoured cream or paste. **b** a flan filled with this. **2** = FRANGIPANI. [French, earlier = a perfume resembling jasmine (as FRANGIPANI)]

frangipani /fran(d)ʒɪ'pani, -'pɑ:ni/ *n.* (*pl.* **frangipanis**) **1** any tree or shrub of the genus *Plumeria*, native to tropical America, esp. *P. rubra* with clusters of fragrant white, pink, or yellow flowers. **2** the perfume from this plant. [named after M. *Frangipani*, 16th-c. Italian marquis, inventor of a perfume for scenting gloves]

franglais /'frɒ̃gleɪ/ *n.* a corrupt version of French using many words and idioms borrowed from English. [French, from *français* 'French' + *anglais* 'English']

Frank /fraŋk/ *n.* **1** a member of the Germanic nation or coalition that conquered Gaul in the 6th c. **2** (in the eastern Mediterranean region) a person of Western nationality. □ **Frankish** *adj. & n.* [Old English *Franca*, Old High German *Franko*, perhaps from the name of a weapon: cf. Old English *franca* 'javelin']

frank /fraŋk/ *adj., v., & n.* ● *adj.* **1** candid, outspoken (*a frank opinion*). **2** undisguised, avowed (*frank admiration*). **3** ingenuous, open (*a frank face*). **4** *Med.* unmistakable. ● *v.tr.* **1** stamp (a letter) with an official mark (esp. other than a normal postage stamp) to record the payment of postage. **2** *hist.* superscribe (a letter etc.) with a signature ensuring conveyance without charge; send without charge. **3** *archaic* facilitate the coming and going of (a person). ● *n.* **1** a franking signature or mark. **2** a franked cover. □ **frankable** *adj.* **franker** *n.* **frankness** *n.* [Middle English via Old French *franc* from medieval Latin *francus* 'free', from FRANK (since only Franks had full freedom in Frankish Gaul)]

Frankenstein /'fraŋk(ə)nstʌɪn/ *n.* (in full **Frankenstein's monster**) a thing that becomes terrifying to its maker; a monster. [Baron *Frankenstein*, a character in and the title of a novel (1818) by Mary Shelley]

frankfurter /'fraŋkfə:tə/ *n.* a seasoned smoked sausage made of beef and pork. [German *Frankfurter Wurst* 'Frankfurt sausage']

frankincense /'fraŋkɪnsɛns/ *n.* an aromatic gum resin obtained from trees of the genus *Boswellia*, used for burning as incense. [Middle English from Old French *franc encens* 'pure incense']

franklin /'fraŋklɪn/ *n. hist.* a landowner of free but not noble birth in the 14th and 15th c. in England. [Middle English *francoleyn* etc. from Anglo-Latin *francalanus*, via *francalis* 'held without dues' from *francus* 'free': see FRANK]

frankly /'fraŋkli/ *adv.* **1** in a frank manner. **2** (qualifying a whole sentence) to be frank.

frantic /'frantɪk/ *adj.* **1** wildly excited; frenzied. **2** characterized by great hurry or anxiety; desperate, violent. **3** *colloq.* extreme; very great. □ **frantically** *adv.* **franticly** *adv.* **franticness** *n.* [Middle English *frentik*, *frantik* via Old French *frenetique* from Latin *phreneticus*: see FRENETIC]

frap /frap/ *v.tr.* (**frapped**, **frapping**) *Naut.* bind tightly. [French *frapper* 'bind, strike']

frappé /'frapeɪ, French frape/ *adj. & n.* ● *adj.* (esp. of wine) iced, cooled. ● *n.* **1** an iced drink. **2** a soft water ice. [French, past part. of *frapper* 'strike, ice' (drinks)]

frascati /fra'skɑ:ti/ *n.* (*pl.* **frascatis**) a usu. white wine produced in the Frascati region of Italy.

frass /fras/ *n.* **1** a fine powdery refuse left by insects boring. **2** the excrement of insect larvae. [German, from *fressen* 'devour' (as FRET[1])]

fraternal /frə'tə:n(ə)l/ *adj.* **1** of a brother or brothers. **2** suitable to a brother; brotherly. **3** (of twins) developed from separate ova and not necessarily closely similar. **4** *N. Amer.* of or concerning a fraternity (see FRATERNITY 3). □ **fraternalism** *n.* **fraternally** *adv.* [medieval Latin *fraternalis* from Latin *fraternus*, from *frater* 'brother']

fraternity /frə'tə:nɪti/ *n.* (*pl.* **-ies**) **1** a religious brotherhood. **2** a group or company with common interests, or of the same professional class. **3** *N. Amer.* a male students' society in a university or college. **4** being fraternal; brotherliness. [Middle English via Old French *fraternité* from Latin *fraternitas -tatis* (as FRATERNAL)]

fraternize /'fratənʌɪz/ *v.intr.* (also **-ise**) (often foll. by *with*) **1** associate; make friends; behave as intimates. **2** (of troops) enter into friendly relations with enemy troops or the inhabitants of an occupied country. □ **fraternization** /-'zeɪʃ(ə)n/ *n.* [French *fraterniser* & medieval Latin *fraternizare* from Latin *fraternus*: see FRATERNAL]

fratricide /'fratrɪsʌɪd/ *n.* **1** the killing of one's brother or sister. **2** a person who does this. □ **fratricidal** /-'sʌɪd(ə)l/ *adj.* [French *fratricide* or Late Latin *fratricidium*, Latin *fratricida*, from *frater fratris* 'brother']

Frau /fraʊ/ *n.* (*pl.* **Frauen** /'fraʊən/) (often as a title) a married or widowed German-speaking woman. [German]

fraud /frɔ:d/ *n.* **1** criminal deception; the use of false representations to gain an unjust advantage. **2** a dishonest artifice or trick. **3** a person or thing not fulfilling what is claimed or expected of him, her, or it. [Middle English via Old French *fraude* from Latin *fraus fraudis*]

fraudster /'frɔ:dstə/ *n.* a person who commits fraud, esp. in business dealings.

fraudulent /'frɔ:djʊl(ə)nt/ *adj.* **1** characterized or achieved by fraud. **2** guilty of fraud; intending to deceive. □ **fraudulence** *n.* **fraudulently** *adv.* [Middle English from Old French *fraudulent* or Latin *fraudulentus* (as FRAUD)]

fraught /frɔ:t/ *adj.* **1** (foll. by *with*) filled or attended with (*fraught with danger*). **2** causing or affected by great anxiety or distress. [Middle English, past part. of obsolete *fraught* 'load with cargo', from Middle Dutch *vrachten* from *vracht* FREIGHT]

Fräulein /'frɔɪlʌɪn/ *n.* often *offens.* (often as a title or form of address) an unmarried (esp. young) German-speaking woman. [German, diminutive of FRAU]

Fraunhofer lines /'fraʊnhəʊfə/ *n.pl.* the dark lines visible in solar and stellar spectra. [named after J. von *Fraunhofer*, Bavarian physicist d. 1826]

fraxinella /fraksɪ'nɛlə/ *n.* an aromatic plant, *Dictamnus albus* (rue family), having foliage that emits an ethereal inflammable oil. Also called DITTANY, BURNING BUSH, *gas plant*. [modern Latin, diminutive of Latin *fraxinus* 'ash tree']

fray[1] /freɪ/ *v.* **1** *tr. & intr.* wear through or become worn, esp. (of woven material) unweave at the edges. **2** *intr.* (of nerves, temper, etc.) become strained; deteriorate. [French *frayer* from Latin *fricare* 'rub']

fray[2] /freɪ/ *n.* **1** conflict, fighting (*eager for the fray*). **2** a noisy quarrel or brawl. [Middle English from *fray* 'to quarrel' from *affray* (*v.*) (as AFFRAY)]

frazil /'freɪz(ə)l, frə'zɪl/ *n. N. Amer.* ice crystals that form in a stream or on its bed. [Canadian French *frasil* 'snow floating in the water'; cf. French *fraisil* 'cinders']

frazzle /'fraz(ə)l/ *n. & v. colloq.* ● *n.* a worn, charred, or exhausted state (esp. in phr. **worn**, **burnt**, etc. **to a frazzle**). ● *v.tr.* (esp. as **frazzled** *adj.*) **1** wear out; exhaust. **2** char; shrivel up with burning. [19th c.: origin uncertain]

freak /fri:k/ *n. & v.* ● *n.* **1** (also **freak of nature**) a monstrosity; an abnormally developed individual or thing. **2** (often *attrib.*) an abnormal, irregular, or bizarre occurrence (*a freak storm*). **3** *colloq.* **a** an unconventional person. **b** a person with a specified enthusiasm or interest (*health freak*). **c** a person who undergoes hallucinations; a drug addict (see sense 2 of *v.*). **4 a** a caprice or vagary. **b** capriciousness. ● *v.* (often foll. by *out*) *colloq.* **1** *intr. & tr.* become or make very angry. **2** *intr. & tr.* undergo or cause to undergo hallucinations or a strong emotional experience, esp. from use of narcotics. **3** *intr.* adopt a wildly unconventional lifestyle. [16th c.: probably from dialect]

freakish /'fri:kɪʃ/ *adj.* **1** of or like a freak. **2** bizarre, unconventional. □ **freakishly** *adv.* **freakishness** *n.*

freak-out *n. colloq.* an act of freaking out; a hallucinatory or strong emotional experience.

freak show *n.* a sideshow at a fair, featuring abnormally developed individuals.

freaky /'fri:ki/ *adj.* (**freakier**, **freakiest**) = FREAKISH. □ **freakily** *adv.* **freakiness** *n.*

freckle /'frɛk(ə)l/ *n. & v.* ● *n.* (often in *pl.*) a small light brown patch on the skin, usu. caused by exposure to the sun. ● *v.* **1** *tr.* (usu. as **freckled** *adj.*) mark with freckles. **2** *intr.* be marked with freckles. □ **freckly** *adj.* [Middle English from Old Norse *freknur* (pl.)]

freckle-faced *adj.* having a freckled face.

free /fri:/ *adj., adv., & v.* ● *adj.* (**freer** /'fri:ə/; **freest** /'fri:ɪst/) **1** not in bondage to or under the control of another; having personal rights and social and political liberty. **2** (of a state, or its citizens or institutions) subject neither to foreign domination nor to despotic government; having national and civil liberty (*a free press; a free society*). **3 a** unrestricted, unimpeded; not restrained or fixed. **b** at liberty; not confined or imprisoned. **c** released from ties or duties; unimpeded. **d** unrestrained as to action; independent (*set free*). **4** (foll. by *of, from*) **a** not subject to; exempt from (*free of tax*). **b** not containing or subject to a specified (usu. undesirable) thing (*free of preservatives*; *free from disease*). **5** (foll. by *to* + infin.) able or permitted to take a specified action (*you are free to choose*). **6** unconstrained (*free gestures*). **7 a** available without charge; costing nothing. **b** not subject to tax, duty, trade-restraint, or fees. **8 a** clear of engagements or obligations (*are you free tomorrow?*). **b** not occupied or in use (*the bathroom is free now*). **c** clear of obstructions. **9** spontaneous, unforced (*free compliments*). **10** open to all comers. **11** lavish, profuse; using or used without restraint (*very free with their money*). **12** frank, unreserved. **13** (of a literary style) not observing the strict laws of form. **14** (of a translation) conveying the broad sense; not literal. **15** forward, familiar, impudent. **16** (of talk, stories, etc.) slightly indecent. **17** *Physics* **a** not modified by an external force. **b** not bound in an atom or molecule. **18** *Chem.* not combined (*free oxygen*). **19** (of power or energy) disengaged or available. ● *adv.* **1** in a free manner. **2** without cost or payment. **3** *Naut.* not close-hauled. ● *v.tr.* **1** make free; set at liberty. **2** (foll. by *of, from*) relieve from (something undesirable). **3** disengage, disentangle. □ **for free** *colloq.* free of charge, gratis. **free and easy** informal, unceremonious. **free on board** (or **rail**) without charge for delivery to a ship or railway wagon. **free up** *colloq.* **1** make available. **2** make less restricted. □ **freely** *adv.* **freeness** *n.* [Old English *frēo*, *frēon*, from Germanic]

-free /fri:/ *comb. form* free of or from (*duty-free*; *trouble-free*).

free agent *n.* a person with freedom of action.

free association *n. Psychol.* a method of investigating a person's unconscious by eliciting from him or her spontaneous associations with ideas proposed by the examiner.

freebase /'fri:beɪs/ *n. & v. slang* ● *n.* cocaine that has been purified by heating with ether, and is taken by inhaling the fumes or smoking the residue. ● *v.tr.* purify (cocaine) for smoking or inhaling.

freebie /'fri:bi/ *n. colloq.* a thing provided free of charge. [arbitrary formation from FREE]

freeboard /'fri:bɔ:d/ *n.* the part of a ship's side between the waterline and the deck.

freebooter /'fri:bu:tə/ *n.* a pirate or lawless adventurer. □ **freeboot** *v.intr.* [Dutch *vrijbuiter* (as FREE, BOOTY): cf. FILIBUSTER]

freeborn /'fri:bɔ:n/ *adj.* inheriting a citizen's rights and liberty.

Free Church *n.* a Church dissenting or seceding from an established Church.

freedman /'fri:dmən/ *n.* (*pl.* **-men**) an emancipated slave.

freedom /'fri:dəm/ *n.* **1** the condition of being free or unrestricted. **2** personal or civic liberty; absence of slave status. **3** the power of self-determination; independence of fate or necessity. **4** the state of being free to act (often foll. by *to* + infin.: *we have the freedom to leave*). **5** frankness, outspokenness; undue familiarity. **6** (foll. by *from*) the condition of being exempt from or not subject to (a defect, burden, etc.). **7** (foll. by *of*) **a** full or honorary participation in (membership, privileges, etc.). **b** unrestricted use of (facilities etc.). **8** a privilege possessed by a city or corporation. **9** facility or ease in action. **10** boldness of conception. [Old English *frēodōm* (as FREE, -DOM)]

freedom fighter *n.* a person who takes part in resistance to an established political system etc.

freedom of conscience *n.* a system allowing all citizens freedom of choice in matters of religion, in moral issues, etc.

freedom of religion *n.* the right to follow whatever religion one chooses.

free enterprise *n.* a system in which private business operates in competition and largely free of state control.

free fall *n. & v.* ● *n.* (usu. hyphenated when *attrib.*) **1** movement under the force of gravity only, esp.: **a** the part of a parachute descent before the parachute opens. **b** the movement of a spacecraft in space without thrust from the engines. **2** any state of falling rapidly (*prices were in free fall*). ● *v.intr.* (**free-fall**) move in a free fall.

free fight *n.* a general fight in which all present join.

Freefone /'fri:fəʊn/ *n.* (also **Freephone, free-**) *Brit.* a telephone service by means of which an organization pays for certain incoming calls.

free-for-all *n.* a free fight, unrestricted discussion, etc.

free-form *attrib.adj.* of an irregular shape or structure.

freehand /'fri:hand/ *adj. & adv.* ● *adj.* (of a drawing or plan etc.) done by hand without special instruments or guides. ● *adv.* in a freehand manner.

free hand *n.* freedom to act at one's own discretion (see also FREEHAND).

free-handed *adj.* generous. □ **free-handedly** *adv.* **free-handedness** *n.*

freehold /'fri:həʊld/ *n. & adj.* ● *n.* **1** tenure of land or property in fee simple or fee tail or for life. **2** esp. *Brit.* land, property, or an office held by such tenure. ● *adj.* held by or having the status of freehold. □ **freeholder** *n.*

free house *n. Brit.* an inn or public house not controlled by a brewery and therefore not restricted to selling particular brands of beer or liquor.

free-kick *n. Football* a set kick allowed to be taken by one side without interference from the other.

free labour *n.* esp. *Brit.* the labour of workers not in a trade union.

freelance /'fri:lɑ:ns/ *n., v., & adv.* ● *n.* **1** (also **freelancer**) a person, usu. self-employed, offering services on a temporary basis, esp. to several businesses etc. for particular assignments (often *attrib.*: *a freelance editor*). **2** (usu. **free lance**) *hist.* a medieval mercenary. ● *v.intr.* act as a freelance. ● *adv.* as a freelance. [19th c.: originally in sense 2 of *n.*]

free-living *adj.* **1** freely indulging in pleasures, esp. that of eating. **2** *Biol.* living freely and independently; not attached to a substrate. □ **free-liver** *n.* (in sense 1).

freeloader /'fri:ləʊdə/ *n.* esp. *N. Amer. slang* a person who eats or drinks at others' expense; a sponger. □ **freeload** /-'ləʊd/ *v.intr.*

free love *n.* sexual relations according to choice and unrestricted by marriage.

freeman /'fri:mən/ *n.* (*pl.* **-men**) **1** a person who has the freedom of a city, company, etc. **2** a person who is not a slave or serf.

free market *n.* a market in which prices are determined by unrestricted competition (usu. hyphenated when *attrib*: *a free-market economy*).

freemartin /'fri:mɑ:tɪn/ *n.* a hermaphrodite or imperfect female calf of oppositely sexed twins. [17th c.: origin unknown]

Freemason /'fri:meɪs(ə)n/ *n.* a member of an international fraternity for mutual help and fellowship (the *Free and Accepted Masons*), with elaborate secret rituals.

Freemasonry /'fri:meɪs(ə)nri/ *n.* **1** the system and institutions of the Freemasons. **2** (**freemasonry**) a secret or tacit fellowship; instinctive sympathy.

free pardon see PARDON *n.* 2.

free pass *n.* an authorization of free admission, travel, etc.

Freephone var. of FREEFONE.

free port *n.* **1** a port area where goods in transit are exempt from customs duty. **2** a port open to all traders.

Freepost /'fri:pəʊst/ *n.* esp. *Brit.* a postal service whereby postage is paid by the addressee.

freer *compar.* of FREE.

free radical *n.* an uncharged atom or group of atoms with one or more unpaired electrons.

free-range *adj.* **1** (of hens etc.) kept in natural conditions with freedom of movement. **2** (of eggs) produced by such birds.

free school *n.* usu. *hist.* **1** a school for which no fees are charged. **2** a school run on the basis of freedom from restriction for the pupils.

free sheet *n.* a free newspaper.

freesia /'fri:zɪə/ *n.* any bulbous plant of the genus *Freesia*, native to Africa, having fragrant coloured flowers. [modern Latin named after F. H. T. *Freese*, German physician d. 1876]

free speech *n.* the right to express opinions freely.

free spirit *n.* an independent or uninhibited person.

free-spoken *adj.* speaking candidly; not concealing one's opinions.

freest *superl.* of FREE.

free-standing *adj.* not supported by another structure.

freestone /'fri:stəʊn/ *n.* **1** any fine-grained stone which can be cut easily, esp. sandstone or limestone. **2** a stone fruit, esp. a peach, in which the stone is loose when the fruit is ripe (cf. CLINGSTONE).

freestyle /'fri:stʌɪl/ *adj. & n.* ● *adj.* (of a race or contest) in which all styles are allowed, esp.: **1** *Swimming* in which any style of stroke may be used. **2** *Wrestling* with few restrictions on the holds permitted. ● *n.* freestyle swimming or wrestling. □ **freestyler** *n.*

freethinker /fri:'θɪŋkə/ *n.* a person who rejects dogma or authority, esp. in religious belief. □ **freethinking** *n. & adj.*

free throw *n.* **1** an unimpeded throw awarded to a player following a foul etc. **2** *Basketball* such a throw allowing a shot at the basket, taken from behind a marked line.

free trade *n.* international trade left to its natural course without restriction on imports or exports.

free verse *n.* = VERS LIBRE.

free vote *n.* a parliamentary vote not subject to party discipline.

freeway /'fri:weɪ/ *n.* esp. *US* **1** an express highway, esp. with controlled access. **2** a toll-free highway.

freewheel /fri:'wi:l/ *v.intr.* **1** ride a bicycle with the pedals at rest, esp. downhill. **2** move or act without constraint or effort.

free wheel *n.* the driving wheel of a bicycle, able to revolve with the pedals at rest.

free will *n.* **1** the power of acting without the constraint of necessity or fate. **2** the ability to act at one's own discretion (*I did it of my own free will*).

free world *n.* esp. *US hist.* non-Communist countries.

freeze /fri:z/ *v. & n.* ● *v.* (*past* **froze** /frəʊz/; *past part.* **frozen** /'frəʊz(ə)n/) **1** *tr. & intr.* **a** turn or be turned into ice or another solid by cold. **b** (often foll. by *over, up*) make or become rigid or solid as a result of the cold. **2** *intr.* be or feel very cold. **3** *tr. & intr.* cover or become covered with ice. **4** *intr.* (foll. by *to, together*) adhere or be fastened by frost (*the curtains froze to the window*). **5** *tr.* preserve (food) by refrigeration below freezing point. **6** *tr. & intr.* **a** make or become motionless or powerless through fear, surprise, etc. **b** react or cause to react with sudden aloofness or detachment. **7** *tr.* stiffen or harden, injure or kill, by chilling (*frozen to death*). **8** *tr.* make (credits, assets, etc.) temporarily or permanently unrealizable. **9** *tr.* fix or stabilize (prices, wages, etc.) at a certain level. **10** *tr.* arrest (an action) at a certain stage of development. **11** *tr.* = FREEZE-FRAME *v.* ● *n.* **1** a state of frost; a period or the coming of frost or very cold weather. **2** the fixing or stabilization of prices, wages, etc. **3** = FREEZE-FRAME *n.* □ **freeze on to** *colloq.* take or keep tight hold of. **freeze out** esp. *US colloq.* exclude from business, society, etc. by competition or boycott etc. **freeze up** obstruct or be obstructed by the formation of ice. □ **freezable** *adj.* **frozenly** *adv.* [Old English *frēosan*, from Germanic]

freeze-dry *v.tr.* (**-dries**, **-dried**) freeze and dry by the sublimation of ice in a high vacuum.

freeze-frame *n.* & *v.* ● *n.* (also *attrib.*) the facility of stopping a film or videotape in order to view a motionless image. ● *v.tr.* use freeze-frame on (an image, a recording, etc.).

freezer /ˈfriːzə/ *n.* a refrigerated cabinet or room for preserving food at very low temperatures; = DEEP-FREEZE *n.*

freeze-up *n.* a period or conditions of extreme cold.

freezing /ˈfriːzɪŋ/ *adj.* (also **freezing cold**) *colloq.* very cold.

freezing-mixture *n.* salt and snow or some other mixture used to freeze liquids.

freezing point *n.* the temperature at which a liquid, esp. water, freezes.

freezing works *n.pl. Austral.* & *NZ* a place where animals are slaughtered and carcasses frozen for export.

freight /freɪt/ *n.* & *v.* ● *n.* **1** the transport of goods more slowly and cheaply than by express delivery. **2** goods transported; cargo. **3** a charge for transportation of goods. **4** the hire of a ship, aircraft, etc., for transporting goods. **5** a load or burden. ● *v.tr.* **1** transport (goods) as freight. **2** load with freight. **3** hire or let out (a ship) for the carriage of goods and passengers. [Middle Dutch, Middle Low German *vrecht*, variant of *vracht*: cf. FRAUGHT]

freightage /ˈfreɪtɪdʒ/ *n.* **1 a** the transportation of freight. **b** the cost of this. **2** freight transported.

freight car *n.* a railway wagon for carrying freight.

freighter /ˈfreɪtə/ *n.* **1** a ship or aircraft designed to carry freight. **2** a person who loads, or charters and loads, a ship. **3** a person whose business is to receive and forward freight. **4** *US hist.* a person who transported freight across the plains by wagon.

Freightliner /ˈfreɪtlʌɪnə/ *n. Brit. propr.* a train carrying goods in containers.

freight ton see TON[1] 4b.

French /frɛn(t)ʃ/ *adj.* & *n.* ● *adj.* **1** of or relating to France or its people or language. **2** having the characteristics attributed to the French people. ● *n.* **1** the language of France, also used in Belgium, Switzerland, Canada, and elsewhere. **2** (prec. by *the*; treated as *pl.*) the people of France. **3** *colloq.* bad language (*excuse my French*). **4** *colloq.* dry vermouth (*gin and French*). □ **Frenchness** *n.* [Old English *frencisc*, from Germanic]

French bean *n. Brit.* **1** a bean plant, *Phaseolus vulgaris*, having many varieties cultivated for their pods and seeds. **2 a** the pod used as food. **b** the seed used as food. Cf. HARICOT, KIDNEY BEAN, STRING BEAN.

French bread *n.* white bread in a long crisp loaf.

French Canadian *n.* & *adj.* ● *n.* a Canadian whose principal language is French. ● *adj.* (**French-Canadian**) of or relating to French-speaking Canadians.

French chalk *n.* a kind of steatite used for marking cloth and removing grease and as a dry lubricant.

French cricket *n.* an informal type of cricket without stumps and played with a soft ball.

French cuff *n.* a cuff designed to be folded back before fastening.

French curve *n.* a template used for drawing curved lines.

French door *n.* = FRENCH WINDOW.

French dressing *n.* **1** esp. *Brit.* a salad dressing of vinegar and oil, usu. seasoned; vinaigrette. **2** *US* a salad dressing made with mayonnaise and ketchup.

French fried potatoes *n.pl.* (*N. Amer.* **French fries**) potato chips.

French horn *n.* a coiled brass wind instrument with a wide bell.

Frenchify /ˈfrɛn(t)ʃɪfʌɪ/ *v.tr.* (**-ies**, **-ied**) (usu. as **Frenchified** *adj.*) make French in form, character, or manners.

French kiss *n.* a kiss with one partner's tongue inserted in the other's mouth.

French knickers *n.pl.* wide-legged knickers.

French leave *n.* absence without permission.

French letter *n. Brit. colloq.* a condom.

French loaf *n.* a loaf of French bread.

Frenchman /ˈfrɛn(t)ʃmən/ *n.* (*pl.* **-men**) a man who is French by birth or descent.

French mustard *n. Brit.* a mild mustard mixed with vinegar.

French polish *n.* & *v.* ● *n.* shellac polish for wood. ● *v.tr.* polish with this.

French roof *n.* a mansard.

French seam *n.* a seam with the raw edges enclosed.

French toast *n.* **1** *Brit.* bread buttered on one side and toasted on the other. **2** bread dipped in egg and milk and fried.

French vermouth *n. Brit.* dry vermouth.

French window *n.* (usu. in *pl.*) a glazed door in an outside wall, serving as a window and door.

Frenchwoman /ˈfrɛn(t)ʃwʊmən/ *n.* (*pl.* **-women**) a woman who is French by birth or descent.

frenetic /frəˈnɛtɪk/ *adj.* **1** frantic, frenzied. **2** fanatic. □ **frenetically** *adv.* [Middle English via Old French *frenetique* and Latin *phreneticus* from Greek *phrenitikos*, via *phrenitis* 'delirium' from *phrēn phrenos* 'mind']

frenulum var. of FRAENULUM.

frenum var. of FRAENUM.

frenzy /ˈfrɛnzi/ *n.* & *v.* ● *n.* (*pl.* **-ies**) **1** mental derangement; wild excitement or agitation. **2** delirious fury. ● *v.tr.* (**-ies**, **-ied**) (usu. as **frenzied** *adj.*) drive to frenzy; infuriate. □ **frenziedly** *adv.* [Middle English via Old French *frenesie* and medieval Latin *phrenesia* from Latin *phrenesis*, from Greek *phrēn* 'mind']

freon /ˈfriːɒn/ *n. propr.* any of a group of halogenated hydrocarbons containing fluorine, chlorine, and sometimes bromine, used in aerosols, refrigerants, etc. (see also CFC).

frequency /ˈfriːkw(ə)nsi/ *n.* (*pl.* **-ies**) **1** commonness of occurrence. **2 a** the state of being frequent; frequent occurrence. **b** the process of being repeated at short intervals. **3** *Physics* the rate of recurrence of a vibration, oscillation, cycle, etc.; the number of repetitions in a given time, esp. per second (abbr.: *f*). **4** *Statistics* the ratio of the number of actual to possible occurrences of an event. [Latin *frequentia* (as FREQUENT)]

frequency band *n. Electronics* = BAND[1] *n.* 4a.

frequency distribution *n. Statistics* a measurement of the frequency of occurrence of the values of a variable.

frequency modulation *n. Electronics* the modulation of a radio wave etc. by variation of its frequency, esp. to carry an audio signal (abbr.: **FM**).

frequency response *n. Electronics* the dependence on signal frequency of the output-input ratio of an amplifier etc.

frequent *adj.* & *v.* ● *adj.* /ˈfriːkw(ə)nt/ **1** occurring often or in close succession. **2** habitual, constant (*a frequent caller*). **3** found near together; numerous, abundant. **4** (of the pulse) rapid. ● *v.tr.* /frɪˈkwɛnt/ attend or go to habitually. □ **frequentation** /friːkwɛnˈteɪʃ(ə)n/ *n.* **frequenter** /frɪˈkwɛntə/ *n.* **frequently** /ˈfriːkw(ə)ntli/ *adv.* [French *fréquent* or Latin *frequens -entis* 'crowded']

frequentative /frɪˈkwɛntətɪv/ *adj.* & *n. Gram.* ● *adj.* expressing frequent repetition or intensity of action. ● *n.* a verb or verbal form or conjugation expressing this (e.g. *chatter*, *twinkle*). [French *fréquentatif -ive* or Latin *frequentativus* (as FREQUENT)]

fresco /ˈfrɛskəʊ/ *n.* (*pl.* **-os** or **-oes**) **1** a painting done in watercolour on a wall or ceiling while the plaster is still wet. **2** this method of painting (esp. *in fresco*). □ **frescoed** *adj.* [Italian, = cool, fresh]

fresco secco *n.* = SECCO.

fresh /frɛʃ/ *adj.*, *adv.*, & *n.* ● *adj.* **1** newly made or obtained (*fresh sandwiches*). **2 a** other, different; not previously known or used (*start a fresh page*; *we need fresh ideas*). **b** additional (*fresh supplies*). **3** (foll. by *from*) lately arrived from (a specified place or situation). **4** not stale or musty or faded (*fresh flowers*; *fresh memories*). **5** (of food) not preserved by salting, tinning, freezing, etc. **6** not salty (*fresh water*). **7 a** pure, untainted, refreshing, invigorating (*fresh air*). **b** bright and pure in colour (*a fresh complexion*). **8** (of the wind) brisk; of fair strength. **9** alert, vigorous, fit (*never felt fresher*). **10** *colloq.* **a** cheeky, presumptuous. **b** amorously impudent. **11** young and inexperienced. ● *adv.* newly, recently (esp. in *comb.*: *fresh-baked*; *fresh-cut*). ● *n.* esp. *literary* the fresh part of the day, year, etc. (*in the fresh of the morning*). □ **freshly** *adv.* **freshness** *n.* [Middle English from Old French *freis fresche*, ultimately from Germanic]

freshen /ˈfrɛʃ(ə)n/ *v.* **1** *tr. & intr.* make or become fresh or fresher. **2** *intr. & tr.* (foll. by *up*) **a** wash, change one's clothes, etc. **b** revive, refresh, renew.

fresher /ˈfrɛʃə/ *n. Brit. colloq.* = FRESHMAN.

freshet /ˈfrɛʃɪt/ *n.* **1** a rush of fresh water flowing into the sea. **2** the flood of a river from heavy rain or melted snow. [probably from Old French *freschete*, from *frais* FRESH]

fresh-faced *adj.* having a clear and young-looking complexion.

freshman /ˈfrɛʃmən/ *n.* (*pl.* **-men**; *fem.* **woman**, *pl.* **-women**) a first-year student at university or *N. Amer.* at high school.

freshwater /ˈfrɛʃwɔːtə/ *adj.* **1** of or found in fresh water; not of the sea. **2** *US* (esp. of a school or college) rustic or provincial.

freshwater flea *n.* = DAPHNIA.

fresnel /freɪˈnɛl/ *n.* (also **F-**) (in full **fresnel lens**) *Photog.* a flat lens made of a number of concentric rings, to reduce spherical aberration. [named after A.J. *Fresnel*, French physicist d. 1827]

fret[1] /frɛt/ *v. & n.* ● *v.* (**fretted**, **fretting**) **1** *intr.* **a** be greatly and visibly worried or distressed. **b** be irritated or resentful. **2** *tr.* **a** cause anxiety or distress to. **b** irritate, annoy. **3** *tr.* wear or consume by gnawing or rubbing. **4** *tr.* form (a channel or passage) by wearing away. **5** *intr.* (of running water) flow or rise in little waves. ● *n.* esp. *Brit.* irritation, vexation, querulousness (esp. *in a fret*). [Old English *fretan* from Germanic, related to EAT]

fret[2] /frɛt/ *n. & v.* ● *n.* **1** an ornamental pattern made of continuous combinations of straight lines joined usu. at right angles. **2** *Heraldry* a device of narrow bands and a diamond interlaced. ● *v.tr.* (**fretted**, **fretting**) **1** embellish or decorate with a fret. **2** adorn (esp. a ceiling) with carved or embossed work. [Middle English from Old French *frete* 'trellis-work' and *freter* (*v.*)]

fret[3] /frɛt/ *n.* each of a sequence of bars or ridges on the fingerboard of some stringed musical instruments (esp. the guitar) fixing the positions of the fingers to produce the desired notes. □ **fretless** *adj.* **fretted** *adj.* [16th c.: origin unknown]

fretboard /ˈfrɛtbɔːd/ *n.* a fretted fingerboard.

fretful /ˈfrɛtfʊl, -f(ə)l/ *adj.* visibly anxious, distressed, or irritated. □ **fretfully** *adv.* **fretfulness** *n.*

fretsaw /ˈfrɛtsɔː/ *n.* a saw consisting of a narrow blade stretched on a frame, for cutting thin wood in patterns.

fretwork /ˈfrɛtwəːk/ *n.* ornamental work in wood, done with a fretsaw.

Freudian /ˈfrɔɪdɪən/ *adj. & n. Psychol.* ● *adj.* of or relating to the Austrian psychologist Sigmund Freud (d. 1939) or his methods of psychoanalysis, esp. with reference to the importance of sexuality in human behaviour. ● *n.* a follower of Freud or his methods. □ **Freudianism** *n.*

Freudian slip *n.* an unintentional error regarded as revealing subconscious feelings.

Fri. *abbr.* Friday.

friable /ˈfrʌɪəb(ə)l/ *adj.* easily crumbled. □ **friability** /-ˈbɪlɪti/ *n.* **friableness** *n.* [French *friable* or Latin *friabilis* from *friare* 'crumble']

friar /ˈfrʌɪə/ *n.* a member of any of certain religious orders of men, esp. the four mendicant orders (Augustinians, Carmelites, Dominicans, and Franciscans). □ **friarly** *adj.* [Middle English & Old French *frere* from Latin *frater fratris* 'brother']

friar's balsam *n.* (also **friars' balsam**) a tincture of benzoin etc. used esp. as an inhalant.

friary /ˈfrʌɪəri/ *n.* (*pl.* **-ies**) a convent of friars.

fricandeau /ˈfrɪkandəʊ/ *n. & v.* ● *n.* (*pl.* **fricandeaux** /-dəʊz/) **1** a slice of meat, esp. veal, cut from the leg. **2** a dish made from this, usu. fried or stewed and served with a sauce. ● *v.tr.* (**fricandeaus**, **fricandeaued**, **fricandeauing**) make into fricandeaux. [French]

fricassee /ˈfrɪkəsiː, frɪkəˈsiː/ *n. & v.* ● *n.* a dish of stewed or fried pieces of meat served in a thick white sauce. ● *v.tr.* (**fricassees**, **fricasseed**) make a fricassee of. [French *fricassée*, fem. past part. of *fricasser* 'cut up and cook in sauce']

fricative /ˈfrɪkətɪv/ *adj. & n. Phonet.* ● *adj.* made by the friction of breath in a narrow opening. ● *n.* a consonant made in this way, e.g. *f* and *th*. [modern Latin *fricativus* from Latin *fricare* 'rub']

friction /ˈfrɪkʃ(ə)n/ *n.* **1** the action of one object rubbing against another. **2** the resistance an object encounters in moving over another. **3** a clash of wills, temperaments, or opinions; mutual animosity arising from disagreement. **4** (in *comb.*) of devices that transmit motion by frictional contact (*friction clutch*; *friction disc*). □ **frictional** *adj.* **frictionless** *adj.* [French from Latin *frictio -onis*, from *fricare frict-* 'rub']

Friday /ˈfrʌɪdeɪ, -di/ *n. & adv.* ● *n.* the sixth day of the week, following Thursday. ● *adv. colloq.* **1** on Friday. **2** (**Fridays**) on Fridays; each Friday. [Old English *frīgedæg* from Germanic (named after *Frigg*, wife of Odin)]

fridge /frɪdʒ/ *n.* (also **frig**) *colloq.* = REFRIGERATOR. [abbreviation]

fridge-freezer *n.* esp. *Brit.* an upright unit comprising a refrigerator and a freezer, each self-contained.

friend /frɛnd/ *n. & v.* ● *n.* **1** a person with whom one enjoys mutual affection and regard (usu. exclusive of sexual or family bonds). **2** a sympathizer, helper, or patron (*no friend to virtue*; *a friend of order*). **3** a person who is not an enemy or who is on the same side (*friend or foe?*). **4 a** a person already mentioned or under discussion (*my friend at the next table then left the room*). **b** a person known by sight. **c** used as a polite or ironic form of address. **5** a regular contributor of money or other assistance to an institution. **6** (**Friend**) a member of the Society of Friends, a Quaker. **7** (in *pl.*) *archaic* one's near relatives, those responsible for one. **8** a helpful thing or quality. ● *v.tr. archaic* or *poet.* befriend, help. □ **be** (or **keep**) **friends with** be friendly with. **friend at court** a friend whose influence may be made use of. **my honourable friend** *Brit.* used in the House of Commons to refer to another member of one's own party. **my learned friend** used by a lawyer in court to refer to another lawyer. **my noble friend** *Brit.* used in the House of Lords to refer to another member of one's own party. □ **friended** *adj.* **friendless** *adj.* [Old English *frēond*, from Germanic]

friendly /ˈfrɛn(d)li/ *adj., n., & adv.* ● *adj.* (**friendlier**, **friendliest**) **1** acting as or like a friend, well disposed, kindly. **2 a** (often foll. by *with*) on amicable terms. **b** not hostile. **3** characteristic of friends, showing or prompted by kindness. **4** favourably disposed, ready to approve or help. **5 a** (of a thing) serviceable, convenient, opportune. **b** = USER-FRIENDLY. **6** (esp. in *comb.*) not harming; helping (*ozone-friendly*; *reader-friendly*). ● *n.* (*pl.* **-ies**) *Brit.* = FRIENDLY MATCH. ● *adv.* in a friendly manner. □ **friendlily** *adv.* **friendliness** *n.*

friendly action *adj. Brit. Law* an action brought merely to get a point decided.

friendly fire *n. Mil.* gunfire coming from one's own side, esp. as the cause of accidental injury to one's own forces.

friendly match *n. Brit. Sport.* a match not played in competition for a cup etc.

Friendly Society *n. Brit.* a mutual association providing sickness benefits, life assurance, and pensions.

friendship /ˈfrɛn(d)ʃɪp/ *n.* **1** being friends, the relationship between friends. **2** a friendly disposition felt or shown. [Old English *frēondscipe* (as FRIEND, -SHIP)]

frier var. of FRYER.

Friesian /ˈfriːzj(ə)n, -ʒ(ə)n/ *n. & adj. Brit.* ● *n.* **1** a large animal of a usu. black and white breed of dairy cattle originally from Friesland. **2** this breed. Also called HOLSTEIN. ● *adj.* of or concerning Friesians. [variant of FRISIAN]

frieze[1] /friːz/ *n.* **1** *Archit.* **a** the part of an entablature between the architrave and the cornice. **b** a horizontal band of sculpture filling this. **2** a band of decoration elsewhere, esp. along a wall near the ceiling. [French *frise* via medieval Latin *frisium*, *frigium* from Latin *Phrygium (opus)* '(work) of Phrygia']

frieze[2] /friːz/ *n.* coarse woollen cloth with a nap, usu. on one side only. [Middle English via French *frise* from medieval Latin, = Frisian wool]

frig[1] /frɪɡ/ *v. & n. coarse slang* ● *vtr. & intr.* (**frigged, frigging**) **1** = FUCK *v.* **2** masturbate. ● *n.* = FUCK *n.* 1a, 2. [earlier senses 'move about, rub': perhaps imitative]

frig[2] var. of FRIDGE.

frigate /ˈfrɪɡət/ *n.* **1 a** *Brit.* a naval escort vessel between a corvette and a destroyer in size. **b** *US* a similar ship between a destroyer and a cruiser in size. **2** *hist.* a warship next in size to ships of the line. [French *frégate* from Italian *fregata*, of unknown origin]

frigate bird *n.* any seabird of the family Fregatidae, found in tropical seas, with a wide wingspan and deeply forked tail. Also called *man-of-war bird*.

fright /frʌɪt/ *n. & v.* ● *n.* **1 a** sudden or extreme fear. **b** an instance of this (*gave me a fright*). **2** a person or thing looking grotesque or ridiculous. ● *v.tr. poet.* frighten. □ **take fright** become frightened. [Old English *fryhto*, metathetic form of *fyrhto*, from Germanic]

frighten /ˈfrʌɪt(ə)n/ *v.* **1** *tr.* fill with fright; terrify (*was frightened at the bang; is frightened of dogs*). **2** *tr.* (foll. by *away, off, out of, into*) drive or force by fright (*frightened it out of the room; frightened them into submission; frightened me into agreeing*). **3** *intr.* become frightened (*he doesn't frighten easily*). □ **frightening** *adj.* **frighteningly** *adv.*

frightener /ˈfrʌɪt(ə)nə/ *n.* a person or thing that frightens. □ **put the frighteners on** *Brit. slang* intimidate.

frightful /ˈfrʌɪtfʊl, -f(ə)l/ *adj.* **1 a** dreadful, shocking, revolting. **b** ugly, hideous. **2** *colloq.* extremely bad (*a frightful idea*). **3** *colloq.* very great, extreme. □ **frightfully** *adv.*

frightfulness /ˈfrʌɪtfʊlnɪs, -f(ə)l-/ *n.* **1** being frightful. **2** the terrorizing of a civilian population as a military resource. [sense 2: translation of German *Schrecklichkeit*]

frigid /ˈfrɪdʒɪd/ *adj.* **1 a** lacking friendliness or enthusiasm; apathetic, formal, forced. **b** dull, flat, insipid. **c** chilling, depressing. **2** (of a woman) sexually unresponsive. **3** (esp. of climate or air) cold. □ **frigidity** /-ˈdʒɪdɪti/ *n.* **frigidly** *adv.* **frigidness** *n.* [Latin *frigidus*, via *frigēre* 'be cold' from *frigus* (*n.*) 'cold']

frigid zone *n.* each of two parts of the earth north of the Arctic Circle and south of the Antarctic Circle.

frijoles /frɪˈhəʊlɛs/ *n.pl.* beans. [Spanish, pl. of *frijol* 'bean', ultimately from Latin *phaseolus*]

frill /frɪl/ *n. & v.* ● *n.* **1 a** a strip of material with one side gathered or pleated and the other left loose with a fluted appearance, used as an ornamental edging. **b** a similar paper ornament on a ham-knuckle, chop, etc. **c** a natural fringe of feathers, hair, etc., on an animal (esp. a bird) or a plant. **2** (in *pl.*) **a** unnecessary embellishments or accomplishments. **b** airs, affectation (*put on frills*). ● *v.tr.* **1** decorate with a frill. **2** form into a frill. □ **frilled** *adj.* **frillery** *n.* [16th c.: from or related to Flemish *frul*]

frilling /ˈfrɪlɪŋ/ *n.* **1** a set of frills. **2** material for frills.

frill lizard *n.* (also **frilled lizard** or **frill-necked lizard**) a large N. Australian lizard, *Chlamydosaurus kingii*, with an erectile membrane round the neck.

frilly /ˈfrɪli/ *adj. & n.* ● *adj.* (**frillier, frilliest**) **1** having a frill or frills. **2** resembling a frill. ● *n.* (*pl.* **-ies**) (in *pl.*) *colloq.* women's underwear. □ **frilliness** *n.*

fringe /frɪn(d)ʒ/ *n. & v.* ● *n.* **1 a** an ornamental bordering of threads left loose or formed into tassels or twists. **b** such a bordering made separately. **c** any border or edging. **2 a** esp. *Brit.* a portion of the front hair hanging over the forehead. **b** a natural border of hair etc. in an animal or plant. **3 a** an outer edge, margin, or limit. **b** (*attrib.*) marginal; taking place on the periphery (*fringe group*). **c** (*attrib.*) unconventional (*fringe theatre*). **d** (usu. **the Fringe**) a secondary festival on the peripherary of a mainstream event. **4** a thing, part, or area of secondary or minor importance. **5 a** a band of contrasting brightness or darkness produced by diffraction or interference of light. **b** a strip of false colour in an optical image. **6** *US* a fringe benefit. ● *v.tr.* **1** adorn or encircle with a fringe. **2** serve as a fringe to. □ **fringeless** *adj.* **fringy** *adj.* [Middle English & Old French *frenge*, ultimately from Late Latin *fimbria* (earlier only in pl.) 'fibres, fringe']

fringe benefit *n.* an employee's benefit supplementing a money wage or salary.

fringe medicine *n.* systems of treatment of disease etc. not regarded as orthodox by the medical profession.

fringing /ˈfrɪn(d)ʒɪŋ/ *n.* material for a fringe or fringes.

fringing reef *n.* a coral reef that fringes the shore.

frippery /ˈfrɪp(ə)ri/ *n. & adj.* ● *n.* (*pl.* **-ies**) **1** showy, tawdry, or unnecessary finery or ornament, esp. in dress. **2** empty display in speech, literary style, etc. **3 a** knick-knacks, trifles. **b** a knick-knack or trifle. ● *adj.* **1** frivolous. **2** contemptible. [French *friperie* from Old French *freperie*, from *frepe* 'rag']

frippet /ˈfrɪpɪt/ *n. Brit. slang* a frivolous or showy young woman. [20th c.: origin unknown]

frisbee /ˈfrɪzbi/ *n. propr.* a concave plastic disc designed for skimming through the air as an outdoor game. [perhaps named after the *Frisbie* bakery (Bridgeport, Conn.), whose pie-tins could be used similarly]

frisée /ˈfriːzeɪ/ *n.* = ENDIVE 1. [French, from *chicorée frisée* 'curly endive']

Frisian /ˈfrɪzɪən/ *n. & adj.* ● *n.* **1** a native or inhabitant of Friesland (an area comprising parts of the NW Netherlands and NW Germany). **2** the language of Friesland. ● *adj.* of or relating to Friesland, its people, or language. [Latin *Frisii* (pl.) from Old Frisian *Frīsa*, *Frēsa*]

frisk /frɪsk/ *v. & n.* ● *v.* **1** *intr.* leap or skip playfully. **2** *tr.* feel over or search (a person) for a weapon etc. (usu. rapidly). ● *n.* **1** a playful leap or skip. **2** the frisking of a person. □ **frisker** *n.* [obsolete *frisk* (*adj.*) from Old French *frisque* 'lively', of unknown origin]

frisket /ˈfrɪskɪt/ *n. Printing* a thin iron frame keeping the sheet in position during printing on a hand-press. [French *frisquette* via Provençal *frisqueto* from Spanish *frasqueta*]

frisky /ˈfrɪski/ *adj.* (**friskier, friskiest**) lively, playful. □ **friskily** *adv.* **friskiness** *n.*

frisson /ˈfriːsɔ̃, ˈfrɪsɒn/ *n.* an emotional thrill. [French, = shiver]

frit[1] /frɪt/ *n. & v.* ● *n.* **1** a calcined mixture of sand and fluxes as material for glass-making. **2** a vitreous composition from which soft porcelain, enamel, etc., are made. ● *v.tr.* (**fritted, fritting**) make into frit, partially fuse, calcine. [Italian *fritta*, fem. past part. of *friggere* FRY[1]]

frit² /frɪt/ *adj. dial.* & *colloq.* frightened.

frit-fly /ˈfrɪtflʌɪ/ *n.* (*pl.* **-flies**) a small black fly, *Oscinella frit*, the larvae of which are destructive to cereals. [Latin *frit* 'particle on an ear of corn' + FLY²]

frith var. of FIRTH.

fritillary /frɪˈtɪl(ə)ri/ *n.* (*pl.* **-ies**) **1** any plant of the genus *Fritillaria* (lily family), esp. snake's head, having pendent bell-like flowers. **2** any of various butterflies, esp. of the genus *Argynnis*, having red-brown wings chequered with black. [modern Latin *fritillaria* from Latin *fritillus* 'dice-box']

frittata /frɪˈtɑːtə/ *n.* an Italian dish made with fried beaten eggs, resembling a Spanish omelette. [Italian]

fritter¹ /ˈfrɪtə/ *v.tr.* **1** (usu. foll. by *away*) waste (money, time, energy, etc.) triflingly, indiscriminately, or on divided aims. **2** *archaic* subdivide. [earlier *fritter(s)* 'fragments', perhaps related to Middle High German *vetze* 'rag']

fritter² /ˈfrɪtə/ *n.* a piece of fruit, meat, etc., coated in batter and deep-fried (*apple fritter*). [Middle English from Old French *friture*, ultimately from Latin *frigere frict-* FRY¹]

fritto misto /frɪtəʊ ˈmɪstəʊ, Italian fritto ˈmisto/ *n.* a dish of various foods, usu. seafood, deep-fried in batter. [Italian, = mixed fry]

fritz /frɪts/ *n.* ▫ **on the fritz** *N. Amer. slang* out of order, unsatisfactory. [20th c.: origin unknown]

frivol /ˈfrɪv(ə)l/ *v.* (**frivolled**, **frivolling**; *US* **frivoled**, **frivoling**) **1** *intr.* be a trifler; trifle. **2** *tr.* (foll. by *away*) spend (money or time) foolishly. [back-formation from FRIVOLOUS]

frivolous /ˈfrɪv(ə)ləs/ *adj.* **1** paltry, trifling, trumpery. **2** lacking seriousness; given to trifling; silly. ▫ **frivolity** /-ˈvɒlɪti/ *n.* (*pl.* **-ies**). **frivolously** *adv.* **frivolousness** *n.* [Latin *frivolus* 'silly, trifling']

frizz /frɪz/ *v.* & *n.* ● *v.* **1 a** *tr.* form (hair) into a mass of small curls. **b** *intr.* (of hair) form itself into small curls. **2** *tr.* dress (wash-leather etc.) with pumice or a scraping-knife. ● *n.* **1 a** frizzed hair. **b** a row of curls. **2** a frizzed state. [Middle English from French *friser*, perhaps from the stem of *frire* FRY¹]

frizzle¹ /ˈfrɪz(ə)l/ *v.intr.* & *tr.* **1** fry, toast, or grill, with a sputtering noise. **2** (often foll. by *up*) burn or shrivel. [FRY¹, with imitative ending + -LE⁴]

frizzle² /ˈfrɪz(ə)l/ *v.* & *n.* ● *v.* **1** *tr.* form (hair) into tight curls. **2** *intr.* (often foll. by *up*) (of hair etc.) curl tightly. ● *n.* frizzled hair. [FRIZZ]

frizzly /ˈfrɪzli/ *adj.* in tight curls.

frizzy /ˈfrɪzi/ *adj.* (**frizzier**, **frizziest**) in a mass of small curls. ▫ **frizziness** *n.*

Frl. *abbr.* Fräulein.

fro /frəʊ/ *adv.* back (now only in *to and fro*: see TO). [Middle English from Old Norse *frá* FROM]

frock /frɒk/ *n.* & *v.* ● *n.* **1** esp. *Brit.* a woman's or girl's dress. **2 a** a monk's or priest's long gown with loose sleeves. **b** priestly office. **3** a smock. **4 a** a frock coat. **b** a military coat of similar shape. **5** a sailor's woollen jersey. ● *v.tr.* invest with priestly office (cf. DEFROCK). [Middle English via Old French *froc* from Frankish]

frock coat *n.* a man's long-skirted coat not cut away in front.

froe /frəʊ/ *n.* (also **frow**) *US* a cleaving tool with a handle at right angles to the blade. [abbreviation of *frower* from FROWARD 'turned away']

Froebel system /ˈfrəʊb(ə)l, ˈfrəːb(ə)l/ *n.* a system of education of children by means of kindergartens. ▫ **Froebelian** /-ˈbiːlɪən/ *adj.* **Froebelism** *n.* [named after F. W. A. *Fröbel*, German teacher d. 1852]

frog¹ /frɒg/ *n.* **1** any of various small tailless amphibians of the order Anura, having a moist smooth skin and legs developed for jumping. **2** (**Frog**) *slang offens.* a French person. **3** a hollow in the top face of a brick for holding the mortar. **4** the nut of a violin bow etc. ▫ **frog in the** (or **one's**) **throat** *colloq.* an irritation or apparent impediment in the throat; hoarseness. [Old English *frogga*, from Germanic]

frog² /frɒg/ *n.* an elastic horny substance in the sole of a horse's foot. [17th c.: origin uncertain (perhaps a use of FROG¹)]

frog³ /frɒg/ *n.* **1** an ornamental coat-fastening of a spindle-shaped button and loop. **2** an attachment to a waist-belt to support a sword, bayonet, etc. ▫ **frogged** *adj.* **frogging** *n.* [18th c.: origin unknown]

frog⁴ /frɒg/ *n.* a grooved piece of iron at a place in a railway where tracks cross. [19th c.: origin unknown]

frogbit /ˈfrɒgbɪt/ *n.* a floating plant of the monocotyledonous family Hydrocharitaceae, found in stagnant water. [FROG¹]

frogfish /ˈfrɒgfɪʃ/ *n.* (*pl.* usu. same) an angler fish, esp. of the family Antennariidae.

froggy /ˈfrɒgi/ *adj.* & *n.* ● *adj.* **1** of or like a frog or frogs. **2** abounding in frogs. **3** *slang offens.* French. ● *n.* (**Froggy**) (*pl.* **-ies**) *slang offens.* a French person.

froghopper /ˈfrɒghɒpə/ *n.* any jumping plant-sucking bug of the family Cercopidae, whose larvae produce a protective mass of froth (see CUCKOO SPIT).

frogman /ˈfrɒgmən/ *n.* (*pl.* **-men**) a person equipped with a rubber suit, flippers, and an oxygen supply for underwater swimming.

frogmarch /ˈfrɒgmɑːtʃ/ *v.* & *n.* esp. *Brit.* ● *v.tr.* **1** hustle (a person) forward holding and pinning the arms from behind. **2** carry (a person) in a frogmarch. ● *n.* the carrying of a person face downwards by four others each holding a limb.

frogmouth /ˈfrɒgmaʊθ/ *n.* any of various birds of Australia and SE Asia of the family Podargidae, having large wide mouths.

frogspawn /ˈfrɒgspɔːn/ *n.* the eggs of a frog, usu. surrounded by transparent jelly.

froideur /frwɒˈdəː, French frwadœr/ *n.* coolness or reserve (between people). [French]

frolic /ˈfrɒlɪk/ *v.*, *n.*, & *adj.* ● *v.intr.* (**frolicked**, **frolicking**) play about cheerfully, gambol. ● *n.* **1** cheerful play. **2** a prank. **3** a merry party. **4** an outburst of gaiety. **5** merriment. ● *adj. archaic* **1** full of pranks, sportive. **2** joyous, mirthful. ▫ **frolicker** *n.* [Dutch *vrolijk* (*adj.*), from *vro* 'glad' + *-lijk* -LY¹]

frolicsome /ˈfrɒlɪks(ə)m/ *adj.* merry, playful. ▫ **frolicsomely** *adv.* **frolicsomeness** *n.*

from /frɒm, frəm/ *prep.* expressing separation or origin, followed by: **1** a person, place, time, etc., that is the starting point of motion or action, or of extent in place or time (*rain comes from the clouds*; *repeated from mouth to mouth*; *dinner is served from 8*; *from start to finish*). **2** a place, object, etc. whose distance or remoteness is reckoned or stated (*ten miles from Rome*; *I am far from admitting it*; *absent from home*; *apart from its moral aspect*). **3 a** a source (*dig gravel from a pit*; *a man from Italy*; *draw a conclusion from data*; *quotations from Shaw*). **b** a giver or sender (*presents from Father Christmas*; *have not heard from her*). **4 a** a thing or person avoided, escaped, lost, etc. (*released him from prison*; *cannot refrain from laughing*; *dissuaded from folly*). **b** a person or thing deprived (*took his gun from him*). **5** a reason, cause, or motive (*died from fatigue*; *suffering from mumps*; *did it from jealousy*; *from his looks you might not believe it*). **6** a thing distinguished or unlike (*know black from white*). **7** a lower limit (*saw from 10 to 20 boats*; *tickets from £5*). **8** a state changed for another (*from being the victim he became the attacker*; *raised the penalty from a fine to imprisonment*). **9** an adverb or preposition of time or place (*from long ago*; *from abroad*; *from under the bed*). **10** the position of a person who observes or considers (*saw it from the roof*; *from his point of view*). **11** a model (*painted it from nature*). ▫ **from a child** since childhood. **from day to day** (or **hour to hour** etc.) daily (or hourly etc.); as the days (or hours etc.) pass. **from home** out, away. **from now on** henceforward. **from time to time** occasionally. **from year to year** each year; as the years pass. [Old English *fram*, *from*, from Germanic]

fromage blanc /frɒmɑːʒ 'blɒ̃/ *n.* a type of soft French cheese made from cow's milk and having a creamy sour taste. [French, literally 'white cheese']

fromage frais /frɒmɑːʒ 'freɪ/ *n.* a type of smooth soft fresh cheese, with the consistency of thick yogurt. [French, literally 'fresh cheese']

frond /frɒnd/ *n.* **1** *Bot.* **a** a large usu. divided foliage leaf in various flowerless plants, esp. ferns and palms. **b** the leaflike thallus of some algae. **2** *Zool.* a leaflike expansion. ▫ **frondage** *n.* **frondose** *adj.* [Latin *frons frondis* 'leaf']

frondeur /frɒn'dɜː/ *n.* a political rebel. [French, = slinger, applied to a party (the Fronde) rebelling during the minority of Louis XIV of France]

front /frʌnt/ *n., adj., & v.* ● *n.* **1** the side or part normally nearer or towards the spectator or the direction of motion (*the front of the car; the front of the chair; the front of the mouth*). **2** any face of a building, esp. that of the main entrance. **3** *Mil.* **a** the foremost line or part of an army etc. **b** line of battle. **c** the part of the ground towards a real or imaginary enemy. **d** a scene of actual fighting (*go to the front*). **e** the direction in which a formed line faces (*change front*). **4 a** a sector of activity regarded as resembling a military front. **b** an organized political group. **5 a** demeanour, bearing (*show a bold front*). **b** outward appearance. **6** a forward or conspicuous position (*come to the front*). **7 a** a bluff. **b** a pretext. **8** a person etc. serving to cover subversive or illegal activities. **9** (prec. by *the*) esp. *Brit.* the promenade of a seaside resort. **10** *Meteorol.* the forward edge of an advancing mass of cold or warm air. **11** (prec. by *the*) *Brit.* the auditorium of a theatre. **12 a** a face. **b** *poet.* or *literary* a forehead. **13 a** the breast of a person's clothes. **b** a false shirt-front. **14** impudence. ● *attrib.adj.* **1** of the front. **2** situated in front. **3** *Phonet.* formed at the front of the mouth. ● *v.* **1** *intr.* (foll. by *on, to, towards, upon*) have the front facing or directed. **2** *intr.* (foll. by *for*) *colloq.* act as a front or cover for. **3** *tr.* furnish with a front (*fronted with stone*). **4** *tr.* lead (a band, organization, etc.). **5** *tr.* **a** stand opposite to, front towards. **b** have its front on the side of (a street etc.). **6** *tr. archaic* confront, meet, oppose. **7** *tr. Broadcasting* act as presenter or host of (a programme). ▫ **in front 1** in an advanced position. **2** facing the spectator. **in front of 1** ahead of, in advance of. **2** in the presence of, confronting. **on the front burner** see BURNER. ▫ **frontless** *adj.* **frontward** *adj. & adv.* **frontwards** *adv.* [Middle English via Old French *front* (*n.*), *fronter* (*v.*) from Latin *frons frontis*]

frontage /'frʌntɪdʒ/ *n.* **1** the front of a building. **2 a** land abutting on a street or on water. **b** the land between the front of a building and the road. **3** extent of front (*a shop with little frontage*). **4 a** the way a thing faces. **b** outlook. ▫ **frontager** *n.*

frontage road *n. N. Amer.* a service road.

frontal[1] /'frʌnt(ə)l/ *adj.* **1 a** of, at, or on the front (*a frontal attack*). **b** of the front as seen by an onlooker (*a frontal view*). **2** of the forehead or front part of the skull (*frontal bone*). ▫ **frontally** *adv.* [modern Latin *frontalis* (as FRONT)]

frontal[2] /'frʌnt(ə)l/ *n.* **1** *Eccl.* a covering for the front of an altar. **2** the façade of a building. [Middle English via Old French *frontel* from Latin *frontale* (as FRONT)]

frontal lobe *n.* each of the paired lobes of the brain lying immediately behind the forehead, including areas concerned with behaviour, learning, and voluntary movement.

front bench *n. Brit.* the foremost seats in the House of Commons, occupied by leading members of the government and opposition. ▫ **frontbencher** /frʌnt'bɛntʃə/ *n.*

front door *n.* **1** the chief entrance of a building. **2** a chief means of approach or access to a place, situation, etc.

frontier /'frʌntɪə, frʌn'tɪə/ *n.* **1 a** the border between two countries. **b** the district on each side of this. **2** the limits of attainment or knowledge in a subject. **3** (in the US) the borders between settled and unsettled country. ▫ **frontierless** *adj.* [Middle English from Anglo-French *frounter*, Old French *frontiere*, ultimately from Latin *frons frontis* FRONT]

frontiersman /'frʌntɪəzmən, -'tɪəzmən/ *n.* (*pl.* **-men**; *fem.* **frontierswoman**, *pl.* **-women**) a person living in the region of a frontier, esp. between settled and unsettled country.

frontispiece /'frʌntɪspiːs/ *n.* **1** an illustration facing the title-page of a book or of one of its divisions. **2** *Archit.* **a** the principal face of a building. **b** a decorated entrance. **c** a pediment over a door etc. [French *frontispice* or Late Latin *frontispicium* 'façade', from Latin *frons frontis* FRONT + *-spicium* from *specere* 'look': assimilated to PIECE]

frontlet /'frʌntlɪt/ *n.* **1** a piece of cloth hanging over the upper part of an altar frontal. **2** a band worn on the forehead. **3** a phylactery. **4** an animal's forehead. [Old French *frontelet* (as FRONTAL[2])]

front line *n.* the foremost part of an army or a group under attack (hyphenated when *attrib.*: *front-line positions*).

front-line states *n.pl. hist.* countries bordering on South Africa and opposed to its policy of apartheid.

frontman /'frʌntman/ *n.* **1** a person acting as a front or cover (see FRONT *n.* 8). **2** *Broadcasting* a programme's presenter or host. **3** the leader of a group of musicians, an organization, etc.

front matter *n. Printing* the title-page, preface, etc. preceding the text proper.

front office *n.* a main office, esp. *Brit.* police headquarters.

fronton /'frʌnt(ə)n/ *n. Archit.* a pediment. [French from Italian *frontone*, from *fronte* 'forehead']

front page *n.* the first page of a newspaper, esp. as containing important or remarkable news (hyphenated when *attrib.*: *front-page headline*).

front passage *n. Brit. colloq.* the vagina.

front runner *n.* **1** the contestant most likely to succeed. **2** an athlete or horse running best when in the lead.

front-wheel drive *n.* drive acting on the front wheels of a motor vehicle (see DRIVE *n.* 6a).

frore /frɔː/ *adj. poet.* frozen, frosty. [archaic past part. of FREEZE]

frost /frɒst/ *n. & v.* ● *n.* **1 a** (also **white frost**) a white frozen dew coating esp. the ground at night (*windows covered with frost*). **b** a consistent temperature below freezing point causing frost to form. **2** a chilling dispiriting atmosphere. **3** *Brit. slang* a failure. ● *v.* **1** *intr.* (usu. foll. by *over, up*) become covered with frost. **2** *tr.* **a** cover with or as if with frost, powder, etc. **b** injure (a plant etc.) with frost. **3** *tr.* give a roughened or finely granulated surface to (glass, metal) (*frosted glass*). **4** *tr. US* cover or decorate (a cake etc.) with icing. ▫ **degrees of frost** *Brit.* degrees below freezing point (*ten degrees of frost tonight*). ▫ **frostless** *adj.* [Old English from Germanic]

frostbite /'frɒs(t)bʌɪt/ *n.* injury to body tissues, esp. the nose, fingers, or toes, due to freezing and often resulting in gangrene.

frosting /'frɒstɪŋ/ *n.* **1** *US* icing. **2** a rough surface on glass etc.

frost-work *n.* tracery made by frost on glass etc.

frosty /'frɒsti/ *adj.* (**frostier**, **frostiest**) **1** cold with frost. **2** covered with or as with hoar frost. **3** unfriendly in manner, lacking in warmth of feeling. ▫ **frostily** *adv.* **frostiness** *n.*

froth /frɒθ/ *n. & v.* ● *n.* **1 a** a collection of small bubbles in liquid, caused by shaking, fermenting, etc.; foam. **b** impure matter on liquid, scum. **2 a** idle talk or ideas. **b** anything insubstantial or of little worth. ● *v.* **1** *intr.* emit or gather froth (*frothing at the mouth*). **2** *tr.* cause (beer etc.) to foam. ▫ **frothily** *adv.* **frothiness** *n.* **frothy** *adj.* (**frothier**, **frothiest**). [Middle English from Old Norse *frotha*, *frauth*, from Germanic]

froth-blower *n. Brit. joc.* a beer drinker (formerly esp. as a designation of a member of a charitable organization).

frottage /ˈfrɒtɑːʒ/ *n.* **1** *Psychol.* the practice of touching or rubbing against the clothed body of another person (usu. in a crowd) as a means of obtaining sexual gratification. **2** *Art* the technique or process of taking a rubbing from an uneven surface to form the basis of a work of art. [French, = rubbing, from *frotter* 'rub' from Old French *froter*]

frou-frou /ˈfruːfruː/ *n.* **1** a rustling, esp. of a dress. **2** frills, frippery. [French, imitative]

frow[1] /fraʊ/ *n. Brit.* **1** a Dutchwoman. **2** a housewife. [Middle English from Dutch *vrouw* 'woman']

frow[2] var. of FROE.

froward /ˈfrəʊəd/ *adj. archaic* perverse; difficult to deal with. □ **frowardly** *adv.* **frowardness** *n.* [Middle English from FRO + -WARD]

frown /fraʊn/ *v. & n.* ● *v.* **1** *intr.* wrinkle one's brows, esp. in displeasure or deep thought. **2** *intr.* (foll. by *at, on, upon*) express disapproval. **3** *intr.* (of a thing) present a gloomy aspect. **4** *tr.* compel with a frown (*frowned them into silence*). **5** *tr.* express (defiance etc.) with a frown. ● *n.* **1** an action of frowning; a vertically furrowed or wrinkled state of the brow. **2** a look expressing severity, disapproval, or deep thought. □ **frowner** *n.* **frowningly** *adv.* [Middle English via Old French *frongnier, froignier*, from *froigne* 'surly look', from Celtic]

frowst /fraʊst/ *n. & v. Brit. colloq.* ● *n.* fusty warmth in a room. ● *v.intr.* stay in or enjoy frowst. □ **frowster** *n.* [back-formation from FROWSTY]

frowsty /ˈfraʊsti/ *adj.* (**frowstier, frowstiest**) *Brit.* fusty, stuffy. □ **frowstiness** *n.* [variant of FROWZY]

frowzy /ˈfraʊzi/ *adj.* (also **frowsy**) (**-ier, -iest**) **1** fusty, musty, ill-smelling, close. **2** slatternly, unkempt, dingy. □ **frowziness** *n.* [17th c.: origin unknown]

froze *past* of FREEZE.

frozen *past part.* of FREEZE.

frozen mitt *n. colloq.* a cool reception.

frozen shoulder *n. Med.* a shoulder joint which is painfully stiff.

FRS *abbr.* (in the UK) Fellow of the Royal Society.

FRSE *abbr.* Fellow of the Royal Society of Edinburgh.

fructiferous /frʌkˈtɪf(ə)rəs/ *adj.* bearing fruit. [Latin *fructifer* from *fructus* FRUIT]

fructification /ˌfrʌktɪfɪˈkeɪʃ(ə)n/ *n. Bot.* **1** the process of fructifying. **2** any spore-bearing structure esp. in ferns, fungi, and mosses. [Late Latin *fructificatio* (as FRUCTIFY)]

fructify /ˈfrʌktɪfʌɪ/ *v.* (**-ies, -ied**) **1** *intr.* bear fruit. **2** *tr.* make fruitful; impregnate. [Middle English via Old French *fructifier* from Latin *fructificare*, from *fructus* FRUIT]

fructose /ˈfrʌktəʊz, -s/ *n. Chem.* a simple sugar found in honey and fruits. Also called *fruit sugar, laevulose*. [Latin *fructus* FRUIT + -OSE[2]]

fructuous /ˈfrʌktjʊəs/ *adj.* full of or producing fruit. [Middle English from Old French *fructuous* or Latin *fructuosus* (as FRUIT)]

frugal /ˈfruːg(ə)l/ *adj.* **1** (often foll. by *of*) sparing or economical, esp. as regards food. **2** sparingly used or supplied, meagre, costing little. □ **frugality** /-ˈgalɪti/ *n.* **frugally** *adv.* **frugalness** *n.* [Latin *frugalis* from *frugi* 'economical']

frugivorous /fruˈdʒɪv(ə)rəs/ *adj.* feeding on fruit. [Latin *frux frugis* 'fruit' + -VOROUS]

fruit /fruːt/ *n. & v.* ● *n.* **1 a** the usu. sweet and fleshy edible product of a plant or tree, containing seed. **b** (in *sing.*) these in quantity (*eats fruit*). **2** the seed of a plant or tree with its covering, e.g. an acorn, pea pod, cherry, etc. **3** (usu. in *pl.*) vegetables, grains, etc. used for food (*fruits of the earth*). **4** (usu. in *pl.*) the result of action etc., esp. as financial reward (*fruits of his labours*). **5** *slang* esp. *US* a male homosexual. **6** *Bibl.* an offspring (*the fruit of the womb; the fruit of his loins*). ● *v.intr. & tr.* bear or cause to bear fruit. □ **fruitage** *n.* **fruited** *adj.* (also in *comb.*). [Middle English via Old French from Latin *fructus* 'fruit, enjoyment', from *frui* 'enjoy']

fruitarian /fruːˈtɛːrɪən/ *n.* a person who eats only fruit. [FRUIT, on the pattern of *vegetarian*]

fruit bar *n. Brit.* a piece of dried and pressed fruit.

fruitbat /ˈfruːtbat/ *n.* any large bat of the suborder Megachiroptera, feeding on fruit.

fruit-body *n.* (*pl.* **-ies**) = FRUITING BODY.

fruit cake *n.* **1** a cake containing dried fruit. **2** (**fruitcake**) *slang* an eccentric or mad person.

fruit cocktail *n.* a finely chopped usu. tinned fruit salad.

fruiter /ˈfruːtə/ *n.* **1** a tree producing fruit, esp. with reference to its quality (*a poor fruiter*). **2** *Brit.* a fruit-grower. **3** a ship carrying fruit. [Middle English from Old French *fruitier* (as FRUIT, -ER[5]): in later use from FRUIT + -ER[1]]

fruiterer /ˈfruːt(ə)rə/ *n.* esp. *Brit.* a dealer in fruit.

fruit fly *n.* (*pl.* **flies**) any of various flies, esp. of the genus *Drosophila*, having larvae that feed on fruit.

fruitful /ˈfruːtfʊl, -f(ə)l/ *adj.* **1** producing much fruit; fertile; causing fertility. **2** producing good results, successful; beneficial, remunerative. **3** producing offspring, esp. prolifically. □ **fruitfully** *adv.* **fruitfulness** *n.*

fruiting body *n.* the spore-bearing part of a fungus.

fruition /frʊˈɪʃ(ə)n/ *n.* **1 a** the bearing of fruit. **b** the production of results. **2** the realization of aims or hopes. **3** enjoyment. [Middle English via Old French from Late Latin *fruitio -onis*, from *frui* 'enjoy', erroneously associated with FRUIT]

fruitless /ˈfruːtlɪs/ *adj.* **1** not bearing fruit. **2** useless, unsuccessful, unprofitable. □ **fruitlessly** *adv.* **fruitlessness** *n.*

fruitlet /ˈfruːtlɪt/ *n.* = DRUPEL.

fruit machine *n. Brit.* a coin-operated gaming machine giving random combinations of symbols often representing fruit.

fruit salad *n.* **1** various fruits cut up and served in syrup, juice, etc. **2** *slang* a display of medals etc.

fruit sugar *n.* fructose.

fruit tree *n.* a tree grown for its fruit.

fruitwood /ˈfruːtwʊd/ *n.* the wood of a fruit tree, esp. when used in furniture.

fruity /ˈfruːti/ *adj.* (**fruitier, fruitiest**) **1 a** of fruit. **b** tasting or smelling like fruit, esp. (of wine) tasting of the grape. **2** (of a voice etc.) of full rich quality. **3** *Brit. colloq.* full of rough humour or (usu. scandalous) interest; suggestive. □ **fruitily** *adv.* **fruitiness** *n.*

frumenty /ˈfruːm(ə)nti/ *n.* (also **furmety** /ˈfəːmɪti/) hulled wheat boiled in milk and seasoned with cinnamon, sugar, etc. [Middle English via Old French *frumentee*, from *frument*, from Latin *frumentum* 'corn']

frump /frʌmp/ *n.* a dowdy unattractive old-fashioned woman. □ **frumpish** *adj.* **frumpishly** *adv.* [16th c.: perhaps from dialect *frumple* 'wrinkle' from Middle Dutch *verrompelen* (as FOR-, RUMPLE)]

frumpy /ˈfrʌmpi/ *adj.* (**frumpier, frumpiest**) dowdy, unattractive, and old-fashioned. □ **frumpily** *adv.* **frumpiness** *n.*

frustrate *v. & adj.* ● *v.tr.* /frʌˈstreɪt, ˈfrʌs-/ **1** make (efforts) ineffective. **2** prevent (a person) from achieving a purpose. **3** (as **frustrated** *adj.*) **a** discontented because unable to achieve one's desire. **b** sexually unfulfilled. **4** disappoint (a hope). ● *adj.* /ˈfrʌstreɪt/ *archaic* frustrated. □ **frustratedly** *adv.* **frustrater** *n.* **frustrating** *adj.* **frustratingly** *adv.* **frustration** /-ˈstreɪʃ(ə)n/ *n.* [Middle English from Latin *frustrari frustrat-*, from *frustra* 'in vain']

frustule /ˈfrʌstjuːl/ *n. Bot.* the siliceous cell wall of a diatom. [French from Latin *frustulum* (as FRUSTUM)]

frustum /ˈfrʌstəm/ *n.* (*pl.* **frusta** /-tə/ or **frustums**) *Geom.* **1** the remainder of a cone or pyramid whose upper part has been cut off by a plane parallel to its base. **2** the part of a cone or pyramid intercepted between two planes. [Latin, = piece cut off]

frutescent /frʊˈtɛs(ə)nt/ *adj. Bot.* of the nature of a shrub. [formed irregularly from Latin *frutex* 'bush, shrub']

frutex /ˈfruːtɛks/ *n.* (*pl.* **frutices** /-tɪsiːz/) *Bot.* a woody-stemmed plant smaller than a tree; a shrub. [Latin *frutex fruticis*]

fruticose /ˈfruːtɪkəʊz, -s/ *adj. Bot.* of the nature of or resembling a shrub. [Latin *fruticosus* (as FRUTEX)]

fry[1] /frʌɪ/ *v. & n.* ● *v.* (**fries**, **fried**) **1** *tr. & intr.* cook or be cooked in hot fat. **2** *tr. & intr.* burn or overheat; frizzle, scorch. **3** *tr. & intr. slang* electrocute or be electrocuted. **4** *tr.* (as **fried** *adj.*) *slang* drunk. ● *n.* (*pl.* **fries**) **1** various internal parts of animals usu. eaten fried (*lamb's fry*). **2 a** a dish of fried food, esp. meat. **b** (in *pl.*) *N. Amer.* = FRENCH FRIED POTATOES. **3** *US* a social gathering where fried food is served. ▫ **fry up** heat or reheat (food) in a frying pan. [Middle English via Old French *frire* from Latin *frigere*]

fry[2] /frʌɪ/ *n.pl.* **1** young or newly hatched fishes. **2** the young of other creatures produced in large numbers, e.g. bees or frogs. [Middle English from Old Norse *frjó*]

fryer /ˈfrʌɪə/ *n.* (also **frier**) **1** a person who fries. **2** a vessel for frying esp. fish. **3** *US* a young chicken suitable for frying.

frying pan *n.* (*N. Amer.* **frypan** /ˈfrʌɪpan/) a shallow pan used in frying. ▫ **out of the frying pan into the fire** from a bad situation to a worse one.

fry-up *n. Brit. colloq.* a dish of miscellaneous fried food.

FS *abbr.* (in the UK) Flight Sergeant.

FSA *abbr. Brit.* Fellow of the Society of Antiquaries.

FSH *abbr.* follicle-stimulating hormone.

f-stop *n. Photog.* a camera setting corresponding to a particular f-number.

Ft. *abbr.* Fort.

ft *abbr.* foot, feet.

FTC *abbr. US* Federal Trade Commission.

FT Index *n. Stock Exch.* any of a number of share indices published by the *Financial Times*.

FTP *abbr. Computing* file-transfer protocol.

FT–SE *abbr.* Financial Times–Stock Exchange index (see also FOOTSIE).

fubsy /ˈfʌbzi/ *adj.* (**fubsier**, **fubsiest**) *Brit.* fat or squat. [obsolete *fubs* 'small fat person' + -Y[1]]

fuchsia /ˈfjuːʃə/ *n.* any shrub of the genus *Fuchsia*, with drooping red, purple, or white flowers. [modern Latin, named after L. *Fuchs*, German botanist d. 1566]

fuchsine /ˈfuːksiːn/ *n.* a deep red aniline dye used in the pharmaceutical and textile-processing industries, rosaniline. [FUCHSIA (from its resemblance to the colour of the flower)]

fuck /fʌk/ *v., int., & n. coarse slang* ● *v.* **1** *tr. & intr.* have sexual intercourse (with). **2** *intr.* (foll. by *about*, *around*) mess about; fool around. **3** *tr.* (usu. as an exclamation) curse, confound (*fuck the thing!*). **4** *intr.* (as **fucking** *adj., adv.*) used as an intensive to express annoyance etc. ● *int.* expressing anger or annoyance. ● *n.* **1 a** an act of sexual intercourse. **b** a partner in sexual intercourse. **2** the slightest amount (*don't give a fuck*). ▫ **fuck all** *Brit.* nothing. **fuck off** go away. **fuck up 1** make a mess of. **2** disturb emotionally. **3** make a blunder. ▫ **fucker** *n.* (often as a term of abuse). [16th c.: origin unknown]

■ **Usage** Although widely used in many sections of society, *fuck* is still generally considered to be one of the most offensive words in the English language. In discussions about bad language it is sometimes referred to euphemistically as *the F-word*.

fuck-up *n. coarse slang* a mess or muddle.

fucus /ˈfjuːkəs/ *n.* (*pl.* **fuci** /ˈfjuːsʌɪ/) any seaweed of the genus *Fucus*, with flat leathery fronds. ▫ **fucoid** *adj.* [Latin, = rock-lichen, from Greek *phukos*, of Semitic origin]

fuddle /ˈfʌd(ə)l/ *v. & n.* ● *v.* **1** *tr.* confuse or stupefy, esp. with alcoholic liquor. **2** *intr. archaic* tipple, booze. ● *n.* **1** confusion. **2** intoxication. **3** a spell of drinking (*on the fuddle*). [16th c.: origin unknown]

fuddy-duddy /ˈfʌdɪdʌdi/ *adj. & n. colloq.* ● *adj.* old-fashioned or quaintly fussy. ● *n.* (*pl.* **-ies**) a fuddy-duddy person. [20th c.: origin unknown]

fudge /fʌdʒ/ *n., v., & int.* ● *n.* **1** a soft toffee-like sweet made with milk, sugar, butter, etc. **2** nonsense. **3** a piece of dishonesty or faking. **4** a piece of late news inserted in a newspaper page. ● *v.* **1** *tr.* put together in a makeshift or dishonest way; fake. **2** *tr.* deal with incompetently. **3** *intr.* practise such methods. ● *int.* expressing disbelief or annoyance. [perhaps from obsolete *fadge* 'to fit']

fuehrer var. of FÜHRER.

fuel /fjʊəl, ˈfjuːəl/ *n. & v.* ● *n.* **1** material, esp. coal, wood, oil, etc., burnt or used as a source of heat or power. **2** food as a source of energy. **3** material used as a source of nuclear energy. **4** anything that sustains or inflames emotion or passion. ● *v.* (**fuelled**, **fuelling**; *US* **fueled**, **fueling**) **1** *tr.* supply with fuel. **2** *tr.* sustain or inflame (an argument, feeling, etc.) (*drink fuelled his anger*). **3** *intr.* take in or get fuel. [Middle English from Anglo-French *fuaille*, *fewaile*, Old French *fouaille*, ultimately from Latin *focus* 'hearth']

fuel cell *n.* a cell producing an electric current direct from a chemical reaction.

fuel element *n.* an element of nuclear fuel etc. for use in a reactor.

fuel injection *n.* the direct introduction of fuel under pressure into the combustion units of an internal-combustion engine. ▫ **fuel-injected** *adj.*

fuel oil *n.* oil used as fuel in an engine or furnace.

fuel rod *n.* a rod-shaped fuel element, esp. in a nuclear reactor.

fug /fʌg/ *n. & v. Brit. colloq.* ● *n.* stuffiness or fustiness of the air in a room. ● *v.intr.* (**fugged**, **fugging**) stay in or enjoy a fug. ▫ **fuggy** *adj.* [19th c.: origin unknown]

fugacious /fjʊˈgeɪʃəs/ *adj. literary* fleeting, evanescent, hard to capture or keep. ▫ **fugaciously** *adv.* **fugaciousness** *n.* **fugacity** /-ˈgasɪti/ *n.* [Latin *fugax fugacis* from *fugere* 'flee']

fugal /ˈfjuːg(ə)l/ *adj.* of the nature of a fugue. ▫ **fugally** *adv.*

-fuge /fjuːdʒ/ *comb. form* forming adjectives and nouns denoting expelling or dispelling (*febrifuge*; *vermifuge*). [from or suggested by modern Latin *-fugus* from Latin *fugare* 'put to flight']

fugitive /ˈfjuːdʒɪtɪv/ *adj. & n.* ● *adj.* **1** fleeing; that runs or has run away. **2** transient, fleeting; of short duration. **3** (of literature) of passing interest, ephemeral. **4** flitting, shifting. ● *n.* **1** (often foll. by *from*) a person who flees, esp. from justice, an enemy, danger, or a master. **2** an exile or refugee. ▫ **fugitively** *adv.* [Middle English via Old French *fugitif -ive* from Latin *fugitivus*, from *fugere fugit-* 'flee']

fugle /ˈfjuːg(ə)l/ *v.intr.* act as a fugleman. [back-formation from FUGLEMAN]

fugleman /ˈfjuːg(ə)lmən/ *n.* (*pl.* **-men**) **1** *hist.* a soldier placed in front of a regiment etc. while drilling to show the motions and time. **2** a leader, organizer, or spokesman. [German *Flügelmann*, from *Flügel* 'wing' + *Mann* 'man']

fugue /fjuːg/ *n. & v.* ● *n.* **1** *Mus.* a contrapuntal composition in which a short melody or phrase (the subject) is introduced by one part and successively taken up by others and developed by interweaving the parts. **2** *Psychol.* loss of awareness of one's identity, often coupled with flight from one's usual environment. ● *v.intr.* (**fugues**, **fugued**, **fuguing**) *Mus.* compose or perform a fugue. ▫ **fuguist** *n.* [French or Italian from Latin *fuga* 'flight']

fugued /fjuːgd/ *adj.* in the form of a fugue.

führer /ˈfjʊərə/ *n.* (also **fuehrer**) a leader, esp. a tyrannical one. [German, = leader: part of the title assumed in 1934 by Hitler (see HITLER)]

-ful /fʊl, f(ə)l/ *suffix* forming: **1** adjectives from nouns, meaning: **a** full of (*beautiful*). **b** having the qualities of (*masterful*). **2** adjectives from adjectives or Latin stems with little change of sense (*direful*; *grateful*). **3** adjectives from verbs, meaning 'apt to', 'able to', 'accustomed to' (*forgetful*; *mournful*; *useful*). **4** nouns (*pl.* **-fuls**) meaning 'the amount needed to fill' (*handful*; *spoonful*).

fulcrum /ˈfʊlkrəm, ˈfʌl-/ *n.* (*pl.* **fulcra** /-rə/ or **fulcrums**) **1** the point against which a lever is placed to get a purchase or on which it turns or is supported. **2** the means by which influence etc. is brought to bear. [Latin, = post of a couch, from *fulcire* 'to prop']

fulfil /fʊlˈfɪl/ *v.tr.* (*US* **fulfill**) (**fulfilled**, **fulfilling**) **1** bring to consummation, carry out (a prophecy or promise). **2 a** satisfy (a desire or prayer). **b** (as **fulfilled** *adj.*) completely happy. **3 a** execute, obey (a command or law). **b** perform, carry out (a task). **4** comply with (conditions). **5** answer (a purpose). **6** bring to an end, finish, complete (a period or piece of work). □ **fulfil oneself** develop one's gifts and character to the full. □ **fulfillable** *adj.* **fulfiller** *n.* **fulfilment** *n.* (*US* **fulfillment**). [Old English *fullfyllan* (as FULL[1], FILL)]

fulgent /ˈfʌldʒ(ə)nt/ *adj. poet.* or *literary* shining, brilliant. [Middle English from Latin *fulgēre* 'shine']

fulguration /fʌlgjʊˈreɪʃ(ə)n/ *n. Surgery* the destruction of tissue by means of high-voltage electric sparks. [Latin *fulguratio* 'sheet lightning' from *fulgur* 'lightning']

fulgurite /ˈfʌlgjʊrʌɪt/ *n. Geol.* a rocky substance of sand fused or vitrified by lightning. [Latin *fulgur* 'lightning']

fuliginous /fjuːˈlɪdʒɪnəs/ *adj. literary* sooty, dusky. [Late Latin *fuliginosus* from *fuligo -ginis* 'soot']

full[1] /fʊl/ *adj., adv., n., & v.* ● *adj.* **1** (often foll. by *of*) holding all its limits will allow (*the bucket is full*; *full of water*). **2** having eaten to one's limits or satisfaction. **3** abundant, copious, satisfying, sufficient (*a full programme of events*; *led a full life*; *turned it to full account*; *give full details*; *the book is very full on this point*). **4** (foll. by *of*) having or holding an abundance of, showing marked signs of (*full of vitality*; *full of interest*; *full of mistakes*). **5** (foll. by *of*) **a** engrossed in thinking about (*full of himself*; *full of his work*). **b** unable to refrain from talking about (*full of the news*). **6 a** complete, perfect, reaching the specified or usual or utmost limit (*full membership*; *full daylight*; *waited a full hour*; *it was full summer*; *in full bloom*). **b** *Bookbinding* used for the entire cover (*full leather*). **7 a** (of tone or colour) deep and clear, mellow. **b** (of light) intense. **c** (of motion etc.) vigorous (*a full pulse*; *at full gallop*). **8** plump, rounded, protuberant (*a full figure*). **9** (of clothes) made of much material arranged in folds or gathers. **10** (of the heart etc.) overcharged with emotion. **11** *Brit. slang* drunk. **12** (foll. by *of*) *archaic* having had plenty of (*full of years and honours*). ● *adv.* **1** very (*you know full well*). **2** quite, fully (*full six miles*; *full ripe*). **3** exactly (*hit him full on the nose*). **4** more than sufficiently (*full early*). ● *n.* **1** height, acme (*season is past the full*). **2** the state or time of full moon. **3** the whole (*cannot tell you the full of it*). ● *v.intr. & tr.* be or become or make (esp. clothes) full. □ **at full length 1** lying stretched out. **2** without abridgement. **come full circle** see CIRCLE. **full and by** *Naut.* close-hauled but with sails filling. **full speed** (or **steam**) **ahead!** an order to proceed at maximum speed or to pursue a course of action energetically. **full up** completely full. **in full 1** without abridgement. **2** to or for the full amount (*paid in full*). **in full swing** at the height of activity. **in full view** entirely visible. **on a full stomach** see STOMACH. **to the full** to the utmost extent. [Old English from Germanic]

full[2] /fʊl/ *v.tr.* cleanse and thicken (cloth). [Middle English, back-formation from FULLER[1]: cf. Old French *fouler* (FOIL[1])]

full age *n. Brit.* adult status (esp. with reference to legal rights and duties).

full-back *n.* a defensive player, or a position near the goal, in football, hockey, etc.

full beam *n.* the brightest setting of a vehicle's headlights.

full-blooded *adj.* **1** vigorous, hearty, sensual. **2** not hybrid. □ **full-bloodedly** *adv.* □ **full-bloodedness** *n.*

full-blown *adj.* fully developed, complete, (of flowers) quite open.

full board *n.* provision of accommodation and all meals at a hotel etc.

full-bodied *adj.* rich in quality, tone, etc.

full-bottomed *adj.* (of a wig) long at the back.

full brother *n.* a brother born of the same parents.

full colour *n.* the full range of colours (usu. hyphenated when *attrib.*: *full-colour brochure*).

full-cream *adj.* of or made from unskimmed milk.

full dress *n. & adj.* ● *n.* formal clothes worn on great occasions. ● *attrib.adj.* (**full-dress**) (of a debate etc.) of major importance.

full dress uniform *n.* military uniform worn for ceremonial parades etc.

full employment *n.* **1** the condition in which there is no idle capital or labour of any kind that is in demand. **2** the condition in which virtually all who are able and willing to work are employed.

fuller[1] /ˈfʊlə/ *n.* a person who fulls cloth. [Old English *fullere* from Latin *fullo*]

fuller[2] /ˈfʊlə/ *n. & v.* ● *n.* **1** a grooved or rounded tool on which iron is shaped. **2** a groove made by this esp. in a horseshoe. ● *v.tr.* stamp with a fuller. [19th c.: origin unknown]

fullerene /ˈfʊləriːn/ *n. Chem.* any of several forms of carbon in which atoms are joined in a hollow structure. [BUCKMINSTERFULLERENE]

fuller's earth *n.* a type of clay used in fulling cloth and as an adsorbent.

full face *adv. & adj.* ● *adv.* (also **in full face**) with all the face visible to the observer. ● *adj.* (**full-face**) with all the face visible to the observer.

full-fashioned *adj.* = FULLY-FASHIONED.

full-fledged *adj.* = FULLY-FLEDGED.

full flood *n.* **1** the tide at its highest. **2** (in phr. **in full flood**) speaking volubly.

full-frontal *attrib.adj.* **1** (of nudity or a nude figure) with full exposure at the front. **2** unrestrained, explicit; with nothing concealed.

full-grown *adj.* having reached maturity.

full growth *n.* the size ultimately attained; maturity.

full hand *n. Brit. Poker* = FULL HOUSE 2.

full-hearted *adj.* full of feeling; confident, zealous. □ **full-heartedly** *adv.* □ **full-heartedness** *n.*

full house *n.* **1** a maximum or large attendance at a theatre, in Parliament, etc. **2** *Poker* a hand with three of a kind and a pair.

full-length *adj.* **1** of normal, standard, or maximum length; not shortened or abbreviated. **2** (of a mirror, portrait, etc.) showing the whole height of the human figure.

full lock see LOCK[1] *n.* 3b.

full marks *n.pl. Brit.* the maximum award in an examination, in assessment of a person, etc.

full moon *n.* **1** the moon with its whole disc illuminated. **2** the time when this occurs.

full-mouthed *adj.* **1** (of cattle or sheep) having a full set of teeth. **2** (of a dog) baying loudly. **3** (of oratory etc.) sonorous, vigorous.

fullness /ˈfʊlnɪs/ *n.* (also **fulness**) **1** being full. **2** (of sound, colour, etc.) richness, volume, body. **3** all that is contained (in the world etc.). □ **the fullness of the heart** emotion, genuine feelings. **the fullness of time** the appropriate or destined time.

full out *adv.* **1** *Printing* flush with the margin. **2** at full power. **3** completely.

full page *n.* an entire page of a newspaper etc. (hyphenated when *attrib.*: *full-page spread*).

full pitch *n.* = FULL TOSS.
full point *n.* = FULL STOP 1.
full professor *n.* a professor of the highest grade in a university etc.
full-scale *adj.* not reduced in size, complete.
full score *n. Mus.* a score giving the parts for all performers on separate staves.
full sister *n.* a sister born of the same parents.
full stop *n.* **1** a punctuation mark (.) used at the end of a sentence or an abbreviation. **2** a complete cessation.
full term *n.* the completion of a normal pregnancy.
full tilt see TILT.
full-time *adj. & adv.* ● *adj.* occupying or using the whole of the available working time (*a full-time job*). ● *adv.* on a full-time basis (*works full-time*).
full time *n.* **1** the total normal duration of work etc. **2** the end of a football etc. match.
full-timer *n.* a person who does a full-time job.
full toss *n. & adv. Cricket* ● *n.* a ball pitched right up to the batsman. ● *adv.* without the ball's having touched the ground.
fully /'fʊli/ *adv.* **1** completely, entirely (*am fully aware*). **2** no less or fewer than (*fully 60*). [Old English *fullīce* (as FULL[1], -LY[2])]
-fully /'fʊli, f(ə)li/ *suffix* forming adverbs corresponding to adjectives in *-ful*.
fully-fashioned *adj.* (of women's clothing) shaped to fit the body.
fully-fledged *adj. Brit.* (or **fully fledged** *predic.*) mature.
fulmar /'fʊlmə/ *n.* any medium-sized seabird of the genus *Fulmarus*, with stout body, robust bill, and rounded tail. [originally Hebridean dialect, from Old Norse *fúll* FOUL (with reference to its habit of regurgitating its stomach contents when disturbed) + *már* 'gull' (cf. MEW[2])]
fulminant /'fʌlmɪnənt, 'fʊl-/ *adj.* **1** fulminating. **2** *Med.* (of a disease or symptom) developing suddenly. [French *fulminant* or Latin *fulminant-* (as FULMINATE)]
fulminate /'fʌlmɪneɪt, 'fʊl-/ *v. & n.* ● *v.intr.* **1** (often foll. by *against*) express censure loudly and forcefully. **2** explode violently; flash like lightning (*fulminating mercury*). **3** *Med.* (of a disease or symptom) develop suddenly. ● *n. Chem.* a salt or ester of fulminic acid. □ **fulmination** /-'neɪʃ(ə)n/ *n.* **fulminatory** *adj.* [Latin *fulminare fulminat-* from *fulmen -minis* 'lightning']
fulminic acid /fʌl'mɪnɪk, fʊl-/ *n. Chem.* an isomer of cyanic acid that is stable only in solution. Chem. formula: HONC. [Latin *fulmen*: see FULMINATE]
fulness var. of FULLNESS.
fulsome /'fʊls(ə)m/ *adj.* **1** disgusting by excess of flattery, servility, or expressions of affection; excessive, cloying. **2** *disp.* copious. □ **fulsomely** *adv.* **fulsomeness** *n.* [Middle English, from FULL[1] + -SOME[1]]

■ **Usage** The original meaning of *fulsome* was 'copious' (see sense 2 above). However, this usage is now considered incorrect, and *fulsome* is used only as a pejorative term, applied to nouns such as *flattery*, *praise*, and *tribute*, meaning 'excessive' or 'cloying'.

fulvous /'fʌlvəs, 'fʊl-/ *adj.* reddish yellow, tawny. □ **fulvescent** /-'vɛs(ə)nt/ *adj.* [Latin *fulvus*]
fumarole /'fju:mərəʊl/ *n.* an opening in or near a volcano, through which hot vapours emerge. □ **fumarolic** /-'rɒlɪk/ *adj.* [French *fumarolle*]
fumble /'fʌmb(ə)l/ *v. & n.* ● *v.* **1** *intr.* (often foll. by *at*, *with*, *for*, *after*) use the hands awkwardly, grope about. **2** *tr.* **a** handle or deal with clumsily or nervously. **b** *Sport* fail to stop (a ball) cleanly. ● *n.* an act of fumbling. □ **fumbler** *n.* **fumblingly** *adv.* [Middle English from Low German *fummeln*, *fommeln*, Dutch *fommelen*]
fume /fju:m/ *n. & v.* ● *n.* **1** (usu. in *pl.*) exuded gas or smoke or vapour, esp. when harmful or unpleasant. **2** a fit of anger (*in a fume*). ● *v.* **1** **a** *intr.* emit fumes. **b** *tr.* give off as fumes. **2** *intr.* (often foll. by *at*) be affected by (esp. suppressed) anger (*was fuming at their inefficiency*). **3** *tr.* **a** fumigate. **b** subject to fumes, esp. those of ammonia (to darken tints in oak, photographic film, etc.). **4** *tr.* perfume with incense. □ **fumeless** *adj.* **fumingly** *adv.* **fumy** *adj.* (in sense 1 of *n.*). [Middle English via Old French *fum* from Latin *fumus* 'smoke', and via Old French *fume*, from *fumer*, from Latin *fumare* 'to smoke']
fume cupboard *n.* (also **fume chamber**) *Brit.* a ventilated structure in a laboratory, for storing or experimenting with noxious chemicals.
fume hood *n.* = FUME CUPBOARD.
fumigate /'fju:mɪgeɪt/ *v.tr.* **1** disinfect or purify with fumes. **2** apply fumes to. □ **fumigant** *n.* **fumigation** /-'geɪʃ(ə)n/ *n.* **fumigator** *n.* [Latin *fumigare fumigat-* from *fumus* 'smoke']
fumitory /'fju:mɪt(ə)ri/ *n.* any plant of the genus *Fumaria*, esp. *F. officinalis*, formerly used against scurvy. [Middle English via Old French *fumeterre* from medieval Latin *fumus terrae* 'earth-smoke', from its greyish leaves]
fun /fʌn/ *n. & adj.* ● *n.* **1** amusement, esp. lively or playful. **2** a source of this. **3** (in full **fun and games**) exciting or amusing goings-on. ● *attrib.adj. disp. colloq.* amusing, entertaining, enjoyable (*a fun thing to do*). □ **be great** (or **good**) **fun** be very amusing. **for fun** (or **for the fun of it**) not for a serious purpose. **have fun** enjoy oneself. **in fun** as a joke, not seriously. **like fun 1** vigorously, quickly. **2** much. **3** *iron.* not at all. **make fun of** mock; ridicule. **what fun!** how amusing! [obsolete *fun*, variant of *fon* 'befool': cf. FOND]

■ **Usage** The use of *fun* as an attributive adjective, e.g. *It was essentially a fun project*, is common in informal use, but is considered incorrect by some people.

funambulist /fju:'nambjʊlɪst/ *n.* a rope-walker. [French *funambule* or Latin *funambulus*, from *funis* 'rope' + *ambulare* 'walk']
funboard /'fʌnbɔ:d/ *n.* a type of windsurfing board that is less stable but faster than a standard board.
function /'fʌŋ(k)ʃ(ə)n/ *n. & v.* ● *n.* **1** **a** an activity proper to a person or institution. **b** a mode of action or activity by which a thing fulfils its purpose. **c** an official or professional duty; an employment, profession, or calling. **2** **a** a public ceremony or occasion. **b** a social gathering, esp. a large, formal, or important one. **3** *Math.* a variable quantity regarded in relation to another or others in terms of which it may be expressed or on which its value depends (*x is a function of y and z*). **4** *Computing* a part of a program that corresponds to a single value. ● *v.intr.* fulfil a function, operate; be in working order. □ **functionless** *adj.* [French *fonction* from Latin *functio -onis*, from *fungi funct-* 'perform']
functional /'fʌŋ(k)ʃ(ə)n(ə)l/ *adj.* **1** of or serving a function. **2** (esp. of buildings) designed or intended to be practical rather than attractive; utilitarian. **3** *Physiol.* **a** (esp. of disease) of or affecting only the functions of an organ etc., not structural or organic. **b** (of mental disorder) having no discernible organic cause. **c** (of an organ) having a function, not functionless or rudimentary. **4** *Math.* of a function. □ **functionality** /-'nalɪti/ *n.* **functionally** *adv.*
functional food *n.* a food containing health-giving additives.
functional group *n. Chem.* a group of atoms that determine the reactions of a compound containing the group.
functionalism /'fʌŋ(k)ʃ(ə)n(ə)lɪz(ə)m/ *n.* belief in or stress on the practical application of a thing. □ **functionalist** *n.*
functionary /'fʌn(k)ʃ(ə)n(ə)ri/ *n.* (*pl.* **-ies**) a person who has to perform official functions or duties; an official.
function key *n. Computing* a key which is used to generate instructions.
fund /fʌnd/ *n. & v.* ● *n.* **1** a permanent stock of something ready to be drawn upon (*a fund of*

knowledge; *a fund of tenderness*). **2** a stock of money, esp. one set apart for a purpose. **3** (in *pl.*) money resources. **4** (in *pl.*; prec. by *the*) *Brit.* the stock of the national debt (as a mode of investment). ● *v.tr.* **1** provide with money. **2** convert (a floating debt) into a more or less permanent debt at fixed interest. **3** put into a fund. □ **in funds** *Brit. colloq.* having money to spend. [Latin *fundus* 'bottom, piece of land']

fundament /'fʌndəm(ə)nt/ *n. joc.* the buttocks. [Middle English via Old French *fondement* from Latin *fundamentum* (as FOUND[2])]

fundamental /fʌndə'mɛnt(ə)l/ *adj. & n.* ● *adj.* of, affecting, or serving as a base or foundation, essential, primary, original (*a fundamental change*; *the fundamental rules*; *the fundamental form*). ● *n.* **1** (usu. in *pl.*) a fundamental rule, principle, or article. **2** *Mus.* a fundamental note or tone. □ **fundamentality** /-'talɪti/ *n.* **fundamentally** *adv.* [Middle English from French *fondamental* or Late Latin *fundamentalis* from Latin *fundamentum* (as FOUND[2])]

fundamentalism /fʌndə'mɛnt(ə)lɪz(ə)m/ *n.* **1** strict maintenance of traditional Protestant beliefs such as the inerrancy of Scripture and literal acceptance of the creeds as fundamentals of Christianity. **2** strict maintenance of ancient or fundamental doctrines of any religion, esp. Islam. □ **fundamentalist** *n. & adj.*

fundamental note *n. Mus.* the lowest note of a chord in its original (uninverted) form.

fundamental particle *n.* a subatomic particle.

fundamental tone *n. Mus.* the tone produced by vibration of the whole of a sonorous body (opp. HARMONIC).

fundholder /'fʌndhəʊldə/ *n.* a GP who is provided with and controls his or her own budget. □ **fundholding** *n. & adj.*

fund-raiser *n.* a person who seeks financial support for a cause, enterprise, etc. □ **fund-raising** *n.*

fundus /'fʌndəs/ *n.* (*pl.* **fundi** /-dʌɪ/) *Anat.* the base of a hollow organ; the part furthest from the opening. [Latin, = bottom]

funeral /'fjuːn(ə)r(ə)l/ *n. & adj.* ● *n.* **1 a** the burial or cremation of a dead person with its ceremonies. **b** a burial or cremation procession. **c** *US* a burial or cremation service. **2** *colloq.* one's (usu. unpleasant) concern (*that's your funeral*). ● *attrib.adj.* of or used etc. at a funeral (*funeral oration*). [Middle English via Old French *funeraille* and medieval Latin *funeralia*, neut. pl. of Late Latin *funeralis*, from Latin *funus -eris* 'funeral': the adjective via Old French from Latin *funeralis*]

funeral director *n.* an undertaker.

funeral parlour *n.* (*N. Amer.* also **funeral home**) an establishment where the dead are prepared for burial or cremation.

funeral pile *n.* (also **funeral pyre**) a pile of wood etc. on which a corpse is burnt.

funeral urn *n.* an urn holding the ashes of a cremated body.

funerary /'fjuːn(ə)(rə)ri/ *adj.* of or used at a funeral or funerals. [Late Latin *funerarius* (as FUNERAL)]

funereal /fjuː'nɪərɪəl/ *adj.* **1** of or appropriate to a funeral. **2** gloomy, dismal, dark. □ **funereally** *adv.* [Latin *funereus* (as FUNERAL)]

funfair /'fʌnfɛː/ *n. Brit.* a fair, or part of one, consisting of amusements and sideshows.

fungi *pl.* of FUNGUS.

fungible /'fʌn(d)ʒɪb(ə)l/ *adj. Law* (of goods etc. contracted for, when an individual specimen is not meant) that can serve for, or be replaced by, another answering to the same definition. □ **fungibility** /-'bɪlɪti/ *n.* [medieval Latin *fungibilis*, from *fungi* (*vice*) 'serve (in place of)']

fungicide /'fʌn(d)ʒɪsʌɪd, 'fʌŋgɪ-/ *n.* a fungus-destroying substance. □ **fungicidal** /-'sʌɪd(ə)l/ *adj.*

fungistatic /fʌn(d)ʒɪ'statɪk/ *adj.* inhibiting the growth of fungi. □ **fungistatically** *adv.*

fungoid /'fʌŋgɔɪd/ *adj. & n.* ● *adj.* **1** resembling a fungus in texture or in rapid growth. **2** of a fungus or fungi. ● *n.* a fungoid plant.

fungous /'fʌŋgəs/ *adj.* **1** having the nature of a fungus. **2** springing up like a mushroom; transitory. [Middle English from Latin *fungosus* (as FUNGUS)]

fungus /'fʌŋgəs/ *n.* (*pl.* **fungi** /-gʌɪ, -(d)ʒʌɪ/ or **funguses**) **1** any of a group of unicellular, multicellular, or syncytial spore-producing organisms feeding on organic matter, including moulds, yeast, mushrooms, and toadstools. **2** anything similar usu. growing suddenly and rapidly. **3** *Med.* a spongy morbid growth. **4** *slang* a beard. □ **fungal** *adj.* **fungiform** /'fʌŋ(d)ʒɪfɔːm/ *adj.* **fungivorous** /-'dʒɪv(ə)rəs/ *adj.* [Latin, perhaps from Greek *sp(h)oggos* SPONGE]

funicular /fjʊ'nɪkjʊlə, fə'nɪk-/ *adj. & n.* ● *adj.* **1** (of a railway, esp. on a mountainside) operating by cable with ascending and descending cars counterbalanced. **2** of a rope or its tension. ● *n.* a funicular railway. [Latin *funiculus* from *funis* 'rope']

funk[1] /fʌŋk/ *n. & v. slang* ● *n.* **1** fear, panic. **2** *Brit.* a coward. ● *v. Brit.* **1** *intr.* flinch, shrink, show cowardice. **2** *tr.* try to evade (an undertaking), shirk. **3** *tr.* be afraid of. □ **in a funk** *US* in a dejected state of mind. [18th-c. Oxford slang: perhaps from FUNK[2] in the slang sense 'tobacco smoke']

funk[2] /fʌŋk/ *n. slang* **1** funky music. **2** *US* a strong smell. [*funk* 'blow smoke on', perhaps from French dialect *funkier* from Latin (as FUMIGATE)]

funkia /'fʌŋkɪə/ *n.* = HOSTA. [modern Latin, named after H. C. *Funck*, Prussian botanist d. 1839]

funky[1] /'fʌŋki/ *adj.* (**funkier**, **funkiest**) *slang* **1** (esp. of jazz or rock music) earthy, bluesy, with a heavy rhythmical beat. **2** fashionable. **3** unconventional; striking. **4** *US* having a strong smell. □ **funkily** *adv.* **funkiness** *n.* [FUNK[2]]

funky[2] /'fʌŋki/ *adj.* (**funkier**, **funkiest**) *Brit. slang* **1** terrified. **2** cowardly. [FUNK[1]]

funnel /'fʌn(ə)l/ *n. & v.* ● *n.* **1** a narrow tube or pipe widening at the top, for pouring liquid, powder, etc., into a small opening. **2** a metal chimney on a steam engine or ship. **3** something resembling a funnel in shape or use. ● *v.tr. & intr.* (**funnelled**, **funnelling**; *US* **funneled**, **funneling**) guide or move through or as through a funnel. □ **funnel-like** *adj.* [Middle English via Provençal *fonilh* and Late Latin *fundibulum* from Latin *infundibulum*, from *infundere* (as IN-[2], *fundere* 'pour')]

funniosity /fʌnɪ'ɒsɪti/ *n.* (*pl.* **-ies**) *Brit. joc.* **1** comicality. **2** a comical thing. [FUNNY + -OSITY]

funny /'fʌni/ *adj. & n.* ● *adj.* (**funnier**, **funniest**) **1** amusing, comical. **2** strange, perplexing, hard to account for. **3** *colloq.* slightly unwell, eccentric, etc. ● *n.* (*pl.* **-ies**) (usu. in *pl.*) *colloq.* **1** a comic strip in a newspaper. **2** a joke. □ **funnily** *adv.* **funniness** *n.* [FUN + -Y[1]]

funny bone *n.* the part of the elbow over which the ulnar nerve passes.

funny business *n.* **1** *slang* misbehaviour or deception. **2** comic behaviour, comedy.

funny-face *n. joc. colloq.* an affectionate form of address.

funny farm *n. slang* a psychiatric hospital.

funny-ha-ha *adj. colloq.* = FUNNY *adj.* 1.

funny man *n.* a clown or comedian, esp. a professional.

funny money *n. colloq.* inflated or counterfeit currency.

funny paper *n.* a newspaper etc. containing humorous matter.

funny-peculiar *adj. colloq.* = FUNNY *adj.* 2, 3.

fun run *n. colloq.* an uncompetitive run, esp. for sponsored runners in support of a charity.

funster /'fʌnstə/ *n. colloq.* a person who makes fun; a joker.

fur /fəː/ *n. & v.* ● *n.* **1 a** the short fine soft hair of certain animals, distinguished from the longer hair. **b** the skin of such an animal with the fur on it; a pelt. **2 a** the coat of certain animals as material for making, trimming, or lining clothes. **b** a trimming or lining made of the dressed coat of such animals, or of material imitating this. **c** a garment made of or trimmed or lined with fur. **3** (*collect.*) furred animals. **4 a** a coating formed on the tongue in sickness. **b** *Brit.* a coating formed on the inside surface of a pipe, kettle, etc., by hard water. **c** a crust adhering to a surface, e.g. a deposit from wine. **5** *Heraldry* a representation of tufts on a plain ground. ● *v.* (**furred**, **furring**) **1** *tr.* (esp. as **furred** *adj.*) **a** line or trim (a garment) with fur. **b** provide (an animal) with fur. **c** clothe (a person) with fur. **d** coat (a tongue, the inside of a kettle) with fur. **2** *intr.* (often foll. by *up*) (of a kettle etc.) become coated with fur. **3** *tr.* level (floor-timbers) by inserting strips of wood. □ **fur and feather** game animals and birds. **the fur will fly** *colloq.* there will be a quarrel or disturbance. □ **furless** *adj.* [Middle English (earlier as verb) via Old French *forrer*, from *forre*, *fuerre* 'sheath', from Germanic]

fur. *abbr.* furlong(s).

furbelow /'fəːbɪləʊ/ *n.* & *v.* ● *n.* **1** a gathered strip or pleated border of a skirt or petticoat. **2** (in *pl.*; esp. in phr. **frills and furbelows**) *derog.* showy ornaments. ● *v.tr.* adorn with a furbelow or furbelows. [18th-c. variant of *falbala* 'flounce, trimming']

furbish /'fəːbɪʃ/ *v.tr.* (often foll. by *up*) **1** remove rust from, polish, burnish. **2** give a new look to, renovate, revive (something antiquated). □ **furbisher** *n.* [Middle English from Old French *forbir*, from Germanic]

furcate *adj.* & *v.* ● *adj.* /'fəːkeɪt, -kət/ forked, branched. ● *v.intr.* /'fəːkeɪt, fəː'keɪt/ form a fork, divide. □ **furcation** /fəː'keɪʃ(ə)n/ *n.* [Latin *furca* 'fork': the adjective via Late Latin *furcatus*]

furcula /'fəːkjʊlə/ *n. Zool.* & *Anat.* a forked organ or structure, esp. the wishbone of a bird. [Latin, diminutive of *furca* 'fork']

furfuraceous /fəːf(j)ə'reɪʃəs/ *adj.* **1** *Med.* (of skin) resembling bran or dandruff; scaly. **2** *Bot.* covered with branlike scales. [*furfur* 'scurf' from Latin *furfur* 'bran']

furious /'fjʊərɪəs/ *adj.* **1** extremely angry. **2** full of fury. **3** raging, violent, intense. □ **furiously** *adv.* **furiousness** *n.* [Middle English via Old French *furieus* from Latin *furiosus* (as FURY)]

furl /fəːl/ *v.* **1** *tr.* roll up and secure (a sail, umbrella, flag, etc.). **2** *intr.* become furled. **3** *tr.* **a** close (a fan). **b** fold up (wings). **c** draw away (a curtain). **d** relinquish (hopes). □ **furlable** *adj.* [French *ferler* via Old French *fer(m)* FIRM[1] + *lier* 'bind' from Latin *ligare*]

furlong /'fəːlɒŋ/ *n.* an eighth of a mile, 220 yards. [originally the length of a furrow in a common field: Old English *furlang* from *furh* FURROW + *lang* LONG[1]]

furlough /'fəːləʊ/ *n.* & *v.* ● *n.* leave of absence, esp. granted to a member of the services or to a missionary. ● *v. US* **1** *tr.* grant furlough to. **2** *intr.* spend furlough. [Dutch *verlof*, modelled on German *Verlaub* (as FOR-, LEAVE[2])]

furmety var. of FRUMENTY.

furnace /'fəːnɪs/ *n.* **1** an enclosed structure for intense heating by fire, esp. of metals or water. **2** a very hot place. [Middle English via Old French *fornais* from Latin *fornax -acis*, from *fornus* 'oven']

furnish /'fəːnɪʃ/ *v.tr.* **1** provide (a house, room, etc.) with all necessary contents, esp. movable furniture. **2** (foll. by *with*) cause to have possession or use of. **3** provide, afford, yield. [Old French *furnir*, ultimately from West Germanic]

furnished /'fəːnɪʃt/ *adj.* (of a house, flat, etc.) let with furniture.

furnisher /'fəːnɪʃə/ *n.* **1** a person who sells furniture. **2** a person who furnishes.

furnishings /'fəːnɪʃɪŋz/ *n.pl.* the furniture and fitments in a house, room, etc.

furniture /'fəːnɪtʃə/ *n.* **1** the movable equipment of a house, room, etc., e.g. tables, chairs, and beds. **2** *Naut.* a ship's equipment, esp. tackle etc. **3** accessories, e.g. the handles and lock of a door. **4** *Printing* pieces of wood or metal placed round or between type to make blank spaces and fasten the matter in the chase. □ **part of the furniture** *colloq.* a person or thing taken for granted. [French *fourniture* from *fournir* (as FURNISH)]

furniture beetle *n.* a beetle, *Anobium punctatum*, the larvae of which bore into wood (see WOODWORM).

furniture van *n. Brit.* a large van used to move furniture, esp. from one house to another.

furore /fjʊ(ə)'rɔːri, fjʊ(ə)'rɔː/ *n.* (*US* **furor** /'fjʊərɔː/) **1** an uproar; an outbreak of fury. **2** a wave of enthusiastic admiration, a craze. [Italian from Latin *furor -oris*, from *furere* 'be mad']

furphy /'fəːfi/ *n.* (*pl.* **-ies**) *Austral. slang* **1** a false report or rumour. **2** an absurd story. [water and sanitary *Furphy carts* of the First World War, made at a foundry set up by the Furphy family]

furrier /'fʌrɪə/ *n.* a dealer in or dresser of furs. [Middle English *furrour* from Old French *forreor*, from *forrer* 'trim with fur', assimilated to -IER]

furriery /'fʌrɪəri/ *n.* the work of a furrier.

furrow /'fʌrəʊ/ *n.* & *v.* ● *n.* **1** a narrow trench made in the ground by a plough. **2** a rut, groove, or deep wrinkle. **3** a ship's track. ● *v.* **1** *tr.* plough. **2** *tr.* **a** make furrows, grooves, etc. in. **b** mark with wrinkles. **3** *intr.* (esp. of the brow) become furrowed. □ **furrowless** *adj.* **furrowy** *adj.* [Old English *furh*, from Germanic]

furrow-slice *n.* the slice of earth turned up by the mould-board of a plough.

furry /'fəːri/ *adj.* (**furrier**, **furriest**) **1** of or like fur. **2** covered with or wearing fur. □ **furriness** *n.*

fur seal *n.* any of several related seals with thick fur on the underside used commercially as sealskin.

further /'fəːðə/ *adv.*, *adj.*, & *v.* ● *adv.* (also **farther** /'fɑːðə/) **1** to or at a more advanced point in space or time (*unsafe to proceed further*). **2** at a greater distance (*nothing was further from his thoughts*). **3** to a greater extent, more (*will enquire further*). **4** in addition; furthermore (*I may add further*). ● *adj.* (also **farther** /'fɑːðə/) **1** more distant or advanced (*on the further side*). **2** more, additional, going beyond what exists or has been dealt with (*threats of further punishment*). ● *v.tr.* promote, favour, help on (a scheme, undertaking, movement, or cause). □ **further to** *formal* following on from (esp. an earlier letter etc.). **till further notice** (or **orders**) to continue until explicitly changed. □ **furtherer** *n.* **furthermost** *adj.* [Old English *furthor* (*adv.*), *furthra* (*adj.*), *fyrthrian* (*v.*), formed as FORTH, -ER[2]]

■ **Usage** The form *farther* is used especially with reference to physical distance, although *further* is preferred by many people even in this sense.

furtherance /'fəːð(ə)r(ə)ns/ *n.* furthering or being furthered; the advancement of a scheme etc.

further education *n. Brit.* education for persons above school age but usu. below degree level.

furthermore /fəːðə'mɔː/ *adv.* in addition, besides (esp. introducing a fresh consideration in an argument).

furthest /'fəːðɪst/ *adj.* & *adv.* (also **farthest** /'fɑːðɪst/) ● *adj.* most distant. ● *adv.* to or at the greatest distance. □ **at the furthest** (or **at furthest**) at the greatest distance; at the latest; at most. [Middle English, superlative from FURTHER]

■ **Usage** The form *farthest* is used especially with reference to physical distance, although *furthest* is preferred by many people even in this sense.

furtive /'fəːtɪv/ *adj.* **1** done by stealth, clandestine, meant to escape notice. **2** sly, stealthy. **3** stolen, taken secretly. □ **furtively** *adv.* **furtiveness** *n.* [French *furtif -ive* or Latin *furtivus*, from *furtum* 'theft']

furuncle /'fjʊərʌŋk(ə)l/ *n. Med.* = BOIL[2]. □ **furuncular** /-'rʌŋkjʊlə/ *adj.* **furunculous** /-'rʌŋkjʊləs/ *adj.* [Latin *furunculus* 'petty thief, knob on a vine' ('stealing' the sap), from *fur* 'thief']

furunculosis /fjʊˌrʌŋkjəˈləʊsɪs/ *n.* **1** a diseased condition in which boils appear. **2** a bacterial disease of salmon and trout. [modern Latin (as FURUNCLE)]

fury /ˈfjʊəri/ *n.* (*pl.* **-ies**) **1 a** wild and passionate anger, rage. **b** a fit of rage (*in a blind fury*). **c** impetuosity in battle etc. **2** violence of a storm, disease, etc. **3** (**Fury**) (usu. in *pl.*) (in Greek mythology) each of usu. three goddesses sent from Tartarus to avenge crime, esp. against kinship. **4** an avenging spirit. **5** an angry or malignant woman, a virago. □ **like fury** *colloq.* with great force or effect. [Middle English via Old French *furie* from Latin *furia*, from *furere* 'be mad']

furze /fəːz/ *n. Brit.* = GORSE. □ **furzy** /ˈfəːzi/ *adj.* [Old English *fyrs*, of unknown origin]

fuscous /ˈfʌskəs/ *adj.* sombre, dark-coloured. [Latin *fuscus* 'dusky']

fuse[1] /fjuːz/ *v.* & *n.* ● *v.* **1** *tr.* & *intr.* melt with intense heat; liquefy. **2** *tr.* & *intr.* blend or amalgamate into one whole by or as by melting. **3** *tr.* provide (a circuit, plug, etc.) with a fuse. **4** *Brit.* **a** *intr.* (of an appliance) cease to function when a fuse blows. **b** *tr.* cause (an appliance) to do this. ● *n.* a device or component for protecting an electric circuit, containing a strip or wire of easily melted metal and placed in the circuit so as to break it by melting when an excessive current passes through. □ **blow a fuse** lose one's temper. [Latin *fundere fus-* 'pour, melt']

fuse[2] /fjuːz/ *n.* & *v.* (also **fuze**) ● *n.* **1** a device for igniting a bomb or explosive charge, consisting of a tube or cord etc. filled or saturated with combustible matter. **2** a component in a shell, mine, etc., designed to detonate an explosive charge on impact, after an interval, or when subjected to a magnetic or vibratory stimulation. ● *v.tr.* fit a fuse to. □ **fuseless** *adj.* [Italian *fuso* from Latin *fusus* 'spindle' (from the shape of the tube in sense 1)]

fuse box *n.* a box housing the fuses for circuits in a building.

fusee /fjuːˈziː/ *n.* (*US* **fuzee**) **1** a conical pulley or wheel esp. in a watch or clock. **2** a large-headed match for lighting a cigar or pipe in a wind. **3** *US* a railway signal-flare. [earlier = a spindle-shaped figure: French *fusée* 'spindle', ultimately from Latin *fusus*]

fuselage /ˈfjuːzəlɑːʒ, -lɪdʒ/ *n.* the body of an aeroplane. [French, via *fuseler* 'cut into a spindle', from *fuseau* 'spindle', from Old French *fusel*, ultimately from Latin *fusus*]

fusel oil /ˈfjuːz(ə)l/ *n.* a mixture of several alcohols, chiefly amyl alcohol, produced usu. in small amounts during alcoholic fermentation. [German *Fusel* 'bad brandy etc.': cf. *fuseln* 'to bungle']

fuse wire *n. Electr.* wire used in a fuse (see FUSE[1] *n.*).

fusible /ˈfjuːzɪb(ə)l/ *adj.* that can be easily fused or melted. □ **fusibility** /-ˈbɪlɪti/ *n.*

fusiform /ˈfjuːzɪfɔːm/ *adj. Bot.* & *Zool.* shaped like a spindle or cigar, tapering at both ends. [Latin *fusus* 'spindle' + -FORM]

fusil /ˈfjuːzɪl/ *n. hist.* a light musket. [French, ultimately from Latin *focus* 'hearth, fire']

fusilier /fjuːzɪˈlɪə/ *n.* (*US* also **fusileer**) **1** a member of any of several British regiments formerly armed with fusils. **2** *hist.* a soldier armed with a fusil. [French (as FUSIL)]

fusillade /fjuːzɪˈleɪd, -ˈlɑːd/ *n.* & *v.* ● *n.* **1 a** a continuous discharge of firearms. **b** a wholesale execution by this means. **2** a sustained outburst of criticism etc. ● *v.tr.* **1** assault (a place) by a fusillade. **2** shoot down (persons) with a fusillade. [French, from *fusiller* 'shoot']

fusilli /fʊˈziːli/ *n.pl.* pasta pieces in the form of short spirals. [Italian, literally 'little spindles', diminutive of *fuso* 'spindle']

fusion /ˈfjuːʒ(ə)n/ *n.* **1** the act or an instance of fusing or melting. **2** a fused mass. **3** the blending of different things into one. **4** a coalition. **5** *Physics* = NUCLEAR FUSION. □ **fusional** *adj.* [French *fusion* or Latin *fusio* (as FUSE[1])]

fusion bomb *n.* a bomb involving nuclear fusion, esp. a hydrogen bomb.

fuss /fʌs/ *n.* & *v.* ● *n.* **1** excited commotion, bustle, ostentatious or nervous activity. **2 a** excessive concern about a trivial thing. **b** abundance of petty detail. **3** a sustained protest or dispute. **4** a person who fusses. ● *v.* **1** *intr.* **a** make a fuss. **b** busy oneself restlessly with trivial things. **c** (often foll. by *about*, *up and down*) move fussily. **2** *tr. Brit.* agitate, worry. □ **make a fuss** complain vigorously. **make a fuss over** (or *Brit.* **of**) treat (a person or animal) with great or excessive attention. □ **fusser** *n.* [18th c.: perhaps Anglo-Irish]

fusspot /ˈfʌspɒt/ *n. colloq.* a person given to fussing.

fussy /ˈfʌsi/ *adj.* (**fussier**, **fussiest**) **1** inclined to fuss. **2** full of unnecessary detail or decoration. **3** fastidious. □ **fussily** *adv.* **fussiness** *n.*

fustanella /fʌstəˈnɛlə/ *n.* a man's stiff white kilt worn in Albania and Greece. [Italian diminutive of modern Greek *phoustani*, probably from Italian *fustagno* FUSTIAN]

fustian /ˈfʌstɪən/ *n.* & *adj.* ● *n.* **1** thick twilled cotton cloth with a short nap, usu. dyed in dark colours. **2** turgid speech or writing, bombast. ● *adj.* **1** made of fustian. **2** bombastic. **3** worthless. [Middle English via Old French *fustaigne* from medieval Latin *fustaneus* 'relating to cloth from *Fostat*' a suburb of Cairo]

fustic /ˈfʌstɪk/ *n.* a yellow dye obtained from either of two kinds of wood, esp. old fustic. See also OLD FUSTIC, YOUNG FUSTIC. [French via Spanish *fustoc* and Arabic *fustuk* from Greek *pistakē* 'pistachio']

fusty /ˈfʌsti/ *adj.* (**fustier**, **fustiest**) **1** stale-smelling, musty, mouldy. **2** stuffy, close. **3** antiquated, old-fashioned. □ **fustily** *adv.* **fustiness** *n.* [Middle English via Old French *fusté* 'smelling of the cask', from *fust* 'cask, tree trunk', from Latin *fustis* 'cudgel']

futhorc /ˈfuːθɔːk/ *n.* the Scandinavian runic alphabet. [its first six letters *f*, *u*, *th*, *ö*, *r*, *k*]

futile /ˈfjuːtʌɪl/ *adj.* **1** useless, ineffectual, vain. **2** frivolous, trifling. □ **futilely** *adv.* **futility** /-ˈtɪlɪti/ *n.* [Latin *futilis* 'leaky, futile', related to *fundere* 'pour']

futon /ˈfuːtɒn/ *n.* **1** a Japanese quilted mattress rolled out on the floor for use as a bed. **2** a type of low wooden sofa bed having such a mattress. [Japanese]

futtock /ˈfʌtək/ *n.* each of the middle timbers of a ship's frame, between the floor and the top timbers. [Middle English: origin uncertain, perhaps from Middle Low German or from FOOT + HOOK]

future /ˈfjuːtʃə/ *adj.* & *n.* ● *adj.* **1 a** going or expected to happen or be or become (*his future career*). **b** that will be something specified (*my future wife*). **c** that will be after death (*a future life*). **2 a** of time to come (*future years*). **b** *Gram.* (of a tense or participle) describing an event yet to happen. ● *n.* **1** time to come (*past, present, and future*). **2** what will happen in the future (*the future is uncertain*). **3** the future condition of a person, country, etc. **4** a prospect of success etc. (*there's no future in it*). **5** *Gram.* the future tense. **6** (in *pl.*) *Stock Exch.* **a** goods and stocks sold for future delivery. **b** contracts for these. □ **for the future** = *in future*. **in future** from now onwards. □ **futureless** *adj.* [Middle English via Old French *futur -ure* from Latin *futurus*, future part. of *esse* 'be' (from the stem *fu-*, ultimately from a base meaning 'grow, become')]

future perfect *n. Gram.* a tense giving the sense *will have done*.

future shock *n.* inability to cope with rapid progress.

futurism /ˈfjuːtʃərɪz(ə)m/ *n.* a movement in art, literature, music, etc., with violent departure from traditional forms so as to express movement and growth. [FUTURE + -ISM, translating Italian *futurismo*, French *futurisme*]

futurist /ˈfjuːtʃərɪst/ *n.* (often *attrib.*) **1** an adherent of futurism. **2** a believer in human progress. **3** a student of the future. **4** *Theol.* a person who believes that eschatological prophecies are still to be fulfilled.

futuristic /fju:tʃə'rɪstɪk/ *adj.* **1** suitable for the future; ultra-modern. **2** of futurism. **3** relating to the future. ▫ **futuristically** *adv.*

futurity /fjʊ'tjʊərɪti, -tʃ-/ *n.* (*pl.* **-ies**) **1** future time. **2** (in *sing.* or *pl.*) future events. **3** future condition; existence after death.

futurity stakes *n.pl. US* stakes raced for long after entries or nominations are made.

futurology /fju:tʃə'rɒlədʒi/ *n.* systematic forecasting of the future esp. from present trends in society. ▫ **futurological** /-rə'lɒdʒɪk(ə)l/ *adj.* **futurologist** *n.*

fuze var. of FUSE².

fuzee *US* var. of FUSEE.

fuzz /fʌz/ *n. & v.* ● *n.* **1** fluff. **2** fluffy or frizzled hair. **3** *slang* **a** the police. **b** a police officer. ● *v.tr. & intr.* make or become fluffy or blurred. [16th c.: probably from Low German or Dutch: sense 3 perhaps a different word]

fuzz-ball *n.* a puffball fungus.

fuzzbox /'fʌzbɒks/ *n.* a device which adds a buzzing quality to the sound of an electric guitar or other instrument.

fuzzy /'fʌzi/ *adj.* (**fuzzier**, **fuzziest**) **1 a** like fuzz. **b** frayed, fluffy. **c** frizzy. **2** blurred, indistinct. **3** *Computing* & *Logic* (of a set) of which membership is determined imprecisely according to probability functions; of or relating to such sets (*fuzzy logic*). ▫ **fuzzily** *adv.* **fuzziness** *n.*

fuzzy-wuzzy /'fʌzɪwʌzi/ *n.* (*pl.* **-ies**) *Brit. slang offens.* **1** *hist.* a Sudanese soldier. **2** a black person, esp. one with tightly curled hair.

fwd *abbr.* forward.

f.w.d. *abbr.* **1** four-wheel drive. **2** front-wheel drive.

F-word *n. colloq.* an unprintable or taboo word beginning with the letter *f*, esp. 'fuck'.

FY *abbr. US* fiscal year.

-fy /fʌɪ/ *suffix* forming: **1** verbs from nouns, meaning: **a** make, produce (*pacify*; *speechify*). **b** make into (*deify*; *petrify*). **2** verbs from adjectives, meaning 'bring or come into such a state' (*Frenchify*; *solidify*). **3** verbs in causative sense (*horrify*; *stupefy*). [from or suggested by French *-fier* from Latin *-ficare*, *-facere*, from *facere* 'do, make']

fylfot /'fɪlfɒt/ *n.* a swastika. [perhaps from *fill-foot* 'pattern to fill the foot of a painted window']

fyrd /fə:d, fɪəd/ *n. hist.* **1** the English militia before 1066. **2** the duty to serve in this. [Old English from Germanic (as FARE)]

fytte var. of FIT³.

Gg

G[1] /dʒiː/ *n.* (also **g**) (*pl.* **Gs** or **G's**) **1** the seventh letter of the alphabet. **2** *Mus.* the fifth note in the diatonic scale of C major.

G[2] *abbr.* (also **G.**) *N. Amer. colloq.* = GRAND *n.* 2.

G[3] *symb.* **1** gauss. **2** giga-. **3** gravitational constant.

g[1] *abbr.* (also **g.**) **1** gelding. **2** gas.

g[2] *symb.* **1** gram(s). **2 a** gravity. **b** acceleration due to gravity.

G7 *attrib.adj.* designating a group of seven leading industrialized nations (Canada, France, Germany, Italy, Japan, UK, US). [Group of *Seven*]

GA *abbr. US* Georgia (in official postal use).

Ga *symb. Chem.* the element gallium.

Ga. *abbr.* Georgia (US).

gab /gab/ *n.* & *v. colloq.* ● *n.* talk, chatter, twaddle. ● *v.intr.* (**gabbed**, **gabbing**) talk, chatter. □ **gift of the gab** the facility of speaking eloquently or profusely. [18th-c. variant of GOB[1]]

gabardine /gabəˈdiːn, ˈgabədiːn/ *n.* (also **gaberdine**) **1** a smooth durable twill-woven cloth esp. of worsted or cotton. **2** *Brit.* a garment made of this, esp. a raincoat. [variant of GABERDINE]

gabble /ˈgab(ə)l/ *v.* & *n.* ● *v.* **1** *intr.* **a** talk volubly or inarticulately. **b** read aloud too fast. **2** *tr.* utter too fast, esp. in reading aloud. ● *n.* fast unintelligible talk. □ **gabbler** *n.* [Middle Dutch *gabbelen* (imitative)]

gabbro /ˈgabrəʊ/ *n.* (*pl.* **-os**) a dark granular plutonic rock of crystalline texture. □ **gabbroic** /-ˈbrəʊɪk/ *adj.* **gabbroid** *adj.* [Italian from Latin *glaber glabr-* 'smooth']

gabby /ˈgabi/ *adj.* (**gabbier**, **gabbiest**) *colloq.* talkative. [GAB + -Y[1]]

gaberdine /gabəˈdiːn, ˈgabədiːn/ *n.* **1** var. of GABARDINE. **2** *hist.* a loose long upper garment worn esp. by Jews and beggars. [Old French *gauvardine*, perhaps from Middle High German *wallevart* 'pilgrimage']

gabion /ˈgeɪbɪən/ *n.* a cylindrical wicker or metal basket for filling with earth or stones, used in engineering or (formerly) in fortification. □ **gabionage** *n.* [French from Italian *gabbione*, from *gabbia* CAGE]

gable /ˈgeɪb(ə)l/ *n.* **1 a** the triangular upper part of a wall at the end of a ridged roof. **b** (in full **gable-end**) a gable-topped wall. **2** a gable-shaped canopy over a window or door. □ **gabled** *adj.* (also in *comb.*). [Middle English *gable* from Old Norse *gafl*]

gad[1] /gad/ *v.* & *n.* ● *v.intr.* (**gadded**, **gadding**) (foll. by *about*, *abroad*, *around*) go about idly or in search of pleasure. ● *n.* idle wandering or adventure (esp. in **on the gad**). [back-formation from obsolete *gadling* 'companion' from Old English *gædeling*, from *gæd* 'fellowship']

gad[2] /gad/ *int.* (also **by gad**) *archaic* an expression of surprise or emphatic assertion. [= *God*]

gadabout /ˈgadəbaʊt/ *n.* a person who gads about; an idle pleasure-seeker.

Gadarene /ˈgadəriːn/ *adj.* involving or engaged in headlong or suicidal rush or flight. [Late Latin *Gadarenus* from Greek *Gadarēnos* 'of Gadara' (in ancient Palestine), with reference to Matthew 8:28–32]

gadfly /ˈgadflʌɪ/ *n.* (*pl.* **-flies**) **1** a cattle-biting fly, esp. a warble fly, horsefly, or botfly. **2** an irritating or harassing person. [from GAD[1] or obsolete *gad* 'goad, spike' from Old Norse *gaddr*, related to YARD[1]]

gadget /ˈgadʒɪt/ *n.* any small and usu. ingenious mechanical device or tool. □ **gadgeteer** /-ˈtɪə/ *n.* **gadgetry** *n.* **gadgety** *adj.* [19th-c. (nautical): origin unknown]

gadoid /ˈgeɪdɔɪd, ˈga-/ *n.* & *adj.* ● *n.* any marine fish of the cod family Gadidae, including haddock and whiting. ● *adj.* belonging to or resembling the Gadidae. [modern Latin *gadus* from Greek *gados* 'cod' + -OID]

gadolinite /ˈgad(ə)lɪnʌɪt, gəˈdəʊlɪnʌɪt/ *n.* a dark crystalline mineral consisting of ferrous silicate of beryllium. [named after J. *Gadolin*, Finnish mineralogist d. 1852]

gadolinium /gadəˈlɪnɪəm/ *n. Chem.* a soft silvery metallic element of the lanthanide series, occurring naturally in gadolinite (symbol **Gd**). [modern Latin, from GADOLINITE]

gadroon /gəˈdruːn/ *n.* a decoration on silverware etc., consisting of convex curves in a series forming an ornamental edge like inverted fluting. □ **gadrooned** *adj.* [French *godron*: probably related to *goder* 'to pucker']

gadwall /ˈgadwɔːl/ *n.* a brownish-grey freshwater duck, *Anas strepera*. [17th c.: origin unknown]

gadzooks /gadˈzuːks/ *int. archaic* an expression of asseveration etc. [GAD[2] + *zooks* of unknown origin]

Gael /geɪl/ *n.* **1** a Scottish Celt. **2** a Gaelic-speaking Celt. □ **Gaeldom** *n.* [Gaelic *Gaidheal*: cf. GOIDEL]

Gaelic /ˈgeɪlɪk, ˈgalɪk/ *n.* & *adj.* ● *n.* a Celtic language spoken in Ireland and Scotland, esp. the Scottish variety. ● *adj.* of or relating to the Gaels or Gaelic.

Gaeltacht /ˈgeɪltəxt/ *n.* any of the regions in Ireland where the vernacular language is Irish. [Irish]

gaff[1] /gaf/ *n.* & *v.* ● *n.* **1 a** a stick with an iron hook for landing large fish. **b** a barbed fishing spear. **2** *Naut.* a spar to which the head of a fore-and-aft sail is bent. ● *v.tr.* seize (a fish) with a gaff. [Middle English from Provençal *gaf* 'hook']

gaff[2] /gaf/ *n. Brit. slang* □ **blow the gaff** let out a plot or secret. [19th c., = nonsense: origin unknown]

gaffe /gaf/ *n.* a blunder; an indiscreet act or remark. [French]

gaffer /ˈgafə/ *n.* **1** an old fellow; an elderly rustic. **2** *Brit. colloq.* a foreman or boss. **3** *colloq.* the chief electrician in a film or television production unit. [probably a contraction of GODFATHER]

gag /gag/ *n.* & *v.* ● *n.* **1** a piece of cloth etc. thrust into or held over the mouth to prevent speaking or crying out, or to hold it open in surgery. **2** a joke or comic scene in a play, film, etc., or as part of a comedian's act. **3** an actor's interpolation in a dramatic dialogue. **4** a thing or circumstance restricting free speech. **5 a** a joke or hoax. **b** a humorous action or situation. **6** an imposture or deception. **7** *Parl.* a closure or guillotine. ● *v.* (**gagged**, **gagging**) **1** *tr.* apply a gag to. **2** *tr.* silence; deprive of free speech. **3** *tr.* apply a gag-bit to (a horse). **4 a** *intr.* choke or retch. **b** *tr.* cause to do this. **5** *intr. Theatr.* make gags. [Middle English, originally as verb: origin uncertain]

gaga /ˈgɑːgɑː, ˈgagə/ *adj. slang* **1** senile. **2** fatuous; slightly crazy. [French, = senile]

gag-bit *n.* a specially powerful bit for horse-breaking.

gage[1] /geɪdʒ/ *n.* & *v.* ● *n.* **1** a pledge; a thing deposited as security. **2** *archaic* **a** a challenge to fight. **b** a symbol of this, esp. a glove thrown down. ● *v.tr. archaic* stake, pledge; offer as a guarantee. [Middle English from Old

French *gage* (*n.*), French *gager* (*v.*), ultimately from Germanic, related to WED]

gage[2] *US* var. of GAUGE.

gage[3] /geɪdʒ/ *n.* = GREENGAGE. [abbreviation]

gaggle /'gag(ə)l/ *n.* & *v.* ● *n.* **1** a flock of geese. **2** *colloq.* a disorderly group of people. ● *v.intr.* (of geese) cackle. [Middle English, imitative: cf. *gabble, cackle*]

gag man *n.* a deviser or performer of theatrical gags.

gagster /'gagstə/ *n.* = GAG MAN.

Gaia /'gʌɪə/ *n.* the earth viewed as a vast self-regulating organism (*Gaia hypothesis*; *Gaia theory*). □ **Gaian** *n.* & *adj.* [Greek, = Earth]

gaiety /'geɪəti/ *n.* **1** the state of being light-hearted or merry; mirth. **2** merrymaking, amusement. **3** a bright appearance. □ **gaiety of nations** *Brit.* the cheerfulness or pleasure of numerous people. [French *gaieté* (as GAY)]

gaijin /gʌɪ'dʒɪn/ *n.* & *adj.* ● *n.* (*pl.* same) (in Japan) a foreigner; an alien. ● *adj.* foreign, alien. [Japanese, contraction of *gaikoku-jin* (*gaikaku* 'foreign country', *jin* 'person')]

gaillardia /geɪ'lɑːdɪə/ *n.* any plant of the genus *Gaillardia* (daisy family), with showy flowers. [modern Latin, named after *Gaillard* de Marentonneau, 18th-c. French botanist]

gaily /'geɪli/ *adv.* **1** in a gay or light-hearted manner. **2** with a bright or colourful appearance.

gain /geɪn/ *v.* & *n.* ● *v.* **1** *tr.* obtain or secure (usu. something desired or favourable) (*gain an advantage*; *gain recognition*). **2** *tr.* acquire (a sum) as profits or as a result of changed conditions; earn. **3** *tr.* obtain as an increment or addition (*gain momentum*; *gain weight*). **4** *tr.* **a** win (a victory). **b** reclaim (land from the sea). **5** *intr.* (foll. by *in*) make a specified advance or improvement (*gained in stature*). **6 a** *intr.* (of a clock etc.) have the fault of becoming fast. **b** *tr.* (of a clock etc.) become fast by (a specific amount of time). **7** *intr.* (often foll. by *on, upon*) come closer to a person or thing pursued. **8** *tr.* **a** bring over to one's interest or views. **b** (foll. by *over*) win by persuasion etc. **9** *tr.* reach or arrive at (a desired place). ● *n.* **1** something gained, achieved, etc. **2** an increase of possessions etc.; a profit, advance, or improvement. **3** the acquisition of wealth. **4** (in *pl.*) sums of money acquired by trade etc., emoluments, winnings. **5** an increase in amount. **6** *Electronics* **a** the factor by which power etc. is increased. **b** the logarithm of this. □ **gain ground** see GROUND[1]. **gain time** improve one's chances by causing or accepting delay. □ **gainable** *adj.* **gainer** *n.* **gainings** *n.pl.* [Old French *gaigner, gaaignier* 'to till, acquire', ultimately from Germanic]

gainful /'geɪnfʊl, -f(ə)l/ *adj.* **1** (of employment) paid. **2** lucrative, remunerative. □ **gainfully** *adv.* **gainfulness** *n.*

gainsay /geɪn'seɪ/ *v.tr.* (*past* and *past part.* **gainsaid** /-'sed/) *archaic* or *literary* deny, contradict. □ **gainsayer** *n.* [Middle English from obsolete *gain-* 'against', via Old Norse *gegn* 'straight' from Germanic, + SAY]

'gainst /geɪnst/ *prep. poet.* = AGAINST. [abbreviation]

gait /geɪt/ *n.* **1** a manner of walking; one's bearing as one walks. **2** the manner of forward motion of a runner, horse, vehicle, etc. □ **go one's** (or **one's own**) **gait** *Brit.* pursue one's own course. [variant of GATE[2]]

gaiter /'geɪtə/ *n.* a covering of cloth, leather, etc. for the leg below the knee, for the ankle, for part of a machine, etc. □ **gaitered** *adj.* [French *guêtre*, probably related to WRIST]

Gal. *abbr.* Galatians (New Testament).

gal[1] /gal/ *n.* esp. *N. Amer. slang* a girl. [representing variant pronunciation]

gal[2] /gal/ *n. Physics* a unit of acceleration for a gravitational field, equal to one centimetre per second per second. [named after *Galileo*: see GALILEAN[1]]

gal. *abbr.* gallon(s).

gala /'gɑːlə, 'geɪlə/ *n.* **1** (often *attrib.*) a festive or special occasion (*a gala performance*). **2** *Brit.* a festive gathering for sports, esp. swimming. [French or Italian via Spanish and Old French *gale* 'rejoicing' from Germanic]

galactagogue /gə'laktəgɒg/ *adj.* & *n.* ● *adj.* inducing a flow of milk. ● *n.* a galactagogue substance. [Greek *gala galaktos* 'milk' + *agōgos* 'leading']

galactic /gə'laktɪk/ *adj.* of or relating to a galaxy or galaxies, esp. the Galaxy. [Greek *galaktias*, variant of *galaxias*: see GALAXY]

galactose /gə'laktəʊz, -s/ *n.* a hexose sugar present in many polysaccharides. [Greek *gala galaktos* 'milk' + -OSE[2]]

galago /gə'leɪgəʊ/ *n.* (*pl.* **-os**) = BUSHBABY. [modern Latin genus name]

galah /gə'lɑː/ *n. Austral.* **1** a small rose-breasted grey-backed cockatoo, *Eulophus roseicapillus*. **2** *slang* a fool or simpleton. [Yuwaalaraay *gilaa*]

Galahad /'galəhad/ *n.* a person characterized by nobility, integrity, courtesy, etc. [name of a knight of the Round Table in Arthurian legend]

galangal var. of GALINGALE.

galantine /'gal(ə)ntiːn/ *n.* white meat or fish boned, cooked, pressed, and served cold in aspic etc. [Middle English from Old French, alteration of *galatine* 'jellied meat' from medieval Latin *galatina*]

galaxy /'galəksi/ *n.* (*pl.* **-ies**) **1** any of many independent systems of stars, gas, dust, etc., held together by gravitational attraction. **2 a** (**the Galaxy**) the galaxy of which the solar system is a part. **b** = MILKY WAY. **3** (foll. by *of*) a brilliant company or gathering. [originally = the Milky Way: Middle English via Old French *galaxie* and medieval Latin *galaxia*, Late Latin *galaxias* from Greek, from *gala galaktos* 'milk']

galbanum /'galbənəm/ *n.* a bitter aromatic gum resin produced from kinds of ferula. [Middle English via Latin from Greek *khalbanē*, probably of Semitic origin]

gale[1] /geɪl/ *n.* **1 a** a very strong wind. **b** *Meteorol.* a wind of force 7 to 9 (or 10) on the Beaufort scale (32–54 or 32–63 m.p.h.). **2** *Naut.* a storm. **3** an outburst, esp. of laughter. [16th c.: origin unknown]

gale[2] /geɪl/ *n.* (in full **sweet gale**) bog myrtle. [Old English *gagel(le)*, related to Middle Dutch *gaghel*]

galea /'geɪlɪə/ *n.* (*pl.* **galeae** /-lɪiː/ or **-as**) *Bot.* & *Zool.* a structure like a helmet in shape, form, or function. □ **galeate** /-ɪət/ *adj.* **galeated** /-ɪeɪtɪd/ *adj.* [Latin, = helmet]

galena /gə'liːnə/ *n.* a bluish, grey or black mineral ore of lead sulphide. Chem. formula: PbS. [Latin, = lead ore (in a partly purified state)]

galenic /gə'lenɪk/ *adj.* & *n.* (also **galenical** /-'lenɪk(ə)l/) ● *adj.* **1** of or relating to Galen, a Greek physician of the 2nd c. AD, or his methods. **2** made of natural as opposed to synthetic components. ● *n.* a drug or medicament produced directly from animal or vegetable tissues.

galenical var. of GALENIC.

galia melon /'gɑːlɪə/ *n.* a small roundish variety of melon with rough skin and orange flesh.

Galibi /gə'liːbi/ *n.* & *adj.* ● *n.* **1** (*pl.* same or **Galibis**) a member of a S. American Indian people inhabiting French Guiana. **2** the Carib language of this people. ● *adj.* of or relating to this people or their language.

Galilean[1] /galɪ'liːən/ *adj.* of or relating to Galileo, Italian astronomer d. 1642, or his methods.

Galilean[2] /galɪ'liːən/ *adj.* & *n.* ● *adj.* **1** of Galilee in Palestine. **2** Christian. ● *n.* **1** a native of Galilee. **2** a Christian. **3** (prec. by *the*) *derog.* Christ.

galingale /'galɪŋgeɪl/ *n.* (also **galangal** /'gal(ə)ŋgal/) **1** the aromatic rhizome of E. Asian plants of the genera *Alpinia* and *Kaempferia*, used in cookery and herbal medicine. **2** (in full **English galingale**) a sedge, *Cyperus longus*, having a root with similar properties. [Old English *gallengar*, Old French *galingal* from Arabic *ḵalanjān*, perhaps from Chinese *gāoliángjiāng*, from *gāoliáng*, a district in Guangdon Province, China + *jiāng* 'ginger']

galiot var. of GALLIOT.

galipot /ˈgalɪpɒt/ *n.* a hardened deposit of resin formed on the stem of the cluster pine. [French: ultimate origin unknown]

gall[1] /gɑːl/ *n.* **1** impudence. **2** asperity, rancour. **3** bitterness; anything bitter (*gall and wormwood*). **4** the bile of animals. **5** the gall bladder and its contents. [Old Norse, corresponding to Old English *gealla*, from Germanic]

gall[2] /gɑːl/ *n.* & *v.* ● *n.* **1** a sore on the skin made by chafing. **2 a** vexation, irritation. **b** a cause of this. **3** a place rubbed bare. ● *v.tr.* **1** rub sore; injure by rubbing. **2** vex, annoy, humiliate. □ **gallingly** *adv.* [Old English *gealla* 'sore on a horse' related to GALL[1]]

gall[3] /gɑːl/ *n.* **1** a growth produced by insects or fungus etc. on plants and trees, esp. on oak. **2** (*attrib.*) of insects producing galls (*gall-fly*). [Middle English via Old French *galle* from Latin *galla*]

gall. *abbr.* gallon(s).

gallant *adj.*, *n.*, & *v.* ● *adj.* /ˈgal(ə)nt/ **1** brave, chivalrous. **2 a** (of a ship, horse, etc.) grand, fine, stately. **b** *archaic* finely dressed. **3** /ˈgal(ə)nt, gəˈlant/ **a** markedly attentive to women. **b** concerned with sexual love; amatory. ● *n.* /ˈgal(ə)nt, gəˈlant/ **1** a ladies' man; a lover or paramour. **2** *archaic* a man of fashion; a fine gentleman. ● *v.* /gəˈlant, ˈgal(ə)nt/ **1** *tr.* flirt with. **2** *tr.* escort (a woman). **3** *intr.* **a** play the gallant. **b** (foll. by *with*) flirt. □ **gallantly** /ˈgal(ə)ntli/ *adv.* [Middle English from Old French *galant*, part. of *galer* 'make merry']

gallantry /ˈgaləntri/ *n.* (*pl.* **-ies**) **1** bravery; dashing courage. **2** courtliness; devotion to women. **3** a polite act or speech. **4** the conduct of a gallant; sexual intrigue; immorality. [French *galanterie* (as GALLANT)]

gall bladder *n.* the vessel storing bile after its secretion by the liver and before release into the intestine.

galleon /ˈgalɪən/ *n. hist.* **1** a ship of war (usu. Spanish). **2** a large Spanish ship used in American trade. **3** a vessel shorter and higher than a galley. [Middle Dutch *galjoen* from French *galion*, from *galie* 'galley', or from Spanish *galeón*]

galleria /galəˈriːə/ *n.* a collection of small shops under a single roof; an arcade. [Italian]

gallery /ˈgal(ə)ri/ *n.* (*pl.* **-ies**) **1** a room or building for showing works of art. **2** a balcony, esp. a platform projecting from the inner wall of a church, hall, etc., providing extra room for spectators etc. or reserved for musicians etc. (*minstrels' gallery*). **3 a** the highest balcony in a theatre. **b** its occupants. **4 a** a covered space for walking in, partly open at the side; a portico or colonnade. **b** a long narrow passage in the thickness of a wall or supported on corbels, open towards the interior of the building. **5** a long narrow room, passage, or corridor. **6** *Mil.* & *Mining* a horizontal underground passage. **7** a group of spectators at a golf match etc. □ **play to the gallery** seek to win approval by appealing to popular taste. □ **galleried** *adj.* [French *galerie* via Italian *galleria* from medieval Latin *galeria*]

galleryite /ˈgal(ə)rɪʌɪt/ *n.* a member of the audience in the gallery of a theatre; a playgoer.

galley /ˈgali/ *n.* (*pl.* **-eys**) **1** *hist.* **a** a low flat single-decked vessel using sails and oars, and usu. rowed by slaves or criminals. **b** an ancient Greek or Roman warship with one or more banks of oars. **c** a large open rowing boat, e.g. that used by the captain of a man-of-war. **2** a ship's or aircraft's kitchen. **3** *Printing* **a** an oblong tray for set type. **b** the corresponding part of a composing machine. **c** (in full **galley proof**) a proof in the form of long single-column strips from type in a galley, not in sheets or pages. [Middle English via Old French *galie* from medieval Latin *galea*, medieval Greek *galaia*]

galley slave *n.* **1** *hist.* a person condemned to row in a galley. **2** a drudge.

galliard /ˈgalɪɑːd, -ɪəd/ *n. hist.* **1** a lively dance usu. in triple time for two persons. **2** the music for this. [Middle English from Old French *gaillard* 'valiant']

Gallic /ˈgalɪk/ *adj.* **1** French or typically French. **2** of the Gauls; Gaulish. □ **Gallicize** /-sʌɪz/ *v.tr.* & *intr.* (also **-ise**). [Latin *Gallicus* from *Gallus* 'a Gaul']

gallic acid /ˈgalɪk/ *n. Chem.* an acid extracted from gallnuts etc., formerly used in making ink. [French *gallique* from *galle* GALL[3]]

gallice /ˈgalɪsi/ *adv.* in French. [Latin, = in Gaulish]

Gallicism /ˈgalɪsɪz(ə)m/ *n.* a French idiom, esp. one adopted in another language. [French *gallicisme* (as GALLIC)]

galligaskins /galɪˈgaskɪnz/ *n.pl. Brit. hist.* or *joc.* breeches, trousers. [originally wide hose of the 16th–17th c., from obsolete French *garguesque*, variant of *greguesque*, from Italian *grechesca*, fem. of *grechesco* 'Greek': origin of first element unknown]

gallimaufry /galɪˈmɔːfri/ *n.* (*pl.* **-ies**) a heterogeneous mixture; a jumble or medley. [French *galimafrée*, of unknown origin]

gallinaceous /galɪˈneɪʃəs/ *adj.* of or relating to the order Galliformes, which includes domestic poultry, pheasants, partridges, etc. [Latin *gallinaceus* via *gallina* 'hen' from *gallus* 'cock']

gallinule /ˈgalɪnjuːl/ *n.* **1** a moorhen. **2** any of various similar birds of the genus *Porphyrula* or *Porphyrio*. [modern Latin *gallinula*, diminutive of Latin *gallina* 'hen', from *gallus* 'cock']

galliot /ˈgalɪət/ *n.* (also **galiot**) **1** a single-masted Dutch cargo boat or fishing vessel. **2** *hist.* a small (usu. Mediterranean) galley. [Middle English via Old French *galiote* and Italian *galeotta* from medieval Latin *galea* 'galley']

gallipot /ˈgalɪpɒt/ *n.* a small pot of earthenware, metal, etc., used for ointments etc. [probably GALLEY + POT[1], because brought in galleys from the Mediterranean]

gallium /ˈgalɪəm/ *n. Chem.* a soft bluish-white metallic element occurring naturally in zinc blende, bauxite, and kaolin (symbol **Ga**). [modern Latin from Latin *Gallia* 'France' (so named patriotically by its discoverer Lecoq de Boisbaudran d. 1912)]

gallivant /ˈgalɪvant, galɪˈvant/ *v.intr. colloq.* **1** gad about. **2** flirt. [19th c.: origin uncertain]

galliwasp /ˈgalɪwɒsp/ *n.* a W. Indian lizard, *Diploglossus monotropis*. [17th c.: origin unknown]

gallnut /ˈgɔːlnʌt/ *n.* = GALL[3] 1.

Gallo- /ˈgaləʊ/ *comb. form* **1** French; French and. **2** Gaul (*Gallo-Roman*). [Latin *Gallus* 'a Gaul']

gallon /ˈgalən/ *n.* **1 a** (in full **imperial gallon**) *Brit.* a measure of capacity equal to eight pints and equivalent to 4.55 litres, used for liquids and corn etc. **b** *US* a measure of capacity equivalent to 3.79 litres, used for liquids. **2** (usu. in *pl.*) *colloq.* a large amount. □ **gallonage** *n.* [Middle English via Old Northern French *galon*, Old French *jalon*, from base of medieval Latin *gallēta*, *gallētum*, perhaps of Celtic origin]

galloon /gəˈluːn/ *n.* a narrow closely woven braid of gold, silver, silk, cotton, nylon, etc., for binding dresses etc. [French *galon* from *galonner* 'trim with braid', of unknown origin]

gallop /ˈgaləp/ *n.* & *v.* ● *n.* **1** the fastest pace of a horse or other quadruped, with all the feet off the ground together in each stride. **2** a ride at this pace. **3** *Brit.* a track or ground for this. ● *v.* (**galloped**, **galloping**) **1 a** *intr.* (of a horse etc. or its rider) go at the pace of a gallop. **b** *tr.* make (a horse etc.) gallop. **2** *intr.* (foll. by *through*, *over*) read, recite, or talk at great speed. **3** *intr.* move or progress rapidly (*galloping inflation*). □ **at a gallop** at the pace of a gallop. □ **galloper** *n.* [Old French *galop*, *galoper*: see WALLOP]

galloway /ˈgaləweɪ/ *n.* **1** an animal of a breed of hornless usu. black beef cattle from Galloway in SW Scotland, or (in full **belted galloway**) of a variety of this marked with a broad white band. **2** this breed.

gallows /ˈgaləʊz/ *n.pl.* (usu. treated as *sing.*) **1** a structure, usu. of two uprights and a crosspiece, for the hanging of criminals. **2** (prec. by *the*) execution by hanging. [Old English *gealga*, reinforced by Old Norse *gálgi*]

gallows humour *n.* grim and ironical humour.

gallstone /'gɔ:lstəʊn/ *n.* a small hard mass formed in the gall bladder or bile ducts from bile pigments, cholesterol, and calcium salts.

Gallup poll /'galəp/ *n.* an assessment of public opinion by questioning a representative sample, esp. as the basis for forecasting the results of voting. [named after G. H. *Gallup*, American statistician d. 1984]

galluses /'galəsɪz/ *n.pl. dial.* & *US* trouser-braces. [pl. of *gallus*, variant of GALLOWS]

gall wasp *n.* a gall-forming insect of the hymenopteran superfamily Cynipoidea. [GALL[3]]

galoot /gə'lu:t/ *n. colloq.* a person, esp. a strange or clumsy one. [19th-c. nautical slang: origin unknown]

galop /'galəp, gə'lɒp/ *n.* & *v.* ● *n.* **1** a lively dance in duple time. **2** the music for this. ● *v.intr.* (**galoped, galoping**) perform this dance. [French: see GALLOP]

galore /gə'lɔ:/ *adv.* in abundance (placed after noun: *flowers galore*). [Irish *go leór* 'to sufficiency']

galosh /gə'lɒʃ/ *n.* (usu. in *pl.*) a waterproof overshoe, usu. of rubber. [Middle English via Old French *galoche* from Late Latin *gallicula* 'small Gallic shoe']

galumph /gə'lʌmf/ *v.intr. colloq.* **1** move noisily or clumsily. **2** go prancing in triumph. [coined by Lewis Carroll (in sense 2), perhaps from GALLOP + TRIUMPH]

galvanic /gal'vanɪk/ *adj.* **1 a** sudden and remarkable (*had a galvanic effect*). **b** stimulating; full of energy. **2** involving electricity produced by chemical action. □ **galvanically** *adv.*

galvanism /'galvənɪz(ə)m/ *n. hist.* **1** electricity produced by chemical action. **2** the therapeutic use of electricity. □ **galvanist** *n.* [French *galvanisme*, named after L. *Galvani*, Italian physiologist d. 1798]

galvanize /'galvənʌɪz/ *v.tr.* (also **-ise**) **1** (often foll. by *into*) rouse forcefully, esp. by shock or excitement (*was galvanized into action*). **2** stimulate by or as if by electricity. **3** coat (iron) with zinc (usu. without the use of electricity) as a protection against rust. □ **galvanization** /-'zeɪʃ(ə)n/ *n.* **galvanizer** *n.* [French *galvaniser*: see GALVANISM]

galvanometer /galvə'nɒmɪtə/ *n.* an instrument for detecting and measuring small electric currents. □ **galvanometric** /-nə'mɛtrɪk/ *adj.*

gambade /gam'beɪd, -'bɑ:d/ *n.* (also **gambado** /-'beɪdəʊ, -'bɑ:dəʊ/) (*pl.* **gambades**; **-os** or **-oes**) **1** a horse's leap or bound. **2** a fantastic movement. **3** an escapade. [French *gambade* & Spanish *gambado* from Italian & Spanish *gamba* 'leg']

gambier /'gambɪə/ *n.* an astringent extract of a tropical Asiatic plant used in tanning etc. [Malay *gambir*, the name of the plant]

gambit /'gambɪt/ *n.* **1** a chess opening in which a player sacrifices a piece or pawn to secure an advantage. **2** an opening move in a discussion etc. **3** a trick or device. [earlier *gambett* from Italian *gambetto* 'tripping up', from *gamba* 'leg']

gamble /'gamb(ə)l/ *v.* & *n.* ● *v.* **1** *intr.* play games of chance for money, esp. for high stakes. **2** *tr.* **a** bet (a sum of money) in gambling. **b** (often foll. by *away*) lose (assets) by gambling. **3** *intr.* take great risks in the hope of substantial gain. **4** *intr.* (foll. by *on*) act in the hope or expectation of (*gambled on fine weather*). ● *n.* **1** a risky undertaking or attempt. **2** a spell or an act of gambling. □ **gambler** *n.* [obsolete *gamel* 'to sport' or *gamen* GAME[1]]

gamboge /gam'bəʊʒ, -'bu:ʒ/ *n.* a gum resin produced by various E. Asian trees and used as a yellow pigment and as a purgative. [modern Latin *gambaugium* from *Cambodia* (now Kampuchea) in SE Asia]

gambol /'gamb(ə)l/ *v.* & *n.* ● *v.intr.* (**gambolled, gambolling**; *US* **gamboled, gamboling**) skip or frolic playfully. ● *n.* a playful frolic. [GAMBADE]

gambrel /'gambr(ə)l/ *n.* (in full **gambrel roof**) **1** *Brit.* a roof like a hipped roof but with gable-like ends. **2** *US* = CURB ROOF. [Old Northern French *gamberel*, via *gambier* 'forked stick' from *gambe* 'leg' (from the resemblance to the shape of a horse's hind leg)]

game[1] /geɪm/ *n., adj., & v.* ● *n.* **1** a form or spell of play or sport, esp. a competitive one played according to rules and decided by skill, strength, or luck. **2** a single portion of play forming a scoring unit in some contests, e.g. bridge or tennis. **3** (in *pl.*) **a** *Brit.* athletics or sports as organized in a school etc. **b** a meeting for athletic etc. contests (*Olympic Games*). **4** a winning score in a game; the state of the score in a game (*the game is two all*). **5** the equipment for a game. **6** one's level of achievement in a game, as specified (*played a good game*). **7 a** a piece of fun; a jest (*was only playing a game with you*). **b** (in *pl.*) dodges, tricks (*none of your games!*). **8** a scheme or undertaking etc. regarded as a game (*so that's your game*). **9** a policy or line of action. **10** (*collect.*) **a** wild animals or birds hunted for sport or food. **b** the flesh of these. **11** a hunted animal; a quarry or object of pursuit or attack. **12** a kept flock of swans. ● *adj.* **1** spirited; eager and willing. **2** (foll. by *for*, or *to* + infin.) having the spirit or energy; eagerly prepared. ● *v.intr.* play at games of chance for money; gamble. □ **the game is up** the scheme is revealed or foiled. **make game** (or **a game**) **of** mock, taunt. **off** (or **on**) **one's game** playing badly (or well). **on the game** *Brit. slang* involved in prostitution or thieving. **play the game** behave fairly or according to the rules. □ **gamely** *adv.* **gameness** *n.* **gamester** *n.* [Old English *gamen*]

game[2] /geɪm/ *adj.* (of a leg, arm, etc.) lame, crippled. [18th-c. dialect: origin unknown]

game bird *n.* **1** a bird shot for sport or food. **2** a bird of the order Galliformes, which includes pheasants, grouse, etc.

gamebook /'geɪmbʊk/ *n.* a book for recording game killed in sport.

Game Boy *n. propr.* a hand-held electronic device with a small screen, used to play cartridge computer games.

gamecock /'geɪmkɒk/ *n.* (also **gamefowl** /-faʊl/) a cock bred and trained for cockfighting.

game fish *n.* a kind of fish caught for sport.

gamekeeper /'geɪmki:pə/ *n.* a person employed to breed and protect game. □ **gamekeeping** *n.*

gamelan /'gaməlan/ *n.* a type of orchestra found in Java and Bali, with a wide range of bronze percussion instruments. [Javanese]

game of chance *n.* a game decided by luck, not skill.

game plan *n.* **1** a winning strategy worked out in advance for a particular match. **2** a plan of campaign, esp. in politics.

game point *n. Tennis* etc. a point which, if won, would win the game.

gamer /'geɪmə/ *n.* a person who plays a game or games.

game show *n.* a television light-entertainment programme in which people compete in a game or quiz, often for prizes.

gamesman /'geɪmzmən/ *n.* (*pl.* **-men**) an exponent of gamesmanship.

gamesmanship /'geɪmzmənʃɪp/ *n.* the art or practice of winning games or other contests by gaining a psychological advantage over an opponent.

gamesome /'geɪms(ə)m/ *adj.* merry, sportive. □ **gamesomely** *adv.* **gamesomeness** *n.*

gametangium /gamɪ'tan(d)ʒɪəm/ *n.* (*pl.* **gametangia** /-dʒɪə/) *Bot.* an organ in which gametes are formed. [as GAMETE + Greek *aggeion* 'vessel']

gamete /'gami:t/ *n. Biol.* a mature germ cell able to unite with another in sexual reproduction. □ **gametic** /gə'mɛtɪk/ *adj.* [modern Latin *gameta* from Greek *gametē* 'wife', from *gamos* 'marriage']

game theory *n.* (also **games theory**) the mathematical analysis of competitive strategies where choices depend on the actions of others, e.g. in war, economics, games of skill, etc.

gameto- /gə'mi:təʊ/ *comb. form Biol.* gamete.

gametocyte /gə'mi:tə(ʊ)sʌɪt/ *n. Biol.* any cell that is in the process of developing into one or more gametes.

gametogenesis /gə,mi:təʊ'dʒɛnɪsɪs/ *n. Biol.* the process by which cells undergo meiosis to form gametes.

gametophyte /gə'mi:tə(ʊ)fʌɪt/ *n.* the gamete-producing form of a plant that has alternation of generations between this and the asexual form (sporophyte). ▫ **gametophytic** /-'fɪtɪk/ *adj.*

game warden *n.* an official locally supervising game and hunting.

gamin /'gamɪn, -mã/ *n.* **1** a street urchin. **2** an impudent child. [French]

gamine /ga'mi:n/ *n.* **1** a girl gamin. **2** a girl with mischievous or boyish charm. [French]

gaming house *n.* a place frequented for gambling; a casino.

gaming table *n.* a table used for gambling.

gamma /'gamə/ *n.* **1** the third letter of the Greek alphabet (Γ, γ). **2** *Brit.* a third-class mark given for a piece of work or in an examination. **3** (**Gamma**) *Astron.* the third (usu. third-brightest) star in a constellation (foll. by Latin genitive: *Gamma Orionis*). **4** the third member of a series. [Middle English from Greek]

gamma globulin *n.* a mixture of blood plasma proteins, mainly immunoglobulins, of relatively low electrophoretic mobility, often given to boost immunity.

gamma radiation *n.* (also **gamma rays**) electromagnetic radiation of very short wavelength emitted by some radioactive substances.

gammer /'gamə/ *n. Brit. archaic* an old woman, esp. as a rustic name. [probably contraction of GODMOTHER: cf. GAFFER]

gammon[1] /'gamən/ *n. & v.* ● *n.* **1** the bottom piece of a flitch of bacon including a hind leg. **2** the ham of a pig cured like bacon. ● *v.tr.* cure (bacon). [Old Northern French *gambon* from *gambe* 'leg': cf. JAMB]

gammon[2] /'gamən/ *n. & v.* ● *n.* a victory in backgammon (carrying a double score) in which the winner removes all his or her pieces before the loser has removed any. ● *v.tr.* defeat in this way. [apparently = Middle English *gamen* GAME[1]]

gammon[3] /'gamən/ *n. & v. Brit. colloq.* ● *n.* humbug, deception. ● *v.* **1** *intr.* **a** talk speciously. **b** pretend. **2** *tr.* hoax, deceive. [18th c.: origin uncertain, perhaps from or related to GAMMON[2]]

gammy /'gami/ *adj.* (**gammier**, **gammiest**) *Brit. colloq.* (esp. of a leg) lame; permanently injured. [dialect form of GAME[2]]

gamp /gamp/ *n. Brit. colloq.* an umbrella, esp. a large unwieldy one. [Mrs *Gamp* in Dickens's *Martin Chuzzlewit*, who carried such an umbrella]

gamut /'gamət/ *n.* **1** the whole series or range or scope of anything (*the whole gamut of crime*). **2** *Mus.* **a** the whole series of notes used in medieval or modern music. **b** a major diatonic scale. **c** a people's or a period's recognized scale. **d** a voice's or instrument's compass. **3** *Mus.* the lowest note in the medieval sequence of hexachords, = modern G on the lowest line of the bass staff. ▫ **run the gamut of** experience or perform the complete range of. [medieval Latin *gamma ut* from GAMMA, taken as the name for a note one tone lower than A of the classical scale, + *ut*, the first of six arbitrary names of notes forming the hexachord, being syllables (*ut*, *re*, *mi*, *fa*, *so*, *la*) of the Latin hymn beginning *Ut queant laxis*)]

gamy /'geɪmi/ *adj.* (**gamier**, **gamiest**) **1** having the flavour or scent of game kept till it is high. **2** *N. Amer.* scandalous, sensational. **3** = GAME[1] *adj.* ▫ **gamily** *adv.* **gaminess** *n.*

gander /'gandə/ *n. & v.* ● *n.* **1** a male goose. **2** *slang* a look, a glance (*take a gander*). ● *v.intr.* look or glance. [Old English *gandra*, related to GANNET]

gang[1] /gaŋ/ *n. & v.* ● *n.* **1 a** a band of persons acting or going about together, esp. for criminal purposes. **b** *colloq.* such a band pursuing a purpose causing disapproval. **2** a set of workers, slaves, or prisoners. **3** a set of tools arranged to work simultaneously. ● *v.tr.* arrange (tools etc.) to work in coordination. ▫ **gang up** *colloq.* **1** (often foll. by *with*) act in concert. **2** (foll. by *on*) combine against. [originally = going, journey, from Old Norse *gangr*, *ganga* GOING, corresponding to Old English *gang*]

gang[2] /gaŋ/ *v.intr. Sc.* go. ▫ **gang agley** (of a plan etc.) go wrong. [Old English *gangan*: cf. GANG[1]]

gang-bang *n. slang* an occasion on which several men successively have sexual intercourse with one woman.

gangboard /'gaŋbɔ:d/ *n.* = GANGPLANK.

ganger /'gaŋə/ *n. Brit.* the foreman of a gang of workers, esp. navvies.

gangland /'gaŋland/ *n.* the world of gangs and gangsters.

gangle /'gaŋg(ə)l/ *v.intr.* move ungracefully. [back-formation from GANGLING]

gangling /'gaŋglɪŋ/ *adj.* (of a person) loosely built; lanky. [frequentative of GANG[2]]

ganglion /'gaŋglɪən/ *n.* (*pl.* **ganglia** /-lɪə/ or **ganglions**) **1 a** an enlargement or knot on a nerve etc. containing an assemblage of nerve cells. **b** a mass of grey matter in the central nervous system forming a nerve-nucleus. **2** *Med.* a cyst, esp. on a tendon sheath. **3** a centre of activity or interest. ▫ **gangliar** *adj.* **gangliform** *adj.* **ganglionated** *adj.* **ganglionic** /-'ɒnɪk/ *adj.* [Greek *gagglion*]

gangly /'gaŋgli/ *adj.* (**ganglier**, **gangliest**) = GANGLING.

gangplank /'gaŋplaŋk/ *n.* a movable plank usu. with cleats nailed on it for boarding or disembarking from a ship etc.

gang rape *n.* the successive rape of a person by a group of people. ▫ **gang-rape** *v.tr.*

gangrene /'gaŋgri:n/ *n. & v.* ● *n.* **1** *Med.* death and decomposition of a part of the body tissue, resulting from either obstructed circulation or bacterial infection. **2** moral corruption. ● *v.tr. & intr.* affect or become affected with gangrene. ▫ **gangrenous** /'gaŋgrɪnəs/ *adj.* [French *gangrène* via Latin *gangraena* from Greek *gaggraina*]

gang show *n. Brit.* a variety show performed annually by members of the Scout Association and Guide Association.

gangsta /'gaŋstə/ *n.* **1** *slang* = GANGSTER. **2** (in full **gangsta rap**) a type of rap music featuring aggressive macho lyrics, often with reference to gang warfare, gun battles, etc. [corruption of GANGSTER]

gangster /'gaŋstə/ *n.* a member of a gang of violent criminals. ▫ **gangsterism** *n.*

gangue /gaŋ/ *n.* valueless earth etc. in which ore is found. [French from German *Gang* 'course, lode', related to GANG[1]]

gangway /'gaŋweɪ/ *n. & int.* ● *n.* **1** *Brit.* a passage, esp. between rows of seats. **2 a** an opening in the bulwarks by which a ship is entered or left. **b** a bridge laid from ship to shore. **c** a passage on a ship, esp. a platform connecting quarterdeck and forecastle. **3** a temporary bridge on a building site etc. ● *int.* make way!

ganister /'ganɪstə/ *n.* a close-grained hard siliceous stone found in the coal measures of northern England, and used for furnace-linings. [19th c.: origin unknown]

ganja /'gan(d)ʒə, 'gɑ:-/ *n.* the flowering tops of Indian hemp used as a narcotic. [Hindi *gāṅjhā*]

gannet /'ganɪt/ *n.* **1** a large seabird of the genus *Sula*, esp. *Sula bassana*, which catches fish by plunge-diving. **2** *Brit. colloq.* a greedy person. ▫ **gannetry** *n.* (*pl.* **-ies**). [Old English *ganot* from Germanic, related to GANDER]

ganoid /'ganɔɪd/ *adj. & n.* ● *adj.* **1** (of fish scales) enamelled; smooth and bright. **2** having ganoid scales. ● *n.* a fish having ganoid scales. [French *ganoïde* from Greek *ganos* 'brightness']

gantlet *US* var. of GAUNTLET[2].

gantry /'gantri/ *n.* (*pl.* **-ies**) **1** an overhead structure with a platform supporting a travelling crane, or railway or road signals. **2** a structure supporting a space rocket prior to launching. **3** (also **gauntry**

/ˈgɔːntri/) a wooden stand for barrels. [probably from *gawn*, dialect form of GALLON, + TREE]

gaol *Brit.* var. of JAIL.

gaoler *Brit.* var. of JAILER.

gap /gap/ *n.* **1** an unfilled space or interval; a blank; a break in continuity. **2** a breach in a hedge, fence, or wall. **3** a wide (usu. undesirable) divergence in views, sympathies, development, etc. (*generation gap*). **4** a gorge or pass. □ **fill** (or **close** etc.) **a gap** make up a deficiency. □ **gapped** *adj.* **gappy** *adj.* [Middle English from Old Norse, = chasm, related to GAPE]

gape /geɪp/ *v.* & *n.* ● *v.intr.* **1 a** open one's mouth wide, esp. in amazement or wonder. **b** be or become wide open. **2** (foll. by *at*) gaze curiously or wondrously. **3** split; part asunder. **4** yawn. ● *n.* **1** an open-mouthed stare. **2** a yawn. **3** (in *pl.*; prec. by *the*) **a** a disease of birds with gaping as a symptom, caused by infestation with gapeworm. **b** *joc.* a fit of yawning. **4 a** the expanse of an open mouth or beak. **b** the part of a beak that opens. **5** a rent or opening. □ **gapingly** *adv.* [Middle English from Old Norse *gapa*]

gaper /ˈgeɪpə/ *n.* **1** any bivalve mollusc of the genus *Mya*, with the shell open at one or both ends. **2** the comber, which gapes when dead. **3** a person who gapes.

gapeworm /ˈgeɪpwəːm/ *n.* a nematode worm of the family Syngamidae that infests the trachea and bronchi of birds and causes the gapes.

gap-toothed *adj.* having gaps between the teeth.

gar /gɑː/ *n.* = GARFISH 2.

garage /ˈgarɑː(d)ʒ, -ɪdʒ, gəˈrɑːʒ/ *n.* & *v.* ● *n.* **1** a building or shed for housing a motor vehicle or vehicles. **2** an establishment which sells petrol etc., or repairs and sells motor vehicles, or does both. **3 a** (also **garage rock**) unpolished energetic rock music associated with suburban amateur bands (often *attrib.*: *garage band*). **b** soul-influenced house music. ● *v.tr.* put or keep (a motor vehicle) in a garage. [French from *garer* 'shelter'; sense 3b from Paradise *Garage*, the name of a Manhattan dance club]

garage sale *n.* esp. *N. Amer.* a sale of miscellaneous household goods, usu. for charity, held in the garage of a private house.

garam masala /gʌrəm məˈsɑːlə/ *n.* a spice mixture used in Indian cookery. [Urdu *garam maṣālaḥ*]

garb /gɑːb/ *n.* & *v.* ● *n.* **1** clothing, esp. of a distinctive kind. **2** the way a person is dressed. ● *v.tr.* **1** (usu. in *passive* or *refl.*) put (esp. distinctive) clothes on (a person). **2** attire. [obsolete French *garbe* from Italian *garbo*, from Germanic, related to GEAR]

garbage /ˈgɑːbɪdʒ/ *n.* **1 a** refuse, filth. **b** domestic waste. **2** foul or rubbishy literature etc. **3 a** nonsense. **b** *Computing* incorrect or useless data (*garbage in, garbage out*). [Anglo-French: origin unknown]

garbage bin *n.* esp. *Austral.* a dustbin.

garbage can *n. N. Amer.* a dustbin.

garble /ˈgɑːb(ə)l/ *v.tr.* **1** unintentionally distort or confuse (facts, messages, etc.). **2 a** mutilate in order to misrepresent. **b** make (usu. unfair or malicious) selections from (facts, statements, etc.). □ **garbler** *n.* [Italian *garbellare* from Arabic *ġarbala* 'sift', perhaps via Late Latin *cribellare* 'to sieve' from Latin *cribrum* 'sieve']

garboard /ˈgɑːbɔːd/ *n.* (in full **garboard strake**) the first range of planks or plates laid on a ship's bottom next to the keel. [Dutch *gaarboord*, perhaps from *garen* GATHER + *boord* BOARD]

garbologist /gɑːˈbɒlədʒɪst/ *n.* **1** a person who studies the discarded rubbish of society. **2** *joc.* a dustman, a refuse collector. □ **garbology** *n.* [GARBAGE + -LOGIST]

garçon /ˈgɑːsɒn, ˈgɑːsɔ̃, French garsɔ̃/ *n.* a waiter in a French restaurant, hotel, etc. [French, literally 'boy']

Garda /ˈgɑːdə/ *n.* **1** the state police force of the Irish Republic. **2** (also **garda**) (*pl.* **-dai** /-diː/) a member of this. [Irish *Garda Síochána* 'Civic Guard']

garden /ˈgɑːd(ə)n/ *n.* & *v.* ● *n.* **1** esp. *Brit.* a piece of ground, usu. partly grassed and adjoining a private house, used for growing flowers, fruit, or vegetables, and as a place of recreation. **2** (esp. in *pl.*) ornamental grounds laid out for public enjoyment (*botanical gardens*). **3** a similar place with the service of refreshments (*tea garden*). **4** (*attrib.*) **a** (of plants) cultivated, not wild. **b** for use in a garden (*garden seat*). **5** (usu. in *pl.* prec. by a name) *Brit.* a street, square, etc. (*Onslow Gardens*). **6** an especially fertile region. **7** *US* a large public hall. **8** (**the Garden**) the philosophy or school of Epicurus. ● *v.intr.* cultivate or work in a garden. □ **gardening** *n.* [Middle English from Old Northern French *gardin* (Old French *jardin*), ultimately from Germanic: cf. YARD[2]]

garden centre *n.* an establishment where plants and garden equipment etc. are sold.

garden city *n.* an industrial or other town laid out systematically with spacious surroundings, parks, etc.

garden cress *n.* a cruciferous plant, *Lepidium sativum*, used in salads.

gardener /ˈgɑːdnə/ *n.* a person who gardens or is employed to tend a garden. [Middle English, ultimately from Old French *jardinier* (as GARDEN)]

gardener-bird *n.* a bowerbird making a 'garden' of moss etc. in front of a bower.

gardenia /gɑːˈdiːnɪə/ *n.* any tree or shrub of the genus *Gardenia*, with large white or yellow flowers and usu. a fragrant scent. [modern Latin, named after Dr A. *Garden*, Scots naturalist d. 1791]

garden party *n.* a social event held on a lawn or in a garden.

garden suburb *n. Brit.* a suburb laid out spaciously with open spaces, parks, etc.

garden warbler *n.* a European woodland songbird, *Sylvia borin*.

garfish /ˈgɑːfɪʃ/ *n.* (*pl.* usu. same) **1** any mainly marine fish of the family Belonidae, esp. *Belone belone*, having long beaklike jaws with sharp teeth; also called *needlefish*. **2** *US* any similar freshwater fish of the genus *Lepisosteus*, with ganoid scales; also called *gar* or *garpike*. **3** *NZ* & *Austral.* either of two marine fish of the genus *Hemiramphus*; also called *half-beak*. [apparently from Old English *gār* 'spear' + *fisc* FISH[1]]

garganey /ˈgɑːg(ə)ni/ *n.* (*pl.* **-eys**) a small duck, *Anas querquedula*, the drake of which has a white stripe from the eye to the neck. [Italian, dialect variant of *garganello*]

gargantuan /gɑːˈgantjʊən/ *adj.* enormous, gigantic. [the name of a giant in Rabelais' book *Gargantua* (1534)]

garget /ˈgɑːgɪt/ *n.* **1** inflammation of a cow's or ewe's udder. **2** *US* pokeweed. [perhaps from obsolete *garget* 'throat', from Old French *gargate*, *-guete*]

gargle /ˈgɑːg(ə)l/ *v.* & *n.* ● *v.* **1** *tr.* (also *absol.*) wash (one's mouth and throat), esp. for medicinal purposes, with a liquid kept in motion by breathing through it. **2** *intr.* make a sound as when doing this. ● *n.* **1** a liquid used for gargling. **2** *Brit. slang* an alcoholic drink. [French *gargouiller* from *gargouille*: see GARGOYLE]

gargoyle /ˈgɑːgɔɪl/ *n.* a grotesque carved human or animal face or figure projecting from the gutter of (esp. a Gothic) building usu. as a spout to carry water clear of a wall. [Old French *gargouille* 'throat, gargoyle']

gargoylism /ˈgɑːgɔɪlɪz(ə)m/ *n. Med.* = HURLER'S SYNDROME.

garibaldi /garɪˈbɔːldi, -ˈbaldi/ *n.* (*pl.* **garibaldis**) **1** *hist.* a kind of loose blouse worn by women and children, originally bright red, imitating the shirts worn by Garibaldi and his followers. **2** *Brit.* a biscuit containing a layer of currants. **3** a small red Californian fish, *Hypsypops rubicundus*. [named after G. *Garibaldi*, Italian patriot d. 1882]

garish /ˈgɛːrɪʃ/ *adj.* **1** obtrusively bright; showy. **2** gaudy; over-decorated. □ **garishly** *adv.* **garishness** *n.* [16th-c. *gaurish*, perhaps from obsolete *gaure* 'stare']

garland /ˈgɑːlənd/ *n.* & *v.* ● *n.* **1** a wreath of flowers, leaves, etc., worn on the head or hung as a decoration. **2** a prize or distinction. **3** a literary anthology or miscellany. ● *v.tr.* **1** adorn with garlands. **2** crown with a garland. [Middle English from Old French *garlande*, of unknown origin]

garlic /'gɑːlɪk/ *n.* **1** any of various alliums, esp. *Allium sativum*. **2** the strong-smelling pungent-tasting bulb of this plant, used as a flavouring in cookery. □ **garlicky** *adj.* [Old English *gārleac*, from *gār* 'spear' + *lēac* LEEK]

garment /'gɑːm(ə)nt/ *n.* & *v.* ● *n.* **1 a** an article of dress. **b** (in *pl.*) clothes. **2** the outward and visible covering of anything. ● *v.tr.* (usu. in *passive*) *literary* attire. [Middle English from Old French *garnement* (as GARNISH)]

garner /'gɑːnə/ *v.* & *n.* ● *v.tr.* **1** collect. **2** store, deposit. ● *n. literary* a storehouse or granary. [Middle English (originally as noun) via Old French *gernier* from Latin *granarium* GRANARY]

garnet /'gɑːnɪt/ *n.* a vitreous silicate mineral, esp. a transparent deep red kind used as a gem. [Middle English via Old French *grenat* from medieval Latin *granatum* POMEGRANATE, from its resemblance to the pulp of the fruit]

garnish /'gɑːnɪʃ/ *v.* & *n.* ● *v.tr.* **1** decorate or embellish (esp. food). **2** *Law* **a** serve notice on (a person) for the purpose of legally seizing money belonging to a debtor or defendant. **b** summon (a person) as a party to litigation started between others. ● *n.* (also **garnishing**) a decoration or embellishment, esp. to food. □ **garnishment** *n.* (in sense 2). [earlier 'to equip or arm': Middle English via Old French *garnir* from a Germanic verb, probably related to WARN]

garnishee /gɑːnɪ'ʃiː/ *n.* & *v.* *Law* ● *n.* a person garnished. ● *v.tr.* (**garnishees**, **garnisheed**) **1** garnish (a person). **2** attach (money etc.) by way of garnishment.

garniture /'gɑːnɪtʃə/ *n.* **1** decoration or trimmings, esp. of food. **2** accessories, appurtenances. [French (as GARNISH)]

garotte var. of GARROTTE.

garpike /'gɑːpʌɪk/ *n.* a gar or garfish (see GARFISH 2). [Old English *gār* 'spear' + PIKE[1]]

garret /'garət, -ɪt/ *n.* **1** a top-floor or attic room, esp. a dismal one. **2** an attic. [Middle English from Old French *garite* 'watchtower', from Germanic]

garrison /'garɪs(ə)n/ *n.* & *v.* ● *n.* **1** the troops stationed in a fortress, town, etc., to defend it. **2** the building occupied by them. ● *v.tr.* **1** provide (a place) with or occupy as a garrison. **2** place on garrison duty. [Middle English via Old French *garison*, from *garir* 'defend, furnish', from Germanic]

garrison town *n.* a town having a permanent garrison.

garrotte /gə'rɒt/ *v.* & *n.* (also **garotte**; *US* **garrote**) ● *v.tr.* **1** execute or kill by strangulation, esp. with an iron collar or with a length of wire etc. **2** throttle in order to rob. ● *n. hist.* **1 a** a Spanish method of execution by garrotting. **b** the apparatus used for this. **2** highway robbery in which the victim is throttled. [French *garrotter* or Spanish *garrotear* from *garrote* 'a cudgel', of unknown origin]

garrulous /'garʊləs, -rjʊl-/ *adj.* **1** talkative, esp. on trivial matters. **2** loquacious, wordy. □ **garrulity** /ga'ruːlɪti/ *n.* **garrulously** *adv.* **garrulousness** *n.* [Latin *garrulus* from *garrire* 'chatter']

garter /'gɑːtə/ *n.* & *v.* ● *n.* **1** a band worn to keep a sock or stocking up. **2** (**the Garter**) *Brit.* **a** = ORDER OF THE GARTER. **b** the badge of this. **c** membership of this. **3** *N. Amer.* a suspender for a sock or stocking. ● *v.tr.* fasten (a stocking) or encircle (a leg) with a garter. [Middle English from Old French *gartier*, from *garet* 'bend of the knee']

garter belt *n. N. Amer.* a suspender belt.

Garter King of Arms *n. Heraldry* (in the UK) the title given to the principal King of Arms.

garter snake *n.* any water snake of the genus *Thamnophis*, native to N. America, having lengthwise stripes.

garter stitch *n.* a plain knitting stitch or pattern, forming ridges in alternate rows.

garth /gɑːθ/ *n. Brit.* **1** an open space within cloisters. **2** *archaic* **a** a close or yard. **b** a garden or paddock. [Middle English from Old Norse *garthr*, related to Old English *geard* YARD[2]]

gas /gas/ *n.* & *v.* ● *n.* (*pl.* **gases** or (esp. *US*) **gasses**) **1** any airlike substance which moves freely to fill any space available, irrespective of its quantity. **2 a** such a substance (esp. found naturally or extracted from coal) used as a domestic or industrial fuel (also *attrib.*: *gas cooker*; *gas fire*). **b** an explosive mixture of firedamp with air. **3** nitrous oxide or another gas used as an anaesthetic (esp. in dentistry). **4** a gas or vapour used as a poisonous agent to disable an enemy in warfare. **5** *N. Amer. colloq.* petrol, gasoline. **6** *slang* pointless idle talk; boasting. **7** *slang* an enjoyable, attractive, or amusing thing or person. ● *v.* (**gases**, **gassed**, **gassing**) **1** *tr.* expose to gas, esp. to kill or make unconscious. **2** *intr.* give off gas. **3** *tr.* (usu. foll. by *up*) *N. Amer. colloq.* fill (the tank of a motor vehicle) with petrol. **4** *intr. colloq.* talk idly or boastfully. [invented by J. B. van Helmont, Belgian chemist d. 1644, suggested by Greek *khaos* 'chaos']

gasbag /'gasbag/ *n.* **1** a container of gas, esp. for holding the gas for a balloon or airship. **2** *slang* an idle talker.

gas chamber *n.* an airtight chamber that can be filled with poisonous gas to kill people or animals.

gas chromatography *n.* chromatography employing gas as the eluent.

Gascon /'gask(ə)n/ *n.* & *adj.* ● *n.* **1** a native or inhabitant of Gascony. **2** (**gascon**) a braggart. ● *adj.* of or relating to Gascony or its people. [French, from Latin *Vasco -onis*]

gas-cooled *adj.* (of a nuclear reactor etc.) cooled by a current of gas.

gaseous /'gasɪəs, 'geɪsɪəs/ *adj.* of or like gas. □ **gaseousness** *n.*

gas field *n.* an area yielding natural gas.

gas fire *n.* a domestic fire using gas as its fuel.

gas-fired *adj.* (of a power station etc.) using gas as its fuel.

gas gangrene *n.* a rapidly spreading gangrene of injured tissue infected by a soil bacterium and accompanied by the evolution of foul-smelling gas.

gash[1] /gaʃ/ *n.* & *v.* ● *n.* **1** a long and deep slash, cut, or wound. **2 a** a cleft such as might be made by a slashing cut. **b** the act of making such a cut. ● *v.tr.* make a gash in; cut. [variant of Middle English *garse* from Old French *garcer* 'scarify', perhaps ultimately from Greek *kharassō*]

gash[2] /gaʃ/ *n.* & *adj. Brit. slang* ● *n.* rubbish, waste. ● *adj.* spare, extra. [20th-c. nautical slang: origin unknown]

gasholder /'gashəʊldə/ *n.* a large receptacle for storing gas; a gasometer.

gasify /'gasɪfʌɪ/ *v.tr.* & *intr.* (**-ies**, **-ied**) convert or be converted into gas. □ **gasification** /-fɪ'keɪʃ(ə)n/ *n.*

gasket /'gaskɪt/ *n.* **1** a sheet or ring of rubber etc., shaped to seal the junction of metal surfaces. **2** *Naut.* a small cord securing a furled sail to a yard. □ **blow a gasket** *slang* lose one's temper. [perhaps from French *garcette* 'thin rope' (originally 'little girl')]

gaskin /'gaskɪn/ *n.* the hinder part of a horse's thigh. [perhaps erroneously from GALLIGASKINS]

gaslight /'gaslʌɪt/ *n.* **1** a jet of burning gas, usu. heating a mantle, to provide light. **2** light emanating from this. □ **gaslit** *adj.*

gasman /'gasman/ *n.* (*pl.* **-men**) a man who installs or services gas appliances, or reads gas meters.

gas mask *n.* a respirator used as a defence against poison gas.

gas meter *n.* an apparatus recording the amount of gas consumed.

gasohol /'gasəhɒl/ *n.* a mixture of petrol and ethyl alcohol used as fuel. [GAS + ALCOHOL]

gas oil *n.* a type of fuel oil distilled from petroleum and heavier than paraffin oil.

gasoline /'gasəli:n/ *n.* (also **gasolene**) **1** a volatile inflammable liquid distilled from petroleum and used for heating and lighting. **2** *N. Amer.* petrol. [GAS + -OL[2] + -INE[4], -ENE]

gasometer /ga'sɒmɪtə/ *n.* a large tank in which gas is stored for distribution by pipes to users. [French *gazomètre*, from *gaz* 'gas' + *-mètre* -METER]

gasp /gɑ:sp/ *v. & n.* ● *v.* **1** *intr.* catch one's breath with an open mouth as in exhaustion or astonishment. **2** *intr.* (foll. by *for*) strain to obtain by gasping (*gasped for air*). **3** *tr.* (often foll. by *out*) utter with gasps. ● *n.* a convulsive catching of breath. □ **at one's last gasp 1** at the point of death. **2** exhausted. [Middle English from Old Norse *geispa* 'yawn', related to *geip* 'idle talk']

gasper /'gɑ:spə/ *n.* **1** a person who gasps. **2** *Brit. slang* a cigarette.

gas-permeable *adj.* (esp. of a contact lens) allowing the diffusion of gases into and out of the cornea.

gas plant *n.* = FRAXINELLA.

gas ring *n.* a hollow ring perforated with gas jets, used esp. for cooking.

gasser /'gasə/ *n.* **1** *colloq.* an idle talker. **2** *slang* a very attractive or impressive person or thing.

gas station *n. N. Amer.* a filling station.

gassy /'gasi/ *adj.* (**gassier**, **gassiest**) **1 a** of or like gas. **b** full of gas. **2** *colloq.* (of talk etc.) pointless, verbose. □ **gassiness** *n.*

Gastarbeiter /'gastɑ:bʌɪtə, German 'gastɑ:rbaɪtər/ *n.* (*pl.* ***Gastarbeiters*** or same) a person with temporary permission to work in another country (esp. in W. Europe). [German, from *Gast* GUEST + *Arbeiter* 'worker']

gasteropod var. of GASTROPOD.

gasthaus /'gasthaʊs/ *n.* (*pl.* ***gasthäuser*** /-hɔɪzə, German -hɔyzər/) a small inn or hotel in German-speaking countries. [German, from *Gast* GUEST + *Haus* HOUSE]

gasthof /'gasthɒf, German 'gastho:f/ *n.* (*pl.* ***gasthofs*** or ***gasthöfe*** /-hə:fə, German -hø:fə/) a hotel in German-speaking countries, usu. larger than a *gasthaus.* [German, from *Gast* GUEST + *Hof* 'hotel, large house']

gas-tight *adj.* proof against the leakage of gas.

gastrectomy /ga'strɛktəmi/ *n.* (*pl.* **-ies**) a surgical operation in which the whole or part of the stomach is removed. [GASTRO- + -ECTOMY]

gastric /'gastrɪk/ *adj.* of the stomach. [modern Latin *gastricus*, from Greek *gastēr gast(e)ros* 'stomach']

gastric flu *n.* a popular name for an intestinal disorder of unknown cause.

gastric juice *n.* a thin clear virtually colourless acid fluid secreted by the stomach glands and active in promoting digestion.

gastritis /ga'strʌɪtɪs/ *n.* inflammation of the lining of the stomach.

gastro- /'gastrəʊ/ *comb. form* (also **gastr-** before a vowel) stomach. [Greek *gastēr gast(e)ros* 'stomach']

gastroenteric /,gastrəʊɛn'tɛrɪk/ *adj.* of or relating to the stomach and intestines.

gastroenteritis /,gastrəʊɛntə'rʌɪtɪs/ *n.* inflammation of the stomach and intestines.

gastroenterology /,gastrəʊɛntə'rɒlədʒi/ *n.* the branch of medicine which deals with disorders of the stomach and intestines. □ **gastroenterological** /-rə'lɒdʒɪk(ə)l/ *adj.* **gastroenterologist** *n.* [GASTRO- + ENTERO- + -LOGY]

gastrointestinal /,gastrəʊɪn'tɛstɪn(ə)l, -ɪntɛs'tʌɪn(ə)l/ *adj.* of or relating to the stomach and the intestines.

gastrolith /'gastrə(ʊ)lɪθ/ *n.* **1** *Zool.* a small stone swallowed by a bird, reptile, or fish, to aid digestion in the gizzard. **2** *Med.* a hard concretion in the stomach. [GASTRO- + -LITH]

gastronome /'gastrənəʊm/ *n.* a gourmet. [French from *gastronomie* GASTRONOMY]

gastronomy /ga'strɒnəmi/ *n.* the practice, study, or art of eating and drinking well. □ **gastronomic** /gastrə'nɒmɪk/ *adj.* **gastronomical** /gastrə'nɒmɪk(ə)l/ *adj.* **gastronomically** /gastrə'nɒmɪk(ə)li/ *adv.* [French *gastronomie* from Greek *gastronomia* (as GASTRO-, *-nomia* from *nomos* 'law')]

gastropod /'gastrəpɒd/ *n.* (also **gasteropod**) any mollusc of the class Gastropoda, most often having a single spiral shell and moving by means of a large muscular foot, e.g. a snail, slug, whelk, etc. □ **gastropodous** /ga'strɒpədəs/ *adj.* [French *gastéropode* from modern Latin *gasteropoda* (as GASTRO-, Greek *pous podos* 'foot')]

gastroscope /'gastrəskəʊp/ *n.* an optical instrument used for inspecting the interior of the stomach.

gastrula /'gastrʊlə/ *n.* (*pl.* **gastrulae** /-li:/) *Zool.* an embryonic stage developing from the blastula. [modern Latin, from Greek *gastēr gast(e)ros* 'belly']

gas turbine *n.* a turbine driven by a flow of gas or by gas from combustion.

gasworks /'gaswə:ks/ *n.pl.* a place where gas is manufactured and processed.

gat[1] /gat/ *n. slang* a revolver or other firearm. [abbreviation of GATLING]

gat[2] *archaic past* of GET *v.*

gate[1] /geɪt/ *n. & v.* ● *n.* **1** a barrier, usu. hinged, used to close an opening made for entrance and exit through a wall, fence, etc. **2** such an opening, esp. in the wall of a city, enclosure, or large building. **3** a means of entrance or exit. **4** a numbered place of access to aircraft at an airport. **5** a mountain pass. **6** an arrangement of slots into which the gear lever of a motor vehicle moves to engage the required gear. **7** a device for holding the frame of a cine film momentarily in position behind the lens of a camera or projector. **8 a** an electrical signal that causes or controls the passage of other signals. **b** an electrical circuit with an output which depends on the combination of several inputs. **9** a device regulating the passage of water in a lock etc. **10 a** the number of people entering by payment at the gates of a sports ground etc. **b** (in full **gate money**) the proceeds taken for admission. **11** *Brit. slang* the mouth. **12** = STARTING GATE. ● *v.tr.* **1** *Brit.* confine to college or school entirely or after certain hours. **2** (as **gated** *adj.*) (of a road) having a gate or gates to control the movement of traffic or animals. □ **get** (or **be given**) **the gate** *N. Amer. slang* be dismissed. [Old English *gæt*, *geat*, pl. *gatu*, from Germanic]

gate[2] /geɪt/ *n. Brit. dial.* a street (preceded by a name: *Westgate*). [Middle English from Old Norse *gata*, from Germanic]

-gate /geɪt/ *comb. form* forming nouns denoting a scandal comparable in some way to the Watergate scandal of 1972 (*Irangate*). [Water*gate*]

gateau /'gatəʊ/ *n.* (*pl.* **gateaus** or **gateaux** /-əʊz/) esp. *Brit.* any of various rich cakes, usu. containing cream or fruit. [French *gâteau* 'cake']

gatecrasher /'geɪtkraʃə/ *n.* an uninvited guest at a party etc. □ **gatecrash** *v.tr. & intr.*

gatefold /'geɪtfəʊld/ *n.* a page in a book or magazine etc. that folds out to be larger than the page-format.

gatehouse /'geɪthaʊs/ *n.* **1** a house standing by a gateway, esp. to a large house or park. **2** *hist.* a room over a city gate, often used as a prison.

gatekeeper /'geɪtki:pə/ *n.* **1** an attendant at a gate, controlling entrance and exit. **2** a brown butterfly, *Pyronia tithonus*, frequenting hedgerows and woodland.

gateleg /'geɪtlɛg/ *n.* (in full **gateleg table**) a table with folding flaps supported by legs swung open like a gate. □ **gatelegged** *adj.*

gateman /'geɪtmən/ *n.* (*pl.* **-men**) = GATEKEEPER 1.

gate money see GATE[1] *n.* 10b.

gatepost /'geɪtpəʊst/ *n.* a post on which a gate is hung or against which it shuts. □ **between you and me and the gatepost** in strict confidence.

gate valve *n.* a valve in which a sliding part controls the extent of the aperture.

gateway /'geɪtweɪ/ *n.* **1** an entrance with or opening for a gate. **2** a frame or structure built over a gate. **3** a means of access or entry (*gateway to Scotland*; *gateway* *to success*). **4** *Computing* a device used to connect two different networks.

gather /ˈgaðə/ *v. & n.* ● *v.* **1** *tr. & intr.* bring or come together; assemble, accumulate. **2** *tr.* (usu. foll. by *up*) **a** bring together from scattered places or sources. **b** take up together from the ground, a surface, etc. **c** draw into a smaller compass. **3** *tr.* acquire by gradually collecting; amass. **4** *tr.* **a** pick a quantity of (flowers etc.). **b** collect (grain etc.) as a harvest. **5** *tr.* (often foll. by *that* + clause) infer or understand. **6** *tr.* be subjected to or affected by the accumulation or increase of (*unread books gathering dust; gather speed; gather strength*). **7** *tr.* (often foll. by *up*) summon up (one's thoughts, energy, etc.) for a purpose. **8** *tr.* gain or recover (one's breath). **9** *tr.* **a** draw (material, or one's brow) together in folds or wrinkles. **b** pucker or draw together (fabric, a garment, etc.) by running a thread through. **10** *intr.* come to a head; develop a purulent swelling. ● *n.* (in *pl.*) a part of a garment that is gathered or drawn in. □ **gather way** (of a ship) begin to move. □ **gatherer** *n.* [Old English *gaderian*, from West Germanic]

gathering /ˈgað(ə)rɪŋ/ *n.* **1** an assembly or meeting. **2** a purulent swelling. **3** a group of leaves taken together in bookbinding.

Gatling /ˈgatlɪŋ/ *n.* (in full **Gatling gun**) a machine-gun with clustered barrels. [named after R. J. *Gatling*, American inventor d. 1903]

GATT /gat/ *abbr.* (also **Gatt**) General Agreement on Tariffs and Trade.

gauche /gəʊʃ/ *adj.* **1** lacking ease or grace; socially awkward. **2** tactless. □ **gauchely** *adv.* **gaucheness** *n.* [French, = left-handed, awkward]

gaucherie /ˈgəʊʃ(ə)riː/ *n.* **1** gauche manners. **2** a gauche action. [French]

gaucho /ˈgaʊtʃəʊ, ˈgɔː-/ *n.* (*pl.* **-os**) a cowboy from the S. American pampas. [Latin American Spanish, from a Chilean or Peruvian language]

gaud /gɔːd/ *n.* **1** a gaudy thing; a showy ornament. **2** (in *pl.*) showy ceremonies. [perhaps via Anglo-French and Old French *gaudir* 'rejoice' from Latin *gaudēre*]

gaudy[1] /ˈgɔːdi/ *adj.* (**gaudier**, **gaudiest**) tastelessly or extravagantly bright or showy. □ **gaudily** *adv.* **gaudiness** *n.* [probably from GAUD + -Y[1]]

gaudy[2] /ˈgɔːdi/ *n.* (*pl.* **-ies**) *Brit.* an annual feast or entertainment, esp. a college dinner for old members etc. [Latin *gaudium* 'joy', or *gaude*, imperative of *gaudēre* 'rejoice']

gauge /geɪdʒ/ *n. & v.* (*US* also **gage**: see also sense 7) ● *n.* **1** a standard measure to which certain things must conform, esp.: **a** the measure of the capacity or contents of a barrel. **b** the fineness of a textile. **c** the diameter of a bullet. **d** the thickness of sheet metal. **2** any of various instruments for measuring or determining this, or for measuring length, thickness, or other dimensions or properties. **3** the distance between a pair of rails or the wheels on one axle. **4** the capacity, extent, or scope of something. **5** a means of estimating; a criterion or test. **6** a graduated instrument measuring the force or quantity of rainfall, stream, tide, wind, etc. **7** (usu. **gage**) *Naut.* a relative position with respect to the wind. ● *v.tr.* **1** measure exactly (esp. objects of standard size). **2** determine the capacity or content of. **3** estimate or form a judgement of (a person, temperament, situation, etc.). **4** make uniform; bring to a standard size or shape. □ **take the gauge of** estimate. □ **gaugeable** *adj.* **gauger** *n.* [Middle English from Old Northern French *gauge*, *gauger*, of unknown origin]

gauge pressure *n. Engin.* the amount by which a pressure measured in a fluid exceeds that of the atmosphere.

gauge theory *n. Physics* a form of quantum theory using mathematical functions to describe subatomic interactions in terms of particles not directly detectable.

Gaul /gɔːl/ *n.* a native or inhabitant of ancient Gaul. [*Gaul*, the name of the country from French *Gaule*, from Germanic]

gauleiter /ˈgaʊlʌɪtə/ *n.* **1** *hist.* an official governing a district under Nazi rule. **2** a local or petty tyrant. [German, from *Gau* 'administrative district' + *Leiter* 'leader']

Gaulish /ˈgɔːlɪʃ/ *adj. & n.* ● *adj.* of or relating to the ancient Gauls. ● *n.* the language of the ancient Gauls.

Gaullism /ˈgəʊlɪz(ə)m/ *n.* **1** the principles and policies of Charles de Gaulle, French military and political leader (d. 1970), characterized by their conservatism, nationalism, and advocacy of centralized government. **2** adherence to these. □ **Gaullist** *n.* [French *Gaullisme*]

gault /gɔːlt/ *n. Geol.* **1** a series of clay and marl beds between the upper and lower greensand in southern England. **2** clay obtained from these beds. [16th c.: origin unknown]

gaunt /gɔːnt/ *adj.* **1** lean, haggard. **2** grim or desolate in appearance. □ **gauntly** *adv.* **gauntness** *n.* [Middle English: origin unknown]

gauntlet[1] /ˈgɔːntlɪt/ *n.* **1** a stout glove with a long loose wrist. **2** *hist.* an armoured glove. **3** the part of a glove covering the wrist. □ **take up the gauntlet** see TAKE. **throw down the gauntlet** see THROW. [Middle English from Old French *gantelet*, diminutive of *gant* 'glove', from Germanic]

gauntlet[2] /ˈgɔːntlɪt/ *n.* (*US* **gantlet** /ˈgant-/) □ **run the gauntlet** **1** be subjected to harsh criticism. **2** pass between two rows of people and receive blows from them, as a punishment or ordeal. [earlier *gantlope* from Swedish *gatlopp*, from *gata* 'lane', *lopp* 'course', assimilated to GAUNTLET[1]]

gauntry var. of GANTRY 3.

gaur /ˈgaʊə/ *n.* a wild species of Indian cattle, *Bos gaurus*. [Hindustani]

gauss /gaʊs/ *n.* (*pl.* same or **gausses**) a unit of magnetic induction, equal to one ten-thousandth of a tesla (abbr.: G). [named after K. *Gauss*, German mathematician d. 1855]

Gaussian distribution /ˈgaʊsɪən/ *n. Statistics* = NORMAL DISTRIBUTION. [as GAUSS]

gauze /gɔːz/ *n.* **1** a thin transparent fabric of silk, cotton, etc. **2** a fine mesh of wire etc. **3** a slight haze. [French *gaze*, perhaps from *Gaza*, a town in Palestine]

gauzy /ˈgɔːzi/ *adj.* (**gauzier**, **gauziest**) **1** like gauze; thin and translucent. **2** flimsy, delicate. □ **gauzily** *adv.* **gauziness** *n.*

gave *past* of GIVE.

gavel /ˈgav(ə)l/ *n. & v.* ● *n.* a small hammer used by an auctioneer, or for calling a meeting to order. ● *v.* (**gavelled**, **gavelling**; *US* **gaveled**, **gaveling**) **1** *intr.* use a gavel. **2** *tr.* (often foll. by *down*) end (a meeting) or dismiss (a speaker) by use of a gavel. [19th c.: origin unknown]

gavial var. of GHARIAL.

gavotte /gəˈvɒt/ *n.* **1** a medium-paced French dance popular in the eighteenth century. **2 a** a piece of music for this, composed in common time beginning on the third beat of the bar. **b** a piece of music in this rhythm as a movement in a suite. [French from Provençal *gavoto* from *Gavot*, a native of a region in the Alps]

Gawd /gɔːd/ *n. slang* (esp. as *int.*) God (see GOD 5). [alteration of GOD]

gawk /gɔːk/ *v. & n.* ● *v.intr. colloq.* stare stupidly. ● *n.* an awkward or bashful person. □ **gawkish** *adj.* [related to obsolete *gaw* 'gaze' from Old Norse *gá* 'heed']

gawky /ˈgɔːki/ *adj.* (**gawkier**, **gawkiest**) awkward or ungainly. □ **gawkily** *adv.* **gawkiness** *n.*

gawp /gɔːp/ *v.intr. Brit. colloq.* stare stupidly or obtrusively. □ **gawper** *n.* [earlier *gaup*, *galp* from Middle English *galpen* 'yawn', related to YELP]

gay /geɪ/ *adj. & n.* ● *adj.* (**gayer**, **gayest**) **1** light-hearted and carefree; mirthful. **2** characterized by cheerfulness or pleasure (*a gay life*). **3** brightly coloured; showy, brilliant (*a gay scarf*). **4** *colloq.* **a** homosexual. **b** intended for or used by homosexuals (*a gay bar*). **5** *colloq.* dissolute, immoral. ● *n. colloq.* a homosexual, esp. male. □ **gayness** *n.* [Middle English from Old French *gai*, of unknown origin]

■ **Usage** The use of *gay* to mean 'homosexual' is favoured by homosexuals with reference to themselves. It still has an informal feel to it but is now well established and in widespread general use. In many instances it is restricted in application to male homosexuals and contrasted with *lesbian* when discussing homosexuals as a group, e.g. *The message from gays and lesbians living in rural Ireland was one of a sense of isolation.*

gayal /gʌɪ'jɑ:l, -'jal/ *n.* a semi-domesticated species of Indian cattle, *Bos frontalis*. [Hindi]

gay liberation *n.* **1** the liberation of homosexuals from social and legal discrimination. **2** (**Gay Liberation**) a movement campaigning for gay liberation.

gay plague *n. slang offens.* Aids (so called because first identified amongst homosexual men).

gay rights *n.pl.* rights for homosexuals, esp. legal and social equality with heterosexuals (often *attrib.*: *gay rights movement*).

gazania /gə'zeɪnɪə/ *n.* any herbaceous plant of the genus *Gazania*, with showy yellow or orange daisy-shaped flowers. [modern Latin, named after Theodore of *Gaza*, Greek scholar d. 1478]

gazar /gə'zɑ:/ *n.* a stiff gauzy kind of silk fabric. [French, from *gaze* GAUZE.]

gaze /geɪz/ *v.* & *n.* ● *v.intr.* (foll. by *at*, *into*, *on*, *upon*, etc.) look fixedly. ● *n.* a fixed or intent look. □ **gazer** *n.* [Middle English: origin unknown, perhaps related to obsolete *gaw* GAWK]

gazebo /gə'zi:bəʊ/ *n.* (*pl.* **-os** or **-oes**) a small building or structure such as a summer house or turret, designed to give a wide view. [perhaps jocular from GAZE, in imitation of Latin future tenses ending in *-ēbo*: cf. LAVABO]

gazelle /gə'zɛl/ *n.* any of various small graceful soft-eyed antelopes of Asia or Africa, esp. of the genus *Gazella*. [French, probably via Spanish *gacela* from Arabic *ġazāl*]

gazette /gə'zɛt/ *n.* & *v.* ● *n.* **1** a newspaper, esp. the official one of an organization or institution (*University Gazette*). **2** *hist.* a news-sheet; a periodical publication giving current events. **3** *Brit.* an official journal with a list of government appointments, bankruptcies, and other public notices (*London Gazette*). ● *v.tr. Brit.* announce or publish in an official gazette. [earliest in sense 2: French from Italian *gazzetta*, originally Venetian *gazeta de la novita* 'a halfpenny-worth of news', because sold for a *gazeta*, a Venetian small coin]

gazetteer /gazɪ'tɪə/ *n.* a geographical index or dictionary. [earlier = journalist, for whom such an index was provided: via French *gazettier* from Italian *gazzettiere* (as GAZETTE)]

gazpacho /gəs'pɑ:tʃəʊ/ *n.* (*pl.* **-os**) a Spanish soup made with tomatoes, peppers, cucumber, garlic, etc., and served cold. [Spanish]

gazump /gə'zʌmp/ *v.tr.* (also *absol.*) *Brit. colloq.* **1** (of a seller) raise the price of a property after having accepted an offer by (an intending buyer). **2** swindle. □ **gazumper** *n.* [20th c.: origin uncertain]

gazunder /gə'zʌndə/ *v.tr.* (also *absol.*) *Brit. colloq.* (of a buyer) lower the amount of an offer made to (the seller) for a property, esp. just before exchange of contracts. [GAZUMP + UNDER]

GB *abbr.* Great Britain.

GBE *abbr.* (in the UK) Knight (or Dame) Grand Cross (of the Order) of the British Empire.

GBH *abbr. Brit.* grievous bodily harm.

GC *abbr.* (in the UK) George Cross.

GCB *abbr.* (in the UK) Knight (or Dame) Grand Cross (of the Order) of the Bath.

GCE *abbr.* (in England, Wales, and Northern Ireland) General Certificate of Education, the O level examination of which was replaced in 1988 by the GCSE.

GCHQ *abbr.* (in the UK) Government Communications Headquarters.

GCMG *abbr.* (in the UK) Knight (or Dame) Grand Cross (of the Order) of St Michael & St George.

GCSE *abbr.* (in England, Wales, and Northern Ireland) General Certificate of Secondary Education.

GCVO *abbr.* (in the UK) Knight (or Dame) Grand Cross of the Royal Victorian Order.

Gd *symb. Chem.* the element gadolinium.

Gdn. *abbr.* Garden.

Gdns. *abbr.* Gardens.

GDP *abbr.* gross domestic product.

GDR *abbr. hist.* German Democratic Republic.

Ge *symb. Chem.* the element germanium.

gean /gi:n/ *n.* **1** the wild sweet cherry, *Prunus avium*. **2** the fruit of this. [Old French *guine* (modern *guigne*)]

gear /gɪə/ *n.* & *v.* ● *n.* **1** (often in *pl.*) **a** a set of toothed wheels that work together to transmit and control motion from an engine, esp. to the road wheels of a vehicle. **b** a mechanism for doing this. **2** a particular function or state of adjustment of engaged gears (*low gear*; *second gear*). **3** a mechanism of wheels, levers, etc., usu. for a special purpose (*winding gear*). **4** a particular apparatus or mechanism, as specified (*landing gear*). **5** equipment or tackle for a special purpose. **6** *colloq.* clothing, esp. when modern or fashionable. **7** goods; household utensils. **8** rigging. **9** a harness for a draught animal. ● *v.* **1** *tr.* (foll. by *to*) adjust or adapt to suit a special purpose or need. **2** *tr.* (often foll. by *up*) equip with gears. **3** *tr.* (foll. by *up*) make ready or prepared. **4** *tr.* put (machinery) in gear. **5** *intr.* **a** be in gear. **b** (foll. by *with*) work smoothly with. □ **be geared** (or **all geared**) **up** (often foll. by *for*, or *to* + infin.) *colloq.* be ready or enthusiastic. **gear down** (or **up**) provide with a low (or high) gear. **in gear** with a gear engaged. **out of gear 1** with no gear engaged. **2** out of order. [Middle English from Old Norse *gervi*, from Germanic]

gearbox /'gɪəbɒks/ *n.* **1** the casing that encloses a set of gears. **2** a set of gears with its casing, esp. in a motor vehicle.

gear change *n.* **1** an act of engaging a different gear in a vehicle. **2** US a gear lever.

gearing /'gɪərɪŋ/ *n.* **1** a set or arrangement of gears in a machine. **2** *Finance* the ratio of a company's loan capital (debt) to the value of its ordinary shares (equity).

gear lever *n. Brit.* a lever used to engage or change gear, esp. in a motor vehicle.

gear shift *n.* esp. *N. Amer.* = GEAR LEVER.

gearstick /'gɪəstɪk/ *n. Brit.* = GEAR LEVER.

gearwheel /'gɪəwi:l/ *n.* **1** a toothed wheel in a set of gears. **2** (in a bicycle) the cogwheel driven directly by the chain.

GEC *abbr.* General Electric Company.

gecko /'gɛkəʊ/ *n.* (*pl.* **-os** or **-oes**) any of various mainly nocturnal lizards found in warm climates, with adhesive feet for climbing vertical surfaces. [Malay *chichak* etc., imitative of its cry]

gee[1] /dʒi:/ *int.* (also **gee whiz** /'wɪz/) *N. Amer. colloq.* a mild expression of surprise, discovery, etc. [perhaps abbreviation of JESUS]

gee[2] /dʒi:/ *int.* & *v.* (often foll. by *up*) ● *int.* a command to a horse etc. to go faster. ● *v.tr.* (**geed**, **geeing**) command (a horse etc.) to go faster. [17th c.: origin unknown]

gee[3] /dʒi:/ *n.* (usu. in *pl.*) *US slang* a thousand dollars. [the letter *G*, as initial of GRAND]

gee-gee /'dʒi:dʒi:/ *n. Brit. colloq.* a horse. [originally a child's word, from GEE[2]]

geek /gi:k/ *n.* **1** *Austral. slang* a look. **2** esp. *US slang* a dull or socially inept person. □ **geeky** *adj.* [sense 1 from British dialect *geck* 'to toss the head scornfully', 'to look proudly (at)'; sense 2 from the related English dialect *geck* 'fool']

geese *pl.* of GOOSE.

gee-string var. of G-STRING 2.

geezer /'gi:zə/ *n. slang* a person, esp. an old man. [dialect pronunciation of *guiser* 'mummer']

Gehenna /gə'hɛnə/ *n.* **1** (in the New Testament) hell. **2** a place of burning, torment, or misery. [ecclesiastical Latin via Greek from Hebrew *gê' hinnōm* 'hell', originally the valley of Hinnom near Jerusalem, where children were sacrificed]

Geiger counter /'gʌɪgə/ *n.* a device for measuring radioactivity by detecting and counting ionizing particles. [named after H. *Geiger*, German physicist d. 1945]

geisha /'geɪʃə/ *n.* (*pl.* same or **geishas**) (also **geisha girl**) **1** a Japanese hostess trained in entertaining men with dance and song. **2** a Japanese prostitute. [Japanese, = entertainer]

Geissler tube /'gʌɪslə/ *n.* a sealed tube of glass or quartz with a central constriction, filled with vapour for the production of a luminous electrical discharge. [named after H. *Geissler*, German mechanic d. 1879]

gel /dʒɛl/ *n. & v.* ● *n.* **1** a semi-solid colloidal suspension or jelly, of a solid dispersed in a liquid. **2** a jelly-like substance used for setting the hair. ● *v.intr.* (**gelled**, **gelling**) **1** form a gel. **2** = JELL *v.* 1b. **3** = JELL *v.* 2. ▫ **gelation** /-'leɪʃ(ə)n/ *n.* [abbreviation of GELATIN]

gelada /dʒə'lɑ:də/ *n.* (*pl.* same or **geladas**) a brownish gregarious baboon, *Theropithecus gelada*, with a bare red patch on its chest, native to Ethiopa. [Amharic *č'ällada*]

gelatin /'dʒɛlətɪn/ *n.* (also **gelatine** /-ti:n/) a virtually colourless tasteless transparent water-soluble protein derived from collagen and used in food preparation, photography, etc. [French *gélatine* from Italian *gelatina*, from *gelata* JELLY]

gelatinous /dʒɪ'latɪnəs/ *adj.* **1** of or like gelatin. **2** of a jelly-like consistency. ▫ **gelatinize** /dʒɪ'latɪnʌɪz/ *v.tr. & intr.* (also **-ise**). **gelatinization** /dʒɪ,latɪnʌɪ'zeɪʃ(ə)n/ *n.* **gelatinously** *adv.*

gelatin paper *n. Brit.* a paper coated with sensitized gelatin for photography.

gelation /dʒə'leɪʃ(ə)n/ *n.* solidification by freezing. [Latin *gelatio* from *gelare* 'freeze']

geld /gɛld/ *v.tr.* **1** deprive (usu. a male animal) of the ability to reproduce. **2** castrate or spay; excise the testicles or ovaries of. [Middle English via Old Norse *gelda*, from *geldr* 'barren', from Germanic]

gelding /'gɛldɪŋ/ *n.* a gelded animal, esp. a male horse. [Middle English from Old Norse *geldingr*: see GELD]

gelid /'dʒɛlɪd/ *adj.* **1** icy, ice-cold. **2** chilly, cool. [Latin *gelidus* from *gelu* 'frost']

gelignite /'dʒɛlɪgnʌɪt/ *n.* a high explosive made from a gel of nitroglycerine and nitrocellulose in a base of wood pulp and sodium or potassium nitrate, much used for rock-blasting. [GELATIN + Latin *ignis* 'fire' + -ITE[1]]

gelly /'dʒɛli/ *n. Brit. slang* gelignite. [abbreviation]

gelsemium /dʒɛl'si:mɪəm/ *n.* a preparation of the rhizome of *Gelsemium sempervivens*, a twining shrub of southern N. America, used medicinally esp. to treat neuralgia. [modern Latin, from Italian *gelsomino* 'jasmine']

gem /dʒɛm/ *n. & v.* ● *n.* **1** a precious stone, esp. when cut and polished or engraved. **2** an object or person of great beauty or worth. ● *v.tr.* (**gemmed**, **gemming**) adorn with or as with gems. ▫ **gemlike** *adj.* **gemmy** *adj.* [Middle English via Old French *gemme* from Latin *gemma* 'bud, jewel']

Gemara /gə'mɑ:rə/ *n.* a rabbinical commentary on the Mishnah, forming the second part of the Talmud. [Aramaic g^{e}*mārâ* 'completion']

geminal /'dʒɛmɪn(ə)l/ *adj. Chem.* (of molecules) having two functional groups attached to the same atom. ▫ **geminally** *adv.* [as GEMINATE + -AL]

geminate *adj. & v.* ● *adj.* /'dʒɛmɪnɪt, -nət/ combined in pairs. ● *v.tr.* /'dʒɛmɪneɪt/ **1** double, repeat. **2** arrange in pairs. ▫ **gemination** /-'neɪʃ(ə)n/ *n.* [Latin *geminatus*, past part. of *geminare*, from *geminus* 'twin']

Gemini /'dʒɛmɪnʌɪ, -ni/ *n.* **1** *Astron.* a northern constellation (the Twins), said to represent the twins Castor and Pollux, whose names are given to its two brightest stars. **2** *Astrol.* **a** the third sign of the zodiac, which the sun enters about 21 May. **b** a person born when the sun is in this sign. ▫ **Geminian** /dʒɛmɪ'ni:ən/ *n. & adj.* [Middle English from Latin, = twins]

gemma /'dʒɛmə/ *n.* (*pl.* **gemmae** /-mi:/) a small cellular body in cryptogams that separates from the mother-plant and starts a new one; an asexual spore. [Latin: see GEM]

gemmation /dʒɛ'meɪʃ(ə)n/ *n.* reproduction by gemmae. [French from *gemmer* 'to bud', *gemme* 'bud']

gemmiferous /dʒɛ'mɪf(ə)rəs/ *adj.* **1** producing precious stones. **2** bearing buds. [Latin *gemmifer* (as GEMMA, -FEROUS)]

gemmiparous /dʒɛ'mɪp(ə)rəs/ *adj.* of or propagating by gemmation. [modern Latin *gemmiparus*, from Latin *gemma* 'bud' + *parere* 'bring forth']

gemmology /dʒɛ'mɒlədʒi/ *n.* the study of gems. ▫ **gemmologist** *n.* [Latin *gemma* 'gem' + -LOGY]

gemmule /'dʒɛmju:l/ *n.* a tough-coated dormant cluster of embryonic cells produced by a freshwater sponge, for development in more favourable conditions. [French *gemmule* or Latin *gemmula* 'little bud' (as GEM)]

gemsbok /'gɛmzbɒk/ *n.* a large antelope, *Oryx gazella*, of SW and E. Africa. [Afrikaans from Dutch, = chamois]

gemstone /'dʒɛmstəʊn/ *n.* a precious stone used as a gem.

gemütlich /gə'mu:tlɪx, German gə'my:tlɪç/ *adj.* **1** pleasant and comfortable. **2** genial, agreeable. [German]

Gen. *abbr.* **1** General. **2** Genesis (Old Testament).

gen /dʒɛn/ *n. & v. Brit. slang* ● *n.* information. ● *v.tr. & intr.* (**genned**, **genning**) (foll. by *up*) provide with or obtain information. [perhaps from first syllable of *general information*]

-gen /dʒ(ə)n/ *comb. form* **1** *Chem.* that which produces (*hydrogen*; *antigen*). **2** *Bot.* growth (*endogen*; *exogen*). [French *-gène* from Greek *-genēs* '-born, of a specified kind', from *gen-*, root of *gignomai* 'be born, become']

genco /'dʒɛnkəʊ/ *n.* a power-generating company, esp. a private company selling electricity. [*gen*erating + *co*mpany]

gendarme /'ʒɒndɑ:m/ *n.* **1** a soldier employed in specific public police duties in French-speaking countries. **2** a rock-tower on a mountain, occupying and blocking an arête. [French from *gens d'armes* 'men of arms']

gendarmerie /ʒɒn'dɑ:məri/ *n.* **1** a force of gendarmes. **2** the headquarters of such a force.

gender /'dʒɛndə/ *n.* **1 a** the grammatical classification of nouns and related words, roughly corresponding to the two sexes and sexlessness. **b** each of the classes of nouns (see MASCULINE, FEMININE, NEUTER, COMMON *adj.* 6). **2** (of nouns and related words) the property of belonging to such a class. **3** esp. *colloq.* or *euphem.* **a** = SEX *n.* 1. **b** = SEX *n.* 2 (often *attrib.*: *gender issues*). **c** = SEX *n.* 3. [Middle English from Old French *gendre*, ultimately from Latin GENUS]

gendered /dʒɛndəd/ *adj.* of or specific to the male or female sex.

gene /dʒi:n/ *n.* a unit of heredity composed of DNA or RNA and forming part of a chromosome etc., that determines a particular characteristic of an individual. [German *Gen*: see -GEN]

genealogical /dʒi:nɪə'lɒdʒɪk(ə)l, dʒɛn-/ *adj.* **1** of or concerning genealogy. **2** tracing family descent. ▫ **genealogically** *adv.* [French *généalogique* from Greek *genealogikos* (as GENEALOGY)]

genealogical tree *n.* a chart like an inverted branching tree showing the descent of a family or of an animal species.

genealogy /dʒiːnɪ'ælədʒi, dʒɛn-/ *n.* (*pl.* **-ies**) **1 a** a line of descent traced continuously from an ancestor. **b** an account or exposition of this. **2** the study and investigation of lines of descent. **3** a plant's or animal's line of development from earlier forms. □ **genealogist** *n.* **genealogize** *v.tr. & intr.* (also **-ise**). [Middle English via Old French *genealogie* and Late Latin *genealogia* from Greek *genealogia*, from *genea* 'race']

gene pool *n.* the whole stock of different genes in an interbreeding population.

genera *pl.* of GENUS.

general /'dʒɛn(ə)r(ə)l/ *adj. & n.* ● *adj.* **1 a** completely or almost universal. **b** including or affecting all or nearly all parts or cases of things. **2** prevalent, widespread, usual. **3** not partial, particular, local, or sectional. **4** not limited in application; relating to whole classes or all cases. **5** including points common to the individuals of a class and neglecting the differences (*a general term*). **6** not restricted or specialized (*general knowledge*). **7 a** roughly corresponding or adequate. **b** sufficient for practical purposes. **8** not detailed (*a general resemblance*; *a general idea*). **9** vague, indefinite (*spoke only in general terms*). **10** chief or principal; having overall authority (*general manager*; *Secretary-General*). ● *n.* **1 a** an army officer ranking next below field marshal or above lieutenant general. **b** a commander of an army. **2** *US* **a** = LIEUTENANT GENERAL, MAJOR GENERAL. **b** a general of the army or air force. **3** a tactician or strategist of specified merit (*a great general*). **4** the head of a religious order, e.g. of the Jesuits or Dominicans or the Salvation Army. **5** (prec. by *the*) *archaic* the public. □ **as a general rule** in most cases. **in general 1** as a normal rule; usually. **2** for the most part. [Middle English via Old French from Latin *generalis* (as GENUS)]

General American *n.* a form of US speech not markedly dialectal or regional.

general anaesthetic *n.* an anaesthetic that affects the whole body, usu. with loss of consciousness.

General Certificate of Education *n.* (in England, Wales, and Northern Ireland) an examination set esp. for secondary-school pupils at advanced level and, formerly, at ordinary level.

General Certificate of Secondary Education *n.* (in England, Wales, and Northern Ireland) an examination replacing and combining the GCE ordinary level and CSE examinations.

general delivery *n. US* the delivery of letters to callers at a post office.

general election *n.* the election of representatives to a legislature (esp. in the UK to the House of Commons) from constituencies throughout the country.

general headquarters *n.* (treated as *sing.* or *pl.*) the headquarters of a military commander.

generalissimo /dʒɛn(ə)rə'lɪsɪməʊ/ *n.* (*pl.* **-os**) the commander of a combined military force consisting of army, navy, and air force units. [Italian, superlative of *generale* GENERAL]

generalist /'dʒɛn(ə)rəlɪst/ *n.* a person competent in several different fields or activities (opp. SPECIALIST).

generality /dʒɛnə'rælɪti/ *n.* (*pl.* **-ies**) **1** a statement or principle etc. having general validity or force. **2** applicability to a whole class of instances. **3** vagueness; lack of detail. **4** the state of being general. **5** (foll. by *of*) the main body or majority. [French *généralité* from Late Latin *generalitas -tatis* (as GENERAL)]

generalization /dʒɛn(ə)rəlʌɪ'zeɪʃ(ə)n/ *n.* (also **-isation**) **1** a general notion or proposition obtained by inference from (esp. limited or inadequate) particular cases. **2** the act or an instance of generalizing. [French *généralisation* (as GENERALIZE)]

generalize /'dʒɛn(ə)rəlʌɪz/ *v.* (also **-ise**) **1** *intr.* **a** speak in general or indefinite terms. **b** form general principles or notions. **2** *tr.* reduce to a general statement, principle, or notion. **3** *tr.* **a** give a general character to. **b** call by a general name. **4** *tr.* infer (a law or conclusion) by induction. **5** *tr. Math. & Philos.* express in a general form; extend the application of. **6** *tr.* (in painting) render only the typical characteristics of. **7** *tr.* bring into general use. □ **generalizable** *adj.* **generalizability** /-zə'bɪlɪti/ *n.* **generalizer** *n.* [French *généraliser* (as GENERAL)]

generally /'dʒɛn(ə)rəli/ *adv.* **1** usually; in most cases. **2** in a general sense; without regard to particulars or exceptions (*generally speaking*). **3** for the most part; extensively (*not generally known*). **4** in most respects (*they were generally well-behaved*).

general meeting *n.* a meeting open to all the members of a society etc.

General National Vocational Qualification *n.* (in the UK) a general qualification offered by schools and colleges to prepare students for specific training or higher education, set at various levels and (at Intermediate and Advanced levels) corresponding in standard to GCSE and GCE A levels.

general practitioner *n.* a doctor working in the community and treating cases of all kinds in the first instance, as distinct from a consultant or specialist. □ **general practice** *n.*

general-purpose *adj.* having a range of potential uses or functions; not specialized in design.

generalship /'dʒɛn(ə)rəlʃɪp/ *n.* **1** the art or practice of exercising military command. **2** military skill; strategy. **3** skilful management; tact, diplomacy.

general staff *n.* the staff assisting a military commander in planning and administration.

general strike *n.* a strike of workers in all or most trades.

General Synod *n.* the highest governing body in the Church of England.

General Thanksgiving *n.* a form of thanksgiving in the Book of Common Prayer or the Alternative Service Book.

general theory of relativity see RELATIVITY 2b.

generate /'dʒɛnəreɪt/ *v.tr.* **1** bring into existence; produce, evolve. **2** produce (electricity). **3** *Math.* (of a point, line, or surface) move and so notionally form or trace out (a line, surface, or solid). **4** *Math. & Linguistics* produce (a set or sequence of items) by performing specified operations on or applying specified rules to an initial set. □ **generable** /-rəb(ə)l/ *adj.* [Latin *generare* 'beget' (as GENUS)]

generation /dʒɛnə'reɪʃ(ə)n/ *n.* **1** all the people born at a particular time, regarded collectively (*my generation*; *the rising generation*). **2** a single step in descent or pedigree (*have known them for three generations*). **3** a stage in (esp. technological) development (*fourth-generation computers*). **4** the average time in which children are ready to take the place of their parents (usu. reckoned at about 30 years). **5** production by natural or artificial process, esp. the production of electricity or heat. **6 a** procreation; the propagation of species. **b** the act of begetting or being begotten. □ **generational** *adj.* [Middle English via Old French from Latin *generatio -onis* (as GENERATE)]

generation gap *n.* differences of outlook or opinion between those of different generations.

generative /'dʒɛn(ə)rətɪv/ *adj.* **1** of or concerning procreation. **2** able to produce, productive. [Middle English from Old French *generatif* or Late Latin *generativus* (as GENERATE)]

generative grammar *n.* a set of rules whereby permissible sentences may be generated from the elements of a language.

generator /'dʒɛnəreɪtə/ *n.* **1** a machine for converting mechanical into electrical energy; a dynamo. **2** an apparatus for producing gas, steam, etc. **3** a person who generates an idea etc.; an originator.

generic /dʒɪˈnɛrɪk/ *adj.* **1** characteristic of or relating to a class; general, not specific or special. **2** *Biol.* characteristic of or belonging to a genus. **3** (of goods, esp. a drug) having no brand name; not protected by a registered trade mark. ▫ **generically** *adv.* [French *générique* from Latin GENUS]

generous /ˈdʒɛn(ə)rəs/ *adj.* **1** giving or given freely. **2** magnanimous, noble-minded, unprejudiced. **3 a** ample, abundant, copious (*a generous portion*). **b** (of wine) rich and full. ▫ **generosity** /-ˈrɒsɪti/ *n.* **generously** *adv.* **generousness** *n.* [Old French *genereus* from Latin *generosus* 'noble, magnanimous' (as GENUS)]

genesis /ˈdʒɛnɪsɪs/ *n.* **1** the origin, or mode of formation or generation, of a thing. **2** (**Genesis**) the first book of the Old Testament, with an account of the creation of the world. [Latin from Greek, from *gen-* 'be produced', root of *gignomai* 'become']

genet /ˈdʒɛnɪt/ *n.* (also **genette** /dʒɪˈnɛt/) **1** any catlike mammal of the genus *Genetta*, native to Africa and S. Europe, with spotted fur and a long ringed bushy tail. **2** the fur of the genet. [Middle English via Old French *genete* from Arabic *jarnaiṭ*]

gene therapy *n. Med.* the introduction of normal genes into cells in place of missing or defective ones in order to correct genetic disorders.

genetic /dʒɪˈnɛtɪk/ *adj.* **1** of genetics or genes; inherited. **2** of, in, or concerning origin; causal. ▫ **genetically** *adv.* [GENESIS, on the pattern of *antithetic*]

genetic code *n. Biochem.* the system of correspondence between triplets of bases in DNA and specific amino acids, by which a gene sequence embodies the instructions for synthesis of a specific protein.

genetic engineering *n.* the deliberate modification of the characters of an organism by the manipulation of the genetic material.

genetic fingerprinting *n.* (also **genetic profiling**) the analysis of characteristic patterns in DNA as a means of identifying individuals.

genetics /dʒɪˈnɛtɪks/ *n.* **1** (usu. treated as *sing.*) the study of heredity and the variation of inherited characteristics. **2** (treated as *sing.* or *pl.*) the genetic properties or features of an organism, characteristic, etc. (*the genetics of disease resistance*). ▫ **geneticist** /-tɪsɪst/ *n.*

genette var. of GENET.

Geneva bands /dʒɪˈniːvə/ *n.pl.* two white cloth strips attached to the collar of some Protestants' clerical dress. [*Geneva* in Switzerland, where originally worn by Calvinists]

Geneva Convention /dʒɪˈniːvə/ *n.* an international agreement first made at Geneva in 1864 and later revised, governing the status and treatment of captured and wounded military personnel in wartime.

genever /dʒɪˈniːvə/ *n.* (also *literary* **geneva**) Dutch gin. [Dutch via Old French *genevre* from alteration of Latin *juniperus*, with assimilation of the variant to the place name *Geneva*]

genial[1] /ˈdʒiːnɪəl/ *adj.* **1** jovial, sociable, kindly, cheerful. **2** (of the climate) mild and warm; conducive to growth. **3** cheering, enlivening. ▫ **geniality** /-ˈalɪti/ *n.* **genially** *adv.* [Latin *genialis* (as GENIUS)]

genial[2] /dʒɪˈniːəl/ *adj. Anat.* of or relating to the chin. [Greek *geneion* 'chin' from *genus* 'jaw']

genic /ˈdʒiːnɪk, ˈdʒɛn-/ *adj.* of or relating to genes.

-genic /ˈdʒɛnɪk/ *comb. form* forming adjectives meaning: **1** producing (*carcinogenic*; *pathogenic*). **2** well suited to (*photogenic*; *radiogenic*). **3** produced by (*iatrogenic*). ▫ **-genically** *suffix* forming adverbs. [-GEN + -IC]

genie /ˈdʒiːni/ *n.* (*pl.* usu. **genii** /ˈdʒiːnɪʌɪ/) a jinnee or spirit of Arabian folklore, esp. one contained within a bottle, lamp, etc., and capable of granting wishes. [French *génie* from Latin GENIUS: cf. JINNEE]

genii *pl.* of GENIE, GENIUS.

genista /dʒɪˈnɪstə, dʒɛ-/ *n.* any almost leafless shrub of the genus *Genista*, with a profusion of yellow pea-shaped flowers, including dyer's greenweed and various brooms. [Latin]

genital /ˈdʒɛnɪt(ə)l/ *adj.* & *n.* ● *adj.* of or relating to the reproductive organs. ● *n.* (in *pl.*) the external organ or organs of reproduction. [Old French *génital* or Latin *genitalis* from *gignere genit-* 'beget']

genitalia /dʒɛnɪˈteɪlɪə/ *n.pl.* the genitals. [Latin, neut. pl. of *genitalis*: see GENITAL]

genitive /ˈdʒɛnɪtɪv/ *n.* & *adj. Gram.* ● *n.* the case of nouns and pronouns (and words in grammatical agreement with them) corresponding to *of*, *from*, and other prepositions and indicating possession or close association. ● *adj.* of or in the genitive. ▫ **genitival** /-ˈtʌɪv(ə)l/ *adj.* **genitivally** /-ˈtʌɪv(ə)li/ *adv.* [Middle English from Old French *genetif*, *-ive* or Latin *genitivus* from *gignere genit-* 'beget']

genito- /ˈdʒɛnɪtəʊ/ *comb. form* genital.

genito-urinary /ˌdʒɛnɪtəʊˈjʊərɪn(ə)ri/ *adj.* of the genital and urinary organs.

genius /ˈdʒiːnɪəs/ *n.* (*pl.* **geniuses** or **genii** /-nɪʌɪ/) **1** (*pl.* **geniuses**) **a** an exceptional intellectual or creative power or other natural ability or tendency. **b** a person having this. **2** the tutelary spirit of a person, place, institution, etc. **3** a person or spirit regarded as powerfully influencing a person for good or evil. **4** the prevalent feeling or associations etc. of a nation, age, etc. [Latin (in sense 2), from the root of *gignere* 'beget']

genizah /gɛˈniːzə/ *n.* a room attached to a synagogue and housing damaged, discarded, or heretical books etc., and sacred relics. [Hebrew *gĕnīzāh*, literally 'hiding place', from *gānaz* 'hide, set aside']

genoa /ˈdʒɛnəʊə, dʒɛˈnəʊə/ *n.* **1** (in full **genoa jib**) a large jib or foresail used esp. on racing yachts. **2** (in full **Genoa cake**) a rich fruit cake with almonds on top. [*Genoa*, a city in Italy]

genocide /ˈdʒɛnəsʌɪd/ *n.* the mass extermination of human beings, esp. of a particular race or nation. ▫ **genocidal** /-ˈsʌɪd(ə)l/ *adj.* [Greek *genos* 'race' + -CIDE]

genome /ˈdʒiːnəʊm/ *n.* **1** the haploid set of chromosomes of an organism. **2** the genetic material of an organism. [GENE + CHROMOSOME]

genotype /ˈdʒɛnətʌɪp, ˈdʒiːn-/ *n. Biol.* the genetic constitution of an individual. ▫ **genotypic** /-ˈtɪpɪk/ *adj.* [German *Genotypus* (as GENE, TYPE)]

-genous /dʒɪnəs/ *comb. form* forming adjectives meaning 'produced' (*endogenous*).

genre /ˈʒɒ̃rə, ˈʒɒnrə/ *n.* **1** a kind or style, esp. of art or literature (e.g. Romantic, drama, satire). **2** (in full **genre painting**) the painting of scenes from ordinary life. [French, = a kind (as GENDER)]

gens /dʒɛnz/ *n.* (*pl.* **gentes** /-tiːz, -teɪz/) **1** *Rom.Hist.* a group of families sharing a name and claiming a common origin. **2** *Anthropol.* a number of people sharing descent through the male line. [Latin, from the root of *gignere* 'beget']

gent /dʒɛnt/ *n. colloq.* **1** a gentleman. **2** (in *pl.*) *Brit.* (in shop titles) men (*gents' outfitters*). **3** (**the Gents**) *Brit.* a men's public lavatory. [abbreviation of GENTLEMAN]

genteel /dʒɛnˈtiːl/ *adj.* **1** affectedly or ostentatiously refined or stylish. **2** often *iron.* of or appropriate to the upper classes. ▫ **genteelly** *adv.* **genteelness** *n.* [earlier *gentile*, readoption of French *gentil* GENTLE]

genteelism /dʒɛnˈtiːlɪz(ə)m/ *n.* a word used because it is thought to be less vulgar than the commoner word (e.g. *perspire* for *sweat*).

gentes *pl.* of GENS.

gentian /ˈdʒɛnʃ(ə)n/ *n.* **1** any plant of the genus *Gentiana* or *Gentianella*, found esp. in mountainous regions, and usu. having violet or vivid blue trumpet-shaped flowers. **2** (in full **gentian bitter**) a liquor extracted from the root of the gentian. [Old English from Latin *gentiana*, named after *Gentius*, king of Illyria]

gentian violet *n.* a violet dye used as an antiseptic, esp. in the treatment of burns.

gentile /ˈdʒɛntʌɪl/ *adj.* & *n.* ● *adj.* **1** (**Gentile**) **a** not Jewish. **b** (of a person) not belonging to one's religious community, esp. *hist.* non-Mormon. **2** of or relating to a nation or tribe. **3** *Gram.* (of a word) indicating nationality. ● *n.* **1** (**Gentile**) a person who is not Jewish. **2** *Gram.* a word indicating nationality. [Middle English from Latin *gentilis*, from *gens gentis* 'family': see GENS]

gentility /dʒɛnˈtɪlɪti/ *n.* **1** social superiority. **2** good manners; habits associated with the nobility. **3** people of noble birth. [Middle English from Old French *gentilité* (as GENTLE)]

gentle /ˈdʒɛnt(ə)l/ *adj.*, *v.*, & *n.* ● *adj.* (**gentler**, **gentlest**) **1** mild or kind in temperament. **2 a** moderate; not harsh (*a gentle rebuke*; *a gentle breeze*). **b** gradual (*gentle progression*; *gentle slope*). **3** *archaic* noble (*of gentle birth*). **4** quiet; requiring patience (*gentle art*). **5** *archaic* generous, courteous. ● *v.* **1** *tr.* & *intr.* make or become gentle or docile. **2** *tr.* handle (a horse etc.) firmly but gently. ● *n.* a maggot, the larva of the meat-fly or bluebottle used as fishing bait. □ **gentleness** *n.* **gently** *adv.* [Middle English via Old French *gentil* from Latin *gentilis*: see GENTILE]

gentlefolk /ˈdʒɛnt(ə)lfəʊk/ *n.pl. literary* people of good family.

gentleman /ˈdʒɛnt(ə)lmən/ *n.* (*pl.* **-men**) **1** a man (in polite or formal use). **2** a chivalrous, courteous, or well-educated man. **3** a man of good social position or of wealth and leisure (*country gentleman*). **4** a man of noble birth attached to a royal household (*gentleman in waiting*). **5** (in *pl.* as a form of address) a male audience or the male part of an audience. [GENTLE + MAN, translating Old French *gentilz hom*]

gentleman-at-arms *n.* one of the bodyguards of the British monarch on ceremonial occasions.

gentleman farmer *n.* (*pl.* **gentlemen farmers**) a country gentleman who farms.

gentlemanly /ˈdʒɛnt(ə)lmənli/ *adj.* like a gentleman in looks or behaviour; befitting a gentleman. □ **gentlemanliness** *n.*

gentleman's agreement *n.* (also **gentlemen's agreement**) one which is binding in honour but not legally enforceable.

gentlewoman /ˈdʒɛnt(ə)lwʊmən/ *n.* (*pl.* **-women**) *archaic* a woman of good birth or breeding.

gentoo /dʒɛnˈtuː/ *n.* a penguin, *Pygoscelis papua*, esp. abundant in the Falkland Islands. [perhaps from Anglo-Indian *Gentoo* = Hindu, from Portuguese *gentio* GENTILE]

gentrify /ˈdʒɛntrɪfʌɪ/ *v.tr.* (**-ies**, **-ied**) convert (a working-class or inner-city district etc.) into an area of middle-class residence. □ **gentrification** /-fɪˈkeɪʃ(ə)n/ *n.* **gentrifier** *n.*

gentry /ˈdʒɛntri/ *n.pl.* **1** the class of people next below the nobility in position and birth. **2** *derog.* people (*these gentry*). [probably from obsolete *gentrice* via Old French *genterise*, variant of *gentelise* 'nobility', from *gentil* GENTLE]

genuflect /ˈdʒɛnjʊflɛkt/ *v.intr.* bend the knee, esp. in worship or as a sign of respect. □ **genuflection** /-ˈflɛkʃ(ə)n/ *n.* (also **genuflexion**). **genuflector** *n.* [ecclesiastical Latin *genuflectere genuflex-*, from Latin *genu* 'the knee' + *flectere* 'bend']

genuine /ˈdʒɛnjʊɪn/ *adj.* **1** really coming from its stated, advertised, or reputed source. **2** properly so called; not sham. **3** pure-bred. □ **genuinely** *adv.* **genuineness** *n.* [Latin *genuinus* from *genu* 'knee', with reference to a father's acknowledging a newborn child by placing it on his knee: later associated with GENUS]

genus /ˈdʒɛnəs, ˈdʒiːnəs/ *n.* (*pl.* **genera** /ˈdʒɛn(ə)rə/) **1** *Biol.* a taxonomic grouping of organisms having common characteristics distinct from those of other genera, usu. containing several or many species and being one of a series constituting a taxonomic family. **2** a kind or class having common characteristics. **3** *Logic* kinds of things including subordinate kinds or species. [Latin *genus -eris* 'birth, race, stock']

-geny /dʒəni/ *comb. form* forming nouns meaning 'mode of production or development of' (*anthropogeny*; *ontogeny*; *pathogeny*). [French *-génie* (as -GEN, -Y³)]

Geo. *abbr.* George.

geo- /ˈdʒiːəʊ/ *comb. form* earth. [Greek *geō-* from *gē* 'earth']

geobotany /dʒiːəʊˈbɒt(ə)ni/ *n.* the study of the geographical distribution of plants. □ **geobotanist** *n.*

geocentric /dʒiːə(ʊ)ˈsɛntrɪk/ *adj.* **1** considered as viewed from the centre of the earth. **2** having or representing the earth as the centre; not heliocentric. □ **geocentrically** *adv.*

geocentric latitude *n.* the latitude at which a planet would appear if viewed from the centre of the earth.

geochemistry /dʒiːəʊˈkɛmɪstri/ *n.* the chemistry of the earth and its rocks, minerals, etc. □ **geochemical** *adj.* **geochemist** *n.*

geochronology /dʒiːəʊkrəˈnɒlədʒi/ *n.* **1** the study and measurement of geological time by means of geological events. **2** the ordering of geological events. □ **geochronological** /-krɒnəˈlɒdʒɪk(ə)l/ *adj.* **geochronologist** *n.*

geode /ˈdʒiːəʊd/ *n.* **1** a small cavity lined with crystals or other mineral matter. **2** a rock containing such a cavity. □ **geodic** /dʒiːˈɒdɪk/ *adj.* [Latin *geodes* from Greek *geōdēs* 'earthy', from *gē* 'earth']

geodesic /dʒiːə(ʊ)ˈdɛsɪk, -ˈdiːsɪk/ *adj.* **1** of or relating to geodesy. Cf. GEODETIC. **2** designating, or designed according to, constructional principles based on spheres and geodesic lines.

geodesic dome *n.* a dome constructed of short struts along geodesic lines.

geodesic line *n.* the shortest possible line between two points on a curved surface.

geodesy /dʒɪˈɒdɪsi/ *n.* the branch of mathematics dealing with the shape and area of the earth or large portions of it. □ **geodesist** *n.* [modern Latin from Greek *geōdaisia* (as GEO-, *daiō* 'divide')]

geodetic /dʒiːə(ʊ)ˈdɛtɪk/ *adj.* of or relating to geodesy, esp. as applied to land surveying. [Greek *geōdaitēs* 'land surveyor', from *geōdaisia* GEODESY]

geographical /dʒɪəˈgrafɪk(ə)l/ *adj.* (also **geographic** /-ˈgrafɪk/) of or relating to geography. □ **geographically** *adv.* [*geographic* from French *géographique* or Late Latin *geographicus* from Greek *geōgraphikos* (as GEO-, -GRAPHIC)]

geographical latitude *n.* the angle made with the plane of the equator by a perpendicular to the earth's surface at any point.

geographical mile *n.* a distance equal to one minute of longitude or latitude at the equator (about 1,850 metres).

geography /dʒɪˈɒgrəfi/ *n.* **1** the study of the earth's physical features, resources, natural and political divisions, climate, population, products, etc. **2** the main physical features of an area. **3** the layout or arrangement of rooms in a building. □ **geographer** *n.* [French *géographie* or Latin *geographia* from Greek *geōgraphia* (as GEO-, -GRAPHY)]

geoid /ˈdʒiːɔɪd/ *n.* **1** the shape of the earth. **2** a shape formed by the mean sea level and its imagined extension under land areas. **3** an oblate spheroid. [Greek *geōeidēs* (as GEO-, -OID)]

geology /dʒɪˈɒlədʒi/ *n.* **1** the science of the earth, including the composition, structure, and origin of its rocks. **2** this science applied to any other planet or celestial body. **3** the geological features of a district. □ **geologic** /dʒiːəˈlɒdʒɪk/ *adj.* **geological** /dʒiːəˈlɒdʒɪk(ə)l/ *adj.* **geologically** /dʒiːəˈlɒdʒɪk(ə)li/ *adv.* **geologist** *n.* **geologize** *v.tr.* & *intr.* (also **-ise**). [medieval Latin *geologia* (as GEO-, -LOGY)]

geomagnetism /dʒiːə(ʊ)ˈmagnɪtɪz(ə)m/ *n.* the study of the magnetic properties of the earth. □ **geomagnetic** /-magˈnɛtɪk/ *adj.* **geomagnetically** /-magˈnɛtɪk(ə)li/ *adv.*

geomancy /ˈdʒiːəmansi/ *n.* **1** the art of siting buildings etc. auspiciously. **2** divination from the configuration of a handful of earth or random dots. □ **geomantic** /-'mantɪk/ *adj.*

geometer /dʒɪ'ɒmɪtə/ *n.* **1** a person skilled in geometry. **2 a** = LOOPER 1. **b** = GEOMETRID. [Middle English via Late Latin *geometra* and Latin *geometres* from Greek *geōmetrēs* (as GEO-, *metrēs* 'measurer')]

geometric /dʒɪə'metrɪk/ *adj.* (also **geometrical**) **1** of, according to, or like geometry. **2** (of a design, architectural feature, etc.) characterized by or decorated with regular lines and shapes. □ **geometrically** *adv.* [French *géometrique* via Latin *geometricus* from Greek *geōmetrikos* (as GEOMETER)]

geometrical series *n.* a series in geometrical progression.

geometric mean *n.* the central number in a geometric progression, also calculable as the nth root of a product of n numbers (as 9 from 3 and 27).

geometric progression *n.* a progression of numbers with a constant ratio between each number and the one before (as 1, 3, 9, 27, 81).

geometric tracery *n.* tracery with openings of geometric form.

geometrid /dʒɪ'ɒmɪtrɪd/ *n. & adj.* ● *n.* a moth of the large family Geometridae, whose twiglike caterpillars (loopers) move by looping and straightening the body as if measuring the ground. ● *adj.* of or relating to this family. [modern Latin genus name *Geometra*, from Latin *geometres* GEOMETER]

geometry /dʒɪ'ɒmɪtri/ *n.* **1** the branch of mathematics concerned with the properties and relations of points, lines, surfaces, and solids. **2** the relative arrangement of objects or parts. □ **geometrician** /ˌdʒiːəmɪ'trɪʃ(ə)n/ *n.* [Middle English via Old French *geometrie* and Latin *geometria* from Greek (as GEO-, -METRY)]

geomorphology /ˌdʒiːə(ʊ)mɔː'fɒlədʒi/ *n.* the study of the physical features of the surface of the earth and their relation to its geological structures. □ **geomorphological** /-fə'lɒdʒɪk(ə)l/ *adj.* **geomorphologist** *n.*

geophagy /dʒɪ'ɒfədʒi/ *n.* the practice of eating earth. [GEO- + Greek *phagō* 'eat']

geophysics /dʒiːə(ʊ)'fɪzɪks/ *n.* the physics of the earth. □ **geophysical** *adj.* **geophysicist** /-sɪst/ *n.*

geopolitics /dʒiːə(ʊ)'pɒlɪtɪks/ *n.* **1** the politics of a country as determined by its geographical features. **2** the study of this. □ **geopolitical** /-pə'lɪtɪk(ə)l/ *adj.* **geopolitically** /-pə'lɪtɪk(ə)li/ *adv.* **geopolitician** /-'tɪʃ(ə)n/ *n.*

Geordie /'dʒɔːdi/ *n. & adj. Brit. colloq.* ● *n.* **1** a native of Tyneside. **2** the dialect spoken on Tyneside. ● *adj.* of or relating to Tyneside, its people, or its dialect. [the name *George* + -IE]

George /dʒɔːdʒ/ *n. Brit. slang* the automatic pilot of an aircraft. [the name *George*]

George Cross /dʒɔːdʒ/ *n.* (also **George Medal**) (in the UK) each of two (different) decorations for bravery awarded esp. to civilians, instituted in 1940 by King George VI.

georgette /dʒɔː'dʒɛt/ *n.* a thin silk or crêpe dress material. [named after *Georgette* de la Plante (*c.* 1900), French dressmaker]

Georgian[1] /'dʒɔːdʒ(ə)n/ *adj.* **1** of or characteristic of the time of Kings George I–IV (1714–1830), esp. of architecture of this period. **2** of or characteristic of the time of Kings George V and VI (1910–52), esp. of the literature of 1910–20.

Georgian[2] /'dʒɔːdʒ(ə)n/ *adj. & n.* ● *adj.* of or relating to Georgia, a country of SE Europe. ● *n.* **1** a native of Georgia; a person of Georgian descent. **2** the language of Georgia.

Georgian[3] /'dʒɔːdʒ(ə)n/ *adj. & n.* ● *adj.* of or relating to Georgia in the US. ● *n.* a native of Georgia.

geoscience /dʒiːəʊ'sʌɪəns/ *n.* earth sciences, esp. geology. □ **geoscientist** *n.*

geosphere /'dʒiːə(ʊ)sfɪə/ *n.* **1** the solid surface of the earth. **2** any of the almost spherical concentric regions of the earth and its atmosphere.

geostationary /dʒiːə(ʊ)'steɪʃ(ə)n(ə)ri/ *adj.* (of an artificial satellite of the earth) moving in such an orbit as to remain above the same point on the earth's surface (cf. GEOSYNCHRONOUS).

geostrophic /dʒiːə(ʊ)'strɒfɪk/ *adj. Meteorol.* depending upon the rotation of the earth. [GEO- + Greek *strophē* 'a turning' from *strephō* 'to turn']

geosynchronous /dʒiːə(ʊ)'sɪŋkrənəs/ *adj.* (of an artificial satellite of the earth) moving in an orbit equal to the earth's period of rotation (cf. GEOSTATIONARY).

geothermal /dʒiːə(ʊ)'θəːm(ə)l/ *adj.* relating to, originating from, or produced by the internal heat of the earth.

geotropism /dʒiːə(ʊ)'trəʊpɪz(ə)m/ *n.* plant growth in relation to gravity. □ **geotropic** /dʒiːə(ʊ)'trəʊpɪk, -'trɒpɪk/ *adj.* [GEO- + Greek *tropikos*, via *tropē* 'a turning' from *trepō* 'to turn']

geranium /dʒɪ'reɪnɪəm/ *n.* **1** any herbaceous plant or shrub of the genus *Geranium* bearing fruit shaped like the bill of a crane, e.g. cranesbill. **2** (in general use) a cultivated pelargonium. **3** the colour of the scarlet geranium. [Latin from Greek *geranion*, from *geranos* 'crane']

gerbera /'dʒəːb(ə)rə, 'gəː-/ *n.* any plant of the genus *Gerbera* (daisy family) of Africa or Asia, esp. the Transvaal daisy. [named after T. *Gerber*, German naturalist d. 1743]

gerbil /'dʒəːbɪl/ *n.* a mouselike desert rodent of the subfamily Gerbillinae, esp. *Meriones unguiculatus*, kept as a pet. [French *gerbille* from modern Latin *gerbillus*, diminutive of *gerbo* JERBOA]

gerenuk /'gɛrənʊk/ *n.* an antelope, *Litocranius walleri*, native to E. Africa, with a very long neck and small head. [Somali]

gerfalcon var. of GYRFALCON.

geriatric /dʒɛrɪ'atrɪk/ *adj. & n.* ● *adj.* **1** of or relating to old people. **2** *colloq.* old, outdated. ● *n.* **1** an old person, esp. one receiving special care. **2** *colloq.* a person or thing considered as relatively old or outdated. [Greek *gēras* 'old age' + *iatros* 'doctor']

■ **Usage** *Geriatric* should be used only in sense 1 of the adjective and noun except in very informal contexts. When applied to people in sense 2, it may cause offence.

geriatrics /dʒɛrɪ'atrɪks/ *n.pl.* (treated as *sing.*) a branch of medicine or social science dealing with the health and care of old people. □ **geriatrician** /-ə'trɪʃ(ə)n/ *n.*

germ /dʒəːm/ *n.* **1** a micro-organism, esp. one which causes disease. **2 a** a portion of an organism capable of developing into a new one; the rudiment of an animal or plant. **b** an embryo of a seed (*wheatgerm*). **3** an original idea etc. from which something may develop; an elementary principle. □ **in germ** not yet developed. □ **germy** *adj.* [French *germe* from Latin *germen germinis* 'sprout']

German /'dʒəːmən/ *n. & adj.* ● *n.* **1** a native or national of Germany; a person of German descent. **2** the language of Germany, also used in Austria and Switzerland. ● *adj.* of or relating to Germany or its people or language. [Latin *Germanus*, with reference to related peoples of central and northern Europe, a name perhaps given by Celts to their neighbours: cf. Old Irish *gair* 'neighbour']

german /'dʒəːmən/ *adj.* (placed after *brother*, *sister*, or *cousin*) **1** having both parents the same (*brother german*). **2** having both grandparents the same on one side (*cousin german*). **3** *archaic* germane. [Middle English via Old French *germain* from Latin *germanus* 'genuine, of the same parents']

germander /dʒə'mandə/ *n.* any plant of the genus *Teucrium*. [Middle English from medieval Latin *germandra*, ultimately via Greek *khamaidrus* from *khamai* 'on the ground' + *drus* 'oak']

germander speedwell *n.* a creeping plant, *Veronica chamaedrys*, with germander-like leaves and blue flowers.

germane /dʒəː'meɪn/ *adj.* (usu. foll. by *to*) relevant (to a subject under consideration). □ **germanely** *adv.* **germaneness** *n.* [variant of GERMAN]

Germanic /dʒəː'manɪk/ *adj. & n.* ● *adj.* **1** having German characteristics. **2** *hist.* of the Germans. **3** of the Scandinavians, Anglo-Saxons, or Germans. **4** of the languages or language group called Germanic. ● *n.* **1** the branch of Indo-European languages including English, German, Dutch, and the Scandinavian languages. **2** the (unrecorded) early language from which other Germanic languages developed. [Latin *Germanicus* (as GERMAN)]

germanic /dʒəː'manɪk/ *adj. Chem.* of or containing germanium, esp. in its tetravalent state.

Germanist /'dʒəːmənɪst/ *n.* an expert in or student of the language, literature, and civilization of Germany, or Germanic languages.

germanium /dʒəː'meɪnɪəm/ *n. Chem.* a lustrous brittle semi-metallic element occurring naturally in sulphide ores and used in semiconductors (symbol **Ge**). [modern Latin, from *Germanus* GERMAN]

Germanize /'dʒəːmənʌɪz/ *v.tr. & intr.* (also **-ise**) make or become German; adopt or cause to adopt German customs etc. □ **Germanization** /-'zeɪʃ(ə)n/ *n.* **Germanizer** *n.*

German measles *n.pl.* (also treated as *sing.*) a contagious disease, rubella, with symptoms like mild measles.

Germano- /dʒəː'manəʊ, 'dʒəːmənəʊ/ *comb. form* German; German and.

germanous /dʒəː'meɪnəs/ *adj. Chem.* containing germanium in the divalent state.

German shepherd *n.* (also **German shepherd dog**) an Alsatian.

German silver *n.* a white alloy of nickel, zinc, and copper.

germ cell *n.* **1** a cell containing half the number of chromosomes of a somatic cell and able to unite with one from the opposite sex to form a new individual; a gamete. **2** any embryonic cell with the potential of developing into a gamete.

germicide /'dʒəːmɪsʌɪd/ *n.* a substance destroying germs, esp. those causing disease. □ **germicidal** /-'sʌɪd(ə)l/ *adj.*

germinal /'dʒəːmɪn(ə)l/ *adj.* **1** relating to or of the nature of a germ or germs (see GERM 1). **2** in the earliest stage of development. **3** productive of new ideas. □ **germinally** *adv.* [Latin *germen germin-* 'sprout']

germinate /'dʒəːmɪneɪt/ *v.* **1 a** *intr.* sprout, bud, or put forth shoots. **b** *tr.* cause to sprout or shoot. **2 a** *tr.* cause (ideas etc.) to originate or develop. **b** *intr.* come into existence. □ **germination** /-'neɪʃ(ə)n/ *n.* **germinative** /-nətɪv/ *adj.* **germinator** *n.* [Latin *germinare germinat-* (as GERM)]

germ layer *n. Biol.* each of the three layers of cells (ectoderm, mesoderm, and endoderm) that are formed in the early embryo.

germ line *n. Biol.* a series of germ cells each descended from earlier cells in the series, regarded as continuing through successive generations of an organism.

germon /'dʒəːmən/ *n.* = ALBACORE 1. [French]

germ plasm *n.* germ cells collectively; their genetic material.

germ warfare *n.* the systematic spreading of micro-organisms to cause disease in an enemy population.

Geronimo /dʒə'rɒnɪməʊ/ *int.* expressing exhilaration when leaping etc. [Name of an Apache chief, used as a slogan by US paratroopers in the Second World War]

gerontocracy /dʒɛrɒn'tɒkrəsi/ *n.* **1** government by old people. **2** a state or society so governed. □ **gerontocrat** /dʒɛ'rɒntəkrat/ *n.* **gerontocratic** /-'kratɪk/ *adj.* [Greek *gerōn -ontos* 'old man' + -CRACY]

gerontology /dʒɛrɒn'tɒlədʒi/ *n.* the scientific study of old age, the process of ageing, and the special problems of old people. □ **gerontological** /-tə'lɒdʒɪk(ə)l/ *adj.* **gerontologist** *n.* [Greek *gerōn -ontos* 'old man' + -LOGY]

-gerous /dʒ(ə)rəs/ *comb. form* forming adjectives meaning 'bearing' (*lanigerous*). [from Latin *-ger* 'bearing' (from root of *gerere* 'to bear') + -OUS]

gerrymander /'dʒɛrɪmandə/ *v. & n.* (also *Brit.* **jerrymander**) ● *v.tr.* **1** manipulate the boundaries of (a constituency etc.) so as to give undue influence to some party or class. **2** manipulate (a situation etc.) to gain advantage. ● *n.* this practice. □ **gerrymanderer** *n.* [the name of Governor *Gerry* of Massachusetts + SALAMANDER, from the shape of a district on a political map drawn when he was in office (1812)]

gerund /'dʒɛrʌnd/ *n. Gram.* a form of a verb functioning as a noun, originally in Latin ending in *-ndum* (declinable), in English ending in *-ing* and used distinctly as a part of a verb (e.g. *do you mind my asking you?*). [Late Latin *gerundium* from *gerundum*, variant of *gerendum*, the gerund of Latin *gerere* 'do']

gerundive /dʒə'rʌndɪv/ *n. Gram.* a form of a Latin verb, ending in *-ndus* (declinable) and functioning as an adjective meaning 'that should or must be done' etc. [Late Latin *gerundivus* (*modus* 'mood') from *gerundium*: see GERUND]

gesso /'dʒɛsəʊ/ *n.* (*pl.* **-oes**) plaster of Paris or gypsum as used in painting or sculpture. [Italian, from Latin *gypsum*: see GYPSUM]

gestalt /gə'ʃtɑːlt, -'ʃtalt/ *n. Psychol.* an organized whole that is perceived as more than the sum of its parts. □ **gestaltism** *n.* **gestaltist** *n.* [German, = form, shape]

gestalt psychology *n.* a system maintaining that perceptions, reactions, etc., are gestalts.

Gestapo /gə'stɑːpəʊ/ *n.* **1** the German secret police under Nazi rule. **2** *derog.* an organization compared to this. [German, from *Ge*heime *Sta*ats*po*lizei]

gestate /dʒɛ'steɪt/ *v.tr.* **1** carry (a foetus) in gestation. **2** develop (an idea etc.).

gestation /dʒɛ'steɪʃ(ə)n/ *n.* **1 a** the process of carrying or being carried in the womb between conception and birth. **b** this period. **2** the private development of a plan, idea, etc. [Latin *gestatio* from *gestare*, frequentative of *gerere* 'carry']

gesticulate /dʒɛ'stɪkjʊleɪt/ *v.* **1** *intr.* use gestures instead of or in addition to speech. **2** *tr.* express with gestures. □ **gesticulation** /-'leɪʃ(ə)n/ *n.* **gesticulative** /-lətɪv/ *adj.* **gesticulator** *n.* **gesticulatory** /-lət(ə)ri/ *adj.* [Latin *gesticulari* from *gesticulus*, diminutive of *gestus* GESTURE]

gesture /'dʒɛstʃə/ *n. & v.* ● *n.* **1** a movement of a limb or the body as an expression of thought or feeling. **2** the use of such movements esp. to convey feeling or as a rhetorical device. **3** an action to evoke a response or convey intention, usu. friendly (*goodwill gesture*). ● *v.tr. & intr.* gesticulate. □ **gestural** *adj.* [Middle English via medieval Latin *gestura* from Latin *gerere gest-* 'wield']

get /gɛt/ *v. & n.* ● *v.* (**getting**; *past* **got** /gɒt/ or *archaic* **gat**/gat/; *past part.* **got** or *N. Amer.* (and in *comb.*) **gotten** /'gɒt(ə)n/) **1** *tr.* come into the possession of; receive or earn (*get a job*; *got £200 a week*; *got first prize*). **2** *tr.* fetch, obtain, procure, purchase (*get my book for me*; *got a new car*). **3** *tr.* go to reach or catch (a bus, train, etc.). **4** *tr.* prepare (a meal etc.). **5** *intr. & tr.* reach or cause to reach a certain state or condition; become or cause to become (*get rich*; *get one's feet wet*; *get to be famous*; *got them ready*; *got him into trouble*). **6** *tr.* obtain as a result of calculation. **7** *tr.* contract (a disease etc.). **8** *tr.* establish or be in communication with via telephone or radio; receive (a radio signal). **9** *tr.* experience or suffer; have inflicted on one; receive as one's lot or penalty (*got four years in prison*). **10 a** *tr.* succeed in bringing, placing, etc. (*get it round the corner*; *cannot get the key into the lock*; *get it on to the agenda*; *flattery will get you nowhere*). **b** *intr. & tr.* succeed or cause to succeed in coming or going (*will get you there somehow*; *got absolutely nowhere*). **11** *tr.* (prec. by *have*) a possess (*have not got a penny*). **b** (foll. by *to* + infin.) be bound or obliged (*have got to see you*). **12** *tr.* (foll. by *to* + infin.) induce; prevail upon (*got them to help me*). **13** *tr. colloq.* understand (a person or an argument) (*have you got that?*; *I get your point*; *do you get me?*). **14** *tr. colloq.* inflict punishment or retribution on, esp. in retaliation (*I'll get you for that*). **15** *tr. colloq.* **a** annoy. **b** move; affect emotionally. **c** attract, obsess. **d** amuse. **16** *tr.* (foll. by *to* + infin.) develop an inclination as specified (*am getting to like it*). **17** *intr.* (foll. by pres. part.) begin (*get going*). **18** *tr.* (esp. in *past* or *perfect*) catch in an argument; corner, puzzle. **19** *tr.* establish (an idea etc.) in one's mind. **20** *intr. slang* be off; go away. **21** *tr. archaic* beget. **22** *tr. archaic* learn; acquire (knowledge) by study. ● *n.* **1 a** an act of begetting (of animals). **b** an offspring (of animals). **2** *Brit. slang* a fool or idiot. □ **be getting on for** be approaching (a specified time, age, etc.). **get about** (or **around**) **1** travel extensively or fast; go from place to place. **2** manage to walk, move about, etc. (esp. after illness). **3** (of news) be circulated, esp. orally. **get across 1** manage to communicate (an idea etc.). **2** (of an idea etc.) be communicated successfully. **3** *Brit. colloq.* annoy, irritate. **get along** (or **on**) **1** (foll. by *together*, *with*) live harmoniously, accord. **2** *Brit. colloq.* **a** (as *imper.*) be off! **b** (as *int.*) nonsense! (expressing scepticism). **get at 1** reach; get hold of. **2** *colloq.* imply (*what are you getting at?*). **3** *colloq.* nag, criticize, bully. **get away 1** escape. **2** (as *int.*) *colloq.* expressing disbelief or scepticism. **3** (foll. by *with*) escape blame or punishment for. **get back 1** move back or away. **2** return, arrive home. **3** recover (something lost). **4** (usu. foll. by *to*) contact later (*I'll get back to you*). **get back at** *colloq.* retaliate against. **get by** *colloq.* **1** just manage, even with difficulty. **2** be acceptable. **get down 1** alight, descend (from a vehicle, ladder, etc.). **2** record in writing. **get a person down** depress or deject him or her. **get down to** begin working on or discussing; turn one's attention seriously to. **get even** (often foll. by *with*) **1** achieve revenge; act in retaliation. **2** equalize the score. **get his** (or **hers** etc.) *slang* **1** be killed. **2** suffer retribution. **get hold of 1** grasp (physically). **2** grasp (intellectually); understand. **3** make contact with (a person). **4** acquire. **get in 1** enter; gain entrance. **2** arrive. **3** be elected. **get into** become interested or involved in. **get it** *slang* be punished or in trouble. **get it into one's head** (foll. by *that* + clause) firmly believe or maintain; realize. **get off 1** *colloq.* be acquitted; escape with little or no punishment. **2** start. **3** alight; alight from (a bus etc.). **4** go, or cause to go, to sleep. **5** (foll. by *with, together*) *Brit. colloq.* form an amorous or sexual relationship, esp. abruptly or quickly. **get a person off** *colloq.* cause a person to be acquitted. **get on 1** make progress; manage. **2** enter (a bus etc.). **3** esp. *Brit.* = *get along* 1. **4** (usu. as **getting on**) *adj. colloq.* grow old. **get on to** *colloq.* **1** make contact with. **2** understand; become aware of. **get out 1** leave or escape. **2** manage to go outdoors. **3** alight from a vehicle. **4** transpire; become known. **5** succeed in uttering, publishing, etc. **6** *Brit.* solve or finish (a puzzle etc.). **7** *Cricket* be dismissed. **get a person out 1** help a person to leave or escape. **2** *Cricket* dismiss (a batsman). **get out of 1** avoid or escape (a duty etc.). **2** abandon (a habit) gradually. **get a thing out of** manage to obtain (esp. information) from (a person) esp. with difficulty. **get outside** (or **outside of**) *Brit. slang* eat or drink. **get over 1** recover from (an illness, upset, etc.). **2** overcome (a difficulty). **3** manage to communicate (an idea etc.). **get a thing over** (or **over with**) complete (a tedious task) promptly. **get one's own back** *Brit. colloq.* have one's revenge. **get-rich-quick** *adj.* designed or concerned to make a lot of money fast. **get rid of** see RID. **get round** (*US* **around**) **1** successfully coax or cajole (a person) esp. to secure a favour. **2** evade (a law etc.). **get round to** deal with (a task etc.) in due course. **get somewhere** make progress; be initially successful. **get there** *colloq.* **1** succeed. **2** understand what is meant. **get through 1** pass or assist in passing (an examination, an ordeal, etc.). **2** finish or use up (esp. resources). **3** (often foll. by *to*) make contact by telephone. **4** (foll. by *to*) succeed in making (a person) listen or understand. **get a thing through** cause it to overcome obstacles, difficulties, etc. **get to 1** reach. **2** = *get down to*. **get together** gather, assemble. **get up 1** rise or cause to rise from sitting etc., or from bed after sleeping or an illness. **2** ascend or mount, e.g. on horseback. **3** (of fire, wind, or the sea) begin to be strong or agitated. **4** prepare or organize. **5** enhance or refine one's knowledge of (a subject). **6** work up (a feeling, e.g. anger). **7** produce or stimulate (*get up steam*; *get up speed*). **8** (often *refl.*) dress or arrange elaborately; make presentable; arrange the appearance of. **9** (foll. by *to*) *Brit. colloq.* indulge or be involved in (*always getting up to mischief*). **get-up-and-go** *colloq.* energy, vim, enthusiasm. **get the wind up** see WIND[1]. **get with child** *archaic* make pregnant. **have got it bad** (or **badly**) *slang* be obsessed or affected emotionally. □ **gettable** *adj.* [Middle English from Old Norse *geta* 'obtain, beget, guess', corresponding to Old English *gietan* (recorded only in compounds), from Germanic]

get-at-able /gɛt'atəb(ə)l/ *adj. colloq.* accessible.

getaway /'gɛtəweɪ/ *n.* an escape, esp. after committing a crime.

get-out *n. Brit.* a means of avoiding something.

getter /'gɛtə/ *n.* & *v.* ● *n.* **1** in senses of GET *v.* **2** *Physics* a substance used to remove residual gas from an evacuated vessel. ● *v.tr. Physics* remove (gas) or evacuate (a vessel) with a getter.

get-together *n. colloq.* a social gathering.

get-up *n. colloq.* a style or arrangement of dress etc., esp. an elaborate one.

geum /'dʒiːəm/ *n.* any plant of the genus *Geum* (rose family) including herb bennet, with rosettes of leaves and yellow, red, or white flowers. [modern Latin, variant of Latin *gaeum*]

GeV *abbr.* gigaelectronvolt (equivalent to 10^9 electronvolts).

gewgaw /'gjuːgɔː/ *n.* a gaudy plaything or ornament; a bauble. [Middle English: origin unknown]

geyser /'giːzə, 'gʌɪ-/ *n.* **1** an intermittently gushing hot spring that throws up a tall column of water. **2** /'giːzə/ *Brit.* an apparatus for heating water rapidly for domestic use. [Icelandic *Geysir*, the name of a particular spring in Iceland, related to *geysa* 'to gush']

GG *abbr. Brit.* Governor-General.

Ghanaian /gɑː'neɪən/ *adj.* & *n.* ● *adj.* of or relating to Ghana in W. Africa. ● *n.* a native or national of Ghana; a person of Ghanaian descent.

gharial /'garɪɑːl, gʌrɪ'ɑːl, 'gɛːrɪəl/ *n.* (also **gavial** /'geɪvɪəl/) a large Indian crocodile, *Gavialis gangeticus*, having a long narrow snout widening at the nostrils. See also FALSE GHARIAL. [Hindustani]

ghastly /gɑːs(t)li/ *adj.* & *adv.* ● *adj.* (**ghastlier, ghastliest**) **1** horrible, frightful. **2** *colloq.* objectionable, unpleasant. **3** deathlike, pallid. ● *adv.* in a ghastly or sickly way (*ghastly pale*). □ **ghastlily** *adv.* **ghastliness** *n.* [Middle English *gastlich* from obsolete *gast* 'terrify': *gh* by analogy with *ghost*]

ghat /gɑːt, gɔːt/ *n.* in India: **1** steps leading down to a river. **2** a landing place. **3** a defile or mountain pass. [Hindi *ghāṭ*]

Ghazi /'gɑːzi/ *n.* (*pl.* **Ghazis**) (often as an honorific title) a Muslim fighter against non-Muslims. [Arabic *al-ġāzī*, part. of *ġazā* 'raid']

GHB *abbr.* gamma hydroxy butyrate, a designer drug with anaesthetic properties, claimed also to be an aphrodisiac.

ghee /giː/ *n.* (also **ghi**) Indian clarified butter esp. from the milk of a buffalo or cow. [Hindi *ghī* from Sanskrit *ghṛitá-* 'sprinkled']

gherao /gɛ'raʊ/ *n.* (*pl.* **-os**) (in India and Pakistan) coercion of employers, by which their workers prevent them from leaving the premises until certain demands are met. [Hindustani *gherna* 'besiege']

gherkin /'gɜːkɪn/ *n.* a small variety of cucumber, or a young green cucumber, used for pickling. [Dutch *gurkje*, diminutive of *gurk*, from Slavonic, ultimately from medieval Greek *aggourion*]

ghetto /'gɛtəʊ/ *n.* & *v.* ● *n.* (*pl.* **-os** or **-oes**) **1** a part of a city, esp. a slum area, occupied by a minority group or groups. **2** *hist.* the Jewish quarter in a city. **3** a segregated group or area. ● *v.tr.* (**-oes**, **-oed**) put or keep (people) in a ghetto. □ **ghettoize** *v.tr.* (also **ghettoise**). [perhaps from Italian *getto* 'foundry' (applied to the site of the first ghetto in Venice in 1516)]

ghetto blaster *n. slang* a large portable radio and cassette player, esp. used to play loud pop music.

ghi var. of GHEE.

ghillie var. of GILLIE.

ghost /gəʊst/ *n.* & *v.* ● *n.* **1** a supposed apparition of a dead person or animal, often as a nebulous image; a disembodied spirit. **2** a mere semblance (*not a ghost of a chance*). **3** a secondary or duplicated image produced by defective television reception or by a telescope. **4** *archaic* a spirit or soul. ● *v.* **1** *intr.* (often foll. by *for*) act as ghost writer. **2** *tr.* act as ghost writer of (a work). □ **ghostlike** *adj.* [Old English *gāst* from West Germanic: *gh-* occurs first in Caxton, probably influenced by Flemish *gheest*]

ghostbuster /'gəʊs(t)bʌstə/ *n. colloq.* a person who professes to banish ghosts, poltergeists, etc.

ghosting /'gəʊstɪŋ/ *n.* the appearance of a 'ghost' (see GHOST *n.* 3) or secondary image in a television picture.

ghostly /'gəʊs(t)li/ *adj.* (**ghostlier**, **ghostliest**) like a ghost; spectral. □ **ghostliness** *n.* [Old English *gāstlic* (as GHOST)]

ghost town *n.* a deserted town with few or no remaining inhabitants.

ghost train *n.* (at a funfair) an open-topped miniature railway in which the rider experiences ghoulish sights, sounds, etc.

ghost writer *n.* a person who writes on behalf of the credited author of a work. □ **ghost-write** *v.tr.* & *intr.*

ghoul /guːl/ *n.* **1** a person morbidly interested in death etc. **2** an evil spirit or phantom. **3** a spirit in Arabic folklore preying on travellers. □ **ghoulish** *adj.* **ghoulishly** *adv.* **ghoulishness** *n.* [Arabic *gūl*, a protean desert demon]

GHQ *abbr.* General Headquarters.

ghyll *Brit.* var. of GILL[3].

GI *n.* & *adj.* ● *n.* (*pl.* **GIs**) a private soldier in the US Army. ● *adj.* of or for US servicemen. [abbreviation of *government* (or *general*) *issue*]

giant /'dʒʌɪənt/ *n.* & *adj.* ● *n.* **1** (*fem.* **giantess** /-tɪs/) an imaginary or mythical being of human form but superhuman size. **2** (in Greek mythology) one of such beings who fought against the gods. **3** an abnormally tall or large person, animal, or plant. **4** a person of exceptional ability, integrity, courage, etc. **5** a star of relatively great size and luminosity. ● *attrib.adj.* **1** of extraordinary size or force, gigantic; monstrous. **2** *colloq.* extra large (*giant packet*). **3** (of a plant or animal) of a very large kind. □ **giantism** *n.* **giant-like** *adj.* [Middle English *geant* (later influenced by Latin) from Old French, ultimately via Latin *gigas gigant-* from Greek]

giant-killer *n.* a person who defeats a seemingly much more powerful opponent.

giant sequoia see SEQUOIA.

giaour /'dʒaʊə/ *n. derog.* a non-Muslim, esp. a Christian (originally a Turkish name). [Persian *gaur*, probably from Arabic *kāfir* KAFFIR]

giardiasis /dʒɪɑː'dʌɪəsɪs/ *n. Med.* infection of the gut with a flagellate protozoan of the genus *Giardia*, esp. *Giardia lamblia*, causing diarrhoea etc. [modern Latin genus name *Giardia* (from A. *Giard*, French biologist d. 1908) + -ASIS]

Gib /dʒɪb/ *n. colloq.* Gibraltar. [abbreviation]

gib /dʒɪb, gɪb/ *n.* a wood or metal bolt, wedge, or pin for holding a machine part etc. in place. [18th c.: origin unknown]

gibber[1] /'dʒɪbə, 'gɪbə/ *v.* & *n.* ● *v.intr.* speak fast and inarticulately; chatter incoherently. ● *n.* such speech or sound. [imitative]

gibber[2] /'gɪbə/ *n. Austral.* a boulder or large stone. [Dharuk *giba* 'stone']

gibberellin /dʒɪbə'rɛlɪn/ *n.* one of a group of plant hormones that stimulate the growth of leaves and shoots. [*Gibberella*, a genus of fungi, diminutive of genus name *Gibbera*, from Latin *gibber* 'hump']

gibberish /'dʒɪb(ə)rɪʃ, 'gɪb-/ *n.* unintelligible or meaningless speech; nonsense. [perhaps from GIBBER[1] (but attested earlier) + -ISH[1] as used in *Spanish*, *Swedish*, etc.]

gibbet /'dʒɪbɪt/ *n.* & *v.* ● *n. hist.* **1 a** a gallows. **b** an upright post with an arm on which the bodies of executed criminals were hung up. **2** (prec. by *the*) death by hanging. ● *v.tr.* (**gibbeted**, **gibbeting**) **1** put to death by hanging. **2 a** expose on a gibbet. **b** hang up as on a gibbet. **3** hold up to contempt. [Middle English from Old French *gibet* 'gallows', diminutive of *gibe* 'club', probably from Germanic]

gibbon /'gɪb(ə)n/ *n.* any small ape of the genus *Hylobates*, native to SE Asia, having a slender body, long arms, and no tail. [French, from a native name]

gibbous /'gɪbəs/ *adj.* **1** convex or protuberant. **2** (of a moon or planet) having the bright part greater than a semicircle and less than a circle. **3** humped or humpbacked. □ **gibbosity** /-'bɒsɪti/ *n.* **gibbously** *adv.* **gibbousness** *n.* [Middle English from Late Latin *gibbosus*, from *gibbus* 'hump']

gibe /dʒʌɪb/ *v.* & *n.* (also **jibe**) ● *v.intr.* (often foll. by *at*) jeer, mock. ● *n.* an instance of gibing; a taunt. □ **giber** *n.* [perhaps from Old French *giber* 'handle roughly']

giblets /'dʒɪblɪts/ *n.pl.* the liver, gizzard, neck, etc., of a bird, usu. removed and kept separate when the bird is prepared for cooking. [Old French *gibelet* 'game stew', perhaps from *gibier* 'game']

Gibson girl /'gɪbs(ə)n/ *n.* a girl typifying the fashionable ideal of around 1900. [as represented in the work of C.D. *Gibson* (d. 1944), US artist]

giddy /'gɪdi/ *adj.* & *v.* ● *adj.* (**giddier**, **giddiest**) **1** having a sensation of whirling and a tendency to fall, stagger, or spin round. **2 a** overexcited as a result of success, pleasurable emotion, etc.; mentally intoxicated. **b** excitable, frivolous. **3** tending to make one giddy. ● *v.tr.* & *intr.* (**-ies**, **-ied**) make or become giddy. □ **giddily** *adv.* **giddiness** *n.* [Old English *gidig* 'insane', literally 'possessed by a god']

giddy-up /'gɪdɪʌp, -'ʌp/ *int.* & *v.* ● *int.* commanding a horse to go or go faster. ● *v.tr.* urge to go or go faster. [reproducing a pronunciation of *get up*]

gie /giː/ *v.tr.* & *intr. Sc.* = GIVE.

GIFT /gɪft/ *n.* gamete intrafallopian transfer, a technique for assisting conception by introducing mixed ova and sperm into a Fallopian tube. [acronym]

gift /gɪft/ *n.* & *v.* ● *n.* **1** a thing given; a present. **2** a natural ability or talent. **3** the power to give (*in his gift*). **4** the act or an instance of giving. **5** *colloq.* an easy task. ● *v.tr.* **1** endow with gifts. **2 a** (foll. by *with*) give to as a gift. **b** bestow as a gift. □ **look a gift-horse in the mouth** (usu. *neg.*) find fault with what has been given. [Middle English from Old Norse *gipt* from Germanic, related to GIVE]

gifted /'gɪftɪd/ *adj.* exceptionally talented or intelligent. □ **giftedly** *adv.* **giftedness** *n.*

gift of the gab see GAB.

gift of tongues see TONGUE.

gift token *n.* (also **gift voucher**) *Brit.* a voucher used as a gift and exchangeable for goods.

giftware /'gɪftwɛː/ *n.* goods sold as being suitable as gifts.

gift-wrap *v. & n.* ● *v.tr.* (**-wrapped**, **-wrapping**) wrap attractively as a gift. ● *n.* (**giftwrap**) decorative paper etc. for wrapping gifts.

gig[1] /gɪg/ *n.* **1** a light two-wheeled one-horse carriage. **2** a light ship's boat for rowing or sailing. **3** a rowing boat esp. for racing. [Middle English, perhaps originally = a flighty girl]

gig[2] /gɪg/ *n. & v. colloq.* ● *n.* **1** an engagement of an entertainer, esp. of musicians to play jazz, pop, or dance music, usu. for a single appearance. **2** a performance of this kind. ● *v.intr.* (**gigged**, **gigging**) perform a gig. [20th c.: origin unknown]

gig[3] /gɪg/ *n.* a kind of fishing spear. [short for *fizgig*, *fishgig*: cf. Spanish *fisga* 'harpoon']

giga- /ˈgʌɪgə, ˈgɪgə, dʒ-/ *comb. form* denoting a factor of 10^9 (*gigawatt*) or (in *Computing*) a factor of 2^{30} (*gigabyte*). [Greek *gigas* 'giant']

gigaflop /ˈgʌɪgəflɒp, ˈgɪgə-, dʒ-/ *n. Computing* a unit of computing speed equal to one thousand million floating-point operations per second.

gigametre /ˈgʌɪgəmiːtə, ˈgɪgə-, dʒ-/ *n.* a metric unit equal to 10^9 metres.

gigantic /dʒʌɪˈgantɪk/ *adj.* **1** very large; enormous. **2** like or suited to a giant. ◻ **gigantesque** /-ˈtɛsk/ *adj.* **gigantically** *adv.* [Latin *gigas gigantis* GIANT]

gigantism /ˈdʒʌɪgantɪz(ə)m, dʒʌɪˈgantɪz(ə)m/ *n.* abnormal largeness, esp. *Med.* excessive growth due to hormonal imbalance, or *Bot.* excessive size due to polyploidy in plants.

giggle /ˈgɪg(ə)l/ *v. & n.* ● *v.intr.* laugh in half-suppressed spasms, esp. in an affected or silly manner. ● *n.* **1** such a laugh. **2** *colloq.* an amusing person or thing; a joke. ◻ **giggler** *n.* **giggly** *adj.* (**gigglier**, **giggliest**). [imitative]

GIGO /ˈgʌɪgəʊ/ *abbr. Computing* garbage in, garbage out.

gigolo /ˈʒɪgələʊ, dʒ-/ *n.* (*pl.* **-os**) **1** a young man paid by an older woman to be her escort or lover. **2** a professional male dancing partner or escort. [French, formed as masc. of *gigole* 'dance hall woman']

gigot /ˈdʒɪgət/ *n.* a leg of mutton or lamb. [French, diminutive of dialect *gigue* 'leg']

gigot sleeve *n.* a leg-of-mutton sleeve.

gigue /ʒiːg/ *n.* **1** = JIG 1. **2** *Mus.* a lively piece of music usu. in a dotted rhythm with two sections each repeated. [French: see JIG]

gild[1] /gɪld/ *v.tr.* (*past part.* **gilded** or as adj. in sense 1 **gilt**) **1** cover thinly with gold. **2** tinge with a golden colour or light. **3** give a specious or false brilliance to. ◻ **gild the lily** try to improve what is already beautiful or excellent. ◻ **gilder** *n.* [Old English *gyldan*, from Germanic]

gild[2] var. of GUILD.

gilded cage *n.* a luxurious but restrictive environment.

gilded youth *n.pl.* young people of wealth, fashion, and flair.

gilding /ˈgɪldɪŋ/ *n.* **1** the act or art of applying gilt. **2** material used in applying gilt.

gilet /dʒɪˈleɪ/ *n. Brit.* **1** a woman's light garment resembling a waistcoat. **2** a sleeveless padded jacket. [French, = waistcoat]

gilgai /ˈgɪlgʌɪ/ *n. Austral.* a saucer-like natural reservoir for rainwater. [Wiradhuri and Kamilaroi *gilgaay*]

gill[1] /gɪl/ *n. & v.* ● *n.* (usu. in *pl.*) **1** the respiratory organ in fishes and other aquatic animals. **2** the vertical radial plates on the underside of mushrooms and other fungi. **3** the flesh below a person's jaws and ears (*green about the gills*). **4** the wattles or dewlap of fowls. ● *v.tr.* **1** gut (a fish). **2** cut off the gills of (a mushroom). **3** catch in a gill-net. ◻ **gilled** *adj.* (also in *comb.*). [Middle English via Old Norse from Germanic]

gill[2] /dʒɪl/ *n.* **1** a unit of liquid measure, equal to a quarter of a pint. **2** *Brit. dial.* half a pint. [Middle English via Old French *gille*, medieval Latin *gillo* from Late Latin *gello*, *gillo* 'water pot']

gill[3] /gɪl/ *n.* (also **ghyll**) *Brit.* **1** a deep usu. wooded ravine. **2** a narrow mountain torrent. [Middle English from Old Norse *gil* 'glen']

gill[4] /dʒɪl/ *n.* (also **Gill**, **jill**, **Jill**) **1** *derog.* a young woman. **2** *Brit. colloq.* or *dial.* a female ferret. [Middle English, abbreviation of *Gillian*]

gill cover *n.* a bony case protecting a fish's gills; an operculum.

gillie /ˈgɪli/ *n.* (also **ghillie**) *Sc.* **1** a man or boy attending a person hunting or fishing. **2** *hist.* a Highland chief's attendant. [Gaelic *gille* 'lad, servant']

gill-net *n.* a net for entangling fishes by the gills.

gillyflower /ˈdʒɪlɪflaʊə/ *n.* **1** (in full **clove gillyflower**) a clove-scented pink (see CLOVE[1] 2). **2** any of various similarly scented flowers such as the wallflower or white stock. [Middle English *gilofre*, *gerofle* via Old French *gilofre*, *girofle*, and medieval Latin from Greek *karuophullon* 'clove', from *karuon* 'nut' + *phullon* 'leaf', assimilated to FLOWER]

gilt[1] /gɪlt/ *adj. & n.* ● *adj.* **1** covered thinly with gold. **2** gold-coloured. ● *n.* **1** gold or a goldlike substance applied in a thin layer to a surface. **2** (often in *pl.*) *Brit.* a gilt-edged security. [past part. of GILD[1]]

gilt[2] /gɪlt/ *n.* a young sow. [Middle English from Old Norse *gyltr*]

gilt-edged *adj.* **1** (of securities, stocks, etc.) having a high degree of reliability as an investment. **2** having a gilded edge.

giltwood /ˈgɪltwʊd/ *adj.* made of wood and gilded.

gimbals /ˈdʒɪmb(ə)lz/ *n.pl.* a contrivance, usu. of rings and pivots, for keeping instruments such as a compass and chronometer horizontal at sea, in the air, etc. ◻ **gimballed** *adj.* [variant of earlier *gimmal*, via Old French *gemel* 'double finger ring' from Latin *gemellus*, diminutive of *geminus* 'twin']

gimcrack /ˈdʒɪmkrak/ *adj. & n.* ● *adj.* showy but flimsy and worthless. ● *n.* a cheap showy ornament; a knick-knack. ◻ **gimcrackery** *n.* **gimcracky** *adj.* [Middle English *gibecrake*, a kind of ornament, of unknown origin]

gimlet /ˈgɪmlɪt/ *n.* **1** a small tool with a screw-tip for boring holes. **2** a cocktail usu. of gin and lime juice. [Middle English from Old French *guimbelet*, diminutive of *guimble*, ultimately from Germanic]

gimlet eye *n.* an eye with a piercing glance.

gimmick /ˈgɪmɪk/ *n. colloq.* a trick or device, esp. to attract attention, publicity, or trade. ◻ **gimmickry** *n.* **gimmicky** *adj.* [20th-c. US: origin unknown]

gimp[1] /gɪmp/ *n.* (also **guimp**, **gymp**) **1** a twist of silk etc. with cord or wire running through it, used esp. as trimming. **2** fishing line of silk etc. bound with wire. **3** a coarser thread outlining the design of lace. [Dutch: origin unknown]

gimp[2] /gɪmp/ *n. & v. slang* ● *n.* **1** a lame person or leg. **2** a stupid or contemptible person. ● *v.intr.* limp, hobble. [20th c. US: origin unknown]

gin[1] /dʒɪn/ *n.* an alcoholic spirit distilled from grain or malt and flavoured with juniper berries. [abbreviation of *geneva* GENEVER]

gin[2] /dʒɪn/ *n. & v.* ● *n.* **1** a snare or trap. **2** a machine for separating cotton from its seeds. **3** a kind of crane and windlass. ● *v.tr.* (**ginned**, **ginning**) **1** treat (cotton) in a gin. **2** trap. ◻ **ginner** *n.* [Middle English from Old French *engin* ENGINE]

gin[3] /dʒɪn/ *n. Austral.* an Aboriginal woman. [Dharuk *diyin* 'woman, wife']

ginger /ˈdʒɪndʒə/ *n., adj., & v.* ● *n.* **1 a** a hot spicy root usu. powdered for use in cooking, or preserved in syrup, or candied. **b** the plant, *Zingiber officinale*, of SE Asia, having this root. **2** a light reddish-yellow colour. **3** spirit, mettle. **4** stimulation. ● *adj.* of a ginger colour. ● *v.tr.* **1** flavour with ginger. **2** (foll. by *up*) rouse or enliven. ◻ **gingery** *adj.* [Middle English from Old English *gingiber* and Old French *gingi(m)bre*, both from medieval Latin *gingiber*, ultimately from Sanskrit *śr̥ṅgaveram* from *śr̥ṅgam* 'horn' + *-vera* 'body', with reference to the antler-shape of the root]

ginger ale *n.* an effervescent non-alcoholic clear drink flavoured with ginger extract.

ginger beer *n.* **1** an effervescent mildly alcoholic cloudy drink, made by fermenting a mixture of ginger and syrup. **2** a non-alcoholic commercial variety of this.

gingerbread /ˈdʒɪndʒəbrɛd/ *n.* **1** a cake made with treacle or syrup and flavoured with ginger. **2** (often *attrib.*) a gaudy or tawdry decoration or ornament. □ **take the gilt off the gingerbread** *Brit.* strip something of its attractive qualities.

ginger group *n. Brit.* a group within a party or movement that presses for stronger or more radical policy or action.

gingerly /ˈdʒɪndʒəli/ *adv. & adj.* ● *adv.* in a careful or cautious manner. ● *adj.* showing great care or caution. □ **gingerliness** *n.* [perhaps from Old French *gensor* 'delicate', comparative of *gent* 'graceful', from Latin *genitus* '(well-)born']

ginger nut *n. Brit.* a ginger-flavoured biscuit.

ginger snap *n.* a thin brittle biscuit flavoured with ginger.

ginger wine *n.* a drink of fermented sugar, water, and bruised ginger.

gingham /ˈgɪŋəm/ *n.* a plain-woven cotton cloth esp. striped or checked. [Dutch *gingang* from Malay *ginggang* (originally an adj. = striped)]

gingili /ˈdʒɪndʒɪli/ *n.* **1** sesame. **2** sesame oil. [Hindi *jinjalī* from Arabic *juljulān*]

gingival /dʒɪnˈdʒʌɪv(ə)l/ *adj. Med.* of or relating to the gums. [Latin *gingiva* 'gum']

gingivitis /dʒɪndʒɪˈvʌɪtɪs/ *n.* inflammation of the gums.

gingko var. of GINKGO.

ginglymus /ˈgɪŋglɪməs/ *n.* (*pl.* **ginglymi** /-mʌɪ/) *Anat.* a hinge-like joint in the body with motion in one plane only, e.g. the elbow or knee. [modern Latin from Greek *gigglumos* 'hinge']

gink /gɪŋk/ *n. slang* often *derog.* a fellow; a man. [20th-c. US: origin unknown]

ginkgo /ˈgɪŋkgəʊ, ˈgɪŋkəʊ/ *n.* (also **gingko** /ˈgɪŋkəʊ/) (*pl.* **-os** or **-oes**) an originally Chinese and Japanese tree, *Ginkgo biloba*, with fan-shaped leaves and yellow flowers. Also called MAIDENHAIR TREE. [Japanese *ginkyo* from Chinese *yinxing* 'silver apricot']

ginormous /dʒʌɪˈnɔːməs/ *adj. Brit. slang* very large; enormous. [GIANT + ENORMOUS]

gin rummy *n.* a form of the card game rummy.

ginseng /ˈdʒɪnsɛŋ/ *n.* **1** any of several medicinal plants of the genus *Panax*, found in E. Asia and N. America. **2** the root of this. [Chinese *renshen*, perhaps = man-image, with allusion to its forked root]

gippy tummy /ˈdʒɪpi/ *n.* (also **gyppy tummy**) *Brit. colloq.* diarrhoea affecting visitors to hot countries. [abbreviation of EGYPTIAN]

gipsy var. of GYPSY.

giraffe /dʒɪˈrɑːf, -ˈraf/ *n.* (*pl.* same or **giraffes**) a ruminant mammal, *Giraffa camelopardalis* of Africa, the tallest living animal, with a long neck and forelegs and a skin of dark patches separated by lighter lines. [French *girafe*, Italian *giraffa*, ultimately from Arabic *zarāfa*]

girandole /ˈdʒɪr(ə)ndəʊl/ *n.* **1** a revolving cluster of fireworks. **2** a branched candle-bracket or candlestick. **3** an earring or pendant with a large central stone surrounded by small ones. [French from Italian *girandola*, from *girare* GYRATE]

girasol /ˈdʒɪrəsɒl, -səʊl/ *n.* (also **girasole** /-səʊl/) a kind of opal reflecting a reddish glow; a fire-opal. [originally = sunflower, from French *girasol* or Italian *girasole*, from *girare* (as GIRANDOLE) + *sole* 'sun']

gird[1] /gəːd/ *v.tr.* (*past* and *past part.* **girded** or **girt**) *literary* **1** encircle, attach, or secure with a belt or band. **2** secure (clothes) on the body with a girdle or belt. **3** enclose or encircle. **4 a** (foll. by *with*) equip with a sword in a belt. **b** fasten (a sword) with a belt. **5** (foll. by *round*) place (cord etc.) round. □ **gird** (or **gird up**) **one's loins** prepare for action. [Old English *gyrdan* from Germanic (as GIRTH)]

gird[2] /gəːd/ *v. & n.* ● *v.intr.* (foll. by *at*) jeer or gibe. ● *n.* a gibe or taunt. [Middle English, = strike etc.: origin unknown]

girder /ˈgəːdə/ *n.* a large iron or steel beam or compound structure for bearing loads, esp. in bridge-building. [GIRD[1] + -ER[1]]

girdle[1] /ˈgəːd(ə)l/ *n. & v.* ● *n.* **1** a belt or cord worn round the waist. **2** a woman's corset extending from waist to thigh. **3** a thing that surrounds like a girdle. **4** the bony support for a limb (*pelvic girdle*). **5** the part of a cut gem dividing the crown from the base and embraced by the setting. **6** a ring round a tree made by the removal of bark. ● *v.tr.* **1** surround with a girdle. **2** remove a ring of bark from (a tree), esp. to make it more fruitful. [Old English *gyrdel*: see GIRD[1]]

girdle[2] /ˈgəːd(ə)l/ *n. Sc. & N.Engl.* = GRIDDLE 1. [metathetic form of GRIDDLE]

girl /gəːl/ *n.* **1** a female child or youth. **2** *colloq.* a young (esp. unmarried) woman. **3** *colloq.* a girlfriend or sweetheart. **4** a female servant. □ **girlhood** *n.* [Middle English *gurle, girle, gerle*, perhaps related to Low German *gör* 'child']

girl Friday *n.* a female helper or follower. [after MAN FRIDAY]

girlfriend /ˈgəːlfrɛnd/ *n.* **1** a regular female companion or lover. **2** a female friend.

Girl Guide *n.* = GUIDE *n.* 10.

girlie /ˈgəːli/ *n. & adj.* (also **girly**) *colloq.* ● *n.* (*pl.* **-ies**) a girl (esp. as a term of endearment). ● *adj.* **1** girlish. **2** (of a magazine etc.) depicting nude or partially nude young women in erotic poses.

girlish /ˈgəːlɪʃ/ *adj.* of or like a girl. □ **girlishly** *adv.* **girlishness** *n.*

Girl Scout *n.* a girl belonging to the Scout Association.

girn var. of GURN.

giro /ˈdʒʌɪrəʊ/ *n. & v. Brit.* ● *n.* (*pl.* **-os**) **1** a system of credit transfer between banks, post offices, etc. **2** a cheque or payment by giro. ● *v.tr.* (**-oes, -oed**) pay by giro. [German from Italian, = circulation (of money)]

girt[1] *past part.* of GIRD[1].

girt[2] var. of GIRTH.

girth /gəːθ/ *n. & v.* (also **girt** /gəːt/) ● *n.* **1** the measurement around the waist, a tree trunk, or a thing of similar shape. **2** a band round the body of a horse to secure the saddle etc. ● *v.* **1** *tr.* **a** secure (a saddle etc.) with a girth. **b** put a girth on (a horse). **2** *tr.* surround, encircle. **3** *intr.* measure (an amount) in girth. [Middle English from Old Norse *gjörth*, Gothic *gairda*, from Germanic]

gismo var. of GIZMO.

gist /dʒɪst/ *n.* **1** the substance or essence of a matter. **2** *Law* the real ground of an action etc. [Old French, 3rd sing. present of *gesir* 'lie', from Latin *jacēre*]

git /gɪt/ *n. Brit. slang* a silly or contemptible person. [variant of GET *n.*]

gîte /ʒiːt, French ʒit/ *n.* a furnished holiday house in France, usu. small and in a rural district. [originally = lodging: French from Old French *giste*, related to *gésir* 'lie']

gittern /ˈgɪtəːn/ *n.* a medieval stringed instrument, a forerunner of the guitar. [Middle English from Old French *guiterne*: cf. CITTERN, GUITAR]

give /gɪv/ *v. & n.* ● *v.* (*past* **gave** /geɪv/; *past part.* **given** /ˈgɪv(ə)n/) **1** *tr.* (also *absol.*; often foll. by *to*) transfer the possession of freely; hand over as a present (*gave them her old curtains*; *gives to cancer research*). **2** *tr.* **a** transfer the ownership of with or without actual delivery; bequeath (*gave him £200 in her will*). **b** transfer, esp. temporarily or for safe keeping; hand over; provide with (*gave him the dog to hold*; *gave them a drink*). **c** administer (medicine). **d** communicate or impart (a message, compliments, etc.) (*give her my best wishes*). **3** *tr.* (usu. foll. by *for*) make over in exchange or payment;

pay; sell (*gave him £30 for the bicycle*). **4** *tr.* **a** confer; grant (a benefit, an honour, etc.). **b** accord; bestow (one's affections, confidence, etc.). **c** award; administer (one's approval, blame, etc.); tell, offer (esp. something unpleasant) (*gave him a talking-to*; *gave him my blessing*; *gave him the sack*). **d** pledge, assign as a guarantee (*gave his word*). **5** *tr.* **a** effect or perform (an action etc.) (*gave him a kiss*; *gave a jump*). **b** utter (*gave a shriek*). **6** *tr.* allot; assign; grant (*was given the contract*). **7** *tr.* (in *passive*; foll. by *to*) be inclined to or fond of (*is given to speculation*). **8** *tr.* yield as a product or result (*the lamp gives a bad light*; *the field gives fodder for twenty cows*). **9** *intr.* **a** yield to pressure; become relaxed; lose firmness (*they pushed hard but the door wouldn't give*; *old elastic gives too much*). **b** collapse (*the roof gave under the pressure*). **10** *intr.* (usu. foll. by *of*) grant; bestow (*gave freely of his time*). **11** *tr.* **a** commit, consign, or entrust (*gave him into custody*; *give her into your care*). **b** sanction the marriage of (a daughter etc.). **12** *tr.* devote; dedicate (*gave his life to table tennis*; *shall give it my attention*). **13** *tr.* (usu. *absol.*) *colloq.* tell what one knows (*What happened? Come on, give!*). **14** *tr.* present; offer; show; hold out (*gives no sign of life*; *gave her his arm*; *give him your ear*). **15** *tr. Theatr.* read, recite, perform, act, etc. (*gave them Hamlet's soliloquy*). **16** *tr.* impart; be a source of (*gave him my sore throat*; *gave its name to the battle*; *gave me much pain*; *gives him a right to complain*). **17** *tr.* allow (esp. a fixed amount of time) (*can give you five minutes*). **18** *tr.* (usu. foll. by *for*) value (something) (*gives nothing for their opinions*). **19** *tr.* concede; yield (*I give you the victory*). **20** *tr.* deliver (a judgement etc.) authoritatively (*gave his verdict*). **21** *tr. Cricket* (of an umpire) declare (a batsman) out or not out. **22** *tr.* toast (a person, cause, etc.) (*I give you our President*). **23** *tr.* provide (a party, meal, etc.) as host (*gave a banquet*). ● *n.* **1** capacity to yield or bend under pressure; elasticity (*there is no give in a stone floor*). **2** ability to adapt or comply (*no give in his attitudes*). □ **give and take** *v.tr.* exchange (words, blows, or concessions). ● *n.* an exchange of words etc.; a compromise. **give as good as one gets** retort adequately in words or blows. **give away 1** transfer as a gift. **2** hand over (a bride) ceremonially to a bridegroom. **3** betray or expose to ridicule or detection. **4** esp. *Sport* give inadvertently to the opposition (*gave away a penalty*). **5** *Austral.* abandon, desist from, lose faith or interest in. **give back** return (something) to its previous owner or in exchange. **give a person** (or **thing**) **best** see BEST. **give birth (to)** see BIRTH. **give chase** pursue a person, animal, etc.; hunt. **give down** (often *absol.*) (of a cow) let (milk) flow. **give forth** emit; publish; report. **give the game** (or **show**) **away** reveal a secret or intention. **give a hand** see HAND. **give a person** (or **the devil**) **his or her due** acknowledge, esp. grudgingly, a person's rights, abilities, etc. **give in 1** cease fighting or arguing; yield. **2** *Brit.* hand in (a document etc.) to an official etc. **give in marriage** sanction the marriage of (one's daughter etc.). **give it to a person** *colloq.* scold or punish. **give me** I prefer or admire (*give me the Greek islands any day*). **give off** emit (vapour etc.). **give oneself** (of a woman) yield sexually. **give oneself airs** act pretentiously or snobbishly. **give oneself up to 1** abandon oneself to an emotion, esp. despair. **2** addict oneself to. **give on to** (or **into**) (of a window, corridor, etc.) overlook or lead into. **give or take** *colloq.* add or subtract (a specified amount or number) in estimating. **give out 1** announce; emit; distribute. **2** cease or break down from exhaustion etc. **3** run short. **give over** *Brit.* **1** *colloq.* cease from doing; abandon (a habit etc.); desist (*give over sniffing*). **2** hand over. **3** devote. **give rise to** cause, induce, suggest. **give tongue 1** speak one's thoughts. **2** (of hounds) bark, esp. on finding a scent. **give a person to understand** inform authoritatively. **give up 1** resign; surrender. **2** part with. **3** deliver (a wanted person etc.). **4** pronounce incurable or insoluble; renounce hope of. **5** renounce or cease (an activity). **give up the ghost** *archaic* or *colloq.* die. **give way** see WAY. **give a person what for** *colloq.* punish or scold severely. **give one's word** (or **word of honour**) promise solemnly. **not give a damn** (or *Brit.* **monkey's** or **toss** etc.) *colloq.* not care at all. **what gives?** *colloq.* what is the news?; what's happening? **would give the world** (or **one's ears, right arm,** etc.) **for** covet or wish for desperately. □ **giveable** *adj.* **giver** *n.* [Old English *g(i)efan*, from Germanic]

give-away *n. colloq.* **1** an inadvertent betrayal or revelation. **2** an act of giving away. **3** a free gift; a low price.

given /ˈgɪv(ə)n/ *adj. & n.* ● *adj.* **1** as previously stated or assumed; granted; specified (*given that he is a liar, we cannot trust him*; *a given number of people*). **2** *Law* (of a document) signed and dated (*given this day the 30th June*). ● *n.* a known fact or situation. [past part. of GIVE]

given name *n. US* = FORENAME.

gizmo /ˈgɪzməʊ/ *n.* (also **gismo**) (*pl.* **-os**) *slang* a gadget. [20th c.: origin unknown]

gizzard /ˈgɪzəd/ *n.* **1** a muscular thick-walled part of a bird's stomach, for grinding food usu. with grit. **2** a muscular stomach of some fish, insects, molluscs, and other invertebrates. □ **stick in one's gizzard** *colloq.* be distasteful. [Middle English *giser* from Old French *giser*, *gesier* etc., ultimately from Latin *gigeria* 'cooked entrails of fowl']

glabella /gləˈbɛlə/ *n.* (*pl.* **glabellae** /-liː/) *Anat.* the smooth part of the forehead above and between the eyebrows. □ **glabellar** *adj.* [modern Latin from Latin *glabellus* (*adj.*), diminutive of *glaber* 'smooth']

glabrous /ˈgleɪbrəs/ *adj.* free from hair or down; smooth-skinned. [Latin *glaber glabri* 'hairless']

glacé /ˈglaseɪ/ *adj.* **1** (of fruit, esp. cherries) preserved in sugar, usu. resulting in a glossy surface. **2** (of cloth, leather, etc.) smooth; polished. [French, past part. of *glacer* 'to ice, gloss', from *glace* 'ice': see GLACIER]

glacé icing *n.* icing made with icing sugar and water.

glacial /ˈgleɪʃ(ə)l, -sɪəl/ *adj.* **1** of ice; icy. **2** *Geol.* characterized or produced by the presence or agency of ice. **3** *Chem.* forming ice-like crystals upon freezing (*glacial acetic acid*). □ **glacially** *adv.* [French *glacial* or Latin *glacialis* 'icy', from *glacies* 'ice']

glacial period *n.* (also **glacial epoch**) a period in the earth's history when ice sheets were exceptionally extensive; an ice age.

glaciated /ˈgleɪsɪeɪtɪd, ˈglas-/ *adj.* **1** marked or polished by the action of ice. **2** covered or having been covered by glaciers or ice sheets. □ **glaciation** /-ˈeɪʃ(ə)n/ *n.* [past part. of *glaciate* from Latin *glaciare* 'freeze', from *glacies* 'ice']

glacier /ˈglasɪə, ˈgleɪs-/ *n.* a slowly-moving mass or river of ice formed by the accumulation and compaction of snow on mountains or near the poles. [French, from *glace* 'ice', ultimately from Latin *glacies*]

glaciology /gleɪsɪˈɒlədʒi/ *n.* the science of the internal dynamics and effects of glaciers. □ **glaciological** /-əˈlɒdʒɪk(ə)l/ *adj.* **glaciologist** *n.* [Latin *glacies* 'ice' + -LOGY]

glacis /ˈglasɪs, -si/ *n.* (*pl.* same /-sɪz, -siːz/) a bank sloping down from a fort, on which attackers are exposed to the defenders' missiles etc. [French from Old French *glacier* 'to slip', from *glace* 'ice': see GLACIER]

glad[1] /glad/ *adj. & v.* ● *adj.* (**gladder**, **gladdest**) **1** (*predic.*; usu. foll. by *about*, *Brit. of*, or *to* + infin.) pleased; willing (*shall be glad to come*; *would be glad of a chance to talk about it*). **2 a** marked by, filled with, or expressing, joy (*a glad expression*). **b** (of news, events, etc.) giving joy (*glad tidings*). ● *v.tr.* (**gladded**, **gladding**) *archaic* make glad. □ **gladly** *adv.* **gladness** *n.* **gladsome** *adj. poet.* [Old English *glæd*, from Germanic]

glad[2] /glad/ *n.* (also *Austral.* **gladdie** /ˈgladi/) *colloq.* a gladiolus. [abbreviation]

gladden /ˈglad(ə)n/ *v.tr.* make glad.

gladdon /ˈglad(ə)n/ *n.* a purple-flowered iris, *Iris foetidissima*, with an unpleasant odour when bruised. Also called *stinking iris*. [Old English *glædene*]

glade /gleɪd/ *n.* an open space in a wood or forest. [Middle English: origin unknown]

glad eye *n.* (prec. by *the*) *colloq.* an amorous glance.

glad hand *n.* & *v.* ● *n.* a warm, often superficial, greeting or welcome. ● *v.tr.* (**glad-hand**) (esp. of a politician, celebrity, etc.) greet or welcome warmly, often superficially. □ **glad-hander** *n.*

gladiator /ˈglædɪeɪtə/ *n.* **1** *hist.* a man trained to fight with a sword or other weapons at ancient Roman shows. **2** a person defending or opposing a cause; a controversialist. □ **gladiatorial** /-ɪəˈtɔːrɪəl/ *adj.* [Latin, from *gladius* 'sword']

gladiolus /glædɪˈəʊləs/ *n.* (*pl.* **gladioli** /-laɪ/ or **gladioluses**) a plant of the genus *Gladiolus* (iris family), with sword-shaped leaves and usu. brightly coloured flower spikes. [Latin, diminutive of *gladius* 'sword']

glad rags *n.pl. colloq.* best clothes; evening dress.

Gladstone bag /ˈglædst(ə)n/ *n.* a bag like a briefcase having two equal compartments joined by a hinge. [named after W. E. *Gladstone*, English statesman d. 1898]

Glagolitic /glægəˈlɪtɪk/ *adj.* of or relating to the alphabet ascribed to St Cyril and formerly used in writing some Slavonic languages. [modern Latin *glagoliticus* via Serbo-Croatian *glagòljica* 'Glagolitic alphabet' from Old Church Slavonic *glagolŭ* 'word']

glair /gleə/ *n.* (also **glaire**) **1** white of egg. **2** an adhesive preparation made from this, used in bookbinding etc. □ **glairy** *adj.* [Middle English from Old French *glaire*, ultimately from Latin *clara*, fem. of *clarus* 'clear']

glaive /gleɪv/ *n. archaic poet.* **1** a broadsword. **2** any sword. [Middle English from Old French, apparently from Latin *gladius* 'sword']

Glam. *abbr.* Glamorgan.

glam /glæm/ *adj., n.,* & *v. colloq.* ● *adj.* glamorous. ● *n.* glamour. ● *v.tr.* (**glammed**, **glamming**) glamorize. [abbreviation]

glamorize /ˈglæməraɪz/ *v.tr.* (also **glamourize**, **-ise**) make glamorous or attractive. □ **glamorization** /-ˈzeɪʃ(ə)n/ *n.*

glamour /ˈglæmə/ *n.* & *v.* (*US* also **glamor**) ● *n.* **1** physical attractiveness, esp. when achieved by make-up etc. **2** alluring or exciting beauty or charm (*the glamour of New York*). ● *v.tr.* **1** *poet.* affect with glamour; bewitch; enchant. **2** *colloq.* make glamorous. □ **cast a glamour over** enchant. □ **glamorous** *adj.* **glamorously** *adv.* [18th c.: variant of GRAMMAR, with reference to the occult practices associated with learning in the Middle Ages]

glamour girl *n.* (also **glamour boy**) an attractive young woman (or man), esp. a model etc.

glance[1] /glɑːns/ *v.* & *n.* ● *v.* **1** *intr.* (often foll. by *down, up*, etc.) cast a momentary look (*glanced up at the sky*). **2** *intr.* (often foll. by *off*) (of a bullet, ball, etc.) bounce (off an object) obliquely. **3** *intr.* (usu. foll. by *over, off, from*) (of talk or a talker) pass quickly over a subject or subjects (*glanced over the question of payment*). **4** *intr.* (of a bright object or light) flash, dart, or gleam; reflect (*the sun glanced off the knife*). **5** *tr.* (esp. of a weapon) strike (an object) obliquely. **6** *tr. Cricket* deflect (the ball) with an oblique stroke. ● *n.* **1** (usu. foll. by *at, into, over*, etc.) a brief look (*took a glance at the paper*; *threw a glance over her shoulder*). **2** a flash or gleam (*a glance of sunlight*). **3** *Cricket* a stroke with the bat's face turned slantwise to deflect the ball. □ **at a glance** immediately upon looking. **glance at 1** give a brief look at. **2** make a passing and usu. sarcastic allusion to. **glance one's eye** (foll. by *at, over*, etc.) look at briefly (esp. a document). **glance over** (or **through**) read cursorily. □ **glancingly** *adv.* [Middle English *glence* etc., probably a nasalized form of obsolete *glace* in the same sense, from Old French *glacier* 'to slip': see GLACIS]

glance[2] /glɑːns/ *n.* any lustrous sulphide ore (*copper glance*; *lead glance*). [German *Glanz* 'lustre']

gland[1] /glænd/ *n.* **1 a** an organ in an animal body secreting substances for use in the body or for ejection. **b** a structure resembling this, such as a lymph gland. **2** *Bot.* a secreting cell or group of cells on the surface of a plant structure. [French *glande* via Old French *glandre* from Latin *glandulae* 'throat-glands']

gland[2] /glænd/ *n.* a sleeve used to produce a seal round a piston rod or other shaft. [19th c.: perhaps a variant of *glam, glan* 'a vice', related to CLAMP[1]]

glanders /ˈglændəz/ *n.pl.* (also treated as *sing.*) **1** a contagious disease of horses, caused by a bacterium and characterized by swellings below the jaw and mucous discharge from the nostrils. **2** this disease in humans or other animals. □ **glandered** *adj.* **glanderous** *adj.* [Old French *glandre*: see GLAND[1]]

glandular /ˈglændjʊlə, ˈglæn(d)ʒʊlə/ *adj.* of or relating to a gland or glands. [French *glandulaire* (as GLAND[1])]

glandular fever *n.* an infectious viral disease characterized by swelling of the lymph glands and prolonged lassitude; infectious mononucleosis (see MONONUCLEOSIS).

glans /glænz/ *n.* (*pl.* **glandes** /ˈglændiːz/) the rounded part forming the end of the penis or clitoris. [Latin, = acorn]

glare[1] /gleə/ *v.* & *n.* ● *v.* **1** *intr.* (usu. foll. by *at, upon*) look fiercely or fixedly. **2** *intr.* shine dazzlingly or disagreeably. **3** *tr.* express (hatred, defiance, etc.) by a look. **4** *intr.* be over-conspicuous or obtrusive. ● *n.* **1 a** strong fierce light, esp. sunshine. **b** oppressive public attention (*the glare of fame*). **2** a fierce or fixed look (*a glare of defiance*). **3** tawdry brilliance. □ **glary** *adj.* [Middle English from Middle Dutch and Middle Low German *glaren* 'gleam, glare': probably ultimately related to GLASS]

glare[2] /gleə/ *adj. N. Amer.* (esp. of ice) smooth and glassy. [19th c.: perhaps from 16th c. *glare* 'frost', of uncertain origin]

glaring /ˈgleərɪŋ/ *adj.* **1** obvious, conspicuous (*a glaring error*). **2** shining oppressively. **3** staring fiercely. □ **glaringly** *adv.*

glasnost /ˈglæznɒst, ˈglɑːs-/ *n.* (in the former Soviet Union) the policy or practice of more open consultative government and wider dissemination of information. [Russian *glasnost'*, literally 'publicity, openness']

glass /glɑːs/ *n., v.,* & *adj.* ● *n.* **1 a** (often *attrib.*) a hard, brittle, usu. transparent, translucent, or shiny substance, made by fusing sand with soda and lime and sometimes other ingredients (cf. CROWN GLASS, FLINT GLASS, PLATE GLASS). **b** any similar substance which has solidified from a molten state without crystallizing (*volcanic glass*). **2** (often *collect.*) an object or objects made from, or partly from, glass, esp.: **a** esp. *Brit.* a drinking vessel. **b** esp. *Brit.* a mirror; a looking-glass. **c** an hourglass. **d** a window. **e** a greenhouse (*rows of lettuce under glass*). **f** glass ornaments. **g** a barometer. **h** *Brit.* a glass disc covering a watch face. **i** a magnifying lens. **j** a monocle. **3** (in *pl.*) **a** spectacles. **b** field glasses; opera glasses. **4** the amount of liquid contained in a glass; a drink (*he likes a glass*). ● *v.tr.* **1** (usu. as **glassed** *adj.*) fit with glass; glaze. **2** *poet.* reflect as in a mirror. **3** *Mil.* look at or for with field glasses. ● *adj.* of or made from glass. □ **glassful** *n.* (*pl.* **-fuls**). **glassless** *adj.* **glasslike** *adj.* [Old English *glæs*, from Germanic: cf. GLAZE]

glass-blowing *n.* the blowing of semi-molten glass to make glassware. □ **glass-blower** *n.*

glass case *n.* an exhibition display case made mostly from glass.

glass ceiling *n.* an unacknowledged barrier to personal advancement.

glass cloth *n.* **1** a linen cloth for drying glasses. **2** *Brit.* a cloth covered with powdered glass or abrasive, like glasspaper. **3** a woven fabric of fine-spun glass.

glass cutter *n.* **1** a worker who cuts glass. **2** a tool used for cutting glass.

glass eye *n.* a false eye made from glass.

glass fibre *n. Brit.* **1** a filament or filaments of glass made into fabric. **2** such filaments embedded in plastic as reinforcement (often *attrib.*: *glass fibre gliders*).

glass-gall *n.* = SANDIVER.

glasshouse /ˈglɑːshaʊs/ *n.* **1** *Brit.* a greenhouse. **2** *Brit. slang* a military prison. **3** a building where glass is made.

glassie var. of GLASSY *n.*

glassine /ˈglɑːsiːn/ *n.* a glossy transparent paper. [GLASS]

glass-making *n.* the manufacture of glass. ◻ **glassmaker** *n.*

glasspaper /ˈglɑːspeɪpə/ *n.* paper covered with powdered glass and used for smoothing and polishing.

glass snake *n.* any snakelike lizard of the genus *Ophisaurus*, with a very brittle tail.

glassware /ˈglɑːswɛː/ *n.* articles made from glass, esp. drinking glasses, tableware, etc.

glass wool *n.* glass in the form of fine fibres used for packing and insulation.

glasswort /ˈglɑːswəːt/ *n.* a salt-marsh plant of the genus *Salicornia* or *Salsola*, formerly burnt for use in glass-making.

glassy /ˈglɑːsi/ *adj.* & *n.* ● *adj.* (**glassier**, **glassiest**) **1** of or resembling glass, esp. in smoothness. **2** (of the eye, the expression, etc.) abstracted; dull; fixed (*fixed her with a glassy stare*). ● *n.* (also **glassie**) *Austral.* a glass marble. ◻ **the** (or **just the**) **glassy** *Austral. colloq.* the most excellent person or thing. ◻ **glassily** *adv.* **glassiness** *n.*

Glaswegian /glazˈwiːdʒ(ə)n, glas-, glɑːz-, glɑːs-/ *adj.* & *n.* ● *adj.* of or relating to Glasgow in Scotland. ● *n.* a native of Glasgow. [*Glasgow*, on the pattern of *Norwegian* etc.]

Glauber's salt /ˈglaʊbəz, ˈglɔː-/ *n.* (also **Glauber's salts**) a crystalline hydrated form of sodium sulphate used esp. as a laxative. [named after J. R. *Glauber*, German chemist d. 1668]

glaucoma /glɔːˈkəʊmə/ *n.* an eye-condition with increased pressure within the eyeball, causing gradual loss of sight. ◻ **glaucomatous** *adj.* [Latin from Greek *glaukōma -atos*, ultimately from *glaukos* GLAUCOUS, from the grey-green haze in the pupil]

glaucous /ˈglɔːkəs/ *adj.* **1** of a dull greyish-green or blue colour. **2** covered with a powdery bloom as of grapes. [Latin *glaucus* from Greek *glaukos*]

glaucous gull *n.* a large grey and white gull, *Larus hyperboreus*, of Arctic coasts.

glaze /gleɪz/ *v.* & *n.* ● *v.* **1** *tr.* **a** fit (a window, picture, etc.) with glass. **b** provide (a building) with glass windows. **2** *tr.* **a** cover (pottery etc.) with a glaze. **b** fix (paint) on pottery with a glaze. **3** *tr.* cover (pastry, meat, etc.) with a glaze. **4** *intr.* (often foll. by *over*) (of the eyes) become fixed or glassy (*his eyes glazed over*). **5** *tr.* cover (cloth, paper, leather, a painted surface, etc.) with a glaze or other similar finish. **6** *tr.* give a glassy surface to, e.g. by rubbing. ● *n.* **1** a vitreous substance, usu. a special glass, used to glaze pottery. **2** a smooth shiny coating of milk, sugar, gelatin, etc., on food. **3** a thin topcoat of transparent paint used to modify the tone of the underlying colour. **4** a smooth surface formed by glazing. **5** *US* a thin coating of ice. ◻ **glaze in** enclose (a building, a window frame, etc.) with glass. ◻ **glazer** *n.* **glazy** *adj.* [Middle English, from an oblique form of GLASS]

glazed frost *n.* a glassy coating of ice caused by frozen rain or a sudden thaw succeeded by a frost.

glazier /ˈgleɪzɪə/ *n.* a person whose trade is glazing windows etc. ◻ **glaziery** *n.*

glazing /ˈgleɪzɪŋ/ *n.* **1** the act or an instance of glazing. **2** windows (see also DOUBLE GLAZING). **3** material used to produce a glaze.

GLC *abbr.* **1** *hist.* (in the UK) Greater London Council. **2** *Chem.* gas-liquid chromatography.

gleam /gliːm/ *n.* & *v.* ● *n.* **1** a faint or brief light (*a gleam of sunlight*). **2** a faint, sudden, intermittent, or temporary show (*not a gleam of hope*). ● *v.intr.* **1** emit gleams. **2** shine with a faint or intermittent brightness. **3** (of a quality) be indicated (*fear gleamed in his eyes*). ◻ **gleamingly** *adv.* **gleamy** *adj.* [Old English *glǣm*, related to GLIMMER]

glean /gliːn/ *v.tr.* **1** collect or scrape together (news, facts, gossip, etc.) in small quantities. **2 a** (also *absol.*) gather (ears of corn etc.) after the harvest. **b** strip (a field etc.) after a harvest. ◻ **gleaner** *n.* [Middle English via Old French *glener* from Late Latin *glennare*, probably of Celtic origin]

gleanings /ˈgliːnɪŋz/ *n.pl.* things gleaned, esp. facts.

glebe /gliːb/ *n.* **1** a piece of land serving as part of a clergyman's benefice and providing income. **2** *poet.* earth; land; a field. [Middle English from Latin *gl(a)eba* 'clod, soil']

glee /gliː/ *n.* **1** mirth; delight (*watched the enemy's defeat with glee*). **2** a song for three or more, esp. adult male, voices, singing different parts simultaneously, usu. unaccompanied. ◻ **gleesome** *adj.* [Old English *glīo*, *glēo* 'minstrelsy, jest', from Germanic]

glee club *n.* a society for singing part-songs.

gleeful /ˈgliːfʊl, -f(ə)l/ *adj.* exuberantly or triumphantly joyful. ◻ **gleefully** *adv.* **gleefulness** *n.*

gleet /gliːt/ *n. Med.* a watery discharge from the urethra caused by gonorrhoeal infection. [Old French *glette* 'slime, secretion']

Gleichschaltung /ˈglʌɪxʃaltʊŋ, German ˈglaɪçʃaltʊŋ/ *n.* the standardization of political, economic, and social institutions in authoritarian states. [German]

glen /glɛn/ *n.* a narrow valley. [Gaelic & Irish *gleann*]

glengarry /glɛnˈgari/ *n.* (*pl.* **-ies**) a brimless Scottish hat with a cleft down the centre and usu. two ribbons hanging at the back, chiefly worn as part of Highland dress. [*Glengarry* in Scotland]

glenoid cavity /ˈgliːnɔɪd/ *n.* a shallow depression on a bone, esp. the scapula and temporal bone, receiving the projection of another bone to form a joint. [French *glénoïde* from Greek *glēnoeidēs*, from *glēnē* 'socket']

gley /gleɪ/ *n.* a sticky waterlogged soil grey to blue in colour. [Ukrainian, = sticky blue clay, related to CLAY]

glia /ˈglʌɪə, ˈgliːə/ *n.* = NEUROGLIA. ◻ **glial** *adj.* [Greek, = glue]

glib /glɪb/ *adj.* (**glibber**, **glibbest**) **1** (of a speaker, speech, etc.) fluent and voluble but insincere and shallow. **2** *archaic* smooth; unimpeded. ◻ **glibly** *adv.* **glibness** *n.* [related to obsolete *glibbery* 'slippery', from Germanic: perhaps imitative]

glide /glʌɪd/ *v.* & *n.* ● *v.* **1** *intr.* (of a stream, bird, snake, ship, train, skater, etc.) move with a smooth continuous motion. **2** *intr.* **a** (of an aircraft) fly without engine power. **b** (of a pilot) fly a glider. **3** *intr.* of time etc.: **a** pass gently and imperceptibly. **b** (often foll. by *into*) pass and change gradually and imperceptibly (*night glided into day*). **4** *intr.* move quietly or stealthily. **5** *tr.* cause to glide (*breezes glided the ship on its course*). ● *n.* **1 a** the act of gliding. **b** an instance of this. **2** *Phonet.* a gradually changing sound made in passing from one position of the speech organs to another. **3** a gliding dance or dance step. **4** a flight in a glider. **5** *Cricket* = GLANCE[1] *n.* 3. [Old English *glīdan*, from West Germanic]

glide path *n.* an aircraft's line of descent to land, esp. as indicated by ground radar.

glider /ˈglʌɪdə/ *n.* **1 a** an aircraft that flies without an engine. **b** a glider pilot. **2** a person or thing that glides.

gliding /ˈglɪdɪŋ/ *n.* the sport of flying in a glider.

glim /glɪm/ *n.* **1** a faint light. **2** *archaic slang* a candle; a lantern. [Middle English: perhaps abbreviation of GLIMMER or GLIMPSE]

glimmer /ˈglɪmə/ *v.* & *n.* ● *v.intr.* shine faintly or intermittently. ● *n.* **1** a feeble or wavering light. **2** (usu. foll. by *of*) a faint gleam (of hope, understanding, etc.). **3** a glimpse. ◻ **glimmeringly** *adv.* [Middle English, probably via Scandinavian from West Germanic: related to GLEAM]

glimmering /ˈglɪm(ə)rɪŋ/ *n.* **1** = GLIMMER *n.* **2** an act of glimmering.

glimpse /glɪm(p)s/ *n.* & *v.* ● *n.* (often foll. by *of*) **1** a momentary or partial view (*caught a glimpse of her*). **2** a faint and transient appearance (*glimpses of the truth*). ● *v.* **1** *tr.* see faintly or partly (*glimpsed his face in the crowd*). **2** *intr.* (often foll. by *at*) cast a passing glance. **3** *intr.* **a** shine faintly or intermittently. **b** *poet.* appear faintly; dawn. [Middle English *glimse*, corresponding to Middle High German *glimsen*, from the West Germanic base of GLIMMER]

glint /glɪnt/ *v.* & *n.* ● *v.intr.* & *tr.* flash or cause to flash; glitter; sparkle; reflect (*eyes glinted with amusement*; *the sword glinted fire*). ● *n.* a brief flash of light; a sparkle. [alteration of Middle English *glent*, probably of Scandinavian origin]

glissade /glɪˈsɑːd, -ˈseɪd/ *n.* & *v.* ● *n.* **1** an act of sliding down a steep slope of snow or ice, usu. on the feet with the support of an ice axe etc. **2** a gliding step in ballet. ● *v.intr.* perform a glissade. [French, from *glisser* 'slip, slide']

glissando /glɪˈsandəʊ/ *n.* (*pl.* **glissandi** /-di/ or **-os**) *Mus.* a continuous slide of adjacent notes upwards or downwards. [Italian from French *glissant* 'sliding' (as GLISSADE)]

glissé /gliːˈseɪ/ *n.* (in full **pas glissé**) (*pl.* **glissés** *pronunc.* same) *Ballet* a sliding step in which the flat of the foot is often used. [French, past part. of *glisser*: see GLISSADE]

glisten /ˈglɪs(ə)n/ *v.* & *n.* ● *v.intr.* shine, esp. like a wet object, snow, etc.; glitter. ● *n.* a glitter; a sparkle. [Old English *glisnian* from *glisian* 'shine']

glister /ˈglɪstə/ *v.* & *n.* *archaic* ● *v.intr.* sparkle; glitter. ● *n.* a sparkle; a gleam. [Middle English from Middle Low German *glistern*, Middle Dutch *glisteren*, related to GLISTEN]

glitch /glɪtʃ/ *n.* *colloq.* a sudden irregularity or malfunction (of equipment etc.). [20th c.: origin unknown]

glitter /ˈglɪtə/ *v.* & *n.* ● *v.intr.* **1** shine, esp. with a bright reflected light; sparkle. **2** (usu. foll. by *with*) **a** be showy or splendid (*glittered with diamonds*). **b** be ostentatious or flashily brilliant (*glittering rhetoric*). ● *n.* **1** a gleam; a sparkle. **2** showiness; splendour. **3** tiny pieces of sparkling material as on Christmas tree decorations. ▫ **glitteringly** *adv.* **glittery** *adj.* [Middle English from Old Norse *glitra*, from Germanic]

glitterati /glɪtəˈrɑːti/ *n.pl.* *slang* the fashionable set of literary or show-business people. [GLITTER + LITERATI]

glitz /glɪts/ *n.* *slang* extravagant but superficial display; show-business glamour. [back-formation from GLITZY]

glitzy /ˈglɪtsi/ *adj.* (**glitzier**, **glitziest**) *slang* extravagant, ostentatious; tawdry, gaudy. ▫ **glitzily** *adv.* **glitziness** *n.* [GLITTER, suggested by RITZY: cf. German *glitzerig* 'glittering']

gloaming /ˈgləʊmɪŋ/ *n.* *poet.* twilight; dusk. [Old English *glōmung* from *glōm* 'twilight', related to GLOW]

gloat /gləʊt/ *v.* & *n.* ● *v.intr.* (often foll. by *on*, *upon*, *over*) consider or contemplate with lust, greed, malice, triumph, etc. (*gloated over his collection*). ● *n.* **1** the act of gloating. **2** a look or expression of triumphant satisfaction. ▫ **gloater** *n.* **gloatingly** *adv.* [16th c.: origin unknown, but perhaps related to Old Norse *glotta* 'grin', Middle High German *glotzen* 'stare']

glob /glɒb/ *n.* a mass or lump of semi-liquid substance, e.g. mud. [20th c.: perhaps from BLOB and GOB[2]]

global /ˈgləʊb(ə)l/ *adj.* **1** worldwide (*global conflict*). **2** **a** relating to or embracing a group of items etc.; total. **b** *Computing* operating or applying through the whole of a file, program, etc. ▫ **globally** *adv.* [French (as GLOBE)]

globalize /ˈgləʊb(ə)lʌɪz/ *v.tr.* (also **-ise**) make global. ▫ **globalization** /-ˈzeɪʃ(ə)n/ *n.*

global village *n.* the world considered as a single community linked by telecommunications.

global warming *n.* a potential increase in temperature of the earth's atmosphere caused by the greenhouse effect.

globe /gləʊb/ *n.* & *v.* ● *n.* **1** **a** (prec. by *the*) the planet earth. **b** a planet, star, or sun. **c** any spherical body; a ball. **2** a spherical representation of the earth or of the constellations with a map on the surface. **3** a golden sphere as an emblem of sovereignty; an orb. **4** any spherical glass vessel, esp. a fishbowl, a lamp, etc. **5** the eyeball. ● *v.tr.* & *intr.* make (usu. in *passive*) or become globular. ▫ **globelike** *adj.* **globoid** *adj.* & *n.* **globose** *adj.* [French *globe* or Latin *globus*]

globe artichoke *n.* the head of the artichoke plant of which parts are edible.

globe-fish *n.* (*pl.* usu. same) any tropical fish of the family Tetraodontidae, able to inflate itself into a spherical form. Also called *puffer fish.*

globeflower /ˈgləʊbflaʊə/ *n.* a plant of the genus *Trollius* (buttercup family), with globular usu. yellow flowers.

globe lightning *n.* = BALL LIGHTNING.

globe-trotter *n.* a person who travels widely. ▫ **globe-trotting** *n.* & *attrib.adj.*

globigerina /ˌgləʊbɪdʒəˈrʌɪnə/ *n.* (*pl.* **globigerinas** or **globigerinae** /-niː/) a planktonic marine foraminiferan of the genus *Globigerina*, having a calcareous shell which collects as a deposit (ooze) over much of the ocean floor. ▫ **globigerinal** *adj.* [modern Latin, from Latin *globus* 'globe' + *-ger* 'carrying' + -INA]

globular /ˈglɒbjʊlə/ *adj.* **1** globe-shaped, spherical. **2** composed of globules. ▫ **globularity** /-ˈlarɪti/ *n.* **globularly** *adv.*

globular cluster *n.* *Astron.* a large compact spherical star cluster usu. of old stars in the outer regions of a galaxy.

globule /ˈglɒbjuːl/ *n.* **1** a small globe or round particle; a drop. **2** a pill. ▫ **globulous** *adj.* [French *globule* or Latin *globulus* (as GLOBE)]

globulin /ˈglɒbjʊlɪn/ *n.* any of a group of single proteins characterized by solubility only in salt solutions and esp. forming a large fraction of blood serum protein.

glockenspiel /ˈglɒk(ə)nspiːl, -ʃpiːl/ *n.* a musical instrument consisting of a series of bells or metal bars or tubes suspended or mounted in a frame and struck by hammers. [German, = bell-play]

glom /glɒm/ *v.* (**glommed**, **glomming**) *US slang* **1** *tr.* steal; grab. **2** *intr.* (usu. foll. by *on to*) steal; grab. [variant of Scots *glaum*, of unknown origin]

glomerate /ˈglɒm(ə)rət/ *adj.* *Bot.* & *Anat.* compactly clustered. [Latin *glomeratus*, past part. of *glomerare*, from *glomus -eris* 'ball']

glomerule /ˈglɒməruːl/ *n.* a clustered flower head.

glomerulus /glɒˈmɛr(j)ʊləs/ *n.* (*pl.* **glomeruli** /-lʌɪ, -liː/) a cluster of nerve endings, spores, or small blood vessels, esp. of capillaries at the end of a kidney tubule. ▫ **glomerular** *adj.* [modern Latin, diminutive of Latin *glomus -eris* 'ball']

gloom /gluːm/ *n.* & *v.* ● *n.* **1** darkness; obscurity. **2** melancholy; despondency. **3** *poet.* a dark place. ● *v.* **1** *intr.* be gloomy or melancholy; frown. **2** *intr.* (of the sky etc.) be dull or threatening; lour. **3** *intr.* appear darkly or obscurely. **4** *tr.* cover with gloom; make dark or dismal. [Middle English *gloum(b)e*, of unknown origin]

gloomy /ˈgluːmi/ *adj.* (**gloomier**, **gloomiest**) **1** dark; unlighted. **2** depressed; sullen. **3** dismal; depressing. ▫ **gloomily** *adv.* **gloominess** *n.*

gloop /gluːp/ *n.* *colloq.* semi-fluid or sticky material. [imitative: cf. GLOP]

glop /glɒp/ *n.* *US slang* a liquid or sticky mess, esp. inedible food. [imitative]

Gloria /ˈglɔːrɪə/ *n.* **1** any of various doxologies beginning with *Gloria*, esp. the hymn beginning with *Gloria in excelsis Deo* (Glory be to God in the highest), as part of the Mass. **2** an aureole. [Latin, = glory]

glorify /ˈglɔːrɪfʌɪ/ *v.tr.* (**-ies, -ied**) **1** exalt to heavenly glory; make glorious. **2** transform into something more splendid. **3** extol; praise. **4** (as **glorified** *adj.*) seeming or pretending to be more splendid than in reality (*just a glorified office boy*). ▫ **glorification** /-fɪˈkeɪʃ(ə)n/ *n.*

glorifier *n.* [Middle English via Old French *glorifier*, ecclesiastical Latin *glorificare*, and Late Latin *glorificus* from Latin *gloria* 'glory']

gloriole /'glɔːrɪəʊl/ *n.* an aureole; a halo. [French from Latin *gloriola*, diminutive of *gloria* 'glory']

glorious /'glɔːrɪəs/ *adj.* **1** possessing glory; illustrious. **2** conferring glory; honourable. **3** *colloq.* splendid; magnificent; delightful (*a glorious day*; *glorious fun*). **4** *iron.* intense; unmitigated (*a glorious muddle*). **5** Brit. *colloq.* happily intoxicated. ▫ **gloriously** *adv.* **gloriousness** *n.* [Middle English via Anglo-French *glorious*, Old French *glorios*, *-eus* from Latin *gloriosus* (as GLORY)]

glory /'glɔːri/ *n.* & *v.* ● *n.* (*pl.* **-ies**) **1** high renown or fame; honour. **2** adoring praise and thanksgiving (*Glory to the Lord*). **3** resplendent majesty or magnificence; great beauty (*the glory of Versailles*; *the glory of the rose*). **4** a thing that brings renown or praise; a distinction. **5** the bliss and splendour of heaven. **6** *colloq.* a state of exaltation, prosperity, happiness, etc. (*is in his glory playing with his trains*). **7** an aureole, a halo. **8** an anthelion. ● *v.intr.* (**-ies**, **-ied**) (often foll. by *in*, or *to* + infin.) pride oneself; exult (*glory in their skill*). ▫ **glory be! 1** expressing enthusiastic piety. **2** *colloq.* an exclamation of surprise or delight. **go to glory** *slang* die; be destroyed. [Middle English via Anglo-French and Old French *glorie* from Latin *gloria*]

glory-box *n. Austral.* & *NZ* a box for women's clothes etc., stored in preparation for marriage.

glory-hole *n.* **1** *colloq.* an untidy room, drawer, or receptacle. **2** *N. Amer.* an open quarry.

glory-of-the-snow *n.* = CHIONODOXA.

Glos. *abbr.* Gloucestershire.

gloss[1] /glɒs/ *n.* & *v.* ● *n.* **1 a** a surface shine or lustre. **b** an instance of this; a smooth finish. **2 a** deceptively attractive appearance. **b** an instance of this. **3** (in full **gloss paint**) paint formulated to give a hard glossy finish (cf. MATT *n.* 2). ● *v.tr.* make glossy. ▫ **gloss over 1** seek to conceal beneath a false appearance. **2** conceal or evade by mentioning briefly or misleadingly. ▫ **glosser** *n.* [16th c.: origin unknown]

gloss[2] /glɒs/ *n.* & *v.* ● *n.* **1 a** an explanatory word or phrase inserted between the lines or in the margin of a text. **b** a comment, explanation, interpretation, or paraphrase. **2** a misrepresentation of another's words. **3 a** a glossary. **b** an interlinear translation or annotation. ● *v.* **1** *tr.* **a** add a gloss or glosses to (a text, word, etc.). **b** read a different sense into; explain away. **2** *intr.* (often foll. by *on*) make (esp. unfavourable) comments. **3** *intr.* write or introduce glosses. [alteration of GLOZE suggested by medieval Latin *glossa*]

glossal /'glɒs(ə)l/ *adj. Anat.* of the tongue; lingual. [Greek *glōssa* 'tongue']

glossary /'glɒs(ə)ri/ *n.* (*pl.* **-ies**) **1** (also **gloss**) an alphabetical list of terms or words found in or relating to a specific subject or text, esp. dialect, with explanations; a brief dictionary. **2** a collection of glosses. ▫ **glossarial** /glɒ'sɛːrɪəl/ *adj.* **glossarist** *n.* [Latin *glossarium* from *glossa* GLOSS[2]]

glossator /glɒ'seɪtə/ *n.* **1** a writer of glosses. **2** *hist.* a commentator on, or interpreter of, medieval law texts. [Middle English from medieval Latin, from *glossare*, from Latin *glossa* GLOSS[2]]

glosseme /'glɒsiːm/ *n.* any meaningful feature of a language that cannot be analysed into smaller meaningful units. [Greek *glōssēma* from *glōssa* 'tongue']

glossitis /glɒ'sʌɪtɪs/ *n.* inflammation of the tongue. [Greek *glōssa* 'tongue' + -ITIS]

glossographer /glɒ'sɒgrəfə/ *n.* a writer of glosses or commentaries. [GLOSS[2] + -GRAPHER]

glossolalia /glɒsə'leɪlɪə/ *n.* = *gift of tongues* (see TONGUE). [modern Latin from Greek *glōssa* 'tongue' + *-lalia* 'speaking']

glossopharyngeal /ˌglɒsəʊfə'rɪn(d)ʒɪəl, -far(ə)n'dʒiːəl/ *adj.* & *n.* ● *adj.* of or relating to the tongue and pharynx. ● *n.* (in full **glossopharyngeal nerve**) either of the ninth pair of cranial nerves, supplying the tongue and pharynx. [Greek *glōssa* 'tongue' + *pharyngeal*: see PHARYNX]

glossy /'glɒsi/ *adj.* & *n.* ● *adj.* (**glossier**, **glossiest**) **1** having a shine; smooth. **2** (of paper etc.) smooth and shiny. **3** (of a magazine etc.) printed on such paper; expensively produced and attractively presented, but sometimes lacking in content or depth. ● *n.* (*pl.* **-ies**) *colloq.* **1** a glossy magazine. **2** a photograph with a glossy surface. ▫ **glossily** *adv.* **glossiness** *n.*

glottal /'glɒt(ə)l/ *adj.* of or produced by the glottis.

glottal stop *n.* a sound produced by the sudden opening or shutting of the glottis.

glottis /'glɒtɪs/ *n.* the space at the upper end of the windpipe and between the vocal cords, affecting voice modulation through expansion or contraction. ▫ **glottic** *adj.* [modern Latin from Greek *glōttis*, from *glōtta*, variant of *glōssa* 'tongue']

glove /glʌv/ *n.* & *v.* ● *n.* **1** a covering for the hand, of wool, leather, cotton, etc., worn esp. for protection against cold or dirt, and usu. having separate fingers. **2** a padded protective glove, esp.: **a** a boxing glove. **b** a glove worn by a wicketkeeper or baseball catcher. ● *v.tr.* cover or provide with a glove or gloves. ▫ **fit like a glove** fit exactly. **throw down** (or **take up**) **the glove** issue (or accept) a challenge. **with the gloves off** mercilessly; unfairly; with no compunction. ▫ **gloveless** *adj.* **glover** *n.* [Old English *glōf*, corresponding to Old Norse *glófi*, perhaps from Germanic]

glovebox /'glʌvbɒks/ *n.* **1** a box for gloves. **2** a closed chamber with sealed-in gloves for handling radioactive material etc. **3** = GLOVE COMPARTMENT.

glove compartment *n.* a recess for small articles in the dashboard of a motor vehicle.

glove puppet *n.* esp. *Brit.* a small cloth puppet fitted on the hand and worked by the fingers.

glow /gləʊ/ *v.* & *n.* ● *v.intr.* **1 a** throw out light and heat without flame; be incandescent. **b** shine like something heated in this way. **2** (of the cheeks) redden, esp. from cold or exercise. **3** (often foll. by *with*) **a** (of the body) be heated, esp. from exertion; sweat. **b** express or experience strong emotion (*glowed with pride*; *glowing with indignation*). **4** show a warm colour (*the painting glows with warmth*). **5** (as **glowing** *adj.*) expressing pride or satisfaction (*a glowing report*). ● *n.* **1** a glowing state. **2** a bright warm colour, esp. the red of cheeks. **3** ardour; passion. **4** a feeling induced by good health, exercise, etc.; well-being. ▫ **in a glow** *colloq.* hot or flushed; sweating. ▫ **glowingly** *adv.* [Old English *glōwan*, from Germanic]

glow discharge *n.* a luminous sparkless electrical discharge from a pointed conductor in a gas at low pressure.

glower /'glaʊə/ *v.* & *n.* ● *v.intr.* (often foll. by *at*) stare or scowl, esp. angrily. ● *n.* a glowering look. ▫ **gloweringly** *adv.* [origin uncertain: perhaps Scots variant of Middle English *glore* from Low German or Scandinavian, or from obsolete (Middle English) *glow* 'stare' + -ER[4]]

glow-worm *n.* a soft-bodied beetle of the genus *Lampyris* whose wingless female emits light from the abdomen.

gloxinia /glɒk'sɪnɪə/ *n.* any tropical plant of the genus *Gloxinia*, native to S. America, with large bell flowers of various colours. [modern Latin, named after B. P. *Gloxin*, 18th-c. German botanist]

gloze /gləʊz/ *v.* **1** *tr.* (also **gloze over**) explain away; extenuate; palliate. **2** *intr. archaic* **a** (usu. foll. by *on*, *upon*) comment. **b** talk speciously; fawn. [Middle English via Old French *gloser*, from *glose*, and medieval Latin *glosa*, *gloza* from Latin *glossa* 'tongue, GLOSS[2]']

glucagon /'gluːkəg(ə)n, -gɒn/ *n.* a polypeptide hormone formed in the pancreas, which aids the breakdown of glycogen to glucose. [Greek *glukus* 'sweet' + *agōn* 'leading']

glucose /'glu:kəʊs, -z/ *n.* **1** a simple sugar containing six carbon atoms, found mainly in its dextrorotatory form (see DEXTROSE), which is an important energy source in living organisms and obtainable from some carbohydrates by hydrolysis. Chem. formula: $C_6H_{12}O_6$. **2** a syrup containing glucose sugars from the incomplete hydrolysis of starch. [French, from Greek *gleukos* 'sweet wine', related to *glukus* 'sweet']

glucoside /'glu:kəsʌɪd/ *n.* a compound giving glucose and other products upon hydrolysis. □ **glucosidic** /-'sɪdɪk/ *adj.*

glue /glu:/ *n.* & *v.* ● *n.* an adhesive substance used for sticking objects or materials together. ● *v.tr.* (**glues**, **glued**, **gluing** or **glueing**) **1** fasten or join with glue. **2** keep or put very close (*an eye glued to the keyhole*). □ **glue-like** *adj.* **gluey** /'glu:i/ *adj.* (**gluier**, **gluiest**). **glueyness** *n.* [Middle English via Old French *glu* (*n.*), *gluer* (*v.*), and Late Latin *glus glutis* from Latin *gluten*]

glue ear *n.* blocking of the Eustachian tube by mucus, esp. in children.

glue-pot *n.* **1** a pot with an outer vessel holding water to heat glue. **2** *colloq.* an area of sticky mud etc.

glue-sniffing *n.* the inhalation of intoxicating fumes from the solvents in adhesives etc. □ **glue-sniffer** *n.*

glühwein /'glu:vʌɪn/ *n.* mulled wine. [German, from *glühen* 'mull' + *Wein* 'wine']

glum /glʌm/ *adj.* (**glummer**, **glummest**) looking or feeling dejected. sullen; morose. □ **glumly** *adv.* **glumness** *n.* [related to dialect verb *glum* 'frown', variant of *gloume* GLOOM *v.*]

glume /glu:m/ *n.* **1** a membranous bract surrounding the spikelet of grasses or the florets of sedges. **2** the husk of grain. □ **glumaceous** /-'meɪʃəs/ *adj.* **glumose** *adj.* [Latin *gluma* 'husk']

gluon /'glu:ɒn/ *n.* *Physics* any of a class of subatomic particles that are thought to bind quarks together. [GLUE + -ON]

glut /glʌt/ *v.* & *n.* ● *v.tr.* (**glutted**, **glutting**) **1** feed (a person, one's stomach, etc.) or indulge (an appetite, a desire, etc.) to the full; satiate; cloy. **2** fill to excess; choke up. **3** *Econ.* overstock (a market) with goods. ● *n.* **1** *Econ.* supply exceeding demand; a surfeit (*a glut in the market*). **2** full indulgence; one's fill. [Middle English, probably via Old French *gloutir* 'swallow' from Latin *gluttire*: cf. GLUTTON]

glutamate /'glu:təmeɪt/ *n.* any salt or ester of glutamic acid, esp. a sodium salt used to enhance the flavour of food.

glutamic acid /glu:'tamɪk/ *n.* *Biochem.* a naturally occurring amino acid, a constituent of many proteins. [GLUTEN + AMINE + -IC]

glutamine /'glu:təmi:n/ *n.* *Biochem.* a hydrophilic amino acid present in many proteins. [GLUTAMIC ACID + AMINE]

gluten /'glu:t(ə)n/ *n.* **1** a mixture of two proteins present in flour, esp. wheat flour. **2** *archaic* a sticky substance. [French from Latin *gluten glutinis* 'glue']

gluteus /'glu:tɪəs, glu:'ti:əs/ *n.* (*pl.* **glutei** /-tɪʌɪ, -'ti:ʌɪ/) any of the three muscles in each buttock. □ **gluteal** *adj.* [modern Latin from Greek *gloutos* 'buttock']

glutinous /'glu:tɪnəs/ *adj.* sticky; like glue. □ **glutinously** *adv.* **glutinousness** *n.* [French *glutineux* or Latin *glutinosus* (as GLUTEN)]

glutton /'glʌt(ə)n/ *n.* **1** an excessively greedy eater. **2** (often foll. by *for*) *colloq.* a person insatiably eager (*a glutton for work*). **3** a voracious animal, *Gulo gulo*, of the weasel family. Also called WOLVERINE. □ **a glutton for punishment** a person eager to take on hard or unpleasant tasks. □ **gluttonize** *v.intr.* (also **-ise**). **gluttonous** *adj.* **gluttonously** *adv.* [Middle English via Old French *gluton*, *gloton* from Latin *glutto -onis*, from *gluttire* 'swallow', *gluttus* 'greedy']

gluttony /'glʌt(ə)ni/ *n.* habitual greed or excess in eating. [Old French *glutonie* (as GLUTTON)]

glyceride /'glɪs(ə)rʌɪd/ *n.* any fatty acid ester of glycerol.

glycerine /'glɪs(ə)ri:n, -ɪn/ *n.* (*US* **glycerin** /-ɪn/) = GLYCEROL. [French *glycerin* from Greek *glukeros* 'sweet']

glycerol /'glɪs(ə)rɒl/ *n.* a colourless sweet viscous liquid formed as a by-product in the manufacture of soap, used as an emollient and laxative, and in explosives, antifreeze, etc. (also called *glycerine*). Chem. formula: $C_3H_8O_3$. [GLYCERINE + -OL[1]]

glycine /'glʌɪsi:n/ *n.* *Biochem.* the simplest naturally occurring amino acid, a general constituent of proteins. [German *Glycin* from Greek *glukus* 'sweet']

glyco- /'glʌɪkəʊ/ *comb. form* sugar. [Greek *glukus* 'sweet']

glycogen /'glʌɪkədʒ(ə)n/ *n.* *Biochem.* a polysaccharide serving as a store of carbohydrates, esp. in animal tissues, and yielding glucose on hydrolysis. □ **glycogenic** /-'dʒɛnɪk/ *adj.*

glycogenesis /glʌɪkəʊ'dʒɛnɪsɪs/ *n.* *Biochem.* the formation of glycogen from sugar.

glycol /'glʌɪkɒl/ *n.* *Chem.* a diol, esp. ethylene glycol. □ **glycolic** /-'kɒlɪk/ *adj.* **glycollic** /-'kɒlɪk/ *adj.* [GLYCERINE + -OL[1], originally as being intermediate between glycerine and alcohol]

glycolysis /glʌɪ'kɒlɪsɪs/ *n.* *Biochem.* the breakdown of glucose by enzymes in most living organisms to release energy and pyruvic acid.

glycoprotein /glʌɪkəʊ'prəʊti:n/ *n.* any of a class of compounds consisting of a protein combined with a carbohydrate.

glycoside /'glʌɪkəsʌɪd/ *n.* any compound giving sugar and other products on hydrolysis. □ **glycosidic** /-'sɪdɪk/ *adj.* [GLYCO-, after GLUCOSIDE]

glycosuria /glʌɪkə'sjʊərɪə/ *n.* a condition characterized by an excess of sugar in the urine, associated with diabetes, kidney disease, etc. □ **glycosuric** *adj.* [French *glycose* 'glucose' + -URIA]

glyph /glɪf/ *n.* **1** a sculptured character or symbol. **2** a vertical groove, esp. that on a Greek frieze. □ **glyphic** *adj.* [French *glyphe* from Greek *gluphē* 'carving', from *gluphō* 'carve']

glyptal /'glɪpt(ə)l/ *n.* an alkyd resin, esp. one formed from glycerine and phthalic acid or anhydride. [perhaps from *gly*cerol + *phthal*ic]

glyptic /'glɪptɪk/ *adj.* of or concerning carving, esp. on precious stones. [French *glyptique* or Greek *gluptikos*, via *gluptēs* 'carver' from *gluphō* 'carve']

glyptodont /'glyptədɒnt/ *n.* any extinct armadillo-like edentate animal of the genus *Glyptodon* native to S. America, having fluted teeth and a body covered in a hard thick bony shell. [modern Latin, from Greek *gluptos* 'carved' + *odous odontos* 'tooth']

glyptography /glɪp'tɒgrəfi/ *n.* the art or scientific study of gem-engraving. [Greek *gluptos* 'carved' + -GRAPHY]

GM *abbr.* **1** (in the UK) George Medal. **2** (in the US) General Motors. **3** general manager. **4** grant-maintained.

gm *abbr.* gram(s).

G-man *n.* (*pl.* **G-men**) **1** *US colloq.* an FBI agent. **2** *Ir.* a political detective. [*G*overnment + MAN]

GMB *abbr.* (in the UK) General and Municipal Boilermakers (Union).

GMPU *abbr.* (in the UK) Graphical, Paper, and Media Union (formed by the merger of the NGA and SOGAT in 1991).

GMS *abbr.* (with reference to schools) grant maintained status.

GMT *abbr.* Greenwich Mean Time.

GMWU *abbr.* (in the UK) General and Municipal Workers' Union.

gnamma /'namə/ *n.* (also **namma**) *Austral.* a natural hole in a rock, containing water; a waterhole. [Nyungar *ngamar*]

gnarled /nɑ:ld/ *adj.* (also **gnarly** /'nɑ:li/) (of a tree, hands, etc.) knobbly, twisted, rugged. □ **gnarl** *n.* [variant of *knarled*, related to KNURL]

gnash /naʃ/ *v. & n.* ● *v.* **1** *tr.* grind (the teeth). **2** *intr.* (of the teeth) strike together; grind. ● *n.* an act of grinding the teeth. [variant of obsolete *gnacche* or *gnast*, related to Old Norse *gnastan* 'a gnashing' (imitative)]

gnashers /ˈnaʃəz/ *n.pl. slang* teeth, esp. false teeth.

gnat /nat/ *n.* **1** any small two-winged biting fly of the genus *Culex*, esp. *C. pipiens*. **2** an insignificant annoyance. **3** a tiny thing. [Old English *gnætt*]

gnathic /ˈnaθɪk, ˈneɪ-/ *adj.* of or relating to the jaws. [Greek *gnathos* 'jaw']

gnaw /nɔː/ *v.* (*past part.* **gnawed** or **gnawn**) **1 a** *tr.* (usu. foll. by *away*, *off*, *in two*, etc.) bite persistently; wear away by biting. **b** *intr.* (often foll. by *at*, *into*) bite, nibble. **2 a** *intr.* (often foll. by *at*, *into*) (of a destructive agent, pain, fear, etc.) corrode; waste away; consume; torture. **b** *tr.* corrode, consume, torture, etc. with pain, fear, etc. (*was gnawed by doubt*). **3** *tr.* (as **gnawing** *adj.*) persistent; worrying. □ **gnawingly** *adv.* [Old English *gnagen*, ultimately imitative]

gneiss /nʌɪs/ *n.* a usu. coarse-grained metamorphic rock foliated by mineral layers, principally of feldspar, quartz, and ferromagnesian minerals. □ **gneissic** *adj.* **gneissoid** *adj.* **gneissose** *adj.* [German]

gnocchi /ˈn(j)ɒki, ˈgnɒki/ *n.pl.* an Italian dish of small dumplings usu. made from potato, semolina flour, etc., often flavoured with spinach and cheese. [Italian, pl. of *gnocco*, from *nocchio* 'knot in wood']

gnome[1] /nəʊm/ *n.* **1 a** a dwarfish legendary creature supposed to guard the earth's treasures underground; a goblin. **b** a figure of a gnome, esp. as a garden ornament. **2** (esp. in *pl.*) *colloq.* a person with sinister influence, esp. financial (*gnomes of Zurich*). □ **gnomish** *adj.* [French, from modern Latin *gnomus* (word invented by Paracelsus)]

gnome[2] /nəʊm, ˈnəʊmi/ *n.* a maxim; an aphorism. [Greek *gnōmē* 'opinion' from *gignōskō* 'know']

gnomic /ˈnəʊmɪk/ *adj.* **1** of, consisting of, or using gnomes or aphorisms; sententious (see GNOME[2]). **2** *Gram.* (of a tense) used without the implication of time to express a general truth, e.g. *men were deceivers ever.* □ **gnomically** *adv.* [Greek *gnōmikos* (as GNOME[2])]

gnomon /ˈnəʊmɒn/ *n.* **1** the rod or pin etc. on a sundial that shows the time by the position of its shadow. **2** *Geom.* the part of a parallelogram left when a similar parallelogram has been taken from its corner. **3** *Astron.* a column etc. used in observing the sun's meridian altitude. □ **gnomonic** /-ˈmɒnɪk/ *adj.* [French or Latin *gnomon* from Greek *gnōmōn* 'indicator' etc., from *gignōskō* 'know']

gnosis /ˈnəʊsɪs/ *n.* knowledge of spiritual mysteries. [Greek *gnōsis* 'knowledge' (as GNOMON)]

gnostic /ˈnɒstɪk/ *adj. & n.* ● *adj.* **1** relating to knowledge, esp. esoteric mystical knowledge. **2** (**Gnostic**) concerning the Gnostics; occult; mystic. ● *n.* (**Gnostic**) (usu. in *pl.*) a Christian heretic of the 1st–3rd c. claiming gnosis. □ **Gnosticism** /-sɪz(ə)m/ *n.* **gnosticize** /-sʌɪz/ *v.tr. & intr.* (also **-ise**). [ecclesiastical Latin *gnosticus* from Greek *gnōstikos* (as GNOSIS)]

GNP *abbr.* gross national product.

Gnr. *abbr. Brit.* Gunner.

gns. *abbr. Brit. hist.* guineas.

gnu /nuː, njuː; gn-/ *n.* any antelope of the genus *Connochaetes*, native to S. Africa, with a large erect head and brown stripes on the neck and shoulders. Also called *wildebeest*. [Bushman *nqu*, probably via Dutch *gnoe*]

GNVQ *abbr.* General National Vocational Qualification.

go[1] /gəʊ/ *v., n., & adj.* ● *v.* (*3rd sing. present* **goes** /gəʊz/; *past* **went** /wɛnt/; *past part.* **gone** /gɒn/) **1** *intr.* **a** start moving or be moving from one place or point in time to another; travel, proceed. **b** (foll. by *to* + infin., or *and* + verb) proceed in order to (*went to find him*; *go and buy some bread*). **c** (foll. by *and* + verb) *colloq.* expressing annoyance (*you went and told him*; *they've gone and broken it*; *she went and won*). **2** *intr.* (foll. by verbal noun) make a special trip for; participate in; proceed to do (*went skiing*; *then went shopping*; *often goes running*). **3** *intr.* lie or extend in a certain direction (*the road goes to London*). **4** *intr.* leave; depart (*they had to go*). **5** *intr.* move, act, work, etc. (*the clock doesn't go*; *his brain is going all the time*). **6** *intr.* **a** make a specified movement (*go like this with your foot*). **b** make a sound (of a specified kind) (*the gun went bang*; *the cow went 'moo'*). **c** (of a bell etc.) make a sound in functioning (*an ambulance with its sirens going*; *the doorbell went*). **d** *colloq.* say (*so he goes to me 'Why didn't you like it?'*). **7** *intr.* be in a specified state (*go hungry*; *went in fear of his life*). **8** *intr.* **a** pass into a specified condition (*gone bad*; *went mad*; *went to sleep*). **b** *colloq.* die. **c** proceed or escape in a specified condition (*the poet went unrecognized*; *the crime went unnoticed*). **9** *intr.* (of time or distance) pass, elapse; be traversed (*ten days to go before Easter*; *the last mile went quickly*). **10** *intr.* **a** (of a document, verse, song, etc.) have a specified content or wording; run (*the tune goes like this*). **b** be current or accepted (*so the story goes*). **c** be suitable; fit; match (*the shoes don't go with the hat*). **d** be regularly kept or put (*the forks go here*). **e** fit; be accommodated (*this won't go into the cupboard*). **11** *intr.* **a** turn out, proceed; take a course or view (*things went well*; *Liverpool went Labour*). **b** be successful (*make the party go*; *went like a bomb*). **c** progress (*we've still a long way to go*). **12** *intr.* **a** be sold (*went for £1*; *went cheap*). **b** (of money) be spent (*£200 went on a new jacket*). **13** *intr.* **a** be relinquished, dismissed, or abolished (*the car will have to go*). **b** fail, decline; give way, collapse (*his sight is going*; *the bulb has gone*). **14** *intr.* be acceptable or permitted; be accepted without question (*anything goes*; *what I say goes*). **15** *intr.* (often foll. by *by*, *with*, *on*, *upon*) be guided by; judge or act on or in harmony with (*have nothing to go on*; *a good rule to go by*). **16** *intr.* attend or visit or travel to regularly (*goes to church*; *goes to school*; *this train goes to Bristol*). **17** *intr.* (foll. by pres. part.) *colloq.* proceed (often foolishly) to do (*went running to the police*; *don't go making him angry*). **18** *intr.* act or proceed to a certain point (*will go so far and no further*; *went as high as £100*). **19** *intr.* (of a number) be capable of being contained in another (*6 into 12 goes twice*; *6 into 5 won't go*). **20** *tr. Cards* bid; declare (*go nap*; *has gone two spades*). **21** *intr.* (usu. foll. by *to*) be allotted or awarded; pass (*first prize went to the girl*; *the job went to his rival*). **22** *intr.* (foll. by *to*, *towards*) amount to; contribute to (*12 inches go to make a foot*; *this will go towards your holiday*). **23** *intr.* (in *imper.*) begin motion (a starter's order in a race) (*ready, steady, go!*). **24** *intr.* (usu. foll. by *to*) refer or appeal (*go to him for help*). **25** *intr.* (often foll. by *on*) take up a specified profession (*went on the stage*; *gone soldiering*; *went to sea*). **26** *intr.* (usu. foll. by *by*, *under*) be known or called (*goes by the name of Droopy*). **27** *tr. colloq.* proceed to (*go jump in the lake*). **28** *intr.* (foll. by *for*) apply to; have relevance for (*that goes for me too*). ● *n.* (*pl.* **goes**) **1** the act or an instance of going. **2** mettle; spirit; dash; animation (*she has a lot of go in her*). **3** vigorous activity (*it's all go*). **4** *colloq.* a success (*made a go of it*). **5** *colloq.* a turn; an attempt (*I'll have a go*; *it's my go*; *all in one go*). **6** esp. *Brit. colloq.* a state of affairs (*a rum go*). **7** esp. *Brit. colloq.* an attack of illness (*a bad go of flu*). **8** esp. *Brit. colloq.* a quantity of liquor, food, etc. served at one time. ● *adj. colloq.* **1** functioning properly (*all systems are go*). **2** fashionable; progressive. □ **all the go** *Brit. colloq.* in fashion. **as** (or **so**) **far as it goes** an expression of caution against taking a statement too positively (*the work is good as far as it goes*). **as (a person or thing) goes** as the average is (*a good actor as actors go*). **from the word go** *colloq.* from the very beginning. **give it a go** *colloq.* make an effort to succeed. **go about 1** busy oneself with; set to work at. **2** be socially active. **3** (foll. by pres. part.) make a habit of doing (*goes about telling lies*). **4** *Naut.* change to an opposite tack. **go against 1** be contrary to (*goes against my principles*). **2** have an unfavourable result for (*decision went against them*). **go ahead** proceed without hesitation. **go along with** agree to; take the same view as. **go around 1** (foll. by *with*) be regularly in the company of. **2** = *go about* 3. **go-as-you-please** untrammelled; free. **go at** take in hand energetically; attack. **go away** depart, esp. from home for a holiday etc. **go back 1** return (to). **2** extend backwards in space or time (*goes back to the 18th century*). **3** (of the hour, a clock, etc.) be set to an earlier standard time (*the clocks go back in the autumn*). **go back on** fail to keep (one's word, promise, etc.). **go bail** see BAIL[1]. **go begging** see BEG. **go by 1** pass. **2** be dependent on; be guided by. **go by default** see DEFAULT. **go down 1 a** (of an amount) become less (*the coffee has gone down a lot*). **b** subside (*the flood went down*). **c** decrease in price; lose value. **2 a** (of a ship) sink. **b** (of the sun) set. **3** (usu. foll. by *to*) be continued to a specified point. **4** deteriorate; fail; (of a computer network etc.) cease to function. **5** be recorded in writing. **6** be swallowed. **7** (often foll. by *with*) find acceptance. **8** *Brit. colloq.* leave university. **9** *Brit. colloq.* be sent to prison (*went down for ten years*). **10** (often foll. by *before*) fall (before a conqueror). **go down with** *Brit.* begin to suffer from (a disease). **go Dutch** see DUTCH. **go far** be very successful. **go for 1** go to fetch. **2** be accounted as or achieve (*went for nothing*). **3** prefer; choose (*that's the one I go for*). **4** *colloq.* strive to attain (*go for it!*). **5** *colloq.* attack (*the dog went for him*). **go forward 1** proceed, progress (*go forward into the next round*). **2** (of the hour, a clock, etc.) be set to a later time, esp. summer time. **go great guns** see GUN. **go halves** (or **shares**) (often foll. by *with*) share equally. **go in 1** enter a room, house, etc. **2** (usu. foll. by *for*) enter as a competitor. **3** *Cricket* take or begin an innings. **4** (of the sun etc.) become obscured by cloud. **go in for** take as one's object, style, pursuit, principle, etc. **going!, gone!** an auctioneer's announcement that bidding is closing or closed. **go into 1** enter (a place); go to stay in (hospital etc.). **2** pass into (a state or condition) (*he has gone into hiding*; *the company went into liquidation*). **3** investigate. **4** (of resources etc.) be invested in (*a lot of effort went into this*). **5** start a career or interest in. **6** dress oneself in (mourning etc.). **go it** *Brit. colloq.* **1** act vigorously, furiously, etc. **2** indulge in dissipation. **go it alone** see ALONE. **go it strong** *Brit. colloq.* go to great lengths; exaggerate. **go a long way 1** (often foll. by *towards*) have a great effect; contribute or progress significantly. **2** (of food, money, etc.) last a long time, buy much. **3** = *go far*. **go off 1** explode. **2** leave the stage. **3** gradually cease to be felt. **4** (esp. of foodstuffs) deteriorate; decompose. **5** go to sleep; become unconscious. **6** begin. **7** (of an alarm) begin to sound. **8** die. **9** be got rid of by sale etc. **10** *Brit. colloq.* begin to dislike (*I've gone off him*). **go off at** *Austral. & NZ slang* reprimand, scold. **go off well** (or **badly** etc.) (of an enterprise etc.) be received or accomplished well (or badly etc.). **go on 1** (often foll. by pres. part.) continue, persevere (*decided to go on with it*; *went on trying*; *unable to go on*). **2** *colloq.* **a** talk at great length. **b** (foll. by *at*) admonish (*went on and on at him*). **3** (foll. by *to* + infin.) proceed (*went on to become a star*). **4** happen. **5** conduct oneself (*shameful, the way they went on*). **6** *Theatr.* appear on stage. **7** *Cricket* begin bowling. **8** (of a garment) be large enough for its wearer. **9** take one's turn to do something. **10** (also **go upon**) *Brit. colloq.* use as evidence (*police don't have anything to go on*). **11** (esp. in *neg.*) *colloq.* **a** concern oneself about. **b** care for (*don't go much on red hair*). **12** become chargeable to (the parish etc.). **go on!** *colloq.* an expression of encouragement or disbelief. **go out 1** leave a room, house, etc. **2** be broadcast. **3** be extinguished. **4** (often foll. by *with*) have a sexual relationship. **5** (of a government) leave office. **6** cease to be fashionable. **7** (usu. foll. by *to*) depart, esp. to a colony etc. **8** *colloq.* lose consciousness. **9** (of workers) strike. **10** (usu. foll. by *to*) (of the heart etc.) expand with sympathy etc. towards (*my heart goes out to them*). **11** *Golf* play the first nine holes in a round. **12** *Cards* be the first to dispose of one's hand. **13** (of a tide) ebb; recede to low tide. **go over 1** inspect the details of; rehearse; retouch. **2** (often foll. by *to*) change one's allegiance or religion. **3** (of a play etc.) be received, esp. favourably (*went over well in Dundee*). **go round** (or *US* **around**) **1** spin, revolve. **2** be long enough to encompass. **3** (of food etc.) suffice for everybody. **4** (usu. foll. by *to*) visit informally. **5** = *go around*. **go slow** *Brit.* deliberately work slowly, as a form of industrial action (cf. GO-SLOW). **go through 1** be dealt with or completed. **2** discuss in detail; scrutinize in sequence. **3** perform (a ceremony, a recitation, etc.). **4** undergo. **5** *colloq.* use up; spend (money etc.). **6** make holes in. **7** (of a book) be successively published (in so many editions). **8** *Austral. slang* abscond. **go through with** not leave unfinished; complete. **go to!** *archaic* an exclamation of disbelief, impatience, admonition, etc. **go to the bar** become a barrister. **go to blazes** (or **hell** or **Jericho** etc.) *slang* an exclamation of dismissal, contempt, etc. **go to the country** see COUNTRY. **go together 1** match; fit. **2** have a sexual relationship. **go to it!** *colloq.* begin work! **go to show** (or **prove**) serve as evidence (or proof) (also *absol.*). **go under** sink; fail; succumb. **go up 1** increase in price. **2** *Brit. colloq.* enter university. **3** be consumed (in flames etc.); explode. **go well** (or **ill** etc.) (often foll. by *with*) turn out well, (or ill etc.). **go with 1** be harmonious with; match. **2** agree to; take the same view as. **3 a** be a pair with. **b** have a sexual relationship. **4** follow the drift of. **go without** manage without; forgo (also *absol.*: *we shall just have to go without*). **go with the tide** (or **times**) do as others do; follow the drift. **have a go at 1** esp. *Brit.* attack, criticize. **2** attempt, try. **on the go** *colloq.* **1** in constant motion. **2** constantly working. **to go 1** still to be dealt with. **2** *N. Amer.* (of refreshments etc.) to be eaten or drunk off the premises. **who goes there?** a sentry's challenge. [Old English *gān*, from Germanic: *went* originally the past tense of WEND]

go[2] /gəʊ/ *n.* a Japanese board game of territorial possession and capture. [Japanese]

goa /ˈgəʊə/ *n.* a Tibetan gazelle, *Procapra picticaudata*, with backward curving horns. [Tibetan *dgoba*]

goad /gəʊd/ *n.* & *v.* ● *n.* **1** a spiked stick used for urging cattle forward. **2** anything that torments, incites, or stimulates. ● *v.tr.* **1** urge on with a goad. **2** (usu. foll. by *on, into*) irritate; stimulate (*goaded him into retaliating*; *goaded me on to win*). [Old English *gād*, related to Lombard *gaida* 'arrowhead', from Germanic]

go-ahead *n.* & *adj.* ● *n.* permission to proceed. ● *adj.* enterprising.

goal /gəʊl/ *n.* **1** the object of a person's ambition or effort; a destination; an aim (*fame is his goal*; *London was our goal*). **2 a** *Football* a pair of posts linked by a crossbar, forming a space into which the ball has to be sent to score. **b** a cage or basket used similarly in other games. **c** a successful attempt to score (*it's a goal!*). **d** a point won (*scored 3 goals*). **3** a point marking the end of a race. □ **in goal** in the position of goalkeeper. □ **goalless** *adj.* [Middle English, in the sense 'limit, boundary': origin unknown]

goal average *n. Football* the ratio of the numbers of goals scored for and against a team in a series of matches.

goalball /ˈgəʊlbɔːl/ *n.* a team ball game for blind and visually handicapped players.

goal difference *n. Football* the difference of goals scored for and against a team.

goalie /ˈgəʊli/ *n. colloq.* = GOALKEEPER.

goalkeeper /ˈgəʊlkiːpə/ *n.* a player stationed to protect the goal in various sports. □ **goalkeeping** *n.*

goal kick *n.* **1** *Football* a kick by the defending side after attackers send the ball over the goal line without scoring. **2** *Rugby* an attempt to kick a goal. □ **goal-kicker** *n. Rugby.* **goal-kicking** *n. Rugby.*

goal line *n.* a line between the posts of a goal, extended to form the end boundary of a field of play or the boundary beyond which a try or touchdown may be scored (cf. TOUCHLINE).

goalmouth /ˈgəʊlmaʊθ/ *n.* the space between or near the posts of a goal in football, hockey, etc.

goalpost /ˈgəʊlpəʊst/ *n.* either of the two upright posts of a goal. □ **move the goalposts** alter the basis or scope of a procedure during its course, so as to fit adverse circumstances encountered.

goalscorer /ˈgəʊlskɔːrə/ *n.* a player who scores a goal. □ **goalscoring** *n. & adj.*

goaltender /ˈgəʊltɛndə/ *n.* (also **goalminder**) *N. Amer.* a goalkeeper at ice hockey. □ **goaltending** *n.*

goanna /gəʊˈanə/ *n.* *Austral.* a monitor lizard. [corruption of IGUANA]

goat /gəʊt/ *n.* **1 a** a hardy lively frisky short-haired domesticated mammal, *Capra aegagrus*, having horns and (in the male) a beard, and kept for its milk and meat. **b** either of two similar mammals, the mountain goat and the Spanish goat. **2** any other mammal of the genus *Capra*, including the ibex. **3** a lecherous man. **4** *Brit. colloq.* a foolish person. **5** (**the Goat**) the zodiacal sign Capricorn or the constellation Capricornus. **6** *US* a scapegoat. □ **get a person's goat** *colloq.* irritate a person. □ **goatish** *adj.* **goaty** *adj.* [Old English *gāt* 'she-goat']

goat-antelope *n.* a ruminant mammal of the subfamily Caprinae, esp. of the tribe Rupicaprini, which includes the chamois, goral, and Rocky Mountain goat.

goatee /gəʊˈtiː/ *n.* (in full **goatee beard**) a small pointed beard like a goat's.

goatherd /ˈgəʊthəːd/ *n.* a person who tends goats.

goat moth *n.* any of various large moths of the family Cossidae, esp. *Cossus cossus*, whose wood-boring caterpillar smells like a goat.

goat's-beard *n.* **1** a yellow-flowered meadow plant, *Tragopogon pratensis* (daisy family). **2** a herbaceous plant of the rose family, *Aruncus dioicus*, with long plumes of white flowers.

goatskin /ˈgəʊtskɪn/ *n.* **1** the skin of a goat. **2** a garment or bottle made out of goatskin.

goatsucker /ˈgəʊtsʌkə/ *n.* = NIGHTJAR.

gob[1] /gɒb/ *n.* esp. *Brit. slang* the mouth. [perhaps from Gaelic & Irish, = beak, mouth]

gob[2] /gɒb/ *n. & v. slang* ● *n.* **1** *Brit.* a clot of slimy matter. **2** *N. Amer.* a small lump. **3** (in *pl.*; foll. by *of*) *N. Amer.* lots of. ● *v.intr.* (**gobbed**, **gobbing**) *Brit.* spit. [Middle English from Old French *go(u)be* 'mouthful']

gob[3] /gɒb/ *n. slang* a US sailor. [20th c.: origin unknown]

gobbet /ˈgɒbɪt/ *n.* **1** a piece or lump of flesh, food, slime, etc. **2** an extract from a text, esp. one set for translation or comment in an examination. [Middle English from Old French *gobet* (as GOB[2])]

gobble[1] /ˈgɒb(ə)l/ *v.tr. & intr.* eat hurriedly and noisily. □ **gobbler** *n.* [probably dialect, from GOB[2]]

gobble[2] /ˈgɒb(ə)l/ *v.intr.* **1** (of a turkeycock) make a characteristic swallowing sound in the throat. **2** make such a sound when speaking, esp. when excited, angry, etc. [imitative: perhaps based on GOBBLE[1]]

gobbledegook /ˈgob(ə)ldɪguːk, -ʊk/ *n.* (also **gobbledygook**) *colloq.* pompous or unintelligible jargon. [probably imitative of a turkeycock]

gobbler /ˈgɒblə/ *n. colloq.* a turkeycock.

Gobelin /ˈgəʊb(ə)lan, ˈgɒb-, -lɪn/ *n.* (in full **Gobelin tapestry**) **1** a tapestry made at the Gobelins factory. **2** a tapestry imitating this. [name of a State factory in Paris, called *Gobelins* after its original owners]

gobemouche /ˈgɒbmuːʃ/ *n.* (*pl.* **gobemouches** *pronunc.* same) a gullible listener. [French *gobe-mouches*, = flycatcher, from *gober* 'swallow' + *mouches* 'flies']

go-between *n.* an intermediary; a negotiator.

goblet /ˈgɒblɪt/ *n.* **1** a drinking vessel with a foot and a stem, usu. of glass. **2 a** *archaic* a metal or glass bowl-shaped drinking cup without handles, sometimes with a foot and a cover. **b** *poet.* any drinking cup. **3** a goblet-shaped receptacle forming part of a liquidizer. [Middle English from Old French *gobelet*, diminutive of *gobel* 'cup', of unknown origin]

goblin /ˈgɒblɪn/ *n.* a mischievous ugly dwarflike creature of folklore. [Middle English, probably from Anglo-French *gobelin*, medieval Latin *gobelinus*, probably diminutive of the name *Gobel*, related to German *Kobold*: see COBALT]

gobsmacked /ˈgɒbsmakt/ *adj. Brit. slang* astounded; utterly astonished. □ **gobsmacking** *adj.* [GOB[1] + SMACK[1]: with reference to clapping a hand to one's mouth in astonishment]

gobstopper /ˈgɒbstɒpə/ *n.* a very large hard sweet.

goby /ˈgəʊbi/ *n.* (*pl.* **-ies**) any small marine fish of the family Gobiidae, having ventral fins joined to form a sucker or disc. [Latin *gobius*, *cobius* from Greek *kōbios* GUDGEON[1]]

go-by *n. colloq.* a snub; a slight (*gave it the go-by*).

GOC *abbr. Brit.* General Officer Commanding.

go-cart *n.* **1** a handcart. **2** a pushchair. **3** var. of GO-KART. **4** *archaic* a baby walker.

god /gɒd/ *n.* **1 a** (in many religions) a superhuman being or spirit worshipped as having power over nature, human fortunes, etc.; a deity. **b** an image, idol, animal, or other object worshipped as divine or symbolizing a god. **2** (**God**) (in Christian and other monotheistic religions) the creator and ruler of the universe; the supreme being. **3 a** an adored, admired, or influential person. **b** something worshipped like a god (*makes a god of success*). **4** (in *pl.*) *Theatr.* **a** the gallery. **b** the people sitting in it. **5** (**God!**) an exclamation of surprise, anger, etc. □ **by God!** an exclamation of surprise etc. **for God's sake!** see SAKE[1]. **God bless** an expression of good wishes on parting. **God bless me** (or **my soul**) see BLESS. **God damn (you, him**, etc.) may (you, he, etc.) be damned. **God the Father, Son, and Holy Ghost** (in the Christian tradition) the persons of the Trinity. **God forbid** (foll. by *that* + clause, or *absol.*) may it not happen! **God grant** (foll. by *that* + clause) may it happen. **God help (you, him**, etc.) an expression of concern for or sympathy with a person. **God knows 1** it is beyond all knowledge (*God knows what will become of him*). **2** I call God to witness that (*God knows we tried hard enough*). **God willing** if Providence allows. **in God's name** an appeal for help. **my** (or **oh**) **God!** an exclamation of surprise, anger, etc. **play God** assume importance or superiority. **with God** dead and in Heaven. □ **godhood** *n.* **godship** *n.* **godward** *adj. & adv.* **godwards** *adv.* [Old English from Germanic]

God-awful *adj. slang* extremely unpleasant, nasty, etc.

godchild /ˈgɒdtʃʌɪld/ *n.* (*pl.* **-children**) a person in relation to a godparent.

goddam /ˈgɒdam/*adj.* (also **goddamned**) *slang* accursed, damnable.

god-daughter *n.* a female godchild.

goddess /ˈgɒdɪs/ *n.* **1** a female deity. **2** a woman who is adored, esp. for her beauty.

godet /gəʊˈdɛt, ˈgəʊdeɪ/ *n.* a triangular piece of material inserted in a dress, glove, etc. [Middle English from Old French]

godetia /gə(ʊ)ˈdiːʃə/ *n.* any plant of the genus *Godetia*, having showy rose-purple or reddish flowers. [modern Latin, named after C. H. *Godet*, Swiss botanist d. 1879]

go-devil *n. US* an instrument used to clean the inside of pipes etc.

godfather /ˈgɒdfɑːθə/ *n.* **1** a male godparent. **2** a person directing an illegal organization, esp. a leader of the American Mafia. □ **my godfathers!** *Brit. euphem.* my God!

God-fearing *adj.* earnestly religious.

godforsaken /ˈgɒdfəseɪk(ə)n/ *adj.* devoid of all merit; dismal; dreary.

God-given *adj.* received as from God; possessed from birth or by divine authority.

godhead /ˈgɒdhɛd/ *n.* (also **Godhead**) **1 a** the state of being God or a god. **b** divine nature. **2** a deity. **3** (**the Godhead**) God.

godless /ˈgɒdlɪs/ *adj.* **1** impious; wicked. **2** without a god. **3** not recognizing God. □ **godlessness** *n.*

godlike /'gɒdlʌɪk/ *adj.* **1** resembling God or a god in some quality, esp. in physical beauty. **2** befitting or appropriate to a god.

godly /'gɒdli/ *adj.* (**-ier, -iest**) religious, pious, devout. □ **godliness** *n.*

godmother /'gɒdmʌθə/ *n.* a female godparent.

godown /'gəʊdaʊn, gəʊ'daʊn/ *n.* a warehouse in parts of E. Asia, esp. in India. [Portuguese *gudão* from Malay *godong*, perhaps from Telugu *gidaṅgi* 'place where goods lie' from *kidu* 'lie']

godparent /'gɒdpɛːr(ə)nt/ *n.* a person who presents a child at baptism and responds on the child's behalf.

God's Acre *n.* a churchyard.

God's book *n.* the Bible.

God's country *n.* (also **God's own country**) an earthly paradise, esp. with reference to the United States.

godsend /'gɒdsɛnd/ *n.* an unexpected but welcome event or acquisition.

God's gift *n.* often *iron.* a godsend.

godson /'gɒdsʌn/ *n.* a male godchild.

Godspeed /gɒd'spiːd/ *int.* an expression of good wishes to a person starting a journey.

God squad *n. slang* **1** a religious organization, esp. an evangelical Christian group. **2** its members.

God's truth *n.* the absolute truth.

godwit /'gɒdwɪt/ *n.* any wading bird of the genus *Limosa*, with long legs and a long straight or slightly upcurved bill. [16th c.: of unknown origin]

Godwottery /gɒd'wɒt(ə)ri/ *n. Brit. joc.* affected, archaic, or excessively elaborate speech or writing, esp. regarding gardens. [*God wot* (in a poem on gardens, by T. E. Brown 1876)]

goer /'gəʊə/ *n.* **1** a person or thing that goes (*a slow goer*). **2** (often in *comb.*) a person who attends, esp. regularly (*a churchgoer*). **3** *Brit. colloq.* **a** a lively or persevering person or animal. **b** a sexually promiscuous person. **4** *colloq.* a project likely to be accepted or to succeed.

goes *3rd sing. present* of GO[1].

goest /'gəʊɪst/ *archaic 2nd sing. present* of GO[1].

goeth /'gəʊɪθ/ *archaic 3rd sing. present* of GO[1].

Goethean /'gəːtɪən/ *adj.* (also **Goethian**) of, relating to, or characteristic of the German writer J. W. von Goethe (d. 1832).

gofer /'gəʊfə/ *n.* esp. *N. Amer slang* a person who runs errands, esp. on a film set or in an office; a dogsbody. [*go for* (see GO[1])]

goffer /'gɒfə/ *v. & n.* ● *v.tr.* **1** make wavy, flute, or crimp (a lace edge, a trimming, etc.) with heated irons. **2** (as **goffered** *adj.*) (of the edges of a book) embossed. ● *n.* **1** an iron used for goffering. **2** ornamental plaiting used for frills etc. [French *gaufrer* 'stamp with a patterned tool' from *gaufre* 'honeycomb', related to WAFER, WAFFLE[2]]

go-getter *n. colloq.* an aggressively enterprising person, esp. a businessman.

goggle /'gɒg(ə)l/ *v., adj., & n.* ● *v.* **1** *intr.* **a** (often foll. by *at*) look with wide-open eyes. **b** (of the eyes) be rolled about; protrude. **2** *tr.* turn (the eyes) sideways or from side to side. ● *adj.* (usu. *attrib.*) (of the eyes) protuberant or rolling. ● *n.* **1** (in *pl.*) **a** spectacles for protecting the eyes from glare, dust, water, etc. **b** *colloq.* spectacles. **2** (in *pl.*) a sheep disease, the staggers. **3** a goggling expression. [Middle English, probably from a base expressive of oscillating movement: related to JOG, JOGGLE[1]]

goggle-box *n. Brit. colloq.* a television set.

goggle-dive *n. Brit.* an underwater dive in goggles.

goggle-eyed *adj.* having staring or protuberant eyes, esp. through astonishment or disbelief.

goglet /'gɒglɪt/ *n. Anglo-Ind.* a long-necked usu. porous earthenware vessel used for keeping water cool. [Portuguese *gorgoleta*]

go-go *adj. colloq.* **1** (of a dancer, music, etc.) in modern style; lively and rhythmic. **2** unrestrained; energetic. **3** (of investment) speculative.

Goidel /'gɔɪd(ə)l/ *n.* a member of the Gaelic people that comprises the Scottish, Irish, and Manx Celts. [Old Irish *Góidel*: cf. GAEL]

Goidelic /gɔɪ'dɛlɪk/ *n. & adj.* ● *n.* the northern group of the Celtic languages, comprising Irish, Scottish Gaelic, and Manx. ● *adj.* of or relating to the Goidelic or the Goidels.

going /'gəʊɪŋ/ *n. & adj.* ● *n.* **1 a** the act or process of going. **b** an instance of this; a departure. **2 a** the condition of the ground for walking, riding, etc. **b** progress affected by this (*found the going hard*). ● *adj.* **1** in or into action (*set the clock going*). **2** esp. *Brit.* existing, available; to be had (*there's cold beef going*; *one of the best fellows going*). **3** current, prevalent (*the going rate*). □ **get going** start steadily talking, working, etc. (*can't stop him when he gets going*). **going for one** *colloq.* acting in one's favour (*he has got a lot going for him*). **going on fifteen** etc. esp. *US* approaching one's fifteenth etc. birthday. **going on for** *Brit.* approaching (a time, an age, etc.) (*must be going on for 6 years*). **going to** intending or intended to; about to; likely to (*it's going to sink!*). **to be going on with** to start with; for the time being. **while the going is good** while conditions are favourable. [GO[1]: in some senses from earlier *a-going*: see A[2]]

going away *n.* a departure, esp. on a honeymoon (often, with hyphen, *attrib.*: *going-away outfit*).

going concern *n.* a thriving business.

going-over *n.* (*pl.* **goings-over**) **1** *colloq.* an inspection or overhaul. **2** *slang* a thrashing. **3** *US colloq.* a scolding.

goings-on *n.pl.* behaviour, esp. of a morally suspect nature.

goitre /'gɔɪtə/ *n.* (*US* **goiter**) *Med.* a swelling of the neck resulting from enlargement of the thyroid gland. □ **goitred** *adj.* **goitrous** *adj.* [French, back-formation from *goitreux* or from Provençal *goitron*, ultimately from Latin *guttur* 'throat']

go-kart *n.* (also **go-cart**) a miniature racing car with a skeleton body. [alteration of GO-CART]

Golconda /gɒl'kɒndə/ *n.* a mine or source of wealth, advantages, etc. [a city near Hyderabad, India, famous for its diamonds]

gold /gəʊld/ *n. & adj.* ● *n.* **1** a yellow malleable ductile high-density metallic element resistant to chemical reaction, occurring naturally in quartz veins and gravel, and precious as a monetary medium, in jewellery, etc. (symbol **Au**). **2** the colour of gold. **3 a** coins or articles made of gold. **b** money in large sums, wealth. **4** something precious, beautiful, or brilliant (*all that glitters is not gold*). **5** = GOLD MEDAL. **6** gold used for coating a surface or as a pigment, gilding. **7** the bull's-eye of an archery target (usu. gilt). ● *adj.* **1** made wholly or chiefly of gold. **2** coloured like gold. [Old English from Germanic]

gold amalgam *n.* an easily-moulded combination of gold with mercury.

gold-beater *n.* a person who beats gold out into gold leaf.

gold-beater's skin *n.* a membrane used to separate leaves of gold during beating, or as a covering for slight wounds.

gold bloc *n. Econ.* a bloc of countries having a gold standard.

gold brick *n. & v. slang* ● *n.* **1** a thing with only a surface appearance of value, a sham or fraud. **2** *US* a lazy person. ● *v.intr.* (**goldbrick**) *US* shirk.

gold card *n.* a charge card issued only to people with a high credit rating and giving benefits not available to holders of the standard card.

goldcrest /'gəʊl(d)krɛst/ *n.* a very small warbler, *Regulus regulus*, with a golden crest.

gold-digger *n.* **1** *slang* a woman who wheedles money out of men. **2** a person who digs for gold.

gold disc *n. Brit.* an award given to a recording artist or group for sales of a record etc. exceeding a specified high figure (which varies from country to country).

gold dust *n.* **1** gold in fine particles as often found naturally. **2** a plant, *Alyssum saxatile*, with many small yellow flowers.

golden /ˈgəʊld(ə)n/ *adj.* **1 a** made or consisting of gold (*golden sovereign*). **b** yielding gold. **2** coloured or shining like gold (*golden hair*). **3** precious; valuable; excellent; important (*a golden memory*; *a golden opportunity*). □ **goldenly** *adv.* **goldenness** /ˈgəʊld(ə)nnɪs/ *n.*

golden age *n.* **1** a supposed past age when people were happy and innocent. **2** the period of a nation's greatest prosperity, literary merit, etc.

golden ager *n. N. Amer.* an old person.

golden balls *n.pl.* a pawnbroker's sign.

golden boy *n.* (*fem.* **golden girl**) *colloq.* a popular or successful person.

golden calf *n.* wealth as an object of worship (Exod. 32).

golden chain *n.* the laburnum.

golden delicious *n.* a greenish-yellow variety of dessert apple.

golden eagle *n.* a large eagle, *Aquila chrysaetos*, with yellow-tipped head-feathers.

golden-eye *n.* any marine duck of the genus *Bucephala*.

Golden Fleece *n.* (in Greek mythology) a fleece of gold sought and won by Jason.

golden girl see GOLDEN BOY.

golden goose *n.* a continuing source of wealth or profit.

golden hamster see HAMSTER.

golden handshake *n. colloq.* a payment given on redundancy or early retirement.

golden hello *n. Brit. colloq.* a payment made by an employer to a keenly-sought recruit.

Golden Horde *n.* the Tartar horde that overran E. Europe in the 13th c. (from the richness of the leader's tent).

Golden Horn *n.* the harbour of Istanbul.

golden jubilee *n.* **1** the fiftieth anniversary of a sovereign's accession. **2** any other fiftieth anniversary.

golden mean *n.* **1** the principle of moderation, as opposed to excess. **2** = GOLDEN SECTION.

golden number *n.* the number of a year in the Metonic lunar cycle, used to fix the date of Easter.

golden oldie *n. colloq.* **1** an old hit record or film etc. that is still well known and popular. **2** a person who is no longer young but is still successful in his or her field.

golden opinions *n.pl. Brit.* high regard.

golden orfe *n.* a yellow variety of orfe, kept in aquaria.

golden oriole *n.* a European oriole, *Oriolus oriolus*, of which the male has yellow and black plumage and the female has mainly green plumage.

golden parachute *n. colloq.* financial compensation guaranteed to company executives dismissed as a result of a merger or takeover.

golden perch *n.* = CALLOP.

golden retriever *n.* a retriever with a thick golden-coloured coat.

golden rod *n.* any plant of the genus *Solidago* with a rodlike stem and a spike of small bright yellow flowers.

golden rule *n.* a basic principle of action, esp. 'do as you would be done by'.

golden section *n.* the division of a line so that the whole is to the greater part as that part is to the smaller part (i.e. in a ratio of 1 to $\frac{1}{2}(\sqrt{5}+1)$).

golden share *n.* a share in a company that controls at least 51 per cent of the voting rights (esp. held by a government in a privatized industry in order to prevent undesirable takeovers).

Golden State *n. US* California.

golden syrup *n. Brit.* a pale treacle.

golden wedding *n.* the fiftieth anniversary of a wedding.

goldfield /ˈgəʊl(d)fiːld/ *n.* a district in which gold is found as a mineral.

goldfinch /ˈgəʊl(d)fɪn(t)ʃ/ *n.* any of various brightly coloured songbirds of the genus *Carduelis*, esp. the Eurasian *C. carduelis*, with a yellow band across each wing. [Old English *goldfinc* (as GOLD, FINCH)]

goldfish /ˈgəʊl(d)fɪʃ/ *n.* (*pl.* usu. same) a small reddish-golden Chinese carp kept for ornament, *Carassius auratus*.

goldfish bowl *n.* **1** a globular glass container for goldfish. **2** a place or situation lacking privacy.

gold foil *n.* gold beaten into a thin sheet.

goldilocks /ˈgəʊldɪlɒks/ *n.* **1** a person with golden hair. **2 a** a kind of buttercup, *Ranunculus auricomus*. **b** a plant of the daisy family, *Aster linosyris*, like the golden rod. [*goldy* from GOLD + LOCK^2]

gold leaf *n.* gold beaten into a very thin sheet.

gold medal *n.* a gold-coloured medal, usu. awarded as first prize.

gold mine *n.* **1** a place where gold is mined. **2** *colloq.* a source of wealth.

gold of pleasure *n.* an annual yellow-flowered plant, *Camelina sativa*.

gold plate *n. & v.* ● *n.* **1** vessels made of gold. **2** material plated with gold. ● *v.tr.* (**gold-plate**) plate with gold.

gold record *n. US* = GOLD DISC.

gold reserve *n.* a reserve of gold coins or bullion held by a central bank etc.

gold rush *n.* a rush to a newly discovered goldfield.

goldsmith /ˈgəʊl(d)smɪθ/ *n.* a worker in gold, a manufacturer of gold articles. [Old English (as GOLD, SMITH)]

gold standard *n. Econ.* a system by which the value of a currency is defined in terms of gold, for which the currency may be exchanged.

Gold Stick *n.* **1** (in the UK) a gilt rod carried on State occasions by the colonel of the Life Guards or the captain of the gentlemen-at-arms. **2** the officer carrying this rod.

gold thread *n.* **1** a thread of silk etc. with gold wire wound round it. **2** a bitter plant, *Coptis trifolia*.

golem /ˈgəʊləm, ˈgɔɪl-/ *n.* **1** a clay figure supposedly brought to life in Jewish legend. **2** an automaton; a robot. [Yiddish *goylem* from Hebrew *gōlem* 'shapeless mass']

golf /gɒlf/ *n. & v.* ● *n.* a game played on a course set in open country, in which a small hard ball is struck with clubs into a series of 18 or 9 holes with the fewest possible strokes. ● *v.intr.* play golf. [Middle English: perhaps related to Dutch *kolf* 'club']

golf bag *n.* a bag used for carrying clubs and balls.

golf ball *n.* **1** a ball used in golf. **2** a small ball used in some electric typewriters to carry the type.

golf cart *n.* **1** a trolley used for carrying clubs in golf. **2** a motorized cart for golfers and equipment.

golf club *n.* **1** a club used in golf. **2** an association for playing golf. **3** the premises used by a golf club.

golf course *n.* the course on which golf is played.

golfer /ˈgɒlfə/ *n.* **1** a golf player. **2** *Brit.* a cardigan.

golf links *n.pl.* = LINKS 1.

Golgi body /ˈgɒldʒi, -gi/ *n.* (also **Golgi apparatus**) *Biol.* an organelle of vesicles and folded membranes within the cytoplasm of most eukaryotic cells, involved esp. in the secretion of substances. [named after C. *Golgi*, Italian cytologist d. 1926]

Goliath beetle /gəˈlʌɪəθ/ *n.* any large beetle of the genus *Goliathus*, esp. *G. giganteus* native to Africa. [Late Latin from Hebrew *golyaṯ*, the name of a giant slain traditionally by David (1 Sam. 17)]

Goliath frog *n.* a giant frog, *Rana goliath*, of central Africa.

golliwog /ˈgɒlɪwɒg/ *n.* a black-faced brightly dressed soft doll with fuzzy hair. [from *Golliwogg*, the name of a doll character in books by B. Upton, US writer d. 1912: perhaps suggested by GOLLY[1] + POLLIWOG]

gollop /ˈgɒləp/ *v.* & *n. colloq.* ● *v.tr.* (**golloped, golloping**) swallow hastily or greedily. ● *n.* a hasty gulp. [perhaps from GULP, influenced by GOBBLE[1]]

golly[1] /ˈgɒli/ *int.* expressing surprise. [euphemism for GOD]

golly[2] /ˈgɒli/ *n.* (*pl.* **-ies**) *colloq.* = GOLLIWOG. [abbreviation]

GOM *abbr. Brit.* Grand Old Man (name originally applied to W. E. Gladstone).

gombeen /gɒmˈbiːn/ *n. Ir.* usury. [Irish *gaimbín*, perhaps from the same Celtic source as medieval Latin *cambire* CHANGE]

gombeen man *n. Ir.* a moneylender.

-gon /g(ə)n, gɒn/ *comb. form* forming nouns denoting plane figures with a specified number of angles (*hexagon*; *polygon*; *n-gon*). [Greek *-gōnos* '-angled']

gonad /ˈgəʊnad/ *n.* an animal organ producing gametes, e.g. the testis or ovary. □ **gonadal** /gə(ʊ)ˈneɪd(ə)l/ *adj.* [modern Latin *gonas gonad-* from Greek *gonē, gonos* 'generation, seed']

gonadotrophic hormone /ˌgəʊnadə(ʊ)ˈtrəʊfɪk, -ˈtrɒfɪk/ *n.* (also **gonadotropic** /-ˈtrəʊpɪk, -ˈtrɒpɪk/) *Biochem.* any of various hormones stimulating the activity of the gonads.

gonadotrophin /ˌgəʊnadə(ʊ)ˈtrəʊfɪn/ *n.* = GONADOTROPHIC HORMONE.

gondola /ˈgɒndələ/ *n.* **1** a light flat-bottomed boat used on Venetian canals, with a central cabin and a high point at each end, worked by one oar at the stern. **2** a car suspended from an airship or balloon. **3** a free-standing block of shelves used to display goods in a supermarket. **4** (also **gondola car**) *US* a flat-bottomed open railway goods wagon. **5** a car attached to a ski lift. [Venetian Italian, from Rhaeto-Romance *gondolà* 'rock, roll']

gondolier /gɒndəˈlɪə/ *n.* the oarsman on a gondola. [French from Italian *gondoliere* (as GONDOLA)]

gone /gɒn/ *past part.* of GO[1]. ● *adj.* **1** *Brit.* (of time) past (*not until gone nine*). **2 a** lost; hopeless. **b** dead. **3** *colloq.* pregnant for a specified time (*already three months gone*). **4** *slang* completely enthralled or entranced, esp. by rhythmic music, drugs, etc. □ **be gone** depart (cf. BEGONE). **gone away!** a huntsman's cry, indicating that a fox has been started. **gone on** *slang* infatuated with.

gone goose *n.* (also **gone gosling**) *colloq.* a person or thing beyond hope.

goner /ˈgɒnə/ *n. slang* a person or thing that is doomed, ended, irrevocably lost, etc.; a dead person.

gonfalon /ˈgɒnf(ə)lən/ *n.* **1** a banner, often with streamers, hung from a crossbar. **2** *hist.* such a banner as the standard of some Italian republics. □ **gonfalonier** /ˌgɒnfələˈnɪə/ *n.* [Italian *gonfalone*, from Germanic (cf. VANE)]

gong /gɒŋ/ *n.* & *v.* ● *n.* **1** a metal disc with a turned rim, giving a resonant note when struck. **2** a saucer-shaped bell. **3** *Brit. slang* a medal; a decoration. ● *v.tr.* summon with a gong. [Malay *gong*, *gung*, of imitative origin]

gongoozler /gɒŋˈguːzlə/ *n. dial.* or *slang* a person who stares curiously at something, an idle spectator. [English dialect]

goniometer /gəʊnɪˈɒmɪtə/ *n.* an instrument for measuring angles. □ **goniometry** *n.* **goniometric** /-əˈmɛtrɪk/ *adj.* **goniometrical** /-əˈmɛtrɪk(ə)l/ *adj.* [French *goniomètre* from Greek *gōnia* 'angle']

gonna /ˈgɒnə/ *contr. colloq.* going to (*we're gonna win*; *it's gonna be tough*). [corruption]

■ **Usage** *Gonna* is non-standard and should generally be avoided in both speech and writing.

gonococcus /gɒnəˈkɒkəs/ *n.* (*pl.* **gonococci** /-k(s)ʌɪ, -k(s)iː/) a bacterium causing gonorrhoea. □ **gonococcal** *adj.* [Greek *gonos* 'generation, semen' + COCCUS]

gonorrhoea /gɒnəˈrɪə/ *n.* (*US* **gonorrhea**) a venereal disease with inflammatory discharge from the urethra or vagina. □ **gonorrhoeal** *adj.* [Late Latin from Greek *gonorrhoia*, from *gonos* 'semen' + *rhoia* 'flux']

gonzo /ˈgɒnzəʊ/ *adj.* esp. *US* **1** of or associated with journalistic writing of an exaggerated, subjective, and fictionalized style. **2** *colloq.* bizarre; crazy. [perhaps from Italian *gonzo* 'foolish' or Spanish *ganso* 'goose, fool']

goo /guː/ *n. colloq.* **1** a sticky or slimy substance. **2** sickly sentiment. [20th c.: perhaps from *burgoo* (nautical slang) = porridge]

good /gʊd/ *adj., n.,* & *adv.* ● *adj.* (**better, best**) **1** having the right or desired qualities; satisfactory, adequate. **2 a** (of a person) efficient, competent (*good at French*; *a good driver*). **b** (of a thing) reliable, efficient (*good brakes*). **c** (of health etc.) strong (*good eyesight*). **3 a** kind, benevolent (*good of you to come*). **b** morally excellent; virtuous (*a good deed*). **c** charitable (*good works*). **d** well-behaved (*a good child*). **4** enjoyable, agreeable (*a good party*; *good news*). **5** thorough, considerable (*gave it a good wash*). **6 a** not less than (*waited a good hour*). **b** considerable in number, quality, etc. (*a good many people*). **7** (usu. foll. by *for*) healthy, beneficial (*good for you*). **8 a** valid, sound (*a good reason*). **b** financially sound (*his credit is good*). **c** (usu. foll. by *for*) *US* (of a ticket) valid. **9** in exclamations of surprise (*good heavens!*). **10** right, proper, expedient (*thought it good to have a try*). **11** fresh, eatable, untainted (*is the meat still good?*). **12** (sometimes patronizing) commendable, worthy (*good old George*; *your good lady wife*; *good men and true*; *my good man*). **13** well-shaped, attractive (*has good legs*; *good looks*). **14** in courteous greetings and farewells (*good morning*; *good afternoon*). ● *n.* **1** (only in *sing.*) that which is good; what is beneficial or morally right (*only good can come of it*; *did it for your own good*; *what good will it do?*). **2** (only in *sing.*) a desirable end or object; a thing worth attaining (*sacrificing the present for a future good*). **3** (in *pl.*) **a** *Law* movable property or merchandise. **b** *Brit.* things to be transported, as distinct from passengers. **c** (prec. by *the*) *colloq.* what one has undertaken to supply (esp. *deliver the goods*). **d** (prec. by *the*) *slang* the real thing; the genuine article. **4** (treated as *pl.*; prec. by *the*) virtuous people. ● *adv. N. Amer. colloq.* well (*doing pretty good*). □ **as good as** practically (*he as good as told me*). **as good as gold** extremely well-behaved. **be so good as** (or **be good enough) to** (often in a request) be kind and do (a favour) (*be so good as to open the window*). **be (a certain amount) to the good** have as net profit or advantage. **do good** show kindness, act philanthropically. **do a person good** be beneficial to. **for good (and all)** finally, permanently. **good and** *colloq.* used as an intensifier before an adj. or adv. (*raining good and hard*; *was good and angry*). **good for 1** beneficial to; having a good effect on. **2** able to perform; inclined for (*good for a ten-mile walk*). **3** able to be trusted to pay (*is good for £100*). **good for you!** (or **him!, her!**, etc.) an exclamation of approval towards a person. **good God!** (or **good Lord!**) an exclamation of surprise, anger, etc. **good oil** *Austral. slang* reliable information. **good on you!** (or **him!** etc.) esp. *Austral.* & *NZ* = *good for you!* **have a good mind** see MIND. **have the goods on a person** *slang* have information about a person which may be used to his or her detriment. **have a good time** enjoy oneself. **in a person's good books** see BOOK. **in good faith** with honest or sincere intentions. **in** (or **on**) **good form** see GOOD FORM. **in good time 1** with no risk of being late. **2** (also **all in good time**) in due course but without haste. **make good 1** make up for, compensate for, pay (an expense). **2** fulfil (a promise); effect (a purpose or an intended action). **3** demonstrate the truth of (a statement); substantiate (a charge). **4** gain and hold (a position). **5** replace or restore (a thing lost or damaged). **6** (*absol.*) accomplish what one intended. **take in good**

part not be offended by. **to the good** having as profit or benefit. ▫ **goodish** *adj.* [Old English *gōd*, from Germanic]

good Book *n.* (prec. by *the*) the Bible.

good breeding *n.* correct or courteous manners.

goodbye /gʊd'bʌɪ/ *int.* & *n.* (*US* also **goodby**) ● *int.* expressing good wishes on parting, ending a telephone conversation, etc., or said with reference to a thing discarded or irrevocably lost. ● *n.* (*pl.* **goodbyes** or *US* also **goodbys**) the saying of 'goodbye'; a parting; a farewell. [contraction of *God be with you!*, with *good* substituted on the pattern of *good morning* etc.]

good company *n.* **1** a pleasant companion. **2** a suitable associate or group of friends.

good faith *n.* honesty or sincerity of intention.

good form *n.* what complies with current social conventions. ▫ **in good form** in a state of good health or training. **on good form** playing or performing well; in good spirits.

good-for-nothing *adj.* & *n.* ● *adj.* worthless. ● *n.* a worthless person.

Good Friday *n.* the Friday before Easter Sunday, commemorating the Crucifixion of Christ.

good-hearted *n.* kindly, well-meaning.

good humour *n.* a genial mood.

good-humoured *adj.* genial, cheerful, amiable. ▫ **good-humouredly** *adv.*

goodie var. of GOODY[1] *n.*

good job *n. Brit.* a fortunate state of affairs (*it's a good job you came early*).

Good King Henry *n.* a weed of the goosefoot family, *Chenopodium bonus-henricus*, of northern regions. [16th c.: origin unknown]

good-looker *n.* a handsome or attractive person.

good-looking *adj.* handsome; attractive.

good luck *n.* & *int.* ● *n.* **1** good fortune. **2** an omen of this. ● *int.* an exclamation of well-wishing.

goodly /'gʊdli/ *adj.* (**goodlier**, **goodliest**) **1** *archaic* comely, handsome. **2** considerable in size or quantity. ▫ **goodliness** *n.* [Old English *gōdlic* (as GOOD, -LY[1])]

goodman /'gʊdmən/ *n.* (*pl.* **-men**) esp. *Sc. archaic* the head of a household.

good money *n.* **1** genuine money; money that might usefully have been spent elsewhere. **2** *colloq.* high wages.

good nature *n.* a friendly disposition.

good-natured /gʊd'neɪtʃəd/ *adj.* kind, patient; easygoing. ▫ **good-naturedly** *adv.*

goodness /'gʊdnɪs/ *n.* & *int.* ● *n.* **1** virtue; excellence, esp. moral. **2** kindness, generosity (*had the goodness to wait*). **3** what is good or beneficial in a thing (*vegetables with all the goodness boiled out*). ● *int.* (as a substitution for 'God') expressing surprise, anger, etc. (*goodness me!*; *goodness knows*; *for goodness' sake!*). [Old English *gōdnes* (as GOOD, -NESS)]

goodnight /gʊd'nʌɪt/ *int.* & *n.* ● *int.* expressing good wishes on parting at night or bedtime. ● *n.* an instance of saying 'goodnight'.

goodo /'gʊdəʊ/ *adj. Austral.* & *NZ* = GOOD *adj.* 10.

good-oh /'gʊdəʊ, gʊd'əʊ/ *int.* good! excellent!

goods and chattels *n.pl.* all kinds of personal property.

Good Shepherd *n.* (prec. by *the*) Christ.

good-tempered *adj.* having a good temper; not easily annoyed. ▫ **good-temperedly** *adv.*

good-time *attrib.adj.* recklessly pursuing pleasure. ▫ **good-timer** *n.*

good times *n.pl.* a period of prosperity.

goodwife /'gʊdwʌɪf/ *n.* (*pl.* **-wives**) *Sc. archaic* the female head of a household.

goodwill /gʊd'wɪl/ *n.* **1** kindly feeling. **2** the established reputation of a business etc. as enhancing its value. **3** cheerful consent or acquiescence; readiness, zeal. **4** (**good will**) the intention and hope that good will result.

good word *n.* (often in phr. **put in a good word for**) words in recommendation or defence of a person.

good works *n.pl.* charitable acts.

goody[1] /'gʊdi/ *n.* & *int.* ● *n.* (also **goodie**) (*pl.* **-ies**) **1** *Brit. colloq.* a good or favoured person, esp. a hero in a story, film, etc. **2** (usu. in *pl.*) something good or attractive, esp. to eat. **3** = GOODY-GOODY *n.* ● *int.* expressing childish delight.

goody[2] /'gʊdi/ *n.* (*pl.* **goodies**) *archaic* (often as a title prefixed to a surname) an elderly woman of humble station (*Goody Blake*). [for GOODWIFE: cf. HUSSY]

goody-goody *n.* & *adj. colloq.* ● *n.* (*pl.* **-ies**) a smug or obtrusively virtuous person. ● *adj.* obtrusively or smugly virtuous.

gooey /'guːi/ *adj.* (**gooier**, **gooiest**) *colloq.* **1** viscous, sticky. **2** sickly, sentimental. ▫ **gooeyness** *n.* (also **gooiness**). [GOO + -Y[2]]

goof /guːf/ *n.* & *v. slang* ● *n.* **1** a foolish or stupid person. **2** a mistake. ● *v.* **1** *tr.* bungle, mess up. **2** *intr.* blunder, make a mistake. **3** *intr.* (often foll. by *off*) idle. **4** *tr.* (as **goofed** *adj.*) stupefied with drugs. [variant of dialect *goff*, from French *goffe* via Italian *goffo* from medieval Latin *gufus* 'coarse']

go-off *n. colloq.* a start (*at the first go-off*).

goofy /'guːfi/ *adj.* (**goofier**, **goofiest**) *slang* **1** stupid, silly, daft. **2** having or displaying protruding or crooked front teeth. ▫ **goofily** *adv.* **goofiness** *n.*

goog /gʊg/ *n. Austral. slang* an egg. ▫ **full as a goog** very drunk. [20th c.: origin unknown]

googly /'guːgli/ *n.* (*pl.* **-ies**) *Cricket* an off-break ball bowled with apparent leg-break action. [20th c.: origin unknown]

googol /'guːgɒl/ *n.* ten raised to the hundredth power (10^{100}). [arbitrary formation]

■ **Usage** *Googol* is a fanciful word, not found in technical use.

googolplex /'guːg(ə)lplɛks/ *n.* ten raised to the power of a googol. [GOOGOL + *-plex* as in MULTIPLEX]

■ **Usage** *Googolplex* is a fanciful word, not found in technical use.

gook /guːk, gʊk/ *n. US slang offens.* a foreigner, esp. a person of E. Asian descent. [20th c.: origin unknown]

goolie /'guːli/ *n.* (also **gooly**) (*pl.* **-ies**) **1** (usu. in *pl.*) *Brit. slang* a testicle. **2** *Austral. slang* a stone or pebble. [apparently of Indian origin; cf. Hindustani *golī* 'bullet, ball, pill']

goombah /guːm'bɑː/ *n. US slang* **1** a member of a criminal gang; a Mafioso. **2** a boss or mentor; a crony. [Italian *compàre* 'godfather, friend, accomplice']

goon /guːn/ *n. slang* **1** a stupid or playful person. **2** esp. *N. Amer.* a person hired by racketeers etc. to terrorize political or industrial opponents. [perhaps from dialect *gooney* 'booby': influenced by the subhuman cartoon character 'Alice the *Goon*', created by US cartoonist E. C. *Segar* (d. 1938)]

goop[1] /guːp/ *n. Brit. slang* a stupid or fatuous person. ▫ **goopy** *adj.* (**goopier**, **goopiest**). **goopiness** *n.* [20th c.: cf. GOOF]

goop[2] /guːp/ *n.* esp. *N. Amer.* = GLOOP. [imitative: cf. GOO, GLOOP]

goosander /guː'sandə/ *n.* a large diving duck, *Mergus merganser*, with a narrow serrated bill. [probably from GOOSE + *-ander* as in *bergander* 'sheldrake']

goose /guːs/ *n.* & *v.* ● *n.* (*pl.* **geese** /giːs/) **1 a** any of various large waterbirds of the family Anatidae, with short legs, webbed feet, and a broad bill. **b** the female of this (opp. GANDER *n.* 1). **c** the flesh of a goose as food. **2** *colloq.* a simpleton. **3** (*pl.* **gooses**) a tailor's smoothing iron, having a handle like a goose's neck. ● *v.tr. slang* poke (a person) in the bottom. [Old English *gōs*, from Germanic]

gooseberry /'gʊzb(ə)ri, 'guːs-/ *n.* (*pl.* **-ies**) **1** a round edible yellowish-green berry with a thin usu. translucent skin enclosing seeds in a juicy flesh. **2** the thorny shrub, *Ribes grossularia*, bearing this fruit. **3** *Brit. colloq.* an unwanted extra (usu. third) person (esp. in phr. **play gooseberry**). [perhaps from GOOSE + BERRY]

goose bumps *n.pl. N. Amer.* = GOOSE-FLESH.

goose egg *n. N. Amer.* a zero score in a game.

goose-flesh *n.* (also **goose pimples** *n.pl.* or **goose-skin**) a pimply state of the skin with the hairs erect, produced by cold, fright, etc.

goosefoot /ˈguːsfʊt/ *n.* (*pl.* **-foots**) any plant of the genus *Chenopodium*, having leaves shaped like the foot of a goose.

goosegog /ˈgʊzgɒg, ˈguːsgɒg/ *n. Brit. colloq.* a gooseberry. [jocular corruption]

goosegrass /ˈguːsgrɑːs/ *n.* = CLEAVERS.

goose pimples see GOOSE-FLESH.

goose-skin see GOOSE-FLESH.

goose-step *n.* & *v.* ● *n.* a military marching step in which the knees are kept stiff. ● *v.intr.* march in this way.

GOP *abbr. US* Grand Old Party (the Republican Party).

gopak /ˈgəʊpak/ *n.* an energetic Ukrainian dance. [Russian, from Ukrainian *hopak*]

gopher[1] /ˈgəʊfə/ *n.* **1** (in full **pocket gopher**) any burrowing rodent of the family Geomyidae, native to N. America, having food-pouches on the cheeks. **2** *N. Amer.* a ground squirrel. **3** (in full **gopher tortoise**) a tortoise, *Gopherus polyphemus*, native to the southern US, that excavates tunnels as shelter from the sun. [18th c.: origin uncertain]

gopher[2] /ˈgəʊfə/ *n.* **1** *Bibl.* a tree from the wood of which Noah's ark was made. **2** (in full **gopher wood**) a tree, *Cladrastis lutea*, yielding yellowish timber. [Hebrew *gōper*]

gopher snake *n.* = INDIGO SNAKE.

goral /ˈgɔːr(ə)l/ *n.* a goat-antelope, *Nemorhaedus goral*, native to mountainous regions of northern India, having short horns curving to the rear. [native name]

gorblimey /gɔːˈblʌɪmi/ *int.* & *n. Brit. colloq.* ● *int.* an expression of surprise, indignation, etc. ● *n.* (*pl.* **-eys**) a soft service cap. [corruption of *God blind me*]

gorcock /ˈgɔːkɒk/ *n. Sc.* & *N.Engl.* the male of the red grouse. [*gor-* (of unknown origin) + COCK[1]]

Gordian knot /ˈgɔːdɪən/ *n.* **1** an intricate knot. **2** a difficult problem or task. □ **cut the Gordian knot** solve a problem by force or by evasion. [named after *Gordius*, king of Phrygia, who tied an intricate knot that remained tied until cut by Alexander the Great]

Gordon setter /ˈgɔːd(ə)n/ *n.* **1** a setter of a black and tan breed, used as a gun dog. **2** this breed. [named after the 4th Duke of *Gordon*, d. 1827, promoter of the breed]

gore[1] /gɔː/ *n.* blood shed, esp. when clotted. [Old English *gor* 'dung, dirt']

gore[2] /gɔː/ *v.tr.* pierce with a horn, tusk, etc. [Middle English: origin unknown]

gore[3] /gɔː/ *n.* & *v.* ● *n.* **1** a wedge-shaped piece in a garment. **2** a triangular or tapering piece in an umbrella etc. ● *v.tr.* shape with a gore. [Old English *gāra* 'triangular piece of land', related to Old English *gār* 'spear', a spearhead being triangular]

gorge /gɔːdʒ/ *n.* & *v.* ● *n.* **1** a narrow opening between hills or a rocky ravine, often with a stream running through it. **2** an act of gorging; a feast. **3** the contents of the stomach; what has been swallowed. **4** the neck of a bastion or other outwork; the rear entrance to a work. **5** *US* a mass of ice etc. blocking a narrow passage. ● *v.* **1** *intr.* feed greedily. **2** *tr.* **a** (often *refl.*) satiate, glut. **b** swallow, devour greedily. □ **cast the gorge at** *Brit.* reject with loathing. **one's gorge rises at** one is sickened by. □ **gorger** *n.* [Middle English from Old French *gorge* 'throat', ultimately from Latin *gurges* 'whirlpool']

gorgeous /ˈgɔːdʒəs/ *adj.* **1** richly coloured, sumptuous, magnificent. **2** *colloq.* very pleasant, splendid (*gorgeous weather*). **3** *colloq.* strikingly beautiful. □ **gorgeously** *adv.* **gorgeousness** *n.* [earlier *gorgayse*, *-yas* from Old French *gorgias* 'fine, elegant', of unknown origin]

gorget /ˈgɔːdʒɪt/ *n.* **1** *hist.* **a** a piece of armour for the throat. **b** a woman's wimple. **2** a patch of colour on the throat of a bird, insect, etc. [Old French *gorgete* (as GORGE)]

Gorgio /ˈgɔːdʒɪəʊ/ *n.* (*pl.* **-os**) the gypsy name for a non-gypsy. [Romany]

gorgon /ˈgɔːg(ə)n/ *n.* **1** (in Greek mythology) each of three snake-haired sisters (esp. Medusa) with the power to turn anyone who looked at them to stone. **2** a frightening or repulsive person, esp. a woman. □ **gorgonian** /gɔːˈgəʊnɪən/ *adj.* [Latin *Gorgo -onis* from Greek *Gorgō*, from *gorgos* 'terrible']

gorgonian /gɔːˈgəʊnɪən/ *n.* & *adj.* ● *n.* a usu. brightly coloured horny coral of the order Gorgonacea, having a treelike skeleton bearing polyps, e.g. a sea fan. ● *adj.* of or relating to the Gorgonacea. [modern Latin (as GORGON), with reference to its petrifaction]

gorgonize /ˈgɔːg(ə)nʌɪz/ *v.tr.* (also **-ise**) **1** stare at like a gorgon. **2** paralyse with terror etc.

Gorgonzola /gɔːg(ə)nˈzəʊlə/ *n.* a type of rich cheese with bluish-green veins. [*Gorgonzola*, a village in Italy, where it was originally made]

gorilla /gəˈrɪlə/ *n.* **1** the largest anthropoid ape, *Gorilla gorilla*, native to central Africa, having a large head, short neck, and prominent mouth. **2** *colloq.* a heavily built man of aggressive demeanour. [adopted as the specific name in 1847 from *Gorillai*, the Greek name of an African tribe noted for hairiness]

gormandize /ˈgɔːm(ə)ndʌɪz/ *v.* & *n.* (also **-ise**) ● *v.* **1** *intr.* & *tr.* eat or devour voraciously. **2** *intr.* indulge in good eating. ● *n.* = GOURMANDISE. □ **gormandizer** *n.* [as GOURMANDISE]

gormless /ˈgɔːmlɪs/ *adj.* esp. *Brit. colloq.* foolish, lacking sense. □ **gormlessly** *adv.* **gormlessness** *n.* [originally *gaumless*, from dialect *gaum* 'understanding']

gorse /gɔːs/ *n.* any spiny yellow-flowered shrub of the genus *Ulex*, esp. growing on European wastelands. Also called *furze*. □ **gorsy** *adj.* [Old English *gors(t)*, related to Old High German *gersta*, Latin *hordeum*, 'barley']

Gorsedd /ˈgɔːsɛð/ *n.* a council of Welsh etc. bards and Druids (esp. as meeting daily before the eisteddfod). [Welsh, literally 'throne']

gory /ˈgɔːri/ *adj.* (**gorier**, **goriest**) **1** involving bloodshed; bloodthirsty (*a gory film*). **2** covered in gore. □ **gory details** *joc.* explicit details. □ **gorily** *adv.* **goriness** *n.*

gosh /gɒʃ/ *int.* expressing surprise. [euphemism for GOD]

goshawk /ˈgɒshɔːk/ *n.* a large short-winged hawk, *Accipiter gentilis*. [Old English *gōs-hafoc* (as GOOSE, HAWK[1])]

gosling /ˈgɒzlɪŋ/ *n.* a young goose. [Middle English, originally *gesling*, from Old Norse *gǽslingr*]

go-slow *n. Brit.* a form of industrial action in which employees deliberately work slowly.

gospel /ˈgɒsp(ə)l/ *n.* **1** the teaching or revelation of Christ. **2** (**Gospel**) **a** the record of Christ's life and teaching in the first four books of the New Testament. **b** each of these books. **c** a portion from one of these read at a church service. **3** (also **gospel truth**) a thing regarded as absolutely true (*take my word as gospel*). **4** a principle one acts on or advocates. **5** (in full **gospel music**) black American evangelical religious singing. [Old English *gōdspel* (as GOOD, *spel* 'news, SPELL[1]'), rendering ecclesiastical Latin *bona annuntiatio*, *bonus nuntius* = *evangelium* EVANGEL: later associated with *God*]

gospeller /ˈgɒsp(ə)lə/ *n.* (*US* **gospeler**) the reader of the Gospel in a Communion service.

Gospel side *n.* the north side of the altar, at which the Gospel is read.

gossamer /ˈgɒsəmə/ *n.* & *adj.* ● *n.* **1** a filmy substance of small spiders' webs. **2** delicate filmy material. **3** a thread of gossamer. ● *adj.* light and flimsy as gossamer. □ **gossamered** *adj.* **gossamery** *adj.* [Middle English *gos(e)somer(e)*, apparently from GOOSE + SUMMER[1] (*goose summer* = St Martin's summer, i.e. early November when geese were eaten, gossamer being common then)]

gossip /'gɒsɪp/ *n. & v.* ● *n.* **1 a** easy or unconstrained talk or writing esp. about persons or social incidents. **b** idle talk; groundless rumour. **2** an informal chat, esp. about persons or social incidents. **3** a person who indulges in gossip. ● *v.intr.* (**gossiped**, **gossiping**) talk or write gossip. □ **gossiper** *n.* **gossipy** *adj.* [earlier sense 'godparent': from Old English *godsibb* 'person related to one in *God*': see SIB]

gossip column *n.* a section of a newspaper devoted to gossip about well-known people. □ **gossip columnist** *n.*

gossip monger /'gɒsɪpmʌŋgə/*n.* a perpetrator of gossip.

gossoon /gɒ'su:n/ *n. Ir.* a lad. [earlier *garsoon* from French *garçon* 'boy']

got *past* and *past part.* of GET.

Goth /gɒθ/ *n.* **1** a member of a Germanic tribe that invaded the Roman Empire in the 3rd–5th c. **2** an uncivilized or ignorant person. **3** (**goth**) **a** a style of rock music derived from punk, often with apocalyptic or mystical lyrics. **b** a member of a subculture favouring black clothing, white and black make-up, metal jewellery, and goth music. [Late Latin *Gothi* (pl.) from Greek *Go(t)thoi*, from Gothic]

Gothic /'gɒθɪk/ *adj. & n.* ● *adj.* **1** of the Goths or their language. **2** in the style of architecture prevalent in W. Europe in the 12th–16th c., characterized by pointed arches. **3** (of a novel etc.) in a style popular in the 18th–19th c., with supernatural or horrifying events. **4** barbarous, uncouth. **5** *Printing* (of type) old-fashioned German, black letter, or sans serif. ● *n.* **1** the Gothic language. **2** Gothic architecture. **3** *Printing* Gothic type. □ **Gothically** *adv.* **Gothicism** /-sɪz(ə)m/ *n.* **Gothicize** /-saɪz/ *v.tr. & intr.* (also **-ise**). [French *gothique* or Late Latin *gothicus* from *Gothi*: see GOTH]

go-to-meeting *attrib.adj.* (of a hat, clothes, etc.) suitable for going to church in.

gotta /'gɒtə/ *colloq.* have got a; have got to (*I gotta pain*; *we gotta go*). [corruption]

■ **Usage** *Gotta* is non-standard and should generally be avoided in both speech and writing.

gotten *US past part.* of GET.

Götterdämmerung /gɒtə'damərʊŋ, gə:t-, -'dɛm-/ *n.* **1** the twilight (i.e. downfall) of the gods. **2** the complete downfall of a regime etc. [German, esp. as the title of an opera by Wagner]

gouache /gu:'ɑ:ʃ, gwɑ:ʃ/ *n.* **1** a method of painting in opaque pigments ground in water and thickened with a glue-like substance. **2** these pigments. **3** a picture painted in this way. [French from Italian *guazzo*]

Gouda /'gaʊdə/ *n.* a flat round usu. Dutch cheese with a yellow rind. [*Gouda*, a town in the Netherlands, where it was originally made]

gouge /gaʊdʒ, gu:dʒ/ *n. & v.* ● *n.* **1** a chisel with a concave blade, used in carpentry, sculpture, and surgery. **2** an indentation or groove made with or as with this. ● *v.* **1** *tr.* cut with or as with a gouge. **2** *tr.* **a** (foll. by *out*) force out (esp. an eye with the thumb) with or as with a gouge. **b** force out the eye of (a person). **3** *tr. N. Amer. colloq.* overcharge, swindle. **4** *intr. Austral.* dig for opal. □ **gouger** *n.* [French, from Late Latin *gubia*, perhaps of Celtic origin]

goujons /'gu:dʒ(ə)nz/ *n.pl.* deep-fried strips of chicken or fish. [French, formed as GUDGEON[1,2]]

goulash /'gu:laʃ/ *n.* **1** a highly-seasoned Hungarian soup or stew of meat and vegetables, flavoured with paprika. **2** (in contract bridge) a dealing again, several cards at a time, of the four hands (unshuffled, but with each hand arranged in suits and order of value) when no player has bid. [Hungarian *gulyás-hús*, from *gulyás* 'herdsman' + *hús* 'meat']

gourami /gʊ(ə)'rɑ:mi, 'gʊərəmi/ *n.* **1** a large freshwater fish, *Osphronemus goramy*, native to SE Asia, used as food. **2** any small brightly coloured freshwater fish of the related families Belontiidae and Helostomatidae, often kept in aquariums. Also called *labyrinth fish*. [Malay *gurāmi*]

gourd /gʊəd, gɔ:d/ *n.* **1 a** a fleshy usu. large fruit with a hard skin. **b** any of various climbing or trailing plants of the family Cucurbitaceae bearing such a fruit; also called *cucurbit*. **2** the hollow hard skin of a gourd, dried and used as a drinking vessel, water container, ornament, etc. □ **gourdful** *n.* (*pl.* **-fuls**). [Middle English from Anglo-French *gurde*, Old French *gourde*, ultimately from Latin *cucurbita*]

gourmand /'gʊəmənd, 'gɔ:-/ *n. & adj.* ● *n.* **1** a glutton. **2** *disp.* a gourmet. ● *adj.* gluttonous; fond of eating, esp. to excess. □ **gourmandism** *n.* [Middle English from Old French, of unknown origin]

■ **Usage** The use of *gourmand* in sense 2 is considered incorrect by some people; it is therefore preferable to use *gourmet*.

gourmandise /gʊəmɒ̃'di:z/ *n.* the habits of a gourmand; gluttony. [French (as GOURMAND)]

gourmet /'gʊəmeɪ, 'gɔ:-/ *n. & adj.* ● *n.* a connoisseur of good food, having a discerning palate. ● *attrib.adj.* **1** of a kind or standard suitable for gourmets. **2** of or relating to a gourmet. [French, = wine taster: sense influenced by GOURMAND]

gout /gaʊt/ *n.* **1** a disease with inflammation of the smaller joints, esp. the toe, as a result of excess uric acid salts in the blood. **2** *archaic* **a** a drop, esp. of blood. **b** a splash or spot. □ **gouty** *adj.* **goutiness** *n.* [Middle English via Old French *goute* from Latin *gutta* 'drop', with reference to the medieval theory of the flowing down of humours]

Gov. *abbr.* **1** Government. **2** Governor.

gov. *abbr.* governor.

govern /'gʌv(ə)n/ *v.* **1 a** *tr.* rule or control (a state, subject, etc.) with authority; conduct the policy and affairs of (an organization etc.). **b** *intr.* be in government. **2 a** *tr.* influence or determine (a person or a course of action). **b** *intr.* be the predominating influence. **3** *tr.* be a standard or principle for; constitute a law for; serve to decide (a case). **4** *tr.* check or control (esp. passions). **5** *tr. Gram.* (esp. of a verb or preposition) have (a noun or pronoun or the case of these) depending on it. **6** *tr.* be in military command of (a fort, town). □ **governable** *adj.* **governability** /-nə'bɪlɪti/ *n.* [Middle English via Old French *governer* and Latin *gubernare* 'steer, rule' from Greek *kubernaō*]

governance /'gʌv(ə)nəns/ *n.* **1** the act or manner of governing. **2** the office or function of governing. **3** sway, control. [Middle English from Old French (as GOVERN)]

governess /'gʌv(ə)nɪs/ *n.* a woman employed to teach children in a private household. [earlier *governeress* from Old French *governeresse* (as GOVERNOR)]

governessy /'gʌv(ə)nɪsi/ *adj.* characteristic of a governess; prim.

governing body *n.* the body of managers of an institution.

government /'gʌv(ə)nm(ə)nt, -vəm(ə)nt/ *n.* **1** the act or manner of governing. **2** the system by which a state or community is governed. **3 a** a body of persons governing a state. **b** (usu. **Government**) a particular ministry in office. **4** the State as an agent. **5** *Gram.* the relation between a governed and a governing word. □ **governmental** /-'mɛnt(ə)l/ *adj.* **governmentally** /-'mɛnt(ə)li/ *adv.* [Middle English from Old French *governement* (as GOVERN)]

Government House *n. Brit.* the official residence of a governor.

government issue *adj. US* (of equipment) provided by the government.

government paper *n.* (also **government securities** *n.pl.*) bonds etc. issued by the government.

government pension see PENSION[1] *n.* 1a.

government surplus *n.* unused equipment sold by the government.

governor /ˈgʌv(ə)nə/ *n.* **1** a person who governs; a ruler. **2 a** an official governing a province, town, etc. **b** *Brit.* a representative of the Crown in a colony. **3** the executive head of each state of the US. **4** an officer commanding a fortress or garrison. **5** the head or a member of a governing body of an institution. **6** *Brit.* the official in charge of a prison. **7** *Brit.* **a** *slang* one's employer. **b** *slang* one's father. **c** *colloq.* (as a form of address) sir. **8** *Mech.* an automatic regulator controlling the speed of an engine etc. □ **governorate** /-rət/ *n.* **governorship** *n.* [Middle English via Anglo-French *gouvernour*, Old French *governëo(u)r* from Latin *gubernator -oris* (as GOVERN)]

Governor-General *n.* (*pl.* **Governors-General**) the representative of the Crown in a Commonwealth country that regards the British Monarch as head of state.

Govt. *abbr.* Government.

gowan /ˈgaʊən/ *n. Sc. & N.Engl.* **1** a daisy. **2** any white or yellow field-flower. [probably a variant of dialect *gollan* 'ranunculus' etc., and related to *gold* in *marigold*]

gowk /gaʊk/ *n. Brit. dial.* **1** a cuckoo. **2** an awkward or half-witted person; a fool. [Middle English from Old Norse *gaukr*, from Germanic]

gown /gaʊn/ *n. & v.* ● *n.* **1** a loose flowing garment, esp. a long dress worn by a woman. **2** the official robe of an alderman, judge, cleric, member of a university, etc. **3** a protective overall worn by a surgeon, a hospital patient, etc. **4** the members of a university as distinct from the permanent residents of the university town (cf. TOWN *n.* 4). ● *v.tr.* (usu. as **gowned** *adj.*) attire in a gown. [Middle English via Old French *goune, gon(n)e* from Late Latin *gunna* 'fur garment': cf. medieval Greek *gouna* 'fur']

goy /gɔɪ/ *n.* (*pl.* **goyim** /ˈgɔɪɪm/ or **goys**) *slang offens.* a Jewish name for a non-Jew. □ **goyish** *adj.* (also **goyisch**). [Hebrew *gōy* 'people, nation']

GP *abbr.* **1** general practitioner. **2** Grand Prix.

Gp. Capt. *abbr.* (in the RAF) Group Captain.

GPI *abbr.* general paralysis of the insane.

GPMU *abbr.* (in the UK) Graphical, Paper, and Media Union. (formed by the merger of the NGA and SOGAT in 1991).

GPO *abbr.* **1** *Brit.* General Post Office. **2** *US* Government Printing Office.

GPS *abbr.* Global Positioning System, an accurate worldwide navigational and surveying facility based on the reception of signals from an array of orbiting satellites.

GR *abbr.* King George. [Latin *Georgius Rex*]

gr *abbr.* (also **gr.**) **1** gram(s). **2** grain(s). **3** gross. **4** grey.

Graafian follicle /ˈgrɑːfɪən/ *n.* a follicle in the mammalian ovary in which an ovum develops prior to ovulation. [named after R. de *Graaf*, Dutch anatomist d. 1673]

grab /grab/ *v. & n.* ● *v.* (**grabbed**, **grabbing**) **1** *tr.* **a** seize suddenly. **b** capture, arrest. **2** *tr.* take greedily or unfairly. **3** *tr. slang* attract the attention of, impress. **4** *intr.* (foll. by *at*) make a sudden snatch at. **5** *intr.* (of the brakes of a motor vehicle) act harshly or jerkily. ● *n.* **1** a sudden clutch or attempt to seize. **2** a mechanical device for clutching. **3** the practice of grabbing; rapacious proceedings esp. in politics and commerce. **4** a children's card game in which certain cards may be snatched from the table. □ **up for grabs** *slang* readily obtainable or available; on offer. □ **grabber** *n.* [Middle Low German, Middle Dutch *grabben*: perhaps related to GRIP, GRIPE, GROPE]

grab bag *n. N. Amer.* a lucky dip.

grabble /ˈgrab(ə)l/ *v.intr.* **1** grope about, feel for something. **2** (often foll. by *for*) sprawl on all fours, scramble (for something). [Dutch & Low German *grabbeln* 'scramble for a thing' (as GRAB)]

grabby /ˈgrabi/ *adj. colloq.* tending to grab; greedy, grasping.

graben /ˈgrɑːb(ə)n/ *n.* (*pl.* same or **grabens**) *Geol.* a depression of the earth's surface between faults. [German, originally = ditch]

grab handle *n.* (also **grab rail** etc.) a handle or rail etc. to steady passengers in a moving vehicle.

grace /greɪs/ *n. & v.* ● *n.* **1** attractiveness, esp. in elegance of proportion or manner or movement; gracefulness. **2** courteous good will (*had the grace to apologize*). **3** an attractive feature; an accomplishment (*social graces*). **4 a** (in Christian belief) the unmerited favour of God; a divine saving and strengthening influence. **b** the state of receiving this. **c** a divinely given talent. **5** goodwill, favour (*fall from grace*). **6** delay granted as a favour (*a year's grace*). **7** a short thanksgiving before or after a meal. **8** (**Grace**) (in Greek mythology) each of three beautiful sister goddesses, bestowers of beauty and charm. **9** (**Grace**) (prec. by *His*, *Her*, *Your*) forms of description or address for a duke, duchess, or archbishop. ● *v.tr.* (often foll. by *with*) lend or add grace to; enhance or embellish; confer honour or dignity on (*a vase graced the table*; *graced us with his presence*). □ **days of grace** the time allowed by law for payment of a sum due. **in a person's good** (or **bad**) **graces** regarded by a person with favour (or disfavour). **with good** (or **bad**) **grace** as if willingly (or reluctantly). [Middle English via Old French from Latin *gratia*, from *gratus* 'pleasing': cf. GRATEFUL]

grace and favour *attrib.adj. Brit.* designating a house etc. occupied by permission of a sovereign etc.

graceful /ˈgreɪsfʊl, -f(ə)l/ *adj.* having or showing grace or elegance. □ **gracefully** *adv.* **gracefulness** *n.*

graceless /ˈgreɪslɪs/ *adj.* lacking grace or elegance or charm. □ **gracelessly** *adv.* **gracelessness** *n.*

grace note *n.* an extra note as an embellishment not essential to the harmony or melody.

gracile /ˈgrasɪl, ˈgrasʌɪl/ *adj.* slender; esp. *Anthropol.* (of hominid species) of slender build. [Latin *gracilis* 'slender']

gracility /grəˈsɪlɪti/ *n.* **1** slenderness. **2** (of literary style) unornamented simplicity.

gracious /ˈgreɪʃəs/ *adj. & int.* ● *adj.* **1** indulgent and beneficent to inferiors. **2** (of God) merciful, benign. **3** kindly, courteous. **4** *Brit.* a polite epithet used of royal persons or their acts (*the gracious speech from the throne*). **5** characterized by elegance and usu. wealth (*gracious grandeur*; *gracious rooms*). ● *int.* expressing surprise. □ **graciosity** /greɪʃɪˈɒsɪti, greɪsɪ-/ *n.* **graciously** *adv.* **graciousness** *n.* [Middle English via Old French from Latin *gratiosus* (as GRACE)]

gracious living *n.* an elegant way of life.

grackle /ˈgrak(ə)l/ *n.* **1** any of various orioles, esp. of the genus *Quiscalus*, native to America, the males of which are shiny black with a blue-green sheen; also called BLACKBIRD. **2** any of various mynas, esp. of the genus *Gracula*, native to Asia. [modern Latin *Gracula* from Latin *graculus* 'jackdaw']

grad /grad/ *n. colloq.* = GRADUATE *n.* 1. [abbreviation]

gradate /grəˈdeɪt/ *v.* **1** *v.intr. & tr.* pass or cause to pass by gradations from one shade to another. **2** *tr.* arrange in steps or grades of size etc. [back-formation from GRADATION]

gradation /grəˈdeɪʃ(ə)n/ *n.* (usu. in *pl.*) **1** a stage of transition or advance. **2 a** a certain degree in rank, intensity, merit, divergence, etc. **b** such a degree; an arrangement in such degrees. **3** (of paint etc.) the gradual passing from one shade, tone, etc., to another. **4** *Philol.* ablaut. □ **gradational** *adj.* **gradationally** *adv.* [Latin *gradatio* from *gradus* 'step']

grade /greɪd/ *n. & v.* ● *n.* **1 a** a certain degree in rank, merit, proficiency, quality, etc. **b** a class of persons or things of the same grade. **2 a** a mark indicating the quality of a student's work. **b** *Brit.* an examination, esp. in music. **3** *N. Amer.* a class in school, concerned with a particular year's work and usu. numbered from the first upwards. **4 a** a gradient or slope. **b** the rate of ascent or descent. **5 a** a variety of cattle produced by crossing native stock with a superior breed. **b** a group of animals at a similar level of development. **6** *Philol.* a relative position in a series of forms involving ablaut. ● *v.* **1** *tr.* arrange in or allocate to grades; class, sort. **2** *intr.* (foll. by *up, down, off, into*, etc.) pass gradually between grades, or into a grade. **3** *tr.* give a grade to (a student). **4** *tr.* blend so as to affect the grade of colour with tints passing into each other. **5** *tr.* reduce (a road etc.) to easy gradients. **6** *tr.* (often foll. by *up*) cross (livestock) with a better breed. □ **at grade** *US* on the same level. **make the grade** *colloq.* succeed; reach the desired standard. [French *grade* or Latin *gradus* 'step']

grade crossing *n. US* = LEVEL CROSSING.

grader /ˈgreɪdə/ *n.* **1** a person or thing that grades. **2** a wheeled machine for levelling the ground, esp. in making roads. **3** (in *comb.*) *N. Amer.* a pupil of a specified grade in a school (*sixth-grader*).

grade school *n. US* elementary school.

gradient /ˈgreɪdɪənt, -djənt/ *n.* **1** esp. *Brit.* **a** a stretch of road, railway, etc., that slopes from the horizontal. **b** the amount of such a slope. **2** the rate of rise or fall of temperature, pressure, etc., in passing from one region to another. [probably formed on GRADE, on the pattern of *salient*]

gradine /grəˈdiːn/ *n.* (also **gradin** /ˈgreɪdɪn/) **1** each of a series of low steps or a tier of seats. **2** a ledge at the back of an altar. [Italian *gradino*, diminutive of *grado* GRADE]

gradual /ˈgradʒʊəl/ *adj. & n.* ● *adj.* **1** taking place or progressing slowly or by degrees. **2** not rapid or steep or abrupt. ● *n. Eccl.* **1** a response sung or recited between the Epistle and Gospel in the Mass. **2** a book of music for the sung Mass service. □ **gradually** *adv.* **gradualness** *n.* [medieval Latin *gradualis, -ale* from Latin *gradus* 'step', the noun referring to the altar steps on which the response is sung]

gradualism /ˈgradʒʊəlɪz(ə)m/ *n.* a policy of gradual reform rather than sudden change or revolution. □ **gradualist** *n.* **gradualistic** /-ˈlɪstɪk/ *adj.*

graduand /ˈgradʒʊand, -dj-, -ənd/ *n. Brit.* a person about to receive an academic degree. [medieval Latin *graduandus*, gerundive of *graduare* GRADUATE]

graduate *n. & v.* ● *n.* /ˈgradʒʊət, -djʊət/ **1** a person who has been awarded an undergraduate or first academic degree (also *attrib.*: *graduate student*). **2** *N. Amer.* a person who has completed a course of study. ● *v.* /ˈgradʒʊeɪt, -djʊeɪt/ **1** *intr.* **a** take an academic degree or (*N. Amer.*) a high school diploma. **b** (foll. by *from*) be a graduate of a specified university. **c** (foll. by *in*) be a graduate in a specified subject. **2** *tr. N. Amer.* confer a degree, diploma, etc. upon; send out as a graduate from a university etc. **3** *intr.* **a** (foll. by *to*) move up to (a higher grade of activity etc.). **b** (foll. by *as, in*) gain specified qualifications. **4** *tr.* mark out in degrees or parts. **5** *tr.* arrange in gradations; apportion (e.g. tax) according to a scale. **6** *intr.* (foll. by *into, away*) pass by degrees. □ **graduator** *n.* [medieval Latin *graduari* 'take a degree' from Latin *gradus* 'step']

graduated pension *n.* (in the UK) a system of pension contributions by employees in proportion to their wages or salary.

graduate school *n.* a department of a university for advanced work by graduates.

graduation /gradʒʊˈeɪʃ(ə)n, -djʊ-/ *n.* **1** the act or an instance of graduating or being graduated. **2** a ceremony at which degrees are conferred. **3** each or all of the marks on a vessel or instrument indicating degrees of quantity etc.

Graecism /ˈgriːsɪz(ə)m, ˈgrʌɪ-/ *n.* (also **Grecism**) **1** a Greek idiom, esp. as imitated in another language. **2 a** the Greek spirit, style, mode of expression, etc. **b** the imitation of these. [French *grécisme* or medieval Latin *Graecismus* from *Graecus* GREEK]

Graecize /ˈgriːsʌɪz, ˈgrʌɪ-/ *v.tr.* (also **Grecize, -ise**) give a Greek character or form to. [Latin *Graecizare* (as GRAECISM)]

Graeco- /ˈgriːkəʊ, ˈgrʌɪ-/ *comb. form* (also **Greco-**) Greek; Greek and. [Latin *Graecus* GREEK]

Graeco-Roman /griːkəʊˈrəʊmən, grʌɪ-/ *adj.* **1** of or relating to the Greeks and Romans. **2** *Wrestling* denoting a style attacking only the upper part of the body.

graffiti /grəˈfiːti/ *n. & v.* ● *n.pl.* (*sing.* **graffito** /-təʊ/) inscriptions or drawings scribbled, scratched, or sprayed on a surface, originally as inscribed on ancient walls. ● *v.tr.* (**graffitied**) **1** cover (a surface) with graffiti. **2** write as graffiti (*graffitied initials*). □ **graffitist** *n.* [Italian, from *graffio* 'a scratch']

■ **Usage** *Graffiti* is, in formal terms, a plural noun and as such should be used with a plural verb. This rule is straightforward when referring to individual inscriptions, e.g. *The graffiti were aggressive and insulting.* The singular form in such examples is *graffito*, e.g. *The graffito on the tombstone said simply 'Jim'.* It is wrong to use the plural form *graffiti* as a singular in such contexts, e.g. *The most common graffiti is 'Vive le roi'.* An alternative to *graffito* is *piece of graffiti*, e.g. *We saw an amusing piece of graffiti.* However, the most common use of *graffiti* is as a collective or mass noun, referring to inscriptions in general or en masse. As such, this word is usually found with a singular verb, e.g. *Graffiti is an increasing problem.* Most people find this use natural and acceptable, as they do the collective use of the word *data*.

graft[1] /grɑːft/ *n. & v.* ● *n.* **1** *Bot.* **a** a shoot or scion inserted into a slit of stock, from which it receives sap. **b** the place where a graft is inserted. **c** an instance or the process of inserting a shoot or scion. **2** *Surgery* **a** a piece of living tissue, organ, etc., transplanted surgically. **b** an instance or the process of doing this. **3** *Brit. slang* work (esp. in phr. **hard graft**). ● *v.* **1** *tr.* **a** (often foll. by *into, on, together*, etc.) insert (a scion) as a graft. **b** insert a graft on (a stock). **2** *intr.* insert a graft. **3** *tr. Surgery* transplant (living tissue). **4** *tr.* (foll. by *in, on*) insert or fix (a thing) permanently to another. **5** *intr. Brit. slang* work hard. □ **grafter** *n.* [Middle English (earlier *graff*) via Old French *grafe, grefe* and Latin *graphium* from Greek *graphion* 'stylus', from *graphō* 'write']

graft[2] /grɑːft/ *n. & v. colloq.* ● *n.* **1** practices, esp. bribery, used to secure illicit gains in politics or business. **2** such gains. ● *v.intr.* seek or make such gains. □ **grafter** *n.* [19th c.: origin unknown]

grafting clay *n.* (also **grafting wax**) a substance for covering the united parts of a graft and stock.

Grail /greɪl/ *n.* (in full **Holy Grail**) **1** (in medieval legend) the cup or platter used by Christ at the Last Supper, and in which Joseph of Arimathea received Christ's blood at the Cross, esp. as the object of quests by medieval knights. **2** any object of a quest. [Middle English via Old French *graal* etc. from medieval Latin *gradalis* 'dish', of unknown origin]

grain /greɪn/ *n. & v.* ● *n.* **1** a fruit or seed of a cereal. **2 a** (*collect.*) wheat or any allied grass used as food, corn. **b** (*collect.*) their fruit. **c** any particular species of corn. **3 a** a small hard particle of salt, sand, etc. **b** a discrete particle or crystal, usu. small, in a rock or metal. **c** a piece of solid propellant for use in a rocket engine. **4** the smallest unit of weight in the troy and avoirdupois systems, equal to $^1/_{5760}$ of a pound troy and $^1/_{7000}$ of a pound avoirdupois (approx. 0.0648 grams). **5** the smallest possible quantity (*not a grain of truth in it*). **6 a** roughness of surface. **b** *Photog.* a granular appearance on a photograph or negative. **7** the texture of skin, wood, stone, fabric, etc.; the arrangement and size of constituent particles. **8 a** a pattern of lines of fibre in wood or paper. **b** lamination or planes of cleavage in stone, coal, etc. **9** nature, temper, tendency. **10 a** *hist.* kermes or cochineal, or dye made from either of these. **b** *poet.* dye; colour. ● *v.* **1** *tr.* paint in imitation of the grain of wood or marble. **2** *tr.* give a granular surface to. **3** *tr.* dye in grain. **4** *tr. & intr.* form into grains. **5** *tr.* remove hair from (hides). □ **against the**

grain (often in phr. **go against the grain**) contrary to one's natural inclination or feeling. **in grain** thorough, genuine, by nature, downright, indelible. □ **grained** *adj.* (also in *comb.*). **grainer** *n.* **grainless** *adj.* [Middle English via Old French from Latin *granum*]

grain leather *n.* leather dressed with grain side out.

grain side *n.* the side of a hide on which the hair was.

grains of Paradise *n.pl.* capsules of a W. African plant (*Aframomum melegueta*), used as a spice and a drug.

grainy /ˈgreɪni/ *adj.* (**grainier**, **grainiest**) **1** granular. **2** resembling the grain of wood. **3** *Photog.* having a granular appearance. □ **graininess** *n.*

grallatorial /graləˈtɔːrɪəl/ *adj. Zool.* of or relating to long-legged wading birds, e.g. storks, flamingos, etc. [modern Latin *grallatorius* from Latin *grallator* 'stilt-walker', from *grallae* 'stilts']

gram[1] /gram/ *n.* (also *Brit.* **gramme**) a metric unit of mass equal to one-thousandth of a kilogram. [French *gramme* from Greek *gramma* 'small weight']

gram[2] /gram/ *n.* any of various pulses used as food. [Portuguese *grão* from Latin *granum* 'grain']

-gram /gram/ *comb. form* forming nouns denoting a thing written or recorded (often in a certain way) (*anagram*; *epigram*; *monogram*; *telegram*). □ **-grammatic** /grəˈmatɪk/ *comb. form* forming adjectives. [from or suggested by Greek *gramma -atos* 'thing written, letter of the alphabet', from *graphō* 'write']

gram-equivalent *n. Chem.* the quantity of a substance equal to its relative atomic or molecular weight in grams.

graminaceous /gramɪˈneɪʃəs/ *adj.* of or like grass; grassy. [Latin *gramen -inis* 'grass']

gramineous /grəˈmɪnɪəs/ *adj.* = GRAMINACEOUS. [Latin *gramineus* from *gramen -inis* 'grass']

graminivorous /gramɪˈnɪv(ə)rəs/ *adj.* feeding on grass, cereals, etc. [Latin *gramen -inis* 'grass' + -VOROUS]

grammalogue /ˈgraməlɒg/ *n.* **1** a word represented by a single shorthand sign. **2** a logogram. [formed irregularly from Greek *gramma* 'letter of the alphabet' + *logos* 'word']

grammar /ˈgramə/ *n.* **1 a** the study or rules of a language's inflections or other means of showing the relation between words, including its phonetic system. **b** a body of form and usages in a specified language (*Latin grammar*). **2** a person's manner or quality of observance or application of the rules of grammar (*bad grammar*). **3** a book on grammar. **4** the elements or rudiments of an art or science. **5** *Brit. colloq.* = GRAMMAR SCHOOL 1. □ **grammarless** *adj.* [Middle English via Anglo-French *gramere*, Old French *gramaire* from Latin *grammatica*, from Greek *grammatikē* (*tekhnē*) '(art) of letters', from *gramma -atos* 'letter of the alphabet']

grammarian /grəˈmɛːrɪən/ *n.* an expert in grammar or linguistics; a philologist. [Middle English from Old French *gramarien*]

grammar school *n.* **1** *Brit.* esp. *hist.* a selective state secondary school with a mainly academic curriculum. **2** *Brit. hist.* a school founded in or before the 16th c. for teaching Latin, later becoming a secondary school teaching academic subjects. **3** *US* = ELEMENTARY SCHOOL 2.

grammatical /grəˈmatɪk(ə)l/ *adj.* **1 a** of or relating to grammar. **b** determined by grammar, esp. by form or inflection (*grammatical gender*). **2** conforming to the rules of grammar, or to the formal principles of an art, science, etc. □ **grammatically** *adv.* **grammaticalness** *n.* [French *grammatical* or Late Latin *grammaticalis* via Latin *grammaticus* from Greek *grammatikos* (as GRAMMAR)]

gramme *Brit.* var. of GRAM[1].

Gram-negative *adj. Biol.* (of bacteria) not retaining the first (violet) dye of Gram stain. [see GRAM STAIN]

gramophone /ˈgraməfəʊn/ *n.* = RECORD PLAYER. □ **gramophonic** /-ˈfɒnɪk/ *adj.* [formed by inversion of PHONOGRAM]

gramophone record see RECORD *n.* 3a.

Gram-positive *adj. Biol.* (of bacteria) retaining the first (violet) dye of Gram stain. [see GRAM STAIN]

grampus /ˈgrampəs/ *n.* (*pl.* **grampuses**) **1 a** a dolphin, *Grampus griseus*, with a blunt snout and long pointed black flippers. **b** the killer whale. **2** *Brit.* a person breathing heavily and loudly. [earlier *graundepose*, *grapeys* from Old French *grapois* etc. via medieval Latin *craspiscis* from Latin *crassus piscis* 'fat fish']

Gram stain /gram/ *n.* (also **Gram's stain**) *Biol.* a technique for identifying bacteria of different cell-wall types by successive application of a violet dye, a decolorizing agent, and a red dye. [named after H.C.J. *Gram*, Danish physician d. 1938]

gran /gran/ *n. colloq.* grandmother (cf. GRANNY). [abbreviation]

granadilla var. of GRENADILLA.

granary /ˈgran(ə)ri/ *n.* (*pl.* **-ies**) **1** a storehouse for threshed grain. **2** a region producing, and esp. exporting, much corn. **3** *propr.* a type of brown bread or flour containing whole grains of wheat. [Latin *granarium* from *granum* 'grain']

grand /grand/ *adj.* & *n.* ● *adj.* **1 a** splendid, magnificent, imposing, dignified. **b** solemn or lofty in conception, execution, or expression; noble. **2** main; of chief importance (*grand staircase*; *grand entrance*). **3** (**Grand**) of the highest rank, esp. in official titles (*Grand Cross*; *Grand Vizier*; *Grand Inquisitor*). **4** *colloq.* excellent, enjoyable (*had a grand time*; *in grand condition*). **5** belonging to high society; displaying opulence (*the grand folk at the big house*; *grand affair*). **6** (in *comb.*) in names of family relationships, denoting the second degree of ascent or descent (*granddaughter*). **7** (**Grand**) (in French phrases or imitations) great (*Grand Monarch*; *Grand Hotel*). **8** *Law* serious, important (*grand larceny*) (cf. COMMON *adj.* 9, PETTY 4). ● *n.* **1** = GRAND PIANO. **2** (*pl.* same) (usu. in *pl.*) *slang* a thousand dollars or pounds. □ **grandly** *adv.* **grandness** *n.* [Middle English via Anglo-French *graunt*, Old French *grant* from Latin *grandis* 'full-grown']

grandad /ˈgrandad/ *n.* (also **granddad**) *colloq.* **1** grandfather. **2** an elderly man.

grandam /ˈgrandam/ *n.* **1** (also **grandame**) *archaic* grandmother. **2** an old woman. **3** an ancestress. [Middle English from Anglo-French *graund dame* (as GRAND, DAME)]

grand-aunt *n.* = GREAT-AUNT.

grandchild /ˈgran(d)tʃʌɪld/ *n.* (*pl.* **-children**) a child of one's son or daughter.

granddad var. of GRANDAD.

granddaughter /ˈgrandɔːtə/ *n.* a female grandchild.

grand duchy *n.* a state ruled by a grand duke or duchess.

grand duke *n.* (also **grand duchess**) **1** a prince (or princess) or noble person ruling over a territory. **2** (**Grand Duke**) *hist.* the son or grandson of a Russian tsar.

grande dame /grɒ̃ dam/ *n.* a dignified lady of high rank. [French]

grandee /granˈdiː/ *n.* **1** a Spanish or Portuguese nobleman of the highest rank. **2** a person of high rank or eminence. [Spanish & Portuguese *grande*, assimilated to -EE]

grandeur /ˈgrandjə, -(d)ʒə/ *n.* **1** majesty, splendour; dignity of appearance or bearing. **2** high rank, eminence. **3** nobility of character. [French from *grand* 'great, GRAND']

grandfather /ˈgran(d)fɑːðə/ *n.* a male grandparent. □ **grandfatherly** *adj.*

grandfather clock *n.* a clock in a tall free-standing wooden case, driven by weights.

Grand Fleet *n. Brit. hist.* **1** (in the 18th c.) the British fleet based at Spithead. **2** the British fleet operating in the North Sea during the First World War.

Grand Guignol /grɒn giːˈnjɒl/ *n.* a dramatic entertainment of a sensational or horrific nature. [the name (= Great Punch) of a theatre in Paris]

grandiflora /grandɪˈflɔːrə/ *adj.* bearing large flowers. [modern Latin (often used in specific names of large-flowered plants), from Latin *grandis* 'great' + FLORA]

grandiloquent /granˈdɪləkwənt/ *adj.* **1** pompous or inflated in language. **2** given to boastful talk. ▫ **grandiloquence** *n.* **grandiloquently** *adv.* [Latin *grandiloquus* (as GRAND, *-loquus* '-speaking' from *loqui* 'speak'), the ending altered on the pattern of *eloquent* etc.]

Grand Inquisitor *n.* the director of the court of Inquisition in some countries.

grandiose /ˈgrandɪəʊs/ *adj.* **1** producing or meant to produce an imposing effect. **2** planned on an ambitious or magnificent scale. ▫ **grandiosely** *adv.* **grandiosity** /-ˈɒsɪti/ *n.* [French from Italian *grandioso* (as GRAND, -OSE[1])]

grand jury *n.* esp. *US Law* a jury selected to examine the validity of an accusation prior to trial.

grandma /ˈgran(d)mɑː/ *n. colloq.* grandmother.

grand mal /grɒn ˈmal/ *n.* **1** a serious form of epilepsy with loss of consciousness (often *attrib.*: *grand mal epilepsy*). **2** an epileptic fit of this kind. Cf. PETIT MAL. [French, = great sickness]

grandmama /ˈgran(d)məmɑː/ *n. archaic colloq.* = GRANDMA.

grand master *n.* **1** a chess player of the highest class. **2** (**Grand Master**) the head of a military order of knighthood, of Freemasons, etc.

grandmother /ˈgran(d)mʌðə/ *n.* a female grandparent. ▫ **teach one's grandmother to suck eggs** presume to advise a more experienced person. ▫ **grandmotherly** *adj.*

grandmother clock *n.* a clock like a grandfather clock but in a smaller case.

Grand National *n.* a steeplechase held annually at Aintree, Liverpool.

grand-nephew *n.* = GREAT-NEPHEW.

grand-niece *n.* = GREAT-NIECE.

grand opera *n.* opera on a serious theme, or in which the entire libretto (including dialogue) is sung.

grandpa /ˈgran(d)pɑː/ *n. colloq.* grandfather.

grandpapa /ˈgran(d)pəpɑː/ *n. archaic colloq.* = GRANDPA.

grandpappy /ˈgran(d)papi/ *n.* (*pl.* **-ies**) *N. Amer. colloq.* = GRANDPA.

grandparent /ˈgran(d)pɛːr(ə)nt/ *n.* a parent of one's father or mother.

Grand Penitentiary *n.* a cardinal presiding over the penitentiary.

Grand Pensionary *n. hist.* the first minister of Holland and Zeeland (1619-1794).

grand piano *n.* a large full-toned piano standing on three legs, with the body, strings, and soundboard arranged horizontally and in line with the keys.

Grand Prix /grɒ̃ ˈpriː/ *n.* (*pl.* **Grands Prix** *pronunc.* same) any of several important international motor or motorcycle racing events. [French, = great or chief prize]

grand seigneur /grɒ̃ seɪˈnjəː/ *n.* a person of high rank or noble presence. [French, literally 'great lord']

grand siècle /grɒ̃ sɪˈɛkl(ə), French grɑ̃ sjɛkl/ *n.* the classical or golden age, esp. the 17th c. in France. [French, = great century or age]

grandsire /ˈgran(d)sʌɪə/ *n. archaic* **1** grandfather, old man, ancestor. **2** (in bell-ringing) a method of change-ringing.

grand slam *n.* **1** *Bridge* the winning of 13 tricks. **2** the winning of all of a group of major championships or matches in a sport. **3** *Baseball* a home run hit when all three bases are occupied by a runner, thus scoring four runs.

grandson /ˈgran(d)sʌn/ *n.* a male grandchild.

grandstand /ˈgran(d)stand/ *n.* the main stand, usu. roofed, for spectators at a racecourse etc.

grandstand finish *n.* a close and exciting finish to a race etc.

grand total *n.* the final amount after everything is added up; the sum of other totals.

grand tour *n.* esp. *hist.* a cultural tour of Europe, made for educational purposes.

grand-uncle *n.* = GREAT-UNCLE.

grand unified theory *n. Physics* a theory attempting to give a single explanation of the strong, weak, and electromagnetic interactions between subatomic particles.

grange /greɪn(d)ʒ/ *n.* **1** *Brit.* a country house with farm buildings. **2** *archaic* a barn. [Middle English via Anglo-French *graunge*, Old French *grange* from medieval Latin *granica (villa)*, ultimately from Latin *granum* 'grain']

graniferous /graˈnɪf(ə)rəs/ *adj.* producing grain or a grainlike seed. ▫ **graniform** /ˈgranɪfɔːm/ *adj.* [Latin *granum* 'grain']

granite /ˈgranɪt/ *n.* **1** a granular crystalline igneous rock of quartz, mica, feldspar, etc., used for building. **2** a determined or resolute quality, attitude, etc. ▫ **granitic** /grəˈnɪtɪk/ *adj.* **granitoid** *adj.* & *n.* [Italian *granito*, literally 'grained', from *grano*, from Latin *granum* 'grain']

graniteware /ˈgranɪtwɛː/ *n.* **1** a speckled form of earthenware imitating the appearance of granite. **2** a kind of enamelled ironware.

granivorous /graˈnɪv(ə)rəs/ *adj.* feeding on grain. ▫ **granivore** /ˈgranɪvɔː/ *n.* [Latin *granum* 'grain']

granny /ˈgrani/ *n.* (also **grannie**) (*pl.* **-ies**) *colloq.* grandmother. [obsolete *grannam* for GRANDAM + -Y[2]]

granny bond *n. Brit. colloq.* a form of National Savings certificate originally available only to pensioners.

granny flat *n.* (also **granny annexe**) *Brit.* part of a house made into self-contained accommodation for an elderly relative.

granny knot *n.* a reef knot crossed the wrong way and therefore insecure.

Granny Smith /granɪ ˈsmɪθ/ *n.* an Australian green variety of apple. [named after Maria Ann ('Granny') Smith d. 1870, who first produced them]

granodiorite /granə(ʊ)ˈdʌɪərʌɪt/ *n. Geol.* a coarse-grained plutonic rock containing quartz and plagioclase, between granite and diorite in composition. [GRANITE + -O- + DIORITE]

grant /grɑːnt/ *v.* & *n.* ● *v.tr.* **1 a** consent to fulfil (a request, wish, etc.) (*granted all he asked*). **b** allow (a person) to have (a thing) (*granted me my freedom*). **c** (as **granted** *adj.*) *Brit. colloq.* apology accepted; pardon given. **2** give (rights, property, etc.) formally; transfer legally. **3** (often foll. by *that* + clause) admit as true; concede, esp. as a basis for argument. ● *n.* **1** the process of granting or a thing granted. **2** a sum of money given by the State for any of various purposes, esp. to finance education. **3** *Law* **a** a legal conveyance by written instrument. **b** formal conferment. ▫ **take for granted 1** assume something to be true or valid. **2** cease to appreciate through familiarity. ▫ **grantable** *adj.* **grantee** /-ˈtiː/ *n.* (esp. in sense 2 of *v.*). **granter** *n.* **grantor** /-ˈtɔː/ *n.* (esp. in sense 2 of *v.*). [Middle English from Old French *gr(e)anter*, variant of *creanter*, ultimately from part. of Latin *credere* 'entrust']

grant aid *n.* & *v.* ● *n.* a grant by central government to local government or an institution. ● *v.tr.* (**grant-aid**) give financial assistance to.

Granth /grʌnt/ *n.* (in full **Granth Sahib**) the sacred scriptures of the Sikhs. [Hindi, = book, code from Sanskrit *grantha* 'tying, literary composition']

grant-in-aid *n.* (*pl.* **grants-in-aid**) = GRANT AID *n.*

grant-maintained *adj.* (of a school) funded by central rather than local government, and self-governing.

gran turismo /gran tə'rɪzməʊ, Italian tu'rizmo/ *n.* (*pl.* ***-os***) a comfortable high-performance model of motor car. [Italian, = great touring]

granular /'granjʊlə/ *adj.* **1** of or like grains or granules. **2** having a granulated surface or structure. □ **granularity** /-'larɪti/ *n.* **granularly** *adv.* [Late Latin *granulum* GRANULE]

granulate /'granjʊleɪt/ *v.* **1** *tr. & intr.* form into grains (*granulated sugar*). **2** *tr.* roughen the surface of. **3** *intr.* (of a wound etc.) form small prominences as the beginning of healing; heal, join. □ **granulation** /-'leɪʃ(ə)n/ *n.* **granulator** *n.*

granule /'granju:l/ *n.* a small grain. [Late Latin *granulum*, diminutive of Latin *granum* 'grain']

granulocyte /'granjʊləsʌɪt/ *n. Physiol.* any of various white blood cells having granules in their cytoplasm. □ **granulocytic** /-'sɪtɪk/ *adj.*

granulometric /,granjʊlə(ʊ)'mɛtrɪk/ *adj.* relating to the distribution of grain sizes in sand etc. [French *granulométrique* (as GRANULE, METRIC)]

grape /greɪp/ *n.* **1** a berry (usu. green, purple, or black) growing in clusters on a vine, used as fruit and in making wine. **2** (prec. by *the*) *colloq.* wine. **3** = GRAPESHOT. **4** (in *pl.*) a diseased growth like a bunch of grapes on the pastern of a horse etc., or on a pleura in cattle. □ **grapey** *adj.* (also **grapy**). [Middle English from Old French *grape* 'bunch of grapes', probably via *graper* 'gather (grapes)' from *grap(p)e* 'hook', ultimately from Germanic]

grapefruit /'greɪpfru:t/ *n.* (*pl.* same) **1** a large round yellow citrus fruit with an acid juicy pulp. **2** the tree, *Citrus paradisi*, bearing this fruit. [GRAPE + FRUIT, probably from the fruits growing in clusters]

grape hyacinth *n.* a plant of the genus *Muscari* (lily family), with clusters of usu. blue flowers.

grapeseed oil /'greɪpsi:d/ *n.* oil extracted from the residue of grapes.

grapeshot /'greɪpʃɒt/ *n. hist.* small balls used as charge in a cannon and scattering when fired.

grape-sugar *n.* dextrose.

grapevine /'greɪpvʌɪn/ *n.* **1** any of various vines of the genus *Vitis*, esp. *Vitis vinifera*. **2** *colloq.* the means of transmission of unofficial information or rumour (*heard it through the grapevine*).

graph[1] /grɑ:f, graf/ *n. & v.* ● *n.* **1** a diagram showing the relation between variable quantities, usu. of two variables, each measured along one of a pair of axes at right angles. **2** *Math.* a collection of points whose coordinates satisfy a given relation. ● *v.tr.* plot or trace on a graph. [abbreviation of *graphic formula*]

graph[2] /grɑ:f, graf/ *n. Linguistics* a visual symbol, esp. a letter or letters, representing a unit of sound or other feature of speech. [Greek *graphē* 'writing']

-graph /grɑ:f, graf/ *comb. form* forming nouns and verbs meaning: **1** a thing written or drawn etc. in a specified way (*autograph*; *photograph*). **2** an instrument that records (*heliograph*; *seismograph*; *telegraph*).

grapheme /'grafi:m/ *n. Linguistics* **1** a class of letters etc. representing a unit of sound. **2** a feature of a written expression that cannot be analysed into smaller meaningful units. □ **graphematic** /-'matɪk/ *adj.* **graphemic** /grə'fi:mɪk/ *adj.* **graphemically** /grə'fi:mɪk(ə)li/ *adv.* [GRAPH[2] + -EME]

-grapher /grəfə/ *comb. form* forming nouns denoting a person concerned with a subject etc. with a name ending in *-graphy* (*geographer*; *radiographer*). [from or suggested by Greek *-graphos* 'writer' + -ER[1]]

graphic /'grafɪk/ *adj. & n.* ● *adj.* **1** of or relating to the visual or descriptive arts, esp. writing and drawing. **2** vividly descriptive; conveying all (esp. unwelcome or unpleasant) details. **3** (of minerals) showing marks like writing on the surface or in a fracture. **4** = GRAPHICAL. ● *n.* a product of the graphic arts (cf. GRAPHICS 1, 3b). □ **graphically** *adv.* **graphicness** *n.* [Latin *graphicus* from Greek *graphikos*, from *graphē* 'writing']

-graphic /'grafɪk/ *comb. form* (also **-graphical**) forming adjectives corresponding to nouns in *-graphy* (see -GRAPHY). □ **-graphically** *comb. form* forming adverbs. [from or suggested by Greek *-graphikos* (as GRAPHIC)]

graphicacy /'grafɪkəsi/ *n.* the ability to read a map, graph, etc., or to present information by means of diagrams. [GRAPHIC, on the pattern of *literacy*, *numeracy*]

graphical /'grafɪk(ə)l/ *adj.* **1** of or in the form of graphs (see GRAPH[1]). **2** graphic. □ **graphically** *adv.*

graphic arts *n.pl.* the visual and technical arts involving design, writing, drawing, printing, etc. □ **graphic artist** *n.*

graphic equalizer *n.* a device for the separate control of the strength and quality of selected frequency bands.

graphic novel *n.* an adult novel published in comic-strip format.

graphics /'grafɪks/ *n.pl.* (usu. treated as *sing.* except in sense 3b) **1** the products of the graphic arts, esp. commercial design or illustration. **2** the use of diagrams in calculation and design. **3** (in full **computer graphics**) *Computing* **a** the use of computers linked to VDUs to generate and manipulate visual images. **b** visual images produced by computer processing.

graphite /'grafʌɪt/ *n.* a grey crystalline allotropic form of carbon used as a solid lubricant, in pencils, and as a moderator in nuclear reactors etc. Also called *plumbago*, *blacklead*. □ **graphitic** /-'fɪtɪk/ *adj.* **graphitize** /-fɪtʌɪz/ *v.tr. & intr.* (also **-ise**). [German *Graphit* from Greek *graphō* 'write']

graphology /gra'fɒlədʒi/ *n.* **1** the study of handwriting esp. as a supposed guide to character. **2** a system of graphic formulae; notation for graphs (see GRAPH[1]). **3** *Linguistics* the study of systems of writing. □ **graphological** /grafə'lɒdʒɪk(ə)l/ *adj.* **graphologist** *n.* [Greek *graphē* 'writing']

graph paper *n.* paper printed with a network of lines as a basis for drawing graphs.

-graphy /grəfi/ *comb. form* forming nouns denoting: **1** a descriptive science (*bibliography*; *geography*). **2** a technique of producing images (*photography*; *radiography*). **3** a style or method of writing, drawing, etc. (*calligraphy*). [from or suggested by French or German *-graphie*, from Latin or Greek *-graphia* 'writing']

grapnel /'grapn(ə)l/ *n.* **1** a device with iron claws, attached to a rope and used for dragging or grasping. **2** a small anchor with several flukes. [Middle English via Anglo-French from Old French *grapon*, from Germanic: cf. GRAPE]

grappa /'grapə/ *n.* a brandy distilled from the fermented residue of grapes after they have been pressed in wine-making. [Italian]

grapple /'grap(ə)l/ *v. & n.* ● *v.* **1** *intr.* (often foll. by *with*) fight at close quarters or in close combat. **2** *intr.* (foll. by *with*) try to manage or overcome a difficult problem etc. **3** *tr.* **a** grip with the hands; come to close quarters with. **b** seize with or as with a grapnel; grasp. ● *n.* **1** **a** a hold or grip in or as in wrestling. **b** a contest at close quarters. **2** a clutching-instrument; a grapnel. □ **grappler** *n.* [Old French *grapil* (*n.*) from Provençal, diminutive of *grapa* 'hook' (as GRAPNEL)]

grappling hook *n.* = GRAPNEL 1.

grappling iron *n.* = GRAPNEL 1.

graptolite /'graptəlʌɪt/ *n.* an extinct marine invertebrate animal found as a fossil in lower Palaeozoic rocks. [Greek *graptos* 'marked with letters' + -LITE]

grasp /grɑ:sp/ *v. & n.* ● *v.* **1** *tr.* **a** clutch at; seize greedily. **b** hold firmly; grip. **2** *intr.* (foll. by *at*) try to seize; accept avidly. **3** *tr.* understand or realize (a fact or meaning). ● *n.* **1** a firm hold; a grip. **2** (foll. by *of*) **a** mastery or control (*a grasp of the situation*). **b** a mental hold or understanding (*a grasp of the facts*). **3** mental agility (*a quick grasp*). □ **grasp at a straw** (or **at straws**) see STRAW. **grasp the nettle** *Brit.* tackle a difficulty boldly. **within one's grasp** capable of being grasped or comprehended by one. □ **graspable** *adj.* **grasper** *n.* [Middle English *graspe, grapse*, perhaps from a Germanic base related to GROPE]

grasping /'grɑːspɪŋ/ *adj.* avaricious, greedy. □ **graspingly** *adv.* **graspingness** *n.*

grass /grɑːs/ *n. & v.* ● *n.* **1 a** a plant of the family Gramineae, with long narrow leaves, jointed stems, and spikes of small wind-pollinated flowers, including cereals, reeds, and bamboos. **b** vegetation consisting of usu. short plants of this family, eaten by cattle, horses, sheep, etc., and used for lawns and playing fields. **2** pastureland. **3** grass-covered ground, a lawn (*keep off the grass*). **4** *slang* marijuana. **5** *Brit. slang* an informer, esp. a police informer. **6** *Brit.* the earth's surface above a mine; the pithead. **7** *slang* asparagus. ● *v.* **1** *tr.* cover with turf. **2** *tr. US* provide with pasture. **3** *Brit. slang* **a** *tr.* betray, esp. to the police. **b** *intr.* inform the police. **4** *tr.* knock down; fell (an opponent). **5** *tr.* **a** bring (a fish) to the bank. **b** bring down (a bird) by a shot. □ **at grass 1** grazing. **2** out of work, on holiday, etc. **not let the grass grow under one's feet** be quick to act or to seize an opportunity. **out to grass 1** out to graze. **2** in retirement. □ **grassless** *adj.* **grasslike** *adj.* [Old English *græs* from Germanic: related to GREEN, GROW]

grass bird *n.* **1** *Austral.* any of various warblers, esp. of the genus *Megalurus*, living among reeds. **2** a southern African warbler, *Sphenoeacus afer*.

grass box *n. Brit.* a receptacle for cut grass on a lawnmower.

grasscloth /'grɑːsklɒθ/ *n.* a linen-like cloth woven from ramie etc.

grass court *n.* a grass-covered tennis court.

grasshopper /'grɑːshɒpə/ *n.* a jumping and chirping plant-eating insect of the order Orthoptera.

grassland /'grɑːsland/ *n.* a large open area of country covered with grass, esp. one used for grazing.

grass of Parnassus *n.* a herbaceous plant, *Parnassia palustris*.

grass parakeet *n. Austral.* a parakeet, esp. of the genus *Neophema*, frequenting grassland.

grass roots *n.pl.* **1** a fundamental level or source. **2** ordinary people, esp. as voters; the rank and file of an organization, esp. a political party (often hyphenated when *attrib.*: *grass-roots support*).

grass ski *n.* each of a pair of short skis with small wheels or rollers for skiing down grass-covered slopes. □ **grass skiing** *n.*

grass skirt *n.* a skirt made of long grass and leaves fastened to a waistband.

grass snake *n.* **1** *Brit.* a common Eurasian snake, *Natrix natrix*, greenish-brown or greenish-grey with a yellow band around the neck. **2** *N. Amer.* the common greensnake, *Opheodrys vernalis*.

grass tree *n.* = BLACKBOY.

grass widow *n.* (*masc.* **grass widower**) a person whose husband (or wife) is away for a prolonged period.

grass-wrack *n.* eelgrass.

grassy /'grɑːsi/ *adj.* (**grassier**, **grassiest**) **1** covered with or abounding in grass. **2** resembling grass. **3** of grass. □ **grassiness** *n.*

grate[1] /greɪt/ *v.* **1** *tr.* reduce to small shreds by rubbing on a serrated surface. **2** *intr.* (often foll. by *against, on*) rub with a harsh scraping sound. **3** *tr.* utter in a harsh tone. **4** *intr.* **a** sound harshly or discordantly. **b** (often foll. by *on*) have an irritating effect. **5** *tr.* grind (one's teeth). **6** *intr.* (of a hinge etc.) creak. [Middle English from Old French *grater*, ultimately from West Germanic]

grate[2] /greɪt/ *n.* **1** the recess of a fireplace or furnace. **2** a metal frame confining fuel in a fireplace etc. [Middle English, = grating, from Old French, ultimately from Latin *cratis* 'hurdle']

grateful /'greɪtfʊl, -f(ə)l/ *adj.* **1** thankful; feeling or showing gratitude (*am grateful to you for helping*). **2** pleasant, acceptable. □ **gratefully** *adv.* **gratefulness** *n.* [obsolete *grate* (*adj.*), from Latin *gratus* + -FUL]

grater /'greɪtə/ *n.* a device for reducing cheese or other food to small shreds.

graticule /'gratɪkjuːl/ *n.* **1** a series of fine lines or fibres incorporated in a telescope or other optical instrument as a measuring scale or as an aid in locating objects. **2** *Surveying* a network of lines on paper representing meridians and parallels. [French from medieval Latin *graticula*, for *craticula* 'gridiron', from Latin *cratis* 'hurdle']

gratify /'gratɪfʌɪ/ *v.tr.* (**-fies**, **-fied**) **1 a** please, delight. **b** please by compliance; assent to the wish of. **2** indulge in or yield to (a feeling or desire). □ **gratification** /-fɪ'keɪʃ(ə)n/ *n.* **gratifier** *n.* **gratifying** *adj.* **gratifyingly** *adv.* [French *gratifier* or Latin *gratificari* 'do a favour to, make a present of', from *gratus* 'pleasing']

gratin /'gratã(ŋ)/ *n. Cookery* **1** a light browned crust usu. of breadcrumbs or melted cheese. **2** a dish cooked with this (cf. AU GRATIN).

gratiné /'gratɪneɪ, French gratine/ *adj. & n.* (also *fem.* ***gratinée***) ● *adj.* = AU GRATIN. ● *n.* = GRATIN.

grating[1] /'greɪtɪŋ/ *adj.* **1** sounding harsh or discordant (*a grating laugh*). **2** having an irritating effect. □ **gratingly** *adv.*

grating[2] /'greɪtɪŋ/ *n.* **1** a framework of parallel or crossed metal bars. **2** *Optics* a set of parallel wires, lines ruled on glass, etc., for producing spectra by diffraction.

gratis /'gratɪs, 'grɑː-, 'greɪ-/ *adv. & adj.* free; without charge. [Latin, contracted ablative pl. of *gratia* 'favour']

gratitude /'gratɪtjuːd/ *n.* being thankful; readiness to show appreciation for and to return kindness. [French *gratitude* or medieval Latin *gratitudo* from *gratus* 'thankful']

gratuitous /grə'tjuːɪtəs/ *adj.* **1** given or done free of charge. **2** uncalled for; unwarranted; lacking good reason (*a gratuitous insult*). □ **gratuitously** *adv.* **gratuitousness** *n.* [Latin *gratuitus* 'spontaneous']

gratuity /grə'tjuːɪti/ *n.* (*pl.* **-ies**) money given in recognition of services; a tip. [Old French *gratuité* or medieval Latin *gratuitas* 'gift' from Latin *gratus* 'grateful']

gratulatory /'gratjʊlət(ə)ri/ *adj.* expressing congratulation. [Late Latin *gratulatorius* from Latin *gratus* 'grateful']

graunch /grɔːn(t)ʃ/ *v.intr. & tr. Brit. colloq.* make or cause to make a crunching or grinding sound. [imitative]

gravadlax var. of GRAVLAX.

gravamen /grə'veɪmɛn/ *n.* (*pl.* **gravamens** or **gravamina** /-mɪnə/) **1** the essence or most serious part of an argument. **2** a grievance. [Late Latin, = inconvenience, from Latin *gravare* 'to load' from *gravis* 'heavy']

grave[1] /greɪv/ *n.* **1 a** a trench dug in the ground to receive a coffin on burial. **b** the place where someone is buried, often marked by a mound or stone. **2** (prec. by *the*) death, esp. as indicating mortal finality. **3** something compared to or regarded as a grave. □ **turn in one's grave** (of a dead person) be thought of in certain circumstances as likely to have been shocked or angry if still alive. [Old English *græf*, from West Germanic]

grave[2] /greɪv/ *adj. & n.* ● *adj.* **1 a** serious, weighty, important (*a grave matter*). **b** dignified, solemn, sombre (*a grave look*). **2** extremely serious or threatening (*grave danger*). **3** /grɑːv/ (of sound) low-pitched, not acute. ● *n.* /grɑːv/ = GRAVE ACCENT. □ **gravely** *adv.* **graveness** *n.* [French *grave* or Latin *gravis* 'heavy, serious']

grave[3] /greɪv/ *v.tr.* (*past part.* **graven** or **graved**) **1** (foll. by *in, on*) fix indelibly (on one's memory). **2** *archaic* engrave, carve. [Old English *grafan* 'dig, engrave', from Germanic: related to GROOVE]

grave[4] /greɪv/ *v.tr.* clean (a ship's bottom) by burning off accretions and by tarring. [perhaps French dialect *grave* = Old French *greve* 'shore']

grave accent /grɑːv/ *n.* a mark (`) placed over a vowel in some languages to denote pronunciation, length, etc., originally indicating low or falling pitch. [GRAVE[2]]

gravedigger /ˈgreɪvdɪgə/ *n.* **1** a person who digs graves. **2** (in full **gravedigger beetle**) a sexton beetle.

gravel /ˈgrav(ə)l/ *n. & v.* ● *n.* **1 a** a mixture of coarse sand and small water-worn or pounded stones, used for paths and roads and as an aggregate. **b** *Geol.* a stratum of this. **2** *Med.* aggregations of crystals formed in the urinary tract. ● *v.tr.* (**gravelled**, **gravelling**; *US* **graveled**, **graveling**) **1** lay or strew with gravel. **2** perplex, puzzle, nonplus (from an obsolete sense 'run (a ship) aground'). □ **gravel-blind** *literary* almost completely blind (from obsolete 'more than sand-blind', in Shakespeare's *Merchant of Venice* II. ii. 33). [Middle English from Old French *gravel(e)*, diminutive of *grave* (as GRAVE[4])]

gravelly /ˈgrav(ə)li/ *adj.* **1** of or like gravel. **2** having or containing gravel. **3** (of a voice) deep and rough-sounding.

graven *past part.* of GRAVE[3].

graven image *n.* an idol.

graver /ˈgreɪvə/ *n.* **1** an engraving tool; a burin. **2** *archaic* an engraver; a carver.

Graves /grɑːv/ *n.* a light usu. white wine from Graves in France.

Graves' disease /greɪvz/ *n.* exophthalmic goitre with characteristic swelling of the neck and protrusion of the eyes, resulting from an overactive thyroid gland. [named after R. J. *Graves*, Irish physician d. 1853]

graveside /ˈgreɪvsʌɪd/ *n.* the ground at the edge of a grave.

gravestone /ˈgreɪvstəʊn/ *n.* a stone (usu. inscribed) marking a grave.

graveyard /ˈgreɪvjɑːd/ *n.* a burial ground, esp. by a church.

gravid /ˈgravɪd/ *adj. literary* or *Zool.* pregnant; carrying eggs or young. [Latin *gravidus* from *gravis* 'heavy']

gravimeter /grəˈvɪmɪtə/ *n.* an instrument for measuring the difference in the force of gravity from one place to another. [French *gravimètre* (Latin *gravis* 'heavy', -METER)]

gravimetric /gravɪˈmɛtrɪk/ *adj.* **1** of or relating to the measurement of weight. **2** denoting chemical analysis based on weighing reagents and products.

gravimetry /grəˈvɪmɪtri/ *n.* the measurement of weight.

graving dock *n.* = DRY DOCK.

gravitas /ˈgravɪtas, -tɑːs/ *n.* solemn demeanour; seriousness. [Latin from *gravis* 'serious']

gravitate /ˈgravɪteɪt/ *v.* **1** *intr.* (foll. by *to*, *towards*) move or be attracted to some source of influence. **2** *tr.* & *intr.* **a** move or tend by force of gravity towards. **b** sink by or as if by gravity. [modern Latin *gravitare* GRAVITAS]

gravitation /gravɪˈteɪʃ(ə)n/ *n. Physics* **1** a force of attraction between any particle of matter in the universe and any other. **2** the effect of this, esp. the falling of bodies to the earth. [modern Latin *gravitatio* (as GRAVITY)]

gravitational /gravɪˈteɪʃ(ə)n(ə)l/ *adj.* of or relating to gravitation. □ **gravitationally** *adv.*

gravitational constant *n.* the constant in Newton's law of gravitation relating gravity to the masses and separation of particles (symbol **G**).

gravitational field *n.* the region of space surrounding a body in which another body experiences a force of attraction.

graviton /ˈgravɪtɒn/ *n. Physics* a hypothetical quantum of gravitational energy. [GRAVITY + -ON]

gravity /ˈgravɪti/ *n.* **1 a** the force that attracts a body towards the centre of the earth or towards any other physical body having mass. **b** the degree of intensity of this measured by acceleration. **c** gravitational force. **2** the property of having weight. **3 a** importance, seriousness; the quality of being grave. **b** solemnity, sobriety; serious demeanour. [French *gravité* or Latin *gravitas* from *gravis* 'heavy']

gravity feed *n.* the supply of material by its fall under gravity.

gravlax /ˈgravlaks/ *n.* (also **gravadlax** /ˈgravədlaks/) a Scandinavian dish of dry-cured salmon marinated in herbs. [Swedish *gravlax*, from *grav* 'trench' + *lax* 'salmon', from the former practice of marinating the salmon in a hole in the ground]

gravure /grəˈvjʊə/ *n.* = PHOTOGRAVURE. [abbreviation]

gravy /ˈgreɪvi/ *n.* (*pl.* **-ies**) **1 a** the juices exuding from meat during and after cooking. **b** a dressing or sauce for food, made from these or from stock etc. **2** *slang* unearned or unexpected money. [Middle English, perhaps from a misreading as *gravé* of Old French *grané*, probably from *grain* 'spice': see GRAIN]

gravy boat *n.* a boat-shaped vessel for serving gravy.

gravy train *n. slang* a source of easy financial benefit.

gray[1] /greɪ/ *n. Physics* the SI unit of the absorbed dose of ionizing radiation, corresponding to one joule per kilogram (abbr.: **Gy**). [named after L. H. *Gray*, English radiobiologist d. 1965]

gray[2] *US* var. of GREY.

graybeard *US* var. of GREYBEARD.

grayling /ˈgreɪlɪŋ/ *n.* **1** any silver-grey freshwater fish of the genus *Thymallus*, with a long high dorsal fin. **2** a butterfly, *Hipparchia semele*, having wings with grey undersides and bright eye-spots on the upper side. [*gray*, variant of GREY + -LING[1]]

graywacke *US* var. of GREYWACKE.

graze[1] /greɪz/ *v.* **1** *intr.* (of cattle, sheep, etc.) eat growing grass. **2** *tr.* **a** feed (cattle etc.) on growing grass. **b** feed on (grass). **3** *intr.* pasture cattle. **4** *intr. colloq.* **a** eat snacks or small meals throughout the day. **b** flick rapidly between television channels. **c** casually sample something. □ **grazer** *n.* [Old English *grasian* from *græs* GRASS]

graze[2] /greɪz/ *v. & n.* ● *v.* **1** *tr.* rub or scrape (a part of the body, esp. the skin) so as to break the surface but cause little or no bleeding. **2 a** *tr.* touch lightly in passing. **b** *intr.* (foll. by *against*, *along*, etc.) move with a light passing contact. ● *n.* an act or instance of grazing; the result of grazing. [perhaps a specific use of GRAZE[1], as if 'take off the grass close to the ground' (of a shot etc.)]

grazier /ˈgreɪzɪə/ *n.* **1** a person who feeds cattle for market. **2** *Austral.* a large-scale sheep farmer or cattle farmer. □ **graziery** *n.* [GRASS + -IER]

grazing /ˈgreɪzɪŋ/ *n.* **1** in senses of GRAZE[1, 2]. **2** grassland suitable for pasturage.

grease /griːs/ *n. & v.* ● *n.* **1** oily or fatty matter, esp. as a lubricant. **2** the melted fat of a dead animal. **3** oily matter in unprocessed wool. ● *v.tr.* /griːs, griːz/ smear or lubricate with grease. □ **grease the palm of** *colloq.* bribe. **like greased lightning** *colloq.* very fast. □ **greaseless** *adj.* [Middle English from Anglo-French *grece*, *gresse*, Old French *graisse*, ultimately from Latin *crassus* (*adj.*) 'fat']

grease gun *n.* a device for pumping grease under pressure to a particular point.

greasepaint /ˈgriːspeɪnt/ *n.* a waxy composition used as make-up for actors.

greaseproof /ˈgriːspruːf/ *adj.* (esp. of paper) impervious to the penetration of grease.

greaser /ˈgriːsə, -z-/ *n.* **1** a person or thing that greases machinery etc. **2** *slang* a member of a gang of youths with long hair and riding motorcycles. **3** *US slang offens.* a Mexican or Spanish American. **4** *Brit. slang* a gentle landing of an aircraft.

greasy /ˈgriːsi, -zi/ *adj.* (**greasier**, **greasiest**) **1 a** of or like grease. **b** smeared or covered with grease. **c** containing or having too much grease. **2 a** slippery. **b** (of a person or manner) unpleasantly unctuous, smarmy. **c** objectionable. □ **greasily** *adv.* **greasiness** *n.*

greasy pole *n. colloq.* a difficult pathway to success.

great /greɪt/ *adj., n., & adv.* ● *adj.* **1 a** of a size, amount, extent, or intensity considerably above the normal or average; big (*made a great hole*; *take great care*; *lived to a great age*). **b** also with implied surprise, admiration, contempt, etc., esp. in exclamations (*you great idiot!*; *great stuff!*; *look at that great wasp*). **c** reinforcing other words denoting size, quantity, etc. (*a great big hole*; *a great many*). **2** important, pre-eminent; worthy or most worthy of consideration (*the great thing is not to get caught*). **3** grand, imposing (*a great occasion*; *the great hall*). **4 a** (esp. of a public or historic figure) distinguished; prominent. **b** (**the Great**) as a title denoting the most important of the name (*Alfred the Great*). **5 a** (of a person) remarkable in ability, character, achievement, etc. (*great men*; *a great thinker*). **b** (of a thing) outstanding of its kind (*the Great Fire*). **6** (foll. by *at*, *on*) competent, skilled, well informed. **7** fully deserving the name of; doing a thing habitually or extensively (*a great reader*; *a great believer in tolerance*; *not a great one for travelling*). **8** (also **greater**) the larger of the name, species, etc. (*great auk*; *greater celandine*). **9** (**Greater**) (of a city etc.) including adjacent urban areas (*Greater Manchester*). **10** *colloq.* **a** very enjoyable or satisfactory; attractive, fine (*had a great time*; *it would be great if we won*). **b** (as an exclamation) fine, very good. **11** (in *comb.*) (in names of family relationships) denoting one degree further removed upwards or downwards (*great-uncle*; *great-great-grandmother*). ● *n.* **1** a great or outstanding person or thing. **2** (in *pl.*) (**Greats**) *colloq.* = LITERAE HUMANIORES. ● *adv. colloq.* excellently, well, successfully. □ **great and small** all classes or types. **the great and the good** often *iron.* distinguished and worthy people. **to a great extent** largely. □ **greatness** *n.* [Old English *grēat*, from West Germanic]

great ape *n.* any of the large apes of the family Pongidae, closely related to humans, including the gorilla, orang-utan, and chimpanzee.

great auk *n.* an extinct flightless auk, *Alca impennis*.

great-aunt *n.* a parent's aunt.

Great Bear *n. Astron.* = URSA MAJOR.

Great Britain *n.* England, Wales, and Scotland.

Great Charter *n.* = MAGNA CARTA.

great circle *n.* any circle on the surface of a sphere which lies in a plane passing through the sphere's centre, and represents the shortest distance between any two points on the circle.

greatcoat /ˈgreɪtkəʊt/ *n.* a long heavy overcoat.

great crested grebe *n.* a large Old World grebe, *Podiceps cristatus*, with a crest and ear-tufts.

Great Dane *n.* **1** a dog of a very large short-haired breed. **2** this breed.

great deal see DEAL[1] *n.* 1.

Great Divide *n.* (prec. by *the*) **1** the boundary between life and death. **2** (usu. **great divide**) *joc.* or *literary* the boundary between two contrasting conditions, cultures, etc.

Greater Bairam *n.* an annual Muslim festival at the end of the Islamic year.

great-grandchild *n.* a grandchild's son or daughter.

great-granddaughter *n.* a grandchild's daughter.

great-grandfather *n.* a grandparent's father.

great-grandmother *n.* a grandparent's mother.

great-grandparent *n.* a grandparent's parent.

great-grandson *n.* a grandchild's son.

great-hearted *adj.* magnanimous; having a noble or generous mind. □ **great-heartedness** *n.*

Great Lakes *n.pl.* (prec. by *the*) the Lakes Superior, Huron, Michigan, Erie, and Ontario, along the boundary of the US and Canada.

greatly /ˈgreɪtli/ *adv.* by a considerable amount; much (*greatly admired*; *greatly superior*).

great majority *n.* (prec. by *the*) **1** much the greater number. **2** *euphem.* the dead (*has joined the great majority*).

great-nephew *n.* a nephew's or niece's son.

great-niece *n.* a nephew's or niece's daughter.

great northern diver *n.* a diving seabird, *Gavia immer*, of the northern hemisphere.

great organ *n.* the chief manual in a large organ, with its related pipes and mechanism.

Great Russian *n. & adj. hist.* ● *n.* **1** a Russian. **2** the Russian language. ● *adj.* Russian.

Great Seal *n.* (in the UK) the seal in the charge of the Lord Chancellor or Lord Keeper used in sealing important state papers.

great tit *n.* a Eurasian songbird, *Parus major*, with black and white head markings.

great toe *n.* esp. *Brit.* the big toe.

great-uncle *n.* a parent's uncle.

great unwashed *n.* (prec. by *the*) *colloq.* the rabble.

Great War *n.* the First World War (1914–18).

great wen *n.* (prec. by *the*) London.

greave /griːv/ *n.* (usu. in *pl.*) a piece of armour for the shin. [Middle English from Old French *greve* 'shin, greave', of unknown origin]

grebe /griːb/ *n.* any diving bird of the family Podicipedidae, with a long neck, lobed toes, and almost no tail. [French *grèbe*, of unknown origin]

grebo /ˈgriːbəʊ/ *n.* (*pl.* **-os**) **1** a British urban youth cult favouring heavy metal and punk rock music, long hair, and an antisocial manner. **2** a member of this. [perhaps from GREASER + *-bo* on the pattern of *dumbo* etc.]

Grecian /ˈgriːʃ(ə)n/ *adj.* (of architecture or facial outline) following Greek models or ideals. [Old French *grecien* or medieval Latin, from Latin *Graecia* 'Greece']

Grecian nose *n.* a straight nose that continues the line of the forehead without a dip.

Grecism var. of GRAECISM.

Grecize var. of GRAECIZE.

Greco- var. of GRAECO-.

greed /griːd/ *n.* intense or excessive desire, esp. for food or wealth. [back-formation from GREEDY]

greedy /ˈgriːdi/ *adj.* (**greedier**, **greediest**) **1** having or showing an excessive appetite for food or drink. **2** wanting wealth or pleasure to excess. **3** (foll. by *for*, or *to* + infin.) very keen or eager; needing intensely (*greedy for affection*; *greedy to learn*). □ **greedily** *adv.* **greediness** *n.* [Old English *grǣdig*, from Germanic]

Greek /griːk/ *n. & adj.* ● *n.* **1 a** a native or national of modern Greece; a person of Greek descent. **b** a native or citizen of any of the ancient states of Greece. **2** the Indo-European language of Greece. ● *adj.* of Greece or its people or language; Hellenic. □ **Greek to me** *colloq.* incomprehensible to me. □ **Greekness** *n.* [Old English *Grēcas* (pl.) via Germanic and Latin *Graecus* 'Greek' from Greek *Graikoi*, according to Aristotle the prehistoric name of the Hellenes]

Greek Church *n.* (also **Greek Orthodox Church**) the Orthodox Church, esp. the national Church of Greece.

Greek cross *n.* a cross with four equal arms.

Greek fire *n. hist.* a combustible composition for igniting enemy ships etc.

green /griːn/ *adj., n., & v.* ● *adj.* **1** of the colour between blue and yellow in the spectrum; coloured like grass, emeralds, etc. **2 a** covered with leaves or grass. **b** mild and without snow (*a green Christmas*). **3** (of fruit etc. or wood) unripe or unseasoned. **4** not dried, smoked, or tanned. **5** inexperienced, naive, gullible. **6 a** (of the complexion) pale, sickly-hued. **b** jealous, envious. **7** young, flourishing. **8** not withered or worn out (*a green old age*). **9** (also **Green**) concerned with or supporting protection of the environment as a political principle. **10** *archaic* fresh; not healed (*a green wound*). ● *n.* **1** a green colour or pigment. **2** green clothes or material (*dressed in green*). **3 a** a piece of public or common grassy land (*village green*). **b** a grassy area used for a special purpose (*putting green*; *bowling green*). **c** *Golf* a putting green. **d** *Golf* a fairway. **4** (in *pl.*) green vegetables. **5** vigour, youth, virility (*in the green*). **6** a green light. **7** a green ball, piece, etc., in a game or sport. **8** (also **Green**) a member or supporter of an environmentalist group or party. **9** (in *pl.*) *Brit. slang* sexual intercourse. **10** *slang* low-grade marijuana. **11** *slang* money. **12** green foliage or growing plants. ● *v.* **1** *tr. & intr.* make or become green. **2** *tr. slang* hoax; take in. □ **green in a person's eye** a sign of gullibility (*do you see any green in my eye?*). □ **greenish** *adj.* **greenly** *adv.* **greenness** /'gri:nnɪs/ *n.* [Old English *grēne* (*adj.* & *n.*), *grēnian* (*v.*), from Germanic: related to GRASS, GROW]

greenback /'gri:nbak/ *n.* **1** *US* a US legal-tender note; the US dollar. **2** any of various green-backed animals.

green belt *n.* an area of open land round a city, on which building is restricted.

Green Beret *n. colloq.* a British or American commando.

greenbottle /'gri:nbɒt(ə)l/ *n.* any fly of the genus *Lucilia*, esp. *L. sericata* which lays eggs in the flesh of sheep.

green card *n.* **1** *Brit.* an international insurance document for motorists. **2** *US* a permit allowing a foreign national to live and work permanently in the US.

green cheese *n.* **1** cheese coloured green with sage. **2** whey cheese. **3** unripened cheese.

Green Cloth *n.* (in full **Board of Green Cloth**) (in the UK) the Lord Steward's department of the Royal Household.

green crop *n. Brit.* a crop used as fodder in a green state rather than as hay etc.

green drake *n. Brit.* the common mayfly.

green earth *n.* a hydrous silicate of potassium, iron, and other metals.

greenery /'gri:n(ə)ri/ *n.* green foliage or growing plants.

green-eyed *adj.* jealous.

green-eyed monster *n.* (prec. by *the*) jealousy.

green fat *n.* part of a turtle, highly regarded by gourmets.

green fee *n. Golf* (*US* also **greens fee**) a charge for playing one round or session on a course.

greenfeed /'gri:nfi:d/ *n. Austral.* & *NZ* forage grown to be fed fresh to livestock.

greenfield /'gri:nfi:ld/ *n.* (*attrib.*) (of a site, in terms of its potential development) having no previous building development on it.

greenfinch /'gri:nfɪn(t)ʃ/ *n.* a finch, *Carduelis chloris*, with green and yellow plumage.

green fingers *n.pl. Brit.* skill in growing plants. □ **green-fingered** *adj.*

greenfly /'gri:nflʌɪ/ *n.* (*pl.* same or **-flies**) *Brit.* a green aphid.

greengage /'gri:ngeɪdʒ/ *n.* a roundish green fine-flavoured variety of plum. [named after Sir W. *Gage* d. 1727]

green goose *n.* a goose killed under four months old and eaten without stuffing.

greengrocer /'gri:ngrəʊsə/ *n. Brit.* a retailer of fruit and vegetables.

greengrocery /'gri:ngrəʊs(ə)ri/ *n.* (*pl.* **-ies**) *Brit.* **1** the business of a greengrocer. **2** goods sold by a greengrocer.

greenhead /'gri:nhɛd/ *n.* **1** any biting fly of the genus *Chrysops*. **2** an Australian ant, *Chalcoponera metallica*, with a painful sting.

greenheart /'gri:nhɑ:t/ *n.* **1** a tropical American evergreen tree, *Ocotea rodiaei* (laurel family). **2** the hard greenish wood of this.

greenhorn /'gri:nhɔ:n/ *n.* an inexperienced or foolish person; a new recruit.

greenhouse /'gri:nhaʊs/ *n.* a light structure with the sides and roof mainly of glass, for rearing delicate plants or hastening the growth of plants.

greenhouse effect *n.* the trapping of the sun's warmth in the lower atmosphere caused by high levels of carbon dioxide and other gases more transparent to incoming solar radiation than to reflected infrared radiation.

greenhouse gas *n.* any of various gases, esp. carbon dioxide, that contribute to the greenhouse effect.

greenie /'gri:ni/ *n. colloq.* a person concerned about environmental issues.

greening[1] /'gri:nɪŋ/ *n.* **1** the process or result of making something green, or becoming green. **2** the planting of trees etc. in urban or desert areas. **3** the process of becoming or making aware of or sensitive to ecological issues.

greening[2] /'gri:nɪŋ/ *n.* a variety of apple that is green when ripe. [probably from Middle Dutch *groeninc* (as GREEN)]

greenkeeper /'gri:nki:pə/ *n.* (*US* also **greenskeeper** /'gri:nzki:pə/) the keeper of a golf course.

green leek *n. Austral.* any of various green or mainly green parrots.

greenlet /'gri:nlɪt/ *n.* = VIREO.

green light *n.* **1** a green light used as a signal to proceed on a road, railway, etc. **2** *colloq.* permission to go ahead with a project.

green linnet *n.* = GREENFINCH.

greenmail /'gri:nmeɪl/ *n. Stock Exch.* the practice of buying enough shares in a company to threaten a takeover, thereby forcing the others to buy them back at a higher price in order to retain control of the business. □ **greenmailer** *n.* [GREEN + BLACKMAIL]

green man *n.* **1** *colloq.* a symbol of a human figure illuminated green at a pedestrian crossing to indicate a time to cross. **2** esp. *hist.* a man dressed up in greenery to represent a wild man of the woods or seasonal fertility. Cf. LITTLE GREEN MAN.

green manure *n.* growing plants ploughed into the soil as fertilizer.

Green Paper *n.* (in the UK) a preliminary report of Government proposals, for discussion.

green pepper *n.* the unripe fruit of *Capsicum annuum*.

green plover *n.* a lapwing.

green pound *n.* the exchange rate for the pound for payments for agricultural produce in the EEC.

green revolution *n.* **1** an increase in crop production, esp. in developing countries, achieved by using artificial fertilizers, pesticides, and high-yield crop varieties. **2** a rise of environmental concern in industrialized countries.

green room *n.* a room in a theatre, studio, etc. in which performers may relax when they are not on stage, on the air, etc.

greensand /'gri:nsand/ *n.* **1** a greenish kind of sandstone, often imperfectly consolidated. **2** a stratum largely formed of this sandstone.

greens fee *US* var. of GREEN FEE.

greenshank /'gri:nʃaŋk/ *n.* a large sandpiper, *Tringa nebularia*, with greenish legs, breeding in northern Eurasia.

green shoots *n.pl.* signs of growth or renewal, esp. of economic recovery.

greensick /'gri:nsɪk/ *adj.* affected with chlorosis. □ **greensickness** *n.*

greenskeeper *US* var. of GREENKEEPER.

green-stick fracture *n.* a bone-fracture, esp. in children, in which one side of the bone is broken and one only bent.

greenstone /'gri:nstəʊn/ *n.* **1** a greenish igneous rock containing feldspar and hornblende. **2** a variety of jade found in New Zealand, used for tools, ornaments, etc.

greenstuff /'gri:nstʌf/ *n.* vegetation; green vegetables.

greensward /'gri:nswɔ:d/ *n. archaic* or *literary* **1** grassy turf. **2** an expanse of this.

green tea *n.* tea made from steam-dried, not fermented, leaves.

green thumb *n.* = GREEN FINGERS.

green turtle *n.* a green-shelled sea turtle, *Chelonia mydas*, highly regarded as food.

green vitriol *n.* = COPPERAS.

greenweed see DYER'S GREENWEED.

Greenwich Mean Time /ˈgrɛnɪtʃ, ˈgrɪnɪdʒ/ *n.* (also **Greenwich Time**) the local time on the meridian of Greenwich, used as an international basis of time-reckoning. [*Greenwich* in London, former site of the Royal Observatory]

greenwood /ˈgriːnwʊd/ *n.* a woodland in summer, esp. as the scene of outlaw life.

green woodpecker *n.* a large green and yellow European woodpecker, *Picus viridis*, with a red crown.

greeny /ˈgriːni/ *adj.* greenish (*greeny yellow*).

greenyard /ˈgriːnjɑːd/ *n. Brit.* an enclosure for stray animals, a pound.

greet[1] /griːt/ *v.tr.* **1** address politely or welcomingly on meeting or arrival. **2** receive or acknowledge in a specified way (*was greeted with derision*). **3** (of a sight, sound, etc.) become apparent to or noticed by. ▫ **greeter** *n.* [Old English *grētan* 'handle, attack, salute', from West Germanic]

greet[2] /griːt/ *v.intr. Sc.* weep. [Old English *grētan*, *grēotan*, of uncertain origin]

greeting /ˈgriːtɪŋ/ *n.* **1** the act or an instance of welcoming or addressing politely. **2** words, gestures, etc., used to greet a person. **3** (often in *pl.*) an expression of goodwill.

greetings card *n.* (*US* **greeting card**) a decorative card sent to convey greetings.

gregarious /grɪˈgɛːrɪəs/ *adj.* **1** fond of company. **2** living in flocks or communities. **3** growing in clusters. ▫ **gregariously** *adv.* **gregariousness** *n.* [Latin *gregarius* from *grex gregis* 'flock']

Gregorian calendar /grɪˈgɔːrɪən/ *n.* the calendar introduced in 1582 by Pope Gregory XIII, as a modification of the Julian calendar.

Gregorian chant /grɪˈgɔːrɪən/ *n.* plainsong church music, named after Pope Gregory I.

Gregorian telescope /grɪˈgɔːrɪən/ *n.* a reflecting telescope in which light reflected from a concave elliptical secondary mirror passes through a hole in the primary mirror. [named after J. *Gregory*, Scots mathematician (d. 1675), who devised it]

Gregory powder /ˈgrɛg(ə)ri/ *n. hist.* a compound powder of rhubarb, magnesia, and ginger, used as a laxative. [named after J. *Gregory*, Scots physician d. 1822]

gremlin /ˈgrɛmlɪn/ *n. colloq.* **1** an imaginary mischievous sprite regarded as responsible for mechanical faults, esp. in aircraft. **2** any similar cause of trouble. [20th c.: origin unknown, but probably suggested by *goblin*]

grenade /grəˈneɪd/ *n.* **1** a small bomb thrown by hand (in full **hand grenade**) or launched mechanically. **2** a glass receptacle containing chemicals which disperse on impact, for testing drains, extinguishing fires, etc. [French, from Old French *grenate* and Spanish *granada* POMEGRANATE]

grenadier /grɛnəˈdɪə/ *n.* **1 a** *Brit.* (**Grenadiers** or **Grenadier Guards**) the first regiment of the royal household infantry. **b** *hist.* a soldier armed with grenades. **2** any deep-sea fish of the family Macrouridae, with a long tapering body and pointed tail, and secreting luminous bacteria when disturbed. [French (as GRENADE)]

grenadilla /grɛnəˈdɪlə/ *n.* (also **granadilla** /gran-/) a passion fruit. [Spanish *granadilla*, diminutive of *granada* POMEGRANATE]

grenadine[1] /ˈgrɛnədiːn/ *n.* a French cordial syrup of pomegranates. [French from *grenade*: see GRENADE]

grenadine[2] /ˈgrɛnədiːn/ *n.* a dress fabric of loosely woven silk or silk and wool. [French, earlier *grenade* 'grained silk' from *grenu* 'grained']

Gresham's law /ˈgrɛʃ(ə)mz/ *n.* the tendency for money of lower intrinsic value to circulate more freely than money of higher intrinsic and equal nominal value. [named after Sir T. *Gresham*, English financier d. 1579]

gressorial /grɛˈsɔːrɪəl/ *adj. Zool.* **1** walking. **2** adapted for walking. [modern Latin *gressorius* from Latin *gradi gress-* 'walk']

grew *past* of GROW.

grey /greɪ/ *adj., n., & v.* (*US* **gray**) ● *adj.* **1** of a colour intermediate between black and white, as of ashes or lead. **2 a** (of the weather etc.) dull, dismal; heavily overcast. **b** bleak, depressing; (of a person) depressed. **3 a** (of hair) turning white with age etc. **b** (of a person) having grey hair. **4** anonymous, nondescript, unidentifiable. ● *n.* **1 a** a grey colour or pigment. **b** grey clothes or material (*dressed in grey*). **2** a cold sunless light. **3** a grey or white horse. ● *v.tr. & intr.* make or become grey. ▫ **greyish** *adj.* **greyly** *adv.* **greyness** *n.* [Old English *grǣg*, from Germanic]

grey area *n.* **1** an ill-defined situation, field, etc., not readily conforming to a category or to an existing set of rules. **2** *Brit.* an area in economic decline.

greybeard /ˈgreɪbɪəd/ *n.* (*US* **graybeard**) **1** an old man. **2** a large stoneware jug for spirits. **3** *dial.* = OLD MAN'S BEARD.

grey economy *n.* the part of the economy conducted by means of informal commercial activity and not accounted for in official statistics.

grey eminence *n.* = ÉMINENCE GRISE.

Grey Friar *n.* a Franciscan friar. [from the colour of the Order's habit]

grey goose *n.* any goose of the genus *Anser*, with mainly grey plumage, esp. the greylag.

greyhen /ˈgreɪhɛn/ *n.* the female of the black grouse (cf. BLACKCOCK).

greyhound /ˈgreɪhaʊnd/ *n.* **1** a dog of a tall slender breed having keen sight and capable of high speed, used in racing and coursing. **2** this breed. [Old English *grīghund* from the Germanic base also of Old Norse *grey* 'bitch' + *hund* 'dog', related to HOUND]

greylag /ˈgreɪlag/ *n.* (in full **greylag goose**) a wild goose, *Anser anser*, native to Europe. [18th c.: probably GREY + obsolete dialect *lag* 'goose']

grey market *n.* unofficial trade esp. in unissued shares or in controlled or scarce goods.

grey matter *n.* **1** the darker tissues of the brain and spinal cord consisting of nerve cell bodies and branching dendrites (cf. WHITE MATTER). **2** *colloq.* intelligence.

grey mullet *n.* any mullet of the family Mugilidae, usu. found near coasts and having a thick body and blunt head, and often used as food.

grey seal *n.* a common large seal, *Halichoerus grypus*, of the N. Atlantic.

grey squirrel *n.* an American squirrel, *Sciurus carolinensis*, introduced in Europe in the 19th c.

greywacke /ˈgreɪwakə/ *n.* (*US* **graywacke**) *Geol.* a dark coarse-grained sandstone, usu. with an admixture of clay. [Anglicized from German *Grauwacke*, from *grau* 'grey': see WACKE]

grid /grɪd/ *n.* **1** a framework of spaced parallel bars; a grating. **2** a system of numbered squares printed on a map and forming the basis of map references. **3** a network of lines, electric power connections, gas-supply lines, etc. **4** a pattern of lines marking the starting places on a motor racing track. **5** the wire network between the filament and the anode of a thermionic valve etc. **6** an arrangement of town streets in a rectangular pattern. ▫ **gridded** *adj.* [back-formation from GRIDIRON]

grid bias *n. Electr.* a fixed voltage applied between the cathode and the control grid of a thermionic valve which determines its operating conditions.

griddle /ˈgrɪd(ə)l/ *n. & v.* ● *n.* **1** a circular iron plate placed over a fire or otherwise heated for baking, toasting, etc. **2** *Brit.* a miner's wire-bottomed sieve. ● *v.tr.* **1** cook with a griddle; grill. **2** sieve with a griddle. [Middle English from Old French *gredil*, *gridil* 'gridiron', ultimately from Latin *craticula*, diminutive of *cratis* 'hurdle'; cf. GRATE[2], GRILL[1]]

gridiron /ˈgrɪdʌɪən/ *n.* **1** a cooking utensil of metal bars for broiling or grilling. **2** a frame of parallel beams for supporting a ship in dock. **3** an American football field (with parallel lines marking out the area of play). **4** *Theatr.* a plank structure over a stage supporting the mechanism for drop curtains etc. **5** = GRID 6. [Middle English *gredire*, variant of *gredil* GRIDDLE, later associated with IRON]

gridlock /ˈgrɪdlɒk/ *n.* **1** a traffic jam affecting a whole network of intersecting streets. **2** = DEADLOCK *n.* 1. □ **gridlocked** *adj.*

grief /gri:f/ *n.* **1** deep or intense sorrow or mourning. **2** the cause of this. **3** *colloq.* trouble; annoyance. □ **come to grief** meet with disaster; fail. **good** (or **great) grief!** an exclamation of surprise, alarm, etc. [Middle English from Anglo-French *gref*, Old French *grief* from *grever* GRIEVE[1]]

grievance /ˈgri:v(ə)ns/ *n.* a real or fancied cause for complaint. [Middle English, = injury, from Old French *grevance* (as GRIEF)]

grieve[1] /gri:v/ *v.* **1** *tr.* cause grief or great distress to. **2** *intr.* suffer grief, esp. at another's death. □ **griever** *n.* [Middle English from Old French *grever*, ultimately via Latin *gravare* from *gravis* 'heavy']

grieve[2] /gri:v/ *n. Sc.* a farm bailiff; an overseer. [Old English *grǣfa*: cf. REEVE[1]]

grievous /ˈgri:vəs/ *adj.* **1** (of pain etc.) severe. **2** causing grief or suffering. **3** injurious. **4** flagrant, heinous. □ **grievously** *adv.* **grievousness** *n.* [Middle English from Old French *grevos* (as GRIEVE[1])]

grievous bodily harm *n.* serious mental or physical injury inflicted intentionally on a person.

griffin /ˈgrɪfɪn/ *n.* (also **gryphon** /-f(ə)n/) a fabulous creature with an eagle's head and wings and a lion's body. [Middle English from Old French *grifoun*, ultimately via Late Latin *gryphus* and Latin *gryps* from Greek *grups*]

griffon /ˈgrɪf(ə)n/ *n.* **1 a** a dog of a small terrier-like breed with coarse or smooth hair. **b** this breed. **2** (in full **griffon vulture**) a large vulture, *Gyps fulvus* of Eurasia and N. Africa. [French (in sense 1), or variant of GRIFFIN]

grift /grɪft/ *n.* & *v. US slang* ● *n.* = GRAFT[2] *n.* ● *v.intr.* = GRAFT[2] *v.* □ **grifter** *n.* [perhaps alteration of GRAFT[2]]

grig /grɪg/ *n.* **1** a small eel. **2** a grasshopper or cricket. □ **merry** (or **lively) as a grig** full of fun; extravagantly lively. [Middle English, originally = dwarf: origin unknown]

Grignard reagent /ˈgri:njɑ:, -jɑ:d/ *n. Chem.* any of a class of organic magnesium compounds used in organic syntheses. [named after V. *Grignard*, French organic chemist d. 1935]

grike /grʌɪk/ *n.* (also **gryke**) *Geol.* a fissure between clints in limestone, enlarged through erosion by rainwater. [18th c. northern dialect: origin unknown]

grill[1] /grɪl/ *n.* & *v.* ● *n.* **1 a** *Brit.* a device on a cooker for radiating heat downwards. **b** = GRIDIRON 1. **2** a dish of food cooked on a grill. **3** (in full **grill room**) a restaurant serving grilled food. ● *v.* **1** *tr.* & *intr. Brit.* cook or be cooked under a grill or on a gridiron. **2** *tr.* & *intr.* subject or be subjected to extreme heat, esp. from the sun. **3** *tr.* subject to severe questioning or interrogation. □ **griller** *n.* **grilling** *n.* (in sense 3 of *v.*). [French *gril* (*n.*), *griller* (*v.*), from Old French forms of GRILLE]

grill[2] var. of GRILLE.

grillage /ˈgrɪlɪdʒ/ *n.* a heavy framework of cross-timbering or metal beams forming a foundation for building on difficult ground. [French (as GRILLE)]

grille /grɪl/ *n.* (also **grill**) **1** a grating or latticed screen, used as a partition or to allow discreet vision. **2** a metal grid, esp. for ventilation (*radiator grille*). [French, via Old French *graïlle* from medieval Latin *graticula*, *craticula*: see GRIDDLE]

grill room see GRILL[1] *n.* 3.

grilse /grɪls/ *n.* a salmon that has returned to fresh water after a single winter at sea. [Middle English: origin unknown]

grim /grɪm/ *adj.* (**grimmer**, **grimmest**) **1** of a stern or forbidding appearance. **2** harsh, merciless, severe. **3** ghastly, joyless, sinister (*has a grim truth in it*). **4** unpleasant, unattractive. □ **like grim death** with great determination. □ **grimly** *adv.* **grimness** *n.* [Old English from Germanic]

grimace /grɪˈmeɪs, ˈgrɪməs/ *n.* & *v.* ● *n.* a distortion of the face made in disgust etc. or to amuse. ● *v.intr.* make a grimace. □ **grimacer** *n.* [French from Spanish *grimazo*, from *grima* 'fright']

grimalkin /grɪˈmalkɪn, -ˈmɔ:l-/ *n. archaic* **1** an old she-cat. **2** a spiteful old woman. [GREY + *Malkin*, diminutive of the name *Matilda*]

grime /grʌɪm/ *n.* & *v.* ● *n.* soot or dirt ingrained in a surface, esp. of buildings or the skin. ● *v.tr.* blacken with grime; befoul. [originally as a verb: from Middle Low German & Middle Dutch]

grimy /ˈgrʌɪmi/ *adj.* (**grimier**, **grimiest**) covered with grime; dirty. □ **grimily** *adv.* **griminess** *n.*

grin /grɪn/ *v.* & *n.* ● *v.* (**grinned**, **grinning**) **1** *intr.* smile broadly, esp. in an unrestrained, forced, or stupid manner. **2** *tr.* express by grinning (*grinned his satisfaction*). ● *n.* the act or action of grinning. □ **grin and bear it** take pain or misfortune stoically. □ **grinner** *n.* **grinningly** *adv.* [Old English *grennian*, from Germanic]

grind /grʌɪnd/ *v.* & *n.* ● *v.* (*past* and *past part.* **ground** /graʊnd/) **1 a** *tr.* reduce to small particles or powder by crushing esp. by passing through a mill. **b** *intr.* (of a mill, machine, etc.) move with a crushing action. **2 a** *tr.* reduce, sharpen, or smooth by friction. **b** *tr.* & *intr.* rub or rub together gratingly (*grind one's teeth*). **3** *tr.* (often foll. by *down*) oppress, wear down; harass with exactions (*grinding poverty*). **4** *intr.* **a** (often foll. by *away*) work or study hard. **b** (foll. by *out*) produce with effort (*grinding out verses*). **c** (foll. by *on*) (of a sound) continue gratingly or monotonously. **5** *tr.* turn the handle of (a barrel organ etc.). **6** *intr. slang* (of a dancer) rotate the hips. **7** *intr. Brit. coarse slang* have sexual intercourse. ● *n.* **1** the act or an instance of grinding. **2** *colloq.* hard dull work; a laborious task (*the daily grind*). **3** the size of ground particles. **4** *slang* a dancer's rotary movement of the hips. **5** *Brit. coarse slang* an act of sexual intercourse. □ **grind to a halt** stop laboriously. □ **grindingly** *adv.* [Old English *grindan*, of unknown origin]

grinder /ˈgrʌɪndə/ *n.* **1** a person or thing that grinds, esp. a machine (often in *comb.*: *coffee grinder*; *organ-grinder*). **2** a molar tooth.

grindstone /ˈgrʌɪn(d)stəʊn/ *n.* **1** a thick revolving disc used for grinding, sharpening, and polishing. **2** a kind of stone used for this. □ **keep one's nose to the grindstone** work hard and continuously.

gringo /ˈgrɪŋgəʊ/ *n.* (*pl.* **-os**) *colloq.* a foreigner, esp. a British or N. American person, in a Spanish-speaking country. [Spanish, = gibberish]

grip /grɪp/ *v.* & *n.* ● *v.* (**gripped**, **gripping**) **1 a** *tr.* grasp tightly; take a firm hold of. **b** *intr.* take a firm hold, esp. by friction. **2** *tr.* (of a feeling or emotion) deeply affect (a person) (*was gripped by fear*). **3** *tr.* compel the attention or interest of (*a gripping story*). ● *n.* **1 a** a firm hold; a tight grasp or clasp. **b** a manner of grasping or holding. **2** the power of holding attention. **3 a** mental or intellectual understanding or mastery. **b** effective control of a situation or one's behaviour etc. (*lose one's grip*). **4 a** a part of a machine that grips or holds something. **b** a part or attachment by which a tool, implement, weapon, etc., is held in the hand. **5** = HAIRGRIP. **6** a travelling bag. **7** an assistant in a theatre, film studio, etc. **8** *Austral. slang* a job or occupation. □ **come** (or **get**) **to grips with** approach purposefully; begin to deal with or understand. **get a grip 1** (foll. by *on*) = *come to grips with*. **2** (in full **get a grip on oneself**) control or discipline oneself. **in the grip of**

dominated or affected by (esp. an adverse circumstance or unpleasant sensation). □ **gripper** *n.* **grippingly** *adv.* **grippy** *adj.* [Old English *gripe*, *gripa* 'handful' (as GRIPE)]

gripe /grʌɪp/ *v.* & *n.* ● *v.* **1** *intr. colloq.* complain, esp. peevishly. **2** *tr.* affect with gastric or intestinal pain. **3** *tr. archaic* clutch, grip. **4** *Naut.* **a** *tr.* secure with gripes. **b** *intr.* turn to face the wind in spite of the helm. ● *n.* **1** (usu. in *pl.*) gastric or intestinal pain; colic. **2** *colloq.* **a** a complaint. **b** the act of griping. **3** a grip or clutch. **4** (in *pl.*) *Naut.* lashings securing a boat in its place. □ **griper** *n.* **gripingly** *adv.* [Old English *grīpan* from Germanic: related to GROPE]

gripe water *n. Brit. propr.* a carminative solution to relieve colic and stomach ailments in infants.

grippe /grɪp/ *n. archaic* or *colloq.* influenza. [French from *gripper* 'seize']

grisaille /grɪ'zeɪl, -li/ *n.* **1** a method of painting in grey monochrome, often to imitate sculpture. **2** a painting or stained-glass window of this kind. [French, from *gris* 'grey']

griseofulvin /ˌgrɪzɪə(ʊ)'fʊlvɪn/ *n.* an antibiotic used against fungal infections of the hair and skin. [modern Latin (*Penicillium*) *griseofulvum* (a micro-organism from which it is obtained), from medieval Latin *griseus* 'grey' + Latin *fulvus* 'reddish yellow']

grisette /grɪ'zɛt/ *n.* a young working-class Frenchwoman. [originally a grey dress material worn by such women: French, from *gris* 'grey']

grisly /'grɪzli/ *adj.* (**grislier**, **grisliest**) causing horror, disgust, or fear. □ **grisliness** *n.* [Old English *grislic* 'terrifying']

grison /'grɪz(ə)n, 'grʌɪs(ə)n/ *n.* any weasel-like mammal of the genus *Galictis*, with dark fur and a white stripe across the forehead. [French, apparently from *grison* 'grey']

grist /grɪst/ *n.* **1** corn to grind. **2** malt crushed for brewing. □ **grist to the** (or **a person's**) **mill** a source of profit or advantage. [Old English from Germanic: related to GRIND]

gristle /'grɪs(ə)l/ *n.* tough cartilaginous tissue, esp. as occurring in meat. □ **gristly** /-sli/ *adj.* [Old English]

grit /grɪt/ *n.* & *v.* ● *n.* **1** particles of stone or sand, esp. as causing discomfort, clogging machinery, etc. **2** coarse sandstone. **3** *colloq.* pluck, endurance; strength of character. ● *v.* (**gritted**, **gritting**) **1** *tr.* spread grit on (icy roads etc.). **2** *tr.* clench (the teeth). **3** *intr.* make or move with a grating sound. □ **gritter** *n.* **gritty** *adj.* (**grittier**, **grittiest**). **grittily** *adv.* **grittiness** *n.* [Old English *grēot* from Germanic: related to GROATS]

grits /grɪts/ *n.pl.* **1** (treated as *sing.* or *pl.*) esp. *US* **a** coarsely ground grain, esp. corn. **b** = HOMINY. **2** oats that have been husked but not ground (or only coarsely). [Old English *grytt(e)*: related to GROATS]

grizzle /'grɪz(ə)l/ *v.intr. Brit. colloq.* **1** (esp. of a child) cry fretfully. **2** complain whiningly. □ **grizzler** *n.* **grizzly** *adj.* [18th c.: origin unknown]

grizzled /'grɪz(ə)ld/ *adj.* having, or streaked with, grey hair. [earlier *grizzle* 'grey' from Old French *grisel*, from *gris* 'grey']

grizzly /'grɪzli/ *adj.* & *n.* ● *adj.* (**grizzlier**, **grizzliest**) grey, greyish, grey-haired. ● *n.* (*pl.* **-ies**) (in full **grizzly bear**) a large variety of brown bear, found in N. America.

groan /grəʊn/ *v.* & *n.* ● *v.* **1 a** *intr.* make a deep sound expressing pain, grief, or disapproval. **b** *tr.* utter with groans. **2** *intr.* complain inarticulately. **3** *intr.* (usu. foll. by *under*, *beneath*, *with*) be loaded or oppressed. ● *n.* the sound made in groaning. □ **groan inwardly** be distressed. □ **groaner** *n.* **groaningly** *adv.* [Old English *grānian* from Germanic: related to GRIN]

groat /grəʊt/ *n. hist.* **1** a silver coin worth four old pence. **2** *archaic* a small sum (*don't care a groat*). [Middle English from Middle Dutch *groot*, originally = great, i.e. thick (penny): cf. GROSCHEN]

groats /grəʊts/ *n.pl.* hulled or crushed grain, esp. oats. [Old English *grotan* (pl.): cf. *grot* 'fragment', *grēot* GRIT, *grytt* 'bran']

grocer /'grəʊsə/ *n.* a dealer in food and household provisions. [Middle English and Anglo-French *grosser*, originally a person who sells in the gross, via Old French *grossier* from medieval Latin *grossarius* (as GROSS)]

grocery /'grəʊs(ə)ri/ *n.* (*pl.* **-ies**) **1** a grocer's trade or shop. **2** (in *pl.*) provisions, esp. food, sold by a grocer.

grockle /'grɒk(ə)l/ *n. Brit. dial.* & *slang* a visitor or holidaymaker, esp. from the North or Midlands to SW England. [invented word, orig. a character in a children's comic]

grog /grɒg/ *n.* **1** a drink of spirit (originally rum) and water. **2** *Austral.* & *NZ colloq.* alcoholic liquor, esp. beer. [said to be from 'Old *Grog*', the reputed nickname (from his GROGRAM cloak) of Admiral Vernon, who in 1740 first had diluted instead of neat rum served out to sailors]

groggy /'grɒgi/ *adj.* (**groggier**, **groggiest**) muzzy or unsteady from being semi-conscious, hung over, etc. □ **groggily** *adv.* **grogginess** *n.*

grogram /'grɒgrəm/ *n.* a coarse fabric of silk, or of mohair and wool, or of a mixture of all these, often stiffened with gum. [French *gros grain* 'coarse grain' (as GROSS, GRAIN)]

groin[1] /grɔɪn/ *n.* & *v.* ● *n.* **1** the depression between the belly and the thigh. **2** *Archit.* **a** an edge formed by intersecting vaults. **b** an arch supporting a vault. ● *v.tr. Archit.* build with groins. [Middle English *grynde*, perhaps from Old English *grynde* 'depression']

groin[2] *US* var. of GROYNE.

grommet /'grɒmɪt/ *n.* **1** a metal, plastic, or rubber eyelet placed in a hole to protect or insulate a rope or cable etc. passed through it. **2** a tube surgically implanted in the eardrum to make a communication with the middle ear. [earlier 'a ring or wreath of rope, used as a fastening': obsolete French *grommette* from *gourmer* 'to curb', of unknown origin]

gromwell /'grɒmw(ə)l/ *n.* any of various plants of the genus *Lithospermum*, with hard seeds formerly used in medicine. [Middle English from Old French *gromil*, probably from a medieval Latin phrase meaning 'crane's millet']

groom /gru:m/ *n.* & *v.* ● *n.* **1** a person employed to take care of horses. **2** = BRIDEGROOM. **3** *Brit. Mil.* any of certain officers of the Royal Household. ● *v.tr.* **1 a** tend to, esp. brush the coat of (a horse, dog, etc). **b** (of an animal) clean and comb the fur of (another) (also refl.). **2 a** give a neat or tidy appearance to (a person etc.). **b** carefully attend to (a lawn, a ski slope, etc.). **3** prepare or train (a person) for a particular purpose or activity (*was groomed for the top job*). [originally = boy: Middle English, origin unknown]

groove /gru:v/ *n.* & *v.* ● *n.* **1 a** a channel or hollow, esp. one made to guide motion or receive a corresponding ridge. **b** a spiral track cut in a gramophone record. **2 a** an established routine or habit. **b** a monotonous routine, a rut. **3** *slang* an established rhythmic pattern (*got a groove going*). ● *v.* **1** *tr.* make a groove or grooves in. **2** *intr. slang* **a** play music (esp. jazz or dance music) rhythmically. **b** dance or move rhythmically to music. **c** enjoy oneself. □ **in the groove** *slang* **1** doing or performing well. **2** fashionable. [Middle English, = mine shaft, via obsolete Dutch *groeve* 'furrow' from Germanic]

groovy /'gru:vi/ *adj.* (**groovier**, **grooviest**) **1** *slang* (often *joc.*) fashionable and exciting; enjoyable, excellent. **2** of or like a groove. □ **groovily** *adv.* **grooviness** *n.*

grope /grəʊp/ *v.* & *n.* ● *v.* **1** *intr.* (usu. foll. by *for*) feel about or search blindly or uncertainly with the hands. **2** *intr.* (foll. by *for*, *after*) search mentally (*was groping for the answer*). **3** *tr.* feel (one's way) towards something. **4** *tr. slang* fondle clumsily, or in an unwelcome advance, for sexual pleasure. ● *n.* the process or an instance of groping. □ **groper** *n.* **gropingly** *adv.* [Old English *grāpian*, from Germanic]

groper /'grəʊpə/ *n.* esp. *Austral.* & *NZ* = GROUPER. [variant of GROUPER]

grosbeak /'grəʊsbi:k/ *n.* any of various finches and cardinals having stout conical bills and usu. brightly coloured plumage. [French *grosbec*, from *gros* as GROSS + *bec* BEAK[1]]

groschen /'grəʊʃ(ə)n, 'grɒʃ(ə)n/ *n.* **1** an Austrian coin and monetary unit equal to one-hundredth of a schilling. **2** *colloq.* a German 10-pfennig piece. **3** *hist.* a small German silver coin. [German via Middle High German *gros, grosse* from medieval Latin (*denarius*) *grossus* 'thick (penny)': cf. GROAT]

grosgrain /'grəʊgreɪn/ *n.* a corded fabric of silk etc. [French, = coarse grain (as GROSS, GRAIN)]

gros point /grəʊ 'pwã/ *n.* cross stitch embroidery on canvas. [French, = large stitch (as GROSS, POINT)]

gross /grəʊs/ *adj., v., & n.* ● *adj.* **1** overfed, bloated; repulsively fat. **2** (of a person, manners, or morals) noticeably coarse, unrefined, or indecent. **3** *slang* very unpleasant, repulsive, disgusting. **4** flagrant; conspicuously wrong (*gross negligence*). **5** total; without deductions; not net (*gross tonnage*; *gross income*). **6 a** luxuriant, rank. **b** thick, solid, dense. **7** (of the senses etc.) dull; lacking sensitivity. ● *v.tr.* produce or earn as gross profit or income. ● *n.* (*pl.* same) an amount equal to twelve dozen. □ **by the gross** in large quantities; wholesale. **gross out** *N. Amer. slang* disgust, esp. by repulsive or obscene behaviour. **gross up** increase (a net amount) to its value before deductions. □ **grossly** *adv.* **grossness** *n.* [Middle English via Old French *gros grosse* 'large' from Late Latin *grossus*: the noun from French *grosse douzaine* 'large dozen']

gross domestic product *n.* the total value of goods produced and services provided in a country in one year.

gross national product *n.* the gross domestic product plus the total of net income from abroad.

gross ton see TON[1] 5a.

grot /grɒt/ *n. & adj. Brit. slang* ● *n.* rubbish, junk. ● *adj.* dirty. [back-formation from GROTTY]

grotesque /grə(ʊ)'tɛsk/ *adj. & n.* ● *adj.* **1** comically or repulsively distorted; monstrous, unnatural. **2** incongruous, ludicrous, absurd. ● *n.* **1** a decorative form interweaving human and animal features. **2** a comically distorted figure or design. **3** *Printing* a family of sans serif typefaces. □ **grotesquely** *adv.* **grotesqueness** *n.* **grotesquerie** /-'tɛsk(ə)ri/ *n.* [earlier *crotesque*, via French from Italian *grottesca* 'grotto-like' (painting etc.), fem. of *grottesco* (as GROTTO, -ESQUE)]

grotto /'grɒtəʊ/ *n.* (*pl.* **-oes** or **-os**) **1** a small picturesque cave. **2** an artificial ornamental cave, e.g. in a park or large garden. □ **grottoed** *adj.* [Italian *grotta*, ultimately via Latin *crypta* from Greek *kruptē* CRYPT]

grotty /'grɒti/ *adj.* (**grottier**, **grottiest**) *Brit. slang* unpleasant, dirty, shabby, unattractive. □ **grottiness** *n.* [shortening of GROTESQUE + -Y[1]]

grouch /graʊtʃ/ *v. & n. colloq.* ● *v.intr.* grumble. ● *n.* **1** a discontented or grumpy person. **2** a fit of grumbling or the sulks. **3** a cause of discontent. [variant of *grutch*: see GRUDGE]

grouchy /'graʊtʃi/ *adj.* (**grouchier**, **grouchiest**) *colloq.* discontented, grumpy. □ **grouchily** *adv.* **grouchiness** *n.*

ground[1] /graʊnd/ *n. & v.* ● *n.* **1 a** the surface of the earth, esp. as contrasted with the air around it. **b** a part of this qualified in some way (*low ground*). **2** the substance of the earth's surface; soil, earth (*stony ground*; *dug deep into the ground*). **3 a** a limited or defined area (*the ground beyond the farm*). **b** the extent of activity etc. achieved or of a subject dealt with (*the book covers a lot of ground*). **4** (often in *pl.*) a foundation, motive, or reason (*there is ground for concern*; *there are grounds for believing*; *excused on the grounds of ill health*). **5** an area of a special kind or designated for special use (often in *comb.*: *cricket ground*; *fishing grounds*). **6** (in *pl.*) an area of usu. enclosed land attached to a house etc. **7** an area or basis for consideration, agreement, etc. (*common ground*; *on firm ground*). **8 a** (in painting) the prepared surface giving the predominant colour or tone. **b** (in embroidery, ceramics, etc.) the undecorated surface. **9** (in full **ground bass**) *Mus.* a short theme in the bass constantly repeated with the upper parts of the music varied. **10** (in *pl.*) solid particles, esp. of coffee, forming a residue. **11** *Electr.* = EARTH *n.* 4. **12** the bottom of the sea (*the ship touched ground*). **13** *Brit.* the floor of a room etc. **14** a piece of wood fixed to a wall as a base for boards, plaster, or joinery. **15** (*attrib.*) **a** (of animals) living on or in the ground; (of fish) living at the bottom of water; (of plants) dwarfish or trailing. **b** relating to or concerned with the ground (*ground staff*). ● *v.* **1** *tr.* **a** refuse authority for (a pilot or an aircraft) to fly. **b** *colloq.* temporarily withdraw permission for (usu. a teenager) to participate socially outside the home. **2 a** *tr.* run (a ship) aground; strand. **b** *intr.* (of a ship) run aground. **3** *tr.* (foll. by *in*) instruct thoroughly (in a subject). **4** *tr.* (often as **grounded** *adj.*) (foll. by *on*) base (a principle, conclusion, etc.) on. **5** *tr. Electr.* = EARTH *v.* 3. **6** *intr.* alight on the ground. **7** *tr.* place or lay (esp. weapons) on the ground. □ **break new** (or **fresh**) **ground** treat a subject previously not dealt with. **cut the ground from under a person's feet** anticipate and pre-empt a person's arguments, plans, etc. **down to the ground** *Brit. colloq.* thoroughly; in every respect. **fall to the ground** (of a plan etc.) fail. **gain** (or **make**) **ground 1** advance steadily; make progress. **2** (foll. by *on*) catch (a person) up. **get in on the ground floor** become part of an enterprise in its early stages. **get off the ground** *colloq.* make a successful start. **give** (or **lose**) **ground 1** retreat, decline. **2** lose the advantage or one's position in an argument, contest, etc. **go to ground 1** (of a fox etc.) enter its earth or burrow etc. **2** (of a person) become inaccessible for a prolonged period. **hold one's ground** not retreat or give way. **on the ground** at the point of production or operation; in practical conditions. **on one's own ground** on one's own territory or subject; on one's own terms. **thin on the ground** not numerous. **work** (or **run** etc.) **oneself into the ground** *colloq.* work etc. to the point of exhaustion. [Old English *grund*, from Germanic]

ground[2] /graʊnd/ *past* and *past part.* of GRIND. ● *adj.* **1 a** reduced to fine particles or powder by crushing (*freshly ground pepper*). **b** (of meat) finely minced. **2** shaped, roughened, or polished by grinding. □ **ground down** exhausted, worn down.

groundage /'graʊndɪdʒ/ *n. Brit.* duty levied on a ship entering a port or lying on a shore.

ground ash *n.* **1** an ash sapling. **2** a stick made from this.

groundbait /'graʊn(d)beɪt/ *n.* bait thrown to the bottom of a fishing ground.

ground bass see GROUND[1] *n.* 9.

ground control *n.* the personnel and equipment that monitor and direct the landing etc. of aircraft or spacecraft.

ground cover *n.* plants covering the surface of the earth, esp. low-growing spreading plants that inhibit the growth of weeds.

ground crew *n.* the people who maintain and service an aircraft on the ground.

ground elder *n.* an umbelliferous plant, *Aegopodium podagraria*, with spreading underground stems, common as a weed.

grounder /'graʊndə/ *n.* (esp. in baseball) a ball that is hit or passed along the ground.

ground floor *n.* the floor of a building at ground level.

ground frost *n.* frost on the surface of the ground or in the top layer of soil.

ground glass *n.* **1** glass made non-transparent by grinding etc. (hyphenated when *attrib.*: *ground-glass screen*). **2** glass ground to a powder.

groundhog /'graʊndhɒg/ *n.* = WOODCHUCK.

grounding /ˈgraʊndɪŋ/ *n.* basic training or instruction in a subject.

ground ivy *n.* a common Eurasian hedge-plant, *Glechoma hederacea*, with bluish-purple flowers.

groundless /ˈgraʊn(d)lɪs/ *adj.* without motive or foundation. □ **groundlessly** *adv.* **groundlessness** *n.* [Old English *grundlēas* (as GROUND[1], -LESS)]

ground level *n.* **1** the level of the ground; the ground floor. **2** *Physics* = GROUND STATE.

groundling /ˈgraʊn(d)lɪŋ/ *n.* **1 a** a creeping or dwarf plant. **b** a fish that lives at the bottom of lakes etc., esp. a gudgeon or a loach. **2** a person on the ground as opposed to one in an aircraft. **3** a spectator or reader of inferior taste (with reference to Shakespeare's *Hamlet* III. ii. 11).

groundnut /ˈgraʊn(d)nʌt/ *n.* **1** *Brit.* = PEANUT 1, 2. **2 a** a N. American wild bean. **b** its edible tuber.

ground plan *n.* **1** the plan of a building at ground level. **2** the general outline of a scheme.

ground rent *n.* esp. *Brit.* rent for land leased for building.

ground rule *n.* a basic principle.

groundsel /ˈgraʊn(d)s(ə)l/ *n.* any plant of the genus *Senecio* (daisy family), with yellow rayless flowers, esp. *S. vulgaris*, common as a weed. [Old English *grundeswylige*, *gundæswelgiæ* (perhaps = pus-absorber, from *gund* 'pus', with reference to use for poultices)]

groundsheet /ˈgraʊn(d)ʃiːt/ *n.* a waterproof sheet for spreading on the ground, esp. in a tent.

groundskeeper /ˈgraʊn(d)zkiːpə/ *n. US* = GROUNDSMAN.

groundsman /ˈgraʊn(d)zmən/ *n.* (*pl.* **-men**) *Brit.* a person who maintains a sports ground.

ground speed *n.* an aircraft's speed relative to the ground.

ground squirrel *n.* any ground-dwelling rodent resembling a squirrel, esp. one of the genus *Spermophilus*.

ground staff *n.* **1** the non-flying personnel of an airport or airbase. **2** the staff employed to maintain a sports ground.

ground state *n. Physics* the lowest energy state of an atom etc.

ground stroke *n. Tennis* a stroke played near the ground after the ball has bounced.

groundswell /ˈgraʊn(d)swɛl/ *n.* **1** a heavy sea caused by a distant or past storm or an earthquake. **2** an increasingly forceful presence (esp. of public opinion).

groundwater /ˈgraʊn(d)wɔːtə/ *n.* water found in soil or in pores, crevices, etc., in rock.

groundwork /ˈgraʊn(d)wəːk/ *n.* **1** preliminary or basic work. **2** a foundation or basis.

ground zero *n.* the point on the ground under an exploding (usu. nuclear) bomb.

group /gruːp/ *n.* & *v.* ● *n.* **1** a number of persons or things located close together, or considered or classed together. **2** (*attrib.*) concerning or done by a group (*a group photograph*; *group sex*). **3** a number of people working together or sharing beliefs, e.g. part of a political party. **4** a number of commercial companies under common ownership. **5** an ensemble playing popular music. **6** a division of an air force or air-fleet. **7** *Math.* a set of elements, together with an associative binary operation, which contains an inverse for each element and an identity element. **8** *Chem.* **a** a set of ions or radicals giving a characteristic qualitative reaction. **b** a set of elements occupying a column in the periodic table and having broadly similar properties. **c** a combination of atoms having a recognizable identity in a number of compounds. ● *v.* **1** *tr.* & *intr.* form or be formed into a group. **2** *tr.* (often foll. by *with*) place in a group or groups. **3** *tr.* form (colours, figures, etc.) into a well-arranged and harmonious whole. **4** *tr.* classify. □ **groupage** *n.* [French *groupe* from Italian *gruppo*, from Germanic, related to CROP]

group captain *n.* an RAF officer next below air commodore.

group dynamics *n.pl.* (also treated as *sing.*) *Psychol.* **1** the interaction of people in groups. **2** the principles perceived as underlying such interaction.

grouper /ˈgruːpə/ *n.* any marine fish of the family Serranidae, with heavy body, big head, and wide mouth. [Portuguese *garupa*, probably from a native name in S. America]

groupie /ˈgruːpi/ *n. colloq.* **1** an ardent follower of touring pop groups, esp. a young woman seeking sexual relations with them. **2** a fan, enthusiast, or follower (*chess groupie*).

grouping /ˈgruːpɪŋ/ *n.* **1** a process or system of allocation to groups. **2** a formation or arrangement in a group or groups.

group practice *n.* a medical practice in which several doctors are associated.

group therapy *n.* therapy in which patients are brought together to assist one another psychologically.

groupthink /ˈgruːpθɪŋk/ *n.* esp. *N. Amer.* the practice of thinking or making decisions as a group, often resulting in poor-quality decision-making. [modelled on DOUBLETHINK]

group velocity *n.* the speed of travel of the energy of a wave or wave-group.

groupware /ˈgruːpwɛː/ *n. Computing* software designed to facilitate collective working by a number of different users.

group work *n.* work done by a group working in close association.

grouse[1] /graʊs/ *n.* (*pl.* same) **1** any of various game birds of the family Tetraonidae, with a plump body and feathered legs. **2** the flesh of a grouse used as food. [16th c.: origin uncertain]

grouse[2] /graʊs/ *v.* & *n. colloq.* ● *v.intr.* grumble or complain pettily. ● *n.* a complaint. □ **grouser** *n.* [19th c.: origin unknown]

grouse moor *n.* (in the UK) an area of managed moorland for the shooting of red grouse.

grout[1] /graʊt/ *n.* & *v.* ● *n.* a thin fluid mortar for filling gaps in tiling etc. ● *v.tr.* provide or fill with grout. □ **grouter** *n.* [perhaps from GROUT[2], but cf. French dialect *grouter* 'grout a wall']

grout[2] /graʊt/ *n. Brit.* sediment, dregs. [Old English *grūt*, related to GRITS, GROATS]

grouter /ˈgraʊtə/ *n. Austral. slang* an unfair advantage. [20th c.: origin uncertain]

grove /grəʊv/ *n.* **1** a small wood or group of trees. **2** an orchard planted for the cultivation of olives, citrus fruit, etc. □ **grovy** *adj.* [Old English *grāf*, related to *grǣfa* 'brushwood']

grovel /ˈgrɒv(ə)l, ˈgrʌv-/ *v.intr.* (**grovelled**, **grovelling**; *US* **groveled**, **groveling**) **1** behave obsequiously in seeking favour or forgiveness. **2** lie prone in abject humility. □ **groveller** *n.* **grovelling** *adj.* **grovellingly** *adv.* [back-formation from obsolete adverb *grovelling* from *gruf* 'face down', in the phrase *on grufe* translating Old Norse *á grúfu*, later taken as pres. part.]

groves of Academe *n.pl.* a university environment.

grow /grəʊ/ *v.* (*past* **grew** /gruː/; *past part.* **grown** /grəʊn/) **1** *intr.* increase in size, height, quantity, degree, or in any way regarded as measurable (e.g. authority or reputation) (often foll. by *in*: *grew in stature*). **2** *intr.* **a** develop or exist as a living plant or natural product. **b** develop in a specific way or direction (*began to grow sideways*). **c** germinate, sprout; spring up. **3** *intr.* be produced; come naturally into existence; arise. **4** *intr.* (as **grown** *adj.*) fully matured; adult. **5** *intr.* **a** become gradually (*grow rich*; *grow less*). **b** (foll. by *to* + infin.) come by degrees (*grew to like it*). **6** *intr.* (foll. by *into*) **a** become, having grown or developed (*the acorn has grown into a tall oak*; *will grow into a fine athlete*). **b** become large enough for or suited to (*will grow into the coat*; *grew into her new job*). **7** *intr.* (foll. by *on*) become gradually more appealing to. **8** *tr.* **a** produce (plants, fruit, wood, etc.) by cultivation. **b** bring forth. **c** allow (a beard etc.) to develop or increase in length. **9** *tr.* (in *passive*; foll. by *over*, *up*) be covered with a growth. □ **grow out of 1** become too large to wear (a garment). **2** become too mature to retain (a childish habit etc.). **3** be the result or development of. **grow together** coalesce. **grow up 1 a** advance to maturity. **b** (esp. in *imper.*) begin to behave sensibly. **2** (of a custom) arise, become common. □ **growable** *adj.* [Old English *grōwan* from Germanic: related to GRASS, GREEN]

growbag /ˈgrəʊbag/ *n.* (also **Gro-bag** *propr.*) = GROWING BAG.

grower /ˈgrəʊə/ *n.* **1** (often in *comb.*) a person growing produce (*fruit-grower*). **2** a plant that grows in a specified way (*a fast grower*).

growing bag *n. Brit.* a bag containing potting compost, in which plants, e.g. tomatoes, may be grown.

growing pains *n.pl.* **1** early difficulties in the development of an enterprise etc. **2** neuralgic pain in children's legs due to fatigue etc.

growl /graʊl/ *v.* & *n.* ● *v.* **1** *intr.* **a** (often foll. by *at*) (esp. of a dog) make a low guttural sound, usu. of anger. **b** murmur angrily. **2** *intr.* rumble. **3** *tr.* (often foll. by *out*) utter with a growl. ● *n.* **1** a growling sound, esp. made by a dog. **2** an angry murmur; complaint. **3** a rumble. □ **growlingly** *adv.* [probably imitative]

growler /ˈgraʊlə/ *n.* **1** a person or thing that growls, esp. *slang* a dog. **2** a small iceberg.

Growmore /ˈgrəʊmɔː/ *n.* vegetable fertilizer of a standard kind.

grown *past part.* of GROW.

grown-up *adj.* & *n.* ● *adj.* adult. ● *n.* an adult person.

growth /grəʊθ/ *n.* **1** the act or process of growing. **2** an increase in size or value. **3** something that has grown or is growing. **4** *Med.* an abnormal formation, esp. a tumour. **5** the cultivation of produce. **6** a crop or yield of grapes.

growth hormone *n.* a substance which stimulates the growth of a plant or animal.

growth industry *n.* an industry that is developing rapidly.

growth ring *n.* a concentric layer of wood, shell, etc., developed during an annual or other regular period of growth.

growth stock *n.* stock that tends to increase in capital value rather than yield high income.

groyne /grɔɪn/ *n.* (*US* **groin**) a timber framework or low broad wall built out from a shore to check erosion of a beach. [dialect *groin* 'snout', via Old French *groign* from Late Latin *grunium* 'pig's snout']

grub /grʌb/ *n.* & *v.* ● *n.* **1** the larva of an insect, esp. of a beetle. **2** *colloq.* food. ● *v.* (**grubbed**, **grubbing**) **1** *tr.* & *intr.* dig superficially. **2** *tr.* **a** clear (the ground) of roots and stumps. **b** clear away (roots etc.). **3** *tr.* (foll. by *up*, *out*) **a** fetch by digging (*grubbing up weeds*). **b** extract (information etc.) by searching in books etc. **4** *intr.* search, rummage. **5** *intr.* (foll. by *on*, *along*, *away*) toil, plod. [Middle English, origin uncertain, perhaps from a Germanic base related to GRAVE[1]]

grubber /ˈgrʌbə/ *n.* **1** (usu. in *comb.*) *derog.* a person devoted to amassing something (*vote-grubber*). Cf. MONEY-GRUBBER. **2** an implement for digging up weeds etc. **3** *Cricket*, *Rugby*, etc. a ball bowled or kicked along the ground. **4** a person who or animal which grubs.

grubby /ˈgrʌbi/ *adj.* (**grubbier**, **grubbiest**) **1** dirty, grimy, slovenly. **2** of or infested with grubs. □ **grubbily** *adv.* **grubbiness** *n.*

grub-screw *n.* a small headless screw, esp. used to attach a handle etc. to a spindle.

grubstake /ˈgrʌbsteɪk/ *n.* & *v. N. Amer. colloq.* ● *n.* material or provisions supplied to an enterprise in return for a share in the resulting profits (originally in prospecting for ore). ● *v.tr.* provide with a grubstake. □ **grubstaker** *n.*

Grub Street /ˈgrʌb/ *n.* (often *attrib.*) the world or class of literary hacks and impoverished authors. [name of a street (later Milton St.) in Moorgate, London, inhabited by these in the 17th c.]

grudge /grʌdʒ/ *n.* & *v.* ● *n.* a persistent feeling of ill will or resentment, esp. one due to an insult or injury (*bears a grudge against me*). ● *v.tr.* **1** be resentfully unwilling to give, grant, or allow (a thing). **2** (foll. by verbal noun or *to* + infin.) be reluctant to do (a thing) (*grudged paying so much*). □ **grudger** *n.* [Middle English *grutch* from Old French *grouchier* 'murmur', of unknown origin]

grudging /ˈgrʌdʒɪŋ/ *adj.* reluctant; not willing (*grudging approval*). □ **grudgingly** *adv.* **grudgingness** *n.*

gruel /ˈgruːəl/ *n.* a liquid food of oatmeal etc. boiled in milk or water chiefly for invalids. [Middle English from Old French, ultimately from Germanic: related to GROUT[1]]

gruelling /ˈgruːəlɪŋ/ *adj.* & *n.* (*US* **grueling**) ● *adj.* extremely demanding, severe, or tiring. ● *n.* a harsh, punishing, or exhausting experience. □ **gruellingly** *adv.* [GRUEL as verb, = exhaust, punish]

gruesome /ˈgruːs(ə)m/ *adj.* horrible, grisly, disgusting. □ **gruesomely** *adv.* **gruesomeness** *n.* [Scots *grue* 'to shudder' from Scandinavian + -SOME[1]]

gruff /grʌf/ *adj.* **1 a** (of a voice) low and harsh. **b** (of a person) having a gruff voice. **2** surly, laconic, rough-mannered. □ **gruffly** *adv.* **gruffness** *n.* [Dutch, Middle Low German *grof* 'coarse' from West Germanic (related to ROUGH)]

grumble /ˈgrʌmb(ə)l/ *v.* & *n.* ● *v.* **1** *intr.* **a** (often foll. by *at, about, over*) complain peevishly. **b** be discontented. **2** *intr.* **a** utter a dull inarticulate sound; murmur, growl faintly. **b** rumble. **3** *tr.* (often foll. by *out*) utter complainingly. **4** *intr.* (as **grumbling** *adj.*) *colloq.* giving intermittent discomfort without causing illness (*a grumbling appendix*). ● *n.* **1** a complaint. **2 a** a dull inarticulate sound; a murmur. **b** a rumble. □ **grumbler** *n.* **grumbling** *adj.* **grumblingly** *adv.* **grumbly** *adj.* [obsolete *grumme*: cf. Middle Dutch *grommen*, Middle Low German *grommelen*, from Germanic (imitative)]

grump /grʌmp/ *n. colloq.* **1** a grumpy person. **2** (in *pl.*) a fit of sulks. □ **grumpish** *adj.* **grumpishly** *adv.* [imitative]

grumpy /ˈgrʌmpi/ *adj.* (**grumpier**, **grumpiest**) morosely irritable; surly. □ **grumpily** *adv.* **grumpiness** *n.*

Grundy /ˈgrʌndi/ *n.* (*pl.* **-ies**) (in full **Mrs Grundy**) a person embodying conventional propriety and prudery. □ **Grundyism** *n.* [a person repeatedly mentioned in T. Morton's comedy *Speed the Plough* (1798)]

grunge /grʌn(d)ʒ/ *n.* **1** esp. *N. Amer.* grime, dirt. **2** (in full **grunge rock**) a relaxed style of rock music characterized by a raucous guitar sound. **3** the fashion associated with this music, including unkempt hair, flannel shirts, and ripped jeans. □ **grungy** *adj.* [perhaps suggested by GRUBBY, DINGY, etc.]

grunion /ˈgrʌnjən/ *n.* a slender Californian silverside fish, *Leuresthes tenuis*, that spawns on beaches. [probably from Spanish *gruñón* 'grunter']

grunt /grʌnt/ *n.* & *v.* ● *n.* **1** a low guttural sound made by a pig. **2** a sound resembling this. **3** any tropical fish of the family Haemulidae that grunts when caught. ● *v.* **1** *intr.* (of a pig) make a grunt or grunts. **2** *intr.* (of a person) make a low inarticulate sound resembling this, esp. to express effort, assent, fatigue, etc. **3** *tr.* utter with a grunt. [Old English *grunnettan*, probably originally imitative]

grunter /ˈgrʌntə/ *n.* **1** a person or animal that grunts, esp. a pig. **2** a fish that grunts when caught.

Gruyère /ˈgruːjɛː/ *n.* a firm pale cheese made from cow's milk. [*Gruyère*, a district in Switzerland where it was first made]

gryke var. of GRIKE.

gryphon var. of GRIFFIN.

grysbok /ˈgrʌɪsbɒk, ˈxreɪs-/ *n.* any small straight-horned antelope of the genus *Raphicerus*, of central and southern Africa. [South African Dutch, from Dutch *grijs* 'grey' + *bok* BUCK[1]]

gs. *abbr. Brit. hist.* guineas.

G-string /ˈdʒiːstrɪŋ/ *n.* **1** *Mus.* a string sounding the note G. **2** (also **gee-string**) a narrow strip of cloth etc. covering only the genitals and attached to a string round the waist, as worn esp. by striptease artistes.

G-suit /ˈdʒiːsuːt/ *n.* a garment with inflatable pressurized pouches, worn by pilots and astronauts to enable them to withstand high acceleration. [*g* = gravity + SUIT]

GT *adj.* designating a high-performance car. [abbreviation of Italian GRAN TURISMO]

Gt. *abbr.* Great.

GTi /dʒiːtiːˈʌɪ/ *adj.* designating a high-performance car with a fuel-injected engine. [GT + *i*njection]

guacamole /gwɑːkəˈməʊli/ *n.* a dish of mashed avocado pears mixed with chopped onion, tomatoes, chilli peppers, and seasoning. [Latin American Spanish from Nahuatl *ahuacamolli*, from *ahuacatl* 'avocado' + *molli* 'sauce']

guacharo /ˈgwɑːtʃərəʊ/ *n.* (*pl.* **-os**) = OIL-BIRD. [Latin American Spanish]

guaiacum /ˈgwʌɪəkəm/ *n.* **1** any tree of the genus *Guaiacum*, native to tropical America. **2** (also **guaiac** /ˈgwʌɪak/) **a** the hard dense oily timber of some of these, esp. of *G. officinale*; also called *lignum vitae*. **b** the resin from this used medicinally. [modern Latin from Spanish *guayaco*, of Haitian origin]

guan /gwɑːn/ *n.* a pheasant-like bird of the family Cracidae, esp. of the genus *Penelope*, of tropical American rainforests. [American Spanish, from Miskito *kwamu*]

guanaco /gwəˈnɑːkəʊ/ *n.* (*pl.* **-os**) an Andean mammal, *Lama guanicoe*, related to the llama, with a coat of soft pale brown hair used for wool. [Spanish, from Quechua *huanacu*]

guanine /ˈgwɑːniːn/ *n. Biochem.* a purine found in all living organisms as a component base of DNA and RNA. [GUANO + -INE[4]]

guano /ˈgwɑːnəʊ/ *n. & v.* ● *n.* (*pl.* **-os**) **1** the excrement of seabirds, found esp. on islands off S. America and used as manure. **2** artificial manure, esp. that made from fish. ● *v.tr.* (**-oes, -oed**) fertilize with guano. [Spanish, from Quechua *huanu* 'dung']

Guarani /gwɑːrəˈniː/ *n. & adj.* ● *n.* **1 a** a member of a S. American Indian people. **b** the language of this people. **2** (**guarani**) the chief monetary unit of Paraguay. ● *adj.* of or relating to the Guarani or their language. [Spanish]

guarantee /gar(ə)nˈtiː/ *n. & v.* ● *n.* **1 a** a formal promise or assurance, esp. that an obligation will be fulfilled or that something is of a specified quality and durability. **b** a document giving such an undertaking. **2** = GUARANTY. **3** a person making a guaranty or giving a security. ● *v.tr.* (**guarantees, guaranteed**) **1 a** give or serve as a guarantee for; answer for the due fulfilment of (a contract etc.) or the genuineness of (an article). **b** assure the permanence etc. of. **c** provide with a guarantee. **2** (foll. by *that* + clause, or *to* + infin.) give a promise or assurance. **3 a** (foll. by *to*) secure the possession of (a thing) for a person. **b** make (a person) secure against a risk or in possession of a thing. [earlier *garante*, perhaps from Spanish *garante* = French *garant* WARRANT: later influenced by French *garantie* 'guaranty']

guarantee fund *n. Brit.* a sum pledged as a contingent indemnity for loss.

guarantor /gar(ə)nˈtɔː/ *n.* a person who gives a guarantee or guaranty.

guaranty /ˈgar(ə)nti/ *n.* (*pl.* **-ies**) **1** a written or other undertaking to answer for the payment of a debt or for the performance of an obligation by another person liable in the first instance. **2** a thing serving as security for a guaranty. [Anglo-French *guarantie*, variant of *warantie* WARRANTY]

guard /gɑːd/ *v. & n.* ● *v.* **1** *tr.* (often foll. by *from*, *against*) watch over and defend or protect from harm. **2** *tr.* keep watch by (a door etc.) so as to control entry or exit. **3** *tr.* supervise (prisoners etc.) and prevent from escaping. **4** *tr.* provide (machinery) with a protective device. **5** *tr.* keep (thoughts or speech) in check. **6** *tr.* provide with safeguards. **7** *intr.* (foll. by *against*) take precautions. **8** *tr.* (in various games) protect (a piece, card, etc.) with set moves. ● *n.* **1** a state of vigilance or watchfulness. **2** a person who protects or keeps watch. **3** a body of soldiers etc. serving to protect a place or person; an escort. **4** *Brit.* an official who rides with and is in general charge of a train. **5** a part of an army detached for some purpose (*advance guard*). **6** (in *pl.*) (usu. **Guards**) any of various bodies of troops nominally employed to guard a monarch. **7** a thing that protects or defends. **8** (often in *comb.*) a device fitted to a machine, vehicle, weapon, etc., to prevent injury or accident to the user (*fireguard*). **9** *N. Amer.* a prison warder. **10** in some sports: **a** a protective or defensive player. **b** a defensive posture or motion. □ **be on** (or **keep** or **stand**) **guard** (of a sentry etc.) keep watch. **lower one's guard** reduce vigilance against attack. **off** (or **off one's**) **guard** unprepared for some surprise or difficulty. **on** (or **on one's**) **guard** prepared for all contingencies; vigilant. **raise one's guard** become vigilant against attack. [Middle English from Old French *garde*, *garder*, ultimately from West Germanic: related to WARD *n.*]

guardant /ˈgɑːd(ə)nt/ *adj. Heraldry* depicted with the body sideways and the face towards the viewer.

guard cell *n. Bot.* either of a pair of cells surrounding the stomata in plants.

guarded /ˈgɑːdɪd/ *adj.* (of a remark etc.) cautious, avoiding commitment. □ **guardedly** *adv.* **guardedness** *n.*

guard hair *n.* each of the long coarse hairs forming an animal's outer fur.

guardhouse /ˈgɑːdhaʊs/ *n.* a building used to accommodate a military guard or to detain prisoners.

guardian /ˈgɑːdɪən/ *n.* **1** a defender, protector, or keeper. **2** a person having legal custody of another person and his or her property when that person is incapable of managing his or her own affairs. **3** the superior of a Franciscan convent. □ **guardianship** *n.* [Middle English via Anglo-French *gardein*, Old French *garden* from Frankish: related to WARD, WARDEN]

guardian angel *n.* a spirit conceived as watching over a person or place.

guard rail *n.* a rail, e.g. a handrail, fitted as a support or to prevent an accident.

guard ring *n.* a ring-shaped electrode used to limit the extent of an electric field, esp. in a capacitor.

guardroom /ˈgɑːdruːm, -rʊm/ *n.* a room with the same purpose as a guardhouse.

guardsman /ˈgɑːdzmən/ *n.* (*pl.* **-men**) **1** a soldier belonging to a body of guards. **2** (in the UK) a soldier of a regiment of Guards.

guard's van *n. Brit.* a railway coach or compartment occupied by a guard.

guava /ˈgwɑːvə/ *n.* **1** a small tropical American tree, *Psidium guajava*, bearing an edible pale orange fruit with pink juicy flesh. **2** this fruit. [Spanish *guayaba*, probably from a S. American name]

guayule /gwʌɪˈuːli/ *n.* **1** a silver-leaved shrub, *Parthenium argentatum*, native to Mexico. **2** a rubber substitute made from the sap of this plant. [Latin American Spanish, from Nahuatl *cuauhuli*]

gubbins /ˈgʌbɪnz/ *n. Brit.* **1** *colloq.* paraphernalia. **2** a gadget. **3** something of little value; rubbish. **4** *archaic* a foolish person. [originally = fragments, from obsolete *gobbon*: perhaps related to GOBBET]

gubernatorial /gjuːbənəˈtɔːrɪəl/ *adj.* esp. *US* of or relating to a governor. [Latin *gubernator* 'governor']

gudgeon[1] /ˈgʌdʒ(ə)n/ *n.* **1** a small European freshwater fish, *Gobio gobio*, often used as bait. **2** a credulous or easily fooled person. [Middle English via Old French *goujon* from Latin *gobio -onis* GOBY]

gudgeon[2] /ˈɡʌdʒ(ə)n/ *n.* **1** any of various kinds of pivot working a wheel, bell, etc. **2** the tubular part of a hinge into which the pin fits to effect the joint. **3** a socket at the stern of a boat, into which a rudder is fitted. **4** a pin holding two blocks of stone etc. together. [Middle English from Old French *goujon*, diminutive of *gouge* GOUGE]

gudgeon pin *n. Brit.* a pin holding a piston rod and a connecting rod together.

guelder rose /ˈɡɛldə/ *n.* a deciduous shrub, *Viburnum opulus*, with round bunches of creamy-white flowers. Also called *snowball tree*. [Dutch *geldersch* from *Gelderland*, a province in the Netherlands]

guenon /ɡəˈnɒn/ *n.* any African monkey of the genus *Cercopithecus*, having a characteristic long tail, e.g. the vervet. [French: ultimate origin unknown]

guerdon /ˈɡəːd(ə)n/ *n. & v. poet.* ● *n.* a reward or recompense. ● *v.tr.* give a reward to. [Middle English via Old French *guerdon* and medieval Latin *widerdonum* from West Germanic *widarlōn* (as WITH, LOAN[1]), assimilated to Latin *donum* 'gift']

Guernsey /ˈɡəːnzi/ *n.* (*pl.* **-eys**) **1 a** an animal of a breed of dairy cattle from Guernsey in the Channel Islands. **b** this breed. **2** (**guernsey**) **a** a thick (originally fisherman's) sweater of esp. oiled dark blue wool. **b** *Austral.* a football shirt. □ **get a guernsey** *Austral. colloq.* **1** be selected for a football team. **2** gain recognition.

Guernsey lily *n.* a nerine, *Nerine sarniensis*, originally from S. Africa, with large pink lily-like flowers.

guerrilla /ɡəˈrɪlə/ *n.* (also **guerilla**) a member of a small independently acting (usu. political) group taking part in irregular fighting, esp. against larger regular forces. [Spanish, diminutive of *guerra* 'war']

guerrilla war *n.* (also **guerrilla warfare**) fighting by or with guerrillas.

guess /ɡɛs/ *v. & n.* ● *v.* **1** *tr.* (often *absol.*) estimate without calculation or measurement, or on the basis of inadequate data. **2** *tr.* (often foll. by *that* etc. + clause, or *to* + infin.) form a hypothesis or opinion about; conjecture; think likely (*cannot guess how you did it*; *guess them to be Italian*). **3** *tr.* conjecture or estimate correctly by guessing (*you have to guess the weight*). **4** *intr.* (foll. by *at*) make a conjecture about. ● *n.* an estimate or conjecture reached by guessing. □ **anybody's** (or **anyone's**) **guess** something very vague or difficult to determine. **I guess** *colloq.* I think it likely; I suppose. **keep a person guessing** *colloq.* withhold information. □ **guessable** *adj.* **guesser** *n.* [Middle English *gesse*, of uncertain origin: cf. Old Swedish *gissa*, Middle Low German, Middle Dutch *gissen*: from the root of GET *v.*]

guess-rope var. of GUEST-ROPE.

guesstimate *n. & v.* (also **guestimate**) *colloq.* ● *n.* /ˈɡɛstɪmət/ an estimate based more on guesswork than calculation. ● *v.tr.* /ˈɡɛstɪmeɪt/ (also *absol.*) form a guesstimate of. [GUESS + ESTIMATE]

guesswork /ˈɡɛswəːk/ *n.* the process of, or results got by, guessing.

guest /ɡɛst/ *n. & v.* ● *n.* **1** a person invited to visit another's house or have a meal etc. at the expense of the inviter. **2** a person lodging at a hotel, boarding house, etc. **3 a** an outside performer invited to take part with a regular body of performers. **b** a person who takes part by invitation in a radio or television programme (often *attrib.*: *guest artist*). **4** (*attrib.*) **a** serving or set aside for guests (*guest room*; *guest night*). **b** acting as a guest (*guest speaker*). **5** an organism living in close association with another. ● *v.intr.* be a guest on a radio or television show or in a theatrical performance etc. □ **be my guest** *colloq.* make what use you wish of the available facilities. **guest of honour** the most important guest at an occasion. □ **guestship** *n.* [Middle English via Old Norse *gestr* from Germanic]

guest beer *n. Brit.* **1** (in a tied public house) a beer offered in addition to those produced by the brewery. **2** (in a free house) a beer available only temporarily.

guest house *n.* a private house offering paid accommodation.

guestimate var. of GUESSTIMATE.

guest-rope *n.* (also **guess-rope**) **1** a second rope fastened to a boat in tow to steady it. **2** a rope slung outside a ship to give a hold for boats coming alongside. [17th c.: origin uncertain]

guest worker *n.* = GASTARBEITER. [translation of German]

guff /ɡʌf/ *n. slang* empty talk; nonsense. [19th c., originally = 'puff': imitative]

guffaw /ɡəˈfɔː/ *n. & v.* ● *n.* a coarse or boisterous laugh. ● *v.* **1** *intr.* utter a guffaw. **2** *tr.* say with a guffaw. [originally Scots: imitative]

guidance /ˈɡʌɪd(ə)ns/ *n.* **1** advice or information aimed at resolving a problem, difficulty, etc. **2** the action or process of guiding or being guided (*missile guidance*).

guide /ɡʌɪd/ *n. & v.* ● *n.* **1** a person who leads or shows the way, or directs the movements of a person or group. **2** a person who conducts visitors or tourists on tours etc. **3** a professional mountain climber in charge of a group. **4** an adviser. **5** a directing principle or standard (*one's feelings are a bad guide*). **6** a book with essential information on a subject, esp. = GUIDEBOOK. **7** a thing marking a position or guiding the eye. **8** a soldier, vehicle, or ship whose position determines the movements of others. **9** *Mech.* **a** a bar, rod, etc., directing the motion of something. **b** a gauge etc. controlling a tool. **10** (**Guide**) *Brit.* a member of the Guides Association, an organization similar to the Scouts. ● *v.tr.* **1 a** act as guide to; lead or direct. **b** arrange the course of (events). **2** be the principle, motive, or ground of (an action, judgement, etc.). **3** direct the affairs of (a state etc.). □ **guidable** *adj.* **guider** *n.* [Middle English from Old French *guide* (*n.*), *guider* (*v.*), earlier *guier*; ultimately from Germanic: related to WIT[2]]

guidebook /ˈɡʌɪdbʊk/ *n.* a book of information about a place for visitors, tourists, etc.

guided missile *n.* a missile directed to its target by remote control or by equipment within itself.

guide dog *n.* a dog trained to guide a blind person.

Guide Guider *n.* the adult leader of a company of Guides (see GUIDE *n.* 10).

guideline /ˈɡʌɪdlʌɪn/ *n.* a principle or criterion guiding or directing action.

guidepost /ˈɡʌɪdpəʊst/ *n.* = SIGNPOST.

Guider /ˈɡʌɪdə/ *n. Brit.* an adult leader in the Guides Association.

guide rope *n.* a rope guiding the movement of a crane, airship, etc.

guideway /ˈɡʌɪdweɪ/ *n.* a groove or track that guides movement.

guidon /ˈɡʌɪd(ə)n/ *n.* a pennant narrowing to a point or fork at the free end, esp. one used as the standard of a regiment of dragoons. [French from Italian *guidone*, from *guida* GUIDE]

guild /ɡɪld/ *n.* (also **gild**) **1** an association of people for mutual aid or the pursuit of a common goal. **2** a medieval association of craftsmen or merchants. [Middle English, probably via Middle Low German, Middle Dutch *gilde* from Germanic: related to Old English *gild* 'payment, sacrifice']

guilder /ˈɡɪldə/ *n.* **1** the chief monetary unit of the Netherlands. **2** *hist.* a gold coin of the Netherlands and Germany. [Middle English, alteration of Dutch *gulden*: see GULDEN]

guildhall /ɡɪldˈhɔːl, ˈɡɪld-/ *n.* **1 a** the meeting place of a guild or corporation. **b** *Brit.* a town hall. **2** (**Guildhall**) the hall of the Corporation of the City of London, used for ceremonial occasions.

guildsman /ˈɡɪldzmən/ *n.* (*pl.* **-men**; *fem.* **guildswoman**, *pl.* **-women**) a member of a guild.

guile /ɡʌɪl/ *n.* treachery, deceit; cunning or sly behaviour. □ **guileful** *adj.* **guilefully** *adv.* **guileless** *adj.*

guilelessly *adv.* **guilelessness** *n.* [Middle English from Old French, probably from Germanic]

guillemot /ˈɡɪlɪmɒt/ *n.* any narrow-billed auk of the genus *Uria* or *Cepphus*, nesting on cliffs or islands. [French, diminutive of *Guillaume* 'William']

guilloche /ɡɪˈləʊʃ, -ˈlɒʃ/ *n.* an architectural or metalwork ornament imitating braided ribbons. [French *guillochis* (or *guilloche*, the tool used)]

guillotine /ˈɡɪlətiːn, ɡɪləˈtiːn/ *n.* & *v.* ● *n.* **1** a machine with a heavy knife blade sliding vertically in grooves, used for beheading. **2** a device for cutting paper, metal, etc., by means of a descending blade. **3** a surgical instrument with a sliding blade for excising the tonsils etc. **4** *Brit. Parl.* a method of preventing delay in the discussion of a legislative bill by fixing times at which various parts of it must be voted on. ● *v.tr.* **1** use a guillotine on. **2** *Brit. Parl.* end discussion of (a bill) by applying a guillotine. □ **guillotiner** *n.* [French, named after J.-I. *Guillotin*, French physician (d. 1814), who recommended its use for executions in 1789]

guilt /ɡɪlt/ *n.* **1** the fact of having committed a specified or implied offence. **2 a** culpability. **b** the feeling of this. [Old English *gylt*, of unknown origin]

guilt complex *n.* a mental obsession with the idea of having done wrong.

guiltless /ɡɪltlɪs/ *adj.* **1** (often foll. by *of* an offence) innocent. **2** (foll. by *of*) not having knowledge or possession of. □ **guiltlessly** *adv.* **guiltlessness** *n.* [Old English *gyltlēas* (as GUILT, -LESS)]

guilty /ɡɪlti/ *adj.* (**guiltier**, **guiltiest**) **1** culpable of or responsible for a wrong. **2** conscious of or affected by guilt (*a guilty conscience*; *a guilty look*). **3** concerning guilt (*a guilty secret*). **4** (often foll. by *of*) **a** having committed a (specified) offence. **b** *Law* adjudged to have committed a specified offence, esp. by a verdict in a trial. □ **guiltily** *adv.* **guiltiness** *n.* [Old English *gyltig* (as GUILT, -Y[1])]

guimp var. of GIMP[1].

guinea /ˈɡɪni/ *n.* **1** *Brit.* the sum of 21 old shillings (£1.05), used esp. in determining professional fees and auction prices. **2** *hist.* a former British gold coin worth 21 shillings, first coined for the African trade. [*Guinea* in W. Africa]

guinea fowl *n.* any African fowl of the family Numididae, esp. *Numida meleagris*, with slate-coloured white-spotted plumage.

guinea pig *n.* **1** a domesticated S. American cavy, *Cavia porcellus*, kept as a pet or for research in biology etc. **2** a person or thing used as a subject for experiment.

Guinea worm *n.* a very long parasitic nematode worm, *Dracunculus medinensis*, which lives under the skin of infected people in rural tropical Africa and Asia.

guipure /ɡɪˈpjʊə/ *n.* a heavy lace of linen pieces joined by embroidery. [French, from *guiper* 'cover with silk etc.', from Germanic]

guise /ɡʌɪz/ *n.* **1** an assumed appearance; a pretence (*in the guise of*; *under the guise of*). **2** external appearance. **3** *archaic* style of attire, garb. [Middle English from Old French, ultimately from Germanic]

guitar /ɡɪˈtɑː/ *n.* a usu. six-stringed musical instrument with a fretted fingerboard, played by plucking with the fingers or a plectrum. □ **guitarist** *n.* [Spanish *guitarra* (partly through French *guitare*) from Greek *kithara*: see CITTERN, GITTERN]

guiver /ˈɡʌɪvə/ *n.* (also **gyver**) *Austral.* & *NZ slang* **1** plausible talk. **2** affectation of speech or manner. [19th c.: origin unknown]

Gujarati /ɡuːdʒəˈrɑːti, ɡʊ-/ *n.* & *adj.* (also **Gujerati**) ● *n.* (*pl.* **Gujaratis**) **1** the language of Gujarat in W. India. **2** a native of Gujarat. ● *adj.* of or relating to Gujarat or its language. [Hindustani: see -I[2]]

gulch /ɡʌltʃ/ *n. N. Amer.* a ravine, esp. one in which a torrent flows. [perhaps from dialect *gulch* 'to swallow']

gulden /ˈɡʊld(ə)n/ *n.* = GUILDER. [Dutch & German, = GOLDEN]

gules /ɡjuːlz/ *n.* & *adj.* (usu. placed after noun) *Heraldry* red. [Middle English from Old French *goules* 'red-dyed fur neck ornaments', from *gole* 'throat']

gulf /ɡʌlf/ *n.* **1** a stretch of sea consisting of a deep inlet with a narrow mouth. **2** (**the Gulf**) **a** the Persian Gulf. **b** the Gulf of Mexico. **3** a deep hollow; a chasm or abyss. **4** a wide difference of feelings, opinion, etc. [Middle English via Old French *golfe* from Italian *golfo*, ultimately from Greek *kolpos* 'bosom, gulf']

Gulf Stream *n.* a warm ocean current flowing from the Gulf of Mexico to Newfoundland, across the North Atlantic Ocean, and along the coast of NW Europe.

gulfweed /ˈɡʌlfwiːd/ *n.* = SARGASSO.

gull[1] /ɡʌl/ *n.* any of various long-winged web-footed seabirds of the family Laridae, typically having white plumage with a grey or black mantle, and a bright bill. □ **gullery** *n.* (*pl.* **-ies**). [Middle English, ultimately from Celtic]

gull[2] /ɡʌl/ *v.tr.* (usu. in *passive*; foll. by *into*) dupe, fool. [perhaps from obsolete *gull* 'yellow', from Old Norse *gulr*]

Gullah /ˈɡʌlə/ *n.* & *adj.* ● *n.* **1** a member of a Negro people living on the coast of S. Carolina or the nearby sea islands. **2** the Creole language spoken by them. ● *adj.* of or relating to the Gullahs or their language. [perhaps a shortening of *Angola*, or from a tribal name *Golas*]

gullet /ˈɡʌlɪt/ *n.* **1** the food-passage extending from the mouth to the stomach; the oesophagus. **2** the throat. [Middle English from Old French, diminutive of *go(u)le* 'throat', from Latin *gula*]

gulley var. of GULLY *n.*

gullible /ˈɡʌlɪb(ə)l/ *adj.* easily persuaded or deceived; credulous. □ **gullibility** /-ˈbɪlɪti/ *n.* **gullibly** *adv.* [GULL[2] + -IBLE]

gully /ˈɡʌli/ *n.* & *v.* ● *n.* (also **gulley**) (*pl.* **-ies** or **-eys**) **1** a water-worn ravine. **2** a deep artificial channel; a gutter or drain. **3** *Austral.* & *NZ* a river valley. **4** *Cricket* **a** the fielding position between point and slips. **b** a fielder in this position. ● *v.tr.* (**-ies**, **-ied**) **1** form (channels) by water action. **2** make gullies in. [French *goulet* 'bottle-neck' (as GULLET)]

gully-hole *n.* an opening in a street to a drain or sewer.

gulp /ɡʌlp/ *v.* & *n.* ● *v.* **1** *tr.* (often foll. by *down*) swallow hastily, greedily, or with effort. **2** *intr.* swallow gaspingly or with difficulty; choke. **3** *tr.* (foll. by *down*, *back*) stifle, suppress (esp. tears). ● *n.* **1** an act of gulping (*drained it in one gulp*). **2** an effort to swallow. **3** a large mouthful of a drink. □ **gulper** *n.* **gulpy** *adj.* [Middle English, probably from Middle Dutch *gulpen* (imitative)]

gum[1] /ɡʌm/ *n.* & *v.* ● *n.* **1 a** a viscous secretion of some trees and shrubs that hardens on drying but is soluble in water (cf. RESIN *n.* 1). **b** *Brit.* an adhesive substance made from this. **2** *N. Amer.* chewing gum. **3** = GUMDROP. **4** = GUM ARABIC. **5** = GUM TREE. **6** a secretion collecting in the corner of the eye. **7** *US* = GUMBOOT. ● *v.* (**gummed**, **gumming**) **1** *tr.* smear or cover with gum. **2** *tr.* (usu. foll. by *down*, *together*, etc.) fasten with gum. **3** *intr.* exude gum. □ **gum up 1** (of a mechanism etc.) become clogged or obstructed with stickiness. **2** *colloq.* interfere with the smooth running of (*gum up the works*). [Middle English from Old French *gomme*, ultimately from Latin *gummi*, *cummi*, via Greek *kommi* from Egyptian *kemai*]

gum[2] /ɡʌm/ *n.* (usu. in *pl.*) the firm flesh around the roots of the teeth. [Old English *gōma*, related to Old High German *guomo*, Old Norse *gómr* 'roof or floor of the mouth']

gum[3] /ɡʌm/ *n. colloq.* □ **by gum!** a mild oath. [corruption of *God*]

gum arabic *n.* a gum exuded by some kinds of acacia and used as glue and in incense.

gum benjamin *n.* = BENZOIN 1.

gumbo /ˈɡʌmbəʊ/ *n.* (*pl.* **-os**) *N. Amer.* **1** okra. **2** a spicy chicken or seafood soup thickened with okra, rice, etc.

3 (**Gumbo**) a patois of blacks and Creoles spoken esp. in Louisiana. [of African origin]

gumboil /ˈgʌmbɔɪl/ *n.* a small abscess on the gums.

gumboot /ˈgʌmbuːt/ *n.* a rubber boot; a wellington.

gum dragon *n.* tragacanth.

gumdrop /ˈgʌmdrɒp/ *n.* a soft coloured sweet made with gelatin or gum arabic.

gum juniper *n.* sandarac.

gumma /ˈgʌmə/ *n.* (*pl.* **gummas** or **gummata** /-mətə/) *Med.* a small soft swelling occurring in the connective tissue of the liver, brain, testes, and heart, and characteristic of the late stages of syphilis. □ **gummatous** *adj.* [modern Latin, from Latin *gummi* GUM[1]]

gummy[1] /ˈgʌmi/ *adj.* (**gummier**, **gummiest**) **1** viscous, sticky. **2** suffused with or exuding gum. □ **gumminess** *n.* [Middle English, from GUM[1] + -Y[1]]

gummy[2] /ˈgʌmi/ *adj.* & *n.* ● *adj.* (**gummier**, **gummiest**) toothless. ● *n.* (*pl.* **-ies**) **1** (also **gummy shark**) a small shark, *Mustelus antarcticus*, of Australasian coasts, having rounded teeth with which it crushes hard-shelled prey. **2** *Austral.* & *NZ* a toothless sheep. □ **gummily** *adv.* [GUM[2] + -Y[1]]

gumption /ˈgʌm(p)ʃ(ə)n/ *n. colloq.* **1** resourcefulness, initiative; enterprising spirit. **2** common sense. [18th-c. Scots: origin unknown]

gum resin *n.* a vegetable secretion of resin mixed with gum, e.g. gamboge.

gumshield /ˈgʌmʃiːld/ *n.* a pad protecting a boxer's teeth and gums.

gumshoe /ˈgʌmʃuː/ *n.* **1** a galosh. **2** *N. Amer. slang* a detective.

gum tree *n.* a tree exuding gum, esp. a eucalyptus. □ **up a gum tree** *Brit. colloq.* in great difficulties.

gum turpentine see TURPENTINE *n.* 1.

gun /gʌn/ *n.* & *v.* ● *n.* **1** a kind of weapon (of any size from a hand-held pistol to a mounted piece of artillery), consisting of a metal tube from which bullets or other missiles are propelled by explosive force. **2** any device imitative of this, e.g. a starting pistol. **3** a device for discharging insecticide, grease, electrons, etc., in the required direction (often in *comb.*: *grease gun*). **4** *Brit.* a member of a shooting party. **5** *N. Amer.* a gunman. **6** the firing of a gun. **7** (in *pl.*) *Naut. slang* a gunnery officer. ● *v.* (**gunned**, **gunning**) **1** *tr.* (usu. foll. by *down*) shoot (a person) with a gun. **2** *tr. colloq.* accelerate (an engine or vehicle). **3** *intr.* go shooting. **4** *intr.* (foll. by *for*) seek out determinedly to attack or rebuke. □ **go great guns** *colloq.* proceed forcefully or vigorously or successfully. **jump the gun** *colloq.* start before a signal is given, or before an agreed time. **stick to one's guns** *colloq.* maintain one's position under attack. □ **gunless** *adj.* **gunned** *adj.* [Middle English *gunne, gonne*, perhaps from the Scandinavian name *Gunnhildr*, from *gunnr* + *hildr*, both meaning 'war']

gunboat /ˈgʌnbəʊt/ *n.* a small vessel of shallow draught and with relatively heavy guns.

gunboat diplomacy *n.* political negotiation supported by the use or threat of military force.

gun carriage *n.* a wheeled support for a gun.

gun cotton *n.* an explosive used for blasting, made by steeping cotton in nitric and sulphuric acids.

gun crew *n.* a team manning a gun.

gun-deck *n.* **1** a deck on a ship on which guns are placed. **2** *hist.* the lowest such deck on a battleship.

gun dog *n.* a dog trained to follow sportsmen using guns and to retrieve game.

gunfight /ˈgʌnfʌɪt/ *n.* a fight with firearms. □ **gunfighter** *n.*

gunfire /ˈgʌnfʌɪə/ *n.* **1** the firing of a gun or guns, esp. repeatedly. **2** the noise from this.

gunge /gʌn(d)ʒ/ *n.* & *v. Brit. colloq.* ● *n.* sticky or viscous matter, esp. when messy or indeterminate. ● *v.tr.* (usu. foll. by *up*) clog or obstruct with gunge. □ **gungy** *adj.* [20th c.: origin uncertain: cf. GOO, GUNK]

gung-ho /gʌŋˈhəʊ/ *adj.* **1** enthusiastic, eager. **2** uninhibited; quick to take action. [Chinese *gonghe* 'work together', slogan adopted by US Marines in 1942]

gunk /gʌŋk/ *n. slang* viscous or liquid material. [20th c.: originally the proprietary name of a detergent]

gunlock /ˈgʌnlɒk/ *n.* a mechanism by which the charge of a gun is exploded.

gunmaker /ˈgʌnmeɪkə/ *n.* a manufacturer of guns.

gunman /ˈgʌnmən/ *n.* (*pl.* **-men**) a man armed with a gun, esp. in committing a crime.

gunmetal /ˈgʌnmɛt(ə)l/ *n.* & *adj.* ● *n.* **1** (in full **gunmetal grey**, **gunmetal blue**) a dull bluish-grey colour. **2** an alloy of copper and tin or zinc (formerly used for guns). ● *adj.* (in full **gunmetal grey**, **gunmetal blue**; hyphenated when *attrib.*) dull bluish grey (*gunmetal-grey wings*).

gunnel[1] /ˈgʌn(ə)l/ *n.* any small eel-shaped marine fish of the family Pholidae, esp. *Pholis gunnellus*. Also called *butterfish*. [17th c.: origin unknown]

gunnel[2] var. of GUNWALE.

gunner /ˈgʌnə/ *n.* **1** *Brit.* an artillery soldier (esp. as an official term for a private). **2** *Naut.* a warrant officer in charge of a battery, magazine, etc. **3** a member of an aircraft crew who operates a gun. **4** a person who hunts game with a gun.

gunnera /ˈgʌn(ə)rə, gʌˈnɪərə/ *n.* any plant of the genus *Gunnera* from S. America and New Zealand, having large leaves and often grown for ornament. [modern Latin, named after J. E. *Gunnerus*, Norwegian botanist d. 1773]

gunnery /ˈgʌnəri/ *n.* **1** the construction and management of large guns. **2** the firing of guns.

gunny /ˈgʌni/ *n.* (*pl.* **-ies**) **1** coarse sacking, usu. of jute fibre. **2** a sack made of this. [Hindi & Marathi *gōnī* from Sanskrit *goṇī* 'sack']

gunplay /ˈgʌnpleɪ/ *n.* the use of guns.

gunpoint /ˈgʌnpɔɪnt/ *n.* □ **at gunpoint** threatened with a gun or an ultimatum etc.

gunpowder /ˈgʌnpaʊdə/ *n.* **1** an explosive made of saltpetre, sulphur, and charcoal. **2** a fine green tea of granular appearance.

gunpower /ˈgʌnpaʊə/ *n.* the strength or quantity of available guns.

gunroom /ˈgʌnruːm, -rʊm/ *n.* **1** a room in a house for storing sporting guns. **2** *Brit.* quarters for junior officers (originally for gunners) in a warship.

gun-runner *n.* a person engaged in the illegal sale or importing of firearms. □ **gun-running** *n.*

gunship /ˈgʌnʃɪp/ *n.* a heavily armed helicopter or other aircraft.

gunshot /ˈgʌnʃɒt/ *n.* **1** a shot fired from a gun. **2** the range of a gun (*within gunshot*).

gun-shy *adj.* (esp. of a sporting dog) alarmed at the report of a gun.

gunsight /ˈgʌnsʌɪt/ *n.* a sight on a gun (see SIGHT *n.* 6a).

gun-site *n. Brit.* a (usu. fortified) emplacement for a gun.

gunslinger /ˈgʌnslɪŋə/ *n. slang* a gunman. □ **gunslinging** *n.* & *adj.*

gunsmith /ˈgʌnsmɪθ/ *n.* a person who makes, sells, and repairs small firearms.

gunstock /ˈgʌnstɒk/ *n.* the wooden mounting of the barrel of a gun.

Gunter's chain /ˈgʌntəz/ *n. Surveying* **1** a measuring chain of 66 ft. **2** this length as a unit. [named after E. *Gunter*, English mathematician d. 1626]

gunwale /ˈgʌn(ə)l/ *n.* (also **gunnel**) the upper edge of the side of a boat or ship. [GUN + WALE (because formerly used to support guns)]

gunyah /ˈgʌnjə/ *n. Austral.* an Aboriginal bush hut. [Dharuk *ganʸi* 'house, hut']

guppy /ˈgʌpi/ *n.* (*pl.* **-ies**) a freshwater fish, *Poecilia reticulata*, of the W. Indies and S. America, giving birth to live young and frequently kept in aquariums. [named after R. J. L. *Guppy*, 19th-c. Trinidadian clergyman who sent the first specimen to the British Museum]

gurdwara /gʊəˈdwɑːrə, gəːˈdwɑːrə/ *n.* a Sikh temple. [Punjabi *gurduārā*, from Sanskrit *guru* 'teacher' + *dvāra* 'door']

gurgle /ˈgəːg(ə)l/ *v. & n.* ● *v.* **1** *intr.* make a bubbling sound as of water from a bottle. **2** *tr.* utter with such a sound. ● *n.* a gurgling sound. [imitative, or from Dutch *gorgelen*, German *gurgeln*, or medieval Latin *gurgulare*, from Latin *gurgulio* 'gullet']

Gurkha /ˈgəːkə, ˈgʊəkə/ *n.* **1** a member of the dominant Hindu race in Nepal. **2** a Nepalese soldier serving in the British army. [native name, from Sanskrit *go* 'cow' + *rakṣ* 'protect']

gurn /gəːn/ *v.intr.* (also **girn**) esp. *dial.* grimace, pull a face (esp. for a competition). □ **gurner** *n.* **gurning** *n.* [dialect variant of GRIN]

gurnard /ˈgəːnəd/ *n.* (also **gurnet** /ˈgəːnɪt/) any marine fish of the family Triglidae, having a large spiny head with mailed sides, and three finger-like pectoral rays used for walking on the seabed etc. [Middle English via Old French *gornart*, from *grondir* 'to grunt', from Latin *grunnire*]

guru /ˈgʊruː, ˈguːruː/ *n.* **1** a Hindu or Sikh spiritual teacher or head of a religious sect. **2 a** an influential teacher. **b** a revered mentor. [Hindi *gurū* 'teacher' from Sanskrit *gurús* 'grave, dignified']

gush /gʌʃ/ *v. & n.* ● *v.* **1** *tr. & intr.* emit or flow in a sudden and copious stream. **2** *intr.* speak or behave with effusiveness or sentimental affectation. ● *n.* **1** a sudden or copious stream. **2** an effusive or sentimental manner. □ **gushing** *adj.* **gushingly** *adv.* [Middle English *gosshe*, *gusche*, probably imitative]

gusher /ˈgʌʃə/ *n.* **1** an oil well from which oil flows without being pumped. **2** an effusive person.

gushy /ˈgʌʃi/ *adj.* (**gushier**, **gushiest**) excessively effusive or sentimental. □ **gushily** *adv.* **gushiness** *n.*

gusset /ˈgʌsɪt/ *n.* **1** a piece let into a garment etc. to strengthen or enlarge a part. **2** a bracket strengthening an angle of a structure. □ **gusseted** *adj.* [Middle English from Old French *gousset* 'flexible piece filling up a joint in armour', from *gousse* 'pod, shell']

gussy /ˈgʌsi/ *v.tr.* (**-ies, -ied**) (esp. in *passive*; foll. by *up*) *colloq.* smarten up, dress up. [perhaps from *Gussie* pet form of the name *Augustus*]

gust /gʌst/ *n. & v.* ● *n.* **1** a sudden strong rush of wind. **2** a burst of rain, fire, smoke, or sound. **3** a passionate or emotional outburst. ● *v.intr.* blow in gusts. [Old Norse *gustr*, related to *gjósa* 'to gush']

gustation /gʌˈsteɪʃ(ə)n/ *n.* the act or capacity of tasting. □ **gustative** /ˈgʌstətɪv/ *adj.* **gustatory** /gʌˈsteɪt(ə)ri, ˈgʌstət(ə)ri/ *adj.* [French *gustation* or Latin *gustatio*, via *gustare* from *gustus* 'taste']

gusto /ˈgʌstəʊ/ *n.* (*pl.* **-os** or **-oes**) **1** zest; enjoyment or vigour in doing something. **2** (foll. by *for*) *archaic* a relish or liking. **3** *archaic* a style of artistic execution. [Italian, from Latin *gustus* 'taste']

gusty /ˈgʌsti/ *adj.* (**gustier**, **gustiest**) **1** characterized by or blowing in gusts. **2** characterized by gusto. □ **gustily** *adv.* **gustiness** *n.*

gut /gʌt/ *n. & v.* ● *n.* **1** the lower alimentary canal or a part of this; the intestine. **2** (in *pl.*) the bowel or entrails, esp. of animals. **3** (in *pl.*) *colloq.* personal courage and determination; vigorous application and perseverance. **4** (in *pl.*) *colloq.* the belly as the source of appetite. **5** (in *pl.*) **a** the contents of anything, esp. representing substantiality. **b** the essence of a thing, e.g. of an issue or problem. **6 a** material for violin or racket strings or surgical use made from the intestines of animals. **b** material for fishing lines made from the silk-glands of silkworms. **7 a** a narrow water-passage; a sound, straits. **b** a defile or narrow passage. **8** (*attrib.*) **a** instinctive (*a gut reaction*). **b** fundamental (*a gut issue*). ● *v.tr.* (**gutted**, **gutting**) **1** remove or destroy (esp. by fire) the internal fittings of (a house etc.). **2** take out the guts of (a fish). **3** (as **gutted** *adj.*) *slang* bitterly disappointed; deeply upset. **4** extract the essence of (a book etc.). □ **hate a person's guts** *colloq.* dislike a person intensely. **sweat** (or **work**) **one's guts out** *colloq.* work extremely hard. [Old English *guttas* (pl.), probably related to *gēotan* 'pour']

gut flora *n.* = INTESTINAL FLORA.

gutless /ˈgʌtlɪs/ *adj.* *colloq.* lacking courage or determination; feeble. □ **gutlessly** *adv.* **gutlessness** *n.*

gut-rot *n. Brit. slang* **1** = ROT-GUT. **2** a stomach upset.

gutsy /ˈgʌtsi/ *adj.* (**gutsier**, **gutsiest**) *colloq.* **1** courageous. **2** greedy. □ **gutsily** *adv.* **gutsiness** *n.*

gutta-percha /gʌtəˈpəːtʃə/ *n.* a tough plastic substance obtained from the latex of various Malaysian trees. [Malay *getah* 'gum' + *percha*, the name of a tree]

guttate /ˈgʌteɪt/ *adj. Biol.* having droplike markings. [Latin *guttatus* 'speckled' from *gutta* 'drop']

gutter /ˈgʌtə/ *n. & v.* ● *n.* **1** a shallow trough below the eaves of a house, or a channel at the side of a street, to carry off rainwater. **2** (prec. by *the*) a poor or degraded background or environment. **3** an open conduit along which liquid flows out. **4** a groove. **5** a track made by the flow of water. ● *v.* **1** *intr.* flow in streams. **2** *tr.* furrow, channel. **3** *intr.* (of a candle) burn unsteadily and melt away rapidly forming channels in the sides. [Middle English from Anglo-French *gotere*, Old French *gotiere*, ultimately from Latin *gutta* 'drop']

guttering /ˈgʌt(ə)rɪŋ/ *n.* **1 a** the gutters of a building etc. **b** a section or length of a gutter. **2** material for gutters.

gutter press *n. Brit.* sensational journalism concerned esp. with the private lives of public figures.

guttersnipe /ˈgʌtəsnʌɪp/ *n.* a street urchin.

guttural /ˈgʌt(ə)r(ə)l/ *adj. & n.* ● *adj.* **1** throaty, harsh-sounding. **2 a** *Phonet.* (of a consonant) produced in the throat or by the back of the tongue and palate. **b** (of a sound) coming from the throat. **c** of the throat. ● *n.* *Phonet.* a guttural consonant (e.g. *k*, *g*). □ **gutturally** *adv.* [French *guttural* or medieval Latin *gutturalis* from Latin *guttur* 'throat']

guv /gʌv/ *n. Brit. slang* = GOVERNOR 7c. [abbreviation]

guy[1] /gʌɪ/ *n. & v.* ● *n.* **1** *colloq.* a man; a fellow. **2** (usu. in *pl.*) *N. Amer.* a person of either sex. **3** *Brit.* an effigy of Guy Fawkes in ragged clothing, burnt on a bonfire on 5 Nov. **4** *Brit.* a grotesquely dressed person. ● *v.tr.* **1** ridicule. **2** *Brit.* exhibit in effigy. [earliest in sense 3, from *Guy* Fawkes, conspirator in the Gunpowder Plot to blow up Parliament in 1605]

guy[2] /gʌɪ/ *n. & v.* ● *n.* a rope or chain to secure a tent or steady a crane-load etc. ● *v.tr.* secure with a guy or guys. [probably of Low German origin]

guzzle /ˈgʌz(ə)l/ *v.tr. & intr.* eat, drink, or consume excessively or greedily. □ **guzzler** *n.* [perhaps from Old French *gosiller* 'chatter, vomit' from *gosier* 'throat']

GWR *abbr. hist.* Great Western Railway.

Gy *abbr.* = GRAY[1].

gybe /dʒʌɪb/ *v. & n.* (*US* **jibe**) ● *v.* **1** *intr.* (of a fore-and-aft sail or boom) swing across in wearing or running before the wind. **2** *tr.* cause (a sail) to do this. **3** *intr.* (of a ship or its crew) change course so that this happens. ● *n.* a change of course causing gybing. [obsolete Dutch *gijben*]

gym /dʒɪm/ *n. colloq.* **1** a gymnasium. **2** gymnastics. [abbreviation]

gymkhana /dʒɪmˈkɑːnə/ *n.* **1** a meeting for competition or display in sport, esp. horse-riding. **2** *Brit.* a public place with facilities for athletics. [Hindustani *gendkhāna* 'ball-house, racket court', assimilated to GYMNASIUM]

gymnasium /dʒɪmˈneɪzɪəm/ *n.* (*pl.* **gymnasiums** or **gymnasia** /-zɪə/) **1** a room or building equipped for gymnastics. **2** /also gɪmˈnɑːzɪəm/ a school in Germany or Scandinavia that prepares pupils for university entrance. □ **gymnasial** *adj.* [Latin from Greek *gumnasion*, via *gumnazō* 'exercise' from *gumnos* 'naked']

gymnast /ˈdʒɪmnast/ *n.* an expert in gymnastics. [French *gymnaste* or Greek *gumnastēs* 'athlete-trainer', from *gumnazō*: see GYMNASIUM]

gymnastic /dʒɪm'nastɪk/ *adj.* of or involving gymnastics. □ **gymnastically** *adv.* [Latin *gymnasticus* from Greek *gumnastikos* (as GYMNASIUM)]

gymnastics /dʒɪm'nastɪks/ *n.pl.* (also treated as *sing.*) **1** exercises developing or displaying physical agility and coordination, usu. in competition. **2** other physical or mental agility of a specified kind (*verbal gymnastics*; *pianistic gymnastics*).

gymno- /'dʒɪmnəʊ/ *comb. form Biol.* bare, naked. [Greek *gumnos* 'naked']

gymnosophist /dʒɪm'nɒsəfɪst/ *n.* a member of an ancient Hindu sect wearing little clothing and devoted to contemplation. □ **gymnosophy** *n.* [Middle English via French *gymnosophiste* and Latin *gymnosophistae* (pl.) from Greek *gumnosophistai*: see GYMNO-, SOPHIST]

gymnosperm /'dʒɪmnə(ʊ)spəːm/ *n.* any of various plants having seeds unprotected by an ovary, including the conifers, cycads, and ginkgo (opp. ANGIOSPERM). □ **gymnospermous** /-'spəːməs/ *adj.*

gymp var. of GIMP[1].

gymslip /'dʒɪmslɪp/ *n. Brit.* a sleeveless tunic, usu. belted, worn by schoolgirls.

gynaeceum var. of GYNOECIUM.

gynaeco- /gʌɪnɪ'kɒ, gʌɪ'niːkəʊ, dʒ-/ *comb. form* (*US* **gyneco-**) woman, women; female. [Greek *gunē gunaikos* 'woman']

gynaecology /gʌɪnɪ'kɒlədʒi, dʒ-/ *n.* (*US* **gynecology**) the science of the physiological functions and diseases of women and girls, esp. those affecting the reproductive system. □ **gynaecological** /-kə'lɒdʒɪk(ə)l/ *adj.* **gynaecologically** /-kə'lɒdʒɪk(ə)li/ *adv.* **gynaecologist** *n.* **gynecologic** /-kə'lɒdʒɪk/ *adj. US.*

gynaecomastia /ˌgʌɪnɪkə(ʊ)'mastɪə/ *n.* (*US* **gynecomastia**) *Med.* enlargement of a man's breasts, usu. due to hormone imbalance or hormone therapy.

gynandromorph /dʒɪ'nandrəmɔːf, gʌɪ-/ *n. Biol.* an individual, esp. an insect, having male and female characteristics. □ **gynandromorphic** /-'mɔːfɪk/ *adj.* **gynandromorphism** /-'mɔːfɪz(ə)m/ *n.* [formed as GYNANDROUS + Greek *morphē* 'form']

gynandrous /dʒɪ'nandrəs, gʌɪ-/ *adj. Bot.* with stamens and pistil united in one column, as in orchids. [Greek *gunandros* 'of doubtful sex', from *gunē* 'woman' + *anēr andros* 'man']

gyneco- *US* var. of GYNAECO-.

gynoecium /gʌɪ'niːsɪəm, dʒ-/ *n.* (also **gynaeceum**) (*pl.* **-cia** /-sɪə/) *Bot.* the carpels of a flower taken collectively. [modern Latin, from Greek *gunaikeion* 'women's apartments' (as GYNAECO-, Greek *oikos* 'house')]

-gynous /'dʒɪnəs, 'gɪnəs/ *comb. form Bot.* forming adjectives meaning 'having specified female organs or pistils' (*monogynous*). [Greek *-gunos* from *gunē* 'woman']

gyp[1] /dʒɪp/ *n. Brit. colloq.* **1** pain or severe discomfort. **2** a scolding (*gave them gyp*). [19th c.: perhaps from *gee-up* (see GEE[2])]

gyp[2] /dʒɪp/ *n. Brit.* a college servant at Cambridge and Durham. [perhaps from obsolete *gippo* 'scullion', originally a man's short tunic, from obsolete French *jupeau*]

gyp[3] /dʒɪp/ *v. & n. slang* ● *v.tr.* (**gypped**, **gypping**) cheat, swindle. ● *n.* an act of cheating; a swindle. [19th c.: origin unknown]

gyppy tummy var. of GIPPY TUMMY.

gypsophila /dʒɪp'sɒfɪlə/ *n.* any plant of the genus *Gypsophila* (daisy family), with a profusion of small usu. white flowers. [modern Latin, from Greek *gupsos* 'chalk' + *philos* 'loving']

gypsum /'dʒɪpsəm/ *n.* a hydrated form of calcium sulphate occurring naturally and used to make plaster of Paris and in the building industry. □ **gypseous** *adj.* **gypsiferous** /-'sɪf(ə)rəs/ *adj.* [Latin from Greek *gupsos*]

gypsy /'dʒɪpsi/ *n.* (also **gipsy**) (*pl.* **-ies**) **1** (also **Gypsy**) a member of a nomadic people of Europe and N. America, of Hindu origin with dark skin and hair, and speaking a language (Romany) related to Hindi. **2** a person resembling or living like this people. □ **gypsyish** *adj.* [earlier *gipcyan*, *gipsen* from EGYPTIAN, from the supposed origin of gypsies when they appeared in England in the early 16th c.]

gypsy moth *n.* a kind of tussock moth, *Lymantria dispar*, whose larvae are very destructive to foliage.

gyrate *v. & adj.* ● *v.intr.* /dʒʌɪ'reɪt/ go in a circle or spiral; revolve, whirl. ● *adj.* /'dʒʌɪrət/ *Bot.* arranged in rings or convolutions. □ **gyration** /-'reɪʃ(ə)n/ *n.* **gyrator** /-'reɪtə/ *n.* **gyratory** /'dʒʌɪrət(ə)ri, -'reɪt(ə)ri/ *adj.* [Latin *gyrare gyrat-* 'revolve', via *gyrus* 'ring' from Greek *guros*]

gyre /'dʒʌɪə, 'gʌɪə/ *v. & n.* esp. *poet.* ● *v.intr.* whirl, gyrate. ● *n.* **1** a whirling, a vortex. **2** a circulatory ocean current. [Latin *gyrus* 'ring' from Greek *guros*]

gyrfalcon /'dʒəːfɔː(l)k(ə)n, -fɒlk(ə)n/ *n.* (also **gerfalcon**) a large falcon, *Falco rusticolus*, of cold northern regions. [Middle English via Old French *gerfaucon* and Frankish *gērfalco* from Old Norse *geirfálki*: see FALCON]

gyro /'dʒʌɪrəʊ/ *n.* (*pl.* **-os**) *colloq.* **1** = GYROSCOPE. **2** = GYROCOMPASS. [abbreviation]

gyro- /'dʒʌɪrəʊ/ *comb. form* **1** rotation. **2** gyroscopic. [Greek *guros* 'ring']

gyrocompass /'dʒʌɪrə(ʊ)kʌmpəs/ *n.* a non-magnetic compass giving true north and bearings from it by means of a gyroscope.

gyromagnetic /ˌdʒʌɪrəʊmag'nɛtɪk/ *adj.* **1** *Physics* of the magnetic and mechanical properties of a rotating charged particle. **2** (of a compass) combining a gyroscope and a normal magnetic compass.

gyropilot /'dʒʌɪrə(ʊ)ˌpʌɪlət/ *n.* a gyrocompass used for automatic steering.

gyroplane /'dʒʌɪrə(ʊ)pleɪn/ *n.* an autogiro or similar aircraft.

gyroscope /'dʒʌɪrəskəʊp/ *n.* a wheel or disc mounted so as to spin rapidly about an axis whose orientation is not fixed but is unperturbed by tilting of the mount, esp. used in stabilizers, gyrocompasses, navigation systems, etc. □ **gyroscopic** /-'skɒpɪk/ *adj.* **gyroscopically** /-'skɒpɪk(ə)li/ *adv.* [French (as GYRO-, -SCOPE)]

gyrostabilizer /'dʒʌɪrəʊˌsteɪbɪlʌɪzə/ *n.* a gyroscopic device for maintaining the equilibrium of a ship, aircraft, platform, etc.

gyrus /'dʒʌɪrəs/ *n.* (*pl.* **gyri** /-rʌɪ/) a fold or convolution, esp. of the brain. [Latin from Greek *guros* 'ring']

gyttja /'jɪtʃə/ *n. Geol.* a lake deposit of a usu. black organic sediment. [Swedish, = mud, ooze]

gyver var. of GUIVER.

H[1] /eɪtʃ/ *n.* (also **h**) (*pl.* **Hs** or **H's**) **1** the eighth letter of the alphabet (see AITCH). **2** anything having the form of an H (esp. in *comb.*: *H-girder*).

H[2] *abbr.* (also **H.**) **1** (of a pencil lead) hard. **2** (water) hydrant. **3** *slang* heroin.

H[3] *symb.* **1** *Chem.* the element hydrogen. **2** henry(s). **3** magnetic field strength.

h[1] *abbr.* (also **h.**) **1** height. **2** hour(s). **3** hot. **4** horse. **5** husband.

h[2] *symb.* **1** hecto-. **2** Planck's constant.

Ha *symb. Chem.* the element hahnium.

ha[1] /hɑː/ *int. & v.* (also **hah**) ● *int.* expressing surprise, suspicion, triumph, etc. (cf. HA HA). ● *v.intr.* (in **hum and ha**): see HUM[1]. [Middle English]

ha[2] *abbr.* hectare(s).

haar /hɑː/ *n.* a cold sea fog on the east coast of England or Scotland. [perhaps from Old Norse *hárr* 'hoar, hoary']

Hab. *abbr.* Habakkuk (Old Testament).

habanera /habəˈnɛːrə, ɑːb-/ *n.* **1** a Cuban dance in slow duple time. **2** the music for this. [Spanish, fem. of *habanero* 'of Havana', the capital of Cuba]

habdabs /ˈhabdabz/ *n.pl.* (usu. in phr. **the screaming habdabs**) *slang* nervous anxiety or irritation; the heebie-jeebies. [20th c.: origin unknown]

habeas corpus /ˌheɪbɪəs ˈkɔːpəs/ *n.* a writ requiring a person to be brought before a judge or into court, esp. to investigate the lawfulness of his or her detention. [Latin, = you must have the body]

haberdasher /ˈhabədaʃə/ *n.* **1** *Brit.* a dealer in dress accessories and sewing goods. **2** *N. Amer.* a dealer in men's clothing. □ **haberdashery** *n.* (*pl.* **-ies**). [Middle English, probably ultimately from Anglo-French *hapertas*, perhaps the name of a fabric]

habergeon /ˈhabədʒ(ə)n, həˈbəːdʒ(ə)n/ *n. hist.* a sleeveless coat of mail. [Middle English from Old French *haubergeon* (as HAUBERK)]

habiliment /həˈbɪlɪm(ə)nt/ *n.* (usu. in *pl.*) **1** clothes suited to a particular purpose. **2** *joc.* ordinary clothes. [Middle English from Old French *habillement*, via *habiller* 'fit out' from *habile* ABLE]

habilitate /həˈbɪlɪteɪt/ *v.intr.* qualify for office (esp. as a teacher in a German university). □ **habilitation** /-ˈteɪʃ(ə)n/ *n.* [medieval Latin *habilitare* (as ABILITY)]

habit /ˈhabɪt/ *n. & v.* ● *n.* **1** a settled or regular tendency or practice (often foll. by *of* + verbal noun: *has a habit of ignoring me*). **2** a practice that is hard to give up. **3** a mental constitution or attitude. **4** *Psychol.* an automatic reaction to a specific situation. **5** *colloq.* an addictive practice, esp. of taking drugs. **6 a** the dress of a particular class, esp. of a religious order. **b** (in full **riding habit**) a woman's riding dress. **c** *archaic* dress, attire. **7** a bodily constitution. **8** *Biol.* & *Crystallog.* a mode of growth. ● *v.tr.* (usu. as **habited** *adj.*) clothe. □ **make a habit of** do regularly. [Middle English via Old French *abit* from Latin *habitus*, from *habēre habit-* 'have, be constituted']

habitable /ˈhabɪtəb(ə)l/ *adj.* that can be inhabited. □ **habitability** /-ˈbɪlɪti/ *n.* [Middle English via Old French from Latin *habitabilis* (as HABITANT)]

habitant *n.* **1** /ˈhabɪt(ə)nt/ an inhabitant. **2** /abiːˈtɒ̃/ **a** an early French settler in Canada or Louisiana. **b** a descendant of these settlers. [French via Old French *habiter* from Latin *habitare* 'inhabit' (as HABIT)]

habitat /ˈhabɪtat/ *n.* **1** the natural home of an organism. **2** a habitation. [Latin, = it dwells: see HABITANT]

habitation /habɪˈteɪʃ(ə)n/ *n.* **1** the process of inhabiting (*fit for human habitation*). **2** a house or home. [Middle English via Old French from Latin *habitatio -onis* (as HABITANT)]

habit-forming *adj.* causing addiction.

habitual /həˈbɪtʃʊəl, -tjʊəl/ *adj.* **1** done constantly or as a habit. **2** regular, usual. **3** given to a (specified) habit (*a habitual smoker*). □ **habitually** *adv.* **habitualness** *n.* [medieval Latin *habitualis* (as HABIT)]

habituate /həˈbɪtʃʊeɪt, -tjʊeɪt/ *v.tr.* (often foll. by *to*) accustom; make used to something. □ **habituation** /-ˈeɪʃ(ə)n/ *n.* [Late Latin *habituare* (as HABIT)]

habitude /ˈhabɪtjuːd/ *n.* **1** a mental or bodily disposition. **2** a custom or tendency. [Middle English via Old French from Latin *habitudo -dinis*, from *habēre habit-* 'have']

habitué /həˈbɪtjʊeɪ/ *n.* a habitual visitor or resident. [French, past part. of *habituer* (as HABITUATE)]

háček /ˈhɑːtʃɛk, ˈha-/ *n.* a diacritic mark (ˇ) placed over letters to modify the sound in some Slavonic and Baltic languages. [Czech, diminutive of *hák* 'hook']

hachures /haˈʃjʊəz/ *n.pl.* parallel lines used in hill-shading on maps, their closeness indicating the steepness of gradient. □ **hachure** *v.tr.* [French from *hacher* HATCH[3]]

hacienda /hasɪˈɛndə/ *n.* in Spanish-speaking countries: **1** an estate or plantation with a dwelling house. **2** a factory. [Spanish, from Latin *facienda* 'things to be done']

hack[1] /hak/ *v. & n.* ● *v.* **1** *tr.* cut or chop roughly; mangle. **2** *tr.* kick the shin of (an opponent at football). **3** *intr.* (often foll. by *at*) deliver cutting blows. **4** *tr.* cut (one's way) through thick foliage etc. **5 a** *intr.* (usu. foll. by *into*) use a computer to gain unauthorized access to data in a system. **b** *tr.* gain unauthorized access to (data in a computer). **6** *tr. slang* **a** manage, cope with. **b** tolerate. ● *n.* **1** a kick with the toe of a boot. **2** a gash or wound, esp. from a kick. **3 a** a mattock. **b** a miner's pick. □ **hacking cough** a short dry frequent cough. [Old English *haccian* 'cut in pieces', from West Germanic]

hack[2] /hak/ *n., adj., & v.* ● *n.* **1 a** a horse for ordinary riding. **b** a horse let out for hire. **c** = JADE[2] 1. **2** a dull, uninspired writer. **3** a person hired to do dull routine work. **4** *N. Amer.* a taxi. ● *attrib.adj.* **1** used as a hack. **2** typical of a hack; commonplace (*hack work*). ● *v.* **1 a** *intr.* use a horse for ordinary riding, esp. for pleasure. **b** *tr.* ride (a horse) in this way. **2** *tr.* make common or trite. [abbreviation of HACKNEY]

hack[3] /hak/ *n.* **1** a board on which a hawk's meat is laid. **2** a rack holding fodder for cattle. □ **at hack** (of a young hawk) not yet allowed to prey for itself. [variant of HATCH[1]]

hackberry /ˈhakb(ə)ri/ *n.* (*pl.* **-ies**) **1** any tree of the genus *Celtis*, native to N. America, bearing purple edible berries. **2** the berry of this tree. [variant of *hagberry*, of Norse origin]

hacker /ˈhakə/ *n.* **1** a person or thing that hacks or cuts roughly. **2** a person who uses computers for a hobby, esp. to gain unauthorized access to data.

hackette /haˈkɛt/ *n. colloq.*, usu. *derog.* a female journalist.

hackle /ˈhak(ə)l/ *n. & v.* ● *n.* **1** a long feather or series of feathers on the neck or saddle of a domestic cock and other birds. **2** *Fishing* an artificial fishing-fly dressed with a hackle. **3** a feather in a Highland soldier's bonnet. **4** (in *pl.*) the erectile hairs along the back of a dog, which rise when it is angry or alarmed. **5** a steel comb for dressing flax. ● *v.tr.* dress or comb with a hackle. □ **make a person's hackles rise** cause a person to be angry or indignant. [Middle English *hechele, hakele*, ultimately from West Germanic: related to HOOK]

hackney /'hakni/ *n.* (*pl.* **-eys**) **1** a light horse with a high-stepping trot, used in harness. **2** (*attrib.*) designating any of various vehicles kept for hire. [Middle English, perhaps from *Hackney* (formerly *Hakenei*) in London, where horses were pastured]

■ **Usage** *Hackney* is no longer used except in *hackney carriage*, still in official use as a term for 'taxi'.

hackneyed /'haknɪd/ *adj.* (of a phrase etc.) made commonplace or trite by overuse.

hacksaw /'hakso:/ *n.* & *v.* ● *n.* a saw with a narrow blade set in a frame, for cutting metal. ● *v.tr.* (*past part.* **-sawn** or **-sawed**) cut using a hacksaw.

had *past* and *past part.* of HAVE.

haddock /'hadək/ *n.* (*pl.* same) an edible marine fish, *Melanogrammus aeglefinus*, of the N. Atlantic, allied to cod, but smaller. [Middle English, probably from Anglo-French *hadoc*, Old French (*h*)*adot*, of unknown origin]

hade /heɪd/ *n.* & *v.* *Geol.* ● *n.* an incline from the vertical. ● *v.intr.* incline from the vertical. [17th c., perhaps a dialect form of *head*]

Hades /'heɪdi:z/ *n.* (in Greek mythology) the underworld, the abode of the spirits of the dead. [Greek *haidēs*, originally a name of Pluto, the god of the dead]

Hadith /ha'di:θ/ *n.* *Relig.* a body of traditions relating to Muhammad. [Arabic *ḥadīṯ* 'tradition']

hadn't /'had(ə)nt/ *contr.* had not.

hadron /'hadrɒn/ *n.* *Physics* any strongly interacting subatomic particle. □ **hadronic** /-'drɒnɪk/ *adj.* [Greek *hadros* 'bulky']

hadrosaur /'hadrəso:/ *n.* a large herbivorous usu. bipedal dinosaur of the family Hadrosauridae, of the late Cretaceous period, with jaws flattened like the bill of a duck. [modern Latin genus name *Hadrosaurus*, from Greek *hadros* 'thick, stout' + *sauros* 'lizard']

hadst /hadst/ *archaic 2nd sing. past* of HAVE.

haecceity /hɛk'si:ɪti, hi:k-/ *n.* *Philos.* **1** the quality of a thing that makes it unique or describable as 'this (one)'. **2** individuality. [medieval Latin *haecceitas* from *haec*, fem. of *hic* 'this']

haem /hi:m/ *n.* (*US* **heme**) a porphyrin compound containing iron, responsible for the red colour of haemoglobin. [Greek *haima* 'blood', or from HAEMOGLOBIN]

haemal /'hi:m(ə)l/ *adj.* (*US* **hemal**) *Anat.* **1** of or concerning the blood. **2** situated on the same side of the body as the heart and major blood vessels (i.e. in chordates, ventral). [Greek *haima* 'blood']

haematic /hi:'matɪk/ *adj.* (*US* **hematic**) *Med.* of or containing blood. [Greek *haimatikos* (as HAEMATIN)]

haematin /'hi:mətɪn/ *n.* (*US* **hematin** /'hi:m-, 'hɛm-/) *Biochem.* a bluish-black derivative of haemoglobin, formed by removal of the protein part and oxidation of the iron atom. [Greek *haima -matos* 'blood']

haematite /'hi:mətʌɪt/ *n.* (*US* **hematite** /'hi:m-, 'hɛm-/) a ferric oxide ore forming dark red or reddish-black masses. [Latin *haematites* from Greek *haimatitēs* (*lithos*) 'bloodlike (stone)' (as HAEMATIN)]

haemato- /'hi:mətəʊ/ *comb. form* (*US* **hemato-**) blood. [Greek *haima haimat-* 'blood']

haematocele /'hi:mətə(ʊ)si:l/ *n.* (*US* **hematocele** /'hi:-, 'hɛ-/) *Med.* a swelling caused by blood collecting in a body cavity.

haematocrit /'hi:mətə(ʊ)krɪt/ *n.* (*US* **hematocrit** /'hi:-, 'hɛ-/) *Physiol.* **1** the ratio of the volume of red blood cells to the total volume of blood. **2** an instrument for measuring this. [HAEMATO- + Greek *kritēs* 'judge']

haematology /hi:mə'tɒlədʒi/ *n.* (*US* **hematology** /hi:-, hɛ-/) the study of the physiology of the blood. □ **haematologic** /-tə'lɒdʒɪk/ *adj.* **haematological** /-tə'lɒdʒɪk(ə)l/ *adj.* **haematologist** *n.*

haematoma /hi:mə'təʊmə/ *n.* (*US* **hematoma** /hi:-, hɛ-/) (*pl.* **haematomas** or **haematomata** /-mətə/) *Med.* a solid swelling of clotted blood within the tissues.

haematophagous /hi:mə'tɒfəgəs/ *adj.* (*US* **hematophagous**) feeding on blood. [HAEMATO- + -PHAGOUS]

haematuria /hi:mə'tjʊərɪə/ *n.* (*US* **hematuria** /hi:-, hɛ-/) *Med.* the presence of blood in urine.

-haemia var. of -AEMIA.

haemo- /'hi:məʊ/ *comb. form* (*US* **hemo-**) = HAEMATO-. [abbreviation]

haemocoel /'hi:məsi:l/ *n.* (*US* **hemocoel** /'hi:m-, 'hɛm-/) *Zool.* the primary body cavity of most invertebrates, containing circulatory fluid. [HAEMO- + Greek *koilos* 'hollow, cavity']

haemocyanin /hi:mə(ʊ)'sʌɪənɪn/ *n.* (*US* **hemocyanin** /hi:-, hɛ-/) an oxygen-carrying protein containing copper, present in the blood plasma of arthropods and molluscs. [HAEMO- + *cyanin*, a blue pigment (as CYAN)]

haemodialysis /ˌhi:məʊdʌɪ'alɪsɪs/ *n.* (*US* **hemodialysis** /ˌhi:-, ˌhɛ-/) = DIALYSIS 2.

haemoglobin /hi:mə'gləʊbɪn/ *n.* (*US* **hemoglobin** /hi:-, hɛ-/) a red oxygen-carrying protein containing iron, present in the red blood cells of vertebrates. [shortened from HAEMATO- + GLOBULIN]

haemolymph /'hi:mə(ʊ)lɪmf/ *n.* (*US* **hemolymph** /'hi:-, 'hɛ-/) a fluid equivalent to blood in invertebrate animals.

haemolysis /hi:'mɒlɪsɪs/ *n.* (*US* **hemolysis** /hi:-, hɛ-/) the rupture of red blood cells leading to loss of haemoglobin. □ **haemolytic** /-mə'lɪtɪk/ *adj.*

haemophilia /hi:mə'fɪlɪə/ *n.* (*US* **hemophilia** /hi:-, hɛ-/) *Med.* a usu. hereditary disorder with a tendency to bleed severely from even a slight injury, through the failure of the blood to clot normally. □ **haemophilic** *adj.* [modern Latin (as HAEMO-, -PHILIA)]

haemophiliac /hi:mə'fɪlɪak/ *n.* (*US* **hemophiliac** /hi:-, hɛ-/) a person suffering from haemophilia.

haemorrhage /'hɛmərɪdʒ/ *n.* & *v.* (*US* **hemorrhage**) ● *n.* **1** an escape of blood from a ruptured blood vessel, esp. when profuse. **2** an extensive damaging loss suffered by a state, organization, etc., esp. of people or assets. ● *v.* **1** *intr.* suffer a haemorrhage; bleed heavily. **2** *intr.* be extensively lost or dissipated. **3** *tr.* expend (money etc.) in large amounts; lose or dissipate, esp. wastefully. □ **haemorrhagic** /hɛmə'radʒɪk/ *adj.* [earlier *haemorrhagy*, from French *hémorr*(*h*)*agie* via Latin *haemorrhagia* from Greek *haimorrhagia*, from *haima* 'blood' + stem of *rhēgnumi* 'burst']

haemorrhoid /'hɛmərɔɪd/ *n.* (*US* **hemorrhoid**) (usu. in *pl.*) swollen veins at or near the anus; piles. □ **haemorrhoidal** /-'rɔɪd(ə)l/ *adj.* [Middle English *emeroudis* (Bibl. *emerods*) via Old French *emeroyde* and Latin from Greek *haimorrhoides* (*phlebes*) 'bleeding (veins)', from *haima* 'blood', *-rhoos* -'flowing']

haemostasis /hi:mə(ʊ)'steɪsɪs/ *n.* (*US* **hemostasis**) the stopping of the flow of blood from a wound etc. □ **haemostatic** /hi:mə'statɪk, hɛ-/ *adj.*

haere mai /'hʌɪrə 'mʌɪ/ *int.* *NZ* welcome. [Maori, literally 'come hither']

hafiz /'hɑ:fɪz/ *n.* a Muslim who knows the Koran by heart. [Persian from Arabic *ḥāfiẓ* 'guardian']

hafnium /'hafnɪəm/ *n.* *Chem.* a silvery lustrous metallic element occurring naturally with zirconium, used in tungsten alloys for filaments and electrodes (symbol **Hf**). [modern Latin from *Hafnia*, the Latinized form of the former name of Copenhagen, capital of Denmark]

haft /hɑ:ft/ *n.* & *v.* ● *n.* the handle of a dagger or knife etc. ● *v.tr.* provide with a haft. [Old English *hæft*, from Germanic]

Hag. *abbr.* Haggai (Old Testament).

hag[1] /hag/ *n.* **1** an ugly old woman. **2** a witch. **3** = HAGFISH. □ **haggish** *adj.* [Middle English *hegge, hagge*, perhaps from Old English *hægtesse*, Old High German *hagazissa*, of unknown origin]

hag[2] /hag/ *n. Sc. & N.Engl.* **1** a soft place on a moor. **2** a firm place in a bog. [Old Norse *högg* 'gap', originally 'cutting blow', related to HEW]

hagfish /ˈhagfɪʃ/ *n.* (*pl.* usu. same) any marine jawless fish of the family Myxinidae, with an eel-like slimy body, a slit-like mouth surrounded by barbels, and a rasp-like tongue used for feeding on dead or dying fish. [HAG[1]]

Haggadah /həˈgɑːdə, hagaˈdɑː/ *n.* **1** a legend etc. used to illustrate a point of the Law in the Talmud; the legendary element of the Talmud. **2** a book recited at the Passover Seder service. □ **Haggadic** /-ˈgadɪk, -ˈgɑːdɪk/ *adj.* [Hebrew, = tale, from *higgiḏ* 'tell']

haggard /ˈhagəd/ *adj. & n.* ● *adj.* **1** looking exhausted and distraught, esp. from fatigue, worry, privation, etc. **2** (of a hawk) caught and trained as an adult. ● *n.* a haggard hawk. □ **haggardly** *adv.* **haggardness** *n.* [French *hagard*, of uncertain origin: later influenced by HAG[1]]

haggis /ˈhagɪs/ *n.* a Scottish dish consisting of a sheep's or calf's offal mixed with suet, oatmeal, etc., and boiled in a bag made from the animal's stomach or in an artificial bag. [Middle English, probably from Scots *hag* 'to hack' (as HAGGLE)]

haggle /ˈhag(ə)l/ *v. & n.* ● *v.intr.* (often foll. by *about, over*) dispute or bargain persistently. ● *n.* a dispute or wrangle. □ **haggler** *n.* [earlier in the sense 'hack': from Old Norse *höggva* HEW]

hagio- /ˈhagɪəʊ/ *comb. form* of saints or holiness. [Greek *hagios* 'holy']

Hagiographa /hagɪˈɒgrəfə/ *n.* the twelve books comprising the last of the three major divisions of the Hebrew Scriptures, additional to the Law and the Prophets.

hagiographer /hagɪˈɒgrəfə/ *n.* **1** a writer of the lives of saints. **2** a writer of any of the Hagiographa.

hagiography /hagɪˈɒgrəfi/ *n.* **1** the writing of the lives of saints. **2** an idealized biography of any person. □ **hagiographic** /-əˈgrafɪk/ *adj.* **hagiographical** /-əˈgrafɪk(ə)l/ *adj.*

hagiolatry /hagɪˈɒlətri/ *n.* the worship of saints.

hagiology /hagɪˈɒlədʒi/ *n.* literature dealing with the lives and legends of saints. □ **hagiological** /-gɪəˈlɒdʒɪk(ə)l/ *adj.* **hagiologist** *n.*

hag-ridden /ˈhagrɪd(ə)n/ *adj.* afflicted by nightmares or anxieties.

hah var. of HA[1].

ha-ha /ˈhɑːhɑː/ *n.* a ditch with a wall on its inner side below ground level, forming a boundary to a park or garden without interrupting the view. [French, perhaps from the cry of surprise on encountering it]

ha ha /hɑː ˈhɑː/ *int.* representing laughter. [Old English: cf. HA[1]]

hahnium /ˈhɑːnɪəm/ *n. Chem.* (a name proposed in the US for) the artificial radioactive element of atomic number 105 (symbol **Ha**). [named after O. *Hahn*, German chemist (d. 1968), + -IUM]

Haida /ˈhʌɪdə/ *n. & adj.* ● *n.* **1** (*pl.* same or **Haidas**) a member of a N. American Indian people living on the west coast of Canada. **2** the language of this people. ● *adj.* of or relating to this people or their language.

haik /heɪk, ˈhɑːɪk/ *n.* (also **haick**) an outer covering for head and body worn by Arabs. [Moroccan Arabic *ḥā'ik*]

haiku /ˈhʌɪkuː/ *n.* (*pl.* same) **1** a Japanese three-part poem of usu. 17 syllables. **2** an English imitation of this. [Japanese]

hail[1] /heɪl/ *n. & v.* ● *n.* **1** pellets of frozen rain falling in showers from cumulonimbus clouds. **2** (foll. by *of*) a barrage or onslaught (of missiles, curses, questions, etc.). ● *v.* **1** *intr.* (prec. by *it* as subject) hail falls (*it is hailing; if it hails*). **2 a** *tr.* pour down (blows, words, etc.). **b** *intr.* come down forcefully. [Old English *hagol, hægl, hagalian*, from Germanic]

hail[2] /heɪl/ *v., int., & n.* ● *v.* **1** *tr.* greet enthusiastically. **2** *tr.* signal to or attract the attention of (*hailed a taxi*). **3** *tr.* (often foll. by *as*) acclaim (*hailed him king; was hailed as a success*). **4** *intr.* (foll. by *from*) have one's home or origins in (a place) (*hails from Mauritius*). ● *int. archaic* or *literary* expressing greeting. ● *n.* **1** a greeting or act of hailing. **2** distance as affecting the possibility of hailing (*was within hail*). □ **hailer** *n.* [elliptical use of obsolete *hail* (*adj.*) from Old Norse *heill* 'sound', WHOLE]

hail-fellow-well-met *adj.* informal; showing usu. excessive familiarity.

Hail Mary *n.* the Ave Maria (see AVE *n.* 1).

hailstone /ˈheɪlstəʊn/ *n.* a pellet of hail.

hailstorm /ˈheɪlstɔːm/ *n.* a period of heavy hail.

hair /hɛː/ *n.* **1 a** any of the fine threadlike strands growing from the skin of mammals, esp. from the human head. **b** these collectively (*his hair is falling out*). **2 a** an artificially produced hairlike strand, e.g. in a brush. **b** a mass of such hairs. **3** anything resembling a hair. **4** an elongated cell growing from the epidermis of a plant. **5** a very small quantity or extent (also *attrib.*: *a hair crack*). □ **get in a person's hair** *colloq.* encumber or annoy a person. **keep one's hair on** *Brit. colloq.* remain calm; not get angry. **let one's hair down** *colloq.* abandon restraint; behave freely or wildly. **make one's hair stand on end** alarm or horrify one. **not turn a hair** remain apparently unmoved or unaffected. □ **haired** *adj.* (also in *comb.*). **hairless** *adj.* **hairlike** *adj.* [Old English *hǣr*, from Germanic]

hairbreadth /ˈhɛːbrɛdθ/ *n.* = HAIR'S BREADTH (esp. *attrib.*: *a hairbreadth escape*).

hairbrush /ˈhɛːbrʌʃ/ *n.* a brush for arranging or smoothing the hair.

haircare /ˈhɛːkɛː/ *n.* the care of the hair.

haircloth /ˈhɛːklɒθ/ *n.* stiff cloth woven from hair, used e.g. in upholstery.

haircut /ˈhɛːkʌt/ *n.* **1** a cutting of the hair. **2** the style in which the hair is cut.

hairdo /ˈhɛːduː/ *n.* (*pl.* **-dos**) *colloq.* the style of or an act of styling a woman's hair.

hairdresser /ˈhɛːdrɛsə/ *n.* **1** a person who cuts and styles hair, esp. professionally. **2** the business or establishment of a hairdresser. □ **hairdressing** *n.*

hairdryer /ˈhɛːdrʌɪə/ *n.* (also **hairdrier**) an electrical device for drying the hair by blowing warm air over it.

hair-grass *n.* any of various grasses, esp. of the genus *Deschampsia*, *Corynephous*, *Aira*, etc., with slender stems.

hairgrip /ˈhɛːgrɪp/ *n. Brit.* a flat hairpin with the ends close together.

hairline /ˈhɛːlʌɪn/ *n.* **1** the edge of a person's hair, esp. on the forehead. **2** (usu. *attrib.*) a very thin line or crack etc.

hairnet /ˈhɛːnɛt/ *n.* a piece of fine mesh-work for confining the hair.

hair of the dog *n.* alcoholic drink to cure the effects of alcoholic drink.

hairpiece /ˈhɛːpiːs/ *n.* a quantity or switch of detached hair used to augment a person's natural hair.

hairpin /ˈhɛːpɪn/ *n.* a U-shaped pin for fastening the hair.

hairpin bend *n.* a sharp U-shaped bend in a road.

hair-raising *adj.* extremely alarming; terrifying.

hair's breadth *n.* a very small amount or margin.

hair shirt *n. & adj.* ● *n.* a shirt of haircloth, worn formerly by penitents and ascetics. ● *attrib.adj.* (**hair-shirt**) austere, harsh, self-sacrificing.

hairslide /ˈhɛːslʌɪd/ *n. Brit.* a (usu. ornamental) clip for keeping the hair in position.

hair-splitting *adj. & n.* making overfine distinctions; quibbling. □ **hair-splitter** *n.*

hairspray /ˈhɛːspreɪ/ *n.* a solution sprayed on to the hair to keep it in place.

hairspring /ˈhɛːsprɪŋ/ *n.* a fine spring regulating the balance wheel in a watch.

hairstreak /ˈhɛːstriːk/ *n.* a butterfly of the genera *Callophrys, Strymonidia*, etc., with fine streaks or rows of spots on its wings.

hairstyle /ˈhɛːstʌɪl/ *n.* a particular way of arranging or dressing the hair. ▫ **hairstyling** *n.* **hairstylist** *n.*

hair-trigger *n.* a trigger of a firearm set for release at the slightest pressure.

hairy /ˈhɛːri/ *adj.* (**hairier**, **hairiest**) **1** made of or covered with hair. **2** having the feel of hair. **3** *slang* **a** alarmingly unpleasant or difficult. **b** crude, clumsy. ▫ **hairily** *adv.* **hairiness** *n.*

haj /hadʒ/ *n.* (also **hajj**) the annual Muslim pilgrimage to Mecca. [Arabic *ḥājj* 'pilgrimage']

haji /ˈhadʒiː/ *n.* (also **hajji**) **1** (*pl.* **-is**) a Muslim who has been to Mecca as a pilgrim. **2** (**Haji**) a title given to such a pilgrim. [Persian *ḥājī* (partly via Turkish *hacı*) from Arabic *ḥājj*: see HAJ]

haka /ˈhɑːkə/ *n.* **1** a Maori ceremonial war dance accompanied by chanting. **2** an imitation of this by members of a New Zealand sports team before a match. [Maori]

hake /heɪk/ *n.* any edible marine fish of the genus *Merluccius*, esp. *M. merluccius* with an elongated body and large head. [Middle English, perhaps ultimately from dialect *hake* 'hook']

hakenkreuz /ˈhɑːk(ə)nkrɔɪts, German ˈhɑːkənkrɔyts/ *n.* a swastika, esp. as a Nazi symbol. [German, from *Haken* 'hook' + *Kreuz* CROSS]

hakim[1] /haˈkiːm/ *n.* (in India and Muslim countries) a physician. [Arabic *ḥakīm* 'wise man, physician']

hakim[2] /ˈhɑːkɪm/ *n.* (in India and Muslim countries) a judge, ruler, or governor. [Arabic *ḥākim* 'governor']

Halacha /halɑːˈxɑː, həˈlɑːkə/ *n.* (also **Halakah**) Jewish law and jurisprudence, based on the Talmud. ▫ **Halachic** *adj.* [Aramaic *hᵃlāḵāh* 'law']

halal /həˈlɑːl/ *v.* & *n.* ● *v.tr.* (**halalled**, **halalling**) kill (an animal) as prescribed by Muslim law. ● *n.* (often *attrib.*) meat prepared in this way; lawful food. [Arabic *ḥalāl* 'lawful']

halation /həˈleɪʃ(ə)n/ *n. Photog.* the spreading of light beyond its proper extent in a developed image, caused by internal reflection in the support of the emulsion. [formed irregularly from HALO + -ATION]

halberd /ˈhalbəːd/ *n.* (also **halbert**) *hist.* a combined spear and battleaxe. [Middle English via French *hallebarde* and Italian *alabarda* from Middle High German *helmbarde*, from *helm* 'handle' + *barde* 'hatchet']

halberdier /halbəˈdɪə/ *n. hist.* a man armed with a halberd. [French *hallebardier* (as HALBERD)]

halcyon /ˈhalsɪən, ˈhalʃ(ə)n/ *adj.* & *n.* ● *adj.* **1** calm, peaceful (*halcyon days*). **2** (of a period) happy, prosperous. ● *n.* **1** any tropical kingfisher of the genus *Halcyon*, with brightly coloured plumage. **2** *Mythol.* a bird thought in antiquity to breed in a nest floating at sea at the winter solstice, charming the wind and waves into calm. [Middle English via Latin *(h)alcyon* from Greek *(h)alkuōn* 'kingfisher']

hale[1] /heɪl/ *adj.* (esp. of an old person) strong and healthy (esp. in **hale and hearty**). ▫ **haleness** *n.* [Old English *hāl* WHOLE]

hale[2] /heɪl/ *v.tr.* drag or draw forcibly. [Middle English via Old French *haler* from Old Norse *hala*]

haler /ˈhɑːlə/ *n.* (*pl.* same or **haleru** /ˈhɑːləruː/) a monetary unit of the Czech Republic and Slovakia, equal to one-hundredth of a koruna. [Czech *haléř* from Middle High German *haller*]

half /hɑːf/ *n., predet., adj.,* & *adv.* ● *n.* (*pl.* **halves** /hɑːvz/) **1** either of two equal or corresponding parts or groups into which a thing, number, or quantity, is or might be divided. **2** *colloq.* = HALF-BACK. **3** *Brit. colloq.* half a pint, esp. of beer etc. **4** either of two equal periods of play in sports. **5** *colloq.* a half-price fare or ticket, esp. for a child. **6** *Golf* a score for an individual hole that is the same as one's opponent's. ● *predet.* of an amount or quantity equal to a half, or loosely to a part thought of as roughly a half (*take half the men*; *spent half the time reading*; *half a pint*). ● *adj.* forming a half (*a half share*). ● *adv.* **1** (often in *comb.*) to the extent of half; partly (*only half-cooked*; *half-frozen*; *half-laughing*). **2** to a certain extent; somewhat (esp. in idiomatic phrases: *half dead*; *am half inclined to agree*). **3** (in reckoning time) by the amount of half (an hour etc.) (*half past two*). ▫ **at half cock** see COCK[1]. **by half** (prec. by *too* + adj.) excessively (*too clever by half*). **by halves** imperfectly or incompletely (*never does things by halves*). **half the battle** see BATTLE. **half a chance** *colloq.* the slightest opportunity (esp. *given half a chance*). **half an eye** the slightest degree of perceptiveness. **have half a mind** see MIND. **the half of it** *colloq.* the rest or more important part of something (usu. after *neg.*: *you don't know the half of it*). **half the time** see TIME. **not half 1** not nearly (*not half long enough*). **2** *colloq.* not at all (*not half bad*). **3** *Brit. slang* to an extreme degree (*he didn't half get angry*). [Old English *half, healf*, from Germanic]

■ **Usage** In sense 3 of the adverb, the word *past* is often omitted in colloquial usage, e.g. *She came at half two.* In some parts of Scotland and Ireland this means 'half past one'.

half a crown var. of HALF-CROWN.

half a dozen var. of HALF-DOZEN.

half-and-half *adv., adj.,* & *n.* ● *adv.* in equal parts. ● *adj.* that is half one thing and half another. ● *n. US* a mixture of milk and cream.

half-back *n.* (in some sports) a player between the forwards and full-backs.

half-baked *adj.* **1** incompletely considered or planned. **2** (of enthusiasm etc.) only partly committed. **3** foolish.

half-beak *n.* any fish of the family Hemirhamphidae, with the lower jaw projecting beyond the upper.

half-binding *n.* a type of bookbinding in which the spine and corners are bound in one material (usu. leather) and the sides in another.

half-blood *n.* **1** a person having one parent in common with another. **2** this relationship. **3** = HALF-BREED.

half-blooded *adj.* born from parents of different races.

half-blue *n. Brit.* **1** a person who has represented a university, esp. Oxford or Cambridge, in a minor sport or as a second choice in a sport but who has not received a full blue (cf. BLUE[1] *n.* 3). **2** this distinction.

half board *n. Brit.* provision of bed, breakfast, and one main meal at a hotel etc.

half-boot *n.* a boot reaching up to the calf.

half-bottle *n.* **1** a bottle that is half the standard size. **2** its contents or the amount that will fill it.

half-breed *n. offens.* a person of mixed race.

half-brother *n.* a brother with only one parent in common.

half-caste *n.* & *adj. offens.* ● *n.* a person whose parents are of different races, esp. the offspring of a European father and an Indian mother. ● *adj.* of or relating to such a person.

half-century *n.* **1** a period of fifty years. **2** a score etc. of fifty in a sporting event, esp. in cricket.

half-crown *n.* (also **half a crown**) *hist.* (in the UK) a former coin and monetary unit equal to 2s. 6d. (12½p).

half-cut *adj. Brit. slang* fairly drunk.

half-deck *n.* the quarters of cadets and apprentices on a merchant vessel.

half-dozen *n.* (also **half a dozen**) *colloq.* six, or about six.

half-duplex *adj.* (of a communications system, computer circuit, etc.) allowing the transmission of signals in both directions but not simultaneously.

half-hardy *adj.* (of a plant) able to grow in the open air at all times except in severe frost.

half-hear *v.tr.* (*past.* and *past part.* **half-heard** /-hɜːd/) hear (a thing) incompletely (*she only half-heard their shouts above the sound of the television*).

half-hearted *adj.* lacking enthusiasm; feeble. □ **half-heartedly** *adv.* **half-heartedness** *n.*

half hitch *n.* a noose or knot formed by passing the end of a rope round its standing part and then through the loop.

half holiday *n.* a day of which half (usu. the afternoon) is taken as a holiday.

half-hose *n.* socks.

half-hour *n.* **1** (also **half an hour**) a period of 30 minutes. **2** a point of time 30 minutes after any hour o'clock. □ **half-hourly** *adj. & adv.*

half-hunter *n.* a watch with a hinged cover in which a small opening allows identification of the approximate position of the hands.

half-inch *n. & v.* ● *n.* a unit of length half as large as an inch. ● *v.tr. Brit. rhyming slang* steal (= *pinch*).

half-integer *n.* a number obtained by dividing an odd integer by two. □ **half-integral** *adj.*

half-landing *n.* a landing part of the way up a flight of stairs, whose length is twice the width of the flight plus the width of the well.

half-lap *n.* = LAP JOINT.

half-length *n.* a canvas depicting a half-length portrait.

half-life *n.* the time taken for the radioactivity or some other property of a substance to fall to half its original value.

half-light *n.* a dim imperfect light.

half-litre *n.* a unit of capacity half as large as a litre.

half-marathon *n.* a long-distance running race, usu. of 13 miles 352 yards (21.243 km).

half mast *n.* the position of a flag halfway down the mast, as a mark of respect for a person who has died. □ **at half mast** often *joc.* (esp. of a garment) having slipped down.

half measures *n.pl.* an unsatisfactory compromise or inadequate policy.

half-moon *n.* **1** the moon when only half its illuminated surface is visible from earth. **2** the time when this occurs. **3** a semicircular object.

half nelson see NELSON.

half note *n.* esp. *N. Amer. Mus.* = MINIM 1.

half pay *n.* reduced income, esp. on retirement.

halfpenny /ˈheɪpni/ *n.* (also **ha'penny** /ˈheɪpni/) (*pl.* **-pennies** or **-pence** /ˈheɪp(ə)ns/) (in the UK) a former bronze coin worth half a penny (withdrawn in 1984). (cf. FARTHING).

halfpennyworth /ˈheɪpəθ, ˈheɪpnɪwəθ/ *n.* (also **ha'p'orth**) *Brit.* **1** as much as could be bought for a halfpenny. **2** *colloq.* a negligible amount (esp. after *neg.*: *doesn't make a halfpennyworth of difference*).

half-pie *adj. NZ slang* imperfect, mediocre.

half-plate *n. Brit.* **1** a photographic plate 16.5 × 10.8 cm. **2** a photograph reproduced from this.

half-relief *n. Sculpture* **1** a method of moulding, carving, or stamping, in relief a design in which figures etc. project to half their true proportions (cf. *high relief*, *low relief* (RELIEF 6a)). **2** a sculpture, carving, etc. in half-relief.

half-seas-over *adj. Brit. slang* fairly drunk.

half-sister *n.* a sister with only one parent in common.

half-sole *n.* the sole of a boot or shoe from the shank to the toe.

half-sovereign *n. hist.* (in the UK) a former gold coin and monetary unit equal to ten shillings (50p).

half-step *n. Mus.* a semitone.

half-term *n. Brit.* a period about halfway through a school term, when a short holiday is usually taken.

half-timbered *adj. Archit.* having walls with a timber frame and a brick or plaster filling. □ **half-timbering** *n.*

half-time *n.* **1** the time at which half of a game or contest is completed. **2** a short interval occurring at this time.

half-title *n.* **1** the title or short title of a book, printed on the recto of the leaf preceding the title-page. **2** the title of a section of a book printed on the recto of the leaf preceding it.

half-tone *n.* **1** a reproduction printed from a block (produced by photographic means) in which the various tones of grey are produced from small and large black dots. **2** esp. *US Mus.* a semitone.

half-track *n.* **1** a propulsion system for land vehicles with wheels at the front and an endless driven belt at the back. **2** a vehicle equipped with this.

half-truth *n.* a statement that (esp. deliberately) conveys only part of the truth.

half-volley *n.* (*pl.* **-eys**) (in ball games) the playing of a ball as soon as it bounces off the ground.

halfway /hɑːfˈweɪ, ˈhɑːfweɪ/ *adv. & adj.* ● *adv.* **1** at a point equidistant between two others (*we were halfway to Rome*). **2** to some extent; more or less (*is halfway decent*). ● *adj.* situated halfway (*reached a halfway point*).

halfway house *n.* **1** a compromise. **2** the halfway point in a progression. **3** a centre for rehabilitating ex-prisoners, mental patients, or others unused to normal life. **4** an inn midway between two towns.

halfway line *n.* a line midway between the ends of a pitch, esp. in football.

halfwit /ˈhɑːfwɪt/ *n.* **1** *colloq.* an extremely foolish or stupid person. **2** a person who is mentally deficient. □ **half-witted** /-ˈwɪtɪd/ *adj.* **half-wittedly** /-ˈwɪtɪdli/ *adv.* **half-wittedness** /-ˈwɪtɪdnɪs/ *n.*

half-yearly *adj. & adv.* esp. *Brit.* at intervals of six months.

halibut /ˈhalɪbət/ *n.* (*pl.* same) any of various large marine flatfishes, esp. *Hippoglossus hippoglossus* of the N. Atlantic, used as food. [Middle English, from *haly* HOLY + BUTT[3] 'flatfish', perhaps because eaten on holy days]

halide /ˈheɪlʌɪd/ *n. Chem.* a binary compound of a halogen with another element or group.

halieutic /halɪˈjuːtɪk/ *adj. formal* of or concerning fishing. [Latin *halieuticus* from Greek *halieutikos*, from *halieutēs* 'fisherman']

haliotis /halɪˈəʊtɪs/ *n.* any edible gastropod mollusc of the genus *Haliotis* with an ear-shaped shell lined with mother-of-pearl. [Greek *hals hali-* 'sea' + *ous ōt-* 'ear']

halite /ˈhalʌɪt/ *n.* rock salt. [modern Latin *halites* from Greek *hals* 'salt']

halitosis /halɪˈtəʊsɪs/ *n.* = BAD BREATH. [modern Latin, from Latin *halitus* 'breath']

hall /hɔːl/ *n.* **1 a** a space or passage into which the front entrance of a house etc. opens. **b** *N. Amer.* a corridor or passage in a building. **2 a** a large room or building for meetings, meals, concerts, etc. **b** (in *pl.*) music halls. **3** *Brit.* a large country house, esp. with a landed estate. **4** (*Brit.* in full **hall of residence**) a university residence for students. **5 a** (in a college etc.) a common dining room. **b** *Brit.* dinner in this. **6** the building of a guild (*Fishmongers' Hall*). **7 a** a large public room in a palace etc. **b** the principal living room of a medieval house. [Old English from Germanic: related to HELL]

hallelujah var. of ALLELUIA.

hallmark /ˈhɔːlmɑːk/ *n. & v.* ● *n.* **1** a mark used by the British assay offices indicating the standard of gold, silver, and platinum. **2** any distinctive feature esp. of excellence. ● *v.tr.* **1** stamp with a hallmark. **2** designate as excellent. [Goldsmiths' *Hall* in London where articles are tested and stamped]

hallo esp. *Brit.* var. of HELLO.

Hall of Fame *n.* **1** esp. *N. Amer.* a building with memorials of people who have excelled, esp. in a particular sport. **2** a group of people famous in a particular sphere.

hall of residence see HALL 4.

halloo /həˈluː, ha-/ *int., n., & v.* ● *int.* **1** inciting dogs to the chase. **2** calling attention. **3** expressing surprise. ● *n.* the cry 'halloo'. ● *v.* (**halloos, hallooed**) **1** *intr.* cry 'halloo', esp. to dogs. **2** *intr.* shout to attract attention. **3** *tr.* urge on (dogs etc.) with shouts. [perhaps from *hallow* 'pursue with shouts', from Old French *halloer* (imitative)]

hallow /ˈhaləʊ/ *v. & n.* ● *v.tr.* **1** make holy, consecrate. **2** honour as holy. ● *n. archaic* a saint or holy person. [Old English *hālgian, hālga*, from Germanic]

Hallowe'en /haləʊˈiːn/ *n.* the eve of All Saints' Day, 31 Oct. [HALLOW + EVEN[2]]

hall porter *n. Brit.* a porter who carries baggage etc. in a hotel.

hallstand /ˈhɔːlstand/ *n.* a stand in the hall of a house, with a mirror, pegs, etc.

Hallstatt /ˈhalʃtat/ *adj. Archaeol.* of or relating to a cultural phase of the late Bronze Age and early Iron Age in Europe, dated to *c.*700–500 BC. [a village in Austria, site of a burial ground of this period]

halluces *pl.* of HALLUX.

hallucinate /həˈluːsɪneɪt, -ˈljuː-/ *v.* **1** *tr.* produce illusions in the mind of (a person). **2** *intr.* experience hallucinations. □ **hallucinant** *adj. & n.* **hallucinator** *n.* [Latin *(h)allucinari* 'wander in mind' from Greek *alussō* 'be uneasy']

hallucination /həluːsɪˈneɪʃ(ə)n, -ljuː-/ *n.* the apparent perception of an object or sense datum not actually present. □ **hallucinatory** /həˈluːsɪnətəri/ *adj.* [Latin *hallucinatio* (as HALLUCINATE)]

hallucinogen /həˈluːsɪnədʒ(ə)n, -ˈljuː-/ *n.* a drug causing hallucinations. □ **hallucinogenic** /-ˈdʒɛnɪk/ *adj.*

hallux /ˈhaləks/ *n.* (*pl.* **halluces** /-jʊsiːz/) **1** the big toe. **2** the innermost digit of the hind foot of vertebrates. [modern Latin from Latin *allex*]

hallway /ˈhɔːlweɪ/ *n.* an entrance hall or corridor.

halm var. of HAULM.

halma /ˈhalmə/ *n.* a game played by two or four persons using a board of 256 squares, with pieces advancing from one corner to the opposite corner by being moved over other pieces into vacant squares. [Greek, = leap]

halo /ˈheɪləʊ/ *n. & v.* ● *n.* (*pl.* **-oes** or **-os**) **1** a disc or circle of light shown surrounding the head of a sacred person. **2** the glory associated with an idealized person etc. **3** a circle of white or coloured light round a luminous body, esp. the sun or moon. **4** a circle or ring. ● *v.tr.* (**-oes, -oed**) surround with a halo. [medieval Latin via Latin from Greek *halōs* 'threshing floor, disc of the sun or moon']

halogen /ˈhalədʒ(ə)n, ˈheɪl-/ *n.* **1** *Chem.* any of a group of reactive non-metallic elements (fluorine, chlorine, bromine, iodine, and astatine) which form strongly acidic compounds with hydrogen from which simple salts can be made. **2** (*attrib.*) (of lamps and radiant heat sources) using a filament surrounded by a halogen, usu. iodine vapour. □ **halogenic** /-ˈdʒɛnɪk/ *adj.* [Greek *hals halos* 'salt']

halogenation /halədʒɪˈneɪʃ(ə)n/ *n.* the introduction of a halogen atom into a molecule. □ **halogenated** /həˈlɒdʒɪneɪtɪd/ *adj.*

halon /ˈheɪlɒn/ *n. Chem.* any of various gaseous compounds of carbon, bromine, and other halogens, used to extinguish fires. [as HALOGEN + -ON]

haloperidol /halə(ʊ)ˈpɛrɪdɒl, heɪlə(ʊ)-/ *n. Pharm.* a drug used to treat psychotic disorders, esp. mania. [HALOGEN + PIPERIDINE + -OL[1]]

halophyte /ˈhaləfʌɪt, ˈheɪlə-/ *n.* a plant adapted to saline conditions. [Greek *hals halos* 'salt' + -PHYTE]

halothane /ˈhaləθeɪn/ *n. Med.* a volatile liquid used as a general anaesthetic, a halogenated derivative of ethane. [HALOGEN + ETHANE]

halt[1] /hɔːlt/ *n. & v.* ● *n.* **1** a stop (usu. temporary); an interruption of progress (*come to a halt*). **2** a temporary stoppage on a march or journey. **3** *Brit.* a minor stopping place on a local railway line, usu. without permanent buildings. ● *v.intr. & tr.* stop; come or bring to a halt. □ **call a halt (to)** decide to stop. [originally in the phrase *make halt* from German *Halt machen*, from *halten* 'hold, stop']

halt[2] /hɔːlt/ *v. & adj.* ● *v.intr.* **1** (esp. as **halting** *adj.*) fail to make smooth progress. **2** hesitate (*halt between two opinions*). **3** walk hesitatingly. **4** *archaic* be lame. ● *adj. archaic* lame or crippled. □ **haltingly** *adv.* [Old English *halt, healt, healtian*, from Germanic]

halter /ˈhɔːltə/ *n. & v.* ● *n.* **1** a rope or strap with a noose or headstall for horses or cattle. **2 a** a strap round the back of a woman's neck holding her dress-top and leaving her shoulders and back bare. **b** a dress-top held by this. **3 a** a rope with a noose for hanging a person. **b** death by hanging. ● *v.tr.* **1** put a halter on (a horse etc.). **2** hang (a person) with a halter. [Old English *hælftre*: cf. HELVE]

halter-break *v.tr.* accustom (a horse) to a halter.

halteres /halˈtɪəriːz/ *n.pl.* the balancing organs of dipterous insects. [Greek, = weights used to aid leaping, from *hallomai* 'to leap']

halter-neck *attrib.adj.* (of a garment) held up by a strap around the neck.

halva /ˈhalvɑː, -və/ *n.* (also **halvah**) a sweet confection of sesame flour and honey. [Yiddish via Turkish *helva* from Arabic *ḥalwa*]

halve /hɑːv/ *v.tr.* **1** divide into two halves or parts. **2** reduce by half. **3** share equally (with another person etc.). **4** *Golf* use the same number of strokes as one's opponent in (a hole or match). **5** fit (crossing timbers) together by cutting out half the thickness of each. [Middle English *halfen* from HALF]

halves *pl.* of HALF.

halyard /ˈhaljəd/ *n. Naut.* a rope or tackle for raising or lowering a sail or yard etc. [Middle English *halier*, from HALE[2] + -IER, associated with YARD[1]]

ham /ham/ *n. & v.* ● *n.* **1 a** the upper part of a pig's leg salted and dried or smoked for food. **b** the meat from this. **2** the back of the thigh; the thigh and buttock. **3** (often *attrib.*) *slang* an inexpert or unsubtle actor or piece of acting. **4** (in full **radio ham**) *colloq.* the operator of an amateur radio station. ● *v.intr. & tr.* (often foll. by *up*) (**hammed, hamming**) *slang* overact; act or treat emotionally or sentimentally. [Old English *ham, hom*, from a Germanic root meaning 'be crooked']

hamadryad /haməˈdrʌɪəd, -ad/ *n.* **1** (in Greek and Roman mythology) a nymph who lives in a tree and dies when it dies. **2** the king cobra, *Naja bungarus.* [Middle English via Latin *hamadryas* from Greek *hamadruas*, from *hama* 'with' + *drus* 'tree']

hamadryas /haməˈdrʌɪəs, -as/ *n.* a large Arabian baboon, *Papio hamadryas*, with a silvery-grey cape of hair over the shoulders, held sacred in ancient Egypt. [modern Latin, as HAMADRYAD]

hamamelis /haməˈmiːlɪs/ *n.* any shrub of the genus *Hamamelis*, e.g. witch hazel. [modern Latin from Greek *hamamēlis* 'medlar']

hamartia /həˈmɑːtɪə/ *n.* (in Greek tragedy) the fatal flaw leading to the destruction of the tragic hero or heroine. [Greek, = fault, failure, guilt]

hamba /ˈhambə/ *int. S.Afr.* be off; go away. [Nguni *-hambe* from *ukuttamba* 'to go']

hamburger /ˈhambəːgə/ *n.* a beefburger, usu. served in a roll. [German, = of Hamburg in Germany]

hames /heɪmz/ *n.pl.* two curved pieces of iron or wood forming the collar or part of the collar of a draught horse, to which the traces are attached. [Middle English from Middle Dutch *hame*]

ham-fisted /hamˈfɪstɪd/ *adj. colloq.* clumsy, heavy-handed, bungling. □ **ham-fistedly** *adv.* **ham-fistedness** *n.*

ham-handed /hamˈhandɪd/ *adj. colloq.* = HAM-FISTED. □ **ham-handedly** *adv.* **ham-handedness** *n.*

Hamitic /həˈmɪtɪk/ *n. & adj.* ● *n.* a group of African languages including ancient Egyptian and Berber. ● *adj.* **1** of or relating to this group of languages. **2** of or relating to the Hamites, a group of peoples in Egypt and N. Africa, by tradition descended from Noah's son Ham (Gen. 10:6 ff.).

hamlet /'hamlɪt/ *n.* a small village, esp. one without a church. [Middle English via Anglo-French *hamelet(t)e*, Old French *hamelet*, diminutive of *hamel*, diminutive of *ham*, from Middle Low German *hamm*]

hammer /'hamə/ *n.* & *v.* ● *n.* **1 a** a tool with a heavy metal head mounted at right angles to the handle, used for breaking, driving nails, etc. **b** a machine with a metal block serving the same purpose. **c** a similar contrivance, as for exploding the charge in a gun, striking the strings of a piano, etc. **2** an auctioneer's mallet for indicating by a sharp tap that an article is sold. **3 a** a metal ball of about 7 kg, attached to a wire for throwing in an athletic contest. **b** the sport of throwing the hammer. **4** a bone of the middle ear; the malleus. ● *v.* **1 a** *tr.* & *intr.* hit or beat with or as with a hammer. **b** *intr.* strike loudly; knock violently (esp. on a door). **2** *tr.* **a** drive in (nails) with a hammer. **b** fasten or secure by hammering (*hammered the lid down*). **3** *tr.* (often foll. by *in*) inculcate (ideas, knowledge, etc.) forcefully or repeatedly. **4** *tr. colloq.* utterly defeat; inflict heavy damage on. **5** *intr.* (foll. by *at*, *away at*) work hard or persistently at. **6** *tr. Brit. Stock Exch.* declare (a person or a firm) a defaulter. □ **come under the hammer** be sold at an auction. **hammer out 1** make flat or smooth by hammering. **2** work out the details of (a plan, agreement, etc.) laboriously. **3** play (a tune, esp. on the piano) loudly or clumsily. □ **hammering** *n.* (esp. in sense 4 of *v.*). **hammerless** *adj.* [Old English *hamor*, *hamer*]

hammer and sickle *n.* the symbols of the industrial worker and the peasant used as the emblem of the former USSR and of international communism.

hammer and tongs *adv. colloq.* with great vigour and commotion.

hammerbeam /'haməbi:m/ *n.* a wooden beam (often carved) projecting from a wall to support the principal rafter or the end of an arch.

hammer drill *n.* a drill with a bit that moves backwards and forwards while rotating.

hammerhead /'haməhɛd/ *n.* **1** (also **hammerhead shark**) any shark of the family Sphyrnidae, with a flattened head and eyes in lateral extensions of it. **2** a long-legged African marsh bird, *Scopus umbretta*, with a thick bill and an occipital crest.

hammerlock /'haməlɒk/ *n. Wrestling* a hold in which the arm is twisted and bent behind the back.

hammer-toe *n.* a deformity in which the toe is bent permanently downwards.

hammock /'hamək/ *n.* a bed of canvas or rope network, suspended by cords at the ends, used esp. on board ship. [earlier *hamaca* from Spanish, from Taino *hamaka*]

hammy /'hami/ *adj.* (**hammier**, **hammiest**) **1** of or like ham. **2** *colloq.* (of an actor or acting) over-theatrical.

hamper[1] /'hampə/ *n.* **1** a large basket usu. with a hinged lid and containing food (*picnic hamper*) or *US* laundry. **2** *Brit.* a selection of food, drink, etc., for an occasion. [Middle English via obsolete *hanaper* from Anglo-French, from Old French *hanapier* 'case for a goblet' from *hanap* 'goblet']

hamper[2] /'hampə/ *v.* & *n.* ● *v.tr.* **1** prevent the free movement or activity of. **2** impede, hinder. ● *n. Naut.* necessary but cumbersome equipment on a ship. [Middle English: origin unknown]

hamsin var. of KHAMSIN.

hamster /'hamstə/ *n.* a Eurasian rodent of the subfamily Cricetinae, having a short tail and large cheek pouches for storing food, esp. (in full **common hamster**) *Cricetus cricetus* and (in full **golden hamster**) *Mesocricetus auratus*, often kept as a pet or as a laboratory animal. [German, from Old High German *hamustro* 'corn-weevil']

hamstring /'hamstrɪŋ/ *n.* & *v. Anat.* ● *n.* **1** each of five tendons at the back of the knee in humans. **2** the great tendon at the back of the hock in quadrupeds. ● *v.tr.* (*past* and *past part.* **hamstrung** or **hamstringed**) **1** cripple by cutting the hamstrings of (a person or animal). **2** prevent the activity or efficiency of (a person or enterprise).

hamulus /'hamjʊləs/ *n.* (*pl.* **hamuli** /-lʌɪ, -li:/) *Anat.*, *Zool.*, & *Bot.* a hooklike projection. [Latin, diminutive of *hamus* 'hook']

hand /hand/ *n.* & *v.* ● *n.* **1 a** the end part of the human arm beyond the wrist, including the fingers and thumb. **b** in other primates, the end part of a forelimb, also used as a foot. **2 a** (often in *pl.*) control, management, custody, disposal (*is in good hands*). **b** agency or influence (*suffered at their hands*). **c** a share in an action; active support. **3** a thing compared with a hand or its functions, esp. the pointer of a clock or watch. **4** the right or left side or direction relative to a person or thing. **5 a** a skill, esp. in something practical (*a hand for making pastry*). **b** a person skilful in some respect. **6** a person who does or makes something, esp. distinctively (*a picture by the same hand*). **7** an individual's writing or the style of this; a signature (*a legible hand*; *in one's own hand*; *witness the hand of* ...). **8** a person etc. as the source of information etc. (*at first hand*). **9** a pledge of marriage. **10** a person as a source of manual labour esp. in a factory, on a farm, or on board ship. **11 a** the playing cards dealt to a player. **b** the player holding these. **c** a round of play. **12** *colloq.* applause (*got a big hand*). **13** the unit of measure of a horse's height, equal to 4 inches (10.16 cm). **14** *Brit.* a forehock of pork. **15** a bunch of bananas. **16** (*attrib.*) **a** operated or held in the hand (*hand drill*; *hand luggage*). **b** done by hand and not by machine (*hand-knitted*). ● *v.tr.* **1** (foll. by *in*, *to*, *over*, etc.) deliver; transfer by hand or otherwise. **2** convey verbally (*handed me a lot of abuse*). **3** *colloq.* give away too readily (*handed them the advantage*). □ **all hands 1** the entire crew of a ship. **2** the entire workforce. **at hand 1** close by. **2** about to happen. **by hand 1** by a person and not a machine. **2** delivered privately and not by the public post. **from hand to mouth** satisfying only one's immediate needs (also *attrib.*: *a hand-to-mouth existence*). **get** (or **have** or **keep**) **one's hand in** become (or be or remain) practised in something. **give** (or **lend**) **a hand** assist in an action or enterprise. **hand and foot** completely; satisfying all demands (*waited on them hand and foot*). **hand down 1** pass the ownership or use of to another, esp. a successor or descendant. **2 a** transmit (a decision) from a higher court etc. **b** *US* express (an opinion or verdict). **hand in glove** in collusion or association. **hand in hand** in close association. **hand it to** *colloq.* acknowledge the merit of (a person). **hand off 1** *Rugby* push off (a tackling opponent) with the hand. **2** *Amer. Football* pass the ball by hand. **hand on** pass (a thing) to the next in a series or succession. **hand out 1** serve, distribute. **2** award, allocate (*the judges handed out stiff sentences*). **hand over** deliver; surrender possession of. **hand over fist** *colloq.* with rapid progress. **hand round** (or *US* **around**) distribute. **hands down** (esp. of winning) with no difficulty. **hands off** a warning not to touch or interfere with something. ● *adj.* (**hands-off**) not involving or requiring direct control or intervention. **hands-on 1** *Computing* of or requiring personal operation at a keyboard. **2** involving or offering active participation rather than theory; direct, practical. **a hand's turn** *colloq.* a stroke of work. **hands up!** an instruction to raise one's hands in surrender or to signify assent or participation. **have** (or **take**) **a hand in** share or take part in. **have one's hands full** be fully occupied. **have one's hands tied** *colloq.* be unable to act. **hold one's hand** = *stay one's hand* (see below). **in hand 1** receiving attention. **2** in reserve; at one's disposal. **3** under one's control. **lay** (or **put**) **one's hands on** see LAY[1]. **off one's hands** no longer one's responsibility. **on every hand** (or **all hands**) to or from all directions. **on hand 1** available. **2** present, in attendance. **on one's hands 1** resting on one as a responsibility. **2** at one's disposal; available (*with time on his hands*). **on the one** (or **the other**) **hand** from one (or another) point of view. **out of hand**

1 out of control. **2** peremptorily (*refused out of hand*). **put** (or **set**) **one's hand to** start work on; engage in. **stay one's hand** *archaic* or *literary* refrain from action. **to hand 1** within easy reach. **2** (of a letter) received. **turn one's hand to** undertake (as a new activity). □ **handless** *adj.* [Old English *hand, hond,* from Germanic]

handbag /ˈhan(d)bag/ *n.* & *v.* ● *n.* a small bag for a purse etc., carried esp. by a woman. ● *v.tr.* treat (a person, idea, etc.) ruthlessly or insensitively. □ **handbagging** *n.*

handball *n.* **1** /ˈhan(d)bɔːl/ **a** *Brit.* a game similar to football in which the ball is thrown rather than kicked. **b** a game in which a ball is hit with the hand in a walled court. **2** /han(d)ˈbɔːl/ *Football* intentional touching of the ball with the hand or arm by a player other than the goalkeeper in the penalty area, constituting a foul.

handbasin /ˈhan(d)beɪs(ə)n/ *n.* a small washbasin.

handbell /ˈhan(d)bɛl/ *n.* a small bell, usu. tuned to a particular note and rung by hand, esp. one of a set giving a range of notes.

handbill /ˈhan(d)bɪl/ *n.* a printed notice distributed by hand.

handbook /ˈhan(d)bʊk/ *n.* a short manual or guidebook.

handbrake /ˈhan(d)breɪk/ *n.* a brake operated by hand.

h. & c. *abbr. Brit.* hot and cold (water).

handcart /ˈhan(d)kɑːt/ *n.* a small cart pushed or drawn by hand.

handclap /ˈhan(d)klap/ *n.* a clapping of the hands.

handcraft /ˈhan(d)krɑːft/ *n.* & *v.* ● *n.* = HANDICRAFT. ● *v.tr.* make by handicraft.

hand cream *n.* an emollient for the hands.

handcuff /ˈhan(d)kʌf/ *n.* & *v.* ● *n.* (in *pl.*) a pair of lockable linked metal rings for securing a prisoner's wrists. ● *v.tr.* put handcuffs on.

-handed /ˈhandɪd/ *adj.* (in *comb.*) **1** for or involving a specified number of hands (in various senses) (*two-handed*). **2** using chiefly the hand specified (*left-handed*). □ **-handedly** *adv.* **-handedness** *n.* (both in sense 2).

handful /ˈhan(d)fʊl, -f(ə)l/ *n.* (*pl.* **-fuls**) **1** a quantity that fills the hand. **2** a small number or amount. **3** *colloq.* a troublesome person or task.

handglass /ˈhan(d)glɑːs/ *n.* **1** a magnifying glass held in the hand. **2** a small mirror with a handle.

hand grenade see GRENADE 1.

handgrip /ˈhan(d)grɪp/ *n.* **1** a grasp with the hand. **2** a handle designed for easy holding.

handgun /ˈhan(d)gʌn/ *n.* a small firearm held in and fired with one hand.

hand-held /ˈhandhɛld/ *adj.* & *n.* ● *adj.* designed to be held in the hand. ● *n.* a small hand-held computer.

handhold /ˈhandhəʊld/ *n.* something for the hands to grip on (in climbing, sailing, etc.).

hand-hot *adj.* (esp. of water) hot, but not too hot to put the hands into.

handicap /ˈhandɪkap/ *n.* & *v.* ● *n.* **1 a** a disadvantage imposed on a superior competitor in order to make the chances more equal. **b** a race or contest in which this is imposed. **2** the number of strokes by which a golfer normally exceeds par for the course. **3** a thing that makes progress or success difficult; an encumbrance or hindrance. **4** a condition that markedly restricts a person's ability to function physically, mentally, or socially. ● *v.tr.* (**handicapped**, **handicapping**) **1** impose a handicap on. **2** place (a person) at a disadvantage. □ **handicapper** *n.* [originally a game in which participants deposited forfeit money in a cap: the name probably from the phrase *hand in cap*]

handicapped /ˈhandɪkapt/ *adj.* suffering from a physical or mental disability.

handicraft /ˈhandɪkrɑːft/ *n.* work that requires both manual and artistic skill. [Middle English, alteration of earlier HANDCRAFT on the pattern of HANDIWORK]

handiwork /ˈhandɪwəːk/ *n.* work done or a thing made by hand, or by a particular person. [Old English *handgeweorc*]

handkerchief /ˈhaŋkətʃɪf/ *n.* (*pl.* **handkerchiefs** or **-chieves** /-tʃiːvz/) a square of cotton, linen, silk, etc., usu. carried in the pocket for wiping one's nose, etc.

handle /ˈhand(ə)l/ *n.* & *v.* ● *n.* **1** the part by which a thing is held, carried, or controlled. **2** a fact that may be taken advantage of (*gave a handle to his critics*). **3** *colloq.* a personal title. **4** the feel of goods, esp. textiles, when handled. ● *v.tr.* **1** touch, feel, operate, or move with the hands. **2** manage or deal with; treat in a particular or correct way (*knows how to handle people*; *unable to handle the situation*). **3** deal in (goods). **4** discuss or write about (a subject). □ **get a handle on** *colloq.* understand the basis of or reason for (a situation, circumstance, etc.). □ **handleable** *adj.* **handleability** /-ˈbɪlɪti/ *n.* **handled** *adj.* (also in *comb.*). [Old English *handle, handlian* (as HAND)]

handlebar /ˈhand(ə)lbɑː/ *n.* (often in *pl.*) the steering bar of a bicycle etc., with a handgrip at each end.

handlebar moustache *n.* a thick moustache extended sideways with curved ends.

handler /ˈhandlə/ *n.* **1** a person who handles or deals in certain commodities. **2** a person who trains and looks after an animal (esp. a police dog).

handlist /ˈhandlɪst/ *n.* a short list of essential reading, reference books, etc.

handmade /han(d)ˈmeɪd/ *adj.* made by hand and not by machine, esp. as designating superior quality.

handmaid /ˈhan(d)meɪd/ *n.* (also **handmaiden** /-meɪd(ə)n/) *archaic* a female servant or helper.

hand-me-down *n.* an article of clothing etc. passed on from another person.

handout /ˈhandaʊt/ *n.* **1** something given free to a needy person. **2** a statement given to the press etc.

handover /ˈhandəʊvə/ *n.* esp. *Brit.* the act or an instance of handing over.

hand-pick *v.tr.* (usu. as **handpicked** *adj.*) choose carefully or personally.

handpump /ˈhan(d)pʌmp/ *n.* a pump operated by hand.

handrail /ˈhandreɪl/ *n.* a narrow rail for holding as a support on stairs etc.

handsaw /ˈhan(d)sɔː/ *n.* a saw worked by one hand.

handsel /ˈhans(ə)l/ *n.* & *v.* (also **hansel**) *archaic* ● *n.* **1** a gift at the beginning of the new year, or on coming into new circumstances. **2** = EARNEST[2] 1. ● *v.tr.* (**handselled**, **handselling**; *US* **handseled**, **handseling**) esp. *Brit.* **1** give a handsel to. **2** inaugurate; be the first to try. [Middle English, corresponding to Old English *handselen* 'giving into a person's hands', Old Norse *handsal* 'giving of the hand (esp. in promise)', formed as HAND + Old English *sellan* SELL]

handset /ˈhan(d)set/ *n.* a telephone mouthpiece and earpiece forming one unit.

handshake /ˈhan(d)ʃeɪk/ *n.* the shaking of a person's hand with one's own as a greeting etc.

handsome /ˈhans(ə)m/ *adj.* (**handsomer**, **handsomest**) **1** (esp. of a man) good-looking. **2** imposing, fine (*handsome building*; *handsome stallion*). **3 a** generous, liberal (*a handsome present*; *handsome treatment*). **b** (of a price, fortune, etc., as assets gained) considerable. □ **handsomeness** *n.* [Middle English, in the sense 'easily handled, handy, suitable' from HAND + -SOME[1]]

handsomely /ˈhans(ə)mli/ *adv.* **1** generously, liberally. **2** finely, beautifully. **3** *Naut.* carefully.

handspike /ˈhan(d)spʌɪk/ *n.* a wooden rod shod with iron, used as a lever on board ship and by artillery soldiers.

handspring /ˈhan(d)sprɪŋ/ *n.* a somersault in which one lands first on the hands and then on the feet.

handstand /ˈhan(d)stand/ *n.* an act of balancing on one's hands with the feet in the air or against a wall.

hand-to-hand *adj.* (of fighting) at close quarters.

hand tool *n.* a tool operated by hand without electricity.

handwork /ˈhandwəːk/ *n.* work done with the hands, esp. as opposed to machinery. □ **handworked** *adj.*

handwriting /ˈhandrʌɪtɪŋ/ *n.* **1** writing with a pen, pencil, etc. **2** a person's particular style of writing. □ **handwritten** /-ˈrɪt(ə)n/ *adj.*

handy /ˈhandi/ *adj.* (**handier**, **handiest**) **1** convenient to handle or use; useful. **2** ready to hand; placed or occurring conveniently. **3** clever with the hands. □ **handily** *adv.* **handiness** *n.*

handyman /ˈhandɪman/ *n.* (*pl.* **-men**) a person able or employed to do occasional domestic repairs and minor renovations.

hang /haŋ/ *v.* & *n.* ● *v.* (*past* and *past part.* **hung** /hʌŋ/ except in sense 7) **1** *tr.* **a** secure or cause to be supported from above, esp. with the lower part free. **b** (foll. by *up*, *on*, *on to*, etc.) attach loosely by suspending from the top. **2** *tr.* set up (a door, gate, etc.) on its hinges so that it moves freely. **3** *tr.* place (a picture) on a wall or in an exhibition. **4** *tr.* attach (wallpaper) in vertical strips to a wall. **5** *tr.* (foll. by *on*) *colloq.* attach the blame for (a thing) to (a person) (*you can't hang that on me*). **6** *tr.* (foll. by *with*) decorate by hanging pictures or decorations etc. (*a hall hung with tapestries*). **7** *tr.* & *intr.* (*past* and *past part.* **hanged**) **a** suspend or be suspended by the neck until dead, esp. as a form of capital punishment. **b** as a mild oath (*hang the expense*; *let everything go hang*). **8** *tr.* let droop (*hang one's head*). **9** *tr.* suspend (meat or game) from a hook and leave it until dry or tender or high. **10** *intr.* be or remain hung (in various senses). **11** *intr.* remain static in the air. **12** *intr.* (often foll. by *over*) be present or imminent, esp. oppressively or threateningly (*a hush hung over the room*). **13** *intr.* (foll. by *on*) **a** be contingent or dependent on (*everything hangs on the discussions*). **b** listen closely to (*hangs on their every word*). ● *n.* **1** the way a thing hangs or falls. **2** a downward droop or bend. □ **be hung up** *slang* be emotionally confused or disturbed. **be hung up on** *slang* have a psychological or emotional obsession or problem about (*is really hung up on her father*). **get the hang of** *colloq.* understand the technique or meaning of. **hang around** (also *Brit.* **about**) **1 a** loiter or dally; not move away. **b** linger near (a person or place). **c** wait. **2** (foll. by *with*) associate with (a person etc.). **hang back 1** show reluctance to act or move. **2** remain behind. **hang fire** be slow in taking action or in progressing. **hang heavily** (or **heavy**) (of time) pass slowly. **hang in** esp. *N. Amer. colloq.* **1** persist, persevere. **2** linger. **hang on 1** *colloq.* continue or persevere, esp. with difficulty. **2** (often foll. by *to*) continue to hold or grasp. **3** (foll. by *to*) retain; fail to give back. **4 a** *colloq.* wait for a short time. **b** (in telephoning) continue to listen during a pause in the conversation. **hang out 1** hang from a window, clothes line, etc. **2** protrude or cause to protrude downwards. **3** (foll. by *of*) lean out of (a window etc.). **4** *slang* reside or be often present. **hang together 1** make sense. **2** remain associated. **hang up 1** hang from a hook, peg, etc. **2** end a telephone conversation, esp. (foll. by *on*) abruptly (*then he hung up on me*). **3 a** cause delay or difficulty to. **b** *slang* confuse or disturb emotionally. **let it all hang out** *slang* be uninhibited or relaxed. **not care** (or **give**) **a hang** *colloq.* not care at all. [partly from Old Norse transitive verb *hanga* = Old English *hōn*, partly from Old English intransitive verb *hangian*, from Germanic]

hangar /ˈhaŋə/ *n.* a building with extensive floor area, for housing aircraft etc. □ **hangarage** *n.* [French, of unknown origin]

hangdog /ˈhaŋdɒg/ *adj.* having a dejected or guilty appearance; shamefaced.

hanger[1] /ˈhaŋə/ *n.* **1** a person or thing that hangs. **2** (in full **coat-hanger**) a shaped piece of wood or plastic etc. from which clothes may be hung.

hanger[2] /ˈhaŋə/ *n. Brit.* a wood on the side of a steep hill. [Old English *hangra* from *hangian* HANG]

hanger-on *n.* (*pl.* **hangers-on**) a follower or dependant, esp. an unwelcome one.

hang-glider /ˈhaŋˌglʌɪdə/ *n.* **1** a frame with a fabric aerofoil stretched over it, from which the operator is suspended and controls flight by body movement. **2** a person who practises hang-gliding. □ **hang-glide** *v.intr.* **hang-gliding** *n.*

hanging /ˈhaŋɪŋ/ *n.* & *adj.* ● *n.* **1 a** the practice or an act of executing by hanging a person. **b** (*attrib.*) meriting or causing this (*a hanging offence*). **2** (usu. in *pl.*) draperies hung on a wall etc. ● *adj.* **1** that hangs or is hung; suspended. **2** situated on a steep slope (*hanging gardens*; *hanging glacier*).

hanging valley *n.* a valley which is cut across by a deeper valley or a cliff.

hangman /ˈhaŋmən/ *n.* (*pl.* **-men**) **1** an executioner who hangs condemned persons. **2** a game for two in which failed attempts to guess the letters of a word are recorded by drawing a gallows and someone hanging on it, line by line.

hangnail /ˈhaŋneɪl/ *n.* = AGNAIL. [alteration of AGNAIL, influenced by HANG and taking *nail* as = NAIL *n.* 2a]

hang-out *n. slang* a place one lives in or frequently visits.

hangover /ˈhaŋəʊvə/ *n.* **1** a severe headache or other after-effects caused by drinking an excess of alcohol. **2** a survival from the past.

Hang Seng index /haŋ ˈsɛŋ/ *n.* a figure indicating the relative price of representative shares on the Hong Kong Stock Exchange. [*Hang Seng*, name of a Hong Kong bank]

hang-up *n. slang* an emotional problem or inhibition.

hank /haŋk/ *n.* **1** a coil or skein of wool or thread etc. **2** any of several measures of length of cloth or yarn, e.g. 840 yards for cotton yarn and 560 yards for worsted. **3** *Naut.* a ring of rope, iron, etc., for securing the staysails to the stays. [Middle English from Old Norse *hönk*: cf. Swedish *hank* 'string', Danish *hank* 'handle']

hanker /ˈhaŋkə/ *v.intr.* (foll. by *for*, *after*, or *to* + infin.) long for; crave. □ **hankerer** *n.* **hankering** *n.* [obsolete *hank*, probably related to HANG]

hanky /ˈhaŋki/ *n.* (also **hankie**) (*pl.* **-ies**) *colloq.* a handkerchief. [abbreviation]

hanky-panky /haŋkɪˈpaŋki/ *n. slang* **1** naughtiness, esp. sexual misbehaviour. **2** dishonest dealing; trickery. [19th c.: perhaps based on *hocus-pocus*]

Hanoverian /hanə(ʊ)ˈvɪərɪən/ *adj.* of or relating to the British sovereigns from George I to Victoria (1714–1901). [*Hanover* in Germany, whose Elector became George I in 1714]

Hansa /ˈhansə/ *n.* (also **Hanse**) **1 a** a medieval guild of merchants. **b** the entrance fee to a guild. **2** (also **Hanseatic League**) a medieval political and commercial league of Germanic towns. □ **Hanseatic** /-sɪˈatɪk/ *adj.* [Middle High German *hanse*, Old High German, Gothic *hansa* 'company']

Hansard /ˈhansɑːd, -səd/ *n.* the official verbatim record of debates in the British Parliament. [named after T. C. *Hansard*, English printer (d. 1833), who first printed it]

hansel var. of HANDSEL.

Hansen's disease /ˈhans(ə)nz/ *n.* = LEPROSY 1. [named after G. H. A. *Hansen*, Norwegian physician d. 1912]

hansom /ˈhans(ə)m/ *n.* (in full **hansom cab**) *hist.* a two-wheeled horse-drawn cab accommodating two inside, with the driver seated behind. [named after J. A. *Hansom*, English architect (d. 1882), who designed it]

Hants /hants/ *abbr.* Hampshire. [Old English *Hantescire*]

Hanukkah /ˈhanʊkə, x-/ *n.* (also **Chanukkah**) the Jewish festival of lights, commemorating the purification of the Temple in 165 BC. [Hebrew *ḥănukkāh* 'consecration']

hanuman /hʌnʊˈmɑːn/ *n.* **1** an Indian langur, *Presbytis entellus*, venerated by Hindus; also called *wanderoo*. **2** (**Hanuman**) *Hinduism* the monkey-god, a loyal helper of Rama. [Hindi]

hap /hap/ *n.* & *v. archaic* ● *n.* **1** chance, luck. **2** a chance occurrence. ● *v.intr.* (**happed**, **happing**) **1** come about by chance. **2** (foll. by *to* + infin.) happen to. [Middle English from Old Norse *happ*]

hapax legomenon /hapaks lɪˈɡɒmɪnɒn/ *n.* (*pl.* **hapax legomena** /-mɪnə/) a word of which only one instance of use is recorded. [Greek, = a thing said once]

ha'penny var. of HALFPENNY.

haphazard /hapˈhazəd/ *adj. & adv.* ● *adj.* done etc. by chance; random. ● *adv.* at random. □ **haphazardly** *adv.* **haphazardness** *n.* [HAP + HAZARD]

hapless /ˈhaplɪs/ *adj.* (esp. of a person) unfortunate. □ **haplessly** *adv.* **haplessness** *n.* [HAP + -LESS]

haplography /hapˈlɒɡrəfi/ *n.* the accidental omission of letters when these are repeated in a word (e.g. *philogy* for *philology*). [Greek *haplous* 'single' + -GRAPHY]

haploid /ˈhaplɔɪd/ *adj. & n.* ● *adj. Biol.* **1** (of a cell) having a single set of unpaired chromosomes. **2** (of an organism) composed of haploid cells. ● *n.* a haploid organism or cell. [German, from Greek *haplous* 'single' + *eidos* 'form']

haplology /hapˈlɒlədʒi/ *n.* the omission of a sound when this is repeated within a word (e.g. *February* pronounced /ˈfebri/). [Greek *haplous* 'single' + -LOGY]

ha'p'orth var. of HALFPENNYWORTH.

happen /ˈhap(ə)n/ *v. & adv.* ● *v.intr.* **1** occur (by chance or otherwise). **2** (foll. by *to* + infin.) have the (good or bad) fortune to (*I happened to meet her*). **3** (foll. by *to*) be the (esp. unwelcome) fate or experience of (*what happened to you?*; *I hope nothing happens to them*). **4** (foll. by *on*) encounter or discover by chance. ● *adv. N.Engl. dial.* perhaps, maybe (*happen it'll rain*). □ **as it happens** in fact; in reality (*as it happens, it turned out well*). [Middle English from HAP + -EN[1]]

happening /ˈhap(ə)nɪŋ/ *n. & adj.* ● *n.* **1** an event or occurrence. **2** an improvised or spontaneous theatrical etc. performance. ● *adj. slang* exciting, fashionable, trendy.

happenstance /ˈhap(ə)nstans/ *n.* esp. *N. Amer.* a thing that happens by chance. [HAPPEN + CIRCUMSTANCE]

happi /ˈhapi/ *n.* (*pl.* **happis**) (also **happi-coat**) a loose informal Japanese coat. [Japanese]

happy /ˈhapi/ *adj.* (**happier**, **happiest**) **1** feeling or showing pleasure or contentment. **2 a** fortunate; characterized by happiness. **b** (of words, behaviour, etc.) apt, pleasing. **3** *colloq.* slightly drunk. **4** (in *comb.*) *colloq.* inclined to use excessively or at random (*trigger-happy*). □ **happy as a sandboy** see SANDBOY. □ **happily** *adv.* **happiness** *n.* [Middle English, from HAP + -Y[1]]

happy event *n. colloq.* the birth of a child.

happy families *n. Brit.* a card game the object of which is to acquire four members of the same 'family'.

happy-go-lucky /ˌhapɪɡəʊˈlʌki/*adj.* cheerfully casual.

happy hour *n.* a period of the day when drinks are sold at reduced prices in bars, hotels, etc.

happy hunting ground *n.* a place where success or enjoyment is obtained.

happy medium *n.* a satisfactory compromise; the avoidance of extremes.

haptic /ˈhaptɪk/ *adj.* relating to the sense of touch. [Greek *haptikos* 'able to touch' from *haptō* 'fasten']

hara-kiri /harəˈkɪri/ *n.* ritual suicide by disembowelment with a sword, formerly practised by Samurai to avoid dishonour. [colloq. Japanese, from *hara* 'belly' + *kiri* 'cutting']

harangue /həˈraŋ/ *n. & v.* ● *n.* a lengthy and earnest speech. ● *v.tr.* lecture or make a harangue to. □ **haranguer** *n.* [Middle English from French via Old French *arenge* from medieval Latin *harenga*, perhaps from Germanic]

harass /ˈharəs, *disp.* həˈras/ *v.tr.* **1** trouble and annoy continually or repeatedly. **2** make repeated attacks on (an enemy or opponent). □ **harasser** *n.* **harassingly** *adv.* **harassment** *n.* [French *harasser* from Old French *harer* 'set a dog on']

■ **Usage** The second pronunciation given, with the stress on the second syllable, is common, but is considered incorrect by some people.

harbinger /ˈhɑːbɪn(d)ʒə/ *n.* **1** a person or thing that announces or signals the approach of another. **2** a forerunner. [earlier = 'a person who provides lodging': Middle English *herbergere* from Old French, from *herberge* 'lodging', from Germanic]

harbour /ˈhɑːbə/ *n. & v.* (*US* **harbor**) ● *n.* **1** a place of shelter for ships. **2** a shelter; a place of refuge or protection. ● *v.* **1** *tr.* give shelter to (esp. a criminal or wanted person). **2** *tr.* keep in one's mind, esp. resentfully (*harbour a grudge*). **3** *intr.* come to anchor in a harbour. □ **harbourless** *adj.* [Old English *herebeorg*, perhaps from Old Norse, related to HARBINGER]

harbourage /ˈhɑːb(ə)rɪdʒ/ *n.* (*US* **harborage**) a shelter or place of shelter, esp. for ships.

harbour master *n.* (*US* **harbormaster**) an official in charge of a harbour.

harbour seal *n. N. Amer.* the common seal, *Phoca vitulina.*

hard /hɑːd/ *adj., adv., & n.* ● *adj.* **1** (of a substance, material, etc.) firm and solid; unyielding to pressure; not easily cut. **2 a** difficult to understand or explain (*a hard problem*). **b** difficult to accomplish (*a hard decision*). **c** (foll. by *to* + infin.) not easy to (*hard to believe*; *hard to please*). **3** difficult to bear; entailing suffering (*a hard life*). **4** (of a person) unfeeling; severely critical. **5** (of a season or the weather) severe, harsh (*a hard winter*; *a hard frost*). **6** harsh or unpleasant to the senses (*a hard voice*; *hard colours*). **7 a** strenuous, enthusiastic, intense (*a hard worker*; *a hard fight*). **b** severe, uncompromising (*a hard blow*; *a hard bargain*; *hard words*). **c** *Polit.* extreme; most radical (*the hard right*). **8 a** (of liquor) strongly alcoholic. **b** (of drugs) potent and addictive. **c** (of radiation) highly penetrating. **d** (of pornography) highly obscene and explicit. **9** (of water) containing mineral salts that make lathering difficult. **10** established; not disputable; reliable (*hard facts*; *hard data*). **11** *Stock Exch.* (of currency, prices, etc.) high; not likely to fall in value. **12** (of a consonant) guttural (as *c* in *cat*, *g* in *go*). ● *adv.* **1** strenuously, intensely, copiously; with one's full effort (*try hard*; *look hard at*; *is raining hard*; *hard-working*). **2** with difficulty or effort (*hard-earned*). **3** so as to be hard or firm (*hard-baked*; *the jelly set hard*). ● *n. Brit.* **1** a sloping roadway across a foreshore. **2** *slang* = HARD LABOUR (*got two years' hard*). □ **be hard on 1** be difficult for. **2** be severe in one's treatment or criticism of. **3** be unpleasant to (the senses). **be hard put to it** (usu. foll. by *to* + infin.) find it difficult. **go hard with** turn out to (a person's) disadvantage. **hard at it** *colloq.* busily working or occupied. **hard by** near; close by. **a hard case 1** *colloq.* **a** an intractable person. **b** *Austral.* & *NZ* an amusing or eccentric person. **2** a case of hardship. **a hard nut to crack** *colloq.* **1** a difficult problem. **2** a person or thing not easily understood or influenced. **hard on** (or **upon**) close to in pursuit etc. **put the hard word on** *Austral.* & *NZ slang* ask a favour (esp. sexual or financial) of. □ **hardish** *adj.* **hardness** *n.* [Old English *hard, heard*, from Germanic]

hard and fast *adj.* (of a rule or a distinction made) definite, unalterable, strict.

hardback /ˈhɑːdbak/ *adj. & n.* ● *adj.* (of a book) bound in stiff covers. ● *n.* a hardback book.

hardball /ˈhɑːdbɔːl/ *n. & v. N. Amer.* ● *n.* **1** = BASEBALL. **2** *slang* uncompromising methods or dealings, esp. in politics (*play hardball*). ● *v.tr. slang* pressure or coerce politically.

hardbitten /hɑːdˈbɪt(ə)n/ *adj. colloq.* tough and cynical.

hardboard /ˈhɑːdbɔːd/ *n.* stiff board made of compressed and treated wood pulp.

hard-boiled *adj.* **1** (of an egg) boiled until the white and the yolk are solid. **2** (of a person) tough, shrewd.

hard cash *n.* negotiable coins and banknotes.

hard cheese see CHEESE[1].

hard coal *n.* anthracite.

hard copy *n.* printed material produced by computer, usu. on paper, suitable for ordinary reading.

hard-core *adj.* **1** forming a nucleus or centre. **2** blatant, uncompromising. **3** (of pornography) explicit, obscene. **4** (of drug addiction) relating to 'hard' drugs, esp. heroin.

hard core *n.* **1** an irreducible nucleus. **2** *colloq.* **a** the most active or committed members of a society etc. **b** a conservative or reactionary minority. **3** (usu. **hardcore**) *Brit.* solid material, esp. rubble, forming the foundation of a road etc. **4** (usu. **hardcore**) popular music that is experimental in nature and usu. characterized by high volume and aggressive presentation.

hardcover /'hɑːdkʌvə/ *adj.* & *n.* esp. *N. Amer.* = HARDBACK.

hard disk *n. Computing* a rigid usu. magnetic disk, having a large data storage capacity.

hard doer see DOER 3.

hard-done-by *adj. Brit.* harshly or unfairly treated.

hard-earned *adj.* that has taken a great deal of effort to earn or acquire.

harden /'hɑːd(ə)n/ *v.* **1** *tr.* & *intr.* make or become hard or harder. **2** *intr.* & *tr.* become, or make (one's attitude etc.), obdurate, uncompromising, or less sympathetic. **3** *intr.* (of prices etc.) cease to fall or fluctuate. ▫ **harden off** inure (a plant) to cold by gradual increase of its exposure. ▫ **hardener** *n.*

hardening /'hɑːd(ə)nɪŋ/ *n.* **1** the process or an instance of becoming hard. **2** (in full **hardening of the arteries**) *Med.* = ARTERIOSCLEROSIS.

hard error *n. Computing* a permanent error.

hard feelings *n.pl.* feelings of resentment.

hard hat *n.* **1** protective headgear worn on building sites etc. **2** *colloq.* a reactionary person.

hard-headed *adj.* practical, realistic; not sentimental. ▫ **hard-headedly** *adv.* **hard-headedness** *n.*

hardheads /'hɑːdhɛdz/ *n.* (also **hardhead** /'hɑːdhɛd/) a tough-stemmed knapweed, *Centaurea nigra*, with dense purple flower heads, native to Europe and widely introduced elsewhere.

hard-hearted *adj.* unfeeling, unsympathetic. ▫ **hard-heartedly** *adv.* **hard-heartedness** *n.*

hard hit *adj.* (hyphenated when *attrib.*) badly affected.

hard-hitting *adj.* aggressively critical.

hardihood /'hɑːdɪhʊd/ *n.* boldness, daring.

hard labour *n.* heavy manual work as a punishment, esp. in a prison.

hard landing *n.* **1** a clumsy or rough landing of an aircraft. **2** an uncontrolled landing in which a spacecraft is destroyed.

hard line *n.* & *adj.* ● *n.* unyielding adherence to a firm policy. ● *attrib.adj.* (**hardline**) unyielding, strict, firm. ▫ **hardliner** *n.*

hard lines *n.pl. Brit. colloq.* = HARD LUCK.

hard luck *n.* worse fortune than one deserves.

hardly /'hɑːdli/ *adv.* **1** scarcely; only just (*we hardly knew them*). **2** only with difficulty (*could hardly speak*). **3** harshly. ▫ **hardly any** almost no; almost none. **hardly ever** very rarely.

▪ **Usage** *Hardly* should not be used with negative constructions. Expressions such as *I couldn't hardly see* are non-standard; the correct form is *I could hardly see.*

hard-nosed *adj. colloq.* realistic, uncompromising.

hard nut *n. slang* a tough, aggressive person.

hard of hearing *adj.* somewhat deaf.

hard-on *n. coarse slang* an erection of the penis.

hard pad *n.* a form of distemper in dogs etc.

hard palate *n.* the front part of the palate.

hardpan /'hɑːdpan/ *n. Geol.* a hardened layer of clay occurring in or below the soil profile.

hard-paste *adj.* denoting a Chinese or 'true' porcelain made of fusible and infusible materials (usu. clay and stone) and fired at a high temperature.

hard-pressed *adj.* **1** closely pursued. **2** burdened with urgent business.

hard rock *n. colloq.* rock music with a heavy beat.

hard roe see ROE[1] 1.

hard sauce *n.* a sauce of butter and sugar, often with brandy etc. added.

hard sell *n.* aggressive salesmanship or advertising.

hardshell /'hɑːdʃɛl/ *adj.* **1** having a hard shell. **2** esp. *US* rigid, orthodox, uncompromising.

hardship /'hɑːdʃɪp/ *n.* **1** severe suffering or privation. **2** the circumstance causing this.

hard shoulder *n. Brit.* a hardened strip alongside a motorway for stopping on in an emergency.

hardstanding /'hɑːdstandɪŋ/ *n.* an area of hard material for a vehicle to stand on when not in use.

hard stuff *n. colloq.* strong alcoholic drink, esp. whisky.

hard tack *n.* a ship's biscuit.

hard-top *n.* a motor car with a rigid (usu. detachable) roof.

hard up *adj.* **1** short of money. **2** (foll. by *for*) at a loss for; lacking.

hardware /'hɑːdwɛː/ *n.* **1** tools and household articles of metal etc. **2** heavy machinery or armaments. **3** the mechanical and electronic components of a computer etc. (cf. SOFTWARE).

hard-wearing *adj.* able to stand much wear.

hard wheat *n.* wheat with a hard grain rich in gluten.

hard-wired *adj.* involving or achieved by permanently connected circuits designed to perform a specific function.

hardwood /'hɑːdwʊd/ *n.* the wood from a deciduous broadleaved tree as distinguished from that of conifers.

hard-working *adj.* diligent.

hardy /'hɑːdi/ *adj.* (**hardier**, **hardiest**) **1** robust; capable of enduring difficult conditions. **2** (of a plant) able to grow in the open air all the year. ▫ **hardily** *adv.* **hardiness** *n.* [Middle English from Old French *hardi*, past part. of *hardir* 'become bold', from Germanic: related to HARD]

hardy annual *n.* **1** an annual plant that may be sown in the open. **2** *Brit. joc.* a subject that comes up at regular intervals.

hare /hɛː/ *n.* & *v.* ● *n.* **1** any of various mammals esp. of the genus *Lepus* resembling a large rabbit, with tawny fur, long ears, short tail, and hind legs longer than forelegs, inhabiting fields, hills, etc. **2** (in full **electric hare**) a dummy hare propelled by electricity, used in greyhound racing. ● *v.intr.* run with great speed. ▫ **run with the hare and hunt with the hounds** *Brit.* try to remain on good terms with both sides. **start a hare** *Brit.* raise a topic of conversation. [Old English *hara*, from Germanic]

hare and hounds *n.* a paperchase.

harebell /'hɛːbɛl/ *n.* a plant, *Campanula rotundifolia*, with slender stems and pale blue bell-shaped flowers. Also (esp. *Sc.*) called *bluebell*.

hare-brained /'hɛːbreɪnd/ *adj.* rash, wild.

Hare Krishna /harɪ 'krɪʃnə, hɑːreɪ/ *n.* **1** a sect devotee to the worship of the Hindu deity Krishna (an incarnation of Vishnu). **2** (*pl.* **Hare Krishnas**) a member of this sect. [Sanskrit, = O Vishnu Krishna (a devotional chant)]

harelip /hɛː'lɪp/ *n.* often *offens.* = CLEFT LIP. ▫ **harelipped** *adj.*

▪ **Usage** *Harelip* is now usually regarded as offensive; *cleft lip* is the preferred term.

harem /'hɑːriːm, hɑː'riːm, 'hɛːrəm/ *n.* **1 a** the women of a Muslim household, living in a separate part of the house. **b** their quarters. **2** a group of female animals sharing a mate. [Arabic *ḥarām*, *ḥarīm*, originally = prohibited, prohibited place, from *ḥarama* 'prohibit']

hare's-foot *n.* (in full **hare's-foot clover**) a clover, *Trifolium arvense*, with soft hair around the flowers.

harewood /'hɛ:wʊd/ *n.* stained sycamore wood used for making furniture. [German dialect *Ehre* (from Latin *acer* 'maple') + WOOD]

haricot /'harɪkəʊ/ *n.* **1** (in full **haricot bean**) a variety of French bean with small white seeds. **2** the dried seed of this used as a vegetable. [French]

Harijan /'hʌrɪdʒ(ə)n, 'harɪdʒan/ *n.* a member of the class of untouchables in India. [Sanskrit, = a person dedicated to Vishnu, from *Hari* 'Vishnu', *jana* 'person']

hark /hɑ:k/ *v.intr.* (usu. in *imper.*) *archaic* listen attentively. ◻ **hark back** revert to a topic discussed earlier. [Middle English *herkien* from Old English, related to HEARKEN: *hark back* was originally a hunting call to retrace steps]

harken var. of HEARKEN.

harl /hɑ:l/ *n.* (also **harle**, **herl** /hə:l/) fibre of flax or hemp. [Middle Low German *herle*, *harle*]

harlequin /'hɑ:lɪkwɪn/ *n.* & *adj.* ● *n.* **1** (**Harlequin**) **a** a mute character in pantomime, usu. masked and dressed in a diamond-patterned costume. **b** *hist.* a stock comic character in Italian *commedia dell'arte*. **2** (in full **harlequin duck**) an Icelandic duck, *Histrionicus histrionicus*, the male of which has grey-blue plumage with chestnut and white markings. ● *adj.* in varied colours; variegated. [French from earlier *Herlequin*, the name of the leader of a legendary troop of demon horsemen]

harlequinade /,hɑ:lɪkwɪ'neɪd/ *n.* **1** the part of a pantomime featuring Harlequin. **2** a piece of buffoonery. [French *arlequinade* (as HARLEQUIN)]

harlot /'hɑ:lət/ *n. archaic* a prostitute. ◻ **harlotry** *n.* [Middle English, in the sense 'lad, knave, vagabond', from Old French *harlot*, *herlot*]

harm /hɑ:m/ *n.* & *v.* ● *n.* hurt, damage. ● *v.tr.* cause harm to. ◻ **out of harm's way** in safety. [Old English *hearm*, *hearmian*, from Germanic]

harmattan /hɑ:'mat(ə)n/ *n.* a parching dusty land-wind of the W. African coast occurring from December to February. [from Twi (the chief Ghanaian language) *haramata*]

harmful /'hɑ:mfʊl, -f(ə)l/ *adj.* causing or likely to cause harm. ◻ **harmfully** *adv.* **harmfulness** *n.*

harmless /'hɑ:mlɪs/ *adj.* **1** not able or likely to cause harm. **2** inoffensive. ◻ **harmlessly** *adv.* **harmlessness** *n.*

harmonic /hɑ:'mɒnɪk/ *adj.* & *n.* ● *adj.* **1** of or characterized by harmony; harmonious. **2** *Mus.* **a** of or relating to harmony. **b** (of a tone) produced by vibration of a string etc. in an exact fraction of its length. **3** *Math.* of or relating to quantities whose reciprocals are in arithmetical progression (*harmonic progression*). ● *n.* **1** *Mus.* an overtone accompanying at a fixed interval (and forming a note with) a fundamental tone. **2** *Physics* a component frequency of wave motion. ◻ **harmonically** *adv.* [Latin *harmonicus* from Greek *harmonikos* (as HARMONY)]

harmonica /hɑ:'mɒnɪkə/ *n.* a small rectangular wind instrument with a row of metal reeds along its length, held against the lips and moved from side to side to produce different notes by blowing or sucking. [Latin, fem. sing. or neut. pl. of *harmonicus*: see HARMONIC]

harmonic motion *n.* (in full **simple harmonic motion**) oscillatory motion under a retarding force proportional to the amount of displacement from an equilibrium position.

harmonic progression *n.* (also **harmonic series**) *Math.* a series of quantities whose reciprocals are in arithmetical progression.

harmonious /hɑ:'məʊnɪəs/ *adj.* **1** sweet-sounding, tuneful. **2** forming a pleasing or consistent whole; concordant. **3** free from disagreement or dissent. ◻ **harmoniously** *adv.* **harmoniousness** *n.*

harmonist /'hɑ:mənɪst/ *n.* a person skilled in musical harmony, a harmonizer. ◻ **harmonistic** /-'nɪstɪk/ *adj.*

harmonium /hɑ:'məʊnɪəm/ *n.* a keyboard instrument in which the notes are produced by air driven through metal reeds by bellows operated by the feet. [French from Latin (as HARMONY)]

harmonize /'hɑ:mənʌɪz/ *v.* (also **-ise**) **1** *tr.* add notes to (a melody) to produce harmony. **2** *tr.* & *intr.* (often foll. by *with*) bring into or be in harmony. **3** *intr.* make or form a pleasing or consistent whole. ◻ **harmonization** /-'zeɪʃ(ə)n/ *n.* [French *harmoniser* (as HARMONY)]

harmony /'hɑ:məni/ *n.* (*pl.* **-ies**) **1 a** a combination of simultaneously sounded musical notes to produce chords and chord progressions, esp. as having a pleasing effect. **b** the study of this. **2 a** an apt or aesthetic arrangement of parts. **b** the pleasing effect of this. **3** agreement, concord. **4** a collation of parallel narratives, esp. of the Gospels. ◻ **in harmony 1** (of singing etc.) producing chords; not discordant. **2** (often foll. by *with*) in agreement. **harmony of the spheres** see SPHERE. [Middle English via Old French *harmonie* and Latin *harmonia* from Greek *harmonia* 'joining, concord', from *harmos* 'joint']

harness /'hɑ:nɪs/ *n.* & *v.* ● *n.* **1** the equipment of straps and fittings by which a horse or other draught animal is fastened to a cart etc. and controlled. **2** a similar arrangement for fastening a thing to a person's body, for restraining a young child, etc. ● *v.tr.* **1 a** put a harness on (esp. a horse). **b** (foll. by *to*) attach by a harness. **2** make use of (natural resources) esp. to produce energy. ◻ **in harness** in the routine of daily work. ◻ **harnesser** *n.* [Middle English via Old French *harneis* 'military equipment' from Old Norse, from *herr* 'army' + *nest* 'provisions']

harp /hɑ:p/ *n.* & *v.* ● *n.* a large upright roughly triangular musical instrument consisting of a frame housing a graduated series of vertical strings, played by plucking with the fingers. ● *v.intr.* **1** (foll. by *on*, *on about*) talk repeatedly and tediously about. **2** play on a harp. ◻ **harper** *n.* **harpist** *n.* [Old English *hearpe*, from Germanic]

harpoon /hɑ:'pu:n/ *n.* & *v.* ● *n.* a barbed spearlike missile with a rope attached, for catching whales etc. ● *v.tr.* spear with a harpoon. ◻ **harpooner** *n.* [French *harpon*, from *harpe* 'clamp' via Latin *harpa* from Greek *harpē* 'sickle']

harpoon gun *n.* a gun for firing a harpoon.

harp seal *n.* a Greenland seal, *Phoca groenlandica*, with a harp-shaped dark mark on its back.

harpsichord /'hɑ:psɪkɔ:d/ *n.* a keyboard instrument with horizontal strings which are plucked mechanically. ◻ **harpsichordist** *n.* [obsolete French *harpechorde*, from Late Latin *harpa* 'harp', + *chorda* 'string', the *-s-* being unexplained]

harpy /'hɑ:pi/ *n.* (*pl.* **-ies**) **1** (in Greek and Roman mythology) a monster with a woman's head and body and bird's wings and claws. **2** a grasping unscrupulous person. [French *harpie* or Latin *harpyia* from Greek *harpuiai* 'snatchers']

harpy eagle *n.* a S. American crested bird of prey, *Harpia harpyja*, one of the largest of eagles.

harquebus /'hɑ:kwɪbəs/ *n.* (also **arquebus** /'ɑ:k-/) *hist.* an early type of portable gun supported on a tripod or on a forked rest. [French *(h)arquebuse*, ultimately from Middle Low German *hakebusse* or Middle High German *hakenbühse*, from *haken* 'hook' + *busse* 'gun']

harridan /'harɪd(ə)n/ *n.* a bad-tempered old woman. [17th-c. slang, perhaps from French *haridelle* 'old horse']

harrier[1] /'harɪə/ *n.* a person who harries or lays waste.

harrier[2] /'harɪə/ *n.* **1 a** a hound used for hunting hares. **b** (in *pl.*) a pack of these with huntsmen. **2** (in *pl.*) (usu. **Harriers** as part of a club's name) cross-country runners as a group or club. [HARE + -IER, assimilated to HARRIER[1]]

harrier[3] /ˈharɪə/ *n.* any bird of prey of the genus *Circus*, with long wings for swooping over the ground. [*harrower* from *harrow* 'harry, rob', assimilated to HARRIER[1]]

Harris tweed /ˈharɪs/ *n. propr.* a kind of tweed woven by hand in the Outer Hebrides, esp. on the island of Lewis with Harris.

harrow /ˈharəʊ/ *n. & v.* ● *n.* a heavy frame with iron teeth dragged over ploughed land to break up clods, remove weeds, cover seed, etc. ● *v.tr.* **1** draw a harrow over (land). **2** (usu. as **harrowing** *adj.*) distress greatly. □ **harrower** *n.* **harrowingly** *adv.* [Middle English from Old Norse *hervi*]

harrumph /həˈrʌmf/ *v.* **1** *intr.* clear the throat or make a similar sound, esp. ostentatiously. **2** *tr.* say gutturally, esp. expressing disapproval. [imitative]

harry /ˈhari/ *v.tr.* (**-ies, -ied**) **1** ravage or despoil. **2** harass, worry. [Old English *herian, hergian* from Germanic: related to Old English *here* 'army']

harsh /hɑːʃ/ *adj.* **1** unpleasantly rough or sharp, esp. to the senses. **2** severe, cruel. □ **harshen** *v.tr. & intr.* **harshly** *adv.* **harshness** *n.* [Middle Low German *harsch* 'rough', literally 'hairy', from *haer* HAIR]

harslet var. of HASLET.

hart /hɑːt/ *n.* the male of the deer (esp. the red deer) usu. over five years old. [Old English *heor(o)t*, from Germanic]

hartal /ˈhɑːtɑːl, ˈhəːtɑːl/ *n.* the closing of shops and offices in India as a mark of protest or sorrow. [Hindustani *hartāl, haṭṭāl*, from Sanskrit *haṭṭa* 'shop' + *tālaka* 'lock']

hartebeest /ˈhɑːtɪbiːst/ *n.* any large African antelope of the genus *Alcelaphus*, with ringed horns bent back at the tips. [Afrikaans, from Dutch *hert* HART + *beest* BEAST]

hartshorn /ˈhɑːtshɔːn/ *n. archaic* **1** an ammonious substance obtained from the horns of a hart. **2** (in full **spirit of hartshorn**) an aqueous solution of ammonia. [Old English (as HART, HORN)]

hart's tongue *n.* a fern, *Phyllitis scolopendrium*, with narrow undivided fronds.

harum-scarum /hɛːrəmˈskɛːrəm/ *adj. & n. colloq.* ● *adj.* wild and reckless. ● *n.* such a person. [rhyming formation on HARE, SCARE]

haruspex /həˈrʌspɛks/ *n.* (*pl.* **haruspices** /-spɪsiːz/) a Roman religious official who interpreted omens from the inspection of animals' entrails. [Latin]

Harvard classification /ˈhɑːvəd/ *n. Astron.* a system of classification of stars based on their spectral types, the chief classes (O, B, A, F, G, K, M) forming a series from very hot bluish-white stars to cool dull red stars. [named after the observatory at Harvard, Massachusetts, where it was devised]

harvest /ˈhɑːvɪst/ *n. & v.* ● *n.* **1 a** the process of gathering in crops etc. **b** the season when this takes place. **2** the season's yield or crop. **3** the product or result of any action. ● *v.tr.* **1** gather as a harvest, reap. **2** experience (consequences). □ **harvestable** *adj.* [Old English *hærfest*, from Germanic]

harvester /ˈhɑːvɪstə/ *n.* **1** a reaper. **2** a reaping machine, esp. with sheaf-binding.

harvest festival *n.* a thanksgiving festival for the harvest, esp. *Brit.* a church service.

harvest home *n.* the close of harvesting or the festival to mark this.

harvestman /ˈhɑːvɪs(t)mən/ *n.* (*pl.* **-men**) any of various arachnids of the order Opiliones, with very long thin legs, found in humus and on tree trunks.

harvest mite *n.* any of various mites or their biting larvae common at harvest time, esp. (in the British Isles) *Trombicula autumnalis*. Cf. CHIGGER 2.

harvest moon *n.* the full moon nearest to the autumn equinox.

harvest mouse *n.* a small mouse, *Micromys minutus*, with a prehensile tail, that nests in the stalks of growing grain.

has *3rd sing. present* of HAVE.

has-been /ˈhazbiːn/ *n. colloq.* a person or thing that has lost a former importance, popularity, or usefulness.

hash[1] /haʃ/ *n. & v.* ● *n.* **1** a dish of cooked meat cut into small pieces and recooked, usu. with potatoes. **2 a** a mixture; a jumble. **b** a mess. **3** reused or recycled material. ● *v.tr.* (often foll. by *up*) **1** make (meat etc.) into a hash. **2** recycle (old material). □ **make a hash of** *colloq.* make a mess of; bungle. **settle a person's hash** *colloq.* deal with and subdue a person. [French *hacher* from *hache* HATCHET]

hash[2] /haʃ/ *n. colloq.* hashish. [abbreviation]

hash[3] /haʃ/ *n.* (also **hash sign**) the symbol #.

hash browns *n.pl.* esp. *N. Amer.* a dish made of chopped cooked potatoes and onions, fried until brown.

hashish /ˈhaʃiːʃ, -ʃɪʃ, haˈʃiːʃ/ *n.* a resinous product of the top leaves and tender parts of hemp, smoked or chewed for its narcotic effects. [Arabic *ḥašīš* 'dry herb, powdered hemp leaves']

Hasid /ˈhasɪd/ *n.* (*pl.* **Hasidim**) a member of any of several mystical Jewish sects, esp. one founded in the 18th c. □ **Hasidic** /-ˈsɪdɪk/ *adj.* [Hebrew *ḥāsîḏ* 'pious']

haslet /ˈheɪzlɪt, ˈhazlɪt/ *n.* (also **harslet** /ˈhɑː-/) pieces of (esp. pig's) offal cooked together and usu. compressed into a meat loaf. [Middle English via Old French *hastelet*, diminutive of *haste* 'roast meat, spit', from Old Low German, Old High German *harst* 'roast']

hasn't /ˈhaz(ə)nt/ *contr.* has not.

hasp /hɑːsp/ *n. & v.* ● *n.* a hinged metal clasp that fits over a staple and can be secured by a padlock. ● *v.tr.* fasten with a hasp. [Old English *hæpse, hæsp*]

hassle /ˈhas(ə)l/ *n. & v. colloq.* ● *n.* **1** a prolonged trouble or inconvenience. **2** an argument or involved struggle. ● *v.* **1** *tr.* harass, annoy; cause trouble to. **2** *intr.* argue, quarrel. [20th c.: originally dialect]

hassock /ˈhasək/ *n.* **1** a thick firm cushion for kneeling on, esp. in church. **2** a tuft of matted grass etc. [Old English *hassuc*]

hast /hast/ *archaic 2nd sing. present* of HAVE.

hastate /ˈhasteɪt/ *adj. Bot.* triangular like the head of a spear. [Latin *hastatus* from *hasta* 'spear']

haste /heɪst/ *n. & v.* ● *n.* **1** urgency of movement or action. **2** excessive hurry. ● *v.intr. archaic* = HASTEN. □ **in haste** quickly, hurriedly. **make haste** hurry; be quick. [Middle English from Old French *haste, haster*, from West Germanic]

hasten /ˈheɪs(ə)n/ *v.* **1** *intr.* (often foll. by *to* + infin.) make haste; hurry. **2** *tr.* cause to occur or be ready or be done sooner.

hasty /ˈheɪsti/ *adj.* (**hastier, hastiest**) **1** hurried; acting too quickly or hurriedly. **2** said, made, or done too quickly or too soon; rash, unconsidered. **3** quick-tempered. □ **hastily** *adv.* **hastiness** *n.* [Middle English from Old French *hasti, hastif* (as HASTE, -IVE)]

hat /hat/ *n. & v.* ● *n.* **1** a covering for the head, often with a brim and worn out of doors. **2** *colloq.* a person's occupation or capacity, esp. one of several (*wearing his managerial hat*). ● *v.tr.* (**hatted, hatting**) cover or provide with a hat. □ **hats off** (as *int.*; foll. by *to*) expressing admiration or appreciation. **keep it under one's hat** *colloq.* keep it secret. **out of a hat** by random selection. **pass the hat** (or *Brit.* **the hat round**) collect contributions of money. **take off one's hat to** *colloq.* acknowledge admiration for. **throw one's hat in the ring** take up a challenge. □ **hatful** *n.* (*pl.* **-fuls**). **hatless** *adj.* [Old English *hætt*, from Germanic]

hatband /ˈhatband/ *n.* a band of ribbon etc. round a hat above the brim.

hatbox /ˈhatbɒks/ *n.* a box to hold a hat, esp. for travelling.

hatch[1] /hatʃ/ *n.* **1** an opening between two rooms, e.g. between a kitchen and a dining room for serving food. **2** an opening or door in an aircraft, spacecraft, etc. **3** *Naut.* **a** = HATCHWAY. **b** a trapdoor or cover for this (often in *pl.*: *batten the hatches*). **4** a floodgate. □ **down the hatch** *colloq.* (as a drinking toast) drink up, cheers!

under hatches 1 below deck. **2 a** down out of sight. **b** brought low; dead. [Old English *hæcc*, from Germanic]

hatch[2] /hatʃ/ *v.* & *n.* ● *v.* **1** *intr.* **a** (often foll. by *out*) (of a young bird or fish etc.) emerge from the egg. **b** (of an egg) produce a young animal. **2** *tr.* incubate (an egg). **3** *tr.* (also foll. by *up*) devise (a plot etc.). ● *n.* **1** the act or an instance of hatching. **2** a brood hatched. [Middle English *hacche*, of unknown origin]

hatch[3] /hatʃ/ *v.tr.* mark (a surface, e.g. a map or drawing, or road surface at a junction) with close parallel lines. [Middle English from French *hacher*, from *hache* HATCHET]

hatchback /ˈhatʃbak/ *n.* a car with a sloping back hinged at the top to form a door.

hatchery /ˈhatʃəri/ *n.* (*pl.* **-ies**) a place for hatching eggs, esp. of fish or poultry.

hatchet /ˈhatʃɪt/ *n.* a light short-handled axe. [Middle English via Old French *hachette*, diminutive of *hache* 'axe', from medieval Latin *hapia*, from Germanic]

hatchet-faced *adj. colloq.* sharp-featured or grim-looking.

hatchet job *n. colloq.* a fierce verbal attack on a person, esp. in print.

hatchet man *n. colloq.* **1** a hired killer. **2** a person employed to carry out a hatchet job.

hatching /ˈhatʃɪŋ/ *n.* close parallel lines forming shading, esp. on a map or an architectural drawing, or on a road surface at a junction.

hatchling /ˈhatʃlɪŋ/ *n.* a bird or fish that has just hatched.

hatchment /ˈhatʃm(ə)nt/ *n.* a large usu. diamond-shaped tablet with a deceased person's armorial bearings, affixed to that person's house, tomb, etc. [contraction of ACHIEVEMENT]

hatchway /ˈhatʃweɪ/ *n.* an opening in a ship's deck for lowering cargo into the hold.

hate /heɪt/ *v.* & *n.* ● *v.tr.* **1** feel hatred or intense dislike towards. **2 a** dislike. **b** (foll. by verbal noun or *to* + infin.) be reluctant (to do something) (*I hate to disturb you*). ● *n.* **1** hatred. **2** *colloq.* a hated person or thing (esp. in phr. **pet hate**). □ **hatable** *adj.* (also **hateable**). **hater** *n.* [Old English *hatian*, from Germanic]

hateful /ˈheɪtfʊl, -f(ə)l/ *adj.* arousing hatred. □ **hatefully** *adv.* **hatefulness** *n.*

hate mail *n.* usu. anonymous letters of hostility towards the recipient.

hath /haθ/ *archaic 3rd sing. present* of HAVE.

hatha yoga /hʌtə ˈjəʊgə, haθə/ *n.* a system of physical exercises and breathing control used in yoga. [Sanskrit *hatha* 'force': see YOGA]

hatpin /ˈhatpɪn/ *n.* a long pin, often decorative, for securing a hat to the hair.

hatred /ˈheɪtrɪd/ *n.* intense dislike or ill will. [Middle English, from HATE + *-red* from Old English *rǣden* 'condition']

hatstand /ˈhatstand/ *n.* a stand with hooks on which to hang hats.

hatter /ˈhatə/ *n.* a maker or seller of hats.

hat-trick *n.* **1** *Cricket* the taking of three wickets by the same bowler with three successive balls. **2 a** the scoring of three goals, points, etc. in other sports by one player or team. **b** three successes.

hauberk /ˈhɔːbəːk/ *n. hist.* a coat of mail. [Middle English via Old French *hau(s)berc* from Frankish, = neck protection, from *hals* 'neck' + *berg-* from *beorg* 'protection']

haughty /ˈhɔːti/ *adj.* (**haughtier**, **haughtiest**) arrogantly self-admiring and disdainful. □ **haughtily** *adv.* **haughtiness** *n.* [extension of *haught* (*adj.*), earlier *haut*, via Old French *haut* from Latin *altus* 'high']

haul /hɔːl/ *v.* & *n.* ● *v.* **1** *tr.* pull or drag forcibly. **2** *tr.* transport by lorry, cart, etc. **3** *intr.* turn a ship's course. **4** *tr.* (usu. foll. by *up*) *colloq.* bring for reprimand or trial. ● *n.* **1** the act or an instance of hauling. **2** an amount gained or acquired. **3** a distance to be traversed (*a short haul*). □ **haul over the coals** see COAL. [variant of HALE[2]]

haulage /ˈhɔːlɪdʒ/ *n.* **1** the commercial transport of goods. **2** a charge for this.

hauler /ˈhɔːlə/ *n.* **1** a person or thing that hauls. **2** = HAULIER.

haulier /ˈhɔːlɪə/ *n. Brit.* **1** a miner who takes coal from the face to the bottom of the shaft. **2** a person or firm engaged in the transport of goods.

haulm /hɔːm/ *n.* (also **halm**) **1** a stalk or stem. **2** the stalks or stems collectively of peas, beans, potatoes, etc., without the pods etc. [Old English *h(e)alm*, from Germanic]

haunch /hɔːn(t)ʃ/ *n.* **1** the fleshy part of the buttock with the thigh, esp. in animals. **2** the leg and loin of a deer etc. as food. **3** the side of an arch between the crown and the pier. [Middle English from Old French *hanche*, of Germanic origin: cf. Low German *hanke* 'hind leg of a horse']

haunt /hɔːnt/ *v.* & *n.* ● *v.* **1** *tr.* **a** (of a ghost) visit (a place) regularly, usu. giving signs of its presence. **b** (as **haunted** *adj.*) frequented by a ghost. **2** *tr.* (of a person or animal) frequent or be persistently in (a place). **3** *tr.* (of a memory etc.) be persistently in the mind of. **4** *intr.* (foll. by *with*, *in*) stay habitually. ● *n.* **1** (often in *pl.*) a place frequented by a person. **2** a place frequented by animals, esp. for food and drink. □ **haunter** *n.* [Middle English from Old French *hanter*, from Germanic]

haunting /ˈhɔːntɪŋ/ *adj.* (of a memory, melody, etc.) poignant, wistful, evocative. □ **hauntingly** *adv.*

Hausa /ˈhaʊsə/ *n.* & *adj.* ● *n.* (*pl.* same or **Hausas**) **1** a member of a people of W. Africa and Sudan. **2** the Hamitic language of this people, widely used in W. Africa. ● *adj.* of or relating to this people or language. [native name]

hausfrau /ˈhaʊsfraʊ/ *n.* a German housewife. [German, from *Haus* 'house' + *Frau* 'woman']

hautboy /ˈ(h)əʊbɔɪ/ *archaic* var. of OBOE.

haute couture /əʊt kʊˈtjʊə/ *n.* high fashion; the leading fashion houses or their products. [French, literally 'high dressmaking']

haute cuisine /əʊt kwɪˈziːn/ *n.* cookery of a high standard, esp. of the French traditional school. [French, literally 'high cookery']

haute école /əʊt eɪˈkɒl, French ot ekɔl/ *n.* the art or practice of advanced classical dressage. [French, literally 'high school']

hauteur /əʊˈtəː/ *n.* haughtiness of manner. [French from *haut* 'high']

haut monde /əʊ ˈmɒnd, French o mɔ̃d/ *n.* fashionable society. [French, literally 'high world']

haut-relief /əʊrɪˈliːf/ *n. Sculpture* **1** = *high relief* (see RELIEF 6a). **2** a sculpture, carving, etc. in high relief. [French, = high relief; cf. BAS-RELIEF]

Havana /həˈvanə/ *n.* a cigar made at Havana or elsewhere in Cuba.

have /hav/ *v.* & *n.* ● *v.* (*3rd sing. present* **has** /haz, has/; *past* and *past part.* **had** /had/) ● *v.tr.* **1** hold in possession as one's property or at one's disposal; be provided with (*has a car*; *had no time to read*; *has nothing to wear*). **2** hold in a certain relationship (*has a sister*; *had no equals*). **3** contain as a part or quality (*house has two floors*; *has green eyes*). **4 a** undergo, experience, enjoy, suffer (*had a good time*; *had a shock*; *has a headache*). **b** be subjected to a specified state (*had my car stolen*; *the book has a page missing*). **c** cause, instruct, or invite (a person or thing) to be in a particular state or take a particular action (*had him dismissed*; *had us worried*; *had my hair cut*; *had a copy made*; *had them to stay*). **5 a** engage in (an activity) (*had an argument*; *had sex*). **b** hold (a meeting, party, etc.). **6** eat or drink (*had a beer*). **7** (usu. in *neg.*) accept or tolerate; permit to (*I won't have it*; *will not have you say such things*). **8 a** let (a feeling etc.) be present (*have no doubt*; *has a lot of sympathy for me*; *have nothing against them*). **b** show or feel (mercy, pity, etc.) towards another person (*have pity on him; have mercy!*). **c** (foll. by *to* + infin.) show by action that one is influenced by (a feeling, quality, etc.) (*have the goodness to leave now*). **9 a** give birth to (offspring). **b** conceive mentally (an idea etc.). **10** receive, obtain (*had a letter from him; not a ticket to be had*). **11** be burdened with or committed to (*has a job to do; have my garden to attend to*). **12 a** have obtained (a qualification) (*has six O levels*). **b** know (a language) (*has no Latin*). **13** *colloq.* **a** get the better of (*I had him there*). **b** (usu. in *passive*) cheat, deceive (*you were had*). **14** *coarse slang* have sexual intercourse with. ● *v.aux.* (with *past part.* or *ellipt.*, to form the perfect, pluperfect, and future perfect tenses, and the conditional mood) (*have worked; had seen; will have been; had I known, I would have gone; have you met her? yes, I have*). ● *n.* **1** (usu. in *pl.*) *colloq.* a person who has wealth or resources. **2** *Brit. slang* a swindle. □ **had best** see BEST. **had better** would find it prudent to. **had rather** see RATHER. **have a care** see CARE. **have done, have done with** see DONE. **have an eye for, have eyes for, have an eye to** see EYE. **have a good mind to** see MIND. **have got to** *colloq.* = *have to*. **have had it** *colloq.* **1** have missed one's chance. **2** have passed one's prime. **3** have been killed, defeated, etc. **have it 1** (foll. by *that* + clause) express the view that. **2** win a decision in a vote etc. **3** have found the answer etc. **have it away** (or **off**) *Brit. coarse slang* have sexual intercourse. **have it both ways** see BOTH. **have it in for** *colloq.* be hostile or ill-disposed towards. **have it out** (often foll. by *with*) *colloq.* attempt to settle a dispute by discussion or argument. **have it one's own way** see WAY. **have nothing to do with** see DO[1]. **have on 1** be wearing (clothes). **2** be committed to (an engagement). **3** *Brit. colloq.* tease; play a trick on. **have one too many** see MANY. **have out** get (a tooth etc.) extracted (*had her tonsils out*). **have something** (or **nothing**) **on a person 1** know something (or nothing) discreditable or incriminating about a person. **2** have an (or no) advantage or superiority over a person. **have to** be obliged to, must. **have to do with** see DO[1]. **have up** *Brit. colloq.* bring (a person) before a court of justice, interviewer, etc. [Old English *habban* from Germanic, probably related to HEAVE]

■ **Usage** See Usage Note at OF.

haven /ˈheɪv(ə)n/ *n.* **1** a harbour or port. **2** a place of refuge. [Old English *hæfen* from Old Norse *höfn*]

have-not *n.* (usu. in *pl.*) *colloq.* a person lacking wealth or resources.

haven't /ˈhav(ə)nt/ *contr.* have not.

haver /ˈheɪvə/ *v. & n.* ● *v.intr. Brit.* **1** talk foolishly; babble. **2** vacillate, hesitate. ● *n.* (usu. in *pl.*) *Sc.* foolish talk; nonsense. [18th c.: origin unknown]

haversack /ˈhavəsak/ *n.* a stout bag for provisions etc., carried on the back or over the shoulder. [French *havresac* from German *Habersack*, from *Haber* 'oats' + *Sack* SACK[1]]

haversine /ˈhavəsʌɪn/ *n.* (also **haversin**) *Math.* half of a versed sine. [contraction of *half versed sine*]

havildar /ˈhavɪldɑː/ *n.* an Indian NCO corresponding to an army sergeant. [Urdu *hawildār* from Persian *ḥawāldār* 'trust-holder']

havoc /ˈhavək/ *n. & v.* ● *n.* widespread destruction; great confusion or disorder. ● *v.tr.* (**havocked, havocking**) devastate. □ **play havoc with** *colloq.* cause great confusion or difficulty to. [Middle English via Anglo-French *havok* from Old French *havo(t)*, of unknown origin]

haw[1] /hɔː/ *n.* **1** the fruit of the hawthorn. **2** = HAWTHORN. [Old English *haga* from Germanic: related to HEDGE]

haw[2] /hɔː/ *n.* the nictitating membrane of a horse, dog, etc., esp. when inflamed. [Middle English: origin unknown]

haw[3] /hɔː/ *int. & v.* ● *int.* expressing hesitation. ● *v.intr.* (in **hum and haw**): see HUM[1]. [imitative: cf. HA[1]]

Hawaiian /həˈwʌɪən/ *n. & adj.* ● *n.* **1 a** a native of Hawaii, an island or island group in the N. Pacific. **b** a person of Hawaiian descent. **2** the Austronesian language of Hawaii. ● *adj.* of or relating to Hawaii or its people or language.

hawfinch /ˈhɔːfɪn(t)ʃ/ *n.* any large stout finch of the genus *Coccothraustes*, with a heavy beak for cracking seeds. [HAW[1] + FINCH]

hawk[1] /hɔːk/ *n. & v.* ● *n.* **1** any of various diurnal birds of prey of the family Accipitridae, having a characteristic curved beak, rounded short wings, and a long tail. **2** *Polit.* a person who advocates an aggressive or warlike policy, esp. in foreign affairs. **3** a rapacious person. ● *v.* **1** *intr.* hunt game with a hawk. **2** *intr.* (often foll. by *at*) & *tr.* attack, as a hawk does. **3** *intr.* (of a bird) hunt on the wing for food. □ **hawkish** *adj.* **hawkishness** *n.* **hawklike** *adj.* [Old English *h(e)afoc, hæbuc*, from Germanic]

hawk[2] /hɔːk/ *v.tr.* **1** carry about or offer around (goods) for sale. **2** (often foll. by *about*) relate (news, gossip, etc.) freely. [back-formation from HAWKER[1]]

hawk[3] /hɔːk/ *v.* **1** *intr.* clear the throat noisily. **2** *tr.* (foll. by *up*) bring (phlegm etc.) up from the throat. [probably imitative]

hawk[4] /hɔːk/ *n.* a plasterer's square board with a handle underneath for carrying plaster or mortar. [Middle English: origin unknown]

hawkbit /ˈhɔːkbɪt/ *n.* a plant of the genus *Leontodon* (daisy family) with yellow florets and rosettes of leaves. [HAWK[1] + DEVIL'S BIT]

hawker[1] /ˈhɔːkə/ *n.* a person who travels about selling goods. [16th c.: probably from Low German or Dutch and related to HUCKSTER]

hawker[2] /ˈhɔːkə/ *n.* a falconer. [Old English *hafocere*]

hawk-eyed *adj.* keen-sighted.

hawkmoth /ˈhɔːkmɒθ/ *n.* any large darting and hovering moth of the family Sphingidae, having narrow forewings and a stout body.

hawk-nosed *adj.* having an aquiline nose.

hawksbill /ˈhɔːksbɪl/ *n.* (in full **hawksbill turtle**) a small tropical turtle, *Eretmochelys imbricata*, with hooked jaws.

hawkweed /ˈhɔːkwiːd/ *n.* any plant of the genus *Hieracium* (daisy family), with yellow flowers.

hawse /hɔːz/ *n.* **1** the part of a ship's bows in which hawse-holes or hawse-pipes are placed. **2** the space between the head of an anchored vessel and the anchors. **3** the arrangement of cables when a ship is moored with port and starboard forward anchors. [Middle English *halse*, probably from Old Norse *háls* 'neck, ship's bow']

hawse-hole *n.* a hole in the side of a ship through which a cable or anchor-rope passes.

hawse-pipe *n.* a metal pipe lining a hawse-hole.

hawser /ˈhɔːzə/ *n. Naut.* a thick rope or cable for mooring or towing a ship. [Middle English via Anglo-French *haucer*, *hauceour* from Old French *haucier* 'hoist', ultimately from Latin *altus* 'high']

hawthorn /ˈhɔːθɔːn/ *n.* any thorny shrub or tree of the genus *Crataegus* (rose family), esp. *C. monogyna*, with white, red, or pink blossom and small dark red fruit or haws. Also called *may, quickthorn, whitethorn*. [Old English *hagathorn* (as HAW[1], THORN)]

hay[1] /heɪ/ *n. & v.* ● *n.* grass mown and dried for fodder. ● *v.* **1** *intr.* make hay. **2** *tr.* put (land) under grass for hay. **3** *tr.* make into hay. □ **hit the hay** *colloq.* go to bed. **make hay of** throw into confusion. **make hay (while the sun shines)** seize opportunities for profit or enjoyment. [Old English *hēg, hīeg, hīg*, from Germanic]

hay[2] /heɪ/ *n.* (also **hey**) **1** a country dance with interweaving steps. **2** a figure in this. [obsolete French *haie*]

haybox /ˈheɪbɒks/ *n.* a box stuffed with hay, in which heated food is left to continue cooking.

haycock /ˈheɪkɒk/ *n.* a conical heap of hay in a field.

hay fever *n.* an allergy with catarrhal and other asthmatic symptoms, caused by pollen or dust.

hayfield /ˈheɪfiːld/ *n.* a field where hay is being or is to be made.

hayloft /ˈheɪlɒft/ *n.* = LOFT *n.* 2.

haymaker /ˈheɪmeɪkə/ *n.* **1** a person who tosses and spreads hay to dry after mowing. **2** an apparatus for shaking and drying hay. **3** *slang* a forceful blow or punch. □ **haymaking** *n.*

haymow /ˈheɪmaʊ/ *n.* hay stored in a stack or barn.

hayrick /ˈheɪrɪk/ *n.* = HAYSTACK.

hayseed /ˈheɪsiːd/ *n.* **1** grass seed obtained from hay. **2** *N. Amer.*, *Austral.*, & *NZ colloq.* a rustic or yokel.

haystack /ˈheɪstak/ *n.* a packed pile of hay with a pointed or ridged top.

haywire /ˈheɪwʌɪə/ *adj. colloq.* **1** badly disorganized, out of control. **2** (of a person) crazy, erratic. [HAY[1] + WIRE, from the use of hay-baling wire in makeshift repairs]

hazard /ˈhazəd/ *n.* & *v.* ● *n.* **1** a danger or risk. **2** a source of this. **3** chance. **4** a dice game with a complicated arrangement of chances. **5** *Golf* an obstruction in playing a shot, e.g. a bunker, water, etc. **6** (in real tennis) each of the winning openings in a court. ● *v.tr.* **1** venture on (*hazard a guess*). **2** run the risk of. **3** expose to hazard. [Middle English via Old French *hasard* and Spanish *azar* from Arabic *az-zahr* 'chance, luck']

hazard light *n.* (usu. in *pl.*) (also **hazard warning light**) a flashing light warning that a vehicle is stationary or unexpectedly slowing or reversing, usu. each of the direction indicators used simultaneously.

hazardous /ˈhazədəs/ *adj.* **1** risky, dangerous. **2** dependent on chance. □ **hazardously** *adv.* **hazardousness** *n.* [French *hasardeux* (as HAZARD)]

hazard pay *n. US* = DANGER MONEY.

haze[1] /heɪz/ *n.* **1** obscuration of the atmosphere near the earth by fine particles of water, smoke, or dust. **2** mental obscurity or confusion. [probably a back-formation from HAZY]

haze[2] /heɪz/ *v.tr.* **1** *Naut.* harass with overwork. **2** *US* bully; seek to disconcert. [origin uncertain: cf. obsolete French *haser* 'tease, insult']

hazel /ˈheɪz(ə)l/ *n.* & *adj.* ● *n.* **1** any shrub or small tree of the genus *Corylus*, esp. *C. avellana* bearing round brown edible nuts. **2 a** wood from the hazel. **b** a stick made of this. **3** a reddish-brown or greenish-brown colour (esp. of the eyes). ● *adj.* (esp. of the eyes) of a reddish- or greenish-brown colour. [Old English *hæsel*, from Germanic]

hazel-grouse *n.* a woodland grouse, *Tetrastes bonasia*.

hazelnut /ˈheɪz(ə)lnʌt/ *n.* the fruit of the hazel, a round brown hard-shelled nut.

hazy /ˈheɪzi/ *adj.* (**hazier**, **haziest**) **1** misty. **2** vague, indistinct. **3** confused, uncertain. □ **hazily** *adv.* **haziness** *n.* [17th c. in nautical use: origin unknown]

HB *abbr.* hard black (pencil lead).

Hb *symb.* haemoglobin.

HBM *abbr.* Her or His Britannic Majesty (or Majesty's).

H-bomb /ˈeɪtʃbɒm/ *n.* = HYDROGEN BOMB. [H[3] + BOMB]

HC *abbr.* **1** Holy Communion. **2** (in the UK) House of Commons.

h.c. *abbr. honoris causa.*

HCF *abbr.* **1** highest common factor. **2** (in the UK) Honorary Chaplain to the Forces.

HCFC *abbr.* hydrochlorofluorocarbon (similar to CFC but thought to be less harmful to the ozone layer).

HDTV *abbr.* high-definition television.

HE *abbr.* **1** His or Her Excellency. **2** His Eminence. **3** high explosive.

He *symb. Chem.* the element helium.

he /hiː/ *pron.* & *n.* ● *pron.* (*obj.* **him** /hɪm/; *poss.* **his** /hɪz/; *pl.* **they** /ðeɪ/) **1** the man or boy or male animal previously named or in question. **2** a person etc. of unspecified sex, esp. referring to one already named or identified (*if anyone comes he will have to wait*). ● *n.* **1** a male; a man. **2** (in *comb.*) male (*he-goat*). **3** *Brit.* a children's chasing game, with the chaser designated 'he'. [Old English from Germanic]

head /hɛd/ *n.*, *adj.*, & *v.* ● *n.* **1** the upper part of the human body, or the foremost or upper part of an animal's body, containing the brain, mouth, and sense organs. **2 a** the head regarded as the seat of intellect or repository of comprehended information. **b** intelligence; imagination (*use your head*). **c** mental aptitude or tolerance (usu. foll. by *for*: *a good head for business*; *no head for heights*). **3** *colloq.* a headache, esp. resulting from a blow or from intoxication. **4** a thing like a head in form or position, esp.: **a** the operative part of a tool. **b** the flattened top of a nail. **c** the ornamented top of a pillar. **d** a mass of leaves or flowers at the top of a stem. **e** the flat end of a drum. **f** the foam on top of a glass of beer etc. **g** the upper horizontal part of a window frame, door frame, etc. **5** life when regarded as vulnerable (*it cost him his head*). **6 a** a person in charge; a director or leader (esp. *Brit.* the principal teacher at a school or college). **b** a position of leadership or command. **7** the front or forward part of something, e.g. a queue. **8** the upper end of something, e.g. a table or bed. **9** the top or highest part of something, e.g. a page, stairs, etc. **10** a person or individual regarded as a numerical unit (*£10 per head*). **11** (*pl.* same) **a** an individual animal as a unit. **b** (treated as *pl.*) a number of cattle or game as specified (*20 head*). **12 a** the side of a coin bearing the image of a head. **b** (usu. in *pl.*) this side as a choice when tossing a coin. **13 a** the source of a river or stream etc. **b** the end of a lake, bay, etc., at which a river enters. **14** the height or length of a head as a measure. **15** the component of a machine that is in contact with or very close to what is being processed or worked on, esp.: **a** the component on a tape recorder that touches the moving tape in play and converts the signals. **b** the part of a record player that holds the playing cartridge and stylus. **c** = PRINTHEAD. **16 a** a confined body of water or steam in an engine etc. **b** the pressure exerted by this. **17** a promontory (esp. in place names: *Beachy Head*). **18** *Naut.* **a** the bows of a ship. **b** (often in *pl.*) a ship's latrine. **19** a main topic or category for consideration or discussion. **20** *Journalism* = HEADLINE *n.* 1. **21** a culmination, climax, or crisis. **22** the fully developed top of a boil etc. **23** *slang* a habitual taker of drugs; a drug addict. ● *attrib.adj.* chief or principal (*head gardener*; *head office*). ● *v.* **1** *tr.* be at the head or front of. **2** *tr.* be in charge of (*headed a small team*). **3** *tr.* **a** provide with a head or heading. **b** (of an inscription, title, etc.) be at the top of, serve as a heading for. **4 a** *intr.* face or move in a specified direction or towards a specified result (often foll. by *for*: *is heading for trouble*). **b** *tr.* direct in a specified direction. **5** *tr. Football* strike (the ball) with the head. **6 a** *tr.* (often foll. by *down*) cut the head off (a plant etc.). **b** *intr.* (of a plant etc.) form a head. □ **above** (or **over**) **one's head** beyond one's ability to understand. **come to a head** reach a crisis. **enter** (or **come into**) **one's head** *colloq.* occur to one. **from head to toe** (or **foot**) all over a person's body. **get into one's head** come, or cause, to realize or understand. **get** (or **take**) **it into one's head** (foll. by *that* + clause or *to* + infin.) form a definite idea or plan, esp. mistakenly or impetuously. **get one's head down** *Brit. slang* **1** go to bed. **2** concentrate on the task in hand. **give a person his** or **her head** allow a person to act freely. **go out of one's head** go mad. **go to one's head 1** (of liquor) make one dizzy or slightly drunk. **2** (of success) make one conceited. **head and shoulders** *colloq.* by a considerable amount. **head back 1** get ahead of so as to intercept and turn back. **2** return home etc. **head off 1** get ahead of so as to intercept and turn aside. **2** forestall. **head over heels 1** turning over completely in forward motion as in a somersault etc. **2** topsy-turvy. **3** utterly, completely (*head over heels in love*). **heads will roll** *colloq.* people will be disgraced or dismissed. **head up** take charge of (a group of people). **hold up one's head** be confident or unashamed. **in one's head 1** in one's thoughts or imagination. **2** by mental process without use of physical aids. **keep one's head** remain calm. **keep one's head above water** *colloq.* **1** keep out of debt. **2** avoid succumbing to difficulties. **keep one's head down** *colloq.* remain inconspicuous in difficult or dangerous times. **lose one's head** lose self-control; panic. **make head or tail of** (usu. with *neg.* or *interrog.*) understand at all. **off one's head** *colloq.* crazy. **off the top of one's head** *colloq.* impromptu; without careful thought or investigation. **on one's** (or **one's own**) **head** as one's sole responsibility. **out of one's head 1** *colloq.* crazy. **2** from one's imagination or memory. **over one's head 1** beyond one's ability to understand. **2** without one's knowledge or involvement, esp. when one has a right to this. **3** with disregard for one's own (stronger) claim (*was promoted over their heads*). **put heads together** consult together. **put into a person's head** suggest to a person. **turn a person's head 1** make a person conceited. **2** distract or sway a person. **with one's head in the clouds** see CLOUD. ◻ **headed** *adj.* (also in *comb.*). **headless** *adj.* **headward** *adj.* & *adv.* [Old English *hēafod*, from Germanic]

-head /hɛd/ *suffix* = -HOOD (*godhead*; *maidenhead*). [Middle English *-hed*, *-hede* = -HOOD]

headache /ˈhɛdeɪk/ *n.* **1** a continuous pain in the head. **2** *colloq.* **a** a worrying problem. **b** a troublesome person. ◻ **headachy** *adj.*

headage /ˈhɛdɪdʒ/ *n.* the number of animals on a farm etc.

headband /ˈhɛdband/ *n.* a band worn round the head as decoration or to keep the hair off the face.

headbanger /ˈhɛdbaŋə/ *n. slang* **1** a young person shaking violently to the rhythm of pop music (esp. heavy metal). **2** a crazy or eccentric person.

headbanging /ˈhɛdbaŋɪŋ/ *n.* (often *attrib.*) **1** violent shaking of the head esp. by young music fans. **2** the brisk forceful disciplining of uncooperative persons.

headboard /ˈhɛdbɔːd/ *n.* an upright panel forming or placed behind the head of a bed.

head-butt *n.* & *v.* ● *n.* a forceful thrust with the top of the head into the head, chin, or body of another person. ● *v.tr.* attack (another person) with a head-butt.

head case *n. colloq.* a mentally ill or unstable person.

headcount /ˈhɛdkaʊnt/ *n.* **1** a counting of individual people. **2** a total number of people, esp. the number of people employed in a particular organization.

headdress /ˈhɛddrɛs/ *n.* an ornamental covering or band for the head.

header /ˈhɛdə/ *n.* **1** *Football* a shot or pass made with the head. **2** *colloq.* a headlong fall or dive. **3** a brick or stone laid at right angles to the face of a wall (cf. STRETCHER 2). **4** (in full **header-tank**) a tank of water etc. maintaining pressure in a plumbing system. **5** a line or block of text appearing at the top of each page of a document etc. (cf. FOOTER[1] 2).

head first *adv.* **1** with the head foremost. **2** precipitately.

headgear /ˈhɛdgɪə/ *n.* a hat or headdress.

headhunting /ˈhɛdhʌntɪŋ/ *n.* **1** the practice among some peoples of collecting the heads of dead enemies as trophies. **2** the practice of filling a (usu. senior) business position by approaching a suitable person employed elsewhere. ◻ **headhunt** *v.tr.* (also *absol.*). **headhunter** *n.*

heading /ˈhɛdɪŋ/ *n.* **1 a** a title at the head of a page or section of a book etc. **b** a division or section of a subject of discourse etc. **2 a** a horizontal passage made in preparation for building a tunnel. **b** *Mining* = DRIFT *n.* 6. **3** material for making cask-heads. **4** the extension of the top of a curtain above the tape that carries the hooks or the pocket for a wire.

headlamp /ˈhɛdlamp/ *n.* = HEADLIGHT.

headland /ˈhɛdlənd, -land/ *n.* **1** a promontory. **2** a strip left unploughed at the end of a field, for machinery to pass along.

headlight /ˈhɛdlʌɪt/ *n.* **1** a strong light at the front of a motor vehicle or railway engine. **2** the beam from this.

headline /ˈhɛdlʌɪn/ *n.* & *v.* ● *n.* **1** a heading at the top of an article or page, esp. in a newspaper. **2** (in *pl.*) the most important items of news in a newspaper or broadcast news bulletin. ● *v.* **1** *tr.* give a headline to. **2** *intr.* appear as the star performer. ◻ **hit** (or **make**) **the headlines** *colloq.* be given prominent attention as news.

headliner /ˈhɛdlʌɪnə/ *n. US* a star performer.

headlock /ˈhɛdlɒk/ *n. Wrestling* a hold with an arm round the opponent's head.

headlong /ˈhɛdlɒŋ/ *adv.* & *adj.* **1** with head foremost. **2** in a rush. [Middle English *headling* (as HEAD, -LING[2]), assimilated to -LONG]

head louse *n.* a louse of the variety which infests the hair of the human head.

headman /ˈhɛdmən/ *n.* (*pl.* **-men**) the chief man of a tribe etc.

headmaster /hɛdˈmɑːstə/ *n.* (*fem.* **headmistress** /-ˈmɪstrɪs/) the principal teacher in charge of a school. ◻ **headmasterly** *adj.*

headmost /ˈhɛdməʊst/ *adj.* (esp. of a ship) foremost.

headnote /ˈhɛdnəʊt/ *n.* **1** a note or comment at the head of a document, page, etc. **2** *Law* a summary giving the principle of a decision and an outline of the facts, prefixed to the report of a decided case.

head of hair *n.* the hair on a person's head, esp. as a distinctive feature.

head of state *n.* (*pl.* **heads of state**) the title of the head of a state, usu. the leader of the ruling party or a monarch.

head-on *adj.* & *adv.* **1** with the front foremost (*a head-on crash*; *hit us head-on*). **2** in direct confrontation.

headphone /ˈhɛdfəʊn/ *n.* (usu. in *pl.*) a pair of earphones joined by a band placed over the head, for listening to audio equipment etc.

headpiece /ˈhɛdpiːs/ *n.* **1** an ornamental engraving at the head of a chapter etc. **2** a helmet. **3** *archaic* intellect.

headquarters /hɛdˈkwɔːtəz/ *n.* (treated as *sing.* or *pl.*) **1** the administrative centre of an organization. **2** the premises occupied by a military commander and the commander's staff.

headrest /ˈhɛdrɛst/ *n.* a support for the head, esp. on a seat or chair.

headroom /ˈhɛdruːm, -rʊm/ *n.* **1** the space or clearance between the top of a vehicle and the underside of a bridge etc. which it passes under. **2** the space above a driver's or passenger's head in a vehicle.

headsail /ˈhɛdseɪl/ *n.* a sail on a ship's foremast or bowsprit.

headscarf /ˈhɛdskɑːf/ *n.* a scarf worn round the head and tied under the chin, instead of a hat.

headset /ˈhɛdsɛt/ *n.* a set of headphones, often with a microphone attached, used esp. in telephony and radio communication.

headship /ˈhɛdʃɪp/ *n.* the position of chief or leader, esp. *Brit.* of a headmaster or headmistress.

headshrinker /ˈhɛdʃrɪŋkə/ *n. slang* a psychiatrist.

headsman /ˈhɛdzmən/ *n.* (*pl.* **-men**) **1** *hist.* an executioner who beheads. **2** a person in command of a whaling boat.

headspring /ˈhɛdsprɪŋ/ *n.* **1** the main source of a stream. **2** a principal source of ideas etc.

headsquare /ˈhɛdskwɛː/ *n. Brit.* a rectangular scarf for wearing on the head.

headstall /ˈhɛdstɔːl/ *n.* the part of a halter or bridle that fits round a horse's head.

head start *n.* an advantage granted or gained at an early stage.

headstock /ˈhɛdstɒk/ *n.* a set of bearings in a machine, supporting a revolving part.

headstone /ˈhɛdstəʊn/ *n.* a (usu. inscribed) stone set up at the head of a grave.

headstrong /ˈhɛdstrɒŋ/ *adj.* self-willed and obstinate.

head teacher *n.* the teacher in charge of a school.

head-to-head *n., adj., & adv.* ● *n.* a conversation, confrontation, or contest between two parties. ● *attrib.adj.* involving two parties confronting each other. ● *adv.* confronting another party. [translation of French *tête-à-tête*]

head-up *adj.* (of instrument readings in an aircraft, vehicle, etc.) shown so as to be visible without lowering the eyes.

head voice *n.* the high register of the voice in speaking or singing.

headwater /ˈhɛdwɔːtə/ *n.* (in *sing.* or *pl.*) streams flowing from the sources of a river.

headway /ˈhɛdweɪ/ *n.* **1** progress. **2** the rate of progress of a ship. **3** = HEADROOM 1.

headwind /ˈhɛdwɪnd/ *n.* a wind blowing from directly in front.

headword /ˈhɛdwəːd/ *n.* a word forming a heading, e.g. of an entry in a dictionary or encyclopedia.

headwork /ˈhɛdwəːk/ *n.* mental work or effort.

heady /ˈhɛdi/ *adj.* (**headier**, **headiest**) **1** (of liquor) potent, intoxicating. **2** (of success etc.) likely to cause conceit. **3** (of a person, thing, or action) impetuous, violent. **4** headachy. □ **headily** *adv.* **headiness** *n.*

heal /hiːl/ *v.* **1** *intr.* (often foll. by *up*) (of a wound or injury) become sound or healthy again. **2** *tr.* cause (a wound, disease, or person) to heal or be cured, or be made sound again. **3** *tr.* put right (differences etc.). **4** *tr.* alleviate (sorrow etc.). □ **healable** *adj.* [Old English *hǣlan* from Germanic: related to WHOLE]

heal-all *n.* **1** a universal remedy, a panacea. **2** a popular name of various medicinal plants.

heald /hiːld/ *n.* = HEDDLE. [Old English *hefel, hefeld*, from Germanic]

healer /ˈhiːlə/ *n.* **1** a person who heals others, esp. a faith healer. **2** a thing which heals or assists in healing.

health /hɛlθ/ *n.* **1** the state of being well in body or mind. **2** a person's mental or physical condition (*has poor health*). **3** soundness, esp. financial or moral (*the health of the nation*). **4** a toast drunk in someone's honour. [Old English *hǣlth*, from Germanic]

health centre *n. Brit.* the headquarters of a group of local medical services.

health certificate *n.* a certificate attesting fitness or good health.

health farm *n.* a residential establishment where people seek improved health by a regimen of dieting, exercise, etc.

health food *n.* natural food thought to have health-giving qualities.

healthful /ˈhɛlθfʊl, -f(ə)l/ *adj.* conducive to good health; beneficial. □ **healthfully** *adv.* **healthfulness** *n.*

health physics *n.* the branch of radiology which deals with the health of people working with radioactive materials.

health service *n. Brit.* a public service providing medical care.

health visitor *n. Brit.* a trained nurse who visits those in need of medical attention in their homes.

healthy /ˈhɛlθi/ *adj.* (**healthier**, **healthiest**) **1** having, showing, or promoting good health. **2** beneficial, helpful (*a healthy respect for experience*). **3** ample, sizeable, considerable (*a healthy portion*). □ **healthily** *adv.* **healthiness** *n.*

heap /hiːp/ *n. & v.* ● *n.* **1** a collection of things lying haphazardly one on another; a pile. **2** (esp. in *pl.*) *colloq.* a large number or amount (*there's heaps of time*; *is heaps better*). **3** *colloq.* an old or dilapidated thing, esp. a motor vehicle or building. ● *v.* **1** *tr. & intr.* (foll. by *up*, *together*, etc.) collect or be collected in a heap. **2** *tr.* (foll. by *with*) load copiously or to excess. **3** *tr.* (foll. by *on*, *upon*) accord or offer copiously to (*heaped insults on them*). **4** *tr.* (as **heaped** *adj.*) *Brit.* (of a spoonful etc.) with the contents piled above the brim. □ **heap coals of fire on a person's head** *Brit.* cause a person remorse by returning good for evil. [Old English *hēap, hēapian*, from Germanic]

hear /hɪə/ *v.* (*past* and *past part.* **heard** /həːd/) **1** *tr.* (also *absol.*) perceive (sound etc.) with the ear. **2** *tr.* listen to (*heard them on the radio*). **3** *tr.* listen judicially to and judge (a case, plaintiff, etc.). **4** *intr.* (foll. by *about*, *of*, or *that* + clause) be told or informed. **5** *intr.* (foll. by *from*) be contacted by, esp. by letter or telephone. **6** *tr.* be ready to obey (an order). **7** *tr.* grant (a prayer). □ **have heard of** be aware of; know of the existence of. **hear! hear!** *int.* expressing agreement (esp. with something said in a speech). **hear a person out** listen to all that a person says. **hear say** (or **tell**) (usu. foll. by *of*, or *that* + clause) be informed. **will not hear of** will not allow or agree to. □ **hearable** *adj.* **hearer** *n.* [Old English *hīeran*, from Germanic]

hearing /ˈhɪərɪŋ/ *n.* **1** the faculty of perceiving sounds. **2** the range within which sounds may be heard; earshot (*within hearing*; *in my hearing*). **3** an opportunity to state one's case (*give them a fair hearing*). **4** the listening to evidence and pleadings in a law court.

hearing aid *n.* a small device to amplify sound, worn by a partially deaf person.

hearken /ˈhɑːk(ə)n/ *v.intr.* (also **harken**) (often foll. by *to*) *archaic* or *literary* listen. [Old English *heorcnian* (as HARK)]

hearsay /ˈhɪəseɪ/ *n.* rumour, gossip.

hearsay evidence *n.* evidence given by a witness based on information received from others rather than personal knowledge.

hearse /həːs/ *n.* a vehicle for conveying the coffin at a funeral. [Middle English via Old French *herse* 'harrow' from medieval Latin *herpica*, ultimately from Latin *hirpex -icis* 'large rake']

heart /hɑːt/ *n.* **1** a hollow muscular organ maintaining the circulation of blood by rhythmic contraction and dilation. **2** the region of the heart; the breast. **3 a** the heart regarded as the centre of thought, feeling, and emotion (esp. love). **b** a person's capacity for feeling emotion (*has no heart*). **4 a** courage or enthusiasm (*take heart*; *lose heart*). **b** one's mood or feeling (*change of heart*). **5 a** the central or innermost part of something. **b** the vital part or essence (*the heart of the matter*). **6** the close compact head of a cabbage, lettuce, etc. **7 a** a heart-shaped thing. **b** a conventional representation of a heart with two equal curves meeting at a point at the bottom and a cusp at the top. **8 a** a playing card of a suit denoted by a red figure of a heart. **b** (in *pl.*) this suit. **c** (in *pl.*) a card game in which players avoid taking tricks containing a card of this suit. **9** condition of land as regards fertility (*in good heart*). □ **after one's own heart** such as one likes or desires. **at heart 1** in one's inmost feelings. **2** basically, essentially. **break a person's heart** overwhelm a person with sorrow. **by heart** in or from memory. **close to** (or **near**) **one's heart 1** dear to one. **2** affecting one deeply. **from the heart** (or **the bottom of one's heart**) sincerely, profoundly. **give** (or **lose**) **one's heart** (often foll. by *to*) fall in love (with). **have a heart** be merciful. **have the heart** (usu. with *neg.*; foll. by *to* + infin.) be insensitive or hard-hearted enough (*didn't have the heart to ask him*). **have** (or **put**) **one's heart in** (or **into**) be (or become) keenly involved in or committed to (an enterprise etc.). **have one's heart in one's mouth** be greatly alarmed or apprehensive. **have one's heart in the right place** be sincere or well-intentioned. **heart of gold** a generous nature. **heart of oak** a courageous nature. **heart of stone** a stern or cruel nature. **heart to heart** candidly, intimately. **in heart** *Brit.* in good spirits. **in one's heart of hearts** in one's inmost feelings. **out of heart** *Brit.* in low spirits. **take to heart** be much affected or distressed by. **to one's heart's content** see CONTENT[1]. **wear one's heart on one's sleeve** make one's feelings apparent. **with all one's heart** sincerely; with all goodwill. **with one's whole heart** with enthusiasm; without doubts or reservations. □ **-hearted** *adj.* [Old English *heorte*, from Germanic]

heartache /ˈhɑːteɪk/ *n.* mental anguish or grief.

heart attack *n.* a sudden occurrence of coronary thrombosis usu. resulting in the death of part of a heart muscle.

heartbeat /ˈhɑːtbiːt/ *n.* a pulsation of the heart.

heartbreak /ˈhɑːtbreɪk/ *n.* overwhelming distress. □ **heartbreaker** *n.* **heartbreaking** *adj.* **heartbreakingly** *adv.* **heartbroken** *adj.*

heartburn /ˈhɑːtbəːn/ *n.* a burning sensation in the chest resulting from indigestion; pyrosis.

hearten /ˈhɑːt(ə)n/ *v.tr. & intr.* make or become more cheerful. □ **heartening** *adj.* **hearteningly** *adv.*

heart failure *n.* severe failure of the heart to function properly, esp. as a cause of death.

heartfelt /ˈhɑːtfɛlt/ *adj.* sincere; deeply felt.

hearth /hɑːθ/ *n.* **1 a** the floor of a fireplace. **b** the area in front of a fireplace. **2** this symbolizing the home. **3** the bottom of a blast furnace where molten metal collects. [Old English *heorth*, from West Germanic]

hearthrug /ˈhɑːθrʌg/ *n.* a rug laid before a fireplace.

hearthstone /ˈhɑːθstəʊn/ *n.* **1** a flat stone forming a hearth. **2** a soft stone used to whiten hearths, doorsteps, etc.

heartily /ˈhɑːtɪli/ *adv.* **1** in a hearty manner; with goodwill, appetite, or vigour. **2** very; to a great degree (esp. with reference to personal feelings) (*am heartily sick of it*; *disliked him heartily*).

heartland /ˈhɑːtland/ *n.* the central or most important part of an area.

heartless /ˈhɑːtlɪs/ *adj.* unfeeling, pitiless. □ **heartlessly** *adv.* **heartlessness** *n.*

heart-lung machine *n.* a machine that temporarily takes over the functions of the heart and lungs, esp. in surgery.

heart-rending *adj.* very distressing. □ **heart-rendingly** *adv.*

heart's-blood *n. Brit.* lifeblood, life.

heart-searching *n.* the thorough examination of one's own feelings and motives.

heartsease /ˈhɑːtsiːz/ *n.* (also **heart's-ease**) a pansy, esp. the wild pansy, *Viola tricolor*.

heartsick /ˈhɑːtsɪk/ *adj.* very despondent. □ **heartsickness** *n.*

heartsore /ˈhɑːtsɔː/ *adj. archaic* or *literary* grieving, heartsick.

heartstrings /ˈhɑːtstrɪŋz/ *n.pl.* one's deepest feelings or emotions.

heart-throb *n.* **1** beating of the heart. **2** *colloq.* a person, usu. a celebrity, for whom one has (esp. immature) romantic feelings.

heart-to-heart *adj. & n.* ● *adj.* (of a conversation etc.) candid, intimate. ● *n.* a candid or personal conversation.

heart-warming *adj.* emotionally rewarding or uplifting.

heartwood /ˈhɑːtwʊd/ *n.* the dense inner part of a tree trunk yielding the hardest timber.

hearty /ˈhɑːti/ *adj. & n.* ● *adj.* (**heartier**, **heartiest**) **1** strong, vigorous. **2** spirited. **3** (of a meal or appetite) large. **4** warm, friendly. ● *n. Brit.* **1** a hearty person, esp. one ostentatiously so. **2** (usu. in *pl.*) (as a form of address) fellows, esp. fellow sailors. □ **heartiness** *n.*

heat /hiːt/ *n. & v.* ● *n.* **1 a** the condition of being hot. **b** the sensation or perception of this. **c** high temperature of the body. **2** *Physics* **a** a form of energy arising from the random motion of the molecules of bodies, which may be transferred by conduction, convection, or radiation. **b** the amount of this needed to cause a specific process, or evolved in a process (*heat of formation*; *heat of solution*). **3** hot weather (*succumbed to the heat*). **4 a** warmth of feeling. **b** anger or excitement (*the heat of the argument*). **5** (foll. by *of*) the most intense part or period of an activity (*in the heat of the battle*). **6** a (usu. preliminary or trial) round in a race or contest. **7** the receptive period of the sexual cycle, esp. in female mammals. **8** redness of the skin with a sensation of heat (*prickly heat*). **9** pungency of flavour. **10** *slang* intensive pursuit, e.g. by the police. ● *v.* **1** *tr. & intr.* make or become hot or warm. **2** *tr.* inflame; excite or intensify. □ **in the heat of the moment** during or resulting from intense activity, without pause for thought. **on heat** (of mammals, esp. females) sexually receptive. **turn the heat on** *colloq.* concentrate an attack or criticism on (a person). [Old English *hǣtu*, from Germanic]

heat barrier *n.* the limitation of the speed of an aircraft etc. by heat resulting from air friction.

heat capacity *n.* thermal capacity.

heat death *n. Physics* a state of uniform distribution of energy, esp. viewed as a possible fate of the universe.

heated /ˈhiːtɪd/ *adj.* **1** (of a person, discussions, etc.) angry; inflamed with passion or excitement. **2** made hot. □ **heatedly** *adv.*

heat engine *n.* a device for producing motive power from heat.

heater /ˈhiːtə/ *n.* **1** a device for warming the air in a room, car, etc. **2** a container with an element etc. for heating the contents (*water heater*). **3** *slang* a gun.

heat-exchanger *n.* a device for the transfer of heat from one medium to another.

heath /hiːθ/ *n.* **1 a** esp. *Brit.* an area of open uncultivated land, usu. on acid sandy soil, with heather, coarse grasses, etc. **b** *Bot.* an area dominated by dwarf ericaceous shrubs. **2** a plant growing on a heath, esp. of the genus *Erica* or *Calluna* (e.g. heather). □ **heathy** *adj.* [Old English *hǣth*, from Germanic]

heathen /ˈhiːð(ə)n/ *n. & adj.* ● *n.* **1** a person who does not belong to a widely held religion (esp. who is not Christian, Jew, or Muslim) as regarded by those that do. **2** an unenlightened person; a person regarded as lacking culture or moral principles. **3** (**the heathen**) heathen people collectively. **4** *Bibl.* a Gentile. ● *adj.* **1** of or relating to heathens. **2** having no religion. □ **heathendom** *n.* **heathenism** *n.* [Old English *hǣthen*, from Germanic]

heather /ˈhɛðə/ *n.* **1** an evergreen shrub, *Calluna vulgaris* (family Ericaceae), with purple bell-shaped flowers. **2** any of various related shrubs of the genus *Erica* or *Daboecia*, growing esp. on moors and heaths. □ **heathery** *adj.* [Middle English, Scots, & northern English *hathir* etc., of unknown origin: assimilated to *heath*]

heather mixture *n. Brit.* **1** a fabric of mixed hues supposed to resemble heather. **2** the colour of this.

heathland /ˈhiːθland/ *n.* an extensive area of heath.

Heath Robinson /hiːθ ˈrɒbɪns(ə)n/ *adj. Brit.* absurdly ingenious and impracticable in design or construction. [named after W. *Heath Robinson*, English cartoonist d. 1944 who drew such contrivances]

heating /ˈhiːtɪŋ/ *n.* **1** the imparting or generation of heat. **2** equipment or devices used to provide heat, esp. to a building.

heat lamp *n.* a lamp used for its heat as well as its light.

heatproof /ˈhiːtpruːf/ *adj. & v.* ● *adj.* able to resist great heat. ● *v.tr.* make heatproof.

heat pump *n.* a device for the transfer of heat from a colder area to a hotter area by using mechanical energy.

heat-resistant *adj.* = HEATPROOF.

heat-seeking *adj.* (of a missile etc.) able to detect infra-red radiation to guide it to its target.

heat shield *n.* a device for protection from excessive heat, esp. fitted to a spacecraft.

heat sink *n.* a device or substance for absorbing excessive or unwanted heat.

heatstroke /ˈhiːtstrəʊk/ *n.* a feverish condition caused by excessive exposure to high temperature.

heat treatment *n.* the use of heat to modify the properties of a metal, ease muscular pains, etc. □ **heat-treat** *v.tr.*

heatwave /ˈhiːtweɪv/ *n.* a prolonged period of abnormally hot weather.

heave /hiːv/ *v.* & *n.* ● *v.* (*past* and *past part.* **heaved** or esp. *Naut.* **hove** /həʊv/) **1** *tr.* lift or haul (a heavy thing) with great effort. **2** *tr.* utter with effort or resignation (*heaved a sigh*). **3** *tr. colloq.* throw. **4** *intr.* rise and fall rhythmically or spasmodically. **5** *tr. Naut.* haul by rope. **6** *intr.* retch. ● *n.* **1** an instance of heaving. **2** *Geol.* a sideways displacement in a fault. **3** (in *pl.*) a disease of horses, with laboured breathing. □ **heave in sight** *Naut.* or *colloq.* come into view. **heave to** esp. *Naut.* bring or be brought to a standstill. □ **heaver** *n.* [Old English *hebban* from Germanic, related to Latin *capere* 'take']

heave-ho *int.* a sailors' cry, esp. on raising the anchor.

heaven /ˈhɛv(ə)n/ *n.* **1** (also **Heaven**) a place regarded in some religions as the abode of God and the angels, and of the good after death, often characterized as above the sky. **2** a place or state of supreme bliss. **3** *colloq.* something delightful. **4** (usu. **Heaven**) God, Providence (often, in *sing.* or *pl.*, as an exclamation or mild oath: *by Heaven*). **5** (**the heavens**) esp. *poet.* the sky as the abode of the sun, moon, and stars and regarded from earth. □ **in seventh heaven** in a state of ecstasy. **move heaven and earth** (foll. by *to* + infin.) make extraordinary efforts. □ **heavenward** *adj.* & *adv.* **heavenwards** *adv.* [Old English *heofon*]

heavenly /ˈhɛv(ə)nli/ *adj.* **1** of heaven; divine. **2** of the heavens or sky. **3** *colloq.* very pleasing; wonderful. □ **heavenliness** *n.* [Old English *heofonlic* (as HEAVEN)]

heavenly body *n.* a natural object in outer space, e.g. the sun, a star, a planet, etc.; a celestial object.

heavenly host see HOST[1] 3.

heaven-sent *adj.* providential; wonderfully opportune.

heavier-than-air *adj.* (of an aircraft) weighing more than the air it displaces.

Heaviside layer /ˈhɛvɪsʌɪd/ *n.* (in full **Heaviside-Kennelly layer** /hɛvɪsʌɪdˈkɛn(ə)li/) = E-LAYER. [named after O. *Heaviside*, English physicist d. 1925, and A. E. *Kennelly*, US physicist d. 1939]

heavy /ˈhɛvi/ *adj.*, *n.*, & *adv.* ● *adj.* (**heavier**, **heaviest**) **1** of great or exceptionally high weight; difficult to lift. **2 a** of great density. **b** *Physics* having a greater than the usual mass (esp. of isotopes and compounds containing them). **3** abundant, considerable (*a heavy crop*). **4** severe, intense, extensive, excessive (*heavy fighting*; *a heavy sleep*). **5** doing something to excess (*a heavy drinker*). **6 a** striking or falling with force (*heavy blows*; *heavy rain*). **b** (of the sea) having large powerful waves. **7** (of rock music etc.) highly amplified with a strong beat. **8** (of machinery, artillery, etc.) very large of its kind; large in calibre etc. **9** causing a strong impact (*a heavy fall*). **10** needing much physical effort (*heavy work*). **11** (foll. by *with*) laden. **12** carrying heavy weapons (*the heavy brigade*). **13 a** (of a speech, writing, etc.) serious or sombre in tone or attitude; dull, tedious. **b** (of a person) sternly repressive (*heavy father*). **14 a** (of food) hard to digest. **b** (of a literary work etc.) hard to read or understand. **15** intellectually slow. **16** (of bread etc.) too dense from not having risen. **17** (of ground) difficult to traverse or work. **18** oppressive; hard to endure (*a heavy fate*; *heavy demands*). **19 a** coarse, ungraceful (*heavy features*). **b** unwieldy. ● *n.* (*pl.* **-ies**) **1** *colloq.* a large violent person; a thug. **2** a villainous or tragic role or actor in a play etc. **3** (usu. in *pl.*) *Brit. colloq.* a serious newspaper. **4** anything large or heavy of its kind, e.g. a vehicle. **5** *slang* strong beer, esp. bitter. ● *adv.* heavily (esp. in *comb.*: *heavy-laden*). □ **heavy on** using a lot of (*heavy on petrol*). **make heavy weather of** see WEATHER. □ **heavily** *adv.* **heaviness** *n.* **heavyish** *adj.* [Old English *hefig* from Germanic: related to HEAVE]

heavy breathing *n.* breathing that is audible through being deep or laboured, esp. as a result of exertion.

heavy chemicals *n.pl.* bulk chemicals used in industry and agriculture.

heavy-duty *adj.* **1** intended to withstand hard use. **2** *US colloq.* significant in size, amount, etc.

heavy-footed *adj.* awkward, ponderous.

heavy going *adj.* slow or difficult to progress with (*found Proust heavy going*).

heavy-handed *adj.* **1** clumsy. **2** overbearing, oppressive. □ **heavy-handedly** *adv.* **heavy-handedness** *n.*

heavy-hearted *adj.* sad, doleful.

heavy hydrogen *n.* = DEUTERIUM.

heavy industry *n.* industry producing metal, machinery, etc.

heavy metal *n.* **1** heavy guns. **2** metal of high density. **3** (often *attrib.*) *colloq.* a type of highly amplified harsh-sounding rock music with a strong beat and frequently theatrical performance.

heavy petting *n.* erotic fondling between two people, stopping short of intercourse.

heavy sleeper *n.* a person who sleeps deeply.

heavy water *n.* a substance composed entirely or mainly of deuterium oxide.

heavyweight /ˈhɛvɪweɪt/ *n.* **1 a** a weight in certain sports, in the amateur boxing scale over 81 kg but differing for professional boxers, wrestlers, and weightlifters. **b** a boxer etc. of this weight. **2** a person, animal, or thing of above average weight. **3** *colloq.* a person of influence or importance.

Heb. *abbr.* Hebrews (New Testament).

hebdomadal /hɛbˈdɒməd(ə)l/ *adj. formal* weekly, esp. meeting weekly. [Late Latin *hebdomadalis* from Greek *hebdomas, -ados*, from *hepta* 'seven']

hebe /hiːbi/ *n.* any flowering shrub of the genus *Hebe*, with usu. overlapping scalelike leaves. [modern Latin, named after the Greek goddess *Hēbē*]

hebetude /ˈhɛbɪtjuːd/ *n. literary* dullness. [Late Latin *hebetudo* from *hebes, -etis* 'blunt']

Hebraic /hɪˈbreɪɪk/ *adj.* of Hebrew or the Hebrews. □ **Hebraically** *adv.* [Late Latin from Greek *Hebraikos* (as HEBREW)]

Hebraism /ˈhiːbreɪɪz(ə)m/ *n.* **1** a Hebrew idiom or expression, esp. in the Greek of the Bible. **2** an attribute of the Hebrews. **3** the Hebrew system of thought or religion. □ **Hebraistic** /-ˈɪstɪk/ *adj.* **Hebraize** *v.tr.* & *intr.* (also **-ise**). [French *hébraïsme* or modern Latin *Hebraismus* from late Greek *Hebraïsmos* (as HEBREW)]

Hebraist /ˈhiːbreɪɪst/ *n.* an expert in Hebrew.

Hebrew /ˈhiːbruː/ *n.* & *adj.* ● *n.* **1** a member of a Semitic people originally centred in ancient Palestine. **2 a** the language of this people. **b** a modern form of this used esp. in Israel. ● *adj.* **1** of or in Hebrew. **2** of the Hebrews or the Jews. [Middle English via Old French *Ebreu*, medieval Latin *Ebreus*, Latin *hebraeus*, Greek *Hebraios* and Aramaic *'iḇray* from Hebrew *'iḇrî* 'one from the other side' (of the river)]

Hebridean /hɛbrɪˈdiːən/ *adj.* & *n.* ● *adj.* of or relating to the Hebrides, an island group off the W. coast of Scotland. ● *n.* a native of the Hebrides.

hecatomb /ˈhɛkətuːm/ *n.* **1** (in ancient Greece or Rome) a great public sacrifice, originally of 100 oxen. **2** any extensive sacrifice. [Latin *hecatombe* from Greek *hekatombē*, from *hekaton* 'hundred' + *bous* 'ox']

heck /hɛk/ *int. colloq.* a mild exclamation of surprise or dismay. [alteration of HELL]

heckelphone /ˈhɛk(ə)lfəʊn/ *n. Mus.* a bass oboe. [German *Heckelphon*, named after W. *Heckel*, 20th-c. German instrument-maker]

heckle /ˈhɛk(ə)l/ *v.* & *n.* ● *v.tr.* **1** interrupt and harass (a public speaker). **2** dress (flax or hemp). ● *n.* an act of heckling. □ **heckler** *n.* [Middle English, northern and eastern form of HACKLE]

hectare /ˈhɛktɛː, -ɑː/ *n.* a metric unit of square measure, equal to 100 ares (2.471 acres or 10,000 square metres) (abbr.: **ha**). □ **hectarage** /ˈhɛktərɪdʒ/ *n.* [French (as HECTO-, ARE[2])]

hectic /ˈhɛktɪk/ *adj. & n.* ● *adj.* **1** busy and confused. **2** *Med. hist.* having a hectic fever; abnormally flushed. ● *n. Med. hist.* **1** a hectic fever or flush. **2** a patient suffering from this. □ **hectically** *adv.* [Middle English *etik* via Old French *etique* and Late Latin *hecticus* from Greek *hektikos* 'habitual', from *hexis* 'habit', assimilated to French *hectique* or Late Latin]

hectic fever *n.* (also **hectic flush**) *Med. hist.* a fever which accompanies consumption and similar diseases, with flushed cheeks and hot dry skin.

hecto- /ˈhɛktəʊ/ *comb. form* a hundred, esp. of a unit in the metric system (abbr.: **h**). [French, formed irregularly from Greek *hekaton* 'hundred']

hectogram /ˈhɛktə(ʊ)gram/ *n.* (also **hectogramme**) a metric unit of mass, equal to one hundred grams.

hectograph /ˈhɛktə(ʊ)grɑːf/ *n.* an apparatus for copying documents by the use of a gelatin plate which receives an impression of the master copy.

hectolitre /ˈhɛktə(ʊ)liːtə/ *n.* (*US* **hectoliter**) a metric unit of capacity, equal to one hundred litres.

hectometre /ˈhɛktə(ʊ)miːtə/ *n.* (*US* **hectometer**) a metric unit of length, equal to one hundred metres.

hector /ˈhɛktə/ *v. & n.* ● *v.tr.* bully, intimidate. ● *n.* a bully. □ **hectoringly** *adv.* [earlier 'a swaggering fellow': Latin *Hector* from Greek *Hektōr*, the name of a Trojan hero and son of Priam in Homer's *Iliad*]

he'd /hiːd, hɪd/ *contr.* **1** he had. **2** he would.

heddle /hɛd(ə)l/ *n.* one of the sets of small cords or wires between which the warp is passed in a loom before going through the reed. [apparently from Old English *hefeld*]

hedge /hɛdʒ/ *n. & v.* ● *n.* **1** a fence or boundary formed by closely growing bushes or shrubs. **2** a protection against possible loss or diminution. ● *v.* **1** *tr.* surround or bound with a hedge. **2** *tr.* (foll. by *in*) enclose. **3 a** *tr.* reduce one's risk of loss on (a bet or speculation) by compensating transactions on the other side. **b** *intr.* avoid a definite decision or commitment. **4** *intr.* make or trim hedges. □ **hedger** *n.* [Old English *hegg*, from Germanic]

hedgehog /ˈhɛdʒ(h)ɒg/ *n.* **1** a small nocturnal mammal of the family Erinaceidae, esp. *Erinaceus europaeus*, having a piglike snout and a coat of spines, eating small invertebrates, and rolling itself up into a ball for defence. **2** a porcupine or other animal similarly covered with spines. [Middle English, from HEDGE (from its habitat) + HOG (from its snout)]

hedge-hop *v.intr.* fly at a very low altitude.

hedgerow /ˈhɛdʒrəʊ/ *n.* a row of bushes etc. forming a hedge.

hedge sparrow *n.* = DUNNOCK.

hedge trimmer *n.* a usu. electric device for trimming hedges.

hedonic /hiːˈdɒnɪk, hɛ-/ *adj.* **1** of or characterized by pleasure. **2** *Psychol.* of pleasant or unpleasant sensations. [Greek *hēdonikos* from *hēdonē* 'pleasure']

hedonism /ˈhiːd(ə)nɪz(ə)m, ˈhɛ-/ *n.* **1** belief in pleasure as the highest good and humankind's proper aim. **2** behaviour based on this. □ **hedonist** *n.* **hedonistic** /-ˈnɪstɪk/ *adj.* [Greek *hēdonē* 'pleasure']

-hedron /ˈhiːdrən, ˈhɛd-/ *comb. form* (*pl.* **-hedra** or **-hedrons**) forming nouns denoting geometrical solids with various numbers or shapes of faces (*dodecahedron*; *rhombohedron*). □ **-hedral** *comb. form* forming adjectives. [Greek *hedra* 'seat']

heebie-jeebies /hiːbɪˈdʒiːbɪz/ *n.pl.* (prec. by *the*) *slang* a state of nervous depression or anxiety. [20th c.: origin unknown]

heed /hiːd/ *v. & n.* ● *v.tr.* attend to; take notice of. ● *n.* careful attention. [Old English *hēdan*, from West Germanic]

heedful /ˈhiːdfʊl/ *adj.* (often foll. by *of*) mindful, attentive; careful, cautious. □ **heedfully** *adv.* **heedfulness** *n.*

heedless /ˈhiːdlɪs/ *adj.* (often foll. by *of*) inattentive, regardless; careless (*went out, heedless of the rain*). □ **headlessly** *adv.* **heedlessness** *n.*

hee-haw /ˈhiːhɔː/ *n. & v.* ● *n.* the bray of a donkey. ● *v.intr.* emit a braying sound. [imitative]

heel[1] /hiːl/ *n. & v.* ● *n.* **1** the back part of the foot below the ankle. **2** the corresponding part in vertebrate animals. **3 a** the part of a sock etc. covering the heel. **b** the part of a shoe or boot supporting the heel. **4** a thing like a heel in form or position, e.g. the part of the palm next to the wrist, the end of a violin bow at which it is held, or the part of a golf club near where the head joins the shaft. **5** the crust of a loaf of bread or the rind of a cheese. **6** *colloq.* a person regarded with contempt or disapproval. **7** (as *int.*) a command to a dog to walk close to its owner's heel. ● *v.* **1** *tr.* fit or renew a heel on (a shoe or boot). **2** *intr.* touch the ground with the heel as in dancing. **3** *intr.* (foll. by *out*) *Rugby* pass the ball with the heel. **4** *tr. Golf* strike (the ball) with the heel of the club. □ **at heel 1** (of a dog) close behind. **2** (of a person etc.) under control. **at** (or **on**) **the heels of** following closely after (a person or event). **cool** (or *Brit.* **kick) one's heels** be kept waiting. **down at heel 1** (of a shoe) with the heel worn down. **2** (of a person) shabby. **take to one's heels** run away. **to heel 1** (of a dog) close behind. **2** (of a person etc.) under control. **turn on one's heel** turn sharply round. □ **heelless** *adj.* [Old English *hēla*, *hǣla*, from Germanic]

heel[2] /hiːl/ *v. & n.* ● *v.* **1** *intr.* (of a ship etc.) lean over owing to the pressure of wind or an uneven load (cf. LIST[2] *v.*). **2** *tr.* cause (a ship etc.) to do this. ● *n.* the act or amount of heeling. [probably via obsolete *heeld*, *hield* 'incline' from Old English *hieldan*, Old Saxon *-heldian*, from Germanic]

heel[3] /hiːl/ *v.tr.* (foll. by *in*) set (a plant) in the ground and cover its roots. [Old English *helian* from Germanic]

heelball /ˈhiːlbɔːl/ *n.* **1** a mixture of hard wax and lampblack used by shoemakers for polishing. **2** this or a similar mixture used in brass rubbing.

heeltap /ˈhiːltap/ *n.* **1** a layer of leather in a shoe heel. **2** liquor left at the bottom of a glass after drinking.

heft /hɛft/ *v. & n.* ● *v.tr.* lift (something heavy), esp. to judge its weight. ● *n. dial.* or *N. Amer.* weight, heaviness. [probably from HEAVE, on the pattern of *cleft*, *weft*]

hefty /ˈhɛfti/ *adj.* (**heftier**, **heftiest**) **1** (of a person) big and strong. **2** (of a thing) large, heavy, powerful. □ **heftily** *adv.* **heftiness** *n.*

Hegelian /heɪˈgiːlɪən, hɪ-, -ˈgeɪl-/ *adj. & n.* ● *adj.* of or relating to the German philosopher G. W. F. Hegel (d. 1831) or his philosophy of objective idealism. ● *n.* an adherent of Hegel or his philosophy. □ **Hegelianism** *n.*

hegemonic /hɛdʒɪˈmɒnɪk, hɛgɪ-/ *adj.* ruling, supreme. [Greek *hēgemonikos* (as HEGEMONY)]

hegemony /hɪˈdʒɛməni, -ˈgɛ-/ *n.* leadership or dominance, esp. by one state of a confederacy. [Greek *hēgemonia*, via *hēgemōn* 'leader' from *hēgeomai* 'lead']

Hegira /ˈhɛdʒɪrə/ *n.* (also **Hejira**, **Hijra** /ˈhɪdʒrə/) **1 a** Muhammad's departure from Mecca to Medina in AD 622. **b** the Muslim era reckoned from this date. **2** (**hegira**) a general exodus or departure. [medieval Latin *hegira* from Arabic *hijra* 'departure from one's country', from *hajara* 'separate']

heifer /ˈhɛfə/ *n.* **1** a female domestic bovine animal that has not borne a calf, or has borne only one calf. Cf. COW[1] 1c. **2** *Brit. slang offens.* a woman. [Old English *heahfore*]

heigh /heɪ/ *int.* expressing encouragement or enquiry. [imitative]

heigh-ho /heɪˈhəʊ/ *int.* expressing boredom, resignation, etc.

height /hʌɪt/ *n.* **1** the measurement from base to top or (of a standing person) from head to foot. **2** the elevation above ground or a recognized level (usu. sea level). **3** any considerable elevation (*situated at a height*). **4 a** a high place or area. **b** rising ground. **5** the top of something. **6** *Printing* the distance from the foot to the face of type. **7 a** the most intense part or period of anything (*the battle was at its height*). **b** an extreme instance or example (*the height of fashion*). [Old English *hēhthu*, from Germanic]

heighten /'hʌɪt(ə)n/ *v.tr. & intr.* make or become higher or more intense.

height of land *n. N. Amer.* a watershed.

heinous /'hemәs, 'hi:nәs/ *adj.* (of a crime or criminal) utterly odious or wicked. □ **heinously** *adv.* **heinousness** *n.* [Middle English from Old French *haïneus*, ultimately from *haïr* 'to hate', from Frankish]

heir /ɛ:/ *n.* **1** a person entitled to property or rank as the legal successor of its former owner (often foll. by *to*: *heir to the throne*). **2** a person deriving or morally entitled to some thing, quality, etc., from a predecessor. □ **heirdom** *n.* **heirless** *adj.* **heirship** *n.* [Middle English via Old French *eir* and Late Latin *herem* from Latin *heres -edis*]

heir apparent *n.* (*pl.* **heirs apparent**) an heir whose claim cannot be set aside by the birth of another heir.

■ **Usage** Note that *heir apparent* does not mean 'seeming heir'.

heir-at-law *n.* (*pl.* **heirs-at-law**) an heir by right of blood, esp. to the real property of an intestate.

heiress /'ɛ:rɪs, ɛ:'rɛs/ *n.* a female heir, esp. to wealth or high title.

heirloom /'ɛ:lu:m/ *n.* **1** a piece of personal property that has been in a family for several generations. **2** a piece of property received as part of an inheritance. [HEIR + LOOM[1] in the sense 'tool']

heir presumptive *n.* (*pl.* **heirs presumptive**) an heir whose claim may be set aside by the birth of another heir.

Heisenberg uncertainty principle see UNCERTAINTY PRINCIPLE.

heist /hʌɪst/ *n. & v. N. Amer. slang* ● *n.* a robbery. ● *v.tr.* rob. [representing a local pronunciation of HOIST]

hei-tiki /heɪ'tɪki/ *n. NZ* a greenstone neck ornament worn by Maoris. [Maori from *hei* 'hang', TIKI]

Hejira var. of HEGIRA.

HeLa cell /'hi:lә/ *n.* (usu. in *pl.*) a human epithelial cell of a strain maintained in tissue culture since 1951 and used in research esp. in virology. [from the name of *He*nrietta *La*cks, whose cervical carcinoma provided the original cells]

held *past* and *past part.* of HOLD[1].

Heldentenor /'hɛld(ә)ntɛnɔ:/ *n.* **1** a powerful tenor voice suitable for heroic roles in opera. **2** a singer with this voice. [German, from *Held* 'hero']

helenium /hɛ'li:nɪәm/ *n.* any plant of the genus *Helenium* (daisy family), with flowers having prominent central discs. [modern Latin from Greek *helenion*, possibly commemorating Helen of Troy]

heli- /'hɛli/ *comb. form* helicopter (*heliport*).

heliacal /hɪ'lʌɪәk(ә)l/ *adj. Astron.* relating to or near the sun. [Late Latin *heliacus* from Greek *hēliakos*, from *hēlios* 'sun']

heliacal rising *n.* (also **heliacal setting**) the first rising (or setting) of a star after (or before) a period of invisibility due to conjunction with the sun.

helianthemum /hi:lɪ'anθɪmәm/ *n.* any evergreen shrub of the genus *Helianthemum*, with saucer-shaped flowers. Also called ROCK ROSE. [modern Latin, from Greek *hēlios* 'sun' + *anthemon* 'flower']

helianthus /hi:lɪ'anθәs/ *n.* any plant of the genus *Helianthus*, including the sunflower and Jerusalem artichoke. [modern Latin, from Greek *hēlios* 'sun' + *anthos* 'flower']

helical /'hɛlɪk(ә)l, 'hi:-/ *adj.* having the form of a helix. □ **helically** *adv.* **helicoid** *adj. & n.*

helices *pl.* of HELIX.

helichrysum /hɛlɪ'krʌɪsәm/ *n.* any plant of the genus *Helichrysum* (daisy family), with flowers retaining their appearance when dried. [Latin from Greek *helikhrusos*, from *helix* 'spiral' + *khrusos* 'gold']

helicity /hi:'lɪsɪti/ *n.* **1** esp. *Biochem.* helical character. **2** *Physics* a combination of the spin and the linear motion of a subatomic particle. [HELICAL + -ITY]

helicon /'hɛlɪk(ә)n/ *n.* a large spiral bass tuba played encircling the player's head and resting on the shoulder. [Latin from Greek *Helikōn*, the name of a mountain sacred to the Muses: later associated with HELIX]

helicopter /'hɛlɪkɒptә/ *n. & v.* ● *n.* a type of aircraft obtaining lift and propulsion from horizontally revolving overhead blades or rotors, and capable of moving vertically and horizontally. ● *v.tr. & intr.* transport or fly by helicopter. [French *hélicoptère*, from Greek *helix* (see HELIX) + *pteron* 'wing']

helio- /'hi:lɪәʊ/ *comb. form* the sun. [Greek *hēlios* 'sun']

heliocentric /ˌhi:lɪә(ʊ)'sɛntrɪk/ *adj.* **1** regarding the sun as centre. **2** considered as viewed from the sun's centre. □ **heliocentrically** *adv.*

heliogram /'hi:lɪә(ʊ)gram/ *n.* a message sent by heliograph.

heliograph /'hi:lɪә(ʊ)grɑ:f/ *n. & v.* ● *n.* **1 a** a signalling apparatus reflecting sunlight in flashes from a movable mirror. **b** a message sent by means of this; a heliogram. **2** an apparatus for photographing the sun. **3** an engraving obtained chemically by exposure to light. ● *v.tr.* send (a message) by heliograph. □ **heliography** /-'ɒgrәfi/ *n.*

heliogravure /ˌhi:lɪәʊgra'vjʊә/ *n.* = PHOTOGRAVURE.

heliolithic /ˌhi:lɪә'lɪθɪk/ *adj.* (of a civilization) characterized by sun-worship and megaliths.

heliometer /hi:lɪ'ɒmɪtә/ *n.* an instrument used for finding the angular distance between two stars (originally used for measuring the diameter of the sun).

heliostat /'hi:lɪәstat/ *n.* an apparatus with a mirror driven by clockwork to reflect sunlight in a fixed direction. □ **heliostatic** /-'statɪk/ *adj.*

heliotherapy /ˌhi:lɪә(ʊ)'θɛrәpi/ *n.* the therapeutic use of sunlight.

heliotrope /'hi:lɪәtrәʊp, 'hɛl-/ *n. & adj.* ● *n.* **1 a** any plant of the genus *Heliotropium* (borage family), with fragrant purple flowers. **b** the scent of these. **2** (**winter heliotrope**) a plant of the daisy family, *Petasites fragrans*, which produces fragrant lilac flowers in winter. **3** a light purple colour. **4** bloodstone. ● *adj.* light purple. [Latin *heliotropium* from Greek *hēliotropion* 'plant turning its flowers to the sun', from *hēlios* 'sun' + *-tropos* from *trepō* 'turn']

heliotropism /ˌhi:lɪә(ʊ)'trәʊpɪz(ә)m/ *n.* the directional growth of a plant in response to sunlight (cf. PHOTOTROPISM). □ **heliotropic** /ˌhi:lɪә'trɒpɪk/ *adj.*

heliotype /'hi:lɪәtʌɪp/ *n.* a picture obtained from a sensitized gelatin film exposed to light.

helipad /'hɛlɪpad/ *n.* a landing pad for helicopters.

heliport /'hɛlɪpɔ:t/ *n.* a place where helicopters take off and land. [HELI-, on the pattern of *airport*]

heli-skiing /'hɛlɪski:ɪŋ/ *n.* skiing in which transport up the mountain is by helicopter.

helium /'hi:lɪәm/ *n. Chem.* a colourless light inert gaseous element occurring in deposits of natural gas, used in airships and as a refrigerant (symbol **He**). [Greek *hēlios* 'sun' (having been first identified in the sun's atmosphere)]

helix /'hi:lɪks/ *n.* (*pl.* **helices** /'hi:lɪsi:z, 'hɛl-/) **1** a spiral curve (like a corkscrew) or a coiled curve (like a watch spring). **2** *Geom.* a curve that cuts a line on a solid cone or cylinder, at a constant angle with the axis. **3** *Archit.* a spiral ornament. **4** *Anat.* the rim of the external ear. [Latin *helix -icis* from Greek *helix -ikos*]

hell /hɛl/ *n. & int.* ● *n.* **1** the abode of the dead; in Christian, Jewish, and Islamic belief, the place of punishment or torment where the souls of the damned are confined after death. **2** a place or state of misery or wickedness. ● *int.* an exclamation of surprise or annoyance. □ **beat** (or **knock** etc.) **the hell out of**

colloq. beat etc. without restraint. **come hell or high water** no matter what the difficulties. **for the hell of it** *colloq.* for fun. **get** (or **catch**) **hell** *colloq.* be severely scolded or punished. **give a person hell** *colloq.* scold or punish or make things difficult for a person. **the hell** (usu. prec. by *what, where, who*, etc.) expressing anger, disbelief, etc. (*who the hell is this?*; *the hell you are!*). **hell for leather** at full speed. **a** (or **one**) **hell of a** *colloq.* an outstanding example of (*a hell of a mess*; *one hell of a party*). **hell to pay** great trouble, resulting from a previous action. **like hell** *colloq.* **1** not at all. **2** recklessly, exceedingly. **not a hope in hell** *colloq.* no chance at all. **play hell** (or *Brit.* **merry hell**) **with** *colloq.* be upsetting or disruptive to. **what the hell** *colloq.* it is of no importance. □ **hell-like** *adj.* **hellward** *adv. & adj.* [Old English *hel, hell*, from Germanic]

he'll /hiːl, hɪl/ *contr.* he will; he shall.

hellacious /hɛˈleɪʃəs/ *adj. US slang* hellish; tremendous. □ **hellaciously** *adv.* [HELL + *-acious*, perhaps suggested by BODACIOUS]

Helladic /hɛˈladɪk/ *adj.* of or belonging to the Bronze Age culture of mainland Greece. [Greek *Helladikos* from *Hellas -ados* 'Greece']

hellbender /ˈhɛlbɛndə/ *n.* a large N. American salamander, *Cryptobranchus alleganiensis*. [HELL + BEND¹ + -ER¹]

hell-bent *adj.* (foll. by *on*) recklessly determined.

hell-cat *n.* a spiteful violent woman.

hellebore /ˈhɛlɪbɔː/ *n.* **1** any evergreen plant of the genus *Helleborus* (buttercup family), having large white, green, or purplish flowers, e.g. the Christmas rose. **2** a plant of the lily family, *Veratrum album*. **3** *hist.* any of various plants supposed to cure madness. [Middle English via Old French *ellebre, elebore* or medieval Latin *eleborus* from Latin *elleborus*, from Greek *(h)elleboros*]

helleborine /ˈhɛlɪbəriːn, -rʌɪn/ *n.* any orchid of the genus *Epipactis* or *Cephalanthera*. [French or Latin *helleborine* from Greek *helleborinē* 'plant like hellebore' (as HELLEBORE)]

Hellene /ˈhɛliːn/ *n.* **1** a native of modern Greece. **2** an ancient Greek. □ **Hellenic** /hɛˈlɛnɪk, -ˈliːnɪk/ *adj.* [Greek *Hellēn* 'a Greek']

Hellenism /ˈhɛlɪnɪz(ə)m/ *n.* **1** Greek character or culture (esp. of ancient Greece). **2** the study or imitation of Greek culture. □ **Hellenize** *v.tr. & intr.* (also **-ise**). **Hellenization** /-nʌɪˈzeɪʃ(ə)n/ *n.* [Greek *hellēnismos* from *hellēnizō* 'speak Greek, make Greek' (as HELLENE)]

Hellenist /ˈhɛlɪnɪst/ *n.* an expert on or admirer of Greek language or culture. [Greek *Hellēnistēs* (as HELLENISM)]

Hellenistic /hɛlɪˈnɪstɪk/ *adj.* of or relating to Greek history, language, and culture from the death of Alexander the Great to the time of Augustus (4th–1st c. BC).

hellfire /ˈhɛlfʌɪə/ *n.* the fire or fires regarded as existing in hell.

hellgrammite /ˈhɛlɡrəmʌɪt/ *n. US* an aquatic larva of an American fly, *Corydalus cornutus*, often used as fishing bait. [19th c.: origin unknown]

hell-hole *n.* an oppressive or unbearable place.

hell-hound *n.* a fiend.

hellion /ˈhɛljən/ *n. N. Amer. colloq.* a mischievous or troublesome person, esp. a child. [perhaps from dialect *hallion* 'a worthless fellow', assimilated to HELL]

hellish /ˈhɛlɪʃ/ *adj. & adv.* ● *adj.* **1** of or like hell. **2** *colloq.* extremely difficult or unpleasant. ● *adv. Brit. colloq.* (as an intensifier) extremely (*hellish expensive*). □ **hellishly** *adv.* **hellishness** *n.*

hello /həˈləʊ, hɛ-/ *int., n., & v.* (also **hullo**, esp. *Brit.* **hallo**) ● *int.* **1 a** an expression of informal greeting, or esp. *Brit.* of surprise. **b** used to begin a telephone conversation. **2** a cry used to call attention. ● *n.* (*pl.* **-os**) a cry of 'hello'. ● *v.intr.* (**-oes, -oed**) cry 'hello'. [variant of earlier HOLLO]

hellraiser /ˈhɛlreɪzə/ *n.* a person who causes trouble or creates chaos. □ **hellraising** *adj. & n.*

Hell's Angel *n.* a member of a gang of male motorcycle enthusiasts notorious for outrageous and violent behaviour.

helm¹ /hɛlm/ *n. & v.* ● *n.* **1** a tiller or wheel by which a ship's rudder is controlled. **2** the amount by which this is turned (*more helm needed*). ● *v.tr.* steer or guide as if with a helm. □ **at the helm** in control; at the head (of an organization etc.). [Old English *helma*, probably related to HELVE]

helm² /hɛlm/ *n. archaic* helmet. □ **helmed** *adj.* [Old English from Germanic]

helmet /ˈhɛlmɪt/ *n.* **1** any of various protective head coverings worn by soldiers, police officers, firefighters, divers, motorcyclists, etc. **2** *Bot.* the arched upper part of the corolla in some flowers. **3** the shell of a gastropod mollusc of the genus *Cassis*, used in jewellery. □ **helmeted** *adj.* [Middle English from Old French, diminutive of *helme*, from West Germanic (as HELM²)]

helminth /ˈhɛlmɪnθ/ *n.* any of various parasitic worms including flukes, tapeworms, and nematodes. □ **helminthic** /-ˈmɪnθɪk/ *adj.* **helminthoid** /-ˈmɪnθɔɪd/ *adj.* **helminthology** /-mɪnˈθɒlədʒi/ *n.* [Greek *helmins -inthos* 'intestinal worm']

helminthiasis /hɛlmɪnˈθʌɪəsɪs/ *n.* a disease characterized by the presence of any of several parasitic worms in the body.

helmsman /ˈhɛlmzmən/ *n.* (*pl.* **-men**) a steersman.

helot /ˈhɛlət/ *n.* a serf, esp. (**Helot**) of a class in ancient Sparta. □ **helotism** *n.* **helotry** *n.* [Latin *helotes* (pl.) from Greek *heilōtes, -ōtai*, erroneously taken as = inhabitants of *Helos*, a Laconian town]

help /hɛlp/ *v. & n.* ● *v.tr.* **1** provide (a person etc.) with the means towards what is needed or sought (*helped me with my work*; *helped me (to) pay my debts*). **2** (foll. by *up, down*, etc.) assist or give support to (a person) in moving etc. as specified (*helped her into the chair*; *helped him on with his coat*). **3** (often *absol.*) be of use or service to (a person) (*does that help?*). **4** contribute to alleviating (a pain or difficulty). **5** prevent or remedy (*it can't be helped*). **6** (usu. with *neg.*) **a** refrain from (*can't help it*; *could not help laughing*). **b** *refl.* refrain from acting (*couldn't help himself*). **7** (often foll. by *to*) serve (a person with food) (*shall I help you to greens?*). ● *n.* **1** the act of helping or being helped (*we need your help*; *came to our help*). **2** a person or thing that helps. **3** a domestic servant or employee, or several collectively. **4** a remedy or escape (*there is no help for it*). □ **help oneself** (often foll. by *to*) **1** serve oneself (with food etc.). **2** take without seeking help or permission. **help a person out** give a person help, esp. in difficulty. **so help me** (or **help me God**) (as an invocation or oath) I am speaking the truth. □ **helper** *n.* [Old English *helpan*, from Germanic]

helpful /ˈhɛlpfʊl, -f(ə)l/ *adj.* **1** giving help; useful. **2** obliging. □ **helpfully** *adv.* **helpfulness** *n.*

helping /ˈhɛlpɪŋ/ *n.* a portion of food, esp. at a meal.

helping hand *n.* assistance.

helpless /ˈhɛlplɪs/ *adj.* **1** lacking help or protection; defenceless. **2** unable to act without help. □ **helplessly** *adv.* **helplessness** *n.*

helpline /ˈhɛlplʌɪn/ *n.* a telephone service providing help with problems.

helpmate /ˈhɛlpmeɪt/ *n.* a helpful companion or partner (usu. a husband or wife).

helter-skelter /hɛltəˈskɛltə/ *adv., adj., & n.* ● *adv.* in disorderly haste; confusedly. ● *adj.* characterized by disorderly haste or confusion; disorganized, confused. ● *n. Brit.* a tall spiral slide round a tower, at a fairground or funfair. [imitative, originally in a rhyming jingle, perhaps from Middle English *skelte* 'hasten']

helve /hɛlv/ *n.* the handle of a weapon or a tool. [Old English *helfe*, from West Germanic]

Helvetian /hɛl'vi:ʃ(ə)n/ *adj. & n.* ● *adj.* Swiss. ● *n.* a native of Switzerland. [Latin *Helvetia* 'Switzerland']

hem[1] /hɛm/ *n. & v.* ● *n.* the border of a piece of cloth, esp. a cut edge turned under and sewn down. ● *v.tr.* (**hemmed, hemming**) turn down and sew in the edge of (a piece of cloth etc.). □ **hem in** confine; restrict the movement of. [Old English, perhaps related to dialect *ham* 'enclosure']

hem[2] /həm, hɛm/ *int., n., & v.* ● *int.* attracting attention or expressing hesitation by a slight cough or clearing of the throat. ● *n.* an utterance of this. ● *v.intr.* (**hemmed, hemming**) say *hem*; hesitate in speech. □ **hem and haw** = *hum and haw* (see HUM[1]). [imitative]

hemal etc. *US* var. of HAEMAL etc.

he-man *n.* (*pl.* **-men**) a masterful or virile man, esp. ostentatiously so.

hemato- etc. *US* var. of HAEMATO- etc.

heme *US* var. of HAEM.

hemerocallis /hɛm(ə)rə(ʊ)'kalɪs/ *n.* = DAY LILY. [Latin *hemerocalles* from Greek *hēmerokalles*, a kind of lily, from *hēmera* 'day' + *kallos* 'beauty']

hemi- /'hɛmi/ *comb. form* half. [Greek *hēmi-* = Latin *semi-*: see SEMI-]

-hemia see -AEMIA.

hemianopsia /hɛmɪə'nɒpsɪə/ *n.* (also **hemianopia** /hɛmɪə'nəʊpɪə/) blindness over half the field of vision.

hemicellulose /hɛmɪ'sɛljʊləʊz, -s/ *n.* any of various polysaccharides forming the matrix of plant cell walls in which cellulose is embedded. [German (as HEMI-, CELLULOSE)]

hemichordate /hɛmɪ'kɔ:deɪt/ *n. & adj. Zool.* ● *n.* a wormlike marine invertebrate of the phylum Hemichordata, comprising the acorn worms, possessing a notochord in the larval stage. ● *adj.* of or relating to this phylum.

hemicycle /'hɛmɪsʌɪk(ə)l/ *n.* a semicircular figure.

hemidemisemiquaver /'hɛmɪdɛmɪˌsɛmɪkweɪvə/ *n. Brit. Mus.* a note having the time value of half a demisemiquaver and represented by a large dot with a four-hooked stem.

hemihedral /hɛmɪ'hi:dr(ə)l/ *adj. Crystallog.* having half the number of planes required for symmetry of the holohedral form.

hemiplegia /hɛmɪ'pli:dʒə/ *n. Med.* paralysis of one side of the body. □ **hemiplegic** *n. & adj.* [modern Latin from Greek *hēmiplēgia* 'paralysis' (as HEMI-, *plēgē* 'stroke')]

hemipterous /hɛ'mɪpt(ə)rəs/ *adj.* of the insect order Hemiptera including aphids, bugs, and cicadas, with piercing or sucking mouthparts. [HEMI- + Greek *pteron* 'wing']

hemisphere /'hɛmɪsfɪə/ *n.* **1** half of a sphere. **2** a half of the earth, esp. as divided by the equator (into *northern* and *southern hemisphere*) or by an imaginary line passing through the poles (into *eastern* and *western hemisphere*). □ **hemispheric** /-'sfɛrɪk/ *adj.* **hemispherical** /-'sfɛrɪk(ə)l/ *adj.* [Old French *emisphere* & Latin *hemisphaerium* from Greek *hēmisphaira* (as HEMI-, SPHERE)]

hemistich /'hɛmɪstɪk/ *n.* half of a line of verse. [Late Latin *hemistichium* from Greek *hēmistikhion* (as HEMI-, *stikhion* from *stikhos* 'line')]

hemline /'hɛmlʌɪn/ *n.* the line or level of the lower edge of a skirt, dress, or coat.

hemlock /'hɛmlɒk/ *n.* **1 a** a poisonous umbelliferous plant, *Conium maculatum*, with fernlike leaves and small white flowers. **b** a poisonous potion obtained from this. **2** (in full **hemlock fir** or **spruce**) **a** any coniferous tree of the genus *Tsuga*, having foliage that smells like hemlock when crushed. **b** the timber or pitch of these trees. [Old English *hymlic(e)*]

hemo- *comb. form US* var. of HAEMO-.

hemp /hɛmp/ *n.* **1** (in full **Indian hemp**) a herbaceous plant, *Cannabis sativa*, native to Asia. **2** its fibre extracted from the stem and used to make rope and stout fabrics. **3** any of several narcotic drugs made from the hemp plant, esp. marijuana or cannabis. **4** any of several other plants yielding fibre, including Manila hemp and sunn hemp. [Old English *henep*, *hænep* from Germanic: related to Greek *kannabis*]

hemp agrimony *n.* a plant of the daisy family, *Eupatorium cannabinum*, with pale purple flowers and hairy leaves.

hempen /'hɛmpən/ *adj.* made from hemp.

hemp-nettle *n.* any of various nettle-like plants of the genus *Galeopsis*.

hemstitch /'hɛmstɪtʃ/ *n. & v.* ● *n.* a decorative stitch used in sewing hems. ● *v.tr.* hem with this stitch.

hen /hɛn/ *n.* **1 a** a female bird, esp. of a domestic fowl. **b** (in *pl.*) domestic fowls of either sex. **2** a female lobster or crab or salmon. [Old English *henn*, from West Germanic]

hen and chickens *n.* any of several plants producing additional small flower heads or offshoots, esp. the houseleek.

henbane /'hɛnbeɪn/ *n.* **1** a poisonous herbaceous plant, *Hyoscyamus niger*, with sticky hairy leaves and an unpleasant smell. **2** a narcotic drug obtained from this.

hence /hɛns/ *adv.* **1** from this time (*two years hence*). **2** for this reason; as a result of inference (*hence we seem to be wrong*). **3** *archaic* from here; from this place. [Middle English *hens*, *hennes*, *henne* from Old English *heonan*, ultimately from the Germanic root of HE]

henceforth /hɛns'fɔ:θ, 'hɛnsfɔ:θ/ *adv.* (also **henceforward** /-'fɔ:wəd/) from this time onwards.

henchman /'hɛn(t)ʃmən/ *n.* (*pl.* **-men**) **1** often *derog.* a trusted supporter or attendant. **2** *hist.* a squire; a page of honour. **3** (in Scotland) the principal attendant of a Highland chief. [Middle English *henxman*, *hengestman* from Old English *hengst* 'male horse']

hen-coop *n.* a coop for keeping fowls in.

hendeca- /'hɛndɛkə, hɛn'dɛkə/ *comb. form* eleven. [Greek *hendeka* 'eleven']

hendecagon /hɛn'dɛkəg(ə)n/ *n.* a plane figure with eleven sides and angles.

hendiadys /hɛn'dʌɪədɪs/ *n.* the expression of an idea by two words connected with 'and', instead of one modifying the other, e.g. *nice and warm* for *nicely warm*. [medieval Latin, from Greek *hen dia duoin* 'one thing by two']

henequen /'hɛnɪkɛn/ *n.* **1** a Mexican agave, *Agave fourcroydes*. **2** the sisal-like fibre obtained from this. [Spanish *jeniquen*, from the local name]

henge /hɛn(d)ʒ/ *n.* a prehistoric monument consisting of a circle of stone or wood uprights. [back-formation from *Stonehenge*, such a monument in S. England]

hen harrier *n.* a common harrier, *Circus cyaneus*, of open country and moorland.

hen house *n.* a small shed for fowls to roost in.

henna /'hɛnə/ *n. & v.* ● *n.* **1** a tropical shrub, *Lawsonia inermis*, having small pink, red, or white flowers. **2** the reddish dye from its shoots and leaves, esp. used to colour hair. ● *v.tr.* (**hennaed, hennaing**) dye (hair) with henna. [Arabic *ḥinnā'*]

henotheism /'hɛnəʊˌθi:ɪz(ə)m/ *n.* belief in or adoption of a particular god in a polytheistic system as the god of a tribe, class, etc. [Greek *heis henos* 'one' + *theos* 'god']

hen-party *n. colloq.* often *derog.* a social gathering of women.

henpeck /'hɛnpɛk/ *v.tr.* (usu. as **henpecked** *adj.*) (of a woman) constantly harass (a man, esp. her husband).

hen-roost *n.* a place where fowls roost at night.

hen-run *n. Brit.* an enclosure for fowls.

henry /'hɛnri/ *n.* (*pl.* **-ies** or **henrys**) *Electr.* the SI unit of inductance which gives an electromotive force of one volt in a closed circuit with a uniform rate of change of current of one ampere per second (abbr.: **H**). [named after J. *Henry*, American physicist d. 1878]

heortology /hɪɔ:'tɒlədʒi/ *n.* the study of Church festivals. [German *Heortologie*, French *héortologie*, from Greek *heortē* 'feast']

hep[1] var. of HIP[3].

hep[2] var. of HIP[2].

heparin /ˈhɛpərɪn/ *n. Biochem.* a sulphur-containing polysaccharide found in the liver and other tissues which inhibits blood coagulation and is used as an anticoagulant in the treatment of thrombosis. □ **heparinize** *v.tr.* (also **-ise**). [Latin, from Greek *hēpar* 'liver']

hepatic /hɪˈpatɪk/ *adj.* **1** of or relating to the liver. **2** dark brownish red; liver-coloured. [Middle English via Latin *hepaticus* from Greek *hēpatikos*, from *hēpar -atos* 'liver']

hepatica /hɪˈpatɪkə/ *n.* any plant of the genus *Hepatica*, with reddish-brown lobed leaves resembling the liver. [medieval Latin, fem. of *hepaticus*: see HEPATIC]

hepatitis /hɛpəˈtʌɪtɪs/ *n.* inflammation of the liver; a disease in which this occurs. [modern Latin: see HEPATIC]

hepatitis A *n.* a form of viral hepatitis transmitted in food, causing fever and jaundice.

hepatitis B *n.* a severe form of viral hepatitis transmitted in infected blood, causing fever, debility, and jaundice.

hepcat /ˈhɛpkat/ *n. slang* a stylish or fashionable person, esp. as regards jazz or popular music. [HEP[1]]

Hepplewhite /ˈhɛp(ə)lwʌɪt/ *n.* a light and graceful style of furniture. [named after G. *Hepplewhite*, English cabinetmaker d. 1786]

hepta- /ˈhɛptə/ *comb. form* seven. [Greek *hepta* 'seven']

heptad /ˈhɛptad/ *n.* a group of seven. [Greek *heptas -ados* from *hepta* 'seven']

heptagon /ˈhɛptəg(ə)n/ *n.* a plane figure with seven sides and angles. □ **heptagonal** /-ˈtag(ə)n(ə)l/ *adj.* [French *heptagone* or medieval Latin *heptagonum* from Greek (as HEPTA-, -GON)]

heptahedron /hɛptəˈhiːdrən, -ˈhɛd-/ *n.* (*pl.* **heptahedra** /-drə/ or **heptahedrons**) a solid figure with seven faces. □ **heptahedral** *adj.* [HEPTA- + -HEDRON, on the pattern of POLYHEDRON]

heptameter /hɛpˈtamɪtə/ *n.* a line or verse of seven metrical feet. [Latin *heptametrum* from Greek (as HEPTA-, -METER)]

heptane /ˈhɛpteɪn/ *n. Chem.* a liquid hydrocarbon of the alkane series, obtained from petroleum. Chem. formula: C_7H_{16}. [HEPTA- + -ANE[2]]

heptarchy /ˈhɛptɑːki/ *n.* (*pl.* **-ies**) **1 a** government by seven rulers. **b** an instance of this. **2** *hist.* the supposed seven kingdoms of the Angles and the Saxons in Britain in the 7th–8th centuries. □ **heptarchic** /-ˈtɑːkɪk/ *adj.* **heptarchical** /-ˈtɑːkɪk(ə)l/ *adj.* [HEPTA-, on the pattern of *tetrarchy*]

Heptateuch /ˈhɛptətjuːk/ *n.* the first seven books of the Old Testament. [Latin from Greek, from *hepta* 'seven' + *teukhos* 'book, volume']

heptathlon /hɛpˈtaθlɒn, -lən/ *n.* an athletic contest, usu. for women, in which each competitor takes part in seven events. □ **heptathlete** /-liːt/ *n.* [HEPTA-, on the pattern of DECATHLON]

heptavalent /hɛptəˈveɪl(ə)nt/ *adj. Chem.* having a valency of seven; septivalent.

her /həː, hə/ *pron. & poss.det.* ● *pron.* **1** *objective case of* SHE (*I like her*). **2** *archaic & US dial.* herself (*she fell and hurt her*). ● *poss.det.* **1** of or belonging to her (*her house; her own business*). **2** (**Her**) (in titles) that she is (*Her Majesty*). □ **her indoors** *Brit. colloq.* a jocular reference to one's wife. [Old English *hi(e)re*, dative and genitive of *hio, hēo*, fem. of HE]

■ **Usage** The use of *her* instead of *she* after the verb 'to be' (as in *It's her all right; I am older than her*) is considered by some to be grammatically incorrect but is normal in ordinary usage. The notion that the subjective rather than the objective case should be used after 'to be' is based partly on logic — the references of the grammatical subject and the complement are the same — and partly on the grammar of languages such as Latin, which are more highly inflected than English, but not on actual English usage. *Him, me, them,* and *us* are used similarly, e.g. *It's them on the phone again; It's us who will have to pay for it.* See also Usage Note at THAN.

herald /ˈhɛr(ə)ld/ *n. & v.* ● *n.* **1** an official messenger bringing news. **2** a forerunner (*spring is the herald of summer*). **3 a** *hist.* an officer responsible for State ceremonial and etiquette. **b** (in the UK) an official of the Heralds' College. ● *v.tr.* proclaim the approach of; usher in (*the storm heralded trouble*). [Middle English from Old French *herau(l)t, herauder*, from Germanic]

heraldic /hɛˈraldɪk/ *adj.* of or concerning heraldry. □ **heraldically** *adv.* [HERALD]

heraldist /ˈhɛr(ə)ldɪst/ *n.* an expert in heraldry. [HERALD]

heraldry /ˈhɛr(ə)ldri/ *n.* **1** the science or art of a herald, esp. in dealing with armorial bearings. **2** heraldic pomp. **3** armorial bearings.

Heralds' College *n. Brit. colloq.* = COLLEGE OF ARMS.

herb /həːb/ *n.* **1** any non-woody seed-bearing plant which dies down to the ground after flowering; a herbaceous plant. **2** any plant with leaves, seeds, or flowers used for flavouring, food, medicine, scent, etc. □ **herbiferous** /-ˈbɪf(ə)rəs/ *adj.* **herblike** *adj.* [Middle English via Old French *erbe* from Latin *herba* 'grass, green crops, herb']

herbaceous /həːˈbeɪʃəs/ *adj.* of, designating, or relating to herbs (see HERB 1). [Latin *herbaceus* 'grassy' (as HERB)]

herbaceous border *n.* a garden border containing esp. perennial flowering plants.

herbaceous perennial *n.* a plant whose growth dies down annually but whose roots etc. survive.

herbage /ˈhəːbɪdʒ/ *n.* **1** herbaceous vegetation. **2** the succulent part of this, esp. as pasture. **3** *Law* the right of pasture on another person's land. [Middle English via Old French *erbage* and medieval Latin *herbaticum, herbagium* 'right of pasture' from Latin *herba* 'herb, grass']

herbal /ˈhəːb(ə)l/ *adj. & n.* ● *adj.* of herbs in medicinal and culinary use. ● *n.* a book with descriptions and accounts of the properties of these. [medieval Latin *herbalis* (as HERB)]

herbalist /ˈhəːb(ə)lɪst/ *n.* **1** a practitioner of herbal medicine; a dealer in medicinal herbs. **2** a collector of or writer on plants, esp. an early botanical writer. □ **herbalism** *n.*

herbarium /həːˈbɛːrɪəm/ *n.* (*pl.* **herbaria** /-rɪə/) **1** a systematically arranged collection of dried plants. **2** a book, room, or building for these. [Late Latin (as HERB)]

herb bennet /ˈbɛnɪt/ *n.* a common yellow-flowered plant, *Geum urbanum*. [probably from medieval Latin *herba benedicta* 'blessed herb' (thought of as expelling the Devil)]

herb Christopher /ˈkrɪstəfə/ *n.* a white-flowered baneberry, *Actaea spicata*.

herb Gerard /ˈdʒɛrɑːd/ *n.* ground elder.

herbicide /ˈhəːbɪsʌɪd/ *n.* a substance toxic to plants and used to destroy unwanted vegetation.

herbivore /ˈhəːbɪvɔː/ *n.* an animal that feeds on plants. □ **herbivorous** /-ˈbɪv(ə)rəs/ *adj.* [Latin *herba* 'herb' + -VORE (see -VOROUS)]

herb Paris /ˈparɪs/ *n.* a plant, *Paris quadrifolia*, with a single flower and four leaves in a cross shape on an unbranched stem.

herb Robert /ˈrɒbət/ *n.* a common cranesbill, *Geranium robertianum*, with red-stemmed leaves and pink flowers.

herb tea *n.* an infusion of herbs.

herb tobacco *n.* a mixture of herbs smoked as a substitute for tobacco.

herby /ˈhəːbi/ *adj.* (**herbier**, **herbiest**) **1** abounding in herbs. **2** of the nature of a culinary or medicinal herb.

Herculean /həːkjʊˈliːən, həːˈkjuːlɪən/ *adj.* having or requiring great strength or effort. [Latin *Herculeus* (as HERCULES)]

Hercules /'hɜːkjʊliːz/ *n.* a man of exceptional strength or size. [Middle English via Latin from Greek *Hēraklēs*, the name of a hero noted for his great strength]

Hercules beetle *n.* a large S. American beetle, *Dynastes hercules*, with two horns extending from its head.

Hercynian /hɜː'sɪnɪən/ *adj. Geol.* of a mountain-forming time in the eastern hemisphere in the late Palaeozoic era. [Latin *Hercynia silva*, the name of an area of forested mountains of central Germany]

herd /hɜːd/ *n. & v.* ● *n.* **1** a large number of animals, esp. cattle, feeding or travelling or kept together. **2** (prec. by *the*) *derog.* a large number of people; a mob (*prefers not to follow the herd*). **3** (esp. in *comb.*) a keeper of herds; a herdsman (*cowherd*). ● *v.* **1** *intr. & tr.* go or cause to go in a herd (*herded together for warmth*; *herded the cattle into the field*). **2** *tr.* tend (sheep, cattle, etc.) (*he herds the goats*). □ **ride herd on** *US* keep watch on. □ **herder** *n.* [Old English *heord*, (in sense 3) *hirdi*, from Germanic]

herd book *n. Brit.* a book recording the pedigrees of cattle or pigs.

herd instinct *n.* the tendency of associating or conforming with one's own kind for support etc.

herdsman /'hɜːdzmən/ *n.* (*pl.* **-men**) the owner or keeper of a herd of domesticated animals.

Herdwick /'hɜːdwɪk/ *n.* **1** an animal of a hardy breed of mountain sheep from N. England. **2** this breed. [obsolete *herdwick* 'pasture-ground' (as HERD, WICK²), perhaps because this breed originated in Furness Abbey pastures]

here /hɪə/ *adv., n., & int.* ● *adv.* **1** in or at or to this place or position (*put it here*; *has lived here for many years*; *comes here every day*). **2** indicating a person's presence or a thing offered (*here is your coat*; *my son here will show you*). **3** at this point in the argument, situation, etc. (*here I have a question*). ● *n.* this place (*get out of here*; *lives near here*; *fill it up to here*). ● *int.* **1** calling attention: short for *come here*, *look here*, etc. (*here, where are you going with that?*). **2** indicating one's presence in a roll-call: short for *I am here*. □ **here and now** at this very moment; immediately. **here and there** in various places. **here goes!** *colloq.* an expression indicating the start of a bold act. **here's to** I drink to the health of. **here we are** said on arrival at one's destination. **here we go again** *colloq.* the same, usu. undesirable, events are recurring. **here you are** said on handing something to somebody. **neither here nor there** of no importance or relevance. [Old English *hēr* from Germanic: related to HE]

hereabouts /hɪərə'baʊts/ *adv.* (also **hereabout**) near this place.

hereafter /hɪər'ɑːftə/ *adv. & n.* ● *adv.* **1** from now on; in the future. **2** in the world to come (after death). ● *n.* **1** the future. **2** life after death.

hereat /hɪər'at/ *adv. archaic* as a result of this.

hereby /hɪə'bʌɪ/ *adv.* by this means; as a result of this.

hereditable /hɪ'rɛdɪtəb(ə)l/ *adj.* that can be inherited. [obsolete French *héréditable* or medieval Latin *hereditabilis* via ecclesiastical Latin *hereditare* from Latin *heres -edis* 'heir']

hereditament /hɛrɪ'dɪtəm(ə)nt, hɪ'rɛdɪt-/ *n. Law* **1** any property that can be inherited. **2** inheritance. [medieval Latin *hereditamentum* (as HEREDITABLE)]

hereditary /hɪ'rɛdɪt(ə)ri/ *adj.* **1** (of disease, instinct, etc.) able to be passed down from one generation to another. **2 a** descending by inheritance. **b** holding a position by inheritance. **3** the same as or resembling what one's parents had (*a hereditary hatred*). **4** of or relating to inheritance. □ **hereditarily** *adv.* **hereditariness** *n.* [Latin *hereditarius* (as HEREDITY)]

heredity /hɪ'rɛdɪti/ *n.* **1 a** the passing on of physical or mental characteristics genetically from one generation to another. **b** these characteristics. **2** the genetic constitution of an individual. [French *hérédité* or Latin *hereditas* 'heirship' (as HEIR)]

Hereford /'hɛrɪfəd/ *n.* **1** an animal of a breed of red and white beef cattle. **2** this breed. [*Hereford*, a city and county in England, where it originated]

herein /hɪər'ɪn/ *adv. formal* in this matter, book, etc.

hereinafter /hɪərɪn'ɑːftə/ *adv.* esp. *Law formal* **1** from this point on. **2** in a later part of this document etc.

hereinbefore /ˌhɪərɪnbɪ'fɔː/ *adv.* esp. *Law formal* in a preceding part of this document etc.

hereof /hɪər'ɒv/ *adv. formal* of this.

heresiarch /hɛ'riːzɪɑːk/ *n.* the leader or founder of a heresy. [ecclesiastical Latin *haeresiarcha* from Greek *hairesiarkhēs* (as HERESY + *arkhēs* 'ruler')]

heresy /'hɛrɪsi/ *n.* (*pl.* **-ies**) **1** esp. *RC Ch.* **a** belief or practice contrary to orthodox doctrine. **b** an instance of this. **2 a** opinion contrary to what is normally accepted or maintained (*it's heresy to suggest that instant coffee is as good as the real thing*). **b** an instance of this. □ **heresiology** /ˌhɛrɪsɪ'ɒlədʒi/ *n.* [Middle English via Old French (*h*)*eresie* and ecclesiastical Latin *haeresis*, in Latin = school of thought, from Greek *hairesis* 'choice, sect', from *haireomai* 'choose']

heretic /'hɛrɪtɪk/ *n.* **1** the holder of an unorthodox opinion. **2** a person believing in or practising religious heresy. □ **heretical** /hɪ'rɛtɪk(ə)l/ *adj.* **heretically** /hɪ'rɛtɪk(ə)li/ *adv.* [Middle English via Old French *heretique* and ecclesiastical Latin *haereticus* from Greek *hairetikos* 'able to choose' (as HERESY)]

hereto /hɪə'tuː/ *adv. formal* to this matter.

heretofore /hɪətʊ'fɔː/ *adv. formal* before this time.

hereunder /hɪər'ʌndə/ *adv. formal* below (in a book, legal document, etc.).

hereunto /hɪərʌn'tuː/ *adv. archaic* to this.

hereupon /hɪərə'pɒn/ *adv.* after this; in consequence of this.

herewith /hɪə'wɪð, -'wɪθ/ *adv.* with this (esp. of an enclosure in a letter etc.).

heriot /'hɛrɪət/ *n. Brit. hist.* a tribute paid to a lord on the death of a tenant, consisting of a live animal, a chattel, or, originally, the return of borrowed equipment. [Old English *heregeatwa*, from *here* 'army' + *geatwa* 'trappings']

heritable /'hɛrɪtəb(ə)l/ *adj.* **1** *Law* **a** (of property) capable of being inherited by heirs-at-law (cf. MOVABLE *adj.* 2). **b** capable of inheriting. **2** *Biol.* (of a characteristic) transmissible from parent to offspring. □ **heritability** /-'bɪlɪti/ *n.* **heritably** *adv.* [Middle English via Old French, from *heriter*, from ecclesiastical Latin *hereditare*: see HEREDITABLE]

heritage /'hɛrɪtɪdʒ/ *n.* **1** anything that is or may be inherited. **2** inherited circumstances, benefits, etc. (*a heritage of confusion*). **3** a nation's historic buildings, monuments, countryside, etc., esp. when regarded as worthy of preservation. **4** *Bibl.* **a** the ancient Israelites. **b** the Church. [Middle English from Old French (as HERITABLE)]

heritage centre *n.* a museum focusing on the cultural heritage of the surrounding area.

heritor /'hɛrɪtə/ *n.* (esp. in Scottish Law) a person who inherits. [Middle English from Anglo-French *heriter*, Old French *heritier* (as HEREDITARY), assimilated to words ending in -OR¹]

herl var. of HARL.

herm /hɜːm/ *n. Gk Antiq.* a squared stone pillar with a head (esp. of Hermes) on top, used as a boundary marker etc. (cf. TERMINUS 6). [Latin *Herma* from Greek *Hermēs*, the name of the messenger of the gods]

hermaphrodite /hɜː'mafrədʌɪt/ *n. & adj.* ● *n.* **1 a** *Zool.* an animal having both male and female sexual organs. **b** *Bot.* a plant having stamens and pistils in the same flower. **2** a human being in which both male and female sex organs are present, or in which the sex organs contain both ovarian and testicular tissue. **3** a person or thing combining opposite qualities or characteristics. ● *adj.* **1** combining both sexes. **2** combining opposite qualities or characteristics. □ **hermaphroditic** /-'dɪtɪk/ *adj.* **hermaphroditical**

/-ˈdɪtɪk(ə)l/ *adj.* **hermaphroditism** *n.* [Latin *hermaphroditus* from Greek *hermaphroditos*, originally the name of a son of Hermes and Aphrodite in Greek mythology, who became joined in one body with the nymph Salmacis]

hermaphrodite brig *n. hist.* a two-masted sailing ship rigged on the foremast as a brig and on the mainmast as a schooner.

hermeneutic /həːmɪˈnjuːtɪk/ *adj.* concerning interpretation, esp. of Scripture or literary texts. □ **hermeneutical** *adj.* **hermeneutically** *adv.* [Greek *hermēneutikos* from *hermēneuō* 'interpret']

hermeneutics /həːmɪˈnjuːtɪks/ *n.pl.* (also treated as *sing.*) *Bibl.* the branch of knowledge that deals with interpretation, esp. of Scripture or literary texts.

hermetic /həːˈmɛtɪk/ *adj.* (also **hermetical**) **1** with an airtight closure. **2** protected from outside agencies. **3 a** of alchemy or other occult sciences (*hermetic art*). **b** esoteric. □ **hermetically** *adv.* **hermetism** /ˈhəːmɪtɪz(ə)m/ *n.* [modern Latin *hermeticus*, formed irregularly from *Hermes Trismegistus* 'thrice-greatest Hermes' (as the founder of alchemy)]

hermetic seal *n.* an airtight seal (originally as used by alchemists).

hermit /ˈhəːmɪt/ *n.* **1** an early Christian recluse. **2** any person living in solitude. □ **hermitic** /-ˈmɪtɪk/ *adj.* [Middle English via Old French (*h*)*ermite* or Late Latin *eremita* from Greek *erēmitēs*, via *erēmia* 'desert' from *erēmos* 'solitary']

hermitage /ˈhəːmɪtɪdʒ/ *n.* **1** a hermit's dwelling. **2** a monastery. **3** a solitary dwelling. [Middle English from Old French (*h*)*ermitage* (as HERMIT)]

hermit crab *n.* a crab of the family Paguridae, living in a cast-off mollusc shell for protection.

hermit thrush *n.* a migratory N. American thrush, *Catharus guttatus.*

hernia /ˈhəːnɪə/ *n.* (*pl.* **hernias** or **herniae** /-nɪiː/) the displacement and protrusion of part of an organ through the wall of the cavity containing it, esp. of the abdomen. □ **hernial** *adj.* **herniated** *adj.* [Latin]

hero /ˈhɪərəʊ/ *n.* (*pl.* **-oes**) **1 a** a person noted or admired for courage, outstanding achievements, etc. (*Newton, a hero of science*). **b** a great warrior. **2** the chief male character in a poem, play, story, etc. **3** *Gk Antiq.* a man of superhuman qualities, favoured by the gods; a demigod. [Middle English via Latin *heros* from Greek *hērōs*]

heroic /hɪˈrəʊɪk/ *adj.* & *n.* ● *adj.* **1 a** (of an act, a quality, etc.) of or fit for a hero. **b** (of a person) like a hero. **2 a** (of language) grand, high-flown, dramatic. **b** (of a work of art) ambitious in scale or subject. **3** (of poetry) dealing with the ancient heroes. ● *n.* (in *pl.*) **1 a** high-flown language or sentiments. **b** unduly bold behaviour. **2** = HEROIC VERSE. □ **heroically** *adv.* [French *héroïque* or Latin *heroicus* from Greek *hērōikos* (as HERO)]

heroic age *n.* (prec. by *the*) the period in Greek history before the return from the Trojan War.

heroic couplet *n.* two lines of rhyming iambic pentameters.

heroi-comic /hɪˌrəʊɪˈkɒmɪk/ *adj.* (also **heroi-comical**) combining the heroic with the comic. [French *héroï-comique* (as HERO, COMIC)]

heroic verse *n.* a type of verse used for heroic poetry, esp. the hexameter, the iambic pentameter, or the alexandrine.

heroin /ˈhɛrəʊɪn/ *n.* a highly addictive crystalline analgesic drug derived from morphine, often used as a narcotic. [German (as HERO, from its effects on the user's self-esteem)]

heroine /ˈhɛrəʊɪn/ *n.* **1** a woman noted or admired for courage, outstanding achievements, etc. **2** the chief female character in a poem, play, story, etc. **3** *Gk Antiq.* a demigoddess. [French *héroïne* or Latin *heroina* from Greek *hērōinē*, fem. of *hērōs* HERO]

heroism /ˈhɛrəʊɪz(ə)m/ *n.* heroic conduct or qualities. [French *héroïsme* from *héros* HERO]

heroize /ˈhɪərəʊʌɪz, ˈhɛr-/ *v.* (also **-ise**) **1** *tr.* **a** make a hero of. **b** make heroic. **2** *intr.* play the hero.

heron /ˈhɛr(ə)n/ *n.* any of various large wading birds of the family Ardeidae, esp. *Ardea cinerea*, with long legs and a long S-shaped neck. □ **heronry** *n.* (*pl.* **-ies**). [Middle English from Old French *hairon*, from Germanic]

hero's welcome *n.* a rapturous welcome, like that given to a successful warrior.

hero-worship *n.* & *v.* ● *n.* **1** idealization of an admired man. **2** *Gk Antiq.* worship of superhuman heroes. ● *v.tr.* (**-worshipped**, **-worshipping**; *US* **-worshiped**, **-worshiping**) worship as a hero; idolize. □ **hero-worshipper** *n.*

herpes /ˈhəːpiːz/ *n.* a virus disease with outbreaks of blisters on the skin etc. □ **herpetic** /-ˈpɛtɪk/ *adj.* [Middle English via Latin from Greek *herpēs -ētos* 'shingles', from *herpō* 'creep']

herpes simplex *n.* a viral infection which may produce cold sores, genital inflammation, or conjunctivitis.

herpesvirus /ˈhəːpiːzˌvʌɪrəs/ *n.* any of a group of viruses causing herpes or other diseases.

herpes zoster /həːpiːz ˈzɒstə/ *n.* = SHINGLES. [Greek *zōstēr* 'belt, girdle']

herpetology /həːpɪˈtɒlədʒi/ *n.* the study of reptiles. □ **herpetological** /-təˈlɒdʒɪk(ə)l/ *adj.* **herpetologist** *n.* [Greek *herpeton* 'reptile' from *herpō* 'creep']

herptile /ˈhəːptʌɪl/ *n.* & *adj.* ● *n.* a reptile or amphibian. ● *adj.* of or relating to both reptiles and amphibians. [HERPETOLOGY + REPTILE]

Herr /hɛː/ *n.* (*pl.* **Herren** /ˈhɛr(ə)n/) **1** the title of a German man; Mr. **2** a German man. [German from Old High German *hērro*, comparative of *hēr* 'exalted']

Herrenvolk /ˈhɛr(ə)nfɒlk, -fəʊk, German ˈhɛrənfɔlk/ *n.* **1** the German nation characterized by the Nazis as born to mastery. **2** a group regarding itself as naturally superior. [German, = master race (as HERR, FOLK)]

herring /ˈhɛrɪŋ/ *n.* a N. Atlantic fish, *Clupea harengus*, coming near the coast in large shoals to spawn. [Old English *hǣring*, *hēring*, from West Germanic]

herringbone /ˈhɛrɪŋbəʊn/ *n.* & *v.* ● *n.* **1** a stitch with a zigzag pattern, resembling the pattern of a herring's bones. **2** this pattern, or cloth woven in it. **3** any zigzag pattern, e.g. in building. **4** *Skiing* a method of ascending a slope with the skis pointing outwards. ● *v.* **1** *tr.* **a** work with a herringbone stitch. **b** mark with a herringbone pattern. **2** *intr. Skiing* ascend a slope using the herringbone technique.

herring gull *n.* a large gull, *Larus argentatus*, with dark wing-tips.

Herrnhuter /ˈhɛːnhuːtə, ˈhɛːr(ə)n-/ *n.* a member of a Moravian Christian sect (see MORAVIAN). [German, from *Herrnhut* (= the Lord's keeping), name of their first German settlement]

hers /həːz/ *poss.pron.* the one or ones belonging to or associated with her (*it is hers; hers are over there*). □ **of hers** of or belonging to her (*a friend of hers*).

herself /həːˈsɛlf/ *pron.* **1 a** *emphat. form* of SHE or HER (*she herself will do it*). **b** *refl. form* of HER (*she has hurt herself*). **2** in her normal state of body or mind (*does not feel quite herself today*). □ **be herself** act in her normal unconstrained manner. **by herself** see *by oneself.* [Old English *hire self* (as HER, SELF)]

Herts. /hɑːts/ *abbr.* Hertfordshire.

hertz /həːts/ *n.* (*pl.* same) the SI unit of frequency, equal to one cycle per second (abbr.: **Hz**). [named after H. R. *Hertz*, German physicist d. 1894]

Hertzian wave /ˈhəːtsɪən/ *n.* an electromagnetic wave of a length suitable for use in radio.

he's /hiːz, hɪz/ *contr.* **1** he is. **2** he has.

hesitant /ˈhɛzɪt(ə)nt/ *adj.* hesitating; irresolute. □ **hesitance** *n.* **hesitancy** *n.* **hesitantly** *adv.*

hesitate /ˈhɛzɪteɪt/ *v.intr.* **1** (often foll. by *about, over*) show or feel indecision or uncertainty; pause in doubt (*hesitated over her choice*). **2** (often foll. by *to* + infin.) be deterred by scruples; be reluctant (*I hesitate to inform against him*). □ **hesitater** *n.* **hesitatingly** *adv.* **hesitation** /-ˈteɪʃ(ə)n/ *n.* **hesitative** *adj.* [Latin *haesitare*, frequentative of *haerēre haes-* 'stick fast']

Hesperian /hɛˈspɪərɪən/ *adj. poet.* **1** western. **2** (in Greek mythology) of or concerning the Hesperides (nymphs who guarded the garden of golden apples at the western extremity of the earth). [Latin *Hesperius* from Greek *Hesperios* (as HESPERUS)]

hesperidium /hɛspəˈrɪdɪəm/ *n.* (*pl.* **hesperidia** /-dɪə/) a fruit with sectioned pulp inside a separable rind, e.g. an orange or grapefruit. [Greek *Hesperides*, the daughters of Hesperus, nymphs in Greek mythology who guarded a tree of golden apples]

Hesperus /ˈhɛspərəs/ *n. poet.* the evening star, Venus. [Middle English from Latin from Greek *hesperos* (*adj.* & *n.*) 'western, evening (star)']

hessian /ˈhɛsɪən/ *n.* & *adj.* ● *n.* **1** a strong coarse sacking made of hemp or jute. **2** (**Hessian**) a native or inhabitant of Hesse in Germany. ● *adj.* (**Hessian**) of or relating to Hesse. [*Hesse* in Germany]

Hessian boot *n.* a tasselled high boot first worn by Hessian troops.

Hessian fly *n.* a midge, *Mayetiola destructor*, whose larva destroys growing wheat (thought to have been brought to America by Hessian troops).

hest /hɛst/ *n. archaic* behest. [Old English *hǣs* (see HIGHT), assimilated to Middle English nouns ending in *-t*]

hetaera /hɪˈtɪərə/ *n.* (also **hetaira** /-ˈtʌɪrə/) (*pl.* **-as**, **hetaerae** /-ˈtɪəriː/, or **hetairai** /-ˈtʌɪrʌɪ/) a courtesan or mistress, esp. in ancient Greece. [Greek *hetaira*, fem. of *hetairos* 'companion']

hetaerism /hɪˈtɪərɪz(ə)m/ *n.* (also **hetairism** /-ˈtʌɪrɪz(ə)m/) **1** a recognized system of concubinage. **2** communal marriage in a tribe. [Greek *hetairismos* 'prostitution' (as HETAERA)]

hetero /ˈhɛt(ə)rəʊ/ *n.* (*pl.* **-os**) *colloq.* a heterosexual. [abbreviation]

hetero- /ˈhɛt(ə)rəʊ/ *comb. form* other, different (often opp. HOMO-). [Greek *heteros* 'other']

heterochromatic /ˌhɛt(ə)rəʊkrə(ʊ)ˈmatɪk/ *adj.* of several colours.

heteroclite /ˈhɛt(ə)rə(ʊ)klʌɪt/ *adj.* & *n.* ● *adj.* **1** abnormal. **2** *Gram.* (esp. of a noun) irregularly declined. ● *n.* **1** an abnormal thing or person. **2** *Gram.* an irregularly declined word, esp. a noun. [Late Latin *heteroclitus* from Greek (as HETERO-, *klitos* from *klinō* 'bend, inflect')]

heterocyclic /hɛt(ə)rə(ʊ)ˈsʌɪklɪk, -ˈsɪklɪk/ *adj. Chem.* (of a compound) with a bonded ring of atoms of more than one kind.

heterodox /ˈhɛt(ə)rə(ʊ)dɒks/ *adj.* (of a person, opinion, etc.) not orthodox. □ **heterodoxy** *n.* [Late Latin *heterodoxus* from Greek (as HETERO-, *doxos* from *doxa* 'opinion')]

heterodyne /ˈhɛt(ə)rə(ʊ)dʌɪn/ *adj.* & *v. Radio* ● *adj.* relating to the production of a lower frequency from the combination of two almost equal high frequencies. ● *v.intr.* produce a lower frequency in this way. [from HETERO- + Greek *dunamis* 'power']

heterogamous /hɛtəˈrɒgəməs/ *adj.* **1** *Bot.* irregular as regards stamens and pistils. **2** *Biol.* characterized by heterogamy or heterogony.

heterogamy /hɛtəˈrɒgəmi/ *n.* **1** the alternation of generations, esp. of a sexual and parthenogenic generation. **2** sexual reproduction by fusion of unlike gametes. **3** *Bot.* a state in which the flowers of a plant are of two types.

heterogeneous /hɛt(ə)rə(ʊ)ˈdʒiːnɪəs, -ˈdʒɛn-/ *adj.* (also *disp.* **heterogenous** /hɛtəˈrɒdʒɪnəs/) **1** diverse in character. **2** varied in content. **3** *Math.* incommensurable through being of different kinds or degrees. □ **heterogeneity** /-dʒɪˈniːɪti/ *n.* **heterogeneously** *adv.* **heterogeneousness** *n.* [medieval Latin *heterogeneus* from Greek *heterogenēs* (as HETERO-, *genos* 'kind')]

■ **Usage** The less common form *heterogenous* is considered incorrect by some people and best avoided. Cf. *homogeneous* and *homogenous* which have quite different senses but are often confused: see Usage Note at HOMOGENEOUS.

heterogenesis /hɛt(ə)rə(ʊ)ˈdʒɛnɪsɪs/ *n.* **1** the birth of a living being otherwise than from parents of the same kind. **2** spontaneous generation from inorganic matter. □ **heterogenetic** /-dʒɪˈnɛtɪk/ *adj.*

heterogony /hɛtəˈrɒgəni/ *n.* the alternation of generations, esp. of a sexual and hermaphroditic generation. □ **heterogonous** *adj.*

heterograft /ˈhɛt(ə)rə(ʊ)grɑːft/ *n.* = XENOGRAFT.

heterologous /hɛtəˈrɒləgəs/ *adj.* not homologous. □ **heterology** *n.*

heteromerous /hɛtəˈrɒm(ə)rəs/ *adj.* not isomerous.

heteromorphic /hɛt(ə)rə(ʊ)ˈmɔːfɪk/ *adj.* (also **heteromorphous** /-ˈmɔːfəs/) *Biol.* **1** of dissimilar forms. **2** (of insects) existing in different forms at different stages in their life cycle.

heteromorphism /hɛt(ə)rə(ʊ)ˈmɔːfɪz(ə)m/ *n.* the quality or condition of existing in various forms.

heteronomous /hɛtəˈrɒnəməs/ *adj.* **1** subject to an external law (cf. AUTONOMOUS). **2** *Biol.* subject to different laws (of growth etc.).

heteronomy /hɛtəˈrɒnəmi/ *n.* **1** the presence of a different law. **2** subjection to an external law.

heteropathic /hɛt(ə)rə(ʊ)ˈpaθɪk/ *adj.* **1** allopathic. **2** differing in effect.

heterophyllous /hɛt(ə)rə(ʊ)ˈfɪləs/ *adj.* bearing leaves of different forms on the same plant. □ **heterophylly** *n.* [HETERO- + Greek *phullon* 'leaf']

heteropolar /hɛtərəʊˈpəʊlə/ *adj.* having dissimilar poles, esp. *Electr.* with an armature passing north and south magnetic poles alternately.

heteropteran /hɛtəˈrɒpt(ə)rən/ *n.* any insect of the suborder Heteroptera, including true bugs with non-uniform forewings having a thickened base and membranous tip (cf. HOMOPTERAN). □ **heteropterous** *adj.* [HETERO- + Greek *pteron* 'wing']

heterosexism /hɛt(ə)rə(ʊ)ˈsɛksɪz(ə)m/ *n.* discrimination or prejudice by heterosexuals against or towards homosexuals. □ **heterosexist** *adj.* & *n.*

heterosexual /hɛt(ə)rə(ʊ)ˈsɛksjʊəl, -ʃʊəl/ *adj.* & *n.* ● *adj.* **1** feeling or involving sexual attraction to persons of the opposite sex. **2** concerning heterosexual relations or people. **3** relating to the opposite sex. ● *n.* a heterosexual person. □ **heterosexuality** /-ˈalɪti/ *n.* **heterosexually** *adv.*

heterosis /hɛtəˈrəʊsɪs/ *n.* the tendency of a cross-bred individual to show qualities superior to those of both parents. [Greek from *heteros* 'different']

heterotaxy /ˈhɛt(ə)rə(ʊ)taksi/ *n.* the abnormal disposition of organs or parts. [HETERO- + Greek *taxis* 'arrangement']

heterotransplant /hɛt(ə)rə(ʊ)ˈtransplɑːnt, -ˈtrɑːns-, -nz-/ *n.* = XENOGRAFT.

heterotrophic /hɛt(ə)rə(ʊ)ˈtrəʊfɪk, -ˈtrɒfɪk/ *adj. Biol.* deriving its nourishment and carbon requirements from organic substances; not autotrophic. [HETERO- + Greek *trophos* 'feeder']

heterozygote /hɛt(ə)rə(ʊ)ˈzʌɪgəʊt/ *n. Biol.* an individual having two different alleles of a particular gene or genes, and so giving rise to varying offspring (cf. HOMOZYGOTE). □ **heterozygous** *adj.*

hetman /ˈhɛtmən/ *n.* (*pl.* **-men**) a Polish or Cossack military commander. [Polish, probably from German *Hauptmann* 'captain']

het up /hɛt ˈʌp/ *adj. colloq.* excited, overwrought. [*het*, dialect past part. of HEAT]

heuchera /ˈhɔɪkərə, ˈhjuːk-/ *n.* any N. American herbaceous plant of the genus *Heuchera*, with dark green round or heart-shaped leaves and tiny flowers. [modern Latin, named after J. H. von *Heucher*, German botanist d. 1747]

heuristic /hjʊ(ə)ˈrɪstɪk/ *adj. & n.* ● *adj.* **1** allowing or assisting to discover. **2** *Computing* proceeding to a solution by trial and error. ● *n.* **1** the science of heuristic procedure. **2** a heuristic process or method. **3** (in *pl.*, usu. treated as *sing.*) *Computing* the study and use of heuristic techniques in data processing. □ **heuristically** *adv.* [formed irregularly from Greek *heuriskō* 'find']

heuristic method *n.* a system of education under which pupils are trained to find out things for themselves.

hevea /ˈhiːvɪə/ *n.* any S. American tree of the genus *Hevea*, yielding a milky sap used for making rubber. [modern Latin from Quechua *hevé*]

HEW *abbr.* (in the US) Department of Health, Education, and Welfare.

hew /hjuː/ *v.* (*past part.* **hewn** /hjuːn/ or **hewed**) **1** *tr.* **a** (often foll. by *down*, *away*, *off*) chop or cut (a thing) with an axe, a sword, etc. **b** cut (a block of wood etc.) into shape. **2** *intr.* (often foll. by *at*, *among*, etc.) strike cutting blows. **3** *intr.* (usu. foll. by *to*) *N. Amer.* conform. □ **hew one's way** make a way for oneself by hewing. [Old English *hēawan*, from Germanic]

hewer /ˈhjuːə/ *n.* **1** a person who hews. **2** a person who cuts coal from a seam. □ **hewers of wood and drawers of water** menial drudges; labourers (Josh. 9:21).

hex[1] /hɛks/ *v. & n.* ● *v.* **1** *intr.* practise witchcraft. **2** *tr.* cast a spell on; bewitch. ● *n.* **1** a magic spell; a curse. **2** a witch. [Pennsylvanian German *hexe* (*v.*), *Hex* (*n.*), from German *hexen*, *Hexe*]

hex[2] /hɛks/ *adj. & n.* esp. *Computing* = HEXADECIMAL. [abbreviation]

hexa- /ˈhɛksə/ *comb. form* six. [Greek *hex* 'six']

hexachord /ˈhɛksəkɔːd/ *n.* a diatonic series of six notes with a semitone between the third and fourth, used at three different pitches in medieval music. [HEXA- + CHORD[1]]

hexad /ˈhɛksad/ *n.* a group of six. [Greek *hexas -ados* from *hex* 'six']

hexadecimal /hɛksəˈdɛsɪm(ə)l/ *adj. & n.* esp. *Computing* ● *adj.* relating to or using a system of numerical notation that has 16 rather than 10 as a base. ● *n.* the hexadecimal system; hexadecimal notation. □ **hexadecimally** *adv.*

hexagon /ˈhɛksəg(ə)n/ *n.* a plane figure with six sides and angles. □ **hexagonal** /-ˈsag(ə)n(ə)l/ *adj.* [Late Latin *hexagonum* from Greek (as HEXA-, -GON)]

hexagram /ˈhɛksəgram/ *n.* **1** a figure formed by two intersecting equilateral triangles. **2** a figure of six lines. [HEXA- + Greek *gramma* 'line']

hexahedron /hɛksəˈhiːdrən, -ˈhɛd-/ *n.* (*pl.* **hexahedra** /-drə/ or **hexahedrons**) a solid figure with six faces. □ **hexahedral** *adj.* [Greek (as HEXA-, -HEDRON)]

hexameter /hɛkˈsamɪtə/ *n.* a line or verse of six metrical feet. □ **hexametric** /-səˈmɛtrɪk/ *adj.* **hexametrist** *n.* [Middle English via Latin from Greek *hexametros* (as HEXA-, *metron* 'measure')]

hexane /ˈhɛkseɪn/ *n. Chem.* a liquid hydrocarbon of the alkane series. Chem. formula: C_6H_{14}. [HEXA- + -ANE[2]]

hexapla /ˈhɛksəplə/ *n.* a sixfold text, esp. of the Old Testament, in parallel columns. [Greek neut. pl. of *hexaploos* (as HEXA-, *ploos* '-fold'), originally of Origen's OT text]

hexapod /ˈhɛksəpɒd/ *n. & adj.* ● *n.* an arthropod with six legs; an insect. ● *adj.* having six legs. [Greek *hexapous, hexapod-* (as HEXA-, *pous pod-* 'foot')]

hexastyle /ˈhɛksəstʌɪl/ *n. & adj.* ● *n.* a six-columned portico. ● *adj.* having six columns. [Greek *hexastulos* (as HEXA-, *stulos* 'column')]

Hexateuch /ˈhɛksətjuːk/ *n.* the first six books of the Old Testament. [Greek *hex* 'six' + *teukhos* 'book']

hexavalent /hɛksəˈveɪl(ə)nt/ *adj.* having a valency of six; sexivalent.

hexose /ˈhɛksəʊz, -s/ *n. Biochem.* a monosaccharide with six carbon atoms in each molecule, e.g. glucose or fructose. [HEXA- + -OSE[2]]

hey[1] /heɪ/ *int.* calling attention or expressing joy, surprise, enquiry, enthusiasm, etc. [Middle English: cf. Old French *hay*, Dutch, German *hei*]

hey[2] var. of HAY[2].

heyday /ˈheɪdeɪ/ *n.* the flush or full bloom of youth, vigour, prosperity, etc. [archaic *heyday*, an expression of joy, surprise, etc.: cf. Low German *heidi*, *heida*, an exclamation denoting gaiety]

hey presto! *int. Brit.* a phrase announcing the successful completion of a trick or other surprising achievement.

HF *abbr.* high frequency.

Hf *symb. Chem.* the element hafnium.

hf. *abbr.* half.

HG *abbr. Brit.* **1** Her or His Grace. **2** Home Guard.

Hg *symb. Chem.* the element mercury. [modern Latin *hydrargyrum*]

hg *abbr.* hectogram(s).

HGV *abbr. Brit.* heavy goods vehicle.

HH *abbr.* **1** *Brit.* Her or His Highness. **2** His Holiness. **3** double-hard (pencil lead).

hh. *abbr.* hands (see HAND *n.* 13).

hhd. *abbr.* hogshead(s).

H-hour *n.* the hour at which an operation is scheduled to begin. [*H* for *hour* + HOUR]

HI *abbr. US* **1** Hawaii (also in official postal use). **2** the Hawaiian Islands.

hi /hʌɪ/ *int.* calling attention or as a greeting. [parallel form to HEY[1]]

hiatus /hʌɪˈeɪtəs/ *n.* (*pl.* **hiatuses**) **1** a break or gap, esp. in a series, account, or chain of proof. **2** *Prosody & Gram.* a break between two vowels coming together but not in the same syllable, as in *though oft the ear*. □ **hiatal** *adj.* [Latin, = gaping, from *hiare* 'gape']

hiatus hernia *n. Med.* the protrusion of an organ, esp. the stomach, through the oesophageal opening in the diaphragm.

Hib /hɪb/ *n. Med.* a bacterium, *Haemophilus influenzae* type B, causing infant meningitis (often *attrib.*: *Hib vaccine*). [acronym]

hibernate /ˈhʌɪbəneɪt/ *v.intr.* **1** (of some animals) spend the winter in a dormant state. **2** remain inactive. □ **hibernation** /-ˈneɪʃ(ə)n/ *n.* **hibernator** *n.* [Latin *hibernare* from *hibernus* 'wintry']

Hibernian /hʌɪˈbəːnɪən/ *adj. & n. archaic poet.* ● *adj.* of or concerning Ireland. ● *n.* a native of Ireland. [Latin *Hibernia*, *Iverna* via Greek *Iernē* from Celtic]

Hibernicism /hʌɪˈbəːnɪsɪz(ə)m/ *n.* **1** an Irish idiom or expression. **2** = BULL[3] 1. [as HIBERNIAN on the pattern of *Anglicism* etc.]

Hiberno- /hʌɪˈbəːnəʊ/ *comb. form* Irish (*Hiberno-British*). [medieval Latin *hibernus* 'Irish' (as HIBERNIAN)]

hibiscus /hɪˈbɪskəs/ *n.* (*pl.* **hibiscuses**) any tree or shrub of the genus *Hibiscus*, cultivated for its large brightly coloured flowers. Also called *rose-mallow*. [Latin from Greek *hibiskos* 'marsh mallow']

hic /hɪk/ *int.* expressing the sound of a hiccup, esp. a drunken hiccup. [imitative]

hiccup /ˈhɪkʌp/ *n. & v.* (also **hiccough** *pronunc.* same) ● *n.* **1 a** an involuntary spasm of the diaphragm and respiratory organs, with sudden closure of the glottis and characteristic coughlike sound. **b** (in *pl.*) an attack of such spasms. **2** a temporary or minor fault or setback. ● *v.* (**hiccuped**, **hiccuping**) **1** *intr.* make a hiccup or series of hiccups. **2** *tr.* utter with a hiccup. □ **hiccupy** *adj.* [imitative]

hic jacet /hɪk ˈdʒeɪsɛt, ˈjakɛt/ *n.* an epitaph. [Latin, = here lies]

hick /hɪk/ *n. colloq.* a country dweller; a provincial. [pet form of the name *Richard*: cf. DICK[1]]

hickey /'hɪki/ *n.* (*pl.* **-eys**) *N. Amer. colloq.* **1** a gadget (cf. DOOHICKEY). **2** a skin blemish, esp. a mark caused by a lovebite. [20th c.: origin unknown]

hickory /'hɪk(ə)ri/ *n.* (*pl.* **-ies**) **1** any N. American tree of the genus *Carya*, yielding tough heavy wood and bearing nutlike edible fruits (see PECAN). **2 a** the wood of these trees. **b** a stick made of this. [local Virginian name *pohickery* from Algonquian *pawcohiccora*]

hid *past* of HIDE[1].

hidalgo /hɪ'dalgəʊ/ *n.* (*pl.* **-os**) a Spanish gentleman. [Spanish from *hijo dalgo*, literally 'son of something']

hidden *past part.* of HIDE[1]. □ **hiddenness** /'hɪd(ə)nnɪs/ *n.*

hidden agenda *n.* a secret or ulterior motive behind an action, statement, etc.

hidden reserves *n.pl.* extra profits, resources, etc. kept concealed in reserve.

hide[1] /hʌɪd/ *v.* & *n.* ● *v.* (*past* **hid**; *past part.* **hidden** /'hɪd(ə)n/ or *archaic* **hid**) **1** *tr.* put or keep out of sight (*hid it under the cushion*; *hid her in the cupboard*). **2** *intr.* conceal oneself. **3** *tr.* (usu. foll. by *from*) keep (a fact) secret (*hid his real motive from her*). **4** *tr.* conceal (a thing) from sight intentionally or not (*trees hid the house*). ● *n. Brit.* a camouflaged shelter used for observing wildlife or hunting animals. □ **hide one's head** keep out of sight, esp. from shame. **hide one's light under a bushel** conceal one's merits (Matthew 5:15). **hide out** (or **up**) remain in concealment. □ **hider** *n.* [Old English *hȳdan*, from West Germanic]

hide[2] /hʌɪd/ *n.* & *v.* ● *n.* **1** the skin of an animal, esp. when tanned or dressed. **2** *joc.* the human skin, esp. on the buttocks (*I'll tan your hide*). ● *v.tr. colloq.* flog. □ **hided** *adj.* (also in *comb.*). [Old English *hȳd*, from Germanic]

hide[3] /hʌɪd/ *n. hist.* (in England) a former measure of land large enough to support a family and its dependants, usu. between 60 and 120 acres. [Old English *hī(gi)d* from *hīw-*, *hīg-* 'household']

hide-and-seek *n.* **1** a children's game in which one or more players seek a child or children hiding. **2** a process of attempting to find an evasive person or thing.

hideaway /'hʌɪdəweɪ/ *n.* a hiding place or place of retreat.

hidebound /'hʌɪdbaʊnd/ *adj.* **1 a** narrow-minded; bigoted. **b** (of the law, rules, etc.) constricted by tradition. **2** (of cattle) with the skin clinging close as a result of bad feeding. [HIDE[2] + BOUND[4]]

hideosity /hɪdɪ'ɒsɪti/ *n.* (*pl.* **-ies**) **1** a hideous object. **2** hideousness.

hideous /'hɪdɪəs/ *adj.* **1** frightful, repulsive, or revolting, to the senses or the mind. **2** *colloq.* unpleasant. □ **hideously** *adv.* **hideousness** *n.* [Middle English *hidous* via Anglo-French *hidous*, Old French *hidos*, *-eus*, from Old French *hide*, *hisde* 'fear', of unknown origin]

hideout /'hʌɪdaʊt/ *n.* a hiding place.

hidey-hole /'hʌɪdɪhəʊl/ *n.* (also **hidy-hole**) *Brit. colloq.* a hiding place.

hiding[1] /'hʌɪdɪŋ/ *n. colloq.* a thrashing. □ **on a hiding to nothing** *Brit.* in a position from which there can be no successful outcome. [HIDE[2] + -ING[1]]

hiding[2] /'hʌɪdɪŋ/ *n.* **1** the act or an instance of hiding. **2** the state of remaining hidden (*go into hiding*). [Middle English, from HIDE[1] + -ING[1]]

hiding place *n.* a place of concealment.

hidrosis /hɪ'drəʊsɪs/ *n. Med.* perspiration. □ **hidrotic** /-'drɒtɪk/ *adj.* [modern Latin from Greek, from *hidrōs* 'sweat']

hie /hʌɪ/ *v.intr.* & *refl.* (**hies**, **hied**, **hieing** or **hying**) *archaic* or *poet.* go quickly (*hie to your chamber*; *hied him to the chase*). [Old English *hīgian* 'strive, pant', of unknown origin]

hierarch /'hʌɪrɑːk/ *n.* **1** a chief priest. **2** an archbishop. [medieval Latin from Greek *hierarkhēs*, from *hieros* 'sacred' + *-arkhēs* 'ruler']

hierarchy /'hʌɪrɑːki/ *n.* (*pl.* **-ies**) **1 a** a system in which grades or classes of status or authority are ranked one above the other (*bottom of a hierarchy*). **b** a hierarchical system (of government, management, etc.). **c** (foll. by *of*) a range in order of importance (*hierarchy of values*). **2 a** priestly government. **b** a priesthood organized in grades. **3** in Christian theology: **a** each of the three divisions of angels. **b** the angels. □ **hierarchic** /-'rɑːkɪk/ *adj.* **hierarchical** /-'rɑːkɪk(ə)l/ *adj.* **hierarchism** *n.* **hierarchize** *v.tr.* (also **-ise**). [Middle English via Old French *ierarchie* and medieval Latin *(h)ierarchia* from Greek *hierarkhia* (as HIERARCH)]

hieratic /hʌɪ'ratɪk/ *adj.* **1** of or concerning priests; priestly. **2** of the ancient Egyptian writing of abridged hieroglyphics as used by priests (cf. DEMOTIC *n.* 2a). **3** of or concerning Egyptian or Greek traditional styles of art. □ **hieratically** *adv.* [Latin from Greek *hieratikos*, via *hieraomai* 'be a priest' from *hiereus* 'priest']

hiero- /'hʌɪrəʊ/ *comb. form* sacred, holy. [Greek *hieros* 'sacred' + -o-]

hierocracy /hʌɪ'rɒkrəsi/ *n.* (*pl.* **-ies**) **1** priestly rule. **2** a body of ruling priests.

hieroglyph /'hʌɪrəglɪf/ *n.* **1 a** a picture of an object representing a word, syllable, or sound, as used in ancient Egyptian and other writing. **b** a writing consisting of characters of this kind. **2** a secret or enigmatic symbol. **3** (in *pl.*) *joc.* writing difficult to read. [back-formation from HIEROGLYPHIC]

hieroglyphic /hʌɪrə'glɪfɪk/ *adj.* & *n.* ● *adj.* **1** of or written in hieroglyphs. **2** symbolical. ● *n.* (in *pl.*) hieroglyphs; hieroglyphic writing. □ **hieroglyphical** *adj.* **hieroglyphically** *adv.* [French *hiéroglyphique* or Late Latin *hieroglyphicus* from Greek *hierogluphikos* (as HIERO-, *gluphikos* from *gluphē* 'carving')]

hierogram /'hʌɪrəgram/ *n.* a sacred inscription or symbol.

hierograph /'hʌɪrəgrɑːf/ *n.* = HIEROGRAM.

hierolatry /hʌɪ'rɒlətri/ *n.* the worship of saints or sacred things.

hierology /hʌɪ'rɒlədʒi/ *n.* sacred literature or lore.

hierophant /'hʌɪrə(ʊ)fant/ *n.* **1** *Gk Antiq.* an initiating or presiding priest; an official interpreter of sacred mysteries. **2** an interpreter of sacred mysteries or any esoteric principle. □ **hierophantic** /-'fantɪk/ *adj.* [Late Latin *hierophantes* from Greek *hierophantēs* (as HIERO-, *phantēs* from *phainō* 'show')]

hi-fi /'hʌɪfʌɪ/ *adj.* & *n. colloq.* ● *adj.* of high fidelity. ● *n.* (*pl.* **hi-fis**) a set of equipment for high-fidelity sound reproduction. [abbreviation]

higgle /'hɪg(ə)l/ *v.intr.* dispute about terms; haggle. [variant of HAGGLE]

higgledy-piggledy /ˌhɪg(ə)ldɪ'pɪg(ə)ldi/ *adv., adj.,* & *n.* ● *adv.* & *adj.* in confusion or disorder. ● *n.* a state of disordered confusion. [rhyming jingle, probably with reference to the irregular herding together of pigs]

high /hʌɪ/ *adj., n.,* & *adv.* ● *adj.* **1 a** of great vertical extent (*a high building*). **b** (*predic.*; often in *comb.*) of a specified height (*one inch high*; *water was waist-high*). **2 a** far above ground or sea level etc. (*a high altitude*). **b** inland, esp. when raised (*High Asia*). **3** extending above the normal or average level (*high boots*; *jersey with a high neck*). **4** of exalted, esp. spiritual, quality (*high minds*; *high principles*; *high art*). **5** of exalted rank (*in high society*; *is high in the Government*). **6 a** great; intense; extreme; powerful (*high praise*; *high temperature*). **b** greater than normal (*high prices*). **c** extreme in religious or political opinion (*high Tory*). **7** (of physical action, esp. athletics) performed at, to, or from a considerable height (*high diving*; *high flying*). **8** (often foll. by *on*) *colloq.* intoxicated by alcohol or esp. drugs. **9** (of a sound or note) of high frequency; shrill; at the top end of the scale. **10** (of a period, an age, a time, etc.) at its peak (*high noon*; *high summer*; *High Renaissance*). **11 a** (of meat etc.) beginning to go bad; off. **b** (of game) well-hung and slightly decomposed. **12** *Geog.* (of latitude) near the North or South Pole. **13** *Phonet.* = CLOSE[1] *adj.* 14. ● *n.* **1** a high, or the highest, level or figure. **2** an area of high barometric pressure; an anticyclone. **3** *slang* a euphoric state, esp. drug-induced (*I'm on a high at the moment*). **4** top gear in a motor vehicle. **5** *N. Amer. colloq.* high school. **6** (**the High**) *Brit. colloq.* a High Street, esp. that in Oxford. ● *adv.* **1** far up; aloft (*flew the flag high*). **2** in or to a high degree. **3** at a high price. **4** (of a sound) at or to a high pitch (*sang high*). □ **ace** (or **king** or **queen** etc.) **high** (in card games) having the ace etc. as the highest-ranking card. **from on high** from heaven or a high place. **high old** (*attrib.*) *colloq.* most enjoyable (*had a high old time*). **high opinion of** a favourable opinion of. **high, wide, and handsome** *colloq.* in a carefree or stylish manner. **in high feather** see FEATHER. **on high** in or to heaven or a high place. **on one's high horse** *colloq.* behaving superciliously or arrogantly. **play high 1** play for high stakes. **2** play a card of high value. **run high 1** (of the sea) have a strong current with high tide. **2** (of feelings) be strong. [Old English *hēah*, from Germanic]

High Admiral *n. Brit.* a chief officer of admiral's rank.

high altar *n.* the chief altar of a church.

high and dry *adv.* (usu. in phr. **left high and dry**) **1** stranded without resources. **2** (of a ship) out of the water, esp. stranded.

high and low *adv.* (esp. in phr. **search high and low**) everywhere.

high and mighty *adj.* **1** *colloq.* arrogant. **2** *archaic* of exalted rank.

highball /ˈhʌɪbɔːl/ *n. N. Amer.* **1** a drink of spirits and soda etc., served with ice in a tall glass. **2** a railway signal to proceed.

highbinder /ˈhʌɪbʌɪndə/ *n. US slang* a ruffian; a swindler; an assassin.

high-born *adj.* of noble birth.

highboy /ˈhʌɪbɔɪ/ *n. N. Amer.* a tall chest of drawers on legs.

highbrow /ˈhʌɪbraʊ/ *adj. & n. colloq.* ● *adj.* intellectual; cultural. ● *n.* an intellectual or cultured person.

high camp *n.* sophisticated camp (cf. CAMP[2]).

high card *n.* a card that outranks others, esp. the ace or a court card.

high chair *n.* an infant's chair with long legs and a tray, for use at meals.

High Church *n. & adj.* ● *n.* a tradition within the Anglican Church emphasizing ritual, priestly authority, sacraments, and historical continuity with Catholic Christianity. ● *adj.* of or relating to this tradition.

High Churchman *n.* (*pl.* **-men**) an advocate of High Church principles.

high-class *adj.* of high quality.

high colour *n.* a flushed complexion.

high command *n.* an army commander-in-chief and associated staff.

High Commission *n.* an embassy from one Commonwealth country to another. □ **High Commissioner** *n.*

High Court *n.* **1** a supreme court of justice, esp. in England (in full **High Court of Justice**) the court of unlimited civil jurisdiction forming part of the Supreme Court. **2** (often **high court**) (in the US) a supreme court in a state.

high day *n.* a festal day.

high enema *n.* an enema delivered into the colon.

Higher /ˈhʌɪə/ *n.* (usu. in *pl.*) (in Scotland) an examination leading to the Scottish Certificate of Education, Higher Grade.

higher animal *n.* an animal showing relatively advanced characteristics, e.g. a placental mammal.

higher court *n.* a court that can overrule the decision of another.

higher criticism *n.* (prec. by *the*) criticism dealing with the origin and character etc. of texts, esp. of biblical writings.

higher education *n.* education at university etc., esp. to degree level.

higher mathematics *n.pl.* (usu. treated as *sing.*) advanced mathematics as taught at university etc.

higher plant *n.* a plant showing relatively advanced characteristics, e.g. a flowering plant.

higher-up *n.* (*pl.* **higher-ups**) *colloq.* a person of higher rank; a superior.

highest common factor /ˈhʌɪɪst/ *n.* the highest number that can be divided exactly into each of two or more numbers.

high explosive *n.* an extremely explosive substance used in shells, bombs, etc.

highfalutin /hʌɪfəˈluːtɪn/ *adj. & n.* (also **highfaluting** /-tɪŋ/) *colloq.* ● *adj.* absurdly pompous or pretentious. ● *n.* speech or writing of this kind. [perhaps from HIGH + *fluting* pres. part. of FLUTE *v.*]

high fashion *n.* = HAUTE COUTURE.

high fidelity *n.* the reproduction of sound with little distortion, giving a result very similar to the original.

high finance *n.* financial transactions involving large sums.

high-five *n. & v. N. Amer. slang* ● *n.* a gesture of celebration or greeting in which two people slap each other's palms with their arms outstretched over their heads. ● *v.tr.* greet with a high-five.

high-flown *adj.* (of language etc.) extravagant, bombastic.

high-flyer *n.* (also **high-flier**) **1** a person with the potential and usu. ambition to succeed, esp. academically or in business. **2** a thing with potential for exceptional, usu. commercial, achievement (*high-flyer of the sports car range*). □ **high-flying** *adj.*

high frequency *n.* a frequency, esp. in radio, of 3–30 megahertz.

high gear *n.* a gear such that the driven end of a transmission revolves faster than the driving end.

High German *n.* a literary and cultured form of German, originally used in the highlands or south of Germany.

high-grade *adj.* of high quality.

high ground *n.* (usu. prec. by *the*) a position of superiority in a debate etc. (*the moral high ground*).

high-handed *adj.* disregarding others' feelings; overbearing. □ **high-handedly** *adv.* **high-handedness** *n.*

high hat *n., adj., & v.* ● *n.* **1** a tall hat; a top hat. **2** a pair of foot-operated cymbals. **3** a snobbish or overbearing person. ● *adj.* (**high-hat**) supercilious; snobbish. ● *v.* (**high-hat**) (**-hatted, -hatting**) *US* **1** *tr.* treat superciliously. **2** *intr.* assume a superior attitude.

high heels *n.pl.* women's shoes with high heels. □ **high-heeled** *adj.*

high holiday *n.* the Jewish New Year or the Day of Atonement.

high-income *attrib.adj.* **1** of or relating to the income group of people earning high salaries. **2** with a high national income. **3** (of an investment) with or offering a high dividend.

high jinks *n.pl.* boisterous joking or merrymaking.

high jump *n.* **1** an athletic event consisting of jumping as high as possible over a bar of adjustable height. **2** *Brit. colloq.* a drastic punishment (*he's for the high jump*). □ **high-jumper** *n.*

high-key *adj. Photog.* consisting of light tones only.

high kick *n.* a dancer's kick high in the air. □ **high-kicking** *attrib.adj.*

highland /ˈhʌɪlənd/ *n. & adj.* ● *n.* (usu. in *pl.*) **1** an area of high or mountainous land. **2** (**the Highlands**) the mountainous part of Scotland. ● *adj.* **1** relating to high or mountainous land. **2** (**Highland**) of or relating to the Highlands. □ **highlander** *n.* (also **Highlander**). **Highlandman** *n.* (*pl.* **-men**). [Old English *hēahlond* 'promontory' (as HIGH, LAND)]

Highland cattle *n.* **1** cattle of a shaggy-haired breed with long curved widely spaced horns. **2** this breed.

Highland dress *n.* the Scottish kilt etc.

Highland fling see FLING *n.* 3.

high latitudes *n.pl.* regions near the poles.

high-level *adj.* **1** (of negotiations etc.) conducted by high-ranking people. **2** *Computing* (of a programming language) that is not machine-dependent and is usu. at a level of abstraction close to natural language.

high life *n.* (also **high living**) a luxurious existence ascribed to the upper classes.

highlight /ˈhʌɪlʌɪt/ *n. & v.* ● *n.* **1** (in a painting etc.) a light area, or one seeming to reflect light. **2** a moment or detail of vivid interest; an outstanding feature. **3** (usu. in *pl.*) a bright tint in the hair, esp. one produced by bleaching or dyeing. ● *v.tr.* **1 a** bring into prominence; draw attention to. **b** mark with a highlighter. **2** create highlights in (the hair).

highlighter /ˈhʌɪlʌɪtə/ *n.* a marker pen which overlays colour on a printed word etc., leaving it legible and emphasized.

high-lows *n.pl. archaic* boots reaching over the ankles.

highly /ˈhʌɪli/ *adv.* **1** in a high degree (*highly amusing*; *highly probable*; *commend it highly*). **2** honourably; favourably (*think highly of him*). [Old English *hēalīce* (as HIGH)]

highly strung *adj.* (hyphenated when *attrib.*) very sensitive or nervous.

High Mass *n.* Mass with incense, music, and usu. the assistance of a deacon and subdeacon.

high-minded *adj.* **1** having high moral principles. **2** *archaic* proud. □ **high-mindedly** *adv.* **high-mindedness** *n.*

high-muck-a-muck /ˈhʌɪmʌkəmʌk/ *n.* (also **high-muckety-muck** /-mʌkətɪmʌk/) *N. Amer.* a person of great self-importance. [perhaps from Chinook *hiu* 'plenty' + *muckamuck* 'food']

highness /ˈhʌɪnɪs/ *n.* **1** the state of being high (*highness of taxation*) (cf. HEIGHT). **2** (**Highness**) a title used in addressing and referring to a prince or princess (*Her Highness*; *Your Royal Highness*). [Old English *hēanes* (as HIGH)]

high-octane *adj.* (of fuel used in internal-combustion engines) having good antiknock properties, not detonating readily during the power stroke.

high-pitched *adj.* **1** (of a sound) high. **2** (of a roof) steep. **3** (of style etc.) lofty.

high places *n.pl.* the upper ranks of an organization etc.

high point *n.* the maximum or best state reached.

high polymer *n.* a polymer having a high molecular weight.

high-powered *adj.* **1** having great power or energy. **2** important or influential.

high pressure *n.* **1** a high degree of activity or exertion. **2** a condition of the atmosphere with the pressure above average e.g. in an anticyclone.

high priest *n.* **1** a chief priest, esp. *hist.* Jewish. **2** (*fem.* **high priestess**) the head of any cult.

high profile *n.* exposure to attention or publicity (usu. hyphenated when *attrib.*: *high-profile event*).

high-quality *adj.* of high quality.

high-ranking *adj.* of high rank, senior.

high relief see RELIEF 6a.

high-rise *adj. & n.* ● *attrib.adj.* (of a building) having many storeys. ● *n.* such a building.

high-risk *attrib.adj.* involving or exposed to danger (*high-risk sports*).

high road *n.* **1** *Brit.* a main road. **2** (usu. foll. by *to*) a direct route (*on the high road to success*).

high roller *n. N. Amer. slang* a person who gambles large sums or spends freely.

high school *n.* **1** *Brit.* a grammar school. **2** *N. Amer.* & *Sc.* a secondary school.

high sea *n.* (also **high seas** *pl.*) open seas not within any country's jurisdiction.

high season *n.* the period of the greatest number of visitors at a resort etc.

high-security *attrib.adj.* **1** (of a prison, lock, etc.) extremely secure. **2** (of a prisoner) kept in a high-security prison.

High Sheriff see SHERIFF 1a.

high sign *n. US colloq.* a surreptitious gesture indicating that all is well or that the coast is clear.

high-sounding *adj.* pretentious, bombastic.

high-speed *attrib.adj.* **1** operating at great speed. **2** (of steel) suitable for tools, cutting so rapidly as to become red-hot.

high spirit *n.* **1** see SPIRIT *n.* 6c. **2** (in *pl.*) cheerfulness. **3** (in *pl.*) = HIGH JINKS. □ **in high spirits** very cheerful; in a very good mood.

high-spirited *adj.* vivacious; cheerful.

high spot *n. colloq.* the most enjoyable feature, moment, or experience. □ **hit the high spots 1** visit the most notable places. **2** go to excess or extremes.

high-stepper *n.* **1** a horse that lifts its feet high when walking or trotting. **2** a stately person. □ **high-stepping** *attrib.adj.*

High Steward see STEWARD *n.* 6.

high street *n. Brit.* a main road, esp. the principal shopping street of a town (usu. hyphenated when *attrib.*: *high-street bank*).

high-strung *adj.* = HIGHLY STRUNG.

hight /hʌɪt/ *adj. archaic, poet.*, or *joc.* called; named. [past part. of Middle English *hight* from Old English *hātan* 'command, call']

high table *n. Brit.* a table on a platform at a public dinner or for the fellows of a college.

hightail /ˈhʌɪteɪl/ *v.intr. N. Amer. colloq.* move at high speed.

high tea *n. Brit.* a main evening meal usu. consisting of a cooked dish, bread and butter, tea, etc.

high-tech *adj. & n.* ● *adj.* **1** (of interior design etc.) imitating styles more usual in industry etc., esp. using steel, glass, or plastic in a functional way. **2** employing, requiring, or involved in high technology. ● *n.* (**high tech**) = HIGH TECHNOLOGY.

high technology *n.* advanced technological development, esp. in electronics.

high-tensile *adj.* (of metal) having great tensile strength.

high tension *n.* = HIGH VOLTAGE.

high tide *n.* **1** the state of the tide when at its highest or fullest level. **2** the time of this.

high time *n.* a time that is late or overdue (*it is high time they arrived*).

high-toned *adj.* stylish; dignified; superior.

high treason see TREASON 1.

high-up *n. colloq.* a person of high rank.

high voltage *n.* electrical potential large enough to cause injury or damage if diverted, as in power transmission cables.

high water *n.* = HIGH TIDE.

high water mark *n.* **1** the level reached by the sea etc. at high tide. **2** the maximum recorded value or highest point of excellence.

highway /ˈhʌɪweɪ/ *n.* **1 a** a public road. **b** a main route (by land or water). **2** a direct course of action (*on the highway to success*).

Highway Code *n.* (in the UK) the official booklet of guidance for road users.

highwayman /ˈhʌɪweɪmən/ *n.* (*pl.* **-men**; *fem.* **highwaywoman**, *pl.* **-women**) *hist.* a robber of passengers, travellers, etc., usu. mounted.

high wire *n.* a high tightrope.

high words *n.pl.* angry talk.

high yellow *n. US offens.* a light-skinned person of mixed black and white parentage.

HIH *abbr. Brit.* Her or His Imperial Highness.

hijack /ˈhʌɪdʒak/ *v. & n.* ● *v.tr.* **1** seize control of (a loaded lorry, an aircraft in flight, etc.), esp. to force it to a different destination. **2** seize (goods) in transit. **3** take over (an organization etc.) by force or subterfuge in order to redirect it. ● *n.* an instance of hijacking. □ **hijacker** *n.* [20th c.: origin unknown]

Hijra var. of HEGIRA.

hike /hʌɪk/ *n.* & *v.* ● *n.* **1** a long country walk, esp. with rucksacks etc. **2** an increase (of prices etc.). ● *v.* **1** *intr.* walk for a long distance, esp. across country with boots, rucksack, etc. **2** (usu. foll. by *up*) **a** *tr.* hitch up (clothing etc.); hoist; shove. **b** *intr.* work upwards out of place, become hitched up. **3** *tr.* increase (prices etc.). □ **hiker** *n.* [19th-c. dialect: origin unknown]

hila *pl.* of HILUM.

hilarious /hɪˈlɛːrɪəs/ *adj.* **1** exceedingly funny. **2** boisterously merry. □ **hilariously** *adv.* **hilariousness** *n.* **hilarity** /-ˈlarɪti/ *n.* [Latin *hilaris* from Greek *hilaros* 'cheerful']

Hilary term /ˈhɪləri/ *n. Brit.* the university term beginning in January, esp. at Oxford. [named after *Hilarius* bishop of Poitiers (d. 367), whose festival is on 13 Jan.]

hill /hɪl/ *n.* & *v.* ● *n.* **1 a** a naturally raised area of land, not as high as a mountain. **b** (as **the hills**) *Anglo-Ind.* = HILL STATION. **2** (often in *comb.*) a heap; a mound (*anthill*; *dunghill*). **3** a sloping piece of road. ● *v.tr.* **1** form into a hill. **2** (usu. foll. by *up*) bank up (plants) with soil. □ **old as the hills** very ancient. **over the hill** *colloq.* **1** past the prime of life; declining. **2** past the crisis. **up hill and down dale** see UP. [Old English *hyll*]

hill-billy *n.* (*pl.* **-ies**) *US* **1** *colloq.*, often *derog.* a person from a remote or mountainous area, esp. in the Appalachians (cf. HICK). **2** country music of or like that of the southern US. [HILL + *Billy*, pet form of the name *William*]

hill climb *n.* a race for vehicles up a steep hill.

hill fort *n.* a fort built on a hill.

hillman /ˈhɪlmən/ *n.* (*pl.* **-men**) an inhabitant of hilly country.

hillock /ˈhɪlək/ *n.* a small hill or mound. □ **hillocky** *adj.*

hillside /ˈhɪlsʌɪd/ *n.* the sloping side of a hill.

hill station *n.* a government settlement, esp. for holidays etc. during the hot season, in the low mountains of the northern Indian subcontinent.

hilltop /ˈhɪltɒp/ *n.* the summit of a hill.

hillwalking /ˈhɪlwɔːkɪŋ/ *n.* the pastime of walking in hilly country. □ **hillwalker** *n.*

hilly /ˈhɪli/ *adj.* (**hillier**, **hilliest**) having many hills. □ **hilliness** *n.*

hilt /hɪlt/ *n.* & *v.* ● *n.* **1** the handle of a sword, dagger, etc. **2** the handle of a tool. ● *v.tr.* provide with a hilt. □ **up to the hilt** completely. [Old English *hilt(e)*, from Germanic]

hilum /ˈhʌɪləm/ *n.* (*pl.* **hila** /-lə/) **1** *Bot.* the point of attachment of a seed to its seed vessel. **2** *Anat.* a notch or indentation where a vessel enters an organ. [Latin, = little thing, trifle]

HIM *abbr. Brit.* Her or His Imperial Majesty.

him /hɪm/ *pron.* **1** *objective case* of HE (*I saw him*). **2** *archaic* himself (*fell and hurt him*). [Old English, masc. and neut. dative sing. of HE, IT[1]]

■ **Usage** See Usage Note at HER.

Himalayan /hɪməˈleɪən/ *adj.* of or relating to the Himalaya mountains in Nepal. [Sanskrit *Himalaya*, from *hima* 'snow' + *ālaya* 'abode']

himation /hɪˈmatɪɒn/ *n. hist.* the outer garment worn by the ancient Greeks over the left shoulder and under the right. [Greek]

himself /hɪmˈsɛlf/ *pron.* **1 a** *emphat. form* of HE or HIM (*he himself will do it*). **b** *refl. form* of HIM (*he has hurt himself*). **2** in his normal state of body or mind (*does not feel quite himself today*). **3** esp. *Ir.* a third party of some importance; the master of the house. □ **be himself** act in his normal unconstrained manner. **by himself** see *by oneself*. [Old English (as HIM, SELF)]

Hinayana /hiːnəˈjɑːnə/ *n.* = THERAVADA. [Sanskrit, from *hīna* 'lesser' + *yāna* 'vehicle']

hind[1] /hʌɪnd/ *adj.* (esp. of parts of the body) situated at the back, posterior (*hind leg*) (opp. FORE *adj.*). □ **on one's hind legs** see LEG. [Middle English, perhaps shortened from Old English *bihindan* BEHIND]

hind[2] /hʌɪnd/ *n.* a female deer (usu. a red deer or sika), esp. in and after the third year. [Old English from Germanic]

hind[3] /hʌɪnd/ *n. hist.* **1** esp. *Sc.* a skilled farmworker, usu. married and with a tied cottage, and formerly having charge of two horses. **2** *Brit.* a steward on a farm. **3** a rustic, a boor. [Middle English *hine* from Old English *hīne* (pl.), apparently from *hī(g)na*, genitive pl. of *hīgan*, *hīwan* 'members of a family' (cf. HIDE[3]): for *-d* cf. SOUND[1]]

hindbrain /ˈhʌɪn(d)breɪn/ *n. Anat.* the lower part of the brainstem, comprising the cerebellum, pons, and medulla oblongata. Also called *rhombencephalon*.

hinder[1] /ˈhɪndə/ *v.tr.* (also *absol.*) impede; delay; prevent (*you will hinder him*; *hindered me from working*). [Old English *hindrian*, from Germanic]

hinder[2] /ˈhʌɪndə/ *adj.* rear, hind (*the hinder part*). [Middle English, perhaps from Old English *hinderweard* 'backward': cf. HIND[1]]

Hindi /ˈhɪndi/ *n.* & *adj.* ● *n.* **1** a group of spoken dialects of northern India. **2** a literary form of Hindustani with a Sanskrit-based vocabulary and the Devanagari script, an official language of India. ● *adj.* of or concerning Hindi. [Urdu *hindī* from *Hind* 'India']

hindmost /ˈhʌɪn(d)məʊst/ *adj.* furthest behind; most remote.

Hindoo *archaic* var. of HINDU.

hindquarters /hʌɪn(d)ˈkwɔːtəz/ *n.pl.* the hind legs and adjoining parts of a quadruped.

hindrance /ˈhɪndr(ə)ns/ *n.* **1** the act or an instance of hindering; the state of being hindered. **2** a thing that hinders; an obstacle.

hindsight /ˈhʌɪn(d)sʌɪt/ *n.* **1** wisdom after the event (*realized with hindsight that they were wrong*). **2** the backsight of a gun.

Hindu /ˈhɪnduː, hɪnˈduː/ *n.* & *adj.* (also *archaic* **Hindoo**) ● *n.* (*pl.* **Hindus**) **1** a follower of Hinduism. **2** *archaic* an Indian. ● *adj.* **1** of or concerning Hindus or Hinduism. **2** *archaic* Indian. [Urdu from Persian, from *Hind* 'India']

Hinduism /ˈhɪnduːɪz(ə)m/ *n.* the main religious and social system of India, including belief in reincarnation, the worship of several gods, and a caste system as the basis of society. □ **Hinduize** *v.tr.* (also **-ise**).

Hindustani /hɪndʊˈstɑːni/ *n.* & *adj.* ● *n. hist.* **1** a group of mutually intelligible languages and dialects spoken in north-west India, principally Hindi and Urdu. **2** the Delhi dialect of Hindi, widely used throughout India as a lingua franca. ● *adj.* of or relating to the culture of north-west India. [Urdu from Persian *hindūstānī* (as HINDU + *-stān* 'country')]

■ **Usage** *Hindustani* was the usual term in the 18th and 19th centuries for the native language of north-west India. The usual modern term is *Hindi*, although *Hindustani* is still sometimes used to refer to the lingua franca.

hinge /hɪn(d)ʒ/ *n.* & *v.* ● *n.* **1 a** a movable, usu. metal, joint or mechanism such as that by which a door is hung on a side post. **b** *Biol.* a natural joint performing a similar function, e.g. that of a bivalve shell. **2** a central point or principle on which everything depends. ● *v.* (**hingeing** or **hinging**) **1** *intr.* (foll. by *on*) **a** depend (on a principle, an event, etc.) (*all hinges on his acceptance*). **b** (of a door etc.) hang and turn (on a post etc.). **2** *tr.* attach with or as if with a hinge. □ **hinged** *adj.* **hingeless** *adj.* **hingewise** *adv.* [Middle English *heng* etc., related to HANG]

hinny[1] /ˈhɪni/ *n.* (*pl.* **-ies**) the offspring of a female donkey and a male horse. [Latin *hinnus* from Greek *hinnos*]

hinny[2] /ˈhɪni/ *n.* (also **hinnie**) (*pl.* **-ies**) *Sc.* & *N.Engl.* (esp. as a form of address) darling, sweetheart. [variant of HONEY]

hint /hɪnt/ *n.* & *v.* ● *n.* **1** a slight or indirect indication or suggestion (*took the hint and left*). **2** a small piece of practical information (*handy hints on cooking*). **3** a very small trace; a suggestion (*a hint of perfume*). ● *v.tr.* (often foll. by *that* + clause) suggest slightly (*hinted the contrary*; *hinted that they were wrong*). □ **hint at** give a hint of; refer indirectly to. [apparently from obsolete *hent* 'grasp, lay hold of', from Old English *hentan*, from Germanic: related to HUNT]

hinterland /ˈhɪntəland/ *n.* **1** the often deserted or uncharted areas beyond a coastal district or a river's banks. **2** an area served by a port or other centre. **3** a remote or fringe area. [German, from *hinter* 'behind' + *Land* LAND]

hip[1] /hɪp/ *n.* **1** a projection of the pelvis and upper thigh bone on each side of the body in human beings and quadrupeds. **2** (often in *pl.*) the circumference of the body at the buttocks. **3** *Archit.* the sharp edge of a roof from ridge to eaves where two sides meet. □ **on the hip** *archaic* at a disadvantage. □ **hipless** *adj.* **hipped** *adj.* (also in comb.). [Old English *hype* from Germanic: related to HOP[1]]

hip[2] /hɪp/ *n.* (also *Brit.* **hep** /hɛp/) the fruit of a rose, esp. a wild kind. [Old English *hēope*, *hīope*, from West Germanic]

hip[3] /hɪp/ *adj.* (also **hep** /hɛp/) (**hipper**, **hippest** or **hepper**, **heppest**) *slang* **1** following the latest fashion in esp. jazz or popular music, clothes, etc.; stylish. **2** (often foll. by *to*) understanding, aware. □ **hipness** *n.* [20th c.: origin unknown]

hip[4] /hɪp/ *int.* introducing a united cheer (*hip, hip, hooray*). [19th c.: origin unknown]

hip bath *n.* a portable bath in which a person sits.

hip bone *n.* a bone forming the hip, esp. the ilium.

hip flask *n.* a flask for spirits etc., carried in a hip pocket.

hip hop *n.* **1** a style of popular music of US black and Hispanic origin, featuring rap with an electronic backing. **2** the subculture associated with this, including graffiti art, break-dancing, etc. [20th c.: perhaps from HIP[1]]

hip joint *n.* the articulation of the head of the thigh bone with the ilium.

hip-length *adj.* (of a garment) reaching down to the hips.

hippeastrum /hɪpɪˈastrəm/ *n.* any S. American bulbous plant of the genus *Hippeastrum*, with showy white or red flowers. [modern Latin, from Greek *hippeus* 'horseman' (the leaves appearing to ride on one another) + *astron* 'star' (from the flower-shape)]

hipped /hɪpt/ *adj.* (usu. foll. by *on*) esp. *US slang* obsessed, infatuated. [past part. of *hip* = make hip (HIP[3])]

hipped roof var. of HIP ROOF.

hippie var. of HIPPY[1].

hippo /ˈhɪpəʊ/ *n.* (*pl.* **-os**) *colloq.* a hippopotamus. [abbreviation]

hippocampus /hɪpə(ʊ)ˈkampəs/ *n.* (*pl.* **hippocampi** /-pi, -pʌɪ/) **1** a sea horse of the genus *Hippocampus*. **2** *Anat.* the elongated ridges on the floor of each lateral ventricle of the brain, thought to be the centre of emotion and the autonomic nervous system. [Latin from Greek *hippokampos*, from *hippos* 'horse' + *kampos* 'sea monster']

hip pocket *n.* a trouser pocket just behind the hip. □ **in one's hip pocket** *N. Amer.* completely under control.

hippocras /ˈhɪpəkras/ *n. hist.* wine flavoured with spices. [Middle English from Old French *ipocras* 'Hippocrates' (see HIPPOCRATIC OATH), probably because strained through a filter called 'Hippocrates' sleeve']

Hippocratic oath /hɪpəˈkratɪk/ *n.* (*hist.* except in revised form in certain medical schools) an oath taken by doctors prior to beginning medical practice, affirming their obligations and proper conduct. [medieval Latin *Hippocraticus* from *Hippocrates*, the name of a Greek physician of the 5th c. BC]

Hippocrene /ˈhɪpəkriːn/ *n. poet.* poetic or literary inspiration. [name of a fountain on Mount Helicon sacred to the Muses: Latin from Greek, from *hippos* 'horse' + *krēnē* 'fountain', as having been produced by a stroke of Pegasus' hoof]

hippodrome /ˈhɪpədrəʊm/ *n.* **1** a music hall, theatre, or dance hall. **2** *Antiq.* a course for chariot races etc. **3** a circus. [French *hippodrome* or Latin *hippodromus* from Greek *hippodromos*, from *hippos* 'horse' + *dromos* 'race, course']

hippogriff /ˈhɪpə(ʊ)ɡrɪf/ *n.* (also **hippogryph**) a mythical griffin-like creature with the body of a horse. [French *hippogriffe* from Italian *ippogrifo*, from Greek *hippos* 'horse' + Italian *grifo* GRIFFIN]

hippopotamus /hɪpəˈpɒtəməs/ *n.* (*pl.* **hippopotamuses** or **hippopotami** /-mʌɪ/) **1** a large thick-skinned four-legged mammal, *Hippopotamus amphibius*, native to Africa, inhabiting rivers, lakes, etc. **2** (in full **pygmy hippopotamus**) a smaller related mammal, *Choeropsis liberiensis*, native to Africa, inhabiting forests and swamps. [Middle English via Latin from Greek *hippopotamos*, from *hippos* 'horse' + *potamos* 'river']

hippy[1] /ˈhɪpi/ *n.* (also **hippie**) (*pl.* **-ies**) (esp. in the 1960s) a person of unconventional appearance, typically with long hair, jeans, beads, etc., often associated with hallucinogenic drugs and a rejection of conventional values. [HIP[3]]

hippy[2] /ˈhɪpi/ *adj.* having large hips.

hip roof *n.* (also **hipped roof**) a roof with the sides and the ends inclined.

hipster[1] /hɪpstə/ *adj.* & *n. Brit.* ● *adj.* (of a garment) hanging from the hips rather than the waist. ● *n.* (in *pl.*) trousers hanging from the hips.

hipster[2] /hɪpstə/ *n. slang* a person who is hip; a hepcat. □ **hipsterism** *n.* [HIP[3]]

hiragana /hɪrəˈɡɑːnə, hɪərə-/ *n.* the cursive form of Japanese syllabic writing or kana (cf. KATAKANA). [Japanese, = plain kana]

hircine /ˈhəːsʌɪn/ *adj.* goatlike. [Latin *hircinus* from *hircus* 'he-goat']

hire /ˈhʌɪə/ *v.* & *n.* ● *v.tr.* **1** (often foll. by *from*) procure the temporary use of (a thing) for an agreed payment (*hired a van from them*). **2** esp. *US* employ (a person) for wages or a fee. ● *n.* **1** hiring or being hired. **2** payment for this. **3** *N. Amer.* a recently recruited employee. □ **for** (or **on**) **hire** ready to be hired. **hire out 1** grant the temporary use of (a thing) for an agreed payment. **2** *refl.* make oneself available for employment. □ **hireable** *adj.* (*US* **hirable**). **hirer** *n.* [Old English *hȳrian*, *hȳr*, from West Germanic]

hire car *n. Brit.* a car available for hire.

hired girl *n.* (also **hired man**) *N. Amer.* a domestic servant, esp. on a farm.

hireling /ˈhʌɪəlɪŋ/ *n.* usu. *derog.* a person who works for hire. [Old English *hȳrling* (as HIRE, -LING[1])]

hire purchase *n. Brit.* a system by which a person may purchase a thing by regular payments while having the use of it.

hirsute /ˈhəːsjuːt/ *adj.* **1** hairy, shaggy. **2** untrimmed. □ **hirsuteness** *n.* [Latin *hirsutus*]

hirsutism /ˈhəːsjuːtɪz(ə)m/ *n.* the excessive growth of hair on the face and body.

hirundine /hɪˈrʌndʌɪn/ *n.* & *adj.* ● *n.* a bird of the swallow family Hirundinidae. ● *adj.* of or relating to swallows. [Latin *hirundo* 'swallow' + -INE[1]]

his /hɪz/ *poss.det.* & *poss.pron.* ● *poss.det.* **1** of or belonging to him (*his house*; *his own business*). **2** (**His**) (in titles) that he is (*His Majesty*). ● *poss.pron.* the one or ones belonging to or associated with him (*it is his*; *his are over there*). □ **his and hers** *joc.* (of matching items) for husband and wife, or men and women. **of his** of or belonging to him (*a friend of his*). [Old English, genitive of HE, IT[1]]

Hispanic /hɪˈspanɪk/ *adj. & n.* ● *adj.* **1** of or relating to Spain or to Spain and Portugal. **2** of Spain and other Spanish-speaking countries. ● *n.* a Spanish-speaking person, esp. one of Latin American descent, living in the US. □ **Hispanicize** /-SAIZ/ *v.tr.* (also **-ise**). [Latin *Hispanicus* from *Hispania* 'Spain']

Hispanist /ˈhɪspənɪst/ *n.* (also **Hispanicist** /hɪˈspanɪsɪst/) an expert in or student of the language, literature, and civilization of Spain.

Hispano- /hɪˈspanəʊ/ *comb. form* Spanish. [Latin *Hispanus* 'Spanish']

hispid /ˈhɪspɪd/ *adj. Bot. & Zool.* **1** rough with bristles; bristly. **2** shaggy. [Latin *hispidus*]

hiss /hɪs/ *v. & n.* ● *v.* **1** *intr.* (of a person, snake, goose, etc.) make a sharp sibilant sound, esp. as a sign of disapproval or derision (*audience booed and hissed*; *the water hissed on the hotplate*). **2** *tr.* express disapproval of (a person etc.) by hisses. **3** *tr.* whisper (a threat etc.) urgently or angrily (*'Get back!' he hissed*). ● *n.* **1** a sharp sibilant sound as of the letter *s*, esp. as an expression of disapproval or derision. **2** *Electronics* unwanted interference at audio frequencies. □ **hiss away** (or **down**) drive off etc. by hisses. **hiss off** drive (an actor etc.) off stage by hissing. [Middle English: imitative]

hist /hɪst/ *int. archaic* used to call attention, enjoin silence, incite a dog, etc. [16th c.: a natural exclamation]

histamine /ˈhɪstəmiːn/ *n. Biochem.* an amine causing contraction of smooth muscle and dilation of capillaries, released by most cells in response to injury and in allergic and inflammatory reactions. □ **histaminic** /-ˈmɪnɪk/ *adj.* [HISTO- + AMINE]

histidine /ˈhɪstɪdiːn/ *n. Biochem.* an amino acid present in proteins and from which histamine is derived. [Greek *histos* 'web, tissue']

histo- /ˈhɪstəʊ/ *comb. form* (also **hist-** before a vowel) *Biol.* tissue. [Greek *histos* 'web, tissue']

histochemistry /hɪstəʊˈkɛmɪstri/ *n.* the study of the identification and distribution of the chemical constituents of tissues by means of stains, indicators, and microscopy. □ **histochemical** *adj.*

histogenesis /hɪstəʊˈdʒɛnɪsɪs/ *n.* the formation of tissues. □ **histogenetic** /-dʒɪˈnɛtɪk/ *adj.*

histogeny /hɪˈstɒdʒɪni/ *n.* = HISTOGENESIS. □ **histogenic** /hɪstəˈdʒɛnɪk/ *adj.*

histogram /ˈhɪstəgram/ *n. Statistics* a chart consisting of rectangles (usu. drawn vertically from a baseline) whose areas and positions are proportional to the value or range of a number of variables. [Greek *histos* 'mast, web' + -GRAM]

histology /hɪˈstɒlədʒi/ *n.* the study of the microscopic structure of tissues. □ **histological** /hɪstəˈlɒdʒɪk(ə)l/ *adj.* **histologist** /hɪˈstɒlədʒɪst/ *n.*

histolysis /hɪˈstɒlɪsɪs/ *n.* the breaking down of tissues. □ **histolytic** /-təˈlɪtɪk/ *adj.*

histone /ˈhɪstəʊn/ *n. Biochem.* any of a group of basic proteins found in chromatin. [German *Histon*, perhaps from Greek *histamai* 'arrest', or as HISTO-]

histopathology /ˌhɪstəʊpəˈθɒlədʒi/ *n.* **1** changes in tissues caused by disease. **2** the study of these. □ **histopathological** /-paθəˈlɒdʒɪk(ə)l/ *adj.* **histopathologist** *n.*

historian /hɪˈstɔːrɪən/ *n.* **1** a writer of history, esp. a critical analyst, rather than a compiler. **2** a person learned in or studying history (*English historian*; *ancient historian*). [French *historien* from Latin (as HISTORY)]

historiated /hɪˈstɔːrɪeɪtɪd/ *adj.* = STORIATED. [medieval Latin *historiare* (as HISTORY)]

historic /hɪˈstɒrɪk/ *adj.* **1** famous or important in history or potentially so (*a historic moment*). **2** *Gram.* (of a tense) normally used in the narration of past events (esp. Latin & Greek imperfect and pluperfect; cf. PRIMARY *adj.* 9). **3** *archaic* or *disp.* = HISTORICAL. [Latin *historicus* from Greek *historikos* (as HISTORY)]

■ **Usage** Note the relatively limited scope of usage of *historic* as compared with *historical*. Apart from the specialist use in grammatical terminology, *historic* is confined to meaning 'famous or important with regards to history', as in *a historic event*.

historical /hɪˈstɒrɪk(ə)l/ *adj.* **1** of or concerning history (*historical evidence*). **2** belonging to history, not to prehistory or legend. **3** (of the study of a subject) based on an analysis of its development over a period. **4** belonging to the past, not the present. **5** (of a novel, a film, etc.) dealing or professing to deal with historical events. **6** in connection with history, from the historian's point of view (*of purely historical interest*). □ **historically** *adv.*

■ **Usage** See Usage Note at HISTORIC.

historic infinitive *n.* the infinitive when used instead of the indicative.

historicism /hɪˈstɒrɪsɪz(ə)m/ *n.* **1 a** the theory that social and cultural phenomena are determined by history. **b** the belief that historical events are governed by laws. **2** the tendency to regard historical development as the most basic aspect of human existence. **3** an excessive regard for past styles etc. □ **historicist** *n.* [HISTORIC, translating German *Historismus*]

historicity /hɪstəˈrɪsɪti/ *n.* the historical genuineness of an event etc.

historic present *n.* the present tense used instead of the past in vivid narration.

historiographer /ˌhɪstɔːrɪˈɒgrəfə, -stɒr-/ *n.* **1** an expert in or student of historiography. **2** a writer of history, esp. an official historian. [Middle English via French *historiographe* or Late Latin *historiographus* from Greek *historiographos* (as HISTORY, -GRAPHER)]

historiography /ˌhɪstɔːrɪˈɒgrəfi, -stɒr-/ *n.* **1** the writing of history. **2** the study of history-writing. □ **historiographic** /-əˈgrafɪk/ *adj.* **historiographical** /-əˈgrafɪk(ə)l/ *adj.* [medieval Latin *historiographia* from Greek (as HISTORY, -GRAPHY)]

history /ˈhɪst(ə)ri/ *n.* (*pl.* **-ies**) **1** a continuous, usu. chronological, record of important or public events. **2 a** the study of past events, esp. human affairs. **b** the total accumulation of past events, esp. relating to human affairs or to the accumulation of developments connected with a particular nation, person, thing, etc. (*our island history*; *the history of astronomy*; *he has a history of illness*). **3** an eventful past (*this house has a history*). **4 a** a systematic or critical account of or research into a past event or events etc. **b** a similar record or account of natural phenomena. **5** a historical play. □ **make history 1** influence the course of history. **2** do something memorable. [Middle English via Latin *historia* from Greek *historia* 'finding out, narrative, history', from *histōr* 'learned, wise man': related to WIT[2]]

histrionic /hɪstrɪˈɒnɪk/ *adj. & n.* ● *adj.* **1** of or concerning actors or acting. **2** (of behaviour) theatrical, dramatic. ● *n.* **1** (in *pl.*) **a** insincere and dramatic behaviour designed to impress. **b** theatricals; theatrical art. **2** *archaic* an actor. □ **histrionically** *adv.* [Late Latin *histrionicus* from Latin *histrio -onis* 'actor']

hit /hɪt/ *v. & n.* ● *v.* (**hitting**; *past* and *past part.* **hit**) **1** *tr.* **a** strike with a blow or a missile. **b** (of a moving body) strike (*the plane hit the ground*). **c** reach (a target, a person, etc.) with a directed missile (*hit the window with the ball*). **2** *tr.* cause to suffer or affect adversely; wound (*the loss hit him hard*). **3** *intr.* (often foll. by *at*, *against*, *upon*) direct a blow. **4** *tr.* (often foll. by *against*, *on*) knock (a part of the body) (*hit his head on the door frame*). **5** *tr.* light upon; get at (a thing aimed at) (*he's hit the truth at last*; *tried to hit the right tone in his apology*) (see *hit on*). **6** *tr. colloq.* **a** encounter (*hit a snag*). **b** arrive at (*hit an all-time low*; *hit the town*). **c** indulge in, esp. liquor etc. (*hit the bottle*). **7** *tr.* esp. *US slang* rob or kill. **8** *tr.* occur forcefully to (*the seriousness of the situation only hit him later*). **9** *tr. Sport* **a** propel (a ball etc.) with a bat etc. to score runs or points. **b** score (runs etc.) in this way. **c** (usu. foll. by *for*) strike (a ball or a bowler) for so many runs (*hit him for six*). **10** *tr.* represent exactly. ● *n.* **1 a** a blow; a stroke. **b** a collision. **2** a shot etc. that hits its target. **3** *colloq.* **a** a popular success, esp. in entertainment. **b** a successful pop record. **4** a stroke of sarcasm, wit, etc. **5** a stroke of good luck. **6** esp. *US slang* **a** a murder or other violent crime. **b** a drug injection etc. **7** a successful attempt. □ **hit-and-miss** aimed or done carelessly or at random. **hit and run** cause (accidental or wilful) damage and escape or leave the scene before being discovered. **hit-and-run** *attrib.adj.* relating to or (of a person) committing an act of this kind. **hit back** retaliate. **hit below the belt 1** esp. *Boxing* give a foul blow. **2** treat or behave unfairly. **hit for six** *Brit.* defeat in argument. **hit the ground running** esp. *N. Amer. colloq.* proceed with enthusiasm and dynamism. **hit the hay** see HAY[1]. **hit the headlines** see HEADLINE. **hit home** make a salutary impression. **hit it off** (often foll. by *with*, *together*) agree or be congenial. **hit the nail on the head** state the truth exactly. **hit on** (or **upon**) find (what is sought), esp. by chance. **hit-or-miss** = *hit-and-miss*. **hit out** deal vigorous physical or verbal blows (*hit out at her enemies*). **hit the road** (*US* **trail**) *slang* depart. **hit the roof** see ROOF. **hit the sack** see SACK[1]. **hit the spot** see SPOT. **hit up** *Cricket* score (runs) energetically. **hit wicket** *Cricket* an infringement involving striking the wicket with the bat etc., resulting in the dismissal of the batsman. **make a hit** (usu. foll. by *with*) be successful or popular. □ **hitter** *n.* [Old English *hittan* from Old Norse *hitta* 'meet with', of unknown origin]

hitch /hɪtʃ/ *v. & n.* ● *v.* **1 a** *tr.* fasten with a loop, hook, etc.; tether (*hitched the horse to the cart*). **b** *intr.* (often foll. by *in*, *on to*, etc.) become fastened in this way (*the rod hitched in to the bracket*). **2** *tr.* move (a thing) with a jerk; shift slightly (*hitched the pillow to a comfortable position*). **3** *colloq.* **a** *intr.* = HITCH-HIKE. **b** *tr.* obtain (a lift) by hitch-hiking. ● *n.* **1** an impediment; a temporary obstacle. **2** an abrupt pull or push; a jerk. **3** a noose or knot of various kinds. **4** *colloq.* a free ride in a vehicle. **5** *N. Amer. slang* a period of service. □ **get hitched** *colloq.* marry. **hitch up** lift (esp. clothing) with a jerk. **hitch one's wagon to a star** make use of powers higher than one's own. □ **hitcher** *n.* [Middle English: origin uncertain]

hitch-hike *v. & n.* ● *v.intr.* travel by seeking free lifts in passing vehicles. ● *n.* a journey made by hitch-hiking. □ **hitch-hiker** *n.*

hi-tech /hʌɪ'tɛk/ *adj.* = HIGH-TECH. [abbreviation]

hither /'hɪðə/ *adv. & adj.* usu. *formal* or *literary* ● *adv.* to or towards this place. ● *adj.* situated on this side; the nearer (of two). [Old English *hider*: cf. THITHER]

hither and thither *adv.* (also **hither and yon**) in various directions; to and fro.

hitherto /hɪðə'tuː, 'hɪðətuː/ *adv.* until this time, up to now.

hitherward /'hɪðəwəd/ *adv. archaic* in this direction.

Hitler /'hɪtlə/ *n.* a person who embodies the authoritarian characteristics of Adolf Hitler, German Nazi dictator d. 1945. □ **Hitlerite** /-rʌɪt/ *n. & adj.*

Hitlerism /'hɪtlərɪz(ə)m/ *n.* the political principles or policy of the Nazi Party in Germany. [HITLER]

hit list *n. slang* a list of prospective victims.

hit man *n.* (*pl.* **hit men**) *slang* a male hired assassin.

hit-out *n. Austral. slang* a brisk gallop.

hit parade *n. colloq.* a list of the current best-selling records of popular music.

Hittite /'hɪtʌɪt/ *n. & adj.* ● *n.* **1** a member of an ancient people of Asia Minor and Syria. **2** the language of the Hittites. ● *adj.* of or relating to the Hittites or their language. [Hebrew *Ḥittīm*]

hit woman *n.* (*pl.* **hit women**) *slang* a female hired assassin.

HIV *abbr.* human immunodeficiency virus, a retrovirus which causes Aids.

hive /hʌɪv/ *n. & v.* ● *n.* **1 a** a beehive. **b** the bees in a hive. **2** a busy swarming place. **3** a swarming multitude. **4** a thing shaped like a hive in being domed. ● *v.* **1** *tr.* **a** place (bees) in a hive. **b** house (people etc.) snugly. **2** *intr.* **a** enter a hive. **b** live together like bees. □ **hive off** esp. *Brit.* **1** separate from a larger group. **2 a** form into or assign (work) to a subsidiary department or company. **b** denationalize or privatize (an industry etc.). **hive up** hoard. [Old English *hȳf*, from Germanic]

hives /hʌɪvz/ *n.pl.* **1** a skin eruption, esp. nettle-rash. **2** *Brit.* inflammation of the larynx etc. [16th c. (originally Scots): origin unknown]

hiya /'hʌɪjə/ *int. colloq.* a word used in greeting. [corruption of *how are you?*]

HK *abbr.* Hong Kong.

HL *abbr.* (in the UK) House of Lords.

hl *abbr.* hectolitre(s).

HM *abbr. Brit.* **1** Her (or His) Majesty('s). **2 a** headmaster. **b** headmistress. **3** *Mus.* heavy metal.

hm *abbr.* hectometre(s).

h'm /hm/ *int. & n.* (also **hmm**) = HEM[2], HUM[2].

HMG *abbr.* (in the UK) Her or His Majesty's Government.

HMI *abbr.* (in the UK) Her or His Majesty's Inspector (of Schools).

HMS *abbr.* (in the UK) Her or His Majesty's Ship.

HMSO *abbr.* (in the UK) Her or His Majesty's Stationery Office.

HMV *abbr.* (in the UK) His Master's Voice.

HNC *abbr.* (in the UK) Higher National Certificate.

HND *abbr.* (in the UK) Higher National Diploma.

Ho *symb. Chem.* the element holmium.

ho /həʊ/ *int.* **1 a** an expression of admiration or (often repeated as **ho! ho!** etc.) derision, surprise, or triumph. **b** (in *comb.*) the second element of various exclamations (*heigh-ho*; *what ho*). **2** a call for attention. **3** (in *comb.*) *Naut.* an addition to the name of a destination etc. (*westward ho*). [Middle English, imitative: cf. Old Norse *hó*]

ho. *abbr.* house.

hoar /hɔː/ *adj. & n. literary* ● *adj.* **1** grey-haired with age. **2** greyish white. **3** (of a thing) grey with age. ● *n.* **1** = HOAR FROST. **2** hoariness. [Old English *hār*, from Germanic]

hoard /hɔːd/ *n. & v.* ● *n.* **1** a stock or store (esp. of money) laid by. **2** an amassed store of facts etc. **3** *Archaeol.* an ancient store of treasure etc. ● *v.* **1** *tr.* (often *absol.*; often foll. by *up*) amass (money etc.) and put away; store. **2** *intr.* accumulate more than one's current requirements of food etc. in a time of scarcity. **3** *tr.* store in the mind. □ **hoarder** *n.* [Old English *hord*, from Germanic]

hoarding /'hɔːdɪŋ/ *n.* **1** *Brit.* a large, usu. wooden, structure used to carry advertisements etc. **2** a board fence erected round a building site etc., often used for displaying posters etc. [obsolete *hoard* via Anglo-French *h(o)urdis* from Old French *hourd*, *hort*, related to HURDLE]

hoar frost *n.* frozen water vapour deposited in clear still weather on vegetation etc.

hoarhound var. of HOREHOUND.

hoarse /hɔːs/ *adj.* **1** (of the voice) rough and deep; husky; croaking. **2** having such a voice. □ **hoarsely** *adv.* **hoarsen** *v.tr. & intr.* **hoarseness** *n.* [Old English *hās*, influenced by Old Norse, from Germanic]

hoarstone /'hɔːstəʊn/ *n. Brit.* an ancient boundary stone.

hoary /'hɔːri/ *adj.* (**hoarier**, **hoariest**) **1 a** (of hair) grey or white with age. **b** having such hair; aged. **2** old and trite (*a hoary joke*). **3** *Bot. & Zool.* covered with short white hairs. □ **hoarily** *adv.* **hoariness** *n.*

hoatzin /həʊ'atsɪn/ *n.* a tropical American bird, *Opisthocomus hoatzin*, whose young climb by means of hooked claws on their wings. [native name, imitative]

hoax /həʊks/ *n. & v.* ● *n.* a humorous or malicious deception; a practical joke. ● *v.tr.* deceive (a person) with a hoax. □ **hoaxer** *n.* [18th c.: probably contraction from HOCUS]

hob[1] /hɒb/ *n.* **1 a** *Brit.* a cooking appliance or the flat top part of a cooker, with hotplates or burners. **b** a flat metal shelf at the side of a fireplace, having its surface level with the top of the grate, used esp. for heating a pan etc. **2** a tool used for cutting gears etc. **3** a peg or pin used as a mark in quoits etc. **4** = HOBNAIL. [perhaps variant of HUB]

hob[2] /hɒb/ *n.* **1** a male ferret. **2** a hobgoblin. □ **play** (or **raise**) **hob** *US* cause mischief. [Middle English, familiar form of *Rob*, short for *Robin* or *Robert*]

hobbit /ˈhɒbɪt/ *n.* a member of an imaginary race similar to humans, of small size and with hairy feet, in stories by J.R.R. Tolkien. □ **hobbitry** *n.* [invented by Tolkien, English writer d. 1973, and said by him to mean 'hole-dweller']

hobble /ˈhɒb(ə)l/ *v.* & *n.* ● *v.* **1** *intr.* **a** walk lamely; limp. **b** proceed haltingly in action or speech (*hobbled lamely to his conclusion*). **2** *tr.* **a** tie together the legs of (a horse etc.) to prevent it from straying. **b** tie (a horse's etc. legs). **3** *tr.* cause (a person etc.) to limp. ● *n.* **1** an uneven or infirm gait. **2** a rope, clog, etc. used for hobbling a horse etc. □ **hobbler** *n.* [Middle English, probably from Low German: cf. HOPPLE and Dutch *hobbelen* 'rock from side to side']

hobbledehoy /ˈhɒb(ə)ldɪˌhɔɪ/ *n.* *colloq.* **1** a clumsy or awkward youth. **2** a hooligan. [16th c.: origin unknown]

hobble skirt *n.* a skirt so narrow at the hem as to impede walking.

hobby[1] /ˈhɒbi/ *n.* (*pl.* **-ies**) **1** a favourite leisure-time activity or occupation. **2** *archaic* a small horse. **3** *hist.* an early type of velocipede. □ **hobbyist** *n.* [Middle English *hobyn*, *hoby*, from pet forms of *Robin*: cf. DOBBIN]

hobby[2] /ˈhɒbi/ *n.* (*pl.* **-ies**) any of several small long-winged falcons, esp. *Falco subbuteo*, catching prey on the wing. [Middle English from Old French *hobé*, *hobet*, diminutive of *hobe* 'falcon']

hobby horse *n.* **1** a child's toy consisting of a stick with a horse's head. **2** a preoccupation; a favourite topic of conversation. **3** a model of a horse, esp. of wicker, used in morris dancing etc. **4** a rocking horse. **5** a horse on a merry-go-round.

hobday /ˈhɒbdeɪ/ *v.tr.* *Brit.* operate on (a horse) to improve its breathing. [named after F. T. *Hobday*, British veterinary surgeon d. 1939]

hobgoblin /ˈhɒbɡɒblɪn/ *n.* a mischievous imp; a bogey; a bugbear. [HOB[2] + GOBLIN]

hobnail /ˈhɒbneɪl/ *n.* a heavy-headed nail used for boot-soles. □ **hobnailed** *adj.* [HOB[1] + NAIL]

hobnail liver *n.* (also **hobnailed liver**) a liver having many small knobbly projections due to cirrhosis.

hobnob /ˈhɒbnɒb/ *v.intr.* (**hobnobbed**, **hobnobbing**) **1** (usu. foll. by *with*) mix socially or informally. **2** drink together. [*hob or nob* = give or take, of alternate drinking; earlier *hab nab*, = have or not have]

hobo /ˈhəʊbəʊ/ *n.* (*pl.* **-oes** or **-os**) *N. Amer.* a wandering worker; a tramp. [19th c.: origin unknown]

Hobson's choice /ˈhɒbs(ə)nz/ *n.* a choice of taking the thing offered or nothing. [from T. *Hobson*, Cambridge carrier (d. 1631), who let out horses on the basis that customers must take the one nearest the door]

hock[1] /hɒk/ *n.* **1** the joint of a quadruped's hind leg between the knee and the fetlock. **2** a knuckle of pork; the lower joint of a ham. [obsolete *hockshin* from Old English *hōhsinu*: see HOUGH]

hock[2] /hɒk/ *n.* *Brit.* a German white wine from the Rhineland (properly that of Hochheim on the river Main). [abbreviation of obsolete *hockamore* from German *Hochheimer*]

hock[3] /hɒk/ *v.* & *n.* esp. *N. Amer. slang* ● *v.tr.* pawn; pledge. ● *n.* a pawnbroker's pledge. □ **in hock 1** in pawn. **2** in debt. **3** in prison. [Dutch *hok* 'hutch, prison, debt']

hockey[1] /ˈhɒki/ *n.* **1** *Brit.* a game played between two teams on a field with curved sticks and a small hard ball. **2** *N. Amer.* = ICE HOCKEY. □ **hockeyist** *n.* *N. Amer.* (in sense 2). [16th c.: origin unknown]

hockey[2] var. of OCHE.

Hocktide /ˈhɒktʌɪd/ *n.* *Brit. hist.* a festival formerly kept on the second Monday and Tuesday after Easter, originally for money-raising. [Middle English: origin unknown]

hocus /ˈhəʊkəs/ *v.tr.* (**hocussed**, **hocussing** or **hocused**, **hocusing**) **1** take in; hoax. **2** stupefy (a person) with drugs. **3** drug (liquor). [obsolete noun *hocus* = HOCUS-POCUS]

hocus-pocus /həʊkəsˈpəʊkəs/ *n.* & *v.* ● *n.* **1** deception; trickery. **2** a typical verbal formula used in conjuring. ● *v.* (**-pocussed**, **-pocussing** or **-pocused**, **-pocusing**) **1** *intr.* (often foll. by *with*) play tricks. **2** *tr.* play tricks on, deceive. [17th-c. sham Latin]

hod /hɒd/ *n.* **1** a V-shaped open trough on a pole used for carrying bricks, mortar, etc. **2** a portable receptacle for coal. [probably = dialect *hot* from Old French *hotte* 'pannier', from Germanic]

hodden /ˈhɒd(ə)n/ *n.* *Sc.* a coarse woollen cloth. [16th c.: origin unknown]

hodden grey *n.* *Sc.* grey hodden; typical rustic clothing.

Hodge /hɒdʒ/ *n.* *Brit.* a typical English agricultural labourer. [pet form of the name *Roger*]

hodgepodge /ˈhɒdʒpɒdʒ/ *n.* = HOTCHPOTCH 1, 2. [Middle English, assimilated to HODGE]

Hodgkin's disease /ˈhɒdʒkɪnz/ *n.* a malignant disease of lymphatic tissues usu. characterized by enlargement of the lymph nodes. [named after T. *Hodgkin*, English physician d. 1866]

hodiernal /hɒdɪˈəːn(ə)l, həʊ-/ *adj.* *formal* of the present day. [Latin *hodiernus* from *hodie* 'today']

hodman /ˈhɒdman/ *n.* (*pl.* **-men**) *Brit.* **1** a labourer who carries a hod. **2** a literary hack. **3** a person who works mechanically.

hodograph /ˈhɒdəɡrɑːf/ *n.* a curve in which the radius vector represents the velocity of a moving particle. [Greek *hodos* 'way' + -GRAPH]

hodometer var. of ODOMETER.

hoe /həʊ/ *n.* & *v.* ● *n.* a long-handled tool with a thin metal blade, used for weeding etc. ● *v.* (**hoes**, **hoed**, **hoeing**) **1** *tr.* weed (crops); loosen (earth); dig up or cut down with a hoe. **2** *intr.* use a hoe. □ **hoe in** *Austral.* & *NZ slang* eat eagerly. **hoe into** *Austral.* & *NZ slang* attack (food, a person, a task). □ **hoer** *n.* [Middle English *howe* from Old French *houe*, from Germanic]

hoecake /ˈhəʊkeɪk/ *n.* *US* a coarse cake of maize flour originally baked on the blade of a hoe.

hoedown /ˈhəʊdaʊn/ *n.* *N. Amer.* **1 a** a lively folk dance. **b** the music for this. **2** a party at which such dancing takes place.

hog /hɒɡ/ *n.* & *v.* ● *n.* **1 a** a domesticated pig, esp. a castrated male reared for slaughter. **b** any of several other pigs of the family Suidae, e.g. a warthog. **2** *colloq.* a greedy person. **3** (also **hogg**) *Brit. dial.* a young sheep before the first shearing. ● *v.* (**hogged**, **hogging**) **1** *tr.* *colloq.* take greedily; hoard selfishly; monopolize. **2** *tr.* & *intr.* raise (the back), or rise in an arch in the centre. □ **go the whole hog** *colloq.* do something completely or thoroughly. **hog-tie** *N. Amer.* **1** secure by fastening the hands and feet or all four feet together. **2** restrain, impede. □ **hogger** *n.* **hoggery** *n.* **hoggish** *adj.* **hoggishly** *adv.* **hoglike** *adj.* [Old English *hogg*, *hocg*, perhaps of Celtic origin]

hogan /ˈhəʊɡ(ə)n/ *n.* an American Indian hut of logs etc. [Navajo]

hogback /ˈhɒɡbak/ *n.* (also **hog's back**) a steep-sided ridge of a hill.

hogg var. of HOG *n.* 3.

hogget /ˈhɒɡɪt/ *n.* *Brit.* a yearling sheep. [HOG]

hoggin /ˈhɒɡɪn/ *n.* **1** a mixture of sand and gravel. **2** sifted gravel. [19th c.: origin unknown]

hogmanay /ˈhɒɡmәneɪ, hɒɡməˈneɪ/ *n.* *Sc.* **1** New Year's Eve. **2** a celebration on this day. **3** a gift of cake etc.

demanded by children at hogmanay. [17th c.: perhaps from Norman French *hoguinané* from Old French *aguillanneuf* (also = new year's gift)]

hog's back var. of HOGBACK.

hogshead /'hɒgzhɛd/ *n.* **1** a large cask. **2** a liquid or dry measure, usu. about 50 imperial gallons. [Middle English from HOG, HEAD: reason for the name unknown]

hogwash /'hɒgwɒʃ/ *n.* **1** *colloq.* nonsense, rubbish. **2** kitchen swill etc. for pigs.

hogweed /'hɒgwi:d/ *n.* any of various coarse weeds of the genus *Heracleum*, esp. *H. sphondylium*.

ho ho *int.* **1** representing deep jolly laughter. **2** expressing surprise, triumph, or derision. [reduplication of HO]

ho-hum /həʊ'hʌm/ *int.* expressing boredom. [imitative of yawn]

hoick[1] /hɔɪk/ *v. & n. Brit. colloq.* ● *v.tr.* (often foll. by *out*) lift or pull, esp. with a jerk. ● *n.* a jerky pull; a jerk. [perhaps a variant of HIKE]

hoick[2] /hɔɪk/ *v.intr. Brit. slang* spit. [probably imitative; perhaps a variant of HAWK[3]]

hoicks var. of YOICKS.

hoi polloi /hɔɪ pɒ'lɔɪ/ *n.* (often prec. by *the* : see note below) **1** the masses; the common people. **2** the majority. [Greek, = the many]

■ **Usage** The use of *hoi polloi* with *the* is strictly unnecessary, since *hoi* = 'the', but this construction is very common.

hoist /hɔɪst/ *v. & n.* ● *v.tr.* **1** raise or haul up. **2** raise by means of ropes and pulleys etc. ● *n.* **1** an act of hoisting, a lift. **2** an apparatus for hoisting. **3 a** the part of a flag nearest the staff. **b** a group of flags raised as a signal. □ **hoist the flag** stake one's claim to discovered territory by displaying a flag. **hoist one's flag** signify that one takes command. **hoist with one's own petard** see PETARD. □ **hoister** *n.* [Middle English: alteration of *hoise*, probably of Low German origin]

hoity-toity /hɔɪtɪ'tɔɪti/ *adj., int., & n.* ● *adj.* **1** haughty; petulant; snobbish. **2** *archaic* frolicsome. ● *int.* expressing surprised protest at presumption etc. ● *n. archaic* riotous or giddy conduct. [obsolete *hoit* 'indulge in riotous mirth', of unknown origin]

hokey /'həʊki/ *adj.* (also **hoky**) (**hokier**, **hokiest**) *N. Amer. slang* sentimental, melodramatic, artificial. □ **hokeyness** *n.* (also **hokiness**). [HOKUM + -Y[2]]

hokey-cokey /həʊkɪ'kəʊki/ *n. Brit.* a communal dance performed in a circle with synchronized shaking of the limbs in turn. [perhaps from HOCUS-POCUS]

hokey-pokey /həʊkɪ'pəʊki/ *n. colloq.* **1** = HOCUS-POCUS *n.* 1. **2** ice cream formerly sold esp. by Italian street vendors. [HOCUS-POCUS: sense 2 of unknown origin]

hoki /'həʊki/ *n.* an edible marine fish, *Macruronus novaezelandiae*, related to the hake and native to the southern coasts of New Zealand. [Maori]

hokku /'hɒku:/ *n.* (*pl.* same) = HAIKU. [Japanese]

hokum /'həʊkəm/ *n.* esp. *US slang* **1** sentimental, popular, sensational, or unreal situations, dialogue, etc., in a film or play etc. **2** bunkum; rubbish. [20th c.: origin unknown]

hoky var. of HOKEY.

Holarctic /hə(ʊ)'lɑ:ktɪk/ *adj. & n.* (also **holarctic**) ● *adj.* of, relating to, or found throughout the Nearctic and Palaearctic regions considered together as a single zoogeographical region. ● *n.* the Holarctic region. [HOLO- + ARCTIC]

hold[1] /həʊld/ *v. & n.* ● *v.* (*past* and *past part.* **held** /hɛld/) **1** *tr.* **a** keep fast; grasp (esp. in the hands or arms). **b** (also *refl.*) keep or sustain (a thing, oneself, one's head, etc.) in a particular position (*hold it to the light*; *held himself erect*). **c** grasp so as to control (*hold the reins*). **2** *tr.* (of a vessel etc.) contain or be capable of containing (*the jug holds two pints*; *the hall holds 900*). **3** *tr.* possess, gain, or have, esp.: **a** be the owner or tenant of (land, property, stocks, etc.) (*holds the farm from the trust*). **b** gain or have gained (a degree, record, etc.) (*holds the long jump record*). **c** have the position of (a job or office). **d** have (a specified playing card) in one's hand. **e** keep possession of (a place, a person's thoughts, etc.), esp. against attack (*held the fort against the enemy*; *held his place in her estimation*). **4** *intr.* remain unbroken; not give way (*the roof held under the storm*). **5** *tr.* observe; celebrate; conduct (a meeting, festival, conversation, etc.). **6** *tr.* **a** keep (a person etc.) in a specified condition, place, etc. (*held him prisoner*; *held him at arm's length*). **b** detain, esp. in custody (*hold him until I arrive*). **7** *tr.* **a** engross (a person or a person's attention) (*the book held him for hours*). **b** dominate (*held the stage*). **8** *tr.* (foll. by *to*) make (a person etc.) adhere to (terms, a promise, etc.). **9** *intr.* (of weather) continue fine. **10** *tr.* (often foll. by *to* + infin., or *that* + clause) think; believe (*held it to be self-evident*; *held that the earth was flat*). **11** *tr.* regard with a specified feeling (*held him in contempt*). **12** *tr.* **a** cease; restrain (*hold your fire*). **b** *US colloq.* withhold; not use (*a burger please, and hold the onions!*). **13** *tr.* keep or reserve (*will you hold our seats please?*). **14** *tr.* be able to drink (liquor) without effect (*can't hold his drink*). **15** *tr.* (usu. foll. by *that* + clause) (of a judge, a court, etc.) lay down; decide. **16** *intr.* keep going (*held on his way*). **17** *tr. Mus.* sustain (a note). **18** *intr.* = *hold the line* 2. **19** *intr. archaic* restrain oneself. ● *n.* **1** a grasp (*catch hold of him*; *keep a hold on him*). **2** (often in *comb.*) a thing to hold by (*seized the handhold*). **3** (foll. by *on, over*) influence over (*has a strange hold over them*). **4** a manner of holding in wrestling etc. **5** *archaic* a fortress. □ **hold (a thing) against (a person)** resent or regard it as discreditable to (a person). **hold aloof** avoid communication with people etc. **hold back 1** impede the progress of; restrain. **2** keep (a thing) to or for oneself. **3** (often foll. by *from*) hesitate; refrain. **hold one's breath** see BREATH. **hold by** (or **to**) adhere to (a choice, purpose, etc.). **hold cheap** *Brit.* not value highly; despise. **hold the clock on** time (a sporting event etc.). **hold court** preside over one's admirers etc., like a sovereign. **hold dear** regard with affection. **hold down 1** repress. **2** *colloq.* be competent enough to keep (one's job etc.). **hold everything!** (or **it!**) cease action or movement. **hold the fort 1** act as a temporary substitute. **2** cope in an emergency. **hold forth 1** offer (an inducement etc.). **2** usu. *derog.* speak at length or tediously. **hold good** (or **true**) be valid; apply. **hold one's ground** see GROUND[1]. **hold one's hand** see HAND. **hold a person's hand** give a person guidance or moral support. **hold hands** grasp one another by the hand as a sign of affection or for support or guidance. **hold hard!** *Brit.* stop!; wait! **hold harmless** *Law* indemnify. **hold one's head high** behave proudly and confidently. **hold one's horses** *colloq.* stop; slow down. **hold in** keep in check, confine. **hold it good** think it advisable. **hold the line 1** not yield. **2** maintain a telephone connection. **hold one's nose** compress the nostrils to avoid inhaling a smell, water, etc. **hold off 1** delay; not begin. **2** keep one's distance. **hold on 1** keep one's grasp on something. **2** wait a moment. **3** (when telephoning) not ring off. **hold out 1** stretch forth (a hand etc.). **2** offer (an inducement etc.). **3** maintain resistance. **4** persist or last. **hold out for** continue to demand. **hold out on** *colloq.* refuse something to (a person). **hold over** postpone. **hold something over** threaten (a person) constantly with something. **hold one's own** see OWN. **hold to bail** *Law* bind by bail. **hold to a draw** *Sport* manage to achieve a draw against (an opponent thought likely to win). **hold together 1** cohere. **2** cause to cohere. **hold one's tongue** *colloq.* be silent. **hold to ransom** *Brit.* **1** keep (a person) prisoner until a ransom is paid. **2** demand concessions from by threats of damaging action. **hold up 1 a** support; sustain. **b** maintain (the head etc.) erect. **2** exhibit; display. **3** arrest the progress of; obstruct. **4** stop and rob by violence or threats. **hold water** (of reasoning) be sound; bear examination. **hold with** (usu. with *neg.*) *colloq.* approve of (*don't hold with motorbikes*). **left holding the baby** (or *US* **bag**) left with unwelcome responsibility. **on hold 1** (when telephoning) holding the line. **2** (esp. in phr. **put on hold**) temporarily inactive or receiving little attention. **take hold** (of a custom or habit) become established. **there is no holding him** (or **her** etc.) he (or she etc.) is restive, high-spirited, determined, etc. **with no holds barred** with no restrictions, all methods being permitted. □ **holdable** *adj.* [Old English *h(e)aldan, heald*]

hold[2] /həʊld/ *n.* a cavity in the lower part of a ship or aircraft in which the cargo is stowed. [obsolete *holl* from Old English *hol* (originally adj. = hollow), related to HOLE, assimilated to HOLD[1]]

holdall /ˈhəʊldɔːl/ *n. Brit.* a portable case or bag for miscellaneous articles.

holdback /ˈhəʊl(d)bak/ *n.* **1** something serving to hold a thing in place. **2** a hindrance.

holder /ˈhəʊldə/ *n.* **1** (often in *comb.*) a device or implement for holding something (*cigarette-holder*). **2 a** the possessor of a title etc. **b** the occupant of an office etc. **3** = SMALLHOLDER.

holdfast /ˈhəʊl(d)fɑːst/ *n.* **1** a firm grasp. **2** a staple or clamp securing an object to a wall etc. **3** the attachment-organ of an alga etc.

holding /ˈhəʊldɪŋ/ *n.* **1 a** land held by lease (cf. SMALLHOLDING). **b** the tenure of land. **2** stocks, property, etc. held.

holding company *n.* a company created to hold the shares of other companies, which it then controls.

holding operation *n.* a manoeuvre designed to maintain the status quo.

holding pattern *n.* **1** *Aeron.* the (usu. circular) flight path maintained by an aircraft awaiting permission to land. **2** a state or period of no progress or change.

holdout /ˈhəʊldaʊt/ *n.* **1** an act of holding out against some trend, or of staying out of some activity. **2** a person who does this, esp. *N. Amer.* a baseball player who refuses to play until paid more.

hold-over *n.* esp. *N. Amer.* a relic.

hold-up *n.* **1** a stoppage or delay by traffic, fog, etc. **2** a robbery, esp. by the use of threats or violence. **3** each of a pair of stockings held up by elasticated tops rather than by suspenders.

hole /həʊl/ *n.* & *v.* ● *n.* **1 a** an empty space in a solid body. **b** an aperture in or through something. **2** an animal's burrow. **3** a cavity or receptacle into which the ball must be propelled in various sports or games, e.g. golf. **4** *colloq.* a small, mean, or dingy abode. **5** *colloq.* an awkward situation. **6** *Golf* **a** a point scored by a player who gets the ball from tee to hole with the fewest strokes. **b** the terrain or distance from tee to hole. **7** a position from which an electron is absent, esp. acting as a mobile positive particle in a semiconductor. ● *v.* **1** *tr.* make a hole or holes in. **2** *tr.* pierce the side of (a ship). **3** *tr.* put into a hole. **4 a** *tr. Golf* send (the ball) into a hole. **b** *intr.* (usu. foll. by *out*) *Golf* send the ball into a hole. **c** *intr.* (foll. by *out*) *Cricket* (of a batsman) be caught. □ **hole up** *N. Amer. colloq.* hide oneself. **in holes** worn so much that holes have formed. **make a hole in** use a large amount of. **a square** (or **round**) **peg in a round** (or **square**) **hole** see PEG. □ **holey** *adj.* [Old English *hol, holian* (as HOLD[2])]

hole-and-corner *adj.* secret; underhand.

hole-in-one *n.* (*pl.* **holes-in-one**) *Golf* a shot that enters the hole from the tee.

hole in the heart *n.* a congenital defect in the heart septum.

hole in the wall *n. Brit.* **1** a small dingy place (esp. of business). **2** *colloq.* an automatic cash dispenser installed in the outside wall of a bank etc.

hole-proof *adj.* (of materials etc.) treated so as to be resistant to wear.

holiday /ˈhɒlɪdeɪ, -di/ *n.* & *v.* ● *n.* **1** (often in *pl.*) esp. *Brit.* an extended period of recreation, esp. away from home or in travelling; a break from work (cf. VACATION *n.* 1, 2). **2** a day of festivity or recreation when no work is done, esp. a religious festival etc. **3** (*attrib.*) (of clothes etc.) festive. ● *v.intr.* esp. *Brit.* spend a holiday. □ **on holiday** (or **one's holidays**) *Brit.* in the course of one's holiday; having a break from work. **take a** (or *archaic* **make**) **holiday** have a break from work. [Old English *hāligdæg* (HOLY, DAY)]

holiday camp *n. Brit.* a camp for holidaymakers with accommodation, entertainment, and facilities on site.

holiday centre *n. Brit.* a place with many tourist attractions.

holidaymaker /ˈhɒlɪdeɪˌmeɪkə, -dɪ-/ *n.* esp. *Brit.* a person on holiday.

holiday village *n. Brit.* a modern holiday camp.

holier-than-thou *adj. colloq.* self-righteous.

holily /ˈhəʊlɪli/ *adv.* in a holy manner. [Old English *hāliglīce* (as HOLY)]

holiness /ˈhəʊlɪnɪs/ *n.* **1** sanctity; the state of being holy. **2** (**Holiness**) a title used when referring to or addressing the pope. [Old English *hālignes* (as HOLY)]

holism /ˈhəʊlɪz(ə)m, ˈhɒl-/ *n.* (also **wholism**) **1** *Philos.* the theory that certain wholes are to be regarded as greater than the sum of their parts (cf. REDUCTIONISM 2). **2** *Med.* the treating of the whole person including mental and social factors rather than just the symptoms of a disease. □ **holist** *adj.* & *n.* **holistic** /-ˈlɪstɪk/ *adj.* **holistically** /-ˈlɪstɪk(ə)li/ *adv.* [as HOLO- + -ISM]

holla /ˈhɒlə/ *int., n.,* & *v.* ● *int.* calling attention. ● *n.* a cry of 'holla'. ● *v.* (**hollas, hollaed** or **holla'd, hollaing**) **1** *intr.* shout. **2** *tr.* call to (hounds). [French *holà* (as HO, *là* 'there')]

holland /ˈhɒlənd/ *n.* a smooth hard-wearing linen fabric. [*Holland* = Netherlands: Dutch, earlier *Holtlant* from *holt* 'wood' + *-lant* 'land', describing the Dordrecht district, where the cloth was made]

hollandaise sauce /hɒlənˈdeɪz, ˈhɒl-/ *n.* a creamy sauce of melted butter, egg yolks, vinegar, etc., served esp. with fish. [French, fem. of *hollandais* 'Dutch', from *Hollande* 'Holland']

Hollander /ˈhɒləndə/ *n.* **1** a native of Holland (the Netherlands). **2** a Dutch ship.

Hollands /ˈhɒləndz/ *n. archaic* Dutch gin. [Dutch *hollandsch genever* 'Dutch gin']

holler /ˈhɒlə/ *v.* & *n. dial.* or *N. Amer. colloq.* ● *v.* **1** *intr.* make a loud cry or noise. **2** *tr.* express with a loud cry or shout. ● *n.* a loud cry, noise, or shout. [variant of HOLLO]

hollo /ˈhɒləʊ/ *int., n.,* & *v.* ● *int.* = HOLLA. ● *n.* (*pl.* **-os**) = HOLLA. ● *v.* (**-oes, -oed**) (also **hollow** *pronunc.* same) = HOLLA. [related to HOLLA]

hollow /ˈhɒləʊ/ *adj., n., v.,* & *adv.* ● *adj.* **1 a** having a hole or cavity inside; not solid throughout. **b** having a depression; sunken (*hollow cheeks*). **2** (of a sound) echoing, as though made in or on a hollow container. **3** empty; hungry. **4** without significance; meaningless (*a hollow triumph*). **5** insincere; cynical; false (*a hollow laugh; hollow promises*). ● *n.* **1** a hollow place; a hole. **2** a valley; a basin. ● *v.tr.* (often foll. by *out*) make hollow; excavate. ● *adv. colloq.* completely (*beaten hollow*). □ **in the hollow of one's hand** entirely subservient to one. □ **hollowly** *adv.* **hollowness** *n.* [Old English *holh* 'cave', related to HOLE]

hollow-cheeked *adj.* with sunken cheeks.

hollow-eyed *adj.* with eyes deep sunk.

hollow-hearted *adj.* insincere.

hollow square *n. hist.* a body of infantry drawn up in a square with a space in the middle.

hollowware /ˈhɒləʊwɛː/ *n.* hollow articles of metal, china, etc., such as pots, kettles, jugs, etc. (opp. FLATWARE 1).

holly /ˈhɒli/ *n.* (*pl.* **-ies**) **1** an evergreen shrub, *Ilex aquifolium*, with prickly usu. dark green leaves, small white flowers, and red berries. **2** its branches and foliage used as decorations at Christmas. [Old English *hole(g)n*]

hollyhock /ˈhɒlɪhɒk/ *n.* a tall plant, *Alcea rosea* (mallow family), with large showy flowers of various colours. [originally = marsh mallow: Middle English from HOLY

+ obsolete *hock* 'mallow', from Old English *hoc*, of unknown origin]

holly oak *n.* a holm-oak.

Hollywood /ˈhɒlɪwʊd/ *n.* the American cinema industry or its products, with its principal centre at Hollywood in California.

holm[1] /həʊm/ *n.* (also **holme**) *Brit.* **1** an islet, esp. in a river or near a mainland. **2** a piece of flat ground by a river, which is submerged in time of flood. [Old Norse *holmr*]

holm[2] /həʊm/ *n.* (in full **holm-oak**) an evergreen oak, *Quercus ilex*, with holly-like young leaves. [Middle English, alteration of obsolete *holin* (as HOLLY)]

holmium /ˈhəʊlmɪəm/ *n. Chem.* a soft silvery metallic element of the lanthanide series occurring naturally in apatite (symbol **Ho**). [modern Latin from *Holmia* 'Stockholm']

holo- /ˈhɒləʊ/ *comb. form* whole (*Holocene*; *holocaust*). [Greek *holos* 'whole']

holocaust /ˈhɒləkɔːst/ *n.* **1** a case of large-scale destruction, esp. by fire or nuclear war. **2** (**the Holocaust**) the mass murder of the Jews by the Nazis 1941–5. **3** a sacrifice wholly consumed by fire. [Middle English via Old French *holocauste* and Late Latin *holocaustum* from Greek *holokauston* (as HOLO-, *kaustos* 'burnt' from *kaiō* 'burn')]

Holocene /ˈhɒləsiːn/ *adj. & n. Geol.* ● *adj.* of or relating to the most recent epoch of the Quaternary period, marked by the development of human culture. Cf. Appendix X. ● *n.* this period or system. Also called *Recent*. [HOLO- + Greek *kainos* 'new']

holoenzyme /hɒləʊˈɛnzʌɪm/ *n. Biochem.* the active complex of an enzyme with a coenzyme.

hologram /ˈhɒləgram/ *n. Physics* **1** a three-dimensional image formed by the interference of light beams from a coherent light source. **2** a photograph of the interference pattern, which when suitably illuminated produces a three-dimensional image.

holograph /ˈhɒləgrɑːf/ *adj. & n.* ● *adj.* wholly written by hand by the person named as the author. ● *n.* a holograph document. [French *holographe* or Late Latin *holographus* from Greek *holographos* (as HOLO-, -GRAPH)]

holography /hɒˈlɒgrəfi/ *n. Physics* the study or production of holograms. □ **holographic** /-ləˈgrafɪk/ *adj.* **holographically** /-ləˈgrafɪk(ə)li/ *adv.*

holohedral /hɒləˈhiːdr(ə)l, -ˈhɛd-/ *adj. Crystallog.* having the full number of planes required by the symmetry of a crystal system.

holophyte /ˈhɒləfʌɪt/ *n.* an organism that synthesizes complex organic compounds by photosynthesis. □ **holophytic** /-ˈfɪtɪk/ *adj.*

holothurian /hɒlə(ʊ)ˈθjʊərɪən/ *n. & adj.* ● *n.* any echinoderm of the class Holothuroidea, with a wormlike body, e.g. a sea cucumber. ● *adj.* of or relating to this class. [modern Latin *Holothuria* (n.pl.) from Greek *holothourion*, a zoophyte]

holotype /ˈhɒlətʌɪp/ *n.* the specimen used for naming and describing a species.

hols /hɒlz/ *n.pl. Brit. colloq.* holidays. [abbreviation]

Holstein /ˈhɒlstʌɪn, -iːn/ *n. & adj. N. Amer.* = FRIESIAN. [*Holstein* in NW Germany]

holster /ˈhəʊlstə, ˈhɒl-/ *n.* a leather case for a pistol or revolver, worn on a belt or under an arm or fixed to a saddle. [17th c., synonymous with Dutch *holster*: origin unknown]

holt[1] /həʊlt/ *n. Brit.* **1** an animal's (esp. an otter's) lair. **2** *colloq.* or *dial.* grip, hold. [variant of HOLD[1]]

holt[2] /həʊlt/ *n. archaic* or *dial.* **1** a wood or copse. **2** a wooded hill. [Old English from Germanic]

holus-bolus /həʊləsˈbəʊləs/ *adv.* all in a lump, altogether. [apparently sham Latin, perhaps = 'whole lump': cf. BOLUS]

holy /ˈhəʊli/ *adj.* (**holier**, **holiest**) **1** morally and spiritually excellent or perfect, and to be revered. **2** belonging to, devoted to, or empowered by, God. **3** consecrated, sacred. **4** used in trivial exclamations (*holy cow!*; *holy mackerel!*; *holy Moses!*; *holy smoke!*). [Old English *hālig* from Germanic: related to WHOLE]

Holy City *n.* **1** a city held sacred by the adherents of a religion, esp. Jerusalem. **2** Heaven.

Holy Communion see COMMUNION 3.

Holy Cross Day *n.* the festival of the Exaltation of the Cross, 14 Sept.

holy day *n.* a religious festival.

Holy Family *n.* the young Jesus with his mother and St Joseph (often with St John the Baptist, St Anne, etc.) as grouped in pictures etc.

Holy Father *n.* the Pope.

Holy Ghost *n.* = HOLY SPIRIT.

Holy Grail see GRAIL.

Holy Innocents' Day var. of INNOCENTS' DAY.

holy Joe *n.* orig. *Naut. slang* **1** a clergyman. **2** a pious person.

Holy Land *n.* **1** W. Palestine, esp. Judaea. **2** a region similarly revered in non-Christian religions.

Holy Name *n. RC Ch.* the name of Jesus as an object of formal devotion.

Holy Office *n.* the Inquisition.

holy of holies *n.* **1** the inner chamber of the sanctuary in the Jewish Temple in Jerusalem, separated by a veil from the outer chamber. **2** an innermost shrine. **3** a thing regarded as most sacred.

holy orders *n.pl.* the status of a member of the clergy, esp. the grades of bishop, priest, and deacon.

holy place *n.* **1** (in *pl.*) places to which religious pilgrimage is made. **2** the outer chamber of the sanctuary in the Jewish Temple in Jerusalem.

holy roller *n. slang* a member of a religious group characterized by frenzied excitement or trances.

Holy Roman Empire *n.* the western part of the Roman Empire as revived by Charlemagne in 800.

Holy Rood Day *n.* **1** the festival of the Invention of the Cross, 3 May. **2** = HOLY CROSS DAY.

Holy Sacrament see SACRAMENT 3.

Holy Saturday *n.* Saturday in Holy Week.

Holy Scripture *n.* the Bible.

Holy See *n.* the papacy or the papal court.

Holy Sepulchre *n.* (prec. by *the*) the tomb in which Christ was laid.

Holy Spirit *n.* the third person of the Trinity, God as spiritually acting.

holystone /ˈhəʊlɪstəʊn/ *n. & v. Naut.* ● *n.* a piece of soft sandstone used for scouring decks. ● *v.tr.* scour with this. [19th c.: probably from HOLY + STONE: the stones were called *bibles* etc., perhaps because used while kneeling]

holy terror see TERROR 2b.

Holy Thursday *n.* **1** (in the Anglican Church) Ascension Day. **2** *RC Ch.* Maundy Thursday.

Holy Trinity see TRINITY 3.

holy war *n.* a war waged in support of a religious cause.

holy water *n.* water dedicated to holy uses, or blessed by a priest.

Holy Week *n.* the week before Easter.

Holy Writ *n.* holy writings collectively, esp. the Bible.

Holy Year *n. RC Ch.* a period of remission from the penal consequences of sin, granted under certain conditions for a year usu. at intervals of 25 years.

hom /həʊm/ *n.* (also **homa** /ˈhəʊmə/) **1** the soma plant. **2** the juice of this plant as a sacred drink of the Parsees. [Persian *hōm*, *hūm*, Avestan *haoma*]

homage /ˈhɒmɪdʒ/ *n.* **1** acknowledgement of superiority, dutiful reverence (*pay homage to*; *do homage to*). **2** *hist.* formal public acknowledgement of feudal allegiance. [Middle English via Old French (*h*)*omage* and medieval Latin *hominaticum* from Latin *homo -minis* man]

hombre /ˈɒmbreɪ/ *n. US slang* a man. [Spanish]

Homburg /ˈhɒmbəːg/ *n.* a man's felt hat with a narrow curled brim and a lengthwise dent in the crown. [*Homburg* in Germany, where first worn]

home /həʊm/ *n., adj., adv., & v.* ● *n.* **1 a** the place where one lives; the fixed residence of a family or household. **b** a dwelling house. **2** the members of a family collectively; one's family background (*comes from a good home*). **3** the native land of a person or of a person's ancestors. **4** an institution for persons needing care, rest, or refuge (*nursing home*). **5** the place where a thing originates or is native or most common. **6 a** the finishing point in a race. **b** (in games) the place where one is free from attack; the goal. **c** *Lacrosse* a player in an attacking position near the opponents' goal. **d** *Baseball* = HOME PLATE. **7** *Sport* a home match or win. ● *attrib.adj.* **1 a** of or connected with one's home. **b** carried on, done, or made, at home. **c** proceeding from home. **2 a** carried on or produced in one's own country (*home industries*; *the home market*). **b** dealing with the domestic affairs of a country. **3** *Sport* played on one's own ground etc. (*home match*; *home win*). **4** in the neighbourhood of home. ● *adv.* **1 a** to one's home or country (*go home*). **b** arrived at home (*is he home yet?*). **c** *N. Amer.* at home (*stay home*). **2 a** to the point aimed at (*the thrust went home*). **b** as far as possible (*drove the nail home*; *pressed his advantage home*). ● *v.* **1** *intr.* (esp. of a trained pigeon) return home (cf. HOMING 1). **2** *intr.* (often foll. by *on*, *in on*) (of a vessel, missile, etc.) be guided towards a destination or target by a landmark, radio beam, etc. **3** *tr.* send or guide homewards. **4** *tr.* provide with a home. □ **at home 1** in one's own house or native land. **2** at ease as if in one's own home (*make yourself at home*). **3** (usu. foll. by *in, on, with*) familiar or well informed. **4** available to callers. **come home to** become fully realized by. **come home to roost** see ROOST[1]. **home and dry** *Brit.* having achieved one's purpose. **home, James!** *joc.* drive home quickly! **near home** affecting one closely. □ **homelike** *adj.* [Old English *hām*, from Germanic]

home away from home *n.* = HOME FROM HOME.

home-bird *n. Brit. colloq.* a person who likes to stay at home.

homebody /ˈhəʊmbɒdi/ *n.* (*pl.* **-ies**) a person who likes to stay at home.

homeboy /ˈhəʊmbɔɪ/ *n.* esp. *US slang* a person from one's own town or neighbourhood.

home-brew *n.* beer or other alcoholic drink brewed at home. □ **home-brewed** *adj.*

homebuyer /ˈhəʊmbʌɪə/ *n.* a person who buys a house, flat, etc.

homecoming /ˈhəʊmkʌmɪŋ/ *n.* arrival at home.

Home Counties *n.pl.* (in the UK) the counties closest to London.

home economics *n.pl.* (often treated as *sing.*) the study of household management.

home farm *n. Brit.* a farm (one of several on an estate) set aside to provide produce for the owner.

home from home *n.* a place other than one's home where one feels at home; a place providing homelike amenities.

home-grown *adj.* grown or produced at home.

Home Guard *n. hist.* **1** the British citizen army organized in 1940 to defend the UK against invasion, and disbanded in 1957. **2** a member of this.

home help *n. Brit.* a person employed to help in another's home, esp. one provided by a local authority.

homeland /ˈhəʊmland/ *n.* **1** one's native land. **2** a partially self-governing area in S. Africa set aside for a particular indigenous African people or peoples under the former policy of separate development (the official name for a Bantustan). **3** any similar semi-autonomous area.

homeless /ˈhəʊmlɪs/ *adj.* lacking a home. □ **homelessness** *n.*

home loan *n.* a loan advanced to a person to assist in buying a house, flat, etc.

homely /ˈhəʊmli/ *adj.* (**homelier**, **homeliest**) **1** *Brit.* **a** simple, plain. **b** unpretentious. **c** primitive. **2** *N. Amer.* (of people or their features) not attractive in appearance, ugly. **3** comfortable in the manner of a home, cosy. **4** skilled at housekeeping. □ **homeliness** *n.*

home-made *adj.* made at home.

home-making *n.* the creation of a (pleasant) home. □ **homemaker** *n.*

home movie *n.* a film made at home or of one's own activities.

Home Office *n.* **1** the British government department dealing with law and order, immigration, etc., in England and Wales. **2** the building used for this.

homeopath esp. *US* var. of HOMOEOPATH.

homeopathy etc. esp. *US* var. of HOMOEOPATHY etc.

homeostasis /həʊmɪəʊˈsteɪsɪs, hɒm-/ *n.* (also **homoeostasis**) (*pl.* **-stases** /-siːz/) the tendency towards a relatively stable equilibrium between interdependent elements, esp. as maintained by physiological processes. □ **homeostatic** /-ˈstatɪk/ *adj.* [modern Latin, from Greek *homoios* 'like' + -STASIS]

homeotherm /ˈhɒmɪəʊθəːm/ *n.* (also **homoeotherm**, **homoiotherm**) an organism that maintains its body temperature at a constant level, usu. above that of the environment, by its metabolic activity; a warm-blooded organism (cf. POIKILOTHERM). □ **homeothermal** /-ˈθəːm(ə)l/ *adj.* **homeothermic** /-ˈθəːmɪk/ *adj.* **homeothermy** *n.* [modern Latin, from Greek *homoios* 'like' + *thermē* 'heat']

homeowner /ˈhəʊməʊnə/ *n.* a person who owns his or her own home.

home perm *n.* a permanent wave made with domestic equipment.

home plate *n. Baseball* a plate beside which the batter stands.

home port *n.* the port from which a ship originates.

homer /ˈhəʊmə/ *n.* **1** a homing pigeon. **2** *Baseball* a home run.

Homeric /həʊˈmɛrɪk/ *adj.* **1** of, or in the style of, Homer or the epic poems ascribed to him. **2** of Bronze Age Greece as described in these poems. **3** epic, large-scale, titanic (*Homeric conflict*). [Latin *Homericus* from Greek *Homērikos* from *Homēros* 'Homer', the name of the traditional author of the *Iliad* and the *Odyssey*]

home rule *n.* the government of a country or region by its own citizens.

home run *n. Baseball* a hit that allows the batter to make a complete circuit of the bases.

Home Secretary *n.* (in the UK) the Secretary of State in charge of the Home Office.

home shopping *n.* shopping carried out from home using catalogues, satellite TV channels, etc.

homesick /ˈhəʊmsɪk/ *adj.* depressed by longing for one's home during absence from it. □ **homesickness** *n.*

home signal *n.* a signal indicating whether a train may proceed into a station or to the next section of the line.

homespun /ˈhəʊmspʌn/ *adj. & n.* ● *adj.* **1 a** (of cloth) made of yarn spun at home. **b** (of yarn) spun at home. **2** plain, simple, unsophisticated, homely. ● *n.* **1** homespun cloth. **2** anything plain or homely.

homestead /ˈhəʊmstɛd/ *n.* **1** a house, esp. a farmhouse, and outbuildings. **2** *Austral.* & *NZ* the owner's residence on a sheep or cattle station. **3** *N. Amer.* an area of land (usu. 160 acres) granted to a settler as a home. □ **homesteader** *n.* **homesteading** *n.* [Old English *hāmstede* (as HOME, STEAD)]

home straight *n.* (also **home stretch**) the concluding stretch of a racecourse.

homestyle /ˈhəʊmstʌɪl/ *adj. N. Amer.* (esp. of food) of a kind made or done at home, homely.

home town *n.* the town of one's birth or early life or present fixed residence.

home trade *n. Brit.* trade carried on within a country.

home truth *n.* basic but unwelcome information concerning oneself.

home unit *n. Austral.* a private residence, usu. occupied by the owner, as one of several in a building.

homeward /ˈhəʊmwəd/ *adv.* & *adj.* ● *adv.* (also **homewards** /-wədz/) towards home. ● *adj.* going or leading towards home. [Old English *hāmweard(es)* (as HOME, -WARD)]

homeward-bound *adv.* & *adj.* (esp. of a ship) preparing to go, or on the way, home.

homework /ˈhəʊmwə:k/ *n.* **1** work to be done at home, esp. by a school pupil. **2** preparatory work or study.

homeworker /ˈhəʊmwə:kə/ *n.* a person who works from home, esp. doing low-paid piecework.

homey /ˈhəʊmi/ *adj.* (also **homy**) (**homier**, **homiest**) suggesting home; cosy. □ **homeyness** *n.* (also **hominess**).

homicide /ˈhɒmɪsʌɪd/ *n.* **1** the killing of a human being by another. **2** a person who kills a human being. □ **homicidal** /-ˈsʌɪd(ə)l/ *adj.* [Middle English via Old French from Latin *homicidium* (sense 1), *homicida* (sense 2), from *homo* 'man']

homiletic /hɒmɪˈlɛtɪk/ *adj.* & *n.* ● *adj.* of homilies. ● *n.* (usu. in *pl.*) the art of preaching. [Late Latin *homileticus* from Greek *homilētikos*, from *homileō* 'hold converse, consort' (as HOMILY)]

homiliary /hɒˈmɪlɪəri/ *n.* (*pl.* **-ies**) a book of homilies. [medieval Latin *homeliarius* (as HOMILY)]

homily /ˈhɒmɪli/ *n.* (*pl.* **-ies**) **1** a sermon. **2** a tedious moralizing discourse. □ **homilist** *n.* [Middle English via Old French *omelie* and ecclesiastical Latin *homilia* from Greek *homilia*, from *homilos* 'crowd']

homing /ˈhəʊmɪŋ/ *attrib.adj.* **1** (of a pigeon) trained to fly home, bred for long-distance racing. **2** (of a device) for guiding to a target etc. **3** that goes home.

homing instinct *n.* the instinct of certain animals to return to the territory which they have left or from which they have been moved.

hominid /ˈhɒmɪnɪd/ *n.* & *adj.* ● *n.* any member of the primate family Hominidae, including humans and their fossil ancestors. ● *adj.* of or relating to this family. [modern Latin *Hominidae* from Latin *homo hominis* 'man']

hominoid /ˈhɒmɪnɔɪd/ *adj.* & *n.* ● *adj.* **1** like a human. **2** hominid or pongid. ● *n.* an animal resembling a human.

hominy /ˈhɒmɪni/ *n.* (esp. in the US) coarsely ground maize kernels boiled with water or milk. [Algonquian]

homo /ˈhəʊməʊ/ *n.* (*pl.* **-os**) *colloq.* a homosexual. [abbreviation]

homo- /ˈhɒməʊ, ˈhəʊməʊ/ *comb. form* same (often opp. HETERO-). [Greek *homos* 'same']

Homo /ˈhəʊməʊ, ˈhɒməʊ/ *n.* any primate of the genus *Homo*, including modern humans and various extinct species. [Latin, = man]

homocentric /həʊmə(ʊ)ˈsɛntrɪk, hɒm-/ *adj.* having the same centre.

homoeopath /ˈhəʊmɪəpaθ, ˈhɒm-/ *n.* (also esp. *US* **homeopath**) a person who practises homoeopathy. [German *Homöopath* (as HOMOEOPATHY)]

homoeopathy /həʊmɪˈɒpəθi, hɒm-/ *n.* (also esp. *US* **homeopathy**) the treatment of disease by minute doses of drugs that in a healthy person would produce symptoms of the disease (cf. ALLOPATHY). □ **homoeopathic** /-ˈpaθɪk/ *adj.* **homoeopathically** /-ˈpaθɪk(ə)li/ *adv.* **homoeopathist** *n.* [German *Homöopathie*, from Greek *homoios* 'like' + *patheia* -PATHY]

homoeostasis etc. var. of HOMEOSTASIS etc.

homoeotherm etc. var. of HOMEOTHERM etc.

homoerotic /ˌhəʊməʊɪˈrɒtɪk, ˌhɒməʊ-/ *adj.* homosexual.

homogametic /hɒməgəˈmɛtɪk, -ˈmi:-; həʊm-/ *adj. Biol.* (of a sex or individuals of a sex) producing gametes that carry the same sex chromosome.

homogamy /hɒˈmɒgəmi/ *n. Bot.* **1** a state in which the flowers of a plant are hermaphrodite or of the same sex. **2** the simultaneous ripening of the stamens and pistils of a flower. □ **homogamous** *adj.* [Greek *homogamos* (as HOMO-, *gamos* 'marriage')]

homogenate /həˈmɒdʒɪneɪt/ *n.* a suspension produced by homogenizing.

homogeneous /hɒmə(ʊ)ˈdʒi:nɪəs, -ˈdʒɛn-; həʊm-/ *adj.* (also *disp.* **homogenous** /həˈmɒdʒənəs/) **1** of the same kind. **2** consisting of parts all of the same kind; uniform. **3** *Math.* containing terms all of the same degree. □ **homogeneity** /-dʒɪˈni:ɪti, -dʒɪˈneɪɪti/ *n.* **homogeneously** *adv.* **homogeneousness** *n.* [medieval Latin *homogeneus* from Greek *homogenēs* (as HOMO-, *genēs* from *genos* 'kind')]

■ **Usage** The variant *homogenous* is considered incorrect by many people and is best avoided. It is found especially in spoken English and arose perhaps under the influence of the verb *homogenize.* The technical term *homogenous* (see HOMOGENOUS[1]) is quite different in meaning and has now been largely replaced by HOMOGENETIC.

homogenetic /ˌhəʊməʊdʒɪˈnɛtɪk, ˌhɒməʊ-/ *adj. Biol.* having a common descent or origin.

homogenize /həˈmɒdʒənʌɪz/ *v.* (also **-ise**) **1** *tr.* & *intr.* make or become homogeneous. **2** *tr.* treat (milk) so that the fat droplets are emulsified and the cream does not separate. □ **homogenization** /-ˈzeɪʃ(ə)n/ *n.* **homogenizer** *n.*

homogenous[1] /həˈmɒdʒɪnəs/ *adj. Biol. archaic* = HOMOGENETIC. [HOMOGENY + -OUS]

homogenous[2] *adj.* see HOMOGENEOUS. [alteration of HOMOGENEOUS, perhaps influenced by HOMOGENIZE]

homogeny /həˈmɒdʒəni/ *n. Biol.* similarity due to common descent.

homograft /ˈhɒməgrɑ:ft, ˈhəʊm-/ *n.* a tissue graft from a donor of the same species as the recipient (cf. ALLOGRAFT).

homograph /ˈhɒməgrɑ:f; ˈhəʊm-/ *n.* a word spelt like another but of different meaning or origin (e.g. POLE[1], POLE[2]).

homoiotherm var. of HOMEOTHERM.

homoiousian /hɒmɔɪˈu:sɪən, -ˈaʊ-, -z-/ *n. hist.* a person who held that God the Father and God the Son are of like but not identical substance (cf. HOMOOUSIAN). [ecclesiastical Latin from Greek *homoiousios*, from *homoios* 'like' + *ousia* 'essence']

homolog *US* var. of HOMOLOGUE.

homologate /həˈmɒləgeɪt/ *v.tr.* **1** acknowledge, admit. **2** confirm, accept. **3** approve (a car, boat, engine, etc.) for use in a particular class of racing. □ **homologation** /-ˈgeɪʃ(ə)n/ *n.* [medieval Latin *homologare* 'agree' from Greek *homologeō* (as HOMO-, *logos* 'word')]

homologize /hɒˈmɒlədʒʌɪz/ *v.* (also **-ise**) **1** *intr.* be homologous; correspond. **2** *tr.* make homologous.

homologous /hɒˈmɒləgəs/ *adj.* **1 a** having the same relation, relative position, etc. **b** corresponding. **2** *Biol.* (of organs etc.) similar in position, structure, and evolutionary origin but not necessarily in function (opp. ANALOGOUS 2). **3** *Biol.* (of chromosomes) pairing at meiosis and having the same structural features and pattern of genes. **4** *Chem.* (of a series of chemical compounds) having the same functional group but differing in composition by a fixed group of atoms. [medieval Latin *homologus* from Greek (as HOMO-, *logos* 'ratio, proportion')]

homologue /ˈhɒməlɒg/ *n.* (*US* **homolog**) a homologous thing. [French from Greek *homologon* (neut. adj.) (as HOMOLOGOUS)]

homology /hɒˈmɒlədʒi/ *n.* a homologous state or relation; correspondence. □ **homological** /hɒməˈlɒdʒɪk(ə)l/ *adj.*

homomorphic /hɒmə(ʊ)ˈmɔ:fɪk, həʊm-/ *adj.* (also **homomorphous**) of the same or similar form. □ **homomorphically** *adv.* **homomorphism** *n.* **homomorphy** *n.*

homonym /ˈhɒmənɪm/ *n.* **1** a word of the same spelling or sound as another but of different meaning; a homograph or homophone. **2** a namesake. □ **homonymic** /-ˈnɪmɪk/ *adj.* **homonymous**

/hə'mɒnɪməs/ *adj.* [Latin *homonymum* from Greek *homōnumon* (neut. adj.) (as HOMO-, *onoma* 'name')]

homoousian /hɒməʊ'u:sɪən, -'aʊ-, -z-; həʊməʊ-/ *n.* (also **homousian** /hɒ'mu:-, hɒ'maʊ-/) *hist.* a person who held that God the Father and God the Son are of the same substance (cf. HOMOIOUSIAN). [ecclesiastical Latin *homoousianus* via Late Latin *homousius* from Greek *homoousios* (as HOMO-, *ousia* 'essence')]

homophobia /hɒmə(ʊ)'fəʊbɪə, həʊmə(ʊ)-/ *n.* a hatred or fear of homosexuals. □ **homophobe** /'hɒm-, 'həʊm-/ *n.* **homophobic** /-'fəʊbɪk/ *adj.*

homophone /'hɒməfəʊn, 'həʊm-/ *n.* **1** a word having the same sound as another but of different meaning, origin, or spelling (e.g. *pair*, *pear*). **2** a symbol denoting the same sound as another.

homophonic /hɒmə'fɒnɪk, həʊm-/ *adj. Mus.* in unison; characterized by movement of all parts to the same melody. □ **homophonically** *adv.*

homophonous /hə'mɒf(ə)nəs/ *adj.* **1** (of music) homophonic. **2** (of a word or symbol) that is a homophone. □ **homophony** *n.*

homopolar /həʊməʊ'pəʊlə, hɒməʊ-/ *adj.* **1** electrically symmetrical. **2** *Electr.* (of a generator) producing direct current without the use of commutators. **3** *Chem.* (of a covalent bond) in which one atom supplies both electrons.

homopteran /hɒ'mɒpt(ə)rən/ *n.* any insect of the suborder Homoptera, including true bugs with wings of a uniform texture, e.g. aphids and cicadas (cf. HETEROPTERAN). □ **homopterous** *adj.* [HOMO- + Greek *pteron* 'wing']

Homo sapiens /həʊməʊ 'sapɪɛnz, hɒməʊ/ *n.* modern humans regarded as a species. [Latin, = wise man]

homosexual /hɒmə(ʊ)'sɛksjʊəl, həʊm-, -ʃʊəl/ *adj. & n.* ● *adj.* **1** feeling or involving sexual attraction to persons of the same sex. **2** concerning homosexual relations or people. **3** relating to the same sex. ● *n.* a homosexual person. □ **homosexuality** /-'alɪti/ *n.* **homosexually** *adv.*

homousian var. of HOMOOUSIAN.

homozygote /hɒmə(ʊ)'zʌɪgəʊt, həʊm-/ *n. Biol.* an individual having two identical alleles of a particular gene or genes and so breeding true for the corresponding characteristic. □ **homozygous** *adj.*

homunculus /hɒ'mʌŋkjʊləs/ *n.* (also **homuncule** /-kju:l/) (*pl.* **homunculi** /-lʌɪ/ or **homuncules**) a little man, a manikin. [Latin *homunculus* from *homo -minis* 'man']

homy var. of HOMEY.

Hon. *abbr.* **1** Honorary. **2** Honourable.

hon /hʌn/ *n. colloq.* = HONEY 5. [abbreviation]

honcho /'hɒn(t)ʃəʊ/ *n. & v. N. Amer. slang* ● *n.* (*pl.* **-os**) **1** a leader or manager, the person in charge. **2** an admirable man. ● *v.tr.* (**-oes**, **-oed**) be in charge of, oversee. [Japanese *han'chō* 'group leader']

hone /həʊn/ *n. & v.* ● *n.* **1** a whetstone, esp. for razors. **2** any of various stones used as material for this. ● *v.tr.* sharpen on or as on a hone. [Old English *hān* 'stone', from Germanic]

honest /'ɒnɪst/ *adj. & adv.* ● *adj.* **1** fair and just in character or behaviour, not cheating or stealing. **2** free of deceit and untruthfulness, sincere. **3** fairly earned (*an honest living*). **4** (of an act or feeling) showing fairness. **5** (with patronizing effect) blameless but undistinguished (cf. WORTHY *adj.* 2). **6** (of a thing) unadulterated, unsophisticated. ● *adv. colloq.* genuinely, really. □ **earn** (or **turn**) **an honest penny** earn money fairly. **make an honest woman of** *colloq.* or *joc.* marry (esp. a pregnant woman). [Middle English via Old French *(h)oneste* from Latin *honestus*, from *honos* HONOUR]

honest broker *n.* a mediator in international, industrial, etc., disputes (originally of Bismarck).

honest Injun *adv. colloq.* genuinely, really.

honestly /'ɒnɪstli/ *adv.* **1** in an honest way. **2** really (*I don't honestly know; honestly, the cheek of it!*).

honest-to-God *adj. & adv.* (also **honest-to-goodness**) *colloq.* ● *adj.* genuine, real. ● *adv.* genuinely, really.

honesty /'ɒnɪsti/ *n.* **1** being honest. **2** truthfulness. **3** a plant of the genus *Lunaria* with purple or white flowers, so called from its flat round semi-transparent seed pods. [Middle English via Old French *(h)onesté* from Latin *honestas -tatis* (as HONEST)]

honey /'hʌni/ *n.* (*pl.* **-eys**) **1** a sweet sticky yellowish fluid made by bees and other insects from nectar collected from flowers. **2** the colour of this. **3 a** sweetness. **b** a sweet thing. **4** a person or thing excellent of its kind. **5** esp. *N. Amer.* (usu. as a form of address) darling, sweetheart. [Old English *hunig*, from Germanic]

honey badger *n.* a ratel.

honey bee *n.* see BEE 1a.

honeybun /'hʌnɪbʌn/ *n.* (also **honeybunch** /-bʌntʃ/) (esp. as a form of address) darling.

honey buzzard *n.* any bird of prey of the genus *Pernis* feeding on the larvae of bees and wasps.

honeycomb /'hʌnɪkəʊm/ *n. & v.* ● *n.* **1** a structure of hexagonal cells of wax, made by bees to store honey and eggs. **2 a** a pattern arranged hexagonally. **b** fabric made with a pattern of raised hexagons etc. **3** tripe from the second stomach of a ruminant. **4** a cavernous flaw in metalwork, esp. in guns. ● *v.tr.* **1** fill with cavities or tunnels, undermine. **2** mark with a honeycomb pattern. [Old English *hunigcamb* (as HONEY, COMB)]

honeycreeper /'hʌni:kri:pə/ *n.* **1** a Hawaiian bird of the family Drepanididae. **2** a tanager of tropical America, feeding on nectar.

honeydew /'hʌnɪdju:/ *n.* **1** a sweet sticky substance found on leaves and stems, excreted by aphids. **2** a variety of melon with smooth pale skin and sweet green flesh. **3** an ideally sweet substance. **4** tobacco sweetened with molasses.

honeyeater *n.* any Australasian bird of the family Meliphagidae with a long tongue used to take nectar from flowers.

honeyed /'hʌnɪd/ *adj.* (also **honied**) **1** of or containing honey. **2** (of words, flattery, etc.) sweet; sweet-sounding.

honey fungus *n.* a parasitic fungus, *Armillaria mellea*, with honey-coloured edible toadstools.

honeyguide /'hʌnɪgʌɪd/ *n.* **1** any small bird of the family Indicatoridae which feeds on beeswax and insects. **2** a marking on the corolla of a flower thought to guide bees to nectar.

honeymoon /'hʌnɪmu:n/ *n. & v.* ● *n.* **1** a holiday spent together by a newly married couple. **2** an initial period of enthusiasm or goodwill. ● *v.intr.* (usu. foll. by *in, at*) spend a honeymoon. □ **honeymooner** *n.* [HONEY + MOON, originally with reference to waning affection, not to a period of a month]

honey pot *n.* **1** a pot for honey. **2** a posture with the hands clasped under the hams. **3** something very attractive or tempting.

honey sac *n.* an enlarged part of a bee's gullet where honey is formed.

honeysuckle /'hʌnɪsʌk(ə)l/ *n.* any climbing shrub of the genus *Lonicera* with fragrant yellow and pink flowers. [Middle English extension of *honeysuck*, from Old English *hunigsūce* (as HONEY, SUCK)]

honey-sweet *adj.* sweet as honey.

honied var. of HONEYED.

honk /hɒŋk/ *n. & v.* ● *n.* **1** the cry of a wild goose. **2** the harsh sound of a car horn. ● *v.* **1** *intr.* emit or give a honk. **2** *tr.* cause to do this. [imitative]

honky /'hɒŋki/ *n.* (*pl.* **-ies**) *US black slang offens.* **1** a white person. **2** white people collectively. [20th c.: origin unknown]

honky-tonk /'hɒŋkɪtɒŋk/ *n. colloq.* **1** ragtime piano music. **2** a cheap or disreputable nightclub, dance hall, etc. [19th c.: origin unknown]

honnête homme /ɒneɪt 'ɒm, French ɔnɛt ɔm/ *n.* a decent, cultivated man of the world. [French]

honor *US* var. of HONOUR.

honorable *US* var. of HONOURABLE.

honorand /ˈɒnərand/ *n.* a person to be honoured, esp. with an honorary degree. [Latin *honorandus* (as HONOUR)]

honorarium /ɒnəˈrɛːrɪəm/ *n.* (*pl.* **honorariums** or **honoraria** /-rɪə/) a fee, esp. a voluntary payment for professional services rendered without the normal fee. [Latin, neut. of *honorarius*: see HONORARY]

honorary /ˈɒn(ə)(rə)ri/ *adj.* **1 a** conferred as an honour, without the usual requirements, functions, etc. (*honorary degree*). **b** holding such a title or position (*honorary colonel*). **2** (of an office or its holder) unpaid (*honorary secretaryship*; *honorary treasurer*). **3** (of an obligation) depending on honour, not legally enforceable. [Latin *honorarius* (as HONOUR)]

honorific /ɒnəˈrɪfɪk/ *adj.* & *n.* ● *adj.* **1** conferring honour. **2** (esp. of oriental forms of speech) implying respect. ● *n.* an honorific form of words. □ **honorifically** *adv.* [Latin *honorificus* (as HONOUR)]

honoris causa /ɒˌnɔːrɪs ˈkaʊzə/ *adv.* (esp. of a degree awarded without examination) as a mark of esteem. [Latin, = for the sake of honour]

honour /ˈɒnə/ *n.* & *v.* (*US* **honor**) ● *n.* **1** high respect; glory; credit, reputation, good name. **2** adherence to what is right or to a conventional standard of conduct. **3** nobleness of mind, magnanimity (*honour among thieves*). **4** a thing conferred as a distinction, esp. an official award for bravery or achievement. **5** (foll. by *of* + verbal noun, or *to* + infin.) privilege, special right (*had the honour of being invited*). **6 a** exalted position. **b** (**Honour**) (prec. by *your, his*, etc.) a title of a circuit judge, *US* a mayor, and *Ir.* or in rustic speech any person of rank. **7** (foll. by *to*) a person or thing that brings honour (*she is an honour to her profession*). **8 a** (of a woman) chastity. **b** the reputation for this. **9** (in *pl.*) **a** special distinction for proficiency in an examination. **b** a course of degree studies more specialized than for an ordinary pass. **10 a** *Bridge* the ace, king, queen, jack, and ten, esp. of trumps, or the four aces at no trumps. **b** *Whist* the ace, king, queen, and jack, esp. of trumps. **11** *Golf* the right of driving off first as having won the last hole (*it is my honour*). ● *v.tr.* **1** respect highly. **2** confer honour on. **3** accept (a bill) or pay (a cheque) when due. **4** acknowledge. □ **do the honours** perform the duties of a host to guests etc. **honour bright** on my honour! **honours are even** *Brit.* there is equality in the contest. **in honour bound** = *on one's honour*. **in honour of** as a celebration of. **on one's honour** (usu. foll. by *to* + infin.) under a moral obligation. **on** (or **upon**) **my honour** an expression of sincerity. [Middle English via Old French *(h)onor* (*n.*), *onorer* (*v.*) from Latin *honor, honorare*]

honourable /ˈɒn(ə)rəb(ə)l/ *adj.* (*US* **honorable**) **1 a** worthy of honour. **b** bringing honour to its possessor. **c** showing honour, not base. **d** consistent with honour. **e** *colloq.* or *joc.* (of the intentions of a man courting a woman) directed towards marriage. **2** (**Honourable**) a title indicating eminence or distinction, given to certain high officials, the children of certain ranks of the nobility, and MPs. □ **honourableness** *n.* **honourably** *adv.* [Middle English via Old French *honorable* from Latin *honorabilis* (as HONOUR)]

honourable mention *n.* an award of merit to a candidate in an examination, a work of art, etc., not awarded a prize.

honour point *n. Heraldry* the point halfway between the top of a shield and the fesse point.

honours list *n.* a list of persons awarded honours.

honours of war *n.pl.* privileges granted to a capitulating force, e.g. that of marching out with colours flying.

honour system *n.* a system of examinations etc. without supervision, relying on the honour of those concerned.

honour-trick *n. Bridge* = QUICK TRICK.

Hon. Sec. *abbr.* Honorary Secretary.

hooch /huːtʃ/ *n.* (also **hootch**) *N. Amer. colloq.* alcoholic liquor, esp. inferior or illicit whisky. [abbreviation of *hoochinoo*, the name of a liquor-making Alaskan tribe]

hood[1] /hʊd/ *n.* & *v.* ● *n.* **1 a** a covering for the head and neck, whether part of a cloak etc. or separate. **b** a separate hoodlike garment worn over a university gown or a surplice to indicate the wearer's degree. **2** *Brit.* a folding waterproof top of a motor car, pram, etc. **3** *N. Amer.* the bonnet of a motor vehicle. **4** a canopy to protect users of machinery or to remove fumes etc. **5** a hoodlike structure or marking on the head or neck of a cobra, seal, etc. **6** a leather covering for a hawk's head. ● *v.tr.* cover with a hood. □ **hoodless** *adj.* **hoodlike** *adj.* [Old English *hōd* from West Germanic: related to HAT]

hood[2] /hʊd/ *n.* esp. *US slang* a gangster or gunman. [abbreviation of HOODLUM]

-hood /hʊd/ *suffix* forming nouns: **1** of condition or state (*childhood*; *falsehood*). **2** indicating a collection or group (*sisterhood*; *neighbourhood*). [Old English *-hād*, originally an independent noun, = person, condition, quality]

hooded /ˈhʊdɪd/ *adj.* having a hood; covered with a hood.

hooded crow *n.* a piebald grey and black crow, of a northern race of the carrion crow.

hoodie /ˈhʊdi/ *n.* = HOODED CROW.

hoodlum /ˈhuːdləm/ *n.* **1** a street hooligan, a young thug. **2** a gangster. [19th c.: origin unknown]

hood-mould *n.* (also **hood-moulding**) *Archit.* a dripstone.

hoodoo /ˈhuːduː/ *n.* & *v.* esp. *US* ● *n.* **1 a** bad luck. **b** a thing or person that brings or causes this. **2** voodoo. **3** a strangely shaped rock pinnacle or column of rock formed by erosion etc. ● *v.tr.* (**hoodoos, hoodooed**) **1** make unlucky. **2** bewitch. [alteration of VOODOO]

hoodwink /ˈhʊdwɪŋk/ *v.tr.* deceive, delude. [originally 'blindfold', from HOOD[1] *n.* + WINK]

hooey /ˈhuːi/ *n.* & *int. colloq.* nonsense, humbug. [20th c.: origin unknown]

hoof /huːf/ *n.* & *v.* ● *n.* (*pl.* **hoofs** or **hooves** /-vz/) the horny part of the foot of a horse, antelope, and other ungulates. ● *v.* **1** *tr.* strike with a hoof. **2** *tr. slang* kick or shove. □ **hoof it** *slang* **1** go on foot. **2** dance. **on the hoof** (of cattle) not yet slaughtered. □ **hoofed** *adj.* (also in *comb.*). [Old English *hōf*, from Germanic]

hoofer /ˈhuːfə/ *n. slang* a professional dancer.

hoo-ha /ˈhuːhɑː/ *n. colloq.* a commotion, a row; uproar, trouble. [20th c.: origin unknown]

hook /hʊk/ *n.* & *v.* ● *n.* **1 a** a piece of metal or other material bent back at an angle or with a round bend, for catching hold or for hanging things on. **b** (in full **fish-hook**) a bent piece of wire, usu. barbed and baited, for catching fish. **2** a curved cutting instrument (*reaping-hook*). **3 a** a sharp bend, e.g. in a river. **b** a projecting point of land (*Hook of Holland*). **c** a sand-spit with a curved end. **4 a** *Cricket* & *Golf* a hooking stroke (see sense 5 of *v.*). **b** *Boxing* a short swinging blow with the elbow bent and rigid. **5** a trap, a snare. **6 a** a curved stroke in handwriting, esp. as made in learning to write. **b** *Mus.* an added stroke transverse to the stem in the symbol for a quaver etc. **7** (in *pl.*) *slang* fingers. ● *v.* **1** *tr.* **a** grasp with a hook. **b** secure with a hook or hooks. **2** (often foll. by *on, up*) **a** *tr.* attach with or as with a hook. **b** *intr.* be or become attached with a hook. **3** *tr.* catch with or as with a hook (*he hooked a fish*; *she hooked a husband*). **4** *tr. slang* steal. **5** *tr.* **a** *Cricket* play (the ball) round from the off to the on side with an upward stroke. **b** (also *absol.*) *Golf* strike (the ball) so that it deviates towards the striker. **6** *tr. Rugby* secure (the ball) and pass it backward with the foot in the scrum. **7** *tr. Boxing* strike (one's opponent) with the elbow bent and rigid. □ **by hook or by crook** by one means or another, by fair means or foul. **hook it** *Brit. slang* make off, run away. **hook, line, and sinker** entirely. **off the hook 1** *colloq.* no longer in difficulty or trouble. **2** (of a telephone receiver) not on its rest, and so preventing incoming calls. **off the hooks** *Brit. slang* dead. **on one's own hook** *slang* on one's own account. **sling** (or **take**) **one's hook** *Brit. slang* = *hook it.* □ **hookless** *adj.* **hooklet** *n.* **hooklike** *adj.* [Old English *hōc*: sense 3 of *n.* probably influenced by Dutch *hoek* 'corner']

hookah /'hʊkə/ *n.* an oriental tobacco pipe with a long tube passing through water for cooling the smoke as it is drawn through. [Urdu from Arabic *ḥukkah* 'casket, jar']

hook and eye *n.* a small metal hook and loop as a fastener on a garment.

hooked /'hʊkt/ *adj.* **1** hook-shaped (*hooked nose*). **2** furnished with a hook or hooks. **3** in senses of HOOK *v.* **4** (of a rug or mat) made by pulling woollen yarn through canvas with a hook. □ **hooked on** *slang* addicted to; captivated by.

hooker[1] /'hʊkə/ *n.* **1** *Rugby* the player in the middle of the front row of the scrum who tries to hook the ball. **2** *slang* a prostitute. **3** a person or thing that hooks.

hooker[2] /'hʊkə/ *n.* **1** a small Dutch or Irish fishing vessel. **2** *derog.* any ship. [Dutch *hoeker* from *hoek* HOOK]

Hooke's law /hʊks/ *n.* the law that the strain in a solid is proportional to the applied stress within the elastic limit of that solid. [named after R. *Hooke*, English scientist d. 1703]

hookey /'hʊki/ *n.* (also **hooky**) *N. Amer.* □ **play hookey** *colloq.* play truant. [19th c.: origin unknown]

hook-nose *n.* an aquiline nose. □ **hook-nosed** *adv.*

hook-up *n.* a connection, esp. an interconnection of broadcasting equipment for special transmissions.

hookworm /'hʊkwɜːm/ *n.* **1** any of various parasitic nematode worms with hooklike mouthparts for attachment and feeding, infesting the gut of humans and animals. **2** a disease caused by an infestation of these, often resulting in severe anaemia.

hooligan /'huːlɪg(ə)n/ *n.* a young ruffian, esp. a member of a gang. □ **hooliganism** *n.* [19th c.: perhaps from *Hooligan*, surname of a fictional rowdy Irish family]

hoop[1] /huːp/ *n.* & *v.* ● *n.* **1** a circular band of metal, wood, etc., esp. for binding the staves of casks etc. or for forming part of a framework. **2 a** a ring bowled along by a child. **b** a large ring, usu. with paper stretched over it, for circus performers to jump through. **3** esp. *Brit.* an arch of iron etc. through which the balls are hit in croquet. **4** *hist.* **a** a circle of flexible material for expanding a woman's petticoat or skirt. **b** (in full **hoop petticoat**) a petticoat expanded with this. **5 a** a band in contrasting colour on a sports shirt, jockey's cap, etc. **b** *Austral. colloq.* a jockey. ● *v.tr.* **1** bind with a hoop or hoops. **2** encircle with or as with a hoop. □ **be put** (or **go**) **through the hoop** (or **hoops**) undergo an ordeal. [Old English *hōp*, from West Germanic]

hoop[2] var. of WHOOP.

hoop-iron *n.* iron in long thin strips for binding casks etc.

hoopla /'huːplɑː/ *n.* **1** *Brit.* a game in which rings are thrown in an attempt to encircle one of various prizes. **2** *colloq.* commotion. **3** *colloq.* pretentious nonsense.

hoopoe /'huːpuː, -pəʊ/ *n.* a salmon-pink bird, *Upupa epops*, with black and white wings and tail, a large erectile crest, and a long decurved bill. [alteration of Middle English *hoop*, via Old French *huppe* from Latin *upupa*, imitative of its cry]

hoop petticoat see HOOP[1] *n.* 4b.

hooray /hʊ'reɪ/ *int.* **1** = HURRAH. **2** *Austral.* & *NZ* goodbye. [variant of HURRAH]

Hooray Henry /ˌhuːreɪ 'hɛnri/ *n. Brit. colloq.* a rich ineffectual young man, esp. one who is fashionable, extroverted, and conventional.

hoosegow /'huːsgaʊ/ *n. US slang* a prison. [Latin American Spanish *juzgao*, Spanish *juzgado* 'tribunal', from Latin *judicatum*, neut. past part. of *judicare* JUDGE]

hoot /huːt/ *n.* & *v.* ● *n.* **1** an owl's cry. **2** the sound made by a motor horn or a steam whistle. **3** a shout expressing scorn or disapproval; an inarticulate shout. **4 a** a short outburst (of laughter). **b** *colloq.* a cause of this (*the escapade was a hoot*). **5** (also **two hoots**) *colloq.* anything at all (*don't care a hoot; don't give a hoot; doesn't matter two hoots*). ● *v.* **1** *intr.* **a** (of an owl) utter its cry. **b** (of a motor horn or steam whistle) make a hoot. **c** (often foll. by *at*) make loud sounds, esp. of scorn, disapproval, or merriment (*hooted with laughter*). **2** *tr.* **a** assail with scornful shouts. **b** (often foll. by *out, away*) drive away by hooting. **3** *tr.* sound (a motor horn or steam whistle). [Middle English *hūten* (*v.*), perhaps imitative]

hootch var. of HOOCH.

hootenanny /'huːt(ə)nani/ *n.* (*pl.* **-ies**) esp. *US colloq.* an informal gathering with folk music. [originally dialect, = 'gadget']

hooter /'huːtə/ *n.* **1** *Brit.* a siren or steam whistle, esp. as a signal for work to begin or cease. **2** *Brit.* the horn of a motor vehicle. **3** *slang* a nose. **4** a person or animal that hoots. **5** (in *pl.*) *N. Amer. coarse slang* a woman's breasts.

hoots /huːts/ *int. Sc.* & *N.Engl.* expressing dissatisfaction or impatience. [a natural exclamation: cf. Swedish *hut* 'begone', Welsh *hwt* 'away', Irish *ut* 'out', all in similar sense]

Hoover /'huːvə/ *n.* & *v. Brit.* ● *n. propr.* a vacuum cleaner (properly one made by the Hoover company). ● *v.* (**hoover**) **1** *tr.* (also *absol.*) clean (a carpet etc.) with a vacuum cleaner. **2** (foll. by *up*) **a** *tr.* suck up with or as with a vacuum cleaner (*hoovered up the crumbs*). **b** *absol.* clean a room etc. with a vacuum cleaner (*decided to hoover up before they arrived*). [named after W. H. *Hoover*, American manufacturer d. 1932]

hooves *pl.* of HOOF.

hop[1] /hɒp/ *v.* & *n.* ● *v.* (**hopped, hopping**) **1** *intr.* (of a bird, frog, etc.) spring with two or all feet at once. **2** *intr.* (of a person) jump on one foot. **3** *intr.* move or go quickly (*hopped over the fence*). **4** *tr.* cross (a ditch etc.) by hopping. **5** *intr. colloq.* **a** make a quick trip. **b** make a quick change of position or location. **6** *tr. colloq.* **a** jump into (a vehicle). **b** obtain (a ride) in this way. **7** *tr.* (usu. as **hopping** *n.*) (esp. of aircraft) pass quickly from one (place of a specified type) to another (*cloud-hopping; hedge-hopping*). ● *n.* **1** a hopping movement. **2** *colloq.* an informal dance. **3** a short flight in an aircraft; the distance travelled by air without landing; a stage of a flight or journey. □ **hop in** (or **out**) *colloq.* get into (or out of) a car etc. **hop it** *Brit. slang* go away. **hop the twig** (or **stick**) *Brit. slang* **1** depart suddenly. **2** die. **on the hop** *Brit. colloq.* **1** unprepared (*caught on the hop*). **2** bustling about. [Old English *hoppian*]

hop[2] /hɒp/ *n.* & *v.* ● *n.* **1** a climbing plant, *Humulus lupulus*, cultivated for the cones borne by the female. **2** (in *pl.*) **a** the ripe cones of this, used to give a bitter flavour to beer. **b** *Austral.* & *NZ colloq.* beer. **3** *US slang* opium or any other narcotic. ● *v.* (**hopped, hopping**) **1** *tr.* flavour with hops. **2** *intr.* produce or pick hops. **3** *tr.* (foll. by *up*) *N. Amer. slang* (as **hopped up** *adj.*) intoxicated; stimulated by or as if by drugs. [Middle English *hoppe* from Middle Low German, Middle Dutch *hoppe*]

hop-bind *n.* (also **hop-bine**) the climbing stem of the hop.

hope /həʊp/ *n.* & *v.* ● *n.* **1** (in *sing.* or *pl.*; often foll. by *of, that*) expectation and desire combined, e.g. for a certain thing to occur (*hope of getting the job*). **2 a** a person, thing, or circumstance that gives cause for hope. **b** ground of hope, promise. **3** what is hoped for. **4** *archaic* a feeling of trust. ● *v.* **1** *intr.* (often foll. by *for*) feel hope. **2** *tr.* expect and desire. **3** *tr.* feel fairly confident. □ **hope against hope** cling to a mere possibility. **not a** (or **some**) **hope!** *colloq.* no chance at all. □ **hoper** *n.* [Old English *hopa*]

hope chest *n. N. Amer.* = BOTTOM DRAWER.

hopeful /'həʊpfʊl, -f(ə)l/ *adj.* & *n.* ● *adj.* **1** feeling hope. **2** causing or inspiring hope. **3** likely to succeed, promising. ● *n.* (in full **young hopeful**) **1** a person likely to succeed. **2** *iron.* a person likely to be disappointed. ▫ **hopefulness** *n.*

hopefully /ˈhəʊpfʊli, -f(ə)li/ *adv.* **1** in a hopeful manner. **2** (qualifying a whole sentence) *disp.* it is to be hoped (*hopefully, the car will be ready by then*).

▪ **Usage** The use of *hopefully* in sense 2 is extremely common, but it is still considered incorrect by some people. The main reason is that other such adverbs, e.g. *regrettably, fortunately*, etc., can be converted to the form *it is regrettable, it is fortunate*, etc., but *hopefully* converts to *it is to be hoped*. This use of *hopefully* probably arose as a translation of German *hoffentlich*, used in the same way, and first became popular in America in the late 1960s. Its use is best restricted to informal contexts.

hopeless /ˈhəʊplɪs/ *adj.* **1** feeling no hope. **2** admitting no hope (*a hopeless case*). **3** inadequate, incompetent (*am hopeless at tennis*). ▫ **hopelessly** *adv.* **hopelessness** *n.*

hophead /ˈhɒphɛd/ *n. slang* **1** *US* a drug addict. **2** *Austral.* & *NZ* a drunkard.

hoplite /ˈhɒplʌɪt/ *n.* a heavily armed foot soldier of ancient Greece. [Greek *hoplitēs* from *hoplon* 'weapon']

hopper[1] /ˈhɒpə/ *n.* **1** a person who hops. **2** a hopping arthropod, esp. a flea or cheese-maggot or young locust. **3 a** a container tapering downward (originally having a hopping motion) through which grain passes into a mill. **b** a similar contrivance in various machines. **4 a** a barge carrying away mud etc. from a dredging machine and discharging it. **b** a railway truck able to discharge coal etc. through its floor.

hopper[2] /ˈhɒpə/ *n.* a hop-picker.

hopping /ˈhɒpɪŋ/ *adj.* esp. *N. Amer. colloq.* very active, lively.

hopping mad *adj. colloq.* very angry.

hopple /ˈhɒp(ə)l/ *v.* & *n.* ● *v.tr.* fasten together the legs of (a horse etc.) to prevent it from straying etc. ● *n.* an apparatus for this. [probably Low German: cf. HOBBLE and early Flemish *hoppelen* = Middle Dutch *hobelen* 'jump, dance']

hopsack /ˈhɒpsak/ *n.* **1 a** a coarse material made from hemp etc. **b** sacking for hops made from this. **2** a coarse clothing fabric of a loose plain weave.

hopscotch /ˈhɒpskɒtʃ/ *n.* a children's game of hopping over squares or oblongs marked on the ground to retrieve a flat stone etc. [HOP[1] + SCOTCH[1]]

hop, skip, and jump *n.* (also **hop, step, and jump**) = TRIPLE JUMP.

horary /ˈhɔːrəri/ *adj. archaic* **1** of the hours. **2** occurring every hour, hourly. [medieval Latin *horarius* from Latin *hora* HOUR]

horde /hɔːd/ *n.* **1 a** usu. *derog.* a large group, a gang. **b** a moving swarm or pack (of insects, wolves, etc.). **2** a troop of Tartar or other nomads. [Polish *horda* from Turkic *ordī, ordū* 'camp': cf. URDU]

horehound /ˈhɔːhaʊnd/ *n.* (also **hoarhound**) **1 a** (in full **white horehound**) a herbaceous plant, *Marrubium vulgare* (mint family), with a white cottony covering on its stem and leaves. **b** its bitter aromatic juice used against coughs etc. **2** (in full **black horehound**) a herbaceous plant, *Ballota nigra* (mint family), with an unpleasant aroma. [Old English *hāre hūne*, from *hār* HOAR + *hūne*, the plant]

horizon /həˈrʌɪz(ə)n/ *n.* **1 a** the line at which the earth and sky appear to meet. **b** (in full **apparent** or **sensible** or **visible horizon**) the line at which the earth and sky would appear to meet but for irregularities and obstructions; a circle where the earth's surface touches a cone whose vertex is at the observer's eye. **c** (in full **celestial** or **rational** or **true horizon**) a great circle of the celestial sphere, the plane of which passes through the centre of the earth and is parallel to that of the apparent horizon of a place. **2** limit of mental perception, experience, interest, etc. **3** a geological stratum or set of strata, or layer of soil, with particular characteristics. **4** *Archaeol.* the level at which a particular set of remains is found. ▫ **on the horizon** (of an event) just imminent or becoming apparent. [Middle English via Old French *orizon(te)* and Late Latin *horizon -ontis* from Greek *horizōn* (*kuklos*) 'limiting (circle)']

horizontal /hɒrɪˈzɒnt(ə)l/ *adj.* & *n.* ● *adj.* **1 a** parallel to the plane of the horizon, at right angles to the vertical (*horizontal plane*). **b** (of machinery etc.) having its parts working in a horizontal direction. **2 a** combining firms engaged in the same stage of production (*horizontal integration*). **b** involving social groups of equal status etc. **3** of or at the horizon. ● *n.* a horizontal line, plane, etc. ▫ **horizontality** /-ˈtalɪti/ *n.* **horizontally** *adv.* [French *horizontal* or modern Latin *horizontalis* (as HORIZON)]

hormone /ˈhɔːməʊn/ *n.* **1** *Physiol.* a regulatory substance produced in an organism and transported in tissue fluids such as blood or sap to stimulate specific cells or tissues into action. **2** a synthetic substance with a similar effect. ▫ **hormonal** /-ˈməʊn(ə)l/ *adj.* [Greek *hormōn*, part. of *hormaō* 'impel']

hormone replacement therapy *n.* treatment with oestrogens to alleviate menopausal symptoms (abbr.: HRT).

horn /hɔːn/ *n.* & *v.* ● *n.* **1 a** a hard permanent outgrowth, often curved and pointed, on the head of cattle, rhinoceroses, giraffes, and other esp. hoofed mammals, found singly, in pairs, or one in front of another. **b** the structure of a horn, consisting of a core of bone encased in keratinized skin. **2** each of two deciduous branched appendages on the head of (esp. male) deer. **3** a hornlike projection on the head of other animals, e.g. a snail's tentacle, the crest of a horned owl, etc. **4** the substance of which horns are composed. **5** anything resembling or compared to a horn in shape. **6** *Mus.* **a** = FRENCH HORN. **b** a wind instrument played by lip vibration, originally made of horn, now usu. of brass. **c** a horn player. **7** an instrument sounding a warning or other signal (*car horn*; *foghorn*). **8** a receptacle or instrument made of horn, e.g. a drinking vessel or powder flask etc. **9** a horn-shaped projection. **10** *US colloq.* a telephone. **11** the extremity of the moon or other crescent. **12 a** an arm or branch of a river, bay, etc. **b** (**the Horn**) Cape Horn. **13** a pyramidal peak formed by glacial action. **14** *Brit. coarse slang* an erect penis. **15** the hornlike emblem of a cuckold. ● *v.tr.* **1** (esp. as **horned** *adj.*) provide with horns. **2** gore with the horns. ▫ **horn in** *slang* **1** (usu. foll. by *on*) intrude. **2** interfere. **horn of plenty** a cornucopia. **on the horns of a dilemma** faced with a decision involving equally unfavourable alternatives. ▫ **hornist** *n.* (in senses 6a and b of *n.*). **hornless** *adj.* **hornlike** *adj.* [Old English from Germanic: related to Latin *cornu*]

hornbeam /ˈhɔːnbiːm/ *n.* any tree of the genus *Carpinus*, with a smooth bark and a hard tough wood.

hornbill /ˈhɔːnbɪl/ *n.* any bird of the tropical family Bucerotidae, with a hornlike excrescence on its large red or yellow curved bill.

hornblende /ˈhɔːnblɛnd/ *n.* a dark brown, black, or green mineral occurring in many igneous and metamorphic rocks, and composed of calcium, magnesium, and iron silicates. [German (as HORN, BLENDE)]

hornbook /ˈhɔːnbʊk/ *n. hist.* a leaf of paper containing the alphabet, the Lord's Prayer, etc., mounted on a wooden tablet with a handle, and protected by a thin plate of horn.

horned /hɔːnd/ *adj.* **1** having a horn or horns. **2** (*attrib.*) crescent-shaped (*horned moon*).

horned owl *n.* an owl, *Bubo virginianus*, with hornlike feathers over the ears.

horned toad *n.* **1** an American lizard, *Phrynosoma cornutum*, covered with spiny scales. **2** any SE Asian toad of the family Pelobatidae, with horn-shaped extensions over the eyes.

hornet /ˈhɔːnɪt/ *n.* a large wasp, *Vespa crabro*, with a brown and yellow striped body, and capable of inflicting a severe sting. □ **stir up a hornets' nest** provoke or cause trouble or opposition. [Old English *hyrnet*, perhaps related to HORN]

hornpipe /ˈhɔːnpʌɪp/ *n.* **1** a lively dance, usu. by one person (esp. associated with sailors). **2** the music for this. [name of an obsolete wind instrument partly of horn: Middle English, from HORN + PIPE]

horn-rimmed *adj.* (esp. of spectacles) having rims made of horn or a substance resembling it.

hornswoggle /ˈhɔːnswɒg(ə)l/ *v.tr. slang* cheat, hoax. [19th c.: origin unknown]

hornwort /ˈhɔːnwəːt/ *n.* any aquatic rootless plant of the genus *Ceratophyllum*, with forked leaves.

horny /ˈhɔːni/ *adj.* (**hornier, horniest**) **1** of or like horn. **2** hard like horn, callous (*horny-handed*). **3** *slang* sexually excited. □ **horniness** *n.*

horologe /ˈhɒrəlɒdʒ/ *n. archaic* a timepiece. [Middle English via Old French *orloge* and Latin *horologium* from Greek *hōrologion*, from *hōra* 'time' + *-logos* '-telling']

horology /hɒˈrɒlədʒi/ *n.* the art of measuring time or making clocks, watches, etc.; the study of this. □ **horologer** *n.* **horologic** /hɒrəˈlɒdʒɪk/ *adj.* **horological** /hɒrəˈlɒdʒɪk(ə)l/ *adj.* **horologist** *n.* [Greek *hōra* 'time' + -LOGY]

horoscope /ˈhɒrəskəʊp/ *n. Astrol.* **1** a forecast of a person's future based on a diagram showing the relative positions of the stars and planets at that person's birth. **2** such a diagram (*cast a horoscope*). **3** observation of the sky and planets at a particular moment, esp. at a person's birth. □ **horoscopic** /-ˈskɒpɪk/ *adj.* **horoscopical** /-ˈskɒpɪk(ə)l/ *adj.* **horoscopy** /hɒˈrɒskəpi/ *n.* [French via Latin *horoscopus* from Greek *hōroskopos*, from *hōra* 'time' + *skopos* 'observer']

horrendous /hɒˈrɛndəs/ *adj.* horrifying; awful. □ **horrendously** *adv.* **horrendousness** *n.* [Latin *horrendus*, gerundive of *horrēre*: see HORRID]

horrent /ˈhɒr(ə)nt/ *adj. poet.* **1** bristling. **2** shuddering. [Latin *horrēre*: see HORRID]

horrible /ˈhɒrɪb(ə)l/ *adj.* **1** causing or likely to cause horror; hideous, shocking. **2** *colloq.* unpleasant, excessive (*horrible weather*; *horrible noise*). □ **horribleness** *n.* **horribly** *adv.* [Middle English via Old French *(h)orrible* from Latin *horribilis*, from *horrēre*: see HORRID]

horrid /ˈhɒrɪd/ *adj.* **1** horrible, revolting. **2** *colloq.* unpleasant, disagreeable (*horrid weather*; *horrid children*). **3** *poet.* rough, bristling. □ **horridly** *adv.* **horridness** *n.* [Latin *horridus* from *horrēre* 'bristle, shudder']

horrific /hɒˈrɪfɪk/ *adj.* horrifying. □ **horrifically** *adv.* [French *horrifique* or Latin *horrificus* from *horrēre*: see HORRID]

horrify /ˈhɒrɪfʌɪ/ *v.tr.* (**-ies, -ied**) arouse horror in; shock, scandalize. □ **horrification** /-fɪˈkeɪʃ(ə)n/ *n.* **horrifiedly** /-fʌɪdli/ *adv.* **horrifying** *adj.* **horrifyingly** *adv.* [Latin *horrificare* (as HORRIFIC)]

horripilation /hɒˌrɪpɪˈleɪʃ(ə)n/ *n. literary* = GOOSE-FLESH. [Late Latin *horripilatio*, from Latin *horrēre* 'to bristle' + *pilus* 'hair']

horror /ˈhɒrə/ *n.* & *adj.* ● *n.* **1** an intense feeling of loathing and fear. **2 a** (often foll. by *of*) intense dislike. **b** (often foll. by *at*) *colloq.* intense dismay. **3 a** a person or thing causing horror. **b** *colloq.* a bad or mischievous person etc. **4** (in *pl.*; prec. by *the*) a fit of horror, depression, or nervousness, esp. as in delirium tremens. **5** a terrified and revolted shuddering. **6** (in *pl.*) an exclamation of dismay. ● *attrib.adj.* (of literature, films, etc.) designed to attract by arousing pleasurable feelings of horror. [Middle English via Old French *(h)orrour* from Latin *horror -oris* (as HORRID)]

horror-struck *adj.* (also **horror-stricken**) horrified, shocked.

hors concours /ɔː kɒ̃ˈkʊə, French ɔr kɔ̃kur/ *adj.* **1** unrivalled, unequalled. **2** (of an exhibit or exhibitor) not competing for a prize. [French, literally 'outside competition']

hors de combat /ɔː də ˈkɒ̃bɑː, French ɔr də kɔ̃ba/ *adj.* out of the fight or the running. [French]

hors d'oeuvre /ɔː ˈdəːv, ɔː ˈdəːvr(ə)/ *n.* (*pl.* same or **hors d'oeuvres** *pronunc.* same or /ˈdəːvz/) an appetizer served at the beginning of a meal or (occasionally) during a meal. [French, literally 'outside the work']

horse /hɔːs/ *n.* & *v.* ● *n.* **1 a** a solid-hoofed plant-eating quadruped, *Equus caballus*, with flowing mane and tail, used for riding and to carry and pull loads. **b** an adult male horse; a stallion or gelding. **c** any other four-legged mammal of the genus *Equus*, including asses and zebras. **d** (*collect.*; treated as *sing.*) cavalry. **e** a representation of a horse. **2** = VAULTING HORSE. **3 a** a frame or structure on which something is mounted or supported. **b** = SAWHORSE. **c** = CLOTHES HORSE 1. **4** *slang* heroin. **5** *colloq.* a unit of horsepower. **6** *Naut.* any of various ropes and bars. **7** *Mining* an obstruction in a vein. ● *v.* **1** *intr.* (foll. by *around*) fool about. **2** *tr.* provide (a person or vehicle) with a horse or horses. **3** *intr.* mount or go on horseback. □ **from the horse's mouth** (of information etc.) from the person directly concerned or another authoritative source. **horses for courses** *Brit.* the matching of tasks and talents. **to horse!** (as a command) mount your horses. □ **horseless** *adj.* **horselike** *adj.* [Old English *hors*, from Germanic]

horse-and-buggy *attrib.adj. N. Amer.* old-fashioned, bygone.

horseback /ˈhɔːsbak/ *n.* the back of a horse, esp. as sat on in riding. □ **on horseback** mounted on a horse.

horsebean /ˈhɔːsbiːn/ *n.* a broad bean used as fodder.

horse-block *n.* a small platform of stone or wood for mounting a horse.

horsebox /ˈhɔːsbɒks/ *n. Brit.* a closed vehicle for transporting a horse or horses.

horse brass see BRASS *n.* 5.

horsebreaker /ˈhɔːsbreɪkə/ *n.* a person who breaks in horses.

horse chestnut /hɔːs ˈtʃɛsnʌt/ *n.* **1** (also **horse chestnut tree**) any large ornamental tree of the genus *Aesculus*, with upright conical clusters of white or pink or red flowers. **2** the smooth dark brown inedible nut of this, enclosed in a spiny fruit (like the edible chestnut). Also called *conker*.

horse-cloth *n.* a cloth used to cover a horse, or as part of its trappings.

horse-coper *n. Brit.* a horse-dealer.

horse-doctor *n.* a veterinary surgeon attending horses.

horse-drawn *adj.* (of a vehicle) pulled by a horse or horses.

horseflesh /ˈhɔːsflɛʃ/ *n.* **1** the flesh of a horse, esp. as food. **2** horses collectively.

horsefly /ˈhɔːsflʌɪ/ *n.* (*pl.* **-flies**) any of various biting dipterous insects of the family Tabanidae troublesome esp. to horses.

Horse Guards *n.pl.* (in the UK) **1** a cavalry brigade of the household troops, now an armoured-car regiment providing a mounted squadron for ceremonial purposes. **2** the headquarters of this brigade in Whitehall.

horsehair /ˈhɔːshɛː/ *n.* hair from the mane or tail of a horse, used for padding etc.

horse latitudes *n.pl.* a belt of calms in each hemisphere between the trade winds and the westerlies.

horseleech /ˈhɔːsliːtʃ/ *n.* **1** a large freshwater leech of the genus *Haemopis*, feeding by swallowing not sucking. **2** an insatiable person (cf. Prov. 30:15).

horseless /ˈhɔːslɪs/ *adj.* without a horse.

horseless carriage *n. archaic* a motor car.

horse mackerel *n.* any large fish of the mackerel type, e.g. the scad or the tunny.

horseman /ˈhɔːsmən/ *n.* (*pl.* **-men**) **1** a rider on horseback. **2** a skilled rider.

horsemanship /ˈhɔːsmənʃɪp/ *n.* the art of riding on horseback; skill in doing this.

horse mushroom *n.* a large edible mushroom, *Agaricus arvensis.*

horse opera *n. N. Amer. slang* a western film.

horse-pistol *n.* a pistol for use by a horseman.

horseplay /ˈhɔːspleɪ/ *n.* boisterous play.

horse-pond *n.* a pond for watering and washing horses, proverbial as a place for ducking obnoxious persons.

horsepower /ˈhɔːspaʊə/ *n.* (*pl.* same) **1** an imperial unit of power equal to 550 foot-pounds per second (about 750 watts) (abbr.: **hp**). **2** the power of an engine etc. measured in terms of this.

horse race *n.* a race between horses with riders. □ **horse racing** *n.*

horseradish /ˈhɔːsradɪʃ/ *n.* **1** a cruciferous plant, *Armoracia rusticana*, with long lobed leaves. **2** the pungent root of this scraped or grated as a condiment, often made into a sauce.

horse sense *n. colloq.* plain common sense.

horseshoe /ˈhɔːsʃuː, -ʃʃ-/ *n.* **1** an iron shoe for a horse shaped like the outline of the hard part of the hoof. **2** a thing of this shape; an object shaped like C or U (e.g. a magnet, a table, a Spanish or Islamic arch).

horseshoe bat *n.* a bat of the Old World family Rhinolophidae, usu. with a horseshoe-shaped ridge on the nose.

horseshoe crab *n.* a large marine arthropod, *Xiphosura polyphemus*, with a horseshoe-shaped shell and a long tail-spine. Also called *king crab*.

horse's neck *n. slang* a drink of flavoured ginger ale usu. with spirits.

horse-soldier *n.* a soldier mounted on a horse.

horsetail /ˈhɔːsteɪl/ *n.* **1** the tail of a horse (formerly used in Turkey as a standard, or as an ensign denoting the rank of a pasha). **2** any cryptogamous plant of the genus *Equisetum*, like a horse's tail, with a hollow jointed stem and scalelike leaves. **3** = PONYTAIL.

horse-trading *n.* **1** *N. Amer.* dealing in horses. **2** shrewd bargaining.

horsewhip /ˈhɔːswɪp/ *n.* & *v.* ● *n.* a whip for driving horses. ● *v.tr.* (**-whipped**, **-whipping**) beat with a horsewhip.

horsewoman /ˈhɔːswʊmən/ *n.* (*pl.* **-women**) **1** a woman who rides on horseback. **2** a skilled woman rider.

horst /hɔːst/ *n. Geol.* a raised elongated block of land bounded by faults on both sides. [German, = heap]

horsy /ˈhɔːsi/ *adj.* (also **horsey**) (**horsier**, **horsiest**) **1** of or like a horse. **2** concerned with or devoted to horses or horse racing. **3** affectedly using the dress and language of a groom or jockey. □ **horsily** *adv.* **horsiness** *n.*

hortatory /ˈhɔːtət(ə)ri/ *adj.* (also **hortative** /ˈhɔːtətɪv/) tending or serving to exhort. □ **hortation** /hɔːˈteɪʃ(ə)n/ *n.* [Latin *hortativus* from *hortari* 'exhort']

hortensia /hɔːˈtɛnsɪə/ *n.* a kind of hydrangea, *Hydrangea macrophylla*, with large rounded infertile flower heads. [modern Latin, named after *Hortense* Lepaute, 18th-c. Frenchwoman]

horticulture /ˈhɔːtɪkʌltʃə/ *n.* the art of garden cultivation. □ **horticultural** /-ˈkʌltʃ(ə)r(ə)l/ *adj.* **horticulturalist** /-ˈkʌltʃ(ə)r(ə)lɪst/ *n.* **horticulturist** /-ˈkʌltʃərɪst/ *n.* [Latin *hortus* 'garden', on the pattern of AGRICULTURE]

hortus siccus /ˌhɔːtəs ˈsɪkəs/ *n.* **1** an arranged collection of dried plants. **2** *Brit.* a collection of uninteresting facts etc. [Latin, = dry garden]

Hos. *abbr.* Hosea (Old Testament).

hosanna /həʊˈzanə/ *n.* & *int.* a shout of adoration (Matt. 21:9, 15, etc.). [Middle English via Late Latin and Greek *hōsanna* from Hebrew *hôšaʻnā*, for *hôšîʻa-nnâ* 'save now!']

hose /həʊz/ *n.* & *v.* ● *n.* **1** a flexible tube conveying water for watering plants etc., putting out fires, etc. **2 a** (*collect.*; treated as *pl.*) stockings and socks (esp. in trade use). **b** *hist.* breeches (*doublet and hose*). ● *v.tr.* **1** (often foll. by *down*) water or spray or drench with a hose. **2** provide with hose. [Old English from Germanic]

hosepipe /ˈhəʊzpʌɪp/ *n. Brit.* = HOSE *n.* 1.

hosier /ˈhəʊzɪə/ *n.* a dealer in hosiery.

hosiery /ˈhəʊzɪəri, -ʒəri/ *n.* **1** stockings and socks. **2** *Brit.* knitted or woven underwear.

hospice /ˈhɒspɪs/ *n.* **1** a home for people who are ill (esp. terminally) or *Brit.* destitute. **2** a lodging for travellers, esp. one kept by a religious order. [French, from Latin *hospitium* (as HOST²)]

hospitable /hɒˈspɪtəb(ə)l, ˈhɒspɪt-/ *adj.* giving or disposed to give welcome and entertainment to strangers or guests. □ **hospitably** *adv.* [French from *hospiter* from medieval Latin *hospitare* 'entertain' (as HOST²)]

hospital /ˈhɒspɪt(ə)l/ *n.* **1** an institution providing medical and surgical treatment and nursing care for ill or injured people. **2** *hist.* **a** a hospice. **b** an establishment of the Knights Hospitallers. **3** *Brit. Law* a charitable institution (also in proper names, e.g. *Christ's Hospital*). [Middle English via Old French from medieval Latin *hospitale*, neut. of Latin *hospitalis* (*adj.*) (as HOST²)]

hospital corners *n.pl.* a way of tucking in sheets, used by nurses.

hospitaler *US* var. of HOSPITALLER.

hospital fever *n.* a kind of typhus formerly prevalent in crowded hospitals.

hospitalism /ˈhɒspɪt(ə)lɪz(ə)m/ *n.* the adverse effects of a prolonged stay in hospital.

hospitality /hɒspɪˈtalɪti/ *n.* the friendly and generous reception and entertainment of guests or strangers. [Middle English via Old French *hospitalité* from Latin *hospitalitas -tatis* (as HOSPITAL)]

hospitalize /ˈhɒspɪt(ə)lʌɪz/ *v.tr.* (also **-ise**) send or admit (a patient) to hospital. □ **hospitalization** /-ˈzeɪʃ(ə)n/ *n.*

hospitaller /ˈhɒspɪt(ə)lə/ *n.* (*US* **hospitaler**) **1** (also **Hospitaller**) a member of a charitable religious order. **2** a chaplain (in some London hospitals). [Middle English via Old French *hospitalier* from medieval Latin *hospitalarius* (as HOSPITAL)]

hospital ship *n.* a ship to receive sick and wounded sailors, or to take sick and wounded soldiers home.

hospital social worker *n.* a social worker attached to a hospital and seeing to the aftercare of patients.

hospital train *n.* a train taking wounded soldiers from a battlefield.

hospital trust *n.* (in the UK) a trust consisting of a National Health Service hospital or hospitals no longer under local authority control.

host¹ /həʊst/ *n.* **1** (usu. foll. by *of*) a large number of people or things. **2** *archaic* an army. **3** (in full **heavenly host**) **a** the sun, moon, and stars. **b** *Bibl.* the angels. □ **host** (or **hosts**) **of heaven** = sense 3 of *n.* **is a host in himself** or **herself** *Brit.* can do as much as several ordinary people. [Middle English via Old French from Latin *hostis* 'stranger, enemy', in medieval Latin 'army']

host² /həʊst/ *n.* & *v.* ● *n.* **1** a person who receives or entertains another as a guest. **2** the landlord of an inn (*mine host*). **3** *Biol.* an animal or plant having a parasite or commensal. **4** an animal or person that has received a transplanted organ etc. **5** the compère of a show, esp. of a television or radio programme. ● *v.tr.* act as host to (a person) or at (an event). [Middle English via Old French *oste* from Latin *hospes -pitis* 'host, guest']

host³ /həʊst/ *n.* the bread consecrated in the Eucharist. [Middle English via Old French (*h*)*oiste* from Latin *hostia* 'victim']

hosta /ˈhɒstə/ *n.* any perennial garden plant of the genus *Hosta* (formerly *Funkia*) with green or variegated ornamental leaves and loose clusters of tubular mauve or white flowers. [modern Latin, named after N. T. *Host*, Austrian physician d. 1834]

hostage /ˈhɒstɪdʒ/ *n.* **1** a person seized or held as security for the fulfilment of a condition. **2** a pledge or security. □ **hostageship** *n.* [Middle English from Old

French *(h)ostage*, ultimately via Late Latin *obsidatus* 'hostageship' from Latin *obses obsidis* 'hostage']

hostage to fortune *n.* an acquisition, commitment, etc., regarded as endangered by unforeseen circumstances.

hostel /'hɒst(ə)l/ *n.* **1** *Brit.* a house of residence or lodging for students, nurses, etc. **2** = YOUTH HOSTEL. **3** *archaic* an inn. [Middle English via Old French *(h)ostel* from medieval Latin (as HOSPITAL)]

hostelling /'hɒst(ə)lɪŋ/ *n.* (*US* **hosteling**) the practice of staying in youth hostels, esp. while travelling. □ **hosteller** *n.*

hostelry /'hɒst(ə)lri/ *n.* (*pl.* **-ies**) *archaic* or *literary* an inn. [Middle English from Old French *(h)ostelerie*, from *(h)ostelier* 'innkeeper' (as HOSTEL)]

hostess /'həʊstɪs, -ɛs, həʊ'stɛs/ *n.* **1** a woman who receives or entertains a guest. **2** a woman employed to welcome and entertain customers at a nightclub etc. **3** a stewardess on an aircraft, train, etc. (*air hostess*). [Middle English from Old French *(h)ostesse* (as HOST[2])]

hostile /'hɒstʌɪl/ *adj.* **1** of an enemy. **2** (often foll. by *to*) unfriendly, opposed. □ **hostilely** *adv.* [French *hostile* or Latin *hostilis* (as HOST[1])]

hostile witness *n. Law* a witness who appears hostile to the party calling him or her and therefore untrustworthy.

hostility /hɒ'stɪlɪti/ *n.* (*pl.* **-ies**) **1** being hostile, enmity. **2** a state of warfare. **3** (in *pl.*) acts of warfare. **4** opposition (in thought etc.). [French *hostilité* or Late Latin *hostilitas* (as HOSTILE)]

hostler /'(h)ɒslə/ *n.* **1** *hist.* = OSTLER. **2** *US* a person in charge of vehicles or machines, esp. railway engines, when they are not in use. [Middle English from *hosteler* (as OSTLER)]

hot /hɒt/ *adj., v., & adv.* ● *adj.* (**hotter**, **hottest**) **1 a** having a relatively or noticeably high temperature. **b** (of food or drink) prepared by heating and served without cooling. **2** producing the sensation of heat (*hot fever*; *hot flush*). **3** (of pepper, spices, etc.) pungent. **4** (of a person) feeling heat. **5 a** (often foll. by *for*, *on*) eager, keen (*in hot pursuit*). **b** (foll. by *on*) *colloq.* strict with. **c** (foll. by *on*) *colloq.* knowledgeable about. **6 a** ardent, passionate, excited. **b** angry or upset. **c** lustful. **d** exciting. **7 a** (of news etc.) fresh, recent. **b** *Brit. colloq.* (of Treasury bills) newly issued. **8** *Hunting* (of the scent) fresh and strong, indicating that the quarry has passed recently. **9 a** (of a player) very skilful. **b** (of a competitor in a race or other sporting event) strongly fancied to win (*a hot favourite*). **c** (of a hit, return, etc., in ball games) difficult for an opponent to deal with. **10** (of music, esp. jazz) strongly rhythmical and emotional. **11** *slang* **a** (of goods) stolen, esp. easily identifiable and hence difficult to dispose of. **b** (of a person) wanted by the police. **12** *slang* radioactive. **13** *colloq.* (of information) unusually reliable (*hot tip*). ● *v.tr. & intr.* (**hotted**, **hotting**) (usu. foll. by *up*) *Brit. colloq.* **1** make or become hot. **2** make or become active, lively, exciting, or dangerous. ● *adv.* **1** *Brit.* angrily, severely (*give it him hot*). **2** eagerly. □ **go hot and cold** feel alternately hot and cold owing to fear etc. **have the hots for** *slang* be sexually attracted to. **hot under the collar** angry, resentful, or embarrassed. **make it** (or **things**) **hot for a person** persecute a person. **not so hot** *colloq.* only mediocre. **sell** (or **go**) **like hot cakes** see CAKE. □ **hotly** *adv.* **hotness** *n.* **hottish** *adj.* [Old English *hāt*, from Germanic]

hot air *n. colloq.* empty, boastful, or excited talk.

hot-air balloon *n.* a balloon (see BALLOON *n.* 2) consisting of a bag in which air is heated by burners located below it, causing it to rise.

hotbed /'hɒtbɛd/ *n.* **1** a bed of earth heated by fermenting manure, for raising or forcing plants. **2** (foll. by *of*) an environment promoting the growth of something, esp. something unwelcome (*hotbed of vice*).

hot blast *n.* a blast of heated air forced into a furnace.

hot-blooded *adj.* ardent, passionate.

hot cathode *n.* a cathode heated to emit electrons.

hotchpotch /'hɒtʃpɒtʃ/ *n.* (also (esp. in sense 3) **hotchpot** /-pɒt/) **1** a confused mixture, a jumble. **2** a dish of many mixed ingredients, esp. a mutton broth or stew with vegetables. **3** *Law* the reunion and blending of properties for the purpose of securing equal division (esp. of the property of an intestate parent). [Middle English from Anglo-French & Old French *hochepot*, from Old French *hocher* 'shake' + POT[1]: *-potch* by assimilation]

hot cross bun *n.* a bun marked with a cross, traditionally eaten on Good Friday.

hot-desking *n.* the practice of sharing workspaces or moving from desk to desk according to need.

hot dog *n., int., & v.* ● *n.* **1** a hot sausage sandwiched in a soft roll. **2** *N. Amer. slang* a person who performs stunts, esp. when skiing or surfing. ● *int. N. Amer. slang* expressing approval. ● *v.intr.* (**hotdog**) (**hotdogged**, **hotdogging**) *N. Amer. slang* perform stunts. □ **hotdogger** *n.*

hotel /həʊ'tɛl, əʊ-/ *n.* **1** an establishment providing accommodation and meals for payment. **2** *Austral.* & *NZ* a public house. [French *hôtel*, later form of HOSTEL]

hotelier /həʊ'tɛlɪeɪ, -ɪə/ *n.* a hotel-keeper. [French *hôtelier* from Old French *hostelier*: see HOSTELRY]

hot flash *n.* esp. *N. Amer.* = HOT FLUSH.

hot flush see FLUSH[1] *n.* 6a.

hotfoot /'hɒtfʊt, hɒt'fʊt/ *adv., v., & adj.* ● *adv.* in eager haste. ● *v.tr.* hurry eagerly (esp. *hotfoot it*). ● *adj.* acting quickly.

hot gospeller *n.* a zealous puritan; a rabid propagandist.

hothead /'hɒthɛd/ *n.* an impetuous person.

hot-headed *adj.* impetuous, excitable. □ **hot-headedly** *adv.* **hot-headedness** *n.*

hothouse /'hɒthaʊs/ *n. & v.* ● *n.* **1** a heated building, usu. largely of glass, for rearing plants out of season or in a climate colder than is natural for them (often attrib.: *hothouse flowers*). **2** an environment that encourages the rapid growth or development of something. ● *v.tr.* raise in or as if in a hothouse; force the development of.

hotline /'hɒtlʌɪn/ *n.* a direct exclusive line of communication, esp. for emergencies.

hot metal *n. Printing* using type made from molten metal.

hot money *n.* capital transferred at frequent intervals.

hot pants *n.pl.* very brief shorts, usu. with a bib, worn as a fashion garment.

hotplate /'hɒtpleɪt/ *n.* a heated metal plate etc. (or a set of these) for cooking food or keeping it hot.

hotpot /'hɒtpɒt/ *n. Brit.* a casserole of meat and vegetables, usu. with a layer of potato on top.

hot potato *n. colloq.* a controversial or awkward matter or situation.

hot-press *n. & v.* ● *n.* a press of glazed boards and hot metal plates for smoothing paper or cloth or making plywood. ● *v.tr.* press (paper etc.) in this.

hot rod *n. & v.* ● *n.* a motor vehicle modified to have extra power and speed. ● *v.* (**hot-rod**) (**-rodded**, **-rodding**) **1** *tr.* soup up (a vehicle, amplifier, etc.). **2** *intr.* drive a hot rod. □ **hot-rodder** *n.*

hot seat *n. slang* **1** a position of difficult responsibility. **2** the electric chair.

hot shoe *n. Photog.* a socket on a camera with electrical contacts for a flashgun etc.

hot-short *adj.* (of metal) brittle in its hot state. [HOT + *short* suggested by the earlier *red-short* from Swedish *rödskör*, from *röd* 'red' + *skör* 'brittle']

hotshot /'hɒtʃɒt/ *n. & adj.* esp. *US colloq.* ● *n.* **1** an important or exceptionally able person. **2** *Sport* a player of football, basketball, etc. with exceptionally good aim. ● *attrib.adj.* important, able, expert, suddenly prominent.

hot spot *n.* **1** a small region that is relatively hot. **2** a lively or dangerous place.

hot spring *n.* a spring of naturally hot water.

hotspur /ˈhɒtspəː, -spə/ *n.* a rash person. [sobriquet of Sir H. Percy, d. 1403]

hot stuff *n. colloq.* **1** a formidably capable person. **2** an important person or thing. **3** a sexually attractive person. **4** a spirited, strong-willed, or passionate person. **5** a book, film, etc. with a strongly erotic content.

hot-tempered *adj.* impulsively angry.

Hottentot /ˈhɒt(ə)ntɒt/ *n. & adj.* often *offens.* ● *n.* (*pl.* same or **Hottentots**) = NAMA *n.* 1, 2. ● *adj.* = NAMA *adj.* [Dutch, probably originally a repetitive formula in a Nama dancing-song, transferred by Dutch sailors to the people themselves]

■ **Usage** *Nama* is now the preferred name for this people and their language.

hottie /ˈhɒti/ *n.* (also **hotty**) (*pl.* **-ies**) *Brit. colloq.* a hot-water bottle.

hotting /ˈhɒtɪŋ/ *n. slang* the practice of driving recklessly in a stolen car. □ **hotter** *n.*

hot tub *n.* a large tub filled with hot aerated water and used by one or several people for recreation or physical therapy.

hot war *n.* an open war, with active hostilities.

hot water *n. colloq.* difficulty, trouble, or disgrace (*be in hot water*; *get into hot water*).

hot-water bottle *n.* (*US* **hot-water bag**) a container, usu. made of rubber, filled with hot water, esp. to warm a bed.

hot well *n.* **1** = HOT SPRING. **2** a reservoir in a condensing steam engine.

hot-wire *adj. & v.* ● *attrib.adj.* operated by the expansion of heated wire. ● *v.tr.* esp. *N. Amer. slang* start the engine of (a car etc.) by bypassing the ignition system.

Houdini /huːˈdiːni/ *n.* **1** an ingenious escape. **2** a person skilled at escaping. [H. *Houdini*, professional name of E. Weiss, American escapologist d. 1926]

hough /hɒk/ *n. & v. Brit.* ● *n.* **1** = HOCK[1]. **2** a cut of beef etc. from this and the leg above it. ● *v.tr.* hamstring. [Middle English *ho(u)gh* = Old English *hōh* 'heel' in *hōhsinu* 'hamstring']

hoummos var. of HUMMUS.

hound /haʊnd/ *n. & v.* ● *n.* **1 a** a dog used for hunting, esp. one able to track by scent. **b** (**the hounds**) *Brit.* a pack of foxhounds. **2** *colloq.* a despicable man. **3** a runner who follows a trail in hare and hounds. **4** a person keen in pursuit of something (usu. in *comb.*: *news-hound*). ● *v.tr.* **1** harass or pursue relentlessly. **2** chase or pursue with a hound. **3** (foll. by *at*) set (a dog or person) on (a quarry). **4** urge on or nag (a person). □ **ride to hounds** go fox-hunting on horseback. [Old English *hund*, from Germanic]

hound's-tongue *n.* a tall plant, *Cynoglossum officinale*, with tongue-shaped leaves.

houndstooth /ˈhaʊn(d)ztuːθ/ *n.* a check pattern with notched corners suggestive of a canine tooth.

hour /ˈaʊə/ *n.* **1** a twenty-fourth part of a day and night, 60 minutes. **2** a time of day, a point in time (*a late hour*; *what is the hour?*). **3** (in *pl.* with preceding numerals in form 18.00, 20.30, etc.) this number of hours and minutes past midnight on the 24-hour clock (*will assemble at 20.00 hours*). **4 a** a period set aside for some purpose (*lunch hour*; *keep regular hours*). **b** (in *pl.*) a fixed period of time for work, use of a building, etc. (*office hours*; *opening hours*). **5** a short indefinite period of time (*an idle hour*). **6** the present time (*question of the hour*). **7** a time for action etc. (*the hour has come*). **8** the distance travelled in one hour (*we are an hour from London*). **9** *RC Ch.* **a** prayers to be said at one of seven fixed times of day (*book of hours*). **b** any of these times. **10** (prec. by *the*) each time o'clock of a whole number of hours (*buses leave on the hour*; *on the half-hour*; *at quarter past the hour*). **11** *Astron.* 15° of longitude or right ascension. □ **after hours** after closing time. **till all hours** till very late. [Middle English *ure* etc. via Anglo-French *ure*, Old French *ore*, *eure* and Latin *hora* from Greek *hōra* 'season, hour']

hourglass /ˈaʊəglɑːs/ *n.* **1** a reversible device with two connected glass bulbs containing sand that takes an hour to pass from the upper to the lower bulb. **2** (*attrib.*) shaped like an hourglass (*hourglass figure*).

hour hand *n.* the hand on a clock or watch which shows the hour.

houri /ˈhʊəri/ *n.* (*pl.* **houris**) a beautiful young woman, esp. in the Muslim Paradise. [French via Persian *ḥūrī* from Arabic *ḥūr*, pl. of *ḥawra'* 'gazelle-like' (of the eyes)]

hour-long *adj. & adv.* ● *adj.* lasting for one hour. ● *adv.* for one hour.

hourly /ˈaʊəli/ *adj. & adv.* ● *adj.* **1** done or occurring every hour. **2** frequent, continual. **3** reckoned hour by hour (*hourly wage*). ● *adv.* **1** every hour. **2** frequently, continually.

house *n. & v.* ● *n.* /haʊs/ (*pl.* /ˈhaʊzɪz/) **1 a** a building for human habitation. **b** (*attrib.*) (of an animal) kept in, frequenting, or infesting houses (*house cat*; *housefly*). **2** a building for a special purpose (*opera house*; *summer house*). **3** a building for keeping animals or goods (*hen house*). **4 a** a religious community. **b** the buildings occupied by it. **5** *Brit.* **a** a body of pupils living in the same building at a boarding school. **b** such a building. **c** a division of a day school for games, competitions, etc. **6** *Brit.* **a** a college of a university. **b** (**the House**) Christ Church, Oxford. **7** (usu. **House**) a family, esp. a royal family; a dynasty (*House of York*). **8 a** a firm or institution. **b** *Brit.* its place of business. **c** (**the House**) *Brit. colloq.* the Stock Exchange. **9 a** a legislative or deliberative assembly. **b** the building where it meets. **c** (**the House**) (in the UK) the House of Commons or Lords; (in the US) the House of Representatives. **10 a** an audience in a theatre, cinema, etc. **b** *Brit.* a performance in a theatre or cinema (*second house starts at 9 o'clock*). **c** a theatre. **11** *Astrol.* a twelfth part of the heavens. **12** (*attrib.*) living in a hospital as a member of staff (*house officer*; *house surgeon*). **13 a** a place of public refreshment, a restaurant or inn (*coffee house*; *public house*). **b** (*attrib.*) (of wine) selected by the management of a restaurant, hotel, etc. to be offered at a special price. **14** a brothel. **15** *Sc.* a dwelling that is one of several in a building. **16** *Brit. slang* = HOUSEY-HOUSEY. **17** an animal's den, shell, etc. **18** (in full **house music**) a style of popular dance music typically using drum machines, synthesized bass lines, sparse repetitive vocals, and a fast beat. **19** (**the House**) *Brit. hist. euphem.* the workhouse. ● *v.tr.* /haʊz/ **1** provide (a person, a population, etc.) with a house or houses or other accommodation. **2** store (goods etc.). **3** enclose or encase (a part or fitting). **4** fix in a socket, mortise, etc. □ **as safe as houses** *Brit.* thoroughly or completely safe. **keep house** provide for or manage a household. **keep** (or **make**) **a House** secure the presence of enough members for a quorum in the House of Commons. **keep to the house** (or **keep the house**) stay indoors. **like a house on fire 1** vigorously, fast. **2** successfully, excellently. **on the house** at the management's expense, free. **play house** play at being a family in its home. **put** (or **set**) **one's house in order** make necessary reforms. **set up house** begin to live in a separate dwelling. □ **houseful** *n.* (*pl.* **-fuls**). **houseless** *adj.* [Old English *hūs*, *hūsian*, from Germanic]

house agent *n. Brit.* an agent for the sale and letting of houses.

house and home *n.* (as an emphatic) home.

house arrest *n.* detention in one's own house etc., not in prison.

houseboat /ˈhaʊsbəʊt/ *n.* a boat fitted up for living in.

housebound /ˈhaʊsbaʊnd/ *adj.* unable to leave one's house through illness etc.

houseboy /ˈhaʊsbɔɪ/ *n.* a boy or man as a servant in a house.

housebreaker /ˈhaʊsbreɪkə/ *n.* **1** a person guilty of housebreaking. **2** *Brit.* a person who is employed to demolish houses.

housebreaking /ˈhaʊsbreɪkɪŋ/ *n.* the act of breaking into a building, esp. in daytime, to commit a crime (in 1968 replaced as a statutory crime in English law by BURGLARY).

house-broken *adj.* = *house-trained* (see HOUSE-TRAIN).

housebuilding /ˈhaʊsbɪldɪŋ/ *n.* the activity of building houses. □ **housebuilder** *n.*

housebuyer /ˈhaʊsbʌɪə/ *n.* a person who buys a house. □ **house-buying** *n. & adj.*

housecarl /ˈhaʊskɑːl/ *n.* (also **housecarle**) *hist.* a member of the bodyguard of a Danish or English king or noble. [Old English *húscarl* from Old Norse *húskarl*, from *hús* HOUSE + *karl* 'man': cf. CARL]

house church *n. Brit.* **1** a charismatic Church independent of traditional denominations. **2** a group meeting in a house as part of the activities of a Church.

housecoat /ˈhaʊskəʊt/ *n.* a woman's garment for informal wear in the house, usu. a long dresslike coat.

housecraft /ˈhaʊskrɑːft/ *n. Brit.* skill in household management.

house dog *n.* a dog kept to guard a house.

house-father *n.* a man in charge of a house, esp. of a home for children.

house finch *n.* a red-breasted finch, *Carpodacus mexicanus*, common in western N. America.

house-flag *n.* a flag indicating to what firm a ship belongs.

housefly /ˈhaʊsflʌɪ/ *n.* (*pl.* **-flies**) any fly of the family Muscidae, esp. *Musca domestica*, breeding in decaying organic matter and often entering houses.

house guest *n.* a guest staying for some days in a private house.

household /ˈhaʊshəʊld/ *n.* **1** the occupants of a house regarded as a unit. **2** a house and its affairs. **3** (prec. by *the*) (in the UK) the royal household.

householder /ˈhaʊshəʊldə/ *n.* **1** a person who owns or rents a house. **2** the head of a household.

household gods *n.pl.* **1** gods presiding over a household, esp. *Rom.Hist.* the lares and penates. **2** the essentials of home life.

household troops *n.pl.* (in the UK) troops nominally employed to guard the sovereign.

household word *n.* (also **household name**) **1** a familiar name or saying. **2** a familiar person or thing.

house-hunting *n.* the process of seeking a house to live in. □ **house-hunt** *v.intr.* **house-hunter** *n.*

house-husband *n.* a husband who carries out the household duties traditionally carried out by a housewife.

housekeep /ˈhaʊskiːp/ *v.intr.* (*past* and *past part.* **-kept**) *colloq.* keep house.

housekeeper /ˈhaʊskiːpə/ *n.* **1** a person, esp. a woman, employed to manage a household. **2** a person in charge of a house, office, etc.

housekeeping /ˈhaʊskiːpɪŋ/ *n.* **1** the management of household affairs. **2** money allowed for this. **3** the operations of a computer, or of an organization etc., which make work possible but do not directly constitute its performance, e.g. maintenance and record-keeping.

houseleek /ˈhaʊsliːk/ *n.* a succulent plant, *Sempervivum tectorum*, with pink flowers, growing on walls and roofs.

house lights *n.pl.* the lights in the auditorium of a theatre.

house magazine *n.* a magazine published by a firm and dealing mainly with its own activities.

housemaid /ˈhaʊsmeɪd/ *n.* a female servant in a house, esp. *Brit.* in charge of reception rooms and bedrooms.

housemaid's knee *n.* inflammation of the kneecap, often due to excessive kneeling.

houseman /ˈhaʊsmən/ *n.* (*pl.* **-men**) **1** *Brit.* a resident doctor at a hospital etc. **2** = HOUSEBOY.

house martin *n.* a black and white swallow-like bird, *Delichon urbica*, which builds a mud nest on house walls etc.

housemaster /ˈhaʊsmɑːstə/ *n.* (*fem.* **housemistress** /ˈhaʊsˌmɪstrɪs/) the teacher in charge of a house at a boarding school.

house-mother *n.* a woman in charge of a house, esp. of a home for children.

house mouse *n.* a usu. grey mouse, *Mus musculus*, very common as a scavenger around human dwellings, and bred as a pet and experimental animal.

house music see HOUSE *n.* 18.

house of cards *n.* **1** an insecure scheme etc. **2** a structure built (usu. by a child) out of playing cards.

House of Commons *n.* (in the UK) the elected chamber of Parliament.

house officer *n.* a hospital doctor of one of the more junior grades.

house of God *n.* a church, a place of worship.

house of ill fame *n. archaic* a brothel.

House of Keys *n.* (in the Isle of Man) the elected chamber of Tynwald.

House of Lords *n.* **1** (in the UK) the chamber of Parliament composed of peers and bishops. **2** a committee of specially qualified members of this appointed as the ultimate judicial appeal court.

House of Representatives *n.* the lower house of the US Congress and other legislatures.

house-parent *n.* a house-mother or house-father.

house party *n.* **1** *Brit.* a group of guests staying at a country house etc. **2** a party at which the guests stay at a house overnight.

house plant *n.* a plant grown indoors.

house-proud *adj.* attentive to, or unduly preoccupied with, the care and appearance of the home.

houseroom /ˈhaʊsruːm, -rʊm/ *n.* space or accommodation in one's house. □ **not give houseroom to** *Brit.* not have in any circumstances.

house-sit *v.intr.* live in and look after a house while its owner is away. □ **housesitter** *n.*

Houses of Parliament *n.pl.* **1** the Houses of Lords and Commons regarded together. **2** the buildings where they meet.

house sparrow *n.* a common brown and grey sparrow, *Passer domesticus*, which nests in the eaves and roofs of houses.

house style *n.* a particular printer's or publisher's etc. preferred way of presentation.

house-to-house *adj., adv., & n.* ● *adj. & adv.* performed at or carried to each house in turn. ● *n.* a house-to-house collection, search, etc.

housetop /ˈhaʊstɒp/ *n.* the roof of a house. □ **proclaim** (or **shout** etc.) **from the housetops** announce publicly.

house-train *v.tr.* (often as **house-trained** *adj.*) *Brit.* **1** train (an animal) to be clean in the house. **2** *colloq.* teach good manners or tidiness to.

house-warming *n.* a party celebrating a move to a new home.

housewife /ˈhaʊswʌɪf/ *n.* (*pl.* **-wives**) **1** a woman (usu. married) managing a household. **2** /ˈhʌzɪf/ *Brit.* a case for needles, thread, etc. □ **housewifely** *adj.* [Middle English *hus(e)wif*, from HOUSE + WIFE]

housewifery /ˈhaʊswɪfri/ *n.* **1** housekeeping. **2** skill in this, housecraft.

housework /ˈhaʊswəːk/ *n.* regular work done in housekeeping, e.g. cleaning and cooking.

housey-housey /haʊsɪˈhaʊsi, haʊzɪˈhaʊzi/ *n.* (also **housie-housie**) *Brit.* a gambling form of lotto.

housing[1] /ˈhaʊzɪŋ/ *n.* **1 a** dwelling houses collectively. **b** the provision of these. **2** shelter, lodging. **3** a rigid casing, esp. for moving or sensitive parts of a machine. **4** the hole or niche cut in one piece of wood to receive some part of another in order to join them.

housing[2] /ˈhaʊzɪŋ/ *n.* a cloth covering put on a horse for protection or ornament. [Middle English = covering, from obsolete *house* via Old French *houce* from medieval Latin *hultia*, from Germanic]

housing estate *n. Brit.* a residential area planned as a unit.

houting /'haʊtɪŋ/ *n.* a freshwater whitefish, *Coregonus lavaretus*, of northern Eurasia. [Dutch *houtic*]

hove *past* of HEAVE.

hovel /'hɒv(ə)l/ *n.* **1** a small miserable dwelling. **2** a conical building enclosing a kiln. **3** an open shed or outhouse. [Middle English: origin unknown]

hover /'hɒvə/ *v. & n.* ● *v.intr.* **1** (of a bird, helicopter, etc.) remain in one place in the air. **2** (often foll. by *about, round*) wait close at hand, linger. **3** remain undecided. ● *n.* **1** hovering. **2** a state of suspense. □ **hoverer** *n.* [Middle English from obsolete *hove* 'hover, linger', of unknown origin]

hovercraft /'hɒvəkrɑːft/ *n.* (*pl.* same) a vehicle or craft that travels over land or water on a cushion of air provided by a downward blast.

hoverfly /'hɒvəflʌɪ/ *n.* (*pl.* **-flies**) any fly of the family Syrphidae, hovering with rapidly beating wings.

hoverport /'hɒvəpɔːt/ *n.* a terminal for hovercraft.

hovertrain /'hɒvətreɪn/ *n.* a train that travels on a cushion of air like a hovercraft.

how[1] /haʊ/ *adv., conj., & n.* ● *interrog.adv.* **1** by what means, in what way (*how do you do it?*; *tell me how you do it*; *how could you behave so disgracefully?*; *but how to bridge the gap?*). **2** in what condition, esp. of health (*how is the patient?*; *how do things stand?*). **3 a** to what extent (*how far is it?*; *how would you like to take my place?*; *how we laughed!*). **b** to what extent good or well, what ... like (*how was the film?*; *how did they play?*). ● *rel. adv.* in whatever way, as (*do it how you can*). ● *conj. colloq.* that (*told us how he'd been in India*). ● *n.* the way a thing is done (*the how and why of it*). □ **and how!** *colloq.* very much so (chiefly used ironically or intensively). **here's how!** I drink to your good health. **how about 1** would you like (*how about a game of chess?*). **2** what is to be done about. **3** what is the news about. **how are you? 1** what is your state of health? **2** = *how do you do?* **how come?** see COME. **how do?** an informal greeting on being introduced to a stranger. **how do you do?** a formal greeting. **how many** what number. **how much 1** what amount (*how much do I owe you?*; *did not know how much to take*). **2** what price (*how much is it?*). **3** (as *interrog.*) *Brit. joc.* what? (*'She is a hedonist.' 'A how much?'*). **how now?** *archaic* what is the meaning of this? **how so?** how can you show that that is so? **how's that? 1** what is your opinion or explanation of that? **2** *Cricket* (said to an umpire) is the batsman out or not? [Old English *hū*, from West Germanic]

how[2] /haʊ/ *int.* a greeting attributed to N. American Indians. [perhaps from Sioux *háo*, Omaha *hau*]

howbeit /haʊ'biːɪt/ *adv. archaic* nevertheless.

howdah /'haʊdə/ *n.* a seat for two or more, usu. with a canopy, for riding on the back of an elephant or camel. [Urdu *hawda* from Arabic *hawdaj* 'litter']

how-do-you-do (or **how-d'ye-do**) *n.* (*pl.* **-dos**) an awkward situation.

howdy /'haʊdi/ *int. US* = *how do you do?* (see HOW[1]). [corruption]

howe'er /haʊ'ɛː/ *poet.* var. of HOWEVER.

however /haʊ'ɛvə/ *adv.* **1 a** in whatever way (*do it however you want*). **b** to whatever extent, no matter how (*must go however inconvenient*). **2** nevertheless. **3** *colloq.* (as an emphatic) in what way, by what means (*however did that happen?*).

howitzer /'haʊɪtsə/ *n.* a short gun for high-angle firing of shells at low velocities. [Dutch *houwitser* via German *Haubitze* from Czech *houfnice* 'catapult']

howl /haʊl/ *n. & v.* ● *n.* **1** a long loud doleful cry uttered by a dog, wolf, etc. **2** a prolonged wailing noise, e.g. as made by a strong wind. **3** a loud cry of pain or rage. **4** a yell of derision or merriment. **5** *Electronics* a howling noise in a loudspeaker due to electrical or acoustic feedback. ● *v.* **1** *intr.* make a howl. **2** *intr.* weep loudly. **3** *tr.* utter (words) with a howl. □ **howl down** prevent (a speaker) from being heard by howls of derision. [Middle English *houle* (*v.*), probably imitative: cf. OWL]

howler /'haʊlə/ *n.* **1** *colloq.* a glaring mistake. **2** a S. American monkey of the genus *Alouatta*. **3** a person or animal that howls.

howling /'haʊlɪŋ/ *adj.* **1** that howls. **2** *colloq.* extreme (*a howling shame*). **3** *archaic* dreary (*howling wilderness*).

howling dervish see WHIRLING DERVISH.

howsoever /haʊsəʊ'ɛvə/ *adv.* (also *poet.* **howsoe'er** /-'ɛː/) **1** in whatsoever way. **2** to whatsoever extent.

howzat /haʊ'zat/ *int. Cricket* = *how's that* 2 (see HOW[1]). [corruption]

hoy[1] /hɔɪ/ *int. & n.* ● *int.* used to call attention, drive animals, or *Naut.* hail or call aloft. ● *n. Austral.* a game of chance resembling bingo, using playing cards. [Middle English: natural cry]

hoy[2] /hɔɪ/ *n. hist.* a small vessel, usu. rigged as a sloop, carrying passengers and goods esp. for short distances. [Middle Dutch *hoei, hoede*, of unknown origin]

hoy[3] /hɔɪ/ *v.tr. Austral. slang* throw. [British dialect: origin unknown]

hoya /'hɔɪə/ *n.* any climbing shrub of the genus *Hoya*, with pink, white, or yellow waxy flowers. [modern Latin, named after T. *Hoy*, English gardener d. 1821]

hoyden /'hɔɪd(ə)n/ *n.* a boisterous girl. □ **hoydenish** *adj.* [originally = rude fellow, probably from Middle Dutch *heiden* (= HEATHEN)]

Hoyle /hɔɪl/ *n.* □ **according to Hoyle** correctly, exactly; according to plan or the rules. [E. *Hoyle*, English writer on card games d. 1769]

h.p. *abbr.* (also **HP**) **1** horsepower. **2** *Brit.* hire purchase. **3** high pressure.

HQ *abbr.* headquarters.

HR *abbr. US* House of Representatives.

hr. *abbr.* hour.

HRH *abbr. Brit.* Her or His Royal Highness.

hrs. *abbr.* hours.

HRT *abbr.* hormone replacement therapy.

HSH *abbr.* Her or His Serene Highness.

HT *abbr.* high tension.

hub /hʌb/ *n.* **1** the central part of a wheel, rotating on or with the axle, and from which the spokes radiate. **2** a central point of interest, activity, etc. [16th c.: perhaps = HOB[1]]

hubble-bubble /'hʌb(ə)lbʌb(ə)l/ *n.* **1** a rudimentary form of hookah. **2** a bubbling sound. **3** confused talk. [reduplication of BUBBLE]

Hubble's constant /'hʌb(ə)lz/ *n. Astron.* **1** the ratio of the speed of recession of a galaxy to its distance from the observer. **2** the reciprocal of this, interpretable as the age of the universe. [named after E.P. *Hubble*, US astronomer (d. 1953)]

hubbub /'hʌbʌb/ *n.* **1** a confused din, esp. from a crowd of people. **2** a disturbance or riot. [perhaps of Irish origin; cf. Gaelic *ubub*, expressing contempt, Irish *abú*, used in battle-cries]

hubby /'hʌbi/ *n.* (*pl.* **-ies**) *colloq.* a husband. [abbreviation]

hubcap /'hʌbkap/ *n.* a cover for the hub of a vehicle's wheel.

hubris /'hjuːbrɪs/ *n.* **1** arrogant pride or presumption. **2** (in Greek tragedy) excessive pride towards or defiance of the gods, leading to nemesis. □ **hubristic** /-'brɪstɪk/ *adj.* [Greek]

huckaback /'hʌkəbak/ *n.* a stout linen or cotton fabric with a rough surface, used for towelling. [17th c.: origin unknown]

huckleberry /'hʌk(ə)lb(ə)ri/ *n.* (*pl.* **-ies**) **1** any low-growing N. American shrub of the genus *Gaylussacia*. **2** the blue or black soft fruit of this plant. [probably alteration of *hurtleberry*, WHORTLEBERRY]

huckster /'hʌkstə/ *n. & v.* ● *n.* **1** a mercenary person. **2** *US* a publicity agent, esp. for broadcast material. **3** a pedlar or hawker. ● *v.* **1** *intr.* bargain, haggle. **2** *tr.* carry on a petty traffic in. **3** *tr.* adulterate.

□ **hucksterism** *n.* [Middle English, probably from Low German: cf. dialect *huck* 'to bargain', HAWKER[1]]

huddle /ˈhʌd(ə)l/ *v. & n.* ● *v.* **1** *tr. & intr.* (often foll. by *up*) crowd together; nestle closely. **2** *intr. & refl.* (often foll. by *up*) coil one's body into a small space. **3** *tr. Brit.* heap together in a muddle. ● *n.* **1** a confused or crowded mass of people or things. **2** *colloq.* a close or secret conference (esp. in **go into a huddle**). **3** confusion, bustle. [16th c.: perhaps from Low German and ultimately related to HIDE[3]]

hue /hjuː/ *n.* **1 a** a colour or tint. **b** a variety or shade of colour caused by the admixture of another. **2** the attribute of a colour by virtue of which it is discernible as red, green, etc. □ **-hued** *adj.* **hueless** *adj.* [Old English *hīew*, *hēw* 'form, beauty', from Germanic]

hue and cry *n.* **1** a loud clamour or outcry. **2** *hist.* **a** a loud cry raised for the pursuit of a wrongdoer. **b** a proclamation for the capture of a criminal. [Anglo-French *hu e cri*, from Old French *hu* 'outcry' (from *huer* 'shout') + *e* 'and' + *cri* 'cry']

huff /hʌf/ *v. & n.* ● *v.* **1** *intr.* give out loud puffs of air, steam, etc. **2** *intr.* bluster loudly or threateningly (*huffing and puffing*). **3** *intr. & tr.* take or cause to take offence. **4** *tr.* (in draughts) remove (an opponent's man that could have made a capture) from the board as a forfeit (originally after blowing on the piece). ● *n.* a fit of petty annoyance. □ **in a huff** annoyed and offended. □ **huffish** *adj.* [imitative of the sound of blowing]

huffy /ˈhʌfi/ *adj.* (**huffier**, **huffiest**) **1** apt to take offence. **2** offended. □ **huffily** *adv.* **huffiness** *n.*

hug /hʌg/ *v. & n.* ● *v.tr.* (**hugged**, **hugging**) **1** squeeze tightly in one's arms, esp. with affection. **2** (of a bear) squeeze (a person) between its forelegs. **3** keep close to (the shore, kerb, etc.). **4** cherish or cling to (prejudices etc.). **5** *refl.* congratulate or be pleased with (oneself). ● *n.* **1** a strong esp. affectionate clasp with the arms. **2** a squeezing grip in wrestling. □ **huggable** *adj.* [16th c.: probably from Scandinavian: cf. Old Norse *hugga* 'console']

huge /hjuːdʒ/ *adj.* **1** extremely large; enormous. **2** (of immaterial things) very great (*a huge success*). □ **hugeness** *n.* [Middle English from Old French *ahuge*, *ahoge*, of unknown origin]

hugely /ˈhjuːdʒli/ *adv.* **1** enormously (*hugely successful*). **2** very much (*enjoyed it hugely*).

hugger-mugger /ˈhʌgəmʌgə/ *adj., adv., n., & v.* ● *adj. & adv.* **1** in secret. **2** confused; in confusion. ● *n.* **1** secrecy. **2** confusion. ● *v.intr.* proceed in a secret or muddled fashion. [probably related to Middle English *hoder* 'huddle', *mokere* 'conceal': cf. 15th-c. *hoder moder*, 16th-c. *hucker mucker* in the same sense]

Huguenot /ˈhjuːgənəʊ, -nɒt/ *n. hist.* a French Protestant. [French, assimilation of *eiguenot* (from Dutch *eedgenot* from Swiss German *Eidgenoss* 'confederate') to the name of a Geneva burgomaster *Hugues*]

huh /hʌ, hə/ *int.* expressing disgust, surprise, etc. [imitative]

hula /huːlə/ *n.* (also **hula-hula**) a dance performed by Hawaiian women, characterized by six basic steps and flowing arm movements. [Hawaiian]

hula hoop *n.* a large hoop for spinning round the body with hula-like movements.

hula skirt *n.* a long grass skirt.

hulk /hʌlk/ *n.* **1 a** the body of a dismantled ship, used as a store vessel etc. **b** (in *pl.*) *hist.* this used as a prison. **2** an unwieldy vessel. **3** *colloq.* a large clumsy-looking person or thing. [Old English *hulc* & Middle Low German, Middle Dutch *hulk*: related to Greek *holkas* 'cargo ship']

hulking /ˈhʌlkɪŋ/ *adj. colloq.* bulky; large and clumsy.

hull[1] /hʌl/ *n. & v.* ● *n.* the body or frame of a ship, airship, flying boat, etc. ● *v.tr.* pierce the hull of (a ship) with gunshot etc. [Middle English, perhaps related to HOLD[2]]

hull[2] /hʌl/ *n. & v.* ● *n.* **1** the outer covering of a fruit, esp. the pod of peas and beans, the husk of grain, or the green calyx of a strawberry. **2** a covering. ● *v.tr.* remove the hulls from (fruit etc.). [Old English *hulu*, ultimately from *helan* 'cover': cf. HEEL[3]]

hullabaloo /hʌləbəˈluː/ *n.* (*pl.* **hullabaloos**) an uproar or clamour. [18th c.: reduplication of *hallo*, *hullo*, etc.]

hullo var. of HELLO.

hum[1] /hʌm/ *v. & n.* ● *v.* (**hummed**, **humming**) **1** *intr.* make a low steady continuous sound like that of a bee. **2** *tr.* (also *absol.*) sing (a wordless tune) with closed lips. **3** *intr.* utter a slight inarticulate sound. **4** *intr. colloq.* be in an active state (*really made things hum*). **5** *intr. Brit. colloq.* smell unpleasantly. ● *n.* **1** a humming sound. **2** an unwanted low-frequency noise caused by variation of electric current, usu. the alternating frequency of the mains, in an amplifier etc. **3** *Brit. colloq.* a bad smell. □ **hum and haw** (or **ha**) *Brit.* hesitate, esp. in speaking. □ **hummable** *adj.* **hummer** *n.* [Middle English, imitative]

hum[2] /hʌm, h(ə)m/ *int.* expressing hesitation or dissent. [imitative]

human /ˈhjuːmən/ *adj. & n.* ● *adj.* **1** of, relating to, or characteristic of humankind or people; of or belonging to the genus *Homo*. **2** consisting of human beings (*the human race*). **3** of or characteristic of humankind as opposed to God or animals or machines, esp. susceptible to the weaknesses of humankind (*is only human*). **4** showing (esp. the better) qualities of humankind (*proved to be very human*). ● *n.* a human being, esp. as distinguished from an animal or (in science fiction and fantasy) a Martian, an elf, etc. □ **humanness** /ˈhjuːmənnɪs/ *n.* [Middle English *humain(e)* via Old French from Latin *humanus*, from *homo* 'human being']

human being *n.* any man or woman or child of the species *Homo sapiens*.

human chain *n.* a line of people formed for passing things along, e.g. buckets of water to the site of a fire.

humane /hjʊˈmeɪn/ *adj.* **1** benevolent, compassionate. **2** inflicting the minimum of pain. **3** (of a branch of learning) tending to civilize or confer refinement. □ **humanely** *adv.* **humaneness** *n.* [variant of HUMAN, differentiated in sense in the 18th c.]

human ecology see ECOLOGY 2.

humane killer *n. Brit.* an instrument for the painless slaughter of animals.

human engineering *n.* **1** the management of industrial labour, esp. as regards man–machine relationships. **2** the study of this.

human geography *n.* the branch of geography dealing with how human activity affects or is influenced by the earth's surface.

human interest *n.* (in a newspaper story etc.) reference to personal experience and emotions etc.

humanism /ˈhjuːmənɪz(ə)m/ *n.* **1** an outlook or system of thought concerned with human rather than divine or supernatural matters. **2** a belief or outlook emphasizing common human needs and seeking solely rational ways of solving human problems, and concerned with humankind as responsible and progressive intellectual beings. **3** (often **Humanism**) literary culture, esp. that of the Renaissance humanists.

humanist /ˈhjuːmənɪst/ *n.* **1** an adherent of humanism. **2** a humanitarian. **3** a student (esp. in the 14th–16th c.) of Roman and Greek literature and antiquities. □ **humanistic** /-ˈnɪstɪk/ *adj.* **humanistically** /-ˈnɪstɪk(ə)li/ *adv.* [French *humaniste* from Italian *umanista* (as HUMAN)]

humanitarian /hjʊˌmænɪˈtɛːrɪən/ *n. & adj.* ● *n.* **1** a person who seeks to promote human welfare. **2** a person who advocates or practises humane action; a philanthropist. ● *adj.* **1** of, relating to, or holding the views of humanitarians. **2** of or relating to human welfare (*released on humanitarian grounds*; *humanitarian aid*). □ **humanitarianism** *n.*

■ **Usage** The adjective *humanitarian* is often used inaccurately by reporters and journalists in conjunction with the noun *disaster*, e.g. *This is the worst humanitarian disaster within living memory*, as if *humanitarian* meant 'of or relating to humanity'. Such use can be avoided by using the adjective *human* instead.

humanity /hjʊˈmanɪti/ *n.* (*pl.* **-ies**) **1 a** the human race. **b** human beings collectively. **c** the fact or condition of being human. **2** humaneness, benevolence. **3** (in *pl.*) human attributes. **4** (in *pl.*) learning or literature concerned with human culture, esp. the study of Roman and Greek literature and philosophy. [Middle English via Old French *humanité* from Latin *humanitas -tatis* (as HUMAN)]

humanize /ˈhjuːmənʌɪz/ *v.tr.* (also **-ise**) **1** make human; give a human character to. **2** make humane. □ **humanization** /-ˈzeɪʃ(ə)n/ *n.* [French *humaniser* (as HUMAN)]

humankind /hjuːmənˈkʌɪnd/ *n.* human beings collectively.

humanly /ˈhjuːmənli/ *adv.* **1** by human means (*I will do it if it is humanly possible*). **2** in a human manner. **3** from a human point of view. **4** with human feelings.

human nature *n.* the general characteristics and feelings of humankind.

humanoid /ˈhjuːmənɔɪd/ *adj.* & *n.* ● *adj.* having human form or character. ● *n.* a humanoid animal or thing. [HUMAN + -OID]

human relations *n.pl.* relations with or between people or individuals.

human rights *n.pl.* rights held to be justifiably belonging to any person.

human shield *n.* a person or group of persons placed near a potential target to deter attack.

humble /ˈhʌmb(ə)l/ *adj.* & *v.* ● *adj.* (**humbler, humblest**) **1 a** having or showing a low estimate of one's own importance. **b** offered with or affected by such an estimate (*if you want my humble opinion*). **2** of low social or political rank (*humble origins*). **3** (of a thing) of modest pretensions, dimensions, etc. ● *v.tr.* **1** make humble; bring low; abase. **2** lower the rank or status of. □ **eat humble pie** make a humble apology; accept humiliation. □ **humbleness** *n.* **humbly** *adv.* [Middle English *umble*, *humble* via Old French *umble* from Latin *humilis* 'lowly', from *humus* 'ground': *humble pie* from UMBLES]

humble-bee /ˈhʌmb(ə)lbiː/ *n.* = BUMBLE-BEE. [Middle English, probably from Middle Low German *hummelbē*, Middle Dutch *hommel*, Old High German *humbal*]

humbug /ˈhʌmbʌg/ *n.* & *v.* ● *n.* **1** deceptive or false talk or behaviour. **2** an impostor. **3** *Brit.* a boiled sweet usu. flavoured with peppermint. ● *v.* (**humbugged, humbugging**) **1** *intr.* be or behave like an impostor. **2** *tr.* deceive, hoax. □ **humbuggery** *n.* [18th c.: origin unknown]

humdinger /hʌmˈdɪŋə/ *n.* *slang* an excellent or remarkable person or thing. [20th c.: origin unknown]

humdrum /ˈhʌmdrʌm/ *adj.* & *n.* ● *adj.* **1** commonplace, dull. **2** monotonous. ● *n.* **1** commonplaceness, dullness. **2** a monotonous routine etc. [16th c.: probably from HUM[1] by reduplication]

humectant /hjʊˈmɛkt(ə)nt/ *adj.* & *n.* ● *adj.* retaining or preserving moisture. ● *n.* a substance, esp. a food additive, used to reduce loss of moisture. [Latin *(h)umectant-*, part. stem of *(h)umectare* 'moisten', from *umēre* 'be moist']

humeral /ˈhjuːm(ə)r(ə)l/ *adj.* **1** of the humerus or shoulder. **2** worn on the shoulder. [French *huméral* & Late Latin *humeralis* (as HUMERUS)]

humerus /ˈhjuːm(ə)rəs/ *n.* (*pl.* **humeri** /-rʌɪ/) **1** the bone of the upper arm in man. **2** the corresponding bone in other vertebrates. [Latin, = shoulder]

humic /ˈhjuːmɪk/ *adj.* of or consisting of humus.

humid /ˈhjuːmɪd/ *adj.* (of the air or climate) warm and damp. □ **humidly** *adv.* [French *humide* or Latin *humidus* from *umēre* 'be moist']

humidifier /hjʊˈmɪdɪfʌɪə/ *n.* a device for keeping the atmosphere moist in a room etc.

humidify /hjʊˈmɪdɪfʌɪ/ *v.tr.* (**-ies, -ied**) make (air etc.) humid or damp. □ **humidification** /-fɪˈkeɪʃ(ə)n/ *n.*

humidity /hjʊˈmɪdɪti/ *n.* (*pl.* **-ies**) **1** a humid state. **2** moisture. **3** the degree of moisture esp. in the atmosphere. [Middle English from Old French *humidité* or Latin *humiditas* (as HUMID)]

humidor /ˈhjuːmɪdɔː/ *n.* a room or container for keeping cigars or tobacco moist. [HUMID, on the pattern of *cuspidor*]

humify /ˈhjuːmɪfʌɪ/ *v.tr.* & *intr.* (**-ies, -ied**) make or be made into humus. □ **humification** /-fɪˈkeɪʃ(ə)n/ *n.*

humiliate /hjʊˈmɪlɪeɪt/ *v.tr.* make humble; injure the dignity or self-respect of. □ **humiliating** *adj.* **humiliatingly** *adv.* **humiliation** /-ˈeɪʃ(ə)n/ *n.* **humiliator** *n.* [Late Latin *humiliare* (as HUMBLE)]

humility /hjʊˈmɪlɪti/ *n.* **1** humbleness, meekness. **2** a humble condition. [Middle English via Old French *humilité* from Latin *humilitas -tatis* (as HUMBLE)]

hummingbird /ˈhʌmɪŋbəːd/ *n.* any small nectar-feeding tropical American bird of the family Trochilidae, that makes a humming sound by the vibration of its wings when it hovers.

humming-top /ˈhʌmɪŋtɒp/ *n.* *Brit.* a child's top which hums as it spins.

hummock /ˈhʌmək/ *n.* **1** a hillock or knoll. **2** *US* a piece of forested ground rising above a marsh. **3** a hump or ridge in an ice field. □ **hummocky** *adj.* [16th c.: origin unknown]

hummus /ˈhʊməs/ *n.* (also **hoummos**) a thick sauce or spread made from ground chickpeas and sesame seeds, olive oil, lemon, and garlic. [Turkish *humus* 'mashed chickpeas']

humongous /hjuːˈmʌŋgəs/ *adj.* (also **humungous**) *slang* huge, enormous. [20th c.: origin unknown; cf. HUGE, MONSTROUS, STUPENDOUS, etc.]

humor *US* var. of HUMOUR.

humoral /ˈhjuːm(ə)r(ə)l/ *adj.* **1** *hist.* of the four bodily humours. **2** *Med.* of or relating to the body fluids, esp. with regard to immune responses involving antibodies in body fluids as distinct from cells. [French *humoral* or medieval Latin *humoralis* (as HUMOUR)]

humoresque /hjuːməˈrɛsk/ *n.* a short lively piece of music. [German *Humoreske* from *Humor* HUMOUR]

humorist /ˈhjuːm(ə)rɪst/ *n.* **1** a facetious person. **2** a humorous talker, actor, or writer. □ **humoristic** /-ˈrɪstɪk/ *adj.*

humorous /ˈhjuːm(ə)rəs/ *adj.* **1** showing humour or a sense of humour. **2** facetious, comic. □ **humorously** *adv.* **humorousness** *n.*

humour /ˈhjuːmə/ *n.* & *v.* (*US* **humor**) ● *n.* **1 a** the quality of being amusing or comic. **b** the expression of humour in literature, speech, etc. **2** (in full **sense of humour**) the ability to perceive or express humour or take a joke. **3** a mood or state of mind (*bad humour*). **4** an inclination or whim (*in the humour for fighting*). **5** (in full **cardinal humour**) *hist.* each of the four chief fluids of the body (blood, phlegm, yellow bile, black bile), thought to determine a person's physical and mental qualities. ● *v.tr.* **1** gratify or indulge (a person or taste etc.). **2** adapt oneself to; make concessions to. □ **out of humour** displeased. □ **-humoured** *adj.* (in *comb.*). **humourless** *adj.* **humourlessly** *adv.* **humourlessness** *n.* [Middle English via Anglo-French *umour*, *humour*, Old French *umor*, *humor* from Latin *humor* 'moisture' (as HUMID)]

humous /ˈhjuːməs/ *adj.* like or consisting of humus.

hump /hʌmp/ *n.* & *v.* ● *n.* **1** a rounded protuberance on the back of a camel etc., or as an abnormality on a person's back. **2** a rounded raised mass of earth etc. **3** a mound over which railway vehicles are pushed so as to run by gravity to the required place in a marshalling yard. **4** a critical point in an undertaking, ordeal, etc. **5** (prec. by *the*) *Brit. slang* a fit of depression or vexation (*it gives me the hump*). ● *v.tr.* **1 a** (often foll. by *about*) *colloq.* lift or carry (heavy objects etc.) with difficulty. **b** esp. *Austral.* hoist up, shoulder (one's pack etc.). **2** make hump-shaped. **3** annoy, depress. **4** *coarse slang* have sexual intercourse with. □ **live on one's hump** *colloq.* be self-sufficient. **over the hump** over the worst; well begun. □ **humped** *adj.* **humpless** *adj.* [17th c.: perhaps related to Low German *humpel* 'hump', Low German *humpe*, Dutch *homp* 'lump, hunk' (of bread)]

humpback /ˈhʌm(p)bak/ *n.* **1 a** a back deformed by a hump. **b** a person having this. **2** a baleen whale, *Megaptera novaeangliae*, with a dorsal fin forming a hump. □ **humpbacked** *adj.*

humpback bridge *n. Brit.* a small bridge with a steep ascent and descent.

hump bridge *n.* = HUMPBACK BRIDGE.

humph /hʌmf, h(ə)mf/ *int. & n.* an inarticulate sound expressing doubt or dissatisfaction. [imitative]

humpty-dumpty /hʌm(p)tɪˈdʌm(p)ti/ *n.* (*pl.* **-ies**) **1** a short dumpy person. **2** a person or thing that once overthrown cannot be restored. [the nursery rhyme *Humpty-Dumpty*, perhaps ultimately from HUMPY[1], DUMPY]

humpy[1] /ˈhʌmpi/ *adj.* (**humpier**, **humpiest**) **1** having a hump or humps. **2** humplike.

humpy[2] /ˈhʌmpi/ *n.* (*pl.* **-ies**) *Austral.* a primitive hut. [Yagara *ngumbi*]

humungous var. of HUMONGOUS.

humus /ˈhjuːməs/ *n.* the organic constituent of soil, usu. formed by the decomposition of plants and leaves by soil bacteria. □ **humusify** *v.tr. & intr.* (**-ies**, **-ied**). [Latin, = soil]

Hun /huːn/ *n.* **1** a member of a warlike Asiatic nomadic people who invaded and ravaged Europe in the 4th–5th c. **2** *offens.* a German (esp. in military contexts). **3** an uncivilized devastator; a vandal. □ **Hunnish** *adj.* [Old English *Hūne* (pl.) via Late Latin *Hunni* and Greek *Hounnoi* from Turkic *Hun-yü*]

hunch /hʌn(t)ʃ/ *v. & n.* ● *v.* **1** *tr.* bend or arch into a hump. **2** *tr.* thrust out or up to form a hump. **3** *intr.* (usu. foll. by *up*) esp. *N. Amer.* sit with the body hunched. ● *n.* **1** an intuitive feeling or conjecture. **2** *US colloq.* a hint. **3** a hump. **4** a thick piece. [Middle English: origin unknown]

hunchback /ˈhʌn(t)ʃbak/ *n.* = HUMPBACK 1. □ **hunchbacked** *adj.*

hundred /ˈhʌndrəd/ *n. & adj.* ● *n.* (*pl.* **hundreds** or (in sense 1) **hundred**) (in *sing.*, prec. by *a* or *one*) **1** the product of ten and ten. **2** a symbol for this (100, c, C). **3** a set of a hundred things. **4** (in *sing.* or *pl.*) *colloq.* a large number. **5** (in *pl.*) the years of a specified century (*the seventeen hundreds*). **6** *Brit. hist.* a subdivision of a county or shire, having its own court. ● *adj.* **1** that amount to a hundred. **2** used to express whole hours in the 24-hour system (*thirteen hundred hours*). □ **a** (or **one**) **hundred per cent** *adv.* entirely, completely. ● *adj.* **1** entire, complete. **2** (usu. with *neg.*) fully recovered. □ **hundredfold** *adj. & adv.* **hundredth** *adj. & n.* [Old English from Germanic]

hundreds and thousands *n.pl. Brit.* tiny coloured sweets used chiefly for decorating cakes etc.

hundredweight /ˈhʌndrədweɪt/ *n.* (*pl.* same or **-weights**) **1** (in full **long hundredweight**) *Brit.* a unit of weight equal to 112 lb avoirdupois (about 50.8 kg). **2** (in full **metric hundredweight**) a unit of weight equal to 50 kg. **3** (in full **short hundredweight**) *US* a unit of weight equal to 100 lb (about 45.4 kg).

hung *past* and *past part.* of HANG.

Hungarian /hʌŋˈgɛːrɪən/ *n. & adj.* ● *n.* **1 a** a native or national of Hungary in central Europe. **b** a person of Hungarian descent. **2** the Finno-Ugric language of Hungary. ● *adj.* of or relating to Hungary or its people or language. [medieval Latin *Hungaria* from *Hungari* 'Magyar nation']

hunger /ˈhʌŋgə/ *n. & v.* ● *n.* **1** a feeling of pain or discomfort, or (in extremes) an exhausted condition, caused by lack of food. **2** (often foll. by *for, after*) a strong desire. ● *v.intr.* **1** (often foll. by *for, after*) have a craving or strong desire. **2** feel hunger. [Old English *hungor, hyngran*, from Germanic]

hunger march *n.* a march undertaken by a body of unemployed etc. to call attention to their condition. □ **hunger marcher** *n.*

hunger strike *n.* the refusal of food as a form of protest, esp. by prisoners. □ **hunger striker** *n.*

hung-over *adj. colloq.* suffering from a hangover.

hung parliament *n.* a parliament in which no party has a clear majority.

hungry /ˈhʌŋgri/ *adj.* (**hungrier**, **hungriest**) **1** feeling or showing hunger; needing food. **2** characterized by hunger (*those were hungry days*). **3 a** (often foll. by *for*) eager, greedy, craving. **b** *Austral.* mean, stingy. **4** (of soil) poor, barren. □ **hungrily** *adv.* **hungriness** *n.* [Old English *hungrig* (as HUNGER)]

hunk /hʌŋk/ *n.* **1 a** a large piece cut off (*a hunk of bread*). **b** a thick or clumsy piece. **2** *colloq.* **a** a very large person. **b** a sexually attractive, ruggedly handsome man. □ **hunky** *adj.* (**hunkier**, **hunkiest**). [19th c.: probably of Low Dutch origin: cf. Flemish *hunke*]

hunker /ˈhʌŋkə/ *v.intr.* (often foll. by *down*) esp. *Sc. & N. Amer.* squat or crouch with the haunches nearly touching the heels, esp. for shelter or concealment. □ **hunker down** apply oneself, knuckle down. [related to Middle Dutch *hucken*, Middle Low German *hūken*, Old Norse *húka*; cf. German *hocken* 'squat']

hunkers /ˈhʌŋkəz/ *n.pl.* the haunches. [originally Scots, from HUNKER]

hunky-dory /hʌŋkɪˈdɔːri/ *adj. colloq.* excellent. [19th c.: origin unknown]

hunt /hʌnt/ *v. & n.* ● *v.* **1** *tr.* (also *absol.*) **a** pursue and kill (wild animals or game) for sport or food. **b** *Brit.* pursue on horseback and usu. kill (a fox) using hounds. **c** *Brit.* use (hounds or a horse) for hunting. **d** (of an animal) chase (its prey). **2** *intr.* (foll. by *after, for*) seek, search (*hunting for a pen*). **3** *intr.* **a** oscillate. **b** *Brit.* (of an engine etc.) run alternately too fast and too slow. **4** *tr.* **a** (foll. by *away* etc.) drive off by pursuit. **b** pursue with hostility. **5** *tr.* scour (a district) in pursuit of game. **6** *tr.* (as **hunted** *adj.*) (of a look etc.) expressing alarm or terror as of one being hunted. **7** *tr.* (foll. by *down, up*) move the place of (a bell) in ringing the changes. ● *n.* **1** the practice of hunting or an instance of this. **2 a** an association of people engaged in hunting with hounds. **b** an area where hunting takes place. **3** an oscillating motion. □ **hunt down** pursue and capture. **hunt out** find by searching; track down. [Old English *huntian*, weak grade of *hentan* 'seize']

huntaway /ˈhʌntəweɪ/ *n. Austral. & NZ* a dog trained to drive sheep forward.

hunter /ˈhʌntə/ *n.* **1 a** (*fem.* **huntress** /-rɪs/) a person or animal that hunts. **b** a horse used in hunting. **2** a person who seeks something. **3** a watch with a hinged cover protecting the glass.

hunter-gatherer *n.* a member of a people whose mode of subsistence is based on hunting animals and gathering plants etc.

hunter's moon *n.* the next full moon after the harvest moon.

hunting /ˈhʌntɪŋ/ *n.* the practice of pursuing and killing wild animals, esp. for sport. [Old English *huntung* (as HUNT)]

hunting crop see CROP *n.* 3.

hunting ground *n.* **1** a place suitable for hunting. **2** a source of information or object of exploitation likely to be fruitful.

hunting horn *n.* a straight horn used in hunting.

hunting pink see PINK[1] *n.* 4.

Huntington's chorea /ˈhʌntɪŋt(ə)nz/ *n.* chorea accompanied by a progressive dementia. [named after G. *Huntington*, American neurologist, d. 1916]

huntress see HUNTER 1a.

hunt saboteur *n.* a person who attempts, usu. with others, to disrupt a hunt.

huntsman /ˈhʌntsmən/ *n.* (*pl.* **-men**) **1** a hunter. **2** a hunt official in charge of hounds.

hurdle /ˈhəːd(ə)l/ *n. & v.* ● *n.* **1 a** each of a series of light frames to be cleared by athletes in a race. **b** (in *pl.*) a hurdle race. **2** an obstacle or difficulty. **3** a portable rectangular frame strengthened with withes or wooden bars, used as a temporary fence etc. **4** *Brit. hist.* a frame on which traitors were dragged to execution. ● *v.* **1 a** *intr.* run in a hurdle race. **b** *tr.* clear (a hurdle) in a race. **2** *tr.* fence off etc. with hurdles. **3** *tr.* overcome (a difficulty). [Old English *hyrdel*, from Germanic]

hurdler /ˈhəːdlə/ *n.* **1** an athlete who runs in hurdle races. **2** a person who makes hurdles.

hurdy-gurdy /ˈhəːdɪgəːdi/ *n.* (*pl.* **-ies**) **1** a musical instrument with a droning sound, played by turning a handle, esp. one with a rosined wheel turned by the right hand to sound the drone strings, and keys played by the left hand. **2** *colloq.* a barrel organ. [probably imitative]

hurl /həːl/ *v. & n.* ● *v.* **1** *tr.* throw with great force. **2** *tr.* utter (abuse etc.) vehemently. **3** *intr.* play hurley. ● *n.* **1** a forceful throw. **2** the act of hurling. [Middle English, probably imitative, but corresponding in form and partly in sense with Low German *hurreln*]

Hurler's syndrome /ˈhəːləz/ *n. Med.* a defect in metabolism resulting in mental retardation, a protruding abdomen, and deformities of the bones, including an abnormally large head. Also called *gargoylism*. [named after G. *Hurler*, German paediatrician fl. 1894]

hurley /ˈhəːli/ *n.* (*pl.* **-eys**) **1** (also **hurling** /ˈhəːlɪŋ/) an Irish game somewhat resembling hockey, played with broad sticks. **2** a stick used in this.

hurly-burly /ˈhəːlɪbəːli/ *n.* boisterous activity; commotion. [reduplication of HURL]

hurrah /hʊˈrɑː/ *int., n., & v.* (also **hurray** /hʊˈreɪ/) ● *int. & n.* an exclamation of joy or approval. ● *v.intr.* cry or shout 'hurrah' or 'hurray'. [alteration of earlier *huzza*, perhaps originally a sailor's cry when hauling]

hurricane /ˈhʌrɪk(ə)n, -keɪn/ *n.* **1** a storm with a violent wind, esp. a tropical cyclone in the Caribbean. **2** *Meteorol.* a wind of force 12 on the Beaufort scale, exceeding 75 m.p.h. (65 knots). **3** a violent commotion. [Spanish *huracan* & Portuguese *furacão*, of Carib origin]

hurricane-bird *n.* a frigate bird.

hurricane deck *n.* a light upper deck on a ship etc.

hurricane lamp *n.* an oil lamp designed to resist a high wind.

hurry /ˈhʌri/ *n. & v.* ● *n.* **1 a** great haste. **b** (with *neg.* or *interrog.*) a need for haste (*there is no hurry*; *what's the hurry?*). **2** (often foll. by *for*, or *to* + infin.) eagerness to get a thing done quickly. ● *v.* (**-ies, -ied**) **1** *intr.* move or act with great or undue haste. **2** *tr.* (often foll. by *away, along*) cause to move or proceed in this way. **3** *tr.* (as **hurried** *adj.*) hasty; done rapidly owing to lack of time. □ **hurry along** (or **up**) make or cause to make haste. **in a hurry 1** hurrying, rushed; in a rushed manner. **2** *colloq.* easily or readily (*you will not beat that in a hurry*; *shall not ask again in a hurry*). □ **hurriedly** *adv.* **hurriedness** *n.* [16th c.: imitative]

hurry-scurry *n., adj., & adv.* ● *n.* disorderly haste. ● *adj. & adv.* in confusion. [jingling reduplication of HURRY]

hurst /həːst/ *n.* **1** a hillock. **2** a sandbank in the sea or a river. **3** a wood or wooded eminence. [Old English *hyrst*, related to Old Saxon, Old High German *hurst*, *horst*]

hurt /həːt/ *v. & n.* ● *v.* (*past* and *past part.* **hurt**) **1** *tr.* (also *absol.*) cause pain, injury, or harm to. **2** *tr.* cause mental pain or distress to (a person, feelings, etc.). **3** *intr.* suffer pain, harm, or misfortune. **4** *intr.* (foll. by *for*) *N. Amer.* have a pressing need for. ● *n.* **1** bodily or material injury. **2** harm, wrong. [Middle English from Old French *hurter*, *hurt*, ultimately perhaps from Germanic]

hurtful /ˈhəːtfʊl, -f(ə)l/ *adj.* causing (esp. mental) hurt. □ **hurtfully** *adv.* **hurtfulness** *n.*

hurtle /ˈhəːt(ə)l/ *v.* **1** *intr. & tr.* move or hurl rapidly or with a clattering sound. **2** *intr.* come with a crash. [HURT in obsolete sense 'strike forcibly']

husband /ˈhʌzbənd/ *n. & v.* ● *n.* a married man esp. in relation to his wife. ● *v.tr.* manage thriftily; use (resources) economically. □ **husbander** *n.* **husbandhood** *n.* **husbandless** *adj.* **husbandly** *adj.* [Old English *hūsbonda* 'house-dweller' from Old Norse *húsbóndi* (as HOUSE, *bóndi* 'a person who has a household')]

husbandman /ˈhʌzbən(d)mən/ *n.* (*pl.* **-men**) a man who cultivates the ground; a farmer.

husbandry /ˈhʌzbəndri/ *n.* **1** farming. **2 a** management of resources. **b** careful management.

hush /hʌʃ/ *v., int., & n.* ● *v.tr. & intr.* make or become silent or quiet. ● *int.* calling for silence. ● *n.* an expectant stillness or silence. □ **hush up** suppress public mention of (an affair). [back-formation from obsolete interjection *husht*, = quiet!, taken as a past part.]

hushaby /ˈhʌʃəbʌɪ/ *int.* (also **hushabye**) used to lull a child.

hush-hush /hʌʃˈhʌʃ/ *adj. colloq.* (esp. of an official plan or enterprise etc.) highly secret or confidential.

hush money *n.* money paid to prevent the disclosure of a discreditable matter.

hush puppy *n. US* quickly fried maize bread.

husk /hʌsk/ *n. & v.* ● *n.* **1** the dry outer covering of some fruits or seeds, esp. of a nut or *N. Amer.* maize. **2** the worthless outside part of a thing. ● *v.tr.* remove a husk or husks from. [Middle English, probably from Low German *hūske* 'sheath', diminutive of *hūs* HOUSE]

husky[1] /ˈhʌski/ *adj.* (**huskier, huskiest**) **1** (of a person or voice) dry in the throat; hoarse. **2** of or full of husks. **3** dry as a husk. **4** tough, strong, hefty. □ **huskily** *adv.* **huskiness** *n.*

husky[2] /ˈhʌski/ *n.* (*pl.* **-ies**) **1** a dog of a powerful breed used in the Arctic for pulling sledges. **2** this breed. [perhaps a contraction, related to ESKIMO]

huss /hʌs/ *n.* dogfish as food. [Middle English *husk*, of unknown origin]

hussar /hʊˈzɑː/ *n.* **1** a soldier of a light cavalry regiment. **2** a Hungarian light horseman of the 15th c. [Hungarian *huszár* via Old Serbian *husar* from Italian *corsaro* CORSAIR]

Hussite /ˈhʌsʌɪt/ *n. hist.* a member or follower of the movement begun by John *Huss*, Bohemian religious and nationalist reformer d. 1415. □ **Hussitism** *n.*

hussy /ˈhʌsi, ˈhʌzi/ *n.* (*pl.* **-ies**) *derog.* an impudent or immoral girl or woman. [phonetic reduction of HOUSEWIFE (the original sense)]

hustings /ˈhʌstɪŋz/ *n.* **1** parliamentary election proceedings. **2** *Brit. hist.* a platform from which (before 1872) candidates for Parliament were nominated and addressed electors. [late Old English *husting* from Old Norse *hústhing* 'house of assembly']

hustle /ˈhʌs(ə)l/ *v. & n.* ● *v.* **1** *tr.* push roughly; jostle. **2** *tr.* **a** (foll. by *into, out of*, etc.) force, coerce, or deal with hurriedly or unceremoniously (*hustled them out of the room*). **b** (foll. by *into*) coerce hurriedly (*was hustled into agreeing*). **3** *intr.* push one's way; hurry, bustle. **4** *tr. colloq.* **a** obtain by forceful action. **b** swindle. **5** *intr. slang* engage in prostitution. ● *n.* **1** an act or instance of hustling. **2** *colloq.* a fraud or swindle. [Middle Dutch *husselen* 'shake, toss', frequentative of *hutsen*, originally imitative]

hustler /'hʌslə/ *n. slang* **1** an active, enterprising, or unscrupulous individual. **2** a prostitute.

hut /hʌt/ *n. & v.* ● *n.* **1** a small simple or crude house or shelter. **2** *Mil.* a temporary wooden etc. house for troops. ● *v.* (**hutted**, **hutting**) **1** *tr.* provide with huts. **2** *tr. Mil.* place (troops etc.) in huts. **3** *intr.* lodge in a hut. ▫ **hut-like** *adj.* [French *hutte* from Middle High German *hütte*]

hutch /hʌtʃ/ *n.* **1** a box or cage, usu. with a wire mesh front, for keeping small pet animals. **2** *derog.* a small house. [Middle English, = coffer, via Old French *huche* from medieval Latin *hutica*, of unknown origin]

hutment /'hʌtm(ə)nt/ *n. Mil.* an encampment of huts.

Hutu /'hu:tu:/ *n. & adj.* ● *n.* (*pl.* same, **Hutus**, or **Bahutu** /bə'hu:tu:/) a member of a Bantu-speaking people forming the majority population in Rwanda and Burundi. ● *adj.* of or relating to the Hutu people. [Bantu]

HWM *abbr.* high water mark.

hwyl /'hu:ɪl/ *n. Brit.* an emotional quality inspiring impassioned eloquence. [Welsh]

Hy. *abbr.* Henry.

hyacinth /'hʌɪəsɪnθ/ *n. & adj.* ● *n.* **1** any bulbous plant of the genus *Hyacinthus* with racemes of usu. purplish-blue, pink, or white bell-shaped fragrant flowers. **2** = GRAPE HYACINTH. **3** the purplish-blue colour of some hyacinth flowers. **4** an orange variety of zircon used as a precious stone. **5** *poet.* hair or locks like the hyacinth flower (as a Homeric epithet of doubtful sense). ● *adj.* purplish blue. ▫ **hyacinthine** /-'sɪnθi:n, -'sɪnθʌɪn/ *adj.* [French *hyacinthe* via Latin *hyacinthus* from Greek *huakinthos*, flower and gem, also the name of a youth loved by Apollo]

Hyades /'hʌɪədi:z/ *n.pl.* a group of stars in Taurus near the Pleiades, whose heliacal rising was once thought to foretell rain. [Middle English from Greek *Huades* (by popular etymology from *huō* 'rain', but perhaps from *hus* 'pig')]

hyaena var. of HYENA.

hyalin /'hʌɪəlɪn/ *n. Anat. & Physiol.* a clear substance esp. produced as a result of the degeneration of certain body tissues. Cf. HYALINE. [Greek *hualos* 'glass' + -IN]

hyaline /'hʌɪəlɪn, -i:n, -ʌɪn/ *adj. & n.* ● *adj.* **1** glasslike, vitreous, transparent. **2** *Anat. & Zool.* characterized by the formation of hyaline material. ● *n.* **1** *literary* a smooth sea, clear sky, etc. **2** *Anat. & Zool.* = HYALIN. [Latin *hyalinus* from Greek *hualinos*, from *hualos* 'glass']

hyaline cartilage *n.* a translucent bluish-white type of cartilage present in the joints and respiratory tract, and in the immature skeleton.

hyalite /'hʌɪəlʌɪt/ *n.* a colourless variety of opal. [Greek *hualos* 'glass']

hyaloid /'hʌɪəlɔɪd/ *adj. Anat.* glassy. [French *hyaloïde* via Late Latin *hyaloides* from Greek *hualoeidēs* (as HYALITE)]

hyaloid membrane *n.* a thin transparent membrane enveloping the vitreous humour of the eye.

hyaluronic acid /ˌhʌɪəljʊə'rɒnɪk/ *n. Biochem.* a viscous fluid carbohydrate found in synovial fluid, the vitreous humour of the eye, etc. [HYALOID + *-uronic* chemical suffix]

hybrid /'hʌɪbrɪd/ *n. & adj.* ● *n.* **1** *Biol.* the offspring of two plants or animals of different species or varieties. **2** *offens.* a person of mixed racial or cultural origin. **3** a thing composed of incongruous elements, e.g. a word with parts taken from different languages. ● *adj.* **1** bred as a hybrid from different species or varieties. **2** *Biol.* heterogeneous. ▫ **hybridism** *n.* **hybridity** /-'brɪdɪti/ *n.* [Latin *hybrida*, (*h*)*ibrida* 'offpring of a tame sow and wild boar, child of a freeman and slave, etc.']

hybridize /'hʌɪbrɪdʌɪz/ *v.* (also **-ise**) **1** *tr.* subject (a species etc.) to cross-breeding. **2** *intr.* **a** produce hybrids. **b** (of an animal or plant) interbreed. ▫ **hybridizable** *adj.* **hybridization** /-'zeɪʃ(ə)n/ *n.*

hybrid vigour *n.* heterosis.

hydatid /'hʌɪdətɪd/ *n. Med.* **1** a cyst containing watery fluid (esp. one formed by, and containing, a tapeworm larva). **2** a tapeworm larva. ▫ **hydatidiform** /-'tɪdɪfɔ:m/ *adj.* [modern Latin *hydatis* from Greek *hudatis -idos* 'watery vesicle', from *hudōr hudatos* 'water']

hydra /'hʌɪdrə/ *n.* **1** a freshwater polyp of the genus *Hydra* with tubular body and tentacles around the mouth. **2** any water snake. **3** something which is hard to destroy. [Middle English via Latin from Greek *hudra* 'water snake', esp. a fabulous one with many heads that grew again when cut off]

hydrangea /hʌɪ'dreɪn(d)ʒə/ *n.* any shrub of the genus *Hydrangea* with large white, pink, or blue flowers. [modern Latin, from Greek *hudōr* 'water' + *aggos* 'vessel' (from the cup-shape of its seed capsule)]

hydrant /'hʌɪdr(ə)nt/ *n.* a pipe (esp. in a street) with a nozzle to which a hose can be attached for drawing water from the main. [formed irregularly from HYDRO- + -ANT]

hydrate /'hʌɪdreɪt/ *n. & v. Chem.* ● *n.* a compound of water combined with another compound or with an element. ● *v.tr.* **1 a** combine chemically with water. **b** (as **hydrated** *adj.*) chemically bonded to water. **2** cause to absorb water. ▫ **hydratable** *adj.* **hydration** /-'dreɪʃ(ə)n/ *n.* **hydrator** *n.* [French, from Greek *hudōr* 'water']

hydraulic /hʌɪ'drɔ:lɪk, -'drɒl-/ *adj.* **1** (of water, oil, etc.) conveyed through pipes or channels usu. by pressure. **2** (of a mechanism etc.) operated by liquid moving in this manner (*hydraulic brakes*; *hydraulic lift*). **3** of or concerned with hydraulics (*hydraulic engineer*). **4** hardening under water (*hydraulic cement*). ▫ **hydraulically** *adv.* **hydraulicity** /-'lɪsɪti/ *n.* [Latin *hydraulicus* from Greek *hudraulikos*, from *hudōr* 'water' + *aulos* 'pipe']

hydraulic press *n.* a device in which the force applied to a fluid creates a pressure which when transmitted to a larger volume of fluid gives rise to a greater force.

hydraulic ram *n.* an automatic pump in which the kinetic energy of a descending column of water raises some of the water above its original level.

hydraulics /hʌɪ'drɔ:lɪks, -'drɒlɪks/ *n.pl.* (usu. treated as *sing.*) the science of the conveyance of liquids through pipes etc. esp. as motive power.

hydrazine /'hʌɪdrəzi:n/ *n. Chem.* a colourless alkaline liquid which is a powerful reducing agent and is used as a rocket propellant. Chem. formula: N_2H_4. [HYDROGEN + AZO- + -INE[4]]

hydride /'hʌɪdrʌɪd/ *n. Chem.* a binary compound of hydrogen with an element, esp. with a metal.

hydriodic acid /hʌɪdrɪ'ɒdɪk, -ʌɪ'ɒdɪk/ *n. Chem.* a strongly acidic solution of the colourless gas hydrogen iodide in water. Chem. formula: HI. [HYDROGEN + IODINE]

hydro /'hʌɪdrəʊ/ *n.* (*pl.* **-os**) *colloq.* **1** a hotel or clinic etc. originally providing hydropathic treatment. **2** a hydroelectric power plant. [abbreviation]

hydro- /'hʌɪdrəʊ/ *comb. form* (also **hydr-** before a vowel) **1** having to do with water (*hydroelectric*). **2** *Med.* affected with an accumulation of serous fluid (*hydrocele*). **3** *Chem.* combined with hydrogen (*hydrochloric*). [Greek *hudro-* from *hudōr* 'water']

hydrobromic acid /hʌɪdrə(ʊ)'brəʊmɪk/ *n. Chem.* a strongly acidic solution of the colourless gas hydrogen bromide in water. Chem. formula: HBr.

hydrocarbon /hʌɪdrə(ʊ)'kɑ:b(ə)n/ *n. Chem.* a compound of hydrogen and carbon.

hydrocele /'hʌɪdrə(ʊ)si:l/ *n. Med.* the accumulation of serous fluid in a body sac.

hydrocephalus /hʌɪdrə'sɛf(ə)ləs, -'kɛf-/ *n. Med.* an accumulation of fluid in the brain, esp. in young children, which makes the head enlarge and can cause mental handicap. ▫ **hydrocephalic** /-sɪ'falɪk, -kɪ'falɪk/ *adj.*

hydrochloric acid /hʌɪdrəˈklɔːrɪk, -ˈklɒrɪk/ *n. Chem.* a solution of the colourless gas hydrogen chloride in water. Chem. formula: HCl.

hydrochloride /hʌɪdrə(ʊ)ˈklɔːrʌɪd/ *n. Chem.* a compound of an organic base with hydrochloric acid.

hydrocortisone /hʌɪdrə(ʊ)ˈkɔːtɪzəʊn/ *n. Biochem.* a steroid hormone produced by the adrenal cortex, used medicinally to treat inflammation and rheumatism.

hydrocyanic acid /hʌɪdrə(ʊ)sʌɪˈanɪk/ *n. Chem.* a highly poisonous volatile liquid with a characteristic odour of bitter almonds (also called *prussic acid*). Chem. formula: HCN.

hydrodynamics /hʌɪdrə(ʊ)dʌɪˈnamɪks/ *n.* the science of forces acting on or exerted by fluids (esp. liquids). □ **hydrodynamic** *adj.* **hydrodynamical** *adj.* **hydrodynamicist** /-sɪst/ *n.* [modern Latin *hydrodynamicus* (as HYDRO-, DYNAMIC)]

hydroelectric /hʌɪdrəʊɪˈlɛktrɪk/ *adj.* **1** generating electricity by utilization of water-power. **2** (of electricity) generated in this way. □ **hydroelectricity** /-ˈtrɪsɪti/ *n.*

hydrofluoric acid /hʌɪdrə(ʊ)ˈflʊərɪk/ *n. Chem.* a solution of the colourless liquid hydrogen fluoride in water. Chem. formula: HF.

hydrofoil /ˈhʌɪdrə(ʊ)fɔɪl/ *n.* **1** a boat equipped with a device consisting of planes for lifting its hull out of the water to increase its speed. **2** this device. [HYDRO-, on the pattern of AEROFOIL]

hydrogel /ˈhʌɪdrə(ʊ)dʒɛl/ *n.* a gel in which the liquid component is water. [HYDRO- + GEL]

hydrogen /ˈhʌɪdrədʒ(ə)n/ *n. Chem.* a colourless gaseous element, without taste or odour, the lightest of the elements and occurring in water and all organic compounds (symbol **H**). □ **hydrogenous** /-ˈdrɒdʒɪnəs/ *adj.* [French *hydrogène* (as HYDRO-, -GEN)]

hydrogenase /hʌɪˈdrɒdʒəneɪz/ *n. Biochem.* any enzyme that catalyses the reduction of a substrate by hydrogen, as in some micro-organisms.

hydrogenate /hʌɪˈdrɒdʒəneɪt, ˈhʌɪdrədʒəneɪt/ *v.tr.* charge with or cause to combine with hydrogen. □ **hydrogenation** /-ˈneɪʃ(ə)n/ *n.*

hydrogen bomb *n.* an immensely powerful nuclear bomb utilizing the explosive fusion of hydrogen nuclei. Also called *H-bomb.*

hydrogen bond *n.* a weak electrostatic interaction between an electronegative atom and a hydrogen atom bonded to a different electronegative atom.

hydrogen peroxide *n.* a colourless viscous unstable liquid with strong oxidizing properties. Chem. formula: H_2O_2.

hydrogen sulphide *n.* a colourless poisonous gas with a disagreeable smell, formed by rotting animal matter. Chem. formula: H_2S.

hydrogeology /hʌɪdrəʊdʒɪˈɒlədʒi/ *n.* the branch of geology dealing with underground and surface water. □ **hydrogeological** /-dʒɪəˈlɒdʒɪk(ə)l/ *adj.* **hydrogeologist** *n.*

hydrography /hʌɪˈdrɒgrəfi/ *n.* the science of surveying and charting seas, lakes, rivers, etc. □ **hydrographer** *n.* **hydrographic** /hʌɪdrəˈgrafɪk/ *adj.* **hydrographical** /hʌɪdrəˈgrafɪk(ə)l/ *adj.* **hydrographically** /hʌɪdrəˈgrafɪk(ə)li/ *adv.*

hydroid /ˈhʌɪdrɔɪd/ *n. & adj. Zool.* ● *n.* a hydrozoan coelenterate of the order Hydroida, in which the polyp phase is predominant, e.g. sea anemones, corals, hydras. ● *adj.* of or relating to this order.

hydrolase /ˈhʌɪdrəleɪz/ *n. Biochem.* any enzyme that catalyses the hydrolysis of a substrate.

hydrology /hʌɪˈdrɒlədʒi/ *n.* the science of the properties of the earth's water, esp. of its movement in relation to land. □ **hydrologic** /hʌɪdrəˈlɒdʒɪk/ *adj.* **hydrological** /hʌɪdrəˈlɒdʒɪk(ə)l/ *adj.* **hydrologically** /hʌɪdrəˈlɒdʒɪk(ə)li/ *adv.* **hydrologist** *n.*

hydrolyse /ˈhʌɪdrəlʌɪz/ *v.tr. & intr.* (also **hydrolyze**) subject to or undergo the chemical action of water.

hydrolysis /hʌɪˈdrɒlɪsɪs/ *n.* the chemical reaction of a substance with water, usu. resulting in decomposition. □ **hydrolytic** /hʌɪdrəˈlɪtɪk/ *adj.*

hydromagnetic /hʌɪdrə(ʊ)magˈnɛtɪk/ *adj.* involving hydrodynamics and magnetism; magnetohydrodynamic.

hydromania /hʌɪdrəˈmeɪnɪə/ *n.* a craving for water.

hydromechanics /hʌɪdrə(ʊ)mɪˈkanɪks/ *n.* the mechanics of liquids; hydrodynamics.

hydrometer /hʌɪˈdrɒmɪtə/ *n.* an instrument for measuring the density of liquids. □ **hydrometric** /hʌɪdrəˈmɛtrɪk/ *adj.* **hydrometry** *n.*

hydronium ion /hʌɪˈdrəʊnɪəm/ *n. Chem.* = HYDROXONIUM ION. [contraction]

hydropathy /hʌɪˈdrɒpəθi/ *n.* the treatment of disorders by external and internal application of water. □ **hydropathic** /hʌɪdrəˈpaθɪk/ *adj.* **hydropathist** *n.* [HYDRO-, on the pattern of HOMOEOPATHY etc.]

hydrophil /ˈhʌɪdrəfɪl/ *adj.* (also **hydrophile** /-fʌɪl/) = HYDROPHILIC. [as HYDROPHILIC]

hydrophilic /hʌɪdrə(ʊ)ˈfɪlɪk/ *adj.* **1** having an affinity for water. **2** readily mixing with or wetted by water. [HYDRO- + Greek *philos* 'loving']

hydrophobia /hʌɪdrə(ʊ)ˈfəʊbɪə/ *n.* **1** a morbid aversion to water, esp. as a symptom of rabies in humans. **2** rabies, esp. in humans. [Late Latin from Greek *hudrophobia* (as HYDRO-, -PHOBIA)]

hydrophobic /hʌɪdrə(ʊ)ˈfəʊbɪk/ *adj.* **1** of or suffering from hydrophobia. **2 a** lacking an affinity for water. **b** not readily wettable.

hydrophone /ˈhʌɪdrəfəʊn/ *n.* a microphone for the detection of sound waves in water.

hydrophyte /ˈhʌɪdrəfʌɪt/ *n.* an aquatic plant, or a plant which needs much moisture.

hydroplane /ˈhʌɪdrəpleɪn/ *n. & v.* ● *n.* **1** a light fast motor boat designed to skim over the surface of water. **2** a finlike attachment which enables a submarine to rise and fall in water. ● *v.intr.* **1** (of a boat) skim over the surface of water with its hull lifted. **2** = AQUAPLANE *v.* 2.

hydroponics /hʌɪdrə(ʊ)ˈpɒnɪks/ *n.* the process of growing plants in sand, gravel, or liquid, without soil and with added nutrients. □ **hydroponic** *adj.* **hydroponically** *adv.* [HYDRO- + Greek *ponos* 'labour']

hydroquinone /hʌɪdrəˈkwɪnəʊn/ *n.* a substance formed by the reduction of benzoquinone, used as a photographic developer.

hydrosphere /ˈhʌɪdrəsfɪə/ *n.* the waters of the earth's surface.

hydrostatic /hʌɪdrə(ʊ)ˈstatɪk/ *adj.* of the equilibrium of liquids and the pressure exerted by liquid at rest. □ **hydrostatical** *adj.* **hydrostatically** *adv.* [probably from Greek *hudrostatēs* 'hydrostatic balance' (as HYDRO-, STATIC)]

hydrostatic press *n.* = HYDRAULIC PRESS.

hydrostatics /hʌɪdrə(ʊ)ˈstatɪks/ *n.* the branch of mechanics concerned with the hydrostatic properties of liquids.

hydrotherapy /hʌɪdrə(ʊ)ˈθɛrəpi/ *n.* the use of water in the treatment of disorders, usu. exercises in swimming pools for arthritic or partially paralysed patients. □ **hydrotherapist** *n.*

hydrothermal /hʌɪdrə(ʊ)ˈθəːm(ə)l/ *adj.* of the action of heated water on the earth's crust. □ **hydrothermally** *adv.*

hydrothorax /hʌɪdrə(ʊ)ˈθɔːraks/ *n.* the condition of having fluid in the pleural cavity.

hydrotropism /hʌɪˈdrɒtrəpɪz(ə)m/ *adj.* a tendency of plant roots etc. to turn to or from moisture.

hydrous /ˈhʌɪdrəs/ *adj. Chem. & Mineral.* containing water. [Greek *hudōr hudro-* 'water']

hydroxide /hʌɪˈdrɒksʌɪd/ *n. Chem.* a metallic compound containing oxygen and hydrogen either in the form of the hydroxide ion (OH^-) or the hydroxyl group (-OH).

hydroxonium ion /hʌɪdrɒkˈsəʊnɪəm/ *n. Chem.* the hydrated hydrogen ion, H_3O^+. [HYDRO- + OXY-[2] + *-onium*]

hydroxy- /hʌɪˈdrɒksi/ *comb. form Chem.* having a hydroxide ion (or ions) or a hydroxyl group (or groups) (*hydroxybenzoic acid*). [HYDROGEN + OXYGEN]

hydroxyl /hʌɪˈdrɒksɪl/ *n. Chem.* the monovalent group containing hydrogen and oxygen, as -OH. [HYDROGEN + OXYGEN + -YL]

hydrozoan /hʌɪdrə(ʊ)ˈzəʊən/ *n. & adj.* ● *n.* any aquatic coelenterate of the class Hydrozoa of mainly marine forms that are often colonial and have both polyp and medusoid phases, including hydras and Portuguese men-of-war. ● *adj.* of or relating to this class. [modern Latin *Hydrozoa* (as HYDRA, Greek *zōion* 'animal')]

hyena /hʌɪˈiːnə/ *n.* (also **hyaena**) any flesh-eating mammal of the family Hyaenidae, with hind limbs shorter than forelimbs. [Middle English via Old French *hyene* & Latin *hyaena* from Greek *huaina*, fem. of *hus* 'pig']

hygiene /ˈhʌɪdʒiːn/ *n.* **1 a** a study, or set of principles, of maintaining health. **b** conditions or practices conducive to maintaining health. **2** sanitary science. [French *hygiène* via modern Latin *hygieina* from Greek *hugieinē* (*tekhnē*) '(art) of health', from *hugiēs* 'healthy']

hygienic /hʌɪˈdʒiːnɪk/ *adj.* conducive to hygiene; clean and sanitary. □ **hygienically** *adv.*

hygienics /hʌɪˈdʒiːnɪks/ *n.* = HYGIENE 1a.

hygienist /ˈhʌɪdʒiːnɪst/ *n.* a specialist in the promotion and practice of cleanliness for the preservation of health.

hygro- /ˈhʌɪgrəʊ/ *comb. form* moisture. [Greek *hugro-* from *hugros* 'wet, moist']

hygrology /hʌɪˈgrɒlədʒi/ *n.* the study of the humidity of the atmosphere etc.

hygrometer /hʌɪˈgrɒmɪtə/ *n.* an instrument for measuring the humidity of the air or a gas. □ **hygrometric** /hʌɪgrəˈmɛtrɪk/ *adj.* **hygrometry** *n.*

hygrophilous /hʌɪˈgrɒfɪləs/ *adj.* (of a plant) growing in a moist environment.

hygrophyte /ˈhʌɪgrəfʌɪt/ *n.* = HYDROPHYTE.

hygroscope /ˈhʌɪgrə(ʊ)skəʊp/ *n.* an instrument which indicates but does not measure the humidity of the air.

hygroscopic /hʌɪgrə(ʊ)ˈskɒpɪk/ *adj.* **1** of the hygroscope. **2** (of a substance) tending to absorb moisture from the air. □ **hygroscopically** *adv.*

hying *pres. part.* of HIE.

hylic /ˈhʌɪlɪk/ *adj.* of matter; material. [Late Latin *hylicus* from Greek *hulikos*, from *hulē* 'matter']

hylo- /ˈhʌɪləʊ/ *comb. form* matter. [Greek *hulo-* from *hulē* 'matter']

hylomorphism /hʌɪlə(ʊ)ˈmɔːfɪz(ə)m/ *n.* the theory that physical objects are composed of matter and form. [HYLO- + Greek *morphē* 'form']

hylozoism /hʌɪlə(ʊ)ˈzəʊɪz(ə)m/ *n.* the doctrine that all matter has life. [HYLO- + Greek *zōē* 'life']

hymen /ˈhʌɪmɛn/ *n. Anat.* a membrane which partially closes the opening of the vagina and is usu. broken at the first occurrence of sexual intercourse. □ **hymenal** *adj.* [Late Latin from Greek *humēn* 'membrane']

hymeneal /hʌɪmɪˈniːəl/ *adj. literary* of or concerning marriage. [*Hymen* (Latin from Greek *Humēn*) the name of the Greek and Roman god of marriage]

hymenium /hʌɪˈmiːnɪəm/ *n.* (*pl.* **hymenia** /-nɪə/) the spore-bearing surface of certain fungi. [modern Latin from Greek *humenion*, diminutive of *humēn* 'membrane']

hymenopteran /hʌɪməˈnɒpt(ə)rən/ *n.* any insect of the order Hymenoptera having four transparent wings, including bees, wasps, and ants. □ **hymenopterous** *adj.* [modern Latin *hymenoptera* from Greek *humenopteros* 'membrane-winged' (as HYMEN, *pteron* 'wing')]

hymn /hɪm/ *n. & v.* ● *n.* **1** a song of praise, esp. to God in Christian worship, usu. a metrical composition sung in a religious service. **2** a song of praise in honour of a god or other exalted being or thing. ● *v.* **1** *tr.* praise or celebrate in hymns. **2** *intr.* sing hymns. □ **hymnic** /ˈhɪmnɪk/ *adj.* [Middle English *ymne* etc. via Old French *ymne* and Latin *hymnus* from Greek *humnos*]

hymnal /ˈhɪmn(ə)l/ *n. & adj.* ● *n.* a hymn book. ● *adj.* of hymns. [Middle English from medieval Latin *hymnale* (as HYMN)]

hymnary /ˈhɪmnəri/ *n.* (*pl.* **-ies**) a hymn book.

hymn book *n.* a book of hymns.

hymnody /ˈhɪmnədi/ *n.* (*pl.* **-ies**) **1 a** the singing of hymns. **b** the composition of hymns. **2** hymns collectively. □ **hymnodist** *n.* [medieval Latin *hymnodia* from Greek *humnōidia*, from *humnos* 'hymn': cf. PSALMODY]

hymnographer /hɪmˈnɒgrəfə/ *n.* a writer of hymns. □ **hymnography** *n.* [Greek *humnographos* from *humnos* 'hymn']

hymnology /hɪmˈnɒlədʒi/ *n.* (*pl.* **-ies**) **1** the composition or study of hymns. **2** hymns collectively. □ **hymnologist** *n.*

hyoid /ˈhʌɪɔɪd/ *n. & adj. Anat.* ● *n.* (in full **hyoid bone**) a U-shaped bone in the neck which supports the tongue. ● *adj.* of or relating to this. [French *hyoïde* via modern Latin *hyoïdes* from Greek *huoeidēs* 'shaped like the letter upsilon' (*hu*)]

hyoscine /ˈhʌɪəsiːn/ *n.* a poisonous alkaloid found in plants of the nightshade family, esp. of the genus *Scopolia*, and used as an antiemetic in motion sickness and a preoperative medication for examination of the eye. Also called *scopolamine*. [HYOSCYAMINE]

hyoscyamine /hʌɪə(ʊ)ˈsʌɪəmiːn/ *n.* a poisonous alkaloid obtained from henbane, having similar properties to hyoscine. [modern Latin *hyoscyamus* from Greek *huoskuamos* 'henbane', from *hus huos* 'pig' + *kuamos* 'bean']

hypaesthesia /hʌɪpiːsˈθiːzjə -pɛs-/ *n.* (*US* **hypesthesia**) a diminished capacity for sensation, esp. of the skin. □ **hypaesthetic** /-ˈθɛtɪk/ *adj.* [modern Latin (as HYPO-, Greek *-aisthēsia* from *aisthanomai* 'perceive')]

hypaethral /hʌɪˈpiːθr(ə)l, hɪ-/ *adj.* (also **hypethral**) **1** open to the sky; roofless. **2** *literary* open-air. [Latin *hypaethrus* from Greek *hupaithros* (as HYPO-, *aithēr* 'air')]

hypallage /hʌɪˈpalədʒiː, hɪ-/ *n. Rhet.* the transposition of the natural relations of two elements in a proposition (e.g. *Melissa shook her doubtful curls*). [Late Latin from Greek *hupallagē* (as HYPO-, *allassō* 'exchange')]

hype[1] /hʌɪp/ *n. & v. slang* ● *n.* **1** extravagant or intensive publicity promotion. **2** cheating; a trick. ● *v.tr.* **1** promote (a product) with extravagant publicity. **2** cheat, trick. [20th c.: origin unknown]

hype[2] /hʌɪp/ *n. slang* **1** a drug addict. **2** a hypodermic needle or injection. □ **hyped up** stimulated by or as if by a hypodermic injection. [abbreviation of HYPODERMIC]

hyper /ˈhʌɪpə/ *adj. slang* hyperactive, highly strung; extraordinarily energetic.

hyper- /ˈhʌɪpə/ *prefix* meaning: **1** over, beyond, above (*hyperphysical*). **2** exceeding (*hypersonic*). **3** excessively; above normal (*hyperbole*; *hypersensitive*; *hyperinflation*). [Greek *huper* 'over, beyond']

hyperactive /hʌɪpərˈaktɪv/ *adj.* (of a person, esp. a child) abnormally active. □ **hyperactivity** /-ˈtɪvɪti/ *n.*

hyperaemia /hʌɪpərˈiːmɪə/ *n.* (*US* **hyperemia**) an excessive quantity of blood in the vessels supplying an organ or other part of the body. □ **hyperaemic** *adj.* [modern Latin (as HYPER-, -AEMIA)]

hyperaesthesia /hʌɪpəriːsˈθiːzjə, -ɛsˈθiː-/ *n.* (*US* **hyperesthesia**) an excessive physical sensibility, esp. of the skin. □ **hyperaesthetic** /-ˈθɛtɪk/ *adj.* [modern Latin (as HYPER-, Greek *-aisthēsia* from *aisthanomai* 'perceive')]

hyperbaric /hʌɪpəˈbarɪk/ *adj.* (of a gas) at a pressure greater than normal. [HYPER- + Greek *barus* 'heavy']

hyperbaton /hʌɪˈpəːbətɒn/ *n. Rhet.* the inversion of the normal order of words, esp. for the sake of emphasis (e.g. *this I must see*). [Latin from Greek *huperbaton* (as HYPER-, *bainō* 'go')]

hyperbola /hʌɪˈpəːbələ/ *n.* (*pl.* **hyperbolas** or **hyperbolae** /-liː/) *Geom.* the plane curve of two equal branches, produced when a cone is cut by a plane that makes a larger angle with the base than the side of the cone (cf. ELLIPSE). [modern Latin from Greek *huperbolē* 'excess' (as HYPER-, *ballō* 'to throw')]

hyperbole /hʌɪˈpəːbəli/ *n. Rhet.* an exaggerated statement not meant to be taken literally. □ **hyperbolical** /-ˈbɒlɪk(ə)l/ *adj.* **hyperbolically** /-ˈbɒlɪk(ə)li/ *adv.* **hyperbolism** *n.* [Latin (as HYPERBOLA)]

hyperbolic /hʌɪpəˈbɒlɪk/ *adj.* **1** *Geom.* of or relating to a hyperbola. **2** *Math.* (of a function, e.g. cosine) having the same relation to a rectangular hyperbola as the trigonometric functions do to a circle.

hyperboloid /hʌɪˈpəːbəlɔɪd/ *n. Geom.* a solid or surface having plane sections that are hyperbolas, ellipses, or circles. □ **hyperboloidal** *adj.*

hyperborean /hʌɪpəbɔːˈriːən, -ˈbɔːrɪən/ *n. & adj.* ● *n.* **1** an inhabitant of the extreme north of the earth. **2** (**Hyperborean**) (in Greek mythology) a member of a race worshipping Apollo and living in a land of sunshine and plenty beyond the north wind. ● *adj.* of the extreme north of the earth. [Late Latin *hyperboreanus* via Latin *hyperboreus* from Greek *huperboreos* (as HYPER-, *Boreas*, the name of the god of the north wind)]

hypercholesterolaemia /ˌhʌɪpəkəˌlɛstərɒˈliːmɪə/ *n.* an excess of cholesterol in the bloodstream. [HYPER- + CHOLESTEROL + -AEMIA]

hyperconscious /hʌɪpəˈkɒnʃəs/ *adj.* (foll. by *of*) acutely or excessively aware.

hypercritical /hʌɪpəˈkrɪtɪk(ə)l/ *adj.* excessively critical, esp. of small faults. □ **hypercritically** *adv.*

hypercube /ˈhʌɪpəkjuːb/ *n.* a geometrical figure in four or more dimensions, analogous to a cube in three dimensions.

hyperemia *US* var. of HYPERAEMIA.

hyperesthesia *US* var. of HYPERAESTHESIA.

hyperfocal distance /hʌɪpəˈfəʊk(ə)l/ *n.* the distance on which a camera lens can be focused to bring the maximum range of object-distances into focus.

hypergamy /hʌɪˈpəːgəmi/ *n.* marriage to a person of equal or superior caste or class. [HYPER- + Greek *gamos* 'marriage']

hyperglycaemia /hʌɪpəglʌɪˈsiːmɪə/ *n.* (*US* **hyperglycemia**) an excess of glucose in the bloodstream, often associated with diabetes mellitus. □ **hyperglycaemic** *adj.* [HYPER- + GLYCO- + -AEMIA]

hypergolic /hʌɪpəˈgɒlɪk/ *adj.* (of a rocket propellant) igniting spontaneously on contact with an oxidant etc. [German *Hypergol* (perhaps as HYPO-, ERG[1], -OL[1])]

hypericum /hʌɪˈpɛrɪkəm/ *n.* any shrub of the genus *Hypericum* with five-petalled yellow flowers. Also called ST JOHN'S WORT. [Latin from Greek *hupereikon* (as HYPER-, *ereikē* 'heath')]

hyperinflation /hʌɪpərɪnˈfleɪʃ(ə)n/ *n.* monetary inflation at a very high rate.

hyperkinesis /hʌɪpəkɪˈniːsɪs, -kʌɪ-/ *n.* (also **hyperkinesia** /-kɪˈniːzɪə, -kʌɪ-/) *Med.* **1** muscle spasm. **2** a disorder of children marked by hyperactivity and inability to attend. □ **hyperkinetic** /-ˈnɛtɪk/ *adj.* [HYPER- + Greek *kinēsis* 'motion']

hypermarket /ˈhʌɪpəmɑːkɪt/ *n. Brit.* a very large self-service store with a wide range of goods and extensive car-parking facilities, usu. outside a town. [translation of French *hypermarché* (as HYPER-, MARKET)]

hypermedia /hʌɪpəˈmiːdɪə/ *n.* = MULTIMEDIA *n.* [HYPER- + MEDIA[1]]

hypermetropia /hʌɪpəmɪˈtrəʊpɪə/ *n.* the condition of having long sight. □ **hypermetropic** /-ˈtrɒpɪk/ *adj.* [modern Latin, from HYPER- + Greek *metron* 'measure', *ōps* 'eye']

hypernym /ˈhʌɪpənɪm/ *n.* a word of general meaning applicable to more specific, related words; a superordinate (e.g. *insect* is a hypernym of *bee* and *wasp*).

hyperon /ˈhʌɪp(ə)rɒn/ *n. Physics* an unstable subatomic particle classified as a baryon, heavier than the neutron and proton. [HYPER- + -ON]

hyperopia /hʌɪpərˈəʊpɪə/ *n.* = HYPERMETROPIA. □ **hyperopic** /-ˈɒpɪk/ *adj.* [modern Latin, from HYPER- + Greek *ōps* 'eye']

hyperphysical /hʌɪpəˈfɪzɪk(ə)l/ *adj.* supernatural. □ **hyperphysically** *adv.*

hyperplasia /hʌɪpəˈpleɪzɪə/ *n.* the enlargement of an organ or tissue from the increased production of cells. [HYPER- + Greek *plasis* 'formation']

hypersensitive /hʌɪpəˈsɛnsɪtɪv/ *adj.* (often foll. by *to*) abnormally or excessively sensitive in character or reaction. □ **hypersensitiveness** *n.* **hypersensitivity** /-ˈtɪvɪti/ *n.*

hypersonic /hʌɪpəˈsɒnɪk/ *adj.* **1** relating to speeds of more than five times the speed of sound (Mach 5). **2** relating to sound frequencies above about a thousand million hertz. □ **hypersonically** *adv.* [HYPER-, on the pattern of SUPERSONIC, ULTRASONIC]

hyperspace /ˈhʌɪpəspeɪs/ *n.* space of more than three dimensions, esp. (in science fiction) a notional space-time continuum in which motion and communication at speeds greater than that of light are supposedly possible.

hypersthene /ˈhʌɪpəsθiːn/ *n.* a rock-forming mineral, magnesium iron silicate, of greenish colour. [French *hyperstène* (as HYPER-, Greek *sthenos* 'strength', from its being harder than hornblende]

hypertension /hʌɪpəˈtɛnʃ(ə)n/ *n.* **1** abnormally high blood pressure. **2** a state of great emotional tension. □ **hypertensive** /-sɪv/ *adj.*

hypertext /ˈhʌɪpətɛkst/ *n. Computing* a software system allowing extensive cross-referencing between related sections of text and associated graphic material.

hyperthermia /hʌɪpəˈθəːmɪə/ *n. Med.* the condition of having a body temperature greatly above normal. □ **hyperthermic** *adj.* [HYPER- + Greek *thermē* 'heat']

hyperthyroidism /hʌɪpəˈθʌɪrɔɪdɪz(ə)m/ *n. Med.* overactivity of the thyroid gland, resulting in rapid heartbeat and an increased rate of metabolism. □ **hyperthyroid** *adj.* **hyperthyroidic** *adj.*

hypertonic /hʌɪpəˈtɒnɪk/ *adj.* **1** (of muscles) having high tension. **2** (of a solution) having a greater osmotic pressure than another solution. □ **hypertonia** /-ˈtəʊnɪə/ *n.* (in sense 1). **hypertonicity** /-təˈnɪsɪti/ *n.*

hypertrophy /hʌɪˈpəːtrəfi/ *n.* the enlargement of an organ or tissue from the increase in size of its cells. □ **hypertrophic** /hʌɪpəˈtrɒfɪk/ *adj.* **hypertrophied** *adj.* [modern Latin *hypertrophia* (as HYPER-, Greek *-trophia* 'nourishment')]

hyperventilation /ˌhʌɪpəvɛntɪˈleɪʃ(ə)n/ *n.* breathing at an abnormally rapid rate, resulting in an increased loss of carbon dioxide. □ **hyperventilate** *v.intr.*

hypethral var. of HYPAETHRAL.

hypha /ˈhʌɪfə/ *n.* (*pl.* **hyphae** /-fiː/) a filament in the mycelium of a fungus. □ **hyphal** *adj.* [modern Latin from Greek *huphē* 'web']

hyphen /ˈhʌɪf(ə)n/ *n. & v.* ● *n.* the sign (-) used to join words semantically or syntactically (as in *pick-me-up*, *rock-forming*), to indicate the division of a word at the end of a line, or to indicate a missing or implied element (as in *man- and womankind*). ● *v.tr.* **1** write (a compound word) with a hyphen. **2** join (words) with a hyphen. [Late Latin from Greek *huphen* 'together', from *hupo* 'under' + *hen* 'one']

hyphenate /ˈhʌɪfəneɪt/ *v.tr.* = HYPHEN *v.* □ **hyphenation** /-ˈneɪʃ(ə)n/ *n.*

hypno- /ˈhɪpnəʊ/ *comb. form* sleep, hypnosis. [Greek *hupnos* 'sleep']

hypnogenesis /hɪpnəʊˈdʒɛnɪsɪs/ *n.* the induction of a hypnotic state.

hypnology /hɪpˈnɒlədʒi/ *n.* the science of the phenomena of sleep. □ **hypnologist** *n.*

hypnopaedia /hɪpnəʊˈpiːdɪə/ *n.* (*US* **hypnopedia**) learning by hearing while asleep.

hypnosis /hɪp'nəʊsɪs/ *n.* **1** a state like sleep in which the subject acts only on external suggestion. **2** artificially produced sleep. [modern Latin, from Greek *hupnos* 'sleep' + -OSIS]

hypnotherapy /hɪpnə(ʊ)'θɛrəpi/ *n.* the treatment of disease by hypnosis. □ **hypnotherapist** *n.*

hypnotic /hɪp'nɒtɪk/ *adj.* & *n.* ● *adj.* **1** of or producing hypnosis. **2** (of a drug) soporific. ● *n.* **1** a thing, esp. a drug, that produces sleep. **2** a person under or open to the influence of hypnotism. □ **hypnotically** *adv.* [French *hypnotique* via Late Latin *hypnoticus* from Greek *hupnōtikos*, from *hupnoō* 'put to sleep']

hypnotism /'hɪpnətɪz(ə)m/ *n.* the study or practice of hypnosis. □ **hypnotist** *n.*

hypnotize /'hɪpnətʌɪz/ *v.tr.* (also **-ise**) **1** produce hypnosis in. **2** fascinate; capture the mind of (a person). □ **hypnotizable** *adj.*

hypo[1] /'hʌɪpəʊ/ *n.* *Photog.* the chemical sodium thiosulphate (incorrectly called hyposulphite) used as a photographic fixer. [abbreviation]

hypo[2] /'hʌɪpəʊ/ *n.* (*pl.* **-os**) *colloq.* = HYPODERMIC *n.* [abbreviation]

hypo[3] /'hʌɪpəʊ/ *n.* (*pl.* **-os**) *colloq.* hyperglycaemia. [abbreviation]

hypo- /'hʌɪpəʊ/ *prefix* (before a vowel or h usu. **hyp-**) **1** under (*hypodermic*). **2** below normal (*hypoxia*). **3** slightly (*hypomania*). **4** *Chem.* containing an element combined in low valence (*hypochlorous*). [Greek from *hupo* 'under']

hypo-allergenic /ˌhʌɪpəʊalə'dʒɛnɪk/ *adj.* having little tendency, or a specially reduced tendency, to cause an allergic reaction.

hypoblast /'hʌɪpə(ʊ)blast/ *n.* *Biol.* = ENDODERM. [modern Latin *hypoblastus* (as HYPO-, -BLAST)]

hypocaust /'hʌɪpə(ʊ)kɔːst/ *n.* a hollow space under the floor in ancient Roman houses, into which hot air was sent for heating a room or bath. [Latin *hypocaustum* from Greek *hupokauston* 'place heated from below' (as HYPO-, *kaiō, kau-* 'burn')]

hypochlorite /hʌɪpə(ʊ)'klɔːrʌɪt/ *n.* *Chem.* a salt of hypochlorous acid.

hypochlorous acid /hʌɪpə(ʊ)'klɔːrəs/ *n.* *Chem.* an unstable acid existing only in dilute solution and used in bleaching and water treatment. Chem. formula: HOCl. [HYPO- + CHLORINE + -OUS]

hypochondria /hʌɪpə(ʊ)'kɒndrɪə/ *n.* **1** abnormal anxiety about one's health. **2** morbid depression without real cause. [Late Latin from Greek *hupokhondria*, the soft parts of the body below the ribs, where melancholy was thought to arise (as HYPO-, *khondros* 'sternal cartilage')]

hypochondriac /hʌɪpə(ʊ)'kɒndrɪak/ *n.* & *adj.* ● *n.* a person suffering from hypochondria. ● *adj.* (also **hypochondriacal** /-'drʌɪək(ə)l/) of or affected by hypochondria. [French *hypocondriaque* from Greek *hupokhondriakos* (as HYPOCHONDRIA)]

hypocoristic /hʌɪpə(ʊ)kə'rɪstɪk/ *adj.* *Gram.* of the nature of a pet name. [Greek *hupokoristikos* from *hupokorizomai* 'call by pet names']

hypocotyl /hʌɪpə'kɒtɪl/ *n.* *Bot.* the part of the stem of an embryo plant beneath the stalks of the seed-leaves or cotyledons and directly above the root.

hypocrisy /hɪ'pɒkrɪsi/ *n.* (*pl.* **-ies**) **1** the assumption or postulation of moral standards to which one's own behaviour does not conform; dissimulation, pretence. **2** an instance of this. [Middle English via Old French *ypocrisie* and ecclesiastical Latin *hypocrisis* from Greek *hupokrisis* 'acting of a part, pretence' (as HYPO-, *krinō* 'decide, judge')]

hypocrite /'hɪpəkrɪt/ *n.* a person given to hypocrisy. □ **hypocritical** /-'krɪtɪk(ə)l/ *adj.* **hypocritically** /-'krɪtɪk(ə)li/ *adv.* [Middle English via Old French *ypocrite* and ecclesiastical Latin from Greek *hupokritēs* 'actor' (as HYPOCRISY)]

hypocycloid /hʌɪpə(ʊ)'sʌɪklɔɪd/ *n.* *Math.* the curve traced by a point on the circumference of a circle rolling on the interior of another circle. □ **hypocycloidal** /-'klɔɪd(ə)l/ *adj.*

hypodermic /hʌɪpə(ʊ)'dəːmɪk/ *adj.* & *n.* ● *adj.* *Med.* **1** of or relating to the area beneath the skin. **2 a** (of a drug etc. or its application) injected beneath the skin. **b** (of a needle, syringe, etc.) used to do this. ● *n.* a hypodermic injection or syringe. □ **hypodermically** *adv.* [HYPO- + Greek *derma* 'skin']

hypogastrium /hʌɪpə(ʊ)'gastrɪəm/ *n.* (*pl.* **hypogastria** /-strɪə/) the part of the central abdomen which is situated below the region of the stomach. □ **hypogastric** *adj.* [modern Latin from Greek *hupogastrion* (as HYPO-, *gastēr* 'belly')]

hypogeal /hʌɪpə(ʊ)'dʒiːəl/ *adj.* **1** esp. *Biol.* (existing or growing) underground. **2** *Bot.* (of seed germination) with the seed-leaves remaining below the ground. [Late Latin *hypogeus* from Greek *hupogeios* (as HYPO-, *gē* 'earth')]

hypogene /'hʌɪpədʒiːn/ *adj.* *Geol.* produced under the surface of the earth. [HYPO- + Greek *gen-* 'produce']

hypogeum /hʌɪpə(ʊ)'dʒiːəm/ *n.* (*pl.* **hypogea** /-'dʒiːə/) an underground chamber. [Latin from Greek *hupogeion*, neut. of *hupogeios*: see HYPOGEAL]

hypoglycaemia /hʌɪpəʊglʌɪ'siːmɪə/ *n.* (*US* **hypoglycemia**) a deficiency of glucose in the bloodstream. □ **hypoglycaemic** *adj.* [HYPO- + GLYCO- + -AEMIA]

hypoid /'hʌɪpɔɪd/ *n.* a gear with the pinion offset from the centre line of the wheel, to connect non-intersecting shafts. [perhaps from HYPERBOLOID]

hypolimnion /hʌɪpə(ʊ)'lɪmnɪən/ *n.* (*pl.* **hypolimnia** /-nɪə/) the lower layer of water in stratified lakes. [HYPO- + Greek *limnion*, diminutive of *limnē* 'lake']

hypomania /hʌɪpə(ʊ)'meɪnɪə/ *n.* a minor form of mania. □ **hypomanic** /-'manɪk/ *adj.* [modern Latin from German *Hypomanie* (as HYPO-, MANIA)]

hyponasty /'hʌɪpə(ʊ)nasti/ *n.* *Bot.* the tendency in plant organs for growth to be more rapid on the underside. □ **hyponastic** /-'nastɪk/ *adj.* [HYPO- + Greek *nastos* 'pressed']

hyponym /'hʌɪpə(ʊ)nɪm/ *n.* a word of more specific meaning than a general or superordinate term applicable to it (e.g. *spoon* is a hyponym of *cutlery*). □ **hyponymy** /hʌɪ'pɒnɪmi/ *n.*

hypophysis /hʌɪ'pɒfɪsɪs/ *n.* (*pl.* **hypophyses** /-siːz/) *Anat.* = *pituitary gland* (see PITUITARY). □ **hypophyseal** /hʌɪpə(ʊ)'fɪzɪəl/ *adj.* (also **-physial**). [modern Latin from Greek *hupophusis* 'offshoot' (as HYPO-, *phusis* 'growth')]

hypostasis /hʌɪ'pɒstəsɪs/ *n.* (*pl.* **hypostases** /-siːz/) **1** *Med.* an accumulation of fluid or blood in the lower parts of the body or organs under the influence of gravity, in cases of poor circulation. **2** *Metaphysics* an underlying substance, as opposed to attributes or to that which is unsubstantial. **3** in Christian theology: **a** the person of Christ, combining human and divine natures. **b** each of the three persons of the Trinity. [ecclesiastical Latin from Greek *hupostasis* (as HYPO-, STASIS 'standing, state')]

hypostasize /hʌɪ'pɒstəsʌɪz/ *v.tr.* (also **-ise**) *Brit.* make into or represent as a substance or concrete reality; embody, personify.

hypostatic /hʌɪpə(ʊ)'statɪk/ *adj.* (also **hypostatical**) (in Christian theology) relating to the three persons of the Trinity.

hypostatic union *n.* the divine and human natures in Christ.

hypostatize /hʌɪ'pɒstətʌɪz/ *v.tr.* *N. Amer.* = HYPOSTASIZE.

hypostyle /'hʌɪpə(ʊ)stʌɪl/ *adj.* *Archit.* having a roof supported by pillars. [Greek *hupostulos* (as HYPO-, STYLE)]

hypotaxis /hʌɪpə(ʊ)'taksɪs/ *n.* *Gram.* the subordination of one clause to another. □ **hypotactic** /-'taktɪk/ *adj.* [Greek *hupotaxis* (as HYPO-, *taxis* 'arrangement')]

hypotension /hʌɪpə(ʊ)'tɛnʃ(ə)n/ *n.* abnormally low blood pressure. □ **hypotensive** *adj.*

hypotenuse /hʌɪˈpɒtɪnjuːz, -s/ *n.* the side opposite the right angle of a right-angled triangle. [Latin *hypotenusa* from Greek *hupoteinousa* (*grammē*) 'subtending (line)', fem. part. of *hupoteinō* (as HYPO-, *teinō* 'stretch')]

hypothalamus /hʌɪpə(ʊ)ˈθaləməs/ *n.* (*pl.* **-mi** /-mʌɪ/) *Anat.* the region of the brain which controls body temperature, thirst, hunger, etc. □ **hypothalamic** *adj.* [modern Latin, formed as HYPO-, THALAMUS]

hypothec /hʌɪˈpɒθɪk, ˈhʌɪ-/ *n.* (in Roman and Scottish law) a right established by law over property belonging to a debtor. □ **hypothecary** /hʌɪˈpɒθɪk(ə)ri/ *adj.* [French *hypothèque* via Late Latin *hypotheca* from Greek *hupothēkē* 'deposit' (as HYPO-, *tithēmi* 'place')]

hypothecate /hʌɪˈpɒθɪkeɪt/ *v.tr.* pledge, mortgage. □ **hypothecation** /-ˈkeɪʃ(ə)n/ *n.* [medieval Latin *hypothecare* (as HYPOTHEC)]

hypothermia /hʌɪpə(ʊ)ˈθəːmɪə/ *n. Med.* the condition of having an abnormally low body temperature. [HYPO- + Greek *thermē* 'heat']

hypothesis /hʌɪˈpɒθɪsɪs/ *n.* (*pl.* **hypotheses** /-siːz/) **1** a proposition made as a basis for reasoning, without the assumption of its truth. **2** a supposition made as a starting point for further investigation from known facts (cf. THEORY 1). **3** a groundless assumption. [Late Latin from Greek *hupothesis* 'foundation' (as HYPO-, THESIS)]

hypothesize /hʌɪˈpɒθɪsʌɪz/ *v.* (also **-ise**) **1** *intr.* frame a hypothesis. **2** *tr.* assume as a hypothesis. □ **hypothesist** /-sɪst/ *n.* **hypothesizer** *n.*

hypothetical /hʌɪpə(ʊ)ˈθɛtɪk(ə)l/ *adj.* **1** of or based on or serving as a hypothesis. **2** supposed but not necessarily real or true. □ **hypothetically** *adv.*

hypothyroidism /hʌɪpəʊˈθʌɪrɔɪdɪz(ə)m/ *n. Med.* subnormal activity of the thyroid gland, resulting in cretinism in children, and mental and physical slowing in adults. □ **hypothyroid** *n.* & *adj.* **hypothyroidic** /-ˈrɔɪdɪk/ *adj.*

hypoventilation /ˌhʌɪpəʊvɛntɪˈleɪʃ(ə)n/ *n.* breathing at an abnormally slow rate, resulting in an increased amount of carbon dioxide in the blood.

hypoxaemia /hʌɪpɒkˈsiːmɪə/ *n.* (*US* **hypoxemia**) *Med.* an abnormally low concentration of oxygen in the blood. [modern Latin (as HYPO-, OXYGEN, -AEMIA)]

hypoxia /hʌɪˈpɒksɪə/ *n. Med.* a deficiency of oxygen reaching the tissues. □ **hypoxic** *adj.* [HYPO- + OX- + -IA[1]]

hypso- /ˈhɪpsəʊ/ *comb. form* height. [Greek *hupsos* 'height']

hypsography /hɪpˈsɒgrəfi/ *n.* a description or mapping of the contours of the earth's surface. □ **hypsographic** /-ˈgrafɪk/ *adj.* **hypsographical** /-ˈgrafɪk(ə)l/ *adj.*

hypsometer /hɪpˈsɒmɪtə/ *n.* **1** a device for calibrating thermometers at the boiling point of water. **2** this instrument when used to estimate height above sea level. □ **hypsometric** /-səˈmɛtrɪk/ *adj.*

hyrax /ˈhʌɪraks/ *n.* any small mammal of the order Hyracoidea, including the rock rabbit and the dassie. [modern Latin from Greek *hurax* 'shrew-mouse']

hyson /ˈhʌɪs(ə)n/ *n.* a kind of green China tea. [Chinese *xichun*, literally 'bright spring']

hyssop /ˈhɪsəp/ *n.* **1** any small bushy aromatic herb of the genus *Hyssopus*, esp. *H. officinalis*, formerly used medicinally. **2** *Bibl.* **a** a plant whose twigs were used for sprinkling in Jewish rites. **b** a bunch of this used in purification. [Old English *(h)ysope* (reinforced in Middle English by Old French *ysope*) via Latin *hyssopus* from Greek *hyssōpos*, of Semitic origin]

hysterectomy /hɪstəˈrɛktəmi/ *n.* (*pl.* **-ies**) the surgical removal of the womb. □ **hysterectomize** *v.tr.* (also **-ise**). [Greek *hustera* 'womb' + -ECTOMY]

hysteresis /hɪstəˈriːsɪs/ *n. Physics* the lagging behind of an effect when its cause varies in amount etc., esp. of magnetic induction behind the magnetizing force. [Greek *husterēsis*, via *hustereō* 'be behind' from *husteros* 'coming after']

hysteria /hɪˈstɪərɪə/ *n.* **1** a wild uncontrollable emotion or excitement. **2** a functional disturbance of the nervous system, of psychoneurotic origin. [modern Latin (as HYSTERIC)]

hysteric /hɪˈstɛrɪk/ *n.* & *adj.* ● *n.* **1** (in *pl.*) **a** a fit of hysteria. **b** *colloq.* overwhelming mirth or laughter (*we were in hysterics*). **2** a hysterical person. ● *adj.* = HYSTERICAL. [Latin from Greek *husterikos* 'of the womb' (from *hustera* 'womb'), hysteria being thought to occur more frequently in women than in men and to be associated with the womb]

hysterical /hɪˈstɛrɪk(ə)l/ *adj.* **1** of or affected with hysteria. **2** morbidly or uncontrolledly emotional. **3** *colloq.* extremely funny or amusing. □ **hysterically** *adv.*

hysteron proteron /ˌhɪstərɒn ˈprɒtərɒn/ *n. Rhet.* a figure of speech in which what should come last is put first; an inversion of the natural order (e.g. *I die! I faint! I fail!*). [Late Latin from Greek *husteron proteron* 'the latter (put in place of) the former']

Hz *abbr.* hertz.

Ii

I[1] /ʌɪ/ *n.* (also **i**) (*pl.* **Is** or **I's**) **1** the ninth letter of the alphabet. **2** (as a Roman numeral) one.

I[2] /ʌɪ/ *pron. & n.* ● *pron.* (*obj.* **me**; *poss.* **my**, **mine**; *pl.* **we**) used by a speaker or writer to refer to himself or herself. ● *n.* (**the I**) *Metaphysics* the ego; the subject or object of self-consciousness. [Old English from Germanic]

I[3] *abbr.* (also **I.**) Island(s), Isle(s).

I[4] *symb.* **1** *Chem.* the element iodine. **2** electric current.

i *symb. Math.* the imaginary square root of minus one.

-i[1] /i, ʌɪ, iː/ *suffix* forming the plural of nouns from Latin ending in *-us* or from Italian ending in *-e* or *-o* (*foci*; *dilettanti*; *timpani*).

■ **Usage** Plurals in *-s* or *-es* are often also possible especially when the word is well established in English, e.g. *cactus*, plural *cacti* or *cactuses*.

-i[2] *suffix* forming adjectives from names of countries or regions in the Near or Middle East (*Israeli*; *Pakistani*). [adjectival suffix in Semitic and Indo-Iranian languages]

-i- /ɪ/ a connecting vowel esp. forming words ending in *-ana*, *-ferous*, *-fic*, *-form*, *-fy*, *-gerous*, *-vorous* (cf. -o-). [from or suggested by French from Latin]

IA *abbr. US* Iowa (in official postal use).

Ia. *abbr.* Iowa.

-ia[1] /ɪə/ *suffix* **1** forming abstract nouns (*mania*; *utopia*), often in *Med.* (*anaemia*; *pneumonia*). **2** *Bot.* forming names of classes and genera (*dahlia*; *fuchsia*). **3** forming names of countries (*Australia*; *India*). [from or suggested by Latin & Greek]

-ia[2] /ɪə/ *suffix* forming plural nouns or the plural of nouns: **1** from Greek ending *-ion* or Latin *-ium* (*paraphernalia*; *regalia*; *amnia*; *labia*). **2** *Zool.* the names of groups (*Mammalia*).

IAA *abbr.* indoleacetic acid.

IAEA *abbr.* International Atomic Energy Agency.

-ial /ɪəl/ *suffix* forming adjectives (*celestial*; *dictatorial*; *trivial*). [from or suggested by French *-iel* or Latin *-ialis*: cf. -AL]

iamb /ˈʌɪam(b)/ *n.* an iambus. [Anglicized from IAMBUS]

iambic /ʌɪˈambɪk/ *adj. & n. Prosody* ● *adj.* of or using iambuses. ● *n.* (usu. in *pl.*) iambic verse. [French *iambique* via Late Latin *iambicus* from Greek *iambikos* (as IAMBUS)]

iambus /ʌɪˈambəs/ *n.* (*pl.* **iambuses** or **-bi** /-bʌɪ/) *Prosody* a foot consisting of one short (or unstressed) followed by one long (or stressed) syllable. [Latin from Greek *iambos* 'iambus, lampoon', from *iaptō* 'assail in words', from its use by Greek satirists]

-ian /ɪən/ *suffix* var. of -AN. [from or suggested by French *-ien* or Latin *-ianus*]

-iasis /ˈʌɪəsɪs/ *suffix* the usual form of -ASIS.

IATA /ʌɪˈɑːtə/ *abbr.* International Air Transport Association.

iatrogenic /ʌɪˌatrə(ʊ)ˈdʒɛnɪk/ *adj.* (of a disease etc.) caused by medical examination or treatment. [Greek *iatros* 'physician' + -GENIC]

ib. var. of IBID.

IBA *abbr.* (in the UK) Independent Broadcasting Authority.

I-beam *n.* a girder of I-shaped section.

Iberian /ʌɪˈbɪərɪən/ *adj. & n.* ● *adj.* of ancient Iberia, the peninsula now comprising Spain and Portugal; of Spain and Portugal. ● *n.* **1** a native of ancient Iberia. **2** any of the languages of ancient Iberia. [Latin *Iberia* from Greek *Ibēres* 'Spaniards']

Ibero- /ʌɪˈbɪərəʊ/ *comb. form* Iberian; Iberian and (*Ibero-American*).

ibex /ˈʌɪbɛks/ *n.* (*pl.* **ibexes**) a wild goat, *Capra ibex*, esp. of mountainous areas of Europe, N. Africa, and Asia, with a beard and thick curved ridged horns. [Latin]

ibid. /ˈɪbɪd/ *abbr.* (also **ib.**) in the same book or passage etc. [Latin *ibidem* 'in the same place']

-ibility /ɪˈbɪlɪti/ *suffix* forming nouns from, or corresponding to, adjectives in *-ible* (*possibility*; *credibility*). [French *-ibilité* or Latin *-ibilitas*]

I.Biol. *abbr.* (in the UK) Institute of Biology.

ibis /ˈʌɪbɪs/ *n.* (*pl.* **ibises**) any wading bird of the family Threskiornithidae with a long down-curved bill, long neck, and long legs, and nesting in colonies. [Middle English via Latin from Greek]

-ible /ɪb(ə)l/ *suffix* forming adjectives meaning 'that may or may be' (see -ABLE) (*terrible*; *forcible*; *possible*). [French *-ible* or Latin *-ibilis*]

-ibly /ɪbli/ *suffix* forming adverbs corresponding to adjectives in *-ible*.

IBM *abbr.* International Business Machines.

Ibo /ˈiːbəʊ/ *n. & adj.* ● *n.* (also **Igbo** /ˈiːgbəʊ/) (*pl.* same or **-os**) **1** a member of a people of SE Nigeria. **2** the Kwa language of this people. ● *adj.* of or relating to this people or their language. [native name]

IBRD *abbr.* International Bank for Reconstruction and Development (also known as the *World Bank*).

ibuprofen /ʌɪbjuːˈprəʊf(ə)n/ *n.* an analgesic and anti-inflammatory drug used esp. as a stronger alternative to aspirin. [ISO- + BUTYL + PROPIONIC ACID + *-fen* representing PHENYL, elements of the chemical name]

IC *abbr.* integrated circuit.

i/c *abbr.* **1** in charge. **2** in command. **3** internal combustion.

-ic /ɪk/ *suffix* **1** forming adjectives (*Arabic*; *classic*; *public*) and nouns (*critic*; *epic*; *mechanic*; *music*). **2** *Chem.* in higher valence or degree of oxidation (*ferric*; *sulphuric*) (see also -OUS). **3** denoting a particular form or instance of a noun in *-ics* (*aesthetic*; *tactic*). [from or suggested by French *-ique*, Latin *-icus*, or Greek *-ikos*: cf. -ATIC, -ETIC, -FIC, -OTIC]

-ical /ɪk(ə)l/ *suffix* **1** forming adjectives corresponding to nouns or adjectives, usu. ending in *-ic* (*classical*; *comical*; *farcical*; *musical*). **2** forming adjectives corresponding to nouns in *-y* (*pathological*).

-ically /ɪk(ə)li/ *suffix* forming adverbs corresponding to adjectives ending in *-ic* or *-ical* (*comically*; *musically*; *tragically*).

ICAO *abbr.* International Civil Aviation Organization.

ICBM *abbr.* intercontinental ballistic missile.

ICE *abbr.* **1** (in the UK) Institution of Civil Engineers. **2** internal-combustion engine.

ice /ʌɪs/ *n. & v.* ● *n.* **1 a** frozen water, a brittle transparent crystalline solid. **b** a sheet of this on the surface of water (*fell through the ice*). **2** *Brit.* a portion of ice cream or water ice (*would you like an ice?*). **3** *slang* diamonds. ● *v.* **1** *tr.* mix with or cool in ice (*iced drinks*). **2** *tr. & intr.* (often foll. by *over*, *up*) **a** cover or become covered with ice. **b** freeze. **3** *tr.* cover (a cake etc.) with icing. **4** *tr. US Sport colloq.* clinch (victory). **5** *tr. US colloq.* murder. □ **on ice 1** (of an entertainment, sport, etc.) performed by skaters. **2** *colloq.* held in reserve; awaiting further attention. **on thin ice** in a risky situation. [Old English *īs*, from Germanic]

-ice /ɪs/ *suffix* forming (esp. abstract) nouns (*avarice; justice; service*) (cf. -ESS², -ISE²).

ice age *n.* a glacial period, esp. in the Pleistocene epoch.

ice axe *n.* a tool used by mountain climbers for cutting footholds.

ice-bag *n.* an ice-filled rubber bag for medical use.

iceberg /ˈʌɪsbəːɡ/ *n.* **1** a large floating mass of ice detached from a glacier or ice sheet and carried out to sea. **2** an unemotional or cold-blooded person. ▫ **the tip of the iceberg** a small perceptible part of something (esp. a difficulty) the greater part of which is hidden. [probably from Dutch *ijsberg*, from *ijs* 'ice' + *berg* 'hill']

iceberg lettuce *n.* any of various crisp lettuces with a freely blanching head.

iceblink /ˈʌɪsblɪŋk/ *n.* a luminous appearance on the horizon, caused by a reflection from ice.

iceblock /ˈʌɪsblɒk/ *n. Austral. & NZ* = ICE LOLLY.

ice blue *n. & adj.* ● *n.* a very pale blue colour. ● *adj.* (hyphenated when *attrib.*) of this colour.

ice-boat *n.* **1** a boat mounted on runners for travelling on ice. **2** a boat used for breaking ice on a river etc.

ice-bound *adj.* confined by ice.

icebox /ˈʌɪsbɒks/ *n.* a compartment in a refrigerator for making and storing ice.

ice-breaker *n.* **1** = ICE-BOAT 2. **2** something that serves to relieve inhibitions, start a conversation, etc.

ice bucket *n.* a bucket-like container with chunks of ice, used either to keep a bottle of wine chilled or to hold ice for drinks.

ice cap *n.* a permanent covering of ice e.g. in polar regions.

ice-cold *adj.* as cold as ice.

ice cream *n.* a sweet creamy frozen food, usu. flavoured.

ice cube *n.* a small block of ice made in a refrigerator.

ice dancing *n.* ice-skating to choreographed dance moves, esp. competitively and in pairs.

iced lolly var. of ICE LOLLY.

icefall /ˈʌɪsfɔːl/ *n.* a steep part of a glacier like a frozen waterfall.

ice field *n.* an expanse of ice, esp. in polar regions.

ice fish *n.* **1** = CAPELIN. **2** a semi-transparent Antarctic fish of the family Chaenichthyidae.

ice floe *n.* = FLOE.

ice hockey *n.* a form of hockey played on ice with a puck.

ice house *n.* a building often partly or wholly underground for storing ice.

Icelander /ˈʌɪsləndə/ *n.* **1** a native or national of Iceland, an island in the N. Atlantic. **2** a person of Icelandic descent.

Icelandic /ʌɪsˈlandɪk/ *adj. & n.* ● *adj.* of or relating to Iceland. ● *n.* the language of Iceland.

Iceland lichen /ˈʌɪslənd/ *n.* (also **Iceland moss**) a mountain and moorland lichen, *Cetraria islandica*, with edible branching fronds.

Iceland poppy /ˈʌɪslənd/ *n.* an Arctic poppy, esp. *Papaver nudicaule*, with white or yellow flowers.

Iceland spar /ˈʌɪslənd/ *n.* a transparent variety of calcite with the optical property of strong double refraction.

ice lolly *n.* (also **iced lolly**) *Brit.* a piece of flavoured ice, often with chocolate or ice cream, on a stick.

iceman /ˈʌɪsmən/ *n.* (*pl.* **-men**) **1** a man skilled in crossing ice. **2** esp. *N. Amer.* a man who sells or delivers ice.

ice milk *n. N. Amer.* a sweet frozen food similar to ice cream but containing less butterfat.

ice pack *n.* **1** a quantity of ice applied to the body for medical etc. purposes. **2** see PACK¹ *n.* 9.

ice pick *n.* **1** a needle-like implement with a handle for splitting up small pieces of ice. **2** a mountaineer's pick.

ice plant *n.* a plant, *Mesembryanthemum crystallinum*, with leaves covered with crystals or vesicles looking like ice specks.

ice rink *n.* = RINK 1.

ice sheet *n.* a permanent layer of ice covering an extensive tract of land.

ice shelf *n.* a floating sheet of ice permanently attached to a landmass.

ice show *n.* a show performed by ice-skaters.

ice-skate *n. & v.* ● *n.* a skate consisting of a boot with a blade beneath, for skating on ice. ● *v.intr.* skate on ice. ▫ **ice-skater** *n.* **ice-skating** *n.*

ice station *n.* a meteorological research centre in polar regions.

ice storm *n.* esp. *N. Amer.* a storm of freezing rain, that leaves a deposit of ice.

ice water *n.* water from, or cooled by the addition of, ice.

I.Chem.E. *abbr.* (in the UK) Institution of Chemical Engineers.

I Ching /iː ˈtʃɪŋ/ *n.* an ancient Chinese manual of divination based on symbolic trigrams and hexagrams. [Chinese *yijing* 'book of changes']

ichneumon /ɪkˈnjuːmən/ *n.* **1** (in full **ichneumon wasp**) any small hymenopterous insect of the family Ichneumonidae, depositing eggs in or on the larva of another insect as food for its own larva. **2** a mongoose of N. Africa, *Herpestes ichneumon*, noted for destroying crocodile eggs. [Latin from Greek *ikhneumōn*, literally 'tracker', a spider-hunting wasp, via *ikhneuō* 'trace' from *ikhnos* 'footstep']

ichnography /ɪkˈnɒɡrəfi/ *n.* (*pl.* **-ies**) **1** the ground plan of a building, map of a region, etc. **2** a drawing of this. [French *ichnographie* or Latin *ichnographia* from Greek *ikhnographia*, from *ikhnos* 'track': see -GRAPHY]

ichor /ˈʌɪkɔː/ *n.* **1** (in Greek mythology) fluid flowing like blood in the veins of the gods. **2** *poet.* bloodlike fluid. **3** *archaic* a watery fetid discharge from a wound etc. ▫ **ichorous** /ˈʌɪk(ə)rəs/ *adj.* [Greek *ikhōr*]

ichthyo- /ˈɪkθɪəʊ/ *comb. form* fish. [Greek *ikhthus* 'fish']

ichthyoid /ˈɪkθɪɔɪd/ *adj. & n.* ● *adj.* fishlike. ● *n.* any fishlike vertebrate.

ichthyolite /ˈɪkθɪəlʌɪt/ *n.* a fossil fish.

ichthyology /ɪkθɪˈɒlədʒi/ *n.* the study of fishes. ▫ **ichthyological** /-əˈlɒdʒɪk(ə)l/ *adj.* **ichthyologist** *n.*

ichthyophagous /ɪkθɪˈɒfəɡəs/ *adj.* fish-eating. ▫ **ichthyophagy** /-fədʒi/ *n.*

ichthyosaurus /ɪkθɪəˈsɔːrəs/ *n.* (also **ichthyosaur** /ˈɪkθɪəsɔː/) any extinct marine reptile of the order Ichthyosauria, with long head, tapering body, four flippers, and usu. a large tail. [ICHTHYO- + Greek *sauros* 'lizard']

ichthyosis /ɪkθɪˈəʊsɪs/ *n.* a skin disease which causes the epidermis to become dry and horny like fish scales. ▫ **ichthyotic** /-ˈɒtɪk/ *adj.* [Greek *ikhthus* 'fish' + -OSIS]

ICI *abbr.* Imperial Chemical Industries.

-ician /ˈɪʃ(ə)n/ *suffix* forming nouns denoting persons skilled in or concerned with subjects having nouns (usu.) in *-ic* or *-ics* (*magician; politician*). [from or suggested by French *-icien* (as -IC, -IAN)]

icicle /ˈʌɪsɪk(ə)l/ *n.* a hanging tapering piece of ice, formed by the freezing of dripping water. [Middle English, from ICE + *ickle* (now dialect) 'icicle']

icing /ˈʌɪsɪŋ/ *n.* **1** a coating of a sugar mixture on a cake or biscuit. **2** the formation of ice on a ship or aircraft. **3 a** (in ice hockey) the act of shooting the puck from one's own end of the rink to the other but not at goal. **b** the penalty for this. ▫ **icing on the cake** an attractive though inessential addition or enhancement.

icing sugar *n. Brit.* finely powdered sugar for making icing for cakes etc.

-icist /ɪsɪst/ *suffix* = -ICIAN (*classicist*). [-IC + -IST]

-icity /ˈɪsɪti/ *suffix* forming abstract nouns esp. from adjectives in *-ic* (*authenticity; publicity*). [-IC + -ITY]

-ick /ɪk/ *suffix archaic* var. of -IC.

icky /ˈɪki/ *adj.* (also **ikky**) *colloq.* **1** sweet, sticky, sickly. **2** (as a general term of disapproval) nasty, repulsive. [20th c.: origin unknown]

-icle /ɪk(ə)l/ *suffix* forming (originally diminutive) nouns (*article*; *particle*). [formed as -CULE]

icon /ˈʌɪkɒn, -k(ə)n/ *n.* (also **ikon**) **1** a devotional painting or carving, usu. on wood, of Christ or another holy figure, esp. in the Eastern Church. **2** an image or statue. **3** *Computing* a symbol or graphic representation on a VDU screen of a program, option, or window, esp. one of several for selection. **4** an object of particular admiration, esp. as a representative symbol of something (*a literary icon of the 1970s*). **5** *Linguistics* a sign which has a characteristic in common with the thing it signifies. [Latin from Greek *eikōn* 'image']

iconic /ʌɪˈkɒnɪk/ *adj.* **1** of or having the nature of an image or portrait. **2** (of a statue) following a conventional type. **3** *Linguistics* that is an icon. □ **iconicity** /-kəˈnɪsɪti/ *n.* (esp. in sense 3). [Latin *iconicus* from Greek *eikonikos* (as ICON)]

icono- /ˈʌɪkənəʊ, ʌɪˈkɒnəʊ/ *comb. form* an image or likeness. [Greek *eikōn*]

iconoclasm /ʌɪˈkɒnəklaz(ə)m/ *n.* **1** the breaking of images. **2** the assailing of cherished beliefs. [ICONOCLAST, on the pattern of *enthusiasm* etc.]

iconoclast /ʌɪˈkɒnəklast/ *n.* **1** a person who attacks cherished beliefs. **2** a person who destroys images used in religious worship, esp. *hist.* during the 8th–9th c. in the Churches of the East, or as a Puritan of the 16th–17th c. □ **iconoclastic** /-ˈklastɪk/ *adj.* **iconoclastically** /-ˈklastɪk(ə)li/ *adv.* [medieval Latin *iconoclastes* from ecclesiastical Greek *eikonoklastēs* (as ICONO-, *klaō* 'break')]

iconography /ʌɪkəˈnɒgrəfi/ *n.* (*pl.* **-ies**) **1** the illustration of a subject by drawings or figures. **2 a** the study of portraits, esp. of an individual. **b** the study of artistic images or symbols. **3** a treatise on pictures or statuary. **4** a book composed essentially of illustrations. □ **iconographer** *n.* **iconographic** /-nəˈgrafɪk/ *adj.* **iconographical** /-nəˈgrafɪk(ə)l/ *adj.* **iconographically** /-nəˈgrafɪk(ə)li/ *adv.* [Greek *eikonographia* 'sketch' (as ICONO- + -GRAPHY)]

iconolatry /ʌɪkəˈnɒlətri/ *n.* the worship of images. [ecclesiastical Greek *eikonolatreia* (as ICONO-, -LATRY)]

iconology /ʌɪkəˈnɒlədʒi/ *n.* **1** the study of visual imagery and its symbolism and interpretation. **2** symbolism.

iconostasis /ʌɪkəˈnɒstəsɪs/ *n.* (*pl.* **iconostases** /-siːz/) (in the Eastern Church) a screen bearing icons and separating the sanctuary from the nave. [modern Greek *eikonostasis* (as ICONO-, STASIS)]

icosahedron /ˌʌɪkɒsəˈhiːdrən, -ˈhɛd-/ *n.* (*pl.* **icosahedra** /-drə/ or **icosahedrons**) a solid figure with twenty faces. □ **icosahedral** *adj.* [Late Latin *icosahedrum* from Greek *eikosaedron*, from *eikosi* 'twenty' + -HEDRON]

-ics /ɪks/ *suffix* (treated as *sing.* or *pl.*) forming nouns denoting arts or sciences or branches of study or action (*athletics*; *politics*) (cf. -IC 3). [from or suggested by French pl. *-iques*, Latin pl. *-ica*, or Greek pl. *-ika*]

■ **Usage** A word ending in *-ics* meaning 'a subject of study or branch of knowledge' will generally be treated as singular, e.g. *Aerodynamics is a mathematical science*, but the same word may be used in the plural to mean 'particular aspects of something considered collectively', e.g. *The aerodynamics of this car are rather primitive*.

icterus /ˈɪkt(ə)rəs/ *n. Med.* = JAUNDICE *n.* 1. □ **icteric** /ɪkˈtɛrɪk/ *adj.* [Latin from Greek *ikteros*]

ictus /ˈɪktəs/ *n.* (*pl.* same or **ictuses**) **1** *Prosody* rhythmical or metrical stress. **2** *Med.* a stroke or seizure; a fit. [Latin, = blow, from *icere* 'strike']

icy /ˈʌɪsi/ *adj.* (**icier, iciest**) **1** very cold. **2** covered with or abounding in ice. **3** (of a tone or manner) unfriendly, hostile (*an icy stare*). □ **icily** *adv.* **iciness** *n.*

ID *abbr.* **1** identification, identity (*ID card*). **2** *US* Idaho (in official postal use).

Id var. of EID.

I'd /ʌɪd/ *contr.* **1** I had. **2** I should; I would.

id /ɪd/ *n. Psychol.* the inherited instinctive impulses of the individual as part of the unconscious. [Latin, = that, translation of German *es*]

id. *abbr.* = IDEM.

i.d. *abbr.* inner diameter.

-id[1] /ɪd/ *suffix* forming adjectives (*arid*; *rapid*). [French *-ide* from Latin *-idus*]

-id[2] /ɪd/ *suffix* forming nouns: **1** general (*pyramid*). **2** *Biol.* of structural constituents (*plastid*). **3** *Bot.* of a plant belonging to a family with a name in *-idaceae* (*orchid*). [from or suggested by French *-ide*, via Latin *-is -idis* from Greek *-is -ida* or *-idos*]

-id[3] /ɪd/ *suffix* forming nouns denoting: **1** *Zool.* an animal belonging to a family with a name in *-idae* or a class with a name in *-ida* (*canid*; *arachnid*). **2** a member of a person's family (*Seleucid* from Seleucus). **3** *Astron.* **a** a meteor in a group radiating from a specified constellation (*Leonid* from Leo). **b** a star of a class like one in a specified constellation (*cepheid*). [from or suggested by Latin *-ides*, pl. *-idae* or *-ida*]

IDA *abbr.* International Development Association.

ide /ʌɪd/ *n.* = ORFE. [modern Latin *idus* from Swedish *id*]

-ide /ʌɪd/ *suffix Chem.* forming nouns denoting: **1** binary compounds of an element (the suffix *-ide* being added to the abbreviated name of the more electronegative element etc.) (*sodium chloride*; *lead sulphide*; *calcium carbide*). **2** various other compounds (*amide*; *anhydride*; *peptide*; *saccharide*). **3** elements of a series in the periodic table (*actinide*; *lanthanide*). [originally in OXIDE]

idea /ʌɪˈdɪə/ *n.* **1** a conception or plan formed by mental effort (*have you any ideas?*; *had the idea of writing a book*). **2 a** a mental impression or notion; a concept. **b** a vague belief or fancy (*had an idea you were married*; *had no idea where you were*). **3** an intention, purpose, or essential feature (*the idea is to make money*). **4** an archetype or pattern as distinguished from its realization in individual cases. **5** *Philos.* **a** (in Platonism) an eternally existing pattern of which individual things in any class are imperfect copies. **b** a concept of pure reason which transcends experience. □ **get** (or **have**) **ideas** *colloq.* be ambitious, rebellious, etc. **have no idea** *colloq.* **1** not know at all. **2** be completely incompetent. **not one's idea of** *colloq.* not what one regards as (*not my idea of a pleasant evening*). **put ideas into a person's head** suggest ambitions etc. he or she would not otherwise have had. **that's an idea** *colloq.* that proposal etc. is worth considering. **the very idea!** *colloq.* an exclamation of disapproval or disagreement. [Greek *idea* 'form, pattern' from stem *id-* 'see']

ideal /ʌɪˈdɪəl, -ˈdiːəl/ *adj.* & *n.* ● *adj.* **1 a** answering to one's highest conception. **b** perfect or supremely excellent. **2 a** existing only in idea. **b** visionary. **3** embodying an idea. **4** relating to or consisting of ideas; dependent on the mind. ● *n.* **1** a perfect type, or a conception of this. **2** an actual thing as a standard for imitation. □ **ideally** *adv.* [Middle English via French *idéal* from Late Latin *idealis* (as IDEA)]

ideal gas *n.* a hypothetical gas consisting of molecules occupying negligible space and without attraction for each other, thereby obeying simple laws.

idealism /ʌɪˈdɪəlɪz(ə)m, -ˈdiːə-/ *n.* **1** the practice of forming or following after ideals, esp. unrealistically (cf. REALISM). **2** the representation of things in ideal or idealized form. **3** imaginative treatment. **4** *Philos.* any of various systems of thought in which the objects of knowledge are held to be in some way dependent on the activity of mind (cf. REALISM). □ **idealist** *n.* **idealistic** /-ˈlɪstɪk/ *adj.* **idealistically** /-ˈlɪstɪk(ə)li/ *adv.* [French *idéalisme* or German *Idealismus* (as IDEAL)]

ideality /ʌɪdɪˈalɪti/ *n.* (*pl.* **-ies**) **1** the quality of being ideal. **2** an ideal thing.

idealize /ʌɪˈdɪəlʌɪz, -ˈdiːə-/ *v.tr.* (also **-ise**) **1** regard or represent (a thing or person) in ideal form or character. **2** exalt in thought to ideal perfection or excellence. ◻ **idealization** /-ˈzeɪʃ(ə)n/ *n.* **idealizer** *n.*

ideate /ˈʌɪdɪeɪt/ *v. Psychol.* **1** *tr.* imagine, conceive. **2** *intr.* form ideas. ◻ **ideation** /-ˈeɪʃ(ə)n/ *n.* **ideational** /-ˈeɪʃ(ə)n(ə)l/ *adj.* **ideationally** /-ˈeɪʃ(ə)n(ə)li/ *adv.* [medieval Latin *ideare* 'form an idea' (as IDEA)]

idée fixe /iːdeɪ ˈfiːks, French ide fiks/ *n.* (*pl.* ***idées fixes*** *pronunc.* same) an idea that dominates the mind; an obsession. [French, literally 'fixed idea']

idée reçue /ˌiːdeɪ rəˈsjuː, French ide rəsy/ *n.* (*pl.* ***idées reçues*** *pronunc.* same) a generally accepted notion or opinion. [French, literally 'received idea']

idem /ˈɪdɛm/ *adv.* & *n.* ● *adv.* in the same author. ● *n.* the same word or author. [Middle English from Latin]

identical /ʌɪˈdɛntɪk(ə)l/ *adj.* **1** (often foll. by *with*) (of different things) agreeing in every detail. **2** (of one thing viewed at different times) one and the same. **3** (of twins) developed from a single fertilized ovum, therefore of the same sex and usu. very similar in appearance. **4** *Logic* & *Math.* expressing an identity. ◻ **identically** *adv.* [medieval Latin *identicus* (as IDENTITY)]

identification /ʌɪˌdɛntɪfɪˈkeɪʃ(ə)n/ *n.* **1** the act or an instance of identifying. **2** a means of identifying a person. **3** (*attrib.*) serving to identify (esp. the bearer) (*identification card*).

identification parade *n. Brit.* an assembly of persons from whom a suspect is to be identified.

identifier /ʌɪˈdɛntɪfʌɪə/ *n.* **1** a person or thing that identifies. **2** *Computing* a sequence of characters used to identify or refer to a set of data.

identify /ʌɪˈdɛntɪfʌɪ/ *v.* (**-ies**, **-ied**) **1** *tr.* establish the identity of; recognize. **2** *tr.* establish or select by consideration or analysis of the circumstances (*identify the best method of solving the problem*). **3** *tr.* (foll. by *with*) associate (a person or oneself) inseparably or very closely (with a party, policy, etc.). **4** *tr.* (often foll. by *with*) treat (a thing) as identical. **5** *intr.* (foll. by *with*) **a** regard oneself as sharing characteristics of (another person). **b** associate oneself. ◻ **identifiable** *adj.* **identifiably** *adv.* [medieval Latin *identificare* (as IDENTITY)]

identikit /ʌɪˈdɛntɪkɪt/ *n.* (often *attrib.*) *propr.* a reconstructed picture of a person (esp. one sought by the police) assembled from transparent strips showing typical facial features according to witnesses' descriptions. [IDENTITY + KIT[1]]

identity /ʌɪˈdɛntɪti/ *n.* (*pl.* **-ies**) **1 a** the quality or condition of being a specified person or thing. **b** individuality, personality (*felt he had lost his identity*). **2** identification or the result of it (*a case of mistaken identity*; *identity card*). **3** the state of being the same in substance, nature, qualities, etc.; absolute sameness (*no identity of interests between them*). **4** *Algebra* **a** the equality of two expressions for all values of the quantities expressed by letters. **b** an equation expressing this, e.g. $(x + 1)^2 = x^2 + 2x + 1$. **5** *Math.* **a** (in full **identity element**) an element in a set, left unchanged by any operation to it. **b** a transformation that leaves an object unchanged. [Late Latin *identitas* from Latin *idem* 'same']

identity crisis *n.* a period during which an individual experiences a feeling of loss or breakdown of his or her identity.

identity parade *n. Brit.* = IDENTIFICATION PARADE.

ideogram /ˈɪdɪə(ʊ)gram, ˈʌɪd-/ *n.* a character symbolizing the idea of a thing without indicating the sequence of sounds in its name (e.g. a numeral, and many Chinese characters). [Greek *idea* 'form' + -GRAM]

ideograph /ˈɪdɪə(ʊ)grɑːf, ˈʌɪd-/ *n.* = IDEOGRAM. ◻ **ideographic** /-ˈgrafɪk/ *adj.* **ideography** /ɪdɪˈɒgrəfi, ʌɪdɪ-/ *n.* [Greek *idea* 'form' + -GRAPH]

ideologue /ˈʌɪdɪəlɒg, ˈɪd-/ *n.* **1** a theorist; a visionary. **2** an adherent of an ideology. [French *idéologue* from Greek *idea* (see IDEA) + -LOGUE]

ideology /ʌɪdɪˈɒlədʒi, ɪd-/ *n.* (*pl.* **-ies**) **1** the system of ideas at the basis of an economic or political theory (*Marxist ideology*). **2** the manner of thinking characteristic of a class or individual (*bourgeois ideology*). **3** visionary speculation. **4** *archaic* the science of ideas. ◻ **ideological** /-əˈlɒdʒɪk(ə)l/ *adj.* **ideologically** /-əˈlɒdʒɪk(ə)li/ *adv.* **ideologist** *n.* [French *idéologie* (as IDEOLOGUE)]

ides /ʌɪdz/ *n.pl.* the eighth day after the nones in the ancient Roman calendar (the 15th day of March, May, July, October, the 13th of other months). [Middle English via Old French from Latin *idus* (pl.), perhaps from Etruscan]

idiocy /ˈɪdɪəsi/ *n.* (*pl.* **-ies**) **1** utter foolishness; idiotic behaviour or an idiotic action. **2** extremely low intelligence. [Middle English from IDIOT, probably on the pattern of *lunacy*]

idiolect /ˈɪdɪəlɛkt/ *n.* the form of language used by an individual person. [Greek *idios* 'own' + *-lect* in DIALECT]

idiom /ˈɪdɪəm/ *n.* **1** a group of words established by usage and having a meaning not deducible from those of the individual words (as in *over the moon, see the light*). **2** a form of expression peculiar to a language, person, or group of people. **3 a** the language of a people or country. **b** the specific character of this. **4** a characteristic mode of expression in music, art, etc. [French *idiome* or Late Latin *idioma* from Greek *idiōma -matos* 'private property', from *idios* 'own, private']

idiomatic /ɪdɪəˈmatɪk/ *adj.* **1** relating to or conforming to idiom. **2** characteristic of a particular language. ◻ **idiomatically** *adv.* [Greek *idiōmatikos* 'peculiar' (as IDIOM)]

idiopathy /ɪdɪˈɒpəθi/ *n. Med.* any disease or condition of unknown cause or that arises spontaneously. ◻ **idiopathic** /ɪdɪəˈpaθɪk/ *adj.* [modern Latin *idiopathia* from Greek *idiopatheia*, from *idios* 'own' + -PATHY]

idiosyncrasy /ɪdɪə(ʊ)ˈsɪŋkrəsi/ *n.* (*pl.* **-ies**) **1** a mental constitution, view or feeling, or mode of behaviour, peculiar to a person. **2** anything highly individualized or eccentric. **3** a mode of expression peculiar to an author. **4** *Med.* a physical constitution peculiar to a person. ◻ **idiosyncratic** /-ˈkratɪk/ *adj.* **idiosyncratically** /-ˈkratɪk(ə)li/ *adv.* [Greek *idiosugkrasia*, from *idios* 'own' + *sun* 'together' + *krasis* 'mixture']

idiot /ˈɪdɪət/ *n.* **1** *colloq.* a stupid person; an utter fool. **2** a person of extremely low intelligence. ◻ **idiotic** /-ˈɒtɪk/ *adj.* **idiotically** /-ˈɒtɪk(ə)li/ *adv.* [Middle English via Old French and Latin *idiota* 'ignorant person' from Greek *idiōtēs* 'private person, layman, ignorant person', from *idios* 'own, private']

idiot board *n.* (also **idiot card**) *colloq.* a board displaying a television script to a speaker as an aid to memory.

idiot savant /iːdjəʊ saˈvɒ̃/ *n.* (*pl.* **idiot savants** or **idiots savants** *pronunc.* same) a person considered mentally retarded but who displays brilliance in a specific area esp. related to memory skills. [French, = learned idiot]

idle /ˈʌɪd(ə)l/ *adj.* & *v.* ● *adj.* (**idler**, **idlest**) **1** lazy, indolent. **2** not in use; not working; unemployed. **3** (of time etc.) unoccupied. **4** having no special basis or purpose (*idle rumour*; *idle curiosity*). **5** useless. **6** (of an action, thought, or word) ineffective, worthless, vain. ● *v.* **1 a** *intr.* (of an engine) run slowly without doing any work. **b** *tr.* cause (an engine) to idle. **2** *intr.* be idle. **3** *tr.* (foll. by *away*) pass (time etc.) in idleness. ◻ **idleness** *n.* **idly** *adv.* [Old English *īdel* 'empty, useless']

idler /ˈʌɪdlə/ *n.* **1** a habitually lazy person. **2** = IDLE WHEEL.

idle wheel *n.* an intermediate wheel between two geared wheels, esp. to allow them to rotate in the same direction.

Ido /ˈiːdəʊ/ *n.* an artificial universal language based on Esperanto. [Ido, = offspring]

idol /ˈʌɪd(ə)l/ *n.* **1** an image of a deity etc. used as an object of worship. **2** *Bibl.* a false god. **3** a person or thing that is the object of excessive or supreme adulation (*cinema idol*). **4** *archaic* a phantom. [Middle English via Old French *idole* and Latin *idolum* from Greek *eidōlon* 'phantom', from *eidos* 'form']

idolater /ʌɪˈdɒlətə/ *n.* (*fem.* **idolatress** /-trɪs/) **1** a worshipper of idols. **2** (often foll. by *of*) a devoted admirer. □ **idolatrous** *adj.* [Middle English *idolatrer* from Old French *idolatrer* or *idolâtre*, or from *idolatry*, ultimately from Greek *eidōlolatrēs* (as IDOL, -LATER)]

idolatry /ʌɪˈdɒlətri/ *n.* **1** the worship of idols. **2** great adulation. [Old French *idolatrie* (as IDOLATER)]

idolize /ˈʌɪd(ə)lʌɪz/ *v.* (also **-ise**) **1** *tr.* venerate or love extremely or excessively. **2** *tr.* make an idol of. **3** *intr.* practise idolatry. □ **idolization** /-ˈzeɪʃ(ə)n/ *n.* **idolizer** *n.*

idyll /ˈɪdɪl/ *n.* (also **idyl**) **1** a short description in verse or prose of a picturesque scene or incident, esp. in rustic life. **2** an episode suitable for such treatment, usu. a love story. **3** a blissful period or scene. □ **idyllist** *n.* **idyllize** *v.tr.* (also **-ise**). [Latin *idyllium* from Greek *eidullion*, diminutive of *eidos* 'form']

idyllic /ɪˈdɪlɪk/ *adj.* **1** blissfully peaceful and happy. **2** of or like an idyll. □ **idyllically** *adv.*

i.e. *abbr.* that is to say. [Latin *id est*]

-ie /i/ *suffix* **1** var. of -Y[2] (*dearie*; *nightie*). **2** *archaic* var. of -Y[1], -Y[3] (*litanie*; *prettie*). [earlier form of -Y[1,2,3]]

IEE *abbr.* (in the UK) Institution of Electrical Engineers.

-ier /ɪə/ *suffix* forming personal nouns denoting an occupation or interest: **1** with stress on the preceding element (*grazier*). **2** with stress on the suffix (*cashier*; *brigadier*). [sense 1 Middle English of various origins; sense 2 French *-ier* from Latin *-arius*]

IF *abbr.* intermediate frequency.

if /ɪf/ *conj.* & *n.* ● *conj.* **1** introducing a conditional clause: **a** on the condition or supposition that; in the event that (*if he comes I will tell him*; *if you are tired we will rest*). **b** (with past tense) implying that the condition is not fulfilled (*if I were you*; *if I knew I would say*). **2** even though (*I'll finish it, if it takes me all day*). **3** whenever (*if I am not sure I ask*). **4** whether (*see if you can find it*). **5 a** expressing wish or surprise (*if I could just try!*; *if it isn't my old hat!*). **b** expressing a request (*if you wouldn't mind opening the door?*). **6** with implied reservation, = and perhaps not (*very rarely if at all*). **7** (with reduction of the protasis to its significant word) if there is or it is etc. (*took little if any*). **8** despite being (*a useful if cumbersome device*). ● *n.* a condition or supposition (*too many ifs about it*). □ **if anything** if any degree, perhaps even (*if anything, it's too large*; *if anything, he finds maths easier*). **if only 1** even if for no other reason than (*I'll come if only to see her*). **2** (often *ellipt.*) an expression of regret (*if only I had thought of it*; *if only I could swim!*). **if so** if that is the case. [Old English *gif*]

IFC *abbr.* International Finance Corporation.

-iferous see -FEROUS.

iff /ɪf/ *conj. Logic* & *Math.* = if and only if. [arbitrary extension of *if*]

iffy /ˈɪfi/ *adj.* (**iffier**, **iffiest**) *colloq.* **1** uncertain, doubtful. **2** of questionable quality.

-ific see -FIC.

-ification see -FICATION.

-iform see -FORM.

Igbo var. of IBO.

igloo /ˈɪgluː/ *n.* an Eskimo dome-shaped dwelling, esp. one built of blocks of snow. [Eskimo, = house]

igneous /ˈɪgnɪəs/ *adj.* **1** of fire; fiery. **2** *Geol.* (esp. of rocks) produced by volcanic or magmatic action. [Latin *igneus* from *ignis* 'fire']

ignimbrite /ˈɪgnɪmbrʌɪt/ *n. Geol.* a volcanic rock, esp. a tuff, formed by the consolidation of material from a *nuée ardente*. [Latin *ignis* 'fire' + *imbr- imber* 'shower of rain, storm cloud' + -ITE[1]]

ignis fatuus /ˌɪgnɪs ˈfatjʊəs/ *n.* (*pl.* **ignes fatui** /ˌɪgniːz ˈfatjʊʌɪ, ˌɪgneɪz, ˈfatjʊiː/) a will-o'-the-wisp. [modern Latin, = foolish fire, because of its erratic movement]

ignite /ɪgˈnʌɪt/ *v.* **1** *tr.* set fire to; cause to burn. **2** *intr.* catch fire. **3** *tr. Chem.* heat to the point of combustion or chemical change. **4** *tr.* provoke or excite (feelings etc.). □ **ignitable** *adj.* **ignitability** /-təˈbɪlɪti/ *n.* [Latin *ignire ignit-* from *ignis* 'fire']

igniter /ɪgˈnʌɪtə/ *n.* **1** a device for igniting a fuel mixture in an engine. **2** a device for causing an electric arc.

ignition /ɪgˈnɪʃ(ə)n/ *n.* **1** a mechanism for, or the action of, starting the combustion of mixture in the cylinder of an internal-combustion engine. **2** the act or an instance of igniting or being ignited. [French *ignition* or medieval Latin *ignitio* (as IGNITE)]

ignition key *n.* a key to operate the ignition of a motor vehicle.

ignitron /ɪgˈnʌɪtrɒn/ *n. Electr.* a kind of rectifier with a mercury cathode, able to carry large currents. [IGNITE + -TRON]

ignoble /ɪgˈnəʊb(ə)l/ *adj.* (**ignobler**, **ignoblest**) **1** dishonourable, mean, base. **2** of low birth, position, or reputation. □ **ignobility** /-nəˈbɪlɪti/ *n.* **ignobly** *adv.* [French *ignoble* or Latin *ignobilis* (as IN-[1], *nobilis* 'noble')]

ignominious /ɪgnəˈmɪnɪəs/ *adj.* **1** causing or deserving ignominy. **2** humiliating. □ **ignominiously** *adv.* **ignominiousness** *n.* [Middle English from French *ignominieux* or Latin *ignominiosus*]

ignominy /ˈɪgnəmɪni/ *n.* **1** dishonour, infamy. **2** *archaic* infamous conduct. [French *ignominie* or Latin *ignominia* (as IN-[1], *nomen* 'name')]

ignoramus /ɪgnəˈreɪməs/ *n.* (*pl.* **ignoramuses**) an ignorant person. [Latin, = we do not know: in legal use (formerly of a grand jury rejecting a bill) 'we take no notice of it'; modern sense perhaps from a character in Ruggle's *Ignoramus* (1615), a satirical comedy exposing lawyers' ignorance]

ignorance /ˈɪgn(ə)r(ə)ns/ *n.* (often foll. by *of*) lack of knowledge (about a thing). [Middle English via Old French from Latin *ignorantia* (as IGNORANT)]

ignorant /ˈɪgn(ə)r(ə)nt/ *adj.* **1 a** lacking knowledge or experience. **b** (foll. by *of*, *in*) uninformed (about a fact or subject). **2** *colloq.* ill-mannered, uncouth. □ **ignorantly** *adv.* [Middle English via Old French from Latin *ignorare ignorant-* (as IGNORE)]

■ **Usage** It is better to follow *ignorant* by *of* (a fact etc.) or *in* (a subject etc.) then *about*, e.g. *I was ignorant of my rights*; *I am ignorant in these matters.*

---

ignore /ɪgˈnɔː/ *v.tr.* **1** refuse to take notice of or accept. **2** intentionally disregard. □ **ignorable** *adj.* **ignorer** *n.* [French *ignorer* or Latin *ignorare* 'not know, ignore' (as IN-[1], *gno-* 'know')]

iguana /ɪˈgwɑːnə/ *n.* any of various large lizards of the family Iguanidae native to America, the W. Indies, and some Pacific islands, having a spiny crest along the back. [Spanish from Taino or Carib *iwana*]

iguanodon /ɪˈgwɑːnədɒn/ *n.* a large, partly bipedal herbivorous dinosaur of the Cretaceous period, with a broad stiff tail and a spike on each thumb. [modern Latin, from IGUANA + Greek *odous odontos* 'tooth', from the resemblance of the teeth to those of the iguana]

i.h.p. *abbr.* indicated horsepower.

IHS *abbr.* Jesus. [Middle English from Late Latin, representing Greek ΙΗΣ = *Iēs*(*ous*) Jesus: often taken as an abbreviation of various Latin words]

ikebana /ɪkɪˈbɑːnə/ *n.* the art of Japanese flower arrangement, with formal display according to strict rules. [Japanese, = living flowers]

ikky var. of ICKY.

ikon var. of ICON.

IL *abbr. US* Illinois (in official postal use).

il- /ɪl/ *prefix* assim. form of IN-[1], IN-[2] before *l*.

-il /əl, ɪl/ *suffix* (also **-ile** /ʌɪl/) forming adjectives or nouns denoting relation (*civil*; *utensil*) or capability (*agile*; *sessile*). [Old French from Latin *-ilis*]

ilang-ilang var. of YLANG-YLANG.

ilea *pl.* of ILEUM.

ileitis /ɪlɪˈʌɪtɪs/ *n. Med.* inflammation of the ileum.

ileostomy /ɪlɪˈɒstəmi/ *n.* (*pl.* **-ies**) a surgical operation in which a damaged part is removed from the ileum and the cut end directed to an artificial opening in the abdominal wall. [ILEUM + Greek *stoma* 'mouth']

ileum /ˈɪlɪəm/ *n.* (*pl.* **ilea** /ɪlɪə/) *Anat.* the third and last portion of the small intestine. □ **ileac** *adj.* [variant of ILIUM]

ileus /ˈɪlɪəs/ *n. Med.* any painful obstruction of the intestine, esp. of the ileum. [Latin from Greek *(e)ileos* 'colic']

ilex /ˈʌɪlɛks/ *n.* **1** any tree or shrub of the genus *Ilex*, esp. the common holly. **2** the holm-oak. [Middle English from Latin]

ilia *pl.* of ILIUM.

iliac /ˈɪlɪak/ *adj.* of the lower body or ilium (*iliac artery*). [Late Latin *iliacus* (as ILIUM)]

ilium /ˈɪlɪəm/ *n.* (*pl.* **ilia** /ˈɪlɪə/) **1** the bone forming the upper part of each half of the human pelvis. **2** the corresponding bone in animals. [Middle English from Latin]

ilk /ɪlk/ *n.* **1** *colloq.*, usu. *derog.* a family, class, sort, or kind (*for John and his ilk there is only one kind of music*). **2** (in **of that ilk**) *Sc.* of the same place, estate, or name (*Guthrie of that ilk* = of Guthrie). [Old English *ilca* 'same']

■ **Usage** *Of that ilk* is a Scots term meaning 'of the same place, estate, or name'. By misunderstanding *ilk* has come to mean 'family' or 'sort'. This should be avoided in formal English.

Ill. *abbr.* Illinois.

I'll /ʌɪl/ *contr.* I shall; I will.

ill /ɪl/ *adj., adv., & n.* ● *adj.* (*attrib.* except in sense 1) **1** (usu. *predic.*; often foll. by *with*) out of health; sick (*is ill*; *was taken ill with pneumonia*; *mentally ill people*). **2** wretched, unfavourable (*ill fortune*; *ill luck*). **3** harmful (*ill effects*). **4** hostile, unkind (*ill feeling*). **5** *archaic* morally bad. **6** faulty, unskilful (*ill taste*; *ill management*). **7** (of manners or conduct) improper. ● *adv.* **1** badly, wrongly (*ill-matched*). **2 a** imperfectly (*ill-provided*). **b** scarcely (*can ill afford to do it*). **3** unfavourably (*it would have gone ill with them*). ● *n.* **1** injury, harm. **2** evil; the opposite of good. □ **do an ill turn to** harm (a person or a person's interests). **ill at ease** embarrassed, uneasy. **speak ill of** say something unfavourable about. [Middle English from Old Norse *illr*, of unknown origin]

■ **Usage** The use of *ill* to mean 'vomiting' or 'tending to vomit', as in *He was outside being ill* is non-standard. See also Usage Note at SICK[1].

ill-advised *adj.* **1** (of a person) foolish or imprudent. **2** (of a plan etc.) not well formed or considered. □ **ill-advisedly** /-zɪdli/ *adv.*

ill-affected *adj.* (foll. by *towards*) not well disposed.

ill-assorted *adj.* not well matched.

illation /ɪˈleɪʃ(ə)n/ *n.* **1** a deduction or conclusion. **2** a thing deduced. [Latin *illatio* from *illatus*, past part. of *inferre* INFER]

illative /ɪˈleɪtɪv/ *adj.* **1 a** (of a word) stating or introducing an inference. **b** inferential. **2** *Gram.* (of a case) denoting motion into. □ **illatively** *adv.* [Latin *illativus* (as ILLATION)]

ill-behaved *adj.* having bad manners or conduct.

ill-bred *adj.* badly brought up; rude. □ **ill breeding** *n.*

ill-conceived *adj.* badly planned or conceived.

ill-considered *adj.* = ILL-ADVISED 2.

ill-defined *adj.* not clearly defined.

ill-disposed *adj.* **1** (often foll. by *towards*) unfavourably disposed. **2** disposed to evil; malevolent.

illegal /ɪˈliːg(ə)l/ *adj.* **1** not legal. **2** contrary to law. □ **illegality** /-ˈgalɪti/ *n.* (*pl.* **-ies**). **illegally** *adv.* [French *illégal* or medieval Latin *illegalis* (as IN-[1], LEGAL)]

illegible /ɪˈlɛdʒɪb(ə)l/ *adj.* not legible. □ **illegibility** /-ˈbɪlɪti/ *n.* **illegibly** *adv.*

illegitimate *adj., n., & v.* ● *adj.* /ɪlɪˈdʒɪtɪmət/ **1** (of a child) born of parents not married to each other. **2 a** not authorized by law; unlawful. **b** not in accordance with a rule; abnormal. **3** improper. **4** wrongly inferred. ● *n.* /ɪlɪˈdʒɪtɪmət/ a person whose position is illegitimate, esp. by birth. ● *v.tr.* /ɪlɪˈdʒɪtɪmeɪt/ declare or pronounce illegitimate. □ **illegitimacy** *n.* **illegitimately** *adv.* [Late Latin *illegitimus* (as IL-, LEGITIMATE)]

ill-equipped *adj.* (often foll. by *to* + infin.) not adequately equipped or qualified.

ill fame *n.* disrepute.

ill-fated *adj.* destined to or bringing bad fortune.

ill-favoured *adj.* (*US* **ill-favored**) unattractive, displeasing, objectionable.

ill feeling *n.* bad feeling; animosity.

ill-fitting *adj.* **1** fitting badly. **2** inappropriate.

ill-founded *adj.* (of an idea etc.) not well founded; baseless.

ill-gotten *adj.* gained by wicked or unlawful means.

ill health *n.* poor physical or mental condition.

ill humour *n.* moroseness, irritability. □ **ill-humoured** *adj.*

illiberal /ɪˈlɪb(ə)r(ə)l/ *adj.* **1** intolerant, narrow-minded. **2** without liberal culture. **3** not generous; stingy. **4** vulgar, sordid. □ **illiberality** /-ˈralɪti/ *n.* (*pl.* **-ies**). **illiberally** *adv.* [French *illibéral* from Latin *illiberalis* 'mean, sordid' (as IN-[1], LIBERAL)]

illicit /ɪˈlɪsɪt/ *adj.* unlawful, forbidden (*illicit dealings*). □ **illicitly** *adv.* **illicitness** *n.* [French *illicite* or Latin *illicitus* (as IN-[1], LICIT)]

illimitable /ɪˈlɪmɪtəb(ə)l/ *adj.* limitless. □ **illimitability** /-ˈbɪlɪti/ *n.* **illimitably** *adv.* [Late Latin *illimitatus* from Latin *limitatus* (as IN-[1], Latin *limitatus*, past part. of *limitare* LIMIT)]

ill-informed *adj.* inadequately informed.

illiquid /ɪˈlɪkwɪd/ *adj.* (of assets) not easily converted into cash. □ **illiquidity** /-ˈkwɪdɪti/ *n.*

illiterate /ɪˈlɪt(ə)rət/ *adj. & n.* ● *adj.* **1** unable to read. **2** uneducated. ● *n.* an illiterate person. □ **illiteracy** *n.* **illiterately** *adv.* **illiterateness** *n.* [Latin *illitteratus* (as IN-[1], *litteratus* LITERATE)]

ill-judged *adj.* unwise; badly considered.

ill-mannered *adj.* having bad manners; rude.

ill-matched *adj.* badly matched; unsuited.

ill nature *n.* churlishness, unkindness. □ **ill-natured** *adj.* **ill-naturedly** *adv.*

illness /ɪlnɪs/ *n.* **1** a disease, ailment, or malady. **2** the state of being ill.

illogical /ɪˈlɒdʒɪk(ə)l/ *adj.* devoid of or contrary to logic. □ **illogicality** /-ˈkalɪti/ *n.* (*pl.* **-ies**). **illogically** *adv.*

ill-omened *adj.* attended by bad omens.

ill-prepared *adj.* badly or inadequately prepared.

ill-starred *adj.* unlucky; destined to failure.

ill-suited *adj.* **1** not suited to doing something; unsuitable. **2** inappropriate.

ill temper *n.* moroseness. □ **ill-tempered** *adj.*

ill-timed *adj.* done or occurring at an inappropriate time.

ill-treat *v.tr.* treat badly; abuse. □ **ill-treatment** *n.*

illude /ɪˈluːd, ɪˈljuːd/ *v.tr. literary* trick or deceive. [Middle English, = mock, from Latin *illudere* (as ILLUSION)]

illume /ɪˈluːm, ɪˈljuːm/ *v.tr. poet.* light up; make bright. [shortening of ILLUMINE]

illuminance /ɪˈluːmɪnəns, ɪˈljuː-/ *n. Physics* the amount of luminous flux per unit area.

illuminant /ɪˈluːmɪnənt, ɪˈljuː-/ *n. & adj.* ● *n.* a means of illumination. ● *adj.* serving to illuminate. [Latin *illuminant-*, part. stem of *illuminare* ILLUMINATE]

illuminate /ɪˈluːmɪneɪt, ɪˈljuː-/ *v.tr.* **1** light up; make bright. **2** decorate (buildings etc.) with lights as a sign of festivity. **3** decorate (an initial letter, a manuscript, etc.) with gold, silver, or brilliant colours. **4** help to explain (a subject etc.). **5** enlighten spiritually or intellectually. **6** shed lustre on. □ **illuminating** *adj.* **illuminatingly** *adv.* **illuminative** /-neɪtɪv, -nətɪv/ *adj.* **illuminator** *n.* [Latin *illuminare* (as IN-[2], *lumen luminis* 'light')]

illuminati /ɪˌluːmɪˈnɑːti, ɪˌljuː-/ *n.pl.* **1** persons claiming to possess special knowledge or enlightenment. **2** (**Illuminati**) *hist.* any of various intellectual movements or societies of illuminati. □ **illuminism** /ɪˈluːmɪnɪz(ə)m, ɪˈljuː-/ *n.* **illuminist** /ɪˈluːmɪnɪst, ɪˈljuː-/ *n.* [pl. of Italian *illuminato* 'enlightened' or Latin *illuminatus*, past part. of *illuminare* (as ILLUMINATE)]

illumination /ɪˌluːmɪˈneɪʃ(ə)n, ɪˌljuː-/ *n.* **1** the act or process of illuminating. **2** (in *pl.*) lights used in decorating a street, building, etc.

illumine /ɪˈluːmɪn, ɪˈljuː-/ *v.tr. literary* **1** light up; make bright. **2** enlighten spiritually. [Middle English via Old French *illuminer* from Latin (as ILLUMINATE)]

ill use *n.* ill-treatment. □ **ill-use** *v.tr.*

illusion /ɪˈluːʒ(ə)n, ɪˈljuː-/ *n.* **1** deception, delusion. **2** a misapprehension of the true state of affairs. **3 a** the faulty perception of an external object. **b** an instance of this. **4** a figment of the imagination. **5** = OPTICAL ILLUSION. □ **be under the illusion** (foll. by *that* + clause) believe mistakenly. □ **illusional** *adj.* [Middle English via French from Latin *illusio -onis*, from *illudere* 'mock' (as IN-[2], *ludere lus-* 'play')]

illusionist /ɪˈluːʒ(ə)nɪst, ɪˈljuː-/ *n.* a person who produces illusions; a conjuror. □ **illusionism** *n.* **illusionistic** /-ˈnɪstɪk/ *adj.*

illusive /ɪˈluːsɪv, ɪˈljuː-/ *adj.* = ILLUSORY. [medieval Latin *illusivus* (as ILLUSION)]

illusory /ɪˈluːs(ə)ri, ɪˈljuː-/ *adj.* **1** deceptive (esp. as regards value or content). **2** having the character of an illusion. □ **illusorily** *adv.* **illusoriness** *n.* [ecclesiastical Latin *illusorius* (as ILLUSION)]

illustrate /ˈɪləstreɪt/ *v.tr.* **1 a** provide (a book, newspaper, etc.) with pictures. **b** elucidate (a description etc.) by drawings or pictures. **2** serve as an example of. **3** explain or make clear, esp. by examples. [earlier = shed light on, light up: Latin *illustrare* (as IN-[2], *lustrare* 'light up')]

illustration /ɪləˈstreɪʃ(ə)n/ *n.* **1** a drawing or picture illustrating a book, magazine article, etc. **2** an example serving to elucidate. **3** the act or an instance of illustrating. □ **illustrational** *adj.* [Middle English via Old French from Latin *illustratio -onis* (as ILLUSTRATE)]

illustrative /ˈɪləstrətɪv, ɪˈlʌst-/ *adj.* (often foll. by *of*) serving as an explanation or example. □ **illustratively** *adv.*

illustrator /ˈɪləstreɪtə/ *n.* a person who makes illustrations, esp. for magazines, books, advertising copy, etc.

illustrious /ɪˈlʌstrɪəs/ *adj.* distinguished, renowned. □ **illustriously** *adv.* **illustriousness** *n.* [Latin *illustris* (as ILLUSTRATE)]

ill will *n.* bad feeling; animosity.

ill wind *n.* an unfavourable or untoward circumstance (with reference to the proverb *it's an ill wind that blows nobody good*).

Illyrian /ɪˈlɪrɪən/ *adj.* & *n.* ● *adj.* **1** of or relating to Illyria on the Balkan coast of the Adriatic (corresponding to parts of modern Albania, Slovenia, and Croatia). **2** of the language group represented by modern Albanian. ● *n.* **1** a native of Illyria; a person of Illyrian descent. **2 a** the language of Illyria. **b** the language group represented by modern Albanian.

illywhacker /ˈɪlɪwakə/ *n. Austral. slang* a professional trickster. [20th c.: origin unknown]

ilmenite /ˈɪlmənʌɪt/ *n.* a black ore of titanium. [*Ilmen* mountains in the Urals]

ILO *abbr.* International Labour Organization.

ILR *abbr.* Independent Local Radio.

-ily /ɪli/ *suffix* forming adverbs corresponding to adjectives in *-y* (see -Y[1], -LY[2]).

I'm /ʌɪm/ *contr.* I am.

im- /ɪm/ *prefix* assim. form of IN-[1], IN-[2] before *b, m, p*.

image /ˈɪmɪdʒ/ *n.* & *v.* ● *n.* **1** a representation of the external form of a person or thing in sculpture, painting, etc. **2** the character or reputation of a person or thing as generally perceived. **3** an optical appearance or counterpart produced by light or other radiation from an object reflected in a mirror, refracted through a lens, etc. **4** semblance, likeness (*God created man in His own image*). **5** a person or thing that closely resembles another (*is the image of his father*). **6** a typical example. **7** a simile or metaphor. **8 a** a mental representation. **b** an idea or conception. **9** *Math.* a set formed by mapping from another set. ● *v.tr.* **1** make an image of; portray. **2** reflect, mirror. **3** describe or imagine vividly. **4** typify. □ **imageable** *adj.* **imageless** *adj.* [Middle English via Old French from Latin *imago -ginis*, related to IMITATE]

image intensifier *n.* a device used to make a brighter version of an image on a photoelectric screen.

image-maker *n.* a person employed to create a public image for a politician, product, etc.

image processing *n.* the analysis and manipulation of an (esp. digitized) image, esp. to improve its quality. □ **image processor** *n.*

imagery /ˈɪmɪdʒ(ə)ri/ *n.* **1** figurative illustration, esp. as used by an author for particular effects. **2** images collectively. **3** statuary, carving. **4** mental images collectively. [Middle English from Old French *imagerie* (as IMAGE)]

imaginable /ɪˈmadʒɪnəb(ə)l/ *adj.* that can be imagined (*the greatest difficulty imaginable*). □ **imaginably** *adv.* [Middle English from Late Latin *imaginabilis* (as IMAGINE)]

imaginal /ɪˈmadʒɪn(ə)l/ *adj.* **1** of an image or images. **2** *Zool.* of or relating to an adult insect or imago. [Latin *imago imagin-*: see IMAGE]

imaginary /ɪˈmadʒɪn(ə)ri/ *adj.* **1** existing only in the imagination. **2** *Math.* being the square root of a negative quantity, and plotted graphically in a direction usu. perpendicular to the axis of real quantities. □ **imaginarily** *adv.* [Middle English from Latin *imaginarius* (as IMAGE)]

imagination /ɪˌmadʒɪˈneɪʃ(ə)n/ *n.* **1** a mental faculty forming images or concepts of external objects not present to the senses. **2** the ability of the mind to be creative or resourceful. **3** the process of imagining. [Middle English via Old French from Latin *imaginatio -onis* (as IMAGINE)]

imaginative /ɪˈmadʒɪnətɪv/ *adj.* **1** having or showing in a high degree the faculty of imagination. **2** given to using the imagination. □ **imaginatively** *adv.* **imaginativeness** *n.* [Middle English via Old French *imaginatif -ive* from medieval Latin *imaginativus* (as IMAGINE)]

imagine /ɪˈmadʒɪn/ *v.tr.* **1 a** form a mental image or concept of. **b** picture to oneself (something non-existent or not present to the senses). **2** (often foll. by *to* + infin.) think or conceive (*imagined them to be soldiers*). **3** guess (*cannot imagine what they are doing*). **4** (often foll. by *that* + clause) suppose; be of the opinion (*I imagine you will need help*). **5** (*absol.*; in *imper.*) as an exclamation of surprise (*just imagine!*). □ **imaginer** *n.* [Middle English via Old French *imaginer* from Latin *imaginari* (as IMAGE)]

imagines *pl.* of IMAGO.

imaginings /ɪˈmadʒɪnɪŋz/ *n.pl.* fancies, fantasies.

imagism /ˈɪmɪdʒɪz(ə)m/ *n.* a movement in early 20th-c. poetry which sought clarity of expression through the use of precise images. □ **imagist** *n.* **imagistic** /-ˈdʒɪstɪk/ *adj.*

imago /ɪˈmeɪgəʊ/ *n.* (*pl.* **-os** or **imagines** /ɪˈmeɪdʒɪniːz/) **1** *Zool.* the final and fully developed stage of an insect after all metamorphoses, e.g. a butterfly or beetle. **2** *Psychol.* an idealized mental picture of oneself or others, esp. a parent. [modern Latin sense of *imago* IMAGE]

imam /ɪ'mɑːm/ *n.* **1** a leader of prayers in a mosque. **2** a title of various Muslim leaders, esp. of one succeeding Muhammad as leader of Islam. □ **imamate** /-meɪt/ *n.* [Arabic *'imām* 'leader' from *'amma* 'precede']

IMAX /'ʌɪmaks/ *n. propr.* a technique of wide-screen cinematography which produces an image approx. ten times larger than that from standard 35 mm film. [from *i-* (probably representing pronunciation of EYE) + MAXIMUM]

imbalance /ɪm'bal(ə)ns/ *n.* **1** lack of balance. **2** disproportion.

imbecile /'ɪmbɪsiːl/ *n. & adj.* ● *n.* **1** a person of abnormally weak intellect, esp. an adult with a mental age of about five. **2** *colloq.* a stupid person. ● *adj.* mentally weak; stupid, idiotic. □ **imbecilic** /-'sɪlɪk/ *adj.* **imbecility** /-'sɪlɪti/ *n.* (*pl.* **-ies**). [in earlier use also = physically weak: French *imbécil(l)e* from Latin *imbecillus* (as IN-[1], *baculum* 'stick') literally 'without supporting staff']

imbed var. of EMBED.

imbibe /ɪm'bʌɪb/ *v.tr.* **1** (also *absol.*) drink (esp. alcoholic liquor). **2 a** absorb or assimilate (ideas etc.). **b** absorb (moisture etc.). **3** inhale (air etc.). □ **imbiber** *n.* **imbibition** /ɪmbɪ'bɪʃ(ə)n/ *n.* [Middle English from Latin *imbibere* (as IN-[2], *bibere* 'drink')]

imbricate *v. & adj.* ● *v.tr. & intr.* /'ɪmbrɪkeɪt/ arrange (leaves, the scales of a fish, etc.), or be arranged, so as to overlap like roof tiles. ● *adj.* /'ɪmbrɪkət/ having scales etc. arranged in this way. □ **imbrication** /-'keɪʃ(ə)n/ *n.* [Latin *imbricare imbricat-* 'cover with rain-tiles', via *imbrex -icis* 'rain-tile' from *imber* 'shower']

imbroglio /ɪm'brəʊlɪəʊ/ *n.* (*pl.* **-os**) **1** a confused or complicated situation. **2** a confused heap. [Italian *imbrogliare* 'confuse' (as EMBROIL)]

imbrue /ɪm'bruː/ *v.tr.* (**imbrues, imbrued, imbruing**) (foll. by *in, with*) *literary* stain (one's hand, sword, etc.). [Old French *embruer* 'bedabble' (as IN-[2], *breu*, ultimately from Germanic, related to BROTH)]

imbue /ɪm'bjuː/ *v.tr.* (**imbues, imbued, imbuing**) (often foll. by *with*) **1** inspire or permeate (with feelings, opinions, or qualities). **2** saturate. **3** dye. [originally as past part., via French *imbu* or Latin *imbutus* from *imbuere* 'moisten']

I.Mech.E. *abbr.* (in the UK) Institution of Mechanical Engineers.

IMF *abbr.* International Monetary Fund.

imide /'ɪmʌɪd/ *n. Chem.* an organic compound containing the group (–CO·NH·CO–) formed by replacing two of the hydrogen atoms in ammonia by carbonyl groups. [originally French: arbitrary alteration of AMIDE]

I.Min.E. *abbr.* (in the UK) Institution of Mining Engineers.

imine /'ɪmiːn/ *n. Chem.* a compound containing the group (–NH–) formed by replacing two of the hydrogen atoms in ammonia by other groups. [German *Imin*, arbitrary alteration of *Amin* AMINE]

imitate /'ɪmɪteɪt/ *v.tr.* **1** follow the example of; copy the action(s) of. **2** mimic. **3** make a copy of; reproduce. **4** be (consciously or not) like. □ **imitable** *adj.* **imitator** *n.* [Latin *imitari imitat-*, related to *imago* IMAGE]

imitation /ɪmɪ'teɪʃ(ə)n/ *n.* **1** the act or an instance of imitating or being imitated. **2** a copy. **3** counterfeit (often *attrib.*: *imitation leather*). **4** *Mus.* the repetition of a phrase etc., usu. at a different pitch, in another part or voice. [French *imitation* or Latin *imitatio* (as IMITATE)]

imitative /'ɪmɪtətɪv/ *adj.* **1** (often foll. by *of*) imitating; following a model or example. **2** counterfeit. **3** of a word: **a** that reproduces a natural sound (e.g. *fizz*). **b** whose sound is thought to correspond to the appearance etc. of the object or action described (e.g. *blob*). □ **imitatively** *adv.* **imitativeness** *n.* [Late Latin *imitativus* (as IMITATE)]

imitative arts *n.pl.* painting and sculpture.

immaculate /ɪ'makjʊlət/ *adj.* **1** pure, spotless; perfectly clean or neat and tidy. **2** perfectly or extremely well executed (*an immaculate performance*). **3** free from fault; innocent. **4** *Biol.* not spotted. □ **immaculacy** *n.* **immaculately** *adv.* **immaculateness** *n.* [Middle English from Latin *immaculatus* (as IN-[1], *maculatus* from *macula* 'spot')]

Immaculate Conception *n. RC Ch.* **1** the doctrine that God preserved the Virgin Mary from the taint of original sin from the moment she was conceived. **2** 8 Dec., the feast of the Immaculate Conception.

immanent /'ɪmənənt/ *adj.* **1** (often foll. by *in*) indwelling, inherent. **2** (of the supreme being) permanently pervading the universe (opp. TRANSCENDENT 4). □ **immanence** *n.* **immanency** *n.* **immanentism** *n.* **immanentist** *n.* [Late Latin *immanēre* (as IN-[2], *manēre* 'remain')]

immaterial /ɪmə'tɪərɪəl/ *adj.* **1** of no essential consequence; unimportant. **2** not material; incorporeal. □ **immateriality** /-'alɪti/ *n.* **immaterialize** *v.tr.* (also **-ise**). **immaterially** *adv.* [Middle English from Late Latin *immaterialis* (as IN-[1], MATERIAL)]

immaterialism /ɪmə'tɪərɪəlɪz(ə)m/ *n.* the doctrine that matter has no objective existence. □ **immaterialist** *n.*

immature /ɪmə'tjʊə/ *adj.* **1** not mature or fully developed. **2** lacking emotional or intellectual development. **3** unripe. □ **immaturely** *adv.* **immaturity** *n.* [Latin *immaturus* (as IN-[1], MATURE)]

immeasurable /ɪ'mɛʒ(ə)rəb(ə)l/ *adj.* not measurable; immense. □ **immeasurability** /-'bɪlɪti/ *n.* **immeasurably** *adv.*

immediate /ɪ'miːdɪət/ *adj.* **1** occurring or done at once or without delay (*an immediate reply*). **2** nearest, next; not separated by others (*the immediate vicinity*; *the immediate future*; *my immediate neighbour*). **3** most pressing or urgent; of current concern (*our immediate concern was to get him to hospital*). **4** (of a relation or action) having direct effect; without an intervening medium or agency (*the immediate cause of death*). **5** (of knowledge, reactions, etc.) intuitive; gained or exhibited without reasoning. □ **immediacy** *n.* **immediateness** *n.* [Middle English from French *immédiat* or Late Latin *immediatus* (as IN-[1], MEDIATE)]

immediately /ɪ'miːdɪətli/ *adv. & conj.* ● *adv.* **1** without pause or delay. **2** without intermediary. ● *conj.* esp. *Brit.* as soon as.

immedicable /ɪ'mɛdɪkəb(ə)l/ *adj.* that cannot be healed or cured. [Latin *immedicabilis* (as IN-[1], MEDICABLE)]

immemorial /ɪmɪ'mɔːrɪəl/ *adj.* **1** ancient beyond memory or record. **2** very old. □ **immemorially** *adv.* [medieval Latin *immemorialis* (as IN-[1], MEMORIAL)]

immense /ɪ'mɛns/ *adj.* **1** immeasurably large or great; huge. **2** very great; considerable (*made an immense difference*). **3** *colloq.* very good. □ **immenseness** *n.* **immensity** *n.* [Middle English from French from Latin *immensus* 'immeasurable' (as IN-[1], *mensus*, past part. of *metiri* 'measure')]

immensely /ɪ'mɛnsli/ *adv.* **1** very much (*enjoyed myself immensely*). **2** to an immense degree.

immerse /ɪ'məːs/ *v.tr.* **1 a** (often foll. by *in*) dip, plunge. **b** cause (a person) to be completely under water. **2** (often *refl.* or in *passive*; often foll. by *in*) absorb or involve deeply. **3** (often foll. by *in*) bury, embed. [Latin *immergere* (as IN-[2], *mergere mers-* 'dip')]

immersion /ɪ'məːʃ(ə)n/ *n.* **1** the act or an instance of immersing; the process of being immersed. **2** baptism by immersing the whole person in water. **3** mental absorption. **4** *Astron.* the disappearance of a celestial body behind another or in its shadow. [Middle English from Late Latin *immersio* (as IMMERSE)]

immersion heater *n.* an electric heater designed for direct immersion in a liquid to be heated, esp. as a fixture in a hot water tank.

immigrant /ˈɪmɪɡr(ə)nt/ *n.* & *adj.* ● *n.* a person who immigrates. ● *adj.* **1** immigrating. **2** of or concerning immigrants.

immigrate /ˈɪmɪɡreɪt/ *v.* **1** *intr.* come as a permanent resident to a country other than one's native land. **2** *tr.* bring in (a person) as an immigrant. □ **immigration** /-ˈɡreɪʃ(ə)n/ *n.* **immigratory** *adj.* [Latin *immigrare* (as IN-², MIGRATE)]

imminent /ˈɪmɪnənt/ *adj.* **1** (of an event, esp. danger) impending; about to happen. **2** *archaic* overhanging. □ **imminence** *n.* **imminently** *adv.* [Latin *imminēre imminent-* 'overhang, project']

immiscible /ɪˈmɪsɪb(ə)l/ *adj.* (often foll. by *with*) that cannot be mixed. □ **immiscibility** /-ˈbɪlɪti/ *n.* **immiscibly** *adv.* [Late Latin *immiscibilis* (as IN-¹, MISCIBLE)]

immitigable /ɪˈmɪtɪɡəb(ə)l/ *adj.* that cannot be mitigated. □ **immitigably** *adv.* [Late Latin *immitigabilis* (as IN-¹, MITIGATE)]

immittance /ɪˈmɪt(ə)ns/ *n.* *Electr.* admittance or impedance (when not distinguished). [*im*pedance + ad*mittance*]

immixture /ɪˈmɪkstʃə/ *n.* **1** the process of mixing up. **2** (often foll. by *in*) being involved.

immobile /ɪˈməʊbʌɪl/ *adj.* **1** not moving. **2** not able to move or be moved. □ **immobility** /-ˈbɪlɪti/ *n.* [Middle English via Old French from Latin *immobilis* (as IN-¹, MOBILE)]

immobilize /ɪˈməʊbɪlʌɪz/ *v.tr.* (also **-ise**) **1** make or keep immobile. **2** make (esp. a vehicle or troops) incapable of being moved. **3** keep (a limb or patient) restricted in movement for healing purposes. **4** restrict the free movement of. **5** withdraw (coins) from circulation to support banknotes. □ **immobilization** /-ˈzeɪʃ(ə)n/ *n.* **immobilizer** *n.* [French *immobiliser* (as IMMOBILE)]

immoderate /ɪˈmɒd(ə)rət/ *adj.* excessive; lacking moderation. □ **immoderately** *adv.* **immoderateness** *n.* **immoderation** /-ˈreɪʃ(ə)n/ *n.* [Middle English from Latin *immoderatus* (as IN-¹, MODERATE)]

immodest /ɪˈmɒdɪst/ *adj.* **1** lacking modesty; forward, impudent. **2** lacking due decency. □ **immodestly** *adv.* **immodesty** *n.* [French *immodeste* or Latin *immodestus* (as IN-¹, MODEST)]

immolate /ˈɪmə(ʊ)leɪt/ *v.tr.* **1** kill or offer as a sacrifice. **2** *literary* sacrifice (a valued thing). □ **immolation** /-ˈleɪʃ(ə)n/ *n.* **immolator** *n.* [Latin *immolare* 'sprinkle with sacrificial meal' (as IN-², *mola* MEAL²)]

immoral /ɪˈmɒr(ə)l/ *adj.* **1** not conforming to accepted standards of morality (cf. AMORAL). **2** morally wrong (esp. in sexual matters). **3** depraved, dissolute. □ **immorality** /ɪməˈralɪti/ *n.* (*pl.* **-ies**). **immorally** *adv.*

immortal /ɪˈmɔːt(ə)l/ *adj.* & *n.* ● *adj.* **1 a** living for ever; not mortal. **b** divine. **2** unfading, incorruptible. **3** likely or worthy to be famous for all time. ● *n.* **1 a** an immortal being. **b** (in *pl.*) the gods of antiquity. **2 a** person (esp. an author) of enduring fame. **3** (**Immortal**) a member of the French Academy. □ **immortality** /ɪmɔːˈtalɪti/ *n.* **immortalize** *v.tr.* (also **-ise**). **immortalization** /-ˈzeɪʃ(ə)n/ *n.* **immortally** *adv.* [Middle English from Latin *immortalis* (as IN-¹, MORTAL)]

immortelle /ɪmɔːˈtɛl/ *n.* a flower of the daisy family with papery texture, retaining its shape and colour after being dried, esp. a helichrysum. [French, fem. of *immortel* IMMORTAL]

immovable /ɪˈmuːvəb(ə)l/ *adj.* & *n.* (also **immoveable**) ● *adj.* **1** that cannot be moved. **2** steadfast, unyielding. **3** emotionless. **4** not subject to change (*immovable law*). **5** motionless. **6** *Law* (of property) consisting of land, houses, etc. ● *n.* (in *pl.*) *Law* immovable property. □ **immovability** /-ˈbɪlɪti/ *n.* **immovably** *adv.*

immovable feast *n.* a religious feast day that occurs on the same date each year.

immune /ɪˈmjuːn/ *adj.* **1 a** (often foll. by *against*, *from*, *to*) *Biol.* resistant to a particular infection, toxin, etc., owing to the presence of specific antibodies or sensitized white blood cells. **b** relating to immunity (*immune mechanism*). **2** (foll. by *from*, *to*) free or exempt from or not subject to (some undesirable factor or circumstance). [Middle English from Latin *immunis* 'exempt from public service or charge' (as IN-¹, *munis* 'ready for service'): sense 1 via French *immun*]

immune response *n.* the reaction of the body to the introduction into it of an antigen.

immunity /ɪˈmjuːnɪti/ *n.* (*pl.* **-ies**) **1** *Biol.* the ability of an organism to resist a specific infection, toxin, etc. **2** freedom or exemption from an obligation, penalty, or unfavourable circumstance. [Middle English from Latin *immunitas* (as IMMUNE): sense 1 via French *immunité*]

immunize /ˈɪmjʊnʌɪz/ *v.tr.* (also **-ise**) make immune, esp. to infection, usu. by inoculation. □ **immunization** /-ˈzeɪʃ(ə)n/ *n.* **immunizer** *n.*

immuno- /ˈɪmjʊnəʊ, ɪˈmjuːnəʊ/ *comb. form* immunity to infection.

immunoassay /ˌɪmjʊnəʊˈaseɪ, ɪˌmjuːnəʊ-/ *n.* *Biochem.* the determination of the presence or quantity of a substance, esp. a protein, through its properties as an antigen or antibody.

immunochemistry /ˌɪmjʊnəʊˈkɛmɪstri, ɪˌmjuːnəʊ-/ *n.* **1** the chemical study of immune systems. **2** the use of specific immune reactions in the study of biological molecules.

immunocompromised /ˌɪmjʊnəʊˈkɒmprəmʌɪzd/ *adj.* *Med.* having an impaired immune system.

immunodeficiency /ˌɪmjʊnəʊdɪˈfɪʃ(ə)nsi, ɪˌmjuːnəʊ-/ *n.* a reduction in a person's normal immune defences.

immunogenic /ˌɪmjʊnəʊˈdʒɛnɪk, ɪˌmjuːnəʊ-/ *adj.* *Biochem.* of, relating to, or possessing the ability to elicit an immune response.

immunoglobulin /ˌɪmjʊnəʊˈɡlɒbjʊlɪn, ɪˌmjuːnəʊ-/ *n.* *Biochem.* any of a group of structurally related blood proteins which function as antibodies.

immunology /ɪmjʊˈnɒlədʒi/ *n.* the scientific study of immunity. □ **immunologic** /-nəˈlɒdʒɪk/ *adj.* **immunological** /-nəˈlɒdʒɪk(ə)l/ *adj.* **immunologically** /-nəˈlɒdʒɪk(ə)li/ *adv.* **immunologist** *n.*

immunosuppressed /ˌɪmjʊnəʊsəˈprɛst, ɪˌmjuːnəʊ-/ *adj.* (of an individual) rendered partially or completely unable to react immunologically.

immunosuppression /ˌɪmjʊnəʊsəˈprɛʃ(ə)n, ɪˌmjuːnəʊ-/ *n.* *Biochem.* the partial or complete suppression of the immune response of an individual, esp. to maintain the survival of an organ after a transplant operation. □ **immunosuppressant** *n.*

immunosuppressive /ˌɪmjʊnəʊsəˈprɛsɪv, ɪˌmjuːnəʊ-/ *adj.* & *n.* ● *adj.* partially or completely suppressing the immune response of an individual. ● *n.* an immunosuppressive drug.

immunotherapy /ˌɪmjʊnəʊˈθɛrəpi, ɪˌmjuːnəʊ-/ *n.* *Med.* the prevention or treatment of disease with substances that stimulate the immune response.

immure /ɪˈmjʊə/ *v.tr.* **1** enclose within walls; imprison. **2** *refl.* shut oneself away. □ **immurement** *n.* [French *emmurer* or medieval Latin *immurare* (as IN-², *murus* 'wall')]

immutable /ɪˈmjuːtəb(ə)l/ *adj.* **1** unchangeable. **2** not subject to variation in different cases. □ **immutability** /-ˈbɪlɪti/ *n.* **immutably** *adv.* [Middle English from Latin *immutabilis* (as IN-¹, MUTABLE)]

imp /ɪmp/ *n.* & *v.* ● *n.* **1** a mischievous child. **2** a small mischievous devil or sprite. ● *v.tr.* **1** add feathers to (the wing of a falcon) to restore or improve its flight. **2** *archaic* enlarge; add by grafting. [Old English *impa*, *impe* 'young shoot, scion', *impian* 'to graft': ultimately from Greek *emphutos* 'implanted', past part. of *emphuō*]

impact *n.* & *v.* ● *n.* /ˈɪmpakt/ **1** (often foll. by *on*, *against*) the action of one body coming forcibly into contact with another. **2** an effect or influence, esp. when strong. ● *v.* /ɪmˈpakt/ **1** *tr.* (often foll. by *in*, *into*) press or fix firmly. **2** *tr.* (as **impacted** *adj.*) **a** (of a tooth) wedged between another tooth and the jaw. **b** (of a fractured bone) with the parts crushed together. **c** (of faeces) lodged in the intestine. **3 a** *intr.* (often foll. by *on*) have an impact. **b** *tr.* have an impact on. □ **impaction** /ɪmˈpakʃ(ə)n/ *n.* [Latin *impact-*, part. stem of *impingere* IMPINGE]

impair /ɪmˈpɛː/ *v.tr.* damage or weaken. □ **impairment** *n.* [Middle English *empeire* from Old French *empeirier* (as IN-[2], Late Latin *pejorare* from Latin *pejor* 'worse')]

impala /ɪmˈpɑːlə, -ˈpalə/ *n.* (*pl.* same) a medium-sized antelope, *Aepyceros melampus*, of S. and E. Africa, capable of long high jumps. [Zulu]

impale /ɪmˈpeɪl/ *v.tr.* **1** (foll. by *on, upon, with*) transfix or pierce with a sharp instrument. **2** *Heraldry* combine (two coats of arms) by placing them side by side on one shield separated by a vertical line down the middle. □ **impalement** *n.* [French *empaler* or medieval Latin *impalare* (as IN-[2], *palus* 'stake')]

impalpable /ɪmˈpalpəb(ə)l/ *adj.* **1** not easily grasped by the mind; intangible. **2** imperceptible to the touch. **3** (of powder) very fine; not containing grains that can be felt. □ **impalpability** /-ˈbɪlɪti/ *n.* **impalpably** *adv.* [French *impalpable* or Late Latin *impalpabilis* (as IN-[1], PALPABLE)]

impanel var. of EMPANEL.

impark /ɪmˈpɑːk/ *v.tr. archaic* **1** enclose (animals) in a park. **2** enclose (land) for a park. [Middle English from Anglo-French *enparker*, Old French *emparquer* (as IN-[2], *parc* PARK)]

impart /ɪmˈpɑːt/ *v.tr.* (often foll. by *to*) **1** communicate (news etc.). **2** give a share of (a thing). □ **impartation** /ɪmpɑːˈteɪʃ(ə)n/ *n.* [Middle English via Old French *impartir* from Latin *impartire* (as IN-[2], *pars* 'part')]

impartial /ɪmˈpɑːʃ(ə)l/ *adj.* treating all sides in a dispute etc. equally; unprejudiced, fair. □ **impartiality** /-ʃɪˈalɪti/ *n.* **impartially** *adv.*

impassable /ɪmˈpɑːsəb(ə)l/ *adj.* that cannot be traversed. □ **impassability** /-ˈbɪlɪti/ *n.* **impassableness** *n.* **impassably** *adv.*

impasse /amˈpɑːs, ˈampɑːs/ *n.* a position from which progress is impossible; deadlock. [French (as IN-[1], *passer* PASS[1])]

impassible /ɪmˈpasɪb(ə)l/ *adj.* **1** impassive. **2** incapable of feeling or emotion. **3** incapable of suffering injury. **4** *Theol.* not subject to suffering. □ **impassibility** /-ˈbɪlɪti/ *n.* **impassibly** *adv.* [Middle English via Old French from ecclesiastical Latin *impassibilis* (as IN-[1], PASSIBLE)]

impassion /ɪmˈpaʃ(ə)n/ *v.tr.* fill with passion; arouse emotionally. [Italian *impassionare* (as IN-[2], PASSION)]

impassioned /ɪmˈpaʃ(ə)nd/ *adj.* deeply felt; ardent (*an impassioned plea*).

impassive /ɪmˈpasɪv/ *adj.* **1 a** deficient in or incapable of feeling emotion. **b** undisturbed by passion; serene. **2** without sensation. **3** not subject to suffering. □ **impassively** *adv.* **impassiveness** *n.* **impassivity** /-ˈsɪvɪti/ *n.*

impasto /ɪmˈpastəʊ/ *n. Art* **1** the process of laying on paint thickly. **2** this technique of painting. [Italian *impastare* (as IN-[2], *pastare* 'paste')]

impatiens /ɪmˈpeɪʃɪɛnz/ *n.* any plant of the genus *Impatiens*, including busy Lizzie, balsam, and touch-me-not. [modern Latin from IMPATIENT]

impatient /ɪmˈpeɪʃ(ə)nt/ *adj.* **1 a** (often foll. by *at, with*) lacking patience or tolerance. **b** (of an action) showing a lack of patience. **2** (often foll. by *for*, or *to* + infin.) restlessly eager. **3** (foll. by *of*) intolerant. □ **impatience** *n.* **impatiently** *adv.* [Middle English via Old French from Latin *impatiens* (as IN-[1], PATIENT)]

impeach /ɪmˈpiːtʃ/ *v.tr.* **1** *Brit.* charge with a crime against the State, esp. treason. **2** esp. *US* charge (the holder of a public office) with misconduct. **3** call in question, disparage (a person's integrity etc.). □ **impeachable** *adj.* **impeachment** *n.* [Middle English via Old French *empecher* 'impede' from Late Latin *impedicare* 'entangle' (as IN-[2], *pedica* 'fetter' from *pes pedis* 'foot')]

impeccable /ɪmˈpɛkəb(ə)l/ *adj.* **1** (of behaviour, performance, etc.) faultless, exemplary. **2** not liable to sin. □ **impeccability** /-ˈbɪlɪti/ *n.* **impeccably** *adv.* [Latin *impeccabilis* (as IN-[1], *peccare* 'sin')]

impecunious /ɪmpɪˈkjuːnɪəs/ *adj.* having little or no money. □ **impecuniosity** /-ˈɒsɪti/ *n.* **impecuniousness** *n.* [IN-[1] + obsolete *pecunious* 'having money' from Latin *pecuniosus*, via *pecunia* 'money' from *pecu* 'cattle']

impedance /ɪmˈpiːd(ə)ns/ *n.* **1** *Electr.* the total effective resistance of an electric circuit etc. to alternating current, arising from ohmic resistance and reactance. **2** an analogous mechanical property. [IMPEDE + -ANCE]

■ **Usage** *Impedance*, a technical term, is sometimes confused with *impediment* which means 'a hindrance' or 'a speech defect'.

impede /ɪmˈpiːd/ *v.tr.* retard by obstructing; hinder. [Latin *impedire* 'shackle the feet of' (as IN-[2], *pes* 'foot')]

impediment /ɪmˈpɛdɪm(ə)nt/ *n.* **1** a hindrance or obstruction. **2** a defect in speech, e.g. a lisp or stammer. □ **impedimental** /-ˈmɛnt(ə)l/ *adj.* [Middle English from Latin *impedimentum* (as IMPEDE)]

■ **Usage** See Usage Note at IMPEDANCE.

impedimenta /ɪmˌpɛdɪˈmɛntə/ *n.pl.* **1** encumbrances. **2** travelling equipment, esp. of an army. [Latin, pl. of *impedimentum*: see IMPEDIMENT]

impel /ɪmˈpɛl/ *v.tr.* (**impelled**, **impelling**) **1** drive, force, or urge into action. **2** drive forward; propel. □ **impeller** *n.* [Middle English from Latin *impellere* (as IN-[2], *pellere puls-* 'drive')]

impend /ɪmˈpɛnd/ *v.intr.* **1** be about to happen. **2** (often foll. by *over*) **a** (of a danger) be threatening. **b** hang; be suspended. □ **impending** *adj.* [Latin *impendēre* (as IN-[2], *pendēre* 'hang')]

impenetrable /ɪmˈpɛnɪtrəb(ə)l/ *adj.* **1** that cannot be penetrated. **2** inscrutable, unfathomable. **3** inaccessible to ideas, influences, etc. **4** *Physics* (of matter) having the property such that a body is incapable of occupying the same place as another body at the same time. □ **impenetrability** /-ˈbɪlɪti/ *n.* **impenetrableness** *n.* **impenetrably** *adv.* [Middle English via French *impénétrable* from Latin *impenetrabilis* (as IN-[1], PENETRATE)]

impenitent /ɪmˈpɛnɪt(ə)nt/ *adj.* not repentant or penitent. □ **impenitence** *n.* **impenitency** *n.* **impenitently** *adv.* [ecclesiastical Latin *impaenitens* (as IN-[1], PENITENT)]

imperative /ɪmˈpɛrətɪv/ *adj.* & *n.* ● *adj.* **1** urgent. **2** obligatory. **3** commanding, peremptory. **4** *Gram.* (of a mood) expressing a command (e.g. *come here!*). ● *n.* **1** *Gram.* the imperative mood. **2** a command. **3** an essential or urgent thing. □ **imperatival** /ɪmˌpɛrəˈtʌɪv(ə)l/ *adj.* **imperatively** *adv.* **imperativeness** *n.* [Late Latin *imperativus* from *imperare* 'command' (as IN-[2], *parare* 'make ready')]

imperator /ɪmpəˈrɑːtɔː/ *n. Rom.Hist.* commander (a title conferred under the Republic on a victorious general and under the Empire on the emperor). □ **imperatorial** /ˌɪmpɛrəˈtɔːrɪəl, ɪmˌpɛrə-/ *adj.* [Latin (as IMPERATIVE)]

imperceptible /ɪmpəˈsɛptɪb(ə)l/ *adj.* **1** that cannot be perceived. **2** very slight, gradual, or subtle. □ **imperceptibility** /-ˈbɪlɪti/ *n.* **imperceptibly** *adv.* [French *imperceptible* or medieval Latin *imperceptibilis* (as IN-[1], PERCEPTIBLE)]

impercipient /ɪmpəˈsɪpɪənt/ *adj.* lacking in perception. □ **impercipience** *n.*

imperfect /ɪmˈpəːfɪkt/ *adj.* & *n.* ● *adj.* **1** not fully formed or done; faulty, incomplete. **2** *Gram.* (of a tense) denoting a (usu. past) action in progress but not completed at the time in question (e.g. *they were singing*). **3** *Mus.* (of a cadence) ending on the dominant chord. ● *n.* the imperfect tense. □ **imperfectly** *adv.* [Middle English *imparfit* etc. via Old French *imparfait* from Latin *imperfectus* (as IN-[1], PERFECT)]

imperfection /ɪmpəˈfɛkʃ(ə)n/ *n.* **1** incompleteness. **2 a** faultiness. **b** a fault or blemish. [Middle English from Old French *imperfection* or Late Latin *imperfectio* (as IMPERFECT)]

imperfective /ɪmpəˈfɛktɪv/ *adj. & n. Gram.* ● *adj.* (of a verb aspect etc.) expressing an action without reference to its completion (opp. PERFECTIVE). ● *n.* an imperfective aspect or form of a verb.

imperfect rhyme *n.* a rhyme that only partly satisfies the usual criteria (e.g. *love* and *move*).

imperforate /ɪmˈpəːf(ə)rət/ *adj.* **1** not perforated. **2** *Anat.* lacking the normal opening. **3** (of a postage stamp) lacking perforations.

imperial /ɪmˈpɪərɪəl/ *adj. & n.* ● *adj.* **1** of or characteristic of an empire or comparable sovereign state. **2 a** of or characteristic of an emperor. **b** supreme in authority. **c** majestic, august. **d** magnificent. **3** (of non-metric weights and measures) used or formerly used by statute in the UK (*imperial gallon*). ● *n.* **1** a former size of paper, 762 × 559 mm (30 × 22 inches). **2** a small pointed beard growing below the lower lip (associated with Napoleon III of France). □ **imperially** *adv.* [Middle English via Old French from Latin *imperialis*, from *imperium* 'command, authority']

imperialism /ɪmˈpɪərɪəlɪz(ə)m/ *n.* **1** an imperial rule or system. **2** usu. *derog.* a policy of acquiring dependent territories or of extending a country's influence through trade, diplomacy, etc. □ **imperialistic** /-ˈlɪstɪk/ *adj.* **imperialistically** /-ˈlɪstɪk(ə)li/ *adv.* **imperialize** *v.tr.* (also **-ise**).

imperialist /ɪmˈpɪərɪəlɪst/ *n. & adj.* ● *n.* usu. *derog.* an advocate or agent of imperial rule or of imperialism. ● *adj.* of or relating to imperialism or imperialists.

imperil /ɪmˈpɛrɪl, -r(ə)l/ *v.tr.* (**imperilled**, **imperilling**; *US* **imperiled**, **imperiling**) bring or put into danger.

imperious /ɪmˈpɪərɪəs/ *adj.* **1** overbearing, domineering. **2** urgent, imperative. □ **imperiously** *adv.* **imperiousness** *n.* [Latin *imperiosus* from *imperium* 'command, authority']

imperishable /ɪmˈpɛrɪʃəb(ə)l/ *adj.* that cannot perish. □ **imperishability** /-ˈbɪlɪti/ *n.* **imperishableness** *n.* **imperishably** *adv.*

imperium /ɪmˈpɪərɪəm/ *n.* absolute power or authority. [Latin, = command, authority]

impermanent /ɪmˈpəːmənənt/ *adj.* not permanent; transient. □ **impermanence** *n.* **impermanency** *n.* **impermanently** *adv.*

impermeable /ɪmˈpəːmɪəb(ə)l/ *adj.* **1** that cannot be penetrated. **2** that does not permit the passage of fluids. □ **impermeability** /-ˈbɪlɪti/ *n.* [French *imperméable* or Late Latin *impermeabilis* (as IN-[1], PERMEABLE)]

impermissible /ɪmpəˈmɪsɪb(ə)l/ *adj.* not allowable. □ **impermissibility** /-ˈbɪlɪti/ *n.*

impersonal /ɪmˈpəːs(ə)n(ə)l/ *adj.* **1** having no personal feeling or reference. **2** having no personality. **3** *Gram.* **a** (of a verb) used only with a formal subject (usu. *it*) and expressing an action not attributable to a definite subject (e.g. *it is snowing*). **b** (of a pronoun) = INDEFINITE 3. □ **impersonality** /-ˈnalɪti/ *n.* **impersonally** *adv.* [Late Latin *impersonalis* (as IN-[1], PERSONAL)]

impersonate /ɪmˈpəːs(ə)neɪt/ *v.tr.* **1** pretend to be (another person) for the purpose of entertainment or fraud. **2** act (a character). □ **impersonation** /-ˈneɪʃ(ə)n/ *n.* **impersonator** *n.* [IN-[2] + Latin *persona* PERSON]

impertinent /ɪmˈpəːtɪnənt/ *adj.* **1** rude or insolent; lacking proper respect. **2** out of place; absurd. **3** esp. *Law* irrelevant, intrusive. □ **impertinence** *n.* **impertinently** *adv.* [Middle English from Old French or Late Latin *impertinens* (as IN-[1], PERTINENT)]

imperturbable /ɪmpəˈtəːbəb(ə)l/ *adj.* not excitable; calm. □ **imperturbability** /-ˈbɪlɪti/ *n.* **imperturbableness** *n.* **imperturbably** *adv.* [Middle English from Late Latin *imperturbabilis* (as IN-[1], PERTURB)]

impervious /ɪmˈpəːvɪəs/ *adj.* (usu. foll. by *to*) **1** not responsive (to an argument, outside influence, etc.). **2** not affording passage to a fluid etc. □ **imperviously** *adv.* **imperviousness** *n.* [Latin *impervius* (as IN-[1], PERVIOUS)]

impetigo /ɪmpɪˈtʌɪgəʊ/ *n.* a contagious bacterial skin infection forming pustules and yellow crusty sores. □ **impetiginous** /ɪmpɪˈtɪdʒɪnəs/ *adj.* [Middle English from Latin *impetigo -ginis*, from *impetere* 'assail' (as IMPETUS)]

impetuous /ɪmˈpɛtjʊəs/ *adj.* **1** acting or done rashly or with sudden energy. **2** moving forcefully or rapidly. □ **impetuosity** /-ˈɒsɪti/ *n.* **impetuously** *adv.* **impetuousness** *n.* [Middle English via Old French *impetueux* from Late Latin *impetuosus* (as IMPETUS)]

impetus /ˈɪmpɪtəs/ *n.* **1** the force or energy with which a body moves. **2** a driving force or impulse. [Latin, = assault, force, from *impetere* 'assail' (as IN-[2], *petere* 'seek')]

impi /ˈɪmpi/ *n.* (*pl.* **impis**) esp. *hist.* a body of Zulu warriors or armed tribesmen. [Zulu, = regiment, armed band]

impiety /ɪmˈpʌɪɪti/ *n.* (*pl.* **-ies**) **1** a lack of piety or reverence. **2** an act etc. showing this. [Middle English from Old French *impieté* or Latin *impietas* (as IN-[1], PIETY)]

impinge /ɪmˈpɪn(d)ʒ/ *v.tr.* (**impinging**) (usu. foll. by *on*, *upon*) **1** make an impact; have an effect. **2** encroach. □ **impingement** *n.* **impinger** *n.* [Latin *impingere* 'drive (a thing) at' (as IN-[2], *pangere* 'fix, drive')]

impious /ˈɪmpɪəs, ɪmˈpʌɪəs/ *adj.* **1** not pious. **2** wicked, profane. □ **impiously** *adv.* **impiousness** *n.* [Latin *impius* (as IN-[1], PIOUS)]

impish /ˈɪmpɪʃ/ *adj.* of or like an imp; mischievous. □ **impishly** *adv.* **impishness** *n.*

implacable /ɪmˈplakəb(ə)l/ *adj.* that cannot be appeased; inexorable. □ **implacability** /-ˈbɪlɪti/ *n.* **implacably** *adv.* [Middle English from French *implacable* or Latin *implacabilis* (as IN-[1], PLACABLE)]

implant *v. & n.* ● *v.tr.* /ɪmˈplɑːnt/ **1** (often foll. by *in*) insert or fix. **2** (often foll. by *in*) instil (a principle, idea, etc.) in a person's mind. **3** plant. **4** *Med.* **a** insert (tissue, a substance, a device, etc.) into the body. **b** (in *passive*) (of a fertilized ovum) become attached to the wall of the womb. ● *n.* /ˈɪmplɑːnt/ **1** a thing implanted. **2** a thing implanted in the body, e.g. a piece of tissue or a capsule containing material for radium therapy. □ **implantation** /-ˈteɪʃ(ə)n/ *n.* [French *implanter* or Late Latin *implantare* 'engraft' (as IN-[2], PLANT)]

implausible /ɪmˈplɔːzɪb(ə)l/ *adj.* not plausible. □ **implausibility** /-ˈbɪlɪti/ *n.* **implausibly** *adv.*

implead /ɪmˈpliːd/ *v.tr. Law* **1** prosecute or take proceedings against (a person). **2** involve (a person etc.) in a suit. [Middle English from Anglo-French *empleder*, Old French *empleidier* (as EM-, IM- + PLEAD)]

implement *n. & v.* ● *n.* /ˈɪmplɪm(ə)nt/ **1** a tool, instrument, or utensil. **2** (in *pl.*) equipment; articles of furniture, dress, etc. **3** *Law* performance of an obligation. ● *v.tr.* /ˈɪmplɪmɛnt/ **1 a** put (a decision, plan, etc.) into effect. **b** fulfil (an undertaking). **2** complete (a contract etc.). **3** fill up; supplement. □ **implementation** /ɪmplɪmɛnˈteɪʃ(ə)n/ *n.* **implementer** *n.* [Middle English from medieval Latin *implementa* (pl.), from *implēre* 'employ' (as IN-[2], Latin *plēre plet-* 'fill')]

implicate *v. & n.* ● *v.tr.* /ˈɪmplɪkeɪt/ **1** (often foll. by *in*) show (a person) to be concerned or involved (in a charge, crime, etc.). **2** (in *passive*; often foll. by *in*) be affected or involved. **3** lead to as a consequence or inference. ● *n.* /ˈɪmplɪkət/ a thing implied. □ **implicative** /ɪmˈplɪkətɪv/ *adj.* **implicatively** /ɪmˈplɪkətɪvli/ *adv.* [Latin *implicatus*, past part. of *implicare* (as IN-[2], *plicare, plicat-* or *plicit-* 'fold')]

implication /ɪmplɪˈkeɪʃ(ə)n/ *n.* **1** what is involved in or implied by something else. **2** the act of implicating or implying. □ **by implication** by what is implied or suggested rather than by formal expression. [Middle English from Latin *implicatio* (as IMPLICATE)]

implicit /ɪmˈplɪsɪt/ *adj.* **1** implied though not plainly expressed. **2** (often foll. by *in*) virtually contained. **3** absolute, unquestioning, unreserved (*implicit obedience*). **4** *Math.* (of a function) not expressed directly in terms of independent variables. □ **implicitly** *adv.* **implicitness** *n.* [French *implicite* or Latin *implicitus* (as IMPLICATE)]

implode /ɪmˈpləʊd/ *v.intr. & tr.* burst or cause to burst inwards. □ **implosion** /ɪmˈpləʊʒ(ə)n/ *n.* **implosive** /-sɪv, -zɪv/ *adj.* [IN-[2] + Latin *-plodere*, on the pattern of EXPLODE]

implore /ɪmˈplɔː/ *v.tr.* **1** (often foll. by *to* + infin.) entreat (a person). **2** beg earnestly for. □ **imploringly** *adv.* [French *implorer* or Latin *implorare* 'invoke with tears' (as IN-[2], *plorare* 'weep')]

imply /ɪmˈplʌɪ/ *v.tr.* (**-ies**, **-ied**) **1** (often foll. by *that* + clause) strongly suggest the truth or existence of (a thing not expressly asserted). **2** insinuate, hint (*what are you implying?*). **3** signify. □ **implied** *adj.* **impliedly** *adv.* [Middle English via Old French *emplier* from Latin *implicare* (as IMPLICATE)]

■ **Usage** See Usage Note at INFER.

impolder /ɪmˈpəʊldə/ *v.tr.* (also **empolder**) *Brit.* **1** make a polder of. **2** reclaim from the sea. [Dutch *inpolderen* (as IN-[2], POLDER)]

impolite /ɪmpəˈlʌɪt/ *adj.* ill-mannered, uncivil, rude. □ **impolitely** *adv.* **impoliteness** *n.* [Latin *impolitus* (as IN-[1], POLITE)]

impolitic /ɪmˈpɒlɪtɪk/ *adj.* **1** inexpedient, unwise. **2** not politic. □ **impoliticly** *adv.*

imponderable /ɪmˈpɒnd(ə)rəb(ə)l/ *adj. & n.* ● *adj.* **1** that cannot be estimated or assessed in any definite way. **2** very light. **3** *Physics* having no weight. ● *n.* (usu. in *pl.*) something difficult or impossible to assess. □ **imponderability** /-ˈbɪlɪti/ *n.* **imponderably** *adv.*

import *v. & n.* ● *v.tr.* /ɪmˈpɔːt, ˈɪm-/ **1** bring in (esp. foreign goods or services) to a country. **2** (often foll. by *that* + clause) **a** imply, indicate, signify. **b** express, make known. ● *n.* /ˈɪmpɔːt/ **1** the process of importing. **2 a** an imported article or service. **b** (in *pl.*) an amount imported (*imports exceeded £50m.*). **3** what is implied; meaning. **4** importance. □ **importable** /ɪmˈpɔːtəb(ə)l/ *adj.* **importation** /ɪmpɔːˈteɪʃ(ə)n/ *n.* **importer** /ɪmˈpɔːtə/ *n.* (all in sense 1 of *v.*). [Middle English from Latin *importare* 'bring in', in medieval Latin = imply, be of consequence (as IN-[2], *portare* 'carry')]

importance /ɪmˈpɔːt(ə)ns/ *n.* **1** the state of being important. **2** import, significance. **3** personal consequence; dignity. [French from medieval Latin *importantia* (as IMPORT)]

important /ɪmˈpɔːt(ə)nt/ *adj.* **1** (often foll. by *to*) of great effect or consequence; momentous. **2** (of a person) having high rank or status, or great authority. **3** pretentious, pompous. **4** (*absol.*, in parenthetic construction prec. by *more* or *most*) what is a more, or most, significant point or matter (*they are willing and, more important, able*). □ **importantly** *adv.* [French from medieval Latin (as IMPORT)]

■ **Usage** Some people use *importantly* in sense 4 above, i.e. *They are wiling and, more importantly, able.* This is considered incorrect in standard English and should be avoided.

importunate /ɪmˈpɔːtjʊnət/ *adj.* **1** making persistent or pressing requests. **2** (of affairs) urgent. □ **importunately** *adv.* **importunity** /ɪmpɔːˈtjuːnɪti/ *n.* [Latin *importunus* 'inconvenient' (as IN-[1], *portunus* from *portus* 'harbour')]

importune /ɪmpɔːˈtjuːn/ *v.tr.* **1** solicit (a person) pressingly. **2** solicit for an immoral purpose. [French *importuner* or medieval Latin *importunari* (as IMPORTUNATE)]

impose /ɪmˈpəʊz/ *v.* **1** *tr.* (often foll. by *on*, *upon*) require (a tax, duty, charge, or obligation) to be paid or undertaken (by a person etc.). **2** *tr.* enforce compliance with. **3** *intr. & refl.* (foll. by *on*, *upon*, or *absol.*) demand the attention or commitment of (a person); take advantage of (*I do not want to impose on you any longer*; *I did not want to impose*). **4** *tr.* (often foll. by *on*, *upon*) palm (a thing) off on (a person). **5** *tr. Printing* lay (pages of type) in the proper order ready for printing. **6** *intr.* (foll. by *on*, *upon*) exert influence by an impressive character or appearance. **7** *tr.* (foll. by *upon*) *archaic* place (a thing). [Middle English via French *imposer* from Latin *imponere imposit-* 'inflict, deceive' (as IN-[2], *ponere* 'put')]

imposing /ɪmˈpəʊzɪŋ/ *adj.* impressive, formidable, esp. in appearance. □ **imposingly** *adv.* **imposingness** *n.*

imposition /ɪmpəˈzɪʃ(ə)n/ *n.* **1** the act or an instance of imposing; the process of being imposed. **2** an unfair or resented demand or burden. **3** a tax or duty. **4** *Brit.* work set as a punishment at school. [Middle English from Old French *imposition* or Latin *impositio*, from *imponere*: see IMPOSE]

impossibility /ɪmˌpɒsɪˈbɪlɪti/ *n.* (*pl.* **-ies**) **1** the fact or condition of being impossible. **2** an impossible thing or circumstance. [French *impossibilité* or Latin *impossibilitas* (as IMPOSSIBLE)]

impossible /ɪmˈpɒsɪb(ə)l/ *adj.* **1** not possible; that cannot occur, exist, or be done (*such a thing is impossible; it is impossible to alter them*). **2** (loosely) not easy; not convenient; not easily believable. **3** *colloq.* (of a person or thing) outrageous, intolerable. □ **impossibly** *adv.* [Middle English from Old French *impossible* or Latin *impossibilis* (as IN-[1], POSSIBLE)]

impost[1] /ˈɪmpəʊst/ *n.* **1** a tax, duty, or tribute. **2** a weight carried by a horse in a handicap race. [French from medieval Latin *impost-*, part. stem of Latin *imponere*: see IMPOSE]

impost[2] /ˈɪmpəʊst/ *n.* the upper course of a pillar, carrying an arch. [French *imposte* or Italian *imposta*, fem. past part. of *imporre*, from Latin *imponere*: see IMPOSE]

impostor /ɪmˈpɒstə/ *n.* (also **imposter**) **1** a person who assumes a false character or pretends to be someone else. **2** a swindler. [French *imposteur* from Late Latin *impostor* (as IMPOST[1])]

imposture /ɪmˈpɒstʃə/ *n.* the act or an instance of fraudulent deception. [French from Late Latin *impostura* (as IMPOST[1])]

impotent /ˈɪmpət(ə)nt/ *adj.* **1 a** powerless; lacking all strength. **b** helpless, decrepit. **2** (esp. of a male) unable, esp. for a prolonged period, to achieve a sexual erection or orgasm. □ **impotence** *n.* **impotency** *n.* **impotently** *adv.* [Middle English via Old French from Latin *impotens* (as IN-[1], POTENT[1])]

impound /ɪmˈpaʊnd/ *v.tr.* **1** confiscate. **2** take possession of. **3** shut up (animals) in a pound. **4** shut up (a person or thing) as in a pound. **5** (of a dam etc.) collect or confine (water). □ **impoundable** *adj.* **impounder** *n.* **impoundment** *n.*

impoverish /ɪmˈpɒv(ə)rɪʃ/ *v.tr.* **1** make poor. **2** exhaust the strength or natural fertility of. □ **impoverishment** *n.* [Middle English from Old French *empoverir* (as EN-[1], *povre* POOR)]

impracticable /ɪmˈpraktɪkəb(ə)l/ *adj.* **1** impossible in practice. **2** (of a road etc.) impassable. **3** (of a person or thing) unmanageable. □ **impracticability** /-ˈbɪlɪti/ *n.* **impracticableness** *n.* **impracticably** *adv.*

impractical /ɪmˈpraktɪk(ə)l/ *adj.* **1** not practical. **2** esp. *US* not practicable. □ **impracticality** /-ˈkalɪti/ *n.* **impractically** *adv.*

imprecation /ɪmprɪˈkeɪʃ(ə)n/ *n.* **1** a spoken curse; a malediction. **2** the act of uttering an imprecation. [Latin *imprecatio* (as IN-[2], *precari* 'pray']

imprecatory /ˈɪmprɪkeɪt(ə)ri, ɪmˈprɛkət(ə)ri/ *adj.* expressing or involving imprecation.

imprecise /ɪmprɪˈsʌɪs/ *adj.* not precise. □ **imprecisely** *adv.* **impreciseness** *n.* **imprecision** /-ˈsɪʒ(ə)n/ *n.*

impregnable[1] /ɪmˈprɛgnəb(ə)l/ *adj.* **1** (of a fortified position) that cannot be taken by force. **2** resistant to attack or criticism. □ **impregnability** /-ˈbɪlɪti/ *n.*

impregnably *adv.* [Middle English from Old French *imprenable* (as IN-[1], *prendre* 'take')]

impregnable[2] /ɪm'prɛgnəb(ə)l/ *adj.* that can be impregnated.

impregnate *v. & adj.* ● *v.tr.* /'ɪmprɛgneɪt/ **1** (often foll. by *with*) fill or saturate. **2** (often foll. by *with*) imbue, fill (with feelings, moral qualities, etc.). **3 a** make (a female) pregnant. **b** *Biol.* fertilize (a female reproductive cell or ovum). ● *adj.* /ɪm'prɛgnət/ **1** pregnant. **2** (often foll. by *with*) permeated. □ **impregnation** /ɪmprɛg'neɪʃ(ə)n/ *n.* [Late Latin *impregnare impregnat-* (as IN-[2], *pregnare* 'be pregnant')]

impresario /ɪmprɪ'sɑːrɪəʊ/ *n.* (*pl.* **-os**) an organizer of public entertainments, esp. the manager of an operatic, theatrical, or concert company. [Italian from *impresa* 'undertaking']

imprescriptible /ɪmprɪ'skrɪptɪb(ə)l/ *adj. Law* (of rights) that cannot be taken away by prescription or lapse of time. [medieval Latin *imprescriptibilis* (as IN-[1], PRESCRIBE)]

impress[1] *v. & n.* ● *v.tr.* /ɪm'prɛs/ **1** (often foll. by *with*) **a** affect or influence deeply. **b** (also *absol.*) evoke a favourable opinion or reaction from (a person) (*was most impressed with your efforts*). **2** (often foll. by *on, upon*) emphasize (an idea etc.) (*must impress on you the need to be prompt*). **3** (often foll. by *on*) **a** imprint or stamp. **b** apply (a mark etc.) with pressure. **4** make a mark or design on (a thing) with a stamp, seal, etc. **5** *Electr.* apply (voltage etc.) from outside. ● *n.* /'ɪmprɛs/ **1** the act or an instance of impressing. **2** a mark made by a seal, stamp, etc. **3** a characteristic mark or quality. **4** = IMPRESSION 1. □ **impressible** /ɪm'prɛsɪb(ə)l/ *adj.* [Middle English from Old French *empresser* (as EN-[1], PRESS[1])]

impress[2] /ɪm'prɛs/ *v.tr. hist.* **1** force (men) to serve in the army or navy. **2** seize (goods etc.) for public service. □ **impressment** *n.* [IN-[2] + PRESS[2]]

impression /ɪm'prɛʃ(ə)n/ *n.* **1** an effect produced (esp. on the mind or feelings). **2** a notion or belief (esp. a vague or mistaken one) (*my impression is they are afraid*). **3** an imitation of a person or sound, esp. done to entertain. **4 a** the impressing of a mark. **b** a mark impressed. **5** esp. *Brit.* an unaltered reprint from standing type or plates (esp. as distinct from *edition*). **6 a** the number of copies of a book, newspaper, etc., issued at one time. **b** the printing of these. **7** a print taken from a wood engraving. **8** *Dentistry* a negative copy of the teeth or mouth made by pressing them into a soft substance. □ **impressional** *adj.* [Middle English via Old French from Latin *impressio -onis*, from *imprimere impress-* (as IN-[2], PRESS[1])]

impressionable /ɪm'prɛʃ(ə)nəb(ə)l/ *adj.* easily influenced; susceptible to impressions. □ **impressionability** /-'bɪlɪti/ *n.* **impressionably** *adv.* [French *impressionnable* from *impressionner* (as IMPRESSION)]

Impressionism /ɪm'prɛʃ(ə)nɪz(ə)m/ *n.* **1** a style or movement in art concerned with expression of feeling by visual impression, esp. from the effect of light on objects. **2** a style of music or writing that seeks to describe a feeling or experience rather than achieve accurate depiction or systematic structure. [French *impressionnisme* (after *Impression*: *Soleil levant*, title of a painting by Monet, 1872)]

impressionist /ɪm'prɛʃ(ə)nɪst/ *n. & adj.* ● *n.* **1** an entertainer who impersonates famous people etc. **2** (**Impressionist**) an adherent or practitioner of Impressionism. ● *adj.* (**Impressionist**) of or relating to Impressionism or Impressionists.

impressionistic /ɪm,prɛʃə'nɪstɪk/ *adj.* **1** in the style of Impressionism. **2** subjective, unsystematic. □ **impressionistically** *adv.*

impressive /ɪm'prɛsɪv/ *adj.* **1** impressing the mind or senses, esp. so as to cause approval or admiration. **2** (of language, a scene, etc.) tending to excite deep feeling. □ **impressively** *adv.* **impressiveness** *n.*

imprest /'ɪmprɛst/ *n.* money advanced to a person for use in State business. [originally *in prest*, from Old French *prest* 'loan, advance pay': see PRESS[2]]

imprimatur /ɪmprɪ'meɪtə, -'mɑːtə, -'mɑːtʊə/ *n.* **1** *RC Ch.* an official licence to print (an ecclesiastical or religious book etc.). **2** official approval. [Latin, = let it be printed]

■ **Usage** *Imprimatur* meaning 'an official licence to print' is sometimes confused with *imprint* 'the name of the publisher or printer etc. printed in a book'.

imprimatura /,ɪmpriːmə'tʊərə, Italian ,imprima'tuːra/ *n.* (in painting) a coloured transparent glaze as a primer. [Italian *imprimitura* from *imprimere* IMPRESS[1]]

imprint *v. & n.* ● *v.tr.* /ɪm'prɪnt/ **1** (often foll. by *on*) impress or establish firmly, esp. on the mind. **2 a** (often foll. by *on*) make a stamp or impression of (a figure etc.) on a thing. **b** make an impression on (a thing) with a stamp etc. **3** (usu. in *passive*; often foll. by *on* or *to*) *Biol.* cause (a young animal etc.) to recognize another as a parent or object of habitual trust. ● *n.* /'ɪmprɪnt/ **1** an impression or stamp. **2** the printer's or publisher's name and other details printed in a book. [Middle English via Old French *empreinter empreint* from Latin *imprimere*: see IMPRESSION]

■ **Usage** See Usage Note at IMPRIMATUR.

imprison /ɪm'prɪz(ə)n/ *v.tr.* **1** put into prison. **2** confine; shut up. □ **imprisonment** *n.* [Middle English from Old French *emprisoner* (as EN-[1], PRISON)]

impro /'ɪmprəʊ/ *n.* (*pl.* **-os**) *colloq.* **1** (often *attrib.*) improvisation, esp. as a theatrical technique. **2** an instance of this. [abbreviation]

improbable /ɪm'prɒbəb(ə)l/ *adj.* **1** not likely to be true or to happen. **2** difficult to believe. □ **improbability** /-'bɪlɪti/ *n.* **improbably** *adv.* [French *improbable* or Latin *improbabilis* (as IN-[1], PROBABLE)]

improbity /ɪm'prəʊbɪti, -'prɒb-/ *n.* (*pl.* **-ies**) **1** wickedness; lack of moral integrity. **2** dishonesty. **3** a wicked or dishonest act. [Latin *improbitas* (as IN-[1], PROBITY)]

impromptu /ɪm'prɒm(p)tjuː/ *adj., adv., & n.* ● *adj. & adv.* extempore, unrehearsed. ● *n.* (*pl.* **impromptus**) **1** an extempore performance or speech. **2** a short piece of usu. solo instrumental music, often songlike. [French from Latin *in promptu* 'in readiness': see PROMPT]

improper /ɪm'prɒpə/ *adj.* **1 a** unseemly; indecent. **b** not in accordance with accepted rules of behaviour. **2** inaccurate, wrong. **3** not properly so called. □ **improperly** *adv.* [French *impropre* or Latin *improprius* (as IN-[1], PROPER)]

improper fraction *n.* a fraction in which the numerator is greater than or equal to the denominator.

impropriate /ɪm'prəʊprɪeɪt/ *v.tr. Brit.* **1** annex (an ecclesiastical benefice) to a corporation or person as property. **2** place (tithes or ecclesiastical property) in lay hands. □ **impropriation** /-'eɪʃ(ə)n/ *n.* [Anglo-Latin *impropriare* (as IN-[2], *proprius* 'own')]

impropriator /ɪm'prəʊprɪeɪtə/ *n. Brit.* a person to whom a benefice is impropriated.

impropriety /ɪmprə'prʌɪəti/ *n.* (*pl.* **-ies**) **1** lack of propriety; indecency. **2** an instance of improper conduct etc. **3** incorrectness. **4** unfitness. [French *impropriété* or Latin *improprietas* (as IN-[1], *proprius* 'proper')]

improv /'ɪmprɒv/ *n.* (also *attrib.*) *colloq.* = IMPRO. [abbreviation]

improvable /ɪm'pruːvəb(ə)l/ *adj.* **1** that can be improved. **2** suitable for cultivation. □ **improvability** /-'bɪlɪti/ *n.*

improve /ɪm'pruːv/ *v.* **1 a** *tr. & intr.* make or become better. **b** *intr.* (foll. by *on, upon*) produce something better than. **2** *absol.* (as **improving** *adj.*) giving moral benefit (*improving literature*). [originally *emprowe, improwe*, via Anglo-French *emprower* from Old French *emprou*, from *prou* 'profit', influenced by PROVE]

improvement /ɪmˈpruːvm(ə)nt/ *n.* **1** the act or an instance of improving or being improved. **2** something that improves, esp. an addition or alteration that adds to value. **3** something that has been improved. [Middle English from Anglo-French *emprowement* (as IMPROVE)]

improver /ɪmˈpruːvə/ *n.* **1** a person who improves. **2** *Brit. hist.* a person who works for low wages while acquiring skill and experience in a trade.

improvident /ɪmˈprɒvɪd(ə)nt/ *adj.* **1** lacking foresight or care for the future. **2** not frugal; thriftless. **3** heedless, incautious. □ **improvidence** *n.* **improvidently** *adv.*

improvise /ˈɪmprəvʌɪz/ *v.tr.* (also *absol.*) **1** compose or perform (music, verse, etc.) extempore. **2** provide or construct (a thing) extempore. □ **improvisation** /-ˈzeɪʃ(ə)n/ *n.* **improvisational** /-ˈzeɪʃ(ə)n(ə)l/ *adj.* **improvisatorial** /-zəˈtɔːrɪəl/ *adj.* **improvisatory** /-ˈzeɪt(ə)ri/ *adj.* **improviser** *n.* [French *improviser* or Italian *improvvisare*, from *improvviso* 'extempore', from Latin *improvisus* 'unforeseen' (as IN-[1], PROVIDE)]

imprudent /ɪmˈpruːd(ə)nt/ *adj.* rash, indiscreet. □ **imprudence** *n.* **imprudently** *adv.* [Middle English from Latin *imprudens* (as IN-[1], PRUDENT)]

impudent /ˈɪmpjʊd(ə)nt/ *adj.* **1** insolently disrespectful; impertinent. **2** shamelessly presumptuous. **3** unblushing. □ **impudence** *n.* **impudently** *adv.* [Middle English from Latin *impudens* (as IN-[1], *pudēre* 'be ashamed')]

impudicity /ɪmpjʊˈdɪsɪti/ *n.* shamelessness, immodesty. [French *impudicité* from Latin *impudicus* (as IMPUDENT)]

impugn /ɪmˈpjuːn/ *v.tr.* challenge or call in question (a statement, action, etc.). □ **impugnable** *adj.* **impugnment** *n.* [Middle English from Latin *impugnare* 'assail' (as IN-[2], *pugnare* 'fight')]

impuissant /ɪmˈpjuːɪs(ə)nt, -ˈpwɪs-/ *adj.* impotent, weak. □ **impuissance** *n.* [French (as IN-[1], PUISSANT)]

impulse /ˈɪmpʌls/ *n.* **1** the act or an instance of impelling; a push. **2** an impetus. **3** *Physics* **a** an indefinitely large force acting for a very short time but producing a finite change of momentum (e.g. the blow of a hammer). **b** the change of momentum produced by this or any force. **4** a wave of excitation in a nerve. **5** mental incitement. **6** a sudden desire or tendency to act without reflection (*did it on impulse*). [Latin *impulsus* (as IMPEL)]

impulse buying *n.* the unpremeditated buying of goods as a result of a whim or impulse.

impulsion /ɪmˈpʌlʃ(ə)n/ *n.* **1** the act or an instance of impelling. **2** a mental impulse. **3** impetus. [Middle English via Old French from Latin *impulsio -onis* (as IMPEL)]

impulsive /ɪmˈpʌlsɪv/ *adj.* **1** (of a person or conduct etc.) apt to be affected or determined by sudden impulse. **2** tending to impel. **3** *Physics* acting as an impulse. □ **impulsively** *adv.* **impulsiveness** *n.* [Middle English from French *impulsif -ive* or Late Latin *impulsivus* (as IMPULSION)]

impunity /ɪmˈpjuːnɪti/ *n.* exemption from punishment or from the injurious consequences of an action. □ **with impunity** without having to suffer the normal injurious consequences (of an action). [Latin *impunitas* from *impunis* (as IN-[1], *poena* 'penalty')]

impure /ɪmˈpjʊə/ *adj.* **1** mixed with foreign matter; adulterated. **2** dirty. **3** unchaste. **4** (of a colour) mixed with another colour. □ **impurely** *adv.* **impureness** *n.* [Middle English from Latin *impurus* (as IN-[1], *purus* 'pure')]

impurity /ɪmˈpjʊərɪti/ *n.* (*pl.* **-ies**) **1** the quality or condition of being impure. **2 a** a thing or constituent which impairs the purity of something. **b** *Electronics* a trace element deliberately added to a semiconductor, a dopant. [French *impurité* or Latin *impuritas* (as IMPURE)]

impute /ɪmˈpjuːt/ *v.tr.* (foll. by *to*) **1** regard (esp. something undesirable) as being done or caused or possessed by. **2** *Theol.* ascribe (righteousness, guilt, etc.) to (a person) by virtue of a similar quality in another. □ **imputable** *adj.* **imputation** /-ˈteɪʃ(ə)n/ *n.* **imputative** /-tətɪv/ *adj.* [Middle English via Old French *imputer* from Latin *imputare* 'enter in the account' (as IN-[2], *putare* 'reckon')]

I.Mun.E. *abbr.* (in the UK) Institution of Municipal Engineers.

IN *abbr. US* Indiana (in official postal use).

In *symb. Chem.* the element indium.

in /ɪn/ *prep., adv., & adj.* ● *prep.* **1** expressing inclusion or position within limits of space, time, circumstance, etc. (*in England*; *in bed*; *in the rain*). **2** during the time of (*in the night*; *in 1989*). **3** within the time of (*will be back in two hours*). **4 a** with respect to (*blind in one eye*; *good in parts*). **b** as a kind of (*the latest thing in luxury*). **5** as a proportionate part of (*one in three failed*; *a gradient of one in six*). **6** with the form or arrangement of (*packed in tens*; *falling in folds*). **7** as a member of (*in the army*). **8** concerned with (*is in politics*). **9** as or regarding the content of (*there is something in what you say*). **10** within the ability of (*does he have it in him?*). **11** having the condition of; affected by (*in bad health*; *in danger*). **12** having as a purpose (*in search of*; *in reply to*). **13** by means of or using as material (*drawn in pencil*; *modelled in bronze*). **14 a** using as the language of expression (*written in French*). **b** (of music) having as its key (*symphony in C*). **15** (of a word) having as a beginning or ending (*words in un-*). **16** wearing as dress (*in blue*; *in a suit*). **17** with the identity of (*found a friend in Mary*). **18** (of an animal) pregnant with (*in calf*). **19** into (with a verb of motion or change: *put it in the box*; *cut it in two*). **20** introducing an indirect object after a verb (*believe in*; *engage in*; *share in*). **21** forming adverbial phrases (*in any case*; *in reality*; *in short*). ● *adv.* expressing position within limits, or motion to such a position: **1** into a room, house, etc. (*come in*). **2** at home, in one's office, etc. (*is not in*). **3** so as to be enclosed or confined (*locked in*). **4** in a publication (*is the advertisement in?*). **5** in or to the inward side (*rub it in*). **6 a** in fashion, season, or office (*long skirts are in*; *strawberries are not yet in*). **b** elected (*the Democrat got in*). **7** exerting favourable action or influence (*their luck was in*). **8** *Sport* **a** (of a shot, serve, etc.) within the boundary of the playing area. **b** *Cricket* (of a player or side) batting. **9** (of transport) at the platform etc. (*the train is in*). **10** (of a season, harvest, order, etc.) having arrived or been received. **11** *Brit.* (of a fire) continuing to burn. **12** denoting effective action (*join in*). **13** (of the tide) at the highest point. **14** (in *comb.*) *colloq.* denoting prolonged or concerted action, esp. by large numbers (*sit-in*; *teach-in*). ● *adj.* **1** internal; living in; inside (*in-patient*). **2** fashionable, esoteric (*the in thing to do*). **3** confined to or shared by a group of people (*in-joke*). □ **in all** see ALL. **in at** present at; contributing to (*in at the kill*). **in between** see BETWEEN *adv.* **in for 1** about to undergo (esp. something unpleasant). **2** competing in or for. **3** involved in; committed to. **in on** sharing in; privy to (a secret etc.). **ins and outs** (often foll. by *of*) all the details (of a procedure etc.). **in so far as** see FAR. **in that** because; in so far as. **in with** on good terms with. [Old English *in*, *inn*, originally as adv. with verbs of motion]

in. *abbr.* inch(es).

in-[1] /ɪn/ *prefix* (also **il-** before *l*, **im-** before *b*, *m*, *p*, **ir-** before *r*) added to: **1** adjectives, meaning 'not' (*inedible*; *insane*). **2** nouns, meaning 'without, lacking' (*inaction*). [Latin]

in-[2] /ɪn/ *prefix* (also **il-** before *l*, **im-** before *b*, *m*, *p*, **ir-** before *r*) in, on, into, towards, within (*induce*; *influx*; *insight*; *intrude*). [IN, or from or suggested by Latin *in* IN *prep.*]

-in /ɪn/ *suffix Chem.* forming names of organic compounds, pharmaceutical products, proteins, etc. (*dioxin*; *fibrin*; *gelatin*; *penicillin*). [-INE[4]]

-ina /ˈiːnə/ *suffix* denoting: **1** feminine names and titles (*Georgina*; *tsarina*). **2** names of musical instruments (*concertina*). **3** names of zoological classification categories (*globigerina*). [Italian, Spanish, or Latin]

inability /mə'bɪlɪti/ *n.* **1** the state of being unable. **2** a lack of power or means.

in absentia /ˌɪn ab'sɛntɪə/ *adv.* in (his, her, or their) absence. [Latin]

inaccessible /mək'sɛsɪb(ə)l/ *adj.* **1** not accessible; that cannot be reached. **2** (of a person) not open to advances or influence; unapproachable. ◻ **inaccessibility** /-'bɪlɪti/ *n.* **inaccessibly** *adv.* [Middle English from French *inaccessible* or Late Latin *inaccessibilis* (as IN-[1], ACCESSIBLE)]

inaccurate /ɪn'akjʊrət/ *adj.* not accurate. ◻ **inaccuracy** *n.* (*pl.* **-ies**). **inaccurately** *adv.*

inaction /ɪn'akʃ(ə)n/ *n.* **1** lack of action. **2** sluggishness, inertness.

inactivate /ɪn'aktɪveɪt/ *v.tr.* make inactive or inoperative. ◻ **inactivation** /-'veɪʃ(ə)n/ *n.*

inactive /ɪn'aktɪv/ *adj.* **1** not active or inclined to act. **2** passive. **3** indolent. ◻ **inactively** *adv.* **inactivity** /-'tɪvɪti/ *n.*

inadequate /ɪn'adɪkwət/ *adj.* (often foll. by *to*) **1** not adequate; insufficient. **2** (of a person) incompetent; unable to deal with a situation. ◻ **inadequacy** *n.* (*pl.* **-ies**). **inadequately** *adv.*

inadmissible /məd'mɪsɪb(ə)l/ *adj.* that cannot be admitted or allowed. ◻ **inadmissibility** /-'bɪlɪti/ *n.* **inadmissibly** *adv.*

inadvertent /məd'vɜ:t(ə)nt/ *adj.* **1** (of an action) unintentional. **2 a** not properly attentive. **b** negligent. ◻ **inadvertence** *n.* **inadvertency** *n.* **inadvertently** *adv.* [IN-[1] + obsolete *advertent* 'attentive' (as ADVERT[2])]

inadvisable /məd'vʌɪzəb(ə)l/ *adj.* not advisable. ◻ **inadvisability** /-'bɪlɪti/ *n.*

inalienable /ɪn'eɪlɪənəb(ə)l/ *adj.* that cannot be transferred to another; not alienable. ◻ **inalienability** /-'bɪlɪti/ *n.* **inalienably** *adv.*

inalterable /ɪn'ɔ:lt(ə)rəb(ə)l, -'ɒl-/ *adj.* not alterable; that cannot be changed. ◻ **inalterability** /-'bɪlɪti/ *n.* **inalterably** *adv.* [medieval Latin *inalterabilis* (as IN-[1], *alterabilis* 'alterable')]

inamorato /ɪˌnamə'rɑ:təʊ/ *n.* (*pl.* **-os**; *fem.* **inamorata** /-tə/) a lover. [Italian, past part. of *inamorare* 'enamour' (as IN-[2], *amore* from Latin *amor* 'love')]

inane /ɪ'neɪn/ *adj.* **1** silly, senseless. **2** empty, void. ◻ **inanely** *adv.* **inaneness** *n.* **inanity** /-'anɪti/ *n.* (*pl.* **-ies**). [Latin *inanis* 'empty, vain']

inanimate /ɪn'anɪmət/ *adj.* **1** not animate; not endowed with (esp. animal) life. **2** lifeless; showing no sign of life. **3** spiritless, dull. ◻ **inanimately** *adv.* **inanimation** /-'meɪʃ(ə)n/ *n.* [Late Latin *inanimatus* (as IN-[1], ANIMATE)]

inanimate nature *n.* everything other than the animal world.

inanition /ɪnə'nɪʃ(ə)n/ *n.* emptiness, esp. exhaustion from lack of nourishment. [Middle English via Late Latin *inanitio* from Latin *inanire* 'make empty' (as INANE)]

inappellable /ɪnə'pɛləb(ə)l/ *adj.* that cannot be appealed against. [obsolete French *inappelable* (as IN-[1], *appeler* APPEAL)]

inapplicable /ɪn'aplɪkəb(ə)l, ɪnə'plɪk-/ *adj.* (often foll. by *to*) not applicable; unsuitable. ◻ **inapplicability** /-'bɪlɪti/ *n.* **inapplicably** *adv.*

inapposite /ɪn'apəzɪt/ *adj.* not apposite; out of place. ◻ **inappositely** *adv.* **inappositeness** *n.*

inappreciable /ɪnə'pri:ʃəb(ə)l, -ʃɪə-/ *adj.* **1** imperceptible; not worth reckoning. **2** that cannot be appreciated. ◻ **inappreciably** *adv.*

inappreciation /ˌɪnəpri:ʃɪ'eɪʃ(ə)n, -sɪ-/ *n.* failure to appreciate. ◻ **inappreciative** /-'pri:ʃ(ɪ)ətɪv/ *adj.*

inappropriate /ɪnə'prəʊprɪət/ *adj.* not appropriate. ◻ **inappropriately** *adv.* **inappropriateness** *n.*

inapt /ɪn'apt/ *adj.* **1** not apt or suitable. **2** unskilful. ◻ **inaptitude** *n.* **inaptly** *adv.*

■ **Usage** See Usage Note at INEPT.

inarch /ɪn'ɑ:tʃ/ *v.tr.* graft (a plant) by connecting a growing branch without separation from the parent stock. [IN-[2] + ARCH[1] *v.*]

inarguable /ɪn'ɑ:gjʊəb(ə)l/ *adj.* that cannot be argued about or disputed. ◻ **inarguably** *adv.*

inarticulate /ɪnɑ:'tɪkjʊlət/ *adj.* **1** unable to speak distinctly or express oneself clearly. **2** (of speech) not articulate; indistinctly pronounced. **3** dumb. **4** esp. *Anat.* not jointed. ◻ **inarticulacy** *n.* **inarticulately** *adv.* **inarticulateness** *n.* [Late Latin *inarticulatus* (as IN-[1], ARTICULATE)]

inartistic /ɪnɑ:'tɪstɪk/ *adj.* **1** not following the principles of art. **2** lacking skill or talent in art; not appreciating art. ◻ **inartistically** *adv.*

inasmuch /ɪnəz'mʌtʃ/ *adv.* (foll. by *as*) **1** since, because. **2** to the extent that. [Middle English, originally *in as much*]

inattentive /ɪnə'tɛntɪv/ *adj.* **1** not paying due attention; heedless. **2** neglecting to show courtesy. ◻ **inattention** *n.* **inattentively** *adv.* **inattentiveness** *n.*

inaudible /ɪn'ɔ:dɪb(ə)l/ *adj.* that cannot be heard. ◻ **inaudibility** /-'bɪlɪti/ *n.* **inaudibly** *adv.*

inaugural /ɪ'nɔ:gjʊr(ə)l/ *adj.* & *n.* ● *adj.* **1** of inauguration. **2** (of a lecture etc.) given by a person being inaugurated. ● *n.* an inaugural speech etc. [French from *inaugurer* (as INAUGURATE)]

inaugurate /ɪ'nɔ:gjʊreɪt/ *v.tr.* **1** admit (a person) formally to office. **2** initiate the public use of (a building etc.). **3** begin, introduce. **4** enter with ceremony upon (an undertaking etc.). ◻ **inauguration** /-'reɪʃ(ə)n/ *n.* **inaugurator** *n.* **inauguratory** *adj.* [Latin *inaugurare* (as IN-[2], *augurare* 'take omens': see AUGUR)]

inauspicious /ɪnɔ:'spɪʃəs/ *adj.* **1** ill-omened, unpropitious. **2** unlucky. ◻ **inauspiciously** *adv.* **inauspiciousness** *n.*

inauthentic /ɪnɔ:'θɛntɪk/ *n.* not authentic; not genuine. ◻ **inauthenticity** /-'tɪsɪti/ *n.*

in-between *attrib.adj. colloq.* intermediate (*at an in-between stage*).

inboard /'ɪnbɔ:d/ *adv.* & *adj.* ● *adv.* within the sides of or towards the centre of a ship, aircraft, or vehicle. ● *adj.* situated inboard.

inborn /'ɪnbɔ:n, ɪn'bɔ:n/ *adj.* existing from birth; implanted by nature.

inbreathe /ɪn'bri:ð/ *v.tr.* **1** breathe in or absorb. **2** inspire (a person).

inbred /ɪn'brɛd, 'ɪnbrɛd/ *adj.* **1** inborn. **2** produced by inbreeding.

inbreeding /'ɪnbri:dɪŋ/ *n.* breeding from closely related animals or persons. ◻ **inbreed** *v.tr.* & *intr.* (*past* and *past part.* **inbred**).

inbuilt /'ɪnbɪlt/ *adj.* incorporated as part of a structure.

Inc. /ɪŋk/ *abbr. N. Amer.* Incorporated.

Inca /'ɪŋkə/ *n.* a member of an American Indian people in Peru before the Spanish conquest. ◻ **Incaic** /ɪŋ'keɪɪk/ *adj.* **Incan** *adj.* [Quechua, = lord, royal person]

incalculable /ɪn'kalkjʊləb(ə)l/ *adj.* **1** too great for calculation. **2** that cannot be reckoned beforehand. **3** (of a person, character, etc.) uncertain. ◻ **incalculability** /-'bɪlɪti/ *n.* **incalculably** *adv.*

in camera see CAMERA.

incandesce /ɪnkan'dɛs/ *v.intr.* & *tr.* glow or cause to glow with heat. [back-formation from INCANDESCENT]

incandescent /ɪnkan'dɛs(ə)nt/ *adj.* **1** glowing with heat. **2** shining brightly. **3** (of an electric or other light) produced by a glowing white-hot filament. ◻ **incandescence** *n.* **incandescently** *adv.* [French from Latin *incandescere* (as IN-[2], *candescere*, inceptive of *candēre* 'be white')]

incantation /ɪnkan'teɪʃ(ə)n/ *n.* **1 a** a magical formula. **b** the use of this. **2** a spell or charm. ◻ **incantational** *adj.* **incantatory** *adj.* [Middle English via Old French from Late Latin *incantatio -onis*, from *incantare* 'chant, bewitch' (as IN-[2], *cantare* 'sing')]

incapable /ɪn'keɪpəb(ə)l/ *adj.* **1** (often foll. by *of*) **a** not capable. **b** lacking the required quality or characteristic (favourable or adverse) (*incapable of hurting anyone*). **2** not capable of rational conduct or of managing one's own affairs (*drunk and incapable*). ▫ **incapability** /-'bılıti/ *n.* **incapably** *adv.* [French *incapable* or Late Latin *incapabilis* (as IN-[1], *capabilis* CAPABLE)]

incapacitate /ınkə'pasıteıt/ *v.tr.* **1** render incapable or unfit. **2** disqualify. ▫ **incapacitant** *n.* **incapacitation** /-'teıʃ(ə)n/ *n.*

incapacity /ınkə'pasıti/ *n.* (*pl.* **-ies**) **1** inability; lack of the necessary power or resources. **2** legal disqualification. **3** an instance of incapacity. [French *incapacité* or Late Latin *incapacitas* (as IN-[1], CAPACITY)]

in-car *attrib.adj.* occurring, situated, or carried in a car.

incarcerate /ın'kɑːsəreıt/ *v.tr.* imprison or confine. ▫ **incarceration** /-'reıʃ(ə)n/ *n.* **incarcerator** *n.* [medieval Latin *incarcerare* (as IN-[2], Latin *carcer* 'prison')]

incarnadine /ın'kɑːnədʌın/ *n., adj., & v. poet.* ● *n.* flesh colour; crimson. ● *adj.* flesh-coloured; crimson. ● *v.tr.* dye incarnadine. [French *incarnadin -ine* from Italian *incarnadino* (for *-tino*), from *incarnato* INCARNATE *adj.*]

incarnate *adj. & v.* ● *adj.* /ın'kɑːnət/ **1** (of a person, spirit, quality, etc.) embodied in flesh, esp. in human form (*the devil incarnate*). **2** represented in a recognizable or typical form (*folly incarnate*). ● *v.tr.* /'ınkɑːneıt, -'kɑːneıt/ **1** embody in flesh. **2** put (an idea etc.) into concrete form; realize. **3** (of a person etc.) be the living embodiment of (a quality). [Middle English from ecclesiastical Latin *incarnare incarnat-* 'make flesh' (as IN-[2], Latin *caro carnis* 'flesh')]

incarnation /ınkɑː'neıʃ(ə)n/ *n.* **1 a** embodiment in (esp. human) flesh. **b** (**the Incarnation**) (in Christian theology) the embodiment of God the Son in human flesh as Jesus Christ. **2** (often foll. by *of*) a living type (of a quality etc.). **3** *Med.* the process of forming new flesh. [Middle English via Old French from ecclesiastical Latin *incarnatio -onis* (as INCARNATE)]

incase var. of ENCASE.

incautious /ın'kɔːʃəs/ *adj.* heedless, rash. ▫ **incaution** *n.* **incautiously** *adv.* **incautiousness** *n.*

incendiary /ın'sɛndjəri/ *adj. & n.* ● *adj.* **1** (of a substance or device, esp. a bomb) designed to cause fires. **2 a** of or relating to the malicious setting on fire of property. **b** guilty of this. **3** tending to stir up strife; inflammatory. ● *n.* (*pl.* **-ies**) **1** an incendiary bomb or device. **2** an incendiary person. ▫ **incendiarism** *n.* [Middle English from Latin *incendiarius*, via *incendium* 'conflagration' from *incendere incens-* 'set fire to']

incense[1] /'ınsɛns/ *n. & v.* ● *n.* **1** a gum or spice producing a sweet smell when burned. **2** the smoke of this, esp. in religious ceremonial. ● *v.tr.* **1** treat or perfume (a person or thing) with incense. **2** burn incense to (a deity etc.). **3** suffuse with fragrance. ▫ **incensation** /-'seıʃ(ə)n/ *n.* [Middle English via Old French *encens*, *encenser* from ecclesiastical Latin *incensum* 'a thing burnt, incense': see INCENDIARY]

incense[2] /ın'sɛns/ *v.tr.* (often foll. by *at, with, against*) enrage; make angry. [Middle English from Old French *incenser* (as INCENDIARY)]

incensory /'ınsɛns(ə)ri/ *n.* (*pl.* **-ies**) = CENSER. [medieval Latin *incensorium* (as INCENSE[1])]

incentive /ın'sɛntıv/ *n. & adj.* ● *n.* **1** (often foll. by *to*) a motive or incitement, esp. to action. **2** a payment or concession to stimulate greater output by workers. ● *adj.* serving to motivate or incite. [Middle English from Latin *incentivus* 'setting the tune', from *incinere incent-* 'sing to' (as IN-[2], *canere* 'sing')]

incept /ın'sɛpt/ *v.* **1** *tr. Biol.* (of an organism) digest (food). **2** *intr. Brit. hist.* take a master's or doctor's degree at a university. ▫ **inceptor** *n.* (in sense 2). [Latin *incipere incept-* 'begin' (as IN-[2], *capere* 'take')]

inception /ın'sɛpʃ(ə)n/ *n.* a beginning. [Middle English from Old French *inception* or Latin *inceptio* (as INCEPT)]

inceptive /ın'sɛptıv/ *adj. & n.* ● *adj.* **1 a** beginning. **b** initial. **2** *Gram.* (of a verb) that denotes the beginning of an action. ● *n.* an inceptive verb. [Late Latin *inceptivus* (as INCEPT)]

incertitude /ın'səːtıtjuːd/ *n.* uncertainty, doubt. [French *incertitude* or Late Latin *incertitudo* (as IN-[1], CERTITUDE)]

incessant /ın'sɛs(ə)nt/ *adj.* unceasing, continual, repeated. ▫ **incessancy** *n.* **incessantly** *adv.* **incessantness** *n.* [French *incessant* or Late Latin *incessans* (as IN-[1], *cessans*, pres. part. of Latin *cessare* CEASE)]

incest /'ınsɛst/ *n.* sexual intercourse between persons regarded as too closely related to marry each other. [Middle English from Latin *incestus* (as IN-[1], *castus* CHASTE)]

incestuous /ın'sɛstjʊəs/ *adj.* **1** involving or guilty of incest. **2** (of human relations generally) excessively restricted or resistant to wider influence. ▫ **incestuously** *adv.* **incestuousness** *n.* [Late Latin *incestuosus* (as INCEST)]

inch[1] /ın(t)ʃ/ *n. & v.* ● *n.* **1** a unit of linear measure equal to one-twelfth of a foot (2.54 cm). **2 a** (as a unit of rainfall) a quantity that would cover a horizontal surface to a depth of 1 inch. **b** (of atmospheric or other pressure) an amount that balances the weight of a column of mercury 1 inch high. **3** (as a unit of map-scale) so many inches representing 1 mile on the ground. **4** a small amount (usu. with *neg.*: *would not yield an inch*). ● *v.tr. & intr.* move gradually in a specified way (*inched forward*). ▫ **every inch 1** entirely (*looked every inch a queen*). **2** the whole distance or area (*combed every inch of the garden*). **give a person an inch and he** or **she will take a mile** (or originally **an ell**) a person once conceded to will demand much. **inch by inch** gradually; bit by bit. **within an inch of** almost to the point of. [Old English *ynce* from Latin *uncia* 'twelfth part': cf. OUNCE[1]]

inch[2] /ın(t)ʃ/ *n.* esp. *Sc.* a small island (esp. in place names). [Middle English from Gaelic *innis*]

-in-chief *comb. form* (as second element) supreme (*commander-in-chief*).

inchoate *adj. & v.* ● *adj.* /ın'kəʊeıt, 'ınk-, -ət/ **1** just begun. **2** undeveloped, rudimentary, unformed. ● *v.tr.* /'ınkəʊeıt/ begin; originate. ▫ **inchoately** *adv.* **inchoateness** *n.* **inchoative** /-'kəʊətıv/ *adj.* [Latin *inchoatus*, past part. of *inchoare* (as IN-[2], *choare* 'begin')]

▪ **Usage** *Inchoate*, meaning 'just begun' or 'undeveloped', should not be confused with *incoherent* or *chaotic*, although all these words can often be found in similar contexts. *Inchoate scribbles* thus means 'undeveloped' rather than 'incoherent' pieces of writing.

inchworm /'ın(t)ʃwəːm/ *n.* = MEASURING WORM.

incidence /'ınsıd(ə)ns/ *n.* **1** (often foll. by *of*) the fact, manner, or rate, of occurrence or action. **2** the range, scope, or extent of influence of a thing. **3** *Physics* the falling of a line, or of a thing moving in a line, upon a surface. **4** the act or an instance of coming into contact with a thing. ▫ **angle of incidence** the angle which an incident line, ray, etc., makes with the perpendicular to the surface at the point of incidence. [Middle English from Old French *incidence* or medieval Latin *incidentia* (as INCIDENT)]

incident /'ınsıd(ə)nt/ *n. & adj.* ● *n.* **1 a** an event or occurrence. **b** a minor or detached event attracting general attention or noteworthy in some way. **2** a hostile clash, esp. of troops of countries at war (*a frontier incident*). **3** a distinct piece of action in a play or a poem. **4** *Law* a privilege, burden, etc., attaching to an obligation or right. ● *adj.* **1 a** (often foll. by *to*) apt or liable to happen; naturally attaching or dependent. **b** (foll. by *to*) *Law* attaching to. **2** (often foll. by *on, upon*) (of light etc.) falling or striking. [Middle English from French *incident* or Latin *incidere* (as IN-[2], *cadere* 'fall')]

incidental /ınsı'dɛnt(ə)l/ *adj. & n.* ● *adj.* **1** (often foll. by *to*) **a** having a minor role in relation to a more important thing, event, etc. **b** not essential. **2** (foll. by *to*) liable to happen. **3** (foll. by *on, upon*) following as a subordinate event. ● *n.* (usu. in *pl.*) a minor detail, expense, event, etc.

incidentally /ɪnsɪˈdɛnt(ə)li/ *adv.* **1** by the way; as an unconnected remark. **2** in an incidental way.

incidental music *n.* music used as a background to the action of a film, broadcast, etc.

incinerate /ɪnˈsɪnəreɪt/ *v.tr.* **1** consume (a body etc.) by fire. **2** reduce to ashes. ▫ **incineration** /-ˈreɪʃ(ə)n/ *n.* [medieval Latin *incinerare* (as IN-², *cinis -eris* 'ashes')]

incinerator /ɪnˈsɪnəreɪtə/ *n.* a furnace or apparatus for burning esp. refuse to ashes.

incipient /ɪnˈsɪpɪənt/ *adj.* **1** beginning. **2** in an initial stage. ▫ **incipience** *n.* **incipiency** *n.* **incipiently** *adv.* [Latin *incipere incipient-* (as INCEPT)]

incise /ɪnˈsʌɪz/ *v.tr.* **1** make a cut in. **2** engrave. [French *inciser* from Latin *incidere incis-* (as IN-², *caedere* 'cut')]

incision /ɪnˈsɪʒ(ə)n/ *n.* **1** a cut; a division produced by cutting; a notch. **2** the act of cutting into a thing. [Middle English from Old French *incision* or Late Latin *incisio* (as INCISE)]

incisive /ɪnˈsʌɪsɪv/ *adj.* **1** mentally sharp; acute. **2** clear and effective. **3** cutting, penetrating. ▫ **incisively** *adv.* **incisiveness** *n.* [medieval Latin *incisivus* (as INCISE)]

incisor /ɪnˈsʌɪzə/ *n.* a narrow-edged tooth at the front of the mouth, adapted for cutting. [medieval Latin, = cutter (as INCISE)]

incite /ɪnˈsʌɪt/ *v.tr.* (often foll. by *to* or *to* + infin.) urge or stir up. ▫ **incitation** /-ˈteɪʃ(ə)n/ *n.* **incitement** *n.* **inciter** *n.* [Middle English via French *inciter* from Latin *incitare* (as IN-², *citare* 'rouse')]

incivility /ɪnsɪˈvɪlɪti/ *n.* (*pl.* **-ies**) **1** rudeness, discourtesy. **2** a rude or discourteous act. [French *incivilité* or Late Latin *incivilitas* (as IN-¹, CIVILITY)]

incl. *abbr.* including.

inclement /ɪnˈklɛm(ə)nt/ *adj.* (of the weather or climate) severe, esp. cold or stormy. ▫ **inclemency** *n.* (*pl.* **-ies**). **inclemently** *adv.* [French *inclément* or Latin *inclemens* (as IN-¹, CLEMENT)]

inclination /ɪnklɪˈneɪʃ(ə)n/ *n.* **1** (often foll. by *to*) a disposition or propensity. **2** (often foll. by *for*) a liking or affection. **3 a** a leaning, slope, or slant. **b** a bending of the body or head in a bow. **4** the difference of direction of two lines or planes, esp. as measured by the angle between them. **5** the dip of a magnetic needle. [Middle English from Old French *inclination* or Latin *inclinatio* (as INCLINE)]

incline *v.* & *n.* ● *v.* /ɪnˈklʌɪn/ **1** *tr.* (usu. in *passive*; often foll. by *to, for,* or *to* + infin.) **a** make (a person, feelings, etc.) willing or favourably disposed (*am inclined to think so*; *does not incline me to agree*). **b** give a specified tendency to (a thing) (*the door is inclined to bang*). **2** *intr.* **a** be disposed (*I incline to think so*). **b** (often foll. by *to, towards*) tend. **3** *intr.* & *tr.* lean or turn away from a given direction, esp. the vertical. **4** *tr.* bend (the head, body, or oneself) forward or downward. ● *n.* /ˈɪnklʌɪn/ **1** a slope. **2** an inclined plane. ▫ **incline one's ear** (often foll. by *to*) listen favourably. ▫ **incliner** *n.* [Middle English *encline* via Old French *encliner* from Latin *inclinare* (as IN-², *clinare* 'bend')]

inclined plane *n.* a sloping plane (esp. as a means of reducing the force needed to raise a load).

inclinometer /ɪnklɪˈnɒmɪtə/ *n.* **1** an instrument for measuring the angle between the direction of the earth's magnetic field and the horizontal. **2** an instrument for measuring the inclination of an aircraft or ship to the horizontal. **3** an instrument for measuring a slope. [Latin *inclinare* INCLINE *v.* + -METER]

inclose var. of ENCLOSE.

inclosure var. of ENCLOSURE.

include /ɪnˈkluːd/ *v.tr.* **1** comprise or reckon in as part of a whole. **2** (as **including** *prep.*) counting in the reckoning (*six members, including the chairman*). **3** treat or regard as so included. **4** (as **included** *adj.*) shut in; enclosed. ▫ **include out** *colloq.* or *joc.* specifically exclude. [Middle English from Latin *includere inclus-* (as IN-², *claudere* 'shut')]

inclusion /ɪnˈkluːʒ(ə)n/ *n.* **1** the act of including something. **2 a** the condition of being included. **b** an instance of this. **3** a thing which is included. **4** a body or particle distinct from the substance in which it is embedded.

inclusive /ɪnˈkluːsɪv/ *adj.* **1** (foll. by *of*) including, comprising. **2** with the inclusion of the extreme limits stated (*pages 7 to 26 inclusive*). **3** including all the normal services etc. (*a hotel offering inclusive terms*). **4 a** not excluding any section of society. **b** (of language) deliberately non-sexist, esp. avoiding the use of masculine pronouns to cover both men and women. ▫ **inclusively** *adv.* **inclusiveness** *n.* [medieval Latin *inclusivus* (as INCLUDE)]

incog /ɪnˈkɒg/ *adj., adv.,* & *n. colloq.* = INCOGNITO. [abbreviation]

incognito /ɪnkɒgˈniːtəʊ, ɪnˈkɒgnɪtəʊ/ *adj., adv.,* & *n.* ● *adj.* & *adv.* with one's name or identity kept secret (*was travelling incognito*). ● *n.* (*pl.* **-os**) **1** a person who is incognito. **2** the pretended identity or anonymous character of such a person. [Italian, = unknown, from Latin *incognitus* (as IN-¹, *cognitus,* past part. of *cognoscere* 'know')]

incognizant /ɪnˈkɒ(g)nɪz(ə)nt/ *adj.* (also **incognisant**) (foll. by *of*) unaware; not knowing. ▫ **incognizance** *n.*

incoherent /ɪnkə(ʊ)ˈhɪər(ə)nt/ *adj.* **1** (of a person) unable to speak intelligibly. **2** (of speech etc.) lacking logic or consistency. **3** *Physics* (of waves) having no definite or stable phase relationship. ▫ **incoherence** *n.* **incoherency** *n.* (*pl.* **-ies**). **incoherently** *adv.*

incombustible /ɪnkəmˈbʌstɪb(ə)l/ *adj.* that cannot be burnt or consumed by fire. ▫ **incombustibility** /-ˈbɪlɪti/ *n.* [Middle English from medieval Latin *incombustibilis* (as IN-¹, COMBUSTIBLE)]

income /ˈɪnkʌm/ *n.* the money or other assets received, esp. periodically or in a year, from one's business, lands, work, investments, etc. [originally = arrival: Middle English, probably from Old Norse *innkoma*: in later use from *come in*]

income group *n.* a section of the population determined by income.

incomer /ˈɪnkʌmə/ *n.* **1** a person who comes in. **2** esp. *Brit.* a person who arrives to settle in a place; an immigrant. **3** an intruder. **4** a successor.

-incomer /ˈɪnkʌmə/ *comb. form Brit.* earning a specified kind or level of income (*middle-incomer*).

income support *n.* a system by which people on low incomes can, according to their circumstances, claim a payment from the state.

income tax *n.* a tax levied on income.

incoming /ˈɪnkʌmɪŋ/ *adj.* & *n.* ● *adj.* **1** coming in (*the incoming tide*; *incoming telephone calls*). **2** succeeding another person or persons (*the incoming tenant*). **3** *Brit.* immigrant. **4** (of profit) accruing. ● *n.* **1** (usu. in *pl.*) revenue, income. **2** the act of arriving or entering.

incommensurable /ɪnkəˈmɛnʃ(ə)rəb(ə)l, -sjə-/ *adj.* & *n.* ● *adj.* **1** having no common standard of measurement; not comparable in respect of magnitude or value. **2** (foll. by *with*) not worthy of being compared with; utterly disproportionate to. **3** *Math.* **a** (often foll. by *with*) (of a magnitude or magnitudes) having no common factor, integral or fractional. **b** irrational. ● *n.* (usu. in *pl.*) an incommensurable quantity. ▫ **incommensurability** /-ˈbɪlɪti/ *n.* **incommensurably** *adv.* [Late Latin *incommensurabilis* (as IN-¹, COMMENSURABLE)]

incommensurate /ɪnkəˈmɛnʃ(ə)rət, -sjə-/ *adj.* **1** (often foll. by *with, to*) out of proportion; inadequate. **2** = INCOMMENSURABLE *adj.* 1. ▫ **incommensurately** *adv.* **incommensurateness** *n.*

incommode /ɪnkəˈməʊd/ *v.tr.* **1** hinder, inconvenience. **2** trouble, annoy. [French *incommoder* or Latin *incommodare* (as IN-¹, *commodus* 'convenient')]

incommodious /ɪnkəˈməʊdɪəs/ *adj.* not affording good accommodation; uncomfortable. ▫ **incommodiously** *adv.* **incommodiousness** *n.*

incommunicable /ɪnkəˈmjuːnɪkəb(ə)l/ *adj.* **1** that cannot be communicated or shared. **2** that cannot be uttered or told. **3** that does not communicate; uncommunicative. □ **incommunicability** /-ˈbɪlɪti/ *n.* **incommunicableness** *n.* **incommunicably** *adv.* [Late Latin *incommunicabilis* (as IN-[1], COMMUNICABLE)]

incommunicado /ˌɪnkəmjuːnɪˈkɑːdəʊ/ *adj.* **1** without or deprived of the means of communication with others. **2** (of a prisoner) in solitary confinement. [Spanish *incomunicado*, past part. of *incomunicar* 'deprive of communication']

incommunicative /ɪnkəˈmjuːnɪkətɪv/ *adj.* not communicative; taciturn. □ **incommunicatively** *adv.* **incommunicativeness** *n.*

incommutable /ɪnkəˈmjuːtəb(ə)l/ *adj.* **1** not changeable. **2** not commutable. □ **incommutably** *adv.* [Middle English from Latin *incommutabilis* (as IN-[1], COMMUTABLE)]

incomparable /ɪnˈkɒmp(ə)rəb(ə)l/ *adj.* **1** without an equal; matchless. **2** (often foll. by *with, to*) not to be compared. □ **incomparability** /-ˈbɪlɪti/ *n.* **incomparably** *adv.* [Middle English via Old French from Latin *incomparabilis* (as IN-[1], COMPARABLE)]

incompatible /ɪnkəmˈpatɪb(ə)l/ *adj.* **1** opposed in character; discordant. **2** (often foll. by *with*) inconsistent. **3** (of persons) unable to live, work, etc., together in harmony. **4** (of drugs) not suitable for taking at the same time. **5** (of equipment, machinery, etc.) not capable of being used in combination. □ **incompatibility** /-ˈbɪlɪti/ *n.* **incompatibleness** *n.* **incompatibly** *adv.* [medieval Latin *incompatibilis* (as IN-[1], COMPATIBLE)]

incompetent /ɪnˈkɒmpɪt(ə)nt/ *adj.* & *n.* ● *adj.* **1 a** (often foll. by *to* + infin.) not qualified or able to perform a particular task or function (*an incompetent builder*). **b** (of a witness, evidence, etc.) not legally qualified or qualifying. **2** showing a lack of skill (*an incompetent performance*). **3** *Med.* (esp. of a valve or sphincter) not able to perform its function. ● *n.* an incompetent person. □ **incompetence** *n.* **incompetency** *n.* **incompetently** *adv.* [French *incompétent* or Late Latin *incompetens* (as IN-[1], COMPETENT)]

incomplete /ɪnkəmˈpliːt/ *adj.* not complete. □ **incompletely** *adv.* **incompleteness** *n.* [Middle English from Late Latin *incompletus* (as IN-[1], COMPLETE)]

incomprehensible /ˌɪnkɒmprɪˈhɛnsɪb(ə)l/ *adj.* (often foll. by *to*) that cannot be understood. □ **incomprehensibility** /-ˈbɪlɪti/ *n.* **incomprehensibleness** *n.* **incomprehensibly** *adv.* [Middle English from Latin *incomprehensibilis* (as IN-[1], COMPREHENSIBLE)]

incomprehension /ˌɪnkɒmprɪˈhɛnʃ(ə)n/ *n.* failure to understand.

incompressible /ɪnkəmˈprɛsɪb(ə)l/ *adj.* that cannot be compressed. □ **incompressibility** /-ˈbɪlɪti/ *n.*

inconceivable /ɪnkənˈsiːvəb(ə)l/ *adj.* **1** that cannot be imagined. **2** *colloq.* unbelievable. □ **inconceivability** /-ˈbɪlɪti/ *n.* **inconceivableness** *n.* **inconceivably** *adv.*

inconclusive /ɪnkənˈkluːsɪv/ *adj.* (of an argument, evidence, or action) not decisive or convincing. □ **inconclusively** *adv.* **inconclusiveness** *n.*

incondensable /ɪnkənˈdɛnsəb(ə)l/ *adj.* that cannot be condensed, esp. that cannot be reduced to a liquid or solid condition.

incongruous /ɪnˈkɒŋgrʊəs/ *adj.* **1** out of place; absurd. **2** (often foll. by *with*) disagreeing; out of keeping. □ **incongruity** /-ˈgruːɪti/ *n.* (*pl.* **-ies**). **incongruously** *adv.* **incongruousness** *n.* [Latin *incongruus* (as IN-[1], CONGRUOUS)]

inconsecutive /ɪnkənˈsɛkjʊtɪv/ *adj.* lacking sequence; inconsequent. □ **inconsecutively** *adv.*

inconsequent /ɪnˈkɒnsɪkw(ə)nt/ *adj.* **1** irrelevant. **2** lacking logical sequence. **3** disconnected. □ **inconsequence** *n.* **inconsequently** *adv.* [Latin *inconsequens* (as IN-[1], CONSEQUENT)]

inconsequential /ˌɪnkɒnsɪˈkwɛnʃ(ə)l/ *adj.* **1** unimportant. **2** = INCONSEQUENT. □ **inconsequentiality** /-ʃɪˈalɪti/ *n.* (*pl.* **-ies**). **inconsequentially** *adv.* **inconsequentialness** *n.*

inconsiderable /ɪnkənˈsɪd(ə)rəb(ə)l/ *adj.* **1** of small size, value, etc. **2** not worth considering. [obsolete French *inconsidérable* or Late Latin *inconsiderabilis* (as IN-[1], CONSIDERABLE)]

inconsiderate /ɪnkənˈsɪd(ə)rət/ *adj.* **1** (of a person or action) thoughtless, rash. **2** lacking in regard for the feelings of others. □ **inconsiderately** *adv.* **inconsiderateness** *n.* **inconsideration** /-ˈreɪʃ(ə)n/ *n.* [Latin *inconsideratus* (as IN-[1], CONSIDERATE)]

inconsistent /ɪnkənˈsɪst(ə)nt/ *adj.* **1** acting at variance with one's own principles or former conduct. **2** (often foll. by *with*) not in keeping; discordant, incompatible. **3** (of a single thing) incompatible or discordant; having self-contradictory parts. □ **inconsistency** *n.* (*pl.* **-ies**). **inconsistently** *adv.*

inconsolable /ɪnkənˈsəʊləb(ə)l/ *adj.* (of a person, grief, etc.) that cannot be consoled or comforted. □ **inconsolability** /-ˈbɪlɪti/ *n.* **inconsolably** *adv.* [French *inconsolable* or Latin *inconsolabilis* (as IN-[1], *consolabilis* from *consolari* CONSOLE[1])]

inconsonant /ɪnˈkɒns(ə)nənt/ *adj.* (often foll. by *with, to*) not harmonious; not compatible. □ **inconsonance** *n.* **inconsonantly** *adv.*

inconspicuous /ɪnkənˈspɪkjʊəs/ *adj.* **1** not conspicuous; not easily noticed. **2** *Bot.* (of flowers) small, pale, or green. □ **inconspicuously** *adv.* **inconspicuousness** *n.* [Latin *inconspicuus* (as IN-[1], CONSPICUOUS)]

inconstant /ɪnˈkɒnst(ə)nt/ *adj.* **1** (of a person) fickle, changeable. **2** frequently changing; variable, irregular. □ **inconstancy** *n.* (*pl.* **-ies**). **inconstantly** *adv.* [Middle English via Old French from Latin *inconstans -antis* (as IN-[1], CONSTANT)]

incontestable /ɪnkənˈtɛstəb(ə)l/ *adj.* that cannot be disputed. □ **incontestability** /-ˈbɪlɪti/ *n.* **incontestably** *adv.* [French *incontestable* or medieval Latin *incontestabilis* (as IN-[1], *contestabilis* from Latin *contestari* CONTEST)]

incontinent /ɪnˈkɒntɪnənt/ *adj.* **1** unable to control movements of the bowels or bladder or both. **2** lacking self-restraint (esp. in regard to sexual desire). **3** (foll. by *of*) unable to control. □ **incontinence** *n.* **incontinently** *adv.* [Middle English from Old French or Latin *incontinens* (as IN-[1], CONTINENT[2])]

incontrovertible /ˌɪnkɒntrəˈvəːtɪb(ə)l/ *adj.* indisputable, indubitable. □ **incontrovertibility** /-ˈbɪlɪti/ *n.* **incontrovertibly** *adv.*

inconvenience /ɪnkənˈviːnɪəns/ *n.* & *v.* ● *n.* **1** lack of suitability to personal requirements or ease. **2** a cause or instance of this. ● *v.tr.* cause inconvenience to. [Middle English via Old French from Late Latin *inconvenientia* (as INCONVENIENT)]

inconvenient /ɪnkənˈviːnɪənt/ *adj.* **1** unfavourable to ease or comfort; not convenient. **2** awkward, troublesome. □ **inconveniently** *adv.* [Middle English via Old French from Latin *inconveniens -entis* (as IN-[1], CONVENIENT)]

inconvertible /ɪnkənˈvəːtɪb(ə)l/ *adj.* **1** not convertible. **2** (esp. of currency) not convertible into another form on demand. □ **inconvertibility** /-ˈbɪlɪti/ *n.* **inconvertibly** *adv.* [French *inconvertible* or Late Latin *inconvertibilis* (as IN-[1], CONVERTIBLE)]

incoordination /ˌɪnkəʊɔːdɪˈneɪʃ(ə)n/ *n.* lack of coordination, esp. of muscular action.

incorporate *v.* & *adj.* ● *v.* /ɪnˈkɔːpəreɪt/ **1** *tr.* (often foll. by *in, with*) unite; form into one body or whole. **2** *intr.* become incorporated. **3** *tr.* combine (ingredients) into one substance. **4** *tr.* admit as a member of a company etc. **5** *tr.* **a** constitute as a legal corporation. **b** (as **incorporated** *adj.*) forming a legal corporation. ● *adj.* /ɪnˈkɔːp(ə)rət/ **1** (of a company etc.) formed into a legal corporation. **2** embodied. □ **incorporation** /-ˈreɪʃ(ə)n/ *n.* **incorporator** *n.* [Middle English from Late Latin *incorporare* (as IN-[2], Latin *corpus -oris* 'body')]

incorporeal /ɪnkɔːˈpɔːrɪəl/ *adj.* **1** not composed of matter. **2** of immaterial beings. **3** *Law* having no physical existence. ▫ **incorporeality** /-ˈalɪti/ *n.* **incorporeally** *adv.* **incorporeity** /-pəˈriːɪti, -pəˈreɪɪti/ *n.* [Latin *incorporeus* (as INCORPORATE)]

incorrect /ɪnkəˈrɛkt/ *adj.* **1** not in accordance with fact; wrong. **2** (of style etc.) improper, faulty. ▫ **incorrectly** *adv.* **incorrectness** *n.* [Middle English from Old French or Latin *incorrectus* (as IN-[1], CORRECT)]

incorrigible /ɪnˈkɒrɪdʒɪb(ə)l/ *adj.* **1** (of a person or habit) incurably bad or depraved. **2** not readily improved. ▫ **incorrigibility** /-ˈbɪlɪti/ *n.* **incorrigibleness** *n.* **incorrigibly** *adv.* [Middle English from Old French *incorrigible* or Latin *incorrigibilis* (as IN-[1], CORRIGIBLE)]

incorruptible /ɪnkəˈrʌptɪb(ə)l/ *adj.* **1** that cannot be corrupted, esp. by bribery. **2** that cannot decay; everlasting. ▫ **incorruptibility** /-ˈbɪlɪti/ *n.* **incorruptibly** *adv.* [Middle English from Old French *incorruptible* or ecclesiastical Latin *incorruptibilis* (as IN-[1], CORRUPT)]

increase *v. & n.* ● *v.* /ɪnˈkriːs/ **1** *tr. & intr.* make or become greater in size, amount, etc., or more numerous. **2** *intr.* advance (in quality, attainment, etc.). **3** *tr.* intensify (a quality). ● *n.* /ˈɪŋkriːs/ **1** the act or process of becoming greater or more numerous; growth, enlargement. **2** (of people, animals, or plants) growth in numbers; multiplication. **3** the amount or extent of an increase. ▫ **on the increase** increasing, esp. in frequency. ▫ **increasable** *adj.* **increasingly** *adv.* [Middle English via Old French *encreiss-*, stem of *encreistre*, from Latin *increscere* (as IN-[2], *crescere* 'grow')]

incredible /ɪnˈkrɛdɪb(ə)l/ *adj.* **1** that cannot be believed. **2** *colloq.* hard to believe; amazing. ▫ **incredibility** /-ˈbɪlɪti/ *n.* **incredibly** *adv.* [Middle English from Latin *incredibilis* (as IN-[1], CREDIBLE)]

incredulous /ɪnˈkrɛdjʊləs/ *adj.* (often foll. by *of*) unwilling to believe. ▫ **incredulity** /ɪnkrɪˈdjuːlɪti/ *n.* **incredulously** *adv.* **incredulousness** *n.* [Latin *incredulus* (as IN-[1], CREDULOUS)]

increment /ˈɪŋkrɪm(ə)nt/ *n.* **1 a** an increase or addition, esp. one of a series on a fixed scale. **b** the amount of this. **2** *Math.* a small amount by which a variable quantity increases. ▫ **incremental** /-ˈmɛnt(ə)l/ *adj.* **incrementally** /-ˈmɛnt(ə)li/ *adv.* [Middle English from Latin *incrementum*, from *increscere* INCREASE]

incriminate /ɪnˈkrɪmɪneɪt/ *v.tr.* **1** (often as **incriminating** *adj.*) tend to prove the guilt of (*incriminating evidence*). **2** involve in an accusation. **3** charge with a crime. ▫ **incrimination** /-ˈneɪʃ(ə)n/ *n.* **incriminatory** *adj.* [Late Latin *incriminare* (as IN-[2], Latin *crimen* 'offence')]

incrust var. of ENCRUST.

incrustation /ɪnkrʌˈsteɪʃ(ə)n/ *n.* (also **encrustation**) **1** the process of encrusting or state of being encrusted. **2** a crust or hard coating, esp. of fine material. **3** a concretion or deposit on a surface. **4** a facing of marble etc. on a building. [French *incrustation* or Late Latin *incrustatio* (as ENCRUST)]

incubate /ˈɪŋkjʊbeɪt/ *v.* **1** *tr.* sit on or artificially heat (eggs) in order to bring forth young birds etc. **2** *tr.* cause the development of (bacteria etc.) by creating suitable conditions. **3** *intr.* sit on eggs; brood. **4** *tr. & intr.* develop slowly. [Latin *incubare* (as IN-[2], *cubare cubit-* or *cubat-* 'lie')]

incubation /ɪŋkjʊˈbeɪʃ(ə)n/ *n.* **1 a** the act of incubating. **b** brooding. **2** *Med.* **a** (in full **incubation period**) the period between exposure to an infection and the appearance of the first symptoms. **b** the processes occurring during this. ▫ **incubative** /ˈɪŋkjʊbeɪtɪv/ *adj.* **incubatory** /ˈɪŋkjʊbeɪt(ə)ri/ *adj.* [Latin *incubatio* (as INCUBATE)]

incubator /ˈɪŋkjʊbeɪtə/ *n.* **1** an apparatus used to provide a suitable temperature and environment for a premature baby or one of low birthweight. **2** an apparatus used to hatch eggs or grow micro-organisms.

incubus /ˈɪŋkjʊbəs/ *n.* (*pl.* **incubi** /-bʌɪ/) **1** a male demon believed to have sexual intercourse with sleeping women. **2** a nightmare. **3** a person or thing that oppresses like a nightmare. [Middle English from Late Latin, = Latin *incubo* 'nightmare' (as INCUBATE)]

incudes *pl.* of INCUS.

inculcate /ˈɪnkʌlkeɪt/ *v.tr.* (often foll. by *upon*, *in*) urge or impress (a fact, habit, or idea) persistently. ▫ **inculcation** /-ˈkeɪʃ(ə)n/ *n.* **inculcator** *n.* [Latin *inculcare* (as IN-[2], *calcare* 'tread' from *calx calcis* 'heel')]

inculpate /ˈɪnkʌlpeɪt/ *v.tr.* **1** involve in a charge. **2** accuse, blame. ▫ **inculpation** /-ˈpeɪʃ(ə)n/ *n.* **inculpative** /ɪnˈkʌlpətɪv/ *adj.* **inculpatory** /ɪnˈkʌlpət(ə)ri/ *adj.* [Late Latin *inculpare* (as IN-[2], *culpare* 'blame' from *culpa* 'fault')]

incumbency /ɪnˈkʌmb(ə)nsi/ *n.* (*pl.* **-ies**) the office, tenure, or sphere of an incumbent.

incumbent /ɪnˈkʌmbənt/ *adj. & n.* ● *adj.* **1** (foll. by *on*, *upon*) resting as a duty (*it is incumbent on you to warn them*). **2** (often foll. by *on*) lying, pressing. **3** currently holding office (*the incumbent president*). ● *n.* the holder of an office or post. [Middle English from Anglo-Latin *incumbens*, pres. part. of Latin *incumbere* 'lie upon' (as IN-[2], *cubare* 'lie')]

incunable /ɪnˈkjuːnəb(ə)l/ *n.* = INCUNABULUM 1. [French, formed as INCUNABULUM]

incunabulum /ɪnkjʊˈnabjʊləm/ *n.* (*pl.* **incunabula** /-lə/) **1** a book printed at an early date, esp. before 1501. **2** (in *pl.*) the early stages of the development of a thing. [Latin *incunabula* 'swaddling-clothes, cradle' (as IN-[2], *cunae* 'cradle')]

incur /ɪnˈkəː/ *v.tr.* (**incurred**, **incurring**) suffer, experience, or become subject to (something unpleasant) as a result of one's own behaviour etc. (*incurred huge debts*). ▫ **incurrable** *adj.* [Middle English from Latin *incurrere incurs-* (as IN-[2], *currere* 'run')]

incurable /ɪnˈkjʊərəb(ə)l/ *adj. & n.* ● *adj.* that cannot be cured. ● *n.* a person who cannot be cured. ▫ **incurability** /-ˈbɪlɪti/ *n.* **incurableness** *n.* **incurably** *adv.* [Middle English from Old French *incurable* or Late Latin *incurabilis* (as IN-[1], CURABLE)]

incurious /ɪnˈkjʊərɪəs/ *adj.* **1** lacking curiosity. **2** heedless, careless. ▫ **incuriosity** /-ˈɒsɪti/ *n.* **incuriously** *adv.* **incuriousness** *n.* [Latin *incuriosus* (as IN-[1], CURIOUS)]

incursion /ɪnˈkəːʃ(ə)n/ *n.* an invasion or attack, esp. when sudden or brief. ▫ **incursive** /-sɪv/ *adj.* [Middle English from Latin *incursio* (as INCUR)]

incurve /ɪnˈkəːv/ *v.tr.* **1** bend into a curve. **2** (as **incurved** *adj.*) curved inwards. ▫ **incurvation** /-ˈveɪʃ(ə)n/ *n.* [Latin *incurvare* (as IN-[2], CURVE)]

incus /ˈɪŋkəs/ *n.* (*pl.* **incudes** /ˈɪŋkjʊdiːz, ɪnˈkjuːdiːz/) the small anvil-shaped bone in the middle ear, in contact with the malleus and stapes. [Latin, = anvil]

incuse /ɪnˈkjuːz/ *n., v., & adj.* ● *n.* an impression hammered or stamped on a coin. ● *v.tr.* **1** mark (a coin) with a figure by stamping. **2** impress (a figure) on a coin by stamping. ● *adj.* hammered or stamped on a coin. [Latin *incusus*, past part. of *incudere* (as IN-[2], *cudere* 'forge')]

Ind. *abbr.* **1** Independent. **2 a** India. **b** Indian. **3** Indiana.

indaba /ɪnˈdɑːbə/ *n.* *S.Afr.* **1** a conference between or with members of southern African native peoples. **2** *colloq.* one's problem or concern. [Zulu, = business]

indebted /ɪnˈdɛtɪd/ *adj.* (usu. foll. by *to*) **1** owing gratitude or obligation. **2** owing money. ▫ **indebtedness** *n.* [Middle English from Old French *endetté*, past part. of *endetter* 'involve in debt' (as EN-[1], *detter* from *dette* DEBT)]

indecent /ɪnˈdiːs(ə)nt/ *adj.* **1** offending against recognized standards of decency. **2** unbecoming; highly unsuitable (*with indecent haste*). ▫ **indecency** *n.* (*pl.* **-ies**). **indecently** *adv.* [French *indécent* or Latin *indecens* (as IN-[1], DECENT)]

indecent assault *n.* a sexual attack not involving rape.

indecent exposure *n.* the intentional act of publicly and indecently exposing one's body, esp. the genitals.

indecipherable /ɪndɪˈsʌɪf(ə)rəb(ə)l/ *adj.* that cannot be deciphered.

indecision /ɪndɪˈsɪʒ(ə)n/ *n.* lack of decision; hesitation. [French *indécision* (as IN-¹, DECISION)]

indecisive /ɪndɪˈsʌɪsɪv/ *adj.* **1** not decisive. **2** undecided, hesitating. □ **indecisively** *adv.* **indecisiveness** *n.*

indeclinable /ɪndɪˈklʌɪnəb(ə)l/ *adj. Gram.* **1** that cannot be declined. **2** having no inflections. [Middle English via French *indéclinable* from Latin *indeclinabilis* (as IN-¹, DECLINE)]

indecorous /ɪnˈdɛk(ə)rəs/ *adj.* **1** improper. **2** in bad taste. □ **indecorously** *adv.* **indecorousness** *n.* [Latin *indecorus* (as IN-¹, *decorus* 'seemly')]

indecorum /ɪndɪˈkɔːrəm/ *n.* **1** lack of decorum. **2** improper behaviour. [Latin, neut. of *indecorus*: see INDECOROUS]

indeed /ɪnˈdiːd/ *adv.* & *int.* ● *adv.* **1** in truth; really (*they are, indeed, a remarkable family*). **2** expressing emphasis or intensification (*I shall be very glad indeed; indeed it is*). **3** admittedly (*there are indeed exceptions*). **4** in point of fact (*if indeed such a thing is possible*). **5** expressing an approving or ironic echo (*who is this Mr Smith? — who is he indeed?*). ● *int.* expressing irony, contempt, incredulity, etc.

indefatigable /ɪndɪˈfatɪgəb(ə)l/ *adj.* (of a person, quality, etc.) that cannot be tired out; unwearying, unremitting. □ **indefatigability** /-ˈbɪlɪti/ *n.* **indefatigably** *adv.* [obsolete French *indéfatigable* or Latin *indefatigabilis* (as IN-¹, *defatigare* 'wear out')]

indefeasible /ɪndɪˈfiːzɪb(ə)l/ *adj. literary* (esp. of a claim, rights, etc.) that cannot be lost. □ **indefeasibility** /-ˈbɪlɪti/ *n.* **indefeasibly** *adv.*

indefectible /ɪndɪˈfɛktɪb(ə)l/ *adj.* **1** unfailing; not liable to defect or decay. **2** faultless. [IN-¹ + *defectible* from Late Latin *defectibilis* (as DEFECT)]

indefensible /ɪndɪˈfɛnsɪb(ə)l/ *adj.* that cannot be defended or justified. □ **indefensibility** /-ˈbɪlɪti/ *n.* **indefensibly** *adv.*

indefinable /ɪndɪˈfʌɪnəb(ə)l/ *adj.* that cannot be defined or exactly described. □ **indefinably** *adv.*

indefinite /ɪnˈdɛfɪnɪt/ *adj.* **1** vague, undefined. **2** unlimited. **3** *Gram.* not determining the person, thing, time, etc., referred to. □ **indefiniteness** *n.* [Latin *indefinitus* (as IN-¹, DEFINITE)]

indefinite article *n. Gram.* a word (*a* and *an* in English) preceding a noun and implying lack of specificity (as in *bought me a book*; *government is an art; went to a public school*).

indefinite integral *n. Math.* an integral expressed without limits, and so having the same derivative if an arbitrary constant is added.

indefinitely /ɪnˈdɛfɪnɪtli/ *adv.* **1** for an unlimited time (*was postponed indefinitely*). **2** in an indefinite manner.

indefinite pronoun *n.* a pronoun indicating a person, amount, etc., without being definite or particular, e.g. *any, some, anyone.*

indehiscent /ɪndɪˈhɪs(ə)nt/ *adj. Bot.* (of fruit) not splitting open when ripe. □ **indehiscence** *n.*

indelible /ɪnˈdɛlɪb(ə)l/ *adj.* **1** that cannot be rubbed out or (in abstract senses) removed. **2** (of ink etc.) that makes indelible marks. □ **indelibility** /-ˈbɪlɪti/ *n.* **indelibly** *adv.* [French *indélébile* or Latin *indelebilis* (as IN-¹, *delebilis* from *delēre* 'efface')]

indelicate /ɪnˈdɛlɪkət/ *adj.* **1** coarse, unrefined. **2** tactless. **3** tending to indecency. □ **indelicacy** *n.* (*pl.* **-ies**). **indelicately** *adv.*

indemnify /ɪnˈdɛmnɪfʌɪ/ *v.tr.* (**-ies, -ied**) **1** (often foll. by *from, against*) protect or secure (a person) in respect of harm, a loss, etc. **2** (often foll. by *for*) secure (a person) against legal responsibility for actions. **3** (often foll. by *for*) compensate (a person) for a loss, expenses, etc. □ **indemnification** /-fɪˈkeɪʃ(ə)n/ *n.* **indemnifier** *n.* [Latin *indemnis* 'unhurt' (as IN-¹, *damnum* 'loss, damage')]

indemnity /ɪnˈdɛmnɪti/ *n.* (*pl.* **-ies**) **1 a** compensation for loss incurred. **b** a sum paid for this, esp. a sum exacted by a victor in war etc. as one condition of peace. **2** security against loss. **3** legal exemption from penalties etc. incurred. [Middle English from French *indemnité* or Late Latin *indemnitas -tatis* (as INDEMNIFY)]

indemonstrable /ɪndɪˈmɒnstrəb(ə)l, ɪnˈdɛmən-/ *adj.* that cannot be proved (esp. of primary or axiomatic truths).

indene /ˈɪndiːn/ *n. Chem.* a colourless flammable liquid hydrocarbon obtained from coal tar and used in making synthetic resins. [INDOLE + -ENE]

indent¹ *v.* & *n.* ● *v.* /ɪnˈdɛnt/ **1** *tr.* start (a line of print or writing) further from the margin than other lines, e.g. to mark a new paragraph. **2** *tr.* **a** divide (a document drawn up in duplicate) into its two copies with a zigzag line dividing them and ensuring identification. **b** draw up (usu. a legal document) in exact duplicate. **3** *Brit.* **a** *intr.* (often foll. by *on, upon* a person, *for* a thing) make a requisition (originally a written order with a duplicate). **b** *tr.* order (goods) by requisition. **4** *tr.* make toothlike notches in. **5** *tr.* form deep recesses in (a coastline etc.). ● *n.* /ˈɪndɛnt/ **1** *Brit.* **a** an order (esp. from abroad) for goods. **b** an official requisition for stores. **2** an indented line. **3** indentation. **4** an indenture. □ **indentor** *n.* [Middle English via Anglo-French *endenter* from Anglo-Latin *indentare* (as IN-², Latin *dens dentis* 'tooth')]

indent² /ɪnˈdɛnt/ *v.tr.* **1** make a dent in. **2** impress (a mark etc.). [Middle English, from IN-² + DENT]

indentation /ɪndɛnˈteɪʃ(ə)n/ *n.* **1** the act or an instance of indenting; the process of being indented. **2** a cut or notch. **3** a zigzag. **4** a deep recess in a coastline etc.

indention /ɪnˈdɛnʃ(ə)n/ *n.* (an) indentation, esp. in printing or writing.

indenture /ɪnˈdɛntʃə/ *n.* & *v.* ● *n.* **1** an indented document (see INDENT¹ *v.* 2). **2** (usu. in *pl.*) a sealed agreement or contract. **3** a formal list, certificate, etc. ● *v.tr. hist.* bind (a person) by indentures, esp. as an apprentice. □ **indentureship** *n.* [Middle English (originally Scots) from Anglo-French *endenture* (as INDENT¹)]

independence /ɪndɪˈpɛnd(ə)ns/ *n.* **1** (often foll. by *of, from*) the fact or process of being independent. **2** independent income.

Independence Day *n.* a day celebrating the anniversary of national independence, esp. 4 July in the US.

independency /ɪndɪˈpɛnd(ə)nsi/ *n.* (*pl.* **-ies**) **1** an independent state. **2** = INDEPENDENCE.

independent /ɪndɪˈpɛnd(ə)nt/ *adj.* & *n.* ● *adj.* **1 a** (often foll. by *of*) not depending on authority or control. **b** self-governing. **2 a** not depending on another person for one's opinion or livelihood. **b** (of income or resources) making it unnecessary to earn one's living. **3** unwilling to be under an obligation to others. **4** *Polit.* not belonging to or supported by a party. **5** not depending on something else for its validity, efficiency, value, etc. (*independent proof*). **6** (of broadcasting, a school, etc.) not supported by public funds. **7** (**Independent**) *hist.* Congregational. ● *n.* **1** a person who is politically independent. **2** (**Independent**) *hist.* a Congregationalist. □ **independently** *adv.*

in-depth *attrib.adj.* thorough; done in depth.

indescribable /ɪndɪˈskrʌɪbəb(ə)l/ *adj.* **1** too unusual or extreme to be described. **2** vague, indefinite. □ **indescribability** /-ˈbɪlɪti/ *n.* **indescribably** *adv.*

indestructible /ɪndɪˈstrʌktɪb(ə)l/ *adj.* that cannot be destroyed. □ **indestructibility** /-ˈbɪlɪti/ *n.* **indestructibly** *adv.*

indeterminable /ɪndɪˈtəːmɪnəb(ə)l/ *adj.* **1** that cannot be ascertained. **2** (of a dispute etc.) that cannot be settled. □ **indeterminably** *adv.* [Middle English from Late Latin *indeterminabilis* (as IN-¹, Latin *determinare* DETERMINE)]

indeterminate /ɪndɪˈtəːmɪnət/ *adj.* **1** not fixed in extent, character, etc. **2** left doubtful; vague. **3** *Math.* (of a quantity) not limited to a fixed value by the value of another quantity. **4** (of a judicial sentence) such that the convicted person's conduct determines the date of release. ◻ **indeterminacy** *n.* **indeterminately** *adv.* **indeterminateness** *n.* [Middle English from Late Latin *indeterminatus* (as IN-[1], DETERMINATE)]

indeterminate vowel *n.* the obscure vowel /ə/ heard in '*a* moment *ago*'; a schwa.

indetermination /ˌɪndɪtəːmɪˈneɪʃ(ə)n/ *n.* **1** lack of determination. **2** the state of being indeterminate.

indeterminism /ɪndɪˈtəːmɪnɪz(ə)m/ *n.* the belief that human action is not wholly determined by motives. ◻ **indeterminist** *n.* **indeterministic** /-ˈnɪstɪk/ *adj.*

index /ˈɪndɛks/ *n.* & *v.* ● *n.* (*pl.* **indexes** or esp. in technical use **indices** /ˈɪndɪsiːz/) **1** an alphabetical list of names, subjects, etc., with references, usu. at the end of a book. **2** = CARD INDEX. **3** (in full **index number**) a number showing the variation of prices or wages as compared with a chosen base period (*retail price index*; *Dow-Jones index*). **4** *Math.* **a** the exponent of a number. **b** the power to which it is raised. **5 a** a pointer, esp. on an instrument, showing a quantity, a position on a scale, etc. **b** an indicator of a trend, direction, tendency, etc. **c** (usu. foll. by *of*) a sign, token, or indication of something. **6** *Physics* a number expressing a physical property etc. in terms of a standard (*refractive index*). **7** *Computing* a set of items each of which specifies one of the records of a file and contains information about its address. **8** (**Index**) *RC Ch. hist.* a list of books forbidden to Roman Catholics to read. **9** *Printing* a symbol shaped like a pointing hand, used to draw attention to a note etc. ● *v.tr.* **1** provide (a book etc.) with an index. **2** enter in an index. **3** relate (wages etc.) to the value of a price index. ◻ **indexation** /-ˈseɪʃ(ə)n/ *n.* **indexer** *n.* **indexible** /ˈɪndɛks-, ɪnˈdɛks-/ *adj.* **indexical** /ɪnˈdɛks-/ *adj.* **indexless** *adj.* [Middle English from Latin *index indicis* 'forefinger, informer, sign': sense 8 from Latin *Index librorum prohibitorum* 'list of prohibited books']

index finger *n.* the forefinger.

index-linked *adj.* related to the value of a retail price index. ◻ **index-linking** *n.*

India ink /ˈɪndɪə/ *n.* esp. *N. Amer.* = INDIAN INK. [*India* in Asia: see INDIAN]

Indiaman /ˈɪndɪəmən/ *n.* (*pl.* **-men**) *Naut. hist.* a ship engaged in trade with India or the East Indies.

Indian /ˈɪndɪən/ *n.* & *adj.* ● *n.* **1 a** a native or national of India. **b** a person of Indian descent. **2** an American Indian. **3** any of the languages of the aboriginal peoples of America. ● *adj.* **1** of or relating to India, or to the subcontinent comprising India, Pakistan, and Bangladesh. **2** of or relating to the aboriginal peoples of America. [Middle English from *India*, ultimately via Greek *Indos*, the River Indus, from Persian *Hind*: cf. HINDU]

▪ **Usage** *Indian* is a misnomer for the native peoples of America, having arisen from the mistaken belief of Christopher Columbus and other Europeans in the 15th–16th centuries that they had reached part of India by a new route. The term is considered to convey an offensive stereotype by some. However, it is used by many Native Americans in the US as a term of pride and respect. The full form *American Indian* (and in Canada, *Canadian Indian*) are unambiguous alternatives. See also Usage Note at NATIVE AMERICAN.

Indian club *n.* each of a pair of bottle-shaped clubs swung to exercise the arms in gymnastics.

Indian corn *n.* maize.

Indian elephant *n.* the elephant, *Elephas maximus*, of India, which is smaller than the African elephant.

Indian file *n.* = SINGLE FILE.

Indian hemp see HEMP 1.

Indian ink *n. Brit.* **1** a black pigment made originally in China and Japan. **2** a dark ink made from this, used esp. in drawing and technical graphics.

Indian Ocean *n.* the ocean between Africa to the west, and Australia to the east.

Indian rope-trick *n.* the supposed Indian feat of climbing an upright unsupported length of rope.

Indian sign *n.* a magic spell, jinx (esp. in **put** (or **have**) **the Indian sign on a person**).

Indian summer *n.* **1** a period of unusually dry warm weather sometimes occurring in late autumn. **2** a late period of life characterized by comparative calm.

India paper /ˈɪndɪə/ *n.* **1** a soft absorbent kind of paper originally imported from China, used for proofs of engravings. **2** a very thin tough opaque printing paper.

India rubber /ˈɪndɪə/ *n.* = RUBBER[1] 2.

Indic /ˈɪndɪk/ *adj.* & *n.* ● *adj.* of or relating to the group of Indo-European languages comprising Sanskrit and its modern descendants. ● *n.* this language group. [Latin *Indicus* from Greek *Indikos* INDIAN]

indicate /ˈɪndɪkeɪt/ *v.* (often foll. by *that* + clause) **1** *tr.* point out; make known; show. **2** *tr.* be a sign or symptom of; express the presence of. **3** *tr.* (often in *passive*) suggest; call for; require or show to be necessary (*stronger measures are indicated*). **4** *tr.* admit to or state briefly (*indicated his disapproval*). **5** *tr.* (of a gauge etc.) give as a reading. **6** *intr.* signal one's intention to turn etc. using an indicator. [Latin *indicare* (as IN-[2], *dicare* 'make known')]

indication /ɪndɪˈkeɪʃ(ə)n/ *n.* **1** the act or an instance of indicating. **2** something indicated or suggested. **3** a reading given by a gauge or instrument. [French from Latin *indicatio* (as INDICATE)]

indicative /ɪnˈdɪkətɪv/ *adj.* & *n.* ● *adj.* **1** (foll. by *of*) suggestive; serving as an indication. **2** *Gram.* (of a mood) denoting simple statement of a fact. ● *n. Gram.* **1** the indicative mood. **2** a verb in this mood. ◻ **indicatively** *adv.* [Middle English via French *indicatif -ive* from Late Latin *indicativus* (as INDICATE)]

indicator /ˈɪndɪkeɪtə/ *n.* **1** a person or thing that indicates esp. performance, change, etc. **2** a device indicating the condition of a machine etc. **3** a recording instrument attached to an apparatus etc. **4** *Brit.* a board in a railway station etc. giving current information. **5** a device (esp. a flashing light) on a vehicle to show that it is about to change direction. **6** *Chem.* a substance which changes to a characteristic colour in the presence of a particular concentration of an ion, so indicating e.g. acidity. **7** *Physics* & *Med.* a radioactive tracer. **8** *Biol.* a species or group which acts as a sign of particular environmental conditions.

indicatory /ɪnˈdɪkət(ə)ri, ˈɪndɪkeɪt(ə)ri/ *adj.* = INDICATIVE *adj.* 1.

indices *pl.* of INDEX.

indicia /ɪnˈdɪʃɪə, -sɪə/ *n.pl.* **1** distinguishing marks. **2** signs, indications. [pl. of Latin *indicium* (as INDEX)]

indicial /ɪnˈdɪʃ(ə)l/ *adj.* **1** of the nature or form of an index. **2** of the nature of indicia; indicative.

indict /ɪnˈdʌɪt/ *v.tr.* accuse (a person) formally by legal process. ◻ **indictee** /-ˈtiː/ *n.* **indicter** *n.* [Middle English via Anglo-French *enditer* 'indict' and Old French *enditier* 'declare' from Romanic (as IN-[2], DICTATE)]

indictable /ɪnˈdʌɪtəb(ə)l/ *adj.* **1** (of an offence) rendering the person who commits it liable to be charged with a crime. **2** (of a person) so liable.

indictment /ɪnˈdʌɪtm(ə)nt/ *n.* **1** the act of indicting. **2 a** a formal accusation. **b** a legal process in which this is made. **c** a document containing a charge. **3** something that serves to condemn or censure. [Middle English from Anglo-French *enditement* (as INDICT)]

indie /ˈɪndi/ *adj.* & *n. colloq.* ● *adj.* (of a pop group or record label) independent, not belonging to one of the major record companies. ● *n.* **1** such a group or label. **2** an independent film company.

Indies /ˈɪndɪz/ *n.pl.* (prec. by *the*) *archaic* India and adjacent regions (see also EAST INDIES, WEST INDIES). [pl. of obsolete *Indy* 'India']

indifference /ɪnˈdɪf(ə)r(ə)ns/ *n.* **1** lack of interest or attention. **2** unimportance (*a matter of indifference*). **3** neutrality. [Latin *indifferentia* (as INDIFFERENT)]

indifferent /ɪn'dɪf(ə)r(ə)nt/ *adj.* **1** neither good nor bad; average, mediocre. **2 a** not especially good. **b** fairly bad. **3** (often prec. by *very*) decidedly inferior. **4** (foll. by *to*) having no partiality for or against; having no interest in or sympathy for. **5** chemically, magnetically, etc., neutral. □ **indifferently** *adv.* [Middle English via Old French *indifferent* or Latin *indifferens* (as IN-[1], DIFFERENT)]

indifferentism /ɪn'dɪf(ə)r(ə)ntɪz(ə)m/ *n.* an attitude of indifference, esp. in religious matters. □ **indifferentist** *n.*

indigenize /ɪn'dɪdʒɪnʌɪz/ *v.tr.* (also **-ise**) **1** make indigenous; subject to native influence. **2** subject to increased use of indigenous people in government etc. □ **indigenization** /-'zeɪʃ(ə)n/ *n.*

indigenous /ɪn'dɪdʒɪnəs/ *adj.* **1 a** (esp. of flora or fauna) originating naturally in a region. **b** (of people) born in a region. **2** (foll. by *to*) belonging naturally to a place. □ **indigenously** *adv.* **indigenousness** *n.* [Latin *indigena*, from *indi-* = IN-[2] + *gen-* 'be born']

indigent /'ɪndɪdʒ(ə)nt/ *adj.* needy, poor. □ **indigence** *n.* [Middle English via Old French from Late Latin *indigēre*, from *indi-* = IN-[2] + *egēre* 'need']

indigested /ɪndɪ'dʒɛstɪd, -dʌɪ-/ *adj.* **1** shapeless. **2** ill-considered. **3** not digested.

indigestible /ɪndɪ'dʒɛstɪb(ə)l, -dʌɪ-/ *adj.* **1** difficult or impossible to digest. **2** too complex or awkward to read or comprehend easily. □ **indigestibility** /-'bɪlɪti/ *n.* **indigestibly** *adv.* [French *indigestible* or Late Latin *indigestibilis* (as IN-[1], DIGEST)]

indigestion /ɪndɪ'dʒɛstʃ(ə)n, -dʌɪ-/ *n.* **1** difficulty in digesting food. **2** pain or discomfort caused by this. □ **indigestive** *adj.* [Middle English from Old French *indigestion* or Late Latin *indigestio* (as IN-[1], DIGESTION)]

indignant /ɪn'dɪgnənt/ *adj.* feeling or showing scornful anger or a sense of injured innocence. □ **indignantly** *adv.* [Latin *indignari indignant-* 'regard as unworthy' (as IN-[1], *dignus* 'worthy')]

indignation /ɪndɪg'neɪʃ(ə)n/ *n.* scornful anger at supposed unjust or unfair conduct or treatment. [Middle English from Old French *indignation* or Latin *indignatio* (as INDIGNANT)]

indignity /ɪn'dɪgnɪti/ *n.* (*pl.* **-ies**) **1** unworthy treatment. **2** a slight or insult. **3** the humiliating quality of something (*the indignity of my position*). [French *indignité* or Latin *indignitas* (as INDIGNANT)]

indigo /'ɪndɪgəʊ/ *n.* & *adj.* ● *n.* (*pl.* **-os**) **1 a** a natural blue dye obtained from the indigo plant. **b** a synthetic form of this dye. **2** any plant of the genus *Indigofera*. **3** (in full **indigo blue**) a colour between blue and violet in the spectrum. ● *adj.* (in full **indigo blue**; hyphenated when *attrib.*) of this colour. □ **indigotic** /-'gɒtɪk/ *adj.* [16th-c. *indico* (from Spanish), *indigo* (from Portuguese), via Latin *indicum* from Greek *indikon* INDIAN (dye)]

indigo snake *n.* a large non-venomous American snake, *Drymarchon corais*, usu. blue-black, brown, or particoloured. Also called *cribo, gopher snake*.

indirect /ɪndɪ'rɛkt, ɪndʌɪ-/ *adj.* **1** not going straight to the point. **2** (of a route etc.) not straight. **3** not directly sought or aimed at (*an indirect result*). **4** (of lighting) from a concealed source and diffusely reflected. □ **indirectly** *adv.* **indirectness** *n.* [Middle English from Old French *indirect* or medieval Latin *indirectus* (as IN-[1], DIRECT)]

indirect object *n. Gram.* a person or thing affected by a verbal action but not primarily acted on (e.g. *him* in *give him the book*).

indirect question *n. Gram.* a question in reported speech (e.g. *they asked who I was*).

indirect speech *n.* = REPORTED SPEECH.

indirect tax *n.* a tax levied on goods and services and not on income or profits.

indiscernible /ɪndɪ'sə:nɪb(ə)l/ *adj.* that cannot be discerned or distinguished from another. □ **indiscernibility** /-'bɪlɪti/ *n.* **indiscernibly** *adv.*

indiscipline /ɪn'dɪsɪplɪn/ *n.* lack of discipline.

indiscreet /ɪndɪ'skri:t/ *adj.* **1** not discreet; revealing secrets. **2** injudicious, unwary. □ **indiscreetly** *adv.* [Middle English from Late Latin *indiscretus* (as IN-[1], DISCREET)]

indiscrete /ɪndɪ'skri:t/ *adj.* not divided into distinct parts. [Latin *indiscretus* (as IN-[1], DISCRETE)]

indiscretion /ɪndɪ'skrɛʃ(ə)n/ *n.* **1** lack of discretion; indiscreet conduct. **2** an indiscreet action, remark, etc. [Middle English from Old French *indiscretion* or Late Latin *indiscretio* (as IN-[1], DISCRETION)]

indiscriminate /ɪndɪ'skrɪmɪnət/ *adj.* **1** making no distinctions. **2** confused, promiscuous. □ **indiscriminately** *adv.* **indiscriminateness** *n.* **indiscrimination** /-'neɪʃ(ə)n/ *n.* **indiscriminative** *adj.* [IN-[1] + *discriminate* (*adj.*) from Latin *discriminatus*, past part. of *discriminare* DISCRIMINATE]

indispensable /ɪndɪ'spɛnsəb(ə)l/ *adj.* **1** (often foll. by *to, for*) that cannot be dispensed with; necessary. **2** (of a law, duty, etc.) that is not to be set aside. □ **indispensability** /-'bɪlɪti/ *n.* **indispensableness** *n.* **indispensably** *adv.* [medieval Latin *indispensabilis* (as IN-[1], DISPENSABLE)]

indispose /ɪndɪ'spəʊz/ *v.tr.* **1** (often foll. by *for*, or *to* + infin.) make unfit or unable. **2** (often foll. by *towards, from*, or *to* + infin.) make averse.

indisposed /ɪndɪ'spəʊzd/ *adj.* **1** slightly unwell. **2** averse or unwilling.

indisposition /ˌɪndɪspə'zɪʃ(ə)n/ *n.* **1** ill health, a slight or temporary ailment. **2** disinclination. **3** aversion. [French *indisposition*, or from IN-[1] + DISPOSITION]

indisputable /ɪndɪ'spju:təb(ə)l, ɪn'dɪspjʊtəb(ə)l/ *adj.* **1** that cannot be disputed. **2** unquestionable. □ **indisputability** /-'bɪlɪti/ *n.* **indisputably** *adv.* [Late Latin *indisputabilis* (as IN-[1], DISPUTABLE)]

indissolubilist /ɪndɪ'sɒljʊbɪlɪst/ *n.* & *adj.* ● *n.* (in the Church of England) a person who believes that the Church should not remarry divorcees. ● *adj.* of or holding this belief.

indissoluble /ɪndɪ'sɒljʊb(ə)l/ *adj.* **1** that cannot be dissolved or decomposed. **2** lasting, stable (*an indissoluble bond*). □ **indissolubility** /-'bɪlɪti/ *n.* **indissolubly** *adv.* [Latin *indissolubilis* (as IN-[1], DISSOLUBLE)]

indistinct /ɪndɪ'stɪŋkt/ *adj.* **1** not distinct. **2** confused, obscure. □ **indistinctly** *adv.* **indistinctness** *n.* [Middle English from Latin *indistinctus* (as IN-[1], DISTINCT)]

indistinctive /ɪndɪ'stɪŋktɪv/ *adj.* not having distinctive features. □ **indistinctively** *adv.* **indistinctiveness** *n.*

indistinguishable /ɪndɪ'stɪŋgwɪʃəb(ə)l/ *adj.* (often foll. by *from*) not distinguishable. □ **indistinguishableness** *n.* **indistinguishably** *adv.*

indite /ɪn'dʌɪt/ *v.tr. formal* or *joc.* **1** put (a speech etc.) into words. **2** write (a letter etc.). [Middle English from Old French *enditier*: see INDICT]

indium /'ɪndɪəm/ *n. Chem.* a soft silvery-white metallic element occurring naturally in zinc blende etc., used for electroplating and in semiconductors (symbol **In**). [Latin *indicum* 'indigo', with reference to its characteristic spectral lines]

indivertible /ɪndʌɪ'və:tɪb(ə)l, ɪndɪ-/ *adj.* that cannot be turned aside. □ **indivertibly** *adv.*

individual /ɪndɪ'vɪdjʊ(ə)l/ *adj.* & *n.* ● *adj.* **1** single. **2** particular, special; not general. **3** having a distinct character. **4** characteristic of a particular person. **5** designed for use by one person. ● *n.* **1** a single member of a class. **2** a single human being as distinct from a family or group. **3** *colloq.* a person (*a most unpleasant individual*). **4** a distinctive person. [Middle English, = indivisible, from medieval Latin *individualis* (as IN-[1], *dividuus* from *dividere* DIVIDE)]

individualism /ɪndɪ'vɪdjʊ(ə)lɪz(ə)m/ *n.* **1** the habit or principle of being independent and self-reliant. **2** a social theory favouring the free action of individuals. **3** self-centred feeling or conduct; egoism. □ **individualist** *n.* **individualistic** /-'lɪstɪk/ *adj.* **individualistically** /-'lɪstɪk(ə)li/ *adv.*

individuality /ˌɪndɪvɪdjʊˈalɪti/ *n.* (*pl.* **-ies**) **1** individual character, esp. when strongly marked. **2** (in *pl.*) individual tastes etc. **3** separate existence.

individualize /ɪndɪˈvɪdjʊ(ə)lʌɪz/ *v.tr.* (also **-ise**) **1** give an individual character to. **2** specify. **3** (esp. as **individualized** *adj.*) personalize or tailor to suit the individual (*individualized notepaper*; *individualized training course*). □ **individualization** /-ˈzeɪʃ(ə)n/ *n.*

individually /ɪndɪˈvɪdjʊ(ə)li/ *adv.* **1** personally; in an individual capacity. **2** in a distinctive manner. **3** one by one; not collectively.

individuate /ɪndɪˈvɪdjʊeɪt/ *v.tr.* individualize; form into an individual. □ **individuation** /-ˈeɪʃ(ə)n/ *n.* [medieval Latin *individuare* (as INDIVIDUAL)]

indivisible /ɪndɪˈvɪzɪb(ə)l/ *adj.* **1** not divisible. **2** not distributable among a number. □ **indivisibility** /-ˈbɪlɪti/ *n.* **indivisibly** *adv.* [Middle English from Late Latin *indivisibilis* (as IN-[1], DIVISIBLE)]

Indo- /ˈɪndəʊ/ *comb. form* Indian; Indian and. [Latin *Indus* from Greek *Indos*]

Indo-Aryan /ɪndəʊˈɛːrɪən/ *n.* & *adj.* ● *n.* **1** a member of any of the Aryan peoples of India. **2** the Indic group of languages. ● *adj.* of or relating to the Indo-Aryans or Indo-Aryan.

Indo-Chinese /ˌɪndəʊtʃʌɪˈniːz/ *adj.* & *n.* ● *adj.* of or relating to Indo-China in SE Asia. ● *n.* (*pl.* same) a native of Indo-China; a person of Indo-Chinese descent.

indocile /ɪnˈdəʊsʌɪl/ *adj.* not docile. □ **indocility** /-də(ʊ)ˈsɪlɪti/ *n.* [French *indocile* or Latin *indocilis* (as IN-[1], DOCILE)]

indoctrinate /ɪnˈdɒktrɪneɪt/ *v.tr.* **1** teach (a person or group) systematically or for a long period to accept (esp. partisan or tendentious) ideas uncritically. **2** teach, instruct. □ **indoctrination** /-ˈneɪʃ(ə)n/ *n.* **indoctrinator** *n.* [IN-[2] + DOCTRINE + -ATE[3]]

Indo-European /ˌɪndəʊjʊərəˈpiːən/ *adj.* & *n.* ● *adj.* **1** of or relating to the family of languages spoken over the greater part of Europe and Asia as far as N. India. **2** of or relating to the hypothetical parent language of this family. ● *n.* **1** the Indo-European family of languages. **2** the hypothetical parent language of all languages belonging to this family. **3** (usu. in *pl.*) a speaker of an Indo-European language.

Indo-Iranian /ˌɪndəʊɪˈreɪnɪən, -ˈrɑː-/ *adj.* & *n.* ● *adj.* of or relating to the subfamily of Indo-European languages spoken chiefly in northern India and Iran. ● *n.* this subfamily.

indole /ˈɪndəʊl/ *n. Chem.* an organic compound with a characteristic odour formed on the reduction of indigo. [INDIGO + Latin *oleum* 'oil']

indoleacetic acid /ˌɪndəʊləˈsiːtɪk, -ˈsɛtɪk/ *n. Biochem.* any of a group of isomeric acetic acid derivatives of indole, esp. one found as a natural growth hormone (auxin) in plants (abbr.: **IAA**). [INDOLE + ACETIC]

indolent /ˈɪnd(ə)l(ə)nt/ *adj.* **1** lazy; wishing to avoid activity or exertion. **2** *Med.* causing no pain (*an indolent tumour*). □ **indolence** *n.* **indolently** *adv.* [Late Latin *indolens* (as IN-[1], *dolēre* 'suffer pain')]

Indology /ɪnˈdɒlədʒi/ *n.* the study of Indian history, literature, etc. □ **Indologist** *n.*

indomitable /ɪnˈdɒmɪtəb(ə)l/ *adj.* **1** that cannot be subdued; unyielding. **2** stubbornly persistent. □ **indomitability** /-ˈbɪlɪti/ *n.* **indomitableness** *n.* **indomitably** *adv.* [Late Latin *indomitabilis* (as IN-[1], Latin *domitare* 'tame')]

Indonesian /ɪndəˈniːzj(ə)n, -ʒ(ə)n/ *n.* & *adj.* ● *n.* **1 a** a native or national of Indonesia in SE Asia. **b** a person of Indonesian descent. **2** a member of the chief pre-Malay population of the E. Indies. **3 a** the western branch of the Austronesian language family. **b** = BAHASA INDONESIA. ● *adj.* of or relating to Indonesia or its people or language(s). [*Indonesia* from INDIES, on the pattern of *Polynesia*]

indoor /ˈɪndɔː/ *adj.* situated, carried on, or used within a building or under cover (*indoor aerial*; *indoor games*). [earlier *within-door*: cf. INDOORS]

indoors /ɪnˈdɔːz/ *adv.* into or within a building. [earlier *within doors*]

indorse var. of ENDORSE.

indorsement var. of ENDORSEMENT.

indraught /ˈɪndrɑːft/ *n.* (*US* **indraft**) **1** the drawing in of something. **2** an inward flow or current.

indrawn /ɪnˈdrɔːn, ˈɪn-/ *adj.* **1** (of breath etc.) drawn in. **2** aloof.

indri /ˈɪndri/ *n.* (*pl.* **indris**) a large lemur, *Indri indri*, of Madagascar. [Malagasy *indry* 'behold', mistaken for its name]

indubitable /ɪnˈdjuːbɪtəb(ə)l/ *adj.* that cannot be doubted. □ **indubitably** *adv.* [French *indubitable* or Latin *indubitabilis* (as IN-[1], *dubitare* 'to doubt')]

induce /ɪnˈdjuːs/ *v.tr.* **1** (often foll. by *to* + infin.) prevail on; persuade. **2** bring about; give rise to. **3** *Med.* bring on (labour) artificially, esp. by use of drugs. **4** *Electr.* produce (a current) by induction. **5** *Physics* cause (radioactivity) by bombardment. **6** infer; derive as a deduction. □ **inducer** *n.* **inducible** *adj.* [Middle English from Latin *inducere induct-* (as IN-[2], *ducere* 'lead')]

inducement /ɪnˈdjuːsm(ə)nt/ *n.* **1** (often foll. by *to*) an attraction that leads one on. **2** a thing that induces.

induct /ɪnˈdʌkt/ *v.tr.* (often foll. by *to*, *into*) **1 a** introduce formally into office. **b** introduce (a member of the clergy) formally into possession of a benefice. **2** introduce, initiate. **3** *US* enlist (a person) for military service. **4** *archaic* lead (to a seat, into a room, etc.); install. □ **inductee** /ɪndʌkˈtiː/ *n.* [Middle English (as INDUCE)]

inductance /ɪnˈdʌkt(ə)ns/ *n. Electr.* the property of an electric circuit that causes an electromotive force to be generated by a change in the current flowing.

induction /ɪnˈdʌkʃ(ə)n/ *n.* **1** the act or an instance of inducting or inducing. **2** *Med.* the process of bringing on (esp. labour) by artificial means. **3** *Logic* **a** the inference of a general law from particular instances (cf. DEDUCTION). **b** *Math.* a means of proving a theorem by showing that if it is true of any particular case it is true of the next case in a series, and then showing that it is indeed true in one particular case. **c** (foll. by *of*) the production of (facts) to prove a general statement. **4** (often *attrib.*) a formal introduction to a new job, position, etc. (*attended an induction course*). **5** *Electr.* **a** the production of an electric or magnetic state by the proximity (without contact) of an electrified or magnetized body. **b** the production of an electric current in a conductor by a change of magnetic field. **6** the drawing of a fuel mixture into the cylinders of an internal-combustion engine. **7** *US* enlistment for military service. [Middle English from Old French *induction* or Latin *inductio* (as INDUCE)]

induction coil *n.* a coil for generating intermittent high voltage from a direct current.

induction heating *n.* heating by an induced electric current.

induction loop *n.* a sound system in which a loop of wire around an area in a building etc. produces an electromagnetic signal received directly by hearing aids for the partially deaf.

inductive /ɪnˈdʌktɪv/ *adj.* **1** (of reasoning etc.) of or based on induction. **2** of electric or magnetic induction. □ **inductively** *adv.* **inductiveness** *n.* [Late Latin *inductivus* (as INDUCE)]

inductor /ɪnˈdʌktə/ *n.* **1** *Electr.* a component (in a circuit) which possesses inductance. **2** a person who inducts a member of the clergy. [Latin (as INDUCE)]

indue var. of ENDUE.

indulge /ɪnˈdʌldʒ/ *v.* **1** *intr.* (often foll. by *in*) take pleasure freely. **2** *tr.* yield freely to (a desire etc.). **3** *tr.* gratify the wishes of; favour (*indulged them with money*). **4** *intr. colloq.* take alcoholic liquor. □ **indulger** *n.* [Latin *indulgēre indult-* 'give free rein to']

indulgence /ɪnˈdʌldʒ(ə)ns/ *n.* **1 a** the act of indulging. **b** the state of being indulgent. **2** something indulged in. **3** *RC Ch.* the remission of temporal punishment in purgatory, still due for sins after absolution. **4** a privilege granted. [Middle English via Old French from Latin *indulgentia* (as INDULGENT)]

indulgent /ɪnˈdʌldʒ(ə)nt/ *adj.* **1** ready or too ready to overlook faults etc. **2** indulging or tending to indulge. □ **indulgently** *adv.* [French *indulgent* or Latin *indulgere indulgent-* (as INDULGE)]

indumentum /ɪndjʊˈmɛntəm/ *n.* (*pl.* **indumenta** /-tə/) *Bot.* the covering of hairs on part of a plant, esp. when dense. [Latin, = garment]

induna /ɪnˈduːnə/ *n. S.Afr.* **1** a tribal councillor or headman. **2 a** an African foreman. **b** a person in authority. [Nguni *inDuna* 'captain, councillor']

indurate /ˈɪndjʊreɪt/ *v.* **1** *tr. & intr.* make or become hard. **2** *tr.* make callous or unfeeling. **3** *intr.* become inveterate. □ **induration** /-ˈreɪʃ(ə)n/ *n.* **indurative** *adj.* [Latin *indurare* (as IN-[2], *durus* 'hard')]

indusium /ɪnˈdjuːzɪəm/ *n.* (*pl.* **indusia** /-zɪə/) **1** a membranous shield covering the fruit-cluster of a fern. **2** a collection of hairs enclosing the stigma of some flowers. **3** the case of a larva. □ **indusial** *adj.* [Latin, = tunic, from *induere* 'put on' (a garment)]

industrial /ɪnˈdʌstrɪəl/ *adj. & n.* ● *adj.* **1** of or relating to industry or industries. **2** designed or suitable for use in industry (*industrial alcohol*). **3** characterized by highly developed industries (*the industrial nations*). ● *n.* (in *pl.*) shares in industrial companies. □ **industrially** *adv.* [INDUSTRY + -AL: in 19th c. partly from French *industriel*]

industrial action *n. Brit.* any action, esp. a strike or work to rule, taken by employees as a protest.

industrial archaeology *n.* the study of machines, factories, bridges, etc., formerly used in industry.

industrial estate *n. Brit.* an area of land developed for the siting of industrial enterprises.

industrialism /ɪnˈdʌstrɪəlɪz(ə)m/ *n.* a social or economic system in which manufacturing industries are prevalent.

industrialist /ɪnˈdʌstrɪəlɪst/ *n.* a person engaged in the management of industry.

industrialize /ɪnˈdʌstrɪəlʌɪz/ *v.* (also **-ise**) **1** *tr.* introduce industries to (a country or region etc.). **2** *intr.* become industrialized. □ **industrialization** /-ˈzeɪʃ(ə)n/ *n.*

industrial park *n. N. Amer.* = INDUSTRIAL ESTATE.

industrial relations *n.pl.* the relations between management and workers in industries.

Industrial Revolution *n.* the rapid development of a nation's industry (esp. in Britain in the late 18th and early 19th c.).

industrial-strength *adj.* (often *attrib.*) often *joc.* strong, powerful (*industrial-strength coffee*).

industrious /ɪnˈdʌstrɪəs/ *adj.* diligent, hard-working. □ **industriously** *adv.* **industriousness** *n.* [French *industrieux* or Late Latin *industriosus* (as INDUSTRY)]

industry /ˈɪndəstri/ *n.* (*pl.* **-ies**) **1 a** a branch of trade or manufacture. **b** trade and manufacture collectively (*incentives to industry*). **2** concerted or copious activity (*the building was a hive of industry*). **3 a** diligence. **b** *colloq.* the diligent study of a particular topic (*the Shakespeare industry*). **4** habitual employment in useful work. [Middle English, = skill, from French *industrie* or Latin *industria* 'diligence']

indwell /ɪnˈdwɛl/ *v.* (*past* and *past part.* **indwelt**) **1 a** *intr.* (often foll. by *in*) be permanently present as a spirit, principle, etc. **b** *tr.* inhabit spiritually. **2** *intr.* (as **indwelling** *adj.*) *Med.* (of a catheter, needle, etc.) fixed in the body over a long period. □ **indweller** *n.*

Indy /ˈɪndi/ *n.* a chiefly American form of motor racing, usu. at very high speeds on oval circuits (often *attrib.*: *Indy racing*). [*Indianapolis* in the US, where the principal Indy race is held]

Indycar /ˈɪndɪkɑː/ *n.* **1** a car used in Indy racing. **2** (*attrib.*) = INDY (*Indycar champion*; *Indycar team*).

-ine[1] /ʌɪn, ɪn, iːn/ *suffix* forming adjectives, meaning 'belonging to, of the nature of' (*Alpine*; *asinine*). [from or suggested by French *-in -ine*, or from Latin *-inus*]

-ine[2] /ʌɪn/ *suffix* forming adjectives esp. from names of minerals, plants, etc. (*crystalline*). [Latin *-inus* from or suggested by Greek *-inos*]

-ine[3] /ɪn, iːn/ *suffix* forming feminine nouns (*heroine*; *margravine*). [French via Latin *-ina* from Greek *-inē*, or from German *-in*]

-ine[4] *suffix* **1** /ɪn/ forming (esp. abstract) nouns (*discipline*; *medicine*). **2** /iːn, ɪn/ *Chem.* forming nouns denoting derived substances, esp. alkaloids, halogens, amines, and amino acids. [French from Latin *-ina* (fem.) = -INE[1]]

inebriate *v., adj., & n.* ● *v.tr.* /ɪˈniːbrɪeɪt/ **1** make drunk; intoxicate. **2** excite. ● *adj.* /ɪˈniːbrɪət/ drunken. ● *n.* /ɪˈniːbrɪət/ a drunken person, esp. a habitual drunkard. □ **inebriation** /-ˈeɪʃ(ə)n/ *n.* **inebriety** /-ˈbrʌɪəti/ *n.* [Middle English from Latin *inebriatus*, past part. of *inebriare* (as IN-[2], *ebrius* 'drunk')]

inedible /ɪnˈɛdɪb(ə)l/ *adj.* not edible, esp. not suitable for eating (cf. UNEATABLE). □ **inedibility** /-ˈbɪlɪti/ *n.*

ineducable /ɪnˈɛdjʊkəb(ə)l, -dʒʊ-/ *adj.* incapable of being educated, esp. through mental handicap. □ **ineducability** /-ˈbɪlɪti/ *n.*

ineffable /ɪnˈɛfəb(ə)l/ *adj.* **1** unutterable; too great for description in words. **2** that must not be uttered. □ **ineffability** /-ˈbɪlɪti/ *n.* **ineffably** *adv.* [Middle English from Old French *ineffable* or Latin *ineffabilis* (as IN-[1], *effari* 'speak out, utter')]

ineffaceable /ɪnɪˈfeɪsəb(ə)l/ *adj.* that cannot be effaced. □ **ineffaceability** /-ˈbɪlɪti/ *n.* **ineffaceably** *adv.*

ineffective /ɪnɪˈfɛktɪv/ *adj.* **1** not producing any effect or the desired effect. **2** (of a person) inefficient; not achieving results. **3** lacking artistic effect. □ **ineffectively** *adv.* **ineffectiveness** *n.*

ineffectual /ɪnɪˈfɛktʃʊəl/ *adj.* **1 a** without effect. **b** not producing the desired or expected effect. **2** (of a person) lacking the ability to achieve results (*an ineffectual leader*). □ **ineffectuality** /-tʃʊˈalɪti/ *n.* **ineffectually** *adv.* **ineffectualness** *n.* [Middle English from medieval Latin *ineffectualis* (as IN-[1], EFFECTUAL)]

inefficacious /ˌɪnɛfɪˈkeɪʃəs/ *adj.* (of a remedy etc.) not producing the desired effect. □ **inefficaciously** *adv.* **inefficaciousness** *n.* **inefficacy** /ɪnˈɛfɪkəsi/ *n.*

inefficient /ɪnɪˈfɪʃ(ə)nt/ *adj.* **1** not efficient. **2** (of a person) not fully capable; not well qualified. □ **inefficiency** *n.* **inefficiently** *adv.*

inelastic /ɪnɪˈlastɪk/ *adj.* **1** not elastic. **2** unadaptable, inflexible, unyielding. **3** *Physics* (of a collision etc.) involving an overall loss of translational kinetic energy. □ **inelastically** *adv.* **inelasticity** /-ˈstɪsɪti/ *n.*

inelegant /ɪnˈɛlɪg(ə)nt/ *adj.* **1** ungraceful. **2 a** unrefined. **b** (of a style) unpolished. □ **inelegance** *n.* **inelegantly** *adv.* [French *inélégant* from Latin *inelegans* (as IN-[1], ELEGANT)]

ineligible /ɪnˈɛlɪdʒɪb(ə)l/ *adj.* **1** not eligible. **2** undesirable. □ **ineligibility** /-ˈbɪlɪti/ *n.* **ineligibly** *adv.*

ineluctable /ɪnɪˈlʌktəb(ə)l/ *adj.* **1** against which it is useless to struggle. **2** that cannot be escaped from. □ **ineluctability** /-ˈbɪlɪti/ *n.* **ineluctably** *adv.* [Latin *ineluctabilis* (as IN-[1], *eluctari* 'struggle out')]

inept /ɪˈnɛpt/ *adj.* **1 a** clumsy, unskilful. **b** absurd, silly. **2** out of place; inappropriate. □ **ineptitude** *n.* **ineptly** *adv.* **ineptness** *n.* [Latin *ineptus* (as IN-[1], APT)]

■ **Usage** *Inept* and *inapt* are easily confused because they have virtually the same meanings and are closely related etymologically. However, *inept* is a far commoner word than *inapt* and is usually used in sense 1a 'clumsy, unskilful'. *Inapt* is more often used to mean 'unsuitable, inappropriate'. This difference is illustrated by the example *His after-dinner speech was both inept and inapt*, i.e. it was both clumsy and inappropriate.

inequable /ɪn'ɛkwəb(ə)l/ *adj.* **1** not fairly distributed. **2** not uniform. [Latin *inaequabilis* 'uneven' (as IN-[1], EQUABLE)]

inequality /ɪnɪ'kwɒlɪti/ *n.* (*pl.* **-ies**) **1 a** lack of equality in any respect. **b** an instance of this. **2** the state of being variable. **3** (of a surface) irregularity. **4** *Math.* a formula affirming that two expressions are not equal. [Middle English from Old French *inequalité* or Latin *inaequalitas* (as IN-[1], EQUALITY)]

inequitable /ɪn'ɛkwɪtəb(ə)l/ *adj.* unfair, unjust. ▫ **inequitably** *adv.*

inequity /ɪn'ɛkwɪti/ *n.* (*pl.* **-ies**) unfairness, bias.

ineradicable /ɪnɪ'radɪkəb(ə)l/ *adj.* that cannot be eradicated. ▫ **ineradicably** *adv.*

inerrant /ɪn'ɛr(ə)nt/ *adj.* not liable to err. ▫ **inerrancy** *n.* [Latin *inerrans* (as IN-[1], ERR)]

inert /ɪ'nəːt/ *adj.* **1** without inherent power of action, motion, or resistance. **2** without active chemical or other properties. **3** sluggish, slow. ▫ **inertly** *adv.* **inertness** *n.* [Latin *iners inert-* (as IN-[1], *ars* ART[1])]

inert gas *n.* = NOBLE GAS.

inertia /ɪ'nəːʃə/ *n.* **1** *Physics* a property of matter by which it continues in its existing state of rest or uniform motion in a straight line, unless that state is changed by an external force. **2 a** inertness, sloth. **b** a tendency to remain unchanged. ▫ **inertial** *adj.* **inertialess** *adj.* [Latin (as INERT)]

inertial guidance *n.* guidance of a missile by internal instruments which measure its acceleration and compare the calculated position with stored data.

inertia reel *n.* a reel device which allows a vehicle seat belt to unwind freely but which locks under force of impact or rapid deceleration.

inertia selling *n. Brit.* the sending of unsolicited goods in the hope of making a sale.

inescapable /ɪnɪ'skeɪpəb(ə)l, ɪnɛ-/ *adj.* that cannot be escaped or avoided. ▫ **inescapability** /-'bɪlɪti/ *n.* **inescapably** *adv.*

-iness /ɪnɪs/ *suffix* forming nouns corresponding to adjectives ending in *-y* (see -Y[1], -LY[2]).

inessential /ɪnɪ'sɛnʃ(ə)l/ *adj.* & *n.* ● *adj.* **1** not necessary. **2** dispensable. ● *n.* an inessential thing.

inestimable /ɪn'ɛstɪməb(ə)l/ *adj.* too great, intense, precious, etc., to be estimated. ▫ **inestimably** *adv.* [Middle English via Old French from Latin *inaestimabilis* (as IN-[1], ESTIMABLE)]

inevitable /ɪn'ɛvɪtəb(ə)l/ *adj.* & *n.* ● *adj.* **1 a** unavoidable. **b** that is bound to occur or appear. **2** *colloq.* that is tiresomely predictable (*the inevitable soap opera romance*). **3** (of the development of a plot, characters, etc.) so true to nature etc. as to preclude alternative treatment or solution; convincing. ● *n.* **1** (prec. by *the*) that which is inevitable. **2** an inevitable fact, event, truth, etc. (*old age and other inevitables*). ▫ **inevitability** /-'bɪlɪti/ *n.* **inevitableness** *n.* **inevitably** *adv.* [Latin *inevitabilis* (as IN-[1], *evitare* 'avoid')]

inexact /ɪnɪg'zakt, ɪnɛg-/ *adj.* not exact. ▫ **inexactitude** *n.* **inexactly** *adv.* **inexactness** *n.*

inexcusable /ɪnɪk'skjuːzəb(ə)l, ɪnɛk-/ *adj.* (of a person, action, etc.) that cannot be excused or justified. ▫ **inexcusably** *adv.* [Middle English from Latin *inexcusabilis* (as IN-[1], EXCUSE)]

inexhaustible /ɪnɪg'zɔːstɪb(ə)l, ɪnɛg-/ *adj.* that cannot be exhausted or used up. ▫ **inexhaustibility** /-'bɪlɪti/ *n.* **inexhaustibly** *adv.*

inexorable /ɪn'ɛks(ə)rəb(ə)l/ *adj.* **1** relentless. **2** (of a person or attribute) that cannot be persuaded by request or entreaty. ▫ **inexorability** /-'bɪlɪti/ *n.* **inexorably** *adv.* [French *inexorable* or Latin *inexorabilis* (as IN-[1], *exorare* 'entreat')]

inexpedient /ɪnɪk'spiːdɪənt, ɪnɛk-/ *adj.* not expedient. ▫ **inexpediency** *n.*

inexpensive /ɪnɪk'spɛnsɪv, ɪnɛk-/ *adj.* not expensive, cheap. ▫ **inexpensively** *adv.* **inexpensiveness** *n.*

inexperience /ɪnɪk'spɪərɪəns, ɪnɛk-/ *n.* lack of experience, or of the resulting knowledge or skill. ▫ **inexperienced** *adj.* [French *inexpérience* from Late Latin *inexperientia* (as IN-[1], EXPERIENCE)]

inexpert /ɪn'ɛkspəːt/ *adj.* unskilful; lacking expertise. ▫ **inexpertly** *adv.* **inexpertness** *n.* [Middle English via Old French from Latin *inexpertus* (as IN-[1], EXPERT)]

inexpiable /ɪn'ɛkspɪəb(ə)l/ *adj.* (of an act or feeling) that cannot be expiated or appeased. ▫ **inexpiably** *adv.* [Latin *inexpiabilis* (as IN-[1], EXPIATE)]

inexplicable /ɪnɪk'splɪkəb(ə)l, ɪnɛk-, ɪn'ɛksplɪ-/ *adj.* that cannot be explained or accounted for. ▫ **inexplicability** /-'bɪlɪti/ *n.* **inexplicably** *adv.* [French *inexplicable* or Latin *inexplicabilis* 'that cannot be unfolded' (as IN-[1], EXPLICABLE)]

inexplicit /ɪnɪk'splɪsɪt, ɪnɛk-/ *adj.* not definitely or clearly expressed. ▫ **inexplicitness** *n.*

inexpressible /ɪnɪk'sprɛsɪb(ə)l, ɪnɛk-/ *adj.* that cannot be expressed. ▫ **inexpressibly** *adv.*

inexpressive /ɪnɪk'sprɛsɪv, ɪnɛk-/ *adj.* not expressive. ▫ **inexpressively** *adv.* **inexpressiveness** *n.*

inexpungible /ɪnɪk'spʌn(d)ʒɪb(ə)l, ɪnɛk-/ *adj.* that cannot be expunged or obliterated.

in extenso /ˌɪn ɛk'stɛnsəʊ/ *adv.* in full; at length. [Latin]

inextinguishable /ɪnɪk'stɪŋgwɪʃəb(ə)l, ɪnɛk-/ *adj.* **1** not quenchable. **2** indestructible. **3** (of laughter etc.) irrepressible.

in extremis /ˌɪn ɛk'striːmɪs/ *adj.* **1** at the point of death. **2** in great difficulties. [Latin]

inextricable /ɪn'ɛkstrɪkəb(ə)l, ɪnɪk'strɪk-, ɪnɛk-/ *adj.* **1** (of a circumstance) that cannot be escaped from. **2** (of a knot, problem, etc.) that cannot be unravelled or solved. **3** intricately confused. ▫ **inextricability** /-'bɪlɪti/ *n.* **inextricably** *adv.* [Middle English from Latin *inextricabilis* (as IN-[1], EXTRICATE)]

INF *abbr.* intermediate-range nuclear force(s).

infallible /ɪn'falɪb(ə)l/ *adj.* **1** incapable of error. **2** (of a method, test, proof, etc.) unfailing; sure to succeed. **3** *RC Ch.* (of the Pope) unable to err in pronouncing dogma as doctrinally defined. ▫ **infallibility** /-'bɪlɪti/ *n.* **infallibly** *adv.* [Middle English from French *infaillible* or Late Latin *infallibilis* (as IN-[1], FALLIBLE)]

infamous /'ɪnfəməs/ *adj.* **1** notoriously bad; having a bad reputation. **2** abominable. **3** (in ancient law) deprived of all or some citizens' rights on account of serious crime. ▫ **infamously** *adv.* **infamy** /'ɪnfəmi/ *n.* (*pl.* **-ies**). [Middle English via medieval Latin *infamosus* from Latin *infamis* (as IN-[1], FAME)]

infancy /'ɪnf(ə)nsi/ *n.* (*pl.* **-ies**) **1** early childhood; babyhood. **2** an early state in the development of an idea, undertaking, etc. **3** *Law* the state of being a minor. [Latin *infantia* (as INFANT)]

infant /'ɪnf(ə)nt/ *n.* **1 a** a child during the earliest period of its life. **b** *Brit.* a schoolchild below the age of seven years. **2** (esp. *attrib.*) a thing in an early stage of its development. **3** *Law* a minor; a person under 18. [Middle English via Old French *enfant* from Latin *infans* 'unable to speak' (as IN-[1], *fans fantis*, pres. part. of *fari* 'speak')]

infanta /ɪn'fantə/ *n. hist.* a daughter of the ruling monarch of Spain or Portugal (usu. the eldest daughter who is not heir to the throne). [Spanish & Portuguese, fem. of INFANTE]

infante /ɪn'fanti/ *n. hist.* the second son of the ruling monarch of Spain or Portugal. [Spanish & Portuguese from Latin (as INFANT)]

infanticide /ɪn'fantɪsʌɪd/ *n.* **1** the killing of an infant soon after birth. **2** the practice of killing newborn infants. **3** a person who kills an infant. ▫ **infanticidal** /-'sʌɪd(ə)l/ *adj.* [French from Late Latin *infanticidium*, *-cida* (as INFANT)]

infantile /'ɪnf(ə)ntʌɪl/ *adj.* **1 a** like or characteristic of a child. **b** childish, immature (*infantile humour*). **2** in its infancy. ▫ **infantility** /-'tɪlɪti/ *n.* (*pl.* **-ies**). [French *infantile* or Latin *infantilis* (as INFANT)]

infantile paralysis *n.* poliomyelitis.

infantilism /ɪnˈfantɪlɪz(ə)m/ *n.* **1** childish behaviour. **2** *Psychol.* the persistence of infantile characteristics or behaviour in adult life.

infant mortality *n.* death before the age of one.

infantry /ˈɪnf(ə)ntri/ *n.* (*pl.* **-ies**) a body of soldiers who march and fight on foot; foot soldiers collectively. [French *infanterie* from Italian *infanteria*, from *infante* 'youth, infantryman' (as INFANT)]

infantryman /ˈɪnf(ə)ntrɪmən/ *n.* (*pl.* **-men**) a soldier of an infantry regiment.

infarct /ˈɪnfɑːkt, ɪnˈfɑːkt/ *n. Med.* a small localized area of dead tissue caused by an inadequate blood supply. ▫ **infarction** /ɪnˈfɑːkʃ(ə)n/ *n.* [modern Latin *infarctus* (as IN-[2], Latin *farcire farct-* 'stuff')]

infatuate /ɪnˈfatjʊət, -tʃʊ-/ *v.tr.* **1** inspire with intense usu. transitory fondness or admiration. **2** affect with extreme folly. ▫ **infatuation** /-ˈeɪʃ(ə)n/ *n.* [Latin *infatuare* (as IN-[2], *fatuus* 'foolish')]

infatuated /ɪnˈfatjʊeɪtɪd, -tʃʊ-/ *adj.* (often foll. by *with*) affected by an intense fondness or admiration.

infauna /ˈɪnfɔːnə/ *n.* the animal life found within the sediments of the ocean floor, river beds, etc. ▫ **infaunal** *adj.* [Danish *ifauna* (as IN-[2], FAUNA)]

infeasible /ɪnˈfiːzɪb(ə)l/ *adj.* not feasible; impractical. ▫ **infeasibility** /-ˈbɪlɪti/ *n.*

infect /ɪnˈfɛkt/ *v.tr.* **1** contaminate (air, water, etc.) with harmful organisms or noxious matter. **2 a** affect (a person) with disease etc. **b** affect (a computer system) with a virus. **3** instil bad feeling or opinion into (a person). ▫ **infector** *n.* [Middle English from Latin *inficere infect-* 'taint' (as IN-[2], *facere* 'make')]

infection /ɪnˈfɛkʃ(ə)n/ *n.* **1 a** the process of infecting or state of being infected. **b** an instance of this; an infectious disease. **c** the presence of a virus in, or its entry into, a computer system. **2** communication of disease, esp. by the agency of air or water etc. **3 a** moral contamination. **b** the diffusive influence of example, sympathy, etc. [Middle English from Old French *infection* or Late Latin *infectio* (as INFECT)]

infectious /ɪnˈfɛkʃəs/ *adj.* **1** infecting with disease. **2** (of a disease) liable to be transmitted by air, water, etc. **3** (of emotions etc.) apt to spread; quickly affecting others. ▫ **infectiously** *adv.* **infectiousness** *n.*

infective /ɪnˈfɛktɪv/ *adj.* **1** capable of infecting with disease. **2** infectious. ▫ **infectiveness** *n.* [Latin *infectivus* (as INFECT)]

infelicitous /ɪnfɪˈlɪsɪtəs/ *adj.* not felicitous; unfortunate. ▫ **infelicitously** *adv.*

infelicity /ɪnfɪˈlɪsɪti/ *n.* (*pl.* **-ies**) **1 a** inaptness of expression etc. **b** an instance of this. **2 a** unhappiness. **b** a misfortune. [Middle English from Latin *infelicitas* (as IN-[1], FELICITY)]

infer /ɪnˈfəː/ *v.tr.* (**inferred**, **inferring**) (often foll. by *that* + clause) **1** deduce or conclude from facts and reasoning. **2** *disp.* imply, suggest. ▫ **inferable** *adj.* (also **inferrable**). [Latin *inferre* (as IN-[2], *ferre* 'bring')]

▪ **Usage** The use of *infer* in sense 2 is considered incorrect by many people since it is the reverse of the primary sense of the verb. It should be avoided by using *imply* or *suggest*.

inference /ˈɪnf(ə)r(ə)ns/ *n.* **1** the act or an instance of inferring. **2** *Logic* **a** the forming of a conclusion from premisses. **b** a thing inferred. ▫ **inferential** /-ˈrɛnʃ(ə)l/ *adj.* **inferentially** /-ˈrɛnʃ(ə)li/ *adv.* [medieval Latin *inferentia* (as INFER)]

inferior /ɪnˈfɪərɪə/ *adj.* & *n.* ● *adj.* **1** (often foll. by *to*) **a** lower; in a lower position. **b** of lower rank, quality, etc. **2** poor in quality. **3** (of a planet) having an orbit closer to the sun than the earth's. **4** *Bot.* situated below an ovary or calyx. **5** (of figures or letters) written or printed below the line. ● *n.* **1** a person inferior to another, esp. in rank. **2** an inferior letter or figure. ▫ **inferiorly** *adv.* [Middle English from Latin, comparative of *inferus* 'that is below']

inferiority /ɪnˌfɪərɪˈɒrɪti/ *n.* the state of being inferior.

inferiority complex *n.* an unrealistic feeling of general inadequacy caused by actual or supposed inferiority in one sphere, sometimes marked by aggressive behaviour in compensation.

infernal /ɪnˈfəːn(ə)l/ *adj.* **1 a** of hell or the underworld. **b** hellish, fiendish. **2** *colloq.* detestable, tiresome. ▫ **infernally** *adv.* [Middle English via Old French and Late Latin *infernalis* from Latin *infernus* 'situated below']

inferno /ɪnˈfəːnəʊ/ *n.* (*pl.* **-os**) **1** a raging fire. **2** a scene of horror or distress. **3** hell, esp. with reference to Dante's *Divine Comedy*. [Italian from Late Latin *infernus* (as INFERNAL)]

infertile /ɪnˈfəːtʌɪl/ *adj.* not fertile. ▫ **infertility** /-ˈtɪlɪti/ *n.* [French *infertile* or Late Latin *infertilis* (as IN-[1], FERTILE)]

infest /ɪnˈfɛst/ *v.tr.* (of harmful persons or things, esp. vermin or disease) overrun (a place) in large numbers. ▫ **infestation** /-ˈsteɪʃ(ə)n/ *n.* [Middle English from French *infester* or Latin *infestare* 'assail', from *infestus* 'hostile']

infibulate /ɪnˈfɪbjʊleɪt/ *v.tr.* (usu. as **infibulated** *adj.*) subject to infibulation. [Latin *infibulat-*, past part. stem of *infibulare* (as IN-[2] + FIBULA)]

infibulation /ɪnˌfɪbjʊˈleɪʃ(ə)n/ *n.* the practice in some cultures of partially stitching together the labia, often after excision of the clitoris, to prevent sexual intercourse.

infidel /ˈɪnfɪd(ə)l/ *n.* & *adj.* ● *n.* **1** a person who does not believe in religion or in a particular religion; an unbeliever. **2** *hist.* an adherent of a religion other than Christianity, esp. a Muslim. ● *adj.* **1** that is an infidel. **2** of unbelievers. [Middle English from French *infidèle* or Latin *infidelis* (as IN-[1], *fidelis* 'faithful')]

infidelity /ɪnfɪˈdɛlɪti/ *n.* (*pl.* **-ies**) **1 a** disloyalty, or esp. unfaithfulness to a sexual partner. **b** an instance of this. **2** disbelief in Christianity or another religion. [Middle English from French *infidélité* or Latin *infidelitas* (as INFIDEL)]

infield /ˈɪnfiːld/ *n.* **1** *Cricket* **a** the part of the ground near the wicket. **b** the fielders stationed there. **2** *Baseball* **a** the area within the four bases. **b** the defensive positions near the bases. **c** the fielders at these positions. **3** farmland around or near a homestead. **4 a** arable land. **b** land regularly manured and cropped. ▫ **infielder** *n.* (in senses 1b, 2c).

infighting /ˈɪnfʌɪtɪŋ/ *n.* **1** hidden conflict or competitiveness within an organization. **2** boxing at closer quarters than arm's length. ▫ **infighter** *n.*

infill *n.* & *v.* ● *n.* /ˈɪnfɪl/ **1** material used to fill a hole, gap, etc. **2** the placing of buildings to occupy the space between existing ones. ● *v.tr.* /ɪnˈfɪl/ fill in (a cavity etc.).

infilling /ˈɪnfɪlɪŋ/ *n.* = INFILL *n.*

infiltrate /ˈɪnfɪltreɪt/ *v.* **1 a** *tr.* & *intr.* penetrate, gain entrance or access (to) surreptitiously and by degrees (as spies etc.). **b** *tr.* cause to do this. **2** *tr.* & *intr.* permeate by filtration. **3** *tr.* & *intr.* (often foll. by *into*, *through*) introduce (fluid) by filtration. ▫ **infiltration** /-ˈtreɪʃ(ə)n/ *n.* **infiltrator** *n.* [IN-[2] + FILTRATE]

infinite /ˈɪnfɪnɪt/ *adj.* & *n.* ● *adj.* **1** boundless, endless. **2** very great. **3** (usu. with *pl.*) innumerable; very many (*infinite resources*). **4** *Math.* **a** greater than any assignable quantity or countable number. **b** (of a series) that may be continued indefinitely. **5** *Gram.* (of a verb part) not limited by person or number, e.g. infinitive, gerund, and participle. ● *n.* **1** (**the Infinite**) God. **2** (**the infinite**) infinite space. ▫ **infinitely** *adv.* **infiniteness** *n.* [Middle English from Latin *infinitus* (as IN-[1], FINITE)]

infinitesimal /ˌɪnfɪnɪˈtɛsɪm(ə)l/ *adj.* & *n.* ● *adj.* infinitely or very small. ● *n.* an infinitesimal amount. ▫ **infinitesimally** *adv.* [modern Latin *infinitesimus* from INFINITE: cf. CENTESIMAL]

infinitesimal calculus *n.* the differential and integral calculuses regarded as one subject.

infinitive /ɪnˈfɪnɪtɪv/ *n. & adj.* ● *n.* a form of a verb expressing the verbal notion without reference to a particular subject, tense, etc. (e.g. *see* in *we came to see, let him see*). ● *adj.* having this form. ▫ **infinitival** /-ˈtʌɪv(ə)l/ *adj.* **infinitivally** /-ˈtʌɪv(ə)li/ *adv.* [Latin *infinitivus* (as IN-[1], *finitivus* 'definite' from *finire finit-* 'define')]

infinitude /ɪnˈfɪnɪtjuːd/ *n.* **1** the state of being infinite; boundlessness. **2** (often foll. by *of*) a boundless number or extent. [Latin *infinitus*: see INFINITE, -TUDE]

infinity /ɪnˈfɪnɪti/ *n.* (*pl.* **-ies**) **1** the state of being infinite. **2** an infinite number or extent. **3** infinite distance. **4** *Math.* infinite quantity (symbol ∞). [Middle English from Old French *infinité* or Latin *infinitas* (as INFINITE)]

infirm /ɪnˈfəːm/ *adj.* **1** physically weak, esp. through age. **2** (of a person, mind, judgement, etc.) weak, irresolute. ▫ **infirmity** *n.* (*pl.* **-ies**). **infirmly** *adv.* [Middle English from Latin *infirmus* (as IN-[1], FIRM[1])]

infirmary /ɪnˈfəːm(ə)ri/ *n.* (*pl.* **-ies**) **1** a hospital. **2** a place for those who are ill in a monastery, school, etc. [medieval Latin *infirmaria* (as INFIRM)]

infix *v. & n.* ● *v.tr.* /ɪnˈfɪks/ **1** (often foll. by *in*) **a** fix (a thing in another). **b** impress (a fact etc. in the mind). **2** *Gram.* insert (a formative element) into the body of a word. ● *n.* /ˈɪnfɪks/ *Gram.* a formative element inserted in a word. ▫ **infixation** /-ˈseɪʃ(ə)n/ *n.* [Latin *infigere infix-* (as IN-[2], FIX): the noun on the pattern of *prefix, suffix*]

in flagrante delicto /ɪn fləˌgrantɪ dɪˈlɪktəʊ/ *adv.* in the very act of committing an offence. [Latin, = in blazing crime]

inflame /ɪnˈfleɪm/ *v.* **1** *tr. & intr.* (often foll. by *with, by*) provoke or become provoked to strong feeling, esp. anger. **2** *Med.* **a** *intr.* become hot, reddened, and sore. **b** *tr.* cause inflammation or fever in (a body etc.); make hot. **3** *tr.* aggravate. **4** *intr. & tr.* catch or set on fire. **5** *tr.* light up with or as if with flames. ▫ **inflamer** *n.* [Middle English via Old French *enflammer* from Latin *inflammare* (as IN-[2], *flamma* 'flame')]

inflammable /ɪnˈflaməb(ə)l/ *adj. & n.* ● *adj.* **1** easily set on fire; flammable. **2** easily excited. ● *n.* (usu. in *pl.*) an inflammable substance. ▫ **inflammability** /-ˈbɪlɪti/ *n.* **inflammableness** *n.* **inflammably** *adv.* [INFLAME, suggested by French *inflammable*]

■ **Usage** See Usage Note at FLAMMABLE.

inflammation /ɪnfləˈmeɪʃ(ə)n/ *n.* **1** the act or an instance of inflaming. **2** *Med.* a localized physical condition with heat, swelling, redness, and usu. pain, esp. as a reaction to injury or infection. [Latin *inflammatio* (as INFLAME)]

inflammatory /ɪnˈflamət(ə)ri/ *adj.* **1** (esp. of speeches, leaflets, etc.) tending to cause anger etc. **2** of or tending to inflammation of the body.

inflatable /ɪnˈfleɪtəb(ə)l/ *adj. & n.* ● *adj.* that can be inflated. ● *n.* an inflatable plastic or rubber object.

inflate /ɪnˈfleɪt/ *v.tr.* **1** distend (a balloon etc.) with air. **2** (usu. foll. by *with*; usu. in *passive*) puff up (a person with pride etc.). **3 a** (often *absol.*) bring about inflation of (a currency). **b** raise (prices) artificially. **4** exaggerate or embellish. **5** (as **inflated** *adj.*) (esp. of language, sentiments, etc.) bombastic. ▫ **inflatedly** *adv.* **inflatedness** *n.* **inflater** *n.* **inflator** *n.* [Latin *inflare inflat-* (as IN-[2], *flare* 'blow')]

inflation /ɪnˈfleɪʃ(ə)n/ *n.* **1 a** the act or condition of inflating or being inflated. **b** an instance of this. **2** *Econ.* **a** a general increase in prices and fall in the purchasing value of money. **b** an increase in available currency regarded as causing this. ▫ **inflationary** *adj.* **inflationism** *n.* **inflationist** *n. & adj.* [Middle English from Latin *inflatio* (as INFLATE)]

inflect /ɪnˈflɛkt/ *v.* **1** *tr.* change the pitch of (the voice, a musical note, etc.). **2** *Gram.* **a** *tr.* change the form of (a word) to express tense, gender, number, mood, etc. **b** *intr.* (of a word, language, etc.) undergo such change. **3** *tr.* bend inwards; curve. ▫ **inflective** *adj.* [Middle English from Latin *inflectere inflex-* (as IN-[2], *flectere* 'bend')]

inflection /ɪnˈflɛkʃ(ə)n/ *n.* (also **inflexion**) **1 a** the act or condition of inflecting or being inflected. **b** an instance of this. **2** *Gram.* **a** the process or practice of inflecting words. **b** an inflected form of a word. **c** a suffix etc. used to inflect, e.g. *-ed*. **3** a modulation of the voice. **4** *Geom.* a change of curvature from convex to concave at a particular point on a curve. ▫ **inflectional** *adj.* **inflectionally** *adv.* **inflectionless** *adj.* [French *inflection* or Latin *inflexio* (as INFLECT)]

inflexible /ɪnˈflɛksɪb(ə)l/ *adj.* **1** unbendable. **2** stiff; immovable; obstinate (*old and inflexible in his attitudes*). **3** unchangeable; inexorable. ▫ **inflexibility** /-ˈbɪlɪti/ *n.* **inflexibly** *adv.* [Latin *inflexibilis* (as IN-[1], FLEXIBLE)]

inflict /ɪnˈflɪkt/ *v.tr.* (usu. foll. by *on, upon*) **1** administer, deal (a stroke, wound, defeat, etc.). **2** (also *refl.*) often *joc.* impose (suffering, a penalty, oneself, one's company, etc.) on (*shall not inflict myself on you any longer*). ▫ **inflictable** *adj.* **inflicter** *n.* **inflictor** *n.* [Latin *infligere inflict-* (as IN-[2], *fligere* 'strike')]

■ **Usage** Care should be taken not to confuse *inflict* with *afflict*. One *inflicts* something *on* or *upon* someone, or one is *afflicted with* or *by* something, e.g. *They were afflicted by a virus* is correct, as is *A virus was inflicted upon them*.

infliction /ɪnˈflɪkʃ(ə)n/ *n.* **1** the act or an instance of inflicting. **2** something inflicted, esp. a troublesome or boring experience. [Late Latin *inflictio* (as INFLICT)]

in-flight /ˈɪnflʌɪt/ *attrib.adj.* occurring or provided during an aircraft flight.

inflorescence /ɪnflɔːˈrɛs(ə)ns, -flə-/ *n.* **1** *Bot.* **a** the complete flower head of a plant including stems, stalks, bracts, and flowers. **b** the arrangement of this. **2** the process of flowering. [modern Latin *inflorescentia* from Late Latin *inflorescere* (as IN-[2], FLORESCENCE)]

inflow /ˈɪnfləʊ/ *n.* **1** a flowing in. **2** something that flows in. ▫ **inflowing** *n. & adj.*

influence /ˈɪnflʊəns/ *n. & v.* ● *n.* **1 a** (usu. foll. by *on, upon*) the effect a person or thing has on another. **b** (usu. foll. by *over, with*) moral ascendancy or power. **c** a thing or person exercising such power (*is a good influence on them*). **2** *Astrol.* an ethereal fluid supposedly flowing from the stars and affecting character and destiny. **3** *Electr. archaic* = INDUCTION 5. ● *v.tr.* exert influence on; have an effect on. ▫ **under the influence** *colloq.* affected by alcoholic drink. ▫ **influenceable** *adj.* **influencer** *n.* [Middle English via Old French *influence* or medieval Latin *influentia* 'inflow' from Latin *influere* 'flow in' (as IN-[2], *fluere* 'flow')]

influent /ˈɪnflʊənt/ *adj. & n.* ● *adj.* flowing in. ● *n.* a tributary stream. [Middle English from Latin (as INFLUENCE)]

influential /ɪnflʊˈɛnʃ(ə)l/ *adj.* having a great influence or power (*influential in the financial world*). ▫ **influentially** *adv.* [medieval Latin *influentia* INFLUENCE]

influenza /ɪnflʊˈɛnzə/ *n.* a highly contagious virus infection causing fever, severe aching, and catarrh, often occurring in epidemics. ▫ **influenzal** *adj.* [Italian from medieval Latin *influentia* INFLUENCE]

influx /ˈɪnflʌks/ *n.* **1** a continual stream of people or things (*an influx of complaints*). **2** (usu. foll. by *into*) a flowing in, esp. of a stream etc. [French *influx* or Late Latin *influxus* (as IN-[2], FLUX)]

info /ˈɪnfəʊ/ *n. colloq.* information. [abbreviation]

infomercial /ɪnfəˈməːʃ(ə)l/ *n.* (also **informercial**) esp. *US* an advertising film, esp. on television, which promotes a product in an informative and purportedly objective style. [INFORMATION + COMMERCIAL]

inform /ɪnˈfɔːm/ *v.* **1** *tr.* (usu. foll. by *of, about, on,* or *that, how* + clause) tell (*informed them of their rights; informed us that the train was late*). **2** *intr.* (usu. foll. by *against, on*) give incriminating information about a person to the authorities. **3** *tr.* (usu. foll. by *with*) *literary* inspire or imbue (a person, heart, or thing) with a feeling, principle, quality, etc. **4** *tr.* impart its quality to; permeate. ▫ **informant** *n.* [Middle English via Old French *enfo(u)rmer* from Latin *informare* 'give shape to, fashion, describe' (as IN-[2], *forma* 'form')]

informal /ɪnˈfɔːm(ə)l/ *adj.* **1** without ceremony or formality (*just an informal chat*). **2** (of language, clothing, etc.) everyday; normal. ▫ **informality** /-ˈmalɪti/ *n.* (*pl.* **-ies**). **informally** *adv.*

informal vote *n. NZ & Austral.* an invalid vote or voting paper.

informatics /ɪnfəˈmatɪks/ *n.* the science of processing data for storage and retrieval; information science. [translation of Russian *informatika* (as INFORMATION, -ICS)]

information /ɪnfəˈmeɪʃ(ə)n/ *n.* **1 a** something told; knowledge. **b** (usu. foll. by *on, about*) items of knowledge; news (*the latest information on the crisis*). **2** (usu. foll. by *against*) *Law* a charge or complaint lodged with a court or magistrate. **3 a** the act of informing or telling. **b** an instance of this. **4** (in information theory) a mathematical quantity expressing the probability of occurrence of a particular sequence of symbols etc. ▫ **informational** *adj.* **informationally** *adv.* [Middle English via Old French from Latin *informatio -onis* (as INFORM)]

information retrieval *n.* the tracing and recovery of information stored in books, computers, etc.

information science *n.* the study of processes for storing and retrieving (esp. scientific or technical) information.

information superhighway see SUPERHIGHWAY.

information technology *n.* the study or use of systems (esp. computers, telecommunications, etc.) for storing, retrieving, and sending information.

information theory *n.* the mathematical study of the coding and transmission of information in the form of sequences of symbols, impulses, etc.

informative /ɪnˈfɔːmətɪv/ *adj.* (also **informatory** /ɪnˈfɔːmət(ə)ri/) giving information; instructive. ▫ **informatively** *adv.* **informativeness** *n.* [medieval Latin *informativus* (as INFORM)]

informed /ɪnˈfɔːmd/ *adj.* **1** with knowledge of the facts (*take an informed decision*). **2** educated; knowledgeable (*informed readers*). ▫ **informedly** /also ɪnˈfɔːmɪdli/ *adv.* **informedness** /also ɪnˈfɔːmɪdnɪs/ *n.*

informer /ɪnˈfɔːmə/ *n.* **1** a person who informs against another. **2** a person who informs or advises.

informercial var. of INFOMERCIAL.

infotainment /ɪnfəˈteɪnm(ə)nt/ *n.* broadcast material intended both to entertain and to inform. [INFORMATION + ENTERTAINMENT]

infra- /ˈɪnfrə/ *comb. form* **1** below (opp. SUPRA-). **2** *Anat.* below or under a part of the body. [from or suggested by Latin *infra* 'below, beneath']

infra /ˈɪnfrə/ *adv.* below, further on (in a book or writing). [Latin, = below]

infraclass /ˈɪnfrəklɑːs/ *n.* a taxonomic category below a subclass.

infraction /ɪnˈfrakʃ(ə)n/ *n.* esp. *Law* a violation or infringement. ▫ **infract** *v.tr.* **infractor** *n.* [Latin *infractio* (as INFRINGE)]

infradian /ɪnˈfreɪdɪən/ *adj. Physiol.* (of a rhythm or cycle) having a period of recurrence longer than a day (cf. ULTRADIAN). [from INFRA-, as having a lower frequency than *circadian*]

infra dig /ɪnfrə ˈdɪɡ/ *predic.adj. colloq.* beneath one's dignity; unbecoming. [abbreviation of Latin *infra dignitatem*]

infrangible /ɪnˈfran(d)ʒɪb(ə)l/ *adj.* **1** unbreakable. **2** inviolable. ▫ **infrangibility** /-ˈbɪlɪti/ *n.* **infrangibly** *adv.* [obsolete French *infrangible* or medieval Latin *infrangibilis* (as IN-[1], FRANGIBLE)]

infra-red /ɪnfrəˈrɛd/ *adj.* (*US & Sci.* **infrared**) of or using electromagnetic radiation having a wavelength just greater than that of the red end of the visible light spectrum but less than that of microwaves.

infrasonic /ɪnfrəˈsɒnɪk/ *adj.* of or relating to sound waves with a frequency below the lower limit of human audibility. ▫ **infrasonically** *adv.*

infrasound /ˈɪnfrəsaʊnd/ *n.* sound waves with frequencies below the lower limit of human audibility.

infrastructure /ˈɪnfrəstrʌktʃə/ *n.* **1 a** the basic structural foundations of a society or enterprise; a substructure or foundation. **b** roads, bridges, sewers, etc., regarded as a country's economic foundation. **2** permanent installations as a basis for military etc. operations. ▫ **infrastructural** *adj.* [French (as INFRA-, STRUCTURE)]

infrequent /ɪnˈfriːkw(ə)nt/ *adj.* not frequent. ▫ **infrequency** *n.* **infrequently** *adv.* [Latin *infrequens* (as IN-[1], FREQUENT)]

infringe /ɪnˈfrɪn(d)ʒ/ *v.* **1** *tr.* **a** act contrary to; violate (a law, an oath, etc.). **b** act in defiance of (another's rights etc.). **2** *intr.* (usu. foll. by *on, upon*) encroach; trespass. ▫ **infringement** *n.* **infringer** *n.* [Latin *infringere infract-* (as IN-[2], *frangere* 'break')]

infula /ˈɪnfjʊlə/ *n.* (*pl.* **infulae** /-liː/) *Eccl.* either of the two ribbons on a bishop's mitre. [Latin, = woollen fillet worn by priest etc.]

infundibular /ɪnfʌnˈdɪbjʊlə/ *adj.* funnel-shaped. [Latin *infundibulum* 'funnel' from *infundere* 'pour in' (as IN-[2], *fundere* 'pour')]

infuriate *v. & adj.* ● *v.tr.* /ɪnˈfjʊərɪeɪt/ fill with fury; enrage. ● *adj.* /ɪnˈfjʊərɪət/ *literary* excited to fury; frantic. ▫ **infuriating** *adj.* **infuriatingly** /ɪnˈfjʊərɪeɪtɪŋli/ *adv.* [medieval Latin *infuriare infuriat-* (as IN-[2], Latin *furia* FURY)]

infuse /ɪnˈfjuːz/ *v.* **1** *tr.* (usu. foll. by *with*) imbue; pervade (*anger infused with resentment*). **2** *tr.* steep (herbs, tea, etc.) in liquid to extract the content. **3** *tr.* (usu. foll. by *into*) instil (grace, spirit, life, etc.). **4** *intr.* undergo infusion (*let it infuse for five minutes*). **5** *tr.* (usu. foll. by *into*) pour (a thing). ▫ **infusable** *adj.* **infuser** *n.* [Middle English from Latin *infundere infus-* (as IN-[2], *fundere* 'pour')]

infusible /ɪnˈfjuːzɪb(ə)l/ *adj.* not able to be fused or melted. ▫ **infusibility** /-ˈbɪlɪti/ *n.*

infusion /ɪnˈfjuːʒ(ə)n/ *n.* **1** a liquid obtained by infusing. **2** an infused element; an admixture. **3** *Med.* a slow injection of a substance into a vein or tissue. **4 a** the act of infusing. **b** an instance of this. [Middle English from French *infusion* or Latin *infusio* (as INFUSE)]

infusoria /ɪnfjʊˈzɔːrɪə, -ˈsɔːrɪə/ *n.pl. Zool. hist.* unicellular organisms of the former group Infusoria (mainly ciliate protozoans). [modern Latin *Infusoria* (as INFUSE), because originally found in infusions of decaying organic matter]

infusorial earth /ɪnfjʊˈzɔːrɪəl, -ˈsɔːrɪəl/ *n. archaic* = KIESELGUHR.

-ing[1] /ɪŋ/ *suffix* forming gerunds and nouns from verbs (or occasionally from nouns), denoting: **1 a** the verbal action or its result (*asking*; *carving*; *fighting*; *learning*). **b** the verbal action as described or classified in some way (*tough going*). **2** material used for or associated with a process etc. (*piping*; *washing*). **3** an occupation or event (*banking*; *wedding*). **4** a set or arrangement of (*colouring*; *feathering*). [Old English *-ung, -ing*, from Germanic]

-ing[2] /ɪŋ/ *suffix* **1** forming the present participle of verbs (*asking*; *fighting*), often as adjectives (*charming*; *strapping*). **2** forming adjectives from nouns (*hulking*). [Middle English, alteration of Old English *-ende*, later *-inde*]

-ing[3] /ɪŋ/ *suffix* forming nouns meaning 'one belonging to' or 'one having the quality of', surviving esp. in names of coins and fractional parts (*farthing*; *gelding*; *riding*). [Old English from Germanic]

ingather /ɪnˈgaðə/ *v.tr.* gather in (esp. harvest); assemble. ▫ **ingathering** *n.*

ingeminate /ɪnˈdʒɛmɪneɪt/ *v.tr. literary* repeat; reiterate. ▫ **ingeminate peace** constantly urge peace. [Latin *ingeminare ingeminat-* (as IN-², GEMINATE)]

ingenious /ɪnˈdʒiːnɪəs/ *adj.* **1** clever at inventing, constructing, organizing, etc.; skilful; resourceful. **2** (of a machine, theory, etc.) cleverly contrived. ▫ **ingeniously** *adv.* **ingeniousness** *n.* [Middle English, = talented, via French *ingénieux* or Latin *ingeniosus* from *ingenium* 'cleverness': cf. ENGINE]

■ **Usage** See Usage Note at INGENUOUS.

ingénue /anʒeɪˈnjuː/ *n.* **1** an innocent or unsophisticated young woman. **2** *Theatr.* **a** such a part in a play. **b** the actress who plays this part. [French, fem. of *ingénu* INGENUOUS]

ingenuity /ɪndʒɪˈnjuːɪti/ *n.* skill in devising or contriving; ingeniousness. [Latin *ingenuitas* 'ingenuousness' (as INGENUOUS): English meaning by confusion of INGENIOUS with INGENUOUS]

ingenuous /ɪnˈdʒɛnjʊəs/ *adj.* **1** innocent; artless. **2** open; frank. ▫ **ingenuously** *adv.* **ingenuousness** *n.* [Latin *ingenuus* 'freeborn, frank' (as IN-², root of *gignere* 'beget')]

■ **Usage** *Ingenuous*, meaning 'open, frank, innocent', is sometimes confused with *ingenious*, which means 'clever at inventing, resourceful'.

ingest /ɪnˈdʒɛst/ *v.tr.* **1** take in (food etc.); eat. **2** absorb (facts, knowledge, etc.). ▫ **ingestion** /ɪnˈdʒɛstʃ(ə)n/ *n.* **ingestive** *adj.* [Latin *ingerere ingest-* (as IN-², *gerere* 'carry')]

inglenook /ˈɪŋg(ə)lnʊk/ *n.* a space within the opening on either side of a large fireplace. [dialect (originally Scots) *ingle* 'fire burning on a hearth', perhaps from Gaelic *aingeal* 'fire, light', + NOOK]

inglorious /ɪnˈglɔːrɪəs/ *adj.* **1** shameful; ignominious. **2** not famous. ▫ **ingloriously** *adv.* **ingloriousness** *n.*

-ingly /ˈɪŋli/ *suffix* forming adverbs esp. denoting manner of action or nature or condition (*dotingly*; *charmingly*; *slantingly*).

in-goal area *n. Rugby* the area between the goal line and the dead ball line (see DEAD *adj.* 11).

ingoing /ˈɪngəʊɪŋ/ *adj.* **1** going in; entering. **2** penetrating; thorough.

ingot /ˈɪŋgət/ *n.* a usu. oblong piece of cast metal, esp. of gold, silver, or steel. [Middle English: perhaps from IN + *goten*, past part. of Old English *geotan* 'cast']

ingraft var. of ENGRAFT.

ingrain /ɪnˈgreɪn/ *v. & adj.* ● *v.tr.* (also **engrain**) **1** (esp. as **ingrained** *adj.*) implant (a habit, belief, or attitude) ineradicably in a person. **2** (as **ingrained** *adj.*) (of dirt etc.) deeply embedded. **3** cause (dye etc.) to sink deeply into a thing. ● *adj.* (also /ˈɪn-/) **1** inherent; ingrained. **2** (of textiles) dyed in the fibre, before being woven. [Middle English from Old French *engrainer* 'dye in grain' (*en greine*): see GRAIN]

ingrain carpet *n.* a reversible carpet, with different colours interwoven.

ingrate /ˈɪngreɪt, ɪnˈgreɪt/ *n. & adj. formal* or *literary* ● *n.* an ungrateful person. ● *adj.* ungrateful. [Middle English from Latin *ingratus* (as IN-¹, *gratus* 'grateful')]

ingratiate /ɪnˈgreɪʃɪeɪt/ *v.refl.* (usu. foll. by *with*) bring oneself into favour. ▫ **ingratiation** /-ˈeɪʃ(ə)n/ *n.* [Latin *in gratiam* 'into favour']

ingratiating /ɪnˈgreɪʃɪeɪtɪŋ/ *adj.* intended to gain grace or favour. ▫ **ingratiatingly** *adv.*

ingratitude /ɪnˈgratɪtjuːd/ *n.* a lack of due gratitude. [Middle English from Old French *ingratitude* or Late Latin *ingratitudo* (as INGRATE)]

ingravescent /ɪngrəˈvɛs(ə)nt/ *adj. Med.* (of a disease etc.) growing worse. ▫ **ingravescence** *n.* [Latin *ingravescere* (as IN-², *gravescere* 'grow heavy' from *gravis* 'heavy')]

ingredient /ɪnˈgriːdɪənt/ *n.* a component part or element in a recipe, mixture, or combination. [Middle English from Latin *ingredi ingress-* 'enter' (as IN-², *gradi* 'step')]

ingress /ˈɪngrɛs/ *n.* **1** the act or right of going in or entering. **2** *Astron.* the start of an eclipse or transit. ▫ **ingression** /ɪnˈgrɛʃ(ə)n/ *n.* [Middle English from Latin *ingressus* (as INGREDIENT)]

in-group *n.* a small exclusive group of people with a common interest.

ingrowing /ˈɪngrəʊɪŋ/ *adj.* growing inwards, esp. (of a toenail) growing into the flesh. ▫ **ingrown** *adj.* **ingrowth** *n.*

inguinal /ˈɪŋgwɪn(ə)l/ *adj.* of the groin. ▫ **inguinally** *adv.* [Latin *inguinalis* from *inguen -inis* 'groin']

ingulf var. of ENGULF.

ingurgitate /ɪnˈgəːdʒɪteɪt/ *v.tr.* **1** swallow greedily. **2** engulf. ▫ **ingurgitation** /-ˈteɪʃ(ə)n/ *n.* [Latin *ingurgitare ingurgitat-* (as IN-², *gurges gurgitis* 'whirlpool')]

inhabit /ɪnˈhabɪt/ *v.tr.* (**inhabited**, **inhabiting**) (of a person or animal) dwell in; occupy (a region, town, house, etc.). ▫ **inhabitable** *adj.* **inhabitability** /-təˈbɪlɪti/ *n.* **inhabitant** *n.* **inhabitation** /-ˈteɪʃ(ə)n/ *n.* [Middle English *inhabite*, *enhabite* from Old French *enhabiter* or Latin *inhabitare* (as IN-², *habitare* 'dwell'): see HABIT]

inhabitancy /ɪnˈhabɪt(ə)nsi/ *n.* (also **inhabitance** /-t(ə)ns/) residence as an inhabitant, esp. during a specified period so as to acquire rights etc.

inhalant /ɪnˈheɪl(ə)nt/ *n. & adj.* ● *n.* **1** a medicinal preparation for inhaling. **2** a substance inhaled by drug-abusers. ● *adj.* of or relating to inhalation or inhalants.

inhale /ɪnˈheɪl/ *v.tr.* (often *absol.*) breathe in (air, gas, tobacco smoke, etc.). ▫ **inhalation** /-həˈleɪʃ(ə)n/ *n.* [Latin *inhalare* 'breathe in' (as IN-², *halare* 'breathe')]

inhaler /ɪnˈheɪlə/ *n.* a portable device used for relieving nasal or bronchial congestion, esp. asthma, by inhaling.

inharmonic /ɪnhɑːˈmɒnɪk/ *adj.* esp. *Mus.* not harmonic.

inharmonious /ɪnhɑːˈməʊnɪəs/ *adj.* esp. *Mus.* not harmonious. ▫ **inharmoniously** *adv.*

inhere /ɪnˈhɪə/ *v.intr.* (often foll. by *in*) *formal* **1** exist essentially or permanently in (*goodness inheres in that child*). **2** (of rights etc.) be vested in (a person etc.). [Latin *inhaerēre inhaes-* (as IN-², *haerēre* 'to stick')]

inherent /ɪnˈhɪər(ə)nt, -ˈhɛr-/ *adj.* (often foll. by *in*) **1** existing in something, esp. as a permanent or characteristic attribute. **2** vested in (a person etc.) as a right or privilege. ▫ **inherence** *n.* **inherently** *adv.* [Latin *inhaerēre inhaerent-* (as INHERE)]

inherit /ɪnˈhɛrɪt/ *v.* (**inherited**, **inheriting**) **1** *tr.* receive (property, rank, title, etc.) by legal descent or succession. **2** *tr.* derive (a quality or characteristic) genetically from one's parents or ancestors. **3** *absol.* succeed as an heir (*a younger son rarely inherits*). ▫ **inheritor** *n.* (*fem.* **inheritress** /-trɪs/or **inheritrix** /-trɪks/). [Middle English via Old French *enheriter* from Late Latin *inhereditare* (as IN-², Latin *heres heredis* 'heir')]

inheritable /ɪnˈhɛrɪtəb(ə)l/ *adj.* **1** capable of being inherited. **2** capable of inheriting. ▫ **inheritability** /-ˈbɪlɪti/ *n.* [Middle English from Anglo-French (as INHERIT)]

inheritance /ɪnˈhɛrɪt(ə)ns/ *n.* **1** something that is inherited. **2 a** the act of inheriting. **b** an instance of this. [Middle English via Anglo-French *inheritaunce* from Old French *enheriter*: see INHERIT]

inheritance tax *n.* a tax levied on property etc. acquired by gift or inheritance (introduced in the UK in 1986 to replace *capital transfer tax*).

inhesion /ɪnˈhiːʒ(ə)n/ *n. formal* the act or fact of inhering. [Late Latin *inhaesio* (as INHERE)]

inhibit /ɪnˈhɪbɪt/ *v.tr.* (**inhibited**, **inhibiting**) **1** hinder, restrain, or prevent (an action or progress). **2** (as **inhibited** *adj.*) subject to inhibition. **3 a** (usu. foll. by *from* + verbal noun) forbid or prohibit (a person etc.). **b** (esp. in ecclesiastical law) forbid (an ecclesiastic) to exercise clerical functions. □ **inhibitive** *adj.* **inhibitor** *n.* **inhibitory** *adj.* [Latin *inhibēre* (as IN-², *habēre* 'hold')]

inhibition /ɪn(h)ɪ'bɪʃ(ə)n/ *n.* **1** *Psychol.* a restraint on the direct expression of an instinct. **2** *colloq.* an emotional resistance to a thought, an action, etc. (*no inhibitions about singing in public*). **3** *Brit. Law* an order forbidding alteration to property rights. **4 a** the act of inhibiting. **b** the process of being inhibited. [Middle English from Old French *inhibition* or Latin *inhibitio* (as INHIBIT)]

inhomogeneous /ˌɪnhɒmə(ʊ)'dʒiːnɪəs, -'dʒɛn-; ˌɪnhəʊm-/ *adj.* not homogeneous. □ **inhomogeneity** /-dʒɪ'niːɪti, -dʒɪ'neɪɪti/ *n.*

inhospitable /ɪnhɒ'spɪtəb(ə)l, ɪn'hɒspɪt-/ *adj.* **1** not hospitable. **2** (of a region, coast, etc.) not affording shelter etc. □ **inhospitableness** *n.* **inhospitably** *adv.* [obsolete French (as IN-¹, HOSPITABLE)]

inhospitality /ˌɪnhɒspɪ'talɪti/ *n.* the act or process of being inhospitable. [Latin *inhospitalitas* (as IN-¹, HOSPITALITY)]

in-house *adj.* & *adv.* ● *adj.* /'ɪnhaʊs/ done or existing within an institution, company, etc. (*an in-house project*). ● *adv.* /ɪn'haʊs/ internally, without outside assistance.

inhuman /ɪn'hjuːmən/ *adj.* **1** (of a person, conduct, etc.) brutal; unfeeling; barbarous. **2** not of a human type. □ **inhumanly** *adv.* [Latin *inhumanus* (as IN-¹, HUMAN)]

inhumane /ɪnhjʊ'meɪn/ *adj.* not humane. □ **inhumanely** *adv.* [Latin *inhumanus* (see INHUMAN), and from IN-¹ + HUMANE, originally = INHUMAN]

inhumanity /ɪnhjʊ'manɪti/ *n.* (*pl.* **-ies**) **1** brutality; barbarousness; callousness. **2** an inhumane act.

inhume /ɪn'hjuːm/ *v.tr. literary* bury. □ **inhumation** /-'meɪʃ(ə)n/ *n.* [Latin *inhumare* (as IN-², *humus* 'ground')]

inimical /ɪ'nɪmɪk(ə)l/ *adj.* (usu. foll. by *to*) **1** hostile. **2** harmful. □ **inimically** *adv.* [Late Latin *inimicalis* from Latin *inimicus* (as IN-¹, *amicus* 'friend')]

inimitable /ɪ'nɪmɪtəb(ə)l/ *adj.* impossible to imitate. □ **inimitability** /-'bɪlɪti/ *n.* **inimitably** *adv.* [French *inimitable* or Latin *inimitabilis* (as IN-¹, *imitabilis* 'imitable')]

iniquity /ɪ'nɪkwɪti/ *n.* (*pl.* **-ies**) **1** wickedness; unrighteousness. **2** a gross injustice. □ **iniquitous** *adj.* **iniquitously** *adv.* **iniquitousness** *n.* [Middle English via Old French *iniquité* from Latin *iniquitas -tatis*, from *iniquus* (as IN-¹, *aequus* 'just')]

initial /ɪ'nɪʃ(ə)l/ *adj.*, *n.*, & *v.* ● *adj.* of, existing, or occurring at the beginning (*initial stage*; *initial expenses*). ● *n.* **1** = INITIAL LETTER. **2** (usu. in *pl.*) the first letter or letters of the words of a (esp. a person's) name or names. ● *v.tr.* (**initialled**, **initialling**; *US* **initialed**, **initialing**) mark or sign with one's initials. □ **initially** *adv.* [Latin *initialis*, via *initium* 'beginning' from *inire init-* 'go in']

initialism /ɪ'nɪʃ(ə)lɪz(ə)m/ *n.* **1** a group of initial letters used as an abbreviation for a name or expression, each letter being pronounced separately (e.g. *BBC*) (cf. ACRONYM). **2** *US* an acronym.

initialize /ɪ'nɪʃ(ə)lʌɪz/ *v.tr.* (also **-ise**) (often foll. by *to*) *Computing* set to the value or put in the condition appropriate to the start of an operation. □ **initialization** /-'zeɪʃ(ə)n/ *n.*

initial letter *n.* (also **initial consonant**) a letter or consonant at the beginning of a word.

initial teaching alphabet *n.* a 44-letter phonetic alphabet used to help those beginning to read and write English.

initiate *v.*, *n.*, & *adj.* ● *v.tr.* /ɪ'nɪʃɪeɪt/ **1** begin; set going; originate. **2 a** (usu. foll. by *into*) admit (a person) into a society, an office, a secret, etc., esp. with a ritual. **b** (usu. foll. by *in*, *into*) instruct (a person) in science, art, etc. ● *n.* /ɪ'nɪʃɪət/ a person who has been newly initiated. ● *adj.* /ɪ'nɪʃɪət/ (of a person) newly initiated (*an initiate member*). □ **initiation** /-'eɪʃ(ə)n/ *n.* **initiator** *n.* **initiatory** /ɪ'nɪʃɪət(ə)ri, ɪˌnɪʃɪ'eɪt(ə)ri/ *adj.* [Latin *initiare* from *initium*: see INITIAL]

initiative /ɪ'nɪʃɪətɪv, -ʃə-/ *n.* & *adj.* ● *n.* **1** the ability to initiate things; enterprise (*I'm afraid he lacks initiative*). **2** a first step; origination (*a peace initiative*). **3** the power or right to begin something. **4** *Polit.* (esp. in Switzerland and some US states) the right of citizens outside the legislature to originate legislation. ● *adj.* beginning; originating. □ **have the initiative** esp. *Mil.* be able to control the enemy's movements. **on one's own initiative** without being prompted by others. **take the initiative** (often foll. by *in* + verbal noun) be the first to take action. [French (as INITIATE)]

inject /ɪn'dʒɛkt/ *v.tr.* **1** *Med.* **a** (usu. foll. by *into*) drive or force (a solution, medicine, etc.) by or as if by a syringe. **b** (usu. foll. by *with*) fill (a cavity etc.) by injecting. **c** administer medicine etc. to (a person) by injection. **2** insert or introduce by way of interruption or as a boost (*may I inject a note of realism?*; *theatres injected with new life*). □ **injectable** *adj.* & *n.* **injector** *n.* [Latin *injicere* (as IN-², *jacere* 'throw')]

injection /ɪn'dʒɛkʃ(ə)n/ *n.* **1 a** the act of injecting. **b** an instance of this. **2** a liquid or solution (to be) injected (*prepare a morphine injection*). [French *injection* or Latin *injectio* (as INJECT)]

injection moulding *n.* the shaping of rubber or plastic articles by injecting heated material into a mould. □ **injection-moulded** *adj.*

in-joke *n.* a joke that is shared exclusively by a group of people.

injudicious /ɪndʒʊ'dɪʃəs/ *adj.* unwise; ill-judged. □ **injudiciously** *adv.* **injudiciousness** *n.*

Injun /'ɪndʒ(ə)n/ *n.* esp. *N. Amer. colloq. offens.* an American Indian. [corruption]

injunction /ɪn'dʒʌŋ(k)ʃ(ə)n/ *n.* **1** an authoritative warning or order. **2** *Law* a judicial order restraining a person from an act or compelling redress to an injured party. □ **injunctive** *adj.* [Late Latin *injunctio* from Latin *injungere* ENJOIN]

injure /'ɪndʒə/ *v.tr.* **1** do physical harm or damage to; hurt (*was injured in a road accident*). **2** harm or impair (*illness might injure her chances*). **3** do wrong to. □ **injurer** *n.* [back-formation from INJURY]

injured /'ɪndʒəd/ *adj.* **1** harmed or hurt (*the injured passengers*). **2** offended; wronged (*in an injured tone*).

injurious /ɪn'dʒʊərɪəs/ *adj.* **1** hurtful. **2** (of language) insulting; libellous. **3** wrongful. □ **injuriously** *adv.* **injuriousness** *n.* [Middle English from French *injurieux* or Latin *injuriosus* (as INJURY)]

injury /'ɪn(d)ʒ(ə)ri/ *n.* (*pl.* **-ies**) **1 a** physical harm or damage. **b** an instance of this (*suffered head injuries*). **2** esp. *Law* **a** wrongful action or treatment. **b** an instance of this. **3** damage to one's good name etc. [Middle English via Anglo-French *injurie* from Latin *injuria* 'a wrong' (as IN-¹, *jus juris* 'right')]

injury time *n. Brit. Football* extra playing time allowed by a referee to compensate for time lost in dealing with injuries.

injustice /ɪn'dʒʌstɪs/ *n.* **1** a lack of fairness or justice. **2** an unjust act. □ **do a person an injustice** judge a person unfairly. [Middle English via Old French from Latin *injustitia* (as IN-¹, JUSTICE)]

ink /ɪŋk/ *n.* & *v.* ● *n.* **1 a** a coloured fluid used for writing with a pen, marking with a rubber stamp, etc. **b** a thick paste used in printing, duplicating, in ballpoint pens, etc. **2** *Zool.* a black liquid ejected by a cuttlefish, octopus, etc. to confuse a predator. ● *v.tr.* **1** (usu. foll. by *in*, *over*, etc.) mark with ink. **2** cover (type etc.) with ink before printing. **3** apply ink to. **4** (as **inked** *adj.*) *Austral. slang* drunk. □ **ink out** obliterate with ink. □ **inker** *n.* [Middle English *enke*, *inke* via Old French *enque* and Late Latin *encau(s)tum* from Greek *egkauston*, purple ink used by Roman emperors for signatures (as EN-², CAUSTIC)]

ink-blot test *n.* = RORSCHACH TEST.

ink-cap *n.* any fungus of the genus *Coprinus*, turning into black liquid when it decays.

inkhorn /ˈɪŋkhɔːn/ *n. hist.* a small portable horn container for ink.

ink-jet printer *n. Computing* a printer in which the characters are formed by minute jets of ink.

inkling /ˈɪŋklɪŋ/ *n.* (often foll. by *of*) a slight knowledge or suspicion; a hint. [Middle English *inkle* 'utter in an undertone', of unknown origin]

ink-pad *n.* an ink-soaked pad, usu. in a box, used for inking a rubber stamp etc.

inkstand /ˈɪŋkstand/ *n.* a stand for one or more ink bottles, often incorporating a pen tray etc.

inkwell /ˈɪŋkwɛl/ *n.* a pot for ink usu. housed in a hole in a desk.

inky /ˈɪŋki/ *adj.* (**inkier, inkiest**) of, as black as, or stained with ink. □ **inkiness** *n.*

inlaid *past* and *past part.* of INLAY.

inland /ˈɪnlənd, -land/ *adj., n., & adv.* ● *adj.* **1** situated in the interior of a country. **2** esp. *Brit.* carried on within the limits of a country; domestic (*inland trade*). ● *n.* the parts of a country remote from the sea or frontiers; the interior. ● *adv.* /also ɪnˈland/ in or towards the interior of a country. □ **inlander** *n.* **inlandish** *adj.*

inland duty *n.* a tax payable on inland trade.

inland navigation *n.* communication by canals and rivers.

inland revenue *n.* **1** *Brit.* revenue consisting of taxes and inland duties. **2** (**Inland Revenue**) (in the UK) the government department responsible for assessing and collecting such taxes.

in-law /ˈɪnlɔː/ *n.* (often in *pl.*) a relative by marriage.

inlay *v. & n.* ● *v.tr.* /ɪnˈleɪ/ (*past* and *past part.* **inlaid** /ɪnˈleɪd/) **1 a** (usu. foll. by *in*) embed (a thing in another) so that the surfaces are even. **b** (usu. foll. by *with*) ornament (a thing with inlaid work). **2** (as **inlaid** *adj.*) (of a piece of furniture etc.) ornamented by inlaying. **3** insert (a page, an illustration, etc.) in a space cut in a larger thicker page. ● *n.* /ˈɪnleɪ/ **1** inlaid work. **2** material inlaid. **3** a filling shaped to fit a tooth cavity. □ **inlayer** *n.* [IN-[2] + LAY[1]]

inlet /ˈɪnlɛt/ *n.* **1** a small arm of the sea, a lake, or a river. **2** a piece inserted, esp. in dressmaking etc. **3** a way of entry. [Middle English from IN + LET[1] *v.*]

inlier /ˈɪnlʌɪə/ *n. Geol.* a structure or area of older rocks completely surrounded by newer rocks. [IN, on the pattern of *outlier*]

in-line /ˈɪnlʌɪn/ *adj.* **1** having parts arranged in a line. **2** constituting an integral part of a continuous sequence of operations or machines.

in loco parentis /ɪn ˌləʊkəʊ pəˈrɛntɪs/ *adv.* in the place or position of a parent (used of a teacher etc. responsible for children). [Latin]

inly /ˈɪnli/ *adv. poet.* **1** inwardly; in the heart. **2** intimately; thoroughly. [Old English *innlīce* (as IN, -LY[2])]

inlying /ˈɪnlʌɪɪŋ/ *adj.* situated within, or near a centre.

inmate /ˈɪnmeɪt/ *n.* (often foll. by *of*) **1** an occupant of a hospital, prison, institution, etc. **2** an occupant of a house etc., esp. one of several. [probably originally INN + MATE[1], associated with IN]

in medias res /ɪn ˌmiːdɪas ˈreɪz/ *adv.* **1** into the midst of things. **2** into the middle of a story, without preamble. [Latin]

in memoriam /ɪn mɪˈmɔːrɪam/ *prep. & n.* ● *prep.* in memory of (a dead person). ● *n.* a written article or notice etc. in memory of a dead person; an obituary. [Latin]

inmost /ˈɪnməʊst/ *adj.* **1** most inward. **2** most intimate; deepest. [Old English *innemest* (as IN, -MOST)]

inn /ɪn/ *n.* **1** a public house providing alcoholic liquor for consumption on the premises, and sometimes accommodation etc. **2** *hist.* a house providing accommodation, esp. for travellers. [Old English *inn* (as IN)]

innards /ˈɪnədz/ *n.pl. colloq.* **1** entrails. **2** internal workings (of an engine etc.). [dialect etc. pronunciation of INWARDS, used as a noun]

innate /ɪˈneɪt, ˈɪneɪt/ *adj.* **1** inborn; natural. **2** *Philos.* originating in the mind. □ **innately** *adv.* **innateness** *n.* [Middle English from Latin *innatus* (as IN-[2], *natus*, past part. of *nasci* 'be born')]

inner /ˈɪnə/ *adj. & n.* ● *adj.* (usu. *attrib.*) **1** further in; inside; interior (*the inner compartment*). **2** (of thoughts, feelings, etc.) deeper; more secret. ● *n. Brit. Archery* **1** a division of the target next to the bull's-eye. **2** a shot that strikes this. □ **innerly** *adv.* **innermost** *adj.* **innerness** *n.* [Old English *innera* (*adj.*), comparative of IN]

inner bar *n. Brit. Law* Queen's or King's Counsel collectively.

inner circle *n.* an exclusive group of friends or associates within a larger group.

inner city *n.* the area near the centre of a city, esp. when densely populated (also, with hyphen, *attrib.*: *inner-city housing*).

inner-directed *adj. Psychol.* governed by standards formed in childhood.

inner ear *n.* the semicircular canals and cochlea, which form the organs of balance and hearing and are embedded in the temporal bone.

inner man *n.* (also **inner woman**) **1** the soul or mind. **2** *joc.* the stomach.

inner planet *n.* a planet whose orbit lies within the asteroid belt (i.e. Mercury, Venus, Earth, Mars).

inner space *n.* **1** the region between the earth and outer space, or below the surface of the sea. **2** the part of the mind not normally accessible to consciousness.

inner-spring *adj. N. Amer.* = INTERIOR-SPRUNG.

Inner Temple *n.* one of the two Inns of Court on the site of the Temple in London (cf. MIDDLE TEMPLE).

inner tube *n.* a separate inflatable tube inside the cover of a pneumatic tyre.

innervate /ˈɪnəveɪt, ɪˈnəːveɪt/ *v.tr.* supply (an organ etc.) with nerves. □ **innervation** /-ˈveɪʃ(ə)n/ *n.* [IN-[2] + Latin *nervus* 'nerve' + -ATE[3]]

inner woman see INNER MAN.

inning /ˈɪnɪŋ/ *n. N. Amer.* each division of a game of baseball during which both sides have a turn at batting. [*in* (*v.*) 'go in' (from IN)]

innings /ˈɪnɪŋz/ *n.* (*pl.* same or *colloq.* **inningses**) **1** esp. *Cricket* **a** the part of a game during which a side is in or batting. **b** the play of or score achieved by a player during a turn at batting. **2** a period during which a government, party, cause, etc. is in office or effective. **3 a** a period during which a person can achieve something. **b** *colloq.* a person's lifespan (*had a good innings and died at 94*).

innkeeper /ˈɪnkiːpə/ *n.* a person who keeps an inn.

innocent /ˈɪnəs(ə)nt/ *adj. & n.* ● *adj.* **1** free from moral wrong; sinless. **2** (usu. foll. by *of*) not guilty (of a crime etc.). **3** free from responsibility for an event yet suffering its consequences (*innocent bystanders*). **4 a** simple; guileless; naive. **b** pretending to be guileless. **5** harmless. **6** (foll. by *of*) *colloq.* without, lacking (*appeared, innocent of shoes*). ● *n.* **1** an innocent person, esp. a young child. **2** (in *pl.*) the young children killed by Herod after the birth of Jesus (Matt. 2:16). **3** a person involved by chance in a situation, esp. a victim of crime or war. □ **innocence** *n.* **innocency** *n.* **innocently** *adv.* [Middle English from Old French *innocent* or Latin *innocens innocent-* (as IN-[1], *nocēre* 'hurt')]

Innocents' Day *n.* (also **Holy Innocents' Day**) the day, 28 Dec., commemorating the massacre of the innocents.

innocuous /ɪˈnɒkjʊəs/ *adj.* **1** not injurious; harmless. **2** inoffensive. □ **innocuously** *adv.* **innocuousness** *n.* [Latin *innocuus* (as IN-[1], *nocuus* from *nocēre* 'hurt')]

Inn of Court *n. Brit. Law* **1** each of the four legal societies having the exclusive right of admitting people to the English bar. **2** any of the sets of buildings in

London belonging to these societies. **3** a similar society in Ireland.

innominate /ɪ'nɒmɪnət/ *adj.* not having a name; unnamed. [Late Latin *innominatus* (as IN-[1], NOMINATE)]

innominate bone *n. Anat.* the bone formed from the fusion of the ilium, ischium, and pubis; the hip bone.

innovate /'ɪnəveɪt/ *v.intr.* **1** bring in new methods, ideas, etc. **2** (often foll. by *in*) make changes. □ **innovation** /-'veɪʃ(ə)n/ *n.* **innovational** /-'veɪʃ(ə)n(ə)l/ *adj.* **innovative** *adj.* **innovator** *n.* **innovatory** /-veɪt(ə)ri/ *adj.* [Latin *innovare* 'make new, alter' (as IN-[2], *novus* 'new')]

Inns of Chancery *n.pl. Brit. hist.* the buildings in London formerly used as hostels for law students.

innuendo /ɪnjʊ'endəʊ/ *n. & v.* ● *n.* (*pl.* **-oes** or **-os**) **1** an allusive or oblique remark or hint, usu. disparaging. **2** a remark with a double meaning, usu. suggestive. ● *v.intr.* (**-oes**, **-oed**) make innuendoes. [Latin, = by nodding at, by pointing to: ablative gerund of *innuere* 'nod at' (as IN-[2], *nuere* 'nod')]

innumerable /ɪ'nju:m(ə)rəb(ə)l/ *adj.* too many to be counted. □ **innumerability** /-'bɪlɪti/ *n.* **innumerably** *adv.* [Middle English from Latin *innumerabilis* (as IN-[1], NUMERABLE)]

innumerate /ɪ'nju:m(ə)rət/ *adj.* having no knowledge of or feeling for mathematical operations; not numerate. □ **innumeracy** /-əsi/ *n.*

innutrition /ɪnjʊ'trɪʃ(ə)n/ *n.* lack of nutrition. □ **innutritious** *adj.*

inobservance /ɪnəb'zə:v(ə)ns/ *n.* **1** inattention. **2** (usu. foll. by *of*) non-observance (of a law etc.). [French *inobservance* or Latin *inobservantia* (as IN-[1], OBSERVANCE)]

inoculate /ɪ'nɒkjʊleɪt/ *v.tr.* **1 a** treat (a person or animal) with a vaccine containing a dead or modified disease-causing agent, usu. by injection, to promote immunity against the disease. **b** introduce (an infective agent) into an organism. **c** introduce (cells or organisms) into a culture medium. **2** instil (a person) with ideas or opinions. □ **inoculable** *adj.* **inoculation** /-'leɪʃ(ə)n/ *n.* **inoculative** /-lətɪv/ *adj.* **inoculator** *n.* [originally in sense 'insert (a bud) into a plant': Latin *inoculare inoculat-* 'engraft' (as IN-[2], *oculus* 'eye, bud')]

inoculum /ɪ'nɒkjʊləm/ *n.* (*pl.* **inocula** /-lə/) any substance used for inoculation. [modern Latin (as INOCULATE)]

inodorous /ɪn'əʊd(ə)rəs/ *adj.* having no smell; odourless.

in-off *n. Billiards* the act of pocketing a ball by bouncing it off another ball.

inoffensive /ɪnə'fensɪv/ *adj.* not objectionable; harmless. □ **inoffensively** *adv.* **inoffensiveness** *n.*

inoperable /ɪn'ɒp(ə)rəb(ə)l/ *adj.* **1** *Surgery* that cannot suitably be operated on (*inoperable cancer*). **2** that cannot be operated; inoperative. **3** impractical, unworkable. □ **inoperability** /-'bɪlɪti/ *n.* **inoperably** *adv.* [French *inopérable* (as IN-[1], OPERABLE)]

inoperative /ɪn'ɒp(ə)rətɪv/ *adj.* not working or taking effect.

inopportune /ɪn'ɒpətju:n, ˌɪnɒpə'tju:n/ *adj.* not appropriate, esp. as regards time; unseasonable. □ **inopportunely** *adv.* **inopportuneness** *n.* [Latin *inopportunus* (as IN-[1], OPPORTUNE)]

inordinate /ɪ'nɔ:dɪnət/ *adj.* **1** immoderate; excessive. **2** intemperate. **3** disorderly. □ **inordinately** *adv.* [Middle English from Latin *inordinatus* (as IN-[1], *ordinatus*, past part. of *ordinare* ORDAIN)]

inorganic /ɪnɔ:'ganɪk/ *adj.* **1** *Chem.* (of a compound) not organic, usu. of mineral origin (opp. ORGANIC). **2** without organized physical structure. **3** not arising by natural growth; extraneous. **4** *Philol.* not explainable by normal etymology. □ **inorganically** *adv.*

inorganic chemistry *n.* the chemistry of inorganic compounds.

inosculate /ɪ'nɒskjʊleɪt/ *v.intr. & tr.* **1** join by running together. **2** join closely. □ **inosculation** /-'leɪʃ(ə)n/ *n.* [IN-[2] + Latin *osculare* 'provide with a mouth' from *osculum*, diminutive of *os* 'mouth']

in-patient /'ɪnpeɪʃ(ə)nt/ *n.* a patient who lives in hospital while under treatment.

in propria persona /ɪn ˌprəʊprɪə pə:'səʊnə/ *adv.* in his or her own person. [Latin]

input /'ɪnpʊt/ *n. & v.* ● *n.* **1** what is put in or taken in, or operated on by any process or system. **2** *Electronics* **a** a place where, or a device through which, energy, information, etc., enters a system (*a tape recorder with inputs for microphone and radio*). **b** energy supplied to a device or system; an electrical signal. **3** the information fed into a computer. **4** the action or process of putting in or feeding in. **5** a contribution of information etc. ● *v.tr.* (**inputting**; *past* and *past part.* **input** or **inputted**) (often foll. by *into*) **1** put in. **2** *Computing* supply (data, programs, etc., to a computer, program, etc.). □ **inputter** *n.*

input-output *attrib.adj.* (also **input/output**) *Computing* etc. of, relating to, or for input and output.

inquest /'ɪnkwest/ *n.* **1** *Law* **a** *Brit.* an inquiry by a coroner's court into the cause of a death. **b** a judicial inquiry to ascertain the facts relating to an incident etc. **c** *Brit.* a coroner's jury. **2** *colloq.* a discussion analysing the outcome of a game, an election, etc. [Middle English from Old French *enqueste* (as ENQUIRE)]

inquietude /ɪn'kwʌɪətju:d/ *n.* uneasiness of mind or body. [Middle English via Old French *inquietude* or Late Latin *inquietudo* from Latin *inquietus* (as IN-[1], *quietus* 'quiet')]

inquiline /'ɪnkwɪlʌɪn/ *n.* an animal living in the home of another; a commensal. [Latin *inquilinus* 'sojourner' (as IN-[2], *colere* 'dwell')]

inquire /ɪn'kwʌɪə/ *v.* **1** *intr.* seek information formally; make a formal investigation. **2** *intr. & tr.* = ENQUIRE. □ **inquirer** *n.* [variant of ENQUIRE]

■ **Usage** See Usage Note at ENQUIRE.

inquiry /ɪn'kwʌɪri/ *n.* (*pl.* **-ies**) **1** an investigation, esp. an official one. **2** = ENQUIRY.

inquiry agent *n. Brit.* a private detective.

inquisition /ɪŋkwɪ'zɪʃ(ə)n/ *n.* **1** usu. *derog.* an intensive search or investigation. **2** a judicial or official inquiry. **3** (**the Inquisition**) *RC Ch. hist.* an ecclesiastical tribunal for the suppression of heresy, esp. in Spain, operating through torture and execution. □ **inquisitional** *adj.* [Middle English via Old French from Latin *inquisitio -onis* 'examination' (as INQUIRE)]

inquisitive /ɪn'kwɪzɪtɪv/ *adj.* **1** unduly curious; prying. **2** seeking knowledge; inquiring. □ **inquisitively** *adv.* **inquisitiveness** *n.* [Middle English via Old French *inquisitif -ive* from Late Latin *inquisitivus* (as INQUISITION)]

inquisitor /ɪn'kwɪzɪtə/ *n.* **1** an official investigator. **2** *hist.* an officer of the Inquisition. [French *inquisiteur* from Latin *inquisitor -oris* (as INQUIRE)]

Inquisitor-General *n.* the head of the Spanish Inquisition.

inquisitorial /ɪnˌkwɪzɪ'tɔ:rɪəl/ *adj.* **1** of or like an inquisitor. **2** offensively prying. **3** *Law* (of a trial etc.) in which the judge has a prosecuting role (opp. ACCUSATORIAL). □ **inquisitorially** *adv.* [medieval Latin *inquisitorius* (as INQUISITOR)]

inquorate /ɪn'kwɔ:rət, -eɪt/ *adj. Brit.* not constituting a quorum.

in re /ɪn 'ri:, 'reɪ/ *prep.* = RE[1]. [Latin, = in the matter of]

INRI *abbr.* Jesus of Nazareth, King of the Jews. [Latin *Iesus Nazarenus Rex Iudaeorum*]

inroad /'ɪnrəʊd/ *n.* **1** (often in *pl.*; usu. foll. by *on, into*) an encroachment; a using up of resources etc. (*makes inroads on my time*). **2** a hostile attack; a raid. [IN + ROAD[1] in the sense 'riding']

inrush /'ɪnrʌʃ/ *n.* a rushing in; an influx. □ **inrushing** *adj. & n.*

ins. *abbr.* **1** inches. **2** insurance.

insalubrious /msəˈluːbrɪəs/ *adj.* (of a climate or place) unhealthy. □ **insalubrity** *n.* [Latin *insalubris* (as IN-[1], SALUBRIOUS)]

insane /ɪnˈseɪn/ *adj.* **1** not of sound mind; mad. **2** *colloq.* extremely foolish; irrational. □ **insanely** *adv.* **insanity** /-ˈsanɪti/ *n.* (*pl.* **-ies**). [Latin *insanus* (as IN-[1], *sanus* 'healthy')]

insanitary /ɪnˈsanɪt(ə)ri/ *adj.* not sanitary; dirty or germ-carrying.

insatiable /ɪnˈseɪʃəb(ə)l/ *adj.* **1** unable to be satisfied. **2** extremely greedy. □ **insatiability** /-ˈbɪlɪti/ *n.* **insatiably** *adv.* [Middle English from Old French *insaciable* or Latin *insatiabilis* (as IN-[1], SATIATE)]

insatiate /ɪnˈseɪʃɪət/ *adj.* never satisfied. [Latin *insatiatus* (as IN-[1], SATIATE)]

inscape /ˈɪnskeɪp/ *n. literary* the unique inner quality or essence of an object etc. as shown in a work of art, esp. a poem. [perhaps from IN-[2] + -SCAPE]

inscribe /ɪnˈskrʌɪb/ *v.tr.* **1 a** (usu. foll. by *in, on*) write or carve (words etc.) on stone, metal, paper, a book, etc. **b** (usu. foll. by *with*) mark (a sheet, tablet, etc.) with characters. **2** (usu. foll. by *to*) write an informal dedication (to a person) in or on (a book etc.). **3** enter the name of (a person) on a list or in a book. **4** *Geom.* draw (a figure) within another so that some or all points of it lie on the boundary of the other (cf. CIRCUMSCRIBE 3). **5** (esp. as **inscribed** *adj.*) *Brit.* issue (stock etc.) in the form of shares with registered holders. □ **inscribable** *adj.* **inscriber** *n.* [Latin *inscribere inscript-* (as IN-[2], *scribere* 'write')]

inscription /ɪnˈskrɪpʃ(ə)n/ *n.* **1** words inscribed, esp. on a monument, coin, stone, or in a book etc. **2 a** the act of inscribing, esp. the informal dedication of a book etc. **b** an instance of this. □ **inscriptional** *adj.* **inscriptive** *adj.* [Middle English from Latin *inscriptio* (as INSCRIBE)]

inscrutable /ɪnˈskruːtəb(ə)l/ *adj.* wholly mysterious, impenetrable. □ **inscrutability** /-ˈbɪlɪti/ *n.* **inscrutableness** *n.* **inscrutably** *adv.* [Middle English from ecclesiastical Latin *inscrutabilis* (as IN-[1], *scrutari* 'search': see SCRUTINY)]

insect /ˈɪnsɛkt/ *n.* **1 a** any arthropod of the class Insecta, having a head, thorax, abdomen, two antennae, three pairs of thoracic legs, and usu. one or two pairs of thoracic wings. **b** (loosely) any other small invertebrate animal esp. with several pairs of legs. **2** an insignificant or contemptible person or creature. □ **insectile** /-ˈsɛktʌɪl/ *adj.* [Latin *insectum* (*animal*) 'notched (animal)' from *insecare insect-* (as IN-[2], *secare* 'cut')]

insectarium /ɪnsɛkˈtɛːrɪəm/ *n.* (also **insectary** /ɪnˈsɛktəri/) (*pl.* **insectariums** or **insectaries**) a place for keeping insects.

insecticide /ɪnˈsɛktɪsʌɪd/ *n.* a substance used for killing insects. □ **insecticidal** /-ˈsʌɪd(ə)l/ *adj.*

insectivore /ɪnˈsɛktɪvɔː/ *n.* **1** any animal that feeds on insects, esp. a mammal of the order Insectivora, including shrews, hedgehogs, and moles. **2** any plant which captures and absorbs insects. □ **insectivorous** /-ˈtɪv(ə)rəs/ *adj.* [French from modern Latin *insectivorus* (as INSECT, -VORE: see -VOROUS)]

insecure /ɪnsɪˈkjʊə/ *adj.* **1** (of a person or state of mind) uncertain; lacking confidence. **2 a** unsafe; not firm or fixed. **b** (of ice, ground, etc.) liable to give way. □ **insecurely** *adv.* **insecurity** /-ˈkjʊərɪti/ *n.*

inselberg /ˈɪns(ə)lbəːg, -z-/ *n.* an isolated hill or mountain rising abruptly from its surroundings. [German, from *Insel* 'island' + *Berg* 'mountain']

inseminate /ɪnˈsɛmɪneɪt/ *v.tr.* **1** introduce semen into (a female) by natural or artificial means. **2** sow (seed etc.). □ **insemination** /-ˈneɪʃ(ə)n/ *n.* **inseminator** *n.* [Latin *inseminare* (as IN-[2], SEMEN)]

insensate /ɪnˈsɛnseɪt, -sət/ *adj.* **1** without physical sensation; unconscious. **2** without sensibility; unfeeling. **3** stupid. □ **insensately** *adv.* [ecclesiastical Latin *insensatus* (as IN-[1], *sensatus* from *sensus* SENSE)]

insensibility /ɪnˌsɛnsɪˈbɪlɪti/ *n.* **1** unconsciousness. **2** a lack of mental feeling or emotion; hardness. **3** (often foll. by *to*) indifference. [French *insensibilité* or Late Latin *insensibilitas* (as INSENSIBLE)]

insensible /ɪnˈsɛnsɪb(ə)l/ *adj.* **1 a** without one's mental faculties; unconscious. **b** (of the extremities etc.) numb; without feeling. **2** (usu. foll. by *of, to*) unaware; indifferent (*insensible of her needs*). **3** without emotion; callous. **4** too small or gradual to be perceived; inappreciable. □ **insensibly** *adv.* [Middle English from Old French *insensible* or Latin *insensibilis* (as IN-[1], SENSIBLE)]

insensitive /ɪnˈsɛnsɪtɪv/ *adj.* (often foll. by *to*) **1** showing or feeling no sympathetic or emotional response. **2** not sensitive to physical stimuli. □ **insensitively** *adv.* **insensitiveness** *n.* **insensitivity** /-ˈtɪvɪti/ *n.*

insentient /ɪnˈsɛnʃ(ə)nt/ *adj.* not sentient; inanimate. □ **insentience** *n.*

inseparable /ɪnˈsɛp(ə)rəb(ə)l/ *adj. & n.* ● *adj.* **1** (esp. of friends) unable or unwilling to be separated. **2** *Gram.* (of a prefix, or a verb in respect of it) unable to be used as a separate word, e.g.: *dis-*, *mis-*, *un-*. ● *n.* (usu. in *pl.*) an inseparable person or thing, esp. a friend. □ **inseparability** /-ˈbɪlɪti/ *n.* **inseparably** *adv.* [Middle English from Latin *inseparabilis* (as IN-[1], SEPARABLE)]

insert *v. & n.* ● *v.tr.* /ɪnˈsəːt/ **1** (usu. foll. by *in, into, between*, etc.) place, fit, or thrust (a thing) into another. **2** (usu. foll. by *in, into*) introduce (a letter, word, article, advertisement, etc.) into a newspaper etc. **3** (as **inserted** *adj.*) *Anat.* etc. (of a muscle etc.) attached (at a specific point). ● *n.* /ˈɪnsəːt/ something inserted, e.g. a loose page in a magazine, a piece of cloth in a garment, a shot in a cinema film. □ **insertable** *adj.* **inserter** *n.* [Latin *inserere* (as IN-[2], *serere sert-* 'join')]

insertion /ɪnˈsəːʃ(ə)n/ *n.* **1** the act or an instance of inserting. **2** an amendment etc. inserted in writing or printing. **3** each appearance of an advertisement in a newspaper etc. **4** an ornamental section of needlework inserted into plain material (*lace insertions*). **5** the manner or place of attachment of a muscle, an organ, etc. **6** the placing of a spacecraft in an orbit. [Late Latin *insertio* (as INSERT)]

in-service /ˈɪnsəːvɪs/ *attrib.adj.* (of training) intended for those actively engaged in the profession or activity concerned.

INSET /ˈɪnsɛt/ *n.* (often *attrib.*) training during term-time for teachers in British state schools. [acronym, from *in*-service *e*ducation and *t*raining]

inset *n. & v.* ● *n.* /ˈɪnsɛt/ **1 a** an extra page or pages inserted in a folded sheet or in a book; an insert. **b** a small map, photograph, etc., inserted within the border of a larger one. **2** a piece let into a dress etc. ● *v.tr.* /ɪnˈsɛt/ (**insetting**; *past* and *past part.* **inset** or **insetted**) **1** put in as an inset. **2** decorate with an inset. □ **insetter** *n.*

inshallah /ɪnˈʃalə/ *int.* if Allah wills it. [Arabic *in šā' Allah*]

inshore /ɪnˈʃɔː, ˈɪnʃɔː/ *adv. & adj.* at sea but close to the shore. □ **inshore of** nearer to shore than.

inside *n., adj., adv., & prep.* ● *n.* /ɪnˈsʌɪd/ **1 a** the inner side or surface of a thing. **b** the inner part; the interior. **2 a** the side of a path next to the wall or away from the road. **b** *Brit.* (of a double-decker bus) the lower section. **3** (usu. in *pl.*) *colloq.* the stomach and bowels (*something wrong with my insides*). **4** *colloq.* a position affording inside information (*knows someone on the inside*). ● *adj.* /ˈɪnsʌɪd/ **1** situated on or in, or derived from, the inside. **2** *Hockey* & (now less often) *Football* nearer to the centre of the field (*inside forward*; *inside left*; *inside right*). ● *adv.* /ɪnˈsʌɪd/ **1** on, in, or to the inside. **2** *slang* in prison. ● *prep.* /ɪnˈsʌɪd/ **1** on the inner side of; within (*inside the house*). **2** in less than (*inside an hour*). □ **inside of** *colloq.* in less than (a week etc.). [IN + SIDE]

inside country *n. Austral.* settled areas near the coast.

inside information *n.* information not accessible to outsiders.

inside job *n. colloq.* a crime committed by a person living or working on the premises burgled etc.

inside out *adv. & adj.* ● *adv.* with the inner surface turned outwards. ● *attrib.adj.* (**inside-out**) in this condition (*an inside-out building with lifts on the outside*). □ **know a thing inside out** know a thing thoroughly. **turn inside out 1** turn the inner surface outwards. **2** *colloq.* cause confusion or a mess in.

insider /ɪn'sʌɪdə/ *n.* **1** a person who is within a society, organization, etc. **2** a person privy to a secret, esp. when using it to gain advantage.

insider dealing *n.* (also **insider trading**) *Stock Exch.* the illegal practice of trading to one's own advantage through having access to confidential information.

inside track *n.* **1** the track which is shorter, because of the curve. **2** a position of advantage.

insidious /ɪn'sɪdɪəs/ *adj.* **1** proceeding or progressing inconspicuously but harmfully (*an insidious disease*). **2** treacherous; crafty. □ **insidiously** *adv.* **insidiousness** *n.* [Latin *insidiosus* 'cunning' from *insidiae* 'ambush' (as IN-[2], *sedēre* 'sit')]

insight /'ɪnsʌɪt/ *n.* (usu. foll. by *into*) **1** the capacity of understanding hidden truths etc., esp. of character or situations. **2** an instance of this. □ **insightful** *adj.* **insightfully** *adv.* [Middle English, probably of Scandinavian and Low German origin (as IN-[2], SIGHT)]

insignia /ɪn'sɪgnɪə/ *n.* (treated as *sing.* or *pl.*; usu. foll. by *of*) **1** badges (*wore his insignia of office*). **2** distinguishing marks. [Latin, pl. of *insigne*, neut. of *insignis* 'distinguished' (as IN-[2], *signis* from *signum* SIGN)]

■ **Usage** *Insignia* is, in origin, a plural noun; its singular form *insigne* is rarely encountered. *Insignia* can be treated as a singular or plural, e.g. *He was wearing camouflage dress and no rank insignia was/were visible*, but should not be used as a countable noun.

insignificant /ɪnsɪg'nɪfɪk(ə)nt/ *adj.* **1** unimportant; trifling. **2** (of a person) undistinguished. **3** meaningless. □ **insignificance** *n.* **insignificancy** *n.* **insignificantly** *adv.*

insincere /ɪnsɪn'sɪə/ *adj.* not sincere; not candid. □ **insincerely** *adv.* **insincerity** /-'sɛrɪti/ *n.* (*pl.* **-ies**). [Latin *insincerus* (as IN-[1], SINCERE)]

insinuate /ɪn'sɪnjʊeɪt/ *v.tr.* **1** (often foll. by *that* + clause) convey indirectly or obliquely; hint (*insinuated that she was lying*). **2** (often *refl.*; usu. foll. by *into*) **a** introduce (oneself, a person, etc.) into favour, office, etc., by subtle manipulation. **b** introduce (a thing, an idea, oneself, etc.) subtly or deviously into a place (*insinuated himself into the Royal Box*). □ **insinuatingly** *adv.* **insinuation** /-'eɪʃ(ə)n/ *n.* **insinuative** *adj.* **insinuator** *n.* [Latin *insinuare insinuat-* (as IN-[2], *sinuare* 'to curve')]

insipid /ɪn'sɪpɪd/ *adj.* **1** lacking vigour or interest; dull. **2** lacking flavour; tasteless. □ **insipidity** /-'pɪdɪti/ *n.* **insipidly** *adv.* **insipidness** *n.* [French *insipide* or Late Latin *insipidus* (as IN-[1], *sapidus* SAPID)]

insist /ɪn'sɪst/ *v.tr.* (usu. foll. by *that* + clause; also *absol.*) maintain or demand positively and assertively (*insisted that he was innocent; give me the bag! I insist!*). □ **insist on** demand or maintain (*I insist on being present; insists on his suitability*). □ **insistingly** *adv.* [Latin *insistere* 'stand on, persist' (as IN-[2], *sistere* 'stand')]

insistent /ɪn'sɪst(ə)nt/ *adj.* **1** (often foll. by *on*) insisting; demanding positively or continually (*is insistent on taking me with him*). **2** obtruding itself on the attention (*the insistent rattle of the window frame*). □ **insistence** *n.* **insistency** *n.* **insistently** *adv.*

in situ /ɪn 'sɪtjuː/ *adv.* **1** in its place. **2** in its original place. [Latin]

insobriety /ɪnsə'brʌɪəti/ *n.* intemperance, esp. in drinking.

insofar /ɪnsə(ʊ)'fɑː/ *adv.* = *in so far* (see FAR).

insolation /ɪnsə'leɪʃ(ə)n/ *n.* exposure to the sun's rays, esp. for bleaching. [Latin *insolatio* from *insolare* (as IN-[2], *solare* from *sol* 'sun')]

insole /'ɪnsəʊl/ *n.* **1** a removable sole worn in a boot or shoe for warmth etc. **2** the fixed inner sole of a boot or shoe.

insolent /'ɪns(ə)l(ə)nt/ *adj.* offensively contemptuous or arrogant; insulting. □ **insolence** *n.* **insolently** *adv.* [Middle English from Latin *insolens* (as IN-[1], *solens*, pres. part. of *solēre* 'be accustomed')]

insoluble /ɪn'sɒljʊb(ə)l/ *adj.* **1** incapable of being solved. **2** incapable of being dissolved. □ **insolubility** /-'bɪlɪti/ *n.* **insolubilize** /-bɪlʌɪz/ *v.tr.* (also **-ise**). **insolubly** *adv.* [Middle English from Old French *insoluble* or Latin *insolubilis* (as IN-[1], SOLUBLE)]

insolvable /ɪn'sɒlvəb(ə)l/ *adj.* = INSOLUBLE.

insolvent /ɪn'sɒlv(ə)nt/ *adj. & n.* ● *adj.* **1** unable to pay one's debts. **2** relating to insolvency (*insolvent laws*). ● *n.* an insolvent person. □ **insolvency** *n.*

insomnia /ɪn'sɒmnɪə/ *n.* habitual sleeplessness; inability to sleep. □ **insomniac** /-ɪak/ *n. & adj.* [Latin from *insomnis* 'sleepless' (as IN-[1], *somnus* 'sleep')]

insomuch /ɪnsə(ʊ)'mʌtʃ/ *adv.* **1** (foll. by *that* + clause) to such an extent. **2** (foll. by *as*) inasmuch. [Middle English, originally *in so much*]

insouciant /ɪn'suːsɪənt/ *adj.* carefree; unconcerned. □ **insouciance** *n.* **insouciantly** *adv.* [French (as IN-[1], *souciant*, pres. part. of *soucier* 'care')]

inspan /ɪn'span/ *v.* (**inspanned**, **inspanning**) *S.Afr.* **1** *tr.* (also *absol.*) **a** yoke (oxen etc.) in a team to a vehicle. **b** harness an animal or animals to (a wagon). **2** *tr.* harness (people or resources) into service. [Dutch *inspannen* 'stretch' (as IN-[2], SPAN[2])]

inspect /ɪn'spɛkt/ *v.tr.* **1** look closely at or into. **2** examine (a document etc.) officially. □ **inspection** *n.* [Latin *inspicere inspect-* (as IN-[2], *specere* 'look at'), or its frequentative *inspectare*]

inspector /ɪn'spɛktə/ *n.* **1** a person who inspects. **2** an official employed to supervise a service, a machine, etc., and make reports. **3** a police officer below a superintendent and (*Brit.*) above a sergeant in rank. □ **inspectorate** /-rət/ *n.* **inspectorial** /-'tɔːrɪəl/ *adj.* **inspectorship** *n.* [Latin (as INSPECT)]

inspector general *n.* a chief inspector.

inspector of taxes *n.* (in the UK) an official of the Inland Revenue responsible for collecting taxes.

inspiration /ɪnspɪ'reɪʃ(ə)n/ *n.* **1 a** a supposed force or influence on poets, artists, musicians, etc., stimulating creativity, ideas, etc. **b** a person, principle, faith, etc. as a source of esp. artistic creativity or moral fervour. **c** a similar divine influence supposed to have led to the writing of Scripture etc. **2** a sudden brilliant, creative, or timely idea. **3** a drawing in of breath; inhalation. □ **inspirational** *adj.* [Middle English via Old French from Late Latin *inspiratio -onis* (as INSPIRE)]

inspirator /'ɪnspɪreɪtə/ *n.* an apparatus for drawing in air or vapour. [Late Latin (as INSPIRE)]

inspire /ɪn'spʌɪə/ *v.tr.* **1** (often foll. by *to*) stimulate or arouse (a person) to esp. creative activity or moral fervour (*inspired her to write; inspired by God*). **2 a** (usu. foll. by *with*) animate (a person) with a feeling. **b** (usu. foll. by *into*) instil (a feeling) into a person etc. **c** (usu. foll. by *in*) create (a feeling) in a person. **3** prompt; give rise to (*the poem was inspired by the autumn*). **4** (as **inspired** *adj.*) **a** (of a work of art etc.) as if prompted by or emanating from a supernatural source; characterized by inspiration (*an inspired speech*). **b** (of a guess) intuitive but accurate. **5** (also *absol.*) breathe in (air etc.); inhale. □ **inspiratory** /-rət(ə)ri/ *adj.* **inspiredly** /-rɪdli/ *adv.* **inspirer** *n.* **inspiring** *adj.* **inspiringly** *adv.* [Middle English via Old French *inspirer* from Latin *inspirare* 'breathe in' (as IN-[2], *spirare* 'breathe')]

inspirit /ɪn'spɪrɪt/ *v.tr.* (**inspirited**, **inspiriting**) **1** put life into; animate. **2** (usu. foll. by *to*, or *to* + infin.) encourage (a person). □ **inspiriting** *adj.* **inspiritingly** *adv.*

inspissate /ɪn'spɪseɪt/ *v.tr. literary* thicken; condense. □ **inspissation** /-'seɪʃ(ə)n/ *n.* [Late Latin *inspissare inspissat-* (as IN-[2], Latin *spissus* 'thick')]

inspissator /'ɪnspɪseɪtə/ *n.* an apparatus for thickening serum etc. by heat.

inst. /ɪnst/ *abbr.* **1** = INSTANT *adj.* 4 (*the 6th inst.*). **2** institute. **3** institution.

instability /ɪnstə'bɪlɪti/ *n.* (*pl.* **-ies**) **1** a lack of stability. **2** *Psychol.* unpredictability in behaviour etc. **3** an instance of instability. [Middle English via French *instabilité* from Latin *instabilitas -tatis* from *instabilis* (as IN-[1], STABLE[1])]

install /ɪn'stɔːl/ *v.tr.* (also **instal**) (**installed, installing**) **1** place (equipment, machinery, etc.) in position ready for use. **2** place (a person) in an office or rank with ceremony (*installed in the office of chancellor*). **3** establish (oneself, a person, etc.) in a place, condition, etc. (*installed herself at the head of the table*). □ **installant** *adj.* & *n.* **installer** *n.* [medieval Latin *installare* (as IN-[2], *stallare* from *stallum* STALL[1])]

installation /ɪnstə'leɪʃ(ə)n/ *n.* **1 a** the act or an instance of installing. **b** the process or an instance of being installed. **2 a** a large piece of equipment etc. installed for use. **b** a subsidiary military or industrial establishment. **3** an art exhibit constructed within a gallery etc. [medieval Latin *installatio* (as INSTALL)]

instalment /ɪn'stɔːlm(ə)nt/ *n.* (*US* **installment**) **1** a sum of money due as one of several usu. equal payments for something, spread over an agreed period of time. **2** any of several parts, esp. of a television or radio serial or a magazine story, published or shown in sequence at intervals. [alteration of obsolete *estallment* from Anglo-French *estalement*, from *estaler* 'fix': probably associated with INSTALLATION]

instalment plan *n.* payment by instalments, esp. hire purchase.

instance /'ɪnst(ə)ns/ *n.* & *v.* ● *n.* **1** an example or illustration of (*just another instance of his lack of determination*). **2** a particular case (*that's not true in this instance*). **3** *Law* a legal suit. ● *v.tr.* cite (a fact, case, etc.) as an instance. □ **at the instance of** at the request or suggestion of. **for instance** as an example. **in the first** (or **second** etc.) **instance** in the first (or second etc.) place; at the first (or second etc.) stage of a proceeding. [Middle English via Old French from Latin *instantia* (as INSTANT)]

instancy /'ɪnst(ə)nsi/ *n.* **1** urgency. **2** pressing nature. [Latin *instantia*: see INSTANCE]

instant /'ɪnst(ə)nt/ *adj.* & *n.* ● *adj.* **1** occurring immediately (*gives an instant result*). **2 a** (of food etc.) processed to allow quick preparation. **b** prepared hastily and with little effort (*I have no instant solution*). **3** urgent; pressing. **4** *Commerce* of the current month (*the 6th instant*). **5** *archaic* of the present moment. ● *n.* **1** a precise moment of time, esp. the present (*come here this instant*; *told you the instant I heard*). **2** a short space of time (*was there in an instant*). [Middle English via French from Latin *instare instant-* 'be present, press upon' (as IN-[2], *stare* 'stand')]

instantaneous /ɪnst(ə)n'teɪnɪəs/ *adj.* **1** occurring or done in an instant or instantly. **2** *Physics* existing at a particular instant. □ **instantaneity** /-tə'niːɪti, -tə'neɪɪti/ *n.* **instantaneously** *adv.* **instantaneousness** *n.* [medieval Latin *instantaneus* from Latin *instans* (as INSTANT), suggested by ecclesiastical Latin *momentaneus*]

instanter /ɪn'stantə/ *adv. archaic* or *joc.* immediately; at once. [Latin from *instans* (as INSTANT)]

instantiate /ɪn'stanʃɪeɪt/ *v.tr.* represent by an instance. □ **instantiation** /-'eɪʃ(ə)n/ *n.* [Latin *instantia*: see INSTANCE]

instantly /'ɪnst(ə)ntli/ *adv.* **1** immediately; at once. **2** *archaic* urgently; pressingly.

instant replay *n.* the immediate repetition of part of a filmed sports event, often in slow motion.

instar /'ɪnstɑː/ *n.* a stage in the life of an insect etc. between two periods of moulting. [Latin, = form]

instate /ɪn'steɪt/ *v.tr.* (often foll. by *in*) install; establish. [IN-[2] + STATE]

in statu pupillari /ɪn ˌstatjuː pjuːpɪ'lɑːri/ *adj.* **1** under guardianship, esp. as a pupil. **2** in a junior position at university; not having a master's degree. [Latin]

instauration /ɪnstɔː'reɪʃ(ə)n/ *n. formal* **1** restoration; renewal. **2** an act of instauration. □ **instaurator** /'ɪnstɔːreɪtə/ *n.* [Latin *instauratio* from *instaurare* (as IN-[2]: cf. RESTORE)]

instead /ɪn'stɛd/ *adv.* **1** (foll. by *of*) as a substitute or alternative to; in place of (*instead of this one*; *stayed instead of going*). **2** as an alternative (*took me instead*) (cf. STEAD). [Middle English, from IN + STEAD]

instep /'ɪnstɛp/ *n.* **1** the inner arch of the foot between the toes and the ankle. **2** the part of a shoe etc. fitting over or under this. **3** a thing shaped like an instep. [Middle English: ultimately formed as IN-[2] + STEP, but immediate origin uncertain]

instigate /'ɪnstɪgeɪt/ *v.tr.* **1** bring about by incitement or persuasion; provoke (*who instigated the inquiry?*). **2** (usu. foll. by *to*) urge on, incite (a person etc.) to esp. an evil act. □ **instigation** /-'geɪʃ(ə)n/ *n.* **instigator** *n.* [Latin *instigare instigat-*]

instil /ɪn'stɪl/ *v.tr.* (*US* **instill**) (**instilled, instilling**) (often foll. by *in* or *into*) **1** introduce (a feeling, idea, etc.) into a person's mind etc. gradually. **2** put (a liquid) into something in drops. □ **instillation** /-'leɪʃ(ə)n/ *n.* **instilment** *n.* [Latin *instillare* (as IN-[2], *stillare* 'drop'): cf. DISTIL]

instinct *n.* & *adj.* ● *n.* /'ɪnstɪŋ(k)t/ **1 a** an innate, usu. fixed, pattern of behaviour in most animals in response to certain stimuli. **b** a similar propensity in human beings to act without conscious intention; innate impulsion. **2** (usu. foll. by *for*) unconscious skill; intuition. ● *predic.adj.* /ɪn'stɪŋ(k)t/ (foll. by *with*) imbued, filled (with life, beauty, force, etc.). □ **instinctual** /-'stɪŋ(k)tjʊəl/ *adj.* **instinctually** /-'stɪŋ(k)tjʊəli/ *adv.* [Middle English, = 'impulse', from Latin *instinctus* from *instinguere* 'incite' (as IN-[2], *stinguere stinct-* 'prick')]

instinctive /ɪn'stɪŋ(k)tɪv/ *adj.* **1** relating to or prompted by instinct. **2** apparently unconscious or automatic (*an instinctive reaction*). □ **instinctively** *adv.*

institute /'ɪnstɪtjuːt/ *n.* & *v.* ● *n.* **1 a** a society or organization for the promotion of science, education, etc. **b** a building used by an institute. **2** *Law* (usu. in *pl.*) a digest of the elements of a legal subject (*Institutes of Justinian*). **3** a principle of instruction. ● *v.tr.* **1** establish; found. **2 a** initiate (an inquiry etc.). **b** begin (proceedings) in a court. **3** (usu. foll. by *to, into*) appoint (a person) as a cleric in a church etc. [Middle English from Latin *institutum* 'design, precept', neut. past part. of *instituere* 'establish, arrange, teach' (as IN-[2], *statuere* 'set up')]

institution /ɪnstɪ'tjuːʃ(ə)n/ *n.* **1** the act or an instance of instituting. **2 a** a society or organization founded esp. for charitable, religious, educational, or social purposes. **b** a building used by an institution. **3** an established law, practice, or custom. **4** *colloq.* (of a person, a custom, etc.) a familiar object. **5** the establishment of a cleric etc. in a church, parish, etc. [Middle English via Old French from Latin *institutio -onis* (as INSTITUTE)]

institutional /ɪnstɪ'tjuːʃ(ə)n(ə)l/ *adj.* **1** of or like an institution. **2** typical of institutions, esp. in being regimented or unimaginative (*the food was dreadfully institutional*). **3** (of religion) expressed or organized through institutions (Churches etc.). **4** (of advertising) intended to create prestige rather than immediate sales. □ **institutionalism** *n.* **institutionally** *adv.*

institutionalize /ɪnstɪ'tjuːʃ(ə)n(ə)lʌɪz/ *v.tr.* (also **-ise**) **1** (as **institutionalized** *adj.*) **a** (of a prisoner, a long-term patient, etc.) made apathetic and dependent after a long period in an institution. **b** established in practice or custom (*institutionalized secrecy*). **2** place or keep (a person) in an institution. **3** convert into an institution; make institutional. □ **institutionalization** /-ˈzeɪʃ(ə)n/ *n.*

in-store /ˈɪnstɔː, -ˈstɔː/ *adj. & adv.* within a store (*in-store bakery*).

Inst.P. *abbr.* (in the UK) Institute of Physics.

instruct /ɪnˈstrʌkt/ *v.tr.* **1** (often foll. by *in*) teach (a person) a subject etc. (*instructed her in French*). **2** (usu. foll. by *to* + infin.) direct; command (*instructed him to fill in the hole*). **3** (often foll. by *of*, or *that* etc. + clause) inform (a person) of a fact etc. **4** *Brit.* **a** (of a client or solicitor) give information to (a solicitor or counsel). **b** authorize (a solicitor or counsel) to act for one. [Middle English from Latin *instruere instruct-* 'build, teach' (as IN-², *struere* 'pile up')]

instruction /ɪnˈstrʌkʃ(ə)n/ *n.* **1** (often in *pl.*) a direction; an order (*gave him his instructions*). **2** teaching; education (*took a course of instruction*). **3** *Brit. Law* (in *pl.*) directions to a solicitor or counsel. **4** *Computing* a direction in a computer program defining and effecting an operation. □ **instructional** *adj.* [Middle English via Old French from Late Latin *instructio -onis* (as INSTRUCT)]

instructive /ɪnˈstrʌktɪv/ *adj.* tending to instruct; conveying a lesson; enlightening (*found the experience instructive*). □ **instructively** *adv.* **instructiveness** *n.*

instructor /ɪnˈstrʌktə/ *n.* (*fem.* **instructress** /-ˈstrʌktrɪs/) **1** a person who instructs; a teacher, demonstrator, etc. **2** *N. Amer.* a university teacher ranking below assistant professor. □ **instructorship** *n.*

instrument /ˈɪnstrʊm(ə)nt/ *n. & v.* ● *n.* **1** a tool or implement, esp. for delicate or scientific work. **2** (in full **musical instrument**) a device for producing musical sounds by vibration, wind, percussion, etc. **3** **a** a thing used in performing an action (*the meeting was an instrument in his success*). **b** a person made use of (*is merely their instrument*). **4** a measuring device, esp. in a car or aircraft, serving to gauge position, speed, etc. **5** a formal, esp. legal, document. ● *v.tr.* **1** arrange (music) for instruments. **2** equip with instruments (for measuring, recording, controlling, etc.). [Middle English from Old French *instrument* or Latin *instrumentum* (as INSTRUCT)]

instrumental /ɪnstrʊˈmɛnt(ə)l/ *adj. & n.* ● *adj.* **1** (usu. foll. by *to*, *in*, or *in* + verbal noun) serving as an instrument or means (*was instrumental in finding the money*). **2** (of music) performed on instruments, without singing (cf. VOCAL). **3** of, or arising from, an instrument (*instrumental error*). **4** *Gram.* of or in the instrumental. ● *n.* **1** a piece of music performed by instruments, not by the voice. **2** *Gram.* the case of nouns and pronouns (and words in grammatical agreement with them) indicating a means or instrument. □ **instrumentalist** /-ˈmɛnt(ə)lɪst/ *n.* **instrumentality** /-ˈtalɪti/ *n.* **instrumentally** *adv.* [Middle English via French from medieval Latin *instrumentalis* (as INSTRUMENT)]

instrumentation /ˌɪnstrʊmɛnˈteɪʃ(ə)n/ *n.* **1** **a** the arrangement or composition of music for a particular group of musical instruments. **b** the instruments used in any one piece of music. **2** **a** the design, provision, or use of instruments in industry, science, etc. **b** such instruments collectively. [French from *instrumenter* (as INSTRUMENT)]

instrument panel *n.* (also **instrument board**) a surface, esp. in a car or aeroplane, containing the dials etc. of measuring devices.

insubordinate /ɪnsəˈbɔːdɪnət/ *adj.* disobedient; rebellious. □ **insubordinately** *adv.* **insubordination** /-ˈneɪʃ(ə)n/ *n.*

insubstantial /ɪnsəbˈstanʃ(ə)l/ *adj.* **1** lacking solidity or substance. **2** not real. □ **insubstantiality** /-ʃɪˈalɪti/ *n.* **insubstantially** *adv.* [Late Latin *insubstantialis* (as IN-¹, SUBSTANTIAL)]

insufferable /ɪnˈsʌf(ə)rəb(ə)l/ *adj.* **1** intolerable. **2** unbearably arrogant or conceited etc. □ **insufferableness** *n.* **insufferably** *adv.*

insufficiency /ɪnsəˈfɪʃ(ə)nsi/ *n.* **1** the condition of being insufficient. **2** *Med.* the inability of an organ to perform its normal function (*renal insufficiency*). [Middle English from Late Latin *insufficientia* (as INSUFFICIENT)]

insufficient /ɪnsəˈfɪʃ(ə)nt/ *adj.* not sufficient; inadequate. □ **insufficiently** *adv.* [Middle English via Old French from Late Latin *insufficiens* (as IN-¹, SUFFICIENT)]

insufflate /ˈɪnsəfleɪt/ *v.tr.* **1** *Med.* **a** blow or breathe (air, gas, powder, etc.) into a cavity of the body etc. **b** treat (the nose etc.) in this way. **2** *Theol.* blow or breathe on (a person) to symbolize spiritual influence. □ **insufflation** /-ˈfleɪʃ(ə)n/ *n.* [Late Latin *insufflare insufflat-* (as IN-², *sufflare* 'blow upon')]

insufflator /ˈɪnsəfleɪtə/ *n.* **1** a device for blowing powder on to a surface in order to make fingerprints visible. **2** an instrument for insufflating.

insular /ˈɪnsjʊlə/ *adj.* **1** **a** of or like an island. **b** separated or remote, like an island. **2** ignorant of or indifferent to cultures, peoples, etc., outside one's own experience; narrow-minded. **3** of a variant of Latin handwriting current in Britain and Ireland in the Middle Ages. **4** (of climate) equable. □ **insularism** *n.* **insularity** /-ˈlarɪti/ *n.* **insularly** *adv.* [Late Latin *insularis* (as INSULATE)]

insulate /ˈɪnsjʊleɪt/ *v.tr.* **1** prevent the passage of electricity, heat, or sound from (a thing, room, etc.) by interposing non-conductors. **2** detach (a person or thing) from its surroundings; isolate. **3** *archaic* make (land) into an island. □ **insulation** /-ˈleɪʃ(ə)n/ *n.* [Latin *insula* 'island' + -ATE³]

insulating tape *n.* an adhesive tape used to cover exposed electrical wires etc.

insulator /ˈɪnsjʊleɪtə/ *n.* **1** a thing or substance used for insulation against electricity, heat, or sound. **2** an insulating device to support telegraph wires etc. **3** a device preventing contact between electrical conductors.

insulin /ˈɪnsjʊlɪn/ *n. Biochem.* a polypeptide hormone produced in the pancreas by the islets of Langerhans, which regulates the amount of glucose in the blood, and the lack of which causes diabetes. [Latin *insula* 'island' + -IN]

insult *v. & n.* ● *v.tr.* /ɪnˈsʌlt/ **1** speak to or treat with scornful abuse or indignity. **2** offend the self-respect or modesty of. ● *n.* /ˈɪnsʌlt/ **1** an insulting remark or action. **2** (often foll. by *to*) something so worthless or contemptible as to be offensive (*an insult to his intelligence*). **3** *Med.* **a** an agent causing damage to the body. **b** such damage. □ **insulter** *n.* **insulting** *adj.* **insultingly** *adv.* [French *insulte* or Latin *insultare* (as IN-², *saltare*, frequentative of *salire salt-* 'leap')]

insuperable /ɪnˈsuːp(ə)rəb(ə)l, -ˈsjuː-/ *adj.* **1** (of a barrier) impossible to surmount. **2** (of a difficulty etc.) impossible to overcome. □ **insuperability** /-ˈbɪlɪti/ *n.* **insuperably** *adv.* [Middle English from Old French *insuperable* or Latin *insuperabilis* (as IN-¹, SUPERABLE)]

insupportable /ɪnsəˈpɔːtəb(ə)l/ *adj.* **1** unable to be endured. **2** unjustifiable. □ **insupportableness** *n.* **insupportably** *adv.* [French (as IN-¹, SUPPORT)]

insurance /ɪnˈʃʊər(ə)ns/ *n.* **1** the act or an instance of insuring. **2** **a** a sum paid for this; a premium. **b** a sum paid out as compensation for theft, damage, loss, etc. **3** the business of providing insurance policies. **4** = INSURANCE POLICY. **5** a measure taken to provide for a possible contingency (*take an umbrella as insurance*). [earlier *ensurance* from Old French *enseürance* (as ENSURE)]

insurance agent *n. Brit.* a person employed to collect premiums door to door.

insurance broker *n.* an agent selling insurance.

insurance company *n.* a company engaged in the business of insurance.

insurance policy *n.* **1** a contract of insurance. **2** a document detailing such a policy and constituting a contract.

insurance stamp *n. Brit.* a stamp certifying the payment of a sum, usu. paid weekly, for National Insurance.

insure /ɪn'ʃʊə/ *v.tr.* **1** (often foll. by *against*; also *absol.*)) secure the payment of a sum of money in the event of loss or damage to (property, life, a person, etc.) by regular payments or premiums (*insured the house for £100,000*; *we have insured against flood damage*) (cf. ASSURE 3). **2** (of the owner of a property, an insurance company, etc.) secure the payment of (a sum of money) in this way. **3** (usu. foll. by *against*) provide for (a possible contingency) (*insured themselves against the rain by taking umbrellas*). **4** *US* = ENSURE. □ **insurable** *adj.* **insurability** /-'bɪlɪti/ *n.* [Middle English, variant of ENSURE]

insured /ɪn'ʃʊəd/ *adj. & n.* ● *adj.* covered by insurance. ● *n.* (usu. prec. by *the*) a person etc. covered by insurance.

insurer /ɪn'ʃʊərə/ *n.* **1** a person or company offering insurance policies for premiums; an underwriter. **2** a person who takes out insurance.

insurgent /ɪn'sɜːdʒ(ə)nt/ *adj. & n.* ● *adj.* **1** rising in active revolt. **2** (of the sea etc.) rushing in. ● *n.* a rebel; a revolutionary. □ **insurgence** *n.* **insurgency** *n.* (*pl.* **-ies**). [French, from Latin *insurgere insurrect-* (as IN-[2], *surgere* 'rise')]

insurmountable /ɪnsə'maʊntəb(ə)l/ *adj.* unable to be surmounted or overcome. □ **insurmountably** *adv.*

insurrection /ɪnsə'rɛkʃ(ə)n/ *n.* a rising in open resistance to established authority; a rebellion. □ **insurrectionary** *adj.* **insurrectionist** *n.* [Middle English via Old French from Late Latin *insurrectio -onis* (as INSURGENT)]

insusceptible /ɪnsə'sɛptɪb(ə)l/ *adj.* (usu. foll. by *of*, *to*) not susceptible (of treatment, to an influence, etc.). □ **insusceptibility** /-'bɪlɪti/ *n.*

in-swinger /'ɪnswɪŋə/ *n.* **1** *Cricket* a ball bowled with a swing towards the batsman. **2** *Football* a pass or kick that sends the ball curving towards the goal.

int. *abbr.* **1** interior. **2** internal. **3** international.

intact /ɪn'takt/ *adj.* **1** entire; unimpaired. **2** untouched. □ **intactness** *n.* [Middle English from Latin *intactus* (as IN-[1], *tactus*, past part. of *tangere* 'touch')]

intagliated /ɪn'talɪeɪtɪd/ *adj.* decorated with surface carving. [Italian *intagliato*, past part. of *intagliare* 'cut into']

intaglio /ɪn'talɪəʊ, -'tɑːl-/ *n. & v.* ● *n.* (*pl.* **-os**) **1** a gem with an incised design (cf. CAMEO). **2** an engraved design. **3** a carving, esp. incised, in hard material. **4** a process of printing from an engraved design. ● *v.tr.* (**-oes**, **-oed**) **1** engrave (material) with a sunk pattern or design. **2** engrave (such a design). [Italian (as INTAGLIATED)]

intake /'ɪnteɪk/ *n.* **1 a** the action of taking in. **b** an instance of this. **2 a** a number (of people etc.) or the amount taken in or received (*this year's intake of students*). **b** such people etc. **3** a place where water is taken into a channel or pipe from a river, or fuel or air enters an engine etc. **4** an airway into a mine. **5** *N.Engl.* land reclaimed from a moor etc.

intangible /ɪn'tan(d)ʒɪb(ə)l/ *adj. & n.* ● *adj.* **1** unable to be touched; not solid. **2** unable to be grasped mentally. ● *n.* something that cannot be precisely measured or assessed. □ **intangibility** /-'bɪlɪti/ *n.* **intangibly** *adv.* [French *intangible* or medieval Latin *intangibilis* (as IN-[1], TANGIBLE)]

intarsia /ɪn'tɑːsɪə/ *n.* **1 a** the craft of using wood inlays, esp. as practised in 15th-c. Italy. **b** similar inlaid work in stone, metal, or glass. **2** a method of knitting with a number of colours in which a separate length or ball of yarn is used for each area of colour (as opposed to different yarns being carried at the back of the work). [Italian *intarsio*]

integer /'ɪntɪdʒə/ *n.* **1** a whole number. **2** a thing complete in itself. [Latin (*adj.*) = untouched, whole: see ENTIRE]

integral *adj. & n.* ● *adj.* /'ɪntɪgr(ə)l, *disp.* ɪn'tɛgr(ə)l/ **1 a** of a whole or necessary to the completeness of a whole. **b** forming a whole (*integral design*). **c** whole, complete. **2** *Math.* **a** of or denoted by an integer. **b** involving only integers, esp. as coefficients of a function. ● *n.* /'ɪntɪgr(ə)l/ *Math.* **1** a quantity of which a given function is the derivative, i.e. which yields that function when differentiated, and which may express the area under the curve of a graph of the function (see DEFINITE INTEGRAL, INDEFINITE INTEGRAL). **2** a function satisfying a given differential equation. □ **integrality** /-'gralɪti/ *n.* **integrally** *adv.* [Late Latin *integralis* (as INTEGER)]

■ **Usage** The alternative pronunciation given for the adjective, with the stress on the second syllable, is considered incorrect by some people.

integral calculus *n.* mathematics concerned with finding integrals, their properties and application, etc. (cf. DIFFERENTIAL CALCULUS).

integrand /'ɪntɪgrand/ *n. Math.* a function that is to be integrated. [Latin *integrandus*, gerundive of *integrare*: see INTEGRATE]

integrant /'ɪntɪgr(ə)nt/ *adj.* (of parts) making up a whole; component. [French *intégrant* from *intégrer* (as INTEGRATE)]

integrate *v. & adj.* ● *v.* /'ɪntɪgreɪt/ **1** *tr.* **a** combine (parts) into a whole. **b** complete (an imperfect thing) by the addition of parts. **2** *tr. & intr.* bring or come into equal participation in or membership of society, a school, etc. **3** *tr.* desegregate, esp. racially (a school etc.). **4** *tr. Math.* **a** find the integral of. **b** (as **integrated** *adj.*) indicating the mean value or total sum of (temperature, an area, etc.). ● *adj.* /'ɪntɪgrət/ **1** made up of parts. **2** whole; complete. □ **integrable** /'ɪntɪgrəb(ə)l/ *adj.* **integrability** /ˌɪntɪgrə'bɪlɪti/ *n.* **integrative** /'ɪntɪgrətɪv/ *adj.* [Latin *integrare integrat-* 'make whole' (as INTEGER)]

integrated circuit *n.* a small chip etc. of material incorporating the functions of several components of an electric circuit.

integrated services digital network *n.* a telecommunications network through which sound, images, and data can be transmitted as digitized signals.

integration /ɪntɪ'greɪʃ(ə)n/ *n.* **1** the act or an instance of integrating. **2** the intermixing of persons previously segregated. **3** *Psychol.* the combination of the diverse elements of perception etc. in a personality. □ **integrationist** *n.* [Latin *integratio* (as INTEGRATE)]

integrator /'ɪntɪgreɪtə/ *n.* **1** an instrument for indicating or registering the total amount or mean value of some physical quality, as area, temperature, etc. **2** a person or thing that integrates.

integrity /ɪn'tɛgrɪti/ *n.* **1** moral uprightness; honesty. **2** wholeness; soundness. [Middle English from French *intégrité* or Latin *integritas* (as INTEGER)]

integument /ɪn'tɛgjʊm(ə)nt/ *n.* a natural outer covering, as a skin, husk, rind, etc. □ **integumental** /-'mɛnt(ə)l/ *adj.* **integumentary** /-'mɛnt(ə)ri/ *adj.* [Latin *integumentum* from *integere* (as IN-[2], *tegere* 'cover')]

intellect /'ɪntəlɛkt/ *n.* **1 a** the faculty of reasoning, knowing, and thinking, as distinct from feeling. **b** the understanding or mental powers (of a particular person etc.) (*his intellect is not great*). **2 a** a clever or knowledgeable person. **b** the intelligentsia regarded collectively (*the combined intellect of four universities*). [Middle English from Old French *intellect* or Latin *intellectus* 'understanding' (as INTELLIGENT)]

intellection /ɪntɪ'lɛkʃ(ə)n/ *n.* the action or process of understanding (opp. IMAGINATION). □ **intellective** *adj.* [Middle English from medieval Latin *intellectio* (as INTELLIGENT)]

intellectual /ɪntɪ'lɛktʃʊəl/ *adj. & n.* ● *adj.* **1** of or relating to the intellect. **2** possessing a high level of understanding or intelligence. **3** requiring, or appealing to, the intellect. ● *n.* a person possessing a highly developed intellect. ▫ **intellectuality** /-'alɪti/ *n.* **intellectualize** /-'lɛktʃʊəlʌɪz/ *v.tr. & intr.* (also **-ise**). **intellectually** *adv.* [Middle English from Latin *intellectualis* (as INTELLECT)]

intellectualism /ɪntɪ'lɛktʃʊəlɪz(ə)m/ *n.* **1** the exercise, esp. when excessive, of the intellect at the expense of the emotions. **2** *Philos.* the theory that knowledge is wholly or mainly derived from pure reason. ▫ **intellectualist** *n.*

intellectual property *n. Law* non-tangible property that is the result of creativity, such as patents, copyrights, etc.

intelligence /ɪn'tɛlɪdʒ(ə)ns/ *n.* **1 a** the intellect; the understanding. **b** (of a person or an animal) quickness of understanding; wisdom. **2 a** the collection of information, esp. of military or political value. **b** people employed in this. **c** information so collected. **d** *archaic* information in general; news. **3** an intelligent or rational being. ▫ **intelligential** /-'dʒɛnʃ(ə)l/ *adj.* [Middle English via Old French from Latin *intelligentia* (as INTELLIGENT)]

intelligence department *n.* a usu. government department engaged in collecting esp. secret information.

intelligence quotient *n.* a number denoting the ratio of a person's intelligence to the statistical norm, 100 being average (abbr.: **IQ**).

intelligence test *n.* a test designed to measure intelligence rather than acquired knowledge.

intelligent /ɪn'tɛlɪdʒ(ə)nt/ *adj.* **1** having or showing intelligence, esp. of a high level. **2** quick of mind; clever. **3 a** (of a device or machine) able to vary its behaviour in response to varying situations and requirements and past experience. **b** (esp. of a computer terminal) having its own data-processing capability; incorporating a microprocessor (opp. DUMB). ▫ **intelligently** *adv.* [Latin *intelligere intellect-* 'understand' (as INTER-, *legere* 'gather, pick out, read')]

intelligentsia /ɪn,tɛlɪ'dʒɛntsɪə/ *n.* **1** the class of intellectuals regarded as possessing culture and political initiative. **2** people doing intellectual work; intellectuals. [Russian via Polish *inteligencja* from Latin *intelligentia* (as INTELLIGENT)]

intelligible /ɪn'tɛlɪdʒɪb(ə)l/ *adj.* **1** (often foll. by *to*) able to be understood; comprehensible. **2** *Philos.* able to be understood only by the intellect, not by the senses. ▫ **intelligibility** /-'bɪlɪti/ *n.* **intelligibly** *adv.* [Latin *intelligibilis* (as INTELLIGENT)]

Intelpost /'ɪntɛlpəʊst/ *n.* the international electronic transmission of messages and graphics by fax, telex, etc. [acronym from *Int*ernational *El*ectronic *Post*]

Intelsat /'ɪntɛlsat/ *n.* an international organization of countries operating a system of commercial communication satellites. [acronym from *Int*ernational *Tel*ecommunications *Sat*ellite Consortium]

intemperate /ɪn'tɛmp(ə)rət/ *adj.* **1** (of a person, conduct, or speech) immoderate; unbridled; violent (*used intemperate language*). **2 a** given to excessive indulgence in alcohol. **b** excessively indulgent in one's appetites. ▫ **intemperance** *n.* **intemperately** *adv.* **intemperateness** *n.* [Middle English from Latin *intemperatus* (as IN-[1], TEMPERATE)]

intend /ɪn'tɛnd/ *v.tr.* **1** have as one's purpose or intention (*we intend to go*; *we intend going*; *we intend that it shall be done*). **2** (usu. foll. by *for*, or *to* + infin.) design or destine (a person or a thing) (*I intend him to go*; *intended him for an academic career*). **3** (often foll. by *as*) mean (*what does he intend by that?*; *intended it as a warning*). **4** (in *passive*; foll. by *for*) **a** be meant for a person to have or use etc. (*they are intended for the children*). **b** be designed for (*intended for a small child's hand*). **5** (as **intending** *adj.*) who intends to be (*an intending visitor*). [Middle English *entende, intende* via Old French *entendre, intendre* from Latin *intendere intent-* or *intens-* 'strain, direct, purpose' (as IN-[2], *tendere* 'stretch, tend')]

intendant /ɪn'tɛnd(ə)nt/ *n.* **1** (esp. as a title of foreign officials) a superintendent or manager of a department of public business etc. **2** the administrator of an opera house or theatre. ▫ **intendancy** *n.* [French from Latin *intendere* (as INTEND)]

intended /ɪn'tɛndɪd/ *adj. & n.* ● *adj.* **1** done on purpose; intentional. **2** designed, meant. ● *n. colloq.* the person one intends to marry; one's fiancé or fiancée (*is this your intended?*). ▫ **intendedly** *adv.*

intense /ɪn'tɛns/ *adj.* (**intenser**, **intensest**) **1** (of a quality, feeling, etc.) existing in a high degree; extreme, forceful (*intense joy*; *intense cold*). **2 a** (of a person) feeling, or apt to feel, strong emotion (*very intense about her music*). **b** expressing strong emotion (*a deeply intense poem*). **3** (of a colour) very strong or deep. **4** (of an action etc.) highly concentrated (*intense thought*). ▫ **intensely** *adv.* **intenseness** *n.* [Middle English from Old French *intens* or Latin *intensus* (as INTEND)]

■ **Usage** *Intense* is sometimes confused with *intensive* and wrongly used to describe a course of study etc.

intensifier /ɪn'tɛnsɪfʌɪə/ *n.* **1** a person or thing that intensifies. **2** *Gram.* a word or prefix used to give force or emphasis.

intensify /ɪn'tɛnsɪfʌɪ/ *v.* (**-ies, -ied**) **1** *tr. & intr.* make or become intense or more intense. **2** *tr. Photog.* increase the opacity of (a negative). ▫ **intensification** /-fɪ'keɪʃ(ə)n/ *n.*

intension /ɪn'tɛnʃ(ə)n/ *n.* **1** *Logic* the internal content of a concept. **2** *formal* the intensity, or high degree, of a quality. **3** *formal* the strenuous exertion of the mind or will. ▫ **intensional** *adj.* **intensionally** *adv.* [Latin *intensio* (as INTEND)]

intensity /ɪn'tɛnsɪti/ *n.* (*pl.* **-ies**) **1** the quality or an instance of being intense. **2** esp. *Physics* the measurable amount of some quality, e.g. force, brightness, a magnetic field, etc.

intensive /ɪn'tɛnsɪv/ *adj. & n.* ● *adj.* **1** thorough, vigorous; directed to a single point, area, or subject (*intensive study*; *intensive bombardment*). **2** of or relating to intensity as opposed to extent; producing intensity. **3** serving to increase production in relation to costs (*intensive farming methods*) (cf. EXTENSIVE 3). **4** (usu. in *comb.*) *Econ.* making much use of (*a labour-intensive industry*). **5** *Gram.* (of an adjective, adverb, etc.) expressing intensity; giving force or emphasis, as *really* in *my feet are really cold*. ● *n. Gram.* an intensive adjective, adverb, etc.; an intensifier. ▫ **intensively** *adv.* **intensiveness** *n.* [French *intensif -ive* or medieval Latin *intensivus* (as INTEND)]

■ **Usage** See Usage Note at INTENSE.

intensive care *n.* **1** medical treatment with constant monitoring etc. of a dangerously ill patient (also, with hyphen, *attrib.*: *intensive-care unit*). **2** a part of a hospital devoted to this.

intent /ɪn'tɛnt/ *n. & adj.* ● *n.* (usu. without article) intention; a purpose (*with intent to defraud*; *my intent to reach the top*; *with evil intent*). ● *adj.* **1** (usu. foll. by *on*) **a** resolved; bent; determined (*was intent on succeeding*). **b** attentively occupied (*intent on his books*). **2** (esp. of a look) earnest; eager; meaningful. ▫ **to all intents and purposes** practically; virtually. ▫ **intently** *adv.* **intentness** *n.* [Middle English *entent* via Old French from Latin *intentus* (as INTEND)]

intention /ɪn'tɛnʃ(ə)n/ *n.* **1** (often foll. by *to* + infin., or *of* + verbal noun) a thing intended; an aim or purpose (*it was not his intention to interfere*; *have no intention of staying*). **2** the act of intending (*done without intention*). **3** (usu. in *pl.*) *colloq.* a person's, esp. a man's, designs in respect to marriage (*are his intentions strictly honourable?*). **4** *Logic* a conception. ▫ **intentioned** *adj.* (usu. in *comb.*). [Middle English *entencion* via Old French from Latin *intentio* 'stretching, purpose' (as INTEND)]

intentional /ɪn'tɛnʃ(ə)n(ə)l/ *adj.* done on purpose. ▫ **intentionality** /-'nalɪti/ *n.* **intentionally** *adv.* [French *intentionnel* or medieval Latin *intentionalis* (as INTENTION)]

intention tremor *n.* a trembling of a part of a body when commencing a movement.

inter /ɪn'tə:/ *v.tr.* (**interred**, **interring**) deposit (a corpse etc.) in the earth, a tomb, etc.; bury. [Middle English via Old French *enterrer* from Romanic (as IN-[2], Latin *terra* 'earth')]

inter. *abbr.* intermediate.

inter- /'ɪntə/ *prefix* **1** between, among (*intercontinental*). **2** mutually, reciprocally (*interbreed*). [Old French *entre-* or Latin *inter* 'between, among']

interact /ɪntər'akt/ *v.intr.* act reciprocally; act on each other. ▫ **interactant** *adj. & n.*

interaction /ɪntər'akʃ(ə)n/ *n.* **1** reciprocal action or influence. **2** *Physics* the action of atomic and subatomic particles on each other. ▫ **interactional** *adj.*

interactive /ɪntər'aktɪv/ *adj.* **1** reciprocally active; acting upon or influencing each other. **2** (of a computer or other electronic device) allowing a two-way flow of information between it and a user, responding to the user's input. ▫ **interactively** *adv.* **interactivity** /-'tɪvɪti/ *n.* [INTERACT, on the pattern of *active*]

inter alia /ɪntər 'eɪlɪə, 'alɪə/ *adv.* among other things. [Latin]

inter-allied /ɪntər'alʌɪd/ *adj.* relating to two or more allies (in war etc.).

interarticular /ɪntərɑ:'tɪkjʊlə/ *adj.* between the contiguous surfaces of a joint.

interatomic /ɪntərə'tɒmɪk/ *adj.* between atoms.

interbank /'ɪntəbaŋk/ *adj.* agreed, arranged, or operating between banks (*interbank loan*).

interbed /ɪntə'bɛd/ *v.tr.* (**-bedded**, **-bedding**) embed (one thing) among others.

interblend /ɪntə'blɛnd/ *v.* **1** *tr.* (usu. foll. by *with*) mingle (things) together. **2** *intr.* blend with each other.

interbreed /ɪntə'bri:d/ *v.* (*past* and *past part.* **-bred** /-'brɛd/) *intr. & tr.* breed or cause to breed with members of a different stock, race, or species to produce a hybrid.

intercalary /ɪn'tə:kəl(ə)ri, ɪntə'kal(ə)ri/ *adj.* **1 a** (of a day or a month) inserted in the calendar to harmonize it with the solar year, e.g. 29 Feb. in leap years. **b** (of a year) having such an addition. **2** interpolated; intervening. [Latin *intercalari(u)s* (as INTERCALATE)]

intercalate /ɪn'tə:kəleɪt/ *v.tr.* **1** (also *absol.*) insert (an intercalary day etc.). **2** interpose (anything out of the ordinary course). **3** (as **intercalated** *adj.*) (of strata etc.) interposed. ▫ **intercalation** /-'leɪʃ(ə)n/ *n.* [Latin *intercalare intercalat-* 'proclaim the insertion of a day etc.' (as INTER-, *calare* 'proclaim')]

intercede /ɪntə'si:d/ *v.intr.* (usu. foll. by *with*) interpose or intervene on behalf of another; plead (*they interceded with the king for his life*). ▫ **interceder** *n.* [French *intercéder* or Latin *intercedere intercess-* 'intervene' (as INTER-, *cedere* 'go')]

intercellular /ɪntə'sɛljʊlə/ *adj. Biol.* located or occurring between cells.

intercensal /ɪntə'sɛns(ə)l/ *adj.* between two censuses.

intercept *v. & n.* ● *v.tr.* /ɪntə'sɛpt/ **1** seize, catch, or stop (a person, message, vehicle, ball, etc.) going from one place to another. **2** (usu. foll. by *from*) cut off (light etc.). **3** check or stop (motion etc.). **4** *Math.* mark off (a space) between two points etc. ● *n.* /'ɪntəsɛpt/ *Math.* the part of a line between two points of intersection with usu. the coordinate axes or other lines. ▫ **interception** /-'sɛpʃ(ə)n/ *n.* **interceptive** /-'sɛptɪv/ *adj.* [Latin *intercipere intercept-* (as INTER-, *capere* 'take')]

interceptor /ɪntə'sɛptə/ *n.* **1** an aircraft used to intercept enemy raiders. **2** a person or thing that intercepts.

intercession /ɪntə'sɛʃ(ə)n/ *n.* **1** the act of interceding, esp. by prayer. **2** an instance of this, esp. a prayer on behalf of another. ▫ **intercessional** *adj.* **intercessor** *n.* **intercessorial** /-sɛ'sɔ:rɪəl/ *adj.* **intercessory** *adj.* [French *intercession* or Latin *intercessio* (as INTERCEDE)]

interchange *v. & n.* ● *v.tr.* /ɪntə'tʃeɪn(d)ʒ/ **1** (of two people) exchange (things) with each other. **2** put each of (two things) in the other's place; alternate. ● *n.* /'ɪntətʃeɪn(d)ʒ/ **1** (often foll. by *of*) a reciprocal exchange between two people etc. **2** alternation (*the interchange of woods and fields*). **3** a road junction designed so that traffic streams do not intersect. ▫ **interchangeable** *adj.* **interchangeability** /-'bɪlɪti/ *n.* **interchangeableness** *n.* **interchangeably** *adv.* [Middle English from Old French *entrechangier* (as INTER-, CHANGE)]

intercity /ɪntə'sɪti/ *adj. & n.* ● *adj.* existing or travelling between cities, esp. (**InterCity** *Brit. propr.*) with reference to train travel. ● *n.* (*pl.* **intercities**) a usu. fast train operating between cities.

inter-class /ɪntə'klɑ:s/ *adj.* existing or conducted between different social classes.

intercollegiate /ɪntəkə'li:dʒ(ɪ)ət/ *adj.* existing or conducted between colleges or universities.

intercolonial /ɪntəkə'ləʊnɪəl/ *adj.* existing or conducted between colonies.

intercom /'ɪntəkɒm/ *n. colloq.* **1** a system of intercommunication by radio or telephone between or within offices, aircraft, etc. **2** an instrument used in this. [abbreviation]

intercommunicate /ɪntəkə'mju:nɪkeɪt/ *v.intr.* **1** communicate reciprocally. **2** (of rooms etc.) have free passage into each other; have a connecting door. ▫ **intercommunication** /-'keɪʃ(ə)n/ *n.* **intercommunicative** /-kətɪv/ *adj.*

intercommunion /ɪntəkə'mju:njən/ *n.* **1** mutual fellowship, esp. mutual sharing of the Eucharist by Christian denominations. **2** mutual action or relationship.

intercommunity /ɪntəkə'mju:nɪti/ *n.* **1** the quality of being common to various groups etc. **2** having things in common.

interconnect /ɪntəkə'nɛkt/ *v.tr. & intr.* connect with each other. ▫ **interconnection** /-'nɛkʃ(ə)n/ *n.*

intercontinental /ˌɪntəkɒntɪ'nɛnt(ə)l/ *adj.* connecting or travelling between continents. ▫ **intercontinentally** *adv.*

interconvert /ɪntəkən'və:t/ *v.tr. & intr.* convert into each other. ▫ **interconversion** *n.* **interconvertible** *adj.*

intercooler /'ɪntəku:lə/ *n.* an apparatus for cooling gas between successive compressions, esp. in a car or truck engine. ▫ **intercool** *v.tr.*

intercorrelate /ɪntə'kɒrəleɪt, -rɪ-/ *v.tr. & intr.* correlate with one another. ▫ **intercorrelation** /-'leɪʃ(ə)n/ *n.*

intercostal /ɪntə'kɒst(ə)l/ *adj.* between the ribs (of the body or a ship). ▫ **intercostally** *adv.*

intercounty /ɪntə'kaʊnti/ *adj.* existing or conducted between counties.

intercourse /'ɪntəkɔ:s/ *n.* **1** communication or dealings between individuals, nations, etc. **2** = SEXUAL INTERCOURSE. **3** communion between human beings and God. [Middle English via Old French *entrecours* 'exchange, commerce', from Latin *intercursus* (as INTER-, *currere curs-* 'run')]

intercrop /ɪntə'krɒp/ *v.tr.* (**-cropped**, **-cropping**) (also *absol.*) raise (a crop) among plants of a different kind, usu. in the space between rows. ▫ **intercropping** *n.*

intercross /ɪntə'krɒs/ *v.* **1** *tr. & intr.* lay or lie across each other. **2 a** *intr.* (of animals) breed with each other. **b** *tr.* cause to do this.

intercrural /ɪntə'krʊər(ə)l/ *adj.* between the legs.

intercurrent /ɪntə'kʌr(ə)nt/ *adj.* **1** (of a time or event) intervening. **2** *Med.* **a** (of a disease) occurring during the progress of another. **b** recurring at intervals. [Latin *intercurrere intercurrent-* (as INTERCOURSE)]

intercut /ɪntə'kʌt/ *v.tr.* (**-cutting**; *past* and *past part.* **-cut**) *Cinematog.* alternate (shots) with contrasting shots by cutting.

interdenominational /ˌɪntədɪnɒmɪ'neɪʃ(ə)n(ə)l/ *adj.* concerning more than one (religious) denomination. ▫ **interdenominationally** *adv.*

interdepartmental /ˌɪntədiːpɑːtˈmɛnt(ə)l/ *adj.* concerning more than one department. □ **interdepartmentally** *adv.*

interdepend /ɪntədɪˈpɛnd/ *v.intr.* depend on each other. □ **interdependence** *n.* **interdependency** *n.* **interdependent** *adj.*

interdict *n. & v.* ● *n.* /ˈɪntədɪkt/ **1** an authoritative prohibition. **2** *RC Ch.* a sentence debarring a person, or esp. a place, from ecclesiastical functions and privileges. **3** *Sc. Law* an injunction. ● *v.tr.* /ɪntəˈdɪkt/ **1** prohibit (an action). **2** forbid the use of. **3** (usu. foll. by *from* + verbal noun) restrain (a person). **4** (usu. foll. by *to*) forbid (a thing) to a person. **5** *US* **a** *Mil.* impede (an enemy force), esp. by bombing lines of communication or supply. **b** intercept (a prohibited commodity); prevent (its movement). □ **interdiction** /-ˈdɪkʃ(ə)n/ *n.* **interdictory** /-ˈdɪkt(ə)ri/ *adj.* [Middle English from Old French *entredit* from Latin *interdictum* past part. of *interdicere* interpose, forbid by decree (as INTER-, *dicere* say)]

interdigital /ɪntəˈdɪdʒɪt(ə)l/ *adj.* between the fingers or toes.

interdigitate /ɪntəˈdɪdʒɪteɪt/ *v.intr.* interlock like clasped fingers. [INTER- + Latin *digitus* finger + -ATE[3]]

interdisciplinary /ɪntəˈdɪsɪplɪn(ə)ri, ˌɪntədɪsɪˈplɪn(ə)ri/ *adj.* of or between more than one branch of learning.

interest /ˈɪnt(ə)rɪst/ *n. & v.* ● *n.* **1 a** concern; curiosity (*have no interest in fishing*). **b** a quality exciting curiosity or holding the attention (*this magazine lacks interest*). **2** a subject, hobby, etc., in which one is concerned (*his interests are gardening and sport*). **3** advantage or profit, esp. when financial (*it is in your interest to go; look after your own interests*). **4** money paid for the use of money lent, or for not requiring the repayment of a debt. **5** (usu. foll. by *in*) **a** a financial stake (in an undertaking etc.). **b** a legal concern, title, or right (in property). **6 a** a party or group having a common concern (*the brewing interest*). **b** a principle in which a party or group is concerned. **7** the selfish pursuit of one's own welfare, self-interest. ● *v.tr.* **1** excite the curiosity or attention of (*your story interests me greatly*). **2** (usu. foll. by *in*) cause (a person) to take a personal interest or share (*can I interest you in a holiday abroad?*). **3** (as **interested** *adj.*) having a private interest; not impartial or disinterested (*an interested party*). □ **at interest** (of money borrowed) on the condition that interest is payable. **declare an** (or **one's**) **interest** make known one's financial etc. interests in an undertaking before it is discussed. **in the interest** (or **interests**) **of** as something that is advantageous to. **lose interest** become bored or boring. **with interest 1** with interest charged or paid. **2** with increased force etc. (*returned the blow with interest*). □ **interestedly** *adv.* **interestedness** *n.* [Middle English, earlier *interesse* from Anglo-French from medieval Latin, alteration apparently after Old French *interest*, both from Latin *interest*, 3rd sing. present of *interesse* matter, make a difference (as INTER-, *esse* be)]

interesting /ˈɪnt(ə)rɪstɪŋ/ *adj.* causing curiosity; holding the attention. □ **in an interesting condition** *archaic* pregnant. □ **interestingly** *adv.* **interestingness** *n.*

interface /ˈɪntəfeɪs/ *n. & v.* ● *n.* **1** esp. *Physics* a surface forming a common boundary between two regions. **2** a point where interaction occurs between two systems, processes, subjects, etc. (*the interface between psychology and education*). **3** esp. *Computing* an apparatus for connecting two pieces of equipment so that they can be operated jointly. ● *v.* (often foll. by *with*) **1** *tr. & intr.* connect with (another piece of equipment etc.) by an interface. **2** *intr.* interact (with another person etc.).

■ **Usage** The use of the noun and the verb in sense 2 is deplored by some people, because it often reduces the word to a high-sounding synonym for *boundary, meeting point, link, liaison, interact*, etc.

interfacial /ɪntəˈfeɪʃ(ə)l/ *adj.* **1** included between two faces of a crystal or other solid. **2** of or forming an interface.

interfacing /ˈɪntəfeɪsɪŋ/ *n.* a stiffish material, esp. buckram, between two layers of fabric in collars etc.

interfaith /ˈɪntəfeɪθ, -ˈfeɪθ/ *adj.* of, relating to, or between different religions or members of different religions.

interfemoral /ɪntəˈfɛm(ə)r(ə)l/ *adj.* between the thighs.

interfere /ɪntəˈfɪə/ *v.intr.* **1** (usu. foll. by *with*) **a** (of a person) meddle; obstruct a process etc. **b** (of a thing) be a hindrance; get in the way. **2** (usu. foll. by *in*) take part or intervene, esp. without invitation or necessity. **3** (foll. by *with*) *Brit. euphem.* molest or assault sexually. **4** *Physics* (of light or other waves) combine so as to cause interference. **5** (of a horse) knock one leg against another. □ **interferer** *n.* **interfering** *adj.* **interferingly** *adv.* [Old French *s'entreferir* 'strike each other' (as INTER-, *ferir* from Latin *ferire* 'strike')]

interference /ɪntəˈfɪər(ə)ns/ *n.* **1** (usu. foll. by *with*) **a** the act of interfering. **b** an instance of this. **2** the fading or disturbance of received radio signals by the interference of waves from different sources, or esp. by atmospherics or unwanted signals. **3** *Physics* the combination of two or more wave motions to form a resultant wave in which the displacement is reinforced or cancelled. □ **interferential** /-fəˈrɛnʃ(ə)l/ *adj.*

interferometer /ɪntəfəˈrɒmɪtə/ *n.* an instrument for measuring wavelengths etc. by means of interference phenomena. □ **interferometric** /-fɛrəˈmɛtrɪk/ *adj.* **interferometrically** /-fɛrəˈmɛtrɪk(ə)li/ *adv.* **interferometry** *n.*

interferon /ɪntəˈfɪərɒn/ *n. Biochem.* any of various proteins released by cells, usu. in response to a virus, and able to inhibit viral replication. [INTERFERE + -ON]

interfibrillar /ɪntəˈfɪbrɪlə/ *adj.* between fibrils.

interfile /ɪntəˈfʌɪl/ *v.tr.* **1** file (two sequences) together. **2** file (one or more items) into an existing sequence.

interflow /ˈɪntəfləʊ/ *v. & n.* ● *v.intr.* flow into each other. ● *n.* the process or result of this.

interfluent /ɪntəˈfluːənt/ *adj.* flowing into each other. [Latin *interfluere interfluent-* (as INTER-, *fluere* 'flow')]

interfuse /ɪntəˈfjuːz/ *v.* **1** *tr.* **a** (usu. foll. by *with*) mix (a thing) with; intersperse. **b** blend (things) together. **2** *intr.* (of two things) blend with each other. □ **interfusion** /-ˈfjuːʒ(ə)n/ *n.* [Latin *interfundere interfus-* (as INTER-, *fundere* 'pour')]

intergalactic /ɪntəgəˈlaktɪk/ *adj.* of or situated between two or more galaxies. □ **intergalactically** *adv.*

interglacial /ɪntəˈgleɪsɪəl, -ʃ(ə)l/ *adj. & n.* ● *adj.* of or relating to a period of milder climate between glacial periods. ● *n.* such a period.

intergovernmental /ˌɪntəgʌv(ə)nˈmɛnt(ə)l/ *adj.* concerning or conducted between two or more governments. □ **intergovernmentally** *adv.*

intergradation /ˌɪntəgrəˈdeɪʃ(ə)n/ *n.* the process of merging together by gradual change of the constituents.

intergrade /ˈɪntəgreɪd/ *v. & n.* ● *v.intr.* pass into another form by intervening grades. ● *n.* such a grade.

intergrowth /ˈɪntəgrəʊθ/ *n.* the growing of things into each other.

interim /ˈɪnt(ə)rɪm/ *n., adj., & adv.* ● *n.* the intervening time (*in the interim he had died*). ● *adj.* intervening; provisional, temporary. ● *adv. archaic* meanwhile. [Latin, as INTER- + adv. suffix *-im*]

interim dividend *n. Brit.* a dividend declared on the basis of less than a full year's results.

interior /ɪnˈtɪəriə/ *adj. & n.* ● *adj.* **1** inner. **2** remote from the coast or frontier; inland. **3** internal; domestic. **4** (usu. foll. by *to*) situated further in or within. **5** existing in the mind or soul; inward. **6** drawn, photographed, etc. within a building. **7** coming from inside. ● *n.* **1** the interior part; the inside. **2** the interior part of a country or region. **3 a** the home affairs of a country. **b** a department dealing with these (*Minister of the Interior*). **4** a representation of the inside of a building or a room (*Dutch interior*). **5** the inner nature; the soul. □ **interiorize** *v.tr.* (also **-ise**). **interiorly** *adv.* [Latin, = inner, comparative adj. from *inter* 'among']

interior angle *n.* the angle between adjacent sides of a rectilinear figure.

interior decoration *n.* (also **interior design**) the decoration or design of the interior of a building, a room, etc.

interior monologue *n.* a form of writing expressing a character's inner thoughts.

interior-sprung *adj. Brit.* (of a mattress etc.) with internal springs.

interject /ɪntəˈdʒɛkt/ *v.tr.* **1** utter (words) abruptly or parenthetically. **2** interrupt with. □ **interjectory** *adj.* [Latin *interjicere* (as INTER-, *jacere* 'throw')]

interjection /ɪntəˈdʒɛkʃ(ə)n/ *n.* an exclamation, esp. as a part of speech (e.g. *ah!, dear me!*). □ **interjectional** *adj.* [Middle English via Old French from Latin *interjectio -onis* (as INTERJECT)]

interknit /ɪntəˈnɪt/ *v.tr. & intr.* (**-knitting**; *past* and *past part.* **-knitted** or **-knit**) knit together; intertwine.

interlace /ɪntəˈleɪs/ *v.* **1** *tr.* bind intricately together; interweave. **2** *tr.* mingle, intersperse. **3** *intr.* cross each other intricately. □ **interlacement** *n.* [Middle English from Old French *entrelacier* (as INTER-, LACE *v.*)]

interlanguage /ˈɪntəlaŋgwɪdʒ/ *n.* a language or use of language having features of two others, often a pidgin or dialect form.

interlap /ɪntəˈlap/ *v.intr.* (**-lapped, -lapping**) overlap.

interlard /ɪntəˈlɑːd/ *v.tr.* (usu. foll. by *with*) mix (writing or speech) with different material, esp. with unusual words or phrases; intersperse. [French *entrelarder* (as INTER-, LARD *v.*)]

interleaf /ˈɪntəliːf/ *n.* (*pl.* **-leaves**) an extra (usu. blank) leaf between the leaves of a book.

interleave /ɪntəˈliːv/ *v.tr.* insert (usu. blank) leaves between the leaves of (a book etc.).

interleukin /ɪntəˈluːkɪn/ *n. Biochem.* any of several glycoproteins produced by leucocytes for regulating immune responses. [INTER- + LEUCOCYTE]

interlibrary /ɪntəˈlʌɪbrəri, -bri/ *adj.* between libraries (esp. *interlibrary loan*).

interline[1] /ɪntəˈlʌɪn/ *v.tr.* **1** insert words between the lines of (a document etc.). **2** insert (words) in this way. □ **interlineation** /-lɪnɪˈeɪʃ(ə)n/ *n.* [Middle English from medieval Latin *interlineare* (as INTER-, LINE[1])]

interline[2] /ɪntəˈlʌɪn/ *v.tr.* put an extra lining between the ordinary lining and the fabric of (a garment etc.).

interlinear /ɪntəˈlɪnɪə/ *adj.* written or printed between the lines of a text. [Middle English from medieval Latin *interlinearis* (as INTER-, LINEAR)]

interlining /ˈɪntəlʌɪnɪŋ/ *n.* material used to interline a garment.

interlink /ɪntəˈlɪŋk/ *v.tr. & intr.* link or be linked together.

interlobular /ɪntəˈlɒbjʊlə/ *adj.* situated between lobes.

interlock *v., adj., & n.* ● *v.* /ɪntəˈlɒk/ **1** *intr.* engage with each other by overlapping or by the fitting together of projections and recesses. **2** *tr.* (usu. in *passive*) lock or clasp within each other. ● *adj.* /ˈɪntəlɒk/ (of a fabric) knitted with closely interlocking stitches. ● *n.* /ˈɪntəlɒk/ a device or mechanism for connecting or coordinating the function of different components. □ **interlocker** *n.*

interlocutor /ɪntəˈlɒkjʊtə/ *n.* (*fem.* **interlocutrix** /-trɪks/) a person who takes part in a dialogue or conversation. □ **interlocution** /-ləˈkjuːʃ(ə)n/ *n.* [modern Latin from Latin *interloqui interlocut-* 'interrupt in speaking' (as INTER-, *loqui* 'speak')]

interlocutory /ɪntəˈlɒkjʊt(ə)ri/ *adj.* **1** of dialogue or conversation. **2** *Law* (of a decree etc.) given provisionally in a legal action. [medieval Latin *interlocutorius* (as INTERLOCUTOR)]

interloper /ˈɪntələʊpə/ *n.* **1** an intruder. **2** a person who interferes in others' affairs, esp. for profit. □ **interlope** *v.intr.* [INTER- + *loper* as in *landloper* 'vagabond' from Middle Dutch *landlooper*]

interlude /ˈɪntəluːd, -ljuːd/ *n.* **1 a** a pause between the acts of a play. **b** something performed or done during this pause. **2 a** an intervening time, space, or event that contrasts with what goes before or after. **b** a temporary amusement or entertaining episode. **3** a piece of music played between other pieces, the verses of a hymn, etc. [originally a light dramatic item between the acts of a morality play: Middle English from medieval Latin *interludium* (as INTER-, *ludus* 'play')]

intermarriage /ɪntəˈmarɪdʒ/ *n.* **1** marriage between people of different races, castes, families, etc. **2** (loosely) marriage between near relations.

intermarry /ɪntəˈmari/ *v.intr.* (**-ies, -ied**) (foll. by *with*) (of races, castes, families, etc.) become connected by marriage.

intermediary /ɪntəˈmiːdjəri/ *n. & adj.* ● *n.* (*pl.* **-ies**) an intermediate person or thing, esp. a mediator. ● *adj.* acting as mediator; intermediate. [French *intermédiaire* via Italian *intermediario* from Latin *intermedius* (as INTERMEDIATE)]

intermediate /ɪntəˈmiːdɪət/ *adj., n., & v.* ● *adj.* coming between two things in time, place, order, character, etc. ● *n.* **1** an intermediate thing. **2** a chemical compound formed by one reaction and then used in another, esp. during synthesis. ● *v.intr.* /-dɪeɪt/ (foll. by *between*) act as intermediary; mediate. □ **intermediacy** /-si/ *n.* **intermediately** *adv.* **intermediateness** *n.* **intermediation** /-ˈeɪʃ(ə)n/ *n.* **intermediator** /-eɪtə/ *n.* [medieval Latin *intermediatus* (as INTER-, *medius* 'middle')]

intermediate frequency *n.* the frequency to which a radio signal is converted during heterodyne reception.

intermediate technology *n.* technology suitable for use in developing countries, esp. by making use of locally available resources.

interment /ɪnˈtəːm(ə)nt/ *n.* the burial of a corpse, esp. with ceremony.

■ **Usage** Do not confuse *interment* meaning 'burial' with *internment* 'confinement' and *internship* 'period of serving as an intern'.

intermesh /ɪntəˈmɛʃ/ *v.tr. & intr.* make or become meshed together.

intermezzo /ɪntəˈmɛtsəʊ/ *n.* (*pl.* **intermezzi** /-tsi/ or **-os**) **1 a** a short connecting instrumental movement in an opera or other musical work. **b** a similar piece performed independently. **c** a short piece for a solo instrument. **2** a short light dramatic or other performance inserted between the acts of a play. [Italian, from Latin *intermedium* 'interval' (as INTERMEDIATE)]

interminable /ɪnˈtəːmɪnəb(ə)l/ *adj.* **1** endless. **2** tediously long or habitual. **3** with no prospect of an end. □ **interminableness** *n.* **interminably** *adv.* [Middle English from Old French *interminable* or Late Latin *interminabilis* (as IN-[1], TERMINATE)]

intermingle /ɪntəˈmɪŋg(ə)l/ *v.tr. & intr.* (often foll. by *with*) mix together; mingle.

intermission /ɪntəˈmɪʃ(ə)n/ *n.* **1** a pause or cessation. **2** an interval between parts of a play, film, concert, etc. **3** a period of inactivity. [French *intermission* or Latin *intermissio* (as INTERMIT)]

intermit /ɪntəˈmɪt/ *v.* (**intermitted, intermitting**) **1** *intr.* esp. *Med.* stop or cease activity briefly (e.g. of a fever, or a pulse). **2** *tr.* suspend; discontinue for a time. [Latin *intermittere intermiss-* (as INTER-, *mittere* 'let go')]

intermittent /ɪntəˈmɪt(ə)nt/ *adj.* occurring at intervals; not continuous or steady. □ **intermittence** /-t(ə)ns/ *n.* **intermittency** /-t(ə)nsi/ *n.* **intermittently** *adv.* [Latin *intermittere intermittent-* (as INTERMIT)]

intermix /ɪntəˈmɪks/ *v.tr. & intr.* mix together. □ **intermixable** *adj.* **intermixture** *n.* [back-formation from *intermixed, intermixt* from Latin *intermixtus*, past part. of *intermiscēre* 'mix together' (as INTER-, *miscēre* 'mix')]

intermodal /ɪntəˈməʊd(ə)l/ *adj.* involving two or more different modes, esp. modes of transport in conveying goods.

intermolecular /ɪntəməˈlɛkjʊlə/ *adj.* between molecules.

intern *n. & v.* ● *n.* /ˈɪntəːn/ (also **interne**) esp. *N. Amer.* a recent graduate or advanced student receiving supervised training in a hospital and acting as an assistant physician or surgeon. ● *v.* **1** *tr.* /ɪnˈtəːn/ confine; oblige (a prisoner, alien, etc.) to reside within prescribed limits. **2** *intr.* /ˈɪntəːn/ esp. *N. Amer.* serve as an intern. ▫ **internment** *n.* (in sense 1 of *v.*). **internship** *n.* esp. *N. Amer.* (in sense 2 of *v.*). [French *interne* from Latin *internus* 'internal']

■ **Usage** See Usage Note at INTERMENT.

internal /ɪnˈtəːn(ə)l/ *adj. & n.* ● *adj.* **1** of or situated in the inside or invisible part. **2** relating or applied to the inside of the body (*internal injuries*). **3** of a nation's domestic affairs. **4** *Brit.* (of a student) attending a university etc. as well as taking its examinations. **5** used or applying within an organization. **6 a** of the inner nature of a thing; intrinsic. **b** of the mind or soul. ● *n.* (in *pl.*) intrinsic qualities. ▫ **internality** /-ˈnalɪti/ *n.* **internally** *adv.* [modern Latin *internalis* (as INTERN)]

internal-combustion engine *n.* an engine in which motive power is generated by the expansion of exhaust gases from the burning of fuel (esp. petrol or diesel) with air inside the engine.

internal energy *n.* the energy in a system arising from the relative positions and interactions of its parts.

internal evidence *n.* evidence derived from the contents of the thing discussed.

internal exile see EXILE *n.* 1.

internalize /ɪnˈtəːn(ə)lʌɪz/ *v.tr.* (also **-ise**) **1** *Psychol.* make (attitudes, behaviour, etc.) part of one's nature by learning or unconscious assimilation. **2** *Econ.* incorporate (costs) as part of the internal structure, esp. social costs resulting from the manufacture and use of a product. ▫ **internalization** /-ˈzeɪʃ(ə)n/ *n.*

internal market *n.* **1** = SINGLE MARKET. **2** (in the UK) a system of decentralized funding in the National Health Service whereby hospital departments purchase each other's services contractually.

internal rhyme *n.* a rhyme involving a word in the middle of a line and another at the end of the line or in the middle of the next.

internat. *abbr.* international.

international /ɪntəˈnaʃ(ə)n(ə)l/ *adj. & n.* ● *adj.* **1** existing, involving, or carried on between two or more nations. **2** agreed on or used by all or many nations (*international driving licence*). ● *n.* **1** *Brit.* **a** a contest, esp. in sport, between teams representing different countries. **b** a member of such a team. **2 a** (**International**) any of four associations founded (1864–1936) to promote socialist or communist action. **b** a member of any of these. ▫ **internationality** /-ˈnalɪti/ *n.* **internationally** *adv.*

International Date Line see DATE LINE 1.

Internationale /ˌɪntənaʃjəˈnɑːl/ *n.* **1** (prec. by *the*) an (originally French) revolutionary song adopted by socialists. **2** = INTERNATIONAL *n.* 2a. [French, fem. of *international* (*adj.*), from INTERNATIONAL]

internationalism /ɪntəˈnaʃ(ə)n(ə)lɪz(ə)m/ *n.* **1** the advocacy of a community of interests among nations. **2** (**Internationalism**) the principles of any of the Internationals. ▫ **internationalist** *n.*

internationalize /ɪntəˈnaʃ(ə)n(ə)lʌɪz/ *v.tr.* (also **-ise**) **1** make international. **2** bring under the protection or control of two or more nations. ▫ **internationalization** /-ˈzeɪʃ(ə)n/ *n.*

international law *n.* a body of rules established by custom or treaty and agreed as binding by nations in their relations with one another.

International Phonetic Alphabet *n.* an internationally recognized set of phonetic symbols used to transcribe the pronunciation of words etc.

international system of units *n.* a system of physical units based on the metre, kilogram, second, ampere, kelvin, candela, and mole, with prefixes to indicate multiplication or division by a power of ten.

international unit *n.* a standard quantity of a vitamin etc.

interne var. of INTERN *n.*

internecine /ɪntəˈniːsʌɪn/ *adj.* mutually destructive. [originally = deadly, from Latin *internecinus*, via *internecio* 'a massacre' from *internecare* 'to slaughter' (as INTER-, *necare* 'kill')]

internee /ˌɪntəːˈniː/ *n.* a person interned.

Internet /ˈɪntənɛt/ *n.* an international computer network linking computers from educational institutions, government agencies, industry, etc. [INTER- + NETWORK]

internist /ɪnˈtəːnɪst/ *n.* esp. *N. Amer. Med.* a specialist in internal diseases.

internode /ˈɪntənəʊd/ *n.* **1** *Bot.* a part of a stem between two of the nodes or knobs from which leaves arise. **2** *Anat.* a slender part between two nodes or joints, e.g. the bone of a finger or toe.

internuclear /ɪntəˈnjuːklɪə/ *adj.* between nuclei.

internuncial /ɪntəˈnʌnʃ(ə)l/ *adj.* (of nerves) communicating between different parts of the system. [Latin *internuntius* (as INTER-, *nuntius* 'messenger')]

interoceanic /ˌɪntərəʊʃɪˈanɪk, -sɪ-/ *adj.* between or connecting two oceans.

interoceptive /ɪntərəʊˈsɛptɪv/ *adj. Biol.* relating to stimuli produced within an organism, esp. in the viscera. [formed irregularly from Latin *internus* 'interior' + RECEPTIVE]

interoperable /ɪntərˈɒp(ə)rəb(ə)l/ *adj.* able to operate in conjunction. ▫ **interoperability** /-əˈbɪlɪti/ *n.*

interosculate /ɪntərˈɒskjʊleɪt/ *v.intr.* = INOSCULATE.

interosseous /ɪntərˈɒsɪəs/ *adj.* between bones.

interparietal /ɪntəpəˈrʌɪət(ə)l/ *adj.* between the right and left parietal bones of the skull. ▫ **interparietally** *adv.*

interpellate /ɪnˈtəːpɪleɪt/ *v.tr.* (in a parliament) interrupt the order of the day by demanding an explanation from (the minister concerned). ▫ **interpellation** /-ˈleɪʃ(ə)n/ *n.* **interpellator** *n.* [Latin *interpellare interpellat-* (as INTER-, *pellere* 'drive')]

interpenetrate /ɪntəˈpɛnɪtreɪt/ *v.* **1** *intr.* (of two things) penetrate each other. **2** *tr.* pervade; penetrate thoroughly. ▫ **interpenetration** /-ˈtreɪʃ(ə)n/ *n.* **interpenetrative** /-trətɪv/ *adj.*

interpersonal /ɪntəˈpəːs(ə)n(ə)l/ *adj.* (of relations) occurring between persons, esp. reciprocally. ▫ **interpersonally** *adv.*

interphase /ˈɪntəfeɪz/ *n. Biol.* the resting phase between successive divisions of a cell.

interplait /ɪntəˈplat/ *v.tr. & intr.* plait together.

interplanetary /ɪntəˈplanɪt(ə)ri/ *adj.* **1** between planets. **2** relating to travel between planets.

interplay /ˈɪntəpleɪ/ *n.* **1** reciprocal action. **2** the operation of two things on each other.

interplead /ɪntəˈpliːd/ *v.* **1** *intr.* litigate with each other to settle a point concerning a third party. **2** *tr.* cause to do this. ▫ **interpleader** *n.* [Middle English from Anglo-French *enterpleder* (as INTER-, PLEAD)]

Interpol /ˈɪntəpɒl/ *n.* the International Criminal Police Commission based in Paris. [abbreviation of *Inter*national *pol*ice]

interpolate /ɪnˈtəːpəleɪt/ *v.tr.* **1 a** insert (words) in a book etc., esp. to give false impressions as to its date etc. **b** make such insertions in (a book etc.). **2** interject (a remark) in a conversation. **3** estimate (intermediate values) from surrounding known values. ▫ **interpolation** /-ˈleɪʃ(ə)n/ *n.* **interpolative** /-lətɪv/ *adj.* **interpolator** *n.* [Latin *interpolare* 'furbish up' (as INTER-, *polire* POLISH)]

interpose /ɪntəˈpəʊz/ *v.* **1** *tr.* (often foll. by *between*) place or insert (a thing) between others. **2** *tr.* say (words) as an interruption. **3** *tr.* exercise or advance (a veto or objection) so as to interfere. **4** *intr.* (often foll. by *between*) intervene (between parties). [French *interposer* from Latin *interponere* 'put in' (as INTER-, POSE[1])]

interposition /ˌɪntəpəˈzɪʃ(ə)n/ *n.* **1** the act of interposing. **2** a thing interposed. **3** an interference. [Middle English from Old French *interposition* or Latin *interpositio* (as INTER-, POSITION)]

interpret /ɪnˈtəːprɪt/ *v.* (**interpreted**, **interpreting**) **1** *tr.* explain the meaning of (foreign or abstruse words, a dream, etc.). **2** *tr.* elucidate or bring out the meaning of (creative work). **3** *intr.* act as an interpreter, esp. of foreign languages. **4** *tr.* explain or understand (behaviour etc.) in a specified manner (*interpreted his gesture as mocking*). □ **interpretable** *adj.* **interpretability** /-təˈbɪlɪti/ *n.* **interpretation** /-ˈteɪʃ(ə)n/ *n.* **interpretational** /-ˈteɪʃ(ə)n(ə)l/ *adj.* **interpretative** /-tətɪv/ *adj.* **interpretatively** /-tətɪvli/ *adv.* **interpretive** *adj.* **interpretively** *adv.* [Middle English from Old French *interpreter* or Latin *interpretari* 'explain, translate' from *interpres -pretis* 'explainer']

interpreter /ɪnˈtəːprɪtə/ *n.* **1** a person who interprets, esp. one who translates speech orally. **2** *Computing* a program that can analyse and execute a program line by line. [Middle English via Anglo-French *interpretour*, Old French *interpreteur* from Late Latin *interpretator -oris* (as INTERPRET)]

interprovincial /ɪntəprəˈvɪnʃ(ə)l/ *adj.* situated or carried on between provinces.

interracial /ɪntəˈreɪʃ(ə)l/ *adj.* existing between or affecting different races. □ **interracially** *adv.*

interregnum /ɪntəˈrɛgnəm/ *n.* (*pl.* **interregnums** or **interregna** /-nə/) **1** an interval when the normal government is suspended, esp. between successive reigns or regimes. **2** an interval or pause. [Latin (as INTER-, *regnum* 'reign')]

interrelate /ɪntərɪˈleɪt/ *v.* **1** *tr.* relate (two or more things) to each other. **2** *intr.* (of two or more things) relate to each other. □ **interrelation** *n.* **interrelationship** *n.*

interrogate /ɪnˈtɛrəgeɪt/ *v.tr.* ask questions of (a person) esp. closely, thoroughly, or formally. □ **interrogator** *n.* [Middle English from Latin *interrogare interrogat-* (as INTER-, *rogare* 'ask')]

interrogation /ɪnˌtɛrəˈgeɪʃ(ə)n/ *n.* **1** the act or an instance of interrogating; the process of being interrogated. **2** a question or enquiry. □ **interrogational** *adj.* [Middle English from French *interrogation* or Latin *interrogatio* (as INTERROGATE)]

interrogation point *n.* (also **interrogation mark** etc.) = QUESTION MARK.

interrogative /ɪntəˈrɒgətɪv/ *adj.* & *n.* ● *adj.* **1 a** of or like a question; used in questions. **b** *Gram.* (of an adjective or pronoun) asking a question (e.g. *who?, which?*). **2** having the form or force of a question. **3** suggesting enquiry (*an interrogative tone*). ● *n.* an interrogative word (e.g. *what?, why?*). □ **interrogatively** *adv.* [Late Latin *interrogativus* (as INTERROGATE)]

interrogatory /ɪntəˈrɒgət(ə)ri/ *adj.* & *n.* ● *adj.* questioning; of or suggesting enquiry (*an interrogatory eyebrow*). ● *n.* (*pl.* **-ies**) a formal set of questions, esp. *Law* one formally put to an accused person etc. [Late Latin *interrogatorius* (as INTERROGATE)]

interrupt /ɪntəˈrʌpt/ *v.tr.* **1** act so as to break the continuous progress of (an action, speech, a person speaking, etc.). **2** obstruct (a person's view etc.). **3** break the continuity of. □ **interruptible** *adj.* **interruption** /-ˈrʌpʃ(ə)n/ *n.* **interruptive** *adj.* **interruptory** *adj.* [Middle English from Latin *interrumpere interrupt-* (as INTER-, *rumpere* 'break')]

interrupter /ɪntəˈrʌptə/ *n.* (also **interruptor**) **1** a person or thing that interrupts. **2** a device for interrupting, esp. an electric circuit.

intersect /ɪntəˈsɛkt/ *v.* **1** *tr.* divide (a thing) by passing or lying across it. **2** *intr.* (of lines, roads, etc.) cross or cut each other. [Latin *intersecare intersect-* (as INTER-, *secare* 'cut')]

intersection /ɪntəˈsɛkʃ(ə)n/ *n.* **1** the act of intersecting. **2** a place where two or more roads intersect. **3** a point or line common to lines or planes that intersect. □ **intersectional** *adj.* [Latin *intersectio* (as INTERSECT)]

interseptal /ɪntəˈsɛpt(ə)l/ *adj.* between septa or partitions.

intersex /ˈɪntəsɛks/ *n.* **1** the abnormal condition of being intermediate between male and female. **2** an individual in this condition.

intersexual /ɪntəˈsɛksjʊəl, -ʃʊəl/ *adj.* **1** existing between the sexes. **2** of or relating to intersex. □ **intersexuality** /-ˈalɪti/ *n.*

interspace *n.* & *v.* ● *n.* /ˈɪntəspeɪs/ an interval of space or time. ● *v.tr.* /ɪntəˈspeɪs/ put interspaces between.

interspecific /ɪntəspəˈsɪfɪk/ *adj.* formed from or occurring between or among individuals of different species.

intersperse /ɪntəˈspəːs/ *v.tr.* **1** (often foll. by *between, among*) scatter; place here and there. **2** (foll. by *with*) diversify (a thing or things with others so scattered). □ **interspersion** *n.* [Latin *interspergere interspers-* (as INTER-, *spargere* 'scatter')]

interspinal /ɪntəˈspʌɪn(ə)l/ *adj.* (also **interspinous** /-nəs/) between spines or spinous processes.

interstadial /ɪntəˈsteɪdɪəl/ *adj.* & *n.* ● *adj.* of or relating to a minor period of ice retreat during a glacial period. ● *n.* such a period. [INTER- + Latin *stadium* 'stage' + -AL]

interstate *adj.* & *n.* ● *adj.* /ɪntəˈsteɪt/ existing or carried on between states, esp. of the US. ● *n.* /ˈɪntəsteɪt/ *US* each motorway of a system of motorways between states.

interstellar /ɪntəˈstɛlə/ *adj.* occurring or situated between stars.

interstice /ɪnˈtəːstɪs/ *n.* **1** an intervening space. **2** a chink or crevice. [Latin *interstitium* (as INTER-, *sistere stit-* 'stand')]

interstitial /ɪntəˈstɪʃ(ə)l/ *adj.* of, forming, or occupying interstices. □ **interstitially** *adv.*

intertextuality /ˌɪntətɛkstjʊˈalɪti/ *n.* the relationship between esp. literary texts.

intertidal /ɪntəˈtʌɪd(ə)l/ *adj.* of or relating to the area which is covered at high tide and uncovered at low tide.

intertribal /ɪntəˈtrʌɪb(ə)l/ *adj.* existing or occurring between different tribes.

intertrigo /ɪntəˈtrʌɪgəʊ/ *n. Med.* inflammation from the rubbing of one area of skin on another. [Latin from *interterere intertrit-* (as INTER-, *terere* 'rub')]

intertwine /ɪntəˈtwʌɪn/ *v.* **1** *tr.* (often foll. by *with*) entwine (together). **2** *intr.* become entwined. □ **intertwinement** *n.*

intertwist /ɪntəˈtwɪst/ *v.tr.* twist together.

interval /ˈɪntəv(ə)l/ *n.* **1** an intervening time or space. **2** *Brit.* a pause or break, esp. between the parts of a theatrical or musical performance. **3** the difference in pitch between two sounds. **4** the distance between persons or things in respect of qualities. □ **at intervals** here and there; now and then. □ **intervallic** /-ˈvalɪk/ *adj.* [Middle English, ultimately from Latin *intervallum* 'space between ramparts, interval' (as INTER-, *vallum* 'rampart')]

intervene /ɪntəˈviːn/ *v.intr.* (often foll. by *between, in*) **1** occur in time between events. **2** interfere; come between so as to prevent or modify the result or course of events. **3** be situated between things. **4** come in as an extraneous factor or thing. **5** *Law* interpose in a lawsuit as a third party. □ **intervener** *n.* **intervenient** *adj.* **intervenor** *n.* [Latin *intervenire* (as INTER-, *venire* 'come')]

intervention /ɪntəˈvɛnʃ(ə)n/ *n.* **1** the act or an instance of intervening. **2** interference, esp. by a state in another's affairs. **3** mediation. [Middle English from French *intervention* or Latin *interventio* (as INTERVENE)]

interventionist /ɪntə'vɛnʃ(ə)nɪst/ *n.* a person who favours intervention. □ **interventionism** *n.*

intervertebral /ɪntə'vəːtɪbr(ə)l/ *adj.* between vertebrae.

interview /'ɪntəvjuː/ *n. & v.* ● *n.* **1** an oral examination of an applicant for employment, a college place, etc. **2** a conversation between a reporter etc. and a person of public interest, used as a basis of a broadcast or publication. **3** a meeting of persons face to face, esp. for consultation. **4** a session of formal questioning by the police. ● *v.* **1** *tr.* hold an interview with. **2** *tr.* question to discover the opinions or experience of (a person). **3** *intr.* participate in an interview; perform (well etc.) at interview. □ **interviewee** /-vjuː'iː/ *n.* **interviewer** *n.* [French *entrevue* from *s'entrevoir* 'see each other' (as INTER-, *voir* from Latin *vidēre* 'see': see VIEW)]

inter-war /ɪntə'wɔː/ *attrib.adj.* existing in the period between two wars, esp. the two world wars.

interweave /ɪntə'wiːv/ *v.tr.* (*past* **-wove** /-'wəʊv/; *past part.* **-woven** /-'wəʊv(ə)n/) **1** (often foll. by *with*) weave together. **2** blend intimately.

interwind /ɪntə'wʌɪnd/ *v.tr. & intr.* (*past* and *past part.* **-wound** /-'waʊnd/) wind together.

interwork /ɪntə'wəːk/ *v.* **1** *intr.* work together or interactively. **2** *tr.* interweave.

intestate /ɪn'tɛsteɪt/ *adj. & n.* ● *adj.* not having made a will before death. ● *n.* a person who has died intestate. □ **intestacy** /-təsi/ *n.* [Middle English from Latin *intestatus* (as IN-[1], *testari testat-* 'make a will' from *testis* 'witness')]

intestinal flora *n.pl.* the symbiotic bacteria naturally inhabiting the gut.

intestine /ɪn'tɛstɪn/ *n.* (in *sing.* or *pl.*) **1** the lower part of the alimentary canal from the end of the stomach to the anus. **2** *Zool.* (esp. in invertebrates) the whole alimentary canal. □ **intestinal** /also ɪntɛ'stʌɪn(ə)l/ *adj.* [Latin *intestinum* from *intestinus* 'internal']

inthrall *US* var. of ENTHRAL.

intifada /ɪntɪ'fɑːdə/ *n.* a movement of Palestinian uprising in the Israeli-occupied West Bank and Gaza Strip, beginning in 1987. [Arabic, = uprising]

intimacy /'ɪntɪməsi/ *n.* (*pl.* **-ies**) **1** close familiarity or friendship; closeness. **2** an intimate act, esp. sexual intercourse. **3** a private cosy atmosphere. **4** an intimate remark; an endearment.

intimate[1] /'ɪntɪmət/ *adj. & n.* ● *adj.* **1** closely acquainted; familiar, close (*an intimate friend*; *an intimate relationship*). **2** private and personal (*intimate thoughts*). **3** (usu. foll. by *with*) having sexual relations. **4** (of knowledge) detailed, thorough. **5** (of a relationship between things) close. **6** (of mixing etc.) thorough. **7** essential, intrinsic. **8** (of a place etc.) friendly; promoting close personal relationships. ● *n.* a very close friend. □ **intimately** *adv.* [Latin *intimus* 'inmost']

intimate[2] /'ɪntɪmeɪt/ *v.tr.* **1** (often foll. by *that* + clause) state or make known. **2** imply, hint. □ **intimation** /-'meɪʃ(ə)n/ *n.* [Late Latin *intimare* 'announce' from Latin *intimus* 'inmost']

intimidate /ɪn'tɪmɪdeɪt/ *v.tr.* frighten or overawe, esp. to subdue or influence. □ **intimidating** *adj.* **intimidation** /-'deɪʃ(ə)n/ *n.* **intimidator** *n.* **intimidatory** /-'deɪt(ə)ri/ *adj.* [medieval Latin *intimidare* (as IN-[2], *timidare* from *timidus* TIMID)]

intinction /ɪn'tɪŋ(k)ʃ(ə)n/ *n. Eccl.* the dipping of the Eucharistic bread in the wine so that the communicant receives both together. [Late Latin *intinctio* from Latin *intingere intinct-* (as IN-[2], TINGE)]

intitule /ɪn'tɪtjuːl/ *v.tr. Brit.* entitle (an Act of Parliament etc.). [Old French *intituler* from Late Latin *intitulare* (as IN-[2], *titulare* from *titulus* 'title')]

into /'ɪntʊ, 'ɪntə/ *prep.* **1** expressing motion or direction to a point on or within (*walked into a tree*; *ran into the house*). **2** expressing direction of attention or concern (*will look into it*). **3** expressing a change of state (*turned into a dragon*; *separated into groups*; *forced into it*). **4** after the beginning of (*five minutes into the game*). **5** *colloq.* interested in; knowledgeable about (*is really into art*). [Old English *intō* (as IN, TO)]

intolerable /ɪn'tɒl(ə)rəb(ə)l/ *adj.* that cannot be endured. □ **intolerably** *adv.* [Middle English from Old French *intolerable* or Latin *intolerabilis* (as IN-[1], TOLERABLE)]

intolerant /ɪn'tɒl(ə)r(ə)nt/ *adj.* not tolerant, esp. of views, beliefs, or behaviour differing from one's own. □ **intolerance** *n.* **intolerantly** *adv.* [Latin *intolerans* (as IN-[1], TOLERANT)]

intonate /'ɪntəneɪt/ *v.tr.* intone. [medieval Latin *intonare*: see INTONE]

intonation /ɪntə'neɪʃ(ə)n/ *n.* **1** modulation of the voice; accent. **2** the act of intoning. **3** accuracy of pitch in playing or singing (*has good intonation*). **4** the opening phrase of a plainsong melody. □ **intonational** *adj.* [medieval Latin *intonatio* (as INTONE)]

intone /ɪn'təʊn/ *v.tr.* **1** recite (prayers etc.) with prolonged sounds, esp. in a monotone. **2** utter with a particular tone. □ **intoner** *n.* [medieval Latin *intonare* (as IN-[2], Latin *tonus* TONE)]

in toto /ɪn 'təʊtəʊ/ *adv.* completely. [Latin]

intoxicant /ɪn'tɒksɪk(ə)nt/ *adj. & n.* ● *adj.* intoxicating. ● *n.* an intoxicating substance.

intoxicate /ɪn'tɒksɪkeɪt/ *v.tr.* **1** make drunk. **2** excite or elate beyond self-control. □ **intoxicatingly** *adv.* **intoxication** /-'keɪʃ(ə)n/ *n.* [medieval Latin *intoxicare* (as IN-[2], *toxicare* 'to poison' from Latin *toxicum*): see TOXIC]

intra- /'ɪntrə/ *prefix* forming adjectives usu. from adjectives, meaning 'on the inside, within' (*intramural*). [Latin *intra* 'inside']

intracellular /ɪntrə'sɛljʊlə/ *adj. Biol.* located or occurring within a cell or cells.

intracranial /ɪntrə'kreɪnɪəl/ *adj.* within the skull. □ **intracranially** *adv.*

intractable /ɪn'traktəb(ə)l/ *adj.* **1** hard to control or deal with. **2** difficult, stubborn. □ **intractability** /-'bɪlɪti/ *n.* **intractableness** *n.* **intractably** *adv.* [Latin *intractabilis* (as IN-[1], TRACTABLE)]

intrados /ɪn'treɪdɒs/ *n. Archit.* the lower or inner curve of an arch (opp. EXTRADOS). [French (as INTRA-, *dos* 'back' from Latin *dorsum*)]

intramolecular /ɪntrəmə'lɛkjʊlə/ *adj.* within a molecule.

intramural /ɪntrə'mjʊər(ə)l/ *adj.* **1** situated or done within walls. **2 a** forming part of normal university or college studies. **b** taking place within a single (esp. educational) institution. □ **intramurally** *adv.*

intramuscular /ɪntrə'mʌskjʊlə/ *adj.* in or into a muscle or muscles.

intransigent /ɪn'transɪdʒ(ə)nt, -'trɑː-, -nz-/ *adj. & n.* ● *adj.* uncompromising, stubborn. ● *n.* an intransigent person. □ **intransigence** /-dʒ(ə)ns/ *n.* **intransigency** /-dʒ(ə)nsi/ *n.* **intransigently** *adv.* [French *intransigeant* from Spanish *los intransigentes*, a name adopted by the extreme republicans in the Cortes, ultimately formed as IN-[1] + Latin *transigere transigent-* 'come to an understanding' (as TRANS-, *agere* 'act')]

intransitive /ɪn'transɪtɪv, -'trɑː-, -nz-/ *adj.* (of a verb or sense of a verb) that does not take or require a direct object (whether expressed or implied), e.g. *look* in *look at the sky* (opp. TRANSITIVE). □ **intransitively** *adv.* **intransitivity** /-'tɪvɪti/ *n.* [Late Latin *intransitivus* (as IN-[1], TRANSITIVE)]

intrapreneur /ɪntrəprə'nəː/ *n.* a company employee who develops innovative products etc. [INTRA- + ENTREPRENEUR]

intrauterine /ɪntrə'juːtərʌɪn, -rɪn/ *adj.* within the womb.

intrauterine device *n.* a contraceptive device fitted inside the uterus and physically preventing the implantation of fertilized ova (abbr.: **IUD**).

intravenous /ɪntrə'viːnəs/ *adj.* in or into a vein or veins. □ **intravenously** *adv.* [INTRA- + Latin *vena* 'vein']

in-tray *n.* esp. *Brit.* a tray for incoming documents, letters, etc.

intrepid /ɪn'trɛpɪd/ *adj.* fearless; very brave. □ **intrepidity** /-trɪ'pɪdɪti/ *n.* **intrepidly** *adv.* [French *intrépide* or Latin *intrepidus* (as IN-[1], *trepidus* 'alarmed')]

intricate /'ɪntrɪkət/ *adj.* very complicated; perplexingly detailed or obscure. □ **intricacy** /-kəsi/ *n.* (*pl.* **-ies**). **intricately** *adv.* [Middle English from Latin *intricare intricat-* (as IN-[2], *tricare* from *tricae* 'tricks')]

intrigant /'ɪntrɪg(ə)nt/ *n.* (*fem.* **intrigante**) an intriguer. [French *intriguant* from *intriguer*: see INTRIGUE]

intrigue *v.* & *n.* ● *v.* /ɪn'tri:g/ (**intrigues, intrigued, intriguing**) **1** *intr.* (foll. by *with*) **a** carry on an underhand plot. **b** use secret influence. **2** *tr.* arouse the curiosity of; fascinate. ● *n.* /ɪn'tri:g, 'ɪn-/ **1** an underhand plot or plotting. **2** *archaic* a secret love affair. □ **intriguer** /ɪn'tri:gə/ *n.* **intriguing** *adj.* (esp. in sense 2 of *v.*). **intriguingly** /ɪn'tri:g-/ *adv.* [French *intrigue* (*n.*), *intriguer* (*v.*) via Italian *intrigo*, *intrigare* from Latin (as INTRICATE)]

intrinsic /ɪn'trɪnsɪk/ *adj.* inherent, essential; belonging naturally (*intrinsic value*) (opp. EXTRINSIC). □ **intrinsically** *adv.* [originally = interior: Middle English via French *intrinsèque* and Late Latin *intrinsecus* from Latin *intrinsecus* 'inwardly']

intro /'ɪntrəʊ/ *n.* (*pl.* **-os**) *colloq.* an introduction. [abbreviation]

intro- /'ɪntrəʊ/ *comb. form* into (*introgression*). [Latin *intro* 'to the inside']

introduce /ɪntrə'dju:s/ *v.tr.* **1** (foll. by *to*) make (a person or oneself) known by name to another, esp. formally. **2** announce or present to an audience. **3 a** bring (a custom, idea, etc.) into use. **b** put on sale for the first time. **4** bring (a piece of legislation) before a legislative assembly. **5** (foll. by *to*) draw the attention or extend the understanding of (a person) to a subject. **6** (often foll. by *into*) **a** insert (*introduce into the tank*; *introduced a note of optimism*). **b** bring in; usher in; bring forward. **7** begin; occur just before the start of. □ **introducer** *n.* **introducible** *adj.* [Middle English from Latin *introducere introduct-* (as INTRO-, *ducere* 'lead')]

introduction /ɪntrə'dʌkʃ(ə)n/ *n.* **1** the act or an instance of introducing; the process of being introduced. **2** a formal presentation of one person to another. **3** an explanatory section at the beginning of a book etc. **4** a preliminary section in a piece of music, often thematically different from the main section. **5** an introductory treatise on a subject. **6** a thing introduced. [Middle English from Old French *introduction* or Latin *introductio* (as INTRODUCE)]

introductory /ɪntrə'dʌkt(ə)ri/ *adj.* serving as an introduction; preliminary. [Late Latin *introductorius* (as INTRODUCTION)]

introit /'ɪntrɔɪt, ɪn'trəʊɪt/ *n.* a psalm or antiphon sung or said while the priest approaches the altar for the Eucharist. [Middle English via Old French from Latin *introitus*, from *introire introit-* 'enter' (as INTRO-, *ire* 'go')]

introjection /ɪntrə(ʊ)'dʒɛkʃ(ə)n/ *n.* the unconscious incorporation of external ideas into one's mind. [INTRO-, on the pattern of *projection*]

intromit /ɪntrə(ʊ)'mɪt/ *v.tr.* (**intromitted, intromitting**) **1** (foll. by *into*) *archaic* let in, admit. **2** insert. □ **intromission** /-'mɪʃ(ə)n/ *n.* **intromittent** *adj.* [Latin *intromittere intromiss-* 'introduce' (as INTRO-, *mittere* 'send')]

introspection /ɪntrə(ʊ)'spɛkʃ(ə)n/ *n.* the examination or observation of one's own mental and emotional processes etc. □ **introspective** *adj.* **introspectively** *adv.* **introspectiveness** *n.* [Latin *introspicere introspect-* 'look inwards' (as INTRO-, *specere* 'look')]

introvert *n.*, *adj.*, & *v.* ● *n.* /'ɪntrəvə:t/ **1** *Psychol.* a person predominantly concerned with his or her own thoughts and feelings rather than with external things. **2** a shy inwardly thoughtful person. ● *adj.* /'ɪntrəvə:t/ (also **introverted** /-tɪd/) typical or characteristic of an introvert. ● *v.tr.* /ɪntrə(ʊ)'və:t/ **1** *Psychol.* direct (one's thoughts or mind) inwards. **2** *Zool.* withdraw (an organ etc.) within its own tube or base, like the finger of a glove. □ **introversion** /-'və:ʃ(ə)n/ *n.* **introversive** /-'və:sɪv/ *adj.* **introverted** *adj.* **introvertive** /-'və:tɪv/ *adj.* [INTRO- + *vert* as in INVERT]

intrude /ɪn'tru:d/ *v.* (foll. by *on*, *upon*, *into*) **1** *intr.* come uninvited or unwanted; force oneself abruptly on others. **2** *tr.* thrust or force (something unwelcome) on a person. [Latin *intrudere intrus-* (as IN-[2], *trudere* 'thrust')]

intruder /ɪn'tru:də/ *n.* a person who intrudes, esp. into a building with criminal intent.

intrusion /ɪn'tru:ʒ(ə)n/ *n.* **1** the act or an instance of intruding. **2** an unwanted interruption etc. **3** *Geol.* an influx of molten rock between or through strata etc. but not reaching the surface. **4** the occupation of a vacant estate etc. to which one has no claim. [Middle English from Old French *intrusion* or medieval Latin *intrusio* (as INTRUDE)]

intrusive /ɪn'tru:sɪv/ *adj.* **1** that intrudes or tends to intrude. **2** characterized by intrusion. **3** *Phonet.* (of a sound) pronounced between words or syllables to facilitate pronunciation, such as the *r* in *saw a film*. □ **intrusively** *adv.* **intrusiveness** *n.*

intrust var. of ENTRUST.

intubate /'ɪntjʊbeɪt/ *v.tr. Med.* insert a tube into the trachea for ventilation, usu. during anaesthesia. □ **intubation** /-'beɪʃ(ə)n/ *n.* [IN-[2] + Latin *tuba* 'tube']

intuit /ɪn'tju:ɪt/ *v.* **1** *tr.* know by intuition. **2** *intr.* receive knowledge by direct perception. □ **intuitable** *adj.* [Latin *intueri intuit-* 'consider' (as IN-[2], *tueri* 'look')]

intuition /ɪntjʊ'ɪʃ(ə)n/ *n.* **1** immediate apprehension by the mind without reasoning. **2** immediate apprehension by a sense. **3** immediate insight. □ **intuitional** *adj.* [Late Latin *intuitio* (as INTUIT)]

intuitionism /ɪntjʊ'ɪʃ(ə)nɪz(ə)m/ *n.* (also **intuitionalism**) *Philos.* the belief that primary truths and principles (esp. of ethics and metaphysics) are known directly by intuition. □ **intuitionist** *n.*

intuitive /ɪn'tju:ɪtɪv/ *adj.* **1** of, characterized by, or possessing intuition. **2** perceived by intuition. □ **intuitively** *adv.* **intuitiveness** *n.* [medieval Latin *intuitivus* (as INTUIT)]

intuitivism /ɪn'tju:ɪtɪvɪz(ə)m/ *n.* the doctrine that ethical principles can be established by intuition. □ **intuitivist** *n.*

intumesce /ɪntjʊ'mɛs/ *v.intr.* swell up. □ **intumescence** *n.* **intumescent** *adj.* [Latin *intumescere* (as IN-[2], *tumescere*, inceptive of *tumēre* 'swell')]

intussusception /ɪntəsə'sɛpʃ(ə)n/ *n.* **1** *Med.* the inversion of one portion of the intestine within another. **2** *Bot.* the deposition of new cellulose particles in a cell wall, to increase the surface area of the cell. [French *intussusception* or modern Latin *intussusceptio*, from Latin *intus* 'within' + *susceptio* from *suscipere* 'take up']

intwine var. of ENTWINE.

Inuit /'ɪnjʊɪt, 'ɪnʊɪt/ *n.* & *adj.* ● *n.* **1** (*pl.* same) an Eskimo, esp. a Canadian Eskimo. **2** any of the languages spoken by these peoples. ● *adj.* of or relating to the Inuit or their languages. [Eskimo *inuit* 'people', pl. of *inuk* 'person']

■ **Usage** See Usage Note at ESKIMO.

inundate /'ɪnʌndeɪt/ *v.tr.* (often foll. by *with*) **1** flood. **2** overwhelm (*inundated with enquiries*). □ **inundation** /-'deɪʃ(ə)n/ *n.* [Latin *inundare* 'flow' (as IN-[2], *unda* 'wave')]

Inupiaq /ɪ'nu:pɪak/ *n.* & *adj.* (also **Inupiat**) (*pl.* same) ● *n.* **1** (a member of) an Inuit people inhabiting areas of northern Alaska along the Arctic slope and inland. **2** the Inuit language spoken by the Inupiaq. ● *adj.* of or relating to the Inupiaq or their language. [Eskimo (Inuit), from *inuk* 'person' + *piaq* 'genuine']

inure /ɪ'njʊə/ *v.* **1** *tr.* (often in *passive*; foll. by *to*) accustom (a person) to something esp. unpleasant. **2**

intr. Law come into operation; take effect. □ **inurement** *n.* [Middle English from an Anglo-French phrase meaning 'in use or practice', from *en* 'in' + Old French *e(u)vre* 'work' from Latin *opera*]

in utero /ɪn ˈjuːtərəʊ/ *adv.* in the womb; before birth. [Latin]

in vacuo /ɪn ˈvakjʊəʊ/ *adv.* in a vacuum. [Latin]

invade /ɪnˈveɪd/ *v.tr.* (often *absol.*) **1** enter (a country etc.) under arms, with intent to control or subdue it. **2** swarm into or onto (*fans invaded the pitch*). **3** (of a disease) attack (a body etc.). **4** encroach upon (a person's rights, esp. privacy). □ **invader** *n.* [Latin *invadere invas-* (as IN-[2], *vadere* 'go')]

invaginate /ɪnˈvadʒɪneɪt/ *v.tr.* **1** put in a sheath. **2** turn (a tube or tubular sheath) inside out. □ **invagination** /-ˈneɪʃ(ə)n/ *n.* [IN-[2] + Latin *vagina* 'sheath']

invalid[1] /ˈɪnvəliːd, -lɪd/ *n.* & *v.* ● *n.* **1** a person enfeebled or disabled by illness or injury. **2** (*attrib.*) **a** of or for invalids (*invalid car; invalid diet*). **b** being an invalid (*caring for her invalid mother*). ● *v.* (**invalided, invaliding**) **1** *tr.* (often foll. by *out* etc.) esp. *Brit.* remove from active service (a person who has become an invalid). **2** *tr.* (usu. in *passive*) disable (a person) by illness. **3** *intr.* esp. *Brit.* become an invalid. □ **invalidism** *n.* [Latin *invalidus* 'weak, infirm' (as IN-[1], VALID)]

invalid[2] /ɪnˈvalɪd/ *adj.* not valid, esp. having no legal force. □ **invalidly** *adv.* [Latin *invalidus* (as INVALID[1])]

invalidate /ɪnˈvalɪdeɪt/ *v.tr.* **1** make (esp. an argument etc.) invalid. **2** remove the validity or force of (a treaty, contract, etc.). □ **invalidation** /-ˈdeɪʃ(ə)n/ *n.* [medieval Latin *invalidare invalidat-* (as IN-[1], *validus* VALID)]

invalidity /ɪnvəˈlɪdɪti/ *n.* **1** lack of validity. **2** bodily infirmity. [French *invalidité* or medieval Latin *invaliditas* (as INVALID[1])]

invaluable /ɪnˈvaljʊ(ə)b(ə)l/ *adj.* above valuation; inestimable. □ **invaluableness** *n.* **invaluably** *adv.*

Invar /ˈɪnvɑː/ *n. propr.* an iron-nickel alloy with a negligible coefficient of expansion, used in the manufacture of clocks and scientific instruments. [abbreviation of INVARIABLE]

invariable /ɪnˈvɛːrɪəb(ə)l/ *adj.* **1** unchangeable; always the same. **2** *Math.* constant, fixed. □ **invariability** /-ˈbɪlɪti/ *n.* **invariableness** *n.* **invariably** *adv.* [French *invariable* or Late Latin *invariabilis* (as IN-[1], VARIABLE)]

invariant /ɪnˈvɛːrɪənt/ *adj.* & *n.* ● *adj.* invariable. ● *n. Math.* a function which remains unchanged when a specified transformation is applied. □ **invariance** *n.*

invasion /ɪnˈveɪʒ(ə)n/ *n.* **1** the act of invading or process of being invaded. **2** an entry of a hostile army into a country. [French *invasion* or Late Latin *invasio* (as INVADE)]

invasive /ɪnˈveɪsɪv/ *adj.* **1** (of weeds, cancer cells, etc.) tending to spread. **2** (of medical procedures etc.) involving the introduction of instruments into the body. **3** tending to encroach on the privacy, rights, etc., of others.

invective /ɪnˈvɛktɪv/ *n.* **1 a** strongly attacking words. **b** the use of these. **2** abusive rhetoric. [Middle English via Old French from Late Latin *invectivus* 'attacking' (as INVEIGH)]

inveigh /ɪnˈveɪ/ *v.intr.* (foll. by *against*) speak or write with strong hostility. [Latin *invehi* 'go into, assail' (as IN-[2], *vehi*, passive of *vehere vect-* 'carry')]

inveigle /ɪnˈviːɡ(ə)l, ɪnˈveɪɡ(ə)l/ *v.tr.* (foll. by *into*, or *to* + infin.) entice; persuade by guile. □ **inveiglement** *n.* [earlier *enve(u)gle* from Anglo-French *envegler*, Old French *aveugler* 'to blind' from *aveugle* 'blind', probably from Romanic]

invent /ɪnˈvɛnt/ *v.tr.* **1** create by thought, devise; originate (a new method, an instrument, etc.). **2** concoct (a false story etc.). [originally = find, discover: Middle English from Latin *invenire invent-* 'find, contrive' (as IN-[2], *venire vent-* 'come')]

invention /ɪnˈvɛnʃ(ə)n/ *n.* **1** the process of inventing. **2** a thing invented; a contrivance, esp. one for which a patent is granted. **3** a fictitious story. **4** inventiveness. **5** *Mus.* a short piece for keyboard, developing a simple idea. [Middle English from Latin *inventio* (as INVENT)]

inventive /ɪnˈvɛntɪv/ *adj.* **1** able or inclined to invent; original in devising. **2** showing ingenuity of devising. □ **inventively** *adv.* **inventiveness** *n.* [Middle English from French *inventif -ive* or medieval Latin *inventivus* (as INVENT)]

inventor /ɪnˈvɛntə/ *n.* (*fem.* **inventress** /-trɪs/) a person who invents, esp. as an occupation.

inventory /ˈɪnv(ə)nt(ə)ri/ *n.* & *v.* ● *n.* (*pl.* **-ies**) **1** a complete list of goods in stock, house contents, etc. **2** the goods listed in this. **3** *US* the total of a firm's commercial assets. ● *v.tr.* (**-ies, -ied**) **1** make an inventory of. **2** enter (goods) in an inventory. [Middle English via medieval Latin *inventorium* from Late Latin *inventarium* (as INVENT)]

inverse /ˈɪnvəːs, ɪnˈvəːs/ *adj.* & *n.* ● *adj.* inverted in position, order, or relation. ● *n.* **1** the state of being inverted. **2** (often foll. by *of*) a thing that is the opposite or reverse of another. **3** *Math.* an element which, when combined with a given element in an operation, produces the identity element for that operation. □ **inversely** *adv.* [Latin *inversus*, past part. of *invertere*: see INVERT]

inverse proportion *n.* (also **inverse ratio**) a relation between two quantities such that one increases in proportion as the other decreases.

inverse square law *n.* a law by which the intensity of an effect, such as gravitational force, illumination, etc., changes in inverse proportion to the square of the distance from the source.

inversion /ɪnˈvəːʃ(ə)n/ *n.* **1** the act of turning upside down or inside out. **2** the reversal of a normal order, position, or relation. **3** the reversal of the order of words, for rhetorical effect. **4** (in full **temperature inversion**) the reversal of the normal variation of air temperature with altitude. **5** the process or result of inverting. **6** the reversal of direction of rotation of a plane of polarized light. **7 a** homosexuality. **b** the adoption of behaviour typical of the opposite sex. □ **inversive** /-sɪv/ *adj.* [Latin *inversio* (as INVERT)]

inversion layer *n. Meteorol.* a layer of air in which temperature increases with height.

invert *v.* & *n.* ● *v.tr.* /ɪnˈvəːt/ **1** turn upside down. **2** reverse the position, order, or relation of. **3** *Mus.* change the relative position of the notes of (a chord or interval) by placing the lowest note higher, usu. by an octave. **4** subject to inversion. ● *n.* /ˈɪnvəːt/ **1** a homosexual. **2** an inverted arch, as at the bottom of a sewer. □ **inverter** /ɪnˈvəːtə/ *n.* **invertible** /ɪnˈvəːtɪb(ə)l/ *adj.* **invertibility** /-ˈbɪlɪti/ *n.* [Latin *invertere invers-* (as IN-[2], *vertere* 'turn')]

invertase /ˈɪnvəːteɪz, ɪnˈvəːt-/ *n. Biochem.* an enzyme from yeast which catalyses the inversion of sucrose to produce invert sugar. [INVERT + -ASE]

invertebrate /ɪnˈvəːtɪbrət/ *adj.* & *n.* ● *adj.* **1** (of an animal) not having a backbone. **2** lacking firmness of character. ● *n.* an invertebrate animal. [modern Latin *invertebrata* (pl.) (as IN-[1], VERTEBRA)]

inverted comma *n.* esp. *Brit.* = QUOTATION MARK.

inverted snob *n.* a person who likes or takes pride in what a snob might be expected to disapprove of.

invert sugar *n.* a mixture of glucose and fructose obtained by the hydrolysis of sucrose.

invest /ɪnˈvɛst/ *v.* **1** *tr.* (often foll. by *in*) apply or use (money), esp. for profit. **2** *intr.* (often foll. by *in*) devote (time, effort, etc.) to an enterprise. **3** *intr.* (foll. by *in*) **a** put money for profit (into stocks etc.). **b** *colloq.* buy (something useful) (*invested in a new car*). **4** *tr.* **a** (foll. by *with*) provide, endue, or credit (a person or thing with qualities, insignia, or rank). **b** (foll. by *in*) attribute or entrust (qualities or feelings to a person or thing). **5** *tr.* cover as a garment. **6** *tr.* lay siege to. □ **investable** *adj.* **investible** *adj.* **investor** *n.* [Middle English from French *investir* or Latin *investire investit-*

(as IN-², *vestire* 'clothe' from *vestis* 'clothing'): sense 1 from Italian *investire*]

investigate /ɪnˈvɛstɪgeɪt/ *v.* **1** *tr.* **a** inquire into; examine; study carefully. **b** make an official inquiry into. **2** *intr.* make a systematic inquiry or search. □ **investigator** *n.* **investigatory** /-gət(ə)ri/ *adj.* [Latin *investigare investigat-* (as IN-², *vestigare* 'track')]

investigation /ɪnˌvɛstɪˈgeɪʃ(ə)n/ *n.* **1** the process or an instance of investigating. **2** a formal examination or study. □ **investigational** *adj.*

investigative /ɪnˈvɛstɪgətɪv, -geɪtɪv/ *adj.* seeking or serving to investigate, esp. (of journalism) inquiring intensively into controversial issues.

investiture /ɪnˈvɛstɪtjə, -tʃə/ *n.* **1** the formal investing of a person with honours or rank, esp. a ceremony at which a sovereign confers honours. **2** (often foll. by *with*) the act of enduing (with attributes). [Middle English from medieval Latin *investitura* (as INVEST)]

investment /ɪnˈvɛs(t)m(ə)nt/ *n.* **1** the act or process of investing. **2** money invested. **3** property etc. in which money is invested. **4** the act of besieging; a blockade.

investment bond *n.* a single-premium life insurance policy linked to a unit trust for long-term investment.

investment trust *n.* a trust that buys and sells shares in selected companies to make a profit for its members.

inveterate /ɪnˈvɛt(ə)rət/ *adj.* **1** (of a person) confirmed in an (esp. undesirable) habit etc. (*an inveterate gambler*). **2 a** (of a habit etc.) long established. **b** (of an activity, esp. an undesirable one) habitual. □ **inveteracy** /-rəsi/ *n.* **inveterately** *adv.* [Middle English from Latin *inveterare inveterat-* 'make old' (as IN-², *vetus veteris* 'old')]

invidious /ɪnˈvɪdɪəs/ *adj.* (of an action, conduct, attitude, etc.) likely to excite resentment or indignation against the person responsible, esp. by real or seeming injustice (*an invidious position*; *an invidious task*). □ **invidiously** *adv.* **invidiousness** *n.* [Latin *invidiosus* from *invidia* ENVY]

invigilate /ɪnˈvɪdʒɪleɪt/ *v.intr. Brit.* supervise candidates at an examination. □ **invigilation** /-ˈleɪʃ(ə)n/ *n.* **invigilator** *n.* [originally = keep watch, from Latin *invigilare invigilat-* (as IN-², *vigilare* 'watch' from *vigil* 'watchful')]

invigorate /ɪnˈvɪgəreɪt/ *v.tr.* give vigour or strength to. □ **invigorating** *adj.* **invigoratingly** *adv.* **invigoration** /-ˈreɪʃ(ə)n/ *n.* **invigorative** /-rətɪv/ *adj.* **invigorator** *n.* [IN-² + medieval Latin *vigorare vigorat-* 'make strong']

invincible /ɪnˈvɪnsɪb(ə)l/ *adj.* unconquerable; that cannot be defeated. □ **invincibility** /-ˈbɪlɪti/ *n.* **invincibleness** *n.* **invincibly** *adv.* [Middle English via Old French from Latin *invincibilis* (as IN-¹, VINCIBLE)]

inviolable /ɪnˈvʌɪələb(ə)l/ *adj.* not to be violated or profaned. □ **inviolability** /-ˈbɪlɪti/ *n.* **inviolably** *adv.* [French *inviolable* or Latin *inviolabilis* (as IN-¹, VIOLATE)]

inviolate /ɪnˈvʌɪələt/ *adj.* **1** not violated or profaned. **2** safe from violation or harm. □ **inviolacy** /-ləsi/ *n.* **inviolately** *adv.* **inviolateness** *n.* [Middle English from Latin *inviolatus* (as IN-¹, *violare, violat-* 'treat violently')]

invisible /ɪnˈvɪzɪb(ə)l/ *adj.* & *n.* ● *adj.* **1** not visible to the eye, either characteristically or because hidden. **2** too small to be seen or noticed. **3** artfully concealed (*invisible mending*). ● *n.* an invisible person or thing, esp. (in *pl.*) invisible exports and imports. □ **invisibility** /-ˈbɪlɪti/ *n.* **invisibleness** *n.* **invisibly** *adv.* [Middle English from Old French *invisible* or Latin *invisibilis* (as IN-¹, VISIBLE)]

invisible exports *n.pl.* (also **invisible imports** etc.) items, esp. services, involving payment between countries but not constituting tangible commodities.

invitation /ɪnvɪˈteɪʃ(ə)n/ *n.* **1** the process of inviting or fact of being invited, esp. to a social occasion. **2** a letter or card used to invite someone.

invitational /ɪnvɪˈteɪʃ(ə)n(ə)l/ *adj.* & *n.* esp. *N. Amer.* ● *adj.* characterized by invitation, esp. (of a contest etc.) open only to those invited. ● *n.* an invitational contest etc.

invite /ɪnˈvʌɪt/ *v.* & *n.* ● *v.* **1** *tr.* (often foll. by *to*, or *to* + infin.) ask (a person) courteously to come, or to do something (*were invited to lunch*; *invited them to reply*). **2** *tr.* make a formal courteous request for (*invited comments*). **3** *tr.* tend to elicit (a negative response) (*invited abuse*). **4 a** *tr.* attract. **b** *intr.* be attractive. ● *n.* /ˈɪnvʌɪt/ *colloq.* an invitation. □ **invitee** /-ˈtiː/ *n.* **inviter** *n.* [French *inviter* or Latin *invitare*]

■ **Usage** Although over three centuries old, the use of *invite* as a noun meaning 'invitation' is still highly informal.

inviting /ɪnˈvʌɪtɪŋ/ *adj.* **1** attractive. **2** enticing, tempting. □ **invitingly** *adv.*

in vitro /ɪn ˈviːtrəʊ/ *adj.* & *adv. Biol.* (of processes or reactions) taking place in a test tube, culture dish, or elsewhere outside a living organism (opp. IN VIVO). [Latin, = in glass]

in vivo /ɪn ˈviːvəʊ/ *adj.* & *adv. Biol.* (of processes) taking place in a living organism (opp. IN VITRO). [Latin, = in a living thing]

invocation /ɪnvə(ʊ)ˈkeɪʃ(ə)n/ *n.* **1** the act or an instance of invoking, esp. in prayer. **2** an appeal to a supernatural being or beings, e.g. the Muses, for psychological or spiritual inspiration. **3** *Eccl.* the words 'In the name of the Father' etc. used as the preface to a sermon etc. □ **invocatory** /ɪnˈvɒkət(ə)ri/ *adj.* [Middle English via Old French from Latin *invocatio -onis* (as INVOKE)]

invoice /ˈɪnvɔɪs/ *n.* & *v.* ● *n.* a list of goods shipped or sent, or services rendered, with prices and charges; a bill. ● *v.tr.* **1** make an invoice of (goods and services). **2** send an invoice to (a person). [earlier *invoyes*, pl. of *invoy* = ENVOY²]

invoke /ɪnˈvəʊk/ *v.tr.* **1** call on (a deity etc.) in prayer or as a witness. **2** appeal to (the law, a person's authority, etc.). **3** summon (a spirit) by charms. **4** ask earnestly for (vengeance, help, etc.). **5** *Computing* cause (a procedure etc.) to be carried out. □ **invocable** *adj.* **invoker** *n.* [French *invoquer* from Latin *invocare* (as IN-², *vocare* 'call')]

involucre /ˈɪnvəl(j)uːkə/ *n.* **1** a covering or envelope. **2** *Anat.* a membranous envelope. **3** *Bot.* a whorl of bracts surrounding an inflorescence. □ **involucral** /-ˈl(j)uːkr(ə)l/ *adj.* [French *involucre* or Latin *involucrum* (as INVOLVE)]

involuntary /ɪnˈvɒlənt(ə)ri/ *adj.* **1** done without conscious control; unintentional. **2** (of a limb, muscle, or movement) not under the control of the will. □ **involuntarily** *adv.* **involuntariness** *n.* [Late Latin *involuntarius* (as IN-¹, VOLUNTARY)]

involute /ˈɪnvəl(j)uːt/ *adj.* & *n.* ● *adj.* **1** involved, intricate. **2** curled spirally. **3** *Bot.* rolled inwards at the edges. ● *n. Geom.* the locus of a point fixed on a straight line that rolls without sliding on a curve and is in the plane of that curve (cf. EVOLUTE). [Latin *involutus*, past part. of *involvere*: see INVOLVE]

involuted /ˈɪnvəl(j)uːtɪd/ *adj.* **1** complicated, abstruse. **2** = INVOLUTE *adj.* 2.

involution /ɪnvəˈl(j)uːʃ(ə)n/ *n.* **1** the process of involving. **2** an entanglement. **3** intricacy. **4** curling inwards. **5** a part that curls inwards. **6** *Math.* the raising of a quantity to any power. **7** *Physiol.* the reduction in size of an organ in old age, or when its purpose has been fulfilled (esp. the uterus after childbirth). □ **involutional** *adj.* [Latin *involutio* (as INVOLVE)]

involve /ɪnˈvɒlv/ *v.tr.* **1** (often foll. by *in*) cause (a person or thing) to participate, or share the experience or effect (of a situation, activity, etc.). **2** imply, entail, make necessary. **3** (foll. by *in*) implicate (a person in a charge, crime, etc.). **4** include or affect in its operations. **5** (as **involved** *adj.*) **a** (often foll. by *in*) concerned or interested. **b** complicated in thought or form. **c**

amorously associated. [Middle English from Latin *involvere involut-* (as IN-[2], *volvere* 'roll')]

involvement /ɪnˈvɒlvm(ə)nt/ *n.* **1** (often foll. by *in, with*) the act or an instance of involving; the process of being involved. **2** a complicated affair or concern.

invulnerable /ɪnˈvʌln(ə)rəb(ə)l/ *adj.* that cannot be wounded or hurt, physically or mentally. ▫ **invulnerability** /-ˈbɪlɪti/ *n.* **invulnerably** *adv.* [Latin *invulnerabilis* (as IN-[1], VULNERABLE)]

inward /ˈɪnwəd/ *adj. & adv.* ● *adj.* **1** directed toward the inside; going in. **2** situated within. **3** mental, spiritual. ● *adv.* (also **inwards**) **1** (of motion or position) towards the inside. **2** in the mind or soul. [Old English *innanweard* (as IN, -WARD)]

inward investment *n.* investment made within a country.

inward-looking *adj.* introverted, self-absorbed, insular.

inwardly /ˈɪnwədli/ *adv.* **1** on the inside. **2** in the mind or soul. **3** (of speaking) not aloud; inaudibly. [Old English *inweardlīce* (as INWARD)]

inwardness /ˈɪnwədnɪs/ *n.* **1** inner nature; essence. **2** the condition of being inward. **3** spirituality.

inwards var. of INWARD *adv.*

inweave /ɪnˈwiːv/ *v.tr.* (also **enweave**) (*past* **-wove** /-ˈwəʊv/; *past part.* **-woven** /-ˈwəʊv(ə)n/) **1** weave (two or more things) together. **2** intermingle.

inwrap var. of ENWRAP.

inwreathe var. of ENWREATHE.

inwrought /ɪnˈrɔːt, *attrib.* ˈɪnrɔːt/ *adj.* **1 a** (often foll. by *with*) (of a fabric) decorated (with a pattern). **b** (often foll. by *in, on*) (of a pattern) wrought (in or on a fabric). **2** closely blended.

in-your-face *adj.* (also **in your face** *predic.*) *slang* aggressively blatant or provocative. [from *in your face* used as a derisive insult]

IOC *abbr.* International Olympic Committee.

iodic /ʌɪˈɒdɪk/ *adj. Chem.* containing iodine in chemical combination (*iodic acid*). ▫ **iodate** /ˈʌɪədeɪt/ *n.*

iodide /ˈʌɪədʌɪd/ *n. Chem.* any compound of iodine with another element or group.

iodinate /ˈʌɪədɪneɪt, ʌɪˈɒdɪneɪt/ *v.tr.* treat or combine with iodine. ▫ **iodination** /-ˈneɪʃ(ə)n/ *n.*

iodine /ˈʌɪədiːn, -ʌɪn, -ɪn/ *n.* **1** *Chem.* a non-metallic element of the halogen group, forming black crystals and a violet vapour, used in medicine and photography, and important as an essential element for living organisms (symbol **I**). **2** a solution of this in alcohol used as a mild antiseptic. [French *iode* from Greek *iōdēs* 'violet-like', from *ion* 'violet' + -INE[4]]

iodism /ˈʌɪədɪz(ə)m/ *n. Med.* a condition caused by an overdose of iodides.

iodize /ˈʌɪədʌɪz/ *v.tr.* (also **-ise**) treat or impregnate with iodine. ▫ **iodization** /-ˈzeɪʃ(ə)n/ *n.*

iodo- /ˈʌɪədəʊ, ʌɪˈəʊdəʊ/ *comb. form* (usu. **iod-** before a vowel) *Chem.* iodine.

iodoform /ʌɪˈəʊdə(ʊ)fɔːm, ˈʌɪədə(ʊ)-, ʌɪˈɒdə(ʊ)-/ *n.* a pale yellow volatile sweet-smelling solid iodine compound with antiseptic properties. Chem. formula: CHI_3. [IODINE, on the pattern of *chloroform*]

IOM *abbr.* Isle of Man.

ion /ˈʌɪən/ *n.* an atom, molecule, or group that has lost one or more electrons (= CATION), or gained one or more electrons (= ANION). [Greek, neut. pres. part. of *eimi* 'go']

-ion /(ə)n, ɪən, jən/*suffix* (usu. as **-sion**, **-tion**, **-xion**; see -ATION, -ITION, -UTION) forming nouns denoting: **1** verbal action (*excision*). **2** an instance of this (*a suggestion*). **3** a resulting state or product (*vexation*; *concoction*). [from or suggested by French *-ion* or Latin *-io -ionis*]

ion exchange *n.* the exchange of ions of the same charge between a usu. aqueous solution and a solid, used in water-softening, separation of chemical compounds, etc. ▫ **ion-exchanger** *n.*

Ionian /ʌɪˈəʊnɪən/ *n. & adj.* ● *n.* a native or inhabitant of ancient Ionia in western Asia Minor. ● *adj.* of or relating to Ionia or the Ionians. [Latin *Ionius* from Greek *Iōnios*]

Ionian mode *n. Mus.* the mode represented by the natural diatonic scale C–C.

Ionic /ʌɪˈɒnɪk/ *adj. & n.* ● *adj.* **1** of the order of Greek architecture characterized by a column with scroll-shapes on either side of the capital. **2** of the ancient Greek dialect used in Ionia. ● *n.* the Ionic dialect. [Latin *Ionicus* from Greek *Iōnikos*]

ionic /ʌɪˈɒnɪk/ *adj.* of, relating to, or using ions. ▫ **ionically** *adv.*

ionization /ʌɪənʌɪˈzeɪʃ(ə)n/ *n.* (also **-isation**) the process of producing ions as a result of solvation, heat, radiation, etc.

ionization chamber *n.* an instrument for detecting ionizing radiation.

ionize /ˈʌɪənʌɪz/ *v.tr. & intr.* (also **-ise**) convert or be converted into an ion or ions. ▫ **ionizable** *adj.*

ionizer /ˈʌɪənʌɪzə/ *n.* any thing which produces ionization, esp. a device used to improve the quality of the air in a room etc.

ionizing radiation *n.* a radiation of sufficient energy to cause ionization in the medium through which it passes.

ionosphere /ʌɪˈɒnəsfɪə/ *n.* an ionized region of the atmosphere above the stratosphere, extending to about 1,000 km above the earth's surface and able to reflect radio waves for long-distance transmission round the earth (cf. TROPOSPHERE). ▫ **ionospheric** /-ˈsfɛrɪk/ *adj.*

-ior[1] /ɪə, jə/ *suffix* forming adjectives of comparison (*senior*; *ulterior*). [Latin]

-ior[2] var. of -IOUR.

iota /ʌɪˈəʊtə/ *n.* **1** the ninth letter of the Greek alphabet (Ι, ι). **2** (usu. with *neg.*) the smallest possible amount. [Greek *iōta* (as the smallest letter): cf. JOT]

IOU *n.* a signed document acknowledging a debt. [abbreviation of I owe you]

-iour /ɪə, jə/ *suffix* (also **-ior**) forming nouns (*saviour*; *warrior*). [-I- (as a stem element) + -OUR[2], -OR[1]]

-ious /ɪəs, əs/ *suffix* forming adjectives meaning 'characterized by, full of', often corresponding to nouns in *-ion* (*cautious*; *curious*; *spacious*). [from or suggested by French *-ieux* from Latin *-iosus*]

IOW *abbr.* Isle of Wight.

IPA *abbr.* International Phonetic Alphabet (or Association).

ipecac /ˈɪpɪkak/ *n. colloq.* ipecacuanha. [abbreviation]

ipecacuanha /ˌɪpɪkakjʊˈanə/ *n.* the root of a S. American shrub, *Cephaelis ipecacuanha*, used as an emetic and expectorant. [Portuguese from Tupi-Guarani *ipekaaguéne* 'emetic creeper']

IPMS *abbr.* (in the UK) Institution of Professionals, Managers, and Specialists.

ipomoea /ɪpəˈmiːə/ *n.* any twining plant of the genus *Ipomoea*, having trumpet-shaped flowers, e.g. the sweet potato and morning glory. [modern Latin, from Greek *ips ipos* 'worm' + *homoios* 'like']

ips *abbr.* (also **i.p.s.**) inches per second.

ipse dixit /ɪpsiː ˈdɪksɪt, ɪpseɪ/ *n.* a dogmatic statement resting merely on the speaker's authority. [Latin, 'he himself said it' (originally of Pythagoras)]

ipsilateral /ɪpsɪˈlat(ə)r(ə)l/ *adj.* belonging to or occurring on the same side of the body. [formed irregularly from Latin *ipse* 'self' + LATERAL]

ipsissima verba /ɪpˌsɪsɪmə ˈvəːbə/ *n.pl.* the precise words. [Latin]

ipso facto /ɪpsəʊ ˈfaktəʊ/ *adv.* **1** by that very fact or act. **2** thereby. [Latin]

IQ *abbr.* = INTELLIGENCE QUOTIENT.

-ique *archaic* var. of -IC.

IR *abbr.* infra-red.

Ir *symb. Chem.* the element iridium.

ir- /ɪ/ *prefix* assim. form of IN-[1], IN-[2] before *r*.

IRA *abbr.* Irish Republican Army.

Iranian /ɪˈreɪnɪən, ɪˈrɑː-/ *adj. & n.* ● *adj.* **1** of or relating to Iran in the Middle East. **2** of or relating to the Indo-European group of languages including Persian, Pashto, Avestan, and Kurdish. ● *n.* **1** a native or national of Iran. **2** a person of Iranian descent.

Iraqi /ɪˈrɑːki/ *adj. & n.* ● *adj.* of or relating to Iraq in the Middle East. ● *n.* (*pl.* **Iraqis**) **1 a** a native or national of Iraq. **b** a person of Iraqi descent. **2** the form of Arabic spoken in Iraq.

irascible /ɪˈrasɪb(ə)l/ *adj.* irritable; hot-tempered. □ **irascibility** /-ˈbɪlɪti/ *n.* **irascibly** *adv.* [Middle English via French and Late Latin *irascibilis* from Latin *irasci* 'grow angry', from *ira* 'anger']

irate /ʌɪˈreɪt/ *adj.* angry, enraged. □ **irately** *adv.* **irateness** *n.* [Latin *iratus* from *ira* 'anger']

IRBM *abbr.* intermediate-range ballistic missile.

ire /ˈʌɪə/ *n. literary* anger. □ **ireful** *adj.* [Middle English via Old French from Latin *ira*]

irenic /ʌɪˈrɛnɪk, -ˈriː-/ *adj.* (also **irenical**, **eirenic**) *literary* aiming or aimed at peace. [Greek *eirēnikos*: see EIRENICON]

irenicon var. of EIRENICON.

iridaceous /ʌɪrɪˈdeɪʃəs, ɪr-/ *adj. Bot.* of or relating to the family Iridaceae of plants growing from bulbs, corms, or rhizomes, e.g. iris, crocus, and gladiolus. [modern Latin *iridaceus* (as IRIS)]

iridescent /ɪrɪˈdɛs(ə)nt/ *adj.* **1** showing rainbow-like luminous or gleaming colours. **2** changing colour with position. □ **iridescence** *n.* **iridescently** *adv.* [Latin *irid-* (as IRIS) + -ESCENT]

iridium /ɪˈrɪdɪəm, ʌɪ-/ *n. Chem.* a hard white metallic element of the transition series used esp. in alloys (symbol **Ir**). [modern Latin, from Latin *irid-* (as IRIS) + -IUM]

iridology /ʌɪrɪˈdɒlədʒi, ɪr-/ *n.* (in alternative medicine) diagnosis by examination of the iris of the eye. □ **iridologist** *n.* [Greek *iris iridos* 'iris' + -LOGY]

iris /ˈʌɪrɪs/ *n.* **1** the flat circular coloured membrane behind the cornea of the eye, with a circular opening (pupil) in the centre. **2** any herbaceous plant of the genus *Iris* (family Iridaceae), usu. with tuberous roots, sword-shaped leaves, and showy flowers. **3** (in full **iris diaphragm**) an adjustable diaphragm of thin overlapping plates for regulating the size of a central hole esp. for the admission of light to a lens. [Middle English via Latin *iris iridis* from Greek *iris iridos* 'rainbow, iris']

Irish /ˈʌɪrɪʃ/ *adj. & n.* ● *adj.* of or relating to Ireland, its people, or its Celtic language. ● *n.* **1** the Celtic language of Ireland. **2** (prec. by *the*; treated as *pl.*) the people of Ireland. □ **Irishness** *n.* [Middle English from Old English *Iras* 'the Irish']

Irish bull *n.* = BULL[3].

Irish coffee *n.* coffee mixed with a dash of Irish whiskey and served with cream on top.

Irishman /ˈʌɪrɪʃmən/ *n.* (*pl.* **-men**) a man who is Irish by birth or descent.

Irish moss *n.* = CARRAGEEN.

Irish stew *n.* a stew of mutton, potato, and onion.

Irish terrier *n.* **1** a terrier of a rough-haired light reddish-brown breed. **2** this breed.

Irish wolfhound *n.* **1** a large, often greyish hound of a rough-coated breed. **2** this breed.

Irishwoman /ˈʌɪrɪʃwʊmən/ *n.* (*pl.* **-women**) a woman who is Irish by birth or descent.

iritis /ʌɪˈrʌɪtɪs/ *n.* inflammation of the iris.

irk /əːk/ *v.tr.* (often prec. by *it* as subject) irritate, bore, annoy. [Middle English: origin unknown]

irksome /ˈəːks(ə)m/ *adj.* tedious, annoying, tiresome. □ **irksomely** *adv.* **irksomeness** *n.*

IRO *abbr.* **1** (in the UK) Inland Revenue Office. **2** International Refugee Organization.

iroko /ɪˈrəʊkəʊ, iː-/ *n.* (*pl.* **-os**) **1** either of two African trees, *Chlorophora excelsa* or *C. regia*. **2** the light-coloured hardwood from these trees. [Ibo]

iron /ˈʌɪən/ *n., adj., & v.* ● *n.* **1** *Chem.* a silver-white ductile metallic element occurring naturally as haematite, magnetite, etc., much used for tools and implements, and an essential element in all living organisms (symbol **Fe**). **2** this as a type of unyieldingness or a symbol of firmness (*man of iron*; *will of iron*). **3** a tool or implement made of iron (*branding iron*; *curling iron*). **4** a household, now usu. electrical, implement with a flat base which is heated to smooth clothes etc. **5** a golf club with an iron or steel sloping head which is angled in order to loft the ball (often in *comb.* with a number indicating the degree of angle: *seven-iron*). **6** (usu. in *pl.*) a fetter (*clapped in irons*). **7** (usu. in *pl.*) a stirrup. **8** (often in *pl.*) *Brit. archaic* an iron support for a malformed leg. **9** a preparation of iron as a tonic or dietary supplement (*iron tablets*). ● *adj.* **1** made of iron. **2** very robust. **3** unyielding, merciless (*iron determination*). ● *v.tr.* **1** smooth (clothes etc.) with an iron. **2** furnish or cover with iron. **3** shackle with irons. □ **in irons** handcuffed, chained, etc. **iron in the fire** an undertaking, opportunity, or commitment (usu. in *pl.*: *too many irons in the fire*). **iron out** remove or smooth over (difficulties etc.). □ **ironer** *n.* **ironless** *adj.* **iron-like** *adj.* [Old English *īren*, *īsern* from Germanic, probably from Celtic]

Iron Age *n.* the period following the Bronze Age when iron replaced bronze in the making of implements and weapons, lasting in Europe until the Roman period.

ironbark /ˈʌɪənbɑːk/ *n.* any of various eucalyptus trees, esp. *Eucalyptus paniculata* and *E. sideroxylon*, with a thick solid bark and hard dense timber.

iron-bound *adj.* **1** bound with iron. **2** rigorous; hard and fast. **3** (of a coast) rock-bound.

ironclad *adj. & n.* ● *adj.* /ʌɪənˈklad/ **1** clad or protected with iron. **2** impregnable; rigorous. ● *n.* /ˈʌɪənklad/ *hist.* an early name for a 19th-c. warship protected by iron plates.

Iron Cross *n.* the highest German military decoration for bravery.

Iron Curtain *n. hist.* a notional barrier to the passage of people and information between the former Soviet bloc and the West.

iron hand *n.* firmness or inflexibility (cf. VELVET GLOVE).

ironic /ʌɪˈrɒnɪk/ *adj.* (also **ironical**) **1** using or displaying irony. **2** in the nature of irony. □ **ironically** *adv.* [French *ironique* or Late Latin *ironicus* from Greek *eirōnikos* 'dissembling' (as IRONY[1])]

ironing /ˈʌɪənɪŋ/ *n.* clothes etc. for ironing or just ironed.

ironing board *n.* a flat surface usu. on legs and of adjustable height on which clothes etc. are ironed.

ironist /ˈʌɪr(ə)nɪst/ *n.* a person who uses irony. □ **ironize** *v.intr.* (also **-ise**). [Greek *eirōn* 'dissembler' + -IST]

iron lung *n.* a rigid case fitted over a patient's body, used for administering prolonged artificial respiration by means of mechanical pumps.

iron maiden *n. hist.* an instrument of torture consisting of a coffin-shaped box lined with iron spikes.

iron man /ˈʌɪən man/ *n.* **1** a brave or robust man, esp. a powerful athlete. **2** a multi-event sporting contest demanding stamina, esp. a consecutive triathlon of swimming, cycling, and running.

ironmaster /ˈʌɪənmɑːstə/ *n.* a manufacturer of iron.

ironmonger /ˈʌɪənmʌŋgə/ *n. Brit.* a dealer in hardware etc. □ **ironmongery** *n.* (*pl.* **-ies**).

iron-mould *n.* (*US* **iron-mold**) a spot caused by iron-rust or an ink-stain, esp. on fabric.

iron-on *adj.* able to be fixed to the surface of a fabric etc. by ironing.

iron pyrites see PYRITES.

iron rations *n.pl.* a small emergency supply of food.

Ironsides /ˈʌɪənsʌɪdz/ *n.* a man of great bravery, esp. (treated as *pl.*) Cromwell's troopers in the English Civil War.

ironstone /ˈʌɪənstəʊn/ *n.* **1** any rock containing a substantial proportion of an iron compound. **2** a kind of hard white opaque stoneware.

ironware /ˈʌɪənwɛː/ *n.* articles made of iron, esp. domestic implements.

ironwork /ˈʌɪənwəːk/ *n.* **1** things made of iron. **2** work in iron.

ironworks /ˈʌɪənwəːks/ *n.* (treated as *sing.* or *pl.*) a place where iron is smelted or iron goods are made.

irony[1] /ˈʌɪrəni/ *n.* (*pl.* **-ies**) **1** an expression of meaning, often humorous or sarcastic, by the use of language of a different or opposite tendency. **2** an ill-timed or perverse arrival of an event or circumstance that is in itself desirable. **3** (also **dramatic irony**) a literary technique in which the audience can perceive hidden meanings unknown to the characters. [Latin *ironia* from Greek *eirōneia* 'simulated ignorance', from *eirōn* 'dissembler']

irony[2] /ˈʌɪəni/ *adj.* of or like iron.

Iroquoian /ɪrəˈkwɔɪən, -ˈkɔɪ-/ *n.* & *adj.* ● *n.* **1** a language family of eastern N. America, including Cherokee and Mohawk. **2** a member of the Iroquois Indians. ● *adj.* of or relating to the Iroquois or the Iroquoian language family or one of its members.

Iroquois /ˈɪrəkwɔɪ, -kɔɪ/ *n.* & *adj.* ● *n.* (*pl.* same) **1 a** a confederacy of six American Indian peoples (Mohawk, Oneida, Seneca, Onondaga, Cayuga, and Tuscarora) formerly inhabiting New York State, now living mainly in Canada. **b** a member of any of these peoples. **2** any of the Iroquoian languages of these peoples. ● *adj.* of or relating to the Iroquois or their languages. [French from Algonquian]

irradiant /ɪˈreɪdɪənt/ *adj. literary* shining brightly. □ **irradiance** *n.*

irradiate /ɪˈreɪdɪeɪt/ *v.tr.* **1** subject to (any form of) radiation. **2** shine upon; light up. **3** throw light on (a subject). □ **irradiative** /-dɪətɪv/ *adj.* [Latin *irradiare irradiat-* (as IN-[2], *radiare* from *radius* RAY[1])]

irradiation /ɪˌreɪdɪˈeɪʃ(ə)n/ *n.* **1** the process of irradiating. **2** the process of exposing food to gamma rays to kill micro-organisms. **3** shining, illumination. **4** the apparent extension of the edges of an illuminated object seen against a dark background. [French *irradiation* or Late Latin *irradiatio* (as IRRADIATE)]

irrational /ɪˈraʃ(ə)n(ə)l/ *adj.* **1** illogical; unreasonable. **2** not endowed with reason. **3** *Math.* (of a root etc.) not rational; not commensurate with the natural numbers (e.g. a non-terminating decimal). □ **irrationality** /-ˈnalɪti/ *n.* **irrationalize** *v.tr.* (also **-ise**). **irrationally** *adv.* [Latin *irrationalis* (as IN-[1], RATIONAL)]

irreclaimable /ɪrɪˈkleɪməb(ə)l/ *adj.* that cannot be reclaimed or reformed. □ **irreclaimably** *adv.*

irreconcilable /ɪˌrɛk(ə)nˈsʌɪləb(ə)l, ɪˈrɛk(ə)nsʌɪləb(ə)l/ *adj.* & *n.* ● *adj.* **1** implacably hostile. **2** (of ideas etc.) incompatible. ● *n.* **1** an uncompromising opponent of a political measure etc. **2** (usu. in *pl.*) any of two or more items, ideas, etc., that cannot be made to agree. □ **irreconcilability** /-ˈbɪlɪti/ *n.* **irreconcilableness** *n.* **irreconcilably** *adv.*

irrecoverable /ɪrɪˈkʌv(ə)rəb(ə)l/ *adj.* that cannot be recovered or remedied. □ **irrecoverably** *adv.*

irrecusable /ɪrɪˈkjuːzəb(ə)l/ *adj.* that must be accepted. [French *irrécusable* or Late Latin *irrecusabilis* (as IN-[1], *recusare* refuse)]

irredeemable /ɪrɪˈdiːməb(ə)l/ *adj.* **1** that cannot be redeemed. **2** hopeless, absolute. **3 a** (of a government annuity) not terminable by repayment. **b** (of paper currency) for which the issuing authority does not undertake ever to pay coin. □ **irredeemability** /-ˈbɪlɪti/ *n.* **irredeemably** *adv.*

irredentist /ɪrɪˈdɛntɪst/ *n.* a person, esp. in 19th-c. Italy, advocating the restoration to his or her country of any territory formerly belonging to it. □ **irredentism** *n.* [Italian *irredentista* from (*Italia*) *irredenta* 'unredeemed (Italy)']

irreducible /ɪrɪˈdjuːsɪb(ə)l/ *adj.* **1** that cannot be reduced or simplified. **2** (often foll. by *to*) that cannot be brought to a desired condition. □ **irreducibility** /-ˈbɪlɪti/ *n.* **irreducibly** *adv.*

irrefragable /ɪˈrɛfrəgəb(ə)l/ *adj.* **1** (of a statement, argument, or person) unanswerable, indisputable. **2** (of rules etc.) inviolable. □ **irrefragably** *adv.* [Late Latin *irrefragabilis* (as IN-[1], *refragari* oppose)]

irrefrangible /ɪrɪˈfran(d)ʒɪb(ə)l/ *adj.* **1** inviolable. **2** *Optics* incapable of being refracted.

irrefutable /ɪˈrɛfjʊtəb(ə)l, ɪrɪˈfjuː-/ *adj.* that cannot be refuted. □ **irrefutability** /-ˈbɪlɪti/ *n.* **irrefutably** *adv.* [Late Latin *irrefutabilis* (as IN-[1], REFUTE)]

irregular /ɪˈrɛgjʊlə/ *adj.* & *n.* ● *adj.* **1** not regular in shape, unsymmetrical; varying in form. **2** (of a surface) uneven. **3** contrary to a rule, moral principle, or custom; abnormal. **4** uneven in duration, order, etc.; not occurring at regular intervals. **5** (of troops) not belonging to the regular army. **6** *Gram.* (of a verb, noun, etc.) not inflected according to the usual rules. **7** disorderly. **8** (of a flower) having unequal petals etc. ● *n.* (in *pl.*) irregular troops. □ **irregularity** /-ˈlarɪti/ *n.* (*pl.* **-ies**). **irregularly** *adv.* [Middle English from Old French *irreguler* from Late Latin *irregularis* (as IN-[1], REGULAR)]

irrelative /ɪˈrɛlətɪv/ *adj.* **1** (often foll. by *to*) unconnected, unrelated. **2** having no relations; absolute. **3** irrelevant. □ **irrelatively** *adv.*

irrelevant /ɪˈrɛlɪv(ə)nt/ *adj.* (often foll. by *to*) not relevant; not applicable (to a matter in hand). □ **irrelevance** *n.* **irrelevancy** *n.* (*pl.* **-ies**). **irrelevantly** *adv.*

irreligion /ɪrɪˈlɪdʒ(ə)n/ *n.* disregard of or hostility to religion. □ **irreligionist** *n.* [French *irréligion* or Latin *irreligio* (as IN-[1], RELIGION)]

irreligious /ɪrɪˈlɪdʒəs/ *adj.* **1** indifferent or hostile to religion. **2** lacking a religion. □ **irreligiously** *adv.* **irreligiousness** *n.*

irremediable /ɪrɪˈmiːdɪəb(ə)l/ *adj.* that cannot be remedied. □ **irremediably** *adv.* [Latin *irremediabilis* (as IN-[1], REMEDY)]

irremissible /ɪrɪˈmɪsɪb(ə)l/ *adj.* **1** unpardonable. **2** unalterably obligatory. [Middle English from Old French *irremissible* or ecclesiastical Latin *irremissibilis* (as IN-[1], REMISSIBLE)]

irremovable /ɪrɪˈmuːvəb(ə)l/ *adj.* that cannot be removed, esp. from office. □ **irremovability** /-ˈbɪlɪti/ *n.* **irremovably** *adv.*

irreparable /ɪˈrɛp(ə)rəb(ə)l/ *adj.* (of an injury, loss, etc.) that cannot be rectified or made good. □ **irreparability** /-ˈbɪlɪti/ *n.* **irreparableness** *n.* **irreparably** *adv.* [Middle English from Old French from Latin *irreparabilis* (as IN-[1], REPARABLE)]

irreplaceable /ɪrɪˈpleɪsəb(ə)l/ *adj.* **1** that cannot be replaced. **2** of which the loss cannot be made good. □ **irreplaceably** *adv.*

irrepressible /ɪrɪˈprɛsɪb(ə)l/ *adj.* that cannot be repressed or restrained. □ **irrepressibility** /-ˈbɪlɪti/ *n.* **irrepressibleness** *n.* **irrepressibly** *adv.*

irreproachable /ɪrɪˈprəʊtʃəb(ə)l/ *adj.* faultless, blameless. □ **irreproachability** /-ˈbɪlɪti/ *n.* **irreproachableness** *n.* **irreproachably** *adv.* [French *irréprochable* (as IN-[1], REPROACH)]

irresistible /ɪrɪˈzɪstɪb(ə)l/ *adj.* **1** too strong or convincing to be resisted. **2** delightful; alluring. □ **irresistibility** /-ˈbɪlɪti/ *n.* **irresistibleness** *n.* **irresistibly** *adv.* [medieval Latin *irresistibilis* (as IN-[1], RESIST)]

irresolute /ɪˈrɛzəluːt/ *adj.* **1** hesitant, undecided. **2** lacking in resoluteness. □ **irresolutely** *adv.* **irresoluteness** *n.* **irresolution** /-ˈluːʃ(ə)n, -ˈljuːʃ(ə)n/ *n.*

irresolvable /ɪrɪˈzɒlvəb(ə)l/ *adj.* **1** that cannot be resolved into its components. **2** (of a problem) that cannot be solved.

irrespective /ɪrɪˈspɛktɪv/ *adj.* (foll. by *of*) not taking into account; regardless of. □ **irrespectively** *adv.*

irresponsible /ɪrɪˈspɒnsɪb(ə)l/ *adj.* **1** acting or done without due sense of responsibility. **2** not responsible for one's conduct. □ **irresponsibility** /-ˈbɪlɪti/ *n.* **irresponsibly** *adv.*

irresponsive /ɪrɪˈspɒnsɪv/ *adj.* (often foll. by *to*) not responsive. □ **irresponsiveness** *n.*

irretrievable /ɪrɪˈtriːvəb(ə)l/ *adj.* that cannot be retrieved or restored. □ **irretrievability** /-ˈbɪlɪti/ *n.* **irretrievably** *adv.*

irreverent /ɪˈrɛv(ə)r(ə)nt/ *adj.* lacking reverence; disrespectful. □ **irreverence** *n.* **irreverential** /-ˈrɛnʃ(ə)l/ *adj.* **irreverently** *adv.* [Latin *irreverens* (as IN-[1], REVERENT)]

irreversible /ɪrɪˈvəːsɪb(ə)l/ *adj.* not reversible or alterable. □ **irreversibility** /-ˈbɪlɪti/ *n.* **irreversibly** *adv.*

irrevocable /ɪˈrɛvəkəb(ə)l/ *adj.* **1** unalterable. **2** gone beyond recall. □ **irrevocability** /-ˈbɪlɪti/ *n.* **irrevocably** *adv.* [Middle English from Latin *irrevocabilis* (as IN-[1], REVOKE)]

irrigate /ˈɪrɪgeɪt/ *v.tr.* **1 a** supply water to (land) by means of channels. **b** (of a stream etc.) supply (land) with water. **2** *Med.* apply a cleansing or cooling flow of water or medication to (a wound etc.). **3** refresh as with moisture. □ **irrigable** *adj.* **irrigation** /-ˈgeɪʃ(ə)n/ *n.* **irrigative** *adj.* **irrigator** *n.* [Latin *irrigare* (as IN-[2], *rigare* 'moisten')]

irritable /ˈɪrɪtəb(ə)l/ *adj.* **1** easily annoyed or angered. **2** (of an organ etc.) very sensitive to contact. **3** *Biol.* responding actively to physical stimulus. □ **irritability** /-ˈbɪlɪti/ *n.* **irritably** *adv.* [Latin *irritabilis* (as IRRITATE)]

irritable bowel syndrome *n.* a condition involving abdominal pain and diarrhoea or constipation and associated with stress, depression, etc.

irritant /ˈɪrɪt(ə)nt/ *adj.* & *n.* ● *adj.* causing irritation. ● *n.* an irritant substance. □ **irritancy** *n.*

irritate /ˈɪrɪteɪt/ *v.tr.* **1** excite to anger; annoy. **2** stimulate discomfort or pain in (a part of the body). **3** *Biol.* stimulate (an organ) to an active response. □ **irritatedly** *adv.* **irritating** *adj.* **irritatingly** *adv.* **irritation** /-ˈteɪʃ(ə)n/ *n.* **irritative** *adj.* **irritator** *n.* [Latin *irritare irritat-*]

irrupt /ɪˈrʌpt/ *v.intr.* (foll. by *into*) enter forcibly or suddenly. [Latin *irrumpere irrupt-* (as IN-[2], *rumpere* 'break')]

irruption /ɪˈrʌpʃ(ə)n/ *n.* **1** the action of irrupting; a sudden incursion. **2** a sudden temporary increase in the local population of a migrant bird or animal species. □ **irruptive** *adj.*

Is. *abbr.* **1 a** Island(s). **b** Isle(s). **2** (also **Isa.**) Isaiah (Old Testament).

is *3rd sing. present* of BE.

isagogic /ʌɪsəˈgɒdʒɪk/ *adj.* introductory. [Latin *isagogicus* from Greek *eisagōgikos*, via *eisagōgē* 'introduction', from *eis* 'into' + *agōgē* 'leading', from *agō* 'lead']

isagogics /ʌɪsəˈgɒdʒɪks/ *n.* an introductory study, esp. of the literary and external history of the Bible.

isatin /ˈʌɪsətɪn/ *n. Chem.* a red crystalline derivative of indole used in the manufacture of dyes. [Latin *isatis* 'woad', from Greek]

ISBN *abbr.* international standard book number.

ischaemia /ɪˈskiːmɪə/ *n.* (*US* **ischemia**) *Med.* a reduction of the blood supply to part of the body. □ **ischaemic** *adj.* [modern Latin from Greek *iskhaimos*, from *iskhō* 'keep back']

ischium /ˈɪskɪəm/ *n.* (*pl.* **ischia** /-kɪə/) the curved bone forming the base of each half of the pelvis. □ **ischial** *adj.* [Latin from Greek *iskhion* 'hip joint': cf. SCIATIC]

ISDN *abbr.* intergrated services digital network.

-ise[1] *suffix* var. of -IZE.

■ **Usage** See Usage Note at -IZE.

-ise[2] /ʌɪz, iːz/ *suffix* forming nouns of quality, state, or function (*exercise*; *expertise*; *franchise*; *merchandise*). [from or suggested by French or Old French *-ise* from Latin *-itia* etc.]

-ise[3] *suffix* var. of -ISH[2].

isentropic /ʌɪsɛnˈtrɒpɪk/ *adj.* having equal entropy. [ISO- + ENTROPY]

-ish[1] /ɪʃ/ *suffix* forming adjectives: **1** from nouns, meaning: **a** having the qualities or characteristics of (*boyish*). **b** of the nationality of (*Danish*). **2** from adjectives, meaning 'somewhat' (*thickish*). **3** *colloq.* denoting an approximate age or time of day (*fortyish*; *six-thirtyish*). [Old English *-isc*]

-ish[2] /ɪʃ/ *suffix* (also **-ise** /ʌɪz/) forming verbs (*vanish*; *advertise*). [from or suggested by French *-iss-* (in extended stems of verbs ending in *-ir*) from Latin inceptive suffix *-isc-*]

isinglass /ˈʌɪzɪŋglɑːs/ *n.* **1** a kind of gelatin obtained from fish, esp. sturgeon, and used in making jellies, glue, etc. and for fining beer. **2** mica. [corruption of obsolete Dutch *huisenblas* 'sturgeon's bladder', assimilated to GLASS]

Islam /ˈɪzlɑːm, ˈɪs-; ɪsˈlɑːm, ɪz-/ *n.* **1** the religion of the Muslims, a monotheistic faith regarded as revealed through Muhammad as the Prophet of Allah. **2** the Muslim world. □ **Islamic** /ɪzˈlamɪk, ɪzˈlɑːmɪk, ɪs-/ *adj.* **Islamism** *n.* **Islamist** *n.* **Islamize** *v.tr.* (also **-ise**). **Islamization** /-ʌɪˈzeɪʃ(ə)n/ *n.* [Arabic *islām* 'submission' (to God) from *aslama* 'resign oneself']

island /ˈʌɪlənd/ *n.* **1** a piece of land surrounded by water. **2** anything compared to an island, esp. in being surrounded in some way. **3** = TRAFFIC ISLAND. **4 a** a detached or isolated thing. **b** *Physiol.* a detached portion of tissue or group of cells (cf. ISLET). **5** *Naut.* a ship's superstructure, bridge, etc. [Old English *īgland*, from *īg* 'island' + LAND: first syllable influenced by ISLE]

islander /ˈʌɪləndə/ *n.* a native or inhabitant of an island.

island-hop *v.tr.* move from one island to another, esp. as a tourist in an area of small islands.

isle /ʌɪl/ *n. poet.* (and in place names) an island or peninsula, esp. a small one. [Middle English *ile* (later *isle*) via Old French *ile*, *isle* from Latin *insula*]

islet /ˈʌɪlɪt/ *n.* **1** a small island. **2** *Anat.* a portion of tissue structurally distinct from surrounding tissues. **3** an isolated place. [Old French, diminutive of *isle* ISLE]

islets of Langerhans /ˈlaŋəhanz/ *n.pl.* groups of pancreatic cells secreting insulin and glucagon. [named after P. *Langerhans* (d. 1888), German physician]

ism /ˈɪz(ə)m/ *n. colloq.* usu. *derog.* any distinctive but unspecified doctrine or practice of a kind with a name in *-ism*.

-ism /ɪz(ə)m/ *suffix* forming nouns, esp. denoting: **1** an action or its result (*baptism*; *organism*). **2** a system, principle, or ideological movement (*Conservatism*; *jingoism*; *feminism*). **3** a state or quality (*heroism*; *barbarism*). **4** a basis of prejudice or discrimination (*racism*; *sexism*). **5** a peculiarity in language (*Americanism*). **6** a pathological condition (*alcoholism*; *Parkinsonism*). [from or suggested by French *-isme*, via Latin *-ismus* from Greek *-ismos* or *-isma* from *-izō* -IZE]

Ismaili /ɪsmʌɪˈiːli, ɪsmɑː-/ *n.* (*pl.* **Ismailis**) a member of a Muslim Shi'ite sect that arose in the 8th c. [*Ismail*, the name of a son of the patriarch Ibrāhim (= Abraham)]

isn't /ˈɪz(ə)nt/ *contr.* is not.

ISO *abbr.* **1** (in the UK) Imperial Service Order. **2** International Organization for Standardization.

iso- /ˈʌɪsəʊ/ *comb. form* **1** equal (*isometric*). **2** *Chem.* isomeric, esp. of a hydrocarbon with a branched chain of carbon atoms (*isobutane*). [Greek *isos* 'equal']

isobar /ˈʌɪsə(ʊ)bɑː/ *n.* **1** a line on a map connecting positions having the same atmospheric pressure at a given time or on average over a given period. **2** a curve for a physical system at constant pressure. **3** each of two or more isotopes of different elements, with the same atomic weight. □ **isobaric** /-ˈbarɪk/ *adj.* [Greek *isobarēs* 'of equal weight' (as ISO-, *baros* 'weight')]

isocheim /ˈʌɪsə(ʊ)kʌɪm/ *n.* a line on a map connecting places having the same average temperature in winter. [ISO- + Greek *kheima* 'winter weather']

isochromatic /ˌʌɪsə(ʊ)krə(ʊ)ˈmatɪk/ *adj.* of the same colour.

isochronous /ʌɪˈsɒkrənəs/ *adj.* **1** occurring at the same time. **2** occupying equal time. □ **isochronously** *adv.* [ISO- + Greek *khronos* 'time']

isoclinal /ʌɪsə(ʊ)ˈklʌɪn(ə)l/ *adj.* (also **isoclinic** /-ˈklɪnɪk/) **1** *Geol.* (of a fold) in which the two limbs are parallel. **2** corresponding to equal values of magnetic dip. [ISO- + CLINE]

isodynamic /ˌʌɪsə(ʊ)dʌɪˈnamɪk/ *adj.* corresponding to equal values of (magnetic) force.

isoelectric /ˌʌɪsəʊɪˈlɛktrɪk/ *adj.* having or involving no net electric charge or difference in electrical potential. [ISO- + ELECTRIC]

isoelectric focusing *n.* (also **isoelectric focussing**) *Biochem.* a form of high-resolution electrophoresis.

isoenzyme /ˈʌɪsəʊˌɛnzʌɪm/ *n. Biochem.* each of two or more enzymes with identical function but different structure.

isogamy /ʌɪˈsɒgəmi/ *n. Biol.* sexual reproduction by fusion of similar gametes. [ISO- + Greek *-gamia* from *gamos* 'marriage']

isogeotherm /ʌɪsə(ʊ)ˈdʒiːə(ʊ)θəːm/ *n.* a line or surface connecting points in the interior of the earth having the same temperature. □ **isogeothermal** /-ˈθəːm(ə)l/ *adj.*

isogloss /ˈʌɪsə(ʊ)glɒs/ *n.* a line on a map marking an area having a distinct linguistic feature.

isogonic /ʌɪsə(ʊ)ˈgɒnɪk/ *adj.* corresponding to equal values of magnetic declination.

isohel /ˈʌɪsə(ʊ)hɛl/ *n.* a line on a map connecting places having the same duration of sunshine. [ISO- + Greek *hēlios* 'sun']

isohyet /ʌɪsə(ʊ)ˈhʌɪɪt/ *n.* a line on a map connecting places having the same amount of rainfall in a given period. [ISO- + Greek *huetos* 'rain']

isokinetic /ˌʌɪsə(ʊ)kɪˈnɛtɪk/ *adj.* **1** characterized by or producing a constant speed. **2** *Physiol.* of or relating to muscular action with a constant rate of movement.

isolate /ˈʌɪsəleɪt/ *v.tr.* **1 a** place apart or alone, cut off from society. **b** place (a patient thought to be contagious or infectious) in quarantine. **2 a** identify and separate for attention (*isolated the problem*). **b** *Chem.* prepare (a substance) in a pure form. **3** insulate (electrical apparatus). □ **isolable** /ˈʌɪs(ə)ləb(ə)l/ *adj.* **isolatable** *adj.* **isolator** *n.* [originally in past part., from French *isolé* via Italian *isolato* and Late Latin *insulatus* from Latin *insula* 'island']

isolated /ˈʌɪsəleɪtɪd/ *adj.* **1** lonely; cut off from society or contact; remote (*feeling isolated*; *an isolated farmhouse*). **2** untypical, exceptional (*an isolated example*).

isolating /ˈʌɪsəleɪtɪŋ/ *adj.* (of a language) having each element as an independent word without inflections.

isolation /ʌɪsəˈleɪʃ(ə)n/ *n.* **1** the act or an instance of isolating; the state of being isolated or separated. **2** (*attrib.*) designating a hospital, ward, etc. for patients with contagious or infectious diseases. □ **in isolation** considered singly and not relatively.

isolationism /ʌɪsəˈleɪʃ(ə)nɪz(ə)m/ *n.* the policy of holding aloof from the affairs of other countries or groups esp. in politics. □ **isolationist** *n.*

isoleucine /ʌɪsə(ʊ)ˈluːsiːn/ *n. Biochem.* a hydrophobic amino acid that is a constituent of proteins and an essential nutrient. [German *Isoleucin* (see ISO-, LEUCINE)]

isomer /ˈʌɪsəmə/ *n.* **1** *Chem.* each of two or more compounds with the same molecular formula but a different arrangement of atoms and different properties. **2** *Physics* each of two or more atomic nuclei that have the same atomic number and the same mass number but different energy states. □ **isomeric** /-ˈmɛrɪk/ *adj.* **isomerism** /ʌɪˈsɒmərɪz(ə)m/ *n.* **isomerize** /ʌɪˈsɒmərʌɪz/ *v.* (also **-ise**). [German, from Greek *isomerēs* 'sharing equally' (as ISO-, *meros* 'share')]

isomerous /ʌɪˈsɒm(ə)rəs/ *adj. Bot.* (of a flower) having the same number of petals in each whorl. [Greek *isomerēs*: see ISOMER]

isometric /ʌɪsə(ʊ)ˈmɛtrɪk/ *adj.* **1** of equal measure. **2** *Physiol.* (of muscle action) developing tension while the muscle is prevented from contracting. **3** (of a drawing etc.) with the plane of projection at equal angles to the three principal axes of the object shown. **4** *Math.* (of a transformation) without change of shape or size. □ **isometrically** *adv.* **isometry** /ʌɪˈsɒmɪtri/ *n.* (in sense 4). [Greek *isometria* 'equality of measure' (as ISO-, -METRY)]

isometrics /ʌɪsə(ʊ)ˈmɛtrɪks/ *n.pl.* a system of physical exercises in which muscles are caused to act against each other or against a fixed object.

isomorph /ˈʌɪsə(ʊ)mɔːf/ *n.* an isomorphic substance or organism. [ISO- + Greek *morphē* 'form']

isomorphic /ʌɪsə(ʊ)ˈmɔːfɪk/ *adj.* (also **isomorphous** /-fəs/) **1** exactly corresponding in form and relations. **2** *Crystallog.* having the same form. □ **isomorphism** *n.*

-ison /ɪs(ə)n/ *suffix* forming nouns, = -ATION (*comparison*; *garrison*; *jettison*; *venison*). [Old French *-aison* etc. from Latin *-atio* etc.: see -ATION]

isophote /ˈʌɪsə(ʊ)fəʊt/ *n.* a line (imaginary or in a diagram) of equal brightness or illumination. [ISO- + Greek *phōs phōtos* 'light']

isopleth /ˈʌɪsə(ʊ)plɛθ/ *n.* a line on a map connecting places having equal incidence of a meteorological feature. [ISO- + Greek *plēthos* 'fullness']

isopod /ˈʌɪsəpɒd/ *n.* any crustacean of the order Isopoda, having a flattened body with seven similar pairs of legs, including woodlice, slaters, and many aquatic species. [French *isopode* from modern Latin *Isopoda* (as ISO-, Greek *pous podos* 'foot')]

isosceles /ʌɪˈsɒsɪliːz/ *adj.* (of a triangle) having two sides equal. [Late Latin from Greek *isoskelēs* (as ISO-, *skelos* 'leg')]

isoseismal /ʌɪsə(ʊ)ˈsʌɪzm(ə)l/ *adj.* & *n.* (also **isoseismic** /-mɪk/) ● *adj.* having equal strength of earthquake shock. ● *n.* a line on a map connecting places having an equal strength of earthquake shock.

isostasy /ʌɪˈsɒstəsi/ *n. Geol.* the equilibrium that exists between parts of the earth's crust, so that they rise if material is removed and sink if it is deposited. □ **isostatic** /ʌɪsə(ʊ)ˈstatɪk/ *adj.* [ISO- + Greek *stasis* 'station']

isothere /ˈʌɪsə(ʊ)θɪə/ *n.* a line on a map connecting places having the same average temperature in the summer. [ISO- + Greek *theros* 'summer']

isotherm /ˈʌɪsə(ʊ)θəːm/ *n.* **1** a line on a map connecting places having the same temperature at a given time or on average over a given period. **2** a curve for changes in a physical system at a constant temperature. □ **isothermal** /-ˈθəːm(ə)l/ *adj.* **isothermally** /-ˈθəːm(ə)li/ *adv.* [French *isotherme* (as ISO-, Greek *thermē* 'heat')]

isotonic /ʌɪsə(ʊ)ˈtɒnɪk/ *adj.* **1** having the same osmotic pressure. **2** *Physiol.* (of muscle action) taking place with normal contraction. □ **isotonically** *adv.* **isotonicity** /-təˈnɪsɪti/ *n.* [Greek *isotonos* (as ISO-, TONE)]

isotope /ˈʌɪsətəʊp/ *n. Chem.* each of two or more forms of an element differing from each other in relative atomic mass, and in nuclear but not chemical properties. □ **isotopic** /-ˈtɒpɪk/ *adj.* **isotopically** /-ˈtɒpɪk(ə)li/ *adv.* **isotopy** /ʌɪˈsɒtəpi/ *n.* [ISO- + Greek *topos* 'place' (i.e. in the periodic table of elements)]

isotropic /ʌɪsə(ʊ)ˈtrɒpɪk/ *adj.* having the same physical properties in all directions (opp. ANISOTROPIC). □ **isotropically** *adv.* **isotropy** /ʌɪˈsɒtrəpi/ *n.* [ISO- + Greek *tropos* 'turn']

I spy *n.* **1** *Brit.* a children's game of guessing a visible object from the initial letter of its name. **2** *US* = HIDE-AND-SEEK.

Israeli /ɪzˈreɪli/ *adj.* & *n.* ● *adj.* of or relating to the modern state of Israel in the Middle East. ● *n.* (*pl.* **Israelis**) **1** a native or national of Israel. **2** a person of Israeli descent. [*Israel*, a later name of Jacob, ultimately from Hebrew *yisrā'ēl* 'he that strives with God' (Gen. 32:28) + -ɪ[2]]

Israelite /'ɪzrəlʌɪt/ *n.* & *adj.* ● *n.* a member of the ancient Hebrew nation or people, esp. an inhabitant of the northern kingdom of the Hebrews (*c.*930–721 BC). ● *adj.* of or relating to the Israelites.

ISSN *abbr.* international standard serial number.

issuant /'ɪʃ(j)ʊənt, 'ɪsjʊ-/ *adj. Heraldry* (esp. of a beast with only the upper part shown) rising from the bottom or top of a bearing.

issue /'ɪʃ(j)uː, 'ɪsjuː/ *n.* & *v.* ● *n.* **1 a** a giving out or circulation of shares, notes, stamps, etc. **b** a quantity of coins, supplies, copies of a newspaper or book etc., circulated or put on sale at one time. **c** an item or amount given out or distributed. **d** each of a regular series of a magazine etc. (*the May issue*). **2 a** an outgoing, an outflow. **b** a way out or outlet, esp. the place of the emergence of a stream etc. **3** a point in question; an important subject of debate or litigation. **4** a result; an outcome; a decision. **5** *Law* children, progeny (*without male issue*). **6** *archaic* a discharge of blood etc. ● *v.* (**issues**, **issued**, **issuing**) **1** *intr.* (often foll. by *out*, *forth*) *literary* go or come out. **2** *tr.* **a** send forth; publish; put into circulation. **b** supply, esp. officially or authoritatively (foll. by *to*, *with*: *issued passports to them*; *issued them with passports*; *issued orders to the staff*). **3** *intr.* **a** (often foll. by *from*) be derived or result. **b** (foll. by *in*) end, result. **4** *intr.* (foll. by *from*) emerge from a condition. □ **at issue 1** under discussion; in dispute. **2** at variance. **join** (or **take**) **issue** (foll. by *with*, *on*) identify an issue for argument. **make an issue of** make a fuss about; turn into a subject of contention. □ **issuable** *adj.* **issuance** *n.* **issueless** *adj.* **issuer** *n.* [Middle English from Old French, ultimately from Latin *exitus*, past part. of *exire* EXIT]

issue of fact *n.* (also **issue of law**) a dispute at law when the significance of a fact or facts is denied or when the application of the law is contested.

-ist /ɪst/ *suffix* forming personal nouns (and in some senses related adjectives) denoting: **1** an adherent of a system etc. in *-ism*: see -ISM 2 (*Marxist*; *fatalist*). **2 a** a member of a profession (*pathologist*). **b** a person concerned with something (*tobacconist*). **3** a person who uses a thing (*violinist*; *balloonist*; *motorist*). **4** a person who does something expressed by a verb in *-ize* (*plagiarist*). **5** a person who subscribes to a prejudice or practises discrimination (*racist*; *sexist*). [Old French *-iste*, Latin *-ista* from Greek *-istēs*]

isthmian /'ɪsθmɪən, 'ɪstm-, 'ɪsm-/ *adj.* of or relating to an isthmus, esp. (**Isthmian**) to the Isthmus of Corinth in southern Greece.

isthmus /'ɪsθməs, 'ɪstməs, 'ɪsməs/ *n.* **1** (*pl.* **isthmuses**) a narrow piece of land connecting two larger bodies of land. **2** (*pl.* **isthmi**) *Anat.* a narrow part connecting two larger parts. [Latin from Greek *isthmos*]

istle /'ɪstli, 'ɪst(ə)l/ *n.* a fibre used for cord, nets, etc., obtained from agave. [Mexican *ixtli*]

IT *abbr.* information technology.

it[1] /ɪt/ *pron.* (*poss.* **its**; *pl.* **they**) **1** the thing (or occasionally the animal or child) previously named or in question (*took a stone and threw it*). **2** the person in question (*Who is it? It is I*; *is it a boy or a girl?*). **3** as the subject of an impersonal verb (*it is raining*; *it is winter*; *it is Tuesday*; *it is two miles to Bath*). **4** as a substitute for a deferred subject or object (*it is intolerable, this delay*; *it is silly to talk like that*; *I take it that you agree*). **5** as a substitute for a vague object (*brazen it out*; *run for it!*). **6** as the antecedent to a relative word (*it was an owl* (*that*) *I heard*). **7** exactly what is needed (*absolutely it*). **8** the extreme limit of achievement. **9** *colloq.* sexual intercourse; sex appeal. **10** (in children's games) a player who has to perform a required feat, esp. to catch the others. □ **that's it** *colloq.* that is: **1** what is required. **2** the difficulty. **3** the end, enough. **this is it** *colloq.* **1** the expected event is at hand. **2** this is the difficulty. [Old English *hit*, neut. of HE]

it[2] /ɪt/ *n. Brit. colloq.* Italian vermouth (*gin and it*). [abbreviation]

i.t.a. *abbr.* (also **ITA**) initial teaching alphabet.

ital. *abbr.* italic (type).

Italian /ɪ'taljən/ *n.* & *adj.* ● *n.* **1 a** a native or national of Italy. **b** a person of Italian descent. **2** the Romance language used in Italy and parts of Switzerland. ● *adj.* of or relating to Italy or its people or language. [Middle English from Italian *Italiano* from *Italia* 'Italy']

Italianate /ɪ'taljəneɪt/ *adj.* of Italian style or appearance. [Italian *Italianato*]

Italian vermouth *n.* a sweet kind of vermouth.

italic /ɪ'talɪk/ *adj.* & *n.* ● *adj.* **1 a** *Printing* of the sloping kind of letters now used esp. for emphasis or distinction and in foreign words. **b** (of handwriting) compact and pointed like 16th-c. Italian handwriting. **2** (**Italic**) of ancient Italy. ● *n.* **1** a letter in italic type. **2** this type. [Latin *italicus* from Greek *italikos* 'Italian' (because introduced by Aldo Manuzio of Venice)]

italicize /ɪ'talɪsʌɪz/ *v.tr.* (also **-ise**) print in italics. □ **italicization** /-'zeɪʃ(ə)n/ *n.*

Italiot /ɪ'talɪət/ *n.* & *adj.* ● *n.* an inhabitant of the Greek colonies in ancient Italy. ● *adj.* of or relating to the Italiots. [Greek *Italiōtēs* from *Italia* 'Italy']

Italo- /'ɪtələʊ, ɪ'taləʊ/ *comb. form* Italian; Italian and.

ITAR-Tass /'ʌɪtɑː/ *n.* the official news agency of Russia. [the initials of Russian *Informatsionnoe telegrafnoe agentstvo Rossii* 'Information Telegraph Agency of Russia' + TASS]

itch /ɪtʃ/ *n.* & *v.* ● *n.* **1** an irritation in the skin. **2** an impatient desire; a hankering. **3** (prec. by *the*) (in general use) scabies. ● *v.intr.* **1** feel an irritation in the skin, causing a desire to scratch it. **2** (usu. foll. by *to* + infin.) (of a person) feel a desire to do something (*I'm itching to tell you the news*). □ **one's fingers itch** (often foll. by *to* + infin.) one is longing or impatient. **itching palm** avarice. [Old English *gycce*, *gyccan*, from West Germanic]

itching powder *n.* powder used to make the skin itch, esp. as a practical joke.

itch mite *n.* a parasitic arthropod, *Sarcoptes scabiei*, which burrows under the skin causing scabies.

itchy /'ɪtʃi/ *adj.* (**itchier**, **itchiest**) having or causing an itch. □ **have itchy feet** *colloq.* **1** be restless. **2** have a strong urge to travel. □ **itchiness** *n.*

it'd /'ɪtəd/ *contr. colloq.* **1** it had. **2** it would.

-ite[1] /ʌɪt/ *suffix* forming nouns meaning 'a person or thing connected with': **1** in names of persons: **a** as natives of a country (*Israelite*). **b** often *derog.* as followers of a movement etc. (*pre-Raphaelite*; *Trotskyite*). **2** in names of things: **a** fossil organisms (*ammonite*). **b** minerals (*graphite*). **c** constituent parts of a body or organ (*somite*). **d** explosives (*dynamite*). **e** commercial products (*ebonite*; *vulcanite*). **f** salts of acids having names in *-ous* (*nitrite*; *sulphite*). [from or suggested by French *-ite*, via Latin *-ita* from Greek *-itēs*]

-ite[2] /ʌɪt, ɪt/ *suffix* **1** forming adjectives (*erudite*; *favourite*). **2** forming nouns (*appetite*). **3** forming verbs (*expedite*; *unite*). [from or suggested by Latin *-itus*, past part. of verbs ending in *-ēre*, *-ere*, and *-ire*]

item /'ʌɪtəm/ *n.* & *adv.* ● *n.* **1 a** any of a number of enumerated or listed things. **b** an entry in an account. **2** an article, esp. one for sale (*household items*). **3** a separate or distinct piece of news, information, etc. **4** *colloq.* a couple in a romantic or sexual relationship. ● *adv. archaic* (introducing the mention of each item) likewise, also. [originally as adv.: Latin, = in like manner, also]

itemize /'ʌɪtəmʌɪz/ *v.tr.* (also **-ise**) state or list item by item. □ **itemization** /-'zeɪʃ(ə)n/ *n.* **itemizer** *n.*

iterate /'ɪtəreɪt/ *v.tr.* repeat; state repeatedly. □ **iteration** /-'reɪʃ(ə)n/ *n.* [Latin *iterare iterat-* from *iterum* 'again']

iterative /'ɪt(ə)rətɪv/ *adj. Gram.* = FREQUENTATIVE. □ **iteratively** *adv.*

ithyphallic /ɪθɪˈfalɪk/ *adj. Gk Hist.* **1 a** of the phallus carried in Bacchic festivals. **b** (of a statue etc.) having an erect penis. **2** lewd, licentious. **3** (of a poem or metre) used for Bacchic hymns. [Late Latin *ithyphallicus* from Greek *ithuphallikos,* from *ithus* 'straight', *phallos* PHALLUS]

-itic /ɪtɪk/ *suffix* forming adjectives and nouns corresponding to nouns in *-ite, -itis,* etc. (*Semitic*; *arthritic*; *syphilitic*). [from or suggested by French *-itique,* via Latin *-iticus* from Greek *-itikos*: see -IC]

itinerant /ɪˈtɪn(ə)r(ə)nt, ʌɪ-/ *adj. & n.* ● *adj.* **1** travelling from place to place. **2** (of a judge, minister, etc.) travelling within a circuit. ● *n.* an itinerant person; a tramp. ◻ **itineracy** *n.* **itinerancy** *n.* [Late Latin *itinerari* 'travel' from Latin *iter itiner-* 'journey']

itinerary /ʌɪˈtɪn(ə)(rə)ri, ɪ-/ *n. & adj.* ● *n.* (*pl.* **-ies**) **1** a detailed route. **2** a record of travel. **3** a guidebook. ● *adj.* of roads or travelling. [Late Latin *itinerarius* (*adj.*), *-um* (*n.*) from Latin *iter*: see ITINERANT]

itinerate /ɪˈtɪnəreɪt, ʌɪ-/ *v.intr.* travel from place to place or (of a minister etc.) within a circuit. ◻ **itineration** /-ˈreɪʃ(ə)n/ *n.* [Late Latin *itinerari*: see ITINERANT]

-ition /ˈɪʃ(ə)n/ *suffix* forming nouns, = -ATION (*admonition*; *perdition*; *position*). [from or suggested by French *-ition* or Latin *-itio -itionis*]

-itious[1] /ˈɪʃəs/ *suffix* forming adjectives corresponding to nouns in *-ition* (*ambitious*; *suppositious*). [Latin *-itio* etc. + -OUS]

-itious[2] /ˈɪʃəs/ *suffix* forming adjectives meaning 'related to, having the nature of' (*adventitious*; *supposititious*). [Latin *-icius* + -OUS, commonly written with *t* in medieval Latin manuscripts]

-itis /ˈʌɪtɪs/ *suffix* forming nouns, esp.: **1** names of inflammatory diseases (*appendicitis*; *bronchitis*). **2** *colloq.* in extended uses with reference to conditions compared to diseases (*electionitis*). [Greek *-itis,* forming fem. of adjectives ending in *-itēs* (with *nosos* 'disease' implied)]

-itive /ɪtɪv/ *suffix* forming adjectives, = -ATIVE (*positive*; *transitive*). [from or suggested by French *-itif -itive* or Latin *-itivus* from participial stems formed with *-it-*: see -IVE]

it'll /ˈɪt(ə)l/ *contr. colloq.* it will; it shall.

ITN *abbr.* (in the UK) Independent Television News .

ITO *abbr.* International Trade Organization.

-itor /ɪtə/ *suffix* forming agent nouns, usu. from Latin words (sometimes via French) (*creditor*). See also -OR[1].

-itory /ɪt(ə)ri/ *suffix* forming adjectives meaning 'relating to or involving (a verbal action)' (*inhibitory*). See also -ORY[2]. [Latin *-itorius*]

-itous /ɪtəs/ *suffix* forming adjectives corresponding to nouns in *-ity* (*calamitous*; *felicitous*). [from or suggested by French *-iteux* from Latin *-itosus*]

its /ɪts/ *poss.det.* of or belonging to it or itself (*can see its advantages*; *the dog injured its paw*).

■ **Usage** Care should be taken not to confuse *its* with *it's. Its,* meaning 'of or belonging to it', does not have an apostrophe, e.g. *Its handle had fallen off.* The apostrophe is used only in the short form of *it is* or *it has*, e.g. *It's raining*; *It's been a long time since we met.*

it's /ɪts/ *contr.* **1** it is. **2** it has.

■ **Usage** See Usage Note at ITS.

itself /ɪtˈsɛlf/ *pron.* emphatic and refl. form of IT[1]. ◻ **by itself** apart from its surroundings, automatically, spontaneously. **in itself** viewed in its essential qualities (*not in itself a bad thing*). [Old English, from IT[1] + SELF, but often treated as ITS + SELF]

itsy-bitsy /ɪtsɪˈbɪtsi/ *adj.* (also **itty-bitty** /ɪtɪˈbɪti/) *colloq.* usu. *derog.* tiny, insubstantial, slight. [reduplication of LITTLE, influenced by BIT[1]]

ITU *abbr.* International Telecommunication Union.

ITV *abbr.* (in the UK) Independent Television.

-ity /ɪti/ *suffix* forming nouns denoting: **1** quality or condition (*authority*; *humility*; *purity*). **2** an instance or degree of this (*a monstrosity*; *capacity*). [from or suggested by French *-ité* from Latin *-itas -itatis*]

IU *abbr.* international unit.

IUD *abbr.* **1** intrauterine device (to prevent pregnancy). **2** intrauterine death (of the foetus before birth).

-ium /ɪəm/ *suffix* forming nouns denoting esp.: **1** (also **-um**) names of metallic elements (*uranium*; *tantalum*). **2** a region of the body (*pericardium*; *hypogastrium*). **3** a biological structure (*mycelium*; *prothallium*). [from or suggested by Latin *-ium* from Greek *-ion*]

IUPAC /ˈjuːpak/ *abbr.* International Union of Pure and Applied Chemistry.

IV *abbr.* intravenous.

I've /ʌɪv/ *contr.* I have.

-ive /ɪv/ *suffix* forming adjectives meaning 'tending to, having the nature of', and corresponding nouns (*suggestive*; *corrosive*; *palliative*; *coercive*; *talkative*). ◻ **-ively** *suffix* forming adverbs. **-iveness** *suffix* forming nouns. [from or suggested by French *-if -ive* from Latin *-ivus*]

IVF *abbr. in vitro* fertilization.

ivied /ˈʌɪvɪd/ *adj.* overgrown with ivy.

ivory /ˈʌɪv(ə)ri/ *n. & adj.* ● *n.* (*pl.* **-ies**) **1** a hard creamy-white substance composing the main part of the tusks of an elephant, hippopotamus, walrus, and narwhal. **2** the colour of this. **3** (usu. in *pl.*) **a** an article made of ivory. **b** *slang* anything made of or resembling ivory, esp. a piano key or a tooth. ● *adj.* of the colour of ivory; creamy white. ◻ **ivoried** *adj.* [Middle English from Old French *yvoire*, ultimately from Latin *ebur eboris*]

ivory black *n.* black pigment from calcined ivory or bone.

ivory-nut *n.* the seed of a corozo palm, *Phytelephas macrocarpa*, which when hardened is a source of vegetable ivory for carving. Also called *corozo-nut*.

ivory tower *n.* a state of seclusion or separation from the ordinary world and the harsh realities of life.

ivy /ˈʌɪvi/ *n.* (*pl.* **-ies**) **1** a climbing evergreen shrub, *Hedera helix*, with usu. dark green shiny five-angled leaves. **2** any of various other climbing or trailing plants including ground ivy and poison ivy. [Old English *īfig*]

Ivy League *n.* a group of universities in the eastern US.

IWW *abbr.* Industrial Workers of the World.

ixia /ˈɪksɪə/ *n.* any plant of the genus *Ixia* (iris family) of S. Africa, with large showy flowers. [Latin from Greek, a kind of thistle]

izard /ˈɪzəd/ *n.* a chamois of the Pyrenean variety. [French *isard*, of unknown origin]

-ize /ʌɪz/ *suffix* (also **-ise**) forming verbs, meaning: **1** make or become such (*Americanize*; *pulverize*; *realize*). **2** treat in such a way (*monopolize*; *pasteurize*). **3 a** follow a special practice (*economize*). **b** have a specified feeling (*sympathize*). **4** affect with, provide with, or subject to (*oxidize*; *hospitalize*). ◻ **-ization** /-ˈzeɪʃ(ə)n/ *suffix* forming nouns. **-izer** *suffix* forming agent nouns. [from or suggested by French *-iser*, via Late Latin *-izare* from Greek *-izō*]

■ **Usage** The form *-ize* has been in use in English since the 16th c.; it is widely used in American English, but is not an Americanism. The alternative spelling *-ise* (reflecting a French influence) is in common use, especially in British English, and is obligatory in certain cases: (*a*) where it forms part of a larger word-element, such as *-mise* (= sending) in *compromise*, and *-prise* (= taking) in *surprise*; and (*b*) in verbs corresponding to nouns with *-s-* in the stem, such as *advertise* and *televise*.

Jj

J^{1} /dʒeɪ/ *n.* (also **j**) (*pl.* **Js** or **J's**) **1** the tenth letter of the alphabet. **2** (as a Roman numeral) = *i* in a final position (*ij*; *vj*).

J^{2} *abbr.* (also **J.**) **1** Judge. **2** Justice. **3** (in cards) jack.

J^{3} *symb.* joule(s).

jab /dʒab/ *v.* & *n.* ● *v.tr.* (**jabbed**, **jabbing**) **1 a** poke roughly. **b** stab. **2** (foll. by *into*) thrust (a thing) hard or abruptly. ● *n.* **1** an abrupt blow with one's fist or a pointed implement. **2** *colloq.* a hypodermic injection, esp. a vaccination. [originally Scots variant of JOB^{2}]

jabber /ˈdʒabə/ *v.* & *n.* ● *v.* **1** *intr.* chatter volubly and incoherently. **2** *tr.* utter (words) fast and indistinctly. ● *n.* meaningless jabbering; a gabble. [imitative]

jabberwocky /ˈdʒabəwɒki/ *n.* (*pl.* **-ies**) a piece of nonsensical writing or speech, esp. for comic effect. [title of a poem in Lewis Carroll's *Through the Looking Glass* (1871)]

jabiru /ˈdʒabɪruː/ *n.* a large black-necked stork of the genus *Ephippiorhynchus*, esp. *E. mycteria* of Central and S. America, with mainly white plumage. [Tupi-Guarani *jabirú*]

jaborandi /dʒabəˈrandi/ *n.* (*pl.* **jaborandis**) **1** any shrub of the genus *Pilocarpus*, of S. America. **2** the dried leaflets of this, having diuretic and diaphoretic properties. [Tupi-Guarani *jaburandi*]

jabot /ˈʒabəʊ/ *n.* an ornamental frill or ruffle of lace etc. on the front of a shirt or blouse. [French, originally = crop of a bird]

jacamar /ˈdʒakəmɑː/ *n.* a small insect-eating bird with partly iridescent plumage, of the tropical S. American family Galbulidae. [French, apparently from Tupi]

jacana /ˈdʒakənə/ *n.* (also **jaçana** /dʒasəˈnɑː/) any of various small tropical wading birds of the family Jacanidae, with elongated toes and hind claws which enable them to walk on floating leaves etc. [Portuguese *jaçanã* from Tupi-Guarani *jasaná*]

jacaranda /dʒakəˈrandə/ *n.* a tropical American tree with fragrant wood, esp. one of the genus *Jacaranda*, with trumpet-shaped blue flowers. [Tupi-Guarani *jacarandá*]

jacinth /ˈdʒasɪnθ, ˈdʒeɪ-/ *n.* a reddish-orange variety of zircon used as a gem. [Middle English *iacynt* etc. via Old French *iacinte* or medieval Latin *jacint(h)us* from Latin *hyacinthus* HYACINTH]

jack^{1} /dʒak/ *n.* & *v.* ● *n.* **1** a device for lifting heavy objects, esp. the axle of a vehicle off the ground while changing a wheel etc. **2** a court card with a picture of a man, esp. a soldier, page, or knave, etc. **3** a ship's flag, esp. one flown from the bow and showing nationality. **4** (in full **jack socket**) a socket designed to receive a jack plug. **5** a small white ball in bowls, at which the players aim. **6 a** = JACKSTONE 1. **b** (in *pl.*) = JACKSTONE 2. **7** (**Jack**) the familiar form of *John* esp. typifying the common man (*I'm all right, Jack*). **8** the figure of a man striking the bell on a clock. **9** *slang* a detective; a police officer. **10** *US slang* money. **11** *N. Amer. colloq.* = LUMBERJACK. **12** = STEEPLEJACK. **13** a device for turning a spit. **14** any of various marine perch-like fish of the family Carangidae, including the amberjack. **15** a device for plucking the string of a harpsichord etc., one being operated by each key. **16** the male of various animals (*jackass*). **17** a species or variety of animal smaller than other similar kinds (*jack snipe*). ● *v.tr.* (usu. foll. by *up*) **1** raise with or as with a jack (in sense 1). **2** *colloq.* raise e.g. prices. □ **every man jack** each and every person. **jack in** (or **up**) *slang* abandon (an attempt etc.). **jack off** *coarse slang* masturbate. **on one's jack** (or **Jack Jones**) *slang* alone; on one's own. [Middle English *Iakke*, a pet name for *John*, erroneously associated with French *Jacques* 'James']

jack^{2} /dʒak/ *n.* **1** = BLACKJACK^{3}. **2** *hist.* a sleeveless padded tunic worn by foot soldiers. [Middle English from Old French *jaque*, of uncertain origin]

jackal /ˈdʒakɔːl, -k(ə)l/ *n.* **1** any of various wild doglike mammals of the genus *Canis*, esp. *C. aureus*, found in Africa and S. Asia, usu. hunting or scavenging for food in packs. **2** *colloq.* **a** a person who does preliminary drudgery for another. **b** a person who assists another's immoral behaviour. [Turkish *çakal* from Persian *šağāl*]

jackanapes /ˈdʒakəneɪps/ *n.* *archaic* **1** a pert or insolent fellow. **2** a mischievous child. **3** a tame monkey. [earliest as *Jack Napes* (1450): supposed to refer to the Duke of Suffolk, whose badge was an ape's clog and chain]

jackaroo /dʒakəˈruː/ *n.* (also **jackeroo**) *Austral. colloq.* a novice on a sheep station or cattle station. [JACK^{1} + KANGAROO]

jackass /ˈdʒakas/ *n.* **1** a male ass. **2** a stupid person.

jackboot /ˈdʒakbuːt/ *n.* **1** a large boot reaching above the knee worn chiefly by soldiers, e.g. those under the Nazi regime. **2** this as a symbol of fascism or military oppression. □ **jackbooted** *adj.*

Jack-by-the-hedge *n.* a white-flowered cruciferous plant, *Alliaria petiolata*, of shady places.

jackdaw /ˈdʒakdɔː/ *n.* a small grey-headed crow, *Corvus monedula*, often frequenting rooftops and nesting in tall buildings, and noted for its inquisitiveness. [JACK^{1} + DAW]

jackeroo var. of JACKAROO.

jacket /ˈdʒakɪt/ *n.* & *v.* ● *n.* **1 a** a sleeved short outer garment. **b** a thing worn esp. round the torso for protection or support (*life jacket*). **2** a casing or covering, e.g. as insulation round a boiler. **3** = DUST JACKET. **4** the skin of a potato, esp. when baked whole. **5** an animal's coat. ● *v.tr.* (**jacketed**, **jacketing**) cover with a jacket. [Middle English from Old French *ja(c)quet*, diminutive of *jaque* JACK^{2}]

jacket potato *n. Brit.* a baked potato served with the skin on.

jackfish /ˈdʒakfɪʃ/ *n.* (*pl.* usu. same) **1** a pike or pikeperch. **2** = JACK^{1} 14.

Jack Frost *n.* frost personified.

jackfruit /ˈdʒakfruːt/ *n.* **1** an East Indian tree, *Artocarpus heterophyllus*, bearing fruit resembling breadfruit. **2** this fruit. [Portuguese *jaca*, from Malayalam *chakka*, + FRUIT]

jackhammer /ˈdʒakhamə/ *n.* esp. *N. Amer.* a portable pneumatic hammer or drill.

jack-in-office *n. Brit.* a self-important minor official.

jack-in-the-box *n.* a toy figure that springs out of a box when it is opened.

Jack-in-the-pulpit *n.* any of several small woodland plants of the arum family, esp. cuckoo pint. [from the erect spadix overarched by the spathe, resembling a person in a pulpit]

jackknife /ˈdʒaknʌɪf/ *n.* & *v.* ● *n.* (*pl.* **-knives**) **1** a large clasp-knife. **2** a dive in which the body is first bent at the waist and then straightened. ● *v.* (**-knifed**, **-knifing**) **1** *intr.* (of an articulated vehicle) fold against itself in an accidental skidding movement. **2** *intr. & tr.* fold like a jackknife. **3** *intr.* perform a jackknife dive.

jack of all trades *n.* a person who can do many different kinds of work.

jack-o'-lantern *n.* **1** a will-o'-the wisp. **2** a lantern made esp. from a pumpkin with holes for facial features.

jack plane *n.* a medium-sized plane for use in rough joinery.

jack plug *n.* a plug for use esp. in sound equipment, consisting of a single shaft used to make a connection which transmits a signal.

jackpot /'dʒakpɒt/ *n.* a large prize or amount of winnings, esp. accumulated in a game or lottery etc. □ **hit the jackpot** *colloq.* **1** win a large prize. **2** have remarkable luck or success. [originally in a form of poker with two jacks as minimum to open the pool: JACK[1] *n.* 2 + POT[1]]

jackrabbit /'dʒakrabɪt/ *n.* any of various large N. American prairie hares of the genus *Lepus* with very long ears and hind legs. [abbreviation of *jackass-rabbit* (so called from the long ears)]

Jack Russell /'rʌs(ə)l/ *n.* (in full **Jack Russell terrier**) **1** a terrier of a small working breed with short legs. **2** this breed. [from Revd. John (*Jack*) *Russell*, English clergyman and dog breeder d. 1883]

jack snipe *n.* any of several waders, esp. a small dark snipe, *Lymnocryptes minimus*.

jack socket see JACK[1] *n.* 4.

jackstaff /'dʒakstɑːf/ *n. Naut.* **1** a staff at the bow of a ship for a jack. **2** a staff carrying the flag that is to show above the masthead.

jackstone /'dʒakstəʊn/ *n.* **1** a small piece of metal etc. used with others in tossing games. Also called *jack*. **2** (in *pl.*) such a tossing game.

jackstraw /'dʒakstrɔː/ *n.* = SPILLIKIN.

Jack tar *n.* a sailor.

Jack the Lad *n. colloq.* a self-assured, carefree, and often brash young man. [nickname of *Jack* Sheppard, 18th c. thief]

Jacobean /dʒakə'biːən/ *adj. & n.* ● *adj.* **1** of or relating to the reign of James I of England. **2** (of furniture) in the style prevalent during this period, esp. of the colour of dark oak. ● *n.* a person of the time of James 1. [modern Latin *Jacobaeus* via ecclesiastical Latin *Jacobus* 'James' from Greek *Iakōbos* 'Jacob']

Jacobin /'dʒakəbɪn/ *n.* **1 a** *hist.* a member of a radical democratic club established in Paris in 1789 in the old convent of the Jacobins (see sense 2). **b** any extreme radical. **2** *archaic* a Dominican friar. **3** (**jacobin**) a pigeon with reversed feathers on the back of its neck like a cowl. □ **Jacobinic** /-'bɪnɪk/ *adj.* **Jacobinical** /-'bɪnɪk(ə)l/ *adj.* **Jacobinism** *n.* [originally in sense 2 by association with the Rue St Jacques in Paris: Middle English via French and medieval Latin *Jacobinus* from ecclesiastical Latin *Jacobus* (as JACOBEAN)]

Jacobite /'dʒakəbʌɪt/ *n. hist.* a supporter of James II of England after his removal from the throne in 1688, or of the Stuarts. □ **Jacobitical** /-'bɪtɪk(ə)l/ *adj.* **Jacobitism** *n.* [ecclesiastical Latin *Jacobus* 'James': see JACOBEAN]

Jacob's ladder /'dʒeɪkəbz/ *n.* **1** a plant, *Polemonium caeruleum*, with corymbs of blue or white flowers, and leaves suggesting a ladder. **2** a rope ladder with wooden rungs. [from Jacob's dream of a ladder reaching to heaven, as described in Gen. 28:12]

Jacob's staff /'dʒeɪkəbz/ *n.* **1** a surveyor's iron-shod rod used instead of a tripod. **2** an instrument for measuring distances and heights. [from the staffs used by Jacob, as described in Gen. 30:37–43]

jaconet /'dʒakənɪt/ *n.* a cotton cloth like cambric, esp. a dyed waterproof kind for poulticing etc. [Urdu *jagannāthi* from *Jagannath* (now Puri) in India, its place of origin: see JUGGERNAUT]

jacquard /'dʒakɑːd, -kəd/ *n.* **1** an apparatus with perforated cards, fitted to a loom to facilitate the weaving of figured fabrics. **2** (in full **jacquard loom**) a loom fitted with this. **3** a fabric or article made with this, with an intricate variegated pattern. [named after J. M. *Jacquard*, French inventor d. 1834]

jactitation /dʒaktɪ'teɪʃ(ə)n/ *n.* **1** *Med.* **a** the restless tossing of the body in illness. **b** the twitching of a limb or muscle. **2** *archaic* the offence of falsely claiming to be a person's spouse. [medieval Latin *jactitatio* 'false declaration' from Latin *jactitare* 'boast', frequentative of *jactare* 'throw': sense 1 from earlier *jactation*]

jacuzzi /dʒə'kuːzi/ *n.* (*pl.* **jacuzzis**) *propr.* a large round bath with underwater jets of water to massage the body. [named after C. *Jacuzzi* (d. 1986), US inventor]

jade[1] /dʒeɪd/ *n. & adj.* ● *n.* **1** a hard usu. green stone composed of silicates of calcium and magnesium, or of sodium and aluminium, used for ornaments and implements. **2** the green colour of jade. ● *adj.* of this colour. [French *le jade* for *l'ejade*, from Spanish *piedra de ijada* 'stone of the flank', i.e. stone for colic (which it was believed to cure)]

jade[2] /dʒeɪd/ *n.* **1** an inferior or worn-out horse. **2** *derog.* a disreputable woman. [Middle English: origin unknown]

jaded /'dʒeɪdɪd/ *adj.* tired or worn out; surfeited. □ **jadedly** *adv.* **jadedness** *n.* [JADE[2]]

jadeite /'dʒeɪdʌɪt/ *n.* a green, blue, or white sodium aluminium silicate form of jade.

j'adoube /ʒɑː'duːb, French ʒadub/ *int. Chess* a declaration by a player intending to adjust the placing of a piece without making a move with it. [French, = I adjust]

jaeger /'dʒeɪgə/ *n. N. Amer.* a seabird of the skua family Stercorariidae, esp. one of the smaller kinds, of the genus *Stercoraria*. [German *Jäger* 'hunter' from *jagen* 'to hunt']

Jaffa /'dʒafə/ *n.* a large oval thick-skinned variety of orange. [*Jaffa*, a city in Israel, near where it was first grown]

jag[1] /dʒag/ *n. & v.* ● *n.* a sharp projection of rock etc. ● *v.tr.* (**jagged, jagging**) **1** cut or tear unevenly. **2** make indentations in. □ **jagger** *n.* [Middle English, probably imitative]

jag[2] /dʒag/ *n.* esp. *US colloq.* **1** a bout (of drinking, laughter, etc.); a spree. **2** a period of indulgence in an activity, emotion, etc. **3** a bundle (of hay, logs, etc.). [originally = load for one horse: 16th c., origin unknown]

jagged /'dʒagɪd/ *adj.* **1** with an unevenly cut or torn edge. **2** deeply indented; with sharp points. □ **jaggedly** *adv.* **jaggedness** *n.* [JAG[1]]

jaggy /'dʒagi/ *adj.* (**jaggier, jaggiest**) **1** = JAGGED. **2** (also **jaggie**) *Sc.* prickly.

jaguar /'dʒagjʊə/ *n.* a large flesh-eating spotted feline, *Panthera onca*, of Central and S. America. [Tupi-Guarani *jaguara*]

jaguarundi /dʒagwə'rʌndi/ *n.* (*pl.* **jaguarundis**) a long-tailed slender feline, *Felis yaguarondi*, of Central and S. America. [Tupi-Guarani]

jai alai /hʌɪ ə'lʌɪ/ *n.* a game like pelota played with large curved wicker baskets. [Spanish, from Basque *jai* 'festival' + *alai* 'merry']

jail /dʒeɪl/ *n. & v.* (also *Brit.* **gaol**) ● *n.* **1** a place to which persons are committed by a court for detention. **2** confinement in a jail. ● *v.tr.* put in jail. [Middle English *gayole* via Old French *jaiole, jeole* & Old Northern French *gaole* from Romanic diminutive of Latin *cavea* CAGE]

jailbait /'dʒeɪlbeɪt/ *n.* (*collect.*) *slang* a girl, or girls, under the age of consent.

jailbird /'dʒeɪlbəːd/ *n.* (also *Brit.* **gaolbird**) a prisoner or habitual criminal.

jailbreak /'dʒeɪlbreɪk/ *n.* (also *Brit.* **gaolbreak**) an escape from jail.

jailer /'dʒeɪlə/ *n.* (also *Brit.* **gaoler**) a person in charge of a jail or of the prisoners in it.

jailhouse /'dʒeɪlhaʊs/ *n.* esp. *US* a prison.

Jain /dʒʌɪn, dʒeɪn/ *n. & adj.* ● *n.* an adherent of a non-Brahminical Indian religion. ● *adj.* of or relating to this religion. □ **Jainism** *n.* **Jainist** *n.* [Hindi, via Sanskrit *jainas* 'saint, victor' from *jīna* 'victorious']

jake /dʒeɪk/ *adj. Austral. & NZ slang* all right; satisfactory. [20th c.: origin uncertain]

jalap /'dʒaləp, 'dʒɒləp/ *n.* a purgative drug obtained esp. from the tuberous roots of a Mexican climbing plant, *Exogonium purga*. [French from Spanish *jalapa*, from *Jalapa*, *Xalapa*, a city in Mexico]

jalapeño /halə'peɪnjəʊ, -'pi:nəʊ/ *n.* (*pl.* **-os**) (also **japaleño pepper**) a very hot green chilli pepper, used esp. in Mexican-style cooking. [Mexican Spanish (*chile*) *jalapeño*]

jalopy /dʒə'lɒpi/ *n.* (*pl.* **-ies**) *colloq.* a dilapidated old motor vehicle. [20th c.: origin unknown]

jalousie /'ʒalʊzi:/ *n.* a blind or shutter made of a row of angled slats to keep out rain etc. and control the influx of light. [French (as JEALOUSY)]

Jam. *abbr.* **1** Jamaica. **2** James (New Testament).

jam[1] /dʒam/ *v. & n.* ● *v.* (**jammed**, **jamming**) **1 a** *tr.* (usu. foll. by *into*) squeeze or wedge into a space. **b** *intr.* become wedged. **2 a** *tr.* cause (machinery or a component) to become wedged or immovable so that it cannot work. **b** *intr.* become jammed in this way. **3** *tr.* push or cram together in a compact mass. **4** *intr.* (foll. by *in*, *on to*) push or crowd (*they jammed on to the bus*). **5** *tr.* **a** block (a passage, road, etc.) by crowding or obstructing. **b** (foll. by *in*) obstruct the exit of (*we were jammed in*). **6** *tr.* (usu. foll. by *on*) apply (brakes etc.) forcefully or abruptly. **7** *tr.* make (a radio transmission) unintelligible by causing interference. **8** *intr. colloq.* (in jazz etc.) extemporize with other musicians. ● *n.* **1** a squeeze or crush. **2** a crowded mass (*traffic jam*). **3** *colloq.* an awkward situation or predicament. **4** a stoppage (of a machine etc.) due to jamming. **5** (in full **jam session**) *colloq.* improvised playing by a group of usu. jazz musicians. □ **jammer** *n.* [imitative]

jam[2] /dʒam/ *n. & v.* ● *n.* **1** a conserve of fruit and sugar boiled to a thick consistency. **2** *Brit. colloq.* something easy or pleasant (*money for jam*). ● *v.tr.* (**jammed**, **jamming**) **1** spread jam on. **2** make (fruit etc.) into jam. □ **jam tomorrow** a pleasant thing often promised but usu. never forthcoming. [perhaps = JAM[1]]

jamb /dʒam/ *n. Archit.* a side post or surface of a doorway, window, or fireplace. [Middle English from Old French *jambe* 'leg, vertical support', ultimately from Late Latin *gamba* 'hoof']

jambalaya /dʒambə'lʌɪə/ *n.* a Cajun dish of rice with shrimps, chicken, etc. [Louisiana French from modern Provençal *jambalaia*]

jamboree /dʒambə'ri:/ *n.* **1** a celebration or merrymaking. **2** a large rally of Scouts. [19th c.: origin unknown]

jam jar /'dʒamdʒɑ:/ *n.* **1** a glass jar for containing jam. **2** *Brit. rhyming slang* a car.

jammy /'dʒami/ *adj.* (**jammier**, **jammiest**) **1** covered with jam. **2** *Brit. colloq.* **a** lucky. **b** profitable.

jam-packed *adj. colloq.* full to capacity.

jam session see JAM[1] *n.* 5.

Jan. *abbr.* January.

jane /dʒeɪn/ *n.* esp. *US slang* a woman. □ **plain jane** an unattractive girl or woman. [the name *Jane*]

jangle /'dʒaŋg(ə)l/ *v. & n.* ● *v.* **1** *intr. & tr.* make, or cause (a bell etc.) to make, a harsh metallic sound. **2** *tr.* irritate (the nerves etc.) by discordant sound or speech etc. ● *n.* a harsh metallic sound. [Middle English from Old French *jangler*, of uncertain origin]

Janglish /'dʒaŋglɪʃ/ *n.* = JAPLISH. [*Japanese* + *English*]

janitor /'dʒanɪtə/ *n.* **1** a doorkeeper. **2** a caretaker of a building. □ **janitorial** /-'tɔ:rɪəl/ *adj.* [Latin, from *janua* 'door']

janizary /'dʒanɪz(ə)ri/ *n.* (also **janissary** /-s(ə)ri/) (*pl.* **-ies**) **1** *hist.* a member of the Turkish infantry forming the Sultan's guard in the 14th–19th c. **2** a devoted follower or supporter. [ultimately from Turkish *yeniçeri*, from *yeni* 'new' + *çeri* 'troops']

jankers /'dʒaŋkəz/ *n. Mil. slang* punishment for defaulters. [20th c.: origin unknown]

January /'dʒanjʊ(ə)ri/ *n.* (*pl.* **-ies**) the first month of the year. [Middle English via Anglo-French *Jenever* from Latin *Januarius* (*mensis*) '(month) of Janus' the guardian god of doors and beginnings]

Jap /dʒap/ *n. & adj. colloq. offens.* = JAPANESE. [abbreviation]

japan /dʒə'pan/ *n. & v.* ● *n.* **1** a hard usu. black varnish, esp. of a kind brought originally from Japan. **2** work in a Japanese style. ● *v.tr.* (**japanned**, **japanning**) **1** varnish with japan. **2** make black and glossy as with japan. [*Japan* in E. Asia]

Japanese /dʒapə'ni:z/ *n. & adj.* ● *n.* (*pl.* same) **1 a** a native or national of Japan. **b** a person of Japanese descent. **2** the language of Japan. ● *adj.* of or relating to Japan, its people, or its language.

Japanese beetle *n.* a chafer, *Popillia japonica*, which is a plant pest in eastern N. America.

Japanese cedar *n.* = CRYPTOMERIA.

Japanese print *n.* a colour print from woodblocks.

Japanese quince *n.* = JAPONICA.

jape /dʒeɪp/ *n. & v.* ● *n.* a practical joke. ● *v.intr.* play a joke. □ **japery** *n.* [Middle English: origin uncertain]

Japlish /'dʒaplɪʃ/ *n.* a blend of Japanese and English, used in Japan. [*Japanese* + *English*]

japonica /dʒə'pɒnɪkə/ *n.* any flowering shrub of the genus *Chaenomeles*, esp. *C. speciosa*, with round white, green, or yellow edible fruits and bright red flowers. Also called *Japanese quince*. [modern Latin, fem. of *japonicus* 'Japanese']

jar[1] /dʒɑ:/ *n.* **1 a** a container of glass, earthenware, plastic, etc., usu. cylindrical. **b** the contents of this. **2** *Brit. colloq.* a glass of beer. □ **jarful** *n.* (*pl.* **-fuls**). [French *jarre* from Arabic *jarra*]

jar[2] /dʒɑ:/ *v. & n.* ● *v.* (**jarred**, **jarring**) **1** *intr.* (often foll. by *on*) (of sound, words, manner, etc.) sound discordant or grating (on the nerves etc.). **2 a** *tr.* (foll. by *against*, *on*) strike or cause to strike with vibration or a grating sound. **b** *intr.* (of a body affected) vibrate gratingly. **3** *tr.* send a shock through (a part of the body) (*the fall jarred his neck*). **4** *intr.* (often foll. by *with*) (of an opinion, fact, etc.) be at variance; be in conflict or in dispute. ● *n.* **1** a jarring sound or sensation. **2** a physical shock or jolt. **3** lack of harmony; disagreement. [Middle English: probably imitative]

jar[3] /dʒɑ:/ *n.* □ **on the jar** ajar. [late form of obsolete *char* 'turn': see AJAR[1], CHAR[2]]

jardinière /ʒɑ:dɪ'njɛ:/ *n.* **1** an ornamental pot or stand for the display of growing plants. **2** a dish of mixed vegetables. [French, literally 'female gardener']

jargon[1] /'dʒɑ:g(ə)n/ *n.* **1** words or expressions used by a particular group or profession (*medical jargon*). **2** barbarous or debased language. **3** gibberish. □ **jargonic** /-'gɒnɪk/ *adj.* **jargonistic** /-'nɪstɪk/ *adj.* **jargonize** *v.tr. & intr.* (also **-ise**). [Middle English from Old French: origin unknown]

jargon[2] /'dʒɑ:g(ə)n/ *n.* (also **jargoon** /dʒɑ:'gu:n/) a translucent, colourless, or smoky variety of zircon. [French from Italian *giargone*, probably ultimately related to ZIRCON]

jargonelle /dʒɑ:gə'nɛl/ *n.* an early-ripening variety of pear. [French, diminutive of JARGON[2]]

jarl /jɑ:l/ *n. hist.* a Norse or Danish chief. [Old Norse, originally = man of noble birth, related to EARL]

jarrah /'dʒarə/ *n.* **1** the western Australian mahogany gum tree, *Eucalyptus marginata*. **2** the durable timber of this. [Nyungar]

Jas. *abbr.* James (also in New Testament).

jasmine /'dʒasmɪn, 'dʒaz-/ *n.* (also **jasmin**, **jessamin** /'dʒɛsəmɪn/, **jessamine** /'dʒɛsəmɪn/) any of various ornamental shrubs of the genus *Jasminum* usu. with white or yellow flowers. [French *jasmin*, *jessemin* via Arabic *yās(a)mīn* from Persian *yāsamīn*]

jasmine tea *n.* a tea perfumed with dried jasmine blossom.

jaspé /ˈdʒaspeɪ/ *adj.* like jasper; randomly coloured (esp. of cotton fabric). [French, past part. of *jasper* 'marble', from *jaspe* JASPER]

jasper /ˈdʒaspə/ *n.* an opaque variety of quartz, usu. red, yellow, or brown in colour. [Middle English via Old French *jasp(r)e* and Latin *iaspis* from Greek, of oriental origin]

Jat /dʒɑːt/ *n.* a member of an Indo-Aryan people widely distributed in NW India. [Hindi *jāṭ*]

jato /ˈdʒeɪtəʊ/ *n.* (*pl.* **-os**) *Aeron.* **1** jet-assisted take-off. **2** an auxiliary power unit providing extra thrust at take-off. [acronym]

jaundice /ˈdʒɔːndɪs/ *n.* & *v.* ● *n.* **1** *Med.* a condition with yellowing of the skin or whites of the eyes, often caused by obstruction of the bile duct or by liver disease. **2** disordered (esp. mental) vision. **3** envy, resentment, jealousy. ● *v.tr.* **1** affect with jaundice. **2** (esp. as **jaundiced** *adj.*) affect (a person) with envy, resentment, or jealousy. [Middle English *iaunes* from Old French *jaunice* 'yellowness', from *jaune* 'yellow']

jaunt /dʒɔːnt/ *n.* & *v.* ● *n.* a short excursion for enjoyment. ● *v.intr.* take a jaunt. [16th c.: origin unknown]

jaunting car *n. hist.* a light two-wheeled horse-drawn vehicle formerly used in Ireland.

jaunty /ˈdʒɔːnti/ *adj.* (**jauntier**, **jauntiest**) **1** cheerful and self-confident. **2** dashing, pert (*jaunty hat*). □ **jauntily** *adv.* **jauntiness** *n.* [earlier *jentee* from French *gentil* GENTLE]

Java man /ˈdʒɑːvə/ *n.* a fossil human of the species *Homo erectus* (formerly *Pithecanthropus*) whose remains were found in Java, Indonesia.

Javan /ˈdʒɑːv(ə)n/ *n.* & *adj.* = JAVANESE.

Javanese /dʒɑːvəˈniːz/ *n.* & *adj.* ● *n.* (*pl.* same) **1 a** a native or inhabitant of Java in Indonesia. **b** a person of Javanese descent. **2** the Austronesian language of central Java. ● *adj.* of or relating to Java, its people, or its language.

Java sparrow /ˈdʒɑːvə/ *n.* a waxbill, *Padda oryzivora*, native to Java and Bali and often kept as an aviary pet.

javelin /ˈdʒav(ə)lɪn/ *n.* **1** a light spear thrown in a competitive sport or as a weapon. **2** the athletic event or sport of throwing the javelin. [French *javeline*, *javelot* from Gallo-Roman *gabalottus*]

jaw /dʒɔː/ *n.* & *v.* ● *n.* **1 a** each of the upper and lower bony structures in vertebrates forming the framework of the mouth and containing the teeth. **b** the parts of certain invertebrates used for the ingestion of food. **2 a** (in *pl.*) the mouth with its bones and teeth. **b** the narrow mouth of a valley, channel, etc. **c** the gripping parts of a tool or machine. **d** gripping-power (*jaws of death*). **3** *colloq.* **a** talkativeness; tedious talk (*hold your jaw*). **b** a sermonizing talk; a lecture. ● *v. colloq.* **1** *intr.* speak esp. at tedious length. **2** *tr.* **a** persuade by talking. **b** admonish or lecture. □ **jawless** *adj.* [Middle English from Old French *joe* 'cheek, jaw', of uncertain origin]

jawbone /ˈdʒɔːbəʊn/ *n.* a bone of the jaw, esp. that of the lower jaw (the mandible), or either half of this.

jaw-breaker *n. colloq.* a word that is very long or hard to pronounce.

jaw-jaw *n.* & *v.* ● *n.* talking, esp. lengthy and pointless discussion. ● *v.intr.* talk, esp. at length or to no purpose. [reduplication of JAW]

jawline /ˈdʒɔːlʌɪn/ *n.* the outline of the jaw.

jay /dʒeɪ/ *n.* **1 a** a noisy chattering European bird, *Garrulus glandarius*, with vivid pinkish-brown, blue, black, and white plumage. **b** any other bird of the subfamily Garrulinae. **2** a person who chatters impertinently. [Middle English via Old French from Late Latin *gaius*, *gaia*, perhaps from Latin praenomen *Gaius*: cf. *jackdaw*, *robin*]

jaywalk /ˈdʒeɪwɔːk/ *v.intr.* cross or walk in the street or road without regard for traffic. □ **jaywalker** *n.*

jazz /dʒaz/ *n.* & *v.* ● *n.* **1** music of African-American origin characterized by improvisation, syncopation, and usu. a regular or forceful rhythm. **2** *colloq.* pretentious talk or behaviour, nonsensical stuff (*all that jazz*). ● *v.intr.* play or dance to jazz. □ **jazz up** brighten or enliven. □ **jazzer** *n.* [20th c.: origin uncertain]

jazzman /ˈdʒazman/ *n.* (*pl.* **-men**) a male jazz musician.

jazzy /ˈdʒazi/ *adj.* (**jazzier**, **jazziest**) **1** of or like jazz. **2** vivid, unrestrained, showy. □ **jazzily** *adv.* **jazziness** *n.*

JCB *n. propr.* a type of mechanical excavator with a shovel at the front and a digging arm at the rear. [*J. C. Bamford*, the makers]

JCL *abbr. Computing* job-control language.

J-cloth *n.* (also **J cloth** *propr.*) a type of cloth used esp. for household cleaning. [*J*ohnson and Johnson, original makers]

JCR *abbr. Brit.* Junior Common (or Combination) Room.

jealous /ˈdʒɛləs/ *adj.* **1** (often foll. by *of*) fiercely protective (of rights etc.). **2** afraid, suspicious, or resentful of rivalry in love or affection. **3** (often foll. by *of*) envious or resentful (of a person or a person's advantages etc.). **4** (of God) intolerant of disloyalty. **5** (of inquiry, supervision, etc.) vigilant. □ **jealously** *adv.* [Middle English via Old French *gelos* from medieval Latin *zelosus* ZEALOUS]

jealousy /ˈdʒɛləsi/ *n.* (*pl.* **-ies**) **1** a jealous state or feeling. **2** an instance of this. [Middle English from Old French *gelosie* (as JEALOUS)]

jeans /dʒiːnz/ *n.pl.* hard-wearing trousers made of denim or other cotton fabric, for informal wear. [from *jean* 'twilled cotton cloth' from Middle English, attributive use of *Jene* from Old French *Janne*, from medieval Latin *Janua* 'Genoa']

jeep /dʒiːp/ *n. propr.* a small sturdy esp. military motor vehicle with four-wheel drive. [originally US, from *GP* = *g*eneral *p*urposes, influenced by 'Eugene the Jeep', an animal in a comic strip]

jeepers /ˈdʒiːpəz/ *int.* (also **jeepers creepers**) *N. Amer. slang* expressing surprise etc. [corruption of JESUS]

jeer /dʒɪə/ *v.* & *n.* ● *v.* **1** *intr.* (usu. foll. by *at*) scoff derisively. **2** *tr.* scoff at; deride. ● *n.* a scoff or taunt. □ **jeeringly** *adv.* [16th c.: origin unknown]

Jeez /dʒiːz/ *int. slang* a mild expression of surprise, discovery, etc. (cf. GEE[1]). [abbreviation of JESUS]

jehad var. of JIHAD.

Jehoshaphat /dʒɪˈhɒʃəfat/ *int.* (also **Jehosaphat**) (often in phr. **jumping Jehoshaphat**) a mild expletive. [a biblical name (2 Sam. 8:16, etc.)]

Jehovah /dʒɪˈhəʊvə/ *n.* the Hebrew name of God in the Old Testament. [medieval Latin *Iehoua(h)* from Hebrew *YHVH* (with the vowels of *adonai* 'my lord' included): see YAHWEH]

Jehovah's Witness *n.* a member of a millenarian Christian sect rejecting the supremacy of the State and religious institutions over personal conscience, faith, etc.

Jehovist /dʒɪˈhəʊvɪst/ *n.* = YAHWIST.

jejune /dʒɪˈdʒuːn/ *adj.* **1** intellectually unsatisfying; shallow. **2** puerile, childish; naive. **3** (of ideas, writings, etc.) meagre, scanty; dry and uninteresting. **4** (of land) barren, poor. □ **jejunely** *adv.* **jejuneness** *n.* [originally = fasting, from Latin *jejunus*]

jejunum /dʒɪˈdʒuːnəm/ *n. Anat.* the part of the small intestine between the duodenum and ileum. [Latin, neut. of *jejunus* 'fasting']

Jekyll and Hyde /ˌdʒɛkɪl (ə)nd ˈhʌɪd/ *n.* a person alternately displaying opposing good and evil personalities. [from R. L. Stevenson's story *The Strange Case of Dr Jekyll and Mr Hyde* (1886)]

jell /dʒɛl/ *v.intr. colloq.* **1 a** set as a jelly. **b** (of ideas etc.) take a definite form. **2** (of people) readily cooperate or reach an understanding. [back-formation from JELLY]

jellaba var. of DJELLABA.

jellify /ˈdʒɛlɪfʌɪ/ *v.tr.* & *intr.* (**-ies**, **-ied**) turn into jelly; make or become like jelly. □ **jellification** /-fɪˈkeɪʃ(ə)n/ *n.*

jello /ˈdʒɛləʊ/ *n.* (also **Jell-O** *propr.*) esp. *N. Amer.* **1** a fruit-flavoured gelatin dessert; jelly. **2** the powder used to make this.

jelly /ˈdʒɛli/ *n.* & *v.* ● *n.* (*pl.* **-ies**) **1 a** a semi-transparent preparation of boiled sugar and fruit juice or milk etc., set to a soft semi-solid consistency, often in a mould, and eaten as a dessert. **b** a similar preparation of fruit juice etc. for use as a jam or a condiment (*redcurrant jelly*). **c** a similar preparation derived from meat, bones, etc., and gelatin (*marrowbone jelly*). **2** any substance of a similar consistency. **3** *Brit. slang* gelignite (cf. GELLY). ● *v.* (**-ies, -ied**) **1** *intr.* & *tr.* set or cause to set as a jelly, congeal. **2** *tr.* set (food) in a jelly (*jellied eels*). □ **jelly-like** *adj.* [Middle English via Old French *gelee* 'frost, jelly' and Romanic *gelata* from Latin *gelare* 'freeze', from *gelu* 'frost']

jelly baby *n. Brit.* a jelly-like sweet in the stylized shape of a baby.

jelly bag *n.* a bag for straining juice for jelly.

jelly bean *n.* a bean-shaped sweet with a jelly-like centre and a hard sugar coating.

jellyfish /ˈdʒɛlɪfɪʃ/ *n.* (*pl.* usu. same) **1** a marine coelenterate of the class Scyphozoa having an umbrella-shaped jelly-like body and stinging tentacles. **2** *colloq.* a feeble person.

jelly roll *n. N. Amer.* = SWISS ROLL.

jemmy /ˈdʒɛmi/ *n.* & *v.* (*N. Amer.* **jimmy** /ˈdʒɪmi/) ● *n.* (*pl.* **-ies**) a burglar's short crowbar, usu. made in sections. ● *v.tr.* (**-ies, -ied**) force open with a jemmy. [pet form of the name *James*]

je ne sais quoi /ʒə nə seɪ ˈkwɑː, dʒə-, French ʒən sɛ kwa/ *n.* an indefinable something. [French, = I do not know what]

jennet /ˈdʒɛnɪt/ *n.* a small Spanish horse. [French *genet* via Spanish *jinete* 'light horseman' from Arabic *zenāta*, the name of a Berber tribe famous as horsemen]

jenny /ˈdʒɛni/ *n.* (*pl.* **-ies**) **1** *hist.* = SPINNING JENNY. **2** a female donkey or ass. **3** a locomotive crane. [pet form of the name *Janet*]

jenny-wren *n.* a popular name for a female wren.

jeopardize /ˈdʒɛpədʌɪz/ *v.tr.* (also **-ise**) endanger; put into jeopardy.

jeopardy /ˈdʒɛpədi/ *n.* **1** danger, esp. of severe harm or loss. **2** *Law* danger resulting from being on trial for a criminal offence. [Middle English *iuparti* from Old French *ieu parti* 'divided (i.e. even) game', from Latin *jocus* 'game' + *partitus*, past part. of *partire* 'divide', from *pars partis* 'part']

Jer. *abbr.* Jeremiah (Old Testament).

jerboa /dʒəːˈbəʊə, ˈdʒəːbəʊə/ *n.* any small desert rodent of the family Dipodidae with long hind legs and the ability to make large jumps. [modern Latin, from Arabic *yarbūʻ* 'flesh of loins, jerboa']

jeremiad /dʒɛrɪˈmʌɪad/ *n.* a doleful complaint or lamentation; a list of woes. [French *jérémiade* from *Jérémie* 'Jeremiah', from ecclesiastical Latin *Jeremias*, with reference to the Lamentations of Jeremiah in the Old Testament]

Jeremiah /dʒɛrɪˈmʌɪə/ *n.* a dismal prophet; a denouncer of the times. [with reference to *Jeremiah* (as JEREMIAD)]

jerk[1] /dʒəːk/ *n.* & *v.* ● *n.* **1** a sharp sudden pull, twist, twitch, start, etc. **2** a spasmodic muscular twitch. **3** (in *pl.*) *Brit. colloq.* exercises (*physical jerks*). **4** *slang* a fool; a stupid person. **5** (in full **clean and jerk**) (prec. by *the*) (in weightlifting) the raising of a weight to above the head following an initial lift to shoulder level. ● *v.* **1** *intr.* move with a jerk. **2** *tr.* pull, thrust, twist, etc., with a jerk. **3** *tr.* throw with a suddenly arrested motion. **4** *tr. Sport* (in weightlifting) raise (a weight) from shoulder level to above the head. □ **jerk off** *coarse slang* masturbate. □ **jerker** *n.* [16th c.: perhaps imitative]

jerk[2] /dʒəːk/ *v.tr.* cure (beef) by cutting it in long slices and drying it in the sun. [Latin American Spanish *charquear*, from *charqui*, from Quechua *echarqui* 'dried flesh']

jerkin /ˈdʒəːkɪn/ *n.* **1** a sleeveless jacket. **2** *hist.* a man's close-fitting jacket, often of leather. [16th c.: origin unknown]

jerky /ˈdʒəːki/ *adj.* (**jerkier, jerkiest**) **1** having sudden abrupt movements. **2** spasmodic. □ **jerkily** *adv.* **jerkiness** *n.*

jeroboam /dʒɛrəˈbəʊəm/ *n.* a wine bottle of 4 times the ordinary size. [named after *Jeroboam* King of Israel (1 Kings 11:28, 14:16)]

Jerry /ˈdʒɛri/ *n.* (*pl.* **-ies**) *Brit. slang* **1** a German (esp. in military contexts). **2** the Germans collectively. [probably alteration of *German*]

jerry /ˈdʒɛri/ *n.* (*pl.* **-ies**) *Brit. slang* a chamber pot. [probably dimunitive of JEROBOAM]

jerry-builder /ˈdʒɛrɪbɪldə/ *n.* a builder of unsubstantial houses with poor-quality materials. □ **jerry-building** *n.* **jerry-built** *adj.* [19th c.: origin unknown]

jerrycan /ˈdʒɛrɪkan/ *n.* (also **jerrican**) a kind of (originally German) petrol can or water can. [JERRY + CAN[2]]

jerrymander *Brit.* var. of GERRYMANDER.

jersey /ˈdʒəːzi/ *n.* (*pl.* **-eys**) **1 a** a knitted usu. woollen pullover or similar garment. **b** a plain-knitted (originally woollen) fabric. **2** (**Jersey**) a light brown dairy cow from Jersey. [*Jersey*, largest of the Channel Islands]

Jerusalem artichoke /dʒəˈruːs(ə)ləm/ *n.* **1** a species of sunflower, *Helianthus tuberosus*, with edible underground tubers. **2** this tuber used as a vegetable. [corruption of Italian *girasole* 'sunflower']

jess /dʒɛs/ *n.* & *v.* ● *n.* a short strap of leather, silk, etc., put round the leg of a hawk in falconry. ● *v.tr.* put jesses on (a hawk etc.). [Middle English *ges* from Old French *ges, get*, ultimately from Latin *jactus* 'a throw' from *jacere jact-* 'to throw']

jessamin (also **jessamine**) var. of JASMINE.

jest /dʒɛst/ *n.* & *v.* ● *n.* **1 a** a joke. **b** fun. **2 a** raillery, banter. **b** an object of derision (*a standing jest*). ● *v.intr.* **1** joke; make jests. **2** fool about; play or act triflingly. □ **in jest** in fun. [originally = exploit: Old French *geste* from Latin *gesta*, neut. pl. past part. of *gerere* 'do']

jester /ˈdʒɛstə/ *n. hist.* a professional joker or 'fool' at a medieval court etc., traditionally wearing a cap and bells and carrying a mock sceptre.

Jesuit /ˈdʒɛzjʊɪt/ *n.* a member of the Society of Jesus, a Roman Catholic order founded by St Ignatius Loyola and others in 1534. [French *jésuite* or modern Latin *Jesuita* from *Jesus*: see JESUS]

Jesuitical /dʒɛzjʊˈɪtɪk(ə)l/ *adj.* **1** of or concerning the Jesuits. **2** *offens.* dissembling or equivocating, in the manner once associated with Jesuits. □ **Jesuitically** *adv.*

Jesus /ˈdʒiːzəs/ *int. colloq.* an exclamation of surprise, dismay, etc. [name of the founder of the Christian religion d. *c.* AD 30]

jet[1] /dʒɛt/ *n.* & *v.* ● *n.* **1** a stream of liquid, gas, or (more rarely) solid particles shot out, esp. from a small opening. **2** a spout or nozzle for emitting water etc. in this way. **3 a** a jet engine. **b** an aircraft powered by one or more jet engines. ● *v.* (**jetted, jetting**) **1** *intr.* spurt out in jets. **2** *tr.* & *intr. colloq.* send or travel by jet plane. [earlier as verb (in sense 1): French *jeter* 'throw', ultimately from Latin *jactare*, frequentative of *jacere jact-* 'throw']

jet[2] /dʒɛt/ *n.* & *adj.* ● *n.* **1 a** a hard black variety of lignite capable of being carved and highly polished. **b** (*attrib.*) made of this. **2** the colour of jet; a deep glossy black. ● *adj.* of this colour. [Middle English via Anglo-French *geet*, Old French *jaiet*, and Latin *gagates* from Greek (*lithos*) *gagatēs* '(stone) from *Gagai*', a town in Asia Minor]

jet black *n.* & *adj.* ● *n.* a black colour like jet; a glossy black. ● *adj.* (hyphenated when *attrib.*) of this colour.

jeté /ʒɛˈteɪ/ *n. Ballet* a spring or leap with one leg forward and the other stretched backwards. [French, past part. of *jeter* 'throw': see JET[1]]

jet engine *n.* an engine using jet propulsion for forward thrust, esp. of an aircraft.

jetfoil /ˈdʒɛtfɔɪl/ *n.* a type of passenger-carrying hydrofoil. [JET[1] + HYDROFOIL]

jet lag *n.* extreme tiredness and other bodily effects felt after a long flight involving marked differences of local time. □ **jet-lagged** *adj.*

jet-propelled *adj.* **1** having jet propulsion. **2** very fast.

jet propulsion *n.* propulsion by the backward ejection of a high-speed jet of gas etc.

jetsam /ˈdʒɛts(ə)m/ *n.* discarded material washed ashore, esp. that thrown overboard to lighten a ship etc. (cf. FLOTSAM). [contraction of JETTISON]

jet set *n. colloq.* wealthy people frequently travelling by air, esp. for pleasure. □ **jet-setter** *n.* **jet-setting** *adj.*

jet ski *n.* & *v.* ● *n.* (*pl.* **skis**) a jet-propelled vehicle like a motorbike, for riding across water. ● *v.intr.* (**jet-ski**) (**-skies**, **-skied**, **skiing**) ride on a jet ski.

jet stream *n.* **1** a narrow current of very strong winds encircling the globe several miles above the earth. **2** the flow of vapour from a jet engine.

jettison /ˈdʒɛtɪs(ə)n, -z(ə)n/ *v.* & *n.* ● *v.tr.* **1 a** throw (esp. heavy material) overboard to lighten a ship, hot-air balloon, etc. **b** drop (goods) from an aircraft. **2** abandon; get rid of (something no longer wanted). ● *n.* the act of jettisoning. [Middle English via Anglo-French *getteson*, Old French *getaison* from Latin *jactatio -onis*, from *jactare* 'throw': see JET[1]]

jetton /ˈdʒɛt(ə)n/ *n.* a counter with a stamped or engraved design, esp. for insertion like a coin to operate a machine etc. [French *jeton* from *jeter* 'throw, add up accounts': see JET[1]]

jetty /ˈdʒɛti/ *n.* (*pl.* **-ies**) **1** a pier or breakwater constructed to protect or defend a harbour, coast, etc. **2** a landing pier. [Middle English from Old French *jetee*, fem. past part. of *jeter* 'throw': see JET[1], JUT]

jeu d'esprit /ʒəː dɛˈspriː, French ʒø dɛspri/ *n.* (*pl.* ***jeux d'esprit*** *pronunc.* same) a witty or humorous (usu. literary) trifle. [French, = game of the spirit]

jeunesse dorée /ʒəːnɛs ˈdɔːreɪ, French ʒœnɛs dɔre/ *n.* = GILDED YOUTH. [French]

Jew /dʒuː/ *n.* a person of Hebrew descent or whose religion is Judaism. [Middle English via Old French *giu* and Latin *judaeus* from Greek *ioudaios*, ultimately via Hebrew *yᵉhûḏî* from *yᵉhûḏâh* Judah]

jewel /ˈdʒuːəl/ *n.* & *v.* ● *n.* **1 a** a precious stone. **b** this as used for its hardness as a bearing in watchmaking. **2** a personal ornament containing a jewel or jewels. **3** a precious person or thing. ● *v.tr.* (**jewelled**, **jewelling**; *US* **jeweled**, **jeweling**) **1** (esp. as **jewelled** *adj.*) adorn or set with jewels. **2** (in watchmaking) set with jewels. □ **jewelly** *adj.* [Middle English from Anglo-French *juel*, *jeuel*, Old French *joel*, of uncertain origin]

jewel-fish *n.* (*pl.* usu. same) a scarlet and green tropical cichlid fish, *Hemichromis bimaculatus*.

jeweller /ˈdʒuːələ/ *n.* (*US* **jeweler**) a maker of or dealer in jewels or jewellery. [Middle English from Anglo-French *jueler*, Old French *juelier* (as JEWEL)]

jeweller's rouge *n.* finely ground rouge for polishing metal.

jewellery /ˈdʒuːəlri/ *n.* (also **jewelry**) jewels or other ornamental objects, esp. for personal adornment, regarded collectively. [Middle English from Old French *juelerie*, and from JEWEL, JEWELLER]

Jewess /ˈdʒuːɛs, -ɪs/ *n. offens.* a female Jew.

jewfish /ˈdʒuːfɪʃ/ *n.* (*pl.* usu. same) **1** a grouper, *Epinephelus itajara*, of N. American, Atlantic, and Pacific coasts. **2** any of various large Australian fish used as food, esp. the mulloway.

Jewish /ˈdʒuːɪʃ/ *adj.* **1** of or relating to Jews. **2** of Judaism. □ **Jewishly** *adv.* **Jewishness** *n.*

Jewry /ˈdʒʊəri/ *n.* (*pl.* **-ies**) **1** Jews collectively. **2** *hist.* a Jews' quarter in a town etc. [Middle English from Anglo-French *juerie*, Old French *juierie* (as JEW)]

Jew's ear *n.* a rubbery cup-shaped fungus, *Auricularia auricula-judae*, growing on trees. [mistranslation of medieval Latin *auricula Judae* 'Judas's ear', from its shape and its occurrence on the elder, said to be the tree from which Judas Iscariot hanged himself]

jew's harp *n.* a small lyre-shaped musical instrument held between the teeth and struck with the finger.

Jezebel /ˈdʒɛzəbɛl/ *n.* a shameless or immoral woman. [*Jezebel*, wife of Ahab in the Old Testament (1 Kings 16, 19, 21)]

jib[1] /dʒɪb/ *n.* & *v.* ● *n.* **1** a triangular staysail extending from the outer end of the jib-boom to the top of the foremast or from the bowsprit to the masthead. **2** the projecting arm of a crane. ● *v.tr.* & *intr.* (**jibbed**, **jibbing**) (of a sail etc.) pull or swing round from one side of the ship to the other; gybe. [17th c.: origin unknown]

jib[2] /dʒɪb/ *v.intr.* (**jibbed**, **jibbing**) **1 a** (of an animal, esp. a horse) stop and refuse to go on; move backwards or sideways instead of going on. **b** (of a person) refuse to continue. **2** (foll. by *at*) show aversion to (a person or course of action). □ **jibber** *n.* [19th c.: origin unknown]

jibba /ˈdʒɪbə/ *n.* (also **jibbah**, **djibba**, **djibbah**) a long coat worn by Muslim men. [Egyptian variant of Arabic *jubba*]

jib-boom *n.* a spar run out from the end of the bowsprit.

jibe[1] var. of GIBE.

jibe[2] *US* var. of GYBE.

jibe[3] /dʒʌɪb/ *v.intr.* (usu. foll. by *with*) *US colloq.* agree; be in accord. [19th c.: origin unknown]

jiff /dʒɪf/ *n.* (also **jiffy**, *pl.* **-ies**) *colloq.* a short time; a moment (*in a jiffy*; *half a jiff*). [18th c.: origin unknown]

Jiffy bag /ˈdʒɪfi/ *n. propr.* a type of padded envelope for postal use.

jig /dʒɪg/ *n.* & *v.* ● *n.* **1 a** a lively dance with leaping movements. **b** the music for this, usu. in triple time. **2** a device that holds a piece of work and guides the tools operating on it. **3** a device for catching fish that is jerked up and down through the water. ● *v.* (**jigged**, **jigging**) **1** *intr.* dance a jig. **2** *tr.* & *intr.* move quickly and jerkily up and down. **3** *tr.* work on or equip with a jig or jigs. **4** *tr.* & *intr.* fish (for) or catch with a jig. □ **jig about** fidget. [16th c.: origin unknown]

jigger[1] /ˈdʒɪgə/ *n.* & *v.* ● *n.* **1** *Naut.* **a** a small tackle consisting of a double and single block with a rope. **b** a small sail at the stern. **c** a small smack having this. **2** *slang* a gadget. **3** *Golf* an iron club with a narrow face. **4** *Billiards colloq.* a cue-rest. **5 a** a measure of spirits etc. **b** a small glass holding this. **6** a person or thing that jigs. ● *v.tr.* **1** (usu. in phr. **I'll be jiggered**) *slang* confound, damn. **2** exhaust; damage, break. [JIG *v.*]

jigger[2] var. of CHIGGER.

jiggery-pokery /ˌdʒɪg(ə)rɪˈpəʊk(ə)ri/ *n.* *Brit.* *colloq.* deceitful or dishonest dealing, trickery. [cf. Scots *joukery-pawkery* from *jouk* 'dodge, skulk']

jiggle /ˈdʒɪg(ə)l/ *v.* & *n.* ● *v.* (often foll. by *about* etc.) **1** *tr.* shake lightly; rock jerkily. **2** *intr.* fidget. ● *n.* a light shake. □ **jiggly** *adj.* [JIG or JOGGLE[1]]

jigsaw /ˈdʒɪgsɔː/ *n.* **1 a** (in full **jigsaw puzzle**) a puzzle consisting of a picture on board or wood etc. cut into irregular interlocking pieces to be reassembled. **b** a mental puzzle resolvable by assembling various pieces of information. **2** a machine saw with a fine blade enabling it to cut curved lines in a sheet of wood, metal, etc.

jihad /dʒɪˈhɑːd, -ˈhad/ *n.* (also **jehad**) a holy war undertaken by Muslims against unbelievers. [Arabic *jihād*]

jill var. of GILL[4].

jilt /dʒɪlt/ *v.* & *n.* ● *v.tr.* abruptly reject or abandon (a lover etc.). ● *n.* a person (esp. a woman) who jilts a lover. [17th c.: origin unknown]

Jim Crow /dʒɪm ˈkrəʊ/ *n.* *US* **1** the practice of segregating blacks. **2** *offens.* a black person. **3** an implement for straightening iron bars or bending rails by screw pressure. □ **Jim Crowism** *n.* (in sense 1).

[from the name of a black character in a 19th c. plantation song]

jim-jams[1] /ˈdʒɪmdʒamz/ *n.pl.* **1** *slang* = DELIRIUM TREMENS. **2** *colloq.* a fit of depression or nervousness. [fanciful reduplication]

jim-jams[2] /ˈdʒɪmdʒamz/ *n.pl. Brit. colloq.* pyjamas. [abbreviation of *pie-jim-jams*, corruption of PYJAMAS]

Jimmy /ˈdʒɪmi/ *n. Brit. slang* an act of urination; a piddle. [abbreviation of *Jimmy Riddle*, rhyming slang]

jimmy *N. Amer.* var. of JEMMY.

jimson /ˈdʒɪms(ə)n/ *n.* (in full **jimson weed**) *US* a highly poisonous tall weed, *Datura stramonium*, with large trumpet-shaped flowers. [*Jamestown* in Virginia]

jingle /ˈdʒɪŋg(ə)l/ *n. & v.* ● *n.* **1** a mixed noise as of bells or light metal objects being shaken together. **2 a** a repetition of the same sound in words, esp. as an aid to memory or to attract attention. **b** a short verse of this kind used in advertising etc. ● *v.* **1** *intr. & tr.* make or cause to make a jingling sound. **2** *intr.* (of writing) be full of alliterations, rhymes, etc. □ **jingly** *adj.* [Middle English: imitative]

jingo /ˈdʒɪŋgəʊ/ *n.* (*pl.* **-oes**) a supporter of policy favouring war; a blustering patriot. □ **by jingo!** a mild oath. □ **jingoism** *n.* **jingoist** *n.* **jingoistic** /-ˈɪstɪk/ *adj.* [17th c.: originally a conjuror's word: political sense from use of *by jingo* in a popular song, first applied to those supporting the sending of a British fleet into Turkish waters to resist Russia in 1878]

jink /dʒɪŋk/ *v. & n.* ● *v.* **1** *intr.* move elusively; dodge. **2** *tr.* elude by dodging. ● *n.* an act of dodging or eluding. [originally Scots: probably imitative of nimble motion]

jinnee /ˈdʒɪni:/ *n.* (also **jinn, djinn** /dʒɪn/) (*pl.* **jinn** or **djinn**) (in Muslim mythology) an intelligent being lower than the angels, able to appear in human and animal forms, and having power over people. [Arabic *jinnī*, pl. *jinn*: cf. GENIE]

jinx /dʒɪŋks/ *n. & v. colloq.* ● *n.* a person or thing that seems to cause bad luck. ● *v.tr.* (often in *passive*) subject (a person or thing) to bad luck; cast an evil spell on. [perhaps variant of *jynx* 'wryneck, charm']

JIT *abbr. Commerce* just-in-time.

jitter /ˈdʒɪtə/ *n. & v. colloq.* ● *n.* (**the jitters**) extreme nervousness. ● *v.intr.* be nervous; act nervously. □ **jittery** *adj.* **jitteriness** *n.* [20th c.: origin unknown]

jitterbug /ˈdʒɪtəbʌg/ *n. & v.* ● *n.* **1** a nervous person. **2** *hist.* **a** a fast dance popular in the 1940s, performed chiefly to swing music. **b** a person fond of dancing this. ● *v.intr.* (**-bugged, -bugging**) dance the jitterbug.

jiu-jitsu var. of JU-JITSU.

jive /dʒʌɪv/ *n. & v.* ● *n.* **1** a jerky lively style of dance esp. popular in the 1950s, performed to jazz or rock and roll music. **2** music for this. ● *v.intr.* **1** dance the jive. **2** play jive music. □ **jiver** *n.* [20th c.: origin uncertain]

jizz /dʒɪz/ *n.* the characteristic impression given by an animal or plant. [20th c.: origin unknown]

Jnr. *abbr.* Junior.

jo /dʒəʊ/ *n.* (*pl.* **joes**) *Sc.* a sweetheart or beloved. [variant of JOY]

job[1] /dʒɒb/ *n. & v.* ● *n.* **1** a piece of work, esp. one done for hire or profit. **2** a paid position of employment. **3** *colloq.* **a** anything one has to do. **b** a specified operation or other matter, esp. an operation involving plastic surgery (*a nose job*; *a respray job*). **4** *colloq.* a difficult task (*had a job to find them*). **5** *slang* a product of work, esp. if well done; an example of its type. **6** *Computing* an item of work regarded separately. **7** *slang* a crime, esp. a robbery. **8** a transaction in which private advantage prevails over duty or public interest. **9** esp. *Brit. colloq.* a state of affairs or set of circumstances (*is a bad job*). ● *v.* (**jobbed, jobbing**) **1** *intr.* do jobs; do piecework. **2 a** *intr.* deal in stocks. **b** *tr.* buy and sell (stocks or goods) as a middleman. **3 a** *intr.* turn a position of trust to private advantage. **b** *tr.* deal corruptly with (a matter). **4** *tr. US slang* swindle. □ **jobs for the boys** *Brit. colloq.* preferment for one's supporters or favourites. **just the job** *Brit. colloq.* exactly what is wanted. **make a job** (or **good job**) **of** *Brit.* do thoroughly or successfully. **on the job** *colloq.* **1** at work; in the course of doing a piece of work. **2** *Brit. euphem.* engaged in sexual intercourse. **out of a job** unemployed. [16th c.: origin unknown]

job[2] /dʒɒb/ *v. & n.* ● *v.* (**jobbed, jobbing**) **1** *tr.* prod; stab slightly. **2** *intr.* (foll. by *at*) thrust. ● *n.* a prod or thrust; a jerk at a horse's bit. [Middle English, apparently imitative: cf. JAB]

job analysis *n.* the analysis of the essential factors of a particular job or task and the qualifications needed to carry it out. □ **job analyst** *n.*

jobber /ˈdʒɒbə/ *n.* **1** (in the UK) a principal or wholesaler dealing on the Stock Exchange (permitted only to deal with brokers, not directly with the public). **2** *US* **a** a wholesaler. **b** *derog.* = BROKER 2. **3** a person who jobs. [JOB[1]]

■ **Usage** The term *jobber* in sense 1 was officially replaced by *broker-dealer* in 1986, broker-dealers being entitled to act as both agents and principals in share dealings.

jobbery /ˈdʒɒb(ə)ri/ *n.* corrupt dealing.

jobbie /ˈdʒɒbi/ *n. slang* = JOB[1] *n.* 5.

jobbing /ˈdʒɒbɪŋ/ *adj.* working on separate or occasional jobs (esp. of a computer, gardener, or printer).

jobcentre /ˈdʒɒbsɛntə/ *n.* (in the UK) any of several government offices displaying information about available jobs.

job-control language *n. Computing* a language enabling the user to determine the tasks to be undertaken by the operating system.

job-hunt *v.intr. colloq.* seek employment.

jobless /ˈdʒɒblɪs/ *adj.* without a job; unemployed. □ **joblessness** *n.*

job lot *n.* a miscellaneous group of articles, esp. sold or bought together.

Job's comforter /dʒəʊbz/ *n.* a person who under the guise of comforting aggravates distress. [the patriarch *Job* in the Old Testament (Job 16:2)]

job-sharing *n.* an arrangement by which a full-time job is done jointly by two or more part-time employees who share the remuneration etc. □ **job-share** *n. & v.intr.*

jobsheet /ˈdʒɒbʃi:t/ *n.* a sheet for recording details of jobs done.

Job's tears /dʒəʊbz/ *n.pl.* the seeds of a grass, *Coix lacryma-jobi*, used as beads. [the patriarch *Job* in the Old Testament]

jobsworth /ˈdʒɒbzwə:θ/ *n. Brit. colloq.* an official who upholds petty rules. [contraction of 'it's more than my *job's worth* (not) to']

jobwork /ˈdʒɒbwə:k/ *n.* work done and paid for by the job.

Jock /dʒɒk/ *n. colloq.* often *offens.* a Scotsman. [Scots form of the name *Jack* (see JACK[1])]

jock[1] /dʒɒk/ *n. colloq.* **1** a jockey. **2** a disc jockey. [abbreviation]

jock[2] /dʒɔk/ *n. N. Amer. colloq.* **1** = JOCKSTRAP. **2** a well-built rugged man. [abbreviation]

jockey /ˈdʒɒki/ *n. & v.* ● *n.* (*pl.* **-eys**) a rider in horse races, esp. a professional one. ● *v.* (**-eys, -eyed**) **1** *tr.* **a** trick or cheat (a person). **b** outwit. **2** *tr.* (foll. by *away*, *out*, *in*, etc.) draw (a person) by trickery. **3** *intr.* cheat. □ **jockey for position** try to gain an advantageous position esp. by skilful manoeuvring or unfair action. □ **jockeydom** *n.* **jockeyship** *n.* [diminutive of JOCK]

jockey cap *n.* a strengthened cap with a long peak, as worn by jockeys.

jockstrap /ˈdʒɒkstrap/ *n.* **1** a support or protection for the male genitals, worn esp. by sportsmen. **2** *N. Amer. colloq.* an athletic person, esp. a student participant in sport. [slang *jock* 'genitals' + STRAP]

jocose /dʒəˈkəʊs/ *adj.* **1** playful in style. **2** fond of joking, jocular. □ **jocosely** *adv.* **jocoseness** *n.* **jocosity** /-ˈkɒsɪti/ *n.* (*pl.* **-ies**). [Latin *jocosus* from *jocus* 'jest']

jocular /ˈdʒɒkjʊlə/ *adj.* **1** merry; fond of joking. **2** of the nature of a joke; humorous. □ **jocularity** /-ˈlarɪti/ *n.* (*pl.* **-ies**). **jocularly** *adv.* [Latin *jocularis* from *joculus*, diminutive of *jocus* 'jest']

jocund /ˈdʒɒk(ə)nd, ˈdʒəʊk-/ *adj. literary* merry, cheerful, sprightly. □ **jocundity** /dʒɒˈkʌndɪti/ *n.* (*pl.* **-ies**). **jocundly** *adv.* [Middle English via Old French from Latin *jocundus, jucundus*, from *juvare* 'delight']

jodhpurs /ˈdʒɒdpəz/ *n.pl.* long breeches for riding etc., close-fitting from the knee to the ankle. [*Jodhpur*, a city in India]

Joe Bloggs /dʒəʊ ˈblɒgz/ *n. Brit. colloq.* a hypothetical average man.

Joe Blow /dʒəʊ ˈbləʊ/ *n. N. Amer. colloq.* = JOE BLOGGS.

Joe Public /dʒəʊ ˈpʌblɪk/ *n. colloq.* **1** (a member of) an audience. **2** (a member of) the general public.

joey /ˈdʒəʊi/ *n.* (*pl.* **-eys**) *Austral.* **1** a young kangaroo. **2** a young animal. [Aboriginal *joè*]

jog /dʒɒg/ *v.* & *n.* ● *v.* (**jogged**, **jogging**) **1** *intr.* run at a slow pace, esp. as physical exercise. **2** *intr.* (of a horse) move at a jogtrot. **3** *intr.* (often foll. by *on, along*) **a** proceed laboriously; trudge. **b** *Brit.* go on one's way. **c** *Brit.* proceed; get through the time (*we must jog on somehow*). **4** *intr.* move up and down with an unsteady motion. **5** *tr.* nudge (a person), esp. to arouse attention. **6** *tr.* shake with a push or jerk. **7** *tr.* stimulate (a person's or one's own memory). ● *n.* **1** a shake, push, or nudge. **2** a slow walk or trot. [Middle English: apparently imitative: cf. GOGGLE]

jogger /ˈdʒɒgə/ *n.* a person who jogs, esp. one who runs for physical exercise.

joggle[1] /ˈdʒɒg(ə)l/ *v.* & *n.* ● *v.tr.* & *intr.* shake or move by or as if by repeated jerks. ● *n.* **1** a slight shake. **2** the act or action of joggling. [frequentative of JOG]

joggle[2] /ˈdʒɒg(ə)l/ *n.* & *v.* ● *n.* **1** a joint of two pieces of stone or timber, contrived to prevent their sliding on one another. **2** a notch in one of the two pieces, a projection in the other, or a small piece let in between the two, for this purpose. ● *v.tr.* join with a joggle. [perhaps from *jog* = JAG[1]]

jogtrot /ˈdʒɒgtrɒt/ *n.* **1** a slow regular trot. **2** a monotonous progression.

john /dʒɒn/ *n.* esp. *N. Amer. slang* **1** a lavatory. **2** a prostitute's client. [the name *John*]

John Bull /dʒɒn ˈbʊl/ *n.* a personification of England or the typical Englishman. [the name of a character representing the English nation in J. Arbuthnot's satire *Law is a Bottomless Pit* (1712)]

John Doe /dʒɒn ˈdəʊ/ *n.* **1** *US Law* an anonymous party, usu. the plaintiff, in a legal action. **2** *N. Amer. colloq.* = JOE BLOGGS.

John Dory /dʒɒn ˈdɔːri/ *n.* (*pl.* **-ies**) a European marine fish, *Zeus faber*, with a laterally flattened body and a black spot on each side.

johnny /ˈdʒɒni/ *n.* (*pl.* **-ies**) *Brit.* **1** *slang* a condom. **2** *colloq.* a fellow; a man. [familiar form of the name *John*]

johnny-come-lately *n. colloq.* a recently arrived person.

Johnsonian /dʒɒnˈsəʊnɪən/ *adj.* **1** of or relating to Samuel Johnson, English man of letters and lexicographer (d. 1784). **2** typical of his style of writing.

joie de vivre /ʒwɑː də ˈviːvrə, French ʒwad vivr/ *n.* a feeling of healthy and exuberant enjoyment of life. [French, = joy of living]

join /dʒɔɪn/ *v.* & *n.* ● *v.* **1** *tr.* (often foll. by *to, together*) put together; fasten, unite (one thing or person to another or several together). **2** *tr.* connect (points) by a line etc. **3** *tr.* become a member of (an association, society, organization, etc.). **4** *tr.* take one's place with or in (a company, group, procession, etc.). **5** *tr.* **a** come into the company of (a person). **b** (foll. by *in*) take part with (others) in an activity etc. (*joined me in condemnation of the outrage*). **c** (foll. by *for*) share the company of for a specified occasion (*may I join you for lunch?*). **6** *intr.* (often foll. by *with, to*) come together; be united. **7** *intr.* (often foll. by *in*) take part with others in an activity etc. **8** *tr.* be or become connected or continuous with (*the Inn joins the Danube at Passau*). ● *n.* a point, line, or surface at which two or more things are joined. □ **join battle** begin fighting. **join forces** combine efforts. **join hands 1 a** clasp each other's hands. **b** clasp one's hands together. **2** combine in an action or enterprise. **join in** (also *absol.*) take part in (an activity). **join up 1** enlist for military service. **2** (often foll. by *with*) unite, connect. □ **joinable** *adj.* [Middle English via Old French *joindre* (stem *joign-*) from Latin *jungere junct-* 'join']

joinder /ˈdʒɔɪndə/ *n. Law* the act of bringing together. [Anglo-French from Old French *joindre* 'to join']

joiner /ˈdʒɔɪnə/ *n.* **1** a person who makes furniture and light woodwork. **2** *colloq.* a person who readily joins societies etc. □ **joinery** *n.* (in sense 1). [Middle English from Anglo-French *joignour*, Old French *joigneor* (as JOIN)]

joint /dʒɔɪnt/ *n., adj.,* & *v.* ● *n.* **1 a** a place at which two things are joined together. **b** a point at which, or a contrivance by which, two parts of an artificial structure are joined. **2** a structure in an animal body by which two bones are fitted together. **3 a** any of the parts into which an animal carcass is divided for food. **b** any of the parts of which a body is made up. **4** *slang* a place of meeting for drinking etc. **5** *slang* a marijuana cigarette. **6** the part of a stem from which a leaf or branch grows. **7** a piece of flexible material forming the hinge of a book cover. **8** *Geol.* a fissure in a mass of rock. ● *adj.* **1** held or done by, or belonging to, two or more persons etc. in conjunction (*a joint mortgage*; *joint action*). **2** sharing with another in some action, state, etc. (*joint author*; *joint favourite*). ● *v.tr.* **1** connect by joints. **2** divide (a body or member) at a joint or into joints. **3** fill up the joints of (masonry etc.) with mortar etc.; trim the surface of (a mortar joint). **4** prepare (a board etc.) for being joined to another by planing its edge. □ **out of joint 1** (of a bone) dislocated. **2** out of order. □ **jointless** *adj.* **jointly** *adv.* [Middle English from Old French, past part. of *joindre* JOIN]

joint account *n.* a bank account held by more than one person, each of whom has the right to deposit and withdraw funds.

joint and several *adj.* (of an obligation etc.) undertaken and signed by two or more people, of whom each is liable for the whole obligation etc.

jointer /ˈdʒɔɪntə/ *n.* **1 a** a plane for jointing. **b** a tool for jointing or pointing masonry. **2** a worker employed in jointing wires, pipes, etc.

jointress /ˈdʒɔɪntrɪs/ *n.* a widow who holds a jointure. [obsolete *jointer* 'joint possessor']

joint stock *n.* capital held jointly; a common fund.

joint-stock company *n.* a company formed on the basis of a joint stock.

jointure /ˈdʒɔɪntʃə/ *n.* & *v.* ● *n.* an estate settled on a wife for the period during which she survives her husband. ● *v.tr.* provide (a wife) with a jointure. [Middle English via Old French from Latin *junctura* (as JOIN)]

joist /dʒɔɪst/ *n.* each of a series of parallel supporting beams of timber, steel, etc., used in floors, ceilings, etc. □ **joisted** *adj.* [Middle English from Old French *giste*, ultimately from Latin *jacēre* 'lie']

jojoba /həˈhəʊbə, həʊ-/ *n.* a plant, *Simmondsia chinensis*, with seeds yielding an oily extract used in cosmetics etc. [Mexican Spanish]

joke /dʒəʊk/ *n.* & *v.* ● *n.* **1 a** a thing said or done to excite laughter. **b** a witticism or jest. **2** a ridiculous thing, person, or circumstance. ● *v.* **1** *intr.* make jokes. **2** *tr.* poke fun at; banter. □ **no joke** *colloq.* a serious matter. □ **jokingly** *adv.* **joky** *adj.* (also **jokey**). **jokily** *adv.* **jokiness** *n.* [17th c. (*joque*), originally slang: perhaps from Latin *jocus* 'jest']

joker /ˈdʒəʊkə/ *n.* **1** a person who jokes. **2** *slang* a fellow; a man. **3** a playing card usu. with a figure of a jester, used in some games esp. as a wild card. **4** *US* a clause unobtrusively inserted in a bill or document and affecting its operation in a way not immediately apparent. **5** an unexpected factor or resource. □ **the joker in the pack** an unpredictable factor or participant.

jolie laide /ʒɒliː ˈleɪd, French ʒɔli lɛd/ *n.* (*pl.* ***jolies laides*** *pronunc.* same) *Brit.* = BELLE LAIDE. [French, from *jolie* 'pretty' + *laide* 'ugly']

jollify /ˈdʒɒlɪfʌɪ/ *v.tr. & intr.* (**-ies**, **-ied**) make or be merry, esp. in drinking. □ **jollification** /-frˈkeɪʃ(ə)n/ *n.*

jollity /ˈdʒɒlɪti/ *n.* (*pl.* **-ies**) **1** merrymaking; festiveness. **2** (in *pl.*) festivities. [Middle English from Old French *jolivetė* (as JOLLY[1])]

jolly[1] /ˈdʒɒli/ *adj., adv., v., & n.* ● *adj.* (**jollier, jolliest**) **1** cheerful and good-humoured; merry. **2** festive, jovial. **3** slightly drunk. **4** *colloq.* (of a person or thing) very pleasant, delightful (often *iron.*: *a jolly shame*). ● *adv. colloq.* very (*they were jolly unlucky*). ● *v.tr.* (**-ies, -ied**) **1** (usu. foll. by *along*) *colloq.* coax or humour (a person) in a friendly way. **2** chaff, banter. ● *n.* (*pl.* **-ies**) *Brit. colloq.* a party or celebration. □ **jollily** *adv.* **jolliness** *n.* [Middle English from Old French *jolif* 'gay, pretty', perhaps from Old Norse *jól* YULE]

jolly[2] /ˈdʒɒli/ *n.* (*pl.* **-ies**) (in full **jolly boat**) a clinker-built ship's boat smaller than a cutter. [18th c.: origin unknown: perhaps related to YAWL]

Jolly Roger *n.* a pirates' black flag, usu. with the skull and crossbones.

jolt /dʒəʊlt, dʒɒlt/ *v. & n.* ● *v.* **1** *tr.* disturb or shake from the normal position (esp. in a moving vehicle) with a jerk. **2** *tr.* give a mental shock to; perturb. **3** *intr.* (of a vehicle) move along with jerks, as on a rough road. ● *n.* **1** such a jerk. **2** a surprise or shock. □ **jolty** *adj.* [16th c.: origin unknown]

Jon. *abbr.* **1** Jonah (Old Testament). **2** Jonathan.

Jonah /ˈdʒəʊnə/ *n.* a person who seems to bring bad luck. [*Jonah* in the Old Testament]

jongleur /dʒɒ̃ˈɡləː, French ʒɔ̃ɡlœr/ *n. hist.* an itinerant minstrel. [French, variant of *jougleur* JUGGLER]

jonquil /ˈdʒʌŋkwɪl, ˈdʒɒn-/ *n.* a bulbous plant, *Narcissus jonquilla*, with clusters of small fragrant yellow flowers. [modern Latin *jonquilla* or French *jonquille* from Spanish *junquillo*, diminutive of *junco*: see JUNCO]

Jordanian /dʒɔːˈdeɪnɪən/ *adj. & n.* ● *adj.* of or relating to the kingdom of Jordan in the Middle East. ● *n.* **1** a native or national of Jordan. **2** a person of Jordanian descent. [*Jordan*, a river flowing into the Dead Sea]

jorum /ˈdʒɔːrəm/ *n.* **1** a large drinking bowl. **2** its contents, esp. punch. [perhaps from *Joram* (2 Sam. 8:10)]

Jos. *abbr.* Joseph.

Josh. *abbr.* Joshua (Old Testament).

josh /dʒɒʃ/ *n. & v. colloq.* ● *n.* a good-natured or teasing joke. ● *v.* **1** *tr.* tease or banter. **2** *intr.* indulge in ridicule. □ **josher** *n.* [19th c.: origin unknown]

Joshua tree /ˈdʒɒʃjʊə/ *n.* a yucca, *Yucca brevifolia*, of arid parts of western N. America. [apparently from *Joshua*, ancient Israelite leader, the plant being likened to a man brandishing a spear (Joshua 8:18)]

joss /dʒɒs/ *n.* a Chinese idol. [perhaps ultimately via Portuguese *deos* from Latin *deus* 'god']

josser /ˈdʒɒsə/ *n. slang* **1** *Brit.* **a** a fool. **b** a fellow. **2** *Austral.* a clergyman. [JOSS + -ER[1]]

joss stick *n.* a stick of fragrant tinder mixed with clay, burnt as incense.

jostle /ˈdʒɒs(ə)l/ *v. & n.* ● *v.* **1** *tr.* push against; elbow. **2** *tr.* (often foll. by *away*, *from*, etc.) push (a person) abruptly or roughly. **3** *intr.* (foll. by *against*) knock or push, esp. in a crowd. **4** *intr.* (foll. by *with*) struggle; have a rough exchange. ● *n.* **1** the act or an instance of jostling. **2** a collision. [Middle English, earlier *justle*, from JOUST + -LE[4]]

jot /dʒɒt/ *v. & n.* ● *v.tr.* (**jotted, jotting**) (usu. foll. by *down*) write briefly or hastily. ● *n.* (usu. with *neg.* expressed or implied) a very small amount (*not one jot*). [earlier as noun: Latin from Greek *iōta*: see IOTA]

jotter /ˈdʒɒtə/ *n. Brit.* a small pad or notebook for making notes etc.

jotting /ˈdʒɒtɪŋ/ *n.* (usu. in *pl.*) a note; something jotted down.

joule /dʒuːl/ *n.* the SI unit of work or energy equal to the work done by a force of one newton when its point of application moves one metre in the direction of action of the force, equivalent to a watt-second (symbol **J**). [named after J. P. *Joule*, English physicist d. 1889]

jounce /dʒaʊns/ *v.tr. & intr.* bump, bounce, jolt. [Middle English: origin unknown]

journal /ˈdʒəːn(ə)l/ *n.* **1** a newspaper or periodical. **2** a daily record of events. **3** *Naut.* a logbook. **4** a book in which business transactions are entered, with a statement of the accounts to which each is to be debited and credited. **5** the part of a shaft or axle that rests on bearings. **6** (**the Journals**) *Parl.* a record of daily proceedings. [Middle English via Old French *jurnal* from Late Latin *diurnalis* DIURNAL]

journalese /dʒəːnəˈliːz/ *n.* a hackneyed style of language characteristic of some newspaper writing.

journalism /ˈdʒəːn(ə)lɪz(ə)m/ *n.* the business or practice of writing and producing newspapers.

journalist /ˈdʒəːn(ə)lɪst/ *n.* a person employed to write for, edit, or report for, a newspaper, journal, or newscast. □ **journalistic** /-ˈlɪstɪk/ *adj.* **journalistically** /-ˈlɪstɪk(ə)li/ *adv.*

journalize /ˈdʒəːn(ə)lʌɪz/ *v.tr.* (also **-ise**) record in a private journal.

journey /ˈdʒəːni/ *n. & v.* ● *n.* (*pl.* **-eys**) **1** an act of going from one place to another, esp. at a long distance. **2** the distance travelled in a specified time (*a day's journey*). **3** the travelling of a vehicle along a route at a stated time. ● *v.intr.* (**-eys, -eyed**) make a journey. □ **journeyer** *n.* [Middle English from Old French *jornee* 'day, day's work or travel', ultimately from Latin *diurnus* 'daily']

journeyman /ˈdʒəːnɪmən/ *n.* (*pl.* **-men**) **1** a qualified mechanic or artisan who works for another. **2** *derog.* **a** a reliable but not outstanding worker. **b** a mere hireling. [JOURNEY in obsolete sense 'day's work' + MAN]

journo /ˈdʒəːnəʊ/ *n.* (*pl.* **-os**) esp. *Austral. slang* a journalist.

joust /dʒaʊst/ *n. & v. hist.* ● *n.* a combat between two knights on horseback with lances, esp. for sport. ● *v.intr.* engage in a joust. □ **jouster** *n.* [Middle English from Old French *juster* 'bring together', ultimately from Latin *juxta* 'near']

Jove /ˈdʒəʊv/ *n.* (in Roman mythology) Jupiter, chief of the gods. □ **by Jove!** an exclamation of surprise or approval. [Middle English from Latin *Jovis*, genitive of Old Latin *Jovis*, used as genitive of JUPITER]

jovial /ˈdʒəʊvɪəl, -vj(ə)l/ *adj.* **1** merry. **2** convivial. **3** hearty and good-humoured. □ **joviality** /-ˈalɪti/ *n.* **jovially** *adv.* [French from Late Latin *jovialis* 'of Jupiter' (as JOVE), with reference to the supposed influence of the planet Jupiter on those born under it]

Jovian /ˈdʒəʊvɪən/ *adj.* **1** (in Roman mythology) of or like Jupiter, chief of the gods. **2** of the planet Jupiter.

jowar /dʒaʊˈɑː/ *n.* = DURRA. [Hindi *jawār*]

jowl[1] /dʒaʊl/ *n.* **1** the jaw or jawbone. **2** the cheek (*cheek by jowl*). □ **-jowled** *adj.* (in *comb.*). [Old English *ceafl*]

jowl[2] /dʒaʊl/ *n.* **1** the external loose skin on the throat or neck when prominent. **2** the dewlap of an ox, wattle of a bird, etc. □ **jowly** *adj.* [Old English *ceole*]

joy /dʒɔɪ/ *n. & v.* ● *n.* **1** (often foll. by *at*, *in*) a vivid emotion of pleasure; extreme gladness. **2** a thing that causes joy. **3** *Brit. colloq.* satisfaction, success (*got no joy*). ● *v.* esp. *poet.* **1** *intr.* rejoice. **2** *tr.* gladden. □ **wish a person joy of** *Brit. iron.* be gladly rid of (what that person has to deal with). □ **joyless** *adj.* **joylessly** *adv.* [Middle English from Old French *joie*, ultimately via Latin *gaudium* from *gaudēre* 'rejoice']

Joycean /ˈdʒɔɪsɪən/ *adj. & n.* ● *adj.* of or characteristic of James Joyce, Irish poet and novelist (d. 1941) or his writings. ● *n.* a specialist in or admirer of Joyce's works.

joyful /'dʒɔɪfʊl, -f(ə)l/ *adj.* full of, showing, or causing joy. □ **joyfully** *adv.* **joyfulness** *n.*

joyous /'dʒɔɪəs/ *adj.* (of an occasion, circumstance, etc.) characterized by pleasure or joy; joyful. □ **joyously** *adv.* **joyousness** *n.*

joyride /'dʒɔɪrʌɪd/ *n. & v. colloq.* ● *n.* a ride for pleasure, esp. one in a stolen motor car. ● *v.intr.* (*past* **-rode** /-rəʊd/; *past part.* **-ridden** /-rɪd(ə)n/) go for a joyride. □ **joyrider** *n.*

joystick /'dʒɔɪstɪk/ *n.* **1** *colloq.* the control column of an aircraft. **2** a lever that can be moved in several directions to control the movement of an image on a VDU screen.

JP *abbr.* (in the UK) Justice of the Peace.

Jr. *abbr.* Junior.

jt. *abbr.* joint.

jube /dʒu:b/ *n. Austral. & NZ* = JUJUBE 2. [abbreviation]

jubilant /'dʒu:bɪl(ə)nt/ *adj.* exultant, rejoicing, joyful. □ **jubilance** *n.* **jubilantly** *adv.* [Latin *jubilare jubilant-* 'shout for joy']

jubilate *v. & n.* ● *v.intr.* /'dʒu:bɪleɪt/ exult; be joyful. ● *n.* /dʒu:bɪ'lɑ:teɪ/ (**Jubilate**) **1** Psalm 100, beginning *Jubilate deo* 'rejoice in God', used as a canticle in the Anglican service of matins. **2** a musical setting of this. □ **jubilation** /-'leɪʃ(ə)n/ *n.* [Latin *jubilare* (as JUBILANT)]

jubilee /'dʒu:bɪli:/ *n.* **1** a time or season of rejoicing. **2** an anniversary of an event, esp. the 25th or 50th. **3** *Jewish Hist.* a year of emancipation and restoration, kept every 50 years. **4** *RC Ch.* a period of remission from the penal consequences of sin, granted under certain conditions for a year usu. at intervals of 25 years. **5** exultant joy. [Middle English via Old French *jubilé* from Late Latin *jubilaeus* (*annus*) '(year) of jubilee', ultimately from Hebrew *yōḇēl*, originally = ram, ram's-horn trumpet, with which the jubilee year was proclaimed]

Jubilee clip *n. propr.* an adjustable steel band secured with a screw.

Jud. *abbr.* Judith (Apocrypha).

Judaeo- /dʒu:'di:əʊ/ *comb. form* (*US* **Judeo-**) Jewish; Jewish and. [Latin *judaeus* 'Jewish']

Judaic /dʒu:'deɪɪk/ *adj.* of or characteristic of the Jews or Judaism. [Latin *Judaicus* from Greek *Ioudaïkos*, from *Ioudaios* JEW]

Judaism /'dʒu:deɪɪz(ə)m/ *n.* **1** the religion of the Jews, with a belief in one God and a basis in Mosaic and rabbinical teachings. **2** the Jews collectively. □ **Judaist** *n.* [Middle English via Late Latin *Judaismus* from Greek *Ioudaïsmos* (as JUDAIC)]

Judaize /'dʒu:deɪʌɪz/ *v.* (also **-ise**) **1** *intr.* follow Jewish customs or rites. **2** *tr.* **a** make Jewish. **b** convert to Judaism. □ **Judaization** /-'zeɪʃ(ə)n/ *n.* [Late Latin *judaizare* from Greek *ioudaïzō* (as JUDAIC)]

Judas /'dʒu:dəs/ *n.* **1** a person who betrays a friend. **2** (**judas**) a peephole in a door. [*Judas* Iscariot who betrayed Christ (Luke 22)]

Judas tree *n.* a Mediterranean tree, *Cercis siliquastrum*, with purple flowers usu. appearing before the leaves.

judder /'dʒʌdə/ *v. & n.* esp. *Brit.* ● *v.intr.* **1** (esp. of a mechanism) vibrate noisily or violently. **2** (of a singer's voice) oscillate in intensity. ● *n.* an instance of juddering. [imitative: cf. SHUDDER]

Judeo- *US* var. of JUDAEO-.

Judg. *abbr.* Judges (Old Testament).

judge /dʒʌdʒ/ *n. & v.* ● *n.* **1** a public officer appointed to hear and try causes in a court of justice. **2** a person appointed to decide in a competition, contest, or dispute. **3 a** a person who decides a question. **b** a person regarded in terms of capacity to decide on the merits of a thing or question (*am no judge of that*; *a good judge of art*). **4** *Jewish Hist.* a leader having temporary authority in ancient Israel in the period between Joshua and the kings. **5** (**Judges**) a book of the Old Testament containing the history of the period of the judges. ● *v.* **1** *tr.* **a** try (a cause) in a court of justice. **b** pronounce sentence on (a person). **2** *tr.* form an opinion about; estimate, appraise. **3** *tr.* act as a judge of (a dispute or contest). **4** *tr.* (often foll. by *to* + infin. or *that* + clause) conclude, consider, or suppose. **5** *intr.* **a** form a judgement. **b** act as judge. □ **judgeship** *n.* [Middle English via Old French *juge* (*n.*), *juger* (*v.*) from Latin *judex judicis*, from *jus* 'law' + *-dicus* 'speaking']

Judge Advocate General *n.* an officer in supreme control of the courts martial in the armed forces.

judgement /'dʒʌdʒm(ə)nt/ *n.* (also **judgment**) **1** the critical faculty; discernment (*an error of judgement*). **2** good sense. **3** an opinion or estimate (*in my judgement*). **4** the sentence of a court of justice; a decision by a judge. **5** often *joc.* a misfortune viewed as a deserved recompense (*it is a judgement on you for getting up late*). **6** criticism. □ **against one's better judgement** contrary to what one really feels to be advisable. [Middle English from Old French *jugement* (as JUDGE)]

judgemental /dʒʌdʒ'mɛnt(ə)l/ *adj.* (also **judgmental**) **1** of or concerning or by way of judgement. **2** condemning, critical. □ **judgementally** *adv.*

judgement by default *n.* judgement given for the plaintiff on the defendant's failure to plead.

Judgement Day *n.* the day on which the Last Judgement is believed to take place.

judgement-seat *n.* a judge's seat; a tribunal.

judge's marshal see MARSHAL *n.* 4.

Judges' Rules *n.pl. Brit.* rules regarding the admissibility of an accused's statements as evidence.

judicature /'dʒu:dɪkətʃə, dʒʊ'dɪk-/ *n.* **1** the administration of justice. **2** a judge's office or term of office. **3** judges collectively. **4** a court of justice. [medieval Latin *judicatura* from Latin *judicare* 'to judge']

judicial /dʒʊ'dɪʃ(ə)l/ *adj.* **1** of, done by, or proper to a court of law. **2** having the function of judgement (*a judicial assembly*). **3** of or proper to a judge. **4** expressing a judgement; critical. **5** impartial. **6** regarded as a divine judgement. □ **judicially** *adv.* [Middle English from Latin *judicialis*, via *judicium* 'judgement' from *judex* JUDGE]

judicial factor *n. Sc.* an official receiver.

judicial separation see SEPARATION 2.

judiciary /dʒʊ'dɪʃ(ə)ri/ *n.* (*pl.* **-ies**) the judges of a state collectively. [Latin *judiciarius* (as JUDICIAL)]

judicious /dʒʊ'dɪʃəs/ *adj.* **1** sensible, prudent. **2** sound in discernment and judgement. □ **judiciously** *adv.* **judiciousness** *n.* [French *judicieux* from Latin *judicium* (as JUDICIAL)]

judo /'dʒu:dəʊ/ *n.* a sport of unarmed combat derived from ju-jitsu. □ **judoist** *n.* [Japanese, from *jū* 'gentle' + *dō* 'way']

judoka /'dʒu:dəʊkə/ *n.* a person who practises or is an expert in judo. [Japanese, from JUDO + *-ka* 'person, profession']

Judy /'dʒu:di/ *n.* (*pl.* **-ies**) **1** see PUNCH[4] 1. **2** (also **judy**) *Brit. slang* a woman. [pet form of the name *Judith*]

jug /dʒʌg/ *n. & v.* ● *n.* **1** *Brit.* **a** a deep vessel for holding liquids, with a handle and often with a spout or lip shaped for pouring. **b** the contents of this; a jugful. **2** *US* a large vessel, esp. for liquids, with a narrow mouth. **3** *slang* prison. **4** (in *pl.*) *N. Amer. coarse slang* a woman's breasts. ● *v.tr.* (**jugged**, **jugging**) **1** (usu. as **jugged** *adj.*) stew or boil (a hare or rabbit) in a covered vessel. **2** *slang* imprison. □ **jugful** *n.* (*pl.* **-fuls**). [perhaps from *Jug*, pet form of the name *Joan* etc.]

Jugendstil /'ju:gənt-ʃti:l/ *n.* the German name for ART NOUVEAU. [German, from *Jugend* 'youth' + *Stil* 'style']

juggernaut /'dʒʌgənɔ:t/ *n.* **1** esp. *Brit.* a large heavy motor vehicle, esp. an articulated lorry. **2** a huge or overwhelming force or object. **3** (**Juggernaut**) an institution or notion to which persons blindly sacrifice themselves or others. [Hindi *Jagannath* from Sanskrit *Jagannātha* = lord of the world: name of an image of

Krishna in Hindu mythology, carried in procession on a huge cart under which devotees are said to have formerly thrown themselves]

juggins /ˈdʒʌgɪnz/ *n. Brit. slang* a simpleton. [perhaps from proper name *Juggins* (as JUG): cf. MUGGINS]

juggle /ˈdʒʌg(ə)l/ *v. & n.* ● *v.* **1 a** *intr.* (often foll. by *with*) perform feats of dexterity, esp. by tossing objects in the air and catching them, keeping several in the air at the same time. **b** *tr.* perform such feats with. **2** *tr.* continue to deal with (several activities) at once, esp. with ingenuity. **3** *intr. & tr.* (foll. by *with*) **a** deceive or cheat. **b** misrepresent (facts). **c** rearrange adroitly. ● *n.* **1** a piece of juggling. **2** a fraud. [Middle English, back-formation from JUGGLER, or via Old French *jogler, jugler* from Latin *joculari* 'jest' from *joculus*, diminutive of *jocus* 'jest']

juggler /ˈdʒʌglə/ *n.* **1 a** a person who juggles. **b** a conjuror. **2** a trickster or impostor. □ **jugglery** *n.* [Middle English via Old French *jouglere -eor* from Latin *joculator -oris* (as JUGGLE)]

Jugoslav var. of YUGOSLAV.

jugular /ˈdʒʌgjʊlə/ *adj. & n.* ● *adj.* **1** of the neck or throat. **2** (of fish) having ventral fins in front of the pectoral fins. ● *n.* = JUGULAR VEIN. [Late Latin *jugularis* from Latin *jugulum* 'collarbone, throat', diminutive of *jugum* YOKE]

jugular vein *n.* any of several large veins of the neck which carry blood from the head.

jugulate /ˈdʒʌgjʊleɪt/ *v.tr.* **1** kill by cutting the throat. **2** arrest the course of (a disease etc.) by a powerful remedy. [Latin *jugulare* from *jugulum* (as JUGULAR)]

juice /dʒuːs/ *n. & v.* ● *n.* **1** the liquid part of vegetables or fruits. **2** the fluid part of an animal body or substance, esp. a secretion (*gastric juice*). **3** the essence or spirit of anything. **4** *colloq.* petrol or electricity as a source of power. ● *v.tr.* extract the juice from (a fruit etc.). □ **juiceless** *adj.* [Middle English via Old French *jus* from Latin *jus* 'broth, juice']

juicy /ˈdʒuːsi/ *adj.* (**juicier**, **juiciest**) **1** full of juice; succulent. **2** *colloq.* substantial or interesting; racy, scandalous. **3** *colloq.* profitable. □ **juicily** *adv.* **juiciness** *n.*

ju-jitsu /dʒuːˈdʒɪtsuː/ *n.* (also **jiu-jitsu**, **ju-jutsu**) a Japanese system of unarmed combat and physical training. [Japanese *jūjutsu*, from *jū* 'gentle' + *jutsu* 'skill']

ju-ju /ˈdʒuːdʒuː/ *n.* **1** a charm or fetish of some W. African peoples. **2** a supernatural power attributed to this. [perhaps from French *joujou* 'toy']

jujube /ˈdʒuːdʒuːb/ *n.* **1 a** any plant of the genus *Zizyphus* bearing edible acidic berry-like fruits. **b** this fruit. **2** a lozenge of gelatin etc. flavoured with or imitating this. [French *jujube* or medieval Latin *jujuba*, ultimately from Greek *zizuphon*]

jukebox /ˈdʒuːkbɒks/ *n.* a machine that automatically plays a selected musical recording when a coin is inserted. [Gullah *juke* 'disorderly' + BOX[1]]

Jul. *abbr.* July.

julep /ˈdʒuːlɛp/ *n.* **1 a** a sweet drink, esp. as a vehicle for medicine. **b** a medicated drink as a mild stimulant etc. **2** *US* iced and flavoured spirits and water (*mint julep*). [Middle English via Old French and Arabic *julāb* from Persian *gulāb*, from *gul* 'rose' + *āb* 'water']

Julian /ˈdʒuːlɪən/ *adj.* of or associated with Julius Caesar. [Latin *Julianus* from *Julius*]

Julian calendar *n.* a calendar introduced by Julius Caesar, in which the year consisted of 365 days, every fourth year having 366 (cf. GREGORIAN CALENDAR).

julienne /dʒuːlɪˈɛn/ *n. & adj.* ● *n.* foodstuff, esp. vegetables, cut into short thin strips. ● *adj.* cut into thin strips. [French, from the name *Jules* or *Julien*]

Juliet cap /ˈdʒuːlɪət/ *n.* a small net ornamental cap worn by brides etc. [the heroine of Shakespeare's *Romeo and Juliet*]

July /dʒʊˈlʌɪ/ *n.* (*pl.* **Julys**) the seventh month of the year. [Middle English via Anglo-French *julie* from Latin *Julius* (*mensis* 'month'), named after Julius Caesar]

jumble /ˈdʒʌmb(ə)l/ *v. & n.* ● *v.* **1** *tr.* (often foll. by *up*) confuse; mix up. **2** *intr.* move about in disorder. ● *n.* **1** a confused state or heap; a muddle. **2** *Brit.* articles collected for a jumble sale. □ **jumbly** *adj.* [probably imitative]

jumble sale *n. Brit.* a sale of miscellaneous usu. second-hand articles, esp. for charity.

jumbo /ˈdʒʌmbəʊ/ *n. & adj. colloq.* ● *n.* (*pl.* **-os**) **1** a large animal (esp. an elephant), person, or thing. **2** (in full **jumbo jet**) a large airliner with capacity for several hundred passengers (usu. applied specifically to the Boeing 747). ● *adj.* **1** very large of its kind. **2** extra large (*jumbo packet*). [19th c. (originally of a person): origin unknown: popularized as the name of a zoo elephant sold in 1882]

jumbuck /ˈdʒʌmbʌk/ *n. Austral. colloq.* a sheep. [19th c. Australian pidgin: origin unknown]

jump /dʒʌmp/ *v. & n.* ● *v.* **1** *intr.* move off the ground or other surface (usu. upward, at least initially) by sudden muscular effort in the legs. **2** *intr.* (often foll. by *up, from, in, out,* etc.) move suddenly or hastily in a specified way (*we jumped into the car*). **3** *intr.* give a sudden bodily movement from shock or excitement etc. **4** *intr.* undergo a rapid change, esp. an advance in status. **5** *intr.* (often foll. by *about*) change or move rapidly from one idea or subject to another. **6 a** *intr.* rise or increase suddenly (*prices jumped*). **b** *tr.* cause to do this. **7** *tr.* **a** pass over (an obstacle, barrier, etc.) by jumping. **b** move or pass over (an intervening thing) to a point beyond. **8** *tr.* skip or pass over (a passage in a book etc.). **9** *tr.* cause (a thing, or an animal, esp. a horse) to jump. **10** *intr.* (foll. by *to, at*) reach a conclusion hastily. **11** *tr.* (of a train) leave (the rails) owing to a fault or error. **12** *tr.* ignore and pass (a red traffic light etc.). **13** *tr.* get on or off (a train etc.) quickly, esp. illegally or dangerously. **14** *tr.* pounce on or attack (a person) unexpectedly. **15** *tr.* take summary possession of (a piece of land) after alleged abandonment or forfeiture by the former occupant. ● *n.* **1** the act or an instance of jumping. **2 a** a sudden bodily movement caused by shock or excitement. **b** (**the jumps**) *colloq.* extreme nervousness or anxiety. **3** an abrupt rise in amount, price, value, status, etc. **4** an obstacle to be jumped, esp. by a horse. **5 a** a sudden transition. **b** a gap in a series, logical sequence, etc. □ **get** (or **have**) **the jump on** *colloq.* get (or have) an advantage over (a person) by prompt action. **jump at** accept eagerly. **jump bail** see BAIL[1]. **jump down a person's throat** *colloq.* reprimand or contradict a person fiercely. **jump the gun** see GUN. **jump on** *colloq.* attack or criticize severely and without warning. **jump out of one's skin** *colloq.* be extremely startled. **jump the queue 1** push forward out of one's turn. **2** take unfair precedence over others. **jump ship** (of a sailor) desert. **jump to it** *Brit. colloq.* act promptly and energetically. **one jump ahead** one stage further on than a rival etc. **on the jump** *colloq.* on the move; in a hurry. □ **jumpable** *adj.* [16th c.: probably imitative of the sound of feet coming to the ground]

jumped-up *adj. Brit. colloq.* upstart; presumptuously arrogant.

jumper[1] /ˈdʒʌmpə/ *n.* **1** *Brit.* a knitted pullover. **2** a loose outer jacket of canvas etc. worn by sailors. **3** *N. Amer.* a pinafore dress. [probably from (17th-c., now dialect) *jump* 'short coat', perhaps via French *jupe* from Arabic *jubba*]

jumper[2] /ˈdʒʌmpə/ *n.* **1** a person or animal that jumps. **2** *Electr.* a short wire used to shorten a circuit or close it temporarily. **3** a rope made fast to keep a yard, mast, etc., from jumping. **4** a heavy chisel-ended iron bar for drilling blast-holes.

jumper cable *n.* esp. *US* a jump lead.

jumping bean /'dʒʌmpɪŋ/ *n.* the seed of a Mexican plant that jumps with the movement of a moth larva inside.

jumping jack /'dʒʌmpɪŋ/ *n.* **1** *Brit.* a small firework producing repeated explosions. **2** a toy figure of a man, with movable limbs.

jumping-off place *n.* (also **jumping-off point**) the place or point of starting.

jump jet *n.* a jet aircraft that can take off and land vertically.

jump lead *n. Brit.* each of a pair of cables for conveying current from the battery of a motor vehicle to boost (or recharge) another.

jump-off *n.* a deciding round in a showjumping competition.

jump rope *n. N. Amer.* a skipping rope.

jump seat *n. US* a folding extra seat in a motor vehicle.

jump-start *v. & n.* ● *v.tr.* start (a motor vehicle) with jump leads. ● *n.* the action of jump-starting.

jumpsuit /'dʒʌmpsu:t, -sju:t/ *n.* a one-piece garment for the whole body, of a kind originally worn by paratroopers.

jumpy /'dʒʌmpi/ *adj.* (**jumpier, jumpiest**) **1** nervous; easily startled. **2** making sudden movements, esp. of nervous excitement. □ **jumpily** *adv.* **jumpiness** *n.*

Jun. *abbr.* **1** June. **2** Junior.

junco /'dʒʌŋkəʊ/ *n.* (*pl.* **-os** or **-oes**) any small American bunting of the genus *Junco*. [originally = reed-bunting: Spanish, from Latin *juncus* 'rush plant']

junction /'dʒʌŋ(k)ʃ(ə)n/ *n.* **1** a point at which two or more things are joined. **2** a place where two or more railway lines or roads meet, unite, or cross. **3** the act or an instance of joining. **4** *Electronics* a region of transition in a semiconductor between regions where conduction is mainly by electrons and regions where it is mainly by holes. [Latin *junctio* (as JOIN)]

junction box *n.* a box containing a junction of electric cables etc.

juncture /'dʒʌŋ(k)tʃə/ *n.* **1** a critical convergence of events; a critical point of time (*at this juncture*). **2** a place where things join. **3** an act of joining. [Middle English from Latin *junctura* (as JOIN)]

June /dʒu:n/ *n.* the sixth month of the year. [Middle English via Old French *juin* from Latin *Junius*, variant of *Junonius* 'sacred to Juno']

June bug *n.* any of various beetles, esp. N. American chafers, appearing in June.

Jungian /'jʊŋɪən/ *adj. & n.* ● *adj.* of the Swiss psychologist Carl Jung (d. 1961) or his system of analytical psychology. ● *n.* a supporter of Jung or of his system.

jungle /'dʒʌŋg(ə)l/ *n.* **1 a** land overgrown with underwood or tangled vegetation, esp. in the tropics. **b** an area of such land. **2** a wild tangled mass. **3** a place of bewildering complexity or confusion, or of a struggle for survival (*blackboard jungle*). **4** (in full **jungle music**) a type of fast dance music with an exaggerated bass line, influenced by reggae and soul. □ **jungled** *adj.* **jungly** *adj.* [Hindi *jangal* from Sanskrit *jangala* 'desert, forest']

jungle fever *n.* a severe form of malaria.

junior /'dʒu:nɪə/ *adj. & n.* ● *adj.* **1** less advanced in age. **2** (foll. by *to*) inferior in age, standing, or position. **3** the younger (esp. appended to a name for distinction from an older person of the same name). **4** of less or least standing; of the lower or lowest position (*junior partner*). **5** *Brit.* (of a school) having pupils in a younger age range, usu. 7–11. **6** *N. Amer.* of the year before the final year at university, high school, etc. ● *n.* **1** a junior person. **2** one's inferior in length of service etc. **3** a junior student. **4** a barrister who is not a QC. **5** *US colloq.* a young male child, esp. in relation to his family. □ **juniority** /-'ɒrɪti/ *n.* [Latin, comparative of *juvenis* 'young']

junior college *n. US* a college offering a two-year course esp. in preparation for completion at senior college.

junior common room *n.* (also **junior combination room**) *Brit.* **1** a room for social use by the junior members of a college. **2** the junior members collectively.

junior high school *n. N. Amer.* a school intermediate between elementary school and high school.

junior lightweight *n.* **1** a weight in professional boxing of 57.1–59 kg. **2** a professional boxer of this weight.

junior management *n.* **1** the lowest level of management in an organization. **2** the managers at this level usu. with supervisory rather than full management responsibility (cf. MIDDLE MANAGEMENT, SENIOR MANAGEMENT).

junior middleweight *n.* **1** a weight in professional boxing of 66.7–69.8 kg. **2** a professional boxer of this weight.

junior technician *n.* an RAF rank next above senior aircraftman.

junior welterweight *n.* **1** a weight in professional boxing of 61.2–63.5 kg. **2** a professional boxer of this weight.

juniper /'dʒu:nɪpə/ *n.* any evergreen shrub or tree of the genus *Juniperus*, esp. *J. communis* with prickly leaves and dark purple berries. [Middle English from Latin *juniperus*]

junk[1] /dʒʌŋk/ *n. & v.* ● *n.* **1** discarded articles; rubbish. **2** anything regarded as of little value. **3** *slang* a narcotic drug, esp. heroin. **4** old cables or ropes cut up for oakum etc. **5** *Brit.* a lump or chunk. **6** *Naut.* hard salt meat. **7** a lump of fibrous tissue in a sperm whale's head, containing spermaceti. ● *v.tr.* discard as junk. [Middle English: origin unknown]

junk[2] /dʒʌŋk/ *n.* a flat-bottomed sailing vessel used in the China seas, with a prominent stem and lugsails. [obsolete French *juncque*, Portuguese *junco*, or Dutch *jonk*, from Javanese *djong*]

junk bond *n.* a high-yielding high-risk security, esp. one issued to finance a take-over.

junker /'jʊŋkə/ *n. hist.* **1** a young German nobleman. **2** a member of an exclusive Prussian aristocratic party. □ **junkerdom** *n.* [German, earlier *Junkher*, from Old High German (as YOUNG, HERR)]

junket /'dʒʌŋkɪt/ *n. & v.* ● *n.* **1** a dish of sweetened and flavoured curds, often served with fruit or cream. **2** a feast. **3** a pleasure outing. **4** *N. Amer.* an official's tour at public expense. ● *v.intr.* (**junketed, junketing**) feast, picnic. □ **junketing** *n.* [Middle English *jonket* via Old French *jonquette* 'rush-basket' (used to carry junket), from *jonc* 'rush', from Latin *juncus*]

junk food *n.* food with low nutritional value.

junkie /'dʒʌŋki/ *n. slang* a drug addict.

junk mail *n.* unsolicited advertising matter sent by post.

junk shop *n.* a shop selling cheap second-hand goods or antiques.

junkyard /'dʒʌŋkjɑ:d/ *n.* = SCRAPYARD.

Junr. *abbr.* Junior.

junta /'dʒʌntə, 'hʊ-/ *n.* **1 a** a political or military clique or faction taking power after a revolution or *coup d'état*. **b** a secretive group; a cabal. **2** a deliberative or administrative council in Spain or Portugal. [Spanish & Portuguese from Latin *juncta*, fem. past part. of *jungere* JOIN]

Jupiter /'dʒu:pɪtə/ *n.* the largest planet of the solar system, orbiting the sun between Mars and Saturn. [Middle English via Latin *Jupiter*, the king of the gods, from Old Latin *Jovis pater*, literally 'Jove father']

jural /'dʒʊər(ə)l/ *adj.* **1** of law. **2** of rights and obligations. [Latin *jus juris* 'law, right']

Jurassic /dʒʊ'rasɪk/ *adj. & n. Geol.* ● *adj.* of or relating to the second period of the Mesozoic era with evidence of many large dinosaurs, the first birds (including

Archaeopteryx), and mammals. Cf. Appendix X. ● *n.* this era or system. [French *jurassique* from *Jura* (Mountains): cf. *Triassic*]

jurat[1] /'dʒʊərat/ *n. Brit.* **1** a municipal officer (esp. of the Cinque Ports) holding a position similar to that of an alderman. **2** an honorary judge or magistrate in the Channel Islands. [Middle English from medieval Latin *juratus* (literally 'sworn man'), past part. of Latin *jurare* 'swear']

jurat[2] /'dʒʊərat/ *n.* a statement of the circumstances in which an affidavit was made. [Latin *juratum*, neut. past part. (as JURAT[1])]

juridical /dʒʊ'rɪdɪk(ə)l/ *adj.* **1** of judicial proceedings. **2** relating to the law. □ **juridically** *adv.* [Latin *juridicus*, from *jus juris* 'law' + *-dicus* 'saying' from *dicere* 'say']

juried /'dʒʊərɪd/ *adj. N. Amer.* judged or selected by a jury or panel.

jurisconsult /ˌdʒʊərɪskən'sʌlt/ *n.* a person learned in law; a jurist. [Latin *jurisconsultus*, from *jus juris* 'law' + *consultus* 'skilled': see CONSULT]

jurisdiction /dʒʊərɪs'dɪkʃ(ə)n/ *n.* **1** (often foll. by *over*, *of*) the administration of justice. **2 a** legal or other authority. **b** the extent of this; the territory it extends over. □ **jurisdictional** *adj.* [Middle English *jurisdiccioun* from Old French *jurediction*, *juridiction*, Latin *jurisdictio*, from *jus juris* 'law' + *dictio* DICTION]

jurisprudence /dʒʊərɪs'pruːd(ə)ns/ *n.* **1** the science or philosophy of law. **2** skill in law. □ **jurisprudent** *adj. & n.* **jurisprudential** /-'dɛnʃ(ə)l/ *adj.* [Late Latin *jurisprudentia*, from Latin *jus juris* 'law' + *prudentia* 'knowledge': see PRUDENT]

jurist /'dʒʊərɪst/ *n.* **1** an expert in law. **2** a legal writer. **3** *US* **a** a lawyer. **b** a judge. □ **juristic** /-'rɪstɪk/ *adj.* **juristical** /-'rɪstɪk(ə)l/ *adj.* [French *juriste* or medieval Latin *jurista* from *jus juris* 'law']

juror /'dʒʊərə/ *n.* **1** a member of a jury. **2** a person who takes an oath (cf. NONJUROR). [Middle English via Anglo-French *jurour*, Old French *jureor* from Latin *jurator -oris*, from *jurare jurat-* 'swear']

jury /'dʒʊəri/ *n.* (*pl.* **-ies**) **1** a body of usu. twelve persons sworn to render a verdict on the basis of evidence submitted to them in a court of justice. **2** a body of persons selected to award prizes in a competition. □ **the jury is** (or **is still**) **out** (often foll. by *on*) a decision has not yet been reached. [Middle English via Anglo-French and Old French *juree* 'oath, inquiry' from *jurata*, fem. past part. of Latin *jurare* 'swear']

jury box *n.* the enclosure for the jury in a law court.

juryman /'dʒʊərɪmən/ *n.* (*pl.* **-men**) a member of a jury.

jury-rigged *adj.* **1** *Naut.* having temporary makeshift rigging. **2** makeshift, improvised. [perhaps ultimately from Old French *ajurie* 'aid']

jurywoman /'dʒʊərɪwʊmən/ *n.* (*pl.* **-women**) a female member of a jury.

jussive /'dʒʌsɪv/ *adj. Gram.* expressing a command. [Latin *jubēre juss-* 'command']

just /dʒʌst/ *adj. & adv.* ● *adj.* **1** acting or done in accordance with what is morally right or fair. **2** (of treatment etc.) deserved (*a just reward*). **3** (of feelings, opinions, etc.) well-grounded (*just resentment*). **4** right in amount etc.; proper. ● *adv.* **1** exactly (*just what I need*). **2** exactly or nearly at this or that moment; a little time ago (*I have just seen them*). **3** *colloq.* simply, merely (*we were just good friends*; *it just doesn't make sense*). **4** barely; no more than (*I just managed it*; *just a minute*). **5** *colloq.* positively (*it is just splendid*). **6** quite (*not just yet*; *it is just as well that I checked*). **7** *colloq.* really, indeed (*won't I just tell him!*). **8** in questions, seeking precise information (*just how did you manage?*). □ **just about** *colloq.* almost exactly; almost completely. **just in case** as a precaution. **just now 1** at this moment. **2** a little time ago. **just so 1** exactly arranged (*they like everything just so*). **2** it is exactly as you say. □ **justly** *adv.* **justness** *n.* [Middle English via Old French *juste* from Latin *justus*, from *jus* 'right']

justice /'dʒʌstɪs/ *n.* **1** just conduct. **2** fairness. **3** the exercise of authority in the maintenance of right. **4** judicial proceedings (*was duly brought to justice*; *the Court of Justice*). **5 a** a magistrate. **b** a judge, esp. (in England) of the Supreme Court of Judicature or (in the US) of the US Supreme Court or a state Supreme Court. □ **do justice to** treat fairly or appropriately; show due appreciation of. **do oneself justice** perform in a manner worthy of one's abilities. **in justice to** out of fairness to. **Mr** (or **Mrs**) **Justice** *Brit.* a form of address or reference to a Supreme Court Judge. **with justice** reasonably. □ **justiceship** *n.* (in sense 5). [Middle English via Old French from Latin *justitia* (as JUST)]

Justice of the Peace *n.* a lay magistrate appointed to preserve the peace in a county, town, etc., hear minor cases, grant licences, etc.

justiciable /dʒʌ'stɪʃəb(ə)l/ *adj.* liable to legal consideration. [Old French from *justicier* 'bring to trial', from medieval Latin *justitiare* (as JUSTICE)]

justiciary /dʒʌ'stɪʃ(ə)ri/ *n. & adj.* ● *n.* (*pl.* **-ies**) an administrator of justice. ● *adj.* of the administration of justice. [medieval Latin *justitiarius* from Latin *justitia*: see JUSTICE]

justifiable /'dʒʌstɪfʌɪəb(ə)l/ *adj.* that can be justified or defended. □ **justifiability** /-'bɪlɪti/ *n.* **justifiableness** *n.* **justifiably** *adv.* [French from *justifier*: see JUSTIFY]

justifiable homicide *n.* killing regarded as lawful and without criminal guilt, esp. the execution of a death sentence.

justify /'dʒʌstɪfʌɪ/ *v.tr.* (**-ies**, **-ied**) **1** show the justice or rightness of (a person, act, etc.). **2** demonstrate the correctness of (an assertion etc.). **3** adduce adequate grounds for (conduct, a claim, etc.). **4 a** (esp. in *passive*) (of circumstances) be such as to justify. **b** vindicate. **5** (as **justified** *adj.*) just, right (*am justified in assuming*). **6** *Theol.* declare (a person) righteous. **7** *Printing* adjust (a line of type) to fill a space evenly. □ **justification** /-fɪ'keɪʃ(ə)n/ *n.* **justificatory** /-fɪkeɪt(ə)ri, -fɪ'keɪt(ə)ri/ *adj.* **justifier** *n.* [Middle English via French *justifier* and Late Latin *justificare* 'do justice to' from Latin *justus* JUST]

just-in-time *n.* (often *attrib.*) **1** a manufacturing system in which production is operated in very small batches. **2** a factory system in which materials are delivered immediately before they are required in order to minimize storage costs.

jut /dʒʌt/ *v. & n.* ● *v.intr.* (**jutted**, **jutting**) (often foll. by *out*, *into*, *through*, etc.) protrude, project. ● *n.* a projection; a protruding point. [variant of JET[1]]

Jute /dʒuːt/ *n.* a member of a Germanic people that settled in Britain in the 5th–6th c. □ **Jutish** *adj.* [representing medieval Latin *Jutae*, *Juti*, in Old English *Eotas*, *Iotas* = Icelandic *Iótar* 'people of Jutland' in Denmark]

jute /dʒuːt/ *n.* **1** a rough fibre made from the bark of a jute plant, used for making twine and rope, and woven into sacking, mats, etc. **2** an Asian plant of the genus *Corchorus* yielding this fibre. [Bengali *jhōṭo* from Sanskrit *jūṭa* = *jaṭā* 'braid of hair']

juvenescence /dʒuːvə'nɛs(ə)ns/ *n.* **1** youth. **2** the transition from infancy to youth. □ **juvenescent** *adj.* [Latin *juvenescere* 'reach the age of youth' from *juvenis* 'young']

juvenile /'dʒuːvənʌɪl/ *adj. & n.* ● *adj.* **1 a** young, youthful. **b** of or for young persons. **2** suited to or characteristic of youth. **3** often *derog.* immature (*behaving in a very juvenile way*). ● *n.* **1** a young person. **2** *Commerce* a book intended for young people. **3** an actor playing the part of a youthful person. □ **juvenilely** *adv.* **juvenility** /-'nɪlɪti/ *n.* [Latin *juvenilis* from *juvenis* 'young']

juvenile court *n.* a court for the trial of children under 17 or (in the US) 18.

juvenile delinquency *n.* the (habitual) committing of offences by a person or persons below the age of legal responsibility. □ **juvenile deliquent** *n.*

juvenilia /dʒuːvəˈnɪlɪə/ *n.pl.* works produced by an author or artist in youth. [Latin, neut. pl. of *juvenilis* (as JUVENILE)]

juxtapose /dʒʌkstəˈpəʊz/ *v.tr.* **1** place (things) side by side. **2** (foll. by *to, with*) place (a thing) beside another. □ **juxtaposition** /-pəˈzɪʃ(ə)n/ *n.* **juxtapositional** /-pəˈzɪʃ(ə)n(ə)l/ *adj.* [French *juxtaposer* from Latin *juxta* 'next': see POSE[1]]

K[1] /keɪ/ *n.* (also **k**) (*pl.* **Ks** or **K's**) the eleventh letter of the alphabet.

K[2] *abbr.* (also **K.**) **1** King, King's. **2** Köchel (catalogue of Mozart's works). **3** (also **k**) (prec. by a numeral) **a** *Computing* a unit of 1,024 (i.e. 2^{10}) bytes or bits, or loosely 1,000. **b** thousand. [sense 3 as abbreviation of KILO-]

K[3] *symb.* **1** *Chem.* the element potassium. **2** kelvin(s). [sense 1 from modern Latin *kalium*]

k[1] *abbr.* (also **k.**) knot(s).

k[2] *symb.* **1** kilo-. **2** *Math.* a constant.

Kaaba /'kɑ:əbə/ *n.* (also **Caaba**) a sacred building at Mecca, the Muslim Holy of Holies containing the sacred black stone. [Arabic *Ka'ba*]

kabbala **1** var. of CABBALA 1. **2** (**Kabbala**) var. of KABBALAH.

Kabbalah /kə'bɑ:lə, 'kabələ/ *n.* (also **Kabbala, Cabbala, Cabala**) the Jewish mystical tradition. □ **Kabbalism** *n.* **Kabbalist** *n.* **Kabbalistic** *adj.* [medieval Latin *cab(b)ala* from Rabbinical Hebrew *ḳabbālâ* 'tradition']

kabuki /kə'bu:ki/ *n.* a form of popular traditional Japanese drama with highly stylized song, acted by males only. [Japanese, from *ka* 'song' + *bu* 'dance' + *ki* 'art']

kachina /kə'tʃi:nə/ *n.* **1** a Pueblo Indian ancestral spirit. **2** (in full **kachina dancer**) a person who represents a kachina in ceremonial dances. [Pueblo Indian word, = supernatural]

kachina doll *n.* a wooden doll representing a kachina.

kadaitcha var. of KURDAITCHA.

Kaddish /'kadɪʃ/ *n.* *Judaism* **1** a Jewish mourner's prayer. **2** a doxology in the synagogue service. [Aramaic *ḳaddîš* 'holy']

kadi var. of CADI.

Kaffir /'kafə/ *n.* **1 a** *hist.* a member of the Xhosa-speaking peoples of S. Africa. **b** the language of these peoples. **2** *S.Afr. offens.* any black African (now an actionable insult). [originally = a non-Muslim: Arabic *kāfir* 'infidel' from *kafara* 'not believe']

kaffiyeh var. of KEFFIYEH.

Kafir /'kafə/ *n.* a native of the Hindu Kush mountains of NE Afghanistan. [formed as KAFFIR]

Kafkaesque /kafkə'esk/ *adj.* (of a situation, atmosphere, etc.) impenetrably oppressive, nightmarish, in a manner characteristic of the fictional world of Franz Kafka, German-speaking novelist (d. 1924).

kaftan /'kaftan/ *n.* (also **caftan**) **1** a long usu. belted tunic worn by men in countries of the Near East. **2 a** a woman's long loose dress. **b** a loose shirt or top. [Turkish *ḳafṭān*, partly through French *cafetan*]

kai /kʌɪ/ *n.* *NZ colloq.* food. [Maori]

kail var. of KALE.

kailyard var. of KALEYARD.

kaiser /'kʌɪzə/ *n.* *hist.* an emperor, esp. the German Emperor, the Emperor of Austria, or the head of the Holy Roman Empire. □ **kaisership** *n.* [in modern English from German *Kaiser* and Dutch *keizer*; in Middle English from Old English *cāsere*, from Germanic adoption (through Greek *kaisar*) of Latin *Caesar*: see CAESAR]

kaizen /kʌɪ'zɛn/ *n.* a Japanese business philosophy of continuous improvement of working practices, personal efficiency, etc. [Japanese, = improvement]

kaka /'kɑ:kɑ:/ *n.* (*pl.* **kakas**) a large New Zealand parrot, *Nestor meridionalis*, with olive-brown plumage. [Maori]

kakapo /'kɑ:kəpəʊ/ *n.* (*pl.* **-os**) an owl-like flightless New Zealand parrot, *Strigops habroptilus*. [Maori, = night kaka]

kakemono /kɑ:kɪ'məʊnəʊ, kakɪ-/ *n.* (*pl.* **-os**) a vertical Japanese unframed wall-picture, usu. painted or inscribed on paper or silk and mounted on rollers. [Japanese, from *kake-* 'hang' + *mono* 'thing']

kala-azar /kɑ:lə-ə'zɑ:/ *n.* a tropical disease caused by the parasitic protozoan *Leishmania donovani*, which is transmitted to man by sandflies. [Assamese, from *kālā* 'black' + *āzār* 'disease']

kalanchoe /kalən'kəʊi/ *n.* a succulent plant of the mainly African genus *Kalanchoe*, which includes several house plants, some producing miniature plants from the edges of the leaves. [modern Latin from French, ultimately from Chinese *gāláncài*]

Kalashnikov /kə'laʃnɪkɒf, -'lɑ:ʃ-/ *n.* a type of rifle or sub-machine gun made in Russia (also *attrib.*: *Kalashnikov rifle*). [named after M.T. *Kalashnikov* (b. 1919), its Russian developer]

kale /keɪl/ *n.* (also **kail**) **1** a variety of cabbage which forms no compact head. See also CURLY KALE. **2** *N. Amer. slang* money. [Middle English, northern form of COLE]

kaleidoscope /kə'lʌɪdəskəʊp/ *n.* **1** a tube containing mirrors and pieces of coloured glass or paper, whose reflections produce changing patterns when the tube is rotated. **2** a constantly changing group of bright or interesting objects. □ **kaleidoscopic** /-'skɒpɪk/ *adj.* **kaleidoscopically** /-'skɒpɪk(ə)li/ *adv.* [Greek *kalos* 'beautiful' + *eidos* 'form' + -SCOPE]

kalends var. of CALENDS.

kaleyard /'keɪljɑ:d/ *n.* (also **kailyard**) *Sc.* a kitchen garden. [KALE + YARD[2]]

kaleyard school *n.* a group of 19th-c. fiction writers including J. M. Barrie, who described local town life in Scotland in a romantic vein and with much use of the vernacular.

kali /'keɪlʌɪ, 'kali/ *n.* a glasswort, *Salsola kali*, with fleshy jointed stems, having a high soda content. [Arabic *kalī* ALKALI]

kalmia /'kalmɪə/ *n.* a N. American evergreen shrub of the genus *Kalmia*, esp. *K. latifolia*, with showy pink flowers. [modern Latin, named after P. *Kalm*, Swedish botanist d. 1779]

Kalmuck /'kalmʌk/ *n.* & *adj.* (also **Kalmyk**) ● *n.* (*pl.* same or **Kalmucks** or **Kalmyks**) **1** a member of a Buddhist Mongolian people living in the west of the former USSR. **2** the Ural-Altaic language of this people. ● *adj.* of or relating to this people or their language. [Russian *kalmyk*]

kalong /'kɑ:lɒŋ/ *n.* any of various fruit-eating bats of the family Pteropodidae, esp. *Pteropus edulis*; a flying fox. [Malay]

kalpa /'kalpə/ *n.* *Hinduism* & *Buddhism* the period between the beginning and the end of the world considered as the day of Brahma (4,320 million human years). [Sanskrit]

Kama /'kɑ:mə/ *n.* the Hindu god of love. [Sanskrit]

Kama Sutra /'su:trə/ *n.* an ancient Sanskrit treatise on the art of erotic love.

kame /keɪm/ *n.* a short ridge of sand and gravel deposited from the water of a melted glacier. [Scots form of COMB]

kamikaze /kamɪ'kɑːzi/ *n. & adj.* ● *n. hist.* **1** a Japanese aircraft loaded with explosives and deliberately crashed by its pilot on its target. **2** the pilot of such an aircraft. ● *adj.* **1** of or relating to a kamikaze. **2** reckless, dangerous, potentially self-destructive. [Japanese, from *kami* 'divinity' + *kaze* 'wind']

Kamilaroi /kə'mɪlərɔɪ/ *n.* an Aboriginal language of New South Wales and S. Queensland, now extinct.

kampong /kam'pɒŋ, 'kampɒŋ/ *n.* a Malayan enclosure or village. [Malay: cf. COMPOUND²]

Kampuchean /kampʊ'tʃiːən/ *n. & adj.* = CAMBODIAN. [*Kampuchea*, native name for Cambodia]

■ **Usage** The term *Kampuchean* was in official use from 1976 to 1989.

Kan. *abbr.* Kansas.

kana /'kɑːnə/ *n.* any of various Japanese syllabaries. [Japanese]

kanaka /kə'nakə, -'nɑːkə/ *n.* a South Sea Islander, esp. *hist.* one employed in forced labour in Australia. [Hawaiian, = man]

Kanarese /kanə'riːz/ *n. & adj.* (also **Canarese**) ● *n.* (*pl.* same) **1** a member of a Dravidian people living in western India. **2** the language of this people. ● *adj.* of or relating to the Kanarese or their language. [*Kanara* in India]

kanban /'kanban/ *n.* **1** (in full **kanban system**) a Japanese just-in-time manufacturing system in which parts etc. are ordered on cards. **2** a card used in this system. [Japanese, = billboard, sign]

kangaroo /kaŋgə'ruː/ *n.* a plant-eating marsupial of the genus *Macropus*, native to Australia and New Guinea, with a long tail and strongly developed hind quarters enabling it to travel by jumping. [*ganurru*, the name of a specific kind of kangaroo in an extinct Aboriginal language of N. Queensland]

kangaroo closure *n. Brit. Parl.* a closure involving the chairperson of a committee selecting some amendments for discussion and excluding others.

kangaroo court *n.* an improperly constituted or illegal court held by strikers etc.

kangaroo mouse *n.* any small rodent of the genus *Microdipodops*, native to N. America, with long hind legs for hopping.

kangaroo paw *n.* any Australian plant of the genus *Anigozanthos* or *Macropidia*, with irregular woolly flowers, esp. *A. manglesii*, the floral emblem of Western Australia.

kangaroo rat *n.* any burrowing rodent of the genus *Dipodomys*, having elongated hind feet.

kangaroo vine *n.* an evergreen climbing plant, *Cissus antarctica*, with serrated leaves.

kanji /'kandʒi, 'kɑːn-/ *n.* Japanese writing using Chinese characters. [Japanese, from *kan* 'Chinese' + *ji* 'character']

Kannada /'kanədə/ *n.* the Kanarese language. [Kanarese *kannada*]

kanoon /kə'nuːn/ *n.* an instrument like a zither, with fifty to sixty strings. [Persian or Arabic *kānūn*]

Kans. *abbr.* Kansas.

KANU /'kɑːnuː/ *abbr.* Kenya African National Union.

kaolin /'keɪəlɪn/ *n.* a fine soft white clay produced by the decomposition of other clays or feldspar, used esp. for making porcelain and in medicines. Also called *china clay.* □ **kaolinic** /-'lɪnɪk/ *adj.* **kaolinize** *v.tr.* (also **-ise**). [French, from Chinese *gaoling*, literally 'high hill', the name of a mountain in Jiangxi province where it is found]

kaon /'keɪɒn/ *n. Physics* a meson having a mass several times that of a pion. [*ka* representing the letter *K* (as symbol for the particle) + -ON]

kapellmeister /kə'pɛlmʌɪstə/ *n.* (*pl.* same) the conductor of an orchestra, opera, choir, etc., esp. in German contexts. [German, from *Kapelle* 'court orchestra' from Italian *cappella* CHAPEL + *Meister* 'master']

kapok /'keɪpɒk/ *n.* **1** a fine fibrous cotton-like substance found surrounding the seeds of a tropical tree, *Ceiba pentandra*, used for stuffing cushions, soft toys, etc. **2** the tree itself. [ultimately from Malay *kāpoq*]

Kaposi's sarcoma /kə'pəʊsɪz/ *n. Med.* a form of cancer involving multiple tumours of the lymph nodes or skin, occurring esp. in people with depressed immune systems, e.g. as a result of Aids. [named after M.K. *Kaposi*, Hungarian dermatologist d. 1902]

kappa /'kapə/ *n.* the tenth letter of the Greek alphabet (Κ, κ). [Greek]

kaput /kə'pʊt/ *predic.adj. colloq.* broken, ruined; done for. [German *kaputt* from French (*être*) *capot* '(be) without tricks in piquet etc.': cf. CAPOT]

karabiner /karə'biːnə/ *n.* a coupling link with safety closure, used by mountaineers. [German *karabiner-haken* 'spring-hook']

karakul /'karəkʊl/ *n.* (also **caracul**) **1** a variety of Asian sheep with a dark curled fleece when young. **2** fur made from or resembling this; also called *Persian lamb.* [Russian]

karaoke /karə'əʊki, karɪ-/ *n.* a form of entertainment in which people sing popular songs as soloists against a pre-recorded backing (often *attrib.*: *karaoke bar*). [Japanese, = empty orchestra]

karat *US* var. of CARAT 2.

karate /kə'rɑːti/ *n.* a Japanese form of kung fu, a system of unarmed combat using the hands and feet as weapons. [Japanese, from *kara* 'empty' + *te* 'hand']

karma /'kɑːmə, 'kəːmə/ *n. Buddhism & Hinduism* **1** the sum of a person's actions in previous states of existence, viewed as deciding his or her fate in future existences. **2** destiny. □ **karmic** *adj.* [Sanskrit, = action, fate]

Karoo /kə'ruː/ *n.* (also **Karroo**) an elevated semi-desert plateau in S. Africa. [Nama]

karri /'kari/ *n.* (*pl.* **karris**) **1** a tall W. Australian tree, *Eucalyptus diversicolor*, with a hard red wood. **2** the timber from this. [Nyungar]

karst /kɑːst/ *n.* a limestone region with underground drainage and many cavities and passages caused by the dissolution of the rock. [German *der Karst*, a limestone region in Slovenia]

karyo- /'karɪəʊ/ *comb. form Biol.* denoting the nucleus of a cell. [Greek *karuon* 'kernel']

karyokinesis /ˌkarɪəʊkɪ'niːsɪs/ *n. Biol.* the division of a cell nucleus during mitosis. [KARYO- + Greek *kinēsis* 'movement' from *kineō* 'move']

karyotype /'karɪətʌɪp/ *n. Biol.* the number and visual appearance of the chromosomes in the nucleus of a cell. □ **karyotypic** /-ə'tɪpɪk/ *adj.*

kasbah /'kazbɑː/ *n.* (also **casbah**) **1** the citadel of a N. African city. **2** an Arab quarter near this. [French *casbah* from Arabic *kas(a)ba* 'citadel']

Kashmiri /kaʃ'mɪəri/ *adj. & n.* ● *adj.* of or relating to Kashmir or its people or language. ● *n.* **1** a native or inhabitant of Kashmir. **2** the Indic language of Kashmir. [*Kashmir* in the western Himalayas + -I²]

katabatic /katə'batɪk/ *adj. Meteorol.* (of wind) caused by local downward motion of esp. cool air (cf. ANABATIC). [Greek *katabatikos* from *katabainō* 'go down']

katabolism var. of CATABOLISM.

katakana /katə'kɑːnə/ *n.* an angular form of Japanese kana. [Japanese, = side kana]

kathode var. of CATHODE.

katydid /'keɪtɪdɪd/ *n.* any of various green grasshoppers of the family Tettigoniidae, native to the US. [imitative of the sound it makes]

kauri /'kaʊri/ *n.* (*pl.* **kauris**) a coniferous New Zealand tree, *Agathis australis*, which produces valuable timber and a resin. [Maori]

kauri gum *n.* resin of the kauri tree.

kava /'kɑ:və/ *n.* **1** a Polynesian shrub, *Piper methysticum.* **2** an intoxicating drink made from the crushed roots of this. [Polynesian]

kawakawa /'kɑ:wəkɑ:wə/ *n.* a New Zealand shrub, *Macropiper excelsum*, with aromatic leaves. [Maori]

kayak /'kʌɪak/ *n. & v.* ● *n.* **1** an Eskimo one-man canoe consisting of a light wooden frame covered with sealskins. **2** a small covered canoe resembling this. ● *v.intr.* (**kayaked, kayaking**) travel by kayak; paddle a kayak. [Eskimo]

kayo /keɪ'əʊ/ *v. & n. colloq.* ● *v.tr.* (**-oes, -oed**) knock out; stun by a blow. ● *n.* (*pl.* **-os**) a knockout. [representing pronunciation of *KO*]

Kazakh /kə'zɑ:k/ *n. & adj.* ● *n.* **1** (*pl.* **Kazakhs**) a member of a Turkic people of central Asia, esp. of Kazakhstan. **2** the language of this people. ● *adj.* of or relating to the Kazakhs or their language.

kazoo /kə'zu:/ *n.* a toy musical instrument into which the player sings or hums. [19th c., apparently with reference to the sound produced]

KB *abbr.* **1** kilobyte(s). **2** (in the UK) King's Bench.

KBE *abbr.* (in the UK) Knight Commander of the Order of the British Empire.

kbyte *abbr.* kilobyte(s).

KC *abbr.* **1** King's College. **2** King's Counsel.

kc *abbr.* kilocycle(s).

kcal *abbr.* kilocalorie(s).

KCB *abbr.* (in the UK) Knight Commander of the Order of the Bath.

KCMG *abbr.* (in the UK) Knight Commander of the Order of St Michael and St George.

kc/s *abbr.* kilocycles per second.

KCVO *abbr.* (in the UK) Knight Commander of the Royal Victorian Order.

KE *abbr.* kinetic energy.

kea /'ki:ə/ *n.* a parrot, *Nestor notabilis*, of New Zealand, with brownish-green and red plumage. [Maori, imitative]

kebab /kɪ'bab, -'bɑ:b/ *n.* small pieces of meat, vegetables, etc., packed closely and cooked on a skewer. [Urdu from Arabic *kabāb*]

ked /kɛd/ *n.* any of various bloodsucking flies of the family Hippoboscidae, esp. *Melophagus ovinus*, a wingless flat-bodied fly infesting sheep. [16th c.: origin unknown]

kedge /kɛdʒ/ *v. & n.* ● *v.* **1** *tr.* move (a ship) by means of a hawser attached to a small anchor. **2** *intr.* (of a ship) move in this way. ● *n.* (in full **kedge anchor**) a small anchor for this purpose. [perhaps a specific use of obsolete *cagge*, dialect *cadge* 'bind, tie']

kedgeree /'kɛdʒəri:/ *n.* **1** an Indian dish of rice, split pulse, onions, eggs, etc. **2** a European dish of fish, rice, hard-boiled eggs, etc. [Hindi *khichṛī*, Sanskrit *k'rsara*, a dish of rice and sesame]

keek /ki:k/ *v. & n. Sc.* ● *v.intr.* peep. ● *n.* a peep. [Middle English *kike*: cf. Middle Dutch, Middle Low German *kīken*]

keel[1] /ki:l/ *n. & v.* ● *n.* **1** the lengthwise timber or steel structure along the base of a ship, airship, or some aircraft, on which the framework of the whole is built up. **2** *poet.* a ship. **3** a ridge along the breastbone of many birds; a carina. **4** *Bot.* a prow-shaped pair of petals in a corolla etc. ● *v.* **1** (often foll. by *over*) **a** *intr.* turn over or fall down. **b** *tr.* cause to do this. **2 a** *intr.* (of a boat) turn keel upwards. **b** *tr.* turn up the keel of (a boat). □ **keelless** *adj.* [Middle English *kele* from Old Norse *kjölr*, from Germanic]

keel[2] /ki:l/ *n. Brit. hist.* **1** a flat-bottomed vessel, esp. of the kind formerly used on the River Tyne etc. for loading coal-ships. **2** an amount carried by such a vessel. [Middle English *kele* from Middle Low German *kēl*, Middle Dutch *kiel* 'ship, boat', from Germanic]

keelboat /'ki:lbəʊt/ *n.* **1** a yacht built with a permanent keel instead of a centreboard. **2** a large flat boat used on American rivers.

keelhaul /'ki:lhɔ:l/ *v.tr.* **1** *hist.* drag (a person) through the water under the keel of a ship as a punishment. **2** scold or rebuke severely.

keelson /'ki:ls(ə)n/ *n.* (also **kelson** /'kɛls(ə)n/) a line of timber fastening a ship's floor-timbers to its keel. [Middle English *kelswayn*, perhaps from Low German *kielswīn*, from *kiel* KEEL[1] + (probably) *swīn* SWINE used as the name of a timber]

keen[1] /ki:n/ *adj.* **1** (of a person, desire, or interest) eager, ardent (*a keen sportsman*). **2** (foll. by *on*) much attracted by; fond of or enthusiastic about. **3** (of the senses) sharp; highly sensitive. **4** intellectually acute. **5 a** having a sharp edge or point. **b** (of an edge etc.) sharp. **6** (of a sound, light, etc.) penetrating, vivid, strong. **7** (of a wind, frost, etc.) piercingly cold. **8** (of a pain etc.) acute, bitter. **9** *Brit.* (of a price) competitive. **10** *colloq.* excellent. □ **keenly** *adv.* **keenness** /'ki:nnɪs/ *n.* [Old English *cēne*, from Germanic]

keen[2] /ki:n/ *n. & v.* ● *n.* an Irish funeral song accompanied with wailing. ● *v.* **1** *intr.* utter the keen. **2** *tr.* bewail (a person) in this way. **3** *tr.* utter in a wailing tone. □ **keener** *n.* [Irish *caoine* from *caoinim* 'wail']

keep /ki:p/ *v. & n.* ● *v.* (*past* and *past part.* **kept** /kɛpt/) **1** *tr.* have continuous charge of; retain possession of. **2** *tr.* (foll. by *for*) retain or reserve for a future occasion or time (*will keep it for tomorrow*). **3** *tr. & intr.* retain or remain in a specified condition, position, course, etc. (*keep cool; keep off the grass; keep them happy*). **4** *tr.* put or store in a regular place (*knives are kept in this drawer*). **5** *tr.* (foll. by *from*) cause to avoid or abstain from something (*will keep you from going too fast*). **6** *tr.* detain; cause to be late (*what kept you?*). **7** *tr.* **a** observe or pay due regard to (a law, custom, etc.). **b** honour or fulfil (a commitment, undertaking, etc.) (*keep one's word*). **c** respect the commitment implied by (a secret etc.). **d** act fittingly on the occasion of (*keep the sabbath*). **8** *tr.* own and look after (animals) for pleasure or profit (*keeps bees*). **9** *tr.* **a** provide for the sustenance of (a person, family, etc.). **b** (foll. by *in*) maintain (a person) with a supply of. **10** *tr.* carry on; manage (a shop, business, etc.). **11 a** *tr.* maintain (accounts, a diary, etc.) by making the requisite entries. **b** *tr.* maintain (a house) in proper order. **12** *tr.* have (a commodity) regularly on sale (*do you keep buttons?*). **13** *tr.* guard or protect (a person or place, a goal in football, etc.). **14** *tr.* preserve in being; continue to have (*keep order*). **15** *intr.* (foll. by verbal noun) continue or do repeatedly or habitually (*why do you keep saying that?*). **16** *tr.* continue to follow (a way or course). **17** *intr.* **a** (esp. of perishable commodities) remain in good condition. **b** (of news or information etc.) admit of being withheld for a time. **18** *tr.* remain in (one's bed, room, house, etc.). **19** *tr.* retain one's place in (a seat or saddle, one's ground, etc.) against opposition or difficulty. **20** *tr.* maintain (a person) in return for sexual favours (*a kept woman*). ● *n.* **1** maintenance or the essentials for it (esp. food) (*hardly earn your keep*). **2** charge or control (*is in your keep*). **3** *hist.* a tower or stronghold. □ **for keeps** *colloq.* (esp. of something received or won) permanently, indefinitely. **how are you keeping?** *Brit.* how are you? **keep at** persist or cause to persist with. **keep away** (often foll. by *from*) **1** avoid being near. **2** prevent from being near. **keep back 1** remain or keep at a distance. **2** retard the progress of. **3** conceal; decline to disclose. **4** retain, withhold (*kept back £50*). **keep one's balance 1** remain stable; avoid falling. **2** retain one's composure. **keep down 1** hold in subjection. **2** keep low in amount. **3** lie low; stay hidden. **4** manage not to vomit (food eaten). **keep one's feet** manage not to fall. **keep one's hair on** see HAIR. **keep one's hand in** see HAND. **keep in 1** confine or restrain (one's feelings etc.). **2** remain or confine indoors. **3** keep (a fire) burning. **keep in with** remain on good terms with. **keep off 1** stay or cause to stay away from. **2** ward off; avert. **3** abstain from. **4** avoid (a subject) (*let's keep off religion*). **keep on 1** continue to do something; do continually (*kept on* *laughing*). **2** continue to use or employ. **3** (foll. by *at*) pester or harass. **keep open house** provide general hospitality. **keep out 1** keep or remain outside. **2** exclude. **keep to 1** adhere to (a course, schedule, etc.). **2** observe (a promise). **3** confine oneself to. **keep to oneself 1** avoid contact with others. **2** refuse to disclose or share. **keep together** remain or keep in harmony. **keep track of** see TRACK[1]. **keep under** hold in subjection. **keep up 1** maintain (progress etc.). **2** prevent (prices, one's spirits, etc.) from sinking. **3** keep in repair, in an efficient or proper state, etc. **4** carry on (a correspondence etc.). **5** prevent (a person) from going to bed, esp. when late. **6** (often foll. by *with*) manage not to fall behind. **keep up with the Joneses** strive to compete socially with one's neighbours. □ **keepable** *adj.* [Old English *cēpan*, of unknown origin]

keeper /ˈkiːpə/ *n.* **1** a person who keeps or looks after something or someone. **2** *Brit.* a custodian of a museum, art gallery, forest, etc. **3 a** = GAMEKEEPER. **b** = ZOOKEEPER 1. **4 a** = WICKETKEEPER. **b** = GOALKEEPER. **5** a fruit, wine, etc. that remains in good condition if stored. **6** a bar of soft iron placed across the poles of a horseshoe magnet to maintain its strength. **7 a** a plain ring to preserve a hole in a pierced ear lobe; a sleeper. **b** a ring worn to guard against the loss of a more valuable one.

keep-fit *n.* (often *attrib.*) esp. *Brit.* regular exercises to promote personal fitness and health.

keeping /ˈkiːpɪŋ/ *n.* **1** custody, charge (*in safe keeping*). **2** agreement, harmony (esp. *in* or *out of keeping*).

keepnet /ˈkiːpnɛt/ *n.* a net for keeping fish alive until they are returned to the water.

keepsake /ˈkiːpseɪk/ *n.* a thing kept for the sake of or in remembrance of the giver or original owner.

keeshond /ˈkeɪshɒnd/ *n.* **1** a dog of a Dutch breed with long thick hair like a large Pomeranian. **2** this breed. [Dutch]

kef /kɛf/ *n.* (also **kif** /kɪf/) **1** a drowsy state induced by marijuana etc. **2** the enjoyment of idleness. **3** a substance, esp. marijuana, smoked to produce kef. [Arabic *kayf* 'enjoyment, well-being']

keffiyeh /kəˈfiː(j)ə/ *n.* (also **kaffiyeh**) a Bedouin Arab's kerchief worn as a headdress. [Arabic *keffiya*, *kūfiyya*, perhaps from Late Latin *cofea* COIF]

keg /kɛg/ *n.* a small barrel, usu. of less than 10 gallons or (in the US) 30 gallons. [Middle English *cag* from Old Norse *kaggi*, of unknown origin]

keg beer *n. Brit.* beer to which carbon dioxide has been added in a sealed metal container, from which it is supplied.

keister /ˈkiːstə, ˈkʌɪstə/ *n. US slang* **1** the buttocks. **2** a suitcase, satchel, handbag, etc. [19th c.: origin unknown]

keloid /ˈkiːlɔɪd/ *n.* fibrous tissue formed at the site of a scar or injury. [Greek *khēlē* 'claw' + -OID]

kelp /kɛlp/ *n.* **1** any of several large broad-fronded brown seaweeds esp. of the genus *Laminaria*, suitable for use as manure, or the American Pacific genus *Macrocystis*. **2** the calcined ashes of seaweed, formerly used in glass-making and soap manufacture because of their high content of sodium, potassium, and magnesium salts. [Middle English *cülp(e)*, of unknown origin]

kelpie /ˈkɛlpi/ *n.* **1** *Sc.* a water spirit, usu. in the form of a horse, reputed to delight in the drowning of travellers etc. **2** an Australian sheepdog originally bred from a Scottish collie. [17th c.: origin unknown: sense 2 apparently from the name of a particular bitch]

kelson var. of KEELSON.

kelt /kɛlt/ *n.* a salmon or sea trout after spawning. [Middle English: origin unknown]

kelter var. of KILTER.

kelvin /ˈkɛlvɪn/ *n.* the SI unit of thermodynamic temperature, equal in magnitude to the degree Celsius (symbol **K**). [named after Lord *Kelvin*, British physicist d. 1907]

Kelvin scale *n.* a scale of temperature with absolute zero as zero, and the triple point of water as exactly 273.16 degrees.

kemp /kɛmp/ *n.* coarse hair in wool. □ **kempy** *adj.* [Middle English from Old Norse *kampr* 'beard, whisker']

kempt /kɛm(p)t/ *adj.* combed; neatly kept. [past part. of (now dialect) *kemb* COMB from Old English *cemban*, from Germanic]

ken /kɛn/ *n. & v.* ● *n.* range of sight or knowledge (*it's beyond my ken*). ● *v.tr.* (**kenning**; *past* and *past part.* **kenned** or **kent**) *Sc.* & *N.Engl.* **1** recognize at sight. **2** know. [Old English *cennan*, from Germanic]

kendo /ˈkɛndəʊ/ *n.* a Japanese form of fencing with two-handed bamboo swords. [Japanese, = sword-way]

kennel /ˈkɛn(ə)l/ *n. & v.* ● *n.* **1** a small shelter for a dog. **2** (in *pl.*) a breeding or boarding establishment for dogs. **3** a mean dwelling. ● *v.* (**kennelled**, **kennelling**; *US* **kenneled**, **kenneling**) **1** *tr.* put into or keep in a kennel. **2** *intr.* live in or go to a kennel. [Middle English from Old French *chenil* via medieval Latin from Latin *canis* 'dog']

kenning /ˈkɛnɪŋ/ *n.* a compound expression in Old English and Old Norse poetry, e.g. *oar-steed* = ship. [Middle English, = 'teaching' etc. from KEN]

kenosis /kɪˈnəʊsɪs/ *n.* (in Christian theology) the renunciation of the divine nature, at least in part, by Christ in the Incarnation. □ **kenotic** /-ˈnɒtɪk/ *adj.* [Greek *kenōsis* via *kenoō* 'to empty' from *kenos* 'empty']

kenspeckle /ˈkɛnspɛk(ə)l/ *adj. Sc.* conspicuous. [*kenspeck* of Scandinavian origin: related to KEN]

kent *past* and *past part.* of KEN.

Kentish /ˈkɛntɪʃ/ *adj.* of Kent in England. [Old English *Centisc*, from *Cent*, from Latin *Cantium*]

Kentish fire *n. Brit.* a prolonged volley of rhythmic applause or a demonstration of dissent.

kentledge /ˈkɛntlɪdʒ/ *n. Naut.* pig-iron etc. used as permanent ballast. [French *quintelage* 'ballast', with assimilation to *kentle*, obsolete variant of QUINTAL]

Kenyan /ˈkɛnjən, ˈkiː-/ *adj. & n.* ● *adj.* of or relating to Kenya in E. Africa. ● *n.* **1** a native or national of Kenya. **2** a person of Kenyan descent.

kepi /ˈkɛpi, ˈkeɪpi/ *n.* (*pl.* **kepis**) a French military cap with a horizontal peak. [French *képi* from Swiss German *käppi*, diminutive of *kappe* 'cap']

Kepler's laws /ˈkɛpləz/ *n.pl.* three theorems describing orbital motion. □ **Keplerian** /-ˈlɪərɪən/ *adj.* [named after J. *Kepler* German astronomer d. 1630]

kept *past* and *past part.* of KEEP.

keratin /ˈkɛrətɪn/ *n.* any of a group of fibrous proteins occurring in hair, feathers, hoofs, claws, horns, etc. [Greek *keras keratos* 'horn' + -IN]

keratinize /ˈkɛrətɪnʌɪz, kəˈrat-/ *v.tr. & intr.* (also **-ise**) cover or become covered with a deposit of keratin. □ **keratinization** /-ˈzeɪʃ(ə)n/ *n.*

keratitis /kɛrəˈtʌɪtɪs/ *n. Med.* inflammation of the cornea of the eye. [*kerat-* denoting the cornea (from Greek *keras keratos* 'horn') + -ITIS]

keratose /ˈkɛrətəʊs, -z/ *adj.* (of sponge) composed of a horny substance. [Greek *keras keratos* 'horn' + -OSE[1]]

keratotomy /kɛrəˈtɒtəmi/ *n. Med.* a surgical operation involving cutting into the cornea of the eye, esp. (in full **radial keratotomy**) to correct myopia. [*kerat-* denoting the cornea (cf. KERATITIS) + -TOMY]

kerb /kəːb/ *n. Brit.* a stone edging to a pavement or raised path. [variant of CURB]

kerb-crawler *n. Brit.* a (usu. male) person who drives slowly near the edge of the road in an attempt to engage a prostitute or harass esp. female passers-by. □ **kerb-crawling** *n.*

kerb drill *n. Brit.* precautions, esp. looking to right and left, before crossing a road.

kerbside /ˈkəːbsʌɪd/ *n. Brit.* the side of a road or pavement nearer the kerb.

kerbstone /ˈkəːbstəʊn/ *n. Brit.* each of a series of stones forming a kerb.

kerchief /ˈkəːtʃɪf/ *n.* **1** a cloth used to cover the head. **2** *poet.* a handkerchief. ▫ **kerchiefed** *adj.* [Middle English *curchef* from Anglo-French *courchef*, Old French *couvrechief*, from *couvrir* COVER + CHIEF 'head']

kerf /kəːf/ *n.* **1** a slit made by cutting, esp. with a saw. **2** the cut end of a felled tree. [Old English *cyrf* from Germanic: related to CARVE]

kerfuffle /kəˈfʌf(ə)l/ *n.* esp. *Brit. colloq.* a fuss or commotion. [Scots *curfuffle* from *fuffle* 'to disorder': imitative]

kermes /ˈkəːmɪz/ *n.* **1** (in full **kermes oak**) a small evergreen oak, *Quercus coccifera*, of the Mediterranean region. **2 a** the female of a scale-insect, *Kermes ilicis*, which forms berry-like galls on the kermes oak. **b** a red dye made from the dried bodies of these insects. **3** (in full **kermes mineral**) a bright red hydrous trisulphide of antimony. [French *kermès* from Arabic & Persian *ḳirmiz*: related to CRIMSON]

kermis /ˈkəːmɪs/ *n.* **1** a periodical country fair, esp. in the Netherlands. **2** *US* a charity bazaar. [Dutch, originally = a Mass on the anniversary of the dedication of a church, when a yearly fair was held: from *kerk* (formed as CHURCH) + *mis, misse* MASS]

kern¹ /kəːn/ *n. & v. Printing* ● *n.* the part of a metal type projecting beyond its body or shank. ● *v.tr.* **1** provide (type) with kerns; make (letters) overlap. **2** adjust the spacing between (characters). ▫ **kerned** *adj.* [perhaps from French *carne* 'corner' via Old French *charne* from Latin *cardo cardinis* 'hinge']

kern² /kəːn/ *n.* (also **kerne**) **1** *hist.* a light-armed Irish foot soldier. **2** *archaic* a peasant; a rustic. [Middle English from Irish *ceithern*]

kernel /ˈkəːn(ə)l/ *n.* **1** a central, softer, usu. edible part within a hard shell of a nut, fruit stone, seed, etc. **2** the whole seed of a cereal. **3** the nucleus or essential part of anything. [Old English *cyrnel*, diminutive of CORN¹]

kerosene /ˈkɛrəsiːn/ *n.* (also **kerosine**) esp. *US* a fuel oil suitable for use in jet engines and domestic heating boilers; paraffin oil. [Greek *kēros* 'wax' + -ENE]

Kerry /ˈkɛri/ *n.* (*pl.* **-ies**) **1** an animal of a breed of small black dairy cattle. **2** this breed. [*Kerry*, a county in Ireland, where the breed originated]

Kerry blue /ˈkɛri/ *n.* **1** a terrier of a breed with a silky blue-grey coat. **2** this breed. [as KERRY]

kersey /ˈkəːzi/ *n.* (*pl.* **-eys**) **1** a kind of coarse narrow cloth woven from short-stapled wool, usu. ribbed. **2** a variety of this. [Middle English, probably from *Kersey* in Suffolk]

kerseymere /ˈkəːzmɪə/ *n.* a twilled fine woollen cloth. [alteration of *cassimere*, variant of CASHMERE, assimilated to KERSEY]

keskidee var. of KISKADEE.

kestrel /ˈkɛstr(ə)l/ *n.* any small falcon, esp. *Falco tinnunculus*, which hovers while searching for its prey. [Middle English *castrell*, perhaps from French dialect *casserelle*, French *créc(er)elle*, perhaps imitative of its cry]

ketamine /ˈkiːtəmiːn/ *n.* an anaesthetic and pain-killing drug, also used (illicitly) as a hallucinogen. [KETONE + AMINE]

ketch /kɛtʃ/ *n.* a two-masted fore-and-aft rigged sailing boat with a mizzen-mast stepped forward of the rudder and smaller than its foremast. [Middle English *catche*, probably from CATCH]

ketchup /ˈkɛtʃəp, -ʌp/ *n.* (also **catchup** /ˈkatʃʌp/, *US* **catsup** /ˈkatsəp/) a spicy sauce made from tomatoes, mushrooms, vinegar, etc., used as a condiment. [perhaps from Cantonese *k'ē chap* 'tomato juice']

ketone /ˈkiːtəʊn/ *n.* any of a class of organic compounds in which two hydrocarbon groups are linked by a carbonyl group, e.g. propanone (acetone). ▫ **ketonic** /kɪˈtɒnɪk/ *adj.* [German *Keton*, alteration of *Aketon* ACETONE]

ketone body *n. Biochem.* each of three related compounds including acetone produced during the metabolism of fats.

ketonuria /kiːtə(ʊ)ˈnjʊərɪə/ *n.* the excretion of abnormally large amounts of ketone bodies in the urine, characteristic of diabetes mellitus, starvation, etc.

ketosis /kɪˈtəʊsɪs/ *n.* a condition characterized by raised levels of ketone bodies in the body, associated with fat metabolism and diabetes mellitus. ▫ **ketotic** /-ˈtɒtɪk/ *adj.*

kettle /ˈkɛt(ə)l/ *n.* a vessel, usu. of metal with a lid, spout, and handle, for boiling water in. ▫ **a different kettle of fish** a different matter altogether. **a pretty** (or **fine**) **kettle of fish** an awkward state of affairs. ▫ **kettleful** *n.* (*pl.* **-fuls**). [Middle English from Old Norse *ketill*, ultimately from Latin *catillus*, diminutive of *catinus* 'deep food-vessel']

kettledrum /ˈkɛt(ə)ldrʌm/ *n.* a large drum shaped like a bowl with a membrane adjustable for tension (and so pitch) stretched across. ▫ **kettledrummer** *n.*

kettle hole *n.* a depression in the ground resulting from the melting of an ice block trapped in glacial deposits.

keV *abbr.* kilo-electronvolt.

Kevlar /ˈkɛvlɑː/ *n. propr.* a synthetic fibre of high tensile strength used esp. as a reinforcing agent in the manufacture of rubber products, e.g. tyres.

kewpie /ˈkjuːpi/ *n.* a small chubby doll with wings and a curl or topknot. [CUPID + -IE]

key¹ /kiː/ *n. & v.* ● *n.* (*pl.* **keys**) **1** an instrument, usu. of metal, for moving the bolt of a lock forwards or backwards to lock or unlock. **2** a similar implement for operating a switch in the form of a lock. **3** an instrument for grasping screws, pegs, nuts, etc., esp. one for winding a clock etc. **4** a lever depressed by the finger in playing the organ, piano, flute, concertina, etc. **5** (often in *pl.*) each of several buttons for operating a typewriter, word processor, computer terminal, etc. **6** a thing that gives or precludes the opportunity for, or access to, something. **7** (*attrib.*) essential; of vital importance (*the key element in the problem*). **8** a place that by its position gives control of a sea, territory, etc. **9 a** a solution or explanation. **b** a word or system for solving a cipher or code. **c** an explanatory list of symbols used in a map, table, etc. **d** a book of solutions to mathematical problems etc. **e** a literal translation of a book written in a foreign language. **f** the first move in a chess problem solution. **10** *Mus.* a group of notes based on a particular note and comprising a scale, regarded as a unit forming the tonal basis of a piece of music (*a study in the key of C major*). **11** a tone or style of thought or expression. **12** a piece of wood or metal inserted between others to secure them. **13** the part of a first coat of wall plaster that passes between the laths and so secures the rest. **14** the roughness of a surface, helping the adhesion of plaster etc. **15** the samara of a sycamore etc. **16** a mechanical device for making or breaking an electric circuit, e.g. in telegraphy. ● *v.tr.* (**keys, keyed**) **1** (foll. by *in, on*, etc.) fasten with a pin, wedge, bolt, etc. **2** (often foll. by *in*) enter (data) by means of a keyboard. **3** roughen (a surface) to help the adhesion of plaster etc. **4** (foll. by *to*) align or link (one thing to another). **5** regulate the pitch of the strings of (a violin etc.). **6** word (an advertisement in a particular periodical) so that answers to it can be identified (usu. by varying the form of address given). ▫ **key up** (often foll. by *to*, or *to* + infin.) make (a person) nervous or tense; excite. ▫ **keyer** *n.* **keyless** *adj.* [Old English *cǣg*, of unknown origin]

key² /kiː/ *n.* a low-lying island or reef, esp. in the W. Indies (cf. CAY). [Spanish *cayo* 'shoal, reef', influenced by QUAY]

keyboard /ˈkiːbɔːd/ *n. & v.* ● *n.* **1** a set of keys on a typewriter, computer, piano, etc. **2** an electronic musical instrument with keys arranged as on a piano. ● *v.* **1** *tr.* enter (data) by means of a keyboard. **2** *intr.* work at a keyboard. ▫ **keyboarder** *n.* (in sense 1 of *n.*). **keyboardist** *n.* (in sense 2 of *n.*).

keyholder /ˈkiːhəʊldə/ *n.* a person who has a key to a place, esp. to an office or factory.

keyhole /ˈkiːhəʊl/ *n.* a hole by which a key is put into a lock.

keyhole surgery *n.* minimally invasive surgery carried out through a very small incision.

key industry *n.* an industry essential to the carrying on of others, e.g. coal mining, dyeing.

key map *n.* a map in bare outline, to simplify the use of a full map.

key money *n. Brit.* a payment demanded from an incoming tenant for the provision of a key to the premises.

Keynesian /ˈkeɪnzɪən/ *adj. & n.* ● *adj.* of or relating to the economic theories of J. M. Keynes (d. 1946), esp. regarding state control of the economy through money and taxation. ● *n.* an adherent of these theories. □ **Keynesianism** *n.*

keynote /ˈkiːnəʊt/ *n.* **1** a prevailing tone or idea (*the keynote of the whole occasion*). **2** (*attrib.*) intended to set the prevailing tone at a meeting or conference (*keynote address*). **3** *Mus.* the note on which a key is based.

keypad /ˈkiːpad/ *n.* a miniature keyboard or set of buttons for operating a portable electronic device, telephone, etc.

keypunch /ˈkiːpʌn(t)ʃ/ *n. & v.* ● *n.* a device for transferring data by means of punched holes or notches on a series of cards or paper tape. ● *v.tr.* transfer (data) by means of a keypunch. □ **keypuncher** *n.*

keyring /ˈkiːrɪŋ/ *n.* a ring for keeping keys on.

key signature *n. Mus.* any of several combinations of sharps or flats after the clef at the beginning of each staff indicating the key of a composition.

keystone /ˈkiːstəʊn/ *n.* **1** the central principle of a system, policy, etc., on which all the rest depends. **2** a central stone at the summit of an arch locking the whole together.

keystroke /ˈkiːstrəʊk/ *n.* a single depression of a key on a keyboard, esp. as a measure of work.

keyway /ˈkiːweɪ/ *n.* a slot for receiving a machined key.

keyword /ˈkiːwəːd/ *n.* **1** the key to a cipher etc. **2 a** a word of great significance. **b** an informative word used in an information retrieval system to indicate the content of a document etc.

KG *abbr.* (in the UK) Knight of the Order of the Garter.

kg *abbr.* kilogram(s).

KGB *n.* the state security police of the former USSR from 1954. [Russian, abbreviation of *Komitet gosudarstvennoĭ bezopasnosti* 'committee of state security']

Kgs. *abbr.* Kings (Old Testament).

khaddar /ˈkadə/ *n.* Indian homespun cloth. [Hindi]

khaki /ˈkɑːki/ *adj. & n.* ● *adj.* dull brownish yellow in colour. ● *n.* (*pl.* **khakis**) **1** khaki fabric of twilled cotton or wool, used esp. in military dress. **2** the dull brownish-yellow colour of this. [Urdu *ḵākī* 'dust-coloured' from *ḵāk* 'dust']

■ **Usage** In the military sense (see sense 1 of the noun above), this term has now been largely replaced by *olive drab*.

khalasi /kəˈlasi/ *n.* (*pl.* **khalasis**) (in the Indian subcontinent) a native servant or labourer, esp. one employed as a seaman. [Hindustani]

khamsin /ˈkamsɪn/ *n.* (also **hamsin** /ˈha-/) an oppressive hot south or south-east wind occurring in Egypt for about 50 days in March, April, and May. [Arabic *ḵamsīn* from *ḵamsūn* 'fifty']

khan[1] /kɑːn, kan/ *n.* **1** a title given to rulers and officials in central Asia, Afghanistan, etc. **2** *hist.* **a** the supreme ruler of the Turkish, Tartar, and Mongol tribes. **b** the emperor of China in the Middle Ages. □ **khanate** *n.* [Turkic *ḵān* 'lord']

khan[2] /kɑːn, kan/ *n.* a caravanserai. [Arabic *ḵān* 'inn']

khat /kɑːt/ *n.* **1** a shrub, *Catha edulis*, grown in Arabia. **2** the leaves of this shrub, chewed or infused as a stimulant. [Arabic *ḳāt*]

Khedive /kɪˈdiːv/ *n. hist.* the title of the viceroy of Egypt under Turkish rule 1867–1914. □ **Khedival** *adj.* **Khedivial** *adj.* [French *khédive*, ultimately from Persian *ḵadīv* 'prince']

Khmer /kmɛː/ *n. & adj.* ● *n.* **1** a native of the ancient Khmer kingdom in SE Asia, or of modern Cambodia. **2** the language of the Khmers. ● *adj.* of the Khmers or their language. [native name]

khus-khus /ˈkʌskʌs/ *n.* (also **cuscus**) the aromatic fibrous root of an Indian grass, *Vetiveria zizanaoides*, used for making fans, screens, etc. [Urdu *ḵaśḵaś*]

kHz *abbr.* kilohertz.

kiang /kɪˈaŋ/ *n.* a wild ass, *Equus hemionus*, of a race native to Tibet with a thick furry coat. [Tibetan *kyang*]

kibble[1] /ˈkɪb(ə)l/ *v. & n.* ● *v.tr.* grind or chop (dried corn, beans, etc.) coarsely. ● *n. N. Amer.* ground meal shaped into pellets esp. for pet food. [18th c.: origin unknown]

kibble[2] /ˈkɪb(ə)l/ *n. Brit.* an iron hoisting bucket used in mines. [German *Kübel* from medieval Latin *cupellus*, 'corn-measure', diminutive of *cuppa* 'cup']

kibbutz /kɪˈbʊts/ *n.* (*pl.* **kibbutzim** /-ˈtsiːm/) a communal esp. farming settlement in Israel. [modern Hebrew *ḳibbūṣ* 'gathering']

kibbutznik /kɪˈbʊtsnɪk/ *n.* a member of a kibbutz. [Yiddish (as KIBBUTZ)]

kibe /kʌɪb/ *n.* an ulcerated chilblain, esp. on the heel. [Middle English, probably from Welsh *cibi*]

kibitka /kɪˈbɪtkə/ *n.* **1** a type of Russian hooded sledge. **2 a** a Tartar's circular tent, covered with felt. **b** a Tartar household. [Russian from Tartar *kibitz*]

kibitz /ˈkɪbɪts/ *v.intr.* esp. *N. Amer. colloq.* act as a kibitzer. [Yiddish from German *kiebitzen* (as KIBITZER)]

kibitzer /ˈkɪbɪtsə, kɪˈbɪtsə/ *n.* esp. *N. Amer. colloq.* **1** an onlooker at cards etc., esp. one who offers unwanted advice. **2** a busybody, a meddler. [Yiddish *kibitser* from German *Kiebitz* 'lapwing, busybody']

kiblah /ˈkɪblə/ *n.* (also **qibla**) **1** the direction of the Kaaba (the sacred building at Mecca), to which Muslims turn at prayer. **2** = MIHRAB. [Arabic *ḳibla* 'that which is opposite']

kibosh /ˈkʌɪbɒʃ/ *n.* (also **kybosh**) *slang* nonsense. □ **put the kibosh on** put an end to; finally dispose of. [19th c.: origin unknown]

kick[1] /kɪk/ *v. & n.* ● *v.* **1** *tr.* strike or propel forcibly with the foot or hoof etc. **2** *intr.* (usu. foll. by *at, against*) **a** strike out with the foot. **b** express annoyance at or dislike of (treatment, a proposal, etc.); rebel against. **3** *tr. colloq.* give up (a habit). **4** *tr.* (often foll. by *out* etc.) expel or dismiss forcibly. **5** *refl.* be annoyed with oneself (*I'll kick myself if I'm wrong*). **6** *tr. Football* score (a goal) by a kick. **7** *intr. Cricket* (of a ball) rise sharply from the pitch. **8** *intr.* (as **kicking** *adj.*) *slang* lively, exciting; excellent. ● *n.* **1 a** a blow with the foot or hoof etc. **b** the delivery of such a blow. **2** *colloq.* **a** a sharp stimulant effect, esp. of alcohol (*has some kick in it; a cocktail with a kick in it*). **b** (often in *pl.*) a pleasurable thrill (*did it just for kicks; got a kick out of flying*). **3** strength, resilience (*have no kick left*). **4** *colloq.* a specified temporary interest or enthusiasm (*on a jogging kick*). **5** the recoil of a gun when discharged. **6** *Brit. Football colloq.* a player of specified kicking ability (*is a good kick*). □ **kick about** (or **around**) *colloq.* **1 a** drift idly from place to place. **b** be unused or unwanted. **2 a** treat roughly or scornfully. **b** discuss (an idea) unsystematically. **kick against the pricks** see PRICK. **kick ass** (or **some ass**) *N. Amer. coarse slang* act forcefully or in a domineering manner (cf. KICK-ASS). **kick the bucket** *slang* die. **kick one's heels** see HEEL[1]. **kick in 1** knock down (a door etc.) by kicking. **2** esp. *US slang* contribute (esp. money); pay one's share. **3** become activated, start. **kick in the pants** (or **teeth**) *colloq.* a humiliating punishment or setback. **kick off 1**

a *Football* begin or resume a match. **b** *colloq.* begin. **2** remove (shoes etc.) by kicking. **kick over the traces** see TRACE². **kick up** (or **kick up a fuss**, **dust**, etc.) *colloq.* create a disturbance; object or register strong disapproval. **kick up one's heels** frolic. **kick a person upstairs** *colloq.* shelve a person by giving him or her ostensible promotion or a title. □ **kickable** *adj.* **kicker** *n.* [Middle English *kike*, of unknown origin]

kick² /kɪk/ *n.* an indentation in the bottom of a glass bottle. [19th c.: origin unknown]

kick-ass *adj. N. Amer. coarse slang* forceful, aggressive, domineering (cf. *kick ass* (KICK¹)).

kickback /ˈkɪkbak/ *n. colloq.* **1** the force of a recoil. **2** payment for collaboration, esp. collaboration for illicit profit.

kickball /ˈkɪkbɔːl/ *n.* esp. *N. Amer.* **1** football (played informally by kicking a ball, as distinct from e.g. American football). **2** a football for kicking.

kick-boxing *n.* a form of boxing characterized by the use of blows with the feet as well as with gloved fists.

kick-down *n. Brit.* a device for changing gear in a motor vehicle by full depression of the accelerator.

kick-off *n.* **1** *Football* the start or resumption of a match. **2** (in phr. **for a kick-off**) *Brit. colloq.* a start (*that's wrong for a kick-off*).

kick-pleat *n.* a pleat in a narrow skirt to allow freedom of movement.

kickshaw /ˈkɪkʃɔː/ *n.* **1** *archaic,* usu. *derog.* a fancy dish in cookery. **2** something elegant but insubstantial; a toy or trinket. [French *quelque chose* 'something']

kicksorter /ˈkɪksɔːtə/ *n. colloq.* a device for analysing electrical pulses according to amplitude.

kickstand /ˈkɪkstand/ *n.* a rod attached to a bicycle or motorcycle and kicked into a vertical position to support the vehicle when stationary.

kick-start *n. & v.* ● *n.* **1** (also **kick-starter**) a device to start the engine of a motorcycle etc. by the downward thrust of a pedal. **2** an act of starting a motorcycle etc. in this way. **3** an impetus given to get a thing started or restarted. ● *v.tr.* **1** start (a motorcycle etc.) in this way. **2** start or restart (a process etc.) by providing some initial impetus.

kick-turn *n.* a standing turn in skiing.

kid¹ /kɪd/ *n. & v.* ● *n.* **1** a young goat. **2** the leather made from its skin. **3** *colloq.* a child or young person. ● *v.intr.* (**kidded**, **kidding**) (of a goat) give birth. □ **handle with kid gloves** handle in a gentle, delicate, or excessively tactful manner. **kids' stuff** *slang* something very simple. [Middle English *kide* from Old Norse *kith*, from Germanic]

kid² /kɪd/ *v.* (**kidded**, **kidding**) *colloq.* **1** *tr. & refl.* deceive, trick (*don't kid yourself*; *kidded his mother that he was ill*). **2** *tr. & intr.* tease (*only kidding*). □ **no kidding** (or **kid**) *slang* that is the truth. □ **kidder** *n.* **kiddingly** *adv.* [perhaps from KID¹]

kid³ /kɪd/ *n. hist.* a small wooden tub, esp. a sailor's mess tub for grog or rations. [perhaps a variant of KIT¹]

kid brother *n.* (also **kid sister**) *colloq.* a younger brother or sister.

Kidderminster carpet /ˈkɪdəmɪnstə/ *n.* a carpet made of two cloths of different colours woven together so that the carpet is reversible. [*Kidderminster* in Hereford and Worcester, England]

kiddie /ˈkɪdi/ *n.* (also **kiddy**) (*pl.* **-ies**) *colloq.* = KID¹ *n.* 3.

kiddle /ˈkɪd(ə)l/ *n.* **1** a barrier in a river, having an opening fitted with nets etc. to catch fish. **2** an arrangement of fishing nets hung on stakes along the seashore. [Middle English from Anglo-French *kidel*, Old French *quidel*, *guidel*]

kiddo /ˈkɪdəʊ/ *n.* (*pl.* **-os**) *colloq.* (esp. as a form of address) = KID¹ *n.* 3.

kiddy var. of KIDDIE.

kid-glove *attrib.adj.* dainty or delicate (*expects kid-glove treatment*).

kidnap /ˈkɪdnap/ *v.tr.* (**kidnapped**, **kidnapping**; *US* **kidnaped**, **kidnaping**) carry off (a person etc.) by illegal force or deception, esp. to obtain a ransom. □ **kidnapper** *n.* [back-formation from *kidnapper*, from KID¹ + *nap* = NAB]

kidney /ˈkɪdni/ *n.* (*pl.* **-eys**) **1** either of a pair of organs in the abdominal cavity of mammals, birds, and reptiles, which remove nitrogenous wastes from the blood and excrete urine. **2** the kidney of a sheep, ox, or pig as food. **3** temperament, nature, kind (*a man of that kidney*; *of the right kidney*). [Middle English *kidnei*, pl. *kidneiren*, apparently partly from *ei* EGG¹]

kidney bean *n.* a kidney-shaped bean, esp. a dark red one from a dwarf French bean plant.

kidney dish *n.* a kidney-shaped dish, esp. one used in surgery.

kidney machine *n.* = ARTIFICIAL KIDNEY.

kidney-shaped *adj.* shaped like a kidney, with one side concave and the other convex.

kidney vetch *n.* a yellow-flowered leguminous plant, *Anthyllis vulneraria*, found in grassland. Also called *lady's finger*.

kid sister see KID BROTHER.

kidskin /ˈkɪdskɪn/ *n.* = KID¹ *n.* 2.

kidvid /ˈkɪdvɪd/ *n. slang* **1** children's television or video entertainment. **2** a children's programme or videotape. [portmanteau word from *kids' video*]

kiekie /ˈkiːkiː/ *n.* a New Zealand climbing plant with edible bracts, and leaves which are used for basket-making etc. [Maori]

kieselguhr /ˈkiːz(ə)lgʊə/ *n.* a soft friable porous form of diatomite used as a filter, filler, insulator, etc., in various manufacturing processes. Also called *diatomaceous earth*. [German, from *Kiesel* 'gravel' + dialect *Guhr* 'earthy deposit']

kif var. of KEF.

kike /kʌɪk/ *n.* esp. *US slang offens.* a Jew. [20th c.: origin uncertain]

Kikuyu /kɪˈkuːjuː/ *n. & adj.* ● *n.* (*pl.* same or **Kikuyus**) **1** a member of an agricultural Negro people, the largest Bantu-speaking group in Kenya. **2** the language of this people. ● *adj.* of or relating to this people or their language. [native name]

kilderkin /ˈkɪldəkɪn/ *n.* **1** a cask for liquids etc., holding 16 or 18 gallons. **2** this measure. [Middle English, alteration of *kinderkin* from Middle Dutch *kinde(r)kin*, *kinneken*, diminutive of *kintal* QUINTAL]

kilim /kɪˈliːm, ˈkiːlɪm/ *n. & adj.* ● *n.* a pileless woven carpet, rug, etc., made in Turkey, Kurdistan, and neighbouring areas. ● *attrib.adj.* designating such a carpet, rug, etc. [Turkish from Persian *gelīm*]

kill /kɪl/ *v. & n.* ● *v.tr.* **1 a** deprive of life or vitality; put to death; cause the death of. **b** (*absol.*) cause or bring about death (*must kill to survive*). **2** destroy; put an end to (feelings etc.) (*overwork killed my enthusiasm*). **3** *refl.* (often foll. by pres. part.) *colloq.* **a** overexert oneself (*don't kill yourself lifting them all at once*). **b** laugh heartily. **4** *colloq.* overwhelm (a person) with amusement, delight, etc. (*the things he says really kill me*). **5** switch off (a spotlight, engine, etc.). **6** *colloq.* delete (a line, paragraph, etc.) from a computer file. **7** *colloq.* cause pain or discomfort to (*my feet are killing me*). **8** pass (time, or a specified amount of it), usu. while waiting for a specific event (*had an hour to kill before the interview*). **9** defeat (a bill in Parliament). **10** *colloq.* consume the entire contents of (a bottle of wine etc.). **11 a** *Tennis* etc. hit (the ball) so skilfully that it cannot be returned. **b** stop (the ball) dead. **12** neutralize or render ineffective (taste, sound, colour, etc.) (*thick carpet killed the sound of footsteps*). ● *n.* **1** an act of killing (esp. an animal). **2** an animal or animals killed, esp. by a hunter. **3** *colloq.* the destruction or disablement of an enemy aircraft, submarine, etc. □ **dressed to kill** dressed showily, seductively, or impressively. **in at the kill** present at or benefiting from the successful conclusion of an enterprise. **kill off 1** get rid of or destroy completely (esp. a number of persons or things). **2** (of an author) bring about the death of (a fictional character). **kill or cure** (usu. *attrib.*) *Brit.* (of a remedy etc.) drastic, extreme. **kill two birds with one stone** achieve two aims at once. **kill with kindness** spoil (a person) with over-indulgence. [Middle English *cülle, kille,* perhaps ultimately related to QUELL]

killdeer /ˈkɪldɪə/ *n.* a large American plover, *Charadrius vociferus*, with a plaintive song. [imitative of its call]

killer /ˈkɪlə/ *n.* **1 a** a person, animal, or thing that kills. **b** a murderer. **2** *colloq.* **a** an impressive, formidable, or excellent person or thing (*this one is quite difficult, but the next one is a real killer*). **b** a hilarious joke. **c** a decisive blow (*his brilliant header proved to be the killer*).

killer bee *n. colloq.* an Africanized honey bee.

killer cell *n. Physiol.* a white blood cell which destroys infected or cancerous cells.

killer instinct *n.* **1** an innate tendency to kill. **2** a ruthless streak.

killer whale *n.* a voracious cetacean, *Orcinus orca*, with a white belly and prominent dorsal fin.

killick /ˈkɪlɪk/ *n.* **1** a heavy stone used by small craft as an anchor. **2** a small anchor. **3** *Brit. Naut. slang* a leading seaman. [17th c.: origin unknown]

killifish /ˈkɪlɪfɪʃ/ *n.* (*pl.* usu. same) any small freshwater or brackish-water fish of the family Cyprinodontidae or Poeciliidae, often brightly coloured and kept in aquaria, esp. one of the genus *Fundulus* of eastern N. America, or *Pterolebias* of the upper Amazon. [perhaps from US dialect *kill* 'stream' from Dutch *kil* + FISH[1]]

killing /ˈkɪlɪŋ/ *n.* & *adj.* ● *n.* **1 a** the causing of death. **b** an instance of this. **2** a great (esp. financial) success (*make a killing*). ● *adj. colloq.* **1** overwhelmingly funny. **2** exhausting; very strenuous. □ **killingly** *adv.*

killing bottle *n.* a bottle containing poisonous vapour to kill insects collected as specimens.

killjoy /ˈkɪldʒɔɪ/ *n.* a person who throws gloom over or prevents other people's enjoyment.

kiln /kɪln/ *n.* a furnace or oven for burning, baking, or drying, esp. for calcining lime or firing pottery etc. [Old English *cylene* from Latin *culina* 'kitchen']

kiln-dry *v.tr.* (**-ies, -ied**) dry in a kiln.

kilo /ˈkiːləʊ/ *n.* (*pl.* **-os**) **1** a kilogram. **2** a kilometre. [French: abbreviation]

kilo- /ˈkɪləʊ, ˈkiːləʊ/ *comb. form* denoting a factor of 1,000 (esp. in metric units) (abbr.: **k**, or **K** in *Computing*). [French from Greek *khilioi* 'thousand']

kilobyte /ˈkɪləbʌɪt/ *n. Computing* 1,024 (i.e. 2^{10}) bytes as a measure of memory size (abbr.: **KB** or **kbyte**).

kilocalorie /ˈkɪləˌkaləri/ *n.* = CALORIE 2.

kilocycle /ˈkɪləsʌɪk(ə)l/ *n.* a former measure of frequency, equivalent to 1 kilohertz (abbr.: **kc**).

kilogram /ˈkɪləgram/ *n.* (also **-gramme**) the SI unit of mass, equivalent to the international standard kept at Sèvres near Paris (approx. 2.205 lb) (abbr.: **kg**). [French *kilogramme* (as KILO-, GRAM[1])]

kilohertz /ˈkɪləhəːts/ *n.* a measure of frequency equivalent to 1,000 cycles per second (abbr.: **kHz**).

kilojoule /ˈkɪlədʒuːl/ *n.* 1,000 joules, esp. as a measure of the energy value of foods (abbr.: **kJ**).

kilolitre /ˈkɪləliːtə/ *n.* (*US* **-liter**) 1,000 litres (equivalent to 220 imperial gallons) (abbr.: **kl**).

kilometre /ˈkɪləmiːtə, kɪˈlɒmɪtə/ *n.* (*US* **kilometer**) a metric unit of measurement equal to 1,000 metres (approx. 0.62 miles) (abbr.: **km**). □ **kilometric** /kɪləˈmɛtrɪk/ *adj.* [French *kilomètre* (as KILO-, METRE[1])]

kiloton /ˈkɪlətʌn/ *n.* (also **kilotonne**) a unit of explosive power equivalent to 1,000 tons of TNT.

kilovolt /ˈkɪləvɒlt/ *n.* 1,000 volts (abbr.: **kV**).

kilowatt /ˈkɪləwɒt/ *n.* 1,000 watts (abbr.: **kW**).

kilowatt-hour *n.* a measure of electrical energy equivalent to a power consumption of 1,000 watts for one hour (abbr.: **kWh**).

kilt /kɪlt/ *n.* & *v.* ● *n.* **1** a skirtlike garment, usu. of pleated tartan cloth and reaching to the knees, as traditionally worn by Highland men. **2** a similar garment worn by women and children. ● *v.tr.* **1** tuck up (skirts) round the body. **2** (esp. as **kilted** *adj.*) gather in vertical pleats. □ **kilted** *adj.* [originally as verb: Middle English, of Scandinavian origin]

kilter /ˈkɪltə/ *n.* (also **kelter** /ˈkɛl-/) good working order (esp. *out of kilter*). [17th c.: origin unknown]

kiltie /ˈkɪlti/ *n.* a wearer of a kilt, esp. a kilted Highland soldier.

kimberlite /ˈkɪmbəlʌɪt/ *n. Mineral.* a rare igneous blue-tinged rock sometimes containing diamonds, found in South Africa and Siberia. Also called *blue ground*. [*Kimberley*, a diamond-mining centre in S. Africa]

kimono /kɪˈməʊnəʊ/ *n.* (*pl.* **-os**) **1** a long loose Japanese robe worn with a sash. **2** a European dressing gown modelled on this. □ **kimonoed** *adj.* [Japanese, from *ki* 'wearing' + *mono* 'thing']

kin /kɪn/ *n.* & *adj.* ● *n.* one's relatives or family. ● *predic.adj.* (of a person) related (*we are kin; he is kin to me*) (see also AKIN). □ **kith and kin** see KITH. **near of kin** closely related by blood, or in character. **next of kin** see NEXT OF KIN. □ **kinless** *adj.* [Old English *cynn*, from Germanic]

-kin /kɪn/ *suffix* forming diminutive nouns (*catkin; manikin*). [from or suggested by Middle Dutch *-kijn, -ken*, Old High German *-chin*]

kina /ˈkiːnə/ *n.* the chief monetary unit of Papua New Guinea. [Tolai]

kinaesthesia /kɪnɪsˈθiːzɪə, kʌɪn-/ *n.* (*US* **kinesthesia**) the brain's awareness of the position and movement of the body, limbs, etc., by means of sensory nerves in the muscles and joints. □ **kinaesthetic** /-ˈθɛtɪk/ *adj.* [Greek *kineō* 'move' + *aisthēsis* 'sensation']

kincob /ˈkɪŋkɒb/ *n.* a rich Indian fabric embroidered with gold or silver. [Urdu from Persian *kamk̲āb*, from *kamk̲ā* 'damask']

kind[1] /kʌɪnd/ *n.* **1 a** a race or species (*human kind*). **b** a natural group of animals, plants, etc. (*the wolf kind*). **2** class, type, sort, variety (*what kind of job are you looking for?*). **3** each of the elements of the Eucharist (*communion under* (or *in*) *both kinds*). **4** the manner or fashion natural to a person etc. (*act after their kind; true to kind*). □ **in kind 1** in the same form, likewise (*was insulted and replied in kind*). **2** (of payment) in goods or labour as opposed to money (*received their wages in kind*). **3** in character or quality (*differ in degree but not in kind*). **kind of** *colloq.* to some extent (*felt kind of sorry; I kind of expected it*). **a kind of** used to imply looseness, vagueness, exaggeration, etc., in the term used (*a kind of Jane Austen of our times; I suppose he's a kind of doctor*). **law of kind** *archaic* nature in general; the natural order. **nothing of the kind 1** not at all like the thing in question. **2** (expressing denial) not at all. **of its kind** within the limitations of its own class (*good of its kind*). **of a kind 1** *derog.* scarcely deserving the name (*a choir of a kind*). **2** similar in some important respect (*they're two of a kind*). **one's own kind** those with whom one has much in common. **something of the kind** something like the thing in question. [Old English *cynd(e), gecynd(e)*, from Germanic]

■ **Usage** In sense 2, *these* (or *those*) *kind* is often encountered when followed by a plural, as in *I don't like these kind of films*, but *this kind* or *these kinds* is usually preferable, e.g. *I don't like this* (or *that*) *kind of film, I don't like these* (or *those*) *kinds of films.*

kind[2] /kʌɪnd/ *adj.* **1** of a friendly, generous, benevolent, or gentle nature. **2** (usu. foll. by *to*) showing friendliness, affection, or consideration. **3 a** affectionate. **b** *archaic* loving. [originally = natural, native: Old English *gecynde* (as KIND[1])]

kinda /ˈkʌɪndə/ *colloq.* = *kind of* (see KIND[1]). [corruption]

kindergarten /ˈkɪndəgɑːt(ə)n/ *n.* an establishment for pre-school learning. [German, = children's garden]

kind-hearted *adj.* of a kind disposition. □ **kind-heartedly** *adv.* **kind-heartedness** *n.*

kindle /ˈkɪnd(ə)l/ *v.* **1** *tr.* light or set on fire (a flame, fire, substance, etc.). **2** *intr.* catch fire, burst into flame. **3** *tr.* arouse or inspire (*kindle enthusiasm for the project*; *kindle jealousy in a rival*). **4** *intr.* (usu. foll. by *to*) respond, react (to a person, an action, etc.) (*kindle to his courage*). **5** *intr.* become animated, glow with passion etc. (*her imagination kindled*). **6** *tr.* & *intr.* make or become bright (*kindle the embers to a glow*). □ **kindler** *n.* [Middle English from Old Norse *kynda*, influenced by Old Norse *kindill* 'candle, torch']

kindling /ˈkɪndlɪŋ/ *n.* small sticks etc. for lighting fires.

kindly[1] /ˈkʌɪndli/ *adv.* **1** in a kind manner (*spoke to the child kindly*). **2** often *iron.* used in a polite request or demand (*kindly acknowledge this letter*; *kindly leave me alone*). □ **look kindly upon** regard sympathetically. **take a thing kindly** like or be pleased by it. **take kindly to** be pleased by or endeared to (a person or thing). **thank kindly** thank very much. [Old English *gecyndelīce* (as KIND[2])]

kindly[2] /ˈkʌɪndli/ *adj.* (**kindlier, kindliest**) **1** kind, kind-hearted. **2** (of climate etc.) pleasant, genial. **3** *archaic* native-born (*a kindly Scot*). □ **kindlily** *adv.* **kindliness** *n.* [Old English *gecyndelic* (as KIND[1])]

kindness /ˈkʌɪn(d)nɪs/ *n.* **1** the state or quality of being kind. **2** a kind act.

kindred /ˈkɪndrɪd/ *n.* & *adj.* ● *n.* **1** one's relations, referred to collectively. **2** a relationship by blood. **3** a resemblance or affinity in character. ● *adj.* **1** related by blood or marriage. **2** allied or similar in character (*other kindred symptoms*). [Middle English, from KIN + *-red* from Old English *rǣden* 'condition']

kindred spirit *n.* a person whose character and outlook have much in common with one's own.

kine /kʌɪn/ *archaic pl.* of COW[1].

kinematics /kɪnɪˈmatɪks, kʌɪn-/ *n.pl.* (usu. treated as *sing.*) the branch of mechanics concerned with the motion of objects without reference to the forces which cause the motion. □ **kinematic** *adj.* **kinematically** *adv.* [Greek *kinēma -matos* 'motion' from *kineō* 'move' + -ICS]

kinematic viscosity *n.* a quantity measuring the dynamic viscosity per unit density.

kinematograph var. of CINEMATOGRAPH.

kinesics /kɪˈniːsɪks, kʌɪ-/ *n.pl.* **1** (usu. treated as *sing.*) the study of body movements and gestures which contribute to communication. **2** (usu. treated as *pl.*) these movements; body language. [Greek *kinēsis* 'motion' (as KINETIC)]

kinesiology /kɪˌniːsɪˈɒlədʒi, kʌɪ-/ *n.* the study of the mechanics of body movements. [Greek *kinēsis* 'movement' + -OLOGY]

kinesis /kɪˈniːsɪs, kʌɪ-/ *n.* **1** movement, motion. **2** *Biol.* undirected movement of an organism in response to a stimulus (cf. TAXIS 2). **3** *Zool.* mobility of the bones of the skull, as in some birds and reptiles. [Greek *kinēsis* 'movement']

kinesthesia *US* var. of KINAESTHESIA.

kinetic /kɪˈnɛtɪk, kʌɪ-/ *adj.* of or due to motion. □ **kinetically** *adv.* [Greek *kinētikos* from *kineō* 'move']

kinetic art *n.* a form of art that depends on movement for its effect.

kinetic energy *n.* energy which a body possesses by virtue of being in motion.

kinetics /kɪˈnɛtɪks, kʌɪ-/ *n.pl.* (usu. treated as *sing.*) **1** = DYNAMICS 1a. **2** the branch of physical chemistry or biochemistry concerned with measuring and studying the rates of chemical or biochemical reactions.

kinetic theory *n.* a theory which explains the physical properties of matter in terms of the motions of its constituent particles.

kinetin /ˈkʌɪnɪtɪn/ *n. Biochem.* a synthetic kinin used to stimulate cell division in plants. [as KINETIC + -IN]

kinfolk *N. Amer.* var. of KINSFOLK.

king /kɪŋ/ *n.* & *v.* ● *n.* **1** (as a title usu. **King**) a male sovereign, esp. the hereditary ruler of an independent state. **2** a person or thing pre-eminent in a specified field or class (*railway king*). **3** (*attrib.*) a large (or the largest) kind of plant, animal, etc. (*king penguin*). **4** *Chess* the piece on each side which the opposing side has to checkmate to win. **5** a piece in draughts with extra capacity for moving, made by crowning an ordinary piece that has reached the opponent's baseline. **6** a court card bearing a representation of a king and usu. ranking next below an ace. **7** (**the King**) (in the UK) the national anthem when there is a male sovereign. **8** (**Kings** or **Books of Kings**) two Old Testament books dealing with history, esp. of the kingdom of Judah. ● *v.tr.* make (a person) king. □ **king it 1** play or act the king. **2** (usu. foll. by *over*) govern, control. □ **kinghood** *n.* **kingless** *adj.* **kinglike** *adj.* **kingly** *adj.* **kingliness** *n.* **kingship** *n.* [Old English *cyning*, *cyng*, from Germanic]

kingbird /ˈkɪŋbəːd/ *n.* any flycatcher of the genus *Tyrannus*, with olive-grey plumage and long pointed wings.

kingbolt /ˈkɪŋbəʊlt/ *n.* = KINGPIN.

King Charles spaniel /tʃɑːlz/ *n.* **1** a spaniel of a small black and tan breed. **2** this breed.

king cobra *n.* a large and venomous hooded Indian snake, *Ophiophagus hannah*.

king crab *n.* **1** = HORSESHOE CRAB. **2** *US* any of various large edible spider crabs.

kingcraft /ˈkɪŋkrɑːft/ *n. archaic* the skilful exercise of kingship.

kingcup /ˈkɪŋkʌp/ *n. Brit.* a marsh marigold.

kingdom /ˈkɪŋdəm/ *n.* **1** an organized community headed by a king. **2** the territory subject to a king. **3 a** the spiritual reign attributed to God (*Thy kingdom come*). **b** the sphere of this (*kingdom of heaven*). **4** a domain belonging to a person, animal, etc. **5** a province of nature (*the vegetable kingdom*). **6** a specified mental or emotional province (*kingdom of the heart*; *kingdom of fantasy*). **7** *Biol.* the highest category in taxonomic classification. □ **come into** (or **to**) **one's kingdom** achieve recognition or supremacy. **kingdom come** *colloq.* eternity; the next world. **till kingdom come** *colloq.* for ever. [Old English *cyningdōm* (as KING)]

kingfish /ˈkɪŋfɪʃ/ *n.* (*pl.* usu. same) any of various large fish, e.g. the opah.

kingfisher /ˈkɪŋfɪʃə/ *n.* any bird of the family Alcedinidae, with a long sharp beak, which dives for fish in rivers etc., esp. *Alcedo atthis*, a small European bird with bright blue plumage.

King in Council *n. Brit.* = QUEEN IN COUNCIL.

King James Bible *n.* (also **King James Version**) = AUTHORIZED VERSION.

kinglet /ˈkɪŋlɪt/ *n.* **1** a petty king. **2** esp. *N. Amer.* any of various small warblers of the family Regulidae, esp. the goldcrest.

kingmaker /ˈkɪŋmeɪkə/ *n.* a person who makes kings, leaders, etc., through the exercise of political influence, originally with reference to the Earl of Warwick in the reigns of Henry VI and Edward IV of England.

King of Arms *n. Heraldry* (in the UK) a chief herald (at the College of Arms: Garter, Clarenceux, and Norroy and Ulster; in Scotland: Lyon).

king of beasts *n.* the lion.

king of birds *n.* the eagle.

King of Kings *n.* **1** God. **2** the title assumed by many eastern kings.

King of the Castle *n. Brit.* a children's game consisting of trying to displace a rival from a mound.

kingpin /ˈkɪŋpɪn/ *n.* **1 a** a main or large bolt in a central position. **b** a vertical bolt used as a pivot. **2** an essential person or thing, esp. in a complex system; the most important person in an organization.

king post *n.* an upright post from the tie-beam of a roof to the apex of a truss.

king prawn *n.* a large edible prawn of the genus *Penaeus*, common esp. in Australasia.

King's Bench *n.* (in the UK) = QUEEN'S BENCH.

king's bishop *n. Chess* the bishop on the king's side of the board at the start of a game.

King's bounty *n. Brit. hist.* a grant made to a mother of three or more children born at a single birth.

King's Champion *n.* (in the UK) = CHAMPION OF ENGLAND.

King's colour *n.* (in the UK) = QUEEN'S COLOUR.

King's Counsel *n.* (in the UK) = QUEEN'S COUNSEL.

King's English *n.* = QUEEN'S ENGLISH.

King's evidence *n. Brit. Law* = QUEEN'S EVIDENCE.

king's evil *n. hist.* scrofula, formerly held to be curable by the royal touch.

King's Guide *n.* (in the UK) = QUEEN'S GUIDE.

King's highway *n. Brit.* = QUEEN'S HIGHWAY.

king-size *adj.* (also **king-sized**) larger than normal; very large.

king's knight *n. Chess* the knight on the king's side of the board at the start of a game.

King's Messenger *n.* (in the UK) = QUEEN'S MESSENGER.

king's pawn *n. Chess* the pawn in front of the king at the start of a game.

King's Proctor *n.* (in the UK) = QUEEN'S PROCTOR.

king's ransom *n.* a fortune.

king's rook *n. Chess* the rook on the king's side of the board at the start of a game.

King's Scout *n.* (in the UK) = QUEEN'S SCOUT.

King's speech *n.* (in the UK) = QUEEN'S SPEECH.

kinin /'kʌɪnɪn/ *n.* **1** any of a group of polypeptides formed in body tissue in response to injury, and causing vasodilation and smooth muscle contraction. **2** any of a group of compounds which promote cell division and inhibit ageing in plants. [Greek *kineō* 'move' + -IN]

kink /kɪŋk/ *n. & v.* ● *n.* **1 a** a short backward twist in wire or tubing etc. such as may cause an obstruction. **b** a tight wave in human or animal hair. **2** a mental twist or quirk. ● *v.intr. & tr.* form or cause to form a kink. [Middle Low German *kinke* (*v.*), probably from Dutch *kinken*]

kinkajou /'kɪŋkədʒuː/ *n.* a Central and S. American nocturnal fruit-eating mammal, *Potos flavus*, with a prehensile tail and living in trees. [French *quincajou* from Algonquian]

kinky /'kɪŋki/ *adj.* (**kinkier**, **kinkiest**) **1** *colloq.* **a** given to or involving bizarre or unusual sexual behaviour. **b** (of clothing etc.) bizarre in a sexually provocative way. **2** strange, eccentric. **3** having kinks or twists. □ **kinkily** *adv.* **kinkiness** *n.* [KINK + -Y[1]]

kino /'kiːnəʊ/ *n.* (*pl.* **-os**) a gum produced by various tropical trees and used in medicine and tanning as an astringent. [West African]

-kins /kɪnz/ *suffix* = -KIN, often with suggestions of endearment (*babykins*).

kinsfolk /'kɪnzfəʊk/ *n.pl.* (also *N. Amer.* **kinfolk** /'kɪnfəʊk/) one's relations by blood.

kinship /'kɪnʃɪp/ *n.* **1** blood relationship. **2** the sharing of characteristics or origins.

kinsman /'kɪnzmən/ *n.* (*pl.* **-men**; *fem.* **kinswoman**, *pl.* **-women**) **1** a blood relation or (loosely) a relation by marriage. **2** a member of one's own tribe or people.

kiosk /'kiːɒsk/ *n.* **1** a light open-fronted booth or cubicle from which food, newspapers, tickets, etc., are sold. **2** a telephone box. **3** *Austral.* a building in which refreshments are served in a park, zoo, etc. **4** a light open pavilion in Turkey and Iran. [French *kiosque* via Turkish *kiūshk* 'pavilion' from Persian *guš*]

kip[1] /kɪp/ *n. & v. Brit. slang* ● *n.* **1** a sleep or nap. **2** a bed or cheap lodging house. **3** a brothel. ● *v.intr.* (**kipped**, **kipping**) sleep, take a nap. [18th *c.*, origin uncertain: cf. Danish *kippe* 'hovel, tavern']

kip[2] /kɪp/ *n.* the hide of a young or small animal as used for leather. [Middle English: origin unknown]

kip[3] /kɪp/ *n.* (*pl.* same or **kips**) the chief monetary unit of Laos. [Thai]

kip[4] /kɪp/ *n. Austral. slang* a small piece of wood from which coins are spun in the game of two-up. [19th *c.*, perhaps from English dialect: cf. *keper* 'a flat piece of wood preventing a horse from eating the corn', or Irish dialect *kippeen* from Irish *cipín* 'a little stick']

kipper /'kɪpə/ *n. & v.* ● *n.* **1** a kippered fish, esp. herring. **2** a male salmon in the spawning season. ● *v.tr.* cure (a herring etc.) by splitting open, salting, and drying in the open air or smoke. [Middle English: origin uncertain]

kipper tie *n.* a brightly coloured and very wide tie.

kipsie /'kɪpsi/ *n.* (also **kipsy**) (*pl.* **-ies**) *Austral. slang* a house, home, lean-to, or shelter. [perhaps from KIP[1]]

Kir /kɪə, kəː/ *n. propr.* a drink made from dry white wine and crème de cassis. [named after Canon Felix *Kir* (d. 1968), said to have invented the recipe]

kirby grip /'kəːbi/ *n.* (also **Kirbigrip** *propr.*) *Brit.* a type of sprung hairgrip. [*Kirby*, part of original manufacturer's name (Kirby, Beard & Co. Ltd)]

Kirghiz var. of KYRGYZ.

kirk /kəːk/ *n. Sc. & N.Engl.* **1** a church. **2** (**the Kirk** or **the Kirk of Scotland**) the Church of Scotland as distinct from the Church of England or from the Episcopal Church in Scotland. [Middle English via Old Norse *kirkja* from Old English *cir(i)ce* CHURCH]

kirkman /'kəːkmən/ *n.* (*pl.* **-men**) *Sc. & N.Engl.* a member of the Church of Scotland.

Kirk-session *n.* **1** the lowest court in the Church of Scotland. **2** *hist.* the lowest court in other Presbyterian Churches, composed of ministers and elders.

kirsch /kɪəʃ/ *n.* (also **kirschwasser** /'kɪəʃvasə/) a brandy distilled from the fermented juice of cherries. [German *Kirsche* 'cherry', *Wasser* 'water']

kirtle /'kəːt(ə)l/ *n. archaic* **1** a woman's gown or outer petticoat. **2** a man's tunic or coat. [Old English *cyrtel* from Germanic, ultimately perhaps from Latin *curtus* 'short']

kiskadee /kɪskə'diː/ *n.* (also **keskidee** /kɛskɪ'diː/) a tyrant flycatcher, *Pitangus sulphuratus*, of Central and S. America, with brown and yellow plumage. [imitative of its cry]

kismet /'kɪzmɛt, -mɪt, -s-/ *n.* destiny, fate. [Turkish from Arabic *ḳisma(t)*, from *ḳasama* 'divide']

kiss /kɪs/ *v. & n.* ● *v.* **1** *tr.* touch with the lips, esp. as a sign of love, affection, greeting, or reverence. **2** *tr.* express (greeting or farewell) in this way. **3** *absol.* (of two persons) touch each others' lips in this way. **4** *tr.* (also *absol.*) (of a snooker ball etc. in motion) lightly touch (another ball). ● *n.* **1** a touch with the lips in kissing. **2** the slight impact when one snooker ball etc. lightly touches another. **3** a small sweetmeat or piece of confectionery. □ **kiss and tell** recount one's sexual exploits. **kiss a person's arse** *coarse slang* act obsequiously towards a person. **kiss away** remove (tears etc.) by kissing. **kiss the dust** submit abjectly; be overthrown. **kiss goodbye to** *colloq.* accept the loss of. **kiss the ground** prostrate oneself as a token of homage. **kiss off** esp. *N. Amer. slang* **1** dismiss, get rid of. **2** go away, die. **kiss the rod** accept chastisement submissively. □ **kissable** *adj.* [Old English *cyssan*, from Germanic]

kiss-curl *n.* a small curl of hair on the forehead, at the nape, or in front of the ear.

kisser /'kɪsə/ *n.* **1** a person who kisses. **2** (orig. *Boxing*) *slang* the mouth; the face.

kissing cousin *n.* (also **kissing kin** or **kind**) a distant relative (given a formal kiss on occasional meetings).

kissing gate *n. Brit.* a gate hung in a V- or U-shaped enclosure, letting one person through at a time.

kiss of death *n.* an apparently friendly act which causes ruin.

kiss-off *n.* esp. *N. Amer. slang* a dismissal from a job.

kiss of life *n.* mouth-to-mouth resuscitation.

kiss of peace *n. Eccl.* a ceremonial kiss, esp. during the Eucharist, as a sign of unity.

kissogram /'kɪsəgram/ *n.* (also **Kissagram** *propr.*) *Brit.* a novelty telegram or greetings message delivered with a kiss.

kissy /ˈkɪsi/ *adj. colloq.* given to kissing (*not the kissy type*).

kist var. of CIST[1].

Kiswahili /ki:swəˈhi:li, kɪswɑ:-/ *n.* a major language of the Bantu family, spoken widely in Kenya, Tanzania, and elsewhere in E. Africa, where it serves as a lingua franca. [native name: *ki-* prefix used in names of languages]

kit[1] /kɪt/ *n. & v.* ● *n.* **1** a set of articles, equipment, or clothing needed for a specific purpose (*first-aid kit; bicycle-repair kit*). **2** *Brit.* the clothing etc. needed for any activity, esp. sport (*football kit*). **3** a set of all the parts needed to assemble an item, e.g. a piece of furniture, a model, etc. **4** *Brit.* a wooden tub. ● *v.tr.* (**kitted**, **kitting**) (often foll. by *out*, *up*) equip with the appropriate clothing or tools. [Middle English from Middle Dutch *kitte* 'wooden vessel', of unknown origin]

kit[2] /kɪt/ *n.* **1** a kitten. **2** a young fox, badger, etc. [abbreviation]

kit[3] /kɪt/ *n. hist.* a small fiddle, esp. as used by a dancing master. [perhaps from Latin *cithara*; see CITTERN]

kitbag /ˈkɪtbag/ *n.* a large, usu. cylindrical bag used for carrying a soldier's, traveller's, or sportsman's equipment.

kit-cat /ˈkɪtkat/ *n.* (in full **kit-cat portrait**) a portrait of less than half the full length, but including one hand; usu. 36 × 28 in. [named after a series of portraits of the members of the *Kit-Cat* Club, an early 18th-c. Whig society]

kitchen /ˈkɪtʃɪn, -tʃ(ə)n/ *n.* **1 a** the room or area where food is prepared and cooked. **b** kitchen fitments or units, esp. as sold together. **2** (*attrib.*) of or belonging to the kitchen (*kitchen knife; kitchen table*). **3** *slang* the percussion section of an orchestra. □ **everything but the kitchen sink** everything imaginable. [Old English *cycene* from Latin *coquere* 'cook']

kitchen cabinet *n.* a group of unofficial advisers thought to be unduly influential.

Kitchener bun /ˈkɪtʃɪnə/ *n. Austral.* a cream-filled bun coated with cinnamon and sugar. [named after 1st Earl *Kitchener* d. 1916]

kitchenette /kɪtʃɪˈnɛt/ *n.* a small kitchen or part of a room fitted as a kitchen.

kitchen garden *n.* a garden where vegetables and sometimes fruit or herbs are grown.

kitchen midden *n.* a prehistoric refuse-heap which marks an ancient settlement, chiefly containing bones, seashells, etc.

kitchen roll *n.* a roll of absorbent paper for cleaning up spillages etc.

kitchen-sink *attrib.adj.* (in art forms) depicting extreme realism, esp. drabness or sordidness (*kitchen-sink school of painting; kitchen-sink drama*).

kitchen tea *n. Austral. & NZ* a party held before a wedding to which female guests bring items of kitchen equipment as presents.

kitchenware /ˈkɪtʃɪnwɛ:, ˈkɪtʃ(ə)n-/ *n.* the utensils used in the kitchen.

kite /kʌɪt/ *n. & v.* ● *n.* **1** a toy consisting of a light framework with thin material stretched over it, flown in the wind at the end of a long string. **2** any of various soaring birds of prey esp. of the genus *Milvus* with long wings and usu. a forked tail. **3** *Brit. slang* an aeroplane. **4** *slang* a fraudulent cheque, bill, or receipt. **5** *Geom.* a quadrilateral figure symmetrical about one diagonal. **6** *slang* a letter or note, esp. one that is illicit or surreptitious. **7** (in *pl.*) the highest sail of a ship, set only in a light wind. **8** *archaic* a dishonest person, a sharper. ● *v.* **1** *intr.* soar like a kite. **2** *tr.* (also *absol.*) *slang* originate or pass (fraudulent cheques, bills, or receipts). **3** *tr.* (also *absol.*) *slang* raise (money by dishonest means) (*kite a loan*). [Old English *cȳta*, of unknown origin]

kite balloon *n.* a sausage-shaped captive balloon for military observations.

kite-flying *n.* fraudulent practice.

Kitemark /ˈkʌɪtmɑ:k/ *n.* an official kite-shaped mark on goods approved by the British Standards Institution.

kit-fox *n.* a small fox *Vulpes velox*, of N. American prairies, esp. the form inhabiting the south west US and Mexico, sometimes regarded as a distinct species (*Vulpes macrotis*). [probably from KIT[2]]

kith /kɪθ/ *n.* □ **kith and kin** friends and relations. [Old English *cȳthth*, from Germanic]

kitsch /kɪtʃ/ *n.* (often *attrib.*) garish, tasteless, or sentimental art (*kitsch plastic models of the royal family*). □ **kitschy** *adj.* (**kitschier**, **kitschiest**). **kitschiness** *n.* [German]

kitten /ˈkɪt(ə)n/ *n. & v.* ● *n.* **1** a young cat. **2** a young ferret etc. ● *v.intr. & tr.* (of a cat etc.) give birth or give birth to. □ **have kittens** *Brit. colloq.* be extremely upset, anxious, or nervous. [Middle English *kito(u)n*, *ketoun* from Old French *chitoun*, *chetoun*, diminutive of *chat* CAT[1]]

kittenish /ˈkɪt(ə)nɪʃ/ *adj.* **1** like a young cat; playful and lively. **2** flirtatious, coy. □ **kittenishly** *adv.* **kittenishness** *n.* [KITTEN]

kittiwake /ˈkɪtɪweɪk/ *n.* a small gull of the genus *Rissa*, nesting on sea cliffs, esp. *Rissa tridactyla* of the N. Atlantic and Arctic Oceans. [imitative of its cry]

kittle /ˈkɪt(ə)l/ *adj.* (also **kittle-cattle** /ˈkɪt(ə)lkat(ə)l/) **1** (of a person) capricious, rash, or erratic in behaviour. **2** difficult to deal with. [Middle English (now Scots & dialect) *kittle* 'tickle', probably from Old Norse *kitla*]

kitty[1] /ˈkɪti/ *n.* (*pl.* **-ies**) **1** a fund of money for communal use. **2** the pool in some card games. **3** the jack in bowls. [19th c.: origin unknown]

kitty[2] /ˈkɪti/ *n.* (*pl.* **-ies**) a pet name or a child's name for a kitten or cat.

kitty-cornered var. of CATER-CORNERED.

kiwi /ˈki:wi:, -wi/ *n.* (*pl.* **kiwis**) **1** a flightless New Zealand bird of the genus *Apteryx* with hairlike feathers and a long bill. **2** (**Kiwi**) *colloq.* a New Zealander, esp. a soldier or member of a national sports team. [Maori]

kiwi fruit *n.* the fruit of a climbing plant, *Actinidia chinensis*, having a thin hairy skin, green flesh, and black seeds. Also called *Chinese gooseberry*.

kJ *abbr.* kilojoule(s).

KKK *abbr. US* Ku Klux Klan.

kl *abbr.* kilolitre(s).

Klansman /ˈklanzmən/ *n.* (*pl.* **-men**; *fem.* **Klanswoman**, *pl.* **-women**) a member of the Ku Klux Klan.

klaxon /ˈklaks(ə)n/ *n. propr.* a horn or warning hooter, originally on a motor vehicle. [name of the manufacturing company]

Kleenex /ˈkli:nɛks/ *n.* (*pl.* same or **Kleenexes**) *propr.* an absorbent disposable paper tissue, used esp. as a handkerchief.

Klein bottle /klʌɪn/ *n. Math.* a closed surface with only one side, formed by passing the neck of a tube through the side of the tube to join the hole in the base. [named after F. *Klein*, German mathematician d. 1925]

klepht /klɛft/ *n.* **1** a member of the original body of Greeks who refused to submit to the Turks in the 15th c. **2** any of their descendants. **3** a brigand or bandit. [modern Greek *klephtēs* from Greek *kleptēs* 'thief']

kleptomania /klɛptə(ʊ)ˈmeɪnɪə/ *n.* a recurrent urge to steal, usu. without regard for need or profit. □ **kleptomaniac** /-nɪak/ *n. & adj.* [Greek *kleptēs* 'thief' + -MANIA]

klieg /kli:g/ *n.* (also **klieg light**) a powerful lamp in a film studio etc. [named after A. T. & J. H. *Kliegl*, American inventors d. 1927, 1959]

klipspringer /ˈklɪpsprɪŋə/ *n.* a S. African dwarf antelope, *Oreotragus oreotragus*, which can bound up and down rocky slopes. [Afrikaans, from *klip* 'rock' + *springer* 'jumper']

Klondike /ˈklɒndʌɪk/ *n.* a source of valuable material. [*Klondike* in Yukon, Canada, where gold was found in 1896]

klong /klɒŋ/ *n.* (in Thailand) a canal. [Thai]

kloof /klu:f/ *n.* a steep-sided ravine or valley in S. Africa. [Dutch, = cleft]

kludge /klʌdʒ/ *n. slang* **1** an ill-assorted collection of poorly matching parts. **2** *Computing* a machine, system, or program that has been badly put together. [invented word, perhaps influenced by BODGE, FUDGE]

klutz /klʌts/ *n.* esp. *N. Amer. colloq.* **1** a clumsy, awkward person. **2** a fool. □ **klutzy** *adj.* [Yiddish, from German *Klotz* 'wooden block']

klystron /'klʌɪstrɒn/ *n.* an electron tube that generates or amplifies microwaves by velocity modulation. [Greek *kluzō klus-* 'wash over']

km *abbr.* kilometre(s).

K-meson /keɪ'mɛzɒn, -'mi:zɒn/ *n.* = KAON. [K (see KAON) + MESON]

kn. *abbr. Naut.* knot(s).

knack /nak/ *n.* **1** an acquired or intuitive faculty of doing a thing adroitly. **2** a trick or habit of action or speech etc. (*has a knack of offending people*). **3** *archaic* an ingenious device (see KNICK-KNACK). [Middle English, probably identical with *knack* 'sharp blow or sound', from Low German, ultimately imitative]

knacker /'nakə/ *n. & v. Brit.* ● *n.* **1** a buyer of usu. old horses, cattle, etc. for slaughter. **2** a buyer of old houses, ships, etc. for the materials. ● *v.tr. slang* **1** kill. **2** (esp. as **knackered** *adj.*) exhaust, wear out. [18th c. in the sense 'old or worn-out horse': perhaps from ealier *knacker* 'harness-maker']

knackery /'nakəri/ *n.* (*pl.* **-ies**) a knacker's yard or business.

knag /nag/ *n.* **1** a knot in wood; the base of a branch. **2** a short dead branch. **3** a peg for hanging things on. [Middle English, perhaps from Low German *Knagge*]

knap[1] /nap/ *n.* chiefly *dial.* the crest of a hill or of rising ground. [Old English *cnæp(p)*, perhaps related to Old Norse *knappr* 'knob']

knap[2] /nap/ *v.tr.* (**knapped**, **knapping**) **1** break (stones for roads or building, flints, or *Austral.* ore) with a hammer. **2** *archaic* knock, rap, snap asunder. □ **knapper** *n.* [Middle English, imitative]

knapsack /'napsak/ *n.* a soldier's or hiker's bag with shoulder straps, carried on the back, and usu. made of canvas or weatherproof material. [Middle Low German, probably from *knappen* 'bite' + SACK[1]]

knapweed /'napwi:d/ *n.* any of various plants of the genus *Centaurea*, having thistle-like purple flowers. [Middle English, originally *knopweed*, from KNOP + WEED]

knar /nɑ:/ *n.* a knot or protuberance in a tree trunk, root, etc. [Middle English *knarre*, related to Middle Low German, Middle Dutch, Middle High German *knorre* 'knobbed protuberance']

knave /neɪv/ *n.* **1** a rogue, a scoundrel. **2** = JACK[1] *n.* 2. □ **knavery** *n.* (*pl.* **-ies**). **knavish** *adj.* **knavishly** *adv.* **knavishness** *n.* [Old English *cnafa* 'boy, servant', from West Germanic]

knawel /'nɔ:ɪl/ *n.* any low-growing plant of the genus *Scleranthus* (pink family). [German *Knauel*]

knead /ni:d/ *v.tr.* **1 a** work (a yeast mixture, clay, etc.) into dough, paste, etc., by pummelling and folding. **b** make (bread, pottery, etc.) in this way. **2** blend or weld together (*kneaded them into a unified group*). **3** massage (muscles etc.) as if kneading. □ **kneadable** *adj.* **kneader** *n.* [Old English *cnedan*, from Germanic]

knee /ni:/ *n. & v.* ● *n.* **1 a** (often *attrib.*) the joint between the thigh and the lower leg in humans. **b** the corresponding joint in other animals. **c** the area around this. **d** the upper surface of the thigh of a sitting person; the lap (*held her on his knee*). **2** the part of a garment covering the knee. **3** anything resembling a knee in shape or position, esp. a piece of wood or iron bent at an angle, a sharp turn in a graph, etc. ● *v.* (**knees, kneed, kneeing**) **1** *tr.* touch or strike with the knee (*kneed the ball past him*; *kneed him in the groin*). **2** *Brit. colloq.* **a** *tr.* cause (trousers etc.) to bulge at the knee. **b** *intr.* (of trousers etc.) bulge at the knee (*tend to knee*). □ **bend** (or **bow**) **the knee 1** kneel in submission, worship, or supplication. **2** submit. **bring to its** (or **his** or **her**) **knees** reduce (a thing or person) to a state of weakness or submission. **on** (or **on one's**) **bended knee** (or **knees**) kneeling, esp. in supplication, submission, or worship. [Old English *cnēo(w)*]

knee-bend *n.* the action of bending the knee, esp. as a physical exercise in which the body is raised and lowered without the use of the hands.

knee-breeches *n.pl.* close-fitting trousers reaching to or just below the knee.

kneecap /'ni:kap/ *n. & v.* ● *n.* **1** the convex bone in front of the knee joint; the patella. **2** a protective covering for the knee. ● *v.tr.* (**-capped, -capping**) *colloq.* shoot (a person) in the knee or leg as a punishment, esp. for betraying a terrorist group. □ **kneecapping** *n.*

knee-deep *adj.* **1** (usu. foll. by *in*) **a** immersed up to the knees. **b** deeply involved. **2** so deep as to reach the knees.

knee-high *adj. & adv.* so high as to reach the knees. □ **knee-high to a grasshopper** very small or very young.

kneehole /'ni:həʊl/ *n.* a space for the knees, esp. under a desk (often *attrib.*: *kneehole desk*).

knee-jerk *n. & adj.* ● *n.* a sudden involuntary kick caused by a blow on the tendon just below the knee. ● *attrib.adj.* predictable, automatic, stereotyped (*a knee-jerk reaction*).

knee joint *n.* **1** = KNEE *n.* 1a, b. **2** a joint made of two pieces hinged together.

kneel /ni:l/ *v.intr.* (*past* and *past part.* **knelt** /nɛlt/ or esp. *US* **kneeled**) fall or rest on the knees or a knee. [Old English *cnēowlian* (as KNEE)]

knee-length *adj.* reaching the knees.

kneeler /'ni:lə/ *n.* **1** a hassock or cushion used for kneeling, esp. in church. **2** a person who kneels.

knee-pan *n.* the kneecap.

knees-up *n. Brit. colloq.* a lively party or gathering.

knee-trembler *n. slang* an act of sexual intercourse between people in a standing position.

knell /nɛl/ *n. & v.* ● *n.* **1** the sound of a bell, esp. when rung solemnly for a death or funeral. **2** an announcement, event, etc., regarded as a solemn warning of disaster. ● *v.* **1** *intr.* **a** (of a bell) ring solemnly, esp. for a death or funeral. **b** make a doleful or ominous sound. **2** *tr.* proclaim by or as by a knell (*knelled the death of all their hopes*). □ **ring the knell of** announce or herald the end of. [Old English *cnyll*, *cnyllan*: perhaps influenced by *bell*]

knelt *past* and *past part.* of KNEEL.

Knesset /'knɛsɛt/ *n.* the parliament of modern Israel. [Hebrew, literally 'gathering']

knew *past* of KNOW.

knickerbocker /'nɪkəbɒkə/ *n.* **1** (in *pl.*) loose-fitting breeches gathered at the knee or calf. **2** (**Knickerbocker**) **a** a New Yorker. **b** a descendant of the original Dutch settlers in New York. [named after Diedrich *Knickerbocker*, pretended author of W. Irving's *History of New York* (1809)]

Knickerbocker Glory *n. Brit.* ice cream served with other ingredients in a tall glass.

knickers /'nɪkəz/ *n.pl.* **1** *Brit.* a woman's or girl's undergarment covering the body from the waist or hips to the top of the thighs and having leg-holes or separate legs. **2** *N. Amer.* **a** knickerbockers. **b** a boy's short trousers. **3** (as *int.*) *Brit. slang* an expression of contempt. [abbreviation of *knickerbockers* (KNICKERBOCKER)]

knick-knack /'nɪknak/ *n.* (also **nick-nack**) **1** a useless and usu. worthless ornament; a trinket. **2** a small, dainty article of furniture, dress, etc. □ **knick-knackery** *n.* **knick-knackish** *adj.* [reduplication of *knack* in obsolete sense 'trinket']

knife /nʌɪf/ *n. & v.* ● *n.* (*pl.* **knives** /nʌɪvz/) **1 a** a metal blade used as a cutting tool with usu. one long sharp edge fixed rigidly in a handle or hinged (cf. PENKNIFE). **b** a similar tool used as a weapon. **2** a cutting blade forming part of a machine. **3** (as **the knife**) *colloq.* a surgical operation or operations. ● *v.* **1** *tr.* cut or stab with a knife. **2** *tr. slang* bring about the defeat of (a person) by underhand means. **3** *intr.* (usu. foll. by *through*) cut or cut its way like a knife. □ **before you can say knife** *colloq.* very quickly or suddenly. **get one's knife into** treat maliciously or vindictively, persecute. **go under the knife** *colloq.* have surgery. **that one could cut with a knife** *colloq.* (of an accent, atmosphere, etc.) very obvious, oppressive, etc. □ **knifelike** *adj.* **knifer** *n.* [Old English *cnīf* from Old Norse *knífr*, from Germanic]

knife-board *n.* a board on which knives are cleaned.

knife-edge *n.* **1** the edge of a knife. **2** a position of extreme danger or uncertainty. **3** a steel wedge on which a pendulum etc. oscillates. **4** = ARÊTE.

knife-grinder *n.* **1** a travelling sharpener of knives etc. **2** a person who grinds knives etc. during their manufacture.

knife machine *n.* a machine for cleaning knives.

knife-pleat *n.* a narrow flat pleat on a skirt etc., usu. overlapping another.

knifepoint /ˈnʌɪfpɔɪnt/ *n.* the pointed end of a knife. □ **at knifepoint** threatened with a knife or an ultimatum etc.

knife rest *n.* a metal or glass support for a carving knife or carving fork at table.

knife-throwing *n.* a circus etc. act in which knives are thrown at targets. □ **knife-thrower** *n.*

knight /nʌɪt/ *n.* & *v.* ● *n.* **1** a man awarded a non-hereditary title (*Sir*) by a sovereign in recognition of merit or service. **2** *hist.* **a** a man, usu. noble, raised esp. by a sovereign to honourable military rank after service as a page and squire. **b** a military follower or attendant, esp. of a lady as her champion in a war or tournament. **3** a man devoted to the service of a woman, cause, etc. **4** *Chess* a piece usu. shaped like a horse's head. **5 a** *Rom.Hist.* a member of the class of *equites*, originally the cavalry of the Roman army. **b** *Gk Hist.* a citizen of the second class in Athens. **6** (in full **knight of the shire**) *hist.* a gentleman representing a shire or county in Parliament. ● *v.tr.* confer a knighthood on. □ **knighthood** *n.* **knightlike** *adj.* **knightly** *adj.* & *adv. poet.* **knightliness** *n.* [Old English *cniht* 'boy, youth, hero', from West Germanic]

knightage /ˈnʌɪtɪdʒ/ *n.* **1** knights collectively. **2** a list and account of knights.

knight bachelor *n.* (*pl.* **knights bachelor**) a knight not belonging to a special order.

knight commander see COMMANDER 3.

knight errant *n.* **1** a medieval knight wandering in search of chivalrous adventures. **2** a man of a chivalrous or quixotic nature. □ **knight-errantry** *n.*

Knight Hospitaller *n.* (*pl.* **Knights Hospitallers**) a member of an order of monks with a military history, founded at Jerusalem *c.*1050.

knight in shining armour *n.* a chivalrous rescuer or helper, esp. of a woman.

knight marshal *n. hist.* an officer of the royal household with judicial functions.

knight of the road *n. colloq.* **1** a highwayman. **2** a commercial traveller. **3** a tramp. **4** a lorry driver or taxi driver.

knight of the shire see KNIGHT *n.* 6.

knight-service *n. hist.* the tenure of land by military service.

Knight Templar *n.* (*pl.* **Knights Templars**) *hist.* a member of a religious and military order for the protection of pilgrims to the Holy Land, suppressed in 1312.

kniphofia /nɪˈfəʊfɪə, nʌɪ-; nɪpˈhəʊfɪə/ *n.* a tall ornamental plant of the genus *Kniphofia* (lily family), native to S. and E. Africa, with long spikes or dense racemes of red, yellow, or orange flowers, e.g. the red-hot poker. [named after J.H. *Kniphof*, German botanist d. 1763]

knish /knɪʃ/ *n.* a dumpling of flaky dough filled with cheese etc. and baked or fried. [Yiddish from Russian]

knit /nɪt/ *v.* & *n.* ● *v.* (**knitting**; *past* and *past part.* **knitted** or (esp. in senses 2–4) **knit**) **1** *tr.* (also *absol.*) **a** make (a garment, blanket, etc.) by interlocking loops of esp. wool with knitting needles. **b** make (a garment etc.) with a knitting machine. **c** make (a plain stitch) in knitting (*knit one, purl one*). **2 a** *tr.* contract (the forehead) in vertical wrinkles. **b** *intr.* (of the forehead) contract; frown. **3** *tr.* & *intr.* (often foll. by *together*) make or become close or compact, esp. through common interests etc. (*a close-knit group*). **4** *intr.* (often foll. by *together*) (of parts of a broken bone) become joined; heal. ● *n.* knitted material or a knitted garment. □ **knit up 1** make or repair by knitting. **2** conclude, finish, or end. □ **knitter** *n.* [Old English *cnyttan* from West Germanic: cf. KNOT[1]]

knitting /ˈnɪtɪŋ/ *n.* **1** a garment etc. in the process of being knitted. **2 a** the act of knitting. **b** an instance of this.

knitting machine *n.* a machine used for knitting garments etc.

knitting needle *n.* a thin pointed rod of steel, wood, plastic, etc., used esp. in pairs for knitting.

knitwear /ˈnɪtwɛː/ *n.* knitted garments.

knives *pl.* of KNIFE.

knob /nɒb/ *n.* & *v.* ● *n.* **1 a** a rounded protuberance, esp. at the end or on the surface of a thing. **b** a handle of a door, drawer, etc., shaped like a knob. **c** a knob-shaped attachment for pulling, turning, etc. (*press the knob under the desk*). **2** a small, usu. round, piece (of butter, coal, sugar, etc.). **3** esp. *N. Amer.* a prominent round hill. **4** *coarse slang* the penis. ● *v.* (**knobbed**, **knobbing**) **1** *tr.* provide with knobs. **2** *intr.* (usu. foll. by *out*) bulge. □ **with knobs on** *Brit. slang* that and more (used as a retort to an insult, in emphatic agreement, etc.) (*and the same to you with knobs on*). □ **knobby** *adj.* **knoblike** *adj.* [Middle English from Middle Low German *knobbe* 'knot, knob, bud': cf. KNOP, NOB[2], NUB]

knobble /ˈnɒb(ə)l/ *n. Brit.* a small knob. □ **knobbly** *adj.* (also *N. Amer.*). [Middle English, diminutive of KNOB: cf. Dutch & Low German *knobbel*]

knobkerrie /ˈnɒbkɛri/ *n.* a short stick with a knobbed head used as a weapon, esp. in S. Africa. [from KNOB + Nama *kieri* 'knob kerrie', suggested by Afrikaans *knopkierie*]

knobstick /ˈnɒbstɪk/ *n.* **1** = KNOBKERRIE. **2** *archaic* = BLACKLEG.

knock /nɒk/ *v.* & *n.* ● *v.* **1 a** *tr.* strike (a hard surface) with an audible sharp blow (*knocked the table three times*). **b** *intr.* strike, esp. a door to gain admittance (*can you hear someone knocking?*; *knocked at the door*). **2** *tr.* make (a hole, a dent, etc.) by knocking (*knock a hole in the fence*). **3** *tr.* (usu. foll. by *in*, *out*, *off*, etc.) drive (a thing, a person, etc.) by striking (*knocked the ball into the hole*; *knocked those ideas out of his head*; *knocked her hand away*). **4** *tr. colloq.* criticize. **5** *intr.* **a** (of a motor or other engine) make a thumping or rattling noise, esp. due to faulty combustion. **b** = PINK[3]. **6** *tr. Brit. slang* make a strong impression on, astonish. **7** *tr. Brit. coarse slang offens.* = *knock off* 7. ● *n.* **1** an act of knocking. **2** a sharp rap, esp. at a door. **3** an audible sharp blow. **4** the sound of knocking in an engine, esp. in a motor engine. **5** *Cricket colloq.* an innings. □ **knock about** (or **around**) **1** strike repeatedly; treat roughly (*knocked her about*). **2** lead a wandering adventurous life; wander aimlessly. **3** be present without design or volition (*there's a cup knocking about somewhere*). **4** (usu. foll. by *with*) be associated socially (*knocks about with his brother*). **knock against 1** collide with. **2** come across casually. **knock back 1** *colloq.* eat or drink, esp. quickly. **2** *Brit. colloq.* disconcert. **3** reverse the progress of. **4** *Austral.* & *NZ colloq.* refuse, rebuff. **knock the bottom out of** see BOTTOM. **knock down 1**

strike (esp. a person) to the ground with a blow. **2** demolish. **3** (usu. foll. by *to*) (at an auction) dispose of (an article) to a bidder by a knock with a hammer (*knocked the Picasso down to him for a million*). **4** *colloq.* lower the price of (an article). **5** take (machinery, furniture, etc.) to pieces for transportation. **6** *US slang* earn as a wage. **7** *Austral.* & *NZ slang* spend (a pay cheque etc.) freely. **knock one's head against** come into collision with (unfavourable facts or conditions). **knock into a cocked hat** see COCKED HAT. **knock into the middle of next week** *colloq.* send (a person) flying, esp. with a blow. **knock into shape** see SHAPE. **knock off 1** strike off with a blow. **2** *colloq.* **a** finish work (*knocked off at 5.30*). **b** finish (work) (*knocked off work early*). **3** *colloq.* dispatch (business). **4** *colloq.* rapidly produce (a work of art, verses, etc.). **5** (often foll. by *from*) deduct (a sum) from a price, bill, etc. **6** *slang* steal. **7** *Brit. coarse slang offens.* have sexual intercourse with (a woman). **8** *slang* kill. **knock on** *Rugby* drive (a ball) with the hand or arm towards the opponents' goal line. **knock on the head 1** stun or kill (a person) by a blow on the head. **2** *Brit. colloq.* put an end to (a scheme etc.). **knock on** (or **knock**) **wood** *N. Amer.* = *touch wood*. **knock out 1** make (a person) unconscious by a blow on the head. **2** knock down (a boxer) for a count of 10, thereby winning the contest. **3** defeat, esp. in a knockout competition. **4** *colloq.* astonish, esp. by unexpected excellence, generosity, etc. **5** (*refl.*) *colloq.* exhaust (*knocked themselves out swimming*). **6** *colloq.* make or write (a plan etc.) hastily. **7** empty (a tobacco pipe) by tapping. **8** *Austral., NZ,* & *US slang* earn. **knock sideways** *colloq.* disconcert; astonish. **knock one's socks off** see SOCK[1]. **knock spots off** *Brit.* defeat easily. **knock together** put together or assemble hastily or roughly. **knock up 1** *Brit.* make or arrange hastily. **2** drive upwards with a blow. **3 a** become exhausted or ill. **b** exhaust or make ill. **4** *Brit.* arouse (a person) by a knock at the door. **5** *Cricket* score (runs) rapidly. **6** esp. *US slang* make pregnant. **7** *Brit.* practise a ball game before formal play begins. **take a** (or **the**) **knock** be hard hit financially or emotionally. [Middle English from Old English *cnocian*: probably imitative]

knockabout /ˈnɒkəbaʊt/ *adj.* & *n.* ● *attrib.adj.* **1** (of comedy) boisterous; slapstick. **2** (of clothes) suitable for rough use. **3** *Austral.* of a farm or station handyman. ● *n.* **1** *Austral.* a farm or station handyman. **2** a knockabout performer or performance.

knock-back *n. Austral.* & *NZ colloq.* a refusal; a rebuff.

knock-down *adj.* & *n.* ● *attrib.adj.* **1** (of a blow, misfortune, argument, etc.) overwhelming. **2** *colloq.* (of a price) very low. **3** (of a price at auction) reserve. **4** (of furniture etc.) easily dismantled and reassembled. **5** (of an insecticide) rapidly immobilizing. ● *n. Austral.* & *NZ slang* an introduction (to a person).

knocker /ˈnɒkə/ *n.* **1** a metal or wooden instrument hinged to a door for knocking to call attention. **2** a person or thing that knocks. **3** (in *pl.*) *coarse slang* a woman's breasts. **4** a person who buys or sells door to door. □ **on the knocker 1** *Brit.* **a** (buying or selling) from door to door. **b** (obtained) on credit. **2** *Austral.* & *NZ colloq.* promptly. **up to the knocker** *Brit. slang* in good condition; to perfection.

knocker-up *n. Brit. hist.* a person employed to rouse early workers by knocking at their doors or windows.

knock for knock agreement *n. Brit.* an agreement between insurance companies by which each pays its own policyholder regardless of liability.

knocking shop *n. Brit. slang* a brothel.

knock knees *n.pl.* an abnormal condition with the legs curved inwards at the knee. □ **knock-kneed** *adj.*

knock-off *n.* (often *attrib.*) *colloq.* a copy or imitation made esp. for commercial gain.

knock-on *n. Rugby* an act of knocking on.

knock-on effect *n.* esp. *Brit.* a secondary, indirect, or cumulative effect.

knockout /ˈnɒkaʊt/ *n.* **1** the act of making unconscious by a blow. **2** *Boxing* etc. a blow that knocks an opponent out. **3** *Brit.* a competition in which the loser in each round is eliminated (also *attrib.*: *a knockout round*). **4** *colloq.* an outstanding or irresistible person or thing.

knockout drops *n.pl.* a drug added to a drink to cause unconsciousness.

knock-up *n. Brit.* a warm-up at tennis etc.

knoll[1] /nəʊl/ *n.* a small hill or mound. [Old English *cnoll* 'hilltop', related to Middle Dutch, Middle High German *knolle* 'clod', Old Norse *knollr* 'hilltop']

knoll[2] /nəʊl/ *v.* & *n. archaic* ● *v.* **1** *tr.* & *intr.* = KNELL. **2** *tr.* summon by the sound of a bell. ● *n.* = KNELL. [Middle English, variant of KNELL: perhaps imitative]

knop /nɒp/ *n.* **1** a knob, esp. ornamental. **2** an ornamental loop or tuft in yarn. **3** *archaic* a flower bud. [Middle English from Middle Low German, Middle Dutch *knoppe*]

knopkierie /ˈknɒpkɪəri/ *n. S.Afr.* = KNOBKERRIE. [Afrikaans]

knot[1] /nɒt/ *n.* & *v.* ● *n.* **1 a** an intertwining of a rope, string, tress of hair, etc., with another, itself, or something else to join or fasten together. **b** a set method of tying a knot (*a reef knot*). **c** a ribbon etc. tied as an ornament and worn on a dress etc. **d** a tangle in hair, knitting, etc. **2 a** a unit of a ship's or aircraft's speed equivalent to one nautical mile per hour (see NAUTICAL MILE). **b** a division marked by knots on a log-line, as a measure of speed. **c** *colloq.* a nautical mile. **3** (usu. foll. by *of*) a group or cluster (*a small knot of journalists at the gate*). **4** something forming or maintaining a union; a bond or tie, esp. of wedlock. **5** a hard lump of tissue in an animal or human body. **6 a** a knob or protuberance in a stem, branch, or root. **b** a hard mass formed in a tree trunk at the intersection with a branch. **c** a round cross-grained piece in timber where a branch has been cut through. **d** a node on the stem of a plant. **7** a difficulty; a problem. **8** a central point in a problem or the plot of a story etc. **9** (in full **porter's knot**) *Brit. hist.* a double shoulder pad and forehead-loop used for carrying loads. ● *v.* (**knotted**, **knotting**) **1** *tr.* tie (a string etc.) in a knot. **2** *tr.* entangle. **3** *tr.* knit (the brows). **4** *tr.* unite closely or intricately (*knotted together in intrigue*). **5 a** *intr.* make knots for fringing. **b** *tr.* make (a fringe) with knots. □ **at a rate of knots** *Brit. colloq.* very fast. **get knotted!** *Brit. slang* an expression of disbelief, annoyance, etc. **tie in knots** *colloq.* baffle or confuse completely. □ **knotless** *adj.* **knotter** *n.* **knotting** *n.* (esp. in sense 5a of *v.*). [Old English *cnotta*, from West Germanic]

knot[2] /nɒt/ *n.* a small sandpiper, *Calidris canutus*. [Middle English: origin unknown]

knot-garden *n.* an intricately designed formal garden.

knotgrass /ˈnɒtgrɑːs/ *n.* **1** a common weed, *Polygonum aviculare*, with creeping stems and small pink flowers. **2** any of various other plants, esp. grasses, with jointed stems.

knot-hole *n.* a hole in a piece of timber where a knot has fallen out.

knotty /ˈnɒti/ *adj.* (**knottier**, **knottiest**) **1** full of knots. **2** hard to explain; puzzling (*a knotty problem*). □ **knottily** *adv.* **knottiness** *n.*

knotweed /ˈnɒtwiːd/ *n.* a polygonum, esp. *Fallopia japonica*, a fast-growing Japanese plant, widely naturalized.

knotwork /ˈnɒtwəːk/ *n.* ornamental work representing or consisting of intertwined cords.

knout /naʊt, nuːt/ *n.* & *v. hist.* ● *n.* a scourge used in imperial Russia, often causing death. ● *v.tr.* flog with a knout. [French via Russian *knut* from Icelandic *knútr*: related to KNOT[1]]

know /nəʊ/ *v.* & *n.* ● *v.* (*past* **knew** /njuː/; *past part.* **known** /nəʊn/) **1** *tr.* (often foll. by *that, how, what,* etc.) **a** have in the mind; have learnt; be able to recall (*knows a lot about cars; knows what to do*). **b** (also *absol.*) be aware of (a fact) (*he knows I am waiting; I think he knows*). **c** have a good command of (a subject or language) (*knew German; knows his tables*). **2** *tr.* be acquainted or friendly with (a person or thing). **3** *tr.* **a** recognize; identify (*I knew him at once; knew him for an American*). **b** (foll. by *to* + infin.) be aware of (a person or thing) as being or doing what is specified (*knew them to be rogues*). **c** (foll. by *from*) be able to distinguish (one from another) (*did not know him from Adam*). **4** *tr.* be subject to (*her joy knew no bounds*). **5** *tr.* have personal experience of (fear etc.). **6** *tr.* (as **known** *adj.*) **a** publicly acknowledged (*a known thief; a known fact*). **b** *Math.* (of a quantity etc.) having a value that can be stated. **7** *intr.* have understanding or knowledge. **8** *tr. archaic* have sexual intercourse with. ● *n.* (in phr. **in the know**) *colloq.* well informed; having special knowledge. □ **all one knows** (or **knows how**) **1** all one can (*did all he knew to stop it*). **2** *adv.* to the utmost of one's power (*tried all she knew*). **before one knows where one is** with baffling speed. **be not to know 1** have no way of learning (*wasn't to know they'd arrive late*). **2** be not to be told (*she's not to know about the party*). **don't I know it!** *colloq.* an expression of rueful assent. **don't you know** *colloq.* or *joc.* an expression used for emphasis (*such a bore, don't you know*). **for all** (or **aught**) **I know** so far as my knowledge extends. **have been known to** have occasionally in the past (*they have been known to turn up late*). **I knew it!** I was sure that this would happen. **I know what** I have a new idea, suggestion, etc. **know about** have information about. **know best** be or claim to be better informed etc. than others. **know better than** (foll. by *that*, or *to* + infin.) be wise, well informed, or well-mannered enough to avoid (specified behaviour etc.). **know by name 1** have heard the name of. **2** be able to give the name of. **know by sight** recognize the appearance (only) of. **know how** know the way to do something. **know of** be aware of; have heard of (*not that I know of*). **know one's own mind** be decisive, not vacillate. **know the ropes** (or **one's stuff**) be fully knowledgeable or experienced. **know a thing or two** be experienced or shrewd. **know what's what** have adequate knowledge of the world, life, etc. **know who's who** be aware of who or what each person is. **not know that ...** *colloq.* be fairly sure that ... not (*I don't know that I want to go*). **not know what hit one** be suddenly injured, killed, disconcerted, etc. **not want to know** refuse to take any notice of. **what do you know** (or **know about that**)? *colloq.* an expression of surprise. **you know** *colloq.* **1** an expression implying something generally known or known to the hearer (*you know, the pub on the corner*). **2** an expression used as a gap-filler in conversation. **you know something** (or **what**)? I am going to tell you something. **you never know** nothing in the future is certain. □ **knowable** *adj.* **knower** *n.* [Old English (*ge*)*cnāwan*, related to CAN[1], KEN]

know-all *n.* esp. *Brit. colloq.* a person who seems to know everything.

know-how *n.* **1** practical knowledge; technique, expertise. **2** natural skill or invention.

knowing /ˈnəʊɪŋ/ *n.* & *adj.* ● *n.* the state of being aware or informed of any thing. ● *adj.* **1** usu. *derog.* cunning; sly. **2** showing knowledge or awareness; shrewd. □ **there is no knowing** no one can tell. □ **knowingness** *n.*

knowingly /ˈnəʊɪŋli/ *adv.* **1** consciously; intentionally (*had never knowingly injured him*). **2** in a knowing manner (*smiled knowingly*).

know-it-all *n.* esp. *N. Amer.* = KNOW-ALL.

knowledge /ˈnɒlɪdʒ/ *n.* **1 a** (usu. foll. by *of*) awareness or familiarity gained by experience (of a person, fact, or thing) (*have no knowledge of that*). **b** a person's range of information (*is not within his knowledge*). **2 a** (usu. foll. by *of*) a theoretical or practical understanding of a subject, language, etc. (*has a good knowledge of Greek*). **b** the sum of what is known (*every branch of knowledge*). **3** *Philos.* true, justified belief; certain understanding, as opposed to opinion. **4** = CARNAL KNOWLEDGE. □ **come to one's knowledge** become known to one. **to my knowledge 1** so far as I know. **2** as I know for certain. [Middle English *knaulege*, with earlier verb *knawlechen* formed as KNOW + Old English *-lǣcan* from *lāc* as in WEDLOCK]

knowledgeable /ˈnɒlɪdʒəb(ə)l/ *adj.* (also **knowledgable**) well informed; intelligent. □ **knowledgeability** /-ˈbɪlɪti/ *n.* **knowledgeableness** *n.* **knowledgeably** *adv.*

known *past part.* of KNOW.

know-nothing *n.* **1** an ignorant person. **2** (also **Know-Nothing**) *US* a person who feigns ignorance or who denies holding an opinion, to avoid controversy (after the American Know-Nothing Party of the 1850s which denied its own existence and hence its opposition to immigrants esp. Catholics). □ **know-nothingism** *n.* (in sense 2 of *n.*).

Knt. *abbr.* Knight.

knuckle /ˈnʌk(ə)l/ *n.* & *v.* ● *n.* **1** the bone at a finger joint, esp. that adjoining the hand. **2 a** a projection of the carpal or tarsal joint of a quadruped. **b** a joint of meat consisting of this with the adjoining parts, esp. of bacon or pork. ● *v.tr.* strike, press, or rub with the knuckles. □ **go the knuckle** *Austral. slang* fight, punch. **knuckle down** (often foll. by *to*) **1** apply oneself seriously (to a task etc.). **2** (also **knuckle under**) give in; submit. **rap on** (or **over**) **the knuckles** see RAP[1]. □ **knuckly** *adj.* [Middle English *knokel* from Middle Low German, Middle Dutch *knökel*, diminutive of *knoke* 'bone']

knuckle-bone *n.* **1** bone forming a knuckle. **2** the bone of a sheep or other animal corresponding to or resembling a knuckle. **3** a knuckle of meat. **4** (in *pl.*) **a** animal knuckle-bones used in the game of jacks. **b** the game of jacks.

knuckleduster /ˈnʌk(ə)ldʌstə/ *n.* a metal guard worn over the knuckles in fighting, esp. to increase the effect of blows.

knucklehead /ˈnʌk(ə)lhɛd/ *n. colloq.* a stupid or dull-witted person.

knuckle sandwich *n. slang* a punch in the mouth.

knur /nəː/ *n.* (also **knurr**) **1** a hard excrescence on the trunk of a tree. **2** a hard concretion. [Middle English *knorre*, variant of KNAR]

knurl /nəːl/ *n.* a small projecting knob, ridge, etc. □ **knurled** /nəːld/ *adj.* [KNUR]

KO *abbr.* **1** knockout. **2** kick-off.

koa /ˈkəʊə/ *n.* **1** a Hawaiian tree, *Acacia koa*, which produces dark red wood. **2** this wood. [Hawaiian]

koala /kəʊˈɑːlə/ *n.* an Australian bearlike marsupial, *Phascolarctos cinereus*, having thick grey fur and feeding on eucalyptus leaves. [Dharuk *gula*, *gulawan*[y]]

■ **Usage** The embellished form, *koala bear*, is now considered incorrect.

koan /ˈkəʊɑːn, ˈkəʊan/ *n.* a paradoxical anecdote or riddle without a solution, used in Zen Buddhism to demonstrate the inadequacy of logical reasoning and provoke enlightenment. [Japanese, = public matter (for thought)]

kob /kɒb/ *n.* (*pl.* same) (in full **kob antelope**) a grazing antelope, *Kobus kob*, native to African savannah. [Wolof (a language of Senegal and the Gambia) *kooba*]

kobold /ˈkəʊbəld/ *n.* (in Germanic mythology): **1** a familiar spirit; a brownie. **2** an underground spirit in mines etc. [German]

Köchel number /ˈkəːx(ə)l/ *n. Mus.* a number given to each of Mozart's compositions in the complete catalogue of his works compiled by Köchel and his successors. [named after L. von *Köchel*, Austrian scientist d. 1877]

KO'd /keɪˈəʊd/ *adj.* knocked out. [abbreviation]

Kodiak /ˈkəʊdɪak/ *n.* (in full **Kodiak bear**) a very large Alaskan race of the brown bear. [*Kodiak* Island, Alaska]

koel /ˈkəʊəl/ *n.* a dark-coloured cuckoo, *Eudynamys scolopacea*. [Hindi *kōīl* from Sanskrit *kokila*]

kofta /ˈkɒftə, ˈkəʊftə/ *n.* (in Indian cookery) a spiced meatball (or fish or vegetable ball). [Urdu and Persian *koftah* 'pounded meat']

kohl /kəʊl/ *n.* a black powder, usu. antimony sulphide or lead sulphide, used as eye make-up esp. in Eastern countries. [Arabic *kuḥl*]

kohlrabi /kəʊlˈrɑːbi/ *n.* (*pl.* **kohlrabies**) a variety of cabbage with an edible turnip-like swollen stem. [German, from Italian *cavoli rape* (pl.) from medieval Latin *caulorapa* (as COLE, RAPE[2])]

koi /kɔɪ/ *n.* (also **koi carp**) (*pl.* same) a carp of a large ornamental variety bred in Japan. [Japanese]

koine /ˈkɔmiː/ *n.* **1** the common language of the Greeks from the close of the classical period to the Byzantine era. **2** a common language shared by various peoples; a lingua franca. [Greek *koinē* (*dialektos*) 'common (language)']

kola var. of COLA.

kolinsky /kəˈlɪnski/ *n.* (*pl.* **-ies**) **1** the Siberian weasel, *Mustela sibirica*, with a rich brown coat. **2** the fur of this. [Russian *kolinskiĭ*, from *Kola* in NW Russia]

kolkhoz /ˈkɒlkɒz, kʌlkˈhɔːz/ *n.* a collective farm in the former USSR. [Russian, from *kollektivnoe khozyaĭstvo* 'collective farm']

komitadji (also **komitaji**) var. of COMITADJI.

Komodo dragon /kəˈməʊdəʊ/ *n.* (also **Komodo monitor**) a large monitor lizard, *Varanus komodoensis*, native to the E. Indies. [*Komodo* Island in Indonesia]

Komsomol /ˈkɒmsəmɒl/ *n. hist.* **1** an organization for Communist youth in the former Soviet Union. **2** a member of this. [Russian, from *Kommunisticheskiĭ soyuz molodezhi* 'Communist League of Youth']

Kongo /ˈkɒŋgəʊ/ *n. & adj.* ● *n.* (*pl.* same or **-os**) **1** a member of a Bantu-speaking people inhabiting the region of the River Congo in west central Africa. **2** the language of this people. ● *adj.* of or relating to this people or their language. [native name]

koodoo var. of KUDU.

kook /kuːk/ *n. & adj. US slang* ● *n.* a crazy or eccentric person. ● *adj.* crazy; eccentric. [20th c.: probably from CUCKOO]

kookaburra /ˈkʊkəbʌrə/ *n.* any Australian kingfisher of the genus *Dacelo*, esp. *D. novaeguineae*, which makes a strange laughing cry. Also called *laughing jackass*. [Wiradhuri *guguburra*]

kooky /ˈkʊki, ˈkuːki/ *adj.* (**kookier**, **kookiest**) *slang* crazy, eccentric, strange. □ **kookily** *adv.* **kookiness** *n.*

kop /kɒp/ *n.* **1** *S.Afr.* a prominent hill or peak. **2** (**Kop**) *Football* a high bank of terracing for standing spectators, esp. those supporting the home side. [Afrikaans from Dutch, = head: cf. COP[2]; sense 2 from *Spioen Kop*, site of a Boer War battle]

kopek (also **kopeck**) var. of COPECK.

kopi /ˈkəʊpi/ *n. Austral.* powdered gypsum. [Baagandji dialect *gabi*]

koppie /ˈkɒpi/ *n.* (also **kopje**) *S.Afr.* a small hill. [Afrikaans *koppie*, Dutch *kopje*, diminutive of *kop* 'head']

koradji /ˈkɒrədʒi, kəˈradʒi/ *n.* (*pl.* **koradjis**) *Austral.* an Aboriginal medicine man. [Dharuk *garraaji* 'doctor']

Koran /kɔːˈrɑːn, kə-/ *n.* (also **Quran**, **Qur'an** /kə-/) the Islamic sacred book, believed to be the word of God as dictated to Muhammad and written down in Arabic. □ **Koranic** /-ˈranɪk, -ˈrɑːnɪk/ *adj.* [Arabic *ḳur'ān* 'recitation' from *ḳara'a* 'read']

Korean /kəˈriːən/ *n. & adj.* ● *n.* **1** a native or national of N. or S. Korea in SE Asia. **2** the language of Korea. ● *adj.* of or relating to Korea or its people or language.

korfball /ˈkɔːfbɔːl/ *n.* a game like basketball played by two teams consisting of six men and six women each. [Dutch *korfbal*, from *korf* 'basket' + *bal* 'ball']

korma /ˈkɔːmə/ *n.* a mildly-spiced Indian curry dish of meat or fish marinaded in yogurt or curds. [Urdu *ḳormā* from Turkish *kavurma*]

koruna /ˈkɒrʊnə, kəˈruːnə/ *n.* the chief monetary unit of the Czech Republic and Slovakia, equal to 100 haleru. [Czech, = crown]

kosher /ˈkəʊʃə/ *adj. & n.* ● *adj.* **1** (of food or premises in which food is sold, cooked, or eaten) fulfilling the requirements of Jewish law. **2** *colloq.* correct; genuine; legitimate. ● *n.* **1** kosher food. **2** a kosher shop. [Hebrew *kāšēr* 'proper']

koto /ˈkəʊtəʊ/ *n.* (*pl.* **-os**) a Japanese musical instrument with 13 long esp. silk strings. [Japanese]

kotow var. of KOWTOW.

koumiss /ˈkuːmɪs/ *n.* (also **kumiss**, **kumis**) a fermented liquor prepared from esp. mare's milk, used by Asian nomads and medicinally. [Tartar *kumiz*]

kouprey /ˈkuːpreɪ/ *n.* a rare grey ox, *Bos sauveli*, native to forests in Indo-China. [Cambodian]

kourbash /ˈkʊəbaʃ/ *n.* (also **kurbash**) a whip, esp. of hippopotamus hide, used as an instrument of punishment in Turkey and Egypt. [Arabic *kurbāj* from Turkish *kırbāç* 'whip']

kowhai /ˈkəʊwʌɪ, ˈkɔːfʌɪ/ *n.* any of several trees or shrubs of the genus *Sophora*, esp. *S. tetraptera* native to New Zealand and Chile with pendant clusters of yellow flowers. [Maori]

kowtow /kaʊˈtaʊ/ *n. & v.* (also **kotow** /kəʊˈtaʊ/) ● *n. hist.* the Chinese custom of kneeling and touching the ground with the forehead in worship or submission. ● *v.intr.* **1** (usu. foll. by *to*) act obsequiously. **2** *hist.* perform the kowtow. [Chinese *ketou*, from *ke* 'knock' + *tou* 'head']

KP *n. US Mil. colloq.* **1** enlisted men detailed to help the cooks. **2** kitchen duty. [abbreviation of *kitchen police*]

k.p.h. *abbr.* kilometres per hour.

Kr *symb. Chem.* the element krypton.

kraal /krɑːl/ *n. S.Afr.* **1** a village of huts enclosed by a fence. **2** an enclosure for cattle or sheep. [Afrikaans via Portuguese *curral* from Nama]

kraft /krɑːft/ *n.* (in full **kraft paper**) a kind of strong smooth brown wrapping paper. [German from Swedish, = strength]

krait /krʌɪt/ *n.* any venomous snake of the genus *Bungarus* of E. Asia. [Hindi *karait*]

kraken /ˈkrɑːk(ə)n/ *n.* a large mythical sea monster said to appear off the coast of Norway. [Norwegian]

krans /krɑːns/ *n. S.Afr.* a precipitous or overhanging wall of rocks. [Afrikaans from Dutch *krans* 'coronet']

Kraut /kraʊt/ *n. slang offens.* a German. [shortening of SAUERKRAUT]

kremlin /ˈkrɛmlɪn/ *n.* **1** a citadel within a Russian town. **2** (**the Kremlin**) **a** the citadel in Moscow. **b** the Russian or (formerly) USSR Government housed within it. [French, from Russian *Kreml'*, of Tartar origin]

Kremlinology /krɛmlɪˈnɒlədʒi/ *n.* the study and analysis of Soviet or Russian policies. □ **Kremlinologist** *n.*

kriegspiel /ˈkriːgspiːl/ *n.* **1** a war game in which blocks representing armies etc. are moved about on maps. **2** a form of chess with an umpire, in which each player has only limited information about the opponent's moves. [German, from *Krieg* 'war' + *Spiel* 'game']

krill /krɪl/ *n.* tiny planktonic crustaceans found in the seas around the Antarctic and eaten by fish and some seals and whales. [Norwegian *kril* 'tiny fish']

krimmer /ˈkrɪmə/ *n.* a grey or black furry fleece of young Crimean lambs. [German, from *Krim* 'Crimea']

kris /kriːs/ *n.* (also **crease**, **creese**) a Malay or Indonesian dagger with a wavy blade. [ultimately from Malay *k(i)rīs*]

Krishnaism /ˈkrɪʃnəɪz(ə)m/ *n. Hinduism* the worship of the Hindu god Krishna as an incarnation of Vishnu.

kromesky /krə(ʊ)ˈmɛski, ˈkrɒmɛski/ *n.* (*pl.* **-ies**) a croquette of minced meat or fish, rolled in bacon and fried. [apparently from Polish *kromeczka* 'small slice']

krona /ˈkrəʊnə/ *n.* **1** (*pl.* **kronor** *pronunc.* same) the chief monetary unit of Sweden. **2** (*pl.* **kronur** *pronunc.* same) the chief monetary unit of Iceland. [Swedish & Icelandic, = CROWN]

krone /ˈkrəʊnə/ *n.* (*pl.* **kroner** *pronunc.* same) the chief monetary unit of Denmark and Norway. [Danish & Norwegian, = CROWN]

Kroo var. of KRU.

Kru /kruː/ *n. & adj.* (also **Kroo**) ● *n.* **1** (*pl.* same) a member of a black seafaring people on the coast of Liberia. **2** the language of this people. ● *adj.* of or relating to the Kru or their language. [West African]

krugerrand /ˈkruːɡərand, -rɑːn, kruːɡəˈrɑːnt/ *n.* a S. African gold coin depicting President Kruger. [S. J. P. *Kruger*, S. African statesman d. 1904, + RAND[1]]

krummhorn /ˈkrʌmhɔːn, ˈkrʊm-/ *n.* (also **crumhorn**) a medieval wind instrument with a double reed and a curved end. [German, from *krumm* 'crooked' + *Horn* HORN]

krypton /ˈkrɪptɒn/ *n. Chem.* an inert gaseous element of the noble gas group, forming a small portion of the earth's atmosphere and used in fluorescent lamps etc. (symbol **Kr**). [Greek *krupton* 'hidden', neut. adj. from *kruptō* 'hide']

KS *abbr.* **1** *US* Kansas (in official postal use). **2** (in the UK) King's Scholar.

Kshatriya /ˈkʃatrɪə/ *n.* a member of the second of the four great Hindu castes, the military caste. [Sanskrit from *kshatra* 'rule']

KStJ *abbr.* Knight of the Order of St John.

KT *abbr.* **1** Knight Templar. **2** (in the UK) Knight of the Order of the Thistle.

Kt. *abbr.* Knight.

kt. *abbr.* knot.

K/T boundary *n. Geol.* the boundary between the Cretaceous and Tertiary periods, marked by the extinction of many groups of organisms, including dinosaurs. [from symbols for Cretaceous and Tertiary]

Ku *symb. Chem.* the element kurchatovium.

kudos /ˈkjuːdɒs/ *n.* **1** glory; renown. **2** (often treated as *pl.*) *US disp.* praise, acclaim. [Greek]

■ **Usage** *Kudos* is not a plural noun and there is no singular *kudo*. Use in sense 2 should therefore be avoided.

kudu /ˈkuːduː, ˈkʊdʊ/ *n.* (also **koodoo**) (*pl.* **-s** or same) either of two African antelopes, *Tragelaphus strepsiceros* or *T. imberbis*, with white stripes and corkscrew-shaped ridged horns. [Afrikaans *koedoe* from Xhosa *i-qudu*]

kudzu /ˈkʊdzuː/ *n.* (in full **kudzu vine**) a quick-growing climbing plant, *Pueraria lobata*, with reddish-purple flowers. [Japanese *kuzu*]

Kufic /ˈkjuːfɪk/ *n. & adj.* (also **Cufic**) ● *n.* an early angular form of the Arabic alphabet found chiefly in decorative inscriptions. ● *adj.* of or in this type of script. [attributed to the scholars of *Kufa*, a city S. of Baghdad in Iraq]

Ku Klux Klan /kuː klʌks ˈklan, kjuː-/ *n.* a secret society of white people in the US, originally founded in the southern states after the Civil War to oppose social change and black emancipation by violence and terrorism. [perhaps from Greek *kuklos* 'circle' + CLAN]

kukri /ˈkʊkri/ *n.* (*pl.* **kukris**) a curved knife broadening towards the point, used by Gurkhas. [Hindi *kukṛī*]

kulak /ˈkuːlak/ *n. hist.* a peasant working for personal profit in Soviet Russia. [Russian, = fist, tight-fisted person]

kulan /ˈkuːlən/ *n.* a wild ass of SW Asia, closely related to the kiang. [Tartar]

Kultur /kʊlˈtʊə, German kʊlˈtuːr/ *n.* esp. *derog.* German civilization and culture, seen as racist, authoritarian, and militaristic. [German from Latin *cultura* CULTURE]

Kulturkampf /kʊlˈtʊəkampf, German kʊlˈtuːrkampf/ *n. hist.* the conflict in 19th-c. Germany between the civil and ecclesiastical authorities, esp. as regards the control of schools. [German (as KULTUR, *Kampf* 'struggle')]

kumara /ˈkuːmərə/ *n. NZ* a sweet potato. [Maori]

kumis (also **kumiss**) var. of KOUMISS.

kümmel /ˈkʊm(ə)l/ *n.* a sweet liqueur flavoured with caraway and cumin seeds. [German (as CUMIN)]

kumquat /ˈkʌmkwɒt/ *n.* (also **cumquat**) **1** an orange-like fruit with a sweet rind and acid pulp, used in preserves. **2** any shrub or small tree of the genus *Fortunella* yielding this. [Cantonese variant of Chinese *kin kü* 'golden orange']

kung fu /kʊŋ ˈfuː, kʌŋ/ *n.* a primarily unarmed Chinese martial art resembling karate. [Chinese *gongfu*, from *gong* 'merit' + *fu* 'master']

kurbash var. of KOURBASH.

kurchatovium /kəːtʃəˈtəʊvɪəm/ *n. Chem.* (a name proposed in the former USSR for) the artificial radioactive element of atomic number 104 (symbol **Ku**). Also called RUTHERFORDIUM. [named after I. V. *Kurchatov*, Russian physicist d. 1960]

Kurd /kəːd/ *n.* a member of a mainly pastoral Aryan Islamic people living in Kurdistan (contiguous areas of Iraq, Iran, and Turkey). [Kurdish]

kurdaitcha /kəˈdʌɪtʃə/ *n.* (also **kadaitcha**) *Austral.* **1** the tribal use of a bone in spells intended to cause sickness or death. **2** a man empowered to point the bone at a victim. [probably Aranda *gʷerdaje*]

Kurdish /ˈkəːdɪʃ/ *adj. & n.* ● *adj.* of or relating to the Kurds or their language. ● *n.* the Iranian language of the Kurds.

kurrajong /ˈkʌrədʒɒŋ/ *n.* (also **currajong**) any of various Australian trees, esp. *Brachychiton populneum*, which produce a tough bast fibre. [Dharuk *garrajung* 'fibre fishing line']

kursaal /ˈkʊəsɑːl, -z-/ *n.* **1** a building for the use of visitors at a health resort, esp. at a German spa. **2** a casino. [German, from *Kur* CURE + *Saal* 'room']

kurta /ˈkəːtə/ *n.* (also **kurtha**) a loose shirt or tunic worn by esp. Hindu men and women. [Hindustani]

kurtosis /kəːˈtəʊsɪs/ *n. Statistics* the sharpness of the peak of a frequency-distribution curve. [modern Latin from Greek *kurtōsis* 'bulging', from *kurtos* 'convex']

kuru /ˈkʊruː/ *n. Med.* a fatal infection of the brain occurring in some peoples in New Guinea and thought to be caused by a virus-like agent such as a prion. [name in New Guinea]

kV *abbr.* kilovolt(s).

kvass /kvɑːs/ *n.* (esp. in Russia) a fermented beverage, low in alcohol, made from rye flour or bread with malt. [Russian *kvas*]

kW *abbr.* kilowatt(s).

Kwa /kwɑː/ *n. & adj.* ● *n.* **1** the group of related languages, spoken from Ivory Coast to Nigeria, which includes Ibo and Yoruba. **2** (*pl.* same) a member of a Kwa-speaking people. ● *adj.* of or relating to this group of languages. [native name]

KWAC /kwak/ *n.* esp. *Computing* keyword and context. [abbreviation]

kwacha /ˈkwɑːtʃə/ *n.* the chief monetary unit of Zambia and Malawi. [native word, = dawn]

kwanza /ˈkwanzə/ *n.* (*pl.* same or **kwanzas**) the chief monetary unit of Angola. [perhaps from Swahili, = first]

kwashiorkor /kwɒʃɪˈɔːkɔː, kwa-/ *n.* a form of malnutrition caused by a protein deficiency of diet, esp. in young children in the tropics. [local name in Ghana]

kWh *abbr.* kilowatt-hour(s).

KWIC /kwɪk/ *n.* esp. *Computing* keyword in context. [abbreviation]

KWOC /kwɒk/ *n.* esp. *Computing* keyword out of context. [abbreviation]

KY *abbr. US* Kentucky (in official postal use).

Ky. *abbr.* Kentucky.

kyanite /ˈkʌɪənʌɪt/ *n.* a blue crystalline mineral of aluminium silicate. □ **kyanitic** /-ˈnɪtɪk/ *adj.* [Greek *kuanos* 'dark blue']

kyanize /ˈkʌɪənʌɪz/ *v.tr.* (also **-ise**) treat (wood) with a solution of corrosive sublimate to prevent decay. [named after J. H. *Kyan*, English inventor d. 1850]

kyat /kiːˈɑːt/ *n.* (*pl.* same or **kyats**) the chief monetary unit of Myanmar (Burma). [Burmese]

kybosh var. of KIBOSH.

kyle /kʌɪl/ *n.* (in Scotland) a narrow channel between islands or between an island and the mainland. [Gaelic *caol* 'strait']

kylie /ˈkʌɪli/ *n. W. Austral.* a boomerang. [Nyungar (and other Aboriginal languages) *garli*]

kylin /ˈkiːlɪn/ *n.* a mythical composite animal figured on Chinese and Japanese ceramics. [Chinese *qilin*, from *qi* 'male' + *lin* 'female']

kyloe /ˈkʌɪləʊ/ *n. Brit.* **1** an animal of a breed of small usu. black long-horned highland cattle. **2** this breed. [Gaelic *gaidhealach* 'Gaelic, Highland']

kymograph /ˈkʌɪmə(ʊ)grɑːf/ *n.* an instrument for recording variations in pressure, e.g. in sound waves or in blood within blood vessels. ▫ **kymographic** /-ˈgrafɪk/ *adj.* [Greek *kuma* 'wave' + -GRAPH]

kyphosis /kʌɪˈfəʊsɪs/ *n. Med.* excessive outward curvature of the spine, causing hunching of the back (opp. LORDOSIS). ▫ **kyphotic** /-ˈfɒtɪk/ *adj.* [modern Latin from Greek *kuphōsis*, from *kuphos* 'bent']

Kyrgyz /kɪəˈgiːz, ˈkəːgɪz/ *n. & adj.* (also **Kirghiz**) ● *n.* (*pl.* same) **1** a member of a Mongol people living in central Asia between the Volga and the Irtysh rivers, chiefly in Kyrgyzstan. **2** the Turkic language of this people. ● *adj.* of or relating to this people or their language. [Kyrgyz]

Kyrie /ˈkɪrɪeɪ/ (in full **Kyrie eleison** /ɪˈleɪɪzɒn, -sɒn, ɛˈleɪ-/) *n.* a short repeated invocation (in Greek or translated) used in many Christian liturgies, esp. at the beginning of the Eucharist or as a response in a litany. [Middle English via medieval Latin from Greek *Kurie eleēson* 'Lord, have mercy']

Ll

L[1] /ɛl/ *n.* (also **l**) (*pl.* **Ls** or **L's**) **1** the twelfth letter of the alphabet. **2** (as a Roman numeral) 50. **3** a thing shaped like an L, esp. a joint connecting two pipes at right angles.

L[2] *abbr.* (also **L.**) **1** Lake. **2** *Brit.* learner driver (cf. L-PLATE). **3** Liberal. **4** *Biol.* Linnaeus. **5** lire. **6** left.

L[3] *symb.* **1** laevorotatory. **2** Avogadro's constant.

l[1] *abbr.* (also **l.**) **1** left. **2** line. **3** liquid. **4** length. **5** *archaic* pound(s) (money).

l[2] *symb.* litre(s).

£ *abbr.* (preceding a numeral) pound or pounds (of money). [Latin *libra*]

LA *abbr.* **1** Library Association. **2** Los Angeles. **3** *US* Louisiana (in official postal use).

La *symb. Chem.* the element lanthanum.

La. *abbr.* Louisiana.

la var. of LAH.

laager /ˈlɑːɡə/ *n. & v.* ● *n.* **1** esp. *S.Afr.* a camp or encampment, esp. formed by a circle of wagons. **2** *Mil.* a park for armoured vehicles. ● *v.* **1** *tr.* **a** form (vehicles) into a laager. **b** encamp (people) in a laager. **2** *intr.* encamp. [Afrikaans from Dutch *leger*: see LEAGUER[2]]

Lab. *abbr.* **1** Labour. **2** Labrador.

lab /lab/ *n. colloq.* a laboratory. [abbreviation]

labarum /ˈlabərəm/ *n.* **1** a symbolic banner. **2** *hist.* Constantine the Great's imperial standard, with Christian symbols added to Roman military symbols. [Late Latin: origin unknown]

labdanum var. of LADANUM.

labefaction /labɪˈfakʃ(ə)n/ *n. literary* a shaking, weakening, or downfall. [Latin *labefacere* 'weaken', from *labi* 'fall' + *facere* 'make']

label /ˈleɪb(ə)l/ *n. & v.* ● *n.* **1** a usu. small piece of paper, card, fabric, metal, etc., for attaching to an object and giving information about it, instructions for use, etc. **2** esp. *derog.* a short classifying phrase or name applied to a person, a work of art, etc. **3** **a** the logo, title, or trade mark of esp. a fashion house or recording company (*brought it out under his own label*). **b** the piece of paper in the centre of a gramophone record describing its contents etc. **c** a record-producing company or part of one. **4** an adhesive stamp on a parcel etc. **5** a word placed before, after, or in the course of a dictionary definition etc. to specify its subject, register, nationality, etc. **6** *Archit.* a dripstone. **7** *Heraldry* the mark of an eldest son, consisting of a superimposed horizontal bar with usu. three downward projections. **8** *Biol.* & *Chem.* a radioactive isotope, fluorescent dye, etc., used to label another substance. ● *v.tr.* (**labelled, labelling**; *US* **labeled, labeling**) **1** attach a label to. **2** (usu. foll. by *as*) assign to a category (*labelled them as irresponsible*). **3** *Biol.* & *Chem.* make (a substance, molecule, or atom) identifiable by replacing an atom with one of a distinctive radioactive isotope, or by attaching a fluorescent dye to the molecule. □ **labeller** *n.* [originally = a strip or band: Middle English from Old French, = ribbon, probably from Germanic (as LAP[1])]

labellum /ləˈbɛləm/ *n.* (*pl.* **labella** /-lə/) **1** *Zool.* each of a pair of lobes at the tip of the proboscis in some insects. **2** *Bot.* a central petal at the base of an orchid flower, usu. large and unlike the others. [Latin, diminutive of *labrum* 'lip']

labia *pl.* of LABIUM.

labial /ˈleɪbɪəl/ *adj. & n.* ● *adj.* **1** **a** of the lips. **b** *Zool.* of, like, or serving as a lip, a liplike part, or a labium. **2** *Dentistry* designating the surface of a tooth adjacent to the lips. **3** *Phonet.* **a** (of a consonant) requiring partial or complete closure of the lips (e.g. *p, b, f, v, m, w*). **b** (of a vowel) requiring rounded lips (e.g. *oo* in moon). ● *n.* *Phonet.* a labial sound. □ **labialize** *v.tr.* (also **-ise**). **labially** *adv.* [medieval Latin *labialis* from Latin *labia* 'lips']

labial pipe *n.* an organ pipe having lips; a flue pipe.

labia majora /məˈdʒɔːrə/ *n.pl.* the larger outer pair of labia of the vulva.

labia minora /mɪˈnɔːrə/ *n.pl.* the smaller inner pair of labia of the vulva.

labiate /ˈleɪbɪət/ *n. & adj.* ● *n.* any plant of the family Labiatae, including mint and rosemary, having square stems and a corolla or calyx divided into two parts suggesting lips. ● *adj.* **1** *Bot.* of or relating to the Labiatae. **2** *Bot.* & *Zool.* like a lip or labium. [modern Latin *labiatus* (as LABIUM)]

labile /ˈleɪbɪl, -ʌɪl/ *adj.* unstable, esp. *Chem.* (of a compound) liable to displacement or change esp. if an atom or group is easily replaced by other atoms or groups. □ **lability** /ləˈbɪlɪti/ *n.* [Middle English from Late Latin *labilis*, from *labi* 'to fall']

labio- /ˈleɪbɪəʊ/ *comb. form* of the lips. [as LABIUM]

labiodental /leɪbɪəʊˈdɛnt(ə)l/ *adj.* (of a sound) made with the lips and teeth, e.g. *f* and *v*.

labiovelar /leɪbɪəʊˈviːlə/ *adj.* (of a sound) made with the lips and soft palate, e.g. *w*.

labium /ˈleɪbɪəm/ *n.* (*pl.* **labia** /-bɪə/) **1** (usu. in *pl.*) *Anat.* each fold of skin of the two pairs that enclose the vulva. **2** the lower lip in the mouthparts of an insect or crustacean. **3** a lip, esp. the lower one of a labiate plant's corolla. [Latin, = lip]

labor etc. *US* & *Austral.* var. of LABOUR etc.

laboratory /ləˈbɒrət(ə)ri, ˈlab(ə)rət(ə)ri/ *n.* (*pl.* **-ies**) a room or building fitted out for scientific experiments, research, teaching, or the manufacture of drugs and chemicals. [medieval Latin *laboratorium* from Latin *laborare* LABOUR]

laborious /ləˈbɔːrɪəs/ *adj.* **1** needing hard work or toil (*a laborious task*). **2** (esp. of literary style) showing signs of toil; pedestrian; not fluent. □ **laboriously** *adv.* **laboriousness** *n.* [Middle English via Old French *laborieus* from Latin *laboriosus* (as LABOUR)]

labour /ˈleɪbə/ *n. & v.* (*US*, *Austral.* **labor**) ● *n.* **1** **a** physical or mental work; exertion; toil. **b** such work considered as supplying the needs of a community. **2** **a** workers, esp. manual, considered as a social class or political force (*a dispute between capital and labour*). **b** (**Labour**) the Labour Party. **3** the process of childbirth, esp. the period from the start of uterine contractions to delivery (*has been in labour for three hours*). **4** a particular task, esp. of a difficult nature. ● *v.* **1** *intr.* work hard; exert oneself. **2** *intr.* (usu. foll. by *for*, or *to* + infin.) strive for a purpose (*laboured to fulfil his promise*). **3** *tr.* **a** treat at excessive length; elaborate needlessly (*I will not labour the point*). **b** (as **laboured** *adj.*) done with great effort; not spontaneous or fluent. **4** *intr.* (often foll. by *under*) suffer under (a disadvantage or delusion) (*laboured under universal disapproval*). **5** *intr.* proceed with trouble or difficulty (*laboured slowly up the hill*). **6** *intr.* (of a ship) roll or pitch heavily. **7** *tr.* *archaic* or *poet.* till (the ground). □ **labour in vain** make a fruitless effort. **labour of love** a task done for pleasure, not reward. [Middle English via Old French *labo(u)r*, *labourer* from Latin *labor*, *-oris*, *laborare*]

labour camp *n.* a prison camp enforcing a regime of hard labour.

Labour Day *n.* May 1 (or in the US and Canada the first Monday in September), celebrated in honour of working people.

labourer /'leɪb(ə)rə/ *n.* (*US* **laborer**) **1** a person doing unskilled, usu. manual, work for wages. **2** a person who labours. [Middle English from Old French *laboureur* (as LABOUR)]

Labour Exchange *n. Brit. colloq.* or *hist.* an employment exchange; a jobcentre.

labour force *n.* the body of workers employed, esp. at a single plant.

labour-intensive *adj.* (of a form of work) needing a large work force or a large amount of work in relation to output.

labourism /'leɪbərɪz(ə)m/ *n.* (*US* **laborism**) the principles of a Labour Party or the Labour movement.

Labourite /'leɪbərʌɪt/ *n.* (*US* **Laborite**) a member or follower of the Labour Party.

labour market *n.* the supply of labour with reference to the demand on it.

labour of Hercules *n.* a task needing enormous strength or effort.

Labour Party *n.* **1** a British political party formed to represent the interests of ordinary working people. **2** any similar political party in other countries.

labour-saving *adj.* (of an appliance etc.) designed to reduce or eliminate work.

labour theory of value *n.* the Marxist theory that the value of a commodity should be determined by the amount of human labour used in its production.

labour union *n. US* a trade union.

labra *pl.* of LABRUM.

Labrador /'labrədɔː/ *n.* (in full **Labrador dog** or **retriever**) **1** a retriever of a breed with a black or golden coat often used as a gun dog or as a guide for a blind person. **2** this breed. [*Labrador*, a large peninsula in NE Canada]

labradorite /labrə'dɔːrʌɪt/ *n.* a kind of plagioclase feldspar, often showing iridescence from internal reflective planes. [*Labrador*, a large peninsula in NE Canada]

labret /'leɪbrɪt/ *n.* a piece of shell, bone, etc., inserted in the lip as an ornament. [LABRUM]

labrum /'leɪbrəm/ *n.* (*pl.* **labra** /-brə/) the upper lip in the mouthparts of an insect. [Latin, = lip: related to LABIUM]

laburnum /lə'bəːnəm/ *n.* any small tree of the genus *Laburnum* with racemes of golden flowers yielding poisonous seeds; also called *golden chain*. [Latin]

labyrinth /'lab(ə)rɪnθ/ *n.* **1** a complicated irregular network of passages or paths etc.; a maze. **2** an intricate or tangled arrangement. **3** *Anat.* the complex arrangement of bony and membranous canals and chambers of the inner ear which constitute the organs of hearing and balance. □ **labyrinthian** /-'rɪnθɪən/ *adj.* **labyrinthine** /-'rɪnθʌɪn/ *adj.* [French *labyrinthe* or Latin *labyrinthus* from Greek *laburinthos*, in earliest use referring to the maze constructed by Daedalus in Greek Mythology to house the Minotaur]

labyrinth fish *n.* = GOURAMI 2.

LAC *abbr.* Leading Aircraftman.

lac[1] /lak/ *n.* a resinous substance secreted as a protective covering by the lac insect, and used to make varnish and shellac. [Middle English from Portuguese *lac(c)a*, ultimately from Hindustani *lākh* via Prakrit *lakkha* from Sanskrit *lākṣā*]

lac[2] var. of LAKH.

Lacanian /lə'keɪmɪən/ *adj.* & *n. Psychol.* ● *adj.* of or relating to the French psychologist Jacques Lacan (d.1981) or his methods of psychoanalysis. ● *n.* a follower of Lacan or his methods. □ **Lacanianism** *n.*

laccolith /'lakəlɪθ/ *n. Geol.* a lens-shaped intrusion of igneous rock which thrusts the overlying strata into a dome. [Greek *lakkos* 'reservoir' + -LITH]

lace /leɪs/ *n.* & *v.* ● *n.* **1** a fine open fabric, esp. of cotton or silk, made by weaving thread in patterns and used esp. for trimming garments. **2** a cord or leather strip passed through eyelets or hooks on opposite sides of a shoe, garment, etc., pulled tight and fastened. **3** braid used for trimming esp. dress uniform (*gold lace*). ● *v.* **1** *tr.* (usu. foll. by *up*) **a** fasten or tighten (a shoe, garment, etc.) with a lace or laces. **b** compress the waist of (a person) with a laced corset. **2** *tr.* (usu. foll. by *with*) **a** add an ingredient to (a drink, dish, substance, etc.) to enhance or adulterate flavour, strength, effect, etc. (*laced with rum*; *lace the potion with strychnine*). **b** intermingle (*ribaldry laced with philosophy*). **3** *tr.* (usu. foll. by *with*) **a** streak (a sky etc.) with colour (*cheek laced with blood*). **b** interlace or embroider (fabric) with thread etc. **4** *tr.* & (foll. by *into*) *intr. colloq.* lash, beat, defeat. **5** *tr.* (often foll. by *through*) pass (a shoelace etc.) through. **6** *tr.* trim with lace. [Middle English from Old French *laz*, *las*, *lacier*, ultimately from Latin *laqueus* 'noose']

lace-glass *n.* Venetian glass with lacelike designs.

lacemaker /'leɪsmeɪkə/ *n.* a person who makes lace, esp. professionally. □ **lacemaking** *n.*

lace-pillow *n.* a cushion placed on the lap and providing support in lacemaking.

lacerate /'lasəreɪt/ *v.tr.* **1** mangle or tear (esp. flesh or tissue). **2** distress or cause pain to (the feelings, the heart, etc.). □ **lacerable** *adj.* **laceration** /-'reɪʃ(ə)n/ *n.* [Latin *lacerare* from *lacer* 'torn']

lacertian /lə'səːtɪən, -ʃ(ə)n/ *n.* & *adj.* (also **lacertilian** /lasə'tɪlɪən/, **lacertine** /'lasətʌɪn/) ● *n.* any reptile of the suborder Lacertilia, including lizards. ● *adj.* of or relating to the Lacertilia; lizard-like, saurian. [Latin *lacerta* 'lizard']

lace-up *n.* & *adj. Brit.* ● *n.* a shoe fastened with a lace. ● *attrib.adj.* (of a shoe etc.) fastened by a lace or laces.

lacewing /'leɪswɪŋ/ *n.* a neuropterous insect.

lacewood /'leɪswʊd/ *n.* the timber of the plane tree.

lacework /'leɪswəːk/ *n.* work done in lace.

laches /'latʃɪz, 'leɪ-/ *n. Law* delay in performing a legal duty, asserting a right, claiming a privilege, etc. [Middle English via Anglo-French *laches(se)*, Old French *laschesse* from *lasche*, ultimately from Latin *laxus* 'loose']

lachryma Christi /ˌlakrɪmə 'krɪstʌɪ, -ti/ *n.* any of various Italian wines originally, but now not exclusively, made from grapes grown on the slopes of Mount Vesuvius. [Latin, = Christ's tear]

lachrymal /'lakrɪm(ə)l/ *adj.* & *n.* (also **lacrimal**, **lacrymal**) ● *adj.* **1** *formal* of or for tears. **2** (usu. as **lacrimal**) *Anat.* concerned in the secretion of tears (*lacrimal canal*; *lacrimal duct*). ● *n.* **1** = LACHRYMAL VASE. **2** (in *pl.*) (usu. as **lacrimals**) the lacrimal organs. [Middle English via medieval Latin *lachrymalis* from Latin *lacrima* 'tear']

lachrymal vase *n. hist.* a phial holding the tears of mourners at a funeral.

lachrymation /lakrɪ'meɪʃ(ə)n/ *n.* (also **lacrimation**, **lacrymation**) *formal* the flow of tears. [Latin *lacrimatio* from *lacrimare* 'weep' (as LACHRYMAL)]

lachrymator /'lakrɪmeɪtə/ *n.* an agent irritating the eyes, causing tears.

lachrymatory /'lakrɪmət(ə)ri/ *adj.* & *n.* ● *adj. formal* of or causing tears. ● *n.* (*pl.* **-ies**) a phial of a kind found in ancient Roman tombs and thought to be a lachrymal vase.

lachrymose /'lakrɪməʊs/ *adj. formal* **1** given to weeping; tearful. **2** melancholy; inducing tears. □ **lachrymosely** *adv.* [Latin *lacrimosus* from *lacrima* 'tear']

lacing /'leɪsɪŋ/ *n.* **1** lace trimming, esp. on a uniform. **2** a laced fastening on a shoe or garment. **3** *colloq.* a beating. **4** a dash of spirits in a beverage.

lacing course *n.* a strengthening course built into an arch or wall.

laciniate /lə'sɪnɪət/ *adj.* (also **laciniated** /-eɪtɪd/) *Bot.* & *Zool.* divided into deep narrow irregular segments; fringed. □ **laciniation** /-'eɪʃ(ə)n/ *n.* [Latin *lacinia* 'flap of a garment']

lac insect *n.* an Asian scale insect, *Laccifer lacca*, living in trees.

lack /lak/ *n.* & *v.* ● *n.* (usu. foll. by *of*) an absence, want, or deficiency (*a lack of talent*; *felt the lack of warmth*). ● *v.tr.* be without or deficient in (*lacks courage*). □ **for lack of** owing to the absence of (*went hungry for lack of money*). **lack for** lack. [Middle English *lac*, *lacen*, corresponding to Middle Dutch, Middle Low German *lak* 'deficiency', Middle Dutch *laken* 'to lack']

lackadaisical /lakə'deɪzɪk(ə)l/ *adj.* **1** unenthusiastic; listless; idle. **2** feebly sentimental and affected. □ **lackadaisically** *adv.* **lackadaisicalness** *n.* [archaic *lackaday*, *-daisy* (int.): see ALACK]

lacker var. of LACQUER.

lackey /'laki/ *n.* & *v.* (also **lacquey**) ● *n.* (*pl.* **-eys**) **1** *derog.* **a** a servile political follower. **b** an obsequious parasitical person. **2 a** a (usu. liveried) footman or manservant. **b** a servant. ● *v.tr.* (**-eys**, **-eyed**) *archaic* behave servilely to; dance attendance on. [French *laquais*, obsolete *alaquais* from Catalan *alacay* = Spanish ALCALDE]

lackey moth *n.* a moth, *Malacosoma neustria*, developing from a brightly striped caterpillar.

lacking /'lakɪŋ/ *adj.* **1** absent or deficient (*money was lacking*; *is lacking in determination*). **2** *colloq.* deficient in intellect; mentally subnormal.

lackland /'laklənd/ *n.* & *adj.* ● *n.* **1** a person having no land. **2** (**Lackland**) a nickname for King John of England. ● *adj.* having no land.

lacklustre /'laklʌstə/ *adj.* (*US* **lackluster**) **1** lacking in vitality, force, or conviction. **2** (of the eye) dull.

Laconian /lə'kəʊnɪən/ *n.* & *adj.* ● *n.* an inhabitant or the dialect of ancient Laconia. ● *adj.* of the Laconian dialect or people; Spartan. [Latin *Laconia* 'Sparta' from Greek *Lakōn* 'Spartan']

laconic /lə'kɒnɪk/ *adj.* **1** (of a style of speech or writing) brief; concise; terse. **2** (of a person) laconic in speech etc. □ **laconically** *adv.* **laconicism** /-ɪsɪz(ə)m/ *n.* [Latin from Greek *Lakōnikos*, from *Lakōn* 'Spartan', the Spartans being known for their terse speech]

laconism /'lakənɪz(ə)m/ *n.* **1** brevity of speech. **2** a short pithy saying. [Greek *lakōnismos* from *lakōnizō* 'behave like a Spartan': see LACONIC]

lacquer /'lakə/ *n.* & *v.* (also **lacker**) ● *n.* **1** a sometimes coloured liquid made of shellac dissolved in alcohol, or of synthetic substances, that dries to form a hard protective coating for wood, brass, etc. **2** *Brit.* a chemical substance sprayed on hair to keep it in place. **3** the sap of the lacquer tree used to varnish wood etc. **4** *Art* decorative ware made of wood coated with lacquer. ● *v.tr.* coat with lacquer. □ **lacquerer** *n.* [obsolete French *lacre* 'sealing wax', from unexplained variant of Portuguese *laca* LAC[1]]

lacquer tree *n.* an E. Asian tree, *Rhus verniciflua*, the sap of which is used as a hard-wearing varnish for wood.

lacquerware /'lakəwɛː/ *n.* decorative lacquered articles.

lacquey var. of LACKEY.

lacrimal var. of LACHRYMAL.

lacrimation var. of LACHRYMATION.

lacrosse /lə'krɒs/ *n.* a game like hockey, but with a ball driven by, caught, and carried in a crosse. [French from *la* 'the' + CROSSE]

lacrymal var. of LACHRYMAL.

lacrymation var. of LACHRYMATION.

lactase /'lakteɪz/ *n. Biochem.* any of a group of enzymes which catalyse the hydrolysis of lactose to glucose and galactose. [French from *lactose* LACTOSE]

lactate[1] /lak'teɪt/ *v.intr.* (of mammals) secrete milk. [as LACTATION]

lactate[2] /'lakteɪt/ *n. Chem.* any salt or ester of lactic acid.

lactation /lak'teɪʃ(ə)n/ *n.* **1** the secretion of milk by the mammary glands. **2** the suckling of young. [Latin *lactare* 'suckle' from *lac lactis* 'milk']

lacteal /'laktɪəl/ *adj.* & *n.* ● *adj.* **1** of milk. **2** *Anat.* (of a vessel) conveying chyle or other milky fluid. ● *n.* (in *pl.*) *Anat.* the lymphatic vessels of the small intestine which absorb digested fats. [Latin *lacteus* from *lac lactis* 'milk']

lactescence /lak'tɛs(ə)ns/ *n.* **1** a milky form or appearance. **2** a milky juice. [Latin *lactescere* from *lactēre* 'be milky' (as LACTIC)]

lactescent /lak'tɛs(ə)nt/ *adj.* **1** milky. **2** yielding a milky juice.

lactic /'laktɪk/ *adj. Chem.* of, relating to, or obtained from milk. [Latin *lac lactis* 'milk']

lactic acid *n.* a clear odourless syrupy carboxylic acid formed in sour milk, and produced in the muscle tissues during strenuous exercise.

lactiferous /lak'tɪf(ə)rəs/ *adj.* yielding milk or milky fluid. [Late Latin *lactifer* (as LACTIC)]

lacto- /'laktəʊ/ *comb. form* milk. [Latin *lac lactis* 'milk']

lactobacillus /laktəʊbə'sɪləs/ *n.* (*pl.* **-bacilli** /-lʌɪ/) *Biol.* any rod-shaped bacterium of the family Lactobacillaceae, producing lactic acid from the fermentation of carbohydrates.

lactometer /lak'tɒmɪtə/ *n.* an instrument for testing the density of milk.

lactone /'laktəʊn/ *n. Chem.* any of a class of cyclic esters formed by the elimination of water from a hydroxy-carboxylic acid. [German *Lacton*]

lactoprotein /laktəʊ'prəʊtiːn/ *n.* the albuminous constituent of milk.

lactose /'laktəʊz, -s/ *n. Chem.* a disaccharide sugar occurring in milk, formed of a glucose and a galactose monomer. [as LACTO-]

lacuna /lə'kjuːnə/ *n.* (*pl.* **lacunae** /-niː/ or **lacunas**) **1** a hiatus, blank, or gap. **2** a missing portion or empty page, esp. in an ancient manuscript, book, etc. **3** *Anat.* a cavity or depression, esp. in bone. □ **lacunal** *adj.* **lacunar** *adj.* **lacunary** *adj.* **lacunose** *adj.* [Latin, = pool, from *lacus* LAKE[1]]

lacustrine /lə'kʌstrʌɪn, -rɪn/ *adj. formal* or *Biol.* **1** of or relating to lakes. **2** living or growing in or beside a lake. [Latin *lacus* LAKE[1], influenced by *palustris* 'marshy']

LACW *abbr.* Leading Aircraftwoman.

lacy /'leɪsi/ *adj.* (**lacier**, **laciest**) of or resembling lace fabric. □ **lacily** *adv.* **laciness** *n.*

lad /lad/ *n.* **1 a** a boy or youth. **b** a young son. **2** (esp. in *pl.*) esp. *Brit. colloq.* a man; a fellow, esp. a workmate, drinking companion, etc. (*he's one of the lads*). **3** *Brit. colloq.* a high-spirited fellow; a rogue (*he's a bit of a lad*). **4** *Brit.* a stable worker (regardless of age or sex). [Middle English *ladde*, of unknown origin]

ladanum /'ladənəm/ *n.* (also **labdanum** /'labdənəm/) a gum resin from plants of the genus *Cistus*, used in perfumery etc. [Latin from Greek *ladanon*, from *lēdon* 'mastic']

ladder /'ladə/ *n.* & *v.* ● *n.* **1** a set of horizontal bars of wood or metal fixed between two uprights and used for climbing up or down. **2** *Brit.* a vertical strip of unravelled fabric in a stocking etc. resembling a ladder. **3 a** a hierarchical structure. **b** such a structure as a means of advancement, promotion, etc. ● *v. Brit.* **1** *intr.* (of a stocking etc.) develop a ladder. **2** *tr.* cause a ladder in (a stocking etc.). [Old English *hlǣd(d)er*, ultimately from Germanic: related to LEAN[1]]

ladder-back *n.* (in full **ladder-back chair**) an upright chair with a back resembling a ladder.

ladder stitch *n.* transverse bars in embroidery.

ladder tournament *n.* a sporting contest with each participant listed and entitled to a higher place by defeating the one above.

laddie /ˈladi/ *n.* esp. *Brit. colloq.* a young boy or lad.

laddish /ˈladɪʃ/ *adj.* of or like a lad or lads. ▫ **laddishness** *n.*

lade /leɪd/ *v.* (*past part.* **laden** /ˈleɪd(ə)n/) **1** *tr.* **a** put cargo on board (a ship). **b** ship (goods) as cargo. **2** *intr.* (of a ship) take on cargo. **3** *tr.* (as **laden** *adj.*) (usu. foll. by *with*) **a** (of a vehicle, animal, person, tree, table, etc.) heavily loaded. **b** (of the conscience, spirit, etc.) painfully burdened with sin, sorrow, etc. [Old English *hladan*]

la-di-da /lɑːdɪˈdɑː/ *adj. & n. colloq.* ● *adj.* pretentious or snobbish, esp. in manner or speech. ● *n.* **1** a la-di-da person. **2** la-di-da speech or manners. [imitative of an affected manner of speech]

ladies *pl.* of LADY.

ladies' chain *n.* a figure in a quadrille etc.

ladies' fingers *n.pl. Brit.* = OKRA (cf. LADY'S FINGER).

Ladies' Gallery *n.* a public gallery in the House of Commons, reserved for women.

ladies' man *n.* (also **lady's man**) a man fond of female company; a seducer.

ladies' night *n.* a function at a men's club etc. to which women are invited.

ladies' room *n.* a women's lavatory in a hotel, office, etc.

ladify var. of LADYFY.

Ladin /ləˈdiːn/ *n.* the Rhaeto-Romanic dialect of the Engadine in Switzerland. [Romansh, from Latin *latinus* LATIN]

lading /ˈleɪdɪŋ/ *n.* **1** a cargo. **2** the act or process of lading.

Ladino /ləˈdiːnəʊ/ *n.* (*pl.* **-os**) **1** the Spanish dialect (written in modified Hebrew characters) of some Sephardic Jews, esp. in Mediterranean countries. **2** a mestizo or Spanish-speaking white person in Central America. [Spanish, originally = Latin, from Latin *latinus* LATIN]

ladino /ləˈdiːnəʊ/ *n.* (*pl.* **-os**) a large variety of white clover (*Trifolium repens*) native to Italy and cultivated esp. in the US for fodder. [Italian]

ladle /ˈleɪd(ə)l/ *n. & v.* ● *n.* **1** a large long-handled spoon with a cup-shaped bowl used for serving esp. soups and gravy. **2** a vessel for transporting molten metal in a foundry. ● *v.tr.* (often foll. by *out*) transfer (liquid) from one receptacle to another. ▫ **ladle out** distribute, esp. lavishly. ▫ **ladleful** *n.* (*pl.* **-fuls**). **ladler** *n.* [Old English *hlædel* from *hladan* LADE]

lad's love *n.* = SOUTHERNWOOD.

lady /ˈleɪdi/ *n.* (*pl.* **-ies**) **1 a** a woman regarded as being of superior social status or as having the refined manners associated with this (cf. GENTLEMAN). **b** (**Lady**) a title used by peeresses, female relatives of peers, the wives and widows of knights, etc. **2** (often *attrib.*) a woman; a female person or animal (*ask that lady over there*; *lady butcher*; *lady dog*). **3** *colloq.* **a** a wife. **b** a man's girlfriend. **4** a ruling woman (*lady of the house*; *lady of the manor*). **5** (in *pl.* as a form of address) a female audience or the female part of an audience. **6** *hist.* a woman to whom a man, esp. a knight, is chivalrously devoted; a mistress. ▫ **find the lady** = THREE-CARD TRICK. **my lady wife** *joc.* my wife. **the Ladies** (or **Ladies'**) *Brit.* a women's public lavatory. ▫ **ladyhood** *n.* [Old English *hlǣfdige* from *hlāf* LOAF[1] + a Germanic base meaning 'knead', related to DOUGH: in *Lady Day* etc. from Old English genitive *hlǣfdigan* '(Our) Lady's']

Lady altar *n.* the altar in a Lady chapel.

ladybird /ˈleɪdɪbəːd/ *n.* a coleopterous insect of the family Coccinellidae, with wing-cases usu. of a reddish-brown colour with black spots.

Lady Bountiful *n.* a charitable but patronizing lady of a neighbourhood (after a character in Farquhar's *The Beaux' Stratagem*, 1707).

ladybug /ˈleɪdɪbʌɡ/ *n. dial. & N. Amer.* = LADYBIRD.

Lady chapel *n.* a chapel in a church or cathedral, usu. to the east of the high altar in a cathedral, to the south in a church, dedicated to the Virgin Mary.

Lady Day *n.* esp. *Brit.* the feast of the Annunciation, 25 Mar.

lady-fern *n.* a slender fern, *Athyrium filix-femina.*

ladyfinger /ˈleɪdɪfɪŋɡə/ *n. N. Amer.* a finger-shaped sponge cake.

ladyfy /ˈleɪdɪfʌɪ/ *v.tr.* (also **ladify**) (**-ies**, **-ied**) esp. *Brit.* **1** make a lady of. **2** call (a person) 'lady'. **3** (as **ladyfied** *adj.*) having the manner of a fine lady.

lady-in-waiting *n.* (*pl.* **ladies-in-waiting**) a lady attending a queen or princess.

ladykiller /ˈleɪdɪkɪlə/ *n.* a practised and habitual seducer.

ladylike /ˈleɪdɪlʌɪk/ *adj.* **1 a** with the modesty, manners, etc., of a lady. **b** befitting a lady. **2** (of a man) effeminate.

lady-love *n.* a man's sweetheart.

Lady Mayoress *n.* the wife of a Lord Mayor.

Lady Muck *n. Brit. slang derog.* a socially pretentious woman.

lady of easy virtue *n.* a sexually promiscuous woman; a prostitute.

lady of the bedchamber *n.* = LADY-IN-WAITING.

lady of the house *n.* the female head of a household.

lady of the night *n.* a prostitute.

lady's bedstraw see BEDSTRAW 2.

lady's companion *n. Brit.* a small case or bag containing needlework items.

lady's finger *n. Brit.* **1** = KIDNEY VETCH. **2** = LADYFINGER (cf. LADIES' FINGERS).

ladyship /ˈleɪdɪʃɪp/ *n. archaic* the state of being a lady. ▫ **her** (or **your**) **Ladyship** (or **ladyship**) (*pl.* **their** (or **your**) **Ladyships**) **1** a respectful form of reference or address to a Lady. **2** *iron.* a form of reference or address to a woman thought to be giving herself airs.

lady's maid *n.* a lady's personal maidservant.

lady's man var. of LADIES' MAN.

lady's mantle *n.* any plant of the genus *Alchemilla* (rose family), with yellowish-green clustered flowers.

lady's slipper *n.* any orchid of the genus *Cypripedium*, with a usu. yellow slipper-shaped lip on its flowers.

lady's smock *n.* = CUCKOO FLOWER 1.

lady's tresses *n.pl.* any white-flowered orchid of the genus *Spiranthes.*

Lady Superior *n.* the head of a convent or nunnery in certain orders.

laevo- /ˈliːvəʊ/ *comb. form* (also **levo-**) on or to the left. [Latin *laevus* 'left']

laevorotatory /liːvəʊˈrəʊtət(ə)ri/ *adj.* (*US* **levorotatory**) *Chem.* having the property of rotating the plane of a polarized light ray to the left (anticlockwise facing the oncoming radiation) (cf. DEXTROROTATORY).

laevulose /ˈliːvjʊləʊz, -s/ *n.* (*US* **levulose**) = FRUCTOSE. [LAEVO- + -ULE + -OSE[2]]

lag[1] /laɡ/ *v. & n.* ● *v.intr.* (**lagged**, **lagging**) **1** (often foll. by *behind*) fall behind; not keep pace. **2** *US Billiards* make the preliminary strokes that decide which player shall begin. ● *n.* **1** a delay. **2** *Physics* **a** retardation in a current or movement. **b** the amount of this. ▫ **lagger** *n.* [originally = hindmost person, hang back: perhaps from a fanciful distortion of LAST[1] in a children's game (*fog, seg, lag*, = 1st, 2nd, last, in dialect)]

lag[2] /laɡ/ *v. & n.* ● *v.tr.* (**lagged**, **lagging**) enclose or cover in lagging. ● *n.* **1** the non-heat-conducting cover of a boiler etc.; lagging. **2** a piece of this. [probably from Scandinavian: cf. Old Norse *lögg* 'barrel-rim', related to LAY[1]]

lag[3] /laɡ/ *n. & v. Brit. slang* ● *n.* (esp. as **old lag**) a habitual convict. ● *v.tr.* (**lagged**, **lagging**) **1** send to prison. **2** apprehend; arrest. [19th c.: origin unknown]

lagan /ˈlag(ə)n/ *n.* goods or wreckage lying on the bed of the sea, sometimes with a marker buoy etc. for later retrieval. [Old French, perhaps of Scandinavian origin, from root of LIE[1], LAY[1]]

lager /ˈlɑːgə/ *n.* a kind of beer, effervescent and light in colour and body. [German *Lagerbier* 'beer brewed for keeping' from *Lager* 'store']

lager lout *n. Brit. colloq.* a youth who behaves badly as a result of excessive drinking.

laggard /ˈlagəd/ *n. & adj.* ● *n.* a dawdler; a person who lags behind. ● *adj.* dawdling; slow. □ **laggardly** *adj. & adv.* **laggardness** *n.* [LAG[1]]

lagging /ˈlagɪŋ/ *n.* material providing heat insulation for a boiler, pipes, etc. [LAG[2]]

lag of tide *n.* the interval by which a tide falls behind mean time at the first and third quarters of the moon (cf. PRIMING[2]).

lagomorph /ˈlagəmɔːf/ *n. Zool.* any mammal of the order Lagomorpha, including hares and rabbits. [Greek *lagōs* 'hare' + *morphē* 'form']

lagoon /ləˈguːn/ *n.* **1** a stretch of salt water separated from the sea by a low sandbank, coral reef, etc. **2** the enclosed water of an atoll. **3** *US, Austral., & NZ* a small freshwater lake near a larger lake or river. **4** an artificial pool for the treatment of effluent or to accommodate an overspill from surface drains during heavy rain. □ **lagoonal** *adj.* [French *lagune* or Italian & Spanish *laguna* from Latin *lacuna*: see LACUNA]

Lagrangian point /ləˈgrɒ̃ʒɪən/ *n.* each of five points in the plane of orbit of one body around another (e.g. the moon around the earth) at which a small third body can remain stationary with respect to both. [named after J.L. *Lagrange*, Italian-born mathematician d. 1813]

lah /lɑː/ *n.* (also **la**) *Mus.* **1** (in tonic sol-fa) the sixth note of a major scale. **2** the note A in the fixed-doh system. [Middle English from Latin *labii*: see GAMUT]

lahar /ˈlɑːhɑː/ *n.* a mudflow composed mainly of volcanic debris. [Javanese]

laic /ˈleɪɪk/ *adj. & n.* ● *adj.* non-clerical; lay; secular; temporal. ● *n. formal* a lay person; a non-cleric. □ **laical** *adj.* **laically** *adv.* [Late Latin from Greek *laïkos*, from *laos* 'people']

laicity /leɪˈɪsɪti/ *n.* the status or influence of the laity.

laicize /ˈleɪɪsʌɪz/ *v.tr.* (also **-ise**) **1** make (an office etc.) tenable by lay people. **2** subject (a school or institution) to the control of lay people. **3** secularize. □ **laicization** /-ˈzeɪʃ(ə)n/ *n.*

laid *past* and *past part.* of LAY[1].

laid-back *adj. colloq.* relaxed, unbothered, easygoing.

laid paper *n.* paper with the surface marked in fine ribs.

laid up *adj.* confined to bed or the house.

lain *past part.* of LIE[1].

lair[1] /lɛː/ *n. & v.* ● *n.* **1 a** a wild animal's resting place. **b** a person's hiding place; a den (*tracked him to his lair*). **2** a place where domestic animals lie down. **3** *Brit.* a shed or enclosure for cattle on the way to market. ● *v.* **1** *intr.* go to or rest in a lair. **2** *tr.* place (an animal) in a lair. □ **lairage** *n.* [Old English *leger* from Germanic: cf. LIE[1]]

lair[2] /lɛː/ *n. & v. Austral. slang* ● *n.* a youth or man who dresses flashily and shows off. ● *v.intr.* (often foll. by *up*) behave or dress like a lair. □ **lairy** *adj.* [*lair* back-formation from *lairy*; *lairy* alteration of LEERY]

laird /lɛːd/ *n. Sc.* a landowner. □ **lairdship** *n.* [Scots form of LORD]

laissez-aller /lɛseɪˈaleɪ/ *n.* unconstrained freedom; an absence of constraint. [French, = let go]

laissez-faire /lɛseɪˈfɛː/ *n.* the theory or practice of governmental abstention from interference in the workings of the market etc. [French, = let act]

laissez-passer /lɛseɪˈpɑːseɪ/ *n.* a document allowing the holder to pass; a permit. [French, = let pass]

laity /ˈleɪɪti/ *n.* (usu. prec. by *the*; usu. treated as *pl.*) **1** lay people, as distinct from the clergy. **2** non-professionals. [Middle English, from LAY[2] + -ITY]

lake[1] /leɪk/ *n.* **1** a large body of water surrounded by land. **2** (**the Lakes**) *pl.* = LAKE DISTRICT. □ **lakeless** *adj.* **lakelet** *n.* [Middle English via Old French *lac* from Latin *lacus* 'basin, pool, lake']

lake[2] /leɪk/ *n.* **1** a reddish colouring originally made from lac (*crimson lake*). **2** a complex formed by the action of dye and mordants applied to fabric to fix colour. **3** any insoluble product of a soluble dye and mordant. [variant of LAC[1]]

Lake District *n.* the region of the English lakes in Cumbria.

lake-dwelling *n.* a prehistoric hut built on piles driven into the bed or shore of a lake. □ **lake-dweller** *n.*

Lakeland /ˈleɪklənd/ *n.* = LAKE DISTRICT.

Lakeland terrier *n.* **1** a terrier of a small stocky breed originating in the Lake District. **2** this breed.

Lake Poets *n.pl.* Coleridge, Southey, and Wordsworth, who lived in and were inspired by the Lake District.

lakeside /ˈleɪksʌɪd/ *attrib.adj.* beside a lake.

lakh /lak, lɑːk/ *n.* (also **lac**) (usu. foll. by *of*) *Anglo-Ind.* a hundred thousand (rupees etc.). [Hindustani *lākh* from Sanskrit *lakṣa*]

lalapalooza var. of LOLLAPALOOZA.

Lallan /ˈlalən/ *n. & adj. Sc.* ● *n.* (now usu. **Lallans**) a Lowland Scots dialect, esp. as a literary language. ● *adj.* of or concerning the Lowlands of Scotland. [variant of LOWLAND]

lallation /laˈleɪʃ(ə)n/ *n.* **1** the pronunciation of *r* as *l*. **2** imperfect speech, esp. the repetition of meaningless sounds by babies. [Latin *lallare lallat-* 'sing a lullaby']

lallygag /ˈlalɪgag/ *v.intr.* (**lallygagged**, **lallygagging**) *N. Amer. slang* **1** loiter. **2** cuddle amorously. [19th c.: origin unknown]

Lam. *abbr.* Lamentations (Old Testament).

lam[1] /lam/ *v.* (**lammed**, **lamming**) *colloq.* **1** *tr.* thrash; hit. **2** *intr.* (foll. by *into*) hit (a person etc.) hard with a stick etc. [perhaps from Scandinavian: cf. Old Norse *lemja* 'beat so as to LAME']

lam[2] /lam/ *n.* □ **on the lam** *N. Amer. slang* in flight, esp. from the police. [19th c.: origin unknown]

lama /ˈlɑːmə/ *n.* a Tibetan or Mongolian Buddhist monk. □ **Lamaism** *n.* **Lamaist** *n. & adj.* [Tibetan *blama* (with silent *b*)]

Lamarckism /ləˈmɑːkɪz(ə)m/ *n.* the theory of evolution devised by Lamarck, French botanist and zoologist (d. 1829), based on the inheritance of acquired characteristics. □ **Lamarckian** *n. & adj.*

lamasery /ˈlɑːməs(ə)ri, ləˈmɑːs(ə)ri/ *n.* (*pl.* **-ies**) a monastery of lamas. [French *lamaserie*, formed irregularly from *lama* LAMA]

lamb /lam/ *n. & v.* ● *n.* **1** a young sheep. **2** the flesh of a lamb as food. **3** a mild or gentle person, esp. a young child. ● *v.* **1 a** *tr.* (in *passive*) (of a lamb) be born. **b** *intr.* (of a ewe) give birth to lambs. **2** *tr.* tend (lambing ewes). □ **the Lamb** (or **Lamb of God**) a name for Christ (see John 1:29) (cf. AGNUS DEI). **like a lamb** meekly, obediently. □ **lamber** *n.* (in sense 2 of *v.*). **lambhood** *n.* **lambkin** *n.* **lamblike** *adj.* [Old English *lamb*, from Germanic]

lambada /lamˈbɑːdə/ *n.* a fast erotic Brazilian dance which couples perform with their stomachs touching. [Portuguese, = a beating]

lambaste /lamˈbeɪst/ *v.tr.* (also **lambast** /-ˈbast/) *colloq.* **1** thrash; beat. **2** criticize severely. [LAM[1] + BASTE[3]]

lambda /ˈlamdə/ *n.* **1** the eleventh letter of the Greek alphabet (Λ, λ). **2** (as λ) **a** the symbol for wavelength. **b** the symbol for celestial longitude. [Middle English from Greek *la(m)bda*]

lambent /ˈlambənt/ *adj.* **1** (of a flame or a light) playing on a surface with a soft radiance but without burning. **2** (of the eyes, sky, etc.) softly radiant. **3** (of wit etc.) lightly brilliant. □ **lambency** *n.* **lambently** *adv.* [Latin *lambere lambent-* 'lick']

lambert /ˈlambət/ *n.* a former unit of luminance, equal to the emission or reflection of one lumen per square centimetre. [named after J. H. *Lambert*, German physicist d. 1777]

lambrequin /'lambrɪkɪn/ *n.* **1** *US* a short piece of drapery hung over the top of a door or a window or draped on a mantelpiece. **2** *Heraldry* = MANTLING. [French from the Dutch diminutive of *lamper* 'veil']

lamb's ears *n.* a garden plant, *Stachys byzantina*, with whitish woolly leaves.

lamb's fry *n. Brit.* lamb's testicles or other offal as food.

lambskin /'lamskɪn/ *n.* a prepared skin from a lamb with the wool on or as leather.

lamb's lettuce *n.* a plant, *Valerianella locusta*, used in salad.

lamb's-tails *n.pl. Brit.* catkins from the hazel tree.

lambswool /'lamzwʊl/ *n. & adj.* (also **lamb's-wool**) ● *n.* soft fine wool from a young sheep used in knitted garments etc. ● *adj.* made of lambswool.

lame /leɪm/ *adj. & v.* ● *adj.* **1** disabled, esp. in the foot or leg; limping; unable to walk normally (*lame in his right leg*). **2 a** (of an argument, story, excuse, etc.) unconvincing; unsatisfactory; weak. **b** (of verse etc.) halting. ● *v.tr.* **1** make lame; disable. **2** harm permanently. □ **lamely** *adv.* **lameness** *n.* **lamish** *adj.* [Old English *lama*, from Germanic]

lamé /'lɑːmeɪ/ *n. & adj.* ● *n.* a fabric with gold or silver threads interwoven. ● *adj.* (of fabric, a dress, etc.) having such threads. [French, from Latin *lamina* LAMINA]

lamebrain /'leɪmbreɪn/ *n. N. Amer. colloq.* a stupid person. □ **lamebrained** *adj.*

lame duck *n.* **1** a disabled or weak person. **2** *Brit.* a defaulter on the Stock Exchange. **3** *Brit.* a firm etc. in financial difficulties. **4** *US* an official (esp. the President) in the final period of office, after the election of a successor.

lamella /lə'mɛlə/ *n.* (*pl.* **lamellae** /-liː/) **1** a thin layer, membrane, scale, or platelike tissue or part, esp. in bone tissue. **2** *Bot.* a membranous fold in a chloroplast. □ **lamellar** *adj.* **lamellate** /'lam(ə)lət/ *adj.* **lamelliform** *adj.* **lamellose** /-ləʊs/ *adj.* [Latin, diminutive of *lamina*: see LAMINA]

lamellibranch /lə'mɛlɪbraŋk/ *n.* = BIVALVE. [LAMELLA + Greek *bragkhia* 'gills']

lamellicorn /lə'mɛlɪkɔːn/ *n. & adj.* ● *n.* any beetle of the superfamily Scarabaeoidea (formerly Lamellicornia), having lamelliform antennae, including the stag beetle, cockchafer, dung-beetle, etc. ● *adj.* of or relating to this superfamily. [modern Latin *lamellicornis*, from Latin *lamella* (see LAMELLA) + *cornu* 'horn']

lament /lə'mɛnt/ *n. & v.* ● *n.* **1** a passionate expression of grief. **2** a song or poem of mourning or sorrow. ● *v.tr.* (also *absol.*) **1** express or feel grief for or about; regret (*lamented the loss of his ticket*). **2** (as **lamented** *adj.*) a conventional expression referring to a recently dead person (*your late lamented father*). □ **lament for** (or **over**) mourn or regret. □ **lamenter** *n.* **lamentingly** *adv.* [Latin *lamentum*]

lamentable /'lamǝntəb(ə)l/ *adj.* **1** (of an event, fate, condition, character, etc.) deplorable; regrettable. **2** *archaic* mournful. □ **lamentably** *adv.* [Middle English from Old French *lamentable* or Latin *lamentabilis* (as LAMENT)]

lamentation /lamən'teɪʃ(ə)n/ *n.* **1** the act or an instance of lamenting. **2** a lament. **3** (**Lamentations** or **Lamentations of Jeremiah**) an Old Testament book concerning the destruction of Jerusalem in the 6th c. BC. [Middle English from Old French *lamentation* or Latin *lamentatio* (as LAMENT)]

lamina /'lamɪnə/ *n.* (*pl.* **laminae** /-niː/) a thin plate, scale, or layer, e.g. of sedimentary rock or organic tissue. □ **laminose** *adj.* [Latin]

laminar /'lamɪnə/ *adj.* **1** consisting of laminae. **2** *Physics* (of a flow) taking place along constant streamlines, not turbulent.

laminate *v., n., & adj.* ● *v.* /'lamɪneɪt/ **1** *tr.* beat or roll (metal) into thin plates. **2** *tr.* overlay with metal plates, a plastic layer, etc. **3** *tr.* manufacture by placing layer on layer. **4** *tr. & intr.* split into layers or leaves. ● *n.* /'lamɪnət/ a laminated structure or material, esp. of layers fixed together to form rigid or flexible material. ● *adj.* /'lamɪnət/ in the form of lamina or laminae. □ **lamination** /-'neɪʃ(ə)n/ *n.* **laminator** *n.* [LAMINA + -ATE[2], -ATE[3]]

laminitis /lamɪ'nʌɪtɪs/ *n.* inflammation of the laminae of the hoof in horses and other animals.

Lammas /'laməs/ *n.* (in full **Lammas Day**) the first day of August, formerly observed as harvest festival. [Old English *hlāfmæsse* (as LOAF[1], MASS)]

lammergeier /'laməgʌɪə/ *n.* (also **lammergeyer**) a large vulture, *Gypaetus barbatus*, with a very large wingspan (often of 3 m) and dark beardlike feathers on either side of its beak. [German *Lämmergeier*, from *Lämmer* 'lambs' + *Geier* 'vulture']

lamp /lamp/ *n. & v.* ● *n.* **1** a device for producing a steady light, esp.: **a** an electric bulb, and usu. its holder and shade or cover (*bedside lamp*; *bicycle lamp*). **b** an oil lamp. **c** a usu. glass holder for a candle. **d** a gas jet and mantle. **2** a source of spiritual or intellectual inspiration. **3** *poet.* the sun, the moon, or a star. **4** a device producing esp. ultraviolet or infra-red radiation as a treatment for various complaints. ● *v.* **1** *intr. poet.* shine. **2** *tr.* supply with lamps; illuminate. □ **lampless** *adj.* [Middle English via Old French *lampe* and Late Latin *lampada* from the accusative of Latin *lampas* 'torch', from Greek]

lampblack /'lampblak/ *n.* a pigment made from soot.

lamp-chimney *n.* a glass cylinder enclosing and making a draught for the flame of an oil lamp.

lampern /'lampən/ *n.* a lamprey, *Lampetra fluviatilis*, of rivers and coasts in NW Europe. [Old French *lampreion*, diminutive of *lampreie* LAMPREY]

lamp holder *n.* a device for supporting a lamp, esp. an electric one.

lamplight /'lamplʌɪt/ *n.* light given by a lamp or lamps. □ **lamplit** *adj.*

lamplighter /'lamplʌɪtə/ *n.* **1** *hist.* a person who lights street lamps. **2** *US* a spill for lighting lamps.

lampoon /lam'puːn/ *n. & v.* ● *n.* a satirical attack on a person etc. ● *v.tr.* satirize. □ **lampooner** *n.* **lampoonery** *n.* **lampoonist** *n.* [French *lampon*, conjectured to be from *lampons* 'let us drink' via *lamper* 'gulp down' from *laper* LAP[3]]

lamp-post *n.* a tall post supporting a street light.

lamprey /'lampri/ *n.* (*pl.* **-eys**) any eel-like fish of the family Petromyzonidae, without scales, paired fins, or jaws, but having a sucker mouth with horny teeth and a rough tongue. [Middle English via Old French *lampreie* from medieval Latin *lampreda*: cf. Late Latin *lampetra*, perhaps from Latin *lambere* 'lick' + *petra* 'stone']

lampshade /'lampʃeɪd/ *n.* a usu. translucent cover for a lamp used to soften or direct its light.

lamp shell *n.* a brachiopod. [from the resemblance to an ancient oil lamp]

lamp standard *n.* = LAMP-POST.

LAN /lan/ *n. Computing* local area network. [abbreviation]

Lancastrian /laŋ'kastrɪən/ *n. & adj.* ● *n.* **1** a native of Lancashire or Lancaster in NW England. **2** *hist.* a follower of the House of Lancaster or of the Red Rose party supporting it in the Wars of the Roses (cf. YORKIST). ● *adj.* of or concerning Lancashire or Lancaster, or the House of Lancaster.

lance /lɑːns/ *n. & v.* ● *n.* **1 a** *hist.* a long weapon with a wooden shaft and a pointed steel head, used by a horseman in charging. **b** a similar weapon used for spearing a fish, killing a harpooned whale, etc. **2** a metal pipe supplying oxygen to burn metal. **3** = LANCER 1. ● *v.tr.* **1** *Surgery* prick or cut open with a lancet. **2** pierce with a lance. **3** *poet.* fling; launch. [Middle

English via Old French *lancier* from Latin *lancea*]

lance bombardier *n.* a rank in the Royal Artillery corresponding to lance corporal in the infantry.

lance corporal *n.* the lowest rank of NCO in the Army. [on analogy of obsolete *lancepesade*, the lowest grade of NCO, ultimately from Italian *lancia spezzata* 'broken lance']

lance-jack *n. Brit. slang* a lance corporal or lance bombardier.

lancelet /'lɑːnslɪt/ *n.* any small non-vertebrate fishlike chordate of the family Branchiostomidae, that burrows in sand. [LANCE *n.* + -LET, with reference to its thin form]

lanceolate /'lɑːnsɪələt/ *adj.* shaped like a lance-head, tapering to each end. [Late Latin *lanceolatus* from *lanceola*, diminutive of *lancea* 'lance']

lancer /'lɑːnsə/ *n.* **1** *hist.* a soldier of a cavalry regiment armed with lances. **2** (in *pl.*) **a** a quadrille for 8 or 16 pairs. **b** the music for this. [French *lancier* (as LANCE)]

lance-sergeant *n.* a corporal acting as sergeant.

lance-snake *n.* = FER DE LANCE.

lancet /'lɑːnsɪt/ *n.* a small broad two-edged surgical knife with a sharp point. ◻ **lanceted** *adj.* [Middle English from Old French *lancette* (as LANCE)]

lancet arch *n.* (also **lancet light**, **lancet window**) a narrow arch or window with a pointed head.

lancewood /'lɑːnswʊd/ *n.* a tough elastic wood from a W. Indian tree *Oxandra lanceolata*, used for carriage shafts, fishing rods, etc.

Lancs. *abbr.* Lancashire.

Land /lant, land/ *n.* (*pl.* **Länder** /'lɛndə/) a province of Germany or Austria. [German (as LAND)]

land /land/ *n.* & *v.* ● *n.* **1** the solid part of the earth's surface, as opposed to the sea or air. **2 a** an expanse of country; ground; soil. **b** such land in relation to its use, quality, etc., or (often prec. by *the*) as a basis for agriculture (*building land*; *this is good land*; *works on the land*). **3** a country, nation, or state (*land of hope and glory*). **4 a** landed property. **b** (in *pl.*) estates. **5** the space between the rifling-grooves in a gun. **6** *Sc.* a building containing several dwellings. **7** *S.Afr.* ground fenced off for tillage. **8** a strip of ploughland or pastureland parted from others by drain-furrows. ● *v.* **1 a** *tr.* & *intr.* set or go ashore. **b** *intr.* (often foll. by *at*) disembark (*landed at the harbour*). **2** *tr.* bring (an aircraft, its passengers, etc.) to the ground or the surface of water. **3** *intr.* (of an aircraft, bird, parachutist, etc.) alight on the ground or water. **4** *tr.* bring (a fish) to land, esp. with a hook or net. **5** *tr.* & *intr.* (also *refl.*; often foll. by *up*) *colloq.* bring to, reach, or find oneself in a certain situation, place, or state (*landed himself in jail*; *landed up in France*; *landed her in trouble*; *landed up penniless*). **6** *tr. colloq.* **a** deal (a person etc. a blow etc.) (*landed him one in the eye*). **b** (foll. by *with*) *Brit.* present (a person) with (a problem, job, etc.). **7** *tr.* set down (a person, cargo, etc.) from a vehicle, ship, etc. **8** *tr. colloq.* win or obtain (a prize, job, etc.) esp. against strong competition. ◻ **how the land lies** what the state of affairs is. **in the land of the living** *joc.* still alive. **land of cakes** Scotland. **land of Nod** sleep (with pun on the phr. in Gen. 4:16). **land on one's feet** attain a good position, job, etc., by luck. ◻ **landless** *adj.* **landward** *adj.* & *adv.* **landwards** *adv.* [Old English from Germanic]

land agent *n. Brit.* **1** the steward of an estate. **2** an agent for the sale of estates. ◻ **land agency** *n.*

landau /'landɔː, -aʊ/ *n.* a four-wheeled enclosed carriage with a removable front cover and a back cover that can be raised and lowered. [*Landau* near Karlsruhe in Germany, where it was first made]

landaulet /landɔː'lɛt, -də-/ *n.* **1** a small landau. **2** *hist.* a car with a folding hood over the rear seats.

land bank *n.* a bank issuing banknotes on the securities of landed property.

land breeze *n.* a breeze blowing towards the sea from the land, esp. at night.

land bridge *n.* a neck of land joining two large land masses.

land crab *n.* a crab, *Cardisoma guanhumi*, that lives in burrows inland and migrates in large numbers to the sea to breed.

land drain *n.* a drain made of porous or perforated piping, placed in a gravel-filled trench, and used for subsoil drainage. ◻ **land drainage** *n.* (hyphenated when *attrib.*).

landed /'landɪd/ *adj.* **1** owning land (*landed gentry*). **2** consisting of, including, or relating to land (*landed property*).

Länder *pl.* of LAND.

lander /'landə/ *n.* a spacecraft designed to land on the surface of a planet or moon.

landfall /'lan(d)fɔːl/ *n.* the approach to land, esp. for the first time on a sea or air journey.

landfill /'lan(d)fɪl/ *n.* **1** waste material etc. used to landscape or reclaim areas of ground. **2** the process of disposing of rubbish in this way. **3** an area filled in by this process.

land force *n.* (also **land forces**) armies, not naval or air forces.

landform /'lan(d)fɔːm/ *n.* a natural feature of the earth's surface.

land girl *n. Brit.* a woman doing farm work, esp. in wartime.

land-grabber *n.* an illegal seizer of land, esp. *hist.* a person who took the land of an evicted Irish tenant.

landgrave /'lan(d)greɪv/ *n.* (*fem.* **landgravine** /-grəviːn/) *hist.* **1** a count having jurisdiction over a territory. **2** the title of certain German princes. ◻ **landgraviate** /-'greɪvɪət/ *n.* [Middle Low German *landgrave*, Middle High German *lantgrāve* (as LAND, German *Graf* COUNT[2])]

landholder /'landhəʊldə/ *n.* the proprietor or, esp., the tenant of land.

landholding /'landhəʊldɪŋ/ *n.* & *adj.* ● *n.* a piece of land owned or, esp., rented. ● *attrib.adj.* of or relating to landholders or the holding of land.

landing /'landɪŋ/ *n.* **1 a** the act or process of coming to land. **b** an instance of this. **c** (also **landing place**) a place where ships etc. land. **2 a** a platform between two flights of stairs, or at the top or bottom of a flight. **b** a passage leading to upstairs rooms.

landing craft *n.* any of several types of craft esp. designed for putting troops and equipment ashore.

landing gear *n.* the undercarriage of an aircraft.

landing net *n.* a net for landing a large fish which has been hooked.

landing pad *n.* a small area designed for helicopters to land and take off from.

landing stage *n.* a platform, often floating, on which goods and passengers are disembarked.

landing strip *n.* an airstrip.

landlady /'lan(d)leɪdi/ *n.* (*pl.* **-ies**) **1** a woman who lets land, a building, part of a building, etc., to a tenant. **2** a woman who keeps a public house, boarding house, or lodgings.

land-law *n.* (usu. in *pl.*) the law of landed property.

ländler /'lɛndlə/ *n.* **1** an Austrian dance in triple time, a precursor of the waltz. **2** the music for a ländler. [German from *Landl* 'Upper Austria']

landline /'lan(d)lʌɪn/ *n.* a means of telecommunication over land.

landlocked *adj.* almost or entirely enclosed by land.

landloper /'landləʊpə/ *n.* esp. *Sc.* a vagabond. [Middle Dutch *landlooper* (as LAND, *loopen* 'run', formed as LEAP)]

landlord /'lan(d)lɔːd/ *n.* **1** a man who lets land, a building, part of a building, etc., to a tenant. **2** a man who keeps a public house, boarding house, or lodgings.

landlubber /'landlʌbə/ *n.* a person unfamiliar with the sea or sailing.

landmark /'lan(d)mɑːk/ *n.* **1 a** a conspicuous object in a district etc. **b** an object marking the boundary of an estate, country, etc. **2** an event, change, etc. marking a stage or turning point in history etc.

land mass *n.* a large area of land.

landmine /ˈlan(d)mʌɪn/ *n.* **1** an explosive mine laid in or on the ground. **2** a parachute mine.

land office *n. US* an office recording dealings in public land.

land-office business *n. US colloq.* enormous trade.

land of the Covenant *n.* Canaan.

landowner /ˈlandəʊnə/ *n.* an owner of land. ▫ **landownership** *n.* **landowning** *adj. & n.*

landrail /ˈlandreɪl/ *n.* = CORNCRAKE.

landscape /ˈlan(d)skeɪp/ *n. & v.* ● *n.* **1** natural or imaginary scenery, as seen in a broad view. **2** (often *attrib.*) a picture representing this; the genre of landscape painting. **3** (in graphic design etc.) a format in which the width of an illustration etc. is greater than the height (cf. PORTRAIT 4). ● *v.tr.* (also *absol.*) improve (a piece of land) by landscape gardening. ▫ **landscapist** *n.* [Middle Dutch *landscap* (as LAND, -SHIP)]

landscape architecture *n.* the art or practice of planning and designing the environment, esp. with reference to fitting buildings, roads, etc. harmoniously into the landscape. ▫ **landscape architect** *n.*

landscape gardening *n.* the art or practice of laying out ornamental grounds or grounds imitating natural scenery. ▫ **landscape gardener** *n.*

landscape-marble *n.* marble with treelike markings.

landscape painter *n.* an artist who paints landscapes.

Land's End *n.* the westernmost point of Cornwall and of England.

landside /ˈlan(d)sʌɪd/ *n.* the side of an airport terminal to which the general public has unrestricted access (opp. AIRSIDE).

landslide /ˈlan(d)slʌɪd/ *n.* **1** the sliding down of a mass of land from a mountain, cliff, etc. **2** an overwhelming majority for one side in an election.

landslip /ˈlan(d)slɪp/ *n. Brit.* = LANDSLIDE 1.

landsman /ˈlan(d)zmən/ *n.* (*pl.* **-men**) a non-sailor.

land tax *n. hist.* a tax assessed on landed property.

land-tie *n.* a rod, beam, or piece of masonry securing or supporting a wall etc. by connecting it with the ground.

land-wind *n.* a wind blowing seaward from the land.

land yacht *n.* a vehicle with wheels and sails for recreational use on a beach etc.

lane /leɪn/ *n.* **1** a narrow, often rural, road, street, or path. **2** a division of a road for a stream of traffic (*three-lane highway*). **3** a strip of track or water for a runner, rower, or swimmer in a race. **4** a path or course prescribed for or regularly followed by a ship, aircraft, etc. (*ocean lane*). **5** a gangway between crowds of people, objects, etc. ▫ **it's a long lane that has no turning** change is inevitable. [Old English: origin unknown]

langlauf /ˈlaŋlaʊf/ *n.* cross-country skiing; a cross-country skiing race. [German, = long run]

langouste /ˈlɒŋguːst/ *n.* a crawfish or spiny lobster. [French]

langoustine /ˈlɒŋgʊstiːn/ *n.* = NORWAY LOBSTER. [French]

lang syne /laŋ ˈsʌɪn/ *adv. & n. Sc.* ● *adv.* in the distant past. ● *n.* the old days (cf. AULD LANG SYNE). [= long since]

language /ˈlaŋgwɪdʒ/ *n.* **1** the method of human communication, either spoken or written, consisting of the use of words in an agreed way. **2** the language of a particular community or country etc. (*speaks several languages*). **3 a** the faculty of speech. **b** a style or the faculty of expression; the use of words, etc. (*his language was poetic; hasn't the language to express it*). **c** (also **bad language**) coarse, crude, or abusive speech (*didn't like his language*). **4** a system of symbols and rules for writing computer programs or algorithms. **5** any method of expression or communication (*the language of mime; sign language*). **6** a professional or specialized vocabulary. **7** literary style. ▫ **speak the same language** have a similar outlook, manner of expression, etc. [Middle English from Old French *langage*, ultimately from Latin *lingua* 'tongue']

language laboratory *n.* a room equipped with tape recorders etc. for learning a foreign language.

language of flowers *n.* a set of symbolic meanings attached to different flowers.

langue de chat /lɑːŋ də ˈʃɑː, French lɑ̃g də ʃa/ *n.* a very thin finger-shaped crisp biscuit or piece of chocolate. [French, = cat's tongue]

langue d'oc /laːŋ ˈdɒk, French lɑ̃g dɔk/ *n.* the form of medieval French spoken south of the Loire, the basis of modern Provençal. [Old French *langue* 'language' from Latin *lingua* 'tongue' + *de* 'of' + *oc* (from Latin *hoc*) the form for *yes*]

langue d'oïl /lɑːŋ ˈdɔɪl, French lɑ̃g dɔjl/ *n.* the form of medieval French spoken north of the Loire, the basis of modern French. [as LANGUE D'OC + *oïl* (from Latin *hoc ille*) the form for *yes*]

languid /ˈlaŋgwɪd/ *adj.* **1** lacking vigour; idle; inert; apathetic. **2** (of ideas etc.) lacking force; uninteresting. **3** (of trade etc.) slow-moving; sluggish. **4** faint; weak. ▫ **languidly** *adv.* **languidness** *n.* [French *languide* or Latin *languidus* (as LANGUISH)]

languish /ˈlaŋgwɪʃ/ *v.intr.* **1** be or grow feeble; lose or lack vitality. **2** put on a sentimentally tender or languid look. ▫ **languish for** droop or pine for. **languish under** suffer under (esp. depression, confinement, etc.). ▫ **languisher** *n.* **languishingly** *adv.* **languishment** *n.* [Middle English from Old French *languir*, ultimately from Latin *languēre*: related to LAX]

languor /ˈlaŋgə/ *n.* **1** lack of energy or alertness; inertia; idleness; dullness. **2** faintness; fatigue. **3** a soft or tender mood or effect. **4** an oppressive stillness (of the air etc.). ▫ **languorous** *adj.* **languorously** *adv.* [Middle English via Old French from Latin *languor -oris* (as LANGUISH)]

langur /ˈlaŋgə, lanˈgʊə/ *n.* any of various Asian long-tailed monkeys esp. of the genus *Presbytis*. [Hindi]

laniary /ˈlanɪəri/ *adj. & n.* ● *adj.* (of a tooth) adapted for tearing; canine. ● *n.* (*pl.* **-ies**) a laniary tooth. [Latin *laniarius* via *lanius* 'butcher' from *laniare* 'to tear']

laniferous /ləˈnɪf(ə)rəs/ *adj.* (also **lanigerous** /ləˈnɪdʒ(ə)rəs/) wool-bearing. [Latin *lanifer*, *-ger* from *lana* 'wool']

lank /laŋk/ *adj.* **1** (of hair, grass, etc.) long, limp, and straight. **2** thin and tall. **3** shrunken; spare. ▫ **lankly** *adv.* **lankness** *n.* [Old English *hlanc*, from Germanic]

lanky /ˈlaŋki/ *adj.* (**lankier**, **lankiest**) (of limbs, a person, etc.) ungracefully thin and long or tall. ▫ **lankily** *adv.* **lankiness** *n.*

lanner /ˈlanə/ *n.* a S. European falcon, *Falco biarmicus*, esp. the female. [Middle English via Old French *lanier* (perhaps from Old French *lanier* 'cowardly', originally = weaver) from Latin *lanarius* 'wool-merchant', from *lana* 'wool']

lanneret /ˈlanərɪt/ *n.* a male lanner, smaller than the female. [Middle English from Old French *laneret* (as LANNER)]

lanolin /ˈlan(ə)lɪn/ *n.* a fat found naturally on sheep's wool and used purified as a base for ointments. [German, from Latin *lana* 'wool' + *oleum* 'oil']

lansquenet /ˈlɑːnskənɛt, ˈlans-/ *n.* **1** a card game of German origin. **2** a German mercenary soldier in the 16th–17th c. [French from German *Landsknecht* (as LAND, *Knecht* 'soldier' from Old High German *kneht*, related to KNIGHT)]

lantana /lanˈtɑːnə, -ˈteɪnə/ *n.* any evergreen shrub of the genus *Lantana*, with usu. yellow or orange flowers. [modern Latin]

lantern /ˈlantən/ *n.* **1 a** a lamp with a transparent usu. glass case protecting a candle flame etc. **b** a similar electric etc. lamp. **c** its case. **2 a** a raised structure on a dome, room, etc., glazed to admit light. **b** a similar structure for ventilation etc. **3** the light-chamber of a lighthouse. **4** = MAGIC LANTERN. [Middle English via Old

French *lanterne* and Latin *lanterna* from Greek *lamptēr* 'torch, lamp']

lantern fish *n.* any marine fish of the family Myctophidae, having small light organs on the head and body.

lantern-fly *n.* (*pl.* **-flies**) any tropical homopterous insect of the family Fulgoridae, formerly thought to be luminous.

lantern jaws *n.pl.* long thin jaws and chin, giving a hollow look to the face. □ **lantern-jawed** *adj.*

lantern slide *n.* a slide for projection by a magic lantern etc. (see SLIDE *n.* 5b).

lantern-wheel *n.* a cylindrical gearwheel.

lanthanide /ˈlanθənʌɪd/ *n.* (also **lanthanoid** /-nɔɪd/) *Chem.* any of a series of fifteen mainly soft, reactive metallic elements with similar chemical properties, from lanthanum to lutetium in the periodic table. Cf. RARE EARTH. [German *Lanthanid* (as LANTHANUM)]

lanthanum /ˈlanθənəm/ *n. Chem.* a silvery metallic element of the lanthanide series which is used in the manufacture of alloys and catalysts (symbol **La**). [Greek *lanthanō* 'escape notice', from having remained undetected in cerium oxide]

lanugo /ləˈnjuːgəʊ/ *n.* fine soft hair, esp. that which covers the body and limbs of a human foetus. [Latin, = down, from *lana* 'wool']

lanyard /ˈlanjəd/ *n.* **1** a cord hanging round the neck or looped round the shoulder, esp. of a Scout or sailor etc., to which a knife, a whistle, etc., may be attached. **2** *Naut.* a short rope or line used for securing, tightening, etc. **3** a cord attached to a breech mechanism for firing a gun. [Middle English from Old French *laniere*, *lasniere*: assimilated to YARD[1]]

Laodicean /ˌleɪə(ʊ)dɪˈsiːən/ *adj. & n.* ● *adj.* lukewarm or half-hearted, esp. in religion or politics. ● *n.* such a person. [Latin *Laodicea* in Asia Minor (with reference to the early Christians there: see Rev. 3:16)]

Laotian /ˈlaʊʃ(ə)n, lɑːˈəʊʃ(ə)n/ *n. & adj.* ● *n.* **1 a** a native or national of Laos in SE Asia. **b** a person of Laotian descent. **2** the language of Laos. ● *adj.* of or relating to Laos or its people or language.

lap[1] /lap/ *n.* **1 a** the front of the body from the waist to the knees of a sitting person (*sat on her lap*; *caught it in his lap*). **b** the clothing, esp. a skirt, covering the lap. **c** the front of a skirt held up to catch or contain something. **2** a hollow among hills. **3** a hanging flap on a garment, a saddle, etc. □ **in** (or **on**) **a person's lap** as a person's responsibility. **in the lap of the gods** (of an event etc.) open to chance; beyond human control. **in the lap of luxury** in extremely luxurious surroundings. □ **lapful** *n.* (*pl.* **-fuls**). [Old English *læppa* 'fold, flap']

lap[2] /lap/ *n. & v.* ● *n.* **1 a** one circuit of a racetrack etc. **b** a section of a journey etc. (*finally we were on the last lap*). **2 a** an amount of overlapping. **b** an overlapping or projecting part. **3 a** a layer or sheet (of cotton etc. being made) wound on a roller. **b** a single turn of rope, silk, thread, etc., round a drum or reel. **4** a rotating disc for polishing a gem or metal. ● *v.* (**lapped**, **lapping**) **1** *tr.* lead or overtake (a competitor in a race) by one or more laps. **2** *tr.* (often foll. by *about*, *round*) coil, fold, or wrap (a garment etc.) round (esp. a person). **3** *tr.* (usu. foll. by *in*) enfold or swathe (a person) in wraps etc. **4** *tr.* (as **lapped** *adj.*) (usu. foll. by *in*) protectively encircled; enfolded caressingly. **5** *tr.* surround (a person) with an influence etc. **6** *intr.* (usu. foll. by *over*) project; overlap. **7** *tr.* cause to overlap. **8** *tr.* polish (a gem etc.) with a lap. [Middle English, probably from LAP[1]]

lap[3] /lap/ *v. & n.* ● *v.* (**lapped**, **lapping**) **1** *tr.* **a** (also *absol.*) (usu. of an animal) drink (liquid) with the tongue. **b** (usu. foll. by *up*, *down*) consume (liquid) greedily. **c** (usu. foll. by *up*) consume (gossip, praise, etc.) greedily. **2 a** *tr.* (of water) move or beat upon (a shore) with a rippling sound as of lapping. **b** *intr.* (of waves etc.) move in ripples; make a lapping sound. ● *n.* **1 a** the process or an act of lapping. **b** the amount of liquid taken up. **2** the sound of wavelets on a beach. **3** liquid food for dogs. **4** *slang* **a** a weak beverage. **b** any liquor. [Old English *lapian*, from Germanic]

laparoscope /ˈlap(ə)rəskəʊp/ *n. Surgery* a fibre optic instrument inserted through the abdominal wall to give a view of the organs in the abdomen. □ **laparoscopy** /-ˈrɒskəpi/ *n.* (*pl.* **-ies**). [Greek *lapara* 'flank' + -SCOPE]

laparotomy /lapəˈrɒtəmi/ *n.* (*pl.* **-ies**) a surgical incision into the abdominal cavity for exploration or diagnosis. [Greek *lapara* 'flank' + -TOMY]

lapdog /ˈlapdɒg/ *n.* a small pet dog.

lapel /ləˈpɛl/ *n.* the part of a coat, jacket, etc., folded back against the front round the neck opening. □ **lapelled** *adj.* [LAP[1] + -EL]

lapicide /ˈlapɪsʌɪd/ *n.* a person who cuts or engraves on stone. [Latin *lapicida*, formed irregularly from *lapis -idis* 'stone': see -CIDE]

lapidary /ˈlapɪd(ə)ri/ *adj. & n.* ● *adj.* **1** concerned with stone or stones. **2** engraved upon stone. **3** (of writing style) dignified and concise, suitable for inscriptions. ● *n.* (*pl.* **-ies**) a cutter, polisher, or engraver of gems. [Middle English from Latin *lapidarius*, from *lapis -idis* 'stone']

lapilli /ləˈpɪlʌɪ/ *n.pl.* stone fragments ejected from volcanoes. [Italian from Latin, pl. diminutive of *lapis* 'stone']

lapis lazuli /ˌlapɪs ˈlazjʊlʌɪ, -li/ *n. & adj.* ● *n.* **1** a blue mineral containing sodium aluminium silicate and sulphur, used as a gemstone. **2** a bright blue pigment formerly made from this. **3** its colour. ● *adj.* of this mineral, pigment, or colour. [Middle English, from Latin *lapis* 'stone' + medieval Latin *lazuli*, genitive of *lazulum*, from Persian (as AZURE)]

lap joint *n.* the joining of rails, shafts, etc., by halving the thickness of each at the joint and fitting them together.

Laplander /ˈlaplandə/ *n.* **1** a native or national of Lapland. **2** a person of this descent. [*Lapland* from Swedish *Lappland* (as LAPP, LAND)]

lap of honour *n. Brit.* a ceremonial circuit of a football pitch, a track, etc., by a winner or winners.

Lapp /lap/ *n. & adj.* ● *n.* **1** a member of the indigenous population of the extreme north of Scandinavia. **2** the language of the Lapps. ● *adj.* of or relating to the Lapps or their language. [Swedish *Lapp*, perhaps originally a term of contempt: cf. Middle High German *lappe* 'simpleton']

■ **Usage** The Lapps' own name for themselves, *Sami*, is now often preferred with reference to the people.

lappet /ˈlapɪt/ *n.* **1** a small flap or fold of a garment etc. **2** a hanging or loose piece of flesh, such as a lobe or wattle. **3** (in full **lappet-moth**) any of various usu. brown velvety moths whose larvae have flaps on their sides, esp. *Gastropacha quercifilia* of Eurasia. □ **lappeted** *adj.* [LAP[1] + -ET[1]]

Lappish /ˈlapɪʃ/ *adj. & n.* ● *adj.* = LAPP *adj.* ● *n.* the Lapp language.

lap robe *n. N. Amer.* a travelling rug.

lapsang souchong /ˈlapsaŋ/ *n.* a variety of souchong tea with a smoky flavour. [from invented first element + SOUCHONG]

lapse /laps/ *n. & v.* ● *n.* **1** a slight error; a slip of memory etc. **2** a weak or careless decline into an inferior state. **3** (foll. by *of*) an interval or passage of time (*after a lapse of three years*). **4** *Law* the termination of a right or privilege through disuse or failure to follow appropriate procedures. ● *v.intr.* **1** fail to maintain a position or standard. **2** (foll. by *into*) fall back into an inferior or previous state. **3** (of a right or privilege etc.) become invalid because it is not used or claimed or renewed. **4** (as **lapsed** *adj.*) (of a person or thing) that has lapsed. [Latin *lapsus* from *labi laps-* 'glide, slip, fall']

lapse rate *n.* the rate at which the temperature falls with increasing altitude.

lapstone /ˈlapstəʊn/ *n.* a shoemaker's stone held in the lap and used to beat leather on.

lap-strake *n.* & *adj.* ● *n.* a clinker-built boat. ● *adj.* clinker-built.

lapsus calami /ˌlapsəs ˈkaləmʌɪ/ *n.* (*pl.* same) a slip of the pen. [Latin: see LAPSE]

lapsus linguae /ˌlapsəs ˈlɪŋgwʌɪ/ *n.* (*pl.* same) a slip of the tongue. [Latin: see LAPSE]

laptop /ˈlaptɒp/ *n.* (often *attrib.*) a microcomputer that is portable and suitable for use while travelling.

lap-weld *v.* & *n.* ● *v.tr.* weld with overlapping edges. ● *n.* such a weld.

lapwing /ˈlapwɪŋ/ *n.* a plover, *Vanellus vanellus*, with black and white plumage, crested head, and a shrill cry. [Old English *hlēapewince* from *hlēapan* LEAP + the base of WINK, meaning 'move from side to side': assimilated to LAP[1], WING (named from its manner of flying)]

larboard /ˈlɑːbɔːd, -bəd/ *n.* & *adj.* *Naut. archaic* = PORT[3]. [Middle English *lade-*, *ladde-*, *lathe-* (perhaps = LADE + BOARD): later assimilated to *starboard*]

larceny /ˈlɑːs(ə)ni/ *n.* (*pl.* **-ies**) the theft of personal property (in 1968 replaced as a statutory crime in English law by *theft*). □ **larcener** *n.* **larcenist** *n.* **larcenous** *adj.* [Old French *larcin* via Latin *latrocinium*, from *latro* 'robber, mercenary', from Greek *latreus*]

larch /lɑːtʃ/ *n.* **1** a deciduous coniferous tree of the genus *Larix*, with bright foliage and producing tough timber. **2** (in full **larchwood** /ˈlɑːtʃwʊd/) its wood. [Middle High German *larche*, ultimately from Latin *larix -icis*]

lard /lɑːd/ *n.* & *v.* ● *n.* the internal fat of the abdomen of pigs, esp. when rendered and clarified for use in cooking and pharmacy. ● *v.tr.* **1** insert strips of fat or bacon in (meat etc.) before cooking. **2** (foll. by *with*) embellish (talk or writing) with foreign or technical terms. [Middle English via Old French *lard* 'bacon' from Latin *lardum*, *laridum*, related to Greek *larinos* 'fat']

larder /ˈlɑːdə/ *n.* **1** a room or large cupboard for storing food. **2** a wild animal's store of food, esp. for winter. [Middle English via Old French *lardier* from medieval Latin *lardarium* (as LARD)]

lardon /ˈlɑːdən/ *n.* (also **lardoon** /-ˈduːn/) a strip of fat bacon used to lard meat. [Middle English from French *lardon* (as LARD)]

lardy /ˈlɑːdi/ *adj.* like or with lard.

lardy-cake *n. Brit.* a cake made with lard, currants, etc.

lares /ˈlɑːriːz/ *n.pl. Rom.Hist.* the household gods. □ **lares and penates** the home. [Latin]

large /lɑːdʒ/ *adj.* & *n.* ● *adj.* **1** of considerable or relatively great size or extent. **2** of the larger kind (*the large intestine*). **3** of wide range; comprehensive. **4** pursuing an activity on a large scale (*large farmer*). ● *n.* (**at large**) **1** at liberty. **2** as a body or whole (*popular with the people at large*). **3** (of a narration etc.) at full length and with all details. **4** without a specific target (*scatters insults at large*). **5** *US* representing a whole area and not merely a part of it (*congressman at large*). □ **in large** on a large scale. **large as life** see LIFE. **larger than life** see LIFE. □ **largeness** *n.* **largish** *adj.* [Middle English via Old French from the fem. of Latin *largus* 'copious']

large calorie see CALORIE 2.

large intestine *n.* the caecum, colon, and rectum collectively.

largely /ˈlɑːdʒli/ *adv.* to a great extent; principally (*is largely due to laziness*).

large-minded *adj.* liberal; not narrow-minded.

large-scale *adj.* made or occurring on a large scale or in large amounts.

largesse /lɑːˈʒɛs, -ˈdʒɛs/ *n.* (also **largess**) **1** money or gifts freely given, esp. on a special occasion, by a person in high position. **2** generosity, beneficence. [Middle English from Old French *largesse*, ultimately from Latin *largus* 'copious']

larghetto /lɑːˈgɛtəʊ/ *adv.*, *adj.*, & *n. Mus.* ● *adv.* & *adj.* in a fairly slow tempo. ● *n.* (*pl.* **-os**) a larghetto passage or movement. [Italian, diminutive of LARGO]

largo /ˈlɑːgəʊ/ *adv.*, *adj.*, & *n. Mus.* ● *adv.* & *adj.* in a slow tempo and dignified in style. ● *n.* (*pl.* **-os**) a largo passage or movement. [Italian, = broad]

lariat /ˈlarɪət/ *n.* **1** a lasso. **2** a tethering-rope, esp. used by cowboys. [Spanish *la reata* from *reatar* 'tie again' (as RE-, Latin *aptare* 'adjust' from *aptus* 'APT, fit')]

lark[1] /lɑːk/ *n.* **1** any small bird of the family Alaudidae with brown plumage, elongated hind claws, and tuneful song, esp. the skylark. **2** any of various similar birds such as the meadowlark. [Old English *lāferce*, *lǣwerce*, of unknown origin]

lark[2] /lɑːk/ *n.* & *v. colloq.* ● *n.* **1** a frolic or spree; an amusing incident; a joke. **2** *Brit.* a type of activity, affair, etc. (*fed up with this digging lark*). ● *v.intr.* (foll. by *about*) play tricks; frolic. □ **larky** *adj.* **larkiness** *n.* [19th c.: origin uncertain]

larkspur /ˈlɑːkspəː/ *n.* **1** a plant of the genus *Consolida* (buttercup family), with spurred flowers. **2** a delphinium.

larn /lɑːn/ *v. colloq.* or *joc.* **1** *intr.* = LEARN. **2** *tr.* teach (*that'll larn you*). [dialect form of LEARN]

larrikin /ˈlarɪkɪn/ *n. Austral.* a hooligan. [also English dialect: perhaps from the name *Larry* (pet form of *Lawrence*) + -KIN]

larrup /ˈlarəp/ *v.tr.* (**larruped**, **larruping**) *colloq.* thrash. [dialect: perhaps from LATHER]

Larry /ˈlari/ *n.* □ **as happy as Larry** *Brit. colloq.* extremely happy. [20th c.: origin uncertain: cf. LARRIKIN]

larva /ˈlɑːvə/ *n.* (*pl.* **larvae** /-viː/) **1** the active immature form of an insect, esp. differing greatly from the adult and forming the stage between egg and pupa, e.g. a caterpillar or grub. **2** an immature form of other animals that undergo some metamorphosis, e.g. a tadpole. □ **larval** *adj.* **larvicide** /ˈlɑːvɪsʌɪd/ *n.* [in earlier use = disembodied spirit: Latin, = ghost, mask]

laryngeal /ləˈrɪn(d)ʒɪəl/ *adj.* **1** of or relating to the larynx. **2** *Phonet.* designating a speech sound made in the larynx with the vocal cords partly closed and partly vibrating (producing, in English, the so-called 'creaky voice' sound).

laryngitis /larɪnˈdʒʌɪtɪs/ *n.* inflammation of the larynx. □ **laryngitic** /-ˈdʒɪtɪk/ *adj.*

laryngoscope /ləˈrɪŋgəskəʊp/ *n.* an instrument for examining the larynx, or for inserting a tube through it.

laryngotomy /larɪŋˈgɒtəmi/ *n.* (*pl.* **-ies**) a surgical incision of the larynx, esp. to provide an air passage when breathing is obstructed.

larynx /ˈlarɪŋks/ *n.* (*pl.* **larynges** /ləˈrɪn(d)ʒiːz/) the hollow muscular organ forming an air passage to the lungs and holding the vocal cords in humans and other mammals; the voice box. [modern Latin from Greek *larugx -ggos*]

lasagne /ləˈzanjə, -ˈsan-, -ˈsɑːn-/ *n.* pasta in the form of sheets or wide strips, esp. as cooked and served with minced meat and cheese sauce. [Italian, pl. of *lasagna*, from Latin *lasanum* 'cooking pot']

Lascar /ˈlaskə/ *n.* a sailor from India or SE Asia. [ultimately from Urdu & Persian *laškar* 'army']

lascivious /ləˈsɪvɪəs/ *adj.* **1** lustful. **2** inciting to or evoking lust. □ **lasciviously** *adv.* **lasciviousness** *n.* [Middle English via Late Latin *lasciviosus* from Latin *lascivia* 'lustfulness', from *lascivus* 'sportive, wanton']

lase /leɪz/ *v.intr.* **1** function as or in a laser. **2** (of a substance) undergo the physical processes employed in a laser. [back-formation from LASER]

laser /ˈleɪzə/ *n.* a device that generates an intense beam of coherent monochromatic radiation in the infra-red, visible, or ultraviolet region of the electromagnetic spectrum, by stimulated emission of photons from an excited source (cf. MASER). [acronym from *l*ight *a*mplification by *s*timulated *e*mission of *r*adiation]

laserdisc /ˈleɪzədɪsk/ *n.* a disc on which signals and data are recorded to be reproduced by directing a laser beam on to the surface and detecting the reflected or transmitted light.

laser printer *n.* a printer in which a laser is used to form a pattern of dots on a photosensitive drum corresponding to the pattern of print required on the page.

LaserVision /ˈleɪzəvɪʒ(ə)n/ *n. propr.* a system for the reproduction of video signals recorded on a disc with a laser. [LASER + VISION, on the pattern of TELEVISION]

lash /laʃ/ *v.* & *n.* ● *v.* **1** *tr.* & *intr.* make a sudden whip-like movement (*lashed his tail*; *lashing backwards and forwards*). **2** *tr.* beat with a whip, rope, etc. **3** *intr.* pour or rush with great force. **4** *intr.* (foll. by *at, against*) strike violently. **5** *tr.* castigate in words. **6** *tr.* urge on as with a lash. **7** *tr.* (foll. by *down, together*, etc.) fasten with a cord, rope, etc. **8** *tr.* (of rain, wind, etc.) beat forcefully upon. ● *n.* **1 a** a sharp blow made by a whip, rope, etc. **b** (prec. by *the*) punishment by beating with a whip etc. **2** the flexible end of a whip. **3** (usu. in *pl.*) an eyelash. □ **lash out 1** (often foll. by *at*) speak or hit out angrily. **2** *Brit.* spend money extravagantly, be lavish. □ **lasher** *n.* **lashless** *adj.* [Middle English: probably imitative]

lashing /ˈlaʃɪŋ/ *n.* **1** a beating. **2** cord used for lashing.

lashings /ˈlaʃɪŋz/ *n.pl.* (foll. by *of*) *Brit. colloq.* plenty; an abundance.

lash-up *n. Brit.* a makeshift or improvised structure or arrangement.

lass /las/ *n.* esp. *Sc.* & *N.Engl.* or *poet.* a girl or young woman. [Middle English *lasce* from Old Norse *laskwa* 'unmarried' (fem.)]

Lassa fever /ˈlasə/ *n.* an acute and often fatal febrile viral disease of tropical Africa. [*Lassa*, a village in Nigeria, where first reported]

lassie /ˈlasi/ *n. colloq.* = LASS.

lassitude /ˈlasɪtjuːd/ *n.* **1** languor, weariness. **2** disinclination to exert or interest oneself. [French *lassitude* or Latin *lassitudo* from *lassus* 'tired']

lasso /ləˈsuː, ˈlasəʊ/ *n.* & *v.* ● *n.* (*pl.* **-os** or **-oes**) a rope with a noose at one end, used esp. in N. America for catching cattle etc. ● *v.tr.* (**-oes**, **-oed**) catch with a lasso. □ **lassoer** *n.* [Spanish *lazo* LACE]

last[1] /lɑːst/ *adj.*, *adv.*, & *n.* ● *adj.* **1** after all others; coming at or belonging to the end. **2 a** most recent; next before a specified time (*last Christmas*; *last week*). **b** preceding; previous in a sequence (*got on at the last station*). **3** only remaining (*the last biscuit*; *our last chance*). **4** (prec. by *the*) least likely or suitable (*the last person I'd want*; *the last thing I'd have expected*). **5** the lowest in rank (*the last place*). ● *adv.* **1** after all others (esp. in *comb.*: *last-mentioned*). **2** on the last occasion before the present (*when did you last see him?*). **3** (esp. in enumerating) lastly. ● *n.* **1** a person or thing that is last, last-mentioned, most recent, etc. **2** (prec. by *the*) the last mention or sight etc. (*shall never hear the last of it*). **3** the last performance of certain acts (*breathed his last*). **4** (prec. by *the*) **a** the end or last moment. **b** death. □ **at last** (or **long last**) in the end; after much delay. **on one's last legs** see LEG. **pay one's last respects** see PAY[1]. **to** (or **till**) **the last** till the end; esp. till death. [Old English *latost*, from the Germanic superlative of the base of LATE]

last[2] /lɑːst/ *v.intr.* **1** remain unexhausted or adequate or alive for a specified or considerable time; suffice (*enough food to last us a week*; *the battery lasts and lasts*). **2** continue for a specified time (*the journey lasts an hour*). □ **last out** remain adequate or in existence for the whole of a period previously stated or implied. [Old English *lǣstan*, from Germanic]

last[3] /lɑːst/ *n.* a shoemaker's model for shaping or repairing a shoe or boot. □ **stick to one's last** not meddle with what one does not understand. [Old English *lǣste* 'last', *lǣst* 'boot', *lāst* 'footprint', from Germanic]

last agony *n.* the pangs of death.

last ditch *n.* a place of final desperate defence (often, with hyphen, *attrib.*: *last-ditch attempt*).

lasting /ˈlɑːstɪŋ/ *adj.* **1** continuing, permanent. **2** durable. □ **lastingly** *adv.* **lastingness** *n.*

Last Judgement *n.* (in some beliefs) the judgement of mankind expected to take place at the end of the world.

lastly /ˈlɑːstli/ *adv.* finally; in the last place.

last man *n. Cricket* the batsman who goes into bat last.

last minute *n.* (also **last moment**) the time just before an important event (often, with hyphen, *attrib.*: *last-minute rush*).

last name *n.* surname.

last offices *n.pl.* (prec. by *the*) rites due to the dead.

last post *n. Brit.* **1** the last of several bugle calls giving notice of the hour of retiring at night. **2** this call blown at military funerals etc.

last rites *n.pl.* sacred rites for a person about to die.

last sleep *n.* death.

last straw *n.* (prec. by *the*) a slight addition to a burden or difficulty that makes it finally unbearable. [from the saying *it was the last straw that broke the camel's back*]

Last Supper *n.* the supper eaten by Christ and his disciples on the eve of the Crucifixion, as recorded in the New Testament.

last thing *adv.* very late, esp. as a final act before going to bed (*took the tablets last thing at night*).

last trump *n.* (prec. by *the*) the trumpet blast to wake the dead on Judgement Day.

last word *n.* (prec. by *the*) **1** a final or definitive statement (*always has the last word*; *is the last word on this subject*). **2** (often foll. by *in*) the latest fashion.

lat. *abbr.* latitude.

latch /latʃ/ *n.* & *v.* ● *n.* **1** a bar with a catch and lever used as a fastening for a gate etc. **2** a spring-lock preventing a door from being opened from the outside without a key after being shut. ● *v.tr.* & *intr.* fasten or be fastened with a latch. □ **latch on** (often foll. by *to*) *colloq.* **1** attach oneself (to). **2** understand. **on the latch** fastened by the latch only, not locked. [probably from *latch* 'seize' (now dialect) from Old English *læccan*, from Germanic]

latchkey /ˈlatʃkiː/ *n.* (*pl.* **-eys**) a key of an outer door.

latchkey child *n.* (also *colloq.* **latchkey kid**) a child who is alone at home after school until a parent returns from work.

late /leɪt/ *adj.* & *adv.* ● *adj.* **1** after the due or usual time; occurring or done after the proper time (*late for dinner*; *a late milk delivery*). **2 a** far on in the day or night or in a specified time or period. **b** far on in development. **3** flowering or ripening towards the end of the season (*late strawberries*). **4** (prec. by *the* or *my*, *his*, etc.) no longer alive or having the specified status (*my late husband*; *the late president*). **5** (esp. in *superl.*) of recent date (*the late storms*; *the latest songs*). ● *adv.* **1** after the due or usual time (*arrived late*). **2** far on in time (*this happened later on*). **3** at or till a late hour. **4** at a late stage of development. **5** formerly but not now (*late of the Scillies*). □ **at the latest** as the latest time envisaged (*will have done it by six at the latest*). **late in the day** at a late stage in the proceedings, esp. too late to be useful. **the latest** the most recent news, fashion, etc. (*have you heard the latest?*). □ **lateness** *n.* [Old English *læt* (*adj.*), *late* (*adv.*), from Germanic]

latecomer /ˈleɪtkʌmə/ *n.* a person who arrives late.

lateen /ləˈtiːn/ *adj.* (of a ship) rigged with a lateen sail. [French (*voile*) *latine* 'Latin (sail)', because common in the Mediterranean]

lateen sail *n.* a triangular sail on a long yard at an angle of 45° to the mast.

Late Latin *n.* Latin of about AD 200–600.

lately /ˈleɪtli/ *adv.* not long ago; recently; in recent times. [Old English *lætlīce* (as LATE, -LY[2])]

La Tène /la 'tɛn/ *adj. Archaeol.* of or relating to the second cultural phase of the Iron Age in central and W. Europe, lasting from the 5th to the 1st centuries BC. [a district in Switzerland, where remains of it were first identified]

latent /'leɪt(ə)nt/ *adj.* **1** concealed, dormant. **2** existing but not developed or manifest. □ **latency** *n.* **latently** *adv.* [Latin *latēre latent-* 'be hidden']

latent heat *n. Physics* the heat required to convert a solid into a liquid or vapour, or a liquid into a vapour, without change of temperature.

latent image *n. Photog.* an image not yet made visible by developing.

-later /lətə/ *comb. form* denoting a person who worships a particular thing or person (*idolater*). [Greek: see LATRIA]

lateral /'lat(ə)r(ə)l/ *adj. & n.* ● *adj.* **1** of, at, towards, or from the side or sides. **2** descended from a brother or sister of a person in direct line. ● *n.* a side part etc., esp. a lateral shoot or branch. □ **laterally** *adv.* [Latin *lateralis* from *latus lateris* 'side']

lateral line *n. Zool.* a visible line along the side of a fish consisting of a series of sense organs acting as vibration receptors.

lateral thinking *n. Brit.* a method of solving problems indirectly or by apparently illogical methods (opp. VERTICAL THINKING).

laterite /'latərʌɪt/ *n.* a red or yellow ferruginous clay, friable and hardening in air, used for making roads in the tropics. □ **lateritic** /-'rɪtɪk/ *adj.* [Latin *later* 'brick' + -ITE[1]]

latex /'leɪtɛks/ *n.* (*pl.* **latexes** or **latices** /-tɪsi:z/) **1** a milky fluid of mixed composition found in various plants and trees, esp. the rubber tree, and used for commercial purposes. **2** a synthetic product resembling this. [Latin, = liquid]

lath /lɑ:θ/ *n. & v.* ● *n.* (*pl.* **laths** /lɑ:θs, lɑ:ðz/) **1** a thin flat strip of wood, esp. each of a series forming a framework or support for plaster etc. **2** (esp. in phr. **lath and plaster**) laths collectively as a building material, esp. as a foundation for supporting plaster. ● *v.tr.* attach laths to (a wall or ceiling). [Old English *lætt*]

lathe /leɪð/ *n.* a machine for shaping wood, metal, etc., by means of a rotating drive which turns the piece being worked on against changeable cutting tools. [probably related to Old Danish *lad* 'structure, frame', from Old Norse *hlath*, related to *hlatha* LADE]

lather /'lɑ:ðə, 'laðə/ *n. & v.* ● *n.* **1** a froth produced by agitating soap etc. and water. **2** frothy sweat, esp. of a horse. **3** a state of agitation. ● *v.* **1** *intr.* (of soap etc.) form a lather. **2** *tr.* cover with lather. **3** *intr.* (of a horse etc.) develop or become covered with lather. **4** *tr. colloq.* thrash. □ **lathery** *adj.* [Old English *lēathor* (*n.*), *lēthran* (*v.*)]

lathi /'lɑ:ti:/ *n.* (*pl.* **lathis**) (in India) a long heavy iron-bound bamboo stick used as a weapon, esp. by police. [Hindi *lāṭhī*]

latices *pl.* of LATEX.

Latin /'latɪn/ *n. & adj.* ● *n.* **1** the Italic language of ancient Rome and its empire, originating in Latium. **2** *Rom.Hist.* an inhabitant of ancient Latium in central Italy. ● *adj.* **1** of or in Latin. **2** of the countries or peoples (e.g. France and Spain) using languages developed from Latin. **3** *Rom.Hist.* of or relating to ancient Latium or its inhabitants. **4** of the Roman Catholic Church. □ **Latinism** *n.* **Latinist** *n.* [Middle English via Old French *Latin* or Latin *Latinus* from *Latium*]

Latina see LATINO *n.*

Latin America *n.* the parts of Central and S. America where Spanish or Portuguese is the main language.

Latin American *n. & adj.* ● *n.* a native of Latin America. ● *adj.* of or relating to Latin America.

Latinate /'latɪneɪt/ *adj.* having the character of Latin.

Latin Church *n.* the Western Church.

Latin cross *n.* a plain cross with the lowest member longer than the other three.

Latinize /'latɪnʌɪz/ *v.* (also **-ise**) **1** *tr.* give a Latin or Latinate form to. **2** *tr.* translate into Latin. **3** *tr.* make conformable to the ideas, customs, etc., of the ancient Romans, Latin peoples, or Latin Church. **4** *intr.* use Latin forms, idioms, etc. □ **Latinization** /-'zeɪʃ(ə)n/ *n.* **Latinizer** *n.* [Late Latin *latinizare* (as LATIN)]

Latino /lə'ti:nəʊ/ *n. & adj. N. Amer.* ● *n.* (*pl.* **-os**; *fem.* **Latina**) a Latin American inhabitant of the United States. ● *adj.* of or relating to these inhabitants. [Latin American Spanish]

latish /'leɪtɪʃ/ *adj. & adv.* fairly late.

latitude /'latɪtju:d/ *n.* **1** *Geog.* **a** the angular distance on a meridian north or south of the equator, expressed in degrees and minutes. **b** (usu. in *pl.*) regions or climes, esp. with reference to temperature (*warm latitudes*). **2** freedom from narrowness; liberality of interpretation. **3** tolerated variety of action or opinion (*was allowed much latitude*). **4** *Astron.* the angular distance of a celestial object or point from the ecliptic. □ **latitudinal** /-'tju:dɪn(ə)l/ *adj.* **latitudinally** /-'tju:dɪn(ə)li/ *adv.* [Middle English, = breadth, via Latin *latitudo -dinis* from *latus* 'broad']

latitudinarian /,latɪtju:dɪ'nɛ:rɪən/ *adj. & n.* ● *adj.* allowing latitude esp. in religion; showing no preference among varying creeds and forms of worship. ● *n.* a person with a latitudinarian attitude. □ **latitudinarianism** *n.* [Latin *latitudo -dinis* 'breadth' + -ARIAN]

latria /lə'trʌɪə, 'latrɪə/ *n. RC Ch.* supreme worship allowed to God alone. [Late Latin from Greek *latreia* 'worship', from *latreuō* 'serve']

latrine /lə'tri:n/ *n.* a communal lavatory, esp. in a camp, barracks, etc. [French from Latin *latrina*, shortening of *lavatrina*, from *lavare* 'wash']

-latry /lətri/ *comb. form* denoting worship (*idolatry*). [Greek *latreia*: see LATRIA]

latten /'lat(ə)n/ *n.* an alloy of copper and zinc, often rolled into sheets, and formerly used for monumental brasses and church articles. [Middle English *latoun* from Old French *laton, leiton*]

latter /'latə/ *adj.* **1** (prec. by *the, this*, etc.; usu. *absol.*) the second-mentioned or *disp.* last-mentioned person or thing (opp. FORMER 3). **2** nearer to the end (*the latter part of the year*). **3** recent. **4** belonging to the end of a period, of the world, etc. [Old English *lætra*, comparative of *læt* LATE]

■ **Usage** The use of *latter* to mean 'last-mentioned of three or more' is considered incorrect by some people.

latter-day *attrib.adj.* modern, contemporary.

Latter-day Saints *n.pl.* the Mormons' name for themselves.

latterly /'latəli/ *adv.* **1** in the latter part of life or of a period. **2** recently.

lattice /'latɪs/ *n.* **1 a** a structure of crossed laths or bars with spaces between, used as a screen, fence, etc. **b** (in full **lattice-work**) laths arranged in lattice formation. **2** *Crystallog.* a regular periodic arrangement of atoms, ions, or molecules in a crystalline solid. □ **latticed** *adj.* **latticing** *n.* [Middle English via Old French *lattis*, from *latte* 'lath', from West Germanic]

lattice frame *n.* (also **lattice girder**) a girder or truss made of top and bottom members connected by struts usu. crossing diagonally.

lattice window *n.* a window with small panes set in diagonally crossing strips of lead.

Latvian /'latvɪən/ *n. & adj.* ● *n.* **1 a** a native of Latvia, a Baltic republic. **b** a person of Latvian descent. **2** the language of Latvia. ● *adj.* of or relating to Latvia or its people or language.

laud /lɔ:d/ *v. & n.* ● *v.tr.* praise or extol, esp. in hymns. ● *n.* **1** *literary* praise; a hymn of praise. **2** (in *pl.*) the office of the first canonical hour of prayer, originally said at daybreak. [Middle English: the noun from Old

French *laude*, the verb from Latin *laudare*, from Latin *laus laudis* 'praise']

laudable /'lɔːdəb(ə)l/ *adj.* commendable, praiseworthy. ▫ **laudability** /-'bɪlɪti/ *n.* **laudably** *adv.* [Middle English from Latin *laudabilis* (as LAUD)]

▪ **Usage** *Laudable* 'praiseworthy' is sometimes confused with *laudatory* 'expressing praise'. The difference is illustrated by the sentence *Her laudable efforts were recognized in the mayor's laudatory speech.*

laudanum /'lɔːd(ə)nəm, 'lɒ-/ *n.* a solution containing morphine and prepared from opium, formerly used as a narcotic painkiller. [modern Latin, the name given by Paracelsus to a costly medicament, later applied to preparations containing opium: perhaps a variant of LADANUM]

laudation /lɔː'deɪʃ(ə)n/ *n. formal* praise. [Latin *laudatio -onis* (as LAUD)]

laudatory /'lɔːdət(ə)ri/ *adj.* (also **laudative** /-tɪv/) expressing praise.

▪ **Usage** See Usage Note at LAUDABLE.

lauds see LAUD *n.* 2.

laugh /lɑːf/ *v. & n.* ● *v.* **1** *intr.* make the spontaneous sounds and movements usual in expressing lively amusement, scorn, derision, etc. **2** *tr.* express by laughing. **3** *tr.* bring (a person) into a certain state by laughing (*laughed them into agreeing*). **4** *intr.* (foll. by *at*) ridicule, make fun of (*laughed at us for going*). **5** *intr.* (in phr. **be laughing**) *colloq.* be in a fortunate or successful position. **6** *intr.* esp. *poet.* make sounds reminiscent of laughing. ● *n.* **1** the sound or act or manner of laughing. **2** *colloq.* a comical or ridiculous person or thing. ▫ **have the last laugh** be ultimately the winner. **laugh in a person's face** show open scorn for a person. **a laugh a minute** very funny or amusing. **laugh off** get rid of (embarrassment or humiliation) by joking. **laugh on the other side of one's face** change from enjoyment or amusement to displeasure, shame, apprehension, etc. **laugh out of court** deprive of a hearing by ridicule. **laugh up one's sleeve** be secretly or inwardly amused. ▫ **laugher** *n.* [Old English *hlæhhan, hliehhan*, from Germanic]

laughable /'lɑːfəb(ə)l/ *adj.* ludicrous; highly amusing. ▫ **laughably** *adv.*

laughing /'lɑːfɪŋ/ *n. & adj.* ● *n.* laughter. ● *adj.* in senses of LAUGH *v.* ▫ **no laughing matter** something serious. ▫ **laughingly** *adv.*

laughing gas *n.* nitrous oxide as an anaesthetic, formerly used without oxygen and causing an exhilarating effect when inhaled.

laughing hyena *n.* a hyena, *Crocuta crocuta*, whose howl is compared to a fiendish laugh.

laughing jackass *n.* = KOOKABURRA.

laughing stock *n.* a person or thing open to general ridicule.

laughter /'lɑːftə/ *n.* the act or sound of laughing. [Old English *hleahtor*, from Germanic]

launce /lɑːns, lans/ *n.* a sand eel. [perhaps from LANCE: cf. *garfish*]

launch[1] /lɔːn(t)ʃ/ *v. & n.* ● *v.* **1 a** *tr.* set (a vessel) afloat. **b** *intr.* (often foll. by *out*) (of a vessel) put out to sea etc. **2** *tr.* hurl or send forth (a weapon, rocket, etc.). **3** *tr.* start or set in motion (an enterprise, a person on a course of action, etc.). **4** *tr.* formally introduce (a new product) with publicity etc. **5** *intr.* **a** (foll. by *out, into*) make a start, esp. on an ambitious enterprise. **b** (foll. by *into*) begin suddenly (a tirade, speech, song, etc.). ● *n.* the act or an instance of launching. [Middle English from Anglo-French *launcher*, Old Northern French *lancher*, Old French *lancier* LANCE *v.*]

launch[2] /lɔːn(t)ʃ/ *n.* **1** a large motor boat, used esp. for pleasure. **2** *hist.* a man-of-war's largest boat. [Spanish *lancha* 'pinnace', perhaps via Malay *lancharan* from *lanchār* 'swift']

launcher /'lɔːn(t)ʃə/ *n.* a structure or device to hold a rocket during launching.

launch pad *n.* (also **launching pad**) a platform with a supporting structure, from which rockets are launched.

launder /'lɔːndə/ *v. & n.* ● *v.tr.* **1** wash and iron (clothes, linen, etc.). **2** *colloq.* transfer (funds) to conceal a dubious or illegal origin. ● *n.* a channel for conveying liquids, esp. water or molten metal. ▫ **launderer** *n.* [Middle English *launder* 'washer of linen', contraction of *lavander* from Old French *lavandier*, ultimately from Latin *lavanda* 'things to be washed', neut. pl. gerundive of *lavare* 'wash']

launderette /lɔːndə'rɛt, lɔːn'drɛt/ *n.* (also **laundrette**) an establishment with coin-operated washing machines and dryers for public use.

laundress /'lɔːndrɪs/ *n.* a woman who launders clothes, linen, etc., esp. professionally.

laundromat /'lɔːndrəmat/ *n.* esp. *N. Amer.* a launderette. [US proprietary name, alteration of *US laundermat*]

laundry /'lɔːndri/ *n.* (*pl.* **-ies**) **1 a** a room or building for washing clothes etc. **b** a firm washing clothes etc. commercially. **2** clothes or linen for laundering or newly laundered. **3** the action of laundering clothes etc. [contraction of *lavendry* (from Old French *lavanderie*), influenced by LAUNDER]

laundryman /'lɔːndrɪmən/ *n.* (*pl.* **-men**; *fem.* **laundrywoman**, *pl.* **-women**) a person who launders clothes etc. or who collects and delivers laundry.

laureate /'lɒrɪət, 'lɔː-/ *adj. & n.* ● *adj.* **1** wreathed with laurel as a mark of honour. **2** consisting of laurel; laurel-like. ● *n.* **1** a person who is honoured for outstanding creative or intellectual achievement (*Nobel laureate*). **2** = POET LAUREATE. ▫ **laureateship** *n.* [Latin *laureatus* via *laurea* 'laurel-wreath' from *laurus* 'laurel']

laurel /'lɒr(ə)l/ *n. & v.* ● *n.* **1** = BAY[2] 1. **2 a** (in *sing.* or *pl.*) the foliage of the bay tree used as an emblem of victory or distinction in poetry, usu. formed into a wreath or crown. **b** (in *pl.*) honour or distinction. **3** any plant with dark green glossy leaves like a bay tree, e.g. cherry laurel, mountain laurel, spurge laurel. ● *v.tr.* (**laurelled**, **laurelling**; *US* **laureled**, **laureling**) wreathe with laurel. ▫ **look to one's laurels** beware of losing one's pre-eminence. **rest on one's laurels** be satisfied with what one has done and not seek further success. [Middle English *lorer* via Old French *lorier* and Provençal *laurier*, from *laur*, from Latin *laurus*]

laurustinus /lɒrə'stʌɪnəs, lɔː-/ *n.* an evergreen winter-flowering shrub, *Viburnum tinus*, with dense glossy green leaves and white or pink flowers. [modern Latin, from Latin *laurus* 'laurel' + *tinus* 'wild laurel']

lav /lav/ *n. colloq.* lavatory. [abbreviation]

lava /'lɑːvə/ *n.* **1** the molten matter which flows from a volcano. **2** the solid substance which it forms on cooling. [Italian from *lavare* 'wash', from Latin]

lavabo *n.* (*pl.* **-os**) **1** /lə'veɪbəʊ, lə'vɑː-/ *RC Ch.* **a** the ritual washing of the celebrant's hands at the offertory of the Mass. **b** a towel or basin used for this. **2** /'lavəbəʊ/ a monastery washing trough. **3** /lə'veɪbəʊ, lə'vɑː-/ a washbasin. [Latin, = I will wash, first word of Psalm 26:6]

lavage /'lavɪdʒ, la'vɑːʒ/ *n. Med.* the washing-out of a body cavity, such as the colon or stomach, with water or a medicated solution. [French from *laver* 'wash': see LAVE]

lavation /lə'veɪʃ(ə)n/ *n. formal* washing. [Latin *lavatio* from *lavare* 'wash']

lavatorial /lavə'tɔːrɪəl/ *adj.* **1** of or relating to lavatories, esp. resembling the architecture or decoration of public lavatories. **2** (of humour etc.) scatological.

lavatory /'lavət(ə)ri/ *n.* (*pl.* **-ies**) **1** a large receptacle for urinating or defecating into, usu. flushed and cleansed by water and connected to a sewage system. **2** a room or compartment containing one or more of these.

[originally = washing vessel: Middle English via Late Latin *lavatorium* from Latin *lavare lavat-* 'wash']

lavatory paper *n. Brit.* = TOILET PAPER.

lave /leɪv/ *v.tr. literary* **1** wash, bathe. **2** (of water) wash against; flow along. [Middle English via Old French *laver* from Latin *lavare* 'wash', perhaps coalescing with Old English *lafian*]

lavender /ˈlav(ə)ndə/ *n., v., & adj.* ● *n.* **1 a** any small evergreen shrub of the genus *Lavandula*, with narrow leaves and blue, purple, or pink aromatic flowers. **b** its flowers and stalks dried and used to scent linen, clothes, etc. **2** a pale blue colour with a trace of mauve. **3** *colloq.* effeminacy, homosexuality. ● *v.tr.* put lavender among (linen etc.). ● *adj.* **1** of the blue-mauve colour or fragrance lavender flowers. **2 a** sentimental, genteel. **b** *colloq.* of or relating to homosexuality. **c** *colloq.* (of a man) effeminate, homosexual. [Middle English from Anglo-French *lavendre*, ultimately from medieval Latin *lavandula*]

lavender-water *n.* a perfume made from distilled lavender and alcohol.

laver[1] /ˈleɪvə, ˈlɑːvə/ *n.* any of various edible seaweeds, esp. *Porphyra umbilicaulis*, having sheetlike fronds. [Latin]

laver[2] /ˈleɪvə/ *n.* **1** *Bibl.* a large brass vessel for Jewish priests' ritual ablutions. **2** *archaic* a washing or fountain basin; a font. [Middle English *lavo(u)r* via Old French *laveo(i)r* from Late Latin (as LAVATORY)]

laver bread *n.* a Welsh dish of laver which is boiled, dipped in oatmeal, and fried. [LAVER[1]]

lavish /ˈlavɪʃ/ *adj. & v.* ● *adj.* **1** giving or producing in large quantities; profuse. **2** generous, unstinting. **3** excessive, over-abundant. ● *v.tr.* (often foll. by *on*) bestow or spend (money, effort, praise, etc.) abundantly. □ **lavishly** *adv.* **lavishness** *n.* [Middle English from obsolete *lavish, lavas* 'profusion', from Old French *lavasse* 'deluge of rain' from *laver* 'wash']

law /lɔː/ *n.* **1 a** a rule enacted or customary in a community and recognized as enjoining or prohibiting certain actions and enforced by the imposition of penalties. **b** a body of such rules (*the law of the land*; *forbidden under Scots law*). **2** the controlling influence of laws; a state of respect for laws (*law and order*). **3** laws collectively as a social system or subject of study (*was reading law*). **4** (with defining word) any of the specific branches or applications of law (*commercial law*; *law of contract*). **5** binding force or effect (*their word is law*). **6** (prec. by *the*) **a** the legal profession. **b** *colloq.* the police. **7** the statute and common law (opp. EQUITY 2). **8** (in *pl.*) jurisprudence. **9 a** the judicial remedy; litigation. **b** the law courts as providing this (*go to law*). **10** a rule of action or procedure, e.g. in a game, social context, form of art, etc. **11** a regularity in natural occurrences, esp. as formulated or propounded in particular instances (*the laws of nature*; *the law of gravity*; *Parkinson's law*). **12 a** the body of divine commandments as expressed in the Bible or other sources. **b** (**Law of Moses**) the precepts of the Pentateuch. **c** (**the Law**) the Pentateuch as distinguished from the other parts of the Hebrew Bible (the Prophets and the Writings). Cf. TORAH. □ **at** (or **in**) **law** according to the laws. **be a law unto oneself** do what one feels is right; disregard custom. **go to law** take legal action; make use of the law courts. **lay down the law** be dogmatic or authoritarian. **take the law into one's own hands** redress a grievance by one's own means, esp. by force. [Old English *lagu* from Old Norse *lag*, something 'laid down' or fixed, related to LAY[1]]

law-abiding *adj.* obedient to the laws. □ **law-abidingness** *n.*

law agent *n.* (in Scotland) a solicitor.

lawbreaker /ˈlɔːbreɪkə/ *n.* a person who breaks the law. □ **lawbreaking** *n. & adj.*

law centre *n. Brit.* an independent publicly-funded advisory service on legal matters.

law court *n.* a court of law.

lawful /ˈlɔːfʊl, -f(ə)l/ *adj.* conforming with, permitted by, or recognized by law; not illegal or (of a child) illegitimate. □ **lawfully** *adv.* **lawfulness** *n.*

lawgiver /ˈlɔːgɪvə/ *n.* a person who lays down laws.

lawks /lɔːks/ *int.* expressing surprise, awe, or consternation. [alteration of LORD]

lawless /ˈlɔːlɪs/ *adj.* **1** having no laws or enforcement of them. **2** disregarding laws. **3** unbridled, uncontrolled. □ **lawlessly** *adv.* **lawlessness** *n.*

Law Lord *n.* a member of the House of Lords qualified to perform its legal work.

lawmaker /ˈlɔːmeɪkə/ *n.* a legislator. □ **law-making** *adj. & n.*

lawman /ˈlɔːmən/ *n.* (*pl.* **-men**) *US* a law-enforcement officer, esp. a sheriff or police officer.

lawn[1] /lɔːn/ *n. & v.* ● *n.* a piece of grass kept mown and smooth in a garden, park, etc. ● *v.tr.* turn into lawn, lay with lawn. [Middle English *laund* 'glade' via Old French *launde* from Celtic: related to LAND]

lawn[2] /lɔːn/ *n.* a fine linen or cotton fabric used for clothes. □ **lawny** *adj.* [Middle English, probably from *Laon*, a city in France important for linen manufacture]

lawnmower /ˈlɔːnməʊə/ *n.* a machine for cutting the grass on a lawn.

lawn tennis *n.* the usual form of tennis, played with a soft ball on an open grass or hard court (cf. REAL TENNIS).

■ **Usage** *Lawn Tennis* has been replaced by *Tennis* as the official international name of the sport.

law of averages *n.* the supposed principle that future events are likely to be such as to counteract any past deviation from a presumed average.

law of diminishing returns *n.* the fact that an increase in expenditure, investment, taxation, etc., beyond a certain point ceases to produce a proportionate yield.

law of mass action *n.* the principle that the rate of a chemical reaction is proportional to the masses of the reacting substances.

law of nations *n. Law* international law.

law of nature *n.* **1** = NATURAL LAW 1, 2. **2** *colloq.* a regularly occurring phenomenon observable in human society (*it seemed to be a law of nature that all her friends married awful men*).

law of parsimony *n.* = OCCAM'S RAZOR.

law of succession *n.* the law regulating inheritance.

law of the jungle *n.* a state of ruthless competition.

lawrencium /lɒˈrɛnsɪəm/ *n. Chem.* an artificially made transuranic radioactive metallic element (symbol **Lr**, formerly **Lw**). [named after E. O. *Lawrence*, American physicist d. 1958]

laws of war *n.pl.* the limitations on belligerents' action recognized by civilized nations.

lawsuit /ˈlɔːsuːt, -sjuːt/ *n.* the process or an instance of making a claim in a law court.

law term *n. Brit.* a period appointed for the sitting of law courts.

lawyer /ˈlɔːjə, ˈlɔɪə/ *n.* a member of the legal profession, esp. a solicitor. □ **lawyerly** *adj.* [Middle English *law(i)er* from LAW]

lax /laks/ *adj.* **1** lacking care, concern, or firmness. **2** loose, relaxed; not compact. **3** *Phonet.* pronounced with the vocal muscles relaxed. □ **laxity** *n.* **laxly** *adv.* **laxness** *n.* [Middle English, = loose, from Latin *laxus*: related to SLACK[1]]

laxative /ˈlaksətɪv/ *adj. & n.* ● *adj.* tending to stimulate or facilitate evacuation of the bowels. ● *n.* a laxative medicine. [Middle English via Old French *laxatif -ive* or Late Latin *laxativus* from Latin *laxare* 'loosen' (as LAX)]

lay[1] /leɪ/ *v. & n.* ● *v.* (*past* and *past part.* **laid** /leɪd/) **1** *tr.* place on a surface, esp. horizontally in a position of rest (*laid the book on the table*). **2** *tr.* put or bring into a certain or the required position or state (*lay a carpet, a cable*). **3** *intr. dial.* lie. **4** *tr.* make by laying (*lay the foundations*). **5** *tr.* (often *absol.*) (of a hen bird) produce (an egg). **6** *tr.* **a** cause to subside or lie flat. **b** deal with to remove (a ghost, fear, etc.). **7** *tr.* place or present for consideration (a case, proposal, etc.). **8** *tr.* set down as a basis or starting point. **9** *tr.* (usu. foll. by *on*) attribute or impute (blame etc.). **10** *tr.* locate (a scene etc.) in a certain place. **11** *tr.* prepare or make ready (a plan or a trap). **12** *tr.* prepare (a table) for a meal. **13** *tr.* place or arrange the material for (a fire). **14** *tr.* put down as a wager; stake. **15** *tr.* (foll. by *with*) coat or strew (a surface). **16** *tr. slang offens.* have sexual intercourse with (esp. a woman). ● *n.* **1** the way, position, or direction in which something lies. **2** *slang offens.* **a** a partner (esp. female) in sexual intercourse. **b** an act of sexual intercourse. **3** the direction or amount of twist in rope-strands. □ **in lay** (of a hen) laying eggs regularly. **lay about one 1** hit out on all sides. **2** criticize indiscriminately. **lay aside 1** put to one side. **2** cease to practise or consider. **3** save (money etc.) for future needs. **lay at the door of** see DOOR. **lay back** cause to slope back from the vertical. **lay bare** expose, reveal. **lay a charge** make an accusation. **lay claim to** claim as one's own. **lay down 1** put on the ground or other surface. **2** relinquish; give up (an office). **3** formulate or insist on (a rule or principle). **4** pay or wager (money). **5** begin to construct (a ship or railway). **6** store (wine) in a cellar. **7** set down on paper. **8** sacrifice (one's life). **9** convert (land) into pasture. **10** record (esp. popular music). **lay down the law** see LAW. **lay hands on 1** seize or attack. **2** place one's hands on or over, esp. in confirmation, ordination, or spiritual healing. **lay one's hands on** obtain, acquire, locate. **lay hold of** seize or grasp. **lay in** provide oneself with a stock of. **lay into** *colloq.* attack violently with words or blows. **lay it on thick** (or **with a trowel**) *colloq.* flatter or exaggerate grossly. **lay low** overthrow, kill, or humble. **lay off 1** discharge (workers) temporarily or permanently because of a shortage of work; make redundant. **2** *colloq.* desist. **lay on 1** esp. *Brit.* provide (a facility, amenity, etc.). **2** impose (a penalty, obligation, etc.). **3** inflict (blows). **4** spread on (paint etc.). **lay on the table** see TABLE. **lay out 1** spread out. **2** expose to view. **3** prepare (a corpse) for burial. **4** *colloq.* knock unconscious. **5** dispose (grounds etc.) according to a plan. **6** expend (money). **7** *refl.* (foll. by *to* + infin.) take pains (to do something) (*laid themselves out to help*). **lay store by** see STORE. **lay to rest** bury in a grave. **lay up 1** store, save. **2** put (a ship etc.) out of service. **lay waste** see WASTE. [Old English *lecgan*, from Germanic]

■ **Usage** The intransitive use of the verb *lay* in sense 3 to mean 'lie' is erroneous in standard English and arises probably as a result of confusion with *lay* as the past of *lie*, as in *The dog lay on the floor* which is correct. *The dog is laying on the floor* is incorrect and in this sentence *laying* should be *lying*.

lay[2] /leɪ/ *adj.* **1 a** non-clerical. **b** not ordained into the clergy. **2 a** not professionally qualified, esp. in law or medicine. **b** of or done by such persons. [Middle English via Old French *lai* and ecclesiastical Latin *laicus* from Greek *laïkos* LAIC]

lay[3] /leɪ/ *n.* **1** a short lyric or narrative poem meant to be sung. **2** a song. [Middle English from Old French *lai*, Provençal *lais*, of unknown origin]

lay[4] *past* of LIE[1].

layabout /'leɪəbaʊt/ *n.* a habitual loafer or idler.

lay brother *n.* (also **lay sister**) a person who has taken the vows of a religious order but is not ordained and is employed in ancillary or manual work.

lay-by *n.* (*pl.* **lay-bys**) **1** *Brit.* an area at the side of an open road where vehicles may stop. **2** a similar arrangement on a canal or railway. **3** *Austral. & NZ* a system of paying a deposit to secure an article for later purchase.

layer /'leɪə/ *n. & v.* ● *n.* **1** a thickness of matter, esp. one of several, covering a surface. **2** a person or thing that lays. **3** a hen that lays eggs, esp. with reference to its productivity (*a good layer*). **4** a shoot fastened down to take root while attached to the parent plant. ● *v.tr.* **1 a** arrange in layers. **b** cut (hair) in layers. **2** propagate (a plant) as a layer. □ **layered** *adj.* [Middle English, from LAY[1] + -ER[1]]

layer cake *n.* esp. *US* = SANDWICH *n.* 2.

layer-out *n.* a person who prepares a corpse for burial.

layette /leɪ'jɛt/ *n.* a set of clothing, toilet articles, and bedclothes for a newborn child. [French, diminutive of Old French *laie* 'drawer', from Middle Dutch *laege*]

lay figure *n.* **1** a dummy or jointed figure of a human body used by artists for arranging drapery on etc. **2** an unrealistic character in a novel etc. **3** a person lacking in individuality. [*lay* from obsolete *layman*, from Dutch *leeman*, from obsolete *led* 'joint']

layman /'leɪmən/ *n.* (*pl.* **-men**; *fem.* **laywoman**, *pl.* **-women**) **1** any non-ordained member of a Church. **2** a person without professional or specialized knowledge in a particular subject.

lay-off *n.* **1** a temporary or permanent discharge of workers; a redundency. **2** a period when this is in force.

lay open *v.tr.* **1** break the skin of. **2** (foll. by *to*) expose (to criticism etc.).

layout /'leɪaʊt/ *n.* **1** the disposing or arrangement of a site, ground, etc. **2** the way in which plans, printed matter, etc., are arranged or set out. **3** something arranged or set out in a particular way. **4** the make-up of a book, newspaper, etc.

layover /'leɪəʊvə/ *n.* a period of rest or waiting before a further stage in a journey etc.; a stopover.

layperson /'leɪpə:s(ə)n/ *n.* a layman or laywoman.

lay reader *n.* (in the Anglican Church) a lay person licensed to preach and to conduct some religious services.

layshaft /'leɪʃɑ:ft/ *n. Brit.* a second or intermediate transmission shaft in a machine.

lay sister see LAY BROTHER.

lay vicar see VICAR 3.

laywoman see LAYMAN.

lazar /'leɪzə, 'lazə/ *n. archaic* a poor and diseased person, esp. a leper. [Middle English from medieval Latin *lazarus*, from the name *Lazarus* in Luke 16:20]

lazaret /lazə'rɛt/ *n.* (also **lazaretto** /-'rɛtəʊ/) (*pl.* **lazarets** or **lazarettos**) **1** a hospital for diseased people, esp. lepers. **2** a building or ship for quarantine. **3** the after part of a ship's hold, used for stores. [French *lazaret* or its source, Italian *lazzaretto*, from *lazzaro* LAZAR]

laze /leɪz/ *v. & n.* ● *v.* **1** *intr.* spend time lazily or idly. **2** *tr.* (often foll. by *away*) pass (time) in this way. ● *n.* a spell of lazing. [back-formation from LAZY]

lazuli /'lazjʊlʌɪ, -li/ *n.* = LAPIS LAZULI. [abbreviation]

lazy /'leɪzi/ *adj.* (**lazier**, **laziest**) **1** disinclined to work, doing little work. **2** of or inducing idleness. **3** (of a river etc.) slow-moving. □ **lazily** *adv.* **laziness** *n.* [earlier *laysie, lasie, laesy*, perhaps from Low German: cf. Low German *lasich* 'idle']

lazybones /'leɪzɪbəʊnz/ *n.* (*pl.* same) *colloq.* a lazy person.

lb *abbr.* a pound or pounds (weight). [Latin *libra*]

l.b. *abbr. Cricket* leg-bye(s), leg-byed.

LBC *abbr.* London Broadcasting Company.

L/Bdr *abbr.* Lance Bombardier.

l.b.w. *abbr. Cricket* leg before wicket.

l.c. *abbr.* **1** in the passage etc. cited. **2** lower case. **3** letter of credit. [sense 1 from Latin *loco citato*]

LCC *abbr. hist.* London County Council.

LCD *abbr.* **1** liquid crystal display. **2** lowest (or least) common denominator.

LCM *abbr.* lowest (or least) common multiple.

L/Cpl *abbr.* Lance Corporal.

LD *abbr.* lethal dose, usu. with a following numeral indicating the percentage of a group of animals or cultured cells or micro-organisms killed by such a dose (LD_{50}).

Ld. *abbr.* Lord.

Ldg. *abbr.* Leading (Seaman etc.).

LDL *abbr.* low-density lipoprotein.

L-dopa *n. Biochem.* the laevorotatory form of dopa, used to treat Parkinson's disease. Also called *levodopa*.

L-driver *n. Brit.* a learner driver.

LDS *abbr.* **1** Licentiate in Dental Surgery. **2** Latter-day Saints.

-le[1] /(ə)l/ *suffix* forming nouns, esp.: **1** names of appliances or instruments (*handle*; *thimble*). **2** names of animals and plants (*beetle*; *thistle*). [ultimately from or representing Old English *-el* etc. from Germanic, with many Indo-European cognates]

■ **Usage** The suffix *-le* has ceased to be syllabic in some words, e.g. *stile*.

-le[2] /(ə)l/ *suffix* (also **-el**) forming nouns with (or originally with) diminutive sense (*angle*; *castle*; *mantle*; *syllable*; *novel*; *tunnel*). [Middle English *-el*, *-elle* from Old French, ultimately from Latin forms *-ellus*, *-ella*, *-alis* (cf. -AL), etc.]

-le[3] /(ə)l/ *suffix* forming adjectives, often with (or originally with) the sense 'apt or liable to' (*brittle*; *fickle*; *little*; *nimble*). [Middle English from Old English *-el* etc. from Germanic, corresponding to Latin *-ulus*]

-le[4] /(ə)l/ *suffix* forming verbs, esp. expressing repeated action or movement or having diminutive sense (*bubble*; *crumple*; *wriggle*). [Old English *-lian*, from Germanic]

LEA *abbr.* (in the UK) Local Education Authority.

lea /liː/ *n. poet.* a piece of meadowland, or pastureland, or arable land. [Old English *lēa(h)*, from Germanic]

leach /liːtʃ/ *v.* **1** *tr.* make (a liquid) percolate through some material. **2** *tr.* subject (bark, ore, ash, or soil) to the action of percolating fluid. **3** *tr. & intr.* (foll. by *away*, *out*) remove (soluble matter) or be removed in this way. [probably representing Old English *leccan* 'to water', from West Germanic]

lead[1] /liːd/ *v. & n.* ● *v.* (*past* and *past part.* **led** /lɛd/) **1** *tr.* cause to go with one, esp. by guiding or showing the way or by going in front and taking a person's hand or an animal's halter etc. **2** *tr.* **a** direct the actions or opinions of. **b** (often foll. by *to*, or *to* + infin.) guide by persuasion or example or argument (*what led you to that conclusion?*; *was led to think you may be right*). **3** *tr.* (also *absol.*) provide access to; bring to a certain position or destination (*this door leads you into a small room*; *the road leads to Lincoln*; *the path leads uphill*). **4** *tr.* pass or go through (a life etc. of a specified kind) (*led a miserable existence*). **5** *tr.* **a** have the first place in (*lead the dance*; *leads the world in sugar production*). **b** (also *absol.*) go first; be ahead in a race or game. **c** (also *absol.*) be pre-eminent in some field. **6** *tr.* be in charge of (*leads a team of researchers*). **7** *tr.* **a** direct by example. **b** set (a fashion). **c** be the principal player of (a group of musicians). **8** *tr.* (also *absol.*) begin a round of play at cards by playing (a card) or a card of (a particular suit). **9** *intr.* (foll. by *to*) have as an end or outcome; result in (*what does all this lead to?*). **10** *intr.* (foll. by *with*) *Boxing* make an attack (with a particular blow). **11 a** *intr.* (foll. by *with*) (of a newspaper) use a particular item as the main story (*led with the Stock Market crash*). **b** *tr.* (of a story) be the main feature of (a newspaper or part of it) (*the royal wedding will lead the front page*). **12** *tr.* (foll. by *through*) make (a liquid, strip of material, etc.) pass through a pulley, channel, etc. ● *n.* **1** guidance given by going in front; example. **2 a** a leading place; the leadership (*is in the lead*; *take the lead*). **b** the amount by which a competitor is ahead of the others (*a lead of ten yards*). **3** a clue, esp. an early indication of the resolution of a problem (*is the first real lead in the case*). **4** a strap or cord for leading a dog etc. **5 a** *Brit.* a conductor (usu. a wire) conveying electric current from a source to an appliance. **b** *US* a conductor used in internal wiring. **6 a** the chief part in a play etc. **b** the person playing this. **c** (*attrib.*) the chief performer or instrument of a specified type (*lead guitar*). **7** (in full **lead story**) the item of news given the greatest prominence in a newspaper or magazine. **8 a** the act or right of playing first in a game or round of cards. **b** the card led. **9** the distance advanced by a screw in one turn. **10 a** an artificial watercourse, esp. one leading to a mill. **b** a channel of water in an ice field. □ **lead astray** cause to err or sin. **lead by the nose** cajole (a person) into compliance. **lead a person a dance** see DANCE. **lead off 1** begin; make a start. **2** *Brit. colloq.* lose one's temper. **lead on 1** entice into going further than was intended. **2** mislead or deceive. **lead up the garden path** *colloq.* mislead. **lead the way** see WAY. □ **leadable** *adj.* [Old English *lǣdan*, from Germanic]

lead[2] /lɛd/ *n. & v.* ● *n.* **1** *Chem.* a heavy bluish-grey soft ductile metallic element occurring naturally in galena and used in building and the manufacture of alloys, both the metal and its compounds being toxic (symbol **Pb**). **2 a** graphite. **b** a thin length of this for use in a pencil. **3** a lump of lead used in sounding water. **4** (in *pl.*) *Brit.* **a** strips of lead covering a roof. **b** a piece of lead-covered roof. **5** (in *pl.*) lead frames holding the glass of a lattice or stained-glass window. **6** *Printing* **a** a metal strip used to create space between lines of type. **b** this space. **7** (*attrib.*) made of lead. ● *v.tr.* **1** cover, weight, or frame (a roof or window panes) with lead. **2** *Printing* separate lines of (printed matter) with leads. **3** add a lead compound to (petrol etc.). □ **swing the lead** see SWING. □ **leaded** *adj.* **leadless** *adj.* [Old English *lēad*, from West Germanic]

leaden /ˈlɛd(ə)n/ *adj.* **1** of or like lead. **2** heavy, slow, burdensome (*leaden limbs*). **3** inert, depressing (*leaden rule*). **4** lead-coloured (*leaden skies*). □ **leadenly** *adv.* **leadenness** /ˈlɛd(ə)nnɪs/ *n.* [Old English *lēaden* (as LEAD[2])]

leaden seal *n.* a stamped piece of lead holding the ends of a wire used as a fastening.

leader /ˈliːdə/ *n.* **1 a** a person or thing that leads. **b** a person followed by others. **2 a** the principal player in a music group. **b** the first violin in an orchestra. **c** *US* a conductor of an orchestra. **3** *Brit.* = LEADING ARTICLE. **4** a short strip of non-functioning material at each end of a reel of film or recording tape for connection to the spool. **5** (in full **Leader of the House**) *Brit.* a member of the government officially responsible for initiating business in Parliament. **6** a shoot of a plant at the apex of a stem or of the main branch. **7** (in *pl.*) *Printing* a series of dots or dashes across the page to guide the eye, esp. in tabulated material. **8** the horse placed at the front in a team or pair. □ **leaderless** *adj.* **leadership** *n.* [Old English *lǣdere* (as LEAD[1])]

leader board *n.* a scoreboard, esp. at a golf course, showing the names etc. of the leading competitors.

leaderene /liːdəˈriːn/ *n. joc.* a female leader, esp. of an autocratic character. [LEADER + *-ene* female ending, on the pattern of forenames like *Marlene*]

lead-free *adj.* (of petrol) without added tetraethyl lead.

lead-in *n.* **1** an introduction, opening, etc. **2** a wire leading in from outside, esp. from an aerial to a receiver or transmitter.

leading[1] /ˈliːdɪŋ/ *adj. & n.* ● *adj.* chief; most important. ● *n.* guidance, leadership.

leading[2] /ˈlɛdɪŋ/ *n. Printing* = LEAD[2] *n.* 6.

leading aircraftman *n.* (*fem.* **leading aircraftwoman**) the rank above aircraftman in the RAF.

leading article *n. Brit.* a newspaper article giving the editorial opinion.

leading counsel *n.* the senior barrister of two or more in a case.

leading edge *n.* **1** the foremost edge of an aerofoil, esp. a wing or propeller blade. **2** the forefront of development, esp. in technology. **3** *Electronics* the part of a pulse in which the amplitude increases.

leading lady *n.* the actress playing the principal part in a play etc.

leading light *n.* a prominent and influential person.

leading man *n.* the actor playing the principal part in a play etc.

leading note *n. Mus.* = SUBTONIC.

leading question *n.* a question that prompts the answer wanted, *e.g. so you never saw the accused hit the officer?*

■ **Usage** Note that *leading question* does not mean a 'principal' or 'loaded' or 'searching' question.

leading-rein *n.* a rein used to lead a horse along, esp. when ridden by an inexperienced rider.

leading seaman *n.* the rank next below NCO in the Royal Navy.

leading tone *n. US Mus.* = LEADING NOTE.

lead-off *n.* an action beginning a process.

lead pencil *n.* a pencil of graphite enclosed in wood.

lead poisoning *n.* acute or chronic poisoning by absorption of lead into the body.

lead shot *n.* = SHOT[1] 3b.

lead story see LEAD[1] *n.* 7.

lead tetraethyl *n.* = TETRAETHYL LEAD.

lead time *n.* the time between the initiation and completion of a production process.

lead wool *n.* a fibrous form of lead, used for jointing water pipes.

leadwort /'lɛdwə:t/ *n.* = PLUMBAGO 2.

leaf /li:f/ *n. & v.* ● *n.* (*pl.* **leaves** /li:vz/) **1 a** each of several flattened usu. green structures of a plant, usu. on the side of a stem or branch and the main organ of photosynthesis. **b** other similar plant structures, e.g. bracts, sepals, and petals (*floral leaf*). **2 a** foliage regarded collectively. **b** the state of having leaves out (*a tree in leaf*). **3** the leaves of tobacco or tea. **4** a single thickness of paper, esp. in a book with each side forming a page. **5** a very thin sheet of metal, esp. gold or silver. **6 a** the hinged part or flap of a door, shutter, table, etc. **b** an extra section inserted to extend a table. ● *v.* **1** *intr.* put forth leaves. **2** *tr.* (foll. by *through*) turn over the pages of (a book etc.). □ **leafage** *n.* **leafed** *adj.* (also in *comb.*). **leafless** *adj.* **leaflessness** *n.* **leaflike** *adj.* [Old English *lēaf*, from Germanic]

leafcutter /'li:fkʌtə/ *n.* **1** (in full **leafcutter ant**) an ant of the mainly tropical American genus *Atta*, which cuts pieces from leaves to cultivate fungus. **2** (in full **leafcutter bee**) a solitary bee of the family Megachilidae which lines its nest with leaf fragments.

leaf green *n. & adj.* ● *n.* the colour of green leaves. ● *adj.* (hyphenated when *attrib.*) of this colour.

leafhopper /'li:fhɒpə/ *n.* any homopterous insect of the superfamily Cicadelloidea, which sucks the sap of plants and often causes damage and spreads disease.

leaf insect *n.* any insect of the family Phylliidae, having a flattened body leaflike in appearance.

leaflet /'li:flɪt/ *n. & v.* ● *n.* **1** a sheet of (usu. printed) paper (sometimes folded but not stitched) giving information, esp. for free distribution. **2** a young leaf. **3** *Bot.* a division of a compound leaf. ● *v.tr.* (**leafleted**, **leafleting**) distribute leaflets to.

leaf miner *n.* any of various insect larvae, esp. of some small moths and flies, that burrow between the surfaces of leaves.

leaf monkey *n.* a langur.

leaf mould *n.* soil consisting chiefly of decayed leaves.

leaf spring *n.* a spring made of strips of metal.

leaf-stalk *n.* a petiole.

leafy /'li:fi/ *adj.* (**leafier**, **leafiest**) **1 a** having many leaves. **b** (of a place) rich in foliage; verdant. **2** resembling a leaf. □ **leafiness** *n.*

league[1] /li:g/ *n. & v.* ● *n.* **1** a collection of people, countries, groups, etc., combining for a particular purpose, esp. mutual protection or cooperation. **2** an agreement to combine in this way. **3** a group of sports clubs which compete over a period for a championship. **4** a class of contestants etc. of comparable ability. ● *v.intr.* (**leagues**, **leagued**, **leaguing**) (often foll. by *together*) join in a league. □ **in league** allied, conspiring. [French *ligue* or Italian *liga*, variant of *lega* from *legare* 'bind', from Latin *ligare*]

league[2] /li:g/ *n. archaic* a varying measure of travelling distance by land, usu. about three miles. [Middle English, ultimately from Late Latin *leuga*, *leuca*, of Gaulish origin]

league football *n. Austral.* Rugby League or Australian Rules football played in leagues.

leaguer[1] /'li:gə/ *n.* esp. *US* a member of a league.

leaguer[2] /'li:gə/ *n. & v.* = LAAGER. [Dutch *leger* 'camp', related to LAIR[1]]

league table *n. Brit.* **1** a listing of competitors as a league, showing their ranking according to performance. **2** any list of ranking order.

leak /li:k/ *n. & v.* ● *n.* **1 a** a hole in a pipe, container, etc. caused by wear or damage, through which matter, esp. liquid or gas, passes accidentally in or out. **b** the matter passing in or out through this. **c** the act or an instance of leaking. **2 a** a similar escape of electrical charge. **b** the charge that escapes. **3** the intentional disclosure of secret information. ● *v.* **1 a** *intr.* (of liquid, gas, etc.) pass in or out through a leak. **b** *tr.* lose or admit (liquid, gas, etc.) through a leak. **2** *tr.* intentionally disclose (secret information). **3** *intr.* (often foll. by *out*) (of a secret, secret information) become known. □ **have** (or **take**) **a leak** *slang* urinate. □ **leaker** *n.* [Middle English, probably from Low German]

leakage /'li:kɪdʒ/ *n.* **1** the action or result of leaking. **2** what leaks in or out. **3** an intentional disclosure of secret information.

leaky /'li:ki/ *adj.* (**leakier**, **leakiest**) **1** having a leak or leaks. **2** given to disclosing secrets. □ **leakiness** *n.*

leal /li:l/ *adj. Sc.* loyal, honest. [Middle English from Anglo-French *leal*, Old French *leel*, *loial* (as LOYAL)]

lean[1] /li:n/ *v. & n.* ● *v.* (*past* and *past part.* **leaned** /li:nd, lɛnt/ or esp. *Brit.* **leant** /lɛnt/) **1** *intr. & tr.* (often foll. by *across*, *back*, *over*, etc.) be or place in a sloping position; incline from the perpendicular. **2** *intr. & tr.* (foll. by *against*, *on*, *upon*) rest or cause to rest for support against etc. **3** *intr.* (foll. by *on*, *upon*) rely on; derive support from. **4** *intr.* (foll. by *to*, *towards*) be inclined or partial to; have a tendency towards. ● *n.* a deviation from the perpendicular; an inclination (*has a decided lean to the right*). □ **lean on** *colloq.* put pressure on (a person) to act in a certain way. **lean over backwards** see BACKWARDS. [Old English *hleonian*, *hlinian*, from Germanic]

lean[2] /li:n/ *adj. & n.* ● *adj.* **1** (of a person or animal) thin; having no superfluous fat. **2** (of meat) containing little fat. **3 a** meagre; of poor quality (*lean crop*). **b** not nourishing (*lean diet*). **4** unremunerative. **5** (of a vaporized fuel mixture) having a high proportion of air. ● *n.* the lean part of meat. □ **leanly** *adv.* **leanness** /'li:nnɪs/ *n.* [Old English *hlǣne*, from Germanic]

lean-burn *adj.* of or relating to an internal-combustion engine designed to run on a lean mixture to reduce pollution.

leaning /'li:nɪŋ/ *n.* a tendency or partiality.

lean-to *n.* (*pl.* **-tos**) a building with its roof leaning against a larger building or a wall.

lean years *n.pl.* years of scarcity.

leap /li:p/ *v. & n.* ● *v.* (*past* and *past part.* **leaped** /li:pt, lɛpt/ or **leapt** /lɛpt/) **1** *intr.* jump or spring forcefully. **2** *tr.* jump across. **3** *intr.* (of prices etc.) increase dramatically. ● *n.* a forceful jump. □ **by leaps and bounds** with startlingly rapid progress. **leap in the dark** a daring step or enterprise whose consequences are unpredictable. **leap to the eye** be immediately apparent. □ **leaper** *n.* [Old English *hlȳp*, *hlēapan*, from Germanic]

leapfrog /'li:pfrɒg/ *n. & v.* ● *n.* a game in which players in turn vault with parted legs over others who are bending down. ● *v.* (**-frogged**, **-frogging**) **1** *intr.* (foll. by *over*) perform such a vault. **2** *tr.* vault over in this way.

3 *tr. & intr.* (of two or more people, vehicles, etc.) overtake alternately.

leap year *n.* a year, occurring once in four, with 366 days (including 29th Feb. as an intercalary day). [probably from the fact that feast days after February in such a year fell two days later (as opposed to one day in other years) than in the previous year]

learn /lə:n/ *v.* (*past* and *past part.* **learned** /lə:nt, lə:nd/ or esp. *Brit.* **learnt** /lə:nt/) **1** *tr.* gain knowledge of or skill in by study, experience, or being taught. **2** *tr.* (foll. by *to* + infin.) acquire or develop a particular ability (*learn to swim*). **3** *tr.* commit to memory (*will try to learn your names*). **4** *intr.* (foll. by *of*) be informed about. **5** *tr.* (foll. by *that, how*, etc. + clause) become aware of by information or from observation. **6** *intr.* receive instruction; acquire knowledge or skill. **7** *tr. archaic* or *slang* teach. □ **learn one's lesson** see LESSON. □ **learnable** *adj.* **learnability** /-nəˈbɪlɪti/ *n.* [Old English *leornian* from Germanic: related to LORE[1]]

■ **Usage** The use of *learn* in sense 7 to mean 'teach', as in *I'll learn you*, is non-standard and to be avoided.

learned /ˈlə:nɪd/ *adj.* **1** having much knowledge acquired by study. **2** showing or requiring learning (*a learned work*). **3** studied or pursued by learned persons. **4** concerned with the interests of learned persons; scholarly (*a learned journal*). **5** *Brit.* as a courteous description of a lawyer in certain formal contexts (*my learned friend*). □ **learnedly** *adv.* **learnedness** *n.* [Middle English, from LEARN in the sense 'teach']

learner /ˈlə:nə/ *n.* **1** a person who is learning a subject or skill. **2** (in full **learner driver**) a person who is learning to drive a motor vehicle and has not yet passed a driving test.

learning /ˈlə:nɪŋ/ *n.* knowledge acquired by study. [Old English *leornung* (as LEARN)]

learning curve *n.* **1** the rate of progress in learning or gaining experience. **2** a graph of this.

lease /li:s/ *n. & v.* ● *n.* an agreement by which the owner of a building or land allows another to use it for a specified time, usu. in return for payment. ● *v.tr.* grant or take on lease. □ **a new lease of** (*N. Amer.* **on**) **life** a substantially improved prospect of living, or of use after repair. □ **leasable** *adj.* **leaser** *n.* [Middle English via Anglo-French *les*, Old French *lais, leis*, from *lesser, laissier* 'leave', via Latin *laxare* 'make loose' from *laxus* 'loose']

leaseback /ˈli:sbak/ *n.* the leasing of a property back to the vendor.

leasehold /ˈli:shəʊld/ *n. & adj.* ● *n.* **1** the holding of property by lease. **2** property held by lease. ● *adj.* held by lease. □ **leaseholder** *n.*

leash /li:ʃ/ *n. & v.* ● *n.* a dog's lead or similar restraint. ● *v.tr.* **1** put a leash on. **2** restrain. □ **straining at the leash** eager to begin. [Middle English from Old French *lesse, laisse* from a specific use of *laisser* 'let run on a slack lead': see LEASE]

least /li:st/ *det., adj., & pron.* ● *det.* (usu. prec. by *the*; often with *neg.*) smallest, slightest, most insignificant (*it doesn't make the least difference; hasn't got the least idea; whoever has least experience*). ● *adj.* (of a species or variety) very small (*least tern*). ● *pron.* (prec. by *the*) the least amount (*the least you could do would be not to interfere*). ● *adv.* in the slightest degree; very little (*this surprised her least*). □ **at least 1** at all events; anyway; even if there is doubt about a more extended statement. **2** (also **at the least**) not less than. **in the least** (or **the least**) (usu. with *neg.*) in the smallest degree; at all (*not in the least offended*). **to say the least** (or **the least of it**) used to imply the moderation of a statement (*that is doubtful to say the least*). [Old English *lǣst, lǣsest*, from Germanic]

least common denominator *n.* = LOWEST COMMON DENOMINATOR.

least common multiple *n.* = LOWEST COMMON MULTIPLE.

least squares *n.* (in full **method** or **principle of least squares**) a method of estimating a quantity or fitting a graph to data so as to minimize the sum of the squares of the differences between the observed values and the estimated values.

leastways /ˈli:stweɪz/ *adv.* (also **leastwise** /-wʌɪz/) *dial.* or *colloq.* or at least, or rather.

leat /li:t/ *n. Brit.* an open watercourse conducting water to a mill etc. [Old English *-gelǣt* (as Y- + root of LET[1])]

leather /ˈlɛðə/ *n. & v.* ● *n.* **1 a** material made from the skin of an animal by tanning or a similar process. **b** (*attrib.*) made of leather. **2** a piece of leather for polishing with. **3** the leather part or parts of something. **4** *slang* a cricket ball or football. **5** (in *pl.*) leather clothes, esp. leggings, breeches, or clothes for wearing on a motorcycle. **6** a thong (*stirrup leather*). ● *v.tr.* **1** cover with leather. **2** polish or wipe with a leather. **3** beat, thrash (originally with a leather thong). [Old English *lether*, from Germanic]

leatherback /ˈlɛðəbak/ *n.* a large marine turtle, *Dermochelys coriacea*, having a thick leathery carapace.

leather-bound *adj.* (esp. of a book) bound in leather.

leathercloth /ˈlɛðəklɒθ/ *n.* strong fabric coated to resemble leather.

leatherette /lɛðəˈrɛt/ *n.* imitation leather.

leatherjacket /ˈlɛðədʒakɪt/ *n.* **1** *Brit.* a crane-fly larva with a tough skin. **2** any of various tough-skinned marine fishes of the families Carangidae and Balistidae.

leathern /ˈlɛð(ə)n/ *n. archaic* made of leather.

leatherneck /ˈlɛðənɛk/ *n. Naut. slang* a soldier or (esp. *US*) a marine (with reference to the leather stock formerly worn by them).

leatherwear /ˈlɛðəwɛ:/ *n.* articles of clothing made of leather.

leathery /ˈlɛð(ə)ri/ *adj.* **1** like leather. **2** (esp. of meat etc.) tough. □ **leatheriness** *n.*

leave[1] /li:v/ *v. & n.* ● *v.* (*past* and *past part.* **left** /lɛft/) **1 a** *tr.* go away from; cease to remain in or on (*left him quite well an hour ago; leave the track; leave here*). **b** *intr.* (often foll. by *for*) depart (*we leave tomorrow; has just left for London*). **2** *tr.* cause to or let remain; depart without taking (*has left his gloves; left a slimy trail; left a bad impression; six from seven leaves one*). **3** *tr.* (also *absol.*) cease to reside at or attend or belong to or work for (*has left the school; I am leaving for another firm*). **4** *tr.* abandon, forsake, desert. **5** *tr.* have remaining after one's death (*leaves a wife and two children*). **6** *tr.* bequeath. **7** *tr.* (foll. by *to* + infin.) allow (a person or thing) to do something without interference or assistance (*leave the future to take care of itself*). **8** *tr.* (foll. by *to*) commit or refer to another person or agent (*leave that to me; nothing was left to chance*). **9** *tr.* **a** abstain from consuming or dealing with. **b** (in *passive*; often foll. by *over*) remain over. **10** *tr.* **a** deposit or entrust (a thing) to be attended to, collected, delivered, etc., in one's absence (*left a message with his secretary*). **b** depute (a person) to perform a function in one's absence. **11** *tr.* allow to remain or cause to be in a specified state or position (*left the door open; the performance left them unmoved; left nothing that was necessary undone*). **12** *tr.* pass (an object) so that it is in a specified relative direction (*leave the church on the left*). ● *n.* the position in which a player leaves the balls in billiards, croquet, etc. □ **be left with 1** retain (a feeling etc.). **2** be burdened with (a responsibility etc.). **be well left** be well provided for by a legacy etc. **get left** *colloq.* be deserted or defeated. **have left** have remaining (*has no friends left*). **leave alone 1** refrain from disturbing, not interfere with. **2** not have dealings with. **leave be** *colloq.* refrain from disturbing, not interfere with. **leave behind 1** go away without. **2** leave as a consequence or a visible sign of passage. **3** pass. **leave a person cold** (or **cool**) not impress or excite a person. **leave go** *colloq.* relax one's hold. **leave hold of** cease holding. **leave it at that** abstain from comment or further action. **leave much** (or **a lot** etc.) **to be desired** be highly unsatisfactory. **leave off 1**

come to or make an end. **2** discontinue (*leave off work*; *leave off talking*). **3** not wear. **leave out** omit, not include. **leave over** *Brit.* leave to be considered, settled, or used later. **leave a person to himself** or **herself 1** not attempt to control a person. **2** leave a person solitary. **left at the post** beaten from the start of a race. **left for dead** abandoned as being beyond rescue. □ **leaver** *n.* [Old English *lǣfan*, from Germanic]

leave[2] /liːv/ *n.* **1** (often foll. by *to* + infin.) permission. **2 a** (in full **leave of absence**) permission to be absent from duty. **b** the period for which this lasts. □ **by** (or **with**) **your leave** often *iron.* an expression of apology for taking a liberty or making an unwelcome statement. **on leave** legitimately absent from duty. **take one's leave** bid farewell. **take one's leave of** bid farewell to. **take leave of one's senses** see SENSE. **take leave to** venture or presume to. [Old English *lēaf* from West Germanic: related to LIEF, LOVE]

leaved /liːvd/ *adj.* **1** having leaves. **2** (in *comb.*) having a leaf or leaves of a specified kind or number (*four-leaved clover*).

leaven /ˈlɛv(ə)n/ *n.* & *v.* ● *n.* **1** a substance added to dough to make it ferment and rise, esp. yeast, or fermenting dough reserved for the purpose. **2 a** a pervasive transforming influence (cf. Matt. 13:33). **b** (foll. by *of*) a tinge or admixture of a specified quality. ● *v.tr.* **1** ferment (dough) with leaven. **2 a** permeate and transform. **b** (foll. by *with*) modify with a tempering element. [Middle English via Old French *levain* from Gallo-Roman use of Latin *levamen* 'relief', from *levare* 'lift']

leave of absence see LEAVE[2] 2a.

leaves *pl.* of LEAF.

leave-taking *n.* the act of taking one's leave. [LEAVE[2]]

leavings /ˈliːvɪŋz/ *n.pl.* things left over, esp. as worthless.

Lebanese /lɛbəˈniːz/ *adj.* & *n.* ● *adj.* of or relating to Lebanon in the Middle East. ● *n.* (*pl.* same) **1** a native or national of Lebanon. **2** a person of Lebanese descent.

Lebensraum /ˈleɪbənzraʊm, German leːbənsraʊm/ *n.* the territory which a state or nation believes is needed for its natural development. [German, = living space (originally with reference to Germany, esp. in the 1930s)]

lech /lɛtʃ/ *v.* & *n. colloq.* ● *v.intr.* feel lecherous; behave lustfully. ● *n.* **1** a strong desire, esp. sexual. **2** a lecher. [back-formation from LECHER: the noun perhaps from *letch* 'longing']

lecher /ˈlɛtʃə/ *n.* a lecherous man; a debauchee. [Middle English via Old French *lecheor* etc., from *lechier* 'live in debauchery or gluttony', from Frankish: related to LICK]

lecherous /ˈlɛtʃ(ə)rəs/ *adj.* lustful, having strong or excessive sexual desire. □ **lecherously** *adv.* **lecherousness** *n.* [Middle English from Old French *lecheros* etc., from *lecheur* LECHER]

lechery /ˈlɛtʃ(ə)ri/ *n.* unrestrained indulgence of sexual desire. [Middle English from Old French *lecherie*, from *lecheur* LECHER]

lecithin /ˈlɛsɪθɪn/ *n.* **1** any of a group of phospholipids found naturally in animals, egg yolk, and some higher plants. **2** a preparation of this used to emulsify foods etc. [Greek *lekithos* 'egg yolk' + -IN]

lectern /ˈlɛkt(ə)n, -ɜːn/ *n.* **1** a stand for holding a book in a church or chapel, esp. for a bible from which lessons are to be read. **2** a similar stand for a lecturer etc. [Middle English *lettorne* from Old French *let(t)run*, medieval Latin *lectrum* from *legere lect-* 'read']

lectin /ˈlɛktɪn/ *n. Biochem.* any of a class of proteins, usu. of plant origin, causing the agglutination of particular cell types. [Latin *legere, lect-* 'choose, select' + -IN]

lection /ˈlɛkʃ(ə)n/ *n.* a reading of a text found in a particular copy or edition. [Latin *lectio* 'reading' (as LECTERN)]

lectionary /ˈlɛkʃ(ə)n(ə)ri/ *n.* (*pl.* **-ies**) **1** a list of portions of Scripture appointed to be read at divine service. **2** a book containing such portions. [Middle English from medieval Latin *lectionarium* (as LECTION)]

lector /ˈlɛktɔː/ *n.* **1** a reader, esp. of lessons in a church service. **2** (*fem.* **lectrice** /lɛkˈtriːs/) a lecturer or reader, esp. one employed in a foreign university to give instruction in his or her native language. [Latin from *legere lect-* 'read']

lecture /ˈlɛktʃə/ *n.* & *v.* ● *n.* **1** a discourse giving information about a subject to a class or other audience. **2** a long serious speech esp. as a scolding or reprimand. ● *v.* **1** *intr.* (often foll. by *on*) deliver a lecture or lectures. **2** *tr.* talk seriously or reprovingly to (a person). **3** *tr.* instruct or entertain (a class or other audience) by a lecture. [Middle English via Old French *lecture* or medieval Latin *lectura* from Latin (as LECTOR)]

lecturer /ˈlɛktʃ(ə)rə/ *n.* a person who lectures, esp. as a teacher in higher education.

lectureship /ˈlɛktʃəʃɪp/ *n.* the office of lecturer.

■ **Usage** The form *lecturership*, which is strictly more regular, is in official use at Oxford University and elsewhere, but is not widely current.

lecture theatre see THEATRE 3.

lecythus /ˈlɛsɪθəs/ *n.* (*pl.* **lecythi** /-θʌɪ/) *Gk Antiq.* a thin narrow-necked vase or flask. [Greek *lēkuthos*]

LED *abbr.* light-emitting diode, a semiconductor diode which glows when a voltage is applied (often *attrib.*: *LED display*).

led *past* and *past part.* of LEAD[1].

lederhosen /ˈleɪdəhəʊz(ə)n/ *n.pl.* leather shorts with braces as worn by men in Bavaria etc. [German, = leather trousers]

ledge /lɛdʒ/ *n.* **1** a narrow horizontal surface projecting from a wall etc. **2** a shelf-like projection on the side of a rock or mountain. **3** a ridge of rocks, esp. below water. **4** *Mining* a stratum of metal-bearing rock. □ **ledged** *adj.* **ledgy** *adj.* [perhaps from Middle English *legge* LAY[1]]

ledger /ˈlɛdʒə/ *n.* **1** the principal book containing a record of all the financial transactions of a company etc., classified under the appropriate headings. **2** a flat gravestone. **3** a horizontal timber in scaffolding, parallel to the face of the building. [Middle English, from senses of Dutch *ligger* and *legger* (from *liggen* LIE[1], *leggen* LAY[1]) and pronunciation of Middle English *ligge, legge*]

ledger line *n. Mus.* = LEGER LINE.

ledger-tackle *n.* a kind of fishing tackle in which a lead weight keeps the bait on the bottom.

lee /liː/ *n.* **1** shelter given by a neighbouring object (*under the lee of*). **2** (in full **lee side**) the sheltered side, the side away from the wind (opp. WEATHER SIDE). [Old English *hlēo*, from Germanic]

lee-board *n.* a plank frame fixed to the side of a flat-bottomed vessel and let down into the water to diminish leeway.

leech[1] /liːtʃ/ *n.* **1** any aquatic or terrestrial annelid worm of the class Hirudinea with suckers at both ends, esp. *Hirudo medicinalis*, a bloodsucking parasite of vertebrates formerly much used medically. **2** a person who extorts profit from or sponges on others. □ **like a leech** persistently or clingingly present. [Old English *lǣce*, assimilated to LEECH[2]]

leech[2] /liːtʃ/ *n. archaic* or *joc.* a physician; a healer. [Old English *lǣce*, from Germanic]

leech[3] /liːtʃ/ *n.* **1** a perpendicular or sloping side of a square sail. **2** the side of a fore-and-aft sail away from the mast or stay. [Middle English, perhaps related to Old Norse *lík*, a nautical term of uncertain meaning]

leechcraft /ˈliːtʃkrɑːft/ *n. archaic* the art of healing. [Old English *lǣcecrǣft* (as LEECH[2], CRAFT)]

leek /liːk/ *n.* **1** an allium, *Allium porrum*, with flat overlapping leaves forming an elongated cylindrical bulb, used as food. **2** this as a Welsh national emblem. [Old English *lēac*, from Germanic]

leer[1] /lɪə/ *v. & n.* ● *v.intr.* look slyly or lasciviously or maliciously. ● *n.* a leering look. □ **leeringly** *adv.* [perhaps from obsolete *leer* 'cheek' from Old English *hlēor*, as though 'to glance over one's cheek']

leer[2] var. of LEHR.

leery /ˈlɪəri/ *adj.* (**leerier, leeriest**) *slang* **1** knowing, sly. **2** (foll. by *of*) wary. □ **leeriness** *n.* [perhaps from obsolete *leer* 'looking askance', from LEER[1] + -Y[1]]

lees /li:z/ *n.pl.* **1** the sediment of wine etc. (*drink to the lees*). **2** dregs, refuse. [pl. of Middle English *lie*, from Old French *lie* via medieval Latin *lia* from Gaulish]

lee shore *n.* the shore to leeward of a ship.

lee side see LEE 2.

leet[1] /li:t/ *n. Brit. hist.* **1** (in full **Court leet**) a yearly or half-yearly court of record that lords of certain manors might hold. **2** its jurisdiction or district. [Middle English from Anglo-French *lete* (= Anglo-Latin *leta*), of unknown origin]

leet[2] /li:t/ *n. Sc.* a selected list of candidates for some office. [Middle English *lite* etc., probably from Anglo-French & Old French *lit(t)e*, variant of *liste* LIST[1]]

leeward /ˈli:wəd, ˈlu:əd/ *adj., adv., & n.* ● *adj. & adv.* on or towards the side sheltered from the wind (opp. WINDWARD). ● *n.* the leeward region, side, or direction (*to leeward*; *on the leeward of*).

leewardly /ˈli:wədli, ˈlu:ədli/ *adj.* (of a ship) apt to drift to leeward.

leeway /ˈli:weɪ/ *n.* **1** the sideways drift of a ship to leeward of the desired course. **2 a** allowable deviation or freedom of action. **b** margin of safety. □ **make up leeway** struggle out of a bad position, recover lost time, etc.

left[1] /lɛft/ *adj., adv., & n.* (opp. RIGHT). ● *adj.* **1** on or towards the side of the human body which is to the west when facing north. **2** on or towards the part of an object which is analogous to a person's left side or (with opposite sense) which is nearer to a spectator's left hand. **3** (also **Left**) *Polit.* of the Left. ● *adv.* on or to the left side. ● *n.* **1** the left-hand part or region or direction. **2** *Boxing* **a** the left hand. **b** a blow with this. **3 a** (often **Left**) *Polit.* a group or section favouring socialist or radical left-wing views (originally the more radical section of a continental legislature, seated on the president's left). **b** the more advanced or innovative section of any group. **4** the side of a stage which is to the left of a person facing the audience. **5** (esp. in marching) the left foot. **6** the left wing of an army. □ **have two left feet** be clumsy. **left and right** (or **left, right, and centre**) = *right and left*. **marry with the left hand** marry morganatically (see LEFT-HANDED 7). □ **leftish** *adj.* [original sense 'weak': Middle English *lüft, lift, left*, from Old English]

left[2] *past* and *past part.* of LEAVE[1].

left-back *n.* (in football, hockey, etc.) a back who plays primarily on the left of the pitch.

left bank *n.* the bank of a river on the left facing downstream.

left bower see BOWER[3].

left field *n. Baseball* the part of the outfield to the left of the batter as he or she faces the pitcher.

left-footed *adj.* **1** using the left foot by preference as more serviceable than the right. **2** (of a kick etc.) done or made with the left foot.

left-hand *adj.* **1** on or towards the left side of a person or thing (*left-hand drive*). **2** done with the left hand (*left-hand blow*). **3 a** (of rope) twisted counter-clockwise. **b** (of a screw) = LEFT-HANDED 4c.

left hand *n.* **1** the hand of the left side. **2** (usu. prec. by *at, on, to*) the region or direction on the left side of a person.

left-handed *adj.* **1** using the left hand by preference as more serviceable than the right. **2** (of a tool etc.) made to be used with the left hand. **3** (of a blow etc.) done or made with the left hand. **4 a** turning to the left; towards the left. **b** (of a racecourse) turning anticlockwise. **c** (of a screw) advanced by turning to the left (anticlockwise). **5** awkward, clumsy. **6 a** (of a compliment) ambiguous. **b** of doubtful sincerity or validity. **7** (of a marriage) morganatic (from a German custom by which the bridegroom gave the bride his left hand in such marriages). □ **left-handedly** *adv.* **left-handedness** *n.*

left-hander *n.* **1** a left-handed person. **2** a left-handed blow.

leftie var. of LEFTY.

leftism /ˈlɛftɪz(ə)m/ *n. Polit.* the principles or policy of the left. □ **leftist** *n. & adj.*

left luggage *n. Brit.* **1** luggage deposited for later retrieval. **2** (in full **left-luggage office**) a place, esp. at a railway station, where such luggage may be left for a small charge.

leftmost /ˈlɛftməʊst/ *adj.* furthest to the left.

leftover /ˈlɛftəʊvə/ *n. & adj.* ● *n.* (usu. in *pl.*) an item (esp. of food) remaining after the rest has been used. ● *adj.* remaining over, surplus.

left turn *n.* a turn that brings one's front to face as one's left side did before; a turn or turning to the left.

leftward /ˈlɛftwəd/ *adv. & adj.* ● *adv.* (also **leftwards** /-wədz/) towards the left. ● *adj.* going towards or facing the left.

left-wing *adj.* **1** socialist; radical. **2** of or relating to the left wing in football etc.

left wing *n.* **1** the radical or socialist section of a political party or system. **2** the left side of a football etc. team on the field. **3** the left side of an army. □ **left-winger** *n.*

lefty /ˈlɛfti/ *n.* (also **leftie**) (*pl.* **-ies**) *colloq.* **1** *Polit.* a left-winger. **2** a left-handed person.

leg /lɛg/ *n. & v.* ● *n.* **1 a** each of the limbs on which a person or animal walks and stands. **b** the part of this from the hip to the ankle. **2** a leg of an animal or bird as food. **3** an artificial leg (*wooden leg*). **4** a part of a garment covering a leg or part of a leg. **5 a** a support of a chair, table, bed, etc. **b** a long thin support or prop, esp. a pole. **6** (in full **leg side**) *Cricket* the half of the field (as divided lengthways through the pitch) away from which the batsman's feet are pointed (opp. OFF *n.* 1). **7 a** a section of a journey. **b** a section of a relay race. **c** a stage in a competition. **d** one of two or more games constituting a round. **e** a single game in darts. **8** one branch of a forked object. **9** *Naut.* a run made on a single tack. **10** *archaic* an obeisance made by drawing back one leg and bending it while keeping the front leg straight. ● *v.tr.* (**legged, legging**) propel (a boat) through a canal tunnel by pushing with one's legs against the tunnel sides. □ **feel** (or **find**) **one's legs** become able to stand or walk. **have the legs of** be able to go further than. **have no legs** *colloq.* (of a golf ball etc.) have not enough momentum to reach the desired point. **keep one's legs** not fall. **leg it** *colloq.* walk or run fast. **not have a leg to stand on** be unable to support one's argument by facts or sound reasons. **on one's last legs** near death or the end of one's usefulness etc. **on one's legs** *Brit.* **1** (also **on one's hind legs**) standing esp. to make a speech. **2** well enough to walk about. **take to one's legs** run away. □ **legged** /lɛgd, ˈlɛgɪd/ *adj.* (also in *comb.*). [Middle English from Old Norse *leggr*, from Germanic]

legacy /ˈlɛgəsi/ *n.* (*pl.* **-ies**) **1** a gift left in a will. **2** something handed down by a predecessor (*legacy of corruption*). [Middle English via Old French *legacie* 'legateship' and medieval Latin *legatia* from Latin *legare* 'bequeath']

legacy-hunter *n.* a person who curries favour with old and rich people in the hope of securing a legacy.

legal /ˈli:g(ə)l/ *adj.* **1** of or based on law; concerned with law; falling within the province of law. **2** appointed or required by law. **3** permitted by law, lawful. **4** recognized by law, as distinct from equity. **5** *Theol.* **a** of the Mosaic Law. **b** of salvation by works rather than by faith. □ **legally** *adv.* [French *légal* or Latin *legalis* from *lex legis* 'law': cf. LEAL, LOYAL]

legal aid *n. Brit.* payment from public funds allowed, in cases of need, to help pay for legal advice or proceedings.

legalese /li:gə'li:z/ *n. colloq.* the technical language of legal documents.

legal fiction *n.* an assertion accepted as true (though probably fictitious) to achieve a useful purpose, esp. in legal matters.

legal holiday *n. US* a public holiday established by law.

legalism /'li:g(ə)lɪz(ə)m/ *n.* **1** excessive adherence to law or formula. **2** *Theol.* **a** adherence to the Mosaic Law rather than to the Gospel. **b** the doctrine of justification by works. □ **legalist** *n. & adj.* **legalistic** /-'lɪstɪk/ *adj.* **legalistically** /-'lɪstɪk(ə)li/ *adv.*

legality /li:'galɪti, lɪ-/ *n.* (*pl.* **-ies**) **1** lawfulness. **2** legalism. **3** (in *pl.*) obligations imposed by law. [French *légalité* or medieval Latin *legalitas* (as LEGAL)]

legalize /'li:g(ə)lʌɪz/ *v.tr.* (also **-ise**) **1** make lawful. **2** bring into harmony with the law. □ **legalization** /-'zeɪʃ(ə)n/ *n.*

legal proceedings see PROCEEDING 2.

legal separation see SEPARATION 2.

legal tender *n.* currency that cannot legally be refused in payment of a debt (usu. up to a limited amount for coins not made of gold).

legate /'lɛgət/ *n.* **1** a member of the clergy representing the Pope. **2** *Rom.Hist.* **a** a deputy of a general. **b** a governor or deputy governor of a province. **3** *archaic* an ambassador or delegate. □ **legateship** *n.* **legatine** /-tʌɪn/ *adj.* [Old English via Old French *legat* from Latin *legatus*, past part. of *legare* 'depute, delegate']

legate a latere /'lɛgət ɑ: 'latəreɪ, -ri/ *n.* a papal legate of the highest class, with full powers. [Latin *latere* = by a third party]

legatee /lɛgə'ti:/ *n.* the recipient of a legacy. [as LEGATOR + -EE]

legation /lɪ'geɪʃ(ə)n/ *n.* **1** a body of deputies. **2** **a** the office and staff of a diplomatic minister (esp. when not having ambassadorial rank). **b** the official residence of a diplomatic minister. **3** a legateship. **4** the sending of a legate or deputy. [Middle English from Old French *legation* or Latin *legatio* (as LEGATE)]

legato /lɪ'gɑ:təʊ/ *adv., adj., & n. Mus.* ● *adv. & adj.* in a smooth flowing manner, without breaks between notes (cf. STACCATO, TENUTO). ● *n.* (*pl.* **-os**) **1** a legato style of performance. **2** a legato passage. [Italian, = bound, past part. of *legare* from Latin *ligare* 'bind']

legator /lɪ'geɪtə/ *n.* the giver of a legacy. [archaic *legate* 'bequeath' from Latin *legare* (as LEGACY)]

leg before *adj., adv., & n.* (in full **leg before wicket**) *Cricket* ● *adj. & adv.* (of a batsman) out because of illegally obstructing the ball with a part of the body. ● *n.* such a dismissal (abbr.: **l.b.w.**).

leg-break *n. Cricket* **1** a ball which deviates from the leg side after bouncing. **2** such deviation.

leg-bye *n.* a run scored from a ball that touches the batsman.

leg-cutter *n. Cricket* a fast leg-break.

legend /'lɛdʒ(ə)nd/ *n.* **1** **a** a traditional story sometimes popularly regarded as historical but unauthenticated; a myth. **b** such stories collectively. **c** a popular but unfounded belief. **d** *colloq.* a person about whom unauthenticated tales are told; a famous or notorious person (*became a legend in his own lifetime*). **2** **a** an inscription, esp. on a coin or medal. **b** *Printing* a caption. **c** wording on a map etc. explaining the symbols used. **3** *hist.* **a** the story of a saint's life. **b** a collection of lives of saints or similar stories. □ **legendry** *n.* [Middle English (in sense 3) via Old French *legende* from medieval Latin *legenda* 'what is to be read', neut. pl. gerundive of Latin *legere* 'read']

legendary /'lɛdʒ(ə)nd(ə)ri/ *adj.* **1** of or connected with legends. **2** described in or based on a legend. **3** *colloq.* remarkable enough to be a subject of legend. □ **legendarily** *adv.* [medieval Latin *legendarius* (as LEGEND)]

legerdemain /lɛdʒədɪ'meɪn/ *n.* **1** sleight of hand; conjuring or juggling. **2** trickery, sophistry. [Middle English from French *léger de main* 'light of hand, dexterous']

leger line /'lɛdʒə/ *n. Mus.* a short line added for notes above or below the range of a staff. [variant of LEDGER]

legging /'lɛgɪŋ/ *n.* (usu. in *pl.*) **1** close-fitting stretch trousers for women or children. **2** a stout protective outer covering for the leg from the knee to the ankle.

leggy /'lɛgi/ *adj.* (**leggier**, **leggiest**) **1** **a** long-legged. **b** (of a woman) having attractively long legs. **2** long-stemmed. □ **legginess** *n.*

leghorn /lɛ'gɔ:n, 'lɛghɔ:n/ *n.* **1** **a** fine plaited straw. **b** a hat of this. **2** (**Leghorn**) **a** a bird of a small hardy breed of domestic fowl. **b** this breed. [Italian *Leghorno*, now Livorno, a port in Italy, from where the straw and fowls were imported]

legible /'lɛdʒɪb(ə)l/ *adj.* (of handwriting, print, etc.) clear enough to read; readable. □ **legibility** /-'bɪlɪti/ *n.* **legibly** *adv.* [Middle English from Late Latin *legibilis*, from *legere* 'read']

legion /'li:dʒ(ə)n/ *n. & adj.* ● *n.* **1** a division of 3,000–6,000 men, including a complement of cavalry, in the ancient Roman army. **2** a large organized body. **3** a vast host, multitude, or number. ● *predic.adj.* great in number (*his good works have been legion*). [Middle English via Old French from Latin *legio -onis*, from *legere* 'choose']

legionary /'li:dʒ(ə)n(ə)ri/ *adj. & n.* ● *adj.* of a legion or legions. ● *n.* (*pl.* **-ies**) a member of a legion. [Latin *legionarius* (as LEGION)]

legioned /'li:dʒ(ə)nd/ *adj. poet.* arrayed in legions.

legionella /li:dʒə'nɛlə/ *n.* the bacterium *Legionella pneumophila*, which causes legionnaires' disease.

legionnaire /li:dʒə'nɛ:/ *n.* **1** a member of a foreign legion. **2** a member of the American Legion or the Royal British Legion. [French *légionnaire* (as LEGION)]

legionnaires' disease *n.* a form of bacterial pneumonia first identified after an outbreak at an American Legion meeting in 1976 and spread esp. by water droplets through air-conditioning systems etc. (cf. LEGIONELLA).

Legion of Honour *n.* a French order of distinction founded in 1802. [French *Légion d'honneur*]

leg-iron *n.* a shackle or fetter for the leg.

legislate /'lɛdʒɪsleɪt/ *v.intr.* **1** make laws. **2** (foll. by *for*) make provision by law. [back-formation from LEGISLATION]

legislation /lɛdʒɪs'leɪʃ(ə)n/ *n.* **1** the process of making laws. **2** laws collectively. [Late Latin *legis latio*, from *lex legis* 'law' + *latio* 'proposing' from *lat-*, past part. stem of *ferre* 'bring']

legislative /'lɛdʒɪslətɪv/ *adj.* of or empowered to make legislation. □ **legislatively** *adv.*

legislator /'lɛdʒɪsleɪtə/ *n.* **1** a member of a legislative body. **2** a lawgiver. [Latin (as LEGISLATION)]

legislature /'lɛdʒɪsleɪtʃə, -lətʃə/ *n.* the legislative body of a state.

legit /lɪ'dʒɪt/ *adj. & n. colloq.* ● *adj.* legitimate. ● *n.* **1** legitimate drama. **2** an actor in legitimate drama. [abbreviation]

legitimate *adj. & v.* ● *adj.* /lɪ'dʒɪtɪmət/ **1** **a** (of a child) born of parents lawfully married to each other. **b** (of a parent, birth, descent, etc.) with, of, through, etc., a legitimate child. **2** lawful, proper, regular, conforming to the standard type. **3** logically admissible. **4** **a** (of a sovereign's title) based on strict hereditary right. **b** (of a sovereign) having a legitimate title. **5** constituting or relating to serious drama as distinct from musical comedy, revue, etc. ● *v.tr.* /lɪ'dʒɪtɪmeɪt/ **1** make legitimate by decree, enactment, or proof. **2** justify, serve as a justification for. □ **legitimacy** /-məsi/ *n.* **legitimately** /-mətli/ *adv.* **legitimation** /-'meɪʃ(ə)n/ *n.*

[medieval Latin *legitimare* from Latin *legitimus* 'lawful', from *lex legis* 'law']

legitimatize /lɪ'dʒɪtɪmətʌɪz/ *v.tr.* (also **-ise**) legitimize. ▫ **legitimatization** /-'zeɪʃ(ə)n/ *n.*

legitimism /lɪ'dʒɪtɪmɪz(ə)m/ *n.* adherence to a sovereign or pretender whose claim is based on direct descent (esp. in French and Spanish history). ▫ **legitimist** *n.* & *adj.* [French *légitimisme* from *légitime* LEGITIMATE]

legitimize /lɪ'dʒɪtɪmʌɪz/ *v.tr.* (also **-ise**) **1** make legitimate. **2** serve as a justification for. ▫ **legitimization** /-'zeɪʃ(ə)n/ *n.*

legless /'lɛglɪs/ *adj.* **1** having no legs. **2** *Brit. slang* drunk, esp. too drunk to stand.

legman /'lɛgman/ *n.* (*pl.* **-men**) a person employed to go about gathering news or running errands etc.

Lego /'lɛgəʊ/ *n. propr.* a construction toy consisting of interlocking plastic building blocks. [Danish *leg godt* 'play well' from *lege* 'to play']

leg-of-mutton sail *n.* a triangular mainsail.

leg-of-mutton sleeve *n.* a sleeve which is full and loose on the upper arm but close-fitting on the forearm.

leg-pull *n. colloq.* a hoax. ▫ **leg-pulling** *n.*

leg-rest *n.* a support for a seated invalid's leg.

legroom /'lɛgru:m, -rʊm/ *n.* space for the legs of a seated person.

leg-show *n. colloq.* a theatrical performance by scantily-dressed women.

leg side see LEG *n.* 6.

leg slip *n. Cricket* a fielder stationed for a ball glancing off the bat to the leg side behind the wicket.

leg spin *n. Cricket* a type of spin which causes the ball to deviate from the leg side after bouncing.

leg-spinner *n. Cricket* **1** a ball bowled with a leg spin. **2** a leg spin bowler.

leg stump *n. Cricket* the stump on the leg side.

leg theory *n. Cricket* bowling to leg with fielders massed on that side.

leg trap *n. Cricket* a group of fielders near the wicket on the leg side.

legume /'lɛgju:m/ *n.* **1** the seed pod of a leguminous plant. **2** any seed, pod, or other edible part of a leguminous plant used as food. [French *légume* from Latin *legumen -minis*, from *legere* 'pick', because pickable by hand]

leguminous /lɪ'gju:mɪnəs/ *adj.* of or relating to the family Leguminosae of plants, including peas and beans, having seeds in pods and usu. root nodules containing symbiotic bacteria able to fix nitrogen. [modern Latin *leguminosus* (as LEGUME)]

leg-up *n.* **1** help to mount a horse etc. **2** help to overcome a difficulty; a boost.

leg warmer *n.* either of a pair of tubular knitted garments covering the leg from ankle to thigh.

legwork /'lɛgwə:k/ *n.* work which involves a lot of walking, travelling, or physical activity.

lehr /lɪə/ *n.* (also **leer**) a furnace used for the annealing of glass. [17th c.: origin unknown]

lei[1] /leɪ, 'leɪi/ *n.* a Polynesian garland of flowers. [Hawaiian]

lei[2] *pl.* of LEU.

Leibnizian /lʌɪb'nɪtsɪən/ *adj.* & *n.* ● *adj.* of or relating to the philosophy of G. W. Leibniz, German philosopher (d. 1716), esp. regarding matter as a multitude of monads and assuming a pre-established harmony between spirit and matter. ● *n.* a follower of this philosophy.

Leicester /'lɛstə/ *n.* (in full **Red Leicester**) a kind of mild firm cheese, usu. orange-coloured and originally made in Leicestershire.

Leics. *abbr.* Leicestershire.

leishmaniasis /li:ʃmə'nʌɪəsɪs/ *n.* any of several diseases caused by parasitic protozoans of the genus *Leishmania* transmitted by the bite of sandflies. [named after W. B. *Leishman*, British physician d. 1926]

leister /'li:stə/ *n.* & *v.* ● *n.* a pronged salmon-spear. ● *v.tr.* pierce with a leister. [Old Norse *ljóstr* from *ljósta* 'to strike']

leisure /'lɛʒə/ *n.* **1** free time; time at one's own disposal. **2** enjoyment of free time. **3** (usu. foll. by *for*, or *to* + infin.) opportunity afforded by free time. ▫ **at leisure 1** not occupied. **2** in an unhurried manner. **at one's leisure** when one has time. ▫ **leisureless** *adj.* [Middle English from Anglo-French *leisour*, Old French *leisir*, ultimately from Latin *licēre* 'be allowed']

leisure centre *n.* a large public building with sports facilities, bars, etc.

leisured /'lɛʒəd/ *adj.* having ample leisure.

leisurely /'lɛʒəli/ *adj.* & *adv.* ● *adj.* having leisure; acting or done at leisure; unhurried, relaxed. ● *adv.* without hurry. ▫ **leisureliness** *n.*

leisurewear /'lɛʒəwɛ:/ *n.* informal clothes, especially tracksuits and other sportswear.

leitmotif /'lʌɪtməʊti:f/ *n.* (also **leitmotiv**) a recurrent theme associated throughout a musical, literary, etc. composition with a particular person, idea, or situation. [German *Leitmotiv* (as LEAD[1], MOTIVE)]

lek[1] /lɛk/ *n.* the chief monetary unit of Albania. [Albanian]

lek[2] /lɛk/ *n.* a patch of ground used by groups of certain birds (esp. black grouse) during the breeding season as a setting for the males' display and their meeting with the females. [perhaps from Swedish *leka* 'to play']

LEM *abbr.* lunar excursion module.

leman /'lɛmən, 'li:-/ *n.* (*pl.* **lemans**) *archaic* **1** a lover or sweetheart. **2** an illicit lover, esp. a mistress. [Middle English *leofman* (as LIEF, MAN)]

lemma /'lɛmə/ *n.* **1** an assumed or demonstrated proposition used in an argument or proof. **2 a** a heading indicating the subject or argument of a literary composition, a dictionary entry, etc. **b** (*pl.* **lemmata** /-mətə/) a heading indicating the subject or argument of an annotation. **3** a motto appended to a picture etc. [Latin from Greek *lēmma -matos* 'thing assumed', from the root of *lambanō* 'take']

lemme /'lɛmi/ *colloq.* let me. [corruption]

lemming /'lɛmɪŋ/ *n.* **1** any small vole-like Arctic rodent of the genus *Lemmus* and related genera, including *L. lemmus* of Norway which is noted for mass migrations during which it attempts to cross large bodies of water. **2** a person who unthinkingly joins a mass movement, esp. a headlong rush to destruction. [Norwegian]

lemon /'lɛmən/ *n.* & *adj.* ● *n.* **1 a** a pale yellow thick-skinned oval citrus fruit with acidic juice. **b** (in full **lemon tree**) a tree of the species *Citrus limon* which produces this fruit. **2** a pale yellow colour. **3** *colloq.* a person or thing regarded as feeble or unsatisfactory or disappointing. ● *adj.* of or resembling the colour, flavour, or fragrance of a lemon; pale yellow. ▫ **lemony** *adj.* [Middle English via Old French *limon* from Arabic *līma*: cf. LIME[2]]

lemonade /lɛmə'neɪd/ *n.* **1** an effervescent or still drink made from lemon juice. **2** a synthetic substitute for this.

lemon balm *n.* a bushy plant, *Melissa officinalis*, with leaves smelling and tasting of lemon.

lemon curd *n.* (also *Brit.* **lemon cheese**) a conserve made from lemons, butter, eggs, and sugar, with the consistency of cream cheese.

lemon drop *n.* a boiled sweet flavoured with lemon.

lemon geranium *n.* a lemon-scented pelargonium, *Pelargonium crispum*.

lemon grass *n.* any fragrant tropical grass of the genus *Cymbopogon*, yielding an oil smelling of lemon.

lemon plant *n.* = LEMON VERBENA.

lemon sole *n.* a flatfish, *Microstomus kitt*, of the plaice family. [French *limande*]

lemon squash *n. Brit.* a soft drink made from lemons, sugar, and other ingredients, often sold in concentrated form.

lemon-squeezer *n.* a device for extracting the juice from a lemon.

lemon thyme *n.* a herb, *Thymus citriodorus*, with lemon-scented leaves.

lemon verbena *n.* a shrub, *Aloysia triphylla*, with lemon-scented leaves.

lemon yellow *n.* & *adj.* ● *n.* a pale yellow colour. ● *adj.* (hyphenated when *attrib.*) of this colour.

lempira /lɛmˈpɪərə/ *n.* the chief monetary unit of Honduras, equal to 100 centavos. [named after *Lempira*, 16th-c. chieftain who opposed the Spanish conquest of Honduras]

lemur /ˈliːmə/ *n.* any arboreal primate of the family Lemuridae native to Madagascar, with a pointed snout and long tail. [modern Latin from Latin *lemures* (pl.) 'spirits of the dead', from its spectre-like face]

lend /lɛnd/ *v.tr.* (*past* and *past part.* **lent** /lɛnt/) **1** (usu. foll. by *to*) grant (to a person) the use of (a thing) on the understanding that it or its equivalent shall be returned. **2** allow the use of (money) at interest. **3** bestow or contribute (something temporary) (*lend assistance*; *lends a certain charm*). □ **lend an ear** (or **one's ears**) listen. **lend a hand** = *give a hand* (see HAND). **lend itself to** (of a thing) be suitable for. **lend oneself to** accommodate oneself to (a policy or purpose). □ **lendable** *adj.* **lender** *n.* **lending** *n.* [Middle English, earlier *lēne(n)*, from Old English *lǣnan* from *lǣn* LOAN¹]

lending library *n.* a library from which books may be temporarily taken away with or without direct payment.

Lend-Lease *n. hist.* an arrangement made in 1941 whereby the US supplied equipment etc. to the UK and its allies, originally as a loan in return for the use of British-owned military bases.

length /lɛŋθ, lɛŋkθ/ *n.* **1** measurement or extent from end to end; the greater of two or the greatest of three dimensions of a body. **2** extent in, of, or with regard to, time (*a stay of some length*; *the length of a speech*). **3** the distance a thing extends (*at arm's length*; *ships a cable's length apart*). **4** the length of a swimming pool as a measure of the distance swum. **5** the length of a horse, boat, etc., as a measure of the lead in a race. **6** a long stretch or extent (*a length of hair*). **7** a degree of thoroughness in action (*went to great lengths*; *prepared to go to any length*). **8** a piece of material of a certain length (*a length of cloth*). **9** *Prosody* the quantity of a vowel or syllable. **10** *Cricket* **a** the distance from the batsman at which the ball pitches (*the bowler keeps a good length*). **b** the proper amount of this. **11** the extent of a garment in a vertical direction when worn. **12** the full extent of one's body. □ **at length 1** (also **at full** or **great** etc. **length**) in detail, without curtailment. **2** after a long time, at last. [Old English *lengthu* from Germanic (as LONG¹)]

lengthen /ˈlɛŋθ(ə)n, -ŋkθ-/ *v.* **1** *tr.* & *intr.* make or become longer. **2** *tr.* make (a vowel) long. □ **lengthener** *n.*

lengthman /ˈlɛŋθmən, ˈlɛŋkθ-/ *n.* (*pl.* **-men**) *Brit.* a person employed to maintain a section of railway or road.

lengthways /ˈlɛŋθweɪz, -ŋkθ-/ *adv.* in a direction parallel with a thing's length.

lengthwise /ˈlɛŋθwʌɪz, -ŋkθ-/ *adv.* & *adj.* ● *adv.* lengthways. ● *adj.* lying or moving lengthways.

lengthy /ˈlɛŋθi, ˈlɛŋkθi/ *adj.* (**lengthier**, **lengthiest**) **1** of unusual length. **2** (of speech, writing, style, a speaker, etc.) tedious, excessively detailed. □ **lengthily** *adv.* **lengthiness** *n.*

lenient /ˈliːnɪənt/ *adj.* **1** merciful, tolerant, not disposed to severity. **2** (of punishment etc.) mild. **3** *archaic* emollient. □ **lenience** *n.* **leniency** *n.* **leniently** *adv.* [Latin *lenire lenit-* 'soothe' from *lenis* 'gentle']

Leninism /ˈlɛnɪnɪz(ə)m/ *n.* Marxism as interpreted and applied by Lenin. □ **Leninist** *n.* & *adj.* **Leninite** *n.* & *adj.* [named after V. I. *Lenin* (name assumed by V. I. Ulyanov), Russian statesman d. 1924]

lenition /lɪˈnɪʃ(ə)n/ *n.* (in Celtic languages) the process or result of articulating a consonant softly. [Latin *lenis* 'soft', suggested by German *Lenierung*]

lenitive /ˈlɛnɪtɪv/ *adj.* & *n.* ● *adj. Med.* soothing. ● *n.* **1** *Med.* a soothing drug or appliance. **2** a palliative. [Middle English from medieval Latin *lenitivus* (as LENIENT)]

lenity /ˈlɛnɪti/ *n.* (*pl.* **-ies**) *literary* **1** mercifulness, gentleness. **2** an act of mercy. [French *lénité* or Latin *lenitas* from *lenis* 'gentle']

leno /ˈliːnəʊ/ *n.* (*pl.* **-os**) an openwork fabric with the warp threads twisted in pairs before weaving. [French *linon* from *lin* 'flax', from Latin *linum*]

lens /lɛnz/ *n.* **1** a piece of a transparent substance with one or (usu.) both sides curved for concentrating or dispersing light rays esp. in optical instruments. **2** a combination of lenses used in photography. **3** *Anat.* = CRYSTALLINE LENS. **4** *Physics* an object or device which focuses or otherwise modifies the direction of movement of light, sound, electrons, etc. **5** = CONTACT LENS. □ **lensed** *adj.* **lensless** *adj.* [Latin *lens lentis* 'lentil' (from the similarity of shape)]

lensman /ˈlɛnzman/ *n.* (*pl.* **-men**) = CAMERAMAN.

Lent /lɛnt/ *n.* **1** *Eccl.* the period from Ash Wednesday to Holy Saturday, of which the 40 weekdays are devoted to fasting and penitence in commemoration of Christ's fasting in the wilderness. **2** (in *pl.*) the boat races held at Cambridge in the Lent term. [Middle English, from LENTEN]

lent *past* and *past part.* of LEND.

-lent /lənt/ *suffix* forming adjectives (*pestilent*; *violent*) (cf. -ULENT). [Latin *-lentus* '-ful']

Lenten /ˈlɛnt(ə)n/ *adj.* of, in, or appropriate to, Lent. [originally as noun, = spring, from Old English *lencten* from Germanic, related to LONG¹, perhaps with reference to lengthening of the day in spring: now regarded as adj. from LENT + -EN²]

Lenten fare *n.* food without meat.

lenticel /ˈlɛntɪsɛl/ *n. Bot.* any of the raised pores in the stems of woody plants that allow gas exchange between the atmosphere and the internal tissues. [modern Latin *lenticella*, diminutive of Latin *lens*: see LENS]

lenticular /lɛnˈtɪkjʊlə/ *adj.* **1** shaped like a lentil or a biconvex lens. **2** of the lens of the eye. [Latin *lenticularis* (as LENTIL)]

lentigo /lɛnˈtʌɪgəʊ/ *n.* (*pl.* **lentigines** /-ˈtɪdʒɪniːz/) **1** a condition marked by small brown patches on the skin, esp. in elderly people. **2** such a patch. [Latin, from *lens lentis* 'lentil']

lentil /ˈlɛnt(ə)l/ *n.* **1** a leguminous plant, *Lens culinaris*, yielding edible biconvex seeds. **2** this seed, esp. used as food with the husk removed. [Middle English via Old French *lentille* from Latin *lenticula* (as LENS)]

Lent lily *n. Brit.* a daffodil, esp. a wild one.

lento /ˈlɛntəʊ/ *adj.* & *adv. Mus.* ● *adj.* slow. ● *adv.* slowly. [Italian]

lentoid /ˈlɛntɔɪd/ *adj.* = LENTICULAR 1. [Latin *lens* (see LENS) + -OID]

Lent term *n. Brit.* the term at a university etc. in which Lent falls.

Leo /ˈliːəʊ/ *n.* (*pl.* **-os**) **1** *Astron.* a large constellation (the Lion), said to represent the lion slain by Hercules. **2** *Astrol.* **a** the fifth sign of the zodiac, which the sun enters about 21 July. **b** a person born when the sun is in this sign. [Old English from Latin, = LION]

Leonid /ˈliːənɪd/ *n.* any of the meteors that seem to radiate from the direction of the constellation Leo. [Latin *leo* (see LEO) *leonis* + -ID³]

Leonine /ˈliːənʌɪn/ *adj.* & *n.* ● *adj.* of or relating to a pope or emperor named Leo. ● *n.* (in *pl.*) leonine verse. [the name *Leo* (as LEONINE)]

leonine /ˈliːənʌɪn/ *adj.* **1** like a lion. **2** of or relating to lions. **3 a** (of medieval Latin verse) in hexameter or elegiac metre with internal rhyme. **b** (of English verse) with internal rhyme. [Middle English from Old French *leonin -ine* or Latin *leoninus* from *leo leonis* 'lion']

leopard /ˈlɛpəd/ *n.* (*fem.* **leopardess** /-dɪs/) **1** a large African or Asian feline mammal, *Panthera pardus*, with either a black-spotted yellowish-fawn or all-black coat; also called PANTHER. **2** *Heraldry* a lion passant guardant as in the arms of England. **3** (*attrib.*) spotted like a leopard (*leopard moth*). [Middle English via Old French and Late Latin from late Greek *leopardos* (as LION, PARD)]

leopard's bane *n.* any plant of the genus *Doronicum* (daisy family), with large yellow daisy-like flowers.

leotard /ˈliːətɑːd/ *n.* a close-fitting one-piece garment, usu. covering the torso and usu. the arms, worn by ballet dancers, acrobats, etc. [named after J. *Léotard*, French trapeze artist d. 1870]

leper /ˈlɛpə/ *n.* **1** a person suffering from leprosy. **2** a person who is shunned for moral or social reasons. [Middle English, probably attributive use of *leper* 'leprosy', from Old French *lepre* via Latin *lepra* from Greek, fem. of *lepros* 'scaly', from *lepos* 'scale']

lepidopterous /lɛpɪˈdɒpt(ə)rəs/ *adj.* of the insect order Lepidoptera, comprising butterflies and moths, with four scale-covered wings often brightly coloured. ▫ **lepidopteran** *adj. & n.* **lepidopterist** *n.* [Greek *lepis -idos* 'scale' + *pteron* 'wing']

leporine /ˈlɛpərʌɪn/ *adj.* of or like hares. [Latin *leporinus* from *lepus -oris* 'hare']

leprechaun /ˈlɛprəkɔːn/ *n.* a small mischievous sprite in Irish folklore. [Old Irish *luchorpán*, from *lu* 'small' + *corp* 'body']

leprosarium /lɛprəˈsɛːrɪəm/ *n.* a hospital for people with leprosy.

leprosy /ˈlɛprəsi/ *n.* **1** a contagious bacterial disease that affects the skin, mucous membranes, and nerves, causing disfigurement. Also called *Hansen's disease.* **2** moral corruption or contagion. [LEPROUS + -Y[3]]

leprous /ˈlɛprəs/ *adj.* **1** suffering from leprosy. **2** like or relating to leprosy. [Middle English via Old French and Late Latin *leprosus* from Latin *lepra*: see LEPER]

lepta *pl.* of LEPTON[1].

lepto- /ˈlɛptəʊ/ *comb. form* small, narrow. [Greek *leptos* 'fine, small, thin, delicate']

leptocephalic /ˌlɛptə(ʊ)sɪˈfalɪk/ *adj.* (also **leptocephalous** /-ˈsɛf(ə)ləs/) narrow-skulled.

leptodactyl /lɛptə(ʊ)ˈdaktɪl/ *adj. & n.* ● *adj.* having long slender toes. ● *n.* a bird having these.

lepton[1] /ˈlɛptɒn/ *n.* (*pl.* **lepta** /-tə/) a Greek coin and monetary unit worth one-hundredth of a drachma. [Greek *lepton* (*nomisma* 'coin'), neut. of *leptos* 'small']

lepton[2] /ˈlɛptɒn/ *n.* (*pl.* **leptons**) *Physics* any of a class of subatomic particles which do not undergo strong interaction, e.g. an electron, muon, or neutrino. [LEPTO- + -ON]

leptospirosis /ˌlɛptə(ʊ)spʌɪˈrəʊsɪs/ *n.* an infectious disease caused by spirochaete bacteria of the genus *Leptospira*, that occurs in rodents, dogs, and other mammals, and can be transmitted to humans. [LEPTO- + SPIRO-[1] + -OSIS]

leptotene /ˈlɛptə(ʊ)tiːn/ *n. Biol.* the first stage of the prophase of meiosis in which each chromosome is apparent as two fine chromatids. [LEPTO- + Greek *tainia* 'band']

lesbian /ˈlɛzbɪən/ *n. & adj.* ● *n.* a homosexual woman. ● *adj.* **1** of homosexuality in women. **2** (**Lesbian**) of Lesbos. ▫ **lesbianism** *n.* [Latin *Lesbius* from Greek *Lesbios* from *Lesbos*, an island in the Aegean Sea, home of the poetess Sappho (see SAPPHIC), from her alleged homosexuality]

■ **Usage** See Usage Note at GAY.

lese-majesty /liːzˈmadʒɪsti/ *n.* (also **lèse-majesté** /leɪz ˈmaʒɛsteɪ/) **1** treason. **2** an insult to a sovereign or ruler. **3** presumptuous conduct. [French *lèse-majesté* from Latin *laesa majestas* 'injured sovereignty', from *laedere laes-* 'injure' + *majestas* MAJESTY]

lesion /ˈliːʒ(ə)n/ *n.* **1** damage. **2** injury. **3** *Med.* a morbid change in the functioning or texture of an organ etc. [Middle English via Old French from Latin *laesio -onis*, from *laedere laes-* 'injure']

less /lɛs/ *det., adj., adv., pron., & prep.* ● *det.* **1** smaller in extent, quantity, degree, or duration (opp. MORE) (*of less importance*; *find less difficulty*; *he eats less red meat than before*). **2** *disp.* fewer in number (*eat less biscuits*). ● *adj. archaic* of lower rank etc. (*no less a person than*; *James the Less*). ● *adv.* to a smaller extent, in a lower degree (*uses it less than she used to*; *goes less frequently than she did*; *a less popular book*; *regards him less as a colleague than as a friend*). ● *pron.* **1** a smaller amount or quantity (*cannot take less*; *for less than £10*; *is little less than disgraceful*). **2** *disp.* fewer (*I don't have many friends, but he has even less*). ● *prep.* minus (*made £1,000 less tax*). ▫ **in less than no time** *joc.* very quickly or soon. **less and less** to an extent that is becoming continuously smaller. **much** (or **still**) **less** with even greater force of denial (*do not suspect him of negligence, much less of dishonesty*). [Old English *lǣssa* (*adj.*), *lǣs* (*adv.*), from Germanic]

■ **Usage** The use of *less* as a determiner with countable nouns, as in sense 2, or as a pronoun in sense 2, is regarded as incorrect in formal English, although it is frequent in informal usage. Strictly, *less* should be used only with uncountable nouns as the comparative of *little*, e.g. *I have little time; she has even less*, but *I have few books; she has even fewer*.

-less /lɪs/ *suffix* forming adjectives and adverbs: **1** from nouns, meaning 'not having, without, free from' (*doubtless*; *powerless*). **2** from verbs, meaning 'not affected by or doing the action of the verb' (*fathomless*; *tireless*). ▫ **-lessly** *suffix* forming adverbs. **-lessness** *suffix* forming nouns. [Old English *-lēas* from *lēas* 'devoid of']

lessee /lɛˈsiː/ *n.* (often foll. by *of*) a person who holds a property by lease. ▫ **lesseeship** *n.* [Middle English from Anglo-French, Old French *lessé*, past part. of *lesser* (as LEASE)]

lessen /ˈlɛs(ə)n/ *v.tr. & intr.* make or become less, diminish.

lesser /ˈlɛsə/ *adj.* (usu. *attrib.*) not so great as the other or the rest (*the lesser evil*; *the lesser celandine*). [double comparative, from LESS + -ER[3]]

Lesser Bairam *n.* an annual Muslim festival at the end of Ramadan.

lesser-known *adj.* known less well than others of the same kind.

lesson /ˈlɛs(ə)n/ *n. & v.* ● *n.* **1 a** an amount of teaching given at one time. **b** the time assigned to this. **2** (in *pl.*; foll. by *in*) systematic instruction (*gives lessons in dancing*; *took lessons in French*). **3** a thing learnt or to be learnt by a pupil; an assignment. **4 a** an occurrence, example, rebuke, or punishment, that serves or should serve to warn or encourage (*let that be a lesson to you*). **b** a thing inculcated by experience or study. **5** a passage from the Bible read aloud during a church service, esp. either of two readings at morning and evening prayer in the Anglican Church. ● *v.tr. archaic* **1** instruct. **2** admonish, rebuke. ▫ **learn one's lesson** profit from or bear in mind a particular (usu. unpleasant) experience. **teach a person a lesson** punish a person, esp. as a deterrent. [Middle English via Old French *leçon* from Latin *lectio -onis*: see LECTION]

lessor /lɛˈsɔː, ˈlɛsɔː/ *n.* a person who lets a property by lease. [Anglo-French from *lesser*: see LEASE]

lest /lɛst/ *conj.* **1** in order that not, for fear that (*lest he forget*). **2** that (*afraid lest we should be late*). [Old English *thȳ lǣs the* 'whereby less that', later *the lǣste*, Middle English *lest(e)*]

■ **Usage** *Lest* is followed by the subjunctive or *should* (see examples above).

let[1] /lɛt/ *v., v.aux., & n.* ● *v.* (**letting**; *past* and *past part.* **let**) **1** *tr.* **a** allow to, not prevent or forbid (*we let them go*). **b** cause to (*let me know*; *let it be known*). **2** *tr.* (foll. by *into*) **a** allow to enter. **b** make acquainted with (a secret etc.). **c** inlay in. **3** *tr.* grant the use of (rooms, land, etc.) for rent or hire (*was let to the new tenant for a year*). **4** *tr.* allow or cause (liquid or air) to escape (*let blood*). **5** *tr.* award (a contract for work). ● *v.aux.* supplying the first and third persons of the imperative in exhortations (*let us pray*), commands (*let it be done at once*; *let there be light*), assumptions (*let AB be equal to CD*), and permission or challenge (*let him do his worst*). ● *n. Brit.* the act or an instance of letting a house, room, etc. (*a long let*). □ **let alone 1** not to mention, far less or more (*hasn't got a television, let alone a video*). **2** = *let be*. **let be** not interfere with, attend to, or do. **let down 1** lower. **2** fail to support or satisfy, disappoint. **3** lengthen (a garment). **4** deflate (a tyre). **let down gently** avoid humiliating abruptly. **let drop** (or **fall**) **1** drop (esp. a word or hint) intentionally or by accident. **2** (foll. by *on, upon, to*) *Geom.* draw (a perpendicular) from an outside point to a line. **let fly 1** (often foll. by *at*) attack physically or verbally. **2** discharge (a missile). **let go 1** release, set at liberty. **2 a** (often foll. by *of*) lose or relinquish one's hold. **b** lose hold of. **3** cease to think or talk about. **let oneself go 1** give way to enthusiasm, impulse, etc. **2** cease to take trouble, neglect one's appearance or habits. **let in 1** allow to enter (*let the dog in*; *let in a flood of light*; *this would let in all sorts of evils*). **2** (usu. foll. by *for*) involve (a person, often oneself) in loss or difficulty. **3** (foll. by *on*) allow (a person) to share privileges, information, etc. **4** inlay (a thing) in another. **let oneself in** enter a building by means of a latchkey. **let loose 1** release from captivity or restraint. **2** (also foll. by *with*) emit abruptly (a scream, tirade, etc.). **let me see** see SEE[1]. **let off 1 a** fire (a gun). **b** explode (a bomb or firework). **2** allow or cause (steam, liquid, etc.) to escape. **3** allow to alight from a vehicle etc. **4 a** not punish or compel. **b** (foll. by *with*) punish lightly. **5** *Brit.* let (part of a house etc.). **let off steam** see STEAM. **let on** *colloq.* **1** reveal a secret. **2** pretend (*let on that he had succeeded*). **let out 1** allow to go out, esp. through a doorway. **2** release from restraint. **3** (often foll. by *that* + clause) reveal (a secret etc.). **4** make (a garment) looser esp. by adjustment at a seam. **5** put out to rent esp. to several tenants, or to contract. **6** exculpate. **let rip** see RIP[1]. **let slip** see SLIP[1]. **let through** allow to pass. **let up** *colloq.* **1** become less intense or severe. **2** relax one's efforts. **to let** available for rent. [Old English *lǣtan* from Germanic: related to LATE]

let[2] /lɛt/ *n. & v.* ● *n.* **1** (in tennis, squash, etc.) an obstruction of a ball or a player in certain ways, requiring the ball to be served again. **2** *archaic* (except in **without let or hindrance**) obstruction, hindrance. ● *v.tr.* (**letting**; *past* and *past part.* **letted** or **let**) *archaic* hinder, obstruct. [Old English *lettan* from Germanic: related to LATE]

-let /lɪt, lət/ *suffix* forming nouns, usu. diminutives (*flatlet*; *leaflet*) or denoting articles of ornament or dress (*anklet*). [originally corresponding (in *bracelet, crosslet*, etc.) to French *-ette* added to nouns ending in *-el*]

let-down *n.* **1** a disappointment. **2** the release of milk from a mammary gland, esp. a cow's udder.

lethal /'li:θ(ə)l/ *adj.* causing or sufficient to cause death. □ **lethality** /lɪ'θalɪti/ *n.* **lethally** *adv.* [Latin *let(h)alis* from *letum* 'death']

lethal chamber *n.* a chamber in which animals may be killed painlessly with gas.

lethal dose *n.* the amount of a toxic compound or drug that causes death in humans, animals, micro-organisms, or cultured cells.

lethargy /'lɛθədʒi/ *n.* **1** lack of energy or vitality; a torpid, inert, or apathetic state. **2** *Med.* morbid drowsiness or prolonged and unnatural sleep. □ **lethargic** /lɪ'θɑ:dʒɪk/ *adj.* **lethargically** /lɪ'θɑ:dʒɪk(ə)li/ *adv.* [Middle English via Old French *litargie* and Late Latin *lethargia* from Greek *lēthargia*, via *lēthargos* 'forgetful' from *lēth-*, *lanthanomai* 'forget']

Lethe /'li:θi, -i:/ *n.* **1** (in Greek mythology) a river in Hades producing forgetfulness of the past. **2** such forgetfulness. □ **Lethean** /li:'θi:ən/ *adj.* [Latin, use of Greek *lēthē* 'forgetfulness' (as LETHARGY)]

let-off *n.* being allowed to escape something.

let-out *n. Brit. colloq.* an opportunity to escape from an awkward situation etc.

let's /lɛts/ *contr.* let us (*let's go now*).

Lett /lɛt/ *n. archaic* = LATVIAN *n.* [German *Lette* from Latvian *Latvi*]

letter /'lɛtə/ *n. & v.* ● *n.* **1 a** a character representing one or more of the simple or compound sounds used in speech; any of the alphabetic symbols. **b** (in *pl.*) *Brit. colloq.* the initials of a degree etc. after the holder's name. **c** *US* a school or college initial as a mark of proficiency in games etc. **2 a** a written, typed, or printed communication, usu. sent by post or messenger. **b** (in *pl.*) an addressed legal or formal document for any of various purposes. **3** the precise terms of a statement, the strict verbal interpretation (opp. SPIRIT *n.* 7) (*according to the letter of the law*). **4** (in *pl.*) **a** literature. **b** acquaintance with books, erudition. **c** authorship (*the profession of letters*). **5** *Printing* **a** types collectively. **b** a font of type. ● *v.tr.* **1 a** inscribe letters on. **b** impress a title etc. on (a book cover). **2** classify with letters. □ **to the letter** with adherence to every detail. □ **letterless** *adj.* [Middle English via Old French *lettre* from Latin *litera, littera* 'letter of alphabet', (in pl.) 'epistle, literature']

letter bomb *n.* a terrorist explosive device in the form of a postal packet.

letter box *n.* esp. *Brit.* a box or slot into which letters are posted or delivered.

letter-card *n. Brit.* a folded card with a gummed edge for posting as a letter.

letter-carrier *n. N. Amer.* a postman or postwoman.

lettered /'lɛtəd/ *adj.* well read or educated.

letterhead /'lɛtəhɛd/ *n.* **1** a printed heading on stationery. **2** stationery with this.

letter-heading *n.* = LETTERHEAD 1.

lettering /'lɛt(ə)rɪŋ/ *n.* **1** the process of inscribing letters. **2** letters inscribed.

letter missive *n.* (also **letters missive**) a letter from a sovereign to a dean and chapter nominating a person to be elected bishop.

letter of comfort *n.* an assurance about a debt, short of a legal guarantee, given to a bank by a third party.

letter of credence *n.* a letter of introduction, esp. of an ambassador.

letter of credit *n.* a letter from a banker authorizing a person to draw money up to a specified amount, usu. from another bank.

letter of marque see MARQUE[2].

letter-perfect *adj. Theatr.* knowing one's part perfectly.

letterpress /'lɛtəprɛs/ *n.* **1** *Brit.* **a** the contents of an illustrated book other than the illustrations. **b** printed matter relating to illustrations. **2** printing from raised type, not from lithography or other planographic processes.

letter-quality *adj.* of the quality of printing suitable for a business letter; producing print of this quality.

letters missive var. of LETTER MISSIVE.

letters of administration *n.pl.* authority to administer the estate of an intestate.

letters patent *n.pl.* an open document from a sovereign or government conferring a patent or other right.

letter-writer *n.* **1** a person who writes letters. **2** a book giving guidance on writing letters.

Lettic /'lɛtɪk/ *adj. & n. archaic* ● *adj.* **1** = LATVIAN *adj.* **2** of or relating to the Baltic branch of languages. ● *n.* = LATVIAN *n.* 2.

letting /ˈlɛtɪŋ/ *n.* a property that is let or available for letting.

Lettish /ˈlɛtɪʃ/ *adj.* & *n.* *archaic* = LATVIAN.

lettuce /ˈlɛtɪs/ *n.* **1** a plant of the daisy family, *Lactuca sativa*, with crisp edible leaves used esp. in salads. **2** any of various plants resembling this. [Middle English from Old French *letuës*, *laituës*, pl. of *laituë*, from Latin *lactuca* from *lac lactis* 'milk', with reference to its milky juice]

let-up *n. colloq.* **1** a reduction in intensity. **2** a relaxation of effort.

leu /ˈleɪuː/ *n.* (*pl.* **lei** /leɪ/) the chief monetary unit of Romania. [Romanian, = lion]

leucine /ˈluːsiːn/ *n. Biochem.* a hydrophobic amino acid present in protein and essential in the diet of vertebrates. [French, from Greek *leukos* 'white' + -IN]

leuco- /ˈluːkəʊ/ *comb. form* white. [Greek *leukos* 'white']

leucocyte /ˈluːkə(ʊ)sʌɪt/ *n.* (also **leukocyte**) a colourless amoeboid cell of blood, lymph, etc., containing a nucleus and important in fighting disease. Also called *white (blood) cell, white corpuscle.* □ **leucocytic** /-ˈsɪtɪk/ *adj.*

leucoma /luːˈkəʊmə/ *n.* a white opacity in the cornea of the eye.

leucorrhoea /luːkəˈriːə/ *n.* (*US* **leucorrhea**) a whitish or yellowish discharge of mucus from the vagina.

leucotomy /luːˈkɒtəmi/ *n.* (*pl.* **-ies**) the surgical cutting of white nerve fibres within the brain, esp. prefrontal lobotomy, formerly used in psychosurgery.

leukaemia /luːˈkiːmɪə/ *n.* (*US* **leukemia**) *Med.* any of a group of malignant diseases in which the bone marrow and other blood-forming organs produce increased numbers of leucocytes. □ **leukaemic** *adj.* [modern Latin from German *Leukämie*, from Greek *leukos* 'white' + *haima* 'blood']

leukocyte var. of LEUCOCYTE.

Lev. *abbr.* Leviticus (Old Testament).

lev /lɛv/ *n.* (also **leva**) (*pl.* **leva**, **levas**, or **levs**) the chief monetary unit of Bulgaria. [Bulgarian, = lion]

Levant /lɪˈvant/ *n.* (prec. by *the*) *archaic* the eastern part of the Mediterranean with its islands and neighbouring countries. [French, pres. part. of *lever* 'rise', used as a noun = point of sunrise, east]

levant /lɪˈvant/ *v.intr. Brit. slang* abscond or bolt, esp. with betting or gaming losses unpaid. [perhaps from LEVANT: cf. French *faire voile en Levant* 'be stolen or spirited away']

levanter[1] /lɪˈvantə/ *n.* **1** a strong easterly Mediterranean wind. **2** (**Levanter**) a native or inhabitant of the Levant.

levanter[2] /lɪˈvantə/ *n. slang* a person who levants.

Levantine /lɪˈvantʌɪn, ˈlɛv(ə)n-, -tɪn/ *adj.* & *n.* ● *adj.* of or trading to the Levant. ● *n.* a native or inhabitant of the Levant.

Levant morocco *n.* high-grade large-grained morocco leather.

Levant storax see STORAX 2.

levator /lɪˈveɪtə/ *n.* a muscle that lifts the structure into which it is inserted. [Latin, = a person who lifts, from *levare* 'raise']

levee[1] /ˈlɛvi, ˈlɛveɪ/ *n.* **1** *archaic* or *N. Amer.* an assembly of visitors or guests, esp. at a formal reception. **2** *hist.* (in the UK) an assembly held by the sovereign or sovereign's representative at which men only were received. **3** *hist.* a reception of visitors on rising from bed. [French *levé*, variant of *lever* 'rising' from *lever* 'to rise': see LEVY]

levee[2] /ˈlɛvi, lɪˈviː/ *n. US* **1** an embankment against river floods. **2** a natural embankment built up by a river. **3** a landing place, a quay. [French *levée*, fem. past part. of *lever* 'raise': see LEVY]

level /ˈlɛv(ə)l/ *n.*, *adj.*, & *v.* ● *n.* **1** a horizontal line or plane. **2** a height or value reached, a position on a real or imaginary scale (*eye level*; *sugar level in the blood*; *danger level*). **3** a social, moral, or intellectual standard. **4** a plane of rank or authority (*discussions at Cabinet level*). **5 a** an instrument giving a line parallel to the plane of the horizon for testing whether things are horizontal. **b** *Surveying* an instrument for giving a horizontal line of sight. **6** a more or less level surface. **7** a flat tract of land. ● *adj.* **1** having a flat and even surface; not bumpy. **2** horizontal; perpendicular to the plumb line. **3** (often foll. by *with*) **a** on the same horizontal plane as something else. **b** having equality with something else. **c** (of a spoonful etc.) with the contents flat with the brim. **4** even, uniform, equable, or well-balanced in quality, style, temper, judgement, etc. **5** esp. *Brit.* (of a race) having the leading competitors close together. ● *v.* (**levelled**, **levelling**; *US* **leveled**, **leveling**) **1** *tr.* make level, even, or uniform. **2** *tr.* (often foll. by *to* (or *with*) the ground) raze or demolish. **3** *tr.* (also *absol.*) aim (a missile or gun). **4** *tr.* (also *absol.*; foll. by *at*, *against*) direct (an accusation, criticism, or satire). **5** *tr.* abolish (distinctions). **6** *intr.* (usu. foll. by *with*) *slang* be frank or honest. **7** *tr.* place on the same level. **8** *tr.* (also *absol.*) *Surveying* ascertain differences in the height of (land). □ **do one's level best** *colloq.* do one's utmost; make all possible efforts. **find its level** (or **find its own level**) **1** (of a liquid) reach the same height in containers etc. which communicate with each other. **2** reach a stable level, value, position, etc. with respect to something else (*the pound found its level against the dollar*). **find one's level** (or **find one's own level**) reach the right social, intellectual, etc. place in relation to others. **level down** *Brit.* bring down to a standard. **level off** make or become level or smooth. **level out** make or become level, remove differences from. **level up** *Brit.* bring up to a standard. **on the level** *colloq.* *adv.* honestly, without deception. ● *adj.* honest, truthful. **on a level with 1** in the same horizontal plane as. **2** equal with. □ **levelly** *adv.* **levelness** *n.* [Middle English from Old French *livel*, ultimately from Latin *libella*, diminutive of *libra* 'scales, balance']

level crossing *n. Brit.* a crossing of a railway and a road, or two railways, at the same level.

level-headed *adj.* mentally well-balanced, cool, sensible. □ **level-headedly** *adv.* **level-headedness** *n.*

leveller /ˈlɛv(ə)lə/ *n.* (*US* **leveler**) **1** a person who advocates the abolition of social distinctions. **2** (**Leveller**) *hist.* an extreme radical dissenter in 17th-c. England. **3** a person or thing that levels.

levelling-screw *n.* a screw for adjusting parts of a machine etc. to an exact level.

level pegging *n. Brit.* equality of scores or achievements.

lever /ˈliːvə/ *n.* & *v.* ● *n.* **1** a bar resting on a pivot, used to help lift a heavy or firmly fixed object. **2** *Mech.* a simple machine consisting of a rigid bar pivoted about a fulcrum (fixed point) which can be acted upon by a force (effort) in order to move a load. **3** a projecting handle moved to operate a mechanism. **4** a means of exerting moral pressure. ● *v.* **1** *intr.* use a lever. **2** *tr.* (often foll. by *away*, *out*, *up*, etc.) lift, move, or act on with a lever. [Middle English from Old French *levier*, *leveor*, from *lever* 'raise': see LEVY]

leverage /ˈliːv(ə)rɪdʒ/ *n.* **1** the action of a lever; a way of applying a lever. **2** the power of a lever; the mechanical advantage gained by use of a lever. **3** a means of accomplishing a purpose; power, influence. **4** a set or system of levers. **5** *US Commerce* = GEARING 2.

leveraged buyout *n.* the buyout of a company by its management using outside capital.

lever escapement *n.* a mechanism in a watch connecting the escape wheel and the balance wheel using two levers.

leveret /ˈlɛv(ə)rɪt/ *n.* a young hare, esp. one in its first year. [Middle English from Anglo-French, diminutive of *levre*, Old French *lievre*, from Latin *lepus leporis* 'hare']

lever watch *n.* a watch with a lever escapement.

leviable see LEVY.

leviathan /lɪˈvʌɪəθ(ə)n/ *n.* **1** *Bibl.* a sea monster. **2** anything very large or powerful, esp. a ship. **3** an autocratic monarch or state (in allusion to a book by Hobbes, 1651). [Middle English via Late Latin from Hebrew *liwyāṯān*]

levigate /ˈlɛvɪgeɪt/ *v.tr.* **1** reduce to a fine smooth powder. **2** make a smooth paste of. □ **levigation** /-ˈgeɪʃ(ə)n/ *n.* [Latin *levigare levigat-* from *levis* 'smooth']

levin /ˈlɛvɪn/ *n. archaic* **1** lightning. **2** a flash of lightning. [Middle English *leven(e)*, probably from Old Norse]

levirate /ˈliːvɪrət, ˈlɛv-/ *n.* a custom of the ancient Hebrews and some other peoples by which a man is obliged to marry his brother's widow. □ **leviratic** /-ˈratɪk/ *adj.* **leviratical** /-ˈratɪk(ə)l/ *adj.* [Latin *levir* 'brother-in-law' + -ATE[1]]

Levis /ˈliːvʌɪz/ *n.pl.* (also **Levi's** *propr.*) a type of (originally blue) denim jeans or overalls reinforced with rivets. [named after *Levi* Strauss, original US manufacturer in 1860s]

levitate /ˈlɛvɪteɪt/ *v.* **1** *intr.* rise and float in the air (esp. with reference to spiritualism). **2** *tr.* cause to do this. □ **levitation** /-ˈteɪʃ(ə)n/ *n.* **levitator** *n.* [Latin *levis* 'light', on the pattern of GRAVITATE]

Levite /ˈliːvʌɪt/ *n.* a member of the tribe of Levi, esp. of that part of it which provided assistants to the priests in the worship in the Jewish temple. [Middle English via Late Latin *levita* and Greek *leuitēs*, from *Leui*, from Hebrew *lēwî* Levi]

Levitical /lɪˈvɪtɪk(ə)l/ *adj.* **1** of the Levites or the tribe of Levi. **2** of the Levites' ritual. **3** of Leviticus. [Late Latin *leviticus* from Greek *leuitikos* (as LEVITE)]

levity /ˈlɛvɪti/ *n.* **1** lack of serious thought; frivolity; unbecoming jocularity. **2** inconstancy. **3** undignified behaviour. **4** *archaic* lightness of weight. [Latin *levitas* from *levis* 'light']

levo- *US* var. of LAEVO-.

levodopa /liːvə(ʊ)ˈdəʊpə/ *n.* = L-DOPA. [abbreviation of *l(a)evorotatory dopa*]

levulose *US* var. of LAEVULOSE.

levy /ˈlɛvi/ *v.* & *n.* ● *v.tr.* (**-ies, -ied**) **1 a** impose (a rate or toll). **b** raise (contributions or taxes). **c** (also *absol.*) raise (a sum of money) by legal execution or process (*the debt was levied on the debtor's goods*). **d** seize (goods) in this way. **e** extort (*levy blackmail*). **2** enlist or enrol (troops etc.). **3** (usu. foll. by *upon, against*) wage, proceed to make (war). ● *n.* (*pl.* **-ies**) **1 a** the collecting of a contribution, tax, etc., or of property to satisfy a legal judgement. **b** a contribution, tax, etc., levied. **2 a** the act or an instance of enrolling troops etc. **b** (in *pl.*) troops enrolled. **c** a body of troops enrolled. **d** the number of troops enrolled. □ **leviable** *adj.* [Middle English via Old French *levee*, fem. past part. of *lever*, from Latin *levare* 'raise', from *levis* 'light']

lewd /luːd, ljuːd/ *adj.* **1** lascivious. **2** indecent, obscene. □ **lewdly** *adv.* **lewdness** *n.* [Old English *lǣwede* LAY[2], of unknown origin]

lewis /ˈluːɪs/ *n.* an iron contrivance for gripping heavy blocks of stone or concrete for lifting. [Middle English, probably from Old French *lous*, pl. of *lou(p)* 'wolf', the name of a kind of siege engine]

Lewis gun /ˈluːɪs/ *n.* a light air-cooled machine-gun with a magazine, operated by gas from its own firing. [named after I. N. *Lewis*, American soldier (d. 1931), its inventor]

lewisite /ˈluːɪsʌɪt/ *n.* an irritant gas that produces blisters, developed for use in chemical warfare. [named after W. L. *Lewis*, American chemist d. 1943 + -ITE[1]]

lex domicilii /ˌlɛks dɒmɪˈsɪlɪʌɪ/ *n. Law* the law of the country in which a person is domiciled. [Latin, = law of the domicile]

lexeme /ˈlɛksiːm/ *n. Linguistics* a basic lexical unit of a language comprising one or several words, the elements of which do not separately convey the meaning of the whole. [LEXICON + -EME]

lex fori /lɛks ˈfɔːrʌɪ/ *n. Law* the law of the country in which an action is brought. [Latin, = law of the court]

lexical /ˈlɛksɪk(ə)l/ *adj.* **1** of the words of a language. **2** of or as of a lexicon. □ **lexically** *adv.* [Greek *lexikos*, *lexikon*: see LEXICON]

lexicography /lɛksɪˈkɒgrəfi/ *n.* the compiling of dictionaries. □ **lexicographer** *n.* **lexicographic** /-kəˈgrafɪk/ *adj.* **lexicographical** /-kəˈgrafɪk(ə)l/ *adj.* **lexicographically** /-kəˈgrafɪk(ə)li/ *adv.*

lexicology /lɛksɪˈkɒlədʒi/ *n.* the study of the form, history, and meaning of words. □ **lexicological** /-kəˈlɒdʒɪk(ə)l/ *adj.* **lexicologically** /-kəˈlɒdʒɪk(ə)li/ *adv.* **lexicologist** *n.*

lexicon /ˈlɛksɪk(ə)n/ *n.* **1** a dictionary, esp. of Greek, Hebrew, Syriac, or Arabic. **2** the vocabulary of a person, language, branch of knowledge, etc. [modern Latin from Greek *lexikon* (*biblion* 'book'), neut. of *lexikos*, via *lexis* 'word' from *legō* 'speak']

lexigraphy /lɛkˈsɪgrəfi/ *n.* a system of writing in which each character represents a word. [Greek *lexis* (see LEXICON) + -GRAPHY]

lexis /ˈlɛksɪs/ *n.* **1** words, vocabulary. **2** the total stock of words in a language. [Greek: see LEXICON]

lex loci /lɛks ˈləʊsʌɪ/ *n. Law* the law of the country in which a transaction is performed, a tort is committed, or a property is situated. [Latin, = law of the place]

lex talionis /ˌlɛks talɪˈəʊnɪs/ *n.* the supposed law of retaliation, whereby a punishment resembles the offence committed, in kind and degree. [Latin, from *lex* 'law' + *talionis* from *talis* 'such']

ley[1] /leɪ/ *n.* a field temporarily under grass. [Middle English (originally *adj.*), from Old English, related to LAY[1], LIE[1]]

ley[2] /leɪ, liː/ *n.* (in full **ley line**) a hypothetical straight line connecting prehistoric sites etc. [variant of LEA]

Leyden jar /ˈlʌɪd(ə)n/ *n.* an early form of capacitor consisting of a glass jar with layers of metal foil on the outside and inside. [*Leyden* (now *Leiden*), a city in the Netherlands, where it was invented (1745)]

ley farming *n.* esp. *Brit.* alternate growing of crops and grass.

LF *abbr.* low frequency.

LH *abbr. Biochem.* luteinizing hormone.

l.h. *abbr.* left hand.

LI *abbr.* **1** Light Infantry. **2** *US* Long Island.

Li *symb. Chem.* the element lithium.

liability /lʌɪəˈbɪlɪti/ *n.* (*pl.* **-ies**) **1** the state of being liable. **2** a person or thing that is troublesome as an unwelcome responsibility; a handicap. **3** what a person is liable for, esp. (in *pl.*) debts or pecuniary obligations.

liable /ˈlʌɪəb(ə)l/ *predic.adj.* **1** legally bound. **2** (foll. by *to*) subject to (a tax or penalty). **3** (foll. by *to* + infin.) under an obligation. **4** (foll. by *to*) exposed or open to (something undesirable). **5** (foll. by *to* + infin.) *disp.* apt, likely (*it is liable to rain*). **6** (foll. by *for*) answerable. [Middle English perhaps from Anglo-French, via Old French *lier* from Latin *ligare* 'bind']

■ **Usage** The use of *liable* in sense 5, though common, is considered incorrect by some people.

liaise /lɪˈeɪz/ *v.intr.* (foll. by *with, between*) establish cooperation, act as a link. [back-formation from LIAISON]

liaison /lɪˈeɪz(ə)n, -zɒn, -zɔ̃/ *n.* **1** communication or cooperation, esp. between military forces or units. **2** an illicit sexual relationship. **3** the binding or thickening agent of a sauce. **4** the sounding of an ordinarily silent final consonant before a word beginning with a vowel (or a mute *h* in French). [French from *lier* 'bind', from Latin *ligare*]

liaison officer *n.* an officer acting as a link between allied forces or units of the same force.

liana /lɪˈɑːnə/ *n.* (also **liane** /-ˈɑːn/) any of several climbing and twining plants of tropical forests. [French *liane*, *lierne* 'clematis', of uncertain origin]

liar /ˈlʌɪə/ *n.* a person who tells a lie or lies, esp. habitually. [Old English *lēogere* (as LIE[2], -AR[4])]

liar dice *n.* a game with poker dice in which the result of a throw may be announced falsely.

lias /ˈlʌɪəs/ *n.* **1** (**Lias**) *Geol.* the lower strata of the Jurassic system of rocks, consisting of shales and limestones rich in fossils. **2** a blue limestone rock found in SW England. □ **liassic** /lʌɪˈasɪk/ *adj.* (in sense 1). [Middle English from Old French *liois* 'hard limestone', probably from Germanic]

Lib. *abbr.* Liberal.

lib /lɪb/ *n. colloq.* (in names of political movements etc.) liberation (*women's lib*). [abbreviation]

libation /lʌɪˈbeɪʃ(ə)n/ *n.* **1 a** the pouring out of a drink-offering to a god. **b** such an offering. **2** *joc.* a drink. [Middle English from Latin *libatio*, from *libare* 'pour as offering']

libber /ˈlɪbə/ *n. colloq.* an advocate of women's liberation.

Lib Dem /lɪb ˈdɛm/ *n. colloq.* a Liberal Democrat. [abbreviation]

libel /ˈlʌɪb(ə)l/ *n.* & *v.* ● *n.* **1** *Law* **a** a published false statement damaging to a person's reputation (cf. SLANDER *n.* 3). **b** the act or crime of publishing this. **2 a** a false and defamatory written statement. **b** (foll. by *on*) a thing that brings discredit by misrepresentation etc. (*the portrait is a libel on him*; *the book is a libel on human nature*). **3 a** (in civil and ecclesiastical law) the plaintiff's written declaration. **b** *Sc. Law* a statement of the grounds of a charge. ● *v.tr.* (**libelled**, **libelling**; *US* **libeled**, **libeling**) **1** defame by libellous statements. **2** accuse falsely and maliciously. **3** *Law* publish a libel against. **4** (in ecclesiastical law) bring a suit against. □ **libeller** *n.* [originally = a formal document: Middle English via Old French from Latin *libellus*, diminutive of *liber* 'book']

libellous /ˈlʌɪb(ə)ləs/ *adj.* containing or constituting a libel. □ **libellously** *adv.*

liberal /ˈlɪb(ə)r(ə)l/ *adj.* & *n.* ● *adj.* **1** given freely; ample, abundant. **2** (often foll. by *of*) giving freely; generous, not sparing. **3** open-minded, not prejudiced. **4** not strict or rigorous; (of interpretation) not literal. **5** for general broadening of the mind, not professional or technical (*liberal studies*). **6 a** favouring individual liberty, free trade, and moderate political and social reform. **b** (**Liberal**) *Polit.* of or characteristic of Liberals or a Liberal Party. **7** *Theol.* regarding many traditional beliefs as dispensable, invalidated by modern thought, or liable to change (*liberal Protestant*; *liberal Judaism*). ● *n.* **1** a person of liberal views. **2** (**Liberal**) *Polit.* a supporter or member of a Liberal Party. □ **liberalism** *n.* **liberalist** *n.* **liberalistic** /-ˈlɪstɪk/ *adj.* **liberally** *adv.* **liberalness** *n.* [originally = befitting a free man: Middle English via Old French from Latin *liberalis*, from *liber* 'free (man)']

liberal arts *n.pl.* **1** esp. *N. Amer.* the arts as distinct from science and technology. **2** *hist.* the medieval trivium and quadrivium.

Liberal Democrat *n.* (in the UK) a member of a party (formerly the *Social and Liberal Democrats*) formed from the Liberal Party and members of the Social Democratic Party.

liberality /lɪbəˈralɪti/ *n.* **1** free giving; munificence. **2** freedom from prejudice; breadth of mind. [Middle English from Old French *liberalite* or Latin *liberalitas* (as LIBERAL)]

liberalize /ˈlɪb(ə)r(ə)lʌɪz/ *v.tr.* & *intr.* (also **-ise**) make or become more liberal or less strict. □ **liberalization** /-ˈzeɪʃ(ə)n/ *n.* **liberalizer** *n.*

Liberal Party *n.* a political party advocating liberal policies (renamed in 1988 when the party regrouped with others to form the Social and Liberal Democrats and known from 1989 as the Liberal Democrats).

liberate /ˈlɪbəreɪt/ *v.tr.* **1** (often foll. by *from*) set at liberty; set free. **2** free (a country etc.) from an oppressor or an enemy occupation. **3** (often as **liberated** *adj.*) free (a person) from rigid social conventions, esp. in sexual behaviour. **4** *slang* steal. **5** *Chem.* release (esp. a gas) from a state of combination. □ **liberator** *n.* [Latin *liberare liberat-* from *liber* 'free']

liberation /lɪbəˈreɪʃ(ə)n/ *n.* the act or an instance of liberating; the state of being liberated. □ **liberationist** *n.* [Middle English from Latin *liberatio*, from *liberare*: see LIBERATE]

liberation theology *n.* a theory which interprets liberation from social, political, and economic oppression as an anticipation of ultimate salvation.

libero /ˈliːbərəʊ/ *n. Football* a player who defends across the back of the field; a sweeper. [Italian, = free (man)]

libertarian /lɪbəˈtɛːrɪən/ *n.* & *adj.* ● *n.* **1** an advocate of liberty. **2** a believer in free will (opp. NECESSITARIAN). ● *adj.* believing in free will. □ **libertarianism** *n.*

libertine /ˈlɪbətiːn, -tɪn, -tʌɪn/ *n.* & *adj.* ● *n.* **1** a dissolute or licentious person. **2** a free thinker on religion. **3** a person who follows his or her own inclinations. ● *adj.* **1** licentious, dissolute. **2** freethinking. **3** following one's own inclinations. □ **libertinage** *n.* **libertinism** *n.* [Latin *libertinus* 'freedman', via *libertus* 'made free' from *liber* 'free']

liberty /ˈlɪbəti/ *n.* (*pl.* **-ies**) **1 a** freedom from captivity, imprisonment, slavery, or despotic control. **b** a personification of this. **2 a** the right or power to do as one pleases. **b** (foll. by *to* + infin.) right, power, opportunity, permission. **c** *Philos.* freedom from control by fate or necessity. **3 a** (usu. in *pl.*) a right, privilege, or immunity, enjoyed by prescription or grant. **b** (in *sing.* or *pl.*) *Brit. hist.* an area having such privileges etc., esp. a district controlled by a city though outside its boundary or an area outside a prison where some prisoners might reside. **4** setting aside of rules or convention. **5** *Naut.* leave of absence. □ **at liberty 1** free, not imprisoned (*set at liberty*). **2** (foll. by *to* + infin.) entitled, permitted. **3** available, disengaged. **take liberties 1** (often foll. by *with*) behave in an unduly familiar manner. **2** (foll. by *with*) deal freely or superficially with rules or facts. **take the liberty** (foll. by *to* + infin., or *of* + verbal noun) presume, venture. [Middle English via Old French *liberté* from Latin *libertas -tatis*, from *liber* 'free']

Liberty Bell *n.* (in the US) a bell in Philadelphia rung at the adoption of the Declaration of Independence.

liberty boat *n. Brit. Naut.* a boat carrying liberty men.

liberty bodice *n.* a close-fitting under-bodice with no stiffening.

liberty hall *n.* a place where one may do as one likes.

liberty horse *n.* a horse performing in a circus without a rider.

liberty man *n. Brit. Naut.* a sailor with leave to go ashore.

liberty of the subject *n.* the rights of a subject under constitutional rule.

Liberty ship *n. hist.* a prefabricated US-built freighter of the Second World War.

libidinous /lɪˈbɪdɪnəs/ *adj.* lustful. □ **libidinously** *adv.* **libidinousness** *n.* [Middle English from Latin *libidinosus*, from *libido -dinis* 'lust']

libido /lɪˈbiːdəʊ, lɪˈbʌɪdəʊ/ *n.* (*pl.* **-os**) *Psychol.* psychic drive or energy, esp. that associated with sexual desire. □ **libidinal** /lɪˈbɪdɪn(ə)l/ *adj.* **libidinally** *adv.* [Latin: see LIBIDINOUS]

Lib-Lab /lɪbˈlab/ *adj. Brit. hist.* Liberal and Labour. [abbreviation]

Libra /ˈliːbrə, ˈlɪb-, ˈlʌɪb/ *n.* **1** *Astron.* a small constellation (the Scales or Balance), said to represent the pair of scales which is the symbol of justice. **2** *Astrol.* **a** the seventh sign of the zodiac, which the sun enters at the northern autumnal equinox (about 22 Sept.). **b** a person born when the sun is in this sign. □ **Libran** *n.* & *adj.* [Middle English from Latin, originally = pound weight]

librarian /lʌɪˈbrɛːrɪən/ *n.* a person in charge of, or an assistant in, a library. □ **librarianship** *n.* [Latin *librarius*: see LIBRARY]

library /ˈlʌɪbrəri, -bri/ *n.* (*pl.* **-ies**) **1 a** a collection of books etc. for use by the public or by members of a group. **b** a person's collection of books. **2** a room or building containing a collection of books (for reading or reference rather than for sale). **3 a** a similar collection of films, records, computer routines, etc. **b** the place where these are kept. **4** a series of books issued by a publisher in similar bindings etc., usu. as a set. **5** a public institution charged with the care of a collection of books, films, etc. [Middle English via Old French *librairie* from Latin *libraria*, fem. of *librarius* 'of books' (used as a noun = bookseller), from *liber libri* 'book']

library edition *n.* a strongly bound edition.

library school *n.* a college or a department in a university or polytechnic teaching librarianship.

library science *n.* the study of librarianship.

libration /laɪˈbreɪʃ(ə)n/ *n.* an apparent oscillation of a celestial body, esp. the moon, by which the parts near the edge of the disc are alternately in view and out of view. [Latin *libratio*, via *librare* from *libra* 'balance']

libretto /lɪˈbrɛtəʊ/ *n.* (*pl.* **libretti** /-ti/ or **-os**) the text of an opera or other long musical vocal work. □ **librettist** *n.* [Italian, diminutive of *libro* 'book', from Latin *liber libri*]

Librium /ˈlɪbrɪəm/ *n. propr.* a benzodiazepine drug used as a tranquillizer.

Libyan /ˈlɪbɪən/ *adj. & n.* ● *adj.* **1** of or relating to modern Libya in N. Africa. **2** of ancient N. Africa west of Egypt. **3** of or relating to the Berber group of languages. ● *n.* **1 a** a native or national of modern Libya. **b** a person of Libyan descent. **2** an ancient language of the Berber group.

lice *pl.* of LOUSE.

licence /ˈlaɪs(ə)ns/ *n.* (*US* **license**) **1** a permit from an authority to own or use something (esp. a dog, gun, television set, or vehicle), do something (esp. marry, print something, preach, or drive on a public road), or carry on a trade (esp. in alcoholic liquor). **2** leave, permission (*have I your licence to remove the fence?*). **3 a** liberty of action, esp. when excessive; disregard of law or propriety; abuse of freedom. **b** licentiousness. **4** a writer's or artist's irregularity in grammar, metre, perspective, etc., or deviation from fact, esp. for effect (*poetic licence*). **5** *Brit.* a university certificate of competence in a faculty. [Middle English via Old French from Latin *licentia*, from *licēre* 'be lawful': *-se* by confusion with LICENSE]

license /ˈlaɪs(ə)ns/ *v.tr.* (also **licence**) **1** grant a licence to (a person). **2** authorize the use of (premises) for a certain purpose, esp. the sale and consumption of alcoholic liquor. **3** authorize the publication of (a book etc.) or the performance of (a play). **4** *archaic* allow. □ **licensable** *adj.* **licenser** *n.* **licensor** *n.* [Middle English from LICENCE: *-se* on analogy of the verbs PRACTISE, PROPHESY, perhaps influenced by ADVISE, where the sound differs from the corresponding noun]

licensed victualler see VICTUALLER 1b.

licensee /laɪs(ə)nˈsiː/ *n.* the holder of a licence, esp. to sell alcoholic liquor.

license plate *n. US* the number plate of a licensed vehicle.

licentiate /laɪˈsɛnʃɪət/ *n.* **1** a holder of a certificate of competence to practise a certain profession, or of a university licence. **2** a licensed preacher not yet having an appointment, esp. in a Presbyterian church. [Middle English via medieval Latin *licentiatus*, past part. of *licentiare*, from Latin *licentia*: see LICENCE]

licentious /laɪˈsɛnʃəs/ *adj.* **1** immoral, esp. in sexual relations. **2** *archaic* disregarding accepted rules or conventions. □ **licentiously** *adv.* **licentiousness** *n.* [Latin *licentiosus* from *licentia*: see LICENCE]

lichee var. of LYCHEE.

lichen /ˈlaɪk(ə)n, ˈlɪtʃ(ə)n/ *n.* **1** any plant organism of the group Lichenes, composed of a fungus and an alga in symbiotic association, usu. of green, grey, or yellow tint and growing on and colouring rocks, tree trunks, roofs, walls, etc. **2** any of several types of skin disease in which small round hard lesions occur close together. □ **lichened** *adj.* (in sense 1). **lichenology** /-ˈnɒlədʒi/ *n.* (in sense 1). **lichenous** *adj.* (in sense 2). [Latin from Greek *leikhēn*]

lich-gate /ˈlɪtʃgeɪt/ *n.* (also **lych-gate**) a roofed gateway to a churchyard, formerly used at burials for sheltering a coffin until the clergyman's arrival. [Middle English from Old English *līc* 'corpse' (from Germanic) + GATE[1]]

licit /ˈlɪsɪt/ *adj.* not forbidden; lawful. □ **licitly** *adv.* [Latin *licitus*, past part. of *licēre* 'be lawful']

lick /lɪk/ *v. & n.* ● *v.* **1** *tr.* pass the tongue over, esp. to taste, moisten, or (of animals) clean. **2** *tr.* bring into a specified condition or position by licking (*licked it all up*; *licked it clean*). **3 a** *tr.* (of a flame, waves, etc.) touch; play lightly over. **b** *intr.* move gently or caressingly (*flames licked at the staircase*). **4** *tr. colloq.* **a** defeat, overcome. **b** excel, surpass. **c** surpass the comprehension of (*has got me licked*). **5** *tr. colloq.* thrash. ● *n.* **1** an act of licking with the tongue. **2** = SALT LICK. **3** *colloq.* a fast pace (*at a lick*; *at full lick*). **4** *colloq.* a small amount; quick treatment with (foll. by *of*: *a lick of paint*). **5** a smart blow with a stick etc. □ **a lick and a promise** *colloq.* a hasty performance of a task, esp. of washing oneself. **lick a person's boots** (or **shoes**) toady; be servile. **lick into shape** see SHAPE. **lick one's lips** (or *colloq.* **chops**) **1** look forward with relish. **2** show one's satisfaction. **lick one's wounds** be in retirement after defeat. □ **licker** *n.* (also in *comb.*). [Old English *liccian*, from West Germanic]

lickerish /ˈlɪkərɪʃ/ *adj.* (also **liquorish**) **1** lecherous. **2 a** fond of fine food. **b** greedy, longing. [Middle English *lickerous* from Old French *lecheros*: see LECHER]

lickety-split /lɪkətɪˈsplɪt/ *adv. colloq.* at full speed; headlong. [probably from LICK (see sense 3) + SPLIT]

licking /ˈlɪkɪŋ/ *n. colloq.* **1** a thrashing. **2** a defeat.

lickspittle /ˈlɪkspɪt(ə)l/ *n.* a toady.

licorice var. of LIQUORICE.

lictor /ˈlɪktə/ *n.* (usu. in *pl.*) *Rom.Hist.* an officer attending the consul or other magistrate, bearing the fasces, and executing sentence on offenders. [Middle English from Latin, perhaps related to *ligare* 'bind']

lid /lɪd/ *n.* **1** a hinged or removable cover, esp. for the top of a container. **2** = EYELID. **3** the operculum of a shell or a plant. **4** *slang* a hat. □ **put the lid** (or **tin lid**) **on** *Brit. colloq.* **1** be the culmination of. **2** put a stop to. **take** (or **blow** etc.) **the lid off** *colloq.* expose (a scandal etc.). □ **lidded** *adj.* (also in *comb.*). **lidless** *adj.* [Old English *hlid*, from Germanic]

lido /ˈliːdəʊ, ˈlaɪ-/ *n.* (*pl.* **-os**) *Brit.* a public open-air swimming pool or bathing beach. [Italian from *Lido*, the name of a bathing beach near Venice, from Latin *litus* 'shore']

lidocaine /ˈlɪdəkeɪn/ *n.* = LIGNOCAINE.

lie[1] /laɪ/ *v. & n.* ● *v.intr.* (**lying** /ˈlaɪɪŋ/; *past* **lay** /leɪ/; *past part.* **lain** /leɪn/) **1** be in or assume a horizontal position on a supporting surface; be at rest on something. **2** (of a thing) rest flat on a surface (*snow lay on the ground*). **3** (of abstract things) remain undisturbed or undiscussed etc. (*let matters lie*). **4 a** be kept or remain or be in a specified, esp. concealed, state or place (*lie hidden*; *lie in wait*; *malice lay behind those words*; *they lay dying*; *the books lay unread*; *the money is lying in the bank*). **b** (of abstract things) exist, reside; be in a certain position or relation (foll. by *in*, *with*, etc.: *the answer lies in education*; *my sympathies lie with the family*). **5 a** be situated or stationed (*the village lay to the east*; *the ships are lying off the coast*). **b** (of a road, route, etc.) lead (*the road lies over mountains*). **c** be spread out to view (*the desert lay before us*). **6** (of the dead) be buried in a grave. **7** (foll. by *with*) *archaic* have sexual intercourse. **8** *Law* be admissible or sustainable (*the objection will not lie*). **9** (of a game bird) not rise. ● *n.* **1 a** the way or direction or position in which a thing lies. **b** *Golf* the position of a golf ball when about to be struck. **2** the place of cover of an animal or a bird. □ **as far as in me lies** to the best of my power. **let lie** not raise (a controversial matter etc.) for discussion etc. **lie about** (or **around**) be left carelessly out of place. **lie ahead** be going to happen; be in store. **lie back** recline so as to rest. **lie down** assume a lying position; have a short rest. **lie down under** *Brit.* accept (an insult etc.) without protest. **lie heavy** cause discomfort or anxiety. **lie in 1** remain in bed in the morning. **2** *archaic* be brought to bed in childbirth. **lie in state** (of a deceased person of high rank) be laid in a public place of honour before burial. **lie low 1** keep quiet or unseen. **2** be discreet about one's intentions. **lie off** *Naut.* stand some distance from shore or from another ship. **lie over** be deferred. **lie to** *Naut.* come almost to a stop facing the wind. **lie up** (of a ship) go into dock or be out of commission. **lie with** (often foll. by *to* + infin.) be the responsibility of (a person) (*it lies with you to answer*). **take lying down** (usu. with *neg.*) accept (defeat, rebuke, etc.) without resistance or protest etc. [Old English *licgan*, from Germanic]

■ **Usage** The transitive use of *lie*, meaning 'lay', as in *Lie him on the bed*, is incorrect and to be avoided.

lie[2] /lʌɪ/ *n. & v.* ● *n.* **1** an intentionally false statement (*tell a lie; pack of lies*). **2** imposture; false belief (*live a lie*). ● *v.* (**lies, lied, lying** /'lʌɪɪŋ/) **1** *intr.* **a** tell a lie or lies (*they lied to me*). **b** (of a thing) be deceptive (*the camera cannot lie*). **2** *tr.* (usu. *refl.*; foll. by *into, out of*) get (oneself) into or out of a situation by lying (*lied themselves into trouble; lied my way out of danger*). □ **give the lie to** serve to show the falsity of (a supposition etc.). [Old English *lyge lēogan*, from Germanic]

Liebfraumilch /'li:bfraʊmɪlk/ *n.* a light white wine from the Rhine region. [German from *Liebfrau*, the Virgin Mary, the patroness of the convent where it was first made + *Milch* 'milk']

lied /li:d, -t/ *n.* (*pl.* **lieder** /'li:də/) a type of German song, esp. of the Romantic period, usu. for solo voice with piano accompaniment. [German]

lie detector *n.* an instrument for determining whether a person is telling the truth by testing for physiological changes considered to be symptomatic of lying.

lie-down *n. Brit.* a short rest.

lief /li:f/ *adv. archaic* gladly, willingly (usu. **had lief, would lief**). [originally as adj. from Old English *lēof* 'dear, pleasant' from Germanic: related to LEAVE[2], LOVE]

liege /li:dʒ/ *adj. & n.* usu. *hist.* ● *adj.* (of a superior) entitled to receive or (of a vassal) bound to give feudal service or allegiance. ● *n.* **1** (in full **liege lord**) a feudal superior or sovereign. **2** (usu. in *pl.*) a vassal or subject. [Middle English via Old French *lige, liege* from medieval Latin *laeticus*, probably from Germanic]

liegeman /'li:dʒmən/ *n.* (*pl.* **-men**) *hist.* a sworn vassal; a faithful follower.

lie-in *n. Brit.* a prolonged stay in bed in the morning.

lien /li:n, 'li:ən, 'lʌɪən/ *n. Law* a right over another's property to protect a debt charged on that property. [French via Old French *loien* from Latin *ligamen* 'bond', from *ligare* 'bind']

lie of the land *n.* (prec. by *the*) esp. *Brit.* the current state of affairs.

lierne /lɪ'ə:n/ *n. Archit.* (in vaulting) a short rib connecting the bosses and intersections of the principal ribs. [Middle English from French: related to LIANA]

lieu /lju:, lu:/ *n.* □ **in lieu 1** instead. **2** (foll. by *of*) in the place of. [Middle English via French from Latin *locus* 'place']

Lieut. *abbr.* Lieutenant.

lieutenant /lɛf'tɛnənt/ *n.* **1** a deputy or substitute acting for a superior. **2 a** an army officer next in rank below captain. **b** a naval officer next in rank below lieutenant commander. **3** *US* a police officer next in rank below captain. **4** *colloq.* the assistant adult leader of a company of Guides, officially termed *Assistant Guide Guider* since 1968. □ **lieutenancy** *n.* (*pl.* **-ies**). [Middle English from Old French (as LIEU, TENANT)]

lieutenant colonel *n.* an army officer ranking next below colonel.

lieutenant commander *n.* a naval officer ranking below a commander and above a lieutenant.

lieutenant general *n.* an army officer ranking below a general and above a major general.

lieutenant-governor *n.* the acting or deputy governor of a state, province, etc., under a governor or Governor-General.

Lieutenant of the Tower *n.* the acting commandant of the Tower of London.

life /lʌɪf/ *n.* (*pl.* **lives** /lʌɪvz/) **1** the condition which distinguishes active animals and plants from inorganic matter, including the capacity for growth, functional activity, and continual change preceding death. **2 a** living things and their activity (*insect life; is there life on Mars?*). **b** human presence or activity (*no sign of life*). **3 a** the period during which life lasts, or the period from birth to the present time or from the present time to death (*have done it all my life; will regret it all my life; life membership*). **b** the duration of a thing's existence or of its ability to function; validity, efficacy, etc. (*the battery has a life of two years*). **4 a** a person's state of existence as a living individual (*sacrificed their lives; took many lives*). **b** a living person (*many lives were lost*). **5 a** an individual's occupation, actions, or fortunes; the manner of one's existence (*that would make life easy; start a new life*). **b** a particular aspect of this (*love life; private life*). **6** the active part of existence; the business and pleasures of the world (*travel is the best way to see life*). **7** man's earthly or supposed future existence (*this life and the next*). **8 a** energy, liveliness, animation (*full of life; put some life into it!*). **b** an animating influence (*was the life of the party*). **9** the living, esp. nude, form or model (*taken from the life*). **10** a written account of a person's life; a biography. **11** *colloq.* a sentence of imprisonment for life (*they were all serving life*). **12** a chance; a fresh start (*cats have nine lives; gave the player three lives*). □ **come to life 1** emerge from unconsciousness or inactivity; begin operating. **2** (of an inanimate object) assume an imaginary animation. **for dear** (or **one's**) **life** as if or in order to escape death; as a matter of extreme urgency (*hanging on for dear life; run for your life*). **for life** for the rest of one's life. **for the life of** (foll. by personal pron.) even if (one's) life depended on it (*cannot for the life of me remember*). **give one's life 1** (foll. by *for*) die; sacrifice oneself. **2** (foll. by *to*) dedicate oneself. **large as life** *colloq.* in person, esp. prominently (*stood there large as life*). **larger than life 1** exaggerated. **2** (of a person) having an exuberant or striking personality. **lose one's life** be killed. **not on your life** *colloq.* most certainly not. **save a person's life 1** prevent a person's death. **2** save a person from serious difficulty. **take one's life in one's hands** take a crucial personal risk. **to the life** true to the original. [Old English *līf*, from Germanic]

life-and-death *adj.* vitally important; desperate (*a life-and-death struggle*).

life assurance *n.* = LIFE INSURANCE.

lifebelt /'lʌɪfbɛlt/ *n. Brit.* a belt of buoyant or inflatable material for keeping a person afloat in water.

lifeblood /'lʌɪfblʌd/ *n.* **1** the blood, as being necessary to life. **2** the vital factor or influence.

lifeboat /'lʌɪfbəʊt/ *n.* **1** a specially constructed boat launched from land to rescue those in distress at sea. **2** a ship's small boat for use in emergency.

lifeboatman /'lʌɪfbəʊtmən/ *n.* (*pl.* **-men**) a man who rescues people using a lifeboat.

lifebuoy /'lʌɪfbɔɪ/ *n.* a buoyant support (usu. a ring) for keeping a person afloat in water.

life cycle *n.* the series of changes in the life of an organism including reproduction.

life expectancy *n.* the average period that a person at a specified age may expect to live.

life-force *n.* inspiration or a driving force or influence.

life form *n.* an organism.

life-giving *adj.* sustaining life or uplifting and revitalizing.

lifeguard /'lʌɪfgɑ:d/ *n.* an expert swimmer employed to rescue bathers from drowning.

Life Guards *n.pl.* (in the UK) a regiment of the royal Household Cavalry.

life history *n.* the story of a person's life, esp. told at tedious length.

life insurance *n.* insurance for a sum to be paid on the death of the insured person.

life jacket *n.* a buoyant or inflatable jacket for keeping a person afloat in water.

lifeless /ˈlʌɪflɪs/ *adj.* **1** lacking life; no longer living. **2** unconscious. **3** lacking movement or vitality. □ **lifelessly** *adv.* **lifelessness** *n.* [Old English *līflēas* (as LIFE, -LESS)]

lifelike /ˈlʌɪflʌɪk/ *adj.* closely resembling the person or thing represented. □ **lifelikeness** *n.*

lifeline /ˈlʌɪflʌɪn/ *n.* **1 a** a rope etc. used for life-saving, e.g. that attached to a lifebuoy. **b** a diver's signalling line. **2** a sole means of communication or transport. **3** a fold in the palm of the hand, regarded as significant in palmistry. **4** *Brit.* an emergency telephone counselling service.

lifelong /ˈlʌɪflɒŋ/ *adj.* lasting a lifetime.

life member *n.* a person who has lifelong membership of a society etc.

life peer *n. Brit.* a peer whose title lapses on death. □ **life peerage** *n.*

life-preserver *n.* **1** *Brit.* a short stick with a heavily loaded end. **2** a life jacket etc.

lifer /ˈlʌɪfə/ *n.* **1** *slang* a person serving a life sentence. **2** *US* a person who serves in one of the armed services as a career.

life-raft *n.* an inflatable or timber etc. raft for use in an emergency instead of a boat.

life-saver *n. colloq.* **1** a thing that saves one from serious difficulty. **2** *Austral.* & *NZ* = LIFEGUARD.

life sciences *n.pl.* biology and related subjects.

life sentence *n.* **1** a sentence of imprisonment for life. **2** an illness or commitment etc. perceived as a continuing threat to one's freedom.

life-size *adj.* & *n.* (also **life-sized**) ● *adj.* of the same size as the person or thing represented. ● *n.* (**life size**) this size.

lifespan /ˈlʌɪʃspan/ *n.* the length of time for which a person or creature lives, or for which a thing exists or is functional.

lifestyle /ˈlʌɪfstʌɪl/ *n.* the particular way of life of a person or group.

life-support *attrib.adj.* (of equipment) allowing vital functions to continue in an adverse environment or during severe disablement.

life-support machine *n. Med.* a ventilator or respirator.

life's work *n.* a task etc. pursued throughout one's lifetime.

life-threatening *adj.* (of an illness etc.) that endangers life.

lifetime /ˈlʌɪftʌɪm/ *n.* **1** the duration of a person's life. **2** the duration of a thing or its usefulness. **3** *colloq.* an exceptionally long time. □ **of a lifetime** such as does not occur more than once in a person's life (*the chance of a lifetime; the journey of a lifetime*).

lift /lɪft/ *v.* & *n.* ● *v.* **1** *tr.* (often foll. by *up, off, out,* etc.) raise or remove to a higher position. **2** *intr.* go up; be raised; yield to an upward force (*the window will not lift*). **3** *tr.* give an upward direction to (the eyes or face). **4** *tr.* **a** elevate to a higher plane of thought or feeling (*the news lifted their spirits*). **b** make less heavy or dull; add interest to (something esp. artistic). **c** enhance, improve (*lifted their game after half-time*). **5** *intr.* (of a cloud, fog, etc.) rise, disperse. **6** *tr.* remove (a barrier or restriction). **7** *tr.* transport (supplies, troops, etc.) by air. **8** *tr. colloq.* **a** steal. **b** plagiarize (a passage of writing etc.). **9** *Phonet.* **a** *tr.* make louder; raise the pitch of. **b** *intr.* (of the voice) rise. **10** *tr.* dig up (esp. potatoes etc. at harvest). **11** *intr.* (of a floor) swell upwards, bulge. **12** *tr.* hold or have on high (*the church lifts its spire*). **13** *tr.* hit (a cricket ball) into the air. **14** *tr.* (usu. in *passive*) perform cosmetic surgery on (esp. the face or breasts) to reduce sagging. ● *n.* **1** the act of lifting or process of being lifted. **2** a free ride in another person's vehicle (*gave them a lift*). **3 a** *Brit.* a platform or compartment housed in a shaft for raising and lowering persons or things to different floors of a building or different levels of a mine etc. **b** a similar apparatus for carrying persons up or down a mountain etc. (see SKI LIFT). **4 a** transport by air (see AIRLIFT *n.*). **b** a quantity of goods transported by air. **5** the upward pressure which air exerts on an aerofoil to counteract the force of gravity. **6** a supporting or elevating influence; a feeling of elation. **7** a layer of leather in the heel of a boot or shoe, esp. to correct shortening of a leg or increase height. **8 a** a rise in the level of the ground. **b** the extent to which water rises in a canal lock. □ **lift down** *Brit.* pick up and bring to a lower position. **lift a finger** (or **hand** etc.) (in *neg.*) make the slightest effort (*didn't lift a finger to help*). **lift off** (of a spacecraft or rocket) rise from the launching pad. **lift up one's head** hold one's head high with pride. **lift up one's voice** sing out. □ **liftable** *adj.* **lifter** *n.* [Middle English from Old Norse *lypta*, from Germanic]

lift-off *n.* the vertical take-off of a spacecraft or rocket.

lig /lɪg/ *v.intr.* (**ligged**, **ligging**) *slang* idle, loaf; sponge, freeload. □ **ligger** *n.* [dialect variant of LIE[1]]

ligament /ˈlɪgəm(ə)nt/ *n.* **1** *Anat.* **a** a short band of tough flexible fibrous connective tissue linking bones together. **b** any membranous fold keeping an organ in position. **2** *archaic* a bond of union. □ **ligamental** /-ˈmɛnt(ə)l/ *adj.* **ligamentary** /-ˈmɛnt(ə)ri/ *adj.* **ligamentous** /-ˈmɛntəs/ *adj.* [Middle English from Latin *ligamentum* 'bond', from *ligare* 'bind']

ligand /ˈlɪg(ə)nd/ *n.* **1** *Chem.* an ion or molecule attached to a metal atom by covalent bonding in which both electrons are supplied by one atom. **2** *Biochem.* a molecule that binds to another (usu. larger) molecule. [Latin *ligandus*, gerundive of *ligare* 'bind']

ligate /lɪˈgeɪt/ *v.tr. Surgery* tie up (a bleeding artery etc.). □ **ligation** /-ˈgeɪʃ(ə)n/ *n.* [Latin *ligare ligat-*]

ligature /ˈlɪgətʃə/ *n.* & *v.* ● *n.* **1** a tie or bandage, esp. in surgery for a bleeding artery etc. **2** *Mus.* a slur; a tie. **3** *Printing* two or more letters joined, e.g. æ. **4** a bond; a thing that unites. **5** the act of tying or binding. ● *v.tr.* bind or connect with a ligature. [Middle English via Late Latin *ligatura* from Latin *ligare ligat-* 'tie, bind']

■ **Usage** See Usage Note at DIGRAPH.

liger /ˈlʌɪgə/ *n.* the offspring of a lion and a tigress (cf. TIGON). [portmanteau word from LION + TIGER]

light[1] /lʌɪt/ *n.*, *v.*, & *adj.* ● *n.* **1** the natural agent (electromagnetic radiation of wavelength between about 390 and 740 nm) that stimulates sight and makes things visible (*step into the light; just enough light to see*). **2** the medium or condition of the space in which this is present. **3** an appearance of brightness (*saw a distant light*). **4 a** a source of light, e.g. the sun, or a lamp, fire, etc. **b** (in *pl.*) illuminations. **5** (often in *pl.*) a traffic light (*went through a red light; stop at the lights*). **6 a** the amount or quality of illumination in a place (*bad light stopped play*). **b** one's fair or usual share of this (*you are standing in my light*). **7 a** a flame or spark serving to ignite (*struck a light*). **b** a device producing this (*have you got a light?*). **8** the aspect in which a thing is regarded or considered (*appeared in a new light*). **9 a** mental illumination; elucidation, enlightenment. **b** hope, happiness; a happy outcome. **c** spiritual illumination by divine truth. **10** vivacity, enthusiasm, or inspiration visible in a person's face, esp. in the eyes. **11** (in *pl.*) a person's mental powers or ability (*according to one's lights*). **12** an eminent person (*a leading light*). **13 a** the bright part of a thing; a highlight. **b** the bright parts of a picture etc. esp. suggesting illumination (*light and shade*). **14 a** a window or opening in a wall to let light in. **b** the perpendicular division of a mullioned window. **c** a pane of glass esp. in the side or roof of a greenhouse. **15** *Brit.* (in a crossword etc.) each of the items filling a space and to be deduced from the clues. **16** *Law* the light falling on windows, the obstruction of which by a neighbour is illegal. ● *v.* (*past* **lit** /lɪt/; *past part.* **lit** or (*attrib.*) **lighted**) **1** *tr. & intr.* set burning or begin to burn; ignite. **2** *tr.* provide with light or lighting; illuminate. **3** *tr.* show (a person) the way or surroundings with a light. **4** *intr.* (usu. foll. by *up*) (of the face or eyes) brighten with animation, pleasure, etc. ● *adj.* **1** well provided with light; not dark. **2** (of a colour) pale (*light blue*; *a light blue ribbon*). □ **bring** (or **come**) **to light** reveal or be revealed. **in a good** (or **bad**) **light** giving a favourable (or unfavourable) impression. **in** (**the**) **light of** having regard to; drawing information from. **light of one's life** usu. *joc.* a much loved person. **light up 1** *colloq.* begin to smoke a cigarette etc. **2** provide with lights or lighting; illuminate (a scene etc.). **lit up** *colloq.* drunk. **out like a light** deeply asleep or unconscious. **throw** (or **shed**) **light on** help to explain. □ **lightish** *adj.* **lightless** *adj.* **lightness** *n.* [Old English *lēoht*, *līht*, *līhtan*, from Germanic]

light[2] /lʌɪt/ *adj.*, *adv.*, *& v.* ● *adj.* **1** of little weight; not heavy; easy to lift. **2 a** relatively low in weight, amount, density, intensity, etc. (*light arms*; *light traffic*; *light metal*; *light rain*; *a light breeze*). **b** deficient in weight (*light coin*). **c** (of an isotope etc.) having not more than the usual mass. **3 a** carrying or suitable for small loads (*light aircraft*; *light railway*). **b** (of a ship) unladen. **c** carrying only light arms, armaments, etc. (*light brigade*; *light infantry*). **d** (of a locomotive) with no train attached. **4 a** (of food, a meal, etc.) small in amount; easy to digest (*had a light lunch*). **b** (of a foodstuff) low in fat, cholesterol, or sugar, etc. **c** (of drink) not heavy on the stomach or not strongly alcoholic. **5 a** (of entertainment, music, etc.) intended for amusement, rather than edification; not profound. **b** frivolous, thoughtless, trivial (*a light remark*). **6** (of sleep or a sleeper) easily disturbed. **7** easily borne or done (*light duties*). **8** nimble; quick-moving (*a light step*; *light of foot*; *a light rhythm*). **9** (of a building etc.) graceful, elegant, delicate. **10** (of type) not heavy or bold. **11 a** free from sorrow; cheerful (*a light heart*). **b** giddy (*light in the head*). **12** (of soil) not dense; porous. **13** (of pastry, a sponge cake, etc.) fluffy and well-aerated during cooking and with the fat fully absorbed. **14** *archaic* (of a woman) unchaste or wanton; fickle. ● *adv.* **1** in a light manner (*tread light*; *sleep light*). **2** with a minimum load or minimum luggage (*travel light*). ● *v.intr.* (*past* and *past part.* **lit** /lɪt/ or **lighted**) **1** (foll. by *on*, *upon*) come upon or find by chance. **2** *archaic* **a** alight, descend. **b** (foll. by *on*) land on (shore etc.). □ **light into** *colloq.* attack. **light out** *colloq.* depart. **make light of** treat as unimportant. **make light work of** do a thing quickly and easily. □ **lightish** *adj.* **lightness** *n.* [Old English *lēoht*, *līht*, *līhtan*, from Germanic, the verbal sense from the idea of relieving a horse etc. of weight]

light air *n. Meteorol.* a very light wind, force 1 on the Beaufort scale (1–3 m.p.h.).

light bulb *n.* a glass bulb containing an inert gas and a metal filament, providing light when an electric current is passed through.

light-emitting diode see LED.

lighten[1] /ˈlʌɪt(ə)n/ *v.* **1 a** *tr. & intr.* make or become lighter in weight. **b** *tr.* reduce the weight or load of. **2** *tr.* bring relief to (the heart, mind, etc.). **3** *tr.* mitigate (a penalty).

lighten[2] /ˈlʌɪt(ə)n/ *v.* **1 a** *tr.* shed light on. **b** *tr. & intr.* make or grow lighter or brighter. **2** *intr.* **a** shine brightly; flash. **b** emit lightning (*it is lightening*).

lightening /ˈlʌɪt(ə)nɪŋ/ *n.* a drop in the level of the womb during the last weeks of pregnancy as the head of the foetus engages in the pelvis.

lighter[1] /ˈlʌɪtə/ *n.* a device for lighting cigarettes etc.

lighter[2] /ˈlʌɪtə/ *n.* a boat, usu. flat-bottomed, for transferring goods from a ship to a wharf or another ship. [Middle English from Middle Dutch *lichter* (as LIGHT[2] in the sense 'unload')]

lighterage /ˈlʌɪt(ə)rɪdʒ/ *n.* **1** the transference of cargo by means of a lighter. **2** a charge made for this.

lighterman /ˈlʌɪtəmən/ *n.* (*pl.* **-men**) a person who works on a lighter.

lighter-than-air *attrib.adj.* (of an aircraft) weighing less than the air it displaces.

lightfast /ˈlʌɪtfɑːst/ *adj.* (of a dye, pigment, etc.) resistant to alteration on exposure to light. □ **lightfastness** *n.*

light-fingered *adj.* given to stealing.

light flyweight *n.* **1** a weight in amateur boxing up to 48 kg. **2** an amateur boxer of this weight.

light-footed *adj.* nimble. □ **light-footedly** *adv.*

light-gun var. of LIGHT-PEN.

light-headed *adj.* giddy, frivolous, delirious. □ **light-headedly** *adv.* **light-headedness** *n.*

light-hearted *adj.* **1** cheerful. **2** (unduly) casual, thoughtless. □ **light-heartedly** *adv.* **light-heartedness** *n.*

light heavyweight *n.* **1** the weight in some sports between middleweight and heavyweight, in the amateur boxing scale 75–81 kg; also called CRUISERWEIGHT. **2** a sportsman of this weight.

lighthouse /ˈlʌɪthaʊs/ *n.* a tower or other structure containing a beacon light to warn or guide ships at sea.

light industry *n.* the manufacture of small or light articles.

lighting /ˈlʌɪtɪŋ/ *n.* **1** equipment in a room or street etc. for producing light. **2** the arrangement or effect of lights.

lighting-up time *n. Brit.* the time during or after which vehicles on the road must show the prescribed lights.

lightly /ˈlʌɪtli/ *adv.* in a light (esp. frivolous or unserious) manner. □ **get off lightly** escape with little or no punishment. **take lightly** not be serious about (a thing).

light meter *n.* an instrument for measuring the intensity of the light, esp. to show the correct photographic exposure.

light middleweight *n.* **1** a weight in amateur boxing of 67–71 kg. **2** an amateur boxer of this weight.

lightning /ˈlʌɪtnɪŋ/ *n. & adj.* ● *n.* a flash of bright light produced by an electric discharge between clouds or between clouds and the ground. ● *attrib.adj.* very quick (*with lightning speed*). [Middle English, differentiated from *lightening*, verbal noun from LIGHTEN[2]]

lightning bug *n. N. Amer.* a firefly.

lightning conductor *n.* (*US* **lightning rod**) a metal rod or wire fixed to an exposed part of a building or to a mast to divert lightning into the earth or sea.

lightning strike *n. Brit.* a strike by workers at short notice, esp. without official union backing.

light of day *n.* **1** daylight, sunlight. **2** general notice; public attention.

light-pen *n.* (also **light-gun**) **1** a penlike or gunlike photosensitive device held to the screen of a computer terminal for passing information on to it. **2** a light-emitting device used for reading bar codes.

light pollution *n.* excessive brightening of the night sky by street lights etc.

lightproof /ˈlʌɪtpruːf/ *adj.* able to resist the harmful effects of (esp. excessive) light.

light railway *n.* a railway constructed for light traffic.

lights /lʌɪts/ *n.pl.* the lungs of sheep, pigs, bullocks, etc., used as a food esp. for pets. [Middle English, use of LIGHT[2] as a noun, so named because of their lightness: cf. LUNG]

lightship /ˈlʌɪtʃɪp/ *n.* a moored or anchored ship with a beacon light.

light show *n.* a display of changing coloured lights for entertainment.

lightsome /ˈlʌɪts(ə)m/ *adj.* **1** gracefully light; nimble. **2** merry. □ **lightsomely** *adv.* **lightsomeness** *n.*

light touch *n.* delicate or tactful treatment.

lightweight /ˈlʌɪtweɪt/ *adj. & n.* ● *adj.* **1** (of a person, animal, garment, etc.) of below average weight. **2** of little importance or influence. ● *n.* **1** a lightweight person, animal, or thing. **2 a** a weight in certain sports intermediate between featherweight and welterweight, in the amateur boxing scale 57–60 kg but differing for professional boxers, wrestlers, and weightlifters. **b** a boxer etc. of this weight.

light welterweight *n.* **1** a weight in amateur boxing of 60–63.5 kg. **2** an amateur boxer of this weight.

lightwood /ˈlʌɪtwʊd/ *n.* **1** a tree with a light wood. **2** *US* wood or a tree with wood that burns with a bright flame.

light year *n.* **1** *Astron.* the distance light travels in one year, nearly 6 million million miles. **2** (in *pl.*) *colloq.* a long distance or great amount.

ligneous /ˈlɪgnɪəs/ *adj.* **1** (of a plant) woody (opp. HERBACEOUS). **2** of the nature of wood. [Latin *ligneus* (as LIGNI-)]

ligni- /ˈlɪgni/ *comb. form* wood. [Latin *lignum* 'wood']

lignify /ˈlɪgnɪfʌɪ/ *v.tr. & intr.* **(-ies, -ied)** *Bot.* make or become woody by the deposition of lignin.

lignin /ˈlɪgnɪn/ *n. Bot.* a complex organic polymer deposited in the cell walls of many plants making them rigid and woody. [as LIGNI- + -IN]

lignite /ˈlɪgnʌɪt/ *n.* a soft brown coal showing traces of plant structure, intermediate between bituminous coal and peat. □ **lignitic** /-ˈnɪtɪk/ *adj.* [French (as LIGNI-, -ITE[1])]

lignocaine /ˈlɪgnəkeɪn/ *n. Pharm.* a local anaesthetic for the gums, mucous membranes, or skin, usu. given by injection. Also called *lidocaine.* [*ligno-* (as LIGNI-) for XYLO- + COCA + -INE[4]]

lignum vitae /lɪgnəm ˈvʌɪti:, ˈvi:tʌɪ/ *n.* = GUAIACUM 2a. [Latin, = wood of life]

ligroin /ˈlɪgrəʊɪn/ *n. Chem.* a volatile hydrocarbon mixture obtained from petroleum and used as a solvent. [19th c.: origin unknown]

ligulate /ˈlɪgjʊlət/ *adj. Bot.* having strap-shaped florets. [LIGULE + -ATE[2]]

ligule /ˈlɪgju:l/ *n. Bot.* a narrow projection from the top of the sheath which encloses a leaf of a grass. [Latin *ligula* 'strap, spoon' from *lingere* 'lick']

ligustrum /lɪˈgʌstrəm/ *n.* = PRIVET. [Latin]

likable var. of LIKEABLE.

like[1] /lʌɪk/ *adj., prep., adv., conj., & n.* ● *adj.* (often governing a noun as if a transitive participle such as *resembling*) (**more like**, **most like**) **1 a** having some or all of the qualities of another or each other or an original; alike (*in like manner*; *as like as two peas*; *is very like her brother*). **b** resembling in some way, such as; in the same class as (*good writers like Dickens*). **c** (usu. in pairs correlatively) as one is so will the other be (*like mother, like daughter*). **2** characteristic of (*it is not like them to be late*). **3** in a suitable state or mood for (doing or having something) (*felt like working*; *felt like a cup of tea*). ● *prep.* in the manner of; to the same degree as (*drink like a fish*; *sell like hot cakes*; *acted like an idiot*). ● *adv.* **1** *archaic* likely (*they will come, like enough*). **2** *archaic* in the same manner (foll. by *as*: *sang like as a nightingale*). **3** *slang* so to speak (*did a quick getaway, like*; *as I said, like, I'm no Shakespeare*). **4** *colloq.* likely, probably (*as like as not*). ● *conj. colloq. disp.* **1** as (*cannot do it like you do*). **2** as if (*ate like they were starving*). ● *n.* **1** a counterpart; an equal; a similar person or thing (*shall not see its like again*; *compare like with like*). **2** (prec. by *the*) a thing or things of the same kind (*will never do the like again*). □ **and the like** and similar things; et cetera (*music, painting, and the like*). **be nothing like** (usu. with compl.) be in no way similar or comparable or adequate. **like anything** see ANYTHING. **like** (or **as like**) **as not** *colloq.* probably. **like so** *colloq.* like this; in this manner. **the likes of** *colloq.* a person such as. **more like it** *colloq.* nearer what is required. **of like** (or **of a like**) **mind** = LIKE-MINDED. **what is he** (or **she** or **it** etc.) **like?** what sort of characteristics does he (or she, or it, etc.) have? [Middle English *līc*, *līk*, shortened form of Old English *gelīc* ALIKE]

■ **Usage** When *like* means 'such as' (see sense 1b of the adjective), some people prefer *such as* to be used in formal contexts when more than one example is mentioned, e.g. *good writers such as Dickens, Shakespeare, and Hardy*.
The use of *like* as a conjunction, e.g. *He did it like he'd never done it before*, is often condemned and is therefore best avoided by using instead *as* or *as if* as appropriate.

like[2] /lʌɪk/ *v. & n.* ● *v.tr.* **1 a** find agreeable or enjoyable or satisfactory (*like reading*; *like the sea*; *like to dance*). **b** be fond of (a person). **2 a** choose to have; prefer (*like my coffee black*; *do not like such things discussed*). **b** wish for or be inclined to (*would like a cup of tea*; *should like to come*). **3** (usu. in *interrog.*; prec. by *how*) feel about; regard (*how would you like it if it happened to you?*). ● *n.* (in *pl.*) the things one likes or prefers. □ **I like that!** *iron.* as an exclamation expressing affront. **like it or not** *colloq.* whether it is acceptable or not. [Old English *līcian*, from Germanic]

-like /lʌɪk/ *comb. form* forming adjectives from nouns, meaning 'similar to, characteristic of' (*doglike*; *shell-like*; *tortoise-like*).

■ **Usage** In formations intended as nonce-words, or not generally current, the hyphen should be used. It may be omitted when the first element is of one syllable, but nouns in *-l* always require it.

likeable /ˈlʌɪkəb(ə)l/ *adj.* (also **likable**) pleasant; easy to like. □ **likeability** *n.* **likeableness** *n.* **likeably** /-bli/ *adv.*

likelihood /ˈlʌɪklɪhʊd/ *n.* probability; the state or fact of being likely. □ **in all likelihood** very probably.

likely /ˈlʌɪkli/ *adj. & adv.* ● *adj.* (**likelier**, **likeliest**) **1** probable; such as well might happen or be true (*it is not likely that they will come*; *the most likely place is London*; *a likely story*). **2** (foll. by *to* + infin.) to be reasonably expected (*he is not likely to come now*). **3** promising; apparently suitable (*three likely lads*; *this is a likely spot*). ● *adv.* probably (*is very likely true*). □ **as likely as not** probably. **not likely!** *colloq.* certainly not; I refuse. □ **likeliness** *n.* [Middle English from Old Norse *líkligr* (as LIKE[1], -LY[1])]

■ **Usage** When used as an adverb, *likely* must be preceded by *more*, *most*, or *very*. Use without the qualifying adverb is standard only in American English, e.g. *They'll likely not come.*

like-minded *adj.* having the same tastes, opinions, etc. □ **like-mindedly** *adv.* **like-mindedness** *n.*

liken /ˈlʌɪk(ə)n/ *v.tr.* (foll. by *to*) point out the resemblance of (a person or thing to another). [Middle English, from LIKE[1] + -EN[1]]

likeness /ˈlʌɪknɪs/ *n.* **1** (usu. foll. by *between*, *to*) resemblance. **2** (foll. by *of*) a semblance or guise (*in the likeness of a ghost*). **3** a portrait or representation (*is a good likeness*). [Old English *gelīknes* (as LIKE[1], -NESS)]

likewise /ˈlʌɪkwʌɪz/ *adv.* **1** also, moreover, too. **2** similarly (*do likewise*). [for *in like wise*]

liking /ˈlʌɪkɪŋ/ *n.* **1** what one likes; one's taste (*is it to your liking?*). **2** (foll. by *for*) regard or fondness; taste or fancy (*had a liking for toffee*). [Old English *līcung* (as LIKE[2], -ING[1])]

lilac /ˈlʌɪlək/ *n. & adj.* ● *n.* **1** any shrub or small tree of the genus *Syringa*, esp. *S. vulgaris* with fragrant pale pinkish-violet or white blossoms. **2** a pale pinkish-violet colour. ● *adj.* of this colour. [obsolete French via Spanish and Arabic *līlāk* from Persian *līlak*, variant of *nīlak* 'bluish' from *nīl* 'blue']

liliaceous /lɪlɪ'eɪʃəs/ *adj.* **1** of or relating to the family Liliaceae of plants with elongated leaves growing from a corm, bulb, or rhizome, e.g. tulip, lily, or onion. **2** lily-like. [Late Latin *liliaceus* from Latin *lilium* 'lily']

lilliputian /lɪlɪ'pjuːʃ(ə)n/ *n. & adj.* ● *n.* a diminutive person or thing. ● *adj.* diminutive. [the imaginary country of *Lilliput* in Swift's *Gulliver's Travels*, inhabited by people 6 inches (15 cm) high]

Lilo /'lʌɪləʊ/ *n.* (also **Li-lo** *propr.*) (*pl.* **-os**) *Brit.* a type of inflatable mattress. [alteration of *lie low*]

lilt /lɪlt/ *n. & v.* ● *n.* **1 a** a light springing rhythm or step. **b** a song or tune marked by this. **2** (of the voice) a characteristic cadence or inflection; a pleasant accent. ● *v.intr.* (esp. as **lilting** *adj.*) move or speak etc. with a lilt (*a lilting step; a lilting melody*). [Middle English *lilte, lülte*, of unknown origin]

lily /'lɪli/ *n.* (*pl.* **-ies**) **1 a** any bulbous plant of the genus *Lilium* (family Liliaceae), with large trumpet-shaped often spotted flowers on a tall slender stem, e.g. the madonna lily and tiger lily. **b** any of various plants of similar appearance, e.g. the arum lily. **c** the water lily. **2** a person or thing of special whiteness or purity. **3** a heraldic fleur-de-lis. **4** (*attrib.*) **a** delicately white (*a lily hand*). **b** pallid. □ **lilied** *adj.* [Old English *lilie* from Latin *lilium*, probably from Greek *leirion*]

lily-livered *adj.* cowardly.

lily of the valley *n.* any plant of the genus *Convallaria* (lily family), with oval leaves in pairs and racemes of white bell-shaped fragrant flowers.

lily pad *n.* a floating leaf of a water lily.

lily-trotter *n.* a jacana, esp. an African one.

lily white *n. & adj.* ● *n.* a pure white colour. ● *adj.* (hyphenated when *attrib.*) **1** of this colour. **2** faultless.

lima bean /'liːmə/ *n.* **1** a tropical American bean plant, *Phaseolus limensis*, having large flat white edible seeds. **2** the seed of this plant. [*Lima*, the capital of Peru]

limb[1] /lɪm/ *n.* **1** a projecting part of a person's or animal's body such as an arm, leg, or wing. **2** a large branch of a tree. **3** a branch of a cross. **4** a spur of a mountain. **5** *Brit.* a clause of a sentence. □ **out on a limb 1** isolated, stranded. **2** at a disadvantage. **tear limb from limb** violently dismember. **with life and limb** (esp. escape) without grave injury. □ **limbed** *adj.* (also in *comb.*). **limbless** *adj.* [Old English *lim*, from Germanic]

limb[2] /lɪm/ *n.* **1 a** *Astron.* a specified edge of the sun, moon, etc. (*eastern limb; lower limb*). **b** the graduated edge of a quadrant etc. **2** *Bot.* the broad part of a petal, sepal, or leaf. [French *limbe* or Latin *limbus* 'hem, border']

limber[1] /'lɪmbə/ *adj. & v.* ● *adj.* **1** lithe, agile, nimble. **2** flexible. ● *v.* (usu. foll. by *up*) **1** *tr.* make (oneself or a part of the body etc.) supple. **2** *intr.* warm up in preparation for athletic etc. activity. □ **limberness** *n.* [16th c.: origin uncertain]

limber[2] /'lɪmbə/ *n. & v.* ● *n.* the detachable front part of a gun carriage, consisting of two wheels, axle, pole, and ammunition box. ● *v.* **1** *tr.* attach a limber to (a gun etc.). **2** *intr.* fasten together the two parts of a gun carriage. [Middle English *limo(u)r*, apparently related to medieval Latin *limonarius* from *limo -onis* 'shaft']

limbic /'lɪmbɪk/ *adj.* of or relating to a part of the brain concerned with basic emotions and instinctive actions. [French *limbique*, from Latin *limbus* 'edge']

limbo[1] /'lɪmbəʊ/ *n.* (*pl.* **-os**) **1** (in some Christian beliefs) the supposed abode of the souls of unbaptized infants, and of the just who died before Christ. **2** an intermediate state or condition of awaiting a decision etc. **3** prison, confinement. **4** a state of neglect or oblivion. [Middle English from the medieval Latin phrase *in limbo*, from *limbus*: see LIMB[2]]

limbo[2] /'lɪmbəʊ/ *n.* (*pl.* **-os**) a W. Indian dance in which the dancer bends backwards to pass under a horizontal bar which is progressively lowered to a position just above the ground. [W. Indian word, perhaps = LIMBER[1]]

Limburger /'lɪmbɜːgə/ *n.* a soft white cheese with a characteristic strong smell, originally made in Limburg. [Dutch and German, from *Limburg*, a province in Belgium]

lime[1] /lʌɪm/ *n. & v.* ● *n.* **1** (in full **quicklime**) a white caustic alkaline substance (calcium oxide) obtained by heating limestone and used for making mortar or as a fertilizer or bleach etc. **2** (in full **slaked lime**) a white substance (calcium hydroxide) made by adding water to quicklime, used esp. in cement. **3** calcium or calcium salts, esp. calcium carbonate in soil etc. **4** *archaic* = BIRDLIME. ● *v.tr.* **1** treat (wood, skins, land, etc.) with lime. **2** *archaic* catch (a bird etc.) with birdlime. □ **limeless** *adj.* **limy** *adj.* (**limier**, **limiest**). [Old English *līm* from Germanic: related to LOAM]

lime[2] /lʌɪm/ *n.* **1 a** a rounded citrus fruit like a lemon but greener, smaller, and more acid. **b** (in full **lime tree**) the tree, *Citrus aurantifolia*, bearing this. **2** (in full **lime juice**) the juice of limes as a drink and formerly given to prevent scurvy on long sea voyages. **3** = LIME GREEN. [French via modern Provençal *limo*, Spanish *lima* from Arabic *līma*: cf. LEMON]

lime[3] /lʌɪm/ *n.* **1** (in full **lime tree**) any ornamental tree of the genus *Tilia*, esp. *T. europaea* with heart-shaped leaves and fragrant yellow blossom; also called LINDEN. **2** the wood of this. [alteration of *line* = Old English *lind* = LINDEN]

lime green *n. & adj.* ● *n.* a bright pale green colour like that of a lime (see LIME[2] 1a). ● *adj.* (hyphenated when *attrib.*) of this colour.

limekiln /'lʌɪmkɪln/ *n.* a kiln for heating limestone to produce quicklime.

limelight /'lʌɪmlʌɪt/ *n.* **1** an intense white light obtained by heating a cylinder of lime in an oxyhydrogen flame, used formerly in theatres. **2** (prec. by *the*) the full glare of publicity; the focus of attention.

limepit /'lʌɪmpɪt/ *n.* a pit containing lime for steeping hides to remove hair.

limerick /'lɪm(ə)rɪk/ *n.* a humorous or comic form of five-line poem with a rhyme scheme *aabba*. [said to be from the chorus 'will you come up to Limerick?' sung between improvised verses at a gathering: from *Limerick*, a town and county in Ireland]

limestone /'lʌɪmstəʊn/ *n. Geol.* a sedimentary rock composed mainly of calcium carbonate, used as building material and in the making of cement.

limewash /'lʌɪmwɒʃ/ *n.* a mixture of lime and water for coating walls.

lime water *n.* an aqueous solution of calcium hydroxide used esp. to detect the presence of carbon dioxide.

Limey /'lʌɪmi/ *n.* (*pl.* **-eys**) *N. Amer. slang offens.* a British person (originally a sailor) or ship. [LIME[2], because of the former enforced consumption of lime juice in the British Navy]

liminal /'lɪmɪn(ə)l/ *adj.* **1 a** of or relating to a transitional or initial stage. **b** marginal, insignificant. **2** occupying a position on, or on both sides of, a boundary or threshold. □ **liminality** /-'nalɪti/ *n.* [Latin *limin-, limen* 'threshold' + -AL]

limit /'lɪmɪt/ *n. & v.* ● *n.* **1** a point, line, or level beyond which something does not or may not extend or pass. **2** (often in *pl.*) the boundary of an area. **3** the greatest or smallest amount permissible or possible (*upper limit; lower limit*). **4** *Math.* a quantity which a function or sum of a series can be made to approach as closely as desired. ● *v.tr.* (**limited**, **limiting**) **1** set or serve as a limit to. **2** (foll. by *to*) restrict. □ **be the limit** *colloq.* be intolerable or extremely irritating. **within limits** moderately; with some degree of freedom. **without limit** with no restriction. □ **limitable** *adj.* **limitative** /-tətɪv/ *adj.* [Middle English from Latin *limes limitis* 'boundary, frontier']

limitary /'lɪmɪt(ə)ri/ *adj.* **1** subject to restriction. **2** of, on, or serving as a limit.

limitation /lɪmɪˈteɪʃ(ə)n/ *n.* **1** the act or an instance of limiting; the process of being limited. **2** (often in *pl.*) a condition of limited ability (*know one's limitations*). **3** (often in *pl.*) a limiting rule or circumstance (*has its limitations*). **4** a legally specified period beyond which an action cannot be brought, or a property right is not to continue. [Middle English from Latin *limitatio* (as LIMIT)]

limited /ˈlɪmɪtɪd/ *adj.* **1** confined within limits. **2** not great in scope or talents (*has limited experience*). **3 a** few, scanty, restricted (*limited accommodation*). **b** restricted to a few examples (*limited edition*). **4** (after a company name) being a limited company. □ **limitedness** *n.*

limited company *n. Brit.* a company whose owners are legally responsible only to a limited amount for its debts.

limited liability *n. Brit.* the status of being legally responsible only to a limited amount for debts of a trading company.

limited liability company *n. Brit.* = LIMITED COMPANY.

limiter /ˈlɪmɪtə/ *n.* **1** a person or thing that limits something. **2** *Electronics* a device whose output is restricted to a certain range of values irrespective of the size of the input.

limitless /ˈlɪmɪtlɪs/ *adj.* **1** extending or going on indefinitely (*a limitless expanse*). **2** unlimited (*limitless generosity*). □ **limitlessly** *adv.* **limitlessness** *n.*

limn /lɪm/ *v.tr.* **1** *archaic* paint (esp. a miniature portrait). **2** *hist.* illuminate (manuscripts). □ **limner** *n.* [obsolete *lumine* 'illuminate' via Old French *luminer* from Latin *luminare*: see LUMEN]

limnology /lɪmˈnɒlədʒi/ *n.* the study of the physical phenomena of lakes and other fresh waters. □ **limnological** /-nəˈlɒdʒɪk(ə)l/ *adj.* **limnologist** *n.* [Greek *limnē* 'lake' + -LOGY]

limo /ˈlɪməʊ/ *n.* (*pl.* **-os**) *colloq.* a limousine. [abbreviation]

limousine /ˈlɪməziːn, lɪməˈziːn/ *n.* a large luxurious motor car, often with a partition behind the driver. [French, originally a caped cloak worn in the former French province of *Limousin*]

limp[1] /lɪmp/ *v.* & *n.* ● *v.intr.* **1** walk lamely. **2** (of a damaged ship, aircraft, etc.) proceed with difficulty. **3** (of verse) be defective. ● *n.* a lame walk. □ **limpingly** *adv.* [related to obsolete *limphalt* 'lame', Old English *lemp-healt*]

limp[2] /lɪmp/ *adj.* **1** not stiff or firm; easily bent. **2** without energy or will. **3** (of a book) having a soft cover. □ **limply** *adv.* **limpness** *n.* [18th c.: origin unknown: perhaps related to LIMP[1] in the sense 'hanging loose']

limpet /ˈlɪmpɪt/ *n.* **1** any of various marine gastropod molluscs, esp. the common limpet *Patella vulgata*, with a shallow conical shell and a broad muscular foot that sticks tightly to rocks. **2** a clinging person. [Old English *lempedu* from medieval Latin *lampreda* 'limpet, LAMPREY']

limpet mine *n.* a mine designed to be attached to a ship's hull and set to explode after a certain time.

limpid /ˈlɪmpɪd/ *adj.* **1** (of water, eyes, etc.) clear, transparent. **2** (of writing) clear and easily comprehended. □ **limpidity** /-ˈpɪdɪti/ *n.* **limpidly** *adv.* **limpidness** *n.* [French *limpide* or Latin *limpidus*, perhaps related to LYMPH]

limpkin /ˈlɪm(p)kɪn/ *n.* a wading marsh bird, *Aramus guarauna*, of tropical America. [LIMP[1], with reference to the bird's limping gait]

limp-wristed *adj. colloq.* **1** effeminate. **2** ineffectual, feeble.

linage /ˈlʌɪnɪdʒ/ *n.* **1** the number of lines in printed or written matter. **2** payment by the line.

linchpin /ˈlɪn(t)ʃpɪn/ *n.* (also **lynchpin**) **1** a pin passed through an axle-end to keep a wheel in position. **2** a person or thing vital to an enterprise, organization, etc. [Middle English *linch* from Old English *lynis* + PIN]

Lincoln green /ˈlɪŋk(ə)n/ *n.* a bright green cloth of a kind originally made at Lincoln in E. England.

Lincs. *abbr.* Lincolnshire.

linctus /ˈlɪŋktəs/ *n.* a syrupy medicine, esp. a soothing cough mixture. [Latin, from *lingere* 'lick']

lindane /ˈlɪndeɪn/ *n. Chem.* a toxic colourless isomer of benzene hexachloride used as an insecticide, though now often avoided owing to its persistence in the environment. [named after T. van der *Linden*, Dutch chemist b. 1884]

linden /ˈlɪndən/ *n.* a lime tree. [originally as adj. from Old English *lind* 'lime tree': cf. LIME[3]]

line[1] /lʌɪn/ *n.* & *v.* ● *n.* **1** a continuous mark or band made on a surface (*drew a line*). **2** use of lines in art, esp. draughtsmanship or engraving (*boldness of line*). **3** a thing resembling such a mark esp. a furrow or wrinkle. **4** *Mus.* **a** each of (usu. five) horizontal marks forming a stave in musical notation. **b** a sequence of notes or tones forming an instrumental or vocal melody. **5 a** a straight or curved continuous extent of length without breadth. **b** the track of a moving point. **6 a** a contour or outline, esp. as a feature of design (*admired the yacht's clean lines*; *the pure line of a tailored jacket*). **b** a facial feature (*the cruel line of his mouth*). **7 a** (on a map or graph) a curve connecting all points having a specified common property. **b** (**the Line**) the equator. **8 a** a limit or boundary. **b** a mark limiting the area of play, the starting or finishing point in a race, etc. **c** the boundary between a credit and a debit in an account. **9 a** a row of persons or things. **b** a direction as indicated by them (*line of march*). **c** *N. Amer.* a queue. **10 a** a row of printed or written words. **b** a portion of verse written in one line. **11** (in *pl.*) **a** a piece of poetry. **b** the words of an actor's part. **c** a specified amount of text etc. to be written out as a school punishment. **12** a short letter or note (*drop me a line*). **13** (in *pl.*) = MARRIAGE LINES. **14** a length of cord, rope, wire, etc., usu. serving a specified purpose, esp. a fishing line or clothes line. **15 a** a wire or cable for a telephone or telegraph. **b** a connection by means of this (*am trying to get a line*). **16 a** a single track of a railway. **b** one branch or route of a railway system, or the whole system under one management. **17 a** a regular succession of buses, ships, aircraft, etc., plying between certain places. **b** a company conducting this (*shipping line*). **18** a connected series of persons following one another in time (esp. several generations of a family); stock, succession (*a long line of craftsmen*; *next in line to the throne*). **19 a** a course or manner of procedure, conduct, thought, etc. (*did it along these lines*; *don't take that line with me*). **b** policy (*the party line*). **c** conformity (*bring them into line*). **20** a direction, course, or channel (*lines of communication*). **21** a department of activity; a province; a branch of business (*not in my line*). **22** a range of commercial goods (*a new line in hats*). **23** *colloq.* a false or exaggerated account or story; a dishonest approach (*gave me a line about missing the bus*). **24 a** a connected series of military fieldworks, defences, etc. (*behind enemy lines*). **b** an arrangement of soldiers or ships in a column or line formation; a line of battle (*ship of the line*). **c** (prec. by *the*) regular army regiments (not auxiliary forces or Guards). **25** each of the very narrow horizontal sections forming a television picture. **26** a narrow range of the spectrum that is noticeably brighter or darker than the adjacent parts. **27** the level of the base of most letters in printing and writing. **28** (as a measure) one-twelfth of an inch. ● *v.tr.* **1** mark with lines. **2** cover with lines (*a face lined with pain*). **3** position or stand at intervals along (*crowds lined the route*). □ **all along the line** at every point. **bring into line** make conform. **come into line** conform. **end of the line** the point at which further effort is unproductive or one can go no further. **get a line on** *colloq.* learn something about. **in line for** likely to receive. **in the line of** in the course of (esp. duty). **in** (or **out of**) **line with** in (or not in) alignment or accordance with. **lay** (or **put**) **it on the line** speak frankly. **line up 1** arrange or be arranged in a line or lines. **2** have ready; organize (*had a job lined up*). **on the line 1** at risk (*put my reputation on the line*). **2** speaking on the telephone. **3** (of a picture in an exhibition) hung with its centre about level with the spectator's eye. **out of line 1** not in alignment; discordant. **2** failing to conform to a rule or convention, behaving inappropriately. [Middle English *line, ligne* from Old French *ligne*, ultimately via Latin *linea* from *linum* 'flax', and from Old English *līne* 'rope, series']

line[2] /lʌɪn/ *v.tr.* **1 a** cover the inside surface of (a garment, box, etc.) with a layer of usu. different material. **b** serve as a lining for. **2** cover as if with a lining (*shelves lined with books*). **3** *colloq.* fill, esp. plentifully. □ **line one's pocket** (or **purse**) make money, usu. by corrupt means. [Middle English from obsolete *line* 'flax', with reference to the use of linen for linings]

lineage /ˈlɪnɪɪdʒ/ *n.* lineal descent; ancestry, pedigree. [Middle English via Old French *linage, lignage* and Romanic from Latin *linea* LINE[1]]

lineal /ˈlɪnɪəl/ *adj.* **1** in the direct line of descent or ancestry. **2** linear; of or in lines. □ **lineally** *adv.* [Middle English via Old French from Late Latin *linealis* (as LINE[1])]

lineament /ˈlɪnɪəm(ə)nt/ *n.* (usu. in *pl.*) a distinctive feature or characteristic, esp. of the face. [Middle English from Latin *lineamentum*, via *lineare* 'make straight' from *linea* LINE[1]]

linear /ˈlɪnɪə/ *adj.* **1 a** of or in lines; in lines rather than masses (*linear development*). **b** of length (*linear extent*). **2** long and narrow and of uniform breadth. **3** involving one dimension only. **4** progressing in a single series of steps or stages; sequential. □ **linearity** /-ˈarɪti/ *n.* **linearize** /ˈlɪnɪərʌɪz/ *v.tr.* (also **-ise**). **linearly** *adv.* [Latin *linearis* from *linea* LINE[1]]

linear accelerator *n. Physics* an accelerator in which particles travel in straight lines, not in closed orbits.

Linear B *n.* a form of Bronze Age writing found in Crete and parts of Greece and recording a form of Mycenaean Greek: an earlier undeciphered form (**Linear A**) also exists.

linear equation *n.* an equation between two variables that gives a straight line when plotted on a graph.

linear motor *n.* a motor producing straight-line (not rotary) motion by means of a magnetic field.

linear programming *n.* a mathematical technique for maximizing or minimizing a linear function of several variables, e.g. output or cost.

lineation /lɪnɪˈeɪʃ(ə)n/ *n.* **1** a marking with or drawing of lines. **2** a division into lines. [Middle English from Latin *lineatio*, from *lineare* 'make straight']

linebacker/ˈlʌɪnbakə/ *n. Amer. Football* a player or position just behind the defensive line.

line drawing *n.* a drawing in which images are produced from variations of lines.

linefeed /ˈlʌɪnfiːd/ *n.* **1** the action of advancing paper in a printing machine by the space of one line. **2** the analogous movement of text on a VDU screen.

lineman /ˈlʌɪnmən/ *n.* (*pl.* **-men**) **1 a** a person who repairs and maintains telephone or electrical etc. lines. **b** a person who tests the safety of railway lines. **2** *Amer. Football* a player in the line formed before a scrimmage.

line manager *n.* a manager to whom an employee is directly responsible.

linen /ˈlɪnɪn/ *n. & adj.* ● *n.* **1 a** cloth woven from flax. **b** a particular kind of this. **2** (*collect.*) articles made, or originally made, of linen, e.g. sheets, cloths, shirts, undergarments, etc. ● *adj.* made of linen or flax (*linen cloth*). □ **wash one's dirty linen in public** be indiscreet about one's domestic quarrels etc. [Old English *līnen* from West Germanic: related to obsolete *line* 'flax']

linen basket *n.* esp. *Brit.* a basket for soiled clothes.

linenfold /ˈlɪnɪnfəʊld/ *n.* (often *attrib.*) a carved or moulded ornament representing a fold or scroll of linen (*linenfold panelling*).

line of credit *n.* an amount of credit extended to a borrower.

line of fire *n.* the expected path of gunfire, a missile, etc.

line of force *n.* an imaginary line which represents the strength and direction of a magnetic, gravitational, or electric field at any point.

line of march *n.* the route taken in marching.

line of scrimmage *n. Amer. Football* the imaginary line separating two teams at the beginning of a scrimmage.

line of sight *n.* a straight line along which an observer has unobstructed vision.

line of vision *n.* the straight line along which an observer looks.

line-out *n.* (in rugby) parallel lines of opposing forwards at right angles to the touchline for the throwing in of the ball.

line printer *n.* a machine that prints output from a computer a line at a time rather than character by character.

liner[1] /ˈlʌɪnə/ *n.* a ship or aircraft etc. carrying passengers on a regular line.

liner[2] /ˈlʌɪnə/ *n.* a removable lining.

-liner /ˈlʌɪnə/ *comb. form* (prec. by a numeral, usu. *one* or *two*) *colloq.* a spoken passage of a specified number of lines in a play etc. (*a one-liner*).

liner train *n. Brit.* a fast goods train with detachable containers on permanently coupled wagons.

lineside /ˈlʌɪnsʌɪd/ *attrib.adj. Brit.* adjacent to a railway line.

linesman /ˈlʌɪnzmən/ *n.* (*pl.* **-men**) **1** (in games played on a pitch or court) an umpire's or referee's assistant who decides whether a ball falls within the playing area or not. **2** = LINEMAN 1.

line-up *n.* **1** a line of people for inspection. **2** an arrangement of persons in a team or nations etc. in an alliance.

ling[1] /lɪŋ/ *n.* a long slender marine fish, *Molva molva*, of the E. Atlantic, related to the cod and used as food. [Middle English *leng(e)*, probably from Middle Dutch: related to LONG[1]]

ling[2] /lɪŋ/ *n.* any of various heathers, esp. *Calluna vulgaris*. □ **lingy** *adj.* [Middle English from Old Norse *lyng*]

-ling[1] /lɪŋ/ *suffix* **1** denoting a person or thing: **a** connected with (*hireling*; *sapling*). **b** having the property of being (*weakling*; *underling*) or undergoing (*starveling*). **2** denoting a diminutive (*duckling*), often derogatory (*lordling*). [Old English (as -LE[1] + -ING[3]): sense 2 from Old Norse]

-ling[2] /lɪŋ/ *suffix* forming adverbs and adjectives (*darkling*) (cf. -LONG). [Old English from Germanic]

linga /ˈlɪŋgə/ *n.* (also **lingam** /ˈlɪŋgam/) a phallus, esp. as the Hindu symbol of Siva. [Sanskrit *lingam*, literally 'mark']

linger /ˈlɪŋgə/ *v.intr.* **1 a** be slow or reluctant to depart. **b** stay about a place. **c** (foll. by *over, on*, etc.) dally (*lingered over dinner*). **2** (foll. by *on*) of an action or condition) be protracted; drag on (*his cold lingered on*; *the memory lingered on*). **3** (foll. by *on*) (of a dying person or custom) be slow in dying; drag on feebly. □ **lingerer** *n.* **lingering** *adj.***lingeringly** *adv.* [Middle English *lenger*, frequentative of *leng*, via Old English *lengan* from Germanic: related to LENGTHEN]

lingerie /ˈlãʒ(ə)ri/ *n.* women's underwear and nightclothes. [French from *linge* 'linen']

lingo /ˈlɪŋgəʊ/ *n.* (*pl.* **-os** or **-oes**) *colloq.* **1** a foreign language. **2** the vocabulary of a special subject or group of people. [probably via Portuguese *lingoa* from Latin *lingua* 'tongue']

lingua franca /lɪŋgwə 'fraŋkə/ *n.* (*pl.* **lingua francas**) **1** a language adopted as a common language between speakers whose native languages are different. **2** a system for mutual understanding. **3** *hist.* a mixture of Italian with French, Greek, Arabic, and Spanish, used in the Levant. [Italian, = Frankish tongue]

lingual /'lɪŋgw(ə)l/ *adj.* **1** of or formed by the tongue. **2** of speech or languages. □ **lingualize** *v.tr.* (also **-ise**). **lingually** *adv.* [medieval Latin *lingualis* from Latin *lingua* 'tongue, language']

linguiform /'lɪŋgwɪfɔ:m/ *adj. Bot., Zool., & Anat.* tongue-shaped. [Latin *lingua* 'tongue' + -FORM]

linguine /lɪŋ'gwi:ni/ *n.pl.* pasta in the form of narrow ribbons. [Italian, pl. of *linguina*, diminutive of *lingua* 'tongue']

linguist /'lɪŋgwɪst/ *n.* a person skilled in languages or linguistics. [Latin *lingua* 'language']

linguistic /lɪŋ'gwɪstɪk/ *adj.* of or relating to language or the study of languages. □ **linguistically** *adv.*

linguistics /lɪŋ'gwɪstɪks/ *n.* the scientific study of language and its structure. □ **linguistician** /-'stɪʃ(ə)n/ *n.* [French *linguistique* or German *Linguistik* (as LINGUIST)]

liniment /'lɪnɪm(ə)nt/ *n.* an embrocation, usu. made with oil. [Late Latin *linimentum* from Latin *linire* 'smear']

lining /'lʌɪnɪŋ/ *n.* **1** a layer of material used to line a surface etc. **2** an inside layer or surface etc. (*stomach lining*).

link[1] /lɪŋk/ *n. & v.* ● *n.* **1** one loop or ring of a chain etc. **2 a** a connecting part, esp. a thing or person that unites or provides continuity; one in a series. **b** a state or means of connection. **3** a means of contact by radio or telephone between two points. **4** a means of travel or transport between two places. **5** = CUFF LINK. **6** a measure equal to one-hundredth of a surveying chain (7.92 inches). ● *v.* **1** *tr.* (foll. by *together*, *to*, *with*) connect or join (two things or one to another). **2** *tr.* clasp or intertwine (hands or arms). **3** *intr.* (foll. by *on*, *to*, *in to*) be joined; attach oneself to (a system, company, etc.). □ **link up** (foll. by *with*) connect or combine. [Middle English via Old Norse from Germanic]

link[2] /lɪŋk/ *n. hist.* a torch of pitch and tow for lighting the way in dark streets. [16th c.: perhaps via medieval Latin *li(n)chinus* 'wick' from Greek *lukhnos* 'light']

linkage /'lɪŋkɪdʒ/ *n.* **1** the action of linking; a link or system of links. **2 a** the linking of different issues in political negotiations. **b** *Genetics* the tendency of genes on the same chromosome to be inherited together.

linkman /'lɪŋkman/ *n.* (*pl.* **-men**) **1** *Brit.* a person providing continuity in a broadcast programme. **2** a player between the forwards and half-backs or strikers and backs in football etc.

links /lɪŋks/ *n.pl.* **1** (treated as *sing.* or *pl.*) a golf course, esp. one having undulating ground, coarse grass, etc. **2** *Sc. dial.* level or undulating sandy ground near a seashore, with turf and coarse grass. [pl. of *link* 'rising ground' from Old English *hlinc*]

link-up *n.* an act or result of linking up.

linn /lɪn/ *n. Sc.* **1 a** a waterfall. **b** a pool below this. **2** a precipice; a ravine. [Gaelic *linne*]

Linnaean /lɪ'ni:ən, lɪ'neɪən/ *adj. & n.* ● *adj.* of or relating to the Swedish naturalist Linnaeus (Linné, d. 1778) or his system of binomial nomenclature in the classification of plants and animals. ● *n.* a follower of Linnaeus.

■ **Usage** This word is spelt *Linnean* in *Linnean Society*.

linnet /'lɪnɪt/ *n.* a finch, *Acanthis cannabina*, with brown and grey plumage. [Old French *linette* from *lin* 'flax' (the bird feeding on flaxseeds)]

lino /'lʌɪnəʊ/ *n.* (*pl.* **-os**) linoleum. [abbreviation]

linocut /'lʌɪnəʊkʌt/ *n.* **1** a design or form carved in relief on a block of linoleum. **2** a print made from this. □ **linocutting** *n.*

linoleic acid /lɪnə(ʊ)'li:ɪk, -'leɪɪk/ *n. Chem.* a polyunsaturated fatty acid occurring as a glyceride in linseed and other oils and essential in the human diet. [Latin *linum* 'flax' + OLEIC ACID]

linolenic acid /lɪnə(ʊ)'lɛnɪk, -'li:nɪk/ *n. Chem.* a polyunsaturated fatty acid (with one more double bond than linoleic acid) occurring as a glyceride in linseed and other oils and essential in the human diet. [German *Linolensaüre* from *Linolsaüre* LINOLEIC ACID with *-ene-* inserted]

linoleum /lɪ'nəʊlɪəm/ *n.* a material consisting of a canvas backing thickly coated with a preparation of linseed oil and powdered cork etc., used esp. as a floor covering. □ **linoleumed** *adj.* [Latin *linum* 'flax' + *oleum* 'oil']

Linotype /'lʌɪnə(ʊ)tʌɪp/ *n. Printing propr.* a composing machine producing lines of words as single strips of metal, used esp. for newspapers. [= *line o' type*]

linsang /'lɪnsaŋ/ *n.* any of various civet-like mammals, esp. of the genera *Prionodon* of SE Asia and *Poiana* of Africa. [Javanese]

linseed /'lɪnsi:d/ *n.* the seed of flax. [Old English *līnsǣd*, from *līn* 'flax' + *sǣd* 'seed']

linseed cake *n.* pressed linseed used as cattle food.

linseed meal *n.* ground linseed.

linseed oil *n.* oil extracted from linseed and used in paint and varnish.

linsey-woolsey /lɪnzɪ'wʊlzi/ *n.* a fabric of coarse wool woven on a cotton warp. [Middle English from *linsey* 'coarse linen', probably from *Lindsey*, a village in Suffolk where the material was first made + WOOL, with jingling ending]

linstock /'lɪnstɒk/ *n. hist.* a match-holder used to fire cannon. [earlier *lintstock* from Dutch *lontstok*, from *lont* 'match' + *stok* 'stick', with assimilation to LINT]

lint /lɪnt/ *n.* **1** *Brit.* a fabric, originally of linen, with a raised nap on one side, used for dressing wounds. **2** fluff. **3** *Sc.* flax. □ **linty** *adj.* [Middle English *lyn(n)et*, perhaps from Old French *linette* 'linseed', from *lin* 'flax']

lintel /'lɪnt(ə)l/ *n. Archit.* a horizontal supporting piece of timber, stone, etc., across the top of a door or window. □ **lintelled** *adj.* (*US* **linteled**). [Middle English via Old French *lintel* 'threshold' from Romanic, influenced by Late Latin *liminare* from Latin *limen* 'threshold']

linter /'lɪntə/ *n. US* **1** a machine for removing the short fibres from cotton seeds after ginning. **2** (in *pl.*) these fibres. [LINT + -ER[1]]

liny /'lʌɪni/ *adj.* (**linier**, **liniest**) marked with lines; wrinkled.

lion /'lʌɪən/ *n.* **1** (*fem.* **lioness** /-nɪs/) a large flesh-eating cat, *Panthera leo*, of Africa and S. Asia, with a tawny coat and, in the male, a flowing shaggy mane. **2** (**the Lion**) the zodiacal sign or constellation Leo. **3** a brave or celebrated person. **4** the lion as a national emblem of Great Britain or as a representation in heraldry. □ **lion-like** *adj.* [Middle English via Anglo-French *liun* and Latin *leo -onis* from Greek *leōn leontos*]

lion-heart *n.* a courageous person (esp. as a sobriquet of Richard I of England).

lion-hearted *adj.* brave and generous.

lionize /'lʌɪənʌɪz/ *v.tr.* (also **-ise**) treat as a celebrity. □ **lionization** /-'zeɪʃ(ə)n/ *n.* **lionizer** *n.*

lion's share *n.* (prec. by *the*) the largest or best part.

lip /lɪp/ *n. & v.* ● *n.* **1 a** either of the two fleshy parts forming the edges of the mouth-opening. **b** a thing resembling these. **c** = LABIUM. **2** the edge of a cup, container, etc., esp. the part shaped for pouring from. **3** *colloq.* impudent talk (*that's enough of your lip!*). ● *v.tr.* (**lipped**, **lipping**) **1 a** touch with the lips; apply the lips to. **b** touch lightly. **2** *Golf* **a** hit a ball just to the edge of (a hole). **b** (of a ball) reach the edge of (a hole) but fail to drop in. □ **bite one's lip** repress an emotion; stifle laughter, a retort, etc. **curl one's lip** express scorn. **hang on a person's lips** listen attentively to a person.

lick one's lips see LICK. **pass a person's lips** be eaten, drunk, spoken, etc. **smack one's lips** part the lips noisily in relish or anticipation, esp. of food. □ **lipless** *adj.* **liplike** *adj.* **lipped** *adj.* (also in *comb.*). [Old English *lippa*, from Germanic]

lipase /ˈlɪpeɪz, ˈlʌɪp-/ *n. Biochem.* any enzyme that catalyses the breakdown of fats. [Greek *lipos* 'fat' + -ASE]

lipid /ˈlɪpɪd/ *n. Chem.* any of a class of organic compounds that are insoluble in water but soluble in organic solvents, including fatty acids, oils, waxes, and steroids. [French *lipide* (as LIPASE)]

lipidosis /lɪpɪˈdəʊsɪs/ *n.* (also **lipoidosis** /lɪpɔɪ-/) (*pl.* **-doses** /-siːz/) any disorder of lipid metabolism in the body tissues.

Lipizzaner /lɪpɪtˈsɑːnə, lɪpɪˈzeɪnə/ *n.* (also **Lippizaner**) **1** a horse of a fine white breed used esp. in displays of dressage. **2** this breed. [German, from *Lippiza* in Slovenia]

lipography /lɪˈpɒɡrəfi/ *n.* the omission of letters or words in writing. [Greek *lip-*, stem of *leipō* 'omit' + -GRAPHY]

lipoid /ˈlɪpɔɪd/ *adj.* resembling fat. [Greek *lipos* 'fat']

lipoprotein /ˈlɪpə(ʊ),prəʊtiːn, ˈlʌɪ-/ *n. Biochem.* any of a group of soluble proteins that combine with and transport fat or other lipids in the blood plasma. [Greek *lipos* 'fat' + PROTEIN]

liposome /ˈlɪpəsəʊm, ˈlʌɪ-/ *n. Biochem.* a minute artificial spherical sac usu. of a phospholipid membrane enclosing an aqueous core, esp. used to carry drugs to specific tissues. [German *Liposom* (as Greek *lipos* 'fat', -SOME[3])]

liposuction /ˈlɪpə(ʊ)sʌkʃ(ə)n, ˈlʌɪ-/ *n.* a technique in cosmetic surgery for removing excess fat from under the skin by suction. [Greek *lipos* 'fat' + SUCTION]

Lippizaner var. of LIPIZZANER.

lippy /ˈlɪpi/ *adj.* (**lippier**, **lippiest**) *colloq.* **1** insolent, impertinent. **2** talkative.

lip-read *v.tr.* (*past* and *past part.* **-read** /red/) (also *absol.*) (esp. of a deaf person) understand (speech) entirely from observing a speaker's lip movements. □ **lip-reader** *n.*

lipsalve /ˈlɪpsalv/ *n. Brit.* **1** a preparation, usu. in stick form, to prevent or relieve sore lips. **2** flattery.

lip-service *n.* an insincere expression of support etc.

lipstick /ˈlɪpstɪk/ *n.* a small stick of cosmetic for colouring the lips.

lip-sync *n.* & *v.* (also **-synch**) ● *n.* (in film acting etc) the movement of a performer's lips in sychronization with a pre-recorded soundtrack. ● *v.tr.* & *intr.* perform (esp. a song) on film using this technique. □ **lip-syncer** *n.* **lip-syncing** *n.*

liquate /lɪˈkweɪt/ *v.tr.* separate or purify (metals) by liquefying. □ **liquation** /-ˈkweɪʃ(ə)n/ *n.* [Latin *liquare* 'melt': related to LIQUOR]

liquefy /ˈlɪkwɪfʌɪ/ *v.tr.* & *intr.* (also **liquify**) (**-ies**, **-ied**) *Chem.* make or become liquid. □ **liquefacient** /-ˈfeɪʃ(ə)nt/ *adj.* & *n.* **liquefaction** /-ˈfakʃ(ə)n/ *n.* **liquefactive** /-ˈfaktɪv/ *adj.* **liquefiable** *adj.* **liquefier** *n.* [French *liquéfier* from Latin *liquefacere*, from *liquēre* 'be liquid']

liquescent /lɪˈkwɛs(ə)nt/ *adj.* becoming or apt to become liquid. [Latin *liquescere* (as LIQUEFY)]

liqueur /lɪˈkjʊə/ *n.* any of several strong sweet alcoholic spirits, variously flavoured, usu. drunk after a meal. [French, = LIQUOR]

liquid /ˈlɪkwɪd/ *adj.* & *n.* ● *adj.* **1** having a consistency like that of water or oil, flowing freely but of constant volume. **2** having the qualities of water in appearance; translucent (*liquid blue*; *a liquid lustre*). **3** (of a gas, e.g. air, hydrogen) reduced to a liquid state by intense cold. **4** (of sounds) clear and pure; harmonious, fluent. **5 a** (of assets) easily converted into cash. **b** having ready cash or liquid assets (*prompting investors to stay liquid*). **6** not fixed; fluid (*liquid opinions*). ● *n.* a liquid substance. □ **liquidly** *adv.* **liquidness** *n.* [Middle English from Latin *liquidus*, from *liquēre* 'be liquid']

liquidambar /lɪkwɪdˈambə/ *n.* **1** any tree of the genus *Liquidambar* yielding a resinous gum. **2** this gum. [modern Latin, apparently from Latin *liquidus* (see LIQUID) + medieval Latin *ambar* 'amber']

liquidate /ˈlɪkwɪdeɪt/ *v.* **1 a** *tr.* wind up the affairs of (a company or firm) by ascertaining liabilities and apportioning assets. **b** *intr.* (of a company) be liquidated. **2** *tr.* clear or pay off (a debt). **3** *tr.* eliminate by killing; wipe out. [medieval Latin *liquidare* 'make clear' (as LIQUID)]

liquidation /lɪkwɪˈdeɪʃ(ə)n/ *n.* **1** the process of liquidating a company etc. **2** elimination by killing. □ **go into liquidation** (of a company etc.) be wound up and have its assets apportioned.

liquidator /ˈlɪkwɪdeɪtə/ *n.* a person called in to wind up the affairs of a company etc.

liquid crystal *n.* a turbid liquid with some order in its molecular arrangement.

liquid crystal display *n.* a form of visual display in electronic devices, in which the reflectivity of a matrix of liquid crystals changes as a signal is applied.

liquidity /lɪˈkwɪdɪti/ *n.* (*pl.* **-ies**) **1** the state of being liquid. **2 a** availability of liquid assets. **b** (in *pl.*) liquid assets. [French *liquidité* or medieval Latin *liquiditas* (as LIQUID)]

liquidize /ˈlɪkwɪdʌɪz/ *v.tr.* (also **-ise**) reduce (esp. food) to a liquid or puréed state.

liquidizer /ˈlɪkwɪdʌɪzə/ *n.* (also **-iser**) a machine for liquidizing.

liquid measure *n.* a unit for measuring the volume of liquids.

liquid paraffin *n.* esp. *Brit.* a colourless odourless oily liquid obtained from petroleum and used as a laxative.

liquid storax see STORAX 2.

liquify var. of LIQUEFY.

liquor /ˈlɪkə/ *n.* & *v.* ● *n.* **1** an alcoholic (esp. distilled) drink. **2** water used in brewing. **3** other liquid, esp. that produced in cooking. **4** *Pharm.* a solution of a specified drug in water. ● *v.tr.* **1** dress (leather) with grease or oil. **2** steep (malt etc.) in water. [Middle English via Old French *lic(o)ur* from Latin *liquor -oris* (as LIQUID)]

liquorice /ˈlɪk(ə)rɪs, -rɪʃ/ *n.* (esp. *US* **licorice**) **1** a black root extract used as a sweet and in medicine. **2** the leguminous plant *Glycyrrhiza glabra* from which it is obtained. [Middle English via Anglo-French *lycorys*, Old French *licoresse*, and Late Latin *liquiritia* from Greek *glukurrhiza*, from *glukus* 'sweet' + *rhiza* 'root']

liquorish /ˈlɪkərɪʃ/ *adj.* **1** = LICKERISH. **2** fond of or indicating a fondness for liquor. □ **liquorishly** *adv.* **liquorishness** *n.* [variant of LICKERISH, misapplied]

lira /ˈlɪərə/ *n.* (*pl.* **lire** /ˈlɪərə, ˈlɪəreɪ, ˈlɪəri/) **1** the chief monetary unit of Italy. **2** the chief monetary unit of Turkey. [Italian, via Provençal *liura* from Latin *libra* 'pound' (weight etc.)]

lisle /lʌɪl/ *n.* (in full **lisle thread**) a fine smooth cotton thread for stockings etc. [*Lisle*, former spelling of *Lille* in France, where originally made]

lisp /lɪsp/ *n.* & *v.* ● *n.* **1** a speech defect in which *s* is pronounced like *th* in *thick* and *z* is pronounced like *th* in *this*. **2** a rippling of waters; a rustling of leaves. ● *v.intr.* & *tr.* speak or utter with a lisp. □ **lisper** *n.* **lispingly** *adv.* [Old English *wlispian* (recorded in *āwlyspian*) from *wlisp* (*adj.*) 'lisping', of uncertain origin]

lissom /ˈlɪs(ə)m/ *adj.* (also **lissome**) lithe, supple, agile. □ **lissomly** *adv.* **lissomness** *n.* [ultimately from LITHE + -SOME[1]]

list[1] /lɪst/ *n.* & *v.* ● *n.* **1** a number of connected items, names, etc., written or printed together usu. consecutively to form a record or aid to memory (*shopping list*). **2** (in *pl.*) *hist.* **a** palisades enclosing an area for a tournament. **b** the scene of a contest. **3** esp. *Brit.* **a** a selvedge or edge of cloth, usu. of different material from the main body. **b** such edges collectively used as a material. ● *v.* **1** *tr.* make a list of. **2** *tr.* enter in a list. **3** *tr.* (as **listed** *adj.*) **a** (of securities) approved for dealings on the Stock Exchange. **b** (of a building in the UK) officially designated as being of historical importance and having protection from demolition or major alterations. **4** *tr. & intr. archaic* enlist. □ **enter the lists** issue or accept a challenge. □ **listable** *adj.* [Old English *liste* 'border, strip', from Germanic]

list[2] /lɪst/ *v. & n.* ● *v.intr.* (of a ship etc.) lean over to one side, esp. owing to a leak or shifting cargo (cf. HEEL[2] *v.* 1). ● *n.* the process or an instance of listing. [17th c.: origin unknown]

listen /ˈlɪs(ə)n/ *v.intr.* **1 a** make an effort to hear something. **b** attentively hear a person speaking. **2** (often foll. by *to*) **a** give attention with the ear (*listened to my story*). **b** take notice of; respond to advice or a request or to the person expressing it. **3** (also **listen out**) (often foll. by *for*) seek to hear or be aware of by waiting alertly. □ **listen in 1** eavesdrop; tap a private (esp. telephone) conversation. **2** use a radio receiving set. [Old English *hlysnan*, from West Germanic]

listenable /ˈlɪs(ə)nəb(ə)l/ *adj.* easy or pleasant to listen to. □ **listenability** /-əˈbɪlɪti/ *n.*

listener /ˈlɪs(ə)nə/ *n.* **1** a person who listens. **2** a person receiving broadcast radio programmes.

listening post *n.* **1 a** a point near an enemy's lines for detecting movements by sound. **b** a station for intercepting electronic communications. **2** a place for the gathering of information from reports etc.

lister /ˈlɪstə/ *n. US* a plough with a double mould-board. [*list* 'prepare land for a crop' (as LIST[1]) + -ER[1]]

listeria /lɪˈstɪərɪə/ *n.* any motile rodlike bacterium of the genus *Listeria*, esp. *L. monocytogenes* infecting humans and animals eating contaminated food. [modern Latin, named after J. *Lister*, English surgeon d. 1912]

listeriosis /lɪˌstɪərɪˈəʊsɪs/ *n.* infection with listeria; a disease resulting from this.

listing /ˈlɪstɪŋ/ *n.* **1** a list or catalogue (see LIST[1] 1). **2 a** the drawing up of a list. **b** an entry in a list or register. **3** *Brit.* selvedge (see LIST[1] *n.* 3).

listless /ˈlɪs(t)lɪs/ *adj.* lacking energy or enthusiasm; disinclined for exertion. □ **listlessly** *adv.* **listlessness** *n.* [Middle English, from obsolete *list* 'appetite, desire' + -LESS]

list price *n.* the price of something as shown in a published list.

lit *past* and *past part.* of LIGHT[1], LIGHT[2].

litany /ˈlɪt(ə)ni/ *n.* (*pl.* **-ies**) **1 a** a series of petitions for use in church services or processions, usu. recited by the clergy and responded to in a recurring formula by the people. **b** (**the Litany**) such petitions and responses contained in the Book of Common Prayer. **2** a tedious recital (*a litany of woes*). [Middle English via Old French *letanie* and ecclesiastical Latin *litania* from Greek *litaneia* 'prayer', from *litē* 'supplication']

litchi var. of LYCHEE.

lit crit /lɪt krɪt/ *abbr.* literary criticism.

lite /lʌɪt/ *adj. & n.* ● *adj.* **1** (also *propr.* **Lite**) applied to low-fat or low-sugar versions of manufactured food or drink products, esp. to low-calorie beer. **2** *US colloq.* lacking in substance; facile, over-simplified. ● *n.* **1** (also *propr.* **Lite**) a light beer with relatively few calories. **2** a light esp. a courtesy light in a motor vehicle. [variant of LIGHT[1,2], now usu. a deliberate respelling]

-lite /lʌɪt/ *suffix* forming names of minerals and fossils (*rhyolite*; *zeolite*). [French, from Greek *lithos* 'stone']

liter *US* var. of LITRE.

literacy /ˈlɪt(ə)rəsi/ *n.* the ability to read and write. [LITERATE + -ACY, on the pattern of *illiteracy*]

literae humaniores /ˌlɪtərʌɪ hjuːˌmanɪˈɔːriːz/ *n. Brit.* the honours course in classics, philosophy, and ancient history at Oxford University. [Latin, = the more humane studies]

literal /ˈlɪt(ə)r(ə)l/ *adj. & n.* ● *adj.* **1** taking words in their usual or primary sense without metaphor or allegory (*literal interpretation*). **2** following the letter, text, or exact or original words (*literal translation*; *a literal transcript*). **3** (in full **literal-minded**) (of a person) prosaic; matter-of-fact. **4 a** not exaggerated (*the literal truth*). **b** so called without exaggeration (*a literal extermination*). **5** *colloq. disp.* so called with some exaggeration or using metaphor (*a literal avalanche of mail*). **6** of, in, or expressed by a letter or the letters of the alphabet. **7** *Algebra* not numerical. ● *n. Brit. Printing* a misprint of a letter. □ **literality** /-ˈralɪti/ *n.* **literalize** *v.tr.* (also **-ise**). **literally** *adv.* **literalness** *n.* [Middle English via Old French *literal* or Late Latin *litteralis* from Latin *littera* (as LETTER)]

■ **Usage** The use of *literal* and *literally* simply as intensifiers (see sense 5 above) should be avoided in writing or formal speech.

literalism /ˈlɪt(ə)r(ə)lɪz(ə)m/ *n.* insistence on a literal interpretation; adherence to the letter. □ **literalist** *n.* **literalistic** /-ˈlɪstɪk/ *adj.*

literary /ˈlɪt(ə)(rə)ri/ *adj.* **1** of, constituting, or occupied with books or literature or written composition, esp. of the kind valued for quality of form. **2** well informed about literature. **3** (of a word or idiom) used chiefly in literary works or other formal writing. □ **literarily** *adv.* **literariness** *n.* [Latin *litterarius* (as LETTER)]

literary criticism *n.* the art or practice of estimating the qualities and character of literary works. □ **literary critic** *n.*

literary executor *n.* a person entrusted with a writer's papers, unpublished works, etc.

literary history *n.* the history of the treatment of a subject in literature.

literate /ˈlɪt(ə)rət/ *adj. & n.* ● *adj.* able to read and write; educated. ● *n.* a literate person. □ **literately** *adv.* [Middle English from Latin *litteratus* (as LETTER)]

literati /lɪtəˈrɑːtiː/ *n.pl.* **1** men of letters. **2** the learned class. [Latin, pl. of *literatus* (as LETTER)]

literatim /lɪtəˈrɑːtɪm, -ˈreɪtɪm/ *adv.* letter for letter; textually, literally. [medieval Latin]

literation /lɪtəˈreɪʃ(ə)n/ *n.* the representation of sounds etc. by a letter or group of letters. [Latin *litera* LETTER]

literature /ˈlɪt(ə)rətʃə/ *n.* **1** written works, esp. those whose value lies in beauty of language or in emotional effect. **2** the realm of letters. **3** the writings of a country or period. **4** literary production. **5** *colloq.* printed matter, leaflets, etc. **6** the material in print on a particular subject (*there is a considerable literature on geraniums*). [Middle English, = literary culture, from Latin *litteratura* (as LITERATE)]

-lith /lɪθ/ *suffix* denoting types of stone (*laccolith*; *monolith*). [Greek *lithos* 'stone']

litharge /ˈlɪθɑːdʒ/ *n.* a red or yellow mineral form of lead monoxide, used as a pigment and in glass and ceramics. [Middle English via Old French *litarge* and Latin *lithargyrus* from Greek *litharguros*, from *lithos* 'stone' + *arguros* 'silver']

lithe /lʌɪð/ *adj.* flexible, supple. □ **lithely** *adv.* **litheness** *n.* **lithesome** *adj.* [Old English *līthe*, from Germanic]

lithia /ˈlɪθɪə/ *n.* lithium oxide, a white alkaline solid. [modern Latin, alteration of earlier *lithion* from Greek neut. of *litheios*, from *lithos* 'stone', on the pattern of *soda* etc.]

lithic /ˈlɪθɪk/ *adj.* **1** of, like, or made of stone. **2** *Med.* of a calculus. [Greek *lithikos*, from *lithos* 'stone']

lithium /ˈlɪθɪəm/ *n. Chem.* a soft silver-white metallic element, the lightest metal, used in alloys and in batteries (symbol **Li**). [LITHIA + -IUM]

litho /ˈlʌɪθəʊ, ˈlɪθ-/ *n. & v. colloq.* ● *n.* (*pl.* **-os**) **1** = LITHOGRAPHY. **2** = LITHOGRAPH. ● *v.tr.* (**-oes, -oed**) produce by lithography. [abbreviation]

litho- /ˈlɪθəʊ/ *comb. form* stone. [Greek *lithos* 'stone']

lithograph /ˈlɪθə(ʊ)grɑːf, ˈlʌɪ-/ *n. & v.* ● *n.* a lithographic print. ● *v.tr.* **1** print by lithography. **2** write or engrave on stone. [back-formation from LITHOGRAPHY]

lithography /lɪˈθɒgrəfi/ *n.* a process of obtaining prints from a stone or metal surface so treated that what is to be printed can be inked but the remaining area rejects ink. ▫ **lithographer** *n.* **lithographic** /lɪθə(ʊ)ˈgrafɪk/ *adj.* **lithographically** /lɪθə(ʊ)ˈgrafɪk(ə)li/ *adv.* [German *Lithographie* (as LITHO-, -GRAPHY)]

lithology /lɪˈθɒlədʒi/ *n.* the science of the general physical characteristics of rocks (cf. PETROLOGY). ▫ **lithological** /-θəˈlɒdʒɪk(ə)l/ *adj.*

lithophyte /ˈlɪθə(ʊ)fʌɪt/ *n. Bot.* a plant that grows on stone.

lithopone /ˈlɪθə(ʊ)pəʊn/ *n.* a white pigment of zinc sulphide, barium sulphate, and zinc oxide. [LITHO- + Greek *ponos* '(thing) produced by work']

lithosphere /ˈlɪθə(ʊ)sfɪə/ *n. Geol.* the rigid outer part of the earth consisting of the crust and upper mantle. ▫ **lithospheric** /-ˈsfɛrɪk/ *adj.*

lithotomy /lɪˈθɒtəmi/ *n.* (*pl.* **-ies**) the surgical removal of a calculus from the bladder or urinary tract. ▫ **lithotomist** *n.* **lithotomize** *v.tr.* (also **-ise**). [Late Latin from Greek *lithotomia* (as LITHO-, -TOMY)]

lithotripsy /ˈlɪθə(ʊ)trɪpsi/ *n.* (*pl.* **-ies**) a treatment using ultrasound to shatter a calculus in the bladder into small particles that can be passed through the urethra. ▫ **lithotripter** *n.* **lithotriptic** *adj.* [LITHO- + Greek *tripsis* 'rubbing' from *tribo* 'rub']

Lithuanian /lɪθjʊˈeɪnɪən, lɪθʊ-/ *n.* & *adj.* ● *n.* **1 a** a native of Lithuania, a Baltic republic. **b** a person of Lithuanian descent. **2** the language of Lithuania. ● *adj.* of or relating to Lithuania, its people, or its language.

litigant /ˈlɪtɪg(ə)nt/ *n.* & *adj.* ● *n.* a party to a lawsuit. ● *adj.* engaged in a lawsuit. [French (as LITIGATE)]

litigate /ˈlɪtɪgeɪt/ *v.* **1** *intr.* go to law; be a party to a lawsuit. **2** *tr.* contest (a point) in a lawsuit. ▫ **litigable** /ˈlɪtɪgəb(ə)l/ *adj.* **litigation** /-ˈgeɪʃ(ə)n/ *n.* **litigator** *n.* [Latin *litigare litigat-* from *lis litis* 'lawsuit']

litigious /lɪˈtɪdʒəs/ *adj.* **1** given to litigation; unreasonably fond of going to law. **2** disputable in a law court; offering matter for a lawsuit. **3** of lawsuits. ▫ **litigiously** *adv.* **litigiousness** *n.* [Middle English from Old French *litigieux* or Latin *litigiosus* from *litigium* 'litigation': see LITIGATE]

litmus /ˈlɪtməs/ *n.* a dye obtained from lichens that is red under acid conditions and blue under alkaline conditions. [Middle English from Old Norse *lit-mosi*, from *litr* 'dye' + *mosi* 'moss']

litmus paper *n.* a paper stained with litmus for use as a test for acids or alkalis.

litmus test *n. colloq.* a real or decisively indicative test.

litotes /lʌɪˈtəʊtiːz/ *n.* ironical understatement, esp. the expressing of an affirmative by the negative of its contrary (e.g. *I shan't be sorry* for *I shall be glad*). [Late Latin from Greek *litotēs*, from *litos* 'plain, meagre']

litre /ˈliːtə/ *n.* (*US* **liter**) a metric unit of capacity, formerly defined as the volume of one kilogram of water under standard conditions, now equal to 1,000 cubic centimetres (about 1.75 pints). ▫ **litreage** /ˈliːt(ə)rɪdʒ/ *n.* [French from *litron*, an obsolete measure of capacity, via medieval Latin from Greek *litra*, a Sicilian monetary unit]

Litt.D. *abbr.* Doctor of Letters. [Latin *Litterarum Doctor*]

litter /ˈlɪtə/ *n.* & *v.* ● *n.* **1 a** refuse, esp. paper, discarded in an open or public place. **b** odds and ends lying about. **c** (*attrib.*) for disposing of litter (*litter bin*). **2** a state of untidiness; disorderly accumulation of papers etc. **3** a number of young animals brought forth at a birth. **4** a vehicle containing a couch shut in by curtains and carried on men's shoulders or by beasts of burden. **5** a framework with a couch for transporting the sick and wounded. **6 a** straw, rushes, etc., as bedding, esp. for animals. **b** straw and dung in a farmyard. **7** granular absorbent material for lining a box for a cat to urinate and defecate in indoors. ● *v.tr.* **1** make (a place) untidy with discarded refuse. **2** scatter untidily and leave lying about. **3** give birth to (whelps etc.). **4** (often foll. by *down*)) **a** provide (a horse etc.) with litter as bedding. **b** spread litter or straw on (a floor) or in (a stable). ▫ **littery** *adj.* (in senses 1a, b, & 2 of *n.*). [Middle English via Anglo-French *litere*, Old French *litiere* from medieval Latin *lectaria*, from Latin *lectus* 'bed']

littérateur /lɪtərɑːˈtəː/ *n.* a literary person. [French]

litterbug /ˈlɪtəbʌg/ *n. colloq.* = LITTER LOUT.

litter lout *n. Brit.* a person who carelessly drops litter in a public place.

little /ˈlɪt(ə)l/ *adj., det., pron., & adv.* ● *adj.* (**littler**, **littlest**; **less** /lɛs/ or **lesser** /ˈlɛsə/; **least** /liːst/) **1** small in size, amount, degree, etc.; not great or big: also used with affectionate or emotional overtones, or condescension, not implied by *small* (*a friendly little chap*; *a silly little fool*; *a nice little car*). **2 a** short in stature (*a little man*). **b** of short distance or duration (*will go a little way with you*; *wait a little while*). **3** trivial; relatively unimportant (*exaggerates every little difficulty*). **4** operating on a small scale (*the little shopkeeper*). **5** as a distinctive epithet: **a** of a smaller or the smallest size etc. (*little finger*). **b** that is the smaller or smallest of the name (*little auk*; *little grebe*). **6** young or younger (*a little boy*; *my little sister*). **7** as of a child, evoking tenderness, condescension, amusement, etc. (*we know their little ways*). **8** mean, paltry, contemptible (*you little sneak*). ● *det.* **1** (prec. by *a*) a certain though small amount of (*give me a little butter*). **2** not much; inconsiderable (*gained little advantage from it*). ● *pron.* **1** not much; only a small amount (*got very little out of it*; *did what little I could*). **2** (usu. prec. by a determiner) **a** a certain but no great amount (*knows a little of everything*; *every little helps*). **b** a short time or distance (*after a little*). ● *adv.* (**less**, **least**) **1** to a small extent only (*little-known authors*; *is little more than speculation*). **2** not at all; hardly (*they little thought*). **3** (prec. by *a*) somewhat (*is a little deaf*). ▫ **in little** on a small scale. **little by little** by degrees; gradually. **little or nothing** hardly anything. **no little** considerable; a good deal of (*took no little trouble over it*). **not a little** *n.* much; a great deal. ● *adv.* extremely (*not a little concerned*). ▫ **littleness** *n.* [Old English *lȳtel*, from Germanic]

little auk *n.* a small Arctic auk, *Plautus alle.*

Little Bear *n.Astron.* = URSA MINOR.

little end *n. Mech.* the smaller end of a connecting rod, attached to the piston.

little finger *n.* the smallest finger, at the outer end of the hand.

little grebe *n.* a small waterbird of the grebe family, *Tachybaptus ruficollis.*

little green man *n.* an imaginary person of peculiar appearance, esp. from outer space. Cf. GREEN MAN.

little man *n.* **1** esp. *joc.* (as a form of address) a boy. **2** the average 'man in the street'.

little ones *n.pl.* young children or animals.

little owl *n.* a small owl, *Athene noctua*, of Africa and Eurasia, with speckled plumage.

little people *n.pl.* (prec. by *the*) fairies.

Little Russian *n.* & *adj. hist.* ● *n.* a Ukrainian. ● *adj.* Ukrainian.

little slam *n. Bridge* = SMALL SLAM.

little woman *n.* (prec. by *the*) *colloq.* often *derog.* one's wife.

littoral /ˈlɪt(ə)r(ə)l/ *adj.* & *n.* ● *adj.* of or on the shore of the sea, a lake, etc. ● *n.* a region lying along a shore. [Latin *littoralis* from *litus litoris* 'shore']

liturgical /lɪˈtəːdʒɪk(ə)l/ *adj.* of or related to liturgies or public worship. ▫ **liturgically** *adv.* **liturgist** /ˈlɪtədʒɪst/ *n.* [medieval Latin from Greek *leitourgikos* (as LITURGY)]

liturgy /ˈlɪtədʒi/ *n.* (*pl.* **-ies**) **1 a** a form of public worship, esp. in the Christian Church. **b** a set of formularies for this. **c** public worship in accordance with a prescribed form. **2** (**Liturgy**) the Communion office of the Orthodox Church. **3** (**the Liturgy**) the Book of Common Prayer. **4** *Gk Hist.* a public office or duty performed voluntarily by a rich Athenian. [French *liturgie* or Late Latin *liturgia* from Greek *leitourgia* 'public service, worship of the gods', via *leitourgos* 'minister' from *leit-* 'public' + *ergon* 'work']

livable var. of LIVEABLE.

live[1] /lɪv/ *v.* **1** *intr.* be or remain alive; have (esp. animal) life. **2** *intr.* (foll. by *on*) subsist or feed (*lives on fruit*). **3** *intr.* (foll. by *on, off*) depend for subsistence (*lives off the family; lives on income from investments*). **4** *intr.* (foll. by *on, by*) sustain one's position or repute (*live on their reputation; lives by his wits*). **5** *tr.* **a** (with compl.) spend, pass, experience (*lived a happy life*). **b** express in one's life (*was living a lie*). **6** *intr.* spend or lead one's life; conduct oneself in a specified way (*live quietly*). **7** *intr.* arrange one's habits, expenditure, feeding, etc. (*live modestly*). **8** *intr.* make or have one's abode. **9** *intr.* (foll. by *in*) spend the daytime (*the room does not seem to be lived in*). **10** *intr.* (of a person or thing) survive. **11** *intr.* (of a ship) escape destruction. **12** *intr.* enjoy life intensely or to the full (*you haven't lived till you've drunk champagne*). □ **live and let live** condone others' failings so as to be similarly tolerated. **live down** (usu. with *neg.*) cause (past guilt, embarrassment, etc.) to be forgotten by different conduct over a period of time (*you'll never live that down!*). **live in** (of a domestic employee, student, etc.) reside on the premises of one's work, college, etc. **live it up** *colloq.* enjoy life in an active and extravagant way. **live out 1** survive (a danger, difficulty, etc.). **2** (of a domestic employee, student, etc.) reside away from one's place of work, college, etc. **live through** survive; remain alive at the end of. **live to** survive and reach (*lived to a great age*). **live to oneself** live in isolation. **live together** (esp. of a man and woman not married to each other) share a home and have a sexual relationship. **live up to** honour or fulfil; put into practice (principles etc.). **live with 1** share a home with. **2** tolerate; find congenial. **long live ...!** an exclamation of loyalty (to a person etc. specified). [Old English *libban, lifian*, from Germanic]

live[2] /lʌɪv/ *adj. & adv.* ● *adj.* **1** (*attrib.*) that is alive; living. **2 a** (of a performance) given in front of a public audience; heard or seen at the time of its performance, not from a recording. **b** (of a recording etc.) made of a live performance. **c** taking place concurrently (*live telephone bidding*). **3** not obsolete or exhausted (*disarmament is still a live issue*). **4** expending or still able to expend energy in various forms, esp.: **a** (of coals) glowing, burning. **b** (of a shell) unexploded. **c** (of a match) unkindled. **d** (of a wire, terminal, device, etc.) connected to a source of electrical power. **5** (of rock) not detached, seeming to form part of the earth's frame. **6** (of a wheel or axle etc. in machinery) moving or imparting motion. ● *adv.* in order to make a live broadcast; as a live performance (*going over live now to the House of Commons; the show went out live*). □ **go live** *Computing* (of a system) become operational. [aphetic form of ALIVE]

liveable /ˈlɪvəb(ə)l/ *adj.* (also **livable**) **1** (of a house, room, climate, etc.) fit to live in. **2** (of a life) worth living. **3** (usu. **liveable with**) *colloq.* (of a person) companionable; easy to live with. □ **liveability** /-ˈbɪlɪti/ *n.* **liveableness** *n.*

live bait *n.* small fish used to entice prey.

lived-in *adj.* **1** (of a room etc.) showing signs of habitation. **2** *colloq.* (of a face) marked by experience.

live-in *attrib.adj.* **1** (of a sexual partner) cohabiting. **2** resident (*live-in nanny*).

livelihood /ˈlʌɪvlɪhʊd/ *n.* a means of living; sustenance. [Old English *līflād*, from *līf* LIFE + *lād* 'course' (see LOAD): assimilated to obsolete *livelihood* 'liveliness']

live load *n.* the weight of persons or goods in a building or vehicle.

livelong[1] /ˈlɪvlɒŋ/ *adj. poet.* or *literary* in its entire length or apparently so (*the livelong day*). [Middle English *lefe longe* (as LIEF, LONG[1]): assimilated to LIVE[1]]

livelong[2] /ˈlɪvlɒŋ/ *n.* = ORPINE. [LIVE[1] + LONG[1]]

lively /ˈlʌɪvli/ *adj.* (**livelier, liveliest**) **1** full of life; vigorous, energetic. **2** brisk (*a lively pace*). **3** vigorous, stimulating (*a lively discussion*). **4** vivacious, jolly, sociable. **5** esp. *Brit. joc.* exciting, dangerous, difficult (*the press is making things lively for them*). **6** (of a colour) bright and vivid. **7** lifelike, realistic (*a lively description*). **8** (of a boat etc.) rising lightly to the waves. □ **look lively** see LOOK. □ **livelily** *adv.* **liveliness** *n.* [Old English *līflic* (as LIFE, -LY[1])]

liven /ˈlʌɪv(ə)n/ *v.tr. & intr.* (often foll. by *up*) *colloq.* make or become more lively.

live oak *n.* an American evergreen tree, *Quercus virginiana.*

liver[1] /ˈlɪvə/ *n.* **1 a** a large lobed glandular organ in the abdomen of vertebrates, functioning in many metabolic processes including the regulation of toxic materials in the blood, secreting bile, etc. **b** a similar organ in other animals. **2** the flesh of an animal's liver as food. **3** (in full **liver colour**) a dark reddish brown. [Old English *lifer*, from Germanic]

liver[2] /ˈlɪvə/ *n.* a person who lives in a specified way (*a clean liver*).

liver chestnut *n.* a dark kind of chestnut horse.

liver-coloured *adj.* of liver colour (see LIVER[1] 3).

liver fluke *n.* either of two types of fluke, esp. *Fasciola hepatica*, the adults of which live within the liver tissues of vertebrates, and the larvae within snails.

liverish /ˈlɪv(ə)rɪʃ/ *adj.* **1** suffering from a disorder of the liver. **2** peevish, glum. □ **liverishly** *adv.* **liverishness** *n.*

liver of sulphur *n.* a liver-coloured mixture containing potassium sulphide etc., used as a lotion in skin disease.

Liverpudlian /lɪvəˈpʌdlɪən/ *n. & adj.* ● *n.* a native of Liverpool in NW England. ● *adj.* of or relating to Liverpool. [jocular from *Liverpool* + PUDDLE]

liver salts *n.pl. Brit.* salts to cure dyspepsia or biliousness.

liver sausage *n.* esp. *Brit.* a sausage containing cooked liver etc.

liverwort /ˈlɪvəwəːt/ *n.* any small leafy or thalloid bryophyte of the class Hepaticae, of which some have liver-shaped parts.

livery[1] /ˈlɪv(ə)ri/ *n.* (*pl.* **-ies**) **1 a** distinctive clothing worn by a member of a City Company, a servant, an official, etc. **b** membership of a City livery company. **2** a distinctive colour scheme in which the vehicles, aircraft, etc., of a particular company or line are painted. **3** *US* = LIVERY STABLE. **4** *hist.* a provision of food or clothing for retainers etc. **5** *Law* **a** the legal delivery of property. **b** a writ allowing this. □ **at livery** (of a horse) kept for the owner and fed and groomed for a fixed charge. □ **liveried** *adj.* (esp. in senses 1a, 2). [Middle English from Anglo-French *liveré*, Old French *livrée*, fem. past part. of *livrer* DELIVER]

livery[2] /ˈlɪvəri/ *adj.* **1** of the consistency or colour of liver. **2** *Brit.* (of soil) heavy, tenacious. **3** *colloq.* liverish.

livery company *n. Brit.* one of the London City Companies that formerly had a distinctive costume.

liveryman /ˈlɪv(ə)rɪmən/ *n.* (*pl.* **-men**) **1** *Brit.* a member of a livery company. **2** a keeper of or attendant in a livery stable.

livery stable *n.* a stable where horses are kept at livery or let out for hire.

lives *pl.* of LIFE.

livestock /ˈlʌɪvstɒk/ *n.* (usu. treated as *pl.*) animals, esp. on a farm, regarded as an asset.

liveware /ˈlʌɪvwɛː/ *n.* working personnel, esp. computer personnel, as distinct from the inanimate or abstract things they work with.

live wire *n. colloq.* an energetic and forceful person.

livid /ˈlɪvɪd/ *adj.* **1** *colloq.* furiously angry. **2 a** of a bluish leaden colour. **b** discoloured as by a bruise. □ **lividity** /lɪˈvɪdɪti/ *n.* **lividly** *adv.* **lividness** *n.* [French *livide* or Latin *lividus* from *livēre* 'be bluish']

living /ˈlɪvɪŋ/ *n. & adj.* ● *n.* **1** a livelihood or means of maintenance (*made my living as a journalist; what does* *she do for a living?*). **2** *Brit. Eccl.* a position as a vicar or rector with an income or property. **3** (prec. by *the*; treated as *pl.*) those who are alive. ● *adj.* **1** contemporary; now existent (*the greatest living poet*). **2** (of a likeness or image of a person) exact. **3** (of a language) still in vernacular use. **4** (of water) perennially flowing. **5** (of rock etc.) = LIVE[2] 5. □ **within living memory** within the memory of people still living.

living death *n.* a state of hopeless misery.

living room *n.* a room for general day use.

living wage *n.* a wage that affords the means of normal subsistence.

living will *n.* a written statement (but not legally binding) of a person's desire not to be kept alive by artificial means in circumstances such as terminal illness or serious accident.

lixiviate /lɪkˈsɪvɪeɪt/ *v.tr.* separate (a substance) into soluble and insoluble constituents by the percolation of liquid; leach. □ **lixiviation** /-ˈeɪʃ(ə)n/ *n.* [Latin *lixivius* 'made into lye' from *lix* 'lye']

lizard /ˈlɪzəd/ *n.* any reptile of the suborder Lacertilia or Sauria, having usu. a long body and tail, four legs, movable eyelids, and a rough or scaly hide. [Middle English via Old French *lesard(e)* from Latin *lacertus*]

LJ *abbr.* (*pl.* **L JJ**) *Brit.* Lord Justice.

LL *abbr. Brit.* Lord Lieutenant.

ll. *abbr.* lines.

'll *abbr. colloq.* (usu. after pronouns) shall, will (*I'll*; *that'll*).

llama /ˈlɑːmə/ *n.* **1** a S. American ruminant, *Lama glama*, kept as a beast of burden and for its soft woolly fleece. **2** the wool from this animal, or cloth made from it. [Spanish, probably from Quechua]

llanero /lɑːˈnɛːrəʊ, lj-/ *n.* (*pl.* **-os**) an inhabitant of a llano. [Spanish]

llano /ˈlɑːnəʊ, ˈljɑː-/ *n.* (*pl.* **-os**) a treeless grassy plain or steppe, esp. in S. America. [Spanish, from Latin *planum* 'plain']

LL B *abbr.* Bachelor of Laws. [Latin *legum baccalaureus*]

LL D *abbr.* Doctor of Laws. [Latin *legum doctor*]

LL M *abbr.* Master of Laws. [Latin *legum magister*]

Lloyd's /lɔɪdz/ *n.* an incorporated society of insurance underwriters in London. [after the original meeting in a coffee house established in 1688 by Edward *Lloyd*]

Lloyd's List *n.* a daily publication devoted to shipping news.

Lloyd's Register *n.* **1** an annual alphabetical list of ships assigned to various classes. **2** a society that produces this.

LM *abbr.* **1** long metre. **2** lunar module.

lm *abbr.* lumen(s).

LMS *abbr.* **1** local management of schools. **2** *hist.* London Midland and Scottish (Railway).

ln *abbr.* natural logarithm. [modern Latin *logarithmus naturalis*]

LNB *abbr.* low noise blocker (on a satellite dish).

LNER *abbr. hist.* London and North-Eastern Railway.

lo /ləʊ/ *int. archaic* calling attention to an amazing sight. □ **lo and behold** *joc.* a formula introducing a surprising or unexpected fact. [Old English *lā*, int. of surprise etc., Middle English *lō* = *lōke* LOOK]

loach /ləʊtʃ/ *n.* any small edible freshwater fish of the family Cobitidae. [Middle English from Old French *loche*, of unknown origin]

load /ləʊd/ *n.* & *v.* ● *n.* **1 a** what is carried or is to be carried; a burden. **b** an amount usu. or actually carried (often in *comb.*: *a busload of tourists*; *a lorry-load of bricks*). **2** a unit of measure or weight of certain substances. **3** a burden or commitment of work, responsibility, care, grief, etc. **4** *colloq.* **a** (in *pl.*; often foll. by *of*) plenty; a lot. **b** (**a load of**) a quantity of (*a load of nonsense*). **5 a** *Electr.* the amount of power supplied by a generating system at any given time. **b** *Electronics* an impedance or circuit that receives or develops the output of a transistor or other device. **6** the weight or force borne by the supporting part of a structure. **7** a material object or force acting as a weight or clog. **8** the resistance of machinery to motive power. ● *v.* **1** *tr.* **a** put a load on or aboard (a person, vehicle, ship, etc.). **b** place (a load or cargo) aboard a ship, on a vehicle, etc. **2** *intr.* (often foll. by *up*) (of a ship, vehicle, or person) take a load aboard, pick up a load. **3** *tr.* (often foll. by *with*) be a weight or burden upon; oppress (*loaded with responsibilities*). **4** *tr.* add material weight to; strain the bearing-capacity of (*loaded the table with food*). **5** *tr.* (also **load up**) (foll. by *with*) **a** supply overwhelmingly (*loaded us with work*). **b** assail overwhelmingly (*loaded us with abuse*). **6** *tr.* charge (a firearm) with ammunition. **7** *tr.* insert (the required operating medium) in a device, e.g. film in a camera, magnetic tape in a tape recorder, a program into a computer, etc. **8** *tr.* add an extra charge to (an insurance premium) in the case of a poorer risk. **9** *tr.* **a** weight with lead. **b** give a bias to (dice, a roulette wheel, etc.) with weights. □ **get a load of** *slang* listen attentively to; notice. [Old English *lād* 'way, journey, conveyance', from Germanic: related to LEAD[1], LODE]

load displacement *n.* (also **load draught**) the displacement of a ship when laden.

loaded /ˈləʊdɪd/ *adj.* **1** bearing or carrying a load. **2** *slang* **a** wealthy. **b** drunk. **c** *US* drugged. **3** (of dice etc.) weighted or given a bias. **4** (of a question or statement) charged with some hidden or improper implication. **5** *N. Amer. colloq.* (of a car etc.) equipped with optional extras; de luxe.

loader /ˈləʊdə/ *n.* **1** a loading machine. **2** (in *comb.*) a gun, machine, lorry, etc., loaded in a specified way (*breech-loader*). **3** an attendant who loads guns at a shoot. □ **-loading** *adj.* (in *comb.*) (in sense 2).

loading /ˈləʊdɪŋ/ *n.* **1** *Electr.* the maximum current or power taken by an appliance. **2** an increase in an insurance premium due to a factor increasing the risk involved (see LOAD *v.* 8). **3** *Austral.* an increment added to a basic wage for special skills etc.

load line *n.* a Plimsoll line.

loadstar var. of LODESTAR.

loadstone var. of LODESTONE.

loaf[1] /ləʊf/ *n.* (*pl.* **loaves** /ləʊvz/) **1** a portion of baked bread, usu. of a standard size or shape. **2** a quantity of other food formed into a particular shape (*sugar loaf*; *meat loaf*). **3** *Brit. slang* the head, esp. as a source of common sense (*use your loaf*). [Old English *hlāf*, from Germanic]

loaf[2] /ləʊf/ *v.* & *n.* ● *v.* **1** *intr.* (often foll. by *about*, *around*) spend time idly; hang about. **2** *tr.* (foll. by *away*) waste (time) idly (*loafed away the morning*). **3** *intr.* saunter. ● *n.* an act or spell of loafing. [probably a back-formation from LOAFER]

loafer /ˈləʊfə/ *n.* **1** an idle person. **2** *propr.* a leather shoe shaped like a moccasin with a flat heel. [perhaps from German *Landläufer* 'vagabond']

loaf sugar *n.* a sugar loaf as a whole or cut into lumps.

loam /ləʊm/ *n.* **1** a fertile soil of clay and sand containing humus. **2** a paste of clay and water with sand, chopped straw, etc., used in making bricks, plastering, etc. □ **loamy** *adj.* **loaminess** *n.* [Old English *lām* from West Germanic: related to LIME[1]]

loan[1] /ləʊn/ *n.* & *v.* ● *n.* **1** something lent, esp. a sum of money to be returned normally with interest. **2** the act of lending or state of being lent. **3** funds acquired by the State, esp. from individuals, and regarded as a debt. **4** a word, custom, etc., adopted by one people from another. ● *v.tr. disp.* lend (esp. money). □ **on loan** acquired or given as a loan. □ **loanable** *adj.* **loanee** /ləʊˈniː/ *n.* **loaner** *n.* [Middle English *lan* from Old Norse *lán*, from Germanic: cf. LEND]

■ **Usage** The use of the verb *loan* to mean 'lend' has some justification where a business loan is in question, e.g. *The gas industry is loaning money to the government*, but is considered incorrect by many people as a mere variant for *lend*.

loan[2] /ləʊn/ *n.* (also **loaning** /ˈləʊnɪŋ/) *Sc.* **1** a lane. **2** an open place where cows are milked. [Middle English variant of LANE]

loanholder /ˈləʊnhəʊldə/ *n.* **1** a person holding securities for a loan. **2** a mortgagee.

loan shark *n. colloq.* a person who lends money at exorbitant rates of interest.

loan-translation *n.* an expression adopted by one language from another in a more or less literally translated form.

loanword /ˈləʊnwəːd/ *n.* a word adopted, usu. with little modification, from a foreign language.

loath /ləʊθ/ *predic.adj.* (also **loth**) (usu. foll. by *to* + infin.) disinclined, reluctant, unwilling (*was loath to admit it*). [Old English *lāth*, from Germanic]

loathe /ləʊð/ *v.tr.* regard with disgust; abominate, detest. ▫ **loather** *n.* **loathing** *n.* [Old English *lāthian* from Germanic, related to LOATH]

loathsome /ˈləʊðs(ə)m/ *adj.* arousing hatred or disgust; offensive, repulsive. ▫ **loathsomely** *adv.* **loathsomeness** *n.* [Middle English, via *loath* 'disgust' from LOATHE]

loaves *pl.* of LOAF[1].

lob /lɒb/ *v. & n.* ● *v.tr.* (**lobbed**, **lobbing**) **1** hit or throw (a ball or missile etc.) slowly or in a high arc. **2** send (an opponent) a lobbed ball. ● *n.* **1 a** a ball struck in a high arc. **b** a stroke producing this result. **2** *Cricket* a slow underarm ball. [earlier as noun, probably from Low Dutch]

lobar /ˈləʊbə/ *adj.* **1** of the lungs (*lobar pneumonia*). **2** of, relating to, or affecting a lobe.

lobate /ˈləʊbeɪt/ *adj. Biol.* having a lobe or lobes. ▫ **lobation** /-ˈbeɪʃ(ə)n/ *n.*

lobby /ˈlɒbi/ *n. & v.* ● *n.* (*pl.* **-ies**) **1** a porch, ante-room, entrance hall, or corridor. **2 a** (in the House of Commons) a large hall used esp. for interviews between MPs and members of the public. **b** (also **division lobby**) each of two corridors to which MPs retire to vote. **3 a** a body of persons seeking to influence legislators on behalf of a particular interest (*the anti-abortion lobby*). **b** an organized attempt by members of the public to influence legislators (*a lobby of MPs*). **4** (prec. by *the*) (in the UK) a group of journalists who receive unattributable briefings from the government (*lobby correspondent*). ● *v.* (**-ies**, **-ied**) **1** *tr.* solicit the support of (an influential person). **2** *tr.* (of members of the public) seek to influence (the members of a legislature). **3** *intr.* frequent a parliamentary lobby. **4** *tr.* (foll. by *through*) get (a bill etc.) through a legislature, by interviews etc. in the lobby. ▫ **lobbyer** *n.* **lobbyist** *n.* [medieval Latin *lobia*, *lobium* LODGE]

lobe /ləʊb/ *n.* **1** a roundish and flattish projecting or pendulous part, often each of two or more such parts divided by a fissure (*lobes of the brain*). **2** = EAR LOBE. ▫ **lobed** *adj.* **lobeless** *adj.* [Late Latin from Greek *lobos* 'lobe, pod']

lobectomy /ləʊbˈɛktəmi/ *n.* (*pl.* **-ies**) the surgical removal of a lobe of an organ such as the thyroid gland, lung, etc.

lobelia /ləˈbiːlɪə/ *n.* any plant of the genus *Lobelia*, with blue, scarlet, white, or purple flowers having a deeply cleft corolla. [named after M. de *Lobel*, Flemish botanist to James I, d. 1616]

lobotomy /ləˈbɒtəmi/ *n.* (*pl.* **-ies**) *Med.* surgical incision into a lobe, esp. the prefrontal lobe of the brain (cf. LEUCOTOMY). ▫ **lobotomize** *v.tr.* (also **-ise**). [LOBE + -O- + -TOMY]

lobscouse /ˈlɒbskaʊs/ *n.* a sailor's dish of meat stewed with vegetables and ship's biscuit. [18th c.: origin unknown: cf. Dutch *lapskous*, Danish, Norwegian, German *Lapskaus*]

lobster /ˈlɒbstə/ *n. & v.* ● *n.* **1** any large marine crustacean of the family Nephropidae, with stalked eyes and two pincer-like claws as the first pair of ten limbs. **2** its flesh as food. ● *v.intr.* catch lobsters. [Old English *lopustre*, corruption of Latin *locusta* 'crustacean, locust']

lobster pot *n.* a basket in which lobsters are trapped.

lobster thermidor /ˈθəːmɪdɔː/ *n.* a mixture of lobster meat, mushrooms, cream, egg yolks, and sherry, cooked in a lobster shell. [*thermidor* from the name of the 11th month of the French revolutionary calendar]

lobule /ˈlɒbjuːl/ *n.* esp. *Anat.* a small lobe. ▫ **lobular** *adj.* **lobulate** /-lət/ *adj.* [LOBE]

lobworm /ˈlɒbwəːm/ *n.* **1** a large earthworm used as fishing bait. **2** = LUGWORM. [LOB in obsolete sense 'pendulous object']

local /ˈləʊk(ə)l/ *adj. & n.* ● *adj.* **1** belonging to or existing in a particular place or places. **2** peculiar to or only encountered in a particular place or places. **3** of or belonging to the neighbourhood (*the local doctor*). **4** of or affecting a part and not the whole, esp. of the body (*local pain*). **5** (of a telephone call) to a nearby place and charged at a lower rate. **6** in regard to place. ● *n.* a local person or thing, esp.: **1** an inhabitant of a particular place regarded with reference to that place. **2** a local train, bus, etc. **3** (often prec. by *the*) *Brit. colloq.* a local public house. **4** a local anaesthetic. **5** *N. Amer.* a local branch of a trade union. ▫ **locally** *adv.* **localness** *n.* [Middle English via Old French and Late Latin *localis* from Latin *locus* 'place']

local anaesthetic *n.* an anaesthetic that affects a restricted area of the body.

local area network *n.* a computer network in which computers in close proximity are able to communicate with each other and share resources.

local authority *n. Brit.* an administrative body in local government.

local bus *n.* **1** a bus service operating over short distances. **2** a computer connection directly from a microprocessor to an adjacent peripheral device such as a video system, allowing rapid transmission of data.

local derby *n.* a match between two teams from the same district.

locale /ləʊˈkɑːl/ *n.* a scene or locality, esp. with reference to an event or occurrence taking place there. [French *local* (*n.*) (as LOCAL), respelt to indicate stress: cf. MORALE]

local government *n.* a system of administration of a county, district, parish, etc. by the elected representatives of those who live there.

localism /ˈləʊk(ə)lɪz(ə)m/ *n.* **1** preference for what is local. **2** a local idiom, custom, etc. **3 a** attachment to a place. **b** a limitation of ideas etc. resulting from this.

locality /lə(ʊ)ˈkalɪti/ *n.* (*pl.* **-ies**) **1** a district or neighbourhood. **2** the site or scene of something, esp. in relation to its surroundings. **3** the position of a thing; the place where it is. [French *localité* or Late Latin *localitas* (as LOCAL)]

localize /ˈləʊk(ə)lʌɪz/ *v.tr.* (also **-ise**) **1** restrict or assign to a particular place. **2** invest with the characteristics of a particular place. **3** attach to districts; decentralize. ▫ **localizable** *adj.* **localization** /-ˈzeɪʃ(ə)n/ *n.*

local option *n.* a choice at local or district level as to whether to accept national legislation.

local preacher *n.* a Methodist lay person authorized to conduct services in a particular circuit.

local time *n.* **1** time measured from the sun's transit over the meridian of a place. **2** time as reckoned in a particular region or time zone, esp. with reference to an event reported from it (*we arrived at one o'clock local time*).

local train *n.* a train stopping at all the stations on its route.

local veto *n.* esp. *US* = LOCAL OPTION.

locate /lə(ʊ)ˈkeɪt/ *v.* **1** *tr.* discover the exact place or position of (*locate the enemy's camp*). **2** *tr.* establish or install in a place or in its proper place. **3** *tr.* state the locality of. **4** *tr.* (in *passive*) be situated. **5** *intr.* (often foll. by *in*) *N. Amer.* take up residence or business (in a place). □ **locatable** *adj.* **locator** *n.* [Latin *locare locat-* from *locus* 'place']

■ **Usage** In standard English, it is not acceptable to use *locate* to mean merely 'find', as in *I couldn't locate my key.*

location /lə(ʊ)'keɪʃ(ə)n/ *n.* **1** a particular place; the place or position in which a person or thing is. **2** the act of locating or process of being located. **3** an actual place or natural setting featured in a film or broadcast, as distinct from a simulation in a studio (*filmed entirely on location*). **4** *S.Afr.* an area where blacks are obliged to live, usu. on the outskirts of a town or city. □ **locational** *adj.* [Latin *locatio* (as LOCATE)]

locative /'lɒkətɪv/ *n.* & *adj. Gram.* ● *n.* the case of nouns, pronouns, and adjectives, expressing location. ● *adj.* of or in the locative. [LOCATE + -IVE, on the pattern of *vocative*]

loc. cit. /lɒk 'sɪt/ *abbr.* in the passage already cited. [Latin *loco citato*]

loch /lɒk, lɒx/ *n. Sc.* **1** a lake. **2** an arm of the sea, esp. when narrow or partially landlocked. [Middle English from Gaelic]

lochia /'lɒkɪə, 'ləʊ-/ *n. Med.* a (normal) discharge from the uterus after childbirth. □ **lochial** *adj.* [modern Latin from Greek *lokhia*, neut. pl. of *lokhios* 'of childbirth']

loci *pl.* of LOCUS.

loci classici *pl.* of LOCUS CLASSICUS.

lock[1] /lɒk/ *n.* & *v.* ● *n.* **1** a mechanism for fastening a door, lid, etc., with a bolt that requires a key of a particular shape, or a combination of movements (see COMBINATION LOCK), to work it. **2** a confined section of a canal or river where the level can be changed for raising and lowering boats between adjacent sections by the use of gates and sluices. **3 a** the turning of the front wheels of a vehicle to change its direction of motion. **b** (in full **full lock**) the maximum extent of this. **4** an interlocked or jammed state. **5** *Wrestling* a hold that prevents an opponent from moving a limb. **6** (in full **lock forward**) *Rugby* a player in the second row of a scrum. **7** an appliance to keep a wheel from revolving or slewing. **8** a mechanism for exploding the charge of a gun. **9** = AIRLOCK 2. ● *v.* **1 a** *tr.* fasten with a lock. **b** *tr.* (foll. by *up*) shut and secure (esp. a building) by locking. **c** *intr.* (of a door, window, box, etc.) have the means of being locked. **2** *tr.* **a** (foll. by *up, in, into*) enclose (a person or thing) by locking or as if by locking. **b** (foll. by *up*) *colloq.* imprison (a person). **3** *tr.* (often foll. by *up, away*) store or allocate inaccessibly (*capital locked up in land*). **4** *tr.* (foll. by *in*) hold fast (in sleep or enchantment etc.). **5** *tr.* (usu. in *passive*) (of land, hills, etc.) enclose. **6** *tr.* & *intr.* make or become rigidly fixed or immovable. **7** *intr.* & *tr.* (often foll. by *into*) become or cause to become jammed or caught (*locked into a cycle of borrowing*). **8** *tr.* (usu. in *passive*; foll. by *in*) entangle in an embrace or struggle (*locked in a legal battle*). **9** *tr.* provide (a canal etc.) with locks. **10** *tr.* (foll. by *up, down*) convey (a boat) through a lock. **11** *intr.* go through a lock on a canal etc. □ **lock on to** locate or cause to locate by radar etc. and then track. **lock out 1** keep (a person) out by locking the door. **2** (of an employer) submit (employees) to a lockout. **lock, stock, and barrel** *n.* the whole of a thing. ● *adv.* completely. **under lock and key** securely locked up. □ **lockable** *adj.* **lockless** *adj.* [Old English *loc*, from Germanic]

lock[2] /lɒk/ *n.* **1 a** a portion of hair that coils or hangs together. **b** (in *pl.*) the hair of the head. **2** a tuft of wool or cotton. □ **-locked** *adj.* (in *comb.*). [Old English *locc*, from Germanic]

lockage /'lɒkɪdʒ/ *n.* **1** the amount of rise and fall effected by canal locks. **2** a toll for the use of a lock. **3** the construction or use of locks. **4** locks collectively; the aggregate of locks constructed.

locker /'lɒkə/ *n.* **1** a small lockable cupboard or compartment, esp. each of several for public use. **2** *Naut.* a chest or compartment for clothes, stores, ammunition, etc. **3** a person or thing that locks.

locker room *n.* a room containing small lockable cupboards, esp. in a pavilion or sports centre.

locket /'lɒkɪt/ *n.* **1** a small ornamental case holding a portrait, lock of hair, etc., and usu. hung from the neck. **2** a metal plate or band on a scabbard. [Old French *locquet*, diminutive of *loc* 'latch, lock', from West Germanic (as LOCK[1])]

lockfast /'lɒkfɑːst/ *adj. Sc.* secured with a lock.

lock forward see LOCK[1] *n.* 6.

lockjaw /'lɒkdʒɔː/ *n.* = TRISMUS.

■ **Usage** The word *lockjaw* is not found in technical use.

lock-keeper *n.* a keeper of a lock on a river or canal.

lock-knit *adj.* & *n.* ● *adj.* (of a fabric) knitted with an interlocking stitch. ● *n.* such a fabric.

locknut /'lɒknʌt/ *n.* **1** a nut screwed down on another to keep it tight. **2** a nut designed so that it cannot be accidentally loosened.

lockout /'lɒkaʊt/ *n.* the exclusion of employees by their employer from their place of work until certain terms are agreed to.

locksman /'lɒksmən/ *n.* (*pl.* **-men**) a lock-keeper.

locksmith /'lɒksmɪθ/ *n.* a maker and mender of locks.

lock step *n.* marching with each person as close as possible to the one in front.

lock stitch *n.* a stitch made by a sewing machine by firmly locking together two threads or stitches.

lock-up *n.* & *adj.* ● *n.* **1** a house or room for the temporary detention of prisoners. **2** *Brit.* non-residential premises etc. that can be locked up, esp. a small shop or storehouse. **3 a** the locking up of premises for the night. **b** the time of doing this. **4 a** the unrealizable state of invested capital. **b** an amount of capital locked up. ● *attrib.adj. Brit.* that can be locked up (*lock-up shop*).

loco[1] /'ləʊkəʊ/ *n.* (*pl.* **-os**) *Brit. colloq.* a locomotive. [abbreviation]

loco[2] /'ləʊkəʊ/ *adj.* & *n.* ● *adj. slang* crazy. ● *n.* (*pl.* **-oes** or **-os**) (in full **loco-weed**) a poisonous leguminous plant of the US, esp. of the genus *Astragalus*, affecting the brains of cattle eating it. [Spanish, = insane]

locomotion /ləʊkə'məʊʃ(ə)n/ *n.* **1** motion or the power of motion from one place to another. **2** travel; a means of travelling, esp. an artificial one. [Latin *loco*, ablative of *locus* 'place' + *motio* MOTION]

locomotive /ləʊkə'məʊtɪv/ *n.* & *adj.* ● *n.* (in full **locomotive engine**) an engine powered by steam, diesel fuel, or electricity, used for pulling trains. ● *adj.* **1** of or relating to or effecting locomotion (*locomotive power*). **2** having the power of or given to locomotion; not stationary.

locomotor /ləʊkə(ʊ)'məʊtə/ *adj.* of or relating to locomotion. [LOCOMOTION + MOTOR]

loco-weed see LOCO[2] *n.*

loculus /'lɒkjʊləs/ *n.* (*pl.* **loculi** /-lʌɪ, -liː/) *Zool., Anat., & Bot.* each of a number of small separate cavities. □ **locular** *adj.* [Latin, diminutive of *locus*: see LOCUS]

locum /'ləʊkəm/ *n. colloq.* = LOCUM TENENS. [abbreviation]

locum tenens /ləʊkəm 'tiːnɛnz, 'tɛn-/ *n.* (*pl.* **locum tenentes** /ˌləʊkəm tɪ'nɛntiːz/) a deputy acting esp. for a cleric or doctor. □ **locum tenency** /ləʊkəm 'tɛnənsi/ *n.* [medieval Latin = one holding a place: see LOCUS, TENANT]

locus /'ləʊkəs/ *n.* (*pl.* **loci** /-sʌɪ, -kʌɪ, -kiː/) **1** a position or point, esp. in a text, treatise, etc. **2** *Math.* a curve etc. formed by all the points satisfying a particular equation of the relation between coordinates, or by a point, line, or surface moving according to mathematically defined conditions. **3** *Biol.* the position of a gene, mutation, etc. on a chromosome. [Latin, = place]

locus classicus /ləʊkəs 'klasɪkəs, lɒkəs/ *n.* (*pl.* ***loci classici*** /ləʊsʌɪ 'klasɪsʌɪ, lɒkiː 'klasɪkiː/) the best known or most authoritative passage on a subject. [Latin, = classical place]

locus standi /ˈləʊkəs ˈstandʌɪ, lɒkəs/ *n.* (*pl.* ***loci standi*** /ˈləʊsʌɪ ˈstandʌɪ, lɒkiː ˈstandiː/) a recognized or identifiable (esp. legal) status. [Latin, = place of standing]

locust /ˈləʊkəst/ *n.* **1** any of various African and Asian grasshoppers of the family Acrididae, migrating in swarms and destroying vegetation. **2** *US* a cicada. **3** (in full **locust bean**) a carob. **4** (in full **locust tree**) **a** a carob tree. **b** = ACACIA 2. **c** = KOWHAI. [Middle English via Old French *locuste* from Latin *locusta* 'lobster, locust']

locust-bird *n.* (also **locust-eater**) any of various birds feeding on locusts.

locution /ləˈkjuːʃ(ə)n/ *n.* **1** a word or phrase, esp. considered in regard to style or idiom. **2** style of speech. [Middle English via Old French *locution* or Latin *locutio* from *loqui locut-* 'speak']

lode /ləʊd/ *n.* a vein of metal ore. [variant of LOAD]

loden /ˈləʊd(ə)n/ *n.* **1** a thick waterproof woollen cloth. **2** the dark green colour in which this is often made. [German]

lodestar /ˈləʊdstɑː/ *n.* (also **loadstar**) **1** a star that a ship etc. is steered by, esp. the pole star. **2 a** a guiding principle. **b** an object of pursuit. [LODE in obsolete sense 'way, journey' + STAR]

lodestone /ˈləʊdstəʊn/ *n.* (also **loadstone**) **1** magnetic oxide of iron, magnetite. **2 a** a piece of this used as a magnet. **b** a thing that attracts.

lodge /lɒdʒ/ *n.* & *v.* ● *n.* **1** a small house at the gates of a park or in the grounds of a large house, occupied by a gatekeeper, gardener, etc. **2** a large house or hotel, esp. in a resort. **3** a house occupied in the hunting or shooting season. **4 a** a porter's room or quarters at the gate of a college or other large building. **b** the residence of a head of a college, esp. at Cambridge. **5** the members or the meeting place of a branch of a society such as the Freemasons. **6** a local branch of a trade union. **7** a beaver's or otter's lair. **8** a N. American Indian's tent or wigwam. ● *v.* **1** *tr.* deposit in court or with an official a formal statement of (complaint or information). **2** *tr.* deposit (money etc.) for security. **3** *tr.* bring forward (an objection etc.). **4** *tr.* (foll. by *in*, *with*) place (power etc.) in a person or group. **5** *tr.* & *intr.* make or become fixed or caught without further movement (*the bullet lodged in his brain*; *the tide lodges mud in the cavities*). **6** *tr.* **a** provide (a person or persons) with sleeping quarters. **b** receive as a guest or inmate. **c** establish as a resident in a house, room, or rooms. **7** *intr.* reside or live, esp. as a guest paying for accommodation. **8** *tr.* serve as a habitation for; contain. **9** *tr.* (in *passive*; foll. by *in*) be contained in. **10 a** *tr.* (of wind or rain) flatten (crops). **b** *intr.* (of crops) be flattened in this way. [Middle English *loge* via Old French *loge* 'arbour, hut', from medieval Latin *laubia*, *lobia* (see LOBBY), from Germanic]

lodgement /ˈlɒdʒm(ə)nt/ *n.* **1** the act of lodging or process of being lodged. **2** the depositing or a deposit of money. **3** an accumulation of matter intercepted in fall or transit. [French *logement* (as LODGE)]

lodger /ˈlɒdʒə/ *n.* a person receiving accommodation in another's house for payment.

lodging /ˈlɒdʒɪŋ/ *n.* **1** temporary accommodation (*a lodging for the night*). **2** (in *pl.*) a room or rooms (other than in a hotel) rented for lodging in. **3** a dwelling place. **4** (in *pl.*) the residence of a head of a college at Oxford.

lodging house *n.* a house in which lodgings are let.

lodicule /ˈlɒdɪkjuːl/ *n. Bot.* a small green or white scale below the ovary of a grass flower. [Latin *lodicula*, diminutive of *lodix* 'coverlet']

loess /ˈləʊɪs, ləːs/ *n.* a deposit of fine light-coloured wind-blown dust found esp. in the basins of large rivers and very fertile when irrigated. □ **loessial** /ləʊˈɛsɪəl, ˈləːsɪəl/ *adj.* [German *Löss* from Swiss German *lösch* 'loose', from *lösen* 'loosen']

loft /lɒft/ *n.* & *v.* ● *n.* **1** the space under the roof of a house, above the ceiling of the top floor; an attic. **2** a room over a stable, esp. for hay and straw. **3** a gallery in a church or hall (*organ loft*). **4** *US* an upstairs room, esp. an unpartitioned area over a warehouse or factory. **5** a pigeon house. **6** *Golf* **a** a backward slope in a club-head. **b** a lofting stroke. ● *v.tr.* **1 a** send (a ball etc.) high up. **b** clear (an obstacle) in this way. **2** (esp. as **lofted** *adj.*) give a loft to (a golf club). [Old English from Old Norse *lopt* 'air, sky, upper room', from Germanic (as LIFT)]

lofter /ˈlɒftə/ *n.* a golf club for lofting the ball.

lofty /ˈlɒfti/ *adj.* (**loftier**, **loftiest**) **1** *literary* (of things) of imposing height, towering, soaring (*lofty heights*). **2** consciously haughty, aloof, or dignified (*lofty contempt*). **3** exalted or noble; sublime (*lofty ideals*). □ **loftily** *adv.* **loftiness** *n.* [Middle English from LOFT, as in *aloft*]

log[1] /lɒg/ *n.* & *v.* ● *n.* **1** an unhewn piece of a felled tree, or a similar rough mass of wood, esp. cut for firewood. **2 a** a float attached to a line wound on a reel for gauging the speed of a ship. **b** any other apparatus for the same purpose. **3** a record of events occurring during and affecting the voyage of a ship or aircraft (including the rate of a ship's progress shown by a log: see sense 2 of *n.*). **4** any systematic record of things done, experienced, etc. **5** = LOGBOOK 1. ● *v.tr.* (**logged**, **logging**) **1 a** enter (the distance made or other details) in a ship's logbook. **b** enter details about (a person or event) in a logbook. **c** (of a ship) achieve (a certain distance). **2 a** enter (information) in a regular record. **b** attain (a cumulative total of time etc. recorded in this way) (*logged 50 hours on the computer*). **3** cut into logs. □ **like a log 1** in a helpless or stunned state (*fell like a log*). **2** without stirring (*slept like a log*). **log in** = *log on*. **log on** (or **off**) go through the procedures to begin (or conclude) use of a computer system. [Middle English: origin unknown]

log[2] /lɒg/ *n.* a logarithm (esp. prefixed to a number or algebraic symbol whose logarithm is to be indicated). [abbreviation]

log. /lɒgˈiː/ *abbr.* natural logarithm.

-log *US* var. of -LOGUE.

logan /ˈlɒg(ə)n, ˈləʊg(ə)n/ *n.* (in full **logan-stone**) = ROCKING-STONE. [= *logging*, from dialect *log* 'to rock' + STONE]

loganberry /ˈləʊg(ə)nbɛri/ *n.* (*pl.* **-ies**) **1** a dull red soft fruit, apparently a hybrid of a raspberry and a dewberry. **2** the plant bearing this, *Rubus loganobaccus*. [from the name of J. H. *Logan*, American horticulturalist d. 1928 + BERRY]

logarithm /ˈlɒgərɪð(ə)m, -rɪθ-/ *n.* a figure representing the power to which a fixed number or base must be raised to produce a given number (*the logarithm of 1,000 to base 10 is 3*), used to simplify calculations as the addition and subtraction of logarithms is equivalent to multiplication and division (abbr.: **log**). □ **logarithmic** /-ˈrɪðmɪk/ *adj.* **logarithmically** /-ˈrɪðmɪk(ə)li/ *adv.* [modern Latin *logarithmus*, from Greek *logos* 'reckoning, ratio' + *arithmos* 'number']

logbook /ˈlɒgbʊk/ *n.* **1** a book containing a detailed record or log. **2** *Brit.* = REGISTRATION DOCUMENT.

log cabin *n.* a hut built of logs.

loge /ləʊʒ/ *n.* a private box or enclosure in a theatre. [French]

-loger /lədʒə/ *comb. form* forming nouns, = -LOGIST. [on the pattern of *astrologer*]

logger /ˈlɒgə/ *n. N. Amer.* a lumberjack.

loggerhead /ˈlɒgəhɛd/ *n.* **1** an iron instrument with a ball at the end heated for melting pitch etc. **2 a** (in full **loggerhead turtle**) a large-headed turtle, *Caretta caretta*, of warm seas. **b** (in full **loggerhead shrike**) a green, black, and white shrike, *Lanius ludovicianus*, of the southern US and Mexico. **3** *archaic* a blockhead or fool. □ **at loggerheads** (often foll. by *with*) disagreeing or disputing. [probably from dialect *logger* 'block of wood for hobbling a horse' + HEAD]

loggia /'ləʊdʒə, 'lɒ-, -dʒɪə/ *n.* **1** an open-sided gallery or arcade. **2** an open-sided extension of a house. [Italian, = LODGE]

logging /'lɒgɪŋ/ *n.* the work of cutting and preparing forest timber.

logia *pl.* of LOGION.

logic /'lɒdʒɪk/ *n.* **1 a** the science of reasoning, proof, thinking, or inference. **b** a particular scheme of or treatise on this. **2 a** a chain of reasoning (*I don't follow your logic*). **b** the correct or incorrect use of reasoning (*your logic is flawed*). **c** ability in reasoning (*argues with great learning and logic*). **d** reasoned argument (*is not governed by logic*). **3 a** the inexorable force or compulsion of a thing (*the logic of events*). **b** the necessary consequence of (an argument, decision, etc.). **4 a** a system or set of principles underlying the arrangements of elements in a computer or electronic device so as to perform a specified task. **b** logical operations collectively. □ **logician** /lə'dʒɪʃ(ə)n/ *n.* [Middle English via Old French *logique* and Late Latin *logica* from Greek *logikē* (*tekhnē*) '(art) of reason', from *logos* 'word, reason']

-logic /'lɒdʒɪk/ *comb. form* (also **-logical** /'lɒdʒɪk(ə)l/) forming adjectives corresponding esp. to nouns in *-logy* (*pathological*; *theological*). [from or suggested by Greek *-logikos*: see -IC, -ICAL]

logical /'lɒdʒɪk(ə)l/ *adj.* **1** of logic or formal argument. **2** not contravening the laws of thought, correctly reasoned. **3** deducible or defensible on the ground of consistency; reasonably to be believed or done. **4** capable of correct reasoning. □ **logicality** /-'kalɪti/ *n.* **logically** *adv.* [medieval Latin *logicalis* from Late Latin *logica* (as LOGIC)]

logical atomism *n. Philos.* the theory that all propositions can be analysed into simple independent elements.

logical necessity *n.* the compulsion to believe that of which the opposite is inconceivable.

logical positivism *n.* (also **logical empiricism**) a form of positivism in which symbolic logic is used and linguistic problems of meaning are emphasized.

logic bomb *n. Computing* a set of instructions secretly incorporated into a program so that if a particular logical condition is satisfied they will be carried out, usu. with harmful effects.

logion /'lɒgɪɒn, 'ləʊ-/ *n.* (*pl.* **logia** /-gɪə/) a saying attributed to Christ, esp. one not recorded in the canonical Gospels. [Greek, = oracle, from *logos* 'word']

-logist /lədʒɪst/ *comb. form* forming nouns denoting a person skilled or involved in a branch of study etc. with a name in *-logy* (*archaeologist*; *etymologist*).

logistics /lə'dʒɪstɪks/ *n.pl.* (often treated as *sing.*) **1** the organization of moving, lodging, and supplying troops and equipment. **2** the detailed organization and implementation of a plan or operation. □ **logistic** *adj.* **logistical** *adj.* **logistically** *adv.* [French *logistique* from *loger* 'lodge']

logjam /'lɒgdʒam/ *n.* **1** a crowded mass of logs in a river. **2** a deadlock.

log-line *n.* a line to which a ship's log (see LOG[1] *n.* 2a) is attached.

logo /'lɒgəʊ, 'ləʊgəʊ/ *n.* (*pl.* **-os**) an emblem or device used as the badge of an organization in display material. [abbreviation]

logogram /'lɒgəgram/ *n.* a sign or character representing a word, as in shorthand or some ancient writing systems. [Greek *logos* 'word' + -GRAM]

logomachy /lə'gɒməki/ *n.* (*pl.* **-ies**) *literary* a dispute about words; controversy turning on merely verbal points. [Greek *logomakhia*, from *logos* 'word' + *makhia* 'fighting']

logorrhoea /lɒgə'rɪə/ *n.* (*US* **logorrhea**) an excessive flow of words esp. in mental illness. [Greek *logos* 'word' + *rhoia* 'flow']

Logos /'lɒgɒs/ *n.* (in Christian theology) the Word of God, or second person of the Trinity. [Greek, = word, reason]

logotype /'lɒgə(ʊ)tʌɪp/ *n.* **1** *Printing* a single piece of type that prints a word or group of separate letters. **2 a** = LOGO. **b** *Printing* a single piece of type that prints this. [Greek *logos* 'word' + TYPE]

logrolling /'lɒgrəʊlɪŋ/ *n. US* **1** *colloq.* the practice of exchanging favours, esp. (in politics) of exchanging votes to mutual benefit. **2** a sport in which two contestants stand on a floating log and try to knock each other off. □ **logroller** *n.* [political sense from the phrase *you roll my log and I'll roll yours*]

-logue /lɒg/ *comb. form* (*US* **-log**) **1** forming nouns denoting talk (*dialogue*) or compilation (*catalogue*). **2** = -LOGIST (*ideologue*). [from or suggested by French *-logue* from Greek *-logos*, *-logon*]

logwood /'lɒgwʊd/ *n.* **1** a W. Indian tree, *Haematoxylon campechianum*. **2** the wood of this, producing a substance used in dyeing.

logy /'ləʊgi/ *adj.* (**logier**, **logiest**) *N. Amer.* dull and heavy in motion or thought. [origin uncertain]

-logy /lədʒi/ *comb. form* forming nouns denoting: **1** (usu. as **-ology**) a subject of study or interest (*archaeology*; *zoology*). **2** a characteristic of speech or language (*tautology*). **3** discourse (*trilogy*). [French *-logie* or medieval Latin *-logia* from Greek (as LOGOS)]

loin /lɔɪn/ *n.* **1** (in *pl.*) the part of the body on both sides of the spine between the false ribs and the hip bones. **2** (in *pl.*) *literary* the source of reproductive power (*fruit of his loins*). **3** a joint of meat that includes the loin vertebrae. [Middle English from Old French *loigne*, ultimately from Latin *lumbus*]

loincloth /'lɔɪnklɒθ/ *n.* a cloth worn round the hips, esp. as a sole garment.

loiter /'lɔɪtə/ *v.* **1** *intr.* hang about; linger idly. **2** *intr.* travel indolently and with long pauses. **3** *tr.* (foll. by *away*) pass (time etc.) in loitering. □ **loiter with intent** *Brit.* hang about in order to commit a felony. □ **loiterer** *n.* [Middle English from Middle Dutch *loteren* 'wag about']

loll /lɒl/ *v.intr.* **1** (often foll. by *about*, *around*) stand, sit, or recline in a lazy attitude. **2** hang loosely. [Middle English: probably imitative]

lollapalooza /lɒləpə'lu:zə/ *n.* (also **lalapalooza** etc.) *US slang* an excellent or attractive person or thing. [fanciful formation]

Lollard /'lɒləd/ *n.* any of the followers of the 14th-c. religious reformer John Wyclif. □ **Lollardism** *n.* **Lollardy** *n.* [Middle Dutch *lollaerd* from *lollen* 'mumble']

lollipop /'lɒlɪpɒp/ *n.* **1** a large usu. flat rounded boiled sweet on a small stick. **2** *Brit.* = ICE LOLLY. [perhaps from dialect *lolly* 'tongue' + POP[1]]

lollipop man *n.* (*fem.* **lollipop lady** or **lollipop woman**) *Brit. colloq.* an official using a circular sign on a stick to stop traffic for children to cross the road, esp. near a school.

lollop /'lɒləp/ *v.intr.* (**lolloped**, **lolloping**) *colloq.* **1** flop about. **2** *Brit.* move or proceed in a lounging or ungainly way. [probably from LOLL, associated with TROLLOP]

lolly /'lɒli/ *n.* (*pl.* **-ies**) **1** *colloq.* **a** esp. *Brit.* = LOLLIPOP. **b** *Austral.* a sweet. **2** *Brit. slang* money. [abbreviation of LOLLIPOP]

Lombard /'lɒmbəd, -bɑ:d/ *n.* & *adj.* ● *n.* **1** a member of a Germanic people who conquered Italy in the 6th c. **2** a native of Lombardy in northern Italy. **3** the dialect of Lombardy. ● *adj.* of or relating to Lombardy, the Lombards, or their dialect. □ **Lombardic** /-'bɑ:dɪk/ *adj.* [Middle English via Old French *lombard* or Middle Dutch *lombaerd* from Italian *lombardo*, medieval Latin *Longobardus* via Latin *Langobardus* from Germanic]

Lombardy poplar /lɒmbədɪ 'pɒplə/ *n.* a variety of poplar with an especially tall slender form.

lomentum /lə(ʊ)ˈmɛntəm/ *n.* (also **loment** /ˈləʊmɛnt/) *Bot.* the pod of some leguminous plants, breaking up when mature into one-seeded joints. ◻ **lomentaceous** /-ˈteɪʃ(ə)s/ *adj.* [Latin *lomentum* 'bean-meal' (originally a cosmetic) from *lavare* 'wash']

London clay /ˈlʌndən/ *n.* a geological formation in the lower division of the Eocene in SE England. [*London*, capital of the UK]

Londoner /ˈlʌndənə/ *n.* a native or inhabitant of London.

London plane /ˈlʌndən/ *n.* a hybrid plane tree, *Platanus* × *hispanica*, resistant to smoke and therefore often planted in streets.

London pride /ˈlʌndən/ *n.* a pink-flowered saxifrage, *Saxifraga urbium*.

lone /ləʊn/ *attrib.adj.* **1** (of a person) solitary; without a companion or supporter. **2** (of a place) unfrequented, uninhabited, lonely. **3** unmarried, single (*lone parent*). **4** *literary* feeling or causing to feel lonely. [Middle English, from ALONE]

lone hand *n.* **1** *Cards* a hand played, or a player playing, against the rest at quadrille and euchre. **2** a person or action without allies.

lonely /ˈləʊnli/ *adj.* (**lonelier**, **loneliest**) **1** (of a person) solitary, companionless, isolated. **2** (of a place) unfrequented; (of a thing) standing apart; isolated. **3 a** sad because without friends or company. **b** imparting a sense of loneliness; dreary. ◻ **loneliness** *n.*

lonely heart *n.* a lonely person, esp. one seeking companionship by advertising in a newspaper etc.

loner /ˈləʊnə/ *n.* a person or animal that prefers not to associate with others.

lonesome /ˈləʊns(ə)m/ *adj.* **1** solitary, lonely. **2** feeling lonely or forlorn. **3** causing such a feeling. ◻ **by** (or **on**) **one's lonesome** *colloq.* all alone. ◻ **lonesomely** *adv.* **lonesomeness** *n.*

lone wolf *n.* a person who prefers to act alone.

long[1] /lɒŋ/ *adj.*, *n.*, & *adv.* ● *adj.* (**longer** /ˈlɒŋgə/; **longest** /ˈlɒŋgɪst/) **1** measuring much from end to end in space or time; not soon traversed or finished (*a long line*; *a long journey*; *a long time ago*). **2** (following a measurement) in length or duration (*2 metres long*; *the vacation is two months long*). **3** relatively great in extent or duration (*a long meeting*). **4 a** consisting of a large number of items (*a long list*). **b** seemingly more than the stated amount; tedious, lengthy (*ten long miles*; *tired after a long day*). **5** of elongated shape. **6 a** lasting or reaching far back or forward in time (*a long friendship*). **b** (of a person's memory) retaining things for a long time. **7** far-reaching; acting at a distance; involving a great interval or difference. **8** *Phonet.* & *Prosody* of a vowel or syllable: **a** having the greater of the two recognized durations. **b** (of a vowel) categorized as long with regard to quality and length (e.g. in standard British English the vowel /uː/ in *food* is long as distinct from the short vowel /ʊ/ in *good*) (cf. SHORT *adj.* 6). **9** (of odds or a chance) reflecting or representing a low level of probability. **10** *Stock Exch.* **a** (of stocks) bought in large quantities in advance, with the expectation of a rise in price. **b** (of a broker etc.) buying etc. on this basis. **11** (of a bill of exchange) maturing at a distant date. **12** (of a cold drink) large and refreshing. **13** *colloq.* (of a person) tall. **14** (foll. by *on*) *colloq.* well supplied with. ● *n.* **1** a long interval or period (*shall not be away for long*; *it will not take long*). **2 a** long-dated stock. **b** a person who buys this. ● *adv.* (**longer** /ˈlɒŋgə/; **longest** /ˈlɒŋgɪst/) **1** by or for a long time (*long before*; *long ago*; *long live the king!*). **2** (following nouns of duration) throughout a specified time (*all day long*). **3** (in *compar.*; with *neg.*) after an implied point of time (*shall not wait any longer*). ◻ **as** (or **so**) **long as 1** during the whole time that. **2** provided that; only if. **at long last** see LAST[1]. **before long** fairly soon (*shall see you before long*). **be long** (often foll. by *pres. part.* or *in* + verbal noun) take a long time; be slow (*was long finding it out*; *the chance was long in coming*; *I shan't be long*). **by a long chalk** see CHALK. **in the long run 1** over a long period. **2** eventually; finally. **long ago** in the distant past. **the long and the short of it 1** all that can or need be said. **2** the eventual outcome. **long in the tooth** rather old (originally of horses, from the recession of the gums with age). **not by a long shot** by no means. ◻ **longish** *adj.* [Old English *long*, *lang*, from Germanic]

long[2] /lɒŋ/ *v.intr.* (foll. by *for* or *to* + infin.) have a strong wish or desire for. [Old English *langian* 'seem long, desire']

long. *abbr.* longitude.

-long /lɒŋ/ *comb. form* forming adjectives and adverbs: **1** for the duration of (*lifelong*). **2** = -LING[2] (*headlong*).

long-ago *attrib.adj.* that is in the distant past.

long-awaited *adj.* that has been awaited for a long time.

longboard /ˈlɒŋbɔːd/ *n. US* a type of surfboard.

longboat /ˈlɒŋbəʊt/ *n.* a sailing ship's largest boat.

longbow /ˈlɒŋbəʊ/ *n.* a bow drawn by hand and shooting a long feathered arrow.

long-case clock *n.* a grandfather clock.

long-chain *attrib.adj.* (of a molecule) containing a chain of many carbon atoms.

long-dated *adj.* (of securities) not due for early payment or redemption.

long-day *attrib.adj.* (of a plant) needing a long daily period of light to cause flowering.

long-dead *adj.* that has been dead for a long time.

long-distance *adj.*, *adv.*, & *n.* ● *adj.* **1** (of a telephone call, public transport, etc.) between distant places. **2** *Brit.* (of a weather forecast) long-range. ● *adv.* (also **long distance**) between distant places (*phone long-distance*). ● *n.* (also **long distance**) (often *attrib.*) *Athletics* a race distance of 6 miles or 10,000 metres (6 miles 376 yds), or longer.

long division *n. Math.* division of numbers with details of the calculations written down.

long dozen *n.* thirteen.

long-drawn *adj.* (also **long-drawn-out**) prolonged, esp. unduly.

longe var. of LUNGE[2].

longeron /ˈlɒn(d)ʒərɒn/ *n.* a longitudinal member of a plane's fuselage. [French, = girder]

longevity /lɒnˈdʒɛvɪti/ *n.* long life. [Late Latin *longaevitas*, from Latin *longus* 'long' + *aevum* 'age']

long face *n.* a dismal or disappointed expression. ◻ **long-faced** *adj.*

long field *n. Cricket* **1** = LONG OFF, LONG ON. **2** the part of the field behind the bowler.

long figure *n.* (also **long price**) a heavy cost.

longhair /ˈlɒŋhɛː/ *n.* **1** a person characterized by the associations of long hair, esp. a hippie or intellectual. **2 a** a breed of long-haired cat. **b** a cat of a long-haired breed.

longhand /ˈlɒŋhand/ *n.* ordinary handwriting (as opposed to shorthand or typing or printing).

long haul *n.* **1** the transport of goods or passengers over a long distance (hyphenated when *attrib.*: *long-haul flights*). **2** a prolonged effort or task.

long-headed *adj.* shrewd, far-seeing, sagacious. ◻ **long-headedness** *n.*

long hop *n.* a short-pitched easily hit ball in cricket.

longhorn /ˈlɒŋhɔːn/ *n.* **1** one of a breed of cattle with long horns. **2** any beetle of the family Cerambycidae with long antennae.

longhouse /ˈlɒŋhaʊs/ *n.* **1** (in Britain) an old type of dwelling housing a family and animals under one roof. **2 a** *hist.* the traditional dwelling of the Iroquois and other N. American Indians. **b** a building on an Iroquois reservation, used as a church and meeting hall. **3** a large communal village house in parts of Malaysia and Indonesia.

long hundredweight see HUNDREDWEIGHT 1.

longicorn /ˈlɒn(d)ʒɪkɔːn/ *n.* a longhorn beetle. [modern Latin *longicornis*, from Latin *longus* 'long' + *cornu* 'horn']

longing /ˈlɒŋɪŋ/ *n. & adj.* ● *n.* a feeling of intense desire. ● *adj.* having or showing this feeling. □ **longingly** *adv.*

longitude /ˈlɒn(d)ʒɪtjuːd, ˈlɒŋɡɪ-/ *n.* **1** *Geog.* the angular distance east or west from a standard meridian such as Greenwich to the meridian of any place. **2** *Astron.* the angular distance of a celestial object north or south of the ecliptic measured along a great circle through the object and the poles of the ecliptic (symbol λ). [Middle English from Latin *longitudo -dinis*, from *longus* 'long']

longitudinal /lɒndʒɪˈtjuːdɪn(ə)l, lɒŋɡɪ-/ *adj.* **1** of or in length. **2** running lengthwise. **3** of longitude. □ **longitudinally** *adv.*

longitudinal wave *n. Physics* a wave vibrating in the direction of propagation.

long johns *n.pl. colloq.* underpants with full-length legs.

long jump *n.* an athletic contest of jumping as far as possible along the ground in one leap. □ **long-jumper** *n.*

long-lasting *adj.* that lasts, or has lasted, for a long time.

long leg *n. Cricket* **1** a fielder far behind the batsman on the leg side. **2** this fielding position.

long-legged *adj.* **1** having long legs. **2** speedy.

long-life *adj.* (of consumable goods) treated to preserve freshness.

long-lived *adj.* having a long life; durable.

long-lost *attrib.adj.* that has been lost or not seen for a long time.

long measure *n.* a measure of length (metres, miles, etc.).

long metre *n.* **1** a hymn stanza of four lines with eight syllables each. **2** a quatrain of iambic tetrameters with alternate lines rhyming.

long off *n.* (also **long on**) *Cricket* **1** a fielder far behind the bowler and towards the off (or on) side. **2** this fielding position.

long-playing *adj.* (of a gramophone record) playing for about 20–30 minutes on each side. □ **long-player** *n. Brit.*

long-range *adj.* **1** (of a missile etc.) having a long range of operation. **2** of or relating to a period of time far into the future.

long-running *adj.* continuing for a long time.

long ship *n. hist.* a long narrow warship with many rowers, used esp. by the Vikings.

longshore /ˈlɒŋʃɔː/ *adj.* **1** existing on or frequenting the shore. **2** directed along the shore. [for *along shore*]

longshore drift /ˈlɒŋʃɔː/ *n.* the movement of material along a coast by waves which approach at an angle to the shore but recede directly away from it.

longshoreman /ˈlɒŋʃɔːmən/ *n.* (*pl.* **-men**) *US* a docker.

long shot *n.* **1** a wild guess or venture. **2** a bet at long odds. **3** *Cinematog.* a shot including objects at a distance.

long sight *n.* the ability to see clearly only what is comparatively distant.

long-sighted *adj.* **1** having long sight. **2** having imagination or foresight. □ **long-sightedly** *adv.* **long-sightedness** *n.*

long-sleeved *adj.* with sleeves reaching to the wrist.

longspur /ˈlɒŋspəː/ *n.* a N. American bunting of the genus *Calcarius*.

long-standing *adj.* that has long existed; not recent.

long-stay *attrib.adj.* **1** staying a long time (*long-stay patients*). **2** for people who are staying a long time (*long-stay car park*).

longstop /ˈlɒŋstɒp/ *n.* **1** *Cricket* **a** a fielder directly behind the wicketkeeper. **b** this fielding position. **2** = BACKSTOP 2.

long-suffering *adj.* bearing provocation patiently. □ **long-sufferingly** *adv.*

long suit *n.* **1** many playing cards of one suit in a hand (esp. more than 3 or 4 in a hand of 13). **2** a thing at which one excels.

long-tailed duck *n.* an Arctic marine duck, *Clangula hyemalis*, the male of which has elongated tail feathers. Also (*N. Amer.*) called *old squaw*.

long-term *adj.* occurring in or relating to a long period of time (*long-term plans*).

long-time *attrib.adj.* that has been such for a long time.

long ton see TON[1] 1.

long tongue *n.* loquacity.

longueur /lɔ̃(ŋ)ˈɡəː, French lɔ̃ɡœr/ *n.* **1** a tedious passage in a book etc. **2** a tedious stretch of time. [French, = length]

long vacation *n. Brit.* the summer vacation of law courts and universities.

long waist *n.* a low or deep waist of a dress or body. □ **long-waisted** *adj.*

long wave *n.* a radio wave of frequency less than 300 kHz.

longways /ˈlɒŋweɪz/ *adv.* (also **longwise** /ˈlɒŋwʌɪz/) = LENGTHWAYS.

long-winded *adj.* **1** (of speech or writing) tediously lengthy. **2** able to run a long distance without rest. □ **long-windedly** *adv.* **long-windedness** *n.*

lonicera /lɒˈnɪs(ə)rə/ *n.* **1** a dense evergreen shrub, *Lonicera nitidum*, much used as hedging. **2** = HONEYSUCKLE. [named after A. *Lonicerus*, German botanist d. 1586]

loo[1] /luː/ *n. Brit. colloq.* a lavatory. [20th c.: origin uncertain]

loo[2] /luː/ *n.* **1** a round card game with penalties paid to the pool. **2** this penalty. [abbreviation of obsolete *lanterloo* from French *lanturlu*, the meaningless refrain of a song]

loof var. of LUFF.

loofah /ˈluːfə/ *n.* (also **luffa** /ˈlʌfə/) **1** a climbing gourdlike plant, *Luffa cylindrica*, native to Asia, producing edible marrow-like fruits. **2** the dried fibrous vascular system of this fruit used as a sponge. [Egyptian Arabic *lūfa*, the plant]

look /lʊk/ *v., n., & int.* ● *v.* **1 a** *intr.* (often foll. by *at*) use one's sight; turn one's eyes in some direction. **b** *tr.* turn one's eyes on; contemplate or examine (*looked me in the eyes*). **2** *intr.* **a** make a visual or mental search (*I'll look in the morning*). **b** (foll. by *at*) consider, examine (*we must look at the facts*). **3** *intr.* (foll. by *for*) **a** search for. **b** hope or be on the watch for. **c** expect. **4** *intr.* inquire (*when one looks deeper*). **5** *intr.* have a specified appearance; seem (*look foolish*). **6** *intr.* (foll. by *to*) **a** consider; take care of; be careful about (*look to the future*). **b** rely on (a person or thing) (*you can look to me for support*). **c** expect; count on; aim at. **7** *intr.* (foll. by *into*) investigate or examine. **8** *tr.* (foll. by *what, where*, etc. + clause) ascertain or observe by sight (*look where we are*). **9** *intr.* (of a thing) face or be turned, or have or afford an outlook, in a specified direction. **10** *tr.* express, threaten, or show (an emotion etc.) by one's looks. **11** *intr.* (foll. by *that* + clause) take care; make sure. **12** *intr.* (foll. by *to* + infin.) expect (*am looking to finish this today*). ● *n.* **1** an act of looking; the directing of the eyes to look at a thing or person; a glance (*a scornful look*). **2** (in *sing.* or *pl.*) the appearance of a face; a person's expression or personal aspect. **3** the (esp. characteristic) appearance of a thing (*the place has a European look*). **4** style, fashion (*this year's look*). ● *int.* (also **look here!**) calling attention, expressing a protest, etc. □ **look after 1** attend to, take care of. **2** follow with the eye. **3** seek for. **look one's age** appear to be as old as one really is. **look alive** (or **lively**) (often in *imper.*) *colloq.* move (more) energetically; be brisk or alert. **look as if** suggest by appearance the belief that (*it looks as if he's gone*). **look back 1** (foll. by *on, upon, to*) turn one's thoughts to (something past). **2** (usu. with *neg.*) cease to progress (*since then we have never looked back*). **3** *Brit.* make a further visit later. **look before you leap** avoid precipitate action. **look daggers** see DAGGER. **look down on** (or **upon** or **look down one's nose at**) regard with contempt or a feeling of superiority. **look for trouble** see TROUBLE. **look forward to** await (an expected event) eagerly or with specified feelings. **look in** make a short visit or call. **look a person in the eye** (or **eyes** or **face**) look directly and unashamedly at him or her. **look like 1** have the appearance of. **2** *Brit.* seem to be (*they look like winning*). **3** threaten or promise (*it looks like rain*). **4** indicate the presence of (*it looks like woodworm*). **look lively** see *look alive*. **look on 1** (often foll. by *as*) regard (*looks on you as a friend*; *looked on them with disfavour*). **2** be a spectator; avoid participation. **look oneself** appear in good health (esp. after illness etc.). **look out 1** direct one's sight or put one's head out of a window etc. **2** (often foll. by *for*) be vigilant or prepared. **3** (foll. by *on*, *over*, etc.) have or afford a specified outlook. **4** *Brit.* search for and produce (*shall look one out for you*). **look over 1** inspect or survey (*looked over the house*). **2** examine (a document etc.) esp. cursorily (*shall look it over*). **look round** (*US* **around**) **1** look in every or another direction. **2** examine the objects of interest in a place (*you must come and look round sometime*). **3** examine the possibilities etc. with a view to deciding on a course of action. **look sharp** act promptly; make haste (originally = keep strict watch). **look small** see SMALL. **look through 1** examine the contents of, esp. cursorily. **2** penetrate (a pretence or pretender) with insight. **3** ignore by pretending not to see (*I waved, but you just looked through me*). **look up 1** search for (esp. information in a book). **2** *colloq.* go to visit (a person) (*had intended to look them up*). **3** raise one's eyes (*looked up when I went in*). **4** improve, esp. in price, prosperity, or well-being (*things are looking up all round*). **look a person up and down** scrutinize a person keenly or contemptuously. **look up to** respect or venerate. **not like the look of** find alarming or suspicious. □ **-looking** *adj.* (in *comb.*). [Old English *lōcian*, from West Germanic]

lookalike /ˈlʊkəlʌɪk/ *n.* a person or thing closely resembling another (*a Prince Charles lookalike*).

looker /ˈlʊkə/ *n.* **1** a person having a specified appearance (*a great looker*). **2** *colloq.* a good-looking person, esp. a woman.

looker-on *n.* a person who is a mere spectator.

look-in *n. colloq.* **1** an informal call or visit. **2** a chance of participation or success (*never gets a look-in*).

looking-glass *n.* a mirror for looking at oneself.

lookout /ˈlʊkaʊt/ *n.* **1** a watch or looking out (*on the lookout for bargains*). **2 a** a post of observation. **b** a person or party or boat stationed to keep watch. **3** a view over a landscape. **4** esp. *Brit.* a prospect of luck (*it's a bad lookout for them*). **5** *colloq.* a person's own concern.

look-see *n. colloq.* a survey or inspection. [from, or in imitation of, pidgin English]

loom[1] /luːm/ *n.* an apparatus for weaving yarn or thread into fabric. [Middle English *lōme* from Old English *gelōma* 'tool']

loom[2] /luːm/ *v.* & *n.* ● *v.intr.* (often foll. by *up*) **1** come into sight dimly, esp. as a vague and often magnified or threatening shape. **2** (of an event or prospect) be ominously close. ● *n.* a vague often exaggerated first appearance of land at sea etc. [probably from Low German or Dutch: cf. East Frisian *lōmen* 'move slowly', Middle High German *lüemen* 'be weary']

loon /luːn/ *n.* **1** *N. Amer.* = DIVER 3. **2** *colloq.* a crazy person (cf. LOONY). [alteration of *loom* from Old Norse *lómr*]

loony /ˈluːni/ *n.* & *adj. slang* ● *n.* (*pl.* **-ies**) a mad or silly person; a lunatic. ● *adj.* (**loonier**, **looniest**) crazy, silly. □ **looniness** *n.* [abbreviation of LUNATIC]

loony-bin *n. slang offens.* a mental home or hospital.

loop /luːp/ *n.* & *v.* ● *n.* **1 a** a figure produced by a curve, or a doubled thread etc., that crosses itself. **b** anything forming this figure. **2** a similarly shaped attachment or ornament formed of cord or thread etc. and fastened at the crossing. **3** a ring or curved piece of material as a handle etc. **4** a contraceptive coil. **5** (in full **loop line**) a railway or telegraph line that diverges from a main line and joins it again. **6** a manoeuvre in which an aeroplane describes a vertical loop. **7** *Skating* a manoeuvre describing a curve that crosses itself, made on a single edge. **8** *Electr.* a complete circuit for a current. **9** an endless strip of tape or film allowing continuous repetition. **10** *Computing* a programmed sequence of instructions that is repeated until or while a particular condition is satisfied. ● *v.* **1** *tr.* form (thread etc.) into a loop or loops. **2** *tr.* enclose with or as with a loop. **3** *tr.* (often foll. by *up*, *back*, *together*) fasten or join with a loop or loops. **4** *intr.* **a** form a loop. **b** move in looplike patterns. **5** *intr.* loop the loop (see LOOP-THE-LOOP). [Middle English: origin unknown]

looper /ˈluːpə/ *n.* **1** a caterpillar of the geometer moth which progresses by arching itself into loops. **2** a device for making loops.

loophole /ˈluːphəʊl/ *n.* & *v.* ● *n.* **1** a means of evading a rule etc. without infringing the letter of it. **2** a narrow vertical slit in a wall for shooting or looking through or to admit light or air. ● *v.tr.* make loopholes in (a wall etc.). [Middle English *loop* in sense 2 + HOLE]

loop-the-loop *n.* & *v. Aeron.* ● *n.* the feat of circling in a vertical loop. ● *v.intr.* (**loop the loop**) perform this feat.

loopy /ˈluːpi/ *adj.* (**loopier**, **loopiest**) **1** *slang* crazy. **2** having many loops.

loose /luːs/ *adj.*, *n.*, & *v.* ● *adj.* **1 a** not or no longer held by bonds or restraint. **b** (of an animal) not confined or tethered etc. **2** detached or detachable from its place (*has come loose*). **3** not held together or contained or fixed. **4** not specially fastened or packaged (*loose papers*; *had her hair loose*). **5** hanging partly free (*a loose end*). **6** slack, relaxed; not tense or tight. **7** not compact or dense (*loose soil*). **8** (of language, concepts, etc.) inexact; conveying only the general sense. **9** (preceding an agent noun) doing the expressed action in a loose or careless manner (*a loose thinker*). **10** morally lax; dissolute (*loose living*). **11** (of the tongue) likely to speak indiscreetly. **12** (of the bowels) tending to diarrhoea. **13** *Sport* **a** (of a ball) in play but not in any player's possession. **b** (of play etc.) with the players not close together. **14** *Cricket* **a** (of bowling) inaccurately pitched. **b** (of fielding) careless or bungling. **15** (in *comb.*) loosely (*loose-fitting*). ● *n. Brit.* **1** a state of freedom or unrestrainedness. **2** loose play in football (*in the loose*). **3** (esp. in phr. **give loose to**) free expression. ● *v.tr.* **1** release; set free; free from constraint. **2** untie or undo (something that constrains). **3** detach from moorings. **4** relax (*loosed my hold on it*). **5** discharge (a gun or arrow etc.). □ **at a loose end** (or *N. Amer.* **at loose ends**) (of a person) unoccupied, esp. temporarily. **on the loose 1** escaped from captivity. **2** having a free enjoyable time. □ **loosely** *adv.* **looseness** *n.* **loosish** *adj.* [Middle English *lōs* from Old Norse *lauss*, from Germanic]

loose box *n. Brit.* a compartment for a horse, in a stable or vehicle, in which it can move about.

loose cannon *n.* a person or thing causing unintentional or misdirected damage.

loose change *n.* money as coins in the pocket etc. for casual use.

loose cover *n. Brit.* a removable cover for a chair or sofa etc.

loose-leaf *adj.* & *n.* ● *adj.* (of a notebook, manual, etc.) with each leaf separate and removable. ● *n.* a loose-leaf notebook etc.

loose-limbed *adj.* having supple limbs.

loosen /ˈluːs(ə)n/ *v.* **1** *tr.* & *intr.* make or become less tight or compact or firm. **2** *tr.* make (a regime etc.) less severe. **3** *tr.* release (the bowels) from constipation. **4** *tr.* relieve (a cough) from dryness. □ **loosen a person's tongue** make a person talk freely. **loosen up** = *limber up* (see LIMBER[1] *v.*). □ **loosener** *n.*

loose order *n.* an arrangement of soldiers etc. with wide intervals.

loosestrife /'lu:sstrʌɪf/ *n.* **1** (in full **yellow loosestrife**) a tall waterside plant, *Lysimachia vulgaris*, of the primrose family, with spikes of yellow flowers. **2** (in full **purple loosestrife**) a tall waterside plant *Lythrum salicaria*, with spikes of star-shaped purple flowers. [LOOSE + STRIFE, taking the Greek name *lusimakhion* (from *Lusimakhos*, its discoverer) as if directly from *luō* 'undo' + *makhē* 'battle']

loot /lu:t/ *n.* & *v.* ● *n.* **1** goods taken from an enemy; spoil. **2** booty; illicit gains made by an official. **3** *slang* money. ● *v.tr.* (also *absol.*) **1** rob (premises) or steal (goods) left unprotected, esp. after a riot. **2** plunder or sack (a city, premises, etc.). **3** carry off as booty. □ **looter** *n.* [Hindi *lūṭ*]

loo table *n.* a circular table for playing loo on or one resembling such a table. [LOO²]

lop¹ /lɒp/ *v.* & *n.* ● *v.* (**lopped, lopping**) **1** *tr.* **a** (often foll. by *off, away*) cut or remove (a part or parts) from a whole, esp. branches from a tree. **b** remove branches from (a tree). **2** *tr.* (often foll. by *off, away*) remove (items) as superfluous. **3** *intr.* (foll. by *at*) make lopping strokes on (a tree etc.). ● *n.* parts lopped off, esp. branches and twigs of trees. □ **lop and top** (or **crop**) the trimmings of a tree. □ **lopper** *n.* [Middle English from Old English: perhaps related to Lithuanian *lùpti* 'to strip or peel']

lop² /lɒp/ *v.* (**lopped, lopping**) **1** *intr.* & *tr.* hang limply. **2** *intr.* (foll. by *about*) slouch, dawdle; hang about. **3** *intr.* move with short bounds. **4** *tr.* (of an animal) let (the ears) hang. □ **loppy** *adj.* [probably imitative]

lope /ləʊp/ *v.* & *n.* ● *v.intr.* (esp. of animals) run with a long bounding stride. ● *n.* a long bounding stride. [Middle English, variant of Scots *loup*, from Old Norse *hlaupa* LEAP]

lop-ears *n.pl.* drooping ears. □ **lop-eared** *adj.*

lopho- /'ləʊfəʊ, 'lɒfəʊ/ *comb. form Zool.* crested. [Greek *lophos* 'crest']

lophodont /'ləʊfə(ʊ)dɒnt, 'lɒf-/ *n.* & *adj.* ● *adj.* having transverse ridges on the grinding surface of molar teeth. ● *n.* an animal with these teeth. [LOPHO- + Greek *odous odont-* 'tooth']

lophophore /'ləʊfə(ʊ)fɔ:, 'lɒf-/ *n.* a horseshoe-shaped structure bearing ciliated tentacles around the mouth of bryozoans, brachiopods, etc. □ **lophophorate** /lə'fɒfəreɪt, ləʊfə'fɔ:reɪt/ *n.* & *adj.*

lopolith /'lɒpəlɪθ/ *n. Geol.* a large saucer-shaped intrusion of igneous rock. [Greek *lopas* 'basin' + -LITH]

lopsided /lɒp'sʌɪdɪd/ *adj.* with one side lower or smaller than the other; unevenly balanced. □ **lopsidedly** *adv.* **lopsidedness** *n.* [LOP² + SIDE]

loquacious /lɒ'kweɪʃəs/ *adj.* **1** talkative. **2** (of birds or water) chattering, babbling. □ **loquaciously** *adv.* **loquaciousness** *n.* **loquacity** /-'kwasɪti/ *n.* [Latin *loquax -acis* from *loqui* 'talk']

loquat /'ləʊkwɒt/ *n.* **1** a tree of the rose family, *Eriobotrya japonica*, bearing small yellow egg-shaped fruits. **2** this fruit. [Chinese dialect *luh kwat* 'rush orange']

loquitur /'lɒkwɪtə/ *v.intr.* (he or she) speaks (with the speaker's name following, as a stage direction or to inform the reader). [Latin from *loqui* 'talk, speak']

lor /lɔ:/ *int. Brit. slang* an exclamation of surprise or dismay. [abbreviation of LORD]

loran /'lɔ:ran, 'lɒ-/ *n.* a system of long-distance navigation in which position is determined from the intervals between signal pulses received from widely spaced radio transmitters. [*lo*ng-*ra*nge *n*avigation]

lord /lɔ:d/ *n., int.,* & *v.* ● *n.* **1** a master or ruler. **2** *hist.* a feudal superior, esp. of a manor. **3** a peer of the realm or a person entitled to the title *Lord*, esp. a marquess, earl, viscount, or baron. **4** (**Lord**) (often prec. by *the*) a name for God or Christ. **5** (**Lord**) **a** prefixed as the designation of a marquess, earl, viscount, or baron. **b** prefixed to the Christian name of the younger son of a duke or marquess. **c** (**the Lords**) = HOUSE OF LORDS. **6** *Astrol.* the ruling planet (of a sign, house, or chart). ● *int.* (**Lord**) expressing surprise, dismay, etc. ● *v.tr.* confer the title of Lord upon. □ **live like a lord** live sumptuously. **lord it over 1** domineer. **2** adopt an attitude of superiority over. **lord over** (usu. in *passive*) rule over. □ **lordless** *adj.* **lordlike** *adj.* [Old English *hlāford* from *hlāfweard* = bread-keeper (as LOAF¹, WARD)]

Lord Advocate *n.* the principal law officer of the Crown in Scotland.

Lord Bishop *n.* the formal title of any bishop.

Lord Chamberlain *n.* (in full **Lord Chamberlain of the Household**) (in the UK) the official in charge of the Royal Household, formerly the licenser of plays.

Lord Chancellor *n.* (in the UK) the highest officer of the Crown, presiding in the House of Lords etc.

Lord Chief Justice *n.* (in the UK) the president of the Queen's Bench Division.

Lord Commissioner *n.* the representative of the Crown at the General Assembly of the Church of Scotland.

Lord God of hosts var. of LORD OF HOSTS.

Lord Great Chamberlain of England *n.* the hereditary holder of a ceremonial office.

Lord High Chancellor *n.* = LORD CHANCELLOR.

Lord High Commissioner *n.* = LORD COMMISSIONER.

Lord Lieutenant *n.* **1** (in the UK) the chief executive authority and head of magistrates in each county. **2** *hist.* the viceroy of Ireland.

lordling /'lɔ:dlɪŋ/ *n.* usu. *derog.* a minor lord.

lordly /'lɔ:dli/ *adj.* (**lordlier, lordliest**) **1** haughty, imperious. **2** suitable for a lord. □ **lordliness** *n.* [Old English *hlāfordlic* (as LORD)]

Lord Mayor *n.* the title of the mayor in London and some other large cities.

Lord of hosts *n.* (also **Lord God of hosts**) God as Lord over earthly or heavenly armies.

Lord Ordinary see ORDINARY *n.* 5.

lordosis /lɔ:'dəʊsɪs/ *n. Med.* inward curvature of the spine (opp. KYPHOSIS). □ **lordotic** /-'dɒtɪk/ *adj.* [modern Latin from Greek *lordōsis*, from *lordos* 'bent backwards']

Lord President of the Council *n.* (in the UK) the Cabinet minister presiding at the Privy Council.

Lord Privy Seal *n.* (in the UK) a senior Cabinet minister without specified official duties.

Lord Protector of the Commonwealth see PROTECTOR 4.

Lord Provost *n.* the head of a municipal corporation or borough in certain Scottish cities.

lords and ladies *n.* = CUCKOO PINT.

Lords Commissioners *n.pl.* the members of a board performing the duties of a high state office put in commission.

Lord's Day *n.* (prec. by *the*) Sunday.

lordship /'lɔ:dʃɪp/ *n.* **1** (foll. by *of, over*) dominion, rule, or ownership. **2** *archaic* the state of being a lord. □ **his** (or **your**) **Lordship** (or **lordship**) (*pl.* **their** (or **your**) **Lordships** or **lordships**) **1** a respectful form of reference or address to a Lord, a judge, or a bishop. **2** *iron.* a form of reference or address to a man thought to give himself airs. [Old English *hlāfordscipe* (as LORD, -SHIP)]

Lords of Session *n.pl.* the judges of the Scottish Court of Session.

Lord's Prayer *n.* the prayer taught by Christ to his disciples, beginning 'Our Father'.

Lords spiritual *n.pl.* the bishops in the House of Lords.

Lord's Supper *n.* the Eucharist.

Lords temporal *n.pl.* the members of the House of Lords other than the bishops.

Lordy /'lɔ:di/ *int.* = LORD *int.*

lore[1] /lɔː/ *n.* a body of traditions and knowledge on a subject or held by a particular group (*herbal lore*; *gypsy lore*). [Old English *lār* from Germanic: related to LEARN]

lore[2] /lɔː/ *n. Zool.* a straplike surface between the eye and upper mandible in birds, or between the eye and nostril in snakes. [Latin *lorum* 'strap']

lorgnette /lɔːn'jɛt/ *n.* (in *sing.* or *pl.*) a pair of eyeglasses or opera glasses held by a long handle. [French, from *lorgner* 'to squint']

loricate /'lɒrɪkeɪt, -kət/ *adj. Zool.* having a defensive armour of bone, plates, scales, etc. [Latin *loricatus* via *lorica* 'breastplate' from *lorum* 'strap']

lorikeet /'lɒrɪkiːt/ *n.* any of various small brightly coloured parrots of the subfamily Loriinae. [diminutive of LORY, on the pattern of *parakeet*]

loris /'lɔːrɪs/ *n.* (*pl.* same) either of two small slow-moving nocturnal primates with small ears and a very short tail, *Loris tardigradus* of southern India (**slender loris**), and *Nycticebus coucang* of the E. Indies (**slow loris**). [French, perhaps from obsolete Dutch *loeris* 'clown']

lorn /lɔːn/ *adj. literary* desolate, forlorn, abandoned. [past part. of obsolete *leese* from Old English *-lēosan* 'lose']

lorry /'lɒri/ *n. Brit.* (*pl.* **-ies**) **1** a large heavy motor vehicle for transporting goods etc. **2** *archaic* a long flat low wagon, esp. a truck used on railways and tramways. [19th c.: origin uncertain]

lory /'lɔːri/ *n.* (*pl.* **-ies**) any of various brightly coloured Australasian and SE Asian parrots of the subfamily Loriinae. [Malay *lūrī*]

Los Angeleno see ANGELENO.

lose /luːz/ *v.* (*past* and *past part.* **lost** /lɒst/) **1** *tr.* be deprived of or cease to have, esp. by negligence or misadventure. **2** *tr.* **a** be deprived of (a person, esp. a close relative) by death. **b** suffer the loss of (a baby) in childbirth. **3** *tr.* become unable to find; fail to keep in sight or follow or mentally grasp (*lose one's way*). **4** *tr.* let or have pass from one's control or reach (*lose one's chance*; *lose one's bearings*). **5** *tr.* be defeated in (a game, race, lawsuit, battle, etc.). **6** *tr.* evade; get rid of (*lost our pursuers*). **7** *tr.* fail to obtain, catch, or perceive (*lose a train*; *lose a word*). **8** *tr.* forfeit (a stake, deposit, right to a thing, etc.). **9** *tr.* spend (time, efforts, etc.) to no purpose (*lost no time in raising the alarm*). **10** *intr.* **a** suffer loss or detriment; incur a disadvantage. **b** be worse off, esp. financially. **11** *tr.* cause (a person) the loss of (*will lose you your job*). **12** *intr.* & *tr.* (of a timepiece) become slow; become slow by (a specified amount of time). **13** *tr.* (in *passive*) disappear, perish; be dead (*was lost in the war*; *is a lost art*). **14** *tr. colloq.* get rid of; discard. **15** *tr.* (as **lost** *adj.*) damned, fallen (*lost souls*). □ **be lost** (or **lose oneself**) **in** be engrossed in. **be lost on** be wasted on, or not noticed or appreciated by. **be lost to** be no longer affected by or accessible to (*is lost to pity*; *is lost to the world*). **be lost without** have great difficulty if deprived of (*am lost without my diary*). **get lost** (usu. in *imper.*) *slang* go away. **lose one's balance 1** fail to remain stable; fall. **2** fail to retain one's composure. **lose one's cool** *colloq.* lose one's composure. **lose face** be humiliated; lose one's credibility. **lose ground** see GROUND[1]. **lose one's head** see HEAD. **lose heart** be discouraged. **lose one's heart** see HEART. **lose one's nerve** become timid or irresolute. **lose out** *colloq.* **1** (often foll. by *on*) be unsuccessful; not get a fair chance or advantage (in). **2** (foll. by *to*) be beaten in competition or replaced by. **lose one's temper** become angry. **lose time** allow time to pass with something unachieved etc. **lose touch** see TOUCH. **lose track of** see TRACK[1]. **lose the** (or **one's**) **way** become lost; fail to reach one's destination. [Old English *losian* 'perish, destroy' from *los* 'loss']

loser /'luːzə/ *n.* **1** a person or thing that loses or has lost (esp. a contest or game) (*is a poor loser*; *the loser pays*). **2** *colloq.* a person who regularly fails.

losing battle *n.* a contest or effort in which failure seems certain (*felt we were fighting a losing battle*).

loss /lɒs/ *n.* **1 a** the act or an instance of losing; the state of being lost. **b** the fact of being deprived of a person by death, estrangement, etc. **2** a person, thing, or amount lost. **3** the detriment or disadvantage resulting from losing (*that is no great loss*). □ **at a loss** (sold etc.) for less than was paid for it. **be at a loss** be puzzled or uncertain. **be at a loss for words** not know what to say. [Middle English *los*, *loss*, probably a back-formation from *lost*, past part. of LOSE]

loss adjuster *n.* an insurance agent who assesses the amount of compensation arising from a loss.

loss-leader *n.* an item sold at a loss to attract customers.

loss-making *adj.* (of a business etc.) making a financial loss. □ **loss-maker** *n.*

lost *past* and *past part.* of LOSE.

lost cause *n.* **1** an enterprise etc. with no chance of success. **2** a person one can no longer hope to influence.

lost generation *n.* **1** a generation with many of its men killed in war, esp. in the First World War. **2** an emotionally and culturally unstable generation coming to maturity, esp. in 1915–25.

lost labour *n.* fruitless effort.

lost soul *n.* **1** a soul that is damned. **2** a person who is unable to cope with everyday life; a bewildered or pitiful person.

lost wax *n.* = CIRE PERDUE.

lot /lɒt/ *n.* & *v.* ● *n.* **1** (prec. by *a* or in *pl.*) *colloq.* **a** a large number or amount (*a lot of people*; *lots of chocolate*). **b** (as *adv.*) much (*a lot warmer*; *smiles a lot*; *is lots better*). **2 a** each of a set of objects used in making a chance selection. **b** this method of deciding (*chosen by lot*). **3** a share, or the responsibility resulting from it. **4** a person's destiny, fortune, or condition. **5** esp. *N. Amer.* a plot; an allotment of land (*parking lot*). **6** an article or set of articles for sale at an auction etc. **7** a number or quantity of associated persons or things. ● *v.tr.* (**lotted**, **lotting**) divide into lots. □ **cast** (or **draw**) **lots** decide by means of lots. **throw in one's lot with** decide to share the fortunes of. **the** (or **the whole**) **lot** esp. *Brit.* the whole number or quantity. **a whole lot** *colloq.* very much (*is a whole lot better*). [Old English *hlot* 'portion, choice', from Germanic]

■ **Usage** In sense 1a of the noun, *a lot of* is somewhat informal, but acceptable in serious writing, whereas *lots of* is not.

loth var. of LOATH.

Lothario /lə'θɛːrɪəʊ, -'θɑː-/ *n.* (*pl.* **-os**) a rake or libertine. [a character in Rowe's *Fair Penitent* (1703)]

lotion /'ləʊʃ(ə)n/ *n.* a medicinal or cosmetic liquid preparation applied externally. [Middle English via Old French *lotion* or Latin *lotio* from *lavare lot-* 'wash']

lotsa /'lɒtsə/ *colloq.* lots of.

lotta /'lɒtə/ *colloq.* lot of. [corruption]

lottery /'lɒt(ə)ri/ *n.* (*pl.* **-ies**) **1** a means of raising money by selling numbered tickets and giving prizes to the holders of numbers drawn at random. **2** an enterprise, process, etc., whose success is governed by chance (*life is a lottery*). [probably from Dutch *loterij* (as LOT)]

lotto /'lɒtəʊ/ *n.* **1** a game of chance like bingo, but with numbers drawn by the players instead of being called. **2** esp. *US* a lottery. [Italian]

lotus /'ləʊtəs/ *n.* **1** (in Greek mythology) a legendary plant inducing luxurious languor when eaten. **2 a** any water lily of the genus *Nelumbo*, esp. *N. nucifera* of India, with large pink flowers. **b** this flower used symbolically in Hinduism and Buddhism. **3** an Egyptian water lily, *Nymphaea lotus*, with white flowers. **4** any plant of the genus *Lotus*, e.g. bird's-foot trefoil. [Latin from Greek *lōtos*, of Semitic origin]

lotus-eater *n.* a person given to indolent enjoyment.

lotus-land *n.* a place of indolent enjoyment.

lotus position *n.* a cross-legged position of meditation with the feet resting on the thighs.

louche /luːʃ/ *adj.* disreputable, shifty. [French, = squinting]

loud /laʊd/ *adj. & adv.* ● *adj.* **1 a** strongly audible, esp. noisily or oppressively so. **b** able or liable to produce loud sounds (*a loud engine*). **c** clamorous, insistent (*loud complaints*). **2** (of colours, design, etc.) gaudy, obtrusive. **3** (of behaviour) aggressive and noisy. ● *adv.* in a loud manner. □ **out loud 1** aloud. **2** loudly (*laughed out loud*). □ **louden** *v.tr. & intr.* **loudish** *adj.* **loudly** *adv.* **loudness** *n.* [Old English *hlūd*, from West Germanic]

loud hailer *n. Brit.* an electronic device for amplifying the sound of the voice so that it can be heard at a distance.

loudmouth /ˈlaʊdmaʊθ/ *n. colloq.* a loud-mouthed person. □ **loud-mouthed** *adj.*

loudspeaker /laʊdˈspiːkə/ *n.* an apparatus that converts electrical impulses into sound, esp. music and voice.

lough /lɒk, lɒx/ *n. Ir.* = LOCH. [Irish *loch* LOCH, assimilated to the related obsolete Middle English form *lough*]

louis /ˈluːi/ *n.* (*pl.* same /ˈluːɪz/) *hist.* (in full **louis d'or** /-ˈdɔː/) a former French gold coin worth about 20 francs. [*Louis*, the name of kings of France]

lounge /laʊn(d)ʒ/ *v. & n.* ● *v.intr.* **1** recline comfortably and casually; loll. **2** stand or move about idly. ● *n.* **1** a place for lounging, esp.: **a** a public room (e.g. in a hotel). **b** a place in an airport etc. with seats for waiting passengers. **c** a sitting room in a house. **2** *Brit.* a spell of lounging. [perhaps from obsolete *lungis* 'lout']

lounge bar *n. Brit.* a more comfortable room for drinking in a public house.

lounge lizard *n. colloq.* an idler in fashionable society.

lounger /ˈlaʊn(d)ʒə/ *n.* **1** a person who lounges. **2** a piece of furniture for relaxing on. **3** a casual garment for wearing when relaxing.

lounge suit *n. Brit.* a man's formal suit for ordinary day wear.

loupe /luːp/ *n.* a small magnifying glass used by jewellers etc. [French]

louping-ill /ˈlaʊpɪŋ,ɪl/ *n.* a viral disease of animals, esp. sheep, transmitted by ticks and causing staggering and jumping. [Scots & N. Engl. dialect *loup* 'leap']

lour /ˈlaʊə/ *v. & n.* (also **lower**) ● *v.intr.* **1** frown; look sullen. **2** (of the sky etc.) look dark and threatening. ● *n.* **1** a scowl. **2** a gloomy look (of the sky etc.). □ **louringly** *adv.* **loury** *adj.* [Middle English *loure*, of unknown origin]

louse /laʊs/ *n. & v.* ● *n.* **1** (*pl.* **lice** /lʌɪs/) **a** a parasitic insect, *Pediculus humanus*, infesting the human hair and skin and transmitting various diseases (*head louse*; *body louse*). **b** any insect of the order Anoplura or Mallophaga, parasitic on mammals or birds. **c** any invertebrate that attaches itself parasitically to an animal, esp. an aquatic one, or that infests plants. **2** (*pl.* **louses**) *slang* a contemptible or unpleasant person. ● *v.tr.* remove lice from. □ **louse up** *slang* make a mess of. [Old English *lūs*, pl. *lȳs*]

lousewort /ˈlaʊswəːt/ *n.* a plant of the genus *Pedicularis* with purple-pink flowers, found in marshes and wet places.

lousy /ˈlaʊzi/ *adj.* (**lousier**, **lousiest**) **1** infested with lice. **2** *colloq.* very bad; disgusting (also as a term of general disparagement). **3** (often foll. by *with*) *colloq.* well supplied; teeming. □ **lousily** *adv.* **lousiness** *n.*

lout /laʊt/ *n.* a rough, crude, or ill-mannered person (usu. a man). □ **loutish** *adj.* **loutishly** *adv.* **loutishness** *n.* [perhaps from archaic *lout* 'to bow']

louvre /ˈluvə/ *n.* (also **louver**) **1** each of a set of overlapping slats designed to admit air and some light and exclude rain. **2** a domed structure on a roof with side openings for ventilation etc. □ **louvred** *adj.* [Middle English from Old French *lover*, *lovier* 'skylight', probably from Germanic]

louvre-board *n.* (usu. in *pl.*) each of the slats or boards making up a louvre.

lovable /ˈlʌvəb(ə)l/ *adj.* (also **loveable**) inspiring or deserving love or affection. □ **lovability** /-ˈbɪlɪti/ *n.* **lovableness** *n.* **lovably** *adv.*

lovage /ˈlʌvɪdʒ/ *n.* **1** a S. European herb, *Levisticum officinale*, used for flavouring etc. **2** a white-flowered umbelliferous plant, *Ligusticum scoticum*. [Middle English *loveache*, alteration of Old French *levesche*, via Late Latin *levisticum* from Latin *ligusticum*, neut. of *ligusticus* 'Ligurian']

lovat /ˈlʌvət/ *n. & adj.* ● *n.* (also **lovat green**) a muted green colour found esp. in tweed and woollen garments. ● *adj.* (also **lovat green**; hyphenated when *attrib.*) of this colour. [*Lovat*, a place in Highland Scotland]

love /lʌv/ *n. & v.* ● *n.* **1** an intense feeling of deep affection or fondness for a person or thing; great liking. **2** sexual passion. **3** sexual relations. **4 a** a beloved one; a sweetheart (often as a form of address). **b** *Brit. colloq.* a familiar form of address regardless of affection. **5** *colloq.* a person of whom one is fond. **6** affectionate greetings (*give him my love*). **7** (often **Love**) a representation of Cupid. **8** (in some games) no score; nil. **9** a formula for ending an affectionate letter etc. ● *v.tr.* **1** (also *absol.*) feel love or deep fondness for. **2** delight in; admire; greatly cherish. **3** *colloq.* like very much (*loves books*). **4** (foll. by verbal noun, or *to* + infin.) be inclined, esp. as a habit; greatly enjoy; find pleasure in (*children love dressing up*; *loves to find fault*). □ **fall in love** (often foll. by *with*) develop a great (esp. sexual) love (for). **for love** for pleasure not profit. **for the love of** for the sake of. **in love** (often foll. by *with*) deeply enamoured (of). **love-hate relationship** an intensely emotional relationship in which one or each party has ambivalent feelings of love and hate for the other. **make love 1** (often foll. by *to, with*) have sexual intercourse (with). **2** (often foll. by *to*) *archaic* pay amorous attention (to). **no love lost between** mutual dislike between (two people etc.). **not for love or money** *colloq.* not in any circumstances. **out of love** no longer in love. □ **loveworthy** *adj.* [Old English *lufu* from Germanic: related to LEAVE[2], LIEF]

loveable var. of LOVABLE.

love affair *n.* **1** a romantic or sexual relationship between two people in love. **2** an intense enthusiasm or liking for something.

love-apple *n. archaic* a tomato.

lovebird /ˈlʌvbəːd/ *n.* **1** any of various African and Madagascan parrots, esp. *Agapornis personata*. **2** (in *pl.*) *colloq.* an affectionate couple; lovers.

lovebite /ˈlʌvbʌɪt/ *n.* a red mark on the skin, caused by biting or sucking during sexual play.

love child *n.* an illegitimate child.

love feast *n.* **1** a meal affirming brotherly love among early Christians. **2** a religious service of Methodists, etc., imitating this.

love game *n.* a game in which the loser makes no score.

love handles *n.pl.* esp. *N. Amer. slang* excess fat at the waist.

love-in-a-mist *n.* a blue-flowered garden plant, *Nigella damascena*, with many delicate green bracts.

loveless /ˈlʌvlɪs/ *adj.* without love; unloving or unloved or both. □ **lovelessly** *adv.* **lovelessness** *n.*

love letter *n.* a letter expressing feelings of sexual love.

love-lies-bleeding *n.* a garden plant, *Amaranthus caudatus*, with drooping spikes of purple-red blooms.

love life *n.* a person's life with regard to relationships with lovers.

lovelock /ˈlʌvlɒk/ *n.* a curl or lock of hair worn on the temple or forehead.

lovelorn /ˈlʌvlɔːn/ *adj.* pining from unrequited love.

lovely /ˈlʌvli/ *adj. & n.* ● *adj.* (**lovelier**, **loveliest**) **1** exquisitely beautiful. **2** *colloq.* pleasing, delightful. ● *n.* (*pl.* **-ies**) *colloq.* a pretty woman. □ **lovely and** *colloq.*

delightfully (*lovely and warm*). □ **lovelily** *adv.* **loveliness** *n.* [Old English *luflic* (as LOVE)]

lovemaking /ˈlʌvmeɪkɪŋ/ *n.* **1** amorous sexual activity, esp. sexual intercourse. **2** *archaic* courtship.

love match *n.* a marriage made for love's sake.

love nest *n.* a secluded retreat for (esp. illicit) lovers.

lover /ˈlʌvə/ *n.* **1** a person in love with another. **2** a person with whom another is having sexual relations. **3** (in *pl.*) a couple in love or having sexual relations. **4** a person who likes or enjoys something specified (*a music lover; a lover of words*). □ **loverless** *adj.*

love seat *n.* an armchair or small sofa for two.

lovesick /ˈlʌvsɪk/ *adj.* languishing with romantic love. □ **lovesickness** *n.*

lovesome /ˈlʌvs(ə)m/ *adj. literary* lovely, lovable.

lovey /ˈlʌvi/ *n.* (*pl.* **-eys**) *Brit. colloq.* love, sweetheart (esp. as a form of address).

lovey-dovey /ˈlʌvɪˌdʌvi, lʌvɪˈdʌvi/ *adj. colloq.* fondly affectionate, esp. in an unduly sentimental way.

loving /ˈlʌvɪŋ/ *adj. & n.* ● *adj.* feeling or showing love; affectionate. ● *n.* affection; active love. □ **lovingly** *adv.* **lovingness** *n.* [Old English *lufiende* (as LOVE)]

loving cup *n.* a two-handled drinking cup passed round at banquets.

loving kindness *n.* tenderness and consideration.

low[1] /ləʊ/ *adj., n., & adv.* ● *adj.* **1** of less than average height; not high or tall or reaching far up (*a low wall*). **2 a** situated close to ground or sea level etc.; not elevated in position (*low altitude*). **b** (of the sun) near the horizon. **c** (of latitude) near the equator. **3** of or in humble rank or position (*of low birth*). **4** of small or less than normal amount or extent or intensity (*low price; low temperature; low in calories*). **5** small or reduced in quantity (*stocks are low*). **6** coming below the normal level (*a dress with a low neck*). **7 a** dejected; lacking vigour (*feeling low; in low spirits*). **b** poorly nourished; indicative of poor nutrition. **8** (of a sound) not shrill or loud or high-pitched. **9** *Phonet.* = OPEN *adj.* 22a. **10** not exalted or sublime; commonplace. **11** unfavourable (*a low opinion*). **12** abject, mean, vulgar (*low cunning; low slang*). ● *n.* **1** a low or the lowest level or number (*the dollar has reached a new low*). **2** an area of low barometric pressure; a depression. ● *adv.* **1** in or to a low position or state. **2** in a low tone (*speak low*). **3** at or to a low pitch (*I can't sing so low*). □ **lowish** *adj.* **lowness** *n.* [Middle English *lāh* from Old Norse *lágr*, from Germanic]

low[2] /ləʊ/ *n. & v.* ● *n.* a sound made by cattle; a moo. ● *v.intr.* utter this sound. [Old English *hlōwan*, from Germanic]

low-born *adj.* of humble birth.

lowboy /ˈləʊbɔɪ/ *n. N. Amer.* a low chest or table with drawers and short legs.

lowbrow /ˈləʊbraʊ/ *adj. & n.* ● *adj.* not highly intellectual or cultured. ● *n.* a lowbrow person. □ **lowbrowed** *adj.*

Low Church *n.* a tradition within the Anglican Church giving little emphasis to ritual, priestly authority, and the sacraments.

low-class *adj.* of low quality or social class.

low comedy *n.* that in which the subject and the treatment border on farce.

Low Countries *n.pl.* the Netherlands, Belgium, and Luxembourg.

low-cut *adj.* (of a dress etc.) made with a low neckline.

low-density lipoprotein *n.* the form of lipoprotein in which cholesterol is transported in the blood (abbr.: LDL).

low-down *adj. & n.* ● *adj.* abject, mean, dishonourable. ● *n.* (usu. foll. by *on*) *colloq.* the relevant information (about).

lower[1] /ˈləʊə/ *adj. & adv.* ● *adj.* (*compar.* of LOW[1]). **1** less high in position or status. **2** situated below another part (*lower lip; lower atmosphere*). **3 a** situated on less high land (*Lower Egypt*). **b** situated to the south (*Lower California*). **4** (of an animal or plant) showing relatively primitive characteristics (e.g. a platypus or a fungus). **5** (often **Lower**) *Geol. & Archaeol.* designating an older, and hence usu. deeper, part of a stratigraphic division, archaeological deposit, etc., or the period in which it was formed or deposited. ● *adv.* in or to a lower position, status, etc. □ **lowermost** *adj.*

lower[2] /ˈləʊə/ *v.* **1** *tr.* let or haul down. **2** *tr. & intr.* make or become lower. **3** *tr.* reduce the height or pitch or elevation of (*lower your voice; lower one's eyes*). **4** *tr.* degrade. **5** *tr. & intr.* diminish. □ **lower the tone** diminish the cultural content, prestige, or moral character (of a conversation, place, etc.).

lower[3] var. of LOUR.

lower case *n.* (hyphenated when *attrib.*) small letters.

lower class *n. & adj.* ● *n.* the members of the working class. ● *adj.* (**lower-class**) of the lower class.

lower criticism *n.* (prec. by *the*) textual criticism of the Bible.

lower deck *n.* **1** the deck of a ship situated immediately over the hold. **2** the petty officers and men of a ship collectively.

Lower House *n.* the larger and usu. elected body in a legislature, esp. (in Britain) the House of Commons.

lower regions *n.pl.* (also **lower world**) hell; the realm of the dead.

lowest common denominator *n.* **1** the lowest common multiple of the denominators of several fractions. **2** the least desirable common feature of members of a group.

lowest common multiple *n.* the lowest quantity that is a multiple of two or more given quantities.

low frequency *n.* (in radio) 30–300 kilohertz.

low gear *n.* a gear such that the driven end of a transmission revolves more slowly than the driving end.

Low German *n.* German dialects other than High German, spoken in the lowlands or north of Germany.

low-grade *adj.* of low quality or strength.

low-income *attrib.adj.* **1** of or relating to the income group comprising low-wage earners. **2** with a low national income (used esp. of poorer Third World countries).

low-key *adj.* lacking intensity or prominence; restrained.

lowland /ˈləʊlənd/ *n. & adj.* ● *n.* **1** (usu. in *pl.*) low-lying country. **2** (**Lowland**) (usu. in *pl.*) the region of Scotland lying south and east of the Highlands. ● *adj.* of or in lowland or (**Lowland**) the Scottish Lowlands. □ **lowlander** *n.* (also **Lowlander**).

Low Latin *n.* medieval and later forms of Latin.

low latitudes *n.pl.* regions near the equator.

low-level *adj. Computing* (of a programming language) close in form to machine language.

low life *n.* **1** degenerate living; life in the criminal underworld. **2** (**lowlife**) **a** a member of the underworld. **b** such people collectively.

lowlight /ˈləʊlʌɪt/ *n.* **1** *joc.* a monotonous or dull period; a feature of little prominence (*one of the lowlights of the evening*). **2** (usu. in *pl.*) a dark tint in the hair produced by dyeing. [on the pattern of HIGHLIGHT]

low-loader *n. Brit.* a lorry with a low floor and no sides, for heavy loads.

lowly /ˈləʊli/ *adj.* (**lowlier**, **lowliest**) **1** humble in feeling, behaviour, or status. **2** modest, unpretentious. **3** (of an organism) evolved to only a slight degree. □ **lowlily** *adv.* **lowliness** *n.*

low-lying *adj.* at low altitude (above sea level etc.).

low Mass *n.* Mass with no music and a minimum of ceremony.

low-minded *adj.* vulgar or ignoble in mind or character. □ **low-mindedness** *n.*

low-pitched *adj.* **1** (of a sound) low. **2** (of a roof) having only a slight slope.

low pressure *n.* **1** little demand for activity or exertion. **2** an atmospheric condition with pressure below average, e.g in a depression.

low profile *n. & adj.* ● *n.* avoidance of attention or publicity. ● *adj.* (**low-profile**) **1** (of a motor vehicle tyre) having a greater width than usual in relation to height. **2** (usu. *attrib.*) avoiding attention or publicity (*a low-profile manager*).

low relief see RELIEF 6a.

low-rise *adj.* (of a building) having few storeys.

low season *n.* the period of fewest visitors at a resort etc.

low spirits *n.pl.* dejection, depression. ▫ **low-spirited** *adj.* **low-spiritedness** *n.*

Low Sunday *n.* the Sunday after Easter.

low tide *n.* **1** the state of the tide when at its lowest level. **2** the time of this.

low water *n.* = LOW TIDE.

low water mark *n.* **1** the level reached by the sea etc. at low tide. **2** the minimum recorded level or value etc.

Low Week *n.* the week beginning with Low Sunday.

lox[1] /lɒks/ *n.* liquid oxygen. [abbreviation]

lox[2] /lɒks/ *n. N. Amer.* smoked salmon. [Yiddish *laks*]

loyal /'lɔɪəl/ *adj.* **1** (often foll. by *to*) true or faithful (to duty, love, or obligation). **2** steadfast in allegiance; devoted to the legitimate sovereign or government of one's country. **3** showing loyalty. ▫ **loyally** *adv.* [French via Old French *loial* etc. from Latin *legalis* LEGAL]

loyalist /'lɔɪəlɪst/ *n.* (often *attrib.*) **1** a person who remains loyal to the legitimate sovereign etc., esp. in the face of rebellion or usurpation. **2** (**Loyalist**) a supporter of union between Great Britain and Northern Ireland. ▫ **loyalism** *n.*

loyal toast *n.* a toast to the sovereign.

loyalty /'lɔɪəlti/ *n.* (*pl.* **-ies**) **1** the state of being loyal. **2** (often in *pl.*) a feeling or application of loyalty.

lozenge /'lɒzɪn(d)ʒ/ *n.* **1** a rhombus or diamond figure. **2** a small sweet or medicinal tablet, originally lozenge-shaped, for dissolving in the mouth. **3** a lozenge-shaped pane in a window. **4** *Heraldry* a lozenge-shaped device. **5** the lozenge-shaped facet of a cut gem. ▫ **lozenged** *adj.* (in sense 4). **lozengy** *adj.* [Middle English from Old French *losenge*, ultimately of Gaulish or Iberian origin]

LP *abbr.* **1** long-playing (gramophone record). **2** low pressure.

LPG *abbr.* liquefied petroleum gas.

L-plate *n. Brit.* a sign bearing the letter L, attached to the front and rear of a motor vehicle to indicate that it is being driven by a learner.

LPO *abbr.* London Philharmonic Orchestra.

Lr *symb. Chem.* the element lawrencium.

LSD *abbr.* lysergic acid diethylamide.

l.s.d. *n.* (also **£.s.d.**) *Brit.* **1** pounds, shillings, and pence (in former British currency). **2** money, riches. [Latin *librae* (= pounds), *solidi*, *denarii* (roman coins)]

LSE *abbr.* London School of Economics.

LSO *abbr.* London Symphony Orchestra.

Lt. *abbr.* **1** Lieutenant. **2** light.

LTA *abbr.* Lawn Tennis Association.

Ltd. *abbr.* Limited.

Lu *symb. Chem.* the element lutetium.

lubber /'lʌbə/ *n. archaic* or *dial.* a big clumsy fellow; a lout. ▫ **lubberlike** *adj.* **lubberly** *adj. & adv.* [Middle English, perhaps via Old French *lobeor* 'swindler, parasite' from *lober* 'deceive']

lubber line *n. Naut.* a line marked on a compass, showing the ship's forward direction.

lubra /'lu:brə, 'lju:-/ *n. Austral. offens.* an Aboriginal woman. [Aboriginal, perhaps Tasmanian]

lubricant /'lu:brɪk(ə)nt, 'lju:-/ *n. & adj.* ● *n.* a substance used to reduce friction. ● *adj.* lubricating.

lubricate /'lu:brɪkeɪt, 'lju:-/ *v.tr.* **1** reduce friction in (machinery etc.) by applying oil or grease etc. **2** make slippery or smooth with oil or grease. ▫ **lubrication** /-'keɪʃ(ə)n/ *n.* **lubricative** /-kətɪv/ *adj.* **lubricator** *n.* [Latin *lubricare lubricat-* from *lubricus* 'slippery']

lubricious /lu:'brɪʃəs, lju:-/ *adj.* (also **lubricous** /'lu:brɪkəs/) **1** slippery, smooth, oily. **2** lewd, prurient. **3** evasive. ▫ **lubricity** *n.* [Latin *lubricus* slippery]

Lucan /'lu:k(ə)n, 'lju:-/ *adj.* of or relating to St Luke. [ecclesiastical Latin *Lucas* from Greek *Loukas* 'Luke']

luce /lu:s, lju:s/ *n.* a pike (fish), esp. when full-grown. [Middle English via Old French *lus*, *luis* from Late Latin *lucius*]

lucent /'lu:s(ə)nt, 'lju:-/ *adj. literary* **1** shining, luminous. **2** translucent. ▫ **lucency** *n.* [Latin *lucēre* 'shine' (as LUX)]

lucerne /lu:'sə:n, lju:-/ *n.* (also **lucern**) *Brit.* = ALFALFA. [French *luzerne* from modern Provençal *luzerno* 'glow-worm', with reference to its shiny seeds]

lucid /'lu:sɪd, 'lju:-/ *adj.* **1** expressing or expressed clearly; easy to understand. **2** of or denoting intervals of sanity between periods of insanity or dementia. **3** *Bot.* with a smooth shiny surface. **4** *poet.* bright. ▫ **lucidity** /-'sɪdɪti/ *n.* **lucidly** *adv.* **lucidness** *n.* [Latin *lucidus* (perhaps via French *lucide* or Italian *lucido*) from *lucēre* 'shine' (as LUX)]

Lucifer /'lu:sɪfə, 'lju:-/ *n.* **1** Satan. **2** *poet.* the morning star (the planet Venus). **3** (**lucifer**) *archaic* a friction match. [Old English from Latin, = light-bringing, morning star (as LUX, *-fer* from *ferre* 'bring')]

luck /lʌk/ *n. & v.* ● *n.* **1** chance regarded as the bringer of good or bad fortune. **2** circumstances of life (beneficial or not) brought by this. **3** good fortune; success due to chance (*in luck*; *out of luck*). ● *v.intr. colloq.* **1** (foll. by *upon*, *up on*) chance to find or meet with. **2** (foll. by *into*) esp. *N. Amer.* acquire by good fortune. **3** (foll. by *out*) esp. *N. Amer.* achieve success or advantage by good luck. ▫ **for luck** to bring good fortune. **no such luck** *colloq.* unfortunately not. **try one's luck** make a venture. **with luck** if all goes well. **worse luck** *colloq.* unfortunately. [Middle English via Low German *luk* from Middle Low German *geluke*]

luckily /'lʌkɪli/ *adv.* **1** (qualifying a whole sentence or clause) fortunately (*luckily there was enough food*). **2** in a lucky or fortunate manner.

luckless /'lʌklɪs/ *adj.* having no luck; unfortunate. ▫ **lucklessly** *adv.* **lucklessness** *n.*

lucky /'lʌki/ *adj.* (**luckier**, **luckiest**) **1** having or resulting from good luck, esp. as distinct from skill or design or merit. **2** bringing good luck (*a lucky mascot*). **3** fortunate, appropriate (*a lucky guess*). ▫ **luckiness** *n.*

lucky dip *n. Brit.* a tub containing different articles concealed in wrapping or bran etc., and chosen at random by participants.

lucrative /'lu:krətɪv, 'lju:-/ *adj.* profitable, yielding financial gain. ▫ **lucratively** *adv.* **lucrativeness** *n.* [Middle English from Latin *lucrativus*, from *lucrari* 'to gain']

lucre /'lu:kə, 'lju:-/ *n. derog.* financial profit or gain. [Middle English from French *lucre* or Latin *lucrum*]

lucubrate /'lu:kjʊbreɪt, 'lju:-/ *v.intr. literary* **1** write or study, esp. by night. **2** express one's meditations in writing. ▫ **lucubrator** *n.* [Latin *lucubrare lucubrat-* 'work by lamplight' (as LUX)]

lucubration /lu:kjʊ'breɪʃ(ə)n, lju:-/ *n. literary* **1** nocturnal study or meditation. **2** (usu. in *pl.*) literary writings, esp. of a pedantic or elaborate character. [Latin *lucubratio* (as LUCUBRATE)]

Lucullan /lu:'kʌlən, lʊ-/ *adj.* profusely luxurious. [from the name of Licinius *Lucullus*, Roman general of 1st c. BC, famous for his lavish banquets]

lud /lʌd/ *n. Brit.* ▫ **m'lud** (or **my lud**) a form of address to a judge in a court of law. [corruption of LORD]

Luddite /'lʌdʌɪt/ *n. & adj.* ● *n.* **1** *hist.* a member of any of the bands of English artisans who rioted against mechanization and destroyed machinery (1811–16). **2** a person opposed to increased industrialization or new technology. ● *adj.* of the Luddites or their beliefs. ▫ **Luddism** /'lʌdɪz(ə)m/ *n.* **Ludditism** /'lʌdɪtɪz(ə)m/ *n.* [perhaps named after Ned *Lud*, who destroyed machinery *c.*1779]

ludicrous /'lu:dɪkrəs, 'lju:-/ *adj.* absurd or ridiculous; laughable. ◻ **ludicrously** *adv.* **ludicrousness** *n.* [Latin *ludicrus*, probably from *ludicrum* 'stage play']

ludo /'lu:dəʊ, 'lju:-/ *n. Brit.* a simple board game in which counters are moved round according to the throw of dice. [Latin, = I play]

lues /'lu:i:z, 'lju:-/ *n.* (in full **lues venerea** /vɪ'nɪərɪə/) syphilis. ◻ **luetic** /lu:'ɛtɪk, lju:-/ *adj.* [Latin, = plague]

luff /lʌf/ *n. & v.* (also **loof** /lu:f/) *Naut.* ● *n.* **1** the edge of the fore-and-aft sail next to the mast or stay. **2** *Brit.* the broadest part of the ship's bow where the sides begin to curve in. ● *v.tr.* (also *absol.*) **1** steer (a ship) nearer the wind. **2** turn (the helm) so as to achieve this. **3** obstruct (an opponent in yacht racing) by sailing closer to the wind. **4** raise or lower (the jib of a crane or derrick). [Middle English *lo(o)f* from Old French *lof*, probably from Low German]

luffa var. of LOOFAH.

Luftwaffe /'lʊftwafə, German 'lʊftvafə/ *n. hist.* the German air force up to the end of the Second World War. [German, from *Luft* 'air' + *Waffe* 'weapon']

lug[1] /lʌg/ *v. & n.* ● *v.* (**lugged**, **lugging**) **1** *tr.* **a** drag or tug (a heavy object) with effort or violence. **b** (usu. foll. by *round*, *about*) carry (something heavy) around with one. **2** *tr.* (usu. foll. by *in*, *into*) introduce (a subject etc.) irrelevantly. **3** *tr.* (usu. foll. by *along*, *to*) force (a person) to join in an activity. **4** *intr.* (usu. foll. by *at*) pull hard. ● *n.* **1** a hard or rough pull. **2** (in *pl.*) *US slang* affectation (*put on lugs*). [Middle English, probably from Scandinavian: cf. Swedish *lugga* 'pull a person's hair' from *lugg* 'forelock']

lug[2] /lʌg/ *n.* **1** *Sc.* or *colloq.* an ear. **2** a projection on an object by which it may be carried, fixed in place, etc. **3** esp. *N. Amer. slang* a lout; a sponger; a stupid or clumsy person. [probably of Scandinavian origin: cf. LUG[1]]

lug[3] /lʌg/ *n.* = LUGWORM. [17th c.: origin unknown]

lug[4] /lʌg/ *n.* = LUGSAIL. [abbreviation]

luge /lu:ʒ/ *n. & v.* ● *n.* a light toboggan for one or two people, ridden in a sitting or supine position. ● *v.intr.* ride on a luge. [Swiss French]

Luger /'lu:gə/ *n.* a type of German automatic pistol. [named after G. *Luger*, German firearms expert d. 1922]

luggage /'lʌgɪdʒ/ *n.* suitcases, bags, etc. to hold a traveller's belongings. [LUG[1] + -AGE]

luggage van *n. Brit.* a railway carriage for travellers' luggage.

lugger /'lʌgə/ *n.* a small ship carrying two or three masts with a lugsail on each. [LUGSAIL + -ER[1]]

lughole /'lʌghəʊl, 'lʌgəʊl/ *n. Brit. slang* the ear orifice. [LUG[2] + HOLE]

lugsail /'lʌgseɪl, -s(ə)l/ *n. Naut.* a quadrilateral sail which is bent on and hoisted from a yard. [probably from LUG[2]]

lugubrious /lʊ'gu:brɪəs/ *adj.* doleful, mournful, dismal. ◻ **lugubriously** *adv.* **lugubriousness** *n.* [Latin *lugubris* from *lugēre* 'mourn']

lugworm /'lʌgwə:m/ *n.* any polychaete worm of the genus *Arenicola*, living in muddy sand and leaving characteristic worm-casts on lower shores, and often used as bait by fishermen. [LUG[3]]

lukewarm /'lu:kwɔ:m, lu:k'wɔ:m, lj-/ *adj.* **1** moderately warm; tepid. **2** unenthusiastic, indifferent. ◻ **lukewarmly** *adv.* **lukewarmness** *n.* [Middle English from (now dialect) *luke*, *lew* from Old English, probably related to LEE]

lull /lʌl/ *v. & n.* ● *v.* **1** *tr.* soothe or send to sleep gently. **2** *tr.* (usu. foll. by *into*) deceive (a person) into confidence (*lulled into a false sense of security*). **3** *tr.* allay (suspicions etc.) usu. by deception. **4** *intr.* (of noise, a storm, etc.) abate or fall quiet. ● *n.* a temporary quiet period in a storm or in any activity. [Middle English, imitative of sounds used to quieten a child]

lullaby /'lʌləbʌɪ/ *n. & v.* ● *n.* (*pl.* **-ies**) **1** a soothing song to send a child to sleep. **2** the music for this. ● *v.tr.* (**-ies**, **-ied**) sing to sleep. [as LULL + *-by* as in BYE-BYE[2]]

lulu /'lu:lu:/ *n. slang* a remarkable or excellent person or thing. [19th c., perhaps from *Lulu*, pet form of *Louise*]

lumbago /lʌm'beɪgəʊ/ *n.* rheumatic pain in the muscles of the lower back. [Latin, from *lumbus* 'loin']

lumbar /'lʌmbə/ *adj. Anat.* relating to the loin, esp. the lower back area. [medieval Latin *lumbaris* from Latin *lumbus* 'loin']

lumbar puncture *n.* the withdrawal of spinal fluid from the lower back with a hollow needle, usu. for diagnosis.

lumber[1] /'lʌmbə/ *v.intr.* (usu. foll. by *along*, *past*, *by*, etc.) move in a slow clumsy noisy way. ◻ **lumbering** *adj.* [Middle English *lomere*, perhaps imitative]

lumber[2] /'lʌmbə/ *n. & v.* ● *n.* **1** *Brit.* disused articles of furniture etc. inconveniently taking up space. **2** useless or cumbersome objects. **3** *N. Amer.* partly or fully prepared timber. ● *v.* **1** *tr. Brit.* **a** (usu. foll. by *with*) leave (a person etc.) with something unwanted or unpleasant (*always lumbering me with the cleaning*). **b** (as **lumbered** *adj.*) in an unwanted or inconvenient situation (*afraid of being lumbered*). **2** *tr.* (usu. foll. by *together*) *Brit.* heap or group together carelessly. **3** *tr.* (usu. foll. by *up*) *Brit.* obstruct. **4** *intr.* cut and prepare forest timber for transport. ◻ **lumberer** *n.* (in sense 4 of *v.*). **lumbering** *n.* (in sense 4 of *v.*). [perhaps from LUMBER[1]: later associated with obsolete *lumber* 'pawnbroker's shop']

lumberjack /'lʌmbədʒak/ *n.* (also **lumberman** *pl.* **-men**) esp. *N. Amer.* a person who fells, prepares, or conveys forest timber.

lumber-jacket *n.* a jacket, usu. of warm checked material, of the kind worn by lumberjacks.

lumber-room *n. Brit.* a room where disused or cumbrous things are kept.

lumbersome /'lʌmbəs(ə)m/ *adj.* unwieldy, awkward.

lumbrical muscle /lʌm'brʌɪk(ə)l, 'lʌmbrɪk(ə)l/ *n.* any of a group of small muscles involved in flexing the fingers or toes. [modern Latin *lumbricalis* from Latin *lumbricus* 'earthworm', with reference to its shape]

lumen /'lu:mɛn, 'lju:-/ *n.* **1** (*pl.* **lumens**) *Physics* the SI unit of luminous flux, equal to the amount of light emitted per second in a unit solid angle of one steradian from a uniform source of one candela (abbr.: lm). **2** (*pl.* **lumina** /-mɪnə/) *Anat.* a cavity within a tube, cell, etc. ◻ **luminal** /'lu:mɪn(ə)l, 'lju:-/ *adj.* [Latin *lumen luminis* 'a light, an opening']

luminaire /'lu:mɪnɛ:, 'lju:-/ *n.* a unit consisting of an electric light and its fittings. [French]

Luminal /'lu:mɪn(ə)l, 'lju:-/ *n. propr.* phenobarbitone. [as LUMEN + *-al* as in *veronal*]

luminance /'lu:mɪn(ə)ns, 'lju:-/ *n. Physics* the intensity of light emitted from a surface per unit area in a given direction. [Latin *luminare* 'illuminate' (as LUMEN)]

luminary /'lu:mɪn(ə)ri, 'lju:-/ *n.* (*pl.* **-ies**) **1** *literary* a natural light-giving body, esp. the sun or moon. **2** a person as a source of intellectual light or moral inspiration. **3** a prominent member of a group or gathering (*a host of show-business luminaries*). [Middle English from Old French *luminarie* or Late Latin *luminarium* from Latin LUMEN]

luminescence /lu:mɪ'nɛs(ə)ns, lju:-/ *n.* the emission of light by a substance other than as a result of incandescence. ◻ **luminescent** *adj.* [as LUMEN + -ESCENCE (see -ESCENT)]

luminiferous /lu:mɪ'nɪf(ə)rəs, lju:-/ *adj.* producing or transmitting light.

luminous /'lu:mɪnəs, 'lju:-/ *adj.* **1** full of or shedding light; radiant, bright, shining. **2** phosphorescent, visible in darkness (*luminous paint*). **3** (esp. of a writer or a writer's work) throwing light on a subject. **4** of visible radiation (*luminous intensity*). ◻ **luminosity** /-'nɒsɪti/ *n.* **luminously** *adj.* **luminousness** *n.* [Middle English from Old French *lumineux* or Latin *luminosus*]

lumme /'lʌmi/ *int. Brit. slang* an expression of surprise or interest. [= (*Lord*) *love me*]

lummox /'lʌməks/ *n. N. Amer. colloq.* a clumsy or stupid person. [19th c. in US & dialect: origin unknown]

lump[1] /lʌmp/ *n. & v.* ● *n.* **1** a compact shapeless or unshapely mass. **2** *slang* a quantity or heap. **3** a tumour, swelling, or bruise. **4** a heavy, dull, or ungainly person. **5** (prec. by *the*) *Brit.* casual workers in the building and other trades. **6** (in *pl.*) *slang.* hard knocks, attacks, defeats (esp. in phr. **take one's lumps**). ● *v.* **1** *tr.* (usu. foll. by *together*, *with*, *in with*, *under*, etc.) mass together or group indiscriminately. **2** *tr. Brit.* carry or throw carelessly (*lumping crates round the yard*). **3** *intr.* become lumpy. **4** *intr.* (usu. foll. by *along*) proceed heavily or awkwardly. **5** *intr.* (usu. foll. by *down*) *Brit.* sit down heavily. ▫ **in the lump** *Brit.* taking things as a whole; in a general manner. **lump in the throat** a feeling of pressure there, caused by emotion. ▫ **lumper** *n.* (in sense 2 of *v.*). [Middle English, perhaps of Scandinavian origin]

lump[2] /lʌmp/ *v.tr. colloq.* endure or suffer (a situation) ungraciously. ▫ **like it or lump it** put up with something whether one likes it or not. [imitative: cf. *dump*, *grump*, etc.]

lumpectomy /lʌm'pɛktəmi/ *n.* (*pl.* **-ies**) the surgical removal of a usu. cancerous lump from the breast.

lumpenproletariat /ˌlʌmpənprəʊlɪ'tɛːrɪət/ *n.* (esp. in Marxist terminology) the unorganized and unpolitical lower orders of society, not interested in revolutionary advancement. ▫ **lumpen** *adj.* [German, from *Lumpen* 'rag, rogue': see PROLETARIAT]

lumpfish /'lʌmpfɪʃ/ *n.* (*pl.* usu. same) a spiny-finned fish, *Cyclopterus lumpus*, of the N. Atlantic, with modified pelvic fins for clinging to objects. Also called LUMPSUCKER. [Middle Low German *lumpen*, Middle Dutch *lumpe* (perhaps = LUMP[1]) + FISH[1]]

lumpish /'lʌmpɪʃ/ *adj.* **1** heavy and clumsy. **2** stupid, lethargic. ▫ **lumpishly** *adv.* **lumpishness** *n.*

lumpsucker /'lʌmpsʌkə/ *n.* a marine fish of the family Cyclopteridae, with a ventral sucker, esp. the lumpfish.

lump sugar *n.* sugar shaped into lumps or cubes.

lump sum *n.* **1** a sum covering a number of items. **2** money paid down at once (opp. INSTALMENT 1).

lumpy /'lʌmpi/ *adj.* (**lumpier**, **lumpiest**) **1** full of or covered with lumps. **2** (of water) cut up by the wind into small waves. ▫ **lumpily** *adv.* **lumpiness** *n.*

lunacy /'luːnəsi/ *n.* (*pl.* **-ies**) **1** insanity (originally of the intermittent kind attributed to changes of the moon); the state of being a lunatic. **2** *Law* such mental unsoundness as interferes with civil rights or transactions. **3** great folly or eccentricity; a foolish act.

luna moth /'luːnə/ *n.* a N. American moth, *Actias luna*, with crescent-shaped spots on its pale green wings. [Latin *luna*, = moon (from its markings)]

lunar /'luːnə/ *adj.* **1** of, relating to, or determined by the moon. **2** concerned with travel to the moon and related research. **3** (of light, glory, etc.) pale, feeble. **4** crescent-shaped; lunate. **5** of or containing silver (from alchemists' use of *luna* (= moon) for 'silver'). [Latin *lunaris* from *luna* 'moon']

lunar caustic *n.* silver nitrate, esp. in stick form.

lunar cycle *n.* = METONIC CYCLE.

lunar distance *n.* the angular distance of the moon from the sun, a planet, or a star, used in finding longitude at sea.

lunar module *n.* (also **lunar excursion module**) a small craft used for travelling between the moon's surface and a spacecraft in orbit around the moon.

lunar month *n.* **1** the period of the moon's revolution, esp. the interval between new moons of about 29½ days. **2** (in general use) a period of four weeks.

lunar node *n.* each of the two points at which the moon's orbit cuts the ecliptic.

lunar observation *n.* the finding of longitude by lunar distance.

lunar orbit *n.* **1** the orbit of the moon round the earth. **2** an orbit round the moon.

lunar year *n.* a period of 12 lunar months.

lunate /'luːneɪt/ *adj. & n.* ● *adj.* crescent-shaped. ● *n.* a crescent-shaped prehistoric implement etc. [Latin *lunatus* from *luna* 'moon']

lunate bone *n.* a crescent-shaped bone in the wrist.

lunatic /'luːnətɪk/ *n. & adj.* ● *n.* **1** an insane person. **2** someone foolish or eccentric. ● *adj.* mad, foolish. [Middle English via Old French *lunatique* from Late Latin *lunaticus* from Latin *luna* 'moon', from the belief that changes of the moon caused intermittent insanity]

lunatic asylum *n. hist.* a mental home or hospital.

lunatic fringe *n.* an extreme or eccentric minority group.

lunation /luː'neɪʃ(ə)n/ *n.* the interval between new moons, about 29½ days. [Middle English from medieval Latin *lunatio* from Latin *luna* 'moon']

lunch /lʌn(t)ʃ/ *n. & v.* ● *n.* **1** the meal eaten in the middle of the day. **2** a light meal eaten at any time. ● *v.* **1** *intr.* eat one's lunch. **2** *tr.* provide lunch for. ▫ **luncher** *n.* [LUNCHEON]

lunch box *n.* a container for a packed meal.

luncheon /'lʌn(t)ʃ(ə)n/ *n. formal* lunch. [16th c.: origin unknown]

luncheonette /lʌn(t)ʃə'nɛt/ *n.* orig. *US* a small restaurant or snack bar serving light lunches.

luncheon meat *n.* a block of ground meat ready to cut and eat.

luncheon voucher *n. Brit.* a voucher or ticket issued to employees and exchangeable for food at many restaurants and shops.

lunch hour *n.* a break from work, when lunch is eaten.

lunchtime /'lʌn(t)ʃtʌɪm/ *n.* the time when lunch is eaten (often *attrib.*: *lunchtime drinking*).

lune /luːn/ *n. Geom.* a crescent-shaped figure formed on a sphere or plane by two arcs intersecting at two points. [French from Latin *luna* 'moon']

lunette /luː'nɛt, ljuː-/ *n.* **1** an arched aperture in a domed ceiling to admit light. **2** a crescent-shaped or semicircular space or alcove which contains a painting, statue, etc. **3** a watch-glass of flattened shape. **4** a ring through which a hook is placed to attach a vehicle to the vehicle towing it. **5** a temporary fortification with two faces forming a salient angle, and two flanks. **6** *RC Ch.* a holder for the consecrated host in a monstrance. [French, diminutive of *lune* (see LUNE)]

lung /lʌŋ/ *n.* each of the pair of respiratory organs situated within the ribcage which bring air into contact with the blood in humans and many other vertebrates. ▫ **lunged** *adj.* **lungful** *n.* (*pl.* **-fuls**). **lungless** *adj.* [Old English *lungen* from Germanic, related to LIGHT[2] (see LIGHTS)]

lunge[1] /lʌn(d)ʒ/ *n. & v.* ● *n.* **1** a sudden movement forward. **2** a thrust with a sword etc., esp. the basic attacking move in fencing. **3** a movement forward by bending the front leg at the knee while keeping the back leg straight. ● *v.* **1** *intr.* make a lunge. **2** *intr.* (usu. foll. by *at*, *out*) deliver a blow from the shoulder in boxing. **3** *tr.* drive (a weapon etc.) violently in some direction. [earlier *allonge* from French *allonger* 'lengthen', from *à* 'to' + *long* LONG[1]]

lunge[2] /lʌn(d)ʒ/ *n. & v.* (also **longe**) ● *n.* **1** a long rope on which a horse is held and made to move in a circle round its trainer. **2** a circular exercise ground for training horses. ● *v.tr.* (**lungeing**) exercise (a horse) with or in a lunge. [French *longe*, *allonge* (as LUNGE[1])]

lungfish /'lʌŋfɪʃ/ *n.* (*pl.* usu. same) any freshwater fish of the order Dipnoi, having gills and a modified swim-bladder used as lungs, and able to aestivate to survive drought.

lungi /'lʊŋgiː/ *n.* (*pl.* **lungis**) a length of cotton cloth, usu. worn as a loincloth in India, or as a skirt in Myanmar (Burma) where it is the national dress for both sexes. [Urdu]

lung-power *n.* the power of one's voice.

lungworm /'lʌŋwəːm/ *n.* a nematode parasitic in the lungs of mammals, esp. of farm and domestic animals.

lungwort /ˈlʌŋwəːt/ *n.* **1** any herbaceous plant of the genus *Pulmonaria*, esp. *P. officinalis* with white-spotted leaves likened to a diseased lung. **2** a lichen, *Lobaria pulmonaria*, formerly believed to be a remedy for lung disease.

lunisolar /luːnɪˈsəʊlə/ *adj.* of or concerning the sun and moon. [Latin *luna* 'moon' + *sol* 'sun']

lunisolar period *n.* a period of 532 years between the repetitions of both solar and lunar cycles.

lunisolar year *n.* a year with divisions regulated by changes of the moon and an average length made to agree with the solar year.

lunula /ˈluːnjʊlə/ *n.* (*pl.* **lunulae** /-liː/) **1** a crescent-shaped mark, esp. the white area at the base of the fingernail. **2** a crescent-shaped Bronze Age ornament. [Latin, diminutive of *luna* 'moon']

lupin /ˈluːpɪn/ *n.* (also **lupine** /-pɪn/) **1** any plant of the genus *Lupinus*, with long tapering spikes of blue, purple, pink, white, or yellow flowers. **2** (in *pl.*) seeds of the lupin. [Middle English from Latin *lupinus*]

lupine /ˈluːpʌɪn/ *adj.* of or like a wolf or wolves. [Latin *lupinus* from *lupus* 'wolf']

lupus /ˈluːpəs/ *n.* any of various ulcerous skin diseases, esp. tuberculosis of the skin. □ **lupoid** *adj.* **lupous** *adj.* [Latin, = wolf]

lupus vulgaris /vʌlˈgɑːrɪs, -ˈgɛːrɪs/ *n.* tuberculosis with dark red patches on the skin, usu. due to direct inoculation of the tuberculosis bacillus into the skin.

lur /lʊə/ *n.* (also **lure** /ljʊə, lʊə/) a bronze S-shaped trumpet dating from prehistoric times, still used in Scandinavia to call cattle. [Danish and Norwegian]

lurch[1] /ləːtʃ/ *n.* & *v.* ● *n.* a sudden unsteady movement or leaning; a stagger. ● *v.intr.* stagger; move suddenly and unsteadily. [originally nautical *lee-lurch*, alteration of *lee-latch* 'drifting to leeward']

lurch[2] /ləːtʃ/ *n.* □ **leave in the lurch** desert (a friend etc.) in difficulties. [originally = a severe defeat in a game, from French *lourche* (also the game itself, like backgammon)]

lurcher /ˈləːtʃə/ *n.* **1** *Brit.* a cross-bred dog, usu. a retriever, collie, or sheepdog crossed with a greyhound, originally used esp. for hunting and by poachers. **2** *archaic* a petty thief, swindler, or spy. [obsolete verb *lurch*, variant of LURK]

lure[1] /lʊə, ljʊə/ *v.* & *n.* ● *v.tr.* **1** (usu. foll. by *away*, *into*) entice (a person, an animal, etc.) usu. with some form of bait. **2** attract back again or recall (a person, animal, etc.) with the promise of a reward. ● *n.* **1** a thing used to entice. **2** (usu. foll. by *of*) the attractive or compelling qualities (of a pursuit etc.). **3** a falconer's apparatus for recalling a hawk, consisting of a bunch of feathers attached to a thong, within which the hawk finds food while being trained. □ **luring** *adj.* **luringly** *adv.* [Middle English from Old French *luere*, from Germanic]

lure[2] var. of LUR.

lurex /ˈljʊərɛks/ *n. propr.* **1** a type of yarn which incorporates a glittering metallic thread. **2** fabric made from this yarn.

lurgy /ˈləːgi/ *n.* (*pl.* **-ies**) (esp. in phr. **the dreaded lurgy**) *joc.* an unspecified illness. [20th c.: origin unknown (frequently referred to in the British radio series *The Goon Show*, of the 1950s and 1960s)]

lurid /ˈlʊərɪd, ˈljʊə-/ *adj.* **1** vivid or glowing in colour (*lurid orange*). **2** of an unnatural glare (*lurid nocturnal brilliance*). **3** sensational, horrifying, or terrible (*lurid details*). **4** showy, gaudy (*paperbacks with lurid covers*). **5** ghastly, wan (*lurid complexion*). **6** *Bot.* of a dingy yellowish brown. □ **cast a lurid light on** explain or reveal (facts or character) in a horrific, sensational, or shocking way. □ **luridly** *adv.* **luridness** *n.* [Latin *luridus* from *luror* 'wan or yellow colour']

lurk /ləːk/ *v.* & *n.* ● *v.intr.* **1** linger furtively or unobtrusively. **2 a** lie in ambush. **b** (usu. foll. by *in*, *under*, *about*, etc.) hide, esp. for sinister purposes. **3** (as **lurking** *adj.*)) latent, semi-conscious (*a lurking suspicion*). ● *n. Austral. slang* a dodge, racket, or scheme; a method of profitable business. □ **lurker** *n.* [Middle English, perhaps from LOUR with frequentative *-k* as in TALK]

luscious /ˈlʌʃəs/ *adj.* **1 a** richly sweet in taste or smell. **b** *colloq.* delicious. **2** (of literary style, music, etc.) over-rich in sound, imagery, or voluptuous suggestion. **3** voluptuously attractive. □ **lusciously** *adv.* **lusciousness** *n.* [Middle English, perhaps an alteration of obsolete *licious* from DELICIOUS]

lush[1] /lʌʃ/ *adj.* **1** (of vegetation, esp. grass) luxuriant and succulent. **2** luxurious. **3** (of colour, sound, etc.) rich, voluptuous. **4** *slang* good-looking, attractive. □ **lushly** *adv.* **lushness** *n.* [Middle English, perhaps a variant of obsolete *lash* 'soft', from Old French *lasche* 'lax' (see LACHES): associated with LUSCIOUS]

lush[2] /lʌʃ/ *n.* & *v.* esp. *N. Amer. slang* ● *n.* **1** alcohol, liquor. **2** an alcoholic; a drunkard. ● *v.* **1** *tr.* & *intr.* drink (alcohol). **2** *tr.* ply with alcohol. [18th c.: perhaps jocular use of LUSH[1]]

lust /lʌst/ *n.* & *v.* ● *n.* **1** strong sexual desire. **2 a** (usu. foll. by *for*, *of*) a passionate desire for (*a lust for power*). **b** (usu. foll. by *of*) a passionate enjoyment of (*the lust of battle*). **3** (usu. in *pl.*) a sensuous appetite regarded as sinful (*the lusts of the flesh*). ● *v.intr.* (usu. foll. by *after*, *for*) have a strong or excessive (esp. sexual) desire. □ **lustful** *adj.* **lustfully** *adv.* **lustfulness** *n.* [Old English from Germanic]

luster *US* var. of LUSTRE[1].

lustra *pl.* of LUSTRUM.

lustral /ˈlʌstr(ə)l/ *adj.* relating to or used in ceremonial purification. [Latin *lustralis* (as LUSTRUM)]

lustrate /ˈlʌstreɪt/ *v.tr.* purify by expiatory sacrifice, ceremonial washing, or other such rite. □ **lustration** /-ˈstreɪʃ(ə)n/ *n.* [Latin *lustrare* (as LUSTRUM)]

lustre[1] /ˈlʌstə/ *n.* & *v.* (*US* **luster**) ● *n.* **1** gloss, brilliance, or sheen. **2** a shiny or reflective surface. **3 a** a thin metallic coating giving an iridescent glaze to ceramics. **b** = LUSTREWARE. **4** a radiance or attractiveness; splendour, glory, distinction (of achievements etc.) (*add lustre to*; *shed lustre on*). **5 a** a prismatic glass pendant on a chandelier etc. **b** a cut-glass chandelier or candelabra. **6 a** *Brit.* a thin dress material with a cotton warp, woollen weft, and a glossy surface. **b** any fabric with a sheen or gloss. ● *v.tr.* put lustre on (pottery, a cloth, etc.). □ **lustreless** *adj.* (*US* **lusterless**). **lustrous** *adj.* **lustrously** *adv.* **lustrousness** *n.* [French via Italian *lustro*, from *lustrare*, from Latin *lustrare* 'illuminate']

lustre[2] /ˈlʌstə/ *n.* (*US* **luster**) = LUSTRUM. [Middle English, Anglicized from LUSTRUM]

lustreware /ˈlʌstəwɛː/ *n.* (*US* **lusterware**) ceramics with an iridescent glaze. [LUSTRE[1]]

lustrum /ˈlʌstrəm/ *n.* (*pl.* **lustra** /-strə/ or **lustrums**) a period of five years. [Latin, an originally purificatory sacrifice after a quinquennial census]

lusty /ˈlʌsti/ *adj.* (**lustier**, **lustiest**) **1** healthy and strong. **2** vigorous or lively. □ **lustily** *adv.* **lustiness** *n.* [Middle English, from LUST + -Y[1]]

lusus /ˈljuːsəs, ˈluː-/ *n.* (*pl.* same /-suːs/ or ***lususes***) (in full ***lusus naturae*** /nəˈtjʊəriː, -ˈtjʊərʌɪ/) a freak of nature. [Latin, = sport of nature]

lutanist var. of LUTENIST.

lute[1] /luːt, ljuːt/ *n.* a guitar-like instrument with a long neck and a pear-shaped body, much used in the 14th–17th c. [Middle English from French *lut*, *leüt*, probably via Provençal *laüt* from Arabic *al-ʿūd*]

lute[2] /luːt, ljuːt/ *n.* & *v.* ● *n.* **1** clay or cement used to stop a hole, make a joint airtight, coat a crucible, protect a graft, etc. **2** a rubber seal for a jar etc. ● *v.tr.* apply lute to. [Middle English via Old French *lut* from Latin *lutum* 'mud, clay']

lutecium var. of LUTETIUM.

lutein /ˈluːtɪɪn, ˈljuː-/ *n. Chem.* a pigment of a deep yellow colour found in egg yolk etc. [Latin *luteum* 'yolk of egg', neut. of *luteus* 'yellow']

luteinizing hormone /ˈluːtənʌɪzɪŋ, ˈljuː-/ *n. Biochem.* a hormone secreted by the anterior pituitary gland that in females stimulates ovulation and in males stimulates the synthesis of androgen (abbr.: **LH**). [LUTEIN]

lutenist /ˈluːt(ə)nɪst, ˈljuː-/ *n.* (also **lutanist**) a lute-player. [medieval Latin *lutanista* from *lutana* LUTE[1]]

luteo- /ˈluːtɪəʊ, ˈljuː-/ *comb. form* orange-coloured. [as LUTEOUS + -O-]

luteofulvous /ˌluːtɪəʊˈfʌlvəs, ˌljuː-/ *adj.* orange-tawny.

luteous /ˈluːtɪəs, ˈljuː-/ *adj.* of a deep orange-yellow or greenish yellow. [Latin *luteus* from *lutum* WELD[2]]

lutestring /ˈluːtstrɪŋ, ˈljuː-/ *n. archaic* a glossy silk fabric. [apparently from *lustring,* from French *lustrine* or Italian *lustrino* from *lustro* LUSTRE[1]]

lutetium /luːˈtiːʃɪəm, -sɪəm, ljuː-/ *n.* (also **lutecium**) *Chem.* a silvery metallic element of the lanthanide series (symbol **Lu**). [French *lutécium* from Latin *Lutetia* the ancient name of Paris, France, the home of its discoveror]

Lutheran /ˈluːθ(ə)r(ə)n, ˈljuː-/ *n. & adj.* ● *n.* **1** a follower of Martin Luther, German religious reformer d. 1546. **2** a member of the Church which accepts the Augsburg confession of 1530, with justification by faith alone as a cardinal doctrine. ● *adj.* of or characterized by the theology of Martin Luther. □ **Lutheranism** *n.* **Lutheranize** *v.tr. & intr.* (also **-ise**).

luthier /ˈluːtɪə, ˈljuː-/ *n.* a maker of stringed instruments, esp. those of the violin family. [French from *luth* LUTE[1]]

Lutine Bell /ˈluːtiːn/ *n.* a bell kept at Lloyd's in London and rung whenever there is an important announcement to be made to the underwriters. [HMS *Lutine,* which sank in 1799, whose bell it was]

luting /ˈluːtɪŋ, ˈljuː-/ *n.* = LUTE[2] *n.* 1.

lutz /lʊts/ *n. Sport* a jump in skating from the backward outside edge of one skate to the backward outside edge of the other, with a full turn in the air. [probably from the name of Gustave *Lussi* (b. 1898), who invented it]

luvvy /ˈlʌvi/ *n.* (also **luvvie**) (*pl.* **-ies**) *Brit. colloq.* **1** (as a form of address) = LOVEY. **2** an actor or actress, esp. one who is particularly effusive or affected.

lux /lʌks/ *n.* (*pl.* same) *Physics* the SI unit of illumination, equivalent to one lumen per square metre (abbr.: **lx**). [Latin *lux lucis* 'light']

luxe /lʌks, lʊks/ *n.* luxury (cf. DE LUXE). [French from Latin *luxus* 'abundance']

Luxembourger /ˈlʌks(ə)mbəːgə/ *n.* **1** a native or national of Luxembourg. **2** a person of Luxembourg descent.

luxuriant /lʌgˈʒʊərɪənt, lʌgˈzjʊə-, lʌkˈsjʊə-/ *adj.* **1** (of vegetation etc.) lush; profuse in growth. **2** prolific, exuberant, rank (*luxuriant imagination*). **3** (of literary or artistic style) florid; richly ornate. □ **luxuriance** *n.* **luxuriantly** *adv.* [Latin *luxuriare* 'grow rank' from *luxuria* LUXURY]

■ **Usage** *Luxuriant,* meaning 'growing profusely, exuberant' is sometimes confused with *luxurious,* the adjective relating to *luxury.*

luxuriate /lʌgˈʒʊərɪeɪt, lʌgˈzjʊə-, lʌkˈsjʊə-/ *v.intr.* **1** (foll. by *in*) take self-indulgent delight in; enjoy in a luxurious manner. **2** take one's ease; relax in comfort.

luxurious /lʌgˈʒʊərɪəs, lʌgˈzjʊə-, lʌkˈsjʊə-/ *adj.* **1** supplied with luxuries; characterized by luxury. **2** extremely comfortable. **3** self-indulgent, voluptuous. □ **luxuriously** *adv.* **luxuriousness** *n.* [Middle English via Old French *luxurios* from Latin *luxuriosus* (as LUXURY)]

■ **Usage** See Usage Note at LUXURIANT.

luxury /ˈlʌkʃ(ə)ri/ *n.* (*pl.* **-ies**) **1** choice or costly surroundings, possessions, food, etc.; luxuriousness (*a life of luxury*). **2** something desirable for comfort or enjoyment, but not indispensable. **3** (*attrib.*) providing great comfort; expensive (*a luxury flat; a luxury holiday*). [Middle English via Old French *luxurie, luxure* from Latin *luxuria,* from *luxus* 'abundance']

LV *abbr. Brit.* luncheon voucher.

Lw *symb. Chem.* former symbol for the element lawrencium (now **Lr**).

LWM *abbr.* low water mark.

lx *abbr.* lux.

LXX *symb.* Septuagint. [Roman numeral for 70]

-ly[1] /lɪ/ *suffix* forming adjectives esp. from nouns, meaning: **1** having the qualities of (*princely; manly*). **2** recurring at intervals of (*daily; hourly*). [from or suggested by Old English *-lic* from Germanic: related to LIKE[1]]

-ly[2] /lɪ/ *suffix* forming adverbs from adjectives, denoting esp. manner or degree (*boldly; happily; miserably; deservedly; amusingly*). [from or suggested by Old English *-līce* from Germanic (as -LY[1])]

lycanthrope /ˈlʌɪk(ə)nθrəʊp/ *n.* **1** a werewolf. **2** a person suffering from lycanthropy. [modern Latin *lycanthropus* from Greek (as LYCANTHROPY)]

lycanthropy /lʌɪˈkanθrəpi/ *n.* **1** the mythical transformation of a person into a wolf (cf. WEREWOLF). **2** a form of madness involving the delusion of being usu. a wolf, with changed appetites, voice, etc. [modern Latin *lycanthropia* from Greek *lukanthrōpia,* from *lukos* 'wolf' + *anthrōpos* 'man']

lycée /ˈliːseɪ, French lise/ *n.* (*pl.* ***lycées***) a state secondary school in France. [French from Latin (as LYCEUM)]

Lyceum /lʌɪˈsiːəm/ *n.* **1 a** the garden at Athens in which Aristotle taught philosophy. **b** Aristotelian philosophy and its followers. **2** (**lyceum**) *US hist.* a literary institution, lecture hall, or teaching place. [Latin from Greek *Lukeion,* neut. of *Lukeios,* epithet of Apollo (from whose neighbouring temple the Lyceum was named)]

lychee /ˈlʌɪtʃiː, ˈlɪ-/ *n.* (also **litchi, lichee**) **1** a sweet fleshy fruit with a thin spiny skin. **2** the tree, *Nephelium litchi,* originally from China, bearing this. [Chinese *lizhi*]

lych-gate var. of LICH-GATE.

lychnis /ˈlɪknɪs/ *n.* any herbaceous plant of the genus *Lychnis,* including ragged robin. [Latin from Greek *lukhnis,* a red flower, from *lukhnos* 'lamp']

lycopod /ˈlʌɪkəpɒd/ *n.* any of various clubmosses, esp. of the genus *Lycopodium.* [Anglicized form of LYCOPODIUM]

lycopodium /lʌɪkəˈpəʊdɪəm/ *n.* **1** = LYCOPOD. **2** a fine powder of spores from this, used as an absorbent in surgery, and in making fireworks etc. [modern Latin, from Greek *lukos* 'wolf' + *pous podos* 'foot']

Lycra /ˈlʌɪkrə/ *n. propr.* an elastic polyurethane fibre or fabric used esp. for close-fitting sports clothing.

Lydian /ˈlɪdɪən/ *adj. & n.* ● *n.* **1** a native or inhabitant of ancient Lydia in western Asia Minor. **2** the language of the Lydians. ● *adj.* of or relating to the people of Lydia or their language. [Latin *Lydius* from Greek *Ludios* 'of Lydia']

Lydian mode *n. Mus.* the mode represented by the natural diatonic scale F–F.

lye /lʌɪ/ *n.* **1** water that has been made alkaline by lixiviation of vegetable ashes. **2** any strong alkaline solution, esp. of potassium hydroxide used for washing or cleansing. [Old English *lēag* from Germanic: related to LATHER]

lying[1] /ˈlʌɪɪŋ/ *pres. part.* of LIE[1]. ● *n.* a place to lie (*a dry lying*).

lying[2] /ˈlʌɪɪŋ/ *pres. part.* of LIE[2]. ● *adj.* deceitful, false. □ **lyingly** *adv.*

lying-in-state *n.* the display of the corpse of a public figure for public tribute before burial or cremation.

lyke wake /ˈlʌɪk weɪk/ *n. Brit.* a night watch over a dead body. [Middle English, perhaps from Old Norse: cf. LICH-GATE, WAKE[1]]

Lyme disease /lʌɪm/ *n.* a form of arthritis caused by spirochaete bacteria transmitted by ticks. [*Lyme,* a town in Connecticut, US, where an outbreak occurred]

lymph /lɪmf/ *n.* **1** *Physiol.* a colourless fluid containing white blood cells, drained from the tissues and conveyed through the body in the lymphatic system. **2** this fluid used as a vaccine. **3** exudation from a sore etc. **4** *poet.* pure water. □ **lymphoid** *adj.* **lymphous** *adj.* [French *lymphe* or Latin *lympha, limpa* 'water']

lymphatic /lɪmˈfatɪk/ *adj. & n.* ● *adj.* **1** of or secreting or conveying lymph. **2** (of a person) pale, flabby, or sluggish. ● *n.* a veinlike vessel conveying lymph. [originally = frenzied, from Latin *lymphaticus* 'mad' from Greek *numpholēptos* 'seized by nymphs': now associated with LYMPH (on the analogy of *spermatic* etc.)]

lymphatic system *n.* a network of vessels conveying lymph.

lymph gland *n.* (also **lymph node**) a small mass of tissue in the lymphatic system where lymph is purified and lymphocytes are formed.

lymphocyte /ˈlɪmfə(ʊ)sʌɪt/ *n.* a form of leucocyte occurring in the blood, in lymph, etc. □ **lymphocytic** /-ˈsɪtɪk/ *adj.*

lymphoma /lɪmˈfəʊmə/ *n.* (*pl.* **lymphomas, lymphomata** /-mətə/) any malignant tumour of the lymph nodes, excluding leukaemia.

lyncean /lɪnˈsiːən/ *adj.* lynx-eyed, keen-sighted. [Latin *lynceus* from Greek *lugkeios*, from *lugx* LYNX]

lynch /lɪn(t)ʃ/ *v.tr.* (of a body of people) put (a person) to death, esp. by hanging, for an alleged offence without a legal trial. □ **lyncher** *n.* **lynching** *n.* [*Lynch's law*, named after Capt. W. *Lynch*, head of a self-constituted judicial tribunal in Virginia *c.*1780]

lynchet /ˈlɪn(t)ʃɪt/ *n.* (in the UK) a ridge or ledge formed by ancient ploughing on a slope. [*linch* from Old English *hlinc*: cf. LINKS]

lynch law *n.* the procedure of a self-constituted illegal court that punishes or executes.

lynchpin var. of LINCHPIN.

lynx /lɪŋks/ *n.* **1** a medium-sized cat, *Felis lynx*, with short tail, spotted fur, and tufted ear-tips. **2** its fur. [Middle English via Latin from Greek *lugx*]

lynx-eyed *adj.* keen-sighted.

Lyon /ˈlʌɪən/ *n.* (in full **Lord Lyon** or **Lyon King of Arms**) the chief herald of Scotland. [archaic formation of LION: named from the lion on the royal shield]

Lyon Court *n.* the court over which the chief herald of Scotland presides.

lyophilic /lʌɪə(ʊ)ˈfɪlɪk/ *adj.* (of a colloid) readily dispersed by a solvent. [Greek *luō* 'loosen, dissolve' + *philos* 'loving']

lyophilize /lʌɪˈɒfɪlʌɪz/ *v.tr.* (also **-ise**) freeze-dry. [as LYOPHILIC]

lyophobic /lʌɪə(ʊ)ˈfəʊbɪk/ *adj.* (of a colloid) not lyophilic. [Greek *luō* 'loosen, dissolve' + -PHOBIC (see -PHOBIA)]

lyrate /ˈlʌɪreɪt/ *adj. Biol.* lyre-shaped.

lyre /lʌɪə/ *n. Gk Antiq.* an ancient stringed instrument like a small U-shaped harp, played usu. with a plectrum and accompanying the voice. [Middle English via Old French *lire* and Latin *lyra* from Greek *lura*]

lyre-bird *n.* any Australian bird of the family Menuridae, the male of which has a lyre-shaped tail.

lyre-flower *n.* = BLEEDING HEART 2.

lyric /ˈlɪrɪk/ *adj. & n.* ● *adj.* **1** (of poetry) expressing the writer's emotions, usu. briefly and in stanzas or recognized forms. **2** (of a poet) writing in this manner. **3** of or for the lyre. **4** meant to be sung, fit to be expressed in song, songlike (*lyric drama; lyric opera*). ● *n.* **1** a lyric poem or verse. **2** (in *pl.*) lyric verses. **3** (usu. in *pl.*) the words of a song. [French *lyrique* or Latin *lyricus* from Greek *lurikos* (as LYRE)]

lyrical /ˈlɪrɪk(ə)l/ *adj.* **1** = LYRIC 1, 2. **2** resembling, couched in, or using language appropriate to, lyric poetry. **3** *colloq.* highly enthusiastic (*wax lyrical about*). □ **lyrically** *adv.*

lyricism /ˈlɪrɪsɪz(ə)m/ *n.* **1** the character or quality of being lyric or lyrical. **2** a lyrical expression. **3** high-flown sentiments.

lyricist /ˈlɪrɪsɪst/ *n.* a person who writes the words to a song.

lyrist *n.* **1** /ˈlʌɪərɪst/ a person who plays the lyre. **2** /ˈlɪrɪst/ a lyric poet. [Latin *lyrista* from Greek *luristēs*, from *lura* 'lyre']

lyse /lʌɪz/ *v.tr. & intr. Biol.* bring about or undergo lysis. [back-formation from LYSIS]

lysergic acid /lʌɪˈsəːdʒɪk/ *n.* a crystalline acid extracted from ergot or prepared synthetically. [hydro*lysis* + *erg*ot + -IC]

lysergic acid diethylamide /dʌɪəˈθʌɪləmʌɪd, dʌɪˌiːθʌɪlˈeɪmʌɪd/ *n.* a powerful hallucinogenic drug (abbr.: **LSD**).

lysin /ˈlʌɪsɪn/ *n. Biol.* a substance, esp. an antibody, able to cause lysis of cells esp. bacteria. [German *Lysine*]

lysine /ˈlʌɪsiːn/ *n. Biochem.* an amino acid present in protein and essential in the diet of vertebrates. [German *Lysin*, ultimately from LYSIS]

lysis /ˈlʌɪsɪs/ *n.* (*pl.* **lyses** /-siːz/) *Biol.* the disintegration of a cell. [Latin from Greek *lusis* 'loosening', from *luō* 'loosen']

-lysis /lɪsɪs/ *comb. form* forming nouns denoting disintegration or decomposition (*electrolysis; haemolysis*).

Lysol /ˈlʌɪsɒl/ *n. propr.* a mixture of cresols and soft soap, used as a disinfectant. [LYSIS + -OL²]

lysosome /ˈlʌɪsəsəʊm/ *n. Biol.* a cytoplasmic organelle in eukaryotic cells containing degradative enzymes enclosed in a membrane. [LYSIS + -SOME³]

lysozyme /ˈlʌɪsəzʌɪm/ *n. Biochem.* an enzyme found in tears and egg white which catalyses the destruction of cell walls of certain bacteria. [LYSIS + ENZYME]

lytic /ˈlɪtɪk/ *adj.* of, relating to, or causing lysis.

-lytic /ˈlɪtɪk/ *comb. form* forming adjectives corresponding to nouns in *-lysis*. [Greek *lutikos* (as LYSIS)]

Mm

M[1] /ɛm/ *n.* (also **m**) (*pl.* **Ms** or **M's**) **1** the thirteenth letter of the alphabet. **2** (as a Roman numeral) 1,000. **3** *Printing* em.

M[2] *abbr.* (also **M.**) **1** *Monsieur*. **2** (in the UK in road designations) motorway. **3** *Chem.* molar.

M[3] *symb.* mega-.

m[1] *abbr.* (also **m.**) **1 a** masculine. **b** male. **2** married. **3** *Cricket* maiden (over). **4** mile(s). **5** million(s). **6** minute(s). **7** mare.

m[2] *symb.* **1** metre(s). **2** milli-. **3** *Physics* mass.

m' *adj.* = MY (*m'lud*).

'm[1] *abbr. colloq.* am (*I'm sorry*).

'm[2] *n. colloq.* madam (in *yes'm* etc.).

MA *abbr.* **1** Master of Arts. **2** *US* Massachusetts (in official postal use).

ma /mɑː/ *n. colloq.* mother. [abbreviation of MAMMA[1]]

ma'am /mɑːm, mam, məm/ *n.* madam (used esp. in addressing royalty). [contraction.]

Mac /mak/ *n. colloq.* **1** a Scotsman. **2** *N. Amer.* a form of address to a male stranger. [*Mac-* as a patronymic prefix in many Scottish and Irish surnames]

mac /mak/ *n.* (also **mack**) *Brit. colloq.* mackintosh. [abbreviation]

macabre /məˈkɑːbr(ə)/ *adj.* grim, gruesome. [Middle English from Old French *macabré*, perhaps from *Macabé* a Maccabee, with reference to a miracle play showing the slaughter of the Maccabees]

macadam /məˈkadəm/ *n.* **1** material for road-making with successive layers of compacted broken stone. **2** = TARMACADAM. ▫ **macadamize** *v.tr.* (also **-ise**). [named after J. L. *McAdam*, British surveyor (d. 1836), who advocated using this material]

macadamia /makəˈdeɪmɪə/ *n.* any Australian evergreen tree of the genus *Macadamia*, esp. *M. integrifolia* and *M. tetraphylla*, bearing edible nutlike seeds. [named after J. *Macadam*, Australian chemist d. 1865]

macaque /məˈkɑːk, -ˈkak/ *n.* a medium-sized monkey of the Old World genus *Macaca*, including the rhesus monkey and Barbary ape and typically having a rather long face with cheek pouches. [French via Portuguese *macaco* from Bantu *makaku* 'some monkeys', from *kaku* 'monkey']

macaroni /makəˈrəʊni/ *n.* **1** a tubular variety of pasta. **2** (*pl.* **macaronies**) *hist.* an 18th-c. British dandy affecting Continental fashions. [Italian *maccaroni* from late Greek *makaria* 'food made from barley']

macaronic /makəˈrɒnɪk/ *n. & adj.* ● *n.* (in *pl.*) burlesque verses containing Latin (or other foreign) words and vernacular words with Latin etc. terminations. ● *adj.* (of verse) of this kind. [earlier = of the nature of a jumble or medley: modern Latin *macaronicus* from obsolete Italian *macaronico*, jocularly formed as MACARONI]

macaroon /makəˈruːn/ *n.* a small light cake or biscuit made with white of egg, sugar, and ground almonds or coconut. [French *macaron* from Italian (as MACARONI)]

Macassar /məˈkasə/ *n.* (in full **Macassar oil**) a kind of oil formerly used as a dressing for the hair. [*Macassar*, now in Indonesia, from where its ingredients were said to come]

macaw /məˈkɔː/ *n.* any long-tailed brightly coloured parrot of the genus *Ara* or *Anodorhynchus*, native to S. and Central America. [Portuguese *macao*, of unknown origin]

Macc. *abbr.* Maccabees (Apocrypha).

Maccabees /ˈmakəbiːz/ *n.pl.* (in full **Books of the Maccabees**) four books of Jewish history and theology, of which the first and second are in the Apocrypha. ▫ **Maccabean** /-ˈbiːən/ *adj.* [the name of a Jewish family that led a revolt *c.*170 BC under Judas *Maccabaeus*]

McCarthyism /məˈkɑːθɪɪz(ə)m/ *n.* (esp. in the US) the policy of hunting out suspected or known Communists and removing them esp. from government departments. [named after J. R. *McCarthy*, US senator (d. 1957), who instigated the policy in 1950 claiming to know of many Communists in the State Department]

McCoy /məˈkɔɪ/ *n. colloq.* ▫ **the** (or **the real**) **McCoy** the real thing; the genuine article. [19th c.: origin uncertain]

Mace /meɪs/ *n. & v.* ● *n.* an aerosol used to immobolize an assailant temporarily. ● *v.tr.* (also **mace**) spray with Mace. [US proprietary name, probably from MACE[1]]

mace[1] /meɪs/ *n.* **1** a staff of office, esp. the symbol of the Speaker's authority in the House of Commons. **2** *hist.* a heavy club usu. having a metal head and spikes. **3** a stick used in the game of bagatelle. **4** = MACE-BEARER. [Middle English via Old French *mace*, *masse* (modern *masse* 'large hammer') from Romanic]

mace[2] /meɪs/ *n.* the dried outer covering of the nutmeg, used as a spice. [Middle English *macis* (taken as pl.) via Old French *macis* from Latin *macir*, a red spicy bark]

mace-bearer *n.* an official who carries a mace on ceremonial occasions.

macédoine /ˈmasɪdwɑːn/ *n.* mixed vegetables or fruit, esp. cut up small or in jelly. [French, = Macedonia, with reference to the mixture of peoples there]

macer /ˈmeɪsə/ *n.* a mace-bearer, esp. *Sc.* an official keeping order in a law court. [Middle English from Old French *massier*, from *masse*: see MACE[1]]

macerate /ˈmasəreɪt/ *v.* **1** *tr. & intr.* make or become soft by soaking. **2** *intr.* waste away by fasting. ▫ **maceration** /-ˈreɪʃ(ə)n/ *n.* **macerator** *n.* [Latin *macerare macerat-*]

Mach /mɑːk, mak/ *n.* (in full **Mach number**) the ratio of the speed of a body to the speed of sound in the surrounding medium; often as **Mach 1**, **2**, etc., indicating the speed of sound, twice the speed of sound, etc. [named after E. *Mach*, Austrian physicist d. 1916]

machete /məˈtʃɛti, -ˈʃɛti/ *n.* (also **matchet** /ˈmatʃɪt/) a broad heavy knife used esp. in Central America and the W. Indies as an implement and weapon. [Spanish from *macho* 'hammer', from Late Latin *marcus*]

machiavellian /ˌmakɪəˈvɛlɪən/ *adj.* elaborately cunning; scheming, unscrupulous. ▫ **machiavellianism** *n.* [from the name of N. dei *Machiavelli*, Florentine statesman and political writer (d. 1527), who advocated resort to morally questionable methods in the interests of the state]

machicolate /məˈtʃɪkəleɪt/ *v.tr.* (usu. as **machicolated** *adj.*) furnish (a parapet etc.) with openings between supporting corbels for dropping stones etc. on attackers. ▫ **machicolation** /-ˈleɪʃ(ə)n/ *n.* [Old French *machicoler*, ultimately from Provençal *machacol*, from *macar* 'crush' + *col* 'neck']

machinable /məˈʃiːnəb(ə)l/ *adj.* capable of being cut by machine tools. ▫ **machinability** /-ˈbɪlɪti/ *n.*

machinate /'makɪneɪt, 'maʃ-/ *v.intr.* lay plots; intrigue. □ **machination** /-'neɪʃ(ə)n/ *n.* **machinator** *n.* [Latin *machinari* 'contrive' (as MACHINE)]

machine /mə'ʃi:n/ *n.* & *v.* ● *n.* **1** an apparatus using or applying mechanical power, having several parts each with a definite function and together performing certain kinds of work. **2** a particular kind of machine, esp. a vehicle, a piece of electrical or electronic apparatus, etc. **3** an instrument that transmits a force or directs its application. **4** the controlling system of an organization etc. (*the party machine*). **5** a person who acts mechanically and with apparent lack of emotion. **6** (esp. in *comb.*) a coin-operated dispenser (*cigarette machine*). ● *v.tr.* make or operate on with a machine (esp. in sewing or manufacturing). [French via Latin *machina* from Greek *makhana*, Doric form of *mēkhanē*, from *mēkhos* 'contrivance']

machine code *n.* (also **machine language**) a computer language that a particular computer can respond to directly.

machine-gun *n.* & *v.* ● *n.* an automatic gun giving continuous fire. ● *v.tr.* (**-gunned**, **-gunning**) shoot at with a machine-gun. □ **machine-gunner** *n.*

machine-minder *n.* a person whose job is to attend to a machine.

machine-readable *adj.* (of data, text, etc.) in a form that a computer can process.

machinery /mə'ʃi:n(ə)ri/ *n.* (*pl.* **-ies**) **1** machines collectively. **2** the components of a machine; a mechanism. **3** (foll. by *of*) an organized system. **4** (foll. by *for*) the means devised or available (*the machinery for decision-making*).

machine tool *n.* a mechanically operated tool for working on metal, wood, or plastics. □ **machine-tooled** *adj.*

machine translation *n.* translation carried out by a computer.

machine-washable *adj.* able to be washed in a washing machine without damage.

machinist /mə'ʃi:nɪst/ *n.* **1** a person who operates a machine, esp. a machine tool or *Brit.* a sewing machine. **2** a person who makes machinery.

machismo /mə'tʃɪzməʊ, -'kɪz-/ *n.* exaggeratedly assertive manliness; a show of masculinity. [Spanish from *macho* MALE, from Latin *masculus*]

Machmeter /'mɑ:kmi:tə, 'mak-/ *n.* an instrument indicating air speed in the form of a Mach number.

Mach number see MACH.

macho /'matʃəʊ/ *adj.* & *n.* ● *adj.* showily manly or virile. ● *n.* (*pl.* **-os**) **1** a macho man. **2** = MACHISMO. [MACHISMO]

Machtpolitik /'mɑ:xtpɒlɪ,ti:k, German 'maxtpoliti:k/ *n.* power politics. [German]

macintosh var. of MACKINTOSH.

mack var. of MAC.

mackerel /'mak(ə)r(ə)l/ *n.* (*pl.* same or **mackerels**) a N. Atlantic marine fish, *Scomber scombrus*, with a greenish-blue body, used for food. [Middle English from Anglo-French *makerel*, Old French *maquerel*]

mackerel shark *n.* a porbeagle.

mackerel sky *n.* a sky dappled with rows of small white fleecy clouds, like the pattern on a mackerel's back.

mackintosh /'makɪntɒʃ/ *n.* (also **macintosh**) **1** *Brit.* a waterproof coat or cloak. **2** cloth waterproofed with rubber. [named after C. *Macintosh*, Scots inventor (d. 1843), who originally patented the cloth]

mackle /'mak(ə)l/ *n.* a blurred impression in printing. [French *macule* from Latin *macula* 'blemish': see MACULA]

macle /'mak(ə)l/ *n.* **1** a twin crystal. **2** a dark spot in a mineral. [French from Latin (as MACKLE)]

McNaughten rules /mək'nɔ:t(ə)n/ *n.pl.* (also **M'Naghten rules**) *Brit.* rules governing the decision as to the criminal responsibility of an insane person. [named after *McNaughten* or *McNaughtan*, name of a 19th-c. accused person, at whose trial the rules were established]

macramé /mə'krɑ:mi/ *n.* **1** the art of knotting cord or string in patterns to make decorative articles. **2** articles made in this way. [French via Turkish *makrama* 'bedspread' from Arabic *mikrama*]

macro /'makrəʊ/ *n.* (also **macro-instruction**) *Computing* a single instruction that expands automatically into a set of instructions to perform a particular task.

macro- /'makrəʊ/ *comb. form* **1** long. **2** large; large-scale. [Greek *makro-* from *makros* 'long, large']

macrobiotic /,makrə(ʊ)bʌɪ'ɒtɪk/ *adj.* & *n.* ● *adj.* relating to or following a diet intended to prolong life, comprising pure vegetable foods, brown rice, etc. ● *n.* (in *pl.*; treated as *sing.*) the use or theory of such a dietary system.

macrocarpa /makrə(ʊ)'kɑ:pə/ *n.* an evergreen tree, *Cupressus macrocarpa*, often cultivated for hedges or windbreaks. [modern Latin, from Greek MACRO- + *karpos* 'fruit']

macrocephalic /,makrə(ʊ)sɪ'falɪk, -kɛ'falɪk/ *adj.* (also **macrocephalous** /-'sɛf(ə)ləs/) having a long or large head. □ **macrocephaly** /-'sɛf(ə)li/ *n.*

macrocosm /'makrə(ʊ)kɒz(ə)m/ *n.* **1** the universe. **2** the whole of a complex structure. □ **macrocosmic** /-'kɒzmɪk/ *adj.* **macrocosmically** /-'kɒzmɪk(ə)li/ *adv.*

macroeconomics /,makrəʊi:kə'nɒmɪks, -ɛk-/ *n.* the study of large-scale or general economic factors, e.g. national productivity. □ **macroeconomic** *adj.*

macroevolution /,makrəʊi:və'lu:ʃ(ə)n, -'lju:ʃ-, -ɛv-/ *n.* *Biol.* major evolutionary change, esp. over a long period. □ **macroevolutionary** *adj.*

macrolepidoptera /,makrəʊlɛpɪ'dɒpt(ə)rə/ *n.pl.* butterflies and moths of interest not only to specialist entomologists, mainly the larger kinds. Cf. MICROLEPIDOPTERA. [MACRO- + modern Latin *Lepidoptera*: see LEPIDOPTEROUS]

■ **Usage** The term *macrolepidoptera* is not used in formal classification.

macromolecule /makrə(ʊ)'mɒlɪkju:l/ *n.* *Biochem.* a molecule containing a very large number of atoms, e.g. a protein or a nucleic acid. □ **macromolecular** /-mə'lɛkjʊlə/ *adj.*

macron /'makrɒn/ *n.* a written or printed mark (¯) over a long or stressed vowel. [Greek *makron*, neut. of *makros* 'long']

macronutrient /makrəʊ'nju:trɪənt/ *n.* a chemical required in relatively large amounts for the growth and development of living organisms.

macrophage /'makrə(ʊ)feɪdʒ/ *n.* a large phagocytic white blood cell usu. occurring at points of infection.

macrophotography /,makrə(ʊ)fə'tɒgrəfi/ *n.* photography producing photographs larger than life.

macropod /'makrə(ʊ)pɒd/ *n.* a plant-eating marsupial mammal of the family Macropodidae native to Australia and New Guinea, including kangaroos and wallabies. [MACRO- + Greek *pous podos* 'foot']

macroscopic /makrə(ʊ)'skɒpɪk/ *adj.* **1** visible to the naked eye. **2** regarded in terms of large units. □ **macroscopically** *adv.*

macula /'makjʊlə/ *n.* (*pl.* **maculae** /-li:/) **1** a dark spot, esp. a permanent one, in the skin. **2** (in full **macula lutea** /'lu:tɪə/) the region of greatest visual acuity in the retina. □ **macular** *adj.* **maculation** /-'leɪʃ(ə)n/ *n.* [Latin, = spot, mesh]

mad /mad/ *adj.* & *v.* ● *adj.* (**madder**, **maddest**) **1** insane; having a disordered mind. **2** (of a person, conduct, or an idea) wildly foolish. **3** (often foll. by *about* or *Brit. on*) wildly excited or infatuated (*mad about football*; *is chess-mad*). **4** (often foll. by *at*, *with*) *colloq.* angry. **5** (of an animal) rabid. **6** wildly light-hearted. ● *v.intr.* (**madded**, **madding**) *archaic* be mad; act madly (*the madding crowd*). □ **like mad** *colloq.* with great energy, intensity, or enthusiasm. **mad keen**

colloq. extremely eager. □ **madness** *n.* [Old English *gemǣded*, participial form related to *gemād* 'mad']

madam /ˈmadəm/ *n.* **1** a polite or respectful form of address or mode of reference to a woman. **2** *Brit. colloq.* a conceited or precocious girl or young woman. **3** a woman brothel-keeper. [Middle English from Old French *ma dame* 'my lady']

Madame /məˈdɑːm, ˈmadəm/ *n.* **1** (*pl.* **Mesdames** /meɪˈdɑːm, -ˈdam/) a title or form of address used of or to a French-speaking woman, corresponding to Mrs or madam. **2** (**madame**) = MADAM 1. [French (as MADAM)]

madcap /ˈmadkap/ *adj.* & *n.* ● *adj.* **1** wildly impulsive. **2** undertaken without forethought. ● *n.* a wildly impulsive person.

mad cow disease *n. colloq.* = BSE.

madden /ˈmad(ə)n/ *v.* **1** *tr.* & *intr.* make or become mad. **2** *tr.* irritate intensely. □ **maddening** *adj.* **maddeningly** *adv.*

madder /ˈmadə/ *n.* **1** a herbaceous plant, *Rubia tinctorum*, with yellowish flowers. **2** a red dye obtained from the root of the madder, or its synthetic substitute. [Old English *mædere*]

made /meɪd/ *past* and *past part.* of MAKE. ● *adj.* (usu. in *comb.*) **1** (of a person or thing) built or formed (*well-made*; *strongly-made*). **2** successful (*a self-made man*). □ **have** (or **have got**) **it made** *colloq.* be sure of success. **made for** ideally suited to. **made of** consisting of. **made of money** *colloq.* very rich.

made dish *n.* a dish prepared from several separate foods.

Madeira /məˈdɪərə/ *n.* **1** a fortified white wine from the island of Madeira off the coast of N. Africa. **2** (in full **Madeira cake**) a kind of rich sponge cake. □ **Madeiran** *n.* & *adj.*

madeleine /ˈmadleɪn/ *n.* a small fancy sponge cake. [French, probably named after *Madeleine* Paulmier, 19th-c. French pastry-cook]

made man *n.* a man who has attained success.

Mademoiselle /madəmwəˈzɛl/ *n.* (*pl.* **Mesdemoiselles**) /meɪd-/ **1** a title or form of address used of or to an unmarried French-speaking woman, corresponding to Miss or madam. **2** (**mademoiselle**) **a** a young Frenchwoman. **b** a French governess. [French, from *ma* 'my' + *demoiselle* DAMSEL]

made road *n. Brit.* a properly surfaced road of tarmac, concrete, etc.

made to measure *adj.* (hyphenated when *attrib.*) (of clothes) made from measurements taken.

made to order *adj.* (hyphenated when *attrib.*) **1** made according to individual requirements. **2** exactly as wanted.

made up *adj.* (hyphenated when *attrib.*) **1** invented, not true. **2** wearing make-up. **3** (of a meal etc.) already prepared. **4** (of a road) surfaced, not rough.

madhouse /ˈmadhaʊs/ *n.* **1** *archaic* or *colloq.* a mental home or hospital. **2** *colloq.* a scene of extreme confusion or uproar.

madly /madli/ *adv.* **1** in a mad manner. **2** *colloq.* **a** passionately. **b** extremely.

madman /ˈmadmən/ *n.* (*pl.* **-men**) a man who is mad.

Madonna /məˈdɒnə/ *n. Eccl.* **1** (prec. by *the*) a name for the Virgin Mary. **2** (usu. **madonna**) a picture or statue of the Madonna. [Italian, from *ma* = *mia* 'my' + *donna* 'lady' from Latin *domina*]

madonna lily *n.* the white *Lilium candidum*, as shown in many pictures of the Madonna.

madras /məˈdrɑːs, -ˈdras/ *n.* **1** a strong cotton fabric with coloured or white stripes, checks, etc. **2** (**Madras**) a hot spiced curry dish usu. made with meat. [*Madras* in India, where it was first produced]

madrepore /ˈmadrɪpɔː/ *n.* **1** a stony coral of the genus *Madrepora*. **2** the polyp producing this. □ **madreporic** /-ˈpɒrɪk/ *adj.* [French *madrépore* or modern Latin *madrepora* from Italian *madrepora*, from *madre* 'mother' (perhaps with reference to its prolific growth) + *poro* PORE[1]]

madrigal /ˈmadrɪg(ə)l/ *n.* **1** a usu. 16th-c. or 17th-c. part-song for several voices, usu. arranged in elaborate counterpoint and without instrumental accompaniment. **2** a short love poem. □ **madrigalian** /-ˈgeɪlɪən/ *adj.* **madrigalist** *n.* [Italian *madrigale* from medieval Latin *carmen matricale* 'simple song', from *matricalis* 'mother, simple', adj. from MATRIX]

madroño /məˈdrəʊnjəʊ/ *n.* (*pl.* **-os**) (also **madroña** /-njə/) an evergreen tree, *Arbutus menziesii*, of western N. America, with white flowers, red berries, and glossy leaves. [Spanish]

madwoman /ˈmadwʊmən/ *n.* (*pl.* **-women**) a woman who is mad.

Maecenas /mʌɪˈsiːnəs/ *n.* a generous patron of literature or art. [Gaius *Maecenas*, Roman statesman d. 8 BC, the patron of Horace and Virgil]

maelstrom /ˈmeɪlstrəm/ *n.* **1** a great whirlpool. **2** a state of confusion. [early modern Dutch, the name of a mythical whirlpool, from *malen* 'grind, whirl' + *stroom* STREAM]

maenad /ˈmiːnad/ *n.* **1** a bacchante. **2** a frenzied woman. □ **maenadic** /-ˈnadɪk/ *adj.* [Latin *Maenas Maenad-* from Greek *Mainas -ados*, from *mainomai* 'rave']

maestoso /mʌɪˈstəʊzəʊ/ *adj.*, *adv.*, & *n. Mus.* ● *adj.* & *adv.* to be performed majestically. ● *n.* (*pl.* **-os**) a piece of music to be performed in this way. [Italian, = majestic]

maestro /ˈmʌɪstrəʊ/ *n.* (*pl.* **maestri** /-stri/ or **-os**) (often as a respectful form of address) **1** a distinguished musician, esp. a conductor or performer. **2** a great performer in any sphere, esp. artistic. [Italian, = master]

Mae West /meɪ ˈwɛst/ *n. slang* an inflatable life jacket. [the name of an American film actress (d. 1980), noted for her large bust]

MAFF *abbr.* (in the UK) Ministry of Agriculture, Fisheries, and Food.

Mafia /ˈmafɪə/ *n.* **1** an organized international body of criminals, originally in Sicily and now esp. in Italy and the US. **2** (**mafia**) a group regarded as exerting a hidden sinister influence. [Italian dialect (Sicilian), = bragging]

Mafioso /mafɪˈəʊsəʊ/ *n.* (*pl.* **Mafiosi** /-si/) **1** a member of the Mafia. **2** (**mafioso**) a member of a group regarded as exerting a hidden sinister influence. [Italian (as MAFIA)]

mag /mag/ *n. colloq.* **1** a magazine (periodical). **2** magnesium. **3** magneto. **4** magnitude. [abbreviation]

magazine /magəˈziːn/ *n.* **1** a periodical publication containing articles, stories, etc., usu. with photographs, illustrations, etc. **2** a chamber for holding a supply of cartridges to be fed automatically to the breech of a gun. **3** a similar device feeding a camera, slide projector, etc. **4** a store for arms, ammunition, and provisions for use in war. **5** a store for explosives. [French *magasin* via Italian *magazzino* from Arabic *makẓāzin*, pl. of *makẓan* 'storehouse', from *ẓazana* 'store up']

magdalen /ˈmagdəlɪn/ *n.* **1** a reformed prostitute. **2** a home for reformed prostitutes. [Mary *Magdalene* of Magdala in Galilee (Luke 8:2), identified (probably wrongly) with the sinner of Luke 7:37: from ecclesiastical Latin *Magdalena* from Greek *Magdalēnē*]

Magdalenian /magdəˈliːnɪən/ *adj.* & *n. Archaeol.* ● *adj.* of or relating to the final palaeolithic culture in Europe, following the Solutrean and dated to c.17,000–11,000 years ago. ● *n.* this culture. [French *Magdalénien* 'of La *Madeleine*', Dordogne, France, where remains were found]

mage /meɪdʒ/ *n. archaic* **1** a magician. **2** a wise and learned person. [Middle English, Anglicized from MAGUS]

Magellanic cloud /madʒɪˈlanɪk/ *n.* each of two galaxies visible in the southern sky. [named after F. *Magellan*, Portuguese explorer d. 1521]

magenta /məˈdʒɛntə/ *n.* & *adj.* ● *n.* **1** a brilliant mauvish-crimson shade. **2** an aniline dye of this colour;

fuchsine. ● *adj.* of or coloured with magenta. [*Magenta* in N. Italy, site of a battle (1859) fought shortly before the dye was discovered (with reference to the dye's blood-like colour)]

maggot /ˈmagət/ *n.* **1** a soft-bodied legless larva, esp. that of a blowfly etc. found in decaying matter. **2** *archaic* a whimsical fancy. □ **maggoty** *adj.* [Middle English, alteration of *maddock*, earlier *mathek*, from Old Norse *mathkr*: cf. MAWKISH]

magi *pl.* of MAGUS.

magian /ˈmeɪdʒɪən/ *adj. & n.* ● *adj.* of the magi or Magi. ● *n.* **1** a magus or Magus. **2** a magician. □ **magianism** *n.* [Latin *magus*: see MAGUS]

magic /ˈmadʒɪk/ *n., adj., & v.* ● *n.* **1 a** the supposed art of influencing the course of events by the occult control of nature or of the spirits. **b** witchcraft. **2** conjuring tricks. **3** an inexplicable or remarkable influence producing surprising results. **4** an enchanting quality or phenomenon. ● *adj.* **1** of or resulting from magic. **2** producing surprising results. **3** *colloq.* wonderful, exciting. ● *v.tr.* (**magicked**, **magicking**) change or create by magic, or apparently so. □ **like magic** very effectively or rapidly. **magic away** cause to disappear as if by magic. [Middle English via Old French *magique* from Latin *magicus* (*adj.*), Late Latin *magica* (*n.*), from Greek *magikē* (*tekhnē*) '(art of) a MAGUS']

magical /ˈmadʒɪk(ə)l/ *adj.* **1** of or relating to magic. **2** resembling magic; produced as if by magic. **3** wonderful, enchanting. □ **magically** *adv.*

magic bullet *n. colloq.* any (usually undiscovered) highly specific medicine or other cure.

magic carpet *n.* a mythical carpet able to transport a person on it to any desired place.

magic eye *n.* a small cathode ray tube used to indicate the correct tuning of a radio receiver.

magician /məˈdʒɪʃ(ə)n/ *n.* **1** a person skilled in or practising magic. **2** a conjuror. **3** a person with exceptional skill. [Middle English via Old French *magicien* from Late Latin *magica* (as MAGIC)]

magic lantern *n.* a simple form of image-projector using photographic slides.

magic mushroom *n.* a mushroom producing psilocybin.

magic square *n.* a square divided into smaller squares each containing a number such that the sums of all vertical, horizontal, or diagonal rows are equal.

magilp var. of MEGILP.

Maginot Line /ˈmaʒɪnəʊ/ *n.* **1** a line of fortifications along the NE border of France begun in 1929, overrun in 1940. **2** a line of defence on which one relies blindly. [named after A. *Maginot*, French minister of war d. 1932]

magisterial /madʒɪˈstɪərɪəl/ *adj.* **1** imperious. **2** invested with authority. **3** of or conducted by a magistrate. **4** (of a work, opinion, etc.) highly authoritative. □ **magisterially** *adv.* [medieval Latin *magisterialis* from Late Latin *magisterius* from Latin *magister* MASTER]

magisterium /madʒɪˈstɪərɪəm/ *n. RC Ch.* the official teaching of a bishop or pope. [Latin, = the office of a master (as MAGISTERIAL)]

magistracy /ˈmadʒɪstrəsi/ *n.* (*pl.* **-ies**) **1** the office or authority of a magistrate. **2** magistrates collectively.

magistral /ˈmadʒɪstr(ə)l, məˈdʒɪstr(ə)l/ *adj.* **1** of a master or masters. **2** *Pharm.* (of a remedy etc.) devised and made up for a particular case (cf. OFFICINAL 1b). [French *magistral* or Latin *magistralis* from *magister* MASTER]

magistrate /ˈmadʒɪstrət, -streɪt/ *n.* a civil officer administering the law, esp. an official conducting a court for minor cases and preliminary hearings; a Justice of the Peace (*magistrates' court*). □ **magistrateship** *n.* **magistrature** /-trətʃə/ *n.* [Middle English from Latin *magistratus* 'administrator']

Maglemosian /magləˈməʊsɪən, -z-/ *adj. & n. Archaeol.* ● *adj.* of or relating to a N. European mesolithic culture, dated to *c.*8300–6500 BC. ● *n.* this culture. [*Maglemose*, a town in Denmark, where articles from this period were found]

maglev /ˈmaglɛv/ *n.* (usu. *attrib.*) a transport system in which trains glide above a track, supported by magnetic repulsion. [abbreviation of *mag*netic *lev*itation]

magma /ˈmagmə/ *n.* (*pl.* **magmas** or **magmata** /-mətə/) **1** fluid or semi-fluid material under the earth's surface from which lava and other igneous rock is formed by cooling. **2** a crude pasty mixture of mineral or organic matter. □ **magmatic** /-ˈmatɪk/ *adj.* [Middle English, = a solid residue, via Latin from Greek *magma -atos*, from the root of *massō* 'knead']

Magna Carta /magnə ˈkɑːtə/ *n.* (also **Magna Charta**) **1** a charter of liberty and political rights obtained from King John of England in 1215. **2** any similar document of rights. [medieval Latin, = great charter]

magnanimous /magˈnanɪməs/ *adj.* nobly generous; not petty in feelings or conduct. □ **magnanimity** /magnəˈnɪmɪti/ *n.* **magnanimously** *adv.* [Latin *magnanimus*, from *magnus* 'great' + *animus* 'soul']

magnate /ˈmagneɪt/ *n.* a wealthy and influential person, esp. in business (*shipping magnate*; *financial magnate*). [Middle English via Late Latin *magnas -atis* 'great man' from Latin *magnus* 'great']

magnesia /magˈniːʒə, -zjə, -ʃə/ *n.* **1** *Chem.* magnesium oxide. **2** (in general use) hydrated magnesium carbonate, a white powder used as an antacid and laxative. □ **magnesian** *adj.* [Middle English via medieval Latin from Greek *Magnēsia* (*lithos*) '(stone) of Magnesia', in Asia Minor]

magnesite /ˈmagnɪsʌɪt/ *n.* a white or grey mineral form of magnesium carbonate.

magnesium /magˈniːzɪəm/ *n. Chem.* a silvery metallic element occurring naturally in magnesite and dolomite, used for making light alloys and important as an essential element in living organisms (symbol Mg).

magnesium flare *n.* (also **magnesium light**) a blinding white light produced by burning magnesium wire.

magnet /ˈmagnɪt/ *n.* **1** a piece of iron, steel, alloy, ore, etc., usu. in the form of a bar or horseshoe, having properties of attracting or repelling iron. **2** a lodestone. **3** a person or thing that attracts. [Middle English via Latin *magnes magnetis* from Greek *Magnēs -ētos* (*lithos*) '(stone) of Magnesia', originally referring to lodestone: cf. MAGNESIA]

magnetic /magˈnɛtɪk/ *adj.* **1 a** having the properties of a magnet. **b** producing, produced by, or acting by magnetism. **2** capable of being attracted by or acquiring the properties of a magnet. **3** very attractive or alluring (*a magnetic personality*). □ **magnetically** *adv.* [Late Latin *magneticus* (as MAGNET)]

magnetic compass *n.* = COMPASS *n.* 1.

magnetic disk see DISC *n.* 4a.

magnetic equator *n.* an imaginary line, passing round the earth near the equator, on which a magnetic needle has no dip (see DIP *n.* 8).

magnetic field *n.* a region of variable force around magnets, magnetic materials, or current-carrying conductors.

magnetic inclination *n.* = DIP *n.* 8.

magnetic mine *n.* a submarine mine detonated by the proximity of a magnetized body such as that of a ship.

magnetic moment *n.* the property of a magnet that interacts with an applied field to give a mechanical moment.

magnetic needle *n.* a piece of magnetized steel used as an indicator on the dial of a compass and in magnetic and electrical apparatus, esp. in telegraphy.

magnetic north *n.* the point indicated by the north end of a compass needle.

magnetic pole *n.* **1** each of the points near the extremities of the axis of rotation of the earth or another body where a magnetic needle dips vertically. **2**

each of the regions of an artificial or natural magnet, from which the magnetic forces appear to originate.

magnetic resonance imaging *n.* a form of medical imaging using the nuclear magnetic resonance of protons in the body (abbr.: **MRI**).

magnetic storm *n.* a disturbance of the earth's magnetic field caused by charged particles from the sun etc.

magnetic tape *n.* = TAPE *n.* 4a.

magnetism /ˈmagnɪtɪz(ə)m/ *n.* **1 a** magnetic phenomena and their laws. **b** the property of producing these phenomena. **2** attraction; personal charm. [modern Latin *magnetismus* (as MAGNET)]

magnetite /ˈmagnɪtʌɪt/ *n.* magnetic iron oxide. [German *Magnetit* (as MAGNET)]

magnetize /ˈmagnɪtʌɪz/ *v.tr.* (also **-ise**) **1** give magnetic properties to. **2** make into a magnet. **3** attract as or like a magnet. ▫ **magnetizable** *adj.* **magnetization** /-ˈzeɪʃ(ə)n/ *n.* **magnetizer** *n.*

magneto /magˈniːtəʊ/ *n.* (*pl.* **-os**) an electric generator using permanent magnets and producing high voltage, esp. for the ignition of an internal-combustion engine. [abbreviation of MAGNETO-ELECTRIC]

magneto- /magˈniːtəʊ/ *comb. form* indicating a magnet or magnetism. [Greek *magnēs*: see MAGNET]

magneto-electric /magˌniːtəʊɪˈlɛktrɪk/ *adj.* (of an electric generator) using permanent magnets. ▫ **magneto-electricity** /-ˈtrɪsɪti/ *n.*

magnetograph /magˈniːtəgrɑːf/ *n.* an instrument for recording measurements of magnetic quantities.

magnetometer /magnɪˈtɒmɪtə/ *n.* an instrument measuring magnetic forces, esp. the earth's magnetism. ▫ **magnetometry** *n.*

magnetomotive /magˌniːtə(ʊ)ˈməʊtɪv/ *adj.* (of a force) being the sum of the magnetizing forces along a circuit.

magneton /ˈmagnɪtɒn/ *n.* a unit of magnetic moment in atomic and nuclear physics. [French *magnéton* (as MAGNETIC)]

magnetosphere /magˈniːtəsfɪə/ *n.* the region surrounding a planet, star, etc., in which its magnetic field is effective.

magnetron /ˈmagnɪtrɒn/ *n.* an electron tube for amplifying or generating microwaves, with the flow of electrons controlled by an external magnetic field. [MAGNET + -TRON]

magnificat /magˈnɪfɪkat/ *n.* **1** a song of praise. **2** (**Magnificat**) the hymn of the Virgin Mary (Luke 1:46–55) used as a canticle. [the opening words *magnificat anima mea Dominum* 'my soul magnifies the Lord']

magnification /ˌmagnɪfɪˈkeɪʃ(ə)n/ *n.* **1** the act or an instance of magnifying; the process of being magnified. **2** the amount or degree of magnification. **3** the apparent enlargement of an object by a lens.

magnificent /magˈnɪfɪs(ə)nt/ *adj.* **1** splendid, stately. **2** sumptuously or lavishly constructed or adorned. **3** *colloq.* fine, excellent. ▫ **magnificence** *n.* **magnificently** *adv.* [French *magnificent* or Latin *magnificus* from *magnus* 'great']

magnifico /magˈnɪfɪkəʊ/ *n.* (*pl.* **-oes**) a magnate or grandee. [Italian, = MAGNIFICENT: originally with reference to Venice]

magnify /ˈmagnɪfʌɪ/ *v.tr.* (**-ies, -ied**) **1** make (a thing) appear larger than it is, as with a lens. **2** exaggerate. **3** intensify. **4** *archaic* extol, glorify. ▫ **magnifiable** *adj.* **magnifier** *n.* [Middle English from Old French *magnifier* or Latin *magnificare* (as MAGNIFICENT)]

magnifying glass *n.* a lens used to produce an enlarged image.

magniloquent /magˈnɪləkwənt/ *adj.* **1** grand or grandiose in speech. **2** boastful. ▫ **magniloquence** *n.* **magniloquently** *adv.* [Latin *magniloquus*, from *magnus* 'great' + *-loquus* '-speaking']

magnitude /ˈmagnɪtjuːd/ *n.* **1** largeness. **2 a** size. **b** a mathematical quantity. **3** importance. **4 a** the degree of brightness of a star (see also ABSOLUTE MAGNITUDE, APPARENT MAGNITUDE). **b** a class of stars arranged according to this (*of the third magnitude*). ▫ **of the first magnitude** very important. [Middle English from Latin *magnitudo*, from *magnus* 'great']

magnolia /magˈnəʊlɪə/ *n.* & *adj.* ● *n.* **1** any tree or shrub of the genus *Magnolia*, cultivated for its dark green foliage and large waxlike flowers in spring. **2** a pale creamy-white colour. ● *adj.* of this colour. [modern Latin, named after P. *Magnol*, French botanist d. 1715]

magnox /ˈmagnɒks/ *n.* a magnesium-based alloy used to enclose uranium fuel elements in a nuclear reactor. [*mag*nesium *no ox*idation]

magnum /ˈmagnəm/ *n.* (*pl.* **magnums**) **1** a wine bottle of about twice the standard size. **2 a** a cartridge or shell that is especially powerful or large. **b** (often *attrib.*) a cartridge or gun adapted so as to be more powerful than its calibre suggests. [Latin, neut. of *magnus* 'great']

magnum opus /magnəm ˈəʊpəs, ˈɒpəs/ *n.* (*pl.* **magnum opuses** or **magna opera** /magnə ˈəʊpərə, ˈɒpərə/) **1** a great and usu. large work of art, literature, etc. **2** the most important work of an artist, writer, etc. [Latin, = great work: see OPUS]

magpie /ˈmagpʌɪ/ *n.* **1** a long-tailed crow, *Pica pica*, of Europe and N. America, with black and white plumage. **2** any of various birds with black and white plumage, esp. *Gymnorhina tibicen* of Australia. **3** an idle chatterer. **4** a person who collects things indiscriminately. **5 a** the division of a circular target next to the outer one. **b** a rifle shot which strikes this. [*Mag*, abbreviation of *Margaret* + PIE²]

magpie lark *n.* any of several Australian birds of the family Grallinidae, esp. a common long-legged black and white bird, *Grallina cyanoleuca*, with a loud piping call (also called *peewee*).

magpie moth *n.* a white geometrid moth with black and yellow spots, *Abraxas grossulariata*, whose caterpillars feed on fruit bushes.

maguey /ˈmagweɪ/ *n.* an agave plant, esp. one yielding pulque. [Spanish from Taino]

magus /ˈmeɪgəs/ *n.* (*pl.* **magi** /ˈmeɪdʒʌɪ/) **1** a member of a priestly caste of ancient Persia. **2** a sorcerer. **3** (**the** (**three**) **Magi**) the 'wise men' from the East who brought gifts to the infant Christ (Matt. 2:1–12). [Middle English via Latin and Greek from Old Persian *magus*]

Magyar /ˈmagjɑː/ *n.* & *adj.* ● *n.* **1** a member of a Ural-Altaic people now predominant in Hungary. **2** the language of this people; Hungarian. ● *adj.* of or relating to this people or language. [native name]

maharaja /mɑː(h)əˈrɑːdʒə, məhɑː-/ *n.* (also **maharajah**) *hist.* a title of some Indian princes. [Hindi *mahārājā*, from *mahā* 'great' + RAJA]

maharanee /mɑː(h)əˈrɑːni, məhɑː-/ *n.* (also **maharani**) *hist.* a maharaja's wife or widow. [Hindi *mahārānī*, from *mahā* 'great' + RANEE]

maharishi /mɑː(h)əˈrɪʃi/ *n.* a great Hindu sage or spiritual leader. [Hindi, from *mahā* 'great' + RISHI]

mahatma /məˈhatmə, məˈhɑː-/ *n.* **1 a** (in India etc.) a person regarded with reverence. **b** a sage. **2** each of a class of persons in India and Tibet supposed by some to have preternatural powers. [Sanskrit *mahātman*, from *mahā* 'great' + *ātman* 'soul']

Mahayana /mɑː(h)əˈjɑːnə, məhɑː-/ *n.* a tradition of Buddhism now practised esp. in China, Japan, and Tibet. [Sanskrit, from *mahā* 'great' + *yāna* 'vehicle']

Mahdi /ˈmɑːdi/ *n.* (*pl.* **Mahdis**) **1** a spiritual and temporal messiah expected by Muslims. **2** esp. *hist.* a leader claiming to be this Messiah. ▫ **Mahdism** *n.* **Mahdist** *n.* & *adj.* [Arabic *mahdīy* 'he who is guided right', past part. of *hadā* 'guide']

mah-jong /mɑːˈdʒɒŋ/ *n.* (also **mah-jongg**) a Chinese game for four resembling rummy and played with 136 or 144 pieces called tiles. [Chinese dialect *ma-tsiang*, literally 'sparrows']

mahlstick var. of MAULSTICK.

mahogany /məˈhɒgəni/ *n.* & *adj.* ● *n.* (*pl.* **-ies**) **1 a** a hard reddish-brown wood used esp. for furniture. **b** the colour of this. **2** any tropical tree of the genus *Swietenia*, esp. *S. mahagoni*, yielding this wood. ● *adj.* of a rich reddish-brown colour. [17th c.: origin unknown]

mahonia /mə'həʊnɪə/ *n.* any evergreen shrub of the genus *Mahonia*, with yellow bell-shaped or globular flowers. [modern Latin, named after B. Mc*Mahon* (d. 1816), US botanist]

mahout /mə'haʊt/ *n.* (in the Indian subcontinent) an elephant driver or elephant keeper. [Hindi *mahāut* from Sanskrit *mahāmātra* 'high official', literally 'great in measure']

Mahratta var. of MARATHA.

Mahratti var. of MARATHI.

mahseer /'mɑːsɪə/ *n.* either of two freshwater Indian fish, *Barbus putitora* or *B. tor*, used as food. [Hindi *mahāsir*]

maid /meɪd/ *n.* **1** a female domestic servant. **2** *Brit. archaic* or *poet.* a girl or young woman. □ **maidish** *adj.* [Middle English, abbreviation of MAIDEN]

maidan /mʌɪ'dɑːn/ *n. Anglo-Ind.* **1** an open space in or near a town. **2** a parade ground. [Urdu from Arabic *maydān*]

maiden /'meɪd(ə)n/ *n.* **1 a** *archaic* or *poet.* a girl; a young unmarried woman. **b** (*attrib.*) unmarried (*maiden aunt*). **2** *Cricket* = MAIDEN OVER. **3** (*attrib.*) (of a female animal) unmated. **4** (often *attrib.*) **a** a horse that has never won a race. **b** a race open only to such horses. **5** (*attrib.*) being or involving the first attempt or occurrence (*maiden speech*; *maiden voyage*). □ **maidenhood** *n.* **maidenish** *adj.* **maidenlike** *adj.* **maidenly** *adj.* [Old English *mægden* from a Germanic diminutive = maid, virgin]

maidenhair /'meɪd(ə)nhɛː/ *n.* (in full **maidenhair fern**) a fern of the genus *Adiantum*, esp. *A. capillus-veneris*, with fine hairlike stalks and delicate fronds.

maidenhair tree *n.* the ginkgo (whose leaves resemble those of the maidenhair fern in shape).

maidenhead /'meɪd(ə)nhɛd/ *n.* **1** virginity. **2** the hymen.

maiden name *n.* a wife's surname before marriage.

maiden over *n. Cricket* an over in which no runs are scored off the bat.

maid of honour *n.* **1** an unmarried lady attending a queen or princess. **2** *Brit.* a kind of small custard tart. **3** *N. Amer.* a principal bridesmaid.

maidservant /'meɪdsəːv(ə)nt/ *n.* a female domestic servant.

maieutic /meɪ'juːtɪk/ *adj.* (of the Socratic mode of enquiry) serving to bring a person's latent ideas into clear consciousness. [Greek *maieutikos*, via *maieuomai* 'act as a midwife' from *maia* 'midwife']

maigre /'meɪgə/ *adj. RC Ch.* **1** (of a day) on which abstinence from meat is ordered. **2** (of food) suitable for eating on maigre days. [French, literally 'lean': cf. MEAGRE]

mail[1] /meɪl/ *n.* & *v.* ● *n.* **1 a** letters and parcels etc. conveyed by post. **b** the postal system. **c** one complete delivery or collection of mail. **d** one delivery of letters to one place, esp. to a business on one occasion. **2** = ELECTRONIC MAIL. **3** a vehicle carrying mail. **4** *hist.* a bag of letters for conveyance by post. ● *v.tr.* send (a letter etc.) by post. [Middle English from Old French *male* 'wallet', from West Germanic]

mail[2] /meɪl/ *n.* & *v.* ● *n.* **1** *hist.* armour made of rings, chains, or plates, joined together flexibly. **2** the protective shell, scales, etc., of an animal. ● *v.tr. poet.* clothe with or as if with mail. □ **mailed** *adj.* [Middle English via Old French *maille* from Latin *macula* 'spot, mesh']

mailable /'meɪləb(ə)l/ *adj.* acceptable for conveyance by post.

mailbag /'meɪlbag/ *n.* a large sack or bag for carrying mail.

mailboat /'meɪlbəʊt/ *n.* a boat carrying mail.

mailbox /'meɪlbɒks/ *n. N. Amer.* a letter box.

mail carrier *n. US* a postman or postwoman.

mail cart *n. Brit. hist.* **1** a cart for carrying mail by road. **2** a light vehicle for carrying children.

mail coach *n.* a railway coach or *hist.* stagecoach used for carrying mail.

mail drop *n. N. Amer.* a receptacle for mail.

mailed fist *n.* (prec. by *the*) physical force.

mailing /'meɪlɪŋ/ *n.* **1** the action or process of sending something by mail. **2** something sent by mail.

mailing list *n.* a list of people to whom advertising matter, information, etc., is to be posted.

maillot /ma'jəʊ/ *n.* (*pl.* **maillots** *pronunc.* same) **1** tights for dancing, gymnastics, etc. **2** a woman's one-piece bathing suit. **3** a jersey. [French]

mailman /'meɪlmən/ *n.* (*pl.* **-men**) *N. Amer.* a postman.

mail order *n.* the ordering of goods by post (also, often with hyphen, *attrib.*: *mail-order catalogue*).

mailshot /'meɪlʃɒt/ *n.* a dispatch of mail, esp. advertising and promotional material, to a large number of addresses.

mail train *n.* a train carrying mail.

maim /meɪm/ *v.tr.* **1** cripple, disable, mutilate. **2** harm, impair (*emotionally maimed by neglect*). [Middle English from Old French *mahaignier*, of unknown origin]

main[1] /meɪn/ *adj.* & *n.* ● *adj.* **1** chief in size, importance, extent, etc.; principal (*the main part*; *the main point*). **2** exerted to the full (*by main force*). ● *n.* **1** a principal channel, duct, etc., for water, sewage, etc. (*water main*). **2** (usu. in *pl.*; prec. by *the*) *Brit.* **a** the central distribution network for electricity, gas, water, etc. **b** a domestic electricity supply as distinct from batteries. **3** *archaic* or *poet.* **a** the ocean or oceans (*the Spanish Main*). **b** the mainland. □ **in the main** for the most part. **with might and main** with all one's force. [Middle English, partly from Old Norse *megenn*, *megn* 'strong, powerful', partly from Old English *mægen* 'physical force', from Germanic]

main[2] /meɪn/ *n.* **1** (in the game of hazard) a number (5, 6, 7, 8, or 9) called by a player before dice are thrown. **2** a match between fighting cocks. [16th c.: probably originally MAIN CHANCE]

main brace *n. Naut.* the brace attached to the main yard.

main chance *n.* (prec. by *the*) one's own interests.

main clause *n. Gram.* a clause that alone forms a complete sentence (cf. SUBORDINATE CLAUSE).

main course *n.* **1** the chief course of a meal. **2** *Naut.* the mainsail.

maincrop /'meɪnkrɒp/ *attrib.adj.* (of a vegetable) produced by the main crop.

main deck *n.Naut.* **1** the deck below the spar-deck in a man-of-war. **2** the upper deck between the poop and the forecastle in a merchantman.

main drag *n. US colloq.* = MAIN STREET.

mainframe /'meɪnfreɪm/ *n.* **1** the central processing unit and primary memory of a computer. **2** (often *attrib.*) a large computer system.

mainland /'meɪnlənd, -land/ *n.* a large continuous extent of land, excluding neighbouring islands etc. □ **mainlander** *n.*

mainline /'meɪnlʌɪn/ *v. slang* **1** *intr.* take drugs intravenously. **2** *tr.* inject (drugs) intravenously. □ **mainliner** *n.*

main line *n.* **1** a chief railway line. **2** *slang* a principal vein, esp. as a site for a drug injection (cf. MAINLINE). **3** *US* a chief road or street.

mainly /'meɪnli/ *adv.* for the most part; chiefly.

mainmast /'meɪnmɑːst/ *n. Naut.* the principal mast of a ship.

mainplane /'meɪnpleɪn/ *n.* the principal supporting surface of an aircraft (cf. TAILPLANE).

mainsail /'meɪnseɪl, -s(ə)l/ *n. Naut.* **1** (in a square-rigged vessel) the lowest sail on the mainmast. **2** (in a fore-and-aft rigged vessel) a sail set on the after part of the mainmast.

mainsheet /ˈmeɪnʃiːt/ *n. Naut.* the rope which controls the boom of the mainsail when set.

mainspring /ˈmeɪnsprɪŋ/ *n.* **1** the principal spring of a mechanical watch, clock, etc. **2** a chief motive power; an incentive.

mainstay /ˈmeɪnsteɪ/ *n.* **1** a chief support (*has been his mainstay since his trouble*). **2** *Naut.* a stay from the maintop to the foot of the foremast.

mainstream /ˈmeɪnstriːm/ *n.* **1** (often *attrib.*) the prevailing trend in opinion, fashion, etc. **2** a type of jazz based on the 1930s swing style and consisting esp. of solo improvisation on chord sequences. **3** the principal current of a river.

Main Street *n.* esp. *US* the materialism, mediocrity, or parochialism, regarded as typical of small-town life (after Sinclair Lewis's novel, 1920).

main street *n.* the principal street of a town.

maintain /meɪnˈteɪn, mənˈteɪn/ *v.tr.* **1** cause to continue; keep up, preserve (a state of affairs, an activity, etc.) (*maintained friendly relations*). **2** (often foll. by *in*; often *refl.*) support (life, a condition, etc.) by work, nourishment, expenditure, etc. (*maintained him in comfort*; *maintained themselves by fishing*). **3** (often foll. by *that* + clause) assert (an opinion, statement, etc.) as true (*maintained that she was the best*; *his story was true, he maintained*). **4** preserve or provide for the preservation of (a building, machine, road, etc.) in good repair. **5** give aid to (a cause, party, etc.). **6** provide means for (a garrison etc. to be equipped). ▫ **maintainable** *adj.* **maintainability** /-ˈbɪlɪti/ *n.* [Middle English from Old French *maintenir*, ultimately from Latin *manu tenēre* 'hold in the hand']

maintained school *n. Brit.* a school supported from public funds.

maintainer /meɪnˈteɪnə, mən-/ *n.* **1** a person or thing that maintains. **2** (also **maintainor**) *Law hist.* a person guilty of maintenance (see MAINTENANCE 3).

maintenance /ˈmeɪnt(ə)nəns, -tɪn-/ *n.* **1** the process of maintaining or being maintained. **2 a** the provision of the means to support life, esp. by work etc. **b** (also **separate maintenance**) a husband's or wife's provision for a spouse after separation or divorce; alimony. **3** *Law hist.* the offence of aiding a party in litigation without lawful cause. [Middle English from Old French, from *maintenir*: see MAINTAIN]

maintop /ˈmeɪntɒp/ *n. Naut.* a platform above the head of the lower mainmast.

maintopmast /meɪnˈtɒpməst/ *n. Naut.* a mast above the head of the lower mainmast.

main yard *n. Naut.* the yard on which the mainsail is extended.

maiolica /məˈjɒlɪkə/ *n.* (also **majolica** /məˈjɒl-, -ˈdʒɒl-/) **1** a white tin-glazed earthenware decorated with metallic colours, originally popular in the Mediterranean area during the Renaissance. **2** a modern imitation of this. [Italian, from the former name of Majorca]

maisonette /meɪzəˈnɛt/ *n.* (also **maisonnette**) **1** a part of a house, block of flats, etc., forming separate living accommodation, usu. on two floors and having a separate entrance. **2** a small house. [French *maisonnette*, diminutive of *maison* 'house']

maître d'hôtel /meɪtrə dəʊˈtɛl/ *n.* (*pl.* **maîtres d'hôtel** *pronunc.* same) **1** the manager, head steward, etc., of a hotel. **2** a head waiter. [French, = master of (the) house]

maize /meɪz/ *n.* **1** a cereal plant, *Zea mays*, native to N. America, yielding large grains set in rows on a cob. **2** the cobs or grains of this (cf. CORN[1] 1). [French *maïs* or Spanish *maíz*, of Carib origin]

Maj. *abbr.* Major.

majestic /məˈdʒɛstɪk/ *adj.* showing majesty; stately and dignified; grand, imposing. ▫ **majestically** *adv.*

majesty /ˈmadʒɪsti/ *n.* (*pl.* **-ies**) **1** impressive stateliness, dignity, or authority, esp. of bearing, language, the law, etc. **2 a** royal power. **b** (**Majesty**) forming part of several titles given to a sovereign or a sovereign's wife or widow or used in addressing them (*Your Majesty*; *Her Majesty the Queen Mother*). **3** a picture of God or Christ enthroned within an aureole. ▫ **Her** (or **His**) **Majesty's** part of the title of several State institutions (*Her Majesty's Stationery Office*). [Middle English via Old French *majesté* from Latin *majestas -tatis* (as MAJOR)]

Majlis /ˈmadʒlɪs, madʒˈlɪs/ *n. Polit.* the parliament of various N. African or Middle Eastern countries, esp. Iran. [Persian, = assembly]

majolica var. of MAIOLICA.

major /ˈmeɪdʒə/ *adj.*, *n.*, & *v.* ● *adj.* **1** important, large, serious, significant (*a major road*; *a major war*; *the major consideration must be their health*). **2** (of an operation) serious or life-threatening. **3** *Mus.* **a** (of a scale) having intervals of a semitone between the third and fourth, and seventh and eighth degrees. **b** (of an interval) greater by a semitone than a minor interval (*major third*). **c** (of a key) based on a major scale, tending to produce a bright or joyful effect (*D major*). **4** of full age. **5** *Brit.* (appended to a surname, esp. in public schools) indicating the elder of two brothers (*Smith major*). **6** *Logic* **a** (of a term) occurring in the predicate or conclusion of a syllogism. **b** (of a premiss) containing a major term. ● *n.* **1** *Mil.* **a** an army officer next below lieutenant colonel and above captain. **b** an officer in charge of a section of band instruments (*drum major*; *pipe major*). **2** a person of full age. **3** *Mus.* a major key etc. **4** *US* **a** a student's special subject or course. **b** a student specializing in a specified subject (*a philosophy major*). **5** *Logic* a major term or premiss. ● *v.intr.* (foll. by *in*) *US* study or qualify in as a special subject (*majored in theology*). ▫ **majorship** *n.* [Middle English from Latin, comparative of *magnus* 'great']

major axis *n.* the axis of a conic, passing through its foci.

Majorcan /məˈdʒɔːk(ə)n, məˈjɔː-/ *n.* & *adj.* ● *n.* a native or inhabitant of Majorca, an island in the Mediterranean. ● *adj.* of or relating to Majorca.

major-domo /meɪdʒəˈdəʊməʊ/ *n.* (*pl.* **-os**) **1** the chief official of an Italian or Spanish princely household. **2** a house-steward; a butler. [originally *mayordome*, via Spanish *mayordomo*, Italian *maggiordomo* from medieval Latin *major domus* 'highest official of the household' (as MAJOR, DOME)]

majorette /meɪdʒəˈrɛt/ *n.* = DRUM MAJORETTE. [abbreviation]

major general *n.* an officer next below a lieutenant general.

majority /məˈdʒɒrɪti/ *n.* (*pl.* **-ies**) **1** (usu. foll. by *of*) the greater number or part. **2** *Polit.* **a** the number by which the votes cast for one party, candidate, etc. exceed those of the next in rank (*won by a majority of 151*). **b** a party etc. receiving the greater number of votes. **3** full legal age (*attained his majority*). **4** the rank of major. ▫ **in the majority** esp. *Polit.* belonging to or constituting a majority party etc. [French *majorité* from medieval Latin *majoritas -tatis* (as MAJOR)]

■ **Usage** In sense 1, *majority* is strictly used only with countable nouns, e.g. *a majority of people*, and not with mass nouns, e.g. *a majority of the work*. When used with countable nouns, it is followed by a plural verb, e.g. *The majority of his books were failures*.

majority rule *n.* the principle that the greater number should exercise greater power.

majority verdict *n.* a verdict given by more than half of the jury, but not unanimous.

major league *n.* (often *attrib.*) *US* a top-ranking league in baseball etc.

major part *n.* (often foll. by *of*) the majority.

major piece *n. Chess* a rook or queen.

major planet *n.* Jupiter, Saturn, Uranus, or Neptune.

major prophet *n.* Isaiah, Jeremiah, or Ezekiel.

major suit *n. Bridge* spades or hearts.

majuscule /ˈmadʒəskjuːl/ *n. & adj.* ● *n.* **1** a large letter, whether capital or uncial. **2** large lettering. ● *adj.* of, written in, or concerning majuscules. □ **majuscular** /məˈdʒʌskjʊlə/ *adj.* [French from Latin *majuscula* (*littera* 'letter'), diminutive of MAJOR]

make /meɪk/ *v. & n.* ● *v.* (*past* and *past part.* **made** /meɪd/) **1** *tr.* construct; create; form from parts or other substances (*made a table*; *made it out of cardboard*; *made him a sweater*). **2** *tr.* (usu. foll. by infin. with or without *to*) cause or compel (a person etc.) to do something (*make him repeat it*; *was made to confess*). **3** *tr.* **a** cause to exist; create; bring about (*made a noise*; *made an enemy*). **b** cause to become or seem (*made an exhibition of myself*; *made him angry*). **c** appoint; designate (*made him a Cardinal*). **4** *tr.* compose; prepare; draw up (*made her will*; *made a film about Japan*). **5** *tr.* constitute; amount to (*makes a difference*; *2 and 2 make 4*; *this makes the tenth time*). **6** *tr.* **a** undertake or agree to (an aim or purpose) (*made a promise*; *make an effort*). **b** execute or perform (a bodily movement, a speech, etc.) (*made a face*; *made a bow*). **7** *tr.* gain, acquire, procure (money, a profit, etc.) (*made £20,000 on the deal*). **8** *tr.* prepare (tea, coffee, a dish, etc.) for consumption (*made egg and chips*). **9** *tr.* **a** arrange bedclothes tidily on (a bed) ready for use. **b** arrange and light materials for (a fire). **10** *intr.* **a** proceed (*made towards the river*). **b** (foll. by *to* + infin.) begin an action (*he made to go*). **11** *tr. colloq.* **a** arrive at (a place) or in time for (a train etc.) (*made the border before dark*; *made the six o'clock train*). **b** manage to attend; manage to attend on (a certain day) or at (a certain time) (*couldn't make the meeting last week*; *can make any day except Friday*). **c** achieve a place in (*made the first eleven*; *made the six o'clock news*). **d** esp. *N. Amer.* achieve the rank of (*made colonel in three years*). **12** *tr.* establish or enact (a distinction, rule, law, etc.). **13** *tr.* consider to be; estimate as (*what do you make the time?*; *do you make that a 1 or a 7?*). **14** *tr.* secure the success or advancement of (*his mother made him*; *it made my day*). **15** *tr.* accomplish (a distance, speed, score, etc.) (*made 60 m.p.h. on the motorway*). **16** *tr.* **a** become by development or training (*made a great leader*). **b** serve as (*a log makes a useful seat*). **17** *tr.* (usu. foll. by *out*) represent as; cause to appear as (*makes him out a liar*). **18** *tr.* form in the mind (*I make no judgement*). **19** *tr.* (foll. by *it* + compl.) **a** determine, establish, or choose (*let's make it Tuesday*; *made it my business to know*). **b** bring to (a chosen value etc.) (*decided to make it a dozen*). **20** *tr. slang* have sexual relations with. **21** *tr. Cards* **a** win (a trick). **b** play (a card) to advantage. **c** win the number of tricks that fulfils (a contract). **d** shuffle (a pack of cards) for dealing. **22** *tr. Cricket* score (runs). **23** *tr. Electr.* complete or close (a circuit) (opp. BREAK[1] *v.* 10). **24** *intr.* (of the tide) begin to flow or ebb. ● *n.* **1** (esp. of a product) a type, origin, brand, etc. of manufacture (*different make of car*; *our own make*). **2** a kind of mental, moral, or physical structure or composition. **3** an act of shuffling cards. **4** *Electr.* **a** the making of contact. **b** the position in which this is made. □ **make after** *archaic* pursue. **make against** be unfavourable to. **make as if** (or **though**) (foll. by *to* + infin. or conditional) act as if the specified circumstances applied (*made as if to leave*; *made as if he would hit me*; *made as if I had not noticed*). **make away** (or **off**) depart hastily. **make away with 1** get rid of; kill. **2** squander. **make believe** pretend. **make a clean breast of** see BREAST. **make conversation** talk politely. **make a day** (or **night** etc.) **of it** devote a whole day (or night etc.) to an activity. **make do 1** manage with the limited or inadequate means available. **2** (foll. by *with*) manage with (something) as an inferior substitute. **make an example of** punish as a warning to others. **make a fool of** see FOOL[1]. **make for 1** tend to result in (happiness etc.). **2** proceed towards (a place). **3** assault; attack. **4** confirm (an opinion). **make friends** (often foll. by *with*) become friendly. **make fun of** see FUN. **make good** see GOOD. **make a habit of** see HABIT. **make a hash of** see HASH[1]. **make hay, make hay of** see HAY[1]. **make head or tail of** see HEAD. **make a House** *Brit. Polit.* secure the presence of enough members for a quorum or support in the House of Commons. **make it** *colloq.* **1** succeed in reaching, esp. in time. **2** be successful. **3** (usu. foll. by *with*) *slang* have sexual intercourse (with). **make it up 1** be reconciled, esp. after a quarrel. **2** fill in a deficit. **make it up to** remedy negligence, an injury, etc. to (a person). **make light of** see LIGHT[2]. **make love** see LOVE. **make a meal of** see MEAL[1]. **make merry** see MERRY. **make money** acquire wealth or an income. **make the most of** see MOST. **make much** (or **little** or **the best**) **of 1** derive much (or little etc.) advantage from. **2** give much (or little etc.) attention, importance, etc., to. **make a name for oneself** see NAME. **make no bones about** see BONE. **make nothing of 1** do without hesitation. **2** treat as a trifle. **3** be unable to understand, use, or deal with. **make of 1** construct from. **2** conclude to be the meaning or character of (*can you make anything of it?*). **make off** = *make away*. **make off with** carry away; steal. **make oneself scarce** see SCARCE. **make or break** (or esp. *Brit.* **mar**) cause the success or ruin of. **make out 1 a** distinguish by sight or hearing. **b** decipher (handwriting etc.). **2** understand (*can't make him out*). **3** assert; pretend; represent as; demonstrate, prove; try to prove (*made out he liked it*; *made him out to be a crook*). **4** *colloq.* make progress; fare (*how did you make out?*). **5** (usu. foll. by *to, in favour of*) draw up; write out (*made out a cheque to her*). **6** *N. Amer. colloq.* indulge in sexual activity usu. stopping short of intercourse; neck, pet. **make over 1** transfer the possession of (a thing) to a person. **2** refashion (a garment etc.). **make a point of** see POINT. **make sail** *Naut.* **1** spread a sail or sails. **2** start a voyage. **make shift** see SHIFT. **make so bold as to** see BOLD. **make time 1** (usu. foll. by *for* or *to* + infin.) find an occasion when time is available. **2** (usu. foll. by *with*) *N. Amer. slang* make sexual advances (to a person). **make up 1** serve or act to overcome (a deficiency). **2** complete (an amount, a party, etc.). **3** compensate. **4** be reconciled. **5** put together; compound; prepare (*made up the medicine*). **6** sew (parts of a garment etc.) together. **7** get (a sum of money, a company, etc.) together. **8** concoct (a story). **9** (of parts) compose (a whole). **10 a** apply cosmetics. **b** apply cosmetics to. **11** settle (a dispute). **12** prepare (a bed) for use with fresh sheets etc. **13** *Printing* arrange (type) in pages. **14** compile (a list, an account, a document, etc.). **15** arrange (a marriage etc.). **make up one's mind** decide, resolve. **make up to** curry favour with; court. **make water 1** urinate. **2** (of a ship) take in water. **make way 1** (often foll. by *for*) allow room for others to proceed. **2** achieve progress. **make one's way** proceed. **make with** *US colloq.* supply; perform; proceed with (*made with the feet and left in a hurry*). **on the make** *colloq.* **1** intent on gain. **2** looking for sexual partners. □ **makable** *adj.* [Old English *macian* from West Germanic: related to MATCH[1]]

make-believe *n. & adj.* (also **make-belief**) ● *n.* pretence. ● *adj.* pretended.

make-over *n.* a complete transformation or remodelling.

maker /ˈmeɪkə/ *n.* **1** (often in *comb.*) a person or thing that makes. **2** (**our, the,** etc. **Maker**) God. **3** *archaic* a poet.

makeshift /ˈmeɪkʃɪft/ *adj. & n.* ● *adj.* temporary; serving for the time being (*a makeshift arrangement*). ● *n.* a temporary substitute or device.

make-up *n.* **1** cosmetics for the face etc., either generally or to create an actor's appearance or disguise. **2** the appearance of the face etc. when cosmetics have been applied (*his make-up was not convincing*). **3** *Printing* the making up of a type. **4** *Printing* the type made up. **5** a person's character, temperament, etc. **6** the composition or constitution (of a thing).

makeweight /ˈmeɪkweɪt/ *n.* **1** a small quantity or thing added to make up the full weight. **2** an unimportant extra person. **3** an unimportant point added to make an argument seem stronger.

making /ˈmeɪkɪŋ/ *n.* **1** in senses of MAKE *v.* **2** (in *pl.*) **a** earnings; profit. **b** (foll. by *of*) essential qualities or ingredients (*has the makings of a general*; *we have the makings of a meal*). **c** *N. Amer.* & *Austral. colloq.* paper and tobacco for rolling a cigarette. □ **be the making of** ensure the success or favourable development of. **in the making** in the course of being made or formed. [Old English *macung* (as MAKE)]

mako[1] /ˈmɑːkəʊ, ˈmakəʊ/ *n.* (*pl.* **-os**) a large bluish shark of the genus *Isurus*, found worldwide. [Maori]

mako[2] /ˈmɑːkəʊ, ˈmakəʊ/ *n.* (*pl.* **-os**) a small New Zealand tree, *Aristotelia racemosa*, with clusters of dark red berries and large racemes of pink flowers. Also called WINEBERRY. [Maori]

Mal. *abbr.* Malachi (Old Testament).

mal- /mal/ *comb. form* **1 a** bad, badly (*malpractice*; *maltreat*). **b** faulty, faultily (*malfunction*). **2** not (*maladroit*). [French *mal* 'badly' from Latin *male*]

malabsorption /maləbˈzɔːpʃ(ə)n/ *n.* imperfect absorption of food material by the small intestine.

malacca /məˈlakə/ *n.* (in full **malacca cane**) a rich-brown cane from the stem of the palm tree *Calamus scipionum*, used for walking sticks etc. [*Malacca*, a town and district on the Malay peninsula]

malachite /ˈmaləkʌɪt/ *n.* a bright green mineral of hydrous copper carbonate, taking a high polish and used for ornament. [Old French *melochite* via Latin *molochites* from Greek *molokhitis*, from *molokhē* = *malakhē* 'mallow']

malaco- /ˈmaləkəʊ/ *comb. form* soft. [Greek *malakos* 'soft']

malacology /maləˈkɒlədʒi/ *n.* the study of molluscs.

malacostracan /maləˈkɒstrək(ə)n/ *n.* & *adj.* ● *n.* any crustacean of the class Malacostraca, including crabs, shrimps, lobsters, and krill. ● *adj.* of or relating to this class. [MALACO- + Greek *ostrakon* 'shell']

maladaptive /maləˈdaptɪv/ *adj.* (of an individual, species, etc.) failing to adjust adequately to the environment, and undergoing emotional, behavioural, physical, or mental repercussions. □ **maladaptation** /maladapˈteɪʃ(ə)n/ *n.*

maladjusted /maləˈdʒʌstɪd/ *adj.* **1** not correctly adjusted. **2** (of a person) unable to cope with the demands of a social environment. □ **maladjustment** *n.*

maladminister /maləd'mɪnɪstə/ *v.tr.* manage or administer inefficiently, badly, or dishonestly. □ **maladministration** /-ˈstreɪʃ(ə)n/ *n.*

maladroit /ˌmaləˈdrɔɪt/ *adj.* clumsy; bungling. □ **maladroitly** *adv.* **maladroitness** *n.* [French (as MAL-, ADROIT)]

malady /ˈmalədi/ *n.* (*pl.* **-ies**) **1** an ailment; a disease. **2** a morbid or depraved condition; something requiring a remedy. [Middle English from Old French *maladie*, from *malade* 'sick', ultimately from Latin *male* 'ill' + *habitus*, past part. of *habēre* 'have']

mala fide /meɪlə ˈfʌɪdiː, malə ˈfiːdeɪ/ *adj.* & *adv.* ● *adj.* acting or done in bad faith. ● *adv.* in bad faith. [Latin]

Malaga /ˈmaləgə/ *n.* a sweet fortified wine from Málaga in southern Spain.

Malagasy /maləˈgasi/ *adj.* & *n.* ● *adj.* of or relating to Madagascar, an island in the Indian Ocean. ● *n.* the Austronesian language of Madagascar. [originally *Malegass*, *Madegass* from *Madagascar*]

malagueña /maləˈgeɪnjə/ *n.* **1** a Spanish dance resembling the fandango. **2** a piece of music for or in the style of a fandango. [Spanish (as MALAGA)]

malaise /maˈleɪz/ *n.* **1** a non-specific bodily discomfort not associated with the development of a disease. **2** a feeling of uneasiness. [French, from Old French *mal* 'bad' + *aise* EASE]

malamute /ˈmaləmjuːt/ *n.* (also **malemute**) an Eskimo dog. [name of an Alaskan Inuit people]

malanders var. of MALLENDERS.

malapert /ˈmaləpəːt/ *adj.* & *n. archaic* ● *adj.* impudent; saucy. ● *n.* an impudent or saucy person. [Middle English from Old French (as MAL-, *apert* = *espert* EXPERT)]

malapropism /ˈmaləprɒpɪz(ə)m/ *n.* (also **malaprop** /ˈmaləprɒp/) the use of a word in mistake for one sounding similar, to comic effect, e.g. dance a *flamingo* (for *flamenco*). [Mrs *Malaprop* (from MALAPROPOS) in Sheridan's play *The Rivals* (1775)]

malapropos /ˌmalaprəˈpəʊ/ *adv.*, *adj.*, & *n.* ● *adv.* inopportunely; inappropriately. ● *adj.* inopportune; inappropriate. ● *n.* something inappropriately said, done, etc. [French *mal à propos* from *mal* 'ill': see APROPOS]

malar /ˈmeɪlə/ *adj.* & *n.* ● *adj.* of the cheek. ● *n.* a bone of the cheek. [modern Latin *malaris* from Latin *mala* 'jaw']

malaria /məˈlɛːrɪə/ *n.* **1** an intermittent and remittent fever caused by a protozoan parasite of the genus *Plasmodium*, introduced by the bite of a mosquito. **2** *archaic* an unwholesome atmosphere caused by the exhalations of marshes, to which this fever was formerly attributed. □ **malarial** *adj.* **malarian** *adj.* **malarious** *adj.* [Italian *mal'aria* 'bad air']

malarkey /məˈlɑːki/ *n. colloq.* humbug; nonsense. [20th c.: origin unknown]

malathion /maləˈθʌɪən/ *n.* an insecticide containing phosphorus, with low toxicity to other animals. [diethyl *male*ate + *thio-* acid + -ON]

Malay /məˈleɪ/ *n.* & *adj.* ● *n.* **1 a** a member of a people inhabiting Malaysia and Indonesia. **b** a person of Malay descent. **2** the Austronesian language of this people, the official language of Malaysia. ● *adj.* of or relating to this people or language. [Malay *Melayu*]

Malayalam /maləˈjɑːləm/ *n.* the Dravidian language of the state of Kerala in southern India. [native word, from *mala* (Tamil *malai*) 'mountain' + *āḷ* 'man']

Malayan /məˈleɪən/ *n.* & *adj.* ● *n.* = MALAY *n.* 1. ● *adj.* of or relating to Malays or Malaya (now part of Malaysia).

Malayo- /məˈleɪəʊ/ *comb. form* Malayan and (*Malayo-Chinese*). [MALAY]

Malaysian /məˈleɪzɪən, -ʒ(ə)n/ *n.* & *adj.* ● *n.* a native or inhabitant of Malaysia in SE Asia. ● *adj.* of or relating to Malaysia or its people.

malcontent /ˈmalkəntɛnt/ *n.* & *adj.* ● *n.* a discontented person; a rebel. ● *adj.* discontented or rebellious. [French (as MAL-, CONTENT[1])]

mal de mer /mal də ˈmɛː, French mal də mɛr/ *n.* seasickness. [French, = sickness of (the) sea]

maldistribution /ˌmaldɪstrɪˈbjuːʃ(ə)n/ *n.* faulty or imperfect distribution. □ **maldistributed** *adj.*

male /meɪl/ *adj.* & *n.* ● *adj.* **1** of the sex that can beget offspring by fertilization or insemination (*male dog*). **2** of men or male animals, plants, etc.; masculine (*the male sex*;). **3** (of plants or their parts) containing only fertilizing organs. **4** (of parts of machinery etc.) designed to enter or fill the corresponding female part (*a male screw*). ● *n.* a male person or animal. □ **maleness** *n.* [Middle English via Old French *ma(s)le* from Latin *masculus*, from *mas* 'a male']

male chauvinist see CHAUVINIST 2.

malediction /malɪˈdɪkʃ(ə)n/ *n.* **1** a curse. **2** the utterance of a curse. □ **maledictive** *adj.* **maledictory** *adj.* [Middle English from Latin *maledictio*, via *maledicere* 'speak evil of' from *male* 'ill' + *dicere dict-* 'speak']

malefactor /ˈmalɪfaktə/ *n.* a criminal; an evildoer. □ **malefaction** /-ˈfakʃ(ə)n/ *n.* [Middle English from Latin *malefacere malefact-*, from *male* 'ill' + *facere* 'do']

male fern *n.* a common lowland fern, *Dryopteris filixmas*. [regarded as male because of its robustness]

malefic /məˈlɛfɪk/ *adj. literary* (of magical arts etc.) harmful; baleful. [Latin *maleficus* from *male* 'ill']

maleficent /məˈlɛfɪs(ə)nt/ *adj. literary* **1** (often foll. by *to*) hurtful. **2** criminal. □ **maleficence** *n.* [*maleficence*, formed as MALEFIC, on the pattern of *malevolence*]

maleic acid /məˈleɪɪk/ *n.* a colourless crystalline organic acid used in making synthetic resins. [French *maléique* (as MALIC ACID)]

male menopause *n.* a crisis of potency, confidence, etc., supposed to afflict men in middle life.

malemute var. of MALAMUTE.

malevolent /məˈlɛv(ə)l(ə)nt/ *adj.* wishing evil to others. □ **malevolence** *n.* **malevolently** *adv.* [Old French *malivolent* or Latin *malevolens*, from *male* 'ill' + *volens* 'willing', part. of *velle*]

malfeasance /malˈfi:z(ə)ns/ *n. Law* evildoing. □ **malfeasant** *n. & adj.* [Anglo-French *malfaisance* from Old French *malfaisant* (as MAL-, *faisant* part. of *faire* 'do', from Latin *facere*): cf. MISFEASANCE]

malformation /malfɔ:ˈmeɪʃ(ə)n/ *n.* faulty formation. □ **malformed** /-ˈfɔ:md/ *adj.*

malfunction /malˈfʌŋ(k)ʃ(ə)n/ *n. & v.* ● *n.* a failure to function in a normal or satisfactory manner. ● *v.intr.* fail to function normally or satisfactorily.

mali /ˈmɑ:li/ *n.* (*pl.* **malis**) (in the Indian subcontinent) a member of a caste whose traditional occupation is gardening; a gardener. [Hindi]

malic acid /ˈmalɪk/ *n.* an organic acid found in unripe apples and other fruits. [French *malique* from Latin *malum* 'apple']

malice /ˈmalɪs/ *n.* **1 a** the intention to do evil. **b** a desire to tease, esp. cruelly. **2** *Law* wrongful intention, esp. as increasing the guilt of certain offences. [Middle English via Old French from Latin *malitia*, from *malus* 'bad']

malice aforethought *n.* (also **malice prepense**) the intention to commit a crime, esp. murder.

malicious /məˈlɪʃəs/ *adj.* characterized by malice; intending or intended to do harm. □ **maliciously** *adv.* **maliciousness** *n.* [Old French *malicius* from Latin *malitiosus* (as MALICE)]

malign /məˈlʌɪn/ *adj. & v.* ● *adj.* **1** (of a thing) injurious. **2** (of a disease) malignant. **3** malevolent. ● *v.tr.* speak ill of; slander. □ **maligner** *n.* **malignity** /məˈlɪgnɪti/ *n.* (*pl.* **-ies**). **malignly** *adv.* [Middle English via Old French *malin maligne*, *malignier* and Late Latin *malignare* 'contrive maliciously' from Latin *malignus*, from *malus* 'bad': cf. BENIGN]

malignant /məˈlɪgnənt/ *adj.* **1 a** (of a disease) very virulent or infectious (*malignant cholera*). **b** (of a tumour) tending to invade normal tissue and recur after removal; cancerous. **2** harmful; feeling or showing intense ill will. □ **malignancy** *n.* (*pl.* **-ies**). **malignantly** *adv.* [Late Latin *malignare* (as MALIGN)]

malignant pustule *n.* a form of anthrax.

malinger /məˈlɪŋgə/ *v.intr.* exaggerate or feign illness in order to escape duty, work, etc. □ **malingerer** *n.* [back-formation from *malingerer*, apparently from French *malingre*, perhaps formed as MAL- + *haingre* 'weak']

mall /mal, mɔ:l/ *n.* **1** a sheltered walk or promenade. **2** an enclosed shopping precinct. **3** *hist.* **a** = PALL-MALL. **b** an alley used for this. [applied to *The Mall* in London (originally a pall-mall alley): variant of MAUL, in the sense 'hammer, mallet']

mallard /ˈmalɑ:d, -ləd/ *n.* (*pl.* same or **mallards**) **1** a wild duck or drake, *Anas platyrhynchos*, of the northern hemisphere. **2** the flesh of the mallard. [Middle English from Old French (probably as MALE, -ARD)]

malleable /ˈmalɪəb(ə)l/ *adj.* **1** (of metal etc.) able to be hammered or pressed permanently out of shape without breaking or cracking. **2** adaptable; pliable, flexible. □ **malleability** /-ˈbɪlɪti/ *n.* **malleably** *adv.* [Middle English via Old French and medieval Latin *malleabilis* from Latin *malleare* 'to hammer', from *malleus* 'hammer']

mallee /ˈmali/ *n. Austral.* **1** any of several types of eucalyptus, esp. *Eucalyptus dumosa*, that flourish in arid areas. **2** an area of scrub formed by mallee. [Aboriginal, probably Wemba-wemba *mali*]

mallee bird *n.* (also **mallee fowl** or **mallee hen**) a megapode, *Leipoa ocellata*, resembling a turkey.

mallei *pl.* of MALLEUS.

mallemuck var. of MOLLYMAWK.

mallenders /ˈmal(ə)ndəz/ *n.pl.* (also **malanders**) a dry scabby eruption behind a horse's knee. [Middle English via Old French *malandre* (sing.) from Latin *malandria* (pl.) 'neck-pustules']

malleolus /məˈli:ələs/ *n.* (*pl.* **malleoli** /-lʌɪ/) *Anat.* a bone with the shape of a hammer head, esp. each of those forming a projection on either side of the ankle. [Latin, diminutive of *malleus* 'hammer']

mallet /ˈmalɪt/ *n.* **1** a hammer, usu. of wood. **2** a long-handled wooden hammer for striking a croquet or polo ball. [Middle English from Old French *maillet*, via *mailler* 'to hammer' from *mail* 'hammer', from Latin *malleus*]

malleus /ˈmalɪəs/ *n.* (*pl.* **mallei** /-lɪʌɪ/) *Anat.* a small bone in the middle ear transmitting the vibrations of the tympanum to the incus. [Latin, = hammer]

mallow /ˈmaləʊ/ *n.* **1** any plant of the genus *Malva* (family Malvaceae), esp. *M. sylvestris*, with hairy stems and leaves and pink or purple flowers. **2** any of several other plants of the family Malvaceae, including marsh mallow and tree mallow. [Old English *meal(u)we* from Latin *malva*]

malm /mɑ:m/ *n.* **1** a soft chalky rock. **2** a loamy soil produced by the disintegration of this rock. **3** a fine-quality brick made originally from malm, marl, or a similar chalky clay. [Old English *mealm-*, from Germanic]

malmsey /ˈmɑ:mzi/ *n.* a strong sweet wine originally from Greece, now chiefly from Madeira. [Middle English from Middle Dutch, Middle Low German *malmesie*, *-eye*, from *Monemvasia*, a port in S. Greece: cf. MALVOISIE]

malnourished /malˈnʌrɪʃt/ *adj.* suffering from malnutrition.

malnourishment /malˈnʌrɪʃm(ə)nt/ *n.* = MALNUTRITION.

malnutrition /malnjʊˈtrɪʃ(ə)n/ *n.* a dietary condition resulting from the absence of some foods or essential elements necessary for health; insufficient nutrition.

malocclusion /maləˈklu:ʒ(ə)n/ *n.* imperfect positioning of the teeth when the jaws are closed.

malodorous /malˈəʊd(ə)rəs/ *adj.* evil-smelling.

Malpighian layer /malˈpɪgɪən/ *n.* a layer of proliferating cells in the epidermis. [named after M. *Malpighi*, Italian physician d. 1694]

malpractice /malˈpraktɪs/ *n.* **1** improper or negligent professional treatment, esp. by a medical practitioner. **2 a** criminal wrongdoing; misconduct. **b** an instance of this.

malt /mɔ:lt, mɒlt/ *n. & v.* ● *n.* **1** barley or other grain that is steeped, germinated, and dried, esp. for brewing or distilling and vinegar-making. **2** esp. *Brit. colloq.* malt whisky; malt liquor. **3** (also **malted**) *US* = MALTED MILK. ● *v.* **1** *tr.* **a** convert (grain) into malt. **b** (as **malted** *adj.*) mixed with malt or a malt extract. **2** *intr.* (of seeds) become malt when germination is checked by drought. [Old English *m(e)alt* from Germanic: related to MELT]

malted milk *n.* **1** a hot drink made from dried milk and a malt preparation. **2** the powdered mixture from which this is made.

Maltese /mɔ:lˈti:z, mɒl-/ *n. & adj.* ● *n.* (*pl.* same) **1 a** a native or national of Malta, an island in the W. Mediterranean. **b** a person of Maltese descent. **2** the language of Malta. ● *adj.* of or relating to Malta or its people or language.

Maltese cross *n.* a cross with arms of equal length broadening from the centre, often indented at the ends.

Maltese dog *n.* (also **Maltese terrier**) a small breed of spaniel or terrier.

maltha /ˈmalθə/ *n.* a cement made of pitch and wax or other ingredients. [Latin from Greek]

malthouse /ˈmɔ:lthaʊs, ˈmɒlt-/*n.* a building used for preparing and storing malt.

Malthusian /mal'θju:zɪən/ *adj. & n.* ● *adj.* of or relating to T. R. Malthus, English clergyman and economist (d. 1834) or his theories, esp. his observation that the uncontrolled increase of populations is checked only by the limits of their means of subsistence. ● *n.* a follower of Malthus. □ **Malthusianism** *n.*

malting /'mɔ:ltɪŋ, 'mɒlt-/ *n.* **1** the process or an instance of brewing or distilling with malt. **2** = MALTHOUSE.

malt liquor *n.* alcoholic liquor made from malt by fermentation, not distillation, e.g. beer, stout.

maltose /'mɔ:ltəʊz, -s, mɒlt-/ *n. Chem.* a sugar produced by the hydrolysis of starch under the action of the enzymes in malt, saliva, etc. [MALT + -OSE²]

maltreat /mal'tri:t/ *v.tr.* ill-treat. □ **maltreater** *n.* **maltreatment** *n.* [French *maltraiter* (as MAL-, TREAT)]

maltster /'mɔ:ltstə, mɒlt-/ *n.* a person who makes malt.

malt whisky *n.* whisky made from malted barley.

malty /'mɔ:lti, 'mɒlti/ *adj.* (**maltier, maltiest**) of, containing, or resembling malt. □ **maltiness** *n.*

malvaceous /mal'veɪʃəs/ *adj. Bot.* of or relating to the genus *Malva* or the family Malvaceae, which includes mallow. [Latin *malvaceus* from *malva* MALLOW]

malversation /malvə'seɪʃ(ə)n/ *n. formal* **1** corrupt behaviour in a position of trust. **2** (often foll. by *of*) corrupt administration (of public money etc.). [French from *malverser*, from Latin *male* 'badly' + *versari* 'behave']

malvoisie /'malvɔɪzi, malvɔɪ'zi:/ *n.* = MALMSEY. [Middle English via Old French *malvesie* from the French form of *Monemvasia*: see MALMSEY]

mam /mam/ *n. colloq.* mother. [formed as MAMMA¹]

mama /'mamə, mə'mɑ:/ *n. colloq.* (esp. as a child's term) = MAMMA¹.

mamba /'mambə/ *n.* any venomous African snake of the genus *Dendroaspis*, esp. the green and black mambas, which are varieties of *D. angusticeps*. [Zulu *imamba*]

mambo /'mambəʊ/ *n. & v.* ● *n.* (*pl.* **-os**) **1** a Latin American dance like the rumba. **2** the music for this. ● *v.intr.* (**-oes, -oed**) perform the mambo. [Latin American Spanish, probably from Haitian Creole]

mamelon /'mamɪlən/ *n.* a small rounded hillock. [French, = nipple, via *mamelle* 'breast' from Latin MAMILLA]

Mameluke /'maməlu:k/ *n. hist.* a member of the military class (originally Caucasian slaves) that ruled Egypt 1254–1811. [French *mameluk*, ultimately via Arabic *mamlūk* 'slave' from *malaka* 'possess']

mamilla /ma'mɪlə/ *n.* (*US* **mammilla**) (*pl.* **-lae** /-li:/) **1** the nipple of a woman's breast. **2** a nipple-shaped organ etc. □ **mamillary** /'mamɪləri/ *adj.* **mamillate** /'mamɪleɪt/ *adj.* [Latin, diminutive of MAMMA²]

mamma¹ /'mamə, mə'mɑ:/ *n.* (also **momma** /'mɒmə/) *colloq.* (esp. as a child's term) mother. [imitative of child's *ma, ma*]

mamma² /'mamə/ *n.* (*pl.* **mammae** /-mi:/) **1** a milk-secreting organ of female mammals. **2** a corresponding non-secretory structure in male mammals. □ **mammiform** *adj.* [Old English from Latin]

mammal /'mam(ə)l/ *n.* any vertebrate of the class Mammalia, usu. a warm-blooded quadruped with hair or fur, the females of which possess milk-secreting mammae for the nourishment of the young, and including human beings, dogs, cats, rodents, cattle, whales, bats, etc. □ **mammalian** /-'meɪlɪən/ *adj. & n.* **mammalogy** /-'malədʒi/ *n.* [modern Latin *mammalia*, neut. pl. of Latin *mammalis* (as MAMMA²)]

mammaliferous /mamə'lɪf(ə)rəs/ *adj. Geol.* containing mammalian remains.

mammary /'maməri/ *adj. & n.* ● *adj.* of the human female breasts or milk-secreting organs of other mammals. ● *n.* (*pl.* **-ies**) *slang* a breast. [MAMMA² + -ARY¹]

mammary gland *n.* the milk-producing gland of female mammals.

mammee /ma'mi:/ *n.* a tropical American tree, *Mammea americana*, with large red-rinded yellow-pulped fruit. [Spanish *mamei* from Taino]

mammilla *US* var. of MAMILLA.

mammogram /'maməgram/ *n.* an image obtained by mammography.

mammography /ma'mɒgrəfi/ *n. Med.* an X-ray technique of diagnosing and locating abnormalities (esp. tumours) of the breasts. [MAMMA² + -GRAPHY]

Mammon /'mamən/ *n.* **1** wealth regarded as a god or as an evil influence. **2** the worldly rich. □ **Mammonism** *n.* **Mammonist** *n.* [Middle English via Late Latin *Mam(m)ona* and Greek *mamōnas* from Aramaic *māmōn* 'riches': see Matt. 6:24, Luke 16:9–13]

mammoth /'maməθ/ *n. & adj.* ● *n.* any large extinct elephant of the genus *Mammuthus*, with a hairy coat and curved tusks. ● *adj.* huge. [Russian *mamo(n)t*]

mammy /'mami/ *n.* (*pl.* **-ies**) **1** a child's word for mother. **2** *US offens.* a black nursemaid or nanny in charge of white children, esp. formerly in the southern United States. [formed as MAMMA¹]

Man. *abbr.* Manitoba.

man /man/ *n. & v.* ● *n.* (*pl.* **men** /mɛn/) **1** an adult human male, esp. as distinct from a woman or boy. **2 a** a human being; a person (*no man is perfect*). **b** human beings in general; the human race (*man is mortal*). **3** a person showing characteristics associated with males (*she's more of a man than he is*). **4 a** a usu. male worker or employee (*the manager spoke to the men*). **b** esp. *Brit.* a manservant or valet. **c** *hist.* a vassal. **5 a** (usu. in *pl.*) soldiers, sailors, etc., esp. non-officers (*was in command of 200 men*). **b** an individual, usu. male, person (*fought to the last man*). **c** (usu. prec. by *the*, or *poss. pron.*) a person regarded as suitable or appropriate in some way; a person fulfilling requirements (*I'm your man*; *not the man for the job*). **6 a** a husband (*man and wife*). **b** *colloq.* a boyfriend or lover. **7 a** a human being of a specified historical period or character (*Renaissance man*). **b** a type of prehistoric human named after the place where the remains were found (*Peking man*). **8** any one of a set of pieces used in playing chess, draughts, etc. **9** (as second element in *comb.*) a man of a specified nationality, profession, skill, etc. (*Dutchman*; *clergyman*; *horseman*; *gentleman*). **10 a** an expression of impatience etc. used in addressing a male (*nonsense, man!*). **b** *colloq.* a general mode of address (*blew my mind, man!*). **11** (prec. by *a*) a person; one (*what can a man do?*). **12** a person pursued; an opponent etc. (*the police have so far not caught their man*). **13** (**the Man**) *US slang* **a** the police. **b** *black slang* a person or group with power or authority. **14** (in *comb.*) a ship of a specified type (*merchantman*; *Indiaman*). ● *v.tr.* (**manned, manning**) **1** supply (a ship, fort, factory, etc.) with a person or people for work or defence etc. **2** work or service or defend (a specified piece of equipment, a fortification, etc.) (*man the pumps*). **3** *Naut.* place men at (a part of a ship). **4** fill (a post or office). **5** (usu. *refl.*) fortify the spirits or courage of (*manned herself for the task*). □ **as one man** in unison; in agreement. **be a man** be courageous; not show fear. **be one's own man 1** be free to act; be independent. **2** be in full possession of one's faculties etc. **man and boy** from childhood. **man enough** sufficiently manly. **man to man** with candour; honestly. **men's** (or **men's room**) a usu. public lavatory for men. **my** (or **my good**) **man** a patronizing mode of address to a man. **separate** (or **sort out**) **the men from the boys** *colloq.* find those who are truly manly, competent, etc. **to a man** all without exception. □ **manless** *adj.* [Old English *man(n)*, pl. *menn*, *mannian*, from Germanic]

mana /'mɑ:nə/ *n.* **1** esp. *NZ* power; authority; prestige. **2** supernatural or magical power. [Maori]

man about town *n.* a fashionable man of leisure.

manacle /'manək(ə)l/ *n. & v.* ● *n.* (usu. in *pl.*) **1** a fetter or shackle for the hand; a handcuff. **2** a restraint. ● *v.tr.* fetter with manacles. [Middle English via Old French *manicle* 'handcuff' from Latin *manicula*, diminutive of *manus* 'hand']

manage /ˈmanɪdʒ/ *v.* & *n.* ● *v.* **1** *tr.* organize; regulate; be in charge of (a business, household, team, a person's career, etc.). **2** *tr.* (often foll. by *to* + infin.) succeed in achieving; contrive (*managed to arrive on time*; *managed a smile*; *managed to ruin the day*). **3** *intr.* **a** (often foll. by *with*) succeed in one's aim, esp. against heavy odds (*managed with one assistant*). **b** meet one's needs with limited resources etc. (*just about manages on a pension*). **4** *tr.* gain influence with or maintain control over (a person etc.) (*cannot manage their teenage son*). **5** *tr.* (also *absol.*; often prec. by *can*, *be able to*) **a** cope with; make use of (*couldn't manage another bite*; *can you manage by yourself?*). **b** be free to attend on (a certain day) or at (a certain time) (*can you manage Thursday?*). **6** *tr.* handle or wield (a tool, weapon, etc.). **7** *tr.* take or have charge or control of (an animal or animals, esp. cattle). ● *n. archaic* **1 a** the training of a horse. **b** the trained movements of a horse. **2** a riding school (cf. MANÈGE). [Italian *maneggiare*, *maneggio*, ultimately from Latin *manus* 'hand']

manageable /ˈmanɪdʒəb(ə)l/ *adj.* able to be managed, controlled, or accomplished etc. without great difficulty. □ **manageability** /-ˈbɪlɪti/ *n.* **manageableness** *n.* **manageably** *adv.*

management /ˈmanɪdʒm(ə)nt/ *n.* **1** the process of managing or being managed; the action of managing. **2 a** the professional administration of business concerns, public undertakings, etc. **b** people engaged in this. **c** (prec. by *the*) the governing body; the board of directors or the people in charge of running a business, regarded collectively. **3** (usu. foll. by *of*) *Med.* the technique of treating a disease etc. **4** trickery; deceit.

management buyout *n.* the purchase of at least a controlling share in a company by its directors.

manager /ˈmanɪdʒə/ *n.* **1** a person controlling or administering a business or part of a business. **2** a person controlling the affairs, training, etc., of a person or team in sports, entertainment, etc. **3** *Brit. Parl.* a member of either House of Parliament appointed with others for some duty in which both Houses are concerned. **4** a person regarded in terms of skill in household or financial or other management (*a good business manager*). □ **managerial** /manɪˈdʒɪərɪəl/ *adj.* **managerially** /-ˈdʒɪərɪəli/ *adv.* **managership** *n.*

manageress /ˌmanɪdʒəˈrɛs, ˈmanɪdʒərɪs/ *n.* a woman manager, esp. of a shop, hotel, theatre, etc.

managing /ˈmanɪdʒɪŋ/ *adj.* **1** (in *comb.*) esp. *Brit.* having executive control or authority (*managing director*). **2** *archaic* economical.

manakin /ˈmanəkɪn/ *n.* any small bird of the family Pipridae of Central and S. America, the males of which are often brightly coloured. [variant of MANIKIN]

mañana /manˈjɑːnə/ *adv.* & *n.* ● *adv.* in the indefinite future (esp. to indicate procrastination). ● *n.* an indefinite future time. [Spanish, = tomorrow]

man-at-arms *n.* (*pl.* **men-at-arms**) *archaic* a soldier, esp. when heavily armed and mounted.

manatee /manəˈtiː, ˈmanətiː/ *n.* any large aquatic plant-eating mammal (sirenian) of the genus *Trichechus*, with paddle-like forelimbs, no hind limbs, and a powerful tail. Also called *sea cow*. [Spanish *manatí* from Carib *manattoui*]

manchineel /man(t)ʃɪˈniːl/ *n.* a W. Indian tree, *Hippomane mancinella*, with a poisonous and caustic milky sap and acrid apple-like fruit. [French *mancenille* from Spanish *manzanilla*, diminutive of *manzana* 'apple']

Manchu /manˈtʃuː/ *n.* & *adj.* ● *n.* **1** a member of a people in China, descended from a Tartar people, who formed the last imperial dynasty (1644–1912). **2** the language of the Manchus, now spoken in part of NE China. ● *adj.* of or relating to the Manchu people or their language. [Manchu, = pure]

manciple /ˈmansɪp(ə)l/ *n.* esp. *Brit.* an officer who buys provisions for a college, an Inn of Court, etc. [Middle English via Anglo-French & Old French from Latin *mancipium* 'purchase', via *manceps* 'buyer' from *manus* 'hand' + *capere* 'take']

Mancunian /maŋˈkjuːnɪən/ *n.* & *adj.* ● *n.* a native or inhabitant of Manchester in NW England. ● *adj.* of or relating to Manchester. [*Mancunium*, the Latin name of Manchester]

-mancy /mansi/ *comb. form* forming nouns meaning 'divination by' (*geomancy*; *necromancy*). □ **-mantic** *comb. form* forming adjectives. [Old French *-mancie* via Late Latin *-mantia* from Greek *manteia* 'divination']

Mandaean /manˈdiːən/ *n.* & *adj.* ● *n.* **1** a member of a Gnostic sect surviving in Iraq who worship John the Baptist. **2** the language of this sect. ● *adj.* of or relating to the Mandaeans or their language. [Aramaic *mandaiia* 'Gnostics' from *manda* 'knowledge']

mandala /ˈmandələ, ˈmʌn-/ *n.* **1** a symbolic circular figure representing the universe in various religions. **2** *Psychol.* such a symbol in a dream, representing the dreamer's search for completeness and self-unity. [Sanskrit *máṇḍala* 'disc']

mandamus /manˈdeɪməs/ *n. Law* a judicial writ issued as a command to an inferior court, or ordering a person to perform a public or statutory duty. [Latin, = we command]

mandarin[1] /ˈmand(ə)rɪn/ *n.* **1** (**Mandarin**) the most widely spoken form of Chinese and the official language of China. **2** *hist.* a Chinese official in any of nine grades of the pre-Communist civil service. **3** a person of importance, esp. a government official or a reactionary or secretive bureaucrat. **4 a** a nodding Chinese figure, usu. of porcelain. **b** porcelain etc. decorated with Chinese figures in mandarin dress. □ **mandarinate** *n.* [Portuguese *mandarim* via Malay and Hindi *mantrī* from Sanskrit *mantrin* 'counsellor']

mandarin[2] /ˈmand(ə)rɪn/ *n.* (also **mandarine** /-riːn/) (in full **mandarin orange**) **1** a small flattish deep-coloured orange with a loose skin. **2** the tree, *Citrus reticulata*, yielding this. Also called TANGERINE. [French *mandarine* (perhaps as MANDARIN[1], with reference to the official's yellow robes)]

mandarin collar *n.* a small close-fitting upright collar.

mandarin duck *n.* a small Chinese duck, *Aix galericulata*, noted for its bright plumage.

mandarin sleeve *n.* a wide loose sleeve.

mandatary /ˈmandət(ə)ri/ *n.* (*pl.* **-ies**) esp. *hist.* a person or state receiving a mandate. [Late Latin *mandatarius* (as MANDATE)]

mandate *n.* & *v.* ● *n.* /ˈmandeɪt/ **1** an official command or instruction by an authority. **2** support for a policy or course of action, regarded by a victorious party, candidate, etc., as derived from the wishes of the people in an election. **3** a commission to act for another. **4** *Law* a commission by which a party is entrusted to perform a service, often gratuitously and with indemnity against loss by that party. **5** *hist.* a commission from the League of Nations to a member state to administer a territory. **6** a papal decree or decision. ● *v.tr.* /manˈdeɪt/ **1** instruct (a delegate) to act or vote in a certain way. **2** (usu. foll. by *to*) *hist.* commit (a territory etc.) to a mandatary. [Latin *mandatum*, neut. past part. of *mandare* 'command', from *manus* 'hand' + *dare* 'give': sense 2 of the noun influenced by French *mandat*]

mandatory /ˈmandət(ə)ri/ *adj.* & *n.* ● *adj.* **1** of or conveying a command. **2** compulsory. ● *n.* (*pl.* **-ies**) = MANDATARY. □ **mandatorily** *adv.* [Late Latin *mandatorius* from Latin (as MANDATE)]

man-day see MAN-HOUR.

Mandelbrot set /ˈmand(ə)lbrɒt/ *n. Math.* a particular set of complex numbers which has a highly convoluted fractal boundary when plotted. [named after B.B. *Mandelbrot*, Polish-born American mathematician b. 1924]

mandible /ˈmandɪb(ə)l/ *n.* **1** the jaw, esp. the lower jaw in mammals and fishes. **2** the upper or lower part of a bird's beak. **3** either half of the crushing organ in an arthropod's mouthparts. □ **mandibular** /-'dɪbjʊlə/ *adj.* **mandibulate** /-'dɪbjʊlət/ *adj.* [Middle English from Old French *mandible* or Late Latin *mandibula* from *mandere* 'chew']

mandolin /'mandəlɪn, mandə'lɪn/ *n.* (also **mandoline**) a musical instrument resembling a lute, having paired metal strings plucked with a plectrum. □ **mandolinist** *n.* [French *mandoline* from Italian *mandolino*, diminutive of *mandola*, an early form of mandolin]

mandorla /man'dɔːlə/ *n.* = VESICA 2. [Italian, = almond]

mandragora /man'dragərə/ *n. hist.* the mandrake, esp. as a type of narcotic (Shakespeare's *Othello* III. iii. 334). [Old English via medieval Latin and Latin from Greek *mandragoras*]

mandrake /'mandreɪk/ *n.* a poisonous plant, *Mandragora officinarum*, with white or purple flowers and large yellow fruit, having emetic and narcotic properties and possessing a root once thought to resemble the human form and to shriek when plucked. [Middle English *mandrag(g)e*, probably via Middle Dutch *mandrag(r)e* from medieval Latin (as MANDRAGORA): associated with MAN + *drake* 'dragon']

mandrel /'mandr(ə)l/ *n.* **1 a** a shaft in a lathe to which work is fixed while being turned. **b** a cylindrical rod round which metal or other material is forged or shaped. **2** *Brit.* a miner's pick. [16th c.: origin unknown]

mandrill /'mandrɪl/ *n.* a large W. African baboon, *Mandrillus sphinx*, the adult of which has a brilliantly coloured face and blue-coloured buttocks. [probably from MAN + DRILL[3]]

manducate /'mandjʊkeɪt/ *v.tr. literary* chew; eat. □ **manducation** /-'keɪʃ(ə)n/ *n.* **manducatory** /-kət(ə)ri, -'keɪt(ə)ri/ *adj.* [Latin *manducare manducat-* 'chew', via *manduco* 'guzzler' from *mandere* 'chew']

mane /meɪn/ *n.* **1** a growth of long hair on the neck of a horse, lion, etc. **2** *colloq.* a person's long hair. □ **maned** *adj.* (also in *comb.*). **maneless** *adj.* [Old English *manu*, from Germanic]

man-eater /'maniːtə/ *n. colloq.* a woman who has many men as lovers.

manège /ma'neɪʒ/ *n.* (also **manege**) **1** a riding school. **2** the movements of a trained horse. **3** horsemanship. [French *manège* from Italian (as MANAGE)]

manes /'mɑːneɪz, 'meɪniːz/ *n.pl.* **1** the deified souls of dead ancestors. **2** (treated as *sing.*) the revered ghost of a dead person. [Middle English from Latin]

maneuver *US* var. of MANOEUVRE.

man Friday *n.* a male helper or follower. [from *Man Friday* in Defoe's novel *Robinson Crusoe* (1719)]

manful /'manfʊl, -f(ə)l/ *adj.* brave; resolute. □ **manfully** *adv.* **manfulness** *n.*

mangabey /'maŋgəbeɪ/ *n.* any small long-tailed W. African monkey of the genus *Cercocebus*. [*Mangabey*, a region of Madagascar]

manganate /'maŋgənət, -neɪt/ *n. Chem.* a salt in which the anion contains both manganese and oxygen, esp. one of the anion MnO_4^{2-}.

manganese /'maŋgəniːz/ *n.* **1** *Chem.* a grey brittle metallic transition element used with steel to make alloys (symbol **Mn**). **2** (in full **manganese oxide**) the black mineral oxide of this used in the manufacture of glass. □ **manganic** /-'ganɪk/ *adj.* **manganous** /'maŋgənəs/ *adj.* [French *manganèse* from Italian *manganese*, alteration of MAGNESIA]

mange /meɪn(d)ʒ/ *n.* a skin disease in hairy and woolly animals, caused by a parasitic mite and occasionally communicated to man. [Middle English *mangie, maniewe* via Old French *manjue, mangeue* 'itch', from *mangier manju-* 'eat', from Latin *manducare* 'chew']

mangel /'maŋg(ə)l/ *n.* (also **mangold** /'maŋg(ə)ld/) (in full **mangel-wurzel, mangold-wurzel** /-'wəːz(ə)l/) a large kind of beet, *Beta vulgaris*, used as cattle food. [German *Mangoldwurzel*, from *Mangold* 'beet' + *Wurzel* 'root']

manger /'meɪn(d)ʒə/ *n.* a long open box or trough in a stable etc., for horses or cattle to eat from. [Middle English from Old French *mangeoire, mangeure*, ultimately from Latin (as MANDUCATE)]

mangetout /'mɒ̃ʒtuː, -'tuː/ *n.* (*pl.* same or **-s** *pronunc.* same) a variety of pea eaten whole including the pod. Also called *snow pea, sugar snap*. [French, = eat all]

mangle[1] /'maŋg(ə)l/ *n. & v.* ● *n.* **1** esp. *Brit. hist.* a machine having two or more cylinders usu. turned by a handle, between which wet clothes etc. are squeezed and pressed. **2** *US* a large machine for ironing usu. damp sheets etc. using heated rollers. ● *v.tr.* press (clothes etc.) in a mangle. [Dutch *mangel(stok)* from *mangelen* 'to mangle', ultimately from Greek *magganon* + *stok* 'staff, STOCK']

mangle[2] /'maŋg(ə)l/ *v.tr.* **1** hack, cut about, or mutilate by blows etc. **2** spoil (a quotation, text, etc.) by misquoting, mispronouncing, etc. **3** cut roughly so as to disfigure. □ **mangler** *n.* [Anglo-French *ma(ha)ngler*, apparently frequentative of *mahaignier* MAIM]

mango /'maŋgəʊ/ *n.* (*pl.* **-oes** or **-os**) **1** a fleshy yellowish-red fruit, eaten ripe or used green for pickles etc. **2** (in full **mango tree**) the Indian evergreen tree, *Mangifera indica*, bearing this. [Portuguese *manga* via Malay *mangā* from Tamil *mānkāy*, from *mān* 'mango tree' + *kāy* 'fruit']

mangold (also **mangold-wurzel**) var. of MANGEL.

mangonel /'maŋgən(ə)l/ *n. Mil. hist.* a military engine for throwing stones etc. [Middle English via Old French *mangonel(le)* from medieval Latin *manganellus*, diminutive of Late Latin *manganum*, from Greek *magganon*]

mangosteen /'maŋgəstiːn/ *n.* **1** a white juicy-pulped fruit with a thick reddish-brown rind. **2** the Malaysian tree, *Garcinia mangostana*, bearing this. [Malay *manggustan*]

mangrove /'maŋgrəʊv/ *n.* any tropical tree or shrub of the genus *Rhizophora*, growing in shore-mud with many tangled roots above ground. [17th c.: origin uncertain: assimilated to GROVE]

mangy /'meɪn(d)ʒi/ *adj.* (**mangier, mangiest**) **1** (esp. of a domestic animal) having mange. **2** squalid; shabby. □ **mangily** *adv.* **manginess** *n.*

manhandle /'manhand(ə)l/ *v.tr.* **1** move (heavy objects) by human effort. **2** *colloq.* handle (a person) roughly.

manhattan /man'hat(ə)n/ *n.* a cocktail made of vermouth and a spirit (e.g. whisky). [*Manhattan*, borough of New York City]

manhole /'manhəʊl/ *n.* a covered opening in a floor, pavement, sewer, etc. for workmen to gain access.

manhood /'manhʊd/ *n.* **1** the state of being a man rather than a child or woman. **2 a** manliness; courage. **b** a man's sexual potency. **c** *colloq. euphem.* the penis. **3** the men of a country etc. **4** the state of being human.

man-hour *n.* (also **man-day** etc.) an hour (or day etc.) regarded in terms of the amount of work that could be done by one person within this period.

manhunt /'manhʌnt/ *n.* an organized search for a person, esp. a criminal.

mania /'meɪnɪə/ *n.* **1** *Psychol.* mental illness marked by periods of great excitement and violence. **2** (often foll. by *for*) excessive enthusiasm; an obsession (*has a mania for jogging*). [Middle English via Late Latin from Greek, = madness, from *mainomai* 'be mad': related to MIND]

-mania /'meɪnɪə/ *comb. form* **1** *Psychol.* denoting a special type of mental abnormality or obsession (*megalomania; nymphomania*). **2** denoting extreme enthusiasm or admiration (*bibliomania; Anglomania*).

maniac /'meɪnɪak/ *n. & adj.* ● *n.* **1** *colloq.* a person exhibiting extreme symptoms of wild behaviour etc.; a madman. **2** *colloq.* an obsessive enthusiast. **3** *Psychol. archaic* a person suffering from mania. ● *adj.* of or behaving like a maniac. □ **maniacal** /mə'nʌɪək(ə)l/ *adj.* **maniacally** /mə'nʌɪək(ə)li/ *adv.* [Late Latin *maniacus* from late Greek *maniakos* (as MANIA)]

-maniac /'meɪnɪæk/ *comb. form* forming adjectives and nouns meaning 'affected with -mania' or 'a person affected with -mania' (*nymphomaniac*).

manic /'mænɪk/ *adj.* of or affected by mania. □ **manically** *adv.*

manic-depressive *adj. & n. Psychol.* ● *adj.* affected by or relating to a mental disorder with alternating periods of elation and depression. ● *n.* a person having such a disorder. □ **manic depression** *n.*

Manichaean /mænɪ'ki:ən/ *n. & adj.* (also **Manichean**) ● *n.* **1** an adherent of a religious system of the 3rd–5th c., representing Satan in a state of everlasting conflict with God. **2** *Theol. & Philos.* a dualist (see DUALISM 2, 3a). ● *adj.* of or relating to Manichaeans. □ **Manichaeism** /-'ki:ɪz(ə)m/ *n.* (also **Manicheism**). [Late Latin *Manichaeus* from late Greek *Manikhaios*, from *Manes* or *Manichaeus*, the name of the Persian founder of the sect]

Manichee /mænɪ'ki:/ *n.* = MANICHAEAN *n.*

manicure /'mænɪkjʊə/ *n. & v.* ● *n.* **1** a usu. professional cosmetic treatment of the hands and fingernails. **2** = MANICURIST. ● *v.tr.* apply a manicure to (the hands or a person). [French, from Latin *manus* 'hand' + *cura* 'care']

manicurist /'mænɪkjʊərɪst/ *n.* a person who manicures hands and fingernails professionally.

manifest[1] /'mænɪfest/ *adj. & v.* ● *adj.* clear or obvious to the eye or mind (*his distress was manifest*). ● *v.* **1** *tr.* display or show (a quality, feeling, etc.) by one's acts etc. **2** *tr.* show plainly to the eye or mind. **3** *tr.* be evidence of; prove. **4** *intr. & refl.* (of a thing) reveal itself. **5** *intr.* (of a ghost) appear. □ **manifestation** /-'steɪʃ(ə)n/ *n.* **manifestly** *adv.* [Middle English from Old French *manifeste* (*adj.*), *manifester* (*v.*) or Latin *manifestus*, *manifestare*, from *manus* 'hand' + *festus* (recorded in compounds) 'struck']

manifest[2] /'mænɪfest/ *n. & v.* ● *n.* **1** a cargo-list for the use of customs officers. **2** a list of passengers in an aircraft or of trucks etc. in a goods train. ● *v.tr.* record (names, cargo, etc.) in a manifest. [Italian *manifesto*: see MANIFESTO]

manifesto /mænɪ'festəʊ/ *n.* (*pl.* **-os**) *Brit.* a public declaration of policy and aims, esp. one issued before an election by a political party, candidate, government, etc. [Italian from *manifestare*, from Latin (as MANIFEST[1])]

manifold /'mænɪfəʊld/ *adj. & n.* ● *adj. literary* **1** many and various (*manifold vexations*). **2** having various forms, parts, applications, etc. **3** performing several functions at once. ● *n.* **1** a thing with many different forms, parts, applications, etc. **2** *Mech.* a pipe or chamber branching into several openings. □ **manifoldly** *adv.* **manifoldness** *n.* [Old English *manigfeald* (as MANY, -FOLD)]

manikin /'mænɪkɪn/ *n.* (also **mannikin**) **1** a little man; a dwarf. **2** an artist's lay figure. **3** an anatomical model of the body. **4** (usu. **mannikin**) any small finchlike bird of the genus *Lonchura*, native to Africa and Australasia. [Dutch *manneken*, diminutive of *man* MAN]

Manila /mə'nɪlə/ *n.* (also **Manilla**) **1** a cigar or cheroot made in Manila. **2** (in full **Manila hemp**) the strong fibre of a Philippine plant, *Musa textilis*, used for rope etc. **3** (also **manila**) a strong brown paper made from Manila hemp or other material and used for wrapping paper, envelopes, etc. [*Manila*, capital and chief port of the Philippines]

manilla /mə'nɪlə/ *n.* a metal bracelet used by some African peoples as a medium of exchange. [Spanish, probably a diminutive of *mano* 'hand', from Latin *manus*]

manille /mə'nɪl/ *n. Cards* the second-best trump or honour in ombre or quadrille. [French, via Spanish *malilla*, diminutive of *mala* 'bad', from Latin *malus*]

man in the moon *n.* the fancied semblance of a face seen on the surface of a full moon.

man in the street *n.* (also *US* **man on the street**) an ordinary average person, as distinct from an expert.

manioc /'mænɪɒk/ *n.* **1** cassava. **2** the flour made from it. [Tupi *mandioca*]

maniple /'mænɪp(ə)l/ *n.* **1** *Rom.Hist.* a subdivision of a legion, containing 120 or 60 men. **2** a Eucharistic vestment consisting of a strip hanging from the left arm. [Old French *maniple* or Latin *manipulus* 'handful, troop' from *manus* 'hand']

manipulate /mə'nɪpjʊleɪt/ *v.tr.* **1** handle, treat, or use, esp. skilfully (a tool, question, material, etc.). **2** manage (a person, situation, etc.) to one's own advantage, esp. unfairly or unscrupulously. **3** manually examine and treat (a part of the body). **4** *Computing* alter, edit, or move (text, data, etc.). **5** sexually stimulate (the genitals). □ **manipulable** /-ləb(ə)l/ *adj.* **manipulability** /-lə'bɪlɪti/ *n.* **manipulatable** *adj.* **manipulation** /-'leɪʃ(ə)n/ *n.* **manipulator** *n.* **manipulatory** /-lət(ə)ri/ *adj.* [back-formation from *manipulation*, via French from modern Latin *manipulatio* (as MANIPLE), influenced by French *manipuler*]

manipulative /mə'nɪpjʊlətɪv/ *adj.* **1** characterized by unscrupulous exploitation of a situation, person, etc., for one's own ends. **2** of or concerning manipulation. □ **manipulatively** *adv.* **manipulativeness** *n.*

Manit. *abbr.* Manitoba.

manitou /'mænɪtu:/ *n.* among some N. American Indians: **1** a good or evil spirit as an object of reverence. **2** something regarded as having supernatural power. [Algonquian *manito*, *-tu* 'he has surpassed']

mankind *n.* **1** /mæn'kaɪnd/ the human species. **2** /'mænkaɪnd/ male people, as distinct from female.

■ **Usage** Some people consider the use of *mankind* in sense 1 as sexist and prefer where possible to use *humankind* or *the human race* instead.

manky /'mæŋki/ *adj.* (**mankier**, **mankiest**) *Brit. colloq.* **1** bad, inferior, defective. **2** dirty. [probably via obsolete *mank* 'mutilated, defective' and Old French *manque* from Latin *mancus* 'maimed']

manlike /'mænlaɪk/ *adj.* **1** having the qualities of a man. **2** (of a woman) mannish. **3** (of an animal, shape, etc.) resembling a human being.

manly /'mænli/ *adj.* (**manlier**, **manliest**) **1** having good qualities associated with men, such as courage, frankness, etc. **2** (of a woman) mannish. **3** (of things, qualities, etc.) befitting a man. □ **manliness** *n.*

man-made *adj.* (esp. of a textile fibre) made by man, artificial, synthetic.

manna /'mænə/ *n.* **1** the substance miraculously supplied as food to the Israelites in the wilderness (Exod. 16). **2** an unexpected benefit (esp. *manna from heaven*). **3** spiritual nourishment, esp. the Eucharist. **4** the sweet dried juice from the manna-ash and other plants, used as a mild laxative. [Old English via Late Latin and Greek from Aramaic *mannā*, from Hebrew *mān*, explained as = *mān hū?* 'what is it?', but probably = Arabic *mann*, an exudation of common tamarisk (*Tamarix gallica*)]

manna-ash *n.* an ash tree native to S. Europe, *Fraxinus ornus*.

manned /mænd/ *adj.* (of an aircraft, spacecraft, etc.) having a human crew. [past part. of MAN]

mannequin /'mænɪkɪn, -kwɪn/ *n.* **1** a model employed by a dressmaker etc. to show clothes to customers. **2** a window dummy. [French, = MANIKIN]

manner /'mænə/ *n.* **1** a way a thing is done or happens (*always dresses in that manner*). **2** (in *pl.*) **a** social behaviour (*it is bad manners to stare*). **b** polite or well-bred behaviour (*he has no manners*). **c** modes of life; conditions of society. **3** a person's outward bearing, way of speaking, etc. (*has an imperious manner*). **4 a** a style in literature, art, etc. (*in the manner of Rembrandt*). **b** = MANNERISM 2a. **5** *archaic* a kind or sort (*what manner of man is he?*). □ **all manner of** many different kinds of. **by all** (or **no**) **manner of means** see

MEANS. **in a manner of speaking** in some sense; to some extent; so to speak. **to the manner born 1** *colloq.* naturally at ease in a specified job, situation, etc. **2** destined by birth to follow a custom or way of life (Shakespeare's *Hamlet* I. iv. 17). □ **mannerless** *adj.* (in sense 2b of *n.*). [Middle English from Anglo-French *manere*, Old French *maniere*, ultimately via Latin *manuarius* 'of the hand' from *manus* 'hand']

mannered /'manəd/ *adj.* **1** (in *comb.*) behaving in a specified way (*ill-mannered*; *well-mannered*). **2** (of a style, artist, writer, etc.) showing idiosyncratic mannerisms. **3** (of a person) eccentrically affected in behaviour.

mannerism /'manərɪz(ə)m/ *n.* **1** a habitual gesture or way of speaking etc.; an idiosyncrasy. **2 a** excessive use of a distinctive style in art or literature. **b** a stylistic trick. **3** a style of Italian art preceding the Baroque, characterized by lengthened figures. □ **mannerist** *n.* **manneristic** /-'rɪstɪk/ *adj.* **manneristical** /-'rɪstɪk(ə)l/ *adj.* **manneristically** /-'rɪstɪk(ə)li/ *adv.*

mannerly /'manəli/ *adj. & adv.* ● *adj.* well-mannered; polite. ● *adv.* politely. □ **mannerliness** *n.*

mannikin var. of MANIKIN.

mannish /'manɪʃ/ *adj.* **1** usu. *derog.* (of a woman) masculine in appearance or manner. **2** characteristic of a man. □ **mannishly** *adv.* **mannishness** *n.* [Old English *mennisc* (as MAN, -ISH[1])]

manoeuvre /mə'nu:və/ *n. & v.* (*US* **maneuver**) ● *n.* **1** a planned and controlled movement or series of moves. **2** (in *pl.*) a large-scale exercise of troops, warships, etc. **3 a** an often deceptive planned or controlled action designed to gain an objective. **b** a skilful plan. ● *v.* **(-ring) 1** *intr. & tr.* perform or cause to perform a manoeuvre (*manoeuvred the car into the space*). **2** *intr. & tr.* perform or cause (troops etc.) to perform military manoeuvres. **3 a** *tr.* (usu. foll. by *into*, *out*, *away*) force, drive, or manipulate (a person, thing, etc.) by scheming or adroitness. **b** *intr.* use artifice. □ **manoeuvrable** *adj.* **manoeuvrability** /-vrə'bɪlɪti/ *n.* **manoeuvrer** *n.* [French *manœuvre*, *manœuvrer* via medieval Latin *manuoperare* from Latin *manus* 'hand' + *operari* 'to work']

man of God *n.* **1** a clergyman. **2** a male saint.

man of honour *n.* a man whose word can be trusted.

man of letters *n.* a scholar or author.

man of sense *n.* (*fem.* **woman of sense**) a sagacious person.

man of straw *n.* **1** an insubstantial person; an imaginary person set up as an opponent. **2** a stuffed effigy. **3** a person undertaking a financial commitment without adequate means. **4** a sham argument set up to be defeated.

man of the cloth *n.* a clergyman.

man of the house *n.* the male head of a household.

man of the moment *n.* a man of importance at a particular time.

man of the world see WORLD.

man-of-war *n.* (*pl.* **men-of-war**) **1** esp. *hist.* an armed ship, esp. of a specified country. **2** a frigate bird.

manometer /mə'nɒmɪtə/ *n.* a pressure gauge for gases and liquids. □ **manometric** /manə'mɛtrɪk/ *adj.* [French *manomètre* from Greek *manos* 'thin']

man on the street *US* var. of MAN IN THE STREET.

ma non troppo see TROPPO[1].

manor /'manə/ *n.* **1** (also **manor house**) **a** a large country house with lands. **b** the house of the lord of the manor. **2** *Brit.* **a** a unit of land consisting of a lord's demesne and lands rented to tenants etc. **b** *hist.* a feudal lordship over lands. **3** *Brit. colloq.* the district covered by a police station. □ **manorial** /mə'nɔ:rɪəl/ *adj.* [Middle English via Anglo-French *maner*, Old French *maneir* 'dwelling', from Latin *manēre* 'remain']

manpower /'manpaʊə/ *n.* **1** the power generated by a man working. **2** the number of people available or required for work, service, etc.

manqué /'mɒŋkeɪ/ *adj.* (placed after noun) that might have been but is not; unfulfilled (*a comic actor manqué*). [French, past part. of *manquer* 'lack']

mansard /'mansɑ:d, -səd/ *n.* a roof which has four sloping sides, each of which becomes steeper halfway down. [French *mansarde*, named after F. *Mansart*, French architect d. 1666]

manse /mans/ *n.* the house of a minister, esp. a Scottish Presbyterian. □ **son** (or **daughter**) **of the manse** the child of a Presbyterian etc. minister. [Middle English from medieval Latin *mansus* 'house', from *manēre mans-* 'remain']

manservant /'mansə:v(ə)nt/ *n.* (*pl.* **menservants**) a male servant.

-manship /mənʃɪp/ *suffix* forming nouns denoting skill in a subject or activity (*craftsmanship*; *gamesmanship*).

mansion /'manʃ(ə)n/ *n.* **1** a large house. **2** (usu. in *pl.*) *Brit.* a large building divided into flats. [Middle English via Old French from Latin *mansio -onis* 'a staying' (as MANSE)]

Mansion House *n.* the official residence of the Lord Mayor of London.

mansion house *n. Brit.* the house of a lord mayor or a landed proprietor.

man-size *adj.* (also **man-sized**) **1** of the size of a man; very large. **2** big enough for a man.

manslaughter /'manslɔ:tə/ *n.* **1** the killing of a human being. **2** *Law* the unlawful killing of a human being without malice aforethought.

mansuetude /'manswɪtju:d/ *n.* *archaic* meekness, docility, gentleness. [Middle English via Old French *mansuetude* or Latin *mansuetudo* from *mansuetus* 'gentle, tame', from *manus* 'hand' + *suetus* 'accustomed']

manta /'mantə/ *n.* a large plankton-eating ray of the family Mobulidae, esp. *Manta birostris*, having winglike pectoral fins and a whip-like tail. [Latin American Spanish, = large blanket]

mantel /'mant(ə)l/ *n.* **1** = MANTELPIECE 1. **2** = MANTELSHELF. [variant of MANTLE]

mantelet /'mant(ə)lɪt/ *n.* (also **mantlet** /'mantlɪt/) **1** *hist.* a woman's short loose sleeveless mantle. **2** a bulletproof screen for gunners. [Middle English from Old French, diminutive of *mantel* MANTLE]

mantelpiece /'mant(ə)lpi:s/ *n.* **1** a structure of wood, marble, etc. above and around a fireplace. **2** = MANTELSHELF.

mantelshelf /'mant(ə)lʃɛlf/ *n.* a shelf above a fireplace.

mantic /'mantɪk/ *adj.* *formal* of or concerning divination or prophecy. [Greek *mantikos* from *mantis* 'prophet']

mantid /'mantɪd/ *n.* = MANTIS.

mantilla /man'tɪlə/ *n.* a lace scarf worn by Spanish women over the hair and shoulders. [Spanish, diminutive of *manta* MANTLE]

mantis /'mantɪs/ *n.* (*pl.* same or **mantises**) any slender predatory insect of the family Mantidae, which waits for prey with its forelegs raised and folded like hands in prayer, esp. *Mantis religiosa* of S. Europe. Also called *praying mantis*. [Greek, = prophet]

mantissa /man'tɪsə/ *n.* the part of a logarithm after the decimal point. [Latin, = makeweight]

mantle /'mant(ə)l/ *n. & v.* ● *n.* **1** a loose sleeveless cloak, esp. of a woman. **2** a covering (*a mantle of snow*). **3** responsibility or authority, esp. as passing from one person to another (see 2 Kings 2:13). **4** a fragile lacelike tube fixed round a gas jet to give an incandescent light. **5** an outer fold of skin enclosing a mollusc's viscera and secreting the shell. **6** a bird's back, scapulars, and wing coverts, esp. if of a distinctive colour. **7** the region between the crust and the core of the earth. ● *v.* **1** *tr.* clothe in or as if in a mantle; cover, conceal, envelop. **2** *intr.* **a** (of the blood) suffuse the cheeks. **b** (of the face) glow with a blush. **3** *intr.* (of a liquid) become covered with a coating or scum. [Middle English via Old French from Latin *mantellum* 'cloak']

mantlet var. of MANTELET.

mantling /'mantlɪŋ/ *n. Heraldry* **1** ornamental drapery etc. behind and around a shield. **2** a representation of this. [MANTLE + -ING[1]]

mantra /'mantrə/ *n.* **1** a word or sound repeated to aid concentration in meditation, originally in Hinduism and Buddhism. **2** a Vedic hymn. [Sanskrit, = instrument of thought, from *man* 'think']

mantrap /'mantrap/ *n.* a trap for catching people, esp. trespassers.

mantua /'mantjʊə/ *n. hist.* a woman's loose gown of the 17th–18th c. [corruption of *manteau* (French, as MANTLE) influenced by *Mantua*, the name of a city in Italy]

manual /'manjʊ(ə)l/ *adj. & n.* ● *adj.* **1** of or done with the hands (*manual labour*). **2** (of a machine etc.) worked by hand, not automatically. ● *n.* **1 a** a book of instructions, esp. for operating a machine or learning a subject; a handbook (*a computer manual*). **b** any small book. **2** an organ keyboard played with the hands not the feet. **3** *colloq.* a vehicle with manual transmission. **4** *Mil.* an exercise in handling a rifle etc. **5** *hist.* a book of the forms to be used by priests in the administration of the sacraments. □ **manually** *adv.* [Middle English from Old French *manuel*, from (and later assimilated to) Latin *manualis*, from *manus* 'hand']

manual alphabet *n.* = FINGER ALPHABET.

manufactory /manjʊ'fakt(ə)ri/ *n.* (*pl.* **-ies**) *archaic* = FACTORY. [MANUFACTURE, on the pattern of *factory*]

manufacture /manjʊ'faktʃə/ *n. & v.* ● *n.* **1 a** the making of articles, esp. in a factory etc. **b** a branch of industry (*woollen manufacture*). **2** esp. *derog.* the merely mechanical production of literature, art, etc. ● *v.tr.* **1** make (articles), esp. on an industrial scale. **2** invent or fabricate (evidence, a story, etc.). **3** esp. *derog.* make or produce (literature, art, etc.) in a mechanical way. □ **manufacturable** *adj.* **manufacturability** /-tʃ(ə)rə'bɪlɪti/ *n.* **manufacturer** *n.* [French, from Italian *manifattura* & Latin *manufactum* 'made by hand']

manuka /'mɑːnʊkə, mə'nuːkə/ *n.* esp. *NZ* a small tree, *Leptospermum scoparium*, with aromatic leaves and hard timber. [Maori]

manumit /manjʊ'mɪt/ *v.tr.* (**manumitted**, **manumitting**) *hist.* set (a slave) free. □ **manumission** /-'mɪʃ(ə)n/ *n.* [Middle English from Latin *manumittere*, literally 'send forth from the hand', from *manus* 'hand' + *emittere* 'send forth']

manure /mə'njʊə/ *n. & v.* ● *n.* **1** animal dung, esp. *Brit.* of horses, used for fertilizing land. **2** any compost or artificial fertilizer. ● *v.tr.* (also *absol.*) apply manure to (land etc.). [originally = to occupy, manage, or cultivate land: Middle English from Anglo-French *mainoverer* = Old French *manouvrer* MANOEUVRE]

manuscript /'manjʊskrɪpt/ *n. & adj.* ● *n.* **1** a book, document, etc. written by hand. **2** an author's handwritten or typed text, submitted for publication. **3** handwritten form (*produced in manuscript*). ● *adj.* written by hand. [medieval Latin *manuscriptus*, from *manu* 'by hand' + *scriptus*, past part. of *scribere* 'write']

manuscript paper *n.* paper printed with staves for writing music on.

Manx /maŋks/ *adj. & n.* ● *adj.* of or relating to the Isle of Man. ● *n.* **1** *hist.* the now extinct Celtic language formerly spoken in the Isle of Man. **2** (prec. by *the*; treated as *pl.*) the Manx people. [Old Norse from Old Irish *Manu* 'Isle of Man']

Manx cat *n.* a cat of a breed having no tail or an extremely short one.

Manxman /'maŋksmən/ *n.* (*pl.* **-men**; *fem.* **Manxwoman**, *pl.* **-women**) a native of the Isle of Man.

Manx shearwater *n.* a brownish-black and white shearwater, *Puffinus puffinus*, of Atlantic and Mediterranean waters.

many /'mɛni/ *det. & pron.* (**more** /mɔː/; **most** /məʊst/) ● *det.* (used with countable nouns) great in number; numerous (*many times*; *many good people*; *many a person*; *his reasons were many*). ● *pron.* (treated as *pl.*) **1** a large number (*many like skiing*; *many went*). **2** (prec. by *the*) the majority of people. □ **a good** (or **great**) **many** a large number. **as many** the same number of (*six mistakes in as many lines*). **as many again** the same number additionally (*sixty here and as many again there*). **be too** (or **one too**) **many for** outwit, baffle. **have one too many** become drunk. **many's the time** often (*many's the time we saw it*). **many a time** many times. [Old English *manig*, ultimately from Germanic]

manyfold /'mɛnɪfəʊld/ *adv.* by many times.

many-sided *adj.* having many sides, aspects, interests, capabilities, etc. □ **many-sidedness** *n.*

manzanilla /manzə'nɪlə, -'niːljə/ *n.* a pale very dry Spanish sherry. [Spanish, literally 'camomile']

manzanita /manzə'niːtə/ *n.* any of several evergreen shrubs of the genus *Arctostaphylos*, esp. *A. manzanita*, native to California. [Spanish, diminutive of *manzana* 'apple']

Maoism /'maʊɪz(ə)m/ *n.* the Communist doctrines of Mao Zedong (d. 1976), Chinese statesman. □ **Maoist** *n. & adj.*

Maori /'maʊri, 'mɑː(ə)ri/ *n. & adj.* ● *n.* (*pl.* same or **Maoris**) **1** a member of the Polynesian aboriginal people of New Zealand. **2** the language of the Maori. ● *adj.* of or concerning the Maori or their language. [native name]

map /map/ *n. & v.* ● *n.* **1 a** a usu. flat representation of the earth's surface, or part of it, showing physical features, cities, etc. **b** a diagrammatic representation of a route etc. (*drew a map of the journey*). **2** a two-dimensional representation of the stars, the heavens, etc., or of the surface of a planet, the moon, etc. **3** a diagram showing the arrangement or components of a thing, esp. *Biol.* of the sequence of genes on a chromosome or of bases in a DNA or RNA molecule. **4** *slang* the face. ● *v.tr.* (**mapped**, **mapping**) **1** represent (a country etc.) on a map. **2** *Math.* associate each element of (a set) with an element of another set. □ **map out** arrange in detail; plan (a course of conduct etc.). **off the map** *colloq.* **1** of no account; obsolete. **2** very distant. **on the map** *colloq.* prominent, important. **wipe off the map** *colloq.* obliterate. □ **mapless** *adj.* **mappable** *adj.* **mapper** *n.* [medieval Latin *mappa mundi*, literally 'sheet of the world', from Latin *mappa* 'napkin' + *mundi*, genitive of *mundus* 'world']

maple /'meɪp(ə)l/ *n.* **1** (also **maple tree**) any tree or shrub of the genus *Acer* grown for shade, ornament, wood, or its sugar. **2** the wood of the maple. [Middle English *mapul* etc. from Old English *mapeltrēow*, *mapulder*]

maple leaf *n.* the leaf of the maple, used as an emblem of Canada.

maple sugar *n.* a sugar produced by evaporating the sap of the sugar maple etc.

maple syrup *n.* a syrup produced from the sap of the sugar maple etc.

map-maker *n.* a person who makes maps; a cartographer. □ **map-making** *n.*

map-read *v.intr.* (esp. as **map-reading** *n.*) consult and interpret a map. □ **map-reader** *n.*

map reference *n.* a set of numbers and letters specifying a location as represented on a map.

maquette /ma'kɛt/ *n.* **1** a sculptor's small preliminary model in wax, clay, etc. **2** a preliminary sketch. [French from Italian *machietta*, diminutive of *macchia* 'spot']

maquillage /makiː'jɑːʒ, French makijaʒ/ *n.* **1** make-up; cosmetics. **2** the application of make-up. [French from *maquiller* 'make up', from Old French *masquiller* 'stain']

Maquis /ma'kiː, 'mɑːkiː/ *n.* (*pl.* same) **1** the French resistance movement during the German occupation (1940–45). **2** a member of this. [French, = brushwood, from Corsican Italian *macchia* 'thicket']

Mar. *abbr.* March.

mar /mɑː/ *v.tr.* (**marred**, **marring**) **1** impair the perfection of; spoil; disfigure. **2** *archaic* ruin. [Old English *merran* 'hinder']

marabou /ˈmarəbuː/ *n.* (also **marabout**) **1** a large W. African stork, *Leptoptilos crumeniferus*. **2** a tuft of down from the wing or tail of the marabou used as a trimming for hats etc. [French from Arabic *murābiṭ* 'holy man' (see MARABOUT), the stork being regarded as holy]

marabout /ˈmarəbuːt/ *n.* **1** a Muslim hermit or monk, esp. in N. Africa. **2** a shrine marking a marabout's burial place. **3** var. of MARABOU. [French via Portuguese *marabuto* from Arabic *murābiṭ* 'holy man', from *ribāṭ* 'frontier station', where merit could be acquired by combat against the infidel]

maraca /məˈrakə/ *n.* a hollow clublike gourd or gourd-shaped container filled with beans etc. and usu. shaken in pairs as a percussion instrument in Latin American music. [Portuguese *maracá*, probably from Tupi]

maraschino /marəˈskiːnəʊ/ *n.* (*pl.* **-os**) a strong sweet liqueur made from small black Dalmatian cherries. [Italian, from *marasca*, the name of the cherry, via *amaro* 'bitter' from Latin *amarus*]

maraschino cherry *n.* a cherry preserved in maraschino or maraschino-flavoured syrup and used to decorate cocktails etc.

marasmus /məˈrazməs/ *n.* a wasting away of the body. □ **marasmic** *adj.* [modern Latin from Greek *marasmos*, from *marainō* 'wither']

Maratha /məˈrɑːtə, -ˈratə/ *n.* (also **Mahratta**) a member of a warrior people native to the modern Indian state of Maharashtra. [Hindi *Marhaṭṭa* from Sanskrit *Māhārāshṭra* 'great kingdom']

Marathi /məˈrɑːti, -ˈrati/ *n.* (also **Mahratti**) the Indic language of the Marathas. [MARATHA]

marathon /ˈmarəθ(ə)n/ *n.* **1** a long-distance running race, usu. of 26 miles 385 yards (42.195 km). **2** a long-lasting or difficult task, operation, etc. (often *attrib.*: *a marathon shopping expedition*). □ **marathoner** *n.* [*Marathon* in Greece, scene of a victory over the Persians in 490 BC: later traditions tell of a messenger supposed to have run to Athens with the news]

maraud /məˈrɔːd/ *v.* **1** *intr.* **a** make a plundering raid. **b** pilfer systematically; plunder. **2** *tr.* plunder (a place). □ **marauder** *n.* [French *marauder* from *maraud* 'rogue']

marble /ˈmɑːb(ə)l/ *n.* & *v.* ● *n.* **1** limestone in a metamorphic crystalline (or granular) state, and capable of taking a polish, used in sculpture and architecture. **2** (often *attrib.*) **a** anything made of marble (*a marble clock*). **b** anything resembling marble in hardness, coldness, durability, etc. (*her features were marble*). **3 a** a small ball of marble, glass, clay, etc., used as a toy. **b** (in *pl.*; treated as *sing.*) a game using these. **4** (in *pl.*) *slang* one's mental faculties (*he's lost his marbles*). **5** (in *pl.*) a collection of sculptures (*Elgin Marbles*). ● *v.tr.* **1** (esp. as **marbled** *adj.*) stain or colour (paper, the edges of a book, soap, etc.) to look like variegated marble. **2** (as **marbled** *adj.*) (of meat) streaked with alternating layers of lean and fat. □ **marbly** *adj.* [Middle English via Old French *marbre*, *marble* and Latin *marmor* from Greek *marmaros* 'shining stone']

marble cake *n.* a cake with a mottled appearance, made of light and dark sponge.

marbled white *n.* a whitish butterfly with black markings, *Melanargia galathea*.

marbling /ˈmɑːblɪŋ/ *n.* **1** colouring or marking like marble. **2** streaks of fat in lean meat.

marc /mɑːk/ *n.* **1** the refuse of pressed grapes etc. **2** a brandy made from this. [French from *marcher* 'tread, MARCH[1]']

Marcan /ˈmɑːk(ə)n/ *adj.* of or relating to St Mark. [Latin *Marcus* 'Mark']

marcasite /ˈmɑːkəsʌɪt, -ziːt/ *n.* a bronze-yellow crystalline iron sulphide mineral, used as a semi-precious stone. [Middle English via medieval Latin *marcasita* and Arabic *marḳašīṯā* from Persian]

marcato /mɑːˈkɑːtəʊ/ *adv.* & *adj.* *Mus.* played with emphasis. [Italian, = marked]

marcel /mɑːˈsɛl/ *n.* & *v.* *hist.* ● *n.* (in full **marcel wave**) a deep artificial wave in the hair. ● *v.tr.* (**marcelled**, **marcelling**) wave (hair) with a deep wave. [named after *Marcel* Grateau, Paris hairdresser d. 1936, who invented the method]

marcescent /mɑːˈsɛs(ə)nt/ *adj.* (of part of a plant) withering but not falling. □ **marcescence** *n.* [Latin *marcescere*, inceptive of *marcēre* 'wither']

March /mɑːtʃ/ *n.* the third month of the year. [Middle English via Old French *march(e)*, dialect variant of *marz*, *mars*, from Latin *Martius* (*mensis*) '(month) of Mars']

march[1] /mɑːtʃ/ *v.* & *n.* ● *v.* **1** *intr.* (usu. foll. by *away*, *off*, *out*, etc.) walk in a military manner with a regular measured tread. **2** *tr.* (often foll. by *away*, *on*, *off*, etc.) cause to march or walk (*marched the army to Moscow*; *marched him out of the room*). **3** *intr.* **a** walk or proceed steadily, esp. across country. **b** (of events etc.) continue unrelentingly (*time marches on*). **4** *intr.* take part in a protest march. ● *n.* **1 a** the act or an instance of marching. **b** the uniform step of troops etc. (*a slow march*). **2** a long difficult walk. **3** a procession as a protest or demonstration. **4** (usu. foll. by *of*) progress or continuity (*the march of events*). **5 a** a piece of music composed to accompany a march. **b** a composition of similar character and form. □ **march on 1** advance towards (a military objective). **2** proceed. **on the march 1** marching. **2** in steady progress. □ **marcher** *n.* [French *marche* (*n.*), *marcher* 'to walk', earlier 'to trample', from Late Latin *marcus* 'hammer']

march[2] /mɑːtʃ/ *n.* & *v.* ● *n.* *hist.* **1** (usu. in *pl.*) a boundary, a frontier (esp. of the borderland between England and Scotland or Wales). **2** a tract of often disputed land between two countries. ● *v.intr.* (foll. by *upon*, *with*) (of a country, an estate, etc.) have a common frontier with, border on. [Middle English from Old French *marche*, *marchir*, ultimately from Germanic: related to MARK[1]]

marcher /ˈmɑːtʃə/ *n.* an inhabitant of a march or border district.

March hare *n.* a hare in the breeding season, characterized by excessive leaping, strange behaviour, etc. (*mad as a March hare*).

marching order *n.* *Mil.* equipment or a formation for marching.

marching orders *n.pl.* **1** *Mil.* the direction for troops to depart for war etc. **2** a dismissal (*gave him his marching orders*).

marchioness /mɑːʃəˈnɛs, ˈmɑːʃ(ə)nɪs/ *n.* **1** the wife or widow of a marquess. **2** a woman holding the rank of marquess in her own right (cf. MARQUISE). [medieval Latin *marchionissa* from *marchio -onis* 'captain of the marches' (as MARCH[2])]

marchpane *archaic* var. of MARZIPAN.

march past *n.* & *v.* ● *n.* the marching of troops past a saluting point at a review. ● *v.intr.* (of troops) carry out a march past.

Mardi Gras /mɑːdɪ ˈgrɑː/ *n.* **1 a** Shrove Tuesday in some Catholic countries. **b** merrymaking on this day. **2** the last day of a carnival etc. **3** *Austral.* a carnival or fair at any time. [French, = fat Tuesday]

mardy /ˈmɑːdi/ *adj.* *dial.* sulky, whining, spoilt. [dialect *mard* 'spoilt', alteration of *marred*: see MAR]

mare[1] /mɛː/ *n.* **1** the female of any equine animal, esp. the horse. **2** *Brit. slang offens.* a woman. [Old English *mearh* 'horse', from Germanic: cf. MARSHAL]

mare[2] /ˈmɑːreɪ, -ri/ *n.* (*pl.* **maria** /ˈmɑːrɪə/ or **mares**) **1** (in full **mare clausum** /ˈklaʊsʊm/) *Law* the sea under the jurisdiction of a particular country. **2** (in full **mare liberum** /ˈliːbərʊm/) *Law* the sea open to all nations. **3 a** any of a number of large dark flat areas on the surface of the moon, once thought to be seas. **b** a similar area on Mars. [Latin, = sea]

maremma /mə'rɛmə/ *n.* (*pl.* **maremme** /-mi/) low marshy unhealthy land near a seashore. [Italian, from Latin *maritima* (as MARITIME)]

mare's nest *n.* **1** an illusory discovery; a fraud. **2** a complex situation or muddle.

mare's tail *n.* **1** a tall slender marsh plant, *Hippuris vulgaris.* **2** (in *pl.*) long straight streaks of cirrus cloud.

margarine /mɑːdʒə'riːn, 'mɑːgəriːn/ *n.* a butter substitute made from vegetable oils or animal fats with milk etc. [French, misapplication of the name of a fatty acid, from Greek *margaron* 'pearl' (from its lustre)]

margay /'mɑːgeɪ/ *n.* a small wild S. American cat, *Felis wiedii.* [French from Tupi *mbaracaïa*]

marge[1] /mɑːdʒ/ *n. Brit. colloq.* margarine. [abbreviation]

marge[2] /mɑːdʒ/ *n. poet.* a margin or edge. [French from Latin *margo* (as MARGIN)]

margin /'mɑːdʒɪn/ *n. & v.* ● *n.* **1** the edge or border of a surface. **2 a** the blank border on each side of the print on a page etc. **b** a line ruled esp. on exercise paper, marking off a margin. **3** an amount (of time, money, etc.) by which a thing exceeds, falls short, etc. (*won by a narrow margin*; *a margin of profit*). **4** the lower limit of possibility, success, etc. (*his effort fell below the margin*). **5** *Austral.* an increment to a basic wage, paid for skill. **6** a sum deposited with a stockbroker to cover the risk of loss on a transaction on account. ● *v.tr.* (**margined**, **margining**) provide with a margin or marginal notes. [Middle English from Latin *margo -ginis*]

marginal /'mɑːdʒɪn(ə)l/ *adj. & n.* ● *adj.* **1 a** of or written in a margin. **b** having marginal notes. **2 a** of or at the edge; not central. **b** not significant or decisive (*the work is of merely marginal interest*). **3** *Brit.* (of a parliamentary seat or constituency) having a small majority at risk in an election. **4** close to the limit, esp. of profitability. **5** (of the sea) adjacent to the shore of a state. **6** (of land) difficult to cultivate; unprofitable. **7** barely adequate; unprovided for. ● *n. Brit.* a marginal constituency or seat. □ **marginality** /-'nælɪti/ *n.* **marginally** *adv.* [medieval Latin *marginalis* (as MARGIN)]

marginal cost *n.* the cost added by making one extra copy etc.

marginalia /mɑːdʒɪ'neɪlɪə/ *n.pl.* marginal notes. [medieval Latin, neut. pl. of *marginalis* (as MARGIN)]

marginalize /'mɑːdʒɪn(ə)lʌɪz/ *v.tr.* (also **-ise**) make or treat as insignificant. □ **marginalization** /-'zeɪʃ(ə)n/ *n.*

marginate *v. & adj.* ● *v.tr.* /'mɑːdʒɪmeɪt/ **1** = MARGINALIZE. **2** provide with a margin or border. ● *adj.* /'mɑːdʒɪmət/ *Biol.* having a distinct margin or border. □ **margination** /-'neɪʃ(ə)n/ *n.*

margin of error *n.* a usu. small difference allowed for miscalculation, change of circumstances, etc.

margin release *n.* a device on a typewriter allowing a word to be typed beyond the margin normally set.

margrave /'mɑːgreɪv/ *n. hist.* the hereditary title of some princes of the Holy Roman Empire (originally of a military governor of a border province). □ **margravate** /'mɑːgrəvət/ *n.* [Middle Dutch *markgrave* 'border count' (as MARK[1], *grave* COUNT[2] from Old Low German *grēve*)]

margravine /'mɑːgrəviːn/ *n. hist.* the wife of a margrave. [Dutch *markgravin* (as MARGRAVE)]

marguerite /mɑːgə'riːt/ *n.* an ox-eye daisy. [French, = Margaret]

maria *pl.* of MARE[2].

mariage de convenance /ˌmarɪɑːʒ də ˌkɒ̃və'nɒ̃s, French marjaʒ də kɔ̃vnɑ̃s/ *n.* (*pl.* ***mariages de convenance*** *pronunc.* same) = MARRIAGE OF CONVENIENCE. [French]

Marian /'mɛːrɪən/ *adj. RC Ch.* of or relating to the Virgin Mary (*Marian vespers*). [Latin *Maria* 'Mary']

marigold /'marɪgəʊld/ *n.* any plant of the genus *Calendula* or *Tagetes*, with golden or bright yellow flowers. [Middle English from *Mary* (probably the Virgin) + dialect *gold*, the corn or garden marigold, from Old English: probably related to GOLD]

marijuana /marɪ'hwɑːnə, marjʊ'ɑːnə/ *n.* (also **marihuana**) **1** the dried leaves, flowering tops, and stems of the hemp, used as an intoxicating or hallucinogenic drug and usu. smoked in cigarettes; cannabis. **2** the plant yielding these (see HEMP 1). [Latin American Spanish]

marimba /mə'rɪmbə/ *n.* **1** a xylophone played by natives of Africa and Central America. **2** a modern orchestral instrument derived from this. [Congolese]

marina /mə'riːnə/ *n.* a specially designed harbour with moorings for pleasure yachts etc. [Italian & Spanish fem. of *marino*, from Latin *marinus* MARINE]

marinade /marɪ'neɪd/ *n. & v.* ● *n.* **1** a mixture of wine, vinegar, oil, spices, etc., in which meat, fish, etc., is soaked before cooking. **2** meat, fish, etc., soaked in such a mixture. ● *v.tr.* = MARINATE. [French from Spanish *marinada*, via *marinar* 'pickle in brine' from *marino* (as MARINA)]

marinate /'marɪneɪt/ *v.tr.* soak (meat, fish, etc.) in a marinade. □ **marination** /-'neɪʃ(ə)n/ *n.* [Italian *marinare* or French *mariner* (as MARINE)]

marine /mə'riːn/ *adj. & n.* ● *adj.* **1** of, found in, or produced by the sea. **2 a** of or relating to shipping or naval matters (*marine insurance*). **b** for use at sea. ● *n.* **1** a country's shipping, fleet, or navy (*mercantile marine*; *merchant marine*). **2 a** a member of a body of troops trained to serve on land or sea. **b** (**Marine**) (in the US) a member of the Marine Corps. **3** a picture of a scene at sea. □ **tell that to the marines** (or **horse marines**) *colloq.* an expression of disbelief. [Middle English via Old French *marin marine* from Latin *marinus*, from *mare* 'sea']

mariner /'marɪnə/ *n.* a sailor. [Middle English via Anglo-French *mariner*, Old French *marinier* and medieval Latin *marinarius* from Latin (as MARINE)]

mariner's compass *n.* a compass showing magnetic or true north and the bearings from it.

marine stores *n.pl.* new or old ships' material etc. sold as merchandise.

marine trumpet *n.* a large single-stringed viol with a trumpet-like tone.

Mariolatry /mɛːrɪ'ɒlətri/ *n. derog.* idolatrous worship of the Virgin Mary. [Latin *Maria* 'Mary' + -LATRY, on the pattern of *idolatry*]

marionette /marɪə'nɛt/ *n.* a puppet worked by strings. [French *marionnette* from *Marion*, diminutive of *Marie* 'Mary']

Marist /'mɛːrɪst, 'marɪst/ *n.* a member of a Roman Catholic missionary and teaching order, esp. the Society of Mary. [French *Mariste* from *Marie* 'Mary']

marital /'marɪt(ə)l/ *adj.* **1** of marriage or the relations between husband and wife. **2** of or relating to a husband. □ **maritally** *adv.* [Latin *maritalis* from *maritus* 'husband']

maritime /'marɪtʌɪm/ *adj.* **1** connected with the sea or seafaring (*maritime insurance*). **2** living or found near the sea. [Latin *maritimus* from *mare* 'sea']

marjoram /'mɑːdʒ(ə)rəm/ *n.* either of two aromatic herbs, *Origanum vulgare* (**wild marjoram**) or *Majorana hortensis* (**sweet marjoram**), the fresh or dried leaves of which are used as a flavouring in cookery. [Middle English & Old French *majorane* from medieval Latin *majorana*, of unknown origin]

mark[1] /mɑːk/ *n. & v.* ● *n.* **1** a trace, sign, stain, scar, etc., on a surface, face, page, etc. **2** (esp. in *comb.*) **a** a written or printed symbol (*exclamation mark*; *question mark*). **b** a numerical or alphabetical award denoting excellence, conduct, proficiency, etc. (*got a good mark for effort*; *gave him a black mark*; *gained 46 marks out of 50*). **3** (usu. foll. by *of*) a sign or indication of quality, character, feeling, etc. (*took off his hat as a mark of respect*). **4 a** a sign, seal, etc., used for distinction or identification. **b** a cross etc. made in place of a signature by an illiterate person. **5 a** a target, object, goal, etc. (*missed the mark with his first play*). **b** a standard for attainment (*his work falls below the mark*). **6** a line etc. indicating a position; a marker. **7** (usu. **Mark**) (followed by a numeral) a particular design, model, etc., of a car, aircraft, etc. (*this is the Mark 2 model*). **8** a runner's starting point in a race. **9** *Naut.* a piece of material etc. used to indicate a position on a sounding line. **10 a** *Rugby* a heel-mark on the ground made by a player who has caught the ball direct from a kick, knock-on, or throw-forward by an opponent. **b** *Austral. Rules* the catching before it reaches the ground of a ball kicked at least ten metres; the spot from which the subsequent kick is taken. **11** *slang* the intended victim of a swindler etc. **12** *Boxing* the pit of the stomach. **13** *hist.* a tract of land held in common by a Teutonic or medieval German village community. ● *v.tr.* **1 a** make a mark on (a thing or person), esp. by writing, cutting, scraping, etc. **b** put a distinguishing or identifying mark, initials, name, etc., on (clothes etc.) (*marked the tree with their initials*). **2 a** allot marks to; correct (a student's work etc.). **b** record (the points gained in games etc.). **3** attach a price to (goods etc.) (*marked the doll at 50p*). **4** (often foll. by *by*) show or manifest (displeasure etc.) (*marked his anger by leaving early*). **5** notice or observe (*she marked his agitation*). **6 a** characterize or be a feature of (*the day was marked by storms*). **b** acknowledge, recognize, celebrate (*marked the occasion with a toast*). **7** name or indicate (a place on a map, the length of a syllable, etc.) by a sign or mark. **8** characterize (a person or a thing) as (*marked them as weak*). **9 a** *Brit.* keep close to so as to prevent the free movement of (an opponent in sport). **b** *Austral. Rules* catch (the ball). **10** (as **marked** *adj.*) having natural marks (*is marked with silver spots*). **11** (of a graduated instrument) show, register (so many degrees etc.). **12** *Austral.* & *NZ* castrate (a lamb). □ **one's mark** *Brit. colloq.* **1** what one prefers. **2** an opponent, object, etc., of one's own size, calibre, etc. (*the little one's more my mark*). **beside** (or **off** or **wide of**) **the mark 1** not to the point; irrelevant. **2** not accurate. **make one's mark** attain distinction. **mark down 1** mark (goods etc.) at a lower price. **2** make a written note of. **3** choose (a person) as one's victim. **4** reduce the examination marks of. **mark off** (often foll. by *from*) separate (one thing from another) by a boundary etc. (*marked off the subjects for discussion*). **mark out 1** plan (a course of action etc.). **2** destine (*marked out for success*). **3** trace out boundaries, a course, etc. **mark time 1** *Mil.* march on the spot, without moving forward. **2** act routinely; go through the motions. **3** await an opportunity to advance. **mark up 1** mark (goods etc.) at a higher price. **2** mark or correct (text etc.) for typesetting or alteration. **mark you** esp. *Brit.* please note (*without obligation, mark you*). **off the mark 1** having made a start. **2** = *beside the mark* (see MARK[1]). **of mark** noteworthy. **on the mark** ready to start. **on your mark** (or **marks**) (as an instruction) get ready to start (esp. a race). **up to the mark** reaching the usual or normal standard, esp. of health. [Old English *me(a)rc* (*n.*), *mearcian* (*v.*), from Germanic]

mark[2] /mɑːk/ *n.* **1 a** = DEUTSCHMARK. **b** *hist.* = OSTMARK. **2** *hist.* **a** a denomination of weight for gold and silver. **b** English money of account. [Old English *marc*, probably related to medieval Latin *marca*, *marcus*]

markdown /ˈmɑːkdaʊn/ *n.* a reduction in price.

marked /mɑːkt/ *adj.* **1** having a visible mark. **2** clearly noticeable; evident (*a marked difference*). **3** (of playing cards) having distinctive marks on their backs to assist cheating. □ **markedly** /-kɪdli/ *adv.* **markedness** /-kɪdnɪs/ *n.* [Old English (past part. of MARK[1])]

marked man *n.* **1** a person whose conduct is watched with suspicion or hostility. **2** a person destined to succeed.

marker /ˈmɑːkə/ *n.* **1** a stone, post, etc., used to mark a position, place reached, etc. **2** a person or thing that marks. **3** a felt-tipped pen with a broad tip. **4** a person who records a score, esp. in billiards. **5** a flare etc. used to direct a pilot to a target. **6** a bookmark. **7** *US slang* a promissory note; an IOU.

market /ˈmɑːkɪt/ *n.* & *v.* ● *n.* **1** the gathering of people for the purchase and sale of provisions, livestock, etc., esp. with a number of different vendors. **2** an open space or covered building used for this. **3 a** (often foll. by *for*) a demand for a commodity or service (*goods find a ready market*). **b** a place or group providing such a demand (*UK market*). **4** conditions as regards, or opportunity for, buying or selling. **5** the rate of purchase and sale, market value (*the market fell*). **6** (prec. by *the*) the trade in a specified commodity (*the corn market; the market in soft drinks*). **7** = STOCK MARKET. ● *v.* (**marketed**, **marketing**) **1** *tr.* sell. **2** *tr.* offer for sale. **3** *intr.* buy or sell goods in a market. □ **be in the market for** wish to buy. **be on** (or **come into**) **the market** be offered for sale. **make a market** *Stock Exch.* induce active dealing in a stock or shares. **put on the market** offer for sale. □ **marketer** *n.* [Middle English, ultimately from Latin *mercatus* from *mercari* 'buy': see MERCHANT]

marketable /ˈmɑːkɪtəb(ə)l/ *adj.* able or fit to be sold. □ **marketability** /-ˈbɪlɪti/ *n.*

market cross *n.* a structure erected in a market place, originally a stone cross, later an arcaded building.

market day *n.* esp. *Brit.* a day on which a market is regularly held, usu. weekly.

marketeer /mɑːkɪˈtɪə/ *n.* **1** *Brit.* a supporter of the EEC and British membership of it. **2** a marketer.

market garden *n.* esp. *Brit.* a place where vegetables and fruit are grown for the market etc. □ **market gardener** *n.*

marketing /ˈmɑːkɪtɪŋ/ *n.* **1** the action or business of promoting and selling products, including market research and advertising. **2** in senses of MARKET *v.*

market maker *n.* *Brit.* a member of the Stock Exchange granted certain privileges and trading to prescribed regulations.

market place *n.* **1** an open space where a market is held in a town. **2** the arena of competitive or commercial dealings, bargaining, etc. (*electoral market place; competition in the film market place*).

market price *n.* the price in current dealings.

market research *n.* the study of consumers' needs and preferences. □ **market researcher** *n.*

market town *n.* *Brit.* a town where a market is held.

market value *n.* value as a saleable thing (opp. BOOK VALUE).

markhor /ˈmɑːkɔː/ *n.* a large spiral-horned wild goat, *Capra falconeri*, of N. India. [Persian *mār-ḵwār*, from *mār* 'serpent' + *ḵwār* '-eating']

marking /ˈmɑːkɪŋ/ *n.* (usu. in *pl.*) **1** an identification mark, esp. a symbol on an aircraft. **2** a mark or pattern of marks on an animal's fur, feathers, skin, etc.

marking ink *n.* *Brit.* indelible ink for marking linen etc.

markka /ˈmɑːkɑː, -kə/ *n.* the chief monetary unit of Finland. [Finnish]

marksman /ˈmɑːksmən/ *n.* (*pl.* **-men**) a person skilled in shooting, esp. with a pistol or rifle. □ **marksmanship** *n.*

mark-up *n.* **1** the amount added to the cost price of goods to cover overhead charges, profit, etc. **2** the corrections made in marking up text.

marl[1] /mɑːl/ *n.* & *v.* ● *n.* soil consisting of clay and lime, with fertilizing properties. ● *v.tr.* apply marl to (the ground). □ **marly** *adj.* [Middle English via Old French *marle* and medieval Latin *margila* from Latin *marga*]

marl[2] /mɑːl/ *n.* **1** a mottled yarn of differently coloured threads. **2** the fabric made from this. [shortening of *marbled*: see MARBLE]

marlin /ˈmɑːlɪn/ *n.* any of various large marine fish of the genera *Makaira* and *Tetrapterus*, with a long pointed upper jaw. [MARLINSPIKE, with reference to its pointed snout]

marline /'mɑːlɪn/ *n. Naut.* a thin line of two strands. [Middle English from Dutch *marlijn*, from *marren* 'bind' + *lijn* LINE[1]]

marlinspike /'mɑːlɪnspʌɪk/ *n.* (also **marline-spike**) *Naut.* a pointed iron tool used to separate strands of rope or wire. [originally apparently *marling-spike*, from *marl* 'fasten with marline' (from Dutch *marlen*, frequentative of Middle Dutch *marren* 'bind') + -ING[1] + SPIKE[1]]

marlite /'mɑːlʌɪt/ *n.* a kind of marl that is not reduced to powder by the action of the air.

marmalade /'mɑːməleɪd/ *n.* a preserve of citrus fruit, usu. bitter oranges, made like jam. [French *marmelade* via Portuguese *marmelada* 'quince jam' from *marmelo* 'quince', ultimately from Greek *melimēlon*, from *meli* 'honey' + *mēlon* 'apple']

marmalade cat *n.* a cat with orange fur.

Marmite /'mɑːmʌɪt/ *n.* **1** *Brit. propr.* a preparation made from yeast extract and vegetable extract, used in sandwiches and for flavouring. **2** (**marmite**) /also mɑː'miːt/ an earthenware cooking vessel. [French, = cooking pot]

marmoreal /mɑː'mɔːrɪəl/ *adj. poet.* of or like marble. □ **marmoreally** *adv.* [Latin *marmoreus* (as MARBLE)]

marmoset /'mɑːməzɛt/ *n.* any of several small tropical American monkeys of the family Callithricidae, having a long silky coat and a bushy tail. [Old French *marmouset* 'grotesque image', of unknown origin]

marmot /'mɑːmət/ *n.* any burrowing rodent of the genus *Marmota*, with a heavy-set body and short bushy tail, living in colonies. [French *marmotte*, probably via Romansh *murmont* from Latin *murem* (nominative *mus*) *montis* 'mountain mouse']

marocain /marə'keɪn/ *n.* a dress fabric of ribbed crêpe. [French, = Moroccan, from *Maroc* 'Morocco']

Maronite /'marənʌɪt/ *n. & adj.* ● *n.* a member of a Christian sect of Syrian origin, living chiefly in Lebanon and in communion with the Roman Catholic Church. ● *adj.* of or relating to the Maronites. [medieval Latin *Maronita* from *Maro*, the name of the 5th-c. Syrian founder]

maroon[1] /mə'ruːn/ *adj. & n.* ● *adj.* brownish crimson. ● *n.* **1** this colour. **2** esp. *Brit.* an explosive device giving a loud report. [French *marron* 'chestnut' via Italian *marrone* from medieval Greek *maraon*]

maroon[2] /mə'ruːn/ *v. & n.* ● *v.tr.* **1** leave (a person) isolated in a desolate place (esp. an island). **2** (of a person or a natural phenomenon) cause (a person) to be unable to leave a place. ● *n.* **1** a person descended from a group of fugitive slaves in the remoter parts of Suriname and the W. Indies. **2** a marooned person. [French *marron* via Spanish *cimarrón* 'wild' (as noun = runaway slave) from *cima* 'peak']

marque[1] /mɑːk/ *n.* a make of motor car, as distinct from a specific model (*the Jaguar marque*). [French, = MARK[1]]

marque[2] /mɑːk/ *n. hist.* reprisals. □ **letter of marque** (in full **letter of marque and reprisal**) **1** a licence to fit out an armed vessel and employ it in the capture of an enemy's merchant shipping. **2** a ship carrying such a licence. [Middle English via French from Provençal *marca*, from *marcar* 'seize as a pledge']

marquee /mɑː'kiː/ *n.* **1** esp. *Brit.* a large tent used for social or commercial functions. **2** *N. Amer.* a rooflike projection over the entrance to a theatre, hotel, etc. [MARQUISE, taken as pl. & assimilated to -EE]

marquess /'mɑːkwɪs/ *n.* a British nobleman ranking between a duke and an earl (cf. MARQUIS). □ **marquessate** /-sət/ *n.* [variant of MARQUIS]

marquetry /'mɑːkɪtri/ *n.* (also **marqueterie**) inlaid work in wood, ivory, etc. [French *marqueterie*, via *marqueter* 'variegate' from MARQUE[1]]

marquis /'mɑːkwɪs/ *n.* a foreign nobleman ranking between a duke and a count (cf. MARQUESS). □ **marquisate** /-sət/ *n.* [Middle English via Old French *marchis* from Romanic (as MARCH[2], -ESE)]

marquise /mɑː'kiːz/ *n.* **1 a** the wife or widow of a marquis. **b** a woman holding the rank of marquis in her own right (cf. MARCHIONESS). **2** a finger ring set with an oval pointed cluster of gems. **3** *archaic* = MARQUEE. [French, fem. of MARQUIS]

marquisette /mɑːkɪ'zɛt/ *n.* a fine light cotton, rayon, or silk fabric for net curtains etc. [French, diminutive of MARQUISE]

marram /'marəm/ *n.* a shore grass, *Ammophila arenaria*, that binds sand with its tough rhizomes. [Old Norse *marálmr*, from *marr* 'sea' + *hálmr* HAULM]

marriage /'marɪdʒ/ *n.* **1** the legal union of a man and a woman in order to live together and often to have children. **2** an act or ceremony establishing this union. **3** one particular union of this kind (*by a previous marriage*). **4** an intimate union (*the marriage of true minds*). **5** *Cards* the union of a king and queen of the same suit. □ **by marriage** as a result of a marriage (*related by marriage*). **in marriage** as husband or wife (*give in marriage*; *take in marriage*). [Middle English from Old French *mariage*, from *marier* MARRY[1]]

marriageable /'marɪdʒəb(ə)l/ *adj.* **1** fit for marriage, esp. old or rich enough to marry. **2** (of age) fit for marriage. □ **marriageability** /-'bɪlɪti/ *n.*

marriage bureau *n.* an establishment arranging introductions between persons wishing to marry.

marriage certificate *n.* a certificate certifying the completion of a marriage ceremony.

marriage guidance *n.* (in the UK) counselling of couples who have problems in married life.

marriage licence *n.* a licence to marry.

marriage lines *n.pl. Brit.* a marriage certificate.

marriage of convenience *n.* a marriage concluded to achieve some practical purpose, esp. financial or political.

marriage settlement *n.* an arrangement securing property between spouses.

married /'marɪd/ *adj. & n.* ● *adj.* **1** united in marriage. **2** of or relating to marriage (*married name*; *married life*). ● *n.* (usu. in *pl.*) a married person (*young marrieds*).

marron glacé /marɒn 'glaseɪ/ *n.* (*pl.* **marrons glacés** *pronunc.* same) a chestnut preserved in and coated with sugar. [French, = iced chestnut: cf. GLACÉ]

marrow /'marəʊ/ *n.* **1** *Brit.* (in full **vegetable marrow**) **a** a large usu. white-fleshed edible gourd used as food. **b** the plant, *Cucurbita pepo*, yielding this. **2** (in full **bone marrow**) a soft fatty substance in the cavities of bones, in which blood cells are produced, often taken as typifying strength and vitality. **3** the essential part. □ **to the marrow** right through. □ **marrowless** *adj.* **marrowy** *adj.* [Old English *mearg*, *mærg*, from Germanic]

marrowbone /'marə(ʊ)bəʊn/ *n.* a bone containing edible marrow.

marrowfat /'marə(ʊ)fat/ *n.* a kind of large pea.

marry[1] /'mari/ *v.* (**-ies**, **-ied**) **1** *tr.* **a** take as one's wife or husband in marriage. **b** (often foll. by *to*) (of a priest etc.) join (persons) in marriage. **c** (of a parent or guardian) give (a son, daughter, etc.) in marriage. **2** *intr.* **a** enter into marriage. **b** (foll. by *into*) become a member of (a family) by marriage. **3** *tr.* **a** unite intimately. **b** correlate (things) as a pair. **c** *Naut.* splice (rope-ends) together without increasing their girth. □ **marry off** find a wife or husband for. **marry up** (often foll. by *with*) link or join up. [Middle English via Old French *marier* from Latin *maritare*, from *maritus* 'husband']

marry[2] /'mari/ *int. archaic* expressing surprise, asseveration, indignation, etc. [Middle English, = (the Virgin) *Mary*]

marrying /'marɪɪŋ/ *adj.* likely or inclined to marry (*not a marrying man*).

Mars /mɑːz/ *n.* a reddish planet, fourth in order of distance from the sun and next beyond the earth. [Latin *Mars Martis*, the name of the Roman god of war]

Marsala /mɑːˈsɑːlə/ *n.* a dark sweet fortified dessert wine. [*Marsala*, a town in Sicily, where originally made]

Marseillaise /mɑːseɪˈjeɪz, -s(ə)ˈleɪz/ *n.* the national anthem of France, first sung in Paris by Marseilles patriots. [French, fem. *adj.* from *Marseille* 'Marseilles']

marsh /mɑːʃ/ *n.* **1** low land flooded in wet weather and usu. watery at all times. **2** (*attrib.*) of or inhabiting marshland. □ **marshy** *adj.* (**marshier**, **marshiest**). **marshiness** *n.* [Old English *mer(i)sc*, from West Germanic]

marshal /ˈmɑːʃ(ə)l/ *n.* & *v.* ● *n.* **1 a** (in titles of ranks) a high-ranking officer in the armed forces (*Marshal of the Royal Air Force*; *Field Marshal*). **b** an officer of the highest rank in the armies of some countries (*Marshal of France*). **c** a high-ranking officer of state (*Earl Marshal*). **2** an officer arranging ceremonies, controlling procedure at races, etc. **3** *US* **a** a federal or municipal law officer. **b** the head of a fire department. **4** (in full **judge's marshal**) (in the UK) an official accompanying a judge on circuit, with secretarial and social duties. ● *v.* (**marshalled**, **marshalling**; *US* **marshaled**, **marshaling**) **1** *tr.* arrange (soldiers, facts, one's thoughts, etc.) in due order. **2** *tr.* (often foll. by *into*, *to*) conduct (a person) ceremoniously. **3** *tr.* *Heraldry* combine (coats of arms). **4** *intr.* take up positions in due arrangement. □ **marshaller** *n.* **marshalship** *n.* [Middle English via Old French *mareschal* and Late Latin *mariscalcus* from Germanic, literally 'horse-servant']

marshalling yard *n.* a railway yard in which goods trains etc. are assembled.

Marshal of the Royal Air Force *n.* an officer of the highest rank in the Royal Air Force.

marsh fever *n.* malaria.

marsh gas *n.* methane.

marsh harrier *n.* a European harrier, *Circus aeruginosus* (see HARRIER[3]).

marsh hawk *n.* *N. Amer.* = HEN HARRIER.

marshland /ˈmɑːʃlənd/ *n.* land consisting of marshes.

marshmallow /mɑːʃˈmæləʊ/ *n.* a soft sweet made of sugar, albumen, gelatin, etc.

marsh mallow *n.* a shrubby herbaceous plant, *Althaea officinalis*, the roots of which were formerly used to make marshmallow.

marsh marigold *n.* a golden-flowered plant, *Caltha palustris* (buttercup family), growing in moist meadows etc. Also called KINGCUP.

marsh tit *n.* a grey tit, *Parus palustris*, inhabiting woods and hedges.

marsh trefoil *n.* the buckbean.

marsupial /mɑːˈsuːpɪəl/ *n.* & *adj.* ● *n.* any mammal of the order Marsupialia, characterized by being born incompletely developed and usu. carried and suckled in a pouch on the mother's belly, and found mainly in Australasia. ● *adj.* **1** of or belonging to this order. **2** of or like a pouch (*marsupial muscle*). [modern Latin *marsupialis* via Latin *marsupium* from Greek *marsupion* 'pouch', diminutive of *marsipos* 'purse']

mart /mɑːt/ *n.* **1** a trade centre. **2** an auction room. **3 a** a market. **b** a market place. [Middle English from obsolete Dutch *mart*, variant of *markt* MARKET]

martagon /ˈmɑːtəg(ə)n/ *n.* a lily, *Lilium martagon*, with small purple turban-like flowers. [French from Turkish *martagān*, a form of turban]

Martello /mɑːˈtɛləʊ/ *n.* (*pl.* **-os**) (also **Martello tower**) a small circular fort, usu. on the coast to prevent a hostile landing. [alteration of the name of Cape *Mortella* in Corsica, where such a tower proved difficult to capture in 1794]

marten /ˈmɑːtɪn/ *n.* any weasel-like carnivore of the genus *Martes*, having valuable fur. [Middle English via Middle Dutch *martren* from Old French (*peau*) *martrine* 'marten (fur)', from *martre*, from West Germanic]

martensite /ˈmɑːtɪnzʌɪt/ *n.* the chief constituent of hardened steel. [named after A. *Martens*, German metallurgist d. 1914 + -ITE[1]]

martial /ˈmɑːʃ(ə)l/ *adj.* **1** of or appropriate to warfare. **2** warlike, brave; fond of fighting. □ **martially** *adv.* [Middle English from Old French *martial* or Latin *martialis* 'of Mars': see MARS]

martial arts *n.pl.* fighting sports such as judo and karate.

martial law *n.* military government, involving the suspension of ordinary law.

Martian /ˈmɑːʃ(ə)n/ *adj.* & *n.* ● *adj.* of the planet Mars. ● *n.* a hypothetical inhabitant of Mars. [Middle English from Old French *martien* or Latin *Martianus* from *Mars*: see MARS]

martin /ˈmɑːtɪn/ *n.* any of several swallows of the family Hirundinidae, esp. the house martin and sand martin. [late Middle English, from the male forename *Martin*]

martinet /mɑːtɪˈnɛt/ *n.* a strict (esp. military or naval) disciplinarian. □ **martinettish** *adj.* (also **martinetish**). [named after J. *Martinet*, 17th-c. French drill-master]

martingale /ˈmɑːtɪŋgeɪl/ *n.* **1** a strap, or set of straps, fastened at one end to the noseband or reins of a horse and at the other end to the girth, to prevent rearing etc. **2** *Naut.* a rope for holding down the jib-boom. **3** a gambling system of continually doubling the stakes in the hope of an eventual win that must yield a net profit. [French, of uncertain origin]

Martini /mɑːˈtiːni/ *n.* **1** *Brit. propr.* a type of vermouth. **2** a cocktail made of gin and French vermouth. [*Martini* & Rossi, Italian firm selling vermouth]

Martinmas /ˈmɑːtɪnməs/ *n.* St Martin's day, 11 Nov. [Middle English from St *Martin*, bishop of Tours in the 4th c., + MASS]

martlet /ˈmɑːtlɪt/ *n.* **1** *Heraldry* an imaginary footless bird borne as a charge. **2** *archaic* **a** a swift. **b** a house martin. [French *martelet*, alteration of *martinet*, diminutive of MARTIN]

martyr /ˈmɑːtə/ *n.* & *v.* ● *n.* **1 a** a person who is put to death for refusing to renounce a faith or belief. **b** a person who suffers for adhering to a principle, cause, etc. **c** a person who suffers or pretends to suffer in order to obtain sympathy or pity. **2** (foll. by *to*) a constant sufferer from (an ailment). ● *v.tr.* **1** put to death as a martyr. **2** torment. □ **make a martyr of oneself** accept or pretend to accept unnecessary discomfort etc. [Old English *martir* via ecclesiastical Latin *martyr* from Greek *martur*, *martus -uros* 'witness']

martyrdom /ˈmɑːtədəm/ *n.* **1** the sufferings and death of a martyr. **2** torment. [Old English *martyrdōm* (as MARTYR, -DOM)]

martyrize /ˈmɑːtərʌɪz/ *v.tr.* & *refl.* (also **-ise**) make a martyr of. □ **martyrization** /-ˈzeɪʃ(ə)n/ *n.*

martyrology /mɑːtəˈrɒlədʒi/ *n.* (*pl.* **-ies**) **1** a list or register of martyrs. **2** the history of martyrs. □ **martyrological** /-rəˈlɒdʒɪk(ə)l/ *adj.* **martyrologist** *n.* [medieval Latin *martyrologium* from ecclesiastical Greek *marturologion* (as MARTYR, *logos* 'account')]

martyry /ˈmɑːtəri/ *n.* (*pl.* **-ies**) a shrine or church erected in honour of a martyr. [Middle English via medieval Latin *martyrium* from Greek *marturion* 'martyrdom' (as MARTYR)]

marvel /ˈmɑːv(ə)l/ *n.* & *v.* ● *n.* **1** a wonderful or astonishing person or thing. **2** (foll. by *of*) a wonderful example of (a quality). ● *v.intr.* (**marvelled**, **marvelling**; *US* **marveled**, **marveling**) *literary* **1** (foll. by *at*, or *that* + clause) feel surprise or wonder. **2** (foll. by *how*, *why*, etc. + clause) wonder. □ **marveller** *n.* [Middle English via Old French *merveille*, *merveiller* from Late Latin *mirabilia*, neut. pl. of Latin *mirabilis*, from *mirari* 'wonder at': see MIRACLE]

marvellous /ˈmɑːv(ə)ləs/ *adj.* (*US* **marvelous**) **1** astonishing. **2** excellent. **3** extremely improbable. □ **marvellously** *adv.* **marvellousness** *n.* [Middle English from Old French *merveillos*, from *merveille*: see MARVEL]

marvel of Peru *n.* a showy garden plant, *Mirabilis jalapa*, with flowers opening at dusk.

Marxism /ˈmɑːksɪz(ə)m/ *n.* the political and economic theories of Karl Marx, German political philosopher (d. 1883), predicting the revolutionary overthrow of capitalism by the proletariat and the eventual attainment of a classless communist society. ◻ **Marxist** *n. & adj.*

Marxism-Leninism *n.* Marxism as developed by Lenin. ◻ **Marxist-Leninist** *n. & adj.*

marzipan /ˈmɑːzɪpan, mɑːzɪˈpan/ *n. & v.* ● *n.* (also *archaic* **marchpane** /ˈmɑːtʃpeɪn/) **1** a paste of ground almonds, sugar, etc., made up into small cakes etc., or used to coat large cakes. **2** a piece of marzipan. ● *v.tr.* (**marzipanned, marzipanning**) cover with or as with marzipan. [German from Italian *marzapane*]

Masai /ˈmɑːsʌɪ, məˈsʌɪ, mɑːˈsʌɪ/ *n. & adj.* ● *n.* (*pl.* same or **Masais**) **1** a member of a pastoral people of mainly Hamitic stock living in Kenya and Tanzania. **2** the Nilotic language of the Masai. ● *adj.* of or relating to the Masai or their language. [Bantu]

masala /məˈsɑːlə/ *n.* **1** any of various spice mixtures ground into a paste or powder for use in Indian cookery. **2** a dish flavoured with this. [Urdu *maṣālaḥ*, ultimately from Arabic *maṣāliḥ* 'ingredients, materials']

mascara /maˈskɑːrə/ *n.* a cosmetic for darkening the eyelashes. [Italian *mascara, maschera* MASK]

mascarpone /maskəˈpəʊni/ *n.* a soft mild Italian cream cheese.

mascle /ˈmɑːsk(ə)l/ *n. Heraldry* a lozenge voided, with a central lozenge-shaped aperture. [Middle English via Anglo-French and Anglo-Latin *ma(s)cula* from Latin MACULA]

mascon /ˈmaskɒn/ *n. Astron.* a concentration of dense matter below the moon's surface, producing a gravitational pull. [*mass concentration*]

mascot /ˈmaskɒt/ *n.* a person, animal, or thing that is supposed to bring good luck. [French *mascotte* from modern Provençal *mascotto*, fem. diminutive of *masco* 'witch']

masculine /ˈmaskjʊlɪn/ *adj. & n.* ● *adj.* **1** of or characteristic of men. **2** manly, vigorous. **3** (of a woman) having qualities considered appropriate to a man. **4** *Gram.* of or denoting the gender proper to words or grammatical forms classified as male. ● *n. Gram.* the masculine gender; a masculine word. ◻ **masculinely** *adv.* **masculinity** /-ˈlɪnɪti/ *n.* **masculinize** *v.tr.* (also **-ise**). [Middle English via Old French *masculin -ine* from Latin *masculinus* (as MALE)]

masculine rhyme *n. Prosody* a rhyme between final stressed syllables (e.g. *blow/flow, confess/redress*) (cf. FEMININE RHYME).

masculinist /ˈmaskjʊlɪnɪst/ *n. & adj.* (also **masculist** /ˈmaskjʊlɪst/) ● *n.* an advocate of the rights of men. ● *adj.* of or relating to the advocacy of the rights of men.

maser /ˈmeɪzə/ *n.* a device using the stimulated emission of radiation by excited atoms to amplify or generate coherent monochromatic electromagnetic radiation in the microwave range (cf. LASER). [*m*icrowave *a*mplification by the *s*timulated *e*mission of *r*adiation]

mash /maʃ/ *n. & v.* ● *n.* **1** a soft mixture. **2** a mixture of boiled grain, bran, etc., given warm to horses etc. **3** *Brit. colloq.* mashed potatoes (*sausage and mash*). **4** a mixture of malt grains and hot water used esp. to form wort for brewing. **5** a soft pulp made by crushing, mixing with water, etc. ● *v.* **1** *tr.* reduce (potatoes etc.) to a uniform mass by crushing. **2** *tr.* crush or pound to a pulp. **3** *tr.* mix (malt) with hot water to form wort. **4** *dial.* **a** *tr.* infuse, brew (tea). **b** *intr.* (of tea) infuse, draw, brew. ◻ **masher** *n.* [Old English *māsc* from West Germanic: perhaps related to MIX]

mashie /ˈmaʃi/ *n. Golf* an iron formerly used for lofting or for medium distances. [perhaps from French *massue* 'club']

mask /mɑːsk/ *n. & v.* ● *n.* **1** a covering for all or part of the face: **a** worn as a disguise, or to appear grotesque and amuse or terrify. **b** made of wire, gauze, etc., and worn for protection (e.g. by a fencer) or by a surgeon to prevent infection of a patient. **c** worn to conceal the face at a ball etc. and usu. made of velvet or silk. **2** a respirator used to filter inhaled air or to supply gas for inhalation. **3** a likeness of a person's face, esp. one made by taking a mould from the face (*death mask*). **4** a disguise or pretence (*throw off the mask*). **5** a hollow model of a human head worn by ancient Greek and Roman actors. **6** *Photog.* a screen used to exclude part of an image. **7** the face or head of an animal, esp. a fox. **8** = FACE PACK. **9** *archaic* a masked person. ● *v.tr.* **1** cover (the face etc.) with a mask. **2** disguise or conceal (a taste, one's feelings, etc.). **3** protect from a process. **4** *Mil.* **a** conceal (a battery etc.) from the enemy's view. **b** hinder (an army etc.) from action by observing with adequate force. **c** hinder (a friendly force) by standing in its line of fire. ◻ **masker** *n.* [French *masque* via Italian *maschera* from Arabic *masḵara* 'buffoon', from *saḵira* 'to ridicule']

masked /mɑːskt/ *adj.* wearing or disguised with a mask.

masked ball *n.* a ball at which masks are worn.

masking tape *n.* adhesive tape used in painting to cover areas on which paint is not wanted.

maskinonge /ˈmaskɪnɒn(d)ʒ, -ˈnɒn(d)ʒi/ *n.* = MUSKELLUNGE. [ultimately from Ojibwa, = great fish]

masochism /ˈmasəkɪz(ə)m/ *n.* **1** a form of (esp. sexual) perversion characterized by gratification derived from one's own pain or humiliation (cf. SADISM). **2** *colloq.* the enjoyment of what appears to be painful or tiresome. ◻ **masochist** *n.* **masochistic** /-ˈkɪstɪk/ *adj.* **masochistically** /-ˈkɪstɪk(ə)li/ *adv.* [named after L. von Sacher-*Masoch*, Austrian novelist d. 1895, who described cases of it]

mason /ˈmeɪs(ə)n/ *n. & v.* ● *n.* **1** a person who builds with stone. **2** (**Mason**) a Freemason. ● *v.tr.* build or strengthen with masonry. [Middle English from Old French *masson, maçonner*, Old Northern French *machun*, probably ultimately from Germanic]

Mason–Dixon Line /meɪs(ə)nˈdɪks(ə)n/ *n.* (in the US) the boundary between Maryland and Pennsylvania, taken as the northern limit of the slave-owning states before the abolition of slavery. [named after C. *Mason* & J. *Dixon*, 18th-c. English astronomers, who surveyed it]

Masonic /məˈsɒnɪk/ *adj.* of or relating to Freemasons.

masonry /ˈmeɪs(ə)nri/ *n.* **1 a** the work of a mason. **b** stonework. **2** (**Masonry**) Freemasonry. [Middle English from Old French *maçonerie* (as MASON)]

mason's mark *n.* a device carved on stone by the mason who dressed it.

Masorah /məˈsɔːrə/ *n.* (also **Massorah**) a body of traditional information and comment on the text of the Hebrew Bible. [Hebrew *māsōreṯ*, perhaps = bond]

Masorete /ˈmasəriːt/ *n.* (also **Massorete**) a Jewish scholar contributing to the Masorah. ◻ **Masoretic** /-ˈrɛtɪk/ *adj.* [French *Massoret* & modern Latin *Massoreta*, originally a misuse of Hebrew (see MASORAH), assimilated to -ETE]

masque /mɑːsk/ *n.* **1** a dramatic and musical entertainment esp. of the 16th and 17th c., originally of pantomime, later with metrical dialogue. **2** a dramatic composition for this. ◻ **masquer** *n.* [variant of MASK]

masquerade /mɑːskəˈreɪd, mas-/ *n. & v.* ● *n.* **1** a false show or pretence. **2** a masked ball. ● *v.intr.* (often foll. by *as*) appear in disguise, assume a false appearance. ◻ **masquerader** *n.* [French *mascarade* from Spanish *mascarada*, from *máscara* 'mask']

Mass /mas/ *n.* (also **mass**) **1** the Eucharist, esp. in the Roman Catholic Church. **2** a celebration of this. **3** the liturgy used in the Mass. **4** a musical setting of parts of this. [Old English *mæsse* via ecclesiastical Latin *missa* from Latin *mittere miss-* 'dismiss', perhaps from the concluding dismissal *Ite, missa est* 'Go, it is the dismissal']

Mass. *abbr.* Massachusetts.

mass /mas/ *n., v., & adj.* ● *n.* **1** a coherent body of matter of indefinite shape. **2** a dense aggregation of objects (*a mass of fibres*). **3** (in *sing.* or *pl.*; foll. by *of*) a large number or amount. **4** (usu. foll. by *of*) an unbroken expanse (of colour etc.). **5** (prec. by *a*; foll. by *of*) covered or abounding in (*was a mass of cuts and bruises*). **6** a main portion (of a painting etc.) as perceived by the eye. **7** (prec. by *the*) **a** the majority. **b** (in *pl.*) the ordinary people. **8** *Physics* the quantity of matter a body contains. **9** (*attrib.*) relating to, done by, or affecting large numbers of people or things; large-scale (*mass audience*; *mass action*; *mass murder*). ● *v.tr. & intr.* **1** assemble into a mass or as one body (*massed bands*). **2** *Mil.* (with reference to troops) concentrate or be concentrated. □ **in the mass** in the aggregate. □ **massless** *adj.* [Middle English via Old French *masse*, *masser* and Latin *massa* from Greek *maza* 'barley-cake': perhaps related to *massō* 'knead']

massacre /'masəkə/ *n. & v.* ● *n.* **1** a general slaughter (of persons, occasionally of animals). **2** *colloq.* an utter defeat or destruction. ● *v.tr.* **1** murder (esp. a large number of people) cruelly or violently. **2** *colloq.* defeat heavily; destroy. [Old French, of unknown origin]

massage /'masɑːʒ, ma'sɑːʒ, -dʒ/ *n. & v.* ● *n.* **1** the rubbing, kneading, etc., of muscles and joints of the body with the hands, to stimulate their action, cure strains, etc. **2** an instance of this. ● *v.tr.* **1** apply massage to. **2** manipulate (statistics) to give an acceptable result. **3** flatter (a person's ego etc.). □ **massager** *n.* [French, from *masser* 'treat with massage', perhaps via Portuguese *amassar* 'knead', from *massa* 'dough': see MASS]

massage parlour *n.* **1** an establishment providing massage. **2** *euphem.* a brothel.

massasauga /masə'sɔːgə/ *n.* a small N. American rattlesnake, *Sistrurus catenatus*. [formed irregularly from the name of the *Mississagi* River, Ontario]

mass defect *n.* the difference between the mass of an isotope and its mass number.

massé /'maseɪ/ *n. Billiards* a stroke made with the cue more or less vertical. [French, past part. of *masser*, to make such a stroke (as MACE[1])]

mass energy *n.* a body's ability to do work according to its mass.

masseter /ma'siːtə/ *n.* (in full **masseter muscle**) either of two chewing muscles which run from the temporal bone to the lower jaw. [Greek *masētēr* from *masaomai* 'chew']

masseur /ma'səː/ *n.* (*fem.* **masseuse** /ma'səːz/) a person who provides massage professionally. [French from *masser*: see MASSAGE]

massicot /'masɪkɒt/ *n.* yellow lead monoxide, used as a pigment. [French, perhaps related to Italian *marzacotto* 'unguent', probably from Arabic *mashakūnyā*]

massif /'masɪf, ma'siːf/ *n.* a compact group of mountain heights. [French *massif* MASSIVE, used as noun]

massive /'masɪv/ *adj.* **1** large and heavy or solid. **2** (of the features, head, etc.) relatively large; of solid build. **3** exceptionally large (*took a massive overdose*). **4** substantial, impressive (*a massive reputation*). **5** *Mineral.* not visibly crystalline. **6** *Geol.* without structural divisions. □ **massively** *adv.* **massiveness** *n.* [Middle English via French *massif -ive* from Old French *massiz*, ultimately from Latin *massa* MASS]

mass market *n. & v.* ● *n.* the market for mass-produced goods. ● *v.tr.* (**mass-market**) market (a product) on a large scale.

mass media *n.* = MEDIA[1] 2.

mass noun *n. Gram.* **1** a noun denoting something which cannot be counted (e.g. a substance or quality), in English usu. a noun which lacks a plural in common usage and is not used with an indefinite article, e.g. *luggage, china, happiness.* Also called *uncountable* or *uncount noun.* **2** a noun denoting something which usually cannot be counted, but is countable when it refers to units or types of something, e.g. *coffee, bread* (*drank some coffee, ordered two coffees*; *ate some bread, stocks several different breads*).

mass number *n.* the total number of protons and neutrons in a nucleus.

mass observation *n. Brit.* esp. *hist.* the study and recording of the social habits and opinions of ordinary people.

Massorah var. of MASORAH.

Massorete var. of MASORETE.

mass production *n.* the production of large quantities of a standardized article by a standardized mechanical process. □ **mass-produce** *v.tr.*

mass spectrograph *n.* a mass spectrometer which uses photographic detection.

mass spectrometer *n.* an apparatus separating isotopes, molecules, and molecular fragments according to mass by their passage in ionic form through electric and magnetic fields.

mass spectrum *n.* the distribution of ions shown by the use of a mass spectrograph or mass spectrometer.

mast[1] /mɑːst/ *n. & v.* ● *n.* **1** a long upright post of timber, iron, etc., set up on a ship's keel, esp. to support sails. **2** a post or lattice-work upright for supporting a radio or television aerial. **3** a flagpole (*half mast*). **4** (in full **mooring-mast**) a strong steel tower to the top of which an airship can be moored. ● *v.tr.* furnish (a ship) with masts. □ **before the mast** serving as an ordinary seaman (quartered in the forecastle). □ **masted** *adj.* (also in *comb.*). **master** *n.* (also in *comb.*). [Old English *mæst*, from West Germanic]

mast[2] /mɑːst/ *n.* the fruit of the beech, oak, chestnut, and other forest trees, esp. as food for pigs, birds, etc. [Old English *mæst* from West Germanic: probably related to MEAT]

mastaba /'mastəbə/ *n.* **1** *Archaeol.* an ancient Egyptian tomb with sloping sides and a flat roof. **2** a bench, usu. of stone, attached to a house in Islamic countries. [Arabic *maṣṭabah*]

mast cell *n.* a cell in connective tissue which releases histamine etc. during inflammatory and allergic reactions.

mastectomy /ma'stɛktəmi/ *n.* (*pl.* **-ies**) the surgical removal of a breast. [Greek *mastos* 'breast' + -ECTOMY]

master /'mɑːstə/ *n., adj., & v.* ● *n.* **1 a** a person having control of persons or things. **b** an employer. **c** a male head of a household (*master of the house*). **d** the owner of a dog, horse, etc. **e** the owner of a slave. **f** *Naut.* the captain of a merchant ship. **g** *Hunting* the person in control of a pack of hounds etc. **2** a male teacher or tutor, esp. a schoolmaster. **3 a** the head of a college, school, etc. **b** the presiding officer of a livery company, Masonic lodge, etc. **4** a person who has or gets the upper hand (*we shall see which of us is master*). **5 a** a person skilled in a particular trade and able to teach others (often *attrib.*: *master carpenter*). **b** a skilled practitioner (*a master of innuendo*). **6** a holder of a university degree originally giving authority to teach in the university (*Master of Arts*; *Master of Science*). **7 a** a revered teacher in philosophy etc. **b** (**the Master**) Christ. **8** a great artist. **9** *Chess* etc. a player of proved ability at international level. **10** an original version (e.g. of a film or gramophone record) from which a series of copies can be made. **11** (**Master**) **a** a title prefixed to the name of a boy not old enough to be called Mr (*Master T. Jones*; *Master Tom*). **b** *archaic* a title for a man of high rank, learning, etc. **12** (in England and Wales) an official of the Supreme Court. **13** a machine or device directly controlling another (cf. SLAVE *n.* 4). **14** (**Master**) a courtesy title of the heir apparent of a Scottish viscount or baron (*the Master of Falkland*). ● *adj.* **1** commanding, superior (*a master spirit*). **2** main, principal (*master bedroom*). **3** controlling others (*master plan*). ● *v.tr.* **1** overcome, defeat. **2** reduce to subjection. **3** acquire complete knowledge of (a subject) or facility in using (an instrument etc.). **4** rule as a master. □ **be master of**

have at one's disposal. **2** know how to control. **be one's own master** be independent or free to do as one wishes. **make oneself master of** acquire a thorough knowledge of or facility in using. □ **masterdom** *n.* **masterhood** *n.* **masterless** *adj.* [Old English *mægester* (later reinforced by Old French *maistre*) from Latin *magister*, probably related to *magis* 'more']

Master Aircrew *n.* an RAF rank equivalent to warrant officer.

master-at-arms *n.* (*pl.* **masters-at-arms**) the chief police officer on a man-of-war or a merchant ship.

masterclass /'mɑːstəklɑːs/ *n.* a class given by a person of distinguished skill, esp. in music.

masterful /'mɑːstəfʊl, -f(ə)l/ *adj.* **1** imperious, domineering. **2** masterly. □ **masterfully** *adv.* **masterfulness** *n.*

■ **Usage** *Masterful* is normally used of a person, whereas *masterly* is used of achievements, abilities, etc.

master hand *n.* **1** a person having commanding power or great skill. **2** the action of such a person.

master key *n.* a key that opens several locks, each of which also has its own key.

masterly /'mɑːstəli/ *adj.* worthy of a master; very skilful (*a masterly piece of work*). □ **masterliness** *n.*

■ **Usage** See Usage Note at MASTERFUL.

master mariner *n.* **1** the captain of a merchant ship. **2** a seaman certified competent to be captain.

master mason *n.* **1** a skilled mason, or one in business on his or her own account. **2** a fully qualified Freemason, who has passed the third degree.

mastermind /'mɑːstəmaɪnd/ *n.* & *v.* ● *n.* **1 a** a person with an outstanding intellect. **b** such an intellect. **2** the person directing an intricate operation. ● *v.tr.* plan and direct (a scheme or enterprise).

Master of Ceremonies *n.* **1** (also **MC**) a person introducing speakers at a banquet, or entertainers in a variety show. **2** a person in charge of ceremonies at a state or public occasion.

Master of the Rolls *n.* (in England and Wales) a judge who presides over the Court of Appeal and was formerly in charge of the Public Record Office.

masterpiece /'mɑːstəpiːs/ *n.* **1** an outstanding piece of artistry or workmanship. **2** a person's best work.

mastership /'mɑːstəʃɪp/ *n.* **1** the position or function of a master, esp. a schoolmaster. **2** dominion, control.

mastersinger /'mɑːstəsɪŋə/ *n.* = MEISTERSINGER.

master stroke *n.* an outstandingly skilful act of policy etc.

master switch *n.* a switch controlling the supply of electricity etc. to an entire system.

master touch *n.* a masterly manner of dealing with something.

masterwork /'mɑːstəwəːk/ *n.* a masterpiece.

mastery /'mɑːst(ə)ri/ *n.* **1** dominion, sway. **2** masterly skill. **3** (often foll. by *of*) comprehensive knowledge or use of a subject or instrument. **4** (prec. by *the*) the upper hand. [Middle English from Old French *maistrie* (as MASTER)]

masthead /'mɑːsthɛd/ *n.* & *v.* ● *n.* **1** the highest part of a ship's mast, esp. that of a lower mast as a place of observation or punishment. **2 a** the title of a newspaper etc. at the head of the front or editorial page. **b** *N. Amer.* the listed details in a newspaper etc. referring to ownership, advertising rates, etc. ● *v.tr.* **1** send (a sailor) to the masthead. **2** raise (a sail) to its position on the mast.

mastic /'mastɪk/ *n.* **1** a gum or resin exuded from the bark of the mastic tree, used in making varnish. **2** (in full **mastic tree**) the evergreen tree, *Pistacia lentiscus*, yielding this. **3** a waterproof filler and sealant used in building. **4** a liquor flavoured with mastic gum. [Middle English via Old French, Late Latin *mastichum*, and Latin *mastiche* from Greek *mastikhē*, perhaps from *mastikhaō* (see MASTICATE) with reference to its use as chewing gum]

masticate /'mastɪkeɪt/ *v.tr.* grind or chew (food) with one's teeth. □ **mastication** /-'keɪʃ(ə)n/ *n.* **masticator** *n.* **masticatory** *adj.* [Late Latin *masticare masticat-* from Greek *mastikhaō* 'gnash the teeth']

mastiff /'mastɪf, -'mɑː-/ *n.* **1** a dog of a large strong breed with drooping ears and pendulous lips. **2** this breed of dog. [Middle English, related to Old French *mastin*, ultimately from Latin *mansuetus* 'tame': see MANSUETUDE]

mastitis /ma'stʌɪtɪs/ *n.* inflammation of the mammary gland (the breast or udder). [Greek *mastos* 'breast' + -ITIS]

mastodon /'mastədɒn/ *n.* a large extinct mammal of the genus *Mammut*, resembling the elephant. □ **mastodontic** /-'dɒntɪk/ *adj.* [modern Latin, from Greek *mastos* 'breast' + *odous odontos* 'tooth' with reference to nipple-shaped tubercles on the crowns of its molar teeth]

mastoid /'mastɔɪd/ *adj.* & *n.* ● *adj.* esp. *Anat.* shaped like a woman's breast. ● *n.* **1** *Anat.* = MASTOID PROCESS. **2** *colloq.* mastoiditis. [French *mastoïde* or modern Latin *mastoides* from Greek *mastoeidēs*, from *mastos* 'breast']

mastoiditis /mastɔɪ'dʌɪtɪs/ *n.* inflammation of the mastoid process.

mastoid process *n.* a conical prominence on the temporal bone behind the ear, to which muscles are attached.

masturbate /'mastəbeɪt/ *v.intr.* & *tr.* arouse oneself sexually or cause (another person) to be aroused by manual stimulation of the genitals. □ **masturbation** /-'beɪʃ(ə)n/ *n.* **masturbator** *n.* **masturbatory** *adj.* [Latin *masturbari masturbat-*]

mat[1] /mat/ *n.* & *v.* ● *n.* **1** a piece of coarse material for wiping shoes on, esp. a doormat. **2** a piece of cork, rubber, plastic, etc., to protect a surface from the heat or moisture of an object placed on it. **3** a piece of resilient material for landing on in gymnastics, wrestling, etc. **4** a piece of coarse fabric of plaited rushes, straw, etc., for lying on, packing furniture, etc. **5** a small rug. ● *v.* (**matted, matting**) **1 a** *tr.* (esp. as **matted** *adj.*) entangle in a thick mass (*matted hair*). **b** *intr.* become matted. **2** *tr.* cover or furnish with mats. □ **on the mat** *slang* being reprimanded (originally in the army, on the orderly room mat before the commanding officer). [Old English *m(e)att(e)* via West Germanic from Late Latin *matta*]

mat[2] /mat/ *n.* = MATRIX 1. [abbreviation]

matador /'matədɔː/ *n.* **1** a bullfighter whose task is to kill the bull. **2** a principal card in ombre, quadrille, etc. **3** a domino game in which the piece played must make a total of seven. [Spanish from *matar* 'kill', from Persian *māt* 'dead']

Mata Hari /mɑːtə 'hɑːri/ *n.* a beautiful and seductive female spy. [name taken by M. G. Zelle, d. 1917, from Malay *mata* 'eye' + *hari* 'day']

match[1] /matʃ/ *n.* & *v.* ● *n.* **1** a contest or game of skill etc. in which persons or teams compete against each other. **2 a** a person able to contend with another as an equal (*meet one's match*; *be more than a match for*). **b** a person equal to another in some quality (*we shall never see his match*). **c** a person or thing exactly like or corresponding to another. **3** a marriage. **4** a person viewed in regard to his or her eligibility for marriage, esp. as to rank or fortune (*an excellent match*). ● *v.* **1 a** *tr.* be equal to or harmonious with; correspond to in some essential respect (*the curtains match the wallpaper*). **b** *intr.* (often foll. by *with*) correspond; harmonize (*his socks do not match*; *does the ribbon match with your hat?*). **2** *tr.* (foll. by *against*, *with*) place (a person etc.) in conflict, contest, or competition with (another). **3** *tr.* find material etc. that matches (another) (*can you match this silk?*). **4** *tr.* find (a person or thing) suitable for another (*matching unemployed workers with vacant posts*). **5** *tr.* prove to be a match for. **6** *tr.* *Electronics* produce or have an adjustment of (circuits) such that maximum power is transmitted between them. **7** *tr.* (usu. foll. by *with*) *archaic* join (a person) with another in marriage. □ **make a match** bring about a marriage. **match up** (often foll. by *with*) fit to form a whole; tally. **match up to** be as good as or equal to. **to match** corresponding in some essential respect with what has been mentioned (*yellow dress with gloves to match*). □ **matchable** *adj.* [Old English *gemæcca* 'mate, companion', from Germanic]

match² /matʃ/ *n.* **1** a short thin piece of wood, wax, etc., tipped with a composition that can be ignited by friction. **2** a piece of wick, cord, etc., designed to burn at a uniform rate, for firing a cannon etc. [Middle English from Old French *mesche*, *meiche*, perhaps from Latin *myxa* 'spout of a lamp', in medieval Latin 'lamp-wick']

matchboard /ˈmatʃbɔːd/ *n.* a board with a tongue cut along one edge and a groove along another, so as to fit with similar boards.

matchbox /ˈmatʃbɒks/ *n.* a box for holding matches.

matchet var. of MACHETE.

matchless /ˈmatʃlɪs/ *adj.* without an equal, incomparable. □ **matchlessly** *adv.*

matchlock /ˈmatʃlɒk/ *n. hist.* **1** an old type of gun with a lock in which a match was placed for igniting the powder. **2** such a lock.

matchmaker /ˈmatʃmeɪkə/ *n.* **1** a person who arranges marriages. **2** a person who schemes to bring couples together. □ **matchmaking** *n.*

matchplay /ˈmatʃpleɪ/ *n. Golf* play in which the score is reckoned by counting the holes won by each side (cf. STROKE PLAY).

match point *n.* **1** *Tennis* etc. **a** the state of a game when one side needs only one more point to win the match. **b** this point. **2** *Bridge* a unit of scoring in matches and tournaments.

matchstick /ˈmatʃstɪk/ *n.* the stem of a match.

matchwood /ˈmatʃwʊd/ *n.* **1** wood suitable for matches. **2** minute splinters. □ **make matchwood of** smash utterly.

mate¹ /meɪt/ *n.* & *v.* ● *n.* **1** a friend or fellow worker. **2** *Brit. colloq.* a general form of address, esp. to another man. **3 a** each of a pair, esp. of birds. **b** *colloq.* a partner in marriage. **c** (in *comb.*) a fellow member or joint occupant of (*team-mate*; *room-mate*). **4** *Naut.* an officer on a merchant ship subordinate to the master. **5** an assistant to a skilled worker (*plumber's mate*). ● *v.* (often foll. by *with*) **1 a** *tr.* bring (animals or birds) together for breeding. **b** *intr.* (of animals or birds) come together for breeding. **2 a** *tr.* join (persons) in marriage. **b** *intr.* (of persons) be joined in marriage. **3** *intr. Mech.* fit well. □ **mateless** *adj.* [Middle English via Middle Low German *mate*, from *gemate* 'messmate', from West Germanic: related to MEAT]

mate² /meɪt/ *n.* & *v.tr. Chess* = CHECKMATE. □ **fool's mate** a series of moves in which the first player is mated at the second player's second move. **scholar's mate** a series of moves in which the second player is mated at the first player's fourth move. [Middle English from French *mat(er)*: see CHECKMATE]

maté /ˈmateɪ/ *n.* **1** an infusion of the leaves of a S. American shrub, *Ilex paraguariensis*. **2** this shrub, or its leaves. **3** a vessel in which these leaves are infused. [Spanish *mate* from Quechua *mati*]

matelot /ˈmatləʊ/ *n.* (also **matlow**, **matlo**) *Brit. slang* a sailor. [French]

matelote /ˈmat(ə)ləʊt, French matlɔt/ *n.* a dish of fish etc. with a sauce of wine and onions. [French (as MATELOT)]

mater /ˈmeɪtə/ *n. Brit. slang* mother. [Latin]

▪ **Usage** *Mater* is now only found in jocular or affected use.

materfamilias /meɪtəfəˈmɪlɪas/ *n.* the woman head of a family or household (cf. PATERFAMILIAS). [Latin, from *mater* 'mother' + *familia* FAMILY]

material /məˈtɪərɪəl/ *n.* & *adj.* ● *n.* **1** the matter from which a thing is made. **2** cloth, fabric. **3** (in *pl.*) things needed for an activity (*building materials*; *cleaning materials*; *writing materials*). **4** a person or thing of a specified kind or suitable for a purpose (*officer material*). **5** (in *sing.* or *pl.*) information etc. to be used in writing a book etc. (*experimental material*; *materials for a biography*). **6** (in *sing.* or *pl.*, often foll. by *of*) the elements or constituent parts of a substance. ● *adj.* **1** of matter; corporeal. **2** concerned with bodily comfort etc. (*material well-being*). **3** (of conduct, points of view, etc.) not spiritual. **4** (often foll. by *to*) important, essential, relevant (*at the material time*; *material witness*). **5** concerned with the matter, not the form, of reasoning. □ **materiality** /-ɪˈalɪti/ *n.* [Middle English via Old French *materiel*, *-al* and Late Latin *materialis* from Latin (as MATTER)]

materialism /məˈtɪərɪəlɪz(ə)m/ *n.* **1** a tendency to consider material possessions and physical comfort to be more important than spiritual values. **2** *Philos.* **a** the opinion that nothing exists but matter and its movements and modifications. **b** the doctrine that consciousness and will are wholly due to material agency. **3** *Art* a tendency to lay stress on the material aspect of objects. □ **materialist** *n.* & *adj.* **materialistic** /-ˈlɪstɪk/ *adj.* **materialistically** /-ˈlɪstɪk(ə)li/ *adv.*

materialize /məˈtɪərɪəlʌɪz/ *v.* (also **-ise**) **1** *intr.* become actual fact. **2 a** *tr.* cause (a spirit) to appear in bodily form. **b** *intr.* (of a spirit) appear in this way. **3** *intr. colloq.* appear or be present when expected. **4** *tr.* represent or express in material form. **5** *tr.* make materialistic. □ **materialization** /-ˈzeɪʃ(ə)n/ *n.*

materially /məˈtɪərɪəli/ *adv.* **1** substantially, considerably. **2** in respect of matter.

materia medica /məˈtɪərɪə ˈmɛdɪkə/ *n.* **1** the remedial substances used in the practice of medicine. **2** the study of the origin and properties of these substances. [modern Latin, translation of Greek *hulē iatrikē* 'healing material']

matériel /mətɪərɪˈɛl, French materjɛl/ *n.* available means, esp. materials and equipment in warfare (opp. PERSONNEL 1). [French (as MATERIAL)]

maternal /məˈtəːn(ə)l/ *adj.* **1** of or like a mother. **2** motherly. **3** related through the mother (*maternal uncle*). **4** of the mother in pregnancy and childbirth. □ **maternalism** *n.* **maternalistic** /-ˈlɪstɪk/ *adj.* **maternally** *adv.* [Middle English from Old French *maternel* or Latin *maternus*, from *mater* 'mother']

maternity /məˈtəːnɪti/ *n.* **1** motherhood. **2** motherliness. **3** (*attrib.*) **a** for women during and just after childbirth (*maternity hospital*; *maternity leave*). **b** suitable for a pregnant woman (*maternity dress*; *maternity wear*). [French *maternité* via medieval Latin *maternitas -tatis* from Latin *maternus*, from *mater* 'mother']

mateship /ˈmeɪtʃɪp/ *n. Austral.* companionship, fellowship.

matey /ˈmeɪti/ *adj.* & *n.* (also **maty**) *Brit.* ● *adj.* (**matier**, **matiest**) (often foll. by *with*) sociable; familiar and friendly. ● *n.* (*pl.* **-eys**) *Brit. colloq.* (usu. as a form of address) mate, companion. □ **mateyness** *n.* (also **matiness**). **matily** *adv.*

math /maθ/ *n. N. Amer. colloq.* mathematics (cf. MATHS). [abbreviation]

mathematical /maθ(ə)ˈmatɪk(ə)l/ *adj.* **1** of or relating to mathematics. **2** (of a proof etc.) rigorously precise. □ **mathematically** *adv.* [French *mathématique* or Latin *mathematicus* from Greek *mathēmatikos*, via *mathēma -matos* 'science' from *manthanō* 'learn']

mathematical induction *n.* = INDUCTION 3b.

mathematical tables *n.pl.* tables of logarithms and trigonometric values etc.

mathematics /maθ(ə)ˈmatɪks/ *n.pl.* **1** (usu. treated as *sing.*) the abstract science of number, quantity, and space studied in its own right (**pure mathematics**), or as applied to other disciplines such as physics, engineering, etc. (**applied mathematics**). **2** (often treated as *pl.*) the mathematical aspects of something. □ **mathematician** /-məˈtɪʃ(ə)n/ *n.* [probably from French *mathématiques* (pl.) via Latin *mathematica* from Greek *mathēmatika*: see MATHEMATICAL]

maths /maθs/ *n. Brit. colloq.* mathematics (cf. MATH). [abbreviation]

Matilda /məˈtɪldə/ *n. Austral. slang* a bushman's bundle; a swag. □ **waltz** (or **walk**) **Matilda** carry a swag. [the name *Matilda*]

matinée /ˈmatɪneɪ/ *n.* (also **matinee**) an afternoon performance in the theatre, cinema, etc. [French, = what occupies a morning, from *matin* 'morning' (as MATINS)]

matinée coat *n.* (also **matinée jacket**) *Brit.* a baby's short coat.

matinée idol *n.* a handsome actor admired chiefly by women.

matins /ˈmatɪnz/ *n.* (also **mattins**) (as *sing* or *pl.*) **1 a** a service of morning prayer in the Anglican Church. **b** the office of one of the canonical hours of prayer, properly a night office, but also recited with lauds at daybreak or on the previous evening. **2** (also **matin**) *poet.* the morning song of birds. [Middle English via Old French *matines* from ecclesiastical Latin *matutinas*, accusative fem. pl. adj. from Latin *matutinus* 'of the morning' from *Matuta*, the name of the dawn-goddess]

matlo (also **matlow**) var. of MATELOT.

matrass /ˈmatrəs/ *n. Chem* a long-necked glass vessel with a round or oval body, used for distilling etc. [French *matras*, of uncertain origin]

matriarch /ˈmeɪtrɪɑːk/ *n.* a woman who is the head of a family or tribe. □ **matriarchal** /-ˈɑːk(ə)l/ *adj.* [Latin *mater* 'mother', on the false analogy of PATRIARCH]

matriarchy /ˈmeɪtrɪɑːki/ *n.* (*pl.* **-ies**) a system of society, government, etc. ruled by a woman or women and with descent through the female line.

matric /məˈtrɪk/ *n. Brit. colloq. hist.* matriculation. [abbreviation]

matrices *pl.* of MATRIX.

matricide /ˈmatrɪsʌɪd, ˈmeɪtrɪ-/ *n.* **1** the killing of one's mother. **2** a person who commits matricide. □ **matricidal** *adj.* [Latin *matricida*, *matricidium* from *mater matris* 'mother']

matriculate /məˈtrɪkjʊleɪt/ *v.* **1** *intr.* be enrolled at a college or university. **2** *tr.* admit (a student) to membership of a college or university. □ **matriculatory** *adj.* [medieval Latin *matriculare matriculat-* 'enrol' from Late Latin *matricula* 'register', diminutive of Latin MATRIX]

matriculation /mətrɪkjʊˈleɪʃ(ə)n/ *n.* **1** the act or an instance of matriculating. **2** *hist.* an examination to qualify for this.

matrilineal /matrɪˈlɪnɪəl/ *adj.* of or based on kinship with the mother or the female line. □ **matrilineally** *adv.* [Latin *mater matris* 'mother' + LINEAL]

matrilocal /matrɪˈləʊk(ə)l/ *adj.* of or denoting a custom in marriage where the husband goes to live with the wife's community. [Latin *mater matris* 'mother' + LOCAL]

matrimony /ˈmatrɪməni/ *n.* (*pl.* **-ies**) **1** the rite of marriage. **2** the state of being married. □ **matrimonial** /-ˈməʊnɪəl/ *adj.* **matrimonially** /-ˈməʊnɪəli/ *adv.* [Middle English via Anglo-French *matrimonie*, Old French *matremoi(g)ne* from Latin *matrimonium*, from *mater matris* 'mother']

matrix /ˈmeɪtrɪks/ *n.* (*pl.* **matrices** /-siːz/ or **matrixes**) **1** a mould in which a thing is cast or shaped, such as a gramophone record, printing type, etc. **2 a** an environment or substance in which a thing is developed. **b** a womb. **3** a mass of fine-grained rock in which gems, fossils, etc., are embedded. **4** *Math.* a rectangular array of elements in rows and columns that is treated as a single entity. **5** *Biol.* the substance between cells or in which structures are embedded. **6** *Computing* a gridlike array of interconnected circuit elements. [Latin, = breeding-female, womb, register, from *mater matris* 'mother']

matrix printer *n.* = DOT MATRIX PRINTER.

matron /ˈmeɪtr(ə)n/ *n.* **1** a married woman, esp. a dignified and sober one. **2** a woman managing the domestic arrangements of a school etc. **3** *Brit.* a woman in charge of the nursing in a hospital. □ **matronhood** *n.* [Middle English via Old French *matrone* from Latin *matrona*, from *mater matris* 'mother']

■ **Usage** In sense 3, *senior nursing officer* is now the official term.

matronly /ˈmeɪtr(ə)nli/ *adj.* like or characteristic of a matron, esp. in respect of staidness or portliness.

matron of honour *n.* a married woman attending the bride at a wedding.

Matt. *abbr.* Matthew (esp. in the New Testament).

matt /mat/ *adj., n., & v.* (also **matte**) ● *adj.* (of a colour, surface, etc.) dull, without lustre. ● *n.* **1** a border of dull gold round a framed picture. **2** (in full **matt paint**) paint formulated to give a dull flat finish (cf. GLOSS[1] *n.* 3). **3** the appearance of unburnished gold. ● *v.tr.* (**matted**, **matting**) **1** make (gilding etc.) dull. **2** frost (glass). [French *mat*, *mater*, identical with *mat* MATE[2]]

matte[1] /mat/ *n.* an impure product of the smelting of sulphide ores, esp. those of copper or nickel. [French, feminine of *mat* MATT *adj.* used as a noun]

matte[2] /mat/ *n. Cinematog.* a mask to obscure part of an image and allow another image to be superimposed, giving a combined effect. [French, variant of MATT]

matte[3] var. of MATT.

matter /ˈmatə/ *n. & v.* ● *n.* **1 a** physical substance in general, as distinct from mind and spirit. **b** that which has mass and occupies space. **2** a particular substance (*colouring matter*). **3** (prec. by *the*; often foll. by *with*) the thing that is amiss (*what is the matter?*; *there is something the matter with him*). **4** material for thought or expression. **5 a** the substance of a book, speech, etc., as distinct from its manner or form. **b** *Logic* the particular content of a proposition, as distinct from its form. **6** a thing or things of a specified kind (*printed matter*; *reading matter*). **7** an affair or situation being considered, esp. in a specified way (*a serious matter*; *a matter for concern*; *the matter of your overdraft*). **8** *Physiol.* **a** any substance in or discharged from the body (*faecal matter*; *grey matter*). **b** pus. **9** (foll. by *of*, *for*) what is or may be a good reason for (complaint, regret, etc.). **10** *Printing* the body of a printed work, as type or as printed sheets. ● *v.intr.* **1** (often foll. by *to*) be of importance; have significance (*it does not matter to me when it happened*). **2** secrete or discharge pus. □ **for that matter** (or **for the matter of that**) **1** as far as that is concerned. **2** and indeed also. **in the matter of** as regards. **a matter of 1** approximately (*for a matter of 40 years*). **2** a thing that relates to, depends on, or is determined by (*a matter of habit*; *only a matter of time before they agree*). **no matter 1** (foll. by *when*, *how*, etc.) regardless of (*will do it no matter what the consequences*). **2** it is of no importance. **what is the matter with** surely there is no objection to. **what matter?** *Brit.* that need not worry us. [Middle English via Anglo-French *mater(i)e*, Old French *matiere* from Latin *materia* 'timber, substance, subject of discourse']

matter of course *n.* the natural or expected thing.

matter of fact *n. & adj.* ● *n.* **1** what belongs to the sphere of fact as distinct from opinion etc. **2** *Law* the part of a judicial inquiry concerned with the truth of alleged facts. ● *adj.* (**matter-of-fact**) **1** unimaginative, prosaic. **2** unemotional. □ **as a matter of fact** in reality (esp. to correct a falsehood or misunderstanding). □ **matter-of-factly** *adv.* **matter-of-factness** *n.*

matter of form *n.* **1** a point of correct procedure. **2** *colloq.* mere routine.

matter of law *n. Law* the part of a judicial inquiry concerned with the interpretation of the law.

matter of life and death *n.* a matter of vital importance.

matter of record see RECORD.

matting /'matɪŋ/ *n.* **1** fabric of hemp, bast, grass, etc., for mats (*coconut matting*). **2** in senses of MAT[1] *v.*

mattins var. of MATINS.

mattock /'matək/ *n.* an agricultural tool shaped like a pickaxe, with an adze and a chisel edge as the ends of the head. [Old English *mattuc*, of unknown origin]

mattress /'matrɪs/ *n.* a fabric case stuffed with soft, firm, or springy material, or a similar case filled with air or water, used on or as a bed. [Middle English via Old French *materas* and Italian *materasso* from Arabic *almaṭraḥ* 'the place, the cushion', from *ṭaraḥa* 'throw']

maturate /'matʃʊreɪt/ *v.intr. Med.* (of a boil etc.) come to maturation. [Latin *maturatus* (as MATURE *v.*)]

maturation /matʃʊ'reɪʃ(ə)n/ *n.* **1 a** the act or an instance of maturing; the state of being matured. **b** the ripening of fruit. **2** *Med.* **a** the formation of purulent matter. **b** the causing of this. □ **maturational** *adj.* **maturative** /mə'tʃʊərətɪv/ *adj.* [Middle English via French *maturation* or medieval Latin *maturatio* from Latin (as MATURE *v.*)]

mature /mə'tʃʊə/ *adj. & v.* ● *adj.* (**maturer**, **maturest**) **1 a** with fully developed powers of body and mind; adult. **b** sensible, wise. **2** complete in natural development; ripe. **3** (of thought, intentions, etc.) duly careful and adequate. **4** (of a bill etc.) due for payment. ● *v.* **1 a** *tr. & intr.* develop fully. **b** *tr. & intr.* ripen. **c** *intr.* come to maturity. **2** *tr.* perfect (a plan etc.). **3** *intr.* (of a bill etc.) become due for payment. □ **maturely** *adv.* **maturity** *n.* [Middle English from Latin *maturus* 'timely, early']

mature student *n.* esp. *Brit.* an adult student who is older than most students.

matutinal /matjʊ'tʌɪn(ə)l, mə'tju:tɪn(ə)l/ *adj.* **1** of or occurring in the morning. **2** early. [Late Latin *matutinalis* from Latin *matutinus*: see MATINS]

maty var. of MATEY.

matzo /'matsə, 'matsəʊ/ *n.* (*pl.* **-os** or **matzoth** /-əʊt/) **1** a wafer of unleavened bread for the Passover. **2** such bread collectively. [Yiddish from Hebrew *maṣṣāh*]

maud /mɔ:d/ *n.* **1** a Scots shepherd's grey striped plaid. **2** a travelling rug like this. [18th c.: origin unknown]

maudlin /'mɔ:dlɪn/ *adj. & n.* ● *adj.* weakly or tearfully sentimental, esp. in a tearful and effusive stage of drunkenness. ● *n.* weak or mawkish sentiment. [Middle English via Old French *Madeleine* from ecclesiastical Latin *Magdalena* MAGDALEN, with reference to pictures of Mary Magdalen weeping]

maul /mɔ:l/ *v. & n.* ● *v.tr.* **1** beat and bruise. **2** (of an animal) tear and mutilate (prey etc.). **3** handle roughly or carelessly. **4** damage by criticism. ● *n.* **1** *Rugby* a loose scrum with the ball off the ground. **2** a brawl. **3** a special heavy hammer, commonly of wood, esp. for driving piles. □ **mauler** *n.* [Middle English via Old French *mail* from Latin *malleus* 'hammer']

maulstick /'mɔ:lstɪk/ *n.* (also **mahlstick**) a light stick with a padded leather ball at one end, held by a painter against the canvas etc. to support the brush hand. [Dutch *maalstok*, from *malen* 'to paint' + *stok* 'stick']

maunder /'mɔ:ndə/ *v.intr.* **1** talk in a dreamy or rambling manner. **2** move or act listlessly or idly. [perhaps from obsolete *maunder* 'beggar, to beg']

Maundy /'mɔ:ndi/ *n.* (in the UK) the distribution of Maundy money on the Thursday before Easter. [Middle English via Old French *mandé* from Latin *mandatum* 'MANDATE, commandment' (see John 13:34)]

Maundy money *n.* specially minted silver coins distributed by the British sovereign on Maundy Thursday.

Maundy Thursday *n.* the Thursday before Easter.

mausoleum /mɔ:sə'lɪəm/ *n.* (*pl.* **mausolea** /-'lɪə/ or **mausoleums**) a large and grand tomb. [Latin from Greek *Mausōleion*, from *Mausōlos* the name of a king of Caria (4th c. BC), to whose tomb the name was originally applied]

mauve /məʊv/ *adj. & n.* ● *adj.* pale purple. ● *n.* **1** this colour. **2** a bright but delicate pale purple dye from aniline. □ **mauvish** *adj.* [French, literally 'mallow', from Latin *malva*]

maven /'meɪv(ə)n/ *n. N. Amer. colloq.* an expert or connoisseur. [Yiddish]

maverick /'mav(ə)rɪk/ *n.* **1** *N. Amer.* an unbranded calf or yearling. **2** an unorthodox or independent-minded person. [named after S. A. *Maverick*, Texas engineer and rancher d. 1870, who did not brand his cattle]

mavis /'meɪvɪs/ *n. poet.* or *dial.* a song thrush. [Middle English from Old French *mauvis*, of uncertain origin]

maw /mɔ:/ *n.* **1 a** the stomach of an animal. **b** the jaws or throat of a voracious animal. **2** *colloq.* the stomach of a greedy person. [Old English *maga*, from Germanic]

mawkish /'mɔ:kɪʃ/ *adj.* **1** sentimental in a feeble or sickly way. **2** having a faint sickly flavour. □ **mawkishly** *adv.* **mawkishness** *n.* [obsolete *mawk* 'maggot' from Old Norse *mathkr*, from Germanic]

max /maks/ *n., adj., adv., & v. N. Amer. colloq.* ● *n.* (a) maximum. ● *adj.* maximal. ● *adv.* maximally. ● *v.* **1** *intr.* (foll. by *out* and often *at*) perform to the limit of one's ability (*the high-jumper maxed out at 6 foot*). **2** *tr.* (as **maxed out** *adj.*) having exhausted one's capabilities or capacity.

max. *abbr.* maximum.

maxi /'maksi/ *n.* (*pl.* **maxis**) *colloq.* a maxi-coat, -skirt, etc. [abbreviation]

maxi- /'maksi/ *comb. form* very large or long (*maxi-coat*). [abbreviation of MAXIMUM: cf. MINI-]

maxilla /mak'sɪlə/ *n.* (*pl.* **maxillae** /-li:/) **1** a jaw or jawbone, esp. the upper jaw in most vertebrates. **2** the mouthpart of many arthropods used in chewing. □ **maxillary** *adj.* [Latin, = jaw]

maxim /'maksɪm/ *n.* a general truth or rule of conduct expressed in a sentence. [Middle English from French *maxime* or medieval Latin *maxima* (*propositio*) 'maximum (proposition)', (as MAXIMUM)]

maxima *pl.* of MAXIMUM.

maximal /'maksɪm(ə)l/ *adj.* being or relating to a maximum; the greatest possible in size, duration, etc. □ **maximally** *adv.*

maximalist /'maksɪm(ə)lɪst/ *n.* a person who rejects compromise and expects a full response to (esp. political) demands (opp. MINIMALIST 1). [MAXIMAL, suggested by Russian *maksimalist*]

maximize /'maksɪmʌɪz/ *v.tr.* (also **-ise**) make as large or great as possible (*need to maximize our income*). □ **maximization** /-'zeɪʃ(ə)n/ *n.* **maximizer** *n.* [Latin *maximus*: see MAXIMUM]

■ **Usage** *Maximize* should not be used in standard English to mean 'make as good as possible' or 'make the most of'.

maximum /'maksɪməm/ *n. & adj.* ● *n.* (*pl.* **maxima** /-mə/ or **maximums**) the highest possible or attainable amount. ● *adj.* that is a maximum. [modern Latin, neut. of Latin *maximus*, superlative of *magnus* 'great']

maxwell /'makswɛl/ *n.* a unit of magnetic flux in the cgs system, equal to that induced through one square centimetre by a perpendicular magnetic field of one gauss. [named after J. C. *Maxwell*, British physicist d. 1879]

May /meɪ/ *n.* **1** the fifth month of the year. **2** (**may**) *Brit.* the hawthorn or its blossom. **3** *poet.* bloom, prime. [Middle English via Old French *mai* from Latin *Maius* (*mensis*) '(month) of the goddess *Maia*']

may /meɪ/ *v.aux.* (*3rd sing. present* **may**; *past* **might** /mʌɪt/) **1** (often foll. by *well* for emphasis) expressing possibility (*it may be true*; *I may have been wrong*; *you may well lose your way*). **2** expressing permission (*you may not go*; *may I come in?*). **3** expressing a wish (*may he live to regret it*). **4** expressing uncertainty or irony in questions (*who may you be?*; *who are you, may I ask?*). **5** in purpose clauses and after *wish*, *fear*, etc. (*take such measures as may avert disaster*; *hope he may succeed*).

□ **be that as it may** despite the fact that it may be so. **may as well** = *might as well* (see MIGHT[1]). **that is as may be** that may or may not be so (implying that there are other factors). [Old English *mæg* from Germanic: related to MAIN[1], MIGHT[2]]

■ **Usage** Both *can* and *may* are used to express permission (see sense 2); in more formal contexts *may* is usual since *can* also denotes capability (*can I move?* = am I physically able to move?; *may I move?* = am I allowed to move?).

Maya /'mʌɪ(j)ə, 'meɪ(j)ə/ *n. & adj.* ● *n.* **1** (*pl.* same or **Mayas**) a member of an ancient Indian people of Central America. **2** the language of this people. ● *adj.* of or relating to this people or language. □ **Mayan** *adj. & n.* [native name]

maya /'mɑːjə/ *n. Hinduism* illusion, magic. [Sanskrit *māyā*]

mayapple /'meɪap(ə)l/ *n.* an American herbaceous plant, *Podophyllum peltatum*, bearing a yellow egg-shaped fruit in May.

maybe /'meɪbiː, -bi/ *adv.* perhaps, possibly. [Middle English, from *it may be*]

May-bug *n.* = COCKCHAFER.

May Day *n.* 1 May esp. as a festival with dancing, or as an international holiday in honour of workers.

mayday /'meɪdeɪ/ *n.* an international radio distress signal used esp. by ships and aircraft. [representing pronunciation of French *m'aidez* 'help me']

mayest /'meɪɪst/ *archaic* = MAYST.

mayflower /'meɪflaʊə/ *n.* any of various flowers that bloom in May, esp. the trailing arbutus, *Epigaea repens*.

mayfly /'meɪflʌɪ/ *n.* (*pl.* **-flies**) **1** any insect of the order Ephemeroptera, with an aquatic nymph and a fragile-winged adult which lives only briefly in spring. **2** an imitation mayfly used by anglers.

mayhap /meɪ'hap, 'meɪhap/ *adv. archaic* perhaps, possibly. [Middle English, from *it may hap*]

mayhem /'meɪhɛm/ *n.* **1** violent or damaging action; disruption, chaos. **2** *hist.* the crime of maiming a person so as to render him or her partly or wholly defenceless. [Anglo-French *mahem*, Old French *mayhem* (as MAIM)]

maying /'meɪɪŋ/ *n. & adj.* participation in May Day festivities. [Middle English, from MAY]

mayn't /'meɪənt/ *contr.* may not.

mayonnaise /meɪə'neɪz/ *n.* **1** a thick creamy dressing made of egg yolks, oil, vinegar, etc. **2** a (usu. specified) dish dressed with this (*chicken mayonnaise*). [French, perhaps from *mahonnais -aise* 'of Port *Mahon*', on Minorca]

mayor /mɛː/ *n.* **1** the head of the municipal corporation of a city or borough. **2** (in England, Wales, and Northern Ireland) the head of a district council with the status of a borough. □ **mayoral** *adj.* **mayorship** *n.* [Middle English via Old French *maire* from Latin (as MAJOR)]

mayoralty /'mɛːr(ə)lti/ *n.* (*pl.* **-ies**) **1** the office of mayor. **2** a mayor's period of office. [Middle English from Old French *mairalté* (as MAYOR)]

mayoress /'mɛːrɪs/ *n.* **1** a woman holding the office of mayor. **2** the wife of a mayor. **3** a woman fulfilling the ceremonial duties of a mayor's wife.

maypole /'meɪpəʊl/ *n.* a pole painted and decked with flowers and ribbons, for dancing round on May Day.

May queen *n.* a girl chosen to preside over celebrations on May Day.

mayst /meɪst/ *archaic 2nd sing. present* of MAY.

mayweed /'meɪwiːd/ *n.* any wild camomile often found as a weed, esp. (**stinking mayweed**) *Anthemis cotula* and (**scentless mayweed**) *Tripleurospermum inodorum*. [earlier *maidwede* via obsolete *maithe(n)* from Old English *magothe*, *mægtha*, + WEED]

mazard /'mazəd/ *n.* (also **mazzard**) **1** the wild sweet cherry, *Prunus avium*, of Europe. **2** *archaic* a head or face. [probably alteration of MAZER in sense 'hardwood']

mazarine /mazə'riːn, 'mazəriːn/ *n. & adj.* ● *n.* a rich deep blue. ● *adj.* of this colour. [17th c., perhaps from the name of Cardinal *Mazarin*, French statesman d. 1661, or the Duchesse de *Mazarin*, French noblewoman d. 1699]

maze /meɪz/ *n. & v.* ● *n.* **1** a network of paths and hedges designed as a puzzle for those who try to penetrate it. **2** a complex network of paths or passages; a labyrinth. **3** (often foll. by *of*) a confused mass, network, etc. ● *v.tr.* (esp. as **mazed** *adj.*) bewilder, confuse. □ **mazy** *adj.* (**mazier, maziest**). [Middle English, originally as *mased* (*adj.*): related to AMAZE]

mazer /'meɪzə/ *n. hist.* a hardwood drinking bowl, usu. silver-mounted. [Middle English from Old French *masere*, from Germanic]

mazuma /mə'zuːmə/ *n.* esp. *US & Austral. slang* money, cash. [Yiddish from Hebrew *mĕzummān*, from *zimmēn* 'prepare']

mazurka /mə'zəːkə, mə'zʊəkə/ *n.* **1** a usu. lively Polish dance in triple time. **2** the music for this. [French *mazurka* or German *Masurka*, from Polish *mazurka*, a woman of the province *Mazovia*]

mazzard var. of MAZARD.

MB *abbr.* **1** Bachelor of Medicine. **2** (also **Mb**) *Computing* megabyte. [sense 1 from Latin *Medicinae Baccalaureus*]

MBA *abbr.* Master of Business Administration.

MBE *abbr.* Member of the Order of the British Empire.

MBO *abbr.* management buyout.

MC *abbr.* **1** Master of Ceremonies. **2** (in the UK) Military Cross. **3** (in the US) Member of Congress. **4** music cassette (of pre-recorded audiotape).

Mc *abbr.* megacycle(s).

MCC *abbr.* Marylebone Cricket Club.

McCarthyism, McCoy see at MACC-.

M.Ch. *abbr.* (also **M.Chir.**) Master of Surgery. [Latin *Magister Chirurgiae*]

mCi *abbr.* millicurie(s).

McNaughten see at MACN-.

M.Com. *abbr.* Master of Commerce.

MCP *abbr. colloq.* male chauvinist pig.

MCR *abbr. Brit.* Middle Common Room.

Mc/s *abbr.* megacycles per second.

MD *abbr.* **1** Doctor of Medicine. **2** Managing Director. **3** *US* Maryland (in official postal use). **4** mentally deficient. **5** musical director. [sense 1 from Latin *Medicinae Doctor*]

Md *symb. Chem.* the element mendelevium.

Md. *abbr.* Maryland.

MDMA *abbr.* methylenedioxymethamphetamine, an amphetamine-based drug that causes euphoric and hallucinatory effects, originally produced as an appetite suppressant. Also called *Ecstasy*.

MDT *abbr.* Mountain Daylight Time (one hour ahead of Mountain Standard Time).

ME *abbr.* **1** *US* Maine (in official postal use). **2** myalgic encephalomyelitis, a condition of unknown cause, with fever, aching, and prolonged tiredness and depression, occurring esp. after a viral infection.

Me. *abbr.* **1** Maine. **2** *Maître* (title of a French advocate).

me[1] /miː/ *pron.* **1** *objective case* of I[2] (*he saw me*). **2** *N. Amer. colloq.* myself; to or for myself (*I got me a gun*). **3** *colloq.* used in exclamations (*ah me!*; *dear me!*; *silly me!*). □ **me and mine** me and my relatives. [Old English *me, mē*, accusative & dative of I[2], from Germanic]

■ **Usage** See Usage Note at HER.

me[2] /miː/ *n.* (also **mi**) *Mus.* **1** (in tonic sol-fa) the third note of a major scale. **2** the note E in the fixed-doh system. [Middle English from Latin *mira*: see GAMUT]

mea culpa /meɪə 'kʊlpə, miːə 'kʌlpə/ *n. & int.* ● *n.* an acknowledgement of one's fault or error. ● *int.* expressing such an acknowledgement. [Latin, = by my fault]

mead[1] /miːd/ *n.* an alcoholic drink of fermented honey and water. [Old English *me(o)du*, from Germanic]

mead[2] /miːd/ *n. poet.* or *archaic* = MEADOW. [Old English *mǣd* from Germanic: related to MOW[1]]

meadow /ˈmɛdəʊ/ *n.* **1** a piece of grassland, esp. one used for hay. **2** a piece of low well-watered ground, esp. near a river. □ **meadowy** *adj.* [Old English *mǣdwe*, oblique case of *mǣd*: see MEAD[2]]

meadow brown *n.* a common brown butterfly, *Maniola jurtina*.

meadow grass *n.* a perennial creeping grass, *Poa pratensis*.

meadowland /ˈmɛdəʊland/ *n.* land used for the cultivation of grass, esp. for hay.

meadowlark /ˈmɛdəʊlɑːk/ *n. N. Amer.* any songbird of the genus *Sturnella*, esp. the yellow-breasted *S. magna* of N. America.

meadow pipit *n.* a common pipit, *Anthus pratensis*, native to Europe, Asia, and Africa.

meadow rue *n.* any plant of the genus *Thalictrum* (buttercup family), esp. *T. flavum* with small yellow flowers.

meadow saffron *n.* a meadow plant, *Colchicum autumnale*, resembling a crocus, and producing lilac flowers in the autumn while still leafless. Also called *autumn crocus*.

meadowsweet /ˈmɛdəʊswiːt/ *n.* **1** a plant of the rose family, *Filipendula ulmaria*, common in meadows and damp places, with creamy-white fragrant flowers. **2** any of several plants of the genus *Spiraea* (rose family), native to N. America.

meagre /ˈmiːgə/ *adj.* (*US* **meager**) **1** lacking in amount or quality (*a meagre salary*). **2** (of literary composition, ideas, etc.) lacking fullness; unsatisfying. **3** (of a person or animal) lean, thin. □ **meagrely** *adv.* **meagreness** *n.* [Middle English via Anglo-French *megre*, Old French *maigre* from Latin *macer*]

meal[1] /miːl/ *n.* **1** an occasion when food is eaten. **2** the food eaten on one occasion. □ **make a meal of 1** *Brit.* treat (a task etc.) too laboriously or fussily. **2** consume as a meal. [Old English *mǣl* 'mark, fixed time, meal', from Germanic]

meal[2] /miːl/ *n.* **1** the edible part of any grain or pulse (usu. other than wheat) ground to powder. **2** *Sc.* oatmeal. **3** *US* maize flour. **4** any powdery substance made by grinding. [Old English *melu*, from Germanic]

meal-beetle *n.* an insect, *Tenebrio molitor*, infesting granaries etc.

mealie /ˈmiːli/ *n.* (also **mielie**) *S.Afr.* **1** (usu. in *pl.*) maize. **2** a corn cob. [Afrikaans *mielie* via Portuguese *milho* 'maize, millet' from Latin *milium*]

meals on wheels *n.pl.* (usu. treated as *sing.*) a service by which meals are delivered to old people, invalids, etc.

meal ticket *n.* **1** a ticket entitling one to a meal, esp. at a specified place with reduced cost. **2** a person or thing that is a source of food or income.

mealtime /ˈmiːltʌɪm/ *n.* a time at which a meal is or is usually eaten.

mealworm /ˈmiːlwəːm/ *n.* the larva of the meal-beetle.

mealy /ˈmiːli/ *adj.* (**mealier**, **mealiest**) **1 a** of or like meal; soft and powdery. **b** containing meal. **2** (of a complexion) pale. **3** (of a horse) spotty. **4** (in full **mealy-mouthed**) not outspoken; afraid to use plain expressions. □ **mealiness** *n.*

mealy bug *n.* any insect of the genus *Pseudococcus*, infesting vines etc., whose body is covered with white powder.

mean[1] /miːn/ *v.tr.* (*past* and *past part.* **meant** /mɛnt/) **1 a** (often foll. by *to* + infin.) have as one's purpose or intention; have in mind (*they really mean mischief*; *I didn't mean to break it*). **b** (foll. by *by*) have as a motive in explanation (*what do you mean by that?*). **2** (often in *passive*) design or destine for a purpose (*mean it to be used*; *mean it for a stopgap*; *is meant to be a gift*). **3** intend to convey or indicate or refer to (a particular thing or notion) (*I mean we cannot go*; *I mean Richmond in Surrey*). **4** entail, involve (*it means catching the early train*). **5** (often foll. by *that* + clause) portend, signify (*this means trouble*; *your refusal means that we must look elsewhere*). **6** (of a word) have as its explanation in the same language or its equivalent in another language. **7** (foll. by *to*) be of some specified importance to (a person), esp. as a source of benefit or object of affection etc. (*that means a lot to me*). □ **mean business** be in earnest. **mean it** not be joking or exaggerating. **mean to say** really admit (usu. in *interrog.*: *do you mean to say you have lost it?*). **mean well** (often foll. by *to, towards, by*) have good intentions. [Old English *mǣnan* from West Germanic: related to MIND]

mean[2] /miːn/ *adj.* **1** niggardly; not generous or liberal. **2** ignoble; uncooperative, unkind, or unfair. **3** (of a person's capacity, understanding, etc.) inferior, poor. **4** (of housing) not imposing in appearance; shabby. **5 a** malicious, ill-tempered. **b** *US* vicious or aggressive in behaviour. **6** *colloq.* skilful, formidable (*is a mean fighter*). □ **no mean** a very good (*that is no mean achievement*). □ **meanly** *adv.* **meanness** /ˈmiːnnɪs/ *n.* [Old English *mǣne*, *gemǣne*, from Germanic]

mean[3] /miːn/ *n. & adj.* ● *n.* **1** a condition, quality, virtue, or course of action equally removed from two opposite (usu. unsatisfactory) extremes. **2** *Math.* **a** the term or one of the terms midway between the first and last terms of an arithmetical or geometrical etc. progression (*2 and 8 have the arithmetic mean 5 and the geometric mean 4*). **b** the quotient of the sum of several quantities and their number; the average. ● *adj.* **1** (of a quantity) equally far from two extremes. **2** calculated as a mean. [Middle English via Anglo-French *meen* and Old French *meien*, *moien* from Latin *medianus* MEDIAN]

meander /mɪˈandə, miː-/ *v. & n.* ● *v.intr.* **1** wander at random. **2** (of a stream) wind about. ● *n.* **1** (in *pl.*) **a** the sinuous windings of a river. **b** winding paths. **2** a circuitous journey. **3** an ornamental pattern of lines winding in and out; a fret. □ **meandering** *adj. & n.* [Latin *maeander* from Greek *Maiandros*, the name of a winding river in Phrygia]

mean free path *n.* the average distance travelled by a gas molecule etc. between collisions.

meanie /ˈmiːni/ *n.* (also **meany**) (*pl.* **-ies**) *colloq.* a mean, niggardly, or small-minded person.

meaning /ˈmiːnɪŋ/ *n. & adj.* ● *n.* **1** what is meant by a word, action, idea, etc. **2** significance. **3** importance. ● *adj.* expressive, significant (*a meaning glance*). □ **meaningly** *adv.*

meaningful /ˈmiːnɪŋfʊl, -f(ə)l/ *adj.* **1** full of meaning; significant. **2** *Logic* able to be interpreted. □ **meaningfully** *adv.* **meaningfulness** *n.*

meaningless /ˈmiːnɪŋlɪs/ *adj.* having no meaning or significance. □ **meaninglessly** *adv.* **meaninglessness** *n.*

means /miːnz/ *n.pl.* **1** (often treated as *sing.*) that by which a result is brought about (*a means of quick travel*). **2 a** money resources (*live beyond one's means*). **b** wealth (*a man of means*). □ **by all means** (or **all manner of means**) **1** certainly. **2** in every possible way. **3** at any cost. **by any means** in any way (*not by any means obtrusive*). **by means of** by the agency or instrumentality of (a thing or action). **by no means** (or **no manner of means**) not at all; certainly not. [pl. of MEAN[3], in the sense 'an intermediary']

mean sea level *n.* the sea level halfway between the mean levels of high and low water.

means test *n. & v.* ● *n.* an official inquiry to establish need before financial assistance from public funds is given. ● *v.tr.* (**means-test**) subject to or base on a means test.

mean sun *n.* an imaginary sun moving in the celestial sphere at the mean rate of the real sun, used in calculating solar time.

meant *past* and *past part.* of MEAN[1].

meantime /ˈmiːntʌɪm/ *adv. & n.* ● *adv.* = MEANWHILE. ● *n.* the intervening period (esp. *in the meantime*). [MEAN³ + TIME]

■ **Usage** As an adverb, *meantime* is less common than *meanwhile.*

mean time *n.* the time based on the movement of the mean sun.

meanwhile /ˈmiːnwʌɪl/ *adv. & n.* ● *adv.* **1** in the intervening period of time. **2** at the same time. ● *n.* the intervening period (esp. in phr. **in the meanwhile**). [MEAN³ + WHILE]

mean white *n.* esp. *US offens.* = POOR WHITE.

meany var. of MEANIE.

measles /ˈmiːz(ə)lz/ *n.pl.* (also treated as *sing.*) **1 a** an acute infectious viral disease marked by red spots on the skin. **b** the spots of measles. **2** a disease of pigs etc. caused by the encysted larvae of the human tapeworm. [Middle English *masele(s)*, probably from Middle Low German *masele*, Middle Dutch *masel* 'pustule' (cf. Dutch *mazelen* 'measles'), Old High German *masala*: change of form probably due to assimilation to Middle English *meser* 'leper']

measly /ˈmiːzli/ *adj.* (**measlier**, **measliest**) **1** *colloq.* inferior, contemptible, worthless. **2** of or affected with measles. **3** (of pork etc.) infested with tapeworm larvae. [MEASLES + -Y¹]

measurable /ˈmɛʒ(ə)rəb(ə)l/ *adj.* that can be measured. □ **within a measurable distance of** getting near (something undesirable). □ **measurability** /-ˈbɪlɪti/ *n.* **measurably** *adv.* [Middle English via Old French *mesurable* and Late Latin *mensurabilis* from Latin *mensurare* (as MEASURE)]

measure /ˈmɛʒə/ *n. & v.* ● *n.* **1** a size or quantity found by measuring. **2** a system of measuring (*liquid measure*; *linear measure*). **3** a rod or tape etc. for measuring. **4** a vessel of standard capacity for transferring or determining fixed quantities of liquids etc. (*a pint measure*). **5 a** the degree, extent, or amount of a thing. **b** (foll. by *of*) some degree of (*there was a measure of wit in her remark*). **6** a unit of capacity, e.g. a bushel (*20 measures of wheat*). **7** a factor by which a person or thing is reckoned or evaluated (*their success is a measure of their determination*). **8** (usu. in *pl.*) suitable action to achieve some end (*took measures to ensure a good profit*). **9** a legislative enactment. **10** a quantity contained in another an exact number of times. **11** a prescribed extent or quantity. **12** *Printing* the width of a page or column of type. **13 a** poetical rhythm; metre. **b** a metrical group of a dactyl or two iambuses, trochees, spondees, etc. **14** *US Mus.* a bar or the time-content of a bar. **15** *archaic* a dance. **16** a mineral stratum (*coal measures*). ● *v.* **1** *tr.* ascertain the extent or quantity of (a thing) by comparison with a fixed unit or with an object of known size. **2** *intr.* be of a specified size (*it measures six inches*). **3** *tr.* ascertain the size and proportion of (a person) for clothes. **4** *tr.* estimate (a quality, person's character, etc.) by some standard or rule. **5** *tr.* (often foll. by *off*) mark (a line etc. of a given length). **6** *tr.* (foll. by *out*) deal or distribute (a thing) in measured quantities. **7** *tr.* (foll. by *with*, *against*) bring (oneself or one's strength etc.) into competition with. **8** *tr. poet.* traverse (a distance). □ **beyond measure** excessively. **for good measure** as something beyond the minimum; as a finishing touch. **in a** (or **some**) **measure** partly. **measure up 1 a** determine the size etc. of by measurement. **b** take comprehensive measurements. **2** (often foll. by *to*) have the necessary qualifications (for). [Middle English via Old French *mesure* from Latin *mensura*, from *metiri mens-* 'measure']

measured /ˈmɛʒəd/ *adj.* **1** rhythmical; regular in movement (*a measured tread*). **2** (of language) carefully considered. □ **measuredly** *adv.*

measureless /ˈmɛʒəlɪs/ *adj.* not measurable; infinite. □ **measurelessly** *adv.*

measurement /ˈmɛʒəm(ə)nt/ *n.* **1** the act or an instance of measuring. **2** an amount determined by measuring. **3** (in *pl.*) detailed dimensions.

measure of capacity *n.* a measure used for vessels and liquids or grains etc.

measuring jug *n. Brit.* (also **measuring cup**) a jug (or cup) marked to measure its contents.

measuring tape *n.* a tape marked to measure length.

measuring worm *n.* the caterpillar of the geometer moth.

meat /miːt/ *n.* **1** the flesh of animals (esp. mammals) as food. **2** (foll. by *of*) the essence or chief part of. **3** esp. *US* the edible part of fruits, nuts, eggs, shellfish, etc. **4** *archaic* **a** food of any kind. **b** a meal. □ **meat and drink** *Brit.* a source of great pleasure. □ **meatless** *adj.* [Old English *mete* 'food', from Germanic]

meat-axe *n.* a butcher's cleaver.

meatball /ˈmiːtbɔːl/ *n.* minced meat compressed into a small round ball.

meat-fly *n.* (*pl.* **-flies**) a fly that breeds in meat.

meat loaf *n.* minced or chopped meat moulded into the shape of a loaf and baked.

meat safe *n. Brit.* a cupboard for storing meat, usu. of wire gauze etc.

meatus /mɪˈeɪtəs/ *n.* (*pl.* same or **meatuses**) *Anat.* a channel or passage in the body or its opening, esp. that leading into the ear. [Latin, = passage from *meare* 'flow, run']

meaty /ˈmiːti/ *adj.* (**meatier**, **meatiest**) **1** full of meat; fleshy. **2** of or like meat. **3** full of substance. □ **meatily** *adv.* **meatiness** *n.*

Mecca /ˈmɛkə/ *n.* **1** a place which attracts people of a particular group (*Mecca for book buyers*). **2** the centre or birthplace of a faith, policy, pursuit, etc. [*Mecca* in Arabia, birthplace of Muhammad and chief place of Muslim pilgrimage]

mechanic /mɪˈkanɪk/ *n.* a skilled worker, esp. one who makes or uses or repairs machinery. [Middle English (originally as adj.) via (Old) French *mécanique* or Latin *mechanicus* from Greek *mēkhanikos* (as MACHINE)]

mechanical /mɪˈkanɪk(ə)l/ *adj. & n.* ● *adj.* **1** of or relating to machines or mechanisms. **2** working or produced by machinery. **3** (of a person or action) like a machine; automatic; lacking originality. **4 a** (of an agency, principle, etc.) belonging to mechanics. **b** (of a theory etc.) explaining phenomena by the assumption of mechanical action. **5** of or relating to mechanics as a science. ● *n.* **1** (in *pl.*) the working parts of a machine, esp. of a motor car. **2** (usu. in *pl.*) *archaic* a manual worker (esp. *Theatr.* with allusion to Shakespeare's *A Midsummer Night's Dream*). □ **mechanicalism** *n.* (in sense 4 of *adj.*). **mechanically** *adv.* **mechanicalness** *n.* [Middle English from Latin *mechanicus* (as MECHANIC)]

mechanical advantage *n.* the ratio of exerted to applied force in a machine.

mechanical drawing *n.* a scale drawing of machinery etc. done with precision instruments.

mechanical engineer *n.* an engineer dealing with the design, construction, and repair of machines. □ **mechanical engineering** *n.*

mechanical equivalent of heat *n.* the conversion factor between heat energy and mechanical energy.

mechanical excavator *n.* a machine for removing soil from the ground by means of a crane to which a scoop is attached.

mechanician /mɛkəˈnɪʃ(ə)n/ *n.* a person skilled in constructing machinery.

mechanics /mɪˈkanɪks/ *n.pl.* **1** (treated as *sing.*) the branch of applied mathematics dealing with motion and tendencies to motion. **2** (treated as *sing.*) the science of machinery. **3** (usu. treated as *pl.*) **a** the construction, workings, or routine operation of a thing (*mechanics of the cochlea*). **b** the practicalities or details of a thing (*mechanics of how money is laundered*).

mechanism /ˈmɛk(ə)nɪz(ə)m/ *n.* **1** the structure or adaptation of parts of a machine. **2** a system of mutually adapted parts working together in or as in a machine. **3** the mode of operation of a process. **4** a means (*defence mechanism*; *no mechanism for complaints*). **5** *Art* mechanical execution; technique. **6** *Philos.* the doctrine that all natural phenomena, including life, allow mechanical explanation by physics and chemistry. [modern Latin *mechanismus* from Greek (as MACHINE)]

mechanist /ˈmɛk(ə)nɪst/ *n.* **1** a mechanician. **2** an expert in mechanics. **3** *Philos.* a person who holds the doctrine of mechanism. □ **mechanistic** /-ˈnɪstɪk/ *adj.* **mechanistically** /-ˈnɪstɪk(ə)li/ *adv.*

mechanize /ˈmɛk(ə)nʌɪz/ *v.tr.* (also **-ise**) **1** give a mechanical character to. **2** introduce machines in. **3** *Mil.* equip with tanks, armoured cars, etc. (originally as a substitute for horse-drawn vehicles and cavalry). □ **mechanization** /-ˈzeɪʃ(ə)n/ *n.* **mechanizer** *n.*

mechano- /ˈmɛk(ə)nəʊ/ *comb. form* mechanical. [Greek *mēkhano-* from *mēkhanē* 'machine']

mechanoreceptor /ˌmɛk(ə)nəʊrɪˈsɛptə/ *n. Biol.* a sensory receptor that responds to mechanical stimuli such as touch or sound.

mechatronics /mɛkəˈtrɒnɪks/ *n.pl.* (usu. treated as *sing.*) technology combining electronics and mechanical engineering, esp. in developing new manufacturing techniques. [*mecha*nics + elec*tronics*]

Mechlin /ˈmɛklɪn/ *n.* (in full **Mechlin lace**) lace made at Mechlin (now Mechelen or Malines) in Belgium.

M.Econ. *abbr.* Master of Economics.

meconium /mɪˈkəʊnɪəm/ *n. Med.* a dark substance forming the first faeces of a newborn infant. [Latin, literally 'poppy-juice', from Greek *mēkōnion*, from *mēkōn* 'poppy']

M.Ed. *abbr.* Master of Education.

Med /mɛd/ *n. Brit. colloq.* the Mediterranean Sea. [abbreviation]

med. *abbr.* medium.

medal /ˈmɛd(ə)l/ *n.* a piece of metal, usu. in the form of a disc, struck or cast with an inscription or device to commemorate an event etc., or awarded as a distinction to a soldier, scholar, athlete, etc., for services rendered, for proficiency, etc. □ **medalled** *adj.* **medallic** /mɪˈdalɪk/ *adj.* [French *médaille* from Italian *medaglia*, ultimately from Latin *metallum* METAL]

medallion /mɪˈdaljən/ *n.* **1** a large medal. **2** a thing shaped like this, e.g. a decorative panel or tablet, portrait, etc. [French *médaillon* from Italian *medaglione*, augmentative of *medaglia* (as MEDAL)]

medallist /ˈmɛd(ə)lɪst/ *n.* (*US* **medalist**) **1** a recipient of a (specified) medal (*gold medallist*). **2** an engraver or designer of medals.

medal play *n. Golf* = STROKE PLAY.

meddle /ˈmɛd(ə)l/ *v.intr.* (often foll. by *with*, *in*) interfere in or busy oneself unduly with others' concerns. □ **meddler** *n.* [Middle English from Old French *medler*, variant of *mesler*, ultimately from Latin *miscēre* 'mix']

meddlesome /ˈmɛd(ə)ls(ə)m/ *adj.* fond of meddling; interfering. □ **meddlesomely** *adv.* **meddlesomeness** *n.*

Mede /miːd/ *n. hist.* a member of an Indo-European people which established an empire in Media in Persia (modern Iran) in the 7th c. BC. □ **Median** *adj.* [Middle English via Latin *Medi* (*pl.*) from Greek *Mēdoi*]

media[1] /ˈmiːdɪə/ *n.pl.* **1** *pl.* of MEDIUM. **2** (usu. prec. by *the*) the main means of mass communication (esp. newspapers and broadcasting) regarded collectively.

■ **Usage** *Media* is commonly used as a mass noun with a singular verb (e.g. *The media is on our side*), but this is not generally accepted (cf. DATA, AGENDA).

media[2] /ˈmiːdɪə/ *n.* (*pl.* **mediae** /-dɪiː/) *Anat.* a middle layer of the wall of an artery or other vessel. [Latin, fem. of *medius* 'middle']

mediaeval var. of MEDIEVAL.

media event *n.* an event primarily intended to attract publicity.

medial /ˈmiːdɪəl/ *adj.* **1** situated in the middle. **2** of average size. □ **medially** *adv.* [Late Latin *medialis* from Latin *medius* 'middle']

median /ˈmiːdɪən/ *adj.* & *n.* ● *adj.* situated in the middle. ● *n.* **1** *Anat.* a median artery, vein, nerve, etc. **2** *Geom.* a straight line drawn from any vertex of a triangle to the middle of the opposite side. **3** *Math.* the middle value of a series of values arranged in order of size. □ **medianly** *adv.* [French *médiane* or Latin *medianus* (as MEDIAL)]

mediant /ˈmiːdɪənt/ *n. Mus.* the third note of a diatonic scale of any key. [French *médiante* from Italian *mediante* part. of obsolete *mediare* 'come between', from Latin (as MEDIATE)]

mediastinum /ˌmiːdɪəˈstʌɪnəm/ *n.* (*pl.* **mediastina** /-nə/) *Anat.* a membranous middle septum, esp. between the lungs. □ **mediastinal** *adj.* [modern Latin from medieval Latin *mediastinus* 'medial', ultimately from Latin *medius* 'middle']

mediate *v.* & *adj.* ● *v.* /ˈmiːdɪeɪt/ **1** *intr.* (often foll. by *between*) intervene (between parties in a dispute) to produce agreement or reconciliation. **2** *tr.* be the medium for bringing about (a result) or for conveying (a gift etc.). **3** *tr.* form a connecting link between. ● *adj.* /ˈmiːdɪət/ **1** connected not directly but through some other person or thing. **2** involving an intermediate agency. □ **mediately** /-ətli/ *adv.* **mediation** /-ˈeɪʃ(ə)n/ *n.* **mediator** /ˈmiːdɪeɪtə/ *n.* **mediatory** /ˈmiːdɪət(ə)ri/ *adj.* [Late Latin *mediare mediat-* from Latin *medius* 'middle']

medic[1] /ˈmɛdɪk/ *n. colloq.* a medical practitioner or student. [Latin *medicus* 'physician' from *medēri* 'heal']

medic[2] var. of MEDICK.

medicable /ˈmɛdɪkəb(ə)l/ *adj.* admitting of remedial treatment. [Latin *medicabilis* (as MEDICATE)]

Medicaid /ˈmɛdɪkeɪd/ *n.* (in the US) a federal system of health insurance for those requiring financial assistance. [MEDICAL + AID]

medical /ˈmɛdɪk(ə)l/ *adj.* & *n.* ● *adj.* **1** of or relating to the science of medicine in general. **2** of or relating to conditions requiring medical and not surgical treatment (*medical ward*). ● *n. colloq.* a medical examination. □ **medically** *adv.* [French *médical* or medieval Latin *medicalis* from Latin *medicus*: see MEDIC[1]]

medical certificate *n.* a certificate of fitness or unfitness to work etc.

medical examination *n.* an examination to determine a person's physical fitness.

medical jurisprudence *n.* the law relating to medicine.

medical officer *n. Brit.* a person in charge of the health services of a local authority or other organization.

medical practitioner *n.* a physician or surgeon.

medicament /mɪˈdɪkəm(ə)nt, ˈmɛdɪk-/ *n.* a substance used for medical treatment. [French *médicament* or Latin *medicamentum* (as MEDICATE)]

Medicare /ˈmɛdɪkɛː/ *n.* **1** (in the US) a federal system of health insurance for persons over 65 years of age. **2** (in Canada and Australia) a national health care scheme financed by taxation. [MEDICAL + CARE]

medicate /ˈmɛdɪkeɪt/ *v.tr.* **1** treat medically. **2** impregnate with a medicinal substance. □ **medicative** /ˈmɛdɪkətɪv/ *adj.* [Latin *medicari medicat-* 'administer remedies to' from *medicus*: see MEDIC[1]]

medication /mɛdɪˈkeɪʃ(ə)n/ *n.* **1** a substance used for medical treatment. **2** treatment using drugs.

Medicean /mɛdɪˈtʃiːən, -ˈsiːən, mɛˈdiːtʃɪən/ *adj.* of the Medici family, rulers of Florence in the 15th c. [modern Latin *Mediceus* from Italian *Medici*]

medicinal /mɪˈdɪsɪn(ə)l/ *adj.* & *n.* ● *adj.* (of a substance) having healing properties. ● *n.* a medicinal substance. □ **medicinally** *adv.* [Middle English via Old French from Latin *medicinalis* (as MEDICINE)]

medicine /ˈmɛds(ə)n; ˈmɛdɪsɪn/ *n.* **1** the science or practice of the diagnosis, treatment, and prevention of disease, esp. as distinct from surgical methods. **2** any drug or preparation used for the treatment or prevention of disease, esp. one taken by mouth. **3** a spell, charm, or fetish which is thought to cure afflictions. □ **a dose** (or **taste**) **of one's own medicine** treatment such as one is accustomed to giving others. **take one's medicine** submit to something disagreeable. [Middle English via Old French *medecine* from Latin *medicina*, from *medicus*: see MEDIC[1]]

medicine ball *n.* a large heavy stuffed usu. leather ball thrown and caught for exercise.

medicine chest *n.* a box containing medicines etc.

medicine man *n.* a person believed, esp. among N. American Indians, to have magical powers of healing.

medick /ˈmiːdɪk/ *n.* (also **medic**) any leguminous plant of the genus *Medicago*, esp. alfalfa. [Middle English via Latin *medica* from Greek *Mēdikē poa* 'Median grass']

medico /ˈmɛdɪkəʊ/ *n.* (*pl.* **-os**) *colloq.* = MEDIC[1]. [Italian from Latin (as MEDIC[1])]

medico- /ˈmɛdɪkəʊ/ *comb. form* medical; medical and (*medico-legal*). [Latin *medicus* (as MEDIC[1])]

medieval /mɛdɪˈiːv(ə)l, miː-/ *adj.* (also **mediaeval**) **1** of, or in the style of, the Middle Ages. **2** *colloq.* old-fashioned, archaic. □ **medievalism** *n.* **medievalist** *n.* **medievalize** *v.tr. & intr.* (also **-ise**). **medievally** *adv.* [modern Latin *medium aevum*, from Latin *medius* 'middle' + *aevum* 'age']

medieval history *n.* the history of the 5th–15th c.

medieval Latin *n.* Latin of about AD 600–1500.

medina /mɪˈdiːnə/ *n.* (also **Medina**) the old Arab or non-European quarter of a N. African town. [Arabic, literally 'town']

mediocre /miːdɪˈəʊkə/ *adj.* **1** of middling quality, neither good nor bad. **2** second-rate. [French *médiocre* or from Latin *mediocris* 'of middle height or degree', from *medius* 'middle' + *ocris* 'rugged mountain']

mediocrity /miːdɪˈɒkrɪti/ *n.* (*pl.* **-ies**) **1** the state of being mediocre. **2** a mediocre person or thing.

meditate /ˈmɛdɪteɪt/ *v.* **1** *intr.* **a** exercise the mind in (esp. religious) contemplation. **b** (usu. foll. by *on*, *upon*) focus on a subject in this manner. **2** *tr.* plan mentally; design. □ **meditation** /-ˈteɪʃ(ə)n/ *n.* **meditator** *n.* [Latin *meditari* 'contemplate']

meditative /ˈmɛdɪtətɪv, -teɪtɪv/ *adj.* **1** inclined to meditate. **2** indicative of meditation. □ **meditatively** *adv.* **meditativeness** *n.*

Mediterranean /ˌmɛdɪtəˈreɪnɪən/ *n. & adj.* ● *n.* **1** a large landlocked sea bordered by southern Europe, SW Asia, and N. Africa. **2** a native of a country bordering on the Mediterranean. ● *adj.* of or characteristic of the Mediterranean, countries bordering it, or their inhabitants (*Mediterranean climate*; *Mediterranean cookery*; *of Mediterranean appearance*). [Latin *mediterraneus* 'inland', from *medius* 'middle' + *terra* 'land']

medium /ˈmiːdɪəm/ *n. & adj.* ● *n.* (*pl.* **media** or **mediums**) **1** the middle quality, degree, etc. between extremes (*find a happy medium*). **2** the means by which something is communicated (*the medium of sound*; *the medium of television*). **3** the intervening substance through which impressions are conveyed to the senses etc. (*light passing from one medium into another*). **4** *Biol.* the physical environment or conditions of growth, storage, or transport of a living organism (*the shape of a fish is ideal for its fluid medium*; *growing mould on the surface of a medium*). **5** an agency or means of doing something (*the medium through which money is raised*). **6** the material or form used by an artist, composer, etc. (*language as an artistic medium*). **7** the liquid (e.g. oil or gel) with which pigments are mixed for use in painting. **8** (*pl.* **mediums**) a person claiming to be in contact with the spirits of the dead and to communicate between the dead and the living. ● *adj.* **1** between two qualities, degrees, etc. **2** average; moderate (*of medium height*). □ **mediumism** *n.* (in sense 8 of *n.*). **mediumistic** /-ˈmɪstɪk/ *adj.* (in sense 8 of *n.*). **mediumship** *n.* (in sense 8 of *n.*). [Latin, = middle, neut. of *medius*]

medium bowler *n.* *Cricket* a bowler who bowls at a medium pace.

medium dry *adj.* (of sherry, wine, etc.) having a flavour intermediate between dry and sweet.

medium frequency *n.* a radio frequency between 300 kHz and 3 MHz.

medium of circulation *n.* something that serves as an instrument of commercial transactions, e.g. coin.

medium-range *adj.* (of an aircraft, missile, etc.) able to travel a medium distance.

medium-sized *adj.* of average size.

medium wave *n.* esp. *Brit.* a radio wave of medium frequency.

medlar /ˈmɛdlə/ *n.* **1** a tree of the rose family, *Mespilus germanica*, bearing small brown apple-like fruits. **2** the fruit of this tree which is eaten when decayed. [Middle English via Old French *medler* and Latin *mespila* from Greek *mespilē, -on*]

medley /ˈmɛdli/ *n., adj., & v.* ● *n.* (*pl.* **-eys**) **1** a varied mixture; a miscellany. **2** a collection of musical items from one work or various sources arranged as a continuous whole. ● *adj. archaic* mixed; motley. ● *v.tr.* (**-eys**, **-eyed**) *archaic* make a medley of; intermix. [Middle English via Old French *medlee*, variant of *meslee*, from Romanic (as MEDDLE)]

medley relay *n.* a relay race between teams in which each member runs a different distance, swims a different stroke, etc.

Medoc /meɪˈdɒk, ˈmɛdɒk/ *n.* a fine red claret from the Médoc region of SW France.

medulla /mɛˈdʌlə/ *n.* **1** *Anat.* the inner region of certain organs or tissues usu. when it is distinguishable from the outer region or cortex, as in hair or a kidney. **2** *Bot.* the soft internal tissue of plants. □ **medullary** *adj.* [Latin, = pith, marrow, probably related to *medius* 'middle']

medulla oblongata /ɒblɒŋˈɡɑːtə/ *n.* the continuation of the spinal cord within the skull, forming the lowest part of the brainstem.

medusa /mɪˈdjuːzə, -sə/ *n.* (*pl.* **medusae** /-ziː, -siː/ or **medusas**) **1** a jellyfish. **2** *Zool.* a free-swimming sexual form of any coelenterate, having tentacles round the edge of a usu. umbrella-shaped jelly-like body, e.g. a jellyfish. □ **medusan** *adj.* [Latin from Greek *Medousa*, the name of a gorgon with snakes instead of hair]

meed /miːd/ *n. literary* or *archaic* **1** reward. **2** merited portion (of praise etc.). [Old English *mēd* from West Germanic: related to Gothic *mizdō*, Greek *misthos* 'reward']

meek /miːk/ *adj.* **1** humble and submissive; suffering injury etc. tamely. **2** piously gentle in nature. □ **meekly** *adv.* **meekness** *n.* [Middle English *me(o)c* from Old Norse *mjúkr* 'soft, gentle']

meerkat /ˈmɪəkat/ *n.* a small African mongoose, esp. (in full **grey meerkat**) *Suricata suricatta*, with grey and black stripes, living gregariously in burrows. Also called *suricate*. [Dutch, = sea-cat]

meerschaum /ˈmɪəʃɔːm, -ʃəm/ *n.* **1** a soft white form of hydrated magnesium silicate, chiefly found in Turkey, which resembles clay. **2** a tobacco pipe with the bowl made from this. [German, = sea-foam, from *Meer* 'sea' + *Schaum* 'foam', translation of Persian *kef-i-daryā*, with reference to its frothiness]

meet[1] /miːt/ *v. & n.* ● *v.* (*past* and *past part.* **met** /mɛt/) **1 a** *tr.* encounter (a person or persons) by accident or design; come face to face with. **b** *intr.* (of two or more people) come into each other's company by accident or design (*decided to meet on the bridge*). **2** *tr.* go to a place to be present at the arrival of (a person, train, etc.). **3 a** *tr.* (of a moving object, line, feature of landscape, etc.) come together or into contact with (*where the road meets the flyover*). **b** *intr.* come together or into contact (*where the sea and the sky meet*). **4 a** *tr.* make the acquaintance of (*delighted to meet you*). **b** *intr.* (of two or more people) make each other's acquaintance. **5** *intr. & tr.* come together or come into contact with for the purposes of conference, business, worship, etc. (*the committee meets every week*; *the union met management yesterday*). **6** *tr.* **a** (of a person or a group) deal with or answer (a demand, objection, etc.) (*met the original proposal with hostility*). **b** satisfy or conform with (proposals, deadlines, a person, etc.) (*agreed to meet the new terms*; *did my best to meet them on that point*). **7** *tr.* pay (a bill etc.); provide the funds required by (a cheque etc.) (*meet the cost of the move*). **8** *tr. &* (foll. by *with*) *intr.* experience, encounter, or receive (success, disaster, a difficulty, etc.) (*met their death*; *met with many problems*). **9** *tr.* oppose in battle, contest, or confrontation. **10** *intr.* (of clothes, curtains, etc.) join or fasten correctly (*my jacket won't meet*). ● *n.* **1** the assembly of riders and hounds for a hunt. **2** the assembly of competitors for various sporting activities, esp. athletics. □ **make ends meet** see END. **meet the case** be adequate. **meet the eye** (or **the ear**) be visible (or audible). **meet a person's eye** check if another person is watching and look into his or her eyes in return. **meet a person halfway** make a compromise; respond in a friendly way to the advances of another person. **meet up** (often foll. by *with*) *colloq.* meet or make contact, esp. by chance. **meet with 1** see sense 8 of *v.* **2** receive (a reaction) (*met with the committee's approval*). **3** esp. *US* = sense 1a of *v.* **more in it than meets the eye** hidden qualities or complications. [Old English *mētan* from Germanic: cf. MOOT]

meet[2] /mi:t/ *adj. archaic* suitable, fit, proper. □ **meetly** *adv.* **meetness** *n.* [Old English *gemǣte* from Germanic: related to METE[1]]

meeting /'mi:tɪŋ/ *n.* **1** in senses of MEET[1]. **2** an assembly of people, esp. the members of a society, committee, etc., for discussion or entertainment. **3** = RACE MEETING. **4** an assembly (esp. of Quakers) for worship. **5** the persons assembled (*address the meeting*).

meeting house *n.* a place of worship, esp. of Quakers etc.

mega /'mɛgə/ *adj. & adv. slang* ● *adj.* **1** brilliant, excellent. **2** enormous. ● *adv.* extremely (*mega famous*).

mega- /'mɛgə/ *comb. form* **1** large. **2** denoting a factor of one million (10^6) in the metric system of measurement (abbr.: **M**). [Greek from *megas* 'great']

megabuck /'mɛgəbʌk/ *n. colloq.* **1** a million dollars. **2** (in *pl.*) a huge sum of money.

megabyte /'mɛgəbʌɪt/ *n. Computing* 1,048,576 (i.e. 2^{20}) bytes as a measure of data capacity, or loosely 1,000,000 (abbr.: **MB**).

megadeath /'mɛgədɛθ/ *n.* the death of one million people (esp. as a unit in estimating the casualties of war).

megaflop /'mɛgəflɒp/ *n.* **1** *Computing* a unit of computing speed equal to one million floating-point operations per second. **2** *slang* a complete failure.

megahertz /'mɛgəhə:ts/ *n.* (*pl.* same) one million hertz, esp. as a measure of frequency of radio transmissions (abbr.: **MHz**).

megalith /'mɛgəlɪθ/ *n. Archaeol.* a large stone, esp. one placed upright as a monument or part of one. [MEGA- + Greek *lithos* 'stone']

megalithic /mɛgə'lɪθɪk/ *adj. Archaeol.* made of or marked by the use of large stones.

megalo- /'mɛgələʊ/ *comb. form* great (*megalomania*). [Greek from *megas megal-* 'great']

megalomania /mɛg(ə)lə(ʊ)'meɪnɪə/ *n.* **1** a mental disorder producing delusions of grandeur. **2** a passion for grandiose schemes. □ **megalomaniac** *adj. & n.* **megalomaniacal** /-mə'nʌɪək(ə)l/ *adj.* **megalomanic** /-'manɪk/ *adj.*

megalopolis /mɛgə'lɒp(ə)lɪs/ *n.* **1** a great city or its way of life. **2** an urban complex consisting of a city and its environs. □ **megalopolitan** /-lə'pɒlɪt(ə)n/ *adj. & n.* [MEGA- + Greek *polis* 'city']

megalosaurus /mɛg(ə)lə(ʊ)'sɔ:rəs/ *n.* (also **megalosaur** /'mɛgələsɔ:/) a large flesh-eating dinosaur of the genus *Megalosaurus*, with stout hind legs and small forelimbs. [MEGALO- + Greek *sauros* 'lizard']

megaphone /'mɛgəfəʊn/ *n.* a large funnel-shaped device for amplifying the sound of the voice.

megapode /'mɛgəpəʊd/ *n.* (also **megapod** /-pɒd/) any bird of the family Megapodidae, native to Australasia, that builds a mound of debris for the incubation of its eggs, e.g. a mallee fowl. [modern Latin genus name *Megapodius*, formed as MEGA- + Greek *pous podos* 'foot']

megaron /'mɛgər(ə)n/ *n.* the central hall of a large Mycenaean house. [Greek, = hall]

megaspore /'mɛgəspɔ:/ *n.* the larger of the two kinds of spores produced by some ferns (cf. MICROSPORE).

megastar /'mɛgəstɑ:/ *n.* a very famous person, esp. in the world of entertainment.

megastore /'mɛgəstɔ:/ *n.* a large shop selling many different types of goods, esp. situated at the edge of a town.

megaton /'mɛgətʌn/ *n.* (also **megatonne**) a unit of explosive power equal to one million tons of TNT.

megavolt /'mɛgəvəʊlt, -vɒlt/ *n.* one million volts, esp. as a unit of electromotive force (abbr.: **MV**).

megawatt /'mɛgəwɒt/ *n.* one million watts, esp. as a measure of electrical power as generated by power stations (abbr.: **MW**).

Megger /'mɛgə/ *n. Electr. propr.* an instrument for measuring electrical insulation resistance. [cf. MEGOHM]

megilp /mə'gɪlp/ *n.* (also **magilp**) a mixture of mastic resin and linseed oil, added to oil paints, much used in the 19th c. [18th c.: origin unknown]

megohm /'mɛgəʊm/ *n. Electr.* one million ohms. [MEGA- + OHM]

megrim[1] /'mi:grɪm/ *n.* **1** *archaic* migraine. **2** a whim, a fancy. **3** (in *pl.*) **a** depression; low spirits. **b** staggers, vertigo in horses etc. [Middle English *mygrane* from Old French MIGRAINE]

megrim[2] /'mi:grɪm/ *n.* either of two European deep-water flatfishes, *Lepidorhombus whiffiagonis* and *Arnoglossus laterna*. Also called *sail-fluke*. [19th c.: origin unknown]

meiosis /mʌɪ'əʊsɪs/ *n.* (*pl.* **meioses** /-si:z/) **1** *Biol.* a type of cell division that results in daughter cells with half the chromosome number of the parent cell (cf. MITOSIS). **2** = LITOTES. □ **meiotic** /-'ɒtɪk/ *adj.* **meiotically** /-'ɒtɪk(ə)li/ *adv.* [modern Latin from Greek *meiōsis*, via *meioō* 'lessen' from *meiōn* 'less']

Meissen /'mʌɪs(ə)n/ *n.* a hard-paste porcelain made since 1710 . [*Meissen* near Dresden in Germany]

Meistersinger /'mʌɪstəzɪŋə, -sɪŋ-/ *n.* (*pl.* same) a member of one of the 14th–16th-c. German guilds for lyric poets and musicians. [German, from *Meister* MASTER + *Singer* SINGER (see SING)]

melamine /'mɛləmi:n/ *n.* **1** a white crystalline compound that can be copolymerized with formaldehyde to give thermosetting resins. **2** (in full **melamine resin**) a plastic made from melamine and used esp. for laminated coatings. [German *melam* (an arbitrary formation) + AMINE]

melancholia /mɛlən'kəʊlɪə/ *n.* **1** a mental illness marked by depression and ill-founded fears. **2** = MELANCHOLY *n.* 1. [Late Latin: see MELANCHOLY]

melancholy /'mɛlənk(ə)li/ *n. & adj.* ● *n.* (*pl.* **-ies**) **1 a** a pensive sadness. **b** a tendency to this. **2** *hist.* = BLACK BILE. **3** *Med. archaic* = MELANCHOLIA 1. ● *adj.* (of a person) sad, gloomy; (of a thing) saddening, depressing; (of words, a tune, etc.) expressing sadness. □ **melancholic** /-'kɒlɪk/ *adj.* **melancholically** /-'kɒlɪk(ə)li/ *adv.* [Middle English via Old French *melancolie* and Late Latin *melancholia* from Greek *melagkholia*, from *melas melanos* 'black' + *kholē* 'bile']

Melanesian /mɛlə'ni:zj(ə)n, -ʒ(ə)n/ *n. & adj.* ● *n.* **1** a member of the dominant Negroid people of Melanesia, an island group in the W. Pacific. **2** any of the Austronesian languages of this people. ● *adj.* of or relating to this people or their language. [*Melanesia* from Greek *melas* 'black' + *nēsos* 'island']

mélange /meɪ'lɒ̃ʒ/ *n.* a mixture; a medley. [French, from *mêler* 'mix' (as MEDDLE)]

melanin /'mɛlənɪn/ *n.* a dark brown to black pigment occurring in the hair, skin, and iris of the eye, that is responsible for tanning of the skin when exposed to sunlight. [Greek *melas melanos* 'black' + -IN]

melanism /'mɛlənɪz(ə)m/ *n.* the unusual darkening of body tissues caused by excessive production of melanin, esp. as a form of colour variation in animals. □ **melanic** /mɪ'lanɪk/ *adj.*

melanoma /mɛlə'nəʊmə/ *n.* a usu. malignant tumour of melanin-forming cells, usu. in the skin. [MELANIN + -OMA]

melanosis /mɛlə'nəʊsɪs/ *n.* **1** = MELANISM. **2** a disorder in the body's production of melanin. □ **melanotic** /-'nɒtɪk/ *adj.* [modern Latin from Greek (as MELANIN)]

Melba /'mɛlbə/ *n.* □ **do a Melba** *Austral. slang* **1** return from retirement. **2** make several farewell appearances. [Dame Nellie *Melba*, Australian operatic soprano d. 1931]

Melba sauce *n.* a sauce made from puréed raspberries thickened with icing sugar.

Melba toast *n.* very thin crisp toast.

meld[1] /mɛld/ *v. & n.* ● *v.tr.* (also *absol.*) (in rummy, canasta, etc.) lay down or declare (one's cards) in order to score points. ● *n.* a completed set or run of cards in any of these games. [German *melden* 'announce']

meld[2] /mɛld/ *v.tr. & intr.* orig. *US* merge, blend, combine. [perhaps from MELT + WELD[1]]

mêlée /'mɛleɪ/ *n.* (*US* **melee**) **1** a confused fight, skirmish, or scuffle. **2** a muddle. [French (as MEDLEY)]

melic /'mɛlɪk/ *adj.* (of a poem, esp. a Greek lyric) meant to be sung. [Latin *melicus* from Greek *melikos*, from *melos* 'song']

melilot /'mɛlɪlɒt/ *n.* a leguminous plant of the genus *Melilotus*, with trifoliate leaves, small flowers, and a scent of hay when dried. [(Old) French *mélilot* via Latin *melilotus* from Greek *melilōtos* 'honey lotus']

meliorate /'miːlɪəreɪt/ *v.tr. & intr. literary* improve (cf. AMELIORATE). □ **melioration** /-'reɪʃ(ə)n/ *n.* **meliorative** /-rətɪv/ *adj.* [Late Latin *meliorare* (as MELIORISM)]

meliorism /'miːlɪərɪz(ə)m/ *n.* a doctrine that the world may be made better by human effort. □ **meliorist** *n.* [Latin *melior* 'better' + -ISM]

melisma /mɪ'lɪzmə/ *n.* (*pl.* **melismata** /-mətə/ or **melismas**) *Mus.* a group of notes sung to one syllable of text. □ **melismatic** /-'matɪk/ *adj.* [Greek]

melliferous /me'lɪf(ə)rəs/ *adj.* yielding or producing honey. [Latin *mellifer* from *mel* 'honey']

mellifluous /me'lɪflʊəs/ *adj.* (of a voice or words) pleasing, musical, flowing. □ **mellifluence** *n.* **mellifluent** *adj.* **mellifluously** *adv.* **mellifluousness** *n.* [Middle English from Old French *melliflue* or Late Latin *mellifluus*, from *mel* 'honey' + *fluere* 'flow']

mellow /'mɛləʊ/ *adj. & v.* ● *adj.* **1** (of sound, colour, light) soft and rich; free from harshness. **2** (of character) softened or matured by age or experience. **3** genial, jovial. **4** slightly drunk. **5** (of fruit) soft, sweet, and juicy. **6** (of wine) well-matured, smooth. **7** (of earth) rich, loamy. ● *v.tr. & intr.* make or become mellow. □ **mellowly** *adv.* **mellowness** *n.* [Middle English, perhaps from attributive use of Old English *melu*, *melw*- MEAL[2]]

melodeon /mɪ'ləʊdɪən/ *n.* (also **melodion**) **1** a small organ popular in the 19th c., similar to the harmonium. **2** a small German accordion, played esp. by folk musicians. [in sense 1, alteration of *melodium*, from MELODY + HARMONIUM; in sense 2, perhaps from MELODY + ACCORDION]

melodic /mɪ'lɒdɪk/ *adj.* **1** of or relating to melody. **2** having or producing melody. □ **melodically** *adv.* [French *mélodique* via Late Latin *melodicus* from Greek *melōidikos* (as MELODY)]

melodic minor *n.* a scale with the sixth and seventh degrees raised when ascending and lowered when descending.

melodious /mɪ'ləʊdɪəs/ *adj.* **1** of, producing, or having melody. **2** sweet-sounding. □ **melodiously** *adv.* **melodiousness** *n.* [Middle English from Old French *melodieus* (as MELODY)]

melodist /'mɛlədɪst/ *n.* **1** a composer of melodies. **2** a singer.

melodize /'mɛlədʌɪz/ *v.* (also **-ise**) **1** *intr.* make a melody or melodies; make sweet music. **2** *tr.* make melodious. □ **melodizer** *n.*

melodrama /'mɛlə(ʊ)drɑːmə/ *n.* **1** a sensational dramatic piece with crude appeals to the emotions and usu. a happy ending. **2** the genre of drama of this type. **3** language, behaviour, or an occurrence suggestive of this. **4** *hist.* a play with songs interspersed and with orchestral music accompanying the action. □ **melodramatic** /-drə'matɪk/ *adj.* **melodramatically** /-drə'matɪk(ə)li/ *adv.* **melodramatist** /-'dramətɪst/ *n.* **melodramatize** /-'dramətʌɪz/ *v.tr.* (also **-ise**). [French *mélodrame*, from Greek *melos* 'music' + French *drame* DRAMA]

melodramatics /mɛlə(ʊ)drə'matɪks/ *n.pl.* melodramatic behaviour, action, or writing.

melody /'mɛlədi/ *n.* (*pl.* **-ies**) **1** an arrangement of single notes in a musically expressive succession. **2** the principal part in harmonized music. **3** a musical arrangement of words. **4** sweet music; tunefulness. [Middle English via Old French *melodie* and Late Latin *melodia* from Greek *melōidia*, from *melos* 'song']

melon /'mɛlən/ *n.* **1** the large round fruit of various plants of the gourd family, with sweet pulpy flesh and many seeds (*honeydew melon*; *watermelon*). **2** the plant producing this. **3** *Zool.* a mass of waxy material in the head of some toothed whales, thought to focus acoustic signals. [Middle English via Old French and Late Latin *melo -onis*, abbreviation of Latin *melopepo*, from Greek *mēlopepōn*, from *mēlon* 'apple' + *pepōn* 'gourd']

melt /mɛlt/ *v. & n.* ● *v.* **1** *intr.* become liquefied by heat. **2** *tr.* change to a liquid condition by heat (see also MOLTEN). **3** *intr. & tr.* soften or liquefy by the action of moisture; dissolve. **4** *intr.* **a** (of a person, feelings, the heart, etc.) be softened as a result of pity, love, etc. **b** dissolve into tears. **5** *tr.* soften (a person, feelings, the heart, etc.) (*a look to melt a heart of stone*). **6** *intr.* (usu. foll. by *into*) change or merge imperceptibly into another form or state (*night melted into dawn*). **7** *intr.* (often foll. by *away*) (of a person) leave or disappear unobtrusively (*melted into the background*; *melted away into the crowd*). **8** *intr.* (usu. as **melting** *adj.*) (of sound) be soft and liquid (*melting chords*). **9** *intr. colloq.* (of a person) suffer extreme heat (*I'm melting in this thick jumper*). ● *n.* **1** liquid metal etc. **2** an amount melted at any one time. **3** the process or an instance of melting. □ **melt away** disappear or make disappear by liquefaction. **melt down 1** melt (esp. metal articles) in order to refuse the raw material. **2** become liquid and lose structure (cf. MELTDOWN). **melt in the mouth** (of food) be delicious and esp. very light. □ **meltable** *adj.* **melter** *n.* **meltingly** *adv.* [Old English *meltan*, *mieltan* from Germanic: related to MALT]

meltdown /'mɛltdaʊn/ *n.* **1** the melting of (and consequent damage to) a structure, esp. the overheated core of a nuclear reactor. **2** a disastrous event, esp. a rapid fall in share prices.

melting point *n.* the temperature at which any given solid will melt.

melting pot *n.* **1** a pot in which metals etc. are melted and mixed. **2** a place where races, theories, etc. are mixed, or an imaginary pool where ideas are mixed together.

melton /'mɛlt(ə)n/ *n.* cloth with a close-cut nap, used for overcoats etc. [*Melton Mowbray*, a town in central England, formerly a centre of manufacture]

melt water *n.* water formed by the melting of snow and ice, esp. from a glacier.

member /ˈmɛmbə/ *n.* **1** a person belonging to a society, team, etc. **2** (**Member**) a person formally elected to take part in the proceedings of certain organizations (*Member of Parliament*; *Member of Congress*). **3** (also *attrib.*) a part or branch of a political body (*member state*; *a member of the Commonwealth*). **4** a constituent portion of a complex structure (*load-bearing member*). **5** a part of a sentence, equation, group of figures, mathematical set, etc. **6 a** any part or organ of the body, esp. a limb. **b** the penis (cf. MEMBRUM VIRILE). **7** used in the title awarded to a person admitted to (usu. the lowest grade of) certain honours (*Member of the British Empire*). □ **membered** *adj.* (also in *comb.*). **memberless** *adj.* [Middle English via Old French *membre* from Latin *membrum* 'limb']

membership /ˈmɛmbəʃɪp/ *n.* **1** being a member. **2** the number of members. **3** the body of members.

membrane /ˈmɛmbreɪn/ *n.* **1** any pliable sheetlike structure acting as a boundary, lining, or partition in an organism. **2** a thin pliable sheet or skin of various kinds. □ **membranaceous** /mɛmbrəˈneɪʃəs/ *adj.* **membraneous** /mɛmˈbreɪnɪəs/ *adj.* **membranous** /ˈmɛmbrənəs/ *adj.* [Latin *membrana* 'skin covering part of the body, parchment' (as MEMBER)]

membrum virile /mɛmbrəm vɪˈrʌɪli, vɪˈriːli/ *n. archaic* the penis. [Latin, = male member]

memento /mɪˈmɛntəʊ/ *n.* (*pl.* **-oes** or **-os**) an object kept as a reminder or a souvenir of a person or an event. [Latin, imperative of *meminisse* 'remember']

memento mori /mɪˌmɛntəʊ ˈmɔːri, -rʌɪ/ *n.* a warning or reminder of death (e.g. a skull). [Latin, = remember you must die]

memo /ˈmɛməʊ/ *n.* (*pl.* **-os**) *colloq.* a memorandum. [abbreviation]

memoir /ˈmɛmwɑː, -wɔː/ *n.* **1** a historical account or biography written from personal knowledge or special sources. **2** (in *pl.*) an autobiography or a written account of one's memory of certain events or people. **3 a** an essay on a learned subject specially studied by the writer. **b** (in *pl.*) the proceedings or transactions of a learned society (*Memoirs of the American Mathematical Society*). □ **memoirist** *n.* [French *mémoire* (masc.), special use of *mémoire* (fem.) MEMORY]

memorabilia /mɛm(ə)rəˈbɪlɪə/ *n.pl.* **1** souvenirs of memorable events, people, etc. **2** *archaic* memorable or noteworthy things. [Latin, neut. pl. (as MEMORABLE)]

memorable /ˈmɛm(ə)rəb(ə)l/ *adj.* **1** worth remembering; not to be forgotten. **2** easily remembered. □ **memorability** /-ˈbɪlɪti/ *n.* **memorableness** *n.* **memorably** *adv.* [Middle English from French *mémorable* or Latin *memorabilis* from *memorare* 'bring to mind', from *memor* 'mindful']

memorandum /mɛməˈrandəm/ *n.* (*pl.* **memoranda** /-də/ or **memorandums**) **1** a note or record made for future use. **2** an informal written message, esp. in business, diplomacy, etc. **3** *Law* a document recording the terms of a contract or other legal details. [Middle English from Latin, neut. sing. gerundive of *memorare*: see MEMORABLE]

memorial /mɪˈmɔːrɪəl/ *n.* & *adj.* ● *n.* **1** an object, institution, or custom established in memory of a person or event (*the Albert Memorial*). **2** (often in *pl.*) *hist.* a statement of facts as the basis of a petition etc.; a record; an informal diplomatic paper. ● *adj.* intending to commemorate a person or thing (*memorial service*). □ **memorialist** *n.* [Middle English from Old French *memorial* or Latin *memorialis* (as MEMORY)]

Memorial Day *n.* (in the US) a day on which those who died on active service are remembered, usu. the last Monday in May.

memorialize /mɪˈmɔːrɪəlʌɪz/ *v.tr.* (also **-ise**) **1** commemorate. **2** address a memorial to (a person or body).

memoria technica /mɪˌmɔːrɪə ˈtɛknɪkə/ *n.* a system or contrivance used to assist the memory. [modern Latin, = artificial memory]

memorize /ˈmɛmərʌɪz/ *v.tr.* (also **-ise**) commit to memory. □ **memorizable** *adj.* **memorization** /-ˈzeɪʃ(ə)n/ *n.* **memorizer** *n.*

memory /ˈmɛm(ə)ri/ *n.* (*pl.* **-ies**) **1** the faculty by which things are recalled to or kept in the mind. **2 a** this faculty in an individual (*my memory is beginning to fail*). **b** one's store of things remembered (*buried deep in my memory*). **3** a recollection or remembrance (*the memory of better times*). **4 a** the part of a computer etc. in which data or instructions can be stored for retrieval. **b** capacity for storing information in this way. **5** the remembrance of a person or thing (*his mother's memory haunted him*). **6 a** the reputation of a dead person (*his memory lives on*). **b** in formulaic phrases used of a dead sovereign etc. (*of blessed memory*). **7** the length of time over which the memory or memories of any given person or group extends (*within living memory*; *within the memory of anyone still working here*). **8** the act of remembering (*a deed worthy of memory*). □ **from memory** without verification in books etc. **in memory of** to keep alive the remembrance of. [Middle English via Old French *memorie*, *memoire* from Latin *memoria*, from *memor* 'mindful, remembering': related to MOURN]

memory bank *n.* **1** the memory device of a computer etc. **2** the store of memories of an individual or group.

memory board *n.* a detachable storage device which can be connected to a computer.

memory lane *n.* (usu. prec. by *down*, *along*) an imaginary and sentimental journey into the past.

memory mapping *n. Computing* a technique whereby a computer treats peripheral devices as if they were located in the main memory.

memsahib /ˈmɛmsɑːɪb, -sɑːb/ *n. Anglo-Ind. hist.* a European married woman in India, as spoken of or to by Indians. [MA'AM + SAHIB]

men *pl.* of MAN.

menace /ˈmɛnəs/ *n.* & *v.* ● *n.* **1** a threat. **2** a dangerous or obnoxious thing or person. **3** *joc.* a pest; a nuisance. ● *v.tr.* & *intr.* threaten, esp. in a malignant or hostile manner. □ **menacer** *n.* **menacingly** *adv.* [Middle English, ultimately from Latin *minax -acis* 'threatening' from *minari* 'threaten']

ménage /meɪˈnɑːʒ/ *n.* the members of a household. [Old French *manaige*, ultimately from Latin (as MANSION)]

ménage à trois /meɪˌnɑːʒ ɑː ˈtrwɑː, French menaʒ a trwɑ/ *n.* (*pl.* ***ménages à trois*** *pronunc.* same) an arrangement in which three people live together, usu. a married couple and the lover of one of them. [French, = household of three (as MÉNAGE)]

menagerie /məˈnadʒ(ə)ri/ *n.* **1** a collection of wild animals in captivity for exhibition etc. **2** the place where these are housed. [French *ménagerie* (as MÉNAGE)]

menaquinone /mɛnəˈkwɪnəʊn/ *n.* one of the K vitamins, produced by bacteria found in the large intestine and essential for the blood-clotting process. Also called *vitamin K_2*. [chemical name *me*thyl-*na*phtho*quinone*]

menarche /mɛˈnɑːki/ *n.* the onset of first menstruation. [modern Latin, formed as MENO- + Greek *arkhē* 'beginning']

mend /mɛnd/ *v.* & *n.* ● *v.* **1** *tr.* restore to a sound condition; repair (a broken article, a damaged road, torn clothes, etc.). **2** *intr.* heal. **3** *tr.* improve (*mend matters*). **4** *tr.* add fuel to (a fire). ● *n.* a darn or repair in material etc. (*a mend in my shirt*). □ **mend one's fences** make peace with a person. **mend one's manners** improve one's behaviour. **mend one's pace** go faster; alter one's pace to another's. **mend one's ways** reform, improve one's habits. **on the mend** improving in health or condition. □ **mendable** *adj.* **mender** *n.* [Middle English from Anglo-French *mender*, from *amender* AMEND]

mendacious /mɛnˈdeɪʃəs/ *adj.* lying, untruthful. □ **mendaciously** *adv.* **mendacity** /-ˈdasɪti/ *n.* (*pl.* **-ies**). [Latin *mendax -dacis*, perhaps from *mendum* 'fault']

mendelevium /mɛndəˈliːvɪəm, -ˈleɪvɪəm/ *n. Chem.* an artificially made transuranic radioactive metallic element (symbol **Md**). [named after D. I. *Mendeleev*, Russian chemist d. 1907]

Mendelism /ˈmɛnd(ə)lɪz(ə)m/ *n.* the theory of heredity based on the recurrence of certain inherited characteristics transmitted by genes. □ **Mendelian** /-ˈdiːlɪən/ *adj. & n.* [from the name of G. J. *Mendel*, Austrian botanist d. 1884, + -ISM]

mendicant /ˈmɛndɪk(ə)nt/ *adj. & n.* ● *adj.* **1** begging. **2** (of a friar) living solely on alms. ● *n.* **1** a beggar. **2** a mendicant friar. □ **mendicancy** *n.* **mendicity** /-ˈdɪsɪti/ *n.* [Latin *mendicare* 'beg' via *mendicus* 'beggar' from *mendum* 'fault']

mending /ˈmɛndɪŋ/ *n.* **1** the action of a person who mends. **2** things, esp. clothes, to be mended.

menfolk /ˈmɛnfəʊk/ *n.pl.* **1** men in general. **2** the men of one's family.

menhaden /mɛnˈheɪd(ə)n/ *n.* any large herring-like fish of the genus *Brevoortia*, of the east coast of N. America, yielding valuable oil and used for manure. [Algonquian]

menhir /ˈmɛnhɪə/ *n. Archaeol.* a tall upright usu. prehistoric monumental stone. [Breton *men* 'stone' + *hir* 'long']

menial /ˈmiːnɪəl/ *adj. & n.* ● *adj.* **1** (esp. of unskilled domestic work) degrading, servile. **2** usu. *derog.* (of a servant) domestic. ● *n.* **1** a menial servant. **2** a servile person. □ **menially** *adv.* [Middle English from Old French *meinee* 'household']

meningitis /mɛnɪnˈdʒʌɪtɪs/ *n.* inflammation of the meninges due to infection by viruses or bacteria. □ **meningitic** /-ˈdʒɪtɪk/ *adj.*

meningococcus /mɪˌnɪŋgəʊˈkɒkəs, -ˌnɪndʒəʊ-/ *n.* (*pl.* **meningococci** /-ˈkɒk(s)ʌɪ, -ˈkɒk(s)iː/) a bacterium, *Neisseria meningitidis*, involved in some forms of meningitis and cerebrospinal infection. □ **meningococcal** *adj.* [from *meninges*, pl. of MENINX, + COCCUS]

meninx /ˈmiːnɪŋks/ *n.* (*pl.* **meninges** /mɪˈnɪndʒiːz/) (usu. in *pl.*) *Anat.* each of three membranes (the dura mater, arachnoid, and pia mater) that line the skull and vertebral canal and enclose the brain and spinal cord. □ **meningeal** /mɪˈnɪndʒɪəl/ *adj.* [modern Latin from Greek *mēnigx -iggos* 'membrane']

meniscus /mɪˈnɪskəs/ *n.* (*pl.* **menisci** /-sʌɪ/) **1** *Physics* the curved upper surface of a liquid in a tube. **2** a lens that is convex on one side and concave on the other. **3** *Anat.* a thin fibrous cartilage between the surfaces of some joints, e.g. the knee. **4** *Math.* a crescent-shaped figure. □ **meniscoid** *adj.* [modern Latin from Greek *mēniskos* 'crescent', diminutive of *mēnē* 'moon']

Mennonite /ˈmɛnənʌɪt/ *n.* a member of a Protestant sect originating in Friesland in the 16th c., emphasizing adult baptism and rejecting Church organization, military service, and public office. [from the name of its founder, *Menno* Simons, d. 1561]

meno- /ˈmɛnəʊ/ *comb. form* menstruation. [Greek *mēn mēnos* 'month']

menology /mɪˈnɒlədʒi/ *n.* (*pl.* **-ies**) a calendar, esp. that of the Greek Church, with biographies of the saints. [modern Latin *menologium* from ecclesiastical Greek *mēnologion*, from *mēn* 'month' + *logos* 'account']

menopause /ˈmɛnə(ʊ)pɔːz/ *n.* **1** the ceasing of menstruation. **2** the period in a woman's life (usu. between 45 and 50) when this occurs (see also MALE MENOPAUSE). □ **menopausal** /-ˈpɔːz(ə)l/ *adj.* [modern Latin *menopausis* (as MENO-, PAUSE)]

menorah /mɪˈnɔːrə/ *n.* a candelabrum having usu. eight branches, used in Jewish worship, esp. as a symbol of Judaism. [Hebrew, = candlestick]

menorrhagia /mɛnəˈreɪdʒɪə/ *n.* abnormally heavy bleeding at menstruation. [MENO- + stem of Greek *rhēgnumi* 'burst']

menorrhoea /mɛnəˈriːə/ *n.* ordinary flow of blood at menstruation. [MENO- + Greek *rhoia* from *rheō* 'flow']

menses /ˈmɛnsiːz/ *n.pl.* **1** blood and other materials discharged from the uterus at menstruation. **2** the time of menstruation. [Latin, pl. of *mensis* 'month']

Menshevik /ˈmɛnʃɪvɪk/ *n. hist.* a member of the non-Leninist wing of the Russian Social Democratic Workers' Party (cf. BOLSHEVIK). [Russian *Men'shevik* 'a member of the minority' from *men'she* 'less']

mens rea /mɛnz ˈriːə/ *n.* criminal intent; the knowledge of wrongdoing. [Latin, = guilty mind]

menstrual /ˈmɛnstrʊəl/ *adj.* of or relating to the menses or menstruation. [Middle English from Latin *menstrualis*, from *mensis* 'month']

menstrual cycle *n.* the process of ovulation and menstruation in female primates.

menstruate /ˈmɛnstrʊeɪt/ *v.intr.* undergo menstruation. [Late Latin *menstruare menstruat-* (as MENSTRUAL)]

menstruation /mɛnstrʊˈeɪʃ(ə)n/ *n.* the process of discharging blood and other materials from the lining of the uterus in sexually mature non-pregnant women at intervals of about one lunar month until the menopause.

menstruous /ˈmɛnstrʊəs/ *adj.* **1** of or relating to the menses. **2** menstruating. [Middle English from Old French *menstrueus* or Late Latin *menstruosus* (as MENSTRUAL)]

menstruum /ˈmɛnstrʊəm/ *n.* (*pl.* **menstrua** /-strʊə/) *archaic* a solvent. [Middle English from Latin, neut. of *menstruus* 'monthly' from *mensis* 'month', from the alchemical parallel between transmutation into gold and the supposed action of menses on the ovum]

mensurable /ˈmɛnʃ(ə)rəb(ə)l, -sjə-/ *adj.* **1** measurable, having fixed limits. **2** *Mus.* = MENSURAL 2. [French *mensurable* or Late Latin *mensurabilis*, from *mensurare* 'to measure', from Latin *mensura* MEASURE]

mensural /ˈmɛnʃ(ə)r(ə)l, -sjə-/ *adj.* **1** of or involving measure. **2** *Mus.* of or involving a fixed rhythm or notes of definite duration (cf. PLAINSONG). [Latin *mensuralis* from *mensura* MEASURE]

mensuration /mɛnʃəˈreɪʃ(ə)n, -sjə-/ *n.* **1** measuring. **2** *Math.* the measuring of geometric magnitudes such as the lengths of lines, areas of surfaces, and volumes of solids. [Late Latin *mensuratio* (as MENSURABLE)]

menswear /ˈmɛnzwɛː/ *n.* clothes for men.

-ment /m(ə)nt/ *suffix* **1** forming nouns expressing the means or result of the action of a verb (*abridgement*; *embankment*). **2** forming nouns from adjectives (*merriment*; *oddment*). [from or suggested by French, from Latin *-mentum*]

mental /ˈmɛnt(ə)l/ *adj.* **1** of or in the mind. **2** done by the mind. **3** *colloq.* **a** insane. **b** mad, crazy, angry, fanatical (*is mental about pop music*). **4** (*attrib.*) of or relating to disorders or illnesses of the mind (*mental hospital*). □ **mentally** *adv.* [Middle English via Old French or Late Latin *mentalis* from Latin *mens mentis* 'mind']

■ **Usage** In sense 4, *psychiatric* is now often preferred to *mental* as it is regarded as a less stigmatizing term.

mental age *n.* the degree of a person's mental development expressed as an age at which the same degree is attained by an average person.

mental arithmetic *n.* arithmetic performed in the mind.

mental block *n.* a particular mental inability due to subconscious emotional factors.

mental cruelty *n.* the infliction of suffering on another's mind, esp. *Law* as grounds for divorce.

mental defective *n. archaic* or *offens.* a person with a mental handicap.

mental deficiency *n. archaic* or *offens.* the condition of having a mental handicap.

mental handicap *n.* a condition in which the intellectual capacity of a person is permanently so much lowered or underdeveloped as to prevent normal function in society. □ **mentally handicapped** *adj.*

■ **Usage** The term *learning difficulties*, which strictly applies to educational problems, is sometimes preferred for or by people with certain mental handicaps.

mental illness *n.* a condition which causes serious abnormality or disorder in a person's behaviour or thinking capacity, esp. irrespective of intelligence; a disorder of the mind.

mentalism /ˈmɛnt(ə)lɪz(ə)m/ *n.* **1** *Philos.* the theory that physical and psychological phenomena are ultimately only explicable in terms of a creative and interpretative mind. **2** *Psychol.* the primitive tendency to personify in spirit form the forces of nature, or endow inert objects with the quality of 'soul'. □ **mentalist** *n.* **mentalistic** /-ˈlɪstɪk/ *adj.*

mentality /mɛnˈtalɪti/ *n.* (*pl.* **-ies**) **1** mental character or disposition. **2** kind or degree of intelligence. **3** what is in or of the mind.

mental nurse *n. Brit.* = PSYCHIATRIC NURSE.

mental patient *n.* = PSYCHIATRIC PATIENT.

mental reservation *n.* a qualification tacitly added in making a statement etc.

mentation /mɛnˈteɪʃ(ə)n/ *n.* **1** mental action. **2** state of mind. [Latin *mens mentis* 'mind']

menthol /ˈmɛnθɒl, -θ(ə)l/ *n.* a mint-tasting organic alcohol found in oil of peppermint etc., used as a flavouring and to relieve local pain. [German, from Latin *mentha* MINT[1]]

mentholated /ˈmɛnθəleɪtɪd/ *adj.* treated with or containing menthol.

mention /ˈmɛnʃ(ə)n/ *v.* & *n.* ● *v.tr.* **1** refer to briefly. **2** specify by name. **3** reveal or disclose (*do not mention this to anyone*). **4** *Brit.* (in dispatches) award (a person) a minor honour for meritorious, usu. gallant, military service. ● *n.* **1** a reference, esp. by name, to a person or thing. **2** *Brit.* (in dispatches) a military honour awarded for outstanding conduct. □ **don't mention it** said in polite dismissal of an apology or thanks. **make mention** (or **no mention**) **of** refer (or not refer) to. **not to mention** introducing a fact or thing of secondary or (as a rhetorical device) of primary importance. □ **mentionable** *adj.* [Old French from Latin *mentio -onis*, from the root of *mens* 'mind']

mentor /ˈmɛntɔː/ *n.* an experienced and trusted adviser. [French, via Latin from Greek *Mentōr*, the name of the adviser of the young Telemachus in Homer's *Odyssey* and Fénelon's *Télémaque*]

menu /ˈmɛnjuː/ *n.* **1 a** a list of dishes available in a restaurant etc. **b** a list of items to be served at a meal. **2** *Computing* a list of options usu. displayed on-screen showing the commands or facilities available. [French, = detailed list (*menu* 'small', used as a noun), from Latin *minutus* MINUTE[2]]

menu-driven *adj.* (of a program or computer) used by making selections from menus.

meow var. of MIAOW.

MEP *abbr.* Member of the European Parliament.

mepacrine /ˈmɛpəkrɪn, -iːn/ *n. Brit.* quinacrine. [*me*thyl + *pa*ludism (malaria) + *acridine*]

meperidine /mɛˈpɛrɪdiːn/ *n.* esp. *US* = PETHIDINE. [METHYL + PIPERIDINE]

Mephistopheles /mɛfɪˈstɒfɪliːz/ *n.* an evil spirit to whom Faust, in the German legend, sold his soul. □ **Mephistophelean** /-ˈfiːlɪən, -ˈliːən/ *adj.* (also **Mephistophelian**).

mephitis /mɪˈfʌɪtɪs/ *n.* **1** a noxious emanation, esp. from the earth. **2** a foul-smelling or poisonous stench. □ **mephitic** /-ˈfɪtɪk/ *adj.* [Latin]

-mer /mə/ *comb. form* denoting a compound or molecule of a specified class, esp. a polymer (*dimer*; *isomer*; *tautomer*). [Greek *meros* 'part, share']

meranti /məˈranti/ *n.* a white, red, or yellow hardwood timber from a Malaysian or Indonesian tree of the genus *Shorea*. [Malay]

mercantile /ˈməːk(ə)ntʌɪl/ *adj.* **1** of trade, trading. **2** commercial. **3** mercenary; fond of bargaining. [French from Italian, from *mercante* MERCHANT]

mercantile marine *n.* shipping employed in commerce not war.

mercantilism /ˈməːk(ə)ntɪlɪz(ə)m/ *n.* an old economic theory that money is the only form of wealth. □ **mercantilist** *n.*

mercaptan /məːˈkapt(ə)n/ *n.* = THIOL. [modern Latin *mercurium captans* 'capturing mercury']

Mercator projection /məːˈkeɪtə/ *n.* (also **Mercator's projection**) a projection of a map of the world on to a cylinder so that all the parallels of latitude have the same length as the equator, first published in 1569 and used esp. for marine charts and certain climatological maps. [*Mercator*, Latinized name of G. Kremer, Flemish-born geographer d. 1594]

mercenary /ˈməːsɪn(ə)ri/ *adj.* & *n.* ● *adj.* primarily concerned with money or other reward (*mercenary motives*). ● *n.* (*pl.* **-ies**) **1** a hired soldier in foreign service. **2** a person available for paid hire (*cricket mercenaries playing abroad*). □ **mercenariness** *n.* [Middle English from Latin *mercenarius*, from *merces -edis* 'reward']

mercer /ˈməːsə/ *n. Brit.* a dealer in textile fabrics, esp. silk and other costly materials. □ **mercery** *n.* (*pl.* **-ies**). [Middle English from Anglo-French *mercer*, Old French *mercier*, ultimately from Latin *merx mercis* 'goods']

mercerize /ˈməːsərʌɪz/ *v.tr.* (also **-ise**) treat (cotton fabric or thread) under tension with caustic alkali to give greater strength and impart lustre. [named after J. *Mercer* d. 1866, alleged inventor of the process]

merchandise /ˈməːtʃ(ə)ndʌɪz/ *n.* & *v.* ● *n.* goods for sale. ● *v.* **1** *intr.* trade, traffic. **2** *tr.* trade or traffic in. **3** *tr.* **a** put on the market, promote the sale of (goods etc.). **b** advertise or publicize (an idea or person). □ **merchandisable** *adj.* **merchandiser** *n.* [Middle English from Old French *marchandise*, from *marchand*: see MERCHANT]

merchant /ˈməːtʃ(ə)nt/ *n.* **1** a wholesale trader, esp. *Brit.* with foreign countries. **2** esp. *US* & *Sc.* a retail trader or in *comb.* (*wine merchant*). **3** *colloq.* usu. *derog.* a person showing a partiality for a specified activity or practice (*speed merchant*). [Middle English from Old French *marchand*, *marchant*, ultimately via Latin *mercari* 'trade' from *merx mercis* 'merchandise']

merchantable /ˈməːtʃ(ə)ntəb(ə)l/ *adj.* saleable, marketable. [Middle English from the verb *merchant* from Old French *marchander* from *marchand*: see MERCHANT]

merchant bank *n.* esp. *Brit.* a bank dealing in commercial loans and finance. □ **merchant banker** *n.*

merchantman /ˈməːtʃ(ə)ntmən/ *n.* (*pl.* **-men**) a ship conveying merchandise.

merchant marine *n. US* = MERCHANT NAVY.

merchant navy *n. Brit.* a nation's commercial shipping.

merchant prince *n.* a wealthy merchant.

merchant ship *n.* = MERCHANTMAN.

merciful /ˈməːsɪfʊl, -f(ə)l/ *adj.* having or showing or feeling mercy. □ **mercifulness** *n.*

mercifully /ˈməːsɪfʊli, -f(ə)li/ *adv.* **1** in a merciful manner. **2** (qualifying a whole sentence) fortunately (*mercifully, the sun came out*).

merciless /ˈməːsɪlɪs/ *adj.* **1** pitiless. **2** showing no mercy. □ **mercilessly** *adv.* **mercilessness** *n.*

mercurial /məːˈkjʊərɪəl/ *adj.* & *n.* ● *adj.* **1** (of a person) sprightly, ready-witted, volatile. **2** of or containing mercury. **3** (**Mercurial**) of the planet Mercury. ● *n.* a drug containing mercury. □ **mercuriality** /-ˈalɪti/ *n.* **mercurially** *adv.* [Middle English from Old French *mercuriel* or Latin *mercurialis* (as MERCURY)]

mercury /ˈməːkjʊri/ *n.* **1** *Chem.* a silvery-white heavy liquid metallic element occurring naturally in cinnabar and used in barometers, thermometers, and amalgams; also called *quicksilver* (symbol **Hg**). **2** (**Mercury**) the planet nearest to the sun. **3** any plant of the genus *Mercurialis*, esp. *M. perenne*. □ **mercuric** /-'kjʊərɪk/ *adj.* **mercurous** *adj.* [Middle English from Latin *Mercurius*, the name of the messenger of the gods and the god of traders, from *merx mercis* 'merchandise']

mercury vapour lamp *n.* a lamp in which light is produced by an electric discharge through mercury vapour.

mercy /'mə:si/ *n. & int.* ● *n.* (*pl.* **-ies**) **1** compassion or forbearance shown to enemies or offenders in one's power. **2** the quality of compassion. **3** an act of mercy. **4** (*attrib.*) administered or performed out of mercy or pity for a suffering person (*mercy killing*). **5** something to be thankful for (*small mercies*). ● *int.* expressing surprise or fear. □ **at the mercy of 1** wholly in the power of. **2** liable to danger or harm from. **have mercy on** (or **upon**) show mercy to. [Middle English via Old French *merci* from Latin *merces -edis* 'reward', in Late Latin 'pity, thanks']

mercy flight *n. Brit.* the transporting by air of an injured or sick person from a remote area to a hospital.

mere[1] /mɪə/ *attrib.adj.* (**merest**) that is solely or no more or better than what is specified (*a mere boy*; *no mere theory*). □ **merely** *adv.* [Middle English via Anglo-French *meer*, Old French *mier* from Latin *merus* 'unmixed']

mere[2] /mɪə/ *n. archaic* or *poet.* a lake or pond. [Old English from Germanic]

mere[3] /'mɛri/ *n.* a Maori war club, esp. one made of greenstone. [Maori]

mere right *n. Law* a right in theory.

meretricious /mɛrɪ'trɪʃəs/ *adj.* **1** (of decorations, literary style, etc.) showily but falsely attractive. **2** of or befitting a prostitute. □ **meretriciously** *adv.* **meretriciousness** *n.* [Latin *meretricius* via *meretrix -tricis* 'prostitute' from *merēri* 'be hired']

merganser /mə:'ganzə, -s-/ *n.* any of various diving fish-eating northern ducks of the genus *Mergus*, with a long narrow serrated hooked bill (cf. GOOSANDER). Also called *sawbill*. [modern Latin, from Latin *mergus* 'diver' (from *mergere* 'dive') + *anser* 'goose']

merge /mə:dʒ/ *v.* **1** *tr. & intr.* (often foll. by *with*) **a** combine or be combined. **b** join or blend gradually. **2** *intr. & tr.* (foll. by *in*) lose or cause to lose character and identity in (something else). **3** *tr.* (foll. by *in*) embody (a title or estate) in (a larger one). □ **mergence** *n.* [earlier = immerse (oneself): Latin *mergere mers-* 'dip, plunge', partly through legal Anglo-French *merger*]

merger /'mə:dʒə/ *n.* **1** the combining of two commercial companies etc. into one. **2** a merging, esp. of one estate in another. **3** *Law* the absorbing of a minor offence in a greater one. [Anglo-French (as MERGE)]

meridian /mə'rɪdɪən/ *n. & adj.* ● *n.* **1** a circle passing through the celestial poles and the zenith of a given place on the earth's surface. **2 a** a circle of constant longitude, passing through a given place and the terrestrial poles. **b** the corresponding line on a map. **3** *archaic* the point at which a sun or star attains its highest altitude. **4** prime; full splendour. ● *adj.* **1** of noon. **2** of the period of greatest splendour, vigour, etc. [Middle English via Old French *meridien* or Latin *meridianus* (*adj.*) from *meridies* 'midday', from *medius* 'middle' + *dies* 'day']

meridian circle *n. Astron.* a telescope mounted so as to move only on a north-south line, for observing the transit of celestial objects across the meridan. Also called *transit-circle*.

meridional /mə'rɪdɪən(ə)l/ *adj. & n.* ● *adj.* **1** of or in the south (esp. of Europe). **2** of or relating to a meridian. ● *n.* an inhabitant of the south (esp. of France). [Middle English via Old French from Late Latin *meridionalis*, formed irregularly from Latin *meridies*: see MERIDIAN]

meringue /mə'raŋ/ *n.* **1** a confection of sugar, the white of eggs, etc., baked crisp. **2** a small cake or shell of this, usu. decorated or filled with whipped cream etc. [French, of unknown origin]

merino /mə'ri:nəʊ/ *n.* (*pl.* **-os**) **1** (in full **merino sheep**) a variety of sheep with long fine wool. **2** a soft woollen or wool-and-cotton material like cashmere, originally of merino wool. **3** a fine woollen yarn. [Spanish, of uncertain origin]

meristem /'mɛrɪstɛm/ *n. Bot.* a plant tissue consisting of actively dividing cells forming new tissue. □ **meristematic** /-stə'matɪk/ *adj.* [Greek *meristos* 'divisible', via *merizō* 'divide' from *meros* 'part': *-em* on the pattern of *xylem*]

merit /'mɛrɪt/ *n. & v.* ● *n.* **1** the quality of deserving well. **2** excellence, worth. **3** (usu. in *pl.*) **a** a thing that entitles one to reward or gratitude. **b** esp. *Law* intrinsic rights and wrongs (*the merits of a case*). **4** *Theol.* good deeds as entitling to a future reward. ● *v.tr.* (**merited**, **meriting**) deserve or be worthy of (reward, punishment, consideration, etc.). □ **make a merit of** regard or represent (one's own conduct) as praiseworthy. **on its merits** with regard only to its intrinsic worth. [Middle English via Old French *merite* from Latin *meritum* 'price, value', past part. of *merēri* 'earn, deserve', used as a noun]

meritocracy /mɛrɪ'tɒkrəsi/ *n.* (*pl.* **-ies**) **1** government by persons selected competitively according to merit. **2** a group of persons selected in this way. **3** a society governed by meritocracy. □ **meritocratic** /-tə'kratɪk/ *adj.*

meritorious /mɛrɪ'tɔ:rɪəs/ *adj.* (of a person or act) having merit; deserving reward, praise, or gratitude. □ **meritoriously** *adv.* **meritoriousness** *n.* [Middle English from Latin *meritorius*, from *merēri merit-* 'earn']

merle /mə:l/ *n. Sc.* or *archaic* a blackbird. [Middle English via French from Latin *merula*]

merlin /'mə:lɪn/ *n.* a small European or N. American falcon, *Falco columbarius*, that hunts small birds. [Middle English via Anglo-French *merilun* from Old French *esmerillon*, augmentative of *esmeril*, from Frankish]

merlon /'mə:lən/ *n.* the solid part of an embattled parapet between two embrasures. [French from Italian *merlone*, from *merlo* 'battlement']

Merlot /'mə:ləʊ, -lɒt/ *n.* **1** a variety of black grape used in wine-making. **2** the vine on which this grape grows. **3** a red wine made from Merlot grapes.

mermaid /'mə:meɪd/ *n.* an imaginary half-human sea creature, with the head and trunk of a woman and the tail of a fish. [Middle English, from MERE[2] (in obsolete sense 'sea') + MAID]

mermaid's purse *n.* the horny egg-case of a skate, ray, or shark; a sea purse.

merman /'mə:man/ *n.* (*pl.* **-men**) the male equivalent of a mermaid.

mero- /'mɛrəʊ/ *comb. form* partly, partial. [Greek *meros* 'part']

-merous /mərəs/ *comb. form* esp. *Bot.* having so many parts (*dimerous*; *5-merous*). [Greek (as MERO-)]

Merovingian /mɛrə'vɪn(d)ʒɪən/ *adj. & n.* ● *adj.* of or relating to the Frankish dynasty founded by Clovis and reigning in Gaul and Germany *c.*500–750. ● *n.* a member of this dynasty. [French *mérovingien* via medieval Latin *Merovingi* from Latin *Meroveus*, the name of the reputed founder]

merriment /'mɛrɪm(ə)nt/ *n.* **1** exuberant enjoyment; being merry. **2** mirth, fun.

merry /'mɛri/ *adj.* (**merrier**, **merriest**) **1 a** joyous. **b** full of laughter or gaiety. **2** *Brit. colloq.* slightly drunk. □ **make merry 1** be festive; enjoy oneself. **2** (foll. by *over*) make fun of. **play merry hell with** see HELL. □ **merrily** *adv.* **merriness** *n.* [Old English *myrige*, from Germanic]

merry andrew *n. hist.* a mountebank's assistant; a clown or buffoon.

merry-go-round /'mɛrɪgə(ʊ)raʊnd/ *n.* **1** a revolving machine with wooden horses or cars for riding on at a fair etc. **2** a cycle of bustling activities.

merrymaking /ˈmɛrɪmeɪkɪŋ/ *n.* revelling, fun. □ **merrymaker** *n.*

merry thought *n.* esp. *Brit.* the wishbone of a bird.

mesa /ˈmeɪsə/ *n.* an isolated flat-topped hill with steep sides, found in landscapes with horizontal strata. [Spanish, literally 'table', from Latin *mensa*]

mésalliance /mɛˈzalɪəns, French mezaljɑ̃s/ *n.* a marriage with a person of a lower social position. [French (as MIS-², ALLIANCE)]

mescal /ˈmɛskal, mɛˈskal/ *n.* **1 a** maguey. **b** liquor obtained from this. **2** a peyote cactus. [Spanish *mezcal* from Nahuatl *mexcalli*]

mescal buttons *n.pl.* disc-shaped dried tops from the peyote cactus, eaten or chewed as an intoxicant.

mescaline /ˈmɛskəliːn/ *n.* (also **mescalin** /-lɪn/) a hallucinogenic alkaloid present in mescal buttons.

Mesdames *pl.* of MADAME.

Mesdemoiselles *pl.* of MADEMOISELLE.

mesembryanthemum /mɪˌzɛmbrɪˈanθɪməm/ *n.* any of various succulent plants of the genus *Mesembryanthemum* of S. Africa, having brightly coloured daisy-like flowers that fully open in sunlight. [modern Latin, from Greek *mesēmbria* 'noon' + *anthemon* 'flower']

mesencephalon /mɛsɛnˈsɛf(ə)lɒn, miːz-, -ˈkɛf-/ *n. Anat.* = MIDBRAIN. [Greek *mesos* 'middle' + ENCEPHALON]

mesentery /ˈmɛs(ə)nt(ə)ri/ *n.* (*pl.* **-ies**) a double layer of peritoneum attaching the stomach, small intestine, pancreas, spleen, and other abdominal organs to the posterior wall of the abdomen. □ **mesenteric** /-ˈtɛrɪk/ *adj.* **mesenteritis** /-ˈrʌɪtɪs/ *n.* [medieval Latin *mesenterium* from Greek *mesenterion* (as MESO-, *enteron* 'intestine')]

mesh /mɛʃ/ *n.* & *v.* ● *n.* **1** a network fabric or structure. **2** each of the open spaces or interstices between the strands of a net or sieve etc. **3** (in *pl.*) **a** a network. **b** a snare. **4** (in *pl.*) *Physiol.* an interlaced structure. ● *v.* **1** *intr.* (often foll. by *with*) (of the teeth of a wheel) be engaged (with others). **2** *intr.* be harmonious. **3** *tr.* catch in or as in a net. □ **in mesh** (of the teeth of wheels) engaged. [earlier *meish* etc. from Middle Dutch *maesche*, from Germanic]

mesial /ˈmiːzɪəl, ˈmɛsɪəl/ *adj. Anat.* of, in, or directed towards the middle line of a body. □ **mesially** *adv.* [formed irregularly from Greek *mesos* 'middle']

mesmerism /ˈmɛzmərɪz(ə)m/ *n.* **1** *Psychol.* **a** a hypnotic state produced in a person by another's influence over the will and nervous system. **b** a doctrine concerning this. **c** an influence or process producing this. **2** fascination. □ **mesmeric** /mɛzˈmɛrɪk/ *adj.* **mesmerically** /-ˈmɛrɪk(ə)li/ *adv.* **mesmerist** *n.* [named after F. A. *Mesmer*, Austrian physician d. 1815]

mesmerize /ˈmɛzmərʌɪz/ *v.tr.* (also **-ise**) **1** *Psychol.* hypnotize; exercise mesmerism on. **2** fascinate, spellbind. □ **mesmerization** /-ˈzeɪʃ(ə)n/ *n.* **mesmerizer** *n.* **mesmerizingly** *adv.*

mesne /miːn/ *adj. Law* intermediate. [Middle English from legal French, variant of Anglo-French *meen*, MEAN³: cf. DEMESNE]

mesne lord *n. hist.* a lord holding an estate from a superior feudal lord.

mesne process *n.* proceedings in a suit intervening between a primary and final process.

mesne profits *n.pl.* profits received from an estate by a tenant between two dates.

meso- /ˈmɛsəʊ, ˈmɛzəʊ, ˈmiːsəʊ, ˈmiːzəʊ/ *comb. form* middle, intermediate. [Greek *mesos* 'middle']

mesoblast /ˈmɛsə(ʊ)blast, ˈmɛz-, ˈmiːs-, ˈmiːz-/ *n. Biol.* the middle germ layer of an embryo.

mesocephalic /ˌmɛsə(ʊ)sɪˈfalɪk, ˌmɛz-, ˌmiːs-, ˌmiːz-, -kɛˈfalɪk/ *adj.* having a medium-sized head, not especially broad or narrow. [MESO- + -CEPHALIC]

mesoderm /ˈmɛsə(ʊ)dəːm, ˈmɛz-, ˈmiːs-, ˈmiːz-/ *n. Zool.* the middle layer of an embryo in early development. □ **mesodermal** /mɛsə(ʊ)ˈdəːm(ə)l, mɛz-, miːs-, miːz-/ *adj.* [MESO- + Greek *derma* 'skin']

mesolithic /mɛsə(ʊ)ˈlɪθɪk, mɛz-, miːs-, miːz-/ *adj.* & *n. Archaeol.* ● *adj.* of or relating to the middle phase of the Stone Age, lasting from the end of the last ice age to the start of agriculture. ● *n.* the mesolithic period. [MESO- + Greek *lithos* 'stone']

mesomorph /ˈmɛsə(ʊ)mɔːf, ˈmɛz-, miːs-, ˈmiːz-/ *n.* a person with a compact and muscular build of body (cf. ECTOMORPH, ENDOMORPH). □ **mesomorphic** /-ˈmɔːfɪk/ *adj.* [MESO- + Greek *morphē* 'form']

meson /ˈmiːzɒn, ˈmɛzɒn/ *n. Physics* any of a class of subatomic particles believed to participate in the forces that hold nucleons together in the atomic nucleus. □ **mesic** /ˈmiːzɪk, ˈmɛz-/ *adj.* **mesonic** /mɪˈzɒnɪk/ *adj.* [as MESO-, -ON]

mesopause /ˈmɛsə(ʊ)pɔːz, ˈmɛz-, ˈmiːs-, ˈmiːz-/ *n.* the boundary in the atmosphere between the mesosphere and the thermosphere, at which the temperature stops decreasing with increasing height and begins to increase.

mesophyll /ˈmɛsə(ʊ)fɪl, ˈmɛz-, ˈmiːs-, ˈmiːz-/ *n. Bot.* the inner tissue of a leaf, containing many chloroplasts. [MESO- + Greek *phullon* 'leaf']

mesophyte /ˈmɛsə(ʊ)fʌɪt, ˈmɛz-, ˈmiːs-, ˈmiːz-/ *n.* a plant needing only a moderate amount of water.

mesosphere /ˈmɛsə(ʊ)sfɪə, ˈmɛz-, ˈmiːs-, ˈmiːz-/ *n.* the region of the atmosphere extending about 80 km from the top of the stratosphere.

Mesozoic /mɛsə(ʊ)ˈzəʊɪk, mɛz-, miːs-, miːz-/ *adj.* & *n. Geol.* ● *adj.* of or relating to an era of geological time marked by the development of dinosaurs, and with evidence of the first mammals, birds, and flowering plants. Cf. Appendix X. ● *n.* this era (cf. CENOZOIC, PALAEOZOIC). [MESO- + Greek *zōion* 'animal']

mesquite /ˈmɛskiːt, mɛˈskiːt/ *n.* (also **mesquit**) any N. American leguminous tree of the genus *Prosopis*, esp. *P. glandulosa*. [Mexican Spanish *mezquite*]

mesquite bean *n.* a pod from the mesquite, used as fodder.

mess /mɛs/ *n.* & *v.* ● *n.* **1** a dirty or untidy state of things (*the room is a mess*). **2** a state of confusion, embarrassment, or trouble. **3** something causing a mess, e.g. spilt liquid etc. **4** a domestic animal's excreta. **5 a** a company of persons who take meals together, esp. in the armed forces. **b** a place where such meals or recreation take place communally. **c** a meal taken there. **6** *derog.* a disagreeable concoction or medley. **7 a** a portion of liquid or pulpy food. **b** *Brit.* a liquid or mixed food for hounds etc. ● *v.* **1** *tr.* (often foll. by *up*) **a** make a mess of; dirty. **b** muddle; make into a state of confusion. **2** *intr.* (foll. by *with*) interfere with. **3** *intr.* take one's meals. **4** *intr.* & *tr. colloq.* defecate or soil by defecating. □ **make a mess of** bungle (an undertaking). **mess about** (or **around**) **1** act desultorily. **2** *colloq.* make things awkward for; cause arbitrary inconvenience to (a person). [Middle English via Old French *mes* 'portion of food' from Late Latin *missus* 'course at dinner', past part. of *mittere* 'send']

message /ˈmɛsɪdʒ/ *n.* & *v.* ● *n.* **1** an oral or written communication sent by one person to another. **2** an inspired or significant communication from a prophet, writer, or preacher. **3** a mission or errand. **4** (in *pl.*) *Sc.* & *N.Engl.* things bought; shopping. ● *v.tr.* **1** send as a message. **2** transmit (a plan etc.) by signalling etc. □ **get the message** *colloq.* understand what is meant. [Middle English from Old French, ultimately from Latin *mittere miss-* 'send']

message stick *n. Austral.* a stick carved with significant marks, carried as identification by Aboriginal messengers.

Messeigneurs *pl.* of MONSEIGNEUR.

messenger /ˈmɛsɪn(d)ʒə/ *n.* **1** a person who carries a message. **2** a person employed to carry messages. [Middle English & Old French *messager* (as MESSAGE): *-n-* as in *harbinger*, *passenger*, etc.]

messenger RNA *n.* the form of RNA in which genetic information transcribed from DNA as a sequence of bases is transferred to a ribosome (abbr.: **mRNA**).

mess hall *n.* a military dining area.

Messiah /mɪˈsʌɪə/ *n.* **1** a liberator or would-be liberator of an oppressed people or country. **2 a** the promised deliverer of the Jews. **b** (usu. prec. by *the*) Christ regarded as this. □ **Messiahship** *n.* [Middle English from Old French *Messie*, ultimately from Hebrew *māšîaḥ* 'anointed']

Messianic /mɛsɪˈanɪk/ *adj.* **1** of the Messiah. **2** inspired by hope or belief in a Messiah. □ **Messianism** /mɪˈsʌɪənɪz(ə)m/ *n.* [French *messianique* (as MESSIAH), on the pattern of *rabbinique* 'rabbinical']

Messieurs *pl.* of MONSIEUR.

mess jacket *n. Mil.* a short close-fitting coat worn at the mess.

mess kit *n.* a soldier's cooking and eating utensils.

messmate /ˈmɛsmeɪt/ *n.* a person with whom one regularly takes meals, esp. in the armed forces.

mess of pottage *n.* a material comfort etc. for which something higher is sacrificed. [with reference to the story of how Jacob tricks his brother Esau into exchanging his birthright for a helping of food (Gen. 25:29–34)]

Messrs /ˈmɛsəz/ *pl.* of MR. [abbreviation of MESSIEURS]

mess tin *n.* a small container as part of a mess kit.

messuage /ˈmɛswɪdʒ/ *n. Law* a dwelling house with outbuildings and land assigned to its use. [Middle English from Anglo-French: perhaps an alternative form of *mesnage* 'dwelling']

messy /ˈmɛsi/ *adj.* (**messier**, **messiest**) **1** untidy or dirty. **2** causing or accompanied by a mess. **3** difficult to deal with; full of awkward complications. □ **messily** *adv.* **messiness** *n.*

mestizo /mɛˈstiːzəʊ/ *n.* (*pl.* **-os**; *fem.* **mestiza** /-zə/, *pl.* **-as**) a Spaniard or Portuguese of mixed race, esp. the offspring of a Spaniard and an American Indian. [Spanish, ultimately from Latin *mixtus*, past part. of *miscēre* 'mix']

met[1] *past* and *past part.* of MEET[1].

met[2] /mɛt/ *adj. colloq.* **1** meteorological. **2** metropolitan. **3** (**the Met**) **a** (in full **the Met Office**) (in the UK) the Meteorological Office. **b** the Metropolitan Police in London. **c** the Metropolitan Opera House in New York. [abbreviation]

meta- /ˈmɛtə/ *comb. form* (usu. **met-** before a vowel or *h*) **1** denoting change of position or condition (*metabolism*). **2** denoting position: **a** behind. **b** after or beyond (*metaphysics*; *metacarpus*). **c** of a higher or second-order kind (*metalanguage*). **3** *Chem.* **a** relating to two carbon atoms separated by one other in a benzene ring. **b** relating to a compound formed by dehydration (*metaphosphate*). [Greek *meta-*, *met-*, *meth-* from *meta* 'with, after']

metabolism /mɪˈtabəlɪz(ə)m/ *n.* all the chemical processes that occur within a living organism, resulting in energy production (**destructive metabolism**) and growth (**constructive metabolism**). □ **metabolic** /mɛtəˈbɒlɪk/ *adj.* **metabolically** /mɛtəˈbɒlɪk(ə)li/ *adv.* [Greek *metabolē* 'change' (as META-, *bolē* from *ballō* 'throw')]

metabolite /mɪˈtabəlʌɪt/ *n. Physiol.* a substance formed in or necessary for metabolism.

metabolize /mɪˈtabəlʌɪz/ *v.tr. & intr.* (also **-ise**) process or be processed by metabolism. □ **metabolizable** *adj.*

metacarpus /mɛtəˈkɑːpəs/ *n.* (*pl.* **metacarpi** /-pʌɪ, -piː/) **1** the set of five bones of the hand that connects the wrist to the fingers. **2** this part of the hand. □ **metacarpal** *adj.* [modern Latin from Greek *metakarpon* (as META-, CARPUS)]

metacentre /ˈmɛtəsɛntə/ *n.* (*US* **metacenter**) the point of intersection between a line (vertical in equilibrium) through the centre of gravity of a floating body and a vertical line through the centre of pressure after a slight angular displacement, which must be above the centre of gravity to ensure stability. □ **metacentric** /-ˈsɛntrɪk/ *adj.* [French *métacentre* (as META-, CENTRE)]

metage /ˈmiːtɪdʒ/ *n.* **1** the official measuring of a load of coal etc. **2** the duty paid for this. [METE[1] + -AGE]

metagenesis /mɛtəˈdʒɛnɪsɪs/ *n.* the alternation of generations between sexual and asexual reproduction. □ **metagenetic** /-dʒɪˈnɛtɪk/ *adj.* [modern Latin (as META-, GENESIS)]

metal /ˈmɛt(ə)l/ *n., adj., & v.* ● *n.* **1 a** any of a class of substances (including many chemical elements) which are in general lustrous, malleable, fusible, ductile solids and good conductors of heat and electricity, e.g. gold, silver, iron, brass, steel. **b** material of this kind. **2** material used for making glass, in a molten state. **3** *Heraldry* gold or silver as tincture. **4** (in *pl.*) the rails of a railway line. **5** = ROAD METAL. ● *adj.* made of metal. ● *v.tr.* (**metalled**, **metalling**; *US* **metaled**, **metaling**) **1** provide or fit with metal. **2** *Brit.* make or mend (a road) with road metal. [Middle English via Old French *metal* or Latin *metallum* from Greek *metallon* 'mine']

metalanguage /ˈmɛtəlaŋgwɪdʒ/ *n.* **1** a form of language used to discuss a language. **2** a system of propositions about propositions.

metal detector *n.* an electronic device giving a signal when it locates metal.

metal fatigue *n.* fatigue (see FATIGUE *n.* 2) in metal.

metalinguistics /mɛtəlɪŋˈgwɪstɪks/ *n.* the branch of linguistics that deals with metalanguages. □ **metalinguistic** *adj.*

metallic /mɪˈtalɪk/ *adj.* **1** of, consisting of, or characteristic of metal or metals. **2** sounding sharp and ringing, like struck metal. **3** having the sheen or lustre of metals. □ **metallically** *adv.* [Latin *metallicus* from Greek *metallikos* (as METAL)]

metalliferous /mɛtəˈlɪf(ə)rəs/ *adj.* bearing or producing metal. [Latin *metallifer* (as METAL, -FEROUS)]

metallize /ˈmɛt(ə)lʌɪz/ *v.tr.* (also **-ise**; *US* **metalize**) **1** render metallic. **2** coat with a thin layer of metal. □ **metallization** /-ˈzeɪʃ(ə)n/ *n.*

metallography /mɛtəˈlɒgrəfi/ *n.* the descriptive science of the structure and properties of metals. □ **metallographic** /mɪˌtaləˈgrafɪk/ *adj.* **metallographical** /mɪˌtaləˈgrafɪk(ə)l/ *adj.* **metallographically** /mɪˌtaləˈgrafɪk(ə)li/ *adv.*

metalloid /ˈmɛt(ə)lɔɪd/ *adj. & n.* ● *adj.* having the form or appearance of a metal. ● *n.* any element intermediate in properties between metals and non-metals, e.g. boron, silicon, and germanium.

metallurgy /mɪˈtalədʒi, ˈmɛt(ə)ləːdʒi/ *n.* the science concerned with the production, purification, and properties of metals and their application. □ **metallurgic** /mɛtəˈləːdʒɪk/ *adj.* **metallurgical** /mɛtəˈləːdʒɪk(ə)l/ *adj.* **metallurgically** /mɛtəˈləːdʒɪk(ə)li/ *adv.* **metallurgist** *n.* [Greek *metallon* 'metal' + *-ourgia* 'working']

metalwork /ˈmɛt(ə)lwəːk/ *n.* **1** the art of working in metal. **2** metal objects collectively. □ **metalworker** *n.* **metalworking** *n. & attrib.adj.*

metamere /ˈmɛtəmɪə/ *n. Zool.* each of several similar body segments containing the same internal structures e.g. in an earthworm. [META- + Greek *meros* 'part']

metameric /mɛtəˈmɛrɪk/ *adj.* **1** *Chem.* having the same proportional composition and molecular weight, but different functional groups and chemical properties. **2** *Zool.* of or relating to metameres. □ **metamer** /ˈmɛtəmə/ *n.* **metamerism** /mɪˈtamərɪz(ə)m/ *n.*

metamorphic /mɛtəˈmɔːfɪk/ *adj.* **1** of or marked by metamorphosis. **2** *Geol.* (of rock) that has undergone transformation by natural agencies such as heat and pressure. □ **metamorphism** *n.* [META- + Greek *morphē* 'form']

metamorphose /mɛtəˈmɔːfəʊz/ *v.tr.* **1** change in form. **2** (foll. by *to*, *into*) **a** turn (into a new form). **b** change the nature of. [French *métamorphoser* from *métamorphose* METAMORPHOSIS]

metamorphosis /mɛtəˈmɔːfəsɪs, mɛtəmɔːˈfəʊsɪs/ *n.* (*pl.* **metamorphoses** /-siːz/) **1** a change of form (by natural or supernatural means). **2** a changed form. **3** a change of character, conditions, etc. **4** *Zool.* the transformation between an immature form and an adult form, e.g. from a pupa to an insect, or from a tadpole to a frog. [Latin from Greek *metamorphōsis*, from *metamorphoō* 'transform' (as META-, *morphoō* from *morphē* 'form')]

metaphase /ˈmɛtəfeɪz/ *n. Biol.* the stage of meiotic or mitotic cell division when the chromosomes become attached to the spindle fibres.

metaphor /ˈmɛtəfə, -fɔː/ *n.* **1 a** the application of a name or descriptive term or phrase to an object or action to which it is imaginatively but not literally applicable (e.g. *a glaring error*). **b** an instance of this. **2** (often foll. by *of* or *for*) a symbol of a usu. abstract thing (*the lark was a metaphor for release*). □ **metaphoric** /-ˈfɒrɪk/ *adj.* **metaphorical** /-ˈfɒrɪk(ə)l/ *adj.* **metaphorically** /-ˈfɒrɪk(ə)li/ *adv.* [French *métaphore* or Latin *metaphora* from Greek *metaphora*, from *metapherō* 'transfer']

metaphrase /ˈmɛtəfreɪz/ *n.* & *v.* ● *n.* literal translation. ● *v.tr.* put into other words. □ **metaphrastic** /-ˈfrastɪk/ *adj.* [modern Latin *metaphrasis* from Greek, from *metaphrazō* 'translate']

metaphysic /mɛtəˈfɪzɪk/ *n.* a system of metaphysics.

metaphysical /mɛtəˈfɪzɪk(ə)l/ *adj.* & *n.* ● *adj.* **1** of or relating to metaphysics. **2** based on abstract general reasoning. **3** excessively subtle or theoretical. **4** incorporeal; supernatural. **5** visionary. **6** (of certain 17th-c. English poets or their poetry) exhibiting subtlety of thought and complex imagery. ● *n.* (**the Metaphysicals**) the metaphysical poets. □ **metaphysically** *adv.*

metaphysics /mɛtəˈfɪzɪks/ *n.pl.* (usu. treated as *sing.*) **1** the theoretical philosophy of being and knowing. **2** the philosophy of mind. **3** *colloq.* abstract or subtle talk; mere theory. □ **metaphysician** /-ˈzɪʃ(ə)n/ *n.* **metaphysicize** /-ˈfɪzɪsʌɪz/ *v.intr.* (also **-ise**). [Middle English *metaphysic* via Old French *metaphysique* from medieval Latin *metaphysica*, ultimately from Greek *ta meta ta phusika* 'the things after the Physics', from the sequence of Aristotle's works]

metaplasia /mɛtəˈpleɪzɪə/ *n. Physiol.* an abnormal change in the nature of a tissue. □ **metaplastic** /-ˈplastɪk/ *adj.* [modern Latin via German *Metaplase* from Greek *metaplasis* (as META-, *plasis* from *plassō* 'to mould')]

metapsychology /mɛtəsʌɪˈkɒlədʒi/ *n.* the study of the nature and functions of the mind beyond what can be studied experimentally. □ **metapsychological** /-kəˈlɒdʒɪk(ə)l/ *adj.*

metastable /mɛtəˈsteɪb(ə)l/ *adj.* **1** (of a state of equilibrium) stable only under small disturbances. **2** (of a substance etc.) technically unstable but so long-lived as to be stable for practical purposes. □ **metastability** /-stəˈbɪlɪti/ *n.*

metastasis /mɪˈtastəsɪs/ *n.* (*pl.* **metastases** /-siːz/) *Med.* **1** the transfer of a disease etc. from one part of the body to another; esp. the development of secondary tumours at a distance from a primary site of cancer. **2** a secondary tumour. □ **metastasize** *v.intr.* (also **-ise**). **metastatic** /mɛtəˈstatɪk/ *adj.* [Late Latin from Greek, from *methistēmi* 'change']

metatarsus /mɛtəˈtɑːsəs/ *n.* (*pl.* **metatarsi** /-sʌɪ, -siː/) **1** the part of the foot between the ankle and the toes. **2** the set of bones in this. □ **metatarsal** *adj.* [modern Latin (as META-, TARSUS)]

metathesis /mɪˈtaθɪsɪs/ *n.* (*pl.* **metatheses** /-siːz/) **1** *Gram.* the transposition of sounds or letters in a word. **2** *Chem.* the interchange of atoms or groups of atoms between two molecules; double decomposition. **3** an instance of either of these. □ **metathetic** /mɛtəˈθɛtɪk/ *adj.* **metathetical** /mɛtəˈθɛtɪk(ə)l/ *adj.* [Late Latin from Greek *metatithēmi* 'transpose']

metazoan /mɛtəˈzəʊən/ *n.* & *adj. Zool.* ● *n.* any animal of the subkingdom Metazoa, having multicellular and differentiated tissues and comprising all animals except protozoa and sponges. ● *adj.* of or relating to the Metazoans. [*Metazoa*, from Greek META- + *zōia*, pl. of *zōion* 'animal']

mete[1] /miːt/ *v.tr.* **1** (usu. foll. by *out*) *literary* apportion or allot (a punishment or reward). **2** *poet.* or *Bibl.* measure. [Old English *metan* from Germanic: related to MEET[1]]

mete[2] /miːt/ *n.* a boundary or boundary stone. [Middle English via Old French from Latin *meta* 'boundary, goal']

metempsychosis /ˌmɛtɛmpsʌɪˈkəʊsɪs/ *n.* (*pl.* **-psychoses** /-siːz/) **1** the supposed transmigration of the soul of a human being or animal at death into a new body of the same or a different species. **2** an instance of this. □ **metempsychosist** *n.* [Late Latin from Greek *metempsukhōsis* (as META-, EN-[2], *psukhē* 'soul')]

meteor /ˈmiːtɪə, -tɪɔː/ *n.* a small body of matter from outer space that becomes incandescent as a result of friction with the earth's atmosphere and is visible as a streak of light. [Middle English via modern Latin *meteorum* from Greek *meteōron*, neut. of *meteōros* 'lofty' (as META-, *aeirō* 'raise')]

meteoric /miːtɪˈɒrɪk/ *adj.* **1 a** of, relating to, or derived from the atmosphere. **b** (of a plant) dependent on atmospheric conditions. **2** of meteors or meteorites. **3** rapid like a meteor; dazzling, transient (*meteoric rise to fame*). □ **meteorically** *adv.*

meteoric stone *n.* a meteorite.

meteorite /ˈmiːtɪərʌɪt/ *n.* a rock or metal fragment formed from a meteor of sufficient size to reach the earth's surface without burning up completely in the atmosphere. □ **meteoritic** /-ˈrɪtɪk/ *adj.*

meteorograph /ˈmiːtɪərəgrɑːf/ *n.* an apparatus that records several meteorological phenomena at the same time. [French *météorographe* (as METEOR, -GRAPH)]

meteoroid /ˈmiːtɪərɔɪd/ *n.* any small body moving in the solar system that becomes visible as it passes through the earth's atmosphere as a meteor. □ **meteoroidal** /-ˈrɔɪd(ə)l/ *adj.*

meteorology /miːtɪəˈrɒlədʒi/ *n.* **1** the study of the processes and phenomena of the atmosphere, esp. as a means of forecasting the weather. **2** the atmospheric character of a region. □ **meteorological** /-rəˈlɒdʒɪk(ə)l/ *adj.* **meteorologically** /-rəˈlɒdʒɪk(ə)li/ *adv.* **meteorologist** *n.* [Greek *meteōrologia* (as METEOR)]

meteor shower *n.* a group of meteors appearing to come from one point in the sky, esp. around a particular date each year.

meter[1] /ˈmiːtə/ *n.* & *v.* ● *n.* **1** a person or thing that measures, esp. an instrument for recording a quantity of gas, electricity, etc. supplied, present, or needed. **2** = PARKING METER. ● *v.tr.* measure by means of a meter. [Middle English, from METE[1] + -ER[1]]

meter[2] *US* var. of METRE[1].

meter[3] *US* var. of METRE[2].

-meter /mɪtə/ *comb. form* **1** forming nouns denoting measuring instruments (*barometer*). **2** *Prosody* forming nouns denoting lines of poetry with a specified number of measures (*pentameter*).

methadone /ˈmɛθədəʊn/ *n.* a potent narcotic analgesic drug used to relieve severe pain, as a linctus to suppress coughs, and as a substitute for morphine or heroin. [chemical name 6-di*methy*lamino-4,4-*d*iphenyl-3-heptan*one*]

methamphetamine /mɛθamˈfɛtəmiːn, -mɪ/ *n.* an amphetamine derivative with quicker and longer action, used as a stimulant. Also called *methedrine.* [METHYL + AMPHETAMINE]

methanal /ˈmɛθənal/ *n. Chem.* = FORMALDEHYDE. [METHANE + ALDEHYDE]

methane /ˈmiːθeɪn, ˈmɛθeɪn/ *n. Chem.* a colourless odourless inflammable gaseous hydrocarbon, the simplest in the alkane series, and the main constituent of natural gas. Also called *marsh gas.* Chem. formula: CH_4. [METHYL + -ANE[2]]

methanoic acid /mɛθəˈnəʊɪk/ *n. Chem.* = FORMIC ACID. [METHANE + -IC]

methanol /ˈmɛθənɒl/ *n. Chem.* a colourless volatile inflammable liquid, used as a solvent (also called *methyl alcohol*). Chem. formula: CH_3OH. [METHANE + -OL[1]]

methedrine /ˈmɛθədrɪn, -driːn/ *n. propr.* = METHAMPHETAMINE. [METHYL + BENZEDRINE]

methinks /mɪˈθɪŋks/ *v.intr.* (*past* **methought** /mɪˈθɔːt/) *archaic* it seems to me. [Old English *mē thyncth*, from *mē*, dative of ME[1] + *thyncth*, 3rd sing. of *thyncan* 'seem, THINK']

methionine /mɪˈθʌɪəniːn/ *n. Biochem.* an amino acid which contains sulphur and is an important constituent of proteins. [METHYL + Greek *theion* 'sulphur']

metho /ˈmɛθəʊ/ *n.* (*pl.* **-os**) *Austral. slang* **1** methylated spirit. **2** a person addicted to drinking methylated spirit. [abbreviation]

method /ˈmɛθəd/ *n.* **1** a special form of procedure esp. in any branch of mental activity. **2** orderliness; regular habits. **3** the orderly arrangement of ideas. **4** a scheme of classification. **5** *Theatr.* a technique of acting based on the actor's thorough emotional identification with the character. □ **method in one's madness** sense in what appears to be foolish or strange behaviour. [French *méthode* or Latin *methodus* from Greek *methodos* 'pursuit of knowledge' (as META-, *hodos* 'way')]

méthode champenoise /meɪˌtəʊd ʃɒ̃pənˈwɑːz/ *n.* **1** the method of introducing a sparkle into wine by allowing the last stage of fermentation to take place in the bottle. **2** a sparkling wine made in this way. [French, = champagne method]

methodical /mɪˈθɒdɪk(ə)l/ *adj.* (also **methodic**) characterized by method or order. □ **methodically** *adv.* [Late Latin *methodicus* from Greek *methodikos* (as METHOD)]

Methodist /ˈmɛθədɪst/ *n. & adj.* ● *n.* **1** a member of any of several Protestant religious bodies (now united) originating in the 18th-c. evangelistic movement of Charles and John Wesley and George Whitefield. **2** (**methodist**) a person who follows or advocates a particular method or system of procedure. ● *adj.* of or relating to Methodists or Methodism. □ **Methodism** *n.* **Methodistic** /-ˈdɪstɪk/ *adj.* **Methodistical** /-ˈdɪstɪk(ə)l/ *adj.* [modern Latin *methodista* (as METHOD): sense 1 probably from following a specified 'method' of devotional study]

methodize /ˈmɛθədʌɪz/ *v.tr.* (also **-ise**) **1** reduce to order. **2** arrange in an orderly manner. □ **methodizer** *n.*

methodology /mɛθəˈdɒlədʒi/ *n.* (*pl.* **-ies**) **1** the science of method. **2** a body of methods used in a particular branch of activity. □ **methodological** /-dəˈlɒdʒɪk(ə)l/ *adj.* **methodologically** /-dəˈlɒdʒɪk(ə)li/ *adv.* **methodologist** *n.* [modern Latin *methodologia* or French *méthodologie* (as METHOD)]

methought *past* of METHINKS.

meths /mɛθs/ *n. Brit. colloq.* methylated spirit. [abbreviation]

Methuselah /mɪˈθ(j)uːz(ə)lə/ *n.* **1** a very old person or thing. **2** (**methuselah**) a wine bottle of about eight times the standard size. [Middle English: the name of a patriarch said to have lived 969 years (Gen. 5:27)]

methyl /ˈmiːθʌɪl, ˈmɛθ-, -θɪl/ *n. Chem.* the monovalent hydrocarbon radical $-CH_3$, present in many organic compounds. □ **methylic** /mɪˈθɪlɪk/ *adj.* [German *Methyl* or French *méthyle*, back-formation from German *Methylen*, French *méthylène*: see METHYLENE]

methyl alcohol *n.* = METHANOL.

methylate /ˈmɛθɪleɪt/ *v.tr.* **1** mix or impregnate with methanol. **2** introduce a methyl group into (a molecule or compound). □ **methylation** /-ˈleɪʃ(ə)n/ *n.*

methylated spirit *n.* (also **methylated spirits**) alcohol saturated with methanol to make it unfit for drinking and exempt from duty.

methylbenzene *n.* /miːθʌɪlˈbɛnziːn/ = TOLUENE.

methylene /ˈmɛθɪliːn/ *n. Chem.* the highly reactive divalent group of atoms CH_2. [French *méthylène*, from Greek *methu* 'wine' + *hulē* 'wood' + -ENE]

metic /ˈmɛtɪk/ *n. Gk Antiq.* an alien living in a Greek city with some privileges of citizenship. [formed irregularly from Greek *metoikos* (as META-, *oikos* 'dwelling')]

meticulous /mɪˈtɪkjʊləs/ *adj.* **1** giving great or excessive attention to details. **2** very careful and precise. □ **meticulously** *adv.* **meticulousness** *n.* [Latin *meticulosus* from *metus* 'fear']

métier /ˈmɛtjeɪ, French metje/ *n.* **1** one's trade, profession, or department of activity. **2** one's forte. [French, ultimately from Latin *ministerium* 'service']

Metis /meɪˈtiːs/ *n.* (*pl.* same) a person of mixed race, esp. the offspring of a white person and an American Indian in Canada. [French *métis*, Old French *mestis*, from Romanic: related to MESTIZO]

metol /ˈmɛtɒl/ *n.* a white soluble phenol derivative used as a photographic developer. [German (arbitrary name)]

Metonic cycle /mɪˈtɒnɪk/ *n.* a period of 19 years (235 lunar months) covering all the changes of the moon's position relative to the sun and the earth. [named after *Metōn*, Athenian astronomer of the 5th c. BC]

metonym /ˈmɛtənɪm/ *n.* a word used in metonymy. [back-formation from METONYMY, on the pattern of *synonym*]

metonymy /mɪˈtɒnɪmi/ *n.* the substitution of the name of an attribute or adjunct for that of the thing meant (e.g. *Crown* for *king*, *the turf* for *horse racing*). □ **metonymic** /mɛtəˈnɪmɪk/ *adj.* **metonymical** /mɛtəˈnɪmɪk(ə)l/ *adj.* **metonymically** /mɛtəˈnɪmɪk(ə)li/ *adv.* [Late Latin *metonymia* from Greek *metōnumia* (as META-, *onoma*, *onuma* 'name')]

metope /ˈmɛtəʊp, ˈmɛtəpi/ *n. Archit.* a square space between triglyphs in a Doric frieze. [Latin *metopa* from Greek *metopē* (as META-, *opē* 'hole for a beam-end')]

metre[1] /ˈmiːtə/ *n.* (*US* **meter**) a metric unit and the base SI unit of linear measure, equal to about 39.4 inches, and reckoned as the length of the path travelled by light in a vacuum during $^{1}/_{299,792,458}$ of a second. □ **metreage** /ˈmiːt(ə)rɪdʒ/ *n.* [French *mètre* from Greek *metron* 'measure']

metre[2] /ˈmiːtə/ *n.* (*US* **meter**) **1 a** any form of poetic rhythm, determined by the number and length of feet in a line. **b** a metrical group or measure. **2** the basic pulse and rhythm of a piece of music. [Old French *metre* via Latin *metrum* from Greek *metron* MEASURE]

metre-kilogram-second *adj.* denoting a system of measure using the metre, kilogram, and second as the basic units of length, mass, and time (abbr.: **mks**).

metric /ˈmɛtrɪk/ *adj. & n.* ● *adj.* **1** of or based on the metre; esp. of or relating to the decimal measuring system with the metre, litre, and gram (or kilogram) as units of length, volume, and mass (*metric system*). See also SI 2. **2** of or relating to measurement; metrical. ● *n.* **1** a system or standard of measurement. **2** a mathematical function based on distances, or on quantities treated as analogous to distances for the purpose of analysis. [French *métrique* (as METRE[1])]

-metric /ˈmɛtrɪk/ *comb. form* (also **-metrical** /-k(ə)l/) forming adjectives corresponding to nouns in *-meter* and *-metry* (*thermometric*; *geometric*). □ **-metrically** *comb. form* forming adverbs. [from or suggested by French *-métrique* from Latin (as METRICAL)]

metrical /ˈmɛtrɪk(ə)l/ *adj.* **1** of, relating to, or composed in metre (*metrical psalms*). **2** of or involving measurement (*metrical geometry*). □ **metrically** *adv.* [Middle English via Latin *metricus* from Greek *metrikos* (as METRE[2])]

metricate /ˈmɛtrɪkeɪt/ *v.intr. & tr.* change or adapt to a metric system of measurement. □ **metrication** /-ˈkeɪʃ(ə)n/ *n.* **metricize** /-sʌɪz/ *v.tr.* (also **-ise**).

metric hundredweight see HUNDREDWEIGHT 2.

metric ton *n.* (also **metric tonne**) 1,000 kilograms (2,205 lb).

metritis /mɪˈtrʌɪtɪs/ *n.* inflammation of the womb. [Greek *mētra* 'womb' + -ITIS]

metro /ˈmɛtrəʊ/ *n.* (*pl.* **-os**) an underground railway system in a city, esp. Paris. [French *métro*, abbreviation of *métropolitain* METROPOLITAN]

metrology /mɪˈtrɒlədʒi/ *n.* the scientific study of measurement. □ **metrologic** /mɛtrəˈlɒdʒɪk/ *adj.* **metrological** /mɛtrəˈlɒdʒɪk(ə)l/ *adj.* [Greek *metron* 'measure' + -LOGY]

metronome /ˈmɛtrənəʊm/ *n. Mus.* a device marking time at a selected rate by giving a regular tick. □ **metronomic** /-ˈnɒmɪk/ *adj.* [Greek *metron* 'measure' + *nomos* 'law']

metronymic /mɛtrəˈnɪmɪk/ *adj. & n.* ● *adj.* (of a name) derived from the name of a mother or female ancestor. ● *n.* a metronymic name. [Greek *mētēr mētros* 'mother', on the pattern of *patronymic*]

metropolis /mɪˈtrɒp(ə)lɪs/ *n.* **1** the chief city of a country; a capital city. **2** a metropolitan bishop's see. **3** a town or city as a centre of activity. [Late Latin from Greek *mētropolis* 'parent state', from *mētēr mētros* 'mother' + *polis* 'city']

metropolitan /mɛtrəˈpɒlɪt(ə)n/ *adj. & n.* ● *adj.* **1** of or relating to a metropolis, esp. as distinct from its environs (*metropolitan New York*). **2** belonging to, forming or forming part of, a mother country as distinct from its colonies etc. (*metropolitan France*). **3** of an ecclesiastical metropolis. ● *n.* **1** (in full **metropolitan bishop**) a bishop having authority over the bishops of a province, in the Western Church equivalent to archbishop, in the Orthodox Church ranking above archbishop and below patriarch. **2** an inhabitant of a metropolis. □ **metropolitanate** *n.* (in sense 1 of *n.*). **metropolitanism** *n.* [Middle English via Late Latin *metropolitanus* from Greek *mētropolitēs* (as METROPOLIS)]

metropolitan county *n. hist.* (in England) each of six units of local government centred on a large urban area (in existence since 1974, although their councils were abolished in 1986).

metropolitan magistrate *n. Brit.* a paid professional magistrate in London (cf. STIPENDIARY MAGISTRATE).

metrorrhagia /miːtrəˈreɪdʒɪə/ *n.* abnormal bleeding from the womb. [modern Latin, from Greek *mētra* 'womb' + stem of *rhēgnumi* 'burst']

-metry /mɪtri/ *comb. form* forming nouns denoting procedures and systems corresponding to instruments in *-meter* (*calorimetry*; *thermometry*). [on the pattern of *geometry* etc. from Greek *-metria*, from *-metrēs* 'measurer']

mettle /ˈmɛt(ə)l/ *n.* **1** the quality of a person's disposition or temperament (*a chance to show your mettle*). **2** natural ardour. **3** spirit, courage. □ **on one's mettle** incited to do one's best. □ **mettled** *adj.* (also in *comb.*). **mettlesome** *adj.* [variant of METAL *n.*]

meu /mjuː/ *n.* (also **meum** /ˈmiːəm/) = SPIGNEL. [formed irregulary from Latin *meum*, from Greek *mēon*]

meunière /məːˈnjɛː/ *adj.* (esp. of fish) cooked or served in lightly browned butter with lemon juice and parsley (*sole meunière*). [French (*à la*) *meunière* '(in the manner of) a miller's wife']

MeV *abbr.* mega-electronvolt(s).

mew[1] /mjuː/ *v. & n.* ● *v.intr.* (of a cat, gull, etc.) utter its characteristic cry. ● *n.* this sound, esp. of a cat. [Middle English: imitative]

mew[2] /mjuː/ *n. & v.* ● *n.* a cage for hawks, esp. while moulting. ● *v.tr.* **1** put (a hawk) in a cage. **2** (often foll. by *up*) shut up; confine. [Middle English via Old French *mue*, from *muer* 'moult', from Latin *mutare* 'change']

mew[3] /mjuː/ *n.* a gull. [Old English *mæw*, from Germanic]

mew gull *n.* esp. *N. Amer.* the common gull, *Larus canus*.

mewl /mjuːl/ *v.intr.* (also **mule**) **1** cry feebly; whimper. **2** mew like a cat. [imitative: cf. MIAUL]

mews /mjuːz/ *n. Brit.* **1** a set of stabling round an open yard or along a lane. **2** such a set of buildings converted into dwellings; a row of houses in the style of a mews. [pl. (now used as sing.) of MEW[2], originally referring to the royal stables on the site of hawks' mews at Charing Cross, London]

Mexican /ˈmɛksɪk(ə)n/ *n. & adj.* ● *n.* **1 a** a native or national of Mexico, a country in southern North America. **b** a person of Mexican descent. **2** an indigenous language of Mexico, esp. Nahuatl. ● *adj.* **1** of or relating to Mexico or its people. **2** of Mexican descent. [Spanish *mexicano*]

Mexican wave *n.* a rising-and-falling effect produced by successive sections of a crowd standing up, raising their arms, lowering them, and sitting down again. [named because it was done repeatedly at the 1986 soccer World Cup finals in Mexico City: the practice itself is older]

mezereon /mɪˈzɪərɪən/ *n.* a small European and Asian shrub, *Daphne mezereum*, with fragrant purplish-red flowers and red berries. [medieval Latin from Arabic *māzaryūn*]

mezuzah /məˈzuːzə/ *n.* (*pl.* **mezuzoth** /-zəʊt/) a parchment inscribed with religious texts and attached in a case to the doorpost of a Jewish house as a sign of faith. [Hebrew *mᵉzûzāh* 'doorpost']

mezzanine /ˈmɛzəniːn, ˈmɛts-/ *n. & adj.* ● *n.* (also *attrib.*) **1** a low storey between two others (usu. between the ground and first floors). **2** *Theatr.* **a** *Brit.* a floor or space beneath the stage. **b** *N. Amer.* a dress circle. ● *adj. Commerce* designating or relating to unsecured, higher-yielding loans that are subordinate to bank and secured loans but rank above equity. [French from Italian *mezzanino*, diminutive of *mezzano* 'middle', from Latin *medianus* MEDIAN]

mezza voce /ˌmɛtsə ˈvəʊtʃeɪ, ˈvɒtʃi/ *adv. Mus.* with less than the full strength of the voice or sound. [Italian, = half voice]

mezzo /ˈmɛtsəʊ/ *adv. & n. Mus.* ● *adv.* half, moderately. ● *n.* (in full **mezzo-soprano**) (*pl.* **-os**) **1 a** a female singing voice between soprano and contralto. **b** a singer with this voice. **2** a part written for mezzo-soprano. [Italian, from Latin *medius* 'middle']

mezzo forte *adj. & adv.* fairly loud.

mezzo piano *adj. & adv.* fairly soft.

mezzo-relievo /ˌmɛtsəʊrɪˈljiːvəʊ/ *n.* (also **mezzo-rilievo** /-rɪˈljeɪvəʊ/) (*pl.* **-os**) *Sculpture* = HALF-RELIEF. [Italian *mezzo-rilievo*]

mezzotint /ˈmɛtsəʊtɪnt, ˈmɛzəʊ-/ *n. & v.* ● *n.* **1** a method of printing or engraving in which the surface of a plate is roughened by scraping so that it produces tones and half-tones. **2** a print produced by this process. ● *v.tr.* engrave in mezzotint. □ **mezzotinter** *n.* [Italian *mezzotinto*, from *mezzo* 'half' + *tinto* 'tint']

MF *abbr.* medium frequency.

mf *abbr.* mezzo forte.

MFH *abbr. Brit.* Master of Foxhounds.

MG *abbr.* **1** machine-gun. **2** Morris Garages (as a make of car).

Mg *symb. Chem.* the element magnesium.

mg *abbr.* milligram(s).

Mgr. *abbr.* **1** Manager. **2** *Monseigneur*. **3** Monsignor.

mho /məʊ/ *n.* (*pl.* **-os**) *Electr.* the reciprocal of an ohm, a former unit of conductance. [OHM reversed]

MHR *abbr.* (in the US and Australia) Member of the House of Representatives.

MHz *abbr.* megahertz.

MI *abbr.* **1** *US* Michigan (in official postal use). **2** *Brit. hist.* Military Intelligence.

mi var. of ME[2].

mi. *abbr.* mile(s).

MI5 *abbr.* (in the UK) the department of Military Intelligence concerned with state security.

■ **Usage** The official term for MI5 is the *Security Service*.

MI6 *abbr.* (in the UK) the department of Military Intelligence concerned with espionage.

■ **Usage** The official term for MI6 is the *Secret Intelligence Service*.

MIA *abbr.* missing in action.

miaow /mɪˈaʊ/ *n.* & *v.* (also **meow**) ● *n.* the characteristic cry of a cat. ● *v.intr.* make this cry. [imitative]

miasma /mɪˈazmə, mʌɪ-/ *n.* (*pl.* **miasmata** /-mətə/ or **miasmas**) *archaic* an infectious or noxious vapour. □ **miasmal** *adj.* **miasmatic** /mɪəzˈmatɪk/ *adj.* **miasmic** *adj.* **miasmically** *adv.* [Greek, = defilement, from *miainō* 'pollute']

miaul /mɪˈɔːl/ *v.intr.* cry like a cat; mew. [French *miauler*: imitative]

Mic. *abbr.* Micah (Old Testament).

mica /ˈmʌɪkə/ *n.* any of a group of silicate minerals with a layered structure, esp. muscovite. □ **micaceous** /-ˈkeɪʃəs/ *adj.* [Latin, = crumb]

mica-schist *n.* (also **mica-slate**) a fissile rock containing quartz and mica.

mice *pl.* of MOUSE.

micelle /mɪˈsɛl, mʌɪˈsɛl/ *n. Chem.* an aggregate of molecules in a colloidal solution, as formed e.g. by detergents. [modern Latin *micella*, diminutive of Latin *mica* 'crumb']

Mich. *abbr.* **1** Michaelmas. **2** Michigan.

Michaelmas /ˈmɪk(ə)lməs/ *n.* the feast of St Michael, 29 September. [Old English *sancte Micheles mæsse* 'Saint Michael's Mass': see MASS]

Michaelmas daisy *n.* an autumn-flowering aster.

Michaelmas term *n. Brit.* (in some universities) the autumn term.

mick /mɪk/ *n. slang offens.* **1** an Irishman. **2** a Roman Catholic. [pet form of the name *Michael*]

mickey /ˈmɪki/ *n.* (also **micky**) □ **take the mickey** (often foll. by *out of*) *Brit. slang* tease, mock, ridicule. □ **mickey-taking** *n.* [20th c.: origin uncertain]

Mickey Finn /mɪkɪ ˈfɪn/ *n. slang* **1** a drink adulterated with a narcotic or laxative. **2** the adulterant itself. [20th c.: origin uncertain]

Mickey Mouse /mɪkɪ ˈmaʊs/*adj. colloq.* **1** of inferior quality. **2** ridiculous, trivial. [mouselike cartoon character created by Walt Disney, American cartoonist d. 1966]

mickle /ˈmɪk(ə)l/ *adj.* & *n.* (also **muckle** /ˈmʌk(ə)l/) *archaic* or *Sc.* ● *adj.* much, great. ● *n.* a large amount. □ **many a little makes a mickle** (also *erroneous* **many a mickle makes a muckle**) many small amounts accumulate to make a large amount. [Middle English from Old Norse *mikell*, from Germanic]

micky var. of MICKEY.

micro /ˈmʌɪkrəʊ/ *n.* (*pl.* **-os**) *colloq.* **1** = MICROCOMPUTER. **2** = MICROPROCESSOR.

micro- /ˈmʌɪkrəʊ/ *comb. form* **1** small (*microchip*). **2** denoting a factor of one-millionth (10^{-6}) (*microgram*) (symbol μ). [Greek *mikro-* from *mikros* 'small']

microanalysis /ˌmʌɪkrəʊəˈnalɪsɪs/ *n.* the quantitative analysis of chemical compounds using a sample of a few milligrams.

microbe /ˈmʌɪkrəʊb/ *n.* a minute living being; a micro-organism (esp. a bacterium causing disease or fermentation). □ **microbial** /-ˈkrəʊbɪəl/ *adj.* **microbic** /-ˈkrəʊbɪk/ *adj.* [French, from Greek *mikros* 'small' + *bios* 'life']

microbiology /ˌmʌɪkrə(ʊ)bʌɪˈɒlədʒi/ *n.* the scientific study of micro-organisms, e.g. bacteria, viruses, and fungi. □ **microbiological** /-bʌɪəˈlɒdʒɪk(ə)l/ *adj.* **microbiologically** /-bʌɪəˈlɒdʒɪk(ə)li/ *adv.* **microbiologist** *n.*

microburst /ˈmʌɪkrə(ʊ)bəːst/ *n.* a particularly strong wind shear, esp. during a thunderstorm.

microcephaly /mʌɪkrəʊˈsɛfəli, ˈkɛ-/ *n.* an abnormal smallness of the head in relation to the rest of the body. □ **microcephalic** /-sɪˈfalɪk, -kɛˈfalɪk/ *adj.* & *n.* **microcephalous** /-ˈsɛf(ə)ləs, -ˈkɛf-/ *adj.*

microchip /ˈmʌɪkrə(ʊ)tʃɪp/ *n.* a tiny wafer of semiconducting material used to make an integrated circuit.

microcircuit /ˈmʌɪkrə(ʊ)ˌsəːkɪt/ *n.* a minute electric circuit, esp. an integrated circuit. □ **microcircuitry** *n.*

microclimate /ˈmʌɪkrə(ʊ)ˌklʌɪmət/ *n.* the climate of a small local area or enclosed space, esp. as differing from the surroundings. □ **microclimatic** /-ˈmatɪk/ *adj.* **microclimatically** /-ˈmatɪk(ə)li/ *adv.*

microcode /ˈmʌɪkrə(ʊ)kəʊd/ *n.* **1** = MICROINSTRUCTION. **2** = MICROPROGRAM.

microcomputer /ˈmʌɪkrə(ʊ)kɒmˌpjuːtə/ *n.* a small computer that contains a microprocessor as its central processor.

microcopy /ˈmʌɪkrə(ʊ)ˌkɒpi/ *n.* & *v.* ● *n.* (*pl.* **-ies**) a copy of printed matter that has been reduced by microphotography. ● *v.tr.* (**-ies**, **-ied**) make a microcopy of.

microcosm /ˈmʌɪkrə(ʊ)kɒz(ə)m/ *n.* **1** (often foll. by *of*) a miniature representation. **2** humankind viewed as the epitome of the universe. **3** any community or complex unity viewed in this way. □ **microcosmic** /-ˈkɒzmɪk/ *adj.* **microcosmically** /-ˈkɒzmɪk(ə)li/ *adv.* [Middle English via French *microcosme* or medieval Latin *microcosmus* from Greek *mikros kosmos* 'little world']

microdot /ˈmʌɪkrə(ʊ)dɒt/ *n.* a microphotograph of a document etc. reduced to the size of a dot.

microeconomics /ˌmʌɪkrəʊiːkəˈnɒmɪks, -ɛkə-/ *n.* the branch of economics dealing with individual commodities, producers, etc. □ **microeconomic** *adj.*

microelectronics /ˌmʌɪkrəʊɪlɛkˈtrɒnɪks/ *n.* the design, manufacture, and use of microchips and microcircuits. □ **microelectronic** *adj.*

microevolution /ˌmʌɪkrəʊiːvəˈluːʃ(ə)n, -ˈljuːʃ(ə)n, -ɛv-/ *n. Biol.* evolutionary change within a species or small group of organisms, esp. over a short period. □ **microevolutionary** *adj.*

microfiche /ˈmʌɪkrə(ʊ)fiːʃ/ *n.* (*pl.* same or **microfiches**) a flat rectangular piece of film bearing microphotographs of the pages of a printed text or document.

microfilm /ˈmʌɪkrə(ʊ)fɪlm/ *n.* & *v.* ● *n.* a length of film bearing microphotographs of documents etc. ● *v.tr.* photograph (a document etc.) on microfilm.

microfloppy /ˈmʌɪkrə(ʊ)ˌflɒpi/ *n.* (*pl.* **-ies**) (in full **microfloppy disk**) *Computing* a floppy disk with a diameter of less than 5¼ inches (usu. 3½ inches).

microform /ˈmʌɪkrə(ʊ)fɔːm/ *n.* microphotographic reproduction on film or paper of a manuscript etc.

microgram /ˈmʌɪkrə(ʊ)gram/ *n.* one-millionth of a gram.

micrograph /ˈmʌɪkrə(ʊ)grɑːf/ *n.* a photograph taken by means of a microscope.

microgravity /ˈmʌɪkrə(ʊ)ˌgravɪti/ *n.* very weak gravity, as in an orbiting spacecraft.

microgroove /ˈmʌɪkrə(ʊ)gruːv/ *n.* a very narrow groove on a long-playing gramophone record.

microinstruction /ˈmʌɪkrəʊɪnˌstrʌkʃ(ə)n/ *n.* a machine-code instruction that effects a basic operation in a computer system.

microlepidoptera /ˌmʌɪkrə(ʊ)lɛpɪˈdɒpt(ə)rə/ *n.pl.* the numerous small moths that are of interest only to specialists. [MICRO- + modern Latin *Lepidoptera*: see LEPIDOPTEROUS]

■ **Usage** The term *microlepidoptera* is not used in formal classification.

microlight /ˈmʌɪkrə(ʊ)lʌɪt/ *n.* a very small, light, low-speed, one- or two-seater aircraft with an open frame.

microlith /ˈmʌɪkrə(ʊ)lɪθ/ *n. Archaeol.* a minute worked flint usu. as part of a composite tool. □ **microlithic** /-ˈlɪθɪk/ *adj.*

micromesh /ˈmʌɪkrə(ʊ)mɛʃ/ *n.* (often *attrib.*) material, esp. nylon, consisting of a very fine mesh.

micrometer /mʌɪˈkrɒmɪtə/ *n.* a gauge for accurately measuring small distances, thicknesses, etc. □ **micrometry** *n.*

micrometre /ˈmʌɪkrə(ʊ),miːtə/ *n.* (*US* **micrometer**) one-millionth of a metre.

microminiaturization /,mʌɪkrəʊ,mɪnɪtʃərʌɪˈzeɪʃ(ə)n/ *n.* (also **-isation**) the manufacture of very small electronic devices by using integrated circuits.

micron /ˈmʌɪkrɒn/ *n.* one-millionth of a metre. [Greek *mikron*, neut. of *mikros* 'small': cf. MICRO-]

Micronesian /mʌɪkrə(ʊ)ˈniːzj(ə)n, -ʒ(ə)n/ *adj.* & *n.* ● *adj.* of or relating to Micronesia, an island group in the W. Pacific. ● *n.* **1** a native of Micronesia. **2** the group of Austronesian languages spoken in Micronesia. [*Micronesia*, formed as MICRO- + Greek *nēsos* 'island']

micronutrient /mʌɪkrə(ʊ)ˈnjuːtrɪənt/ *n.* a chemical element or substance required in trace amounts for the growth and development of living organisms.

micro-organism /mʌɪkrəʊˈɔːg(ə)nɪz(ə)m/ *n.* a microscopic organism, esp. a bacterium or virus.

microphone /ˈmʌɪkrəfəʊn/ *n.* an instrument for converting sound waves into electrical energy variations which may be reconverted into sound after transmission by wire or radio or after recording. □ **microphonic** /-ˈfɒnɪk/ *adj.*

microphotograph /mʌɪkrə(ʊ)ˈfəʊtəgrɑːf/ *n.* a photograph reduced to a very small size.

microphyte /ˈmʌɪkrə(ʊ)fʌɪt/ *n.* a microscopic plant.

microprocessor /mʌɪkrə(ʊ)ˈprəʊsɛsə/ *n.* an integrated circuit that contains all the functions of a central processing unit of a computer and often all the other functions as well.

microprogram /ˈmʌɪkrə(ʊ),prəʊgram/ *n.* a microinstruction program that controls the functions of a central processing unit of a computer.

micropyle /ˈmʌɪkrə(ʊ)pʌɪl/ *n. Bot.* a small opening in the surface of an ovule, through which pollen passes. [MICRO- + Greek *pulē* 'gate']

microscope /ˈmʌɪkrəskəʊp/ *n.* an instrument for magnifying small objects by means of a lens or lenses so as to reveal details invisible to the naked eye. [modern Latin *microscopium* (as MICRO-, -SCOPE)]

microscopic /mʌɪkrəˈskɒpɪk/ *adj.* **1** so small as to be visible only with a microscope. **2** extremely small. **3** regarded in terms of small units. **4** of the microscope. □ **microscopical** *adj.* (in sense 4). **microscopically** *adv.*

microscopy /mʌɪˈkrɒskəpi/ *n.* the use of the microscope. □ **microscopist** *n.*

microsecond /ˈmʌɪkrə(ʊ),sɛkənd/ *n.* one-millionth of a second.

microsome /ˈmʌɪkrəsəʊm/ *n. Biol.* a small particle of organelle fragments obtained by centrifugation of homogenized cells. [MICRO- + -SOME³]

microspore /ˈmʌɪkrə(ʊ)spɔː/ *n. Bot.* the smaller of the two kinds of spore produced by some ferns (cf. MEGASPORE).

microstructure /ˈmʌɪkrə(ʊ),strʌktʃə/ *n.* (in a metal or other material) the arrangement of crystals etc. which can be made visible and examined with a microscope.

microsurgery /mʌɪkrə(ʊ)ˈsəːdʒ(ə)ri/ *n.* intricate surgery performed using microscopes, enabling the tissue to be operated on with miniaturized precision instruments. □ **microsurgical** /-ˈsəːdʒɪk(ə)l/ *adj.*

microswitch /ˈmʌɪkrə(ʊ)swɪtʃ/ *n.* a switch that can be operated rapidly by a small movement.

microtome /ˈmʌɪkrə(ʊ)təʊm/ *n.* an instrument for cutting extremely thin sections of material for examination under a microscope.

microtone /ˈmʌɪkrə(ʊ)təʊn/ *n. Mus.* an interval smaller than a semitone.

microtubule /mʌɪkrə(ʊ)ˈtjuːbjuːl/ *n. Biol.* a minute protein filament occurring in cytoplasm and involved in forming the spindles during cell division etc.

microwave /ˈmʌɪkrə(ʊ)weɪv/ *n.* & *v.* ● *n.* **1** an electromagnetic wave with a wavelength in the range 0.001–0.3m. **2** (in full **microwave oven**) an oven that uses microwaves to cook or heat food. ● *v.tr.* cook in a microwave oven. □ **microwaveable** *adj.* (also **microwavable**).

micrurgy /ˈmʌɪkrəːdʒi/ *n.* the manipulation of individual cells etc. under a microscope. [MICRO- + Greek *-ourgia* 'work']

micturition /mɪktjʊˈrɪʃ(ə)n/ *n. formal* or *Med.* urination. [Latin *micturire micturit-*, desiderative from *mingere mict-* 'urinate']

mid /mɪd/ *prep. poet.* = AMID. [abbreviation from AMID]

mid- /mɪd/ *comb. form* **1** that is the middle of (*in mid-air*; *from mid-June to mid-July*). **2** that is in the middle; medium, half. **3** *Phonet.* (of a vowel) pronounced with the tongue neither high nor low. [Old English *midd* (recorded only in oblique cases), related to Latin *medius*, Greek *mesos*]

Midas touch /ˈmʌɪdəs/ *n.* the ability to turn one's activities to financial advantage. [*Midas*, king of Phrygia, whose touch was said to turn all things to gold]

midbrain /ˈmɪdbreɪn/ *n. Anat.* a small central part of the brainstem, developing from the middle of the primitive or embryonic brain; also called *mesencephalon*.

midday /mɪdˈdeɪ/ *n.* the middle of the day; noon. [Old English *middæg* (as MID-, DAY)]

midden /ˈmɪd(ə)n/ *n.* **1** a dunghill. **2** a refuse heap near a dwelling. **3** = KITCHEN MIDDEN. [Middle English *myddyng*, of Scandinavian origin: cf. Danish *mødding* 'muck heap']

middle /ˈmɪd(ə)l/ *adj.*, *n.*, & *v.* ● *attrib.adj.* **1** at an equal distance from the extremities of a thing. **2** (of a member of a group) so placed as to have the same number of members on each side. **3** intermediate in rank, quality, etc. **4** average (*of middle height*). **5** (of a language) of the period between the old and modern forms. **6** *Gram.* designating the voice of (esp. Greek) verbs that expresses reciprocal or reflexive action. ● *n.* **1** (often foll. by *of*) the middle point or position or part. **2** a person's waist. **3** *Gram.* the middle form or voice of a verb. **4** = MIDDLE TERM. ● *v.tr.* **1** place in the middle. **2** *Football* return (the ball) from the wing to the midfield. **3** *Cricket* strike (the ball) with the middle of the bat. **4** *Naut.* fold in the middle. □ **in the middle of** (often foll. by verbal noun) in the process of; during. [Old English *middel*, from Germanic]

middle age *n.* the period between youth and old age, about 45 to 60. □ **middle-aged** *adj.*

Middle Ages *n.pl.* the period of European history from the fall of the Roman Empire in the West (5th c.) to the fall of Constantinople (1453), or more narrowly from *c.*1000 to 1453.

middle-age spread *n.* (also **middle-aged spread**) the increased bodily girth often associated with middle age.

Middle America *n.* **1** Mexico and Central America. **2** the middle class in the US, esp. as a conservative political force.

middlebrow /ˈmɪd(ə)lbraʊ/ *adj.* & *n. colloq.* ● *adj.* claiming to be or regarded as only moderately intellectual. ● *n.* a middlebrow person.

middle C *n. Mus.* the C near the middle of the piano keyboard, the note between the treble and bass staves, at about 260 Hz.

middle class *n.* & *adj.* ● *n.* the class of society between the upper and the lower, including professional and business workers and their families. ● *adj.* (**middle-class**) of the middle class.

middle common room *n. Brit.* a common room for the use of graduate members of a college who are not fellows.

middle course *n.* a compromise between two extremes.

middle distance *n.* **1** (in a painted or actual landscape) the part between the foreground and the background. **2** *Athletics* a race distance of esp. between 800 and 5,000 metres.

middle ear *n.* the cavity of the central part of the ear behind the drum.

Middle East *n.* (prec. by *the*) an extensive area of SW Asia and northern Africa, stretching from the Mediterranian to Pakistan and including the Arabian peninsular. □ **Middle Eastern** *adj.*

Middle English *n.* the English language from *c.*1150 to 1500.

middle finger *n.* the finger next to the forefinger.

middle game *n.* the central phase of a chess game, when strategies are developed.

middle ground *n.* **1** the thought, area, or path, tending to moderation and compromise. **2** the people regarded as holding moderate views.

middle-income *attrib.adj.* **1** of or relating to the group of people earning average salaries. **2** with an average national income (used esp. of certain Third World countries).

middleman /ˈmɪd(ə)lman/ *n.* (*pl.* **-men**) **1** a trader who handles a commodity between its producer and its consumer. **2** an intermediary.

middle management *n.* **1** the level in an organization between senior and junior management. **2** the managers at this level (cf. SENIOR MANAGEMENT, JUNIOR MANAGEMENT).

middle name *n.* **1** a person's name placed after the first name and before the surname. **2** a person's most characteristic quality (*sobriety is my middle name*).

middle-of-the-road *adj.* **1** (of a person, course of action, etc.) moderate; avoiding extremes. **2** (of music) intended to appeal to a wide audience; unadventurous.

middle passage *n.* the sea journey between W. Africa and the W. Indies (with reference to the slave trade).

middle school *n.* a school for children from about 9 to 13 years old.

middle-sized *adj.* of medium size.

Middle Temple *n.* one of the two Inns of Court on the site of the Temple in London (cf. INNER TEMPLE).

middle term *n. Logic* the term common to both premisses of a syllogism.

middle watch *n.* the watch from midnight to 4 a.m.

middle way *n.* **1** = MIDDLE COURSE. **2** the eightfold path of Buddhism between indulgence and asceticism.

middleweight /ˈmɪd(ə)lweɪt/ *n.* **1** a weight in certain sports intermediate between welterweight and light heavyweight, in the amateur boxing scale 71–5 kg but differing for professionals, wrestlers, and weightlifters. **2** a boxer etc. of this weight.

Middle West *n.* = MIDWEST.

middling /ˈmɪd(ə)lɪŋ/ *adj., n., & adv.* ● *adj.* **1 a** moderately good (esp. *fair to middling*). **b** *colloq.* (of a person's health) fairly well. **c** second-rate. **2** (of goods) of the second of three grades. ● *n.* (in *pl.*) middling goods, esp. flour of medium fineness. ● *adv.* fairly or moderately (*middling good*). □ **middlingly** *adv.* [Middle English, of Scots origin: probably from MID- + -LING²]

Middx. *abbr.* Middlesex.

middy¹ /ˈmɪdi/ *n.* (*pl.* **-ies**) **1** *colloq.* a midshipman. **2** (in full **middy blouse**) a woman's or child's loose blouse with a collar like that worn by sailors.

middy² /ˈmɪdi/ *n.* (*pl.* **-ies**) *Austral. slang* a measure of beer of varying size. [20th c.: origin unknown]

Mideast /mɪdˈiːst/ *n. US* = MIDDLE EAST.

midfield /mɪdˈfiːld, ˈmɪdfiːld/ *n. Football* the central part of the pitch, away from the goals. □ **midfielder** *n.*

midge /mɪdʒ/ *n.* **1 a** any small gnatlike dipterous fly of the family Chironomidae, often seen in dancing swarms near water. **b** any similar fly, esp. a tiny biting fly of the family Ceratopogonidae, with piercing mouthparts. **2** *colloq.* a small person. [Old English *mycg(e)*, from Germanic]

midget /ˈmɪdʒɪt/ *n.* **1** an extremely small person or thing. **2** (*attrib.*) very small. [MIDGE + -ET¹]

midgut /ˈmɪdgʌt/ *n.* the middle part of the alimentary canal, including (in vertebrates) the small intestine.

MIDI /ˈmɪdi/ *n.* a system for using combinations of electronic equipment, esp. audio and computer equipment. [acronym from *m*usical *i*nstrument *d*igital *i*nterface]

midi /ˈmɪdi/ *n.* (*pl.* **midis**) a garment of medium length, usu. reaching to mid-calf. [MID-, on the pattern of MINI]

midi- /ˈmɪdi/ *comb. form* medium-sized; of medium length.

midibus /ˈmɪdɪbʌs/ *n.* a bus seating up to about 25 passengers. [MID- + BUS, on the pattern of *minibus*]

midinette /mɪdɪˈnet/ *n.* a Parisian shop girl, esp. a milliner's assistant. [French, from *midi* 'midday' + *dînette* 'light dinner']

midiron /ˈmɪdʌɪən/ *n. Golf* an iron with a medium degree of loft.

midi system *n.* a set of compact stacking hi-fi equipment components.

midland /ˈmɪdlənd/ *n. & adj.* ● *n.* **1** (**the Midlands**) the inland counties of central England. **2** the middle part of a country. ● *adj.* **1** (also **Midland**) of or in the Midlands. **2** of or in the midland. **3** Mediterranean. □ **Midlander** *n.*

mid-life /mɪdˈlʌɪf/ *n.* middle age (often *attrib.*: *mid-life planning*).

mid-life crisis *n.* an emotional crisis of self-confidence that can occur in early middle age.

midline /ˈmɪdlʌɪn/ *n.* a median line, or plane of bilateral symmetry.

midmost /ˈmɪdməʊst/ *adj. & adv.* in the very middle.

midnight /ˈmɪdnʌɪt/ *n.* **1** the middle of the night; 12 o'clock at night. **2** intense darkness. [Old English *midniht* (as MID-, NIGHT)]

midnight blue *n. & adj.* ● *n.* a very dark blue. ● *adj.* (hyphenated when *attrib.*) of this colour.

midnight sun *n.* the sun visible at midnight during the summer in polar regions.

mid-off *n. Cricket* a fielder or fielding position near the bowler on the off side.

mid-on *n. Cricket* a fielder or fielding position near the bowler on the on side.

Midrash /ˈmɪdraʃ, -rʌʃ/ *n.* (*pl.* **Midrashim** /-ˈʃɪm/) an ancient commentary on part of the Hebrew scriptures. [Bibl. Hebrew *midrāš* 'commentary']

midrib /ˈmɪdrɪb/ *n.* the central rib of a leaf.

midriff /ˈmɪdrɪf/ *n.* **1 a** the region of the front of the body between the thorax and abdomen. **b** the diaphragm. **2** a garment or part of a garment covering the abdomen. [Old English *midhrif* (as MID-, *hrif* 'belly')]

midship /ˈmɪdʃɪp/ *n.* the middle part of a ship or boat.

midshipman /ˈmɪdʃɪpmən/ *n.* (*pl.* **-men**) **1** *Brit.* a naval officer of rank between naval cadet and sub lieutenant. **2** *US* a naval cadet.

midships /ˈmɪdʃɪps/ *adv.* = AMIDSHIPS.

midst /mɪdst/ *prep. & n.* ● *prep. poet.* amidst. ● *n.* middle (now only in phrs. as below). □ **in the midst of** among; in the middle of. **in our** (or **your** or **their**) **midst** among us (or you or them). [Middle English *middest, middes*, from *in middes, in middan* (as IN, MID-)]

midstream /mɪdˈstriːm/ *n. & adv.* ● *n.* the middle of a stream, river, etc. ● *adv.* (also **in midstream**) in the middle of an action etc. (*abandoned the project midstream*).

midsummer /mɪdˈsʌmə/ *n.* the period of or near the summer solstice. [Old English *midsumor* (as MID-, SUMMER¹)]

Midsummer Day *n.* (also **Midsummer's Day**) 24 June.

midsummer madness *n.* extreme folly.

midtown /ˈmɪdtaʊn/ *n. US* the central part of a city between the downtown and uptown areas.

midway /ˈmɪdweɪ, mɪdˈweɪ/ *adv. & n.* ● *adv.* in or towards the middle of the distance between two points. ● *n. N. Amer.* a fair or an area with sideshows etc.

midweek /mɪdˈwiːk/ *n., adj., & adv.* ● *n.* the middle of the week. ● *adj. & adv.* occurring at this time.

Midwest /mɪd'wɛst/ *n.* (in the US) the region of northern states from Ohio west to the Rocky mountains. □ **Midwestern** *adj.*

midwicket /mɪd'wɪkɪt/ *n. Cricket* a fielder or fielding position on the leg side opposite the middle of the pitch.

midwife /'mɪdwʌɪf/ *n.* (*pl.* **-wives** /-wʌɪvz/) **1** a person (usu. a woman) trained to assist women in childbirth. **2** a person or thing that brings about change (*act as a midwife to emergent culture*). □ **midwifery** /-wɪfri/ *n.* [Middle English, probably from obsolete prep. *mid* 'with' + WIFE 'woman', in the sense of 'a person who is with the mother']

midwife toad *n.* a European toad, *Alytes obstetricans*, in which the male carries the developing eggs on his hind legs.

midwinter /mɪd'wɪntə/ *n.* the period of or near the winter solstice. [Old English (as MID-, WINTER)]

mielie var. of MEALIE.

mien /miːn/ *n. literary* a person's look or bearing, as showing character or mood. [probably via obsolete *demean* from DEMEAN², assimilated to French *mine* 'expression']

miff /mɪf/ *v. & n. colloq.* ● *v.tr.* (usu. in *passive*) put out of humour; offend. ● *n.* **1** a petty quarrel. **2** a huff. [perhaps imitative: cf. German *muff*, an exclamation of disgust]

miffy /'mɪfi/ *adj.* easily offended or irritated. [MIFF + -Y¹]

might¹ /mʌɪt/ *past* of MAY, used esp.: **1** in reported speech, expressing possibility (*said he might come*) or permission (*asked if I might leave*) (cf. MAY 1, 2). **2** (foll. by perfect infin.) expressing a possibility based on a condition not fulfilled (*if you'd looked you might have found it; but for the radio we might not have known*). **3** (foll. by present infin. or perfect infin.) expressing complaint that an obligation or expectation is not or has not been fulfilled (*you might help instead of watching; they might have asked; you might have known they wouldn't come*). **4** expressing a request (*you might call in at the butcher's*). **5** *colloq.* **a** = MAY 1 (*it might be true*). **b** (in tentative questions) = MAY 2 (*might I have the pleasure of this dance?*). **c** = MAY 4 (*who might you be?*). □ **might as well** expressing that it is probably at least as desirable to do a thing as not to do it (*finished the work and decided they might as well go to lunch; won't win but might as well try*).

might² /mʌɪt/ *n.* **1** great bodily or mental strength. **2** power to enforce one's will (usu. in contrast with *right*). □ **with all one's might** to the utmost of one's power. **with might and main** see MAIN¹. [Old English *miht, mieht* from Germanic: related to MAY]

might-have-been *n. colloq.* **1** a past possibility that no longer applies. **2** a person who could have been more eminent.

mightn't /'mʌɪt(ə)nt/ *contr.* might not.

mighty /'mʌɪti/ *adj. & adv.* ● *adj.* (**mightier, mightiest**) **1** powerful or strong, in body, mind, or influence. **2** massive, bulky. **3** *colloq.* great, considerable. ● *adv. colloq.* very (*a mighty difficult task*). □ **mightily** *adv.* **mightiness** *n.* [Old English *mihtig* (as MIGHT²)]

mignonette /mɪnjə'nɛt/ *n.* **1 a** any of various plants of the genus *Reseda*, esp. *R. odorata*, with fragrant grey-green flowers. **b** the colour of these. **2** a light fine narrow pillow lace. [French *mignonnette*, diminutive of *mignon* 'small']

migraine /'miːgreɪn, 'mʌɪ-/ *n.* a recurrent throbbing headache that usually affects one side of the head, often accompanied by nausea and disturbance of vision. □ **migrainous** *adj.* [originally referring to a headache confined to one side of the head: French via Late Latin *hemicrania* from Greek *hēmikrania* (as HEMI-, CRANIUM)]

migrant /'mʌɪgr(ə)nt/ *adj. & n.* ● *adj.* that migrates. ● *n.* a migrant person or animal, esp. a bird.

migrate /mʌɪ'greɪt, 'mʌɪgreɪt/ *v.intr.* **1** (of people) move from one place of abode to another, esp. in a different country. **2** (of an animal, esp. a bird or fish) change its area of habitation with the seasons. **3** move under natural forces. □ **migration** /-'greɪʃ(ə)n/ *n.* **migrational** /-'greɪʃ(ə)n(ə)l/ *adj.* **migrator** *n.* **migratory** /'mʌɪgrət(ə)ri, mʌɪ'greɪt(ə)ri/ *adj.* [Latin *migrare migrat-*]

mihrab /'miːrɑːb/ *n.* a niche or slab in a mosque, used to show the direction of Mecca. [Arabic *miḥrāb* 'praying-place']

mikado /mɪ'kɑːdəʊ/ *n.* (*pl.* **-os**) *hist.* the emperor of Japan. [Japanese, from *mi* 'august' + *kado* 'gate']

Mike /mʌɪk/ *n. slang* □ **for the love of Mike** an exclamation of entreaty or dismay. [abbreviation of the name *Michael*]

mike¹ /mʌɪk/ *n. colloq.* a microphone. [abbreviation]

mike² /mʌɪk/ *v. & n. Brit. slang* ● *v.intr.* shirk work; idle. ● *n.* an act of shirking. [19th c.: origin unknown]

mil /mɪl/ *n.* one-thousandth of an inch, as a unit of measure for the diameter of wire etc. [Latin *millesimum* 'thousandth' from *mille* 'thousand']

milady /mɪ'leɪdi/ *n.* (*pl.* **-ies**) **1** an English noblewoman or great lady. **2** a form used in speaking of or to such a person. [French from English *my lady*: cf. MILORD]

milage var. of MILEAGE.

Milanese /mɪlə'niːz/ *adj. & n.* ● *adj.* of or relating to Milan in N. Italy. ● *n.* (*pl.* same) a native of Milan.

Milanese silk *n.* a finely woven silk or rayon.

milch /mɪltʃ/ *adj.* (of a domestic mammal) giving or kept for milk. [Middle English, representing the second syllable of Old English *thrimilce* 'May' (when cows could be milked three times a day), from the Germanic base of MILK]

milch cow *n.* a source of easy profit, esp. a person.

mild /mʌɪld/ *adj. & n.* ● *adj.* **1** (esp. of a person) gentle and conciliatory. **2** (of a rule, punishment, illness, feeling, etc.) moderate; not severe. **3** (of the weather, esp. in winter) moderately warm. **4** (of food, tobacco, etc.) not sharp or strong in taste etc. **5** (of medicine) operating gently. **6** tame, feeble; lacking energy or vivacity. ● *n. Brit.* beer not strongly flavoured with hops (cf. BITTER *n.* 1). □ **milden** *v.tr. & intr.* **mildish** *adj.* **mildness** *n.* [Old English *milde*, from Germanic]

mildew /'mɪldjuː/ *n. & v.* ● *n.* **1** a destructive growth of minute fungi on plants. **2** a similar growth on paper, leather, etc. exposed to damp. ● *v.tr. & intr.* taint or be tainted with mildew. □ **mildewy** *adj.* [Old English *mildēaw*, from Germanic]

mildly /'mʌɪldli/ *adv.* in a mild fashion. □ **to put it mildly** as an understatement (implying the reality is more extreme).

mild-mannered *adj.* = MILD *adj.* 1.

mild steel *n.* steel containing a small percentage of carbon, strong and tough but not readily tempered.

mile /mʌɪl/ *n.* **1** (also **statute mile**) a unit of linear measure equal to 1,760 yards (approx. 1.609 kilometres). **2** *hist.* a Roman measure of 1,000 paces (approx. 1,620 yards). **3** (in *pl.*) *colloq.* a great distance or amount (*miles better; beat them by miles*). **4** a race extending over a mile. □ **miles away** *colloq.* lost in thought; preoccupied. [Old English *mīl*, ultimately from Latin *mil(l)ia*, pl. of *mille* 'thousand' (see sense 2)]

mileage /'mʌɪlɪdʒ/ *n.* (also **milage**) **1 a** a number of miles travelled, used, etc. **b** the number of miles travelled by a vehicle per unit of fuel. **2** travelling expenses (per mile). **3** *colloq.* benefit, profit, advantage.

milepost /'mʌɪlpəʊst/ *n.* **1** a post one mile from the finishing post of a race etc. **2** esp. *N. Amer. & Austral.* = MILESTONE.

miler /'mʌɪlə/ *n. colloq.* a person or horse qualified or trained specially to run a mile.

milestone /'mʌɪlstəʊn/ *n.* **1** a stone set up beside a road to mark a distance in miles. **2** a significant event or stage in a life, history, project, etc.

milfoil /'mɪlfɔɪl/ *n.* **1** the common yarrow, *Achillea millefolium*, with small white flowers and finely divided leaves. **2** (in full **water milfoil**) an aquatic plant of the genus *Myriophyllum* with whorls of fine leaves. [Middle

English via Old French from Latin *millefolium*, from *mille* 'thousand' + *folium* 'leaf', suggested by Greek *muriophullon*]

miliary /ˈmɪlɪəri/ *adj.* **1** like a millet seed in size or form. **2** (of a disease) having as a symptom a rash with lesions resembling millet seed. [Latin *miliarius* from *milium* 'millet']

milieu /ˈmiːljəː, mɪˈljəː/ *n.* (*pl.* **milieux** or **milieus** /-ljəːz/) one's environment or social surroundings. [French, from *mi* MID- + *lieu* 'place']

militant /ˈmɪlɪt(ə)nt/ *adj.* & *n.* ● *adj.* **1** combative; aggressively active esp. in support of a (usu. political) cause. **2** engaged in warfare. ● *n.* a militant person, esp. a political activist. □ **militancy** *n.* **militantly** *adv.* [Middle English via Old French from Latin (as MILITATE)]

militaria /mɪlɪˈtɛːrɪə/ *n.pl.* military articles of historical interest. [MILITARY + -IA²]

militarism /ˈmɪlɪt(ə)rɪz(ə)m/ *n.* **1** the spirit or tendencies of a professional soldier. **2** undue prevalence of the military spirit or ideals. □ **militaristic** /-ˈrɪstɪk/ *adj.* **militaristically** /-ˈrɪstɪk(ə)li/ *adv.* [French *militarisme* (as MILITARY)]

militarist /ˈmɪlɪt(ə)rɪst/ *n.* **1** a person dominated by militaristic ideas. **2** a student of military science.

militarize /ˈmɪlɪt(ə)rʌɪz/ *v.tr.* (also **-ise**) **1** equip with military resources. **2** make military or warlike. **3** imbue with militarism. □ **militarization** /-ˈzeɪʃ(ə)n/ *n.*

military /ˈmɪlɪt(ə)ri/ *adj.* & *n.* ● *adj.* of, relating to, or characteristic of soldiers or armed forces. ● *n.* (treated as *sing.* or *pl.*; prec. by *the*) members of the armed forces, as distinct from civilians and the police. □ **militarily** *adv.* **militariness** *n.* [French *militaire* or Latin *militaris* from *miles militis* 'soldier']

military honours *n.pl.* marks of respect paid by troops at the burial of a soldier, to royalty, etc.

military police *n.* (treated as *pl.*) a corps responsible for police and disciplinary duties in the army. □ **military policeman** *n.*

military tribune see TRIBUNE¹ 2b.

militate /ˈmɪlɪteɪt/ *v.intr.* (usu. foll. by *against*) (of facts or evidence) have force or effect (*what you say militates against our opinion*). [Latin *militare militat-* from *miles militis* 'soldier']

■ **Usage** Care should be taken not to confuse *militate* 'have force or effect' with *mitigate* 'make less intense or severe'. Both words are illustrated by the sentence *The heavy rains militated against their attempts to mitigate the problem of flooding*.

militia /mɪˈlɪʃə/ *n.* a military force, esp. one raised from the civil population and supplementing a regular army in an emergency. [Latin, = military service, from *miles militis* 'soldier']

militiaman /mɪˈlɪʃəmən/ *n.* (*pl.* **-men**) a member of a militia.

milk /mɪlk/ *n.* & *v.* ● *n.* **1** an opaque white fluid secreted by female mammals for the nourishment of their young. **2** the milk of cows, goats, or sheep as food. **3** the milklike juice of plants, e.g. in the coconut. **4** a milklike preparation of herbs, drugs, etc. ● *v.tr.* **1** draw milk from (a cow, ewe, goat, etc.). **2 a** exploit (a person) esp. financially. **b** get all possible advantage from (a situation). **3** extract sap, venom, etc. from. **4** *Brit. slang* tap (telegraph or telephone wires etc.). □ **cry over spilt** (or *US* **spilled**) **milk** lament an irremediable loss or error. **in milk** secreting milk. [Old English *milc*, *milcian*, from Germanic]

milk and honey *n.* abundance, prosperity.

milk and water *n.* & *adj.* ● *n.* a feeble or insipid or mawkish discourse or sentiment. ● *attrib.adj.* (**milk-and-water**) feeble, insipid.

milk bar *n.* a snack bar selling milk drinks and other refreshments.

milk chocolate *n.* chocolate for eating, made with milk.

milker /ˈmɪlkə/ *n.* **1** an animal, esp. a cow, yielding milk or kept for milking. **2** a person who, or a machine which, milks cows.

milk fever *n.* **1** an acute illness in female cows, goats, etc. that have just produced young, caused by calcium deficiency. **2** *Med.* a fever in women caused by infection after childbirth (formerly supposed to be due to the swelling of the breasts with milk).

milk float *n. Brit.* a small usu. electric vehicle used in delivering milk.

milk-leg *n.* a painful swelling, esp. of the legs, after childbirth.

milk-loaf *n. Brit.* a loaf of bread made with milk.

milkmaid /ˈmɪlkmeɪd/ *n.* a girl or woman who milks cows or works in a dairy.

milkman /ˈmɪlkmən/ *n.* (*pl.* **-men**) a person who sells or delivers milk.

milk of human kindness *n.* kindness regarded as natural to humanity.

Milk of Magnesia *n. Brit. propr.* a white suspension of hydrated magnesium carbonate usu. in water as an antacid or laxative.

milk of sulphur *n.* the amorphous powder of sulphur formed by precipitation.

milk powder *n.* milk dehydrated by evaporation.

milk pudding *n. Brit.* a pudding of rice, sago, tapioca, etc., baked with milk in a dish.

milk round *n.* **1** a fixed route on which milk is delivered regularly. **2** a regular trip or tour involving calls at several places.

milk run *n.* a routine expedition or service journey.

milk shake *n.* a drink of milk, flavouring, etc., mixed by shaking or whisking.

milksop /ˈmɪlksɒp/ *n.* a spiritless man or youth.

milk sugar *n.* lactose.

milk tooth *n.* a temporary tooth in young mammals.

milk train *n.* a train chiefly transporting milk, usu. very early in the morning.

milk-vetch *n.* a leguminous plant of the large genus *Astragalus*.

milkweed /ˈmɪlkwiːd/ *n.* any of various plants with milky sap, esp. a poisonous N. American plant of the genus *Asclepias*.

milk white *n.* & *adj.* ● *n.* a white colour like that of milk. ● *adj.* (hyphenated when *attrib.*) of this colour.

milkwort /ˈmɪlkwəːt/ *n.* any plant of the genus *Polygala*, formerly supposed to increase women's milk.

milky /ˈmɪlki/ *adj.* (**milkier**, **milkiest**) **1** of, like, or mixed with milk. **2** (of a gem or liquid) cloudy; not clear. **3** effeminate; weakly amiable. □ **milkiness** *n.*

Milky Way *n.* a faint band of light crossing the night sky, made up of many distant stars forming the bulk of our Galaxy.

mill¹ /mɪl/ *n.* & *v.* ● *n.* **1 a** a building fitted with a mechanical apparatus for grinding corn. **b** such an apparatus. **2** an apparatus for grinding any solid substance to powder or pulp (*pepper mill*). **3 a** a building fitted with machinery for manufacturing processes etc. (*cotton mill*). **b** such machinery. **4 a** a boxing match. **b** a fist fight. ● *v.* **1** *tr.* process in a mill, esp. grind (corn), produce (flour), or hull (seeds) in a mill. **2** *tr.* produce regular ribbed markings on the edge of (a coin). **3** *tr.* cut or shape (metal) with a rotating tool. **4** *intr.* (often foll. by *about*, *around*) (of people or animals) move in an aimless manner, esp. in a confused mass. **5** *tr.* thicken (cloth etc.) by fulling. **6** *tr.* beat (chocolate etc.) to froth. **7** *tr. slang* beat, strike, fight. □ **go** (or **put**) **through the mill** undergo (or cause to undergo) intensive work or training etc. □ **millable** *adj.* [Old English *mylen*, ultimately from Late Latin *molinum* via Latin *mola* 'grindstone, mill' from *molere* 'grind']

mill² /mɪl/ *n. N. Amer.* one-thousandth of a dollar as money of account. [Latin *millesimum* 'thousandth': cf. CENT]

millboard /ˈmɪlbɔːd/ *n.* stout pasteboard for bookbinding etc.

mill-dam *n.* a dam put across a stream to make it usable by a mill.

millefeuille /miːlˈfəːj, French milfœj/ *n.* a rich confection of puff pastry split and filled with jam, cream, etc. [French, = thousand-leaf]

millenarian /mɪlɪˈnɛːrɪən/ *adj. & n.* ● *adj.* **1** of or related to the millennium. **2** believing in the millennium. ● *n.* a person who believes in the millennium. ◻ **millenarianism** *n.* [as MILLENARY]

millenary /mɪˈlɛnəri, ˈmɪlɪnəri/ *n. & adj.* ● *n.* (*pl.* **-ies**) **1** a period of 1,000 years. **2** the festival of the 1,000th anniversary of a person or thing. **3** = MILLENARIAN *n.* ● *adj.* of or relating to a millenary. [Late Latin *millenarius* 'consisting of a thousand' from *milleni*, distributive of *mille* 'thousand']

millennium /mɪˈlɛnɪəm/ *n.* (*pl.* **millenniums** or **millennia** /-nɪə/) **1** a period of 1,000 years. **2** *Theol.* the prophesied 1,000-year reign of Christ in person (Rev. 20:1–5). **3** a period of good government, great happiness, and prosperity. ◻ **millennial** *adj.* **millennialism** *n.* **millennialist** *n. & adj.* [modern Latin from Latin *mille* 'thousand', on the pattern of BIENNIUM]

millepede var. of MILLIPEDE.

millepore /ˈmɪlɪpɔː/ *n.* a reef-building coral of the order Milleporina, with polyps protruding through pores in the calcareous exoskeleton. [French *millépore* or modern Latin *millepora*, from Latin *mille* 'thousand' + *porus* PORE[1]]

miller /ˈmɪlə/ *n.* **1** the proprietor or tenant of a corn mill. **2** a person who works or owns a mill. [Middle English *mylnere*, probably via Middle Low German, Middle Dutch *molner*, *mulner*, Old Saxon *mulineri* from Late Latin *molinarius*, from *molina* MILL[1], assimilated to MILL[1]]

miller's thumb *n.* a small spiny freshwater fish, *Cottus gobio*, with a large head. Also called BULLHEAD.

millesimal /mɪˈlɛsɪm(ə)l/ *adj. & n.* ● *adj.* **1** thousandth. **2** of or belonging to a thousandth. **3** of or dealing with thousandths. ● *n.* a thousandth part. ◻ **millesimally** *adv.* [Latin *millesimus* from *mille* 'thousand']

millet /ˈmɪlɪt/ *n.* **1** any of various cereal plants, esp. *Panicum miliaceum*, bearing a large crop of small nutritious seeds. **2** the seed of this. [Middle English from French, diminutive of *mil*, from Latin *milium*]

millet-grass *n.* a tall woodland grass, *Milium effusum*.

millhand /ˈmɪlhand/ *n.* a worker in a mill or factory.

milli- /ˈmɪli/ *comb. form* a thousand, esp. denoting a factor of one-thousandth (abbr.: **m**). [Latin *mille* 'thousand']

milliammeter /mɪlɪˈamɪtə/ *n.* an instrument for measuring electrical current in milliamperes.

milliamp /ˈmɪlɪamp/ *n.* *colloq.* = MILLIAMPERE. [abbreviation]

milliampere /mɪlɪˈampɛː/ *n.* one-thousandth of an ampere, a measure for small electrical currents.

milliard /ˈmɪlɪɑːd/ *n.* *Brit.* one thousand million. [French, from *mille* 'thousand']

■ **Usage** The term *milliard* has been largely superseded by *billion*.

millibar /ˈmɪlɪbɑː/ *n.* one-thousandth of a bar, the cgs unit of atmospheric pressure equivalent to 100 pascals.

milligram /ˈmɪlɪgram/ *n.* (also **milligramme**) one-thousandth of a gram.

millilitre /ˈmɪlɪliːtə/ *n.* (*US* **milliliter**) one-thousandth of a litre (0.002 pint).

millimetre /ˈmɪlɪmiːtə/ *n.* (*US* **millimeter**) one-thousandth of a metre (0.039 in.).

milliner /ˈmɪlɪnə/ *n.* a person who makes or sells women's hats. ◻ **millinery** *n.* [originally = vendor of fancy goods from *Milan*]

million /ˈmɪljən/ *n. & adj.* ● *n.* (*pl.* same or (in sense 2) **millions**) (in *sing.* prec. by *a* or *one*) **1** a thousand thousand (1,000,000). **2** (in *pl.*) *colloq.* a very large number (*millions of years*). **3** (prec. by *the*) the bulk of the population. **4 a** *Brit.* a million pounds. **b** *N. Amer.* a million dollars. ● *adj.* that amount to a million. ◻ **gone a million** *Austral. slang* completely defeated. ◻ **millionfold** *adj. & adv.* **millionth** *adj. & n.* [Middle English from Old French, probably from Italian *millione*, from *mille* 'thousand' + augmentative suffix *-one*]

millionaire /mɪljəˈnɛː/ *n.* (*fem.* **millionairess** /-rɪs/) **1** a person whose assets are worth at least one million pounds, dollars, etc. **2** a person of great wealth. [French *millionnaire* (as MILLION)]

millipede /ˈmɪlɪpiːd/ *n.* (also **millepede**) any arthropod of the class Diplopoda, having a long segmented body with two pairs of legs on each segment. [Latin *millepeda* 'woodlouse', from *mille* 'thousand' + *pes pedis* 'foot']

millisecond /ˈmɪlɪsɛk(ə)nd/ *n.* one-thousandth of a second.

millivolt /ˈmɪlɪvəʊlt, -vɒlt/ *n.* one-thousandth of a volt.

millpond /ˈmɪlpɒnd/ *n.* a pool of water retained by a mill-dam for the operation of a mill. ◻ **like a millpond** (of a stretch of water) very calm.

mill-race *n.* a current of water that drives a mill-wheel.

Mills bomb /mɪlz/ *n.* an oval hand grenade. [invented by Sir W. *Mills* (d. 1932), English engineer]

millstone /ˈmɪlstəʊn/ *n.* **1** each of two circular stones used for grinding corn. **2** a heavy burden or responsibility (cf. Matt. 18:6).

millstream /ˈmɪlstriːm/ *n.* = MILL-RACE.

mill-wheel *n.* a wheel used to drive a watermill.

millworker /ˈmɪlwəːkə/ *n.* a factory worker.

millwright /ˈmɪlrʌɪt/ *n.* a person who designs or builds mills.

milometer /mʌɪˈlɒmɪtə/ *n.* *Brit.* an instrument for measuring the number of miles travelled by a vehicle.

milord /mɪˈlɔːd/ *n.* *hist.* an Englishman travelling in Europe in aristocratic style. [French from English *my lord*: cf. MILADY]

milt /mɪlt/ *n.* **1** the spleen in mammals. **2** an analogous organ in other vertebrates. **3 a** a sperm-filled reproductive gland of a male fish. **b** the semen of a male fish. [Old English *milt(e)* from Germanic, perhaps related to MELT]

milter /ˈmɪltə/ *n.* a male fish in spawning-time.

mimbar /ˈmɪmbɑː/ *n.* (also **minbar** /ˈmɪn-/) a stepped platform for preaching in a mosque. [Arabic *minbar*]

mime /mʌɪm/ *n. & v.* ● *n.* **1** the theatrical technique of suggesting action, character, etc. by gesture and expression without using words. **2** a theatrical performance using this technique. **3** *Gk & Rom. Antiq.* a simple farcical drama including mimicry. **4** (also **mime artist**) a practitioner of mime. ● *v.* **1** *tr.* (also *absol.*) convey (an idea or emotion) by gesture without words. **2** *intr.* (often foll. by *to*) (of singers etc.) mouth the words of a song etc. along with a soundtrack (*mime to a record*). ◻ **mimer** *n.* [Latin *mimus* from Greek *mimos*]

mimeograph /ˈmɪmɪəgrɑːf/ *n. & v.* ● *n.* **1** (often *attrib.*) a duplicating machine which produces copies from a stencil. **2** a copy produced in this way. ● *v.tr.* reproduce (text or diagrams) by this process. [formed irregularly from Greek *mimeomai* 'imitate': see -GRAPH]

mimesis /mɪˈmiːsɪs, mʌɪ-/ *n.* *Biol.* = MIMICRY 3. [Greek *mimēsis* from *mimeisthai* 'to imitate']

mimetic /mɪˈmɛtɪk, mʌɪ-/ *adj.* **1** relating to or habitually practising imitation or mimicry. **2** *Biol.* of or exhibiting mimicry. ◻ **mimetically** *adv.* [Greek *mimētikos* 'imitation' (as MIMESIS)]

mimic /ˈmɪmɪk/ *v., n., & adj.* ● *v.tr.* (**mimicked**, **mimicking**) **1** imitate (a person, gesture, etc.) esp. to entertain or ridicule. **2** copy minutely or servilely. **3** (of a thing) resemble closely. ● *n.* a person skilled in imitation. ● *adj.* having an aptitude for mimicry; imitating; imitative of a thing, esp. for amusement. ◻ **mimicker** *n.* [Latin *mimicus* from Greek *mimikos* (as MIME)]

mimicry /ˈmɪmɪkri/ *n.* (*pl.* **-ies**) **1** the act or art of mimicking. **2** a thing that mimics another. **3** *Biol.* a close external resemblance of an animal (or part of one) to another animal or to a plant or inanimate object; a similar resemblance in a plant. See also BATESIAN MIMICRY, MÜLLERIAN MIMICRY.

miminy-piminy /ˌmɪmɪnɪˈpɪmɪni/ *adj.* over-refined, finicky (cf. NIMINY-PIMINY, NAMBY-PAMBY). [imitative]

mimosa /mɪˈməʊzə, -sə/ *n.* **1** any leguminous shrub of the genus *Mimosa*, esp. *M. pudica*, having globular usu. yellow flowers and sensitive leaflets which droop when touched. **2** any of various acacia plants with showy yellow flowers. [modern Latin, apparently from Latin (as MIME, from its 'imitating' the sensitivity of animals) + fem. suffix *-osa*]

mimulus /ˈmɪmjʊləs/ *n.* any flowering plant of the genus *Mimulus*, including musk and the monkey flower. [modern Latin, apparently diminutive of Latin (as MIME, perhaps with reference to its masklike flowers)]

Min /mɪn/ *n.* any of the Chinese languages or dialects spoken in the Fukien province in SE China. [Chinese]

Min. *abbr.* **1** Minister. **2** Ministry.

min. *abbr.* **1** minute(s). **2** minimum. **3** minim (fluid measure).

mina var. of MYNAH.

minaret /ˈmɪnərɛt, mɪnəˈrɛt/ *n.* a slender turret connected with a mosque and having a balcony from which the muezzin calls at hours of prayer. □ **minareted** *adj.* [French *minaret* or Spanish *minarete* via Turkish *minare* from Arabic *manār(a)* 'lighthouse, minaret', from *nār* 'fire, light']

minatory /ˈmɪnət(ə)ri/ *adj.* threatening, menacing. [Late Latin *minatorius* from *minari minat-* 'threaten']

minbar var. of MIMBAR.

mince /mɪns/ *v.* & *n.* ● *v.* **1** *tr.* cut up or grind (esp. meat) into very small pieces. **2** *tr.* (usu. with *neg.*) restrain (one's words etc.) within the bounds of politeness. **3** *intr.* (usu. as **mincing** *adj.*) speak or walk with an affected delicacy. ● *n.* esp. *Brit.* minced meat. □ **mince matters** (usu. with *neg.*) use polite expressions etc. □ **mincer** *n.* **mincingly** *adv.* (in sense 3 of *v.*). [Middle English from Old French *mincier*, ultimately from Latin (as MINUTIA)]

mincemeat /ˈmɪnsmiːt/ *n.* a mixture of currants, raisins, sugar, apples, candied peel, spices, and often suet. □ **make mincemeat of** utterly defeat (a person, argument, etc.).

mince pie *n.* a usu. small round pie containing mincemeat.

mind /mʌɪnd/ *n.* & *v.* ● *n.* **1 a** the seat of awareness, thought, volition, and feeling. **b** attention, concentration (*my mind keeps wandering*). **2** the intellect; intellectual powers. **3** remembrance, memory (*it went out of my mind*; *I can't call it to mind*). **4** one's opinion (*we're of the same mind*). **5** a way of thinking or feeling (*shocking to the Victorian mind*). **6** the focus of one's thoughts or desires (*put one's mind to it*). **7** the state of normal mental functioning (*lose one's mind*; *in one's right mind*). **8** a person as embodying mental faculties (*a great mind*). ● *v.tr.* **1** (usu. with *neg.* or *interrog.*) object to (*do you mind if I smoke?*; *I don't mind your being late*). **2 a** remember; take care to (*mind you come on time*). **b** (often foll. by *out*) *Brit.* take care; be careful. **3** have charge of temporarily (*mind the house while I'm away*). **4** apply oneself to, concern oneself with (business, affairs, etc.) (*I try to mind my own business*). **5** give heed to; notice (*mind the step*; *don't mind the expense*; *mind how you go*). **6** *N. Amer.* & *Ir.* be obedient to (*mind what your mother says*). □ **be in** (or esp. *N. Amer.* **of**) **two minds** be undecided. **cast one's mind back** think back; recall an earlier time. **come into a person's mind** be remembered. **come** (or **spring**) **to mind** (of a thought, idea, etc.) suggest itself. **don't mind me** often *iron.* do as you please. **do you mind!** *iron.* an expression of annoyance. **give a person a piece of one's mind** scold or reproach a person. **have a good** (or **great** or **half a**) **mind to** (often as a threat, usu. unfulfilled) feel tempted to (*I've a good mind to report you*). **have (it) in mind** intend. **have a mind of one's own** be capable of independent opinion or action. **have on one's mind** be troubled by the thought of. **in one's mind's eye** in one's imagination or mental view. **mind out for** *Brit.* guard against, avoid. **mind over matter** the power of the mind asserted over the physical universe. **mind one's Ps & Qs** be careful in one's behaviour. **mind the shop** have charge of affairs temporarily. **mind you** an expression used to qualify a previous statement (*I found it quite quickly; mind you, it wasn't easy*). **mind your back** (or **backs**) *colloq.* an expression to indicate that a person wants to get past. **never mind 1** an expression used to comfort or console. **2** (also **never you mind**) an expression used to evade a question. **open** (or **close**) **one's mind to** be receptive (or unreceptive) to (changes, new ideas, etc.). **out of one's mind** insane. **put a person in mind of** remind a person of. **put** (or **set**) **a person's mind at rest** reassure a person. **put a person or thing out of one's mind** deliberately forget. **read a person's mind** discern a person's thoughts. **spring to mind** = *come to mind*. **to my mind** in my opinion. [Old English *gemynd*, from Germanic]

mind-bending *adj. colloq.* (esp. of a psychedelic drug) influencing or altering one's state of mind.

mind-blowing *adj. slang* **1** confusing, shattering. **2** (esp. of drugs etc.) inducing hallucinations.

mind-boggling *adj.colloq.* overwhelming, startling.

minded /ˈmʌɪndɪd/ *adj.* **1** (in *comb.*) **a** inclined to think in some specified way (*mathematically minded*; *fair-minded*). **b** having a specified kind of mind (*high-minded*). **c** interested in or enthusiastic about a specified thing (*car-minded*). **2** (usu. foll. by *to* + infin.) disposed or inclined (to an action).

minder /ˈmʌɪndə/ *n.* **1 a** a person whose job it is to attend to a person or thing. **b** (in *comb.*: *childminder*; *machine-minder*). **2** esp. *Brit.slang* a bodyguard employed to protect a criminal, celebrity, etc.

mind-expanding *adj.* giving a sense of heightened or broader awareness.

mindful /ˈmʌɪn(d)fʊl, -f(ə)l/ *adj.* (often foll. by *of*) taking heed or care; being conscious. □ **mindfully** *adv.* **mindfulness** *n.*

mindless /ˈmʌɪndlɪs/ *adj.* **1** lacking intelligence; stupid. **2** not requiring thought or skill (*totally mindless work*). **3** (usu. foll. by *of*) heedless of (advice etc.). □ **mindlessly** *adv.* **mindlessness** *n.*

mind-numbing *adj.* (esp. of tedium) that numbs the mind. □ **mind-numbingly** *adv.*

mind-read *v.tr.* discern the thoughts of (another person). □ **mind-reader** *n.*

mindset /ˈmʌɪn(d)sɛt/ *n.* a fixed opinion or state of mind formed by earlier events.

mine[1] /mʌɪn/ *poss.pron.* & *poss.det.* ● *poss.pron.* the one or ones belonging to or associated with me (*it is mine*; *mine are over there*). ● *poss.det.* (before a vowel) *archaic* = MY (*mine eyes have seen*; *mine host*). □ **of mine** of or belonging to me (*a friend of mine*). [Old English *mīn*, from Germanic]

mine[2] /mʌɪn/ *n.* & *v.* ● *n.* **1** an excavation in the earth for extracting metal, coal, salt, etc. **2** an abundant source (of information etc.). **3** a receptacle filled with explosive and placed in the ground or in the water for destroying enemy personnel, ships, etc. **4 a** a subterranean gallery in which explosive is placed to blow up fortifications. **b** *hist.* a subterranean passage under the wall of a besieged fortress. ● *v.tr.* **1** obtain (metal, coal, etc.) from a mine. **2** (also *absol.*, often foll. by *for*) dig in (the earth etc.) for ore etc. **3 a** dig or burrow in (usu. the earth). **b** make (a hole, passage, etc.) underground. **4** lay explosive mines under or in. **5** = UNDERMINE. □ **mining** *n.* [Middle English from Old French *mine*, *miner*, perhaps from Celtic]

mine-detector *n.* an instrument for detecting the presence of military mines.

minefield /ˈmʌɪnfiːld/ *n.* **1** an area planted with explosive mines. **2** a subject or situation presenting unseen hazards.

mine hunter *n.* = MINESWEEPER.

minelayer /ˈmʌɪnleɪə/ *n.* a ship or aircraft for laying mines.

miner /ˈmʌɪnə/ *n.* **1** a person who works in a mine. **2** any burrowing insect or grub. [Middle English from Old French *minëor*, *minour* (as MINE[2])]

mineral /ˈmɪn(ə)r(ə)l/ *n. & adj.* ● *n.* **1** any of the species into which inorganic substances are classified. **2** a substance obtained by mining. **3** (often in *pl.*) *Brit.* an artificial mineral water or other effervescent drink. ● *adj.* **1** of or containing a mineral or minerals. **2** obtained by mining. [Middle English from Old French *mineral* or medieval Latin *mineralis*, from *minera* 'ore', from Old French *miniere* 'mine']

mineralize /ˈmɪn(ə)rəlʌɪz/ *v.* (also **-ise**) **1** *v.tr. & intr.* change wholly or partly into a mineral. **2** *v.tr.* impregnate (water etc.) with a mineral substance.

mineralogy /mɪnəˈralədʒi/ *n.* the scientific study of minerals. □ **mineralogical** /-rəˈlɒdʒɪk(ə)l/ *adj.* **mineralogist** *n.*

mineral oil *n.* petroleum or one of its distillation products.

mineral water *n.* **1** water found in nature with some dissolved salts present. **2** an artificial imitation of this, esp. soda water. **3** *Brit.* any effervescent non-alcoholic drink.

mineral wax *n.* a fossil resin, esp. ozocerite.

mineral wool *n.* a wool-like substance made from inorganic material, used for packing etc.

miner's right *n. Austral.* a licence to dig for gold etc. on private or public land.

mine shaft *n.* a shaft giving access to a mine.

minestrone /mɪnɪˈstrəʊni/ *n.* a soup containing vegetables, pasta, and beans. [Italian]

minesweeper /ˈmʌɪnswiːpə/ *n.* a ship for clearing away floating and submarine mines.

minever var. of MINIVER.

mineworker /ˈmʌɪnwəːkə/ *n.* a person who works in a mine, esp. a coal mine.

Ming /mɪŋ/ *n.* **1** the dynasty ruling China 1368–1644. **2** Chinese porcelain made during the rule of this dynasty. [Chinese]

mingle /ˈmɪŋg(ə)l/ *v.tr. & intr.* mix, blend. □ **mingle their** etc. **tears** *literary* weep together. **mingle with** go about among. [Middle English, via obsolete *meng* from Old English *mengan*: related to AMONG]

mingy /ˈmɪn(d)ʒi/ *adj.* (**mingier**, **mingiest**) *Brit. colloq.* mean, stingy. □ **mingily** *adv.* [perhaps from MEAN[2] and STINGY]

mini /ˈmɪni/ *n.* (*pl.* **minis**) **1** *colloq.* a miniskirt, minidress, etc. **2** (**Mini**) *Brit. propr.* a make of small car. [abbreviation]

mini- /ˈmɪni/ *comb. form* miniature; very small or minor of its kind (*minibus*; *mini-budget*). [abbreviation of MINIATURE]

miniature /ˈmɪnɪtʃə/ *adj., n., & v.* ● *adj.* **1** much smaller than normal. **2** represented on a small scale. ● *n.* **1** any object reduced in size. **2** a small-scale minutely finished portrait. **3** this branch of painting. **4** a picture or decorated letters in an illuminated manuscript. ● *v.tr.* represent on a smaller scale. □ **in miniature** on a small scale. □ **miniaturist** *n.* (in senses 2, 3 of *n.*). [Italian *miniatura* via medieval Latin from Latin *miniare* 'rubricate, illuminate' from *minium* 'red lead, vermilion']

miniature camera *n.* a camera producing small negatives.

miniaturize /ˈmɪnɪtʃərʌɪz/ *v.tr.* (also **-ise**) produce in a smaller version; make small. □ **miniaturization** /-ˈzeɪʃ(ə)n/ *n.*

minibar /ˈmɪnɪbɑː/ *n.* a selection of mainly alcoholic drinks placed in a hotel room for the use of guests and charged on the bill if used.

minibus /ˈmɪnɪbʌs/ *n.* a small bus for about twelve passengers.

minicab /ˈmɪnɪkab/ *n. Brit.* a car used as a taxi, but not licensed to ply for hire.

minicomputer /ˈmɪnɪkəm,pjuːtə/ *n.* a computer of medium power, more than a microcomputer but less than a mainframe.

minigolf /ˈmɪnɪgɒlf/ *n. Sport* a game in which a club is used to knock a small ball into a series of holes in a lawn.

minikin /ˈmɪnɪkɪn/ *adj. & n.* ● *adj.* **1** diminutive. **2** affected, mincing. ● *n.* a diminutive person or thing. [obsolete Dutch *minneken*, from *minne* 'love' + *-ken*, *-kijn* -KIN]

minim /ˈmɪnɪm/ *n.* **1** esp. *Brit.Mus.* a note having the time value of two crotchets or half a semibreve and represented by a hollow ring with a stem. **2** one-sixtieth of a fluid drachm; about one drop of liquid. **3** an object or portion of the smallest size or importance. **4** a single downstroke of the pen. [Middle English from Latin *minimus* 'smallest']

minima *pl.* of MINIMUM.

minimal /ˈmɪnɪm(ə)l/ *adj.* **1** very minute or slight. **2** being or related to a minimum. **3** the least possible in size, duration, etc. **4 a** *Art* etc. characterized by the use of simple or primary forms or structures etc., often geometric or massive (*huge minimal forms in a few colours*). **b** *Mus.* characterized by the repetition of short phrases. □ **minimally** *adv.* (in senses 1–3). [Latin *minimus* 'smallest']

minimalist /ˈmɪnɪm(ə)lɪst/ *n. & adj.* ● *n.* **1** a person advocating minor or moderate reform in politics (opp. MAXIMALIST). **2** a person who advocates or practises minimal art or music. ● *adj.* **1** advocating moderate policies. **2** of or relating to minimal art or music. □ **minimalism** *n.* [first used with reference to the Russian Mensheviks]

minimax /ˈmɪnɪmaks/ *n.* **1** *Math.* the lowest of a set of maximum values. **2** (usu. *attrib.*) **a** a strategy that minimizes the greatest risk to a participant in a game etc. **b** the theory that in a game with two players, a player's smallest possible maximum loss is equal to the same player's greatest possible minimum gain. [MINIMUM + MAXIMUM]

minimize /ˈmɪnɪmʌɪz/ *v.* (also **-ise**) **1** *tr.* reduce to, or estimate at, the smallest possible amount or degree. **2** *tr.* estimate or represent at less than the true value or importance. **3** *intr.* attain a minimum value. □ **minimization** /-ˈzeɪʃ(ə)n/ *n.* **minimizer** *n.*

minimum /ˈmɪnɪməm/ *n. & adj.* (*pl.* **minima** /-mə/ or **minimums**) ● *n.* the least possible or attainable amount (*reduced to a minimum*). ● *adj.* that is a minimum. [Latin, neut. of *minimus* 'least']

minimum lending rate *n. hist.* (in the UK) the announced minimum percentage at which a central bank will discount bills (abolished in 1981). Cf. BASE RATE.

minimum wage *n.* the lowest wage permitted by law or special agreement.

minion /ˈmɪnjən/ *n. derog.* **1** a servile agent; a slave. **2** a favourite servant, animal, etc. **3** a favourite of a sovereign etc. [French *mignon*, Old French *mignot*, of Gaulish origin]

minipill /ˈmɪnɪpɪl/ *n.* a contraceptive pill containing a progestogen only (not oestrogen).

miniscule var. of MINUSCULE.

miniseries /ˈmɪnɪ,sɪəriːz/ *n.* (*pl.* same) a short series of television programmes on a common theme.

miniskirt /ˈmɪnɪskəːt/ *n.* a very short skirt.

minister /ˈmɪnɪstə/ *n. & v.* ● *n.* **1** (often **Minister**) *Brit.* a head of a government department. **2** (in full **minister of religion**) a member of the clergy, esp. in the Presbyterian and Nonconformist Churches. **3** a diplomatic agent, usu. ranking below an ambassador. **4** (usu. foll. by *of*) a person employed in the execution of (a purpose, will, etc.) (*a minister of justice*). **5** (in full **minister general**) the superior of some religious orders. ● *v.* **1** *intr.* (usu. foll. by *to*) render aid or service (to a person, cause, etc.). **2** *tr. archaic* furnish, supply, etc. □ **ministership** *n.* **ministrable** *adj.* [Middle English via Old French *ministre* from Latin *minister* 'servant', from *minus* 'less']

ministerial /mɪnɪ'stɪərɪəl/ *adj.* **1** of a minister of religion or a minister's office. **2** instrumental or subsidiary in achieving a purpose (*ministerial in bringing about a settlement*). **3** *Brit.* **a** of a government minister or ministry. **b** supporting the Government against the Opposition. □ **ministerialist** *n.* (in sense 3b). **ministerially** *adv.* [French *ministériel* or Late Latin *ministerialis* from Latin *ministerium* 'ministry' (as MINISTER)]

ministering angel *n.* also *joc.* a kind-hearted person, esp. a woman, who nurses or comforts others (with reference to Mark 1:13).

Minister of State *n.* a government minister, in the UK usu. regarded as holding a rank below that of Head of Department.

Minister of the Crown *n. Brit. Parl.* a member of the Cabinet.

Minister without Portfolio *n.* a government minister who has Cabinet status, but is not in charge of a specific department of state.

ministration /mɪnɪ'streɪʃ(ə)n/ *n.* **1** (usu. in *pl.*) aid or service (*the kind ministrations of his neighbours*). **2** ministering, esp. in religious matters. **3** (usu. foll. by *of*) the supplying (of help, justice, etc.). □ **ministrant** /'mɪnɪstr(ə)nt/ *adj. & n.* **ministrative** /'mɪnɪstrətɪv/ *adj.* [Middle English from Old French *ministration* or Latin *ministratio* (as MINISTER)]

ministry /'mɪnɪstri/ *n.* (*pl.* **-ies**) **1** (often **Ministry**) **a** a government department headed by a minister. **b** the building which it occupies (*the Ministry of Defence*). **2 a** (prec. by *the*) the vocation or profession of a religious minister (*called to the ministry*). **b** the office of a religious minister, priest, etc. **c** the period of tenure of this. **3** (prec. by *the*) the body of ministers of a government or of a religion. **4** a period of government under one Prime Minister. **5** ministering, ministration. [Middle English from Latin *ministerium* (as MINISTER)]

miniver /'mɪnɪvə/ *n.* (also **minever**) plain white fur used in ceremonial costume. [Middle English from Anglo-French *menuver*, Old French *menu vair* (as MENU, VAIR)]

mink /mɪŋk/ *n.* **1** either of two small semiaquatic stoatlike animals of the genus *Mustela*, *M. vison* of N. America and *M. introeola* of Europe. **2** the thick brown fur of these. **3** a coat made of this. [Middle English, origin uncertain: cf. Swedish *mänk*, *menk*]

minke /'mɪŋkə, -ki/ *n.* a small baleen whale, *Balaenoptera acutorostrata*, with a pointed snout. [probably from *Meincke*, the name of a Norwegian whaler]

Minn. *abbr.* Minnesota.

minnesinger /'mɪnəsɪŋə/ *n.* a German lyric poet and singer of the 12th–14th c. [German *Minnesinger*, = love-singer]

minnow /'mɪnəʊ/ *n.* any of various small freshwater fish of the carp family, esp. Phoxinus phoxinus. [late Middle English *menow*, perhaps representing Old English *myne*: influenced by Middle English *menuse*, *menise* from Old French *menuise*, ultimately related to MINUTIA]

Minoan /mɪ'nəʊən/ *adj. & n. Archaeol.* ● *adj.* of or relating to the Bronze Age civilization centred on Crete (*c.*3000–1100 BC). ● *n.* **1** an inhabitant of Minoan Crete or the Minoan world. **2** the language or scripts associated with the Minoans. [named after the legendary Cretan king *Minos* (Greek *Minōs*), to whom the palace excavated at Knossos was attributed]

minor /'maɪnə/ *adj., n., & v.* ● *adj.* **1** lesser or comparatively small in size or importance (*minor poet*; *minor operation*). **2** *Mus.* **a** (of a scale) having intervals of a semitone between the second and third, fifth and sixth, and seventh and eighth degrees. **b** (of an interval) less by a semitone than a major interval. **c** (of a key) based on a minor scale, tending to produce a melancholy effect. **3** *Brit.* (appended to a surname, esp. in public schools) indicating the younger of two brothers (*Smith minor*). **4** *Logic* **a** (of a term) occurring as the subject of the conclusion of a categorical syllogism. **b** (of a premiss) containing the minor term in a categorical syllogism. ● *n.* **1** a person under the legal age limit or majority (*no unaccompanied minors*). **2** *Mus.* a minor key etc. **3** *US* a student's subsidiary subject or course. **4** *Logic* a minor term or premiss. ● *v.intr.* (foll. by *in*) *US* (of a student) undertake study in (a subject) as a subsidiary to a main subject. □ **in a minor key** (of novels, events, people's lives, etc.) understated, uneventful. [Latin, = smaller, less, related to *minuere* 'lessen']

minor axis *n. Geom.* (of a conic) the axis perpendicular to the major axis.

Minorcan /mɪ'nɔːk(ə)n/ *adj. & n.* ● *adj.* of or relating to Minorca, an island in the western Mediterranean. ● *n.* a native or inhabitant of Minorca.

minor canon *n.* a cleric who is not a member of the chapter, who assists in daily cathedral services.

minority /maɪ'nɒrɪti, mɪ-/ *n.* (*pl.* **-ies**) **1** (often foll. by *of*) a smaller number or part, esp. within a political party or structure. **2** the number of votes cast for this (*a minority of two*). **3** the state of having less than half the votes or of being supported by less than half of the body of opinion (*in the minority*). **4** a relatively small group of people differing from others in the society of which they are a part in race, religion, language, political persuasion, etc. **5** (*attrib.*) relating to or done by the minority (*minority interests*). **6 a** the state of being under full legal age. **b** the period of this. [French *minorité* or medieval Latin *minoritas* from Latin *minor*: see MINOR]

minor league *n. N. Amer.* (in baseball, football, etc.) a league of professional clubs other than the major leagues.

minor orders *n.pl. RC Ch. hist.* the grades of members of the clergy below that of deacon.

minor piece *n. Chess* a bishop or a knight.

minor planet *n.* an asteroid.

minor prophet *n.* any of the prophets from Hosea to Malachi, whose surviving writings are not lengthy.

minor suit *n. Bridge* diamonds or clubs.

Minotaur /'maɪnətɔː, 'maɪ-/ *n.* (in Greek mythology) a man with a bull's head, kept in a Cretan labyrinth and fed with human flesh. [Middle English via Old French and Latin *Minotaurus* from Greek *Minōtauros*, from *Minōs*, the name of a legendary king of Crete (see MINOAN) + *tauros* 'bull']

minster /'mɪnstə/ *n.* **1** a large or important church (*York Minster*). **2** the church of a monastery. [Old English *mynster* via ecclesiastical Latin *monasterium* from Greek *monastērion* MONASTERY]

minstrel /'mɪnstr(ə)l/ *n.* **1** *hist.* a medieval singer or musician, esp. singing or reciting poetry. **2** *hist.* a person who entertained patrons with singing, buffoonery, etc. **3** (usu. in *pl.*) a member of a band of public entertainers with blackened faces etc., performing songs and music ostensibly of black American origin. [Middle English via Old French *menestral* 'entertainer, servant' and Provençal *menest(ai)ral* 'officer, employee, musician', from Late Latin *ministerialis* 'official, officer': see MINISTERIAL]

minstrelsy /'mɪnstr(ə)lsi/ *n.* (*pl.* **-ies**) **1** the minstrel's art. **2** a body of minstrels. **3** minstrel poetry. [Middle English from Old French *menestralsie* (as MINSTREL)]

mint[1] /mɪnt/ *n.* **1** any aromatic plant of the genus *Mentha* (family Labiateae). **2** a peppermint sweet or lozenge. □ **minty** *adj.* (**mintier, mintiest**). [Old English *minte*, ultimately via Latin *ment(h)a* from Greek *minthē*]

mint[2] /mɪnt/ *n. & v.* ● *n.* **1** a place where money is coined, usu. under State authority. **2** *colloq.* a vast sum of money (*making a mint*). **3** a source of invention etc. (*a mint of ideas*). ● *v.tr.* **1** make (coin) by stamping metal. **2** invent, coin (a word, phrase, etc.). □ **in mint condition** (or **state**) freshly minted; (of books etc.) as new. □ **mintage** *n.* [Old English *mynet* via West Germanic from Latin *moneta* MONEY]

mint julep *n. US* a sweet iced alcoholic drink of bourbon flavoured with mint.

mint mark *n.* a mark on a coin to indicate the mint at which it was struck.

mint master *n.* the superintendent of coinage at a mint.

mint par *n.* (in full **mint parity**) **1** the ratio between the gold equivalents of currency in two countries. **2** their rate of exchange based on this.

mint sauce *n.* chopped spearmint in vinegar and sugar, usu. eaten with lamb.

minuend /ˈmɪnjʊɛnd/ *n. Math.* a quantity or number from which another is to be subtracted. [Latin *minuendus*, gerundive of *minuere* 'diminish']

minuet /mɪnjʊˈɛt/ *n. & v.* ● *n.* **1** a slow stately dance for two in triple time. **2** *Mus.* the music for this, or music in the same rhythm and style, often as a movement in a suite, sonata, or symphony. ● *v.intr.* (**minueted**, **minueting**) dance a minuet. [French *menuet* = fine, delicate (used as a noun), diminutive of *menu*: see MENU]

minus /ˈmʌɪnəs/ *prep., adj., & n.* ● *prep.* **1** with the subtraction of (*7 minus 4 equals 3*) (symbol −). **2** (of temperature) below zero (*minus 2°*). **3** *colloq.* lacking; deprived of (*returned minus their dog*). ● *adj.* **1** *Math.* negative. **2** *Electronics* having a negative charge. ● *n.* **1** = MINUS SIGN. **2** *Math.* a negative quantity. **3** a disadvantage. [Latin, neut. of *minor* 'less']

minuscule /ˈmɪnəskjuːl/ *n. & adj.* (also *disp.* **miniscule** /ˈmɪnɪs-/) ● *n.* **1** a kind of cursive script developed in the 7th c. **2** a lower-case letter. ● *adj.* **1** lower case. **2** *colloq.* extremely small or unimportant. □ **minuscular** /mɪˈnʌskjʊlə/ *adj.* [French from Latin *minuscula* (*littera* 'letter'), diminutive of *minor*: see MINOR]

minus sign *n.* the symbol −, indicating subtraction or a negative value.

minute[1] /ˈmɪnɪt/ *n. & v.* ● *n.* **1** a sixtieth of an hour. **2** a distance covered in one minute (*twenty minutes from the station*). **3 a** a moment; an instant; a point of time (*expecting her any minute*; *the train leaves in a minute*). **b** (prec. by *the*) *colloq.* the present time (*what are you doing at the minute?*). **c** (foll. by *clause*) as soon as (*call me the minute you get back*). **4** a sixtieth of a degree of angular distance (symbol: ′). **5** (in *pl.*) a brief summary of the proceedings at a meeting. **6** an official memorandum authorizing or recommending a course of action. ● *v.tr.* **1** record (proceedings) in the minutes. **2** send the minutes of a meeting to (a person). □ **just** (or **wait**) **a minute 1** a request to wait for a short time. **2** as a prelude to a query or objection. [Middle English via Old French from Late Latin *minuta* (*n.*), from fem. of *minutus* MINUTE[2]: senses 1 & 4 of noun from medieval Latin *pars minuta prima* 'first minute part' (cf. SECOND[2]): senses 5 & 6 perhaps from medieval Latin *minuta scriptura* 'draft in small writing']

minute[2] /mʌɪˈnjuːt/ *adj.* (**minutest**) **1** very small. **2** trifling, petty. **3** (of an inquiry, inquirer, etc.) accurate, detailed, precise. □ **minutely** *adv.* **minuteness** *n.* [Middle English from Latin *minutus*, past part. of *minuere* 'lessen']

minute-gun *n.* a gun fired at intervals of a minute at funerals etc.

minute hand *n.* the hand on a watch or clock which indicates minutes.

Minuteman /ˈmɪnɪtman/ *n.* (*pl.* **-men**) *US* **1** a type of US three-stage intercontinental ballistic missile. **2** *hist.* an American militiaman of the revolutionary period (ready to march at a minute's notice).

minute steak *n.* a thin slice of steak to be cooked quickly.

minutia /mɪˈnjuːʃɪə, mʌɪ-/ *n.* (*pl.* **-iae** /-ʃɪiː, -ʃɪʌɪ/) (usu. in *pl.*) a precise, trivial, or minor detail. [Latin, = smallness, in pl. 'trifles', from *minutus*: see MINUTE[2]]

minx /mɪŋks/ *n.* a pert, sly, or playful girl. □ **minxish** *adj.* [16th c.: origin unknown]

Miocene /ˈmʌɪəsiːn/ *adj. & n. Geol.* ● *adj.* of or relating to the fourth epoch of the Tertiary period with evidence for the diversification of primates, including early apes. Cf. Appendix X. ● *n.* this epoch or system. [formed irregularly from Greek *meiōn* 'less' + *kainos* 'new']

miosis /mʌɪˈəʊsɪs/ *n.* (also **myosis**) excessive constriction of the pupil of the eye. □ **miotic** /mʌɪˈɒtɪk/ *adj.* [Greek *muō* 'shut the eyes' + -OSIS]

MIPS /mɪps/ *n.* a unit of computing speed equivalent to a million instructions per second. [acronym]

mirabelle /mɪrəˈbɛl/ *n.* **1 a** a European variety of plum tree, *Prunus insititia*, bearing small round yellow fruit. **b** a fruit from this tree. **2** a liqueur distilled from this fruit. [French]

miracidium /mʌɪrəˈsɪdɪəm/ *n.* (*pl.* **miracidia** /-dɪə/) *Zool.* a free-swimming ciliated larval stage in which a parasitic fluke passes from the egg to its first host (esp. a snail) (cf. CERCARIA). [Greek *meirakidion* diminutive of *meirakion* 'boy, stripling']

miracle /ˈmɪrək(ə)l/ *n.* **1** an extraordinary event attributed to some supernatural agency. **2 a** any remarkable occurrence. **b** a remarkable development in some specified area (*an economic miracle*; *the German miracle*). **3** (usu. foll. by *of*) a remarkable or outstanding specimen (*the plan was a miracle of ingenuity*). [Middle English via Old French from Latin *miraculum* 'object of wonder', via *mirari* 'wonder' from *mirus* 'wonderful']

miracle drug *n.* a drug which represents a breakthrough in medical science.

miracle play *n.* a mystery play.

miraculous /mɪˈrakjʊləs/ *adj.* **1** of the nature of a miracle. **2** supernatural. **3** remarkable, surprising. □ **miraculously** *adv.* **miraculousness** *n.* [French *miraculeux* or medieval Latin *miraculosus* from Latin (as MIRACLE)]

mirador /mɪrəˈdɔː/ *n.* a turret or tower etc. attached to a building, and commanding an excellent view. [Spanish, from *mirar* 'to look']

mirage /ˈmɪrɑːʒ, mɪˈrɑːʒ/ *n.* **1** an optical illusion caused by atmospheric conditions, esp. the appearance of a sheet of water in a desert or on a hot road from the reflection of light. **2** an illusory thing. [French, from *se mirer* 'be reflected', from Latin *mirare* 'look at']

MIRAS /ˈmʌɪras/ *abbr.* (also **Miras**) (in the UK) mortgage interest relief at source.

mire /mʌɪə/ *n. & v.* ● *n.* **1** a stretch of swampy or boggy ground. **2** mud, dirt. ● *v.* **1** *tr. & intr.* plunge or sink in a mire. **2** *tr.* involve in difficulties. □ **in the mire** in difficulties. □ **miry** *adj.* [Middle English from Old Norse *mýrr*, from Germanic: related to MOSS]

mirepoix /mɪəˈpwɑː, French mirpwa/ *n.* a mixture of sautéd chopped vegetables, used in sauces etc. [French, named after the Duc de *Mirepoix*, French general d. 1757]

mirid /ˈmɪrɪd, ˈmʌɪərɪd/ *n. & adj. Zool.* ● *n.* a heteropteran bug of the family Miridae (formerly Capsidae), which includes numerous plant pests. ● *adj.* of or relating to this family. Also called *capsid*. [modern Latin *Miris* genus name, from *mirus* 'wonderful']

mirk var. of MURK.

mirky var. of MURKY.

mirror /ˈmɪrə/ *n. & v.* ● *n.* **1** a polished surface, usu. of amalgam-coated glass or metal, which reflects an image; a looking-glass. **2** anything regarded as giving an accurate reflection or description of something else. ● *v.tr.* reflect as in a mirror. [Middle English from Old French *mirour*, ultimately from Latin *mirare* 'look at']

mirror carp *n.* a breed of carp with large shiny scales.

mirror finish *n.* a reflective surface.

mirror image *n.* an identical image, but with the structure reversed, as in a mirror.

mirror symmetry *n.* symmetry as of an object and its reflection.

mirror writing *n.* reversed writing, like ordinary writing reflected in a mirror.

mirth /mə:θ/ *n.* merriment, laughter. □ **mirthful** *adj.* **mirthfully** *adv.* **mirthfulness** *n.* **mirthless** *adj.* **mirthlessly** *adv.* **mirthlessness** *n.* [Old English *myrgth* (as MERRY)]

MIRV /mə:v/ *abbr.* multiple independently-targeted re-entry vehicle (a type of missile).

MIS *abbr. Computing* management information systems.

mis-[1] /mɪs/ *prefix* added to verbs and verbal derivatives: meaning 'amiss', 'badly', 'wrongly', 'unfavourably' (*mislead*; *misshapen*; *mistrust*). [Old English from Germanic]

mis-[2] /mɪs/ *prefix* occurring in a few words adopted from French meaning 'badly', 'wrongly', 'amiss', 'ill-', or having a negative force (*misadventure*; *mischief*). [Old French *mes-*, ultimately from Latin *minus* (see MINUS): assimilated to MIS-[1]]

misaddress /mɪsə'drɛs/ *v.tr.* **1** address (a letter etc.) wrongly. **2** address (a person) wrongly, esp. impertinently.

misadventure /mɪsəd'vɛntʃə/ *n.* **1** *Law* an accident without concomitant crime or negligence (*death by misadventure*). **2** bad luck. **3** a misfortune. [Middle English from Old French *mesaventure*, from *mesavenir* 'turn out badly' (as MIS-[2], ADVENT: cf. ADVENTURE)]

misalign /mɪsə'lʌɪn/ *v.tr.* give the wrong alignment to. □ **misalignment** *n.*

misalliance /mɪsə'lʌɪəns/ *n.* an unsuitable alliance, esp. an unsuitable marriage. □ **misally** *v.tr.* (**-ies, -ied**). [MIS-[1] + ALLIANCE, after MÉSALLIANCE]

misandry /mɪ'sandri/ *n.* the hatred of men. [Greek *misos* 'hatred' + *andr- aner* 'man', on the pattern of MISOGYNY]

misanthrope /'mɪz(ə)nθrəʊp, mɪs-/ *n.* (also **misanthropist** /mɪ'zanθrəpɪst, mɪs'an-/) **1** a person who hates humankind. **2** a person who avoids human society. □ **misanthropic** /-'θrɒpɪk/ *adj.* **misanthropical** /-'θrɒpɪk(ə)l/ *adj.* **misanthropically** /-'θrɒpɪk(ə)li/ *adv.* **misanthropy** /mɪ'zanθrəpi, mɪs'an-/ *n.* **misanthropize** /mɪ'zanθrəpʌɪz, mɪs'an-/ *v.intr.* (also **-ise**). [French from Greek *misanthrōpos*, from *misos* 'hatred' + *anthrōpos* 'man']

misapply /mɪsə'plʌɪ/ *v.tr.* (**-ies, -ied**) apply (esp. funds) wrongly. □ **misapplication** /mɪs,aplɪ'keɪʃ(ə)n/ *n.*

misapprehend /,mɪsaprɪ'hɛnd/ *v.tr.* misunderstand (words, a person). □ **misapprehension** /-'hɛnʃ(ə)n/ *n.* **misapprehensive** *adj.*

misappropriate /mɪsə'prəʊprɪeɪt/ *v.tr.* apply (usu. another's money) to one's own use, or to a wrong use. □ **misappropriation** /-prɪ'eɪʃ(ə)n/ *n.*

misbegotten /mɪsbɪ'gɒt(ə)n/ *adj.* **1** illegitimate, bastard. **2** contemptible, disreputable.

misbehave /mɪsbɪ'heɪv/ *v.intr. & refl.* (of a person or machine) behave badly. □ **misbehaviour** *n.*

misbelief /mɪsbɪ'li:f/ *n.* **1** wrong or unorthodox religious belief. **2** a false opinion or notion.

misc. *abbr.* miscellaneous.

miscalculate /mɪs'kalkjʊleɪt/ *v.tr.* (also *absol.*) calculate (amounts, results, etc.) wrongly. □ **miscalculation** /-'leɪʃ(ə)n/ *n.*

miscall /mɪs'kɔ:l/ *v.tr.* **1** call by a wrong or inappropriate name. **2** *archaic* or *dial.* call (a person) names.

miscarriage /mɪs'karɪdʒ, 'mɪskarɪdʒ/ *n.* **1** a spontaneous abortion, esp. before the 28th week of pregnancy. **2** the failure (of a letter, freight, etc.) to reach its destination. [MISCARRY + -AGE]

miscarriage of justice *n.* any failure of the judicial system to attain the ends of justice.

miscarry /mɪs'kari/ *v.intr.* (**-ies, -ied**) **1** (of a woman) have a miscarriage. **2** (of a letter etc.) fail to reach its destination. **3** (of a business, plan, etc.) fail; be unsuccessful.

miscast /mɪs'kɑ:st/ *v.tr.* (*past* and *past part.* **-cast**) allot an unsuitable part to (an actor).

miscegenation /,mɪsɪdʒɪ'neɪʃ(ə)n/ *n.* the interbreeding of races, esp. of whites and non-whites. [formed irregularly from Latin *miscēre* 'mix' + *genus* 'race']

miscellanea /mɪsə'leɪnɪə/ *n.pl.* **1** a literary miscellany. **2** a collection of miscellaneous items. [Latin, neut. pl. of *miscellaneus* (as MISCELLANEOUS)]

miscellaneous /mɪsə'leɪnɪəs/ *adj.* **1** of mixed composition or character. **2** (foll. by pl. noun) of various kinds. **3** (of a person) many-sided. □ **miscellaneously** *adv.* **miscellaneousness** *n.* [Latin *miscellaneus* via *miscellus* 'mixed' from *miscēre* 'mix']

miscellany /mɪ'sɛləni/ *n.* (*pl.* **-ies**) **1** a mixture; a medley. **2** a book containing a collection of stories etc., or various literary compositions. □ **miscellanist** *n.* [French *miscellanées* (fem. pl.) or Latin MISCELLANEA]

mischance /mɪs'tʃɑ:ns/ *n.* **1** bad luck. **2** an instance of this. [Middle English from Old French *mesch(e)ance*, from *mescheoir* (as MIS-[2], CHANCE)]

mischief /'mɪstʃɪf/ *n.* **1** conduct which is troublesome, but not malicious, esp. in children. **2** pranks, scrapes (*get into mischief*; *keep out of mischief*). **3** playful malice; archness, satire (*eyes full of mischief*). **4** harm or injury caused by a person or thing. **5** a person or thing responsible for harm or annoyance (*that loose connection is the mischief*). **6** (prec. by *the*) the annoying part or aspect (*the mischief of it is that* etc.). □ **do a person a mischief** wound or kill a person. **get up to** (or **make**) **mischief** create discord. [Middle English from Old French *meschief* from *meschever* (as MIS-[2], *chever* 'come to an end' from *chef* 'head': see CHIEF)]

mischief-maker *n.* a person who encourages discord, esp. by gossip etc. □ **mischief-making** *n.*

mischievous /'mɪstʃɪvəs/ *adj.* **1** (of a person) disposed to mischief. **2** (of conduct) playfully malicious. **3** (of a thing) having harmful effects. □ **mischievously** *adv.* **mischievousness** *n.* [Middle English via Anglo-French *meschevous* from Old French *meschever*: see MISCHIEF]

misch metal /mɪʃ/ *n.* an alloy of lanthanide metals, usu. added to iron to improve its malleability. [German *mischen* 'mix' + *Metall* 'metal']

miscible /'mɪsɪb(ə)l/ *adj.* (often foll. by *with*) capable of being mixed. □ **miscibility** /-'bɪlɪti/ *n.* [medieval Latin *miscibilis* from Latin *miscēre* 'mix']

misconceive /mɪskən'si:v/ *v.* **1** *intr.* (often foll. by *of*) have a wrong idea or conception. **2** *tr.* (as **misconceived** *adj.*) badly planned, organized, etc. **3** *tr.* misunderstand (a word, person, etc.). □ **misconceiver** *n.* **misconception** /-'sɛpʃ(ə)n/ *n.*

misconduct *n.* & *v.* ● *n.* /mɪs'kɒndʌkt/ **1** improper or unprofessional behaviour. **2** bad management. ● *v.* /mɪskən'dʌkt/ **1** *refl.* misbehave. **2** *tr.* mismanage.

misconstrue /mɪskən'stru:/ *v.tr.* (**-construes, -construed, -construing**) **1** interpret (a word, action, etc.) wrongly. **2** mistake the meaning of (a person). □ **misconstruction** /-'strʌkʃ(ə)n/ *n.*

miscopy /mɪs'kɒpi/ *v.tr.* (**-ies, -ied**) copy (text etc.) incorrectly.

miscount /mɪs'kaʊnt/ *v.* & *n.* ● *v.tr.* (also *absol.*) count wrongly. ● *n.* /also 'mɪs-/ a wrong count.

miscreant /'mɪskrɪənt/ *n.* & *adj.* ● *n.* **1** a wretch; a villain. **2** *archaic* a heretic. ● *adj.* **1** depraved, villainous. **2** *archaic* heretical. [Middle English from Old French *mescreant* (as MIS-[2], *creant*, part. of *croire*, from Latin *credere* 'believe')]

miscue /mɪs'kju:/ *n.* & *v.* ● *n.* (in snooker etc.) the failure to strike the ball properly with the cue. ● *v.intr.* (**-cues, -cued, -cueing** or **-cuing**) make a miscue.

misdate /mɪs'deɪt/ *v.tr.* date (an event, a letter, etc.) wrongly.

misdeal /mɪs'di:l/ *v.* & *n.* ● *v.tr.* (*past* and *past part.* **-dealt** /-'dɛlt/) (also *absol.*) make a mistake in dealing (cards). ● *n.* /also 'mɪs-/ **1** a mistake in dealing cards. **2** a misdealt hand.

misdeed /mɪs'di:d/ *n.* an evil deed; a wrongdoing; a crime. [Old English *misdǣd* (as MIS-[1], DEED)]

misdemeanant /mɪsdɪ'mi:nənt/ *n.* a person convicted of a misdemeanour or guilty of misconduct. [archaic *misdemean* 'misbehave']

misdemeanour /mɪsdɪ'mi:nə/ *n.* (*US* **misdemeanor**) **1** an offence, a misdeed. **2** *Law* an indictable offence, (in the UK formerly) less heinous than a felony.

misdescribe /mɪsdɪ'skrʌɪb/ *v.tr.* describe inaccurately. □ **misdescription** /-'skrɪpʃ(ə)n/ *n.*

misdiagnose /mɪs'dʌɪəgnəʊz/ *v.tr.* diagnose incorrectly. □ **misdiagnosis** /-'nəʊsɪs/ *n.*

misdial /mɪs'dʌɪəl/ *v.tr.* (**-dialled**, **-dialling**; *US* **-dialed**, **-dialing**) (also *absol.*) dial (a telephone number etc.) incorrectly.

misdirect /mɪsdʌɪ'rɛkt, -dɪ-/ *v.tr.* **1** direct (a person, letter, blow, etc.) wrongly. **2** (of a judge) instruct (the jury) wrongly. □ **misdirection** *n.*

misdoing /mɪs'du:ɪŋ/ *n.* a misdeed.

misdoubt /mɪs'daʊt/ *v.tr.* **1** have doubts or misgivings about the truth or existence of. **2** be suspicious about; suspect that.

miseducation /mɪs,ɛdjʊ'keɪʃ(ə)n/ *n.* wrong or faulty education. □ **miseducate** /-'ɛdjʊkeɪt/ *v.tr.*

mise en scène /mi:z ɒ̃ 'sɛn, French miz ɑ̃ sɛn/ *n.* **1** *Theatr.* the scenery and properties of a play. **2** the setting or surroundings of an event. [French, literally 'putting on stage']

misemploy /mɪsɪm'plɔɪ, -ɛm-/ *v.tr.* employ or use wrongly or improperly. □ **misemployment** *n.*

miser /'mʌɪzə/ *n.* **1** a person who hoards wealth and lives miserably. **2** an avaricious person. [Latin, = wretched]

miserable /'mɪz(ə)rəb(ə)l/ *adj.* **1** wretchedly unhappy or uncomfortable (*felt miserable in a suit*). **2** contemptible, inadequate, mean (*a miserable attempt*). **3** causing wretchedness or discomfort (*miserable weather*). **4** *Sc.*, *Austral.*, & *NZ* (of a person) stingy, mean. **5** *colloq.* (of a person) gloomy, morose. □ **miserableness** *n.* **miserably** *adv.* [Middle English via French *misérable* from Latin *miserabilis* 'pitiable', via *miserari* 'to pity' from *miser* 'wretched']

misère /mɪ'zɛ:/ *n. Cards* (in solo whist etc.) a declaration undertaking to win no tricks. [French, = poverty, MISERY]

miserere /mɪzə'rɪəri, -'rɛ:-/ *n.* **1** a cry for mercy. **2** = MISERICORD 1. [Middle English from Latin, imperative of *miserēri* 'have mercy' (as MISER); first word of Ps. 51 in Latin]

misericord /mɪ'zɛrɪkɔ:d/ *n.* **1** a shelving projection on the underside of a hinged seat in a choir stall serving (when the seat is turned up) to help support a person standing. **2** an apartment in a monastery in which some relaxations of discipline are permitted. **3** a dagger for dealing the death stroke. [Middle English via Old French *misericorde* from Latin *misericordia*, via *misericors* 'compassionate' from stem of *miserēri* 'pity' + *cor cordis* 'heart']

miserly /'mʌɪzəli/ *adj.* like a miser; niggardly. □ **miserliness** *n.* [MISER]

misery /'mɪz(ə)ri/ *n.* (*pl.* **-ies**) **1** a wretched state of mind, or of outward circumstances. **2** a thing causing this. **3** *Brit. colloq.* a constantly depressed or discontented person. **4** = MISÈRE. □ **put out of its** etc. **misery 1** release (a person, animal, etc.) from suffering or suspense. **2** kill (an animal in pain). [Middle English from Old French *misere* or Latin *miseria* (as MISER)]

misfeasance /mɪs'fi:z(ə)ns/ *n. Law* a transgression, esp. the wrongful exercise of lawful authority. [Middle English from Old French *mesfaisance*, from *mesfaire* 'misdo' (as MIS-[2], *faire* 'do' from Latin *facere*): cf. MALFEASANCE]

misfield /mɪs'fi:ld/ *v.* & *n.* ● *v.tr.* (also *absol.*) (in cricket, baseball, etc.) field (the ball) badly. ● *n.* /also 'mɪs-/ *Brit.* an instance of this.

misfire /mɪs'fʌɪə/ *v.* & *n.* ● *v.intr.* **1** (of a gun, motor engine, etc.) fail to go off or start or function regularly. **2** (of an action etc.) fail to have the intended effect. ● *n.* /also 'mɪs-/ a failure of function or intention.

misfit /'mɪsfɪt/ *n.* **1** a person unsuited to a particular kind of environment, occupation, etc. **2** a garment etc. that does not fit.

misfit stream *n. Geog.* a stream not corresponding in size to its valley.

misfortune /mɪs'fɔ:tʃu:n, -tʃ(ə)n/ *n.* **1** bad luck. **2** an instance of this.

misgive /mɪs'gɪv/ *v.tr.* (*past* **-gave** /-'geɪv/; *past part.* **-given** /-'gɪv(ə)n/) (often foll. by *about*, *that*) (of a person's mind, heart, etc.) fill (a person) with suspicion or foreboding.

misgiving /mɪs'gɪvɪŋ/ *n.* (usu. in *pl.*) a feeling of mistrust or apprehension.

misgovern /mɪs'gʌv(ə)n/ *v.tr.* govern (a state etc.) badly. □ **misgovernment** *n.*

misguide /mɪs'gʌɪd/ *v.tr.* **1** (as **misguided** *adj.*) mistaken in thought or action. **2** mislead, misdirect. □ **misguidance** *n.* **misguidedly** *adv.* **misguidedness** *n.*

mishandle /mɪs'hand(ə)l/ *v.tr.* **1** deal with incorrectly or ineffectively. **2** handle (a person or thing) roughly or rudely; ill-treat.

mishap /'mɪshap/ *n.* an unlucky accident.

mishear /mɪs'hɪə/ *v.tr.* (*past* and *past part.* **-heard** /-'hə:d/) hear incorrectly or imperfectly.

mishit *v.* & *n.* ● *v.tr.* /mɪs'hɪt/ (**-hitting**; *past* and *past part.* **-hit**) hit (a ball etc.) faultily. ● *n.* /'mɪshɪt/ a faulty or bad hit.

mishmash /'mɪʃmaʃ/ *n.* a confused mixture. [Middle English, reduplication of MASH]

Mishnah /'mɪʃnə/ *n.* a collection of precepts forming the basis of the Talmud, and embodying Jewish oral law. □ **Mishnaic** /-'neɪɪk/ *adj.* [Hebrew *mišnāh* '(teaching by) repetition']

misidentify /mɪsʌɪ'dɛntɪfʌɪ/ *v.tr.* (**-ies**, **-ied**) identify erroneously. □ **misidentification** /-fɪ'keɪʃ(ə)n/ *n.*

misinform /mɪsɪn'fɔ:m/ *v.tr.* give wrong information to; mislead. □ **misinformation** /-fə'meɪʃ(ə)n/ *n.*

misinterpret /mɪsɪn'tə:prɪt/ *v.tr.* (**-interpreted**, **-interpreting**) **1** interpret wrongly. **2** draw a wrong inference from. □ **misinterpretation** /-'teɪʃ(ə)n/ *n.* **misinterpreter** *n.*

misjudge /mɪs'dʒʌdʒ/ *v.tr.* (also *absol.*) **1** judge wrongly. **2** have a wrong opinion of. □ **misjudgement** *n.* (also **misjudgment**).

miskey /mɪs'ki:/ *v.tr.* (**-keys**, **-keyed**) (also *absol.*) key (data) wrongly.

miskick *v.* & *n.* ● *v.tr.* /mɪs'kɪk/ (also *absol.*) kick (a ball etc.) badly or wrongly. ● *n.* /'mɪskɪk/ an instance of this.

Miskito /mɪ'ski:təʊ/ *n.* & *adj.* ● *n.* (*pl.* same or **-os**) **1** a member of a native people of the Atlantic coast of Nicaragua and Honduras. **2** the language of this people. ● *adj.* of or relating to the Miskito or their language. [American Indian name]

mislay /mɪs'leɪ/ *v.tr.* (*past* and *past part.* **-laid** /-leɪd/) **1** unintentionally put (a thing) where it cannot readily be found. **2** *euphem.* lose.

mislead /mɪs'li:d/ *v.tr.* (*past* and *past part.* **-led** /-'lɛd/) **1** cause (a person) to go wrong, in conduct, belief, etc. **2** lead astray or in the wrong direction. □ **misleader** *n.*

misleading /mɪs'li:dɪŋ/ *adj.* causing to err or go astray; imprecise, confusing. □ **misleadingly** *adv.* **misleadingness** *n.*

mislike /mɪs'lʌɪk/ *v.tr.* & *n. archaic* dislike. [Old English *mislīcian* (as MIS-[1], LIKE[2])]

mismanage /mɪs'manɪdʒ/ *v.tr.* manage badly or wrongly. □ **mismanagement** *n.*

mismarriage /mɪs'marɪdʒ/ *n.* an unsuitable marriage or alliance. [MIS-[1] + MARRIAGE]

mismatch *v.* & *n.* ● *v.tr.* /mɪs'matʃ/ match unsuitably or incorrectly, esp. in marriage. ● *n.* /'mɪsmatʃ/ a bad match.

mismated /mɪsˈmeɪtɪd/ *adj.* **1** (of people) not suited to each other, esp. in marriage. **2** (of objects) not matching.

mismeasure /mɪsˈmɛʒə/ *v.tr.* (also *absol.*) measure or estimate incorrectly. □ **mismeasurement** *n.*

misname /mɪsˈneɪm/ *v.tr.* = MISCALL 1.

misnomer /mɪsˈnəʊmə/ *n.* **1** a name or term used wrongly. **2** the wrong use of a name or term. [Middle English via Anglo-French from Old French *mesnom(m)er* (as MIS-[2], *nommer* 'name' from Latin *nominare* NOMINATE)]

miso /ˈmiːsəʊ/ *n.* a paste made from fermented soya beans and barley or rice malt, used in Japanese cookery. [Japanese]

misogamy /mɪˈsɒgəmi, mʌɪ-/ *n.* the hatred of marriage. □ **misogamist** *n.* [Greek *misos* 'hatred' + *gamos* 'marriage']

misogyny /mɪˈsɒdʒ(ə)ni, mʌɪ-/ *n.* the hatred of women. □ **misogynist** *n.* **misogynistic** /-ˈnɪstɪk/ *adj.* **misogynous** *adj.* [Greek *misos* 'hatred' + *gunē* 'woman']

mispickel /ˈmɪspɪk(ə)l/ *n. Mineral.* an arsenide and sulphide of iron which is a major source of arsenic compounds. [German]

misplace /mɪsˈpleɪs/ *v.tr.* **1** put in the wrong place. **2** bestow (affections, confidence, etc.) on an inappropriate object. **3** time (words, actions, etc.) badly. □ **misplacement** *n.*

misplay /mɪsˈpleɪ/ *v. & n.* ● *v.tr.* play (a ball, card, etc.) in a wrong or ineffective manner. ● *n.* /also ˈmɪs-/ an instance of this.

misprint *n. & v.* ● *n.* /ˈmɪsprɪnt/ a mistake in printing. ● *v.tr.* /mɪsˈprɪnt/ print wrongly.

misprision[1] /mɪsˈprɪʒ(ə)n/ *n. Law* **1** (in full **misprision of a felony** or **of treason**) the deliberate concealment of one's knowledge of a crime, treason, etc. **2** a wrong action or omission. [Middle English via Anglo-French *mesprisioun* from Old French *mesprison* 'error', from *mesprendre* 'to mistake' (as MIS-[2], *prendre* 'take')]

misprision[2] /mɪsˈprɪʒ(ə)n/ *n.* **1** a misreading, misunderstanding, etc. **2** (usu. foll. by *of*) a failure to appreciate the value of a thing. **3** *archaic* contempt. [MISPRIZE, influenced by MISPRISION[1]]

misprize /mɪsˈprʌɪz/ *v.tr. literary* despise, scorn; fail to appreciate. [Middle English from Old French *mesprisier* (as MIS-[1], PRIZE[1])]

mispronounce /mɪsprəˈnaʊns/ *v.tr.* pronounce (a word etc.) wrongly. □ **mispronunciation** /-nʌnsɪˈeɪʃ(ə)n/ *n.*

misquote /mɪsˈkwəʊt/ *v.tr.* quote wrongly. □ **misquotation** /-ˈteɪʃ(ə)n/ *n.*

misread /mɪsˈriːd/ *v.tr.* (*past* and *past part.* **-read** /-ˈrɛd/) read or interpret (text, a situation, etc.) wrongly.

misremember /mɪsrɪˈmɛmbə/ *v.tr.* remember imperfectly or incorrectly.

misreport /mɪsrɪˈpɔːt/ *v. & n.* ● *v.tr.* give a false or incorrect report of. ● *n.* a false or incorrect report.

misrepresent /ˌmɪsrɛprɪˈzɛnt/ *v.tr.* represent wrongly; give a false or misleading account or idea of. □ **misrepresentation** /-ˈteɪʃ(ə)n/ *n.* **misrepresentative** *adj.*

misrule /mɪsˈruːl/ *n. & v.* ● *n.* bad government; disorder. ● *v.tr.* govern badly.

Miss. *abbr.* Mississippi.

miss[1] /mɪs/ *v. & n.* ● *v.* **1** *tr.* (also *absol.*) fail to hit, reach, find, catch, etc. (an object or goal). **2** *tr.* fail to catch (a bus, train, etc.). **3** *tr.* fail to experience, see, or attend (an occurrence or event). **4** *tr.* fail to meet (a person); fail to keep (an appointment). **5** *tr.* fail to seize (an opportunity etc.) (*I missed my chance*). **6** *tr.* fail to hear or understand (*I'm sorry, I missed what you said*). **7** *tr.* **a** regret the loss or absence of (a person or thing) (*did you miss me while I was away?*). **b** notice the loss or absence of (an object or person) (*bound to miss the key if it isn't there*). **8** *tr.* avoid (*go early to miss the traffic*). **9** *tr.* = *miss out* 1. **10** *intr.* (of an engine etc.) fail, misfire. ● *n.* **1** a failure to hit, reach, attain, connect, etc. **2** *colloq.* = MISCARRIAGE 1. □ **be missing** not have, lack (an integral part etc.) (*the coat is missing its belt*) (see also MISSING *adj.*). **give (a thing) a miss** *Brit.* avoid; leave alone (*gave the party a miss*). **miss out 1** *Brit.* omit; leave out (*missed out my name from the list*). **2** (usu. foll. by *on*) *colloq.* fail to get or experience (*always misses out on the good times*). **miss the boat** (or **bus**) lose an opportunity. **a miss is as good as a mile** the fact of failure or escape is not affected by the narrowness of the margin. **not miss much** be alert. **not miss a trick** never fail to seize an opportunity, advantage, etc. □ **missable** *adj.* [Old English *missan*, from Germanic]

miss[2] /mɪs/ *n.* **1** a girl or unmarried woman. **2** (**Miss**) **a** the title of an unmarried woman or girl, or of a married woman retaining her maiden name for professional purposes. **b** the title of a beauty queen (*Miss World*). **3** usu. *derog.* or *joc.* a girl, esp. a schoolgirl, with implications of silliness etc. **4** the title used to address a female schoolteacher, shop assistant, etc. □ **missish** *adj.* (in sense 3). [abbreviation of MISTRESS]

missal /ˈmɪs(ə)l/ *n. RC Ch.* **1** a book containing the texts used in the service of the Mass throughout the year. **2** a book of prayers, esp. an illuminated one. [Middle English from medieval Latin *missale*, neut. of ecclesiastical Latin *missalis* 'of the Mass', from *missa* MASS]

missel thrush var. of MISTLE THRUSH.

misshape /mɪsˈʃeɪp/ *v.tr.* give a bad shape or form to; distort.

misshapen /mɪsˈʃeɪp(ə)n/ *adj.* ill-shaped, deformed, distorted. □ **misshapenly** *adv.* **misshapenness** /mɪsˈʃeɪp(ə)nnɪs/ *n.*

missile /ˈmɪsʌɪl/ *n.* **1** an object or weapon suitable for throwing at a target or for discharge from a machine. **2** a weapon, esp. a nuclear weapon, directed by remote control or automatically. □ **missilery** /-lri/ *n.* [Latin *missilis* from *mittere miss-* 'send']

missing /ˈmɪsɪŋ/ *adj.* **1** not in its place; lost. **2** (of a person) not yet traced or confirmed as alive but not known to be dead. **3** not present.

missing link *n.* **1** a thing lacking to complete a series. **2** a hypothetical intermediate type, esp. between humans and apes.

mission /ˈmɪʃ(ə)n/ *n.* **1 a** a particular task or goal assigned to a person or group. **b** a journey undertaken as part of this. **c** a person's vocation (*mission in life*). **2** a military or scientific operation or expedition for a particular purpose. **3** a body of persons sent, esp. to a foreign country, to conduct negotiations etc. **4 a** a body sent to propagate a religious faith. **b** a field of missionary activity. **c** a missionary post or organization. **d** a place of worship attached to a mission. **5** a particular course or period of preaching, services, etc., undertaken by a parish or community. [French *mission* or Latin *missio* from *mittere miss-* 'send']

missionary /ˈmɪʃ(ə)n(ə)ri/ *adj. & n.* ● *adj.* of, concerned with, or characteristic of, religious missions. ● *n.* (*pl.* **-ies**) a person doing missionary work. [modern Latin *missionarius* from Latin (as MISSION)]

missionary position *n. colloq.* a position for sexual intercourse with the woman lying on her back and the man lying on top and facing her.

missioner /ˈmɪʃ(ə)nə/ *n.* **1** a missionary. **2** a person in charge of a religious mission.

mission statement *n.* a declaration made by a company etc. of its general principles of operation.

missis /ˈmɪsɪs, -ɪz/ *n.* (also **missus** /-səz/) *slang* or *joc.* **1** a form of address to a woman. **2** a wife. □ **the missis** my or your wife. [corruption of MISTRESS: cf. MRS]

missive /ˈmɪsɪv/ *n.* **1** *joc.* a letter, esp. a long and serious one. **2** an official letter. [Middle English via medieval Latin *missivus* from Latin (as MISSION)]

misspell /mɪsˈspɛl/ *v.tr.* (*past* and *past part.* **-spelt** or **-spelled**) spell wrongly. □ **misspelling** *n.*

misspend /mɪsˈspɛnd/ *v.tr.* (*past* and *past part.* **-spent** /-ˈspɛnt/) (esp. as **misspent** *adj.*) spend amiss or wastefully.

misstate /mɪsˈsteɪt/ *v.tr.* state wrongly or inaccurately. □ **misstatement** *n.*

misstep /mɪsˈstɛp/ *n.* **1** a wrong step or action. **2** a faux pas.

missus var. of MISSIS.

missy /ˈmɪsi/ *n.* (*pl.* **-ies**) an affectionate or derogatory form of address to a young girl.

mist /mɪst/ *n.* & *v.* ● *n.* **1 a** water vapour near the ground in minute droplets limiting visibility. **b** condensed vapour settling on a surface and obscuring glass etc. **2** dimness or blurring of the sight caused by tears etc. **3** a cloud of particles resembling mist. ● *v.tr.* & *intr.* (usu. foll. by *up, over*) cover or become covered with mist or as with mist. [Old English from Germanic]

mistake /mɪˈsteɪk/ *n.* & *v.* ● *n.* **1** an incorrect idea or opinion; a thing incorrectly done or thought. **2** an error of judgement. ● *v.tr.* (*past* **mistook** /-ˈstʊk/; *past part.* **mistaken** /-ˈsteɪk(ə)n/) **1** misunderstand the meaning or intention of (a person, a statement, etc.). **2** (foll. by *for*) wrongly take or identify (*mistook me for you*). **3** choose wrongly (*mistake one's vocation*). □ **and** (or **make**) **no mistake** *colloq.* undoubtedly. **by mistake** accidentally; in error. **there is no mistaking** one is sure to recognize (a person or thing). □ **mistakable** *adj.* **mistakably** *adv.* [Middle English from Old Norse *mistaka* (as MIS-[1], TAKE)]

mistaken /mɪˈsteɪk(ə)n/ *adj.* **1** wrong in opinion or judgement. **2** based on or resulting from this (*mistaken loyalty; mistaken identity*). □ **mistakenly** *adv.* **mistakenness** /mɪˈsteɪk(ə)nnɪs/ *n.*

misteach /mɪsˈtiːtʃ/ *v.tr.* (*past* and *past part.* **-taught** /-ˈtɔːt/) teach wrongly or incorrectly.

mister /ˈmɪstə/ *n.* **1** a man without a title of nobility etc. (*a mere mister*). **2** *slang* or *joc.* a form of address to a man. [weakened form of MASTER in unstressed use before a name: cf. MR]

mistigris /ˈmɪstɪgrɪs/ *n.* *Cards* **1** a blank card used as a wild card in a form of draw poker. **2** this game. [French *mistigri* 'jack of clubs']

mistime /mɪsˈtaɪm/ *v.tr.* say or do at the wrong time. [Old English *mistīmian* (as MIS-[1], TIME)]

mistitle /mɪsˈtaɪt(ə)l/ *v.tr.* give the wrong title or name to.

mistle thrush /ˈmɪs(ə)l/ *n.* (also **missel thrush**) a large thrush, *Turdus viscivorus*, with a spotted breast, that feeds on mistletoe berries. [Old English *mistel* 'basil, mistletoe', of unknown origin]

mistletoe /ˈmɪs(ə)ltəʊ/ *n.* **1** a parasitic plant, *Viscum album*, growing on apple and other trees and bearing white glutinous berries in winter. **2** a related plant of the genus *Phoradendron*, native to N. America. [Old English *misteltān* (as MISTLE THRUSH, *tān* 'twig')]

mistook *past* of MISTAKE.

mistral /ˈmɪstr(ə)l, mɪˈstrɑːl/ *n.* a cold northerly wind that blows down the Rhône valley and southern France into the Mediterranean. [French & Provençal from Latin *magistralis* (*ventus*), literally 'master wind' (as MAGISTRAL)]

mistranslate /mɪstransˈleɪt, -trɑːns-, -nz-/ *v.tr.* translate incorrectly. □ **mistranslation** *n.*

mistreat /mɪsˈtriːt/ *v.tr.* treat badly. □ **mistreatment** *n.*

mistress /ˈmɪstrɪs/ *n.* **1** a female head of a household. **2 a** a woman in authority over others. **b** the female owner of a pet. **3** a woman with power to control etc. (often foll. by *of*: *mistress of the situation*). **4** *Brit.* **a** a female teacher (*music mistress*). **b** a female head of a college etc. **5 a** a woman (other than his wife) with whom a married man has a (usu. prolonged) sexual relationship. **b** *archaic* or *poet.* a woman loved and courted by a man. **6** *archaic* or *dial.* (as a title) = MRS. [Middle English from Old French *maistresse*, from *maistre* MASTER]

Mistress of the Robes *n.* (in the UK) a lady in charge of the Queen's wardrobe.

mistrial /mɪsˈtraɪəl, ˈmɪstraɪəl/ *n.* **1** a trial rendered invalid through some error in the proceedings. **2** *US* a trial in which the jury cannot agree on a verdict.

mistrust /mɪsˈtrʌst/ *v.* & *n.* ● *v.tr.* **1** be suspicious of. **2** feel no confidence in (a person, oneself, one's powers, etc.). ● *n.* **1** suspicion. **2** lack of confidence.

mistrustful /mɪsˈtrʌstfʊl, -f(ə)l/ *adj.* **1** (foll. by *of*) suspicious. **2** lacking confidence or trust. □ **mistrustfully** *adv.* **mistrustfulness** *n.*

misty /ˈmɪsti/ *adj.* (**mistier**, **mistiest**) **1** of or covered with mist. **2** indistinct or dim in outline. **3** obscure, vague (*a misty idea*). □ **mistily** *adv.* **mistiness** *n.* [Old English *mistig* (as MIST)]

mistype /mɪsˈtaɪp/ *v.tr.* type wrongly. [MIS-[1] + TYPE]

misunderstand /ˌmɪsʌndəˈstand/ *v.tr.* (*past* and *past part.* **misunderstood** /-ˈstʊd/) **1** fail to understand correctly. **2** (usu. as **misunderstood** *adj.*) misinterpret the words or actions of (a person).

misunderstanding /ˌmɪsʌndəˈstandɪŋ/ *n.* **1** a failure to understand correctly. **2** a slight disagreement or quarrel.

misusage /mɪsˈjuːsɪdʒ/ *n.* **1** wrong or improper usage. **2** ill-treatment.

misuse *v.* & *n.* ● *v.tr.* /mɪsˈjuːz/ **1** use wrongly; apply to the wrong purpose. **2** ill-treat. ● *n.* /mɪsˈjuːs/ wrong or improper use or application. □ **misuser** *n.*

MIT *abbr.* Massachusetts Institute of Technology.

mite[1] /maɪt/ *n.* a very small arachnid of the order Acarina, having four pairs of legs when adult. [Old English *mīte*, from Germanic]

mite[2] /maɪt/ *n.* & *adv.* ● *n.* **1** *hist.* a Flemish copper coin of small value. **2** any small monetary unit. **3** a small object or person, esp. a child. **4** a modest contribution; the best one can do (*offered my mite of comfort*). ● *adv.* (usu. prec. by *a*) *colloq.* somewhat (*is a mite shy*). [Middle English via Middle Low German, Middle Dutch *mīte* from Germanic: probably the same as MITE[1]]

miter *US* var. of MITRE.

Mithraism /ˈmɪθrəɪz(ə)m, ˈmɪθreɪ-/ *n.* the cult of the ancient Persian god Mithras associated with the sun. □ **Mithraic** /-ˈθreɪɪk/ *adj.* **Mithraist** *n.* [Latin *Mithras* via Greek *Mithras* and Old Persian *Mithra* from Sanskrit *Mitra*]

mithridatize /mɪˈθrɪdətaɪz/ *v.tr.* (also **-ise**) render proof against a poison by administering gradually increasing doses of it. □ **mithridatic** /-ˈdatɪk/ *adj.* **mithridatism** /-dətɪz(ə)m/ *n.* [from the name of *Mithridates* VI, King of Pontus (d. 63 BC), who reputedly made himself immune to poisons by constantly taking antidotes]

mitigate /ˈmɪtɪgeɪt/ *v.tr.* make milder or less intense or severe; moderate (*your offer certainly mitigated their hostility*). □ **mitigable** *adj.* **mitigation** /-ˈgeɪʃ(ə)n/ *n.* **mitigator** *n.* **mitigatory** *adj.* [Middle English from Latin *mitigare mitigat-*, from *mitis* 'mild']

■ **Usage** See Usage Note at MILITATE.

mitigating circumstance *n.* (usu. in *pl.*) *Law* a circumstance permitting greater leniency.

mitochondrion /maɪtəˈkɒndrɪən/ *n.* (*pl.* **mitochondria** /-drɪə/) *Biol.* an organelle found in most eukaryotic cells, containing enzymes for respiration and energy production. [modern Latin, from Greek *mitos* 'thread' + *khondrion*, diminutive of *khondros* 'granule']

mitosis /maɪˈtəʊsɪs/ *n.* *Biol.* a type of cell division that results in two daughter cells each having the same number and kind of chromosomes as the parent nucleus (cf. MEIOSIS 1). □ **mitotic** /-ˈtɒtɪk/ *adj.* [modern Latin from Greek *mitos* 'thread']

mitral /ˈmaɪtr(ə)l/ *adj.* of or like a mitre. [modern Latin *mitralis* from Latin *mitra* 'girdle']

mitral valve *n.* a two-cusped valve between the left atrium and the left ventricle of the heart.

mitre /ˈmaɪtə/ *n.* & *v.* (*US* **miter**) ● *n.* **1** a tall deeply cleft headdress worn by bishops and abbots, esp. as a symbol of office. **2** (in full **mitre joint**) the joint of two pieces of wood or other material at an angle of 90°, such that the line of junction bisects this angle. **3** a diagonal join of two pieces of fabric that meet at a corner, made by folding. ● *v.* **1** *tr.* bestow the mitre on (a bishop or abbot). **2** *tr. & intr.* join with a mitre. ▫ **mitred** *adj.* [Middle English via Old French and Latin *mitra* from Greek *mitra* 'girdle, turban']

mitre box *n.* (also **mitre block**, **mitre board**) each of various types of guide for a saw in cutting mitre joints.

mitre wheel *n.* either of a pair of bevelled cogwheels with teeth set at 45° and axes at right angles.

mitt /mɪt/ *n.* **1** = MITTEN 1. **2** a glove leaving the fingers and thumb exposed. **3** *slang* a hand or fist. **4** a baseball glove for catching the ball. [abbreviation of MITTEN]

mitten /ˈmɪt(ə)n/ *n.* **1** a glove with two sections, one for the thumb and the other for all four fingers. **2** (in *pl.*) *slang* boxing gloves. ▫ **mittened** *adj.* [Middle English from Old French *mitaine*, ultimately from Latin *medietas* 'half': see MOIETY]

mittimus /ˈmɪtɪməs/ *n.* a warrant committing a person to prison. [Middle English from Latin, = we send]

mitzvah /ˈmɪtsvə/ *n.* (*pl.* **mitzvoth** /-vɒt/) in Judaism: **1** a precept or commandment. **2** a good deed done from religious duty. [Hebrew *miṣwāh* 'commandment']

mix /mɪks/ *v. & n.* ● *v.* **1** *tr.* combine or put together (two or more substances or things) so that the constituents of each are diffused among those of the other(s). **2** *tr.* prepare (a compound, cocktail, etc.) by combining the ingredients. **3** *tr.* combine (an activity etc.) with another simultaneously (*mix business and pleasure*). **4** *intr.* **a** join, be mixed, or combine, esp. readily (*oil and water will not mix*). **b** be compatible. **c** be sociable (*must learn to mix*). **5** *intr.* **a** (foll. by *with*) (of a person) be harmonious or sociable with; have regular dealings with. **b** (foll. by *in*) participate in. **6** *tr.* drink different kinds of (alcoholic liquor) in close succession. **7** *tr.* combine (two or more sound signals) into one. **8** *tr. Mus.* produce (a recording) by combining a number of separate recordings or soundtracks. ● *n.* **1** **a** the act or an instance of mixing; a mixture. **b** the proportion of materials etc. in a mixture. **2** *colloq.* a group of persons of different types (*social mix*). **3** the ingredients prepared commercially for making a cake etc. or for a process such as making concrete. **4** the merging of film pictures or sound. ▫ **be mixed up in** (or **with**) be involved in or with (esp. something undesirable). **mix and match** select from a range of alternative combinations. **mix in** be harmonious or sociable. **mix it** (*US* **mix it up**) *colloq.* start fighting. **mix up 1** mix thoroughly. **2** confuse; mistake the identity of. ▫ **mixable** *adj.* [back-formation from MIXED (taken as past part.)]

mixed /mɪkst/ *adj.* **1** of diverse qualities or elements. **2** containing persons from various backgrounds etc. **3** for or involving persons of both sexes (*a mixed school*; *mixed bathing*). ▫ **mixedness** *n.* [Middle English *mixt* via Old French *mixte* from Latin *mixtus*, past part. of *miscēre* 'mix']

mixed bag *n.* (also **mixed bunch**) a diverse assortment of things or persons.

mixed blessing *n.* a thing having advantages and disadvantages.

mixed crystal *n.* a crystal formed from more than one substance.

mixed doubles *n.pl. Tennis* etc. a doubles game with a man and a woman as partners on each side.

mixed economy *n.* an economic system combining private and State enterprise.

mixed farming *n.* farming of both crops and livestock.

mixed feelings *n.pl.* a mixture of pleasure and dismay about something.

mixed grill *n.* a dish of various grilled meats and vegetables etc.

mixed marriage *n.* a marriage between persons of different races or religions.

mixed media *n. & adj.* ● *n.* the use of a variety of mediums in an entertainment, work of art, etc. ● *attrib.adj.* (also **mixed-media**) = MULTIMEDIA.

mixed metaphor *n.* a combination of inconsistent metaphors (e.g. *this tower of strength will forge ahead*).

mixed number *n.* an integer and a proper fraction.

mixed-up *adj. colloq.* mentally or emotionally confused; socially ill-adjusted.

mixer /ˈmɪksə/ *n.* **1** a device for mixing foods etc. or for processing other materials. **2** a person who manages socially in a specified way (*a good mixer*). **3** a (usu. soft) drink to be mixed with another. **4** *Broadcasting* & *Cinematog.* **a** a device for merging input signals to produce a combined output in the form of sound or pictures. **b** a person who operates this.

mixer tap *n. Brit.* a tap through which mixed hot and cold water is drawn by means of separate controls.

mixture /ˈmɪkstʃə/ *n.* **1** the process of mixing or being mixed. **2** the result of mixing; something mixed; a combination. **3** *Chem.* the product of the random distribution of one substance through another without any chemical reaction taking place between the components, as distinct from a chemical compound. **4** ingredients mixed together to produce a substance, esp. a medicine (*cough mixture*). **5** a person regarded as a combination of qualities and attributes. **6** gas or vaporized petrol or oil mixed with air, forming an explosive charge in an internal-combustion engine. ▫ **the mixture as before** *Brit.* the same treatment repeated. [Middle English from French *mixture* or Latin *mixtura* (as MIXED)]

mix-up *n.* a confusion, misunderstanding, or mistake.

mizzen /ˈmɪz(ə)n/ *n.* (in full **mizzen-sail**) *Naut.* the lowest fore-and-aft sail of a fully rigged ship's mizzen-mast. [Middle English via French *misaine* from Italian *mezzana* 'mizzen-sail', fem. of *mezzano* 'middle': see MEZZANINE]

mizzen-mast *n.* the mast next aft of the mainmast.

mizzen yard *n.* the yard on which the mizzen is extended.

mizzle¹ /ˈmɪz(ə)l/ *n. & v.intr.* esp. *dial.* drizzle. ▫ **mizzly** *adj.* [Middle English, probably from Low German *miseln*: cf. Middle Dutch *miezelen*]

mizzle² /ˈmɪz(ə)l/ *v.intr. Brit. slang* run away; decamp. [18th c.: origin unknown]

Mk. *abbr.* **1** the German mark. **2** Mark (esp. in the New Testament).

mks *abbr.* metre-kilogram-second.

Mkt. *abbr.* Market.

ml *abbr.* **1** millilitre(s). **2** mile(s).

MLA *abbr.* **1** Member of the Legislative Assembly. **2** Modern Language Association (of America).

MLC *abbr.* Member of the Legislative Council.

MLD *abbr.* minimum lethal dose.

MLF *abbr.* multilateral nuclear force.

M.Litt. *abbr.* Master of Letters. [Latin *Magister Litterarum*]

Mlle *abbr.* (*pl.* **Mlles**) *Mademoiselle*.

MLR *abbr.* minimum lending rate.

m'lud see LUD.

MM *abbr.* **1** *Messieurs*. **2** (in the UK) Military Medal. **3** Maelzel's metronome (an indication of tempo in music, from the original metronome invented by J.N. *Maezel* (d. 1838)).

mm *abbr.* millimetre(s).

Mme *abbr.* (*pl.* **Mmes**) *Madame*.

m.m.f. *abbr.* magnetomotive force.

M.Mus. *abbr.* Master of Music.

MN *abbr.* **1** *Brit.* Merchant Navy. **2** *US* Minnesota (in official postal use).

Mn *symb. Chem.* the element manganese.

M'Naghten rules var. of MCNAUGHTEN RULES (see at MACN-).

mnemonic /nɪ'mɒnɪk, ni:-/ *adj.* & *n.* ● *adj.* of or designed to aid the memory. ● *n.* a mnemonic device. □ **mnemonically** *adv.* **mnemonist** /'ni:mənɪst/ *n.* [medieval Latin *mnemonicus* from Greek *mnēmonikos*, from *mnēmōn* 'mindful']

mnemonics /nɪ'mɒnɪks, ni:-/ *n.pl.* (usu. treated as *sing.*) **1** the art of improving memory. **2** a system for this.

MO *abbr.* **1** Medical Officer. **2** money order. **3** *US* Missouri (in official postal use).

Mo *symb. Chem.* the element molybdenum.

Mo. *abbr.* Missouri.

mo /məʊ/ *n.* (*pl.* **mos**) *colloq.* a moment (*wait a mo*). [abbreviation]

mo. *abbr. US* month.

-mo /məʊ/ *suffix* forming nouns denoting a book size by the number of leaves into a sheet of paper has been folded. [the final syllable of terms derived from the ablative sing. masc. of Latin ordinal numbers, e.g. DUODECIMO]

moa /'məʊə/ *n.* (*pl.* **moas**) any extinct flightless New Zealand bird of the family Dinornithidae, resembling the ostrich. [Maori]

moan /məʊn/ *n.* & *v.* ● *n.* **1** a long murmur expressing physical or mental suffering or pleasure. **2** a low plaintive sound of wind etc. **3** a complaint; a grievance. ● *v.* **1** *intr.* make a moan or moans. **2** *intr. colloq.* complain or grumble. **3** *tr.* **a** utter with moans. **b** lament. □ **moaner** *n.* **moanful** *adj.* **moaningly** *adv.* [Middle English from Germanic (probably present, but unrecorded, in Old English)]

moat /məʊt/ *n.* & *v.* ● *n.* a deep defensive ditch round a castle, town, etc., usu. filled with water. ● *v.tr.* surround with or as with a moat. [Middle English *mot(e)* from Old French *mote, motte* 'mound']

mob /mɒb/ *n.* & *v.* ● *n.* **1** a disorderly crowd; a rabble. **2** (prec. by *the*) usu. *derog.* the populace. **3** *colloq.* **a** *Brit.* a gang; an associated group of persons. **b** (**the Mob**) the Mafia or a similar criminal organization. **4** *Austral.* a flock or herd. ● *v.tr.* & *intr.* (**mobbed, mobbing**) **1** *tr.* **a** crowd round in order to attack or admire. **b** (of a mob) attack. **c** *US* crowd into (a building). **2** *intr.* assemble in a mob. □ **mobber** *n.* & *adj.* [abbreviation of *mobile*, short for Latin *mobile vulgus* 'excitable crowd': see MOBILE]

mob cap *n. hist.* a woman's large indoor cap covering all the hair, worn in the 18th and early 19th c. [obsolete (18th c.) *mob*, originally = slut, + CAP]

mobile /'məʊbaɪl/ *adj.* & *n.* ● *adj.* **1** movable; not fixed; free or able to move or flow easily. **2** (of the face etc.) readily changing its expression. **3** (of a shop, library, etc.) accommodated in a vehicle so as to serve various places. **4** (of a person) able to change his or her social status. ● *n.* a decorative structure that may be hung so as to turn freely. □ **mobility** /mə(ʊ)'bɪlɪti/ *n.* [Middle English via French from Latin *mobilis*, from *movēre* 'move']

mobile home *n.* a large caravan permanently parked and used as a residence.

mobile phone *n.* (also **mobile telephone**) a portable radio telephone.

mobile sculpture *n.* a sculpture having moving parts.

mobilize /'məʊbɪlaɪz/ *v.* (also **-ise**) **1 a** *tr.* organize for service or action (esp. troops in time of war). **b** *intr.* be organized in this way. **2** *tr.* render movable; bring into circulation. □ **mobilizable** *adj.* **mobilization** /-'zeɪʃ(ə)n/ *n.* **mobilizer** *n.* [French *mobiliser* (as MOBILE)]

Möbius strip /'mə:bɪəs/ *n. Math.* a one-sided surface formed by joining the ends of a rectangle after twisting one end through 180°. [named after A. F. *Möbius*, German mathematician d. 1868]

mob law *n.* (also **mob rule**) law or rule imposed and enforced by a mob.

mobocracy /mɒb'ɒkrəsi/ *n.* (*pl.* **-ies**) *colloq.* **1** rule by a mob. **2** a ruling mob.

mobster /'mɒbstə/ *n. slang* a gangster.

moccasin /'mɒkəsɪn/ *n.* **1** a type of soft leather slipper or shoe with combined sole and heel, as originally worn by N. American Indians. **2** a poisonous American snake of the genus *Agkistrodon*, esp. (in full **water moccasin**) the semiaquatic *A. piscivorus* of the south-eastern US. [American Indian *mockasin, makisin*]

mocha /'mɒkə/ *n.* **1** a coffee of fine quality. **2** a beverage or flavouring made with this, often with chocolate added. **3** a soft kind of leather made from sheepskin. [*Mocha*, a port on the Red Sea, from where the coffee first came]

mock /mɒk/ *v.*, *adj.*, & *n.* ● *v.* **1 a** *tr.* ridicule; scoff at. **b** *intr.* (foll. by *at*) act with scorn or contempt for. **2** *tr.* mimic contemptuously. **3** *tr.* jeer, defy, or delude contemptuously. ● *attrib.adj.* sham, imitation (esp. without intention to deceive); pretended (*a mock battle*; *mock cream*). ● *n.* **1** a thing deserving scorn. **2** (in *pl.*) *colloq.* mock examinations. □ **make mock** (or **a mock**) **of** ridicule. □ **mockable** *adj.* **mockingly** *adv.* [Middle English *mokke, mocque* via Old French *mo(c)quer* 'deride' from Romanic]

mocker /'mɒkə/ *n.* a person who mocks. □ **put the mockers on** *Brit. slang* **1** bring bad luck to. **2** put a stop to.

mockery /'mɒk(ə)ri/ *n.* (*pl.* **-ies**) **1 a** derision, ridicule. **b** a subject or occasion of this. **2** (often foll. by *of*) a counterfeit or absurdly inadequate representation. **3** a ludicrously or insultingly futile action etc. [Middle English from Old French *moquerie* (as MOCK)]

mock-heroic *adj.* & *n.* ● *adj.* (of a literary style) burlesquing a heroic style. ● *n.* such a style.

mockingbird /'mɒkɪŋbə:d/ *n.* a long-tailed songbird of the American family Mimidae, noted as a mimic of other birds' calls, etc., esp. *Mimus polyglottos*.

mock moon *n. Astron.* paraselene.

mock orange *n.* a white-flowered heavy-scented shrub, *Philadelphus coronarius*.

mock sun *n. Astron.* parhelion.

mock turtle soup *n.* soup made from a calf's head etc. to resemble turtle soup.

mock-up *n.* an experimental model or replica of a proposed structure etc.

MOD *abbr.* (in the UK) Ministry of Defence.

mod[1] /mɒd/ *adj.* & *n. colloq.* ● *adj.* modern, esp. in style of dress. ● *n. Brit.* a young person (esp. in the 1960s) of a group aiming at sophistication and smart modern dress. [abbreviation]

mod[2] /mɒd/ *prep. Math.* = MODULO. [abbreviation]

mod[3] /mɒd/ *n.* a Highland Gaelic meeting for music and poetry. [Gaelic *mōd*]

modal /'məʊd(ə)l/ *adj.* **1** of or relating to mode or form as opposed to substance. **2** *Gram.* **a** of or denoting the mood of a verb. **b** (of an auxiliary verb, e.g. *would*) used to express the mood of another verb. **c** (of a particle) denoting manner. **3** *Statistics* of or relating to a mode; occurring most frequently in a sample or population. **4** *Mus.* denoting a style of music using a particular mode. **5** *Logic* (of a proposition) in which the predicate is affirmed of the subject with some qualification, or which involves the affirmation of possiblity, impossibility, necessity, or contingency. □ **modally** *adv.* [medieval Latin *modalis* from Latin (as MODE)]

modality /mə(ʊ)'dalɪti/ *n.* (*pl.* **-ies**) **1** the state of being modal. **2** (in *sing.* or *pl.*) a prescribed method of procedure. [medieval Latin *modalitas* (as MODAL)]

mod cons /kɒnz/ *n.pl. Brit.* modern conveniences.

mode /məʊd/ *n.* **1** a way or manner in which a thing is done; a method of procedure. **2** a prevailing fashion or custom. **3** *Computing* a way of operating or using a system (*print mode*). **4** *Statistics* the value that occurs most frequently in a given set of data. **5** *Mus.* **a** each of the scale systems that result when the white notes of the piano are played consecutively over an octave (*Lydian mode*). **b** each of the two main modern scale systems, the major and minor (*minor mode*). **6** *Logic* **a** the character of a modal proposition. **b** = MOOD[2] 2. **7**

Physics any of the distinct kinds or patterns of vibration of an oscillating system. **8** *N. Amer. Gram.* = MOOD² 1. [French *mode* and Latin *modus* 'measure']

model /'mɒd(ə)l/ *n. & v.* ● *n.* **1** a representation in three dimensions of an existing person or thing or of a proposed structure, esp. on a smaller scale (often *attrib.*: *a model train*). **2** a simplified (often mathematical) description of a system etc., to assist calculations and predictions. **3** a figure in clay, wax, etc., to be reproduced in another material. **4** a particular design or style of a structure or commodity, esp. of a car. **5 a** (foll. by *of*) an exemplary person or thing (*a model of self-discipline*). **b** (*attrib.*) ideal, exemplary (*a model student*). **6** (often foll. by *for*) a person or thing used, or for use, as an example to copy or imitate (*an unlikely model for emulation*). **7 a** a person employed to pose for an artist, photographer, etc. **b** a person employed to display clothes etc. by wearing them. **8** a garment etc. by a well-known designer, or a copy of this. ● *v.* (**modelled**, **modelling**; *US* **modeled**, **modeling**) **1** *tr.* **a** fashion or shape (a figure) in clay, wax, etc. **b** (foll. by *after*, *on*, etc.) form (a thing in imitation of). **2 a** *intr.* act or pose as a model. **b** *tr.* (of a person acting as a model) display (a garment). **3** *tr.* devise a (usu. mathematical) model of (a phenomenon, system, etc.). **4** *tr. Art* cause to appear three-dimensional. □ **modeller** *n.* [French *modelle* from Italian *modello*, ultimately from Latin *modulus*: see MODULUS]

modem /'məʊdɛm/ *n.* a combined device for modulation and demodulation, e.g. between a computer and a telephone line. [*mod*ulator + *dem*odulator]

moderate *adj., n., & v.* ● *adj.* /'mɒd(ə)rət/ **1** avoiding extremes; temperate in conduct or expression. **2** fairly or tolerably large or good. **3** (of the wind) of medium strength. **4** (of prices) fairly low. ● *n.* /'mɒd(ə)rət/ a person who holds moderate views, esp. in politics. ● *v.* /'mɒdəreɪt/ **1** *tr. & intr.* make or become less violent, intense, rigorous, etc. **2** *tr.* (also *absol.*) act as a moderator of or to. **3** *tr. Physics* retard (neutrons) with a moderator. □ **moderately** /-rətli/ *adv.* **moderateness** /-rətnɪs/ *n.* **moderatism** /'mɒd(ə)rətɪz(ə)m/ *n.* [Middle English from Latin *moderatus*, past part. of *moderare* 'reduce, control': related to MODEST]

moderation /mɒdə'reɪʃ(ə)n/ *n.* **1** the process or an instance of moderating. **2** the quality of being moderate. **3** *Physics* the retardation of neutrons by a moderator (see MODERATOR 5). **4** (in *pl.*) (**Moderations**) the first public examination in some faculties for the Oxford BA degree. □ **in moderation** in a moderate manner or degree. [Middle English via Old French from Latin *moderatio -onis* (as MODERATE)]

moderato /mɒdə'rɑːtəʊ/ *adj., adv., & n. Mus.* ● *adj. & adv.* performed at a moderate pace. ● *n.* (*pl.* **-os**) a piece of music to be performed in this way. [Italian (as MODERATE)]

moderator /'mɒdəreɪtə/ *n.* **1** an arbitrator or mediator. **2** a presiding officer. **3** *Eccl.* a Presbyterian minister presiding over an ecclesiastical body. **4** an examiner for Moderations. **5** *Physics* a substance used in a nuclear reactor to retard neutrons. □ **moderatorship** *n.* [Middle English from Latin (as MODERATE)]

modern /'mɒd(ə)n/ *adj. & n.* ● *adj.* **1** of the present and recent times. **2** in current fashion; not antiquated. ● *n.* (usu. in *pl.*) a person living in modern times. □ **modernity** /mə'dəːnɪti/ *n.* **modernly** *adv.* **modernness** /'mɒd(ə)nnɪs/ *n.* [French *moderne* or Late Latin *modernus* from Latin *modo* 'just now']

modern English *n.* English from about 1500 onwards.

modern history *n.* history from the end of the Middle Ages to the present day.

modernism /'mɒd(ə)nɪz(ə)m/ *n.* **1 a** modern ideas or methods. **b** the tendency of religious belief to harmonize with modern ideas. **2** a modern term or expression. □ **modernist** *n.* **modernistic** /-'nɪstɪk/ *adj.* **modernistically** /-'nɪstɪk(ə)li/ *adv.*

modernize /'mɒd(ə)nʌɪz/ *v.* (also **-ise**) **1** *tr.* make modern; adapt to modern needs or habits. **2** *intr.* adopt modern ways or views. □ **modernization** /-'zeɪʃ(ə)n/ *n.* **modernizer** *n.*

modern Latin *n.* Latin since 1500, used esp. in scientific classification.

modest /'mɒdɪst/ *adj.* **1** having or expressing a humble or moderate estimate of one's own merits or achievements. **2** diffident, bashful, retiring. **3** decorous in manner and conduct. **4** moderate or restrained in amount, extent, severity, etc.; not excessive or exaggerated (*a modest sum*). **5** (of a thing) unpretentious in appearance etc. □ **modestly** *adv.* [French *modeste* from Latin *modestus* 'keeping due measure']

modesty /'mɒdɪsti/ *n.* the quality of being modest.

modicum /'mɒdɪkəm/ *n.* (foll. by *of*) a small quantity. [Latin, = short distance or time, neut. of *modicus* moderate from *modus* measure]

modification /ˌmɒdɪfɪ'keɪʃ(ə)n/ *n.* **1** the act or an instance of modifying or being modified. **2** a change made. [French or from Latin *modificatio* (as MODIFY)]

modifier /'mɒdɪfʌɪə/ *n.* **1** a person or thing that modifies. **2** *Gram.* a word, esp. an adjective or noun used attributively, that qualifies the sense of another word (e.g. *good* and *family* in *a good family house*).

modify /'mɒdɪfʌɪ/ *v.tr.* (**-ies**, **-ied**) **1** make less severe or extreme; tone down (*modify one's demands*). **2** make partial changes in; make different. **3** *Gram.* qualify or expand the sense of (a word etc.). **4** *Phonet.* change (a linguistic unit). **5** *Chem.* change or replace all the substituent radicals of a polymer, thereby changing its physical properties such as solubility etc. (*modified starch*). □ **modifiable** *adj.* **modificatory** /-fɪkeɪt(ə)ri/ *adj.* [Middle English via Old French *modifier* from Latin *modificare* (as MODE)]

modillion /mə'dɪljən/ *n. Archit.* a projecting bracket under the corona of a cornice in the Corinthian and other orders. [French *modillon* from Italian *modiglione*, ultimately from Latin *mutulus* 'mutule']

modish /'məʊdɪʃ/ *adj.* fashionable. □ **modishly** *adv.* **modishness** *n.*

modiste /mɒ'diːst/ *n.* a milliner; a dressmaker. [French (as MODE)]

Mods /mɒdz/ *n.pl. colloq.* Moderations (see MODERATION 4). [abbreviation]

modular /'mɒdjʊlə/ *adj.* of or consisting of modules or moduli. □ **modularity** /-'larɪti/ *n.* [modern Latin *modularis* from Latin *modulus*: see MODULUS]

modulate /'mɒdjʊleɪt/ *v.* **1** *tr.* **a** regulate or adjust. **b** moderate. **2** *tr.* adjust or vary the tone or pitch of (the speaking voice). **3** *tr.* alter the amplitude or frequency of (a wave) by a wave of a lower frequency to convey a signal. **4** *intr. & tr.* (often foll. by *from*, *to*) *Mus.* change or cause to change from one key to another. □ **modulation** /-'leɪʃ(ə)n/ *n.* **modulator** *n.* [Latin *modulari modulat-* 'to measure' from *modus* 'measure']

module /'mɒdjuːl/ *n.* **1** a standardized part or independent unit used in construction, esp. of furniture, a building, or an electronic system. **2** an independent self-contained unit of a spacecraft (*lunar module*). **3** a unit or period of training or education. **4 a** a standard or unit of measurement. **b** *Archit.* a unit of length for expressing proportions, e.g. the semidiameter of a column at the base. [French *module* or Latin *modulus*: see MODULUS]

modulo /'mɒdjʊləʊ/ *prep. & adj. Math.* using, or with respect to, a modulus (see MODULUS 2). [Latin, ablative of MODULUS]

modulus /'mɒdjʊləs/ *n.* (*pl.* **moduli** /-lʌɪ, -liː/) *Math.* **1 a** the magnitude of a real number without regard to its sign. **b** the positive square root of the sum of the squares of the real and imaginary parts of a complex number. **2** a constant factor or ratio. **3** (in number theory) a number used as a divisor for considering numbers in sets giving the same remainder when divided by it. **4** a constant indicating the relation between a physical effect and the force producing it. [Latin, = measure, diminutive of *modus*]

modus operandi /ˌməʊdəs ɒpəˈrandiː, -daɪ/ *n.* (*pl.* **modi operandi** /ˌməʊdi/) **1** the particular way in which a person performs a task or action. **2** the way a thing operates. [Latin, = way of operating: see MODE]

modus vivendi /ˌməʊdəs vɪˈvɛndiː, -daɪ/ *n.* (*pl.* **modi vivendi** /ˌməʊdi/) **1** a way of living or coping. **2 a** an arrangement whereby those in dispute can carry on pending a settlement. **b** an arrangement between people who agree to differ. [Latin, = way of living: see MODE]

mofette /mɒˈfɛt/ *n.* **1** a fumarole. **2** an exhalation of vapour from this. [French *mofette* or Neapolitan Italian *mofetta*]

mog /mɒg/ *n.* (also **moggie** /ˈmɒgi/) *Brit. slang* a cat. [20th c.: variant of *Mag, Maggie*, pet form of the name *Margaret*]

Mogadon /ˈmɒgədɒn/ *n. propr.* a benzodiazepine drug used to treat insomnia.

mogul[1] /ˈməʊg(ə)l/ *n.* **1** *colloq.* an important or influential person. **2** (**Mogul**) *hist.* **a** = MUGHAL. **b** (often **the Great Mogul**) any of the emperors of Delhi in the 16th–19th c. [Persian *muġul*: see MUGHAL]

mogul[2] /ˈməʊg(ə)l/ *n.* a mound on a ski slope formed by skiers turning. [probably from southern German dialect *Mugel, Mugl*]

MOH *abbr.* Medical Officer of Health.

mohair /ˈməʊhɛː/ *n.* **1** the hair of the angora goat. **2** a yarn or fabric from this, either pure or mixed with wool or cotton. [ultimately from Arabic *mukayyar*, literally 'choice, select', assimilated to HAIR]

Mohammedan var. of MUHAMMADAN.

Mohawk /ˈməʊhɔːk/ *n. & adj.* ● *n.* **1 a** (*pl.* same or **Mohawks**) a member of a N. American Indian people. **b** the Iroquoian language of this people. **2** *Skating* a step from either edge of the skate to the same edge on the other foot in the opposite direction. **3** esp. *US* a Mohican hairstyle. ● *adj.* **1** of or relating to the Mohawks or their language. **2** esp. *US* = MOHICAN *adj.* 2. [Narragansett *mohowawog*, literally 'man-eaters']

Mohican /məʊˈhiːk(ə)n, ˈməʊɪk(ə)n/ *n. & adj.* ● *n.* **1** a member of a N. American Indian people of Connecticut. **2** a Mohican hairstyle. ● *adj.* **1** of or relating to this people. **2** (of a hairstyle) with the head shaved except for a strip of hair from the middle of the forehead to the back of the neck, often worn in long spikes. [native name]

Moho /ˈməʊhəʊ/ *n. Geol.* a boundary of discontinuity separating the earth's crust and mantle. [named after A. *Mohorovičić*, Croatian seismologist d. 1936]

moidore /ˈmɔɪdɔː/ *n. hist.* a Portuguese gold coin, current in England in the 18th c. [Portuguese *moeda d'ouro* 'money of gold']

moiety /ˈmɔɪɪti/ *n.* (*pl.* **-ies**) *Law* or *literary* **1** a half. **2** each of the two parts into which a thing is divided. [Middle English via Old French *moité, moitié* from Latin *medietas -tatis* 'middle' from *medius* 'mid, middle']

moil /mɔɪl/ *v. & n. archaic* ● *v.intr.* drudge (esp. *toil and moil*). ● *n.* drudgery. [Middle English from Old French *moillier* 'moisten, paddle in mud', ultimately from Latin *mollis* 'soft']

moire /mwɑː/ *n.* (in full **moire antique**) watered fabric, originally mohair, now usu. silk. [French (earlier *mouaire*) from MOHAIR]

moiré /ˈmwɑːreɪ/ *adj. & n.* ● *adj.* **1** (of silk) watered. **2** (of metal) having a patterned appearance like watered silk. ● *n.* **1** this patterned appearance. **2** = MOIRE. [French, past part. of *moirer* (as MOIRE)]

moist /mɔɪst/ *adj.* **1 a** slightly wet; damp. **b** (of the season etc.) rainy. **2** (of a disease) marked by a discharge of matter etc. □ **moistly** *adv.* **moistness** *n.* [Middle English from Old French *moiste*, ultimately from or related to Latin *mucidus* (see MUCUS) and *musteus* 'fresh' (see MUST[2])]

moisten /ˈmɔɪs(ə)n/ *v.tr. & intr.* make or become moist.

moisture /ˈmɔɪstʃə/ *n.* water or other liquid diffused in a small quantity as vapour, or within a solid, or condensed on a surface. □ **moistureless** *adj.* [Middle English from Old French *moistour* (as MOIST)]

moisturize /ˈmɔɪstʃəraɪz/ *v.tr.* (also **-ise**) make less dry (esp. the skin by use of a cosmetic). □ **moisturizer** *n.*

moke /məʊk/ *n. slang* **1** *Brit.* a donkey. **2** *Austral.* a very poor horse. [19th c.: origin unknown]

moksha /ˈmɒkʃə/ *n.* (in Hinduism and Jainism) release from the cycle of rebirth. [Sanskrit *mokṣa*]

mol /məʊl/ *abbr.* = MOLE[4].

molal /ˈməʊləl/ *adj. Chem.* (of a solution) containing one mole of solute per kilogram of solvent. □ **molality** /məˈlalɪti/ *n.* [MOLE[4] + -AL]

molar[1] /ˈməʊlə/ *adj. & n.* ● *adj.* (usu. of a mammal's back teeth) serving to grind. ● *n.* a molar tooth. [Latin *molaris* from *mola* 'millstone']

molar[2] /ˈməʊlə/ *adj.* **1** of or relating to mass. **2** acting on or by means of large masses or units. [Latin *moles* mass]

molar[3] /ˈməʊlə/ *adj. Chem.* **1** of or relating to one mole of a substance (*molar latent heat*). **2** (of a solution) containing one mole of solute per litre of solvent. □ **molarity** /məˈlarɪti/ *n.* [MOLE[4] + -AR[1]]

molasses /məˈlasɪz/ *n.pl.* (treated as *sing.*) **1** uncrystallized syrup extracted from raw sugar during refining. **2** *N. Amer.* treacle. [Portuguese *melaço* from Late Latin *mellaceum* MUST[2], from *mel* 'honey']

mold *US* var. of MOULD[1], MOULD[2], MOULD[3].

molder *US* var. of MOULDER.

molding *US* var. of MOULDING.

moldy *US* var. of MOULDY.

mole[1] /məʊl/ *n.* **1** any small burrowing insect-eating mammal of the family Talpidae, esp. *Talpa europaea*, with dark velvety fur and very small eyes. **2** *colloq.* **a** a spy established deep within an organization and usu. dormant for a long period while attaining a position of trust. **b** a betrayer of confidential information. [Middle English *molle*, probably from Middle Dutch *moll(e), mol*, Middle Low German *mol, mul*]

mole[2] /məʊl/ *n.* a small often slightly raised dark blemish on the skin caused by a high concentration of melanin. [Old English *māl*, from Germanic]

mole[3] /məʊl/ *n.* **1** a massive structure serving as a pier, breakwater, or causeway. **2** an artificial harbour. [French *môle* from Latin *moles* 'mass']

mole[4] /məʊl/ *n. Chem.* the SI unit of amount of substance equal to the quantity containing as many elementary units as there are atoms in 0.012 kg of carbon-12. [German *Mol* from *Molekül* MOLECULE]

mole[5] /məʊl/ *n. Med.* an abnormal mass of tissue in the uterus. [French *môle* from Latin *mola* 'millstone']

mole cricket *n.* a large burrowing nocturnal cricket-like insect of the family Gryllotalpidae.

molecular /məˈlɛkjʊlə/ *adj.* of, relating to, or consisting of molecules. □ **molecularity** /-ˈlarɪti/ *n.* **molecularly** *adv.*

molecular biology *n.* the study of the structure and function of large molecules associated with living organisms.

molecular sieve *n.* a crystalline substance with pores of molecular dimensions which permit the passage of molecules below a certain size.

molecular weight *n.* = RELATIVE MOLECULAR MASS.

molecule /ˈmɒlɪkjuːl/ *n.* **1** *Chem.* the smallest fundamental unit (usu. a group of atoms) of a chemical compound that can take part in a chemical reaction. **2** (in general use) a small particle. [French *molécule* from modern Latin *molecula*, diminutive of Latin *moles* 'mass']

molehill /ˈməʊlhɪl/ *n.* a small mound thrown up by a mole in burrowing. □ **make a mountain out of a molehill** exaggerate the importance of a minor difficulty.

mole rat *n.* any of various ratlike rodents with reduced eyes which live underground, esp. of the African family Bathyergidae, often living communally.

moleskin /ˈməʊlskɪn/ *n.* **1** the skin of a mole used as fur. **2 a** a kind of cotton fustian with its surface shaved before dyeing. **b** (in *pl.*) clothes, esp. trousers, made of this.

molest /məˈlɛst/ *v.tr.* **1** annoy or pester (a person) in a hostile or injurious way. **2** attack or interfere with (a person), esp. sexually. □ **molestation** /mɒlɛˈsteɪʃ(ə)n, məʊl-/ *n.* **molester** *n.* [Old French *molester* or Latin *molestare* 'annoy' from *molestus* 'troublesome']

moline /məˈlʌɪn/ *adj. Heraldry* (of a cross) having each extremity broadened and curved back. [probably from Anglo-French *moliné* from *molin* MILL[1], because of the resemblance to the iron support of a millstone]

moll /mɒl/ *n. slang* **1** a gangster's female companion. **2** a prostitute. [pet form of the name *Mary*]

mollify /ˈmɒlɪfʌɪ/ *v.tr.* (**-ies**, **-ied**) **1** appease, pacify. **2** reduce the severity of; soften. □ **mollification** /-fɪˈkeɪʃ(ə)n/ *n.* **mollifier** *n.* [Middle English from French *mollifier* or Latin *mollificare*, from *mollis* 'soft']

mollusc /ˈmɒləsk/ *n.* (*US* also **mollusk**) any invertebrate of the phylum Mollusca, with a soft body and usu. a hard shell, including limpets, snails, cuttlefish, oysters, mussels, etc. □ **molluscan** /məˈlʌskən/ *adj.* **molluscoid** /məˈlʌskɔɪd/ *adj.* **molluscous** /məˈlʌskəs/ *adj.* [modern Latin *mollusca*, neut. pl. of Latin *molluscus*, from *mollis* 'soft']

molly /ˈmɒli/ *n.* (also **mollie**) a small American freshwater fish of the genus *Poecilia*, bearing live young, esp. *P. sphenops*, bred in many colours for aquaria. [from modern Latin *Mollienisia* (former genus name), from Count *Mollien*, French statesman (d. 1850)]

mollycoddle /ˈmɒlɪkɒd(ə)l/ *v. & n.* ● *v.tr.* coddle, pamper. ● *n.* an effeminate man or boy; a milksop. [formed as MOLL + CODDLE]

mollymawk /ˈmɒlɪmɔːk/ *n.* (also **mallemuck** /ˈmalɪmʌk/) any of various fulmars, petrels, and esp. small albatrosses of the genus *Diomedea*. [Dutch *mallemok*, from *mal* 'foolish' + *mok* 'gull']

Moloch /ˈməʊlɒk/ *n.* **1 a** a Canaanite idol to whom children were sacrificed. **b** a tyrannical object of sacrifices. **2** (**moloch**) a grotesque spiny slow-moving Australian lizard, *Moloch horridus*. [Late Latin via Greek *Molokh* from Hebrew *mōlek̲*]

Molotov cocktail /ˈmɒlətɒf/ *n.* a crude incendiary device usu. consisting of a bottle filled with inflammable liquid. [named after V. M. *Molotov*, Russian statesman d. 1986]

molt *US* var. of MOULT.

molten /ˈməʊlt(ə)n/ *adj.* (usu of materials that need a great deal of heat to melt them) melted, esp. made liquid by heat (*molten lava*; *molten lead*). [past part. of MELT]

molto /ˈmɒltəʊ/ *adv. Mus.* very (*molto sostenuto*; *allegro molto*). [Italian, from Latin *multus* 'much']

moly /ˈməʊli/ *n.* (*pl.* **-ies**) **1** an allium, *Allium moly*, with small yellow flowers. **2** a mythical herb with white flowers and black roots, endowed with magic properties. [Latin from Greek *mōlu*]

molybdenite /məˈlɪbdənʌɪt/ *n.* molybdenum disulphide as an ore.

molybdenum /məˈlɪbdənəm/ *n. Chem.* a silver-white brittle metallic transition element occurring naturally in molybdenite and used in steel to give strength and resistance to corrosion (symbol **Mo**). [modern Latin, earlier *molybdena*, originally = molybdenite, lead ore: Latin *molybdena* from Greek *molubdaina* 'plummet', from *molubdos* 'lead']

mom /mɒm/ *n. N. Amer. colloq.* mother. [abbreviation of MOMMA]

moment /ˈməʊm(ə)nt/ *n.* **1** a very brief portion of time; an instant. **2** a short period of time (*wait a moment*) (see also MINUTE[1] 3a). **3** an exact or particular point of time (*at last the moment arrived*; *I came the moment you called*). **4** importance (*of no great moment*). **5** *Physics & Mech.* etc. **a** the turning effect produced by a force acting at a distance on an object. **b** this effect expressed as the product of the force and the distance from its line of action to a point. □ **at the moment** at this time; now. **have one's moments** be impressive, happy, etc., on occasions. **in a moment 1** very soon. **2** instantly. **man** (or **woman** etc.) **of the moment** the one of importance at the time in question. **not for a** (or **one**) **moment** never; not at all. **this moment** immediately; at once (*come here this moment*). [Middle English via Old French from Latin *momentum*: see MOMENTUM]

momenta *pl.* of MOMENTUM.

momentarily /ˈməʊm(ə)nt(ə)rɪli, məʊm(ə)nˈtɛrɪli/ *adv.* **1** for a moment. **2** *N. Amer.* **a** at any moment. **b** instantly.

momentary /ˈməʊm(ə)nt(ə)ri/ *adj.* **1** lasting only a moment. **2** short-lived; transitory. □ **momentariness** *n.* [Latin *momentarius* (as MOMENT)]

momently /ˈməʊm(ə)ntli/ *adv. literary* **1** from moment to moment. **2** every moment. **3** for a moment.

moment of inertia *n. Physics* the quantity by which the angular acceleration of a body must be multiplied to give corresponding torque.

moment of truth *n.* a time of crisis or test (originally the final sword-thrust in a bullfight).

momentous /mə(ʊ)ˈmɛntəs/ *adj.* having great importance. □ **momentously** *adv.* **momentousness** *n.*

momentum /məˈmɛntəm/ *n.* (*pl.* **momenta** /-tə/) **1** *Physics* the quantity of motion of a moving body, measured as a product of its mass and velocity. **2** the impetus gained by movement. **3** strength or continuity derived from an initial effort. [Latin from *movimentum*, from *movēre* 'move']

momma *n.* var. of MAMMA[1].

mommy /ˈmɒmi/ *n.* (*pl.* **-ies**) esp. *US colloq.* = MUMMY[1].

Mon. *abbr.* Monday.

monad /ˈmɒnad, ˈməʊ-/ *n.* **1** the number one; a unit. **2** *Philos.* any ultimate unit of being (e.g. a soul, an atom, a person, God). **3** *Biol.* a simple organism, e.g. one assumed as the first in the genealogy of living beings. □ **monadic** /mɒˈnadɪk/ *adj.* **monadism** *n.* (in sense 2). [French *monade* or Late Latin *monas monad-* from Greek *monas -ados* 'unit', from *monos* 'alone']

monadelphous /mɒnəˈdɛlfəs/ *adj. Bot.* **1** (of stamens) having filaments united into one bundle. **2** (of a plant) with such stamens. [Greek *monos* 'one' + *adelphos* 'brother']

monadnock /məˈnadnɒk/ *n.* a steep-sided isolated hill resistant to erosion and rising above a plain. [named after Mount *Monadnock* in New Hampshire, US]

monandry /mɒˈnandri/ *n.* **1** the custom of having only one husband at a time. **2** *Bot.* the state of having a single stamen. □ **monandrous** *adj.* [MONO-, on the pattern of *polyandry*]

monarch /ˈmɒnək/ *n.* **1** a sovereign with the title of king, queen, emperor, empress, or the equivalent. **2** a supreme ruler. **3** a powerful or pre-eminent person. **4** (in full **monarch butterfly**) a large orange and black butterfly, *Danaus plexippus*, found mainly in the Americas. **5** (in full **monarch flycatcher**) a flycatcher of the Old World family Monarchidae. □ **monarchal** /məˈnɑːk(ə)l/ *adj.* **monarchic** /məˈnɑːkɪk/ *adj.* **monarchical** /məˈnɑːkɪk(ə)l/ *adj.* **monarchically** /məˈnɑːkɪk(ə)li/ *adv.* [Middle English via French *monarque* or Late Latin *monarcha* from Greek *monarkhēs, -os*, from *monos* 'alone' + *arkhō* 'to rule']

monarchism /ˈmɒnəkɪz(ə)m/ *n.* the advocacy of or the principles of monarchy. □ **monarchist** *n.* [French *monarchisme* (as MONARCHY)]

monarchy /ˈmɒnəki/ *n.* (*pl.* **-ies**) **1** a form of government with a monarch at the head. **2** a state with this. □ **monarchial** /məˈnɑːkɪəl/ *adj.* [Middle English via Old French *monarchie* and Late Latin *monarchia* from Greek *monarkhia* 'the rule of one' (as MONARCH)]

monastery /ˈmɒnəst(ə)ri/ *n.* (*pl.* **-ies**) the residence of a religious community, esp. of monks living in seclusion.

[Middle English via ecclesiastical Latin *monasterium* from ecclesiastical Greek *monastērion*, via *monazō* 'live alone' from *monos* 'alone']

monastic /mə'nastɪk/ *adj. & n.* ● *adj.* **1** of or relating to monasteries or the religious communities living in them. **2** resembling these or their way of life; solitary and celibate. ● *n.* a monk or other follower of a monastic rule. □ **monastically** *adv.* **monasticism** /-sɪz(ə)m/ *n.* **monasticize** /-sʌɪz/ *v.tr.* (also **-ise**). [French *monastique* or Late Latin *monasticus* from Greek *monastikos* (as MONASTERY)]

monatomic /mɒnə'tɒmɪk/ *adj. Chem.* **1** (esp. of a molecule) consisting of one atom. **2** having one replaceable atom or radical.

monaural /mɒn'ɔːr(ə)l/ *adj.* **1** = MONOPHONIC 1. **2** of or involving one ear. □ **monaurally** *adv.* [MONO- + AURAL]

monazite /'mɒnəzʌɪt/ *n.* a phosphate mineral containing rare-earth elements and thorium. [German *Monazit* from Greek *monazō* 'live alone' (because of its rarity)]

mondaine /mɔ̃'dɛn, French mɔ̃dɛn/ *adj. & n.* ● *adj.* **1** of the fashionable world. **2** worldly. ● *n.* a worldly or fashionable woman. [French, fem. of *mondain*: see MUNDANE]

Monday /'mʌndeɪ, -di/ *n. & adv.* ● *n.* the second day of the week, following Sunday. ● *adv. colloq.* **1** on Monday. **2** (**Mondays**) on Mondays; each Monday. [Old English *mōnandæg* 'day of the moon', translation of Late Latin *lunae dies*]

Monel /'məʊn(ə)l/ *n.* (in full **Monel metal**) *propr.* a nickel-copper alloy with high tensile strength and resisting corrosion. [named after A. *Monell*, American businessman d. 1921]

monetarism /'mʌnɪt(ə)rɪz(ə)m/ *n.* the theory or practice of controlling the supply of money as the chief method of stabilizing the economy.

monetarist /'mʌnɪt(ə)rɪst/ *n. & adj.* ● *n.* an advocate of monetarism. ● *adj.* in accordance with the principles of monetarism.

monetary /'mʌnɪt(ə)ri/ *adj.* **1** of the currency in use. **2** of or consisting of money. □ **monetarily** *adv.* [French *monétaire* or Late Latin *monetarius* from Latin (as MONEY)]

monetize /'mʌnɪtʌɪz/ *v.tr.* (also **-ise**) **1** give a fixed value as currency. **2** put (a metal) into circulation as money. □ **monetization** /-'zeɪʃ(ə)n/ *n.* [French *monétiser* from Latin (as MONEY)]

money /'mʌni/ *n.* **1 a** a current medium of exchange in the form of coins and banknotes. **b** a particular form of this (*silver money*). **2** (*pl.* **-eys** or **-ies**) (in *pl.*) sums of money. **3 a** wealth; property viewed as convertible into money. **b** wealth as giving power or influence (*money speaks*). **c** a rich person or family (*has married into money*). **4 a** money as a resource (*time is money*). **b** profit, remuneration (*in it for the money*). □ **for my money** in my opinion or judgement; for my preference (*is too aggressive for my money*). **have money to burn** see BURN[1]. **in the money** *colloq.* having or winning a lot of money. **money for jam** (or **old rope**) *Brit. colloq.* profit for little or no trouble. **put money into** invest in. □ **moneyless** *adj.* [Middle English via Old French *moneie* from Latin *moneta* 'mint, money', originally a title of the goddess Juno, in whose temple at Rome money was minted]

moneybags /'mʌnɪbagz/ *n.pl.* (treated as *sing.*) *colloq.* usu. *derog.* a wealthy person.

money box *n. Brit.* a box for saving money dropped through a slit.

money broker *n.* a person who deals in money in the way of exchange, banking, lending, etc.

money changer *n.* a person whose business it is to change money, esp. at an official rate.

moneyed /'mʌnɪd/ *adj.* **1** having much money; wealthy. **2** consisting of money (*moneyed assistance*).

money-grubber *n. colloq.* a person greedily intent on amassing money. □ **money-grubbing** *adj. & n.*

moneylender /'mʌnɪlɛndə/ *n.* a person who lends money, esp. as a business, at interest. □ **moneylending** *n. & adj.*

moneymaker /'mʌnɪmeɪkə/ *n.* **1** a person who earns much money. **2** a thing, idea, etc., that produces much money. □ **moneymaking** *n. & adj.*

money market *n. Stock Exch.* trade in short-term stocks, loans, etc.

money of account see ACCOUNT.

money order *n.* an order for payment of a specified sum, issued by a bank or Post Office.

money spider *n.* a small household spider supposed to bring financial luck.

money-spinner *n.* esp. *Brit.* a thing that brings in a profit.

money supply *n.* the total amount of money in circulation or in being in a country.

money's-worth *n.* (prec. by *your*, *my*, *one's*, etc.) good value for one's money.

moneywort /'mʌnɪwəːt/ *n.* a trailing evergreen plant, *Lysimachia nummularia*, with round glossy leaves and yellow flowers.

monger /'mʌŋgə/ *n.* (usu. in *comb.*) **1** a dealer or trader (*fishmonger*; *ironmonger*). **2** usu. *derog.* a person who promotes or deals in something specified (*warmonger*; *scaremonger*). [Old English *mangere* from *mangian* 'to traffic', from Germanic, ultimately from Latin *mango* 'dealer']

Mongol /'mɒŋg(ə)l/ *adj. & n.* ● *adj.* **1** of or relating to the Asian people now inhabiting Mongolia in central Asia. **2** resembling this people, esp. in appearance. **3** (**mongol**) *offens.* suffering from Down's syndrome. ● *n.* **1** a Mongolian. **2** (**mongol**) *offens.* a person suffering from Down's syndrome. [Mongolian: perhaps from *mong* 'brave']

■ **Usage** In sense 3 of the adjective and sense 2 of the noun, *Down's syndrome* should be used in place of *mongol* in order to avoid offence, e.g. *a Down's syndrome baby*; *She suffers from Down's syndrome.*

Mongolian /mɒŋ'gəʊlɪən/ *n. & adj.* ● *n.* **1** a native or inhabitant of Mongolia. **2** the language of Mongolia. ● *adj.* of or relating to Mongolia or its people or language.

mongolism /'mɒŋg(ə)lɪz(ə)m/ *n. offens.* = DOWN'S SYNDROME. [MONGOL + -ISM, because its physical characteristics were thought to be reminiscent of Mongolians]

■ **Usage** The term *Down's syndrome* is now much preferred to *mongolism* which can cause offence.

Mongoloid /'mɒŋg(ə)lɔɪd/ *adj. & n.* ● *adj.* **1** characteristic of the Mongolians, esp. in having a broad flat yellowish face. **2** (**mongoloid**) *offens.* affected with Down's syndrome. ● *n.* a Mongoloid or *offens.* mongoloid person.

mongoose /'mɒŋguːs/ *n.* (*pl.* **mongooses**) any of various small flesh-eating civet-like mammals of the family Viverridae, esp. of the genus *Herpestes*. [Marathi *mangūs*]

mongrel /'mʌŋgr(ə)l/ *n. & adj.* ● *n.* **1** a dog of no definable type or breed. **2** any other animal or plant resulting from the crossing of different breeds or types. **3** *offens.* a person of mixed race. ● *adj.* of mixed origin, nature, or character. □ **mongrelism** *n.* **mongrelize** *v.tr.* (also **-ise**). **mongrelization** /-'zeɪʃ(ə)n/ *n.* [earlier *meng-*, *mang-* from Germanic: probably related to MINGLE]

'mongst *poet.* var. of AMONGST (see AMONG).

monial /'məʊnɪəl/ *n.* a mullion. [Middle English from Old French *moinel* 'middle', from *moien* MEAN[3]]

monies see MONEY 2.

moniker /'mɒnɪkə/ *n.* (also **monicker**, **monniker**) *slang* a name. [19th c.: origin unknown]

moniliform /mə'nɪlɪfɔːm/ *adj.* esp. *Anat. & Zool.* with a form suggesting a string of beads. [French *moniliforme* or modern Latin *moniliformis* from Latin *monile* 'necklace']

monism /'mɒnɪz(ə)m, 'məʊ-/ *n.* **1** any theory denying the duality of matter and mind. **2** *Philos. & Theol.* the doctrine that only one supreme being exists (cf. PLURALISM 3). □ **monist** *n.* **monistic** /-'nɪstɪk/ *adj.* [modern Latin *monismus* from Greek *monos* 'single']

monition /mə'nɪʃ(ə)n/ *n.* **1** (foll. by *of*) *literary* a warning (of danger). **2** *Eccl.* a formal notice from a bishop or ecclesiastical court admonishing a person not to commit an offence. [Middle English via Old French from Latin *monitio -onis* (as MONITOR)]

monitor /'mɒnɪtə/ *n. & v.* ● *n.* **1** any of various persons or devices for checking or warning about a situation, operation, etc. **2** a school pupil with disciplinary or other special duties. **3 a** a television receiver used in a studio to select or verify the picture being broadcast. **b** = VISUAL DISPLAY UNIT. **4** a person who listens to and reports on foreign broadcasts etc. **5** a detector of radioactive contamination. **6** *Zool.* any tropical lizard of the genus *Varanus*, supposed to give warning of the approach of crocodiles. **7** *hist.* a heavily armed warship of shallow draught. ● *v.tr.* **1** act as a monitor of. **2** maintain regular surveillance over. **3** regulate the technical quality of (a radio transmission, television signal, etc.). □ **monitorial** /-'tɔːrɪəl/ *adj.* **monitorship** *n.* [Latin, from *monēre monit-* 'warn']

monitory /'mɒnɪt(ə)ri/ *adj. & n.* ● *adj. literary* giving or serving as a warning. ● *n.* (*pl.* **-ies**) *Eccl.* a letter of admonition from the Pope or a bishop. [Latin *monitorius* (as MONITION)]

monk /mʌŋk/ *n.* a member of a religious community of men living under certain vows esp. of poverty, chastity, and obedience. □ **monkish** *adj.* [Old English *munuc*, ultimately via Greek *monakhos* 'solitary' from *monos* 'alone']

monkey /'mʌŋki/ *n. & v.* ● *n.* (*pl.* **-eys**) **1** any of various mainly long-tailed agile tree-dwelling primates of the families Cebidae, Callithricidae, and Cercopithecidae. **2** a mischievous person, esp. a child (*young monkey*). **3** *Brit. slang* £500. **4** (in full **monkey engine**) a machine hammer for piledriving etc. ● *v.* (**-eys**, **-eyed**) **1** *tr.* mimic or mock. **2** *intr.* (often foll. by *with*) tamper or play mischievous tricks. **3** *intr.* (foll. by *around, about*) fool around. □ **have a monkey on one's back** *slang* be a drug addict. **make a monkey of** humiliate by making appear ridiculous. □ **monkeyish** *adj.* [16th c.: origin unknown (perhaps Low German)]

monkey bars *n.pl. N. Amer.* = CLIMBING FRAME.

monkey bread *n.* the baobab tree or its fruit.

monkey business *n. colloq.* mischief.

monkey engine see MONKEY *n.* 4.

monkey flower *n.* a mimulus, esp. *Mimulus guttatus* with bright yellow flowers.

monkey-jacket *n.* a short close-fitting jacket worn by sailors etc. or at a mess.

monkey-nut *n. Brit.* a peanut.

monkey-puzzle *n.* (in full **monkey-puzzle tree**) a coniferous tree, *Araucaria araucana*, native to Chile, with downward-pointing branches and small close-set leaves.

monkeyshine /'mʌŋkɪʃʌɪn/ *n.* (usu. in *pl.*) *US colloq.* = MONKEY TRICKS.

monkey suit *n. colloq.* evening dress.

monkey tricks *n.pl. Brit. colloq.* mischief.

monkey wrench *n. & v.* ● *n.* a wrench with an adjustable jaw. ● *v.tr.* (**monkeywrench**) sabotage, esp. as a means of environmentalist protest. □ **monkeywrenching** *n.*

monkfish /'mʌŋkfɪʃ/ *n.* (*pl.* usu. same) **1** an angler fish, esp. *Lophius piscatorius*, often used as food. **2** a large cartilaginous fish, *Squatina squatina*, with a flattened body and large pectoral fins; also called *angel-shark*.

monkshood /'mʌŋkshʊd/ *n.* a poisonous garden plant *Aconitum napellus*, with hood-shaped blue or purple flowers.

monniker var. of MONIKER.

mono /'mɒnəʊ/ *adj. & n.* ● *adj.* monophonic. ● *n.* (*pl.* **-os**) a monophonic record, reproduction, etc. [abbreviation]

mono- /'mɒnəʊ/ *comb. form* (usu. **mon-** before a vowel) **1** one, alone, single. **2** *Chem.* (forming names of compounds) containing one atom or group of a specified kind. [Greek from *monos* 'alone']

monoacid /mɒnəʊ'asɪd/ *adj. Chem.* (of a base) having one replaceable hydroxide ion.

monobasic /mɒnə(ʊ)'beɪsɪk/ *adj. Chem.* (of an acid) having one replaceable hydrogen atom.

monocarpic /mɒnə(ʊ)'kɑːpɪk/ *adj.* (also **monocarpous** /-'kɑːpəs/) *Bot.* bearing fruit only once. [MONO- + Greek *karpos* 'fruit']

monocausal /mɒnəʊ'kɔːz(ə)l/ *adj.* in terms of a sole cause.

monocephalous /mɒnə(ʊ)'sɛf(ə)ləs, -'kɛf-/ *adj. Bot.* having only one head.

monochord /'mɒnə(ʊ)kɔːd/ *n. Mus.* an instrument with a single string and a movable bridge, used esp. to determine intervals. [Middle English via Old French *monocorde* and Late Latin *monochordon* from Greek *monokhordon* (as MONO-, CHORD[1])]

monochromatic /mɒnə(ʊ)krə'matɪk/ *adj.* **1** *Physics* (of light or other radiation) of a single wavelength or frequency. **2** containing only one colour. □ **monochromatically** *adv.*

monochromatism /mɒnə(ʊ)'krəʊmətɪz(ə)m/ *n.* complete colour-blindness in which all colours appear as shades of one colour.

monochrome /'mɒnəkrəʊm, mɒnə(ʊ)'krəʊm/ *n. & adj.* ● *n.* a photograph or picture done in one colour or different tones of this, or in black and white only. ● *adj.* having or using only one colour or in black and white only. □ **monochromic** /-'krəʊmɪk/ *adj.* [ultimately from Greek *monokhrōmatos* (as MONO-, *khrōmatos* from *khrōma* 'colour')]

monocle /'mɒnək(ə)l/ *n.* a single eyeglass. □ **monocled** *adj.* [French, originally *adj.*, from Late Latin *monoculus* 'one-eyed' (as MONO-, *oculus* 'eye')]

monocline /'mɒnə(ʊ)klʌɪn/ *n. Geol.* a bend in rock strata that are otherwise uniformly dipping or horizontal. □ **monoclinal** /-'klʌɪn(ə)l/ *adj.* [MONO- + Greek *klinō* 'lean, dip']

monoclinic /mɒnə(ʊ)'klɪnɪk/ *adj.* (of a crystal) having one axial intersection oblique. [MONO- + Greek *klinō* 'lean, slope']

monoclonal /mɒnə(ʊ)'kləʊn(ə)l/ *adj.* forming a single clone; derived from a single individual or cell.

monoclonal antibody *n.* an antibody produced by a single clone of cells or cell line and consisting of identical antibody molecules.

monocoque /'mɒnə(ʊ)kɒk/ *n.* an aircraft or vehicle structure in which the chassis is integral with the body. [French (as MONO-, *coque* 'shell')]

monocot /'mɒnə(ʊ)kɒt/ *n.* = MONOCOTYLEDON. [abbreviation]

monocotyledon /ˌmɒnə(ʊ)kɒtɪ'liːd(ə)n/ *n. Bot.* any flowering plant with a single cotyledon. □ **monocotyledonous** *adj.*

monocracy /mə'nɒkrəsi/ *n.* (*pl.* **-ies**) government by one person only. □ **monocratic** /-'kratɪk/ *adj.*

monocular /mə'nɒkjʊlə/ *adj.* with or for one eye. □ **monocularly** *adj.* [Late Latin *monoculus* 'having one eye']

monoculture /'mɒnə(ʊ)kʌltʃə/ *n.* the cultivation of a single crop.

monocycle /'mɒnə(ʊ)sʌɪk(ə)l/ *n.* = UNICYCLE.

monocyte /'mɒnə(ʊ)sʌɪt/ *n. Biol.* a large leucocyte with a simple nucleus, developing into a macrophage.

monodactylous /mɒnə(ʊ)'daktɪləs/ *adj.* having one finger, toe, or claw.

monodrama /'mɒnə(ʊ)drɑːmə, mɒnə(ʊ)'drɑːmə/ *n.* a dramatic piece for one performer.

monody /'mɒnədi/ *n.* (*pl.* **-ies**) **1** an ode sung by a single actor in a Greek tragedy. **2** a poem lamenting a person's death. **3** *Mus.* a composition with only one melodic line. □ **monodic** /mə'nɒdɪk/ *adj.* **monodist** *n.* [Late Latin *monodia* from Greek *monōidia*, from *monōidos* 'singing alone' (as MONO-, ODE)]

monoecious /mə'ni:ʃəs/ *adj.* **1** *Bot.* with unisexual male and female organs on the same plant. **2** *Zool.* hermaphrodite. [modern Latin *Monoecia*, the class of such plants (Linnaeus), from Greek *monos* 'single' + *oikos* 'house']

monofilament /'mɒnə(ʊ)fɪləm(ə)nt/ *n.* **1** a single strand of man-made fibre. **2** a type of fishing line using this.

monogamy /mə'nɒgəmi/ *n.* **1** the practice or state of being married to one person at a time. **2** *Zool.* the habit of having only one mate at a time. □ **monogamist** *n.* **monogamous** *adj.* **monogamously** *adv.* [French *monogamie* via ecclesiastical Latin from Greek *monogamia* (as MONO-, *gamos* 'marriage')]

monogenesis /mɒnə(ʊ)'dʒɛnɪsɪs/ *n.* (also **monogeny** /mə'nɒdʒɪni/) **1** the theory of the development of all beings from a single cell. **2** the theory that humankind descended from one pair of ancestors. □ **monogenetic** /-dʒɪ'nɛtɪk/ *adj.*

monoglot /'mɒnə(ʊ)glɒt/ *adj.* & *n.* ● *adj.* using only one language. ● *n.* a monoglot person. [Greek *monoglōttos* (as MONO-, *glōtta* 'tongue')]

monogram /'mɒnəgram/ *n.* two or more letters, esp. a person's initials, interwoven as a device. □ **monogrammatic** /-grə'matɪk/ *adj.* **monogrammed** *adj.* [French *monogramme* via Late Latin *monogramma* from Greek (as MONO-, -GRAM)]

monograph /'mɒnəgrɑ:f/ *n.* & *v.* ● *n.* a separate treatise on a single subject or an aspect of it. ● *v.tr.* write a monograph on. □ **monographer** /mə'nɒgrəfə/ *n.* **monographist** /mə'nɒgrəfɪst/ *n.* **monographic** /mɒnə'grafɪk/ *adj.* [earlier *monography*: modern Latin *monographia* from *monographus* 'writer on a single genus or species' (as MONO-, -GRAPH, -GRAPHY)]

monogynous /mə'nɒdʒɪnəs/ *adj.* *Bot.* having only one pistil.

monogyny /mə'nɒdʒɪni/ *n.* the custom of having only one wife at a time. [MONO- + Greek *gunē* 'woman, wife']

monohull /'mɒnə(ʊ)hʌl/ *n.* a boat with a single hull.

monohybrid /mɒnə(ʊ)'hʌɪbrɪd/ *n.* & *adj.* ● *n.* *Biol.* a hybrid that is heterozygous for alleles of one gene. ● *adj.* of or relating to inheritance of alleles of one gene.

monohydric /mɒnə(ʊ)'hʌɪdrɪk/ *adj.* *Chem.* containing one hydroxyl group. [MONO- + HYDROGEN + -IC]

monokini /mɒnə(ʊ)'ki:ni/ *n.* a woman's one-piece beach garment equivalent to the lower half of a bikini. [MONO- + BIKINI, by false association with BI-]

monolayer /'mɒnəleɪə/ *n.* **1** *Chem.* a layer only one molecule in thickness. **2** *Biol.* & *Med.* a cell culture in a layer one cell thick.

monolingual /mɒnə(ʊ)'lɪŋgw(ə)l/ *adj.* speaking or using only one language.

monolith /'mɒn(ə)lɪθ/ *n.* **1** a single block of stone, esp. shaped into a pillar or monument. **2** a person or thing like a monolith in being massive, immovable, or solidly uniform. **3** a large block of concrete. □ **monolithic** /-'lɪθɪk/ *adj.* [French *monolithe* from Greek *monolithos* (as MONO-, *lithos* 'stone')]

monologue /'mɒn(ə)lɒg/ *n.* **1 a** a scene in a drama in which a person speaks alone. **b** a dramatic composition for one performer. **2** a long speech by one person in a conversation etc. □ **monologic** /-'lɒdʒɪk/ *adj.* **monological** /-'lɒdʒɪk(ə)l/ *adj.* **monologist** /mə'nɒlədʒɪst/ *n.* (also **-loguist** /-gɪst/). **monologize** /mə'nɒlədʒʌɪz/ *v.intr.* (also **-ise**). [French, from Greek *monologos* 'speaking alone' (as MONO-, -LOGUE)]

monomania /mɒnə(ʊ)'meɪnɪə/ *n.* obsession of the mind by one idea or interest. □ **monomaniac** *n.* & *adj.* **monomaniacal** /-mə'nʌɪək(ə)l/ *adj.* [French *monomanie* (as MONO-, -MANIA)]

monomer /'mɒnəmə/ *n.* *Chem.* **1** a unit in a dimer, trimer, or polymer. **2** a molecule or compound that can be polymerized (cf. DIMER). □ **monomeric** /-'mɛrɪk/ *adj.*

monomial /mə'nəʊmɪəl/ *adj.* & *n.* *Math.* ● *adj.* (of an algebraic expression) consisting of one term. ● *n.* a monomial expression. [MONO-, on the pattern of *binomial*]

monomolecular /ˌmɒnə(ʊ)mə'lɛkjʊlə/ *adj.* *Chem.* (of a layer) only one molecule in thickness.

monomorphic /mɒnə(ʊ)'mɔ:fɪk/ *adj.* (also **monomorphous** /-'mɔ:fəs/) *Biochem.* not changing form during development. □ **monomorphism** *n.* [MONO- + Greek *morphē* 'form']

mononucleosis /ˌmɒnə(ʊ)nju:klɪ'əʊsɪs/ *n.* an abnormally high proportion of monocytes in the blood, esp. = GLANDULAR FEVER. [MONO- + NUCLEO- + -OSIS]

monopetalous /mɒnə(ʊ)'pɛt(ə)ləs/ *adj.* *Bot.* having the corolla in one piece, or the petals united into a tube.

monophonic /mɒnə(ʊ)'fɒnɪk/ *adj.* **1** (of sound reproduction) using only one channel of transmission (cf. STEREOPHONIC). **2** *Mus.* homophonic. □ **monophonically** *adv.* [MONO- + Greek *phōnē* 'sound']

monophthong /'mɒnəfθɒŋ/ *n.* *Phonet.* a single vowel sound. □ **monophthongal** /-'θɒŋg(ə)l/ *adj.* [Greek *monophthoggos* (as MONO-, *phthoggos* 'sound')]

monophyletic /ˌmɒnə(ʊ)fʌɪ'lɛtɪk/ *adj.* *Biol.* (of a group of organisms) descended from a common evolutionary ancestor or ancestral group, esp. one not shared with any other group. [MONO- + PHYLETIC]

Monophysite /mə'nɒfɪsʌɪt/ *n.* a person who holds that there is only one nature (partly divine, partly and subordinately human) in the person of Christ. [ecclesiastical Latin *monophysita* from ecclesiastical Greek *monophusitēs* (as MONO-, *phusis* 'nature')]

monoplane /'mɒnəpleɪn/ *n.* an aeroplane with one set of wings (cf. BIPLANE).

monopod /'mɒnə(ʊ)pɒd/ *n.* a structure having only one foot, esp. a one-legged support for a camera. [Latin *monopodium* from Greek *monopodion* (as MONO-, *pod*, *pous* 'foot')]

monopole[1] /'mɒnəpəʊl/ *n.* **1** *Physics* a single electric charge or magnetic pole, esp. a hypothetical isolated magnetic pole. **2** a radio aerial, pylon, etc. consisting of a single pole or rod. [MONO- + (in sense 1) POLE[2], (in sense 2) POLE[1]]

monopole[2] /'mɒnəpəʊl/ *n.* (also **Monopole**) a champagne exclusive to one shipper. [French *monopole* MONOPOLY]

monopolist /mə'nɒp(ə)lɪst/ *n.* a person who has or advocates a monopoly. □ **monopolistic** /-'lɪstɪk/ *adj.*

monopolize /mə'nɒpəlʌɪz/ *v.tr.* (also **-ise**) **1** obtain exclusive possession or control of (a trade or commodity etc.). **2** dominate or prevent others from sharing in (a conversation, person's attention, etc.). □ **monopolization** /-'zeɪʃ(ə)n/ *n.* **monopolizer** *n.*

monopoly /mə'nɒp(ə)li/ *n.* (*pl.* **-ies**) **1 a** the exclusive possession or control of the trade in a commodity or service. **b** this conferred as a privilege by the State. **2 a** a commodity or service that is subject to a monopoly. **b** a company etc. that possesses a monopoly. **3** (foll. by *of*, *on*) exclusive possession, control, or exercise. [Latin *monopolium* from Greek *monopōlion* (as MONO-, *pōleō* 'sell')]

monorail /'mɒnə(ʊ)reɪl/ *n.* a railway in which the track consists of a single rail, usu. elevated with the train units suspended from it.

monosaccharide /mɒnə(ʊ)'sakərʌɪd/ *n.* *Chem.* a sugar that cannot be hydrolysed to give a simpler sugar, e.g. glucose.

monosodium glutamate /mɒnə(ʊ)'səʊdɪəm/ *n.* *Chem.* a sodium salt of glutamic acid used to flavour food (cf. GLUTAMATE).

monospermous /mɒnə(ʊ)'spə:məs/ *adj.* *Bot.* having one seed. [MONO- + Greek *sperma* 'seed']

monostichous /mə'nɒstɪkəs, mɒnə(ʊ)'stʌɪkəs/ *adj. Bot. & Zool.* arranged in or consisting of one layer or row. [MONO- + Greek *stikhos* 'row']

monosyllabic /ˌmɒnə(ʊ)sɪ'labɪk/ *adj.* **1** (of a word) having one syllable. **2** (of a person or statement) using or expressed in monosyllables. ▫ **monosyllabically** *adv.*

monosyllable /'mɒnə(ʊ)sɪləb(ə)l/ *n.* a word of one syllable. ▫ **in monosyllables** in simple direct words.

monotheism /'mɒnə(ʊ)ˌθiːɪz(ə)m/ *n.* the doctrine that there is only one God. ▫ **monotheist** *n.* **monotheistic** /-'ɪstɪk/ *adj.* **monotheistically** /-'ɪstɪk(ə)li/ *adv.* [MONO- + Greek *theos* 'god']

monotint /'mɒnə(ʊ)tɪnt/ *n.* = MONOCHROME.

monotone /'mɒnətəʊn/ *n. & adj.* ● *n.* **1** a sound or utterance continuing or repeated on one note without change of pitch. **2** sameness of style in writing. ● *adj.* without change of pitch. [modern Latin *monotonus* from late Greek *monotonos* (as MONO-, TONE)]

monotonic /mɒnə(ʊ)'tɒnɪk/ *adj.* **1** uttered in a monotone. **2** *Math.* (of a function or quantity) varying in such a way that it either never decreases or never increases. ▫ **monotonically** *adv.*

monotonous /mə'nɒt(ə)nəs/ *adj.* **1** lacking in variety; tedious through sameness. **2** (of a sound or utterance) without variation in tone or pitch. ▫ **monotonize** *v.tr.* (also **-ise**). **monotonously** *adv.* **monotonousness** *n.*

monotony /mə'nɒt(ə)ni/ *n.* **1** the state of being monotonous. **2** dull or tedious routine.

monotreme /'mɒnə(ʊ)triːm/ *n.* any mammal of the order Monotremata, native to Australia and New Guinea, including the duckbill and spiny anteater, laying large yolky eggs through a common opening for urine, faeces, etc. [MONO- + Greek *trēma -matos* 'hole']

monotype /'mɒnə(ʊ)tʌɪp/ *n.* **1** (**Monotype**) *Printing propr.* a typesetting machine that casts and sets up types in individual characters. **2** an impression on paper made from an inked design painted on glass or metal.

monotypic /mɒnə(ʊ)'tɪpɪk/ *adj.* having only one type or representative.

monounsaturated /ˌmɒnəʊʌn'satʃʊreɪtɪd, -tjʊreɪtɪd/ *adj. Chem.* (of a compound, esp. a fat) saturated except for one multiple bond.

monovalent /mɒnə(ʊ)'veɪl(ə)nt/ *adj. Chem.* having a valency of one; univalent.

monoxide /mə'nɒksʌɪd/ *n. Chem.* an oxide containing one oxygen atom (*carbon monoxide*). [MONO- + OXIDE]

Monroe doctrine /mən'rəʊ, 'mʌnrəʊ/ *n.* the US policy of objecting to intervention by European powers in the affairs of Latin America. [named after J. *Monroe*, US President d. 1831, who formulated it]

Monseigneur /mɒnsɛ'njəː, French mɔ̃sɛɲœr/ *n.* (*pl.* ***Messeigneurs*** /mɛsɛ'njəː/, French mesɛɲœr/) a title given to an eminent French person, esp. a prince, cardinal, archbishop, or bishop. [French, from *mon* 'my' + *seigneur* 'lord']

Monsieur /mə'sjəː/ *n.* (*pl.* **Messieurs** /mɛ'sjəː/) **1** the title or form of address used of or to a French-speaking man, corresponding to Mr or sir. **2** a Frenchman. [French, from *mon* 'my' + *sieur* 'lord']

Monsignor /mɒn'siːnjə, mɒnsiː'njɔː/ *n.* (*pl.* **Monsignori** /-'njɔːri/) the title of various Roman Catholic prelates, officers of the papal court, etc. [Italian, suggested by MONSEIGNEUR: see SIGNOR]

monsoon /mɒn'suːn/ *n.* **1** a wind in S. Asia, esp. in the Indian Ocean, blowing from the south-west in summer (**wet monsoon**) and the north-east in winter (**dry monsoon**). **2** a rainy season accompanying a wet monsoon. **3** any other wind with periodic alternations. ▫ **monsoonal** *adj.* [obsolete Dutch *monssoen* via Portuguese *monção* from Arabic *mawsim* 'fixed season', from *wasama* 'to mark']

mons pubis /mɒnz 'pjuːbɪs/ *n.* the rounded mass of fatty tissue lying over the joint of the pubic bones, esp. = MONS VENERIS. [Latin, = mount of the pubes]

monster /'mɒnstə/ *n.* **1** an imaginary creature, usu. large and frightening, compounded of incongruous elements. **2** an inhumanly cruel or wicked person. **3** a misshapen animal or plant. **4** a large usu. ugly animal or thing (e.g. a building). **5** (*attrib.*) huge; extremely large of its kind. [Middle English via Old French *monstre* from Latin *monstrum* 'portent, monster', from *monēre* 'warn']

monstera /mɒn'stɪərə/ *n.* any climbing plant of the genus *Monstera*, including Swiss cheese plant. [modern Latin, perhaps from Latin *monstrum* 'monster' (from the odd appearance of its leaves)]

monstrance /'mɒnstr(ə)ns/ *n. RC Ch.* an open or transparent receptacle in which the consecrated Host is exposed for veneration. [Middle English, = demonstration, via medieval Latin *monstrantia* from Latin *monstrare* 'show']

monstrosity /mɒn'strɒsɪti/ *n.* (*pl.* **-ies**) **1** a huge or outrageous thing. **2** monstrousness. **3** = MONSTER 3. [Late Latin *monstrositas* (as MONSTROUS)]

monstrous /'mɒnstrəs/ *adj.* **1** like a monster; abnormally formed. **2** huge. **3 a** outrageously wrong or absurd. **b** atrocious. ▫ **monstrously** *adv.* **monstrousness** *n.* [Middle English from Old French *monstreux* or Latin *monstrosus* (as MONSTER)]

mons Veneris /mɒnz 'vɛnərɪs/ *n.* the rounded mass of fatty tissue on a woman's abdomen above the vulva. [Latin, = mount of Venus]

Mont. *abbr.* Montana.

montage /mɒn'tɑːʒ, 'mɒntɑːʒ/ *n.* **1 a** a process of selecting, editing, and piecing together separate sections of cinema or television film to form a continuous whole. **b** a sequence of such film as a section of a longer film. **2 a** the technique of producing a new composite whole from fragments of pictures, words, music, etc. **b** a composition produced in this way. [French, from *monter* MOUNT[1]]

Montagu's harrier /'mɒntəgjuːz/ *n.* a slender migratory Eurasian bird of prey, *Circus pygarguas*. [named after G. *Montagu*, British naturalist d. 1815]

montane /'mɒnteɪn/ *adj.* of or inhabiting mountainous country. [Latin *montanus* (as MOUNT[2], -ANE[1])]

montbretia /mɒn(t)'briːʃə/ *n.* a hybrid plant of the genus *Crocosmia*, with bright orange-yellow trumpet-shaped flowers . [modern Latin, named after A. F. E. Coquebert de *Montbret*, French botanist d. 1801]

monte /'mɒnti/ *n. Cards* **1** a Spanish game of chance, played with 45 cards. **2** (in full **three-card monte**) a game of Mexican origin played with three cards, similar to three-card trick. [Spanish, = mountain, heap of cards]

Monte Carlo method /mɒntɪ 'kɑːləʊ/ *n. Statistics* a method of using the random sampling of numbers in order to estimate the solution to a numerical problem. [*Monte Carlo* in Monaco, famous for its gambling casino]

Montessori /mɒntɪ'sɔːri/ *n.* (usu. *attrib.*) a system of education (esp. of young children) that seeks to develop natural interests and activities rather than use formal teaching methods. [named after Maria *Montessori*, Italian educationist d. 1952, who initiated it]

Montezuma's revenge /mɒntɪ'zuːməz/ *n. slang* or *joc.* diarrhoea suffered by travellers, esp. visitors to Mexico. [referring to *Montezuma* II, Aztec emperor d. 1520]

month /mʌnθ/ *n.* **1** (in full **calendar month**) **a** each of usu. twelve periods into which a year is divided. **b** a period of time between the same dates in successive calendar months. **2** a period of 28 days or of four weeks. **3** = LUNAR MONTH. ▫ **month of Sundays** a very long period. [Old English *mōnath* from Germanic: related to MOON]

monthly /'mʌnθli/ *adj., adv., & n.* ● *adj.* done, produced, or occurring once a month. ● *adv.* once a month; from month to month. ● *n.* (*pl.* **-ies**) **1** a monthly periodical. **2** (in *pl.*) *colloq.* a menstrual period.

monticule /'mɒntɪkju:l/ *n.* **1** a small hill. **2** a small mound caused by a volcanic eruption. [French from Late Latin *monticulus*, diminutive of *mons* MOUNT[2]]

montmorillonite /mɒntmə'rɪlənʌɪt/ *n. Mineral.* any of a group of clay minerals which undergo reversible expansion on absorbing water, including the main constituents of fuller's earth and bentonite. [*Montmorillon*, a town in France]

monument /'mɒnjʊm(ə)nt/ *n.* **1** anything enduring that serves to commemorate or make celebrated, esp. a structure or building. **2** a stone or other structure placed over a grave or in a church etc. in memory of the dead. **3** an ancient building or site etc. that has survived or been preserved. **4** (foll. by *of, to*) a typical or outstanding example (*a monument of indiscretion*). **5** a lasting reminder. **6** a written record. [Middle English via French from Latin *monumentum*, from *monēre* 'remind']

monumental /mɒnjʊ'mɛnt(ə)l/ *adj.* **1 a** extremely great; stupendous (*a monumental achievement*). **b** (of a literary work) massive and permanent. **2** of or serving as a monument. □ **monumentality** /-'talɪti/ *n.* **monumentally** *adv.*

monumentalism /mɒnjʊ'mɛnt(ə)lɪz(ə)m/ *n.* **1** a monumental style. **2** a building on a grand scale.

monumentalize /mɒnjʊ'mɛnt(ə)lʌɪz/ *v.tr.* (also **-ise**) record or commemorate by or as by a monument.

monumental mason *n.* a maker of tombstones etc.

-mony /məni/ *suffix* forming nouns esp. denoting an abstract state or quality (*acrimony; testimony*). [Latin *-monia, -monium*, related to -MENT]

moo /mu:/ *v. & n.* ● *v.intr.* (**moos, mooed**) make the characteristic vocal sound of cattle; = LOW[2]. ● *n.* (*pl.* **moos**) this sound. [imitative]

mooch /mu:tʃ/ *v. colloq.* **1** *intr. Brit.* loiter or saunter desultorily. **2** *tr.* esp. *N. Amer.* **a** steal. **b** beg. □ **moocher** *n.* [Middle English, probably from Old French *muchier* 'hide, skulk']

moo-cow *n.* a childish name for a cow.

mood[1] /mu:d/ *n.* **1** a state of mind or feeling. **2** a fit of melancholy or bad temper. **3** (*attrib.*) inducing a particular mood (*mood music*). □ **in the** (or **no**) **mood** (foll. by *for*, or *to* + infin.) inclined (or disinclined) (*was in no mood to agree*). [Old English *mōd* 'mind, thought', from Germanic]

mood[2] /mu:d/ *n.* **1** *Gram.* **a** a form or set of forms of a verb serving to indicate whether it is to express fact, command, wish, etc. (*subjunctive mood*). **b** the distinction of meaning expressed by different moods. **2** *Logic* any of the classes into which each of the figures of a valid categorical syllogism is subdivided. [variant of MODE, associated with MOOD[1]]

moody /'mu:di/ *adj. & n.* ● *adj.* (**moodier, moodiest**) given to changes of mood; gloomy, sullen. ● *n.* (*pl.* **-ies**) *colloq.* a bad mood; a tantrum. □ **moodily** *adv.* **moodiness** *n.* [Old English *mōdig* 'brave' (as MOOD[1])]

Moog /məʊg, mu:g/ *n.* (in full **Moog synthesizer**) an electronic instrument with a keyboard, for producing a wide variety of musical sounds: see SYNTHESIZER. [named after R. A. *Moog*, American engineer b. 1934, who invented it]

moolah /'mu:lə/ *n. slang* money. [20th c.: origin unknown]

mooli /'mu:li/ *n.* a kind of long white radish used esp. in eastern cookery. [Hindi *mūlī* from Sanskrit *mūla* 'root']

moolvi /'mu:lvi/ *n.* (also **moolvie**) **1** a Muslim doctor of the law. **2** a learned person or teacher (esp. as a term of respect among Muslims in India). [Urdu *mulvī* from Arabic *mawlawīy* 'judicial': cf. MULLAH]

moon /mu:n/ *n. & v.* ● *n.* **1 a** the natural satellite of the earth, orbiting it monthly, illuminated by the sun and reflecting some light to the earth. **b** this regarded in terms of its waxing and waning in a particular month (*new moon*). **c** the moon when visible (*there is no moon tonight*). **2** a satellite of any planet. **3** (prec. by *the*) *colloq.* something desirable but unattainable (*promised them the moon*). **4** *poet.* a month. ● *v.* **1** *intr.* (often foll. by *about, around*, etc.) move or look listlessly. **2** *tr.* (foll. by *away*) spend (time) in a listless manner. **3** *intr.* (foll. by *over*) act aimlessly or inattentively from infatuation for (a person). **4** *intr. slang* expose one's buttocks. □ **many moons ago** a long time ago. **over the moon** extremely happy or delighted. □ **moonless** *adj.* [Old English *mōna* from Germanic: related to MONTH]

moonbeam /'mu:nbi:m/ *n.* a ray of moonlight.

moon boot *n.* a thickly-padded boot designed for low temperatures.

mooncalf /'mu:nkɑ:f/ *n.* (*pl.* **mooncalves**) a born fool.

moon-faced *adj.* having a round face.

moonfish /'mu:nfɪʃ/ *n.* (*pl.* usu. same) = OPAH.

Moonie /'mu:ni/ *n. colloq. offens.* a member of the Unification Church. [from the name of its founder, Sun Myung *Moon*]

moonlight /'mu:nlʌɪt/ *n. & v.* ● *n.* **1** the light of the moon. **2** (*attrib.*) lit by the moon. ● *v.intr.* (*past* and *past part.* **-lighted**) *colloq.* have two paid occupations, esp. one by day and one by night. □ **moonlighter** *n.*

moonlight flit *n. Brit.* a hurried departure by night, esp. to avoid paying a debt.

moonlit /'mu:nlɪt/ *adj.* lit by the moon.

moonquake /'mu:nkweɪk/ *n.* a tremor of the moon's surface.

moonrise /'mu:nrʌɪz/ *n.* **1** the rising of the moon. **2** the time of this.

moonscape /'mu:nskeɪp/ *n.* **1** the surface or landscape of the moon. **2** an area resembling this; a wasteland.

moonset /'mu:nsɛt/ *n.* **1** the setting of the moon. **2** the time of this.

moonshee /'mu:nʃi:/ *n.* (also **munshi**) a secretary or language teacher in India. [Urdu *munshī* from Arabic *munšī* 'writer']

moonshine /'mu:nʃʌɪn/ *n.* **1** foolish or unrealistic talk or ideas. **2** *slang* smuggled spirit or esp. *N. Amer.* illicitly distilled liquor.

moonshiner /'mu:nʃʌɪnə/ *n. US slang* a smuggler, or esp. *N. Amer.* an illicit distiller of alcoholic liquor.

moonshot /'mu:nʃɒt/ *n.* the launching of a spacecraft to the moon.

moonstone /'mu:nstəʊn/ *n.* feldspar of pearly appearance.

moonstruck /'mu:nstrʌk/ *adj.* mentally deranged.

moony /'mu:ni/ *adj.* (**moonier, mooniest**) **1** listless; stupidly dreamy. **2** of or like the moon.

Moor /mʊə, mɔ:/ *n.* a member of a Muslim people of mixed Berber and Arab descent, inhabiting NW Africa. [Middle English via Old French *More* and Latin *Maurus* from Greek *Mauros* 'inhabitant of Mauretania', a region of N. Africa]

moor[1] /mʊə, mɔ:/ *n.* **1** a tract of open uncultivated upland, esp. when covered with heather. **2** a tract of such land preserved for shooting. **3** *US* or *dial.* a fen. □ **moorish** *adj.* **moory** *adj.* [Old English *mōr* 'waste land, marsh, mountain', from Germanic]

moor[2] /mʊə, mɔ:/ *v.* **1** *tr.* make fast (a boat, buoy, etc.) by attaching a cable etc. to a fixed object. **2** *intr.* (of a boat) be moored. □ **moorage** *n.* [Middle English *more*, probably from Low German or Middle Low German *mōren*]

moorcock /'mʊəkɒk, 'mɔ:-/ *n.* a male moorfowl.

moorfowl /'mʊəfaʊl, 'mɔ:-/ *n.* a red grouse.

moorhen /'mʊəhɛn, 'mɔ:-/ *n.* **1** a small aquatic bird, *Gallinula chloropus*, with mainly blackish plumage and a short red-yellow bill. **2** a female moorfowl.

mooring /'mʊərɪŋ, 'mɔ:-/ *n.* **1 a** a fixed object to which a boat, buoy, etc., is moored. **b** (often in *pl.*) a place where a boat etc. is moored. **2** (in *pl.*) a set of permanent anchors and chains laid down for ships to be moored to.

mooring-mast see MAST[1] *n.* 4.

Moorish /'mʊərɪʃ, 'mɔ:-/ *adj.* of or relating to the Moors.

Moorish idol *n.* a brightly coloured Pacific fish of the genus *Zanclus*.

moorland /ˈmʊələnd, ˈmɔː-/ *n.* an extensive area of moor.

moose /muːs/ *n.* (*pl.* same) esp. *N. Amer.* the elk, *Alces alces*. [Narragansett *moos*]

moot /muːt/ *adj., v., & n.* ● *adj.* (originally the noun used *attrib.*) **1** debatable, undecided (*a moot point*). **2** *US Law* having no practical significance. ● *v.tr.* raise (a question) for discussion. ● *n.* **1** *hist.* an assembly. **2** *Law* a discussion of a hypothetical case as an academic exercise. [Old English *mōt*, and *mōtian* 'converse', from Germanic: related to MEET[1]]

■ **Usage** *Moot* 'debatable, undecided' is sometimes confused with *mute* 'silent, dumb', especially in the phrase *moot point*.

mop[1] /mɒp/ *n. & v.* ● *n.* **1** a wad or bundle of cotton or synthetic material fastened to the end of a stick, for cleaning floors etc. **2** a similarly-shaped large or small implement for various purposes. **3** anything resembling a mop, esp. a thick mass of hair. **4** an act of mopping or being mopped (*gave it a mop*). ● *v.tr.* (**mopped, mopping**) **1** wipe or clean with or as with a mop. **2 a** wipe tears or sweat etc. from (one's face or brow etc.). **b** wipe away (tears etc.). □ **mop up 1** wipe up with or as with a mop. **2** *colloq.* absorb (profits etc.). **3** dispatch; make an end of. **4** *Mil.* **a** complete the occupation of (a district etc.) by capturing or killing enemy troops left there. **b** capture or kill (stragglers). □ **moppy** *adj.* [Middle English *mappe*, perhaps ultimately related to Latin *mappa* 'napkin']

mop[2] /mɒp/ *n. Brit. hist.* an autumn fair or gathering at which farmhands and servants were formerly hired. [perhaps = *mop-fair*, at which a mop was carried by a maidservant seeking employment]

mope /məʊp/ *v. & n.* ● *v.intr.* **1** be gloomily depressed or listless; behave sulkily. **2** wander about listlessly. ● *n.* **1** a person who mopes. **2** (**the mopes**) low spirits. □ **moper** *n.* **mopy** *adj.* (**mopier, mopiest**). **mopily** *adv.* **mopiness** *n.* [16th c.: related to *mope, mopp(e)* 'fool', perhaps from Scandinavian]

moped /ˈməʊpɛd/ *n.* a motorized bicycle with an engine capacity below 50 cc. [Swedish, perhaps a contraction of *motorvelociped*]

mophead /ˈmɒphɛd/ *n.* a person with thick matted hair.

mopoke /ˈməʊpəʊk/ *n.* (also **morepork** /ˈmɔːpɔːk/) **1** a boobook. **2** an Australian nocturnal insect-eating bird, *Podargus strigoides*; also called FROGMOUTH. [imitative of the bird's cry]

moppet /ˈmɒpɪt/ *n. colloq.* (esp. as a term of endearment) a baby or small child. [obsolete *moppe* 'baby, doll']

moquette /mɒˈkɛt/ *n.* a thick pile or looped material used for carpets and upholstery. [French, perhaps from obsolete Italian *mocaiardo* 'mohair']

mor /mɔː/ *n.* humus formed under acid conditions. [Danish]

moraine /məˈreɪn/ *n.* an area covered by rocks and debris carried down and deposited by a glacier. □ **morainal** *adj.* **morainic** *adj.* [French via Italian dialect *morena*, from French dialect *mor(re)* 'snout', from Romanic]

moral /ˈmɒr(ə)l/ *adj. & n.* ● *adj.* **1 a** concerned with goodness or badness of human character or behaviour, or with the distinction between right and wrong. **b** concerned with accepted rules and standards of human behaviour. **2 a** conforming to accepted standards of general conduct. **b** capable of moral action (*man is a moral agent*). **3** (of rights or duties etc.) founded on moral law. **4 a** concerned with morals or ethics (*moral philosophy*). **b** (of a literary work etc.) dealing with moral conduct. **5** concerned with or leading to a psychological effect associated with confidence in a right action (*moral courage; moral support; moral victory*). ● *n.* **1 a** a moral lesson (esp. at the end) of a fable, story, event, etc. **b** a moral maxim or principle. **2** (in *pl.*) moral behaviour, e.g. in sexual conduct. □ **morally** *adv.* [Middle English from Latin *moralis*, from *mos moris* 'custom', pl. *mores* 'morals']

moral certainty *n.* probability so great as to allow no reasonable doubt.

morale /məˈrɑːl/ *n.* the mental attitude or bearing of a person or group, esp. as regards confidence, discipline, etc. [French *moral*, respelt to preserve the pronunciation]

moralism /ˈmɒr(ə)lɪz(ə)m/ *n.* **1** a natural system of morality. **2** religion regarded as moral practice.

moralist /ˈmɒr(ə)lɪst/ *n.* **1** a person who practises or teaches morality. **2** a person who follows a natural system of ethics. □ **moralistic** /-ˈlɪstɪk/ *adj.* **moralistically** /-ˈlɪstɪk(ə)li/ *adv.*

morality /məˈralɪti/ *n.* (*pl.* **-ies**) **1** the degree of conformity of an idea, practice, etc., to moral principles. **2** right moral conduct. **3** a lesson in morals. **4** the science of morals. **5** a particular system of morals (*commercial morality*). **6** (in *pl.*) moral principles; points of ethics. **7** (in full **morality play**) *hist.* a kind of drama with personified abstract qualities as the main characters and inculcating a moral lesson, popular in the 16th c. [Middle English via Old French *moralité* or Late Latin *moralitas* from Latin (as MORAL)]

moralize /ˈmɒr(ə)lʌɪz/ *v.* (also **-ise**) **1** *intr.* (often foll. by *on*) indulge in moral reflection or talk. **2** *tr.* interpret morally; point the moral of. **3** *tr.* make moral or more moral. □ **moralization** /-ˈzeɪʃ(ə)n/ *n.* **moralizer** *n.* **moralizingly** *adv.* [French *moraliser* or medieval Latin *moralizare* from Latin (as MORAL)]

moral law *n.* the conditions to be satisfied by any right course of action.

moral majority *n.* the majority of people, regarded as favouring firm moral standards (originally *Moral Majority*, name of a right-wing US movement).

moral philosophy *n.* the branch of philosophy concerned with ethics.

moral pressure *n.* persuasion by appealing to a person's moral sense.

Moral Rearmament *n.* **1** = OXFORD GROUP. **2** the beliefs of this organization, esp. as applied to international relations.

moral science *n.* systematic knowledge as applied to morals.

moral sense *n.* the ability to distinguish right and wrong.

morass /məˈras/ *n.* **1** an entanglement; a disordered situation, esp. one impeding progress. **2** *literary* a bog or marsh. [Dutch *moeras* (assimilated to *moer* MOOR[1]) via Middle Dutch *marasch* and Old French *marais* 'marsh' from medieval Latin *mariscus*]

moratorium /mɒrəˈtɔːrɪəm/ *n.* (*pl.* **moratoriums** or **moratoria** /-rɪə/) **1** (often foll. by *on*) a temporary prohibition or suspension (of an activity). **2 a** a legal authorization to debtors to postpone payment. **b** the period of this postponement. [modern Latin, neut. of Late Latin *moratorius* 'delaying', from Latin *morari morat-* 'to delay', from *mora* 'delay']

Moravian /məˈreɪvɪən/ *n. & adj.* ● *n.* **1** a native of Moravia, now part of the Czech Republic. **2** a member of a Protestant sect founded in Saxony by emigrants from Moravia, holding views derived from the Hussites and accepting the Bible as the only source of faith. ● *adj.* **1** of or relating to Moravia or its people. **2** of or relating to the Moravian sect.

moray /mɒˈreɪ, ˈmɒreɪ/ *n.* any voracious eel-like fish of the family Muraenidae, of warm seas, esp. *Muraena helena* of the Mediterranean and E. Atlantic. [Portuguese *moreia* via Latin from Greek *muraina*]

morbid /ˈmɔːbɪd/ *adj.* **1 a** (of the mind, ideas, etc.) macabre, unwholesome, sickly. **b** given to morbid feelings. **2** *colloq.* melancholy. **3** *Med.* of the nature of or indicative of disease. □ **morbidity** /-ˈbɪdɪti/ *n.* **morbidly** *adv.* **morbidness** *n.* [Latin *morbidus* from *morbus* 'disease']

morbid anatomy *n.* the anatomy of diseased organs, tissues, etc.

morbific /mɔːˈbɪfɪk/ *adj.* causing disease. [French *morbifique* or modern Latin *morbificus* from Latin *morbus* 'disease']

morbilli /mɔːˈbɪlʌɪ, -liː/ *n.pl.* **1** measles. **2** the spots characteristic of measles. [Latin, pl. of *morbillus* 'pustule', from *morbus* 'disease']

mordant /ˈmɔːd(ə)nt/ *adj.* & *n.* ● *adj.* **1** (of sarcasm etc.) caustic, biting. **2** pungent, smarting. **3** corrosive or cleansing. **4** (of a substance) serving to fix colouring matter or gold leaf on another substance. ● *n.* **1** a substance that enables a dye or stain to become fixed in a fabric etc. **2** an adhesive compound for fixing gold leaf. **3** a corrosive liquid used to etch the lines on a printing plate. ▫ **mordancy** *n.* **mordantly** *adv.* [Middle English from French, part. of *mordre* 'bite', from Latin *mordēre*]

mordent /ˈmɔːd(ə)nt/ *n. Mus.* **1** an ornament consisting of one rapid alternation of a written note with the note immediately below it. **2** a pralltriller. [German from Italian *mordente*, part. of *mordēre* 'bite']

more /mɔː/ *det., pron., & adv.* ● *det.* existing in a greater or additional quantity, amount, or degree (*more problems than last time*; *bring some more water*). ● *pron.* a greater quantity, number, or amount (*more than three people*; *more to it than meets the eye*). ● *adv.* **1** in a greater degree (*do it more carefully*). **2** to a greater extent (*people like to walk more these days*). **3** forming the comparative of adjectives and adverbs, esp. those of more than one syllable (*more absurd*; *more easily*). **4** again (*once more*; *never more*). **5** moreover. ▫ **more and more** in an increasing degree. **more like it** see LIKE[1]. **more of** to a greater extent (*more of a poet than a musician*). **more or less 1** in a greater or smaller degree. **2** approximately; as an estimate. **more so** of the same kind to a greater degree. [Old English *māra*, from Germanic]

moreen /məˈriːn/ *n.* a strong ribbed woollen or cotton material for curtains etc. [perhaps fanciful from MOIRE]

moreish /ˈmɔːrɪʃ/ *adj.* (also **morish**) *Brit. colloq.* pleasant to eat, causing a desire for more.

morel[1] /məˈrɛl/ *n.* an edible fungus, *Morchella esculenta*, with ridged mushroom caps. [French *morille* from Dutch *morilje*]

morel[2] /məˈrɛl/ *n.* nightshade. [Middle English from Old French *morele*, fem. of *morel* 'dark brown', ultimately from Latin *Maurus* MOOR]

morello /mɒˈrɛləʊ/ *n.* (*pl.* **-os**) a sour kind of dark cherry. [Italian *morello* 'blackish' via medieval Latin *morellus* from Latin (as MOREL[2])]

moreover /mɔːrˈəʊvə/ *adv.* (introducing or accompanying a new statement) further, besides.

morepork var. of MOPOKE.

mores /ˈmɔːreɪz, -riːz/ *n.pl.* customs or conventions regarded as essential to or characteristic of a community. [Latin, pl. of *mos* 'custom']

Moresco var. of MORISCO.

Moresque /məˈrɛsk/ *adj.* (of art or architecture) Moorish in style or design. [French from Italian *moresco*, from *Moro* MOOR]

morganatic /mɔːgəˈnatɪk/ *adj.* **1** (of a marriage) between a person of high rank and another of lower rank, the spouse and children having no claim to the possessions or title of the person of higher rank. **2** (of a wife) married in this way. ▫ **morganatically** *adv.* [French *morganatique* or German *morganatisch* from medieval Latin *matrimonium ad morganaticam* 'marriage with a morning gift', the husband's gift to the wife after consummation being his only obligation in such a marriage]

morgue /mɔːg/ *n.* **1** a mortuary. **2** (in a newspaper office) a room or file of miscellaneous information, esp. for future obituaries. [French, originally the name of a Paris mortuary]

moribund /ˈmɒrɪbʌnd/ *adj.* **1** at the point of death. **2** lacking vitality. ▫ **moribundity** /-ˈbʌndɪti/ *n.* [Latin *moribundus* from *mori* 'die']

Morisco /məˈrɪskəʊ/ *n.* & *adj.* (also **Moresco** /-ˈrɛskəʊ/) ● *n.* (*pl.* **-os** or **-oes**) **1** a Moor, esp. in Spain. **2** a morris dance. ● *adj.* Moorish. [Spanish, from *Moro* MOOR]

morish var. of MOREISH.

Mormon /ˈmɔːmən/ *n.* a member of the Church of Jesus Christ of Latter-Day Saints, a millenary religion founded in 1830 by Joseph Smith on the basis of revelations in the Book of Mormon. ▫ **Mormonism** *n.* [the name of the reputed author]

morn /mɔːn/ *n. poet.* morning. [Old English *morgen*, from Germanic]

mornay /ˈmɔːneɪ/ *n.* a cheese-flavoured white sauce. [20th c.: origin uncertain]

morning /ˈmɔːnɪŋ/ *n.* & *int.* ● *n.* **1** the early part of the day, esp. from sunrise to noon (*this morning*; *during the morning*; *morning coffee*). **2** this time spent in a particular way (*had a busy morning*). **3** sunrise, daybreak. **4** a time compared with the morning, esp. the early part of one's life etc. ● *int. colloq.* = *good morning* (see GOOD *adj.* 14). ▫ **in the morning 1** during or in the course of the morning. **2** *colloq.* tomorrow. [Middle English *mor(we)ning* from *morwen* MORN + -ING[1], on the pattern of *evening*]

morning after *n. colloq.* a hangover.

morning-after pill *n.* a contraceptive pill effective when taken some hours after intercourse.

morning coat *n.* a coat with tails, and with the front cut away below the waist.

morning dress *n.* a man's morning coat and striped trousers.

morning glory *n.* any of various twining plants of the genus *Ipomoea*, with trumpet-shaped flowers.

morning room *n.* a sitting room for the morning.

morning sickness *n.* nausea felt in the morning in pregnancy.

morning star *n.* a planet, esp. Venus, when visible in the east before sunrise.

morning watch *n. Naut.* the 4–8 a.m. watch.

Moro /ˈmɔːrəʊ/ *n.* (*pl.* **-os**) a Muslim living in the Philippines. [Spanish, = MOOR]

Moroccan /məˈrɒk(ə)n/ *n.* & *adj.* ● *n.* **1** a native or national of Morocco in N. Africa. **2** a person of Moroccan descent. ● *adj.* of or relating to Morocco.

morocco /məˈrɒkəʊ/ *n.* (*pl.* **-os**) **1** a fine flexible leather made (originally in Morocco) from goatskins tanned with sumac, used esp. in bookbinding and shoemaking. **2** an imitation of this in grained calf etc.

moron /ˈmɔːrɒn/ *n.* **1** *colloq.* a very stupid or foolish person. **2** an adult with a mental age of about 8–12. ▫ **moronic** /məˈrɒnɪk/ *adj.* **moronically** /məˈrɒnɪk(ə)li/ *adv.* [Greek *mōron*, neut. of *mōros* 'foolish']

morose /məˈrəʊs/ *adj.* sullen and ill-tempered. ▫ **morosely** *adv.* **moroseness** *n.* [Latin *morosus* 'peevish' etc. from *mos moris* 'manner']

morph[1] /mɔːf/ *n.* = ALLOMORPH. [back-formation]

morph[2] /mɔːf/ *n.* a variant form of an animal or plant. [Greek *morphē* 'form']

morpheme /ˈmɔːfiːm/ *n. Linguistics* **1** a morphological element considered in respect of its functional relations in a linguistic system. **2** a meaningful morphological unit of a language that cannot be further divided (e.g. *in, come, -ing*, forming *incoming*). ▫ **morphemic** /-ˈfiːmɪk/ *adj.* **morphemically** /-ˈfiːmɪk(ə)li/ *adv.* [French *morphème* from Greek *morphē* 'form', on the pattern of PHONEME]

morphemics /mɔːˈfiːmɪks/ *n.pl.* (usu. treated as *sing.*) *Linguistics* the study of word structure.

morphia /ˈmɔːfɪə/ *n.* (in general use) = MORPHINE.

morphine /ˈmɔːfiːn/ *n.* an analgesic and narcotic drug obtained from opium and used medicinally to relieve pain. ▫ **morphinism** /-fɪnɪz(ə)m/ *n.* [German *Morphin* and modern Latin *morphia* from *Morpheus*, the name of the god of sleep]

morphing /ˈmɔːfɪŋ/ *n.* a technique that changes a film image into a numerical code, enabling it to be manipulated by a computer so that the effect can be created of transforming an image smoothly into a different one. [shortened from METAMORPHOSIS + -ING[1]]

morphogenesis /mɔːfə(ʊ)ˈdʒɛnɪsɪs/ *n. Biol.* the development of form in organisms. □ **morphogenetic** /-dʒɪˈnɛtɪk/ *adj.* **morphogenic** *adj.* [modern Latin, from Greek *morphē* 'form' + GENESIS]

morphology /mɔːˈfɒlədʒi/ *n.* the study of the forms of things, esp.: **1** *Biol.* the study of the forms of organisms. **2** *Philol.* **a** the study of the forms of words. **b** the system of forms in a language. □ **morphological** /mɔːfəˈlɒdʒɪk(ə)l/ *adj.* **morphologically** /-fəˈlɒdʒɪk(ə)li/ *adv.* **morphologist** *n.* [Greek *morphē* 'form' + -LOGY]

Morris chair /ˈmɒrɪs/ *n.* a type of plain easy chair with an adjustable back. [named after William *Morris*, English poet and craftsman d. 1896]

morris dance /ˈmɒrɪs/ *n.* a lively traditional English dance performed by groups of people in distinctive costume, often using bells, handkerchiefs, or sticks. □ **morris dancer** *n.* **morris dancing** *n.* [*morys*, variant of MOORISH]

morrow /ˈmɒrəʊ/ *n.* (usu. prec. by *the*) *literary* **1** the following day. **2** the time following an event. [Middle English *morwe*, *moru* (as MORN)]

Morse /mɔːs/ *n.* & *v.* ● *n.* (in full **Morse code**) an alphabet or code in which letters are represented by combinations of long and short light or sound signals. ● *v.tr.* & *intr.* signal by Morse code. [named after S. F. B. *Morse*, American electrician d. 1872, who devised it]

morsel /ˈmɔːs(ə)l/ *n.* a mouthful; a small piece (esp. of food). [Middle English from Old French, diminutive of *mors* 'a bite', from *mordēre mors-* 'to bite']

mort /mɔːt/ *n. Hunting* a note sounded when the quarry is killed. [Middle English via Old French from Latin *mors mortis* 'death']

mortadella /mɔːtəˈdɛlə/ *n.* (*pl.* **mortadelle** /-ˈdɛli/) a large spiced pork sausage. [Italian diminutive, formed irregularly from Latin *murtatum* 'seasoned with myrtle berries']

mortal /ˈmɔːt(ə)l/ *adj.* & *n.* ● *adj.* **1** (of a living being, esp. a human) subject to death. **2** (often foll. by *to*) causing death; fatal. **3** (of a battle) fought to the death. **4** associated with death (*mortal agony*). **5** (of an enemy) implacable. **6** (of pain, fear, an affront, etc.) intense, very serious. **7** *colloq.* **a** very great (*in a mortal hurry*). **b** long and tedious (*for two mortal hours*). **8** *colloq.* conceivable, imaginable (*every mortal thing*; *of no mortal use*). ● *n.* **1** a mortal being, esp. a human. **2** *joc.* a person described in some specified way (*a thirsty mortal*). □ **mortally** *adv.* [Middle English from Old French *mortal*, *mortel* or Latin *mortalis* from *mors mortis* 'death']

mortality /mɔːˈtalɪti/ *n.* (*pl.* **-ies**) **1** the state of being subject to death. **2** loss of life on a large scale. **3 a** the number of deaths in a given period etc. **b** (in full **mortality rate**) a death rate. [Middle English via Old French *mortalité* from Latin *mortalitas -tatis* (as MORTAL)]

mortal sin *n. Theol.* a grave sin that is regarded as depriving the soul of divine grace.

mortar /ˈmɔːtə/ *n.* & *v.* ● *n.* **1** a mixture of lime with cement, sand, and water, used in building to bond bricks or stones. **2** a short large-bore cannon for firing bombs at high angles. **3** a contrivance for firing a lifeline or firework. **4** a usu. cup-shaped receptacle made of hard material, in which ingredients are pounded with a pestle. ● *v.tr.* **1** plaster or join with mortar. **2** attack or bombard with mortars. □ **mortarless** *adj.* (in sense 1 of *n.*). **mortary** *adj.* (in sense 1 of *n.*). [Middle English via Anglo-French *morter*, Old French *mortier* from Latin *mortarium*: partly from Low German]

mortarboard /ˈmɔːtəbɔːd/ *n.* **1** an academic cap with a stiff flat square top. **2** a flat board with a handle on the undersurface, for holding mortar in bricklaying etc.

mortgage /ˈmɔːgɪdʒ/ *n.* & *v.* ● *n.* **1 a** a conveyance of property by a debtor to a creditor as security for a debt (esp. one incurred by the purchase of the property), on the condition that it shall be returned on payment of the debt within a certain period. **b** a deed effecting this. **2 a** a debt secured by a mortgage. **b** a loan resulting in such a debt. ● *v.tr.* **1** convey (a property) by mortgage. **2** (often foll. by *to*) pledge (oneself, one's powers, etc.). □ **mortgageable** *adj.* [Middle English from Old French, = dead pledge, *mort* (from Latin *mortuus* 'dead') + *gage* GAGE[1]]

mortgagee /mɔːgɪˈdʒiː/ *n.* the creditor in a mortgage, usu. a bank or building society.

mortgager /ˈmɔːgɪdʒə/ *n.* (also **mortgagor** /-ˈdʒɔː/) the debtor in a mortgage.

mortgage rate *n.* the rate of interest charged by a mortgagee.

mortice var. of MORTISE.

mortician /mɔːˈtɪʃ(ə)n/ *n. N. Amer.* an undertaker; a manager of funerals. [Latin *mors mortis* 'death' + -ICIAN]

mortify /ˈmɔːtɪfʌɪ/ *v.* (**-ies**, **-ied**) **1** *tr.* **a** cause (a person) to feel shamed or humiliated. **b** wound (a person's feelings). **2** *tr.* bring (the body, the flesh, the passions, etc.) into subjection by self-denial or discipline. **3** *intr.* (of flesh) be affected by gangrene or necrosis. □ **mortification** /-fɪˈkeɪʃ(ə)n/ *n.* **mortifying** *adj.* **mortifyingly** *adv.* [Middle English via Old French *mortifier* from ecclesiastical Latin *mortificare* 'kill, subdue', from *mors mortis* 'death']

mortise /ˈmɔːtɪs/ *n.* & *v.* (also **mortice**) ● *n.* a hole in a framework designed to receive the end of another part, esp. a tenon. ● *v.tr.* **1** join securely, esp. by mortise and tenon. **2** cut a mortise in. [Middle English via Old French *mortoise* from Arabic *murtazz* 'fixed in']

mortise lock *n.* a lock recessed into a mortise in the frame of a door or window etc.

mortmain /ˈmɔːtmeɪn/ *n. Law* **1** the status of lands or tenements held inalienably by an ecclesiastical or other corporation. **2** the land or tenements themselves. [Middle English via Anglo-French, Old French *mortemain* from medieval Latin *mortua manus* 'dead hand', probably in allusion to impersonal ownership]

mortuary /ˈmɔːtjʊəri, -tʃʊ-/ *n.* & *adj.* ● *n.* (*pl.* **-ies**) a room or building in which dead bodies may be kept until burial or cremation. ● *adj.* of or concerning death or burial. [Middle English via Anglo-French *mortuarie* and medieval Latin *mortuarium* from Latin *mortuarius*, from *mortuus* 'dead']

morula /ˈmɔːr(j)ʊlə/ *n.* (*pl.* **morulae** /-liː/) *Zool.* a solid ball of cells resulting from division of an ovum, and from which a blastula is formed. [modern Latin, diminutive of Latin *morum* 'mulberry']

morwong /ˈmɔːwɒŋ/ *n.* any of various fish of the family Cheilodactylidae, native to Australasia, used as food. [probably Aboriginal]

Mosaic /məʊˈzeɪɪk/ *adj.* of or associated with Moses (in the Hebrew Bible). [French *mosaïque* or modern Latin *Mosaicus* from *Moses*, from Hebrew *Mōšeh*]

mosaic /mə(ʊ)ˈzeɪɪk/ *n.* & *v.* ● *n.* **1 a** a picture or pattern produced by an arrangement of small variously coloured pieces of glass or stone etc. **b** work of this kind as an art form. **2** a diversified thing. **3** an arrangement of photosensitive elements in a television camera. **4** *Biol.* a chimera. **5** (in full **mosaic disease**) a virus disease causing leaf-mottling in plants, esp. tobacco, maize, and sugar cane. **6** (*attrib.*) **a** of or like a mosaic. **b** diversified. ● *v.tr.* (**mosaicked**, **mosaicking**) **1** adorn with mosaics. **2** combine into or as into a mosaic. □ **mosaicist** /-ɪsɪst/ *n.* [Middle English via French *mosaïque*, Italian *mosaico*, and medieval Latin *mosaicus*, *musaicus* from Greek *mous(e)ion* 'mosaic work', from *mousa* MUSE[1]]

mosaic gold *n.* **1** tin disulphide. **2** an alloy of copper and zinc used in cheap jewellery etc.

Mosaic Law *n.* the laws attributed to Moses and listed in the Pentateuch.

mosasaurus /məʊsəˈsɔːrəs/ *n.* any of a group of large extinct marine reptiles of the late Cretaceous period, esp. of the genus *Mosasaurus*, with a long slender body and paddle-like limbs. [modern Latin, from *Mosa*, the river Meuse (near which it was first discovered) + Greek *sauros* 'lizard']

moschatel /mɒskəˈtɛl/ *n.* a small plant, *Adoxa moschatellina*, with pale green flowers and a musky smell. [French *moscatelle* from Italian *moscatella*, from *moscato* 'musk']

Moselle /mə(ʊ)ˈzɛl/ *n.* (also **Mosel**) a light medium dry white wine produced in the valley of the river Moselle. [French *Moselle*, German *Mosel*]

mosey /ˈməʊzi/ *v.intr.* (**-eys, -eyed**) (often foll. by *along*) *slang* walk in a leisurely or aimless manner. [19th c.: origin unknown]

moshav /ˈməʊʃɑːv, məʊˈʃɑːv/ *n.* (*pl.* **moshavim**) a cooperative association of Israeli smallholders. [Hebrew *mošāḇ*, literally 'dwelling']

Moslem var. of MUSLIM.

mosque /mɒsk/ *n.* a Muslim place of worship. [French *mosquée* via Italian *moschea* from Arabic *masjid*]

mosquito /mɒˈskiːtəʊ/ *n.* (*pl.* **-oes**) any slender biting dipterous fly of the family Culicidae, esp. of the genus *Culex*, *Anopheles*, or *Aedes*, the female of which punctures the skin of humans and other animals with a long proboscis to suck their blood, transmitting diseases such as filariasis and malaria. [Spanish and Portuguese, diminutive of *mosca*, from Latin *musca* 'fly']

mosquito-boat *n. US* a motor torpedo boat.

mosquito net *n.* a net to keep off mosquitoes.

moss /mɒs/ *n.* & *v.* ● *n.* **1** any small cryptogamous plant of the class Musci, growing in dense clusters on the surface of the ground, in bogs, on trees, stones, etc. **2** *Sc.* & *N.Engl.* a bog, esp. a peatbog. ● *v.tr.* cover with moss. □ **mosslike** *adj.* [Old English *mos* 'bog, moss', from Germanic]

moss agate *n.* agate with mosslike dendritic markings.

moss-grown *adj.* overgrown with moss.

moss-hag *n. Sc.* broken ground from which peat has been taken.

mosso /ˈmɒsəʊ/ *adv. Mus.* with animation or speed. [Italian, past part. of *muovere* 'move']

moss stitch *n.* alternate plain and purl in knitting.

mosstrooper /ˈmɒstruːpə/ *n. hist.* a freebooter of the Scottish Border in the 17th c.

mossy /ˈmɒsi/ *adj.* (**mossier, mossiest**) **1** covered in or resembling moss. **2** *US slang* antiquated, old-fashioned. □ **mossiness** *n.*

most /məʊst/ *det., pron.,* & *adv.* ● *det.* **1** existing in the greatest quantity or degree (*most brilliant schemes have a flaw*; *see who can make the most noise*). **2** the majority of; nearly all of (*most people think so*). ● *pron.* **1** the majority (*most of them are missing*). **2** the greatest quantity or number (*this is the most I can do*). **3** (**the most**) *slang* the best of all (*you are the most*). ● *adv.* **1** in the highest degree (*this is most interesting*; *what most annoys me*). **2** forming the superlative of adjectives and adverbs, esp. those of more than one syllable (*most certain*; *most easily*). **3** *US colloq.* almost (*most everyone I know agrees*). □ **at most** no more or better than (*this is at most a makeshift*). **at the most 1** as the greatest amount. **2** not more than. **for the most part 1** as regards the greater part. **2** usually. **make the most of 1** employ to the best advantage. **2** represent at its best or worst. [Old English *māst*, from Germanic]

-most /məʊst/ *suffix* forming superlative adjectives and adverbs from prepositions and other words indicating relative position (*foremost*; *uttermost*). [Old English *-mest*, from Germanic]

Most High *n.* (prec. by *the*) God.

Most Honourable *n.* a title given to marquesses and to members of the Privy Council and the Order of the Bath.

mostly /ˈməʊs(t)li/ *adv.* **1** as regards the greater part. **2** usually.

Most Reverend *n.* the title of an archbishop or of an Irish Roman Catholic bishop.

MOT *abbr.* **1** *hist.* (in the UK) Ministry of Transport. **2** (in full **MOT test**) a compulsory annual test of motor vehicles of more than a specified age.

mot /məʊ, French mo/ *n.* (*pl.* ***mots*** *pronunc.* same or /məʊz/) a witty saying. [French, = word, ultimately via Latin *muttum* 'uttered sound' from *muttire* 'murmur']

mote /məʊt/ *n.* a speck of dust. [Old English *mot*, corresponding to Dutch *mot* 'dust, sawdust', of unknown origin]

motel /məʊˈtɛl/ *n.* a roadside hotel providing accommodation for motorists and parking for their vehicles. [portmanteau word from MOTOR + HOTEL]

motet /məʊˈtɛt/ *n. Mus.* a short sacred choral composition. [Middle English from Old French, diminutive of *mot*: see MOT]

moth /mɒθ/ *n.* **1** any usu. nocturnal insect of the order Lepidoptera, often drably coloured, and distinguished from butterflies as having a stout body, lacking clubbed antennae, and folding the wings flat when at rest. **2** (in full **clothes-moth**) any small lepidopterous insect of the family Tineidae breeding in cloth etc., on which its larva feeds. [Old English *moththe*]

mothball /ˈmɒθbɔːl/ *n.* & *v.* ● *n.* a ball of naphthalene etc. placed in stored clothes to keep away moths. ● *v.tr.* **1** place in mothballs. **2** leave unused. □ **in mothballs** stored unused for a considerable time.

moth-eaten *adj.* **1** damaged or destroyed by moths. **2** antiquated, time-worn.

mother /ˈmʌðə/ *n.* & *v.* ● *n.* **1 a** a woman in relation to a child or children to whom she has given birth. **b** (in full **adoptive mother**) a woman who has continuous care of a child, esp. by adoption. **2** any female animal in relation to its offspring. **3** a quality or condition etc. that gives rise to another (*necessity is the mother of invention*). **4** (in full **Mother Superior**) the head of a female religious community. **5** *archaic* (esp. as a form of address) an elderly woman. **6** (*attrib.*) **a** designating an institution etc. regarded as having maternal authority (*Mother Church*; *mother earth*). **b** designating the main ship, spacecraft, etc., in a convoy or mission (*the mother craft*). ● *v.tr.* **1** give birth to; be the mother of. **2** protect as a mother. **3** give rise to; be the source of. **4** acknowledge or profess oneself the mother of. □ **motherhood** *n.* **motherless** *adj.* **motherlessness** *n.* **motherlike** *adj.* & *adv.* [Old English *mōdor*, from Germanic]

motherboard /ˈmʌðəbɔːd/ *n. Computing* a printed circuit board containing the principal components of a microcomputer etc.

Mother Carey's chicken *n.* = STORM PETREL 1. [18th c.: origin unknown]

mother country *n.* a country in relation to its colonies.

mothercraft /ˈmʌðəkrɑːft/ *n.* skill in or knowledge of looking after children as a mother.

mother figure *n.* an older woman who is regarded as a source of nurture, support, etc.

motherfucker /ˈmʌðəfʌkə/ *n.* esp. *N. Amer. coarse slang* an obnoxious or very unpleasant person or thing. □ **motherfucking** *adj.*

Mother Goose rhyme *n. N. Amer.* a nursery rhyme. [from the name of the imaginary author of a collection of children's rhymes (1781)]

Mothering Sunday /ˈmʌð(ə)rɪŋ/ *n. Brit.* the fourth Sunday in Lent, traditionally a day for honouring mothers with gifts.

mother-in-law *n.* (*pl.* **mothers-in-law**) the mother of one's husband or wife.

mother-in-law's tongue *n.* a plant, *Sansevieria trifasciata*, with long erect pointed leaves.

motherland /ˈmʌðəland/ *n.* one's native country.

mother lode *n. Mining* the main vein of a system.

motherly /ˈmʌðəli/ *adj.* **1** like or characteristic of a mother in affection, care, etc. **2** of or relating to a mother. □ **motherliness** *n.* [Old English *mōdorlic* (as MOTHER)]

mother-naked *adj.* stark naked.

mother-of-pearl *n.* a smooth iridescent substance forming the inner layer of the shell of some molluscs.

Mother's Day *n.* **1** *Brit.* = MOTHERING SUNDAY. **2** *N. Amer.* an equivalent day on the second Sunday in May.

mother's ruin *n. colloq.* gin.

mother's son *n. colloq.* a man (*every mother's son of you*).

Mother Superior see MOTHER *n.* 4.

mother-to-be *n.* a woman who is expecting a baby.

mother tongue *n.* **1** one's native language. **2** a language from which others have evolved.

mother wit *n.* native wit; common sense.

mothproof /ˈmɒθpruːf/ *adj.* & *v.* ● *adj.* (of clothes) treated so as to repel moths. ● *v.tr.* treat (clothes) in this way.

mothy /ˈmɒθi/ *adj.* (**mothier**, **mothiest**) infested with moths.

motif /məʊˈtiːf/ *n.* **1** a distinctive feature or dominant idea in artistic or literary composition. **2** *Mus.* = FIGURE *n.* 10. **3** a decorative design or pattern. **4** an ornament of lace etc. sewn separately on a garment. **5** *Brit.* an ornament on a vehicle identifying the maker, model, etc. [French (as MOTIVE)]

motile /ˈməʊtʌɪl/ *adj. Zool.* & *Bot.* capable of motion. □ **motility** /-ˈtɪlɪti/ *n.* [Latin *motus* 'motion' (as MOVE)]

motion /ˈməʊʃ(ə)n/ *n.* & *v.* ● *n.* **1** the act or process of moving or of changing position. **2** a particular manner of moving the body in walking etc. **3** a change of posture. **4** a gesture. **5** a formal proposal put to a committee, legislature, etc. **6** *Law* an application for a rule or order of court. **7** *Brit.* **a** an evacuation of the bowels. **b** (in *sing.* or *pl.*) faeces. **8** a piece of moving mechanism. ● *v.* (often foll. by *to* + infin.) **1** *tr.* direct (a person) by a sign or gesture. **2** *intr.* (often foll. by *to* a person) make a gesture directing (*motioned to me to leave*). □ **go through the motions 1** make a pretence; do something perfunctorily or superficially. **2** simulate an action by gestures. **in motion** moving; not at rest. **put** (or **set**) **in motion** set going or working. □ **motional** *adj.* **motionless** *adj.* **motionlessly** *adv.* [Middle English via Old French from Latin *motio -onis* (as MOVE)]

motion picture *n.* (often, with hyphen, *attrib.*) a film (see FILM *n.* 3) with the illusion of movement.

motion sickness *n.* nausea induced by motion, esp. by travelling in a vehicle.

motivate /ˈməʊtɪveɪt/ *v.tr.* **1** supply a motive to; be the motive of. **2** cause (a person) to act in a particular way. **3** stimulate the interest of (a person in an activity). □ **motivation** /-ˈveɪʃ(ə)n/ *n.* **motivational** /-ˈveɪʃ(ə)n(ə)l/ *adj.* **motivationally** /-ˈveɪʃ(ə)n(ə)li/ *adv.* **motivator** *n.*

motive /ˈməʊtɪv/ *n.*, *adj.*, & *v.* ● *n.* **1** a factor or circumstance that induces a person to act in a particular way. **2** a motif in art, literature, or music. ● *adj.* **1** tending to initiate movement. **2** concerned with movement. ● *v.tr.* = MOTIVATE. □ **motiveless** *adj.* **motivelessly** *adv.* **motivelessness** *n.* **motivity** /-ˈtɪvɪti/ *n.* [Middle English via Old French *motif* (*adj.* & *n.*) from Late Latin *motivus* (*adj.*) (as MOVE)]

motive power *n.* a moving or impelling power, esp. a source of energy used to drive machinery.

mot juste /ʒuːst, French ʒyst/ *n.* (*pl.* ***mots justes*** *pronunc.* same) the most appropriate expression.

motley /ˈmɒtli/ *adj.* & *n.* ● *adj.* (**motlier**, **motliest**) **1** diversified in colour. **2** of varied character (*a motley crew*). ● *n.* **1** an incongruous mixture. **2** *hist.* the particoloured costume of a jester. □ **wear motley** play the fool. [Middle English *mottelay*, perhaps ultimately related to MOTE]

motmot /ˈmɒtmɒt/ *n.* a bird of the tropical American family Momotidae, some members of which have two long tail feathers like rackets. [Latin American Spanish, imitative]

motocross /ˈməʊtə(ʊ)krɒs/ *n.* cross-country racing on motorcycles. [MOTOR + CROSS-]

moto perpetuo /ˌməʊtəʊ pəˈpɛtjʊəʊ/ *n. Mus.* a usu. fast-moving instrumental composition consisting mainly of notes of equal value. [Italian, = perpetual motion]

motor /ˈməʊtə/ *n.* & *v.* ● *n.* **1** a thing that imparts motion. **2** a machine (esp. one using electricity or internal combustion) supplying motive power for a vehicle etc. or for some other device with moving parts. **3** *Brit.* = MOTOR CAR. **4** (*attrib.*) **a** giving, imparting, or producing motion. **b** driven by a motor (*motor mower*). **c** of or for motor vehicles. **d** *Anat.* relating to muscular movement or the nerves activating it. ● *v.intr.* & *tr.* go or (*Brit.*) convey in a motor vehicle. □ **motorial** /məʊˈtɔːrɪəl/ *adj.* (in sense 4a of *n.*). **motory** *adj.* (in sense 4a of *n.*). [Latin, = mover (as MOVE)]

motorable /ˈməʊt(ə)rəb(ə)l/ *adj. Brit.* (of a road) that can be used by motor vehicles.

motor area *n.* the part of the frontal lobe of the brain associated with the initiation of muscular action.

motor bicycle *n.* a motorcycle or moped.

motorbike /ˈməʊtəbʌɪk/ *n. colloq.* = MOTORCYCLE.

motor boat *n.* a motor-driven boat.

motorcade /ˈməʊtəkeɪd/ *n.* a procession of motor vehicles. [MOTOR, on the pattern of *cavalcade*]

motor car see CAR 1.

motor caravan *n.* a van equipped with beds, cooking facilities, etc., like a caravan.

motor coach *n.* **1** = COACH *n.* 1. **2** a railway passenger carriage with its own motor.

motorcycle /ˈməʊtəsʌɪk(ə)l/ *n.* a two-wheeled motor-driven road vehicle without pedal propulsion. □ **motorcycling** *n.* **motorcyclist** *n.*

motorhome /ˈməʊtəhəʊm/ *n.* esp. *N. Amer.* a large motor vehicle equipped as a self-contained home.

motorist /ˈməʊt(ə)rɪst/ *n.* the driver of a motor car.

motorize /ˈməʊtərʌɪz/ *v.tr.* (also **-ise**) **1** equip (troops etc.) with motor transport. **2** provide with a motor for propulsion etc. □ **motorization** /-ˈzeɪʃ(ə)n/ *n.*

motorman /ˈməʊtəman/ *n.* (*pl.* **-men**) the driver of an underground train, tram, etc.

motormouth /ˈməʊtəməʊθ/ *n. N. Amer. slang* a person who talks incessantly and trivially.

motor nerve *n.* a nerve carrying impulses from the brain or spinal cord to a muscle.

motor neurone disease *n. Med.* a progressive disease involving degeneration of the motor neurones and wasting of the muscles.

motor racing *n.* the racing of motorized vehicles, esp. cars, as a sport.

motor scooter see SCOOTER *n.* 2.

motor sport *n.* = MOTOR RACING.

motor vehicle *n.* a road vehicle powered by an internal-combustion engine.

motorway /ˈməʊtəweɪ/ *n. Brit.* a main road with separate carriageways and limited access, specially constructed and controlled for fast motor traffic.

motor yacht *n.* a motor-driven yacht.

Motown /ˈməʊtaʊn/ *n.* music with rhythm-and-blues and soul elements, associated with Detroit. [abbreviation of *Tamla Motown*, the proprietary name of a record label, *Motown* being a name for Detroit, a shortening of *Motor Town* (from its car manufacturing industry)]

motte /mɒt/ *n.* a mound forming the site of a castle, camp, etc. [Middle English from Old French *mote* (as MOAT)]

mottle /ˈmɒt(ə)l/ *v.* & *n.* ● *v.tr.* (esp. as **mottled** *adj.*) mark with spots or smears of colour. ● *n.* **1** an irregular arrangement of spots or patches of colour. **2** any of these spots or patches. [probably a back-formation from MOTLEY]

motto /ˈmɒtəʊ/ *n.* (*pl.* **-oes** or **-os**) **1** a maxim adopted as a rule of conduct. **2** a phrase or sentence accompanying a coat of arms or crest. **3** a sentence inscribed on some object and expressing an appropriate sentiment. **4** verses etc. in a paper cracker. **5** a quotation prefixed to a book or chapter. **6** *Mus.* a recurrent phrase having some symbolical significance. [Italian (as MOT)]

moue /muː/ *n.* = POUT[1] *n.* [French]

mouflon /ˈmuːflɒn/ *n.* (also **moufflon**) a wild mountain sheep, *Ovis orientalis*, of S. Europe. [French *mouflon* via Italian *muflone* from Romanic]

mouillé /ˈmuːjeɪ, French muje/ *adj. Phonet.* (of a consonant) palatalized. [French, = wetted]

moujik var. of MUZHIK.

mould[1] /məʊld/ *n.* & *v.* (*US* **mold**) ● *n.* **1** a hollow container into which molten metal etc. is poured or soft material is pressed to harden into a required shape. **2 a** a hollow vessel, esp. of metal or earthenware, used to give shape to puddings etc. **b** a pudding etc. made in this way. **3** a form or shape, esp. of an animal body. **4** *Archit.* a moulding or group of mouldings. **5** a frame or template for producing mouldings. **6** character or disposition (*in heroic mould*). ● *v.tr.* **1** make (an object) in a required shape or from certain ingredients (*was moulded out of clay*). **2** give a shape to. **3** influence the formation or development of (*consultation helps to mould policies*). **4** (esp. of clothing) fit closely to (*the gloves moulded his hands*). □ **mouldable** *adj.* **moulder** *n.* [Middle English *mold(e)*, apparently via Old French *modle* from Latin *modulus*: see MODULUS]

mould[2] /məʊld/ *n.* (*US* **mold**) a woolly or furry growth of minute fungi occurring esp. in moist warm conditions. [Middle English, probably from obsolete *mould*, past part. of *moul* 'grow mouldy' from Old Norse *mygla*]

mould[3] /məʊld/ *n.* (*US* **mold**) **1** esp. *Brit.* loose earth. **2** the upper soil of cultivated land, esp. when rich in organic matter. [Old English *molde* from Germanic: related to MEAL[2]]

mould-board *n.* the board in a plough that turns over the furrow-slice.

moulder /ˈməʊldə/ *v.intr.* (*US* **molder**) **1** decay to dust. **2** (foll. by *away*) rot or crumble. **3** deteriorate. [perhaps from MOULD[3], but cf. Norwegian dialect *muldra* 'crumble']

moulding /ˈməʊldɪŋ/ *n.* (*US* **molding**) **1 a** an ornamentally shaped outline as an architectural feature, esp. in a cornice. **b** a strip of material in wood or stone etc. for use as moulding. **2** similar material in wood or plastic etc. used for other decorative purposes, e.g. in picture framing.

mouldy /ˈməʊldi/ *adj.* (*US* **moldy**) (**-ier**, **-iest**) **1** covered with mould. **2** stale; out of date. **3** *colloq.* (as a general term of disparagement) dull, miserable, boring. □ **mouldiness** *n.*

moulin /ˈmuːlɪn, French mulɛ̃/ *n.* a nearly vertical shaft in a glacier, formed by surface water percolating through a crack in the ice. [French, literally 'mill']

moult /məʊlt/ *v.* & *n.* (*US* **molt**) ● *v.* **1** *intr.* shed feathers, hair, a shell, skin, etc., in the process of renewing plumage, acquiring a new growth, etc. **2** *tr.* (of an animal) shed (feathers, hair, etc.). ● *n.* the act or an instance of moulting (*is in moult once a year*). [Middle English *moute* from Old English, from Latin *mutare* 'change': for intrusive *-l-* cf. *fault* etc.]

mound[1] /maʊnd/ *n.* & *v.* ● *n.* **1** a raised mass of earth, stones, or other compacted material. **2** a heap or pile. **3** a hillock. **4** *Baseball* a slight elevation on which the pitcher stands. ● *v.tr.* **1** heap up in a mound or mounds. **2** enclose with mounds. [16th c. (originally = hedge or fence): origin unknown]

mound[2] /maʊnd/ *n. Heraldry* a ball of gold etc. representing the earth, and usu. surmounting a crown. [Middle English via Old French *monde* from Latin *mundus* 'world']

mount[1] /maʊnt/ *v.* & *n.* ● *v.* **1** *tr.* ascend or climb (a hill, stairs, etc.). **2** *tr.* **a** get up on (an animal, esp. a horse) to ride it. **b** set (a person) on horseback. **c** provide (a person) with a horse. **d** (as **mounted** *adj.*) serving on horseback (*mounted police*). **3** *tr.* go up or climb on to (a raised surface). **4** *intr.* **a** move upwards. **b** (often foll. by *up*) increase, accumulate. **c** (of a feeling) become stronger or more intense (*excitement was mounting*). **d** (of the blood) rise into the cheeks. **5** *tr.* (esp. of a male animal) get on to (a female) to copulate. **6** *tr.* (often foll. by *on*) place (an object) on an elevated support. **7** *tr.* **a** set in or attach to a backing, setting, or other support. **b** attach (a picture etc.) to a mount or frame. **c** fix (an object for viewing) on a microscope slide. **8** *tr.* **a** arrange (a play, exhibition, etc.) or present for public view or display. **b** take action to initiate (a programme, campaign, etc.). **9** *tr.* prepare (specimens) for preservation. **10** *tr.* **a** bring into readiness for operation. **b** raise (guns) into position on a fixed mounting. **11** *intr.* rise to a higher level of rank, power, etc. ● *n.* **1** a backing or setting on which a photograph, work of art, gem, etc. is set for display. **2** a support for a gun, camera, etc. **3** a glass microscope slide for securing a specimen etc. to be viewed. **4** a stamp hinge. **5 a** a horse available for riding. **b** an opportunity to ride a horse, esp. as a jockey. □ **mount guard** (often foll. by *over*) perform the duty of guarding; take up sentry duty. □ **mountable** *adj.* **mounter** *n.* [Middle English from Old French *munter*, *monter*, ultimately from Latin (as MOUNT[2])]

mount[2] /maʊnt/ *n. archaic* (except before a name): mountain, hill (*Mount Everest*; *Mount of Olives*). [Old English *munt* from Latin *mons montis* 'mountain', reinforced in Middle English by Old French *mont*]

mountain /ˈmaʊntɪn/ *n.* **1** a large natural elevation of the earth's surface rising abruptly from the surrounding level; a large or high and steep hill. **2** a large heap or pile; a huge quantity (*a mountain of work*). **3** a large surplus stock of a commodity (*butter mountain*). □ **make a mountain out of a molehill** see MOLEHILL. **move mountains 1** achieve spectacular results. **2** make every possible effort. □ **mountainy** *adj.* [Middle English from Old French *montaigne*, ultimately from Latin *mons montis*]

mountain ash *n.* **1** a tree, *Sorbus aucuparia*, with delicate pinnate leaves and scarlet berries; also called ROWAN. **2** any of several Australian eucalypts.

mountain avens *n.* a creeping alpine plant, *Dryas octopetala* (rose family), with white flowers.

mountain bike *n.* a bicycle with a light sturdy frame, broad deep-treaded tyres, and multiple gears, originally designed for riding on mountainous terrain.

mountain chain *n.* a connected series of mountains.

mountaineer /maʊntɪˈnɪə/ *n.* & *v.* ● *n.* **1** a person skilled in mountain climbing. **2** a person living in an area of high mountains. ● *v.intr.* climb mountains as a sport. □ **mountaineering** *n.*

mountain goat *n.* **1** a goat which lives on mountains, proverbial for agility. **2** (in full **Rocky Mountain goat**) a white goatlike animal, *Oreamnos americanus*, of mountains in western N. America.

mountain laurel *n.* a N. American shrub, *Kalmia latifolia*.

mountain lion *n.* a puma.

mountainous /ˈmaʊntɪnəs/ *adj.* **1** (of a region) having many mountains. **2** huge.

mountain panther *n.* = OUNCE[2].

mountain range *n.* a line of mountains connected by high ground.

mountain sickness *n.* a sickness caused by breathing the rarefied air at great heights.

mountainside /ˈmaʊntɪnsʌɪd/ *n.* the slope of a mountain below the summit.

Mountain Standard Time *n.* (also **Mountain Time**) the standard time in a zone including parts of Canada and the US in or near the Rocky Mountains, seven hours behind GMT.

mountebank /ˈmaʊntɪbaŋk/ *n.* **1** a swindler; a charlatan. **2** a clown. **3** *hist.* an itinerant quack appealing to an audience from a platform. □ **mountebankery** *n.* [Italian *montambanco* = *monta in banco* 'climb on bench': see MOUNT[1], BENCH]

Mountie /ˈmaʊnti/ *n. colloq.* a member of the Royal Canadian Mounted Police.

mounting /ˈmaʊntɪŋ/ *n.* **1** = MOUNT[1] *n.* 1. **2** in senses of MOUNT[1] *v.*

mounting block *n.* a block of stone placed to help a rider mount a horse.

mourn /mɔːn/ *v.* **1** *tr.* & (foll. by *for*) *intr.* feel or show deep sorrow or regret for (a dead person, a lost thing, a past event, etc.). **2** *intr.* show conventional signs of grief after a person's death. [Old English *murnan*]

mourner /ˈmɔːnə/ *n.* **1** a person who mourns, esp. at a funeral. **2** a person hired to attend a funeral.

mournful /ˈmɔːnfʊl, -f(ə)l/ *adj.* **1** doleful, sad, sorrowing. **2** expressing or suggestive of mourning. □ **mournfully** *adv.* **mournfulness** *n.*

mourning /ˈmɔːnɪŋ/ *n.* **1** the expression of deep sorrow, esp. for a dead person, by the wearing of solemn dress. **2** the clothes worn in mourning. □ **in mourning** assuming the signs of mourning, esp. in dress.

mourning-band *n.* a band of black crape etc. round a person's sleeve or hat as a token of mourning.

mourning cloak *n. N. Amer.* = CAMBERWELL BEAUTY.

mourning dove *n.* an American dove with a plaintive note, *Zenaida macroura.*

mourning-paper *n.* notepaper with a black edge.

mourning ring *n.* a ring worn as a memorial of a deceased person.

mousaka var. of MOUSSAKA.

mouse /maʊs/ *n.* & *v.* ● *n.* (*pl.* **mice** /mʌɪs/) **1 a** any of various small rodents esp. of the family Muridae, usu. having a pointed snout and relatively large ears and eyes. **b** any of several similar small mammals, such as a shrew or vole. **2** a timid or feeble person. **3** (*pl.* also **mouses**) *Computing* a small hand-held device which controls the cursor on a VDU screen. **4** *slang* a black eye. ● *v.intr.* /also maʊz/ **1** (esp. of a cat, owl, etc.) hunt for or catch mice. **2** (foll. by *about*) search industriously; prowl about as if searching. □ **mouselike** *adj.* & *adv.* **mouser** *n.* [Old English *mūs*, pl. *mȳs*, from Germanic]

mouse-coloured *adj.* of a nondescript shade of light brown, mid brown, or grey.

mouse deer *n.* a chevrotain.

mouse hare *n.* a pika.

mousetrap /ˈmaʊstrap/ *n.* **1** a sprung trap with bait for catching and usu. killing mice. **2** (often *attrib.*) *Brit.* cheese of poor quality.

mousey var. of MOUSY.

moussaka /muːˈsɑːkə, muːsəˈkɑː/ *n.* (also **mousaka**) a Greek dish of minced meat, aubergine, etc. with a cheese sauce. [modern Greek or Turkish]

mousse /muːs/ *n.* **1 a** a dessert of whipped cream, eggs, etc., usu. flavoured with fruit or chocolate. **b** a meat or fish purée made with whipped cream etc. **2** a preparation applied to the hair enabling it to be styled more easily. **3** a mixture of oil and sea water forming a froth on the surface of the sea after an oil-spill. [French, = moss, froth]

mousseline /ˈmuːsliːn/ *n.* **1** a muslin-like fabric of silk etc. **2 a** a soft light mousse. **b** hollandaise sauce made frothy with whipped cream or egg white. [French: see MUSLIN]

moustache /məˈstɑːʃ/ *n.* (*US* **mustache**) **1** hair left to grow above a man's upper lip. **2** a similar growth round the mouth of some animals. □ **moustached** *adj.* [French, via Italian *mostaccio* from Greek *mustax -akos*]

moustache cup *n.* a cup with a partial cover to protect the moustache when drinking.

Mousterian /muːˈstɪərɪən/ *adj.* & *n. Archaeol.* ● *adj.* of or relating to the main culture of the middle palaeolithic period, associated with Neanderthal peoples and dated to *c.*80,000–35,000 BC. ● *n.* this culture. [French *moustiérien* from *Le Moustier* a cave in SW France, where remains were found]

mousy /ˈmaʊsi/ *adj.* (also **mousey**) (**mousier**, **mousiest**) **1** of or like a mouse. **2** (of a person) shy or timid; ineffectual. **3** = MOUSE-COLOURED. □ **mousily** *adv.* **mousiness** *n.*

mouth *n.* & *v.* ● *n.* /maʊθ/ (*pl.* **mouths** /maʊðz/) **1 a** an external opening in the head, through which most animals admit food and emit communicative sounds. **b** (in humans and some animals) the cavity behind it containing the means of biting and chewing and the vocal organs. **2 a** the opening of a container such as a bag or sack. **b** the opening of a cave, volcano, etc. **c** the open end of a woodwind or brass instrument. **d** the muzzle of a gun. **3** the place where a river enters the sea. **4** *colloq.* **a** talkativeness. **b** impudent talk; cheek. **5** an individual regarded as needing sustenance (*an extra mouth to feed*). **6** a horse's readiness to feel and obey the pressure of the bit. ● *v.* /maʊð/ **1** *tr.* & *intr.* utter or speak solemnly or with affectations; rant, declaim (*mouthing platitudes*). **2** *tr.* utter very distinctly. **3** *intr.* **a** move the lips silently. **b** grimace. **4** *tr.* say (words) with movement of the mouth but no sound. **5** *tr.* take (food) in the mouth. **6** *tr.* touch with the mouth. **7** *tr.* train the mouth of (a horse). □ **give mouth** (of a dog) bark, bay. **keep one's mouth shut** *colloq.* not reveal a secret. **put words into a person's mouth** represent a person as having said something in a particular way. **take the words out of a person's mouth** say what another was about to say. □ **mouthed** /maʊðd/ *adj.* (also in *comb.*). **mouther** /ˈmaʊðə/ *n.* **mouthless** /ˈmaʊθlɪs/ *adj.* [Old English *mūth*, from Germanic]

mouthbrooder /ˈmaʊθbruːdə/ *n.* a fish which protects its eggs (and sometimes its young) by carrying them in its mouth.

mouthful /ˈmaʊθfʊl, -f(ə)l/ *n.* (*pl.* **-fuls**) **1** a quantity, esp. of food, that fills the mouth. **2** a small quantity. **3** a long or complicated word or phrase. **4** *US colloq.* something important said.

mouth organ *n.* = HARMONICA.

mouthpart /ˈmaʊθpɑːt/ *n.* any of the (usu. paired) organs surrounding the mouth of an insect or other arthropod and adapted for feeding.

mouthpiece /ˈmaʊθpiːs/ *n.* **1 a** the part of a musical instrument placed between or against the lips. **b** the part of a telephone for speaking into. **c** the part of a tobacco pipe placed between the lips. **2 a** a person who speaks for another or others. **b** *colloq.* a lawyer. **3** a part attached as an outlet.

mouth-to-mouth *adj.* (of resuscitation) in which a person breathes into a subject's lungs through the mouth.

mouthwash /ˈmaʊθwɒʃ/ *n.* **1** a liquid antiseptic etc. for rinsing the mouth or gargling. **2** *colloq.* nonsense.

mouth-watering *adj.* **1** (of food etc.) having a delicious smell or appearance. **2** tempting, alluring.

mouthy /ˈmaʊði/ *adj.* (**mouthier**, **mouthiest**) **1** ranting, railing, bombastic. **2** *colloq.* impudent, cheeky.

movable /ˈmuːvəb(ə)l/ *adj.* & *n.* (also **moveable**) ● *adj.* **1** that can be moved. **2** *Law* (of property) of the nature of a chattel, as distinct from land or buildings (cf. HERITABLE 1a). **3** (of a feast or festival) variable in date from year to year. ● *n.* **1** an article of furniture that may be removed from a house, as distinct from a fixture. **2** (in *pl.*) personal property. □ **movability** /-ˈbɪlɪti/ *n.* **movableness** *n.* **movably** *adv.* [Middle English from Old French (as MOVE)]

movable-doh *attrib.adj.* designating a system of sight-singing in which doh is the keynote of any major scale (cf. FIXED-DOH).

movable feast *n.* **1** a religious feast day that occurs on a different date each year. **2** an event which takes place at no regular time.

move /mu:v/ *v. & n.* ● *v.* **1** *intr. & tr.* change one's position or posture, or cause to do this. **2** *tr. & intr.* put or keep in motion; rouse, stir. **3 a** *intr.* make a move in a board game. **b** *tr.* change the position of (a piece) in a board game. **4** *intr.* (often foll. by *about, away,* etc.) go or pass from place to place. **5** *intr.* take action, esp. promptly (*moved to reduce unemployment*). **6** *intr.* make progress (*the project is moving fast*). **7** *tr.* (also *absol.*) change (one's place of residence or work). **8** *intr.* (foll. by *in*) live or be socially active in (a specified place or group etc.) (*moves in the best circles*). **9** *tr.* affect (a person) with (usu. tender or sympathetic) emotion. **10** *tr.* **a** (foll. by *in*) stimulate (laughter, anger, etc., in a person). **b** (foll. by *to*) provoke (a person to laughter etc.). **11** *tr.* (foll. by *to,* or *to* + infin.) prompt or incline (a person to a feeling or action). **12** *tr. & intr.* (cause to) change in attitude or opinion (*nothing can move me on this issue*). **13 a** *tr.* cause (the bowels) to be evacuated. **b** *intr.* (of the bowels) be evacuated. **14** *tr.* (often foll. by *that* + clause) propose in a meeting, deliberative assembly, etc. **15** *intr.* (foll. by *for*) make a formal request or application. **16 a** *intr.* (of merchandise) be sold. **b** *tr.* sell. ● *n.* **1** the act or an instance of moving. **2** a change of house, business premises, etc. **3** a step taken to secure some action or effect; an initiative. **4 a** the changing of the position of a piece in a board game. **b** a player's turn to do this. □ **get a move on** *colloq.* **1** hurry up. **2** make a start. **make a move** take action. **move along** (or **on**) change to a new position, esp. to avoid crowding, getting in the way, etc. **move away** go to live in another area. **move heaven and earth** see HEAVEN. **move in 1** take possession of a new house etc. **2** get into a position of influence, interference, etc. **3** (often foll. by *on*) get into a position of readiness or proximity (for an offensive action etc.). **move in with** start to share accommodation with (an existing resident). **move mountains** see MOUNTAIN. **move out 1** leave one's home; change one's place of residence. **2** leave a position, job, etc. **move over** (or **up**) adjust one's position to make room for another. **on the move 1** progressing. **2** moving about. [Middle English via Anglo-French *mover,* Old French *moveir* from Latin *movēre mot-*]

moveable var. of MOVABLE.

movement /ˈmu:vm(ə)nt/ *n.* **1** the act or an instance of moving or being moved. **2 a** the moving parts of a mechanism (esp. a clock or watch). **b** a particular group of these. **3 a** a body of persons with a common object (*the peace movement*). **b** a campaign undertaken by such a body. **4** (usu. in *pl.*) a person's activities and whereabouts, esp. at a particular time. **5** *Mus.* a principal division of a longer musical work, self-sufficient in terms of key, tempo, structure, etc. **6** the progressive development of a poem, story, etc. **7** motion of the bowels. **8 a** an activity in a market for some commodity. **b** a rise or fall in price. **9** a mental impulse. **10** a development of position by a military force or unit. [Middle English via Old French from medieval Latin *movimentum* (as MOVE)]

mover /ˈmu:və/ *n.* **1** a person or thing that moves. **2** a person who moves a proposition. **3** *N. Amer.* a remover of furniture. **4** the author of a fruitful idea.

movie /ˈmu:vi/ *n.colloq.* **1** esp. *N. Amer.* a motion-picture film. **2** *US* a cinema.

movie-goer *n.* esp. *N. Amer.* = FILM-GOER. □ **movie-going** *n.*

movie-maker *n.* esp. *N. Amer.* = FILM-MAKER. □ **movie-making** *n.*

movie theatre *n.* (also **movie house**) esp. *N. Amer.* a cinema.

moving /ˈmu:vɪŋ/ *adj.* **1** that moves or causes to move. **2** affecting with emotion. □ **movingly** *adv.* (in sense 2).

moving-coil *adj.* (of an electrical device) containing a wire coil suspended in a magnetic field, so that the coil either moves in response to a current, or produces a current when it is made to move.

moving pavement *n. Brit.* a structure like a conveyor belt for pedestrians.

moving picture *n.* a continuous picture of events obtained by projecting a sequence of photographs taken at very short intervals.

moving staircase *n. Brit.* an escalator.

mow[1] /məʊ/ *v.tr.* (*past part.* **mowed** or **mown**) **1** cut down (grass, hay, etc.) with a scythe or machine. **2** cut down the produce of (a field) or the grass etc. of (a lawn) by mowing. □ **mow down** kill or destroy randomly or in great numbers. □ **mower** *n.* [Old English *māwan* from Germanic: related to MEAD[2]]

mow[2] /maʊ/ *n. N. Amer.* or *dial.* **1** a stack of hay, corn, etc. **2** a place in a barn where hay etc. is heaped. [Old English *mūga*]

moxa /ˈmɒksə/ *n.* a downy substance from the dried leaves of an Asian plant, *Crossostephium artemisioides,* burnt on or near the skin in oriental medicine as a counterirritant. [Japanese *mogusa* from *moe kusa* 'burning herb']

moxibustion /mɒksɪˈbʌstʃ(ə)n/ *n.* the burning of moxa on or near the skin. [MOXA + COMBUSTION]

moxie /ˈmɒksi/ *n. N. Amer. slang* force of character, energy, wit. [proprietary name of a soft drink]

mozzarella /mɒtsəˈrɛlə/ *n.* an Italian curd cheese originally of buffalo milk. [Italian]

MP *abbr.* **1** Member of Parliament. **2 a** military police. **b** military policeman.

mp *abbr.* mezzo piano.

m.p. *abbr.* melting point.

m.p.g. *abbr.* miles per gallon.

m.p.h. *abbr.* miles per hour.

M.Phil. *abbr.* Master of Philosophy.

mpingo /(ə)mˈpɪŋgəʊ/ *n.* (*pl.* **-os**) **1** an E. African leguminous tree, *Dalbergia melanoxylon.* **2** its dense black wood used for carvings and musical instruments. [Swahili]

MR *abbr.* Master of the Rolls.

Mr /ˈmɪstə/ *n.* (*pl.* **Messrs**) **1** the title of a man without a higher or honorific or professional title (*Mr Jones*). **2** a title prefixed to a designation of office etc. (*Mr President; Mr Speaker*). [abbreviation of MISTER]

MRA *abbr.* Moral Rearmament.

MRBM *abbr.* medium-range ballistic missile.

MRC *abbr.* (in the UK) Medical Research Council.

MRCA *abbr.* multi-role combat aircraft.

MRCP *abbr.* Member of the Royal College of Physicians.

MRCVS *abbr.* Member of the Royal College of Veterinary Surgeons.

MRI *abbr.* magnetic resonance imaging.

MRIA *abbr.* Member of the Royal Irish Academy.

mRNA *abbr. Biol.* messenger RNA.

MRPhS *abbr.* Member of the Royal Pharmaceutical Society.

Mr Right *n. joc.* a woman's destined husband.

Mrs /ˈmɪsɪz, -s/ *n.* (*pl.* same or **Mesdames**) the title of a married woman without a higher or honorific or professional title (*Mrs Jones*). [abbreviation of MISTRESS: cf. MISSIS]

Mrs Grundy see GRUNDY.

MS *abbr.* **1** manuscript. **2** Master of Science. **3** Master of Surgery. **4** *US* Mississippi (in official postal use). **5** *US* motor ship. **6** multiple sclerosis.

Ms /mɪz/ *n.* the title of a woman without a higher or honorific or professional title, used regardless of marital status. [combination of MRS, MISS[2]]

MSC *abbr.* (in the UK) Manpower Services Commission.

M.Sc. *abbr.* Master of Science.

MS-DOS /ɛmɛsˈdɒs/ *abbr. Computing propr.* Microsoft disk operating system.

MSF *abbr.* (in the UK) Manufacturing, Science, and Finance (Union).

MSG *abbr.* monosodium glutamate.

Msgr. *abbr. US* **1** *Monseigneur.* **2** Monsignor.

MSS /ɛmˈɛsɪz/ *abbr.* manuscripts.

MST *abbr.* Mountain Standard Time.

MT *abbr.* **1** mechanical transport. **2** *US* Montana (in official postal use).

Mt. *abbr.* Mount.

MTB *abbr.* motor torpedo boat.

M.Tech. *abbr.* Master of Technology.

mu /mju:/ *n.* **1** the twelfth letter of the Greek alphabet (Μ, μ). **2** (μ, as a symbol) = MICRO- 2. [Greek]

much /mʌtʃ/ *det., pron., & adv.* (**more**, **most**) ● *det.* (used with uncountable nouns) existing or occurring in a great quantity (*much trouble*; *not much rain*; *too much noise*). ● *pron.* **1** a great quantity (*much of that is true*). **2** (usu. in *neg.*) a noteworthy or outstanding example (*not much to look at*; *not much of a party*). ● *adv.* **1 a** in a great degree (*much to my surprise*; *is much the same*). **b** (modifying a verb or past participle) greatly (*they much regret the mistake*; *I was much annoyed*). **c** modifying a comparative or superlative adjective (*much better*; *much the most likely*). **2** for a large part of one's time (*is much away from home*). □ **as much** the extent or quantity just specified; the idea just mentioned (*I thought as much*; *as much as that?*). **a bit much** *colloq.* somewhat excessive or immoderate. **make much of** see MAKE. **much as** even though (*cannot come, much as I would like to*). **much less** see LESS. **not much** *colloq.* **1** *iron.* very much. **2** certainly not. **not much in it** little difference between things being compared. **too much** *colloq.* an intolerable situation or circumstance (*that really is too much*). **too much for 1** more than a match for. **2** beyond what is endurable by. □ **muchly** *adv. joc.* [Middle English from *muchel* MICKLE: for loss of *el* cf. BAD, WENCH]

muchness /ˈmʌtʃnɪs/ *n.* greatness in quantity or degree. □ **much of a muchness** very nearly the same or alike.

much obliged see OBLIGE.

mucilage /ˈmju:sɪlɪdʒ/ *n.* **1** a viscous or gelatinous solution obtained from plant roots, seeds, etc., used in medicines and adhesives. **2** *N. Amer.* a solution of gum. **3** a viscous secretion, e.g. mucus. □ **mucilaginous** /-ˈladʒɪnəs/ *adj.* [Middle English via French from Late Latin *mucilago -ginis* 'musty juice' (MUCUS)]

muck /mʌk/ *n. & v.* ● *n.* **1** farmyard manure. **2** *colloq.* dirt or filth; anything disgusting. **3** *colloq.* an untidy state; a mess. ● *v.tr.* **1** (usu. foll. by *up*) *colloq.* bungle (a job), spoil, ruin. **2** (foll. by *out*) remove muck from. **3** make dirty or untidy. **4** manure with muck. □ **make a muck of** *colloq.* bungle. **muck about** (or **around**) *Brit. colloq.* **1** potter or fool about. **2** (foll. by *with*) fool or interfere with. **muck in** (often foll. by *with*) *Brit.* share tasks etc. equally. [Middle English *muk*, probably from Scandinavian: cf. Old Norse *myki* 'dung', from a Germanic base meaning 'soft', whence also MEEK]

mucker /ˈmʌkə/ *n. slang* **1** *Brit.* a friend or companion. **2** *US* a rough or coarse person. **3** *Brit.* a heavy fall. [probably from *muck in*: see MUCK]

muckle var. of MICKLE.

muckrake /ˈmʌkreɪk/ *v.intr.* search out and reveal scandal, esp. among famous people. □ **muckraker** *n.* **muckraking** *n.*

muck-spreader *n.* a machine for spreading manure on fields. □ **muck-spreading** *n.*

muck sweat *n. Brit. colloq.* a profuse sweat.

mucky /ˈmʌki/ *adj.* (**muckier**, **muckiest**) **1** covered with muck. **2** dirty. □ **muckiness** *n.*

muco- /ˈmju:kəʊ/ *comb. form Biochem.* mucus, mucous.

mucopolysaccharide /ˌmju:kəʊpɒlɪˈsakərʌɪd/ *n. Biochem.* any of a group of polysaccharides whose molecules contain sugar residues and are often found as components of connective tissue.

mucosa /mju:ˈkəʊsə/ *n.* (*pl.* **mucosae** /-si:/) a mucous membrane. [modern Latin, fem. of *mucosus*: see MUCOUS]

mucous /ˈmju:kəs/ *adj.* of or covered with mucus. □ **mucosity** /-ˈkɒsɪti/ *n.* [Latin *mucosus* (as MUCUS)]

mucous membrane *n.* an epithelial tissue lining many body cavities and tubular organs and secreting mucus.

mucro /ˈmju:krəʊ/ *n.* (*pl.* **mucrones** /-ˈkrəʊni:z/ or **-os**) *Bot.* & *Zool.* a sharp-pointed part or organ. □ **mucronate** /-krənət, -neɪt/ *adj.* [Latin *mucro -onis* 'sharp point']

mucus /ˈmju:kəs/ *n.* **1** a slimy substance, usu. not miscible with water, secreted by a mucous membrane or gland. **2** a gummy substance found in plants. [Latin]

mud /mʌd/ *n.* **1** wet soft earthy matter. **2** hard ground from the drying of an area of this. **3** what is worthless or polluting. □ **as clear as mud** *colloq.* not at all clear. **drag through the mud** denigrate publicly. **fling** (or **sling** or **throw**) **mud** speak disparagingly or slanderously. **here's mud in your eye!** *colloq.* a drinking toast. **one's name is mud** one is unpopular or in disgrace. [Middle English *mode*, *mudde*, probably from Middle Low German *mudde*, Middle High German *mot* 'bog']

mudbank /ˈmʌdbaŋk/ *n.* a bank of mud on the bed of a river or the bottom of the sea.

mudbath /ˈmʌdbɑ:θ/ *n.* **1** a bath in the mud of mineral springs, esp. to relieve rheumatism etc. **2** a muddy scene or occasion.

mudbrick /ˈmʌdbrɪk/ *n.* a brick made from baked mud.

muddle /ˈmʌd(ə)l/ *v. & n.* ● *v.* **1** *tr.* (often foll. by *up*, *together*) bring into disorder. **2** *tr.* bewilder, confuse. **3** *tr.* mismanage (an affair). **4** *tr. US* crush and mix (the ingredients for a drink). **5** *intr.* (often foll. by *with*) busy oneself in a confused and ineffective way. ● *n.* **1** disorder. **2** a muddled condition. □ **make a muddle of 1** bring into disorder. **2** bungle. **muddle along** (or **on**) progress in a haphazard way. **muddle through** succeed by perseverance rather than skill or efficiency. **muddle up** confuse (two or more things). □ **muddler** *n.* **muddlingly** *adv.* [perhaps from Middle Dutch *moddelen*, frequentative of *modden* 'dabble in mud' (as MUD)]

muddle-headed *adj.* stupid, confused. □ **muddle-headedness** *n.*

muddy /ˈmʌdi/ *adj. & v.* ● *adj.* (**muddier**, **muddiest**) **1** like mud. **2** covered in or full of mud. **3** (of liquid) turbid. **4** mentally confused. **5** obscure. **6** (of light) dull. **7** (of colour) impure. ● *v.tr.* (**-ies**, **-ied**) make muddy. □ **muddily** *adv.* **muddiness** *n.*

mudfish /ˈmʌdfɪʃ/ *n.* (*pl.* usu. same) any fish that burrows in mud, esp. the bowfin.

mudflap /ˈmʌdflap/ *n.* a flap hanging behind the wheel of a vehicle, to catch mud and stones etc. thrown up from the road.

mudflat /ˈmʌdflat/ *n.* a stretch of muddy land left uncovered at low tide.

mudflow /ˈmʌdfləʊ/ *n.* **1** a fluid or hardened stream or avalanche of mud. **2** the flow or motion of such a stream.

mudguard /ˈmʌdgɑ:d/ *n.* a curved strip or cover over a wheel of a bicycle or motorcycle to reduce the amount of mud etc. thrown up from the road.

mudlark /ˈmʌdlɑ:k/ *n. Brit. hist.* **1** a person who scavenges in river mud for objects of value. **2** a street urchin.

mud pack *n.* a cosmetic paste applied thickly to the face.

mud pie *n.* mud made into a pie shape by a child.

mud puppy *n. US* a large neotenous aquatic salamander, esp. *Necturus maculosus*, of the eastern US.

mudskipper /ˈmʌdskɪpə/ *n.* any small goby of the family Periophthalmidae, able to leave the water and scramble over mud etc.

mud-slinger *n. colloq.* one given to making abusive or disparaging remarks. □ **mud-slinging** *n.*

mudstone /ˈmʌdstəʊn/ *n.* a dark clay rock.

mud volcano *n.* a volcano discharging mud.

muesli /'mu:zli, 'mju:zli/ *n.* (*pl.* **-is**) a breakfast food of crushed cereals, dried fruits, nuts, etc., eaten with milk. [Swiss German]

muezzin /mu:'ɛzɪn/ *n.* a Muslim crier who proclaims the hours of prayer usu. from a minaret. [Arabic *mu'aḏḏin*, part. of *'aḏḏana* 'proclaim']

muff[1] /mʌf/ *n.* a fur or other covering, usu. in the form of a tube with an opening at each end for the hands to be inserted for warmth. [Dutch *mof*, Middle Dutch *moffel*, *muffel* from medieval Latin *muff(u)la*, of unknown origin]

muff[2] /mʌf/ *v. & n.* ● *v.tr.* **1** bungle; deal clumsily with. **2** fail to catch or receive (a ball etc.). **3** blunder in (a theatrical part etc.). ● *n.* **1** esp. *Brit.* a person who is awkward or stupid, originally in some athletic sport. **2** a failure, esp. to catch a ball at cricket etc. [19th c.: origin unknown]

muffin /'mʌfɪn/ *n.* **1** *Brit.* a circular spongy cake made from yeast dough and eaten toasted and buttered. **2** *N. Amer.* a small spongy cake made with eggs and baking powder. [18th c.: origin unknown]

muffin man *n. Brit. hist.* a seller of muffins in the street.

muffle[1] /'mʌf(ə)l/ *v. & n.* ● *v.tr.* **1** (often foll. by *up*) wrap or cover for warmth. **2** cover or wrap up (a source of sound) to reduce its loudness. **3** (usu. as **muffled** *adj.*) stifle (an utterance, e.g. a curse). **4** prevent from speaking. ● *n.* **1** a receptacle in a furnace where substances may be heated without contact with combustion products. **2** a similar chamber in a kiln for baking painted pottery. [Middle English: the noun from Old French *moufle* 'thick glove'; the verb perhaps from Old French *enmoufler* from *moufle*]

muffle[2] /'mʌf(ə)l/ *n.* the thick part of the upper lip and nose of ruminants and rodents. [French *mufle*, of unknown origin]

muffler /'mʌflə/ *n.* **1** a wrap or scarf worn for warmth. **2** any of various devices used to deaden sound in musical instruments. **3** *N. Amer.* the silencer of a motor vehicle.

mufti[1] /'mʌfti/ *n.* a Muslim legal expert empowered to give rulings on religious matters. [Arabic *muftī*, part. of *'aftā* 'decide a point of law']

mufti[2] /'mʌfti/ *n.* plain clothes worn by a person who also wears (esp. military) uniform (*in mufti*). [19th c.: perhaps from MUFTI[1]]

mug[1] /mʌg/ *n. & v.* ● *n.* **1 a** a drinking vessel, usu. cylindrical and with a handle and used without a saucer. **b** its contents. **2** *slang* the face or mouth of a person. **3** *Brit. slang* **a** a simpleton. **b** a gullible person. **4** *US slang* a hoodlum or thug. ● *v.* (**mugged**, **mugging**) **1** *tr.* rob (a person) with violence, esp. in a public place. **2** *tr.* fight; thrash. **3** *tr.* strangle. **4** *intr. slang* make faces, esp. before an audience, a camera, etc. □ **a mug's game** *Brit. colloq.* a foolish or unprofitable activity. □ **mugger** *n.* (esp. in sense 1 of *v.*). **mugful** *n.* (*pl.* **-fuls**). **mugging** *n.* (in sense 1 of *v.*). [probably from Scandinavian: sense 2 of *n.* probably from the representation of faces on mugs, sense 3 probably from sense 2]

mug[2] /mʌg/ *v.tr.* (**mugged**, **mugging**) (usu. foll. by *up* or *up on*) *Brit. slang* learn (a subject) by concentrated study. [19th c.: origin unknown]

mugger[1] see MUG[1].

mugger[2] /'mʌgə/ *n.* a broad-nosed Indian crocodile, *Crocodylus palustris*, venerated by many Hindus. [Hindi *magar*]

muggins /'mʌgɪnz/ *n.* (*pl.* same or **mugginses**) *Brit.* **1** *colloq.* **a** a simpleton. **b** a person who is easily outwitted (often with allusion to oneself: *so muggins had to pay*). **2** a card game like snap. [perhaps the surname *Muggins*, with allusion to MUG[1]]

muggy /'mʌgi/ *adj.* (**muggier**, **muggiest**) (of the weather, a day, etc.) oppressively damp and warm; humid. □ **mugginess** *n.* [dialect *mug* 'mist, drizzle' from Old Norse *mugga*]

Mughal /'mu:gɑ:l/ *n.* **1** a Mongolian. **2** (*attrib.*) denoting the Muslim dynasty in India in the 16th–19th c. (cf. MOGUL[1] 2b). [Persian *muġūl* MONGOL]

mugshot /'mʌgʃɒt/ *n. slang* a photograph of a face, esp. for official purposes.

mugwort /'mʌgwə:t/ *n.* any of various plants of the genus *Artemisia*, esp. *A. vulgaris*, with silver-grey aromatic foliage. [Old English *mucgwyrt* (as MIDGE, WORT)]

mugwump /'mʌgwʌmp/ *n. N. Amer.* **1** a great man; a boss. **2** a person who holds aloof, esp. from party politics. [Algonquian *mugquomp* 'great chief']

Muhammadan /mʊ'hamәd(ә)n/ *n. & adj.* (also **Mohammedan**) *offens.* = MUSLIM. □ **Muhammadanism** *n.* [*Muhammad*, Arabian prophet d. 632]

■ **Usage** The term *Muhammadan* is not used or favoured by Muslims, and is often regarded as offensive.

mujahedin /,mʊdʒɑ:hɪ'di:n/ *n.pl.* (also **mujahidin**, **mujahideen**) guerrilla fighters in Islamic countries, esp. supporting Islamic fundamentalism. [Persian & Arabic *mujāhidīn*, pl. of *mujāhid*, a person who fights a JIHAD]

mulatto /mju:'latəʊ/ *n. & adj.* ● *n.* (*pl.* **-os** or **-oes**) a person of mixed white and black parentage. ● *adj.* of the colour of the skin of mulattos; tawny. [Spanish *mulato* 'young mule, mulatto', formed irregularly from *mulo* MULE[1]]

mulberry /'mʌlb(ə)ri/ *n. & adj.* ● *n.* (*pl.* **-ies**) **1** (also **mulberry tree** or **bush**) any deciduous tree of the genus *Morus* (family Moraceae), esp. *M. alba* (**white mulberry**), grown originally for feeding silkworms, and *M. nigra* (**black mulberry**), grown for its fruit. **2** the dark red or white berry of such a tree. **3** a dark red or purple colour. ● *adj.* of this colour. [Middle English *mol-*, *mool-*, *mulberry*, with dissimilation from *murberie* from Old English *mōrberie*, from Latin *morum*: see BERRY]

mulch /mʌl(t)ʃ/ *n. & v.* ● *n.* a mixture of wet straw, leaves, etc., spread around or over a plant to enrich or insulate the soil. ● *v.tr.* treat with mulch. [probably *mulsh* 'soft', used as a noun: related to *melsh* 'mild' from Old English *melsc*]

mulct /mʌlkt/ *v. & n.* ● *v.tr.* **1** extract money from by fine or taxation. **2 a** (often foll. by *of*) deprive by fraudulent means; swindle. **b** obtain by swindling. ● *n.* a fine. [earlier *mult(e)* from Latin *multa*, *mulcta*: the verb via French *mulcter* & Latin *mulctare*]

mule[1] /mju:l/ *n.* **1** the offspring (usu. sterile) of a male donkey and a female horse, or (in general use) of a female donkey and a male horse (cf. HINNY[1]), used as a beast of burden. **2** a stupid or obstinate person. **3** (often *attrib.*) a hybrid and usu. sterile plant or animal (*mule canary*). **4** (in full **spinning mule**) a kind of spinning machine producing yarn on spindles. [Middle English via Old French *mul(e)* from Latin *mulus mula*]

mule[2] /mju:l/ *n.* a light shoe or slipper without a back. [French, = slipper]

mule[3] var. of MEWL.

mule deer *n.* a long-eared black-tailed deer of western N. America, *Odocoileus hemionus*. [MULE[1]]

muleteer /mju:lɪ'tɪə/ *n.* a mule driver. [French *muletier* from *mulet*, diminutive of Old French *mul* MULE[1]]

mulga /'mʌlgə/ *n. Austral.* **1** a small spreading tree, *Acacia aneura*. **2** the wood of this tree. **3** scrub or bush. **4** *colloq.* the outback. [Kamilaroi (and other Aboriginal languages) *malga*]

muliebrity /mju:lɪ'ɛbrɪti/ *n. literary* **1** womanhood. **2** the normal characteristics of a woman. **3** softness, effeminacy. [Late Latin *muliebritas* from Latin *mulier* 'woman']

mulish /'mju:lɪʃ/ *adj.* **1** like a mule. **2** stubborn. □ **mulishly** *adv.* **mulishness** *n.*

mull[1] /mʌl/ *v.tr. & intr.* (often foll. by *over*) ponder or consider. [perhaps from *mull* 'grind to powder', Middle English *mul* 'dust', from Middle Dutch]

mull[2] /mʌl/ *v.tr.* (esp. as **mulled** *adj.*) warm (wine or beer) with added sugar, spices, etc. [17th c.: origin unknown]

mull[3] /mʌl/ *n. Sc.* a promontory. [Middle English: cf. Gaelic *maol*, Icelandic *múli*]

mull[4] /mʌl/ *n.* humus formed under non-acid conditions. [German, from Danish *muld*]

mull[5] /mʌl/ *n.* a thin soft plain muslin. [abbreviation of *mulmull* from Hindi *malmal*]

mullah /'mʌlə, 'mʊlə/ *n.* a Muslim learned in Islamic theology and sacred law. [Persian, Turkish, Urdu *mullā* from Arabic *mawlā*]

mullein /'mʌlm/ *n.* any herbaceous plant of the genus *Verbascum*, with woolly leaves and yellow flowers. [Middle English via Old French *moleine* from Gaulish]

muller /'mʌlə/ *n.* a stone or other heavy weight used for grinding material on a slab. [Middle English, perhaps from Anglo-French *moldre* 'grind']

Müllerian mimicry /mʊ'lɪərɪən/ *n. Zool.* a form of mimicry in which two or more noxious animals develop similar patterns of coloration etc. as a shared protective device. [named after J.F.T. *Müller*, German zoologist d. 1897]

mullet /'mʌlɪt/ *n.* a fish of the family Mullidae (see RED MULLET) or (esp. *US*) the family Mugilidae (see GREY MULLET). [Middle English via Old French *mulet*, diminutive of Latin *mullus* 'red mullet', from Greek *mollos*]

mulligatawny /ˌmʌlɪgə'tɔ:ni/ *n.* a highly seasoned soup originally from India. [Tamil *milagutannir* 'pepper-water']

mullion /'mʌljən/ *n.* (also **munnion** /'mʌn-/) a vertical bar dividing the lights in a window (cf. TRANSOM 1). □ **mullioned** *adj.* [probably an altered form of MONIAL]

mullock /'mʌlək/ *n.* **1** *Austral.* or *dial.* refuse, rubbish. **2** *Austral.* **a** rock containing no gold. **b** refuse from which gold has been extracted. **3** *Austral.* ridicule. [Middle English diminutive of *mul* 'dust, rubbish', from Middle Dutch]

mulloway /'mʌləweɪ/ *n.* a large Australian marine fish, *Argyrosomos hololepidotus*, used as food. [Aboriginal (S. Australia) *malowe*]

multangular /mʌl'taŋgjʊlə/ *adj.* having many angles. [medieval Latin *multangularis* (as MULTI-, ANGULAR)]

multi- /'mʌlti/ *comb. form* many; more than one. [Latin from *multus* 'much, many']

multi-access /mʌltɪ'aksɛs/ *n.* (often *attrib.*) the simultaneous connection to a computer of a number of terminals.

multiaxial /mʌltɪ'aksɪəl/ *adj.* of or involving several axes.

multicellular /mʌltɪ'sɛljʊlə/ *adj. Biol.* having many cells.

multichannel /mʌltɪ'tʃan(ə)l/ *adj.* employing or possessing many communication or television channels.

multicolour /'mʌltɪkʌlə/ *adj.* (also **multicoloured**) (*US* **-color, -colored**) of many colours.

multicultural /mʌltɪ'kʌltʃ(ə)r(ə)l/ *adj.* of or relating to or constituting several cultural or ethnic groups within a society. □ **multiculturalism** *n.* **multiculturalist** *n. & adj.* **multiculturally** *adv.*

multidimensional /ˌmʌltɪdɪ'mɛnʃ(ə)n(ə)l, -dʌɪ-/ *adj.* of or involving more than three dimensions. □ **multidimensionality** /-'nalɪti/ *n.* **multidimension-ally** *adv.*

multidirectional /ˌmʌltɪdɪ'rɛkʃ(ə)n(ə)l, -dʌɪ-/ *adj.* of, involving, or operating in several directions.

multi-ethnic *adj.* composed of or involving several ethnic groups.

multifaceted /mʌltɪ'fasɪtɪd/ *adj.* having several facets.

multifarious /mʌltɪ'fɛ:rɪəs/ *adj.* **1** (foll. by pl. noun) many and various. **2** having great variety. □ **multifariously** *adv.* **multifariousness** *n.* [Latin *multifarius*]

multifid /'mʌltɪfɪd/ *adj. Bot. & Zool.* divided into many parts. [Latin *multifidus* (as MULTI-, *fid-* stem of *findere* 'cleave')]

multifoil /'mʌltɪfɔɪl/ *n. Archit.* an ornament consisting of more than five foils.

multiform /'mʌltɪfɔ:m/ *adj.* **1** having many forms. **2** of many kinds. □ **multiformity** /-'fɔ:mɪti/ *n.*

multifunctional /mʌltɪ'fʌŋ(k)ʃ(ə)n(ə)l/ *adj.* (also **multifunction** /mʌltɪ-/) having or fulfilling several functions.

multigrade /'mʌltɪgreɪd/ *n.* (usu. *attrib.*) an engine oil etc. meeting the requirements of several standard grades.

multihull /'mʌltɪhʌl/ *adj. & n.* ● *adj.* having more than one hull. ● *n.* a multihull boat.

multilateral /mʌltɪ'lat(ə)r(ə)l/ *adj.* **1 a** (of an agreement, treaty, conference, etc.) in which three or more parties participate. **b** performed by more than one party (*multilateral disarmament*). **2** having many sides. □ **multilateralism** *n.* **multilateralist** *n. & adj.* **multilaterally** *adv.*

multilingual /mʌltɪ'lɪŋgw(ə)l/ *adj.* in or using several languages. □ **multilingualism** *n.* **multilingually** *adv.*

multimedia /'mʌltɪmi:dɪə/ *adj. & n.* ● *attrib.adj.* (of art, education, etc.) using more than one medium of expression, communication, etc. ● *n.* an extension of hypertext allowing the provision of audio and video material cross-referenced to a computer text (also *attrib.*: *multimedia applications*). Also called *hypermedia*.

multimillion /'mʌltɪmɪljən/ *attrib.adj.* costing or involving several million (pounds, dollars, etc.) (*multimillion dollar fraud*).

multimillionaire /ˌmʌltɪmɪljə'nɛ:/ *n.* a person with a fortune of several millions.

multinational /mʌltɪ'naʃ(ə)n(ə)l/ *adj. & n.* ● *adj.* **1** (of a business organization) operating in several countries. **2** relating to or including several nationalities or ethnic groups. ● *n.* a multinational company. □ **multi-nationally** *adv.*

multinomial /mʌltɪ'nəʊmɪəl/ *adj. & n. Math.* = POLYNOMIAL. [MULTI-, on the pattern of *binomial*]

multiparous /mʌl'tɪp(ə)rəs/ *adj.* **1** bringing forth many young at a birth. **2** having borne more than one child.

multipartite /mʌltɪ'pɑ:tʌɪt/ *adj.* divided into many parts.

multi-party /'mʌltɪˌpɑ:ti/ *attrib.adj.* of or involving several esp. political parties.

multiphase /'mʌltɪfeɪz/ *adj. Electr.* = POLYPHASE.

multiple /'mʌltɪp(ə)l/ *adj. & n.* ● *adj.* **1** having several or many parts, elements, or individual components. **2** (foll. by pl. noun) many and various. ● *n.* **1** a number that may be divided by another a certain number of times without a remainder (*56 is a multiple of 7*). **2** a multiple shop or store. □ **multiply** *adv.* [French via Late Latin *multiplus* from Latin (as MULTIPLEX)]

multiple-choice *adj.* (of a question in an examination) accompanied by several possible answers from which the correct one has to be chosen.

multiple fruit *n. Bot.* a fruit formed from carpels derived from several flowers (e.g. pineapple).

multiple personality *n. Psychol.* two or more distinct personalities apparently existing in one individual.

multiple sclerosis see SCLEROSIS 2.

multiple shop *n.* (also **multiple store**) *Brit.* a shop or store with branches in several places.

multiple standard *n.* a standard of value obtained by averaging the prices of a number of products.

multiple star *n.* several stars so close as to seem one, esp. when forming a connected system.

multiplex /'mʌltɪplɛks/ *adj., n., & v.* ● *adj.* **1** manifold; of many elements. **2** involving simultaneous transmission of several messages along a single channel of communication. **3** of or relating to a single-site complex of two or more cinemas. ● *n.* **1** a multiplex system or signal. **2** a multiplex cinema. ● *v.tr.* incorporate into a multiplex signal or system. □ **multiplexer** *n.* (also **multiplexor**). **multiplexing** *n.* [Latin (as MULTI-, *-plex -plicis* '-fold')]

multipliable /'mʌltɪplʌɪəb(ə)l/ *adj.* that can be multiplied.

multiplicable /'mʌltɪplɪkəb(ə)l/ *adj.* = MULTIPLIABLE. [Old French *multiplicable* or medieval Latin *multiplicabilis* from Latin (as MULTIPLY)]

multiplicand /ˌmʌltɪplɪ'kand, 'mʌltɪplɪkand/ *n.* a quantity to be multiplied by a multiplier. [medieval Latin *multiplicandus*, gerundive of Latin *multiplicare* (as MULTIPLY)]

multiplication /ˌmʌltɪplɪ'keɪʃ(ə)n/ *n.* **1** the arithmetical process of multiplying. **2** the act or an instance of multiplying. □ **multiplicative** /-'plɪkətɪv/ *adj.* [Middle English from Old French *multiplication* or Latin *multiplicatio* (as MULTIPLY)]

multiplication sign *n.* the sign (×) to indicate that one quantity is to be multiplied by another, as in $2 \times 3 = 6$.

multiplication table *n.* a list of multiples of a particular number, usu. from 1 to 12.

multiplicity /mʌltɪ'plɪsɪti/ *n.* (*pl.* **-ies**) **1** manifold variety. **2** (foll. by *of*) a great number. [Late Latin *multiplicitas* (as MULTIPLEX)]

multiplier /'mʌltɪplʌɪə/ *n.* **1** a quantity by which a given number is multiplied. **2** *Econ.* a factor by which an increment of income exceeds the resulting increment of saving or investment. **3** *Electr.* an instrument for increasing by repetition the intensity of a current, force, etc.

multiply /'mʌltɪplʌɪ/ *v.* (**-ies**, **-ied**) **1** *tr.* (also *absol.*) obtain from (a number) another that is a specified number of times its value (*multiply 6 by 4 and you get 24*). **2** *intr.* increase in number esp. by procreation. **3** *tr.* produce a large number of (instances etc.). **4** *tr.* **a** breed (animals). **b** propagate (plants). [Middle English via Old French *multiplier* from Latin *multiplicare* (as MULTIPLEX)]

multipolar /mʌltɪ'pəʊlə/ *adj.* having many poles (see POLE[2]).

multiprocessing /mʌltɪ'prəʊsɛsɪŋ/ *n.* *Computing* processing by a number of processors sharing a common memory and common peripherals.

multiprocessor /mʌltɪ'prəʊsɛsə/ *n.* a computer capable of performing multiprocessing.

multiprogramming /mʌltɪ'prəʊgramɪŋ/ *n.* *Computing* the execution of two or more independent programs concurrently.

multi-purpose /mʌltɪ'pə:pəs/ *adj.* having several purposes.

multiracial /mʌltɪ'reɪʃ(ə)l/ *adj.* relating to or made up of many human races. □ **multiracially** *adv.*

multi-role /mʌltɪ'rəʊl/ *adj.* having several roles or functions.

multi-stage /'mʌltɪsteɪdʒ/ *attrib.adj.* (of a rocket etc.) having several stages of operation.

multi-storey /mʌltɪ'stɔ:ri/ *adj.* & *n.* ● *attrib.adj.* (of a building) having several (esp. similarly designed) storeys. ● *n. colloq.* a multi-storey car park.

multitasking /mʌltɪ'tɑ:skɪŋ/ *n.* *Computing* the execution of a number of tasks at the same time. □ **multitask** *v.tr.* & *intr.*

multi-track *adj.*, *n.*, & *v.* ● *attrib.adj.* relating to or made by the mixing of separately recorded soundtracks. ● *n.* a multi-track recording. ● *v.tr.* & *intr.* record using multi-track recording. □ **multi-tracked** *adj.* **multi-tracking** *n.*

multitude /'mʌltɪtju:d/ *n.* **1** (often foll. by *of*) a great number. **2** a large gathering of people; a crowd. **3** (**the multitude**) the common people. **4** the state of being numerous. [Middle English via Old French from Latin *multitudo -dinis*, from *multus* 'many']

multitudinous /mʌltɪ'tju:dɪnəs/ *adj.* **1** very numerous. **2** consisting of many individuals or elements. **3** (of an ocean etc.) vast. □ **multitudinously** *adv.* **multitudinousness** *n.* [Latin (as MULTITUDE)]

multi-user /mʌltɪ'ju:zə/ *attrib.adj.* (of a computer system) having a number of simultaneous users (cf. MULTI-ACCESS).

multivalent /mʌltɪ'veɪl(ə)nt/ *adj.* **1** *Chem.* **a** having a valency of more than two. **b** having a variable valency. **2** having many applications, meanings, or values. □ **multivalency** *n.*

multivalve /'mʌltɪvalv/ *attrib.adj.* (of a shell etc.) having several valves.

multivariate /mʌltɪ'vɛ:rɪət/ *adj.* *Statistics* involving two or more variable quantities.

multiversity /mʌltɪ'və:sɪti/ *n.* (*pl.* **-ies**) a large university with many different departments. [MULTI- + UNIVERSITY]

multivocal /mʌl'tɪvək(ə)l/ *adj.* having many meanings.

multi-way /'mʌltɪweɪ/ *attrib.adj.* having several paths of communication etc.

mum[1] /mʌm/ *n. Brit. colloq.* mother. [abbreviation of MUMMY[1]]

mum[2] /mʌm/ *adj. colloq.* silent (*keep mum*). □ **mum's the word** say nothing. [Middle English: imitative of closed lips]

mum[3] /mʌm/ *v.intr.* (**mummed**, **mumming**) act in a traditional masked mime. [cf. MUM[2] and Middle Low German *mummen*]

mumble /'mʌmb(ə)l/ *v.* & *n.* ● *v.* **1** *intr.* & *tr.* speak or utter indistinctly. **2** *tr.* bite or chew with or as with toothless gums. ● *n.* an indistinct utterance. □ **mumbler** *n.* **mumblingly** *adv.* [Middle English *momele*, as MUM[2]: cf. Low German *mummelen*]

mumbo-jumbo /mʌmbəʊ'dʒʌmbəʊ/ *n.* (*pl.* **-jumbos**) **1** meaningless or ignorant ritual. **2** language or action intended to mystify or confuse. **3** an object of senseless veneration. [*Mumbo Jumbo*, a supposed African idol]

mu-meson *n.* = MUON.

mummer /'mʌmə/ *n.* **1** an actor in a traditional masked mime or folk play. **2** *archaic* or *derog.* an actor in the theatre. [Middle English from Old French *momeur*, from *momer* MUM[3]]

mummery /'mʌm(ə)ri/ *n.* (*pl.* **-ies**) **1** ridiculous (esp. religious) ceremonial. **2** a performance by mummers. [Old French *momerie* (as MUMMER)]

mummify /'mʌmɪfʌɪ/ *v.tr.* (**-ies**, **-ied**) **1** embalm and preserve (a body) in the form of a mummy (see MUMMY[2]). **2** (usu. as **mummified** *adj.*) shrivel or dry up (tissues etc.). □ **mummification** /-fɪ'keɪʃ(ə)n/ *n.*

mummy[1] /'mʌmi/ *n.* (*pl.* **-ies**) *Brit. colloq.* mother. [imitative of a child's pronunciation: cf. MAMMA[1]]

mummy[2] /'mʌmi/ *n.* (*pl.* **-ies**) **1** a body of a human being or animal embalmed for burial, esp. in ancient Egypt. **2** a dried-up body. **3** *Brit.* a pulpy mass (*beat it to a mummy*). **4** a rich brown pigment. [French *momie* via medieval Latin *mumia* and Arabic *mūmiyā* from Persian *mūm* 'wax']

mumps /mʌmps/ *n.pl.* **1** (treated as *sing.*) a contagious and infectious viral disease with swelling of the parotid salivary glands in the face, and a risk of sterility in adult males. **2** *Brit.* a fit of sulks. □ **mumpish** *adj.* (in sense 2). [archaic *mump* 'be sullen']

mumsy /'mʌmzi/ *adj.* & *n. colloq.* ● *adj.* maternal; homely; unfashionable. ● *n.* = MUMMY[1]. [jocular variant of MUMMY[1]]

munch /mʌn(t)ʃ/ *v.tr.* eat steadily with a marked action of the jaws. [Middle English, imitative: cf. CRUNCH]

Munchausen's syndrome /'mʌn(t)ʃaʊz(ə)nz/ *n. Med.* a mental illness in which a person repeatedly feigns severe illness so as to obtain hospital treatment. □ **Munchausen by proxy** (in full **Munchausen's syndrome by proxy**) a mental condition in which a person seeks attention by inducing illness in another person, esp. a child. [Baron *Munchausen*, hero of a book of fantastic tales (1785) by R.E. Raspe]

mundane /ˈmʌndeɪn, mʌnˈdeɪn/ *adj.* **1** dull, routine. **2** of this world; worldly. □ **mundanely** *adv.* **mundaneness** *n.* **mundanity** /-ˈdanɪti/ *n.* (*pl.* **-ies**). [Middle English via Old French *mondain* and Late Latin *mundanus* from Latin *mundus* 'world']

mung /mʌŋ, muːŋ/ *n.* (in full **mung bean**) a leguminous plant of the genus *Vigna*, native to India and yielding a small bean used as food. [Hindi *mūng*]

mungo /ˈmʌŋgəʊ/ *n.* the short fibres recovered from heavily felted material. [19th c.: origin uncertain]

municipal /mjʊˈnɪsɪp(ə)l/ *adj.* of or concerning a municipality or its self-government. □ **municipalize** *v.tr.* (also **-ise**). **municipalization** /-ˈzeɪʃ(ə)n/ *n.* **municipally** *adv.* [Latin *municipalis* (from *municipium* 'free city' via *municeps -cipis* 'citizen with privileges' from *munia* 'civic offices') + *capere* 'take']

municipality /mjʊˌnɪsɪˈpalɪti/ *n.* (*pl.* **-ies**) **1** a town or district having local government. **2** the governing body of this area. [French *municipalité* from *municipal* (as MUNICIPAL)]

munificent /mjʊˈnɪfɪs(ə)nt/ *adj.* (of a giver or a gift) splendidly generous, bountiful. □ **munificence** *n.* **munificently** *adv.* [Latin *munificent-*, variant stem of *munificus*, from *munus* 'gift']

muniment /ˈmjuːnɪm(ə)nt/ *n.* (usu. in *pl.*) **1** a document kept as evidence of rights or privileges etc. **2** an archive. [Middle English via Old French from Latin *munimentum* 'defence', in medieval Latin 'title deed' from *munire munit-* 'fortify']

munition /mjʊˈnɪʃ(ə)n/ *n. & v.* ● *n.* (usu. in *pl.*) military weapons, ammunition, equipment, and stores. ● *v.tr.* supply with munitions. [French from Latin *munitio -onis* 'fortification' (as MUNIMENT)]

munitioner /mjuːˈnɪʃ(ə)nə/ *n.* a person who makes or supplies munitions.

munnion var. of MULLION.

munshi var. of MOONSHEE.

munt /mʊnt/ *n. S.Afr. slang offens.* a black African. [Bantu *umuntu* 'person']

muntjac /ˈmʌntdʒak/ *n.* (also **muntjak**) any small deer of the genus *Muntiacus* native to SE Asia, the male having tusks and small antlers. [local name in western Java]

Muntz metal /mʌnts/ *n.* an alloy (60% copper, 40% zinc) used for sheathing ships etc. [named after G. F. *Muntz*, English manufacturer d. 1857]

muon /ˈmjuːɒn/ *n. Physics* an unstable subatomic particle like an electron, but with a much greater mass. [μ (see MU), as the symbol for it]

murage /ˈmjʊərɪdʒ/ *n. Brit. hist.* a tax levied for building or repairing the walls of a town. [Middle English from Old French (in medieval Latin *muragium*) from Old French *mur*, from Latin *murus* 'wall']

mural /ˈmjʊər(ə)l/ *n. & adj.* ● *n.* a painting executed directly on a wall. ● *adj.* **1** of or like a wall. **2** on a wall. □ **muralist** *n.* [French from Latin *muralis*, from *murus* 'wall']

mural crown *n. Rom. Antiq.* a crown or garland given to the soldier who was first to scale the wall of a besieged town.

murder /ˈməːdə/ *n. & v.* ● *n.* **1** the unlawful premeditated killing of a human being by another (cf. MANSLAUGHTER). **2** *colloq.* an unpleasant, troublesome, or dangerous state of affairs (*it was murder here on Saturday*). ● *v.tr.* **1** kill (a human being) unlawfully, esp. wickedly or inhumanly. **2** *Law* kill (a human being) unlawfully with a premeditated motive. **3** *colloq.* **a** utterly defeat. **b** spoil by a bad performance, mispronunciation, etc. (*murdered the soliloquy in the second act*). □ **cry** (or **scream**) **blue** (*N. Amer.* **bloody**) **murder** *slang* make an extravagant outcry. **get away with murder** *colloq.* do whatever one wishes and escape punishment. **murder will out** murder cannot remain undetected. □ **murderer** *n.* **murderess** *n.* [Old English *morthor* & Old French *murdre*, from Germanic]

murderous /ˈməːd(ə)rəs/ *adj.* **1** (of a person, weapon, action, etc.) capable of, intending, or involving murder or great harm. **2** *colloq.* extremely arduous or unpleasant. □ **murderously** *adv.* **murderousness** *n.*

mure /mjʊə/ *v.tr. archaic* **1** immure. **2** (foll. by *up*) wall up or shut up in an enclosed space. [Middle English from Old French *murer*, from *mur*: see MURAGE]

murex /ˈmjʊərɛks/ *n.* (*pl.* **murices** /-rɪsiːz/ or **murexes**) any gastropod mollusc of the genus *Murex*, yielding a purple dye. [Latin]

muriatic acid /mjʊərɪˈatɪk/ *n.* = HYDROCHLORIC ACID. □ **muriate** /ˈmjʊərɪət, -ɪeɪt/ *n.* [Latin *muriaticus* from *muria* 'brine']

■ **Usage** The term *muriatic acid* is regarded as archaic in technical use.

murine /ˈmjʊəraɪn, -rɪn/ *adj.* of or like a mouse or mice. [Latin *murinus* from *mus muris* 'mouse']

murk /məːk/ *n. & adj.* (also **mirk**) ● *n.* **1** darkness, poor visibility. **2** air obscured by fog etc. ● *adj. archaic* (of night, day, place, etc.) = MURKY. [probably from Scandinavian: cf. Old Norse *myrkr*]

murky /ˈməːki/ *adj.* (also **mirky**) (**-ier**, **-iest**) **1** dark, gloomy. **2** (of darkness, liquid, etc.) thick, dirty. **3** suspiciously obscure (*murky past*). □ **murkily** *adv.* **murkiness** *n.*

murmur /ˈməːmə/ *n. & v.* ● *n.* **1** a subdued continuous sound, as made by waves, a brook, etc. **2** a softly spoken or nearly inarticulate utterance. **3** *Med.* a recurring sound heard in the auscultation of the heart and usu. indicating abnormality. **4** a subdued expression of discontent. ● *v.* **1** *intr.* make a subdued continuous sound. **2** *tr.* utter (words) in a low voice. **3** *intr.* (usu. foll. by *at*, *against*) complain in low tones, grumble. □ **murmurer** *n.* **murmuringly** *adv.* **murmurous** *adj.* [Middle English via Old French *murmurer* from Latin *murmurare*: related to Greek *mormurō* (of water) 'roar', Sanskrit *marmaras* 'noisy']

murphy /ˈməːfi/ *n.* (*pl.* **-ies**) *slang* a potato. [Irish surname]

Murphy's Law /ˈməːfɪz/ *n. joc.* the maxim that anything that can go wrong will go wrong.

murrain /ˈmʌrɪn/ *n.* **1** an infectious disease of cattle, carried by parasites. **2** *archaic* a plague, esp. the potato blight during the Irish famine in the mid-19th c. [Middle English via Anglo-French *moryn*, Old French *morine*, from *morir*, from Latin *mori* 'die']

murre /məː/ *n.* esp. *N. Amer.* an auk or guillemot. [16th c.: origin unknown]

murrelet /ˈməːlɪt/ *n.* any of several small auks of the N. Pacific, of the genera *Brachyramphus* and *Synthliboramphus*.

murrey /ˈmʌri/ *n. & adj. archaic* ● *n.* the colour of a mulberry; a deep red or purple. ● *adj.* of this colour. [Middle English via Old French *moré* from medieval Latin *moratus*, from *morum* 'mulberry']

murther /ˈməːðə/ *archaic* var. of MURDER.

Mus.B. *abbr.* (also **Mus. Bac.**) Bachelor of Music. [Latin *Musicae Baccalaureus*]

muscadel var. of MUSCATEL.

Muscadet /ˈmʌskədeɪ, ˈmʊsk-/ *n.* **1** a white wine from the Loire region of France. **2** a variety of grape from which the wine is made. [French from *muscade* 'nutmeg' from *musc* MUSK + -ET[1]]

muscadine /ˈmʌskədɪn, -aɪn/ *n.* a variety of grape with a musk flavour, used chiefly in wine-making. [probably alteration of MUSCATEL]

muscarine /ˈmʌskəriːn, -ɪn/ *n.* a poisonous alkaloid from the fungus *Amanita muscaria*. [Latin *muscarius* from *musca* 'fly']

muscat /ˈmʌskat/ *n.* **1** a sweet fortified white wine made from muscadines. **2** a muscadine. [French from Provençal *muscat muscade* (*adj.*), from *musc* MUSK]

muscatel /mʌskəˈtɛl/ *n.* (also **muscadel** /-ˈdɛl/) **1** = MUSCAT. **2** a raisin from a muscadine grape. [Middle

English via Old French from Provençal diminutive of *muscat*: see MUSCAT]

muscle /ˈmʌs(ə)l/ *n.* & *v.* ● *n.* **1** a fibrous tissue with the ability to contract, producing movement in or maintaining the position of an animal body. **2** the part of an animal body that is composed of muscles. **3** physical power or strength. ● *v.intr.* (usu. foll. by *in*) *colloq.* force oneself on others; intrude by forceful means. □ **not move a muscle** be completely motionless. □ **muscled** *adj.* (usu. in *comb.*). **muscleless** *adj.* **muscly** *adj.* [French from Latin *musculus*, diminutive of *mus* 'mouse', from the fancied mouselike form of some muscles]

muscle-bound *adj.* with muscles stiff and inelastic through excessive exercise or training.

muscle-man *n.* a man with highly developed muscles, esp. one employed as an intimidator.

muscology /mʌˈskɒlədʒi/ *n.* the study of mosses. □ **muscologist** *n.* [modern Latin *muscologia* from Latin *muscus* 'moss']

muscovado /mʌskəˈvɑːdəʊ/ *n.* (*pl.* **-os**) an unrefined sugar made from the juice of sugar cane by evaporation and draining off the molasses. [Spanish *mascabado* (*azucar*) '(sugar) of the lowest quality']

Muscovite /ˈmʌskəvʌɪt/ *n.* & *adj.* ● *n.* **1** a native or citizen of Moscow. **2** *archaic* a Russian. ● *adj.* **1** of or relating to Moscow. **2** *archaic* of or relating to Russia. [modern Latin *Muscovita* from *Muscovia*, = MUSCOVY]

muscovite /ˈmʌskəvʌɪt/ *n.* a silver-grey form of mica with a sheetlike crystalline structure that is used in the manufacture of electrical equipment etc. [obsolete *Muscovy glass* (in the same sense) + -ITE[1]]

Muscovy /ˈmʌskəvi/ *n. archaic* Russia. [obsolete French *Muscovie* via modern Latin *Moscovia* from Russian *Moskva* 'Moscow']

Muscovy duck *n.* a tropical American duck, *Cairina moschata*, having a small crest and red markings on its head.

muscular /ˈmʌskjʊlə/ *adj.* **1** of or affecting the muscles. **2** having well-developed muscles. **3** robust. □ **muscularity** /-ˈlarɪti/ *n.* **muscularly** *adv.* [earlier *musculous* (as MUSCLE)]

muscular Christianity *n.* a Christian life of cheerful physical activity as described in the writings of Charles Kingsley d. 1975.

muscular dystrophy *n.* a hereditary progressive weakening and wasting of the muscles.

muscular rheumatism *n.* = MYALGIA.

muscular stomach *n.* any organ that grinds or squeezes to aid digestion, such as a gizzard.

musculature /ˈmʌskjʊlətʃə/ *n.* the muscular system of a body or organ. [French from Latin (as MUSCLE)]

musculoskeletal /ˌmʌskjʊləʊˈskɛlɪt(ə)l/ *adj.* of or relating to the musculature and skeleton together.

Mus.D. *abbr.* (also **Mus. Doc.**) Doctor of Music. [Latin *Musicae Doctor*]

muse[1] /mjuːz/ *n.* **1 a** (**Muse**) (in Greek and Roman mythology) each of nine goddesses, the daughters of Zeus and Mnemosyne, who inspire poetry, music, drama, etc. **b** a source of inspiration for creativity. **2** (usu. prec. by *the*) **a** a poet's inspiring goddess. **b** a poet's genius. [Middle English via Old French *muse* or Latin *musa* from Greek *mousa*]

muse[2] /mjuːz/ *v.* & *n.* ● *v. literary* **1** *intr.* **a** (usu. foll. by *on, upon*) ponder, reflect. **b** (usu. foll. by *on*) gaze meditatively (on a scene etc.). **2** *tr.* say meditatively. ● *n. archaic* a fit of abstraction. □ **musingly** *adv.* [Middle English via Old French *muser* 'to waste time' from Romanic, perhaps from medieval Latin *musum* 'muzzle']

museology /mjuːzɪˈɒlədʒi/ *n.* the science or practice of organizing and managing museums.

musette /mjuːˈzɛt/ *n.* **1 a** a kind of small bagpipe with bellows, common in the French court in the 17th–18th c. **b** a tune imitating the sound of this. **2** a small oboe-like double-reed instrument in 19th-c. France. **3** a popular dance in the courts of Louis XIV and XV. **4** *US* a small knapsack. [Middle English from Old French, diminutive of *muse* 'bagpipe']

museum /mjuːˈzɪəm/ *n.* a building used for storing and exhibiting objects of historical, scientific, or cultural interest. [Latin from Greek *mouseion* 'seat of the Muses': see MUSE[1]]

museum piece *n.* **1** a specimen of art etc. fit for a museum. **2** *Brit. derog.* an old-fashioned or quaint person or object.

mush[1] /mʌʃ/ *n.* **1** soft pulp. **2** feeble sentimentality. **3** *N. Amer.* maize porridge. [apparently a variant of MASH]

mush[2] /mʌʃ/ *v.* & *n. N. Amer.* ● *v.intr.* **1** (in *imper.*) used as a command to dogs pulling a sledge to urge them forward. **2** go on a journey across snow with a dog sled. ● *n.* a journey across snow with a dog sled. [probably a corruption from French *marchons*, imperative of *marcher* 'advance']

mushroom /ˈmʌʃruːm, -rʊm/ *n.*, *v.*, & *adj.* ● *n.* **1** the usu. edible spore-producing body of various fungi, esp. *Agaricus campestris*, with a stem and domed cap, proverbial for its rapid growth. **2** the pale pinkish-brown colour of this. **3** any item resembling a mushroom in shape (*darning mushroom*). **4** (usu. *attrib.*) something that appears or develops suddenly or is ephemeral; an upstart. ● *v.intr.* **1** appear or develop rapidly. **2** expand and flatten like a mushroom cap. **3** gather mushrooms. ● *adj.* mushroom-coloured; of a pale pinkish-brown colour. □ **mushroomy** *adj.* [Middle English via Old French *mousseron* from Late Latin *mussirio -onis*]

mushroom cloud *n.* a cloud suggesting the shape of a mushroom, esp. from a nuclear explosion.

mushroom growth *n.* **1** a sudden development or expansion. **2** anything undergoing this.

mushy /ˈmʌʃi/ *adj.* (**mushier**, **mushiest**) **1** like mush, soft and pulpy. **2** feebly sentimental. □ **mushily** *adv.* **mushiness** *n.*

music /ˈmjuːzɪk/ *n.* **1** the art of combining vocal or instrumental sounds (or both) to produce beauty of form, harmony, and expression of emotion. **2** the sounds so produced. **3** musical compositions. **4** the written or printed score of a musical composition. **5** certain pleasant sounds, e.g. birdsong, the sound of a stream, etc. □ **music of the spheres** see SPHERE. **music to one's ears** something very pleasant to hear. [Middle English via Old French *musique* and Latin *musica* from Greek *mousikē* (*tekhnē*) '(art) of the Muses', from *mousa* MUSE[1]]

musical /ˈmjuːzɪk(ə)l/ *adj.* & *n.* ● *adj.* **1** of or relating to music. **2** (of sounds, a voice, etc.) melodious, harmonious. **3** fond of or skilled in music (*the musical one of the family*). **4** set to or accompanied by music. ● *n.* a musical film or comedy. □ **musicality** /-ˈkalɪti/ *n.* **musicalize** *v.tr.* (also **-ise**). **musically** *adv.* **musicalness** *n.* [Middle English via Old French and medieval Latin *musicalis* from Latin *musica*: see MUSIC]

musical box *n. Brit.* a mechanical musical instrument in a box, typically incorporating a toothed cylinder which plucks a row of tuned metal strips as it revolves.

musical bumps *n.pl. Brit.* a game similar to musical chairs, with players sitting on the floor and the one left standing eliminated.

musical chairs *n.pl.* **1** a party game in which the players compete in successive rounds for a decreasing number of chairs. **2** a series of changes or political manoeuvring etc. after the manner of the game.

musical comedy *n.* a light dramatic entertainment of songs, dialogue, and dancing, connected by a slender plot.

musical director *n.* the person responsible for the musical aspects of a performance or production, often the conductor or leader of a music group.

musicale /mjuːzɪˈkɑːl/ *n. US* a musical party. [French fem. adj. (as MUSICAL)]

musical film *n.* a film in which music is an important feature.

musical glasses *n.pl.* an instrument in which notes are produced by rubbing graduated glass bowls or tubes.

musical instrument see INSTRUMENT *n.* 2.

musical saw *n.* a bent saw played with a violin bow.

musical sound see SOUND[1] *n.* 6.

music box *n. N. Amer.* = MUSICAL BOX.

music centre *n. Brit.* equipment combining radio, record player, tape recorder, etc.

music drama *n.* Wagnerian-type opera without formal arias etc. and governed by dramatic considerations.

music hall *n.* (usu. hyphenated when *attrib.*) *Brit.* **1** variety entertainment, popular *c.*1850–1914, consisting of singing, dancing, and novelty acts. **2** a theatre where this took place.

musician /mju:'zɪʃ(ə)n/ *n.* a person who plays a musical instrument, esp. professionally, or is otherwise musically gifted. ▫ **musicianly** *adj.* **musicianship** *n.* [Middle English from Old French *musicien*, from *musique* (as MUSIC, -ICIAN)]

musicology /mju:zɪ'kɒlədʒi/ *n.* the study of music other than that directed to proficiency in performance or composition. ▫ **musicologist** *n.* **musicological** /-kə'lɒdʒɪk(ə)l/ *adj.* [French *musicologie*, or MUSIC + -LOGY]

music paper *n.* = MANUSCRIPT PAPER.

music stand *n.* a rest or frame on which sheet music or a score is supported.

music stool *n.* a stool for a pianist, usu. with adjustable height.

music theatre *n.* in late 20th-c. music, the combination of elements from music and drama in new forms distinct from traditional opera, esp. as designed for small groups of performers.

musique concrète /mju:ˌzi:k kɒn'krɛt, French myzik kɔ̃krɛt/ *n.* music constructed by mixing recorded sounds. [French]

musk /mʌsk/ *n.* **1** a strong-smelling reddish-brown substance produced by a gland in the male musk deer and used as an ingredient in perfumes. **2** the plant, *Mimulus moschatus*, with pale green ovate leaves and yellow flowers (originally with a smell of musk which is no longer perceptible in modern varieties). ▫ **musky** *adj.* (**muskier**, **muskiest**). **muskiness** *n.* [Middle English via Late Latin *muscus* from Persian *mušk*, perhaps from Sanskrit *muṣka* 'scrotum' (from the shape of the musk deer's gland)]

musk deer *n.* any small Asian deer of the genus *Moschus*, having no antlers and in the male having long protruding canine teeth.

musk duck *n.* the Australian duck *Biziura lobata*, having a musky smell.

muskeg /'mʌskɛg/ *n.* a level swamp or bog in Canada. [Cree]

muskellunge /'mʌskəlʌn(d)ʒ/ *n.* a large N. American pike, *Esox masquinongy*, esp. of the Great Lakes. [Algonquian]

musket /'mʌskɪt/ *n. hist.* an infantryman's (esp. smooth-bored) light gun, often supported on the shoulder. [French *mousquet* from Italian *moschetto* 'crossbow bolt', from *mosca* 'a fly']

musketeer /mʌskɪ'tɪə/ *n. hist.* a soldier armed with a musket.

musketry /'mʌskɪtri/ *n.* **1** muskets, or soldiers armed with muskets, referred to collectively. **2** the knowledge of handling muskets.

musket shot *n. hist.* **1** a shot fired from a musket. **2** the range of this shot.

musk melon *n.* the common yellow or green melon, *Cucumis melo*, usu. with a raised network of markings on the skin. [from the aromatic flesh of some varieties]

musk ox *n.* a large goat-antelope, *Ovibos moschatus*, native to N. America, with a thick shaggy coat and small curved horns. [from the strong smell emitted by the male during rutting]

muskrat /'mʌskrat/ *n.* **1** a large aquatic rodent, *Ondatra zibethicus*, native to N. America, having a musky smell. **2** the fur of this. Also called MUSQUASH.

musk-rose *n.* a rambling rose, *Rosa moschata*, with large white flowers smelling of musk.

musk thistle *n.* a nodding thistle, *Carduus nutans*, whose flowers have a musky fragrance.

musk tree *n.* an Australian tree with a musky smell, esp. *Olearia argyrophylla*.

muskwood /'mʌskwʊd/ *n.* wood with a musky smell, esp. that of a musk tree or of certain W. Indian trees.

Muslim /'mʊzlɪm, 'mʌz-, -s-/ *n. & adj.* (also **Moslem** /'mɒzləm/) ● *n.* a follower of the Islamic religion. ● *adj.* of or relating to the Muslims or their religion. [Arabic *muslim*, part. of *aslama*: see ISLAM]

muslin /'mʌzlɪn/ *n.* **1** a fine delicately woven cotton fabric. **2** *US* a cotton cloth in plain weave. ▫ **muslined** *adj.* [French *mousseline* from Italian *mussolina*, from *Mussolo* Mosul in Iraq, where it was made]

musmon /'mʌsmɒn, 'mʌzmən/ *n. Zool.* = MOUFLON. [Latin *musimo* from Greek *mousmōn*]

muso /'mju:zəʊ/ *n.* (*pl.* **-os**) *Brit. slang* a musician, esp. a professional. [abbreviation]

musquash /'mʌskwɒʃ/ *n.* = MUSKRAT. [Algonquian]

muss /mʌs/ *v. & n. N. Amer. colloq.* ● *v.tr.* (often foll. by *up*) disarrange; throw into disorder. ● *n.* a state of confusion; untidiness, mess. ▫ **mussy** *adj.* [apparently a variant of MESS]

mussel /'mʌs(ə)l/ *n.* **1** any bivalve mollusc of the genus *Mytilus*, living in sea water and often used for food. **2** any similar freshwater mollusc of the genus *Margaritifer* or *Anodonta*, forming pearls. [Old English *mus(c)le*, superseded by forms from Middle Low German *mussel*, ultimately related to Latin *musculus* (as MUSCLE)]

Mussulman /'mʌs(ə)lmən/ *n. & adj. archaic* ● *n.* (*pl.* **-mans** or **-men**) a Muslim. ● *adj.* of or concerning Muslims. [Persian *musulmān* (originally *adj.*) from *muslim* (as MUSLIM)]

must[1] /mʌst/ *v. & n.* ● *v.aux.* (*3rd sing. present* **must**; *past* **had to** or in indirect speech **must**) (foll. by infin., or *absol.*) **1 a** be obliged to (*you must go to school*; *must we leave now?*; *said he must go*; *I must away*). **b** in ironic questions (*must you slam the door?*). **2** be certain to (*we must win in the end*; *you must be her sister*; *he must be mad*; *they must have left by now*; *seemed as if the roof must blow off*). **3** ought to (*we must see what can be done*; *it must be said that*). **4** expressing insistence (*I must ask you to leave*). **5** (foll. by *not* + infin.) **a** not be permitted to, be forbidden to (*you must not smoke*). **b** ought not; need not (*you mustn't think he's angry*; *you must not worry*). **c** expressing insistence that something should not be done (*they must not be told*). **6** (as past or historic present) expressing the perversity of destiny (*what must I do but break my leg*). ● *n. colloq.* a thing that cannot or should not be overlooked or missed (*if you go to London St Paul's is a must*). ▫ **I must say** often *iron.* I cannot refrain from saying (*I must say he made a good attempt*; *a fine way to behave, I must say*). **must needs** see NEEDS. [Old English *mōste*, past of *mōt* 'may']

■ **Usage** In sense 1a, the negative (i.e. lack of obligation) is expressed by *not have to* or *need not*; *must not* denotes positive forbidding, as in *you must not smoke*.

must[2] /mʌst/ *n.* grape juice before fermentation is complete. [Old English from Latin *mustum*, neut. of *mustus* 'new']

must[3] /mʌst/ *n.* mustiness, mould. [back-formation from MUSTY]

must[4] /mʌst/ *adj. & n.* (also **musth**) ● *adj.* (of a male elephant or camel) in a state of frenzy associated with the breeding season. ● *n.* this state. [Urdu from Persian *mast* 'intoxicated']

mustache *US* var. of MOUSTACHE.

mustachio /mə'stɑːʃɪəʊ, -ʃəʊ/ *n.* (*pl.* **-os**) (often in *pl.*) *archaic* a moustache. □ **mustachioed** *adj.* [Spanish *mostacho* & Italian *mostaccio* (as MOUSTACHE)]

mustang /'mʌstaŋ/ *n.* a small wild horse native to Mexico and California. [Spanish *mestengo* (from *mesta* 'company of graziers') & Spanish *mostrenco*, both meaning 'wild or masterless cattle']

mustang grape *n.* a grape from the wild vine *Vitis candicans*, of the southern US, used for making wine.

mustard /'mʌstəd/ *n.* & *adj.* ● *n.* **1 a** any of various plants of the genus *Brassica* with slender pods and yellow flowers, esp. *B. nigra*. **b** any of various plants of the genus *Sinapis*, esp. *S. alba*, eaten at the seedling stage, often with cress. **2** the seeds of these which are crushed, made into a paste, and used as a spicy condiment. **3** the brownish-yellow colour of this condiment. **4** *slang* a thing which adds piquancy or zest. ● *adj.* of a brownish-yellow colour. [Middle English from Old French *mo(u)starde*: originally the condiment as prepared with MUST[2]]

mustard gas *n.* a colourless oily liquid, whose vapour is a powerful irritant and vesicant.

mustard plaster *n.* a poultice made with mustard.

mustard seed *n.* **1** the seed of the mustard plant. **2** a small thing capable of great development (Matt. 13:31).

mustelid /'mʌstɪlɪd, mʌ'stɛlɪd/ *n.* & *adj.* ● *n.* a mammal of the family Mustelidae, including weasels, stoats, badgers, skunks, martens, etc. ● *adj.* of or relating to this family. [modern Latin *Mustelidae* from Latin *mustela* 'weasel']

muster /'mʌstə/ *v.* & *n.* ● *v.* **1** *tr.* collect (originally soldiers) for inspection, to check numbers, etc. **2** *tr.* & *intr.* collect, gather together. **3** *tr.* (often foll. by *up*) summon up (courage, strength, etc.). **4** *tr. Austral.* round up (livestock). ● *n.* **1** the assembly of persons for inspection. **2** an assembly, a collection. **3** *Austral.* a rounding up of livestock. **4** *Austral. slang* the number of people attending (a meeting etc.) (*had a good muster*). □ **muster in** *US* enrol (recruits). **muster out** *US* discharge (soldiers etc.). **pass muster** bear inspection; come up to a required standard. □ **musterer** *n.* (in sense 3 of *n.* & 4 of *v.*). [Middle English from Old French *mo(u)stre*, ultimately from Latin *monstrare* 'show']

muster-book *n.* a book for registering military personnel.

muster-roll *n.* an official list of officers and men in a regiment or ship's company.

musth var. of MUST[4].

mustn't /'mʌs(ə)nt/ *contr.* must not.

musty /'mʌsti/ *adj.* (**mustier**, **mustiest**) **1** mouldy. **2** of a mouldy or stale smell or taste. **3** stale, antiquated (*musty old books*). □ **mustily** *adv.* **mustiness** *n.* [perhaps alteration of *moisty* (MOIST), by association with MUST[2]]

mutable /'mjuːtəb(ə)l/ *adj. literary* **1** liable to change. **2** fickle. □ **mutability** /-'bɪlɪti/ *n.* [Latin *mutabilis* from *mutare* 'change']

mutagen /'mjuːtədʒ(ə)n/ *n.* an agent promoting mutation, e.g. radiation. □ **mutagenic** /-'dʒɛnɪk/ *adj.* **mutagenesis** /-'dʒɛnɪsɪs/ *n.* [MUTATION + -GEN]

mutant /'mjuːt(ə)nt/ *adj.* & *n.* ● *adj.* resulting from mutation. ● *n.* a mutant form. [Latin *mutant-*, part. stem of *mutare* 'change']

mutate /mjuː'teɪt/ *v.intr.* & *tr.* undergo or cause to undergo mutation. [back-formation from MUTATION]

mutation /mjuː'teɪʃ(ə)n/ *n.* **1** the process or an instance of change or alteration. **2** a genetic change which, when transmitted to offspring, gives rise to heritable variations. **3** a mutant. **4 a** an umlaut. **b** (in a Celtic language) a change of a consonant etc. determined by a preceding word. □ **mutational** *adj.* **mutationally** *adv.* [Middle English from Latin *mutatio*, from *mutare* 'change']

mutatis mutandis /muː,tɑːtɪs muː'tandɪs, mjuː-, -iːs/ *adv.* (in comparing cases) making the necessary alterations. [Latin]

mutch /mʌtʃ/ *n. dial.* a woman's or child's linen cap. [Middle English via Middle Dutch *mutse*, Middle High German *mütze* from medieval Latin *almucia* AMICE[2]]

mute /mjuːt/ *adj.*, *n.*, & *v.* ● *adj.* **1** silent, refraining from or temporarily bereft of speech. **2** not emitting articulate sound. **3** (of a person or animal) dumb. **4** not expressed in speech (*mute protest*). **5 a** (of a letter) not pronounced. **b** (of a consonant) plosive. **6** (of hounds) not giving tongue. ● *n.* **1** a dumb person (*a deaf mute*). **2** *Mus.* **a** a clamp for damping the resonance of the strings of a violin etc. **b** a pad or cone for damping the sound of a wind instrument. **3** an unsounded consonant. **4** an actor whose part is in a dumbshow. **5** a dumb servant in oriental countries. **6** a hired mourner. ● *v.tr.* **1** deaden, muffle, or soften the sound of (a thing, esp. a musical instrument). **2 a** tone down, make less intense. **b** (as **muted** *adj.*) (of colours etc.) subdued (*a muted green*). □ **mutely** *adv.* **muteness** *n.* [Middle English from Old French *muet*, diminutive of *mu*, from Latin *mutus*, assimilated to Latin]

■ **Usage** See Usage Note at MOOT.

mute button *n.* a device on a telephone etc. to temporarily prevent the caller from hearing what is being said at the receiver's end.

mute swan *n.* the commonest Eurasian swan, *Cygnus olor*, having white plumage and an orange-red bill with a swollen black base.

mutilate /'mjuːtɪleɪt/ *v.tr.* **1 a** deprive (a person or animal) of a limb or organ. **b** destroy the use of (a limb or organ). **2** render (a book etc.) imperfect by excision or some act of destruction. □ **mutilation** /-'leɪʃ(ə)n/ *n.* **mutilator** *n.* [Latin *mutilare* from *mutilus* 'maimed']

mutineer /mjuːtɪ'nɪə/ *n.* a person who mutinies. [French *mutinier*, via *mutin* 'rebellious' from *muete* 'movement', ultimately from Latin *movēre* 'move']

mutinous /'mjuːtɪnəs/ *adj.* rebellious; tending to mutiny. □ **mutinously** *adv.* [obsolete *mutine* 'rebellion' from French *mutin*: see MUTINEER]

mutiny /'mjuːtɪni/ *n.* & *v.* ● *n.* (*pl.* **-ies**) an open revolt against constituted authority, esp. by soldiers or sailors against their officers. ● *v.intr.* (**-ies**, **-ied**) (often foll. by *against*) revolt; engage in mutiny. [obsolete *mutine* (as MUTINOUS)]

mutism /'mjuːtɪz(ə)m/ *n.* muteness; silence; dumbness. [French *mutisme* from Latin (as MUTE)]

muton /'mjuːtɒn/ *n. Biol.* the smallest element of genetic material capable of giving rise to a mutant individual.

mutt /mʌt/ *n.* **1** *slang* an ignorant, stupid, or blundering person. **2 a** *Brit. derog.* or *joc.* a dog. **b** *US* a mongrel. [abbreviation of *mutton-head*]

mutter /'mʌtə/ *v.* & *n.* ● *v.* **1** *intr.* speak low in a barely audible manner. **2** *intr.* (often foll. by *against*, *at*) murmur or grumble about. **3** *tr.* utter (words etc.) in a low tone. **4** *tr.* say in secret. ● *n.* **1** muttered words or sounds. **2** muttering. □ **mutterer** *n.* **mutteringly** *adv.* [Middle English, related to MUTE]

mutton /'mʌt(ə)n/ *n.* **1** the flesh of sheep used for food. **2** *joc.* a sheep. □ **mutton dressed as lamb** *Brit. colloq. derog.* a usu. middle-aged or elderly woman dressed or made up to appear younger. □ **muttony** *adj.* [Middle English via Old French *moton* from medieval Latin *multo -onis*, probably from Gaulish]

mutton-bird *n. Austral.* **1** any bird of the genus *Puffinus*, esp. the short-tailed shearwater, *P. tenuirostris*. **2** any of various petrels. [from the flavour of the cooked flesh of some species, said to resemble mutton]

mutton chop *n.* **1** a piece of mutton, usu. the rib and half vertebra to which it is attached. **2** (in full **mutton chop whisker**) a side whisker shaped like this.

mutton-head *n. colloq.* a dull, stupid person. □ **mutton-headed** *adj.*

mutual /'mjuːtʃʊəl, -tjʊəl/ *adj.* **1** (of feelings, actions, etc.) experienced or done by each of two or more parties with reference to the other or others (*mutual affection*). **2** *disp.* common to two or more persons (*a* *mutual friend*; *a mutual interest*). **3** standing in (a specified) relation to each other (*mutual well-wishers*; *mutual beneficiaries*). □ **mutuality** /-ˈalɪti/ *n.* **mutually** *adv.* [Middle English via Old French *mutuel* from Latin *mutuus* 'mutual, borrowed', related to *mutare* 'change']

■ **Usage** The use of *mutual* in sense 2, although often found, is considered incorrect by some people, for whom *common* is preferable.

mutual fund *n. N. Amer.* a unit trust.

mutual inductance *n.* the property of an electric circuit that causes an electromotive force to be generated in it by change in the current flowing through a magnetically linked circuit.

mutual induction *n.* the production of an electromotive force between adjacent circuits that are magnetically linked.

mutual insurance *n.* insurance in which some or all of the profits are divided among the policyholders.

mutualism /ˈmjuːtʃʊəlɪz(ə)m, -tjʊə-/ *n.* **1** the doctrine that mutual dependence is necessary to social well-being. **2** mutually beneficial symbiosis. □ **mutualist** *n. & adj.* **mutualistic** /-ˈlɪstɪk/ *adj.* **mutualistically** /-ˈlɪstɪk(ə)li/ *adv.*

mutuel /ˈmjuːtʃʊəl, -tjʊəl/ *n.* esp. *US* a totalizator; a pari-mutuel. [abbreviation of PARI-MUTUEL]

mutule /ˈmjuːtjuːl/ *n. Archit.* a block derived from the ends of wooden beams projecting under a Doric cornice. [French from Latin *mutulus*]

muu-muu /ˈmuːmuː/ *n.* a woman's loose brightly coloured dress. [Hawaiian]

muzak /ˈmjuːzak/ *n.* **1** *propr.* a system of music transmission for playing in public places. **2** recorded light background music. [alteration of MUSIC]

muzhik /muːˈʒɪk, ˈmuːʒɪk/ *n.* (also **moujik**) *hist.* a Russian peasant. [Russian *muzhik*]

muzzle /ˈmʌz(ə)l/ *n. & v.* ● *n.* **1** the projecting part of an animal's face, including the nose and mouth. **2** a guard, usu. made of straps or wire, fitted over an animal's nose and mouth to stop it biting or feeding. **3** the open end of a firearm. ● *v.tr.* **1** put a muzzle on (an animal etc.). **2** impose silence upon. **3** *Naut.* take in (a sail). [Middle English from Old French *musel*, ultimately from medieval Latin *musum*: cf. MUSE[2]]

muzzle-loader *n.* a gun that is loaded through the muzzle.

muzzle velocity *n.* the velocity with which a projectile leaves the muzzle of a gun.

muzzy /ˈmʌzi/ *adj.* (**muzzier**, **muzziest**) **1 a** mentally hazy; dull, spiritless. **b** esp. *Brit.* confused from drinking alcohol. **2** blurred, indistinct. □ **muzzily** *adv.* **muzziness** *n.* [18th c.: origin unknown]

MV *abbr.* **1** motor vessel. **2** muzzle velocity. **3** megavolt(s).

MVO *abbr.* (in the UK) Member of the Royal Victorian Order.

MVP *abbr. US Sport* most valuable player.

MW *abbr.* **1** megawatt(s). **2** medium wave.

mW *abbr.* milliwatt(s).

Mx. *abbr.* **1** maxwell(s). **2** Middlesex (a former county in England).

MY *abbr.* motor yacht.

my /mʌɪ/ *poss.det.* **1** of or belonging to me (*my house*; *my own business*). **2** as a form of address in affectionate, sympathetic, jocular, or patronizing contexts (*my dear boy*). **3** in various expressions of surprise (*my God!*; *oh my!*). **4** *colloq.* indicating the speaker's husband, wife, child, etc. (*my Johnny's ill again*). □ **my Lady** (or **Lord**) the form of address to certain titled persons. [Middle English *mī*, reduced from *mīn* MINE[1]]

my- *comb. form* var. of MYO-.

myalgia /mʌɪˈaldʒə/ *n.* a pain in a muscle or group of muscles. □ **myalgic** *adj.* [modern Latin from Greek *mus* 'muscle']

myalgic encephalomyelitis see ME 2.

myalism /ˈmʌɪəlɪz(ə)m/ *n.* a kind of sorcery akin to obeah, practised esp. in the W. Indies. [*myal*, probably of West African origin]

myall /ˈmʌɪəl/ *n.* **1 a** any tree of the genus *Acacia*, esp. *A. pendula*, native to Australia. **b** the hard scented wood of this, used for fences and tobacco pipes. **2** an Australian Aboriginal living in a traditional way. [Dharuk *mayal*, *miyal* 'stranger, person of another tribe'; origin of sense 1 uncertain]

myasthenia /mʌɪəsˈθiːnɪə/ *n.* a condition causing abnormal weakness of certain muscles, esp. (in full **myasthenia gravis** /ˈgrɑːvɪs, ˈgravɪs/) a rare chronic autoimmune disease marked by muscular weakness without atrophy. [modern Latin from Greek *mus* 'muscle': cf. ASTHENIA]

mycelium /mʌɪˈsiːlɪəm/ *n.* (*pl.* **mycelia** /-lɪə/) the vegetative part of a fungus, consisting of microscopic threadlike hyphae. □ **mycelial** *adj.* [modern Latin from Greek *mukēs* 'fungus', on the pattern of EPITHELIUM]

Mycenaean /mʌɪsɪˈniːən/ *adj. & n.* ● *adj. Archaeol.* of or relating to the late Bronze Age civilization in Greece (*c.*1580–1100 BC), depicted in the Homeric poems and represented by finds at Mycenae and elsewhere. ● *n.* an inhabitant of Mycenae or the Mycenaean world. [Latin *Mycenaeus*]

-mycin /ˈmʌɪsɪn/ *comb. form* used to form the names of antibiotic compounds derived from fungi. [Greek *mukēs* 'fungus' + -IN]

myco- /ˈmʌɪkəʊ/ *comb. form* fungus. [Greek *mukēs* 'fungus, mushroom']

mycology /mʌɪˈkɒlədʒi/ *n.* **1** the study of fungi. **2** the fungi of a particular region. □ **mycological** /-kəˈlɒdʒɪk(ə)l/ *adj.* **mycologically** /-kəˈlɒdʒɪk(ə)li/ *adv.* **mycologist** *n.* [MYCO- + -LOGY]

mycoplasma /mʌɪkə(ʊ)ˈplazmə/ *n.* (*pl* **mycoplasmas**, **mycoplasmata** /-mətə/) any of a group of mainly parasitic micro-organisms smaller than bacteria and without a cell wall. [MYCO- + PLASMA]

mycoprotein /ˈmʌɪkə(ʊ)prəʊtiːn/ *n.* protein derived from fungi, esp. as produced for human consumption.

mycorrhiza /mʌɪkə(ʊ)ˈrʌɪzə/ *n.* (*pl.* **mycorrhizae** /-ziː/) a symbiotic association of a fungus and the roots of a plant. □ **mycorrhizal** *adj.* [modern Latin from MYCO- + *rhiza* 'root']

mycosis /mʌɪˈkəʊsɪs/ *n. Med.* any disease caused by a fungus, e.g. ringworm. □ **mycotic** /-ˈkɒtɪk/ *adj.* [MYCO- + -OSIS]

mycotoxin /mʌɪkə(ʊ)ˈtɒksɪn/ *n.* any toxic substance produced by a fungus.

mycotrophy /mʌɪˈkɒtrəfi/ *n.* the condition of a plant which has mycorrhizae and is perhaps helped to assimilate nutrients as a result. [MYCO- + Greek *trophē* 'nourishment']

mydriasis /mɪdrɪˈeɪsɪs, mɪˈdrʌɪəsɪs/ *n.* excessive dilation of the pupil of the eye. [Latin from Greek *mudriasis*]

myelin /ˈmʌɪəlɪn/ *n.* a white fatty substance which forms an insulating sheath around certain nerve fibres. □ **myelination** /-ˈneɪʃ(ə)n/ *n.* [Greek *muelos* 'marrow' + -IN]

myelitis /mʌɪəˈlʌɪtɪs/ *n.* inflammation of the spinal cord. [modern Latin, from Greek *muelos* 'marrow']

myeloid /ˈmʌɪəlɔɪd/ *adj.* of or relating to bone marrow or the spinal cord. [Greek *muelos* 'marrow']

myeloma /mʌɪəˈləʊmə/ *n.* (*pl.* **myelomas** or **myelomata** /-mətə/) a malignant tumour of the bone marrow. [modern Latin, as MYELITIS + -OMA]

mylodon /ˈmʌɪləd(ə)n/ *n.* an extinct gigantic ground sloth of the genus *Mylodon*, with cylindrical teeth and found in deposits formed during the ice age of the Pleistocene epoch in South America. [modern Latin, from Greek *mulē* 'mill, molar' + *odous odontos* 'tooth']

mynah /ˈmʌɪnə/ *n.* (also **myna**, **mina**) any of various SE Asian starlings, esp. *Gracula religiosa* able to mimic the human voice. [Hindi *mainā*]

myo- /ˈmʌɪəʊ/ *comb. form* (also **my-** before a vowel) muscle. [Greek *mus muos* 'muscle']

myocardium /mʌɪə(ʊ)ˈkɑːdɪəm/ *n.* (*pl.* **myocardia** /-dɪə/) the muscular tissue of the heart. ◻ **myocardial** *adj.* **myocarditis** /-ˈdʌɪtɪs/ *n.* [MYO- + Greek *kardia* 'heart']

myofibril /mʌɪə(ʊ)ˈfʌɪbrɪl/ *n.* any of the elongated contractile threads found in striated muscle cells.

myogenic /mʌɪə(ʊ)ˈdʒɛnɪk/ *adj.* originating in muscle tissue.

myoglobin /mʌɪə(ʊ)ˈgləʊbɪn/ *n.* an oxygen-carrying protein containing iron and found in muscle cells.

myology /mʌɪˈɒlədʒi/ *n.* the study of the structure and function of muscles.

myope /ˈmʌɪəʊp/ *n.* a short-sighted person. [French via Late Latin *myops* from Greek *muōps*, from *muō* 'shut' + *ōps* 'eye']

myopia /mʌɪˈəʊpɪə/ *n.* **1** short-sightedness. **2** lack of imagination or intellectual insight. ◻ **myopic** /-ˈɒpɪk/ *adj.* **myopically** /-ˈɒpɪk(ə)li/ *adv.* [modern Latin (as MYOPE)]

myosin /ˈmʌɪə(ʊ)sɪn/ *n.* a protein which with actin forms the contractile filaments of muscle. [MYO- + -OSE² + -IN]

myosis var. of MIOSIS.

myosotis /mʌɪə(ʊ)ˈsəʊtɪs/ *n.* (also **myosote** /ˈmʌɪəsəʊt/) any plant of the genus *Myosotis* with blue, pink, or white flowers, esp. a forget-me-not. [Latin from Greek *muosōtis*, from *mus muos* 'mouse' + *ous ōtos* 'ear']

myotonia /mʌɪə(ʊ)ˈtəʊnɪə/ *n.* the inability to relax voluntary muscle after vigorous effort. ◻ **myotonic** /-ˈtɒnɪk/ *adj.* [MYO- + Greek *tonos* 'tone']

myriad /ˈmɪrɪəd/ *n.* & *adj. literary* ● *n.* **1** an indefinitely great number. **2** ten thousand. ● *adj.* of an indefinitely great number. [Late Latin *mirias miriad-* from Greek *murias -ados*, from *murioi* '10,000']

myriapod /ˈmɪrɪəpɒd/ *n.* & *adj.* ● *n.* any land-living arthropod of the class Myriapoda, with numerous leg-bearing segments, e.g. centipedes and millipedes. ● *adj.* of or relating to this group. [modern Latin *Myriapoda* (as MYRIAD, Greek *pous podos* 'foot')]

myrmecology /məːmɪˈkɒlədʒi/ *n.* the scientific study of ants. ◻ **myrmecological** /-ˈlɒdʒɪk(ə)l/ *adj.* **myrmecologist** *n.* [Greek *murmēk- murmēx* 'ant']

myrmidon /ˈməːmɪd(ə)n/ *n.* **1** a hired ruffian. **2** a lowly servant. [Latin *Myrmidones* (pl.) from Greek *Murmidones*, warlike Thessalian people who went with Achilles to Troy]

myrobalan /mʌɪˈrɒbələn/ *n.* **1** (in full **myrobalan plum**) = CHERRY PLUM. **2** (in full **myrobalan nut**) the fruit of an Asian tree, *Terminalia chebula*, used in medicines, for tanning leather, and to produce inks and dyes. [French *myrobolan* or Latin *myrobalanum* from Greek *murobalanos*, from *muron* 'unguent' + *balanos* 'acorn']

myrrh¹ /məː/ *n.* a gum resin from several trees of the genus *Commiphora* used, esp. in the Near East, in perfumery, medicine, incense, etc. ◻ **myrrhic** *adj.* **myrrhy** *adj.* [Old English *myrra, myrre* via Latin *myrr(h)a* from Greek *murra*, of Semitic origin]

myrrh² /məː/ *n.* = SWEET CICELY. [Latin *myrris* from Greek *murris*]

myrtaceous /məːˈteɪʃəs/ *adj.* of or relating to the plant family Myrtaceae, including myrtles.

myrtle /ˈməːt(ə)l/ *n.* **1** an evergreen shrub of the genus *Myrtus* with aromatic foliage and white flowers, esp. *M. communis*, bearing purple-black ovoid berries. **2** *US* = PERIWINKLE¹ 1. [Middle English via medieval Latin *myrtilla, -us*, diminutive of Latin *myrta, myrtus*, from Greek *murtos*]

myself /mʌɪˈsɛlf, mɪˈsɛlf/ *pron.* **1** *emphat. form* of I² or ME¹ (*I saw it myself; I like to do it myself*). **2** *refl. form* of ME¹ (*I was angry with myself; able to dress myself*). **3** in my normal state of body and mind (*I'm not myself today*). **4** *poet.* = I² (*myself when young did often wander in the woods*). ◻ **by myself** see *by oneself*. **I myself** I for my part (*I myself am doubtful*). [ME¹ + SELF: *my-* partly after *herself*, with *her* regarded as possessive pronoun]

mysterious /mɪˈstɪərɪəs/ *adj.* **1** full of or wrapped in mystery. **2** (of a person) delighting in mystery. ◻ **mysteriously** *adv.* **mysteriousness** *n.* [French *mystérieux*, from *mystère*, from Old French (as MYSTERY¹)]

mystery¹ /ˈmɪst(ə)ri/ *n.* (*pl.* **-ies**) **1** a secret, hidden, or inexplicable matter (*the reason remains a mystery*). **2** secrecy or obscurity (*wrapped in mystery*). **3** (*attrib.*) secret, undisclosed (*mystery guest*). **4** the practice of making a secret of (esp. unimportant) things (*engaged in mystery and intrigue*). **5** (in full **mystery story**) a fictional work dealing with a puzzling event, esp. a crime (*a well-known mystery writer*). **6 a** a religious truth divinely revealed, esp. one beyond human reason. **b** *RC Ch.* a decade of the rosary. **7** (in *pl.*) **a** the secret religious rites of the ancient Greeks, Romans, etc. **b** *archaic* the Eucharist. ◻ **make a mystery of** treat as an impressive secret. [Middle English via Old French *mistere* or Latin *mysterium* from Greek *mustērion*, related to MYSTIC]

mystery² /ˈmɪst(ə)ri/ *n.* (*pl.* **-ies**) *archaic* a handicraft or trade, esp. as referred to in indentures etc. (*art and mystery*). [Middle English from medieval Latin *misterium*, contraction of *ministerium* MINISTRY, associated with MYSTERY¹]

mystery play *n.* a medieval play based on the Bible or the lives of the saints.

mystery tour *n. Brit.* a pleasure excursion to an unspecified destination.

mystic /ˈmɪstɪk/ *n.* & *adj.* ● *n.* a person who seeks by contemplation and self-surrender to obtain unity or identity with or absorption into the Deity or the ultimate reality, or who believes in the spiritual apprehension of truths that are beyond the understanding. ● *adj.* **1** mysterious and awe-inspiring. **2** spiritually allegorical or symbolic. **3** occult, esoteric. **4** of hidden meaning. ◻ **mysticism** /-sɪz(ə)m/ *n.* [Middle English via Old French *mystique* or Latin *mysticus* from Greek *mustikos*, via *mustēs* 'initiated person' from *muō* 'close the eyes or lips, initiate']

mystical /ˈmɪstɪk(ə)l/ *adj.* of mystics or mysticism. ◻ **mystically** *adv.*

mystify /ˈmɪstɪfʌɪ/ *v.tr.* (**-ies, -ied**) **1** bewilder, confuse. **2** hoax, take advantage of the credulity of. **3** wrap up in mystery. ◻ **mystification** /-fɪˈkeɪʃ(ə)n/ *n.* **mystifying** *adj.* **mystifyingly** *adv.* [French *mystifier*, formed irregularly from *mystique* MYSTIC or *mystère* MYSTERY¹]

mystique /mɪˈstiːk/ *n.* **1** an atmosphere of mystery and veneration attending some activity or person. **2** any skill or technique impressive or mystifying to the layman. [French from Old French (as MYSTIC)]

myth /mɪθ/ *n.* **1** a traditional narrative usu. involving supernatural or imaginary persons and often embodying popular ideas on natural or social phenomena etc. **2** such narratives collectively. **3** a widely held but false notion. **4** a fictitious person, thing, or idea. **5** an allegory (*the Platonic myth*). ◻ **mythic** *adj.* **mythical** *adj.* **mythically** *adv.* [modern Latin *mythus* via Late Latin *mythos* from Greek *muthos*]

mythi *pl.* of MYTHUS.

mythicize /ˈmɪθɪsʌɪz/ *v.tr.* (also **-ise**) treat (a story etc.) as a myth; interpret mythically. ◻ **mythicism** /-sɪz(ə)m/ *n.* **mythicist** /-sɪst/ *n.*

mytho- /ˈmɪθəʊ/ *comb. form* myth. [Greek *muthos*, or from MYTH]

mythogenesis /mɪθə(ʊ)ˈdʒɛnɪsɪs/ *n.* the production of myths.

mythographer /mɪˈθɒgrəfə/ *n.* a compiler of myths.

mythography /mɪˈθɒgrəfi/ *n.* the representation of myths in plastic art.

mythology /mɪˈθɒlədʒi/ *n.* (*pl.* **-ies**) **1** a body of myths (*Greek mythology*). **2** the study of myths. ◻ **mythologer** *n.* **mythologic** /-θəˈlɒdʒɪk/ *adj.* **mythological** /-θəˈlɒdʒɪk(ə)l/ *adj.* **mythologically** /-θəˈlɒdʒɪk(ə)li/ *adv.* **mythologist** *n.* **mythologize** *v.tr.* & *intr.* (also **-ise**). **mythologizer** *n.* [Middle English via French *mythologie* or Late Latin *mythologia* from Greek *muthologia* (as MYTHO-, -LOGY)]

mythomania /mɪθə(ʊ)'meɪnɪə/ *n.* an abnormal tendency to exaggerate or tell lies. □ **mythomaniac** /-ɪak/ *n. & adj.*

mythopoeia /mɪθə(ʊ)'piːə/ *n.* the making of myths. □ **mythopoeic** *adj.* (also **mythopoetic** /-pəʊ'ɛtɪk/). [Greek *muthopoiia* (as MYTHO-, *poiein* 'make']

mythos /'mʌɪθɒs, 'mɪθɒs/ *n.* (*pl.* **mythoi** /-θɔɪ/) **1** *literary* a myth; a body of myths. **2** a narrative theme or pattern. [Late Latin: see MYTH]

mythus /'mʌɪθəs, 'mɪθəs/ *n.* (*pl.* **mythi** /-θʌɪ/) *literary* a myth. [modern Latin: see MYTH]

myxo- /'mɪksəʊ/ *comb. form* (also **myx-** before a vowel) mucus. [Greek *muxa* 'mucus']

myxoedema /mɪksɪ'diːmə/ *n.* (*US* **myxedema**) a syndrome caused by hypothyroidism, resulting in thickening of the skin, weight gain, mental dullness, loss of energy, and sensitivity to cold.

myxoma /mɪk'səʊmə/ *n.* (*pl.* **myxomas** or **myxomata** /-mətə/) a benign tumour of mucous or gelatinous tissue. □ **myxomatous** /-'sɒmətəs/ *adj.* [modern Latin (as MYXO-, -OMA)]

myxomatosis /mɪksəmə'təʊsɪs/ *n.* an infectious usu. fatal viral disease in rabbits, causing swelling of the mucous membranes.

myxomycete /mɪksə(ʊ)'mʌɪsiːt/ *n.* a slime mould of the class Myxomycetes, usu. forming a mobile plasmodium. [from MYXO- + Greek *mukēs -ētos* 'fungus']

myxovirus /'mɪksə(ʊ)vʌɪrəs/ *n.* any of a group of viruses including the influenza virus.

Nn

N[1] /ɛn/ *n.* (also **n**) (*pl.* **Ns** or **N's**) **1** the fourteenth letter of the alphabet. **2** *Printing* en.

N[2] *abbr.* (also **N.**) **1** North; Northern. **2** *Chess* knight. **3** New. **4** nuclear.

N[3] *symb.* **1** *Chem.* the element nitrogen. **2** newton(s).

n[1] *abbr.* (also **n.**) **1** name. **2** neuter. **3** noon. **4** note.

n[2] *symb.* **1** *Math.* an indefinite number. **2** nano-. □ **to the nth** (or **nth degree**) **1** *Math.* to any required power. **2** to any extent; to the utmost.

'n /(ə)n/ *conj.* (also **'n'**) *colloq.* and. [abbreviation]

-n[1] *suffix* see -EN[2].

-n[2] *suffix* see -EN[3].

Na *symb. Chem.* the element sodium. [modern Latin *natrium*]

na /nə/ *adv.* (in *comb.*; usu. with an auxiliary verb) *Sc.* = NOT (*I canna do it*; *they didna go*).

n/a *abbr.* **1** not applicable. **2** not available.

NAAFI /'nafi/ *abbr. Brit.* **1** Navy, Army, and Air Force Institutes. **2** a canteen for service personnel run by the NAAFI.

naan var. of NAN[2].

nab /nab/ *v.tr.* (**nabbed**, **nabbing**) *slang* **1** arrest; catch in wrongdoing. **2** seize, grab. [17th c., also *napp*, as in KIDNAP: origin unknown]

nabob /'neɪbɒb/ *n.* **1** *hist.* a Muslim official or governor under the Mughal empire. **2** a person of conspicuous wealth or high rank, esp. *hist.* one returned from India with a fortune. [Portuguese *nababo* or Spanish *nabab*, from Urdu (as NAWAB)]

nacelle /nə'sɛl/ *n.* **1** the outer casing of the engine of an aircraft. **2** the car of an airship. [French, from Late Latin *navicella*, diminutive of Latin *navis* 'ship']

nacho /'nɑːtʃəʊ, 'natʃəʊ/ *n.* (*pl.* **-os**) (usu. in *pl.*) a tortilla chip, usu. topped with melted cheese and spices etc. [20th c.: origin uncertain]

NACODS /'neɪkɒds/ *abbr.* (in the UK) National Association of Colliery Overmen, Deputies, and Shot-firers.

nacre /'neɪkə/ *n.* mother-of-pearl from any shelled mollusc. □ **nacreous** /'neɪkrɪəs/ *adj.* [French]

NAD *abbr. Biochem.* nicotinamide adenine dinucleotide, a coenzyme important in many biological oxidation reactions.

nadir /'neɪdɪə/ *n.* **1** the part of the celestial sphere directly below an observer (opp. ZENITH). **2** the lowest point in one's fortunes; a time of deep despair. [Middle English via Old French from Arabic *naẓīr* (*as-samt*) 'opposite (to the zenith)']

naevus /'niːvəs/ *n.* (*US* **nevus**) (*pl.* **naevi** /-vʌɪ/) **1** a birthmark in the form of a raised red patch on the skin. **2** = MOLE[2]. [Latin]

naff[1] /naf/ *v.intr. Brit. slang* **1** (in *imper.*, foll. by *off*) go away. **2** (as **naffing** *adj.*) used as an intensive to express annoyance etc. [probably euphemism for FUCK: cf. EFF]

naff[2] /naf/ *adj. Brit. slang* **1** unfashionable, tasteless. **2** worthless, rubbishy. [20th c.: origin unknown]

Naffy /'nafi/ *n. slang* = NAAFI. [phonetic spelling]

nag[1] /nag/ *v.* & *n.* ● *v.* (**nagged**, **nagging**) **1 a** *tr.* annoy or irritate (a person) with persistent fault-finding or continuous urging. **b** *intr.* (often foll. by *at*) find fault, complain, or urge, esp. persistently. **2** *intr.* (of a pain) ache dully but persistently. **3 a** *tr.* worry or preoccupy (a person, the mind, etc.) (*his mistake nagged him*). **b** *intr.* (often foll. by *at*) worry or gnaw. ● *n.* a persistently nagging person. □ **nagger** *n.* **naggingly** *adv.* [of dialect, perhaps Scandinavian or Low German, origin: cf. Norwegian & Swedish *nagga* 'gnaw, irritate', Low German *(g)naggen* 'provoke']

nag[2] /nag/ *n.* **1** *colloq.* a horse. **2** a small riding-horse or pony. [Middle English: origin unknown]

Nah. *abbr.* Nahum (Old Testament).

Nahuatl /'nɑːwɑːt(ə)l, nɑː'wɑːt(ə)l/ *n.* & *adj.* ● *n.* **1** a member of a group of peoples native to southern Mexico and Central America, including the Aztecs. **2** the language of these people. ● *adj.* of or relating to the Nahuatl peoples or language. □ **Nahuatlan** *adj.* [Spanish from Nahuatl]

naiad /'nʌɪad/ *n.* (*pl.* **naiads** or **-des** /-əˌdiːz/) **1** *Mythol.* a water nymph. **2** the larva of a dragonfly etc. **3** any aquatic plant of the genus *Najas*, with narrow leaves and small flowers. [Latin *Naïas Naïad-* from Greek *Naias -ados*, from *naō* 'flow']

naïf /nʌɪ'iːf, nɑː'iːf/ *adj.* & *n.* ● *adj.* = NAIVE. ● *n.* a naive person.

nail /neɪl/ *n.* & *v.* ● *n.* **1** a small usu. sharpened metal spike with a broadened flat head, driven in with a hammer to join things together or to serve as a peg, protection (cf. HOBNAIL), or decoration. **2 a** a horny covering on the upper surface of the tip of the finger and toe in humans and other primates. **b** a claw or talon. **c** a hard growth on the upper mandible of some soft-billed birds. **3** *hist.* a measure of cloth length (equal to 2¼ inches). ● *v.tr.* **1** fasten with a nail or nails (*nailed it to the beam*; *nailed the planks together*). **2** fix or keep (a person, attention, etc.) fixed. **3 a** secure, catch, or get hold of (a person or thing). **b** expose or discover (a lie or a liar). □ **hard as nails 1** callous; unfeeling. **2** in good physical condition. **nail one's colours to the mast** persist; refuse to give in. **nail down 1** bind (a person) to a promise etc. **2** define precisely. **3** fasten (a thing) with nails. **nail in a person's coffin** something thought to increase the risk of death. **nail up 1** close (a door etc.) with nails. **2** fix (a thing) at a height with nails. **on the nail** (esp. of payment) without delay (*cash on the nail*). □ **nailed** *adj.* (also in *comb.*). **nailless** *adj.* [Old English *nægel*, *næglan*, from Germanic]

nail-biting *adj.* causing severe anxiety or tension.

nail brush *n.* a small brush for cleaning the nails.

nail enamel *n. N. Amer.* = NAIL POLISH.

nailer /'neɪlə/ *n.* a nail-maker. □ **nailery** *n.*

nail file *n.* a roughened metal or emery strip used for smoothing the nails.

nail head *n. Archit.* an ornament like the head of a nail.

nail polish *n.* a varnish applied to the nails to colour them or make them shiny.

nail punch *n.* (also **nail set**) a tool for sinking the head of a nail below a surface.

nail scissors *n.pl.* small curved scissors for trimming the nails.

nail varnish *n. Brit.* = NAIL POLISH.

nainsook /'neɪnsʊk/ *n.* a fine soft cotton fabric, originally Indian. [Hindi *nainsukh*, from *nain* 'eye' + *sukh* 'pleasure']

naira /'nʌɪrə/ *n.* the chief monetary unit of Nigeria. [contraction of *Nigeria*]

naive /nʌɪˈiːv, nɑːˈiːv/ *adj.* (also **naïve**) **1** artless; innocent; unaffected. **2** foolishly credulous; simple. **3** (of art etc.) produced in a sophisticated society but deliberately rejecting conventional expertise. □ **naively** *adv.* **naiveness** *n.* [French, fem. of *naïf*, from Latin *nativus* NATIVE]

naivety /nʌɪˈiːvti, nɑːˈiːvti/ *n.* (also **naïvety**, ***naïveté*** /nʌɪˈiːvteɪ, nɑː-, French naivte/) (*pl.* **-ies** or ***naïvetés***) **1** the state or quality of being naive. **2** a naive action. [French *naïveté* (as NAIVE)]

naked /ˈneɪkɪd/ *adj.* **1** without clothes; nude. **2** plain; undisguised; exposed (*the naked truth*; *his naked soul*). **3** (of a light, flame, etc.) unprotected from the wind etc.; unshaded. **4** defenceless. **5** without addition, comment, support, evidence, etc. (*his naked word*; *naked assertion*). **6 a** (of landscape) barren; treeless. **b** (of rock) exposed; without soil etc. **7** (of a sword etc.) unsheathed. **8** (usu. foll. by *of*) devoid; without. **9** without leaves, hairs, scales, shell, etc. **10** (of a room, wall, etc.) without decoration, furnishings, etc.; empty, plain. □ **nakedly** *adv.* **nakedness** *n.* [Old English *nacod*, from Germanic]

naked ape *n.* (prec. by *the*) present-day man.

naked eye *n.* (prec. by *the*) unassisted vision, e.g. without a telescope, microscope, etc.

naked ladies *n.pl.* (also **naked boys**) the meadow saffron or autumn crocus.

naker /ˈneɪkə/ *n. hist.* a kettledrum. [Middle English via Old French *nacre nacaire* from Arabic *naḳḳāra* 'drum']

NALGO /ˈnalgəʊ/ *abbr. hist.* (in the UK) National and Local Government Officers' Association, merged with COHSE and NUPE in 1993 to form UNISON.

Nama /ˈnɑːmə/ *n. & adj.* ● *n.* (*pl.* same or **Namas**) **1** a member of a people of S. Africa and Namibia. **2** the language of this people. ● *adj.* of or relating to this people or their language. [Nama]

■ **Usage** The term *Hottentot* is sometimes used for this people and language, but it is often considered to be offensive.

namby-pamby /nambɪˈpambi/ *adj. & n.* ● *adj.* **1** lacking vigour or drive; weak. **2** insipidly pretty or sentimental. ● *n.* (*pl.* **-ies**) **1** a namby-pamby person. **2** namby-pamby talk. [fanciful formulation on name of *Ambrose* Philips, English pastoral writer d. 1749]

name /neɪm/ *n. & v.* ● *n.* **1 a** the word by which an individual person, animal, place, or thing is known, spoken of, etc. (*mentioned him by name*; *her name is Joanna*). **b** all who go under one name; a family, clan, or people in terms of its name (*all the clans hostile to the name of Campbell*). **2 a** a usu. abusive term used of a person etc. (*called him names*). **b** a word denoting an object or esp. a class of objects, ideas, etc. (*what is the name of that kind of vase?*; *that sort of behaviour has no name*). **3** a famous person (*many great names were there*). **4** a reputation, esp. a good one (*has a name for honesty*; *their name is guarantee enough*). **5** something existing only nominally (opp. FACT, REALITY). **6** (*attrib.*) widely known (*a name brand of shampoo*). **7** an underwriter of a Lloyd's syndicate. ● *v.tr.* **1** give a usu. specified name to (*named the dog Spot*). **2** call (a person or thing) by the right name (*named the man in the photograph*). **3** mention; specify; cite (*named his requirements*). **4** nominate, appoint, etc. (*was named the new chairman*). **5** specify as something desired (*named it as her dearest wish*). **6** *Brit. Parl.* (of the Speaker) mention (an MP) as disobedient to the chair. □ **by name** called (*Tom by name*). **have to one's name** possess. **in all but name** virtually. **in name** (or **name only**) as a mere formality; hardly at all (*is the leader in name only*). **in a person's name** = *in the name of*. **in the name of** calling to witness; invoking (*in the name of goodness*). **in one's own name** independently; without authority. **make a name for oneself** become famous. **name after** (*N. Amer.* also **for**) call (a person) by the name of (a specified person) (*named him after his uncle Roger*). **name the day** arrange a date (esp. of a woman fixing the date for her wedding). **name names** mention specific names, esp. in accusation. **name of the game** *colloq.* the purpose or essence of an action etc. **of** (or **by**) **the name of** called. **put one's name down for 1** apply for. **2** promise to subscribe (a sum). **what's in a name?** names are arbitrary labels. **you name it** *colloq.* no matter what; whatever you like. □ **nameable** *adj.* [Old English *nama, noma, (ge)namian* from Germanic: related to Latin *nomen*, Greek *onoma*]

name-calling *n.* abusive language.

name-child *n.* (usu. foll. by *of*) *Brit.* one named after another person.

name-day *n.* **1** the feast day of a saint after whom a person is named. **2** *Brit.* = TICKET-DAY.

name-dropping *n.* the familiar mention of famous people as a form of boasting. □ **name-drop** *v.intr.* (**-dropped**, **-dropping**). **name-dropper** *n.*

nameless /ˈneɪmlɪs/ *adj.* **1** having no name or name-inscription. **2** inexpressible; indefinable (*a nameless sensation*). **3** unnamed; anonymous, esp. deliberately (*our informant, who shall be nameless*). **4** too loathsome or horrific to be named (*nameless vices*). **5** obscure; inglorious. **6** illegitimate. □ **namelessly** *adv.* **namelessness** *n.*

namely /ˈneɪmli/ *adv.* that is to say; in other words.

name part *n.* the title role in a play etc.

nameplate /ˈneɪmpleɪt/ *n.* a plate or panel bearing the name of an occupant of a room etc.

namesake /ˈneɪmseɪk/ *n.* a person or thing having the same name as another (*was her aunt's namesake*). [probably from the phrase *for the name's sake*]

name-tape *n.* a tape fixed to a garment etc. and bearing the name of the owner.

namma var. of GNAMMA.

nan[1] /nan/ *n. Brit. colloq.* grandmother. [childish pronunciation]

nan[2] /nɑːn/ *n.* (also **naan**) (in Indian cookery) a type of leavened bread cooked esp. in a clay oven. [Persian & Urdu *nān*]

nana[1] /ˈnɑːnə/ *n. slang* a silly person; a fool. [perhaps from BANANA]

nana[2] /ˈnanə/ *n.* (also *Brit.* **nanna**) *colloq.* grandmother. [as NAN[1]]

nancy /ˈnansi/ *n. & adj. offens.* (also **nance** /nans/) *slang* ● *n.* (*pl.* **-ies**) (in full **nancy boy**) an effeminate man, esp. a homosexual. ● *adj.* effeminate. [pet form of the name *Ann*]

nankeen /naŋˈkiːn, nan-/ *n. & adj.* ● *n.* **1** a yellowish cotton cloth. **2** a yellowish-buff colour. **3** (in *pl.*) trousers of nankeen. ● *adj.* **1** made of nankeen. **2** of the yellowish-buff colour of nankeen. [*Nankin(g)* in China, where originally made]

nanna var. of NANA[2].

nanny /ˈnani/ *n. & v.* ● *n.* (*pl.* **-ies**) **1 a** a child's nurse. **b** *Brit.* an unduly protective person, institution, etc. (*the nanny state*). **2** = NAN[1]. **3** (in full **nanny goat**) a female goat. ● *v.tr.* (**-ies**, **-ied**) be unduly protective towards. [formed as NANCY]

nano- /ˈnanəʊ/ *comb. form* denoting a factor of 10^{-9} (*nanosecond*). [Latin, from Greek *nanos* 'dwarf']

nanometre /ˈnanə(ʊ)miːtə/ *n.* (*US* **nanometer**) one thousand-millionth of a metre.

nanosecond /ˈnanə(ʊ)sɛkənd/ *n.* one thousand-millionth of a second.

nanotechnology /ˌnanə(ʊ)tɛkˈnɒlədʒi/ *n.* the branch of technology that deals with dimensions and tolerances of less than 100 nanometres, esp. the manipulation of individual atoms and molecules. □ **nanotechnological** /ˌnanə(ʊ)tɛknəˈlɒdʒɪk(ə)l/ *adj.* **nanotechnologist** *n.*

naos /ˈneɪɒs/ *n.* (*pl.* **naoi** /ˈneɪɔɪ/) *Gk Antiq.* the inner part of a temple. [Greek, = temple]

nap[1] /nap/ *v. & n.* ● *v.intr.* (**napped**, **napping**) sleep lightly or briefly. ● *n.* a short sleep or doze, esp. by day (*took a nap*). □ **catch a person napping 1** find a person asleep or off guard. **2** detect in negligence or error. [Old

English *hnappian*, related to Old High German (*h*)*naffezan* 'to slumber']

nap[2] /nap/ *n.* & *v.* ● *n.* **1** the raised pile on textiles, esp. velvet. **2** a soft downy surface. **3** *Austral. colloq.* blankets, bedding, swag. ● *v.tr.* (**napped**, **napping**) raise a nap on (cloth). □ **napless** *adj.* [Middle English *noppe* from Middle Dutch, Middle Low German *noppe* 'nap', *noppen* 'trim nap from']

nap[3] /nap/ *n.* & *v.* ● *n.* **1 a** a form of whist in which players declare the number of tricks they expect to take, up to five. **b** a call of five in this game. **2** *Brit.* **a** the betting of all one's money on one horse etc. **b** a tipster's choice for this. ● *v.tr.* (**napped**, **napping**) *Brit.* name (a horse etc.) as a probable winner. □ **go nap 1** attempt to take all five tricks in nap. **2** risk everything in one attempt. **3** win all the matches etc. in a series. **not go nap on** *Austral. colloq.* not be too keen on; not care much for. [abbreviation of NAPOLEON, the original name of the game]

napa var. of NAPPA.

napalm /'neɪpɑːm, 'na-/ *n.* & *v.* ● *n.* **1** a thickening agent produced from naphthenic acid, other fatty acids, and aluminium. **2** a jellied petrol made from this, used in incendiary bombs. ● *v.tr.* attack with napalm bombs. [NAPHTHENIC + PALMITIC ACID]

nape /neɪp/ *n.* (in full **nape of the neck**) the back of the neck. [Middle English: origin unknown]

napery /'neɪp(ə)ri/ *n. Sc.* or *archaic* household linen, esp. table linen. [Middle English from Old French *naperie*, from *nape* (as NAPKIN)]

nap hand *n.* a good winning position worth risking in a venture.

naphtha /'nafθə/ *n.* an inflammable oil obtained by the dry distillation of organic substances such as coal, shale, or petroleum. [Latin from Greek, = inflammable volatile liquid issuing from the earth, of oriental origin]

naphthalene /'nafθəliːn/ *n.* a white crystalline aromatic substance produced by the distillation of coal tar and used in mothballs and the manufacture of dyes etc. □ **naphthalic** /-'θalɪk/ *adj.* [NAPHTHA + -ENE]

naphthene /'nafθiːn/ *n. Chem.* any of a group of cycloalkanes (including cyclohexane) obtained from petroleum. [NAPHTHA + -ENE]

naphthenic /naf'θiːnɪk/ *adj.* of a naphthene or its radical.

naphthenic acid *n.* any carboxylic acid resulting from the refining of petroleum.

Napierian logarithm /neɪ'pɪərɪən/ *n.* = NATURAL LOGARITHM. [named after J. *Napier*, Scots mathematician d. 1617]

napkin /'napkɪn/ *n.* **1** (in full **table napkin**) a square piece of linen, paper, etc. used for wiping the lips, fingers, etc. at meals, or serving fish etc. on; a serviette. **2** *Brit.* a baby's nappy. **3** a small towel. **4** (in full **sanitary napkin**) *N. Amer.* = SANITARY TOWEL. [Middle English via Old French *nappe* from Latin *mappa*: see MAP]

napkin ring *n.* a ring used to hold (and distinguish) a person's table napkin when not in use.

napoleon /nə'pəʊlɪən/ *n.* **1** *hist.* a gold twenty-franc piece minted in the reign of Napoleon I. **2** *hist.* a 19th-c. high boot. **3** = NAP[3]. **4** *N. Amer.* = MILLEFEUILLE. [French *napoléon* from *Napoléon*, name of 19th-c. French emperors]

Napoleonic /nəpəʊlɪ'ɒnɪk/ *adj.* of, relating to, or characteristic of Napoleon I or his time.

nappa /'napə/ *n.* (also **napa**) a soft leather made by a special process from the skin of sheep or goats. [*Napa* in California]

nappe /nap/ *n. Geol.* a sheet of rock that has moved sideways over neighbouring strata, usu. as a result of overthrust. [French *nappe* 'tablecloth']

napper /'napə/ *n. Brit. slang* the head. [18th c.: origin uncertain]

nappy /'napi/ *n.* (*pl.* **-ies**) *Brit.* a piece of towelling or other absorbent material wrapped round a baby to absorb or retain urine and faeces. [abbreviation of NAPKIN]

nappy rash *n.* inflammation of a baby's skin, caused by prolonged contact with a damp nappy.

narc /nɑːk/ *n.* esp. *N. Amer. slang* an official narcotics agent. [abbreviation of NARCOTIC]

narceine /'nɑːsiːiːn, -siːn/ *n.* a narcotic alkaloid obtained from opium. [French *narcéine* from Greek *narkē* 'numbness']

narcissism /'nɑːsɪsɪz(ə)m, nɑː'sɪs-/ *n. Psychol.* excessive or erotic interest in oneself, one's physical features, etc. □ **narcissist** *n.* **narcissistic** /-'sɪstɪk/ *adj.* **narcissistically** /-'sɪstɪk(ə)li/ *adv.* [Latin *Narcissus* from Greek *Narkissos*, the name of a youth who fell in love with his reflection in a pool]

narcissus /nɑː'sɪsəs/ *n.* (*pl.* **narcissi** /-sʌɪ/ or **narcissuses**) any bulbous plant of the genus *Narcissus*, esp. *N. poeticus* bearing a heavily scented single flower with an undivided corona edged with crimson and yellow. [Latin from Greek *narkissos*, perhaps from *narkē* 'numbness', with reference to its narcotic effects]

narcolepsy /'nɑːkəlɛpsi/ *n. Med.* a disease with fits of sleepiness and drowsiness. □ **narcoleptic** /-'lɛptɪk/ *adj.* & *n.* [Greek *narkoō* 'make numb', on the pattern of EPILEPSY]

narcosis /nɑː'kəʊsɪs/ *n.* **1** *Med.* the working or effects of soporific narcotics. **2** a state of insensibility. [Greek *narkōsis* from *narkoō* 'make numb']

narcoterrorism /nɑːkəʊ'tɛrərɪz(ə)m/ *n.* terrorism associated with illicit drugs, esp. directed against law enforcement. □ **narcoterrorist** *n.* [*narco-* *comb. form* from Greek *narkē* 'numbness', or from NARCOTIC, + TERRORISM (see TERRORIST)]

narcotic /nɑː'kɒtɪk/ *adj.* & *n.* ● *adj.* **1** (of a substance) inducing drowsiness, sleep, stupor, or insensibility. **2** (of a drug etc.) affecting the mind. **3** of or involving narcosis. **4** soporific. ● *n.* a narcotic substance, drug, or influence. □ **narcotically** *adv.* **narcotism** /'nɑːkətɪz(ə)m/ *n.* **narcotize** /'nɑːkətʌɪz/ *v.tr.* (also **-ise**). **narcotization** /nɑːkətʌɪ'zeɪʃ(ə)n/ *n.* [Middle English via Old French *narcotique* or medieval Latin from Greek *narkōtikos* (as NARCOSIS)]

nard /nɑːd/ *n.* **1** any of various aromatic plants of the valerian family, esp. (in full **Celtic nard**) *Valeriana celtica* of European mountains. **2** = SPIKENARD 1. [Middle English via Latin *nardus* from Greek *nardos*, from Sanskrit *nalada*, *narada*]

nardoo /nɑː'duː, 'nɑːduː/ *n.* **1** a clover-like plant, *Marsilea quadrifolia*, native to Australia. **2** a food made from the spores of this plant. [various Aboriginal languages *ngardu*, *nhaadu*]

nares /'nɛːriːz/ *n.pl. Anat.* the nostrils. □ **narial** *adj.* [pl. of Latin *naris*]

narghile /'nɑːgɪleɪ, -li/ *n.* an oriental tobacco pipe with the smoke drawn through water; a hookah. [Persian *nārgīl* 'coconut, hookah' from Sanskrit *narikela* 'coconut', partly via French *nargileh* and Turkish *nargile*]

nark /nɑːk/ *n.* & *v. slang* ● *n.* **1** *Brit.* a police informer or decoy. **2** *Austral.* an annoying person or thing. ● *v.tr.* (usu. in *passive*) *Brit.* annoy; infuriate (*was narked by their attitude*). □ **nark it!** stop that! [Romany *nāk* 'nose']

narky /'nɑːki/ *adj.* (**narkier**, **narkiest**) *Brit. slang* bad-tempered, irritable. [NARK]

Narragansett /narə'gansət/ *n.* an Algonquian language of Rhode Island, US, now virtually extinct. [Algonquian, = people of the small point (of land)]

narrate /nə'reɪt/ *v.tr.* (also *absol.*) **1** give a continuous story or account of. **2** provide a spoken commentary or accompaniment for (a film etc.). □ **narratable** *adj.* **narration** /nə'reɪʃ(ə)n/ *n.* [Latin *narrare narrat-*]

narrative /'narətɪv/ *n.* & *adj.* ● *n.* **1** a spoken or written account of connected events in order of happening. **2** the practice or art of narration. ● *adj.* in the form of, or concerned with, narration (*narrative verse*).

□ **narratively** *adv.* [French *narratif -ive* from Late Latin *narrativus* (as NARRATE)]

narratology /narəˈtɒlədʒi/ *n.* the branch of knowledge that deals with the structure and function of narrative. □ **narratological** /-təˈlɒdʒɪk(ə)l/ *adj.* **narratologist** *n.*

narrator /nəˈreɪtə/ *n.* **1** a person who narrates, esp. a character who recounts the events of a novel or narrative poem. **2** an actor, announcer, etc. who delivers a commentary in a film, broadcast, etc. [Latin (as NARRATE)]

narrow /ˈnarəʊ/ *adj., n., & v.* ● *adj.* (**narrower**, **narrowest**) **1 a** of small width in proportion to length; lacking breadth. **b** confined or confining; constricted (*within narrow bounds*). **2** of limited scope; restricted (*in the narrowest sense*). **3** with little margin (*a narrow escape*). **4** searching; precise; exact (*a narrow examination*). **5** = NARROW-MINDED. **6** (of a vowel) tense. **7** of small size. ● *n.* (usu. in *pl.*) **1** the narrow part of a strait, river, sound, etc. **2** a narrow pass or street. ● *v.* **1** *intr.* become narrow; diminish; contract; lessen. **2** *tr.* make narrow; constrict; restrict. □ **narrowish** *adj.* **narrowly** *adv.* **narrowness** *n.* [Old English *nearu nearw-*, from Germanic]

narrow boat *n. Brit.* a canal boat, esp. one less than 7 ft (2.1 metres) wide.

narrowcast /ˈnarə(ʊ)kɑːst/ *v. & n.* esp. *N. Amer.* ● *v.intr. & tr.* (*past* and *past part.* **narrowcast** or **narrowcasted**) transmit (a television programme etc.), esp. by cable, to an audience targeted by interests or location. ● *n.* **1** transmitting in this way. **2** a transmission or programme of this kind. □ **narrowcaster** *n.* **narrowcasting** *n.*

narrow circumstances *n.pl.* poverty.

narrow gauge *n.* a railway track that has a smaller gauge than the standard one.

narrow-minded *adj.* rigid or restricted in one's views, intolerant, prejudiced, illiberal. □ **narrow-mindedly** *adv.* **narrow-mindedness** *n.*

narrow seas *n.pl.* the English Channel and the Irish Sea.

narrow squeak *n. Brit.* **1** a narrow escape. **2** a success barely attained.

narthex /ˈnɑːθɛks/ *n.* **1** a railed-off antechamber or porch etc. at the western entrance of some early Christian churches, used by catechumens, penitents, etc. **2** a similar antechamber in a modern church. [Latin from Greek *narthēx* 'giant fennel, stick, casket, narthex']

narwhal /ˈnɑːw(ə)l/ *n.* a small Arctic whale, *Monodon monoceros*, the male of which has a long straight spirally twisted tusk developed from one of its teeth. [Dutch *narwal* from Danish *narhval*, from *hval* 'whale': cf. Old Norse *náhvalr* (from *nár* 'corpse', with reference to its skin colour)]

nary /ˈnɛːri/ *adj. colloq.* or *dial.* not a; no (*nary a one*). [*ne'er a*]

NAS *abbr. Brit.* Noise Abatement Society.

NASA /ˈnasə/ *abbr.* (in the US) National Aeronautics and Space Administration.

nasal /ˈneɪz(ə)l/ *adj. & n.* ● *adj.* **1** of, for, or relating to the nose. **2** *Phonet.* (of a speech sound) pronounced with the breath passing through the nose, e.g. *m*, *n*, *ng*, or French *en*, *un*. **3** (of the voice or speech) having an intonation caused by breathing through the nose. ● *n.* **1** *Phonet.* a nasal sound. **2** *hist.* a nose-piece on a helmet. □ **nasality** /-ˈzalɪti/ *n.* **nasalize** *v.intr. & tr.* (also **-ise**). **nasalization** /-ˈzeɪʃ(ə)n/ *n.* **nasally** *adv.* [French *nasal* or medieval Latin *nasalis* from Latin *nasus* 'nose']

nascent /ˈnas(ə)nt, ˈneɪ-/ *adj.* **1** in the act of being born. **2** just beginning to be; not yet mature. **3** *Chem.* just being formed and therefore unusually reactive (*nascent hydrogen*). □ **nascency** /ˈnas(ə)nsi, ˈneɪ-/ *n.* [Latin *nasci nascent-* 'be born']

naseberry /ˈneɪzb(ə)ri/ *n.* (*pl.* **-ies**) a sapodilla. [Spanish & Portuguese *néspera* 'medlar': assimilated to BERRY]

naso- /ˈneɪzəʊ/ *comb. form* nose. [Latin *nasus* 'nose']

nasogastric /neɪzəʊˈgastrɪk/ *adj. Med.* supplying the stomach via the nose (*nasogastric tube*).

nastic /ˈnastɪk/ *adj. Bot.* (of the movement of plant parts) caused by an external stimulus but unaffected in direction by it. [Greek *nastos* 'squeezed together' from *nassō* 'to press']

nasturtium /nəˈstəːʃ(ə)m/ *n.* **1** (in general use) a trailing plant, *Tropaeolum majus*, with rounded edible leaves and bright orange, yellow, or red flowers. **2** any cruciferous plant of the genus *Nasturtium*, including watercress. [Latin]

nasty /ˈnɑːsti/ *adj. & n.* ● *adj.* (**nastier**, **nastiest**) **1 a** highly unpleasant (*a nasty experience*). **b** annoying; objectionable (*the car has a nasty habit of breaking down*). **2** difficult to negotiate; dangerous, serious (*a nasty fence*; *a nasty question*; *a nasty illness*). **3** (of a person or animal) ill-natured, ill-tempered, spiteful; violent, offensive (*nasty to his mother*; *turns nasty when he's drunk*). **4** (of the weather) foul, wet, stormy. **5 a** disgustingly dirty, filthy. **b** unpalatable; disagreeable (*nasty smell*). **c** (of a wound) septic. **6 a** obscene. **b** delighting in obscenity. ● *n.* (*pl.* **-ies**) *colloq.* **1** a nasty person, object, or event. **2** a video nasty. □ **a nasty bit** (or **piece**) **of work** *Brit. colloq.* an unpleasant or contemptible person. **a nasty one 1** a rebuff; a snub. **2** an awkward question. **3** a disabling blow etc. □ **nastily** *adv.* **nastiness** *n.* [Middle English: origin unknown]

NASUWT *abbr.* (in the UK) National Association of Schoolmasters and Union of Women Teachers.

Nat. *abbr.* **1** National. **2** Nationalist. **3** Natural.

natal /ˈneɪt(ə)l/ *adj.* of or from one's birth. [Middle English from Latin *natalis* (as NATION)]

natality /nəˈtalɪti/ *n.* (*pl.* **-ies**) birth rate. [French *natalité* (as NATAL)]

natation /nəˈteɪʃ(ə)n/ *n. formal* or *literary* the act or art of swimming. [Latin *natatio* from *natare* 'swim']

natatorial /neɪtəˈtɔːrɪəl/ *adj.* (also **natatory** /ˈneɪtət(ə)ri, nəˈteɪt(ə)ri/) *formal* **1** swimming. **2** of or concerning swimming. [Late Latin *natatorius* from Latin *natator* 'swimmer' (as NATATION)]

natatorium /neɪtəˈtɔːrɪəm/ *n. N. Amer.* a swimming pool, esp. indoors. [Late Latin, neut. of *natatorius* (see NATATORIAL)]

natch /natʃ/ *adv. colloq.* = NATURALLY. [abbreviation]

nates /ˈneɪtiːz/ *n.pl. Anat.* the buttocks. [Latin]

NATFHE *abbr.* (in the UK) National Association of Teachers in Further and Higher Education.

nathless /ˈneɪθlɪs/ *adv.* (also **natheless**) *archaic* nevertheless. [Middle English from Old English *nā* 'not' (from *ne* 'not' + *ā* 'ever') + THE + *lǣs* LESS]

nation /ˈneɪʃ(ə)n/ *n.* **1** a community of people of mainly common descent, history, language, etc., forming a state or inhabiting a territory. **2** a tribe or confederation of tribes of N. American Indians. □ **nationhood** *n.* [Middle English via Old French from Latin *natio -onis*, from *nasci nat-* 'be born']

national /ˈnaʃ(ə)n(ə)l/ *adj. & n.* ● *adj.* **1** of or common to a nation or the nation. **2** peculiar to or characteristic of a particular nation. ● *n.* **1** a citizen of a specified country, usu. entitled to hold that country's passport (*French nationals*). **2** a fellow countryman. **3** (**the National**) = GRAND NATIONAL. □ **nationally** *adv.* [French (as NATION)]

national anthem *n.* a song adopted by a nation, expressive of its identity etc. and intended to inspire patriotism.

National Assembly *n.* **1** an elected house of legislature in various countries. **2** *hist.* the elected legislature in France 1789–91.

National Assistance *n. hist.* **1** (in Britain) the former official name for supplementary benefits under National Insurance. **2** such benefits.

national bank *n. US* a bank chartered under the federal government.

national convention *n. US* a convention of a major political party, nominating candidates for the presidency etc.

national curriculum *n.* a common programme of study laid down for pupils in the maintained schools of England and Wales with tests at specified ages.

national debt *n.* the money owed by a state because of loans to it.

national football *n. Austral.* Australian Rules football.

National Front *n.* a UK political party with extreme reactionary views on immigration etc.

national grid *n. Brit.* **1** the network of high-voltage electric power lines between major power stations. **2** the metric system of geographical coordinates used in maps of the British Isles.

National Guard *n.* (in the US) the primary reserve force partly maintained by the states but available for federal use.

National Health *n.* (also **National Health Service**) (in the UK) a system of national medical care paid for mainly by taxation and started in 1948.

national income *n.* the total money earned within a nation.

National Insurance *n.* (in the UK) the system of compulsory payments by employed persons (supplemented by employers) to provide state assistance in sickness, unemployment, retirement, etc.

nationalism /ˈnaʃ(ə)n(ə)lɪz(ə)m/ *n.* **1 a** patriotic feeling, principles, etc. **b** an extreme form of this; chauvinism. **2** a policy of national independence. □ **nationalist** *n. & adj.* **nationalistic** /-ˈlɪstɪk/ *adj.* **nationalistically** /-ˈlɪstɪk(ə)li/ *adv.*

nationality /naʃəˈnalɪti/ *n.* (*pl.* **-ies**) **1 a** the status of belonging to a particular nation (*what is your nationality?*; *has British nationality*). **b** a nation (*people of all nationalities*). **2** the condition of being national; distinctive national qualities. **3** an ethnic group forming a part of one or more political nations. **4** existence as a nation; nationhood. **5** patriotic sentiment.

nationalize /ˈnaʃ(ə)n(ə)lʌɪz/ *v.tr.* (also **-ise**) **1** take over (railways, coal mines, the steel industry, land, etc.) from private ownership on behalf of the State. **2 a** make national. **b** make into a nation. **3** naturalize (a foreigner). □ **nationalization** /-ˈzeɪʃ(ə)n/ *n.* **nationalizer** *n.* [French *nationaliser* (as NATIONAL)]

national park *n.* an area of natural beauty protected by the State for the use of the general public.

national service *n. Brit. hist.* service in the army etc. under conscription.

National Socialism *n. hist.* the doctrines of nationalism, racial purity, etc., adopted by the Nazis. □ **National Socialist** *n.*

National Trust *n.* (in the UK, Australia, etc.) an organization for maintaining and preserving historic buildings etc.

National Vocational Qualification *n.* (in the UK) a qualification in a vocational subject set at various levels and (at levels two and three) corresponding in standard to GCSE and GCE A levels.

nation state *n.* a sovereign state of which most of the citizens or subjects are united also by factors such as language, common descent, etc., which define a nation.

nationwide /ˈneɪʃ(ə)nwʌɪd, -ˈwʌɪd/ *adj. & adv.* extending over the whole nation.

native /ˈneɪtɪv/ *n. & adj.* ● *n.* **1 a** (usu. foll. by *of*) a person born in a specified place, or whose parents are domiciled in that place at the time of the birth (*a native of Bristol*). **b** a local inhabitant. **2** *offens.* a member of a non-white indigenous people, as regarded by the colonial settlers. **3** (usu. foll. by *of*) an indigenous animal or plant. **4** an oyster reared in British waters, esp. in artificial beds (*a Whitstable native*). **5** *Austral.* a white person born in Australia. ● *adj.* **1** (usu. foll. by *to*) belonging to a person or thing by nature; inherent; innate (*spoke with the facility native to him*). **2** of one's birth or birthplace (*native dress*; *native country*). **3** belonging to one by right of birth. **4** (usu. foll. by *to*) belonging to a specified place (*the anteater is native to S. America*). **5 a** (esp. of a non-European) indigenous; born in a place. **b** of the natives of a place (*native customs*). **6** unadorned; simple; artless. **7** *Geol.* (of metal etc.) found in a pure or uncombined state. **8** *Austral. & NZ* resembling an animal or plant familiar elsewhere (*native cat*; *native oak*). □ **go native** (of a settler) adopt the local way of life, esp. in a non-European country. □ **natively** *adv.* **nativeness** *n.* [Middle English (earlier as *adj.*) via Old French *natif -ive* or Latin *nativus* from *nasci nat-* 'be born']

Native American *n.* an American Indian, esp. of the US.

■ **Usage** The term *Native American* is now often preferred to *American Indian*. However, when used to include the aboriginal peoples of Canada as well as of the US, it can cause offence. Ambiguity can be avoided by using *American Indian* or *Canadian Indian* as appropriate. See also Usage Note at INDIAN.

---

native bear *n. Austral.* = KOALA.

native rock *n.* rock in its original place.

native speaker *n.* a person who has spoken a language from early childhood.

nativism /ˈneɪtɪvɪz(ə)m/ *n. Philos.* the doctrine of innate ideas. □ **nativist** *n.*

nativity /nəˈtɪvɪti/ *n.* (*pl.* **-ies**) **1** (esp. **the Nativity**) **a** the birth of Christ. **b** the festival of Christ's birth; Christmas. **2** a picture of the Nativity. **3** birth. **4** the horoscope at a person's birth. **5 a** the birth of the Virgin Mary or St John the Baptist. **b** the festival of the nativity of the Virgin (8 Sept.) or St John (24 June). [Middle English via Old French *nativité* and Late Latin *nativitas -tatis* from Latin (as NATIVE)]

nativity play *n.* a play, usu. performed by children at Christmas, dealing with the birth of Christ.

NATO /ˈneɪtəʊ/ *abbr.* (also **Nato**) North Atlantic Treaty Organization.

natron /ˈneɪtr(ə)n, ˈnat-/ *n.* a mineral form of hydrated sodium salts found in dried lake beds. [French via Spanish *natrón* and Arabic *natrūn* from Greek *nitron* NITRE]

natter /ˈnatə/ *v. & n.* esp. *Brit. colloq.* ● *v.intr.* **1** chatter idly. **2** grumble; talk fretfully. ● *n.* **1** aimless chatter. **2** grumbling talk. □ **natterer** *n.* [originally Scots, imitative]

natterjack /ˈnatədʒak/ *n.* a toad, *Bufo calamita*, with a bright yellow stripe down its back, and moving by running not hopping. [perhaps from NATTER, from its loud croak, + JACK[1]]

nattier blue /ˈnatjeɪ/ *n. & adj.* ● *n.* a soft shade of blue. ● *adj.* (hyphenated when *attrib.*) of this colour. [much used by J. M. *Nattier*, French painter d. 1766]

natty /ˈnati/ *adj.* (**nattier**, **nattiest**) *colloq.* **1 a** smartly or neatly dressed, dapper. **b** spruce; trim; smart (*a natty blouse*). **2** deft. □ **nattily** *adv.* **nattiness** *n.* [originally slang, perhaps related to NEAT[1]]

natural /ˈnatʃ(ə)r(ə)l/ *adj. & n.* ● *adj.* **1 a** existing in or caused by nature; not artificial (*natural landscape*). **b** uncultivated; wild (*existing in its natural state*). **2** in the course of nature; not exceptional or miraculous (*died of natural causes*; *a natural occurrence*). **3** (of human nature etc.) not surprising; to be expected (*natural for her to be upset*). **4 a** (of a person or a person's behaviour) unaffected, easy, spontaneous. **b** (foll. by *to*) spontaneous, easy (*friendliness is natural to him*). **5 a** (of qualities etc.) inherent; innate (*a natural talent for music*). **b** (of a person) having such qualities (*a natural linguist*). **6** not disguised or altered (as by make-up etc.). **7** lifelike; as if in nature (*the portrait looked very natural*). **8** likely by its or their nature to be such (*natural enemies*; *the natural antithesis*). **9** having a physical existence as opposed to what is spiritual, intellectual, etc. (*the natural world*). **10 a** related genetically (*her natural son*). **b** illegitimate (*a natural child*). **11** based on the innate moral sense; instinctive (*natural justice*). **12** *Mus.* **a** (of a note) not sharpened or flattened (*B natural*). **b** (of a scale) not containing any sharps or flats. **c** (of a key) having no sharps or flats. **13** not enlightened by revelation (*the natural man*). **14** (of cotton, silk, etc.) having a colour characteristic of the unbleached and undyed state; off-white, creamy beige. ● *n.* **1** (usu. foll. by *for*) *colloq.* a person or thing naturally suitable, adept, expert, etc. (*a natural for the championship*). **2** *archaic* a person mentally deficient from birth. **3** *Mus.* **a** a sign (♮) denoting a return to natural pitch after a sharp or a flat. **b** a natural note. **c** a white key on a piano. **4 a** *Cards* a hand making 21 in the first deal in pontoon. **b** a throw of 7 or 11 at craps. **5** a pale fawn colour. □ **naturalness** *n.* [Middle English via Old French *naturel* from Latin *naturalis* (as NATURE)]

natural-born *adj.* (usu. *attrib.*) having a character or position by birth.

natural childbirth *n. Med.* childbirth with minimal medical or technological intervention.

natural classification *n.* a scientific classification according to natural features.

natural death *n.* death by age or disease, not by accident, poison, violence, etc.

natural food *n.* food without preservatives etc.

natural gas *n.* an inflammable mainly methane gas found in the earth's crust, not manufactured.

natural history *n.* **1** the study of animals or plants, esp. as set forth for popular use. **2** an aggregate of the facts concerning the flora and fauna etc. of a particular place or class (*a natural history of the Isle of Wight*). □ **natural historian** *n.*

naturalism /ˈnatʃ(ə)rəlɪz(ə)m/ *n.* **1** the theory or practice in art and literature of representing nature, character, etc. realistically and in great detail. **2 a** *Philos.* a theory of the world that excludes the supernatural or spiritual. **b** any moral or religious system based on this theory. **3** action based on natural instincts. **4** indifference to conventions. [NATURAL, in Philos. translating French *naturalisme*]

naturalist /ˈnatʃ(ə)rəlɪst/ *n. & adj.* ● *n.* **1** an expert in natural history. **2** a person who believes in or practises naturalism. ● *adj.* = NATURALISTIC.

naturalistic /natʃ(ə)rəˈlɪstɪk/ *adj.* **1** imitating nature closely; lifelike. **2** of or according to naturalism. **3** of natural history. □ **naturalistically** *adv.*

naturalize /ˈnatʃ(ə)rəlʌɪz/ *v.* (also **-ise**) **1** *tr.* admit (a foreigner) to the citizenship of a country. **2** *tr.* introduce (an animal, plant, etc.) into another region so that it flourishes in the wild. **3** *tr.* adopt (a foreign word, custom, etc.). **4** *intr.* become naturalized. **5** *tr. Philos.* exclude from the miraculous; explain naturalistically. **6** *tr.* free from conventions; make natural. **7** *tr.* cause to appear natural. **8** *intr.* study natural history. □ **naturalization** /-ˈzeɪʃ(ə)n/ *n.* [French *naturaliser* (as NATURAL)]

natural language *n.* a language that has developed naturally.

natural law *n.* **1** *Philos.* unchanging moral principles common to all people by virtue of their nature as human beings. **2 a** an observable law relating to natural phenomena. **b** these collectively (*where they saw chance, we see natural law*).

natural life *n.* the duration of one's life on earth.

natural logarithm *n.* a logarithm to the base *e* (2.71828.....) (abbr.: **ln** or $\mathbf{log_e}$).

naturally /ˈnatʃ(ə)rəli/ *adv.* **1** in a natural manner. **2** as a natural result. **3** (qualifying a whole sentence) as might be expected; of course.

natural magic *n.* magic involving nature spirits, healing, the use of herbs, etc.

natural note *n. Mus.* a note that is neither sharp nor flat.

natural numbers *n.pl.* the integers 1, 2, 3, etc.

natural philosophy *n. hist.* natural science, esp. physical science. □ **natural philosopher** *n.*

natural religion *n.* a religion based on reason (opp. REVEALED RELIGION); deism.

natural resources *n.pl.* materials or conditions occurring in nature and capable of economic exploitation.

natural science *n.* the sciences used in the study of the physical world, e.g. physics, chemistry, geology, biology, botany.

natural selection *n.* the Darwinian theory of the survival and propagation of organisms best adapted to their environment.

natural theology *n.* the knowledge of God as gained by the light of natural reason.

natural uranium *n.* unenriched uranium.

natural virtues *n.pl. Philos.* justice, prudence, temperance, fortitude.

natural wastage *n.* = WASTAGE 3.

natural year *n.* the time taken by one revolution of the earth round the sun, 365 days, 5 hours, and 48 minutes.

nature /ˈneɪtʃə/ *n.* **1** a thing's or person's innate or essential qualities or character (*not in their nature to be cruel*; *is the nature of iron to rust*). **2** (often **Nature**) **a** the physical power causing all the phenomena of the material world (*Nature is the best physician*). **b** these phenomena, including plants, animals, landscape, etc. **3** a kind, sort, or class (*things of this nature*). **4** = HUMAN NATURE. **5 a** a specified element of human character (*the rational nature*; *our animal nature*). **b** a person of a specified character (*even strong natures quail*). **6 a** an uncultivated or wild area, condition, community, etc. **b** the countryside, esp. when picturesque. **7** inherent impulses determining character or action. **8** heredity as an influence on or determinant of personality (opp. NURTURE *n.* 3). **9** a living thing's vital functions or needs (*such a diet will not support nature*). □ **against nature** unnatural; immoral. **against** (or **contrary to**) **nature** miraculous; miraculously. **back to nature** returning to a pre-civilized or natural state. **by nature** innately. **from nature** *Art* using natural objects as models. **in nature 1** actually existing. **2** anywhere; at all. **in** (or **of**) **the nature of** characteristically resembling or belonging to the class of (*the answer was in the nature of an excuse*). **in the nature of things** inevitable. ● *adv.* inevitably. **in a state of nature 1** in an uncivilized or uncultivated state. **2** totally naked. **3** in an unregenerate state. [Middle English via Old French from Latin *natura*, from *nasci nat-* 'be born']

nature cure *n.* = NATUROPATHY.

natured /ˈneɪtʃəd/ *adj.* (in *comb.*) having a specified disposition (*good-natured*; *ill-natured*).

nature printing *n.* a method of producing a print of leaves etc. by pressing them on a prepared plate.

nature reserve *n.* a tract of land managed so as to preserve its flora, fauna, physical features, etc.

nature study *n.* the practical study of plant and animal life etc. as a school subject.

nature trail *n.* a signposted path through the countryside designed to draw attention to natural phenomena.

naturism /ˈneɪtʃ(ə)rɪz(ə)m/ *n.* **1** nudism. **2** naturalism in regard to religion. **3** the worship of natural objects. □ **naturist** *n. & adj.*

naturopathy /neɪtʃəˈrɒpəθi/ *n.* **1** the treatment of disease etc. without drugs, usu. involving diet, exercise, massage, etc. **2** this regimen used preventively. □ **naturopath** /ˈneɪtʃ(ə)rəpaθ/ *n.* **naturopathic** /neɪtʃ(ə)rəˈpaθɪk/ *adj.*

naught /nɔːt/ *n. & adj.* ● *n.* **1** *archaic* or *literary* nothing, nought. **2** *US* = NOUGHT 1. ● *adj.* (usu. *predic.*) *archaic* or *literary* worthless; useless. □ **bring to naught** ruin; baffle. **come to naught** be ruined or baffled. **set at naught** disregard; despise. [Old English *nāwiht*, *-wuht*, from *nā* (see NO²) + *wiht* WIGHT]

naughty /ˈnɔːti/ *adj.* (**naughtier, naughtiest**) **1** (esp. of children) disobedient; badly behaved. **2** *colloq. joc.* indecent (*a naughty postcard*). **3** *archaic* wicked. □ **naughtily** *adv.* **naughtiness** *n.* [Middle English, from NAUGHT + -Y[1]]

nauplius /ˈnɔːplɪəs/ *n.* (*pl.* **nauplii** /-plɪʌɪ, -plɪiː/) the first larval stage of some crustaceans. [Latin, = a kind of shellfish, or from Greek *Nauplios*, the son of Poseidon]

nausea /ˈnɔːsɪə, -z-/ *n.* **1** a feeling of sickness with an inclination to vomit. **2** loathing; revulsion. [Latin from Greek *nausia*, from *naus* 'ship']

nauseate /ˈnɔːsɪeɪt, -z-/ *v.* **1** *tr.* affect with nausea; disgust (*was nauseated by the smell*). **2** *intr.* (usu. foll. by *at*) loathe food, an occupation, etc.; feel sick. □ **nauseating** *adj.* **nauseatingly** *adv.* [Latin *nauseare* (as NAUSEA)]

nauseous /ˈnɔːsɪəs, -z-/ *adj.* **1** affected with nausea, sick (*felt nauseous all day*). **2** causing nausea, offensive to the taste or smell. **3** disgusting; loathsome. □ **nauseously** *adv.* **nauseousness** *n.* [Latin *nauseosus* (as NAUSEA)]

nautch /nɔːtʃ/ *n.* a performance of professional Indian dancing girls. [Hindi *nāch* via Prakrit *nachcha* from Sanskrit *nṛitja* 'dancing']

nautch girl *n.* a professional Indian dancing girl.

nautical /ˈnɔːtɪk(ə)l/ *adj.* of or concerning sailors or navigation; naval; maritime. □ **nautically** *adv.* [French *nautique*, or via Latin *nauticus* from Greek *nautikos*, via *nautēs* 'sailor' from *naus* 'ship']

nautical almanac *n.* a yearbook containing astronomical and tidal information for navigators etc.

nautical mile *n.* a unit of approx. 2,025 yards (1,852 metres).

nautilus /ˈnɔːtɪləs/ *n.* (*pl.* **nautiluses** or **nautili** /-lʌɪ, -liː/) **1** any cephalopod of the genus *Nautilus* with a light brittle spiral shell, esp. (**pearly nautilus**) one having a chambered shell with nacreous septa. **2** (in full **paper nautilus**) any small floating octopus of the genus *Argonauta*, of which the female has a very thin shell and webbed sail-like arms. [Latin from Greek *nautilos*, literally 'sailor' (as NAUTICAL)]

NAV *abbr.* net asset value.

Navajo /ˈnavəhəʊ/ *n.* & *adj.* (also **Navaho**) ● *n.* (*pl.* same or **-os**) **1** a member of an American Indian people native to New Mexico and Arizona. **2** the language of this people. ● *adj.* of this people or their language. [Spanish, = pueblo]

naval /ˈneɪv(ə)l/ *adj.* **1** of, in, for, etc. the navy or a navy. **2** of or concerning ships (*a naval battle*). □ **navally** *adv.* [Latin *navalis* from *navis* 'ship']

naval academy *n.* a college for training naval officers.

naval architecture *n.* the designing of ships. □ **naval architect** *n.*

naval officer *n.* an officer in a navy.

naval stores *n.pl.* all materials used in shipping.

navarin /ˈnav(ə)rɪn/ *n.* a casserole of mutton or lamb with vegetables. [French]

nave[1] /neɪv/ *n.* the central part of a church, usu. from the west door to the chancel and excluding the side aisles. [medieval Latin *navis* from Latin *navis* 'ship']

nave[2] /neɪv/ *n.* the hub of a wheel. [Old English *nafu*, *nafa* from Germanic, related to NAVEL]

navel /ˈneɪv(ə)l/ *n.* **1** a rounded knotty depression in the centre of the belly caused by the detachment of the umbilical cord; the umbilicus. **2** a central point. [Old English *nafela* from Germanic, related to NAVE[2]]

navel-gazing *n.* usu. profitless meditation; complacent introversion.

navel orange *n.* a large seedless orange with a navel-like formation at the top.

navelwort /ˈneɪv(ə)lwəːt/ *n.* a pennywort.

navicular /nəˈvɪkjʊlə/ *adj.* & *n.* ● *adj.* boat-shaped. ● *n.* (in full **navicular bone**) a boat-shaped bone in the foot or hand. [French *naviculaire* or Late Latin *navicularis* from Latin *navicula*, diminutive of *navis* 'ship']

navicular disease *n.* an inflammatory disease of the navicular bone in horses, causing lameness.

navigable /ˈnavɪgəb(ə)l/ *adj.* **1** (of a river, the sea, etc.) affording a passage for ships. **2** (of a ship etc.) seaworthy (*in navigable condition*). **3** (of a balloon, airship, etc.) steerable. □ **navigability** /-ˈbɪlɪti/ *n.* [French *navigable* or Latin *navigabilis* (as NAVIGATE)]

navigate /ˈnavɪgeɪt/ *v.* **1 a** *tr.* manage or direct the course of (a ship, aircraft, etc.). **b** *intr.* find one's way; steer the correct course. **2** *tr.* **a** sail on or across (a sea, river, etc.). **b** travel or fly through (the air). **3** *intr.* (of a passenger in a vehicle) assist the driver by map-reading etc. **4** *intr.* sail a ship; sail in a ship. **5** *tr.* (often *refl.*) *colloq.* steer (oneself, a course, etc.) through a crowd etc. [Latin *navigare*, from *navis* 'ship' + *agere* 'drive']

navigation /navɪˈgeɪʃ(ə)n/ *n.* **1** the act or process of navigating. **2** any of several methods of determining or planning a ship's or aircraft's position and course by geometry, astronomy, radio signals, etc. **3** a voyage. □ **navigational** *adj.* [French, or from Latin *navigatio* (as NAVIGATE)]

navigation light *n.* a light on a ship or aircraft at night, indicating its position and direction.

navigator /ˈnavɪgeɪtə/ *n.* **1** a person skilled or engaged in navigation. **2** an explorer by sea. [Latin (as NAVIGATE)]

navvy /ˈnavi/ *n.* & *v.* *Brit.* ● *n.* (*pl.* **-ies**) a labourer employed in building or excavating roads, canals, etc. ● *v.intr.* (**-ies, -ied**) work as a navvy. [abbreviation of NAVIGATOR]

navy /ˈneɪvi/ *n.* & *adj.* ● *n.* (*pl.* **-ies**) **1** (often **the Navy**) **a** the whole body of a state's ships of war, including crews, maintenance systems, etc. **b** the officers and men of a navy. **2** (in full **navy blue**) a dark blue colour as used in naval uniform. **3** *poet.* a fleet of ships. ● *adj.* (in full **navy blue**; hyphenated when *attrib.*) dark blue. [Middle English, = fleet, via Old French *navie* 'ship, fleet' and Romanic & popular Latin *navia* 'ship' from Latin *navis*]

navy bean *n.* = HARICOT.

Navy Department *n.* (in the US) the government department in charge of the navy.

Navy List *n.* *Brit.* an official list containing the names of all naval officers etc.

navy yard *n.* *US* a government shipyard with civilian labour.

nawab /nəˈwɑːb, -ˈwɔːb/ *n.* **1** the title of a distinguished Muslim in Pakistan. **2** *hist.* the title of a governor or nobleman in India. [Urdu *nawwāb* pl. from Arabic *nā'ib* 'deputy': cf. NABOB]

nay /neɪ/ *adv.* & *n.* ● *adv.* **1** or rather; and even; and more than that (*impressive, nay, magnificent*). **2** *archaic* = NO[2] *adv.* 1. ● *n.* **1** the word 'nay'. **2** a negative vote (*counted 16 nays*). [Middle English from Old Norse *nei*, from *ne* 'not' + *ei* AYE[2]]

naysay /ˈneɪseɪ/ *v.* (*3rd sing. present* **-says**; *past* and *past part.* **-said**) esp. *US* **1** *intr.* utter a denial or refusal. **2** *tr.* refuse or contradict. □ **naysayer** *n.*

Nazarene /ˈnazəriːn, nazəˈriːn/ *n.* & *adj.* ● *n.* **1 a** (prec. by *the*) Christ. **b** (esp. in Jewish or Muslim use) a Christian. **2** a native or inhabitant of Nazareth. **3 a** a member of an early Jewish-Christian sect. **b** a member of a Protestant sect known as the Church of the Nazarene. ● *adj.* of or concerning Nazareth, the Nazarenes, etc. [Middle English via Late Latin *Nazarenus* from Greek *Nazarēnos*, from *Nazaret* 'Nazareth']

Nazarite /ˈnazərʌɪt/ *n.* (also **Nazirite**) *hist.* a Hebrew who had taken certain vows of abstinence; an ascetic (Num. 6). [Late Latin *Nazaraeus* from Hebrew *nāzīr*, from *nāzar* 'to separate or consecrate oneself']

Nazi /ˈnɑːtsi, ˈnɑːzi/ *n.* & *adj.* ● *n.* (*pl.* **Nazis**) **1** *hist.* a member of the German National Socialist party. **2** *derog.* a person holding extreme racist or authoritarian views or behaving brutally. **3** a person belonging to any organization similar to the Nazis. ● *adj.* of or concerning the Nazis, Nazism, etc. □ **Nazidom** *n.* **Nazify** /-fʌɪ/ *v.tr.* (**-ies, -ied**). **Naziism** /-iːɪz(ə)m/ *n.*

Nazism /ˈnɑːtsɪz(ə)m/ *n.* [representing pronunciation of *Nati-* in German *Nationalsozialist*]

NB *abbr.* **1** New Brunswick. **2** *Cricket* no-ball. **3** Scotland (North Britain). **4** *nota bene*.

Nb *symb. Chem.* the element niobium.

NBC *abbr.* (in the US) National Broadcasting Company.

N. by E. *abbr.* North by East.

N. by W. *abbr.* North by West.

NC *abbr.* North Carolina (also in official postal use).

NCB *abbr. hist.* (in the UK) National Coal Board (since 1987 officially called *British Coal*).

NCO *abbr.* non-commissioned officer.

NCP *abbr.* National Car Parks.

NCU *abbr.* (in the UK) National Communications Union.

ND *abbr. US* North Dakota (in official postal use).

Nd *symb. Chem.* the element neodymium.

n.d. *abbr.* no date.

-nd[1] *suffix* forming nouns (*fiend*; *friend*). [Old English *-ond*, originally participial ending]

-nd[2] *suffix* see -AND, -END.

N.Dak. *abbr.* North Dakota.

Ndebele /(ə)ndəˈbiːli, -ˈbeɪli/ *n. & adj.* ● *n.* **1** (*pl.* same or **Ndebeles**) a member of a Nguni people. **2** the Bantu language of this people. ● *adj.* of or relating to this people or their language. [Bantu from Ndebele sing. prefix *n-* + Sesotho (*lè*)*tèbèlè* 'Nguni', from prefix *le-* + *tēbèla* 'drive away']

NE *abbr.* **1** north-east. **2** north-eastern. **3** *US* Nebraska (in official postal use).

Ne *symb. Chem.* the element neon.

né /neɪ/ *adj.* born (indicating a man's previous name) (*Lord Beaconsfield, né Benjamin Disraeli*). [French, past part. of *naître* 'be born': cf. NÉE]

Neanderthal /nɪˈandətɑːl/ *adj.* of or belonging to a type of fossil human widely distributed in palaeolithic Europe, with a retreating forehead and prominent brow-ridges. [*Neanderthal*, a region in Germany where remains were found]

neap /niːp/ *n. & v.* ● *n.* (in full **neap tide**) a tide just after the first and third quarters of the moon when there is least difference between high and low water. ● *v.* **1** *intr.* (of a tide) tend towards or reach the highest point of a neap tide. **2** *tr.* (in *passive*) (of a ship) be kept aground, in harbour, etc., by a neap tide. [Old English *nēpflōd* (cf. FLOOD), of unknown origin]

Neapolitan /nɪəˈpɒlɪt(ə)n/ *n. & adj.* ● *n.* a native or citizen of Naples in Italy. ● *adj.* of or relating to Naples. [Middle English via Latin *Neapolitanus* and Latin *Neapolis* Naples from Greek, from *neos* 'new' + *polis* 'city']

Neapolitan ice cream *n.* ice cream made in layers of different colours.

Neapolitan violet *n.* a sweet-scented double viola.

neap tide see NEAP *n.*

near /nɪə/ *adv., prep., adj., & v.* ● *adv.* **1** (often foll. by *to*) to or at a short distance in space or time; close by (*the time drew near*; *dropped near to them*). **2** closely (*as near as one can guess*). **3** *archaic* almost, nearly (*very near died*). **4** *archaic* parsimoniously; meanly. ● *prep.* (compar. & superl. also used) **1** to or at a short distance (in space, time, condition, or resemblance) from (*stood near the back*; *occurs nearer the end*; *the sun is near setting*). **2** (in *comb.*) **a** that is almost (*near-hysterical*; *a near-Communist*). **b** intended as a substitute for; resembling (*near-beer*). ● *adj.* **1** close at hand; close to, in place or time (*the end is near*; *in the near future*). **2 a** closely related (*a near relation*). **b** intimate (*a near friend*). **3** (of a part of a vehicle, animal, or road) left (*the near foreleg* (originally of the side from which one mounted)) (opp. OFF *adj.* 2). **4** close; narrow (*a near escape*; *a near guess*). **5** (of a road or way) direct. **6** similar (to) (*is nearer the original*). **7** niggardly, mean. ● *v.* **1** *tr.* approach; draw near to (*neared the harbour*). **2** *intr.* draw near (*could distinguish them as they neared*). □ **come** (or **go**) **near** (foll. by verbal noun, or *to* + verbal noun) be on the point of, almost succeed in (*came near to falling*). **go near** (foll. by *to* + infin.) narrowly fail. **near at hand 1** within easy reach. **2** in the immediate future. **nearest and dearest** one's closest friends and relatives collectively. **near the knuckle** *Brit. colloq.* verging on the indecent. **near upon** *archaic* not far in time from. □ **nearish** *adj.* **nearness** *n.* [Middle English from Old Norse *nær*, originally comparative of *ná* = Old English *nēah* NIGH]

nearby *adj. & adv.* ● *adj.* /ˈnɪəbʌɪ/ situated in a near position (*a nearby hotel*). ● *adv.* /nɪəˈbʌɪ/ (also **near by**) close; not far away.

Nearctic /nɪˈɑːktɪk/ *adj. & n.* (also **nearctic**) ● *adj.* of or relating to the Arctic and the temperate parts of N. America as a zoogeographical region. ● *n.* the Nearctic region. [NEO- + ARCTIC]

near-death experience *n.* an out-of-body experience taking place on the brink of death, recounted by a person on recovery.

Near East *n.* (prec. by *the*) **1** = MIDDLE EAST. **2** the Balkans (see BALKAN). □ **Near Eastern** *adj.*

near go *n. Brit. colloq.* a narrow escape.

nearly /ˈnɪəli/ *adv.* **1** almost (*we are nearly there*). **2** closely (*they are nearly related*). □ **not nearly** nothing like; far from (*not nearly enough*).

near miss *n.* **1** a bomb etc. falling close to the target. **2** a situation in which a collision is narrowly avoided. **3** an attempt that is almost but not quite successful.

nearside /ˈnɪəsʌɪd/ *n.* (often *attrib.*) esp. *Brit.* the left side of a vehicle, animal, etc. (cf. OFFSIDE *n.*).

near sight *n.* esp. *US* = SHORT SIGHT.

near-sighted /nɪəˈsʌɪtɪd/ *adj.* esp. *US* = SHORT-SIGHTED. □ **near-sightedly** *adv.* **near-sightedness** *n.*

near thing *n. Brit.* a narrow escape.

neat[1] /niːt/ *adj.* **1** tidy and methodical. **2** elegantly simple in form etc.; well-proportioned. **3** (of language, style, etc.) brief, clear, and pointed; epigrammatic. **4 a** cleverly executed (*a neat piece of work*). **b** deft; dexterous. **5** (of esp. alcoholic liquor) undiluted. **6** *N. Amer. slang* (as a general term of approval) good, pleasing, excellent. □ **neatly** *adv.* **neatness** *n.* [French *net* from Latin *nitidus* 'shining', from *nitēre* 'shine']

neat[2] /niːt/ *n. archaic* **1** a bovine animal. **2** (treated as *pl.*) cattle. [Old English *nēat*, from Germanic]

neaten /ˈniːt(ə)n/ *v.tr.* make neat.

neath /niːθ/ *prep. poet.* beneath. [BENEATH]

neat's-foot oil *n.* oil made from boiled cow-heel and used to dress leather.

NEB *abbr.* **1** (in the UK) National Enterprise Board. **2** New English Bible.

Neb. *abbr.* Nebraska.

neb /nɛb/ *n. Sc. & N.Engl.* **1** a beak or bill. **2** a nose; a snout. **3** a tip, spout, or point. [Old English *nebb*, ultimately from Germanic: cf. NIB]

nebbish /ˈnɛbɪʃ/ *n. & adj. colloq.* ● *n.* a submissive or timid person. ● *adj.* submissive; timid. [Yiddish *nebach* 'poor thing!']

Nebr. *abbr.* Nebraska.

Nebuchadnezzar /ˌnɛbjʊkədˈnɛzə/ *n.* a wine bottle of about 20 times the standard size. [name of a king of Babylon (6th c. BC)]

nebula /ˈnɛbjʊlə/ *n.* (*pl.* **nebulae** /-liː/ or **nebulas**) **1** *Astron.* **a** a cloud of gas and dust, sometimes glowing and sometimes appearing as a dark silhouette against other glowing matter. **b** a bright area caused by a galaxy, or a large cloud of distant stars. **2** *Med.* a clouded spot on the cornea causing defective vision. [Latin, = mist]

nebular /ˈnɛbjʊlə/ *adj.* of or relating to a nebula or nebulae.

nebular theory *n.* (also **nebular hypothesis**) the theory that the solar and stellar systems were developed from a primeval nebula.

nebulizer /ˈnɛbjʊlʌɪzə/ *n.* (also **-iser**) a device for producing a fine spray of liquid. □ **nebulize** *v.tr.* (also **-ise**). [Latin *nebula* 'mist' + -IZER (see -IZE)]

nebulous /'nɛbjʊləs/ *adj.* **1** cloudlike. **2 a** formless, clouded. **b** hazy, indistinct, vague (*put forward a few nebulous ideas*). **3** *Astron.* of or like a nebula or nebulae. □ **nebulosity** /-'lɒsɪti/ *n.* **nebulously** *adv.* **nebulousness** *n.* [Middle English from French *nébuleux* or Latin *nebulosus* (as NEBULA)]

nebulous star *n.* a small cluster of indistinct stars, or a star in a luminous haze.

nebuly /'nɛbjʊli/ *adj. Heraldry* wavy in form; cloudlike. [French *nébulé* via medieval Latin *nebulatus* from Latin NEBULA]

NEC *abbr.* National Executive Committee.

necessarian /nɛsɪ'sɛːrɪən/ *n. & adj.* = NECESSITARIAN. □ **necessarianism** *n.*

necessarily /'nɛsəs(ə)rɪli, -'sɛrɪli/ *adv.* as a necessary result; inevitably.

necessary /'nɛsəs(ə)ri/ *adj. & n.* ● *adj.* **1** requiring to be done, achieved, etc.; requisite, essential (*it is necessary to work*; *lacks the necessary documents*). **2** determined, existing, or happening by natural laws, predestination, etc., not by free will; inevitable (*mathematically necessary*). **3** *Philos.* (of a concept or a mental process) inevitably resulting from or produced by the nature of things etc., so that the contrary is impossible. **4** *Philos.* (of an agent) having no independent volition. ● *n.* (*pl.* **-ies**) (usu. in *pl.*) any of the basic requirements of life, such as food, warmth, etc. □ **the necessary** *colloq.* **1** *Brit.* money. **2** an action, item, etc., needed for a purpose (*they will do the necessary*). [Middle English via Old French *necessaire* from Latin *necessarius*, from *necesse* 'needful']

necessitarian /nɪˌsɛsɪ'tɛːrɪən/ *n. & adj. Philos.* ● *n.* a person who holds that all action is predetermined and free will is impossible (opp. LIBERTARIAN *n.* 2). ● *adj.* of or concerning such a person or theory. □ **necessitarianism** *n.*

necessitate /nɪ'sɛsɪteɪt/ *v.tr.* **1** make necessary (esp. as a result) (*will necessitate some sacrifice*). **2** (usu. foll. by *to* + infin.) *US* force or compel (a person) to do something. [medieval Latin *necessitare* 'compel' (as NECESSITY)]

necessitous /nɪ'sɛsɪtəs/ *adj.* poor; needy. [French *nécessiteux*, or from NECESSITY + -OUS]

necessity /nɪ'sɛsɪti/ *n.* (*pl.* **-ies**) **1 a** an indispensable thing; a necessary (*central heating is a necessity*). **b** (usu. foll. by *of*) indispensability (*the necessity of a warm overcoat*). **2** a state of things or circumstances enforcing a certain course (*there was a necessity to hurry*). **3** imperative need (*necessity is the mother of invention*). **4** want; poverty; hardship (*stole because of necessity*). **5** constraint or compulsion regarded as a natural law governing all human action. □ **of necessity** unavoidably. [Middle English via Old French *necessité* from Latin *necessitas -tatis*, from *necesse* 'needful']

neck /nɛk/ *n. & v.* ● *n.* **1 a** the part of the body connecting the head to the shoulders. **b** the part of a shirt, dress, etc. round or close to the neck. **2 a** something resembling a neck, such as the narrow part of a cavity or vessel, a passage, channel, pass, isthmus, etc. **b** the narrow part of a bottle near the mouth. **3** the part of a violin etc. bearing the fingerboard. **4** the length of a horse's head and neck as a measure of its lead in a race. **5** the flesh of an animal's neck (*neck of lamb*). **6** *Geol.* solidified lava or igneous rock in an old volcano crater or pipe. **7** *Archit.* the lower part of a capital. **8** *Brit. slang* impudence (*you've got a neck, asking that*). ● *v.* **1** *intr. & tr. colloq.* kiss and caress amorously. **2 a** *tr.* form a narrowed part in. **b** *intr.* form a narrowed part. □ **get it in the neck** *colloq.* **1** receive a severe reprimand or punishment. **2** suffer a fatal or severe blow. **neck and neck** running level in a race etc. **neck or nothing** risking everything on success. **up to one's neck** (often foll. by *in*) *colloq.* very deeply involved; very busy. □ **necked** *adj.* (also in *comb.*). **necker** *n.* (in sense 1 of *v.*). **neckless** *adj.* [Old English *hnecca*, ultimately from Germanic]

neckband /'nɛkband/ *n.* a strip of material round the neck of a garment.

neckcloth /'nɛkklɒθ/ *n. hist.* a cravat.

neckerchief /'nɛkətʃɪf/ *n.* a square of cloth worn round the neck.

necking /'nɛkɪŋ/ *n. Archit.* = NECK *n.* 7.

necklace /'nɛklɪs/ *n. & v.* ● *n.* **1** a chain or string of beads, precious stones, links, etc., worn as an ornament round the neck. **2** *S.Afr.* a tyre soaked or filled with petrol, placed round a victim's neck, and set alight. ● *v.tr. S.Afr.* kill with a 'necklace'.

necklet /'nɛklɪt/ *n.* **1** = NECKLACE *n.* 1. **2** a strip of fur worn round the neck.

neckline /'nɛklʌɪn/ *n.* the edge or shape of the opening of a garment at the neck (*a square neckline*).

neck of the woods *n. colloq.* a locality, esp. *Brit.* a remote one.

necktie /'nɛktʌɪ/ *n.* esp. *US* = TIE *n.* 2.

necktie party *n. slang* a lynching or hanging.

neckwear /'nɛkwɛː/ *n.* collars, ties, etc.

necro- /'nɛkrəʊ/ *comb. form* corpse. [from or suggested by Greek *nekro-* from *nekros* 'corpse']

necrobiosis /nɛkrə(ʊ)bʌɪ'əʊsɪs/ *n.* decay in the tissues of the body, esp. swelling of the collagen bundles in the dermis. □ **necrobiotic** /-'ɒtɪk/ *adj.*

necrolatry /nɛ'krɒlətri/ *n.* worship of, or excessive reverence towards, the dead.

necrology /nɛ'krɒlədʒi/ *n.* (*pl.* **-ies**) **1** a list of recently dead people. **2** an obituary notice. □ **necrological** /-rə'lɒdʒɪk(ə)l/ *adj.*

necromancy /'nɛkrə(ʊ)mansi/ *n.* **1** the prediction of the future by the supposed communication with the dead. **2** witchcraft. □ **necromancer** *n.* **necromantic** /-'mantɪk/ *adj.* [Middle English via Old French *nigromancie* from medieval Latin *nigromantia*, changed (by association with Latin *niger nigri* 'black') from Late Latin *necromantia*, from Greek *nekromanteia* (as NECRO-, -MANCY)]

necrophilia /nɛkrə(ʊ)'fɪlɪə/ *n.* (also **necrophily** /nɛ'krɒfɪli/) a morbid and esp. erotic attraction to corpses. □ **necrophile** /'nɛkrəfʌɪl/ *n.* **necrophiliac** /-'fɪlɪak/ *n.* **necrophilic** *adj.* **necrophilism** /-'krɒfɪlɪz(ə)m/ *n.* **necrophilist** /-'krɒfɪlɪst/ *n.* [NECRO- + Greek *-philia* 'loving']

necrophobia /nɛkrə(ʊ)'fəʊbɪə/ *n.* an abnormal fear of death or dead bodies. [NECRO- + PHOBIA]

necropolis /nɛ'krɒpəlɪs/ *n.* an ancient cemetery or burial place. [Greek, formed as NECRO- + *polis* 'city']

necropsy /'nɛkrɒpsi, nɛ'krɒpsi/ *n.* (also **necroscopy** /-'krɒskəpi/) (*pl.* **-ies**) = AUTOPSY 1. [NECRO-, on the pattern of AUTOPSY, or + -SCOPY]

necrosis /nɛ'krəʊsɪs/ *n. Med. & Physiol.* the death of tissue caused by disease or injury, esp. as one of the symptoms of gangrene or pulmonary tuberculosis. □ **necrotic** /-'krɒtɪk/ *adj.* **necrotize** /'nɛkrətʌɪz/ *v.intr.* (also **-ise**). [modern Latin from Greek *nekrōsis* (as NECRO-, -OSIS)]

nectar /'nɛktə/ *n.* **1** a sugary substance produced by plants to attract pollinating insects and made into honey by bees. **2** (in Greek and Roman mythology) the drink of the gods. **3** a drink compared to this. □ **nectarean** /-'tɛːrɪən/ *adj.* **nectareous** /-'tɛːrɪəs/ *adj.* **nectariferous** /-'rɪf(ə)rəs/ *adj.* **nectarous** *adj.* [Latin from Greek *nektar*]

nectarine /'nɛktərɪn, -iːn/ *n.* **1** a variety of peach with a thin brightly coloured smooth skin and firm flesh. **2** the tree bearing this. [originally as *adj.*, = nectar-like, from NECTAR + -INE[4]]

nectary /'nɛkt(ə)ri/ *n.* (*pl.* **-ies**) the nectar-secreting organ of a flower or plant. [modern Latin *nectarium* (as NECTAR)]

NEDC *abbr. hist.* (in the UK) National Economic Development Council.

neddy /'nɛdi/ *n.* (*pl.* **-ies**) *Brit. colloq.* **1** a donkey. **2** (**Neddy**) *hist.* = NEDC. [diminutive of *Ned*, pet form of the name *Edward*]

née /neɪ/ *adj.* (*US* also **nee**) (used in adding a married woman's maiden name after her surname) born (*Mrs Ann Smith, née Jones*). [French, fem. past part. of *naître* 'be born']

need /ni:d/ *v. & n.* ● *v.* **1** *tr.* stand in want of; require (*needs a new coat*). **2** *tr.* (foll. by *to* + infin.; *3rd sing. present neg. or interrog.* **need** without *to*) be under the necessity or obligation (*it needs to be done carefully*; *he need not come*; *need you ask?*). **3** *intr. archaic* be necessary. ● *n.* **1 a** a want or requirement (*my needs are few*; *the need for greater freedom*). **b** a thing wanted (*my greatest need is a car*). **2** circumstances requiring some course of action; necessity (*there is no need to worry*; *if need arise*). **3** destitution; poverty. **4** a crisis; an emergency (*failed them in their need*). □ **at need** in time of need. **had need** *archaic* ought to (*had need remember*). **have need of** require; want. **have need to** require to (*has need to be warned*). **in need** requiring help. **in need of** requiring. **need not have** did not need to (but did). [Old English *nēodian, nēd*, from Germanic]

needful /'ni:dfʊl, -f(ə)l/ *adj.* **1** requisite; necessary; indispensable. **2** (prec. by *the*) **a** what is necessary. **b** *colloq.* money or action needed for a purpose. □ **needfully** *adv.* **needfulness** *n.*

needle /'ni:d(ə)l/ *n. & v.* ● *n.* **1 a** a very thin small piece of smooth steel etc. pointed at one end and with a slit (eye) for thread at the other, used in sewing. **b** a larger plastic, wooden, etc. slender stick without an eye, used in knitting. **c** a slender hooked stick used in crochet. **2** a pointer on a dial (see MAGNETIC NEEDLE). **3** any of several small thin pointed instruments, esp.: **a** a surgical instrument for stitching. **b** the end of a hypodermic syringe. **c** = STYLUS 1. **d** an etching tool. **e** a steel pin exploding the cartridge of a breech-loading gun. **4 a** an obelisk (*Cleopatra's Needle*). **b** a pointed rock or peak. **5** the leaf of a fir or pine tree. **6** a beam used as a temporary support during underpinning. **7** (usu. prec. by *the*) *Brit. slang* a fit of bad temper or nervousness (*got the needle while waiting*). ● *v.tr.* **1** *colloq.* incite or irritate; provoke (*refused to be needled by him*). **2** sew, pierce, or operate on with a needle. □ **needle in a haystack** something almost impossible to find because it is concealed by so many other similar things. [Old English *nǣdl*, from Germanic]

needlecord /'ni:d(ə)lkɔ:d/ *n. Brit.* a fine-ribbed corduroy fabric.

needlecraft /'ni:d(ə)lkrɑ:ft/ *n.* skill in needlework.

needlefish /'ni:d(ə)lfɪʃ/ *n.* (*pl.* usu. same) a garfish.

needleful /'ni:d(ə)lfʊl, -f(ə)l/ *n.* (*pl.* **-fuls**) the length of thread etc. put into a needle at one time.

needle game *n.* (also **needle match** etc.) *Brit.* a contest that is very close or arouses personal grudges.

needle-lace *n.* lace made with needles not bobbins.

needlepoint /'ni:d(ə)lpɔɪnt/ *n.* **1** a very sharp point. **2** = NEEDLE-LACE. **3** = GROS POINT OR PETIT POINT 1.

needle's eye *n.* (also **eye of a needle**) the least possible aperture, esp. with reference to Matt. 19:24.

needless /'ni:dlɪs/ *adj.* **1** unnecessary. **2** uncalled for; gratuitous. □ **needless to say** of course; it goes without saying. □ **needlessly** *adv.* **needlessness** *n.*

needle time *n. Brit.* an agreed maximum allowance of time for broadcasting recorded music, originally music from records.

needle valve *n.* a valve closed by a thin tapering part.

needlewoman /'ni:d(ə)lwʊmən/ *n.* (*pl.* **-women**) **1** a seamstress. **2** a woman or girl with specified sewing skill (*a good needlewoman*).

needlework /'ni:d(ə)lwə:k/ *n.* sewing or embroidery.

needn't /'ni:d(ə)nt/ *contr.* need not.

needs /ni:dz/ *adv.* (usu. prec. or foll. by *must*) *archaic* of necessity (*must needs decide*). [Old English *nēdes* (as NEED, -s^3)]

needy /'ni:di/ *adj.* (**needier, neediest**) **1** (of a person) poor; destitute. **2** (of circumstances) characterized by poverty. □ **neediness** *n.*

neem /ni:m/ *n.* a tree, *Azadirachta indica* (mahogany family), whose leaves and bark are used medicinally in the Indian subcontinent. [Hindi *nīm*]

neep /ni:p/ *n. Sc. & N.Engl.* a turnip, now esp. a swede. [Old English *nǣp* from Latin *napus*]

ne'er /nɛ:/ *adv. poet.* = NEVER. [Middle English contraction of NEVER]

ne'er-do-well *n. & adj.* ● *n.* a good-for-nothing person. ● *adj.* good-for-nothing.

nefarious /nɪ'fɛ:rɪəs/ *adj.* wicked; iniquitous. □ **nefariously** *adv.* **nefariousness** *n.* [Latin *nefarius* from *nefas* 'wrong', from *ne-* 'not' + *fas* 'divine law']

neg /nɛg/ *n. colloq.* a photographic negative.

neg. *abbr.* negative.

negate /nɪ'geɪt/ *v.tr.* **1** nullify, make ineffective, invalidate, destroy. **2** deny, deny the existence of. **3** *Gram.* make (a clause, sentence, etc.) negative in meaning. [Latin *negare negat-* 'deny']

negation /nɪ'geɪʃ(ə)n/ *n.* **1** (often foll. by *of*) **a** the act of contradicting or denying a statement or allegation; the act of refusing. **b** an instance of this; a contradiction, denial, or refusal; a negative statement or doctrine. **2** the absence or opposite of something actual or positive (*death is the negation of life*). **3** *Gram.* **a** the grammatical process by which the truth of a clause or sentence is denied, involving the use of a negative word, e.g. *not, no, never*. **b** an instance of this. **4** a negative or unreal thing; a nonentity. **5** *Logic* the assertion that a certain proposition is false. □ **negatory** /'nɛgət(ə)ri/ *adj.* [French *negation* or Latin *negatio* (as NEGATE)]

negative /'nɛgətɪv/ *adj., n., & v.* ● *adj.* **1** expressing or implying denial, prohibition, or refusal (*a negative vote*; *a negative answer*). **2** (of a person or attitude): **a** lacking positive attributes; apathetic; pessimistic. **b** opposing or resisting; uncooperative. **3** marked by the absence of qualities (*a negative reaction*; *a negative result from the test*). **4** of the opposite nature to a thing regarded as positive (*debt is negative capital*). **5** *Gram.* (of a word, clause, etc.) expressing negation. **6** (of a quantity) less than zero, to be subtracted from others or from zero (opp. POSITIVE *adj.* 9). **7** *Electr.* **a** of the kind of charge carried by electrons (opp. POSITIVE *adj.* 10). **b** containing or producing such a charge. **8** *Logic* expressing negation or denial of a proposition. ● *n.* **1** a negative statement or reply (*hard to prove a negative*). **2** *Photog.* **a** an image with black and white reversed or colours replaced by complementary ones, from which positive pictures are obtained. **b** a developed film or plate bearing such an image. **3** *Gram.* = NEGATOR 2. **4** (prec. by *the*) the side or aspect of a question which is opposed to the affirmative or positive. **5** a negative quality or characteristic. **6** *Logic* = NEGATION 5. ● *v.tr.* **1** refuse to accept or countenance; veto; reject. **2** disprove (an inference or hypothesis). **3** contradict (a statement). **4** neutralize (an effect). □ **in the negative** with negative effect; so as to reject a proposal etc.; no (*the answer was in the negative*). □ **negatively** *adv.* **negativeness** *n.* **negativity** /-'tɪvɪti/ *n.* [Middle English from Old French *negatif -ive* or Late Latin *negativus* (as NEGATE)]

negative equity *n.* the indebtedness arising when the market value of a property falls below the outstanding amount of a mortgage secured on it.

negative evidence *n.* evidence of the non-occurrence of something.

negative feedback *n.* **1** the return of part of an output signal to the input, tending to decrease the amplification etc. **2** esp. *Biol.* the diminution or counteraction of an effect by its own influence on the process giving rise to it. **3** a negative response to a questionnaire, an experiment, etc.

negative geotropism *n.* the tendency of stems etc. to grow away from the centre of the earth.

negative income tax *n.* an amount credited as allowance to a taxed income, and paid as benefit when it exceeds debited tax.

negative instance *n.* = NEGATIVE EVIDENCE.

negative pole *n.* the south-seeking pole of a magnet.

negative prescription *n.* the time limit within which an action or claim can be raised.

negative proposition *n. Logic* = NEGATION 5.

negative quantity *n. joc.* nothing.

negative sign *n.* a symbol (−) indicating subtraction or a value less than zero.

negative virtue *n.* abstention from vice.

negativism /ˈnɛgətɪvɪz(ə)m/ *n.* **1** a negative position or attitude; extreme scepticism, criticism, etc. **2** denial of accepted beliefs. □ **negativist** *n.* **negativistic** /-ˈvɪstɪk/ *adj.*

negator /nɪˈgeɪtə/ *n.* **1** a person who denies something. **2** *Gram.* a word or particle expressing negation, e.g. *not, don't.*

neglect /nɪˈglɛkt/ *v. & n.* ● *v.tr.* **1** fail to care for or to do; be remiss about (*neglected their duty*; *neglected his children*). **2** (foll. by verbal noun, or *to* + infin.) fail; overlook or forget the need to (*neglected to inform them*; *neglected telling them*). **3** not pay attention to; disregard (*neglected the obvious warning*). ● *n.* **1** lack of caring; negligence (*the house suffered from neglect*). **2 a** the act of neglecting. **b** the state of being neglected (*the house fell into neglect*). **3** (usu. foll. by *of*) disregard. □ **neglectful** *adj.* **neglectfully** *adv.* **neglectfulness** *n.* [Latin *neglegere neglect-*, from *neg-* 'not' + *legere* 'choose, pick up']

negligée /ˈnɛglɪʒeɪ/ *n.* (also **negligee**, **néglige**) **1** (usu. **negligee**) a woman's dressing gown of thin fabric. **2** unceremonious or informal attire. [French, past part. of *négliger* NEGLECT]

negligence /ˈnɛglɪdʒ(ə)ns/ *n.* **1 a** a lack of proper care and attention; carelessness. **b** an act of carelessness. **2** *Law* = CONTRIBUTORY NEGLIGENCE. **3** *Art* freedom from restraint or artificiality. □ **negligent** *adj.* **negligently** *adv.* [Middle English via Old French *negligence* or Latin *negligentia* from *negligere* = *neglegere*: see NEGLECT]

negligible /ˈnɛglɪdʒɪb(ə)l/ *adj.* not worth considering; insignificant. □ **negligibility** /-ˈbɪlɪti/ *n.* **negligibly** *adv.* [obsolete French from *négliger* NEGLECT]

negligible quantity *n.* a person etc. that need not be considered.

negotiable /nɪˈgəʊʃəb(ə)l, -ʃɪə-/ *adj.* **1** open to discussion or modification. **2** able to be negotiated. □ **negotiability** /-ˈbɪlɪti/ *n.*

negotiate /nɪˈgəʊʃɪeɪt/ *v.* **1** *intr.* (usu. foll. by *with*) confer with others in order to reach a compromise or agreement. **2** *tr.* arrange (a matter) or bring about (a result) by negotiating (*negotiated a settlement*). **3** *tr.* find a way over, through, etc. (an obstacle, difficulty, fence, etc.). **4** *tr.* **a** transfer (a cheque etc.) to another for a consideration. **b** convert (a cheque etc.) into cash or notes. **c** get or give value for (a cheque etc.) in money. □ **negotiant** /-ʃɪənt/ *n.* **negotiation** /-ʃɪˈeɪʃ(ə)n/ *n.* **negotiator** *n.* [Latin *negotiari* from *negotium* 'business', from *neg-* 'not' + *otium* 'leisure']

Negress /ˈniːgrɪs/ *n.* a female Negro.

■ **Usage** The term *Negress* is now often considered offensive; *black* is usually preferred.

Negrillo /nɪˈgrɪləʊ/ *n.* (*pl.* **-os**) a member of a very small Negroid people native to central and southern Africa. [Spanish, diminutive of NEGRO]

Negrito /nɪˈgriːtəʊ/ *n.* (*pl.* **-os**) a member of a small Negroid people native to the Austronesian region. [as NEGRILLO]

Negritude /ˈnɛgrɪtjuːd/ *n.* **1** the quality or state of being black. **2** the affirmation or consciousness of the value of black culture. [French *négritude* NIGRITUDE]

Negro /ˈniːgrəʊ/ *n. & adj.* ● *n.* (*pl.* **-oes**) a member of a dark-skinned race originally native to Africa. ● *adj.* of or concerning Negroes. [Spanish & Portuguese, from Latin *niger nigri* 'black']

■ **Usage** The term *Negro* is now often considered offensive; *black* is usually preferred.

negro /ˈniːgrəʊ/ *adj. Zool.* black or dark (*negro ant*). [NEGRO]

Negroid /ˈniːgrɔɪd/ *adj. & n.* ● *adj.* **1** (of features etc.) characteristic of a black person of African ethnic origin, esp. in having dark skin, tightly curled hair, and a broad flattish nose. **2** of or concerning blacks. ● *n.* a black person. [NEGRO]

Negro spiritual *n.* a religious song derived from the musical traditions of black people in the southern US.

Negus /ˈniːgəs/ *n. hist.* the title of the ruler of Ethiopia. [Amharic *n'gus* 'king']

negus /ˈniːgəs/ *n. hist.* a hot drink of port, sugar, lemon, and spice. [named after Col. F. *Negus* (d. 1732), its inventor]

Neh. *abbr.* Nehemiah (Old Testament).

neigh /neɪ/ *n. & v.* ● *n.* **1** the high whinnying sound of a horse. **2** any similar sound, e.g. a laugh. ● *v.* **1** *intr.* make such a sound. **2** *tr.* say, cry, etc. with such a sound. [Old English *hnægan*, of imitative origin]

neighbour /ˈneɪbə/ *n. & v.* (*US* **neighbor**) ● *n.* **1** a person living next door to or near or nearest another (*my next-door neighbour*; *they are neighbours*; *his nearest neighbour is 12 miles away*). **2 a** a person regarded as having the duties or claims of friendliness, consideration, etc., of a neighbour. **b** a fellow human being, esp. as having claims on friendship. **3** a person or thing near or next to another (*my neighbour at dinner*). **4** (*attrib.*) neighbouring. ● *v.* **1** *tr.* border on; adjoin. **2** *intr.* (often foll. by *on, upon*) border; adjoin. □ **neighbouring** *adj.* **neighbourless** *adj.* **neighbourship** *n.* [Old English *nēahgebūr*, from *neah* NIGH + *gebūr*, a tenant farmer, cf. BOOR]

neighbourhood /ˈneɪbəhʊd/ *n.* (*US* **neighborhood**) **1 a** a district, esp. one forming a community within a town or city. **b** the people of a district; one's neighbours. **2** neighbourly feeling or conduct. □ **in the neighbourhood of** roughly; about (*paid in the neighbourhood of £100*).

neighbourhood watch *n.* systematic local vigilance by householders to discourage crime, esp. against property.

neighbourly /ˈneɪbəli/ *adj.* (*US* **neighborly**) characteristic of a good neighbour; friendly; kind. □ **neighbourliness** *n.*

neither /ˈnʌɪðə, ˈniː-/ *det., pron., adv., & conj.* ● *det. & pron.* (with a sing. verb) not the one nor the other (of two things); not either (*neither wish was granted*; *neither of the accusations is true*; *neither of them knows*; *neither went to the fair*). ● *adv.* **1** not either; not on the one hand (foll. by *nor*; introducing the first of two or more things in the negative: *neither knowing nor caring*; *would neither come in nor go out*; *neither the teachers nor the parents nor the children*). **2** not either; also not (*if you do not, neither shall I*). **3** (with *neg.*) *disp.* either (*I don't know that neither*). ● *conj. archaic* nor yet; nor (*I know not, neither can I guess*). [Middle English *naither, neither* from Old English *nowther*, contraction of *nōhwæther* (as NO², WHETHER): assimilated to EITHER]

■ **Usage** It is generally considered wrong to use *neither* instead of *either* in sense 3 of the adverb to strengthen a preceding negative. A double negative, though standard in languages such as Spanish, is unacceptable in standard English.

nek /nɛk/ *n. S.Afr.* = COL 1. [Dutch, = NECK]

nekton /ˈnɛkt(ə)n, -tɒn/ *n. Zool.* aquatic animals able to swim and move independently (cf. PLANKTON). [German from Greek *nēkton*, neut. of *nēktos* 'swimming', from *nēkhō* 'swim']

nelly /ˈnɛli/ *n.* (*pl.* **-ies**) a silly or effeminate person. □ **not on your nelly** *Brit. slang* certainly not. [perhaps from the name *Nelly*: idiom from rhyming slang *Nelly Duff* = puff = breath: cf. *not on your life*]

nelson /ˈnɛls(ə)n/ *n.* a wrestling hold in which one arm is passed under the opponent's arm from behind and the hand is applied to the neck (**half nelson**), or both arms and hands are applied (**full nelson**). [apparently from the name *Nelson*]

Nelson touch *n.* (prec. by *the*) *Brit.* a masterly or sympathetic approach to a problem. [from H. *Nelson* (d. 1805), British Admiral at Trafalgar]

nelumbo /nɪˈlʌmbəʊ/ *n.* (*pl.* **-os**) = LOTUS 2a. [modern Latin from Sinhalese *neḷum(bu)*]

nematic /nɪˈmatɪk/ *adj. & n.* ● *adj.* designating or involving a state of a liquid crystal in which the molecules are oriented in parallel but not arranged in well-defined planes (cf. SMECTIC). ● *n.* a nematic substance. [Greek *nēma nēmat-* 'thread' + -IC]

nematocyst /nɪˈmatə(ʊ)sɪst, ˈnɛmət-/ *n.* a specialized cell in the tentacles of a jellyfish or other coelenterate, containing a barbed or venomous coiled thread that can be projected in self-defence or to capture prey. [as NEMATIC + CYST]

nematode /ˈnɛmətəʊd/ *n.* any parasitic or free-living worm of the phylum Nematoda, with a slender unsegmented cylindrical shape. Also called ROUNDWORM. [Greek *nēma nēmat-* 'thread' + -ODE[1]]

Nembutal /ˈnɛmbjʊt(ə)l, -tɑːl/ *n. propr.* a sodium salt of pentobarbitone, used as a sedative and anticonvulsant. [*Na* (= sodium) + ETHYL, METHYL, BUTYL (elements of the systematic name) + -AL]

nem. con. /nɛm ˈkɒn/ *abbr.* with no one dissenting. [Latin *nemine contradicente*]

nemertean /nɪˈməːtɪən, nɛməˈtiːən, ˈnɛmətiːn/ *n. & adj.* (also **nemertine** /-tʌɪn/) ● *n.* any aquatic worm of the phylum Nemertea, often very long, brightly coloured, and tangled into knots, found in coastal waters of Europe and the Mediterranean. Also called *ribbon worm.* ● *adj.* of or relating to this phylum. [modern Latin *Nemertes* from Greek *Nēmertēs*, the name of a sea nymph]

nemesia /nɪˈmiːʒə/ *n.* any S. African plant of the genus *Nemesia*, cultivated for its variously coloured and irregular flowers. [modern Latin from Greek *nemesion*, the name of a similar plant]

nemesis /ˈnɛmɪsɪs/ *n.* (*pl.* **nemeses** /-ˌsiːz/) **1** retributive justice. **2 a** a downfall caused by this. **b** an agent of such a downfall. [Greek, = righteous indignation, personified as goddess of retribution, from *nemō* 'give what is due']

neo- /ˈniːəʊ/ *comb. form* **1** new, modern. **2** a new or revived form of. [Greek from *neos* 'new']

neoclassical /niːəʊˈklasɪk(ə)l/ *adj.* (also **neoclassic** /-sɪk/) of or relating to a revival of a classical style or treatment in art, literature, music, etc. ▫ **neoclassicism** /-sɪz(ə)m/ *n.* **neoclassicist** /-sɪst/ *n.*

neocolonialism /ˌniːəʊkəˈləʊnɪəlɪz(ə)m/ *n.* the use of economic, political, or other pressures to control or influence other countries, esp. former dependencies. ▫ **neocolonialist** *n. & adj.*

Neo-Darwinian /ˌniːəʊdɑːˈwɪnɪən/ *adj. & n.* ● *adj.* of or relating to the modern version of Darwin's theory of evolution by natural selection, incorporating the findings of genetics. ● *n.* an adherent of this theory. ▫ **Neo-Darwinism** /niːəʊˈdɑː-/ *n.* **Neo-Darwinist** /niːəʊˈdɑː-/ *n.*

neodymium /niːə(ʊ)ˈdɪmɪəm/ *n. Chem.* a silver-grey naturally occurring metallic element of the lanthanide series used in colouring glass etc. (symbol **Nd**). [NEO- + DIDYMIUM]

neo-fascist /niːəʊˈfaʃɪst/ *n. & adj.* ● *n.* a person belonging to an organization based on the Italian Fascist movement of the early 20th century. ● *adj.* of or relating to neo-fascists or neo-fascism. ▫ **neo-fascism** *n.*

neo-Georgian /niːəʊˈdʒɔːdʒ(ə)n/ *adj.* of or relating to a revival of a Georgian style in architecture. [GEORGIAN[1]]

neolithic /niːə(ʊ)ˈlɪθɪk/ *adj. & n. Archaeol.* ● *adj.* of or relating to the later Stone Age, when ground or polished stone weapons and implements prevailed. ● *n.* the neolithic period. [NEO- + Greek *lithos* 'stone']

neologism /nɪˈɒlədʒɪz(ə)m/ *n.* **1** a new word or expression. **2** the coining or use of new words. ▫ **neologist** *n.* **neologize** /-dʒʌɪz/ *v.intr.* (also **-ise**). [French *néologisme* (as NEO-, -LOGY, -ISM)]

neomycin /niːəʊˈmʌɪsɪn/ *n.* an antibiotic related to streptomycin.

neon /ˈniːɒn/ *n. Chem.* an inert gaseous element occurring in traces in the atmosphere and giving an orange glow when electricity is passed through it in a sealed low-pressure tube, used in lights and illuminated advertisements (*neon light*; *neon sign*) (symbol **Ne**). [Greek, neut. of *neos* 'new']

neonate /ˈniːə(ʊ)neɪt/ *n.* a newborn child (or mammal). ▫ **neonatal** /-ˈneɪt(ə)l/ *adj.* [modern Latin *neonatus* (as NEO-, Latin *nasci nat-* 'be born')]

neo-Nazi /niːə(ʊ)ˈnɑːtsi, -ˈnɑːzi/ *n. & adj.* ● *n.* (*pl.* **neo-Nazis**) a person belonging to an organization based on or deriving from the German National Socialist Party, or holding extreme racist views. ● *adj.* of or relating to neo-Nazis or neo-Nazism. ▫ **neo-Nazism** *n.*

neophobia /niːəʊˈfəʊbɪə/ *n.* a fear or dislike of what is new.

neophyte /ˈniːə(ʊ)fʌɪt/ *n.* **1** a new convert, esp. to a religious faith. **2** *RC Ch.* **a** a novice of a religious order. **b** a newly ordained priest. **3** a beginner; a novice. [ecclesiastical Latin *neophytus* from NT Greek *neophutos* 'newly planted' (as NEO- *phuton* 'plant')]

neoplasm /ˈniːə(ʊ)plaz(ə)m/ *n.* a new and abnormal growth of tissue in some part of the body, esp. a tumour. ▫ **neoplastic** /-ˈplastɪk/ *adj.* [NEO- + Greek *plasma* 'formation': see PLASMA]

Neoplatonism /niːəʊˈpleɪt(ə)nɪz(ə)m/ *n.* a philosophical and religious system developed by the followers of Plotinus in the third c., combining Platonic thought with oriental mysticism. ▫ **Neoplatonic** /-pləˈtɒnɪk/ *adj.* **Neoplatonist** *n.*

neoprene /ˈniːə(ʊ)priːn/ *n.* a synthetic rubber-like polymer. [NEO- + *prene* on the pattern of *chloroprene* etc. (perhaps from PROPYL + -ENE)]

neoteny /niːˈɒt(ə)ni/ *n. Zool.* **1** the retention of juvenile features in the adult; paedomorphosis. **2** sexual maturity of an animal still in a larval stage, e.g. an axolotl. ▫ **neotenic** /-ˈtɛnɪk/ *adj.* **neotenous** *adj.* [German *Neotenie* (as NEO- + Greek *teinō* 'extend')]

neoteric /niːə(ʊ)ˈtɛrɪk/ *adj. literary* recent; newfangled; modern. [Late Latin *neotericus* from Greek *neōterikos* from *neōteros*, comparative of *neos* 'new']

neotropical /niːəʊˈtrɒpɪk(ə)l/ *adj.* of or relating to tropical and S. America as a biogeographical region.

Nepalese /nɛpəˈliːz, -pɔː-/ *adj. & n.* (*pl.* same) = NEPALI.

Nepali /nɪˈpɔːli, -ˈpɑːli/ *n. & adj.* ● *n.* (*pl.* same or **Nepalis**) **1 a** a native or national of Nepal in central Asia. **b** a person of Nepali descent. **2** the language of Nepal. ● *adj.* of or relating to Nepal or its language or people.

nepenthe /nɪˈpɛnθi/ *n. poet.* = NEPENTHES 1. [variant of NEPENTHES, after Italian *nepente*]

nepenthes /nɪˈpɛnθiːz/ *n.* **1** *poet.* a drug causing forgetfulness of grief. **2** any pitcher plant of the genus *Nepenthes*. [Latin from Greek *nēpenthes* (*pharmakon* 'drug'), neut. of *nēpenthēs*, from *nē-* 'not' + *penthos* 'grief']

nephelometer /nɛfəˈlɒmɪtə/ *n.* an instrument for measuring the size and concentration of particles suspended in a liquid or gas, esp. by means of the light they scatter. [Greek *nephelē* 'cloud' + -METER]

nephew /ˈnɛfjuː, ˈnɛvjuː/ *n.* a son of one's brother or sister, or of one's brother-in-law or sister-in-law. [Middle English via Old French *neveu* from Latin *nepos nepotis* 'grandson, nephew']

nephology /nɪˈfɒlədʒi/ *n.* the study of clouds. [Greek *nephos* 'cloud' + -LOGY]

nephrite /ˈnɛfrʌɪt/ *n.* a green, yellow, or white calcium magnesium silicate form of jade. [German *Nephrit* from Greek *nephros* 'kidney', with reference to its supposed efficacy in treating kidney disease]

nephritic /nɪˈfrɪtɪk/ *adj.* **1** of or in the kidneys; renal. **2** of or relating to nephritis. [Late Latin *nephriticus* from Greek *nephritikos* (as NEPHRITIS)]

nephritis /nɪˈfrʌɪtɪs/ *n.* inflammation of the kidneys. Also called *Bright's disease.* [Late Latin from Greek *nephros* 'kidney']

nephro- /ˈnɛfrəʊ/ *comb. form* (usu. **nephr-** before a vowel) kidney. [Greek from *nephros* 'kidney']

ne plus ultra /neɪ plʊs ˈʊltrɑː/ *n.* **1** the furthest attainable point. **2** the culmination, acme, or perfection. [Latin, = not further beyond, the supposed inscription on the Pillars of Hercules (the Strait of Gibraltar) prohibiting passage by ships]

nepotism /ˈnɛpətɪz(ə)m/ *n.* favouritism shown to relatives or friends in conferring offices or privileges. □ **nepotist** *n.* **nepotistic** /-ˈtɪstɪk/ *adj.* [French *népotisme* from Italian *nepotismo*, from *nepote* NEPHEW: originally with reference to popes with illegitimate sons who were called 'nephews']

Neptune /ˈnɛptjuːn/ *n.* a distant planet of the solar system, eighth from the sun, discovered in 1846 from mathematical computations. [Middle English from French *Neptune* or Latin *Neptunus*, the god of the sea]

neptunium /nɛpˈtjuːnɪəm/ *n. Chem.* a radioactive transuranic metallic element produced when uranium atoms absorb bombarding neutrons (symbol **Np**). [NEPTUNE, on the pattern of URANIUM, being the next planet beyond Uranus]

NERC *abbr.* (in the UK) Natural Environment Research Council.

nerd /nəːd/ *n.* (also **nurd**) orig. *US slang* a foolish, feeble, or uninteresting person. □ **nerdy** *adj.* [20th c.: origin uncertain]

nereid /ˈnɪərɪɪd/ *n.* **1** *Mythol.* a sea nymph. **2** *Zool.* a carnivorous marine polychaete worm of the ragworm family Nereidae. [Latin *Nereïs Nereïd-* from Greek *Nērēis -idos*, the daughter of the sea-god Nereus]

nerine /nɪˈrʌɪni, nəˈriːnə/ *n.* any S. African plant of the genus *Nerine*, bearing flowers with usu. six narrow strap-shaped petals, often crimped and twisted. [modern Latin from the Latin name of a water nymph]

neroli /ˈnɪərəli/ *n.* (in full **neroli oil**) an essential oil from the flowers of the Seville orange, used in perfumery. [French *néroli* from Italian *neroli*, perhaps from the name of an Italian princess]

nervation /nəːˈveɪʃ(ə)n/ *n. Bot.* the arrangement of nerves in a leaf.

nerve /nəːv/ *n. & v.* ● *n.* **1 a** a fibre or bundle of fibres that transmits impulses of sensation or motion between the brain or spinal cord and other parts of the body. **b** the tissue constituting these. **2 a** coolness in danger; bravery; assurance. **b** *colloq.* impudence, audacity (*they've got a nerve*). **3** (in *pl.*) **a** the bodily state in regard to physical sensitiveness and the interaction between the brain and other parts. **b** a state of heightened nervousness or sensitivity; a condition of mental or physical stress (*need to calm my nerves*). **4** a rib of a leaf, esp. the midrib. **5** *poet. archaic* a sinew or tendon. ● *v.tr.* **1** (usu. *refl.*) brace (oneself) to face danger, suffering, etc. **2** give strength, vigour, or courage to. □ **get on a person's nerves** irritate or annoy a person. **have nerves of iron** (or **steel**) (of a person etc.) be not easily upset or frightened. **hit** (or **touch**) **a nerve** remark on or draw attention to a sensitive subject or point. □ **nerved** *adj.* (also in *comb.*). [Middle English, = sinew, from Latin *nervus*, related to Greek *neuron*]

nerve cell *n.* an elongated branched cell transmitting impulses in nerve tissue.

nerve centre *n.* **1** a group of closely connected nerve cells associated in performing some function. **2** the centre of control of an organization etc.

nerve gas *n.* a poisonous gas affecting the nervous system.

nerveless /ˈnəːvlɪs/ *adj.* **1** inert, lacking vigour or spirit. **2** confident; not nervous. **3** (of style) diffuse. **4** without nervures. **5** *Anat.* & *Zool.* without nerves. □ **nervelessly** *adv.* **nervelessness** *n.*

nerve-racking *adj.* stressful, frightening; straining the nerves.

nervine /ˈnəːvʌɪn, -iːn/ *adj. & n.* ● *adj.* relieving nerve disorders. ● *n.* a nervine drug. [French *nervin* or medieval Latin *nervinus* (as NERVE)]

nervo- /ˈnəːvəʊ/ *comb. form* (also **nerv-** before a vowel) a nerve or the nerves.

nervous /ˈnəːvəs/ *adj.* **1** having delicate or disordered nerves. **2** timid or anxious. **3 a** excitable; highly strung; easily agitated. **b** resulting from this temperament (*nervous tension*; *a nervous headache*). **4** affecting or acting on the nerves. **5** (foll. by *of* + verbal noun) reluctant, afraid (*am nervous of meeting them*). □ **nervously** *adv.* **nervousness** *n.* [Middle English from Latin *nervosus* (as NERVE)]

nervous breakdown *n.* a period of mental illness, usu. resulting from severe depression or anxiety.

nervous system *n.* the body's network of specialized cells which transmit nerve impulses between parts of the body (cf. CENTRAL NERVOUS SYSTEM, PERIPHERAL NERVOUS SYSTEM).

nervous wreck *n. colloq.* a person suffering from mental stress, exhaustion, etc.

nervure /ˈnəːvjʊə/ *n.* **1** each of the hollow tubes that form the framework of an insect's wing; a venule. **2** the principal vein of a leaf. [French *nerf* 'nerve']

nervy /ˈnəːvi/ *adj.* (**nervier**, **nerviest**) **1** esp. *Brit.* nervous; easily excited or disturbed. **2** *N. Amer. colloq.* bold, impudent. **3** *archaic* or *poet.* sinewy, strong. □ **nervily** *adv.* **nerviness** *n.*

nescient /ˈnɛsɪənt/ *adj.* (foll. by *of*) *literary* lacking knowledge; ignorant. □ **nescience** *n.* [Late Latin *nescientia* from Latin *nescire* 'not know', from *ne-* 'not' + *scire* 'know']

ness /nɛs/ *n.* a headland or promontory. [Old English *næs*, related to Old English *nasu* NOSE]

-ness /nɪs/ *suffix* forming nouns from adjectives, and occasionally other words, expressing: **1** state or condition, or an instance of this (*bitterness*; *conceitedness*; *happiness*; *a kindness*). **2** something in a certain state (*wilderness*). [Old English *-nes, -ness*, from Germanic]

nest /nɛst/ *n. & v.* ● *n.* **1** a structure or place where a bird lays eggs and shelters its young. **2** an animal's or insect's breeding place or lair. **3** a snug or secluded retreat or shelter. **4** (often foll. by *of*) a place fostering something undesirable (*a nest of vice*). **5** a brood or swarm. **6** a group or set of similar objects, often of different sizes and fitting together for storage (*a nest of tables*). ● *v.* **1** *intr.* use or build a nest. **2** *intr.* take wild birds' nests or eggs. **3** *intr.* (of objects) fit together or one inside another. **4** *tr.* (usu. as **nested** *adj.*) establish in or as in a nest. □ **nestful** *n.* (*pl.* **-fuls**). **nesting** *n.* **nestlike** *adj.* [Old English *nest*]

nest box *n.* (also **nesting box**) a box provided for a domestic fowl or other bird to make its nest in.

nest egg *n.* **1** a sum of money saved for the future. **2** a real or artificial egg left in a nest to induce hens to lay eggs there.

nestle /ˈnɛs(ə)l/ *v.* **1** *intr.* (often foll. by *down, in*, etc.) settle oneself comfortably. **2** *intr.* press oneself against another in affection etc. **3** *tr.* (foll. by *in, into*, etc.) push (a head or shoulder etc.) affectionately or snugly. **4** *intr.* lie half hidden or embedded. [Old English *nestlian* (as NEST)]

nestling /ˈnɛs(t)lɪŋ/ *n.* a bird that is too young to leave its nest.

Nestorian /nɛˈstɔːrɪən/ *adj. & n.* ● *adj.* of or relating to an early Christian doctrine that there were distinct divine and human persons in Christ, maintained by some ancient Churches of the Middle East. ● *n.* a member of such a Church. □ **Nestorianism** *n.* [*Nestorius*, patriarch of Constantinople 428–31]

net[1] /nɛt/ *n. & v.* ● *n.* **1** an open-meshed fabric of cord, rope, fibre, etc.; a structure resembling this. **2** a piece of net used esp. to restrain, contain, or delimit, or to catch fish or other animals. **3** a structure with net to enclose an area of ground, esp. in sport. **4 a** a structure with net used in various games, esp. forming the goal in football, netball, etc., and dividing the court in tennis etc. **b** (often in *pl.*) a practice-ground in cricket, surrounded by nets. **5** a system or procedure for catching or entrapping a person or persons. **6 a** a network of spies. **b** a broadcasting network. **c** *Computing* a network of interconnected computers. **d** (**the net**) = INTERNET. ● *v.* (**netted**, **netting**) **1** *tr.* **a** cover, confine, or catch with a net. **b** acquire as with a net. **2** *tr.* hit (a ball) into the net, esp. of a goal. **3** *intr.* make netting. **4** *tr.* make (a purse, hammock, etc.) by knotting etc. threads together to form a net. **5** *tr.* fish with nets, or set nets, in (a river). **6** *tr.* (usu. as **netted** *adj.*) mark with a netlike pattern; reticulate. □ **netful** *n.* (*pl.* **-fuls**). [Old English *net*, *nett*]

net[2] /nɛt/ *adj. & v.* (also *Brit.* **nett**) ● *adj.* **1** (esp. of money) remaining after all necessary deductions, or free from deductions. **2** (of a price) to be paid in full; not reducible. **3** (of a weight) excluding that of the packaging or container etc. **4** (of an effect, result, etc.) ultimate, effective. ● *v.tr.* (**netted**, **netting**) gain or yield (a sum) as net profit. [French *net* NEAT[1]]

netball /ˈnɛtbɔːl/ *n.* a team game in which goals are scored by throwing a ball through a high horizontal ring with a net suspended from it.

Net Book Agreement *n.* (in the UK) the agreement of 1900 between booksellers and publishers, by which booksellers will not offer books, with certain exceptions, below the price marked on the cover.

nether /ˈnɛðə/ *adj. archaic* = LOWER[1]. □ **nethermost** *adj.* [Old English *nithera* etc., from Germanic]

Netherlander /ˈnɛðəlandə/ *n.* **1** a native or national of the Netherlands. **2** a person of Dutch descent. □ **Netherlandish** *adj.* [Dutch *Nederlander*, *Nederlandsch*]

Netherlands /ˈnɛðələndz/ *n.* **1** (usu. prec. by *the*) Holland. **2** *hist.* the Low Countries. [Dutch *Nederland* (as NETHER, LAND)]

nether regions *n.pl.* (also **nether world** *n.sing.*) hell; the underworld.

net profit *n.* the effective profit; the actual gain after working expenses have been paid.

netsuke /ˈnɛtski, ˈnɛtsʊki/ *n.* (*pl.* same or **netsukes**) (in Japan) a carved button-like ornament, esp. of ivory or wood, formerly worn to suspend articles from a girdle. [Japanese]

nett *Brit.* var. of NET[2].

netting /ˈnɛtɪŋ/ *n.* **1** netted fabric. **2** a piece of this.

nettle /ˈnɛt(ə)l/ *n. & v.* ● *n.* **1** any plant of the genus *Urtica*, esp. *U. dioica*, with jagged leaves covered with stinging hairs. **2** any of various plants resembling this. ● *v.tr.* **1** irritate, provoke, annoy. **2** sting with nettles. [Old English *netle*, *netele*, from Germanic]

nettle-rash *n. Med.* a rash of itching red spots on the skin caused by allergic reaction to food etc. Also called *urticaria*.

net ton see TON[1] 5b.

network /ˈnɛtwəːk/ *n. & v.* ● *n.* **1** an arrangement of intersecting horizontal and vertical lines, like the structure of a net. **2** a complex system of railways, roads, canals, etc. **3** a group of people who exchange information, contacts, and experience for professional or social purposes. **4** a chain of interconnected computers, machines, or operations. **5** a system of connected electrical conductors. **6** a group of broadcasting stations connected for a simultaneous broadcast of a programme. ● *v.* **1** *tr. Brit.* broadcast on a network. **2** *intr.* establish a network. **3** *tr.* link (machines, esp. computers) to operate interactively. **4** *intr.* communicate with other people as a member of a group to exchange information, establish new links, etc. (see sense 3 of *n.*). □ **networking** *n.*

networker /ˈnɛtwəːkə/ *n.* **1** *Computing* a member of an organization or computer network who operates from home or from an external office. **2** a member of a professional or social network.

neume /njuːm/ *n.* (also **neum**) *Mus.* a sign in plainsong indicating a note or group of notes to be sung to a syllable. [Middle English via Old French *neume* and medieval Latin *neu(p)ma* from Greek *pneuma* 'breath']

neural /ˈnjʊər(ə)l/ *adj.* of or relating to a nerve or the central nervous system. □ **neurally** *adv.* [Greek *neuron* 'nerve']

neuralgia /njʊˈraldʒə/ *n.* an intense intermittent pain along the course of a nerve, esp. in the head or face. □ **neuralgic** *adj.* [as NEURAL + -ALGIA]

neural network *n.* (also **neural net**) a computer system modelled on the human brain and nervous system.

neurasthenia /njʊərəsˈθiːnɪə/ *n.* a general term for fatigue, anxiety, listlessness, etc. (not in medical use). □ **neurasthenic** /-ˈθɛnɪk/ *adj. & n.* [Greek *neuron* 'nerve' + ASTHENIA]

neuritis /njʊəˈrʌɪtɪs/ *n.* inflammation of a nerve or nerves. □ **neuritic** /-ˈrɪtɪk/ *adj.* [formed as NEURO- + -ITIS]

neuro- /ˈnjʊərəʊ/ *comb. form* a nerve or the nerves. [Greek *neuron* 'nerve']

neuroanatomy /ˌnjʊərəʊəˈnatəmi/ *n.* the anatomy of the nervous system. □ **neuroanatomical** /-anəˈtɒmɪk(ə)l/ *adj.* **neuroanatomist** *n.*

neurobiology /ˌnjʊərəʊbʌɪˈɒlədʒi/ *n.* the biology of the nervous system. □ **neurobiological** /-bʌɪəˈlɒdʒɪk(ə)l/ *adj.* **neurobiologist** *n.*

neurogenesis /njʊərə(ʊ)ˈdʒɛnɪsɪs/ *n.* the growth and development of nervous tissue.

neurogenic /njʊərə(ʊ)ˈdʒɛnɪk/ *adj.* caused by or arising in nervous tissue.

neuroglia /njʊəˈrɒglɪə/ *n.* the connective tissue supporting the central nervous system. [NEURO- + Greek *glia* 'glue']

neurohormone /njʊərəʊˈhɔːməʊn/ *n.* a hormone produced by nerve cells and secreted into the circulation.

neurolinguistics /ˌnjʊərəʊlɪŋˈgwɪstɪks/ *n.* the branch of linguistics dealing with the relationship between language and the structure and functioning of the brain. □ **neurolinguistic** *adj.*

neurology /njʊəˈrɒlədʒi/ *n.* the scientific study of nerve systems. □ **neurological** /-rəˈlɒdʒɪk(ə)l/ *adj.* **neurologically** /-rəˈlɒdʒɪk(ə)li/ *adv.* **neurologist** *n.* [modern Latin *neurologia* from modern Greek (as NEURO-, -LOGY)]

neuroma /njʊəˈrəʊmə/ *n.* (*pl.* **neuromas** or **neuromata** /-mətə/) a tumour on a nerve or in nerve tissue. [Greek *neuron* 'nerve' + -OMA]

neuromuscular /njʊərəʊˈmʌskjʊlə/ *adj.* of or relating to nerves and muscles.

neurone /ˈnjʊərəʊn/ *n.* (also **neuron** /-rɒn/) a specialized cell transmitting nerve impulses; a nerve cell. □ **neuronal** /-ˈrəʊn(ə)l/ *adj.* **neuronic** /-ˈrɒnɪk/ *adj.* [Greek *neuron* 'nerve']

■ **Usage** The spelling *neuron* is often preferred to *neurone* in technical use.

neuropath /ˈnjʊərə(ʊ)paθ/ *n.* a person affected by nervous disease, or with an abnormally sensitive nervous system. □ **neuropathic** /-ˈpaθɪk/ *adj.*

neuropathology /ˌnjʊərəʊpəˈθɒlədʒi/ *n.* the pathology of the nervous system. □ **neuropathologist** *n.*

neuropathy /njʊəˈrɒpəθi/ *n.* a disease or dysfunction of one or more peripheral nerves, typically causing numbness or weakness.

neurophysiology /ˌnjʊərəʊfɪzɪˈɒlədʒi/ *n.* the physiology of the nervous system. □ **neurophysiological** /-zɪəˈlɒdʒɪk(ə)l/ *adj.* **neurophysiologist** *n.*

neuropsychology /ˌnjʊərə(ʊ)sʌɪˈkɒlədʒi/ *n.* the study of the relationship between the nervous system (esp. the brain) and behaviour. ▫ **neuropsychological** /-kəˈlɒdʒɪk(ə)l/ *adj.* **neuropsychologist** *n.*

neuropteran /njʊəˈrɒpt(ə)rən/ *n.* any insect of the order Neuroptera, including lacewings, having four finely veined membranous leaflike wings. ▫ **neuropterous** *adj.* [NEURO- + Greek *pteron* 'wing']

neuroscience /ˈnjʊːrəʊsʌɪəns/ *n.* any or all of the sciences dealing with the structure and function of the nervous system and brain. ▫ **neuroscientist** /-ˈsʌɪəntɪst/ *n.*

neurosis /njʊəˈrəʊsɪs/ *n.* (*pl.* **neuroses** /-siːz/) a relatively mild mental illness involving symptoms of stress (e.g. depression, anxiety, obsessive behaviour) without loss of contact with reality, and not caused by organic disease. [modern Latin (as NEURO-, -OSIS)]

neurosurgery /njʊərəʊˈsəːdʒəri/ *n.* surgery performed on the nervous system, esp. the brain and spinal cord. ▫ **neurosurgeon** *n.* **neurosurgical** *adj.*

neurotic /njʊəˈrɒtɪk/ *adj.* & *n.* ● *adj.* **1** caused by or relating to neurosis. **2** (of a person) suffering from neurosis. **3** *colloq.* abnormally sensitive or obsessive. ● *n.* a neurotic person. ▫ **neurotically** *adv.* **neuroticism** /-sɪz(ə)m/ *n.*

neurotomy /njʊəˈrɒtəmi/ *n.* (*pl.* **-ies**) the operation of cutting a nerve, esp. to produce sensory loss.

neurotoxin /njʊərəʊˈtɒksɪn/ *n.* any poison which acts on the nervous system.

neurotransmitter /ˌnjʊərəʊtranzˈmɪtə/ *n.* *Biochem.* a chemical substance released from a nerve fibre that effects the transfer of an impulse to another nerve or muscle.

neuter /ˈnjuːtə/ *adj., n.,* & *v.* ● *adj.* **1** *Gram.* (of a noun etc.) neither masculine nor feminine. **2** (of a plant) having neither pistils nor stamen. **3** (of an insect, animal, etc.) sexually undeveloped; castrated or spayed. ● *n.* **1** *Gram.* a neuter word. **2 a** a non-fertile insect, esp. a worker bee or ant. **b** a castrated animal. ● *v.tr.* castrate or spay. [Middle English from Old French *neutre* or Latin *neuter* 'neither', from *ne-* 'not' + *uter* 'either']

neutral /ˈnjuːtr(ə)l/ *adj.* & *n.* ● *adj.* **1** not helping or supporting either of two opposing sides, esp. states at war or in dispute; impartial. **2** belonging to a neutral party, state, etc. (*neutral ships*). **3** indistinct, vague, indeterminate. **4** (of a gear) in which the engine is disconnected from the driven parts. **5** (of colours) not strong or positive; grey or beige. **6** *Chem.* neither acid nor alkaline. **7** *Electr.* neither positive nor negative. **8** *Biol.* sexually undeveloped; asexual. ● *n.* **1 a** a neutral state or person. **b** a subject of a neutral state. **2** a neutral gear. ▫ **neutrality** /-ˈtralɪti/ *n.* **neutrally** *adv.* [Middle English from obsolete French *neutral* or Latin *neutralis* 'of neuter gender' (as NEUTER)]

neutralism /ˈnjuːtrəlɪz(ə)m/ *n.* a policy of political neutrality. ▫ **neutralist** *n.*

neutralize /ˈnjuːtrəlʌɪz/ *v.tr.* (also **-ise**) **1** make neutral. **2** counterbalance; render ineffective by an opposite force or effect. **3** exempt or exclude (a place) from the sphere of hostilities. **4** *euphem.* make (a person) harmless or ineffective; kill. ▫ **neutralization** /-ˈzeɪʃ(ə)n/ *n.* **neutralizer** *n.* [French *neutraliser* from medieval Latin *neutralizare* (as NEUTRAL)]

neutrino /njuːˈtriːnəʊ/ *n.* (*pl.* **-os**) any of a class of stable neutral subatomic particles with almost zero mass, which travel at the speed of light and rarely interact with normal matter. [Italian, diminutive of *neutro* 'neutral' (as NEUTER)]

neutron /ˈnjuːtrɒn/ *n.* a subatomic particle of about the same mass as a proton but without an electric charge, present in all atomic nuclei except those of ordinary hydrogen. [NEUTRAL + -ON]

neutron bomb *n.* a bomb producing neutrons and little blast, causing damage to life but little destruction to property.

neutron star *n.* a very dense star composed mainly of neutrons.

Nev. *abbr.* Nevada.

névé /ˈnɛveɪ/ *n.* an expanse of granular snow not yet compressed into ice at the head of a glacier. [Swiss French, = glacier, ultimately from Latin *nix nivis* 'snow']

never /ˈnɛvə/ *adv.* **1 a** at no time; on no occasion; not ever (*have never been to Paris*; *never saw them again*). **b** *colloq.* as an emphatic negative (*I never heard you come in*). **2** not at all (*never fear*). **3** *Brit. colloq.* (expressing surprise) surely not (*you never left the key in the lock!*). ▫ **never-never land** an imaginary utopian place. **never a one** none. **never say die** see DIE[1]. **well I never!** *colloq.* expressing great surprise. [Old English *nǣfre*, from *ne* 'not' + *ǣfre* EVER]

never-ending *adj.* never coming to an end, endless.

nevermore /nɛvəˈmɔː/ *adv.* at no future time.

never-never *n.* (often prec. by *the*) *Brit. colloq.* hire purchase.

nevertheless /nɛvəðəˈlɛs/ *adv.* in spite of that; notwithstanding; all the same.

nevus *US* var. of NAEVUS.

new /njuː/ *adj.* & *adv.* ● *adj.* **1 a** of recent origin or arrival. **b** made, invented, discovered, acquired, or experienced recently or now for the first time (*a new star*; *has many new ideas*). **2** in original condition; not worn or used. **3 a** renewed or reformed (*a new life*; *the new order*). **b** reinvigorated (*felt like a new person*). **4** different from a recent previous one (*has a new job*). **5** in addition to others already existing (*have you been to the new supermarket?*). **6** (often foll. by *to*) unfamiliar or strange (*a new sensation*; *the idea was new to me*). **7** (often foll. by *at*) (of a person) inexperienced, unaccustomed (to doing something) (*am new at this business*). **8** (usu. prec. by *the*) often *derog.* **a** later, modern (*the new morality*). **b** newfangled. **c** recently affected by social change (*the new rich*). **9** (often prec. by *the*) advanced in method or theory (*the new formula*). **10** (in place names) discovered or founded later than and named after (*New York*; *New Zealand*). ● *adv.* (usu. in *comb.*) **1** newly, recently (*new-found*; *new-baked*). **2** anew, afresh. ▫ **a new one** (often foll. by *on*) *colloq.* an account or idea not previously encountered (by a person). ▫ **newish** *adj.* **newness** *n.* [Old English *nīwe*, from Germanic]

New Age *n.* a broad movement characterized by alternative approaches to traditional Western culture, with interest in spiritual matters, mysticism, holistic ideas, environmentalism, etc. (often *attrib.*: *New Age travellers*).

New Age music *n.* a style of chiefly instrumental music characterized by light melodic harmonies, improvisation, and the reproduction of sounds from the natural world, intended to promote serenity.

new arrival *n. colloq.* a newborn child.

new birth *n. Theol.* spiritual regeneration.

newborn /njuːˈbɔːn, ˈnjuːbɔːn/ *adj.* **1** (of a child etc.) recently born. **2** spiritually reborn; regenerated.

new broom *n.* a newly appointed person eager to make changes.

Newcastle disease /ˈnjuːkɑːs(ə)l/ *n.* an acute infectious viral fever affecting birds, esp. poultry. [*Newcastle* upon Tyne, a city in N. England]

newcomer /ˈnjuːkʌmə/ *n.* **1** a person who has recently arrived. **2** a beginner in some activity.

new deal *n.* new arrangements or conditions, esp. when better than the earlier ones.

newel /ˈnjuːəl/ *n.* **1** the supporting central post of winding stairs. **2** the top or bottom supporting post of a stair-rail. [Middle English via Old French *noel*, *nouel* 'knob' from medieval Latin *nodellus*, diminutive of Latin *nodus* 'knot']

newfangled /njuːˈfaŋg(ə)ld/ *adj. derog.* different from what one is used to; objectionably new. [Middle English *newfangle* (now dialect) 'liking what is new', from *newe*

NEW *adv.* + *-fangel* from an Old English word meaning 'inclined to take']

Newfoundland /'nju:f(ə)n(d)lənd, -land, nju:'faʊndlənd/ *n.* (in full **Newfoundland dog**) **1** a dog of a very large breed with a thick coarse coat. **2** this breed. [the name of an island at the mouth of the St Lawrence river and a Canadian province consisting of this island and Labrador]

Newfoundlander /'nju:f(ə)n(d)ləndə, nju:f(ə)n(d)'landə/ *n.* a native or inhabitant of Newfoundland.

new-laid *adj.* (of an egg) freshly laid.

new look *n. & adj.* ● *n.* **1** a new or revised appearance or presentation, esp. of something familiar. **2** (often **New Look**) a style of women's clothing introduced after the Second World War, featuring long full skirts and a generous use of material in contrast to wartime austerity. ● *attrib.adj.* (**new-look**) having a new image; restyled.

newly /'nju:li/ *adv.* **1** recently (*a friend newly arrived*; *a newly discovered country*). **2** afresh, anew (*newly painted*). **3** in a new or different manner (*newly arranged*).

newly-wed *n.* a recently married person.

new man *n.* a man who rejects sexist attitudes and the traditional male role.

Newmarket /'nju:mɑ:kɪt/ *n.* a gambling card game in which players seek to play cards that match those on the table. [*Newmarket* in S. England]

new mathematics *n.pl.* (also *Brit.* **new maths**) (often treated as *sing.*) a system of teaching mathematics to children, with emphasis on investigation by them and on set theory.

new moon *n.* **1** the moon when first seen as a crescent after conjunction with the sun. **2** the time of its appearance.

new potatoes *n.pl.* the earliest potatoes of a new crop.

news /nju:z/ *n.pl.* (usu. treated as *sing.*) **1** information about important or interesting recent events, esp. when published or broadcast. **2** (prec. by *the*) a broadcast report of news. **3** newly received or noteworthy information. **4** (foll. by *to*) *colloq.* information not previously known (to a person) (*that's news to me*). □ **newsless** *adj.* [Middle English, pl. of NEW, translating Old French *noveles* or medieval Latin *nova*, neut. pl. of *novus* 'new']

news agency *n.* an organization that collects and distributes news items.

newsagent /'nju:zeɪdʒ(ə)nt/ *n. Brit.* a seller of or shop selling newspapers and usu. related items, e.g. stationery.

newsboy /'nju:zbɔɪ/ *n.* a boy who sells or delivers newspapers.

newsbrief /'nju:zbri:f/ *n.* a short item of news, esp. on television; a newsflash.

news bulletin *n. Brit.* a collection of items of news, esp. for broadcasting.

newscast /'nju:zkɑ:st/ *n.* a radio or television broadcast of news reports.

newscaster /'nju:zkɑ:stə/ *n.* = NEWSREADER.

news conference *n.* a press conference.

newsflash /'nju:zflaʃ/ *n.* a single item of important news broadcast separately and often interrupting other programmes.

news-gatherer *n.* a person who researches news items, esp. those for broadcast or publication. □ **news-gathering** *n.* this process.

newsgirl /'nju:zgə:l/ *n.* a girl who sells or delivers newspapers.

news hound *n. colloq.* a newspaper reporter.

newsletter /'nju:zlɛtə/ *n.* an informal printed report issued periodically to the members of a society, business, organization, etc.

newsman /'nju:zman/ *n.* (*pl.* **-men**) a newspaper reporter; a journalist.

newsmonger /'nju:zmʌŋgə/ *n.* a gossip.

newspaper /'nju:zpeɪpə, 'nju:s-/ *n.* **1** a printed publication (usu. daily or weekly) containing news, advertisements, correspondence, etc. **2** the sheets of paper forming this (*wrapped in newspaper*).

newspaperman /'nju:zpeɪpə,man, -'nju:s-/ *n.* (*pl.* **-men**) a journalist.

Newspeak /'nju:spi:k/ *n.* ambiguous euphemistic language used esp. in political propaganda. [an artificial official language in George Orwell's *Nineteen Eighty-Four* (1949)]

newsprint /'nju:zprɪnt/ *n.* a type of low-quality paper on which newspapers are printed.

newsreader /'nju:zri:də/ *n. Brit.* a person who reads out broadcast news bulletins.

newsreel /'nju:zri:l/ *n.* a short cinema film of news and current affairs.

newsroom /'nju:zru:m, -rʊm/ *n.* a room in a newspaper or broadcasting office where news is processed.

news-sheet *n.* a simple form of newspaper; a newsletter.

news-stand *n.* a stall for the sale of newspapers.

new star *n.* a nova.

New Style *n.* dating reckoned by the Gregorian calendar (superseding the Julian calendar in 1752 in England and Wales).

new-style *attrib.adj.* having a new style (*new-style contracts*).

news-vendor *n. Brit.* a newspaper-seller.

newsworthy /'nju:zwə:ði/ *adj.* topical; noteworthy as news. □ **newsworthiness** *n.*

newsy /'nju:zi/ *adj.* (**newsier**, **newsiest**) *colloq.* full of news.

newt /nju:t/ *n.* any of various small amphibians, esp. of the genus *Triturus*, having a well-developed tail. [Middle English from *ewt*, with *n* from *an* (cf. NICKNAME): variant of *evet* EFT]

New Testament *n.* the second part of the Christian Bible, concerned with the life and teachings of Christ and his earliest followers.

newton /'nju:t(ə)n/ *n. Physics* the SI unit of force that, acting on a mass of one kilogram, increases its velocity by one metre per second every second along the direction that it acts (abbr.: **N**). [named after Sir Isaac *Newton*, English scientist d. 1727]

Newtonian /nju:'təʊnɪən/ *adj.* of or devised by Isaac Newton (see NEWTON).

Newtonian mechanics *n.pl.* (usu. treated as *sing.*) the system of mechanics which relies on Newton's laws of motion concerning the relations between forces acting and motions occurring.

Newtonian telescope *n.* a reflecting telescope with a small secondary mirror at 45° to the main beam of light to reflect it into a magnifying eyepiece.

new town *n.* a town established as a completely new settlement with government sponsorship.

new wave *n.* **1** = NOUVELLE VAGUE. **2** a style of rock music popular in the 1970s.

New World *n.* North and South America regarded collectively in relation to Europe.

new year *n.* **1** the calendar year just begun or about to begin. **2** the first few days of a year.

New Year's Day *n.* 1 January.

New Year's Eve *n.* 31 December.

New Yorker /'jɔ:kə/ *n.* a native or inhabitant of the state or city of New York in the US.

New Zealander /'zi:ləndə/ *n.* **1** a native or national of New Zealand, an island group in the Pacific. **2** a person of New Zealand descent.

next /nɛkst/ *adj., adv., n., & prep.* ● *adj.* **1** (often foll. by *to*) being or positioned or living nearest (*in the next house*; *the chair next to the fire*). **2** the nearest in order of time; the first or soonest encountered or considered (*next Friday*; *ask the next person you see*). ● *adv.* **1** (often foll. by *to*) in the nearest place or degree (*put it next to mine*; *came next to last*). **2** on the first or soonest occasion (*when we next meet*). ● *n.* the next person or thing. ● *prep. colloq.* next to. □ **next to** almost (*next to nothing left*). [Old English *nēhsta*, superlative of *nēah* NIGH]

next-best *adj.* the next in order of preference.

next door *adv. & adj.* (as adj. often hyphenated) in or to the next house or room. □ **next door to 1** in the next house to. **2** nearly, almost, near to.

next of kin *n.sing. & pl.* the closest living relative or relatives.

next world *n.* a supposed life after death.

nexus /'nɛksəs/ *n.* (*pl.* **nexuses**) **1** a connected group, series, or network. **2** a bond; a connection. [Latin from *nectere nex-* 'bind']

NF *abbr.* (in the UK) National Front.

NFL *abbr. US* National Football League.

Nfld *abbr.* (also **NF**) Newfoundland.

NFU *abbr.* (in the UK) National Farmers' Union.

n.g. *abbr.* no good.

NGA *abbr. hist.* (in the UK) National Graphical Association.

ngaio /'nʌɪəʊ/ *n.* (*pl.* **-os**) a small New Zealand tree, *Myoporum laetum*, with edible fruit and light white timber. [Maori]

NGO *abbr.* non-governmental organization.

Nguni /(ə)ŋ'gu:ni/ *n. & adj.* ● *n.* **1** (*pl.* same) a member of a group of Bantu-speaking peoples living mainly in southern Africa. **2** the group of closely related Bantu languages spoken by these peoples. ● *adj.* of or relating to these peoples or this group of languages. [Zulu]

NH *abbr. US* New Hampshire (also in official postal use).

NHI *abbr.* (in the UK) National Health Insurance.

NHS *abbr.* (in the UK) National Health Service.

NI *abbr.* **1** (in the UK) National Insurance. **2** Northern Ireland.

Ni *symb. Chem.* the element nickel.

niacin /'nʌɪəsɪn/ *n.* = NICOTINIC ACID. [*nic*otinic *ac*id + -IN]

nib /nɪb/ *n. & v.* ● *n.* **1** the point of a pen, which touches the writing surface. **2** (in *pl.*) shelled and crushed coffee or cocoa beans. **3** the point of a tool etc. ● *v.* (**nibbed, nibbing**) **1** *tr.* provide with a nib. **2** *tr.* mend the nib of. **3** *tr. & intr.* nibble. [probably from Middle Dutch *nib* or Middle Low German *nibbe*, variant of *nebbe* NEB]

nibble /'nɪb(ə)l/ *v. & n.* ● *v.* **1** *tr.* & (foll. by *at*) *intr.* **a** take small bites at. **b** eat in small amounts. **c** bite at gently or cautiously or playfully. **2** *intr.* (foll. by *at*) show cautious interest in. ● *n.* **1** an instance of nibbling. **2** (usu. in *pl.*) a morsel or titbit of food. **3** *Computing* half a byte, i.e. 4 bits. □ **nibbler** *n.* [probably of Low German or Dutch origin: cf. Low German *nibbeln* 'gnaw']

niblet /'nɪblɪt/ *n.* a small piece or portion, esp. of food. [probably from NIBBLE + -LET]

niblick /'nɪblɪk/ *n. Golf* an iron with a large round heavy head, used esp. for playing out of bunkers. [19th c.: origin unknown]

nibs /'nɪbz/ *n.* □ **his nibs** *joc. colloq.* a mock title used with reference to an important or self-important person. [19th c.: origin unknown (cf. earlier *nabs*)]

nicad /'nʌɪkad/ *n.* (often *attrib.*) a battery, often rechargable, with a nickel anode and a cadmium cathode. [NICKEL + CADMIUM]

Nicam /'nʌɪkam/ *n.* a digital system used in British television to provide video signals with high-quality stereo sound. [*n*ear *i*nstantaneously *c*ompanded (compressed and expanded) *a*udio *m*ultiplex]

nice /nʌɪs/ *adj.* **1** pleasant, agreeable, satisfactory. **2** (of a person) kind, good-natured. **3** *iron.* bad or awkward (*a nice mess you've made*). **4 a** fine or subtle (*a nice distinction*). **b** requiring careful thought or attention (*a nice problem*). **5** fastidious; delicately sensitive. **6** punctilious, scrupulous (*were not too nice about their methods*). **7** (foll. by an adj., often with *and*) satisfactory or adequate in terms of the quality described (*a nice long time*; *nice and warm*). □ **nice one** *colloq.* expressing approval or commendation. **nice work** *colloq.* expressing approval of a task well done. □ **nicely** *adv.* **niceness** *n.* **nicish** *adj.* (also **niceish**). [Middle English originally = stupid, wanton: via Old French, = silly, simple, from Latin *nescius* 'ignorant' (as *nescience*: see NESCIENT)]

Nicene Creed /nʌɪ'si:n, 'nʌɪ-/ *n.* a formal statement of Christian belief based on that adopted at the first Council of Nicaea in 325, and used in the Roman Mass and other Christian liturgies. [*Nicene* Middle English from Late Latin *Nicenus* 'of Nicaea', a town in Asia Minor]

nicety /'nʌɪsɪti/ *n.* (*pl.* **-ies**) **1** a subtle distinction or detail. **2** precision, accuracy. **3** intricate or subtle quality (*a point of great nicety*). **4** (in *pl.*) **a** minutiae; fine details. **b** refinements, trimmings. □ **to a nicety** with exactness. [Middle English from Old French *niceté* (as NICE)]

niche /nɪtʃ, ni:ʃ/ *n. & v.* ● *n.* **1** a shallow recess, esp. in a wall to contain a statue etc. **2** a comfortable or suitable position in life or employment. **3** a specialized but profitable corner of the market. **4** *Ecol.* a position or role taken by a kind of organism within its community. ● *v.tr.* (often as **niched** *adj.*) **1** place in a niche. **2** ensconce (esp. oneself) in a recess or corner. [French from *nicher* 'make a nest', ultimately from Latin *nidus* 'nest']

Nichrome /'nʌɪkrəʊm/ *n. propr.* a group of nickel-chromium alloys used for making wire in heating elements etc. [NICKEL + CHROME]

nick[1] /nɪk/ *n. & v.* ● *n.* **1** a small cut or notch. **2** *Brit. slang* **a** a prison. **b** a police station. **3** (prec. by *in* with adj.) *Brit. colloq.* condition (*in reasonable nick*). **4** the junction between the floor and walls in a squash court. ● *v.tr.* **1** make a nick or nicks in. **2** *Brit. slang* **a** steal. **b** arrest, catch. □ **in the nick of time** only just in time; just at the right moment. [Middle English: origin uncertain]

nick[2] /nɪk/ *v.intr.* (foll. by *off*, *in*, etc.) *Austral. slang* move quickly or furtively. [19th c.: origin uncertain (cf. NIP[1] 4)]

nickel /'nɪk(ə)l/ *n. & v.* ● *n.* **1** *Chem.* a malleable ductile silver-white metallic transition element, occurring naturally in various minerals and used in special steels, in magnetic alloys, and as a catalyst (symbol **Ni**). **2** *N. Amer. colloq.* a five-cent coin. ● *v.tr.* (**nickelled, nickelling**; *US* **nickeled, nickeling**) coat with nickel. □ **nickelic** *adj.* **nickelous** *adj.* [abbreviation of German *Kupfernickel*, the copper-coloured ore from which nickel was first obtained, from *Kupfer* 'copper' + *Nickel* 'demon', with reference to the ore's failure to yield copper]

nickel brass *n.* an alloy of copper, zinc, and a small amount of nickel.

nickelodeon /nɪkə'ləʊdɪən/ *n. US* **1** *colloq.* a jukebox. **2** *hist.* a cinema with an admission fee of one nickel. [NICKEL + MELODEON]

nickel-plated *adj.* coated with nickel by plating.

nickel silver *n.* = GERMAN SILVER.

nickel steel *n.* a type of stainless steel with chromium and nickel.

nicker /'nɪkə/ *n.* (*pl.* same) *Brit. slang* a pound (in money). [20th c.: origin unknown]

nick-nack var. of KNICK-KNACK.

nickname /'nɪkneɪm/ *n. & v.* ● *n.* a familiar or humorous name given to a person or thing instead of or as well as the real name. ● *v.tr.* **1** give a nickname to. **2** call (a person or thing) by a nickname. [Middle English from *eke-name*, with *n* from *an* (cf. NEWT): *eke* = addition, from Old English *ēaca* (as EKE)]

nicol /'nɪk(ə)l/ *n.* (in full **nicol prism**) a device for producing plane-polarized light, consisting of two pieces of cut calcite cemented together with Canada balsam. [named after W. *Nicol*, Scots physicist d. 1851, its inventor]

nicotiana /ˌnɪkɒtɪ'ɑ:nə, -kəʊʃ-/ *n.* = TOBACCO PLANT. [modern Latin *nicotiana* (*herba*) 'tobacco plant', named after J. *Nicot*, 16th-c. French diplomat who introduced tobacco to France]

nicotinamide /nɪkəˈtɪnəmʌɪd/ *n. Biochem.* the amide of nicotinic acid, having a similar role in the diet, and important as a constituent of NAD.

nicotinamide adenine dinucleotide see NAD.

nicotine /ˈnɪkətiːn/ *n.* a colourless poisonous narcotic alkaloid present in tobacco. □ **nicotinism** *n.* **nicotinize** *v.tr.* (also **-ise**). [French, from NICOTIANA + -INE[4]]

nicotinic acid /nɪkəˈtɪnɪk/ *n.* a vitamin of the B complex, found in milk, liver, and yeast, a deficiency of which causes pellagra. Also called *niacin*.

nictitate /ˈnɪktɪteɪt/ *v.intr.* esp. *Zool.* close and open the eyes; blink or wink. □ **nictitation** /-ˈteɪʃ(ə)n/ *n.* [medieval Latin *nictitare*, frequentative of Latin *nictare* 'blink']

nictitating membrane *n.* a clear membrane forming a third eyelid in amphibians, birds, and some other animals, that can be drawn across the eye to give protection without loss of vision.

nide /nʌɪd/ *n.* (*archaic* **nye** /nʌɪ/) a brood of pheasants. [French *nid* or Latin *nidus*: see NIDUS]

nidificate /ˈnɪdɪfɪkeɪt/ *v.intr.* = NIDIFY.

nidify /ˈnɪdɪfʌɪ/ *v.intr.* (**-ies**, **-ied**) (of a bird) build a nest. □ **nidification** /-fɪˈkeɪʃ(ə)n/ *n.* [Latin *nidificare* from *nidus* 'nest']

nidus /ˈnʌɪdəs/ *n.* (*pl.* **nidi** /-dʌɪ/ or **niduses**) **1** a place in which an insect etc. deposits its eggs, or in which spores or seeds develop. **2** a place in which something is nurtured or developed. [Latin, = nest]

niece /niːs/ *n.* a daughter of one's brother or sister, or of one's brother-in-law or sister-in-law. [Middle English from Old French, ultimately from Latin *neptis* 'granddaughter']

niello /nɪˈɛləʊ/ *n.* (*pl.* **nielli** /-liː/ or **-os**) **1** a black composition of sulphur with silver, lead, or copper, for filling engraved lines in silver or other metal. **2 a** such ornamental work. **b** an object decorated with this. □ **nielloed** *adj.* [Italian, from Latin *nigellus*, diminutive of *niger* 'black']

niff /nɪf/ *n.* & *v. Brit. colloq.* ● *n.* a smell, esp. an unpleasant one. ● *v.intr.* smell, stink. □ **niffy** *adj.* (**niffier**, **niffiest**). [originally dialect, perhaps from SNIFF]

nifty /ˈnɪfti/ *adj.* (**niftier**, **niftiest**) *colloq.* **1** clever, adroit. **2** smart, stylish. □ **niftily** *adv.* **niftiness** *n.* [19th c.: origin uncertain]

nigella /nʌɪˈdʒɛlə/ *n.* a plant of the genus *Nigella* (buttercup family), with showy flowers and finely cut leaves, esp. love-in-a-mist, *N. damascena*. [modern Latin use as genus name of Latin *nigellus*, diminutive of *niger* 'black']

niggard /ˈnɪgəd/ *n.* & *adj.* ● *n.* a mean or stingy person. ● *adj. archaic* = NIGGARDLY. [Middle English, alteration of earlier (obsolete) *nigon*, probably of Scandinavian origin: cf. NIGGLE]

niggardly /ˈnɪgədli/ *adj.* & *adv.* ● *adj.* **1** stingy, parsimonious. **2** meagre, scanty. ● *adv.* in a stingy or meagre manner. □ **niggardliness** *n.*

nigger /ˈnɪgə/ *n. offens.* **1** a black person. **2** a dark-skinned person. □ **a nigger in the woodpile** a hidden cause of trouble or inconvenience. [earlier *neger*, via French *nègre* from Spanish *negro* NEGRO]

niggle /ˈnɪg(ə)l/ *v.* & *n.* ● *v.* **1** *intr.* be over-attentive to details. **2** *intr.* find fault in a petty way. **3** *tr.* irritate; nag pettily. ● *n.* a trifling complaint or criticism; a worry or annoyance. [apparently of Scandinavian origin: cf. Norwegian *nigla*]

niggling /ˈnɪglɪŋ/ *adj.* **1** troublesome or irritating in a petty way. **2** trifling or petty. □ **nigglingly** *adv.*

nigh /nʌɪ/ *adv.*, *prep.*, & *adj. archaic* or *dial.* near. [Old English *nēh*, *nēah*]

night /nʌɪt/ *n.* & *int.* ● *n.* **1** the period of darkness between one day and the next; the time from sunset to sunrise. **2** nightfall (*shall not reach home before night*). **3** the darkness of night (*as black as night*). **4** a night or evening appointed for some activity, or spent or regarded in a certain way (*last night of the Proms*; *a great night out*). ● *int. colloq.* = GOODNIGHT *int.* □ **nightless** *adj.* [Old English *neaht*, *niht*, from Germanic]

nightbird /ˈnʌɪtbəːd/ *n.* a person habitually active at night.

night-blindness *n.* = NYCTALOPIA.

nightcap /ˈnʌɪtkap/ *n.* **1** *hist.* a cap worn in bed. **2** a hot or alcoholic drink taken at bedtime.

nightclothes /ˈnʌɪtkləʊðz/ *n.* clothes worn in bed.

nightclub /ˈnʌɪtklʌb/ *n.* a club that is open at night and provides refreshment and entertainment.

night-commode var. of COMMODE 2.

nightdress /ˈnʌɪtdrɛs/ *n.* a woman's or child's loose garment worn in bed.

nightfall /ˈnʌɪtfɔːl/ *n.* the onset of night; the end of daylight.

night fighter *n.* an aeroplane used for interception at night.

nightgown /ˈnʌɪtgaʊn/ *n.* **1** = NIGHTDRESS. **2** *hist.* a dressing gown.

nighthawk /ˈnʌɪthɔːk/ *n.* **1** a nocturnal prowler, esp. a thief. **2** an American nightjar, esp. of the genus *Chordeiles*.

nightie /ˈnʌɪti/ *n. colloq.* a nightdress. [abbreviation]

nightingale /ˈnʌɪtɪŋgeɪl/ *n.* a small brownish migratory thrush, *Luscinia megarhynchos*, the male of which has a melodious song heard esp. at night. [Old English *nihtegala* from Germanic (as NIGHT + base meaning 'sing'): for *-n-* cf. FARTHINGALE]

nightjar /ˈnʌɪtdʒɑː/ *n.* any nocturnal insectivorous bird of the family Caprimulgidae, with grey-brown plumage and often a characteristic chirring call. [NIGHT + JAR[2]]

nightlife /ˈnʌɪtlʌɪf/ *n.* entertainment available at night in a town.

night light *n.* a dim light kept burning in a bedroom at night.

night-long *adj.* & *adv.* throughout the night.

nightly /ˈnʌɪtli/ *adj.* & *adv.* ● *adj.* **1** happening, done, or existing in the night. **2** recurring every night. ● *adv.* every night. [Old English *nihtlic* (as NIGHT)]

nightmare /ˈnʌɪtmɛː/ *n.* **1** a frightening or unpleasant dream. **2** *colloq.* a terrifying or very unpleasant experience or situation. **3** a haunting or obsessive fear. □ **nightmarish** *adj.* **nightmarishly** *adv.* [an evil spirit (incubus) once thought to lie on and suffocate sleepers: Middle English (as NIGHT, Old English *mære* 'incubus')]

night monkey *n.* = DOUROUCOULI.

night nurse *n.* a nurse on duty during the night.

night owl *n. colloq.* a person habitually active or wakeful at night.

night safe *n. Brit.* a safe with access from the outer wall of a bank for the deposit of money etc. when the bank is closed.

night school *n.* an institution providing evening classes for those working by day.

nightshade /ˈnʌɪtʃeɪd/ *n.* any of various poisonous plants of the family Solanaceae, esp. of the genus *Solanum*, including *S. nigrum* (**black nightshade**) with black berries, and *S. dulcamara* (**woody nightshade**) with red berries. [Old English *nihtscada*, apparently formed as NIGHT + SHADE, probably with reference to its poisonous properties]

night shift *n.* a shift of workers employed during the night.

nightshirt /ˈnʌɪtʃəːt/ *n.* a long shirt worn in bed.

night-soil *n.* excrement removed at night from cesspools etc., esp. for use as manure.

nightspot /ˈnʌɪtspɒt/ *n. colloq.* a nightclub.

nightstick /ˈnʌɪtstɪk/ *n. US* a police officer's truncheon.

night terrors *n.pl.* feelings of great fear experienced on suddenly waking in the night, esp. by children.

night-time *n.* the time of darkness.

nightwatchman /nʌɪtˈwɒtʃmən/ *n.* **1** a person whose job is to keep watch by night. **2** *Cricket* an inferior batsman sent in near the close of a day's play.

nightwear /ˈnʌɪtwɛː/ *n.* clothing suitable for wearing in bed.

nigrescent /nɪˈgrɛs(ə)nt, nʌɪ-/ *adj.* blackish. □ **nigrescence** *n.* [Latin *nigrescere* 'grow black' from *niger nigri* 'black']

nigritude /ˈnɪgrɪtjuːd/ *n.* blackness. [Latin *nigritudo* (as NIGRESCENT)]

nihilism /ˈnʌɪ(h)ɪlɪz(ə)m/ *n.* **1** the rejection of all religious and moral principles. **2** an extreme form of scepticism characterized by the assertion that nothing really exists. □ **nihilist** *n.* **nihilistic** /-ˈlɪstɪk/ *adj.* [Latin *nihil* 'nothing']

nihility /nɪˈhɪlɪti, nʌɪ-/ *n.* (*pl.* **-ies**) **1** non-existence, nothingness. **2** a mere nothing; a trifle. [medieval Latin *nihilitas* (as NIHILISM)]

nihil obstat /nʌɪhɪl ˈɒbstat, nɪhɪl/ *n.* **1** *RC Ch.* a certificate that a book is not open to objection on doctrinal or moral grounds. **2** an authorization or official approval. [Latin, = nothing hinders]

-nik /nɪk/ *suffix* forming nouns denoting a person associated with a specified thing or quality (*beatnik*; *refusenik*). [Russian (as SPUTNIK) and Yiddish]

Nikkei index /ˈnɪkeɪ/ *n.* (also **Nikkei average**) a figure indicating the relative price of representative shares on the Tokyo Stock Exchange. [*Nikkei* from Japanese abbreviation of the name of a financial newspaper]

nil /nɪl/ *n.* nothing; no number or amount (esp. *Brit.* as a score in games). [Latin, = *nihil* 'nothing']

nil desperandum /nɪl dɛspəˈrandəm/ *int.* do not despair, never despair. [Latin *nil desperandum* (*Teucro duce*) 'no need to despair (with Teucer as your leader)', from Horace *Odes*]

Nile /nʌɪl/ *n.* & *adj.* (in full **Nile blue, Nile green**) ● *n.* pale greenish blue or green. ● *adj.* (hyphenated when *attrib.*) of this colour. [the river *Nile* in NE Africa]

nilgai /ˈnɪlgʌɪ/ *n.* a large short-horned Indian antelope, *Boselaphus tragocamelus.* [Hindi *nīlgāī*, from *nīl* 'blue' + *gāī* 'cow']

Nilotic /nʌɪˈlɒtɪk/ *adj.* **1** of or relating to the Nile or the Nile region of Africa. **2** of or relating to a group of E. African Negroid peoples, or the languages spoken by them. [Latin *Niloticus* from Greek *Neilōtikos*, from *Neilos* 'Nile']

nim /nɪm/ *n.* a game in which two players must alternately take one or more objects from one of several heaps and seek either to avoid taking or to take the last remaining object. [20th c.: perhaps from archaic *nim* 'take' (as NIMBLE), or German *nimm*, imperative of *nehmen* 'take']

nimble /ˈnɪmb(ə)l/ *adj.* (**nimbler, nimblest**) **1** quick and light in movement or action; agile. **2** (of the mind) quick to comprehend; clever, versatile. □ **nimbleness** *n.* **nimbly** *adv.* [Old English *nǣmel* 'quick to seize' from *niman* 'take', from Germanic, with *-b-* as in THIMBLE]

nimbostratus /nɪmbə(ʊ)ˈstrɑːtəs, -ˈstreɪtəs/ *n. Meteorol.* cloud forming a low dense grey layer, from which rain or snow often falls. [modern Latin, from NIMBUS + STRATUS]

nimbus /ˈnɪmbəs/ *n.* (*pl.* **nimbi** /-bʌɪ/ or **nimbuses**) **1 a** a bright cloud or halo investing a deity or person or thing. **b** the halo of a saint etc. **2** *Meteorol.* a rain cloud. □ **nimbused** *adj.* [Latin, = cloud, aureole]

Nimby /ˈnɪmbi/ *adj.* & *n.* ● *adj.* objecting to the siting of unpleasant (though often necessary) developments in one's own locality. ● *n.* (*pl.* **-ies**) a person who so objects. [*n*ot *i*n *m*y *b*ack *y*ard]

niminy-piminy /ˌnɪmɪnɪ ˈpɪmɪni/ *adj.* feeble, affected; lacking in vigour. [cf. MIMINY-PIMINY, NAMBY-PAMBY]

Nimrod /ˈnɪmrɒd/ *n.* a great hunter or sportsman. [Hebrew *Nimrōd* 'valiant': see Gen. 10:8-9]

nincompoop /ˈnɪŋkəmpuːp/ *n.* a simpleton; a fool. [17th c.: origin unknown]

nine /nʌɪn/ *n.* & *adj.* ● *n.* **1** one more than eight, or one less than ten; the sum of five units and four units. **2** a symbol for this (9, ix, IX). **3** a size etc. denoted by nine. **4** a set or team of nine individuals. **5** nine o'clock. **6** a card with nine pips. **7** (**the Nine**) the nine muses. ● *adj.* that amount to nine. □ **dressed to** (or *Brit.* **up to**) **the nines** dressed very elaborately. **nine points** (or **nine-tenths**) nearly all (*possession is nine points of the law*). **nine times out of ten** nearly always. **nine to five** a designation of typical office hours. [Old English *nigon*, from Germanic]

nine days' wonder *n.* a person or thing that is briefly famous.

ninefold /ˈnʌɪnfəʊld/ *adj.* & *adv.* **1** nine times as much or as many. **2** consisting of nine parts.

ninepin /ˈnʌɪnpɪn/ *n.* **1** = SKITTLE *n.* 1. **2** (in *pl.*; usu. treated as *sing.*) the usual form of skittles, using nine pins. □ **go down** (or **drop** or **fall**) **like ninepins** topple or succumb in large numbers.

nineteen /nʌɪnˈtiːn, ˈnʌɪntiːn/ *n.* & *adj.* ● *n.* **1** one more than eighteen, nine more than ten. **2** the symbol for this (19, xix, XIX). **3** a size etc. denoted by nineteen. ● *adj.* that amount to nineteen. □ **talk nineteen to the dozen** see DOZEN. □ **nineteenth** *adj.* & *n.* [Old English *nigontȳne*]

nineteenth hole *n. Golf slang* the bar at a golf club (as reached after a standard round of 18 holes).

nine-to-five *attrib.adj.* of or involving standard office hours (typically 9 a.m. to 5 p.m.).

ninety /ˈnʌɪnti/ *n.* & *adj.* ● *n.* (*pl.* **-ies**) **1** the product of nine and ten. **2** a symbol for this (90, xc, XC). **3** (in *pl.*) the numbers from 90 to 99, esp. the years of a century or of a person's life. ● *adj.* that amount to ninety. □ **ninety-first, -second**, etc. the ordinal numbers between ninetieth and a hundredth. **ninety-one, -two**, etc. the cardinal numbers between ninety and a hundred. □ **ninetieth** *adj.* & *n.* **ninetyfold** *adj.* & *adv.* [Old English *nigontig*]

ninja /ˈnɪndʒə/ *n.* a person skilled in ninjutsu. [Japanese]

ninjutsu /nɪnˈdʒʌtsuː/ *n.* one of the Japanese martial arts, characterized by stealthy movement and camouflage. [Japanese, from *nin* 'stealth' + *jutsu* 'art, science']

ninny /ˈnɪni/ *n.* (*pl.* **-ies**) *colloq.* a foolish or simple-minded person. [perhaps from *innocent*]

ninon /ˈniːnɒn/ *n.* a lightweight silk dress fabric. [French]

ninth /ˈnʌɪnθ/ *n.* & *adj.* ● *n.* **1** the position in a sequence corresponding to the number 9 in the sequence 1–9. **2** something occupying this position. **3** each of nine equal parts of a thing. **4** *Mus.* **a** an interval or chord spanning nine consecutive notes in the diatonic scale (e.g. C to D an octave higher). **b** a note separated from another by this interval. ● *adj.* that is the ninth. □ **ninthly** *adv.*

niobium /nʌɪˈəʊbɪəm/ *n. Chem.* a rare grey-blue metallic transition element occurring naturally in several minerals and used in alloys for superconductors (symbol Nb). □ **niobic** *adj.* **niobous** *adj.* [named after *Niobe*, the daughter of Tantalus: so called because first found in TANTALITE]

Nip /nɪp/ *n. slang offens.* a Japanese person. [abbreviation of NIPPONESE]

nip[1] /nɪp/ *v.* & *n.* ● *v.* (**nipped, nipping**) **1** *tr.* pinch, squeeze, or bite sharply. **2** *tr.* (often foll. by *off*) remove by pinching etc. **3** *tr.* (of the cold, frost, etc.) cause pain or harm to. **4** *intr.* (foll. by *in, out,* etc.) *Brit. colloq.* go nimbly or quickly. **5** *tr. US slang* steal, snatch. ● *n.* **1 a** a pinch, a sharp squeeze. **b** a bite. **2 a** biting cold. **b** a check to vegetation caused by this. □ **nip in the bud** suppress or destroy (esp. an idea) at an early stage. □ **nipping** *adj.* [Middle English, probably of Low German or Dutch origin]

nip[2] /nɪp/ *n.* & *v.* ● *n.* a small quantity of spirits. ● *v.intr.* (**nipped, nipping**) drink spirits. [probably an abbreviation of *nipperkin* 'small measure': cf. Low German, Dutch *nippen* 'to sip']

nipa /'ni:pə, 'nʌɪpə/ *n.* **1** an E. Indian palm tree, *Nipa fruticans*, with a creeping trunk and large feathery leaves. **2** an alcoholic drink made from its sap. [Spanish & Portuguese from Malay *nīpah*]

nip and tuck *n. & adv.* ● *n. colloq.* a cosmetic surgical operation. ● *adv. N. Amer.* neck and neck.

nipper /'nɪpə/ *n.* **1** a person or thing that nips. **2** the claw of a crab, lobster, etc. **3** *Brit. colloq.* a young child. **4** (in *pl.*) any tool for gripping or cutting, e.g. forceps or pincers. **5** *Austral.* a burrowing prawn of the order Thalassinidea, used as bait; also called YABBY.

nipple /'nɪp(ə)l/ *n.* **1 a** a small projection in which the mammary ducts of female mammals terminate and from which milk is secreted for the young. **b** an analogous structure in the male. **2** the teat of a feeding bottle. **3** a device like a nipple in function, e.g. the tip of a grease gun. **4** a nipple-like protuberance. **5** *US* a short section of pipe with a screw-thread at each end for coupling. [16th c., also *neble, nible*, perhaps diminutive of NEB]

nipplewort /'nɪp(ə)lwə:t/ *n.* a yellow-flowered weed, *Lapsana communis*.

Nipponese /nɪpə'ni:z/ *n. & adj.* ● *n.* (*pl.* same) a Japanese person. ● *adj.* Japanese. [Japanese *Nippon* 'Japan', literally 'place the sun comes from' (i.e. 'land of the rising sun'), from *nip* 'sun', *pon* 'origin']

nippy /'nɪpi/ *adj.* (**nippier, nippiest**) *colloq.* **1** quick, nimble, active. **2** chilly, cold. □ **nippily** *adv.* [NIP[1] + -Y[1]]

NIREX /'nʌɪrɛks/ *abbr.* (in the UK) Nuclear Industry Radioactive Waste Executive.

nirvana /nɪə'vɑ:nə/ *n.* (in Buddhism) perfect bliss and release from karma, attained by the extinction of individuality. [Sanskrit *nirvāṇa* from *nirvā* 'be extinguished', from *nis* 'out' + *vā-* 'to blow']

nisei /'ni:seɪ, ni:'seɪ/ *n.* (also **Nisei**) *US* an American whose parents were immigrants from Japan. [Japanese, literally 'second generation']

nisi /'nʌɪsʌɪ/ *adj. Law* that takes effect only on certain conditions (*decree nisi*). [Latin, = unless]

Nissen hut /'nɪs(ə)n/ *n.* a tunnel-shaped hut of corrugated iron with a cement floor. [named after P. N. *Nissen*, British engineer d. 1930, its inventor]

nit[1] /nɪt/ *n.* **1** the egg or young form of a louse or other parasitic insect, esp. of human head lice or body lice. **2** *Brit. colloq.* a stupid person. [Old English *hnitu*, from West Germanic]

nit[2] /nɪt/ *int. Austral. slang* used as a warning that someone is approaching. □ **keep nit** keep watch; act as guard. [19th c.: origin unknown: cf. NIX[3]]

niter *US* var. of NITRE.

nitinol /'nɪtɪnɒl/ *n.* an alloy of nickel and titanium. [*Ni* + *Ti* + *N*aval *O*rdnance *L*aboratory, Maryland, US]

nit-picking *n. & adj. colloq.* fault-finding in a petty manner. □ **nit-pick** *v.intr.* **nit-picker** *n.*

nitrate *n. & v.* ● *n.* /'nʌɪtreɪt/ **1** any salt or ester of nitric acid. **2** potassium or sodium nitrate when used as a fertilizer. ● *v.tr.* /nʌɪ'treɪt/ *Chem.* treat, combine, or impregnate with nitric acid. □ **nitration** /-'treɪʃ(ə)n/ *n.* [French (as NITRE, -ATE[1])]

nitre /'nʌɪtə/ *n.* (*US* **niter**) saltpetre, potassium nitrate. [Middle English via Old French and Latin *nitrum* from Greek *nitron*, of Semitic origin]

nitric /'nʌɪtrɪk/ *adj.* of or containing nitrogen, esp. in the pentavalent state. [French *nitrique* (as NITRE)]

nitric acid *n.* a colourless or pale yellow corrosive poisonous liquid acid. Chem. formula: HNO_3.

nitric oxide *n.* a colourless toxic gas, involved in physiological processes in minute quantities, and forming nitrogen dioxide in air. Chem. formula: NO.

nitride /'nʌɪtrʌɪd/ *n. Chem.* a binary compound of nitrogen with a more electropositive element. [NITRE + -IDE]

nitrify /'nʌɪtrɪfʌɪ/ *v.tr.* (**-ies, -ied**) **1** impregnate with nitrogen. **2** convert (nitrogen, usu. in the form of ammonia) into nitrites or nitrates. □ **nitrifiable** *adj.* **nitrification** /-fɪ'keɪʃ(ə)n/ *n.* [French *nitrifier* (as NITRE)]

nitrile /'nʌɪtrʌɪl/ *n. Chem.* an organic compound consisting of an alkyl radical bound to a cyanide radical.

nitrite /'nʌɪtrʌɪt/ *n.* any salt or ester of nitrous acid.

nitro- /'nʌɪtrəʊ/ *comb. form* **1** of or containing nitric acid, nitre, or nitrogen. **2** made with or by use of any of these. **3** of or containing the monovalent $-NO_2$ group (*the nitro groups in TNT*). [Greek (as NITRE)]

nitrobenzene /nʌɪtrəʊ'bɛnzi:n/ *n.* a yellow oily liquid made by the nitration of benzene and used to make aniline etc.

nitrocellulose /nʌɪtrəʊ'sɛljʊləʊz, -ləʊs/ *n.* a highly flammable material made by treating cellulose with concentrated nitric acid, used in the manufacture of explosives and celluloid.

nitrogen /'nʌɪtrədʒ(ə)n/ *n. Chem.* a colourless odourless unreactive gaseous element that forms four-fifths of the earth's atmosphere and is an essential constituent of proteins, nucleic acids, and other biological molecules (symbol N). □ **nitrogenous** /-'trɒdʒməs/ *adj.* [French *nitrogène* (as NITRO-, -GEN)]

nitrogen cycle *n. Ecol.* the series of processes by which nitrogen is absorbed from and returned to the atmosphere by biological systems, including nitrogen fixation and decomposition.

nitrogen dioxide *n.* a reddish-brown poisonous gas. Chem. formula: NO_2.

nitrogen fixation *n.* a chemical process in which atmospheric nitrogen is assimilated into organic compounds, esp. naturally by certain micro-organisms as part of the nitrogen cycle.

nitroglycerine /nʌɪtrə(ʊ)'glɪs(ə)ri:n -rɪn/ *n.* (also **nitroglycerin**) an explosive yellow liquid made by reacting glycerol with a mixture of concentrated sulphuric and nitric acids.

nitrosamine /nʌɪ'trəʊsəmi:n/ *n. Chem.* any of a group of carcinogenic substances containing the chemical group :N-N:O.

nitrous /'nʌɪtrəs/ *adj.* of, like, or impregnated with nitrogen, esp. in the trivalent state. [Latin *nitrosus* (as NITRE), partly through French *nitreux*]

nitrous acid *n.* a weak acid existing only in solution and in the gaseous state. Chem. formula: HNO_2.

nitrous oxide *n.* a colourless gas used as an anaesthetic (= LAUGHING GAS) and as an aerosol propellant. Chem. formula: N_2O.

nitty-gritty /nɪtɪ'grɪti/ *n. slang* the realities or practical details of a matter. [20th c.: origin uncertain]

nitwit /'nɪtwɪt/ *n. colloq.* a stupid person. □ **nitwittery** /-'wɪtəri/ *n.* [perhaps from NIT[1] + WIT[1]]

nitwitted /nɪt'wɪtɪd/ *adj.* stupid. □ **nitwittedness** *n.*

nix[1] /nɪks/ *n. & v. slang* ● *n.* **1** nothing. **2** a denial or refusal. ● *v.tr.* **1** cancel. **2** reject. [German, colloq. variant of *nichts* nothing]

nix[2] /nɪks/ *n.* (*fem.* **nixie** /'nɪksi/) a water elf. [German *Nix* (fem. *Nixe*)]

nix[3] /nɪks/ *int. Brit. slang* giving warning to confederates etc. that a person in authority is approaching. [19th c.: perhaps = NIX[1]]

NJ *abbr. US* New Jersey (also in official postal use).

NM *abbr. US* New Mexico (in official postal use).

nm *abbr.* **1** nautical mile. **2** nanometre.

n.m. *abbr.* nautical mile.

N.Mex. *abbr.* New Mexico.

NMR *abbr.* (also **nmr**) nuclear magnetic resonance.

NNE *abbr.* north-north-east.

NNW *abbr.* north-north-west.

No[1] *symb. Chem.* the element nobelium.

No[2] var. of NOH.

No. *abbr.* **1** number. **2** *US* North. [sense 1 from Latin *numero*, ablative of *numerus* 'number']

no[1] /nəʊ/ *det.* **1** not any (*there is no excuse; no circumstances could justify it; no two of them are alike*).

2 not a, quite other than (*is no fool*; *is no part of my plan*; *caused no slight inconvenience*). **3** hardly any (*is no distance*; *did it in no time*). **4** used elliptically as a slogan, notice, etc., to forbid, reject, or deplore the thing specified (*no parking*; *no surrender*). ◻ **by no means** see MEANS. **no dice** see DICE. **no doubt** see DOUBT. **no end** see END. **no fear** see FEAR. **no joke** see JOKE. **no joy** see JOY *n.* 3. **no little** see LITTLE. **no man** no person, nobody. **no place** *US* nowhere. **no small** see SMALL. **no sweat** *colloq.* no bother, no trouble. **no thoroughfare** an indication that passage along a street, path, etc., is blocked or prohibited. **no through road** = *no thoroughfare*. **no time** see TIME. **no way** *colloq.* **1** it is impossible. **2** I will not agree etc. **no whit** see WHIT. **no wonder** see WONDER. **... or no ...** regardless of the ... (*rain or no rain, I shall go out*). **there is no ...ing** it is impossible to ... (*there is no accounting for tastes*; *there was no mistaking what he meant*). [Middle English from *nān*, *nōn* NONE[1], originally only before consonants]

no[2] /nəʊ/ *int.*, *adv.*, *& n.* ● *int.* equivalent to a negative sentence: the answer to your question is negative, your request or command will not be complied with, the statement made or course of action intended or conclusion arrived at is not correct or satisfactory, the negative statement made is correct. ● *adv.* **1** (foll. by *compar.*) by no amount; not at all (*no better than before*). **2** *Sc.* not (*will ye no come back again?*). ● *n.* (*pl.* **noes**) **1** an utterance of the word *no*. **2** a denial or refusal. **3** a negative vote. ◻ **is no more** has died or ceased to exist. **no better than one should be** morally suspect. **no can do** *colloq.* I am unable to do it. **no less** (often foll. by *than*) **1** as much (*gave me £50, no less*; *gave me no less than £50*; *is no less than a scandal*; *a no less fatal victory*). **2** as important (*no less a person than the President*). **3** *disp.* no fewer (*no less than ten people have told me*). **no longer** not now or henceforth as formerly. **the noes have it** the negative voters are in the majority. **no, no** an emphatic equivalent of a negative sentence (cf. sense 1 of *adv.*). **no sooner ... than** see SOON. **not take no for an answer** persist in spite of refusals. **or no** or not (*pleasant or no, it is true*). **whether or no 1** in either case. **2** (as an indirect question) which of a case and its negative (*tell me whether or no*). [Old English *nō*, *nā*, from *ne* 'not' + *ō*, *ā* 'ever']

n.o. *abbr. Cricket* not out.

no-account *attrib.adj.* unimportant, worthless.

Noah's ark /ˈnəʊəz/ *n.* **1 a** the ship in which (according to the Bible) Noah, his family, and the animals were saved. **b** an imitation of this as a child's toy. **2** a large or cumbrous or old-fashioned trunk or vehicle. **3** a small bivalve mollusc, *Arca noae*, with a boat-shaped shell. [*Noah*, Hebrew patriarch in Gen. 6]

nob[1] /nɒb/ *n. Brit. slang* a person of wealth or high social position. [originally Scots *knabb*, *nab*; 17th c., of unknown origin]

nob[2] /nɒb/ *n. slang* the head. [perhaps variant of KNOB]

no-ball *n. & v. Cricket* ● *n.* an unlawfully delivered ball (counting one to the batting side if not otherwise scored from). ● *v.tr.* pronounce (a bowler) to have bowled a no-ball.

nobble /ˈnɒb(ə)l/ *v.tr. Brit. slang* **1** tamper with (a racehorse) to prevent its winning. **2** try to influence, esp. unfairly. **3** steal (money). **4** seize, catch. [probably = dialect *knobble*, *knubble* 'knock, beat', from KNOB]

nobbler /ˈnɒblə/ *n. Austral. slang* a glass or drink of liquor. [19th c.: origin unknown]

Nobelist /nəʊˈbɛlɪst/ *n. US* a winner of a Nobel Prize.

nobelium /nə(ʊ)ˈbiːlɪəm, -ˈbɛl-/ *n. Chem.* an artificially produced radioactive transuranic metallic element (symbol No). [*Nobel* (see NOBEL PRIZE) + -IUM]

Nobel Prize /ˈnəʊbɛl, -ˈbɛl/ *n.* any of six international prizes awarded annually for physics, chemistry, physiology or medicine, literature, economics, and the promotion of peace. ◻ **Nobel prizewinner** *n.* [named after Alfred *Nobel* (d. 1896), Swedish chemist and engineer, who endowed them]

nobiliary /nə(ʊ)ˈbɪljərɪ/ *adj.* of the nobility. [French *nobiliaire* (as NOBLE)]

nobiliary particle *n.* a preposition forming part of a title of nobility (e.g. French *de*, German *von*).

nobility /nə(ʊ)ˈbɪlɪtɪ/ *n.* (*pl.* **-ies**) **1** nobleness of character, mind, birth, or rank. **2** (prec. by *a*, *the*) a class of nobles, an aristocracy. [Middle English from Old French *nobilité* or Latin *nobilitas* (as NOBLE)]

noble /ˈnəʊb(ə)l/ *adj. & n.* ● *adj.* (**nobler**, **noblest**) **1** belonging by rank, title, or birth to the aristocracy. **2** of excellent character; having lofty ideals; free from pettiness and meanness, magnanimous. **3** of imposing appearance, splendid, magnificent, stately. **4** excellent, admirable (*noble horse*; *noble cellar*). ● *n.* **1** a nobleman or noblewoman. **2** *hist.* a former English gold coin first issued in 1351. ◻ **the noble art of self-defence** see SELF-DEFENCE. ◻ **nobleness** *n.* **nobly** *adv.* [Middle English via Old French from Latin *(g)nobilis*: related to KNOW]

noble gas *n.* any gaseous element of a group that almost never combine with other elements.

nobleman /ˈnəʊb(ə)lmən/ *n.* (*pl.* **-men**) a man of noble rank or birth, a peer.

noble metal *n.* a metal (e.g. gold, silver, or platinum) that resists chemical action, does not corrode or tarnish in air or water, and is not easily attacked by acids.

noble rot *n.* **1** the condition of grapes affected by the mould *Botrytis cinerea* (see BOTRYTIS). **2** the mould itself. [translation of French *pourriture noble*]

noble savage *n.* primitive man idealized as in Romantic literature.

noble science *n.* (prec. by *the*) boxing.

noblesse /nəʊˈblɛs, French nɔblɛs/ *n.* the class of nobles (esp. of a foreign country). ◻ ***noblesse oblige*** /ɒˈbliːʒ, French ɔbliʒ/ privilege entails responsibility. [Middle English = nobility, from Old French (as NOBLE)]

noblewoman /ˈnəʊb(ə)lwʊmən/ *n.* (*pl.* **-women**) a woman of noble rank or birth, a peeress.

nobody /ˈnəʊbədɪ/ *pron. & n.* ● *pron.* no person. ● *n.* (*pl.* **-ies**) a person of no importance, authority, or position. ◻ **like nobody's business** see BUSINESS. **nobody's fool** see FOOL[1]. [Middle English, from NO[1] + BODY (= person)]

nock /nɒk/ *n. & v.* ● *n.* **1** a notch at either end of a bow for holding the string. **2 a** a notch at the butt-end of an arrow for receiving the bowstring. **b** a notched piece of horn serving this purpose. ● *v.tr.* set (an arrow) on the string. [Middle English, perhaps = *nock*, the forward upper corner of some sails, from Middle Dutch *nocke*]

no-claims bonus *n.* (also **no-claim bonus**, **no-claim(s) discount**) *Brit.* a reduction of the insurance premium charged when the insured has not made a claim under the insurance during an agreed preceding period.

noctambulist /nɒkˈtambjʊlɪst/ *n.* a sleepwalker. ◻ **noctambulism** *n.* [Latin *nox noctis* 'night' + *ambulare* 'walk']

noctuid /ˈnɒktjʊɪd/ *adj. & n.* ● *adj.* of or relating to the family Noctuidae of mainly large brownish nocturnal moths, often with an eye-spot on the forewings. ● *n.* a moth of this family. [modern Latin genus name *Noctua*, from Latin, = night owl]

noctule /ˈnɒktjuːl/ *n.* a large W. European bat, *Nyctalus noctula*. [French from Italian *nottola* 'bat']

nocturn /ˈnɒktəːn/ *n. RC Ch.* a part of matins originally said at night. [Middle English from Old French *nocturne* or ecclesiastical Latin *nocturnum*, neut. of Latin *nocturnus*: see NOCTURNAL]

nocturnal /nɒkˈtəːn(ə)l/ *adj.* of or in the night; done or active by night. ◻ **nocturnally** *adv.* [Late Latin *nocturnalis* from Latin *nocturnus* 'of the night', from *nox noctis* 'night']

nocturnal emission *n.* involuntary emission of semen during sleep.

nocturne /ˈnɒktəːn/ *n.* **1** *Mus.* a short composition of a romantic nature, usu. for piano. **2** a picture of a night scene. [French (as NOCTURN)]

nocuous /ˈnɒkjʊəs/ *adj. literary* noxious, harmful. [Latin *nocuus* from *nocēre* 'hurt']

nod /nɒd/ *v. & n.* ● *v.* (**nodded**, **nodding**) **1** *intr.* incline one's head slightly and briefly in greeting, assent, or command. **2** *intr.* let one's head fall forward in drowsiness; be drowsy. **3** *tr.* incline (one's head). **4** *tr.* signify (assent etc.) by a nod. **5** *intr.* (of flowers, plumes, etc.) bend downwards and sway, or move up and down. **6** *intr.* make a mistake due to a momentary lack of alertness or attention. ● *n.* a nodding of the head. □ **get the nod** *N. Amer.* be chosen or approved. **nod off** *colloq.* fall asleep. **nod through** *colloq.* **1** approve on the nod. **2** *Brit. Parl.* formally count (a Member of Parliament) as if having voted when unable to do so. **on the nod** *Brit. colloq.* **1** with merely formal assent and no discussion. **2** on credit. [Middle English *nodde*, perhaps of Low German origin]

nodding acquaintance *n.* (usu. foll. by *with*) a very slight acquaintance with a person or subject.

noddle[1] /ˈnɒd(ə)l/ *n. colloq.* the head. [Middle English *nodle*, of unknown origin]

noddle[2] /ˈnɒd(ə)l/ *v.tr.* nod or wag (one's head). [NOD + -LE[4]]

noddy /ˈnɒdi/ *n.* (*pl.* **-ies**) **1** a simpleton. **2** any usu. dark-coloured tropical tern of the genus *Anous* or *Procelsterna*. [probably from obsolete *noddy* 'foolish', which is perhaps from NOD]

node /nəʊd/ *n.* **1** *Bot.* **a** the part of a plant stem from which one or more leaves emerge. **b** a knob on a root or branch. **2** *Anat.* **a** a small mass of differentiated tissue, esp. a lymph gland. **b** an interruption of the myelin sheath of a nerve. **3** *Astron.* either of two points at which a planet's orbit intersects the plane of the ecliptic or the celestial equator. **4** *Physics* a point of minimum disturbance in a standing wave system. **5** *Electr.* a point of zero current or voltage. **6** *Math.* **a** a point at which a curve intersects itself. **b** a vertex in a graph. **7** a component in a computer network. □ **nodal** *adj.* **nodical** *adj.* (in sense 3). [Latin *nodus* 'knot']

nodose /nəʊˈdəʊs/ *adj.* knotty, knotted. □ **nodosity** /-ˈdɒsɪti/ *n.* [Latin *nodosus* (as NODE)]

nodule /ˈnɒdjuːl/ *n.* **1** a small rounded lump of anything, e.g. flint in chalk, carbon in cast iron, or a mineral on the seabed. **2** a small swelling or aggregation of cells, e.g. a small tumour, node, or ganglion, or a swelling on a root of a legume containing bacteria. □ **nodular** *adj.* **nodulated** *adj.* **nodulation** /-ˈleɪʃ(ə)n/ *n.* **nodulose** *adj.* **nodulous** *adj.* [Latin *nodulus*, diminutive of *nodus*: see NODUS]

nodus /ˈnəʊdəs/ *n.* (*pl.* **nodi** /-dʌɪ/) a knotty point, a difficulty, a complication in the plot of a story etc. [Latin, = knot]

Noel /nəʊˈɛl/ *n.* (also **Noël**, *archaic* **Nowel**, **Nowell**) Christmas (esp. as a refrain in carols). [French from Latin (as NATAL)]

noetic /nəʊˈɛtɪk/ *adj. & n.* ● *adj.* **1** of the intellect. **2** purely intellectual or abstract. **3** given to intellectual speculation. ● *n.* (in *sing.* or *pl.*) the science of the intellect. [Greek *noētikos*, via *noētos* 'intellectual' from *noeō* 'apprehend']

no-fault *attrib.adj.* esp. *N. Amer.* involving no fault or blame, esp. designating an insurance policy that is valid regardless of whether the policy-holder was at fault.

no-fly zone *n.* a zone in which aircraft are forbidden to fly.

no-frills *attrib.adj.* lacking ornament or embellishment.

nog[1] /nɒg/ *n. & v.* ● *n.* **1** a small block or peg of wood. **2** a snag or stump on a tree. **3** nogging. ● *v.tr.* (**nogged**, **nogging**) **1** secure with nogs. **2** build in the form of nogging. [17th c.: origin unknown]

nog[2] /nɒg/ *n.* **1** *Brit.* a strong beer brewed in East Anglia. **2** an egg-flip. [17th c.: origin unknown]

noggin /ˈnɒgɪn/ *n.* **1** a small mug. **2** a small measure, usu. ¼ pint, of spirits. **3** *slang* the head. [17th c.: origin unknown]

nogging /ˈnɒgɪŋ/ *n.* brickwork or timber braces in a timber frame. [NOG[1] + -ING[1]]

no go *adj.* (usu. hyphenated when *attrib.*) impossible, hopeless; forbidden.

no-go area *n. Brit.* an area forbidden to unauthorized people.

no-good *adj. & n. colloq.* ● *attrib.adj.* useless. ● *n.* a useless person or thing.

no good *n. & adj.* ● *n.* mischief (*is up to no good*). ● *predic.adj.* useless; to no advantage (*it is no good arguing*; *said my idea was no good*).

Noh /nəʊ/ *n.* (also **No**) traditional Japanese drama with dance and song, evolved from Shinto rites. [Japanese *nō*]

no-hitter *n. Baseball* a match in which a pitcher yields no hits.

no-hoper *n. slang* a useless person; a person or thing doomed to failure.

nohow /ˈnəʊhaʊ/ *adv.* **1** *US* in no way; by no means. **2** *dial.* out of order; out of sorts.

noil /nɔɪl/ *n.* (in *sing.* or *pl.*) short wool-combings. [perhaps via Old French *noel* from medieval Latin *nodellus*, diminutive of Latin *nodus* 'knot']

noise /nɔɪz/ *n. & v.* ● *n.* **1** a sound, esp. a loud or unpleasant or undesired one. **2** a series of loud sounds, esp. shouts; a confused sound of voices and movements. **3** irregular fluctuations accompanying a transmitted signal but not relevant to it. **4** (in *pl.*) conventional remarks, or speechlike sounds without actual words (*made sympathetic noises*). ● *v.* **1** *tr.* (usu. in *passive*) make public; spread abroad (a person's fame or a fact). **2** *intr. archaic* make much noise. □ **make a noise 1** (usu. foll. by *about*) talk or complain much. **2** be much talked of; attain notoriety. [Middle English via Old French from Latin *nausea*: see NAUSEA]

noiseless /ˈnɔɪzlɪs/ *adj.* **1** silent. **2** characterized by the absence of extraneous noise. □ **noiselessly** *adv.* **noiselessness** *n.*

noise-maker *n.* a device for making a loud noise at a festivity etc.

noise pollution *n.* harmful or annoying noise.

noises off *n.pl.* sounds made off stage to be heard by the audience of a play.

noisette /nwɑːˈzɛt/ *n.* **1** a small round piece of meat etc. **2** a chocolate made with hazelnuts. [French, diminutive of *noix* 'nut']

noisome /ˈnɔɪs(ə)m/ *adj. literary* **1** harmful, noxious. **2** evil-smelling. **3** objectionable, offensive. □ **noisomeness** *n.* [Middle English from obsolete *noy*, from ANNOY]

noisy /ˈnɔɪzi/ *adj.* (**noisier**, **noisiest**) **1** full of or attended with noise. **2** making or given to making much noise. **3** clamorous, turbulent. **4** (of a colour, garment, etc.) loud, conspicuous. □ **noisily** *adv.* **noisiness** *n.*

nolens volens /nəʊlɛnz ˈvəʊlɛnz/ *adv. literary* willy-nilly, perforce. [Latin participles, = unwilling, willing]

nolle prosequi /nɒlɪ ˈprɒsɪkwʌɪ/ *n. Law* **1** the relinquishment by a plaintiff or prosecutor of all or part of a suit. **2** the entry of this on record. [Latin, = refuse to pursue]

nom. *abbr.* nominal.

nomad /ˈnəʊmad/ *n. & adj.* ● *n.* **1** a member of a people roaming from place to place for fresh pasture. **2** a wanderer. ● *adj.* **1** living as a nomad. **2** wandering. □ **nomadic** /-ˈmadɪk/ *adj.* **nomadically** /-ˈmadɪk(ə)li/ *adv.* **nomadism** *n.* **nomadize** *v.intr.* (also **-ise**). [French *nomade* via Latin *nomas nomad-* from Greek *nomas -ados*, from *nemō* 'to pasture']

no man's land *n.* **1** *Mil.* the space between two opposing armies. **2** an area not assigned to any owner. **3** an area not clearly belonging to any one subject etc.

nombril /ˈnɒmbrɪl/ *n. Heraldry* the point halfway between fess point and the base of the shield. [French, = navel]

nom de guerre /nɒm də 'gɛː, French nɔ̃ də gɛr/ *n.* (*pl.* ***noms de guerre*** *pronunc.* same) an assumed name under which a person fights, plays, writes, etc. [French, = war-name]

nom de plume /nɒm də 'pluːm/ *n.* (*pl.* **noms de plume** *pronunc.* same) an assumed name under which a person writes. [formed in English of French words, = pen-name, on the pattern of NOM DE GUERRE]

nomen /'nəʊmən/ *n.* an ancient Roman's second name, indicating the gens, as in Marcus *Tullius* Cicero. [Latin, = name]

nomenclature /nə(ʊ)'mɛŋklətʃə, 'nəʊmənkleɪtʃə/ *n.* **1** a person's or community's system of names for things. **2** the terminology of a science etc. **3** systematic naming. **4** a catalogue or register. □ **nomenclative** *adj.* **nomenclatural** /-'klatʃ(ə)r(ə)l, -klə'tʃʊər(ə)l/ *adj.* [French from Latin *nomenclatura*, from *nomen* 'name' + *calare* 'call']

nominal /'nɒmɪn(ə)l/ *adj.* **1** existing in name only; not real or actual (*nominal and real prices*; *nominal ruler*). **2** (of a sum of money, rent, etc.) virtually nothing; much below the actual value of a thing. **3** of or in names (*nominal and essential distinctions*). **4** consisting of or giving the names (*nominal list of officers*). **5** of or as or like a noun. □ **nominally** *adv.* [Middle English via French *nominal* or Latin *nominalis* from *nomen -inis* 'name']

nominal definition *n.* a statement of all that is connoted in the name of a concept.

nominalism /'nɒmɪn(ə)lɪz(ə)m/ *n. Philos.* the doctrine that universals or general ideas are mere names (opp. REALISM 3a). □ **nominalist** *n.* **nominalistic** /-'lɪstɪk/ *adj.* [French *nominalisme* (as NOMINAL)]

nominalize /'nɒmɪn(ə)lʌɪz/ *v.tr.* (also **-ise**) form a noun from (a verb, adjective, etc.), e.g. *output, truth*, from *put out, true*. □ **nominalization** /-'zeɪʃ(ə)n/ *n.*

nominal value *n.* the face value (of a coin, shares, etc.).

nominate /'nɒmɪneɪt/ *v.tr.* **1** propose (a candidate) for election. **2** appoint to an office (*a board of six nominated and six elected members*). **3** name or appoint (a date or place). **4** mention by name. **5** call by the name of, designate. □ **nominator** *n.* [Latin *nominare nominat-* (as NOMINAL)]

nomination /nɒmɪ'neɪʃ(ə)n/ *n.* **1** the act or an instance of nominating; the state of being nominated. **2** the right of nominating for an appointment (*have a nomination at your disposal*). [Middle English from Old French *nomination* or Latin *nominatio* (as NOMINATE)]

nominative /'nɒmɪnətɪv/ *n. & adj.* ● *n. Gram.* **1** the case of nouns, pronouns, and adjectives, expressing the subject of a verb. **2** a word in this case. ● *adj.* **1** *Gram.* of or in this case. **2** /-neɪtɪv/ of, or appointed by, nomination (as distinct from election). □ **nominatival** /-'tʌɪv(ə)l/ *adj.* [Middle English from Old French *nominatif -ive* or Latin *nominativus* (as NOMINATE), translation of Greek *onomastikē* (*ptōsis* 'case')]

nominee /nɒmɪ'niː/ *n.* **1** a person who is nominated for an office or as the recipient of a grant etc. **2** *Commerce* a person (not necessarily the owner) in whose name a stock etc. is registered. [NOMINATE]

nomogram /'nɒməgram, 'nəʊm-/ *n.* (also **nomograph** /-grɑːf/) a graphical presentation of relations between quantities whereby the value of one may be found by simple geometrical construction (e.g. drawing a straight line) from those of others. □ **nomographic** /-'grafɪk/ *adj.* **nomographically** /-'grafɪk(ə)li/ *adv.* **nomography** /nə'mɒgrəfi/ *n.* [Greek *nomo-* from *nomos* 'law' + -GRAM]

no more *n., adj., & adv.* ● *n.* nothing further (*have no more to say*; *want no more of it*). ● *adj.* not any more (*no more wine?*). ● *adv.* **1** no longer. **2** never again. **3** to no greater extent (*is no more a lord than I am*; *could no more do it than fly in the air*). **4** just as little, neither (*you did not come, and no more did he*).

nomothetic /nɒmə'θɛtɪk, 'nəʊm-/ *adj.* **1** stating (esp. scientific) laws. **2** legislative. [obsolete *nomothete* 'legislator' from Greek *nomothetēs*]

-nomy /nəmi/ *comb. form* denoting an area of knowledge or the laws governing it (*aeronomy*; *economy*). [representing Greek *-nomia*, related to *nomos* 'law' *nemein* 'distribute']

non- /nɒn/ *prefix* giving the negative sense of words with which it is combined, esp.: **1** not doing or having or involved with (*non-attendance*; *non-payment*; *non-productive*). **2 a** not of the kind or class described (*non-alcoholic*; *non-member*; *non-event*). **b** forming terms used adjectivally (*non-union*; *non-party*). **3** a lack of (*non-access*). **4** (with adverbs) not in the way described (*non-aggressively*). **5** forming adjectives from verbs, meaning 'that does not' or 'that is not meant to (or to be)' (*non-skid*; *non-iron*). **6** used to form a neutral negative sense when a form in *in-* or *un-* has a special sense or (usu. unfavourable) connotation (*non-controversial*; *non-effective*; *non-human*). [from or suggested by Middle English *no(u)n-* via Anglo-French *noun-*, Old French *non-*, *nom-* from Latin *non* 'not']

■ **Usage** The number of words that can be formed with the prefix *non-* is unlimited; consequently only a selection, considered the most current or semantically noteworthy, can be given here.

nona- /'nɒnə, 'nəʊnə/ *comb. form* nine. [Latin from *nonus* 'ninth']

non-abstainer /nɒnəb'steɪnə/ *n.* a person who does not abstain (esp. from alcohol).

non-acceptance /nɒnək'sɛpt(ə)ns/ *n.* a lack of acceptance.

non-access /nɒn'aksɛs/ *n.* a lack of access.

non-addictive /nɒnə'dɪktɪv/ *adj.* (of a drug, habit, etc.) not causing addiction.

nonage /'nəʊnɪdʒ, 'nɒn-/ *n.* **1** *hist.* the state of being under full legal age, minority. **2** a period of immaturity. [Middle English from Anglo-French *nounage*, Old French *nonage* (as NON-, AGE)]

nonagenarian /nɒnədʒɪ'nɛːrɪən, nəʊn-/ *n. & adj.* ● *n.* a person from 90 to 99 years old. ● *adj.* of this age. [Latin *nonagenarius* from *nonageni*, distributive of *nonaginta* 'ninety']

non-aggression /nɒnə'grɛʃ(ə)n/ *n.* lack of or restraint from aggression (often *attrib.*: *non-aggression pact*).

nonagon /'nɒnəg(ə)n/ *n.* a plane figure with nine sides and angles. [Latin *nonus* 'ninth', on the pattern of HEXAGON]

non-alcoholic /ˌnɒnalkə'hɒlɪk/ *adj.* (of a drink etc.) not containing alcohol.

non-aligned /nɒnə'lʌɪnd/ *adj.* (of states etc.) not aligned with another (esp. major) power. □ **non-alignment** *n.*

non-allergic /nɒnə'ləːdʒɪk/ *adj.* not causing allergy; not allergic.

non-ambiguous /nɒnam'bɪgjʊəs/ *adj.* not ambiguous.

■ **Usage** *Non-ambiguous* is neutral in sense: see NON- 6, UNAMBIGUOUS.

non-appearance /nɒnə'pɪər(ə)ns/ *n.* failure to appear or be present.

non-art /nɒn'ɑːt/ *n.* something that avoids the normal forms of art.

nonary /'nəʊnəri/ *adj. & n.* ● *adj. Math.* (of a scale of notation) having nine as its base. ● *n.* (*pl.* **-ies**) a group of nine. [Latin *nonus* 'ninth']

non-Aryan /nɒn'ɛːrɪən/ *adj. & n.* ● *adj.* (of a person or language) not Aryan or of Aryan descent. ● *n.* a non-Aryan person.

non-attached /nɒnə'tatʃd/ *adj.* that is not attached.

■ **Usage** *Non-attached* is neutral in sense: see NON- 6, UNATTACHED.

non-attendance /nɒnə'tɛnd(ə)ns/ *n.* failure to attend.

non-attributable /nɒnə'trɪbjʊtəb(ə)l/ *adj.* that cannot or may not be attributed to a particular source etc. □ **non-attributably** *adv.*

non-availability /ˌnɒnəveɪləˈbɪlɪti/ *n.* a state of not being available.

non-believer /nɒnbɪˈliːvə/ *n.* a person who does not believe or has no (esp. religious) faith.

non-belligerency /nɒnbɪˈlɪdʒ(ə)r(ə)nsi/ *n.* a lack of belligerency.

non-belligerent /nɒnbɪˈlɪdʒ(ə)r(ə)nt/ *adj. & n.* ● *adj.* not engaged in hostilities. ● *n.* a non-belligerent nation, state, etc.

non-biological /ˌnɒnbʌɪəˈlɒdʒɪk(ə)l/ *adj.* **1** not relating to biology or living organisms. **2** (of a detergent etc.) not containing enzymes.

non-black /nɒnˈblak/ *adj. & n.* ● *adj.* **1** (of a person) not black. **2** of or relating to non-black people. ● *n.* a non-black person.

non-breakable /nɒnˈbreɪkəb(ə)l/ *adj.* not breakable.

non-capital /nɒnˈkapɪt(ə)l/ *adj.* (of an offence) not punishable by death.

non-Catholic /nɒnˈkaθ(ə)lɪk/ *adj. & n.* ● *adj.* not Roman Catholic. ● *n.* a non-Catholic person.

nonce /nɒns/ *n.* □ **for the nonce** for the time being; for the present occasion. [Middle English *than anes* = for the one, altered by wrong division (cf. NEWT)]

nonce-word *n.* a word coined for one occasion.

nonchalant /ˈnɒnʃ(ə)l(ə)nt/ *adj.* calm and casual, unmoved, unexcited, indifferent. □ **nonchalance** *n.* **nonchalantly** *adv.* [French, part. of *nonchaloir* (as NON-, *chaloir* 'be concerned')]

non-Christian /nɒnˈkrɪstʃ(ə)n, -ˈkrɪstɪən/ *adj. & n.* ● *adj.* not Christian. ● *n.* a non-Christian person.

non-citizen /nɒnˈsɪtɪz(ə)n/ *n.* a person who is not a citizen (of a particular state, town, etc.).

non-classified /nɒnˈklasɪfʌɪd/ *adj.* (esp. of information) that is not classified.

■ **Usage** *Non-classified* is neutral in sense: see NON- 6, UNCLASSIFIED.

non-clerical /nɒnˈklɛrɪk(ə)l/ *adj.* not doing or involving clerical work.

non-collegiate /nɒnkəˈliːdʒ(ɪ)ət/ *adj.* **1** not attached to a college. **2** not having colleges.

non-com /ˈnɒnkɒm/ *n. colloq.* a non-commissioned officer. [abbreviation]

non-combatant /nɒnˈkɒmbət(ə)nt/ *n.* a person not fighting in a war, esp. a civilian, army chaplain, etc.

non-commissioned /nɒnkəˈmɪʃ(ə)nd/ *adj. Mil.* (of an officer) not holding a commission.

non-committal /nɒnkəˈmɪt(ə)l/ *adj.* avoiding commitment to a definite opinion or course of action. □ **non-committally** *adv.*

non-communicant /nɒnkəˈmjuːnɪk(ə)nt/ *n.* a person who is not a communicant (esp. in the religious sense).

non-communicating /nɒnkəˈmjuːnɪkeɪtɪŋ/ *adj.* that does not communicate.

non-communist /nɒnˈkɒmjʊnɪst/ *adj. & n.* (also **non-Communist** with reference to a particular party) ● *adj.* not advocating or practising communism. ● *n.* a non-communist person.

non-compliance /nɒnkəmˈplʌɪəns/ *n.* failure to comply; a lack of compliance.

non compos mentis /ˌnɒn kɒmpɒs ˈmɛntɪs/ *adj.* (also **non compos**) not in one's right mind. [Latin, = not having control of one's mind]

non-conductor /nɒnkənˈdʌktə/ *n.* a substance that does not conduct heat or electricity. □ **non-conducting** *adj.*

non-confidential /ˌnɒnkɒnfɪˈdɛnʃ(ə)l/ *adj.* not confidential. □ **non-confidentially** *adv.*

nonconformist /nɒnkənˈfɔːmɪst/ *n. & adj.* ● *n.* **1** a person who does not conform to the doctrine or discipline of an established Church, esp. (**Nonconformist**) a member of a (usu. Protestant) Church dissenting from the Anglican Church. **2** a person who does not conform to a prevailing principle. ● *adj.* of or relating to a nonconformist or to Nonconformism. □ **nonconformism** *n.* (also *Relig.* **Nonconformism**).

nonconformity /nɒnkənˈfɔːmɪti/ *n.* **1 a** nonconformists as a body, esp. (**Nonconformity**) Protestants dissenting from the Anglican Church. **b** the principles or practice of nonconformists, esp. (**Nonconformity**) Protestant dissent. **2** (usu. foll. by *to*) failure to conform to a rule etc. **3** lack of correspondence between things.

non-contagious /nɒnkənˈteɪdʒəs/ *adj.* not contagious.

non-content /ˈnɒnkəntɛnt/ *n. Brit.* a negative voter in the House of Lords.

non-contentious /nɒnkənˈtɛnʃəs/ *adj.* not contentious.

non-contributory /nɒnkənˈtrɪbjʊt(ə)ri/ *adj.* not contributing or (esp. of a pension scheme) involving contributions.

non-controversial /ˌnɒnkɒntrəˈvəːʃ(ə)l/ *adj.* not controversial.

■ **Usage** *Non-controversial* is neutral in sense: see NON- 6, UNCONTROVERSIAL.

non-cooperation /ˌnɒnkəʊɒpəˈreɪʃ(ə)n/ *n.* failure to cooperate; a lack of cooperation.

non-delivery /nɒndɪˈlɪv(ə)ri/ *n.* failure to deliver.

non-denominational /ˌnɒndɪnɒmɪˈneɪʃ(ə)n(ə)l/ *adj.* not restricted as regards religious denomination.

nondescript /ˈnɒndɪskrɪpt/ *adj. & n.* ● *adj.* lacking distinctive characteristics, not easily classified, neither one thing nor another. ● *n.* a nondescript person or thing. □ **nondescriptly** *adv.* **nondescriptness** *n.* [NON- + *descript* 'described' from Latin *descriptus* (as DESCRIBE)]

non-destructive /nɒndɪˈstrʌktɪv/ *adj.* that does not involve destruction or damage.

non-drinker /nɒnˈdrɪŋkə/ *n.* a person who does not drink alcoholic liquor.

non-driver /nɒnˈdrʌɪvə/ *n.* a person who does not drive a motor vehicle.

none[1] /nʌn/ *pron., adj., & adv.* ● *pron.* **1** (foll. by *of*) **a** not any of (*none of this concerns me*; *none of them have found it*; *none of your impudence!*). **b** not any one of (*none of them has come*). **2 a** no persons (*none but fools have ever believed it*). **b** no person (*none can tell*). ● *adj.* (usu. with a preceding noun implied) **1** no; not any (*you have money and I have none*; *would rather have a bad reputation than none at all*). **2** not to be counted in a specified class (*his understanding is none of the clearest*; *if a linguist is wanted, I am none*). ● *adv.* (foll. by *the* + *compar.*, or *so*, *too*) by no amount; not at all (*am none the wiser*; *are none too fond of him*). □ **none the less** see NONETHELESS. **none other** (usu. foll. by *than*) no other person. [Old English *nān*, from *ne* 'not' + *ān* ONE]

■ **Usage** In sense 1 of the pronoun, *none* can be followed by a singular or plural verb according to the sense. If the sense is 'not any one of' a singular verb is used, e.g. *None of them is any good*, while if the sense is simply 'not any of' a plural verb is used, e.g. *None of them want to come*. The use of the singular verb is more emphatic.

none[2] /nəʊn/ *n.* (also in *pl.*) the office of the fifth canonical hour of prayer, originally said at the ninth hour of the day (3 p.m.). [French from Latin *nona*, fem. sing. of *nonus* 'ninth': cf. NOON]

non-earning /nɒnˈəːnɪŋ/ *adj.* not earning (esp. a regular wage or salary).

non-effective /nɒnɪˈfɛktɪv/ *adj.* that does not have an effect.

■ **Usage** *Non-effective* is neutral in sense: see NON- 6, INEFFECTIVE.

non-ego /nɒnˈiːgəʊ/ *n. Philos.* all that is not the conscious self.

nonentity /nɒˈnɛntɪti/ *n.* (*pl.* **-ies**) **1** a person or thing of no importance. **2 a** non-existence. **b** a non-existent thing, a figment. [medieval Latin *nonentitas* 'non-existence']

nones /nəʊnz/ *n.pl.* in the ancient Roman calendar, the ninth day before the ides by inclusive reckoning, i.e. the 7th day of March, May, July, October, the 5th of other months. [Old French *nones* from Latin *nonae*, fem. pl. of *nonus* 'ninth']

none-so-pretty *n.* London Pride.

non-essential /nɒnɪ'sɛnʃ(ə)l/ *adj.* & *n.* ● *adj.* not essential. ● *n.* a non-essential thing.

■ **Usage** *Non-essential* is neutral in sense: see NON- 6, INESSENTIAL.

nonesuch var. of NONSUCH.

nonet /nəʊ'nɛt, nɒ'nɛt/ *n.* **1** *Mus.* **a** a composition for nine voices or instruments. **b** the performers of such a piece. **2** a group of nine. [Italian *nonetto* from *nono* 'ninth', from Latin *nonus*]

nonetheless /nʌnðə'lɛs, 'nʌnðəlɛs/ *adv.* (also **none the less**) nevertheless.

non-Euclidean /nɒnju:'klɪdɪən/ *adj.* denying or going beyond Euclidean principles in geometry, esp. contravening the postulate that only one line through a given point can be parallel to a given line.

non-European /,nɒnjʊərə'pɪən/ *adj.* & *n.* ● *adj.* not European. ● *n.* a non-European person.

non-event /nɒnɪ'vɛnt/ *n.* an unimportant or anticlimactic occurrence.

non-existent /nɒnɪg'zɪst(ə)nt, -ɛg-/ *adj.* not existing. ▫ **non-existence** *n.*

non-explosive /nɒnɪk'spləʊsɪv, -ɛk-/ *adj.* (of a substance) that does not explode.

non-fattening /nɒn'fat(ə)nɪŋ/ *adj.* (of food) that does not make the consumer fat when eaten in normal amounts.

nonfeasance /nɒn'fi:z(ə)ns/ *n.* failure to perform an act required by law. [NON-: see MISFEASANCE]

non-ferrous /nɒn'fɛrəs/ *adj.* (of a metal) other than iron or steel.

non-fiction /nɒn'fɪkʃ(ə)n/ *n.* literary work other than fiction, including biography and reference books. ▫ **non-fictional** *adj.*

non-flam /nɒn'flam/ *adj.* = NON-FLAMMABLE.

non-flammable /nɒn'flaməb(ə)l/ *adj.* not inflammable.

■ **Usage** See Usage Note at FLAMMABLE.

non-fulfilment /nɒnfʊl'fɪlm(ə)nt/ *n.* failure to fulfil (an obligation).

non-functional /nɒn'fʌŋ(k)ʃ(ə)n(ə)l/ *adj.* not having a function.

nong /nɒŋ/ *n. Austral. slang* a foolish or stupid person. [20th c.: origin unknown]

non-governmental /,nɒngʌv(ə)n'mɛnt(ə)l/ *adj.* not belonging to or associated with a government.

non-human /nɒn'hju:mən/ *adj.* & *n.* ● *adj.* (of a being) not human. ● *n.* a non-human being.

■ **Usage** *Non-human* is neutral in sense: see NON- 6, INHUMAN, UNHUMAN.

non-infectious /nɒnɪn'fɛkʃəs/ *adj.* (of a disease) not infectious.

non-inflected /nɒnɪn'flɛktɪd/ *adj.* (of a language) not having inflections.

non-interference /,nɒnɪntə'fɪər(ə)ns/ *n.* a lack of interference.

non-intervention /,nɒnɪntə'vɛnʃ(ə)n/ *n.* the principle or practice of not becoming involved in others' affairs, esp. by one state in regard to another. ▫ **non-interventionist** *adj.* & *n.*

non-intoxicating /nɒnɪn'tɒksɪkeɪtɪŋ/ *adj.* (of drink) not causing intoxication.

non-invasive /nʌnɪn'veɪsɪv/ *adj.* **1** (of a medical procedure) not requiring incision into the body or the removal of tissue. **2** (of an infection etc.) not tending to spread.

non-iron /nɒn'ʌɪən/ *adj.* (of a fabric) that needs no ironing.

nonjoinder /nɒn'dʒɔɪndə/ *n. Law* the failure of a partner etc. to become a party to a suit.

nonjuror /nɒn'dʒʊərə/ *n.* a person who refuses to take an oath, esp. *hist.* a member of the clergy refusing to take the oath of allegiance to William and Mary in 1689. ▫ **nonjuring** *adj.*

non-jury /nɒn'dʒʊəri/ *adj.* (of a trial) without a jury.

non-linear /nɒn'lɪnɪə/ *adj.* not linear, esp. with regard to dimension.

non-literary /nɒn'lɪt(ə)(rə)ri/ *adj.* (of writing, a text, etc.) not literary in character.

non-logical /nɒn'lɒdʒɪk(ə)l/ *adj.* not involving logic. ▫ **non-logically** *adv.*

■ **Usage** *Non-logical* is neutral in sense: see NON- 6, ILLOGICAL.

non-magnetic /nɒnmag'nɛtɪk/ *adj.* (of a substance) not magnetic.

non-member /nɒn'mɛmbə/ *n.* a person who is not a member (of a particular association, club, etc.). ▫ **non-membership** *n.*

non-metal /nɒn'mɛt(ə)l/ *adj.* not made of metal. ▫ **non-metallic** /-mɪ'talɪk/ *adj.*

non-militant /nɒn'mɪlɪt(ə)nt/ *adj.* not militant.

non-military /nɒn'mɪlɪt(ə)ri/ *adj.* not military; not involving armed forces, civilian.

non-ministerial /,nɒnmɪnɪ'stɪərɪəl/ *adj.* not ministerial (esp. in political senses).

non-moral /nɒn'mɒr(ə)l/ *adj.* not concerned with morality. ▫ **non-morally** *adv.*

■ **Usage** *Non-moral* is neutral in sense: see NON- 6, AMORAL, IMMORAL.

non-natural /nɒn'natʃ(ə)r(ə)l/ *adj.* not involving natural means or processes.

■ **Usage** *Non-natural* is neutral in sense: see NON- 6, UNNATURAL.

non-negotiable /nɒnnɪ'gəʊʃəb(ə)l, -ʃɪə-/ *adj.* that cannot be negotiated (esp. in financial senses).

non-net /nɒn'nɛt/ *adj. Brit.* (of a book) not subject to a minimum selling price.

non-nuclear /nɒn'nju:klɪə/ *adj.* **1** not involving nuclei or nuclear energy. **2** (of a state etc.) not having nuclear weapons.

no-no /'nəʊnəʊ/*n.* (*pl.* **no-nos**) *colloq.* a thing that is not possible or acceptable.

non-objective /nɒnəb'dʒɛktɪv/ *adj.* **1** not objective. **2** *Art* abstract.

non-observance /nɒnəb'zə:v(ə)ns/ *n.* failure to observe (esp. an agreement, requirement, etc.).

no-nonsense *attrib.adj.* serious, sensible, without flippancy.

non-operational /,nɒnɒpə'reɪʃ(ə)n(ə)l/ *adj.* **1** that does not operate. **2** out of order.

non-organic /nɒnɔ:'ganɪk/ *adj.* not organic.

■ **Usage** *Non-organic* is neutral in sense: see NON- 6, INORGANIC.

nonpareil /nɒnpə'reɪl/ *adj.* & *n.* ● *adj.* unrivalled or unique. ● *n.* such a person or thing. [French as NON- + *pareil* 'equal' from popular Latin *pariculus*, diminutive of Latin *par*]

non-participating /nɒnpɑ:'tɪsɪpeɪtɪŋ/ *adj.* not taking part.

non-partisan /,nɒnpɑ:tɪ'zan/ *adj.* not partisan.

non-party /nɒn'pɑ:ti/ *adj.* independent of political parties.

non-payment /nɒn'peɪm(ə)nt/ *n.* failure to pay; a lack of payment.

non-penetrative /nɒn'pɛnɪtrətɪv/ *adj.* (of sexual activity) in which penetration does not take place.

non-person /nɒn'pə:s(ə)n/ *n.* a person regarded as non-existent or insignificant (cf. UNPERSON).

non-personal /nɒn'pə:s(ə)n(ə)l/ *adj.* not personal.

■ **Usage** *Non-personal* is neutral in sense: see NON- 6, IMPERSONAL.

non-physical /nɒn'fɪzɪk(ə)l/ *adj.* not physical. ▫ **non-physically** *adv.*

non placet /nɒn ˈpleɪsɛt/ *n.* a negative vote in a Church or university assembly. [Latin, = it does not please]

non-playing /nɒnˈpleɪɪŋ/ *adj.* that does not play or take part (in a game etc.).

nonplus /nɒnˈplʌs/ *v.* & *n.* ● *v.tr.* (**nonplussed**, **nonplussing**) completely perplex. ● *n.* a state of perplexity, a standstill (*at a nonplus*; *reduce to a nonplus*). [Latin *non plus* 'not more']

non-poisonous /nɒnˈpɔɪz(ə)nəs/ *adj.* (of a substance, plant, etc.) not poisonous.

non-political /nɒnpəˈlɪtɪk(ə)l/ *adj.* not political; not involved in politics.

non-porous /nɒnˈpɔːrəs/ *adj.* (of a substance) not porous.

non possumus /nɒn ˈpɒsjʊməs/ *n.* a statement of inability to act in a matter. [Latin, = we cannot]

non-productive /nɒnprəˈdʌktɪv/ *adj.* not productive. □ **non-productively** *adv.*

■ **Usage** *Non-productive* is neutral in sense: see NON- 6, UNPRODUCTIVE.

non-professional /nɒnprəˈfɛʃ(ə)n(ə)l/ *adj.* not professional (esp. in status).

■ **Usage** *Non-professional* is neutral in sense: see NON- 6, UNPROFESSIONAL.

non-profit /nɒnˈprɒfɪt/ *adj.* not involving or making a profit.

non-profit-making /nɒnˈprɒfɪtmeɪkɪŋ/ *adj. Brit.* (of an enterprise) not conducted primarily to make a profit.

non-proliferation /ˌnɒnprəlɪfəˈreɪʃ(ə)n/ *n.* the prevention of an increase in something, esp. possession of nuclear weapons (usu. *attrib.*; *non-proliferation agreement*).

non-racial /nɒnˈreɪʃ(ə)l/ *adj.* not involving race or racial factors.

non-reader /nɒnˈriːdə/ *n.* a person who cannot read.

non-resident /nɒnˈrɛzɪd(ə)nt/ *adj.* & *n.* ● *adj.* **1** not residing in a particular place, esp. (of a member of the clergy) not residing where his or her duties require. **2** (of a post) not requiring the holder to reside at the place of work. ● *n. Brit.* a non-resident person, esp. a person using some of the facilities of a hotel. □ **non-residence** *n.* **non-residential** /-ˈdɛnʃ(ə)l/ *adj.*

non-resistance /nɒnrɪˈzɪst(ə)ns/ *n.* failure to resist; a lack of resistance.

non-returnable /nɒnrɪˈtəːnəb(ə)l/ *adj.* that will or need or may not be returned.

non-rigid /nɒnˈrɪdʒɪd/ *adj.* (esp. of materials) not rigid.

non-scientific /ˌnɒnsʌɪənˈtɪfɪk/ *adj.* not involving science or scientific methods. □ **non-scientist** /-ˈsʌɪəntɪst/ *n.*

■ **Usage** *Non-scientific* is neutral in sense: see NON- 6, UNSCIENTIFIC.

non-sectarian /nɒnsɛkˈtɛːrɪən/ *adj.* not sectarian.

nonsense /ˈnɒns(ə)ns/ *n.* **1 a** (often as *int.*) absurd or meaningless words or ideas; foolish or extravagant conduct. **b** an instance of this. **2** a scheme, arrangement, etc., that one disapproves of. **3** (often *attrib.*) a form of literature meant to amuse by absurdity (*nonsense verse*). □ **nonsensical** /-ˈsɛnsɪk(ə)l/ *adj.* **nonsensicality** /nɒnˌsɛnsɪˈkalɪti/ *n.* (*pl.* **-ies**). **nonsensically** /-ˈsɛnsɪk(ə)li/ *adv.*

non sequitur /nɒn ˈsɛkwɪtə/ *n.* a conclusion that does not logically follow from the premisses. [Latin, = it does not follow]

non-sexual /nɒnˈsɛksjʊəl, -ʃʊəl/ *adj.* not based on or involving sex. □ **non-sexually** *adv.*

non-skid /nɒnˈskɪd/ *adj.* **1** that does not skid. **2** that inhibits skidding.

non-slip /nɒnˈslɪp/ *adj.* **1** that does not slip. **2** that inhibits slipping.

non-smoker /nɒnˈsməʊkə/ *n.* **1** a person who does not smoke. **2** a train compartment etc. in which smoking is forbidden. □ **non-smoking** *adj.* & *n.*

non-soluble /nɒnˈsɒljʊb(ə)l/ *adj.* (esp. of a substance) not soluble.

■ **Usage** *Non-soluble* is neutral in sense: see NON- 6, INSOLUBLE.

non-specialist /nɒnˈspɛʃ(ə)lɪst/ *n.* a person who is not a specialist (in a particular subject).

non-specific /nɒnspəˈsɪfɪk/ *adj.* not specific or not restricted in extent, effect, cause, etc.

non-specific urethritis *n. Med.* inflammation of the urethra due to infection other than by gonococci, esp. by chlamydiae (abbr.: **NSU**).

non-standard /nɒnˈstandəd/ *adj.* not standard.

non-starter /nɒnˈstɑːtə/ *n.* **1** a person or animal that does not start in a race. **2** *colloq.* a person or thing that is unlikely to succeed or be effective.

non-stick /nɒnˈstɪk/ *adj.* **1** that does not stick. **2** that does not allow things to stick to it.

non-stop /nɒnˈstɒp/ *adj., adv.,* & *n.* ● *adj.* **1** (of a train etc.) not stopping at intermediate places. **2** (of a journey, performance, etc.) done without a stop or intermission. ● *adv.* without stopping or pausing. ● *n.* a non-stop train etc.

non-subscriber /nɒnsəbˈskrʌɪbə/ *n.* a person who is not a subscriber.

nonsuch /ˈnɒnsʌtʃ/ *n.* (also **nonesuch**) **1** a person or thing that is unrivalled, a paragon. **2** a leguminous plant, *Medicago lupulina*, with black pods. [NONE[1] + SUCH, usu. now assimilated to NON-]

nonsuit /nɒnˈsuːt, -ˈsjuːt/ *n.* & *v. Law* ● *n.* the stoppage of a suit by the judge when the plaintiff fails to make out a legal case or to bring sufficient evidence. ● *v.tr.* subject (a plaintiff) to a nonsuit. [Middle English from Anglo-French *no(u)nsuit* (as NON-, SUIT)]

non-swimmer /nɒnˈswɪmə/ *n.* a person who cannot swim.

non-technical /nɒnˈtɛknɪk(ə)l/ *adj.* **1** not technical. **2** without technical knowledge.

non-toxic /nɒnˈtɒksɪk/ *adj.* not toxic.

non-transferable /nɒntransˈfəːrəb(ə)l, -ˈtransf(ə)r-, -trɑː-, -nz-/ *adj.* that may not be transferred.

non-U /nɒnˈjuː, ˈnɒnjuː/ *adj.* esp. *Brit. colloq.* not characteristic of the upper class. [NON- + U[2]]

non-uniform /nɒnˈjuːnɪfɔːm/ *adj.* not uniform.

non-union /nɒnˈjuːnjən, -ɪən/ *adj.* **1** not belonging to a trade union. **2** not done or produced by members of a trade union.

non-usage /nɒnˈjuːsɪdʒ/ *n.* = NON-USE.

non-use /nɒnˈjuːs/ *n.* failure to use. □ **non-user** *n.*

non-verbal /nɒnˈvəːb(ə)l/ *adj.* not involving words or speech. □ **non-verbally** *adv.*

non-vintage /nɒnˈvɪntɪdʒ/ *adj.* (of wine etc.) not vintage.

non-violence /nɒnˈvʌɪələns/ *n.* the avoidance of violence, esp. as a principle. □ **non-violent** *adj.*

non-volatile /nɒnˈvɒlətʌɪl/ *adj.* (esp. of a substance) not volatile.

non-voting /nɒnˈvəʊtɪŋ/ *adj.* not having or using a vote. □ **non-voter** *n.*

non-white /nɒnˈwʌɪt/ *adj.* & *n.* ● *adj.* **1** (of a person) not white. **2** of or relating to non-white people. ● *n.* a non-white person.

non-word /ˈnɒnwəːd/ *n.* an unrecorded or unused word.

noodle[1] /ˈnuːd(ə)l/ *n.* a strip or ring of pasta. [German *Nudel*, of unknown origin]

noodle[2] /ˈnuːd(ə)l/ *n.* **1** a simpleton. **2** *slang* the head. [18th c.: origin unknown]

nook /nʊk/ *n.* a corner or recess; a secluded place. [Middle English *nok(e)* 'corner', of unknown origin]

nooky /ˈnʊki/ *n.* (also **nookie**) *slang* sexual activity. [20th c.: perhaps from NOOK]

noon /nuːn/ *n.* **1** twelve o'clock in the day, midday. **2** the culminating point. [originally = 3 p.m.: Old English *nōn* from Latin *nona* (*hora*) 'ninth hour' (cf. NONE[2])]

noonday /ˈnuːndeɪ/ *n.* midday.

no one *n.* no person; nobody.

noontide /'nu:ntʌɪd/ *n.* (also **noontime** /-tʌɪm/) midday.

noose /nu:s/ *n.* & *v.* ● *n.* **1** a loop with a running knot, tightening as the rope or wire is pulled, esp. in a snare, lasso, or hangman's halter. **2** a snare or bond. **3** *joc.* the marriage tie. ● *v.tr.* **1** catch with or enclose in a noose, ensnare. **2 a** make a noose on (a cord). **b** (often foll. by *round*) arrange (a cord) in a noose. □ **put one's head in a noose** bring about one's own downfall. [Middle English *nose*, perhaps via Old French *no(u)s* from Latin *nodus* 'knot']

Nootka /'nu:tkə, 'nʊt-/ *n.* an American Indian language of Vancouver Island, Canada.

nopal /'nəʊp(ə)l/ *n.* any American cactus of the genus *Nopalea*, esp. *N. cochinellifera* grown in plantations for breeding cochineal. [French & Spanish from Nahuatl *nopalli* 'cactus']

nope /nəʊp/ *adv. colloq.* = NO[2] *adv.* 1. [NO[2]]

nor /nɔ:, nə/ *conj.* **1** and not; and not either (*neither one thing nor the other*; *not a man nor a child was to be seen*; *I said I had not seen it, nor had I*; *all that is true, nor must we forget ...*; *can neither read nor write*). **2** and no more; neither (*'I cannot go' – 'Nor can I'*). □ **nor ... nor ...** *poet.* or *archaic* neither ... nor ... [Middle English, contraction from obsolete *nother* from Old English *nawther*, *nāhwæther* (as NO[2], WHETHER)]

nor' /nɔ:/ *n.*, *adj.*, & *adv.* (esp. in compounds) = NORTH (*nor'ward*). [abbreviation]

noradrenalin /nɔ:rə'drɛn(ə)lɪn/ *n.* (also **noradrenaline**) a hormone released by the adrenal medulla and by sympathetic nerve endings as a neurotransmitter. Also called *norepinephrine*. [*nor*mal + ADRENALIN]

Nordic /'nɔ:dɪk/ *adj.* & *n.* ● *adj.* **1** of or relating to the tall blond dolichocephalic Germanic people found in N. Europe, esp. in Scandinavia. **2** of or relating to Scandinavia or Finland. **3** (of skiing) with cross-country work and jumping. ● *n.* a Nordic person, esp. a native of Scandinavia or Finland. [French *nordique* from *nord* 'north']

norepinephrine /ˌnɔ:rɛpɪ'nɛfrɪn, -ri:n/ *n.* = NORADRENALIN. [*nor*mal + EPINEPHRINE]

Norfolk jacket /'nɔ:fək/ *n.* a man's loose belted jacket, with box pleats. [*Norfolk*, a county in S. England]

nork /nɔ:k/ *n.* (usu. in *pl.*) *Austral. slang* a woman's breast. [20th c.: origin uncertain]

norland /'nɔ:lənd/ *n. Brit.* a northern region. [contraction of NORTHLAND]

norm /nɔ:m/ *n.* **1** a standard or pattern or type. **2** a standard quantity to be produced or amount of work to be done. **3** customary behaviour etc. [Latin *norma* 'carpenter's square']

normal /'nɔ:m(ə)l/ *adj.* & *n.* ● *adj.* **1** conforming to a standard; regular, usual, typical. **2** free from mental or emotional disorder. **3** *Geom.* (of a line) at right angles, perpendicular. **4** *Chem.* (of a solution) containing one gram-equivalent of solute per litre. ● *n.* **1 a** the normal value of a temperature etc., esp. blood-heat. **b** the usual state, level, etc. **2** *Geom.* a line at right angles. □ **normalcy** *n.* esp. *N. Amer.* **normality** /-'malɪti/ *n.* [French *normal* or Latin *normalis* (as NORM)]

normal distribution *n. Statistics* a function that represents the distribution of many random variables as a symmetrical bell-shaped graph.

normalize /'nɔ:m(ə)lʌɪz/ *v.* (also **-ise**) **1** *tr.* make normal. **2** *intr.* become normal. **3** *tr.* cause to conform. □ **normalization** /-'zeɪʃ(ə)n/ *n.* **normalizer** *n.*

normally /'nɔ:m(ə)li/ *adv.* **1** in a normal manner. **2** usually.

normally aspirated *adj.* (of an engine) not turbocharged or supercharged.

normal school *n.* (in the US, France, etc.) a school or college for training teachers.

Norman /'nɔ:mən/ *n.* & *adj.* ● *n.* **1** a native or inhabitant of medieval Normandy. **2** a descendant of the people of mixed Scandinavian and Frankish origin established there in the 10th c., who conquered England in 1066. **3** Norman French. **4** *Archit.* the style of Romanesque architecture found in Britain under the Normans. **5** any of the English kings from William I to Stephen. ● *adj.* **1** of or relating to the Normans. **2** of or relating to the Norman style of architecture. □ **Normanesque** /-'nɛsk/ *adj.* **Normanism** *n.* **Normanize** *v.tr.* & *intr.* (also **-ise**). [Old French *Normans*, pl. of *Normant*, from Old Norse *Northmathr* (as NORTH, MAN)]

Norman Conquest see CONQUEST.

Norman English *n.* English as spoken or influenced by the Normans.

Norman French *n.* French as spoken by the Normans or (after 1066) in English law courts.

normative /'nɔ:mətɪv/ *adj.* of or establishing a norm. □ **normatively** *adv.* **normativeness** *n.* [French *normatif -ive* from Latin *norma* (see NORM)]

Norn /'nɔ:n/ *n.* any of three goddesses of destiny in Scandinavian mythology. [Old Norse: origin unknown]

Norroy /'nɒrɔɪ/ *n.* (in full **Norroy and Ulster**) *Heraldry* (in the UK) the title given to the third King of Arms, with jurisdiction north of the Trent and (since 1943) in Northern Ireland (cf. CLARENCEUX, KING OF ARMS). [Middle English via Anglo-French from Old French *nord* 'north', *roi* 'king']

Norse /nɔ:s/ *n.* & *adj.* ● *n.* **1 a** the Norwegian language. **b** the Scandinavian language group. **2** (prec. by *the*; treated as *pl.*) **a** the Norwegians. **b** the Vikings. ● *adj.* **1** of or relating to Norway or the Norse language. **2** of or relating to ancient Scandinavia or its inhabitants. □ **Norseman** *n.* (*pl.* **-men**). [Dutch *noor(d)sch* from *noord* 'north']

north /nɔ:θ/ *n.*, *adj.*, & *adv.* ● *n.* **1 a** the point of the horizon 90° anticlockwise from east. **b** the compass point corresponding to this. **c** the direction in which this lies. **2** (usu. **the North**) **a** the part of the world or a country or a town lying to the north, esp. = NORTH COUNTRY or NORTHERN STATES. **b** the Arctic. **c** the industrialized nations. **3** (**North**) *Bridge* a player occupying the position designated 'north'. ● *adj.* **1** towards, at, near, or facing north. **2** coming from the north (*north wind*). ● *adv.* **1** towards, at, or near the north. **2** (foll. by *of*) further north than. □ **north and south** lengthwise along a line from north to south. **north by east** (or **west**) between north and north-north-east (or north-north-west). **to the north** (often foll. by *of*) in a northerly direction. [Old English from Germanic]

North American *adj.* & *n.* ● *adj.* of North America. ● *n.* a native or inhabitant of North America, esp. a citizen of the US or Canada.

Northants /nɔ:'θants/ *abbr.* Northamptonshire.

northbound /'nɔ:θbaʊnd/ *adj.* travelling or leading northwards.

North Country *n.* (also **north country**) the northern part of England (north of the Humber) (also (often hyphenated) *attrib.*: *a north-country lad*).

north-countryman *n.* (*pl.* **-men**) a native of the North Country.

North-East *n.* the part of a country or town lying to the north-east.

north-east *n.*, *adj.*, & *adv.* ● *n.* **1** the point of the horizon midway between north and east. **2** the compass point corresponding to this. **3** the direction in which this lies. ● *adj.* of, towards, or coming from the north-east. ● *adv.* towards, at, or near the north-east. □ **north-eastern** *adj.*

northeaster /nɔ:θ'i:stə/ *n.* a north-east wind.

north-easterly *adj.* & *adv.* = NORTH-EAST.

north-east passage *n.* a passage for ships along the northern coast of Europe and Asia, formerly thought of as a possible route to the East.

north-eastward *adj.* & *adv.* (also **north-eastwards**) towards the north-east.

norther /ˈnɔːθə/ *n. US* a strong cold north wind blowing in autumn and winter over Texas, Florida, and the Gulf of Mexico.

northerly /ˈnɔːðəli/ *adj., adv., & n.* ● *adj. & adv.* **1** in a northern position or direction. **2** (of wind) blowing from the north. ● *n.* (*pl.* **-ies**) (usu. in *pl.*) a wind blowing from the north.

northern /ˈnɔːð(ə)n/ *adj.* **1** of or in the north; inhabiting the north. **2** lying or directed towards the north. □ **northernmost** *adj.* [Old English *northerne* (as NORTH, -ERN)]

northerner /ˈnɔːð(ə)nə/ *n.* a native or inhabitant of the north.

northern hemisphere *n.* the half of the earth north of the equator.

northern lights *n.pl.* the aurora borealis.

Northern States *n.pl.* the states in the north of the US.

North Germanic *n. & adj.* ● *n.* the northern group of Germanic languages, comprising the Scandinavian languages. ● *adj.* of or relating to North Germanic.

northing /ˈnɔːθɪŋ/ *n. Naut.* the distance travelled or measured northward.

Northland /ˈnɔːθlənd/ *n. poet.* the northern lands; the northern part of a country. [Old English (as NORTH, LAND)]

north light *n.* good natural light without direct sun, esp. as desired by painters and in factory design.

Northman /ˈnɔːθmən/ *n.* (*pl.* **-men**) a native of Scandinavia, esp. of Norway. [Old English]

north-north-east *n.* the point or direction midway between north and north-east.

north-north-west *n.* the point or direction midway between north and north-west.

North Pole *n.* **1** the northernmost point of the earth's axis of rotation. **2** the point in the northern sky about which the stars appear to revolve.

north-south *attrib.adj.* of or relating to countries of the north and south (*north-south divide*).

North Star *n.* the pole star.

Northumb. *abbr.* Northumberland.

Northumbrian /nɔːˈθʌmbrɪən/ *adj. & n.* ● *adj.* of or relating to ancient Northumbria (England north of the Humber) or modern Northumberland. ● *n.* **1** a native of ancient Northumbria or modern Northumberland. **2** the dialect of ancient Northumbria or modern Northumberland. [obsolete *Northumber*, 'persons living beyond the Humber', from Old English *Northhymbre*]

northward /ˈnɔːθwəd/ *adj., adv., & n.* ● *adj. & adv.* (also **northwards**) towards the north. ● *n.* a northward direction or region.

North-West *n.* the part of a country or town lying to the north-west.

north-west *n., adj., & adv.* ● *n.* **1** the point of the horizon midway between north and west. **2** the compass point corresponding to this. **3** the direction in which this lies. ● *adj.* of, towards, or coming from the north-west. ● *adv.* towards, at, or near the north-west. □ **north-western** *adj.*

northwester /nɔːθˈwɛstə/ *n.* a north-west wind.

north-westerly *adj. & adv.* = NORTH-WEST.

north-west passage *n.* a passage for ships along the northern coast of America, formerly thought of as a possible route from the Atlantic to the Pacific.

north-westward *adj. & adv.* (also **north-westwards**) towards the north-west.

Norway lobster /ˈnɔːweɪ/ *n.* a small European lobster, *Nephrops norvegicus*. [*Norway* in N. Europe]

Norway rat /ˈnɔːweɪ/ *n.* the common brown rat, *Rattus norvegicus*.

Norwegian /nɔːˈwiːdʒ(ə)n/ *n. & adj.* ● *n.* **1 a** a native or national of Norway. **b** a person of Norwegian descent. **2** the language of Norway. ● *adj.* of or relating to Norway or its people or language. [medieval Latin *Norvegia* from Old Norse *Norvegr* (as NORTH, WAY), assimilated to *Norway*]

nor'wester /nɔːˈwɛstə/ *n.* **1** a northwester. **2** a glass of strong liquor. **3** an oilskin hat, a sou'wester. [contraction]

Nos. *abbr.* numbers. [cf. No.]

no-score draw *n.* a draw in football in which no goals are scored.

nose /nəʊz/ *n. & v.* ● *n.* **1** an organ above the mouth on the face or head of a human or animal, containing nostrils and used for smelling and breathing. **2 a** the sense of smell (*dogs have a good nose*). **b** the ability to detect a particular thing (*a nose for scandal*). **3** the odour or perfume of wine, tea, tobacco, hay, etc. **4** the open end or nozzle of a tube, pipe, pair of bellows, retort, etc. **5 a** the front end or projecting part of a thing, e.g. of a car or aircraft. **b** = NOSING. **6** *slang* an informer of the police. ● *v.* **1** *tr.* (often foll. by *out*) **a** perceive the smell of, discover by smell. **b** detect. **2** *tr.* thrust or rub one's nose against or into, esp. in order to smell. **3** *intr.* (usu. foll. by *about, around*, etc.) pry or search. **4 a** *intr.* make one's way cautiously forward. **b** *tr.* make (one's or its way). □ **as plain as the nose on your face** easily seen. **by a nose** by a very narrow margin (*won the race by a nose*). **count noses** count those present, one's supporters, etc.; decide a question by mere numbers. **cut off one's nose to spite one's face** disadvantage oneself in the course of trying to disadvantage another. **get up a person's nose** *slang* annoy a person. **keep one's nose clean** *slang* stay out of trouble, behave properly. **keep one's nose to the grindstone** see GRINDSTONE. **on the nose 1** *N. Amer. slang* precisely. **2** *Austral. slang* annoying. **put a person's nose out of joint** *colloq.* embarrass, disconcert, frustrate, or supplant a person. **rub a person's nose in it** see RUB[1]. **see no further than one's nose** be short-sighted, esp. in foreseeing the consequences of one's actions etc. **speak through one's nose** pronounce words with a nasal twang. **turn up one's nose** (usu. foll. by *at*) *colloq.* show disdain. **under a person's nose** *colloq.* right before a person (esp. of defiant or unnoticed actions). **with one's nose in the air** haughtily. □ **nosed** *adj.* (also in *comb.*). **noseless** *adj.* [Old English *nosu*]

nosebag /ˈnəʊzbag/ *n.* a bag containing fodder, hung on a horse's head.

noseband /ˈnəʊzband/ *n.* the lower band of a bridle, passing over the horse's nose.

nosebleed /ˈnəʊzbliːd/ *n.* an instance of bleeding from the nose.

nose-cone *n.* the cone-shaped nose of a rocket etc.

nosedive /ˈnəʊzdʌɪv/ *n. & v.* ● *n.* **1** a steep downward plunge by an aeroplane. **2** a sudden plunge or drop. ● *v.intr.* make a nosedive.

no-see-em /nəʊˈsiːəm/*n.* (also **no-see-um**) *N. Amer.* a small bloodsucking insect, esp. a biting midge.

nose flute *n.* a musical instrument blown with the nose in Fiji etc.

nosegay /ˈnəʊzgeɪ/ *n.* a bunch of flowers, esp. a sweet-scented posy. [NOSE + GAY in obsolete sense 'ornament']

nose leaf *n.* a fleshy part on the nostrils of some bats, used for echolocation.

nose-piece *n.* **1** = NOSEBAND. **2** the part of a helmet etc. protecting the nose. **3** the part of a microscope to which the objective lenses are attached.

nosepipe /ˈnəʊzpʌɪp/ *n.* a piece of piping used as a nozzle.

nose-rag *n. slang* a pocket handkerchief.

nosering /ˈnəʊzrɪŋ/ *n.* a ring fixed in the nose of an animal (esp. a bull) for leading it, or of a person for ornament.

nose tackle *n. Amer. Football* **1** the defensive player who lines up in the centre of the linemen in formation. **2** this field position.

nose-to-tail *adj. & adv. Brit.* (of vehicles) moving or stationary one close behind another, esp. in heavy traffic.

nose wheel *n.* a landing wheel under the nose of an aircraft.

nosey var. of NOSY.

nosh /nɒʃ/ *v.* & *n.* *slang* ● *v.tr.* & *intr.* **1** eat or drink. **2** *N. Amer.* eat between meals. ● *n.* **1** food or drink. **2** *N. Amer.* a snack. [Yiddish]

noshery /ˈnɒʃəri/ *n.* (*pl.* **-ies**) *slang* a restaurant or snack bar.

no-show *n.* a person who has reserved a seat etc. but neither uses it nor cancels the reservation.

nosh-up *n. Brit.* a large meal.

no side *n. Rugby* **1** the end of a game. **2** the referee's announcement of this.

nosing /ˈnəʊzɪŋ/ *n.* a rounded edge of a step, moulding, etc., or a metal shield for it.

nosography /nɒˈsɒɡrəfi/ *n.* the systematic description of diseases. [Greek *nosos* 'disease' + -GRAPHY]

nosology /nɒˈsɒlədʒi/ *n.* the branch of medical science dealing with the classification of diseases. □ **nosological** /nɒsəˈlɒdʒɪk(ə)l/ *adj.* [Greek *nosos* 'disease' + -LOGY]

nostalgia /nɒˈstaldʒə, -dʒɪə/ *n.* **1** (often foll. by *for*) sentimental yearning for a period of the past; regretful or wistful memory of an earlier time. **2** a thing or things which evoke a former era. **3** severe homesickness. □ **nostalgic** *adj.* **nostalgically** *adv.* [modern Latin, from Greek *nostos* 'return home']

nostoc /ˈnɒstɒk/ *n.* any gelatinous blue-green unicellular alga of the genus *Nostoc*, that can fix nitrogen from the atmosphere. [name invented by Paracelsus]

Nostradamus /nɒstrəˈdɑːməs, -ˈdeɪ-/ *n.* a person who claims to foretell future events. [Latinized form of the name of M. de *Nostredame*, French astrologer and physician d. 1566]

nostril /ˈnɒstr(ə)l/ *n.* either of two external openings of the nasal cavity in vertebrates that admit air to the lungs and smells to the olfactory nerves. □ **nostrilled** *adj.* (also in *comb.*). [Old English *nosthyrl*, *nosterl* from *nosu* NOSE + *thȳr(e)l* 'hole': cf. THRILL]

nostrum /ˈnɒstrəm/ *n.* **1** a quack remedy, a patent medicine, esp. one prepared by the person recommending it. **2** a pet scheme, esp. for political or social reform. [Latin, neut. of *noster* 'our', used in sense 'of our own make']

nosy /ˈnəʊzi/ *adj.* & *n.* (also **nosey**) ● *adj.* (**nosier**, **nosiest**) **1** *colloq.* inquisitive, prying. **2** having a large nose. **3** having a distinctive (good or bad) smell. ● *n.* (*pl.* **-ies**) a person with a large nose. □ **nosily** *adv.* **nosiness** *n.*

Nosy Parker *n.* esp. *Brit. colloq.* a busybody.

not /nɒt/ *adv.* expressing negation, esp.: **1** (also **n't** joined to a preceding verb) following an auxiliary verb or *be* or (in a question) the subject of such a verb (*I cannot say*; *she isn't there*; *didn't you tell me?*; *am I not right?*; *aren't we smart?*). **2** used elliptically for a negative sentence or verb or phrase (*Is she coming? — I hope not*; *Do you want it? — Certainly not!*). **3** used to express the negative of other words (*not a single one was left*; *Are they pleased? — Not they*; *he is not my cousin, but my nephew*). **4** *colloq.* following and emphatically negating an affirmative statement (*great party ... not!*). □ **not at all** (in polite reply to thanks) there is no need for thanks. **not but what** *archaic* **1** all the same; nevertheless (*I cannot do it; not but what a stronger man might*). **2** not such ... or so ... that ... not (*not such a fool but what he can see it*). **not half** see HALF. **not least** with considerable importance, notably. **not much** see MUCH. **not quite 1** almost (*am not quite there*). **2** noticeably not (*not quite proper*). **not in the slightest** not at all. **not a thing** nothing at all. **not that** (foll. by clause) it is not to be inferred that (*if he said so — not that he ever did — he lied*). **not very** see VERY. [Middle English contraction of NOUGHT]

■ **Usage** The use of *not* with verbs other than auxiliaries or *be* is now archaic (e.g. *I know not*; *fear not*), except with participles and infinitives (e.g. *not realizing her mistake*; *I cannot say*; *We asked them not to come*).

nota bene /nəʊtə ˈbɛneɪ/ *v.tr.* (as *imper.*) observe what follows, take notice (usu. drawing attention to a following qualification of what has preceded). [Latin, = note well]

notability /nəʊtəˈbɪlɪti/ *n.* (*pl.* **-ies**) **1** the state of being notable (*names of no historical notability*). **2** a prominent person. [Middle English from Old French *notabilité* or Late Latin *notabilitas* (as NOTABLE)]

notable /ˈnəʊtəb(ə)l/ *adj.* & *n.* ● *adj.* worthy of note; striking, remarkable, eminent. ● *n.* an eminent person. □ **notably** *adv.* [Middle English via Old French from Latin *notabilis* (as NOTE)]

notarize /ˈnəʊtərʌɪz/ *v.tr.* (also **-ise**) *N. Amer.* certify (a document) as a notary.

notary /ˈnəʊt(ə)ri/ *n.* (*pl.* **-ies**) (in full **notary public**, *pl.* **notaries public**) a person authorized to perform certain legal formalities, esp. to draw up or certify contracts, deeds, etc. □ **notarial** /nəʊˈtɛːrɪəl/ *adj.* **notarially** /nəʊˈtɛːrɪəli/ *adv.* [Middle English from Latin *notarius* 'secretary' (as NOTE)]

notate /nəʊˈteɪt/ *v.tr.* write in notation. [back-formation from NOTATION]

notation /nəʊˈteɪʃ(ə)n/ *n.* **1 a** the representation of numbers, quantities, pitch and duration etc. of musical notes, etc. by symbols. **b** any set of such symbols. **2** a set of symbols used to represent chess moves, dance steps, etc. **3** *US* **a** a note or annotation. **b** a record. **4** = *scale of notation* (see SCALE³ *n.* 5). □ **notational** *adj.* [French *notation* or Latin *notatio* (as NOTE)]

notch /nɒtʃ/ *n.* & *v.* ● *n.* **1** a V-shaped indentation on an edge or surface. **2** a nick made on a stick etc. in order to keep count. **3** *colloq.* a step or degree (*move up a notch*). **4** *N. Amer.* a deep narrow mountain pass. ● *v.tr.* **1** make notches in. **2** (foll. by *up*) record or score with or as with notches. **3** secure or insert by notches. □ **notched** *adj.* **notcher** *n.* **notchy** *adj.* (**notchier**, **notchiest**). [Anglo-French *noche* perhaps from a verb related to *anoccer* 'add a notch to', of uncertain origin]

note /nəʊt/ *n.* & *v.* ● *n.* **1** a brief record of facts, topics, thoughts, etc., as an aid to memory, for use in writing, public speaking, etc. (often in *pl.*: *make notes*; *spoke without notes*). **2** an observation, usu. unwritten, of experiences etc. (*compare notes*). **3** a short or informal letter. **4** a formal diplomatic or parliamentary communication. **5** a short annotation or additional explanation in a book etc.; a footnote. **6 a** *Brit.* = BANKNOTE (*a five-pound note*). **b** a written promise or notice of payment of various kinds. **7 a** notice, attention (*worthy of note*). **b** distinction, eminence (*a person of note*). **8 a** a written sign representing the pitch and duration of a musical sound. **b** a single tone of definite pitch made by a musical instrument, the human voice, etc. **c** a key of a piano etc. **9 a** a bird's song or call. **b** a single tone in this. **10** a quality or tone of speaking, expressing mood or attitude etc.; a hint or suggestion (*sound a note of warning*; *ended on a note of optimism*). **11** a characteristic; a distinguishing feature. ● *v.tr.* **1** observe, notice; give or draw attention to. **2** (often foll. by *down*) record as a thing to be remembered or observed. **3** (in *passive*; often foll. by *for*) be famous or well known (for a quality, activity, etc.) (*were noted for their generosity*). □ **hit** (or **strike**) **the right note** speak or act in exactly the right manner. **of note** important, distinguished (*a person of note*). **take note** (often foll. by *of*) observe; pay attention (to). □ **noted** *adj.* (in sense 3 of *v.*). **noteless** *adj.* [Middle English via Old French *note* (*n.*), *noter* (*v.*) from Latin *nota* 'mark']

notebook /ˈnəʊtbʊk/ *n.* **1** a small book for making or taking notes. **2** a portable computer smaller than a laptop.

notecase /ˈnəʊtkeɪs/ *n. Brit.* a wallet for holding banknotes.

notelet /ˈnəʊtlɪt/ *n.* a small folded sheet of paper, usu. with a decorative design, for an informal letter.

notepad /ˈnəʊtpad/ *n.* a pad of paper for writing notes on.

notepaper /ˈnəʊtpeɪpə/ *n.* paper for writing letters.

noteworthy /ˈnəʊtwəːði/ *adj.* worthy of attention; remarkable. ▫ **noteworthiness** *n.*

nothing /ˈnʌθɪŋ/ *n. & adv.* ● *n.* **1** not anything (*nothing has been done; have nothing to do*). **2** no thing (often foll. by compl.: *I see nothing that I want; can find nothing useful*). **3 a** a person or thing of no importance or concern; a trivial event or remark (*was nothing to me; the little nothings of life*). **b** (*attrib.*) *colloq.* of no value; indeterminate (*a nothing sort of day*). **4** non-existence; what does not exist. **5** (in calculations) no amount; nought (*a third of nothing is nothing*). ● *adv.* **1** not at all, in no way (*helps us nothing; is nothing like enough*). **2** *US colloq.* not at all (*Is he ill? — Ill nothing, he's dead.*). ▫ **be nothing to 1** not concern. **2** not compare with. **be** (or **have**) **nothing to do with 1** have no connection with. **2** not be involved or associated with. **for nothing 1** at no cost; without payment. **2** to no purpose. **have nothing on 1** be naked. **2** have no engagements. **no nothing** *colloq.* (concluding a list of negatives) nothing at all. **nothing doing** *colloq.* **1 a** there is no prospect of success or agreement. **b** I refuse. **2** nothing (is) happening. **nothing** (or **nothing else**) **for it** (often foll. by *but to* + infin.) *Brit.* no alternative (*nothing for it but to pay up*). **nothing less than** at least (*nothing less than a disaster*). **nothing loath** quite willing. **nothing** (or **not much**) **to it** (or *Brit.* **in it**) **1** untrue or unimportant. **2** simple to do. **3** no (or little) advantage to be seen in one possibility over another. **think nothing of it** do not apologize or feel bound to show gratitude. [Old English *nān thing* (as NO[1], THING)]

nothingness /ˈnʌθɪŋnɪs/ *n.* **1** non-existence; the non-existent. **2** worthlessness, triviality, insignificance.

notice /ˈnəʊtɪs/ *n. & v.* ● *n.* **1** attention, observation (*it escaped my notice*). **2** a displayed sheet etc. bearing an announcement or other information. **3 a** an intimation or warning, esp. a formal one to allow preparations to be made (*give notice; at a moment's notice*). **b** (often foll. by *to* + infin.) a formal announcement or declaration of intention to end an agreement or leave employment at a specified time (*hand in one's notice; notice to quit*). **4** a short published review or comment about a new play, book, etc. ● *v.tr.* **1** (often foll. by *that, how*, etc. + clause) perceive, observe; take notice of. **2** remark upon; speak of. ▫ **at short** (or **a moment's**) **notice** with little warning. **take notice** (or **no notice**) show signs (or no signs) of interest. **take notice of 1** observe; pay attention to. **2** act upon. **under notice** served with a formal notice. [Middle English via Old French from Latin *notitia* 'being known', from *notus*, past part. of *noscere* 'know']

noticeable /ˈnəʊtɪsəb(ə)l/ *adj.* **1** easily seen or noticed; perceptible. **2** noteworthy. ▫ **noticeably** *adv.*

noticeboard /ˈnəʊtɪsbɔːd/ *n. Brit.* a board for displaying notices.

notifiable /ˈnəʊtɪfʌɪəb(ə)l/ *adj.* (of a disease, crop pest, etc.) that must be notified to the appropriate authorities.

notify /ˈnəʊtɪfʌɪ/ *v.tr.* (**-ies, -ied**) **1** (often foll. by *of*, or *that* + clause) inform or give notice to (a person). **2** make known; announce or report (a thing). ▫ **notification** /-fɪˈkeɪʃ(ə)n/ *n.* [Middle English via Old French *notifier* from Latin *notificare*, from *notus* 'known': see NOTICE]

notion /ˈnəʊʃ(ə)n/ *n.* **1 a** a concept or idea; a conception (*it was an absurd notion*). **b** an opinion (*has the notion that people are honest*). **c** a vague view or understanding (*have no notion what you mean*). **2** an inclination, impulse, or intention (*has no notion of conforming*). **3** (in *pl.*) small, useful articles, esp. haberdashery. [Latin *notio* 'idea' from *notus*, past part. of *noscere* 'know']

notional /ˈnəʊʃ(ə)n(ə)l/ *adj.* **1 a** hypothetical, imaginary. **b** (of knowledge etc.) speculative; not based on experiment etc. **2** *Gram.* (of a verb) conveying its own meaning, not auxiliary. ▫ **notionally** *adv.* [obsolete French *notional* or medieval Latin *notionalis* (as NOTION)]

notochord /ˈnəʊtəkɔːd/ *n.* a cartilaginous skeletal rod supporting the body in all embryo and some adult chordate animals. [Greek *nōton* 'back' + CHORD[2]]

notorious /nə(ʊ)ˈtɔːrɪəs/ *adj.* well known, esp. unfavourably (*a notorious criminal; notorious for its climate*). ▫ **notoriety** /-təˈrʌɪəti/ *n.* **notoriously** *adv.* [medieval Latin *notorius* from Latin *notus* (as NOTION)]

notornis /nə(ʊ)ˈtɔːnɪs/ *n.* a rare flightless New Zealand bird, *Porphyrio mantelli*, with a large bill and brightly coloured plumage. Also called *takahe*. [Greek *notos* 'south' + *ornis* 'bird']

no-trumper *n. Bridge* a hand on which a no-trump bid can suitably be, or has been, made.

no trumps *n.* (also **no trump**) *Bridge* a declaration or bid involving playing without a trump suit.

Notts. /nɒts/ *abbr.* Nottinghamshire.

notwithstanding /nɒtwɪðˈstandɪŋ, -wɪθ-/ *prep., adv., & conj.* ● *prep.* in spite of; without prevention by (*notwithstanding your objections; this fact notwithstanding*). ● *adv.* nevertheless; all the same. ● *conj.* (usu. foll. by *that* + clause) although. [Middle English, from NOT + WITHSTAND + -ING[2]]

nougat /ˈnuːgɑː, ˈnʌgət/ *n.* a sweet made from sugar or honey, nuts, and egg white. [French from Provençal *nogat*, from *noga* 'nut']

nought /nɔːt/ *n.* **1** the digit 0; a cipher. **2** *poet.* or *archaic* (in certain phrases) nothing (cf. NAUGHT). [Old English *nōwiht*, from *ne* 'not' + *ōwiht* variant of *āwiht* AUGHT[1]]

noughts and crosses *n.pl.* esp. *Brit.* a game in which players seek to complete a row of three noughts or three crosses drawn alternately in the spaces of a grid of nine squares.

noun /naʊn/ *n. Gram.* a word (other than a pronoun) or group of words used to name or identify any of a class of persons, places, or things (**common noun**), or a particular one of these (**proper noun**). ▫ **nounal** *adj.* [Middle English via Anglo-French from Latin *nomen* 'name']

nourish /ˈnʌrɪʃ/ *v.tr.* **1 a** sustain with food. **b** enrich; promote the development of (the soil etc.). **c** provide with intellectual or emotional sustenance or enrichment. **2** foster or cherish (a feeling etc.). ▫ **nourisher** *n.* [Middle English via Old French *norir* from Latin *nutrire*]

nourishing /ˈnʌrɪʃɪŋ/ *adj.* (esp. of food) containing much nourishment; sustaining. ▫ **nourishingly** *adv.*

nourishment /ˈnʌrɪʃm(ə)nt/ *n.* sustenance, food.

nous /naʊs/ *n.* **1** *Brit. colloq.* common sense; gumption. **2** *Philos.* the mind or intellect. [Greek]

nouveau riche /nuːvəʊ ˈriːʃ/ *n.* (*pl.* **nouveaux riches** *pronunc.* same) a person who has recently acquired (usu. ostentatious) wealth. [French, = new rich]

nouvelle cuisine /ˌnuːvɛl kwɪˈziːn/ *n.* a modern style of cookery avoiding heaviness and emphasizing presentation. [French, = new cookery]

nouvelle vague /ˌnuːvɛl ˈvɑːg, French nuvɛl vag/ *n.* a new trend, esp. in French film-making of the early 1960s. [French, fem. of *nouveau* 'new' + *vague* 'wave']

Nov. *abbr.* November.

nova /ˈnəʊvə/ *n.* (*pl.* **novae** /-viː/ or **novas**) a star showing a sudden large increase of brightness and then subsiding. [Latin, fem. of *novus* 'new', because originally thought to be a new star]

novel[1] /ˈnɒv(ə)l/ *n.* **1** a fictitious prose story of book length. **2** (prec. by *the*) this type of literature. [Italian *novella* (*storia* 'story'), fem. of *novello* 'new', from Latin *novellus* from *novus* 'new']

novel² /ˈnɒv(ə)l/ *adj.* of a new kind or nature; strange; previously unknown. □ **novelly** *adv.* [Middle English via Old French from Latin *novellus*, from *novus* 'new']

novelese /nɒvəˈliːz/ *n. derog.* a style characteristic of inferior novels.

novelette /nɒvəˈlɛt/ *n.* **1 a** a short novel. **b** esp. *Brit. derog.* a light romantic novel. **2** *Mus.* a piano piece in free form with several themes.

novelettish /nɒvəˈlɛtɪʃ/ *adj. derog.* in the style of a light romantic novel; sentimental.

novelist /ˈnɒv(ə)lɪst/ *n.* a writer of novels. □ **novelistic** /-ˈlɪstɪk/ *adj.*

novelize /ˈnɒv(ə)lʌɪz/ *v.tr.* (also **-ise**) make into a novel. □ **novelization** /-ˈzeɪʃ(ə)n/ *n.*

novella /nə(ʊ)ˈvɛlə/ *n.* (*pl.* **novellas**) a short novel or narrative story; a tale. [Italian: see NOVEL¹]

novelty /ˈnɒv(ə)lti/ *n.* (*pl.* **-ies**) **1 a** newness; new character. **b** originality. **2** a new or unusual thing or occurrence. **3** a small toy or decoration etc. of novel design. **4** (*attrib.*) having novelty (*novelty toys*). [Middle English from Old French *novelté* (as NOVEL²)]

November /nə(ʊ)ˈvɛmbə/ *n.* the eleventh month of the year. [originally the ninth month of the Roman year: Middle English via Old French *novembre* from Latin *November*, from *novem* 'nine']

novena /nə(ʊ)ˈviːnə/ *n. RC Ch.* a devotion consisting of special prayers or services on nine successive days. [medieval Latin from Latin *novem* 'nine']

novice /ˈnɒvɪs/ *n.* **1 a** a probationary member of a religious order, before the taking of vows. **b** a new convert. **2** a beginner; an inexperienced person. **3** a horse, dog, etc. that has not won a major prize in a competition (also *attrib.*: *novice hurdle*). [Middle English via Old French from Latin *novicius*, from *novus* 'new']

noviciate /nə(ʊ)ˈvɪʃɪət, -ɪeɪt/ *n.* (also **novitiate**) **1** the period of being a novice. **2** a religious novice. **3** novices' quarters. [French *noviciat* or medieval Latin *noviciatus* (as NOVICE)]

Novocaine /ˈnəʊvəkeɪn/ *n.* (also **novocaine**) a local anaesthetic derived from benzoic acid. [Latin *novus* 'new' + COCAINE]

no-vote *n.* a vote in opposition to a proposal etc.

now /naʊ/ *adv., conj., & n.* ● *adv.* **1** at the present or mentioned time. **2** immediately (*I must go now*). **3** by this or that time (*it was now clear*). **4** under the present circumstances (*I cannot now agree*). **5** on this further occasion (*what do you want now?*). **6** in the immediate past (*just now*). **7** (esp. in a narrative or discourse) then, next (*the police now arrived*; *now to consider the next point*). **8** (without reference to time, giving various tones to a sentence) surely, I insist, I wonder, etc. (*now what do you mean by that?*; *oh come now!*). ● *conj.* (often foll. by *that* + clause) as a consequence of the fact (*now that I am older*; *now you mention it*). ● *n.* this time; the present (*should be there by now*; *has happened before now*). □ **as of now** from or at this time. **for now** until a later time (*goodbye for now*). **now and again** (or **then**) from time to time; intermittently. **now or never** an expression of urgency. [Old English *nū*]

nowadays /ˈnaʊədeɪz/ *adv. & n.* ● *adv.* at the present time or age; in these times. ● *n.* the present time.

noway /ˈnəʊweɪ/ *adv.* = NOWISE (cf. *no way* (NO¹)).

Nowel (also **Nowell**) *archaic* var. of NOEL.

nowhere /ˈnəʊwɛː/ *adv. & pron.* ● *adv.* in or to no place. ● *pron.* no place. □ **be** (or **come in**) **nowhere** be unplaced in a race or competition. **come from nowhere** be suddenly evident or successful. **get nowhere** make or cause to make no progress. **in the middle of nowhere** *colloq.* remote from urban life. **nowhere near** not nearly. [Old English *nāhwǣr* (as NO¹, WHERE)]

no-win *attrib.adj.* of or designating a situation in which success is impossible.

nowise /ˈnəʊwʌɪz/ *adv.* in no manner; not at all.

nowt /naʊt/ *n. colloq.* or *dial.* nothing. [variant of NOUGHT]

noxious /ˈnɒkʃəs/ *adj.* harmful, unwholesome. □ **noxiously** *adv.* **noxiousness** *n.* [Latin *noxius* from *noxa* 'harm']

noyau /nwɑːˈjəʊ/ *n.* (*pl.* **noyaux** /-jəʊz/) a liqueur of brandy flavoured with fruit-kernels. [French, = kernel, ultimately from Latin *nux nucis* 'nut']

nozzle /ˈnɒz(ə)l/ *n.* a spout on a hose etc. from which a jet issues. [NOSE + -LE²]

NP *abbr.* Notary Public.

Np *symb. Chem.* the element neptunium.

n.p. *abbr.* **1** new paragraph. **2** no place of publication.

NPA *abbr.* (in the UK) Newspaper Publishers' Association.

NPL *abbr.* (in the UK) National Physical Laboratory.

NPV *abbr.* net present value.

nr. *abbr.* near.

NRA *abbr.* (in the UK) National Rivers Authority.

NS *abbr.* **1** new style. **2** new series. **3** Nova Scotia.

ns *abbr.* nanosecond.

NSA *abbr.* (in the US) National Security Agency.

NSB *abbr.* (in the UK) National Savings Bank.

NSC *abbr.* (in the US) National Security Council.

NSF *abbr.* (in the US) National Science Foundation.

NSPCC *abbr.* (in the UK) National Society for the Prevention of Cruelty to Children.

NSU *abbr. Med.* non-specific urethritis.

NSW *abbr.* New South Wales.

NT *abbr.* **1** New Testament. **2** Northern Territory (of Australia). **3** National Trust. **4** no trumps.

n't /(ə)nt/ *adv.* (in *comb.*) = NOT 1 (usu. with *is, are, have, must,* and the auxiliary verbs *can, do, should, would*: *isn't*; *mustn't*) (see also CAN'T, DON'T, WON'T). [contraction]

Nth. *abbr.* North.

nth see N².

NTP *abbr.* normal temperature and pressure.

nu /njuː/ *n.* the thirteenth letter of the Greek alphabet (Ν, ν). [Greek]

nuance /ˈnjuːɑːns/ *n. & v.* ● *n.* a subtle difference in or shade of meaning, feeling, colour, etc. ● *v.tr.* give a nuance or nuances to. [French from *nuer* 'to shade', ultimately from Latin *nubes* 'cloud']

nub /nʌb/ *n.* **1** the point or gist (of a matter or story). **2** a small lump, esp. of coal. **3** a stub; a small residue. □ **nubby** *adj.* [apparently a variant of *knub*, from Middle Low German *knubbe, knobbe* KNOB]

nubble /ˈnʌb(ə)l/ *n.* a small knob or lump. □ **nubbly** *adj.* [diminutive of NUB]

nubile /ˈnjuːbʌɪl/ *adj.* (of a woman) marriageable or sexually attractive. □ **nubility** /-ˈbɪlɪti/ [Latin *nubilis* from *nubere* 'become the wife of']

nuchal /ˈnjuːk(ə)l/ *adj.* of or relating to the nape of the neck. [*nucha* 'nape' via medieval Latin *nucha* 'medulla oblongata' from Arabic *nuḵā'* 'spinal marrow']

nuci- /ˈnjuːsi/ *comb. form* nut. [Latin *nux nucis* 'nut']

nuciferous /njuːˈsɪf(ə)rəs/ *adj. Bot.* bearing nuts.

nuclear /ˈnjuːklɪə/ *adj.* **1** of, relating to, or constituting a nucleus. **2** using nuclear energy (*nuclear reactor*). **3** having nuclear weapons. [NUCLEUS + -AR¹]

nuclear bomb *n.* a bomb using the release of energy by nuclear fission or fusion or both.

nuclear disarmament *n.* the gradual or total reduction by a state of its nuclear weapons.

nuclear energy *n.* energy obtained by nuclear fission or fusion.

nuclear family *n.* a couple and their children, regarded as a basic social unit.

nuclear fission *n.* a nuclear reaction in which a heavy nucleus splits spontaneously or on impact with another particle, with the release of energy.

nuclear force *n.* a strong attractive force between nucleons in the atomic nucleus that holds the nucleus together.

nuclear-free *adj.* free from nuclear weapons, power, etc.

nuclear fuel *n.* a substance that will sustain a fission chain reaction so that it can be used as a source of nuclear energy.

nuclear fusion *n.* a nuclear reaction in which atomic nuclei of low atomic number fuse to form a heavier nucleus with the release of energy.

nuclear magnetic resonance *n.* the absorption of electromagnetic radiation by a nucleus having a magnetic moment when in an external magnetic field, used mainly as an analytical technique and in body imaging for diagnosis (abbr.: **NMR**, **nmr**).

nuclear physics *n.* the physics of atomic nuclei and their interactions, esp. in the generation of nuclear energy.

nuclear power *n.* **1** electric or motive power generated by a nuclear reactor. **2** a country that has nuclear weapons. □ **nuclear-powered** *adj.*

nuclear reactor see REACTOR *n.* 2.

nuclear umbrella *n.* supposed protection afforded by an alliance with a country possessing nuclear weapons.

nuclear warfare *n.* warfare in which nuclear weapons are used.

nuclear waste *n.* radioactive waste material e.g. from the use or reprocessing of nuclear fuel.

nuclear weapon *n.* a missile, bomb, etc., using the release of energy by nuclear fission or fusion or both.

nuclear winter *n.* a period of abnormal cold and darkness predicted to follow a nuclear war, caused by a layer of smoke and dust in the atmosphere blocking the sun's rays.

nuclease /ˈnjuːklɪeɪz/ *n.* any enzyme that catalyses the breakdown of nucleic acids.

nucleate *adj.* & *v.* ● *adj.* /ˈnjuːklɪət/ having a nucleus. ● *v.intr.* & *tr.* /ˈnjuːklɪeɪt/ form or form into a nucleus. □ **nucleation** /-ˈeɪʃ(ə)n/ *n.* [Late Latin *nucleare nucleat-* 'form a kernel' (as NUCLEUS)]

nuclei *pl.* of NUCLEUS.

nucleic acid /njuːˈkliːɪk, -ˈkleɪɪk/ *n.* either of two complex organic substances (DNA and RNA), whose molecules consists of many nucleotides linked in a long chain, and present in all living cells.

nucleo- /ˈnjuːklɪəʊ/ *comb. form* nucleus; nucleic acid (*nucleoprotein*).

nucleolus /njuːklɪˈəʊləs/ *n.* (*pl.* **nucleoli** /-lʌɪ/) *Biol.* a small dense spherical structure in the nucleus of a cell during interphase. □ **nucleolar** *adj.* [Late Latin, diminutive of Latin *nucleus*: see NUCLEUS]

nucleon /ˈnjuːklɪɒn/ *n. Physics* a proton or neutron.

nucleonics /njuːklɪˈɒnɪks/ *n.pl.* (treated as *sing.*) the branch of science and technology concerned with atomic nuclei and nucleons, esp. the exploitation of nuclear power. □ **nucleonic** *adj.* [NUCLEAR, on the pattern of *electronics*]

nucleoprotein /ˌnjuːklɪə(ʊ)ˈprəʊtiːn/ *n.* a complex of nucleic acid and protein.

nucleoside /ˈnjuːklɪəsʌɪd/ *n. Biochem.* an organic compound consisting of a purine or pyrimidine base linked to a sugar, e.g. adenosine.

nucleosynthesis /ˌnjuːklɪəʊˈsɪnθɪsɪs/ *n. Astron.* the cosmic formation of atoms more complex than the hydrogen atom. □ **nucleosynthetic** /-ˈθɛtɪk/ *adj.*

nucleotide /ˈnjuːklɪətʌɪd/ *n. Biochem.* an organic compound consisting of a nucleoside linked to a phosphate group.

nucleus /ˈnjuːklɪəs/ *n.* (*pl.* **nuclei** /-lɪʌɪ/) **1 a** the central part or thing round which others are collected. **b** the kernel of an aggregate or mass. **2** an initial part meant to receive additions. **3** *Astron.* the solid part of a comet's head. **4** *Physics* the positively charged central core of an atom that contains most of its mass. **5** *Biol.* a large dense organelle in a eukaryotic cell, containing the genetic material. **6** a discrete mass of grey matter in the central nervous system. [Latin, = kernel, inner part, diminutive of *nux nucis* 'nut']

nuclide /ˈnjuːklʌɪd/ *n. Physics* a distinct kind of atom or nucleus characterized by a specific number of protons and neutrons. □ **nuclidic** /njuːˈklɪdɪk/ *adj.* [NUCLEUS + Greek *eidos* 'form']

nuddy /ˈnʌdi/ *n. colloq.* □ **in the nuddy** in the nude. [jocular alteration of NUDE]

nude /njuːd/ *adj.* & *n.* ● *adj.* naked, bare, unclothed. ● *n.* **1** a painting, sculpture, photograph, etc. of a nude human figure; such a figure. **2** a nude person. **3** (prec. by *the*) **a** an unclothed state. **b** the representation of an undraped human figure as a genre in art. [Latin *nudus*]

nudge /nʌdʒ/ *v.* & *n.* ● *v.tr.* **1** prod gently with the elbow to attract attention. **2** push gently or gradually. **3** give a gentle reminder or encouragement to (a person). ● *n.* the act or an instance of nudging; a gentle push. □ **nudger** *n.* [17th c.: origin unknown: cf. Norwegian dialect *nugga*, *nyggja* 'to push, rub']

nudibranch /ˈnjuːdɪbraŋk/ *n.* & *adj.* ● *n.* a marine gastropod of the order Nudibranchia, with exposed gills and a vestigial shell; a sea slug. ● *adj.* of or relating to this order. □ **nudibranchiate** /-ˈbraŋkɪət/ *n.* & *adj.* [modern Latin *Nudibranchia*, from Latin *nudus* NUDE + BRANCHIA]

nudist /ˈnjuːdɪst/ *n.* a person who advocates or practises going unclothed. □ **nudism** *n.*

nudity /ˈnjuːdɪti/ *n.* the state of being nude; nakedness.

nuée ardente /ˌnjʊeɪ ɑːˈdɒ̃t, French nɥɛ ardɑ̃t/ *n. Geol.* a hot cloud of gas, ash, and lava fragments ejected from a volcano, usu. accompanying a pyroclastic flow. [French, literally 'burning cloud']

nugatory /ˈnjuːgət(ə)ri, ˈnuː-/ *adj.* **1** futile, trifling, worthless. **2** inoperative; not valid. [Latin *nugatorius*, via *nugari* 'to trifle' from *nugae* 'jests']

nugget /ˈnʌgɪt/ *n.* **1 a** a lump of gold, platinum, etc., as found in the earth. **b** a lump of anything compared to this. **2** something valuable for its size (often abstract in sense: *a little nugget of information*). [apparently from dialect *nug* 'lump' etc., of unknown origin]

nuisance /ˈnjuːs(ə)ns/ *n.* **1** a person, thing, or circumstance causing trouble or annoyance. **2** anything harmful or offensive to the community or a member of it and for which a legal remedy exists. [Middle English via Old French, = hurt, from *nuire nuis-* 'hurt, injure', from Latin *nocēre*]

nuisance value *n.* an advantage resulting from the capacity to harass or frustrate.

NUJ *abbr.* (in the UK) National Union of Journalists.

nuke /njuːk/ *n.* & *v. colloq.* ● *n.* a nuclear weapon. ● *v.tr.* bomb or destroy with nuclear weapons. [abbreviation]

null /nʌl/ *adj.* & *n.* ● *adj.* **1** (esp. **null and void**) invalid; not binding. **2** non-existent; amounting to nothing. **3** having or associated with the value zero. **4** *Computing* **a** empty; having no elements (*null list*). **b** all the elements of which are zeros (*null matrix*). **5** without character or expression. ● *n.* a dummy letter in a cipher. [French *nul nulle* or Latin *nullus* 'none', from *ne* 'not' + *ullus* 'any']

nullah /ˈnʌlə/ *n. Anglo-Ind.* a dry river bed or ravine. [Hindi *nālā*]

nulla-nulla /ˈnʌlənʌlə/ *n.* (also **nulla**) *Austral.* a hardwood club used by Aboriginals. [Dharuk *ngalla-ngalla*]

null character *n. Computing* a character denoting nothing, usu. represented by a zero.

null hypothesis *n.* a hypothesis suggesting that the difference between statistical samples does not imply a difference between populations.

nullify /ˈnʌlɪfʌɪ/ *v.tr.* (**-ies**, **-ied**) make null; neutralize, invalidate, cancel. □ **nullification** /-fɪˈkeɪʃ(ə)n/ *n.* **nullifier** *n.*

null instrument *n.* (also **null indicator**) an instrument used to measure an electrical quantity by adjusting known quantities in the circuit until a reading of zero is obtained.

nullipara /nʌˈlɪp(ə)rə/ *n.* a woman who has never borne a child. □ **nulliparous** *adj.* [modern Latin, from Latin *nullus* 'none' + *-para*, fem. of *-parus*, from *parere* 'bear children']

nullipore /'nʌlɪpɔː/ *n.* any of various seaweeds able to secrete lime. [Latin *nullus* 'none' + PORE[1]]

nullity /'nʌlɪti/ *n.* (*pl.* **-ies**) **1** *Law* **a** being null; invalidity, esp. of marriage. **b** an act, document, etc., that is null. **2 a** nothingness. **b** a mere nothing; a nonentity. [French *nullité* or medieval Latin *nullitas* from Latin *nullus* 'none']

null link *n. Computing* a reference incorporated into the last item in a list to indicate there are no further items in the list.

NUM *abbr.* (in the UK) National Union of Mineworkers.

Num. *abbr.* Numbers (Old Testament).

numb /nʌm/ *adj. & v.* ● *adj.* (often foll. by *with*) deprived of feeling or the power of motion (*numb with cold*). ● *v.tr.* **1** make numb. **2** stupefy, paralyse. □ **numbly** *adv.* **numbness** *n.* [Middle English *nome(n)*, past part. of *nim* 'take': for *-b* cf. THUMB]

numbat /'nʌmbat/ *n.* a small Australian marsupial, *Myrmecobius fasciatus*, with a bushy tail and black and white striped back. [Nyungar *numbad*]

number /'nʌmbə/ *n. & v.* ● *n.* **1 a** an arithmetical value representing a particular quantity and used in counting and making calculations. **b** a word, symbol, or figure representing this; a numeral. **c** an arithmetical value showing position in a series, esp. for identification, reference, etc. (*registration number*). **2** (often foll. by *of*) the total count or aggregate (*the number of accidents has decreased*; *twenty in number*). **3 a** the study of the behaviour of numbers; numerical reckoning (*the laws of number*). **b** (in *pl.*) arithmetic (*not good at numbers*). **4 a** (in *sing.* or *pl.*) a quantity or amount; a total; a count (*a large number of people*; *only in small numbers*). **b** (**a number of**) several (of), some (of). **c** (in *pl.*) numerical preponderance (*force of numbers*; *there is safety in numbers*). **5 a** a person or thing having a place in a series, esp. a single issue of a magazine, an item in a programme, etc. **b** a song, dance, musical item, etc. **6** company, collection, group (*among our number*). **7** *Gram.* **a** the classification of words by their singular or plural forms. **b** a particular form so classified. **8** *colloq.* a person or thing regarded familiarly or affectionately (usu. qualified in some way: *an attractive little number*). **9** (**Numbers**) the Old Testament book containing a census. ● *v.tr.* **1** include (*I number you among my friends*). **2** assign a number or numbers to. **3** have or amount to (a specified number). **4 a** count. **b** comprise (*numbering forty thousand men*). □ **any number of 1** any particular whole quantity of. **2** *colloq.* a large unspecified number of. **by numbers** following simple instructions (as if) identified by numbers. **one's days are numbered** one does not have long to live. **have a person's number** *colloq.* understand a person's real motives, character, etc. **have a person's number on it** (of a bomb, bullet, etc.) be destined to hit a specified person. **one's number is up** *colloq.* one is finished or doomed to die. **without number** innumerable. [Middle English via Old French *nombre* (*n.*), *nombrer* (*v.*) from Latin *numerus*, *numerare*]

■ **Usage** In sense 4b of the noun, *a number of* is normally used with a plural verb, e.g. *A number of problems remain.*

number cruncher *n. Computing & Math. slang* a machine capable of complex calculations etc. □ **number crunching** *n.*

numberless /'nʌmbəlɪs/ *adj.* innumerable.

number one *n. & adj. colloq.* ● *n.* oneself (*always takes care of number one*). ● *adj.* most important (*the number one priority*).

number plate *n.* a plate on a vehicle displaying its registration number.

numbers game *n.* **1** usu. *derog.* action involving only arithmetical work. **2** *N. Amer.* a lottery based on the occurrence of unpredictable numbers in the results of races etc. **3** a comparison, contest, etc., regarded merely in terms of numerical statistics.

Number Ten *n.* 10 Downing Street, the official London home of the British Prime Minister.

number two *n.* a second in command.

numb-fish *n.* (*pl.* usu. same) = ELECTRIC RAY.

numbles /'nʌmb(ə)lz/ *n.pl. Brit. archaic* a deer's entrails. [originally = the back and loins of a deer: Middle English via Old French *numbles*, *nombles* from Latin *lumbulus*, diminutive of *lumbus* 'loin': cf. UMBLES]

numbskull var. of NUMSKULL.

numdah /'nʌmdə/ *n.* an embroidered felt rug from India etc. [Urdu *namdā* from Persian *namad* 'carpet']

numen /'njuːmən/ *n.* (*pl.* **numina** /-mɪnə/) a presiding deity or spirit. [Latin *numen -minis*]

numerable /'njuːm(ə)rəb(ə)l/ *adj.* that can be counted. □ **numerably** *adv.* [Latin *numerabilis* from *numerare* NUMBER *v.*]

numeral /'njuːm(ə)r(ə)l/ *n. & adj.* ● *n.* a word, figure, or group of figures denoting a number. ● *adj.* of or denoting a number. [Late Latin *numeralis* from Latin (as NUMBER)]

numerate /'njuːm(ə)rət/ *adj.* acquainted with the basic principles of mathematics. □ **numeracy** *n.* [Latin *numerus* 'number' + -ATE[2] on the pattern of *literate*]

numeration /njuːmə'reɪʃ(ə)n/ *n.* **1 a** a method or process of numbering or computing. **b** calculation. **2** the expression in words of a number written in figures. [Middle English from Latin *numeratio* 'payment', in Late Latin 'numbering' (as NUMBER)]

numerator /'njuːməreɪtə/ *n.* **1** the number above the line in a vulgar fraction showing how many of the parts indicated by the denominator are taken (e.g. 2 in ⅔). **2** a person or device that numbers. [French *numérateur* or Late Latin *numerator* (as NUMBER)]

numerical /njuː'mɛrɪk(ə)l/ *adj.* (also **numeric**) of or relating to a number or numbers (*numerical superiority*). □ **numerically** *adv.* [medieval Latin *numericus* (as NUMBER)]

numerical analysis *n.* the branch of mathematics that deals with the development and use of numerical methods for solving problems.

numerology /njuːmə'rɒlədʒi/ *n.* the study of the supposed occult significance of numbers. □ **numerological** /-rə'lɒdʒɪk(ə)l/ *adj.* **numerologist** *n.* [Latin *numerus* 'number' + -LOGY]

numerous /'njuːm(ə)rəs/ *adj.* **1** (with *pl.*) great in number (*received numerous gifts*). **2** consisting of many (*a numerous family*). □ **numerously** *adv.* **numerousness** *n.* [Latin *numerosus* (as NUMBER)]

numina *pl.* of NUMEN.

numinous /'njuːmɪnəs/ *adj.* **1** indicating the presence of a divinity. **2** spiritual. **3** awe-inspiring. [Latin *numen*: see NUMEN]

numismatic /njuːmɪz'matɪk/ *adj.* of or relating to coins or medals. □ **numismatically** *adv.* [French *numismatique* via Latin *numisma* from Greek *nomisma -atos* 'current coin', from *nomizō* 'use currently']

numismatics /njuːmɪz'matɪks/ *n.* the study of coins or medals. □ **numismatist** /-'mɪzmətɪst/ *n.*

numismatology /ˌnjuːmɪzmə'tɒlədʒi, njuːˌmɪz-/ *n.* = NUMISMATICS.

nummulite /'nʌmjʊlʌɪt/ *n.* a disc-shaped fossil shell of a foraminiferous protozoan found in Tertiary strata. [Latin *nummulus*, diminutive of *nummus* 'coin']

numnah /'nʌmnə/ *n.* a saddle-cloth or pad placed under a saddle. [Urdu *namdā*: see NUMDAH]

numskull /'nʌmskʌl/ *n.* (also **numbskull**) a stupid or foolish person. [NUMB + SKULL]

nun /nʌn/ *n.* a member of a community of women living apart under religious vows. □ **nunhood** *n.* **nunlike** *adj.* **nunnish** *adj.* [Middle English via Old English *nunne* and Old French *nonne* from ecclesiastical Latin *nonna*, fem. of *nonnus* 'monk', originally a title given to an elderly person]

nunatak /ˈnʌnətak/ *n.* an isolated peak of rock projecting above a surface of inland ice or snow e.g. in Greenland. [Eskimo]

nun-buoy /ˈnʌnbɔɪ/ *n.* a buoy circular in the middle and tapering to each end. [obsolete *nun* 'child's top' + BUOY]

Nunc Dimittis /nʌŋk dɪˈmɪtɪs/ *n.* the Song of Simeon (Luke 2:29–32) used as a canticle. [the opening words *nunc dimittis* 'now let (your servant) depart']

nunciature /ˈnʌnʃətjʊə/ *n. RC Ch.* the office or tenure of a nuncio. [Italian *nunziatura* (as NUNCIO)]

nuncio /ˈnʌnsɪəʊ, ˈnʌnʃɪəʊ/ *n.* (*pl.* **-os**) *RC Ch.* a papal ambassador. [Italian from Latin *nuntius* 'messenger']

nuncupate /ˈnʌŋkjʊpeɪt/ *v.tr.* declare (a will or testament) orally, not in writing. □ **nuncupation** /-ˈpeɪʃ(ə)n/ *n.* **nuncupative** /-pətɪv/ *adj.* [Latin *nuncupare nuncupat-* 'name']

nunnery /ˈnʌn(ə)ri/ *n.* (*pl.* **-ies**) a religious house of nuns; a convent.

NUPE /ˈnju:pi/ *abbr. hist.* (in the UK) National Union of Public Employees, merged with COHSE and NALGO in 1993 to form UNISON.

nuptial /ˈnʌpʃ(ə)l/ *adj.* & *n.* ● *adj.* of or relating to marriage or weddings. ● *n.* (usu. in *pl.*) a wedding. [French *nuptial* or Latin *nuptialis*, via *nuptiae* 'wedding' from *nubere nupt-* 'wed']

NUR *abbr. hist.* (in the UK) National Union of Railwaymen (merged in 1990 with the National Union of Seamen to form the RMT).

nurd var. of NERD.

nurse[1] /nə:s/ *n.* & *v.* ● *n.* **1** a person trained to care for the sick or infirm. **2** (formerly) a person employed or trained to take charge of young children. **3** *archaic* = WET-NURSE. **4** *Forestry* a tree planted as a shelter to others. **5** *Zool.* a worker bee, ant, etc., caring for a young brood. ● *v.* **1 a** *intr.* work as a nurse. **b** *tr.* attend to (a sick person). **c** *tr.* give medical attention to (an illness or injury). **2** *tr.* & *intr.* feed or be fed at the breast. **3** *tr.* (in *passive*; foll. by *in*) be brought up in (a specified condition) (*nursed in poverty*). **4** *tr.* esp. *Brit.* hold or treat carefully or caressingly (*sat nursing my feet*). **5** *tr.* **a** foster; promote the development of (the arts, plants, etc.). **b** harbour or nurture (a grievance, hatred, etc.). **c** esp. *Brit.* pay special attention to (*nursed the voters*). **6** *tr.* consume (a drink) slowly. **7** *tr. Billiards* keep (the balls) together for a series of cannons. [reduced from Middle English and Old French *norice*, *nurice*, via Late Latin *nutricia*, fem. of Latin *nutricius* from *nutrix -icis*, from *nutrire* NOURISH]

nurse[2] /nə:s/ *n.* any of various dogfishes and sharks, esp. (in full **nurse hound**) a large dogfish of the NE Atlantic, *Scyliorhinus stellaris*, and (in full **nurse shark**) a slow-swimming brownish shark, *Ginglymostoma cirratum*, of warm Atlantic waters. [originally *nusse*, perhaps derived by wrong division of *an huss* (cf. ADDER)]

nurseling var. of NURSLING.

nursemaid /ˈnə:smeɪd/ *n.* **1** a woman in charge of a child or children. **2** a person who watches over or guides another carefully.

nursery /ˈnə:s(ə)ri/ *n.* (*pl.* **-ies**) **1 a** a room or place equipped for young children. **b** = DAY NURSERY. **2** a place where plants, trees, etc., are reared for sale or transplantation. **3** any sphere or place in or by which qualities or types of people are fostered or bred. **4** *Billiards* **a** grouped balls (see NURSE[1] *v.* 7). **b** (in full **nursery cannon**) *Brit.* a cannon on three close balls.

nurseryman /ˈnə:s(ə)rɪmən/ *n.* (*pl.* **-men**) an owner of or worker in a plant nursery.

nursery nurse *n. Brit.* a person trained to take charge of babies and young children.

nursery rhyme *n.* a simple traditional song or story in rhyme for children.

nursery school *n.* a school for children between the ages of usu. three and five.

nursery slopes *n.pl. Brit. Skiing* gentle slopes suitable for beginners.

nursery stakes *n.pl. Brit.* a race for two-year-old horses.

nursing /ˈnə:sɪŋ/ *n.* **1** the practice or profession of caring for the sick as a nurse. **2** (*attrib.*) concerned with or suitable for nursing the sick or elderly etc. (*nursing home*; *nursing sister*).

nursing officer *n. Brit.* a senior nurse (see SENIOR NURSING OFFICER).

nursling /ˈnə:slɪŋ/ *n.* (also **nurseling**) an infant that is being suckled.

nurture /ˈnə:tʃə/ *n.* & *v.* ● *n.* **1** the process of bringing up or training (esp. children); fostering care. **2** nourishment. **3** sociological factors as an influence on or determinant of personality (opp. NATURE 8). ● *v.tr.* **1** bring up; rear. **2** nourish. □ **nurturer** *n.* [Middle English from Old French *nour(e)ture* (as NOURISH)]

NUS *abbr.* **1** (in the UK) National Union of Students. **2** *hist.* (in the UK) National Union of Seamen (merged in 1990 with the NUR to form the RMT).

NUT *abbr.* (in the UK) National Union of Teachers.

nut /nʌt/ *n.* & *v.* ● *n.* **1 a** a fruit consisting of a hard or tough shell around an edible kernel. **b** this kernel. **2** a pod containing hard seeds. **3** a small usu. square or hexagonal flat piece of metal or other material with a threaded hole through it for screwing on the end of a bolt to secure it. **4** *slang* a person's head. **5** *slang* **a** a crazy or eccentric person. **b** an obsessive enthusiast or devotee (*a health-food nut*). **6** a small lump of coal, butter, etc. **7 a** a screw fitted to the bow of a violin etc. for adjusting its tension. **b** the fixed ridge on the neck of a stringed instrument over which the strings pass. **8** (in *pl.*) *coarse slang* the testicles. ● *v.* (**nutted**, **nutting**) **1** *intr.* seek or gather nuts (*go nutting*). **2** *tr. slang* butt with the head. □ **do one's nut** *Brit. slang* be extremely angry or agitated. **for nuts** *Brit. colloq.* even tolerably well (*cannot sing for nuts*). **nuts and bolts** *colloq.* the practical details. **off one's nut** *slang* crazy. □ **nutlike** *adj.* [Old English *hnutu*, from Germanic]

nutant /ˈnju:t(ə)nt/ *adj. Bot.* nodding, drooping. [Latin *nutare* 'nod']

nutation /nju:ˈteɪʃ(ə)n/ *n.* **1** the act or an instance of nodding. **2** *Astron.* a periodic oscillation of the earth's poles. **3** oscillation of a spinning top. **4** the spiral movement of a plant organ during growth. [Latin *nutatio* (as NUTANT)]

nut brown *n.* & *adj.* ● *n.* a dark brown colour. ● *adj.* (hyphenated when *attrib.*) of this colour.

nutcase /ˈnʌtkeɪs/ *n. slang* a crazy or foolish person.

nutcracker /ˈnʌtkrakə/ *n.* **1** (usu. in *pl.*) a device for cracking nuts. **2** a crow of the genus *Nucifraga*.

nut cutlet *n. Brit.* a cutlet-shaped portion of meat-substitute, made from nuts etc.

nutgall /ˈnʌtgɔ:l/ *n.* a gall found on dyer's oak, used in dyeing.

nuthatch /ˈnʌthatʃ/ *n.* any small songbird of the genus *Sitta* and family Sittidae, climbing up and down tree trunks and feeding on nuts, insects, etc., esp. the Eurasian *S. europaea*. [NUT + *hatch* related to HACK[1], from the bird's habit of hacking with the beak at nuts wedged in a crevice]

nuthouse /ˈnʌthaʊs/ *n. slang* a mental home or hospital.

nutlet /ˈnʌtlɪt/ *n.* a small nut or nutlike fruit.

nutmeg /ˈnʌtmɛg/ *n.* **1** an evergreen tree, *Myristica fragrans*, native to the Moluccas, yielding a hard aromatic spheroidal seed. **2** the seed of this grated and used as a spice. [Middle English: partial translation of Old French *nois mug(u)ede*, ultimately from Latin *nux* 'nut' + Late Latin *muscus* MUSK]

nutmeg-apple *n.* the fruit of the nutmeg tree, yielding mace and nutmeg.

nut oil *n.* an oil obtained from hazelnuts and walnuts and used in paints and varnishes.

nutria /'nju:trɪə/ *n.* the skin or fur of a coypu. [Spanish, = otter]

nutrient /'nju:trɪənt/ *n. & adj.* ● *n.* any substance that provides essential nourishment for the maintenance of life. ● *adj.* serving as or providing nourishment. [Latin *nutrire* 'nourish']

nutriment /'nju:trɪm(ə)nt/ *n.* **1** nourishing food. **2** an intellectual or artistic etc. nourishment or stimulus. □ **nutrimental** /-'mɛnt(ə)l/ *adj.* [Latin *nutrimentum* (as NUTRIENT)]

nutrition /njʊ'trɪʃ(ə)n/ *n.* **1 a** the process of providing or receiving nourishing substances. **b** food, nourishment. **2** the study of nutrients and nutrition. □ **nutritional** *adj.* **nutritionally** *adv.* [French *nutrition* or Late Latin *nutritio* (as NUTRIENT)]

nutritionist /njʊ'trɪʃ(ə)nɪst/ *n.* a person who studies or is an expert on the processes of human nourishment.

nutritious /njʊ'trɪʃəs/ *adj.* efficient as food; nourishing. □ **nutritiously** *adv.* **nutritiousness** *n.* [Latin *nutritius* (as NURSE[1])]

nutritive /'nju:trɪtɪv/ *adj. & n.* ● *adj.* **1** of or concerned in nutrition. **2** serving as nutritious food. ● *n.* a nutritious article of food. [Middle English via French *nutritif -ive* from medieval Latin *nutritivus* (as NUTRIENT)]

nuts /nʌts/ *adj. & int.* ● *predic.adj. slang* crazy, mad, eccentric. ● *int. slang* an expression of contempt or derision (*nuts to you*). □ **be nuts about** (or *Brit.* **on**) *colloq.* be enthusiastic about or very fond of.

nutshell /'nʌtʃɛl/ *n.* the hard exterior covering of a nut. □ **in a nutshell** in a few words.

nutter /'nʌtə/ *n. Brit. slang* a crazy or eccentric person.

nut tree *n.* any tree bearing nuts, esp. a hazel.

nutty /'nʌti/ *adj.* (**nuttier, nuttiest**) **1 a** full of nuts. **b** tasting like nuts. **2** *slang* crazy, mad, eccentric. □ **nuttiness** *n.*

nux vomica /nʌks 'vɒmɪkə/ *n.* **1** a southern Asian tree, *Strychnos nux-vomica*, with a poisonous fruit. **2** the seeds of this tree, containing strychnine. [medieval Latin, from Latin *nux* 'nut' + *vomicus* from *vomere* 'vomit']

nuzzle /'nʌz(ə)l/ *v.* **1** *tr.* prod or rub gently with the nose. **2** *intr.* (foll. by *into, against, up to*) press the nose gently. **3** *tr.* (also *refl.*) nestle; lie snug. [Middle English, from NOSE + -LE[4]]

NV *abbr. US* Nevada (in official postal use).

NVQ *abbr.* (in the UK) National Vocation Qualification.

NW *abbr.* **1** north-west. **2** north-western.

NY *abbr. US* New York (also in official postal use).

nyala/'njɑ:lə/ *n.* (*pl.* same) a large antelope, *Tragelaphus angasi*, native to S. Africa, with curved horns having a single complete turn. [Zulu]

NYC *abbr.* New York City.

nyctalopia /nɪktə'ləʊpɪə/ *n. Med.* inability to see in dim light or at night. Also called *night-blindness*. [Late Latin from Greek *nuktalōps*, from *nux nuktos* 'night' + *alaos* 'blind' + *ōps* 'eye']

nyctitropic /nɪktɪ'trəʊpɪk, -'trɒpɪk/ *adj. Bot.* (of plant movements) occurring at night and caused by changes in light and temperature. [Greek *nukti-*, comb. form of *nux nuktos* 'night' + *tropos* 'turn']

nye var. of NIDE.

nylon /'nʌɪlɒn/ *n.* **1** any of various synthetic polyamide fibres having a protein-like structure, with tough, lightweight, elastic properties, used in industry and for textiles etc. **2** a nylon fabric. **3** (in *pl.*) stockings made of nylon. [invented word, on the pattern of *cotton, rayon*]

nymph /nɪmf/ *n.* **1** any of various mythological semi-divine spirits regarded as maidens and associated with aspects of nature, esp. rivers and woods. **2** *poet.* a beautiful young woman. **3** an immature form of an insect that does not undergo complete metamorphosis, e.g. a dragonfly, mayfly, or locust. □ **nymphal** *adj.* **nymphean** /-'fi:ən/ *adj.* **nymphlike** *adj.* [Middle English via Old French *nimphe* and Latin *nympha* from Greek *numphē*]

nymphae /'nɪmfi:/ *n.pl. Anat.* the labia minora. [Latin, pl. of *nympha*: see NYMPH]

nymphalid /nɪm'falɪd/ *adj. & n.* ● *adj.* of or relating to the large family Nymphalidae of butterflies with degenerate forelegs. ● *n.* a butterfly of this family. [modern Latin genus name *Nymphalis*, from Latin *nympha* NYMPH]

nymphet /'nɪmfɛt, nɪm'fɛt/ *n.* **1** a young nymph. **2** *colloq.* a sexually attractive (esp. precocious) young woman.

nympho /'nɪmfəʊ/ *n.* (*pl.* **-os**) *colloq.* a nymphomaniac. [abbreviation]

nympholepsy /'nɪmfəlɛpsi/ *n.* ecstasy or frenzy caused by desire of the unattainable. [NYMPHOLEPT, on the pattern of *epilepsy*]

nympholept /'nɪmfəlɛpt/ *n.* a person inspired by violent enthusiasm esp. for an ideal. □ **nympholeptic** /-'lɛptɪk/ *adj.* [Greek *numpholēptos* 'caught by nymphs' (as NYMPH, *lambanō* 'take')]

nymphomania /nɪmfə'meɪnɪə/ *n.* excessive sexual desire in a woman. □ **nymphomaniac** *n. & adj.* [modern Latin (as NYMPH, -MANIA)]

nystagmus /nɪ'stagməs/ *n.* rapid involuntary movements of the eyes. □ **nystagmic** *adj.* [Greek *nustagmos* 'nodding, drowiness' from *nustazō* 'nod, be sleepy']

nystatin /'nʌɪstətɪn, 'nɪs-/ *n.* an antibiotic used esp. to treat fungal infections. [*N*ew *Y*ork *Stat*e (where developed) + -IN]

Nyungar /'njʊŋə/ *n.* an Aboriginal language of SW Australia, now extinct.

NZ *abbr.* New Zealand.

Oo

O[1] /əʊ/ *n.* (also **o**) (*pl.* **Os** or **O's**) **1** the fifteenth letter of the alphabet. **2** (**0**) nought, zero (in a sequence of numerals esp. when spoken). **3** a human blood type of the ABO system.

O[2] *symb. Chem.* the element oxygen.

O[3] /əʊ/ *int.* **1** var. of OH[1]. **2** prefixed to a name in the vocative (*O God*). [Middle English, a natural exclamation]

O' /əʊ, ə/ *prefix* of Irish patronymic names (*O'Connor*). [Irish *ó*, *ua*, 'descendant']

o' /əʊ, ə/ *prep.* of, on (esp. in phrs.: *o'clock*; *will-o'-the-wisp*). [abbreviation]

-o /əʊ/ *suffix* forming usu. *slang* or *colloq.* variants or derivatives (*beano*; *wino*). [perhaps OH[1] as jocular suffix]

-o- /əʊ/ *suffix* the terminal vowel of combining forms (*spectro-*; *chemico-*; *Franco-*). [originally Greek]

■ **Usage** This suffix is often elided before a vowel, as in *neuralgia*.

oaf /əʊf/ *n.* (*pl.* **oafs**) **1** an awkward lout. **2** a stupid person. □ **oafish** *adj.* **oafishly** *adv.* **oafishness** *n.* [originally = elf's child, variant of obsolete *auf* from Old Norse *álfr* 'elf']

oak /əʊk/ *n.* **1** (also **oak tree**) any tree of the genus *Quercus* usu. having lobed leaves and bearing acorns. **2** the durable wood of this tree, used esp. for furniture and in building. **3** (*attrib.*) made of oak (*oak table*). **4** *Brit.* a heavy outer door of a set of university college rooms. **5** (**the Oaks**) (treated as *sing.*) an annual race at Epsom for three-year-old fillies (from the name of a nearby estate). □ **oaken** *adj.* [Old English *āc*, from Germanic]

oak-apple *n.* a spongy round gall found on oak trees, formed by the gall wasp *Biorhiza pallida*.

oakum /ˈəʊkəm/ *n.* a loose fibre obtained by picking old rope to pieces and used esp. in caulking. [Old English *ǣcumbe*, *ācumbe*, literally 'off-combings']

O. & M. *abbr.* organization and methods.

OAP *abbr. Brit.* old-age pensioner.

oar /ɔː/ *n.* **1** a pole with a blade used for rowing or steering a boat by leverage against the water. **2** a rower. □ **put** (or **stick**) **one's oar in** interfere, meddle. **rest** (*US* **lay**) **on one's oars** relax one's efforts. □ **oared** *adj.* (also in *comb.*). **oarless** *adj.* [Old English *ār* from Germanic: perhaps related to Greek *eretmos* 'oar']

oarfish /ˈɔːfɪʃ/ *n.* (*pl.* usu. same) a ribbonfish, *Regalecus glesne*.

oarlock /ˈɔːlɒk/ *n. N. Amer.* a rowlock.

oarsman /ˈɔːzmən/ *n.* (*pl.* **-men**; *fem.* **oarswoman**, *pl.* **-women**) a rower. □ **oarsmanship** *n.*

oarweed /ˈɔːwiːd/ *n.* (also **oreweed**) any large marine alga esp. of the genus *Laminaria*, often growing along rocky shores.

OAS *abbr.* **1** Organization of American States. **2** on active service.

oasis /əʊˈeɪsɪs/ *n.* (*pl.* **oases** /-siːz/) **1** a fertile spot in a desert, where water is found. **2** an area or period of calm in the midst of turbulence. [Late Latin from Greek, apparently of Egyptian origin]

oast /əʊst/ *n.* a kiln for drying hops. [Old English *āst*, from Germanic]

oast house *n.* a building containing an oast.

oat /əʊt/ *n.* **1 a** a cereal plant, *Avena sativa*, cultivated in cool climates. **b** (in *pl.*) the grain yielded by this, used as food. **2** any related grass esp. the wild oat, *A. fatua*. **3** *poet.* the oat-stem used as a musical pipe by shepherds etc., usu. in pastoral or bucolic poetry. **4** (in *pl.*) *slang* sexual gratification. □ **feel one's oats** *colloq.* **1** be lively. **2** *US* feel self-important. **off one's oats** *colloq.* lacking an appetite. **sow one's oats** (or **wild oats**) indulge in youthful excess or promiscuity. □ **oaten** *adj.* **oaty** *adj.* [Old English *āte*, pl. *ātan*, of unknown origin]

oatcake /ˈəʊtkeɪk/ *n.* a thin unleavened biscuit-like food made of oatmeal, common in Scotland and northern England.

oat-grass *n.* any of various grasses, esp. of the genus *Arrhenatherum* or *Helictotrichon*.

oath /əʊθ/ *n.* (*pl.* **oaths** /əʊðz/) **1** a solemn declaration or undertaking (often naming God) as to the truth of something or as a commitment to future action. **2** a statement or promise contained in an oath (*oath of allegiance*). **3** a profane or blasphemous utterance; a curse. □ **take** (or **swear**) **an oath** make such a declaration or undertaking. **under** (or *Brit.* **on**) **oath** having sworn a solemn oath. [Old English *āth*, from Germanic]

oatmeal /ˈəʊtmiːl/ *n.* & *adj.* ● *n.* **1** meal made from ground oats used esp. in porridge and oatcakes. **2** a greyish-fawn colour flecked with brown. ● *adj.* of this colour.

OAU *abbr.* Organization of African Unity.

OB *abbr. Brit.* outside broadcast.

ob. *abbr.* he or she died. [Latin *obiit*]

ob- /ɒb/ *prefix* (also **oc-** before *c*, **of-** before *f*, **op-** before *p*) occurring mainly in words of Latin origin, meaning: **1** exposure, openness (*object*; *obverse*). **2** meeting or facing (*occasion*; *obvious*). **3** direction (*oblong*; *offer*). **4** opposition, hostility, or resistance (*obstreperous*; *opponent*; *obstinate*). **5** hindrance, blocking, or concealment (*obese*; *obstacle*; *occult*). **6** finality or completeness (*obsolete*; *occupy*). **7** (in modern technical words) inversely; in a direction or manner contrary to the usual (*obconical*; *obovate*). [Latin from *ob* 'towards, against, in the way of']

Obad. *abbr.* Obadiah (Old Testament).

obbligato /ɒblɪˈgɑːtəʊ/ *n.* (*pl.* **-os**) *Mus.* an accompaniment, usu. special and unusual in effect, forming an integral part of a composition (*with violin obbligato*). [Italian, = obligatory, from Latin *obligatus*, past part. of *obligare* (as OBLIGE)]

obconical /ɒbˈkɒnɪk(ə)l/ *adj.* (also **obconic**) in the form of an inverted cone.

obcordate /ɒbˈkɔːdeɪt/ *adj. Biol.* in the shape of a heart with the pointed end at the base.

obdurate /ˈɒbdjʊrət/ *adj.* **1** stubborn. **2** hardened against persuasion or influence. □ **obduracy** *n.* **obdurately** *adv.* **obdurateness** *n.* [Middle English from Latin *obduratus* past part. of *obdurare* (as OB-, *durare* 'harden' from *durus* 'hard')]

OBE *abbr.* (in the UK) Officer of the Order of the British Empire.

obeah /ˈəʊbɪə/ *n.* (also **obi** /ˈəʊbi/) a kind of sorcery practised esp. in the West Indies. [West African]

obeche /əʊˈbiːtʃi/ *n.* **1** a West African tree, *Triplochiton scleroxylon*. **2** the light-coloured timber from this. [Nigerian name]

obedience /əˈbiːdɪəns/ *n.* **1** the practice or quality of being obedient. **2** submission to another's rule or authority. **3** compliance with a law or command. **4** *Eccl.*

a compliance with a monastic rule. **b** a sphere of authority (*the Roman obedience*). □ **in obedience to** actuated by or in accordance with. [Middle English via Old French from Latin *obedientia* (as OBEY)]

obedient /əˈbiːdɪənt/ *adj.* **1** obeying or ready to obey. **2** (often foll. by *to*) submissive to another's will; dutiful (*obedient to the law*). □ **obediently** *adv.* [Middle English via Old French from Latin *obediens -entis* (as OBEY)]

obeisance /ə(ʊ)ˈbeɪs(ə)ns/ *n.* **1** a bow, curtsy, or other respectful or submissive gesture (*make an obeisance*). **2** homage, submission, deference (*pay obeisance*). □ **obeisant** *adj.* [Middle English from Old French *obeissance* (as OBEY)]

obeli *pl.* of OBELUS.

obelisk /ˈɒb(ə)lɪsk/ *n.* **1 a** a tapering usu. four-sided stone pillar set up as a monument or landmark etc. **b** a mountain, tree, etc., of similar shape. **2** = OBELUS. [Latin *obeliscus* from Greek *obeliskos*, diminutive of *obelos* SPIT[2]]

obelize /ˈɒb(ə)lʌɪz/ *v.tr.* (also **-ise**) mark with an obelus as spurious etc. [Greek *obelizō* from *obelos* SPIT[2]]

obelus /ˈɒb(ə)ləs/ *n.* (*pl.* **obeli** /-lʌɪ, -liː/) **1** a symbol (†) used as a reference mark in printed matter or to indicate that a person is deceased. **2** a mark (- or ÷) used in ancient manuscripts to mark a word or passage, esp. as spurious. [Latin from Greek *obelos* SPIT[2]]

obese /ə(ʊ)ˈbiːs/ *adj.* very overweight; corpulent. □ **obeseness** *n.* **obesity** *n.* [Latin *obesus* (as OB-, *edere* 'eat')]

obey /ə(ʊ)ˈbeɪ/ *v.* **1** *tr.* **a** carry out the command of (*you will obey me*). **b** carry out (a command) (*obey orders*). **2** *intr.* do what one is told to do. **3** *tr.* be actuated by (a force or impulse). □ **obeyer** *n.* [Middle English via Old French *obeir* from Latin *obedire* (as OB-, *audire* 'hear')]

obfuscate /ˈɒbfʌskeɪt/ *v.tr.* **1** obscure or confuse (a mind, topic, etc.). **2** stupefy, bewilder. □ **obfuscation** /-ˈkeɪʃ(ə)n/ *n.* **obfuscatory** *adj.* [Late Latin *obfuscare* (as OB-, *fuscus* 'dark')]

obi[1] var. of OBEAH.

obi[2] /ˈəʊbi/ *n.* (*pl.* **obis**) a broad sash worn with a Japanese kimono. [Japanese *obi* 'belt']

obit /ˈɒbɪt, ˈəʊ-/ *n. colloq.* an obituary. [abbreviation]

obiter dictum /ˌɒbɪtə ˈdɪktəm/ *n.* (*pl.* ***obiter dicta*** /-tə/) **1** a judge's expression of opinion uttered in court or giving judgement, but not essential to the decision and therefore without binding authority. **2** an incidental remark. [Latin, from *obiter* 'by the way' + *dictum* 'a thing said']

obituary /ə(ʊ)ˈbɪtʃʊəri/ *n.* (*pl.* **-ies**) **1** a notice of a death or deaths esp. in a newspaper. **2** an account of the life of a deceased person. **3** (*attrib.*) of or serving as an obituary. □ **obituarial** /-tʃʊˈɛːrɪəl/ *adj.* **obituarist** *n.* [medieval Latin *obituarius* from Latin *obitus* 'death', from *obire obit-* 'die' (as OB-, *ire* 'go')]

object *n.* & *v.* ● *n.* /ˈɒbdʒɪkt/ **1** a material thing that can be seen or touched. **2** (foll. by *of*) a person or thing to which action or feeling is directed (*the object of attention*; *the object of our study*). **3** a thing sought or aimed at; a purpose. **4** *Gram.* a noun or its equivalent governed by an active transitive verb or by a preposition. **5** *Philos.* a thing external to the thinking mind or subject. **6** *derog.* a person or thing of esp. a pathetic or ridiculous appearance. **7** *Computing* a package of information and a description of its manipulation. ● *v.* /əbˈdʒɛkt/ **1** *intr.* (often foll. by *to* or *Brit. against*) express or feel opposition, disapproval, or reluctance; protest (*I object to being treated like this*; *objecting against government policies*). **2** *tr.* (foll. by *that* + clause) state as an objection (*objected that they were kept waiting*). **3** *tr.* (foll. by *to*, *against*, or *that* + clause) adduce (a quality or fact) as contrary or damaging (to a case). □ **no object** not forming an important or restricting factor (*money no object*). **object of the exercise** the main point of an activity. □ **objectless** /ˈɒbdʒɪk(t)lɪs/ *adj.* **objector** /əbˈdʒɛktə/ *n.* [Middle English from medieval Latin *objectum* 'thing presented to the mind', past part. of Latin *objicere* (as OB-, *jacere ject-* 'throw')]

object-ball *n. Billiards* etc. the ball at which a player aims the cue ball.

object-glass *n.* = OBJECTIVE *n.* 3.

objectify /ɒbˈdʒɛktɪfʌɪ/ *v.tr.* (**-ies**, **-ied**) **1** make objective; express in a concrete form. **2** present as an object of perception. □ **objectification** /-fɪˈkeɪʃ(ə)n/ *n.*

objection /əbˈdʒɛkʃ(ə)n/ *n.* **1** an expression or feeling of opposition or disapproval. **2** the act of objecting. **3** an adverse reason or statement. [Middle English from Old French *objection* or Late Latin *objectio* (as OBJECT)]

objectionable /əbˈdʒɛkʃ(ə)nəb(ə)l/ *adj.* **1** open to objection. **2** unpleasant, offensive. □ **objectionableness** *n.* **objectionably** /-bli/ *adv.*

objective /əbˈdʒɛktɪv/ *adj.* & *n.* ● *adj.* **1** external to the mind; actually existing; real. **2** (of a person, writing, art, etc.) dealing with outward things or exhibiting facts uncoloured by feelings or opinions; not subjective. **3** *Gram.* (of a case or word) constructed as or appropriate to the object of a transitive verb or preposition (cf. ACCUSATIVE). **4** aimed at (*objective point*). **5** (of symptoms) observed by another and not only felt by the patient. ● *n.* **1** something sought or aimed at; an objective point. **2** *Gram.* the objective case. **3** (in full **objective lens**) the lens in a telescope, microscope, etc., nearest to the object observed. Also called *object-glass*. □ **objectival** /ɒbdʒɛkˈtʌɪv(ə)l/ *adj.* **objectively** *adv.* **objectiveness** *n.* **objectivity** /ɒbdʒɛkˈtɪvɪti/ *n.* **objectivize** /əbˈdʒɛktɪvʌɪz/ *v.tr.* (also **-ise**). **objectivization** /əbˌdʒɛktɪvʌɪˈzeɪʃ(ə)n/ *n.* [medieval Latin *objectivus* (as OBJECT)]

objectivism /əbˈdʒɛktɪvɪz(ə)m/ *n.* **1** the tendency to lay stress on what is objective. **2** *Philos.* the belief that certain things (esp. moral truths) exist apart from human knowledge or perception of them. □ **objectivist** *n.* **objectivistic** /-ˈvɪstɪk/ *adj.*

object language *n.* **1** a language described by means of another language (see METALANGUAGE 1). **2** *Computing* a language into which a program is translated by means of a compiler or assembler.

object lesson *n.* a striking practical example of some principle.

object of virtu *n.* object interesting because of its workmanship, antiquity, rarity, etc.

objet d'art /ɒbʒeɪ ˈdɑː/ *n.* (*pl.* **objets d'art** *pronunc.* same) a small decorative object. [French, literally 'object of art']

objurgate /ˈɒbdʒəgeɪt/ *v.tr. literary* chide or scold. □ **objurgation** /-ˈgeɪʃ(ə)n/ *n.* **objurgatory** /ɒbˈdʒəːgət(ə)ri/ *adj.* [Latin *objurgare objurgat-* (as OB-, *jurgare* 'quarrel' from *jurgium* 'strife')]

oblanceolate /ɒbˈlɑːnsɪələt/ *adj. Bot.* (esp. of leaves) lanceolate with the more pointed end at the base.

oblate[1] /ˈɒbleɪt/ *n.* a person dedicated to a monastic or religious life or work. [French via medieval Latin *oblatus* from Latin *offerre oblat-* 'offer' (as OB-, *ferre* 'bring')]

oblate[2] /ˈɒbleɪt/ *adj. Geom.* (of a spheroid) flattened at the poles (cf. PROLATE 1). [modern Latin *oblatus* (as OBLATE[1])]

oblation /əˈbleɪʃ(ə)n/ *n. Relig.* **1** a thing offered to a divine being. **2** the presentation of bread and wine to God in the Eucharist. □ **oblational** *adj.* **oblatory** /ˈɒblət(ə)ri/ *adj.* [Middle English from Old French *oblation* or Late Latin *oblatio* (as OBLATE[1])]

obligate *v.* & *adj.* ● *v.tr.* /ˈɒblɪgeɪt/ **1** (usu. in *passive*; foll. by *to* + infin.) bind (a person) legally or morally. **2** *US* commit (assets) as security. ● *adj.* /ˈɒblɪgət/ *Biol.* that has to be as described (*obligate parasite*). □ **obligator** *n.* [Latin *obligare obligat-* (as OBLIGE)]

obligation /ɒblɪˈgeɪʃ(ə)n/ *n.* **1** the constraining power of a law, precept, duty, contract, etc. **2** a duty; a burdensome task. **3** a binding agreement, esp. one enforceable under legal penalty; a written contract or bond. **4 a** a service or benefit; a kindness done or received (*repay an obligation*). **b** indebtedness for this (*be under an obligation*). □ **of obligation** obligatory. □ **obligational** *adj.* [Middle English via Old French from Latin *obligatio -onis* (as OBLIGE)]

obligatory /əˈblɪɡət(ə)ri/ *adj.* **1** legally or morally binding. **2** compulsory and not merely permitted. **3** constituting an obligation. □ **obligatorily** *adv.* [Middle English from Late Latin *obligatorius* (as OBLIGE)]

oblige /əˈblʌɪdʒ/ *v.tr.* **1** (foll. by *to* + infin.) constrain, compel. **2** be binding on. **3 a** make indebted by conferring a favour. **b** (foll. by *with*, or *by* + verbal noun; also *absol.*) gratify, perform a service for (*oblige me by leaving*; *obliged with a song*; *will you oblige?*). **4** (in *passive*; foll. by *to*) be indebted (*am obliged to you for your help*). **5** (foll. by *to*, or *to* + infin.) *archaic* or *Law* bind by oath, promise, contract, etc. □ **much obliged** an expression of thanks. □ **obliger** *n.* [Middle English via Old French *obliger* from Latin *obligare* (as OB-, *ligare* 'bind')]

obligee /ɒblɪˈdʒiː/ *n. Law* a person to whom another is bound by contract or other legal procedure (cf. OBLIGOR).

obliging /əˈblʌɪdʒɪŋ/ *adj.* courteous, accommodating; ready to do a service or kindness. □ **obligingly** *adv.* **obligingness** *n.*

obligor /ˈɒblɪɡɔː, ɒblɪˈɡɔː/ *n. Law* a person who is bound to another by contract or other legal procedure (cf. OBLIGEE).

oblique /əˈbliːk/ *adj., n., & v.* ● *adj.* **1 a** slanting; declining from the vertical or horizontal. **b** diverging from a straight line or course. **2** not going straight to the point; roundabout, indirect. **3** *Geom.* **a** (of a line, plane figure, or surface) inclined at other than a right angle. **b** (of an angle) acute or obtuse. **c** (of a cone, cylinder, etc.) with an axis not perpendicular to the plane of its base. **4** *Anat.* (esp. of a muscle) neither parallel nor perpendicular to the long axis of a body or limb. **5** *Bot.* (of a leaf) with unequal sides. **6** *Gram.* denoting any case other than the nominative or vocative. ● *n.* **1** *Brit.* an oblique stroke (/). **2** an oblique muscle. ● *v.intr.* (**obliques**, **obliqued**, **obliquing**) esp. *Mil.* advance obliquely. □ **obliquely** *adv.* **obliqueness** *n.* **obliquity** /əˈblɪkwɪti/ *n.* [Middle English via French from Latin *obliquus*]

oblique oration *n.* (also **oblique speech**) = REPORTED SPEECH.

obliterate /əˈblɪtəreɪt/ *v.tr.* **1 a** blot out; efface, erase, destroy. **b** leave no clear traces of. **2** deface (a postage stamp etc.) to prevent further use. □ **obliteration** /-ˈreɪʃ(ə)n/ *n.* **obliterative** /-rətɪv/ *adj.* **obliterator** *n.* [Latin *obliterare* (as OB-, *litera* LETTER)]

oblivion /əˈblɪvɪən/ *n.* **1 a** the state of forgetting or having forgotten. **b** the state of being forgotten (*return to oblivion*). **2** an amnesty or pardon. □ **fall into oblivion** be forgotten or disused. [Middle English via Old French from Latin *oblivio -onis*, from *oblivisci* 'forget']

oblivious /əˈblɪvɪəs/ *adj.* **1** (often foll. by *of*) forgetful, unmindful. **2** (foll. by *to*, *of*) unaware or unconscious of. □ **obliviously** *adv.* **obliviousness** *n.* [Middle English from Latin *obliviosus* (as OBLIVION)]

oblong /ˈɒblɒŋ/ *adj. & n.* ● *adj.* **1** deviating from a square form by having one long axis, esp. rectangular with adjacent sides unequal. **2** greater in breadth than in height. ● *n.* an oblong figure or object. [Middle English from Latin *oblongus* 'longish' (as OB-, *longus* 'long')]

obloquy /ˈɒbləkwi/ *n.* **1** the state of being generally ill spoken of. **2** abuse, detraction. [Middle English via Late Latin *obloquium* 'contradiction' from Latin *obloqui* 'deny' (as OB-, *loqui* 'speak')]

obnoxious /əbˈnɒkʃəs/ *adj.* offensive, objectionable, disliked. □ **obnoxiously** *adv.* **obnoxiousness** *n.* [originally = vulnerable (to harm), from Latin *obnoxiosus* or *obnoxius* (as OB-, *noxa* 'harm': associated with NOXIOUS)]

obo *abbr. N. Amer.* or best offer.

oboe /ˈəʊbəʊ/ *n.* **1 a** a woodwind double-reed instrument of treble pitch and plaintive incisive tone. **b** an oboe-player. **2** an organ stop with a quality resembling an oboe. □ **oboist** /ˈəʊbəʊɪst/ *n.* [Italian *oboe* or French *hautbois*, from *haut* 'high' + *bois* 'wood']

oboe d'amore /ˌəʊbəʊ daˈmɔːreɪ/ *n.* an oboe wth a pear-shaped bell and mellow tone, pitched a minor third below a normal oboe, commonly used in baroque music. [Italian, literally 'oboe of love']

obol /ˈɒb(ə)l/ *n.* an ancient Greek coin, equal to one-sixth of a drachma. [Latin *obolus* from Greek *obolos*, variant of *obelos* OBELUS]

obovate /ɒbˈəʊveɪt/ *adj. Biol.* (of a leaf) ovate with the narrower end at the base.

obscene /əbˈsiːn/ *adj.* **1** offensively or repulsively indecent, esp. by offending accepted sexual morality. **2** *colloq.* highly offensive or repugnant (*an obscene accumulation of wealth*). **3** *Brit. Law* (of a publication) tending to deprave or corrupt. □ **obscenely** *adv.* [French *obscène* or Latin *obsc(a)enus* 'ill-omened, abominable']

obscenity /əbˈsɛnɪti/ *n.* (*pl.* **-ies**) **1** the state or quality of being obscene. **2** an obscene action, word, etc. [Latin *obscaenitas* (as OBSCENE)]

obscurantism /ɒbskjʊˈrantɪz(ə)m/ *n.* opposition to knowledge and enlightenment. □ **obscurant** /ɒbˈskjʊər(ə)nt/ *n.* **obscurantist** *n. & adj.* [from *obscurant*, via German from Latin *obscurans*, from *obscurare*: see OBSCURE]

obscure /əbˈskjʊə/ *adj. & v.* ● *adj.* **1** not clearly expressed or easily understood. **2** vague, uncertain. **3** dark, dim. **4** indistinct; not clear. **5** hidden; remote from observation. **6 a** unnoticed. **b** (of a person) undistinguished, hardly known. **7** (of a colour) dingy, dull, indefinite. ● *v.tr.* **1** make obscure, dark, indistinct, or unintelligible. **2** dim the glory of; outshine. **3** conceal from sight. □ **obscuration** /-ˈreɪʃ(ə)n/ *n.* **obscurely** *adv.* [Middle English via Old French *obscur* from Latin *obscurus* 'dark']

obscure vowel *n.* = INDETERMINATE VOWEL.

obscurity /əbˈskjʊərɪti/ *n.* (*pl.* **-ies**) **1** the state of being obscure. **2** an obscure person or thing. [French *obscurité* from Latin *obscuritas* (as OBSCURE)]

obsecration /ɒbsɪˈkreɪʃ(ə)n/ *n.* earnest entreaty. [Middle English from Latin *obsecratio*, from *obsecrare* 'entreat' (as OB-, *sacrare* from *sacer sacri* 'sacred')]

obsequies /ˈɒbsɪkwɪz/ *n.pl.* **1** funeral rites. **2** a funeral. □ **obsequial** /əbˈsiːkwɪəl/ *adj.* [Middle English, pl. of obsolete *obsequy*, from Anglo-French *obsequie*, Old French *obseque* via medieval Latin *obsequiae* from Latin *exsequiae* 'funeral rites' (see EXEQUIES): associated with *obsequium* (see OBSEQUIOUS)]

obsequious /əbˈsiːkwɪəs/ *adj.* servilely obedient or attentive. □ **obsequiously** *adv.* **obsequiousness** *n.* [Middle English from Latin *obsequiosus*, from *obsequium* 'compliance' (as OB-, *sequi* 'follow')]

observance /əbˈzəːv(ə)ns/ *n.* **1** the act or process of keeping or performing a law, duty, custom, ritual, etc. **2** an act of a religious or ceremonial character; a customary rite. **3** the rule of a religious order. **4** *archaic* respect, deference. [Middle English via Old French from Latin *observantia* (as OBSERVE)]

observant /əbˈzəːv(ə)nt/ *adj. & n.* ● *adj.* **1** acute or diligent in taking notice. **2** attentive in esp. religious observances (*an observant Jew*). ● *n.* (**Observant**) a member of the branch of the Franciscan order that observes the strict rule. □ **observantly** *adv.* [French (as OBSERVE)]

observation /ɒbzəˈveɪʃ(ə)n/ *n.* **1** the act or an instance of noticing; the condition of being noticed. **2** perception; the faculty of taking notice. **3** a remark or statement, esp. one that is of the nature of a comment. **4 a** the accurate watching and noting of a phenomenon etc. for the purpose of scientific investigation. **b** a measurement or other result so obtained. **c** the noting of the symptoms of a patient, the behaviour of a suspect, etc. **5** the taking of the sun's or another celestial body's altitude to find a latitude or longitude. **6** *Mil.* the watching of a fortress or hostile position or movements. □ **under observation** being watched or monitored. □ **observational** *adj.* **observationally** *adv.* [Middle English from Latin *observatio* (as OBSERVE)]

observation car *n.* esp. *N. Amer.* a carriage in a train built so as to afford good views.

observation post *n. Mil.* a post for watching the effect of artillery fire etc.

observatory /əbˈzəːvət(ə)ri/ *n.* (*pl.* **-ies**) a room or building equipped for the observation of natural, esp. astronomical or meteorological, phenomena. [modern Latin *observatorium* from Latin *observare* (as OBSERVE)]

observe /əbˈzəːv/ *v.* **1** *tr.* (often foll. by *that, how* + clause) perceive, note; take notice of; become conscious of. **2** *tr.* watch carefully. **3** *tr.* **a** follow or adhere to (a law, command, method, principle, etc.). **b** keep or adhere to (an appointed time). **c** maintain (silence). **d** duly perform (a rite). **e** celebrate (an anniversary). **4** *tr.* examine and note (phenomena) without the aid of experiment. **5** *tr.* (often foll. by *that* + clause) say, esp. by way of comment. **6** *intr.* (foll. by *on*) make a remark or remarks about. □ **observable** *adj.* **observably** *adv.* [Middle English via Old French *observer* from Latin *observare* 'watch' (as OB-, *servare* 'keep')]

observer /əbˈzəːvə/ *n.* **1** a person who observes. **2** an interested spectator. **3** a person who attends a conference etc. to note the proceedings but does not participate. **4 a** a person trained to notice and identify aircraft. **b** a person carried in an aeroplane to note the enemy's position etc.

obsess /əbˈsɛs/ *v.* **1** *tr.* (often in *passive*) preoccupy, haunt; fill the mind of (a person) continually. **2** *intr. US* (foll. by *on, over*) be continually preoccupied with. □ **obsessive** *adj. & n.* **obsessively** *adv.* **obsessiveness** *n.* [Latin *obsidēre obsess-* (as OB-, *sedēre* 'sit')]

obsession /əbˈsɛʃ(ə)n/ *n.* **1** the act of obsessing or the state of being obsessed. **2** a persistent idea or thought dominating a person's mind. **3** a condition in which such ideas are present. □ **obsessional** *adj.* **obsessionalism** *n.* **obsessionally** *adv.* [Latin *obsessio* (as OBSESS)]

obsidian /əbˈsɪdɪən/ *n.* a dark glassy volcanic rock formed from hardened lava. [Latin *obsidianus*, error for *obsianus*, from *Obsius*, the name (in Pliny) of the discoverer of a similar stone]

obsolescent /ɒbsəˈlɛs(ə)nt/ *adj.* becoming obsolete; going out of use or date. □ **obsolescence** *n.* [Latin *obsolescere obsolescent-* (as OB-, *solēre* 'be accustomed')]

obsolete /ˈɒbsəliːt/ *adj.* **1** disused, discarded, antiquated. **2** *Biol.* less developed than formerly or than in a cognate species; rudimentary. □ **obsoletely** *adv.* **obsoleteness** *n.* **obsoletism** *n.* [Latin *obsoletus*, past part. of *obsolescere* (as OBSOLESCENT)]

obstacle /ˈɒbstək(ə)l/ *n.* a person or thing that obstructs progress. [Middle English via Old French from Latin *obstaculum*, from *obstare* 'impede' (as OB-, *stare* 'stand')]

obstacle race *n.* a race in which various obstacles have to be negotiated.

obstetric /əbˈstɛtrɪk/ *adj.* (also **obstetrical**) of or relating to childbirth and associated processes. □ **obstetrically** *adv.* **obstetrician** /-stəˈtrɪʃ(ə)n/ *n.* [modern Latin *obstetricus* for Latin *obstetricius*, via *obstetrix* 'midwife' from *obstare* 'be present' (as OB-, *stare* 'stand')]

obstetrics /əbˈstɛtrɪks/ *n.* the branch of medicine and surgery concerned with childbirth and midwifery.

obstinate /ˈɒbstɪnət/ *adj.* **1** stubborn, intractable. **2** firmly adhering to one's chosen course of action or opinion despite dissuasion. **3** inflexible, self-willed. **4** unyielding; not readily responding to treatment etc. □ **obstinacy** *n.* **obstinately** *adv.* [Middle English from Latin *obstinatus*, past part. of *obstinare* 'persist' (as OB-, *stare* 'stand')]

obstreperous /əbˈstrɛp(ə)rəs/ *adj.* **1** turbulent, unruly; noisily resisting control. **2** noisy, vociferous. □ **obstreperously** *adv.* **obstreperousness** *n.* [Latin *obstreperus* from *obstrepere* (as OB-, *strepere* 'make a noise')]

obstruct /əbˈstrʌkt/ *v.tr.* **1** block up; make hard or impossible to pass along or through. **2** prevent or retard the progress of; impede. □ **obstructor** *n.* [Latin *obstruere obstruct-* (as OB-, *struere* 'build')]

obstruction /əbˈstrʌkʃ(ə)n/ *n.* **1** the act or an instance of blocking; the state of being blocked. **2** the act of making or the state of becoming more or less impassable. **3** an obstacle or blockage. **4** the retarding of progress by deliberate delays, esp. of parliamentary business. **5** *Sport* the act of unlawfully obstructing another player. **6** *Med.* a blockage in a bodily passage, esp. in an intestine. □ **obstructionism** *n.* (in sense 4). **obstructionist** *n.* (in sense 4). [Latin *obstructio* (as OBSTRUCT)]

obstructive /əbˈstrʌktɪv/ *adj. & n.* ● *adj.* causing or intended to cause an obstruction. ● *n.* an obstructive person or thing. □ **obstructively** *adv.* **obstructiveness** *n.*

obtain /əbˈteɪn/ *v.* **1** *tr.* acquire, secure; have granted to one. **2** *intr.* be prevalent or established or in vogue. □ **obtainable** *adj.* **obtainability** /-ˈbɪlɪti/ *n.* **obtainer** *n.* **obtainment** *n.* **obtention** /əbˈtɛnʃ(ə)n/ *n.* [Middle English via Old French *obtenir* from Latin *obtinēre obtent-* 'keep' (as OB-, *tenēre* 'hold')]

obtrude /əbˈtruːd/ *v.* **1** *intr.* be or become obtrusive. **2** *tr.* (often foll. by *on, upon*) thrust forward (oneself, one's opinion, etc.) importunately. □ **obtruder** *n.* **obtrusion** /-ˈtruːʒ(ə)n/ *n.* [Latin *obtrudere obtrus-* (as OB-, *trudere* 'push')]

obtrusive /əbˈtruːsɪv/ *adj.* **1** unpleasantly or unduly noticeable. **2** obtruding oneself. □ **obtrusively** *adv.* **obtrusiveness** *n.* [as OBTRUDE]

obtund /əbˈtʌnd/ *v.tr.* blunt or deaden (a sense or faculty). [Middle English from Latin *obtundere obtus-* (as OB-, *tundere* 'beat')]

obtuse /əbˈtjuːs/ *adj.* **1** dull-witted; slow to understand. **2** of blunt form; not sharp-pointed or sharp-edged. **3** (of an angle) more than 90° and less than 180°. **4** (of pain or the senses) dull; not acute. □ **obtusely** *adv.* **obtuseness** *n.* **obtusity** *n.* [Latin *obtusus*, past part. of *obtundere* (as OBTUND)]

obverse /ˈɒbvəːs/ *n. & adj.* ● *n.* **1 a** the side of a coin or medal etc. bearing the head or principal design. **b** this design (cf. REVERSE). **2** the front or proper or top side of a thing. **3** the counterpart of a fact or truth. ● *adj.* **1** *Biol.* narrower at the base or point of attachment than at the apex or top (see OB- 7). **2** answering as the counterpart to something else. □ **obversely** *adv.* [Latin *obversus*, past part. of *obvertere* (as OBVERT)]

obvert /əbˈvəːt/ *v.tr. Logic* alter (a proposition) so as to infer another proposition with a contradictory predicate, e.g. *no men are immortal* to *all men are mortal.* □ **obversion** *n.* [Latin *obvertere obvers-* (as OB-, *vertere* 'turn')]

obviate /ˈɒbvɪeɪt/ *v.tr.* get round or do away with (a need, inconvenience, etc.). □ **obviation** /-ˈeɪʃ(ə)n/ *n.* [Late Latin *obviare* 'oppose' (as OB-, *via* 'way')]

obvious /ˈɒbvɪəs/ *adj.* easily seen or recognized or understood; palpable, indubitable. □ **obviously** *adv.* **obviousness** *n.* [Latin *obvius*, from *ob viam* 'in the way']

OC *abbr.* Officer Commanding.

oc- /ɒk/ *prefix* assim. form of OB- before *c*.

ocarina /ɒkəˈriːnə/ *n.* a small egg-shaped ceramic (usu. terracotta) or metal wind instrument. [Italian, from *oca* 'goose' (from its shape)]

Occam's razor /ˈɒkəmz/ *n.* the principle attributed to the English philosopher William of Occam (d. *c.*1350) that the fewest possible assumptions are to be made in explaining a thing.

occasion /əˈkeɪʒ(ə)n/ *n. & v.* ● *n.* **1 a** a special or noteworthy event or happening (*dressed for the occasion*). **b** the time or occurrence of this (*on the* *occasion of their marriage*). **2** (often foll. by *for*, or *to* + infin.) a reason, ground, or justification (*there is no occasion to be angry*). **3** a juncture suitable for doing something; an opportunity. **4** an immediate but subordinate or incidental cause (*the assassination was the occasion of the war*). ● *v.tr.* **1** be the occasion or cause of; bring about esp. incidentally. **2** (foll. by *to* + infin.) cause (a person or thing to do something). □ **on occasion** now and then; when the need arises. **rise to the occasion** produce the necessary will, energy, ability, etc., in unusually demanding circumstances. **take occasion** (foll. by *to* + infin.) make use of the opportunity. [Middle English from Old French *occasion* or Latin *occasio* 'juncture, reason', from *occidere occas-* 'go down' (as OB-, *cadere* 'fall')]

occasional /əˈkeɪʒ(ə)n(ə)l/ *adj.* **1** happening irregularly and infrequently. **2** made or meant for, or associated with, a particular occasion (*occasional hymn*). **3** employed for a particular occasion or on an irregular basis (*career as an occasional soloist*). □ **occasionality** /-ˈnalɪti/ *n.* **occasionally** *adv.*

occasional cause *n.* a secondary cause; an occasion (see OCCASION *n.* 4).

occasional table *n.* a small table for infrequent and varied use.

Occident /ˈɒksɪd(ə)nt/ *n. poet.* or *literary* (prec. by *the*) **1** the West. **2** western Europe. **3** Europe, America, or both, as distinct from the Orient. **4** European or Western in contrast to oriental civilization. [Middle English via Old French from Latin *occidens -entis* 'setting, sunset, west' (as OCCASION)]

occidental /ɒksɪˈdɛnt(ə)l/ *adj. & n.* ● *adj.* **1** of the Occident, as distinct from oriental. **2** western. **3** of western Europe. **4** relating to European or Western (in contrast to oriental) civilization. ● *n.* (**Occidental**) a native or inhabitant of the Occident. □ **occidentalism** *n.* **occidentalist** *n.* **occidentalize** *v.tr.* (also **-ise**). **occidentally** *adv.* [Middle English from Old French *occidental* or Latin *occidentalis* (as OCCIDENT)]

occipito- /ɒkˌsɪpɪtəʊ/ *comb. form* the back of the head. [as OCCIPUT]

occiput /ˈɒksɪpʌt/ *n.* the back of the head. □ **occipital** /-ˈsɪpɪt(ə)l/ *adj.* [Middle English from Latin *occiput* (as OB-, *caput* 'head')]

Occitan /ˈɒksɪt(ə)n/ *n.* (also *attrib.*) the Provençal language. □ **Occitanian** /-ˈteɪnɪən/ *n. & adj.* [French: cf. LANGUE D'OC]

occlude /əˈkluːd/ *v.tr.* **1** stop up or close (pores or an orifice); obstruct (a passage). **2** *Chem.* absorb and retain (gases or impurities). [Latin *occludere occlus-* (as OB-, *claudere* 'shut')]

occluded front *n. Meteorol.* a front resulting from occlusion.

occlusion /əˈkluːʒ(ə)n/ *n.* **1** the act or process of occluding. **2** *Meteorol.* a phenomenon in which the cold front of a depression overtakes the warm front, causing upward displacement of warm air between them. **3** *Dentistry* the position of the teeth when the jaws are closed. **4** the blockage or closing of a hollow organ etc. (*coronary occlusion*). □ **occlusive** *adj.*

occult *adj. & v.* ● *adj.* /ɒˈkʌlt, ˈɒkʌlt/ **1** involving the supernatural; mystical, magical. **2** kept secret; esoteric. **3** recondite, mysterious; beyond the range of ordinary knowledge. **4** *Med.* not obvious on inspection. ● *v.tr.* /ɒˈkʌlt/ *Astron.* (of a celestial body) conceal (an apparently smaller body) from view by passing or being in front of it. □ **the occult** occult phenomena generally. □ **occultation** /-ˈteɪʃ(ə)n/ *n.* **occultism** *n.* **occultist** *n.* **occultly** *adv.* **occultness** *n.* [Latin *occulere occult-* (as OB-, *celare* 'hide')]

occulting light *n.* a lighthouse light that is cut off at regular intervals.

occupant /ˈɒkjʊp(ə)nt/ *n.* **1** a person who occupies, resides in, or is in a place etc. (*both occupants of the car were unhurt*). **2** a person holding property, esp. land, in actual possession. **3** a person who establishes a title by taking possession of something previously without an established owner. □ **occupancy** *n.* (*pl.* **-ies**). [French *occupant* or Latin *occupans -antis* (as OCCUPY)]

occupation /ɒkjʊˈpeɪʃ(ə)n/ *n.* **1** what occupies one; a means of passing one's time. **2** a person's temporary or regular employment; a business, calling, or pursuit. **3** the act of occupying or state of being occupied. **4 a** the act of taking or holding possession of (a country, district, etc.) by military force. **b** the state or time of this. **5** tenure, occupancy. **6** (*attrib.*) for the sole use of the occupiers of the land concerned (*occupation road*). [Middle English via Anglo-French *ocupacioun*, Old French *occupation* from Latin *occupatio -onis* (as OCCUPY)]

occupational /ɒkjʊˈpeɪʃ(ə)n(ə)l/ *adj.* **1** of or in the nature of an occupation or occupations. **2** (of a disease, hazard, etc.) rendered more likely by one's occupation.

occupational therapy *n.* mental or physical activity designed to assist recovery from disease or injury. □ **occupational therapist** *n.*

occupier /ˈɒkjʊpʌɪə/ *n. Brit.* a person residing in a property as its owner or tenant.

occupy /ˈɒkjʊpʌɪ/ *v.tr.* (**-ies**, **-ied**) **1** reside in; be the tenant of. **2** take up or fill (space or time or a place). **3** hold (a position or office). **4** take military possession of (a country, region, town, strategic position). **5** place oneself in (a building etc.) forcibly or without authority. **6** (usu. *refl.* or in *passive*; often foll. by *in*, *with*) keep busy or engaged. [Middle English via Old French *occuper* from Latin *occupare* 'seize' (as OB-, *capere* 'take')]

occur /əˈkəː/ *v.intr.* (**occurred**, **occurring**) **1** come into being as an event or process at or during some time; happen. **2** exist or be encountered in some place or conditions. **3** (foll. by *to*; usu. foll. by *that* + clause) come into the mind of, esp. as an unexpected or casual thought (*it occurred to me that you were right*). [Latin *occurrere* 'go to meet, present itself' (as OB-, *currere* 'run')]

occurrence /əˈkʌr(ə)ns/ *n.* **1** the act or an instance of occurring. **2** an incident or event. □ **of frequent occurrence** often occurring. [*occurrent* 'that occurs', via French from Latin *occurrens -entis* (as OCCUR)]

ocean /ˈəʊʃ(ə)n/ *n.* **1 a** a large expanse of sea, esp. each of the main areas called the Atlantic, Pacific, Indian, Arctic, and Southern Oceans. **b** these regarded cumulatively as the body of water surrounding the land of the globe. **2** (usu. prec. by *the*) the sea. **3** (often in *pl.*) a very large expanse or quantity of anything (*oceans of time*). □ **oceanward** *adv.* (also **-wards**). [Middle English via Old French *occean* and Latin *oceanus* from Greek *ōkeanos* 'the great stream encircling the earth's disc, the Atlantic']

oceanarium /əʊʃəˈnɛːrɪəm/ *n.* (*pl.* **oceanariums** or **oceanaria** /-rɪə/) a large sea water aquarium for keeping sea animals. [OCEAN + -ARIUM, on the pattern of *aquarium*]

ocean-going *adj.* (of a ship) designed to cross oceans.

Oceania /əʊsɪˈɑːnɪə, əʊʃɪ-/ *n.* the islands of the Pacific and adjacent seas. □ **Oceanian** *adj. & n.* [modern Latin via French *Océanie* from Latin (as OCEAN)]

oceanic /əʊʃɪˈanɪk, əʊsɪ-/ *adj.* **1** of, like, or near the ocean. **2** (of a climate) governed by the ocean. **3** of the part of the ocean distant from the continents. **4** (**Oceanic**) of Oceania.

Oceanid /əʊˈsiːənɪd, ˈəʊʃ(ə)nɪd/ *n.* (*pl.* **Oceanids** or **Oceanides** /əʊsɪˈanɪdiːz, əʊʃɪ-/) (in Greek mythology) an ocean nymph. [Greek *ōkeanis -idos* 'daughter of *Oceanus*', the god of the sea]

oceanography /əʊʃəˈnɒgrəfi/ *n.* the study of the oceans. □ **oceanographer** *n.* **oceanographic** /-nəˈgrafɪk/ *adj.* **oceanographical** /-nəˈgrafɪk(ə)l/ *adj.*

ocean tramp *n.* a merchant ship, esp. a steamer, running on no regular line or route.

ocellus /əˈsɛləs/ *n.* (*pl.* **ocelli** /-lʌɪ, -liː/) *Zool.* **1** = SIMPLE EYE. **2** = EYE-SPOT 1a. □ **ocellar** *adj.* **ocellate** /ˈɒsɪlət/

adj. **ocellated** /'ɒsɪleɪtɪd/ *adj.* [Latin, diminutive of *oculus* 'eye']

ocelot /'ɒsɪlɒt, 'əʊs-/ *n.* **1** a medium-sized cat, *Felis pardalis,* native to S. and Central America, having a deep yellow or orange coat with black striped and spotted markings. **2** its fur. [French from Nahuatl *ocelotl* 'jaguar']

och /ɒk, ɒx/ *int. Sc. & Ir.* expressing surprise or regret. [Gaelic & Irish]

oche /'ɒki/ *n.* (also **hockey** /'ɒki, 'hɒki/) *Darts* the line behind which the players stand when throwing. [20th c.: origin uncertain (perhaps connected with Old French *ocher* 'cut a deep notch in')]

ocher *US* var. of OCHRE.

ochlocracy /ɒk'lɒkrəsi/ *n.* (*pl.* **-ies**) mob rule. ▫ **ochlocrat** /'ɒkləkrat/ *n.* **ochlocratic** /ɒklə'kratɪk/ *adj.* [French *ochlocratie* from Greek *okhlokratia,* from *okhlos* 'mob']

ochone /əʊ'həʊn, ɒ'xəʊn/ *int.* (also **ohone**) *Sc. & Ir.* expressing regret or lament. [Gaelic & Irish *ochóin*]

ochre /'əʊkə/ *n. & adj.* (*US* **ocher**) ● *n.* **1** a mineral of clay and ferric oxide, used as a pigment varying from light yellow to brown or red. **2** a pale brownish yellow. ● *adj.* of the colour of ochre, esp. pale brownish yellow. ▫ **ochreish** *adj.* **ochreous** /'əʊkrɪəs/ *adj.* **ochrous** /'əʊkrəs/ *adj.* **ochry** /'əʊkri/ *adj.* [Middle English via Old French *ocre* and Latin *ochra* from Greek *ōkhra* 'yellow ochre']

-ock /ək/ *suffix* forming nouns originally with diminutive sense (*hillock*; *bullock*). [from or suggested by Old English *-uc, -oc*]

ocker /'ɒkə/ *n. Austral. slang* a boorish or aggressive Australian (esp. as a stereotype). [alteration of *Oscar,* used as the name of a character in an Australian television series]

o'clock /ə'klɒk/ *adv.* of the clock (used to specify the hour) (*6 o'clock*).

ocotillo /əʊkə'ti:jəʊ/ *n.* (*pl.* **-os**) esp. *US* a spiny scarlet-flowered desert shrub, *Fouquiera splendens,* of Mexico and the south-western US. [American Spanish, diminutive from Nahuatl *ocotl* 'torch']

OCR *abbr.* optical character recognition.

Oct. *abbr.* October.

oct. *abbr.* octavo.

oct- /ɒkt/ *comb. form* assim. form of OCTA-, OCTO- before a vowel.

octa- /'ɒktə/ *comb. form* (also **oct-** before a vowel) eight. [Greek *okta-* from *oktō* 'eight']

octad /'ɒktad/ *n.* a group of eight. [Late Latin *octas octad-* from Greek *oktas -ados,* from *oktō* 'eight']

octagon /'ɒktəg(ə)n/ *n.* **1** a plane figure with eight sides and angles. **2** an object or building with this cross-section. ▫ **octagonal** /-'tag(ə)n(ə)l/ *adj.* **octagonally** /-'tag(ə)n(ə)li/ *adv.* [Latin *octagonos* from Greek *octagōnos* (as OCTA-, -GON)]

octahedron /ɒktə'hi:drən, -'hɛd-/ *n.* (*pl.* **octahedra** /-drə/ or **octahedrons**) **1** a solid figure contained by eight (esp. triangular) plane faces. **2** a body, esp. a crystal, in the form of a regular octahedron. ▫ **octahedral** *adj.* [Greek *oktaedron* (as OCTA-, -HEDRON)]

octal /'ɒkt(ə)l/ *adj.* reckoning or proceeding by eights (*octal scale*).

octamerous /ɒk'tam(ə)rəs/ *adj.* **1** esp. *Bot.* having eight parts. **2** *Zool.* having organs arranged in eights.

octane /'ɒkteɪn/ *n.* a colourless inflammable hydrocarbon of the alkane series. Chem. formula: C_8H_{18}. [OCT- + -ANE²]

octane number *n.* (also **octane rating**) a figure indicating the antiknock properties of a fuel.

octant /'ɒkt(ə)nt/ *n.* **1** an arc of a circle equal to one-eighth of the circumference. **2** such an arc with two radii, forming an area equal to one-eighth of the circle. **3** each of eight parts into which three planes intersecting (esp. at right angles) at a point divide the space or the solid body round it. **4** an instrument in the form of a graduated eighth of a circle, used in astronomy and navigation. [Latin *octans octant-* 'half-quadrant', from *octo* 'eight']

octaroon var. of OCTOROON.

octastyle /'ɒktəstʌɪl/ *adj. & n.* ● *adj.* having eight columns at the end or in front. ● *n.* an octastyle portico or building. [Latin *octastylus* from Greek *oktastulos* (as OCTA- + *stulos* 'pillar')]

octavalent /ɒktə'veɪl(ə)nt/ *adj. Chem.* having a valency of eight. [OCTA- + VALENCE¹]

octave /'ɒktɪv/ *n.* **1** *Mus.* **a** a series of eight notes occupying the interval between (and including) two notes, one having twice or half the frequency of vibration of the other. **b** this interval. **c** each of the two notes at the extremes of this interval. **d** these two notes sounding together. **2** a group or stanza of eight lines; an octet. **3 a** the seventh day after a festival. **b** a period of eight days including a festival and its octave. **4** a group of eight. **5** the last of eight parrying positions in fencing. **6** *Brit.* a wine cask holding an eighth of a pipe. [Middle English via Old French from Latin *octava dies* 'eighth day' (reckoned inclusively)]

octave coupler see COUPLER 1b.

octavo /ɒk'tɑ:vəʊ, -'teɪ-/ *n.* (*pl.* **-os**) **1** a size of book or page given by folding a standard sheet three times to form a quire of eight leaves. **2** a book or sheet of this size (abbr.: **8vo**). [Latin *in octavo* 'in an eighth', from *octavus* 'eighth']

octennial /ɒk'tɛnɪəl/ *adj.* **1** lasting eight years. **2** occurring every eight years. [Late Latin *octennium* 'period of eight years' (as OCT-, *annus* 'year')]

octet /ɒk'tɛt/ *n.* (also **octette**) **1** *Mus.* **a** a composition for eight voices or instruments. **b** the performers of such a piece. **2** a group of eight. **3** the first eight lines of a sonnet. **4** *Chem.* a stable group of eight electrons. [Italian *ottetto* or German *Oktett*: assimilated to OCT-, DUET, QUARTET]

octo- /'ɒktəʊ/ *comb. form* (also **oct-** before a vowel) eight. [Latin *octo* or Greek *oktō* 'eight']

October /ɒk'təʊbə/ *n.* the tenth month of the year. [Old English from Latin (as OCTO-): originally the eighth month of the Roman year]

Octobrist /ɒk'təʊbrɪst/ *n. hist.* a member of the moderate party in the Russian Duma, supporting the Imperial Constitutional Manifesto of 30 Oct. 1905. [OCTOBER, suggested by Russian *oktyabríst*]

octocentenary /,ɒktəʊsɛn'ti:nəri, -'tɛn-, ɒktəʊ'sɛntɪn-/ *n. & adj.* ● *n.* (*pl.* **-ies**) **1** an eight-hundredth anniversary. **2** a celebration of this. ● *adj.* of or relating to an octocentenary.

octodecimo /ɒktəʊ'dɛsɪməʊ/ *n.* (*pl.* **-os**) **1** a size of book in which each leaf is one-eighteenth the size of a printing-sheet. **2** a book of this size. [*in octodecimo* from Latin *octodecimus* 'eighteenth']

octogenarian /,ɒktə(ʊ)dʒɪ'nɛ:rɪən/ *n. & adj.* ● *n.* a person from 80 to 89 years old. ● *adj.* of this age. [Latin *octogenarius* from *octogeni,* distributive of *octoginta* 'eighty']

octopod /'ɒktəpɒd/ *n.* any cephalopod of the order Octopoda, with eight arms usu. having suckers, and a round saclike body, including octopuses. [Greek *oktōpous -podos,* from *oktō* 'eight' + *pous* 'foot']

octopus /'ɒktəpəs/ *n.* (*pl.* **octopuses**) **1** any cephalopod mollusc of the genus *Octopus* having eight suckered arms, a soft saclike body, and strong beaklike jaws. **2** an organized and usu. harmful ramified power or influence. [Greek *oktōpous*: see OCTOPOD]

octoroon /ɒktə'ru:n/ *n.* (also **octaroon**) the offspring of a quadroon and a white person; a person of one-eighth Negro blood. [OCTO-, on the pattern of QUADROON]

octosyllabic /,ɒktəʊsɪ'labɪk/ *adj. & n.* ● *adj.* having eight syllables. ● *n.* an octosyllabic verse. [Late Latin *octosyllabus* (as OCTO-, SYLLABLE)]

octosyllable /'ɒktə(ʊ),sɪləb(ə)l/ *n. & adj.* ● *n.* an octosyllabic verse or word. ● *adj.* = OCTOSYLLABIC.

octroi /'ɒktrwɑ:/ *n.* **1** a duty levied in some European countries on goods entering a town. **2 a** the place where this is levied. **b** the officials by whom it is levied. [French from *octroyer* 'grant', from medieval Latin *auctorizare*: see AUTHORIZE]

octuple /ˈɒktjʊp(ə)l, ɒkˈtjuːp(ə)l/ *adj., n., & v.* ● *adj.* eightfold. ● *n.* an eightfold amount. ● *v.tr. & intr.* multiply by eight. [French *octuple* or Latin *octuplus* (*adj.*), from *octo* 'eight': cf. DOUBLE]

ocular /ˈɒkjʊlə/ *adj. & n.* ● *adj.* of or connected with the eyes or sight; visual. ● *n.* the eyepiece of an optical instrument. □ **ocularly** *adv.* [French *oculaire* via Late Latin *ocularis* from Latin *oculus* 'eye']

ocularist /ˈɒkjʊlərɪst/ *n.* a maker of artificial eyes. [French *oculariste* (as OCULAR)]

ocular spectrum see SPECTRUM 6.

oculate /ˈɒkjʊlət/ *adj.* = OCELLATE (see OCELLUS). [Latin *oculatus* from *oculus* 'eye']

oculist /ˈɒkjʊlɪst/ *n.* a person who specializes in the medical treatment of eye disorders or defects. □ **oculistic** /-ˈlɪstɪk/ *adj.* [French *oculiste* from Latin *oculus* 'eye']

oculo- /ˈɒkjʊləʊ/ *comb. form* eye (*oculo-nasal*). [Latin *oculus* 'eye']

OD[1] *abbr.* ordnance datum.

OD[2] *n. & v.* esp. *N. Amer. slang* ● *n.* an overdose, esp. of a narcotic drug. ● *v.intr.* (**OD's**, **OD'd**, **OD'ing**) take an overdose. [abbreviation]

od[1] /ɒd/ *n.* a hypothetical power once thought to pervade nature and account for various scientific phenomena. [arbitrary term coined in German by Baron von Reichenbach, German scientist d. 1869]

od[2] /ɒd/ *n.* (as *int.* or in oaths) *archaic* God (see GOD 5). [corruption]

o.d. *abbr.* outer diameter.

odal var. of UDAL.

odalisque /ˈəʊd(ə)lɪsk/ *n. hist.* an Eastern female slave or concubine, esp. in the Turkish Sultan's seraglio. [French from Turkish *odalik*, from *oda* 'chamber' + *lik* 'function']

odd /ɒd/ *adj. & n.* ● *adj.* **1** extraordinary, strange, queer, remarkable, eccentric. **2** casual, occasional, unconnected (*odd jobs*; *odd moments*). **3** not normally noticed or considered; unpredictable (*in some odd corner*; *picks up odd bargains*). **4** additional; beside the reckoning (*earned the odd pound*). **5 a** (of numbers such as 3 and 5) not integrally divisible by two. **b** (of things or persons numbered consecutively) bearing such a number (*no parking on odd dates*). **6** left over when the rest have been distributed or divided into pairs (*have got an odd sock*). **7** detached from a set or series (*a few odd volumes*). **8** (appended to a number, sum, weight, etc.) somewhat more than (*forty odd*; *forty-odd people*). **9** by which a round number, given sum, etc., is exceeded (*we have 102 – what shall we do with the odd 2?*). ● *n.* *Golf* **1** *Brit.* a handicap of one stroke at each hole. **2** *US* a score one stroke higher than that of one's opponent. □ **oddish** *adj.* **oddly** *adv.* **oddness** *n.* [Middle English from Old Norse *odda-* in *odda-mathr* 'third man, odd man', from *oddi* 'angle']

oddball /ˈɒdbɔːl/ *n. colloq.* **1** an odd or eccentric person. **2** (*attrib.*) strange, bizarre.

odd bod *n. slang* a strange or eccentric person.

Oddfellow /ˈɒdfɛləʊ/ *n.* a member of a fraternity similar to the Freemasons.

oddity /ˈɒdɪti/ *n.* (*pl.* **-ies**) **1** a strange person, thing, or occurrence. **2** a peculiar trait. **3** the state of being odd.

odd job *n.* a casual isolated piece of work.

odd-job man *n.* (also **odd jobber**) a person who does odd jobs.

odd man out *n.* **1** a person or thing differing from all the others in a group in some respect. **2** a method of selecting one of three or more persons e.g. by tossing a coin.

oddment /ˈɒdm(ə)nt/ *n.* **1** an odd article; something left over. **2** (in *pl.*) miscellaneous articles. **3** (in *pl.*) *Brit. Printing* matter other than the main text.

odds /ɒdz/ *n.pl.* **1** the ratio between the amounts staked by the parties to a bet, based on the expected probability either way. **2** the chances or balance of probability in favour of or against some result (*the odds are against it*; *the odds are that it will rain*). **3** the balance of advantage (*the odds are in your favour*; *won against all the odds*). **4** an equalizing allowance to a weaker competitor. **5** a difference giving an advantage (*it makes no odds*). □ **at odds** (often foll. by *with*) in conflict or at variance. **by all odds** certainly. **lay** (or **give**) **odds** offer a bet with odds favourable to the other better. **over the odds** above a generally agreed price etc. **take odds** offer a bet with odds unfavourable to the other better. **what's the odds?** *colloq.* what does it matter? [apparently pl. of ODD *n.*: cf. NEWS]

odds and ends *n.pl.* (also *colloq.* **odds and sods**) miscellaneous articles or remnants.

odds-on *n. & adj.* ● *n.* a state when success is more likely than failure, esp. as indicated by the betting odds. ● *adj.* (of a chance) better than even; likely.

ode /əʊd/ *n.* **1** a lyric poem, usu. rhymed and in the form of an address, in varied or irregular metre. **2** *hist.* a poem meant to be sung. [French via Late Latin *oda* from Greek *ōidē*, Attic form of *aoidē* 'song', from *aeidō* 'sing']

-ode[1] /əʊd/ *suffix* forming nouns meaning 'thing of the nature of' (*geode*; *trematode*). [Greek adjectival ending *-ōdēs*]

-ode[2] /əʊd/ *comb. form Electr.* forming names of electrodes, or devices having them (*cathode*; *diode*). [Greek *hodos* 'way']

odeum /ˈəʊdɪəm/ *n.* (*pl.* **odeums** or **odea** /-dɪə/) a building for musical performances, esp. among the ancient Greeks and Romans. [French *odéum* or Latin *odeum* from Greek *ōideion* (as ODE)]

odious /ˈəʊdɪəs/ *adj.* hateful, repulsive. □ **odiously** *adv.* **odiousness** *n.* [Middle English via Old French *odieus* from Latin *odiosus* (as ODIUM)]

odium /ˈəʊdɪəm/ *n.* a general or widespread dislike or reprobation incurred by a person or associated with an action. [Latin, = hatred, from *odi* 'to hate']

odometer /əʊˈdɒmɪtə/ *n.* (also **hodometer** /hɒ-/) esp. *US* an instrument for measuring the distance travelled by a wheeled vehicle. □ **odometry** *n.* [French *odomètre*, from Greek *hodos* 'way': see -METER]

odonto- /ɒˈdɒntəʊ, əʊ-/ *comb. form* tooth. [Greek *odous odont-* 'tooth']

odontoglossum /ə(ʊ)ˌdɒntəˈglɒsəm/ *n.* any of various orchids bearing flowers with jagged edges like tooth marks. [ODONTO- + Greek *glōssa* 'tongue']

odontoid /ə(ʊ)ˈdɒntɔɪd/ *adj.* toothlike. [Greek *odontoeidēs* (as ODONTO- + Greek *eidos* 'form')]

odontoid process *n.* a projection from the second cervical vertebra.

odontology /ɒdɒnˈtɒlədʒi, əʊdɒn-/ *n.* the scientific study of the structure and diseases of teeth. □ **odontological** /-təˈlɒdʒɪk(ə)l/ *adj.* **odontologist** *n.*

odor *US* var. of ODOUR.

odoriferous /əʊdəˈrɪf(ə)rəs/ *adj.* diffusing a scent, esp. an agreeable one; fragrant. □ **odoriferously** *adv.* [Middle English from Latin *odorifer* (as ODOUR)]

odorous /ˈəʊd(ə)rəs/ *adj.* **1** having a scent. **2** = ODORIFEROUS. □ **odorously** *adv.* [Latin *odorus* 'fragrant' (as ODOUR)]

odour /ˈəʊdə/ *n.* (*US* **odor**) **1** the property of a substance that has an effect on the nasal sense of smell. **2** a lasting quality or trace attaching to something (*an odour of intolerance*). **3** regard, repute (*in bad odour*). □ **odourless** *adj.* (in sense 1). [Middle English via Anglo-French *odour*, Old French *odor* from Latin *odor -oris* 'smell, scent']

odyssey /ˈɒdɪsi/ *n.* (*pl.* **-eys**) a series of wanderings; a long adventurous journey. □ **Odyssean** *adj.* [Latin *Odyssea* from Greek *Odusseia*, title of an epic poem attributed to Homer describing the adventures of Odysseus (Ulysses) on his journey home from Troy]

OECD *abbr.* Organization for Economic Cooperation and Development.

OED *abbr.* Oxford English Dictionary.

oedema /ɪ'diːmə/ *n.* (*US* **edema**) a condition characterized by an excess of watery fluid collecting in the cavities or tissues of the body. Also called DROPSY. □ **oedematous** *adj.* [Late Latin from Greek *oidēma -atos*, from *oideō* 'swell']

Oedipus complex /'iːdɪpəs/ *n. Psychol.* (according to Freud etc.) the complex of emotions aroused in a young (esp. male) child by a subconscious sexual desire for the parent of the opposite sex and wish to exclude the parent of the same sex. □ **Oedipal** *adj.* [Greek *Oidipous*, the name of a legendary king of Thebes who unknowingly killed his father and married his mother]

oenology /iː'nɒlədʒi/ *n.* (*US* **enology**) the study of wines. □ **oenological** /iːnə'lɒdʒɪk(ə)l/ *adj.* **oenologist** *n.* [Greek *oinos* 'wine']

oenophile /'iːnəfʌɪl/ *n.* a connoisseur of wines. □ **oenophilist** /iː'nɒfɪlɪst/ *n.* [as OENOLOGY]

o'er /'əʊə/ *adv. & prep. poet.* = OVER. [contraction]

oersted /'əːstɛd/ *n.* a unit of magnetic field strength equivalent to 79.58 amperes per metre. [named after H. C. *Oersted*, Danish physicist d. 1851]

oesophagus /ɪ'sɒfəgəs/ *n.* (*US* **esophagus**) (*pl.* **oesophagi** /-dʒʌɪ/ or **-guses**) the part of the alimentary canal from the mouth to the stomach; the gullet. □ **oesophageal** /iːˌsɒfə'dʒiːəl, iːsə'fadʒɪəl/ *adj.* [Middle English from Greek *oisophagos*]

oestradiol /iːstrə'dʌɪɒl, ɛstrə-/ *n. Biochem.* a major oestrogen produced in the ovaries. [OESTRUS + DI-[1] + -OL[1]]

oestrogen /'iːstrədʒ(ə)n, 'ɛstrə-/ *n.* (*US* **estrogen**) **1** any of various steroid hormones developing and maintaining female characteristics of the body. **2** this hormone produced artificially for use in oral contraceptives etc. □ **oestrogenic** /-'dʒɛnɪk/ *adj.* **oestrogenically** /-'dʒɛnɪk(ə)li/ *adv.* [OESTRUS + -GEN]

oestrus /'iːstrəs, 'ɛstrəs/ *n.* (also **oestrum**, *US* **estrus**, **estrum**) a recurring period of sexual receptivity in many female mammals; heat. □ **oestrous** *adj.* [Greek *oistros* 'gadfly, frenzy']

oeuvre /'əːvrə/ *n.* the works of an author, painter, composer, etc., esp. regarded collectively. [French, = work, from Latin *opera*]

of /ɒv, (ə)v/ *prep.* connecting a noun (often a verbal noun) or pronoun with a preceding noun, adjective, adverb, or verb, expressing a wide range of relations broadly describable as follows: **1** origin, cause, or authorship (*paintings of Turner*; *people of Rome*; *died of malnutrition*). **2** the material or substance constituting or identifying a thing (*a house of cards*; *was built of bricks*). **3** belonging, connection, or possession (*a thing of the past*; *articles of clothing*; *the head of the business*; *the tip of the iceberg*). **4** identity or close relation (*the city of Rome*; *a pound of apples*; *a fool of a man*). **5** removal, separation, or privation (*north of the city*; *got rid of them*; *robbed us of £1,000*). **6** reference, direction, or respect (*beware of the dog*; *suspected of lying*; *very good of you*; *short of money*; *the selling of goods*). **7** objective relation (*love of music*; *in search of peace*). **8** partition, classification, or inclusion (*no more of that*; *part of the story*; *a friend of mine*; *this sort of book*; *some of us will stay*). **9** description, quality, or condition (*the hour of prayer*; *a person of tact*; *a girl of ten*; *on the point of leaving*). **10** *N. Amer.* time in relation to the following hour (*a quarter of three*). □ **be of** possess intrinsically; give rise to (*is of great interest*). **of all** designating the (nominally) least likely or expected example (*you of all people!*). **of all the nerve** (or **cheek** etc.) an exclamation of indignation at a person's impudence etc. **of an evening** (or **morning** etc.) *colloq.* **1** on most evenings (or mornings etc.). **2** at some time in the evenings (or mornings etc.). **of late** recently. **of old** formerly; long ago. [Old English, unaccented form of *æf*, from Germanic]

■ **Usage** *Of* should not be used instead of *have* in constructions such as *You should have asked*; *He couldn't have known*, although in rapid speech they sound the same.

of- /ɒf/ *prefix* assim. form of OB- before *f*.

ofay /'əʊfeɪ/ *n. US slang offens.* a white person (esp. used by blacks). [20th c.: probably of African origin]

Off. *abbr.* **1** Office. **2** Officer.

off /ɒf/ *adv., prep., adj., & n.* ● *adv.* **1** away; at or to a distance (*drove off*; *is three miles off*). **2** out of position; not on or touching or attached; loose, separate, gone (*has come off*; *take your coat off*). **3** so as to be rid of (*sleep it off*). **4** so as to break continuity or continuance; discontinued, stopped (*turn off the radio*; *take a day off*; *the game is off*). **5** not available as a choice, e.g. on a menu (*chips are off*). **6** to the end; entirely; so as to be clear (*clear off*; *finish off*; *pay off*). **7** situated as regards money, supplies, etc. (*is badly off*; *is not very well off*). **8** off stage (*noises off*). **9** esp. *Brit.* (with preceding numeral) denoting a quantity produced or made at one time (esp. *one-off*). ● *prep.* **1 a** from; away or down or up from (*fell off the chair*; *took something off the price*; *jumped off the edge*). **b** not on (*was already off the pitch*). **2 a** (temporarily) relieved of or abstaining from (*off duty*; *am off my diet*). **b** not attracted by for the time being (*off their food*; *off smoking*). **c** not achieving or doing one's best in (*off form*; *off one's game*). **3** using as a source or means of support (*live off the land*). **4** leading from; not far from (*a street off the Strand*). **5** at a short distance to sea from (*sank off Cape Horn*). ● *adj.* **1** far, further (*the off side of the wall*). **2** (of a part of a vehicle, animal, or road) right (*the off front wheel*) (opp. NEAR *adj.* 3). **3** (*predic.*) *Brit. colloq.* **a** annoying or unfair. **b** unwell (*am feeling a bit off*). **c** (of food etc.) unfit for consumption; no longer fresh. ● *n.* **1** (in full **off side**) *Cricket* the half of the field (as divided lengthways through the pitch) towards which the batsman's feet are pointed (opp. LEG *n.* 6). **2** *Brit. colloq.* the start of a race; the beginning, the departure. □ **off and on** intermittently; now and then. **off one's feet** see FOOT. **off form** see FORM. **off guard** see GUARD. **off one's hands** see HAND. **off one's head** see HEAD. **off of** *slang disp.* = OFF *prep.* 1a (*picked it up off of the floor*). **off the peg** see PEG. **off the point** *adj.* irrelevant. ● *adv.* irrelevantly. **off the record** see RECORD. [originally variant of OF, to distinguish the sense]

■ **Usage** The use of *off of* for the preposition *off* (sense 1a), e.g. *lifted it up off of the table*, is non-standard and should be avoided.

off-air *adj. & adv.* involving or by the transmission of programmes by broadcasting.

offal /'ɒf(ə)l/ *n.* **1** the less valuable edible parts of a carcass, esp. the entrails and internal organs. **2** refuse or waste stuff. **3** carrion; putrid flesh. [Middle English from Middle Dutch *afval*, from *af* OFF + *vallen* FALL]

offbeat *adj. & n.* ● *adj.* /'ɒfbiːt, ɒf'biːt/ **1** *Mus.* not coinciding with the beat. **2** eccentric, unconventional. ● *n.* /'ɒfbiːt/ *Mus.* any of the normally unaccented beats in a bar.

off-break *n. Cricket* **1** a ball which deviates from the off side after bouncing. **2** such deviation.

off-centre *adj. & adv.* not quite coinciding with a central position.

off chance *n.* (prec. by *the*) the slight possibility.

off colour *predic.adj.* **1** *Brit.* not in good health. **2** *N. Amer.* somewhat indecent.

offcut /'ɒfkʌt/ *n.* a remnant of timber, paper, etc., after cutting.

off day *n.* a day when one is not at one's best.

off-drive *v. & n. Cricket* ● *v.tr.* drive (the ball) to the off side. ● *n.* a drive to the off side.

offence /ə'fɛns/ *n.* (*US* **offense**) **1** an illegal act; a transgression or misdemeanour. **2** a wounding of the feelings (*no offence was meant*). **3** the act of attacking or taking the offensive; aggressive action. ▫ **give offence** cause hurt feelings. **take offence** suffer hurt feelings; take umbrage. ▫ **offenceless** *adj.* [originally = stumbling, stumbling block: Middle English & Old French *offens* from Latin *offensus* 'annoyance', and Middle English & French *offense* from Latin *offensa* 'a striking against, hurt, displeasure', both from *offendere* (as OB-, *fendere fens-* 'strike')]

offend /ə'fɛnd/ *v.* **1** *tr.* cause offence to or resentment in; wound the feelings of. **2** *tr.* displease or anger. **3** *intr.* commit an illegal act. **4** *intr.* (often foll. by *against*) do wrong; transgress. ▫ **offendedly** *adv.* **offender** *n.* **offending** *adj.* [Middle English via Old French *offendre* from Latin (as OFFENCE)]

offense *US* var. of OFFENCE.

offensive /ə'fɛnsɪv/ *adj. & n.* ● *adj.* **1** giving or meant or likely to give offence; insulting (*offensive language*). **2** disgusting, foul-smelling, nauseous, repulsive. **3 a** aggressive, attacking. **b** (of a weapon) meant for use in attack. **4** esp. *N. Amer.* of or relating to a team in possession of the ball, puck, etc. (*offensive line*). ● *n.* **1** an aggressive action or attitude (*take the offensive*). **2** an attack, an offensive campaign or stroke. **3** aggressive or forceful action in pursuit of a cause (*a peace offensive*). ▫ **offensively** *adv.* **offensiveness** *n.* [French *offensif -ive* or medieval Latin *offensivus* (as OFFENCE)]

OFFER /'ɒfə/ *n.* (in the UK) Office of Electricity Regulation, a regulatory body supervising the operation of the electricity industry. [acronym]

offer /'ɒfə/ *v. & n.* ● *v.* **1** *tr.* present for acceptance or refusal or consideration (*offered me a drink*; *was offered a lift*; *offer one's services*; *offer no apology*). **2** *intr.* (foll. by *to* + infin.) express readiness or show intention (*offered to take the children*). **3** *tr.* provide; give an opportunity for. **4** *tr.* make available for sale. **5** *tr.* (of a thing) present to one's attention or consideration (*each day offers new opportunities*). **6** *tr.* present (a sacrifice, prayer, etc.) to a deity. **7** *intr.* present itself; occur (*as opportunity offers*). **8** *tr.* give an opportunity for (battle) to an enemy. **9** *tr.* attempt, or try to show (violence, resistance, etc.). ● *n.* **1** an expression of readiness to do or give if desired, or to buy or sell (for a certain amount). **2** an amount offered. **3** a proposal (esp. of marriage). **4** a bid. ▫ **on offer** *Brit.* for sale at a certain (esp. reduced) price. ▫ **offerer** *n.* **offeror** *n.* [Old English *offrian* in religious sense, from Latin *offerre* (as OB-, *ferre* 'bring')]

offering /'ɒf(ə)rɪŋ/ *n.* **1** a contribution, esp. of money, to a Church. **2** a thing offered as a religious sacrifice or token of devotion. **3** anything, esp. money, contributed or offered.

offertory /'ɒfət(ə)ri/ *n.* (*pl.* **-ies**) **1** *Eccl.* **a** the offering of the bread and wine at the Eucharist. **b** an anthem accompanying this. **2 a** the collection of money at a religious service. **b** the money collected. [Middle English via ecclesiastical Latin *offertorium* 'offering' from Late Latin *offert-*, for Latin *oblat-*, past part. stem of *offerre* OFFER]

offhand *adj. & adv.* ● *adj.* /ɒf'hand, 'ɒfhand/ curt or casual in manner. ● *adv.* /ɒf'hand/ **1** in an offhand manner. **2** without preparation or premeditation. ▫ **offhanded** *adj.* **offhandedly** *adv.* **offhandedness** *n.*

office /'ɒfɪs/ *n.* **1** a room or building used as a place of business, esp. for clerical or administrative work. **2** a room or department or building for a particular kind of business (*ticket office*; *post office*). **3** the local centre of a large business (*our London office*). **4** *N. Amer.* the consulting room of a professional person. **5** a position with duties attached to it; a place of authority or trust or service, esp. of a public nature. **6** tenure of an official position, esp. that of a Minister of State or of the party forming the Government (*hold office*; *out of office for 13 years*). **7** (**Office**) *Brit.* the quarters or staff or collective authority of a Government department etc. (*Foreign Office*). **8** a duty attaching to one's position; a task or function. **9** (usu. in *pl.*) a piece of kindness or attention; a service (esp. *through the good offices of*). **10** *Eccl.* **a** an authorized form of worship (*Office for the Dead*). **b** (in full **divine office**) the daily service of the Roman Catholic breviary (*say the office*). **11** a ceremonial duty. **12** (in *pl.*) *Brit.* the parts of a house devoted to household work, storage, etc. **13** *slang* a hint or signal. [Middle English via Old French from Latin *officium* 'performance of a task' (in medieval Latin also 'office, divine service'), from *opus* 'work' + *facere fic-* 'do']

office-bearer *n.* an official or officer.

office block *n.* a large building designed to contain business offices.

office boy *n.* (also **office girl**) a young man (or woman) employed to do minor jobs in a business office.

office hours *n.pl.* the hours during which business is normally conducted.

office of arms *n.* the College of Arms, or a similar body in another country.

officer /'ɒfɪsə/ *n. & v.* ● *n.* **1** a person holding a position of authority or trust, esp. one with a commission in the armed services, in the mercantile marine, or on a passenger ship. **2** a policeman or policewoman. **3** a holder of a post in a society or organization (e.g. the president or secretary). **4** a holder of a public, civil, or ecclesiastical office; a sovereign's minister; an appointed or elected functionary (usu. with a qualifying word: *medical officer*; *probation officer*; *returning officer*). **5** a bailiff (*the sheriff's officer*). **6** a member of the grade below commander in the Order of the British Empire etc. ● *v.tr.* **1** provide with officers. **2** act as the commander of. [Middle English via Anglo-French *officer*, Old French *officier* and medieval Latin *officiarius* from Latin *officium*: see OFFICE]

officer of arms *n.* a herald or pursuivant.

office worker *n.* an employee in a business office.

official /ə'fɪʃ(ə)l/ *adj. & n.* ● *adj.* **1** of or relating to an office (see OFFICE *n.* 5, 6) or its tenure or duties. **2** (often *derog.*) characteristic of officials and bureaucracy. **3** emanating from or attributable to a person in office; properly authorized. **4** holding office; employed in a public capacity. **5** *Med.* according to the pharmacopoeia, officinal. ● *n.* **1** a person holding office or engaged in official duties. **2** (in full **official principal**) *Brit.* the presiding officer or judge of an archbishop's, bishop's, or esp. archdeacon's court. ▫ **officialdom** *n.* **officialism** *n.* **officially** *adv.* [Middle English via Old French from Latin *officialis* (as OFFICE)]

official birthday *n.* (in the UK) a day in June chosen for the observance of the sovereign's birthday.

officialese /əfɪʃə'li:z/ *n. derog.* the formal precise language characteristic of official documents.

official receiver see RECEIVER 3.

official secrets *n.pl.* (esp. in phr. **Official Secrets Act**) *Brit.* confidential information involving national security.

officiant /ə'fɪʃɪənt, -ʃ(ə)nt/ *n.* a person who officiates at a religious ceremony.

officiate /ə'fɪʃɪeɪt/ *v.intr.* **1** act in an official capacity, esp. on a particular occasion. **2** perform a divine service or ceremony. ▫ **officiation** /-'eɪʃ(ə)n/ *n.* **officiator** *n.* [medieval Latin *officiare* 'perform a divine service', from *officium*: see OFFICE]

officinal /ə'fɪsɪn(ə)l, ɒfɪ'si:n(ə)l/ *adj.* **1 a** (of a medicine) kept ready for immediate dispensing. **b** made from the pharmacopoeia recipe (cf. MAGISTRAL 2). **c** (of a name) adopted in the pharmacopoeia. **2** (of a herb or drug) used in medicine. ▫ **officinally** *adv.* [medieval Latin *officinalis* 'storeroom for medicines etc.' from Latin *officina* 'workshop']

officious /ə'fɪʃəs/ *adj.* **1** asserting one's authority aggressively; domineering. **2** intrusive or excessively enthusiastic in offering help etc.; meddlesome. **3** *Diplomacy* informal, unofficial. ▫ **officiously** *adv.* **officiousness** *n.* [Latin *officiosus* 'obliging', from *officium*: see OFFICE]

offing /ˈɒfɪŋ/ *n.* the more distant part of the sea in view. □ **in the offing** not far away; likely to appear or happen soon. [perhaps from OFF + -ING[1]]

offish /ˈɒfɪʃ/ *adj. colloq.* inclined to be aloof. □ **offishly** *adv.* **offishness** *n.* [OFF: cf. UPPISH]

off-key *adj & adv.* **1** out of tune. **2** not quite suitable or fitting.

off-licence *n. Brit.* **1** a shop selling alcoholic drink for consumption elsewhere. **2** a licence for this.

off-limits *adj.* out of bounds.

off-line *adj. & adv. Computing* ● *adj.* (of a computer terminal or process) not directly controlled by or connected to a central processor. ● *adv.* with a delay between the production of data and its processing; while not directly controlled by or connected to a central processor.

offload /ˈɒfləʊd, ɒfˈləʊd/ *v.tr.* **1** get rid of (esp. something unpleasant) by giving it to someone else. **2** unload (cargo etc.)

off-peak *adj. & adv.* ● *adj.* used or for use at times other than those of greatest demand. ● *adv.* at times other than those of greatest demand.

off-piste *attrib.adj. & adv. Skiing* away from prepared ski runs.

off-price *adj. N. Amer.* involving merchandise sold at a lower price than that recommended by the manufacturer.

offprint /ɒfˈprɪnt, ˈɒfprɪnt/ *n.* a printed copy of an article etc. originally forming part of a larger publication.

off-putting *adj.* **1** disconcerting. **2** repellent. □ **off-puttingly** *adv.*

off-road *attrib.adj.* **1** away from the road, on rough terrain. **2** (of a vehicle etc.) designed for rough terrain or for cross-country driving.

off-roading *n.* the activity of driving over rough terrain, esp. as a sport. □ **off-roader** *n.*

off-screen *adj. & adv.* ● *adj.* **1** not appearing on a cinema, television, or VDU screen. **2** (*attrib.*) in one's private life or in real life as opposed to a film or television role. ● *adv.* **1** without use of a screen. **2** outside the view presented by a cinema film scene. **3** in one's private life or in real life as opposed to a film or television role.

off-season *n.* a time when business etc. is slack (often *attrib.*: *off-season prices*).

offset *n. & v.* ● *n.* /ˈɒfsɛt/ **1** a side shoot from a plant serving for propagation. **2** an offshoot or scion. **3** a compensation; a consideration or amount diminishing or neutralizing the effect of a contrary one. **4** *Archit.* a sloping ledge in a wall etc. where the thickness of the part above is diminished. **5** a mountain spur. **6** a bend in a pipe etc. to carry it past an obstacle. **7** (often *attrib.*) a method of printing in which ink is transferred from a plate or stone to a uniform rubber surface and from there to paper etc. (*offset litho*). **8** *Surveying* a short distance measured perpendicularly from the main line of measurement. ● *v.tr.* /ˈɒfsɛt, ɒfˈsɛt/ (**-setting**; *past* and *past part.* **-set**) **1** counterbalance, compensate. **2** place out of line. **3** print by the offset process.

offshoot /ˈɒfʃuːt/ *n.* **1** a side shoot or branch. **2** a derivative (*an offshoot of a right-wing group*).

offshore *adj. & adv.* ● *adj.* /ˈɒfʃɔː/ **1** situated at sea some distance from the shore. **2** (of the wind) blowing seawards. **3** (of goods, funds, etc.) made or registered abroad. ● *adv.* /ɒfˈʃɔː/ **1** at some distance from the shore. **2** in a direction away from the shore. **3** abroad.

offside *adj. & n.* ● *adj.* /ɒfˈsʌɪd/ *Sport* (of a player in a field game) in a position, usu. ahead of the ball, that is not allowed if it affects play. ● *n.* /ˈɒfsʌɪd/ (often *attrib.*) esp. *Brit.* the right side of a vehicle, animal, etc. (cf. NEARSIDE).

off side see OFF *n.* 1.

offsider /ˈɒfsʌɪdə/ *n. Austral. colloq.* a partner, assistant, or deputy.

offspring /ˈɒfsprɪŋ/ *n.* (*pl.* same) **1** a person's child or children or descendant(s). **2** an animal's young or descendant(s). **3** a result. [Old English *ofspring*, from OF 'from' + *springan* SPRING *v.*]

off-stage *attrib.adj.* not on the stage and so not visible or not audible to the audience.

off-street *adj.* (esp. of parking vehicles) other than on a street.

off the cuff *adv. & adj. colloq.* ● *adv.* without preparation, extempore. ● *adj.* (hyphenated when *attrib.*) made without preparation, extempore.

off-the-shelf *adj. & adv.* ● *attrib.adj.* (of goods) supplied ready-made; available from existing stock. ● *adv.* (**off the shelf**) ready-made; from existing stock.

off-the-shoulder *attrib.adj.* (of a dress etc.) leaving the shoulders bare.

off the wall *adj.* (hyphenated when *attrib.*) esp. *N. Amer. slang* unorthodox, unconventional.

off-time *n.* a time when business etc. is slack.

off-white *n. & adj.* ● *n.* a white colour with a grey or yellowish tinge. ● *adj.* of this colour.

Ofgas /ˈɒfgas/ *n.* (in the UK) Office of Gas Supply, a regulatory body supervising the operation of the gas industry. [acronym]

OFSTED /ˈɒfstɛd/ *n.* (in the UK) Office for Standards in Education, an organization monitoring standards in schools by means of regular inspections. [acronym]

oft /ɒft/ *adv. archaic* or *literary* often (usu. in *comb.*: *oft-recurring*; *oft-quoted*). [Old English]

Oftel /ˈɒftɛl/ *n.* (in the UK) Office of Telecommunications, a regulatory body supervising the operation of the telecommunications industry. [acronym]

often /ˈɒf(ə)n, ˈɒft(ə)n/ *adv.* (**oftener**, **oftenest**) **1 a** frequently; many times. **b** at short intervals. **2** in many instances. □ **as often as not** in roughly half the instances. [Middle English: extended from OFT, probably influenced by *selden* = SELDOM]

oftentimes /ˈɒf(ə)ntʌɪmz, ˈɒft(ə)n-/ *adv.* (also **oft-times**) *archaic* or *literary* often.

Ofwat /ˈɒfwɒt/ *n.* (in the UK) Office of Water Services, a regulatory body supervising the operation of the water industry. [acronym]

ogam var. of OGHAM.

ogdoad /ˈɒgdəʊad/ *n.* a group of eight. [Late Latin *ogdoas ogdoad-* from Greek *ogdoas -ados*, via *ogdoos* 'eighth' from *oktō* 'eight']

ogee /ˈəʊdʒiː, əʊˈdʒiː/ *adj. & n. Archit.* ● *adj.* showing in section a double continuous S-shaped curve. ● *n.* an S-shaped line or moulding. □ **ogee'd** *adj.* [apparently from OGIVE, as being the usual moulding in groin-ribs]

ogee arch *n.* an arch with two ogee curves meeting at the apex.

ogham /ˈɒgəm/ *n.* (also **ogam**) **1** an ancient British and Irish alphabet of twenty characters formed by parallel strokes on either side of or across a continuous line. **2** an inscription in this alphabet. **3** each of its characters. [Old Irish *ogam*, connected with *Ogma*, the name of its mythical inventor]

ogive /ˈəʊdʒʌɪv, əʊˈdʒʌɪv/ *n.* **1** a pointed or Gothic arch. **2** one of the diagonal groins or ribs of a vault. **3** an S-shaped line. **4** *Statistics* a cumulative frequency graph. □ **ogival** *adj.* [Middle English from French, of unknown origin]

ogle /ˈəʊg(ə)l/ *v. & n.* ● *v.* **1** *tr.* eye amorously or lecherously. **2** *intr.* look amorously. ● *n.* an amorous or lecherous look. □ **ogler** *n.* [probably Low German or Dutch: cf. Low German *oegeln*, frequentative of *oegen* 'look at']

O grade *n.* = ORDINARY GRADE. [abbreviation]

ogre /ˈəʊgə/ *n.* (*fem.* **ogress** /-grɪs/) **1** a man-eating giant in folklore etc. **2** a terrifying person. □ **ogreish** *adj.* (also **ogrish**). [French, first used by Perrault in 1697, of unknown origin]

OH *abbr. US* Ohio (in official postal use).

oh[1] /əʊ/ *int.* (also **O**) expressing surprise, pain, entreaty, etc. (*oh, what a mess; oh for a holiday*). □ **oh boy** expressing surprise, excitement, etc. **oh well** expressing resignation. [variant of O[3]]

oh[2] /əʊ/ *n.* = O[1] 2.

o.h.c. *abbr.* overhead camshaft.

ohm /əʊm/ *n. Electr.* the SI unit of resistance, transmitting a current of one ampere when subjected to a potential difference of one volt (symbol Ω). □ **ohmic** *adj.* [named after G. S. *Ohm*, German physicist d. 1854]

ohmmeter /ˈəʊm,miːtə/ *n.* an instrument for measuring electrical resistance.

OHMS *abbr.* on Her (or His) Majesty's Service.

Ohm's law /əʊmz/ *n. Electr.* a law stating that current is proportional to voltage and inversely proportional to resistance. [see OHM]

oho /əʊˈhəʊ/ *int.* expressing surprise or exultation. [Middle English, from O[3] + HO]

ohone var. of OCHONE.

OHP *abbr.* overhead projector.

o.h.v. *abbr.* overhead valve.

oi /ɔɪ/ *int.* calling attention or expressing alarm etc. [variant of HOY[1]]

-oid /ɔɪd/ *suffix* forming adjectives and nouns, denoting form or resemblance (*asteroid; rhomboid; thyroid*). □ **-oidal** *suffix* forming adjectives. **-oidally** *suffix* forming adverbs. [modern Latin *-oides* from Greek *-oeidēs*, from *eidos* 'form']

oidium /əʊˈɪdɪəm/ *n.* (*pl.* **oidia** /-dɪə/) any of several kinds of fungal spore, formed by the breaking up of fungal hyphae into cells. [modern Latin, from Greek *ōion* 'egg' + diminutive suffix *-idion*]

OIEO *abbr. Brit.* offers in excess of.

oik /ɔɪk/ *n. colloq.* an uncouth or obnoxious person; an idiot. [20th c.: origin unknown]

oil /ɔɪl/ *n. & v.* ● *n.* **1** any of various thick, viscous, usu. inflammable liquids insoluble in water but soluble in organic solvents (see also ESSENTIAL OIL, FIXED OIL, MINERAL OIL). **2** petroleum. **3** (in *comb.*) using oil as fuel (*oil-heater*). **4 a** (usu. in *pl.*) = OIL PAINT. **b** *colloq.* a picture painted in oil paints. **5** (in *pl.*) = OILSKIN. ● *v.* **1** *tr.* apply oil to; lubricate. **2** *tr.* impregnate or treat with oil (*oiled silk*). **3** *tr. & intr.* supply with or take on oil as fuel. **4** *tr. & intr.* make (butter, grease, etc.) into or (of butter etc.) become an oily liquid. □ **oil a person's hand** (or **palm**) bribe a person. **oil the wheels** help make things go smoothly. □ **oilless** *adj.* [Middle English *oli, oile* via Anglo-French, Old Northern French *olie*, Old French *oile* from Latin *oleum* '(olive) oil', from *olea* 'olive']

oil-bird *n.* a nocturnal fruit-eating bird, *Steatornis caripensis*, resembling a nightjar and living in caves in Central and S. America. Also called *guacharo*.

oilcake /ˈɔɪlkeɪk/ *n.* a mass of compressed linseed etc. left after oil has been extracted, used as fodder or manure.

oil can *n.* a can containing oil, esp. one with a long nozzle for oiling machinery.

oilcloth /ˈɔɪlklɒθ/ *n.* **1** a fabric waterproofed with oil. **2** an oilskin. **3** a canvas coated with linseed or other oil and used to cover a table or floor.

oil colour *n.* = OIL PAINT.

oil drum *n.* a metal drum used for transporting oil.

oiled silk *n.* silk made waterproof with oil.

oil engine *n.* an engine driven by the explosion of vaporized oil mixed with air.

oiler /ˈɔɪlə/ *n.* **1** an oil can for oiling machinery. **2** an oil tanker. **3** *US* **a** an oil well. **b** (in *pl.*) oilskin.

oilfield /ˈɔɪlfiːld/ *n.* an area yielding mineral oil.

oil-fired *adj.* using oil as fuel.

oil lamp *n.* a lamp using oil as fuel.

oilman /ˈɔɪlmən/ *n.* (*pl.* **-men**) a person who deals in oil.

oil-meal *n.* ground oilcake.

oil of juniper *n.* oil from juniper cones used in medicine and in flavouring gin etc.

oil of turpentine see TURPENTINE *n.* 2.

oil of vitriol *n.* concentrated sulphuric acid.

oil paint *n.* a mix of ground colour pigment and oil.

oil painting *n.* **1** the art of painting in oils. **2** a picture painted in oils. □ **is no oil painting** is physically unattractive.

oil-palm *n.* a palm tree from which palm oil is extracted, esp. *Elaeis guineensis* of W. Africa.

oil pan *n.* an engine sump.

oil-paper *n.* a paper made transparent or waterproof by soaking in oil.

oil platform *n.* a structure designed to stand on the seabed to provide a stable base above water for the drilling and regulation of oil wells.

oil-press *n.* an apparatus for pressing oil from seeds etc.

oil rig *n.* a structure with equipment for drilling an oil well; an oil platform.

oil-sand *n.* a stratum of porous rock yielding petroleum.

oilseed /ˈɔɪlsiːd/ *n.* any of various seeds from cultivated crops yielding oil, e.g. rape, peanut, or cotton.

oil-shale *n.* a fine-grained rock from which oil can be extracted.

oilskin /ˈɔɪlskɪn/ *n.* **1** cloth waterproofed with oil. **2 a** a garment made of this. **b** (in *pl.*) a suit made of this.

oil slick *n.* a smooth patch of oil, esp. one on the sea.

oilstone /ˈɔɪlstəʊn/ *n.* a fine-grained flat stone used with oil for sharpening flat tools, e.g. chisels, planes, etc. (cf. WHETSTONE 1).

oil tanker *n.* a ship designed to carry oil in bulk.

oil well *n.* a well from which mineral oil is drawn.

oily /ˈɔɪli/ *adj.* (**oilier, oiliest**) **1** of, like, or containing much oil. **2** covered or soaked with oil. **3** (of a manner etc.) fawning, insinuating, unctuous. □ **oilily** *adv.* **oiliness** *n.*

oink /ɔɪŋk/ *v.intr.* (of a pig) make its characteristic grunt. [imitative]

ointment /ˈɔɪntm(ə)nt/ *n.* a smooth greasy healing or cosmetic preparation for the skin. [Middle English *oignement, ointment*, from Old French *oignement*, ultimately from Latin (as UNGUENT): influenced by obsolete *oint* 'anoint' from Old French, past part. of *oindre* ANOINT]

Oireachtas /ˈɛrəktəs; Irish ˈɛrəxtəs/ *n.* the legislature of the Irish Republic: the President, Dáil, and Seanad. [Irish, = assembly, convocation]

OIRO *abbr. Brit.* offers in the region of.

Ojibwa /ə(ʊ)ˈdʒɪbweɪ/ *n. & adj.* ● *n.* (*pl.* same or **Ojibwas**) **1** a member of an Algonquian people inhabiting the lands around Lake Superior and certain adjacent areas. **2** the Algonquian language of this people. ● *adj.* of or relating to the Ojibwa or their language. [Ojibwa, from a root meaning 'puckered', with reference to their moccasins]

OK[1] /əʊˈkeɪ/ *adj., adv., n., & v.* (also **okay**) *colloq.* ● *adj.* (often as *int.* expressing agreement or acquiescence) all right; satisfactory. ● *adv.* well, satisfactorily (*that worked out OK*). ● *n.* (*pl.* **OKs**) approval, sanction. ● *v.tr.* (**OK's, OK'd, OK'ing**) give an OK to; approve, sanction. [originally US: probably abbreviation of *orl* (or *oll*) *korrect*, jocular form of 'all correct']

OK[2] *abbr. US* Oklahoma (in official postal use).

okapi /ə(ʊ)ˈkɑːpi/ *n.* (*pl.* same or **okapis**) a ruminant mammal, *Okapia johnstoni*, native to N. and NE Zaïre, with a head resembling that of a giraffe and a body resembling that of a zebra, having a dark chestnut coat and transverse stripes on the hindquarters and upper legs only. [African name]

okay var. of OK[1].

okey-dokey /əʊkɪˈdəʊki/ *adj. & adv.* (also **okey-doke** /-ˈdəʊk/) *slang* = OK[1]. [reduplication]

Okla. *abbr.* Oklahoma.

okra /ˈɒkrə, ˈəʊkrə/ *n.* **1** an African plant, *Abelmoschus esculentus* (mallow family), yielding long ridged seed pods. **2** the seed pods eaten as a vegetable and used to thicken soups and stews. Also called GUMBO, LADIES' FINGERS. [West African native name]

okta /'ɒktə/ *n.* (*pl.* **oktas** or same) *Meteorol.* a unit of cloud cover, equal to one eighth of the sky.

-ol[1] /ɒl/ *suffix Chem.* forming names of alcohols, phenols, and their derivatives (*glycerol*; *methanol*; *retinol*). [from ending of ALCOHOL]

-ol[2] /ɒl/ *suffix Chem.* forming names of oils and oil-derived compounds (*cresol*; *Lysol*). [Latin *oleum* 'oil': cf. -OLE]

old /əʊld/ *adj.* (**older**, **oldest**) (cf. ELDER[1], ELDEST). **1 a** advanced in age; far on in the natural period of existence. **b** not young or near its beginning. **2** made long ago. **3** long in use. **4** worn or dilapidated or shabby from the passage of time. **5** having the characteristics (experience, feebleness, etc.) of age (*the child has an old face*). **6** practised, inveterate (*an old offender*; *old in crime*). **7** belonging only or chiefly to the past; lingering on; former (*old times*; *haunted by old memories*). **8** dating from far back; long established or known; ancient, primeval (*old as the hills*; *old friends*; *an old family*). **9** (appended to a period of time) **a** (often in *comb.*) of age (*is four years old*; *a four-year-old boy*). **b** (in *comb.*, as noun) a person or animal of the age specified (*our four-year-old is ill*). **10** (of language) as used in former or earliest times. **11** *colloq.* as a term of affection or casual reference (*good old Charlie*; *old shipmate*). **12** the former or first of two or more similar things (*our old house*; *wants his old job back*). □ **an old one** a familiar joke. □ **oldish** *adj.* **oldness** *n.* [Old English *ald*, from West Germanic]

old age *n.* the later part of normal life.

old-age pension *n.* = RETIREMENT PENSION. □ **old-age pensioner** *n.*

Old Bailey *n.* the Central Criminal Court in London.

Old Bill *n. Brit. slang* the police.

old bird *n. slang* a wary person.

old boy *n.* **1** a former male pupil of a school. **2** *colloq.* **a** an elderly man. **b** an affectionate form of address to a boy or man.

old boy network *n. Brit. colloq.* preferment in employment of those from a similar social background, esp. fellow ex-pupils of public schools.

Old Church Slavonic *n.* the earliest written Slavonic language, surviving as a liturgical language in the Orthodox Church.

old country *n.* (prec. by *the*) the native country of colonists etc.

old dear *n. colloq.* **1** an elderly woman. **2** one's mother.

olden /'əʊld(ə)n/ *adj. archaic* of old; of a former age (esp. *in the olden days*).

Old English *n.* the English language up to *c.*1150.

Old English sheepdog *n.* **1** a large sheepdog with a shaggy blue-grey and white coat. **2** this breed

olde worlde /əʊldɪ 'wə:ldi/ *adj.* often *derog.* old and quaint, often in a mock old style.

old-fashioned *adj.* in or according to a fashion or tastes no longer current; antiquated.

Old French *n.* the French language of the period before *c.*1400.

old fruit *n.* a familiar form of address to a man.

old fustic *n.* **1** a tropical tree, *Chlorophora tinctoria*, native to America. **2** the wood of this tree.

old girl *n.* **1** a former female pupil of a school. **2** *colloq.* **a** an elderly woman. **b** an affectionate term of address to a girl or woman.

Old Glory *n. US* the US national flag.

old gold *n. & adj.* ● *n.* a dull brownish-gold colour. ● *adj.* (hyphenated when *attrib.*) of this colour.

old guard *n.* the original or past or conservative members of a group.

old hand *n.* a person with much experience.

old hat *adj. colloq.* tediously familiar or out of date.

Old High German *n.* High German (see GERMAN) up to *c.*1200.

Old Icelandic *n.* Icelandic up to the 16th c., a form of Old Norse.

oldie /'əʊldi/ *n. colloq.* an old person or thing.

old lady *n. colloq.* one's mother or wife.

old lag see LAG[3].

old leaven *n.* (prec. by *the*) traces of the unregenerate state (cf. 1 Cor. 5:6–8).

old maid *n.* **1** *derog.* an elderly unmarried woman. **2** a prim and fussy person. **3** a card game in which players try not to be left with an unpaired queen. □ **old-maidish** *n.*

old man *n. colloq.* **1** one's husband or father. **2** one's employer or other person in authority over one. **3** *Brit.* an affectionate form of address to a boy or man.

old man's beard *n.* traveller's joy, esp. in seed. [so called from the grey fluffy hairs round the seeds]

old master *n.* **1** a great artist of former times, esp. of the 13th–17th c. in Europe. **2** a painting by such a painter.

old moon *n.* the moon in its last quarter, before the new moon.

Old Nick *n. colloq.* the Devil. [probably from a pet form of the name *Nicholas*]

Old Norse *n.* the North Germanic language of Norway and its colonies until the 14th c., from which the Scandinavian languages are derived.

Old Pals Act *n. Brit. colloq.* the principle that friends should always help one another.

Old Pretender *n.* James Stuart (1688–1766), son of James II and claimant to the British throne.

Old Prussian *n.* the Baltic language spoken in Prussia until the 17th c.

old retainer see RETAINER 3b.

old school *n.* **1** traditional attitudes. **2** people having such attitudes.

old school tie *n.* esp. *Brit.* **1** a necktie with a characteristic pattern worn by the pupils of a particular (usu. public) school. **2** the group loyalty and traditionalism associated with wearing such a tie.

old soldier *n.* = OLD-TIMER.

old squaw *n. N. Amer.* the long-tailed duck, *Clangula hyemalis*.

old stager *n.* = OLD-TIMER.

oldster /'əʊldstə/ *n.* an old person. [OLD + -STER, on the pattern of *youngster*]

Old Style *adj.* dating reckoned by the Julian calendar.

old-style *attrib.adj.* of an old style, outmoded (*old-style communists*).

Old Testament *n.* the first part of the Christian Bible, containing the scriptures of the Hebrews.

old-time *attrib.adj.* belonging to former times.

old-timer *n.* a person with long experience or standing.

old wives' tale *n.* a foolish or unscientific tradition or belief.

old woman *n. colloq.* **1** one's wife or mother. **2** a fussy or timid man. □ **old-womanish** *adj.*

Old World *n.* Europe, Asia, and Africa.

old-world *adj.* belonging to or associated with old times.

old year *n.* the year just ended or about to end.

-ole /əʊl/ *comb. form* forming names of esp. heterocyclic compounds (*indole*). [Latin *oleum* 'oil': cf. -OL[2]]

oleaceous /əʊlɪ'eɪʃəs/ *adj.* of the plant family Oleaceae, including olive and jasmine. [modern Latin *Oleaceae* from Latin *olea* 'olive tree']

oleaginous /əʊlɪ'adʒɪnəs/ *adj.* **1** having the properties of or producing oil. **2** oily, greasy. **3** obsequious, ingratiating. [French *oléagineux* from Latin *oleaginus*, from *oleum* 'oil']

oleander /əʊlɪ'andə/ *n.* an evergreen poisonous shrub, *Nerium oleander*, native to the Mediterranean and bearing clusters of white, pink, or red flowers. [medieval Latin]

oleaster /əʊlɪ'astə/ *n.* any of various trees of the genus *Elaeagnus*, often thorny and with evergreen leathery foliage, esp. *E. angustifolia* bearing olive-shaped yellowish fruits. Also called *Russian olive*. [Middle English from Latin, from *olea* 'olive tree': see -ASTER]

olecranon /əʊ'lɛkrənɒn, əʊlɪ'kreɪmən/ *n.* a bony prominence on the upper end of the ulna at the elbow. [Greek *ōle(no)kranon*, from *ōlenē* 'elbow' + *kranion* 'head']

olefin /'əʊlɪfɪn/ *n.* (also **olefine**) *Chem.* = ALKENE. [French *oléfiant* 'oil-forming' (with reference to oily ethylene dichloride)]

oleic acid /əʊ'li:ɪk/ *n.* an unsaturated fatty acid present in many fats and soaps. ▫ **oleate** /'əʊlɪət/ *n.* [Latin *oleum* 'oil']

oleiferous /əʊlɪ'ɪf(ə)rəs/ *adj.* yielding oil. [Latin *oleum* 'oil' + -FEROUS]

oleo- /'əʊlɪəʊ, 'ɒlɪəʊ/ *comb. form* oil. [Latin *oleum* 'oil']

oleograph /'əʊlɪəgrɑ:f/ *n.* a print made to resemble an oil painting.

oleomargarine /ˌəʊlɪəʊ'mɑ:dʒəri:n, -'mɑ:gəri:n/ *n.* **1** a fatty substance extracted from beef fat and often used in margarine. **2** *US* margarine.

oleometer /əʊlɪ'ɒmɪtə/ *n.* an instrument for determining the density and purity of oils.

oleoresin /ˌəʊlɪəʊ'rɛzɪn/ *n.* a natural or artificial mixture of essential oils and a resin, e.g. balsam.

oleum /'əʊlɪəm/ *n.* concentrated sulphuric acid containing excess sulphur trioxide in solution forming a dense corrosive liquid. [Latin, = oil]

O level /əʊ/ *n. hist.* = ORDINARY LEVEL. [abbreviation]

olfaction /ɒl'fakʃ(ə)n/ *n.* the act or capacity of smelling; the sense of smell. ▫ **olfactive** *adj.* [Latin *olfactus* 'a smell', from *olēre* 'to smell' + *facere fact-* 'make']

olfactory /ɒl'fakt(ə)ri/ *adj.* of or relating to the sense of smell (*olfactory nerves*). [Latin *olfactare*, frequentative of *olfacere* (as OLFACTION)]

olibanum /ɒ'lɪbənəm/ *n.* a kind of frankincense. [Middle English via medieval Latin and Late Latin *libanus* from Greek *libanos* 'frankincense', of Semitic origin]

oligarch /'ɒlɪgɑ:k/ *n.* a member of an oligarchy. [Greek *oligarkhēs*, from *oligoi* 'few' + *arkhō* 'to rule']

oligarchy /'ɒlɪgɑ:ki/ *n.* (*pl.* **-ies**) **1** government by a small group of people. **2** a state governed in this way. **3** the members of such a government. ▫ **oligarchic** /-'gɑ:kɪk/ *adj.* **oligarchical** /-'gɑ:kɪk(ə)l/ *adj.* **oligarchically** /-'gɑ:kɪk(ə)li/ *adv.* [French *oligarchie* or medieval Latin *oligarchia* from Greek *oligarkhia* (as OLIGARCH)]

oligo- /'ɒlɪgəʊ/ *comb. form* few, slight; containing a relatively small number of units etc. [Greek *oligos* 'small', *oligoi* 'few']

Oligocene /'ɒlɪgəsi:n/ *adj. & n. Geol.* ● *adj.* of or relating to the third epoch of the Tertiary period, with evidence of the first primates. Cf. Appendix X. ● *n.* this epoch or system. [as OLIGO- + Greek *kainos* 'new']

oligochaete /'ɒlɪgəki:t/ *n. & adj. Zool.* ● *n.* an annelid worm of the division Oligochaeta, which includes the earthworms. ● *adj.* of or relating to this division. [OLIGO- + Greek *khaitē* 'long hair' (taken as 'bristle'), so called as having fewer bristles than polychaetes]

oligopoly /ɒlɪ'gɒp(ə)li/ *n.* (*pl.* **-ies**) a state of limited competition between a small number of producers or sellers. ▫ **oligopolist** *n.* **oligopolistic** /-'lɪstɪk/ *adj.* [OLIGO-, on the pattern of MONOPOLY]

oligosaccharide /ˌɒlɪgəʊ'sakərʌɪd/ *n.* any carbohydrate whose molecules are composed of a relatively small number of monosaccharide units.

oligotrophic /ˌɒlɪgə'trəʊfɪk, -'trɒf-/ *adj.* (of a lake etc.) relatively poor in plant nutrients. ▫ **oligotrophy** /ɒlɪ'gɒtrəfi/ *n.*

olio /'əʊlɪəʊ/ *n.* (*pl.* **-os**) **1** a mixed dish; a stew of various meats and vegetables. **2** a hotchpotch or miscellany. [Spanish *olla* 'stew' from Latin *olla* 'cooking pot']

olivaceous /ɒlɪ'veɪʃəs/ *adj.* olive green; of a dusky yellowish green.

olivary /'ɒlɪv(ə)ri/ *adj. Anat.* olive-shaped; oval. [Latin *olivarius* (as OLIVE)]

olive /'ɒlɪv/ *n. & adj.* ● *n.* **1** (in full **olive tree**) any evergreen tree of the genus *Olea*, having dark green lance-shaped leathery leaves with silvery undersides, esp. *O. europaea* of the Mediterranean, and *O. africana* native to S. Africa. **2** the small oval fruit of this, having a hard stone and bitter flesh, green when unripe and bluish black when ripe. **3** (in full **olive green**) the greyish-green colour of an unripe olive. **4** the wood of the olive tree. **5** *Anat.* each of a pair of olive-shaped swellings in the medulla oblongata. **6 a** any olive-shaped gastropod of the genus *Oliva*. **b** the shell of this. **7** a slice of beef or veal made into a roll with stuffing inside and stewed. **8** a metal ring or fitting which is tightened under a threaded nut to form a seal, as in a compression joint. ● *adj.* **1** (in full **olive green**; hyphenated when *attrib.*) coloured like an unripe olive. **2** (of the complexion) yellowish brown, sallow. [Middle English via Old French and Latin *oliva* from Greek *elaia*, from *elaion* 'oil']

olive branch *n.* **1** the branch of an olive tree as a symbol of peace. **2** a gesture of reconciliation or friendship.

olive crown *n.* a garland of olive leaves as a sign of victory.

olive drab *adj. & n.* ● *n.* the dull olive-green colour used in certain army uniforms. ● *adj.* (hyphenated when *attrib.*) of this colour.

olive green see OLIVE *n.* 3, *adj.* 1.

olive oil *n.* an oil extracted from olives, used esp. in cookery.

olivine /'ɒlɪvi:n, -ʌɪn/ *n. Mineral.* a naturally occurring form of magnesium-iron silicate, usu. olive green and found in igneous rocks.

olla podrida /ˌɒlə pə(ʊ)'dri:də/ *n.* = OLIO. [Spanish, literally 'rotten pot' (as OLIO + Latin *putridus*: cf. PUTRID]

olm /əʊlm, ɒlm/ *n.* a blind cave-dwelling salamander, *Proteus anguinus*, native to SE Europe, usu. transparent but turning brown in light and having external gills. [German]

-ology *comb. form* see -LOGY.

oloroso /ɒlə'rəʊsəʊ/ *n.* (*pl.* **-os**) a heavy dark medium-sweet sherry. [Spanish, literally 'fragrant']

Olympiad /ə'lɪmpɪad/ *n.* **1 a** a period of four years between Olympic Games, used by the ancient Greeks in dating events. **b** a four-yearly celebration of the ancient Olympic Games. **2** a celebration of the modern Olympic Games. **3** a regular international contest in chess etc. [Middle English via French *Olympiade* and Latin *Olympias Olympiad-* from Greek *Olumpias Olumpiad-*, from *Olumpios*: see OLYMPIAN, OLYMPIC]

Olympian /ə'lɪmpɪən/ *adj. & n.* ● *adj.* **1 a** of or associated with Mount Olympus in NE Greece, traditionally the home of the Greek gods. **b** celestial, godlike. **2** (of manners etc.) magnificent, condescending, superior. **3 a** of or relating to ancient Olympia in southern Greece. **b** = OLYMPIC. ● *n.* **1** any of the pantheon of twelve gods regarded as living on Olympus. **2** a person of great attainments or of superhuman calm and detachment. **3** a competitor in the Olympic Games. [Latin *Olympus* or *Olympia*: see OLYMPIC]

Olympic /ə'lɪmpɪk/ *adj. & n.* ● *adj.* of ancient Olympia or the Olympic Games. ● *n.pl.* (**the Olympics**) the Olympic Games. [Latin *Olympicus* from Greek *Olumpikos* 'of Olympus or Olympia' (the latter being named from the games in honour of Zeus of *Olympus*)]

Olympic Games *n.pl.* **1** an ancient Greek festival held at Olympia every four years, with athletic, literary, and musical competitions. **2** a modern international revival of this as a sports festival held every four years since 1896 in different venues.

OM *abbr.* (in the UK) Order of Merit.

-oma /'əʊmə/ *suffix* forming nouns denoting tumours and other abnormal growths (*carcinoma*). [modern

Latin from Greek *-ōma*, a suffix denoting the result of verbal action]

omasum /əʊˈmeɪsəm/ *n.* (*pl.* **omasa** /-sə/) the third stomach of a ruminant. [Latin, = bullock's tripe]

ombre /ˈɒmbə, ˈɒmbreɪ/ *n.* a card game for three, popular in Europe in the 17th–18th c. [Spanish *hombre* 'man', with reference to one player seeking to win the pool]

ombré /ˈɔ̃breɪ/ *adj.* (of a fabric etc.) having gradual shading of colour from light to dark. [French, past part. of *ombrer* 'to shadow' (as UMBER)]

ombro- /ˈɒmbrəʊ/ *comb. form* rain. [Greek *ombros* 'rain-shower']

ombudsman /ˈɒmbʊdzmən/ *n.* (*pl.* **-men**) an official appointed by a government to investigate individuals' complaints against public authorities etc. [Swedish, = legal representative]

-ome /əʊm/ *suffix* forming nouns denoting objects or parts of a specified nature (*rhizome*; *trichome*). [variant of -OMA]

omega /ˈəʊmɪgə/ *n.* **1** the last (24th) letter of the Greek alphabet (Ω, ω). **2** the last of a series; the final development. [Greek, *ō mega* = great O]

omelette /ˈɒmlɪt/ *n.* (also **omelet**) a dish of beaten eggs cooked in a frying pan and served plain or with a savoury or sweet filling. [French, earlier *amelette* by metathesis from *alumette*, variant of *alumelle*, from *lemele* 'knife blade' (probably with reference to the thin flat shape of an omelette) from Latin *lamella*: see LAMELLA]

omen /ˈəʊmən/ *n.* & *v.* ● *n.* **1** an occurrence or object regarded as portending good or evil. **2** prophetic significance (*of good omen*). ● *v.tr.* (usu. in *passive*) portend; foreshow. ▫ **omened** *adj.* (also in *comb.*). [Latin *omen ominis*]

omentum /əʊˈmɛntəm/ *n.* (*pl.* **omenta** /-tə/) a fold of peritoneum connecting the stomach with other abdominal organs. ▫ **omental** *adj.* [Latin]

omertà /əʊmɛːˈtɑː, Italian omerˈta/ *n.* a code of silence, esp. as practised by the Mafia. [Italian, = conspiracy of silence]

omicron /ə(ʊ)ˈmʌɪkrɒn/ *n.* the fifteenth letter of the Greek alphabet (Ο, ο). [Greek, *o mikron* = small o]

ominous /ˈɒmɪnəs/ *adj.* **1** threatening; indicating disaster or difficulty. **2** of evil omen; inauspicious. **3** giving or being an omen. ▫ **ominously** *adv.* **ominousness** *n.* [Latin *ominosus* (as OMEN)]

omission /ə(ʊ)ˈmɪʃ(ə)n/ *n.* **1** the act or an instance of omitting or being omitted. **2** something that has been omitted or overlooked. ▫ **omissive** *adj.* [Middle English from Old French *omission* or Late Latin *omissio* (as OMIT)]

omit /ə(ʊ)ˈmɪt/ *v.tr.* (**omitted**, **omitting**) **1** leave out; not insert or include. **2** leave undone. **3** (foll. by verbal noun or *to* + infin.) fail or neglect (*omitted saying anything*; *omitted to say*). ▫ **omissible** *adj.* [Middle English from Latin *omittere omiss-* (as OB-, *mittere* 'send')]

ommatidium /ɒməˈtɪdɪəm/ *n.* (*pl.* **ommatidia** /-dɪə/) a structural element in the compound eye of an insect. [modern Latin from Greek *ommatidion*, diminutive of *omma ommat-* 'eye']

omni- /ˈɒmni/ *comb. form* **1** all; of all things. **2** in all ways or places. [Latin from *omnis* 'all']

omnibus /ˈɒmnɪbəs/ *n.* & *adj.* ● *n.* **1** *formal* = BUS *n.* 1. **2 a** a volume containing several novels etc. previously published separately. **b** a single edition of two or more consecutive programmes previously broadcast separately. ● *adj.* **1** serving several purposes at once. **2** comprising several items. [French from Latin (dative pl. of *omnis*), = for all]

omnicompetent /ɒmnɪˈkɒmpɪt(ə)nt/ *adj.* **1** able to deal with all matters. **2** having jurisdiction in all cases. ▫ **omnicompetence** *n.*

omnidirectional /ˌɒmnɪdɪˈrɛkʃ(ə)n(ə)l, -dʌɪ-/ *adj.* (of an aerial etc.) receiving or transmitting in all directions.

omnifarious /ɒmnɪˈfɛːrɪəs/ *adj.* of all sorts or varieties. [Late Latin *omnifarius* (as OMNI-): cf. MULTIFARIOUS]

omnipotent /ɒmˈnɪpət(ə)nt/ *adj.* **1** having great or absolute power. **2** having great influence. ▫ **omnipotence** *n.* **omnipotently** *adv.* [Middle English via Old French from Latin *omnipotens* (as OMNI-, POTENT[1])]

omnipresent /ɒmnɪˈprɛz(ə)nt/ *adj.* **1** present everywhere at the same time. **2** widely or constantly encountered. ▫ **omnipresence** *n.* [medieval Latin *omnipraesens* (as OMNI-, PRESENT[1])]

omniscient /ɒmˈnɪsɪənt/ *adj.* knowing everything or much. ▫ **omniscience** *n.* **omnisciently** *adv.* [medieval Latin *omnisciens -entis* (as OMNI-, *scire* 'know')]

omnium gatherum /ˌɒmnɪəm ˈgaðərəm/ *n. colloq.* a miscellany or strange mixture. [mock Latin, from Latin *omnium* 'of all' + GATHER]

omnivorous /ɒmˈnɪv(ə)rəs/ *adj.* **1** feeding on many kinds of food, esp. on both plants and flesh. **2** making use of everything available. ▫ **omnivore** /ˈɒmnɪvɔː/ *n.* **omnivorously** *adv.* **omnivorousness** *n.* [Latin *omnivorus* (as OMNI-, -VOROUS)]

omphalo- /ˈɒmfələʊ/ *comb. form* navel. [Greek (as OMPHALOS)]

omphalos /ˈɒmfəlɒs/ *n.* **1** *Gk Antiq.* a conical stone (esp. that at Delphi) representing the navel of the earth. **2** *Gk Antiq.* a boss on a shield. **3** a centre or hub. [Greek, = navel, boss, hub]

on /ɒn/ *prep., adv.,* & *n.* ● *prep.* **1** (so as to be) supported by or attached to or covering or enclosing (*sat on a chair*; *stuck on the wall*; *rings on her fingers*; *leaned on his elbow*). **2** carried with; about the person of (*have you a pen on you?*). **3** (of time) exactly at; during; contemporaneously with (*on 29 May*; *on the hour*; *on schedule*; *working on Tuesday*). **4** immediately after or before (*I saw them on my return*). **5** as a result of (*on further examination I found this*). **6** having, or so as to have, membership etc. of, or residence at or in (*she is on the board of directors*; *lives on the Continent*). **7** supported financially by (*lives on £50 a week*; *lives on his wits*). **8** close to; just by (*a house on the sea*; *lives on the main road*). **9** in the direction of; against. **10** so as to threaten; touching or striking (*advanced on him*; *pulled a knife on me*; *a punch on the nose*). **11** having as an axis or pivot (*turned on his heels*). **12** having as a basis or motive (*works on a ratchet*; *arrested on suspicion*). **13** having as a standard, confirmation, or guarantee (*had it on good authority*; *did it on purpose*; *I promise on my word*). **14** concerning or about (*writes on frogs*). **15** using or engaged with (*is on the pill*; *here on business*). **16** so as to affect (*walked out on her*). **17** at the expense of (*the drinks are on me*; *the joke is on him*). **18** added to (*disaster on disaster*; *ten pence on a pint of beer*). **19** in a specified manner or style (often foll. by *the* + adj. or noun: *on the cheap*; *on the run*). ● *adv.* **1** (so as to be) covering or in contact with something, esp. of clothes (*put your boots on*). **2** in the appropriate direction; towards something (*look on*). **3** further forward; in an advanced position or state (*time is getting on*; *it happened later on*). **4** with continued movement or action (*went plodding on*; *keeps on complaining*). **5** in operation or activity (*the light is on*; *the chase was on*). **6** due to take place as planned (*is the party still on?*). **7** *colloq.* **a** (of a person) willing to participate or approve, or make a bet. **b** esp. *Brit.* (of an idea, proposal, etc.) practicable or acceptable (*that's just not on*). **8** being shown or performed (*a good film on tonight*). **9** (of an actor) on stage. **10** (of an employee) on duty. **11** forward (*head on*). ● *n.* (in full **on side**) *Cricket* = LEG *n.* 6. ▫ **be on about** *Brit.* refer to or discuss esp. tediously or persistently (*what are they on about?*). **be on at** *Brit. colloq.* nag or grumble at. **be on to 1** realize the significance or intentions of. **2** get in touch with (esp. by telephone). **on and off** intermittently; now and then. **on and on** continually; at tedious length. **on time** punctual, punctually. **on to** to a position or state on or in contact with (cf. ONTO). [Old English *on, an,* from Germanic]

-on /ɒn/ *suffix Physics, Biochem., & Chem.* forming nouns denoting: **1** subatomic particles (*meson*; *neutron*). **2** quanta (*photon*). **3** molecular units (*codon*). **4** substances (*interferon*; *parathion*). [ION, originally in *electron*]

onager /ˈɒnəgə/ *n.* **1** a wild ass, esp. *Equus hemionus* of a race native to central Asia. **2** *hist.* an ancient military engine for throwing rocks. [Middle English via Latin from Greek *onagros,* from *onos* 'ass' + *agrios* 'wild']

onanism /ˈəʊnənɪz(ə)m/ *n.* **1** masturbation. **2** coitus interruptus. □ **onanist** *n.* **onanistic** /-ˈnɪstɪk/ *adj.* [French *onanisme* or modern Latin *onanismus,* from the name *Onan* (Gen. 38:9)]

on-board *attrib.adj.* available or situated on board a ship, aircraft, etc. (*on-board facilities*). Cf. *on board* (see BOARD).

ONC *abbr. hist.* (in the UK) Ordinary National Certificate.

once /wʌns/ *adv., conj., & n.* ● *adv.* **1** on one occasion or for one time only (*once is not enough*; *have read it once*). **2** at some point or period in the past (*could once play chess*). **3** ever or at all (*if you once forget it*). **4** multiplied by one; by one degree. ● *conj.* as soon as (*once they have gone we can relax*). ● *n.* one time or occasion (*just the once*). □ **all at once 1** without warning; suddenly. **2** all together. **at once 1** immediately. **2** simultaneously. **for once** on this (or that) occasion, even if at no other. **once again** (or **more**) another time. **once and for all** (or **once for all**) (done) in a final or conclusive manner, esp. so as to end hesitation or uncertainty. **once** (or **every once**) **in a while** from time to time; occasionally. **once or twice** a few times. **once upon a time 1** at some vague time in the past. **2** formerly. [Middle English *ānes, ōnes,* genitive of ONE]

once-over *n. colloq.* a rapid preliminary inspection or piece of work.

oncer /ˈwʌnsə/ *n.* **1** *Brit. hist. slang* a one-pound note. **2** *Brit. colloq.* a thing that occurs only once. **3** *Austral. colloq.* **a** an election of an MP likely to serve only one term. **b** such an MP.

onchocerciasis /ˌɒŋkəʊsəːˈsʌɪəsɪs, -ˈkʌɪəsɪs/ *n. Med.* infestation with parasitic threadworms of the genus *Onchocerca*; esp. river blindness, caused by *O. volvulus.* [genus name *Onchocerca* (Greek *ogkos* 'barb' + *kerkos* 'tail') + -IASIS]

onco- /ˈɒŋkəʊ/ *comb. form Med.* tumour. [Greek *ogkos* 'mass']

oncogene /ˈɒŋkədʒiːn/ *n.* a gene which can transform a cell into a tumour cell.

oncogenic /ɔŋkə(ʊ)ˈdʒɛnɪk/ *adj. Med.* causing development of a tumour or tumours. □ **oncogenicity** /-ˈnɪsɪti/ *n.*

oncology /ɒŋˈkɒlədʒi/ *n. Med.* the study and treatment of tumours. □ **oncologist** *n.*

oncoming /ˈɒnkʌmɪŋ/ *adj. & n.* ● *adj.* approaching from the front. ● *n.* an approach or onset.

oncost /ˈɒnkɒst/ *n. Brit.* an overhead expense.

OND *abbr. hist.* (in the UK) Ordinary National Diploma.

ondes martenot /ɔ̃ːd ˈmɑːt(ə)nəʊ/ *n.* (*pl.* same) *Mus.* an electronic keyboard producing one note of variable pitch. [French *ondes musicales,* literally 'musical waves' (original name of the instrument) + the name of its French inventor, M. *Martenot* d. 1980]

on dit /ɒ̃ ˈdiː, French ɔ̃ di/ *n.* (*pl.* ***on dits*** *pronunc.* same) a piece of gossip or hearsay. [French, = they say]

one /wʌn/ *adj., n., & pron.* ● *adj.* **1** single and integral in number. **2** (with a noun implied) a single person or thing of the kind expressed or implied (*one of the best*; *a nasty one*). **3 a** particular but undefined, esp. as contrasted with another (*that is one view*; *one thing after another*). **b** *colloq.* (as an emphatic) a noteworthy example of (*that is one difficult question*). **4** only such (*the one man who can do it*). **5** forming a unity (*one and undivided*). **6** identical; the same (*of one opinion*). ● *n.* **1 a** the lowest cardinal number. **b** a symbol for this (1, i, I). **2** unity; a unit (*one is half of two*; *came in ones and twos*). **3** a single thing or person or example (often referring to a noun previously expressed or implied: *the big dog and the small one*). **4** one o'clock. **5** *colloq.* an alcoholic drink (*have a quick one*; *have one on me*). **6** a story or joke (*the one about the frog*). ● *pron.* **1** a person of a specified kind (*loved ones*; *like one possessed*). **2** any person, as representing people in general (*one is bound to lose in the end*). **3** any person; the speaker or writer as representing people in general; I, me (*one would like to help*). □ **at one** in agreement. **for one** being one, even if the only one (*I for one do not believe it*). **for one thing** as a single consideration, ignoring others. **one and all** everyone. **and only 1** unique. **2** superb, unequalled. **one by one** singly, successively. **one day 1** on an unspecified day. **2** at some unspecified future date. **one or two** see OR[1]. [Old English *ān,* from Germanic]

■ **Usage** The use of the pronoun *one* to mean 'any person', 'I', or 'me' (see sense 3 of the pronoun) is often regarded as an affectation, but can be useful when a less personal statement is being made, e.g. *One never knows what might happen.* However, it should not be mixed with *he* (*him, his,* etc.), and repeated use in a long sentence may seem clumsy, e.g. *One never knows how one would react if one's house were to burn down.* The less formal *you* can usually replace it successfully and is safer when one is launching into a long statement.

-one /əʊn/ *suffix Chem.* forming nouns denoting various compounds, esp. ketones (*acetone*). [Greek fem. patronymic *-ōnē*]

one another *pron.* each the other or others (as a formula of reciprocity: *love one another*).

one-armed bandit *n. Brit. colloq.* a fruit machine worked by a long handle at the side.

one flesh *n.* (of two people) intimately united, esp. by virtue of marriage (Gen. 2:24).

onefold /ˈwʌnfəʊld/ *adj.* consisting of only one member or element; simple.

one-horse *attrib.adj.* **1** using a single horse. **2** *colloq.* small, poorly equipped.

one-horse race *n.* a competition etc. in which one competitor is clearly superior to all the others.

oneiric /ə(ʊ)ˈnʌɪrɪk/ *adj.* of or relating to dreams or dreaming. [Greek *oneiros* 'dream']

oneiro- /ə(ʊ)ˈnʌɪrəʊ/ *comb. form* dream. [Greek *oneiros* 'dream']

oneiromancy /əˈnʌɪrəmansi/ *n.* the interpretation of dreams.

one-liner *n. colloq.* a single brief sentence, often witty or apposite.

one-man *attrib.adj.* involving, done, or operated by only one man.

oneness /ˈwʌnnɪs/ *n.* **1** the fact or state of being one; singleness. **2** uniqueness. **3** agreement; unity of opinion. **4** identity, sameness.

one-night stand *n.* **1** a single performance of a play etc. in a place. **2** *colloq.* a sexual liaison lasting only one night.

one-off *adj. & n.* esp. *Brit. colloq.* ● *attrib.adj.* made or done as the only one; not repeated. ● *n.* a one-off product, event, etc.

one-piece *adj.* made in one piece, esp. (of a bathing suit etc.) made as a single garment.

oner /ˈwʌnə/ *n. Brit. slang* **1** one pound (of money). **2** a remarkable person or thing.

onerous /ˈəʊn(ə)rəs, ˈɒn-/ *adj.* **1** burdensome; causing or requiring trouble. **2** *Law* involving heavy obligations. □ **onerously** *adv.* **onerousness** *n.* [Middle English via Old French *onereus* from Latin *onerosus,* from *onus oneris* 'burden']

oneself /wʌn'sɛlf/ *pron.* the reflexive and (in apposition) emphatic form of *one* (*kill oneself*; *one has to do it oneself*).

one-sided *adj.* **1** favouring one side in a dispute; unfair, partial. **2** having or occurring on one side only. **3** larger or more developed on one side. □ **one-sidedly** *adv.* **one-sidedness** *n.*

one-step *n.* a vigorous kind of foxtrot in duple time.

one-time *attrib.adj.* former.

one-to-one *adj.* & *adv.* with one member of one group corresponding to one of another.

one-track mind *n.* a mind preoccupied with one subject.

one-two *n. colloq.* **1** *Boxing* the delivery of two punches in quick succession. **2** *Football* etc. a series of reciprocal passes between two advancing players.

one-up *adj. colloq.* having a particular advantage.

one-upmanship *n. colloq.* the art of gaining or maintaining a psychological advantage.

one-way *adj.* allowing movement or travel in one direction only.

onflow /'ɒnfləʊ/ *n.* an onward flow.

onglaze /'ɒngleɪz/ *adj.* (of painting etc.) done on a glazed surface.

ongoing /'ɒngəʊɪŋ/ *adj.* **1** continuing to exist or be operative etc. (*an ongoing problem*). **2** that is or are in progress (*ongoing discussions*). □ **ongoingness** *n.*

■ **Usage** The vague or tautologous use of *ongoing*, as in the cliché *an ongoing situation*, should be avoided.

onion /'ʌnjən/ *n.* **1** an allium, *Allium cepa*, having a swollen bulb with many concentric layers and bearing greenish-white flowers. **2** the bulb of this, used for its pungent taste in cooking, pickling, etc. □ **know one's onions** be fully knowledgeable or experienced. □ **oniony** *adj.* [Middle English from Anglo-French *union*, Old French *oignon*, ultimately from Latin *unio -onis*]

onion dome *n.* a dome which bulges in the middle and rises to a point, used esp. in Russian church architecture.

onion-skin *n.* **1** the brown outermost skin or any outer skin of an onion. **2** thin smooth translucent paper.

on-line *adj.* & *adv. Computing* ● *adj.* (of equipment or a process) directly controlled by or connected to a central processor. ● *adv.* while thus controlled or connected.

onlooker /'ɒnlʊkə/ *n.* a non-participating observer; a spectator. □ **onlooking** *adj.*

only /'əʊnli/ *adv., adj., & conj.* ● *adv.* **1** solely, merely, exclusively; and no one or nothing more besides (*I only want to sit down*; *will only make matters worse*; *needed six only*; *is only a child*). **2** no longer ago than (*saw them only yesterday*). **3** not until (*arrives only on Tuesday*). **4** with no better result than (*hurried home only to find her gone*). ● *attrib.adj.* **1** existing alone of its or their kind (*their only son*). **2** best or alone worth knowing (*the only place to eat*). ● *conj. colloq.* **1** except that; but for the fact that (*I would go, only I feel ill*). **2** but then (as an extra consideration) (*he always makes promises, only he never keeps them*). □ **only too** extremely (*is only too willing*). [Old English *ānlic*, *ǣnlic*, Middle English *onliche* (as ONE, -LY[2])]

■ **Usage** In informal English *only* is usually placed between the subject and verb regardless of what it refers to (e.g. *I only want to talk to you*); in more formal English it is often placed more exactly, especially to avoid ambiguity (e.g. *I want to talk only to you*). In speech, intonation usually serves to clarify the sense.

only-begotten *adj. literary* begotten as the only child.

o.n.o. *abbr. Brit.* or near offer.

on-off *adj.* **1** (of a switch) having two positions, 'on' and 'off'. **2** = *on and off* (see ON).

onomastic /ɒnə'mastɪk/ *adj.* relating to names or nomenclature. [Greek *onomastikos* from *onoma* 'name']

onomastics /ɒnə'mastɪks/ *n.pl.* (treated as *sing.*) the study of the origin and formation of (esp. personal) proper names.

onomatopoeia /ˌɒnə(ʊ)matə'pi:ə/ *n.* **1** the formation of a word from a sound associated with what is named (e.g. *cuckoo*, *sizzle*). **2** the use of such words. □ **onomatopoeic** *adj.* **onomatopoeically** *adv.* [Late Latin from Greek *onomatopoiia* 'word-making', from *onoma -matos* 'name' + *poieō* 'make']

onrush /'ɒnrʌʃ/ *n.* an onward rush.

on-screen *adj.* & *adv.* ● *attrib.adj.* appearing on a cinema, television, or VDU screen. ● *adv.* **1** on or by means of a screen. **2** within the view presented by a cinema film scene.

onset /'ɒnsɛt/ *n.* **1** an attack. **2** a beginning, esp. an energetic or determined one.

on-set *attrib.adj.* taking place or occurring on the set of a play or film.

onshore *adj.* & *adv.* ● *adj.* /'ɒnʃɔ:/ **1** on the shore. **2** (of the wind) blowing from the sea towards the land. ● *adv.* /ɒn'ʃɔ:/ on or towards the land.

onside /ɒn'sʌɪd, 'ɒnsʌɪd/ *adj.* & *adv.* (of a player in a field game) in a lawful position; not offside.

on side see ON *n.*

on-site *attrib.adj.* taking place or available on a site or premises.

onslaught /'ɒnslɔ:t/ *n.* a fierce attack. [earlier *anslaight* from Middle Dutch *aenslag*, from *aen* 'on' + *slag* 'blow', with assimilation to obsolete *slaught* 'slaughter']

on-stage *attrib.adj.* on the stage; visible to the audience.

on-street *attrib.adj.* (with reference to parking vehicles) at the side of a street.

Ont. *abbr.* Ontario.

-ont /ɒnt/ *comb. form Biol.* denoting an individual of a specified type (*symbiont*). [Greek *ōn ont-* 'being', pres. part. of *eimi* 'be']

onto /'ɒntu:/ *prep. disp.* to a position or state on or in contact with (cf. *on to*).

■ **Usage** The form *onto* is still not fully accepted in the way that *into* is, although it is in wide use. It is however useful in distinguishing sense as between *We drove on to the beach* (i.e. in that direction) and *We drove onto the beach* (i.e. in contact with it).

ontogenesis /ɒntə(ʊ)'dʒɛnɪsɪs/ *n.* the origin and development of an individual (cf. PHYLOGENESIS). □ **ontogenetic** /-dʒɪ'nɛtɪk/ *adj.* **ontogenetically** /-dʒɪ'nɛtɪk(ə)li/ *adv.* [formed as ONTOGENY + Greek *genesis* 'birth']

ontogeny /ɒn'tɒdʒəni/ *n.* = ONTOGENESIS. □ **ontogenic** /-tə'dʒɛnɪk/ *adj.* **ontogenically** /-tə'dʒɛnɪk(ə)li/ *adv.* [Greek *ōn ont-* 'being' (see -ONT) + -GENY]

ontology /ɒn'tɒlədʒi/ *n.* the branch of metaphysics dealing with the nature of being. □ **ontological** /-tə'lɒdʒɪk(ə)l/ *adj.* **ontologically** /-tə'lɒdʒɪk(ə)li/ *adv.* **ontologist** *n.* [modern Latin *ontologia*, from Greek *ōn ont-* 'being' (see -ONT) + -LOGY]

onus /'əʊnəs/ *n.* (*pl.* **onuses**) a burden, duty, or responsibility. [Latin]

onward /'ɒnwəd/ *adv.* & *adj.* ● *adv.* (also **onwards**) **1** further on. **2** towards the front. **3** with advancing motion. **4** into the future (*from 1996 onward*). ● *adj.* directed onwards.

onychophoran /ɒnɪ'kɒf(ə)rən/ *n.* & *adj. Zool.* ● *n.* a soft-bodied arthropod of the class Onychophora, with a long body and stubby legs, sometimes regarded as intermediate between annelids and arthropods. ● *adj.* of or relating to this class. [Greek *onux onukh-* 'nail, claw' + *-phoros* 'bearing']

onyx /'ɒnɪks, 'əʊnɪks/ *n.* a semi-precious variety of agate with different colours in layers. [Middle English via Old French *oniche*, *onix* and Latin from Greek *onux* 'fingernail, onyx']

onyx marble *n.* banded calcite etc. used as a decorative material.

oo- /ˈəʊə/ *comb. form* egg, ovum. [Greek *ōion* ‘egg’]

oocyte /ˈəʊəsʌɪt/ *n.* an immature ovum in an ovary.

oodles /ˈu:d(ə)lz/ *n.pl. colloq.* a very great amount. [19th-c. US: origin unknown]

oof /u:f/ *n. slang* money, cash. [Yiddish *ooftisch*, German *auf dem Tische* ‘on the table’ (of money in gambling)]

oofy /ˈu:fi/ *adj. slang* rich, wealthy. □ **oofiness** *n.*

oogamous /əʊˈɒgəməs/ *adj.* esp. *Bot.* reproducing by the union of mobile male and immobile female cells. □ **oogamy** *n.*

oogenesis /əʊəˈdʒɛnɪsɪs/ *n.* the production or development of an ovum.

ooh /u:/ *int.* expressing surprise, delight, pain, etc. [a natural exclamation.]

oolite /ˈəʊəlʌɪt/ *n.* **1** a sedimentary rock, usu. limestone, consisting of rounded grains made up of concentric layers. **2** = OOLITH. □ **oolitic** /-ˈlɪtɪk/ *adj.* [French *oölithe* (as OO-, -LITE)]

oolith /ˈəʊəlɪθ/ *n.* any of the rounded grains making up oolite.

oology /əʊˈɒlədʒi/ *n.* the study or collecting of birds' eggs. □ **oological** /əʊəˈlɒdʒɪk(ə)l/ *adj.* **oologist** *n.*

oolong /ˈu:lɒŋ/ *n.* a dark kind of cured China tea. [Chinese *wulong* ‘black dragon’]

oomiak var. of UMIAK.

oompah /ˈu:mpɑ:/ *n. colloq.* the rhythmical sound of deep-toned brass instruments in a band. [imitative]

oomph /ʊmf, u:mf/ *n. slang* **1** energy, enthusiasm. **2** attractiveness, esp. sexual appeal. [20th c.: origin uncertain]

-oon /u:n/ *suffix* forming nouns, originally from French words in stressed *-on* (*balloon*; *buffoon*). [Latin *-o -onis*, sometimes via Italian *-one*]

■ **Usage** The suffix *-oon* has been replaced by *-on* in recent borrowings and those with unstressed *-on* (e.g. *baron*).

oophorectomy /ˌəʊəfəˈrɛktəmi/ *n.* (*pl.* **-ies**) *Med.* the surgical removal of one or both ovaries. [modern Latin *oophoron* ‘ovary’ (from Greek *ōophoros* ‘egg-bearing’) + -ECTOMY]

oops /u:ps, ʊps/ *int. colloq.* expressing surprise or apology, esp. on making an obvious mistake. [a natural exclamation]

oops-a-daisy var. of UPSY-DAISY.

Oort cloud /ɔ:t, ʊət/ *n. Astron.* a cloud of small rocky and icy bodies thought to orbit the sun beyond the orbit of Pluto, acting as a reservoir of comets. [named after J.H. *Oort*, Dutch astronomer d. 1992]

ooze[1] /u:z/ *v.* & *n.* ● *v.* **1** *intr.* (of fluid) pass slowly through the pores of a body. **2** *intr.* trickle or leak slowly out. **3** *intr.* (of a substance) exude moisture. **4** *tr.* exude or exhibit (a feeling) liberally (*oozed sympathy*). ● *n.* **1** a sluggish flow or exudation. **2** an infusion of oak-bark or other vegetable matter, used in tanning. □ **oozy** *adj.* [originally as noun (sense 2), from Old English *wōs* ‘juice, sap’]

ooze[2] /u:z/ *n.* **1** a deposit of wet mud or slime, esp. at the bottom of a river, lake, or sea. **2** a bog or marsh; soft muddy ground. □ **oozy** *adj.* [Old English *wāse*]

OP *abbr.* **1** *RC Ch. Ordo Praedicatorum* Order of Preachers (Dominican). **2** observation post. **3** opposite prompt.

op /ɒp/ *n. colloq.* operation (in surgical and military senses).

op. /ɒp/ *abbr.* **1** *Mus.* opus. **2** operator.

op- /ɒp/ *prefix* assim. form of OB- before *p*.

o.p. *abbr.* **1** out of print. **2** overproof.

opacify /ə(ʊ)ˈpasɪfʌɪ/ *v.tr.* & *intr.* (**-ies**, **-ied**) make or become opaque. □ **opacifier** *n.*

opacity /ə(ʊ)ˈpasɪti/ *n.* **1** the state or degree of being opaque. **2** obscurity of meaning. **3** obtuseness of understanding. [French *opacité* from Latin *opacitas -tatis* (as OPAQUE)]

opah /ˈəʊpə/ *n.* a large rare deep-sea fish, *Lampris guttatus*, usu. having a silver-blue back with white spots and crimson fins. Also called *moonfish*. [West African name]

opal /ˈəʊp(ə)l/ *n.* a quartzlike form of hydrated silica, usu. white or colourless and sometimes showing changing colours, often used as a gemstone. [French *opale* or Latin *opalus*, probably ultimately from Sanskrit *upalas* ‘precious stone’]

opalescent /əʊpəˈlɛs(ə)nt/ *adj.* showing changing colours like an opal. □ **opalesce** *v.intr.* **opalescence** *n.*

opal glass *n.* a semi-translucent white glass.

opaline /ˈəʊp(ə)lʌɪn, -lɪn/ *adj.* & *n.* ● *adj.* opal-like, opalescent, iridescent. ● *n.* opal glass.

opaque /ə(ʊ)ˈpeɪk/ *adj.* & *n.* ● *adj.* (**opaquer**, **opaquest**) **1** not transmitting light. **2** impenetrable to sight. **3** obscure; not lucid. **4** obtuse, dull-witted. ● *n.* **1** an opaque thing or substance. **2** a substance for producing opaque areas on negatives. □ **opaquely** *adv.* **opaqueness** *n.* [Middle English *opak* from Latin *opacus*: spelling now assimilated to French]

op art /ɒp/ *n.* a form of abstract art that gives the illusion of movement by the precise use of pattern and colour. [abbreviation of OPTICAL ART, after POP ART]

op. cit. /ɒp ˈsɪt/ *abbr.* in the work already quoted. [Latin *opere citato*]

OPEC /ˈəʊpɛk/ *abbr.* Organization of Petroleum Exporting Countries.

open /ˈəʊp(ə)n/ *adj.*, *v.*, & *n.* ● *adj.* **1** not closed or locked or blocked up; allowing entrance or passage or access. **2 a** (of a room, field, or other area) having its door or gate in a position allowing access, or part of its confining boundary removed. **b** (of a container) not fastened or sealed; in a position or with the lid etc. in a position allowing access to the inside part. **3** unenclosed, unconfined, unobstructed (*the open road*; *open views*). **4 a** uncovered, bare, exposed (*open drain*; *open wound*). **b** *Sport* (of a goalmouth or other object of attack) unprotected, vulnerable. **5** undisguised, public, manifest; not exclusive or limited (*open scandal*; *open hostilities*). **6** expanded, unfolded, or spread out (*had the map open on the table*). **7** (of a fabric) not close; with gaps or intervals. **8 a** (of a person) frank and communicative. **b** (of the mind) accessible to new ideas; unprejudiced or undecided. **9 a** (of an exhibition, shop, etc.) accessible to visitors or customers; ready for business. **b** (of a meeting) admitting all, not restricted to members etc. **10** (also **Open**) **a** (of a race, competition, scholarship, etc.) unrestricted as to who may compete. **b** (of a champion, scholar, etc.) having won such a contest. **11** (of government) conducted in an informative manner receptive to enquiry, criticism, etc., from the public. **12** (foll. by *to*) **a** willing to receive (*is open to offers*). **b** (of a choice, offer, or opportunity) still available (*there are three courses open to us*). **c** likely to suffer from or be affected by (*open to abuse*). **13 a** (of the mouth) with lips apart, esp. in surprise or incomprehension. **b** (of the ears or eyes) eagerly attentive. **14** *Mus.* **a** (of a string) allowed to vibrate along its whole length. **b** (of a pipe) unstopped at each end. **c** (of a note) sounded from an open string or pipe. **15** (of an electrical circuit) having a break in the conducting path. **16** (of the bowels) not constipated. **17** (of a return ticket) not restricted as to day of travel. **18** *Brit.* (of a cheque) not crossed. **19** (of a boat) without a deck. **20** (of a river or harbour) free of ice. **21** (of the weather or winter) free of frost. **22 a** (of a vowel) produced with a relatively wide opening of the mouth keeping the tongue low. **b** (of a syllable) ending in a vowel. **23** (of a town, city, etc.) not defended even if attacked. ● *v.* **1** *tr.* & *intr.* make or become open or more open. **2 a** *tr.* change from a closed or fastened position so as to allow access (*opened the door*; *opened the box*). **b** *intr.* (of a door, lid, etc.) have its position changed to allow access (*the door opened slowly*). **3** *tr.* remove the sealing or fastening element of (a container) to get access to the contents (*opened the envelope*). **4** *intr.* (foll. by *into*, *on to*, etc.) (of a door, room, etc.) afford access as specified (*opened on to a large garden*).

5 a *tr.* start or establish or set going (a business, activity, etc.). **b** *intr.* be initiated; make a start (*the session opens tomorrow; the story opens with a murder*). **c** *tr.* (of a counsel in a law court) make a preliminary statement in (a case) before calling witnesses. **6** *tr.* **a** spread out or unfold (a map, newspaper, etc.). **b** (often *absol.*) find and refer to (the contents of a book (*open at the first soliloquy*). **7** *intr.* (often foll. by *with*) (of a person) begin speaking, writing, etc. (*he opened with a warning*). **8** *intr.* (of a prospect) come into view; be revealed. **9** *tr.* reveal or communicate (one's feelings, intentions, etc.). **10** *tr.* make (one's mind, heart, etc.) more sympathetic or enlightened. **11** *tr.* ceremonially declare (a building etc.) to be completed and in use. **12** *tr.* break up (ground) with a plough etc. **13** *tr.* cause evacuation of (the bowels). **14** *Naut.* **a** *tr.* get a view of by change of position. **b** *intr.* come into full view. ● *n.* **1** (prec. by *the*) **a** open space or country or air. **b** public notice or view; general attention (esp. *into the open*). **2** (**Open**) an open championship, competition, or scholarship. □ **be open with** speak frankly to. **open-and-shut** (of an argument, case, etc.) straightforward and conclusive. **open the door to** see DOOR. **open a person's eyes** see EYE. **open out 1** unfold; spread out. **2** develop, expand. **3** esp. *Brit.* become communicative. **4** accelerate. **open up 1** unlock (premises). **2** make accessible. **3** reveal; bring to notice. **4** accelerate esp. a motor vehicle. **5** begin shooting or sounding. **6** talk or speak openly. **with open arms** see ARM[1]. □ **openable** *adj.* **openness** /ˈəʊp(ə)nnɪs/ *n.* [Old English *open*, from Germanic]

open air *n.* & *adj.* ● *n.* (usu. prec. by *the*) a free or unenclosed space outdoors. ● *attrib.adj.* (**open-air**) out of doors.

open-armed *adj.* cordial; warmly receptive.

open book *n.* a person who is easily understood.

opencast /ˈəʊp(ə)nkɑːst/ *adj. Brit.* (of a mine or mining) with removal of the surface layers and working from above, not from shafts.

open college *n.* an adult-education college offering training and vocational courses mainly by correspondence.

open day *n.* a day when the public may visit a place normally closed to them.

open door *n.* & *adj.* ● *n.* free admission of foreign trade and immigrants. ● *attrib.adj.* (**open-door**) open, accessible, public.

open-ended *adj.* having no predetermined limit or boundary.

opener /ˈəʊp(ə)nə/ *n.* **1** a device for opening tins, bottles, etc. **2** *colloq.* the first item on a programme etc. **3** *Cricket* an opening batsman. **4** *Cards* the player who opens the betting or bidding. □ **for openers** *colloq.* to start with.

open-eyed *adj.* **1** with the eyes open. **2** alert, watchful.

open-faced *adj.* having a frank or ingenuous expression.

open-handed *adj.* generous. □ **open-handedly** *adv.* **open-handedness** *n.*

open-hearted *adj.* frank and kindly. □ **open-heartedness** *n.*

open-hearth process *n.* a process of steel manufacture, using a shallow reverberatory furnace.

open-heart surgery *n.* surgery with the heart exposed and the blood made to bypass it.

open house *n.* **1** welcome or hospitality for all visitors. **2** *N. Amer.* = OPEN DAY.

open ice *n.* ice through which navigation is possible.

opening /ˈəʊp(ə)nɪŋ/ *n.* & *adj.* ● *n.* **1** an aperture or gap, esp. allowing access. **2** a favourable situation or opportunity. **3** a beginning; an initial part. **4** *Chess* a recognized sequence of moves at the beginning of a game. **5** a counsel's preliminary statement of a case in a law court. ● *adj.* initial, first.

opening time *n. Brit.* the time at which public houses may legally open for custom.

open letter *n.* a letter, esp. of protest, addressed to an individual and published in a newspaper or journal.

openly /ˈəʊp(ə)nli/ *adv.* **1** frankly, honestly. **2** publicly; without concealment. [Old English *openlīce* (as OPEN, -LY[2])]

open market *n.* an unrestricted market with free competition of buyers and sellers.

open-minded *adj.* accessible to new ideas; unprejudiced. □ **open-mindedly** *adv.* **open-mindedness** *n.*

open-mouthed *adv.* & *adj.* with the mouth open, esp. in surprise.

open-plan *adj.* (of a house, office, etc.) having large undivided rooms.

open prison *n.* a prison with the minimum of physical restraints on prisoners.

open question *n.* a matter on which differences of opinion are legitimate.

open-reel *adj.* (of a tape recorder) having reels of tape requiring individual threading, as distinct from a cassette.

open sandwich *n.* a sandwich without a top slice of bread.

open sea *n.* an expanse of sea away from land.

open season *n.* **1** the season when restrictions on the killing of game etc. are lifted. **2** (often foll. by *on*) a time of no restrictions or restraint (*appears to be open season on union-bashing*).

open secret *n.* a supposed secret that is known to many people.

open sesame see SESAME.

open shop *n.* **1** a business etc. where employees do not have to be members of a trade union (opp. CLOSED SHOP). **2** this system.

open-side *attrib.adj. Rugby* of or relating to the side of the scrum on which the main line of the backs is ranged.

open society *n.* a society with wide dissemination of information and freedom of belief.

open-top *adj.* (also **open-topped**) (of a bus, sports car, etc.) not having a fixed top.

Open University *n.* (in the UK) a university that teaches mainly by broadcasting and correspondence, and is open to those without formal academic qualifications.

open verdict *n.* a verdict affirming that a crime has been committed but not specifying the criminal or (in case of violent death) the cause.

openwork /ˈəʊp(ə)nwəːk/ *n.* a pattern with intervening spaces in metal, leather, lace, etc.

opera[1] /ˈɒp(ə)rə/ *n.* **1 a** a dramatic work in one or more acts, set to music for singers (usu. in costume) and instrumentalists. **b** works of this kind as a genre. **2** a building for the performance of opera. [Italian from Latin, = labour, work]

opera[2] *pl.* of OPUS.

operable /ˈɒp(ə)rəb(ə)l/ *adj.* **1** that can be operated. **2** suitable for treatment by surgical operation. □ **operability** /-ˈbɪlɪti/ *n.* [Late Latin *operabilis* from Latin (as OPERATE)]

opera buffa /ɒp(ə)rə ˈbuːfə/ *n.* (esp. Italian) comic opera, esp. with characters drawn from everyday life. [Italian]

opéra comique /ˌɒp(ə)rə kɒˈmiːk, French ɔpera kɔmik/ *n.* (esp. French) opera on a light-hearted theme, with spoken dialogue. [French, = comic opera]

opera glasses *n.pl.* small binoculars for use at the opera or theatre.

opera hat *n.* a man's tall collapsible hat.

opera house *n.* a theatre for the performance of opera.

operand /ˈɒpərand/ *n. Math.* the quantity etc. on which an operation is to be done. [Latin *operandum*, neut. gerundive of *operari*: see OPERATE]

opera seria /ɒp(ə)rə ˈsɪərɪə/ *n.* (esp. 18th-c. Italian) opera on a serious, usu. classical or mythological theme. [Italian, = serious opera]

operate /ˈɒpəreɪt/ *v.* **1** *tr.* manage, work, control; put or keep in a functional state. **2** *intr.* be in action; function. **3** *intr.* produce an effect; exercise influence (*the tax operates to our disadvantage*). **4** *intr.* (often foll. by *on*) **a** perform a surgical operation. **b** conduct a military or naval action. **c** be active in business etc., esp. dealing in stocks and shares. **5** *intr.* (foll. by *on*) influence or affect (feelings etc.). **6** *tr.* bring about; accomplish. [Latin *operari* 'to work' from *opus operis* 'work']

operatic /ɒpəˈratɪk/ *adj.* **1** of or relating to opera. **2** resembling or characteristic of opera. □ **operatically** *adv.* [formed irregularly from OPERA[1], on the pattern of *dramatic*]

operatics /ɒpəˈratɪks/ *n.pl.* **1** (often treated as *sing.*) the production and performance of operas. **2** = DRAMATICS 2.

operating system *n.* the basic software that enables the running of a computer program.

operating table *n.* a table on which surgical operations are performed.

operating theatre *n.* (*N. Amer.* **operating room**) a room for surgical operations.

operation /ɒpəˈreɪʃ(ə)n/ *n.* **1 a** the action or process or method of working or operating. **b** the state of being active or functioning (*not yet in operation*). **c** the scope or range of effectiveness of a thing's activity. **2** an active process; a discharge of a function (*the operation of breathing*). **3** a piece of work, esp. one in a series (often in *pl.*: *begin operations*). **4** an act of surgery performed on a patient. **5 a** a strategic movement of troops, ships, etc. for military action. **b** preceding a code name (*Operation Overlord*). **6** a financial transaction. **7** *Math.* the subjection of a number or quantity or function to a process affecting its value or form, e.g. multiplication, differentiation. [Middle English via Old French from Latin *operatio -onis* (as OPERATE)]

operational /ɒpəˈreɪʃ(ə)n(ə)l/ *adj.* **1 a** of or used for operations. **b** engaged or involved in operations. **2** able or ready to function. □ **operationally** *adv.*

operationalize /ɒpəˈreɪʃ(ə)n(ə)lʌɪz/ *v.tr.* (also **-ise**) express in operational terms.

operational research *n.* (also **operations research**) the application of scientific principles to business management, providing a quantitative basis for complex decisions.

operative /ˈɒp(ə)rətɪv/ *adj.* & *n.* ● *adj.* **1** in operation; having effect. **2** having the principal relevance (*'may' is the operative word*). **3** of or by surgery. **4** *Law* expressing an intent to perform a transaction. ● *n.* **1** a worker, esp. a skilled one. **2** *US* a private detective or secret agent. □ **operatively** *adv.* **operativeness** *n.* [Late Latin *operativus* from Latin (as OPERATE)]

operator /ˈɒpəreɪtə/ *n.* **1** a person operating a machine etc., esp. making connections of lines in a telephone exchange. **2** a person operating or engaging in business. **3** *colloq.* a person acting in a specified way (*a smooth operator*). **4** *Math.* a symbol or function denoting an operation (e.g. ×, +). [Late Latin from Latin *operari* (as OPERATE)]

operculum /ə(ʊ)ˈpəːkjʊləm/ *n.* (*pl.* **opercula** /-lə/) **1** *Zool.* **a** a flaplike structure covering the gills in a fish. **b** a platelike structure closing the aperture of a gastropod mollusc's shell when the organism is retracted. **c** any of various other parts covering or closing an aperture, such as a flap over the nostrils in some birds. **2** *Bot.* a lidlike structure of the spore-containing capsule of mosses. □ **opercular** *adj.* **operculate** /-lət/ *adj.* **operculi-** *comb. form.* [Latin from *operire* 'cover']

operetta /ɒpəˈrɛtə/ *n.* **1** a one-act or short opera. **2** a light opera. [Italian, diminutive of *opera*: see OPERA[1]]

operon /ˈɒpərɒn/ *n. Biol.* a unit made up of linked genes thought to regulate other genes responsible for protein synthesis. [from French *opérer* 'effect, work' + -ON]

ophicleide /ˈɒfɪklʌɪd/ *n.* **1** an obsolete usu. bass brass wind instrument with keys, developed from the serpent. **2** a powerful organ reed-stop. [French *ophicléide*, from Greek *ophis* 'serpent' + *kleis kleidos* 'key']

ophidian /ɒˈfɪdɪən/ *n.* & *adj.* ● *n.* a reptile of the suborder Serpentes (formerly Ophidia), comprising snakes. ● *adj.* **1** of or relating to this suborder. **2** snakelike. [modern Latin *Ophidia* from Greek *ophis* 'snake']

ophio- /ˈɒfɪəʊ/ *comb. form* snake. [Greek *ophis* 'snake']

ophthalmia /ɒfˈθalmɪə/ *n.* inflammation of the eye, esp. conjunctivitis. [Late Latin from Greek, from *ophthalmos* 'eye']

ophthalmic /ɒfˈθalmɪk/ *adj.* of or relating to the eye and its diseases. [Latin *ophthalmicus* from Greek *ophthalmikos* (as OPHTHALMIA)]

ophthalmic optician *n. Brit.* an optician qualified to prescribe and dispense spectacles and contact lenses and to detect eye diseases.

ophthalmo- /ɒfˈθalməʊ/ *comb. form Optics* denoting the eye. [Greek *ophthalmos* 'eye']

ophthalmology /ɒfθalˈmɒlədʒi/ *n.* the scientific study of the eye. □ **ophthalmological** /-məˈlɒdʒɪk(ə)l/ *adj.* **ophthalmologist** *n.*

ophthalmoscope /ɒfˈθalməskəʊp/ *n.* an instrument for inspecting the retina and other parts of the eye. □ **ophthalmoscopic** /-ˈskɒpɪk/ *adj.*

-opia /ˈəʊpɪə/ *comb. form* denoting a visual disorder (*myopia*). [Greek from *ōps* 'eye']

opiate *adj.*, *n.*, & *v.* ● *adj.* /ˈəʊpɪət/ **1** containing, derived from, or resembling opium. **2** narcotic, soporific. ● *n.* /ˈəʊpɪət/ **1** a drug containing, derived from, or resembling opium, usu. to ease pain or induce sleep. **2** a thing which soothes or stupefies. ● *v.tr.* /ˈəʊpɪeɪt/ **1** mix with opium. **2** stupefy. [medieval Latin *opiatus*, *-um*, *opiare* from Latin *opium*: see OPIUM]

opine /ə(ʊ)ˈpʌɪn/ *v.tr.* (often foll. by *that* + clause) hold or express as an opinion. [Latin *opinari* 'think, believe']

opinion /əˈpɪnjən/ *n.* **1** a belief or assessment based on grounds short of proof. **2** a view held as probable. **3** (often foll. by *on*) what one thinks about a particular topic or question (*my opinion on capital punishment*). **4 a** a formal statement of professional advice (*will get a second opinion*). **b** *Law* a formal statement of reasons for a judgement given. **5** an estimation (*had a low opinion of it*). □ **be of the opinion that** believe or maintain that. **in one's opinion** according to one's view or belief. **a matter of opinion** a disputable point. [Middle English via Old French from Latin *opinio -onis* (as OPINE)]

opinionated /əˈpɪnjəneɪtɪd/ *adj.* conceitedly assertive or dogmatic in one's opinions. [obsolete *opinionate* (in the same sense) from OPINION]

opinion poll *n.* = GALLUP POLL.

opioid /ˈəʊpɪɔɪd/ *n.* & *adj. Pharm.* & *Biochem.* ● *n.* any compound resembling cocaine and morphine in its addictive properties or physiological effects. ● *adj.* of or relating to such a compound. [OPIUM + -OID]

opium /ˈəʊpɪəm/ *n.* **1** a reddish-brown heavy-scented addictive drug prepared from the juice of the opium poppy, used in medicine as an analgesic and narcotic. **2** anything regarded as soothing or stupefying. [Middle English via Latin from Greek *opion* 'poppy-juice', from *opos* 'juice']

opium den *n.* a haunt of opium-smokers.

opium poppy *n.* a poppy, *Papaver somniferum*, native to Europe and E. Asia, with white, red, pink, or purple flowers.

opopanax /ə(ʊ)ˈpɒpənaks/ *n.* **1 a** an umbelliferous plant, *Opopanax chironium*, with yellow flowers. **b** a fetid gum resin obtained from the roots of this plant. **2 a** a gum resin obtained from the tree *Commiphora kataf*. **b** a perfume made from this. **3** = SPONGE TREE. [Middle English via Latin from Greek, from *opos* 'juice' + *panax*, formed as PANACEA]

opossum /əˈpɒs(ə)m/ *n.* **1** any mainly tree-living marsupial of the family Didelphidae, native to America, having a prehensile tail and hind feet with an opposable thumb. **2** *Austral.* = POSSUM 2. [Virginian Indian *āpassūm*]

opp. *abbr.* opposite.

oppo /'ɒpəʊ/ *n.* (*pl.* **-os**) *Brit. colloq.* a colleague or friend. [abbreviation of *opposite number*]

opponent /ə'pəʊnənt/ *n.* & *adj.* ● *n.* a person who opposes, or who belongs to an opposing side. ● *adj.* opposing, contrary, opposed. ▫ **opponency** *n.* [Latin *opponere opponent-* (as OB-, *ponere* 'place')]

opponent muscle *n.* a muscle enabling the thumb to be placed front to front against a finger of the same hand.

opportune /'ɒpətju:n, ɒpə'tju:n/ *adj.* **1** (of a time) well chosen or especially favourable or appropriate (*an opportune moment*). **2** (of an action or event) well timed; done or occurring at a favourable or useful time. ▫ **opportunely** *adv.* **opportuneness** *n.* [Middle English via Old French *opportun -une* from Latin *opportunus* (as OB-, *portus* 'harbour'), originally of the wind driving towards the harbour]

opportunism /ɒpə'tju:nɪz(ə)m, 'ɒpətju:n-/ *n.* **1** the adaptation of policy or judgement to circumstances or opportunity, esp. regardless of principle. **2** the seizing of opportunities when they occur. ▫ **opportunist** *n.* & *adj.* [OPPORTUNE, suggested by Italian *opportunismo* and French *opportunisme* used in political senses]

opportunistic /ɒpətju:'nɪstɪk/ *adj.* **1** of or relating to opportunism. **2** *Ecol.* (of a species) able to spread quickly in a previously unexploited habitat. **3** *Med.* **a** (of a micro-organism) rarely causing disease except in unusual circumstances, e.g. in patients with depressed immune systems. **b** (of an infection) caused by such a micro-organism. ▫ **opportunistically** /-'nɪstɪk(ə)li/ *adv.*

opportunity /ɒpə'tju:nɪti/ *n.* (*pl.* **-ies**) **1** a good chance; a favourable occasion. **2** a chance or opening offered by circumstances. **3** good fortune. ▫ **opportunity knocks** an opportunity occurs. [Middle English via Old French *opportunité* from Latin *opportunitas -tatis* (as OPPORTUNE)]

opposable /ə'pəʊzəb(ə)l/ *adj.* **1** able to be opposed. **2** *Zool.* (of the thumb in primates) capable of facing and touching the other digits on the same hand.

oppose /ə'pəʊz/ *v.tr.* (often *absol.*) **1** set oneself against; resist, argue against. **2** be hostile to. **3** take part in a game, sport, etc., against (another competitor or team). **4** (foll. by *to*) place in opposition or contrast. ▫ **as opposed to** in contrast with. ▫ **opposer** *n.* [Middle English via Old French *opposer* from Latin *opponere*: see OPPONENT]

opposite /'ɒpəzɪt, -sɪt/ *adj.*, *n.*, *adv.*, & *prep.* ● *adj.* **1** (often foll. by *to*) having a position on the other or further side, facing or back to back. **2** (often foll. by *to*, *from*) **a** of a contrary kind; diametrically different. **b** being the other of a contrasted pair. **3** (of angles) between opposite sides of the intersection of two lines. **4** *Bot.* (of leaves etc.) placed at the same height on the opposite sides of the stem, or placed straight in front of another organ. ● *n.* an opposite thing or person or term. ● *adv.* in an opposite position (*the tree stands opposite*). ● *prep.* **1** in a position opposite to (*opposite the house is a tree*). **2** (of a leading theatrical etc. part) in a complementary role to (another performer). ▫ **oppositely** *adv.* **oppositeness** *n.* [Middle English via Old French from Latin *oppositus*, past part. of *opponere*: see OPPONENT]

opposite number *n.* a person holding an equivalent position in another group or organization.

opposite prompt *n. Brit.* the side of a theatre stage usually to an actor's right.

opposite sex *n.* (prec. by *the*) the female sex (or women) in relation to the male sex (or men), or vice versa.

opposition /ɒpə'zɪʃ(ə)n/ *n.* **1** resistance, antagonism. **2** the state of being hostile or in conflict or disagreement. **3** contrast or antithesis. **4 a** a group or party of opponents or competitors. **b** (**the Opposition**) *Brit.* the principal parliamentary party opposed to that in office. **5** the act of opposing or placing opposite. **6 a** diametrically opposite position. **b** *Astrol.* & *Astron.* the position of two celestial bodies when their longitude differs by 180°, as seen from the earth. ▫ **oppositional** *adj.* [Middle English via Old French from Latin *oppositio* (as OB-, POSITION)]

oppress /ə'prɛs/ *v.tr.* **1** keep in subservience by coercion. **2** govern or treat harshly or with cruel injustice. **3** weigh down (with cares or unhappiness). ▫ **oppressor** *n.* [Middle English via Old French *oppresser* from medieval Latin *oppressare* (as OB-, PRESS[1])]

oppression /ə'prɛʃ(ə)n/ *n.* **1** the act or an instance of oppressing; the state of being oppressed. **2** prolonged harsh or cruel treatment or control. **3** mental distress. [Old French from Latin *oppressio* (as OPPRESS)]

oppressive /ə'prɛsɪv/ *adj.* **1** oppressing; harsh or cruel. **2** difficult to endure. **3** (of weather) close and sultry. ▫ **oppressively** *adv.* **oppressiveness** *n.* [French *oppressif -ive* from medieval Latin *oppressivus* (as OPPRESS)]

opprobrious /ə'prəʊbrɪəs/ *adj.* (of language) severely scornful; abusive. ▫ **opprobriously** *adv.* [Middle English from Late Latin *opprobriosus* (as OPPROBRIUM)]

opprobrium /ə'prəʊbrɪəm/ *n.* **1** disgrace or bad reputation attaching to some act or conduct. **2** a cause of this. [Latin from *opprobrum* (as OB-, *probrum* 'disgraceful act')]

oppugn /ə'pju:n/ *v.tr. literary* call into question; controvert. ▫ **oppugner** *n.* [Middle English from Latin *oppugnare* 'attack, besiege' (as OB-, Latin *pugnare* 'fight')]

oppugnant /ə'pʌgnənt/ *adj. literary* antagonistic; opposing. ▫ **oppugnance** *n.* **oppugnancy** *n.* **oppugnation** /-'neɪʃ(ə)n/ *n.*

opsimath /'ɒpsɪmaθ/ *n. literary* a person who learns only late in life. ▫ **opsimathy** /-'sɪməθi/ *n.* [Greek *opsimathēs*, from *opse* 'late' + *math-* 'learn']

opsonin /'ɒpsənɪn/ *n. Biol.* & *Med.* a substance, esp. an antibody, which binds to foreign micro-organisms etc., making them more susceptible to phagocytosis. ▫ **opsonic** /ɒp'sɒnɪk/ *adj.* [Greek *opsōnion* 'victuals' + -IN]

opt /ɒpt/ *v.intr.* (usu. foll. by *for*, *between*) exercise an option; make a choice. ▫ **opt out** (often foll. by *of*) **1** choose not to participate (*opted out of the race*). **2** (in the UK) (of a school or hospital) decide to withdraw from local authority control. [French *opter* from Latin *optare* 'choose, wish']

optative /'ɒptətɪv, ɒp'teɪtɪv/ *adj.* & *n. Gram.* ● *adj.* expressing a wish. ● *n.* the optative mood. ▫ **optatively** *adv.* [French *optatif -ive* from Late Latin *optativus* (as OPT)]

optative mood *n.* a set of verb forms expressing a wish etc., distinct esp. in Sanskrit and Greek.

optic /'ɒptɪk/ *adj.* & *n.* ● *adj.* of or relating to the eye or vision (*optic nerve*). ● *n.* **1** a lens etc. in an optical instrument. **2** *archaic* or *joc.* the eye. **3** *Brit. propr.* a device fastened to the neck of an inverted bottle for measuring out spirits etc. [French *optique* or medieval Latin *opticus* from Greek *optikos*, from *optos* 'seen']

optical /'ɒptɪk(ə)l/ *adj.* **1** of sight; visual. **2 a** of or concerning sight or light in relation to each other. **b** belonging to optics. **3** (esp. of a lens) constructed to assist sight or on the principles of optics. ▫ **optically** *adv.*

optical activity *n. Chem.* the property of rotating the plane of polarization of plane-polarized light.

optical art *n. formal* = OP ART.

optical brightener *n.* any fluorescent substance used to produce a whitening effect on laundry.

optical character recognition *n.* the identification of printed characters using photoelectric devices.

optical disc see DISC 4b.

optical fibre *n.* thin glass fibre through which light can be transmitted.

optical glass *n.* a very pure kind of glass used for lenses etc.

optical illusion *n.* **1** a thing having an appearance so resembling something else as to deceive the eye. **2** an instance of mental misapprehension caused by this.

optical isomer *n. Chem.* each of two or more forms of a chemical substance which have the same structure but a different spatial arrangement of atoms, and so usu. differ in optical activity. □ **optical isomerism** *n.*

optical microscope *n.* a microscope using the direct perception of light (cf. ELECTRON MICROSCOPE).

optic angle *n.* the angle formed by notional lines from the extremities of an object to the eye, or by lines from the eyes to a given point.

optic axis *n.* **1** a line passing through the centre of curvature of a lens or spherical mirror and parallel to the axis of symmetry. **2** the direction in a doubly refracting crystal for which no double refraction occurs.

optician /ɒpˈtɪʃ(ə)n/ *n.* **1** a maker or seller of optical instruments. **2** (in full **dispensing optician**) a person qualified to make and supply spectacles and contact lenses. **3** = OPHTHALMIC OPTICIAN. [French *opticien* from medieval Latin *optica* (as OPTIC)]

optic lobe *n.* the dorsal lobe in the brain from which the optic nerve arises.

optic nerve *n.* each of the second pair of cranial nerves, transmitting impulses to the brain from the retina at the back of the eye.

optics /ˈɒptɪks/ *n.pl.* (treated as *sing.*) the scientific study of sight and the behaviour of light, or of other radiation or particles (*electron optics*).

optima *pl.* of OPTIMUM.

optimal /ˈɒptɪm(ə)l/ *adj.* best or most favourable, esp. under a particular set of circumstances. □ **optimally** *adv.* [Latin *optimus* 'best']

optimism /ˈɒptɪmɪz(ə)m/ *n.* **1** an inclination to hopefulness and confidence. **2** *Philos.* **a** the doctrine, esp. as set forth by Leibniz, that this world is the best of all possible worlds. **b** the theory that good must ultimately prevail over evil in the universe. Opp. PESSIMISM. □ **optimist** *n.* **optimistic** /-ˈmɪstɪk/ *adj.* **optimistically** /-ˈmɪstɪk(ə)li/ *adv.* [French *optimisme* from Latin OPTIMUM]

optimize /ˈɒptɪmʌɪz/ *v.* (also **-ise**) **1** *tr.* make the best or most effective use of (a situation, an opportunity, etc.). **2** *intr.* be an optimist. □ **optimization** /-ˈzeɪʃ(ə)n/ *n.* [Latin *optimus* 'best']

optimum /ˈɒptɪməm/ *n. & adj.* ● *n.* (*pl.* **optima** /-mə/ or **optimums**) **1 a** the most favourable conditions (for growth, reproduction, etc.). **b** the best or most favourable situation. **2** the best possible compromise between opposing tendencies. ● *adj.* = OPTIMAL. [Latin, neut. of *optimus* 'best' used as a noun]

option /ˈɒpʃ(ə)n/ *n.* **1 a** the act or an instance of choosing; a choice. **b** a thing that is or may be chosen (*those are the options*). **2** the liberty of choosing; freedom of choice. **3** *Stock Exch.* etc. the right, obtained by, or as, payment, to buy, sell, etc. specified stocks etc. at a specified price within a set time. □ **have no option but to** must. **keep** (or **leave**) **one's options open** not commit oneself. [French, or from Latin *optio*, stem of *optare* 'choose']

optional /ˈɒpʃ(ə)n(ə)l/ *adj.* being an option only; not obligatory. □ **optionality** /-ˈnalɪti/ *n.* **optionally** *adv.*

optional extra *n.* an accessory or other additional item which is available for purchase.

optoelectronics /ˌɒptəʊɪlɛkˈtrɒnɪks, -ɛl-/ *n.* the branch of technology concerned with the combined use of electronics and light. □ **optoelectronic** *adj.*

optometer /ɒpˈtɒmɪtə/ *n.* an instrument for testing the refractive power of the eye. [Greek *optos* 'seen' + -METER]

optometrist /ɒpˈtɒmɪtrɪst/ *n.* esp. *US* a person who practises optometry, an ophthalmic optician.

optometry /ɒpˈtɒmɪtri/ *n.* the occupation of measuring eyesight, prescribing corrective lenses, detecting eye disease, etc. □ **optometric** /ɒptəˈmɛtrɪk/ *adj.*

optophone /ˈɒptəfəʊn/ *n.* an instrument converting light into sound, and so enabling the blind to read print etc. by ear. [Greek *optos* 'seen' + -PHONE]

opt-out *n.* **1** the action of opting out of something, esp. of a school or hospital opting out of local-authority control. **2** an instance of this.

opulent /ˈɒpjʊl(ə)nt/ *adj.* **1** ostentatiously rich; wealthy. **2** luxurious (*opulent surroundings*). **3** abundant; profuse. □ **opulence** *n.* **opulently** *adv.* [Latin *opulens*, *opulent-* from *opes* 'wealth']

opuntia /ɒˈpʌnʃɪə, ə(ʊ)-/ *n.* = PRICKLY PEAR 1. [Latin plant-name from *Opus -untis*, the name of a city in Locris in ancient Greece]

opus /ˈəʊpəs, ˈɒp-/ *n.* (*pl.* **opuses** or **opera** /ˈɒp(ə)rə/) **1** *Mus.* **a** a separate musical composition or set of compositions of any kind. **b** (also **op.**) used before a number given to a composer's work, usu. indicating the order of publication (*Beethoven, op. 15*). **2** any artistic work (cf. MAGNUM OPUS). [Latin, = work]

opuscule /əˈpʌskjuːl/ *n.* (also **opusculum** /əˈpʌskjʊləm/) (*pl.* **opuscules** or **opuscula** /-lə/) a minor (esp. musical or literary) work. [French from Latin *opusculum*, diminutive of OPUS]

opus Dei /ɒpəs ˈdeɪiː/ *n. Eccl.* **1** liturgical worship regarded as man's primary duty to God. **2** (**Opus Dei**) a Roman Catholic organization of laymen and priests founded in Spain in 1928 with the aim of re-establishing Christian ideals in society. [medieval Latin, = work of God]

OR *abbr.* **1** operational research. **2** *US* Oregon (in official postal use). **3** *Brit.* other ranks (as opposed to commissioned officers).

or[1] /ɔː/ *conj.* **1 a** introducing the second of two alternatives (*white or black*). **b** introducing all but the first, or only the last, of any number of alternatives (*white or grey or black*; *white, grey, or black*). **2** (often prec. by *either*) introducing the only remaining possibility or choice given (*take it or leave it*; *either come in or go out*). **3** (prec. by *whether*) introducing the second part of an indirect question or conditional clause (*ask him whether he was there or not*; *must go whether I like or dislike the prospect*). **4** introducing a synonym or explanation of a preceding word etc. (*suffered from vertigo or giddiness*). **5** introducing a significant afterthought (*he must know — or is he bluffing?*). **6** = *or else* (*run or you'll be late*). **7** *poet.* each of two; either (*or in the heart or in the head*). □ **not A or B** not A, and also not B. **one or two** (or **two or three** etc.) *colloq.* a few. **or else 1** otherwise (*do it now, or else you will have to do it tomorrow*). **2** *colloq.* expressing a warning or threat (*hand over the money or else*). **or rather** introducing a rephrasing or qualification of a preceding statement etc. (*he was there, or rather I heard that he was*). **or so** (after a quantity or a number) or thereabouts (*send me ten or so*). [reduced form of obsolete conj. *other* (which superseded Old English *oththe* 'or'), of uncertain origin]

or[2] /ɔː/ *n. & adj. Heraldry* ● *n.* a gold or yellow colour. ● *adj.* (usu. following noun) gold or yellow (*a crescent or*). [French, from Latin *aurum* 'gold']

-or[1] /ə, ɔː/ *suffix* forming nouns denoting a person or thing performing the action of a verb, or an agent more generally (*actor*; *escalator*; *tailor*; *guarantor*) (see also -ATOR, -ITOR). [Latin *-or*, *-ator*, etc., sometimes via Anglo-French *-eour*, Old French *-ëor*, *-ëur*]

-or[2] /ə/ *suffix* forming nouns denoting state or condition (*error*; *horror*). [Latin *-or -oris*, sometimes via (or suggested by) Old French *-or*, *-ur*]

-or[3] /ə/ *suffix* forming adjectives with comparative sense (*major*; *senior*). [Anglo-French *-our* from Latin *-or*]

-or[4] /ə/ *suffix US* = -OUR[1].

orache /ˈɒrətʃ/ *n.* (also **orach**) an edible plant, *Atriplex hortensis*, with red, yellow, or green leaves sometimes used as a substitute for spinach or sorrel. Also called *saltbush.* [Middle English *arage* via Anglo-French *arasche* and Latin *atriplex* from Greek *atraphaxus*]

oracle /ˈɒrək(ə)l/ *n.* **1 a** a place at which advice or prophecy was sought from the gods in classical antiquity. **b** the usu. ambiguous or obscure response given at an oracle. **c** a prophet or prophetess at an oracle. **2 a** a person or thing regarded as an infallible guide to future action etc. **b** a saying etc. regarded as infallible guidance. **3** divine inspiration or revelation. [Middle English via Old French from Latin *oraculum*, from *orare* 'speak']

oracular /ɒˈrakjʊlə/ *adj.* **1** of or concerning an oracle or oracles. **2** (esp. of advice etc.) mysterious or ambiguous. **3** prophetic. □ **oracularity** /-ˈlarɪti/ *n.* **oracularly** *adv.* [Latin (as ORACLE)]

oracy /ˈɔːrəsi/ *n.* the ability to express oneself fluently in speech. [Latin *os oris* 'mouth', on the pattern of *literacy*]

oral /ˈɔːr(ə)l/ *adj. & n.* ● *adj.* **1** by word of mouth; spoken; not written (*the oral tradition*). **2** done or taken by the mouth (*oral contraceptive*). **3** of or relating to the mouth. **4** *Psychol.* of or concerning a supposed stage of infant emotional and sexual development, in which the mouth is of central interest. ● *n. colloq.* a spoken examination, test, etc. □ **orally** *adv.* [Late Latin *oralis* from Latin *os oris* 'mouth']

oralism /ˈɔːr(ə)lɪz(ə)m/ *n.* the principle that profoundly deaf people should learn to communicate by speech and lip-reading without the use of sign language. □ **oralist** *adj. & n.*

oral sex *n.* sexual activity in which the genitals of one partner are stimulated by the mouth of the other.

oral society *n.* a society that has not reached the stage of literacy.

Orange /ˈɒrɪn(d)ʒ/ *adj.* of or relating to Orangemen or their activities. □ **Orangeism** *n.*

orange /ˈɒrɪn(d)ʒ/ *n. & adj.* ● *n.* **1 a** a large roundish juicy citrus fruit with a bright reddish-yellow tough rind. **b** (also **orange tree**) any of various trees or shrubs of the genus *Citrus*, esp. *C. sinensis* or *C. aurantium*, bearing fragrant white flowers and yielding this fruit. **2** a fruit or plant resembling this. **3 a** the reddish-yellow colour of an orange. **b** orange pigment. ● *adj.* orange-coloured; reddish yellow. [Middle English from Old French *orenge*, ultimately via Arabic *nāranj* from Persian *nārang*]

orangeade /ɒrɪn(d)ʒˈeɪd/ *n. Brit.* a usu. fizzy non-alcoholic drink flavoured with orange.

orange blossom *n.* the flowers of the orange tree, traditionally worn by the bride at a wedding.

orange flower water *n.* a solution of neroli in water.

Orangeman /ˈɒrɪn(d)ʒmən/ *n.* (*pl.* **-men**) a member of a political society formed in 1795 to support Protestantism in Ireland. [after the Protestant William of *Orange* (William III)]

orange peel *n.* **1** the skin of an orange. **2** a rough surface resembling this.

orange pekoe *n.* a type of black tea made from very small leaves.

orangery /ˈɒrɪn(d)ʒ(ə)ri/ *n.* (*pl.* **-ies**) a place, esp. a special structure, where orange trees are cultivated.

orange squash *n. Brit.* a soft drink made from oranges and other ingredients, often sold in concentrated form.

orange stick *n.* a thin stick, pointed at one end and usu. of orange-wood, for manicuring the fingernails.

orange-wood *n.* the wood of the orange tree.

orang-utan /ɔːˌraŋuːˈtan, əˈraŋuːtan/ *n.* (also **orangutan**, **orang-outang** /-uːˈtaŋ/) a large red long-haired tree-living ape, *Pongo pygmaeus*, native to Borneo and Sumatra, with characteristic long arms and hooked hands and feet. [Malay *orang huan* 'forest person']

orate /ˈɔːreɪt, ɒˈreɪt/ *v.intr.* esp. *joc.* or *derog.* make a speech or speak, esp. pompously or at length. [back-formation from ORATION]

oration /ɒˈreɪʃ(ə)n/ *n.* **1** a formal speech, discourse, etc., esp. when ceremonial. **2** *Gram.* a way of speaking; language. [Middle English, via Latin *oratio* 'discourse, prayer' from *orare* 'speak, pray']

orator /ˈɒrətə/ *n.* **1 a** a person making a speech. **b** an eloquent public speaker. **2** (in full **public orator**) an official speaking for a university on ceremonial occasions. □ **oratorial** /-ˈtɔːrɪəl/ *adj.* [Middle English via Anglo-French *oratour*, Old French *orateur* from Latin *orator -oris* 'speaker, pleader' (as ORATION)]

oratorio /ɒrəˈtɔːrɪəʊ/ *n.* (*pl.* **-os**) a semi-dramatic work for orchestra and voices esp. on a sacred theme, performed without costume, scenery, or action. □ **oratorial** *adj.* [Italian from ecclesiastical Latin *oratorium* ORATORY, originally of musical services at Church of the Oratory of St Philip Neri in Rome]

oratory /ˈɒrət(ə)ri/ *n.* (*pl.* **-ies**) **1** the art or practice of formal speaking, esp. in public. **2** exaggerated, eloquent, or highly coloured language. **3** a small chapel, esp. for private worship. **4** (**Oratory**) *RC Ch.* **a** a religious society of priests without vows founded in Rome in 1564 and providing plain preaching and popular services. **b** a branch of this in England etc. □ **oratorian** /-ˈtɔːrɪən/ *adj. & n.* **oratorical** /-ˈtɒrɪk(ə)l/ *adj.* [senses 1 and 2 from Latin *ars oratoria* 'art of speaking'; senses 3 and 4 Middle English via Anglo-French *oratorie*, Old French *oratoire* from ecclesiastical Latin *oratorium*: both via Latin *oratorius* from *orare* 'pray, speak']

orb /ɔːb/ *n. & v.* ● *n.* **1** a globe surmounted by a cross, esp. carried by a sovereign at a coronation. **2** a sphere; a globe. **3** *poet.* a celestial body. **4** *poet.* an eyeball; an eye. ● *v.* esp. *poet.* **1** *tr.* enclose in (an orb); encircle. **2** *intr.* form or gather into an orb. [Latin *orbis* 'ring']

orbicular /ɔːˈbɪkjʊlə/ *adj. formal* **1** circular and flat; disc-shaped; ring-shaped. **2** spherical; globular; rounded. **3** forming a complete whole. □ **orbicularity** /-ˈlarɪti/ *n.* **orbicularly** *adv.* [Middle English via Late Latin *orbicularis* from Latin *orbiculus*, diminutive of *orbis* 'ring']

orbiculate /ɔːˈbɪkjʊlət/ *adj. Bot.* (of a leaf etc.) circular.

orbit /ˈɔːbɪt/ *n. & v.* ● *n.* **1 a** the curved, usu. closed course of a planet, satellite, etc. **b** (prec. by *in*, *into*, *out of*, etc.) the state of motion in an orbit. **c** one complete passage around an orbited body. **2** the path of an electron round an atomic nucleus. **3** a range or sphere of action. **4 a** the eye socket. **b** the area around the eye of a bird or insect. ● *v.* (**orbited**, **orbiting**) **1** *intr.* **a** (of a satellite etc.) go round in orbit. **b** fly in a circle. **2** *tr.* move in orbit round. **3** *tr.* put into orbit. [Latin *orbita* 'course, track' (in medieval Latin 'eye-cavity'), fem. of *orbitus* 'circular' from *orbis* 'ring']

orbital /ˈɔːbɪt(ə)l/ *adj. & n.* ● *adj.* **1** *Anat.*, *Astron.*, & *Physics* of an orbit or orbits. **2** *Brit.* (of a road) passing round the outside of a town. ● *n. Physics* each of the actual or potential patterns of electron density which may be formed around an atomic nucleus by one or more electrons, represented as a wave function.

orbital sander *n.* a sander having a circular and not oscillating motion.

orbiter /ˈɔːbɪtə/ *n.* a spacecraft designed to travel and esp. remain in orbit.

orca /ˈɔːkə/ *n.* the killer whale. [French *orque* or Latin *orca*, a kind of whale]

Orcadian /ɔːˈkeɪdɪən/ *adj. & n.* ● *adj.* of or relating to the Orkney Islands off the N. coast of Scotland. ● *n.* a native of the Orkney Islands. [*Orcades*, the Latin name of the Orkney Islands]

orch. *abbr.* **1** orchestrated by. **2** orchestra.

orchard /ˈɔːtʃəd/ *n.* a piece of enclosed land with fruit trees. □ **orchardist** *n.* [Old English *ortgeard*, from Latin *hortus* 'garden' + YARD[2]]

orcharding /ˈɔːtʃədɪŋ/ *n.* the cultivation of fruit trees.

orchardman /ˈɔːtʃədmən/ *n.* (*pl.* **-men**) a fruit-grower.

orchestra /ˈɔːkɪstrə/ *n.* **1** a usu. large group of instrumentalists, esp. combining strings, woodwinds, brass, and percussion (*symphony orchestra*). **2 a** (in full

orchestra pit) the part of a theatre, opera house, etc., where the orchestra plays, usu. in front of the stage and on a lower level. **b** *N. Amer.* the stalls in a theatre. **3** the semicircular space in front of an ancient Greek theatre stage where the chorus danced and sang. □ **orchestral** /-ˈkɛstr(ə)l/ *adj.* **orchestrally** /-ˈkɛstrəli/ *adv.* [Latin from Greek *orkhēstra*, from *orkheomai* 'to dance' (see sense 3)]

orchestra stalls *n.pl. Brit.* the front of the stalls.

orchestrate /ˈɔːkɪstreɪt/ *v.tr.* **1** arrange, score, or compose for orchestral performance. **2** arrange, combine, or direct the elements of (a situation etc.) for maximum effect. □ **orchestration** /-ˈstreɪʃ(ə)n/ *n.* **orchestrator** *n.*

orchid /ˈɔːkɪd/ *n.* **1** a plant of the family Orchidaceae, often epiphytic, bearing flowers in fantastic shapes and brilliant colours, usu. having one petal larger than the others and variously spurred, lobed, pouched, etc. **2** a flower of such a plant. □ **orchidaceous** /-ˈdeɪʃəs/ *adj.* **orchidist** *n.* **orchidology** /-ˈdɒlədʒi/ *n.* [modern Latin *Orchid(ac)eae*, formed irregularly from Latin *orchis*: see ORCHIS]

orchido- /ˈɔːkɪdəʊ/ *comb. form* (also **orchid-** before a vowel) *Med.* of a testicle or the testicles (*orchidectomy*). [modern Latin, from Greek *orkhis* 'testicle']

orchil /ˈɔːtʃɪl/ *n.* (also **orchilla** /ɔːˈtʃɪlə/, **archil** /ˈɑːtʃɪl/) **1** a red or violet dye from lichen, esp. from *Roccella tinctoria*, often used in litmus. **2** the tropical lichen yielding this. [Middle English from Spanish, of unknown origin]

orchis /ˈɔːkɪs/ *n.* **1** any orchid of the genus *Orchis*, with a tuberous root and an erect fleshy stem having a spike of usu. purple or red flowers. **2** any of various wild orchids. [Latin from Greek *orkhis*, originally = testicle (with reference to the shape of its tuber)]

orchitis /ɔːˈkʌɪtɪs/ *n. Med.* inflammation of the testicles. [modern Latin, from Greek *orkhis* 'testicle']

orcin /ˈɔːsɪn/ *n.* (also **orcinol** /ˈɔːsɪnɒl/) a crystalline substance, becoming red in air, extracted from any of several lichens and used to make dyes. [modern Latin *orcina* from Italian *orcello* 'orchil']

ord. *abbr.* ordinary.

ordain /ɔːˈdeɪn/ *v.tr.* **1** confer holy orders on; appoint to the Christian ministry (*ordained him priest*; *was ordained in 1970*). **2 a** (often foll. by *that* + clause) decree (*ordained that he should go*). **b** (of God, fate, etc.) destine; appoint (*has ordained us to die*). □ **ordainer** *n.* **ordainment** *n.* [Middle English via Anglo-French *ordeiner*, Old French *ordein-*, stressed stem of *ordener*, from Latin *ordinare*, from *ordo -inis* 'order']

ordeal /ɔːˈdiːəl/ *n.* **1** a painful or horrific experience; a severe trial. **2** *hist.* an ancient esp. Germanic test of guilt or innocence by subjection of the accused to severe pain or torture, survival of which was taken as divine proof of innocence. [Old English *ordāl*, *ordēl*, from Germanic]

order /ˈɔːdə/ *n.* & *v.* ● *n.* **1 a** the condition in which every part, unit, etc. is in its right place; tidiness (*restored some semblance of order*). **b** a usu. specified sequence, succession, etc. (*alphabetical order*; *the order of events*). **2** (in *sing.* or *pl.*) an authoritative command, direction, instruction, etc. (*only obeying orders*; *gave orders for it to be done*; *the judge made an order*). **3** a state of peaceful harmony under a constituted authority (*order was restored*; *law and order*). **4** (esp. in *pl.*) esp. *Brit.* a social class, rank, etc., constituting a distinct group in society (*the lower orders*; *the order of baronets*). **5** a kind; a sort (*talents of a high order*). **6 a** a usu. written direction to a manufacturer, tradesman, waiter, etc. to supply something. **b** the quantity of goods etc. supplied. **7** the constitution or nature of the world, society, etc. (*the moral order*; *the order of things*). **8** *Biol.* a taxonomic rank below a class and above a family. **9** (also **Order**) a fraternity of monks or friars, or formerly of knights, bound by a common rule of life (*the Franciscan order*; *the Order of Templars*). **10 a** any of the grades of the Christian ministry. **b** (in *pl.*) the status of a member of the clergy (*Anglican orders*). **11 a** any of the five classical styles of architecture (Doric, Ionic, Corinthian, Tuscan, and Composite) based on the proportions of columns, amount of decoration, etc. **b** any style or mode of architecture subject to uniform established proportions. **12** (esp. **Order**) **a** a company of distinguished people instituted esp. by a sovereign to which appointments are made as an honour or reward (*Order of the Garter*; *Order of Merit*). **b** the insignia worn by members of an order. **13** *Math.* **a** a degree of complexity of a differential equation (*equation of the first order*). **b** the order of the highest derivative in the equation. **14** *Math.* **a** the size of a matrix. **b** the number of elements of a finite group. **15** *Eccl.* the stated form of divine service (*the order of confirmation*). **16** the principles of procedure, decorum, etc., accepted by a meeting, legislative assembly, etc. or enforced by its president. **17** *Mil.* **a** a style of dress and equipment (*review order*). **b** (prec. by *the*) the position of a company etc. with arms ordered (see *order arms*). **18** a Masonic or similar fraternity. **19** any of the nine grades of angelic beings (seraphim, cherubim, thrones, dominations, principalities, powers, virtues, archangels, angels). **20** *Brit.* a pass admitting the bearer to a theatre, museum, private house, etc. free or cheap or as a privilege. ● *v.tr.* **1** (usu. foll. by *to* + infin., or *that* + clause) command; bid; prescribe (*ordered him to go*; *ordered that they should be sent*). **2** command or direct (a person) to a specified destination (*was ordered to Singapore*; *ordered them home*). **3** direct a manufacturer, waiter, tradesman, etc. to supply (*ordered a new suit*; *ordered dinner*). **4** arrange; regulate (*ordered her affairs*). **5** (of God, fate, etc.) ordain (*fate ordered it otherwise*). **6** *US* command (a thing) done or (a person) dealt with (*ordered it settled*; *ordered him expelled*). □ **by order** according to the proper authority. **in bad** (or **good** etc.) **order** not working (or working properly etc.). **in order 1** one after another according to some principle. **2** ready or fit for use. **3** according to the rules (of procedure at a meeting etc.). **in order that** with the intention; so that. **in order to** with the purpose of doing; with a view to. **keep order** enforce orderly behaviour. **not in order** not working properly. **of** (or **in** or **on**) **the order of 1** approximately. **2** having the order of magnitude specified by (*of the order of one in a million*). **on order** (of goods etc.) ordered but not yet received. **order about 1** dominate; command officiously. **2** send hither and thither. **order arms** *Mil.* hold a rifle with its butt on the ground close to one's right side. **Order! Order!** *Parl.* a call for silence or calm, esp. by the Speaker of the House of Commons. **order to view** *Brit.* a house agent's request for a client to be allowed to inspect premises. **out of order 1** not working properly. **2** not in the correct sequence. **3** not according to the rules (of a meeting, organization, etc.). **4** *colloq.* **a** not behaving in an acceptable fashion. **b** (of behaviour) not acceptable. **take orders 1** accept commissions. **2** accept and carry out commands. **3** (also **take holy orders**) be ordained. [Middle English via Old French *ordre* from Latin *ordo ordinis* 'row, array, degree, command', etc.]

order book *n.* **1** a book in which a tradesman enters orders. **2** the level of incoming orders.

order form *n.* a printed form in which details are entered by a customer.

Order in Council *n. Brit.* a sovereign's order on an administrative matter given by the advice of the Privy Council.

orderly /ˈɔːd(ə)li/ *adj.* & *n.* ● *adj.* **1** methodically arranged; regular. **2** obedient to discipline; well-behaved; not unruly. **3** *Mil.* **a** of or concerned with orders. **b** charged with the conveyance or execution of orders. ● *n.* (*pl.* **-ies**) **1** an esp. male cleaner in a hospital. **2** a soldier who carries orders for an officer etc. □ **orderliness** *n.*

orderly book *n. Brit. Mil.* a regimental or company book for entering orders.

orderly officer *n. Brit. Mil.* the officer of the day.

orderly room *n. Brit. Mil.* a room in a barracks used for company business.

order of magnitude *n.* a class in a system of classification determined by size, usu. by powers of 10.

Order of Merit *n.* (in the UK) an order founded in 1902, for distinguished achievement.

Order of the Bath *n.* (in the UK) an order of knighthood. [so called from the ceremonial bath which originally preceded installation]

order of the day *n.* **1** the prevailing state of things. **2** a principal topic of action or a procedure decided upon. **3** business set down for treatment; a programme.

Order of the Garter *n.* the highest order of English knighthood. [so called from the traditional story of the order's founding, that the garter was that of the Countess of Salisbury which Edward III placed on his own leg after it fell off while she was dancing]

order paper *n.* esp. *Parl.* a written or printed order of the day; an agenda.

ordinal /ˈɔːdɪn(ə)l/ *n. & adj.* ● *n.* **1** (in full **ordinal number**) a number defining a thing's position in a series, e.g. 'first', 'second', 'third', etc. (cf. CARDINAL NUMBER). **2** *Eccl.* a service book, esp. one with the forms of service used at ordinations. ● *adj.* **1 a** of or relating to an ordinal number. **b** defining a thing's position in a series etc. **2** *Biol.* of or concerning an order (see ORDER *n.* 8). [Middle English via Late Latin *ordinalis* from Latin (as ORDER: sense 2 of noun from medieval Latin *ordinale* (*liber* 'book'))]

ordinance /ˈɔːdɪnəns/ *n.* **1** an authoritative order; a decree. **2** an enactment by a local authority. **3** a religious rite. **4** *archaic* = ORDONNANCE. [Middle English via Old French *ordenance* and medieval Latin *ordinantia* from Latin *ordinare* ORDAIN]

■ **Usage** Care should be taken not to confuse *ordinance* meaning 'a decree' or 'a religious rite' with *ordnance* meaning 'mounted guns' or 'the government service dealing with military stores and materials'. Note also *ordonnance* and *Ordnance Survey*.

ordinand /ˈɔːdɪnand, ɔːdɪˈnand/ *n. Eccl.* a candidate for ordination. [Latin *ordinandus*, gerundive of *ordinare* ORDAIN]

ordinary /ˈɔːdɪn(ə)ri, -d(ə)n-/ *adj. & n.* ● *adj.* **1 a** regular, normal, customary, usual (*in the ordinary course of events*). **b** boring; commonplace (*an ordinary little man*). **2** *Brit. Law* (esp. of a judge) having immediate or ex officio jurisdiction, not deputed. ● *n.* (*pl.* **-ies**) **1** *Brit. Law* a person, esp. a judge, having immediate or ex officio jurisdiction. **2** (**the Ordinary**) **a** an archbishop in a province. **b** a bishop in a diocese. **3** (usu. **Ordinary**) *RC Ch.* **a** those parts of a service, esp. the Mass, which do not vary from day to day. **b** a rule or book laying down the order of divine service. **4** *Heraldry* a charge of the earliest, simplest, and commonest kind (esp. chief, pale, bend, fess, bar, chevron, cross, saltire). **5** (**Ordinary**) (also **Lord Ordinary**) any of the judges of the Court of Session in Scotland, constituting the Outer House. **6** esp. *US hist.* an early type of bicycle with one large and one very small wheel; a penny-farthing. **7** *Brit. hist.* **a** a public meal provided at a fixed time and price at an inn etc. **b** an establishment providing this. □ **in ordinary** *Brit.* by permanent appointment (esp. to the royal household) (*physician in ordinary*). **in the ordinary way** if the circumstances are or were not exceptional. **out of the ordinary** unusual. □ **ordinarily** /ˈɔːd(ə)n(ə)rɪli, -d(ə)ˈnɛrɪli/ *adv.* **ordinariness** *n.* [Middle English from Latin *ordinarius* 'orderly' (as ORDER)]

ordinary grade *n.* (in Scotland) the lower of two main levels of examination leading to the Scottish Certificate of Education).

ordinary level *n. hist.* (in the UK except Scotland) the lower of the two main levels of the GCE examination.

ordinary scale *n.* = DECIMAL SCALE.

ordinary seaman *n.* a sailor of the lowest rank, that below able-bodied seaman.

ordinary share *n. Brit.* a share entitling the holder to a dividend from net profits (cf. PREFERENCE SHARE).

ordinate /ˈɔːdɪnət/ *n. Math.* a straight line from any point drawn parallel to one coordinate axis and meeting the other, usually a coordinate measured parallel to the vertical (cf. ABSCISSA). [Latin *linea ordinata applicata* 'line applied parallel', from *ordinare* ORDAIN]

ordination /ɔːdɪˈneɪʃ(ə)n/ *n.* **1 a** the act of conferring holy orders, esp. on a priest or deacon. **b** the admission of a priest etc. to Church ministry. **2** the arrangement of things etc. in ranks; classification. **3** the act of decreeing or ordaining. [Middle English from Old French *ordination* or Latin *ordinatio* (as ORDAIN)]

ordnance /ˈɔːdnəns/ *n.* **1** mounted guns; cannon. **2** a branch of government service dealing esp. with military stores and materials. [Middle English, variant of ORDINANCE]

■ **Usage** See Usage Note at ORDINANCE.

ordnance datum *n. Brit.* mean sea level as defined for Ordnance Survey.

Ordnance Survey *n.* (in the UK) an official survey organization, originally under the Master of the Ordnance, preparing large-scale detailed maps of the whole country.

Ordnance Survey map *n.* (also **Ordnance map**) *Brit.* a map produced by Ordnance Survey.

ordonnance /ˈɔːdənəns/ *n.* the systematic arrangement esp. of literary or architectural work. [French from Old French *ordenance*: see ORDINANCE]

Ordovician /ɔːdəˈvɪʃɪən/ *adj. & n. Geol.* ● *adj.* of or relating to the second period of the Palaeozoic era, with evidence of the first vertebrates and an abundance of marine invertebrates. Cf. Appendix X. ● *n.* this period or system. [*Ordovices*, the Latin name of an ancient British tribe in N. Wales]

ordure /ˈɔːdjʊə/ *n.* **1** excrement; dung. **2** obscenity; filth; foul language. [Middle English via Old French, from *ord* 'foul', from Latin *horridus*: see HORRID]

Ore. *abbr.* Oregon.

ore /ɔː/ *n.* a naturally occurring solid material from which metal or other valuable minerals may be extracted. [Old English *ōra* 'unwrought metal', *ār* 'bronze', related to Latin *aes* 'crude metal, bronze']

øre /ˈəːrə/ *n.* (*pl.* same) a Danish and Norwegian monetary unit equal to one-hundredth of a krone. [Danish and Norwegian]

öre /ˈəːrə/ *n.* (*pl.* same) a Swedish monetary unit equal to one-hundredth of a krona. [Swedish]

oread /ˈɔːrɪad/ *n.* (in Greek and Roman mythology) a mountain nymph. [Middle English via Latin *oreas -ados* from Greek *oreias*, from *oros* 'mountain']

orectic /ɒˈrɛktɪk/ *adj. Philos. & Med.* of or concerning desire or appetite. [Greek *orektikos* from *oregō* 'stretch out, reach for']

Oreg. *abbr.* Oregon.

oregano /ɒrɪˈɡɑːnəʊ, əˈrɛɡənəʊ/ *n.* the dried leaves of wild marjoram used as a culinary herb (cf. MARJORAM). [Spanish, = ORIGANUM]

oreography var. of OROGRAPHY.

oreweed var. of OARWEED.

orfe /ɔːf/ *n.* a usu. silvery freshwater fish, *Leuciscus idus*, of the carp family, fished commercially in northern Eurasia. Also called *ide*. See also GOLDEN ORFE. [German: perhaps related to French *orphe*, Latin *orphus*, from Greek *orphos* 'sea-perch']

organ /ˈɔːɡ(ə)n/ *n.* **1 a** a usu. large musical instrument having pipes supplied with air from bellows, sounded by keys, and distributed into sets or stops which form partial organs, each with a separate keyboard (*choir organ*; *pedal organ*). **b** a smaller instrument without pipes, producing similar sounds electronically. **c** a smaller keyboard wind instrument with metal reeds; a harmonium. **d** = BARREL ORGAN. **2 a** a usu. self-contained part of an organism having a special vital function (*vocal organs*; *digestive organs*). **b** esp. *joc.* the penis. **3** a medium of communication, esp. a newspaper or periodical which serves as the mouthpiece of a movement, political party, etc. **4** *archaic* a professionally trained singing voice. **5** *archaic* a region of the brain formerly held to be the seat of a particular faculty. [Middle English from Old English *organa* & Old French *organe*, via Latin *organum* from Greek *organon* 'tool']

organ-blower *n.* a person or mechanism working the bellows of an organ.

organdie /'ɔːg(ə)ndi, ɔː'gandi/ *n.* (*US* **organdy**) (*pl.* **-ies**) a fine translucent cotton muslin, usu. stiffened. [French *organdi*, of unknown origin]

organelle /ɔːgə'nɛl/ *n. Biol.* any of various organized or specialized structures which form part of a cell. [modern Latin *organella*, diminutive of *organum*: see ORGAN, -LE[2]]

organ-grinder *n.* the player of a barrel organ.

organic /ɔː'ganɪk/ *adj.* **1 a** *Physiol.* of or relating to a bodily organ or organs. **b** *Med.* (of a disease) affecting the structure of an organ. **2** (of a plant or animal) having organs or an organized physical structure. **3** produced or involving production without the use of chemical fertilizers, pesticides, etc. (*organic crop*; *organic farming*). **4** *Chem.* (of a compound etc.) containing carbon (opp. INORGANIC). **5 a** structural, inherent. **b** constitutional, fundamental. **6** organized, systematic, coordinated (*an organic whole*). **7** characterized by or designating continuous or natural development (*the company expanded through organic growth rather than acquisitions*). □ **organically** *adv.* [French *organique* via Latin *organicus* from Greek *organikos* (as ORGAN)]

organic chemistry *n.* the chemistry of carbon compounds (other than simple salts such as carbonates).

organic law *n.* a law stating the formal constitution of a country.

organism /'ɔːg(ə)nɪz(ə)m/ *n.* **1** a living individual consisting of a single cell or of a group of interdependent parts sharing the life processes. **2 a** an individual live plant or animal. **b** the material structure of this. **3** a whole with interdependent parts compared to a living being. [French *organisme* (as ORGANIZE)]

organist /'ɔːg(ə)nɪst/ *n.* the player of an organ.

organization /ɔːg(ə)nʌɪ'zeɪʃ(ə)n/ *n.* (also **-isation**) **1** the act or an instance of organizing; the state of being organized. **2** an organized body, esp. a business, government department, charity, etc. **3** systematic arrangement; tidiness. □ **organizational** *adj.* **organizationally** *adv.*

organization man *n.* a man who subordinates his individuality and his personal life to the organization he serves.

organize /'ɔːg(ə)nʌɪz/ *v.tr.* (also **-ise**) **1 a** give an orderly structure to, systematize. **b** bring the affairs of (another person or oneself) into order; make arrangements for (a person). **2** *Brit.* **a** arrange for or initiate (a scheme etc.). **b** provide; take responsibility for (*organized some sandwiches*). **3** (often *absol.*) **a** enrol (new members) in a trade union, political party, etc. **b** form (a trade union or other political group). **4 a** form (different elements) into an organic whole. **b** form (an organic whole). **5** (esp. as **organized** *adj.*) make organic; make into a living being or tissue. □ **organizable** *adj.* [Middle English via Old French *organiser* and medieval Latin *organizare* from Latin (as ORGAN)]

organizer /'ɔːg(ə)nʌɪzə/ *n.* **1 a** a thing used for organizing objects, such as a handbag or folder with many compartments. **b** = PERSONAL ORGANIZER. **2** in senses of ORGANIZE.

organ loft *n.* a gallery in a church or concert room for an organ.

organo- /'ɔːg(ə)nəʊ, ɔː'ganəʊ/ *comb. form* **1** esp. *Biol.* organ. **2** *Chem.* organic, esp. in naming classes of organic compounds containing a particular element (*organochlorine*; *organophosphorus*). [Greek (as ORGAN)]

organ of Corti *n. Anat.* a structure in the inner ear of mammals, responsible for converting sound signals into nerve impulses. [named after A. *Corti*, Italian anatomist d. 1876]

organoleptic /ɔːg(ə)nə(ʊ)'lɛptɪk/ *adj.* affecting the organs of sense. [ORGANO- + Greek *lēptikos* 'disposed to take' from *lambanō* 'take']

organometallic /ɔː,ganəʊmɪ'talɪk/ *adj.* (of a compound) organic and containing a metal.

organon /'ɔːg(ə)nɒn/ *n.* an instrument of thought, esp. a means of reasoning or a system of logic. [Greek *organon* & Latin *organum* (as ORGAN): *Organon* was the title of Aristotle's logical writings, and *Novum* (new) *Organum* that of Bacon's]

organotherapy /ɔːg(ə)nəʊ'θɛrəpi/ *n.* the treatment of disease with extracts from animal organs, esp. glands.

organ pipe *n.* any of the pipes on an organ.

organ-screen *n.* an ornamental screen usu. between the choir and the nave of a church, cathedral, etc., on which the organ is placed.

organ stop *n.* **1** a set of pipes of a similar tone in an organ. **2** the handle of the mechanism that brings it into action.

organum /'ɔːg(ə)nəm/ *n.* (*pl.* **organa** /-nə/) *Mus.* (in medieval music) a part sung as an accompaniment below or above a melody.

organza /ɔː'ganzə/ *n.* a thin stiff transparent silk or synthetic dress fabric. [probably from *Lorganza* (US trade name)]

organzine /'ɔːg(ə)nziːn, -'ganziːn/ *n.* a silk thread in which the main twist is in a contrary direction to that of the strands. [French *organsin* from Italian *organzino*, of unknown origin]

orgasm /'ɔːgaz(ə)m/ *n. & v.* ● *n.* **1 a** the climax of sexual excitement, esp. during sexual intercourse. **b** an instance of this. **2** violent excitement; rage. ● *v.intr.* experience a sexual orgasm. □ **orgasmic** /-'gazmɪk/ *adj.* **orgasmically** /-'gazmɪk(ə)li/ *adv.* **orgastic** /-'gastɪk/ *adj.* **orgastically** /-'gastɪk(ə)li/ *adv.* [French *orgasme* or modern Latin from Greek *orgasmos*, from *orgaō* 'swell, be excited']

orgeat /'ɔːdʒɪət/ *n.* a cooling drink made from barley or almonds and orange flower water. [French via Provençal *orjat*, from *ordi* 'barley', from Latin *hordeum* 'barley']

orgiastic /ɔːdʒɪ'astɪk/ *adj.* of or resembling an orgy. □ **orgiastically** *adv.* [Greek *orgiastikos* from *orgiastēs*, agent noun from *orgiazō* 'hold an orgy']

orgulous /'ɔːgjʊləs/ *adj. archaic* haughty; splendid. [Middle English via Old French *orguillus*, from *orguill* 'pride', from Frankish]

orgy /'ɔːdʒi/ *n.* (*pl.* **-ies**) **1** a wild drunken festivity, esp. one at which indiscriminate sexual activity takes place. **2** excessive indulgence in an activity. **3** (usu. in *pl.*) *Gk & Rom. Hist.* secret rites used in the worship of esp. Bacchus, celebrated with dancing, drunkenness, singing, etc. [originally pl., from French *orgies* via Latin *orgia* from Greek *orgia* 'secret rites']

oribi /'ɒrɪbi/ *n.* (*pl.* same or **oribis**) a small S. African grazing antelope, *Ourebia ourebi*, having a reddish-fawn back and white underparts. [probably Nama or Bushman]

oriel /'ɔːrɪəl/ *n.* **1** a large polygonal recess built out usu. from an upper storey and supported from the ground or on corbels. **2** (in full **oriel window**) **a** any of the windows in an oriel. **b** the projecting window of an upper storey. [Middle English from Old French *oriol* 'gallery', of unknown origin]

orient *n., adj., & v.* ● *n.* /'ɔːrɪənt, 'ɒr-/ **1** (**the Orient**) **a** *poet.* the east. **b** the countries east of the Mediterranean, esp. E. Asia; the East. **2** an orient pearl. ● *adj.* /'ɔːrɪənt, 'ɒr-/ **1** *poet.* oriental. **2** (of precious stones and esp. the finest pearls coming originally from the East) lustrous; sparkling; precious. **3** *archaic* **a** radiant. **b** (of the sun, daylight, etc.) rising. ● *v.* /ˈɔːrɪɛnt, ˈɒr-/ **1** *tr.* **a** place or exactly determine the position of with the aid of a compass; settle or find the bearings of. **b** (often foll. by *towards*) bring (oneself, different elements, etc.) into a clearly understood position or relationship; direct. **2** *tr.* **a** place or build (a church, building, etc.) facing towards the east. **b** bury (a person) with the feet towards the east. **3** *intr.* turn eastward or in a specified direction. □ **orient oneself** determine how one stands in relation to one's surroundings. [Middle English via Old French *orient, orienter* from Latin *oriens -entis* 'rising, sunrise, east', from *oriri* 'rise']

oriental /ɔːrɪˈɛnt(ə)l, ɒr-/ *adj. & n.* ● *adj.* **1** (often **Oriental**) **a** of or characteristic of Eastern civilization etc. **b** of or concerning the East, esp. E. Asia. **2** (of a pearl etc.) orient. ● *n.* (esp. **Oriental**) a person of Oriental, esp. E. Asian descent. □ **orientalism** *n.* **orientalist** *n.* **orientalize** *v.intr. & tr.* (also **-ise**). **orientally** *adv.* [Middle English from Old French *oriental* or Latin *orientalis* (as ORIENT)]

■ **Usage** The term *Oriental*, when applied to people, may be considered offensive, especially in the United States where *Asian* is preferred.

orientate /ˈɔːrɪɛnteɪt, ˈɒr-/ *v.tr. & intr.* = ORIENT *v.* [probably a back-formation from ORIENTATION]

orientation /ˌɔːrɪənˈteɪʃ(ə)n, ˌɒr-/ *n.* **1** the act or an instance of orienting; the state of being oriented. **2 a** a relative position. **b** a person's attitude or adjustment in relation to circumstances, esp. politically or psychologically. **3** an introduction to a subject or situation; a briefing. **4** the faculty by which birds etc. find their way home from a distance. □ **orientational** *adj.* [apparently from ORIENT]

orientation course *n.* esp. *N. Amer.* a course giving information to newcomers to a university etc.

orienteering /ˌɔːrɪɛnˈtɪərɪŋ, ˌɒr-/ *n.* a competitive sport in which runners cross open country with a map, compass, etc. □ **orienteer** *n. & v.intr.* [Swedish *orientering*, originally = orienting]

orifice /ˈɒrɪfɪs/ *n.* an opening, esp. the mouth of a cavity, a bodily aperture, etc. [French from Late Latin *orificium*, from *os oris* 'mouth' + *facere* 'make']

oriflamme /ˈɒrɪflam/ *n.* **1** *hist.* the sacred scarlet silk banner of St Denis given to early French kings by the abbot of St Denis on setting out for war. **2** a standard, a principle, or an ideal as a rallying point in a struggle. **3** a bright conspicuous object, colour, etc. [Middle English from Old French, from Latin *aurum* 'gold' + *flamma* 'flame']

origami /ɒrɪˈɡɑːmi/ *n.* the Japanese art of folding paper into decorative shapes and figures. [Japanese, from *oru* 'fold' + *kami* 'paper']

origanum /ɒˈrɪɡ(ə)nəm/ *n.* any plant of the genus *Origanum*, esp. wild marjoram (see MARJORAM). [Middle English via Latin *origanum* from Greek *origanon*]

origin /ˈɒrɪdʒɪn/ *n.* **1** a beginning or starting point; a derivation; a source (*a word of Latin origin*). **2** (often in *pl.*) a person's ancestry (*what are his origins?*). **3** *Anat.* **a** a place at which a muscle is firmly attached. **b** a place where a nerve or blood vessel begins or branches from a main nerve or blood vessel. **4** *Math.* a fixed point from which coordinates are measured. [French *origine*, or via Latin *origo -ginis* from *oriri* 'rise']

original /əˈrɪdʒɪn(ə)l, ɒ-/ *adj. & n.* ● *adj.* **1** existing from the beginning; innate. **2** novel; inventive; creative (*has an original mind*). **3** serving as a pattern; not derivative or imitative; first-hand (*in the original Greek*; *has an original Rembrandt*). ● *n.* **1** an original model, pattern, picture, etc. from which another is copied or translated (*kept the copy and destroyed the original*). **2** an eccentric or unusual person. **3 a** a garment specially designed for a fashion collection. **b** a copy of such a garment made to order. □ **originally** *adv.* [Middle English from Old French *original* or Latin *originalis* (as ORIGIN)]

original instrument *n.* a musical instrument, or a copy of one, dating from the time the music played on it was composed.

originality /əˌrɪdʒɪˈnalɪti/ *n.* (*pl.* **-ies**) **1** the power of creating or thinking creatively. **2** newness or freshness (*this vase has originality*). **3** an original act, thing, trait, etc.

original print *n.* a print made directly from an artist's own woodcut, etching, etc., and printed under the artist's supervision.

original sin *n.* the innate depravity of all mankind held to be a consequence of the Fall.

originate /əˈrɪdʒɪneɪt, ɒ-/ *v.* **1** *tr.* cause to begin; initiate. **2** *intr.* (usu. foll. by *from, in, with*) have as an origin; begin. □ **origination** /-ˈneɪʃ(ə)n/ *n.* **originative** /-nətɪv/ *adj.* **originator** *n.* [medieval Latin *originare* (as ORIGIN)]

Orimulsion /ɒrɪˈmʌlʃ(ə)n/ *n. propr.* (also **orimulsion**) an emulsion of bitumen in water, used as a fuel. [from *Orinoco* in Venezuela (the original source of the bitumen) + EMULSION]

orinasal /ɔːrɪˈneɪz(ə)l/ *adj.* (esp. of French nasalized vowels) sounded with both the mouth and the nose. [Latin *os oris* 'mouth' + NASAL]

O-ring *n.* a gasket in the form of a ring with a circular cross-section.

oriole /ˈɔːrɪəʊl, ˈɔːrɪəl/ *n.* **1** any Old World bird of the genus *Oriolus*, many of which have brightly coloured plumage (see GOLDEN ORIOLE). **2** any New World bird of the genus *Icterus*, with similar coloration. [medieval Latin *oriolus* via Old French *oriol* from Latin *aureolus*, diminutive of *aureus* 'golden', from *aurum* 'gold']

Orion /əˈrʌɪən/ *n.* a brilliant constellation on the celestial equator visible from most parts of the earth. [Middle English via Latin from Greek *Ōriōn*, the name of a legendary hunter]

Orion's belt *n.* three bright stars in a short line across the middle of the constellation.

Orion's hound *n.* = DOG-STAR.

orison /ˈɒrɪz(ə)n, -s(ə)n/ *n.* (usu. in *pl.*) *archaic* a prayer. [Middle English via Anglo-French *ureison*, Old French *oreison* from Latin (as ORATION)]

-orium /ˈɔːrɪəm/ *suffix* forming nouns denoting a place for a particular function (*auditorium*; *crematorium*). [Latin, neut. of adjectives ending in *-orius*: see -ORY[1]]

Oriya /ɒˈriːjə/ *n.* **1** a native of the state of Orissa in India. **2** the Indo-European language of the Oriyas. [Hindi]

orle /ɔːl/ *n. Heraldry* a narrow band or border of charges near the edge of a shield. [French *o(u)rle* from *ourler* 'to hem', ultimately from Latin *ora* 'edge']

Orlon /ˈɔːlɒn/ *n. propr.* a man-made fibre and fabric for textiles and knitwear. [invented word, on the pattern of NYLON]

orlop /ˈɔːlɒp/ *n.* the lowest deck of a ship with three or more decks. [Middle English from Middle Dutch *overloop* 'covering', from *overloopen* 'run over' (as OVER-, LEAP)]

ormer /ˈɔːmə/ *n.* an edible abalone (mollusc), esp. *Haliotis tuberculata*, used as food in the Channel Islands. Also called *sea-ear*. [Channel Islands French from French *ormier*, from Latin *auris maris* 'ear of sea']

ormolu /ˈɔːməluː/ *n.* **1** (often *attrib.*) gilded bronze; a gold-coloured alloy of copper, zinc, and tin used to decorate furniture, make ornaments, etc. **2** articles made of or decorated with this. [French *or moulu* 'powdered gold' (for use in gilding)]

ornament *n. & v.* ● *n.* /ˈɔːnəm(ə)nt/ **1 a** a thing used or serving to adorn, esp. a small trinket, vase, figure, etc. (*a mantelpiece crowded with ornaments*; *her only ornament was a brooch*). **b** a quality or person conferring adornment, grace, or honour (*an ornament to her profession*). **2** decoration added to embellish esp. a building (*a tower rich in ornament*). **3** (in *pl.*) *Mus.* embellishments and decorations made to a melody. **4**

(usu. in *pl.*) the accessories of worship, e.g. the altar, chalice, sacred vessels, etc. ● *v.tr.* /'ɔːnəmɛnt/ adorn; beautify. □ **ornamentation** /-m(ə)n'teɪʃ(ə)n, -mɛn-/ *n.* [Middle English via Anglo-French *urnement*, Old French *o(u)rnement* from Latin *ornamentum* 'equipment, ornament', from *ornare* 'adorn']

ornamental /ɔːnə'mɛnt(ə)l/ *adj.* & *n.* ● *adj.* serving as an ornament; decorative. ● *n.* a thing considered to be ornamental, esp. a cultivated plant. □ **ornamentalism** *n.* **ornamentalist** *n.* **ornamentally** *adv.*

ornate /ɔː'neɪt/ *adj.* **1** elaborately adorned; highly decorated. **2** (of literary style) convoluted; flowery. □ **ornately** *adv.* **ornateness** *n.* [Middle English from Latin *ornatus*, past part. of *ornare* 'adorn']

ornery /'ɔːnəri/ *adj. N. Amer. colloq.* **1** cantankerous; unpleasant. **2** of poor quality. □ **orneriness** *n.* [variant of ORDINARY]

ornithischian /ɔːnɪ'θɪskiən, -'θɪʃɪən/ *adj.* & *n.* ● *adj.* of or relating to the order Ornithischia, including dinosaurs with a pelvic structure like that of birds. ● *n.* a dinosaur of this order. [modern Latin, from Greek *ornis ornithos* 'bird' + *iskhion* 'hip joint']

ornitho- /'ɔːnɪθəʊ/ *comb. form* bird. [Greek from *ornis ornithos* 'bird']

ornithology /ɔːnɪ'θɒlədʒi/ *n.* the scientific study of birds. □ **ornithological** /-θə'lɒdʒɪk(ə)l/ *adj.* **ornithologically** /-θə'lɒdʒɪk(ə)li/ *adv.* **ornithologist** *n.* [modern Latin *ornithologia* from Greek *ornithologos* 'treating of birds' (as ORNITHO-, -LOGY)]

ornithopod /'ɔːnɪθəpɒd/ *n.* & *adj.* ● *n.* a bipedal herbivorous ornithischian dinosaur of the suborder Ornithopoda. ● *adj.* of or relating to this suborder. [modern Latin, from Greek *ornis ornith-* 'bird' + *pous pod-* 'foot']

ornithorhynchus /ˌɔːnɪθə'rɪŋkəs/ *n.* = PLATYPUS. [ORNITHO- + Greek *rhugkhos* 'bill']

oro- /'ɒrəʊ/ *comb. form* mountain. [Greek *oros* 'mountain']

orogeny /ɒ'rɒdʒəni/ *n.* (also **orogenesis** /ɒrə(ʊ)'dʒɛnɪsɪs/) the process of the formation of mountains. □ **orogenetic** /ɒrə(ʊ)dʒɪ'nɛtɪk/ *adj.* **orogenic** /ɒrə(ʊ)'dʒɛnɪk/ *adj.*

orography /ɒ'rɒgrəfi/ *n.* (also **oreography** /ɒrɪ'ɒgrəfi/) the branch of physical geography dealing with mountains. □ **orographic** /-rə'grafɪk/ *adj.* **orographical** /-'grafɪk(ə)l/ *adj.*

orotund /'ɒrə(ʊ)tʌnd, 'ɔːr-/ *adj.* **1** (of the voice or phrasing) full, round; imposing. **2** (of writing, style, expression, etc.) pompous; pretentious. [Latin *ore rotundo* 'with rounded mouth']

orphan /'ɔːf(ə)n/ *n.* & *v.* ● *n.* (often *attrib.*) **1** a child bereaved of a parent or usu. both parents. **2** a person bereft of previous protection, advantages, etc. **3** *Printing* the first line of a paragraph at the foot of a page or column. ● *v.tr.* bereave (a child) of its parents or a parent. □ **orphanhood** *n.* **orphanize** *v.tr.* (also **-ise**). [Middle English via Late Latin *orphanus* from Greek *orphanos* 'bereaved']

orphanage /'ɔːf(ə)nɪdʒ/ *n.* **1** a usu. residential institution for the care and education of orphans. **2** orphanhood.

Orphean /ɔː'fiːən/ *adj.* like the music of Orpheus, a legendary Greek poet and lyre-player; melodious; entrancing. [Latin *Orpheus* (*adj.*) from Greek *Orpheios*, from *Orpheus*]

Orphic /'ɔːfɪk/ *adj.* **1** of or concerning Orpheus or the mysteries, doctrines, etc. associated with him; oracular; mysterious. **2** = ORPHEAN. □ **Orphism** *n.* [Latin *Orphicus* from Greek *Orphikos*, from *Orpheus* (see ORPHEAN)]

orphrey /'ɔːfri/ *n.* (*pl.* **-eys**) an ornamental stripe or border or separate piece of ornamental needlework, esp. on ecclesiastical vestments. [Middle English *orfreis* (taken as pl.) '(gold) embroidery' via Old French and medieval Latin *aurifrisium* etc. from Latin *aurum* 'gold' + *Phrygius* 'Phrygian', also 'embroidered']

orpiment /'ɔːpɪm(ə)nt/ *n.* **1** a mineral form of arsenic trisulphide, formerly used as a dye and artist's pigment; also called *yellow arsenic*. **2** (in full **red orpiment**) = REALGAR. [Middle English via Old French from Latin *auripigmentum*, from *aurum* 'gold' + *pigmentum* 'pigment']

orpine /'ɔːpɪn/ *n.* (also **orpin**) a succulent herbaceous purple-flowered plant, *Sedum telephium*. Also called *livelong*. [Middle English from Old French *orpine*, probably alteration of ORPIMENT, originally applied to a yellow-flowered sedum]

orra /'ɒrə/ *adj. Sc.* **1** not matched; odd. **2** occasional; extra. [16th c.: origin unknown]

orrery /'ɒrəri/ *n.* (*pl.* **-ies**) a clockwork model of the solar system. [named after the fourth Earl of *Orrery*, for whom one was made]

orris /'ɒrɪs/ *n.* **1** any plant of the genus *Iris*, esp. *I. florentina*. **2** = ORRIS ROOT. [16th c.: apparently an unexplained alteration of IRIS]

orris-powder *n.* powdered orris root.

orris root *n.* the fragrant rootstock of the orris, used in perfumery and formerly in medicine.

ortanique /ɔːtə'niːk/ *n.* a citrus fruit produced by crossing an orange and a tangerine. [*or*ange + *tan*gerine + un*ique*]

ortho- /'ɔːθəʊ/ *comb. form* **1 a** straight, rectangular, upright. **b** right, correct. **2** *Chem.* **a** relating to two adjacent carbon atoms in a benzene ring. **b** relating to acids and salts (e.g. *orthophosphates*) giving *meta-* compounds on removal of water. [Greek *orthos* 'straight']

orthocephalic /ˌɔːθəʊsɪ'falɪk, -kɛ'falɪk/ *adj.* having a head with a medium ratio of breadth to height.

orthochromatic /ˌɔːθəʊkrə'matɪk/ *adj.* giving fairly correct relative intensity to colours in photography by being sensitive to all except red.

orthoclase /'ɔːθəkleɪz/ *n.* a common alkali feldspar usu. occurring as variously coloured crystals, used in ceramics and glass-making. [ORTHO- + Greek *klasis* 'breaking']

orthodontics /ɔːθə'dɒntɪks/ *n.pl.* (treated as *sing.*) (also **orthodontia** /-'dɒntɪə/) the treatment of irregularities in the teeth and jaws. □ **orthodontic** *adj.* **orthodontist** *n.* [ORTHO- + Greek *odous odont-* 'tooth']

orthodox /'ɔːθədɒks/ *adj.* **1 a** holding correct or currently accepted opinions, esp. on religious doctrine, morals, etc. **b** not independent-minded; unoriginal; unheretical. **2** (of religious doctrine, standards of morality, etc.) generally accepted as right or true; authoritatively established; conventional. **3** (also **Orthodox**) (of Judaism) strictly keeping to traditional doctrine and ritual. **4** (**Orthodox**) of or relating to the Orthodox Church. □ **orthodoxly** *adv.* [ecclesiastical Latin *orthodoxus* from Greek *orthodoxos* (as ORTHO-, *doxa* 'opinion')]

Orthodox Church *n.* a Christian Church or federation of Churches acknowledging the authority of the patriarch of Constantinople, originating in the church of the Byzantine empire and including the national Churches of Greece, Russia, Bulgaria, Romania, etc. Also called *Eastern Orthodox Church*.

orthodoxy /'ɔːθədɒksi/ *n.* (*pl.* **-ies**) **1** the state of being orthodox. **2 a** the orthodox practice of Judaism. **b** the body of Orthodox Jews or Orthodox Christians. **3** esp. *Relig.* an authorized or generally accepted theory, doctrine, etc. [Late Latin *orthodoxia* from late Greek *orthodoxia* 'sound doctrine' (as ORTHODOX)]

orthoepy /'ɔːθəʊɛpi, -iːpi, ɔː'θəʊɪpi/ *n.* the study of the (correct) pronunciation of words. □ **orthoepic** /-'ɛpɪk/ *adj.* **orthoepist** *n.* [Greek *orthoepeia* 'correct speech' (as ORTHO-, *epos* 'word')]

orthogenesis /ɔːθə(ʊ)'dʒɛnɪsɪs/ *n.* a theory of evolution which proposes that variations follow a defined direction and are not merely sporadic and fortuitous.

□ **orthogenetic** /-dʒɪ'nɛtɪk/ *adj.* **orthogenetically** /-dʒɪ'nɛtɪk(ə)li/ *adv.*

orthognathous /ɔ:θəg'neɪθəs, ɔ:'θɒgnəθəs/ *adj.* (of mammals, including humans) having a jaw which does not project forwards and a facial angle approaching a right angle. [ORTHO- + Greek *gnathos* 'jaw']

orthogonal /ɔ:'θɒg(ə)n(ə)l/ *adj.* of or involving right angles; at right angles. [French from *orthogone* (as ORTHO-, -GON)]

orthography /ɔ:'θɒgrəfi/ *n.* (*pl.* **-ies**) **1 a** correct or conventional spelling. **b** spelling with reference to its correctness (*dreadful orthography*). **c** the study or science of spelling. **2 a** perspective projection used in maps and elevations in which the projection lines are parallel. **b** a map etc. so projected. □ **orthographer** *n.* **orthographic** /-'grafɪk/ *adj.* **orthographical** /-'grafɪk(ə)l/ *adj.* **orthographically** /-'grafɪk(ə)li/ *adv.* [Middle English via Old French *ortografie* and Latin *orthographia* from Greek *orthographia* (as ORTHO-, -GRAPHY)]

orthopaedics /ɔ:θə'pi:dɪks/ *n.pl.* (*US* **-pedics**) (treated as *sing.*) the branch of medicine dealing with the treatment of disorders of the bones and joints, and with the correction of deformities, originally in children. □ **orthopaedic** *adj.* **orthopaedist** *n.* [French *orthopédie* (as ORTHO-, *pédie* from Greek *paideia* 'rearing of children')]

orthopteran /ɔ:'θɒpt(ə)rən/ *n.* any insect of the order Orthoptera, with straight narrow forewings, and hind legs modified for jumping etc., including grasshoppers and crickets. □ **orthopterous** *adj.* [ORTHO- + Greek *pteros* 'wing']

orthoptic /ɔ:'θɒptɪk/ *adj.* relating to the correct or normal use of the eyes. □ **orthoptist** *n.* [ORTHO- + Greek *optikos* 'of sight': see OPTIC]

orthoptics /ɔ:'θɒptɪks/ *n. Med.* the study or treatment of irregularities of the eyes, esp. with reference to the eye muscles.

orthorhombic /ɔ:θə'rɒmbɪk/ *adj. Crystallog.* (of a crystal) characterized by three mutually perpendicular axes which are unequal in length, as in topaz and talc.

orthotone /'ɔ:θətəʊn/ *adj.* & *n.* ● *adj.* (of a word) having an independent stress pattern, not enclitic nor proclitic. ● *n.* a word of this kind.

ortolan /'ɔ:t(ə)lən/ *n.* (in full **ortolan bunting**) *Zool.* a small European bird, *Emberiza hortulana*, formerly eaten as a delicacy. [French from Provençal, literally 'gardener', via Latin *hortulanus* from *hortulus*, diminutive of *hortus* 'garden']

Orwellian /ɔ:'wɛlɪən/ *adj.* of or characteristic of the writings of George Orwell (E. A. Blair), English writer d. 1950, esp. with reference to the totalitarian development of the State as depicted in *Nineteen Eighty-Four* and *Animal Farm*.

-ory[1] /əri/ *suffix* forming nouns denoting a place for a particular function (*dormitory*; *refectory*). □ **-orial** /'ɔ:rɪəl/ *suffix* forming adjectives. [Latin *-oria*, *-orium*, sometimes via Old Northern French and Anglo-French *-orie*, Old French *-oire*]

-ory[2] /əri/ *suffix* forming adjectives (and occasionally nouns) relating to or involving a verbal action (*accessory*; *compulsory*; *directory*). [Latin *-orius*, sometimes via Anglo-French *-ori(e)*, Old French *-oir(e)*]

oryx /'ɒrɪks/ *n.* any large straight-horned antelope of the genus *Oryx*, native to Africa and Arabia. [Middle English via Latin from Greek *orux* 'stonemason's pickaxe', from its pointed horns]

OS *abbr.* **1** Old Style. **2** ordinary seaman. **3** (in the UK) Ordnance Survey. **4** outsize. **5** out of stock.

Os *symb. Chem.* the element osmium.

Osage orange /'əʊseɪdʒ/ *n.* **1** a hardy thorny tree, *Maclura pomifera*, of the US, bearing inedible wrinkled orange-like fruit. **2** the durable orange-coloured timber from this. [name of a N. American Indian tribe]

Oscan /'ɒsk(ə)n/ *n.* & *adj.* ● *n.* the ancient language of Campania in Italy, related to Latin and surviving only in inscriptions. ● *adj.* relating to or written in Oscan. [Latin *Oscus*]

Oscar /'ɒskə/ *n.* any of the statuettes awarded by the US Academy of Motion Picture Arts and Sciences for excellence in film acting, directing, etc. [apparently from the supposed resemblance of the statuette to an Academy employee's Uncle *Oscar*]

oscillate /'ɒsɪleɪt/ *v.* **1** *intr.* & *tr.* **a** swing to and fro like a pendulum. **b** move to and fro between points. **2** *intr.* vacillate; vary between extremes of opinion, action, etc. **3** *intr. Physics* move with periodic regularity. **4** *intr. Electr.* (of a current) undergo high-frequency alternations as across a spark-gap or in a valve-transmitter circuit. **5** *intr.* (of a radio receiver) radiate electromagnetic waves owing to faulty operation. □ **oscillation** /-'leɪʃ(ə)n/ *n.* **oscillatory** /ɒ'sɪlət(ə)ri, 'ɒsɪleɪt(ə)ri/ *adj.* [Latin *oscillare oscillat-* 'swing']

oscillator /'ɒsɪleɪtə/ *n.* an apparatus for generating oscillatory electric currents by non-mechanical means.

oscillo- /ə'sɪləʊ/ *comb. form* oscillation, esp. of electric current.

oscillogram /ə'sɪləgram/ *n.* a record obtained from an oscillograph.

oscillograph /ə'sɪləgrɑ:f/ *n.* a device for recording oscillations. □ **oscillographic** /-'grafɪk/ *adj.* **oscillography** /-'lɒgrəfi/ *n.*

oscilloscope /ə'sɪləskəʊp/ *n.* a device for viewing oscillations by a display on the screen of a cathode ray tube. □ **oscilloscopic** /-'skɒpɪk/ *adj.*

oscine /'ɒsʌɪn, -sɪn/ *adj.* (also **oscinine** /'ɒsɪnʌɪn, -ni:n/) of or relating to the suborder Oscines of passerine birds including many of the songbirds. [Latin *oscen -cinis* 'songbird' (as OB-, *canere* 'sing')]

oscitation /ɒsɪ'teɪʃ(ə)n/ *n. formal* **1** yawning; drowsiness. **2** inattention; negligence. [Latin *oscitatio* from *oscitare* 'gape', from *os* 'mouth' + *citare* 'move']

oscula *pl.* of OSCULUM.

oscular /'ɒskjʊlə/ *adj.* **1** of or relating to the mouth. **2** of or relating to kissing. [Latin *osculum* 'mouth, kiss', diminutive of *os* 'mouth']

osculate /'ɒskjʊleɪt/ *v.* **1** *tr. Math.* (of a curve or surface) have contact of at least the second order with; have two branches with a common tangent, with each branch extending in both directions of the tangent. **2** *v.intr.* & *tr. joc.* kiss. □ **osculant** *adj.* **osculation** /-'leɪʃ(ə)n/ *n.* **osculatory** /'ɒskjʊlət(ə)ri/ *adj.* [Latin *osculari* 'kiss' (as OSCULAR)]

osculum /'ɒskjʊləm/ *n.* (*pl.* **oscula** /-lə/) *Zool.* a pore or orifice, esp. a large opening in a sponge through which water is expelled. [Latin: see OSCULAR]

-ose[1] /əʊs, əʊz/ *suffix* forming adjectives denoting possession of a quality (*grandiose*; *verbose*). □ **-osely** *suffix* forming adverbs. **-oseness** *suffix* forming nouns (cf. -OSITY). [from or suggested by Latin *-osus*]

-ose[2] /əʊz, əʊs/ *suffix Chem.* forming names of carbohydrates (*cellulose*; *sucrose*). [on the pattern of GLUCOSE]

osier /'əʊzɪə/ *n.* **1** any of various willows, esp. *Salix viminalis*, with long flexible shoots used in basketwork. **2** a shoot of a willow. [Middle English via Old French from medieval Latin *auseria* 'osier bed']

osier bed *n.* a place where osiers are grown.

-osis /'əʊsɪs/ *suffix* (*pl.* **-oses** /'əʊsi:z/) denoting a process or condition (*apotheosis*; *metamorphosis*), esp. a pathological state (*acidosis*; *neurosis*; *thrombosis*). [Latin from Greek *-ōsis*, suffix of verbal nouns]

-osity /'ɒsɪti/ *suffix* forming nouns from adjectives in *-ose* (see -OSE[1]) and *-ous* (*verbosity*; *curiosity*). [French *-osité* or Latin *-ositas -ositatis*: cf. -ITY]

Osmanli /ɒz'manli/ *adj.* & *n.* (*pl.* same or **Osmanlis**) = OTTOMAN. [Turkish from the name *Osman*, from Arabic *'uṯmān* (see OTTOMAN) + adj. suffix *-li*]

osmic[1] /'ɒzmɪk/ *adj.* of or relating to odours or the sense of smell. □ **osmically** *adv.* [Greek *osmē* 'smell, odour']

osmic[2] /'ɒzmɪk/ *adj. Chem.* containing osmium.

osmium /ˈɒzmɪəm/ *n. Chem.* a hard bluish-white transition element, the heaviest known metal, occurring naturally in association with platinum and used in certain alloys (symbol **Os**). [Greek *osmē* 'smell' (from the pungent smell of its tetroxide)]

osmoregulation /ˌɒzməʊrɛgjʊˈleɪʃ(ə)n/ *n. Biol.* the maintenance of constant osmotic pressure in the fluids of an organism by control of water and salt levels etc.

osmosis /ɒzˈməʊsɪs/ *n.* **1** *Biol. & Chem.* the passage of a solvent through a semi-permeable partition into a more concentrated solution. **2** any process by which something is acquired by absorption. ▫ **osmotic** /-ˈmɒtɪk/ *adj.* **osmotically** /-ˈmɒtɪk(ə)li/ *adv.* [Latinized form of earlier *osmose*, from Greek *ōsmos* 'push']

osmund /ˈɒsmənd, ɒz-/ *n.* (also **osmunda** /-də/) = ROYAL FERN. [Middle English from Anglo-French, of uncertain origin]

osprey /ˈɒspri, -preɪ/ *n.* (*pl.* **-eys**) **1** a large bird of prey, *Pandion haliaetus*, with a brown back and white markings, feeding on fish; also called *fish-hawk*. **2** a plume on a woman's hat. [Middle English from Old French *ospres*, apparently ultimately from Latin *ossifraga* 'lammergeyer, osprey' from *os* 'bone' + *frangere* 'break', probably referring to the lammergeyer's habit of dropping bones from a height in order to break them and get at the marrow]

ossein /ˈɒsɪɪn/ *n.* the collagen of bones. [Latin *osseus* (as OSSEOUS)]

osseous /ˈɒsɪəs/ *adj.* **1** consisting of bone. **2** having a bony skeleton. **3** ossified. [Latin *osseus* from *os ossis* 'bone']

ossicle /ˈɒsɪk(ə)l/ *n.* **1** *Anat.* any small bone, esp. of the middle ear. **2** a small piece of bonelike substance. [Latin *ossiculum*, diminutive of *os ossis* 'bone']

Ossie var. of AUSSIE.

ossify /ˈɒsɪfʌɪ/ *v.tr. & intr.* (**-ies**, **-ied**) **1** turn into bone; harden. **2** make or become rigid, callous, or unprogressive. ▫ **ossific** /ɒˈsɪfɪk/ *adj.* **ossification** /-fɪˈkeɪʃ(ə)n/ *n.* [French *ossifier* from Latin *os ossis* 'bone']

osso bucco /ɒsəʊ ˈbuːkəʊ/ *n.* shin of veal containing marrowbone stewed in wine with vegetables. [Italian, = marrowbone]

ossuary /ˈɒsjʊəri/ *n.* (*pl.* **-ies**) **1** a receptacle or urn for the bones of the dead; a charnel house. **2** a cave in which ancient bones are found. [Late Latin *ossuarium*, formed irregularly from *os ossis* 'bone']

osteitis /ɒstɪˈʌɪtɪs/ *n.* inflammation of the substance of a bone. [Greek *osteon* 'bone' + -ITIS]

ostensible /ɒˈstɛnsɪb(ə)l/ *adj.* apparent but not necessarily real; professed (*his ostensible function was that of interpreter*). ▫ **ostensibly** *adv.* [French via medieval Latin *ostensibilis* from Latin *ostendere ostens-* 'stretch out to view' (as OB-, *tendere* 'stretch')]

ostensive /ɒˈstɛnsɪv/ *adj.* **1** directly demonstrative. **2** (of a definition) indicating by direct demonstration that which is signified by a term. ▫ **ostensively** *adv.* **ostensiveness** *n.* [Late Latin *ostensivus* (as OSTENSIBLE)]

ostensory /ɒˈstɛns(ə)ri/ *n.* (*pl.* **-ies**) *RC Ch.* a receptacle for displaying the host to the congregation; a monstrance. [medieval Latin *ostensorium* (as OSTENSIBLE)]

ostentation /ɒstɛnˈteɪʃ(ə)n/ *n.* **1** a pretentious and vulgar display esp. of wealth and luxury. **2** the attempt or intention to attract notice; showing off. ▫ **ostentatious** *adj.* **ostentatiously** *adv.* [Middle English via Old French from Latin *ostentatio -onis*, from *ostentare*, frequentative of *ostendere*: see OSTENSIBLE]

osteo- /ˈɒstɪəʊ/ *comb. form* bone. [Greek *osteon*]

osteoarthritis /ˌɒstɪəʊɑːˈθrʌɪtɪs/ *n.* degeneration of joint cartilage, esp. from middle age onward, causing pain and stiffness. ▫ **osteoarthritic** /-ˈθrɪtɪk/ *adj.*

osteogenesis /ɒstɪəˈdʒɛnɪsɪs/ *n.* the formation of bone. ▫ **osteogenetic** /-dʒɪˈnɛtɪk/ *adj.*

osteology /ɒstɪˈɒlədʒi/ *n.* the study of the structure and function of the skeleton and bony structures. ▫ **osteological** /-əˈlɒdʒɪk(ə)l/ *adj.* **osteologically** /-əˈlɒdʒɪk(ə)li/ *adv.* **osteologist** *n.*

osteomalacia /ˌɒstɪəʊməˈleɪʃɪə/ *n.* softening of the bones, often through a deficiency of vitamin D and calcium. ▫ **osteomalacic** /-ˈlasɪk/ *adj.* [modern Latin (as OSTEO-, Greek *malakos* 'soft')]

osteomyelitis /ˌɒstɪəʊmʌɪɪˈlʌɪtɪs/ *n.* inflammation of the bone or of bone marrow, usu. due to infection.

osteopathy /ɒstɪˈɒpəθi/ *n.* the treatment of medical disorders through the manipulation and massage of the skeleton and musculature. ▫ **osteopath** /ˈɒstɪəpaθ/ *n.* **osteopathic** /ɒstɪəˈpaθɪk/ *adj.*

osteoporosis /ˌɒstɪəʊpəˈrəʊsɪs/ *n.* a condition of brittle and fragile bones caused by loss of bony tissue, esp. as a result of hormonal changes, or deficiency of calcium or vitamin D. [OSTEO- + Greek *poros* 'passage, pore']

ostinato /ɒstɪˈnɑːtəʊ/ *n.* (*pl.* **-os** or **ostinati** /-ti/) (often *attrib.*) *Mus.* a persistent phrase or rhythm repeated through all or part of a piece. [Italian, = OBSTINATE]

ostium /ˈɒstɪəm/ *n.* (*pl.* **ostia** /ˈɒstɪə/) *Anat. & Zool.* an opening into a vessel or body cavity. [Latin, = door, opening]

ostler /ˈɒslə/ *n. Brit. hist.* a stableman at an inn. [earlier HOSTLER, *hosteler* from Anglo-French *hostiler*, Old French *(h)ostelier* (as HOSTEL)]

Ostmark /ˈɒstmɑːk/ *n. hist.* the chief monetary unit of the Democratic Republic of Germany. [German, = east mark: see MARK²]

Ostpolitik /ˈɒstpɒlɪˌtiːk/ *n. hist.* the foreign policy (esp. of détente) of many western European countries with reference to the former Communist bloc. [German, from *Ost* 'east' + *Politik* 'politics']

ostracize /ˈɒstrəsʌɪz/ *v.tr.* (also **-ise**) **1** exclude (a person) from a society, favour, common privileges, etc.; refuse to associate with. **2** (esp. in ancient Athens) banish (a powerful or unpopular citizen) for five or ten years by popular vote. ▫ **ostracism** /-sɪz(ə)m/ *n.* [Greek *ostrakizō* from *ostrakon* 'shell, potsherd' (used to write a name on in voting)]

ostrich /ˈɒstrɪtʃ/ *n.* **1** a large African swift-running flightless bird, *Struthio camelus*, with long legs and two toes on each foot. **2** a person who refuses to accept facts (from the belief that ostriches bury their heads in the sand when pursued). [Middle English from Old French *ostric(h)e*, from Latin *avis* 'bird' + Late Latin *struthio* (via Greek *strouthiōn* 'ostrich' from *strouthos* 'sparrow, ostrich')]

ostrich farm *n.* a place where ostriches are bred for their feathers, or for their flesh as food.

ostrich plume *n.* a feather or bunch of feathers of an ostrich.

Ostrogoth /ˈɒstrəgɒθ/ *n. hist.* a member of the eastern branch of the Goths, who conquered Italy in the 5th–6th c. AD. ▫ **Ostrogothic** /-ˈgɒθɪk/ *adj.* [Late Latin *Ostrogothi* (pl.) from Germanic base of 'east' + Late Latin *Gothi* 'Goths': see GOTH]

OT *abbr.* Old Testament.

-ot¹ /ət/ *suffix* forming nouns, originally diminutives (*ballot*; *chariot*; *parrot*). [French]

-ot² /ət/ *suffix* forming nouns denoting persons (*patriot*), e.g. natives of a place (*Cypriot*). [French *-ote*, Latin *-ota*, Greek *-ōtēs*]

OTC *abbr.* (in the UK) Officers' Training Corps.

other /ˈʌðə/ *adj., n.* or *pron., & adv.* ● *adj.* **1** not the same as one or some already mentioned or implied; separate in identity or distinct in kind (*other people*; *use other means*; *I assure you, my reason is quite other*). **2 a** further; additional (*a few other examples*). **b** alternative of two (*open your other eye*) (cf. *every other*). **3** (prec. by *the*) that remains after all except the one or ones in question have been considered, eliminated, etc. (*must be in the other pocket*; *where are the other two?*; *the other three men left*). **4** (foll. by *than*) apart from; excepting (*any person other than you*). ● *n.* or *pron.* (originally an elliptical use of the adj., now with pl. in *-s*) **1** an additional, different, or extra person, thing, example, etc. (*one or other of us will be there*; *some others have come*) (see also ANOTHER, EACH OTHER). **2** (in *pl.*; prec. by *the*) the ones remaining (*where are the others?*). **3** (prec. by *the*) *slang* sexual intercourse (*a bit of the other*). **4** (usu. **Other** or in quotation marks, prec. by *the*) *Philos. & Sociol.* that which is distinct from, different from, or opposite to something or oneself (*fear of the 'other'*). ● *adv.* (usu. foll. by *than*) *disp.* otherwise (*cannot react other than angrily*). □ **no other** *archaic* nothing else (*I can do no other*). **of all others** out of the many possible or likely (*on this night of all others*). **on the other hand** see HAND. **the other day** (or **night** or **week** etc.) a few days etc. ago (*heard from him the other day*). **the other thing** esp. *joc.* an unexpressed alternative (*if you don't like it, do the other thing*). **other things being equal** if conditions are or were alike in all but the point in question. **someone** (or **something** or **somehow** etc.) **or other** some unspecified person, thing, manner, etc. [Old English *ōther*, from Germanic]

■ **Usage** The use of *other* as an adverb (see example above) is non-standard. *Otherwise* should be used instead, e.g. *It is impossible to do the job otherwise than very superficially in the time allotted.*

other-directed *adj.* governed by external circumstances and trends.

other half *n. colloq.* one's wife or husband.

otherness /ˈʌðənɪs/ *n.* **1** the state of being different; diversity. **2** a thing or existence other than the thing mentioned and the thinking subject.

other place *n.* (prec. by *the*) *Brit. joc.* **1** hell (as opposed to heaven). **2** Oxford University as regarded by Cambridge, and vice versa. **3** *Brit.* the House of Lords as regarded by the House of Commons and vice versa.

other ranks *n.pl. Brit.* soldiers other than commissioned officers.

otherwhere /ˈʌðəwɛː/ *adj. archaic* or *poet.* elsewhere.

otherwise /ˈʌðəwʌɪz/ *adv. & adj.* ● *adv.* **1** else; or else; in the circumstances other than those considered etc. (*bring your umbrella, otherwise you will get wet*). **2** in other respects (*he is untidy, but otherwise very suitable*). **3** (often foll. by *than*) in a different way (*could not have acted otherwise*; *cannot react otherwise than angrily*). **4** as an alternative (*otherwise known as Jack*). ● *adj.* **1** (*predic.*) in a different state (*the matter is quite otherwise*). **2** *archaic* that would otherwise exist (*their otherwise dullness*). □ **and** (or **or**) **otherwise** the negation or opposite (of a specified thing) (*the merits or otherwise of the Bill*; *experiences pleasant and otherwise*). [Old English *on ōthre wisan* (as OTHER, WISE[2])]

■ **Usage** See Usage Note at OTHER.

other woman *n.* (*masc.* **other man**) (prec. by *the*) the lover of a married or similarly attached woman or man.

other world *n.* (prec. by *the*) = NEXT WORLD.

other-worldly *adj.* **1** not of this world; of an imaginary other world. **2** relating to life after death etc. □ **other-worldliness** *n.*

otic /ˈəʊtɪk, ˈɒtɪk/ *adj.* of or relating to the ear. [Greek *ōtikos* from *ous ōtos* 'ear']

-otic /ˈɒtɪk/ *suffix* forming adjectives and nouns corresponding to nouns in *-osis*, meaning 'affected with or producing or resembling a condition in *-osis*' or 'a person affected with this' (*narcotic*; *neurotic*; *osmotic*). □ **-otically** *suffix* forming adverbs. [from or suggested by French *-otique*, via Latin from Greek adj. suffix *-ōtikos*]

otiose /ˈəʊtɪəʊs, ˈəʊʃɪ-, -əʊz/ *adj.* **1** serving no practical purpose; not required; functionless. **2** *archaic* indolent; futile. □ **otiosely** *adv.* **otioseness** *n.* [Latin *otiosus* from *otium* 'leisure']

otitis /ə(ʊ)ˈtʌɪtɪs/ *n.* inflammation of the ear, esp. (in full **otitis media**) of the middle ear. [modern Latin (as OTO-)]

oto- /ˈəʊtəʊ/ *comb. form* ear. [Greek *ōto-* from *ous ōtos* 'ear']

otolaryngology /ˌəʊtə(ʊ)larɪŋˈgɒlədʒi/ *n.* the study of diseases of the ear and throat. □ **otolaryngological** /-gəˈlɒdʒɪk(ə)l/ *adj.* **otolaryngologist** *n.*

otolith /ˈəʊtəlɪθ/ *n.* any of the small particles of calcium carbonate in the inner ear of vertebrates, involved in sensing gravity and movement. □ **otolithic** /-ˈlɪθɪk/ *adj.*

otology /əʊˈtɒlədʒi/ *n.* the study of the anatomy and diseases of the ear. □ **otological** /-təˈlɒdʒɪk(ə)l/ *adj.* **otologist** *n.*

otorhinolaryngology /ˌəʊtərʌɪnəʊˌlarɪŋˈgɒlədʒi/ *n.* the study of diseases of the ear, nose, and throat.

otoscope /ˈəʊtəskəʊp/ *n.* an apparatus for examining the eardrum and the passage leading to it from the ear. □ **otoscopic** /-ˈskɒpɪk/ *adj.*

OTT *abbr. colloq.* over-the-top.

ottava rima /ɒˌtɑːvə ˈriːmə/ *n.* a stanza of eight lines of 10 or 11 syllables, rhyming *abababcc*. [Italian, literally 'eighth rhyme']

otter /ˈɒtə/ *n.* **1 a** any of several semiaquatic fish-eating mammals of the genus *Lutra* or a related genus of the weasel family, with dense fur and webbed feet. **b** its fur or pelt. **2** = SEA OTTER. **3** a piece of board used to carry fishing bait in water. **4** a type of paravane, esp. as used on non-naval craft. [Old English *otr, ot(t)or*, from Germanic]

otter-board *n.* a device for keeping the mouth of a trawl net open.

otter-dog *n.* (also **otter-hound**) a dog of a breed used in otter-hunting.

otto var. of ATTAR.

Ottoman /ˈɒtəmən/ *adj. & n.* ● *adj. hist.* **1** of or relating to: **a** the dynasty of Osman I (Othman I). **b** the branch of the Turks to which he belonged. **c** the empire ruled by his descendants. **2** Turkish. ● *n.* (*pl.* **Ottomans**) an Ottoman person; a Turk. [French or Italian *Ottomano*, ultimately from Arabic *'uṯmānī*, adj. from *'uṯmān* 'Othman', name of the founder of the dynasty]

ottoman /ˈɒtəmən/ *n.* (*pl.* **ottomans**) **1 a** an upholstered seat, usu. square and without a back or arms, sometimes a box with a padded top. **b** a footstool of similar design. **2** a heavy silken fabric with a mixture of cotton or wool. [French *ottomane*, fem. of *ottoman* OTTOMAN]

Ottoman Porte see PORTE.

OU *abbr. Brit.* **1** Open University. **2** Oxford University.

oubliette /uːblɪˈɛt/ *n.* a secret dungeon with access only through a trapdoor. [French from *oublier* 'forget']

ouch /aʊtʃ/ *int.* expressing pain. [a natural exclamation]

ought[1] /ɔːt/ *v.aux.* (usu. foll. by *to* + infin.; present and past indicated by the following infin.) **1** expressing duty or rightness (*we ought to love our neighbours*). **2** expressing shortcoming (*it ought to have been done long ago*). **3** expressing advisability or prudence (*you ought to go for your own good*). **4** expressing esp. strong probability (*he ought to be there by now*). □ **ought not** the negative form of *ought* (*he ought not to have stolen it*). [Old English *āhte*, past of *āgan* OWE]

ought[2] /ɔːt/ *n.* (also **aught**) *colloq.* a figure denoting nothing; nought. [perhaps from *an ought* for a NOUGHT; cf. ADDER]

ought[3] var. of AUGHT[1].

oughtn't /ˈɔːt(ə)nt/ *contr.* ought not.

Ouija /ˈwiːdʒə/ *n.* (in full **Ouija board**) *propr.* a board having letters or signs at its rim to which a planchette, movable pointer, or upturned glass supposedly points in answer to questions from attenders at a seance etc. [French *oui* 'yes' + German *ja* 'yes']

ounce[1] /aʊns/ *n.* **1 a** a unit of weight of one-sixteenth of a pound avoirdupois (approx. 28 grams) (abbr.: **oz**). **b** a unit of one-twelfth of a pound troy or apothecaries' measure, equal to 480 grains (approx. 31 grams). **2** a small quantity. [Middle English & Old French *unce* from Latin *uncia* 'twelfth part' (of pound or foot): cf. INCH[1]]

ounce[2] /aʊns/ *n.* an Asian wild cat, *Panthera uncia*, with leopard-like markings on a cream-coloured coat.

Also called *mountain panther, snow leopard.* [Middle English from Old French *once* (earlier *lonce*) = Italian *lonza*, ultimately from Latin *lynx*: see LYNX]

OUP *abbr.* Oxford University Press.

our /aʊə/ *poss.det.* **1** of or belonging to us or ourselves (*our house*; *our own business*). **2** of or belonging to all people (*our children's future*). **3** (esp. as **Our**) of Us the royal, imperial, etc., personage (*given under Our seal*) (cf. ROYAL 'WE'). **4** of us, the editorial staff of a newspaper etc. (*a foolish adventure in our view*). **5** *Brit. colloq.* indicating a relative, acquaintance, or colleague of the speaker (*our Barry works there*). [Old English *ūre*, originally genitive pl. of 1st person pronoun = of us, later treated as possessive adj.]

-our[1] /ə/ *suffix* var. of -OR[2] surviving in some nouns (*ardour*; *colour*; *valour*).

-our[2] /ə/ *suffix* var. of -OR[1] (*saviour*).

Our Father *n.* **1** the Lord's Prayer. **2** God.

Our Lady *n.* the Virgin Mary.

Our Lady's bedstraw *n.* = BEDSTRAW 2.

Our Lord *n.* **1** Jesus Christ. **2** God.

ours /aʊəz/ *poss.pron.* the one or ones belonging to or associated with us (*it is ours*; *ours are over there*). □ **of ours** of or belonging to us (*a friend of ours*).

Our Saviour *n.* Jesus Christ.

ourself /aʊə'sɛlf/ *pron.* **1** *archaic* a word formerly used instead of *myself* by a sovereign, newspaper editorial staff, etc. (cf. OUR 3, 4). **2** *disp.* = OURSELVES.

■ **Usage** The use of *ourself* rather than *ourselves* in contexts such as *We see ourself as the biggest club in Britain*, is considered incorrect by some people.

ourselves /aʊə'sɛlvz/ *pron.* **1 a** *emphat. form* of WE or US (*we ourselves did it*; *made it ourselves*; *for our friends and ourselves*). **b** *refl. form* of US (*are pleased with ourselves*). **2** in our normal state of body or mind (*not quite ourselves today*). □ **be ourselves** act in our normal unconstrained manner. **by ourselves** see *by oneself*.

-ous /əs/ *suffix* **1** forming adjectives meaning 'abounding in, characterized by, of the nature of' (*envious*; *glorious*; *mountainous*; *poisonous*). **2** *Chem.* denoting a state of lower valence than the corresponding word in *-ic* (*ferrous*). □ **-ously** *suffix* forming adverbs. **-ousness** *suffix* forming nouns. [from or suggested by Anglo-French *-ous*, Old French *-eus*, from Latin *-osus*]

ousel var. of OUZEL.

oust /aʊst/ *v.tr.* **1** (usu. foll. by *from*) drive out or expel, esp. by forcing oneself into the place of. **2** (usu. foll. by *of*) *Law* put (a person) out of possession; deprive. [Anglo-French *ouster*, Old French *oster* 'take away', from Latin *obstare* 'oppose, hinder' (as OB-, *stare* 'stand')]

ouster /'aʊstə/ *n.* **1** ejection as a result of physical action, judicial process, or political upheaval. **2** esp. *N. Amer.* dismissal, expulsion.

out /aʊt/ *adv., prep., n., adj., int., & v.* ● *adv.* **1** away from or not in or at a place etc. (*keep him out*; *get out of here*; *my son is out in Canada*). **2** (forming part of phrasal verbs) **a** indicating dispersal away from a centre etc. (*hire out*; *share out*; *board out*). **b** indicating a progression to a conclusion or resolution (*die out*; *fit it out*). **c** indicating coming or bringing into the open for public attention etc. (*call out*; *send out*; *shine out*; *stand out*). **d** indicating a need for attentiveness (*watch out*; *look out*; *listen out*). **3 a** not in one's house, office, etc. (*went out for a walk*). **b** occupied elsewhere, esp. socially (*out with friends*). **c** no longer detained in prison. **4 a** completely; thoroughly (*tired out*). **b** in its entirety (*typed it out*). **5** (of a fire, light, etc.) not burning; no longer lit. **6** in error (*was 3% out in my calculations*). **7** *colloq.* unconscious (*she was out for five minutes*). **8 a** (of a tooth) extracted. **b** (of a joint, bone, etc.) dislocated (*put his shoulder out*). **9** (of a party, politician, etc.) not in office. **10** (of a jury) considering its verdict in secrecy. **11** (of workers) on strike. **12** (of a secret) revealed. **13** (of a flower) blooming, open. **14** (of a book) published. **15** (of a star) visible after dark. **16** unfashionable (*turn-ups are out*). **17 a** (of a batsman, batter, etc.) no longer taking part as such, having been caught, stumped, etc. **b** (of a shot, serve, etc.) outside the boundary of the playing area. **18** not worth considering; rejected (*that idea is out*). **19** (prec. by *superl.*) *colloq.* known to exist (*the best game out*). **20** (of a stain, mark, etc.) not visible, removed (*painted out the sign*). **21** (of time) not spent working (*took five minutes out*). **22** (of a rash, bruise, etc.) visible. **23** (of the tide) at the lowest point. **24** *Boxing* unable to rise from the floor (*out for the count*). **25 a** at an end; over (*before the week is out*). **b** (in a radio conversation etc.) transmission ends (*over and out*). **26** *archaic* (of a young upper-class woman) introduced into society. ● *prep.* **1** *disp.* out of (*looked out the window*). **2** *archaic* outside; beyond the limits of. ● *n.* **1** *colloq.* a way of escape; an excuse. **2** (**the outs**) the political party out of office. **3** *Baseball* the action or an act of putting a player out. ● *adj.* **1** *Brit.* (of a match) played away. **2** (of an island) away from the mainland. ● *int.* a peremptory dismissal, reproach, etc. (*out, you scoundrel!*). ● *v.* **1** *tr.* **a** put out. **b** *colloq.* eject forcibly. **2** *intr.* come or go out; emerge (*murder will out*). **3** *tr. Boxing* knock out. **4** *tr. colloq.* reveal the homosexuality of (a prominent person). □ **at outs** at variance or enmity. **not out** *Cricket* (of a side or a batsman) not having been caught, bowled, etc. **out and about** (of a person, esp. after an illness) engaging in normal activity. **out and away** by far. **out at elbows** see ELBOW. **out for** having one's interest or effort directed to; intent on. **out of 1** from within (*came out of the house*). **2** not within (*I was never out of England*). **3** from among (*nine people out of ten*; *must choose out of these*). **4** beyond the range of (*is out of reach*). **5** without or so as to be without (*was swindled out of his money*; *out of breath*; *out of sugar*). **6** from (*get money out of him*). **7** owing to; because of (*asked out of curiosity*). **8** by the use of (material) (*what did you make it out of?*). **9** at a specified distance from (a town, port, etc.) (*seven miles out of Liverpool*). **10** beyond (*something out of the ordinary*). **11** *Racing* (of an animal, esp. a horse) born of. **out of bounds** see BOUND[2]. **out of date** see DATE[1]. **out of doors** see DOOR. **out of drawing** see DRAWING. **out of hand** see HAND. **out of it 1** not included; forlorn. **2** *colloq.* unaware of what is happening, due to excessive drinking etc. **out of order** see ORDER. **out of pocket** see POCKET. **out of the question** see QUESTION. **out of sorts** see SORT. **out of temper** see TEMPER. **out of this world** see WORLD. **out of the way** see WAY. **out to** keenly striving to do. **out with** an exhortation to expel or dismiss (an unwanted person). **out with it** say what you are thinking. [Old English *ūt*, Old High German *ūz*, related to Sanskrit *ud-*]

■ **Usage** The use of *out* as a preposition, as in *He threw it out the window* or *I jumped out the boat*, is considered incorrect by some people. *Out of* is preferable in formal contexts.

out- /aʊt/ *prefix* added to verbs and nouns, meaning: **1** so as to surpass or exceed (*outdo*; *outnumber*). **2** external, separate (*outline*; *outhouse*; *outdoors*). **3** out of; away from; outward (*outspread*; *outgrowth*).

outact /aʊt'akt/ *v.tr.* surpass in acting or performing.

outage /'aʊtɪdʒ/ *n.* a period of time during which a power supply etc. is not operating.

out and out *adj. & adv.* ● *adj.* thorough; surpassing. ● *adv.* thoroughly; surpassingly.

out-and-outer *n. slang* **1** a thorough or supreme person or thing. **2** an extremist.

outback /'aʊtbak/ *n.* esp. *Austral.* the remote and usu. uninhabited inland districts. □ **outbacker** *n.*

outbalance /aʊt'baləns/ *v.tr.* **1** count as more important than. **2** outweigh.

outbid /aʊt'bɪd/ *v.tr.* (**-bidding**; *past* and *past part.* **-bid**) **1** bid higher than (another person) at an auction. **2** surpass in exaggeration etc.

outblaze /aʊtˈbleɪz/ *v.* **1** *intr.* blaze out or outwards. **2** *tr.* blaze more brightly than.

outboard /ˈaʊtbɔːd/ *adj., adv., & n.* ● *adj.* **1** (of a motor) portable and attachable to the outside of the stern of a boat. **2** (of a boat) having an outboard motor. ● *adj. & adv.* on, towards, or near the outside of esp. a ship, an aircraft, etc. ● *n.* **1** an outboard engine. **2** a boat with an outboard engine.

outbound /ˈaʊtbaʊnd/ *adj.* outward bound.

outbrave /aʊtˈbreɪv/ *v.tr.* **1** outdo in bravery. **2** face defiantly.

outbreak /ˈaʊtbreɪk/ *n.* **1** a usu. sudden eruption of war, disease, rebellion, etc. **2** an outcrop.

outbreeding /ˈaʊtbriːdɪŋ/ *n.* the theory or practice of breeding from animals not closely related. □ **outbreed** *v.intr. & tr.* (*past* and *past part.* **-bred**).

outbuilding /ˈaʊtbɪldɪŋ/ *n.* a detached shed, barn, garage, etc. within the grounds of a main building; an outhouse.

outburst /ˈaʊtbəːst/ *n.* **1** an explosion of anger etc., expressed in words. **2** an act or instance of bursting out. **3** an outcrop.

outcast /ˈaʊtkɑːst/ *n. & adj.* ● *n.* **1** a person cast out from or rejected by his or her home, country, society, etc. **2** a tramp or vagabond. ● *adj.* rejected; homeless; friendless.

outcaste *n. & v.* ● *n.* /ˈaʊtkɑːst/ (also *attrib.*) **1** a person who has no caste, esp. in Hindu society. **2** a person who has lost his or her caste. ● *v.tr.* /-ˈkɑːst/ cause (a person) to lose his or her caste.

outclass /aʊtˈklɑːs/ *v.tr.* **1** belong to a higher class than. **2** defeat easily.

outcome /ˈaʊtkʌm/ *n.* a result; a visible effect.

outcrop /ˈaʊtkrɒp/ *n. & v.* ● *n.* **1 a** the emergence of a stratum, vein, or rock, at the surface. **b** a stratum etc. emerging. **2** a noticeable manifestation or occurrence. ● *v.intr.* (**-cropped**, **-cropping**) appear as an outcrop; crop out.

outcry /ˈaʊtkrʌɪ/ *n.* (*pl.* **-ies**) **1** the act or an instance of crying out. **2** an uproar. **3** a noisy or prolonged public protest.

outdance /aʊtˈdɑːns/ *v.tr.* surpass in dancing.

outdare /aʊtˈdɛː/ *v.tr.* **1** outdo in daring. **2** overcome by daring.

outdated /aʊtˈdeɪtɪd/ *adj.* out of date; obsolete.

outdistance /aʊtˈdɪst(ə)ns/ *v.tr.* leave (a competitor) behind completely.

outdo /aʊtˈduː/ *v.tr.* (*3rd sing. present* **-does**; *past* **-did**; *pres. part.* **-doing**; *past part.* **-done**) exceed or excel in doing or performance; surpass.

outdoor /ˈaʊtdɔː/ *attrib.adj.* **1** done, existing, or used out of doors. **2** fond of the open air (*an outdoor type*).

outdoor pursuits *n.pl.* usu. organized sporting or leisure activities undertaken out of doors (also *attrib.*: *outdoor pursuits centre*).

outdoors /aʊtˈdɔːz/ *adv. & n.* ● *adv.* in or into the open air; out of doors. ● *n.* the world outside buildings; the open air.

outer /ˈaʊtə/ *adj. & n.* ● *adj.* **1** outside; external (*pierced the outer layer*). **2** farther from the centre or inside; relatively far out. **3** objective or physical, not subjective or psychical. ● *n.* **1** *Brit.* **a** the division of a target furthest from the bull's-eye. **b** a shot that strikes this. **2** *Brit.* an outer garment or part of one. **3** *Austral. slang* the part of a racecourse outside the enclosure. **4** *Brit.* an outer container for transport or display. [Middle English from OUT, replacing UTTER[1]]

outer Bar *n.* (prec. by *the*) barristers who are not Queen's Counsels.

outer garments *n.pl.* clothes worn over other clothes or outdoors.

Outer House *n. Law* (in Scotland) the hall where judges of the Court of Session sit singly.

outer man *n.* (also **outer woman**) (prec. by *the*) personal appearance; dress.

outermost /ˈaʊtəməʊst/ *adj.* furthest from the inside; the most far out.

outer planet *n.* a planet with an orbit outside the asteroid belt (i.e. Jupiter, Saturn, Uranus, Neptune, Pluto).

outer space see SPACE *n.* 3a.

outerwear /ˈaʊtəwɛː/ *n.* = OUTER GARMENTS.

outer woman see OUTER MAN.

outer world *n.* (prec. by *the*) people outside one's own circle.

outface /aʊtˈfeɪs/ *v.tr.* disconcert or defeat by staring or by a display of confidence.

outfall /ˈaʊtfɔːl/ *n.* the mouth of a river, drain, etc., where it empties into the sea etc.

outfield /ˈaʊtfiːld/ *n.* **1** the outer part of a cricket or baseball field. **2** outlying land. □ **outfielder** *n.*

outfight /aʊtˈfʌɪt/ *v.tr.* fight better than; beat in a fight.

outfit /ˈaʊtfɪt/ *n. & v.* ● *n.* **1** a set of clothes worn or esp. designed to be worn together. **2** a complete set of equipment etc. for a specific purpose. **3** *colloq.* a group of people regarded as a unit, organization, etc.; a team. ● *v.tr.* (**-fitted**, **-fitting**) (also *refl.*) provide with an outfit, esp. of clothes.

outfitter /ˈaʊtfɪtə/ *n.* a supplier of equipment, esp. (*Brit.*) of conventional styles of clothing or (*N. Amer.*) of equipment for outdoor expeditions.

outflank /aʊtˈflaŋk/ *v.tr.* **1 a** extend one's flank beyond that of (an enemy). **b** outmanoeuvre (an enemy) in this way. **2** get the better of; confound (an opponent).

outflow /ˈaʊtfləʊ/ *n.* **1** an outward flow. **2** the amount that flows out.

outflung /ˈaʊtflʌŋ, *predic.* -ˈflʌŋ/ *adj.* (esp. of an arm) flung out to one side.

outfly /aʊtˈflʌɪ/ *v.tr.* (**-flies**; *past* **-flew**; *past part.* **-flown**) **1** surpass in flying. **2** fly faster or farther than.

outfox /aʊtˈfɒks/ *v.tr. colloq.* outwit.

outgas /aʊtˈgas/ *v.* (**outgases**, **outgassed**, **outgassing**) **1** *intr.* release or give off a dissolved or adsorbed gas or vapour. **2** *tr.* **a** release or give off (a substance) as a gas or vapour. **b** drive off a gas or vapour from.

outgeneral /aʊtˈdʒɛn(ə)r(ə)l/ *v.tr.* (**-generalled**, **-generalling**; *US* **-generaled**, **-generaling**) **1** outdo in generalship. **2** get the better of by superior strategy or tactics.

outgo *v. & n.* ● *v.tr.* /aʊtˈgəʊ/ (*3rd sing. present* **-goes** /-ˈgəʊz/; *past* **-went** /-ˈwɛnt/; *past part.* **-gone** /-ˈgɒn/) *archaic* go faster than; surpass. ● *n.* /ˈaʊtgəʊ/ (*pl.* **-goes**) expenditure of money, effort, etc.

outgoing /ˈaʊtgəʊɪŋ/ *adj. & n.* ● *adj.* **1** friendly; sociable; extrovert. **2** retiring from office. **3** going out or away. ● *n. Brit.* **1** (in *pl.*) expenditure. **2** the act or an instance of going out.

outgrow /aʊtˈgrəʊ/ *v.tr.* (*past* **-grew**; *past part.* **-grown**) **1** grow too big for (one's clothes). **2** leave behind (a childish habit, taste, ailment, etc.) as one matures. **3** grow faster or taller than (a person, plant, etc.). □ **outgrow one's strength** *Brit.* (esp. of a plant) become lanky and weak through too rapid growth.

outgrowth /ˈaʊtgrəʊθ/ *n.* **1** something that grows out. **2** an offshoot; a natural product. **3** the process of growing out.

outguess /aʊtˈgɛs/ *v.tr.* guess correctly what is intended by (another person).

outgun /aʊtˈgʌn/ *v.tr.* (**-gunned**, **-gunning**) **1** surpass in military or other power or strength. **2** shoot better than.

outhouse /ˈaʊthaʊs/ *n. & v.* ● *n.* **1** esp. *Brit.* a building, esp. a shed, lean-to, barn, etc. built next to or in the grounds of a house. **2** *N. Amer.* an outdoor lavatory. ● *v.tr.* store (books etc.) away from the main collection.

outing /ˈaʊtɪŋ/ *n.* **1** a short holiday away from home, esp. of one day or part of a day; a pleasure trip, an excursion. **2** any brief journey from home. **3** an appearance in an outdoor match, race, etc. **4** *colloq.* the practice or policy of revealing the homosexuality of a prominent person. [OUT *v.* + -ING[1]]

outjockey /aʊt'dʒɒki/ *v.tr.* (**-eys**, **-eyed**) outwit by adroitness or trickery.

outjump /aʊt'dʒʌmp/ *v.tr.* surpass in jumping.

outlander /'aʊtlandə/ *n.* a foreigner, alien, or stranger.

outlandish /aʊt'landɪʃ/ *adj.* **1** looking or sounding foreign. **2** bizarre, strange, unfamiliar. □ **outlandishly** *adv.* **outlandishness** *n.* [Old English *ūtlendisc* from *ūtland* 'foreign country', from OUT + LAND]

outlast /aʊt'lɑːst/ *v.tr.* last longer than (a person, thing, or duration) (*outlasted its usefulness*).

outlaw /'aʊtlɔː/ *n. & v.* ● *n.* **1** a fugitive from the law. **2** *hist.* a person deprived of the protection of the law. ● *v.tr.* **1** declare (a person) an outlaw. **2** make illegal; proscribe (a practice etc.). □ **outlawry** *n.* [Old English *ūtlaga*, *ūtlagian* from Old Norse *útlagi*, from *útlagr* 'outlawed': related to OUT, LAW]

outlay /'aʊtleɪ/ *n.* the money spent on something.

outlet /'aʊtlɛt/ *n.* **1** a means of exit or escape. **2** (usu. foll. by *for*) a means of expression (of a talent, emotion, etc.) (*find an outlet for tension*). **3** an agency, distributor, or market for goods (*a new retail outlet in China*). **4** *US* a power point. [Middle English, from OUT- + LET[1]]

outlier /'aʊtlʌɪə/ *n.* **1** (also *attrib.*) an outlying part or member. **2** *Geol.* a younger rock formation isolated in older rocks. **3** *Brit. Statistics* a result differing greatly from others in the same sample.

outline /'aʊtlʌɪn/ *n. & v.* ● *n.* **1** a rough draft of a diagram, plan, proposal, etc. **2 a** a précis of a proposed novel, article, etc. **b** a verbal description of essential parts only; a summary. **3** a sketch containing only contour lines. **4** (in *sing.* or *pl.*) **a** lines enclosing or indicating an object (*the outline of a shape under the blankets*). **b** a contour. **c** an external boundary. **5** (in *pl.*) the main features or general principles (*the outlines of a plan*). **6** the representation of a word in shorthand. ● *v.tr.* **1** draw or describe in outline. **2** mark the outline of. □ **in outline** sketched or represented as an outline.

outlive /aʊt'lɪv/ *v.tr.* **1** live longer than (another person). **2** live beyond (a specified date or time). **3** live through (an experience).

outlook /'aʊtlʊk/ *n.* **1** the prospect for the future (*the outlook is bleak*). **2** one's mental attitude or point of view (*narrow in their outlook*). **3** what is seen on looking out.

outlying /'aʊtlʌɪɪŋ/ *attrib.adj.* situated far from a centre; remote.

outmanoeuvre /aʊtmə'nuːvə/ *v.tr.* (*US* **-maneuver**) **1** use skill and cunning to secure an advantage over (a person). **2** outdo in manoeuvring.

outmatch /aʊt'matʃ/ *v.tr.* be more than a match for (an opponent etc.); surpass.

outmeasure /aʊt'mɛʒə/ *v.tr.* exceed in quantity or extent.

outmoded /aʊt'məʊdɪd/ *adj.* **1** no longer in fashion. **2** obsolete. □ **outmodedly** *adv.* **outmodedness** *n.*

outmost /'aʊtməʊst/ *adj.* **1** outermost, furthest. **2** uttermost. [Middle English, variant of *utmest* UTMOST]

outnumber /aʊt'nʌmbə/ *v.tr.* exceed in number.

out-of-body experience *n.* a sensation of being outside one's body, esp. of floating and being able to observe onself from a distance.

out-of-court *attrib.adj.* (esp. of a settlement) made or done outside or without the intervention of a court.

out of date *adj.* (hyphenated when *attrib.*) old-fashioned, obsolete.

out of doors *adj. & adv.* in or into the open air.

out-of-pocket expenses *n.pl.* the actual outlay of cash incurred.

out-of-town *attrib.adj.* (esp. of a large store or development) situated or taking place outside a town.

outpace /aʊt'peɪs/ *v.tr.* **1** go faster than. **2** outdo in a contest.

outpatient /'aʊtpeɪʃ(ə)nt/ *n.* a patient who attends a hospital without staying there overnight.

outperform /aʊtpə'fɔːm/ *v.tr.* **1** perform better than. **2** surpass in a specified field or activity. □ **outperformance** *n.*

outplacement /'aʊtpleɪsm(ə)nt/ *n.* the act or process of finding new employment for esp. executive workers who have been dismissed or made redundant.

outplay /aʊt'pleɪ/ *v.tr.* surpass in playing; play better than.

outpoint /aʊt'pɔɪnt/ *v.tr.* (in various sports, esp. boxing) score more points than.

outport /'aʊtpɔːt/ *n.* **1** a subsidiary port. **2** *Canad.* a small remote fishing village.

outpost /'aʊtpəʊst/ *n.* **1** a detachment set at a distance from the main body of an army, esp. to prevent surprise. **2** a distant branch or settlement. **3** the furthest territory of an (esp. the British) empire.

outpouring /'aʊtpɔːrɪŋ/ *n.* **1** (usu. in *pl.*) a copious spoken or written expression of emotion. **2** what is poured out.

outpsych /aʊt'sʌɪk/ *v.tr.* esp. *US colloq.* defeat (a person) by psychological influence.

output /'aʊtpʊt/ *n. & v.* ● *n.* **1** the product of a process, esp. of manufacture, or of mental or artistic work. **2** the quantity or amount of this. **3** the printout, results, etc. supplied by a computer. **4** the power etc. delivered by an apparatus. **5** a place where energy, information, etc. leaves a system. ● *v.tr.* (**-putting**; *past* and *past part.* **-put** or **-putted**) **1** put or send out. **2** (of a computer) supply (results etc.).

outrage /'aʊtreɪdʒ/ *n. & v.* ● *n.* **1** an extreme or shocking violation of others' rights, sentiments, etc. **2** a gross offence or indignity. **3** fierce anger or resentment (*a feeling of outrage*). ● *v.tr.* **1** subject to outrage. **2** injure, insult, etc. flagrantly. **3** shock and anger. [Middle English via Old French *outrage*, via *outrer* 'exceed' from *outre*, from Latin *ultra* 'beyond']

outrageous /aʊt'reɪdʒəs/ *adj.* **1** immoderate. **2** shocking. **3** grossly cruel. **4** immoral, offensive. □ **outrageously** *adv.* **outrageousness** *n.* [Middle English from Old French *outrageus* (as OUTRAGE)]

outran *past* of OUTRUN.

outrange /aʊt'reɪn(d)ʒ/ *v.tr.* (of a gun or its user) have a longer range than.

outrank /aʊt'raŋk/ *v.tr.* **1** be superior in rank to. **2** take priority over.

outré /'uːtreɪ/ *adj.* **1** outside the bounds of what is usual or proper. **2** eccentric or indecorous. [French, past part. of *outrer*: see OUTRAGE]

outreach *v. & n.* ● *v.tr.* /aʊt'riːtʃ/ **1** reach further than. **2** surpass. **3** *poet.* stretch out (one's arms etc.). ● *n.* /'aʊtriːtʃ/ **1 a** any organization's involvement with or influence in the community, esp. in the context of social welfare. **b** the extent of this. **2** the extent or length of reaching out (*an outreach of 38 metres*).

out-relief *n. Brit. hist.* assistance given to very poor people not living in a workhouse etc.

outride /aʊt'rʌɪd/ *v.tr.* (*past* **-rode**; *past part.* **-ridden**) **1** ride better, faster, or further than. **2** (of a ship) come safely through (a storm etc.).

outrider /'aʊtrʌɪdə/ *n.* **1** a mounted attendant riding ahead of, or with, a carriage etc. **2** a motorcyclist acting as a guard in a similar manner. **3** *US* a cowboy keeping cattle within bounds. □ **outriding** *n.*

outrigged /'aʊtrɪgd/ *adj.* (of a boat etc.) having outriggers.

outrigger /'aʊtrɪgə/ *n.* **1** a beam, spar, or framework, rigged out and projecting from or over a ship's side for various purposes. **2** a similar projecting beam etc. in a building. **3** a log etc. fixed parallel to a canoe to stabilize it. **4 a** an extension of the splinter-bar of a carriage etc. to enable another horse to be harnessed outside the shafts. **b** a horse harnessed in this way. **5 a** an iron bracket bearing a rowlock attached horizontally to a boat's side to increase the leverage of the oar. **b** a boat fitted with these. **6** a chassis extension supporting the body of a motor vehicle. [OUT- + RIG[1]: perhaps influenced by obsolete (nautical) *outligger*]

outright *adv. & adj.* ● *adv.* /aʊt'rʌɪt/ **1** altogether, entirely (*proved outright*). **2** not gradually, nor by degrees, nor by instalments (*bought it outright*). **3** without reservation, openly (*denied the charge outright*). ● *attrib.adj.* /'aʊtrʌɪt/ **1** downright, direct, complete (*their resentment turned to outright anger*). **2** undisputed, clear (*the outright winner*). □ **outrightness** *n.*

outrival /aʊt'rʌɪv(ə)l/ *v.tr.* (**-rivalled**, **-rivalling**; *US* **-rivaled**, **-rivaling**) outdo as a rival.

outro /'aʊtrəʊ/ *n.* (*pl.* **-os**) *colloq.* a concluding section, esp. of a broadcast programme or a piece of music. [OUT, on the pattern of INTRO]

outrode *past* of OUTRIDE.

outrun *v. & n.* ● *v.tr.* /aʊt'rʌn/ (**-running**; *past* **-ran**; *past part.* **-run**) **1 a** run faster or farther than. **b** escape from. **2** go beyond (a specified point or limit). ● *n.* /'aʊtrʌn/ *Austral.* a sheep-run distant from its homestead.

outrush /'aʊtrʌʃ/ *n.* **1** a rushing out. **2** a violent overflow.

outsail /aʊt'seɪl/ *v.tr.* sail better or faster than.

outsat *past* and *past part.* of OUTSIT.

outsell /aʊt'sɛl/ *v.tr.* (*past* and *past part.* **-sold**) **1** sell more than. **2** be sold in greater quantities than.

outset /'aʊtsɛt/ *n.* the start, beginning. □ **at** (or **from**) **the outset** at or from the beginning.

outshine /aʊt'ʃʌɪn/ *v.tr.* (*past* and *past part.* **-shone**) **1** shine brighter than. **2** surpass in ability, excellence, etc.

outshoot /aʊt'ʃu:t/ *v.tr.* (*past* and *past part.* **-shot**) **1** shoot better or further than (another person). **2** esp. *US* attempt or score more goals, points, etc. than (another player or team).

outside *n., adj., adv., & prep.* ● *n.* /aʊt'sʌɪd, 'aʊtsʌɪd/ **1** the external side or surface; the outer parts (*painted blue on the outside*). **2** the external appearance; the outward aspect of a building etc. **3** the side of a path away from the wall or next to the road. **4** (also *attrib.*) all that is without; the world as distinct from the thinking subject (*learn about the outside world*; *viewed from the outside the problem is simple*). **5** a position on the outer side (*the gate opens from the outside*). **6** *colloq.* the highest computation (*it is a mile at the outside*). **7** *Brit.* an outside player in football etc. **8** (in *pl.*) the outer sheets of a ream of paper. ● *adj.* /'aʊtsʌɪd/ **1** of or on or nearer the outside; outer. **2 a** not of or belonging to some circle or institution (*outside help*; *outside work*). **b** (of a broker) not a member of the Stock Exchange. **3** (of a chance etc.) remote; very unlikely. **4** (of an estimate etc.) the greatest or highest possible (*the outside price*). **5** (of a player in football etc.) positioned nearest to the edge of the field. ● *adv.* /aʊt'sʌɪd/ **1** on or to the outside. **2** in or to the open air. **3** not within or enclosed or included. **4** *slang* not in prison. ● *prep.* /aʊt'sʌɪd/ (also *disp.* foll. by *of*) **1** not in; to or at the exterior of (*meet me outside the post office*). **2** external to, not included in, beyond the limits of (*outside the law*). □ **at the outside** (of an estimate etc.) at the most. **get outside of** *slang* eat or drink. **outside and in** outside and inside. **outside in** = INSIDE OUT. **outside of** esp. *N. Amer. colloq.* apart from.

■ **Usage** The use of *outside of* as a preposition, e.g. *There is nothing like it outside of Japan* is considered incorrect by some people. *Outside* on its own is preferable.

outside broadcast *n. Brit.* a broadcast made on location and not in a studio.

outside edge *n.* (on an ice-skate) each of the edges facing outwards when both feet are together.

outside interest *n.* a hobby; an interest not connected with one's work or normal way of life.

outsider /aʊt'sʌɪdə/ *n.* **1 a** a non-member of some circle, party, profession, etc. **b** an uninitiated person, a layman. **2** a person without special knowledge, breeding, etc., or not fit to mix with good society. **3** a competitor, applicant, etc. thought to have little chance of success.

outside track *n.* the outside lane of a sports track etc. which is longer because of the curve.

outsit /aʊt'sɪt/ *v.tr.* (**-sitting**; *past* and *past part.* **-sat**) sit longer than (another person or thing).

outsize /'aʊtsʌɪz/ *adj. & n.* ● *adj.* **1** unusually large. **2** (of garments etc.) of an exceptionally large size. ● *n.* an exceptionally large person or thing, esp. a garment. □ **outsizeness** *n.*

outskirts /'aʊtskə:ts/ *n.pl.* the outer border or fringe of a town, district, subject, etc.

outsmart /aʊt'smɑ:t/ *v.tr. colloq.* outwit, be cleverer than.

outsold *past* and *past part.* of OUTSELL.

outsource /aʊt'sɔ:s/ *v.tr.* esp. *N. Amer. Commerce* **1** obtain (goods etc.) by contract from an outside source. **2** contract (work) out. □ **outsourcing** /'aʊtsɔ:sɪŋ/ *n.*

outspan /'aʊtspan/ *v. & n. S.Afr.* ● *v.* (**-spanned**, **-spanning**) **1** *tr.* (also *absol.*) unharness (animals) from a cart, plough, etc. **2** *intr.* break a wagon journey. ● *n.* a place for grazing or encampment. [South African Dutch *uitspannen* 'unyoke']

outspend /aʊt'spɛnd/ *v.tr.* (*past* and *past part.* **-spent**) spend more than (one's resources or another person).

outspoken /aʊt'spəʊk(ə)n/ *adj.* given to or involving plain speaking; frank in stating one's opinions. □ **outspokenly** *adv.* **outspokenness** /aʊt'spəʊk(ə)nnɪs/ *n.*

outspread *adj. & v.* ● *adj.* /aʊt'sprɛd, 'aʊtsprɛd/ spread out; fully extended or expanded. ● *v.tr. & intr.* /aʊt'sprɛd/ (*past* and *past part.* **-spread**) spread out; expand.

outstanding /aʊt'standɪŋ/ *adj.* **1 a** conspicuous, eminent, esp. because of excellence. **b** (usu. foll. by *at*, *in*) remarkable in (a specified field). **2** (esp. of a debt) not yet settled (*£200 still outstanding*). □ **outstandingly** *adv.*

outstare /aʊt'stɛ:/ *v.tr.* **1** outdo in staring. **2** abash by staring.

outstation /'aʊtsteɪʃ(ə)n/ *n.* **1** a branch of an organization, enterprise, or business in a remote area or at a considerable distance from headquarters. **2** esp. *Austral.* & *NZ* part of a farming estate separate from the main estate.

outstay /aʊt'steɪ/ *v.tr.* **1** stay beyond the limit of (one's welcome, invitation, etc.). **2** stay or endure longer than (another person etc.).

outstep /aʊt'stɛp/ *v.tr.* (**-stepped**, **-stepping**) step outside or beyond.

outstretch /aʊt'strɛtʃ/ *v.tr.* **1** (usu. as **outstretched** *adj.*) reach out or stretch out (esp. one's hands or arms). **2** reach or stretch further than.

outstrip /aʊt'strɪp/ *v.tr.* (**-stripped**, **-stripping**) **1** pass in running etc. **2** surpass in competition or relative progress or ability.

out-swinger /'aʊtswɪŋə/ *n. Cricket* a ball that swings away from the batsman.

out-take /'aʊtteɪk/ *n.* a length of film or tape rejected in editing.

out-talk /aʊt'tɔ:k/ *v.tr.* outdo or overcome in talking.

out-think /aʊt'θɪŋk/ *v.tr.* (*past* and *past part.* **-thought**) outwit; outdo in thinking.

out-thrust *adj., v., & n.* ● *adj.* /'aʊtθrʌst/ extended; projected (*ran forward with out-thrust arms*). ● *v.tr.* /aʊt'θrʌst/ (*past* and *past part.* **-thrust**) thrust out. ● *n.* /'aʊtθrʌst/ **1** the act or an instance of thrusting forcibly outward. **2** the act or an instance of becoming prominent or noticeable.

out to lunch *adj. colloq.* crazy, mad.

out-top /aʊt'tɒp/ *v.tr.* (**-topped**, **-topping**) surmount, surpass in height, extent, etc.

out-tray /'aʊttreɪ/ *n.* a tray for outgoing documents, letters, etc.

out-turn /ˈaʊttəːn/ *n.* **1** the quantity produced. **2** the result of a process or sequence of events.

outvalue /aʊtˈvaljuː/ *v.tr.* (**-values**, **-valued**, **-valuing**) be of greater value than.

outvote /aʊtˈvəʊt/ *v.tr.* defeat by a majority of votes.

outwalk /aʊtˈwɔːk/ *v.tr.* **1** outdo in walking. **2** walk beyond.

outward /ˈaʊtwəd/ *adj., adv., & n.* ● *adj.* **1** situated on or directed towards the outside. **2** going out (*on the outward voyage*). **3** bodily, external, apparent, superficial (*in all outward respects*). **4** *archaic* outer (*the outward man*). ● *adv.* (also **outwards**) in an outward direction; towards the outside. ● *n.* the outward appearance of something; the exterior. □ **to outward seeming** apparently. □ **outwardly** *adv.* [Old English *ūtweard* (as OUT, -WARD)]

outward bound *adj. & n.* ● *adj.* (of a ship, passenger, etc.) going away from home. ● *n.* (**Outward Bound**) *propr.* a movement to provide adventure training, naval training, and other outdoor activities for young people.

outward form *n.* appearance.

outwardness /ˈaʊtwədnɪs/ *n.* **1** external existence; objectivity. **2** an interest or belief in outward things, objective-mindedness.

outwards var. of OUTWARD *adv.*

outward things *n.pl.* the world around us.

outwash /ˈaʊtwɒʃ/ *n.* the material carried from a glacier by melt water and deposited beyond the moraine.

outwatch /aʊtˈwɒtʃ/ *v.tr.* **1** watch more than or longer than. **2** *archaic* keep awake beyond the end of (night etc.).

outwear *v. & n.* ● *v.tr.* /aʊtˈwɛː/ (*past* **-wore**; *past part.* **-worn**) **1** exhaust; wear out; wear away. **2** live or last beyond the duration of. **3** (as **outworn** *adj.*) out of date, obsolete. ● *n.* /ˈaʊtwɛː/ *Brit.* outer clothing.

outweigh /aʊtˈweɪ/ *v.tr.* exceed in weight, value, importance, or influence.

outwent *past* of OUTGO.

outwit /aʊtˈwɪt/ *v.tr.* (**-witted**, **-witting**) be too clever or crafty for; deceive by greater ingenuity.

outwith /aʊtˈwɪθ/ *prep. Sc.* outside, beyond.

outwore *past* of OUTWEAR.

outwork /ˈaʊtwəːk/ *n.* **1** an advanced or detached part of a fortification. **2** *Brit.* work done outside the shop or factory which supplies it. □ **outworker** *n.* (in sense 2).

outworking /ˈaʊtwəːkɪŋ/ *n.* (usu. foll. by *of*) the action or process of working out; practical operation.

outworn *past part.* of OUTWEAR.

ouzel /ˈuːz(ə)l/ *n.* (also **ousel**) **1** = RING OUZEL. **2** = WATER OUZEL. **3** *archaic* a blackbird. [Old English *ōsle* 'blackbird', of unknown origin]

ouzo /ˈuːzəʊ/ *n.* (*pl.* **-os**) a Greek aniseed-flavoured spirit. [modern Greek]

ova *pl.* of OVUM.

oval /ˈəʊv(ə)l/ *adj. & n.* ● *adj.* **1** egg-shaped, ellipsoidal. **2** having the outline of an egg, elliptical. ● *n.* **1** an egg-shaped or elliptical closed curve. **2** any object with an oval outline. **3** a sports ground with an oval field, esp. *Austral.* a ground for Australian Rules football. □ **ovality** /-ˈvalɪti/ *n.* **ovally** *adv.* **ovalness** *n.* [medieval Latin *ovalis* (as OVUM)]

Oval Office *n.* the office of the US President in the White House.

ovary /ˈəʊv(ə)ri/ *n.* (*pl.* **-ies**) **1** each of the female reproductive organs in which ova are produced. **2** the hollow base of the carpel of a flower, containing one or more ovules. □ **ovarian** /əʊˈvɛːrɪən/ *adj.* **ovariectomy** /-rɪˈɛktəmi/ *n.* (*pl.* **-ies**) (in sense 1). **ovariotomy** /-rɪˈɒtəmi/ *n.* (*pl.* **-ies**) (in sense 1). **ovaritis** /-ˈrʌɪtɪs/ *n.* (in sense 1). [modern Latin *ovarium* (as OVUM)]

ovate /ˈəʊveɪt/ *adj.* esp. *Biol.* egg-shaped as a solid or in outline; oval. [Latin *ovatus* (as OVUM)]

ovation /ə(ʊ)ˈveɪʃ(ə)n/ *n.* **1** an enthusiastic reception, esp. spontaneous and sustained applause. **2** *Rom. Antiq.* a lesser form of triumph. □ **ovational** *adj.* [Latin *ovatio* from *ovare* 'exult']

oven /ˈʌv(ə)n/ *n.* **1** an enclosed compartment of brick, stone, or metal for cooking food. **2** a chamber for heating or drying. **3** a small furnace or kiln used in chemistry, metallurgy, etc. [Old English *ofen*, from Germanic]

ovenbird /ˈʌv(ə)nbəːd/ *n.* any Central or S. American bird of the family Furnariidae, many of which make domed nests.

ovenproof /ˈʌv(ə)npruːf/ *adj.* suitable for use in an oven; heat-resistant.

oven-ready *adj.* (of food) prepared before sale so as to be ready for immediate cooking in the oven.

ovenware /ˈʌv(ə)nwɛː/ *n.* dishes that can be used for cooking food in the oven.

over /ˈəʊvə/ *adv., prep., n., & adj.* ● *adv.* expressing movement or position or state above or beyond something stated or implied: **1** outward and downward from a brink or from any erect position (*knocked the man over*). **2** so as to cover or touch a whole surface (*paint it over*). **3** so as to produce a fold, or reverse a position; with the effect of being upside down. **4 a** across a street or other space (*decided to cross over*; *came over from America*). **b** for a visit etc. (*invited them over last night*). **5** with transference or change from one hand or part to another (*went over to the enemy*; *swapped them over*). **6** with motion above something; so as to pass across something (*climb over*; *fly over*; *boil over*). **7** from beginning to end with repetition or detailed concentration (*think it over*; *did it six times over*). **8** in excess; more than is right or required (*left over*). **9** for or until a later time (*hold it over*). **10** at an end; settled (*the crisis is over*; *all is over between us*). **11** (in full **over to you**) (as *int.*) (in radio conversations etc.) said to indicate that it is the other person's turn to speak. **12** (as *int.*) *Cricket* an umpire's call to change ends. ● *prep.* **1** above, in, or to a position higher than; upon. **2** out and down from; down from the edge of (*fell over the cliff*). **3** so as to cover (*a hat over his eyes*). **4** above and across; so as to clear (*flew over the North Pole*; *a bridge over the Thames*). **5** concerning; engaged with; as a result of; while occupied with (*laughed over a good joke*; *fell asleep over the newspaper*). **6 a** in superiority of; superior to; in charge of (*a victory over the enemy*; *reign over three kingdoms*). **b** in preference to. **7** *Math.* divided by. **8 a** throughout; covering the extent of (*travelled over most of Africa*; *a blush spread over his face*). **b** so as to deal with completely (*went over the plans*). **9 a** for the duration of (*stay over Saturday night*). **b** at any point during the course of (*I'll do it over the weekend*). **10** beyond; more than (*bids of over £50*; *are you over 18?*). **11** transmitted by (*heard it over the radio*). **12** in comparison with (*gained 20% over last year*). **13** having recovered from (*am now over my cold*; *will get over it in time*). ● *n. Cricket* **1** a sequence of balls (now usu. six), bowled from one end of the pitch. **2** the period of play during which such a sequence is bowled. ● *adj.* (see also OVER-). **1** upper, outer. **2** superior. **3** extra. □ **begin** (or **start** etc.) **over** *N. Amer.* begin again. **get it over with** do or undergo something unpleasant etc. so as to be rid of it. **give over** (usu. as *int.*) *colloq.* desist. **not over** not very; not at all (*not over friendly*). **over again** once again, again from the beginning. **over against** in an opposite situation to; adjacent to, in contrast with. **over all** taken as a whole. **over and above** in addition to; not to mention (*£100 over and above the asking price*). **over and over** so that the same thing or the same point comes up again and again (*said it over and over*; *rolled it over and over*). **over the fence** *Austral. & NZ slang* unreasonable; unfair; indecent. **over one's head** see HEAD. **over the hill** see HILL. **over the moon** see MOON. **over to you** see OVER *adv.* 11. **over the way** (in a street etc.) facing or opposite. [Old English *ofer*, from Germanic]

over- /ˈəʊvə/ *prefix* added to verbs, nouns, adjectives, and adverbs, meaning: **1** excessively; to an unwanted

O PQ

degree (*overheat*; *overdue*). **2** upper, outer, extra (*overcoat*; *overtime*). **3** 'over' in various senses (*overhang*; *overshadow*). **4** completely, utterly (*overawe*; *overjoyed*).

over-abundant /əʊv(ə)rə'bʌnd(ə)nt/ *adj.* in excessive quantity. □ **over-abundance** *n.* **over-abundantly** *adv.*

overachieve /əʊv(ə)rə'tʃi:v/ *v.* **1** *intr.* do more than might be expected (esp. scholastically). **2** *tr.* achieve more than (an expected goal or objective etc.). □ **overachievement** *n.* **overachiever** *n.*

overact /əʊvər'akt/ *v.tr.* & *intr.* act (a role) in an exaggerated manner.

overactive /əʊvər'aktɪv/ *adj.* excessively active. □ **overactivity** /-'tɪvɪti/ *n.*

overage /'əʊv(ə)rɪdʒ/ *n.* a surplus or excess, esp. an amount greater than estimated.

over age *adj.* (usu. hyphenated when *attrib.*) over a certain age limit; too old.

overall *adj., adv.,* & *n.* ● *adj.* /'əʊvərɔ:l/ **1** total, inclusive of all (*overall cost*). **2** taking everything into account, general (*overall improvement*). **3** from end to end (*overall length*). ● *adv.* /əʊvər'ɔ:l/ in all parts; taken as a whole (*overall, the performance was excellent*). ● *n.* /'əʊvərɔ:l/ **1** *Brit.* an outer garment worn to keep out dirt, wet, etc. **2** (in *pl.*) protective trousers, dungarees, or a combination suit, worn by workmen etc. **3** *Brit.* close-fitting trousers worn as part of army uniform. □ **overalled** /'əʊvərɔ:ld/ *adj.*

overambitious /əʊvəram'bɪʃəs/ *adj.* excessively ambitious. □ **overambition** *n.* **overambitiously** *adv.*

over-anxious /əʊvər'aŋkʃəs/ *adj.* excessively anxious. □ **over-anxiety** /-aŋ'zʌɪɪti/ *n.* **over-anxiously** *adv.*

overarch /əʊvər'ɑ:tʃ/ *v.tr.* form an arch over. □ **overarching** *adj.*

overarm /'əʊvərɑ:m/ *adj.* & *adv.* **1** *Cricket* & *Tennis* etc. with the hand above the shoulder (*bowl it overarm*; *an overarm service*). **2** *Swimming* with one or both arms lifted out of the water during a stroke.

overate *past* of OVEREAT.

overawe /əʊvər'ɔ:/ *v.tr.* **1** restrain by awe. **2** keep in awe.

overbalance /əʊvə'bal(ə)ns/ *v.* & *n.* ● *v.* **1** *tr.* esp. *Brit.* cause (a person or thing) to lose its balance and fall. **2** *intr.* fall over, capsize. **3** *tr.* outweigh. ● *n.* **1** an excess. **2** the amount of this.

overbear /əʊvə'bɛ:/ *v.tr.* (*past* **-bore**; *past part.* **-borne**) **1** (as **overbearing** *adj.*) **a** domineering, masterful. **b** overpowering. **2** bear down; upset by weight, force, or emotional pressure. **3** put down or repress by power or authority. **4** surpass in importance etc., outweigh. □ **overbearingly** *adv.* **overbearingness** *n.*

overbid *v.* & *n.* ● *v.* /əʊvə'bɪd/ (**-bidding**; *past* and *past part.* **-bid**) **1** *tr.* make a higher bid than. **2** *tr.* (also *absol.*) *Bridge* **a** bid more on (one's hand) than warranted. **b** overcall. ● *n.* /'əʊvəbɪd/ a bid that is higher than another, or higher than is justified. □ **overbidder** *n.*

overbite /'əʊvəbʌɪt/ *n.* *Dentistry* the overlapping of the lower teeth by the upper.

overblouse /'əʊvəblaʊz/ *n.* a garment like a blouse, but worn without tucking it into a skirt or trousers.

overblown /əʊvə'bləʊn/ *adj.* **1** excessively inflated or pretentious. **2** (of a flower or a woman's beauty etc.) past its prime.

overboard /'əʊvəbɔ:d/ *adv.* from on a ship into the water (*fall overboard*). □ **go overboard 1** be highly enthusiastic. **2** behave immoderately; go too far. **throw overboard** abandon, discard.

overbold /əʊvə'bəʊld/ *adj.* excessively bold.

overbook /əʊvə'bʊk/ *v.tr.* (also *absol.*) make too many bookings for (an aircraft, hotel, etc.) in respect of the space available.

overboot /'əʊvəbu:t/ *n.* a boot worn over another boot or shoe.

overbore *past* of OVERBEAR.

overborne *past part.* of OVERBEAR.

overbought *past* and *past part.* of OVERBUY.

overbrim /əʊvə'brɪm/ *v.* (**-brimmed**, **-brimming**) **1** *tr.* flow over the brim of. **2** *intr.* (of a vessel or liquid) overflow at the brim.

overbuild /əʊvə'bɪld/ *v.tr.* (*past* and *past part.* **-built**) **1** build over or upon. **2** place too many buildings on (land etc.).

overburden *v.* & *n.* ● *v.tr.* /əʊvə'bə:d(ə)n/ burden (a person, thing, etc.) to excess. ● *n.* /'əʊvəbə:d(ə)n/ **1** rock etc. that must be removed prior to mining the mineral deposit beneath it. **2** an excessive burden. □ **overburdensome** /əʊvə'bə:d(ə)ns(ə)m/ *adj.*

overbusy /əʊvə'bɪzi/ *adj.* excessively busy.

overbuy /əʊvə'bʌɪ/ *v.tr.* & *intr.* (*past* and *past part.* **-bought**) buy (a commodity etc.) in excess of immediate need.

overcall *v.* & *n.* ● *v.tr.* /əʊvə'kɔ:l/ (also *absol.*) *Bridge* **1** make a higher bid than (a previous bid or opponent). **2** *Brit.* = OVERBID *v.* 2a. ● *n.* /'əʊvəkɔ:l/ an act or instance of overcalling.

overcame *past* of OVERCOME.

overcapacity /əʊvəkə'pasɪti/ *n.* a state of saturation or an excess of productive capacity.

overcapitalize /əʊvə'kapɪt(ə)lʌɪz/ *v.tr.* (also **-ise**) fix or estimate the capital of (a company etc.) too high.

overcareful /əʊvə'kɛ:fʊl, -f(ə)l/ *adj.* excessively careful. □ **overcarefully** *adv.*

overcast *adj., v.,* & *n.* ● *adj.* /'əʊvəkɑ:st/ **1** (of the sky, weather, etc.) covered with cloud; dull and gloomy. **2** (in sewing) edged with stitching to prevent fraying. ● *v.tr.* /əʊvə'kɑ:st/ (*past* and *past part.* **-cast**) **1** cover (the sky etc.) with clouds or darkness. **2** stitch over (a raw edge etc.) to prevent fraying. ● *n.* /'əʊvəkɑ:st/ cloud covering a large part of the sky.

overcautious /əʊvə'kɔ:ʃəs/ *adj.* excessively cautious. □ **overcaution** *n.* **overcautiously** *adv.* **overcautiousness** *n.*

overcharge *v.* & *n.* ● *v.tr.* /əʊvə'tʃɑ:dʒ/ **1 a** charge too high a price to (a person) for a thing. **b** charge (a specified sum) beyond the right price. **2** put too much charge into (a battery, gun, etc.). **3** put exaggerated or excessive detail into (a description, picture, etc.). ● *n.* /'əʊvətʃɑ:dʒ/ an excessive charge (of explosive, money, etc.).

overcheck /'əʊvətʃɛk/ *n.* **1** a combination of two different-sized check patterns. **2** a cloth with this pattern.

overcloud /əʊvə'klaʊd/ *v.tr.* **1** cover with cloud. **2** mar, spoil, or dim, esp. as the result of anxiety etc. (*overclouded by uncertainties*). **3** make obscure.

overcoat /'əʊvəkəʊt/ *n.* **1** a heavy coat, esp. one worn over indoor clothes for warmth outdoors in cold weather. **2** a protective coat of paint etc.

overcome /əʊvə'kʌm/ *v.* (*past* **-came**; *past part.* **-come**) **1** *tr.* prevail over, master, conquer. **2** *tr.* (as **overcome** *adj.*) **a** exhausted, made helpless. **b** (usu. foll. by *with*, *by*) affected by (emotion etc.). **3** *intr.* be victorious. [Old English *ofercuman* (as OVER-, COME)]

overcommit /əʊvəkə'mɪt/ *v.tr.* (**overcommitted**, **overcommitting**) (usu. *refl.*) commit (esp. oneself) to an excessive degree. □ **overcommitment** *n.*

overcompensate /əʊvə'kɒmpɛnseɪt/ *v.* **1** *tr.* (usu. foll. by *for*) compensate excessively for (something). **2** *intr.* *Psychol.* strive for power etc. in an exaggerated way, esp. to make allowance or amends for a real or fancied grievance, defect, handicap, etc. □ **overcompensation** /-pɛn'seɪʃ(ə)n/ *n.* **overcompensatory** /-'seɪtəri/ *adj.*

overconfident /əʊvə'kɒnfɪd(ə)nt/ *adj.* excessively confident. □ **overconfidence** *n.* **overconfidently** *adv.*

overcook /əʊvə'kʊk/ *v.tr.* cook too much or for too long. □ **overcooked** *adj.*

overcritical /əʊvə'krɪtɪk(ə)l/ *adj.* excessively critical; quick to find fault.

overcrop /əʊvə'krɒp/ *v.tr.* (**-cropped**, **-cropping**) exhaust (the land) by the continuous growing of crops.

overcrowd /əʊvəˈkraʊd/ *v.tr.* fill (a space, object, etc.) beyond what is usual or comfortable. □ **overcrowding** *n.*

over-curious /əʊvəˈkjʊərɪəs/ *adj.* excessively curious. □ **over-curiosity** /ˌəʊvəkjʊərɪˈɒsɪti/ *n.*

over-delicate /əʊvəˈdɛlɪkət/ *adj.* excessively delicate. □ **over-delicacy** *n.*

overdetermine /əʊvədɪˈtəːmɪn/ *v.tr.* **1** determine, account for, or cause in more than one way, or with more conditions than are necessary. **2** (as **overdetermined** *adj.*) have more determining factors than the minimum necessary; have more than one cause. □ **overdetermination** /ˈ-neɪʃ(ə)n/ *n.*

overdevelop /əʊvədɪˈvɛləp/ *v.tr.* (**-developed**, **-developing**) **1** develop too much. **2** *Photog.* treat with developer for too long.

overdo /əʊvəˈduː/ *v.tr.* (*3rd sing. present* **-does**; *past* **-did**; *past part.* **-done**) **1** carry to excess, take too far, exaggerate (*I think you overdid the sarcasm*). **2** (esp. as **overdone** *adj.*) overcook. □ **overdo it** (or **things**) exhaust oneself. [Old English *oferdōn* (as OVER-, DO[1])]

overdose /ˈəʊvədəʊs/ *n.* & *v.* ● *n.* an excessive dose (of a drug etc.). ● *v.* **1** *tr.* give an overdose of a drug etc. to (a person). **2** *intr.* (often foll. by *on*) take on overdose of a drug. □ **overdosage** /əʊvəˈdəʊsɪdʒ/ *n.*

overdraft /ˈəʊvədrɑːft/ *n.* **1** a deficit in a bank account caused by drawing more money than is credited to it. **2** the amount of this.

overdramatize /əʊvəˈdramətʌɪz/ *v.tr.* (also **-ise**) (also *absol.*) express or react to in an excessively dramatic way. □ **overdramatic** /-drəˈmatɪk/ *adj.*

overdraw /əʊvəˈdrɔː/ *v.* (*past* **-drew**; *past part.* **-drawn**) **1** *tr.* **a** draw a sum of money in excess of the amount credited to (one's bank account). **b** (as **overdrawn** *adj.*) having overdrawn one's account. **2** *intr.* overdraw one's account. **3** *tr.* exaggerate in describing or depicting. □ **overdrawer** *n.* (in senses 1 & 2).

overdress *v.* & *n.* ● *v.* /əʊvəˈdrɛs/ **1** *tr.* dress with too much display or formality. **2** *intr.* overdress oneself. ● *n.* /ˈəʊvədrɛs/ esp. *Brit.* a dress worn over another dress or a blouse etc.

overdrink /əʊvəˈdrɪŋk/ *v.intr.* & *refl.* (*past* **-drank**; *past part.* **-drunk**) drink too much.

overdrive /ˈəʊvədrʌɪv/ *n.* **1 a** a mechanism in a motor vehicle providing a gear ratio higher than that of the usual gear. **b** an additional speed-increasing gear. **2** (usu. prec. by *in*, *into*) a state of high or excessive activity.

overdub *v.* & *n.* ● *v.tr.* /əʊvəˈdʌb/ (**-dubbed**, **-dubbing**) (also *absol.*) impose (additional sounds) on an existing recording. ● *n.* /ˈəʊvədʌb/ the act or an instance of overdubbing.

overdue /əʊvəˈdjuː/ *adj.* **1** past the time when due or ready. **2** not yet paid, arrived, born, etc., though after the expected time. **3** (of a library book etc.) retained longer than the period allowed.

overeager /əʊvərˈiːgə/ *adj.* excessively eager. □ **overeagerly** *adv.* **overeagerness** *n.*

overeat /əʊvərˈiːt/ *v.intr.* & *refl.* (*past* **-ate**; *past part.* **-eaten**) eat too much.

over-elaborate *adj.* & *v.* ● *adj.* /əʊv(ə)rɪˈlab(ə)rət/ excessively elaborate. ● *v.tr.* /əʊv(ə)rɪˈlabəreɪt/ (also *absol.*) explain in excessive detail. □ **over-elaborately** *adv.* **over-elaborateness** *n.* **over-elaboration** *n.*

over-emotional /əʊv(ə)rɪˈməʊʃ(ə)n(ə)l/ *adj.* excessively emotional. □ **over-emotionally** *adv.*

overemphasis /əʊvərˈɛmfəsɪs/ *n.* excessive emphasis. □ **overemphasize** /-fəsʌɪz/ *v.tr.* & *intr.* (also **-ise**).

overenthusiasm /əʊv(ə)rɪnˈθjuːzɪaz(ə)m, -rɛn-/ *n.* excessive enthusiasm. □ **overenthusiastic** /-ˈastɪk/ *adj.* **overenthusiastically** /-ˈastɪk(ə)li/ *adv.*

overestimate *v.* & *n.* ● *v.tr.* /əʊvərˈɛstɪmeɪt/ (also *absol.*) form too high an estimate of (a person, ability, cost, etc.). ● *n.* /əʊvərˈɛstɪmət/ too high an estimate. □ **overestimation** /-ˈmeɪʃ(ə)n/ *n.*

overexcite /əʊv(ə)rɪkˈsʌɪt, -rɛk-/ *v.tr.* excite excessively. □ **overexcitement** *n.*

over-exercise /əʊvərˈɛksəsʌɪz/ *v.* & *n.* ● *v.* **1** *tr.* use or exert (a part of the body, one's authority, etc.) too much. **2** *intr.* take too much exercise; overexert oneself. ● *n.* excessive exercise.

overexert /əʊv(ə)rɪgˈzəːt, -rɛk-/ *v.tr.* & *refl.* exert too much. □ **overexertion** /-ɪgˈzəːʃ(ə)n/ *n.*

overexpose /əʊv(ə)rɪkˈspəʊz, -rɛk-/ *v.tr.* (also *absol.*) **1** expose too much, esp. to the public eye. **2** *Photog.* expose (film) for too long a time. □ **overexposure** *n.*

overextend /əʊv(ə)rɪkˈstɛnd, -rɛk-/ *v.tr.* **1** extend (a thing) too far. **2** (also *refl.*) take on (oneself) or impose on (another person) an excessive burden of work.

overfall /ˈəʊvəfɔːl/ *n.* **1** a turbulent stretch of sea etc. caused by a strong current or tide over a submarine ridge, or by a meeting of currents. **2** a place provided on a dam, weir, etc. for the overflow of surplus water.

overfamiliar /əʊvəfəˈmɪlɪə/ *adj.* excessively familiar. □ **overfamiliarity** /-lɪˈarɪti/ *n.*

overfatigue /əʊvəfəˈtiːg/ *n.* excessive fatigue.

overfeed /əʊvəˈfiːd/ *v.tr.* (*past* and *past part.* **-fed**) feed excessively.

overfill /əʊvəˈfɪl/ *v.tr.* & *intr.* fill to excess or to overflowing.

overfine /əʊvəˈfʌɪn/ *adj.* excessively fine; too precise.

overfish /əʊvəˈfɪʃ/ *v.tr.* deplete (a stream, stock of fish, etc.) by too much fishing.

overflow *v.* & *n.* ● *v.* /əʊvəˈfləʊ/ **1** *tr.* **a** flow over (the brim, limits, etc.). **b** flow over the brim or limits of. **2** *intr.* **a** (of a receptacle etc.) be so full that the contents overflow it (*until the cup was overflowing*). **b** (of contents) overflow a container. **3** *tr.* (of a crowd etc.) extend beyond the limits of (a room etc.). **4** *tr.* flood (a surface or area). **5** *intr.* (foll. by *with*) be full of. **6** *intr.* (of kindness, a harvest, etc.) be very abundant. ● *n.* /ˈəʊvəfləʊ/ (also *attrib.*) **1** what overflows or is superfluous (*mop up the overflow*; *put the overflow audience in another room*). **2** an instance of overflowing (*overflow occurs when both systems are run together*). **3** (esp. in a bath or sink) an outlet for excess water etc. **4** *Computing* the generation of a number having more digits than the assigned location. [Old English *oferflōwan* (as OVER-, FLOW)]

overflow meeting *n.* a meeting for those who cannot be accommodated at the main gathering.

overfly /əʊvəˈflʌɪ/ *v.tr.* (**-flies**; *past* **-flew**; *past part.* **-flown**) fly over or beyond (a place or territory). □ **overflight** /ˈəʊvəflʌɪt/ *n.*

overfold /ˈəʊvəfəʊld/ *n.* a series of strata folded so that the middle part is upside down.

overfond /əʊvəˈfɒnd/ *adj.* (often foll. by *of*) having too great an affection or liking (for a person or thing) (*overfond of chocolate*; *an overfond parent*). □ **overfondly** *adv.* **overfondness** *n.*

overfulfil /əʊvəfʊlˈfɪl/ *v.tr.* (*US* **-fulfill**) (**-fulfilled**, **-fulfilling**) fulfil (a plan, quota, etc.) beyond expectation or before the appointed time. □ **overfulfilment** *n.*

overfull /əʊvəˈfʊl/ *adj.* filled excessively or to overflowing.

overgarment /ˈəʊvəgɑːm(ə)nt/ *n.* a garment worn over others; an outer garment.

overgeneralize /əʊvəˈdʒɛn(ə)rəlʌɪz/ *v.* (also **-ise**) **1** *intr.* draw general conclusions from inadequate data etc. **2** *intr.* argue more widely than is justified by the available evidence, by circumstances, etc. **3** *tr.* draw an excessively general conclusion from (data, circumstances, etc.). □ **overgeneralization** /-ˈzeɪʃ(ə)n/ *n.*

overgenerous /əʊvəˈdʒɛn(ə)rəs/ *adj.* excessively generous. □ **overgenerously** *adv.*

overglaze /ˈəʊvəgleɪz/ *n.* & *adj.* ● *n.* **1** a second glaze applied to ceramic ware. **2** decoration on a glazed surface. ● *adj.* (of painting etc.) done on a glazed surface.

overgraze /əʊvəˈgreɪz/ *v.tr.* allow (grassland) to be so heavily grazed, or (of livestock) feed on (grassland) so heavily, that the vegetation is damaged and ground becomes liable to erosion. □ **overgrazing** *n.*

overground /ˈəʊvəgraʊnd, -ˈgraʊnd/ *adv. & adj.* **1** above the ground. **2** in or into the open; unconcealed.

overgrow /əʊvəˈgrəʊ/ *v.tr.* (*past* **-grew**; *past part.* **-grown**) **1** (as **overgrown** *adj.* /əʊvəˈgrəʊn, ˈəʊvəgrəʊn/) **a** abnormally large in stature (*a great overgrown child*). **b** wild; grown over with vegetation (*an overgrown pond*). **2** grow over, overspread, esp. so as to choke (*nettles have overgrown the pathway*). **3** *archaic* grow too big for (one's strength etc.). □ **overgrowth** *n.*

overhand /ˈəʊvəhand/ *adj. & adv.* **1** (in cricket, tennis, baseball, etc.) with the hand above the shoulder (*an overhand service*; *pitch it overhand*). **2** *Swimming* = OVERARM 2. **3 a** with the palm of the hand downward or inward. **b** with the hand above the object held.

overhand knot *n.* a simple knot made by forming a loop and passing the free end through it.

overhang *v. & n.* ● *v.* /əʊvəˈhaŋ/ (*past* and *past part.* **-hung**) **1** *tr. & intr.* project or hang over. **2** *tr.* menace, preoccupy, threaten. ● *n.* /ˈəʊvəhaŋ/ **1** an instance of overhanging. **2** the overhanging part of a structure or rock formation. **3** the amount by which a thing overhangs.

overhaste /əʊvəˈheɪst/ *n.* excessive haste. □ **overhasty** *adj.* **overhastily** *adv.*

overhaul *v. & n.* ● *v.tr.* /əʊvəˈhɔːl/ **1 a** take to pieces in order to examine. **b** examine the condition of (and repair if necessary). **2** overtake. ● *n.* /ˈəʊvəhɔːl/ a thorough examination, with repairs if necessary. [originally nautical, = release (rope-tackle) by slackening]

overhead *adv., adj., & n.* ● *adv.* /əʊvəˈhɛd/ **1** above one's head. **2** in the sky or in the storey above. ● *adj.* /ˈəʊvəhɛd/ **1** placed overhead. **2** (of a driving mechanism etc.) above the object driven. **3** (of expenses) arising from general running costs, as distinct from particular business transactions. ● *n.* /ˈəʊvəhɛd/ (in *pl.* or *N. Amer.* in *sing.*) overhead expenses.

overhead projector *n.* a device that projects an enlarged image of a transparency on to a surface above and behind the user.

overhear /əʊvəˈhɪə/ *v.tr.* (*past* and *past part.* **-heard**) (also *absol.*) hear as an eavesdropper or as an unperceived or unintentional listener.

overheat /əʊvəˈhiːt/ *v.* **1** *tr. & intr.* make or become too hot. *intr. & tr.* suffer, or cause to suffer, from marked inflation, as a result of placing excessive pressure on resources at a time of expanding demand. **3** *tr.* (as **overheated** *adj.*) too passionate about a matter.

over-indulge /əʊv(ə)rɪnˈdʌldʒ/ *v.tr. & intr.* indulge to excess. □ **over-indulgence** *n.* **over-indulgent** *adj.*

over-inflated /əʊv(ə)rɪnˈfleɪtɪd/ *adj.* excessively large or aggrandized; exaggerated.

over-insure /əʊv(ə)rɪnˈʃʊə/ *v.tr.* insure (property etc.) for more than its real value; insure excessively. □ **over-insurance** *n.*

overissue /əʊvərˈɪʃ(j)uː, -ˈɪsjuː/ *v. & n.* ● *v.tr.* (**-issues**, **-issued**, **-issuing**) issue (notes, shares, etc.) beyond the authorized amount, or the ability to pay. ● *n.* the notes, shares, etc., or the amount so issued.

overjoyed /əʊvəˈdʒɔɪd/ *adj.* (often foll. by *at*, *to hear*, etc.) filled with great joy.

overkill *n. & v.* ● *n.* /ˈəʊvəkɪl/ **1** the amount by which destruction or the capacity for destruction exceeds what is necessary for victory or annihilation. **2** excessive behaviour; unwarranted thoroughness of treatment. ● *v.tr. & intr.* /ˈəʊvəkɪl, əʊvəˈkɪl/ kill or destroy to a greater extent than necessary.

overladen /əʊvəˈleɪd(ə)n/ *adj.* bearing or carrying too large a load.

overlaid *past* and *past part.* of OVERLAY[1].

overlain *past part.* of OVERLIE.

overland /ˈəʊvəland/ *adj., adv., & v.* ● *adj. & adv.* /also əʊvəˈland/ by land; not by sea. ● *v. Austral.* **1** *tr.* drive (livestock) overland. **2** *intr.* go a long distance overland.

overlander /ˈəʊvəlandə/ *n. Austral. & NZ* **1** a person who drives livestock overland. **2** *slang* a tramp, a sundowner.

overlap *v. & n.* ● *v.* /əʊvəˈlap/ (**-lapped**, **-lapping**) **1** *tr.* (of part of an object) partly cover (another object). **2** *tr.* cover and extend beyond. **3** *intr.* (of two things) partly coincide; not be completely separate (*where psychology and philosophy overlap*). ● *n.* /ˈəʊvəlap/ **1** an instance of overlapping. **2** the amount of this.

over-large /əʊvəˈlɑːdʒ/ *adj.* too large.

overlay[1] *v. & n.* ● *v.tr.* /əʊvəˈleɪ/ (*past* and *past part.* **-laid**) **1** lay over. **2** (foll. by *with*) cover the surface of (a thing) with (a coating etc.). **3** overlie. ● *n.* /ˈəʊvəleɪ/ **1** a thing laid over another. **2** (in printing, map-reading, etc.) a transparent sheet to be superimposed on another sheet. **3** *Computing* **a** the process of transferring a block of data etc. to replace what is already stored. **b** a section so transferred. **4** a coverlet, small tablecloth, etc.

overlay[2] *past* of OVERLIE.

overleaf /əʊvəˈliːf/ *adv.* on the other side of the leaf (of a book) (*the diagram overleaf*).

overleap /əʊvəˈliːp/ *v.tr.* (*past* and *past part.* **-leaped** or **-leapt**) **1** leap over, surmount. **2** omit, ignore. [Old English *oferhlēapan* (as OVER, LEAP)]

overlie /əʊvəˈlʌɪ/ *v.tr.* (**-lying**; *past* **-lay**; *past part.* **-lain**) **1** lie on top of. **2** smother (a child etc.) by lying on top.

overload *v. & n.* ● *v.tr.* /əʊvəˈləʊd/ load excessively; force (a person, thing, etc.) beyond normal or reasonable capacity. ● *n.* /ˈəʊvələʊd/ an excessive quantity; a demand etc. which surpasses capability or capacity.

overlong /əʊvəˈlɒŋ/ *adj. & adv.* too or excessively long.

overlook *v. & n.* ● *v.tr.* /əʊvəˈlʊk/ **1** fail to notice; ignore, condone (an offence etc.). **2** have a view from above, be higher than. **3** supervise, oversee. **4** bewitch with the evil eye. ● *n.* /ˈəʊvəlʊk/ *US* a commanding position or view. □ **overlooker** /ˈəʊvəlʊkə/ *n.*

overlord /ˈəʊvəlɔːd/ *n.* a supreme lord. □ **overlordship** *n.*

overly /ˈəʊvəli/ *adv.* excessively; too.

overlying *pres. part.* of OVERLIE.

overman *v. & n.* ● *v.tr.* /əʊvəˈman/ (**-manned**, **-manning**) provide with too large a crew, staff, etc. ● *n.* /ˈəʊvəman/ (*pl.* **-men**) **1** an overseer in a colliery. **2** *Philos.* = SUPERMAN 1.

overmantel /ˈəʊvəmant(ə)l/ *n.* ornamental shelves etc. over a mantelpiece.

over-many /əʊvəˈmɛni/ *adj.* too many; an excessive number.

overmaster /əʊvəˈmɑːstə/ *v.tr.* master completely, conquer. □ **overmastering** *adj.* **overmastery** *n.*

overmatch /əʊvəˈmatʃ/ *v.tr.* be more than a match for; defeat by superior strength etc.

overmeasure /ˈəʊvəmɛʒə/ *n.* an amount beyond what is proper or sufficient.

over-mighty /əʊvəˈmʌɪti/ *adj.* excessively powerful.

overmuch /əʊvəˈmʌtʃ/ *adv. & adj.* ● *adv.* to too great an extent; excessively. ● *adj.* excessive; superabundant.

overnice /əʊvəˈnʌɪs/ *adj.* excessively fussy, punctilious, particular, etc. □ **overniceness** *n.* **overnicety** *n.*

overnight /əʊvəˈnʌɪt/ *adv. & adj.* ● *adv.* **1** for the duration of a night (*stay overnight*). **2** during the course of a night. **3** suddenly, immediately (*the situation changed overnight*). ● *adj.* **1** for use overnight (*an overnight bag*). **2** done etc. overnight (*an overnight stop*).

overnighter /əʊvəˈnʌɪtə/ *n.* **1** a person who stops at a place overnight. **2** an overnight bag.

over-optimistic /ˌəʊvə(r)ɒptɪˈmɪstɪk/ *adj.* excessively or unjustifiably optimistic. □ **over-optimism** *n.*

overpaid *past* and *past part.* of OVERPAY.

overpaint /əʊvə'peɪnt/ *v.tr.* cover with another colour or layer of paint.

overparted /əʊvə'pɑːtɪd/ *adj.* esp. *Brit. Theatr.* having too demanding a part to play; cast beyond one's ability.

over-particular /əʊvəpə'tɪkjʊlə/ *adj.* excessively particular or fussy.

overpass *n. & v.* ● *n.* /'əʊvəpɑːs/ a road or railway line that passes over another by means of a bridge. ● *v.tr.* /əʊvə'pɑːs/ **1** pass over or across or beyond. **2** get to the end of; surmount. **3** (as **overpassed** or **overpast** *adj.*) that has gone by, past.

overpay /əʊvə'peɪ/ *v.tr.* (*past* and *past part.* **-paid**) recompense (a person, service, etc.) too highly. ▫ **overpayment** *n.*

overpitch /əʊvə'pɪtʃ/ *v.tr.* **1** (often *absol.*) *Cricket* bowl (a ball) so that it pitches or would pitch too near the stumps. **2** *Brit.* exaggerate.

overplay /əʊvə'pleɪ/ *v.tr.* play (a part) to excess; give undue importance to; overemphasize. ▫ **overplay one's hand 1** be unduly optimistic about one's capabilities. **2** spoil a good case by exaggerating its value.

overplus /'əʊvəplʌs/ *n.* a surplus, a superabundance. [Middle English, partial translation of Anglo-French *surplus* or medieval Latin *su(pe)rplus*]

overpopulated /əʊvə'pɒpjʊleɪtɪd/ *adj.* having too large a population. ▫ **overpopulation** /-'leɪʃ(ə)n/ *n.*

overpower /əʊvə'paʊə/ *v.tr.* **1** reduce to submission, subdue. **2** make (a thing) ineffective or imperceptible by greater intensity. **3** (of heat, emotion, etc.) be too intense for, overwhelm. ▫ **overpowering** *adj.* **overpoweringly** *adv.*

over-prescribe /əʊvəprɪ'skrʌɪb/ *v.tr.* (also *absol.*) prescribe an excessive amount of (a drug) or too many (drugs). ▫ **over-prescription** /-'skrɪpʃ(ə)n/ *n.*

overprice /əʊvə'prʌɪs/ *v.tr.* price (a thing) too highly.

overprint *v. & n.* ● *v.tr.* /əʊvə'prɪnt/ **1** print further matter on (a surface already printed, esp. a postage stamp). **2** print (further matter) in this way. **3** *Photog.* print (a positive) darker than was intended. **4** (also *absol.*) print too many copies of (a work). ● *n.* /'əʊvəprɪnt/ **1** the words etc. overprinted. **2** an overprinted postage stamp.

overproduce /əʊvəprə'djuːs/ *v.tr.* (usu. *absol.*) **1** produce more of (a commodity) than is wanted. **2** produce to an excessive degree. ▫ **overproduction** *n.*

overproof /əʊvə'pruːf/ *adj.* containing more alcohol than proof spirit does.

overprotective /əʊvəprə'tɛktɪv/ *adj.* excessively protective, esp. of a person in one's charge.

overqualified /əʊvə'kwɒlɪfʌɪd/ *adj.* too highly qualified (esp. for a particular job etc.).

overran *past* of OVERRUN.

overrate /əʊvə'reɪt/ *v.tr.* (often as **overrated** *adj.*) assess or value too highly.

overreach /əʊvə'riːtʃ/ *v.tr.* circumvent, outwit; get the better of by cunning or artifice. ▫ **overreach oneself 1** strain oneself by reaching too far. **2** defeat one's object by going too far.

overreact /əʊvərɪ'akt/ *v.intr.* respond more forcibly etc. than is justified. ▫ **overreaction** *n.*

over-refine /əʊvərɪ'fʌɪn/ *v.tr.* (also *absol.*) **1** refine too much. **2** make too subtle distinctions in (an argument etc.). ▫ **over-refinement** *n.*

override *v. & n.* ● *v.tr.* /əʊvə'rʌɪd/ (*past* **-rode**; *past part.* **-ridden**) **1** have or claim precedence or superiority over (*an overriding consideration*). **2 a** intervene and make ineffective. **b** interrupt the action of (an automatic device) esp. to take manual control. **3 a** trample down or underfoot. **b** supersede arrogantly. **4** extend over, esp. (of a part of a fractured bone) overlap (another part). **5** ride over (enemy country). **6** exhaust (a horse etc.) by hard riding. ● *n.* /'əʊvərʌɪd/ **1** the action or process of suspending an automatic function. **2** a device for this.

overrider /'əʊvərʌɪdə/ *n.* *Brit.* each of a pair of projecting pieces on the bumper of a car.

overripe /əʊvə'rʌɪp/ *adj.* (esp. of fruit etc.) past its best; excessively ripe; full-blown.

overrode *past* of OVERRIDE.

overruff *v. & n.* *Cards* ● *v.tr.* /əʊvə'rʌf/ (also *absol.*) overtrump. ● *n.* /'əʊvərʌf/ an instance of this.

overrule /əʊvə'ruːl/ *v.tr.* **1** set aside (a decision, argument, proposal, etc.) by exercising a superior authority. **2** annul a decision by or reject a proposal of (a person) in this way.

overrun *v. & n.* ● *v.tr.* /əʊvə'rʌn/ (**-running**; *past* **-ran**; *past part.* **-run**) **1** (of vermin, weeds, etc.) swarm or spread over. **2** conquer or ravage (territory) by force. **3** (of time, expenditure, production, etc.) exceed (a fixed limit). **4** *Printing* carry over (a word etc.) to the next line or page. **5** *Mech.* rotate faster than. **6** (of water) flood (land). ● *n.* /'əʊvərʌn/ **1** an instance of overrunning. **2** the amount of this. **3** the movement of a vehicle at a speed greater than is imparted by the engine. [Old English *oferyrnan* (as OVER-, RUN)]

oversailing /'əʊvəseɪlɪŋ/ *adj.* (of a part of a building) projecting beyond what is below. [OVER + French *saillir* SALLY[1]]

oversaw *past* of OVERSEE.

overscrupulous /əʊvə'skruːpjʊləs/ *adj.* excessively scrupulous or particular.

overseas *adv. & adj.* ● *adv.* /əʊvə'siːz/ (also **oversea**) abroad (*was sent overseas for training*). ● *attrib.adj.* /'əʊvəsiːz/ (also **oversea**) **1** foreign; across or beyond the sea. **2** of or connected with movement or transport over the sea (*overseas postage rates*). ▫ **from overseas** from abroad.

oversee /əʊvə'siː/ *v.tr.* (**-sees**; *past* **-saw**; *past part.* **-seen**) officially supervise (workers, work, etc.). [Old English *oferseōn* 'look at from above' (as OVER-, SEE[1])]

overseer /'əʊvəsɪə/ *n.* a person who supervises others, esp. workers. [OVERSEE]

overseer of the poor *n.* *Brit. hist.* a parish official who administered funds to the poor.

oversell /əʊvə'sɛl/ *v.tr.* (*past* and *past part.* **-sold**) (also *absol.*) **1** sell more of (a commodity etc.) than one can deliver. **2** exaggerate the merits of.

oversensitive /əʊvə'sɛnsɪtɪv/ *adj.* excessively sensitive; easily hurt by, or too quick to react to, outside influences. ▫ **oversensitiveness** *n.* **oversensitivity** /-'tɪvɪti/ *n.*

overset /əʊvə'sɛt/ *v.tr.* (**-setting**; *past* and *past part.* **-set**) **1** esp. *Brit.* overturn, upset. **2** *Printing* set up (type) in excess of the available space.

oversew /'əʊvəsəʊ/ *v.tr.* (*past part.* **-sewn** or **-sewed**) **1** sew (two edges) with every stitch passing over the join. **2** join the sections of (a book) by a stitch of this type.

oversexed /əʊvə'sɛkst/ *adj.* having unusually strong sexual desires.

overshadow /əʊvə'ʃadəʊ/ *v.tr.* **1** appear much more prominent or important than. **2** cast into the shade; shelter from the sun. [Old English *ofersceadwian* (as OVER-, SHADOW)]

overshoe /'əʊvəʃuː/ *n.* a shoe of rubber, felt, etc., worn over another as protection from wet, cold, etc.

overshoot *v. & n.* ● *v.tr.* /əʊvə'ʃuːt/ (*past* and *past part.* **-shot**) **1** pass or send beyond (a target or limit). **2** (of an aircraft) fly beyond or taxi too far along (the runway) when landing or taking off. ● *n.* /'əʊvəʃuːt/ **1** the act of overshooting. **2** the amount of this. ▫ **overshoot the mark** go beyond what is intended or proper; go too far.

overshot wheel *n.* a waterwheel operated by the weight of water falling into buckets attached to its periphery.

overside /əʊvə'sʌɪd/ *adv.* over the side of a ship (into a smaller boat, or into the sea).

oversight /'əʊvəsʌɪt/ *n.* **1** a failure to notice something. **2** an inadvertent mistake. **3** supervision.

oversimplify /əʊvə'sɪmplɪfʌɪ/ *v.tr.* (**-ies**, **-ied**) (also *absol.*) distort (a problem etc.) by stating it in too simple terms. ▫ **oversimplification** /-fɪ'keɪʃ(ə)n/ *n.*

oversize /ˈəʊvəsʌɪz/ *adj.* (also **-sized** /-ˈsʌɪzd/) of more than the usual size.

overskirt /ˈəʊvəskəːt/ *n.* an outer or second skirt.

overslaugh /ˈəʊvəslɔː/ *n. & v.* ● *n. Brit. Mil.* the passing over of one's turn of duty. ● *v.tr.* **1** *Brit. Mil.* pass over (one's duty) in consideration of another duty that takes precedence. **2** *US* pass over in favour of another. **3** *US* omit to consider. [Dutch *overslag* (*n.*) from *overslaan* 'omit' (as OVER, *slaan* 'strike')]

oversleep /əʊvəˈsliːp/ *v.intr. & refl.* (*past* and *past part.* **-slept**) continue sleeping beyond the intended time of waking; sleep too long.

oversleeve /ˈəʊvəsliːv/ *n.* a protective sleeve covering an ordinary sleeve.

oversold *past* and *past part.* of OVERSELL.

oversolicitous /əʊvəsəˈlɪsɪtəs/ *adj.* excessively worried, anxious, eager, etc. □ **oversolicitude** *n.*

oversoul /ˈəʊvəsəʊl/ *n.* God as a spirit animating the universe and including all human souls.

overspecialize /əʊvəˈspɛʃ(ə)lʌɪz/ *v.intr.* (also **-ise**) concentrate too much on one aspect or area. □ **overspecialization** /-ˈzeɪʃ(ə)n/ *n.*

overspend *v. & n.* ● *v.* /əʊvəˈspɛnd/ (*past* and *past part.* **-spent**) **1** *intr. & refl.* spend too much. **2** *tr.* spend more than (a specified amount). ● *n.* /ˈəʊvəspɛnd/ **1** the act of overspending a limit. **2** an instance of this. **3** the amount by which a limit is overspent.

overspill /ˈəʊvəspɪl/ *n.* **1** what is spilt over or overflows. **2** *Brit.* the surplus population leaving a country or city to live elsewhere.

overspread /əʊvəˈsprɛd/ *v.tr.* (*past* and *past part.* **-spread**) **1** become spread or diffused over. **2** cover or occupy the surface of. **3** (as **overspread** *adj.*) (usu. foll. by *with*) covered (*high mountains overspread with trees*). [Old English *ofersprǣdan* (as OVER-, SPREAD)]

overstaff /əʊvəˈstɑːf/ *v.tr.* provide with too large a staff.

overstate /əʊvəˈsteɪt/ *v.tr.* **1** state (esp. a case or argument) too strongly. **2** exaggerate. □ **overstatement** *n.*

overstay /əʊvəˈsteɪ/ *v.tr.* stay longer than (one's welcome, a time limit, etc.).

oversteer *v. & n.* ● *v.intr.* /əʊvəˈstɪə/ (of a motor vehicle) have a tendency to turn more sharply than was intended. ● *n.* /ˈəʊvəstɪə/ this tendency.

overstep /əʊvəˈstɛp/ *v.tr.* (**-stepped**, **-stepping**) **1** pass beyond (a boundary or mark). **2** violate (certain standards of behaviour etc.). □ **overstep the mark** violate conventions of behaviour.

overstitch /ˈəʊvəstɪtʃ/ *n. & v. Needlework* ● *n.* a stitch made over an edge or another stitch. ● *v.tr.* sew with an overstitch.

overstock *v. & n.* ● *v.tr.* /əʊvəˈstɒk/ stock excessively. ● *n.* /ˈəʊvəstɒk/ esp. *US* a supply in excess of demand or requirement.

overstrain /əʊvəˈstreɪn/ *v.tr.* strain too much.

overstress *v. & n.* ● *v.tr.* /əʊvəˈstrɛs/ stress too much. ● *n.* /ˈəʊvəstrɛs/ an excessive degree of stress.

overstretch /əʊvəˈstrɛtʃ/ *v.tr.* **1** stretch too much. **2** (esp. as **overstretched** *adj.*) make excessive demands on (resources, a person, etc.).

overstrung *adj.* **1** /əʊvəˈstrʌŋ/ (of a person, disposition, etc.) intensely strained, highly strung. **2** /ˈəʊvəstrʌŋ/ (of a piano) with strings in sets crossing each other obliquely.

overstudy /əʊvəˈstʌdi/ *v.tr.* (**-ies**, **-ied**) **1** study beyond what is necessary or desirable. **2** (as **overstudied** *adj.*) excessively deliberate; affected.

overstuff /əʊvəˈstʌf/ *v.tr.* **1** stuff more than is necessary. **2** (as **overstuffed** *adj.*) (of furniture) made soft and comfortable by thick upholstery.

oversubscribe /əʊvəsəbˈskrʌɪb/ *v.tr.* (usu. as **oversubscribed** *adj.*) subscribe for more than the amount available of (a commodity offered for sale etc.) (*the offer was oversubscribed*).

oversubtle /əʊvəˈsʌt(ə)l/ *adj.* excessively subtle; not plain or clear.

oversupply /əʊvəsəˈplʌɪ/ *v. & n.* ● *v.tr.* (**-ies**, **-ied**) supply with too much. ● *n.* an excessive supply.

oversusceptible /əʊvəsəˈsɛptɪb(ə)l/ *adj.* too susceptible or vulnerable.

overt /əʊˈvəːt, ˈəʊvət/ *adj.* unconcealed; done openly. □ **overtly** *adv.* **overtness** *n.* [Middle English via Old French, past part. of *ovrir* 'open', from Latin *aperire*]

overtake /əʊvəˈteɪk/ *v.tr.* (*past* **-took**; *past part.* **-taken**) **1** (also (*Brit.*) *absol.*) catch up with and pass while travelling in the same direction. **2** (of a storm, misfortune, etc.) come suddenly or unexpectedly upon. **3** become level with and exceed (a compared value etc.).

overtask /əʊvəˈtɑːsk/ *v.tr.* **1** give too heavy a task to. **2** be too heavy a task for.

overtax /əʊvəˈtaks/ *v.tr.* **1** make excessive demands on (a person's strength etc.). **2** tax too heavily.

over-the-counter *attrib.adj.* obtainable from a shop, esp. (of drugs) without a prescription (see also *over the counter* (COUNTER[1])).

over-the-top see *over the top* 2 (TOP[1]).

overthrow *v. & n.* ● *v.tr.* /əʊvəˈθrəʊ/ (*past* **-threw**; *past part.* **-thrown**) **1** remove forcibly from power. **2** put an end to (an institution etc.). **3** conquer, overcome. **4** knock down, upset. ● *n.* /ˈəʊvəθrəʊ/ **1** a defeat or downfall. **2** *Cricket* **a** a fielder's return of the ball, not stopped near the wicket and so allowing further runs. **b** such a run. **3** *Archit.* a panel of decorated wrought-iron work in an arch or gateway.

overthrust /ˈəʊvəθrʌst/ *n. Geol.* the thrust of esp. lower strata on one side of a fault over those on the other side.

overtime /ˈəʊvətʌɪm/ *n. & adv.* ● *n.* **1** the time during which a person works at a job in addition to the regular hours. **2** payment for this. **3** *N. Amer. Sport* = EXTRA TIME. ● *adv.* in addition to regular hours.

overtire /əʊvəˈtʌɪə/ *v.tr. & refl.* exhaust or wear out (esp. an invalid etc.).

overtone /ˈəʊvətəʊn/ *n.* **1** *Mus.* any of the tones above the lowest in a harmonic series. **2** a subtle or elusive quality or implication (*sinister overtones*). [OVER- + TONE, suggested by German *Oberton*]

overtop /əʊvəˈtɒp/ *v.tr.* (**-topped**, **-topping**) **1** be or become higher than. **2** surpass.

overtrain /əʊvəˈtreɪn/ *v.tr. & intr.* subject to or undergo too much (esp. athletic) training with a consequent loss of proficiency.

overtrick /ˈəʊvətrɪk/ *n. Bridge* a trick taken in excess of one's contract.

overtrump /əʊvəˈtrʌmp/ *v.tr.* (also *absol.*) *Cards* play a higher trump than (another player).

overture /ˈəʊvətj(ʊ)ə/ *n.* **1** an orchestral piece opening an opera etc. **2** a one-movement composition in this style. **3** (usu. in *pl.*) **a** an opening of negotiations. **b** a formal proposal or offer initiating negotiation, cooperation, etc. (esp. *make overtures to*). **4** the beginning of a poem etc. [Middle English via Old French from Latin *apertura* APERTURE]

overturn *v. & n.* ● *v.* /əʊvəˈtəːn/ **1** *tr.* cause to fall down or turn over; upset. **2** *tr.* reverse; subvert; abolish; invalidate. **3** *intr.* fall down; turn over. ● *n.* /ˈəʊvətəːn/ a subversion, an act of upsetting.

overuse *v. & n.* ● *v.tr.* /əʊvəˈjuːz/ use too much. ● *n.* /əʊvəˈjuːs/ excessive use.

overvalue /əʊvəˈvaljuː/ *v.tr.* (**-values**, **-valued**, **-valuing**) value too highly; have too high an opinion of.

overview /ˈəʊvəvjuː/ *n.* a general survey.

overwater *v. & adj.* ● *v.tr.* /əʊvəˈwɔːtə/ (also *absol.*) water (a plant etc.) too much. ● *attrib.adj.* /ˈəʊvəwɔːtə/ situated above the water.

overweening /əʊvəˈwiːnɪŋ/ *adj.* arrogant, presumptuous, conceited, self-confident. □ **overweeningly** *adv.* **overweeningness** *n.* [OVER- + WEEN]

overweight *adj., n., & v.* ● *adj.* /əʊvəˈweɪt/ **1** in excess of a weight considered normal or desirable. **2** beyond an allowed or suitable weight. ● *n.* /ˈəʊvəweɪt/ excessive or extra weight; preponderance. ● *v.tr.* /əʊvəˈweɪt/ (usu. foll. by *with*) load unduly.

overwhelm /əʊvəˈwɛlm/ *v.tr.* **1** overpower with emotion. **2** (usu. foll. by *with*) overpower with an excess of business etc. **3** bring to sudden ruin or destruction; crush. **4** bury or drown beneath a huge mass, submerge utterly.

overwhelming /əʊvəˈwɛlmɪŋ/ *adj.* irresistible by force of numbers, influence, amount, etc. □ **overwhelmingly** *adv.* **overwhelmingness** *n.*

overwind *v.* & *n.* ● *v.tr.* /əʊvəˈwʌɪnd/ (*past* and *past part.* **-wound**) wind (a mechanism, esp. a watch) beyond the proper stopping point. ● *n.* /ˈəʊvəwʌɪnd/ an instance of this.

overwinter /əʊvəˈwɪntə/ *v.* **1** *intr.* (usu. foll. by *at, in*) spend the winter. **2** *intr.* (of insects, fungi, etc.) live through the winter. **3** *tr.* keep (animals, plants, etc.) alive through the winter.

overwork /əʊvəˈwəːk/ *v.* & *n.* ● *v.* **1** *intr.* work too hard. **2** *tr.* cause (another person) to work too hard. **3** *tr.* weary or exhaust with too much work. **4** *tr.* (esp. as **overworked** *adj.*) make excessive use of. **5** *tr.* (as **overworked** *adj.*) = OVERWROUGHT 2. ● *n.* excessive work.

overwound *past* and *past part.* of OVERWIND.

overwrite /əʊvəˈrʌɪt/ *v.* (*past* **-wrote**; *past part.* **-written**) **1** *tr.* write on top of (other writing). **2** *tr. Computing* destroy (data) in (a file etc.) by entering new data. **3** *intr.* (esp. as **overwritten** *adj.*) write too elaborately or too ornately. **4** *intr.* & *refl.* write too much; exhaust oneself by writing. **5** *tr.* write too much about. **6** *intr.* (esp. as **overwriting** *n.*) in shipping insurance, accept more risk than the premium income limits allow.

overwrought /əʊvəˈrɔːt/ *adj.* **1** overexcited, nervous, distraught. **2** overdone; too elaborate.

overzealous /əʊvəˈzɛləs/ *adj.* too zealous in one's attitude, behaviour, etc.; excessively enthusiastic.

ovi-[1] /ˈəʊvi/ *comb. form* egg, ovum. [Latin *ovum* 'egg']

ovi-[2] /ˈəʊvi/ *comb. form* sheep. [Latin *ovis* 'sheep']

ovibovine /əʊvɪˈbəʊvʌɪn/ *adj.* & *n. Zool.* ● *adj.* having characteristics intermediate between those of a sheep and an ox. ● *n.* such an animal, e.g. a musk-ox.

oviduct /ˈəʊvɪdʌkt/ *n.* the tube through which an ovum passes from the ovary. □ **oviducal** /-ˈdjuːk(ə)l/ *adj.* **oviductal** /-ˈdʌkt(ə)l/ *adj.*

oviform /ˈəʊvɪfɔːm/ *adj.* egg-shaped.

ovine /ˈəʊvʌɪn/ *adj.* of or like sheep. [Late Latin *ovinus* from Latin *ovis* 'sheep']

oviparous /əʊˈvɪp(ə)rəs/ *adj. Zool.* producing young by means of eggs expelled from the body before they are hatched (cf. VIVIPAROUS). □ **oviparity** /-ˈparɪti/ *n.* **oviparously** *adv.*

oviposit /əʊvɪˈpɒzɪt/ *v.intr.* (**oviposited**, **ovipositing**) lay an egg or eggs, esp. with an ovipositor. □ **oviposition** /-pəˈzɪʃ(ə)n/ *n.* [OVI-[1] + Latin *ponere posit-* 'to place']

ovipositor /əʊvɪˈpɒzɪtə/ *n.* a pointed tubular organ with which a female insect deposits her eggs. [modern Latin, from OVI-[1] + Latin *positor* from *ponere posit-* 'to place']

ovoid /ˈəʊvɔɪd/ *adj.* & *n.* ● *adj.* **1** (of a solid or of a surface) egg-shaped. **2** oval, with one end more pointed than the other. ● *n.* an ovoid body or surface. [French *ovoïde* from modern Latin *ovoides* (as OVUM)]

ovolo /ˈəʊvələʊ/ *n.* (*pl.* **ovoli** /-liː/) *Archit.* a rounded convex moulding. [Italian, diminutive of *ovo* 'egg', from Latin OVUM]

ovotestis /əʊvəʊˈtɛstɪs/ *n.* (*pl.* **-testes** /-tiːz/) *Zool.* an organ producing both ova and spermatozoa. [OVUM + TESTIS]

ovoviviparous /ˌəʊvəʊvɪˈvɪp(ə)rəs/ *adj. Zool.* producing young by means of eggs hatched within the body (cf. OVIPAROUS, VIVIPAROUS). □ **ovoviviparity** /-ˈparɪti/ *n.* [OVUM + VIVIPAROUS]

ovulate /ˈɒvjʊleɪt/ *v.intr.* produce ova or ovules, or discharge them from the ovary. □ **ovulation** /-ˈleɪʃ(ə)n/ *n.* **ovulatory** *adj.* [modern Latin *ovulum* (as OVULE)]

ovule /ˈɒvjuːl, ˈəʊ-/ *n.* the part of the ovary of seed plants that contains the germ cell; an unfertilized seed. □ **ovular** *adj.* [French from medieval Latin *ovulum*, diminutive of OVUM]

ovum /ˈəʊvəm/ *n.* (*pl.* **ova** /ˈəʊvə/) **1** a mature reproductive cell of female animals, produced by the ovary. **2** the egg cell of plants. [Latin, = egg]

ow /aʊ/ *int.* expressing sudden pain. [a natural exclamation]

owe /əʊ/ *v.tr.* **1 a** be under obligation (to a person etc.) to pay or repay (money etc.) (*we owe you five pounds*; *owe more than I can pay*). **b** (*absol.*, usu. foll. by *for*) be in debt (*still owe for my car*). **2** (often foll. by *to*) be under obligation to render (gratitude etc., a person honour, gratitude, etc.) (*owe grateful thanks to*). **3** (usu. foll. by *to*) be indebted to a person or thing for (*we owe to Newton the principle of gravitation*). □ **owe a person a grudge** cherish resentment against a person. **owe it to oneself** (often foll. by *to* + infin.) need (to do) something to protect one's own interests. [Old English *āgan*, from Germanic]

owing /ˈəʊɪŋ/ *predic.adj.* **1** owed; yet to be paid (*the balance owing*). **2** (foll. by *to*) **a** caused by; attributable to (*the cancellation was owing to ill health*). **b** (as *prep.*) because of (*trains are delayed owing to bad weather*).

■ **Usage** The use of *owing to* as a preposition meaning 'because of' is entirely acceptable (see example above), unlike this use of *due to*.

owl /aʊl/ *n.* **1** any nocturnal bird of prey of the order Strigiformes, with large eyes and a hooked beak, including barn owls, tawny owls, etc. **2** *colloq.* a person compared to an owl, esp. in looking solemn or wise. □ **owlery** *n.* (*pl.* **-ies**). **owlish** *adj.* **owlishly** *adv.* **owlishness** *n.* (in sense 2). **owl-like** *adj.* [Old English *ūle*, from Germanic]

owlet /ˈaʊlɪt/ *n.* **1** a young owl. **2** a small owl esp. of the genus *Glaucidium*, *Xenoglaux*, or *Athene*.

owl-light *n.* dusk, twilight.

owl monkey *n.* (*pl.* **-eys**) = DOUROUCOULI.

own /əʊn/ *adj.* & *v.* ● *adj.* (prec. by possessive) **1 a** belonging to oneself or itself; not another's (*saw it with my own eyes*). **b** individual, peculiar, particular (*has its own charm*). **2** used to emphasize identity rather than possession (*cooks his own meals*). **3** (*absol.*) **a** private property (*is it your own?*). **b** kindred (*among my own*). ● *v.* **1** *tr.* have as property; possess. **2 a** *tr.* confess; admit as valid, true, etc. (*own their faults*; *owns he did not know*). **b** *intr.* (foll. by *to*) confess to (*owned to a prejudice*). **3** *tr.* acknowledge paternity, authorship, or possession of. □ **come into one's own 1** receive one's due. **2** achieve recognition. **get one's own back** (often foll. by *on*) *colloq.* get revenge. **hold one's own** maintain one's position; not be defeated or lose strength. **of one's own** belonging to oneself alone. **on one's own 1** alone. **2** independently, without help. **own up** (often foll. by *to*) confess frankly. □ **-owned** *adj.* (in *comb.*). [Old English *āgen*, *āgnian*, past part. of *agan* OWE]

own brand *n. Brit.* **1** a make of goods manufactured specially for a retailer and bearing the retailer's name (hyphenated when *attrib.*: *own-brand cosmetics*). **2** (foll. by *of*) a kind particular to a person or group (*own brand of gay activism*).

owner /ˈəʊnə/ *n.* **1** a person who owns something. **2** *slang* the captain of a ship. □ **ownerless** *adj.* **ownership** *n.*

owner-occupier *n. Brit.* a person who owns the house etc. he or she lives in. □ **owner-occupied** *adj.*

own goal *n. Brit.* **1** a goal scored (usu. by mistake) against the scorer's own side. **2** *colloq.* an act or initiative that unintentionally harms one's own interests.

owt /aʊt/ *n. Brit. colloq.* or *dial.* anything. [variant of AUGHT[1]]

ox /ɒks/ *n.* (*pl.* **oxen** /'ɒks(ə)n/) **1** any bovine animal, esp. a large usu. horned domesticated ruminant used for draught, for supplying milk, and for eating as meat. **2** a castrated male of a domesticated species of cattle, *Bos taurus*. [Old English *oxa*, from Germanic]

ox- var. of OXY-[2].

oxalic acid /ɒk'salɪk/ *n. Chem.* a very poisonous and sour acid found in sorrel and rhubarb leaves. Chem. formula: $(COOH)_2$. □ **oxalate** /'ɒksəleɪt/ *n.* [French *oxalique* via Latin *oxalis* from Greek *oxalis* 'wood sorrel']

oxalis /'ɒksəlɪs, ɒk'sɑːlɪs/ *n.* any plant of the genus *Oxalis*, with trifoliate leaves and white, yellow, or pink flowers, e.g. wood sorrel. [Latin from Greek, from *oxus* 'sour']

oxbow /'ɒksbəʊ/ *n.* **1** a U-shaped collar of an ox-yoke. **2 a** a loop formed by a horseshoe bend in a river. **b** a lake formed when the river cuts across the narrow end of the loop.

Oxbridge /'ɒksbrɪdʒ/ *n. Brit.* **1** (also *attrib.*) Oxford and Cambridge universities regarded together, esp. in contrast to newer institutions. **2** (often *attrib.*) the characteristics of these universities. [portmanteau word from *Ox*(ford) + (Cam)*bridge*]

oxen *pl.* of ox.

oxer /'ɒksə/ *n.* **1** an ox-fence. **2** a similar fence used in showjumping.

ox-eye *n.* any of various plants of the daisy family with conspicuously rayed flowers, e.g. (in full **ox-eye daisy**) *Leucanthemum vulgare*, which has large white flowers with yellow centres; also called *white ox-eye*.

Oxf. *abbr.* Oxford.

Oxfam /'ɒksfam/ *abbr.* Oxford Committee for Famine Relief.

ox-fence *n.* a strong fence for keeping in cattle, consisting of railings, a hedge, and often a ditch.

Oxford bags /'ɒksfəd/ *n. Brit.* wide baggy trousers. [*Oxford* in S. England]

Oxford blue /'ɒksfəd/ *n.* & *adj.* ● *n.* **1** a dark blue, sometimes with a purple tinge. **2** = BLUE[1] *n.* 3a. ● *adj.* (hyphenated when *attrib.*) of this colour. [adopted by *Oxford* University in S. England]

Oxford Group /'ɒksfəd/ *n.* a Christian movement founded at Oxford in 1921, with discussion of personal problems by groups.

Oxford Movement /'ɒksfəd/ *n.* an Anglican High Church movement started in Oxford in 1833, advocating traditional forms of worship.

oxherd /'ɒkshəːd/ *n.* a cowherd.

oxhide /'ɒkshʌɪd/ *n.* **1** the hide of an ox. **2** leather made from this.

oxidant /'ɒksɪd(ə)nt/ *n.* an oxidizing agent. [French, participle of *oxider* (cf. OXIDE)]

oxidation /ɒksɪ'deɪʃ(ə)n/ *n.* the process or result of oxidizing or being oxidized. □ **oxidational** /-'deɪʃ(ə)n(ə)l/ *adj.* **oxidative** /'ɒksɪdeɪtɪv/ *adj.* [French, from *oxider* (cf. OXIDE)]

oxidation number *n.* (also **oxidation state**) *Chem.* **1** a number indicating the number of electrons actually or notionally lost or gained by an atom of an element when chemically combined. **2** the state represented by a value of this.

oxide /'ɒksʌɪd/ *n.* a binary compound of oxygen. [French, from *oxygène* OXYGEN + *-ide* as in *acide* ACID]

oxidize /'ɒksɪdʌɪz/ *v.* (also **-ise**) **1** *intr.* & *tr.* combine or cause to combine with oxygen. **2** *tr.* & *intr.* cover (metal) or (of metal) become covered with a coating of oxide etc.; make or become rusty or tarnished. **3** *intr.* & *tr. Chem.* undergo or cause to undergo a loss of electrons (opp. REDUCE 12b). □ **oxidizable** *adj.* **oxidization** /-'zeɪʃ(ə)n/ *n.* **oxidized** *adj.* **oxidizer** *n.*

oxidizing agent *n. Chem.* a substance that brings about oxidation by being reduced and gaining electrons.

oxlip /'ɒkslɪp/ *n.* **1** a woodland primula, *Primula elatior*. **2** (in general use) a natural hybrid between a primrose and a cowslip.

Oxon /'ɒks(ə)n, -sɒn/ *abbr.* **1** Oxfordshire. **2** of Oxford University (esp. in degree titles). [abbreviation of medieval Latin *Oxoniensis* from *Oxonia*: see OXONIAN]

Oxonian /ɒk'səʊnɪən/ *adj.* & *n.* ● *adj.* of or relating to Oxford or Oxford University. ● *n.* **1** a member of Oxford University. **2** a native or inhabitant of Oxford. [*Oxonia*, Latinized name of *Ox(en)ford*]

ox-pecker *n.* any African bird of the genus *Buphagus*, feeding on skin parasites living on animals.

oxtail /'ɒksteɪl/ *n.* the tail of an ox, esp. as an ingredient in soup.

oxter /'ɒkstə/ *n. Sc.* & *N.Engl.* the armpit. [Old English *ōhsta*, *ōxta*]

ox-tongue /'ɒkstʌŋ/ *n.* **1** the tongue of an ox, esp. cooked as food. **2** any plant of the genus *Picris* (daisy family), with bright yellow flowers.

oxy-[1] /'ɒksi/ *comb. form* denoting sharpness (*oxytone*). [Greek *oxu-* from *oxus* 'sharp']

oxy-[2] /'ɒksi/ *comb. form* (also **ox-** /ɒks/) *Chem.* oxygen (*oxyacetylene*). [abbreviation]

oxyacetylene /ɒksɪə'sɛtɪliːn/ *adj.* of or using oxygen and acetylene, esp. in cutting or welding metals (*oxyacetylene burner*).

oxyacid /'ɒksɪˌasɪd/ *n. Chem.* an acid containing oxygen.

oxygen /'ɒksɪdʒ(ə)n/ *n. Chem.* a colourless tasteless odourless gaseous element, occurring naturally in air, water, and most minerals and organic substances, and essential to plant and animal life (symbol **O**). □ **oxygenous** /ɒk'sɪdʒɪnəs/ *adj.* [French *oxygène* 'acidifying principle' (as OXY-[1]): it was at first held to be the essential principle in the formation of acids]

oxygenate /'ɒksɪdʒəneɪt, ɒk'sɪdʒ-/ *v.tr.* supply or treat with oxygen, esp. charge or enrich (blood, water, etc.) with oxygen. □ **oxygenation** /-'neɪʃ(ə)n/ *n.* [French *oxygéner* (as OXYGEN)]

oxygenator /'ɒksɪdʒəneɪtə/ *n.* **1** an apparatus for oxygenating the blood. **2** an aquatic plant which enriches the surrounding water with oxygen.

oxygenize /'ɒksɪdʒənʌɪz/ *v.tr.* (also **-ise**) = OXYGENATE.

oxygen mask *n.* a mask placed over the nose and mouth to supply oxygen from an attached cylinder for breathing.

oxygen tent *n.* a tentlike enclosure supplying a patient with air rich in oxygen.

oxyhaemoglobin /ˌɒksɪhiːmə'gləʊbɪn/ *n. Biochem.* a bright red complex formed when haemoglobin combines with oxygen.

oxymoron /ɒksɪ'mɔːrɒn/ *n. Rhet.* a figure of speech in which apparently contradictory terms appear in conjunction (e.g. *faith unfaithful kept him falsely true*). [Greek *oxumōron*, neut. of *oxumōros* 'pointedly foolish', from *oxus* 'sharp' + *mōros* 'foolish']

oxytetracycline /ˌɒksɪtɛtrə'sʌɪkliːn/ *n.* an antibiotic related to tetracycline.

oxytocin /ɒksɪ'təʊsɪn/ *n.* **1** a hormone released by the pituitary gland that causes increased contraction of the womb during labour and stimulates the ejection of milk into the ducts of the breasts. **2** a synthetic form of this used to induce labour etc. [*oxytocic* 'accelerating parturition' from Greek *oxutokia* 'sudden delivery' (as OXY-[1], *tokos* 'childbirth')]

oxytone /'ɒksɪtəʊn/ *adj.* & *n.* ● *adj.* (esp. in ancient Greek) having an acute accent on the last syllable. ● *n.* a word of this kind. [Greek *oxutonos* (as OXY-[1], *tonos* 'tone')]

oyer and terminer /ˌɔɪə(r) (ə)n(d) 'təːmɪnə/ *n. hist.* a commission issued to judges on a circuit to hold courts. [Middle English from Anglo-French *oyer et terminer*, from Latin *audire* 'hear' + *et* 'and' + *terminare* 'determine']

oyez /əʊ'jɛs, -'jɛz, -'jeɪ/ *int.* (also **oyes**) uttered, usu. three times, by a public crier or a court officer to command silence and attention. [Middle English via Anglo-French, Old French *oiez*, *oyez*, imperative pl. of *oïr* 'hear', from Latin *audire* 'hear']

oyster /ˈɔɪstə/ *n.* **1** any of various bivalve molluscs of the families Ostreidae and Aviculidae, esp. an edible kind, *Ostrea edulis*, of European waters. **2** an oyster-shaped morsel of meat in a fowl's back. **3** something regarded as containing all that one desires (*the world is my oyster*). **4** = OYSTER WHITE. [Middle English & Old French *oistre* via Latin *ostrea*, *ostreum* from Greek *ostreon*]

oyster bed *n.* a part of the sea bottom where oysters breed or are bred.

oystercatcher /ˈɔɪstəkatʃə/ *n.* any usu. coastal wading bird of the genus *Haematopus*, with a strong orange-coloured bill, feeding on shellfish.

oyster-farm *n.* an area of the seabed used for breeding oysters.

oyster mushroom *n.* an edible fungus, *Pleurotus ostreatus*, which grows on trees.

oyster-plant *n.* **1** = SALSIFY. **2** a blue-flowered plant, *Mertensia maritima*, growing on beaches.

oyster white *n.* & *adj.* ● *n.* a greyish-white colour. ● *adj.* (hyphenated when *attrib.*) of this colour.

Oz /ɒz/ *adj.* & *n.* *Austral. slang* ● *adj.* Australian. ● *n.* **1** Australia. **2** an Australian. [abbreviation of the pronunciation]

oz *abbr.* ounce(s). [Italian from *onza* 'ounce']

ozocerite /əʊˈzəʊkərʌɪt, -sərʌɪt, əʊzə(ʊ)ˈsɪərʌɪt/ *n.* (also **ozokerite** /-k-/) a waxlike fossil paraffin used for candles, insulation, etc. [German *Ozokerit*, from Greek *ozō* 'smell' + *kēros* 'wax']

ozone /ˈəʊzəʊn/ *n.* **1** *Chem.* a colourless unstable toxic gas with a pungent odour and powerful oxidizing properties, formed from normal oxygen by electrical discharges or ultraviolet light. Chem. formula: O_3. **2** *colloq.* invigorating air at the seaside etc. □ **ozonic** /əʊˈzɒnɪk/ *adj.* **ozonize** *v.tr.* (also **-ise**). **ozonization** /-ˈzeɪʃ(ə)n/ *n.* **ozonizer** *n.* [German *Ozon* from Greek, neut. pres. part. of *ozō* 'smell']

ozone-friendly *adj.* (of manufactured articles) containing chemicals that are not destructive to the ozone layer.

ozone hole *n.* a region of marked thinning of the ozone layer, esp. above each pole.

ozone layer *n.* a layer in the stratosphere containing a high concentration of ozone that absorbs most of the sun's ultraviolet radiation.

Ozzie var. of AUSSIE.

Pp

P[1] /piː/ *n.* (also **p**) (*pl.* **Ps** or **P's**) the sixteenth letter of the alphabet.

P[2] *abbr.* (also **P.**) **1** (on road signs) parking. **2** *Chess* pawn. **3** (also Ⓟ) proprietary.

P[3] *symb.* **1** *Chem.* the element phosphorus. **2** *Physics* poise (unit).

p *abbr.* (also **p.**) **1** *Brit.* penny, pence. **2** page. **3** pico-. **4** *Mus.* piano (softly).

PA *abbr.* **1** *Brit.* personal assistant. **2** public address (esp. *PA system*). **3** Press Association. **4** *US* Pennsylvania (in official postal use).

Pa *symb. Chem.* the element protactinium.

pa /pɑː/ *n. colloq.* father. [abbreviation of PAPA]

p.a. *abbr.* per annum.

pabulum /ˈpabjʊləm/ *n.* **1** food, esp. for the mind. **2** bland or insipid intellectual fare, entertainment, etc.; pap. [Latin, from *pascere* 'feed']

PABX *abbr. Brit.* private automatic branch exchange.

paca /ˈpakə/ *n.* a tailless rodent of the genus *Agouti*, of S. and Central America, esp. *A. paca*, hunted for food. [Spanish & Portuguese, from Tupi]

pace[1] /peɪs/ *n. & v.* ● *n.* **1 a** a single step in walking or running. **b** the distance covered in this (about 75 cm or 30 in.). **c** the distance between two successive stationary positions of the same foot in walking. **2** speed in walking or running. **3** *Theatr. & Mus.* speed or tempo in theatrical or musical performance (*played with great pace*). **4 a** the rate at which something progresses (*the pace of technological change*). **b** the speed at which life is led (*the pace of city life*). **5 a** a manner of walking or running. **b** any of various gaits, esp. of a trained horse etc. (*rode at an ambling pace*). ● *v.* **1** *intr.* **a** walk (esp. repeatedly or methodically) with a slow or regular pace (*pacing up and down*). **b** (of a horse) = AMBLE. **2** *tr.* traverse by pacing. **3** *tr.* set the pace for (a rider, runner, etc.). **4** *tr.* (often foll. by *out*) measure (a distance) by pacing. □ **keep pace** (often foll. by *with*) advance at an equal rate (as). **put a person through his** (or **her**) **paces** test a person's qualities in action etc. **set the pace** determine the speed, esp. by leading. **stand** (or **stay**) **the pace** be able to keep up with others. □ **-paced** *adj.* **pacer** *n.* [Middle English via Old French *pas* from Latin *passus*, from *pandere pass-* 'stretch']

pace[2] /ˈpɑːtʃeɪ, ˈpeɪsi/ *prep.* (in stating a contrary opinion) with due deference to (the person named). [Latin, ablative of *pax* 'peace']

■ **Usage** *Pace* means 'despite (someone's) opinion', e.g. *I was not* (pace *Mr Smith*) *defending the legalization of drugs.* It does not mean 'according to (someone)' or 'notwithstanding (something)'.

pace bowler *n. Cricket* a fast bowler.

pacemaker /ˈpeɪsmeɪkə/ *n.* **1** a competitor who sets the pace in a race. **2** a natural or artificial device for stimulating the heart muscle and regulating its contractions. □ **pacemaking** *n. & adj.*

paceman /ˈpeɪsman/ *n.* (*pl.* **-men**) = PACE BOWLER.

pace-setter *n.* **1** a leader. **2** = PACEMAKER 1. □ **pace-setting** *adj. & n.*

pacey var. of PACY.

pacha var. of PASHA.

pachinko /pəˈtʃɪŋkəʊ/ *n.* a Japanese form of pinball. [Japanese]

pachisi /pəˈtʃiːzi/ *n.* a four-handed Indian board game with six cowries used like dice. [Hindi, = of 25 (the highest throw)]

pachyderm /ˈpakɪdəːm/ *n.* any thick-skinned mammal, esp. an elephant or rhinoceros. □ **pachydermatous** /-ˈdəːmətəs/ *adj.* [French *pachyderme* from Greek *pakhudermos*, from *pakhus* 'thick' + *derma -matos* 'skin']

pachytene /ˈpakɪtiːn/ *n. Biol.* a stage during the prophase of meiosis when the chromosomes thicken and may exchange genes by crossing over. [Greek *pakhus* 'thick' + *tainia* 'band']

pacific /pəˈsɪfɪk/ *adj. & n.* ● *adj.* **1** characterized by or tending to peace; tranquil. **2** (**Pacific**) of or adjoining the Pacific. ● *n.* (**the Pacific**) = PACIFIC OCEAN. □ **pacifically** *adv.* [French *pacifique* or Latin *pacificus*, from *pax pacis* 'peace']

pacification /ˌpasɪfɪˈkeɪʃ(ə)n/ *n.* the act of pacifying or the process of being pacified. □ **pacificatory** /pəsɪfɪˈkeɪt(ə)ri, pəˈsɪfɪkət(ə)ri/ *adj.* [French from Latin *pacificatio -onis* (as PACIFY)]

Pacific Ocean *n.* the largest of the world's oceans, lying between America to the east and Asia and Australasia to the west.

Pacific Rim *n.* (usu. prec. by *the*) the countries and regions bordering the Pacific Ocean, esp. the small nations of eastern Asia.

Pacific Standard Time *n.* (also **Pacific Time**) the standard time in a zone including the Pacific coastal region of Canada and the US, eight hours behind GMT.

pacifier /ˈpasɪfʌɪə/ *n.* **1** a person or thing that pacifies. **2** *N. Amer.* a baby's dummy.

pacifism /ˈpasɪfɪz(ə)m/ *n.* the belief that war and violence are morally unjustified and that all disputes should be settled by peaceful means. □ **pacifist** *n. & adj.* [French *pacifisme* from *pacifier* PACIFY]

pacify /ˈpasɪfʌɪ/ *v.tr.* (**-ies, -ied**) **1** appease (a person, anger, etc.). **2** bring (a country etc.) to a state of peace. [Middle English from Old French *pacifier* or Latin *pacificare* (as PACIFIC)]

pack[1] /pak/ *n. & v.* ● *n.* **1 a** a collection of things wrapped up or tied together for carrying. **b** = BACKPACK. **2** a set of items packaged for use or disposal together. **3** usu. *derog.* a lot or set (of similar things or persons) (*a pack of lies; a pack of thieves*). **4** *Brit.* a set of playing cards. **5 a** a group of hounds esp. for foxhunting. **b** a group of wild animals, esp. wolves, hunting together. **6** an organized group of Cub Scouts or Brownies. **7 a** *Rugby* a team's forwards. **b** *Sport* the main body of competitors following the leader or leaders esp. in a race. **8 a** a medicinal or cosmetic substance applied to the skin; = FACE PACK. **b** a hot or cold pad of absorbent material for treating a wound etc. **9** (also **ice pack**) an area of pack ice. **10** a quantity of fish, fruit, etc., packed in a season etc. **11** *Med.* **a** the wrapping of a body or part of a body in a wet sheet etc. **b** a sheet etc. used for this. ● *v.* **1** *tr.* (often foll. by *up*) **a** fill (a suitcase, bag, etc.) with clothes and other items. **b** put (things) together in a bag or suitcase, esp. for travelling. **2** *intr. & tr.* come or put closely together; crowd or cram (*packed a lot into a few hours; passengers packed like sardines*). **3** *tr.* (in *passive*; often foll. by *with*) be filled (with); contain extensively (*the restaurant was packed; the book is packed with information*). **4** *tr.* fill (a hall, theatre, etc.) with an audience etc. **5** *tr.*

cover (a thing) with something pressed tightly round. **6** *intr.* be suitable for packing. **7** *tr. colloq.* **a** carry (a gun etc.). **b** be capable of delivering (a punch) with skill or force. **8** *intr.* (of animals or rugby forwards) form a pack. □ **pack in** *colloq.* stop, give up (*packed in his job*). **pack it in** (or **up**) *colloq.* end or stop it. **pack off** *colloq.* send (a person) away, esp. abruptly or promptly. **pack up** *Brit. colloq.* **1** (esp. of a machine) stop functioning; break down. **2** retire from an activity, contest, etc. **send packing** *colloq.* dismiss (a person) summarily. □ **packable** *adj.* [Middle English from Middle Dutch, Middle Low German *pak, pakken,* of unknown origin]

pack[2] /pak/ *v.tr.* select (a jury etc.) or fill (a meeting) so as to secure a decision in one's favour. [probably via an obsolete verb *pact* from PACT]

package /ˈpakɪdʒ/ *n.* & *v.* ● *n.* **1 a** a bundle of things packed. **b** a parcel, box, etc., in which things are packed. **2** (in full **package deal**) a set of proposals or items offered or agreed to as a whole. **3** *Computing* a piece of software suitable for various applications rather than one which is custom-built. **4** *colloq.* = PACKAGE HOLIDAY. ● *v.tr.* **1** make up into or enclose in a package. **2** present (a product, person, or message) so as to appeal to the public. □ **packager** *n.* [PACK[1] + -AGE]

package holiday *n.* (also **package tour** etc.) a holiday or tour etc. with all arrangements made at an inclusive price.

packaging /ˈpakɪdʒɪŋ/ *n.* **1** a wrapping or container for goods. **2** the process of packing goods.

pack animal *n.* an animal for carrying packs.

pack drill *n.* a military punishment of marching up and down carrying full equipment. □ **no names, no pack drill** discretion will prevent punishment.

packed lunch *n.* a lunch carried in a bag, box, etc., esp. to work, school, etc.

packed out *adj. Brit. colloq.* full, crowded.

packer /ˈpakə/ *n.* a person or thing that packs, esp. a dealer who prepares and packs food for transportation and sale.

packet /ˈpakɪt/ *n.* & *v.* ● *n.* **1** a small package. **2** esp. *Brit. colloq.* a large sum of money won, lost, or spent. **3** (in full **packet-boat**) *hist.* a mailboat or passenger ship. ● *v.tr.* make up into or wrap up in a packet. [PACK[1] + -ET[1]]

packet switching *n.* a method of data transmission in which parts of a message are sent independently by the optimum route for each part and then reassembled.

packhorse /ˈpakhɔːs/ *n.* a horse for carrying loads.

pack ice *n.* an area of large crowded pieces of floating ice in the sea.

packing /ˈpakɪŋ/ *n.* **1** the act or process of packing. **2** material used to fill up a space around or in something, esp. to protect a fragile article in transit. **3** material used to seal a join or assist in lubricating an axle.

packing case *n.* a case (usu. wooden) or framework for packing goods in.

pack rat *n.* **1** a N. American wood rat, esp. *Neotoma cinerea,* with a long bushy tail. **2** a person who hoards things.

packsaddle /ˈpaksad(ə)l/ *n.* a horse's saddle adapted for supporting packs.

packthread /ˈpakθrɛd/ *n.* stout thread for sewing or tying up packs.

pact /pakt/ *n.* an agreement or a treaty. [Middle English via Old French *pact(e)* from Latin *pactum,* neut. past part. of *pacisci* 'agree']

pacy /ˈpeɪsi/ *adj.* (also **pacey**) (**pacier, paciest**) fast-moving.

pad[1] /pad/ *n.* & *v.* ● *n.* **1** a piece of soft material used to reduce friction or jarring, fill out hollows, hold or absorb liquid, etc. **2** a number of sheets of blank paper fastened together at one edge, for writing or drawing on. **3** = INK-PAD. **4** the fleshy underpart of an animal's foot or of a human finger. **5** a guard for the leg and ankle in sports. **6** a flat surface for helicopter take-off or rocket-launching. **7** *colloq.* a lodging, esp. a bedsitter or flat. **8** the floating leaf of a water lily. ● *v.tr.* (**padded, padding**) **1** provide with a pad or padding; stuff. **2** (foll. by *out*) lengthen or fill out (a book etc.) with unnecessary material. [probably of Low German or Dutch origin]

pad[2] /pad/ *v.* & *n.* ● *v.* (**padded, padding**) **1** *intr.* walk with a soft dull steady step. **2 a** *tr.* tramp along (a road etc.) on foot. **b** *intr.* travel on foot. ● *n.* the sound of soft steady steps. [Low German *padden* 'tread', *pad* PATH]

padded cell *n.* a room with padded walls in a psychiatric hospital.

padding /ˈpadɪŋ/ *n.* soft material used to pad or stuff with.

paddle[1] /ˈpad(ə)l/ *n.* & *v.* ● *n.* **1** a short broad-bladed oar used without a rowlock. **2** a paddle-shaped instrument. **3** *Zool.* a fin or flipper. **4** each of the boards fitted round the circumference of a paddle wheel or mill-wheel. **5** the action or a spell of paddling. ● *v.* **1** *intr.* & *tr.* move on water or propel a boat by means of paddles. **2** *intr.* & *tr.* row gently. **3** *tr.* esp. *N. Amer. colloq.* spank. □ **paddler** *n.* [Middle English: origin unknown]

paddle[2] /ˈpad(ə)l/ *v.* & *n.* ● *v.intr.* **1** *Brit.* walk, esp. barefoot, in shallow water. **2** dabble the feet or hands in shallow water. ● *n.* the action or a spell of paddling. □ **paddler** *n.* [probably of Low German or Dutch origin: cf. Low German *paddeln* 'tramp about']

paddle boat *n.* (also **paddle steamer** etc.) a boat, steamer, etc., propelled by a paddle wheel.

paddle wheel *n.* a wheel for propelling a ship, with boards round the circumference so as to press backwards against the water.

paddock /ˈpadək/ *n.* & *v.* ● *n.* **1** a small field, esp. for keeping horses in. **2** an enclosure adjoining a racecourse or racetrack where horses or cars are assembled before a race. **3** *Austral.* & *NZ* a field; a plot of land. ● *v.tr.* keep or enclose in a paddock. [apparently variant of (now dialect) *parrock* from Old English *pearruc*: see PARK]

Paddy /ˈpadi/ *n.* (*pl.* **-ies**) *colloq.* often *offens.* an Irishman. [pet form of the Irish name *Padraig* (= Patrick)]

paddy[1] /ˈpadi/ *n.* (*pl.* **-ies**) **1** (in full **paddy field**) a field where rice is grown. **2** rice before threshing or in the husk. [Malay *pādī*]

paddy[2] /ˈpadi/ *n.* (*pl.* **-ies**) *Brit. colloq.* a rage; a fit of temper. [PADDY]

paddy wagon *n. N. Amer. slang* a police van. [Paddy]

pademelon /ˈpadɪmelən/ *n.* any small wallaby of the genus *Thylogale,* inhabiting the coastal scrub of Australia. [earlier *paddymelon,* probably alteration of Dharuk *badimaliyan*]

padlock /ˈpadlɒk/ *n.* & *v.* ● *n.* a detachable lock hanging by a pivoted or sliding hook on the object fastened. ● *v.tr.* secure with a padlock. [Middle English from LOCK[1]: first element unexplained]

padouk /paˈdaʊk, pəˈduːk/ *n.* **1** any leguminous timber tree of the genus *Pterocarpus,* of Africa and Asia. **2** the wood of this tree, resembling rosewood. [Burmese]

padre /ˈpɑːdri, -dreɪ/ *n.* a chaplain in any of the armed services. [Italian, Spanish, & Portuguese, = father, priest, from Latin *pater patris* 'father']

padsaw /ˈpadsɔː/ *n.* a saw with a narrow blade, for cutting curves.

paean /ˈpiːən/ *n.* a song of praise or triumph. [Latin from Doric Greek *paian* 'hymn of thanksgiving to Apollo' (invoked by the name *Paian,* originally the Homeric name for the physician of the gods)]

paederast var. of PEDERAST.

paederasty var. of PEDERASTY.

paediatrics /piːdɪˈatrɪks/ *n.pl.* (*US* **pediatrics**) (treated as *sing.*) the branch of medicine dealing with children and their diseases. □ **paediatric** *adj.* **paediatrician** /-əˈtrɪʃ(ə)n/ *n.* [PAEDO- + Greek *iatros* 'physician']

paedo- /ˈpiːdəʊ/ *comb. form* (*US* **pedo-**) child. [Greek *pais paid-* 'child']

paedomorphosis /piːdə(ʊ)ˈmɔːfəsɪs, -mɔːˈfəʊsɪs/ *n. Biol.* = NEOTENY 1. [PAEDO- + *-morphosis* (cf. METAMORPHOSIS)]

paedophile /ˈpiːdə(ʊ)fʌɪl/ *n.* (*US* **pedophile**) a person who displays paedophilia.

paedophilia /piːdə(ʊ)ˈfɪlɪə/ *n.* (*US* **pedophilia**) sexual desire directed towards children.

paella /pʌɪˈɛlə, pɑː-/ *n.* a Spanish dish of rice, saffron, chicken, seafood, etc., cooked and served in a large shallow pan. [Catalan, via Old French *paele* from Latin *patella* 'pan']

paeon /ˈpiːən/ *n.* a metrical foot of one long syllable and three short syllables in any order. □ **paeonic** /piːˈɒnɪk/ *adj.* [Latin from Greek *paiōn*, the Attic form of *paian* PAEAN]

paeony var. of PEONY.

pagan /ˈpeɪɡ(ə)n/ *n.* & *adj.* ● *n.* a person not subscribing to any of the main religions of the world, esp. formerly regarded by Christians as unenlightened or heathen. ● *adj.* **1 a** of or relating to or associated with pagans. **b** irreligious. **2** identifying divinity or spirituality in nature; pantheistic. □ **paganish** *adj.* **paganism** *n.* **paganize** *v.tr.* & *intr.* (also **-ise**). [Middle English from Latin *paganus* 'villager, rustic', from *pagus* 'country district': in Christian Latin = 'civilian, heathen']

page[1] /peɪdʒ/ *n.* & *v.* ● *n.* **1 a** a leaf of a book, periodical, etc. **b** each side of this. **c** what is written or printed on this. **2** *Computing* a section of the stored data, esp. that can be displayed on a screen at one time. **3 a** an episode that might fill a page in written history etc.; a record. **b** a memorable event. ● *v.* **1** *tr.* paginate. **2** *intr.* **a** (foll. by *through*) leaf through (a book etc.). **b** (foll. by *through, up, down*) *Computing* display (text etc.) one page at a time. [French from Latin *pagina*, from *pangere* 'fasten']

page[2] /peɪdʒ/ *n.* & *v.* ● *n.* **1** a boy or man, usu. in livery, employed to run errands, attend to a door, etc. **2** a boy employed as a personal attendant of a person of rank, a bride, etc. **3** *hist.* a boy in training for knighthood and attached to a knight's service. ● *v.tr.* **1** (in hotels, airports, etc.) summon by making an announcement or by sending a messenger. **2** summon by means of a pager. [Middle English from Old French, perhaps via Italian *paggio* from Greek *paidion*, diminutive of *pais paidos* 'boy']

pageant /ˈpadʒ(ə)nt/ *n.* **1 a** a brilliant spectacle, esp. an elaborate parade. **b** a spectacular procession, or play performed in the open, illustrating historical events. **c** a tableau etc. on a fixed stage or moving vehicle. **2** an empty or specious show. [Middle English *pagyn*, of unknown origin]

pageantry /ˈpadʒ(ə)ntri/ *n.* (*pl.* **-ies**) **1** elaborate or sumptuous show or display. **2** an instance of this.

page-boy *n.* **1** = PAGE[2] *n.* 2. **2** a woman's hairstyle with the hair reaching to the shoulder and rolled under at the ends.

pager /ˈpeɪdʒə/ *n.* a radio device with a bleeper, activated from a central point to alert the person wearing it.

paginal /ˈpadʒɪn(ə)l/ *adj.* **1** of pages (of books etc.). **2** corresponding page for page. □ **paginary** *adj.* [Late Latin *paginalis* (as PAGE[1])]

paginate /ˈpadʒɪneɪt/ *v.tr.* assign numbers to the pages of a book etc. □ **pagination** /-ˈneɪʃ(ə)n/ *n.* [French *paginer* from Latin *pagina* PAGE[1]]

pagoda /pəˈɡəʊdə/ *n.* **1** a Hindu or Buddhist temple or sacred building, esp. a many-tiered tower, in India and the Far East. **2** an ornamental imitation of this. [Portuguese *pagode*, probably ultimately from Persian *butkada* 'idol temple']

pagoda tree *n.* a Chinese leguminous tree, *Sophora japonica*, with hanging clusters of cream flowers.

pah /pɑː/ *int.* expressing disgust or contempt. [natural utterance]

Pahlavi /ˈpɑːləvi/ *n.* (also **Pehlevi** /ˈpeɪləvi/) **1** an Aramaic-based writing system used in Persia from the 2nd c. BC to the advent of Islam in the 7th c. AD. **2** the form of the Middle Persian language written in this. [Persian *pahlawī*, via *pahlav* from *parthava* 'Parthia']

pahoehoe /pəˈhəʊɪhəʊi/ *n. Geol.* lava forming smooth undulating or ropy masses (cf. AA). [Hawaiian]

paid *past* and *past part.* of PAY[1].

paid holidays *n.pl.* an agreed holiday period for which wages are paid as normal.

paid-up member *n.* **1** (esp. of a trade-union member) a person who has paid the subscriptions in full. **2** *colloq.* a fully committed supporter of a cause, organization, etc.

pail /peɪl/ *n.* **1** a bucket. **2** an amount contained in this. □ **pailful** *n.* (*pl.* **-fuls**). [Old English *pægel* 'gill' (cf. Middle Dutch *pegel* 'gauge'), associated with Old French *paelle*: see PAELLA]

paillasse var. of PALLIASSE.

paillette /palˈjɛt, pʌɪˈjɛt/ *n.* **1** a piece of bright metal used in enamel painting. **2** a spangle. [French, diminutive of *paille*, from Latin *palea* 'straw, chaff']

pain /peɪn/ *n.* & *v.* ● *n.* **1 a** a strongly unpleasant bodily sensation such as is produced by illness, injury, or other harmful physical contact etc.; the condition of hurting. **b** a particular kind or instance of this (often in *pl.*: *suffering from stomach pains*). **2** mental suffering or distress. **3** (in *pl.*) careful effort; trouble taken (*take pains*; *got nothing for my pains*). **4** (also **pain in the neck** etc.) *colloq.* a troublesome person or thing; a nuisance. ● *v.tr.* **1** cause pain to. **2** (as **pained** *adj.*) expressing pain (*a pained expression*). □ **be at** (or **take**) **pains** (usu. foll. by *to* + infin.) take great care in doing something. **in pain** suffering pain. **on** (or **under**) **pain of** with (death etc.) as the penalty. [Middle English via Old French *peine* from Latin *poena* 'penalty']

painful /ˈpeɪnfʊl, -f(ə)l/ *adj.* **1** causing bodily or mental pain or distress. **2** (esp. of part of the body) suffering pain. **3** causing trouble or difficulty; laborious (*a painful climb*). □ **painfully** *adv.* **painfulness** *n.*

painkiller /ˈpeɪnkɪlə/ *n.* a medicine or drug for alleviating pain. □ **painkilling** *adj.*

painless /ˈpeɪnlɪs/ *adj.* not causing or suffering pain. □ **painlessly** *adv.* **painlessness** *n.*

painstaking /ˈpeɪnzteɪkɪŋ/ *adj.* careful, industrious, thorough. □ **painstakingly** *adv.* **painstakingness** *n.*

paint /peɪnt/ *n.* & *v.* ● *n.* **1 a** colouring matter, esp. in liquid form for imparting colour to a surface. **b** this as a dried film or coating (*the paint peeled off*). **2** *joc.* or *archaic* cosmetic make-up, esp. rouge or nail varnish. ● *v.tr.* **1 a** cover the surface of (a wall, object, etc.) with paint. **b** apply paint of a specified colour to (*paint the door green*). **2** depict (an object, scene, etc.) with paint; produce (a picture) by painting. **3** describe vividly as if by painting (*painted the scene in vivid terms*). **4** apply a liquid or (*joc.* or *archaic*) cosmetics to (the face, skin, etc.). **5** apply (a liquid) to a surface with a brush etc. □ **paint out** efface with paint. **paint the town red** *colloq.* enjoy oneself flamboyantly. □ **paintable** *adj.* [Middle English, via *peint*, past part. of Old French *peindre*, from Latin *pingere pict-* 'paint']

paintball /ˈpeɪntbɔːl/ *n.* a game in which participants simulate military combat using airguns to shoot capsules of paint at each other. □ **paintballer** *n.*

paintbox /ˈpeɪntbɒks/ *n.* a box holding dry paints for painting pictures.

paintbrush /ˈpeɪntbrʌʃ/ *n.* a brush for applying paint.

painted lady *n.* an orange-red butterfly, esp. *Cynthia cardui*, with black and white spots.

painter[1] /ˈpeɪntə/ *n.* a person who paints, esp. an artist or decorator. [Middle English from Old French *peintour*, ultimately from Latin *pictor* (as PAINT)]

painter[2] /ˈpeɪntə/ *n.* a rope attached to the bow of a boat for tying it to a quay etc. [Middle English, probably from Old French *penteur* 'rope from a masthead': cf. German *Pentertakel* from *pentern* 'fish the anchor']

painterly /ˈpeɪntəli/ *adj.* **1 a** using paint well; artistic. **b** characteristic of a painter or paintings. **2** (of a painting) lacking clearly defined outlines. □ **painterliness** *n.*

painting /ˈpeɪntɪŋ/ *n.* **1** the process or art of using paint. **2** a painted picture.

paint shop *n.* the part of a factory where goods are painted, esp. by spraying.

paintstick /ˈpeɪntstɪk/ *n.* a stick of water-soluble paint used like a crayon.

paintwork /ˈpeɪntwəːk/ *n.* **1** esp. *Brit.* a painted surface or area in a building etc. **2** the work of painting.

painty /ˈpeɪnti/ *adj.* (**paintier**, **paintiest**) **1** of or covered in paint. **2** (of a picture etc.) overcharged with paint.

pair /pɛː/ *n.* & *v.* ● *n.* **1** a set of two persons or things used together or regarded as a unit (*a pair of gloves*; *a pair of eyes*). **2** an article (e.g. scissors, trousers, or tights) consisting of two joined or corresponding parts not used separately. **3 a** an engaged or married couple. **b** a mated couple of animals. **4** two horses harnessed side by side (*a coach and pair*). **5** the second member of a pair in relation to the first (*cannot find its pair*). **6** two playing cards of the same denomination. **7** *Parl.* either or both of two members of a legislative assembly on opposite sides absenting themselves from voting by mutual arrangement. ● *v.tr.* & *intr.* **1** (often foll. by *off*) arrange or be arranged in couples. **2 a** join or be joined in marriage. **b** (of animals) mate. **3** *Parl.* form a pair (see sense 7 of *n.*). □ **in pairs** in twos. [Middle English via Old French *paire* from Latin *paria*, neut. pl. of *par* 'equal']

paired /pɛːd/ *adj.* occurring in pairs or as a pair.

pairing /ˈpɛːrɪŋ/ *n.* an arrangement or match resulting from organizing or forming into pairs.

pair of scales *n.* a simple balance.

pair production *n. Physics* the conversion of a radiation quantum into an electron and a positron.

pair royal *n.* (in cribbage etc.) a set of three cards of the same denomination.

paisa /ˈpʌɪsɑː, -sə/ *n.* (*pl.* **paise** /-seɪ or -sə/) a coin and monetary unit of India, Pakistan, Nepal, and Bangladesh, equal to one-hundredth of a rupee or taka. [Hindi]

Paisley /ˈpeɪzli/ *n.* (often *attrib.*) **1** a distinctive intricate pattern of curved feather-shaped figures. **2** a soft woollen garment having this pattern. [*Paisley* in Scotland, the original place of manufacture]

pajamas *US* var. of PYJAMAS.

pakeha /ˈpɑːkɪhɑː/ *n.* & *adj. NZ* ● *n.* a white person as opposed to a Maori. ● *adj.* of or relating to white people. [Maori]

Paki /ˈpaki/ *n.* (*pl.* **Pakis**) *Brit. slang offens.* a Pakistani, esp. an immigrant in Britain. [abbreviation]

Pakistani /pɑːkɪˈstɑːni, pak-/ *n.* & *adj.* ● *n.* (*pl.* **-is**) **1** a native or national of Pakistan. **2** a person of Pakistani descent. ● *adj.* of or relating to Pakistan. [Hindustani]

pakora /pəˈkɔːrə/ *n.* a piece of cauliflower, carrot, or other vegetable, coated in seasoned batter and deep-fried. [Hindustani]

pal /pal/ *n.* & *v.* ● *n. colloq.* a friend, mate, or comrade. ● *v.intr.* (**palled**, **palling**) (usu. foll. by *up*) associate; form a friendship. [Romany = brother, mate, ultimately from Sanskrit *bhrātr* BROTHER]

palace /ˈpalɪs/ *n.* **1** the official residence of a sovereign, president, archbishop, or bishop. **2** a splendid mansion; a spacious building. [Middle English via Old French *palais* from Latin *Palatium*, the Palatine hill, in Rome, where the house of the emperor was situated]

palace revolution *n.* (also **palace coup**) the (usu. non-violent) overthrow of a sovereign, government, etc. at the hands of senior officials.

paladin /ˈpalədɪn/ *n. hist.* **1** any of the twelve peers of Charlemagne's court, of whom the Count Palatine was the chief. **2** a knight errant; a champion. [French *paladin* via Italian *paladino* from Latin *palatinus*: see PALATINE[1]]

Palaearctic /palɪˈɑːktɪk, peɪ-/ *adj.* & *n.* (*US* **Palearctic**) (also **pal-**) ● *adj.* of or relating to the Arctic and temperate parts of the Old World. ● *n.* the Palaearctic region. [PALAEO- + ARCTIC]

palaeo- /palɪəʊ, peɪlɪəʊ/ *comb. form* (*US* **paleo-**) ancient, old; of ancient (esp. prehistoric) times. [Greek *palaios* 'ancient']

palaeoanthropology /ˌpalɪəʊanθrəˈpɒlədʒi, ˌpeɪ-/ *n.* (*US* **paleoanthropology**) the branch of anthropology concerned with fossil hominids. □ **palaeoanthropological** /-pəˈlɒdʒɪk(ə)l/ *adj.* **palaeoanthropologist** *n.*

palaeobotany /ˌpalɪəʊˈbɒtəni, ˌpeɪ-/ *n.* (*US* **paleobotany**) the study of fossil plants. □ **palaeobotanical** /-bəˈtanɪk(ə)l/ *adj.* **palaeobotanist** *n.*

Palaeocene /ˈpalɪəsiːn, ˈpeɪ-/ *adj.* & *n.* (*US* **Paleocene**) *Geol.* ● *adj.* of or relating to the earliest epoch of the Tertiary period with evidence of the emergence and development of mammals. ● *n.* this epoch or system. Cf. Appendix X. [PALAEO- + Greek *kainos* 'new']

palaeoclimatology /ˌpalɪəʊklʌɪməˈtɒlədʒi, ˌpeɪ-/ *n.* (*US* **paleoclimatology**) the study of the climate in geologically past times. □ **palaeoclimatological** /-təˈlɒdʒɪk(ə)l/ *adj.* **palaeoclimatologist** *n.*

palaeoecology /ˌpalɪəʊɪˈkɒlədʒi, ˌpeɪ-/ *n.* (*US* **paleoecology**) the ecology of extinct and prehistoric organisms. □ **palaeoecological** /-kəˈlɒdʒɪk(ə)l/ *adj.* **palaeoecologist** *n.*

palaeogeography /ˌpalɪəʊdʒɪˈɒgrəfi, ˌpeɪ-/ *n.* (*US* **paleogeography**) the study of the geographical features at periods in the geological past. □ **palaeogeographer** *n.* **palaeogeographical** /-ˈgrafɪk(ə)l/ *adj.*

palaeography /palɪˈɒgrəfi, peɪ-/ *n.* (*US* **paleography**) the study of writing and documents from the past. □ **palaeographer** *n.* **palaeographic** /-əˈgrafɪk/ *adj.* **palaeographical** /-əˈgrafɪk(ə)l/ *adj.* **palaeographically** /-əˈgrafɪk(ə)li/ *adv.* [French *paléographie* from modern Latin *palaeographia* (as PALAEO-, -GRAPHY)]

palaeolithic /ˌpalɪə(ʊ)ˈlɪθɪk, ˌpeɪ-/ *adj.* & *n.* (*US* **paleolithic**) *Archaeol.* ● *adj.* of or relating to the early phase of the Stone Age, lasting for about 2.5 million years until the end of the last ice age. ● *n.* the palaeolithic period. [PALAEO- + Greek *lithos* 'stone']

palaeomagnetism /ˌpalɪə(ʊ)ˈmagnɪtɪz(ə)m, ˌpeɪ-/ *n.* (*US* **paleomagnetism**) the study of the magnetism remaining in rocks. □ **palaeomagnetic** /-magˈnɛtɪk/ *adj.*

palaeontology /ˌpalɪɒnˈtɒlədʒi, ˌpeɪ-/ *n.* (*US* **paleontology**) the branch of science that deals with extinct and fossil animals and plants. □ **palaeontological** /-təˈlɒdʒɪkəl/ *adj.* **palaeontologist** *n.* [PALAEO- + Greek *onta*, neut. pl. of *ōn* 'being', part. of *eimi* 'be' + -LOGY]

Palaeozoic /ˌpalɪə(ʊ)ˈzəʊɪk, ˌpeɪ-/ *adj.* & *n.* (*US* **Paleozoic**) *Geol.* ● *adj.* of or relating to an era of geological time marked by the appearance of marine and terrestrial plants and animals, esp. invertebrates. Cf. Appendix X. ● *n.* this era (cf. CENOZOIC, MESOZOIC). [PALAEO- + Greek *zōē* 'life', *zōos* 'living']

palaestra /pəˈliːstrə, pəˈlʌɪstrə/ *n.* (also **palestra** /-ˈlɛstrə/) *Gk & Rom. Antiq.* a wrestling school or gymnasium. [Middle English via Latin *palaestra* from Greek *palaistra*, from *palaiō* 'wrestle']

palais /ˈpaleɪ/ *n. Brit. colloq.* a public hall for dancing. [French *palais* (*de danse*) '(dancing) hall']

palanquin /palənˈkiːn/ *n.* (also **palankeen**) (in India and the East) a covered litter for one passenger. [Portuguese *palanquim*, ultimately via Hindi *pālkī* from Sanskrit *palyanka* 'bed, couch']

palatable /ˈpalətəb(ə)l/ *adj.* **1** pleasant to taste. **2** (of an idea, suggestion, etc.) acceptable, satisfactory. □ **palatability** /-ˈbɪlɪti/ *n.* **palatableness** *n.* **palatably** *adv.*

palatal /ˈpalət(ə)l/ *adj.* & *n.* ● *adj.* **1** of the palate. **2** (of a speech sound) made by placing the surface of the tongue against the hard palate (e.g. *y* in *yes*). ● *n.* a palatal sound. □ **palatalize** *v.tr.* (also **-ise**). **palatalization** /-ˈzeɪʃ(ə)n/ *n.* **palatally** *adv.* [French (as PALATE)]

palate /ˈpalət/ *n.* **1** the roof of the mouth in vertebrates, separating the cavities of the mouth and nose. **2** the sense of taste. **3** a mental taste or inclination; liking. [Middle English from Latin *palatum*]

palatial /pəˈleɪʃ(ə)l/ *adj.* (of a building) like a palace, esp. spacious and splendid. □ **palatially** *adv.* [Latin (as PALACE)]

palatinate /pəˈlatɪnət/ *n.* a territory under the jurisdiction of a Count Palatine.

palatine[1] /ˈpalətʌɪn, -tɪn/ *adj.* (also **Palatine**) *hist.* **1** (of an official or feudal lord) having local authority that elsewhere belongs only to a sovereign (*Count Palatine*). **2** (of a territory) subject to this authority. [Middle English via French *palatin -ine* from Latin *palatinus* 'of the PALACE']

palatine[2] /ˈpalətʌɪn, -tɪn/ *adj.* & *n.* ● *adj.* of or connected with the palate. ● *n.* (in full **palatine bone**) each of two bones forming the hard palate. [French *palatin -ine* (as PALATE)]

palaver /pəˈlɑːvə/ *n.* & *v.* ● *n.* **1** fuss and bother, esp. prolonged. **2** profuse or idle talk. **3** cajolery. **4** *colloq.* a prolonged or tiresome affair or business. **5** *hist.* a parley between African or other natives and traders. ● *v.* **1** *intr.* talk profusely. **2** *tr.* flatter, wheedle. [Portuguese *palavra* 'word' from Latin (as PARABLE)]

pale[1] /peɪl/ *adj.* & *v.* ● *adj.* **1** (of a person or complexion) of a whitish or ashen appearance. **2 a** (of a colour) faint; not dark or deep. **b** faintly coloured. **3** of faint lustre; dim. ● *v.* **1** *intr.* & *tr.* grow or make pale. **2** *intr.* (often foll. by *before, beside*) become feeble in comparison (with). □ **palely** *adv.* **paleness** *n.* **palish** *adj.* [Middle English via Old French *pale, palir* from Latin *pallidus*, from *pallēre* 'be pale']

pale[2] /peɪl/ *n.* **1** a pointed piece of wood for fencing etc.; a stake. **2** a boundary. **3** an enclosed or delimited area. **4** *Heraldry* a vertical stripe in the middle of a shield. □ **beyond the pale** outside the bounds of acceptable behaviour. **in pale** *Heraldry* arranged vertically. [Middle English via Old French *pal* from Latin *palus* 'stake']

palea /ˈpeɪlɪə/ *n.* (*pl.* **paleae** /-lɪiː/) *Bot.* a chafflike bract, esp. in the flower of a grass. [Latin, = chaff]

paled /peɪld/ *adj.* having palings.

paleface /ˈpeɪlfeɪs/ *n.* a name supposedly used by the N. American Indians for a white person.

paleo- *US* var. of PALAEO-.

Paleocene *US* var. of PALAEOCENE.

Paleozoic *US* var. of PALAEOZOIC.

Palestinian /paləˈstɪnɪən/ *adj.* & *n.* ● *adj.* of or relating to Palestine, a region (in ancient and modern times) and former mandated territory on the E. Mediterranean coast. ● *n.* **1** a native of Palestine in ancient or modern times. **2** an Arab, or a descendant of one, born or living in the area formerly called Palestine.

palestra var. of PALAESTRA.

palette /ˈpalɪt/ *n.* **1** a thin board or slab or other surface, usu. with a hole for the thumb, on which an artist lays and mixes colours. **2** the range of colours used by an artist. [French, diminutive of *pale* 'shovel', from Latin *pala* 'spade']

palette knife *n.* **1** a thin steel blade with a handle for mixing colours or applying or removing paint. **2** *Brit.* a kitchen knife with a long blunt round-ended flexible blade.

palfrey /ˈpɔːlfri, ˈpal-/ *n.* (*pl.* **-eys**) *archaic* a horse for ordinary riding, esp. for women. [Middle English via Old French *palefrei* and medieval Latin *palefredus*, Late Latin *paraveredus* from Greek *para* 'beside, extra' + Latin *veredus* 'light horse', of Gaulish origin]

Pali /ˈpɑːliː/ *n.* & *adj.* ● *n.* an Indic language used in the canonical books of Buddhists. ● *adj.* of or relating to this language. [Pali *pāli-bhāsā*, from *pāli* 'line, canon' + *bhāsā* 'language']

palimony /ˈpalɪməni/ *n.* esp. *US colloq.* an allowance made by one member of an unmarried couple to the other after separation. [PAL + ALIMONY]

palimpsest /ˈpalɪm(p)sɛst/ *n.* **1** a piece of writing material or manuscript on which later writing has been written over the effaced original writing. **2** a monumental brass turned and re-engraved on the reverse side. [Latin *palimpsestus* from Greek *palimpsēstos*, from *palin* 'again' + *psēstos* 'rubbed smooth']

palindrome /ˈpalɪndrəʊm/ *n.* a word or phrase that reads the same backwards as forwards (e.g. *rotator, nurses run*). □ **palindromic** /-ˈdrɒmɪk/ *adj.* **palindromist** *n.* [Greek *palindromos* 'running back again', from *palin* 'again' + *drom-* 'run']

paling /ˈpeɪlɪŋ/ *n.* **1** a fence of pales. **2** a pale.

palingenesis /palɪnˈdʒɛnɪsɪs/ *n.* *Biol.* the exact reproduction of ancestral characteristics in ontogenesis. □ **palingenetic** /-dʒɪˈnɛtɪk/ *adj.* [Greek *palin* 'again' + *genesis* 'birth, GENESIS']

palinode /ˈpalɪnəʊd/ *n.* **1** a poem in which the writer retracts a view or sentiment expressed in a former poem. **2** a recantation. [French *palinode* or Late Latin *palinodia* from Greek *palinōidia*, from *palin* 'again' + *ōidē* 'song']

palisade /palɪˈseɪd/ *n.* & *v.* ● *n.* **1 a** a fence of pales or iron railings. **b** a strong pointed wooden stake used in a close row for defence. **2** (in *pl.*) *US* a line of high cliffs. ● *v.tr.* enclose or provide with a palisade. [French *palissade* from Provençal *palissada*, from *palissa* 'paling', ultimately from Latin *palus* 'stake']

palisade layer *n.* *Bot.* a layer of elongated cells below the epidermis of a leaf.

pall[1] /pɔːl/ *n.* **1** a cloth spread over a coffin, hearse, or tomb. **2** a shoulder band with pendants, worn as an ecclesiastical vestment and sign of authority. **3** a dark covering (*a pall of darkness; a pall of smoke*). **4** *Heraldry* a Y-shaped bearing charged with crosses representing the front of an ecclesiastical pall. [Old English *pæll*, from Latin *pallium* 'cloak']

pall[2] /pɔːl/ *v.* **1** *intr.* (often foll. by *on*) become uninteresting (to). **2** *tr.* satiate, cloy. [Middle English, from APPAL]

palladia *pl.* of PALLADIUM[2].

Palladian /pəˈleɪdɪən/ *adj.* *Archit.* in the neoclassical style of Palladio. □ **Palladianism** *n.* [from the name of A. *Palladio*, Italian architect d. 1580]

palladium[1] /pəˈleɪdɪəm/ *n.* *Chem.* a white ductile metallic element occurring naturally in various ores and used in chemistry as a catalyst and for making jewellery (symbol **Pd**). [modern Latin from *Pallas*, the name given to an asteroid discovered (1803) just before the element, + -IUM; cf. CERIUM]

palladium[2] /pəˈleɪdɪəm/ *n.* (*pl.* **palladia** /-dɪə/) a safeguard or source of protection. [Middle English via Latin from Greek *palladion* 'image of Pallas (Athene)', a protecting deity]

pall-bearer *n.* a person helping to carry or officially escorting a coffin at a funeral.

pallet[1] /ˈpalɪt/ *n.* **1** a straw mattress. **2** a crude or makeshift bed. [Middle English *pailet, paillet* via Anglo-French *paillete* 'straw' and Old French *paille* from Latin *palea*]

pallet[2] /ˈpalɪt/ *n.* **1** a portable platform for transporting and storing loads. **2** a flat wooden blade with a handle, used in ceramics to shape clay. **3** = PALETTE. **4** (in a clock or watch) a projection transmitting motion from an escapement to a pendulum or balance wheel. **5** a projection on a machine part, serving to change the mode of motion of a wheel. □ **palletize** *v.tr.* (also **-ise**) (in sense 1). [French *palette*: see PALETTE]

pallia *pl.* of PALLIUM.

palliasse /ˈpalɪas/ *n.* (also **paillasse**) a straw mattress. [French *paillasse* from Italian *pagliaccio*, ultimately from Latin *palea* 'straw']

palliate /ˈpalɪeɪt/ *v.tr.* **1** alleviate (disease) without curing it. **2** excuse, extenuate. □ **palliation** /-ˈeɪʃ(ə)n/ *n.* **palliator** *n.* [Late Latin *palliare* 'to cloak' from *pallium* 'cloak']

palliative /ˈpalɪətɪv/ *n. & adj.* ● *n.* something used to alleviate pain, anxiety, etc. ● *adj.* serving to alleviate. □ **palliatively** *adv.* [French *palliatif -ive* or medieval Latin *palliativus* (as PALLIATE)]

pallid /ˈpalɪd/ *adj.* pale, esp. from illness. □ **pallidity** /-ˈlɪdɪti/ *n.* **pallidly** *adv.* **pallidness** *n.* [Latin *pallidus* PALE[1]]

pallium /ˈpalɪəm/ *n.* (*pl.* **palliums** or **pallia** /-lɪə/) **1** an ecclesiastical pall, esp. that sent by the Pope to an archbishop as a symbol of authority. **2** *hist.* a man's large rectangular cloak esp. as worn in antiquity. **3** *Zool.* the mantle of a mollusc or brachiopod. [Latin]

pall-mall /palˈmal, pɛlˈmɛl/ *n. hist.* a game in which a ball was driven through an iron ring suspended in a long alley. [obsolete French *pallemaille* from Italian *pallamaglio*, from *palla* 'ball' + *maglio* 'mallet']

pallor /ˈpalə/ *n.* pallidness, paleness. [Latin, from *pallēre* 'be pale']

pally /ˈpali/ *adj.* (**pallier**, **palliest**) *colloq.* like a pal; friendly.

palm[1] /pɑːm/ *n.* **1** (in full **palm tree**) a tree of the mainly tropical family Palmae, with no branches and a mass of large pinnate or fan-shaped leaves at the top. **2** the leaf of this tree as a symbol of victory. **3 a** supreme excellence. **b** a prize for this. **4** a branch of various trees used instead of a palm in non-tropical countries, esp. in celebrating Palm Sunday. □ **palmaceous** /palˈmeɪʃəs/ *adj.* [Old English *palm(a)*, via Germanic from Latin *palma* PALM[2], its leaf being likened to a spread hand]

palm[2] /pɑːm/ *n. & v.* ● *n.* **1** the inner surface of the hand between the wrist and fingers. **2** the part of a glove that covers this. **3** the palmate part of an antler. ● *v.tr.* **1** conceal in the hand. **2** *slang* steal by concealing in the hand. □ **in the palm of one's hand** under one's control or influence. **palm off 1** (often foll. by *on*) **a** impose or thrust fraudulently (on a person). **b** cause a person to accept unwillingly or unknowingly (*palmed my old typewriter off on him*). **2** (often foll. by *with*) cause (a person) to accept unwillingly or unknowingly (*palmed him off with my old typewriter*). □ **palmar** /ˈpalmə/ *adj.* **palmed** *adj.* **palmful** *n.* (*pl.* **-fuls**). [Middle English *paume* via Old French *paume* from Latin *palma*: later assimilated to Latin]

palmate /ˈpalmeɪt/ *adj. Bot. & Zool.* **1** shaped like an open hand. **2** having lobes etc. like spread fingers. [Latin *palmatus* (as PALM[2])]

palmer /ˈpɑːmə/ *n.* **1** *hist.* **a** a pilgrim returning from the Holy Land with a palm branch or leaf. **b** an itinerant monk under a vow of poverty. **2** a hairy artificial fly used in angling. **3** (in full **palmer-worm**) a destructive hairy caterpillar of a European moth, *Euproctis chrysorrhoea*. [Middle English via Anglo-French *palmer*, Old French *palmier* from medieval Latin *palmarius* 'pilgrim']

palmette /palˈmɛt/ *n. Archaeol.* an ornament of radiating petals like a palm leaf. [French, diminutive of *palme* PALM[1]]

palmetto /palˈmɛtəʊ/ *n.* (*pl.* **-os**) a small palm tree, e.g. any of various fan palms of the genus *Sabal* or *Chamaerops*. [Spanish *palmito*, diminutive of *palma* PALM[1], assimilated to Italian words ending in *-etto*]

palmier /ˈpalmɪeɪ, French palmje/ *n.* (*pl.* ***palmiers*** *pronunc.* same) a sweet crisp pastry shaped like a palm leaf. [French, = palm tree]

palmiped /ˈpalmɪpɛd/ *adj. & n.* (also **palmipede** /-piːd/) ● *adj.* web-footed. ● *n.* a web-footed bird. [Latin *palmipes -pedis* (as PALM[2], *pes pedis* 'foot')]

palmistry /ˈpɑːmɪstri/ *n.* supposed divination from lines and other features on the palm of the hand. □ **palmist** *n.* [Middle English (originally *palmestry*) from PALM[2]: second element unexplained]

palmitic acid /palˈmɪtɪk/ *n. Chem.* a saturated fatty acid, solid at room temperature, found in palm oil and other vegetable and animal fats. □ **palmitate** /ˈpalmɪteɪt/ *n.* [French *palmitique*, from *palme* PALM[1]]

palm oil *n.* oil from the fruit of any of various palms, esp. *Elaeis guineensis* of W. Africa.

Palm Sunday *n.* the Sunday before Easter, celebrating Christ's entry into Jerusalem.

palmtop /ˈpɑːmtɒp/ *n.* a computer small and light enough to be held in one hand.

palm wine *n.* an alcoholic drink made from fermented palm sap.

palmy /ˈpɑːmi/ *adj.* (**palmier**, **palmiest**) **1** of or like or abounding in palms. **2** triumphant, flourishing (*palmy days*).

palmyra /palˈmʌɪrə/ *n.* an Asian palm, *Borassus flabellifer*, with fan-shaped leaves used for matting etc. [Portuguese *palmeira* 'palm tree', assimilated to *Palmyra*, the name of an ancient city in Syria]

palomino /paləˈmiːnəʊ/ *n.* (*pl.* **-os**) a golden or tan-coloured horse with a light-coloured mane and tail, originally bred in the south-western US. [Latin American Spanish from Spanish *palomino* 'young pigeon', from *paloma* 'dove', from Latin *palumba*]

paloverde /paləʊˈvəːdi/ *n.* any yellow-flowered thorny tree of the genus *Cercidium* in Arizona etc. [Latin American Spanish, = green tree]

palp /palp/ *n.* (also **palpus** /ˈpalpəs/) (*pl.* **palps** or **palpi** /-pʌɪ, -piː/) a segmented sense organ at the mouth of an arthropod; a feeler. □ **palpal** *adj.* [Latin *palpus* from *palpare* 'feel']

palpable /ˈpalpəb(ə)l/ *adj.* **1** that can be touched or felt. **2** readily perceived by the senses or mind. □ **palpability** /-ˈbɪlɪti/ *n.* **palpably** *adv.* [Middle English from Late Latin *palpabilis* (as PALPATE)]

palpate /palˈpeɪt/ *v.tr.* examine (esp. medically) by touch. □ **palpation** /-ˈpeɪʃ(ə)n/ *n.* [Latin *palpare palpat-* 'touch gently']

palpebral /ˈpalpɪbr(ə)l/ *adj.* of or relating to the eyelids. [Late Latin *palpebralis* from Latin *palpebra* 'eyelid']

palpitate /ˈpalpɪteɪt/ *v.intr.* **1** (of the heart) beat strongly and rapidly; undergo palpitations. **2** throb, tremble. □ **palpitant** *adj.* [Latin *palpitare*, frequentative of *palpare* 'touch gently']

palpitation /palpɪˈteɪʃ(ə)n/ *n.* **1** throbbing, trembling. **2** (often in *pl.*) a noticeably rapid, strong, or irregular heartbeat due to exertion, agitation, or disease. [Latin *palpitatio* (as PALPITATE)]

palpus var. of PALP.

palsgrave /ˈpɔːlzgreɪv/ *n.* a Count Palatine. [Dutch *paltsgrave*, from *palts* 'palatinate' + *grave* 'count']

palstave /ˈpɔːlsteɪv/ *n. Archaeol.* a type of chisel made of bronze etc. shaped to fit into a split handle. [Danish *paalstav* from Old Norse *pálstavr*, from *páll* 'hoe' (cf. Latin *palus* 'stake') + *stafr* STAFF[1]]

palsy /ˈpɔːlzi, ˈpɒl-/ *n. & v.* ● *n.* (*pl.* **-ies**) **1** paralysis, esp. with involuntary tremors. **2 a** a condition of utter helplessness. **b** a cause of this. ● *v.tr.* (**-ies, -ied**) **1** affect with palsy. **2** render helpless. [Middle English *pa(r)lesi* from Old French *paralisie*, ultimately from Latin *paralysis*: see PARALYSIS]

palter /ˈpɔːltə, ˈpɒl-/ *v.intr.* **1** haggle or equivocate. **2** trifle. □ **palterer** *n.* [16th c.: origin unknown]

paltry /ˈpɔːltri, ˈpɒl-/ *adj.* (**paltrier**, **paltriest**) worthless, contemptible, trifling. □ **paltriness** *n.* [16th c.: from *paltry* 'trash', apparently from *palt*, *pelt* 'rubbish' + -RY (cf. *trumpery*): cf. Low German *paltrig* 'ragged']

paludal /pəˈljuːd(ə)l, -ˈluː-, ˈpaljʊd(ə)l, -lʊ-/ *adj.* **1** of a marsh. **2** malarial. □ **paludism** *n.* (in sense 2). [Latin *palus -udis* 'marsh' + -AL]

paly /ˈpeɪli/ *adj. Heraldry* divided into equal vertical stripes. [Old French *palé* from *pal* PALE[2]]

palynology /palɪˈnɒlədʒi/ *n.* the study of pollen grains and other spores, esp. from archaeological or geological deposits etc., e.g. for carbon dating and the investigation of past environments. □ **palynological** /-nəˈlɒdʒɪk(ə)l/ *adj.* **palynologist** *n.* [Greek *palunō* 'sprinkle' + -LOGY]

pampas /ˈpampəs, -z/ *n.pl.* large treeless plains in S. America. [Spanish from Quechua *pampa* 'plain']

pampas grass *n.* a tall grass, *Cortaderia selloana*, from S. America, with silky flowering plumes.

pamper /'pampə/ *v.tr.* **1** over-indulge (a person, taste, etc.), cosset. **2** spoil (a person) with luxury. [Middle English, probably of Low German or Dutch origin]

pampero /pam'pɛːrəʊ/ *n.* (*pl.* **-os**) a strong cold SW wind in S. America, blowing from the Andes towards the Atlantic. [Spanish (as PAMPAS)]

pamphlet /'pamflɪt/ *n.* & *v.* ● *n.* a small usu. unbound booklet or leaflet containing information or a short treatise. ● *v.tr.* (**pamphleted**, **pamphleting**) distribute pamphlets to. [Middle English from *Pamphilet*, the familiar name of the 12th-c. Latin love poem *Pamphilus seu de Amore*]

pamphleteer /pamflə'tɪə/ *n.* & *v.* ● *n.* a writer of (esp. political) pamphlets. ● *v.intr.* write pamphlets.

pan[1] /pan/ *n.* & *v.* ● *n.* **1 a** a vessel of metal, earthenware, or plastic, usu. broad and shallow, used for cooking and other domestic purposes. **b** the contents of this. **2** a panlike vessel in which substances are heated etc. **3** any similar shallow container such as the bowl of a pair of scales or that used for washing gravel etc. to separate gold. **4** *Brit.* the bowl of a lavatory. **5** part of the lock that held the priming in old guns. **6** a hollow in the ground (*salt pan*). **7** a hard substratum of soil. **8** *US slang* the face. **9 a** a metal drum in a steel band. **b** steel-band music and the associated culture. ● *v.* (**panned**, **panning**) **1** *tr. colloq.* criticize severely. **2** *tr. slang* hit or punch (a person). **3 a** *tr.* (often foll. by *off*, *out*) wash (gold-bearing gravel) in a pan. **b** *intr.* search for gold by panning gravel. **c** *intr.* (foll. by *out*) (of gravel) yield gold. □ **pan out** (of an action etc.) turn out well or in a specified way. □ **panful** *n.* (*pl.* **-fuls**). **panlike** *adj.* [Old English *panne*, perhaps ultimately from Latin *patina* 'dish']

pan[2] /pan/ *v.* & *n.* ● *v.* (**panned**, **panning**) **1** *tr.* swing (a camera) horizontally to give a panoramic effect or to follow a moving object. **2** *intr.* (of a camera) be moved in this way. ● *n.* a panning movement. [abbreviation of PANORAMA]

pan[3] /pɑːn/ *n.* **1** a leaf of the betel. **2** this enclosing lime and areca-nut parings, chewed in India etc. [Hindi, from Sanskrit *parna* 'feather, leaf']

pan- /pan/ *comb. form* **1** all; the whole of. **2** relating to the whole or all the parts of a continent, racial group, religion, etc. (*pan-American*; *pan-African*; *pan-Hellenic*; *pan-Anglican*). [Greek from *pan*, neut. of *pas* 'all']

panacea /panə'siːə/ *n.* a universal remedy. □ **panacean** *adj.* [Latin from Greek *panakeia*, from *panakēs* 'all-healing' (as PAN-, *akos* 'remedy')]

■ **Usage** The phrase *universal panacea* should be avoided since it is tautologous.

panache /pə'naʃ/ *n.* **1** flamboyant confidence of style or manner. **2** *hist.* a tuft or plume of feathers, esp. as a headdress or on a helmet. [French via Italian *pennacchio* from Late Latin *pinnaculum*, diminutive of *pinna* 'feather']

panada /pə'nɑːdə/ *n.* **1** a thick paste of flour etc. **2** bread boiled to a pulp and flavoured. [Spanish, ultimately from Latin *panis* 'bread']

panama /'panəmɑː, panə'mɑː/ *n.* a hat of strawlike material made from the leaves of a pine tree. [*Panama* in Central America]

Panamanian /panə'meɪnɪən/ *n.* & *adj.* ● *n.* **1** a native or national of the Republic of Panama in Central America. **2** a person of Panamanian descent. ● *adj.* of or relating to Panama.

panatella /panə'tɛlə/ *n.* a long thin cigar. [Latin American Spanish *panatela*, = long thin biscuit, from Italian *panatella*, diminutive of *panata* (as PANADA)]

pancake /'pankeɪk/ *n.* & *v.* ● *n.* **1** a thin flat cake of batter usu. fried and turned in a pan and often rolled up with a filling. **2** (also **Pan Cake** *propr.*) a flat cake of make-up etc. ● *v.* **1** *intr.* make a pancake landing. **2** *tr.* cause (an aircraft) to pancake. □ **flat as a pancake** completely flat. [Middle English, from PAN[1] + CAKE]

Pancake Day *n.* Shrove Tuesday (on which pancakes are traditionally eaten).

pancake landing *n.* an emergency landing in which an aircraft levels out close to the ground and drops vertically with its undercarriage still retracted.

panchayat /pʌn'tʃʌɪjət/ *n.* a village council in India. [originally consisting of five members: Hindi, from Sanskrit *pancha* 'five' + *āyatta* 'depending upon']

Panchen Lama /pantʃ(ə)n 'lɑːmə/ *n.* a Tibetan lama ranking next after the Dalai Lama. [Tibetan *panchen* 'great learned one']

panchromatic /pankrə(ʊ)'matɪk/ *adj. Photog.* (of a film etc.) sensitive to all visible colours of the spectrum.

pancreas /'paŋkrɪəs/ *n.* a gland near the stomach supplying the duodenum with digestive enzymes and secreting insulin into the blood. □ **pancreatic** /-'atɪk/ *adj.* **pancreatitis** /-'tʌɪtɪs/ *n.* [modern Latin from Greek *pagkreas* (as PAN-, *kreas -atos* 'flesh')]

pancreatin /'paŋkrɪətɪn/ *n.* a digestive extract containing pancreatic enzymes, prepared from animal pancreases.

panda /'pandə/ *n.* **1** (also **giant panda**) a large rare bearlike mammal, *Ailuropoda melanoleuca*, native to certain mountain forests in China and Tibet, having characteristic black and white markings. **2** (also **red panda**) a Himalayan raccoon-like mammal, *Ailurus fulgens*, with reddish-brown fur and a long bushy tail. [Nepali name]

panda car *n. Brit.* a police patrol car (originally black and white or blue and white).

pandanus /pan'deɪnəs, -'dan-/ *n.* **1** a tropical tree or shrub of the genus *Pandanus*, with a twisted stem, aerial roots, and spiral tufts of long narrow leaves at the top; also called *screw pine*. **2** fibre from the leaves of such a plant, or material woven from this. [modern Latin from Malay *pandan*]

pandect /'pandɛkt/ *n.* (usu. in *pl.*) **1** a complete body of laws. **2** *hist.* a compendium in 50 books of the Roman civil law made by order of Justinian in the 6th c. [French *pandecte* or Latin *pandecta pandectes* from Greek *pandektēs* 'all-receiver' (as PAN-, *dektēs* from *dekhomai* 'receive')]

pandemic /pan'dɛmɪk/ *adj.* & *n.* ● *adj.* (of a disease) prevalent over a whole country or the world. ● *n.* an outbreak of such a disease. [Greek *pandēmos* (as PAN-, *dēmos* 'people')]

pandemonium /pandɪ'məʊnɪəm/ *n.* **1** uproar; utter confusion. **2** a scene of this. [modern Latin (place of all demons in Milton's *Paradise Lost*), from PAN- + Greek *daimōn* DEMON]

pander /'pandə/ *v.* & *n.* ● *v.intr.* (foll. by *to*) gratify or indulge a person, a desire or weakness, etc. ● *n.* **1** a go-between in illicit love affairs; a procurer. **2** a person who encourages coarse desires. [*Pandare*, a character in Boccaccio and in Chaucer's *Troilus and Criseyde*, via Latin *Pandarus* from Greek *Pandaros*]

pandit var. of PUNDIT 1.

P. & O. *abbr.* Peninsular and Oriental Shipping Company (or Line).

Pandora's box /pan'dɔːrəz/ *n.* a process that once activated will generate many unmanageable problems. [in Greek mythology, the box from which the ills of humankind were released by Pandora, the first mortal woman, Hope alone remaining: from Greek *Pandōra* 'all-gifted' (as PAN-, *dōron* 'gift'), each god and goddess having contributed a quality to Pandora]

p. & p. *abbr. Brit.* postage and packing.

pane /peɪn/ *n.* **1** a single sheet of glass in a window or door. **2** a rectangular division of a chequered pattern etc. [Middle English in the sense 'piece of cloth, part of a garment': via Old French *pan* from Latin *pannus* 'piece of cloth']

panegyric /panɪ'dʒɪrɪk/ *n.* a laudatory discourse; a eulogy. □ **panegyrical** *adj.* [French *panégyrique* via Latin *panegyricus* from Greek *panēgurikos* 'of public assembly' (as PAN-, *ēguris* = *agora* 'assembly')]

panegyrize /ˈpanɪdʒɪrʌɪz/ *v.tr.* (also **-ise**) speak or write in praise of; eulogize. □ **panegyrist** /-ˈdʒɪrɪst/ *n.* [Greek *panēgurizō* (as PANEGYRIC)]

panel /ˈpan(ə)l/ *n.* & *v.* ● *n.* **1 a** a distinct, usu. rectangular, section of a surface (e.g. of a wall, door, or vehicle). **b** a control panel (see CONTROL *n.* 5). **c** = INSTRUMENT PANEL. **2** a strip of material as part of a garment. **3** a group of people forming a team in a broadcast game, discussion, etc. **4** *Brit.* a list of medical practitioners registered in a district as accepting patients under the National Health Service or *hist.* the National Insurance Act. **5 a** a list of available jurors; a jury. **b** *Sc.* a person or persons accused of a crime. ● *v.tr.* (**panelled, panelling**; *US* **paneled, paneling**) **1** fit or provide with panels. **2** cover or decorate with panels. [Middle English & Old French, = piece of cloth, ultimately from Latin *pannus*: see PANE]

panel beater *n. Brit.* a person whose job is to beat out the metal panels of motor vehicles.

panel game *n.* a broadcast quiz etc. played by a panel.

panel heating *n.* the heating of rooms by panels in the wall etc. containing the sources of heat.

panelling /ˈpan(ə)lɪŋ/ *n.* (*US* **paneling**) **1** panelled work. **2** wood for making panels.

panellist /ˈpan(ə)lɪst/ *n.* (*US* **panelist**) a member of a panel (esp. in broadcasting).

panel pin *n. Brit.* a thin nail with a very small head.

panel saw *n.* a saw with small teeth for cutting thin wood for panels.

panel truck *n. US* a small enclosed delivery truck.

pan-fry *v.tr.* fry in a pan in shallow fat.

pang /paŋ/ *n.* (often in *pl.*) a sudden sharp pain or painful emotion. [variant of PRONG]

panga /ˈpaŋgə/ *n.* a bladed African tool like a machete. [native name in E. Africa]

pangolin /paŋˈgəʊlɪn/ *n.* a mammal of the genus *Manis* (native to Asia) or *Phataginus* (native to Africa), having a small head with elongated snout and tongue with which it feeds on ants, and a tapering tail. Also called *scaly anteater*. [Malay *peng-gōling* 'roller' (from its habit of rolling itself up)]

panhandle /ˈpanhand(ə)l/ *n.* & *v. N. Amer.* ● *n.* a narrow strip of territory projecting from the main territory of one state into another. ● *v.tr.* & *intr. colloq.* beg for money in the street. □ **panhandler** *n.*

panic[1] /ˈpanɪk/ *n.* & *v.* ● *n.* **1** sudden uncontrollable fear or alarm. **2** infectious apprehension or fright esp. in commercial dealings. **3** (*attrib.*) characterized or caused by panic (*panic measure*; *panic buying*). ● *v.tr.* & *intr.* (**panicked, panicking**) (often foll. by *into*) affect or be affected with panic (*was panicked into buying*). □ **panicky** *adj.* [French *panique* via modern Latin *panicus* from Greek *panikos*, from *Pan*, the name of a rural god causing terror]

panic[2] /ˈpanɪk/ *n.* any grass of the genus *Panicum*, including millet and other cereals. [Old English via Latin *panicum*, from *panus* 'thread on bobbin, millet-ear', from Greek *pēnos* 'web']

panic button *n.* **1** a button for summoning help in an emergency. **2** a means of expressing panic or alarm (*pushed the national panic button*).

panicle /ˈpanɪk(ə)l/ *n. Bot.* a loose branching cluster of flowers, as in oats. □ **panicled** *adj.* [Latin *paniculum*, diminutive of *panus* 'thread']

panicmonger /ˈpanɪkmʌŋgə/ *n.* a person who fosters a panic.

panic stations *n.pl. Brit.* a state of emergency.

panic-stricken *adj.* (also **panic-struck**) affected with panic; very apprehensive.

panjandrum /panˈdʒandrəm/ *n.* **1** a mock title for an important person. **2** a pompous or pretentious official etc. [apparently invented in a nonsense composition (1755) by S. Foote]

panne /pan/ *n.* (in full **panne velvet**) a velvet-like fabric of silk or rayon with a flattened pile. [French]

pannier /ˈpanɪə/ *n.* **1** a basket, esp. one of a pair carried by a beast of burden. **2** each of a pair of bags or boxes on either side of the rear wheel of a bicycle or motorcycle. **3** *hist.* **a** part of a skirt looped up round the hips. **b** a frame supporting this. [Middle English via Old French *panier* from Latin *panarium* 'bread basket', from *panis* 'bread']

pannikin /ˈpanɪkɪn/ *n. Brit.* **1** a small metal drinking cup. **2** the contents of this. [PAN[1] + -KIN, on the pattern of *cannikin*]

panoply /ˈpanəpli/ *n.* (*pl.* **-ies**) **1** a complete or splendid array. **2** a complete suit of armour. □ **panoplied** *adj.* [French *panoplie* or modern Latin *panoplia* 'full armour' from Greek (as PAN-, *oplia* from *hopla* 'arms')]

panoptic /paˈnɒptɪk/ *adj.* showing or seeing the whole at one view. [Greek *panoptos* 'seen by all', *panoptēs* 'all-seeing']

panorama /panəˈrɑːmə/ *n.* **1** an unbroken view of a surrounding region. **2** a complete survey or presentation of a subject, sequence of events, etc. **3** a picture or photograph containing a wide view. **4** a continuous passing scene. □ **panoramic** /-ˈramɪk/ *adj.* **panoramically** /-ˈramɪk(ə)li/ *adv.* [PAN- + Greek *horama* 'view' from *horaō* 'see']

pan pipes *n.pl.* a musical instrument originally associated with the Greek rural god Pan, made of a series of short pipes graduated in length and fixed together with the mouthpieces in line.

pansy /ˈpanzi/ *n.* (*pl.* **-ies**) **1** any garden plant of the genus *Viola*, with flowers of various rich colours. **2** *colloq. offens.* **a** an effeminate man. **b** a male homosexual. [French *pensée* 'thought, pansy', from *penser* 'think', from Latin *pensare*, frequentative of *pendere pens-* 'weigh']

pant[1] /pant/ *v.* & *n.* ● *v.* **1** *intr.* breathe with short quick breaths. **2** *tr.* (often foll. by *out*) utter breathlessly. **3** *intr.* (often foll. by *for*) yearn or crave. **4** *intr.* (of the heart etc.) throb violently. ● *n.* **1** a panting breath. **2** a throb. □ **pantingly** *adv.* [Middle English from Old French *pantaisier* 'be agitated, gasp', ultimately from Greek *phantasioō* 'cause to imagine' (as FANTASY)]

pant[2] /pant/ *n.* esp. *US* = PANTS. [back-formation from PANTS]

pantalets /pantəˈlɛts/ *n.pl.* (also **pantalettes**) *hist.* **1** long underpants worn by women and girls in the 19th c., with a frill at the bottom of each leg. **2** women's cycling trousers. [diminutive of PANTALOON]

pantaloon /pantəˈluːn/ *n.* **1** (in *pl.*) **a** *hist.* men's close-fitting breeches fastened below the calf or at the foot. **b** *colloq.* trousers. **c** baggy trousers (esp. for women) gathered at the ankles. **2** (**Pantaloon**) a character in Italian comedy wearing pantaloons (in sense 1a). [French *pantalon* from Italian *pantalone*, a character in Italian comedy]

pantechnicon /panˈtɛknɪk(ə)n/ *n. Brit.* a large van for transporting furniture. [PAN- + TECHNIC, originally as the name of a bazaar for all kinds of artistic work, later converted into a furniture warehouse]

pantheism /ˈpanθiːɪz(ə)m/ *n.* **1** the belief that God is identifiable with the forces of nature and with natural substances. **2** worship that admits or tolerates all gods. □ **pantheist** *n.* **pantheistic** /-ˈɪstɪk/ *adj.* **pantheistical** /-ˈɪstɪk(ə)l/ *adj.* **pantheistically** /-ˈɪstɪk(ə)li/ *adv.* [PAN- + Greek *theos* 'god']

pantheon /ˈpanθɪən/ *n.* **1** a building in which illustrious dead are buried or have memorials. **2** the deities of a people collectively. **3** a temple dedicated to all the gods, esp. the circular one at Rome. **4** a group of individuals who are admired, respected, or distinguished. [Middle English via Latin from Greek *pantheion* (as PAN-, *theion* 'holy' from *theos* 'god')]

panther /ˈpanθə/ *n.* **1** a leopard, esp. with black fur. **2** *US* a puma. [Middle English via Old French *pantere* and Latin *panthera* from Greek *panthēr*]

panties /ˈpantɪz/ *n.pl. colloq.* short-legged or legless underpants worn by women and girls. [diminutive of PANTS]

pantihose var. of PANTYHOSE.

pantile /ˈpantʌɪl/ *n.* a roof tile curved to form an S-shaped section, fitted to overlap. ▫ **pantiled** *adj.* [PAN[1] + TILE]

panto /ˈpantəʊ/ *n.* (*pl.* **-os**) *Brit. colloq.* = PANTOMIME 1. [abbreviation]

panto- /ˈpantəʊ/ *comb. form* all, universal. [Greek *pas pantos* 'all']

pantograph /ˈpantə(ʊ)grɑːf/ *n.* **1** an instrument for copying a plan or drawing etc. on a different scale by a system of jointed rods. **2** a jointed framework conveying a current to an electric vehicle from overhead wires. ▫ **pantographic** /-ˈgrafɪk/ *adj.* [PANTO- + Greek *-graphos* 'writing']

pantomime /ˈpantəmʌɪm/ *n.* **1** *Brit.* a theatrical entertainment based on a fairy tale, with music, topical jokes, etc., usu. produced around Christmas. **2** the use of gestures and facial expression to convey meaning, esp. in drama and dance. **3** *colloq.* an absurd or outrageous piece of behaviour. ▫ **pantomimic** /-ˈmɪmɪk/ *adj.* [French *pantomime* or Latin *pantomimus* from Greek *pantomimos* (as PANTO-, MIME)]

pantothenic acid /pantə(ʊ)ˈθɛnɪk/ *n.* a vitamin of the B complex, found in rice, bran, and many other foods, and essential for the oxidation of fats and carbohydrates. [Greek *pantothen* 'from every side' with allusion to its widespread occurrence]

pantry /ˈpantri/ *n.* (*pl.* **-ies**) **1** a small room or cupboard in which crockery, cutlery, table linen, etc., are kept. **2** a larder. [Middle English from Anglo-French *panetrie*, Old French *paneterie*, from *panetier* 'baker', ultimately via Late Latin *panarius* 'bread-seller' from Latin *panis* 'bread']

pantryman /ˈpantrɪmən/ *n.* (*pl.* **-men**) a butler or a butler's assistant.

pants /pan(t)s/ *n.pl.* **1** *Brit.* underpants or knickers. **2** *N. Amer.* trousers or slacks. ▫ **bore** (or **scare** etc.) **the pants off** *colloq.* bore, scare, etc., to an intolerable degree. **with one's pants down** *colloq.* in an embarrassingly unprepared state. [abbreviation of *pantaloons* (see PANTALOON)]

pants suit *n.* (also **pant suit**) esp. *N. Amer.* a trouser suit.

panty girdle *n.* a woman's girdle with a crotch shaped like pants.

pantyhose /ˈpantɪhəʊz/ *n.* (also **pantihose**) (usu. treated as *pl.*) esp. *N. Amer.* women's usu. sheer tights. [PANTIES + HOSE]

panzer /ˈpanzə/ *n.* **1 a** (in *pl.*) (esp. German) armoured troops. **b** a German tank. **2** (*attrib.*) heavily armoured (*panzer division*). [German, = coat of mail]

pap[1] /pap/ *n.* **1 a** soft or semi-liquid food for infants or invalids. **b** a mash or pulp. **2** light or trivial reading matter; nonsense. ▫ **pappy** *adj.* [Middle English probably from Middle Low German, Middle Dutch *pappe*, probably ultimately from Latin *pappare* 'eat']

pap[2] /pap/ *n. archaic* or *dial.* the nipple of a breast. [Middle English, of Scandinavian origin: ultimately imitative of sucking]

papa /pəˈpɑː, ˈpɑːpə/ *n. US* or *archaic* father (esp. as a child's word). [French via Late Latin from Greek *papas*]

papabile /pəˈpɑːbɪleɪ, -li, Italian papaˈbiːle/ *adj. Brit.* suitable for high office. [Italian, = suitable to be pope, from Latin *papa* 'pope']

papacy /ˈpeɪpəsi/ *n.* (*pl.* **-ies**) **1** a pope's office or tenure. **2** the papal system. [Middle English from medieval Latin *papatia*, from *papa* 'pope']

papain /pəˈpeɪɪn, pəˈpʌɪɪn/ *n.* a protein-digesting enzyme obtained from unripe pawpaws, used to tenderize meat and as a food supplement to aid digestion. [PAPAYA + -IN]

papal /ˈpeɪp(ə)l/ *adj.* of or relating to a pope or to the papacy. ▫ **papally** *adv.* [Middle English via Old French and medieval Latin *papalis* from ecclesiastical Latin *papa* POPE[1]]

Papal States *n.pl. hist.* the temporal dominions belonging to the Pope, esp. in central Italy.

paparazzo /papəˈratsəʊ/ *n.* (*pl.* **paparazzi** /-tsi/) a freelance photographer who pursues celebrities to get photographs of them. [Italian, from the name of a character in Fellini's film *La Dolce Vita* (1960)]

papaveraceous /pəpeɪvəˈreɪʃəs/ *adj.* of or relating to the poppy family Papaveraceae. [modern Latin *Papaveraceae* from Latin *papaver* 'poppy']

papaw var. of PAWPAW.

papaya see PAWPAW.

paper /ˈpeɪpə/ *n.* & *v.* ● *n.* **1** a material manufactured in thin sheets from the pulp of wood or other fibrous substances, used for writing or drawing or printing on, or as wrapping material etc. **2** (*attrib.*) **a** made of or using paper. **b** flimsy like paper. **3** = NEWSPAPER. **4 a** a document printed on paper. **b** (in *pl.*) documents attesting identity or credentials. **c** (in *pl.*) documents belonging to a person or relating to a matter. **5** *Commerce* **a** negotiable documents, e.g. bills of exchange. **b** (*attrib.*) recorded on paper though not existing (*paper profits*). **6 a** a set of questions to be answered at one session in an examination. **b** the written answers to these. **7** = WALLPAPER. **8** an essay or dissertation, esp. one read to a learned society or published in a learned journal. **9** a piece of paper, esp. as a wrapper etc. **10** *Theatr. slang* free tickets or the people admitted by them (*the house is full of paper*). ● *v.tr.* **1** apply paper to, esp. decorate (a wall etc.) with wallpaper. **2** (foll. by *over*) **a** cover (a hole or blemish) with paper. **b** disguise or try to hide (a fault etc.). **3** *Theatr. slang* fill (a theatre) by giving free passes. ▫ **on paper 1** in writing. **2** in theory; to judge from written or printed evidence. ▫ **paperer** *n.* **paperless** *adj.* [Middle English via Anglo-French *papir*, = Old French *papier* from Latin *papyrus*: see PAPYRUS]

paperback /ˈpeɪpəbak/ *adj.* & *n.* ● *adj.* (of a book) bound in stiff paper not boards. ● *n.* a paperback book.

paper boy *n.* (*fem.* **paper girl**) a boy or girl who delivers or sells newspapers.

paperchase /ˈpeɪpətʃeɪs/ *n.* a cross-country run in which the runners follow a trail marked by torn-up paper.

paper clip *n.* a clip of bent wire or of plastic for holding several sheets of paper together.

paperhanger /ˈpeɪpəhaŋgə/ *n.* a person who decorates with wallpaper, esp. professionally.

paperknife /ˈpeɪpənʌɪf/ *n.* (*pl.* **paperknives**) *Brit.* a blunt knife for opening letters etc.

papermaker /ˈpeɪpəmeɪkə/ *n.* a person who makes paper for a living. ▫ **papermaking** *n.* & *adj.*

paper mill *n.* a mill in which paper is made.

paper money *n.* money in the form of banknotes.

paper mulberry *n.* a small Asiatic tree, *Broussonetia papyrifera*, of the mulberry family, whose bark is used for making paper and cloth.

paper nautilus see NAUTILUS 2.

paper round *n.* (*N. Amer.* **paper route**) **1** a job of regularly delivering newspapers. **2** a route taken doing this.

paper tape *n. Computing* tape made of paper, esp. having holes punched in it for conveying data or instructions to a computer.

paper-thin *adj.* & *adv.* ● *adj.* very thin; of no substance (*paper-thin slices*). ● *adv.* very thinly.

paper tiger *n.* an apparently threatening, but ineffectual, person or thing.

paperweight /ˈpeɪpəweɪt/ *n.* a small heavy object for keeping loose papers in place.

paperwork /ˈpeɪpəwəːk/ *n.* routine clerical or administrative work.

papery /ˈpeɪp(ə)ri/ *adj.* like paper in thinness or texture.

papier mâché /ˌpapɪeɪ ˈmaʃeɪ/ *n.* paper pulp used for moulding into boxes, trays, etc. [French, = chewed paper]

papilionaceous /pəpɪlɪəˈneɪʃəs/ *adj. Bot.* (of a plant or flower) having a corolla resembling a butterfly, as in many leguminous plants. [modern Latin *papilionaceus* from Latin *papilio -onis* 'butterfly']

papilla /pəˈpɪlə/ *n.* (*pl.* **papillae** /-liː/) **1** a small nipple-like protuberance in a part or organ of the body. **2** a small fleshy projection on a plant. □ **papillary** *adj.* **papillate** /ˈpapɪleɪt, pəˈpɪlət/ *adj.* **papillose** /ˈpapɪləʊs/ *adj.* [Latin, = nipple, diminutive of *papula*: see PAPULE]

papilloma /papɪˈləʊmə/ *n.* (*pl.* **papillomas** or **papillomata** /-mətə/) a wartlike usu. benign tumour.

papillon /ˈpapɪlɒn, ˈpapɪjɒ̃/ *n.* **1** a toy dog of a breed with ears suggesting the form of a butterfly. **2** this breed. [French, = butterfly, from Latin *papilio -onis*]

papist /ˈpeɪpɪst/ *n.* & *adj.* often *derog.* ● *n.* **1** a Roman Catholic. **2** *hist.* an advocate of papal supremacy. ● *adj.* of or relating to Roman Catholics. □ **papism** *n.* **papistic** /pəˈpɪstɪk/ *adj.* **papistical** /pəˈpɪstɪk(ə)l/ *adj.* **papistry** *n.* [French *papiste* or modern Latin *papista* from ecclesiastical Latin *papa* POPE[1]]

papoose /pəˈpuːs/ *n.* a young N. American Indian child. [Algonquian]

pappus /ˈpapəs/ *n.* (*pl.* **pappi** /-pʌɪ, -piː/) a group of hairs on the fruit of thistles, dandelions, etc. □ **pappose** *adj.* [Latin from Greek *pappos*]

pappy /ˈpapi/ *n.* (*pl.* **-ies**) a child's word for father.

paprika /ˈpaprɪkə, pəˈpriːkə/ *n.* **1** *Bot.* a red pepper. **2** a condiment made from it. [Hungarian]

Pap test /pap/ *n.* (also **pap test**) a test carried out on a cervical smear to detect cancer of the cervix or womb. [named after G. N. *Papanicolaou*, US scientist d. 1962]

papule /ˈpapjuːl/ *n.* (also **papula** /-jʊlə/; *pl.* **papulae** /-jʊliː/ or **papulas**) **1** a pimple. **2** a small fleshy projection on a plant. □ **papular** *adj.* **papulose** *adj.* **papulous** *adj.* [Latin *papula*]

papyrology /papɪˈrɒlədʒi/ *n.* the study of ancient papyri. □ **papyrological** /-rəˈlɒdʒɪk(ə)l/ *adj.* **papyrologist** *n.*

papyrus /pəˈpʌɪrəs/ *n.* (*pl.* **papyri** /-rʌɪ, -riː/) **1** an aquatic plant, *Cyperus papyrus*, with dark green stems topped with fluffy inflorescences. **2 a** a writing material prepared in ancient Egypt from the pithy stem of this. **b** a document written on this. [Middle English via Latin from Greek *papuros*]

par[1] /pɑː/ *n.* **1** the average or normal amount, degree, condition, etc. (*feel below par*; *be up to par*). **2** equality; an equal status or footing (*on a par with*). **3** *Golf* the number of strokes a first-class player should normally require for a hole or course. **4** *Stock Exch.* the face value of stocks and shares etc. (*at par*). **5** (in full **par of exchange**) the recognized value of one country's currency in terms of another's. □ **above** (or **below**) **par** *Stock Exch.* at a premium (or discount). **at par** *Stock Exch.* at face value. **par for the course** *colloq.* what is normal or expected in any given circumstances. [Latin (*adj.* & *n.*) = equal, equality]

par[2] /pɑː/ *n. Brit.* esp. *Journalism colloq.* paragraph. [abbreviation]

par. *abbr.* (also **para.**) paragraph.

par- /pər, par, pɑː/ *prefix* var. of PARA-[1] before a vowel or *h* (*paraldehyde*; *parody*; *parhelion*).

para /ˈparə/ *n. colloq.* **1** a paratrooper. **2** a paragraph. [abbreviation]

para-[1] /ˈparə/ *prefix* (also **par-**) **1** beside, adjacent to (*parathyroid*). **2** beyond or distinct from, but analogous to (*paramilitary*; *paranormal*). **3** *Chem.* (usu. in *italics*) relating to diametrically opposite carbon atoms in a benzene ring (*paradichlorobenzene*). [from or suggested by Greek *para-* from *para* 'beside, past, beyond']

para-[2] /ˈparə/ *comb. form* protect, ward off (*parachute*; *parasol*). [French via Italian from Latin *parare* 'defend']

parabiosis /parəbʌɪˈəʊsɪs/ *n. Biol.* the natural or artificial joining of two individuals. □ **parabiotic** /-ˈɒtɪk/ *adj.* [modern Latin, formed as PARA-[1] + Greek *biōsis* 'mode of life' from *bios* 'life']

parable /ˈparəb(ə)l/ *n.* **1** a narrative of imagined events used to illustrate a moral or spiritual lesson. **2** an allegory. [Middle English via Old French *parabole* from a Late Latin sense 'allegory, discourse' of Latin *parabola* 'comparison']

parabola /pəˈrab(ə)lə/ *n.* (*pl.* **parabolas** or **parabolae** /-liː/) a symmetrical open plane curve formed by the intersection of a cone with a plane parallel to its side, resembling the path of a projectile under the action of gravity. [modern Latin from Greek *parabolē* 'placing side by side, comparison' (as PARA-[1], *bolē* 'a throw' from *ballō*)]

parabolic /parəˈbɒlɪk/ *adj.* **1** of or expressed in a parable. **2** of or like a parabola. □ **parabolically** *adv.* [Late Latin *parabolicus* from Greek *parabolikos* (as PARABOLA)]

parabolical /parəˈbɒlɪk(ə)l/ *adj.* = PARABOLIC 1.

paraboloid /pəˈrab(ə)lɔɪd/ *n.* **1** (in full **paraboloid of revolution**) a solid generated by the rotation of a parabola about its axis of symmetry. **2** a solid having two or more non-parallel parabolic cross-sections. □ **paraboloidal** *adj.*

paracetamol /parəˈsiːtəmɒl, -ˈsɛt-/ *n. Brit.* **1** a drug used to relieve pain and reduce fever. **2** a tablet of this. [*para-acetylaminophenol*]

parachronism /pəˈrakrənɪz(ə)m/ *n.* an error in chronology, esp. by assigning too late a date. [PARA-[1] + Greek *khronos* 'time', perhaps suggested by *anachronism*]

parachute /ˈparəʃuːt/ *n.* & *v.* ● *n.* **1** a rectangular or umbrella-shaped apparatus allowing a person or heavy object attached to it to descend slowly from a height, esp. from an aircraft, or to retard motion in other ways. **2** (*attrib.*) dropped or to be dropped by parachute (*parachute troops*; *parachute flare*). ● *v.tr.* & *intr.* convey or descend by parachute. [French (as PARA-[2], CHUTE[1])]

parachutist /ˈparəʃuːtɪst/ *n.* **1** a person who uses a parachute. **2** (in *pl.*) parachute troops.

Paraclete /ˈparəkliːt/ *n.* the Holy Spirit as advocate or counsellor (John 14:16, 26, etc.). [Middle English via Old French *paraclet* and Late Latin *paracletus* from Greek *paraklētos* 'called in aid' (as PARA-[1], *klētos* from *kaleō* 'call')]

parade /pəˈreɪd/ *n.* & *v.* ● *n.* **1 a** a formal or ceremonial muster of troops for inspection. **b** = PARADE GROUND. **2** a public procession. **3** ostentatious display (*made a parade of their wealth*). **4** *Brit.* a public square, promenade, or row of shops. ● *v.* **1** *intr.* assemble for parade. **2 a** *tr.* march through (streets etc.) in procession. **b** *intr.* march ceremonially. **3** *tr.* display ostentatiously. □ **on parade 1** taking part in a parade. **2** on display. □ **parader** *n.* [French, = show, from Spanish *parada* and Italian *parata*, ultimately from Latin *parare* 'prepare, furnish']

parade ground *n.* a place for the muster of troops.

paradiddle /ˈparədɪd(ə)l/ *n.* one of the rudiments of drumming, consisting of four beats played in the pattern left right left left or right left right right. [imitative]

paradigm /ˈparədʌɪm/ *n.* **1** an example or pattern, esp. one underlying a theory or methodology. **2** a representative set of the inflections of a noun, verb, etc. □ **paradigmatic** /-dɪgˈmatɪk/ *adj.* **paradigmatically** /-dɪgˈmatɪk(ə)li/ *adv.* [Late Latin *paradigma* from Greek *paradeigma*, from *paradeiknumi* 'show side by side' (as PARA-[1], *deiknumi* 'show')]

paradigm shift *n.* a fundamental change (in approach, philosophy, etc.).

paradise /ˈparədʌɪs/ *n.* **1** (in some religions) heaven as the ultimate abode of the just. **2** a place or state of complete happiness. **3** (in full **earthly paradise**) the abode of Adam and Eve in the biblical account of the Creation; the garden of Eden. □ **paradisaical** /-dɪˈseɪɪk(ə)l/ *adj.* **paradisal** /parəˈdʌɪs(ə)l/ *adj.* **paradisiacal** /-dɪˈsʌɪək(ə)l/ *adj.* **paradisical** /-ˈdɪsɪk(ə)l/ *adj.* [Middle English via Old French *paradis*, Late Latin *paradisus*, and Greek *paradeisos* from Avestan *pairidaēza* 'park']

parador /'parədɔ:/ *n.* (*pl.* **paradors** or **paradores** /-dɔ:rɛz/) a hotel owned and administered by the Spanish government. [Spanish]

parados /'paradɒs/ *n.* an elevation of earth behind a fortified place as a protection against attack from the rear, esp. a mound along the back of a trench. [French (as PARA-[2], *dos* 'back' from Latin *dorsum*)]

paradox /'parədɒks/ *n.* **1 a** a seemingly absurd or contradictory statement, even if actually well-founded. **b** a self-contradictory or essentially absurd statement. **2** a person or thing conflicting with a preconceived notion of what is reasonable or possible. **3** a paradoxical quality or character. [originally = a statement contrary to accepted opinion, from Late Latin *paradoxum* from Greek *paradoxon* neut. adj. used as a noun (as PARA-[1], *doxa* 'opinion')]

paradoxical /parə'dɒksɪk(ə)l/ *adj.* **1** of or like or involving paradox. **2** fond of paradox. □ **paradoxically** *adv.*

paraesthesia /parɪs'θi:zɪə/ *n.* (*US* **paresthesia**) (*pl.* **-siae** /-zɪi:/) (in *sing.* or *pl.*) *Med.* abnormal sensations caused esp. by pressure on or damage to peripheral nerves. [PARA-[1] + Greek *aisthēsis* 'sensation' + -IA[1]]

paraffin /'parəfɪn/ *n.* **1** *Brit.* an inflammable waxy or oily substance obtained by distillation from petroleum or shale, used in liquid form (also **paraffin oil**) esp. as a fuel. **2** *Chem.* = ALKANE. [German, from Latin *parum* 'little' + *affinis* 'related', from its low reactivity]

paraffin wax *n.* paraffin in its solid form.

paragliding /'parəglʌɪdɪŋ/ *n.* a sport resembling hang-gliding, using a wide parachute-like canopy attached to the body by a harness, allowing a person to glide after jumping from or being hauled to a height. □ **paraglide** *v.intr.* **paraglider** *n.*

paragoge /parə'gəʊdʒi/ *n.* the addition of a letter or syllable to a word in some contexts or as a language develops (e.g. *t* in *peasant*). □ **paragogic** /-'gɒdʒɪk/ *adj.* [Late Latin from Greek *paragōgē* 'derivation' (as PARA-[1], *agōgē* from *agō* 'lead')]

paragon /'parəg(ə)n/ *n.* **1 a** a model of excellence. **b** a supremely excellent person or thing. **2** (foll. by *of*) a model (of virtue etc.). **3** a perfect diamond of 100 carats or more. [obsolete French via Italian *paragone* 'touchstone' from medieval Greek *parakonē* 'whetstone']

paragraph /'parəgrɑ:f/ *n.* & *v.* ● *n.* **1** a distinct section of a piece of writing, beginning on a new usu. indented line. **2** a symbol (usu. ¶) used to mark a new paragraph, and also as a reference mark. **3** a short item in a newspaper, usu. of only one paragraph. ● *v.tr.* arrange (a piece of writing) in paragraphs. □ **paragraphic** /-'grafɪk/ *adj.* [French *paragraphe* or medieval Latin *paragraphus* from Greek *paragraphos* 'short stroke marking a break in sense' (as PARA-[1], *graphō* 'write')]

parakeet /'parəki:t/ *n.* any of various small usu. long-tailed parrots. [Old French *paroquet*, Italian *parrocchetto*, Spanish *periquito*, perhaps ultimately from diminutive of *Pierre* etc. 'Peter': cf. PARROT]

paralanguage /'parəlaŋgwɪdʒ/ *n.* elements or factors in communication that are ancillary to language proper, e.g. intonation and gesture.

paraldehyde /pə'raldɪhʌɪd/ *n. Chem.* & *Pharm.* a cyclic polymer of acetaldehyde, used as a narcotic and sedative. [PARA-[1] (PAR-) + ALDEHYDE]

paralegal /parə'li:g(ə)l/ *adj.* & *n.* esp. *N. Amer.* ● *adj.* of or relating to auxiliary aspects of the law. ● *n.* a person trained in subsidiary legal matters. [PARA-[1] + LEGAL]

paralipomena /parəlɪ'pɒmɪnə/ *n.pl.* (also **para-leipomena** /-lʌɪ'pɒmɪnə/) **1** things omitted from a work and added as a supplement. **2** *Bibl.* the books of Chronicles in the Old Testament, containing particulars omitted from Kings. [Middle English via ecclesiastical Latin from Greek *paraleipomena*, from *paraleipō* 'omit' (as PARA-[1], *leipō* 'leave')]

paralipsis /parə'lɪpsɪs/ *n.* (also **paraleipsis** /-'lʌɪpsɪs/) (*pl.* **-ses** /-si:z/) *Rhet.* **1** the device of giving emphasis by professing to say little or nothing of a subject, as in *not to mention their unpaid debts of several millions*. **2** an instance of this. [Late Latin from Greek *paraleipsis* 'passing over' (as PARA-[1], *leipsis* from *leipō* 'leave')]

parallax /'parəlaks/ *n.* **1** the apparent difference in the position or direction of an object when viewed from different positions, e.g. through the viewfinder and the lens of a camera. **2** the angular amount of this. □ **parallactic** /-'laktɪk/ *adj.* [French *parallaxe* via modern Latin *parallaxis* from Greek *parallaxis* 'change', from *parallassō* 'to alternate' (as PARA-[1], *allassō* 'exchange' from *allos* 'other')]

parallel /'parəlɛl/ *adj.*, *n.*, & *v.* ● *adj.* **1 a** (of lines or planes) side by side and having the same distance continuously between them. **b** (foll. by *to*, *with*) (of a line or plane) having this relation (to another). **2** (of circumstances etc.) precisely similar, analogous, or corresponding. **3 a** (of processes etc.) occurring or performed simultaneously. **b** *Computing* involving the simultaneous performance of operations. ● *n.* **1** a person or thing precisely analogous or equal to another. **2** a comparison (*drew a parallel between the two situations*). **3** (in full **parallel of latitude**) *Geog.* **a** each of the imaginary parallel circles of constant latitude on the earth's surface. **b** a corresponding line on a map (*the 49th parallel*). **4** *Printing* two parallel lines (| |) as a reference mark. ● *v.tr.* (**paralleled**, **paralleling**) **1** be parallel to; correspond to. **2** represent as similar; compare. **3** adduce as a parallel instance. □ **in parallel** (of electric circuits) arranged so as to join at common points at each end. □ **parallelism** *n.* [French *parallèle* via Latin *parallelus* from Greek *parallēlos* (as PARA-[1], *allēlos* 'one another')]

parallel bars *n.pl.* a pair of parallel rails on posts for gymnastics.

parallelepiped /ˌparəlɛlə'pʌɪpɛd, parəlɛ'lɛpɪpɛd/ *n.* *Geom.* a solid body of which each face is a parallelogram. [Greek *parallēlepipedon* (as PARALLEL, *epipedon* 'plane surface')]

parallelogram /parə'lɛləgram/ *n.* a four-sided plane rectilinear figure with opposite sides parallel. □ **parallelogram of forces 1** a parallelogram illustrating the theorem that if two forces acting at a point are represented in magnitude and direction by two sides of a parallelogram meeting at that point, their resultant is represented by the diagonal drawn from that point. **2** this theorem. [French *parallélogramme* via Late Latin *parallelogrammum* from Greek *parallēlogrammon* (as PARALLEL, *grammē* 'line')]

parallel parking *n.* the parking of a vehicle or vehicles parallel to the roadside.

paralogism /pə'ralədʒɪz(ə)m/ *n. Logic* **1** a fallacy. **2** illogical reasoning (esp. of which the reasoner is unconscious). □ **paralogist** *n.* **paralogize** *v.intr.* (also **-ise**). [French *paralogisme* via Late Latin *paralogismus* from Greek *paralogismos*, via *paralogizomai* 'reason falsely' from *paralogos* 'contrary to reason' (as PARA-[1], *logos* 'reason')]

Paralympics /parə'lɪmpɪks/ *n.pl.* an international athletic competition for disabled athletes. □ **Paralympic** *attrib.adj.* [PARAPLEGIC (see PARAPLEGIA) + OLYMPIC]

paralyse /'parəlʌɪz/ *v.tr.* (*US* **paralyze**) **1** affect with paralysis. **2** render powerless; cripple. **3** bring to a standstill. □ **paralysation** /-'zeɪʃ(ə)n/ *n.* **paralysingly** *adv.* [French *paralyser* from *paralysie*: cf. PALSY]

paralysis /pə'ralɪsɪs/ *n.* (*pl.* **paralyses** /-si:z/) **1** a nervous condition with impairment or loss of esp. the motor function of the nerves. **2** a state of utter powerlessness. [Latin from Greek *paralusis*, from *paraluō* 'disable' (as PARA-[1], *luō* 'loosen')]

paralytic /parə'lɪtɪk/ *adj.* & *n.* ● *adj.* **1** affected by paralysis. **2** esp. *Brit. slang* very drunk. ● *n.* a person affected by paralysis. □ **paralytically** *adv.* [Middle

English via Old French *paralytique* and Latin *paralyticus* from Greek *paralutikos* (as PARALYSIS)]

paramagnetic /parəmag'nɛtɪk/ *adj.* (of a body or substance) tending to become weakly magnetized so as to lie parallel to a magnetic field force. ▫ **paramagnetism** /-'magnɪtɪz(ə)m/ *n.*

paramatta var. of PARRAMATTA.

paramecium /parə'mi:sɪəm/ *n.* (also *Brit.* **paramoecium**) any freshwater protozoan of the genus *Paramecium*, of a characteristic slipper-like shape covered with cilia. [modern Latin, from Greek *paramēkēs* 'oval' (as PARA-[1], *mēkos* 'length')]

paramedic /parə'mɛdɪk/ *n.* a paramedical worker.

paramedical /parə'mɛdɪk(ə)l/ *adj.* (of services etc.) supplementing and supporting medical work.

parameter /pə'ramɪtə/ *n.* **1** *Math.* a quantity constant in the case considered but varying in different cases. **2 a** an (esp. measurable or quantifiable) characteristic or feature (*the three major parameters of colour — brightness, hue, and saturation*). **b** *disp.* (loosely) a constant element or factor, esp. serving as a limit or boundary (*within the parameters of the inquiry*). ▫ **parametric** /parə'mɛtrɪk/ *adj.* **parametrize** *v.tr.* (also **-ise**). [modern Latin, from Greek *para* 'beside' + *metron* 'measure']

■ **Usage** The use of *parameter* in sense 2b is a popular dilution of the word's meaning, probably influenced by *perimeter*. Although very common, it is frowned upon by some people.

paramilitary /parə'mɪlɪt(ə)ri/ *adj.* & *n.* ● *adj.* (of forces) organized similarly to military forces. ● *n.* (*pl.* **-ies**) a member of an unofficial paramilitary organization, esp. in Northern Ireland.

paramnesia /parəm'ni:zjə/ *n.* *Psychol.* = DÉJÀ VU. [PARA-[1] + AMNESIA]

paramo /'parəməʊ/ *n.* (*pl.* **-os**) a high treeless plateau in tropical S. America. [Spanish & Portuguese, from Latin *paramus*]

paramoecium *Brit.* var. of PARAMECIUM.

paramount /'parəmaʊnt/ *adj.* **1** supreme; requiring first consideration; pre-eminent (*of paramount importance*). **2** in supreme authority. ▫ **paramountcy** *n.* **paramountly** *adv.* [Anglo-French *paramont*, from Old French *par* 'by' + *amont* 'above': cf. AMOUNT]

paramour /'parəmʊə/ *n.* *archaic* or *derog.* an illicit lover of a married person. [Middle English from Old French *par amour* 'by love']

parang /'pɑ:raŋ, 'par-/ *n.* a large heavy Malayan knife used for clearing vegetation etc. [Malay]

paranoia /parə'nɔɪə/ *n.* **1** a mental disorder esp. characterized by delusions of persecution and self-importance. **2** an abnormal tendency to suspect and mistrust others. ▫ **paranoiac** *adj.* & *n.* **paranoiacally** *adv.* **paranoic** /-'nəʊɪk, -'nɔɪɪk/ *adj.* **paranoically** /-'nəʊɪk(ə)li, -'nɔɪɪk(ə)li/ *adv.* **paranoid** /'parənɔɪd/ *adj.* & *n.* [modern Latin from Greek, from *paranoos* 'distracted' (as PARA-[1], *noos* 'mind')]

paranormal /parə'nɔ:m(ə)l/ *adj.* beyond the scope of normal objective investigation or explanation. ▫ **paranormally** *adv.*

parapet /'parəpɪt/ *n.* **1** a low wall at the edge of a roof, balcony, etc., or along the sides of a bridge. **2** a defence of earth or stone to conceal and protect troops. ▫ **parapeted** *adj.* [French *parapet* or Italian *parapetto* 'breast-high wall' (as PARA-[2], *petto* 'breast' from Latin *pectus*)]

paraph /'paraf/ *n.* a flourish after a signature, originally as a precaution against forgery. [Middle English via French *paraphe* from medieval Latin *paraphus* for *paragraphus* PARAGRAPH]

paraphernalia /parəfə'neɪlɪə/ *n.pl.* (also treated as *sing.*) miscellaneous belongings, items of equipment, accessories, etc. [originally = property owned by a married woman, from medieval Latin via Late Latin *parapherna* from Greek *parapherna* 'property apart from a dowry' (as PARA-[1], *pherna* from *phernē* 'dower')]

paraphrase /'parəfreɪz/ *n.* & *v.* ● *n.* a free rendering or rewording of a passage. ● *v.tr.* express the meaning of (a passage) in other words. ▫ **paraphrastic** /-'frastɪk/ *adj.* [French *paraphrase* or Latin *paraphrasis* from Greek *paraphrasis*, from *paraphrazō* (as PARA-[1], *phrazō* 'tell')]

paraplegia /parə'pli:dʒə/ *n.* paralysis of the legs and part or the whole of the trunk. ▫ **paraplegic** *adj.* & *n.* [modern Latin from Greek *paraplēgia*, from *paraplēssō* (as PARA-[1], *plēssō* 'strike')]

parapsychology /parəsʌɪ'kɒlədʒi/ *n.* the study of mental phenomena outside the sphere of ordinary psychology (hypnosis, telepathy, etc.). ▫ **parapsychological** /-sʌɪkə'lɒdʒɪk(ə)l/ *adj.* **parapsychologist** *n.*

paraquat /'parəkwɒt, -kwat/ *n.* a toxic fast-acting herbicide, rapidly deactivated by the soil. [PARA-[1] + QUATERNARY (from the position of the bond between the two parts of the molecule relative to quaternary nitrogen atoms)]

parasailing /'parəseɪlɪŋ/ *n.* a sport in which participants wearing open parachutes glide through the air attached to the back of a motor boat. ▫ **parasail** *v.intr.* & *n.*

parascending /'parəsɛndɪŋ/ *n.* *Brit.* = PARAGLIDING, PARASAILING. ▫ **parascend** *v.intr.* **parascender** *n.*

paraselene /parəsɪ'li:ni/ *n.* (*pl.* **paraselenae** /-ni:/) a bright spot, esp. an image of the moon, on a lunar halo. Also called *mock moon*. [modern Latin (as PARA-[1], Greek *selēnē* 'moon')]

parasite /'parəsʌɪt/ *n.* **1** an organism living in or on another and benefiting at the expense of the other. **2** a person who lives off or exploits another or others. **3** *Philol.* an inorganic sound or letter developing from an adjacent one. ▫ **parasitic** /-'sɪtɪk/ *adj.* **parasitical** /-'sɪtɪk(ə)l/ *adj.* **parasitically** /-'sɪtɪk(ə)li/ *adv.* **parasiticide** /-'sɪtɪsʌɪd/ *n.* **parasitism** *n.* **parasitology** /-'tɒlədʒi/ *n.* **parasitologist** /-'tɒlədʒɪst/ *n.* [Latin *parasitus* from Greek *parasitos* 'a person who eats at another's table' (as PARA-[1], *sitos* 'food')]

parasitize /'parəsʌɪtʌɪz, -sɪ-/ *v.tr.* (also **-ise**) infest as a parasite. ▫ **parasitization** /-'zeɪʃ(ə)n/ *n.*

parasitoid /'parəsɪtɔɪd/ *n.* & *adj.* *Zool.* ● *n.* an insect whose larvae live as parasites which eventually kill their hosts, e.g. an ichneumon wasp. ● *adj.* of, relating to, or designating such an insect. [PARASITE + -OID]

parasol /'parəsɒl/ *n.* **1** a light umbrella used to give shade from the sun. **2** (in full **parasol mushroom**) a tall fungus of the genus *Lepiota* with a broad shaggy domed cap, esp. the edible *L. procera*. [French from Italian *parasole* (as PARA-[2], *sole* 'sun' from Latin *sol*)]

parastatal /parə'steɪt(ə)l/ *adj.* & *n.* ● *adj.* (of an industrial organization etc.) having some political authority and serving the State indirectly, esp. in some African countries. ● *n.* a parastatal organization. [PARA-[1] + STATE *n.* + -AL]

parasuicide /parə'su:ɪsʌɪd, -'sju:-/ *n.* *Psychol.* **1** apparent attempted suicide without the actual intention of killing oneself. **2** a person who has carried out or is considered likely to carry out such action.

parasympathetic /ˌparəsɪmpə'θɛtɪk/ *adj.* *Anat.* of or relating to the part of the automatic nervous system consisting of nerves arising from the brain and the lower end of the spinal cord that supply the internal organs, blood vessels, and glands, and balance the action of the sympathetic nerves (cf. SYMPATHETIC 9). [PARA-[1] + SYMPATHETIC, because some of these nerves run alongside sympathetic nerves]

parasynthesis /parə'sɪnθɪsɪs/ *n.* *Philol.* a derivation from a compound, e.g. *black-eyed* from *black eye(s)* + *-ed*. ▫ **parasynthetic** /-'θɛtɪk/ *adj.* [Greek *parasunthesis* (as PARA-[1], SYNTHESIS)]

parataxis /parə'taksɪs/ *n.* *Gram.* the placing of clauses etc. one after another, without words to indicate coordination or subordination, e.g. *Tell me, how are you?* □ **paratactic** /-'taktɪk/ *adj.* **paratactically** /-'taktɪk(ə)li/ *adv.* [Greek *parataxis* (as PARA-[1], *taxis* 'arrangement' from *tassō* 'arrange')]

paratha /pə'rɑːtə/ *n.* (in esp. Indian cookery) a piece of flat unleavened bread fried on a griddle. [Hindi *parāṭhā*]

parathion /parə'θʌɪən/ *n.* a highly toxic organic compound of phosphorus and sulphur used as an agricultural insecticide. [PARA-[1] + THIO- + -ON]

parathyroid /parə'θʌɪrɔɪd/ *n. & adj. Anat.* ● *n.* a gland next to the thyroid, secreting a hormone that regulates calcium levels in the body. ● *adj.* of or associated with this gland.

paratrooper /'parətruːpə/ *n.* a member of a body of paratroops.

paratroops /'parətruːps/ *n.pl.* troops equipped to be dropped by parachute from aircraft. □ **paratroop** *attrib.adj.* [contraction of PARACHUTE + TROOP]

paratyphoid /parə'tʌɪfɔɪd/ *n. & adj.* ● *n.* a fever resembling typhoid but caused by various different though related bacteria. ● *adj.* of, relating to, or caused by this fever.

paravane /'parəveɪn/ *n.* a torpedo-shaped device towed at a depth regulated by its vanes or planes, used esp. for cutting the moorings of submerged mines.

par avion /pɑːr a'vjõ, French par avjõ/ *adv.* by airmail. [French, = by aeroplane]

parboil /'pɑːbɔɪl/ *v.tr.* partly cook by boiling. [Middle English via Old French *parbo(u)illir* from Late Latin *perbullire* 'boil thoroughly' (as PER-, *bullire* 'boil': confused with PART)]

parbuckle /'pɑːbʌk(ə)l/ *n. & v.* ● *n.* a rope arranged like a sling, for raising or lowering casks and cylindrical objects. ● *v.tr.* raise or lower with this. [earlier *parbunkle*, of unknown origin: associated with BUCKLE]

parcel /'pɑːs(ə)l/ *n. & v.* ● *n.* **1 a** goods etc. wrapped up in a single package. **b** a bundle of things wrapped up, usu. in paper. **2** a piece of land, esp. as part of an estate. **3** a quantity dealt with in one commercial transaction. **4** *archaic* part. ● *v.tr.* (**parcelled, parcelling**; *US* **parceled, parceling**) **1** (foll. by *up*) wrap as a parcel. **2** (foll. by *out*) divide into portions. **3** cover (rope) with strips of canvas. □ **part and parcel** see PART. [Middle English from Old French *parcelle*, ultimately from Latin *particula* (as PART)]

parcel post *n.* the branch of the postal service dealing with parcels.

parch /pɑːtʃ/ *v.* **1** *tr. & intr.* make or become hot and dry. **2** *tr.* roast (peas, corn, etc.) slightly. [Middle English *perch, parche*, of unknown origin]

parched /pɑːtʃt/ *adj.* **1** hot and dry; dried out with heat. **2** *colloq.* thirsty.

parchment /'pɑːtʃm(ə)nt/ *n.* **1 a** an animal skin, esp. that of a sheep or goat, prepared as a writing or painting surface. **b** a manuscript written on this. **2** (in full **vegetable parchment**) high-grade paper made to resemble parchment. [Middle English from Old French *parchemin*, ultimately a blend of Late Latin *pergamina* 'writing material from Pergamum' (in Asia Minor) with *Parthica pellis* 'Parthian skin' (leather)]

parclose /'pɑːkləʊz/ *n.* a screen or railing in a church, separating a side chapel. [Middle English from Old French *parclos -ose*, past part. of *parclore* 'enclose']

pard /pɑːd/ *n. archaic* or *poet.* a leopard. [Middle English via Old French and Latin *pardus* from Greek *pardos*]

pardalote /'pɑːdələʊt/ *n.* any small brightly coloured Australian bird of the genus *Pardalotus*, with spotted plumage. Also called *diamond-bird*. [modern Latin *Pardalotus* from Greek *pardalōtos* 'spotted like a leopard' (as PARD)]

pardner /'pɑːdnə/ *n. US dial.* or *joc.* a partner or comrade. [corruption]

pardon /'pɑːd(ə)n/ *n., v., & int.* ● *n.* **1** the act of excusing or forgiving an offence, error, etc. **2** (in full **free pardon**) *Brit.* a remission of the legal consequences of a crime or conviction. **3** *RC Ch.* an indulgence. ● *v.tr.* **1** release from the consequences of an offence, error, etc. **2** forgive or excuse a person for (an offence etc.). **3** make (esp. courteous) allowances for; excuse. ● *int.* (also **pardon me** or **I beg your pardon**) **1** a formula of apology or disagreement. **2** a request to a speaker to repeat something said. □ **pardonable** *adj.* **pardonably** *adv.* [Middle English via Old French *pardun, pardoner* from medieval Latin *perdonare* 'concede, remit' (as PER-, *donare* 'give')]

pardoner /'pɑːd(ə)nə/ *n. hist.* a person licensed to sell papal pardons or indulgences. [Middle English from Anglo-French (as PARDON)]

pare /pɛː/ *v.tr.* **1 a** trim or shave (esp. fruit and vegetables) by cutting away the surface or edge. **b** (often foll. by *off, away*) cut off (the surface or edge). **2** (often foll. by *away, down*) diminish little by little. □ **parer** *n.* [Middle English via Old French *parer* 'adorn, peel (fruit)', from Latin *parare* 'prepare']

paregoric /parɪ'gɒrɪk/ *n.* (in full **paregoric elixir**) *hist.* a camphorated tincture of opium used to reduce pain. [Late Latin *paregoricus* from Greek *parēgorikos* 'soothing' (as PARA-[1], *-agoros* 'speaking' from *agora* 'assembly')]

pareira /pə'rɛːrə/ *n.* a drug from the root of a Brazilian shrub, *Chondrodendron tomentosum*, used as a muscle relaxant in surgery etc. [Portuguese *parreira* 'vine trained against a wall']

paren /pə'rɛn/ *n.* (usu. in *pl.*) a round bracket, each of a pair of parentheses. [abbreviation of PARENTHESIS]

parenchyma /pə'rɛŋkɪmə/ *n.* **1** *Anat.* the functional part of an organ as distinguished from the connective and supporting tissue. **2** *Bot.* the cellular material, usu. soft and succulent, found esp. in the softer parts of leaves, pulp of fruits, bark and pith of stems, etc. □ **parenchymal** *adj.* **parenchymatous** /-'kɪmətəs/ *adj.* [Greek *paregkhuma* 'something poured in besides' (as PARA-[1], *egkhuma* 'infusion' from *egkheō* 'pour in')]

parent /'pɛːr(ə)nt/ *n. & v.* ● *n.* **1** a person who has begotten or borne offspring; a father or mother. **2** a person who has adopted a child or who holds the position or exercises the function of a parent. **3** *archaic* a forefather. **4** an animal or plant from which others are derived. **5** a source or origin. **6** an initiating organization or enterprise. ● *v.tr.* (also *absol.*) be a parent of. □ **parent–teacher association** a local organization of parents and teachers for promoting closer relations and improving educational facilities at a school. □ **parental** /pə'rɛnt(ə)l/ *adj.* **parentally** /pə'rɛnt(ə)li/ *adv.* **parenthood** *n.* [Middle English via Old French from Latin *parens parentis*, from *parere* 'bring forth']

parentage /'pɛːr(ə)ntɪdʒ/ *n.* lineage; descent from or through parents (*their parentage is unknown*). [Middle English from Old French (as PARENT)]

parent company *n.* a company of which other companies are subsidiaries.

parenteral /pə'rɛnt(ə)r(ə)l/ *adj. Med.* administered or occurring elsewhere in the body than in the alimentary canal. □ **parenterally** *adv.* [PARA-[1] + Greek *enteron* 'intestine']

parenthesis /pə'rɛnθɪsɪs/ *n.* (*pl.* **parentheses** /-siːz/) **1 a** a word, clause, or sentence inserted as an explanation or afterthought into a passage which is grammatically complete without it, and usu. marked off by brackets or dashes or commas. **b** (in *pl.*) a pair of round brackets () used for this. **2** an interlude or interval. □ **in parenthesis** as a parenthesis or afterthought. [Late Latin from Greek, from *parentithēmi* 'put in beside']

parenthesize /pə'rɛnθɪsʌɪz/ *v.tr.* (also **-ise**) **1** (also *absol.*) insert as a parenthesis. **2** put into brackets or similar punctuation.

parenthetic /par(ə)n'θɛtɪk/ *adj.* **1** of or by way of a parenthesis. **2** interposed. □ **parenthetical** *adj.* **parenthetically** *adv.* [PARENTHESIS, on the pattern of *synthesis, synthetic*, etc.]

parenting /ˈpɛːr(ə)ntɪŋ/ *n.* the occupation or concerns of parents.

Parent's Charter *n.* a British government document explaining the structure and aims of education in schools and the rights of parents and children within that system.

parergon /pəˈrəːgɒn/ *n.* (*pl.* **parerga** /-gə/) **1** work subsidiary to one's main employment. **2** an ornamental accessory. [Latin from Greek *parergon* (as PARA-[1], *ergon* 'work')]

paresis /pəˈriːsɪs, ˈparɪsɪs/ *n.* (*pl.* **pareses** /-siːz/) *Med.* partial paralysis. □ **paretic** /-ˈrɛtɪk/ *adj.* [modern Latin from Greek, from *pariēmi* 'let go' (as PARA-[1], *hiēmi* 'let go')]

paresthesia *US* var. of PARAESTHESIA.

par excellence /pɑːr ˈɛks(ə)l(ə)ns/ *adv.* as having special excellence; being the supreme example of its kind (*the short story par excellence*). [French, = by excellence]

parfait /ˈpɑːfeɪ/ *n.* **1** a rich iced pudding of whipped cream, eggs, etc. **2** layers of ice cream, meringue, etc., served in a tall glass. [French *parfait* PERFECT *adj.*]

pargana /pəˈgʌnə/ *n.* (also **pergunnah**, **pergana**) (in India) a group of villages or a subdivision of a district. [Urdu *pargana* 'district']

parget /ˈpɑːdʒɪt/ *v. & n.* ● *v.tr.* (**pargeted**, **pargeting**) **1** plaster (a wall etc.) esp. with an ornamental pattern. **2** roughcast. ● *n.* **1** plaster applied in this way; ornamental plasterwork. **2** roughcast. [Middle English from Old French *pargeter*, *parjeter*, from *par* 'all over' + *jeter* 'throw']

parhelion /pɑːˈhiːlɪən/ *n.* (*pl.* **parhelia** /-lɪə/) a bright spot on the solar halo. Also called *mock sun*, *sun-dog*. □ **parheliacal** /-hɪˈlʌɪək(ə)l/ *adj.* **parhelic** *adj.* [Latin *parelion* from Greek (as PARA-[1], *hēlios* 'sun')]

pariah /pəˈrʌɪə/ *n.* **1** a social outcast. **2** *hist.* a member of a low caste or of no caste in southern India. [Tamil *paraiyar*, pl. of *paraiyan* 'hereditary drummer', from *parai* 'drum']

pariah dog *n.* = PYE-DOG.

parietal /pəˈrʌɪɪt(ə)l/ *adj.* **1** *Anat.* of the wall of the body or any of its cavities. **2** *Bot.* of the wall of a hollow structure etc. **3** *US* relating to residence within a college. [French *pariétal* or Late Latin *parietalis* from Latin *paries -etis* 'wall']

parietal bone *n.* either of a pair of bones forming the central part of the sides and top of the skull.

parietal lobe *n.* either of the paired lobes of the brain at the top of the head, including areas concerned with the reception and correlation of sensory information.

pari-mutuel /pɑːrɪˈmjuːtʃʊəl, -ˈtjʊəl/ *n.* **1** a form of betting in which those backing the first three places divide the losers' stakes (less the operator's commission). **2** a totalizator. [French, = mutual stake]

paring /ˈpɛːrɪŋ/ *n.* a strip or piece cut off.

pari passu /pɑːrɪ ˈpasuː, parɪ/ *adv.* **1** with equal speed. **2** simultaneously and equally. [Latin]

Paris commune see COMMUNE[1] 3.

Paris green /ˈparɪs/ *n.* a vivid green toxic compound containing copper and arsenic, used as a pigment and insecticide. [*Paris* in France]

parish /ˈparɪʃ/ *n.* **1** an area having its own church and clergy. **2** (in full **civil parish**) *Brit.* a district constituted for purposes of local government. **3** the inhabitants of a parish. **4** *US* a county in Louisiana. [Middle English *paroche*, *parosse* via Old French *paroche*, *paroisse* and ecclesiastical Latin *parochia*, *paroechia* from Greek *paroikia* 'sojourning', from *paroikos* (as PARA-[1], *-oikos* '-dwelling' from *oikeō* 'dwell')]

parish clerk *n.* an official performing various duties concerned with the church.

parish council *n. Brit.* the administrative body in a civil parish.

parishioner /pəˈrɪʃ(ə)nə/ *n.* an inhabitant of a parish.

parish pump *n.* (often *attrib.*) *Brit.* a symbol of a parochial or restricted outlook.

parish register *n.* a book recording christenings, marriages, and burials, at a parish church.

Parisian /pəˈrɪzɪən/ *adj. & n.* ● *adj.* of or relating to Paris in France. ● *n.* **1** a native or inhabitant of Paris. **2** the kind of French spoken in Paris. [French *parisien*]

parison /ˈparɪs(ə)n/ *n.* a rounded mass of glass formed by rolling immediately after removal from the furnace. [French *paraison*, from *parer* 'prepare', from Latin *parare*]

parity[1] /ˈparɪti/ *n.* **1** equality or equivalence, esp. as regards status or pay. **2** parallelism or analogy (*parity of reasoning*). **3** equivalence of one currency with another; being at par. **4** (of a number) the fact of being even or odd. **5** *Physics* (of a quantity) the fact of changing its sign or remaining unaltered under a given transformation of coordinates etc. [French *parité* or Late Latin *paritas* (as PAR[1])]

parity[2] /ˈparɪti/ *n. Med.* **1** the fact or condition of having borne children. **2** the number of children previously borne. [formed as -PAROUS + -ITY]

park /pɑːk/ *n. & v.* ● *n.* **1** a large public garden in a town, for recreation. **2** a large enclosed piece of ground, usu. with woodland and pasture, attached to a country house etc. **3 a** a large area of land kept in its natural state for public recreational use. **b** a large enclosed area of land used to accommodate wild animals in captivity (*wildlife park*). **4** esp. *Brit.* an area for motor vehicles etc. to be left in (*car park*). **5** the gear position or function in automatic transmission in which the gears are locked, preventing the vehicle's movement. **6** an area devoted to a specified purpose (*industrial park*). **7 a** *N. Amer.* an enclosed sports ground. **b** (usu. prec. by *the*) *Brit. colloq.* a football pitch. ● *v.tr.* **1** (also *absol.*) leave (a vehicle) usu. temporarily, in a car park, by the side of the road, etc. **2** *colloq.* deposit and leave, usu. temporarily. □ **park oneself** *colloq.* sit down. [Middle English via Old French *parc* from medieval Latin *parricus*, of Germanic origin, related to *pearruc*: see PADDOCK]

parka /ˈpɑːkə/ *n.* **1** a skin jacket with a hood, worn by Eskimos. **2** a windproof fabric garment of similar design worn in cold weather. [Aleut from Russian]

parkin /ˈpɑːkɪn/ *n. Brit.* a cake or biscuit made with oatmeal, ginger, and treacle or molasses. [perhaps from the name *Parkin*, diminutive of *Peter*]

parking light *n.* a small light on the side of a vehicle, for use when the vehicle is parked at night.

parking lot *n. US* an outdoor area for parking vehicles.

parking meter *n.* a coin-operated meter which receives fees for vehicles parked in the street and indicates the time available.

parking ticket *n.* a notice, usu. attached to a vehicle, of a penalty imposed for parking illegally.

Parkinsonism /ˈpɑːkɪns(ə)nɪz(ə)m/ *n.* = PARKINSON'S DISEASE.

Parkinson's disease /ˈpɑːkɪns(ə)nz/ *n.* a progressive disease of the nervous system with tremor, muscular rigidity, and emaciation. Also called *Parkinsonism*. [named after J. *Parkinson*, English surgeon d. 1824]

Parkinson's law /ˈpɑːkɪns(ə)nz/ *n.* the notion that work expands so as to fill the time available for its completion. [named after C.N. *Parkinson*, English writer b. 1909]

parkland /ˈpɑːkland/ *n.* open grassland with clumps of trees etc.

parkway /ˈpɑːkweɪ/ *n.* **1** *US* an open landscaped highway. **2** *Brit.* a railway station with extensive parking facilities, used esp. in names (*Bristol Parkway*).

parky /ˈpɑːki/ *adj.* (**parkier**, **parkiest**) *Brit. colloq.* chilly. [19th c.: origin unknown]

Parl. *abbr. Brit.* **1** Parliament. **2** Parliamentary.

parlance /ˈpɑːl(ə)ns/ *n.* a particular way of speaking, esp. as regards choice of words, idiom, etc. [Old French, from *parler* 'speak', ultimately from Latin *parabola* (see PARABLE): in Late Latin = 'speech']

parlay /'pɑːleɪ/ *v. & n. N. Amer.* ● *v.tr.* **1** use (money won on a bet) as a further stake. **2** increase in value by or as if by parlaying. ● *n.* **1** an act of parlaying. **2** a bet made by parlaying. [French *paroli* from Italian, from *paro* 'like', from Latin *par* 'equal']

parley /'pɑːli/ *n. & v.* ● *n.* (*pl.* **-eys**) a conference for debating points in a dispute, esp. a discussion of terms for an armistice etc. ● *v.intr.* (**-leys, -leyed**) (often foll. by *with*) hold a parley. [perhaps from Old French *parlee*, fem. past part. of *parler* 'speak': see PARLANCE]

parliament /'pɑːləm(ə)nt/ *n.* **1** (**Parliament**) (in the UK) **a** the highest legislature, consisting of the Sovereign, the House of Lords, and the House of Commons. **b** the members of this legislature for a particular period, esp. between one dissolution and the next. **2** a similar legislature in other nations and states. [Middle English from Old French *parlement* 'speaking' (as PARLANCE)]

parliamentarian /pɑːləm(ə)n'tɛːrɪən, -mɛn-/ *n. & adj.* ● *n.* **1** a member of a parliament, esp. one well-versed in its procedures. **2** *hist.* an adherent of Parliament in the English Civil War of the 17th c. ● *adj.* = PARLIAMENTARY.

parliamentary /pɑːlə'mɛnt(ə)ri/ *adj.* **1** of or relating to a parliament. **2** enacted or established by a parliament. **3** (of language) admissible in a parliament; polite.

Parliamentary Commissioner for Administration *n.* the official title of the ombudsman in the UK.

parliamentary private secretary *n.* a Member of Parliament assisting a government minister.

parlour /'pɑːlə/ *n.* (*US* **parlor**) **1** a sitting room in a private house. **2** a room in a hotel, convent, etc., for the private use of residents. **3** esp. *US* a shop providing specified goods or services (*beauty parlour*; *ice-cream parlour*). **4** a room or building equipped for milking cows. **5** (*attrib.*) *derog.* denoting support for political views by those who do not try to practise them (*parlour socialist*). [Middle English from Anglo-French *parlur*, Old French *parleor*, *parleur*: see PARLANCE]

parlour game *n.* an indoor game, esp. a word game.

parlourmaid /'pɑːləmeɪd/ *n. hist.* a maid who waits at table.

parlous /'pɑːləs/ *adj. & adv. archaic* or *joc.* ● *adj.* **1** dangerous or difficult. **2** hard to deal with. ● *adv.* extremely. □ **parlously** *adv.* **parlousness** *n.* [Middle English, = PERILOUS]

Parma ham /'pɑːmə/ *n.* a type of ham which is eaten uncooked. [*Parma*, a city and province in Italy]

Parma violet /'pɑːmə/ *n.* a variety of sweet violet with heavy scent and lavender-coloured flowers often crystallized for food decoration. [*Parma*, a city and province in Italy]

Parmesan /pɑːmɪ'zan/ *n.* a kind of hard dry cheese made originally at Parma and used esp. in grated form. [French from Italian *parmegiano* 'of Parma' a city and province in Italy]

Parnassian /pɑː'nasɪən/ *adj. & n.* ● *adj.* **1** of Parnassus, a mountain in central Greece, in antiquity sacred to the Muses. **2** poetic. **3** of or relating to a group of French poets in the late 19th c., emphasizing strictness of form, named from the anthology *Le Parnasse contemporain* (1866). ● *n.* a member of this group.

parochial /pə'rəʊkɪəl/ *adj.* **1** of or concerning a parish. **2** (of affairs, views, etc.) merely local, narrow or restricted in scope. □ **parochialism** *n.* **parochiality** /-'alɪti/ *n.* **parochially** *adv.* [Middle English via Anglo-French *parochiel*, Old French *parochial* from ecclesiastical Latin *parochialis* (as PARISH)]

parody /'parədi/ *n. & v.* ● *n.* (*pl.* **-ies**) **1 a** a humorous exaggerated imitation of an author, literary work, style, etc. **b** a work of this kind. **2** a feeble imitation; a travesty. ● *v.tr.* (**-ies, -ied**) **1** compose a parody of. **2** mimic humorously. □ **parodic** /pə'rɒdɪk/ *adj.* **parodist** *n.* [Late Latin *parodia* or Greek *parōidia* 'burlesque poem' (as PARA-[1], *ōidē* 'ode')]

par of exchange see PAR[1] 5.

parol /pə'rəʊl, 'par(ə)l/ *adj. & n. Law* ● *adj.* **1** given orally. **2** (of a document) not given under seal. ● *n.* an oral declaration. [Old French *parole* (as PAROLE)]

parole /pə'rəʊl/ *n. & v.* ● *n.* **1 a** the release of a prisoner temporarily for a special purpose or completely before the expiry of a sentence, on the promise of good behaviour. **b** such a promise. **2** a word of honour. ● *v.tr.* put (a prisoner) on parole. □ **on parole** released on the terms of parole. □ **parolee** /-'liː/ *n.* [French, = word: see PARLANCE]

paronomasia /parənə'meɪzɪə/ *n.* a play on words; a pun. [Latin from Greek *paronomasia* (as PARA-[1], *onomasia* 'naming', via *onomazō* 'to name' from *onoma* 'a name')]

paronym /'parənɪm/ *n.* **1** a word cognate with another. **2** a word formed from a foreign word. □ **paronymous** /pə'rɒnɪməs/ *adj.* [Greek *parōnumon*, neut. of *parōnumos* (as PARA-[1], *onuma* 'name')]

parotid /pə'rɒtɪd/ *adj. & n. Anat.* ● *adj.* situated near the ear. ● *n.* (in full **parotid gland**) a salivary gland in front of the ear. [French *parotide* or Latin *parotis parotid-* from Greek *parōtis -idos* (as PARA-[1], *ous ōtos* 'ear')]

parotid duct *n.* a duct opening from the parotid gland into the mouth.

parotitis /parə'tʌɪtɪs/ *n. Med.* **1** inflammation of the parotid gland. **2** mumps. [PAROTID + -ITIS]

-parous /pərəs/ *comb. form* bearing offspring of a specified number or kind (*multiparous*; *viviparous*). [Latin *-parus* '-bearing' from *parere* 'bring forth']

Parousia /pə'ruːzɪə/ *n. Theol.* the second coming of Christ. [Greek, = presence, coming]

paroxysm /'parəksɪz(ə)m/ *n.* **1** (often foll. by *of*) a sudden attack or outburst (of rage, laughter, etc.). **2** a fit of disease. □ **paroxysmal** /-'sɪzm(ə)l/ *adj.* [French *paroxysme* via medieval Latin *paroxysmus* from Greek *paroxusmos*, from *paroxunō* 'exasperate' (as PARA-[1], *oxunō* 'sharpen' from *oxus* 'sharp')]

paroxytone /pə'rɒksɪtəʊn/ *adj. & n.* ● *adj.* (esp. in ancient Greek) having an acute accent on the last syllable but one. ● *n.* a word of this kind. [modern Latin from Greek *paroxutonos* (as PARA-[1], OXYTONE)]

parpen /'pɑːp(ə)n/ *n.* a stone passing through a wall from side to side, with two smooth vertical faces. [Middle English from Old French *parpain*, probably ultimately from Latin *per* 'through' + *pannus* 'piece of cloth', in Romanic 'piece of wall']

parquet /'pɑːki, 'pɑːkeɪ/ *n. & v.* ● *n.* **1** (often *attrib.*) a flooring of wooden blocks arranged in a pattern. **2** *US* **a** the ground floor of a theatre auditorium. **b** the front part of this. ● *v.tr.* (**parqueted** /-keɪd/; **parqueting** /-keɪɪŋ/) furnish (a room) with a parquet floor. [French, = small compartment, floor, diminutive of *parc* PARK]

parquetry /'pɑːkɪtri/ *n.* the use of wooden blocks to make floors or inlay for furniture.

parr /pɑː/ *n.* a young salmon with blue-grey finger-like markings on its sides, younger than a smolt. [18th c.: origin unknown]

parramatta /parə'matə/ *n.* (also **paramatta**) a light dress fabric of wool and silk or cotton. [*Parramatta*, a city in New South Wales, Australia, where it was originally produced]

parricide /'parɪsʌɪd/ *n.* **1** the killing of a near relative, esp. of a parent. **2** a person who commits parricide. □ **parricidal** /-'sʌɪd(ə)l/ *adj.* [French *parricide* or Latin *parricida* (= sense 2), *parricidium* (= sense 1), of uncertain origin, associated in Latin with *pater* 'father' and *parens* 'parent']

■ **Usage** *Parricide*, the killing of a near relative, especially of a parent, is sometimes confused with *patricide*, the killing of one's father.

parrot /'parət/ *n. & v.* ● *n.* **1** any of various mainly tropical birds of the order Psittaciformes, with a short hooked bill, often having vivid plumage and sometimes able to mimic the human voice. **2** a person who mechanically repeats the words or actions of another. ● *v.tr.* (**parroted**, **parroting**) repeat mechanically. [probably from obsolete or dialect French *perrot* 'parrot', diminutive of *Pierre* 'Peter': cf. PARAKEET]

parrot-fashion *adv.* (learning or repeating) mechanically without understanding.

parrotfish /ˈparətfɪʃ/ *n.* (*pl.* usu. same) any fish of the genus *Scarus*, with a mouth like a parrot's bill and forming a protective mucous cocoon against predators.

parry /ˈpari/ *v. & n.* ● *v.tr.* (**-ies**, **-ied**) **1** avert or ward off (a weapon or attack), esp. with a countermove. **2** deal skilfully with (an awkward question etc.). ● *n.* (*pl.* **-ies**) an act of parrying. [probably representing French *parez*, imperative of *parer*, from Italian *parare* 'ward off']

parse /pɑːz/ *v.tr.* **1** describe (a word in context) grammatically, stating its inflection, relation to the sentence, etc. **2** resolve (a sentence) into its component parts and describe them grammatically. **3** *Computing* analyse (a string) into syntactic components, esp. to test conformability to a grammar. □ **parser** *n.* (esp. in sense 3). [perhaps from Middle English *pars* 'parts of speech' from Old French *pars*, pl. of *part* PART, influenced by Latin *pars* 'part']

parsec /ˈpɑːsɛk/ *n.* a unit of astronomical distance, equal to about 3.25 light years (3.08×10^{16} metres), the distance at which the mean radius of the earth's orbit subtends an angle of one second of arc. [PARALLAX + SECOND[2]]

Parsee /pɑːˈsiː, ˈpɑːsiː/ *n.* **1** an adherent of Zoroastrianism, esp. a descendant of those Zoroastrians who fled to India from Muslim persecution in Persia during the 7th–8th c. **2** = PAHLAVI. □ **Parseeism** *n.* [Persian *pārsī* 'Persian' from *pārs* 'Persia']

parsimony /ˈpɑːsɪməni/ *n.* **1** carefulness in the use of money or other resources. **2** meanness, stinginess. □ **parsimonious** /-ˈməʊnɪəs/ *adj.* **parsimoniously** /-ˈməʊnɪəsli/ *adv.* **parsimoniousness** /-ˈməʊnɪəsnɪs/ *n.* [Middle English from Latin *parsimonia*, *parcimonia*, from *parcere pars-* 'spare']

parsley /ˈpɑːsli/ *n.* a biennial herb, *Petroselinum crispum*, with white flowers and crinkly aromatic leaves, used for seasoning and garnishing food. [Middle English *percil*, *per(e)sil* from Old French *peresil*, and Old English *petersilie*, ultimately via Latin *petroselinum* from Greek *petroselinon*]

parsley fern *n.* a fern, *Cryptogramma crispa*, with leaves like parsley.

parsley-piert /pɑːslɪˈpɪət/ *n.* a dwarf annual plant, *Aphanes arvensis*, of the rose family. [probably corruption of French *perce-pierre* 'pierce stone']

parsnip /ˈpɑːsnɪp/ *n.* **1** a biennial umbelliferous plant, *Pastinaca sativa*, with yellow flowers and a large pale yellow tapering root. **2** this root eaten as a vegetable. [Middle English *pas(se)nep* (with assimilation to *nep* 'turnip') via Old French *pasnaie* from Latin *pastinaca*]

parson /ˈpɑːs(ə)n/ *n.* **1** a rector. **2** a vicar or any beneficed member of the clergy. **3** *colloq.* any (esp. Protestant) member of the clergy. □ **parsonical** /-ˈsɒnɪk(ə)l/ *adj.* [Middle English *person(e)*, *parson* via Old French *persone* from Latin *persona* PERSON (in medieval Latin 'rector')]

parsonage /ˈpɑːs(ə)nɪdʒ/ *n.* a church house provided for a parson.

parson's nose *n.* the piece of fatty flesh at the rump of a fowl.

part /pɑːt/ *n., v., & adv.* ● *n.* **1** some but not all of a thing or number of things. **2** an essential member or constituent of anything (*part of the family*; *a large part of the job*). **3** a component of a machine etc. (*spare parts*; *needs a new part*). **4 a** a portion of a human or animal body. **b** (in *pl.*) *colloq.* = PRIVATE PARTS. **5** a division of a book, broadcast serial, etc., esp. as much as is issued or broadcast at one time. **6 a** each of several equal portions of a whole (*the recipe has 3 parts sugar to 2 parts flour*). **b** (prec. by ordinal number) a specified fraction of a whole (*each received a fifth part*). **7 a** a portion allotted; a share. **b** a person's share in an action or enterprise (*will have no part in it*). **c** one's duty (*was not my part to interfere*). **8 a** a character assigned to an actor. **b** the words spoken by an actor. **c** a copy of these. **9** *Mus.* **a** a melody or other constituent of harmony assigned to a particular voice or instrument (often in *comb.*: *four-part harmony*). **b** a copy of the music for a particular musician. **10** each of the sides in an agreement or dispute. **11** (in *pl.*) a region or district (*am not from these parts*). **12** (in *pl.*) abilities (*a man of many parts*). **13** *US* = PARTING 2. ● *v.* **1** *tr. & intr.* divide or separate into parts (*the crowd parted to let them through*). **2** *intr.* **a** leave one another's company (*they parted the best of friends*). **b** (foll. by *from*) say goodbye to. **3** *tr.* cause to separate (*they fought hard and had to be parted*). **4** *intr.* (foll. by *with*) give up possession of; hand over. **5** *tr.* separate (the hair of the head on either side of the parting) with a comb. ● *adv.* to some extent; partly (*is part iron and part wood*; *a lie that is part truth*). □ **for the most part** see MOST. **for one's part** as far as one is concerned. **in part** (or **parts**) to some extent; partly. **look the part** appear suitable for a role. **on the part of** proceeding from, on the initiative of (*a long struggle on the part of the scholars*; *no objection on my part*). **part and parcel** (usu. foll. by *of*) an essential part. **part company** see COMPANY. **play a part 1** be significant or contributory. **2** act deceitfully. **3** perform a dramatic role. **take in good part** see GOOD. **take part** (often foll. by *in*) assist or have a share (in). **take the part of** support; back up. [Middle English via Old French from Latin *pars partis* (*n.*), *partire*, *partiri* (*v.*)]

■ **Usage** See Usage Note at BEHALF.

partake /pɑːˈteɪk/ *v.intr.* (*past* **partook** /-ˈtʊk/; *past part.* **partaken** /-ˈteɪk(ə)n/) **1** (foll. by *of*, *in*) take a share or part. **2** (foll. by *of*) eat or drink some or *colloq.* all (of a thing). **3** (foll. by *of*) have some (of a quality etc.) (*their manner partook of insolence*). □ **partakable** *adj.* **partaker** *n.* [16th c.: back-formation from Middle English *partaker*, *partaking* = part-taker, etc.]

parterre /pɑːˈtɛː/ *n.* **1** a level space in a garden occupied by flower beds arranged formally. **2** *US* the ground floor of a theatre auditorium, esp. the pit overhung by balconies. [French, = *par terre* 'on the ground']

part exchange *n. & v.* ● *n. Brit.* a transaction in which goods are given as part of the payment for other goods, with the balance in money. ● *v.tr.* (**part-exchange**) give (goods) in such a transaction.

parthenogenesis /ˌpɑːθɪnəˈdʒɛnɪsɪs/ *n. Biol.* reproduction from an ovum without fertilization, esp. as a normal process in invertebrates and lower plants. □ **parthenogenetic** /-dʒɪˈnɛtɪk/ *adj.* **parthenogenetically** /-dʒɪˈnɛtɪk(ə)li/ *adv.* [modern Latin, from Greek *parthenos* 'virgin' + *genesis* GENESIS]

Parthian shot /ˈpɑːθɪən/ *n.* a remark or glance etc. reserved for the moment of departure. [*Parthia*, an ancient kingdom in W. Asia: from the custom of a retreating Parthian horseman firing a shot at the enemy]

partial /ˈpɑːʃ(ə)l/ *adj. & n.* ● *adj.* **1** not complete; forming only part (*a partial success*). **2** biased, unfair. **3** (foll. by *to*) having a liking for. ● *n. Mus.* any of the constituents of a musical sound. □ **partially** *adv.* **partialness** *n.* [Middle English via Old French *parcial* from Late Latin *partialis* (as PART)]

partial derivative *n. Math.* a derivative of a function of two or more variables with respect to one variable, the other(s) being treated as constant.

partial differential equation *n. Math.* an equation containing a partial derivative.

partial eclipse *n.* an eclipse in which only part of the luminary is covered or darkened.

partiality /pɑːʃɪˈalɪti/ *n.* **1** bias, favouritism. **2** (foll. by *for*) fondness. [Middle English via Old French *parcialité* from medieval Latin *partialitas* (as PARTIAL)]

partial pressure *n. Physics* the pressure that would be exerted by one of the gases in a mixture if it occupied the same volume on its own.

partial verdict *n.* a verdict finding a person guilty of part of a charge.

participant /pɑːˈtɪsɪp(ə)nt/ *n.* a participator.

participate /pɑːˈtɪsɪpeɪt/ *v.intr.* **1** (usu. foll. by *in*) share or take part (in). **2** (foll. by *of*) *literary* or *archaic* have a certain quality (*the speech participated of wit*). □ **participation** /-ˈpeɪʃ(ə)n/ *n.* **participative** *adj.* **participator** *n.* **participatory** *adj.* [Latin *participare* from *particeps -cipis* 'taking part' (as PART + *-cip-* = *cap-*, stem of *capere* 'take')]

participle /ˈpɑːtɪsɪp(ə)l/ *n. Gram.* a word formed from a verb (e.g. *going, gone, being, been*) and used in compound verb forms (e.g. *is going, has been*) or as an adjective (e.g. *working woman, burnt toast*). □ **participial** /-ˈsɪpɪəl/ *adj.* **participially** /-ˈsɪpɪəli/ *adv.* [Middle English from Old French, by-form of *participe*, from Latin *participium* (as PARTICIPATE)]

particle /ˈpɑːtɪk(ə)l/ *n.* **1** a minute portion of matter. **2** the least possible amount (*not a particle of sense*). **3** *Gram.* **a** a minor part of speech, esp. a short indeclinable one. **b** a common prefix or suffix such as *in-, -ness.* [Middle English from Latin *particula* (as PART)]

particle board *n.* = CHIPBOARD.

particle physics *n.* the branch of physics concerned with the properties and interactions of subatomic particles.

particoloured /ˈpɑːtɪkʌləd/ *adj.* (*US* **particolored**) partly of one colour, partly of another or others. [PARTY[2] + COLOURED]

particular /pəˈtɪkjʊlə/ *adj. & n.* ● *adj.* **1** relating to or considered as one thing or person as distinct from others; individual (*in this particular instance*). **2** more than is usual; special, noteworthy (*took particular trouble*). **3** scrupulously exact; fastidious. **4** detailed (*a full and particular account*). **5** *Logic* (of a proposition) in which something is asserted of some but not all of a class (opp. UNIVERSAL *adj.* 2). ● *n.* **1** a detail; an item. **2** (in *pl.*) points of information; a detailed account. □ **in particular** especially, specifically. [Middle English via Old French *particuler* from Latin *particularis* (as PARTICLE)]

particular intention *n.* = SPECIAL INTENTION.

particularism /pəˈtɪkjʊlərɪz(ə)m/ *n.* **1** exclusive devotion to one party, sect, etc. **2** the principle of leaving political independence to each state in an empire or federation. **3** the theological doctrine of individual election or redemption. □ **particularist** *n.* [French *particularisme*, modern Latin *particularismus*, and German *Partikularismus* (as PARTICULAR)]

particularity /pətɪkjʊˈlarɪti/ *n.* (*pl.* **-ies**) **1** the quality of being individual or particular. **2** fullness or minuteness of detail in a description. **3** (usu. in *pl.*) detail, particular.

particularize /pəˈtɪkjʊlərʌɪz/ *v.tr.* (also **-ise**) (also *absol.*) **1** name specially or one by one. **2** specify (items). □ **particularization** /-ˈzeɪʃ(ə)n/ *n.* [French *particulariser* (as PARTICULAR)]

particularly /pəˈtɪkjʊləli/ *adv.* **1** especially, very. **2** specifically (*they particularly asked for you*). **3** in a particular or fastidious manner.

particulate /pɑːˈtɪkjʊlət, -eɪt, pə-/ *adj. & n.* ● *adj.* in the form of separate particles. ● *n.* (usu. in *pl.*) matter in this form. [Latin *particula* PARTICLE]

parting /ˈpɑːtɪŋ/ *n.* **1** a leave-taking or departure (often *attrib.*: *parting words*). **2** *Brit.* the dividing line of combed hair. **3** a division; an act of separating.

parting shot *n.* = PARTHIAN SHOT.

parti pris /pɑːti ˈpriː, French parti pri/ *n. & adj.* ● *n.* (*pl.* ***partis pris*** *pronunc.* same) a preconceived view; a bias. ● *adj.* prejudiced, biased. [French, = side taken]

partisan /ˈpɑːtɪzan, -ˈzan/ *n. & adj.* (also **partizan**) ● *n.* **1** a strong, esp. unreasoning, supporter of a party, cause, etc. **2** *Mil.* a guerrilla in wartime. ● *adj.* **1** of or characteristic of partisans. **2** loyal to a particular cause; biased. □ **partisanship** *n.* [French from Italian dialect *partigiano* etc., from *parte* PART]

partita /pɑːˈtiːtə/ *n.* (*pl.* **partitas** or **partite** /-teɪ, -ti/) *Mus.* **1** a suite. **2** an air with variations. [Italian, fem. past part. of *partire* 'divide', formed as PART]

partite /ˈpɑːtʌɪt/ *adj.* **1** divided (esp. in *comb.*: *tripartite*). **2** *Bot. & Zool.* divided to or nearly to the base. [Latin *partitus*, past part. of *partiri* PART *v.*]

partition /pɑːˈtɪʃ(ə)n/ *n. & v.* ● *n.* **1** division into parts, esp. of a country with separate areas of government. **2** a structure dividing a space into two parts, esp. a light interior wall. ● *v.tr.* **1** divide into parts. **2** (foll. by *off*) separate (part of a room etc.) with a partition. □ **partitioned** *adj.* **partitioner** *n.* **partitionist** *n.* [Middle English via Old French from Latin *partitio -onis* (as PARTITE)]

partitive /ˈpɑːtɪtɪv/ *adj. & n. Gram.* ● *adj.* (of a word, form, etc.) denoting part of a collective group or quantity. ● *n.* a partitive word (e.g. *some, any*) or form. □ **partitively** *adv.* [French *partitif -ive* or medieval Latin *partitivus* (as PARTITE)]

partitive genitive *n.* a genitive used to indicate a whole divided into or regarded in parts, expressed in English by *of* as in *most of us*.

partizan var. of PARTISAN.

partly /ˈpɑːtli/ *adv.* **1** with respect to a part or parts. **2** to some extent.

partner /ˈpɑːtnə/ *n. & v.* ● *n.* **1** a person who shares or takes part with another or others, esp. in a business firm with shared risks and profits. **2** a companion in dancing. **3** a player (esp. one of two) on the same side in a game. **4** either member of a married couple, or of an established unmarried couple. ● *v.tr.* **1** be the partner of. **2** associate as partners. □ **partnerless** *adj.* [Middle English, alteration of *parcener* 'joint heir', influenced by PART]

partnership /ˈpɑːtnəʃɪp/ *n.* **1** the state of being a partner or partners. **2** a joint business. **3** a pair or group of partners.

part of speech *n.* each of the categories to which words are assigned in accordance with their grammatical and semantic functions (in English esp. noun, pronoun, adjective, adverb, verb, preposition, conjunction, and interjection).

partook *past* of PARTAKE.

partridge /ˈpɑːtrɪdʒ/ *n.* (*pl.* same or **partridges**) **1** any game bird of the genus *Perdix*, esp. *P. perdix* of Europe and Asia. **2** any similar bird of the family Phasianidae (*snow partridge*). [Middle English *partrich* etc. via Old French *perdriz* etc. from Latin *perdix -dicis*]

part-song *n.* a song with three or more voice parts, often without accompaniment, and harmonic rather than contrapuntal in character.

part-time *adj. & adv.* occupying or using only part of the usual working week (*a part-time gardener*; *he only works part-time*). □ **part-timer** *n.*

parturient /pɑːˈtjʊərɪənt/ *adj.* about to give birth. [Latin *parturire* 'be in labour', inceptive of *parere part-* 'bring forth']

parturition /pɑːtjʊəˈrɪʃ(ə)n/ *n. formal* the act of bringing forth young; childbirth. [Late Latin *parturitio* (as PARTURIENT)]

part-way *adv.* **1** part of the way. **2** partly.

part-work *n. Brit.* a publication appearing in several parts over a period of time.

party[1] /ˈpɑːti/ *n. & v.* ● *n.* (*pl.* **-ies**) **1** a social gathering, usu. of invited guests. **2** a body of persons engaged in an activity or travelling together (*fishing party*; *search party*). **3** a group of people united in a cause, opinion, etc., esp. a political group organized on a national basis. **4** a person or persons forming one side in an agreement or dispute. **5** (foll. by *to*) *Law* an accessory (to an action). **6** *colloq.* a person. ● *v.tr. & intr.* (**-ies, -ied**) entertain at or attend a party. [Middle English from Old French *partie*, ultimately from Latin *partire*: see PART]

party[2] /'pɑːti/ *adj. Heraldry* divided into parts of different colours. [Middle English via Old French *parti* from Latin (as PARTY[1])]

party-goer *n.* a person who attends a party or who frequents parties.

party line *n.* **1** the policy adopted by a political party. **2** a telephone line shared by two or more subscribers.

party political *adj. & n.* ● *adj.* of or relating to party politics. ● *n.* (in full **party political broadcast**) a television or radio programme on which a representative of a political party presents material intended to foster support for it.

party politics *n.pl.* (also treated as *sing.*) politics as it relates to political parties.

party-poop *n.* (also **party-pooper**) esp. *N. Amer. slang* a person who throws gloom over social enjoyment. □ **party-pooping** *n.*

party popper *n.* a device which rapidly ejects a paper streamer, used as an amusement at parties.

party wall *n.* a wall common to two adjoining buildings or rooms.

parure /pə'rʊə/ *n.* a set of jewels or other ornaments intended to be worn together. [Old French from *parer* (see PARE) + -URE]

parvenu /'pɑːvənuː, -njuː/ *n. & adj.* ● *n.* (*fem.* **parvenue**) **1** a person of obscure origin who has gained wealth or position. **2** an upstart. ● *adj.* **1** associated with or characteristic of such a person. **2** upstart. [French, past part. of *parvenir* 'arrive', from Latin *pervenire* (as PER-, *venire* 'come')]

parvis /'pɑːvɪs/ *n.* (also **parvise**) **1** an enclosed area in front of a cathedral, church, etc. **2** a room over a church porch. [Middle English from Old French *parvis*, ultimately from Late Latin *paradisus* PARADISE, in the Middle Ages denoting a court in front of St Peter's, Rome]

parvovirus /'pɑːvəʊvʌɪrəs/ *n.* any of a class of small viruses affecting vertebrate animals, esp. one which causes contagious disease in dogs. [Latin *parvus* 'small' + VIRUS]

pas /pɑː/ *n.* (*pl.* same) a step in dancing, esp. in classical ballet. [French, = step]

pascal *n.* **1** /'pask(ə)l/ the SI unit of pressure, equal to one newton per square metre. **2** (**Pascal**) /pa'skɑːl/ *Computing* a programming language esp. used in education. [named after B. *Pascal*, French scientist d. 1662: in sense 2 because he built a calculating machine]

paschal /'pask(ə)l, 'pɑːs-/ *adj.* **1** of or relating to the Jewish Passover. **2** of or relating to Easter. [Middle English via Old French *pascal* and ecclesiastical Latin *paschalis*, from *pascha* via Greek *paskha*, from Aramaic *pasḥa*, related to Hebrew *pesaḥ* PASSOVER]

paschal lamb *n.* **1** a lamb sacrificed at Passover. **2** Christ.

pas de chat /pɑː də 'ʃa/ *n.* (*pl.* same) a leap in which each foot in turn is raised to the opposite knee. [French, = (dance) step of a cat]

pas de deux /pɑː də 'dəː/ *n.* (*pl.* same) a dance for two persons. [French]

pas glissé see GLISSÉ.

pash /paʃ/ *n. slang* a brief infatuation. [abbreviation of PASSION]

pasha /'pɑːʃə/ *n.* (also **pacha**) *hist.* the title (placed after the name) of a Turkish officer of high rank, e.g. a military commander, the governor of a province, etc. [Turkish *paşa*, probably = *başa*, from *baş* 'head, chief']

pashm /'paʃ(ə)m/ *n.* the under-fur of some Tibetan animals, esp. that of goats as used for cashmere shawls. [Persian *pašm* 'wool']

Pashto /'pʌʃtəʊ/ *n. & adj.* ● *n.* the official language of Afghanistan, also spoken in areas of Pakistan. ● *adj.* of or in this language. [Pashto]

paskha /'pɑːskə, 'paskə, 'pasxə/ *n.* a rich Russian dessert containing curd cheese and dried fruit, traditionally eaten at Easter. [Russian, = Easter]

paso doble /ˌpasə(ʊ) 'dəʊbleɪ/ *n.* **1** a ballroom dance based on a Latin American style of marching. **2** this style of marching. [Spanish, = double step]

pasque flower /pask, pɑːsk/ *n.* a plant of the buttercup family, *Pulsatilla vulgaris*, with bell-shaped purple flowers and fernlike foliage. [earlier *passe-flower* from French *passe-fleur*: assimilated to *pasque* = obsolete *pasch* (as PASCHAL) 'Easter']

pasquinade /paskwɪ'neɪd/ *n.* a lampoon or satire, originally one displayed in a public place. [Italian *pasquinata* from *Pasquino*, the name of a statue in Rome on which abusive Latin verses were annually posted]

pass[1] /pɑːs/ *v. & n.* ● *v.* (*past part.* **passed**) (see also PAST). **1** *intr.* (often foll. by *along, by, down, on*, etc.) move onward; proceed, esp. past some point of reference (*saw the procession passing*). **2** *tr.* **a** go past; leave (a thing etc.) on one side or behind in proceeding. **b** overtake, esp. in a vehicle. **c** go across (a frontier, mountain range, etc.). **3** *intr. & tr.* be transferred or cause to be transferred from one person or place to another (*pass the butter; the title passes to his son*). **4** *tr.* surpass; be too great for (*it passes my comprehension*). **5** *intr.* get through; effect a passage. **6** *intr.* **a** be accepted as adequate; go uncensured (*let the matter pass*). **b** (foll. by *as, for*) be accepted or currently known as. **c** *US* (of a person with some black ancestry) be accepted as white. **7** *tr.* move; cause to go (*passed her hand over her face; passed a rope round it*). **8 a** *intr.* (of a candidate in an examination) be successful. **b** *tr.* be successful in (an examination or course). **c** *tr.* (of an examiner) judge the performance of (a candidate) to be satisfactory. **9 a** *tr.* (of a bill) be examined and approved by (a parliamentary body or process). **b** *tr.* cause or allow (a bill) to proceed to further legislative processes. **c** *intr.* (of a bill or proposal) be approved. **10** *intr.* **a** occur, elapse (*the remark passed unnoticed; time passes slowly*). **b** happen; be done or said (*heard what passed between them*). **11 a** *intr.* circulate; be current. **b** *tr.* put into circulation (*was passing forged cheques*). **12** *tr.* spend or use up (a certain time or period) (*passed the afternoon reading*). **13** *tr.* (also *absol.*) (in field games) send (the ball) to another player of one's own side. **14** *intr.* forgo one's turn or chance in a game etc. **15** *intr.* (foll. by *to, into*) change from one form (to another). **16** *intr.* come to an end. **17** *tr.* discharge from the body as or with excreta. **18** *tr.* (foll. by *on, upon*) **a** utter (criticism) about. **b** pronounce (a judicial sentence) on. **19** *intr.* (often foll. by *on, upon*) adjudicate. **20** *tr.* not declare or pay (a dividend). **21** *tr.* cause (troops etc.) to go by esp. ceremonially. ● *n.* **1** an act or instance of passing. **2** *Brit.* **a** success in an examination. **b** the status of a university degree without honours. **3** written permission to pass into or out of a place, or to be absent from quarters. **4 a** a ticket or permit giving free entry or access etc. **b** = FREE PASS. **5** (in field games) a transference of the ball to another player on the same side. **6** a thrust in fencing. **7** a juggling trick. **8** an act of passing the hands over anything, as in conjuring or hypnotism. **9** a critical position (*has come to a fine pass*). □ **in passing 1** by the way. **2** in the course of speech, conversation, etc. **make a pass at** *colloq.* make amorous or sexual advances to. **pass away 1** *euphem.* die. **2** cease to exist; come to an end. **pass the buck** see BUCK[3]. **pass by 1** go past. **2** disregard, omit. **pass one's eye over** read (a document etc.) cursorily. **pass the hat round** see HAT. **pass muster** see MUSTER. **pass off 1** (of feelings etc.) disappear gradually. **2** (of proceedings) be carried through (in a specified way). **3** (foll. by *as*) misrepresent (a person or thing) as something else. **4** evade or lightly dismiss (an awkward remark etc.). **pass on 1** proceed on one's way. **2** *euphem.* die. **3** transmit to the next person in a series. **pass out 1** become unconscious. **2** *Brit. Mil.* complete one's training as a cadet. **3** distribute. **pass over 1** omit, ignore, or disregard. **2** ignore the claims of (a person) to promotion or advancement. **3** *euphem.* die. **pass round** (*US* **around**) **1** distribute. **2** send or give to each of a number in turn. **pass through** experience. **pass the time of day** see TIME. **pass up** *colloq.* refuse or neglect (an opportunity etc.). **pass water** urinate. ▫ **passer** *n.* [Middle English from Old French *passer*, ultimately from Latin *passus* PACE[1]]

pass[2] /pɑːs/ *n.* **1** a narrow passage through mountains. **2** a navigable channel, esp. at the mouth of a river. ▫ **sell the pass** *Brit.* betray a cause. [Middle English, variant of PACE[1], influenced by French *pas* 'step, passage' and by PASS[1]]

passable /'pɑːsəb(ə)l/ *adj.* **1** barely satisfactory; just adequate. **2** (of a road, pass, etc.) that can be passed. ▫ **passableness** *n.* **passably** *adv.* [Middle English from Old French (as PASS[1])]

passacaglia /pasə'kɑːlɪə/ *n. Mus.* an instrumental piece usu. with a ground bass. [Italian from Spanish *pasacalle*, from *pasar* 'pass' + *calle* 'street': originally often played in the streets]

passage[1] /'pasɪdʒ/ *n.* **1** the process or means of passing; transit. **2** = PASSAGEWAY. **3** the liberty or right to pass through. **4 a** the right of conveyance as a passenger by sea or air. **b** a journey by sea or air. **5** a transition from one state to another. **6 a** a short extract from a book etc. **b** a section of a piece of music. **7** the passing of a bill etc. into law. **8** (in *pl.*) an interchange of words etc. **9** *Anat.* a duct etc. in the body. ▫ **passage of** (or **at**) **arms** a fight or dispute. **work one's passage** earn a right (originally of passage) by working for it. [Middle English from Old French (as PASS[1])]

passage[2] /'pasɪdʒ/ *v.* **1** *intr.* (of a horse or rider) move sideways, by the pressure of the rein on the horse's neck and of the rider's leg on the opposite side. **2** *tr.* make (a horse) do this. [French *passager*, earlier *passéger*, via Italian *passeggiare* 'to walk, pace' from Latin *passus* PACE[1]]

passageway /'pasɪdʒweɪ/ *n.* a narrow way for passing along, esp. with walls on either side; a corridor.

passant /'pas(ə)nt/ *adj. Heraldry* (of an animal) walking and looking to the dexter side, with three paws on the ground and the right forepaw raised. [Middle English from Old French, part. of *passer* PASS[1]]

passband /'pɑːsband/ *n.* a frequency band within which signals are transmitted by a filter without attenuation.

passbook /'pɑːsbʊk/ *n.* a book issued by a bank or building society etc. to an account-holder recording sums deposited and withdrawn.

passé /'paseɪ/ *adj.* **1** no longer fashionable; out of date. **2** *archaic* past one's prime. [French, past part. of *passer* PASS[1]]

passed pawn *n. Chess* a pawn that has no enemy pawn that can hinder it from queening.

passementerie /'pasm(ə)ntri/ *n.* a trimming of gold or silver lace, braid, beads, etc. [French, from *passement* 'gold lace' etc. from *passer* PASS[1]]

passenger /'pasɪndʒə/ *n.* **1** a traveller in or on a public or private conveyance (other than the driver, pilot, crew, etc.). **2** *colloq.* a member of a team, crew, etc., who does no effective work. **3** (*attrib.*) for the use of passengers (*passenger seat*). [Middle English via Old French *passager* (*n.*) from Old French *passager* (*adj.*) 'passing' (as PASSAGE[1]): *-n-* as in *messenger* etc.]

passenger-mile *n.* one mile travelled by one passenger, as a unit of traffic.

passenger pigeon *n.* an extinct wild pigeon of N. America, noted for migrating in huge flocks and hunted to extinction by 1914.

passepartout /paspɑː'tuː, pɑːs-/ *n.* **1** a master key. **2** a simple picture frame (esp. for mounted photographs), esp. one consisting of a piece of glass stuck to a backing by adhesive tape along the edges. **3** adhesive tape or paper used for this. [French, = passes everywhere]

passepied /paspjeɪ/ *n.* a Breton dance like a quick minuet, popular in the 17th–18th c. [French, from *passer* 'pass' + *pied* 'foot']

passer-by /pɑːsə'bʌɪ/ *n.* (*pl.* **passers-by**) a person who goes past, esp. by chance.

passerine /'pasərʌɪn, -riːn/ *n. & adj.* ● *n.* any bird of the order Passeriformes, comprising the perching birds, having feet with three toes pointing forward and one pointing backwards, including sparrows and other songbirds. ● *adj.* **1** of or relating to this order. **2** of the size of a sparrow. [Latin *passer* 'sparrow']

pas seul /'səːl/ *n.* a solo dance. [French]

passible /'pasɪb(ə)l/ *adj. Theol.* capable of feeling or suffering. ▫ **passibility** /-'bɪlɪti/ *n.* [Middle English via Old French *passible* or Late Latin *passibilis* from Latin *pati pass-* 'suffer']

passim /'pasɪm/ *adv.* (of allusions or references in a published work) to be found at various places throughout the text. [Latin, via *passus* 'scattered' from *pandere* 'spread']

passing /'pɑːsɪŋ/ *adj. & n.* ● *adj.* **1** in senses of PASS[1] *v.* **2** transient, fleeting (*a passing glance*). **3** cursory, incidental (*a passing reference*). ● *n.* **1** in senses of PASS[1] *v.* **2** *euphem.* the death of a person (*mourned his passing*). ▫ **passingly** *adv.*

passing note *n. Mus.* a note not belonging to the harmony but interposed to secure a smooth transition.

passing shot *n. Tennis* etc. a shot aiming the ball beyond and out of reach of the other player.

passion /'paʃ(ə)n/ *n.* **1** strong barely controllable emotion. **2** an outburst of anger (*flew into a passion*). **3** intense sexual love. **4 a** strong enthusiasm (*has a passion for football*). **b** a thing arousing this. **5** (**the Passion**) **a** the suffering of Christ during his last days. **b** a narrative of this from the Gospels. **c** a musical setting of any of these narratives. ▫ **passionless** *adj.* [Middle English via Old French and Late Latin *passio -onis* from Latin *pati pass-* 'suffer']

passional /'paʃ(ə)n(ə)l/ *adj. & n.* ● *adj. literary* of or marked by passion. ● *n.* a book of the sufferings of saints and martyrs.

passionate /'paʃ(ə)nət/ *adj.* **1** dominated by or easily moved to strong feeling, esp. love or anger. **2** showing or caused by passion. ▫ **passionately** *adv.* **passionateness** *n.* [Middle English from medieval Latin *passionatus* (as PASSION)]

passion flower *n.* any climbing plant of the genus *Passiflora*, with a flower that was supposed to suggest the instruments of the Crucifixion.

passion fruit *n.* the edible fruit of some species of passion flower, esp. *Passiflora edulis*. Also called *grenadilla*.

passion play *n.* a miracle play representing Christ's Passion.

Passion Sunday *n.* the fifth Sunday in Lent.

Passiontide /'paʃ(ə)ntʌɪd/ *n.* the last two weeks of Lent.

Passion Week *n.* **1** the week between Passion Sunday and Palm Sunday. **2** = HOLY WEEK.

passivate /'pasɪveɪt/ *v.tr.* make (esp. metal) passive (see PASSIVE 3b). ▫ **passivation** /-'veɪʃ(ə)n/ *n.*

passive /'pasɪv/ *adj.* **1** suffering action; acted upon. **2** offering no opposition; submissive. **3 a** not active; inert. **b** (of a metal) abnormally unreactive owing to a surface coating of oxide. **4** *Gram.* designating the voice in which the subject undergoes the action of the verb (e.g. in *they were killed*). **5** (of a debt) incurring no interest payment. ▫ **passively** *adv.* **passiveness** *n.* **passivity** /-'sɪvɪti/ *n.* [Middle English from Old French *passif -ive* or Latin *passivus* (as PASSION)]

passive obedience *n.* **1** surrender to another's will without cooperation. **2** compliance with commands irrespective of their nature.

passive resistance *n.* non-violent refusal to cooperate.

passive smoking *n.* the involuntary inhaling, esp. by a non-smoker, of smoke from others' cigarettes etc.

pass-key *n.* **1** a private key to a gate etc. for special purposes. **2** a master key.

pass laws *n.pl. hist.* (in South Africa) laws (now repealed) which determined the passes to be carried by Africans, and restricted the free movement of African citizens.

pass-mark *n. Brit.* the minimum mark needed to pass an examination.

Passover /ˈpɑːsəʊvə/ *n.* **1** the Jewish spring festival commemorating the liberation of the Israelites from Egyptian bondage, held from the 14th to the 21st day of the seventh month of the Jewish year. **2** = PASCHAL LAMB. [*pass over* = pass without touching, with reference to the exemption of the Israelites from the death of the first-born (Exod. 12)]

passport /ˈpɑːspɔːt/ *n.* **1** an official document issued by a government certifying the holder's identity and citizenship, and entitling the holder to travel under its protection to and from foreign countries. **2** (foll. by *to*) a thing that ensures admission or attainment (*a passport to success*). [French *passeport* (as PASS[1], PORT[1])]

password /ˈpɑːswəːd/ *n.* a selected word, phrase, or string of characters, securing recognition, admission, access to a computing system, etc., when used by those to whom it is disclosed.

past /pɑːst/ *adj., n., prep., & adv.* ● *adj.* **1** gone by in time and no longer existing (*in past years*; *the time is past*). **2** recently completed or gone by (*the past month*; *for some time past*). **3** relating to a former time (*past president*). **4** *Gram.* expressing a past action or state. ● *n.* **1** (prec. by *the*) **a** a past time. **b** what has happened in past time (*cannot undo the past*). **2** a person's past life or career, esp. if discreditable (*a man with a past*). **3** a past tense or form. ● *prep.* **1** beyond in time or place (*is past two o'clock*; *ran past the house*). **2** beyond the range, duration, or compass of (*past belief*; *past endurance*). ● *adv.* so as to pass by (*hurried past*). □ **not put it past a person** believe it possible of a person. **past it** *colloq.* old and useless. [past part. of PASS[1] *v.*]

pasta /ˈpastə/ *n.* **1** a type of dough extruded or stamped into various shapes for cooking (e.g. lasagne, spaghetti), and used fresh or dried. **2** a dish made from this. [Italian, = PASTE]

paste /peɪst/ *n. & v.* ● *n.* **1** a moist fairly stiff mixture, esp. of powder and liquid. **2** a dough of flour with fat, water, etc., used in baking. **3** an adhesive of flour, water, etc., esp. for sticking paper and other light materials. **4** an easily spread preparation of ground meat, fish, etc. (*anchovy paste*). **5 a** a hard vitreous composition used in making imitation gems. **b** imitation jewellery made of this. **6** a mixture of clay, water, etc., used in making ceramic ware, esp. a mixture of low plasticity used in making porcelain. ● *v.tr.* **1** fasten or coat with paste. **2** *slang* **a** beat or thrash. **b** bomb or bombard heavily. □ **pasting** *n.* (esp. in sense 2 of *v.*). [Middle English via Old French and Late Latin *pasta* 'small square medicinal lozenge' from Greek *pastē*, from *pastos* 'sprinkled']

pasteboard /ˈpeɪs(t)bɔːd/ *n.* **1** a sheet of stiff material made by pasting together sheets of paper. **2** (*attrib.*) **a** flimsy, unsubstantial. **b** fake.

pastel /ˈpast(ə)l/ *n. & adj.* ● *n.* **1** a crayon consisting of powdered pigments bound with a gum solution. **2** a work of art in pastel. **3** a light and subdued shade of a colour. ● *adj.* of a light and subdued shade or colour. □ **pastelist** *n.* **pastellist** *n.* [French *pastel* or Italian *pastello*, diminutive of *pasta* PASTE]

pastern /ˈpast(ə)n/ *n.* **1** the part of a horse's foot between the fetlock and the hoof. **2** a corresponding part in other animals. [Middle English *pastron* from Old French *pasturon*, from *pasture* 'hobble', ultimately from Latin *pastorius* 'of a shepherd': see PASTOR]

paste-up *n.* a document prepared for copying etc. by combining and pasting various sections on a backing.

pasteurize /ˈpɑːstʃəraɪz, -stjə-, ˈpas-/ *v.tr.* (also **-ise**) subject (milk etc.) to the process of partial sterilization by heating. □ **pasteurization** /-ˈzeɪʃ(ə)n/ *n.* **pasteurizer** *n.* [named after L. *Pasteur*, French chemist d. 1895]

pasticcio /paˈstɪtʃəʊ/ *n.* (*pl.* **-os**) = PASTICHE. [Italian: see PASTICHE]

pastiche /paˈstiːʃ/ *n.* **1** a medley, esp. a picture or a musical composition, made up from or imitating various sources. **2** a literary or other work of art composed in the style of a well-known writer, artist, etc. [French from Italian *pasticcio*, ultimately from Late Latin *pasta* PASTE]

pastille /ˈpast(ə)l, -tɪl/ *n.* **1** a small sweet or lozenge. **2** a small roll of aromatic paste burnt as a fumigator etc. [French from Latin *pastillus* 'little loaf, lozenge', from *panis* 'loaf']

pastille-burner *n.* an ornamental ceramic container in which an aromatic pastille may be burnt.

pastime /ˈpɑːstʌɪm/ *n.* **1** a recreation or hobby. **2** a sport or game. [PASS[1] + TIME]

pastis /ˈpastɪs, paˈstiːs/ *n.* (*pl.* same) an aniseed-flavoured aperitif. [French]

past master *n.* **1** a person who is especially adept or expert in an activity, subject, etc. **2** a person who has been a master in a guild, Freemason's lodge, etc.

pastor /ˈpɑːstə/ *n. & v.* ● *n.* **1** a minister in charge of a church or a congregation. **2** a person exercising spiritual guidance. **3** a pink starling, *Sturnus roseus*, of E. Europe and Asia. ● *v.* **1** *tr.* **a** be minister of (a church). **b** have the spiritual care of (a congregation). **2** *intr.* be a pastor. □ **pastorship** *n.* [Middle English via Anglo-French & Old French *pastour* from Latin *pastor -oris* 'shepherd', from *pascere past-* 'feed, graze']

pastoral /ˈpɑːst(ə)r(ə)l/ *adj. & n.* ● *adj.* **1** of, relating to, or associated with shepherds or flocks and herds. **2** (of land) used for pasture. **3** (of a poem, picture, etc.) portraying country life, usu. in a romantic or idealized form. **4** of or appropriate to a pastor. **5** of or relating to a teacher's responsibility for the general well-being of pupils or students. ● *n.* **1** a pastoral poem, play, picture, etc. **2** a letter from a pastor (esp. a bishop) to the clergy or people. □ **pastoralism** *n.* **pastorality** /-ˈralɪti/ *n.* **pastorally** *adv.* [Middle English from Latin *pastoralis* (as PASTOR)]

pastorale /pastəˈrɑːl, -ˈrɑːli/ *n.* (*pl.* **pastorales** or **pastorali** /-liː/) **1** a slow instrumental composition in compound time, usu. with drone notes in the bass. **2** a simple musical play with a rural subject. [Italian (as PASTORAL)]

pastoralist /ˈpɑːst(ə)r(ə)lɪst/ *n. Austral.* a farmer of sheep or cattle.

pastoral staff *n.* a bishop's crosier.

pastoral theology *n.* theology that considers religious truth in relation to spiritual needs.

pastorate /ˈpɑːst(ə)rət/ *n.* **1** the office or tenure of a pastor. **2** a body of pastors.

past perfect *adj. & n.* = PLUPERFECT.

pastrami /paˈstrɑːmi/ *n.* seasoned smoked beef. [Yiddish]

pastry /ˈpeɪstri/ *n.* (*pl.* **-ies**) **1** a dough of flour, fat, and water, used as a base and covering for pies etc. **2 a** food, esp. cake, made wholly or partly of this. **b** a piece or item of this food. [PASTE, influenced by Old French *pastaierie*]

pastry-cook *n.* a cook who specializes in pastry, esp. for public sale.

pasturage /ˈpɑːstʃərɪdʒ/ *n.* **1** land for pasture. **2** the process of pasturing cattle etc. [Old French (as PASTURE)]

pasture /ˈpɑːstʃə/ *n. & v.* ● *n.* **1** land covered with grass etc. suitable for grazing animals, esp. cattle or sheep. **2** herbage for animals. ● *v.* **1** *tr.* put (animals) to graze in a pasture. **2** *intr.* & *tr.* (of animals) graze. [Middle English via Old French from Late Latin *pastura* (as PASTOR)]

pastureland /ˈpɑːstʃəland/ *n.* = PASTURE *n.* 1.

pasty[1] /ˈpasti/ *n.* (*pl.* **-ies**) esp. *Brit.* a pastry case with a usu. savoury filling, baked without a dish to shape it.

[Middle English from Old French *pasté*, ultimately from Late Latin *pasta* PASTE]

pasty[2] /ˈpeɪsti/ *adj.* (**pastier**, **pastiest**) **1** of or like or covered with paste. **2** unhealthily pale (esp. in complexion) (*pasty-faced*). □ **pastily** *adv.* **pastiness** *n.*

Pat /pat/ *n. Brit. slang* often *offens.* a nickname for an Irishman. [abbreviation of the name *Patrick*]

Pat. *abbr.* Patent.

pat[1] /pat/ *v. & n.* ● *v.* (**patted**, **patting**) **1** *tr.* strike gently with the hand or a flat surface. **2** *tr.* flatten or mould by patting. **3** *tr.* strike gently with the inner surface of the hand, esp. as a sign of affection, sympathy, or congratulation. **4** *intr.* (foll. by *on*, *upon*) beat lightly. ● *n.* **1** a light stroke or tap, esp. with the hand in affection etc. **2** the sound made by this. **3** a small mass (esp. of butter) formed by patting. □ **pat on the back** a gesture of approval or congratulation. **pat a person on the back** congratulate a person. [Middle English, probably imitative]

pat[2] /pat/ *adj. & adv.* ● *adj.* **1** known thoroughly and ready for any occasion. **2** apposite or opportune, esp. unconvincingly so (*gave a pat answer*). ● *adv.* **1** in a pat manner. **2** appositely, opportunely. □ **have off** (or **down**) **pat** know or have memorized perfectly. **stand pat** esp. *N. Amer.* **1** stick stubbornly to one's opinion or decision. **2** *Poker* retain one's hand as dealt; not draw other cards. □ **patly** *adv.* **patness** *n.* [16th c.: related to PAT[1]]

pat[3] /pat/ *n.* □ **on one's pat** *Austral. slang* on one's own. [*Pat Malone*, rhyming slang for *own*]

pat-a-cake *n.* a child's game with the patting of hands (the first words of a nursery rhyme).

patagium /patəˈdʒʌɪəm/ *n.* (*pl.* **patagia** /-ˈdʒʌɪə/) *Zool.* **1** the wing membrane of a bat or similar animal. **2** a scale covering the wing joint in moths and butterflies. [medieval Latin use of Latin *patagium*, from Greek *patageion* 'gold edging']

patball /ˈpatbɔːl/ *n. Brit.* **1** a simple game in which a ball is hit back and forth between two players. **2** *derog.* tennis, esp. when played at a slow pace.

patch /patʃ/ *n. & v.* ● *n.* **1** a piece of material or metal etc. used to mend a hole or as reinforcement. **2** a pad or shield worn over an eye or eye socket. **3** a dressing etc. put over a wound. **4** a large or irregular distinguishable area. **5** *Brit. colloq.* a period of time in terms of its characteristic quality (*went through a bad patch*). **6** a piece of ground. **7** *Brit. colloq.* an area assigned to or patrolled by an authorized person, esp. a police officer. **8** a number of plants growing in one place (*brier patch*). **9** a scrap or remnant. **10 a** a temporary electrical connection. **b** *Computing* a small piece of code inserted to correct or enhance a program. **11** *hist.* a small disc etc. of black silk attached to the face, worn esp. by women in the 17th–18th c. for adornment. **12** *Mil.* a piece of cloth on a uniform as the badge of a unit. ● *v.* **1** *tr.* (often foll. by *up*) repair with a patch or patches; put a patch or patches on. **2** *tr.* (of material) serve as a patch to. **3** *tr.* (often foll. by *up*) put together, esp. hastily or in a makeshift way. **4** *tr.* (foll. by *up*) settle (a quarrel etc.) esp. hastily or temporarily. **5** *tr. & intr.* (often foll. by *through*, *into*) connect or be connected by a temporary electrical, radio, etc. connection. **6** *tr. Computing* correct or enhance (a routine, program, etc.) by inserting a patch. □ **not a patch on** *Brit. colloq.* greatly inferior to. □ **patcher** *n.* [Middle English *pacche*, *patche*, perhaps variant of *peche*, from Old French *pieche* a dialect variant of *piece* PIECE]

patchboard /ˈpatʃbɔːd/ *n.* a board with electrical sockets linked to enable changeable permutations of connection.

patch cord *n.* an insulated lead with a plug at each end, for use with a patchboard.

patchouli /ˈpatʃʊli, pəˈtʃuːli/ *n.* **1** a strongly scented S. Asian shrub of the genus *Pogostemon*. **2** the perfume obtained from this. [Tamil *pacculi*]

patch panel *n.* = PATCHBOARD.

patch pocket *n.* one made of a piece of cloth sewn on a garment.

patch test *n.* a test for allergy by applying to the skin patches containing allergenic substances.

patchwork /ˈpatʃwəːk/ *n. & adj.* ● *n.* **1** needlework in which small pieces of cloth in different designs are sewn together to form one article such as a quilt. **2** a thing composed of various small pieces or fragments. ● *attrib.adj.* **1** composed of patchwork pieces. **2 a** resembling patchwork (*patchwork fields*). **b** pieced together with lack of uniformity (*patchwork political philosophy*).

patchy /ˈpatʃi/ *adj.* (**patchier**, **patchiest**) **1** uneven in quality. **2** having or existing in patches. □ **patchily** *adv.* **patchiness** *n.*

pate /peɪt/ *n. archaic* or *joc.* the head, esp. representing the seat of intellect. [Middle English: origin unknown]

pâte /pɑːt/ *n.* the paste of which porcelain is made. [French, = PASTE]

pâté /ˈpateɪ/ *n.* a rich paste or spread of mashed and spiced meat or fish etc. [French from Old French *pasté* (as PASTY[1])]

pâté de foie gras /də fwɑː ˈgrɑː/ *n.* a smooth rich paste of fatted goose liver. [French]

patella /pəˈtɛlə/ *n.* (*pl.* **patellae** /-liː/) the kneecap. □ **patellar** *adj.* **patellate** /-lət/ *adj.* [Latin, diminutive of *patina*: see PATEN]

paten /ˈpat(ə)n/ *n.* **1** a shallow dish used for the bread at the Eucharist. **2** a thin circular plate of metal. [Middle English, ultimately via Old French *patene* or Latin *patena*, *patina* 'shallow dish' from Greek *patanē* 'a plate']

patent /ˈpeɪt(ə)nt, ˈpat-/ *n., adj., & v.* ● *n.* **1** a government authority to an individual or organization conferring a right or title, esp. the sole right to make or use or sell some invention. **2** a document granting this authority. **3** an invention or process protected by it. ● *adj.* **1** /ˈpeɪt(ə)nt/ obvious, plain. **2** conferred or protected by patent. **3 a** made and marketed under a patent; proprietary. **b** to which one has a proprietary claim. **4** such as might be patented; ingenious, well-contrived. **5** (of an opening etc.) allowing free passage. ● *v.tr.* obtain a patent for (an invention). □ **patency** *n.* **patentable** *adj.* **patently** /ˈpeɪt(ə)ntli/ *adv.* (in sense 1 of *adj.*). [Middle English from Old French *patent* and Latin *patēre* 'lie open': the noun an ellipsis for LETTERS PATENT]

patentee /peɪt(ə)nˈtiː, pat-/ *n.* **1** a person who takes out or holds a patent. **2** a person for the time being entitled to the benefit of a patent.

patent leather *n.* leather with a glossy varnished surface.

patent medicine *n.* medicine made and marketed under a patent and available without prescription.

patent office *n.* an office from which patents are issued.

patentor /ˈpeɪt(ə)ntə/ *n.* a person or body that grants a patent.

Patent Roll *n.* (in the UK) a list of patents issued in a year.

pater /ˈpeɪtə/ *n. Brit. slang* father. [Latin]

■ **Usage** *Pater* is now only found in jocular or affected use.

paterfamilias /peɪtəfəˈmɪlɪas, patə-/ *n.* the male head of a family or household. [Latin, = father of the family]

paternal /pəˈtəːn(ə)l/ *adj.* **1** of or like or appropriate to a father. **2** fatherly. **3** related through the father. **4** (of a government etc.) limiting freedom and responsibility by well-meant regulations. □ **paternally** *adv.* [Late Latin *paternalis* from Latin *paternus*, from *pater* 'father']

paternalism /pəˈtəːn(ə)lɪz(ə)m/ *n.* the policy or practice of governing in a paternal way, or behaving paternally to one's associates or subordinates. □ **paternalist** *n.* **paternalistic** /-ˈlɪstɪk/ *adj.* **paternalistically** /-ˈlɪstɪk(ə)li/ *adv.*

paternity /pə'tə:nɪti/ *n.* **1** fatherhood. **2** one's paternal origin. **3** the source or authorship of a thing. [Middle English from Old French *paternité* or Late Latin *paternitas*]

paternity suit *n.* a lawsuit held to determine whether a certain man is the father of a certain child.

paternity test *n.* a blood test to determine whether a man may be or cannot be the father of a particular child.

paternoster /patə'nɒstə/ *n.* **1 a** the Lord's Prayer, esp. in Latin. **b** a rosary bead indicating that this is to be said. **2** a lift consisting of a series of linked doorless compartments moving continuously on a circular belt. [Old English from Latin *pater noster* 'our father', the first words of the prayer]

path /pɑ:θ/ *n.* (*pl.* **paths** /pɑ:ðz/) **1** a way or track laid down for walking or made by continual treading. **2** the line along which a person or thing moves (*flight path*). **3** a course of action or conduct. **4** a sequence of movements or operations taken by a system. ▫ **pathless** *adj.* [Old English *pæth*, from West Germanic]

-path /paθ/ *comb. form* forming nouns denoting: **1** a practitioner of curative treatment (*homoeopath*; *osteopath*). **2** a person who suffers from a disease (*psychopath*). [back-formation from -PATHY, or from Greek *-pathēs* '-sufferer' (as PATHOS)]

Pathan /pə'tɑ:n/ *n.* a member of a Pashto-speaking people inhabiting NW Pakistan and SE Afghanistan. [Hindi]

pathetic /pə'θɛtɪk/ *adj.* **1** arousing pity or sadness or contempt. **2** *colloq.* miserably inadequate. **3** *archaic* of the emotions. ▫ **pathetically** *adv.* [French *pathétique* via Late Latin *patheticus* from Greek *pathētikos* (as PATHOS)]

pathetic fallacy *n.* the attribution of human feelings and responses to inanimate things, esp. in art and literature.

pathfinder /'pɑ:θfʌɪndə/ *n.* **1** a person who explores new territory, investigates a new subject, etc. **2** an aircraft or its pilot sent ahead to locate and mark the target area for bombing.

patho- /'paθəʊ/ *comb. form* disease. [Greek *pathos* 'suffering': see PATHOS]

pathogen /'paθədʒ(ə)n/ *n.* an agent causing disease. ▫ **pathogenic** /-'dʒɛnɪk/ *adj.* **pathogenous** /-'θɒdʒɪnəs/ *adj.* [PATHO- + -GEN]

pathogenesis /paθə'dʒɛnɪsɪs/ *n.* (also **pathogeny** /pə'θɒdʒɪni/) the manner of development of a disease. ▫ **pathogenetic** /-dʒɪ'nɛtɪk/ *adj.*

pathological /paθə'lɒdʒɪk(ə)l/ *adj.* **1** of pathology. **2** of or caused by a physical or mental disorder (*a pathological fear of spiders*). ▫ **pathologically** *adv.*

pathology /pə'θɒlədʒi/ *n.* **1** the science of bodily diseases. **2** the symptoms of a disease. ▫ **pathologist** *n.* [French *pathologie* or modern Latin *pathologia* (as PATHO-, -LOGY)]

pathos /'peɪθɒs/ *n.* a quality in speech, writing, events, etc., that excites pity or sadness. [Greek *pathos* 'suffering', related to *paskhō* 'suffer', *penthos* 'grief']

pathway /'pɑ:θweɪ/ *n.* **1** a path or its course. **2** *Biochem.* etc. a sequence of reactions undergone in a living organism.

-pathy /pəθi/ *comb. form* forming nouns denoting: **1** curative treatment (*allopathy*; *homoeopathy*). **2** feeling (*telepathy*). [Greek *patheia* 'suffering']

patience /'peɪʃ(ə)ns/ *n.* **1** calm endurance of hardship, provocation, pain, delay, etc. **2** tolerant perseverance or forbearance. **3** the capacity for calm self-possessed waiting. **4** esp. *Brit.* a game for one player in which cards taken in random order have to be arranged in certain groups or sequences. ▫ **have no patience with 1** be unable to tolerate. **2** be irritated by. [Middle English via Old French from Latin *patientia* (as PATIENT)]

patient /'peɪʃ(ə)nt/ *adj.* & *n.* ● *adj.* having or showing patience. ● *n.* a person receiving or registered to receive medical treatment. ▫ **patiently** *adv.* [Middle English via Old French from Latin *patiens -entis*, pres. part. of *pati* 'suffer']

patina /'patɪnə/ *n.* (*pl.* **patinas**) **1** a film, usu. green, formed on the surface of old bronze. **2** a similar film on other surfaces. **3** a gloss produced by age on woodwork. ▫ **patinated** /-neɪtɪd/ *adj.* **patination** /-'neɪʃ(ə)n/ *n.* [Italian from Latin *patina* 'dish']

patio /'patɪəʊ/ *n.* (*pl.* **-os**) **1** a paved usu. roofless area adjoining and belonging to a house. **2** an inner court open to the sky in a Spanish or Spanish-American house. [Spanish]

patio rose *n.* a miniature floribunda rose.

patisserie /pə'ti:s(ə)ri/ *n.* **1** a shop where pastries are made and sold. **2** pastries collectively. [French *pâtisserie* from medieval Latin *pasticium* 'pastry', from *pasta* PASTE]

Patna rice /'patnə/ *n.* a variety of rice with long firm grains. [*Patna*, a district in India, where it was originally grown]

patois /'patwɑ:/ *n.* (*pl.* same /-wɑ:z/) the dialect of the common people in a region, differing fundamentally from the literary language. [French, = rough speech, perhaps from Old French *patoier* 'treat roughly' from *patte* 'paw']

patrial /'peɪtrɪəl/ *adj.* & *n. Brit. hist.* ● *adj.* having the right to live in the UK through the British birth of a parent or a grandparent. ● *n.* a person with this right. ▫ **patriality** /-'alɪti/ *n.* [obsolete French *patrial* or medieval Latin *patrialis*, via Latin *patria* 'fatherland' from *pater* 'father']

patriarch /'peɪtrɪɑ:k/ *n.* **1** a man who is the head of a family or tribe. **2** (often in *pl.*) *Bibl.* any of those regarded as fathers of the human race, esp. the sons of Jacob, or Abraham, Isaac, and Jacob, and their forefathers. **3** *Eccl.* **a** the title of a chief bishop, esp. those presiding over the Churches of Antioch, Alexandria, Constantinople, and (formerly) Rome; now also the title of the heads of certain autocephalous Orthodox Churches. **b** (in the Roman Catholic Church) a bishop ranking next above primates and metropolitans, and immediately below the Pope. **c** the head of a Uniate community. **4 a** the founder of an order, science, etc. **b** a venerable old man. **c** the oldest member of a group. ▫ **patriarchal** /-'ɑ:k(ə)l/ *adj.* **patriarchally** /-'ɑ:k(ə)li/ *adv.* [Middle English via Old French *patriarche* and ecclesiastical Latin *patriarcha* from Greek *patriarkhēs*, via *patria* 'family' from *patēr* 'father' + *-arkhēs* '-ruler']

patriarchate /'peɪtrɪɑ:kət/ *n.* **1** the office, see, or residence of an ecclesiastical patriarch. **2** the rank of a tribal patriarch. [medieval Latin *patriarchatus* (as PATRIARCH)]

patriarchy /'peɪtrɪɑ:ki/ *n.* (*pl.* **-ies**) a form of social organization or government etc. in which a man or men rule and descent is reckoned through the male line. ▫ **patriarchism** *n.* [medieval Latin *patriarchia* from Greek *patriarkhia* (as PATRIARCH)]

patrician /pə'trɪʃ(ə)n/ *n.* & *adj.* ● *n.* **1** *hist.* a member of the ancient Roman nobility (cf. PLEBEIAN *n.* 1). **2** *hist.* a nobleman in some Italian republics. **3** an aristocrat. **4** *N. Amer.* a refined or well-bred person. ● *adj.* **1** noble, aristocratic. **2** *hist.* of the ancient Roman nobility. **3** *N. Amer.* refined, well-bred. [Middle English via Old French *patricien* from Latin *patricius* 'having a noble father', from *pater patris* 'father']

patriciate /pə'trɪʃɪət/ *n.* **1** a patrician order; an aristocracy. **2** the rank of patrician. [Latin *patriciatus* (as PATRICIAN)]

patricide /'patrɪsʌɪd/ *n.* **1** the killing of one's father. **2** a person who commits patricide. ▫ **patricidal** /-'sʌɪd(ə)l/ *adj.* [Late Latin *patricida*, *patricidium*, alteration of Latin *parricida*, *parricidium* (see PARRICIDE) by association with *pater* 'father']

■ **Usage** See Usage Note at PARRICIDE.

patrilineal /patrɪˈlɪnɪəl/ *adj.* of or relating to, or based on kinship with, the father or descent through the male line. [Latin *pater patris* 'father' + LINEAL]

patrimony /ˈpatrɪməni/ *n.* (*pl.* **-ies**) **1** property inherited from one's father or ancestor. **2** a heritage. **3** the endowment of a Church etc. □ **patrimonial** /-ˈməʊnɪəl/ *adj.* [Middle English *patrimoigne* via Old French *patrimoine* from Latin *patrimonium*, from *pater patris* 'father']

patriot /ˈpatrɪət, ˈpeɪt-/ *n.* a person who is devoted to and ready to support or defend his or her country. □ **patriotic** /-ˈɒtɪk/ *adj.* **patriotically** /-ˈɒtɪk(ə)li/ *adv.* **patriotism** *n.* [French *patriote* via Late Latin *patriota* from Greek *patriōtēs*, via *patrios* 'of one's fathers' from *patris* 'fatherland']

patristic /pəˈtrɪstɪk/ *adj.* of the early Christian theologians or their writings. □ **patristics** *n.pl.* (usu. treated as *sing.*). [German *patristisch* from Latin *pater patris* 'father']

patrol /pəˈtrəʊl/ *n.* & *v.* ● *n.* **1** the act of walking or travelling around an area, esp. at regular intervals, in order to protect or supervise it. **2** one or more persons or vehicles assigned or sent out on patrol, esp. a detachment of guards, police, etc. **3 a** a detachment of troops sent out to reconnoitre. **b** such reconnaissance. **4** a routine operational voyage of a ship or aircraft. **5** a routine monitoring of astronomical or other phenomena. **6** *Brit.* an official controlling traffic where children cross the road. **7** a unit of six to eight Scouts or Guides. ● *v.* (**patrolled**, **patrolling**) **1** *tr.* carry out a patrol of. **2** *intr.* act as a patrol. □ **patroller** *n.* [French *patrouiller* 'paddle in mud' from *patte* 'paw': the noun via German *Patrolle* from French *patrouille*]

patrol car *n.* a police car used in patrolling roads and streets.

patrolman /pəˈtrəʊlmən/ *n.* (*pl.* **-men**) *US* a police officer of the lowest rank.

patrology /pəˈtrɒlədʒi/ *n.* (*pl.* **-ies**) **1** the study of the writings of the Fathers of the Church. **2** a collection of such writings. □ **patrological** /patrəˈlɒdʒɪk(ə)l/ *adj.* **patrologist** *n.* [Greek *patēr patros* 'father']

patrol wagon *n.* esp. *N. Amer.* a police van for transporting prisoners.

patron /ˈpeɪtr(ə)n/ *n.* (*fem.* **patroness** /-nɪs/) **1** a person who gives financial or other support to a person, cause, work of art, etc., esp. one who buys works of art, or takes an honorary position in a charity etc. **2** a usu. regular customer of a shop etc. **3** *Rom. Antiq.* **a** the former owner of a freed slave. **b** the protector of a client. **4** *Brit.* a person or institution with the right to present a member of the clergy to a benefice. [Middle English via Old French from Latin *patronus* 'protector of clients, defender', from *pater patris* 'father']

patronage /ˈpatr(ə)nɪdʒ, ˈpeɪt-/ *n.* **1** the support, promotion, or encouragement given by a patron. **2** the control of appointments to office, privileges, etc. **3** a patronizing or condescending manner. **4** *Rom. Antiq.* the rights and duties or position of a patron. **5** a customer's support for a shop etc. [Middle English from Old French (as PATRON)]

patronal /pəˈtrəʊn(ə)l/ *adj.* of or relating to a patron saint (*the patronal festival*). [French *patronal* or Late Latin *patronalis* (as PATRON)]

patronize /ˈpatrənʌɪz/ *v.tr.* (also **-ise**) **1** treat condescendingly. **2** act as a patron towards (a person, cause, artist, etc.); support; encourage. **3** frequent (a shop etc.) as a customer. □ **patronization** /-ˈzeɪʃ(ə)n/ *n.* **patronizer** *n.* **patronizing** *adj.* **patronizingly** *adv.* [obsolete French *patroniser* or medieval Latin *patronizare* (as PATRON)]

patron saint *n.* the protecting or guiding saint of a person, place, etc.

patronymic /patrəˈnɪmɪk/ *n.* & *adj.* ● *n.* a name derived from the name of a father or ancestor, e.g. *Johnson, O'Brien, Ivanovich.* ● *adj.* (of a name) so derived. [Late Latin *patronymicus* from Greek *patrōnumikos*, via *patrōnumos* from *patēr patros* 'father' + *onuma, onoma* 'name']

patroon /pəˈtruːn/ *n.* *US hist.* a landowner with manorial privileges under the Dutch governments of New York and New Jersey. [Dutch, = PATRON]

patsy /ˈpatsi/ *n.* (*pl.* **-ies**) esp. *N. Amer. slang* a person who is deceived, ridiculed, tricked, etc. [19th c.: origin unknown]

pattée /ˈpateɪ, -ti/ *adj.* (of a cross) having almost triangular arms becoming very broad at the ends so as to form a square. [French, from *patte* 'paw']

patten /ˈpat(ə)n/ *n.* *hist.* a shoe or clog with a raised sole or set on an iron ring, for walking in mud etc. [Middle English from Old French *patin*, from *patte* 'paw']

patter[1] /ˈpatə/ *v.* & *n.* ● *v.* **1** *intr.* make a rapid succession of taps, as of rain on a window pane. **2** *intr.* run with quick short steps. **3** *tr.* cause (water etc.) to patter. ● *n.* a rapid succession of taps, short light steps, etc. [PAT[1]]

patter[2] /ˈpatə/ *n.* & *v.* ● *n.* **1 a** the rapid speech used by a comedian or introduced into a song. **b** the words of a comic song. **2** the words used by a person selling or promoting a product; a sales pitch. **3** the special language or jargon of a profession, class, etc. ● *v.* **1** *tr.* repeat (prayers etc.) in a rapid mechanical way. **2** *intr.* talk glibly or mechanically. [Middle English, from *pater* = PATERNOSTER]

pattern /ˈpat(ə)n/ *n.* & *v.* ● *n.* **1** a repeated decorative design on wallpaper, cloth, a carpet, etc. **2** a regular or logical form, order, or arrangement of parts (*behaviour pattern; the pattern of one's daily life*). **3** a model or design, e.g. of a garment, from which copies can be made. **4** an example of excellence; an ideal; a model (*a pattern of elegance*). **5** a wooden or metal figure from which a mould is made for a casting. **6** a sample (of cloth, wallpaper, etc.). **7** the marks made by shots, bombs, etc. on a target or target area. **8** a random combination of shapes or colours. ● *v.tr.* **1** (usu. foll. by *after, on*) model (a thing) on a design etc. **2** decorate with a pattern. [Middle English *patron* (see PATRON): differentiated in sense and spelling since the 16th–17th c.]

pattern bombing *n.* bombing over a large area, not on a single target.

patty /ˈpati/ *n.* (*pl.* **-ies**) **1** a little pie or pastry. **2** a small flat cake of minced meat etc. **3** esp. *N. Amer.* a small round flat sweet. [French *pâté* PASTY[1]]

pattypan /ˈpatɪpan/ *n.* a pan for baking a patty.

patulous /ˈpatjʊləs/ *adj.* **1** *Bot.* or *literary* (of branches etc.) spreading. **2** *formal* open; expanded. [Latin *patulus* from *patēre* 'be open']

patzer /ˈpɑːtsə, ˈpat-/ *n.* a poor player at chess. [perhaps related to German *patzen* 'bungle']

paua /ˈpɑːwə, ˈpaʊə/ *n.* **1** a large edible New Zealand shellfish of the genus *Haliotis*. **2** its ornamental shell. **3** a fish-hook made from this. [Maori]

paucity /ˈpɔːsɪti/ *n.* smallness of number or quantity. [Middle English from Old French *paucité*, or from Latin *paucitas* from *paucus* 'few']

Pauli exclusion principle /ˈpaʊli/ *n.* *Physics* the assertion that no two fermions can have the same quantum number. [named after W. *Pauli*, Austrian physicist d. 1958]

Pauline /ˈpɔːlʌɪn/ *adj.* of or relating to St Paul (*the Pauline Epistles*). [Middle English via medieval Latin *Paulinus* from Latin *Paulus* 'Paul']

Paul Jones /pɔːl ˈdʒəʊnz/ *n.* a ballroom dance in which partners are exchanged according to a pattern. [the name of an American naval officer d. 1792]

paulownia /pɔːˈləʊnɪə, -ˈlɒvnɪə/ *n.* any Chinese tree of the genus *Paulownia*, with fragrant purple flowers. [named after Anna *Paulovna*, Russian princess d. 1865]

paunch /pɔːn(t)ʃ/ *n.* & *v.* ● *n.* **1** the belly or stomach, esp. when protruding. **2** *Naut.* a thick strong mat used to give protection from chafing, esp. on a mast or spar.

● *v.tr.* disembowel (an animal). □ **paunchy** *adj.* (**paunchier, paunchiest**). **paunchiness** *n.* [Middle English from Anglo-French *pa(u)nche*, Old Northern French *panche*, ultimately from Latin *pantex panticis* 'bowels']

pauper /'pɔːpə/ *n.* **1** a person without means; a beggar. **2** *hist.* a recipient of poor-law relief. **3** *Law* a person who may sue *in forma pauperis*. □ **pauperdom** /-dəm/ *n.* **pauperism** /-rɪz(ə)m/ *n.* **pauperize** *v.tr.* (also **-ise**). **pauperization** /-'zeɪʃ(ə)n/ *n.* [Latin, = poor]

pause /pɔːz/ *n.* & *v.* ● *n.* **1** an interval of inaction, esp. when due to hesitation; a temporary stop. **2** a break in speaking or reading; a silence. **3** *Mus.* a mark (⌒) over a note or rest that is to be lengthened by an unspecified amount. **4** a control allowing the interruption of the operation of a tape recorder etc. ● *v.intr.* **1** make a pause; wait. **2** (usu. foll. by *upon*) linger over (a word etc.). □ **give pause to** cause (a person) to hesitate. [Middle English via Old French *pause* or Latin *pausa* from Greek *pausis*, from *pauō* 'stop']

pavage /'peɪvɪdʒ/ *n.* **1** paving. **2** *hist.* a tax or toll towards the paving of streets. [Middle English from Old French, from *paver* PAVE]

pavane /pə'van, -'vɑːn/ *n.* (also **pavan** /'pav(ə)n/) **1** *hist.* a stately dance in slow duple time, performed in elaborate clothing. **2** the music for this. [French *pavane* from Spanish *pavana*, perhaps from *pavon* 'peacock']

pave /peɪv/ *v.tr.* **1 a** cover (a street, floor, etc.) with asphalt, stone, etc. **b** cover or strew (a floor etc.) with anything (*paved with flowers*). **2** prepare (*paved the way for her arrival*). □ **paver** *n.* **paving** *n.* **pavior** /'peɪvɪə/ *n.* (also **paviour**). [Middle English from Old French *paver*, back-formation (as PAVEMENT)]

pavé /'paveɪ, French pave/ *n.* **1** a paved street, road, or path. **2** a setting of jewels placed closely together. [French, past part. of *paver*: see PAVE]

pavement /'peɪvm(ə)nt/ *n.* **1** *Brit.* a paved path for pedestrians at the side of and a little higher than a road. **2** the covering of a street, floor, etc., made of tiles, wooden blocks, asphalt, and esp. of rectangular stones. **3** *N. Amer.* a roadway. **4** *Zool.* a pavement-like formation of close-set teeth, scales, etc. [Middle English via Old French from Latin *pavimentum*, from *pavire* 'beat, ram']

pavement artist *n. Brit.* an artist who draws with coloured chalks on paving stones or paper laid on a pavement, hoping to be given money by passers-by.

pavilion /pə'vɪljən/ *n.* & *v.* ● *n.* **1** *Brit.* a building at a cricket or other sports ground used for changing, refreshments, etc. **2** a summer house or other decorative building in a garden. **3** a tent, esp. a large one with crenellated decorations at a show, fair, etc. **4** a building used for entertainments. **5** a temporary stand at an exhibition. **6** a detached building at a hospital. **7** a usu. highly decorated projecting subdivision of a building. **8** the part of a cut gemstone below the girdle. ● *v.tr.* enclose in or provide with a pavilion. [Middle English via Old French *pavillon* from Latin *papilio -onis* 'butterfly, tent']

paving stone *n.* a large flat usu. rectangular piece of stone etc. for paving.

pavior, paviour see PAVE.

pavlova /'pavləvə, pav'ləʊvə/ *n.* a meringue cake with cream and fruit. [named after A. *Pavlova*, Russian ballerina d. 1931]

Pavlovian /pav'ləʊvɪən/ *adj.* of or relating to I. P. Pavlov, Russian physiologist d. 1936, or his work, esp. on conditioned reflexes.

pavonine /'pavənʌɪn/ *adj.* of or like a peacock. [Latin *pavoninus* from *pavo -onis* 'peacock']

paw /pɔː/ *n.* & *v.* ● *n.* **1** a foot of an animal having claws or nails. **2** *colloq.* a person's hand. ● *v.* **1** *tr.* strike or scrape with a paw or foot. **2** *intr.* scrape the ground with a paw or hoof. **3** *tr. colloq.* fondle awkwardly or indecently. [Middle English *pawe, powe* from Old French *poue* etc., ultimately from Frankish]

pawky /'pɔːki/ *adj.* (**pawkier, pawkiest**) *Sc.* & *dial.* **1** drily humorous. **2** shrewd. □ **pawkily** *adv.* **pawkiness** *n.* [Scots & northern English dialect *pawk* 'trick', of unknown origin]

pawl /pɔːl/ *n.* & *v.* ● *n.* **1** a lever with a catch for the teeth of a wheel or bar. **2** *Naut.* a short bar used to lock a capstan, windlass, etc., to prevent it from recoiling. ● *v.tr.* secure (a capstan etc.) with a pawl. [perhaps from Low German & Dutch *pal*, related to *pal* 'fixed']

pawn[1] /pɔːn/ *n.* **1** *Chess* a piece of the smallest size and value. **2** a person used by others for their own purposes. [Middle English via Anglo-French *poun*, Old French *peon* and medieval Latin *pedo -onis* 'foot soldier' from Latin *pes pedis* 'foot': cf. PEON]

pawn[2] /pɔːn/ *v.* & *n.* ● *v.tr.* **1** deposit an object, esp. with a pawnbroker, as security for money lent. **2** pledge or wager (one's life, honour, word, etc.). ● *n.* an object left as security for money etc. lent. □ **in** (or **at**) **pawn** (of an object etc.) held as security. [Middle English from Old French *pan, pand, pant*, 'pledge, security', from West Germanic]

pawnbroker /'pɔːnbrəʊkə/ *n.* a person who lends money at interest on the security of personal property pawned. □ **pawnbroking** *n.*

pawnshop /'pɔːnʃɒp/ *n.* a shop where pawnbroking is conducted.

pawpaw /'pɔːpɔː/ *n.* (also **papaw** /pə'pɔː/) **1** (also **papaya** /pə'pʌɪə/) **a** an elongated melon-shaped fruit with edible orange flesh and small black seeds. **b** a tropical tree, *Carica papaya*, bearing this and producing a milky sap from which papain is obtained. **2** a N. American tree, *Asimina triloba*, with purple flowers and edible fruit. [earlier *papay(a)* from Spanish & Portuguese *papaya*, of Carib origin]

PAX *abbr.* esp. *Brit.* private automatic (telephone) exchange.

pax /paks/ *n.* **1** the kiss of peace. **2** (as *int.*) *Brit. slang* a call for a truce (used esp. by schoolchildren). [Middle English from Latin, = peace]

pay[1] /peɪ/ *v.* & *n.* ● *v.tr.* (*past* and *past part.* **paid** /peɪd/) **1** (also *absol.*) give (a person etc.) what is due for services done, goods received, debts incurred, etc. (*paid him in full; I assure you I have paid*). **2 a** give (a usu. specified amount) for work done, a debt, a ransom, etc. (*they pay £6 an hour*). **b** (foll. by *to*) hand over the amount of (a debt, wages, recompense, etc.) to (*paid the money to the assistant*). **3 a** give, bestow, or express (attention, respect, a compliment, etc.) (*paid them no heed*). **b** make (a visit, a call, etc.) (*paid a visit to their uncle*). **4** (also *absol.*) (of a business, undertaking, attitude, etc.) be profitable or advantageous to (a person etc.). **5** reward or punish (*can never pay you for what you have done for us; I shall pay you for that*). **6** (usu. as **paid** *adj.*) recompense (work, time, etc.) (*paid holiday*). **7** (usu. foll. by *out, away*) let out (a rope) by slackening it. ● *n.* wages; payment. □ **in the pay of** employed by. **pay back 1** return (money). **2** take revenge on (a person). **pay dearly** (usu. foll. by *for*) **1** obtain at a high cost, great effort, etc. **2** suffer for a wrongdoing etc. **pay one's dues** esp. *US* **1** fulfil one's obligations. **2** undergo hardship to succeed or gain experience. **pay for 1** hand over the price of. **2** bear the cost of. **3** suffer or be punished for (a fault etc.). **pay in** pay (money) into a bank account. **pay its** (or **one's**) **way** cover costs; not be indebted. **pay one's last respects** show respect towards a dead person by attending the funeral. **pay off 1** dismiss (workers) with a final payment. **2** *colloq.* yield good results; succeed. **3** pay (a debt) in full. **4** (of a ship) turn to leeward through the movement of the helm. **pay out 1** pay (money) from funds under one's control; spend. **2** punish, take revenge on (a person). **pay the piper and call the tune** pay for, and therefore have control over, a proceeding. **pay one's respects** make a polite visit. **pay through the nose** *colloq.* pay much more than a fair price. **pay up** pay the full amount, or the full amount of. **put paid to** *Brit. colloq.* **1** deal effectively with (a person). **2** terminate (hopes etc.). □ **payee** /peɪˈiː/ *n.* **payer** *n.* [Middle English via Old French *paie, payer* from Latin *pacare* 'appease', from *pax pacis* 'peace']

pay[2] /peɪ/ *v.tr.* (*past* and *past part.* **payed**) *Naut.* smear (a ship) with pitch, tar, etc. as a defence against wet. [Old French *peier* from Latin *picare*, from *pix picis* PITCH[2]]

payable /ˈpeɪəb(ə)l/ *adj. & n.* ● *adj.* **1** that must be paid; due (*payable in April*). **2** that may be paid. **3** (of a mine etc.) profitable. ● *n.* (in *pl.*) debts owed by a business; liabilities.

pay-as-you-earn *n.* (often *attrib.*) *Brit.* the deduction of income tax from wages at source.

pay-as-you-go *n.* (often *attrib.*) a system or the practice of paying debts and meeting costs as they arise.

payback /ˈpeɪbak/ *n.* **1** a financial return; a reward. **2** the profit from an investment etc., esp. one equal to the initial outlay.

payback period *n.* the length of time required for an investment to pay for itself in terms of profits or savings.

pay bed *n. Brit.* a hospital bed for private patients.

pay claim *n. Brit.* a demand for an increase in pay, esp. by a trade union.

pay day *n.* a day on which payment, esp. of wages, is made or expected to be made.

pay dirt *n. US* **1** *Mineral.* ground worth working for ore. **2** a financially promising situation.

PAYE *abbr. Brit.* pay-as-you-earn.

pay envelope *n. N. Amer.* = PAY PACKET.

paying guest *n.* a boarder.

payload /ˈpeɪləʊd/ *n.* **1** the part of an aircraft's load from which revenue is derived. **2 a** the explosive warhead carried by an aircraft or rocket. **b** the instruments etc. carried by a spaceship. **3** the goods carried by a road vehicle.

paymaster /ˈpeɪmɑːstə/ *n.* **1** an official who pays troops, workers, etc. **2** a person, organization, etc., to whom another owes duty or loyalty because of payment given. **3** (in full **Paymaster General**) *Brit.* the minister at the head of the Treasury department responsible for payments.

payment /ˈpeɪm(ə)nt/ *n.* **1** the act or an instance of paying. **2** an amount paid. **3** reward, recompense. [Middle English from Old French *paiement* (as PAY[1])]

paynim /ˈpeɪnɪm/ *n. archaic* **1** a pagan. **2** a non-Christian, esp. a Muslim. [Middle English via Old French *pai(e)nime* from ecclesiastical Latin *paganismus* 'heathenism' (as PAGAN)]

pay-off *n. colloq.* **1** an act of payment, esp. a bribe. **2** return on investment or on a bet. **3** a final outcome.

payola /peɪˈəʊlə/ *n.* esp. *US* **1** a bribe offered in return for unofficial promotion of a product etc. in the media. **2** the practice of such bribery. [PAY[1] + *-ola* as in *Victrola*, the name of a make of gramophone]

pay-out *n.* an instance of money being paid out, esp. compensation or dividends.

pay packet *n. Brit.* a packet or envelope containing an employee's wages.

payphone /ˈpeɪfəʊn/*n.* a coin box telephone.

payroll /ˈpeɪrəʊl/ *n.* a list of employees receiving regular pay.

paysage /peɪˈzɑːʒ, French peizaʒ/ *n.* **1** a rural scene; a landscape. **2** landscape painting. □ **paysagist** /ˈpeɪzədʒɪst/ *n.* [French from *pays* 'country': see PEASANT]

payslip /ˈpeɪslɪp/ *n.* a note given to an employee when paid detailing the amount of pay, and of tax and insurance deducted.

pay station *n. US* = PAYPHONE.

Pb *symb. Chem.* the element lead. [Latin *plumbum*]

PBX *abbr.* private branch exchange (private telephone switchboard).

PC *abbr.* **1** police constable. **2** Privy Counsellor. **3** personal computer. **4** politically correct; political correctness.

p.c. *abbr.* **1** per cent. **2** postcard.

PCAS /ˈpiːkas/ *abbr. hist.* (in the UK) Polytechnics Central Admissions System (incorporated into UCAS in the 1993–4 academic year).

PCB *abbr.* **1** *Computing* printed circuit board. **2** *Chem.* polychlorinated biphenyl, any of several toxic aromatic compounds containing two benzene molecules in which hydrogens have been replaced by chlorine atoms, formed as waste in industrial processes.

PCM *abbr.* pulse code modulation.

PCMCIA *abbr. Computing* Personal Computer Memory Card International Association, denoting a standard specification for memory cards and interfaces in small portable computers.

PCP *abbr.* **1** = PHENCYCLIDINE. **2** *Med.* pneumocystis carinii pneumonia, a fatal lung infection esp. of immunodeficient patients.

pct. *abbr. US* per cent.

PD *abbr. US* Police Department.

Pd *symb. Chem.* the element palladium.

pd. *abbr.* paid.

p.d.q. *abbr. colloq.* pretty damn quick.

PDSA *abbr. Brit.* People's Dispensary for Sick Animals.

PDT *abbr.* Pacific Daylight Time (one hour ahead of Pacific Standard Time).

PE *abbr.* physical education.

p/e *abbr.* market price/earnings (ratio per share).

pea /piː/ *n.* **1 a** a hardy climbing plant, *Pisum sativum* (family Leguminosae), with seeds growing in pods and used for food. **b** its seed. **2** any of several similar leguminous plants (*sweet pea*; *chickpea*). [back-formation from PEASE (taken as pl.: cf. CHERRY)]

pea-brain *n. colloq.* a stupid or dim-witted person. □ **pea-brained** *adj.*

peace /piːs/ *n.* **1 a** quiet; tranquillity (*needs peace to work well*). **b** mental calm; serenity (*peace of mind*). **2 a** (often *attrib.*) freedom from or the cessation of war (*peace talks*). **b** (esp. **Peace**) a treaty of peace between states etc. at war. **3** freedom from civil disorder. **4** *Eccl.* a ritual liturgical greeting. **5** (**the peace**) (also *Brit.* **the queen's** or **king's peace**) peace existing within a realm; civil order. □ **at peace 1** in a state of friendliness. **2** serene. **3** *euphem.* dead. **hold one's peace** keep silence. **keep the peace** prevent, or refrain from, strife. **make one's peace** (often foll. by *with*) re-establish friendly relations. **make peace** bring about peace; reconcile. [Middle English via Anglo-French *pes*, Old French *pais* from Latin *pax pacis*]

peaceable /ˈpiːsəb(ə)l/ *adj.* **1** disposed to peace; unwarlike. **2** free from disturbance; peaceful. □ **peaceableness** *n.* **peaceably** *adv.* [Middle English via Old French *peisible, plaisible* and Late Latin *placibilis* 'pleasing' from Latin *placēre* 'please']

Peace Corps *n. US* an organization sending young people to work as volunteers in developing countries.

peace dividend *n.* public money which becomes available when spending on defence is reduced.

peaceful /ˈpiːsfʊl, -f(ə)l/ *adj.* **1** characterized by peace; tranquil. **2** not violating or infringing peace (*peaceful coexistence*). **3** belonging to a state of peace. □ **peacefully** *adv.* **peacefulness** *n.*

peacekeeper /ˈpiːskiːpə/ *n.* a person or organization that keeps or maintains peace. □ **peacekeeping** *n. & attrib.adj.*

peacemaker /ˈpiːsmeɪkə/ *n.* a person who brings about peace. □ **peacemaking** *n. & adj.*

peace-offering *n.* **1** a propitiatory or conciliatory gift. **2** *Bibl.* an offering presented as a thanksgiving to God.

peace pipe *n.* a tobacco pipe as a token of peace among N. American Indians.

peacetime /ˈpiːstʌɪm/ *n.* a period when a country is not at war.

peach[1] /piːtʃ/ *n. & adj.* ● *n.* **1 a** a round juicy stone fruit with downy cream or yellow skin flushed with red. **b** (in full **peach tree**) the tree, *Prunus persica*, bearing it. **2** the yellowish-pink colour of a peach. **3**

colloq. **a** a person or thing of superlative quality. **b** an attractive young woman. ● *adj.* of a yellowish-pink colour. □ **peaches and cream** (of a complexion) creamy skin with downy pink cheeks. □ **peachy** *adj.* (**peachier, peachiest**). **peachiness** *n.* [Middle English via Old French *peche, pesche,* and medieval Latin *persica* from Latin *persicum* (*malum*), literally 'Persian apple']

peach[2] /piːtʃ/ *v.* esp. *Brit.* **1** *intr.* (usu. foll. by *against, on*) *colloq.* turn informer; inform. **2** *tr. archaic* inform against. [Middle English from *appeach,* from Anglo-French *enpecher,* Old French *empechier* IMPEACH]

peach-bloom *n.* an oriental porcelain-glaze of reddish pink, usu. with green markings.

peach-blow *n.* & *adj.* ● *n.* **1** a delicate purplish-pink colour. **2 a** = PEACH-BLOOM. **b** a type of glass of similar colour. ● *adj.* of a purplish-pink colour.

pea-chick /ˈpiːtʃɪk/ *n.* a young peafowl. [formed as PEACOCK + CHICK[1]]

peach Melba *n.* a dish of ice cream and peaches with liqueur or sauce. [named after Nellie *Melba* (see MELBA SAUCE)]

peacock /ˈpiːkɒk/ *n.* **1** a male peafowl, having brilliant plumage and a tail (with eyelike markings) that can be expanded erect in display like a fan. **2** an ostentatious strutting person. [Middle English *pecock,* from Old English *pēa* (from Latin *pavo*) + COCK[1]]

peacock blue *n.* & *adj.* ● *n.* the lustrous greenish blue of a peacock's neck. ● *adj.* (hyphenated when *attrib.*) of this colour.

peacock butterfly *n.* a butterfly, *Inachis io,* with eyelike markings on its wings.

peafowl /ˈpiːfaʊl/ *n.* a pheasant of the genus *Pavo,* a peacock or peahen.

pea green *n.* & *adj.* ● *n.* a bright green colour. ● *adj.* (hyphenated when *attrib.*) of this colour.

peahen /ˈpiːhɛn/ *n.* a female peafowl.

pea-jacket /ˈpiːdʒakɪt/ *n.* a sailor's short double-breasted overcoat of coarse woollen cloth. [probably from Dutch *pijjakker,* from *pij* 'coat of coarse cloth' + *jekker* 'jacket': assimilated to JACKET]

peak[1] /piːk/ *n., v.,* & *adj.* ● *n.* **1** a projecting usu. pointed part, esp.: **a** the pointed top of a mountain. **b** a mountain with a peak. **c** a stiff brim at the front of a cap. **d** a pointed beard. **e** the narrow part of a ship's hold at the bow or stern (*forepeak; after-peak*). **f** *Naut.* the upper outer corner of a sail extended by a gaff. **2 a** the highest point in a curve (*on the peak of the wave*). **b** the time of greatest success (in a career etc.). **c** the highest point on a graph etc. ● *v.intr.* reach the highest value, quality, etc. (*output peaked in September*). ● *attrib.adj.* of or at the highest value, quality, frequency, rate, level, etc. (*peak shopping times*). □ **peaked** *adj.* **peaky** *adj.* **peakiness** *n.* [probably a back-formation from *peaked,* variant of dialect *picked* 'pointed' (PICK[2])]

peak[2] /piːk/ *v.intr.* **1** waste away. **2** (as **peaked** *adj.*) sharp-featured; pinched; sickly-looking. [Middle English: origin unknown]

peak hour *n.* esp. *Brit.* the time of the most intense traffic etc.

peak load *n.* the maximum of electric power demand etc.

peaky /ˈpiːki/ *adj.* (**peakier, peakiest**) **1** sickly; puny. **2** white-faced.

peal[1] /piːl/ *n.* & *v.* ● *n.* **1 a** the loud ringing of a bell or bells, esp. a series of changes. **b** a set of bells. **2** a loud repeated sound, esp. of thunder, laughter, etc. ● *v.* **1** *intr.* sound forth in a peal. **2** *tr.* utter sonorously. **3** *tr.* ring (bells) in peals. [Middle English *pele,* from *apele* APPEAL]

peal[2] /piːl/ *n. Brit.* a salmon grilse. [16th c.: origin unknown]

pean /piːn/ *n. Heraldry* fur represented as sable spotted with or (see OR[2]). [16th c.: origin unknown]

peanut /ˈpiːnʌt/ *n.* **1** a leguminous plant, *Arachis hypogaea,* bearing pods that ripen underground and contain seeds used as food and yielding oil. **2** the seed of this plant. **3** (in *pl.*) *colloq.* a paltry or trivial thing or amount, esp. of money.

peanut butter *n.* a paste of ground roasted peanuts.

pear /pɛː/ *n.* **1** a yellowish or brownish-green fleshy fruit, tapering towards the stalk. **2** (in full **pear tree**) any of various trees of the genus *Pyrus* bearing it, esp. *P. communis.* [Old English *pere, peru,* ultimately from Latin *pirum*]

pear drop *n.* a small sweet with the shape of a pear.

pearl[1] /pəːl/ *n., adj.,* & *v.* ● *n.* **1 a** (often *attrib.*) a usu. white or bluish-grey hard mass formed within the shell of a pearl-oyster or other bivalve mollusc, highly prized as a gem for its lustre (*pearl necklace*). **b** an imitation of this. **c** (in *pl.*) a necklace of pearls. **d** (usu. *attrib.*) = MOTHER-OF-PEARL. **2** a precious thing; the finest example. **3** anything resembling a pearl, e.g. a dewdrop, tear, etc. **4** a bluish-grey colour. ● *adj.* of the colour of pearl; bluish grey. ● *v.* **1** *tr. poet.* **a** sprinkle with pearly drops. **b** make pearly in colour etc. **2** *tr.* reduce (barley etc.) to small rounded grains. **3** *intr.* fish for pearl-oysters. **4** *intr. poet.* form pearl-like drops. □ **cast pearls before swine** offer a treasure to a person unable to appreciate it. □ **pearler** *n.* [Middle English from Old French *perle,* probably from Latin *perna* 'leg' (applied to leg-of-mutton-shaped bivalve)]

pearl[2] /pəːl/ *n. Brit.* = PICOT. [variant of PURL[1]]

pearl ash *n.* commercial potassium carbonate.

pearl barley *n.* barley reduced to small round grains by grinding.

pearl bulb *n. Brit.* a translucent electric light bulb.

pearl button *n.* a button made of mother-of-pearl or an imitation of it.

pearl-diver *n.* a person who dives for pearl-oysters.

pearled /pəːld/ *adj.* **1** adorned with pearls. **2** formed into pearl-like drops or grains. **3** pearl-coloured.

pearlescent /pəːˈlɛs(ə)nt/ *adj.* having or producing the appearance of mother-of-pearl.

pearlite var. of PERLITE.

pearlized /ˈpəːlʌɪzd/ *adj.* (also **-ised**) treated so as to resemble mother-of-pearl.

pearl millet *n.* a tall cereal, *Pennisetum typhoides.*

pearl onion *n.* a very small onion used in pickles.

pearl-oyster *n.* any of various marine bivalve molluscs of the genus *Pinctada,* bearing pearls.

pearlware /ˈpəːlwɛː/ *n.* a fine white glazed earthenware.

pearlwort /ˈpəːlwəːt/ *n.* any small herbaceous plant of the genus *Sagina,* inhabiting rocky and sandy areas.

pearly /ˈpəːli/ *adj.* & *n.* ● *adj.* (**pearlier, pearliest**) **1** resembling a pearl; lustrous. **2** containing pearls or mother-of-pearl. **3** adorned with pearls. ● *n.* (*pl.* **-ies**) (in *pl.*) *Brit.* **1** pearly kings and queens. **2** a pearly king's or queen's clothes or pearl buttons. **3** *slang* teeth. □ **pearliness** *n.*

Pearly Gates *n.pl. colloq.* the gates of Heaven.

pearly king *n.* (also **pearly queen**) *Brit.* a London costermonger (or his wife) wearing clothes covered with pearl buttons.

pearly nautilus see NAUTILUS 1.

pearmain /ˈpɛːmeɪn, ˈpəː-, pəˈmeɪn/ *n.* a variety of apple with firm white flesh. [Middle English, = warden pear, from Old French *parmain, permain,* probably ultimately from Latin *parmensis* 'of *Parma*', a city and province in Italy]

peart /pəːt/ *adj. US dial.* lively; cheerful. [variant of PERT]

peasant /ˈpɛz(ə)nt/ *n.* **1** a worker on the land, a farm labourer or small farmer, esp. a member of an agricultural class dependent on subsistence farming. **2** *derog.* a boor, a lout; a person of low social status. □ **peasantry** *n.* (*pl.* **-ies**). **peasanty** *adj.* [Middle English via Anglo-French *paisant,* Old French *païsent,* from *païs* 'country', ultimately from Latin *pagus* 'canton']

pease /piːz/ *n.pl. archaic* peas. [Old English *pise* 'pea', pl. *pisan,* via Late Latin *pisa* and Latin *pisum* from Greek *pison*: cf. PEA]

pease pudding *n.* esp. *Brit.* a dish of split peas boiled with onion and carrot and mashed to a pulp (served esp. with boiled ham).

pea-shooter *n.* a small tube for blowing dried peas through as a toy.

pea-souper *n. Brit. colloq.* a thick yellowish fog.

peat /piːt/ *n.* **1** vegetable matter partly decomposed in wet acid conditions to form a brown deposit like soil, used for fuel, in gardening, etc. **2** a cut piece of this. □ **peaty** *adj.* [Middle English from Anglo-Latin *peta*, perhaps from Celtic]

peatbog /ˈpiːtbɒg/ *n.* a bog composed of peat.

peatland /ˈpiːtland/ *n.* land consisting largely of peat.

peatmoss /ˈpiːtmɒs/ *n.* **1** a peatbog. **2** = SPHAGNUM.

peau-de-soie /pəʊdəˈswɑː/ *n.* a smooth finely ribbed satiny fabric of silk or rayon. [French, = skin of silk]

pebble /ˈpɛb(ə)l/ *n.* **1** a small smooth stone worn by the action of water. **2 a** a type of colourless transparent rock crystal used for spectacles. **b** a lens of this. **c** (*attrib.*) *colloq.* (of a spectacle lens) very thick and convex. **3** an agate or other gem, esp. when found as a pebble in a stream etc. □ **not the only pebble on the beach** (esp. of a person) easily replaced. □ **pebbled** *adj.* **pebbly** *adj.* [Old English *papel-stān* 'pebble-stone', *pyppelrīþig* 'pebble-stream', of unknown origin]

pebble-dash *n.* esp. *Brit.* mortar with pebbles in it used as a coating for external walls. □ **pebble-dashed** *adj.*

p.e.c. *abbr.* photoelectric cell.

pecan /ˈpiːk(ə)n, prˈkan, prˈkɑːn/ *n.* **1** a pinkish-brown smooth nut with an edible kernel. **2** a hickory, *Carya illinoensis*, of the southern US, producing this. [earlier *paccan*, of Algonquian origin]

peccable /ˈpɛkəb(ə)l/ *adj. formal* liable to sin. □ **peccability** /-ˈbɪlɪti/ *n.* [French, via medieval Latin *peccabilis* from *peccare* 'sin']

peccadillo /pɛkəˈdɪləʊ/ *n.* (*pl.* **-oes** or **-os**) a trifling offence; a venial sin. [Spanish *pecadillo*, diminutive of *pecado* 'sin', from Latin *peccare*]

peccant /ˈpɛk(ə)nt/ *adj. formal* **1** sinning. **2** inducing disease; morbid. □ **peccancy** *n.* [French *peccant* or Latin *peccare* 'sin']

peccary /ˈpɛk(ə)ri/ *n.* (*pl.* **-ies**) any American wild piglike mammal of the family Tayassuidae, esp. *Tayassu tajacu* and *T. pecari*. [Carib *pakira*]

peccavi /pɛˈkɑːviː/ *int. & n.* ● *int.* expressing guilt. ● *n.* (*pl.* **peccavis**) a confession of guilt. [Latin, = I have sinned]

pêche Melba /pɛʃ ˈmɛlbə/ *n.* = PEACH MELBA. [French]

peck[1] /pɛk/ *v. & n.* ● *v.tr.* **1** strike or bite (something) with a beak. **2** kiss (esp. a person's cheek) hastily or perfunctorily. **3 a** make (a hole) by pecking. **b** (foll. by *out, off*) remove or pluck out by pecking. **4** (also *absol.*) *colloq.* eat (food) listlessly; nibble at. **5** mark with short strokes. **6** (usu. foll. by *up, down*) break with a pick etc. **7** (also foll. by *away, out*) type at a typewriter etc. ● *n.* **1 a** a stroke or bite with a beak. **b** a mark made by this. **2** a hasty or perfunctory kiss. **3** *archaic slang* food. □ **peck at 1** eat (food) listlessly; nibble. **2** carp at; nag. **3** strike (a thing) repeatedly with a beak. [Middle English, probably from Middle Low German *pekken*, of unknown origin]

peck[2] /pɛk/ *n.* **1** a measure of capacity for dry goods, equal to a quarter of a bushel. **2** a vessel used to contain this amount. □ **a peck of** a large number or amount of (troubles, dirt, etc.). [Middle English from Anglo-French *pek*, of unknown origin]

pecker /ˈpɛkə/ *n.* **1** a bird that pecks (*woodpecker*). **2** *N. Amer. coarse slang* the penis. □ **keep your pecker up** *Brit. colloq.* remain cheerful.

pecking order *n.* (also **peck order**) a social hierarchy, originally as observed among hens.

peckish /ˈpɛkɪʃ/ *adj. colloq.* **1** esp. *Brit.* hungry. **2** *US* irritable.

pecorino /pɛkəˈriːnəʊ/ *n.* (*pl.* **-os**) an Italian cheese made from ewes' milk. [Italian from *pecorino* 'of ewes', from *pecora* 'sheep']

pecten /ˈpɛktɛn/ *n.* (*pl.* **pectens** or **pectines** /-tɪniːz/) *Zool.* **1** a comblike structure of various kinds in animal bodies. **2** any bivalve mollusc of the genus *Pecten*; a scallop. □ **pectinate** /-nət/ *adj.* **pectinated** /-neɪtɪd/ *adj.* **pectination** /-ˈneɪʃ(ə)n/ *n.* (all in sense 1). [Latin *pecten pectinis* 'comb']

pectin /ˈpɛktɪn/ *n. Biochem.* any of various soluble gelatinous polysaccharides found in ripe fruits etc. and used as a setting agent in jams and jellies. □ **pectic** *adj.* [Greek *pēktos* 'congealed' from *pēgnumi* 'make solid']

pectoral /ˈpɛkt(ə)r(ə)l/ *adj. & n.* ● *adj.* **1** of or relating to the breast or chest; thoracic (*pectoral fin*; *pectoral muscle*). **2** worn on the chest (*pectoral cross*). ● *n.* **1** (esp. in *pl.*) a pectoral muscle. **2** a pectoral fin. **3** an ornamental breastplate, esp. of a Jewish high priest. [Middle English via Old French from Latin *pectorale* (*n.*), *pectoralis* (*adj.*), from *pectus pectoris* 'breast, chest']

pectose /ˈpɛktəʊs, -z/ *n. Biochem.* an insoluble polysaccharide derivative found in unripe fruits and converted into pectin by ripening, heating, etc. [*pectic* (see PECTIN) + -OSE[2]]

peculate /ˈpɛkjʊleɪt/ *v.tr. & intr.* embezzle (money). □ **peculation** /-ˈleɪʃ(ə)n/ *n.* **peculator** *n.* [Latin *peculari*, related to *peculium*: see PECULIAR]

peculiar /prˈkjuːlɪə/ *adj. & n.* ● *adj.* **1** strange; odd; unusual (*a peculiar flavour*; *is a little peculiar*). **2 a** (usu. foll. by *to*) belonging exclusively (*a fashion peculiar to the time*). **b** belonging to the individual (*in their own peculiar way*). **3** particular; special (*a point of peculiar interest*). ● *n.* **1** *archaic* a peculiar property, privilege, etc. **2** esp. *Brit.* a parish or church exempt from the jurisdiction of the diocese in which it lies. [Middle English from Latin *peculiaris* 'of private property', via *peculium* from *pecu* 'cattle']

peculiarity /prˌkjuːlɪˈarɪti/ *n.* (*pl.* **-ies**) **1 a** idiosyncrasy; unusualness; oddity. **b** an instance of this. **2** a characteristic or habit (*meanness is his peculiarity*). **3** the state of being peculiar.

peculiarly /prˈkjuːlɪəli/ *adv.* **1** more than usually; especially (*peculiarly annoying*). **2** oddly. **3** as regards oneself alone; individually (*does not affect him peculiarly*).

pecuniary /prˈkjuːnɪəri/ *adj.* **1** of, concerning, or consisting of, money (*pecuniary aid*; *pecuniary considerations*). **2** (of an offence) entailing a money penalty or fine. □ **pecuniarily** *adv.* [Latin *pecuniarius*, via *pecunia* 'money' from *pecu* 'cattle']

pedagogue /ˈpɛdəgɒg/ *n.* **1** *archaic* a schoolmaster. **2** a usu. strict or pedantic teacher. □ **pedagogic** /-ˈgɒgɪk, -ˈgɒdʒɪk/ *adj.* **pedagogical** /-ˈgɒgɪk(ə)l, -ˈgɒdʒɪk(ə)l/ *adj.* **pedagogically** /-ˈgɒgɪk(ə)li, -ˈgɒdʒɪk(ə)li/ *adv.* **pedagogism** *n.* (also **pedagoguism**). [Middle English via Latin *paedagogus* from Greek *paidagōgos*, from *pais paidos* 'boy' + *agōgos* 'guide']

pedagogy /ˈpɛdəgɒgi, -gɒdʒi/ *n.* the science of teaching. □ **pedagogics** /-ˈgɒdʒɪks, -ˈgəʊdʒɪks/ *n.* [French *pédagogie* from Greek *paidagōgia* (as PEDAGOGUE)]

pedal[1] /ˈpɛd(ə)l/ *n. & v.* ● *n.* **1** any of several types of foot-operated levers or controls for mechanisms, esp.: **a** either of a pair of levers for transmitting power to a bicycle or tricycle wheel etc. **b** any of the foot-operated controls in a motor vehicle. **c** any of the foot-operated keys of an organ used for playing notes, or for drawing out several stops at once etc. **d** each of the foot-levers on a piano etc. for making the tone fuller or softer. **e** each of the foot-levers on a harp for altering the pitch of the strings. **2** a note sustained in one part, usu. the bass, through successive harmonies, some of which are independent of it. ● *v.* (**pedalled**, **pedalling**; *US* **pedaled**, **pedaling**) **1** *intr.* operate a cycle, organ, etc. by using the pedals. **2** *tr.* work (a bicycle etc.) with the pedals. □ **pedaller** *n.* (*US* **pedaler**). [French *pédale* via Italian *pedale* from Latin (as PEDAL[2])]

pedal[2] /ˈpɛd(ə)l, ˈpiː-/ *adj. Zool.* of the foot or feet (esp. of a mollusc). [Latin *pedalis* from *pes pedis* 'foot']

pedal bin *n.* a rubbish bin with a lid opened by a pedal.

pedal cycle *n.* a bicycle.

pedalo /ˈpɛdələʊ/ *n. Brit.* (*pl.* **-os** or **-oes**) a pedal-operated pleasure boat.

pedal-pusher *n.* **1** *colloq.* a cyclist. **2** (in *pl.*) women's calf-length trousers.

pedant /ˈpɛd(ə)nt/ *n.* **1** a person who insists on strict adherence to formal rules or literal meaning at the expense of a wider view. **2** a person who rates academic learning or technical knowledge above everything. **3** a person who is obsessed by a theory; a doctrinaire. □ **pedantic** /prˈdantɪk/ *adj.* **pedantically** /prˈdantɪk(ə)li/ *adv.* **pedantize** *v.intr. & tr.* (also **-ise**). **pedantry** *n.* (*pl.* **-ies**). [French *pédant* from Italian *pedante*: apparently formed as PEDAGOGUE]

pedate /ˈpɛdeɪt/ *adj.* **1** *Zool.* having feet. **2** *Bot.* (of a leaf) having divisions like toes or a bird's claws. [Latin *pedatus* from *pes pedis* 'foot']

peddle /ˈpɛd(ə)l/ *v.* **1** *tr.* **a** sell (goods), esp. in small quantities, as a pedlar. **b** advocate or promote (ideas, a philosophy, a way of life, etc.). **2** *tr.* sell (drugs) illegally. **3** *intr.* engage in selling, esp. as a pedlar. [back-formation from PEDLAR]

peddler /ˈpɛdlə/ *n.* **1** a person who sells drugs illegally. **2** *US* var. of PEDLAR.

pederast /ˈpɛdərast/ *n.* (also **paederast**) a man who performs pederasty.

pederasty /ˈpɛdərasti/ *n.* (also **paederasty**) anal intercourse between a man and a boy. [modern Latin *paederastia* from Greek *paiderastia*, from *pais paidos* 'boy' + *erastēs* 'lover']

pedestal /ˈpɛdɪst(ə)l/ *n. & v.* ● *n.* **1** the part of a column below the base, comprising the plinth and the dado if present. **2** the stone etc. base of a statue etc. **3** either of the two supports of a kneehole desk or table, usu. containing drawers. **4 a** an upright support of a machine or apparatus. **b** the column supporting a washbasin. **c** a lavatory pan or its base. ● *v.tr.* (**pedestalled**, **pedestalling**; *US* **pedestaled**, **pedestaling**) set or support on a pedestal. □ **put** (or **set**) **on a pedestal** admire disproportionately, idolize. [French *piédestal* via Italian *piedestallo*, from *piè* 'foot' (from Latin *pes pedis*) + *di* 'of' + *stallo* STALL[1]]

pedestal table *n.* a table with a single central support.

pedestrian /prˈdɛstrɪən/ *n. & adj.* ● *n.* **1** (often *attrib.*) a person who is walking, esp. in a town (*pedestrian crossing*). **2** a person who walks competitively. ● *adj.* prosaic; dull; uninspired. □ **pedestrianism** *n.* **pedestrianize** *v.tr. & intr.* (also **-ise**). **pedestrianization** /-ˈzeɪʃ(ə)n/ *n.* [French *pédestre* or Latin *pedester -tris*]

pedestrian crossing *n.* a specified part of a road where pedestrians have right of way to cross.

pedestrian precinct *n.* an area of a town restricted to pedestrians.

pediatrics *US* var. of PAEDIATRICS.

pedicab /ˈpɛdɪkab/ *n.* a pedal-operated rickshaw.

pedicel /ˈpɛdɪs(ə)l/ *n.* **1** *Bot.* a small stalk, esp. one bearing an individual flower in an inflorescence (cf. PEDUNCLE 1). **2** *Anat. & Zool.* a small stalklike structure (cf. PEDICLE 2). □ **pedicellate** /-s(ə)leɪt/ *adj.* [modern Latin *pedicellus*, diminutive of *pes pedis* 'foot']

pedicle /ˈpɛdɪk(ə)l/ *n.* **1** *Med.* part of a graft, esp. a skin graft, left temporarily attached to its original site. **2** *Anat. & Zool.* a small stalklike structure (cf. PEDICEL 2). □ **pediculated** /prˈdɪkjʊleɪtɪd/ *adj.* [Latin *pediculus*, diminutive of *ped pedis* 'foot']

pedicular /prˈdɪkjʊlə/ *adj.* (also **pediculous** /-ləs/) infested with lice. □ **pediculosis** /-ˈləʊsɪs/ *n.* [Latin *pedicularis*, *-losus* from *pediculus* 'louse']

pedicure /ˈpɛdɪkjʊə/ *n. & v.* ● *n.* **1** the care or treatment of the feet, esp. of the toenails. **2** a person practising this, esp. professionally. ● *v.tr.* treat (the feet) by removing corns etc. [French *pédicure*, from Latin *pes pedis* 'foot' + *curare*: see CURE]

pedigree /ˈpɛdɪgriː/ *n.* **1** (often *attrib.*) a recorded line of descent of a person or esp. a pure-bred domestic or pet animal. **2** the derivation of a word. **3** a genealogical table. **4** *colloq.* the history of a person, thing, idea, etc. □ **pedigreed** *adj.* [Middle English *pedegru* etc. from Anglo-French *pé de grue* 'crane's foot', a mark denoting succession in pedigrees]

pediment /ˈpɛdɪm(ə)nt/ *n.* **1 a** the triangular front part of a building in classical style, surmounting esp. a portico of columns. **b** a similar part of a building in baroque or mannerist style. **2** *Geol.* a broad flattish rock surface at the foot of a mountain slope. □ **pedimental** /-ˈmɛnt(ə)l/ *adj.* **pedimented** *adj.* [earlier *pedament*, *periment*, perhaps corruption of PYRAMID]

pedlar /ˈpɛdlə/ *n.* (*US* **peddler**) **1** a travelling seller of small items esp. carried in a pack etc. **2** (usu. foll. by *of*) a retailer of gossip etc. □ **pedlary** *n.* [Middle English *pedlere*, alteration of *pedder*, from *ped* 'pannier', of unknown origin]

pedo- *US* var. of PAEDO-.

pedology /prˈdɒlədʒi, pɛ-/ *n.* the scientific study of soil, esp. its formation, nature, and classification. □ **pedological** /pɛdəˈlɒdʒɪk(ə)l/ *adj.* **pedologist** *n.* [Greek *pedon* 'ground' + -LOGY]

pedometer /prˈdɒmɪtə, pɛ-/ *n.* an instrument for estimating the distance travelled on foot by recording the number of steps taken. [French *pédomètre* from Latin *pes pedis* 'foot']

peduncle /prˈdʌŋk(ə)l/ *n.* **1** *Bot.* the stalk of a flower, fruit, or cluster, esp. a main stalk bearing a solitary flower or subordinate stalks (cf. PEDICEL 1). **2** *Zool.* a stalklike part by which an organ etc. is attached, or by which an animal (e.g. a barnacle) is attached to the substrate. □ **peduncular** /-kjʊlə/ *adj.* [modern Latin *pedunculus* from Latin *pes pedis* 'foot': see -UNCLE]

pedunculate /prˈdʌŋkjʊlət/ *adj. Bot. & Zool.* having a peduncle.

pedunculate oak *n.* a common oak, *Quercus robur*, in which clusters of acorns are borne on long stalks.

pedway /ˈpɛdweɪ/ *n.* esp. *N. Amer.* a footway built for pedestrians in an urban area. [PEDESTRIAN + WAY]

pee /piː/ *v. & n. colloq.* ● *v.* (**pees**, **peed**) **1** *intr.* urinate. **2** *tr.* pass (urine, blood, etc.) from the bladder. ● *n.* **1** an act of urinating. **2** urine. [initial letter of PISS]

peek /piːk/ *v. & n.* ● *v.intr.* (usu. foll. by *in*, *out*, *at*) look quickly or slyly; peep. ● *n.* a quick or sly look. [Middle English *pike*, *pyke*, of unknown origin]

peekaboo /piːkəˈbuː/ *adj. & n.* ● *adj.* **1** (of a garment etc.) transparent or having a pattern of holes which reveal the skin below. **2** (of a hairstyle) concealing one eye with a fringe or wave. ● *n.* a game of hiding and suddenly reappearing, played with a young child (also as *int.*). [PEEK + BOO]

peel[1] /piːl/ *v. & n.* ● *v.* **1** *tr.* **a** strip the skin, rind, bark, wrapping, etc. from (a fruit, vegetable, tree, etc.). **b** (usu. foll. by *off*) strip (skin, peel, wrapping, etc.) from a fruit etc. **2** *intr.* **a** (of a tree, an animal's or person's body, a painted surface, etc.) become bare of bark, skin, paint, etc. **b** (often foll. by *off*) (of bark, a person's skin, paint, etc.) flake off. **3** *intr.* (often foll. by *off*) *colloq.* (of a person) strip for exercise etc. **4** *tr. Croquet* send (another player's ball) through the hoops. ● *n.* the outer covering of a fruit, vegetable, prawn, etc.; rind. □ **peel off 1** veer away and detach oneself from a group of marchers, a formation of aircraft, etc. **2** *colloq.* strip off one's clothes. □ **peeler** *n.* (in sense 1 of *v.*). [earlier *pill*, *pele* (originally = plunder), from Middle English *pilien* etc. via Old English from Latin *pilare* 'to strip hair from', from *pilus* 'hair']

peel[2] /piːl/ *n.* a shovel, esp. a baker's shovel for bringing loaves etc. into or out of an oven. [Middle English & Old French *pele* from Latin *pala*, related to *pangere* 'fix']

peel[3] /piːl/ *n.* (also **pele**) *hist.* a small square tower built in the 16th c. in the border counties of England and Scotland for defence against raids. [Middle English *pel* 'stake, palisade', via Anglo-French & Old French *pel* from Latin *palus* 'stake': cf. PALE[2]]

peeler /ˈpiːlə/ *n. Brit. archaic slang* or *dial.* a police officer. [originally = a member of the Irish constabulary, founded by Sir Robert *Peel*, English statesman d. 1850]

peeling /ˈpiːlɪŋ/ *n.* a strip of the outer skin of a vegetable, fruit, etc. (*potato peelings*).

peen /piːn/ *n. & v.* ● *n.* the wedge-shaped or thin or curved end of a hammer head (opp. FACE *n.* 5a). ● *v.tr.* **1** hammer with a peen. **2** treat (sheet metal) with a stream of metal shot in order to shape it. [16th c.: probably of Scandinavian origin]

peep[1] /piːp/ *v. & n.* ● *v.intr.* **1** (usu. foll. by *at, in, out, into*) look through a narrow opening; look furtively. **2** (usu. foll. by *out*) **a** (of daylight, a flower beginning to bloom, etc.) come slowly into view; emerge. **b** (of a quality etc.) show itself unconsciously. ● *n.* **1** a furtive or peering glance. **2** the first appearance (*at peep of day*). [Middle English: cf. PEEK, PEER[1]]

peep[2] /piːp/ *v. & n.* ● *v.intr.* make a shrill feeble sound as of young birds, mice, etc.; squeak; chirp. ● *n.* **1** such a sound. **2** a slight sound, utterance, or complaint (*not a peep out of them*). [imitative: cf. CHEEP]

peep-bo *n.* = PEEKABOO *n.*

peeper[1] /ˈpiːpə/ *n.* **1** a person who peeps. **2** *colloq.* an eye. **3** *US slang* a private detective. [PEEP[1] + -ER[1]]

peeper[2] /ˈpiːpə/ *n. US* a small tree frog of the genus *Hyla*. [PEEP[2] + -ER[1]]

peephole /ˈpiːphəʊl/ *n.* a small hole that may be looked through.

peeping Tom *n.* a furtive voyeur.

peep-show *n.* a small exhibition of pictures etc. viewed through a lens or hole set into a box etc.

peep-sight *n.* the aperture backsight of some rifles.

peep-toe *attrib.adj.* (also **peep-toed**) *Brit.* (of a shoe) leaving the toes partly exposed.

peepul /ˈpiːp(ə)l/ *n.* (also **pipal**) = BO TREE. [Hindi *pīpal* from Sanskrit *pippala*]

peer[1] /pɪə/ *v.intr.* **1** (usu. foll. by *into, at,* etc.) look keenly or with difficulty (*peered into the fog*). **2** peep out. **3** *archaic* come into view, appear. [variant of *pire*, Low German *pīren*; perhaps partly from APPEAR]

peer[2] /pɪə/ *n. & v.* ● *n.* **1 a** (*fem.* **peeress** /-rɪs/) a member of one of the degrees of the nobility in Britain or Ireland, i.e. a duke, marquess, earl, viscount, or baron. **b** a noble of any country. **2** a person who, or thing which, is equal in ability, standing, age, rank, or value (*tried by a jury of his peers*). ● *v.intr. & tr.* (usu. foll. by *with*) rank or cause to rank equally. □ **peerless** *adj.* (in sense 2 of *n.*). [Middle English via Anglo-French & Old French *pe(e)r, perer* from Late Latin *pariare* and Latin *par* 'equal']

peerage /ˈpɪərɪdʒ/ *n.* **1** peers as a class; the nobility. **2** the rank of peer or peeress (*was given a life peerage*). **3** a book containing a list of peers with their genealogy etc.

peer group *n.* a group of people of the same age, status, interests, etc.

peer of the realm *n.* (also **peer of the United Kingdom**) any of the class of peers whose adult members may all sit in the House of Lords.

peer pressure *n.* influence from members of one's peer group.

peeve /piːv/ *v. & n. colloq.* ● *v.tr.* (usu. as **peeved** *adj.*) annoy; vex; irritate. ● *n.* **1** a cause of annoyance. **2** vexation. [back-formation from PEEVISH]

peevish /ˈpiːvɪʃ/ *adj.* querulous; irritable. □ **peevishly** *adv.* **peevishness** *n.* [Middle English, = foolish, mad, spiteful, etc., of unknown origin]

peewee /ˈpiːwiː/ *n.* **1** *Sc.* a lapwing. **2** *Austral.* a magpie lark. [imitative of its call (cf. PEWEE)]

peewit /ˈpiːwɪt/ *n.* (also **pewit**) **1** a lapwing. **2** its cry. [imitative]

peg /pɛg/ *n. & v.* ● *n.* **1 a** a usu. cylindrical pin or bolt of wood, metal, etc., often tapered at one end, and used for holding esp. two things together. **b** such a peg attached to a wall etc. and used for hanging garments etc. on. **c** a peg driven into the ground and attached to a rope for holding up a tent. **d** a bung for stoppering a cask etc. **e** each of several pegs used to tighten or loosen the strings of a violin etc. **f** a small peg, matchstick, etc. stuck into holes in a board for calculating the scores at cribbage. **2** *Brit.* = CLOTHES-PEG. **3** *Brit.* a measure of spirits or wine. **4** a place allotted to a competitor to fish etc. from (usu. marked by a numbered peg). ● *v.tr.* (**pegged**, **pegging**) **1** (usu. foll. by *down, in, out,* etc.) fix (a thing) with a peg. **2** *Econ.* **a** stabilize (prices, wages, exchange rates, etc.). **b** prevent the price of (stock etc.) from falling or rising by freely buying or selling at a given price. **3** mark (the score) with pegs on a cribbage board. □ **off the peg** esp. *Brit.* (of clothes) ready-made. **peg away** (often foll. by *at*) *Brit.* work consistently and esp. for a long period. **peg down** restrict (a person etc.) to rules, a commitment, etc. **peg on** = *peg away*. **peg out 1** *Brit. slang* die. **2** score the winning point at cribbage. **3** *Croquet* hit the peg with the ball as the final stroke in a game. **4** mark the boundaries of (land etc.). **a peg to hang an idea** etc. **on** a suitable occasion or pretext etc. for it. **a square peg in a round hole** a misfit. **take a person down a peg or two** humble a person. [Middle English, probably of Low German or Dutch origin: cf. Middle Dutch *pegge*, Dutch dialect *peg*, Low German *pigge*]

pegboard /ˈpɛgbɔːd/ *n.* a board having a regular pattern of small holes for pegs, used for commercial displays, games, etc.

pegged /pɛgd/ *adj.* **1** in senses of the verb. **2** (*attrib.*) *N. Amer.* = PEGTOP *adj.*

peg-leg *n. colloq.* **1** an artificial leg. **2** a person with an artificial leg.

pegmatite /ˈpɛgmətʌɪt/ *n.* a coarsely crystalline type of granite. [Greek *pēgma -atos* 'thing joined together' from *pēgnumi* 'fasten']

pegtop /ˈpɛgtɒp/ *n. & adj.* ● *n.* a pear-shaped spinning top with a metal pin or peg forming the point, spun by the rapid uncoiling of a string wound round it. ● *adj.* (of a garment) wide at the top and narrow at the bottom.

Pehlevi var. of PAHLAVI.

PEI *abbr.* Prince Edward Island.

peignoir /ˈpeɪnwɑː/ *n.* a woman's loose dressing gown. [French, from *peigner* 'to comb']

pejorative /pɪˈdʒɒrətɪv/ *adj. & n.* ● *adj.* (of a word, an expression, etc.) depreciatory. ● *n.* a depreciatory word. □ **pejoratively** *adv.* [French *péjoratif -ive* via Late Latin *pejorare* 'make worse' from Latin *pejor* 'worse']

pekan /ˈpɛk(ə)n/ *n.* an American marten (see FISHER 1). [Canadian French from Algonquian]

peke /piːk/ *n. colloq.* a Pekinese dog. [abbreviation]

Pekingese /piːkɪˈniːz/ *n. & adj.* (also **Pekinese**) ● *n.* (*pl.* same) **1** (usu. **Pekinese**) **a** a lapdog of a short-legged breed with long hair and a snub nose. **b** this breed. **2** a citizen of Beijing (Peking) in China. **3** the form of the Chinese language used in Beijing. ● *adj.* of or concerning Beijing or its language or citizens.

pekoe /ˈpiːkəʊ, ˈpɛ-/ *n.* a superior kind of black tea. [Chinese dialect *pek-ho*, from *pek* 'white' + *ho* 'down', leaves being picked young with down on them]

pelage /ˈpɛlɪdʒ/ *n.* the fur, hair, wool, etc. of a mammal. [French, from Old French *pel* (modern *poil*) 'hair']

Pelagian /pɪˈleɪdʒɪən/ *adj. & n.* ● *adj.* of or concerning the monk Pelagius (4th–5th c.) or his theory denying the doctrine of original sin. ● *n.* a follower of Pelagius. □ **Pelagianism** *n.* [ecclesiastical Latin *Pelagianus* from *Pelagius*]

pelagian /pɪˈleɪdʒɪən/ *adj. & n.* ● *adj.* inhabiting the open sea. ● *n.* an inhabitant of the open sea. [Latin *pelagius* from Greek *pelagios* 'of the sea', from *pelagos* 'level surface of the sea']

pelagic /pɪˈladʒɪk/ *adj.* **1** of or performed on the open sea (*pelagic whaling*). **2** (of marine life) belonging to the upper layers of the open sea. [Latin *pelagicus* from Greek *pelagikos* (as PELAGIAN)]

pelargonium /pɛləˈgəʊnɪəm/ *n.* a plant of the genus *Pelargonium*, with red, pink, or white flowers and often fragrant leaves. Also called GERANIUM. [modern Latin, from Greek *pelargos* 'stork': cf. GERANIUM]

pele var. of PEEL[3].

pelf /pɛlf/ *n. derog.* or *joc.* money; wealth. [Middle English via Old Northern French from Old French *pelfre, peufre* 'spoils', of unknown origin: cf. PILFER]

pelham /ˈpɛləm/ *n.* a horse's bit combining a curb and a snaffle. [the surname *Pelham*]

pelican /ˈpɛlɪk(ə)n/ *n.* any large gregarious waterbird of the family Pelecanidae, with a long bill below which hangs a pouch for storing fish. [Old English *pellican* & Old French *pelican* via Late Latin *pelicanus* from Greek *pelekan*, probably from *pelekus* 'axe', with reference to its bill]

pelican crossing *n.* (in the UK) a pedestrian crossing with traffic lights operated by pedestrians. [from *pe*destrian *li*ght *con*trolled, respelt after the bird name]

pelisse /pɪˈliːs/ *n. hist.* **1** a woman's cloak with armholes or sleeves, reaching to the ankles. **2** a fur-lined cloak, esp. as part of a hussar's uniform. [French from medieval Latin *pellicia* (*vestis*) '(garment) of fur', from *pellis* 'skin']

pelite /ˈpiːlʌɪt/ *n. Geol.* a rock composed of claylike sediment. [Greek *pēlos* 'clay, mud']

pellagra /pɛˈlagrə, -ˈleɪgrə/ *n.* a disease caused by deficiency of nicotinic acid, characterized by cracking of the skin and often resulting in insanity. □ **pellagrous** *adj.* [Italian, from *pelle* 'skin', on the pattern of PODAGRA]

pellet /ˈpɛlɪt/ *n. & v.* ● *n.* **1** a small compressed ball of paper, bread, etc. **2** a pill. **3 a** a small mass of bones, feathers, etc. regurgitated by a bird of prey. **b** a small hard piece of animal, usu. rodent, excreta. **4 a** a piece of small shot. **b** an imitation bullet for a toy gun. ● *v.tr.* (**pelleted**, **pelleting**) **1** make into a pellet or pellets. **2** hit with (esp. paper) pellets. □ **pelletize** *v.tr.* (also **-ise**). [Middle English via Old French *pelote* from Latin *pila* 'ball']

pellicle /ˈpɛlɪk(ə)l/ *n.* a thin skin, membrane, or film. □ **pellicular** /-ˈlɪkjʊlə/ *adj.* [French *pellicule* from Latin *pellicula*, diminutive of *pellis* 'skin']

pellitory /ˈpɛlɪtəri/ *n.* any of several wild plants, esp.: **1** (in full **pellitory of Spain**) a plant of the daisy family, *Anacyclus pyrethrum*, with a pungent-flavoured root, used as a local irritant etc. **2** (in full **pellitory of the wall**) a low bushy plant, *Parietaria judaica* (nettle family), with greenish flowers growing on or at the foot of walls. [(sense 1) Middle English via Old French *peletre, peretre* and Latin *pyrethrum* from Greek *purethron* 'feverfew': (sense 2) ultimately via Old French *paritaire* and Late Latin *parietaria* from Latin *paries -etis* 'wall']

pell-mell /pɛlˈmɛl/ *adv., adj., & n.* ● *adv.* **1** headlong, recklessly (*rushed pell-mell out of the room*). **2** in disorder or confusion (*stuffed the papers together pell-mell*). ● *adj.* confused, tumultuous. ● *n.* confusion; a mixture. [French *pêle-mêle*, Old French *pesle mesle, mesle pesle*, etc., reduplication of *mesle* from *mesler* 'mix']

pellucid /pɪˈluːsɪd, pɛ-, -ˈljuːsɪd/ *adj.* **1** (of water, light, etc.) transparent, clear. **2** (of style, speech, sound, etc.) not confused; clear. **3** mentally clear. □ **pellucidity** /-ˈsɪdɪti/ *n.* **pellucidly** *adv.* [Latin *pellucidus* from *perlucēre* (as PER-, *lucēre* 'shine')]

Pelmanism /ˈpɛlmənɪz(ə)m/ *n.* **1** a system of memory-training originally devised by the Pelman Institute in London. **2** a card game based on this. □ **Pelmanize** *v.tr.* (also **-ise**).

pelmet /ˈpɛlmɪt/ *n.* a narrow border of cloth, wood, etc. above esp. a window, concealing the curtain rail. [probably from French PALMETTE]

pelorus /pɪˈlɔːrəs/ *n.* a sighting device like a ship's compass for taking bearings. [perhaps from *Pelorus*, reputed name of Hannibal's pilot]

pelota /pɪˈlɒtə, -ˈləʊtə/ *n.* **1** a Basque or Spanish game played in a walled court with a ball and basket-like rackets attached to the hand. **2** the ball used in this. [Spanish, = ball, augmentative of *pella*, from Latin *pila*]

pelt[1] /pɛlt/ *v. & n.* ● *v.* **1** *tr.* (usu. foll. by *with*) **a** hurl many small missiles at. **b** strike repeatedly with missiles. **c** assail (a person etc.) with insults, abuse, etc. **2** *intr.* (usu. foll. by *down*) (of rain etc.) fall quickly and torrentially. **3** *intr.* run fast. **4** *intr.* (often foll. by *at*) fire repeatedly. ● *n.* the act or an instance of pelting. □ **at full pelt** as fast as possible. [Middle English: origin unknown]

pelt[2] /pɛlt/ *n.* **1** the undressed skin of a fur-bearing mammal. **2** the skin of a sheep, goat, etc. with short wool, or stripped ready for tanning. **3** *joc.* the human skin. □ **peltry** *n.* [Middle English from obsolete *pellet* 'skin', diminutive of *pel* from Anglo-French *pell*, Old French *pel*, or back-formation from *peltry*, Anglo-French *pelterie*, Old French *peleterie* from *peletier* 'furrier', ultimately from Latin *pellis* 'skin']

pelta /ˈpɛltə/ *n.* (*pl.* **peltae** /-tiː/) **1** *hist.* a small light shield used by the ancient Greeks, Romans, etc. **2** *Bot.* a shieldlike structure, esp. in a lichen. □ **peltate** *adj.* [Latin from Greek *peltē*]

pelvic /ˈpɛlvɪk/ *adj.* of or relating to the pelvis or the organs it encloses (e.g. the uterus) (*pelvic fin*; *pelvic infection*).

pelvic girdle *n.* the bony or cartilaginous structure in vertebrates to which the posterior limbs are attached.

pelvis /ˈpɛlvɪs/ *n.* (*pl.* **pelvises** or **pelves** /-viːz/) **1** a basin-shaped cavity at the lower end of the torso of most vertebrates, formed from the innominate bone with the sacrum and other vertebrae. **2** the basin-like cavity of the kidney. [Latin, = basin]

Pembs. *abbr.* Pembrokeshire (a former county in Wales).

pemmican /ˈpɛmɪk(ə)n/ *n.* **1** a cake of dried pounded meat mixed with melted fat, originally made by N. American Indians. **2** beef so treated and flavoured with currants etc. for use by Arctic travellers etc. [Cree *pimecan* from *pime* 'fat']

pemphigus /ˈpɛmfɪgəs/ *n. Med.* the formation of watery blisters or eruptions on the skin. □ **pemphigoid** *adj.* **pemphigous** *adj.* [modern Latin from Greek *pemphix -igos* 'bubble']

PEN *abbr.* International Association of Poets, Playwrights, Editors, Essayists, and Novelists.

Pen. *abbr.* Peninsula.

pen[1] /pɛn/ *n. & v.* ● *n.* **1** an instrument for writing or drawing with ink, originally consisting of a shaft with a sharpened quill or metal nib, now more widely applied. **2 a** (usu. prec. by *the*) the occupation of writing. **b** a style of writing. **3** *Zool.* the tapering internal cartilaginous shell of a squid. ● *v.tr.* (**penned**, **penning**) **1** write. **2** compose and write. □ **put pen to paper** begin writing. [Middle English via Old French *penne* from Latin *penna* feather]

pen[2] /pɛn/ *n. & v.* ● *n.* **1** a small enclosure for cows, sheep, poultry, etc. **2** a place of confinement. **3** an enclosure for sheltering submarines. **4** a Jamaican farm or plantation. ● *v.tr.* (**penned**, **penning**) (often foll. by *in, up*) enclose or shut up, esp. in a pen. [Old English *penn*, of unknown origin]

pen[3] /pɛn/ *n.* a female swan. [16th c.: origin unknown]

pen[4] /pɛn/ *n. US slang* = PENITENTIARY *n.* 1. [abbreviation]

penal /ˈpiːn(ə)l/ *adj.* **1 a** of or concerning punishment or its infliction (*penal laws*; *a penal sentence*; *a penal* *colony*). **b** (of an offence) punishable, esp. by law. **2** extremely severe (*penal taxation*). ◻ **penally** *adv.* [Middle English from Old French *penal* or Latin *poenalis*, from *poena* PAIN]

penalize /ˈpiːn(ə)lʌɪz/ *v.tr.* (also **-ise**) **1** subject (a person) to a penalty or comparative disadvantage. **2** make or declare (an action) penal. ◻ **penalization** /-ˈzeɪʃ(ə)n/ *n.*

penal servitude *n. hist.* imprisonment with compulsory labour.

penalty /ˈpɛn(ə)lti/ *n.* (*pl.* **-ies**) **1 a** a punishment, esp. a fine, for a breach of law, contract, etc. **b** a fine paid. **2** a disadvantage, loss, etc., esp. as a result of one's own actions (*paid the penalty for his carelessness*). **3 a** a disadvantage imposed on a competitor or side in a game etc. for a breach of the rules etc. **b** (*attrib.*) awarded against a side incurring a penalty (*penalty kick*; *penalty goal*). **4** *Bridge* etc. points gained by opponents when a contract is not fulfilled. ◻ **the penalty of** a disadvantage resulting from (a quality etc.). **under** (or **on**) **penalty of** under the threat of (dismissal etc.). [Anglo-French via Old French *pénalité* from medieval Latin *penalitas* (as PENAL)]

penalty area *n. Football* the ground in front of the goal in which a foul by defenders involves the award of a penalty kick.

penalty box *n. Ice Hockey* an area reserved for penalized players and some officials.

penalty kick *n. Football* a free-kick at the goal, given after a foul in the penalty area.

penalty rate *n. Austral.* an increased rate of pay for overtime.

penalty shoot-out see SHOOT-OUT 2.

penalty spot see SPOT *n.* 2c.

penance /ˈpɛnəns/ *n.* & *v.* ● *n.* **1** an act of self-punishment as reparation for guilt. **2 a** (in the RC and Orthodox Church) a sacrament including confession of and absolution for a sin. **b** a penalty imposed esp. by a priest, or undertaken voluntarily, for a sin. ● *v.tr.* impose a penance on. ◻ **do penance** perform a penance. [Middle English via Old French from Latin *paenitentia* (as PENITENT)]

pen and ink *n.* & *adj.* ● *n.* **1** the instruments of writing. **2** writing. ● *adj.* (**pen-and-ink**) drawn or written with ink.

penannular /pɛˈnanjʊlə/ *adj.* almost ringlike. [Latin *paene* 'almost' + ANNULAR]

penates /pɪˈnɑːtiːz, -ˈneɪt-/ *n.pl. Rom.Hist.* the household gods, esp. of the storeroom (see LARES). [Latin, from *penus* 'provision of food']

pence /pɛns/ *n.* **1** *pl.* of PENNY. **2** *colloq.* = PENNY 1.

penchant /ˈpɒ̃ʃɒ̃/ *n.* an inclination or liking (*has a penchant for old films*). [French, pres. part. of *pencher* 'incline']

pencil /ˈpɛns(ə)l, -sɪl/ *n.* & *v.* ● *n.* **1** (often *attrib.*) **a** an instrument for writing or drawing, usu. consisting of a thin rod of graphite etc. enclosed in a wooden cylinder (*a pencil sketch*). **b** a similar instrument with a metal or plastic cover and retractable lead. **c** a cosmetic in pencil form. **2** (*attrib.*) resembling a pencil in shape (*pencil skirt*). **3** *Optics* a set of rays meeting at a point. **4** *Geom.* a figure formed by a set of straight lines meeting at a point. **5** a draughtsman's art or style. ● *v.tr.* (**pencilled**, **pencilling**; *US* **penciled**, **penciling**) **1** tint or mark with or as if with a pencil. **2** (usu. foll. by *in*) **a** write, esp. tentatively or provisionally (*have pencilled in the 29th for our meeting*). **b** (esp. as **pencilled** *adj.*) fill (an area) with soft pencil strokes (*a perfectly pencilled eyebrow*). ◻ **penciller** *n.* [Middle English from Old French *pincel*, ultimately from Latin *penicillum* 'paintbrush', diminutive of *peniculus* 'brush', diminutive of *penis* 'tail']

pencil box *n.* a box for pencils etc.

pencil case *n.* a container for pencils etc.

pencil sharpener *n.* a device for sharpening a pencil by rotating it against a cutting edge.

pendant /ˈpɛnd(ə)nt/ *n.* **1** a hanging jewel etc., esp. one attached to a necklace, bracelet, etc. **2** a light fitting, ornament, etc., hanging from a ceiling. **3** *Naut.* **a** a short rope hanging from the head of a mast etc., used for attaching tackles. **b** *Brit.* = PENNANT 1. **4** the shank and ring of a pocket watch by which it is suspended. **5** /ˈpɛnd(ə)nt, ˈpɒ̃dɒ̃/ (usu. foll. by *to*) a match, companion, parallel, complement, etc. [Middle English from Old French, from *pendre* 'hang', from Latin *pendere*]

pendent /ˈpɛnd(ə)nt/ *adj.* (also **pendant**) **1 a** hanging. **b** overhanging. **2** undecided; pending. **3** *Gram.* (esp. of a sentence) incomplete; not having a finite verb (*pendent nominative*). ◻ **pendency** *n.* [Middle English (as PENDANT)]

pendente lite /pɛnˌdɛntɪ ˈlʌɪti/ *adv. Law* during the progress of a suit. [Latin]

pendentive /pɛnˈdɛntɪv/ *n. Archit.* a curved triangle of vaulting formed by the intersection of a dome with its supporting arches. [French *pendentif -ive* (*adj.*) (as PENDANT)]

pending /ˈpɛndɪŋ/ *adj.* & *prep.* ● *predic.adj.* **1** awaiting decision or settlement, undecided (*a settlement was pending*). **2** about to come into existence (*patent pending*). ● *prep.* **1** during (*pending these negotiations*). **2** until (*pending his return*). [suggested by French *pendant* (see PENDENT)]

pending tray *n. Brit.* a tray for documents, letters, etc., awaiting attention.

pendragon /pɛnˈdrag(ə)n/ *n. hist.* an ancient British or Welsh prince (often as a title). [Welsh, = chief war-leader, from *pen* 'head' + *dragon* 'standard']

penduline /ˈpɛndjʊlʌɪn/ *adj.* **1** (of a nest) suspended. **2** (of a bird) of a kind that builds such a nest. [French (as PENDULOUS)]

pendulous /ˈpɛndjʊləs/ *adj.* **1** (of ears, breasts, flowers, branches, etc.) hanging down; drooping. **2** swinging; oscillating. ◻ **pendulously** *adv.* [Latin *pendulus* from *pendēre* 'hang']

pendulum /ˈpɛndjʊləm/ *n.* a weight suspended so as to swing freely, esp. a rod with a weighted end regulating the movement of a clock's works. ◻ **swing of the pendulum** the tendency of public opinion to oscillate between extremes, esp. between political parties. [Latin, neut. of *pendulus* PENDULOUS, used as a noun]

peneplain /ˈpiːnɪpleɪn/ *n. Geol.* a fairly flat area of land produced by erosion. [Latin *paene* 'almost' + PLAIN[1]]

penetralia /pɛnɪˈtreɪlɪə/ *n.pl.* **1** innermost shrines or recesses. **2** secret or hidden parts; mysteries. [Latin, neut. pl. of *penetralis* 'interior' (as PENETRATE)]

penetrate /ˈpɛnɪtreɪt/ *v.* **1** *tr.* **a** find access into or through, esp. forcibly. **b** (usu. foll. by *with*) imbue (a person or thing) with; permeate. **2** *tr.* see into, find out, or discern (a person's mind, the truth, a meaning, etc.). **3** *tr.* see through (darkness, fog, etc.) (*could not penetrate the gloom*). **4** *intr.* be absorbed by the mind (*my hint did not penetrate*). **5** *tr.* (as **penetrating** *adj.*) **a** having or suggesting sensitivity or insight (*a penetrating remark*). **b** (of a voice etc.) easily heard through or above other sounds; piercing. **6** *tr.* (of a man) put the penis into the vagina of (a woman). **7** *intr.* (usu. foll. by *into*, *through*, *to*) make a way. ◻ **penetrable** /-trəb(ə)l/ *adj.* **penetrability** /-trəˈbɪlɪti/ *n.* **penetrant** *adj.* & *n.* **penetratingly** *adv.* **penetration** /-ˈtreɪʃ(ə)n/ *n.* **penetrative** /-trətɪv/ *adj.* **penetrator** *n.* [Latin *penetrare* 'place or enter within' from *penitus* 'interior']

pen-feather *n.* a quill-feather of a bird's wing.

penfriend /ˈpɛnfrɛnd/ *n. Brit.* a friend communicated with by letter only.

penguin /ˈpɛŋgwɪn/ *n.* any flightless seabird of the family Spheniscidae of the southern hemisphere, with black upper parts and white underparts, and wings developed into scaly flippers for swimming underwater. [16th c., originally = great auk: origin unknown]

pen holder *n.* the esp. wooden shaft of a pen with a metal nib.

penicillate /ˈpɛnɪsɪlət, -ˈsɪlət/ *adj. Biol.* **1** having or forming a small tuft or tufts. **2** marked with streaks as of a pencil or brush. [Latin *penicillum*: see PENCIL]

penicillin /pɛnɪˈsɪlɪn/ *n.* any of various antibiotics produced naturally by moulds of the genus *Penicillium*, or synthetically, and able to prevent the growth of certain disease-causing bacteria. [modern Latin genus name *Penicillium* from Latin *penicillum*: see PENCIL]

penile /ˈpiːnʌɪl/ *adj.* of or concerning the penis. [modern Latin *penilis*]

peninsula /pɪˈnɪnsjʊlə/ *n.* a piece of land almost surrounded by water or projecting far into a sea or lake etc. □ **peninsular** *adj.* [Latin *paeninsula*, from *paene* 'almost' + *insula* 'island']

penis /ˈpiːnɪs/ *n.* (*pl.* **penises** or **penes** /-niːz/) **1** the male organ of copulation and (in mammals) urination. **2** the male copulatory organ in lower vertebrates. [Latin, = tail, penis]

penitent /ˈpɛnɪt(ə)nt/ *adj. & n.* ● *adj.* regretting and wishing to atone for sins etc.; repentant. ● *n.* **1** a repentant sinner. **2** a person doing penance under the direction of a confessor. **3** (in *pl.*) various RC orders associated for mutual discipline and the giving of aid to criminals, prostitutes, etc. □ **penitence** *n.* **penitently** *adv.* [Middle English via Old French from Latin *paenitens*, from *paenitēre* 'repent']

penitential /pɛnɪˈtɛnʃ(ə)l/ *adj.* of or concerning penitence or penance. □ **penitentially** *adv.* [Old French *penitencial* from Late Latin *paenitentialis*, from *paenitentia* 'penitence' (as PENITENT)]

penitential psalms *n.pl.* seven psalms (6, 32, 38, 51, 102, 130, 143) expressing penitence.

penitentiary /pɛnɪˈtɛnʃ(ə)ri/ *n. & adj.* ● *n.* (*pl.* **-ies**) **1** *N. Amer.* a reformatory prison. **2** an office in the papal court deciding questions of penance, dispensations, etc. ● *adj.* **1** of or concerning penance. **2** of or concerning reformatory treatment. **3** *US* (of an offence) making a culprit liable to a prison sentence. [Middle English from medieval Latin *paenitentiarius* (*adj.* & *n.*) (as PENITENT)]

penknife /ˈpɛnnʌɪf/ *n.* (*pl.* **penknives**) a small folding knife, esp. for carrying in a pocket.

penlight /ˈpɛnlʌɪt/ *n.* a small electric torch shaped like a fountain pen.

penman /ˈpɛnmən/ *n.* (*pl.* **-men**) **1** a person who writes by hand with a specified skill (*a good penman*). **2** an author. □ **penmanship** *n.*

Penn. *abbr.* (also **Penna.**) Pennsylvania.

pen-name *n.* a literary pseudonym.

pennant /ˈpɛnənt/ *n.* **1** *Naut.* a tapering flag, esp. that flown at the masthead of a vessel in commission. **2** = PENDANT 3a. **3** = PENNON. **4** *N. Amer.* a flag denoting a sports championship etc. [blend of PENDANT and PENNON]

penne /ˈpɛni/ *n.* pasta in the form of short wide tubes. [Italian, pl. of *penna* 'quill']

penniless /ˈpɛnɪlɪs/ *adj.* having no money; destitute. □ **pennilessly** *adv.* **pennilessness** *n.*

pennon /ˈpɛnən/ *n.* **1** a long narrow flag, triangular or swallow-tailed, esp. as the military ensign of lancer regiments. **2** *Naut.* a long pointed streamer on a ship. **3** a flag. □ **pennoned** *adj.* [Middle English via Old French from Latin *penna* 'feather']

penn'orth var. of PENNYWORTH.

Pennsylvania Dutch /pɛnsɪlˈveɪnɪə/ *n.* **1** a dialect of High German spoken by descendants of 17th–18th-c. German and Swiss immigrants to Pennsylvania etc. **2** (treated as *pl.*) these settlers or their descendants.

Pennsylvanian /pɛnsɪlˈveɪnɪən/ *n. & adj.* ● *n.* **1** a native or inhabitant of Pennsylvania, a state of the US. **2** (prec. by *the*) esp. *N. Amer. Geol.* the upper Carboniferous period or system. ● *adj.* **1** of or relating to Pennsylvania. **2** esp. *N. Amer. Geol.* of or relating to the upper Carboniferous period or system.

penny /ˈpɛni/ *n.* (*pl.* for separate coins **-ies**, for a sum of money **pence** /pɛns/) **1** a British bronze coin and monetary unit equal to one-hundredth of a pound (abbr.: **p**). **2** *hist.* a former British coin and monetary unit equal to one two-hundred-and-fortieth of a pound (abbr.: **d**). **3** *N. Amer.* a one-cent coin. **4** *Bibl.* a denarius. □ **in for a penny, in for a pound** an exhortation to total commitment to an undertaking. **like a bad penny** continually returning when unwanted. **pennies from heaven** unexpected benefits. **the penny drops** *Brit. colloq.* one begins to understand at last. **a penny for your thoughts** a request to a thoughtful person to confide in the speaker. **a pretty penny** a large sum of money. **two a penny** almost worthless though easily obtained. [Old English *penig*, *penning* from Germanic: perhaps related to PAWN[2]]

-penny /pəni/ *comb. form Brit.* forming attributive adjectives meaning 'costing ... pence' (esp. in pre-decimal currency) (*fivepenny*).

penny black *n. hist.* the first adhesive postage stamp (1840, value one penny).

penny cress *n.* a plant, *Thlaspi arvense*, with flat round pods.

penny dreadful *n. Brit.* a cheap sensational comic or story book.

penny-farthing *n. Brit. hist.* an early type of bicycle with one large and one small wheel.

penny-in-the-slot *attrib.adj. Brit.* (of a machine) activated by a coin pushed into a slot.

penny-pinching *n. & adj.* ● *n.* meanness. ● *adj.* mean. □ **penny-pincher** *n.*

penny post *n. Brit. hist.* the system of carrying letters etc. at a standard charge of 1d. regardless of distance.

pennyroyal /pɛnɪˈrɔɪəl/ *n.* **1** a creeping mint, *Mentha pulegium*, cultivated for its supposed medicinal properties. **2** *N. Amer.* an aromatic plant, *Hedeoma pulegioides*. [apparently from earlier *puliol(e) ryall* from Anglo-French *puliol*, Old French *pouliol* (ultimately from Latin *pulegium*) + *real* ROYAL]

pennyweight /ˈpɛnɪweɪt/ *n.* a unit of weight, 24 grains or one-twentieth of an ounce troy.

penny whistle *n.* a tin pipe with six holes giving different notes.

penny wise *adj.* careful in saving small amounts. □ **penny wise and pound foolish** mean in small expenditures but wasteful of large amounts.

pennywort /ˈpɛnɪwəːt/ *n.* any of several wild plants with rounded leaves, esp.: **1** (**wall pennywort**) *Umbilicus rupestris*, growing in crevices. **2** (**marsh** or **water pennywort**) *Hydrocotyle vulgaris*, growing in marshy places. [Middle English, from PENNY + WORT]

pennyworth /ˈpɛnɪwəːθ/ *n.* (also **penn'orth** /ˈpɛnəθ/) esp. *Brit.* **1** as much as can be bought for a penny. **2** a bargain of a specified kind (*a bad pennyworth*). □ **not a pennyworth** not the least bit.

penology /piːˈnɒlədʒi, pɪ-/ *n.* the study of the punishment of crime and of prison management. □ **penological** /-nəˈlɒdʒɪk(ə)l/ *adj.* **penologist** *n.* [Latin *poena* 'penalty' + -LOGY]

pen pal *n. colloq.* = PENFRIEND.

pen-pushing *n. colloq. derog.* clerical work. □ **pen-pusher** *n.*

pensée /pɒ̃ˈseɪ, French pɑ̃se/ *n.* a thought or reflection put into literary form; an aphorism. [French]

pensile /ˈpɛnsʌɪl/ *adj.* **1** hanging down; pendulous. **2** (of a bird etc.) building a pensile nest. [Latin *pensilis* from *pendēre pens-* 'hang']

pension[1] /ˈpɛnʃ(ə)n/ *n. & v.* ● *n.* **1 a** (in full *Brit.* **state pension** or *US* **government pension**) a regular payment made by a government to people above a specified age, to widows, or to the disabled. **b** similar payments made by an employer etc. on the retirement of an employee. **2 a** a regular payment paid to a scientist, artist, etc. for services to the state, or to fund work. **b** any regular payment paid esp. by a government on charitable grounds. ● *v.tr.* **1** grant a pension to. **2** bribe with a pension. □ **pension off 1** dismiss with a pension. **2** cease to employ or use. □ **pensionless** *adj.* [Middle English via Old French from Latin *pensio -onis* 'payment', from *pendere pens-* 'pay']

pension[2] /pɒ̃'sjɒ̃, French pɑ̃sjɔ̃/ *n.* a boarding house in France or continental Europe etc., providing full or half board at a fixed rate. □ ***en pension*** /ɒ̃, French ɑ̃/ as a boarder. [French: see PENSION[1]]

pensionable /'pɛnʃ(ə)nəb(ə)l/ *adj.* **1** entitled to a pension. **2** (of a service, job, etc.) entitling an employee to a pension. □ **pensionability** /-'bɪlɪti/ *n.*

pensionary /'pɛnʃ(ə)n(ə)ri/ *adj. & n.* ● *adj.* of or concerning a pension. ● *n.* (*pl.* **-ies**) **1** a pensioner. **2** a creature; a hireling. [medieval Latin *pensionarius* (as PENSION[1])]

pensioner /'pɛnʃ(ə)nə/ *n.* a recipient of a pension, esp. the retirement pension. [Middle English from Anglo-French *pensionner*, Old French *pensionnier* (as PENSION[1])]

pensive /'pɛnsɪv/ *adj.* **1** deep in thought. **2** sorrowfully thoughtful. □ **pensively** *adv.* **pensiveness** *n.* [Middle English via Old French *pensif, -ive*, from *penser* 'think', from Latin *pensare*, frequentative of *pendere pens-* 'weigh']

penstemon /pɛn'stiːmən, -'stɛmən, 'pɛnstɪmən/ *n.* (also **pentstemon** /pɛnt'stiːmən, -'stɛmən, 'pɛntstɪmən/) any American herbaceous plant of the genus *Penstemon*, with showy flowers and five stamens, one of which is sterile. [modern Latin, formed irregularly from PENTA- + Greek *stēmōn* 'warp', used to mean 'stamen']

penstock /'pɛnstɒk/ *n.* **1** a sluice; a floodgate. **2** *US* a channel for conveying water to a waterwheel. [PEN[2], in the sense 'mill-dam', + STOCK]

pent /pɛnt/ *adj.* (often foll. by *in, up*) closely confined; shut in (*pent-up feelings*). [past part. of *pend*, variant of PEN[2] *v.*]

penta- /'pɛntə/ *comb. form* **1** five. **2** *Chem.* (forming the names of compounds) containing five atoms or groups of a specified kind (*pentachloride*; *pentoxide*). [Greek from *pente* 'five']

pentachord /'pɛntəkɔːd/ *n.* **1** a musical instrument with five strings. **2** a series of five musical notes.

pentacle /'pɛntək(ə)l/ *n.* a pentagram or similar figure used as a mystic or magical symbol. [medieval Latin *pentaculum* (as PENTA-)]

pentad /'pɛntad/ *n.* **1** the number five. **2** a group of five. [Greek *pentas -ados* from *pente* 'five']

pentadactyl /pɛntə'daktɪl/ *adj. Zool.* having five toes or fingers.

pentagon /'pɛntəg(ə)n/ *n.* **1** a plane figure with five sides and angles. **2** (**the Pentagon**) **a** the pentagonal headquarters of the US defence forces in Washington, DC. **b** the leaders of the US defence forces. □ **pentagonal** /-'tag(ə)n(ə)l/ *adj.* [French *pentagone*, or via Late Latin *pentagonus* from Greek *pentagōnon* (as PENTA-, -GON)]

pentagram /'pɛntəgram/ *n.* a five-pointed star formed by extending the sides of a pentagon both ways until they intersect, used as a mystic symbol. [Greek *pentagrammon* (as PENTA-, -GRAM)]

pentagynous /pɛn'tadʒɪnəs/ *adj. Bot.* having five pistils.

pentahedron /pɛntə'hiːdr(ə)n, -'hɛd-/ *n.* (*pl.* **pentahedra** /-drə/ or **pentahedrons**) a solid figure with five faces. □ **pentahedral** *adj.*

pentamerous /pɛn'tam(ə)rəs/ *adj.* **1** *Bot.* having five parts in a flower-whorl. **2** *Zool.* having five joints or parts.

pentameter /pɛn'tamɪtə/ *n.* **1** a verse of five feet, e.g. English iambic verse of ten syllables. **2** a form of Greek or Latin dactylic verse composed of two halves each of two feet and a long syllable, used in elegiac verse. [Latin from Greek *pentametros* (as PENTA-, -METER)]

pentandrous /pɛn'tandrəs/ *adj. Bot.* having five stamens.

pentane /'pɛnteɪn/ *n. Chem.* a hydrocarbon of the alkane series. Chem. formula: C_5H_{12}. [Greek *pente* 'five' + ALKANE]

pentangle /'pɛntaŋg(ə)l/ *n.* = PENTAGRAM. [Middle English, perhaps from medieval Latin *pentaculum* PENTACLE, assimilated to Latin *angulus* ANGLE[1]]

pentanoic acid /pɛntə'nəʊɪk/ *n. Chem.* a colourless liquid carboxylic acid used in making perfumes. [PENTANE]

pentaprism /'pɛntəprɪz(ə)m/ *n.* a five-sided prism with two silvered surfaces used in a viewfinder to obtain a constant deviation of all rays of light through 90°.

Pentateuch /'pɛntətjuːk/ *n.* the first five books of the Old Testament, traditionally ascribed to Moses. □ **Pentateuchal** /-'tjuːk(ə)l/ *adj.* [ecclesiastical Latin *pentateuchus* from ecclesiastical Greek *pentateukhos* (as PENTA-, *teukhos* 'implement, book')]

pentathlon /pɛn'taθlɒn, -lən/ *n.* an athletic event comprising five different events for each competitor. □ **pentathlete** /-liːt/ *n.* [Greek, from *pente* 'five' + *athlon* 'contest']

pentatonic /pɛntə'tɒnɪk/ *adj. Mus.* **1** consisting of five notes. **2** relating to such a scale.

pentavalent /pɛntə'veɪl(ə)nt/ *adj. Chem.* having a valency of five; quinquevalent.

Pentecost /'pɛntɪkɒst/ *n.* **1 a** Whit Sunday. **b** a festival celebrating the descent of the Holy Spirit on Whit Sunday. **2 a** the Jewish harvest festival, on the fiftieth day after the second day of Passover (Lev. 23:15–16). **b** a synagogue ceremony on the anniversary of the giving of the Torah on Mount Sinai. [Old English *pentecosten* & Old French *pentecoste*, via ecclesiastical Latin *pentecoste* from Greek *pentēkostē* (*hēmera*) 'fiftieth (day)']

Pentecostal /pɛntɪ'kɒst(ə)l/ *adj. & n.* ● *adj.* (also **pentecostal**) **1** of or relating to Pentecost. **2** of or designating Christian sects and individuals who emphasize baptism in the Holy Spirit evidenced by 'speaking in tongues', who are often fundamentalist in doctrine, and who are exuberant in worship. ● *n.* a Pentecostalist. □ **Pentecostalism** *n.* **Pentecostalist** *adj. & n.*

penthouse /'pɛnthaʊs/ *n.* **1** a house or flat on the roof or the top floor of a tall building. **2** a sloping roof, esp. of an outhouse built on to another building. **3** an awning, a canopy. [Middle English *pentis* via Old French *apentis, -dis*, and medieval Latin *appendicium* (in Late Latin = appendage) from Latin (as APPEND): influenced by HOUSE]

pentimento /pɛntɪ'mɛntəʊ/ *n.* (*pl.* **pentimenti** /-tiː/) the phenomenon of earlier painting showing through a layer or layers of paint on a canvas. [Italian, = repentance]

pentobarbitone /pɛntə'bɑːbɪtəʊn/ *n.* (*US* **pentobarbital** /-t(ə)l/) a narcotic and sedative barbiturate drug formerly used to relieve insomnia. [PENTA-, BARBITONE, BARBITAL]

pentode /'pɛntəʊd/ *n.* a thermionic valve having five electrodes. [Greek *pente* 'five' + *hodos* 'way']

pentose /'pɛntəʊz, -s/ *n. Biochem.* any monosaccharide containing five carbon atoms, including ribose. [PENTA- + -OSE[2]]

Pentothal /'pɛntəθal/ *n. propr.* = THIOPENTONE.

pent roof *n.* a roof sloping in one direction only. [PENTHOUSE + ROOF]

pentstemon var. of PENSTEMON.

pentyl /'pɛntʌɪl, -tɪl/ *n.* = AMYL. [PENTANE + -YL]

penult /pɪ'nʌlt, 'pɛnʌlt/ *n. & adj.* ● *n.* the last but one (esp. syllable). ● *adj.* last but one. [abbreviation of Latin *paenultimus* (see PENULTIMATE) or of PENULTIMATE]

penultimate /pɪ'nʌltɪmət/ *adj. & n.* ● *adj.* last but one. ● *n.* **1** the last but one. **2** the last syllable but one. [Latin *paenultimus*, from *paene* 'almost' + *ultimus* 'last', on the pattern of *ultimate*]

penumbra /pɪ'nʌmbrə/ *n.* (*pl.* **penumbrae** /-briː/ or **penumbras**) **1 a** the partly shaded outer region of the shadow cast by an opaque object, esp. (*Astron.*) that of the shadow cast by the earth or moon over an area experiencing a partial eclipse. **b** *Astron.* the less dark outer part of a sunspot. **2 a** a partial shadow. **b** an area of obscurity or uncertainty. □ **penumbral** *adj.* [modern Latin, from Latin *paene* 'almost' + UMBRA 'shadow']

penurious /pɪˈnjʊərɪəs/ *adj.* **1** poor; destitute. **2** stingy; grudging. **3** scanty. □ **penuriously** *adv.* **penuriousness** *n.* [medieval Latin *penuriosus* (as PENURY)]

penury /ˈpɛnjʊri/ *n.* (*pl.* **-ies**) **1** destitution; poverty. **2** a lack; scarcity. [Middle English from Latin *penuria*, perhaps related to *paene* 'almost']

peon /ˈpiːən/ *n.* **1** /also peɪˈɒn/ a Spanish-American day labourer or farmworker. **2** /also pjuːn/ an Indian office messenger, attendant, or orderly. **3** a bullfighter's assistant. **4** *hist.* a worker held in servitude in the south-western US. **5** *N. Amer.* a menial or drudge. □ **peonage** *n.* [Portuguese *peão* & Spanish *peon* via medieval Latin *pedo -onis* 'walker, foot soldier' from Latin *pes pedis* 'foot': cf. PAWN[1]]

peony /ˈpiːəni/ *n.* (also **paeony**) (*pl.* **-ies**) any herbaceous plant of the genus *Paeonia*, with large globular red, pink, or white flowers, often double in cultivated varieties. [Old English *peonie* via Latin *peonia* from Greek *paiōnia*, from *Paiōn*, the name of the physician of the gods]

people /ˈpiːp(ə)l/ *n.* & *v.* ● *n.* **1** (usu. treated as *pl.*) **a** persons composing a community, tribe, race, nation, etc. (*the English people*; *a warlike people*; *the peoples of the Commonwealth*). **b** a group of persons of a usu. specified kind (*the chosen people*; *these people here*; *right-thinking people*). **2** (prec. by *the*; treated as *pl.*) **a** the mass of people in a country etc. not having special rank or position. **b** these considered as an electorate (*the people will reject it*). **3 a** *Brit.* parents or other relatives (*my people disapprove*). **b** *US* ancestors. **4 a** subjects, armed followers, a retinue, etc. **b** a congregation of a parish priest etc. **5** persons in general (*people do not like rudeness*). ● *v.tr.* (usu. foll. by *with*) **1** fill with people, animals, etc.; populate. **2** (esp. as **peopled** *adj.*) inhabit; occupy; fill (*thickly peopled*). [Middle English via Anglo-French *poeple*, *people*, Old French *pople*, *peuple*, from Latin *populus*]

people's democracy *n.* a political system, formerly esp. in E. Europe, with power regarded as invested in the people.

PEP *abbr. Brit.* **1** Political and Economic Planning. **2** /pɛp/ Personal Equity Plan.

pep /pɛp/ *n.* & *v. colloq.* ● *n.* vigour; go; spirit. ● *v.tr.* (**pepped**, **pepping**) (usu. foll. by *up*) fill with vigour. [abbreviation of PEPPER]

peperino /pɛpəˈriːnəʊ/ *n.* a light porous (esp. brown) volcanic rock formed of small grains of sand, cinders, etc. [Italian from *pepere* 'pepper']

peperoni var. of PEPPERONI.

peplum /ˈpɛpləm/ *n.* **1** a short flounce etc. at waist level, esp. of a blouse or jacket over a skirt. **2** *Gk Antiq.* a woman's outer garment. [Latin from Greek *peplos*]

pepo /ˈpiːpəʊ/ *n.* (*pl.* **-os**) any fleshy fruit of the melon or cucumber type, with numerous seeds and surrounded by a hard skin. [Latin, = pumpkin, from Greek *pepōn*, abbreviation of *pepōn sikuos* 'ripe gourd']

pepper /ˈpɛpə/ *n.* & *v.* ● *n.* **1 a** a hot aromatic condiment from the dried berries of certain plants used whole or ground. **b** any climbing vine of the genus *Piper*, esp. *P. nigrum*, yielding these berries. **2** anything hot or pungent. **3 a** = CAPSICUM. **b** = CAYENNE. ● *v.tr.* **1** sprinkle or treat with or as if with pepper. **2 a** pelt with missiles. **b** hurl abuse etc. at. **3** punish severely. [Old English *piper*, *pipor* via Latin *piper* and Greek *peperi* from Sanskrit *pippalī-* 'berry, peppercorn']

pepperbox /ˈpɛpəbɒks/ *n.* **1** = PEPPER POT 1. **2** a gun or artillery piece with a revolving set of barrels.

peppercorn /ˈpɛpəkɔːn/ *n.* **1** the dried berry of *Piper nigrum* as a condiment. **2** (in full **peppercorn rent**) *Brit.* a nominal rent.

pepper mill *n.* a device for grinding pepper by hand.

peppermint /ˈpɛpəmɪnt/ *n.* **1 a** a mint plant, *Mentha piperita*, grown for the strong-flavoured oil obtained from its leaves. **b** the oil from this. **2** a sweet flavoured with peppermint. **3** *Austral.* any of various eucalyptuses yielding oil with a similar flavour. □ **pepperminty** *adj.*

pepperoni /pɛpəˈrəʊni/ *n.* (also **peperoni**) beef and pork sausage seasoned with pepper. [Italian *peperone* 'chilli']

pepper pot *n.* **1** *Brit.* a small container with a perforated lid for sprinkling pepper. **2** a W. Indian dish of meat etc. stewed with cayenne pepper.

pepper shaker *n. N. Amer.* = PEPPER POT 1.

pepperwort /ˈpɛpəwəːt/ *n.* any cruciferous plant of the genus *Lepidium*, esp. garden cress.

peppery /ˈpɛp(ə)ri/ *adj.* **1** of, like, or containing much pepper. **2** hot-tempered. **3** pungent; stinging. □ **pepperiness** *n.*

pep pill *n.* a pill containing a stimulant drug.

peppy /ˈpɛpi/ *adj.* (**peppier**, **peppiest**) *colloq.* vigorous, energetic, bouncy.

Pepsi-Cola /pɛpsɪˈkəʊlə/ *n. propr.* (also **Pepsi**) a carbonated non-alcoholic drink. [arbitrary formation + COLA]

pepsin /ˈpɛpsɪn/ *n.* a digestive enzyme contained in the gastric juice, which hydrolyses proteins under acid conditions. [German, from Greek *pepsis* 'digestion']

pep talk *n.* a usu. short talk intended to enthuse, encourage, etc.

peptic /ˈpɛptɪk/ *adj.* concerning or promoting digestion. [Greek *peptikos* 'able to digest' (as PEPTONE)]

peptic gland *n.* a gland secreting gastric juice.

peptic ulcer *n.* an ulcer in the stomach or duodenum caused by the action of pepsin and stomach acid.

peptide /ˈpɛptʌɪd/ *n. Biochem.* a compound consisting of two or more amino acids linked in sequence. [German *Peptid*, back-formation from *Polypeptid* POLYPEPTIDE]

peptone /ˈpɛptəʊn/ *n.* a protein fragment formed by hydrolysis in the process of digestion. □ **peptonize** /-tənʌɪz/ *v.tr.* (also **-ise**). [German *Pepton* from Greek *peptos*, neut. *pepton*, 'cooked']

per /pəː/ *prep.* **1** for each; for every (*two sweets per child*; *five miles per hour*). **2** by means of; by; through (*per post*; *per rail*). **3** (in full **as per**) in accordance with (*as per instructions*). **4** *Heraldry* in the direction of. □ **as per usual** *colloq.* as usual. [Latin]

per- /pəː, pə/ *prefix* **1** forming verbs, nouns, and adjectives meaning: **a** through; all over (*perforate*; *perforation*; *pervade*). **b** completely; very (*perfervid*; *perturb*). **c** to destruction; to the bad (*perdition*; *pervert*). **2** *Chem.* having the maximum of some element in combination, esp.: **a** in the names of binary compounds in *-ide* (*peroxide*). **b** in the names of oxides, acids, etc. in *-ic* (*perchloric*; *permanganic*). **c** in the names of salts of these acids (*perchlorate*; *permanganate*). [Latin *per-* (as PER)]

peradventure /p(ə)rədˈvɛntʃə, pəːr-/ *adv.* & *n. archaic* or *joc.* ● *adv.* perhaps. ● *n.* uncertainty; chance; conjecture; doubt (esp. *beyond* or *without peradventure*). [Middle English from Old French *per* or *par auenture* 'by chance' (as PER, ADVENTURE)]

perambulate /pəˈrambjʊleɪt/ *v.* **1** *tr.* walk through, over, or about (streets, the country, etc.). **2** *intr.* walk from place to place. **3** *tr.* **a** travel through and inspect (territory). **b** formally establish the boundaries of (a parish etc.) by walking round them. □ **perambulation** /-ˈleɪʃ(ə)n/ *n.* **perambulatory** *adj.* [Latin *perambulare perambulat-* (as PER-, *ambulare* 'walk')]

perambulator /pəˈrambjʊleɪtə/ *n. Brit. formal* = PRAM[1]. [PERAMBULATE]

per annum /pər ˈanəm/ *adv.* for each year. [Latin]

percale /pəˈkeɪl/ *n.* a closely woven cotton fabric like calico. [French, of uncertain origin]

per capita /pə ˈkapɪtə/ *adv.* & *adj.* (also **per caput** /ˈkapʊt/) for each person. [Latin, = by heads]

perceive /pəˈsiːv/ *v.tr.* **1** apprehend, esp. through the sight; observe. **2** (usu. foll. by *that*, *how*, etc. + clause) apprehend with the mind; understand. **3** regard mentally in a specified manner (*perceives the universe as* *infinite*). ◻ **perceivable** *adj.* **perceiver** *n.* [Middle English via Old French *perçoivre* from Latin *percipere* (as PER-, *capere* 'take')]

per cent /pə 'sɛnt/ *adv. & n.* (*US* **percent**) ● *adv.* in every hundred. ● *n.* **1** percentage. **2** one part in every hundred (*half a per cent*). **3** (in *pl.*) *Brit.* public securities yielding interest of so much per cent (*three per cents*). [PER + CENT]

percentage /pə'sɛntɪdʒ/ *n.* **1** a rate or proportion per cent. **2** a proportion. **3** *colloq.* personal benefit or advantage; probability of a successful outcome (often *attrib.*: *played percentage shots*). ◻ **play the percentages** *colloq.* play safely or methodically with regard to the odds in favour of success.

percentile /pə'sɛntʌɪl/ *n. Statistics* one of 99 values of a variable dividing a population into 100 equal groups as regards the value of that variable.

percept /'pəːsɛpt/ *n. Philos.* **1** an object of perception. **2** a mental concept resulting from perceiving, esp. by sight. [Latin *perceptum* 'perceived' (thing), neut. past part. of *percipere* PERCEIVE, on the pattern of *concept*]

perceptible /pə'sɛptɪb(ə)l/ *adj.* capable of being perceived by the senses or intellect. ◻ **perceptibility** /-'bɪlɪti/ *n.* **perceptibly** *adv.* [Old French *perceptible* or Late Latin *perceptibilis* from Latin (as PERCEIVE)]

perception /pə'sɛpʃ(ə)n/ *n.* **1 a** the faculty of perceiving. **b** an instance of perceiving. **2** (often foll. by *of*) **a** the intuitive recognition of a truth, aesthetic quality, etc. **b** an instance of this (*a sudden perception of the true position*). **3** an interpretation or impression based on one's understanding of something. **4** *Philos.* the ability of the mind to refer sensory information to an external object as its cause. ◻ **perceptional** *adj.* **perceptual** /pə'sɛptjʊəl/ *adj.* **perceptually** /pə'sɛptjʊəli/ *adv.* [Middle English from Latin *perceptio* (as PERCEIVE)]

perceptive /pə'sɛptɪv/ *adj.* **1** capable of perceiving. **2** sensitive; discerning; observant (*a perceptive remark*). ◻ **perceptively** *adv.* **perceptiveness** *n.* **perceptivity** /-'tɪvɪti/ *n.* [medieval Latin *perceptivus* (as PERCEIVE)]

perch[1] /pəːtʃ/ *n. & v.* ● *n.* **1** a usu. horizontal bar, branch, etc. used by a bird to rest on. **2** a usu. high or precarious place for a person or thing to rest on. **3** esp. *Brit. hist.* a measure of length, esp. for land, of 5½ yards; also called *pole* (cf. ROD 6). ● *v.intr. & tr.* (usu. foll. by *on*) settle or rest, or cause to settle or rest on or as if on a perch etc. (*the bird perched on a branch*; *a town perched on a hill*). ◻ **knock a person off his** (or **her**) **perch 1** vanquish, destroy. **2** make less confident or secure. [Middle English via Old French *perche, percher* from Latin *pertica* 'pole']

perch[2] /pəːtʃ/ *n.* (*pl.* same or **perches**) any spiny-finned freshwater edible fish of the genus *Perca*, esp. *P. fluviatilis* of Europe. [Middle English via Old French *perche* and Latin *perca* from Greek *perkē*]

perchance /pə'tʃɑːns/ *adv. archaic* or *poet.* **1** by chance. **2** possibly; maybe. [Middle English from Anglo-French *par chance*, from *par* 'by', CHANCE]

percher /'pəːtʃə/ *n.* any bird with feet adapted for perching; a passerine.

percheron /'pəːʃ(ə)rɒn/ *n.* a powerful breed of carthorse. [French, originally bred in le *Perche*, a district of northern France]

perchlorate /pə'klɔːreɪt/ *n. Chem.* a salt or ester of perchloric acid.

perchloric acid /pə'klɔːrɪk/ *n. Chem.* a fuming toxic liquid containing heptavalent chlorine, used as a strong oxidizing agent. [PER- + CHLORINE]

percipient /pə'sɪpɪənt/ *adj. & n.* ● *adj.* **1** able to perceive; conscious. **2** discerning; observant. ● *n.* a person who perceives, esp. something outside the range of the senses. ◻ **percipience** *n.* **percipiently** *adv.* [Latin (as PERCEIVE)]

percolate /'pəːkəleɪt/ *v.* **1** *intr.* (often foll. by *through*) **a** (of liquid etc.) filter or ooze gradually (esp. through a porous surface). **b** (of an idea etc.) permeate gradually. **2** *tr.* prepare (coffee) by repeatedly passing boiling water through ground beans. **3** *tr.* ooze through; permeate. **4** *tr.* strain (a liquid, powder, etc.) through a fine mesh etc. ◻ **percolation** /-'leɪʃ(ə)n/ *n.* [Latin *percolare* (as PER-, *colare* 'strain' from *colum* 'strainer')]

percolator /'pəːkəleɪtə/ *n.* a machine for making coffee by circulating boiling water through ground beans.

per contra /pəː 'kɒntrə/ *adv.* on the opposite side (of an account, assessment, etc.); on the other hand. [Italian]

percuss /pə'kʌs/ *v.tr. Med.* tap (a part of the body) gently with a finger or an instrument as part of a diagnosis. [Latin *percutere percuss-* 'strike' (as PER-, *cutere* = *quatere* 'shake')]

percussion /pə'kʌʃ(ə)n/ *n.* **1** *Mus.* **a** (often *attrib.*) the playing of music by striking instruments with sticks etc. (*a percussion band*). **b** the section of such instruments in an orchestra (*asked the percussion to stay behind*). **2** *Med.* the act or an instance of percussing. **3** the forcible striking of one esp. solid body against another. ◻ **percussionist** *n.* **percussive** *adj.* **percussively** *adv.* **percussiveness** *n.* [French *percussion* or Latin *percussio* (as PERCUSS)]

percussion cap *n.* a small amount of explosive powder contained in metal or paper and exploded by striking, used esp. in toy guns and formerly in some firearms.

percutaneous /pəːkjʊ'teɪnɪəs/ *adj.* esp. *Med.* made or done through the skin. [Latin *per cutem* 'through the skin']

per diem /pəː 'diːɛm, 'dʌɪɛm/ *adv., adj. & n.* ● *adv. & adj.* for each day. ● *n.* an allowance or payment for each day. [Latin]

perdition /pə'dɪʃ(ə)n/ *n.* eternal death; damnation. [Middle English via Old French *perdiciun* or ecclesiastical Latin *perditio* from Latin *perdere* 'destroy' (as PER-, *dere dit-* = *dare* 'give')]

perdurable /pə'djʊərəb(ə)l/ *adj. formal* permanent; eternal; durable. ◻ **perdurability** /-'bɪlɪti/ *n.* **perdurably** *adv.* [Middle English via Old French from Late Latin *perdurabilis* (as PER-, DURABLE)]

père /pɛː, French pɛr/ *n.* (added to a surname to distinguish a father from a son of the same name) the father, senior (cf. FILS[2]). [French, = father]

Père David's deer /pɛː 'deɪvɪdz/ *n.* a large slender-antlered deer, *Elaphurus davidianus*. [named after Father A. *David*, French missionary and naturalist, d. 1900]

peregrinate /'pɛrɪgrɪneɪt/ *v.intr. archaic* or *joc.* travel; journey, esp. extensively or at leisure. ◻ **peregrination** /-'neɪʃ(ə)n/ *n.* **peregrinator** *n.* [Latin *peregrinari* (as PEREGRINE)]

peregrine /'pɛrɪgrɪn/ *n. & adj.* ● *n.* (in full **peregrine falcon**) a powerful falcon, *Falco peregrinus*, breeding esp. on coastal cliffs and much used for falconry. ● *adj. archaic* imported from abroad; foreign; outlandish. [Latin *peregrinus* from *peregre* 'abroad', from *per* 'through' + *ager* 'field']

peremptory /pə'rɛm(p)t(ə)ri, 'pɛrɪm-/ *adj.* **1** (of a statement or command) admitting no denial or refusal. **2** (of a person, a person's manner, etc.) dogmatic; imperious; dictatorial. **3** *Law* not open to appeal or challenge; final. **4** absolutely fixed; essential. ◻ **peremptorily** *adv.* **peremptoriness** *n.* [Anglo-French *peremptorie*, Old French *peremptoire* from Latin *peremptorius* 'deadly, decisive', from *perimere perempt-* 'destroy, cut off' (as PER-, *emere* 'take, buy')]

peremptory challenge *n. Law* a defendant's objection to a proposed juror, made without needing to give a reason.

perennial /pə'rɛnɪəl/ *adj. & n.* ● *adj.* **1** lasting through a year or several years. **2** (of a plant) lasting several years (cf. ANNUAL *adj.* 3). **3** lasting a long time or for ever. **4** (of a stream) flowing through all seasons of the year. ● *n.* a perennial plant (*a herbaceous perennial*). ◻ **perenniality** /-'alɪti/ *n.* **perennially** *adv.* [Latin *perennis* (as PER-, *annus* 'year')]

perestroika /pɛrɪ'strɔɪkə/ *n.* (in the former Soviet Union) the policy or practice of restructuring or reforming the economic and political system. [Russian *perestroĭka* = restructuring]

perfect *adj., v., & n.* ● *adj.* /ˈpəːfɪkt/ **1** complete; not deficient. **2** faultless (*a perfect diamond*). **3** very satisfactory (*a perfect evening*). **4** exact; precise (*a perfect circle*). **5** entire; unqualified (*a perfect stranger*). **6** *Math.* (of a number) equal to the sum of its divisors. **7** *Gram.* (of a tense) denoting a completed action or event in the past, formed in English with *have* or *has* and the past participle, as in *they have eaten*. **8** *Mus.* (of pitch) absolute. **9** *Bot.* **a** (of a flower) having all four types of whorl. **b** (of a fungus) in the stage where the sexual spores are formed. **10** (often foll. by *in*) *archaic* thoroughly trained or skilled (*is perfect in geometry*). ● *v.tr.* /pəˈfɛkt/ **1** make perfect; improve. **2** carry through; complete. **3** complete (a sheet) by printing the other side. ● *n.* /ˈpəːfɪkt/ *Gram.* the perfect tense. □ **perfecter** /ˈpəːfɛktə/ *n.* **perfectible** /pəˈfɛktɪb(ə)l/ *adj.* **perfectibility** /pəˌfɛktɪˈbɪlɪti/ *n.* **perfectness** *n.* [Middle English and Old French *parfit, perfet* from Latin *perfectus*, past part. of *perficere* 'complete' (as PER-, *facere* 'do')]

perfecta /pəˈfɛktə/ *n. US* a form of betting in which the first two places in a race must be predicted in the correct order. [Latin American Spanish *quiniela perfecta* 'perfect quinella']

perfect binding *n.* a form of bookbinding in which the leaves are attached to the spine by gluing rather than sewing.

perfect interval *n. Mus.* a fourth or fifth as it would occur in a major or minor scale starting on the lower note of the interval, or octave.

perfection /pəˈfɛkʃ(ə)n/ *n.* **1** the act or process of making perfect. **2** the state of being perfect; faultlessness, excellence. **3** a perfect person, thing, or example. **4** an accomplishment. **5** full development; completion. □ **to perfection** exactly; completely. [Middle English via Old French from Latin *perfectio -onis* (as PERFECT)]

perfectionism /pəˈfɛkʃ(ə)nɪz(ə)m/ *n.* **1** the uncompromising pursuit of excellence. **2** *Philos.* the belief that religious or moral perfection is attainable. □ **perfectionist** *n. & adj.* [PERFECTION]

perfective /pəˈfɛktɪv/ *adj. & n. Gram.* ● *adj.* (of an aspect of a verb etc.) expressing the completion of an action (opp. IMPERFECTIVE). ● *n.* the perfective aspect or form of a verb. [medieval Latin *perfectivus* (as PERFECT)]

perfectly /ˈpəːfɪk(t)li/ *adv.* **1** completely; absolutely (*I understand you perfectly*). **2** quite, completely (*is perfectly capable of doing it*). **3** in a perfect way.

perfecto /pəˈfɛktəʊ/ *n.* (*pl.* **-os**) orig. *US* a large thick cigar pointed at each end. [Spanish, = perfect]

perfect pitch *n.* = ABSOLUTE PITCH 1.

perfect square *n.* = SQUARE NUMBER.

perfervid /pəˈfəːvɪd/ *adj. literary* very fervid. □ **perfervidly** *adv.* **perfervidness** *n.* [modern Latin *perfervidus* (as PER-, FERVID)]

perfidy /ˈpəːfɪdi/ *n.* breach of faith; treachery. □ **perfidious** /-ˈfɪdɪəs/ *adj.* **perfidiously** /-ˈfɪdɪəsli/ *adv.* [Latin *perfidia* from *perfidus* 'treacherous' (as PER-, *fidus* from *fides* 'faith')]

perfin /ˈpəːfɪn/ *n.* a postage stamp perforated with the initials or insignia of an organization. [*perf*orated *in*itials]

perfoliate /pəˈfəʊlɪət/ *adj.* (of a plant) having the stalk apparently passing through the leaf. [modern Latin *perfoliatus* (as PER-, FOLIATE)]

perforate *v. & adj.* ● *v.* /ˈpəːfəreɪt/ **1** *tr.* make a hole or holes through; pierce. **2** *tr.* make a row of small holes in (paper etc.) so that a part may be torn off easily. **3** *tr.* make an opening into; pass into or extend through. **4** *intr.* (usu. foll. by *into, through*, etc.) penetrate. ● *adj.* /ˈpəːf(ə)rət/ perforated. □ **perforation** /-ˈreɪʃ(ə)n/ *n.* **perforative** /ˈpəːf(ə)rətɪv/ *adj.* **perforator** /ˈpəːfəreɪtə/ *n.* [Latin *perforare* (as PER-, *forare* 'pierce')]

perforce /pəˈfɔːs/ *adv. archaic* unavoidably; necessarily. [Middle English from Old French *par force* 'by FORCE[1]']

perform /pəˈfɔːm/ *v.* **1** *tr.* (also *absol.*) carry into effect; be the agent of; do (a command, promise, task, etc.). **2** *tr.* (also *absol.*) go through, execute (a public function, play, piece of music, etc.). **3** *intr.* act in a play; play music, sing, etc. (*likes performing*). **4** *intr.* (of a trained animal) execute tricks etc. at a public show. **5** *intr.* function, esp. satisfactorily (*the car performs well at speed*). **6** *intr.* (of an investment) yield a return, esp. a profit. **7** *intr. slang* have sexual intercourse (esp. satisfactorily). □ **performable** *adj.* **performability** /-ˈbɪlɪti/ *n.* **performatory** *adj. & n.* (*pl.* **-ies**). **performer** *n.* **performing** *adj.* [Middle English via Anglo-French *parfourmer* from Old French *parfournir* (assimilated to *forme* FORM), from *par* PER- + *fournir* FURNISH]

performance /pəˈfɔːm(ə)ns/ *n.* **1** (usu. foll. by *of*) **a** the act or process of performing or carrying out. **b** the execution or fulfilment (of a duty etc.). **2** a staging or production (of a drama, piece of music, etc.) (*the afternoon performance*). **3** a person's achievement under test conditions etc. (*put up a good performance*). **4** *colloq.* a fuss; a scene; a public exhibition (*made such a performance about leaving*). **5 a** the capabilities of a machine, esp. a car or aircraft. **b** (*attrib.*) of high capability (*a performance car*). **6** the return on an investment, esp. in stocks and shares etc.

performance art *n.* a kind of visual art in which the activity of the artist forms a central feature. □ **performance artist** *n.*

performative /pəˈfɔːmətɪv/ *adj. & n.* ● *adj.* **1** of or relating to performance. **2** denoting an utterance that effects an action by being spoken or written (e.g. *I bet, I apologize*). ● *n.* a performative utterance.

performing arts /pəˈfɔːmɪŋ/ *n.pl.* the arts, such as drama, music, and dance, that require performance for their realization.

perfume /ˈpəːfjuːm/ *n. & v.* ● *n.* **1** a sweet smell. **2** fluid containing the essence of flowers etc.; scent. ● *v.tr.* /also pəˈfjuːm/ (usu. as **perfumed** *adj.*) impart a sweet scent to; impregnate with a sweet smell. □ **perfumy** *adj.* [originally of smoke from a burning substance: French *parfum, parfumer* from obsolete Italian *parfumare, perfumare* (as PER-, *fumare* 'smoke, FUME')]

perfumer /pəˈfjuːmə/ *n.* a maker or seller of perfumes. □ **perfumery** *n.* (*pl.* **-ies**).

perfunctory /pəˈfʌŋ(k)t(ə)ri/ *adj.* **1** done merely for the sake of getting through a duty. **2** superficial; mechanical. □ **perfunctorily** *adv.* **perfunctoriness** *n.* [Late Latin *perfunctorius* 'careless' from Latin *perfungi perfunct-* (as PER-, *fungi* 'perform')]

perfuse /pəˈfjuːz/ *v.tr.* **1** (often foll. by *with*) **a** besprinkle (with water etc.). **b** cover or suffuse (with radiance etc.). **2** pour or diffuse (water etc.) through or over. **3** *Med.* cause a fluid to pass through (an organ etc.). □ **perfusion** /-ʒ(ə)n/ *n.* **perfusive** /-sɪv/ *adj.* [Latin *perfundere perfus-* (as PER-, *fundere* 'pour')]

pergana var. of PARGANA.

pergola /ˈpəːgələ/ *n.* an arbour or covered walk, formed of growing plants trained over trellis-work. [Italian from Latin *pergula* 'projecting roof', from *pergere* 'proceed']

pergunnah var. of PARGANA.

perhaps /pəˈhaps/ *adv.* **1** it may be; possibly (*perhaps it is lost*). **2** introducing a polite request (*perhaps you would open the window?*). [PER + HAP]

peri /ˈpɪəri/ *n.* (*pl.* **peris**) **1** (in Persian mythology) a fairy; a good (originally evil) genius. **2** a beautiful or graceful being. [Persian *pārī*]

peri- /ˈpɛri/ *prefix* **1** round, about. **2** *Astron.* the point nearest to (*perigee; perihelion*). [Greek *peri* 'around, about']

perianth /ˈpɛrɪanθ/ *n.* the outer part of a flower. [French *périanthe* from modern Latin *perianthium* (as PERI- + Greek *anthos* 'flower')]

periapt /'pɛrɪapt/ *n.* a thing worn as a charm; an amulet. [French *périapte* from Greek *periapton* (as PERI-, *haptō* 'fasten')]

pericardium /pɛrɪ'kɑ:dɪəm/ *n.* (*pl.* **pericardia** /-dɪə/) the membranous sac enclosing the heart. □ **pericardiac** /-dɪak/ *adj.* **pericardial** *adj.* **pericarditis** /-'dʌɪtɪs/ *n.* [modern Latin from Greek *perikardion* (as PERI- + *kardia* 'heart')]

pericarp /'pɛrɪkɑ:p/ *n.* the part of a fruit formed from the wall of the ripened ovary. [French *péricarpe* from Greek *perikarpion* 'pod, shell' (as PERI-, *karpos* 'fruit')]

perichondrium /pɛrɪ'kɒndrɪəm/ *n.* the membrane enveloping cartilage tissue (except at the joints). [PERI- + Greek *khondros* 'cartilage']

periclase /'pɛrɪkleɪz, -s/ *n.* a pale mineral consisting of magnesia. [modern Latin *periclasia*, erroneously from Greek *peri* 'exceedingly' + *klasis* 'breaking', from its perfect cleavage]

periclinal /pɛrɪ'klʌɪn(ə)l/ *adj. Geol.* (of a mound etc.) sloping down in all directions from a central point. [Greek *periklinēs* 'sloping on all sides' (as PERI-, CLINE)]

pericope /pə'rɪkəpi/ *n.* a short passage or paragraph, esp. a portion of Scripture read in public worship. [Late Latin from Greek *perikopē* (as PERI-, *kopē* 'cutting' from *koptō* 'cut')]

pericranium /pɛrɪ'kreɪnɪəm/ *n.* the membrane enveloping the skull. [modern Latin from Greek (as PERI-, *kranion* 'skull')]

peridot /'pɛrɪdɒt/ *n.* a green variety of olivine, used esp. as a semi-precious stone. [Middle English from Old French *peritot*, of unknown origin]

perigee /'pɛrɪdʒi:/ *n.* the point in a body's orbit at which it is nearest the earth (opp. APOGEE 1). □ **perigean** /pɛrɪ'dʒi:ən/ *adj.* [French *périgée* via modern Latin from Greek *perigeion* 'round the earth' (as PERI-, *gē* 'earth')]

periglacial /pɛrɪ'gleɪʃ(ə)l, -sɪəl/ *adj.* of or characteristic of a region adjoining a glacier or ice sheet.

perigynous /pə'rɪdʒɪnəs/ *adj.* (of stamens) situated around the pistil or ovary. [modern Latin *perigynus* (as PERI-, -GYNOUS)]

perihelion /pɛrɪ'hi:lɪən/ *n.* (*pl.* **perihelia** /-lɪə/) the point in the orbit of a planet, comet, etc. at which it is closest to the sun (opp. APHELION). [Graecized from modern Latin *perihelium* (as PERI-, Greek *hēlios* 'sun')]

peril /'pɛrɪl, -r(ə)l/ *n.* & *v.* ● *n.* serious and immediate danger. ● *v.tr.* (**perilled**, **perilling**; *US* **periled**, **periling**) threaten; endanger. □ **at one's peril** at one's own risk. **in peril of** with great risk to (*in peril of your life*). [Middle English via Old French from Latin *peric(u)lum*]

perilous /'pɛrɪləs/ *adj.* **1** full of risk; dangerous; hazardous. **2** exposed to imminent risk of destruction etc. □ **perilously** *adv.* **perilousness** *n.* [Middle English via Old French *perillous* from Latin *periculosus*, from *periculum* PERIL]

perilune /'pɛrɪlu:n, -lju:n/ *n.* the point in a body's lunar orbit at which it is closest to the moon (opp. APOLUNE). [PERI- + Latin *luna* 'moon', on the pattern of *perigee*]

perilymph /'pɛrɪlɪmf/ *n.* the fluid in the labyrinth of the ear.

perimeter /pə'rɪmɪtə/ *n.* **1 a** the circumference or outline of a closed figure. **b** the length of this. **2 a** the outer boundary of an enclosed area. **b** a defended boundary. **3** an instrument for measuring a field of vision. □ **perimetric** /pɛrɪ'mɛtrɪk/ *adj.* [French *périmètre*, or via Latin *perimetrus* from Greek *perimetros* (as PERI-, *metros* from *metron* 'measure')]

perinatal /pɛrɪ'neɪt(ə)l/ *adj.* of or relating to the time immediately before and after birth.

perineum /pɛrɪ'ni:əm/ *n.* the region of the body between the anus and the scrotum or vulva. □ **perineal** *adj.* [Late Latin from Greek *perinaion*]

period /'pɪərɪəd/ *n.* & *adj.* ● *n.* **1** a length or portion of time (*showers and bright periods*). **2** a distinct portion of history, a person's life, etc. (*the Georgian period*; *Picasso's Blue Period*). **3** *Geol.* a time forming part of a geological era (*the Quaternary period*). **4 a** an interval between recurrences of an astronomical or other phenomenon. **b** the time taken by a planet etc. to rotate about its axis. **c** the time taken by a planet or satellite to make one circuit of its orbit. **5** the time allowed for a lesson in school. **6** an occurrence of menstruation. **7 a** a complete sentence, esp. one consisting of several clauses. **b** (in *pl.*) rhetorical language. **8** esp. *N. Amer.* **a** = FULL STOP 1. **b** used at the end of a sentence etc. to indicate finality, absoluteness, etc. (*we want the best, period*). **9 a** a set of figures marked off in a large number to assist in reading. **b** a set of figures repeated in a recurring decimal. **c** the smallest interval over which a function takes the same value. **10** *Chem.* a sequence of elements between two noble gases forming a row in the periodic table. ● *adj.* belonging to or characteristic of some past period (*period furniture*). [Middle English via Old French *periode* and Latin *periodus* from Greek *periodos* 'orbit, recurrence, course' (as PERI-, *odos* = *hodos* 'way')]

periodate /pə'rʌɪədeɪt/ *n. Chem.* a salt or ester of periodic acid.

periodic /pɪərɪ'ɒdɪk/ *adj.* **1** appearing or occurring at esp. regular intervals. **2** of or concerning the period of a celestial body (*periodic motion*). **3** (of diction etc.) expressed in periods (see PERIOD *n.* 7a). □ **periodicity** /-rɪə'dɪsɪti/ *n.* [French *périodique* or Latin *periodicus* from Greek *periodikos* (as PERIOD)]

periodic acid /pə:rʌɪ'ɒdɪk/ *n. Chem.* a hygroscopic solid acid containing heptavalent iodine. [PER- + IODINE]

periodical /pɪərɪ'ɒdɪk(ə)l/ *n.* & *adj.* ● *n.* a newspaper, magazine, etc. issued at regular intervals, usu. monthly or weekly. ● *adj.* **1** published at regular intervals. **2** periodic, occasional. □ **periodically** *adv.*

periodic decimal *n. Math.* a set of figures repeated in a recurring decimal.

periodic function *n. Math.* a function returning to the same value at regular intervals.

periodic table *n.* a table of the chemical elements arranged in order of atomic number, usu. in rows, so that elements with similar atomic structure (and hence similar chemical properties) appear in vertical columns.

periodization /,pɪərɪədʌɪ'zeɪʃ(ə)n/ *n.* (also **-isation**) the division of history into periods.

periodontics /pɛrɪə'dɒntɪks/ *n.* the branch of dentistry concerned with the structures surrounding and supporting the teeth. □ **periodontal** *adj.* **periodontist** *n.* [PERI- + Greek *odous odont-* 'tooth']

periodontology /,pɛrɪədɒn'tɒlədʒi/ *n.* = PERIODONTICS.

period piece *n.* an object or work whose main interest lies in its historical etc. associations.

perioperative /pɛrɪ'ɒp(ə)rətɪv/ *adj. Med.* occurring or performed around the time of an operation.

periosteum /pɛrɪ'ɒstɪəm/ *n.* (*pl.* **periostea** /-tɪə/) a membrane enveloping the bones where no cartilage is present. □ **periosteal** *adj.* **periostitis** /-'stʌɪtɪs/ *n.* [modern Latin from Greek *periosteon* (as PERI-, *osteon* 'bone')]

peripatetic /,pɛrɪpə'tɛtɪk/ *adj.* & *n.* ● *adj.* **1** (of a teacher) working in more than one school or college etc. **2** going from place to place; itinerant. **3** (**Peripatetic**) Aristotelian (from Aristotle's habit of walking in the Lyceum while teaching). ● *n.* a peripatetic person, esp. a teacher. □ **peripatetically** *adv.* **peripateticism** /-sɪz(ə)m/ *n.* [Middle English via Old French *peripatetique* or Latin *peripateticus* from Greek *peripatētikos*, from *peripateō* (as PERI-, *pateō* 'walk')]

peripeteia /,pɛrɪpɪ'tʌɪə, -'ti:ə/ *n.* a sudden change of fortune in a drama or in life. [Greek (as PERI-, *pet-* from *piptō* 'fall')]

peripheral /pə'rɪf(ə)r(ə)l/ *adj.* & *n.* ● *adj.* **1** of minor importance; marginal. **2** of the periphery; on the fringe. **3** *Anat.* near the surface of the body, with special reference to the circulation and nervous system. **4** (of equipment) used with a computer etc. but not an integral part of it. ● *n. Computing* a peripheral device or piece of equipment. □ **peripherality** /-ˈralɪti/ *n.* **peripherally** *adv.*

peripheral nervous system *n. Anat.* the nervous system outside the brain and spinal cord.

periphery /pəˈrɪf(ə)ri/ *n.* (*pl.* **-ies**) **1** the boundary of an area or surface. **2** an outer or surrounding region (*built on the periphery of the old town*). [Late Latin *peripheria* from Greek *periphereia* 'circumference' (as PERI-, *phereia* from *phero* 'bear')]

periphrasis /pəˈrɪfrəsɪs/ *n.* (*pl.* **periphrases** /-siːz/) **1** a roundabout way of speaking; circumlocution. **2** a roundabout phrase. [Latin from Greek, from *periphrazō* (as PERI-, *phrazō* 'declare')]

periphrastic /pɛrɪˈfrastɪk/ *adj.* **1** of or involving periphrasis. **2** *Gram.* (of a case, tense, etc.) formed by combination of words rather than by inflection (e.g. *did go, of the people* rather than *went, the people's*). □ **periphrastically** *adv.* [Greek *periphrastikos* (as PERIPHRASIS)]

peripteral /pəˈrɪpt(ə)r(ə)l/ *adj.* (of a temple) surrounded by a single row of columns. [Greek *peripteron* (as PERI-, Greek *pteron* 'wing')]

periscope /ˈpɛrɪskəʊp/ *n.* an apparatus with a tube and mirrors or prisms, by which an observer in a trench, submerged submarine, or at the rear of a crowd etc., can see things otherwise out of sight.

periscopic /pɛrɪˈskɒpɪk/ *adj.* of a periscope. □ **periscopically** *adv.*

periscopic lens *n.* a lens allowing distinct vision over a wide angle.

perish /ˈpɛrɪʃ/ *v.* **1** *intr.* be destroyed; suffer death or ruin. **2 a** *intr.* (esp. of rubber, a rubber object, etc.) lose its normal qualities; deteriorate, rot. **b** *tr. Brit.* cause to rot or deteriorate. **3** *tr.* (in *passive*) *Brit.* suffer from cold or exposure (*we were perished standing outside*). □ **perish the thought** an exclamation of horror against an unwelcome idea. □ **perishless** *adj.* [Middle English via Old French *perir* from Latin *perire* 'pass away' (as PER-, *ire* 'go')]

perishable /ˈpɛrɪʃəb(ə)l/ *adj.* & *n.* ● *adj.* liable to perish; subject to decay. ● *n.* a thing, esp. a foodstuff, subject to speedy decay. □ **perishability** /-ˈbɪlɪti/ *n.* **perishableness** *n.*

perisher /ˈpɛrɪʃə/ *n. Brit. slang* an annoying person.

perishing /ˈpɛrɪʃɪŋ/ *adj.* & *adv. Brit. colloq.* ● *adj.* **1** confounded. **2** freezing cold, extremely chilly. ● *adv.* confoundedly. □ **perishingly** *adv.*

perisperm /ˈpɛrɪspəːm/ *n.* a mass of nutritive material outside the embryo-sac in some seeds. [PERI- + Greek *sperma* 'seed']

perissodactyl /pərɪsə(ʊ)ˈdaktɪl/ *adj.* & *n. Zool.* ● *adj.* of or relating to the order Perissodactyla of ungulate mammals with one main central toe, or a single toe, on each foot, including horses, rhinoceroses, and tapirs. ● *n.* an animal of this order. [modern Latin *Perissodactyla*, from Greek *perissos* 'uneven' + *daktulos* 'finger, toe']

peristalsis /pɛrɪˈstalsɪs/ *n.* an involuntary muscular wavelike movement by which the contents of the alimentary canal etc. are propelled along. □ **peristaltic** *adj.* **peristaltically** *adv.* [modern Latin, from Greek *peristellō* 'wrap around' (as PERI-, *stellō* 'place')]

peristome /ˈpɛrɪstəʊm/ *n.* **1** *Bot.* a fringe of small projections around the mouth of a capsule in mosses and certain fungi. **2** *Zool.* the parts surrounding the mouth of various invertebrates. [modern Latin *peristoma*, from PERI- + Greek *stoma* 'mouth']

peristyle /ˈpɛrɪstʌɪl/ *n.* a row of columns surrounding a temple, court, cloister, etc.; a space surrounded by columns. [French *péristyle* via Latin *peristylum* from Greek *peristulon* (as PERI-, *stulos* 'pillar')]

peritoneum /ˌpɛrɪtəˈniːəm/ *n.* (*pl.* **peritoneums** or **peritonea** /-ˈniːə/) the serous membrane lining the cavity of the abdomen. □ **peritoneal** *adj.* [Late Latin from Greek *peritonaion* (as PERI-, *tonaion* from *-tonos* 'stretched')]

peritonitis /ˌpɛrɪtəˈnʌɪtɪs/ *n.* an inflammatory disease of the peritoneum.

periwig /ˈpɛrɪwɪg/ *n.* esp. *hist.* a wig. □ **periwigged** *adj.* [alteration of PERUKE, with *-wi-* for French *-u-* sound]

periwinkle[1] /ˈpɛrɪwɪŋk(ə)l/ *n.* **1** any plant of the genus *Vinca*, esp. an evergreen trailing plant with blue or white flowers. **2** a tropical shrub, *Catharanthus roseus*, native to Madagascar. [Middle English via Anglo-French *pervenke*, Old French *pervenche* from Late Latin *pervinca*, assimilated to PERIWINKLE[2]]

periwinkle[2] /ˈpɛrɪwɪŋk(ə)l/ *n.* = WINKLE. [16th c.: origin unknown]

perjure /ˈpəːdʒə/ *v.refl. Law* **1** wilfully tell an untruth when on oath. **2** (as **perjured** *adj.*) guilty of or involving perjury. □ **perjurer** *n.* [Middle English via Old French *parjurer* from Latin *perjurare* (as PER-, *jurare* 'swear')]

perjury /ˈpəːdʒ(ə)ri/ *n.* (*pl.* **-ies**) *Law* **1** a breach of an oath, esp. the act of wilfully telling an untruth when on oath. **2** the practice of this. □ **perjurious** /-ˈdʒʊərɪəs/ *adj.* [Middle English via Anglo-French *perjurie* and Old French *parjurie* from Latin *perjurium* (as PERJURE)]

perk[1] /pəːk/ *v.* & *adj.* ● *v.tr.* (often foll. by *up*) raise (one's head etc.) briskly. ● *adj.* perky; pert. □ **perk up 1** recover confidence, courage, life, or zest. **2** restore confidence or courage or liveliness in (esp. another person). **3** smarten up. [Middle English, perhaps from a variant of PERCH[1]]

perk[2] /pəːk/ *n. colloq.* a perquisite. [abbreviation]

perk[3] /pəːk/ *v. colloq.* **1** *intr.* (of coffee) percolate, make a bubbling sound in the percolator. **2** *tr.* percolate (coffee). [abbreviation of PERCOLATE]

perky /ˈpəːki/ *adj.* (**perkier**, **perkiest**) **1** self-assertive; saucy; pert. **2** lively; cheerful. □ **perkily** *adv.* **perkiness** *n.*

perlite /ˈpəːlʌɪt/ *n.* (also **pearlite**) a glassy type of vermiculite, expandable to a solid form by heating, used for insulation etc. [French from *perle* 'pearl']

perm[1] /pəːm/ *n.* & *v.* ● *n.* a permanent wave. ● *v.tr.* give a permanent wave to (a person or a person's hair). [abbreviation]

perm[2] /pəːm/ *n.* & *v. Brit. colloq.* ● *n.* a permutation. ● *v.tr.* make a permutation of. [abbreviation]

permaculture /ˈpəːməkʌltʃə/ *n.* the development of agricultural ecosystems intended to be complete and self-sustaining. [PERMANENT + AGRICULTURE]

permafrost /ˈpəːməfrɒst/ *n.* subsoil which remains below freezing point throughout the year, as in polar regions. [PERMANENT + FROST]

permalloy /ˈpəːməlɔɪ/ *n.* an alloy of nickel and iron that is easily magnetized and demagnetized. [PERMEABLE + ALLOY]

permanent /ˈpəːm(ə)nənt/ *adj.* lasting, or intended to last or function, indefinitely (opp. TEMPORARY). □ **permanence** *n.* **permanency** *n.* **permanentize** *v.tr.* (also **-ise**). **permanently** *adv.* [Middle English from Old French *permanent* or Latin *permanēre* (as PER-, *manēre* 'remain')]

permanent hardness *n.* hardness of water which is not removed by boiling.

permanent magnet *n.* a magnet retaining its magnetic properties in the absence of an inducing field or current.

Permanent Secretary *n. Brit.* a senior civil servant, usu. a permanent adviser to a minister.

permanent set *n.* **1** the irreversible deformation of a substance after being subjected to stress. **2** the amount of this.

permanent tooth *n.* a tooth succeeding a milk tooth in a mammal, and lasting most of the mammal's life.

Permanent Under-Secretary *n. Brit.* **1** a senior permanent adviser to a Secretary of State. **2** a senior civil servant below the rank of Permanent Secretary, usu. the head of a division within a department of state.

permanent wave *n.* an artificial wave in the hair, intended to last for some time.

permanent way *n. Brit.* the finished roadbed of a railway.

permanganate /pəˈmaŋgənət, -eɪt/ *n. Chem.* any salt of permanganic acid, esp. potassium permanganate.

permanganic acid /pəːmaŋˈganɪk/ *n. Chem.* an acid containing heptavalent manganese. [PER- + MANGANIC: see MANGANESE]

permeability /pəːmɪəˈbɪlɪti/ *n.* **1** the state or quality of being permeable. **2** a quantity measuring the influence of a substance on the magnetic flux in the region it occupies.

permeable /ˈpəːmɪəb(ə)l/ *adj.* capable of being permeated. [Latin *permeabilis* (as PERMEATE)]

permeate /ˈpəːmɪeɪt/ *v.* **1** *tr.* penetrate throughout; pervade; saturate. **2** *intr.* (usu. foll. by *through*, *among*, etc.) diffuse itself. □ **permeance** *n.* **permeant** *adj.* **permeation** /-ˈeɪʃ(ə)n/ *n.* **permeator** *n.* [Latin *permeare permeat-* (as PER-, *meare* 'pass, go')]

permethrin /pəˈmiːθrɪn/ *n.* a synthetic pyrethroid used as an insecticide, esp. against disease-carrying insects. [from PER- + *-m-* + PYRETHRIN]

Permian /ˈpəːmɪən/ *adj. & n. Geol.* ● *adj.* of or relating to the last period of the Palaeozoic era with evidence of the development of reptiles and amphibians, and deposits of sandstone. Cf. Appendix X. ● *n.* this period or system. [*Perm*, a province in Russia, from the extensive development of such strata there]

per mille /pəː ˈmɪli/ *adv.* (also **per mil** /mɪl/) in every thousand. [Latin]

permissible /pəˈmɪsɪb(ə)l/ *adj.* allowable. □ **permissibility** /-ˈbɪlɪti/ *n.* **permissibly** *adv.* [Middle English from French, or from medieval Latin *permissibilis* (as PERMIT)]

permission /pəˈmɪʃ(ə)n/ *n.* (often foll. by *to* + infin.) consent; authorization. [Middle English from Old French, or from Latin *permissio* (as PERMIT)]

permissive /pəˈmɪsɪv/ *adj.* **1** tolerant; liberal, esp. in sexual matters (*the permissive society*). **2** giving permission. □ **permissively** *adv.* **permissiveness** *n.* [Middle English from Old French (*-if -ive*) or medieval Latin *permissivus* (as PERMIT)]

permissive legislation *n.* legislation giving powers but not enjoining their use.

permit *v. & n.* ● *v.* /pəˈmɪt/ (**permitted**, **permitting**) **1** *tr.* give permission or consent to; authorize (*permit me to say*). **2 a** *tr.* allow; give an opportunity to (*permit the traffic to flow again*). **b** *intr.* give an opportunity (*circumstances permitting*). **3** *intr.* (foll. by *of*) admit; allow for. ● *n.* /ˈpəːmɪt/ **1 a** a document giving permission to act in a specified way (*was granted a work permit*). **b** a document etc. which allows entry into a specified zone. **2** *formal* permission. □ **permittee** /pəːmɪˈtiː/ *n.* **permitter** *n.* [Latin *permittere* (as PER-, *mittere miss-* 'let go')]

permittivity /pəːmɪˈtɪvɪti/ *n. Electr.* a quantity measuring the ability of a substance to store electrical energy in an electric field.

permutate /ˈpəːmjʊteɪt/ *v.tr.* change the order or arrangement of. [as PERMUTE, or back-formation from PERMUTATION]

permutation /pəːmjʊˈteɪʃ(ə)n/ *n.* **1 a** an ordered arrangement or grouping of a set of numbers, items, etc. **b** any one of the range of possible groupings. **2** any combination or selection of a specified number of things from a larger group, esp. *Brit.* matches in a football pool. □ **permutational** *adj.* [Middle English from Old French, or from Latin *permutatio* (as PERMUTE)]

permute /pəˈmjuːt/ *v.tr.* alter the sequence or arrangement of. [Middle English from Latin *permutare* (as PER-, *mutare* 'change')]

Permutit /ˈpəːmjʊtɪt/ *n. propr.* an artificial zeolite used as an ion exchanger esp. for the softening of water. [German, from Latin *permutare* (as PERMUTE)]

pernicious /pəˈnɪʃəs/ *adj.* destructive; ruinous; fatal. □ **perniciously** *adv.* **perniciousness** *n.* [Latin *perniciosus*, via *pernicies* 'ruin' from *nex necis* 'death']

pernicious anaemia *n.* a defective formation of red blood cells through a lack of vitamin B_{12} or folic acid.

pernickety /pəˈnɪkɪti/ *adj. colloq.* **1** fastidious. **2** precise or over-precise. **3** requiring tact or careful handling. [19th-c. Scots: origin unknown]

pernoctate /ˈpəːnɒkteɪt, pəˈnɒkteɪt/ *v.intr. formal* pass or spend the night. □ **pernoctation** /-ˈteɪʃ(ə)n/ *n.* [Late Latin *pernoctatio* from Latin *pernoctare pernoctat-* (as PER-, *noctare* from *nox noctis* 'night')]

Pernod /ˈpəːnəʊ/ *n. propr.* an aniseed-flavoured aperitif. [*Pernod* Fils, the manufacturing firm]

peroneal /pɛrə(ʊ)ˈniːəl/ *adj. Anat.* relating to or near the fibula. [modern Latin *peronaeus* 'peroneal muscle', from *perone* 'fibula', from Greek *peronē* 'pin, fibula']

perorate /ˈpɛrəreɪt/ *v.intr.* **1** sum up and conclude a speech. **2** speak at length. [Latin *perorare perorat-* (as PER-, *orare* 'speak')]

peroration /pɛrəˈreɪʃ(ə)n/ *n.* the concluding part of a speech, forcefully summing up what has been said.

peroxidase /pəˈrɒksɪdeɪz/ *n. Biochem.* any of a class of enzymes which catalyse the oxidation of a substrate by hydrogen peroxide.

peroxide /pəˈrɒksʌɪd/ *n. & v.* ● *n. Chem.* **1 a** = HYDROGEN PEROXIDE. **b** (often *attrib.*) a solution of hydrogen peroxide used to bleach the hair or as an antiseptic. **2** a compound of oxygen with another element containing the greatest possible proportion of oxygen. **3** any salt or ester of hydrogen peroxide. ● *v.tr.* bleach (the hair) with peroxide. [PER- + OXIDE]

perpendicular /pəːp(ə)nˈdɪkjʊlə/ *adj. & n.* ● *adj.* **1 a** at right angles to the plane of the horizon. **b** (usu. foll. by *to*) *Geom.* at right angles (to a given line, plane, or surface). **2** upright, vertical. **3** (of a slope etc.) very steep. **4** (**Perpendicular**) *Archit.* of the third stage of English Gothic (15th–16th c.) with vertical tracery in large windows. **5** *joc.* in a standing position. ● *n.* **1** a perpendicular line. **2** a plumb rule or a similar instrument. **3** (prec. by *the*) a perpendicular line or orientation (*is out of the perpendicular*). □ **perpendicularity** /-ˈlarɪti/ *n.* **perpendicularly** *adv.* [Middle English from Latin *perpendicularis*, via *perpendiculum* 'plumb line' from PER- + *pendēre* 'hang']

perpetrate /ˈpəːpɪtreɪt/ *v.tr.* commit or perform (a crime, blunder, or anything outrageous). □ **perpetration** /-ˈtreɪʃ(ə)n/ *n.* **perpetrator** *n.* [Latin *perpetrare perpetrat-* (as PER-, *patrare* 'effect')]

perpetual /pəˈpɛtʃʊəl, -tjʊəl/ *adj.* **1** eternal; lasting for ever or indefinitely. **2** continuous, uninterrupted. **3** frequent, much repeated (*perpetual interruptions*). **4** permanent during life (*perpetual secretary*). □ **perpetualism** *n.* **perpetually** *adv.* [Middle English via Old French *perpetuel* from Latin *perpetualis*, via *perpetuus* from *perpes -etis* 'continuous']

perpetual calendar *n.* a calendar which can be adjusted to show any combination of day, month, and year.

perpetual check *n. Chess* the position of play when a draw is obtained by repeated checking of the king.

perpetual motion *n.* the motion of a hypothetical machine which once set in motion would run for ever unless subject to an external force or to wear.

perpetuate /pəˈpɛtʃʊeɪt, -tjʊeɪt/ *v.tr.* **1** make perpetual. **2** preserve from oblivion. □ **perpetuance** *n.* **perpetuation** /-ˈeɪʃ(ə)n/ *n.* **perpetuator** *n.* [Latin *perpetuare* (as PERPETUAL)]

perpetuity /pəːpɪˈtjuːɪti/ *n.* (*pl.* **-ies**) **1** the state or quality of being perpetual. **2** a perpetual annuity. **3** a perpetual possession or position. □ **in** (or **to** or **for**) **perpetuity** for ever. [Middle English via Old French *perpetuité* from Latin *perpetuitas -tatis* (as PERPETUAL)]

perpetuum mobile /pəːˌpɛtjʊəm ˈməʊbɪli, pəːˌpɛtjʊʊm, ˈməʊbɪleɪ/ *n.* **1** = PERPETUAL MOTION. **2** *Mus.* = MOTO

PERPETUO. [Latin *perpetuus* 'continuous' + *mobilis* 'movable', on the pattern of PRIMUM MOBILE]

perplex /pəˈplɛks/ *v.tr.* **1** puzzle, bewilder, or disconcert (a person, a person's mind, etc.). **2** complicate or confuse (a matter). **3** (as **perplexed** *adj.*) *archaic* entangled, intertwined. □ **perplexedly** /-ɪdli/ *adv.* **perplexing** *adj.* **perplexingly** *adv.* [back-formation from *perplexed*, from obsolete adj. *perplex*, from Old French *perplexe* or Latin *perplexus* (as PER-, *plexus*, past part. of *plectere* 'plait')]

perplexity /pəˈplɛksɪti/ *n.* (*pl.* **-ies**) **1** bewilderment; the state of being perplexed. **2** a thing which perplexes. **3** *archaic* an entangled state. [Middle English from Old French *perplexité* or Late Latin *perplexitas* (as PERPLEX)]

per pro. /pəː ˈprəʊ/ *abbr.* through the agency of (used in signatures). [Latin *per procurationem*]

■ **Usage** The correct sequence of signatures is A *per pro.* B, where B is signing on behalf of A. The abbreviation *p.p.* is commonly used instead, e.g. *C. Smith p.p. J. Carter* where J. Carter is signing on behalf of C. Smith.

perquisite /ˈpəːkwɪzɪt/ *n.* **1** an extra profit or allowance additional to a main income etc. **2** a customary extra right or privilege. **3** an incidental benefit attached to employment etc. **4** a thing which has served its primary use and to which a subordinate or employee has a customary right. [Middle English via medieval Latin *perquisitum* from Latin *perquirere* 'search diligently for' (as PER-, *quaerere* 'seek')]

■ **Usage** *Perquisite* is sometimes confused with *prerequisite*, which means 'a thing required as a precondition'.

Perrier /ˈpɛrɪə/ *n. propr.* an effervescent natural mineral water. [the name of a spring at Vergèze, France, its source]

perron /ˈpɛrən/ *n.* an exterior staircase leading up to a main entrance to a church or other (usu. large) building. [Middle English from Old French, ultimately from Latin *petra* 'stone']

perry /ˈpɛri/ *n.* (*pl.* **-ies**) *Brit.* a drink like cider, made from the fermented juice of pears. [Middle English *pereye* etc. from Old French *peré*, ultimately from Latin *pirum* 'pear']

per se /pəː ˈseɪ/ *adv.* by or in itself; intrinsically. [Latin]

persecute /ˈpəːsɪkjuːt/ *v.tr.* **1** subject (a person etc.) to hostility or ill-treatment, esp. on the grounds of political or religious belief. **2** harass; worry. **3** (often foll. by *with*) bombard (a person) with questions etc. □ **persecutor** *n.* **persecutory** *adj.* [Middle English from Old French *persecuter*, back-formation from *persecuteur* 'persecutor', via Late Latin *persecutor* from Latin *persequi* (as PER-, *sequi secut-* 'follow, pursue')]

persecution /pəːsɪˈkjuːʃ(ə)n/ *n.* the act or an instance of persecuting; the state of being persecuted.

persecution complex *n.* (also **persecution mania**) an irrational obsessive fear that others are scheming against one.

perseverance /pəːsɪˈvɪər(ə)ns/ *n.* **1** the steadfast pursuit of an objective. **2** (often foll. by *in*) constant persistence (in a belief etc.). [Middle English via Old French from Latin *perseverantia* (as PERSEVERE)]

perseverate /pəˈsɛvəreɪt/ *v.intr.* **1** continue action etc. for an unusually or excessively long time. **2** *Psychol.* tend to prolong or repeat a response after the original stimulus has ceased. □ **perseveration** /-ˈreɪʃ(ə)n/ *n.* [Latin *perseverare* (as PERSEVERE)]

persevere /pəːsɪˈvɪə/ *v.intr.* (often foll. by *in, at, with*) continue steadfastly or determinedly; persist. [Middle English via Old French *perseverer* from Latin *perseverare* 'persist', from *perseverus* 'very strict' (as PER-, *severus* 'severe')]

Persian /ˈpəːʒ(ə)n, -ʃ(ə)n/ *n.* & *adj.* ● *n.* **1 a** a native or inhabitant of ancient or modern Persia (now Iran). **b** a person of Persian descent. **2** the language of ancient Persia or modern Iran. **3** (in full **Persian cat**) **a** a cat of a breed with long silky hair and a thick tail. **b** this breed. ● *adj.* of or relating to Persia or its people or language. [Middle English via Old French *persien* from medieval Latin]

■ **Usage** The preferred terms for the language (see sense 2 of the noun) are *Iranian* and *Farsi* respectively.

Persian carpet *n.* (also **Persian rug**) a carpet or rug of a traditional pattern made in Persia.

Persian lamb *n.* the silky tightly curled fur of a young karakul, used in clothing.

persiennes /pəːsɪˈɛnz/ *n.pl.* window shutters, or outside blinds, with louvres. [French, fem. pl. of obsolete *persien* 'Persian']

persiflage /ˈpəːsɪflɑːʒ/ *n.* light raillery, banter. [French *persifler* 'banter' (as PER- + *siffler* 'whistle')]

persimmon /pəˈsɪmən/ *n.* **1** any evergreen tree of the genus *Diospyros* bearing edible orange pulpy fruits. **2** the fruit of this. [corruption of Algonquian *pessemmins*]

persist /pəˈsɪst/ *v.intr.* **1** (often foll. by *in*) continue firmly or obstinately (in an opinion or a course of action) esp. despite obstacles, remonstrance, etc. **2** (of an institution, custom, phenomenon, etc.) continue in existence; survive. [Latin *persistere* (as PER-, *sistere* 'stand')]

persistent /pəˈsɪst(ə)nt/ *adj.* **1** continuing obstinately; persisting. **2** enduring. **3** constantly repeated (*persistent nagging*). **4** *Biol.* (of horns, leaves, etc.) remaining instead of falling off in the normal manner. □ **persistence** *n.* **persistency** *n.* **persistently** *adv.*

persistent vegetative state *n. Med.* the state of a person whose body is kept functioning by medical means but who manifests no sign of higher brain functions.

persnickety /pəˈsnɪkɪti/ *adj. N. Amer. colloq.* = PERNICKETY. [alteration of PERNICKETY]

person /ˈpəːs(ə)n/ *n.* **1** an individual human being (*a cheerful and forthright person*). **2** the living body of a human being (*hidden about your person*). **3** *Gram.* a category used in the classification of pronouns, verb forms, etc., according to whether they indicate the speaker (**first person**); the addressee (**second person**); a third party (**third person**). **4** (in *comb.*) used to replace *-man* in offices open to either sex (*salesperson*). **5** (in Christianity) God as Father, Son, or Holy Ghost (*three persons in one God*). **6** *euphem.* the genitals (*expose one's person*). **7** a character in a play or story. **8** a type of person who enjoys something specified (*not a party person*). □ **in one's own person** oneself; as oneself. **in person** physically present. [Middle English via Old French *persone* from Latin *persona* 'actor's mask, character in a play, human being']

persona /pəˈsəʊnə, pəː-/ *n.* (*pl.* **personas** or **personae** /-niː/) **1** an aspect of the personality as shown to or perceived by others (opp. ANIMA 1). **2** *Literary Criticism* an author's assumed character in his or her writing. [Latin (as PERSON)]

personable /ˈpəːs(ə)nəb(ə)l/ *adj.* pleasing in appearance and behaviour. □ **personableness** *n.* **personably** *adv.*

personage /ˈpəːs(ə)nɪdʒ/ *n.* **1** a person, esp. of rank or importance. **2** a character in a play etc. [Middle English, from PERSON + -AGE, influenced by medieval Latin *personagium* 'effigy' & French *personnage*]

persona grata /ˈgrɑːtə/ *n.* (*pl.* ***personae gratae*** /ˈgrɑːtiː/) a person, esp. a diplomat, acceptable to certain others. [Latin, as PERSONA + *grata*, fem. of *gratus* 'pleasing']

personal /ˈpəːs(ə)n(ə)l/ *adj.* & *n.* ● *adj.* **1** one's own; individual; private. **2** done or made in person (*made a personal appearance*; *my personal attention*). **3** directed to or concerning an individual (*a personal letter*). **4** referring (esp. in a hostile way) to an individual's private life or concerns (*making personal remarks*; *no need to be personal*). **5** of the body and clothing (*personal hygiene*; *personal appearance*). **6** existing as a person, not as an abstraction or thing (*a personal God*). **7** *Gram.* of or denoting one of the three persons (*personal pronoun*). ● *n.* esp. *N. Amer.* an advertisement or notice in the personal column of a newspaper. [Middle English via Old French from Latin *personalis* (as PERSON)]

personal ad *n.* esp. *US colloq.* = PERSONAL *n.*

personal column *n.* the part of a newspaper devoted to private advertisements or messages.

personal computer *n.* a computer designed for use by a single individual, esp. in an office or business environment .

personal equity plan *n. Brit.* a scheme for limited personal investment in shares, unit trusts, etc.

personal estate *n.* = PERSONAL PROPERTY.

personal identification number *n.* a number allocated to an individual, serving as a password esp. for a cash dispenser, computer, etc.

personality /pə:sə'nalɪti/ *n.* (*pl.* **-ies**) **1 a** the distinctive character or qualities of a person, often as distinct from others (*an attractive personality*). **b** socially attractive qualities (*was clever but had no personality*). **2** a famous person; a celebrity (*a TV personality*). **3** a person who stands out from others by virtue of his or her character (*is a real personality*). **4** personal existence or identity; the condition of being a person. **5** (usu. in *pl.*) personal remarks. [Middle English via Old French *personalité* from Late Latin *personalitas -tatis* (as PERSONAL)]

personality cult *n.* the extreme adulation of an individual.

personalize /'pə:s(ə)n(ə)lʌɪz/ *v.tr.* (also **-ise**) **1** make personal, esp. by marking with one's name etc. **2** personify. □ **personalization** /-'zeɪʃ(ə)n/ *n.*

personally /'pə:s(ə)n(ə)li/ *adv.* **1** in person (*see to it personally*). **2** for one's own part (*speaking personally*). **3** as a person (*a God existing personally*). **4** in a personal manner (*took the criticism personally*).

personal organizer *n.* **1** a loose-leaf notebook with sections for various kinds of information, including a diary etc. **2** a hand-held microcomputer serving the same purpose.

personal pronoun *n.* each of the pronouns (*I, you, he, she, it, we, they, me, him, her, us, them*) comprising a set that shows contrast of person, gender, number, and case.

■ **Usage** Reflexive pronouns (*myself, ourselves,* etc.) and possessive pronouns (*my, your,* etc.) are sometimes included in the category of personal pronouns.

personal property *n. Law* all one's property except land and those interests in land that pass to one's heirs (cf. REAL[1] *adj.* 3).

personal service *n.* individual service given to a customer.

personal space *n.* **1** the immediate area around an individual where any encroachment is considered threatening or uncomfortable. **2** space for the use of an individual.

personal stereo *n.* a small portable audio cassette player, often with radio, or compact disc player, used with lightweight headphones.

personal touch *n.* a characteristic or individual approach to a situation.

personalty /'pə:s(ə)n(ə)lti/ *n.* (*pl.* **-ies**) *Law* one's personal property or estate (opp. REALTY). [Anglo-French *personalté* (as PERSONAL)]

persona non grata /nɒn, nəʊn 'grɑ:tə/ *n.* (*pl.* ***personae non gratae*** /'grɑ:ti:/) an unacceptable or unwelcome person. [Latin, as PERSONA GRATA + *non* 'not']

personate /'pə:s(ə)neɪt/ *v.tr.* **1** play the part of (a character in a drama etc.; another type of person). **2** pretend to be (another person), esp. for fraudulent purposes; impersonate. □ **personation** /-'neɪʃ(ə)n/ *n.* **personator** *n.* [Late Latin *personare personat-* (as PERSON)]

personhood /'pə:s(ə)nhʊd/ *n.* the quality or condition of being an individual person.

personification /pə,sɒnɪfɪ'keɪʃ(ə)n/ *n.* **1** the act of personifying. **2** (foll. by *of*) a person or thing viewed as a striking example of (a quality etc.) (*the personification of ugliness*).

personify /pə'sɒnɪfʌɪ/ *v.tr.* (**-ies**, **-ied**) **1** attribute a personal nature to (an abstraction or thing). **2** symbolize (a quality etc.) by a figure in human form. **3** (usu. as **personified** *adj.*) embody (a quality) in one's own person; exemplify typically (*has always been kindness personified*). □ **personifier** *n.* [French *personnifier* (as PERSON)]

personnel /pə:sə'nɛl/ *n.* **1** a body of employees, persons involved in a public undertaking, armed forces, etc. **2** = PERSONNEL DEPARTMENT. [French, originally *adj.* = personal]

personnel carrier *n.* an armoured vehicle for transporting troops etc.

personnel department *n.* the part of an organization concerned with the appointment, training, and welfare of employees.

person-to-person *adj.* & *adv.* ● *attrib.adj.* **1** between individuals. **2** (of a phone call) booked through the operator to a specified person. ● *adv.* between individuals.

perspective /pə'spɛktɪv/ *n.* & *adj.* ● *n.* **1 a** the art of drawing solid objects on a two-dimensional surface so as to give the right impression of relative positions, size, etc. **b** a picture drawn in this way. **2** the apparent relation between visible objects as to position, distance, etc. **3** a mental view of the relative importance of things (*keep the right perspective*). **4** a geographical or imaginary prospect. ● *adj.* of or in perspective. □ **in** (or **out of**) **perspective 1** drawn or viewed according (or not according) to the rules of perspective. **2** correctly (or incorrectly) regarded in terms of relative importance. □ **perspectival** /-'tʌɪv(ə)l/ *adj.* **perspectively** *adv.* [Middle English, in the sense 'the science of sight, optics', from medieval Latin *perspectiva* (*ars* 'art'), from *perspicere perspect-* 'look at closely, look through' (as PER-, *specere spect-* 'to look')]

perspex /'pə:spɛks/ *n. Brit. propr.* a tough light transparent acrylic thermoplastic used instead of glass. [Latin *perspicere* 'look through' (as PER-, *specere* 'to look')]

perspicacious /pə:spɪ'keɪʃəs/ *adj.* having mental penetration or discernment. □ **perspicaciously** *adv.* **perspicaciousness** *n.* **perspicacity** /-'kasɪti/ *n.* [Latin *perspicax -acis* (as PERSPEX)]

■ **Usage** *Perspicacious*, meaning 'having or showing insight', is sometimes confused with *perspicuous*, meaning 'expressing things clearly' or 'clearly expressed'.

perspicuous /pə'spɪkjʊəs/ *adj.* **1** easily understood; clearly expressed. **2** (of a person) expressing things clearly. □ **perspicuity** /pə:spɪ'kju:ɪti/ *n.* **perspicuously** *adv.* **perspicuousness** *n.* [Middle English, = transparent, from Latin *perspicuus* (as PERSPECTIVE)]

■ **Usage** See Usage Note at PERSPICACIOUS.

perspiration /pə:spɪ'reɪʃ(ə)n/ *n.* **1** = SWEAT *n.* 1. **2** sweating. □ **perspiratory** /-'spɪrət(ə)ri/ *adj.* [French (as PERSPIRE)]

perspire /pə'spʌɪə/ *v.* **1** *intr.* sweat or exude perspiration, esp. as the result of heat, exercise, anxiety, etc. **2** *tr.* sweat or exude (fluid etc.). [French *perspirer* from Latin *perspirare* (as PER-, *spirare* 'breathe')]

persuade /pə'sweɪd/ *v.tr.* & *refl.* **1** (often foll. by *of*, or *that* + clause) cause (another person or oneself) to believe; convince (*persuaded them that it would be helpful; tried to persuade me of its value*). **2 a** (often foll. by *to* + infin.) induce (another person or oneself) (*persuaded us to join them; managed to persuade them at last*). **b** (foll. by *away from, down to,* etc.) lure, attract, entice, etc. (*persuaded them away from the pub*). □ **persuadable** *adj.* **persuadability** /-də'bɪlɪti/ *n.* **persuasible** *adj.* [Latin *persuadēre* (as PER-, *suadēre suas-* 'advise')]

persuader /pəˈsweɪdə/ *n.* **1** a person who persuades. **2** *slang* a gun or other weapon.

persuasion /pəˈsweɪʒ(ə)n/ *n.* **1** persuading (*yielded to persuasion*). **2** persuasiveness (*use all your persuasion*). **3** a belief or conviction (*my private persuasion*). **4** a religious belief, or the group or sect holding it (*of a different persuasion*). **5** *colloq.* or *joc.* any group or party (*the male persuasion*). [Middle English from Latin *persuasio* (as PERSUADE)]

persuasive /pəˈsweɪsɪv/ *adj.* able to persuade. □ **persuasively** *adv.* **persuasiveness** *n.* [French *persuasif -ive* or medieval Latin *persuasivus* (as PERSUADE)]

PERT *abbr.* programme evaluation and review technique.

pert /pəːt/ *adj.* **1** saucy or impudent, esp. in speech or conduct. **2** (of clothes etc.) neat and suggestive of jauntiness. **3** = PEART. □ **pertly** *adv.* **pertness** *n.* [Middle English via Old French *apert* from Latin *apertus*, past part. of *aperire* 'open' and via Old French *aspert* from Latin *expertus* EXPERT]

pertain /pəˈteɪn/ *v.intr.* **1** (foll. by *to*) **a** relate or have reference to. **b** belong to as a part or appendage or accessory. **2** (usu. foll. by *to*) be appropriate to. [Middle English via Old French *partenir* from Latin *pertinēre* (as PER-, *tenēre* 'hold')]

pertinacious /pəːtɪˈneɪʃəs/ *adj.* stubborn; persistent; obstinate (in a course of action etc.). □ **pertinaciously** *adv.* **pertinaciousness** *n.* **pertinacity** /-ˈnasɪti/ *n.* [Latin *pertinax* (as PER-, *tenax* 'tenacious')]

pertinent /ˈpəːtɪnənt/ *adj.* **1** (often foll. by *to*) relevant to the matter in hand; apposite. **2** to the point. □ **pertinence** *n.* **pertinency** *n.* **pertinently** *adv.* [Middle English from Old French *pertinent* or Latin *pertinēre* (as PERTAIN)]

perturb /pəˈtəːb/ *v.tr.* **1** throw into confusion or disorder. **2** disturb mentally; agitate. **3** *Physics & Math.* subject (a physical system, or a set of equations, or its solution) to a perturbation. □ **perturbable** *adj.* **perturbative** /pəˈtəːbətɪv, ˈpəːtəbeɪtɪv/ *adj.* **perturbingly** *adv.* [Middle English via Old French *pertourber* from Latin (as PER-, *turbare* 'disturb')]

perturbation /pəːtəˈbeɪʃ(ə)n/ *n.* **1** the act or an instance of perturbing; the state of being perturbed. **2** a cause of disturbance or agitation. **3** *Physics* a slight alteration of a physical system, e.g. of the electrons in an atom, caused by a secondary influence. **4** *Astron.* a minor deviation in the course of a celestial body, caused by the attraction of a neighbouring body.

pertussis /pəˈtʌsɪs/ *n.* whooping cough. [modern Latin, from PER- + Latin *tussis* 'cough']

peruke /pəˈruːk/ *n. hist.* a wig. [French *perruque* from Italian *perrucca parrucca*, of unknown origin]

peruse /pəˈruːz/ *v.tr.* **1** (also *absol.*) read or study, esp. thoroughly or carefully. **2** examine (a person's face etc.) carefully. □ **perusal** *n.* **peruser** *n.* [Middle English, in the sense 'use up', probably via Anglo-Latin from Romanic (as PER-, USE)]

Peruvian /pəˈruːvɪən/ *n. & adj.* ● *n.* **1** a native or national of Peru. **2** a person of Peruvian descent. ● *adj.* of or relating to Peru. [modern Latin *Peruvia* 'Peru']

Peruvian bark *n.* the bark of the cinchona tree.

pervade /pəˈveɪd/ *v.tr.* **1** spread throughout, permeate. **2** (of influences etc.) become widespread among or in. **3** be rife among or through. □ **pervasion** /-ʒ(ə)n/ *n.* [Latin *pervadere* (as PER-, *vadere vas-* 'go')]

pervasive /pəˈveɪsɪv/ *adj.* **1** pervading. **2** able to pervade. □ **pervasively** *adv.* **pervasiveness** *n.*

perve /pəːv/ *n. & v. slang* ● *n.* (also **perv**) **1** *Brit.* a sexual pervert. **2** *Austral.* an erotic gaze. ● *v.intr.* **1** act like a sexual pervert. **2** (foll. by *at, on*) *Austral.* gaze with erotic interest. [abbreviation]

perverse /pəˈvəːs/ *adj.* **1** (of a person or action) deliberately or stubbornly departing from what is reasonable or required. **2** persistent in error. **3** wayward; intractable; peevish. **4** perverted; wicked. **5** (of a verdict etc.) against the weight of evidence or the judge's direction. □ **perversely** *adv.* **perverseness** *n.* **perversity** *n.* (*pl.* **-ies**). [Middle English via Old French *pervers perverse* from Latin *perversus* (as PERVERT)]

perversion /pəˈvəːʃ(ə)n/ *n.* **1** an act of perverting; the state of being perverted. **2** a perverted form of an act or thing. **3 a** preference for an abnormal form of sexual activity. **b** such an activity. [Middle English from Latin *perversio* (as PERVERT)]

pervert *v. & n.* ● *v.tr.* /pəˈvəːt/ **1** turn (a person or thing) aside from its proper use or nature. **2** misapply or misconstrue (words etc.). **3** lead astray (a person, a person's mind, etc.) from right opinion or conduct, or esp. religious belief. **4** (as **perverted** *adj.*) showing perversion. ● *n.* /ˈpəːvəːt/ **1** a perverted person. **2** a person showing sexual perversion. □ **perversive** /pəˈvəːsɪv/ *adj.* **pervertedly** /pəˈvəːtɪdli/ *adv.* **perverter** /-ˈvəːtə/ *n.* [Middle English from Old French *pervertir* or from Latin *pervertere* (as PER-, *vertere vers-* 'turn'): cf. CONVERT]

pervious /ˈpəːvɪəs/ *adj.* **1** permeable. **2** (usu. foll. by *to*) **a** affording passage. **b** accessible (to reason etc.). □ **perviousness** *n.* [Latin *pervius* (as PER-, *vius* from *via* 'way')]

Pesach /ˈpeɪsɑːx/ *n.* the Passover festival. [Hebrew *Pesaḥ*]

peseta /pəˈseɪtə/ *n.* **1** the chief monetary unit of Spain. **2** *hist.* a silver coin. [Spanish, diminutive of *pesa* 'weight', from Latin *pensa*, pl. of *pensum*: see POISE[1]]

pesky /ˈpɛski/ *adj.* (**peskier**, **peskiest**) esp. *US colloq.* troublesome; confounded; annoying. □ **peskily** *adv.* **peskiness** *n.* [18th c.: perhaps related to PEST]

peso /ˈpeɪsəʊ/ *n.* (*pl.* **-os**) **1** the chief monetary unit of several Latin American countries and of the Philippines. **2** a note or coin worth one peso. [Spanish, = weight, from Latin *pensum*: see POISE[1]]

pessary /ˈpɛs(ə)ri/ *n.* (*pl.* **-ies**) *Med.* **1** a device worn in the vagina to support the uterus or as a contraceptive. **2** a vaginal suppository. [Middle English via Late Latin *pessarium*, *pessulum*, from *pessum*, *pessus*, from Greek *pessos* 'oval stone']

pessimism /ˈpɛsɪmɪz(ə)m/ *n.* **1** a tendency to take the worst view or expect the worst outcome. **2** *Philos.* a belief that this world is as bad as it could be or that all things tend to evil. Opp. OPTIMISM. □ **pessimist** *n.* **pessimistic** /-ˈmɪstɪk/ *adj.* **pessimistically** /-ˈmɪstɪk(ə)li/ *adv.* [Latin *pessimus* 'worst', on the pattern of OPTIMISM]

pest /pɛst/ *n.* **1** a troublesome or annoying person or thing; a nuisance. **2** a destructive animal, esp. an insect which attacks crops, livestock, etc. **3** *archaic* a pestilence; a plague. [French *peste* or Latin *pestis* 'plague']

pester /ˈpɛstə/ *v.tr.* trouble or annoy, esp. with frequent or persistent requests. □ **pesterer** *n.* [French *empestrer* 'encumber', influenced by PEST]

pest-house *n. hist.* a hospital for sufferers from the plague etc.

pesticide /ˈpɛstɪsʌɪd/ *n.* a substance used for destroying insects or other organisms harmful to cultivated plants or to animals. □ **pesticidal** /-ˈsʌɪd(ə)l/ *adj.*

pestiferous /pɛˈstɪf(ə)rəs/ *adj.* **1** noxious; pestilent. **2** harmful; pernicious; bearing moral contagion. [Latin *pestifer, -ferus* (as PEST)]

pestilence /ˈpɛstɪl(ə)ns/ *n.* a fatal epidemic disease, esp. bubonic plague. [Middle English via Old French from Latin *pestilentia* (as PESTILENT)]

pestilent /ˈpɛstɪl(ə)nt/ *adj.* **1** destructive to life, deadly. **2** harmful or morally destructive. **3** *colloq.* troublesome; annoying. □ **pestilently** *adv.* [Latin *pestilens*, *pestilentus* from *pestis* 'plague']

pestilential /pɛstɪˈlɛnʃ(ə)l/ *adj.* **1** of or relating to pestilence. **2** dangerous; troublesome; pestilent. □ **pestilentially** *adv.* [Middle English via medieval Latin *pestilentialis* from Latin *pestilentia* (as PESTILENT)]

pestle /ˈpɛs(ə)l/ *n.* & *v.* ● *n.* **1** a club-shaped instrument for pounding substances in a mortar. **2** an appliance for pounding etc. ● *v.* **1** *tr.* pound with a pestle or in a similar manner. **2** *intr.* use a pestle. [Middle English via Old French *pestel* from Latin *pistillum*, from *pinsare pist-* 'to pound']

pesto /ˈpɛstəʊ/ *n.* an Italian sauce of crushed basil leaves, pine nuts, garlic, Parmesan cheese, and olive oil, usu. served with pasta. [Italian, from *pestare* 'pound, crush']

pestology /pɛˈstɒlədʒi/ *n.* the scientific study of pests (esp. harmful insects) and of methods of dealing with them. □ **pestological** /-stəˈlɒdʒɪk(ə)l/ *adj.* **pestologist** *n.*

PET *abbr.* **1** positron emission tomography, a form of tomography used esp. for brain scans. **2** polyethylene terephthalate, a plastic used in recyclable packaging.

Pet. *abbr.* Peter (New Testament).

pet[1] /pɛt/ *n.*, *adj.*, & *v.* ● *n.* **1** a domestic or tamed animal kept for pleasure or companionship. **2** a darling, a favourite (often as a term of endearment). ● *attrib.adj.* **1** kept as a pet (*pet lamb*). **2** of or for pet animals (*pet food*). **3** often *joc.* favourite or particular (*my pet hate is filling in forms*). **4** expressing fondness or familiarity (*pet form*). ● *v.tr.* (**petted**, **petting**) **1** treat as a pet. **2** (also *absol.*) fondle, esp. erotically. □ **petter** *n.* [16th-c. Scots & northern English dialect: origin unknown]

pet[2] /pɛt/ *n.* a feeling of petty resentment or ill humour (esp. *be in a pet*). [16th c.: origin unknown]

peta- /ˈpɛtə/ *comb. form* denoting a factor of 10^{15}. [perhaps from PENTA-]

petal /ˈpɛt(ə)l/ *n.* each of the parts of the corolla of a flower. □ **petaline** /-ʌɪn, -ɪn/ *adj.* **petalled** *adj.* (also in *comb.*). **petal-like** *adj.* **petaloid** *adj.* [modern Latin *petalum*, in Late Latin 'metal plate', via Greek *petalon* 'leaf' from *petalos* 'outspread']

pétanque /pəˈtaŋk, French petɑ̃k/ *n.* a game similar to boule. [French]

petard /pɪˈtɑːd/ *n. hist.* **1** a small bomb used to blast down a door etc. **2** a kind of firework or cracker. □ **hoist with** (or **by**) **one's own petard** affected adversely by one's schemes against others. [French *pétard* from *péter* 'break wind']

petasus /ˈpɛtəsəs/ *n.* **1** an ancient Greek hat with a low crown and broad brim, esp. (in Greek mythology) as worn by Hermes. **2** the winged hat of Hermes. [Latin from Greek *petasos*]

Pete /piːt/ *n.* □ **for Pete's sake** see SAKE[1]. [abbreviation of the name *Peter*]

petechia /pɪˈtiːkɪə/ *n.* (*pl.* **petechiae** /-kɪiː/) *Med.* a small red or purple spot as a result of bleeding into the skin. □ **petechial** *adj.* [modern Latin from Italian *petecchia*, a freckle or spot on one's face]

peter[1] /ˈpiːtə/ *v.* & *n.* ● *v.intr.* **1** (foll. by *out*) (originally of a vein of ore etc.) diminish, come to an end. **2** *Bridge* play an echo. ● *n. Bridge* an echo. [19th c.: origin unknown]

peter[2] /ˈpiːtə/ *n. slang* **1** a prison cell. **2** a safe. [perhaps from the name *Peter*]

peterman /ˈpiːtəmən/ *n.* (*pl.* **-men**) *slang* a safe-breaker.

Peter Pan /piːtə ˈpan/ *n.* a person who retains youthful features, or who is immature. [hero of J. M. Barrie's play of the same name (1904)]

Peter Principle /ˈpiːtə/ *n. joc.* the principle that members of a hierarchy are promoted until they reach the level at which they are no longer competent. [named after L. J. *Peter*, its propounder, b. 1919]

petersham /ˈpiːtəʃ(ə)m/ *n.* thick corded silk ribbon used for stiffening in dressmaking etc. [named after Lord *Petersham*, English army officer d. 1851]

Peter's pence /ˈpiːtəz/ *n.pl. Eccl.* **1** *hist.* an annual tax of one penny, formerly paid to the papal see. **2** (since 1860) a voluntary payment by Roman Catholics to the papal treasury. [St *Peter*, as first pope]

pethidine /ˈpɛθɪdiːn/ *n.* esp. *Brit.* a synthetic analgesic drug used esp. in childbirth. Also called *meperidine.* [perhaps from PIPERIDINE (from which the drug is derived) + ETHYL]

petiole /ˈpɛtɪəʊl/ *n.* the slender stalk joining a leaf to a stem. □ **petiolar** *adj.* **petiolate** /-lət/ *adj.* [French *pétiole* from Latin *petiolus* 'little foot, stalk']

petit /ˈpɛti/ *adj.* esp. *Law* petty; small; of lesser importance. [Middle English via Old French, = small, from Romanic, perhaps imitative of child's speech]

petit bourgeois /pɛti ˈbʊəʒwɑː, pəˌtiː/ *n.* (*pl.* **petits bourgeois** *pronunc.* same) a member of the lower middle classes. [French]

petite /pəˈtiːt/ *adj.* (of a woman) of small and dainty build. [French, fem. of PETIT]

petite bourgeoisie /pəˌtiːt bʊəʒwɑːˈziː/ *n.* the lower middle classes.

petit four /pɛti ˈfɔː/ *n.* (*pl.* **petits fours** /ˈfɔːz/) a very small fancy cake, biscuit, or sweet. [French, = little oven]

petition /pɪˈtɪʃ(ə)n/ *n.* & *v.* ● *n.* **1** a supplication or request. **2** a formal written request, esp. one signed by many people, appealing to authority in some cause. **3** *Law* an application to a court for a writ etc. ● *v.* **1** *tr.* make or address a petition to (*petition your MP*). **2** *intr.* (often foll. by *for*, *to*) appeal earnestly or humbly. □ **petitionable** *adj.* **petitionary** *adj.* **petitioner** *n.* [Middle English via Old French from Latin *petitio -onis*]

Petition of Right *n.* **1** *hist.* a parliamentary declaration of rights and liberties of the people assented to by Charles I in 1628. **2** *Law* a common-law remedy against the crown for the recovery of property.

petitio principii /pɪˌtɪʃɪəʊ prɪnˈsɪpɪʌɪ, prɪŋˈkɪp-/ *n. Logic* a fallacy in which a conclusion is taken for granted in the premiss; begging the question. [Latin, = assuming a principle: see PETITION]

petit jury *n.* = PETTY JURY.

petit-maître /pətɪˈmeɪtr(ə), French pətimɛtr/ *n.* a dandy or coxcomb. [French, = little master]

petit mal /pəti ˈmal/ *n.* **1** a mild form of epilepsy with only momentary loss of consciousness (often *attrib.*: *petit mal epilepsy*). **2** an epileptic fit of this kind. Cf. GRAND MAL. [French, = little sickness]

petit point /pəti ˈpwã, pɛti ˈpɔɪnt/ *n.* **1** embroidery on canvas using small stitches. **2** tent stitch. [French, = little point]

petits pois /pɛti ˈpwɑː/ *n.pl.* small green peas. [French]

pet name *n.* a name expressing fondness or familiarity.

Petrarchan /pɪˈtrɑːk(ə)n/ *adj.* denoting a sonnet of the kind used by the Italian poet Petrarch (d. 1374), with an octave rhyming abbaabba, and a sestet usu. rhyming cdcdcd or cdecde.

petrel /ˈpɛtr(ə)l/ *n.* any of various seabirds of the family Procellariidae or Hydrobatidae, usu. flying far from land. [17th c. (also *pitteral*), of uncertain origin: later associated with St Peter (from the bird's habit of flying low with legs dangling, appearing to walk on the water: Matt. 14:30)]

Petri dish /ˈpɛtri, ˈpiːtri/ *n.* a shallow covered dish used for the culture of bacteria etc. [named after J. R. *Petri*, German bacteriologist d. 1921]

petrifaction /pɛtrɪˈfakʃ(ə)n/ *n.* **1** the process of fossilization whereby organic matter is turned into a stony substance. **2** a petrified substance or mass. **3** a state of extreme fear or terror. [PETRIFY, on the pattern of *stupefaction*]

petrify /ˈpɛtrɪfʌɪ/ *v.* (**-ies**, **-ied**) **1** *tr.* paralyse with fear, astonishment, etc. **2** *tr.* change (organic matter) into a stony substance. **3** *intr.* become like stone. **4** *tr.* deprive (the mind, a doctrine, etc.) of vitality; deaden. [French *pétrifier* via medieval Latin *petrificare* and Latin *petra* 'rock' from Greek]

petro- /ˈpɛtrəʊ/ *comb. form* **1** rock. **2** petroleum (*petrochemistry*). [Greek *petros* 'stone' or *petra* 'rock']

petrochemical /pɛtrə(ʊ)ˈkɛmɪk(ə)l/ *n.* & *adj.* ● *n.* a substance industrially obtained from petroleum or natural gas. ● *adj.* of or relating to petrochemistry or petrochemicals.

petrochemistry /pɛtrə(ʊ)'kɛmɪstri/ *n.* **1** the chemistry of rocks. **2** the chemistry of petroleum.

petrodollar /'pɛtrəʊˌdɒlə/ *n.* a notional unit of currency earned by a country exporting petroleum.

petroglyph /'pɛtrə(ʊ)glɪf/ *n.* a rock-carving, esp. a prehistoric one. [PETRO- + Greek *glyphē* 'carving']

petrography /pɛ'trɒgrəfi/ *n.* the scientific description of the composition and formation of rocks. □ **petrographer** *n.* **petrographic** /-'grafɪk/ *adj.* **petrographical** /-'grafɪk(ə)l/ *adj.*

petrol /'pɛtr(ə)l/ *n. Brit.* **1** refined petroleum used as a fuel in motor vehicles, aircraft, etc. **2** (*attrib.*) concerned with the supply of petrol (*petrol pump*; *petrol station*). [French *pétrole* from medieval Latin *petroleum*: see PETROLEUM]

petrolatum /pɛtrə'leɪtəm/ *n. US* petroleum jelly. [modern Latin, from PETROL + *-atum*]

petrol bomb *n. Brit.* a simple bomb made of a petrol-filled bottle and a wick.

petroleum /pɪ'trəʊlɪəm/ *n.* a hydrocarbon oil found in the upper strata of the earth, refined for use as a fuel for heating and in internal-combustion engines, for lighting, dry-cleaning, etc. [medieval Latin, from Latin *petra* 'rock' (from Greek) + Latin *oleum* 'oil']

petroleum ether *n.* a volatile liquid distilled from petroleum, consisting of a mixture of hydrocarbons.

petroleum jelly *n.* a translucent solid mixture of hydrocarbons used as a lubricant, ointment, etc.

petrolic /pɪ'trɒlɪk/ *adj.* of or relating to petrol or petroleum.

petrology /pɪ'trɒlədʒi/ *n.* the study of the origin, structure, composition, etc., of rocks (cf. LITHOLOGY). □ **petrologic** /pɛtrə'lɒdʒɪk/ *adj.* **petrological** /pɛtrə'lɒdʒɪk(ə)l/ *adj.* **petrologist** *n.*

petrous /'pɛtrəs/ *adj.* **1** *Anat.* denoting the hard part of the temporal bone protecting the inner ear. **2** *Geol.* of, like, or relating to rock. [Latin *petrosus* from *petra* 'rock', from Greek]

petticoat /'pɛtɪkəʊt/ *n.* **1** a woman's or girl's undergarment in the form of a skirt or a skirt and bodice. **2** *slang* a woman or girl. **3** (*attrib.*) often *derog.* feminine; associated with women (*petticoat pedantry*). □ **petticoated** *adj.* **petticoatless** *adj.* [Middle English, from *petty coat*]

pettifog /'pɛtɪfɒg/ *v.intr.* (**pettifogged**, **pettifogging**) **1** practise legal deception or trickery. **2** quibble or wrangle about petty points. [back-formation from PETTIFOGGER]

pettifogger /'pɛtɪfɒgə/ *n.* **1** a rascally lawyer; an inferior legal practitioner. **2** a petty practitioner in any activity. □ **pettifoggery** *n.* **pettifogging** *adj.* [PETTY + *fogger* 'underhand dealer', probably from *Fugger*, the name of a family of merchants in Augsburg in the 15th–16th c.]

pettish /'pɛtɪʃ/ *adj.* peevish, petulant; easily put out. □ **pettishly** *adv.* **pettishness** *n.* [PET[2] + -ISH[1]]

petty /'pɛti/ *adj.* (**pettier**, **pettiest**) **1** unimportant; trivial. **2** mean, small-minded; contemptible. **3** minor; inferior; on a small scale (*petty princes*). **4** *Law* (of a crime) of lesser importance (*petty larceny*) (cf. COMMON *adj.* 9, GRAND *adj.* 8). □ **pettily** *adv.* **pettiness** *n.* [Middle English *pety*, variant of PETIT]

petty bourgeois *n.* = PETIT BOURGEOIS.

petty bourgeoisie *n.* = PETITE BOURGEOISIE.

petty cash *n.* money from or for small items of receipt or expenditure.

petty jury *n.* a jury of 12 persons who try the final issue of fact in civil or criminal cases and pronounce a verdict.

petty officer *n.* a naval NCO.

petty sessions *n.* (in the UK): **1** a meeting of two or more magistrates for the summary trial of certain offences. **2** = QUARTER SESSIONS.

petty treason see TREASON 2.

petulant /'pɛtjʊl(ə)nt/ *adj.* peevishly impatient or irritable. □ **petulance** *n.* **petulantly** *adv.* [French *pétulant* from Latin *petulans -antis*, from *petere* 'seek']

petunia /pɪ'tju:nɪə/ *n.* any plant of the genus *Petunia* with white, purple, red, etc., funnel-shaped flowers. [modern Latin via French *petun* from Guarani *petȳ* 'tobacco' (to which these plants are related)]

petuntse /peɪ'tʊntsə, pɪ'tʌntsə/ *n.* a white variable feldspathic mineral used for making porcelain. [Chinese *baidunzi*, from *bai* 'white' + *dun* 'stone' + suffix *-zi*]

pew /pju:/ *n. & v.* ● *n.* **1** (in a church) a long bench with a back; an enclosed compartment. **2** *Brit. colloq.* a seat (esp. *take a pew*). ● *v.tr.* furnish with pews. □ **pewage** *n.* **pewless** *adj.* [originally a place in a church with a seat (often raised) for particular worshippers: Middle English *pywe*, *puwe* via Old French *puye* 'balcony' from Latin *podia*, pl. of PODIUM]

pewee /'pi:wi:/ *n.* a N. American tyrant flycatcher of the genus *Contopus*. [imitative (cf. PEEWEE)]

pewit var. of PEEWIT.

pewter /'pju:tə/ *n.* **1** a grey alloy of tin with copper and antimony (formerly, tin and lead). **2** utensils made of this. **3** *Brit. slang* a tankard etc. as a prize. □ **pewterer** *n.* [Middle English via Old French *peutre*, *peualtre* from Romanic, of unknown origin]

peyote /peɪ'əʊti/ *n.* **1** a Mexican cactus, *Lophophora williamsii*, having no spines and button-like tops when dried; also called MESCAL. **2** a hallucinogenic drug containing mescaline prepared from this. [Latin American Spanish from Nahuatl *peyotl*]

Pf. *abbr.* pfennig.

Pfc. *abbr. US* Private First Class.

pfennig /'(p)fɛnɪg/ *n.* **1** a German monetary unit, equal to one-hundredth of a mark. **2** a coin of this value. [German, related to PENNY]

PG *abbr.* **1** (of films) classified as suitable for children subject to parental guidance. **2** paying guest.

pH *n. Chem.* a logarithm of the reciprocal of the hydrogen ion concentration in moles per litre of a solution, giving a measure of its acidity or alkalinity. [German, from *Potenz* 'power' + *H* (symbol for hydrogen)]

phaeton /'feɪt(ə)n/ *n.* **1** a light open four-wheeled carriage, usu. drawn by a pair of horses. **2** *US* a vintage touring car. [French *phaéton* via Latin *Phaethon* from Greek *Phaethōn*, son of Helios the sun-god, who was allowed to drive the sun-chariot for a day, with disastrous results]

phage /feɪdʒ/ *n.* = BACTERIOPHAGE. [abbreviation]

phagocyte /'fagə(ʊ)sʌɪt/ *n.* a type of cell capable of engulfing and absorbing foreign matter, esp. a leucocyte ingesting bacteria in the body. □ **phagocytic** /-'sɪtɪk/ *adj.* [Greek *phag-* 'eat' + -CYTE]

phagocytosis /fagəsʌɪ'təʊsɪs/ *n.* the ingestion of bacteria etc. by phagocytes. □ **phagocytize** /'fagə-/ *v.tr.* (also **-ise**). **phagocytose** /'fagə-/ *v.tr.*

-phagous /fəgəs/ *comb. form* that eats (as specified) (*ichthyophagous*). [Latin *-phagus* from Greek *-phagos*, from *phagein* 'eat']

-phagy /fədʒi/ *comb. form* the eating of (specified food) (*ichthyophagy*). [Greek *-phagia* (as -PHAGOUS)]

phalange /'falan(d)ʒ/ *n.* **1** *Anat.* = PHALANX 3. **2** (**Phalange**) a right-wing activist Maronite party in Lebanon (cf. FALANGE). [French from Latin *phalanx*: see PHALANX]

phalangeal /fə'lan(d)ʒɪəl/ *adj. Anat.* of or relating to a phalanx.

phalanger /fə'lan(d)ʒə/ *n.* any of various arboreal marsupials of the family Phalangeridae, including cuscuses and brush-tailed possums. [French from Greek *phalaggion* 'spider's web', from the webbed toes of their hind feet]

Phalangist /fə'lan(d)ʒɪst, 'falən(d)ʒɪst/ *n. & adj.* ● *n.* a member of the Phalange party in Lebanon. ● *adj.* of or relating to the Phalangists. [PHALANGE]

phalanx /ˈfalaŋks/ *n.* (*pl.* **phalanxes** or **phalanges** /fəˈlan(d)ʒiːz/) **1** *Gk Antiq.* a line of battle, esp. a body of Macedonian infantry drawn up in close order. **2** a set of people etc. forming a compact mass, or banded for a common purpose. **3** a bone of the finger or toe. **4** *Bot.* a bundle of stamens united by filaments. [Latin from Greek *phalagx -ggos*]

phalarope /ˈfalərəʊp/ *n.* any small wading or swimming bird of the subfamily Phalaropodidae, with a straight bill and lobed feet. [French from modern Latin *Phalaropus*, formed irregularly from Greek *phalaris* 'coot' + *pous podos* 'foot']

phalli *pl.* of PHALLUS.

phallic /ˈfalɪk/ *adj.* **1** of, relating to, or resembling a phallus. **2** *Psychol.* denoting the stage of male sexual development characterized by preoccupation with the genitals. □ **phallically** *adv.* [French *phallique* & Greek *phallikos* (as PHALLUS)]

phallocentric /faləʊˈsɛntrɪk/ *adj.* centred on the phallus or on male attitudes. □ **phallocentricity** /-ˈtrɪsɪti/ *n.* **phallocentrism** /-trɪz(ə)m/ *n.*

phallus /ˈfaləs/ *n.* (*pl.* **phalli** /-lʌɪ, -liː/ or **phalluses**) **1** the (esp. erect) penis. **2** an image of this as a symbol of generative power in nature. □ **phallicism** /-lɪsɪz(ə)m/ *n.* **phallism** *n.* [Late Latin from Greek *phallos*]

phanariot /fəˈnarɪət/ *n. hist.* a member of a class of Greek officials in Constantinople under the Ottoman Empire. [modern Greek *phanariōtēs* from *Phanar*, the part of the city where they lived, from Greek *phanarion* 'lighthouse (on the Golden Horn)']

phanerogam /ˈfan(ə)rə(ʊ)gam/ *n. Bot.* a plant that has stamens and pistils, a flowering plant (cf. CRYPTOGAM). □ **phanerogamic** /-ˈgamɪk/ *adj.* **phanerogamous** /-ˈrɒgəməs/ *adj.* [French *phanérogame*, from Greek *phaneros* 'visible' + *gamos* 'marriage']

phantasize var. of FANTASIZE.

phantasm /ˈfantaz(ə)m/ *n.* **1** an illusion, a phantom. **2** (usu. foll. by *of*) an illusory likeness. **3** a supposed vision of an absent (living or dead) person. □ **phantasmal** /-ˈtazm(ə)l/ *adj.* **phantasmic** /-ˈtazmɪk/ *adj.* [Middle English via Old French *fantasme* and Latin from Greek *phantasma*, from *phantazō* 'make visible' from *phainō* 'show']

phantasmagoria /ˌfantazməˈgɒrɪə, -gɔːr-/ *n.* **1** a shifting series of real or imaginary figures as seen in a dream. **2** an optical device for rapidly varying the size of images on a screen. □ **phantasmagoric** /-ˈgɒrɪk/ *adj.* **phantasmagorical** /-ˈgɒrɪk(ə)l/ *adj.* [probably from French *fantasmagorie* (as PHANTASM + fanciful ending)]

phantast var. of FANTAST.

phantasy var. of FANTASY.

phantom /ˈfantəm/ *n.* & *adj.* ● *n.* **1** a ghost; an apparition; a spectre. **2** a form without substance or reality; a mental illusion. **3** *Med.* a model of the whole or part of the body used to practise or demonstrate operative or therapeutic methods. ● *adj.* merely apparent; illusory. [Middle English from Old French *fantosme*, ultimately from Greek *phantasma* (as PHANTASM)]

phantom circuit *n.* an arrangement of telegraph or other electrical wires equivalent to an extra circuit.

phantom limb *n.* a continuing sensation of the presence of a limb which has been amputated.

phantom pregnancy *n. Med.* the symptoms of pregnancy in a person not actually pregnant.

Pharaoh /ˈfɛːrəʊ/ *n.* **1** the ruler of ancient Egypt. **2** the title of this ruler. □ **Pharaonic** /fɛːreɪˈɒnɪk/ *adj.* [Old English via ecclesiastical Latin *Pharao*, Greek *Pharaō*, and Hebrew *parʻōh* from Egyptian *pr-ʻo* 'great house']

Pharaoh's ant *n.* a small reddish ant, *Monomorium pharaonis*, native to warm regions and also a pest of heated buildings elsewhere.

Pharaoh's serpent *n.* an indoor firework burning and uncoiling in serpentine form.

Pharisee /ˈfarɪsiː/ *n.* **1** a member of an ancient Jewish sect, distinguished by strict observance of the traditional and written law, and commonly held to have pretensions to superior sanctity (cf. SADDUCEE). **2** a self-righteous person; a hypocrite. □ **Pharisaic** /farɪˈseɪɪk/ *adj.* **Pharisaical** /farɪˈseɪɪk(ə)l/ *adj.* **Pharisaism** /ˈfarɪseɪɪz(ə)m/ *n.* [Old English *fariseus* & Old French *pharise*, via ecclesiastical Latin *pharisaeus* and Greek *Pharisaios* from Aramaic *p'rīšayyâ* 'separated ones', from Hebrew *pārûš* 'separated']

pharmaceutical /fɑːməˈsjuːtɪk(ə)l/ *adj.* **1** of or engaged in pharmacy. **2** of the use or sale of medicinal drugs. □ **pharmaceutically** *adv.* **pharmaceutics** *n.* [Late Latin *pharmaceuticus* from Greek *pharmakeutikos*, via *pharmakeutēs* 'druggist' from *pharmakon* 'drug']

pharmacist /ˈfɑːməsɪst/ *n.* a person qualified to prepare and dispense drugs.

pharmacognosy /fɑːməˈkɒgnəsi/ *n.* the science of drugs, esp. relating to medicinal products in their natural or unprepared state. [Greek *pharmakon* 'drug' + *gnōsis* 'knowledge']

pharmacology /fɑːməˈkɒlədʒi/ *n.* the branch of medicine that deals with the uses, effects, and modes of action of drugs. □ **pharmacological** /-kəˈlɒdʒɪk(ə)l/ *adj.* **pharmacologically** /-kəˈlɒdʒɪk(ə)li/ *adv.* **pharmacologist** *n.* [modern Latin *pharmacologia* (as Greek *pharmakon* 'drug', -LOGY)]

pharmacopoeia /fɑːməkəˈpiːə/ *n.* **1** a book, esp. one officially published, containing a list of drugs with directions for use. **2** a stock of drugs. □ **pharmacopoeial** *adj.* [modern Latin from Greek *pharmakopoiia*, from *pharmakopoios* 'drug-maker' (as PHARMACOLOGY + *-poios* 'making')]

pharmacy /ˈfɑːməsi/ *n.* (*pl.* **-ies**) **1** the preparation and the (esp. medicinal) dispensing of drugs. **2** a pharmacist's shop, a dispensary. [Middle English via Old French *farmacie* and medieval Latin *pharmacia* from Greek *pharmakeia* 'practice of the druggist', via *pharmakeus* from *pharmakon* 'drug']

pharos /ˈfɛːrɒs/ *n.* a lighthouse or a beacon to guide sailors. [Latin from Greek *Pharos*, the name of an island off Alexandria where a famous lighthouse stood]

pharyngo- /fəˈrɪŋgəʊ/ *comb. form* denoting the pharynx.

pharyngotomy /farɪŋˈgɒtəmi/ *n.* (*pl.* **-ies**) an incision into the pharynx.

pharynx /ˈfarɪŋks/ *n.* (*pl.* **pharynges** /-ˈrɪn(d)ʒiːz/) **1** *Anat.* & *Zool.* a membrane-lined cavity behind the nose and mouth, connecting them to the oesophagus. **2** *Zool.* a part of the alimentary canal immediately behind the mouth in invertebrates. □ **pharyngal** /-ˈrɪŋg(ə)l/ *adj.* **pharyngeal** /-ˈdʒiːəl/ *adj.* **pharyngitis** /-ˈdʒʌɪtɪs/ *n.* [modern Latin from Greek *pharugx -ggos*]

phase /feɪz/ *n.* & *v.* ● *n.* **1** a distinct period or stage in a process of change or development. **2** each of the aspects of the moon or a planet, according to the amount of its illumination, esp. the new moon, the first quarter, the full moon, and the last quarter. **3** *Physics* a stage in a periodically recurring sequence, esp. of alternating electric currents or light vibrations. **4** a difficult or unhappy period, esp. in adolescence. **5** a genetic or seasonal variety of an animal's coloration etc. **6** *Chem.* a distinct and homogeneous form of matter separated by its surface from other forms. ● *v.tr.* carry out (a programme etc.) in phases or stages. □ **in phase** having the same phase at the same time. **out of phase** not in phase. **phase in** (or **out**) bring gradually into (or out of) use. □ **phasic** *adj.* [French *phase* and earlier *phasis*, from Greek *phasis* 'appearance' from *phainō phan-* 'show']

phase rule *n. Chem.* a rule relating numbers of phases, constituents, and degrees of freedom.

phatic /ˈfatɪk/ *adj.* (of speech etc.) used to convey general sociability rather than to communicate a specific meaning, e.g. 'nice morning, isn't it?'. [Greek *phatos* 'spoken' from *phēmi phan-* 'speak']

Ph.D. *abbr.* Doctor of Philosophy. [Latin *philosophiae doctor*]

pheasant /ˈfɛz(ə)nt/ *n.* any of several long-tailed game birds of the family Phasianidae, originally from Asia. [Middle English via Anglo-French *fesaunt*, Old French *faisan*, and Latin *phasianus* from Greek *phasianos* '(bird) of *Phasis*', a river in Asia Minor]

pheasantry /ˈfɛz(ə)ntri/ *n.* (*pl.* **-ies**) a place where pheasants are reared or kept.

phenacetin /fɪˈnasɪtɪn/ *n.* an acetyl derivative of phenol used to treat fever etc. [PHENO- + ACETYL + -IN]

phencyclidine /fɛnˈsʌɪklɪdiːn/ *n.* a piperidine derivative used as a veterinary anaesthetic and a hallucinogenic drug (abbr.: **PCP**).

pheno- /ˈfiːnəʊ, ˈfɛnəʊ/ *comb. form* **1** *Chem.* derived from benzene (*phenol*; *phenyl*). **2** showing (*phenocryst*). [Greek *phainō* 'shine' (with reference to substances used for illumination), 'show']

phenobarbitone /fiːnə(ʊ)ˈbɑːbɪtəʊn, fɛn-/ *n.* (*US* **phenobarbital** /-t(ə)l/) a narcotic and sedative barbiturate drug used esp. to treat epilepsy.

phenocryst /ˈfiːnə(ʊ)krɪst, ˈfɛn-/ *n.* a large or conspicuous crystal in porphyritic rock. [French *phénocryste* (as PHENO-, CRYSTAL)]

phenol /ˈfiːnɒl/ *n. Chem.* **1** a white hygroscopic mildly acidic crystalline solid, used in dilute form as an antiseptic and disinfectant (also called *carbolic*). Chem. formula: C_6H_5OH. **2** any hydroxyl derivative of an aromatic hydrocarbon. □ **phenolic** /fɪˈnɒlɪk/ *adj.* [French *phénole* from *phène* 'benzene' (formed as PHENO-) + -OL[1]]

phenolphthalein /fiːnɒlˈ(f)θaliːn, -ˈ(f)θeɪl-/ *n. Chem.* a white crystalline solid used in solution as an acid-base indicator and medicinally as a laxative. [PHENOL + *phthal* from NAPHTHALENE + -IN]

phenom /ˈfiːnɒm/ *n. US colloq.* an unusually gifted person, a prodigy. [abbreviation of PHENOMENON 2]

phenomena *pl.* of PHENOMENON.

phenomenal /fɪˈnɒmɪn(ə)l/ *adj.* **1** of the nature of a phenomenon. **2** extraordinary, remarkable, prodigious. **3** perceptible by, or perceptible only to, the senses. □ **phenomenalize** *v.tr.* (also **-ise**). **phenomenally** *adv.*

phenomenalism /fɪˈnɒmɪn(ə)lɪz(ə)m/ *n. Philos.* **1** the doctrine that human knowledge is confined to the appearances presented to the senses. **2** the doctrine that appearances are the foundation of all our knowledge. □ **phenomenalist** *n. & adj.* **phenomenalistic** /-ˈlɪstɪk/ *adj.*

phenomenology /fɪˌnɒmɪˈnɒlədʒi/ *n. Philos.* **1** the science of phenomena as distinct from that of being (ontology). **2** a philosophical approach concentrating on the study of consciousness and the objects of direct experience. □ **phenomenological** /-nəˈlɒdʒɪk(ə)l/ *adj.* **phenomenologically** /-nəˈlɒdʒɪk(ə)li/ *adv.* **phenomenologist** *n.*

phenomenon /fɪˈnɒmɪnən/ *n.* (*pl.* **phenomena** /-nə/) **1** a fact or occurrence that appears or is perceived, esp. one of which the cause is in question. **2** a remarkable person or thing. **3** *Philos.* the object of a person's perception; what the senses or the mind notice. [Late Latin from Greek *phainomenon*, neut. pres. part. of *phainomai* 'appear', from *phainō* 'show']

■ **Usage** The plural form of *phenomenon*, *phenomena*, is often used mistakenly for the singular. This should be avoided, i.e. *This is a strange phenomenon* is correct, as is *many strange phenomena*.

phenotype /ˈfiːnə(ʊ)tʌɪp/ *n. Biol.* a set of observable characteristics of an individual or group resulting from the interaction of its genotype with its environment. □ **phenotypic** /-ˈtɪpɪk/ *adj.* **phenotypical** /-ˈtɪpɪk(ə)l/ *adj.* **phenotypically** /-ˈtɪpɪk(ə)li/ *adv.* [German *Phaenotypus* (as PHENO-, TYPE)]

phenyl /ˈfiːnʌɪl, ˈfɛnɪl/ *n. Chem.* the monovalent radical C_6H_5- formed from benzene by the removal of a hydrogen atom. [PHENO- + -YL]

phenylalanine /fiːnʌɪlˈaləniːn, fɛnɪl-/ *n. Biochem.* an amino acid widely distributed in plant proteins and essential in the human diet. [PHENYL + ALANINE]

phenylketonuria /ˌfiːnʌɪlkiːtəˈnjʊəriə, -nɪl-, ˌfɛnɪl-/ *n.* an inherited inability to metabolize phenylalanine, ultimately leading to mental handicap if untreated. [PHENYL + KETONE + -URIA]

pheromone /ˈfɛrəməʊn/ *n.* a chemical substance secreted and released by an animal for detection and response by another usu. of the same species. □ **pheromonal** /-ˈməʊn(ə)l/ *adj.* [Greek *pherō* 'convey' + HORMONE]

phew /fjuː, fjʊ/ *int.* an expression of impatience, discomfort, relief, astonishment, or disgust. [imitative of puffing]

phi /fʌɪ/ *n.* the twenty-first letter of the Greek alphabet (Φ, ϕ). [Greek]

phial /ˈfʌɪəl/ *n.* a small glass bottle, esp. for liquid medicine. [Middle English via Old French *fiole* and Latin *phiola phiala* from Greek *phialē*, a broad flat vessel: cf. VIAL]

Phi Beta Kappa /ˌfʌɪ ˌbiːtə ˈkapə/ *n.* **1** (in the US) an intercollegiate honorary society to which distinguished scholars may be elected (from the initial letters of a Greek motto, = philosophy is the guide to life). **2** a member of this society.

Phil. *abbr.* **1** Philadelphia. **2** Philharmonic. **3** Philippians (New Testament). **4** Philosophy.

phil- var. of PHILO-.

-phil var. of -PHILE.

philabeg var. of FILIBEG.

philadelphus /fɪləˈdɛlfəs/ *n.* a highly-scented deciduous flowering shrub of the genus *Philadelphus*, esp. the mock orange. [modern Latin from Greek *philadelphon*]

philander /fɪˈlandə/ *v.intr.* (often foll. by *with*) flirt or have casual affairs with women; womanize. □ **philanderer** *n.* [*philander* (*n.*), used in Greek literature as the proper name of a lover, from Greek *philandros* 'fond of men' from *anēr* 'male person': see PHIL-]

philanthrope /ˈfɪlənθrəʊp/ *n.* a philanthropist (see PHILANTHROPY). [Greek *philanthrōpos* (as PHIL-, *anthrōpos* 'human being')]

philanthropic /fɪlənˈθrɒpɪk/ *adj.* loving one's fellow men; benevolent. □ **philanthropically** *adv.* [French *philanthropique* (as PHILANTHROPE)]

philanthropy /fɪˈlanθrəpi/ *n.* **1** a love of humankind. **2** practical benevolence, esp. charity on a large scale. □ **philanthropism** *n.* **philanthropist** *n.* **philanthropize** *v.tr. & intr.* (also **-ise**). [Late Latin *philanthropia* from Greek *philanthrōpia* (as PHILANTHROPE)]

philately /fɪˈlat(ə)li/ *n.* the collection and study of postage stamps. □ **philatelic** /ˌfɪləˈtɛlɪk/ *adj.* **philatelically** /fɪləˈtɛlɪk(ə)li/ *adv.* **philatelist** *n.* [French *philatélie* (as PHILO-), Greek *ateleia* 'exemption from payment', from *a-* 'not' + *telos* 'toll, tax', used to mean a franking mark or postage stamp exempting the recipient from payment]

-phile /fʌɪl/ *comb. form* (also **-phil** /fɪl/) forming nouns and adjectives denoting fondness for what is specified (*bibliophile*; *Francophile*). [Greek *philos* 'dear, loving']

Philem. *abbr.* Philemon (New Testament).

philharmonic /fɪlhɑːˈmɒnɪk/ *adj.* **1** fond of music. **2** used characteristically in the names of orchestras, choirs, etc. (*Royal Philharmonic Orchestra*). [French *philharmonique* from Italian *filarmonico* (as PHIL-, HARMONIC)]

philhellene /ˈfɪlhɛliːn, fɪlˈhɛliːn/ *n.* (often *attrib.*) **1** a lover of Greece and Greek culture. **2** *hist.* a supporter of the cause of Greek independence. □ **philhellenic** /-ˈliːnɪk/ *adj.* **philhellenism** /-ˈhɛlɪnɪz(ə)m/ *n.* **philhellenist** /-ˈhɛlɪnɪst/ *n.* [Greek *philellēn* (as PHIL-, HELLENE)]

-philia /ˈfɪlɪə/ *comb. form* **1** denoting (esp. abnormal) fondness or love for what is specified (*necrophilia*). **2** denoting undue inclination (*haemophilia*). □ **-philiac** /-lɪak/ *comb. form* forming nouns and adjectives. **-philic** *comb. form* forming adjectives. **-philous** *comb. form* forming adjectives. [Greek, from *philos* 'loving']

philippic /fɪ'lɪpɪk/ *n.* a bitter verbal attack or denunciation. [Latin *philippicus* from Greek *philippikos*, the name of Demosthenes' speeches against Philip II of Macedon and Cicero's against Mark Antony]

Philippine /'fɪlɪpi:n/ *adj.* of or relating to the Philippine Islands or their people; Filipino. [from the name of *Philip* II of Spain]

Philistine /'fɪlɪstʌɪn/ *n.* & *adj.* ● *n.* **1** a member of a people opposing the Israelites in ancient Palestine. **2** (usu. **philistine**) a person who is hostile or indifferent to culture, or one whose interests or tastes are commonplace or material. ● *adj.* (usu. **philistine**) hostile or indifferent to culture, commonplace, prosaic. ▫ **philistinism** /-stɪnɪz(ə)m/ *n.* [Middle English via French *Philistin* or Late Latin *Philistinus* from Greek *Philistinos* = *Palaistinos*, from Hebrew *pᵉlištī*]

Phillips /'fɪlɪps/ *n.* (usu. *attrib.*) *propr.* denoting a screw with a cross-shaped slot for turning, or a corresponding screwdriver. [name of the original US manufacturer]

phillumenist /fɪ'lu:mənɪst, -'lju:-/ *n.* a collector of matchbox labels. ▫ **phillumeny** *n.* [PHIL- + Latin *lumen* 'light']

Philly /'fɪli/ *n.* *US slang* Philadelphia. [abbreviation]

philo- /'fɪləʊ/ *comb. form* (also **phil-** before a vowel or *h*) denoting a liking for what is specified.

philodendron /fɪlə'dɛndrən/ *n.* (*pl.* **philodendrons** or **philodendra** /-drə/) a tropical American climbing plant of the genus *Philodendron* (arum family). [PHILO- + Greek *dendron* 'tree']

philogynist /fɪ'lɒdʒmɪst/ *n.* a person who likes or admires women. [PHILO- + Greek *gunē* 'woman']

philology /fɪ'lɒlədʒi/ *n.* **1** the science of language, esp. in its historical and comparative aspects. **2** the love of learning and literature. ▫ **philologian** /-lə'ləʊdʒ(ə)n/ *n.* **philological** /-lə'lɒdʒɪk(ə)l/ *adj.* **philologically** /-lə'lɒdʒɪk(ə)li/ *adv.* **philologist** *n.* **philologize** *v.intr.* (also **-ise**). [French *philologie* via Latin *philologia* 'love of learning' from Greek (as PHILO-, -LOGY)]

Philomel /'fɪlə(ʊ)mɛl/ *n.* (also **Philomela** /fɪlə'mi:lə/) *poet.* the nightingale. [earlier *philomene* from medieval Latin *philomena* via Latin *philomela* 'nightingale' from Greek *philomēla*: initial capital with reference to the myth of *Philomela*, an Athenian princess who was changed into a nightingale]

philoprogenitive /ˌfɪlə(ʊ)prə(ʊ)'dʒɛnɪtɪv/ *adj.* **1** prolific. **2** loving one's offspring.

philosopher /fɪ'lɒsəfə/ *n.* **1** a person engaged or learned in philosophy or a branch of it. **2** a person who shows philosophic calmness in trying circumstances. [Middle English from Anglo-French *philosofre*, variant of Old French *philosophe*, via Latin *philosophus* from Greek *philosophos* (as PHILO-, *sophos* 'wise')]

philosophers' stone *n.* (also **philosopher's stone**) the supreme object of alchemy, a substance supposed to change other metals into gold or silver.

philosophical /fɪlə'sɒfɪk(ə)l/ *adj.* (also **philosophic**) **1** of or according to philosophy. **2** skilled in or devoted to philosophy or learning; learned (*philosophical society*). **3** wise; serene; temperate. **4** calm in adverse circumstances. ▫ **philosophically** *adv.* [Late Latin *philosophicus* from Latin *philosophia* (as PHILOSOPHY)]

philosophize /fɪ'lɒsəfʌɪz/ *v.* (also **-ise**) **1** *intr.* reason like a philosopher. **2** *intr.* moralize. **3** *intr.* speculate; theorize. **4** *tr.* render philosophic. ▫ **philosophizer** *n.* [apparently from French *philosopher*]

philosophy /fɪ'lɒsəfi/ *n.* (*pl.* **-ies**) **1** the use of reason and argument in seeking truth and knowledge of reality, esp. of the causes and nature of things and of the principles governing existence, the material universe, perception of physical phenomena, and human behaviour. **2 a** a particular system or set of beliefs reached by this. **b** a personal rule of life. **3** advanced learning in general (*doctor of philosophy*). **4** serenity; calmness; conduct governed by a particular philosophy. [Middle English from Old French *filosofie* via Latin *philosophia* 'wisdom' from Greek (as PHILO-, *sophos* 'wise')]

philtre /'fɪltə/ *n.* (*US* **philter**) a drink supposed to excite sexual love in the drinker. [French *philtre* via Latin *philtrum* from Greek *philtron*, from *phileō* 'to love']

-phily /fɪli/ *comb. form* = -PHILIA.

phimosis /fʌɪ'məʊsɪs/ *n.* a constriction of the foreskin, making it difficult to retract. ▫ **phimotic** /-'mɒtɪk/ *adj.* [modern Latin from Greek, = muzzling]

phiz /fɪz/ *n.* (also **phizog** /'fɪzɒg/) *Brit. colloq.* **1** the face. **2** the expression on a face. [abbreviation of *phiznomy* = PHYSIOGNOMY]

phlebitis /flɪ'bʌɪtɪs/ *n.* inflammation of the walls of a vein. ▫ **phlebitic** /-'bɪtɪk/ *adj.* [modern Latin from Greek, from *phleps phlebos* 'vein']

phlebotomy /flɪ'bɒtəmi/ *n.* **1** the surgical opening or puncture of a vein. **2** esp. *hist.* bloodletting as a medical treatment. ▫ **phlebotomist** *n.* **phlebotomize** *v.tr.* (also **-ise**). [Middle English via Old French *flebothomi* and Late Latin *phlebotomia* from Greek, from *phleps phlebos* 'vein' + -TOMY]

phlegm /flɛm/ *n.* **1** the thick viscous substance secreted by the mucous membranes of the respiratory passages, discharged by coughing. **2** phlegmatic character or behaviour. **3** *hist.* one of the four bodily humours, characterized as cold and moist, and associated with a calm, stolid or apathetic temperament (see HUMOUR *n.* 5). ▫ **phlegmy** *adj.* [Middle English & Old French *fleume* via Late Latin *phlegma* from Greek *phlegma -atos* 'inflammation', from *phlegō* 'burn']

phlegmatic /flɛg'matɪk/ *adj.* stolidly calm; unexcitable, unemotional. ▫ **phlegmatically** *adv.*

phloem /'fləʊɛm/ *n.* *Bot.* the tissue conducting food material in plants (cf. XYLEM). [Greek *phloos* 'bark']

phlogiston /flə'dʒɪstən, -'gɪst-/ *n.* *hist.* a substance formerly supposed to exist in all combustible bodies, and to be released in combustion. [modern Latin from Greek *phlogizō* 'set on fire', from *phlox phlogos* 'flame']

phlox /flɒks/ *n.* any cultivated plant of the genus *Phlox*, with scented clusters of esp. white, blue, or red flowers. [Latin from Greek, the name of a plant (literally 'flame')]

-phobe /fəʊb/ *comb. form* forming nouns and adjectives denoting a person having a fear or dislike of what is specified (*xenophobe*). [French via Latin *-phobus* from Greek *-phobos*, from *phobos* 'fear']

phobia /'fəʊbɪə/ *n.* an abnormal or morbid fear or aversion. ▫ **phobic** *adj.* & *n.* [-PHOBIA used as a separate word]

-phobia /'fəʊbɪə/ *comb. form* forming abstract nouns denoting a fear or dislike of what is specified (*agoraphobia*; *xenophobia*). ▫ **-phobic** *comb. form* forming adjectives. [Latin from Greek]

phoebe /'fi:bi/ *n.* any American flycatcher of the genus *Sayornis*. [imitative: influenced by the name]

Phoenician /fə'nɪʃ(ə)n, -'ni:-/ *n.* & *adj.* ● *n.* a member of a Semitic people of ancient Phoenicia in S. Syria or of its colonies. ● *adj.* of or relating to Phoenicia. [Middle English via Old French *phenicien* and Latin *Phoenicia*, from *Phoenice*, from Greek *Phoinikē* 'Phoenicia']

phoenix /'fi:nɪks/ *n.* **1** a mythical bird, the only one of its kind, that after living for five or six centuries in the Arabian desert, burnt itself on a funeral pyre and rose from the ashes with renewed youth to live through another cycle. **2** a unique person or thing. [Old English & Old French *fenix* via Latin *phoenix* from Greek *phoinix* 'Phoenician, purple, phoenix']

pholas /'fəʊləs/ *n.* a piddock, esp. of the genus *Pholas*. [modern Latin from Greek *phōlas* 'that lurks in a hole', from *phōleos* 'hole']

phon /fɒn/ *n.* a unit of the perceived loudness of sounds. [Greek *phōnē* 'sound']

phonate /fə(ʊ)'neɪt/ *v.intr.* utter a vocal sound. ▫ **phonation** /-'neɪʃ(ə)n/ *n.* **phonatory** /'fəʊnət(ə)ri/ *adj.* [Greek *phōnē* 'voice']

phone[1] /fəʊn/ *n.* & *v.* = TELEPHONE. [abbreviation]

phone[2] /fəʊn/ *n.* a simple vowel or consonant sound. [formed as PHONEME]

-phone /fəʊn/ *comb. form* forming nouns and adjectives meaning: **1** an instrument using or connected with sound (*telephone*; *xylophone*). **2** a person who uses a specified language (*anglophone*). [Greek *phōnē* 'voice, sound']

phone book *n.* = TELEPHONE DIRECTORY.

phonecard /ˈfəʊnkɑːd/ *n.* esp. *Brit.* a card containing prepaid units for use with a cardphone.

phone-in *n.* a broadcast programme during which the listeners or viewers telephone the studio etc. and participate.

phoneme /ˈfəʊniːm/ *n.* any of the units of sound in a specified language that distinguish one word from another (e.g. *p*, *b*, *d*, *t* in the English words pad, pat, bad, bat). □ **phonemic** /-ˈniːmɪk/ *adj.* **phonemics** /-ˈniːmɪks/ *n.* [French *phonème* from Greek *phōnēma* 'sound, speech', from *phōneō* 'speak']

phonetic /fəˈnɛtɪk/ *adj.* **1** representing vocal sounds. **2** (of a system of spelling etc.) having a direct correspondence between symbols and sounds. **3** of or relating to phonetics. □ **phonetically** *adv.* **phoneticism** /-sɪz(ə)m/ *n.* **phoneticist** /-sɪst/ *n.* **phoneticize** /-sʌɪz/ *v.tr.* (also **-ise**). [modern Latin *phoneticus* from Greek *phōnētikos*, from *phōneō* 'speak']

phonetics /fəˈnɛtɪks/ *n.pl.* (usu. treated as *sing.*) **1** vocal sounds and their classification. **2** the study of these. □ **phonetician** /fəʊnɪˈtɪʃ(ə)n, fɒn-/ *n.*

phonetist /ˈfəʊnɪtɪst/ *n.* **1** a person skilled in phonetics. **2** an advocate of phonetic spelling.

phoney /ˈfəʊni/ *adj.* & *n.* (also **phony**) *colloq.* ● *adj.* (**phonier**, **phoniest**) **1** sham; counterfeit. **2** fictitious; fraudulent. ● *n.* (*pl.* **-eys** or **-ies**) a phoney person or thing. □ **phonily** *adv.* **phoniness** *n.* [19th c.: origin unknown]

phonic /ˈfəʊnɪk, ˈfɒnɪk/ *adj.* & *n.* ● *adj.* of sound; acoustic; of vocal sounds. ● *n.* (in *pl.*) a method of teaching reading based on sounds. □ **phonically** *adv.* [Greek *phōnē* 'voice']

phono /ˈfəʊnəʊ/ *attrib.adj.* designating a type of plug (and the corresponding socket) used with audio and video equipment, in which one conductor is cylindrical and the other is a central part that extends beyond it. [abbreviation of PHONOGRAPH]

phono- /ˈfəʊnəʊ, ˈfɒn-/ *comb. form* denoting sound. [Greek *phōnē* 'voice, sound']

phonogram /ˈfəʊnəgram/ *n.* a symbol representing a spoken sound.

phonograph /ˈfəʊnəgrɑːf/ *n.* **1** *Brit.* an early form of gramophone using cylinders and able to record as well as reproduce sound. **2** *N. Amer.* a gramophone.

phonography /fəˈnɒgrəfi/ *n.* **1** writing in esp. shorthand symbols, corresponding to the sounds of speech. **2** the recording of sounds by phonograph. □ **phonographic** /fəʊnəˈgrafɪk/ *adj.*

phonology /fəˈnɒlədʒi/ *n.* the study of sounds in a language. □ **phonological** /fəʊnəˈlɒdʒɪk(ə)l, fɒn-/ *adj.* **phonologically** /fəʊnəˈlɒdʒɪk(ə)li, fɒn-/ *adv.* **phonologist** *n.*

phonon /ˈfəʊnɒn/ *n.* *Physics* a quantum of sound or elastic vibrations. [Greek *phōnē* 'sound', on the pattern of PHOTON]

phony var. of PHONEY.

phooey /ˈfuːi/ *int.* *colloq.* an expression of disgust or disbelief. [imitative]

-phore /fɔː/ *comb. form* forming nouns meaning 'bearer' (*ctenophore*; *semaphore*). □ **-phorous** /fərəs/ *comb. form* forming adjectives. [modern Latin from Greek *-phoros -phoron* 'bearing, bearer', from *pherō* 'bear']

phoresy /fəˈriːsi, ˈfɒrəsi/ *n.* *Zool.* an association in which one organism is carried by another, without being a parasite. □ **phoretic** /fəˈrɛtɪk/ *adj.* [French *phorésie* from Greek *phorēsis* 'being carried']

phormium /ˈfɔːmɪəm/ *n.* a fibre-yielding New Zealand plant of the genus *Phormium* (agave family), esp. New Zealand flax, *P. tenax*. [modern Latin from Greek *phormion*, a species of plant]

phosgene /ˈfɒzdʒiːn/ *n.* a colourless poisonous gas (carbonyl chloride), formerly used in warfare. Chem. formula: $COCl_2$. [Greek *phōs* 'light' + -GEN, with reference to its original production by the action of sunlight on chlorine and carbon monoxide]

phosphatase /ˈfɒsfəteɪz/ *n.* *Biochem.* any enzyme that catalyses the synthesis or hydrolysis of an organic phosphate.

phosphate /ˈfɒsfeɪt/ *n.* **1** any salt or ester of phosphoric acid, esp. used as a fertilizer. **2** an effervescent soft drink containing a small amount of phosphate. □ **phosphatic** /-ˈfatɪk/ *adj.* [French, from *phosphore* PHOSPHORUS]

phosphene /ˈfɒsfiːn/ *n.* the sensation of rings of light produced by pressure on the eyeball due to irritation of the retina. [formed irregularly from Greek *phōs* 'light' + *phainō* 'show']

phosphide /ˈfɒsfʌɪd/ *n.* *Chem.* a binary compound of phosphorus with another element or group.

phosphine /ˈfɒsfiːn/ *n.* *Chem.* a colourless foul-smelling gas, phosphorus trihydride. Chem. formula: PH_3. □ **phosphinic** /-ˈfɪnɪk/ *adj.* [PHOSPHO- + -INE[4], on the pattern of *amine*]

phosphite /ˈfɒsfʌɪt/ *n.* *Chem.* any salt or ester of phosphorous acid. [French (as PHOSPHO-)]

phospho- /ˈfɒsfəʊ/ *comb. form* denoting phosphorus. [abbreviation]

phospholipid /fɒsfə(ʊ)ˈlɪpɪd/ *n.* *Biochem.* any lipid consisting of a phosphate group and one or more fatty acids, including those forming cell membranes.

phosphor /ˈfɒsfə/ *n.* **1** = PHOSPHORUS. **2** a synthetic fluorescent or phosphorescent substance esp. used in cathode ray tubes. [German from Latin *phosphorus* PHOSPHORUS]

phosphorate /ˈfɒsfəreɪt/ *v.tr.* combine or impregnate with phosphorus.

phosphor bronze *n.* a tough hard bronze alloy containing a small amount of phosphorus, used esp. for bearings.

phosphorescence /fɒsfəˈrɛs(ə)ns/ *n.* **1** radiation similar to fluorescence but detectable after excitation ceases. **2** the emission of light without combustion or perceptible heat. □ **phosphoresce** *v.intr.* **phosphorescent** *adj.*

phosphoric /fɒsˈfɒrɪk/ *adj.* **1** *Chem.* containing phosphorus, esp. in its higher valency of five. **2** phosphorescent.

phosphoric acid *n.* a crystalline solid which has many commercial uses, e.g. in fertilizer and soap manufacture and food processing. Chem. formula: H_3PO_4.

phosphorite /ˈfɒsfərʌɪt/ *n.* a non-crystalline form of apatite.

phosphorous /ˈfɒsf(ə)rəs/ *adj.* **1** *Chem.* containing phosphorus, esp. in its lower valency of three (*phosphorous acid*). **2** phosphorescent.

phosphorus /ˈfɒsf(ə)rəs/ *n.* *Chem.* a non-metallic element occurring naturally in various phosphate rocks and existing in allotropic forms, esp. as a poisonous whitish waxy substance burning slowly at ordinary temperatures and so appearing luminous in the dark, and a reddish form used in matches, fertilizers, etc. (symbol **P**). [Latin, = morning star, from Greek *phōsphoros*, from *phōs* 'light' + *-phoros* '-bringing']

phosphorylate /fɒsˈfɒrɪleɪt/ *v.tr.* *Chem.* introduce a phosphate group into (an organic molecule etc.). □ **phosphorylation** /-ˈleɪʃ(ə)n/ *n.*

phossy jaw /ˈfɒsi/ *n.* *colloq.* *hist.* gangrene of the jawbone caused by phosphorus poisoning. [abbreviation]

phot /fəʊt/ *n.* a unit of illumination equal to one lumen per square centimetre. [Greek *phōs phōtos* 'light']

photic /ˈfəʊtɪk/ *adj.* **1** of or relating to light. **2** (of ocean layers) reached by sunlight.

photism /'fəʊtɪz(ə)m/ *n.* a hallucinatory sensation or vision of light. [Greek *phōtismos* via *phōtizō* 'shine' from *phōs phōtos* 'light']

photo /'fəʊtəʊ/ *n. & v.* ● *n.* (*pl.* **-os**) = PHOTOGRAPH *n.* ● *v.tr.* (**-oes, -oed**) = PHOTOGRAPH *v.* [abbreviation]

photo- /'fəʊtəʊ/ *comb. form* denoting: **1** light (*photosensitive*). **2** photography (*photocomposition*). [Greek *phōs phōtos* 'light', or as abbreviation of PHOTOGRAPH]

photobiology /ˌfəʊtəʊbʌɪ'ɒlədʒi/ *n.* the study of the effects of light on living organisms.

photocall /'fəʊtəʊkɔːl/ *n. Brit.* an occasion on which theatrical performers, famous personalities, etc., pose for photographers by arrangement.

photocell /'fəʊtəʊsɛl/ *n.* = PHOTOELECTRIC CELL.

photochemical /fəʊtəʊ'kɛmɪk(ə)l/ *adj.* of or relating to the chemical action of light. □ **photochemically** *adv.*

photochemical smog *n.* a condition of the atmosphere caused by the action of sunlight on pollutants, resulting in haze and high levels of ozone and nitrogen oxide.

photochemistry /fəʊtəʊ'kɛmɪstri/ *n.* the study of the chemical effects of light.

photochromic /fəʊtə(ʊ)'krəʊmɪk/ *adj.* changing colour or shade reversibly in light of a particular frequency or intensity (*photochromic lens*). [PHOTO- + Greek *khrōma* 'colour']

photocomposition /ˌfəʊtəʊkɒmpə'zɪʃ(ə)n/ *n.* = FILMSETTING.

photoconductivity /ˌfəʊtəʊkɒndʌk'tɪvɪti/ *n.* conductivity due to the action of light. □ **photoconductive** /-kən'dʌktɪv/ *adj.* **photoconductor** /-kən'dʌktə/ *n.*

photocopier /'fəʊtəʊkɒpɪə/ *n.* a machine for producing photocopies.

photocopy /'fəʊtəʊkɒpi/ *n. & v.* ● *n.* (*pl.* **-ies**) a photographic copy of printed or written material produced by a process involving the action of light on a specially prepared surface. ● *v.tr.* (**-ies, -ied**) make a photocopy of. □ **photocopiable** *adj.*

photodegradable /ˌfəʊtəʊdɪ'greɪdəb(ə)l/ *adj.* capable of being decomposed by the action of light, esp. sunlight.

photodiode /fəʊtəʊ'dʌɪəʊd/ *n.* a semiconductor diode responding electrically to illumination.

photoelectric /ˌfəʊtəʊɪ'lɛktrɪk/ *adj.* marked by or using emissions of electrons from substances exposed to light. □ **photoelectricity** /-'trɪsɪti/ *n.*

photoelectric cell *n.* a device using this effect to generate current.

photoelectron /'fəʊtəʊɪlɛktrɒn/ *n.* an electron emitted from an atom by interaction with a photon, esp. one emitted from a solid surface by the action of light.

photoemission /'fəʊtəʊmɪʃ(ə)n/ *n.* the emission of electrons from a surface by the action of light incident on it. □ **photoemitter** *n.*

photo finish *n.* a close finish of a race or contest, esp. one where the winner is distinguishable only from a photograph.

photofit /'fəʊtə(ʊ)fɪt/ *n. Brit.* a reconstructed picture of a person (esp. one sought by the police) made from composite photographs of facial features (cf. IDENTIKIT).

photogenic /fəʊtə(ʊ)'dʒɛnɪk, -'dʒiːn-/ *adj.* **1** (esp. of a person) having an appearance that looks pleasing in photographs. **2** *Biol.* producing or emitting light. □ **photogenically** *adv.*

photogram /'fəʊtəgram/ *n.* **1** a picture produced with photographic materials but without a camera. **2** *archaic* a photograph.

photogrammetry /fəʊtə(ʊ)'gramɪtri/ *n.* the use of photography for surveying. □ **photogrammetrist** *n.*

photograph /'fəʊtəgrɑːf/ *n. & v.* ● *n.* a picture formed by means of the chemical action of light or other radiation on sensitive film. ● *v.* **1** *tr.* (also *absol.*) take a photograph of (a person etc.). **2** *intr.* appear (in a particular way) when in a photograph. □ **photographable** *adj.* **photographer** /fə'tɒgrəfə/ *n.* **photographic** /-'grafɪk/ *adj.* **photographically** /-'grafɪk(ə)li/ *adv.*

photographic memory *n.* a memory allowing the recall of visual images with great accuracy.

photography /fə'tɒgrəfi/ *n.* the taking and processing of photographs.

photogravure /ˌfəʊtəʊgra'vjʊə/ *n.* **1** an image produced from a photographic negative transferred to a metal plate and etched in. **2** this process . [French (as PHOTO-, *gravure* 'engraving')]

photojournalism /fəʊtəʊ'dʒəːn(ə)lɪz(ə)m/ *n.* the art or practice of relating news by photographs, with or without an accompanying text, esp. in magazines etc. □ **photojournalist** *n.*

photolithography /ˌfəʊtəʊlɪ'θɒgrəfi/ *n.* (also **photolitho** /-'lʌɪθəʊ/) lithography using plates made photographically. □ **photolithographer** *n.* **photolithographic** /-θə'grafɪk/ *adj.* **photolithographically** /-θə'grafɪk(ə)li/ *adv.*

photolysis /fə(ʊ)'tɒlɪsɪs/ *n.* decomposition or dissociation of molecules by the action of light. □ **photolyse** /'fəʊtəlʌɪz/ *v.tr. & intr.* **photolytic** /-tə'lɪtɪk/ *adj.*

photometer /fə(ʊ)'tɒmɪtə/ *n.* an instrument for measuring light. □ **photometric** /fəʊtə(ʊ)'mɛtrɪk/ *adj.* **photometry** /-'tɒmɪtri/ *n.*

photomicrograph /fəʊtəʊ'mʌɪkrəgrɑːf/ *n.* a photograph of an image produced by a microscope. □ **photomicrography** /-'krɒgrəfi/ *n.*

photomontage /ˌfəʊtəʊmɒn'tɑːʒ/ *n.* **1** the technique of constructing a montage from photographic images. **2** a composite picture so produced.

photomultiplier /fəʊtəʊ'mʌltɪplʌɪə/ *n.* an instrument containing a photocell and a series of electrodes, used to detect and amplify the light from very faint sources.

photon /'fəʊtɒn/ *n.* a quantum of electromagnetic radiation energy (e.g. light), proportional to the frequency of radiation. [Greek *phōs phōtos* 'light', on the pattern of *electron*]

photonics /fəʊ'tɒnɪks/ *n.* the branch of technology concerned with the properties and transmission of photons (e.g. in fibre optics).

photonovel /'fəʊtəʊnɒv(ə)l/ *n.* a novel told in a series of photographs with superimposed speech bubbles.

photo-offset /fəʊtəʊ'ɒfsɛt/ *n.* offset printing with plates made photographically.

photo op *n. N. Amer. colloq.* = PHOTO OPPORTUNITY.

photo opportunity *n.* = PHOTOCALL.

photoperiod /'fəʊtəʊpɪərɪəd/ *n.* the period of daily illumination which an organism receives. □ **photoperiodic** /-ɪ'ɒdɪk/ *adj.*

photoperiodism /fəʊtəʊ'pɪərɪədɪz(ə)m/ *n.* the response of an organism to changes in the lengths of the daily periods of light.

photophobia /fəʊtə(ʊ)'fəʊbɪə/ *n.* an abnormal fear of or aversion to light. □ **photophobic** *adj.*

photorealism /fəʊtəʊ'rɪəlɪz(ə)m/ *n.* detailed and unidealized representation in art, esp. of banal, mundane, or sordid aspects of life. □ **photorealist** *n.* **photorealistic** /-'lɪstɪk/ *adj.*

photoreceptor /'fəʊtəʊrɪˌsɛptə/ *n.* a structure in a living organism, esp. a sensory cell or sense organ, that responds to incident light.

photosensitive /fəʊtəʊ'sɛnsɪtɪv/ *adj.* reacting chemically, electrically, etc., to light. □ **photosensitivity** /-'tɪvɪti/ *n.*

photo session *n.* a pre-arranged session in which a photographer takes photographs of a person for use in advertising etc.

photosetting /'fəʊtəʊsɛtɪŋ/ *n.* = FILMSETTING. □ **photoset** *v.tr.* (*past* and *past part.* **-set**). **photosetter** *n.*

photo shoot *n.* = PHOTO SESSION.

photosphere /'fəʊtəsfɪə/ *n.* the luminous envelope of a star from which its light and heat radiate. □ **photospheric** /-'sfɛrɪk/ *adj.*

photostat /ˈfəʊtə(ʊ)stat/ *n. & v.* ● *n. propr.* **1** a type of machine for making photocopies. **2** a copy made by this means. ● *v.tr.* (**-statted**, **-statting**) make a photostat of. □ **photostatic** /-ˈstatɪk/ *adj.*

photosynthesis /fəʊtəʊˈsɪnθɪsɪs/ *n.* the process by which the energy of sunlight is used by organisms, esp. green plants, to synthesize carbohydrates from carbon dioxide and water. □ **photosynthesize** *v.tr. & intr.* (also **-ise**). **photosynthetic** /-ˈθɛtɪk/ *adj.* **photosynthetically** /-ˈθɛtɪk(ə)li/ *adv.*

phototransistor /ˌfəʊtəʊtranˈzɪstə, -trɑːnˈzɪstə, -ˈsɪstə/ *n.* a transistor that responds to incident light by generating and amplifying an electric current.

phototropism /fəʊtə(ʊ)ˈtrəʊpɪz(ə)m, fəʊˈtɒtrəpɪz(ə)m/ *n.* the tendency of a plant etc. to bend or turn towards or away from a source of light. □ **phototropic** /-ˈtrɒpɪk/ *adj.*

phototypesetter /fəʊtəʊˈtʌɪpsɛtə/ *n.* a machine for filmsetting. □ **phototypeset** *adj.* **phototypesetting** *n.*

photovoltaic /ˌfəʊtəʊvɒlˈteɪɪk/ *adj.* relating to the production of electric current at the junction of two substances exposed to light.

phrasal /ˈfreɪz(ə)l/ *adj. Gram.* consisting of a phrase.

phrasal verb *n.* an idiomatic phrase consisting of a verb and an adverb (e.g. *break down*) or a verb and a preposition (e.g. *see to*), or a combination of both (e.g. *look down on*).

phrase /freɪz/ *n. & v.* ● *n.* **1** a group of words forming a conceptual unit, but not a sentence. **2** an idiomatic or short pithy expression. **3** a manner or mode of expression (*a nice turn of phrase*). **4** *Mus.* a group of notes forming a distinct unit within a larger piece. ● *v.tr.* **1** express in words (*phrased the reply badly*). **2** (esp. when reading aloud or speaking) divide (sentences etc.) into units so as to convey the meaning of the whole. **3** *Mus.* divide (music) into phrases, esp. in performance. □ **phrasing** *n.* [earlier *phrasis*, via Latin from Greek, from *phrazō* 'declare, tell']

phrase book *n.* a book for tourists etc. listing useful expressions with their equivalent in a foreign language.

phraseogram /ˈfreɪzɪəgram/ *n.* a written symbol representing a phrase, esp. in shorthand.

phraseology /freɪzɪˈɒlədʒi/ *n.* (*pl.* **-ies**) **1** a choice or arrangement of words. **2** a mode of expression. □ **phraseological** /-zɪəˈlɒdʒɪk(ə)l/ *adj.* [modern Latin *phraseologia* from Greek *phraseōn*, genitive pl. of *phrasis* PHRASE]

phreatic /frɪˈatɪk/ *adj. Geol.* **1** (of water) situated underground in the zone of saturation; of or relating to groundwater. **2** (of a volcanic eruption or explosion) caused by the heating and expansion of underground water. [Greek *phrear phreatos* 'well']

phrenic /ˈfrɛnɪk/ *adj. Anat.* of or relating to the diaphragm. [French *phrénique* from Greek *phrēn phrenos* 'diaphragm, mind']

phrenology /frɪˈnɒlədʒi/ *n. hist.* the study of the shape and size of the cranium as a supposed indication of character and mental faculties. □ **phrenological** /-nəˈlɒdʒɪk(ə)l/ *adj.* **phrenologist** *n.*

Phrygian /ˈfrɪdʒɪən/ *n. & adj.* ● *n.* **1** a native or inhabitant of ancient Phrygia in central Asia Minor. **2** the language of the Phrygians. ● *adj.* of or relating to Phrygia or its people or language.

Phrygian bonnet *n.* (also **Phrygian cap**) an ancient conical cap with the top bent forwards, now identified with the cap of liberty.

Phrygian mode *n. Mus.* the mode represented by the natural diatonic scale E–E.

phthalic acid /ˈfθalɪk/ *n. Chem.* each of three isomeric dicarboxylic acids derived from benzene. □ **phthalate** /-leɪt/ *n.* [abbreviation of NAPHTHALIC: see NAPHTHALENE]

phthisis /ˈ(f)θʌɪsɪs, ˈtʌɪ-/ *n.* any progressive wasting disease, esp. pulmonary tuberculosis. □ **phthisic** *adj.* **phthisical** *adj.* [Latin from Greek, from *phthinō* 'to decay']

phut /fʌt/ *n.* a dull abrupt sound as of an impact or explosion. □ **go phut** *colloq.* (esp. of a scheme or plan) collapse, break down. [perhaps from Hindi *phaṭnā* 'to burst']

phycology /fʌɪˈkɒlədʒi/ *n.* the study of algae. □ **phycological** /-kəˈlɒdʒɪk(ə)l/ *adj.* **phycologist** *n.* [Greek *phukos* 'seaweed' + -LOGY]

phycomycete /fʌɪkəʊˈmʌɪsiːt/ *n.* any of various fungi which typically form a non-septate mycelium. [Greek *phukos* 'seaweed' + modern Latin *-mycetes* from Greek *mucēs mukētos* 'fungus']

phyla *pl.* of PHYLUM.

phylactery /fɪˈlakt(ə)ri/ *n.* (*pl.* **-ies**) **1** a small leather box containing Hebrew texts on vellum, worn by Jewish men at morning prayer as a reminder to keep the law. **2** an amulet; a charm. **3** a usu. ostentatious religious observance. **4** a fringe; a border. [Middle English via Old French and Late Latin *phylacterium* from Greek *phulaktērion* 'amulet', from *phulassō* 'guard']

phyletic /fʌɪˈlɛtɪk/ *adj. Biol.* of or relating to the development of a species or other group. □ **phyletically** *adv.* [Greek *phuletikos*, via *phuletēs* 'tribesman' from *phulē* 'tribe']

phyllo var. of FILO.

phyllo- /ˈfɪləʊ/ *comb. form* leaf. [Greek *phullo-* from *phullon* 'leaf']

phyllode /ˈfɪləʊd/ *n.* a flattened leaf-stalk resembling a leaf. [modern Latin *phyllodium* from Greek *phullōdēs* 'leaflike' (as PHYLLO-)]

phyllophagous /fɪˈlɒfəgəs/ *adj.* feeding on leaves.

phylloquinone /fʌɪləʊˈkwɪnəʊn/ *n.* one of the K vitamins, found in cabbage, spinach, and other leafy green vegetables, and essential for the blood-clotting process. Also called *vitamin K_1*.

phyllotaxis /fɪlə(ʊ)ˈtaksɪs/ *n.* (also **phyllotaxy** /-ˈtaksi/) the arrangement of leaves on an axis or stem. □ **phyllotactic** *adj.*

phylloxera /fɪlɒkˈsɪərə, fɪˈlɒksərə/ *n.* any plant-louse of (or formerly of) the genus *Phylloxera*, esp. *Daktulosphaira vitifoliae*, a pest of vines. [modern Latin, from Greek *phullon* 'leaf' + *xēros* 'dry']

phylogenesis /fʌɪlə(ʊ)ˈdʒɛnɪsɪs/ *n.* (also **phylogeny** /fʌɪˈlɒdʒ(ə)ni/) the evolutionary development and diversification of groups of organisms, or particular features of organisms. □ **phylogenetic** /-dʒɪˈnɛtɪk/ *adj.* **phylogenetically** /-dʒɪˈnɛtɪk(ə)li/ *adv.* **phylogenic** /-ˈdʒɛnɪk/ *adj.* [Greek *phulon*, *phulē* 'race, tribe' + GENESIS]

phylum /ˈfʌɪləm/ *n.* (*pl.* **phyla** /-lə/) **1** *Biol.* a taxonomic rank below kingdom comprising a class or classes and subordinate taxa. **2** *Linguistics* a group of languages related to each other less closely than those of a family. [modern Latin from Greek *phulon* 'race']

physalis /ˈfʌɪsəlɪs, ˈfɪs-, fʌɪˈseɪlɪs/ *n.* any plant of the genus *Physalis*, bearing fruit surrounded by lantern-like calyxes (see CHINESE LANTERN 2). [Greek *physallis* 'bladder', with reference to the inflated calyx]

physic /ˈfɪzɪk/ *n. & v. archaic* ● *n.* **1** a medicine (*a dose of physic*). **2** the art of healing. **3** the medical profession. ● *v.tr.* (**physicked**, **physicking**) dose with physic. [Middle English via Old French *fisique* 'medicine' and Latin *physica* from Greek *phusikē* (*epistēmē*) '(knowledge) of nature']

physical /ˈfɪzɪk(ə)l/ *adj. & n.* ● *adj.* **1** of or concerning the body (*physical exercise*; *physical education*). **2** of matter; material (*both mental and physical force*). **3 a** of, or according to, the laws of nature (*a physical impossibility*). **b** belonging to physics (*physical science*). ● *n.* (in full **physical examination**) a medical examination to determine physical fitness. □ **physicality** /-ˈkalɪti/ *n.* **physically** *adv.* **physicalness** *n.* [Middle English via medieval Latin *physicalis* from Latin *physica* (as PHYSIC)]

physical chemistry *n.* the application of physics to the study of chemical behaviour.

physical education *n.* instruction in physical exercise and games, esp. in schools.

physical geography *n.* geography dealing with natural features.

physicalism /ˈfɪzɪk(ə)lɪz(ə)m/ *n. Philos.* the theory that all reality must eventually be expressible in the language of physics. □ **physicalist** *n.* & *adj.* **physicalistic** /-ˈlɪstɪk/ *adj.*

physical jerks *n.pl. Brit. colloq.* physical exercises.

physical science *n.* the sciences used in the study of inanimate natural objects, e.g. physics, chemistry, astronomy, etc.

physical training *n.* exercises promoting bodily fitness and strength.

physic garden *n.* a garden for cultivating medicinal herbs etc.

physician /fɪˈzɪʃ(ə)n/ *n.* **1 a** a person legally qualified to practise medicine and surgery. **b** a specialist in medical diagnosis and treatment. **c** any medical practitioner. **2** a healer (*work is the best physician*). [Middle English from Old French *fisicien* (as PHYSIC)]

physicist /ˈfɪzɪsɪst/ *n.* a person skilled or qualified in physics.

physico- /ˈfɪzɪkəʊ/ *comb. form* **1** physical (and). **2** of physics (and). [Greek *phusikos* (as PHYSIC)]

physico-chemical /ˌfɪzɪkəʊˈkɛmɪk(ə)l/ *adj.* relating to physics and chemistry or to physical chemistry.

physics /ˈfɪzɪks/ *n.* the science dealing with the properties and interactions of matter and energy. [pl. of *physic* 'physical (thing)', suggested by Latin *physica*, Greek *phusika* 'natural things' from *phusis* 'nature']

physio /ˈfɪzɪəʊ/ *n.* (*pl.* **-os**) *colloq.* a physiotherapist. [abbreviation]

physio- /ˈfɪzɪəʊ/ *comb. form* nature; what is natural. [Greek *phusis* 'nature']

physiocracy /fɪzɪˈɒkrəsi/ *n.* (*pl.* **-ies**) *hist.* **1** government according to the natural order, esp. as advocated by some 18th-c. economists. **2** a society based on this. □ **physiocrat** /ˈfɪzɪəkrat/ *n.* **physiocratic** /-ɪəˈkratɪk/ *adj.* [French *physiocratie* (as PHYSIO-, -CRACY)]

physiognomy /fɪzɪˈɒ(g)nəmi/ *n.* (*pl.* **-ies**) **1 a** the cast or form of a person's features, expression, body, etc. **b** the art of supposedly judging character from facial characteristics etc. **2** the external features of a landscape etc. **3** a characteristic, esp. moral, aspect. □ **physiognomic** /-zɪəˈnɒmɪk/ *adj.* **physiognomical** /-zɪəˈnɒmɪk(ə)l/ *adj.* **physiognomically** /-zɪəˈnɒmɪk(ə)li/ *adv.* **physiognomist** *n.* [Middle English *fisnomie* etc. from Old French *phisonomie* via medieval Latin *phisonomia* from Greek *phusiognōmonia* 'judging of a man's nature' (by his features) (as PHYSIO-, *gnōmōn* 'judge')]

physiography /fɪzɪˈɒgrəfi/ *n.* the description of nature, of natural phenomena, or of a class of objects; physical geography. □ **physiographer** *n.* **physiographic** /-zɪəˈgrafɪk/ *adj.* **physiographical** /-zɪəˈgrafɪk(ə)l/ *adj.* **physiographically** /-zɪəˈgrafɪk(ə)li/ *adv.* [French *physiographie* (as PHYSIO-, -GRAPHY)]

physiological /ˌfɪzɪəˈlɒdʒɪk(ə)l/ *adj.* (also **physiologic**) of or concerning physiology. □ **physiologically** *adv.*

physiological saline *n.* a solution of salts that is isotonic with the body fluids.

physiology /fɪzɪˈɒlədʒi/ *n.* **1** the science of the functions of living organisms and their parts. **2** these functions. □ **physiologist** *n.* [French *physiologie* or Latin *physiologia* from Greek *phusiologia* (as PHYSIO-, -LOGY)]

physiotherapy /ˌfɪzɪə(ʊ)ˈθɛrəpi/ *n.* the treatment of disease, injury, deformity, etc., by physical methods including manipulation, massage, infra-red heat treatment, remedial exercise, etc., rather than by drugs or surgery. □ **physiotherapist** *n.*

physique /fɪˈziːk/ *n.* the bodily structure, development, and organization of an individual (*an undernourished physique*). [French, originally *adj.* (as PHYSIC)]

-phyte /fʌɪt/ *comb. form* forming nouns denoting a vegetable or plantlike organism (*saprophyte*; *zoophyte*). □ **-phytic** /ˈfɪtɪk/ *comb. form* forming adjectives. [Greek *phuton* 'plant' from *phuō* 'come into being']

phyto- /ˈfʌɪtəʊ/ *comb. form* denoting a plant.

phytochemistry /fʌɪtəʊˈkɛmɪstri/ *n.* the chemistry of plant products. □ **phytochemical** *adj.* **phytochemist** *n.*

phytochrome /ˈfʌɪtəkrəʊm/ *n. Biochem.* a blue-green pigment found in many plants, and regulating various developmental processes according to the nature and timing of the light it absorbs. [PHYTO- + Greek *khrōma* 'colour']

phytogenesis /fʌɪtəʊˈdʒɛnɪsɪs/ *n.* (also **phytogeny** /-ˈtɒdʒɪni/) the science of the origin or evolution of plants.

phytogeography /ˌfʌɪtəʊdʒɪˈɒgrəfi/ *n.* the geographical distribution of plants.

phytopathology /ˌfʌɪtəʊpəˈθɒlədʒi/ *n.* the study of plant diseases.

phytophagous /fʌɪˈtɒfəgəs/ *adj.* feeding on plants.

phytoplankton /ˈfʌɪtəʊplaŋktən/ *n.* the component of plankton consisting of microscopic plants.

phytotomy /fʌɪˈtɒtəmi/ *n.* the dissection of plants.

phytotoxic /fʌɪtə(ʊ)ˈtɒksɪk/ *adj.* poisonous to plants.

phytotoxin /fʌɪtəʊˈtɒksɪn/ *n.* **1** any toxin derived from a plant. **2** a substance poisonous or injurious to plants, esp. one produced by a parasite.

pi[1] /pʌɪ/ *n.* **1** the sixteenth letter of the Greek alphabet (Π, π). **2** (as π) the symbol of the ratio of the circumference of a circle to its diameter (approx. 3.14159). [Greek: sense 2 from Greek *periphereia* 'circumference']

pi[2] /pʌɪ/ *adj. Brit. slang* pious. [abbreviation]

pi[3] *US* var. of PIE[3].

piacular /pʌɪˈakjʊlə/ *adj. formal* **1** expiatory. **2** needing expiation. [Latin *piacularis*, via *piaculum* 'expiation' from *piare* 'appease']

piaffe /pɪˈaf/ *v.intr.* (of a horse etc.) move as in a trot, but slower. [French *piaffer* 'to strut']

piaffer /pɪˈafə/ *n.* the action of piaffing.

pia mater /pʌɪə ˈmeɪtə/ *n. Anat.* the delicate innermost membrane enveloping the brain and spinal cord (see MENINX). [medieval Latin, = tender mother, translation of Arabic *al-'umm al-raḳīka*: cf. DURA MATER]

piani *pl.* of PIANO[2].

pianism /ˈpɪənɪz(ə)m/ *n.* **1** the art or technique of piano playing. **2** the skill or style of a composer of piano music. □ **pianistic** /-ˈnɪstɪk/ *adj.* **pianistically** /-ˈnɪstɪk(ə)li/ *adv.*

pianissimo /pɪəˈnɪsɪməʊ/ *adj., adv.,* & *n. Mus.* ● *adj.* performed very softly. ● *adv.* very softly. ● *n.* (*pl.* **-os** or **pianissimi** /-mi/) a passage to be performed very softly. [Italian, superlative of PIANO[2]]

pianist /ˈpɪənɪst/ *n.* the player of a piano. [French *pianiste* (as PIANO[1])]

piano[1] /pɪˈanəʊ/ *n.* (*pl.* **-os**) a large musical instrument played by pressing down keys on a keyboard and causing hammers to strike metal strings, the vibration from which is stopped by dampers when the keys are released. [Italian, abbreviation of PIANOFORTE]

piano[2] /ˈpjɑːnəʊ/ *adj., adv.,* & *n.* ● *adj.* **1** *Mus.* performed softly. **2** subdued. ● *adv.* **1** *Mus.* softly. **2** in a subdued manner. ● *n.* (*pl.* **-os** or **piani** /-ni/) *Mus.* a passage to be performed softly. [Italian from Latin *planus* 'flat', (of sound) 'soft']

piano accordion *n.* an accordion with the melody played on a small vertical keyboard like that of a piano.

pianoforte /pɪˌanəʊˈfɔːti/ *n. Mus. formal* or *archaic* a piano. [Italian, earlier *piano e forte* 'soft and loud', expressing its gradation of tone]

pianola /pɪəˈnəʊlə/ *n.* **1** *propr.* a kind of automatic piano; a player-piano. **2** *Bridge* an easy hand needing no skill. **3** an easy task. [apparently diminutive of PIANO[1]]

piano nobile /pjɑːnəʊ ˈnəʊbɪleɪ, Italian ˌpjano ˈnoːbile/ *n. Archit.* the main storey of a large house. [Italian, = noble floor]

piano organ *n.* a mechanical piano constructed like a barrel organ.

piano player *n.* **1** a pianist. **2** a contrivance for playing a piano automatically.

piano trio *n.* a trio for piano and two stringed instruments, usu. violin and cello.

piano-tuner *n.* a person who tunes pianos for a living.

piassava /piːəˈsɑːvə/ *n.* **1** a stout fibre obtained from the leaf-stalks of various American and African palm trees. **2** any of these trees. [Portuguese from Tupi *piaçába*]

piastre /pɪˈastə/ *n.* (*US* also **piaster**) a small coin and monetary unit of several Middle Eastern countries. [French *piastre* from Italian *piastra* (*d'argento*) 'plate (of silver)', formed as PLASTER]

piazza /pɪˈatsə/ *n.* **1** a public square or market place esp. in an Italian town. **2** *US* the veranda of a house. [Italian, formed as PLACE]

pibroch /ˈpiːbrɒk, -brɒx/ *n.* a series of esp. martial or funerary variations on a theme for the bagpipes. [Gaelic *piobaireachd* 'art of piping' via *piobair* 'piper' from *piob*, from English PIPE]

pic /pɪk/ *n. colloq.* a picture, esp. a cinema film. [abbreviation]

pica[1] /ˈpʌɪkə/ *n. Printing* **1** a unit of type size (1/6 inch). **2** a size of letters in typewriting (10 per inch). [Anglo-Latin *pica*, a 15th-c. book of rules about Church feasts, perhaps formed as PIE[2]]

pica[2] /ˈpʌɪkə/ *n. Med.* the eating of substances other than normal food, such as earth or stones. [modern Latin or medieval Latin, = magpie]

picador /ˈpɪkədɔː/ *n.* (in bullfighting) a person on horseback who goads the bull with a lance. [Spanish, from *picar* 'prick']

picaresque /pɪkəˈrɛsk/ *adj.* (of a style of fiction) dealing with the episodic adventures of rogues etc. [French from Spanish *picaresco*, from *pícaro* 'rogue']

■ **Usage** *Picaresque* is sometimes used to mean 'transitory' or 'roaming', but this is considered incorrect in standard English.

picaroon /pɪkəˈruːn/ *n. archaic* **1 a** a rogue. **b** a thief. **2 a** a pirate. **b** a pirate ship. [Spanish *picarón* (as PICARESQUE)]

picayune /pɪkəˈjuːn/ *n. & adj. N. Amer.* ● *n.* **1** a small coin of little value, esp. a 5-cent piece. **2** *colloq.* an insignificant person or thing. ● *adj. colloq.* mean; contemptible; petty; trivial. [French *picaillon*, a Piedmontese coin, also used to mean cash, from Provençal *picaioun*, of unknown origin]

piccalilli /ˈpɪkəlɪli, pɪkəˈlɪli/ *n.* (*pl.* **piccalillis**) a pickle of chopped vegetables, mustard, and hot spices. [18th c.: perhaps from PICKLE + CHILLI]

piccaninny /ˈpɪkənɪni/ *n. & adj.* (*US* **pickaninny**) ● *n.* (*pl.* **-ies**) often *offens.* a small black or Australian Aboriginal child. ● *adj. archaic* very small. [West Indian creole from Spanish *pequeño* or Portuguese *pequeno* 'little']

piccolo /ˈpɪkələʊ/ *n.* (*pl.* **-os**) **1** a small flute sounding an octave higher than the ordinary one. **2** a piccolo-player. [Italian, = small (flute)]

pichiciago /pɪtʃɪˈsjeɪgəʊ/ *n.* (also **pichiciego**) (*pl.* **-os**) a fairy armadillo, esp. *Chlamyphorus truncatus*. [Spanish *pichiciego*, perhaps from Guarani *pichey* 'armadillo' + Spanish *ciego* 'blind' from Latin *caecus*]

pick[1] /pɪk/ *v. & n.* ● *v.tr.* **1** (also *absol.*) choose carefully from a number of alternatives (*picked the pink one*; *picked a team*; *picked the right moment to intervene*). **2** detach or pluck (a flower, fruit, etc.) from a stem, tree, etc. **3 a** probe (the teeth, nose, ears, a pimple, etc.) with the finger, an instrument, etc. to remove unwanted matter. **b** clear (a bone, carcass, etc.) of scraps of meat etc. **4** (also *absol.*) (of a person) eat (food, a meal, etc.) in small bits; nibble without appetite. **5** (also *absol.*) esp. *N. Amer.* pluck the strings of (a banjo etc.). **6** remove stalks etc. from (esp. soft fruit) before cooking. **7 a** select (a route or path) carefully over difficult terrain on foot. **b** place (one's steps etc.) carefully. **8** pull apart (*pick oakum*). **9** (of a bird) take up (grains etc.) in the beak. ● *n.* **1** the act or an instance of picking. **2 a** a selection or choice. **b** the right to select (*had first pick of the prizes*). **3** (usu. foll. by *of*) the best (*the pick of the bunch*). □ **pick and choose** select carefully or fastidiously. **pick at 1** eat (food) without interest; nibble. **2** = *pick on* 1 (see PICK[1]). **pick a person's brains** extract ideas, information, etc., from a person for one's own use. **pick a fight** = *pick a quarrel*. **pick holes** (or **a hole**) **in 1** make holes in (material etc.) by plucking, poking, etc. **2** find fault with (an idea etc.). **pick a lock** open a lock with an instrument other than the proper key, esp. with intent to steal. **pick off 1** pluck (leaves etc.) off. **2** shoot (people etc.) one by one without haste. **3** eliminate (opposition etc.) singly. **4** *Baseball* put out (a runner) by throwing the ball to a base. **pick on 1** find fault with; nag at. **2** select. **pick out 1** take from a larger number (*picked him out from the others*). **2** distinguish from surrounding objects or at a distance (*can just pick out the church spire*). **3** play (a tune) by ear on the piano etc. **4** (often foll. by *in*, *with*) esp. *Brit.* **a** highlight (a painting etc.) with touches of another colour. **b** accentuate (decoration, a painting, etc.) with a contrasting colour (*picked out the handles in red*). **5** make out (the meaning of a passage etc.). **pick over** select the best from. **pick a person's pockets** steal the contents of a person's pockets. **pick a quarrel** start an argument or a fight deliberately. **pick to pieces** = *take to pieces* (see PIECE). **pick up 1** grasp and raise (from the ground etc.) (*picked up his hat*). **2** gain or acquire by chance or without effort (*picked up a cold*; *picked up French easily*). **3 a** fetch (a person, animal, or thing) left in another person's charge. **b** stop for and take along with one, esp. in a vehicle (*pick me up on the corner*). **4** make the acquaintance of (a person) casually, esp. as a sexual overture. **5** (of one's health, the weather, share prices, etc.) recover, prosper, improve. **6** (of a motor engine etc.) recover speed; accelerate. **7** (of the police etc.) take into charge; arrest. **8** detect by scrutiny or with a telescope, searchlight, radio, etc. (*picked up most of the mistakes*; *picked up a distress signal*). **9 a** (often foll. by *with*) form or renew a friendship. **b** resume, take up anew (*pick up where we left off*). **10** (esp. in phr. **pick up the tab**) accept the responsibility of paying (a bill etc.). **11** (*refl.*) raise (oneself etc.) after a fall etc. **12** raise (the feet etc.) clear of the ground. **13** *Golf* pick up one's ball, esp. when conceding a hole. **take one's pick** make a choice. □ **pickable** *adj.* [Middle English, earlier *pike*, of unknown origin]

pick[2] /pɪk/ *n. & v.* ● *n.* **1** a long-handled tool having a usu. curved iron bar pointed at one or both ends, used for breaking up hard ground, masonry, etc. **2** *colloq.* a plectrum. **3** any instrument for picking, such as a toothpick. ● *v.tr.* **1** break the surface of (the ground etc.) with or as if with a pick. **2** make (holes etc.) in this way. [Middle English, apparently variant of PIKE[2]]

pickaback var. of PIGGYBACK.

pickaninny *US* var. of PICCANINNY.

pickaxe /ˈpɪkaks/ *n. & v.* (*US* **pickax**) ● *n.* = PICK[2] *n.* 1. ● *v.* **1** *tr.* break (the ground etc.) with a pickaxe. **2** *intr.* work with a pickaxe. [Middle English *pikois* from Old French *picois*, related to PIKE[2]: assimilated to AXE]

pickelhaube /ˈpɪk(ə)l(h)aʊbə/ *n. hist.* a German soldier's spiked helmet. [German]

picker /ˈpɪkə/ *n.* **1** a person or thing that picks something. **2** (often in *comb.*) a person who gathers or collects something (*hop-picker*; *ragpicker*).

pickerel /ˈpɪk(ə)r(ə)l/ *n.* (*pl.* same or **pickerels**) a young pike. [Middle English, diminutive of PIKE[1]]

picket /ˈpɪkɪt/ *n. & v.* ● *n.* **1** a person or group of people outside a place of work, intending to persuade esp. workers not to enter during a strike etc. **2** a pointed stake or peg driven into the ground to form a fence or palisade, to tether a horse, etc. **3** (also **picquet**, **piquet**)

Mil. **a** a small body of troops or a single soldier sent out to watch for the enemy, held in readiness, etc. **b** a party of sentries. **c** an outpost. **d** a camp guard on police duty in a garrison town etc. ● *v.* (**picketed**, **picketing**) **1 a** *tr. & intr.* station or act as a picket. **b** *tr.* beset or guard (a factory, workers, etc.) with a picket or pickets. **2** *tr.* secure with stakes. **3** *tr.* tether (an animal). □ **picketer** *n.* [French *piquet* 'pointed stake' via *piquer* 'prick', from *pic* PICK[2]]

picket line *n.* a boundary established by workers on strike, esp. at the entrance to the place of work, which others are asked not to cross.

pickings /'pɪkɪŋz/ *n.pl.* **1** perquisites; pilferings (*rich pickings*). **2** remaining scraps; gleanings.

pickle /'pɪk(ə)l/ *n. & v.* ● *n.* **1 a** (often in *pl.*) food, esp. vegetables, preserved in brine, vinegar, mustard, etc. and used as a relish. **b** the brine, vinegar, etc. in which food is preserved. **c** *US* a cucumber preserved thus. **2** *colloq.* a plight (*a fine pickle we are in!*). **3** *Brit. colloq.* a mischievous child. **4** an acid solution for cleaning metal etc. ● *v.tr.* **1** preserve in pickle. **2** treat with pickle. **3** (as **pickled** *adj.*) *slang* drunk. [Middle English *pekille*, *pykyl*, from Middle Dutch, Middle Low German *pekel*, of unknown origin]

pickler /'pɪklə/ *n.* **1** a person who pickles vegetables etc. **2** a vegetable suitable for pickling.

picklock /'pɪklɒk/ *n.* **1** a person who picks locks. **2** an instrument for this.

pick-me-up *n.* **1** a tonic for the nerves etc. **2** a good experience, good news, etc. that cheers.

pickpocket /'pɪkpɒkɪt/ *n.* a person who steals from the pockets of others. □ **pickpocketing** *n.*

pick-up *n.* **1** (in full **pick-up truck**) a small open motor truck. **2** a device that produces an electrical signal in response to some other kind of signal or change, esp.: **a** the part of a record player carrying the stylus. **b** a device on a musical instrument which converts sound vibrations into electrical signals for amplification. **3** *slang* a person met casually, esp. for sexual purposes. **4** the act of picking up, esp. of giving a person a lift. **5** an increase in, or recovery of, speed or prosperity. **6** *Mus.* a series of introductory notes leading into the opening part of a tune. **7** *Fishing* a semicircular loop of metal for guiding the line back on to the spool as it is reeled in.

Pickwickian /pɪk'wɪkɪən/ *adj.* **1** of or like Mr Pickwick in Dickens's *Pickwick Papers*, esp. in being jovial, plump, etc. **2** (of words or their sense) misunderstood or misused, esp. to avoid offence.

picky /'pɪki/ *adj.* (**pickier**, **pickiest**) *colloq.* excessively fastidious; choosy. □ **pickiness** *n.*

pick-your-own *adj.* (usu. *attrib.*) (of commercially grown fruit and vegetables) dug or picked by the customer at the place of production.

picnic /'pɪknɪk/ *n. & v.* ● *n.* **1** an outing or excursion taking a packed meal to be eaten out of doors. **2** any meal eaten out of doors or without preparation, tables, chairs, etc. **3** (usu. with *neg.*) *colloq.* something agreeable or easily accomplished etc. (*it was no picnic organizing the meeting*). ● *v.intr.* (**picnicked**, **picnicking**) take part in a picnic. □ **picnicker** *n.* **picnicky** *adj. colloq.* [French *pique-nique*, of unknown origin]

pico- /'pi:kəʊ, 'pʌɪkəʊ/ *comb. form* denoting a factor of 10^{-12} (*picometre*; *picosecond*). [Spanish *pico* 'beak, peak, little bit']

picot /'pi:kəʊ/ *n.* a small loop of twisted thread in a lace edging etc. [French, diminutive of *pic* 'peak, point']

picotee /pɪkə'ti:/ *n.* a type of carnation of which the flowers have a light ground and dark-edged petals. [French *picoté -ée*, past part. of *picoter* 'prick' (as PICOT)]

picquet var. of PICKET *n.* 3.

picric acid /'pɪkrɪk/ *n.* a very bitter yellow compound used in dyeing and surgery and in explosives. □ **picrate** /-reɪt/ *n.* [Greek *pikros* 'bitter']

Pict /pɪkt/ *n.* a member of an ancient people of N. Britain. □ **Pictish** *adj.* [Middle English from Late Latin *Picti*, perhaps from *pingere pict-* 'paint, tattoo']

pictograph /'pɪktə(ʊ)grɑ:f/ *n.* (also **pictogram** /'pɪktə(ʊ)gram/) **1 a** a pictorial symbol for a word or phrase. **b** an ancient record consisting of these. **2** a pictorial representation of statistics etc. on a chart, graph, etc. □ **pictographic** /-'grafɪk/ *adj.* **pictography** /-'tɒgrəfi/ *n.* [Latin *pingere pict-* 'paint']

pictorial /pɪk'tɔ:rɪəl/ *adj. & n.* ● *adj.* **1** of or expressed in a picture or pictures. **2** illustrated. **3** picturesque. ● *n.* a journal, postage stamp, etc., with a picture or pictures as the main feature. □ **pictorially** *adv.* [Late Latin *pictorius* from Latin *pictor* 'painter' (as PICTURE)]

picture /'pɪktʃə/ *n. & v.* ● *n.* **1 a** (often *attrib.*) a painting, drawing, photograph, etc., esp. as a work of art (*picture frame*). **b** a portrait, esp. a photograph, of a person (*does not like to have her picture taken*). **c** a beautiful object (*her hat is a picture*). **2 a** a total visual or mental impression produced; a scene (*the picture looks bleak*). **b** a written or spoken description (*drew a vivid picture of moral decay*). **3 a** a film. **b** (in *pl.*; prec. by *the*) a showing of films at a cinema (*went to the pictures*). **c** (in *pl.*) films in general. **4** an image on a television screen. **5** *colloq.* **a** esp. *iron.* a person or thing exemplifying something (*he was the picture of innocence*). **b** a person or thing resembling another closely (*the picture of her aunt*). **c** *iron.* a striking expression, pose, etc.; a comic or striking sight (*her face was a picture*). ● *v.tr.* **1** represent in a picture. **2** (also *refl.*; often foll. by *to*) imagine, esp. visually or vividly (*pictured it to herself*). **3** describe graphically. □ **get the picture** *colloq.* grasp the tendency or drift of circumstances, information, etc. **in the picture** fully informed or noticed. **out of the picture** uninvolved, inactive; irrelevant. [Middle English from Latin *pictura*, from *pingere pict-* 'paint']

picture book *n.* a book containing many illustrations.

picture card *n.* a court card.

picture frame *n.* a frame made to hold a picture.

picture gallery *n.* a place containing an exhibition or collection of pictures.

picturegoer /'pɪktʃəgəʊə/ *n.* a person who frequents the cinema.

picture hat *n.* a woman's wide-brimmed highly decorated hat as in pictures by 18th-c. English painters such as Reynolds and Gainsborough.

picture-moulding *n.* **1** woodwork etc. used for framing pictures. **2** a rail on a wall used for hanging pictures from.

picture palace *n. Brit. archaic* a cinema.

picture postcard *n.* a postcard with a picture on one side.

picture rail *n.* a horizontal rail on a wall for hanging pictures from.

picturesque /pɪktʃə'rɛsk/ *adj.* **1** (of landscape etc.) beautiful or striking, as in a picture. **2** (of language etc.) strikingly graphic; vivid. □ **picturesquely** *adv.* **picturesqueness** *n.* [French *pittoresque* via Italian *pittoresco*, from *pittore* 'painter', from Latin (as PICTORIAL): assimilated to PICTURE]

picture theatre see THEATRE 1b.

picture window *n.* a very large window consisting of one pane of glass, usu facing an attractive view.

picture-writing *n.* a mode of recording events etc. by pictorial symbols as in early hieroglyphics etc.

piddle /'pɪd(ə)l/ *v. & n.* ● *v.intr.* **1** *colloq.* urinate (used esp. to or by children). **2** work or act in a trifling way. **3** (as **piddling** *adj.*) *colloq.* trivial; trifling. ● *n. colloq.* (used esp. to or by children) **1** an act of urinating. **2** urine. □ **piddler** *n.* [noun and sense 1 of verb probably from PISS + PUDDLE: senses 2 and 3 of the verb perhaps from PEDDLE]

piddock /'pɪdək/ *n.* any rock-boring bivalve mollusc of the family Pholadidae, used for bait. [19th c.: origin unknown]

pidgin /ˈpɪdʒɪn/ *n.* a simplified language containing vocabulary from two or more languages, used for communication between people not having a common language. [corruption of *business*]

pidgin English *n.* a pidgin in which the chief language is English, used originally between Chinese and Europeans.

pi-dog var. of PYE-DOG.

pie[1] /pʌɪ/ *n.* **1** a baked dish of meat, fish, fruit, etc., usu. with a top and base of pastry. **2** anything resembling a pie in form (*a mud pie*). □ **easy as pie** *colloq.* very easy. **pie in the sky** *colloq.* an unrealistic prospect of future happiness after present suffering; a misleading promise. [Middle English, perhaps = PIE[2], from miscellaneous contents compared to objects collected by a magpie]

pie[2] /pʌɪ/ *n. archaic* **1** a magpie. **2** a pied animal. [Middle English via Old French from Latin *pica* 'magpie']

pie[3] /pʌɪ/ *n. & v.* (*US* **pi**) ● *n.* **1** a confused mass of printers' type. **2** chaos. ● *v.tr.* (**pieing**) muddle up (type). [perhaps translation of French PÂTÉ = PIE[1]]

pie[4] /pʌɪ/ *n. hist.* a former monetary unit of India equal to one-twelfth of an anna. [Hindustani etc. *pā'ī* from Sanskrit *pad, padī* 'quarter']

piebald /ˈpʌɪbɔːld/ *adj. & n.* ● *adj.* **1** (usu. of an animal, esp. a horse) having irregular patches of two colours, esp. black and white. **2** motley; mongrel. ● *n.* a piebald animal, esp. a horse. [as PIE[2], BALD]

piece /piːs/ *n. & v.* ● *n.* **1 a** (often foll. by *of*) one of the distinct portions forming part of or broken off from a larger object; a bit; a part (*a piece of string*). **b** each of the parts of which a set or category is composed (*a five-piece band*; *a piece of furniture*). **2** a coin of specified value (*50p piece*). **3 a** a usu. short literary or musical composition or a picture. **b** a theatrical play. **4** an item, instance, or example (*a piece of impudence*; *a piece of news*). **5 a** any of the objects used to make moves in board games. **b** a chessman (strictly, other than a pawn). **6** a definite quantity in which a thing is sold. **7** (often foll. by *of*) an enclosed portion (of land etc.). **8** *slang offens.* a woman. **9** (foll. by *of*) *colloq.* a share in, involvement in; a financial share or investment in (*has a piece of the new production*). **10** esp. *N. Amer. slang* a portable firearm; a handgun. ● *v.tr.* **1** (usu. foll. by *together*) form into a whole; put together; join (*finally pieced his story together*). **2** (usu. foll. by *out*) **a** eke out. **b** form (a theory etc.) by combining parts etc. **3** (usu. foll. by *up*) patch. **4** join (threads) in spinning. □ **break to pieces** break into fragments. **by the piece** (paid) according to the quantity of work done. **go to pieces** collapse emotionally; suffer a breakdown. **in one piece** **1** unbroken. **2** unharmed. **in pieces** broken. **of a piece** (often foll. by *with*) uniform, consistent, in keeping. **a piece of the action** *slang* **1** a share in the profits accruing from something. **2** a share in the excitement. **a piece of cake** see CAKE. **a piece of one's mind** a sharp rebuke or lecture. **say one's piece** give one's opinion or make a prepared statement. **take to pieces** **1** break up or dismantle. **2** criticize harshly. □ **piecer** *n.* (in sense 4 of *v.*). [Middle English via Anglo-French *pece*, Old French *piece* from Romanic, probably of Gaulish origin]

pièce de résistance /ˌpjɛs də rɛˈzɪstɒ̃s/ *n.* (*pl.* **pièces de résistance** *pronunc.* same) **1** the most important or remarkable item. **2** the most substantial dish at a meal. [French]

piece-goods *n.pl.* fabrics, esp. Lancashire cottons, woven in standard lengths.

piecemeal /ˈpiːsmiːl/ *adv. & adj.* ● *adv.* piece by piece; gradually. ● *adj.* partial; gradual; unsystematic. [Middle English, from PIECE + *-meal* from Old English *mǣlum* (instrumental dative pl. of *mǣl* MEAL[1])]

piece of eight *n. hist.* a Spanish dollar, equivalent to 8 reals.

piece of goods *n. Brit. archaic slang offens.* a woman.

piece of water *n.* a small lake etc.

piece of work *n.* a thing made by working (cf. *nasty piece of work*).

piece-rate *n.* a rate of payment for piecework.

piecework /ˈpiːswəːk/ *n.* work paid for by the amount produced.

pie chart *n.* a circle divided into sectors to represent relative quantities.

piecrust /ˈpʌɪkrʌst/ *n.* the baked pastry crust of a pie.

piecrust table *n.* a table with an indented edge like a piecrust.

pied /pʌɪd/ *adj.* particoloured. [Middle English from PIE[2]]

pied-à-terre /pjeɪdɑːˈtɛː/ *n.* (*pl.* **pieds-à-terre** *pronunc.* same) a usu. small flat, house, etc. kept for occasional use. [French, literally 'foot to earth']

piedmont /ˈpiːdmɒnt/ *n.* a gentle slope leading from the foot of mountains to a region of flat land. [Italian *piemonte* 'mountain foot', the name of a region at the foot of the Alps]

pie-dog var. of PYE-DOG.

Pied Piper *n.* a person enticing followers, esp. to their doom.

pied wagtail *n.* a small black and white wagtail, of a race of *Motacilla alba* found mainly in the British Isles.

pie-eater *n. Austral. slang* a person of little account.

pie-eyed *adj. slang* drunk.

pieman /ˈpʌɪmən/ *n.* (*pl.* **-men**) a pie seller.

pier /pɪə/ *n.* **1 a** a structure of iron or wood raised on piles and leading out to sea, a lake, etc., used as a promenade and landing stage, and *Brit.* often with entertainment arcades etc. **b** a breakwater; a mole. **2 a** a support of an arch or of the span of a bridge; a pillar. **b** solid masonry between windows etc. **3** a long narrow structure projecting from the main body of an airport terminal, along which passengers walk to and from their aircraft. [Middle English *per* from Anglo-Latin *pera*, of unknown origin]

pierce /pɪəs/ *v.* **1** *tr.* **a** (of a sharp instrument etc.) penetrate the surface of. **b** (often foll. by *with*) prick with a sharp instrument, esp. to make a hole in. **c** make a hole, opening, or tunnel into or through (something), bore through. **d** make (a hole etc.) (*pierced a hole in the belt*). **e** (of cold, grief, etc.) affect keenly or sharply. **f** (of a light, glance, sound, etc.) penetrate keenly or sharply. **2** *intr.* (as **piercing** *adj.*) (of a glance, intuition, high noise, bright light, etc.) keen, sharp, or unpleasantly penetrating. **3** *tr.* force a way etc. through or into (something); break through or into (*pierced the German line*). **4** *intr.* (usu. foll. by *through, into*) penetrate. □ **piercer** *n.* **piercingly** *adv.* [Middle English via Old French *percer* from Latin *pertundere* 'bore through' (as PER-, *tundere tus-* 'thrust')]

pier glass *n.* a large mirror, used originally to fill wall-space between windows.

pierrot /ˈpɪərəʊ, ˈpjɛrəʊ/ *n.* (*fem.* **pierrette** /pɪəˈrɛt, pjɛˈrɛt/) *Theatr.* **1** a white-faced entertainer in pier shows etc. with a loose white clown's costume. **2** a French pantomime character so dressed. [French, diminutive of *Pierre* 'Peter']

pietà /pɪeɪˈtɑː, Italian pjeˈta/ *n.* a picture or sculpture of the Virgin Mary holding the dead body of Christ on her lap or in her arms. [Italian from Latin (as PIETY)]

pietas /ˈpʌɪətɑːs, piːˈeɪtɑːs/ *n.* respect due to an ancestor, a forerunner, etc. [Latin: see PIETY]

pietism /ˈpʌɪətɪz(ə)m/ *n.* **1 a** a pious sentiment. **b** an exaggerated or affected piety. **2** (esp. as **Pietism**) *hist.* a movement for the revival of piety in the Lutheran Church in the 17th c. □ **pietist** *n.* **pietistic** /-ˈtɪstɪk/ *adj.* **pietistical** /-ˈtɪstɪk(ə)l/ *adj.* [German *Pietismus* (as PIETY)]

piety /ˈpʌɪəti/ *n.* (*pl.* **-ies**) **1** the quality of being pious. **2** a pious act. [Middle English via Old French *pieté* from Latin *pietas -tatis* 'dutifulness' (as PIOUS)]

piezoelectricity /pʌɪˌiːzəʊɪlɛkˈtrɪsɪti, ˌpiːzəʊ-/ *n.* electric polarization in a substance resulting from the application of mechanical stress, esp. in certain crystals. □ **piezoelectric** /-ɪ'lɛktrɪk/ *adj.* **piezoelectrically** /-ɪ'lɛktrɪk(ə)li/ *adv.* [Greek *piezō* 'press' + ELECTRICITY (see ELECTRIC)]

piezometer /pʌɪɪ'zɒmɪtə/ *n.* an instrument for measuring the magnitude or direction of pressure.

piffle /'pɪf(ə)l/ *n.* & *v. colloq.* ● *n.* nonsense; empty speech. ● *v.intr.* talk or act feebly; trifle. □ **piffler** *n.* [imitative]

piffling /'pɪflɪŋ/ *adj. colloq.* trivial; worthless.

pig /pɪg/ *n.* & *v.* ● *n.* **1 a** any omnivorous hoofed broad-snouted bristly mammal of the family Suidae, esp. a domesticated kind, *Sus scrofa.* **b** *US* a young pig; a piglet. **c** (often in *comb.*) any similar animal (*guinea pig*). **2** the flesh of esp. a young or sucking pig as food (*roast pig*). **3** *colloq.* **a** a greedy, dirty, obstinate, sulky, or annoying person. **b** an unpleasant, awkward, or difficult thing, task, etc. **4** an oblong mass of metal (esp. iron or lead) from a smelting furnace. **5** *slang offens.* a police officer. **6** *Sc. dial.* an earthenware hot-water bottle. ● *v.* (**pigged**, **pigging**) **1** *tr.* (also *absol.*) (of a sow) bring forth (piglets). **2** *tr. colloq.* eat (food) greedily. **3** *intr.* herd together or behave like pigs. □ **bleed like a pig** (or **stuck pig**) bleed copiously. **buy a pig in a poke** buy, accept, etc. something without knowing its value or esp. seeing it. **in pig** (of a sow) pregnant. **in a pig's eye** *colloq.* certainly not. **make a pig of oneself** overeat. **make a pig's ear of** *colloq.* make a mess of; bungle. **pig it** live in a disorderly, untidy, or filthy fashion. **pig out** (often foll. by *on*) esp. *N. Amer. slang* make a pig of oneself; overeat. **pigs might fly** esp. *Brit. iron.* an expression of disbelief. □ **piglet** *n.* **piglike** *adj.* **pigling** *n.* [Middle English *pigge*, probably from Old English]

pigeon[1] /'pɪdʒɪn, 'pɪdʒ(ə)n/ *n.* **1** any of several large usu. grey and white birds of the family Columbidae, esp. *Columba livia*, often domesticated and bred and trained to carry messages etc.; a dove (cf. ROCK-PIGEON). **2** *slang* a person easily swindled; a simpleton. □ **pigeonry** *n.* (*pl.* **-ies**). [Middle English via Old French *pijon* from Late Latin *pipio -onis* (imitative)]

pigeon[2] /'pɪdʒɪn/ *n.* **1** = PIDGIN. **2** *colloq.* a particular concern, job, or business (*that's not my pigeon*).

pigeon-breast *n.* (also **pigeon-chest**) a deformed human chest with a projecting breastbone. □ **pigeon-breasted** *adj.* (also **pigeon-chested**).

pigeon fancier *n.* a person who keeps and breeds fancy pigeons. □ **pigeon-fancying** *n.*

pigeon-hawk *n.* = MERLIN.

pigeon-hearted *adj.* cowardly.

pigeon-hole *n.* & *v.* ● *n.* **1** each of a set of compartments in a cabinet or on a wall for papers, letters, etc. **2** a small recess for a pigeon to nest in. ● *v.tr.* **1** assign (a person or thing) to a preconceived category. **2** put (a matter) aside for future consideration or to forget it. **3** deposit (a document) in a pigeon-hole.

pigeon pair *n. Brit.* **1** boy and girl twins. **2** a boy and girl as sole children.

pigeon's milk *n.* **1** a secretion from the oesophagus with which pigeons feed their young. **2** an imaginary article for which children are sent on a fool's errand.

pigeon-toed *adj.* (of a person) having the toes turned inwards.

piggery /'pɪg(ə)ri/ *n.* (*pl.* **-ies**) **1** a pig-breeding farm etc. **2** = PIGSTY. **3** piggishness.

piggish /'pɪgɪʃ/ *adj.* **1** of or relating to pigs. **2** having a quality associated with pigs; greedy; dirty; selfish; mean; stubborn. □ **piggishness** *n.*

piggy /'pɪgi/ *n.* & *adj.* ● *n.* (also **piggie**) (*pl.* **piggies**) *colloq.* **1** a little pig. **2 a** a child's word for a pig. **b** a child's word for a toe. **3** *Brit.* the game of tipcat. ● *adj.* (**piggier**, **piggiest**) **1** like a pig. **2** (of features etc.) like those of a pig (*little piggy eyes*). □ **piggy in the middle** = PIG IN THE MIDDLE.

piggyback /'pɪgɪbak/ *n.*, *v.*, & *adv.* (also **pickaback** /'pɪkəbak/) ● *n.* a ride on the back and shoulders of another person. ● *v.* **1** *intr.* ride (as if) on a person's back and shoulders. **2** *tr.* **a** give a piggyback to. **b** carry or mount on top of another thing. ● *adv.* **1** on the back and shoulders of another person. **2** on the back or top of a larger object. [16th c.: origin unknown]

piggy bank *n.* a pig-shaped money box.

pig-headed *adj.* obstinate. □ **pig-headedly** *adv.* **pig-headedness** *n.*

pightle /'pʌɪt(ə)l/ *n.* chiefly *dial.* a small field or enclosure. [Middle English: origin unknown]

pig-ignorant *adj. colloq.* extremely ignorant.

pig in the middle *n.* esp. *Brit.* a person who is placed in an awkward situation between two others (after a ball game for three with one in the middle).

pig-iron *n.* crude iron from a smelting furnace.

Pig Island *n. Austral.* & *NZ slang* New Zealand.

pig-jump *n.* & *v. Austral. slang* ● *n.* a jump made by a horse from all four legs. ● *v.intr.* (of a horse) jump in this manner.

pig Latin *n.* a made-up jargon.

pig meat *n. Brit.* pork, ham, or bacon.

pigment /'pɪgm(ə)nt/ *n.* & *v.* ● *n.* **1** colouring matter used as paint or dye, usu. as an insoluble suspension. **2** the natural colouring matter of animal or plant tissue, e.g. chlorophyll, haemoglobin. ● *v.tr.* colour with or as if with pigment. □ **pigmental** /-'mɛnt(ə)l/ *adj.* **pigmentary** *adj.* [Middle English from Latin *pigmentum*, from *pingere* 'paint']

pigmentation /pɪgm(ə)n'teɪʃ(ə)n/ *n.* **1** the natural colouring of plants, animals, etc. **2** the excessive colouring of tissue by the deposition of pigment.

pigmy var. of PYGMY.

pignut /'pɪgnʌt/ *n.* = EARTH-NUT.

pigpen /'pɪgpɛn/ *n. US* = PIGSTY.

pigskin /'pɪgskɪn/ *n.* **1** the hide of a pig. **2** leather made from this. **3** *N. Amer.* a football.

pig-sticker *n.* a long sharp knife.

pigsticking /'pɪgstɪkɪŋ/ *n.* **1** the hunting of wild boar with a spear on horseback. **2** the butchering of pigs.

pigsty /'pɪgstʌɪ/ *n.* (*pl.* **-ies**) **1** a pen or enclosure for a pig or pigs. **2** a filthy house, room, etc.

pig's wash *n.* = PIGSWILL.

pigswill /'pɪgswɪl/ *n.* kitchen refuse and scraps fed to pigs.

pigtail /'pɪgteɪl/ *n.* **1** a plait of hair hanging from the back of the head, or either of a pair at the sides. **2** a thin twist of tobacco. □ **pigtailed** *adj.*

pigwash /'pɪgwɒʃ/ *n.* = PIGSWILL.

pigweed /'pɪgwi:d/ *n.* a plant used for fodder, esp. fat hen or a weedy amaranth.

pi jaw *n.* a long moralizing lecture or reprimand. [PI[2] + JAW]

pika /'pʌɪkə, 'pi:kə/ *n.* any small rabbit-like mammal of the genus *Ochotona*, with small ears, short legs, and a very short tail. Also called *mouse hare.* [Tungus *piika*]

pike[1] /pʌɪk/ *n.* (*pl.* same) **1** a large voracious freshwater fish of the family Esocidae, with a long narrow snout and sharp teeth, esp. the common *Esox lucius.* **2** a similar fish, e.g. the garpike. [Middle English, = PIKE[2] (because of its pointed jaw)]

pike[2] /pʌɪk/ *n.* & *v.* ● *n.* **1** *hist.* an infantry weapon with a pointed steel or iron head on a long wooden shaft. **2** *N.Engl.* the peaked top of a hill, esp. in names of hills in the Lake District. ● *v.tr. hist.* thrust through or kill with a pike. □ **pike on** esp. *Austral. colloq.* withdraw timidly from. [Old English *pīc* 'point, prick': sense 2 perhaps from Old Norse]

pike[3] /pʌɪk/ *n.* **1** a toll gate; a toll. **2** a turnpike road. □ **come down the pike** *US* appear on the scene, come to notice. [abbreviation of TURNPIKE]

pike[4] /pʌɪk/ *n.* a jackknife position in diving or gymnastics. [20th c.: origin unknown]

pikelet /'pʌɪklɪt/ *n. N.Engl.* a thin kind of crumpet. [Welsh (*bara*) *pyglyd* 'pitchy (bread)']

pikeman /'pʌɪkmən/ *n.* (*pl.* **-men**) the keeper of a turnpike.

pikeperch /ˈpʌɪkpəːtʃ/ *n.* (*pl.* same) any of various pikelike perches of the genus *Lucioperca* or *Stizostedion*.

piker /ˈpʌɪkə/ *n.* a cautious, timid, or mean person. [PIKE²]

pikestaff /ˈpʌɪkstɑːf/ *n.* **1** *hist.* the wooden shaft of a pike. **2** a walking stick with a metal point. ▫ **plain as a pikestaff** quite plain or obvious (originally *packstaff*, a smooth staff used by a pedlar).

pilaf /pɪˈlaf/ *n.* (also **pilaff**, **pilau** /pɪˈlaʊ/, **pilaw** /pɪˈlɔː/) a Middle Eastern or Indian dish of spiced rice or wheat with meat, fish, vegetables, etc. [Turkish *pilâv*]

pilaster /pɪˈlastə/ *n.* a rectangular column, esp. one projecting from a wall. ▫ **pilastered** *adj.* [French *pilastre* via Italian *pilastro* and medieval Latin *pilastrum* from Latin *pila* 'pillar']

pilchard /ˈpɪltʃəd/ *n.* a small marine fish, *Sardinia pilchardus* of the herring family (see SARDINE¹). [16th-c. *pilcher* etc.: origin unknown]

pile¹ /pʌɪl/ *n.* & *v.* ● *n.* **1** a heap of things laid or gathered upon one another (*a pile of leaves*). **2 a** a large imposing building (*a stately pile*). **b** a large group of tall buildings. **3** *colloq.* **a** a large quantity. **b** a large amount of money; a fortune (*made his pile*). **4 a** a series of plates of dissimilar metals laid one on another alternately to produce an electric current. **b** = ATOMIC PILE. **5** a funeral pyre. ● *v.* **1** *tr.* **a** (often foll. by *up*, *on*) heap up (*piled the plates on the table*). **b** (foll. by *with*) load (*piled the bed with coats*). **2** *intr.* (usu. foll. by *in*, *into*, *on*, *out of*, etc.) crowd hurriedly or tightly (*all piled into the car*; *piled out of the restaurant*). ▫ **pile arms** place (usu. four) rifles with their butts on the ground and the muzzles together. **pile it on** *colloq.* exaggerate. **pile on the agony** *colloq.* exaggerate for effect or to gain sympathy etc. **pile up 1** accumulate; heap up. **2** *colloq.* run (a ship) aground or cause (a vehicle etc.) to crash. [Middle English via Old French from Latin *pila* 'pillar, pier, mole']

pile² /pʌɪl/ *n.* & *v.* ● *n.* **1** a heavy beam driven vertically into the bed of a river, soft ground, etc., to support the foundations of a superstructure. **2** a pointed stake or post. **3** *Heraldry* a wedge-shaped device. ● *v.tr.* **1** provide with piles. **2** drive (piles) into the ground etc. [Old English *pīl* from Latin *pilum* 'javelin']

pile³ /pʌɪl/ *n.* **1** the soft projecting surface on velvet, plush, etc., or esp. on a carpet; nap. **2** soft hair or down, or the wool of a sheep. ▫ **pileless** *adj.* [Middle English, probably via Anglo-French *pyle*, *peile*, Old French *poil* from Latin *pilus* 'hair']

pileated woodpecker /ˈpʌɪlɪeɪtɪd/ *n.* a large N. American woodpecker, *Dryocopus pileatus*, with a red-topped head. [Latin *pileatus* 'capped', from *peilus* 'felt cap']

piledriver /ˈpʌɪldrʌɪvə/ *n.* a machine for driving piles into the ground. ▫ **piledriving** *n.* & *attrib.adj.*

pile dwelling *n.* a dwelling built on piles, esp. in a lake.

piles /pʌɪlz/ *n.pl. colloq.* haemorrhoids. [Middle English, probably from Latin *pila* 'ball', from the globular form of external piles]

pile-up *n. colloq.* a multiple crash of road vehicles.

pileus /ˈpʌɪlɪəs/ *n.* (*pl.* **pilei** /-lɪʌɪ/) the caplike part of a mushroom or other fungus. ▫ **pileate** /-lɪət/ *adj.* **pileated** /-lɪeɪtɪd/ *adj.* [Latin, = felt cap]

pilewort /ˈpʌɪlwəːt/ *n.* the lesser celandine. [PILES, from its reputed efficacy against piles]

pilfer /ˈpɪlfə/ *v.tr.* (also *absol.*) steal (objects) esp. in small quantities. ▫ **pilferage** /-rɪdʒ/ *n.* **pilferer** *n.* [Middle English from Anglo-French & Old French *pelfrer* 'pillage', of unknown origin: associated with archaic *pill* 'plunder': cf. PELF]

pilgrim /ˈpɪlgrɪm/ *n.* & *v.* ● *n.* **1** a person who journeys to a sacred place for religious reasons. **2** a person regarded as journeying through life etc. **3** a traveller. **4** *hist.* a member of the Pilgrim Fathers. ● *v.intr.* (**pilgrimed**, **pilgriming**) wander like a pilgrim. ▫ **pilgrimize** *v.intr.* (also **-ise**). [Middle English *pilegrim* via Provençal *pelegrin* from Latin *peregrinus* 'stranger': see PEREGRINE]

pilgrimage /ˈpɪlgrɪmɪdʒ/ *n.* & *v.* ● *n.* **1** a pilgrim's journey (*go on a pilgrimage*). **2** life viewed as a journey. **3** any journey taken for nostalgic or sentimental reasons. ● *v.intr.* go on a pilgrimage. [Middle English from Provençal *pilgrinatge* (as PILGRIM)]

Pilgrim Fathers *n.pl.* English Puritans who founded the colony of Plymouth, Massachusetts, in 1620.

Pilipino /pɪlɪˈpiːnəʊ/ *n.* the national language of the Philippines. [Tagalog from Spanish *Filipino*]

pill /pɪl/ *n.* **1 a** a ball or disc etc. of solid medicine for swallowing whole. **b** (usu. prec. by *the*) a contraceptive pill. **2** an unpleasant or painful necessity; a humiliation (*a bitter pill*; *must swallow the pill*). **3** *colloq.* or *joc.* a ball, e.g. a football, a bullet or bomb. ▫ **sugar** (or **sweeten**) **the pill** make an unpleasant necessity acceptable. [Middle Dutch, Middle Low German *pille*, probably from Latin *pilula*, diminutive of *pila* 'ball']

pillage /ˈpɪlɪdʒ/ *v.* & *n.* ● *v.tr.* (also *absol.*) plunder; sack (a place or a person). ● *n.* the act or an instance of pillaging, esp. in war. ▫ **pillager** *n.* [Middle English from Old French, from *piller* 'plunder']

pillar /ˈpɪlə/ *n.* **1 a** a usu. slender vertical structure of wood, metal, or esp. stone used as a support for a roof etc. **b** a similar structure used for ornament. **c** a post supporting a structure. **2** a person regarded as a mainstay or support (*a pillar of the faith*; *a pillar of strength*). **3** an upright mass of ice, rock, etc. (*pillar of flame*). **4** a solid mass of coal etc. left to support the roof of a mine. ▫ **from pillar to post** (driven etc.) from one place to another; to and fro. ▫ **pillared** *adj.* **pillaret** *n.* [Middle English & Anglo-French *piler*, Old French *pilier*, ultimately from Latin *pila* 'pillar']

pillar box *n. Brit.* a public postbox shaped like a pillar.

pillar-box red *adj.* & *n. Brit.* ● *n.* a bright red colour, as of pillar boxes. ● *adj.* of this colour.

Pillars of Hercules *n.pl.* two rocks on either side of the Strait of Gibraltar.

pillbox /ˈpɪlbɒks/ *n.* **1** a small shallow cylindrical box for holding pills. **2** a hat of a similar shape. **3** *Mil.* a small partly underground enclosed concrete fort used as an outpost.

pillion /ˈpɪljən/ *n.* **1** seating for a passenger behind a motorcyclist. **2** *hist.* **a** a woman's light saddle. **b** a cushion attached to the back of a saddle for a usu. female passenger. ▫ **ride pillion** travel seated behind a motorcyclist etc. [Gaelic *pillean*, *pillin*, diminutive of *pell* 'cushion', from Latin *pellis* 'skin']

pilliwinks /ˈpɪlɪwɪŋks/ *n. hist.* an instrument of torture used for squeezing the fingers. [Middle English *pyrwykes*, *pyrewinkes*, of unknown origin]

pillock /ˈpɪlək/ *n. Brit. slang* a stupid person; a fool. [16th c., = penis (variant of *pillicock*): 20th c. in sense defined]

pillory /ˈpɪləri/ *n.* & *v.* ● *n.* (*pl.* **-ies**) *hist.* a wooden framework with holes for the head and hands, enabling the public to assault or ridicule a person so imprisoned. ● *v.tr.* (**-ies**, **-ied**) **1** expose (a person) to ridicule or public contempt. **2** *hist.* put in the pillory. [Middle English via Anglo-Latin *pillorium* from Old French *pilori* etc.: probably from Provençal *espilori* of uncertain origin]

pillow /ˈpɪləʊ/ *n.* & *v.* ● *n.* **1 a** a usu. oblong support for the head, esp. in bed, with a cloth cover stuffed with feathers, flock, foam rubber, etc. **b** any pillow-shaped block or support. **2** = LACE-PILLOW. ● *v.tr.* **1** rest (the head etc.) on or as if on a pillow (*pillowed his head on his arms*). **2** serve as a pillow for (*moss pillowed her head*). ▫ **pillowy** *adj.* [Old English *pyle*, *pylu*, ultimately from Latin *pulvinus* 'cushion']

pillowcase /ˈpɪləʊkeɪs/ *n.* a washable cotton etc. cover for a pillow.

pillow-fight *n.* a mock fight with pillows, esp. by children.

pillow lace *n.* lace made on a lace-pillow.

pillow lava *n.* lava forming rounded masses.

pillowslip /ˈpɪləʊslɪp/ *n.* = PILLOWCASE.

pillow talk *n.* romantic or intimate conversation in bed.

pill-popper *n. colloq.* **1** a person who takes pills freely. **2** a drug addict. □ **pill-popping** *n. & attrib.adj.*

pillule var. of PILULE.

pillwort /ˈpɪlwəːt/ *n.* an aquatic fern, *Pilularia globulifera*, with small globular spore-producing bracts.

pilose /ˈpʌɪləʊz/ *adj.* (also **pilous** /ˈpʌɪləs/) covered with hair. □ **pilosity** /pʌɪˈlɒsɪti/ *n.* [Latin *pilosus* from *pilus* 'hair']

pilot /ˈpʌɪlət/ *n. & v.* ● *n.* **1** a person who operates the flying controls of an aircraft. **2** a person qualified to take charge of a ship entering or leaving harbour. **3** (usu. *attrib.*) an experimental undertaking or test, esp. in advance of a larger one (*a pilot project*). **4** a guide; a leader. **5** *archaic* a steersman. ● *v.tr.* (**piloted, piloting**) **1** act as a pilot on (a ship) or of (an aircraft). **2** conduct, lead, or initiate as a pilot (*piloted the new scheme*). □ **pilotage** *n.* **pilotless** *adj.* [French *pilote* via medieval Latin *pilotus, pedot(t)a* from Greek *pēdon* 'oar', in pl. 'rudder']

pilot balloon *n.* a small balloon used to track air currents etc.

pilot-bird *n.* a rare dark brown Australian warbler, *Pycnoptilus floccosus*, with a distinctive loud cry.

pilot chute *n.* a small parachute used to bring the main one into operation.

pilot-cloth *n.* thick blue woollen cloth for seamen's coats etc.

pilot fish *n.* a small fish, *Naucrates ductor*, said to act as a pilot leading a shark to food.

pilot house *n.* = WHEELHOUSE.

pilot-jacket *n.* = PEA-JACKET.

pilot light *n.* **1** a small gas burner kept alight to light another. **2** an electric indicator light or control light.

pilot officer *n.* a rank in the RAF above acting pilot officer.

pilot whale *n.* a small whale of the genus *Globicephalus*, of temperate or subtropical waters.

Pilsner /ˈpɪlznə, ˈpɪls-/ *n.* (also **Pilsener**) a lager beer brewed or like that brewed at *Pilsen* (Plzeň) in the Czech Republic.

pilule /ˈpɪljuːl/ *n.* (also **pillule**) a small pill. □ **pilular** *adj.* **pilulous** *adj.* [French from Latin *pilula*: see PILL]

pimento /pɪˈmɛntəʊ/ *n.* (*pl.* **-os**) **1** = PIMIENTO. **2** esp. *W. Indies* = ALLSPICE 1. [Spanish *pimiento* (as PIMIENTO)]

pi-meson /pʌɪˈmiːzɒn, -ˈmɛzɒn/ *n.* = PION.

pimiento /pɪmɪˈɛntəʊ, pɪmˈjɛn-/ *n.* (*pl.* **-os**) a red pepper (capsicum). [Spanish from Latin *pigmentum* PIGMENT, in medieval Latin = spice]

pimp /pɪmp/ *n. & v.* ● *n.* a man who lives off the earnings of a prostitute or a brothel; a pander; a ponce. ● *v.intr.* act as a pimp. [16th c.: origin unknown]

pimpernel /ˈpɪmpənɛl/ *n.* any plant of the genus *Anagallis*, esp. = SCARLET PIMPERNEL. [Middle English from Old French *pimpernelle, piprenelle*, ultimately from Latin *piper* PEPPER]

pimping /ˈpɪmpɪŋ/ *adj.* **1** small or mean. **2** sickly. [17th c.: origin unknown]

pimple /ˈpɪmp(ə)l/ *n.* **1** a small hard inflamed spot on the skin. **2** anything resembling a pimple, esp. in relative size. □ **pimpled** *adj.* **pimply** *adj.* [Middle English, nasalized from Old English *piplian* 'break out in pustules']

PIN /pɪn/ *n.* (also **PIN number**) personal identification number. [abbreviation]

> ■ **Usage** The variant *PIN number* is common, even though the element *number* is redundant. The reason is probably that it is more readily understood than *PIN* in examples such as *He'd forgotten his PIN*.

pin /pɪn/ *n. & v.* ● *n.* **1 a** a small thin pointed piece of esp. steel wire with a round or flattened head used (esp. in sewing) for holding things in place, attaching one thing to another, etc. **b** any of several types of pin (*drawing pin*; *safety pin*; *hairpin*). **c** a small brooch (*diamond pin*). **d** a badge fastened with a pin. **2** a peg of wood or metal for various purposes, e.g. a wooden skittle in bowling. **3** something of small value (*don't care a pin*; *for two pins I'd resign*). **4** (in *pl.*) *colloq.* legs (*quick on his pins*). **5** *Med.* a steel rod used to join the ends of fractured bones while they heal. **6** *Chess* a position in which a piece is pinned to another. **7** *Golf* a stick with a flag placed in a hole to mark its position. **8** *Mus.* a peg round which one string of a musical instrument is fastened. **9** *Brit.* a half-firkin cask for beer. ● *v.tr.* (**pinned, pinning**) **1 a** (often foll. by *to, up, together*) fasten with a pin or pins (*pinned up the hem*; *pinned the papers together*). **b** transfix with a pin, lance, etc. **2** (usu. foll. by *on*) fix (blame, responsibility, etc.) on a person etc. (*pinned the blame on his friend*). **3** (often foll. by *against, on,* etc.) seize and hold fast. **4** *Chess* prevent (an opposing piece) from moving except by exposing a more valuable piece to capture. □ **on pins and needles** in an agitated state of suspense. **pin down 1** (often foll. by *to*) bind (a person etc.) to a promise, arrangement, etc. **2** force (a person) to declare his or her intentions. **3** restrict the actions or movement of (an enemy etc.). **4** specify (a thing) precisely (*could not pin down his unease to a particular cause*). **5** hold (a person etc.) down by force. **pin one's faith** (or **hopes** etc.) **on** rely implicitly on. [Old English *pinn* from Latin *pinna* 'point' etc., associated with *penna* PEN[1]]

pina colada /ˌpiːnə kəˈlɑːdə/ *n.* a drink made from pineapple juice, rum, and coconut. [Spanish, literally 'strained pineapple']

pinafore /ˈpɪnəfɔː/ *n.* **1 a** *Brit.* an apron, esp. with a bib. **b** a woman's sleeveless wraparound washable covering for the clothes, tied at the back. **2** (in full **pinafore dress**) a collarless sleeveless dress usu. worn over a blouse or jumper. [PIN + AFORE (because originally pinned on the front of a dress)]

pinaster /pʌɪˈnastə/ *n.* = CLUSTER PINE. [Latin, = wild pine, from *pinus* 'pine' + -ASTER]

pinball /ˈpɪnbɔːl/ *n.* a game in which small metal balls are shot across a board and score points by striking pins with lights etc.

pince-nez /pansˈneɪ/ *n.* (*pl.* same) a pair of eyeglasses with a nose clip instead of side pieces. [French, literally 'pinch-nose']

pincer movement *n. Mil.* a movement by two wings of an army converging on the enemy.

pincers /ˈpɪnsəz/ *n.pl.* **1** (also **pair of pincers** *sing.*) a gripping-tool resembling scissors but with blunt usu. concave jaws to hold a nail etc. for extraction. **2** the front claws of lobsters and some other crustaceans. [Middle English *pinsers, pinsours* via Anglo-French from Old French *pincier* PINCH]

pincette /pɪnˈsɛt, pãˈsɛt/ *n.* small pincers; tweezers. [French]

pinch /pɪn(t)ʃ/ *v. & n.* ● *v.* **1** *tr.* **a** grip (esp. the skin of part of the body or of another person) tightly, esp. between finger and thumb (*pinched my finger in the door*; *stop pinching me*). **b** (often *absol.*) (of a shoe, garment, etc.) constrict (the flesh) painfully. **2** *tr.* (of cold, hunger, etc.) grip (a person) painfully (*she was pinched with cold*). **3** *tr.* **a** esp. *Brit. colloq.* steal; take without permission. **b** *slang* arrest (a person) (*pinched him for loitering*). **4** *tr.* (as **pinched** *adj.*) (of the features) drawn, as with cold, hunger, worry, etc. **5 a** *tr.* (usu. foll. by *in, of, for,* etc.) stint (a person). **b** *intr.* be niggardly with money, food, etc. **6** *tr.* (usu. foll. by *out, back, down*) remove (leaves, buds, etc.) to encourage bushy growth. **7** *intr.* sail very close to the wind. ● *n.* **1** the act or an instance of pinching etc. the flesh. **2** an amount that can be taken up with fingers and thumb (*a pinch of snuff*). **3** the stress or pain caused by poverty, cold, hunger, etc. **4** *slang* **a** an arrest. **b** a theft. □ **at** (or **in**) **a pinch** in an emergency; if necessary. **feel the pinch** experience the effects of poverty. [Middle English via an Anglo-French and Old Northern French variant of Old French *pincier*, ultimately from Latin *pungere punct-* 'prick']

pinchbeck /ˈpɪn(t)ʃbɛk/ *n. & adj.* ● *n.* an alloy of copper and zinc resembling gold and used in cheap jewellery etc. ● *adj.* **1** counterfeit; sham. **2** cheap; tawdry. [named after C. *Pinchbeck*, English watchmaker d. 1732]

pinch-hitter *n.* **1** a baseball player who bats instead of another. **2** *US* a person acting as a substitute. □ **pinch-hit** *v.intr.*

pinchpenny /ˈpɪn(t)ʃpɛni/ *n.* (*pl.* **-ies**) (also *attrib.*) a miserly person.

pinch-run *v.intr. Baseball* substitute as a runner between bases, esp. at a critical point in the game. □ **pinch-runner** *n.*

pincushion /ˈpɪnkʊʃ(ə)n/ *n.* a small cushion for holding pins.

pin-down *n.* the action or policy of putting children in care into solitary confinement for long periods of time.

pine[1] /pʌɪn/ *n.* **1** (in full **pine tree**) any evergreen tree of the genus *Pinus* native to northern temperate regions, with needle-shaped leaves growing in clusters. **2** the soft timber of this, often used to make furniture (cf. DEAL[2] 1). **3** (*attrib.*) made of pine. **4** = PINEAPPLE. □ **pinery** *n.* (*pl.* **-ies**). [Middle English via Old English *pīn* & Old French *pin* from Latin *pinus*]

pine[2] /pʌɪn/ *v.intr.* **1** (often foll. by *away*) decline or waste away, esp. from grief, disease, etc. **2** (usu. foll. by *for*, *after*, or *to* + infin.) long eagerly; yearn. [earlier = (cause to) suffer: Old English *pīnian*, related to obsolete *pine* 'punishment', via Germanic from medieval Latin *pena*, Latin *poena*]

pineal /ˈpɪnɪəl, ˈpʌɪ-/ *adj.* shaped like a pine cone. [French *pinéal* from Latin *pinea* 'pine cone': see PINE[1]]

pineal body *n.* (also **pineal gland**) a pea-sized conical mass of tissue behind the third ventricle of the brain, secreting a hormone-like substance in some mammals.

pineapple /ˈpʌɪnap(ə)l/ *n.* **1** a tropical plant, *Ananas comosus*, with a spiral of sword-shaped leaves and a thick stem bearing a large fruit developed from many flowers. **2** the fruit of this, consisting of yellow flesh surrounded by a tough segmented skin and topped with a tuft of stiff leaves. [PINE[1], from the fruit's resemblance to a pine cone]

pine cone *n.* the cone-shaped fruit of the pine tree.

pine marten *n.* a weasel-like mammal, *Martes martes*, native to N. Eurasia, having a dark brown coat with a yellowish throat.

pine nut *n.* the edible seed of various pine trees.

pinetum /pʌɪˈniːtəm/ *n.* (*pl.* **pineta** /-tə/) a plantation of pine trees or other conifers for scientific or ornamental purposes. [Latin, from *pinus* 'pine']

pinewood /ˈpʌɪnwʊd/ *n.* **1** the timber of the pine. **2** (**pine wood**) a forest of pines.

piney var. of PINY.

pin-feather *n. Zool.* an ungrown feather.

pinfold /ˈpɪnfəʊld/ *n. & v.* esp. *hist.* ● *n.* a pound for stray cattle etc. ● *v.tr.* confine (cattle) in a pinfold. [Old English *pundfald* (as POUND[3], FOLD[2])]

ping /pɪŋ/ *n. & v.* ● *n.* a single short high ringing sound. ● *v.* **1** *intr. & tr.* make or cause to make a ping. **2** *intr. US* = PINK[3]. [imitative]

pinger /ˈpɪŋə/ *n.* **1** a device that transmits pings at short intervals for purposes of detection or measurement etc. **2** *Brit.* a timer that pings after a pre-set time.

pingo /ˈpɪŋgəʊ/ *n.* (*pl.* **-os**) *Geol.* a dome-shaped mound found in permafrost areas. [Eskimo]

ping-pong /ˈpɪŋpɒŋ/ *n.* = TABLE TENNIS. [imitative of the sound of a bat striking a ball]

pinguid /ˈpɪŋgwɪd/ *adj. formal* or *joc.* fat, oily, or greasy. [Latin *pinguis* 'fat']

pinhead /ˈpɪnhɛd/ *n.* **1** the flattened head of a pin. **2** a very small thing. **3** *colloq.* a stupid or foolish person.

pinheaded /pɪnˈhɛdɪd/ *adj. colloq.* stupid, foolish. □ **pinheadedness** *n.*

pin-high *adj. Golf* (of a ball) at the same distance ahead as the pin.

pinhole /ˈpɪnhəʊl/ *n.* **1** a hole made by a pin. **2** a hole into which a peg fits.

pinhole camera *n.* a camera with a pinhole aperture and no lens.

pinion[1] /ˈpɪnjən/ *n. & v.* ● *n.* **1** the outer part of a bird's wing, usu. including the flight feathers. **2** *poet.* a wing; a flight feather. ● *v.tr.* **1** cut off the pinion of (a wing or bird) to prevent flight. **2 a** bind the arms of (a person). **b** (often foll. by *to*) bind (the arms, a person, etc.) esp. to a thing. [Middle English from Old French *pignon*, ultimately from Latin *pinna*: see PIN]

pinion[2] /ˈpɪnjən/ *n.* **1** a small cogwheel engaging with a larger one. **2** a cogged spindle engaging with a wheel. [French *pignon*, alteration of obsolete *pignol* from Latin *pinea* 'pine cone' (as PINE[1])]

pink[1] /pɪŋk/ *n. & adj.* ● *n.* **1** a pale red colour (*decorated in pink*). **2** any cultivated plant of the genus *Dianthus*, with sweet-smelling white, pink, crimson, etc. flowers. **3** (prec. by *the*) the most perfect condition etc. (*the pink of elegance*). **4** (also **hunting pink**) **a** a fox-hunter's red coat. **b** the cloth for this. **c** a fox-hunter. **5** *colloq.* often *derog.* a person with socialist tendencies. ● *adj.* **1** (often in *comb.*) of a pale red colour of any of various shades (*rose pink*; *salmon pink*). **2** *colloq.* often *derog.* tending to socialism. **3** (of wine) rosé. □ **in the pink** *colloq.* in very good health. □ **pinkish** *adj.* **pinkly** *adv.* **pinkness** *n.* **pinky** *adj.* [earliest in sense 2 of the noun: perhaps from dialect *pink-eyed* 'having small eyes']

pink[2] /pɪŋk/ *v.tr.* **1** pierce slightly with a sword etc. **2** cut a scalloped or zigzag edge on. **3** (often foll. by *out*) ornament (leather etc.) with perforations. **4** *archaic* adorn; deck. [Middle English, perhaps from Low German or Dutch: cf. Low German *pinken* 'strike, peck']

pink[3] /pɪŋk/ *v.intr. Brit.* (of a vehicle engine) emit a series of high-pitched explosive sounds caused by faulty combustion. [imitative]

pink[4] /pɪŋk/ *n. hist.* a sailing ship, esp. one with a narrow stern, originally small and flat-bottomed. [Middle English from Middle Dutch *pin(c)ke*, of unknown origin]

pink[5] /pɪŋk/ *n.* a yellowish lake pigment made by combining vegetable colouring matter with a white base (*brown pink*; *French pink*). [17th c.: origin unknown]

pink[6] /pɪŋk/ *n. Brit.* **1** a young salmon. **2** *dial.* a minnow. [15th c. *penk*, of unknown origin]

pink-collar *adj.* (usu. *attrib.*) (of a profession etc.) traditionally associated with women (cf. WHITE-COLLAR, BLUE-COLLAR).

pink disease *n.* a disease of young children with pink discoloration of the extremities.

pink elephants *n.pl. colloq.* hallucinations experienced in a drunken state.

pink-eye *n.* **1** a contagious fever in horses. **2** conjunctivitis in humans and some livestock.

pink gin *n. Brit.* gin flavoured with Angostura Bitters.

pinkie /ˈpɪŋki/ *n.* esp. *US & Sc. colloq.* the little finger. [partly from PINK[1], partly from Dutch *pink* 'the little finger']

pinking shears *n.pl.* (also **pinking scissors**) a dressmaker's serrated shears for cutting a zigzag edge.

pinko /ˈpɪŋkəʊ/ *n.* (*pl.* **-os** or **-oes**) esp *US slang* often *derog.* a socialist.

pink slip *n.* esp. *N. Amer.* a notice of dismissal from employment.

Pinkster /ˈpɪŋ(k)stə/ *n. US dial.* Whitsuntide. [Dutch, = Pentecost]

pinkster flower *n.* the pink azalea, *Rhododendron periclymenoides*.

pin money *n.* **1** *hist.* an allowance to a woman for dress etc. from her husband. **2** a small sum of money, esp. for spending on inessentials (*only works for pin money*).

pinna /ˈpɪnə/ *n.* (*pl.* **pinnae** /-niː/ or **pinnas**) **1** the auricle; the external part of the ear. **2** a primary division of a pinnate leaf. **3** a fin or finlike structure, feather, wing, etc. [Latin, = *penna* 'feather, wing, fin']

pinnace /ˈpɪnɪs/ *n. Naut.* a warship's or other ship's small boat, usu. motor-driven, originally schooner-rigged or eight-oared. [French *pinnace*, *pinasse*, ultimately from Latin *pinus* PINE[1]]

pinnacle /ˈpɪnək(ə)l/ *n. & v.* ● *n.* **1** the culmination or climax (of endeavour, success, etc.). **2** a natural peak. **3** a small ornamental turret usu. ending in a pyramid or cone, crowning a buttress, roof, etc. ● *v.tr.* **1** set on or as if on a pinnacle. **2** form the pinnacle of. **3** provide with pinnacles. [Middle English *pinacle* via Old French *pin(n)acle* from Late Latin *pinnaculum*, from *pinna* 'wing, point' (as PIN, -CULE)]

pinnae *pl.* of PINNA.

pinnate /ˈpɪneɪt/ *adj.* **1** (of a compound leaf) having leaflets arranged on either side of the stem, usu. in pairs opposite each other. **2** having branches, tentacles, etc., on each side of an axis. □ **pinnated** *adj.* **pinnately** *adv.* **pinnation** /-ˈneɪʃ(ə)n/ *n.* [Latin *pinnatus* 'feathered' (as PINNA)]

pinni- /ˈpɪni/ *comb. form* wing, fin. [Latin *pinna*]

pinniped /ˈpɪnɪpɛd/ *adj. & n.* ● *adj.* denoting any aquatic mammal with limbs ending in flippers, e.g. a seal. ● *n.* a pinniped mammal. [Latin *pinna* 'fin' + *pes ped-* 'foot']

pinnule /ˈpɪnjuːl/ *n.* **1** the secondary division of a pinnate leaf. **2** a part or organ like a small wing or fin. □ **pinnular** *adj.* [Latin *pinnula*, diminutive of *pinna* 'fin, wing']

PIN number var. of PIN.

pinny /ˈpɪni/ *n.* (*pl.* **-ies**) *colloq.* a pinafore. [abbreviation]

pinochle /ˈpiːnɒk(ə)l/ *n. N. Amer.* **1** a card game with a double pack of 48 cards (nine to ace only). **2** the combination of queen of spades and jack of diamonds in this game. [19th c.: origin unknown]

pinocytosis /ˌpiːnəʊsʌɪˈtəʊsɪs, ˌpɪnəʊ-, ˌpʌɪnəʊ-/ *n. Biol.* the ingestion of liquid into a cell by the budding of small vesicles from the cell membrane. [Greek *pino* 'drink' + *-cytosis* on the pattern of PHAGOCYTOSIS]

pinole /piːˈnəʊleɪ, -li/ *n. US* flour made from parched cornflour, esp. mixed with sweet flour made of mesquite beans, sugar, etc. [Latin American Spanish from Nahuatl *pinolli*]

piñon /pɪˈnjɒn, ˈpɪnjəʊn/ *n.* (also **pinyon**) **1** any of several small N. American pines, esp. *Pinus edulis*, with edible seeds. **2** the seed of such a tree, a type of pine nut. [Spanish, from Latin *pinea* 'pine cone']

pinpoint /ˈpɪnpɔɪnt/ *n. & v.* ● *n.* **1** the point of a pin. **2** something very small or sharp. **3** (*attrib.*) **a** very small. **b** precise, accurate. ● *v.tr.* locate with precision (*pinpointed the target*).

pinprick /ˈpɪnprɪk/ *n.* **1** a prick caused by a pin. **2** a trifling irritation.

pins and needles *n.pl.* a tingling sensation in a limb recovering from numbness.

pinstripe /ˈpɪnstrʌɪp/ *n.* **1** (often *attrib.*) a very narrow stripe in (esp. worsted or serge) cloth (*pinstripe suit*). **2** (in *sing* or *pl.*) a pinstripe suit (*came wearing his pinstripes*). □ **pinstriped** *adj.*

pint /pʌɪnt/ *n.* **1** a unit of liquid or dry capacity equal to one-eighth of a gallon: **a** (in full **imperial pint**) (in Britain) 20 fluid oz, 34.66 cu. in., or 0.565 litre. **b** (in full **US pint**) (in the US) 28.87 cu. in. or 0.473 litre (for liquid measure), or 33.60 cu. in. or 0.551 litre (for dry measure). **2** *Brit.* **a** *colloq.* a pint of beer. **b** a pint of a liquid, esp. milk. **3** *Brit.* a measure of shellfish, being the amount containable in a pint mug (*bought a pint of whelks*). [Middle English from Old French *pinte*, of unknown origin]

pinta /ˈpʌɪntə/ *n. Brit. colloq.* a pint of milk. [corruption of *pint of*]

pin-table *n. Brit.* a table used in playing pinball.

pintail /ˈpɪnteɪl/ *n.* a duck, esp. *Anas acuta*, or grouse with a pointed tail.

pintle /ˈpɪnt(ə)l/ *n.* a pin or bolt, esp. one on which some other part turns. [Old English *pintel* 'penis', of unknown origin: related to Old Frisian Dutch, German *pint*]

pinto /ˈpɪntəʊ/ *adj. & n. N. Amer.* ● *adj.* piebald. ● *n.* (*pl.* **-os**) a piebald horse. [Spanish, = mottled, ultimately from Latin *pictus*, past part. of *pingere* 'paint']

pint pot *n.* a pot, esp. of pewter, holding one pint, esp. of beer.

pint-sized *adj. colloq.* very small, esp. of a person.

pin-tuck *n.* a very narrow ornamental tuck.

pin-up *n.* **1** a photograph of a popular or sexually attractive person, designed to be hung on the wall. **2** a person shown in such a photograph.

pinwheel /ˈpɪnwiːl/ *n. & v.* ● *n.* **1** a small Catherine wheel (firework). **2** a thing which looks or works like a Catherine wheel; a flat rotating spiral. ● *v.intr.* spin or rotate like a pinwheel.

pinworm /ˈpɪnwəːm/ *n.* a small parasitic nematode worm, *Enterobius vermicularis*, of which the female has a pointed tail.

piny /ˈpʌɪni/ *adj.* (also **piney**) of, like, or full of pines (*a piny smell*).

Pinyin /pɪnˈjɪn/ *n.* a system of romanized spelling for transliterating Chinese. [Chinese *pīn-yīn*, literally 'spell sound']

pinyon var. of PIÑON.

piolet /pjəʊˈleɪ/ *n.* a two-headed ice axe for mountaineering. [French]

pion /ˈpʌɪɒn/ *n. Physics* a meson having a mass approximately 270 times that of an electron. Also called *pi-meson*. □ **pionic** /pʌɪˈɒnɪk/ *adj.* [PI[1] (the letter used as a symbol for the particle) + -ON]

pioneer /pʌɪəˈnɪə/ *n. & v.* ● *n.* **1** an initiator of a new enterprise, an inventor, etc. **2** an explorer or settler; a colonist. **3** *Mil.* a member of an infantry group preparing roads, terrain, etc. for the main body of troops. ● *v.* **1 a** *tr.* initiate or originate (an enterprise etc.). **b** *intr.* act or prepare the way as a pioneer. **2** *tr. Mil.* open up (a road etc.) as a pioneer. **3** *tr.* go before, lead, or conduct (another person or persons). [French *pionnier* 'foot soldier, pioneer', Old French *paonier*, *peon(n)ier* (as PEON)]

pious /ˈpʌɪəs/ *adj.* **1** devout; religious. **2** hypocritically virtuous; sanctimonious. **3** dutiful. □ **piously** *adv.* **piousness** *n.* [Latin *pius* 'dutiful, pious']

pious fraud *n.* a deception intended to benefit those deceived, esp. religiously.

pip[1] /pɪp/ *n. & v.* ● *n.* the seed of an apple, pear, orange, grape, etc. ● *v.tr.* (**pipped**, **pipping**) remove the pips from (fruit etc.). □ **pipless** *adj.* [abbreviation of PIPPIN]

pip[2] /pɪp/ *n. Brit.* a short high-pitched sound, usu. mechanically produced, esp. as a radio time signal. [imitative]

pip[3] /pɪp/ *n.* **1** any of the spots on a playing card, dice, or domino. **2** *Brit.* a star (1–3 according to rank) on the shoulder of an army officer's uniform. **3** a single blossom of a clustered head of flowers. **4** a diamond-shaped segment of the surface of a pineapple. **5** an image of an object on a radar screen. [16th c. *peep*, of unknown origin]

pip[4] /pɪp/ *n.* **1** a disease of poultry etc. causing thick mucus in the throat and white scale on the tongue. **2** *colloq.* a fit of disgust or bad temper (esp. *give one the pip*). [Middle English from Middle Dutch *pippe*, Middle Low German *pip*, probably ultimately from corruption of Latin *pituita* 'slime']

pip[5] /pɪp/ *v.tr.* (**pipped**, **pipping**) *Brit. colloq.* **1** hit with a shot. **2** defeat. **3** blackball. □ **pip at** (or **to**) **the post** defeat at the last moment. **pip out** die. [PIP[2] or PIP[1]]

pipa /pɪˈpɑː, ˈpʌɪpə, ˈpɪpə/ *n.* = SURINAME TOAD. [probably from Galibi]

pipal var. of PEEPUL.

pipe /pʌɪp/ *n. & v.* ● *n.* **1** a tube of metal, plastic, wood, etc. used to convey water, gas, etc. **2 a** (also **tobacco pipe**) a narrow wooden or clay etc. tube with a bowl at one end containing burning tobacco, the smoke from which is drawn into the mouth. **b** the quantity of tobacco held by this (*smoked a pipe*). **3** *Mus.* **a** a wind instrument consisting of a single tube. **b** any of the tubes by which sound is produced in an organ. **c** (in *pl.*) bagpipes (see BAGPIPE). **d** (in *pl.*) a set of pipes joined together, e.g. pan pipes. **4** a tubal organ, vessel, etc. in an animal's body. **5** a high note or song, esp. of a bird. **6** a cylindrical vein of ore. **7** a cavity in cast metal. **8 a** a boatswain's whistle. **b** the sounding of this. **9** a cask for wine, esp. as a measure of two hogsheads, usu. equivalent to 105 gallons (about 477 litres). **10** *archaic* the voice, esp. in singing. ● *v.tr.* **1** (also *absol.*) play (a tune etc.) on a pipe or pipes. **2 a** convey (oil, water, gas, etc.) by pipes. **b** provide with pipes. **3** transmit (music, a radio programme, etc.) by wire or cable. **4** (usu. foll. by *up, on, to*, etc.) *Naut.* **a** summon (a crew) to a meal, work, etc. **b** signal the arrival of (an officer etc.) on board. **5** utter in a shrill voice; whistle. **6 a** arrange (icing, cream, etc.) in decorative lines or twists on a cake etc. **b** ornament (a cake etc.) with piping. **7** trim (a dress etc.) with piping. **8** lead or bring (a person etc.) by the sound of a pipe. **9** propagate (pinks etc.) by taking cuttings at the joint of a stem. □ **pipe away** give a signal for (a boat) to start. **pipe down 1** *colloq.* be quiet or less insistent. **2** *Naut.* dismiss from duty. **pipe up** begin to play, sing, speak, etc. **put that in your pipe and smoke it** *colloq.* a challenge to another to accept something frank or unwelcome. □ **pipeful** *n.* (*pl.* **-fuls**). **pipeless** *adj.* **pipy** *adj.* [Old English *pīpe*, *pīpian* & Old French *piper* from Germanic, ultimately from Latin *pipare* 'peep, chirp']

pipe band *n.* a (esp. military) band consisting of bagpipe players, drummers, and a drum major.

pipeclay /ˈpʌɪpkleɪ/ *n.* & *v.* ● *n.* a fine white clay used for tobacco pipes, whitening leather, etc. ● *v.tr.* **1** whiten (leather etc.) with this. **2** put in order.

pipe-cleaner *n.* a piece of flexible covered wire for cleaning a tobacco pipe.

piped music *n.* pre-recorded background music played through loudspeakers in a public place.

pipe dream *n.* an unattainable or fanciful hope or scheme. [originally as experienced when smoking an opium pipe]

pipefish /ˈpʌɪpfɪʃ/ *n.* (*pl.* usu. same) any of various long slender fish of the family Syngnathidae, with an elongated snout.

pipe-light *n.* a spill for lighting a pipe.

pipeline /ˈpʌɪplʌɪn/ *n.* **1** a long, usu. underground, pipe for conveying esp. oil. **2** a channel supplying goods, information, etc. □ **in the pipeline** awaiting completion or processing.

pipe major *n.* an NCO commanding regimental pipers.

pip emma /pɪp ˈɛmə/ *adv.* & *n.* *Brit. colloq.* = P.M. [formerly signallers' names for letters PM]

pipe organ *n.* *Mus.* an organ using pipes instead of or as well as reeds.

piper /ˈpʌɪpə/ *n.* **1** a bagpipe-player. **2** a person who plays a pipe, esp. an itinerant musician. [Old English *pīpere* (as PIPE)]

pipe-rack *n.* a rack for holding tobacco pipes.

piperidine /pɪˈpɛrɪdiːn, pʌɪ-/ *n.* *Chem.* a peppery-smelling liquid formed by the reduction of pyridine. [Latin *piper* 'pepper' + -IDE + -INE[4]]

pipe roll *n.* *hist.* the annual records of the British Exchequer from the 12th–19th c. (probably because subsidiary documents were rolled in pipe form).

pipe-stem *n.* the shaft of a tobacco pipe.

pipe-stone *n.* a hard red clay used by N. American Indians for tobacco pipes.

pipette /pɪˈpɛt/ *n.* & *v.* ● *n.* a slender tube for transferring or measuring small quantities of liquids esp. in chemistry. ● *v.tr.* transfer or measure (a liquid) using a pipette. [French, diminutive of *pipe* PIPE]

pipework /ˈpʌɪpwəːk/ *n.* pipes collectively.

piping /ˈpʌɪpɪŋ/ *n.* & *adj.* ● *n.* **1** the act or an instance of piping, esp. whistling or singing. **2** a thin pipelike fold used to edge hems or frills on clothing, seams on upholstery, etc. **3** ornamental lines of icing, cream, potato, etc. on a cake or other dish. **4** lengths of pipe, or a system of pipes, esp. in domestic use. ● *adj.* (of a noise) high; whistling.

piping hot *adj.* & *adv.* very or suitably hot (esp. as required of food, water, etc.).

pipistrelle /pɪpɪˈstrɛl, ˈpɪp-/ *n.* any bat of the genus *Pipistrellus*, native to temperate regions and feeding on insects. [French from Italian *pipistrello*, *vip-*, via Latin *vespertilio* 'bat' from *vesper* 'evening']

pipit /ˈpɪpɪt/ *n.* any of various mainly ground-dwelling songbirds of the genus *Anthus*, having brown-streaked plumage, e.g. the meadow pipit. [probably imitative]

pipkin /ˈpɪpkɪn/ *n.* a small earthenware pot or pan. [16th c.: origin unknown]

pippin /ˈpɪpɪn/ *n.* **1 a** an apple grown from seed. **b** a red and yellow dessert apple. **2** *colloq.* an excellent person or thing; a beauty. [Middle English from Old French *pepin*, of unknown origin]

pipsqueak /ˈpɪpskwiːk/ *n.* *colloq.* an insignificant or contemptible person or thing. [imitative]

piquant /ˈpiːk(ə)nt, -kɑːnt/ *adj.* **1** agreeably pungent, sharp, or appetizing. **2** pleasantly stimulating, or disquieting, to the mind. □ **piquancy** *n.* **piquantly** *adv.* [French, pres. part. of *piquer* (as PIQUE[1])]

pique[1] /piːk/ *v.* & *n.* ● *v.tr.* (**piques**, **piqued**, **piquing**) **1** wound the pride of, irritate. **2** arouse (curiosity, interest, etc.). **3** (*refl.*; usu. foll. by *on*) pride or congratulate oneself. ● *n.* ill feeling; enmity; resentment (*in a fit of pique*). [French *piquer* 'prick, irritate', from Romanic]

pique[2] /piːk/ *n.* & *v.* ● *n.* the winning of 30 points on cards and play in piquet before one's opponent scores anything. ● *v.* (**piques**, **piqued**, **piquing**) **1** *tr.* score a pique against. **2** *intr.* score a pique. [French *pic*, of unknown origin]

piqué /ˈpiːkeɪ/ *n.* a stiff ribbed cotton or other fabric. [French, past part. of *piquer*: see PIQUE[1]]

piquet[1] /pɪˈkɛt/ *n.* a game for two players with a pack of 32 cards (seven up to ace only). [French, of unknown origin]

piquet[2] var. of PICKET *n.* 3.

piracy /ˈpʌɪrəsi/ *n.* (*pl.* **-ies**) **1** the practice or an act of robbery of ships at sea. **2** a similar practice or act in other forms, esp. hijacking. **3** the infringement of copyright by unauthorized reproduction or use of something. [medieval Latin *piratia* from Greek *pirateia* (as PIRATE)]

piragua /pɪˈragwə/ *n.* = PIROGUE. [Spanish from Carib, = dugout]

piranha /pɪˈrɑːnə, -njə/ *n.* (also **piraya** /-ˈrɑːjə/) a predatory S. American freshwater fish, esp. of the genus *Serrasalmus*, noted for its voracity and sharp teeth. [Portuguese from Tupi, variant of *piraya* 'scissors']

pirate /ˈpʌɪrət/ *n.* & *v.* ● *n.* **1 a** a person who commits piracy. **b** a ship used by pirates. **2** a person who infringes another's copyright or other business rights; a plagiarist. **3** (often *attrib.*) a person, organization, etc., that broadcasts without official authorization (*pirate radio station*). ● *v.tr.* **1** appropriate or reproduce (the work or ideas etc. of another) without permission, for one's own benefit. **2** plunder. □ **piratic** /-ˈratɪk/ *adj.* **piratical** /-ˈratɪk(ə)l/ *adj.* **piratically** /-ˈratɪk(ə)li/ *adv.* [Middle English via Latin *pirata* from Greek *peiratēs*, from *peiraō* 'attempt, assault']

piraya var. of PIRANHA.

piripiri /ˈpɪrɪpɪri/ *n.* (*pl.* **piripiris**) *NZ* a plant of the rose family, *Acaena anserinifolia*, native to New Zealand and having prickly burs. [Maori]

pirogue /pɪˈrəʊg/ *n.* **1** a long narrow canoe made from a single tree trunk. **2** a two-masted sailing barge. [French, probably from Galibi]

pirouette /pɪrʊˈɛt/ *n.* & *v.* ● *n.* a dancer's spin on one foot or the point of the toe. ● *v.intr.* perform a pirouette. [French, = spinning top]

pis aller /piːz 'alei, French piz ale/ *n.* a course of action followed as a last resort. [French, from *pis* 'worse' + *aller* 'go']

piscary /'pɪskəri/ *n.* □ **common of piscary** the right of fishing in another's water in common with the owner and others. [Middle English from medieval Latin *piscaria*, neut. pl. of Latin *piscarius*, from *piscis* 'fish']

piscatorial /pɪskə'tɔːrɪəl/ *adj.* = PISCATORY 1. □ **piscatorially** *adv.*

piscatory /'pɪskət(ə)ri/ *adj.* **1** of or concerning fishermen or fishing. **2** *formal* enthusiastic about fishing. [Latin *piscatorius* via *piscator* 'fisherman' from *piscis* 'fish']

Pisces /'pʌɪsiːz, 'pɪskiːz/ *n.* (*pl.* same) **1** *Astron.* a large constellation (the Fish or Fishes), said to represent a pair of fishes tied together by their tails. **2** *Astrol.* **a** the twelfth sign of the zodiac, which the sun enters about 20 Feb. **b** a person born when the sun is in this sign. □ **Piscean** /'pʌɪsɪən/ *n.* & *adj.* [Middle English from Latin, pl. of *piscis* 'fish']

pisciculture /'pɪsɪkʌltʃə/ *n.* the artificial rearing of fish. □ **piscicultural** /-'kʌltʃ(ə)r(ə)l/ *adj.* **pisciculturist** /-'kʌltʃərɪst/ *n.* [Latin *piscis* 'fish', on the pattern of *agriculture* etc.]

piscina /pɪ'siːnə, pɪ'sʌɪnə/ *n.* (*pl.* **piscinae** /-niː/ or **piscinas**) **1** a stone basin near the altar in RC and pre-Reformation churches for draining water used in the Mass. **2** a fish pond. **3** *hist.* a Roman bathing pond. [Latin, from *piscis* 'fish']

piscine /'pɪsʌɪn/ *adj.* of or concerning fish. [Latin *piscis* 'fish']

piscivorous /pɪ'sɪv(ə)rəs/ *adj.* fish-eating. [Latin *piscis* 'fish' + -VOROUS]

pish /pɪʃ/ *int.* an expression of contempt, impatience, or disgust. [imitative]

pisiform /'pʌɪsɪfɔːm, 'pɪzɪ-/ *adj.* pea-shaped. [modern Latin *pisiformis* from *pisum* 'pea']

pisiform bone *n.* a small bone in the wrist in the upper row of the carpus.

pismire /'pɪsmʌɪə/ *n. dial.* an ant. [Middle English, from PISS (from smell of anthill) + obsolete *mire* 'ant']

piss /pɪs/ *v.* & *n. coarse slang* ● *v.* **1** *intr.* urinate. **2** *tr.* **a** discharge (blood etc.) when urinating. **b** wet with urine. **3** *tr.* (as **pissed** *adj.*) *Brit.* drunk. **4** *refl.* **a** wet one's clothing with urine. **b** be very frightened, amused, or excited. **5** *tr.* (as **pissed** *adj.*) *N. Amer.* annoyed; depressed. ● *n.* **1** urine. **2** an act of urinating. □ **piss about** *Brit.* fool or mess about. **piss down** rain heavily. **piss in the wind** do something to no effect or against one's own interests. **piss off** *Brit.* **1** go away. **2** (often as **pissed off** *adj.*) annoy; depress. **piss on** show utter contempt for, esp. by humiliating; defeat heavily. **take the piss** (often foll. by *out of*) *Brit.* mock; deride. [Middle English from Old French *pisser* (imitative)]

piss artist *n. Brit. coarse slang* **1** a drunkard. **2** a person who fools about. **3** a glib person.

pissoir /piː'swɑː, 'pɪswɑː, French piswar/ *n.* a public urinal. [French]

pisspot /'pɪspɒt/ *n. coarse slang* a chamber pot.

piss-take *n. Brit. coarse slang* a parody.

piss-taker *n. Brit. coarse slang* a person who mocks. □ **piss-taking** *n.*

piss-up *n. Brit. coarse slang* a drinking spree.

pistachio /pɪ'stɑːʃɪəʊ, pɪ'statʃəʊ/ *n.* & *adj.* ● *n.* (*pl.* **-os**) **1** an evergreen tree, *Pistacia vera*, bearing small brownish-green flowers and ovoid reddish fruit. **2** (in full **pistachio nut**) the edible pale green seed of this. **3** (in full **pistachio green**) a pale green colour. ● *adj.* (in full **pistachio green**; hyphenated when *attrib.*) pale green. [Italian *pistaccio* and Spanish *pistacho*, via Latin *pistacium* and Greek *pistakion* from Persian *pistah*]

piste /piːst/ *n.* a ski run of compacted snow. [French, = racetrack]

pisteur /piː'stəː/ *n.* a person employed to prepare the snow on a skiing piste. [French]

pistil /'pɪstɪl/ *n.* the female organs of a flower, comprising the stigma, style, and ovary. □ **pistillary** *adj.* **pistilliferous** /-'lɪf(ə)rəs/ *adj.* **pistilline** /-lʌɪn/ *adj.* [French *pistile* or Latin *pistillum* PESTLE]

pistillate /'pɪstɪlət/ *adj.* **1** having pistils. **2** having pistils but no stamens.

pistol /'pɪst(ə)l/ *n.* & *v.* ● *n.* **1** a small hand-held firearm. **2** anything of a similar shape. ● *v.tr.* (**pistolled**, **pistolling**; *US* **pistoled**, **pistoling**) shoot with a pistol. □ **hold a pistol to a person's head** coerce a person by threats. [obsolete French, via German *Pistole* from Czech *pišťal*]

pistole /pɪ'stəʊl/ *n. hist.* a foreign (esp. Spanish) gold coin. [French *pistole* abbreviation of *pistolet* (with the same meaning), of uncertain origin]

pistoleer /pɪstə'lɪə/ *n.* a soldier armed with a pistol.

pistol grip *n.* a handle shaped like a pistol-butt.

pistol shot *n.* **1** the range of a pistol. **2** a shot fired from a pistol.

pistol-whip *v.tr.* (**-whipped**, **-whipping**) beat with a pistol.

piston /'pɪst(ə)n/ *n.* **1** a disc or short cylinder fitting closely within a tube in which it moves up and down against a liquid or gas, used in an internal-combustion engine to derive motion, or in a pump to impart motion. **2** a sliding valve in a trumpet etc. [French from Italian *pistone*, variant of *pestone*, augmentative of *pestello* PESTLE]

piston engine *n.* an engine, esp. in a aircraft, in which motion is derived from a piston. □ **piston-engined** *adj.*

piston ring *n.* a ring on a piston sealing the gap between the piston and the cylinder wall.

piston rod *n.* a rod or crankshaft attached to a piston to drive a wheel or to impart motion.

pit[1] /pɪt/ *n.* & *v.* ● *n.* **1 a** a usu. large deep hole in the ground. **b** a hole made in digging for industrial purposes, esp. for coal (*chalk pit*; *gravel pit*). **c** a covered hole as a trap for esp. wild animals. **2 a** an indentation left after smallpox, acne, etc. **b** a hollow in a plant or animal body or on any surface. **3 a** = ORCHESTRA 2a. **b** *Brit. Theatr.* (usu. *hist.*) seating at the back of the stalls, or the people seated there. **4 a** (**the pit** or **bottomless pit**) hell. **b** (**the pits**) *slang* a wretched or the worst imaginable place, situation, person, etc. **5 a** an area at the side of a track where racing cars are serviced and refuelled. **b** a sunken area in a workshop floor for access to a car's underside. **6** *N. Amer.* the part of the floor of an exchange allotted to special trading (*wheat-pit*). **7** an enclosure in which animals are made to fight (cf. COCKPIT 3). **8** *Brit. slang* a bed. ● *v.* (**pitted**, **pitting**) **1** *tr.* (usu. foll. by *against*) **a** set (one's wits, strength, etc.) in opposition or rivalry. **b** set (a cock, dog, etc.) to fight, originally in a pit, against another. **2** *tr.* (usu. as **pitted** *adj.*) make pits, esp. scars, in. **3** *intr.* (of the flesh etc.) retain the impression of a finger etc. when touched. **4** *tr.* put (esp. vegetables for storage) into a pit. □ **dig a pit for** try to ensnare. [Old English *pytt*, ultimately from Latin *puteus* 'well']

pit[2] /pɪt/ *n.* & *v.* esp. *US* ● *n.* the stone of a fruit. ● *v.tr.* (**pitted**, **pitting**) remove pits from (fruit). [perhaps Dutch, related to PITH]

pita var. of PITTA[1].

pit-a-pat /'pɪtəpat/ *adv.* & *n.* (also **pitter-patter** /'pɪtəpatə/) ● *adv.* **1** with a sound like quick light steps. **2** with a faltering sound (*heart went pit-a-pat*). ● *n.* such a sound. [imitative]

pit bull *n.* (in full **pit bull terrier**) a dog of an American variety of bull terrier, noted for its ferocity.

pitch[1] /pɪtʃ/ *v.* & *n.* ● *v.* **1** *tr.* (also *absol.*) erect and fix (a tent, camp, etc.). **2** *tr.* **a** throw; fling. **b** (in games) throw (a flat object) towards a mark. **3** *tr.* fix or plant (a thing) in a definite position. **4** *tr.* express in a particular style or at a particular level (*pitched his argument at the most basic level*). **5** *intr.* (often foll. by *against*, *into*, etc.) fall heavily, esp. headlong. **6** *intr.* (of a moving ship etc.) rock or oscillate so that the front moves up and down (cf. ROLL v. 8a). **7** *tr. Mus.* set at a particular pitch. **8** *intr.* (of a roof etc.) slope downwards. **9** *intr.* (often foll. by *about*) move with a vigorous jogging motion, as in a train, carriage, etc. **10** *Cricket* **a** *tr.* cause (a bowled ball) to strike the ground at a specified point etc. **b** *intr.* (of a bowled ball) strike the ground. **11** *tr. colloq.* tell (a yarn or a tale). **12** *tr. Golf* play (a ball) with a pitch shot. **13** *tr.* pave (a road) with stones. ● *n.* **1 a** *Brit.* the area of play in a field game. **b** *Cricket* the area between the creases. **2** height, degree, intensity, etc. (*the pitch of despair*; *nerves were strung to a pitch*). **3 a** the steepness of a slope, esp. of a roof, stratum, etc. **b** the degree of such a pitch. **4** *Mus.* **a** that quality of a sound which is governed by the rate of vibrations producing it; the degree of highness or lowness of a tone. **b** a standard scale of this used in performance etc. (cf. CONCERT PITCH 1). **5** the pitching motion of a ship etc. **6** *Cricket* the act or mode of delivery in bowling, or the spot where the ball bounces. **7** *colloq.* a salesman's advertising or selling approach. **8** *Brit.* a place where a street vendor sells wares, has a stall, etc. **9** (also **pitch shot**) *Golf* a high approach shot with a short run. **10** *Mech.* the distance between successive corresponding points or lines, e.g. between the teeth of a cogwheel etc. **11** the height to which a falcon etc. soars before swooping on its prey. **12** the delivery of a baseball by a pitcher. □ **pitch in** *colloq.* set to work vigorously. **pitch into** *colloq.* **1** attack forcibly with blows, words, etc. **2** assail (food, work, etc.) vigorously. **pitch on** (or **upon**) *Brit.* happen to select. **pitch up** *Cricket* bowl (a ball) to bounce near the batsman. **pitch wickets** *Cricket* fix the stumps in the ground and place the bails. [earlier = thrust a stake etc. into the ground: Middle English *pic(c)he*, perhaps related to Old English *picung* 'stigmata']

pitch[2] /pɪtʃ/ *n.* & *v.* ● *n.* **1** a sticky resinous black or dark brown substance obtained by distilling tar or turpentine, semi-liquid when hot, hard when cold, and used for caulking the seams of ships etc. **2** any of various bituminous substances including asphalt. ● *v.tr.* cover, coat, or smear with pitch. [Old English *pic* via Germanic from Latin *pix picis*]

pitch-and-toss *n.* a gambling game in which coins are pitched at a mark and then tossed.

pitch-black *adj.* (also **pitch-dark**) very or completely dark.

pitchblende /ˈpɪtʃblɛnd/ *n.* a mineral form of uranium oxide occurring in pitchlike masses and also containing radium. [German *Pechblende* (as PITCH[2], BLENDE)]

pitched battle *n.* **1** a vigorous argument etc. **2** *Mil.* a battle planned beforehand and fought on chosen ground.

pitched roof *n.* a sloping roof.

pitcher[1] /ˈpɪtʃə/ *n.* **1 a** *Brit.* a large usu. earthenware jug with a lip and a handle, for holding liquids. **b** *US* = JUG *n.* 1. **2** the modified leaf of a pitcher plant. **3** (in *pl.*) broken pottery crushed and reused. □ **pitcherful** *n.* (*pl.* **-fuls**). [Middle English from Old French *pichier*, *pechier*, from Frankish]

pitcher[2] /ˈpɪtʃə/ *n.* **1** a person or thing that pitches. **2** *Baseball* a player who delivers the ball to the batter. **3** a stone used for paving.

pitcher plant *n.* any of various plants of the families Nepenthaceae and Sarraceniaceae with leaves modified into deep pouches that can hold liquids, trap insects, etc.

pitchfork /ˈpɪtʃfɔːk/ *n.* & *v.* ● *n.* a long-handled two-pronged fork for pitching hay etc. ● *v.tr.* **1** throw with or as if with a pitchfork. **2** (usu. foll. by *into*) thrust (a person) forcibly into a position, office, etc. [in Middle English *pickfork*, probably from PICK[2] + FORK, associated with PITCH[1]]

pitch pine *n.* any of various pine trees with very resinous wood, esp. *Pinus rigida* or *P. palustris* of N. America.

pitch-pipe *n. Mus.* a small pipe blown to set the pitch for singing or tuning.

pitchstone /ˈpɪtʃstəʊn/ *n.* a dull vitreous rock resembling pitch.

pitchy /ˈpɪtʃi/ *adj.* (**pitchier**, **pitchiest**) of, like, or dark as pitch.

piteous /ˈpɪtɪəs/ *adj.* deserving or causing pity; wretched. □ **piteously** *adv.* **piteousness** *n.* [Middle English *pito(u)s* etc. via Anglo-French *pitous*, Old French *pitos* from Romanic (as PIETY)]

pitfall /ˈpɪtfɔːl/ *n.* **1** an unsuspected snare, danger, or drawback. **2** a covered pit for trapping animals etc.

pith /pɪθ/ *n.* & *v.* ● *n.* **1** spongy white tissue lining the rind of an orange, lemon, etc. **2** the essential part; the quintessence (*came to the pith of his argument*). **3** *Bot.* the spongy cellular tissue in the stems and branches of dicotyledonous plants. **4 a** physical strength; vigour. **b** force; energy. **5** *archaic* spinal marrow. ● *v.tr.* **1** remove the pith or marrow from. **2** slaughter or immobilize (an animal) by severing the spinal cord. □ **pithless** *adj.* [Old English *pitha*, from West Germanic]

pithead /ˈpɪthɛd/ *n.* **1** the top of a mine shaft. **2** the area surrounding this.

pith helmet *n.* a lightweight sun-helmet made from the dried pith of the sola etc.

pithos /ˈpɪθɒs/ *n.* (*pl.* **pithoi** /-θɔɪ/) *Archaeol.* a large storage jar. [Greek]

pithy /ˈpɪθi/ *adj.* (**pithier**, **pithiest**) **1** (of style, speech, etc.) condensed, terse, and forcible. **2** of, like, or containing much pith. □ **pithily** *adv.* **pithiness** *n.*

pitiable /ˈpɪtɪəb(ə)l/ *adj.* **1** deserving or causing pity. **2** contemptible. □ **pitiableness** *n.* **pitiably** *adv.* [Middle English from Old French *piteable*, *pitoiable* (as PITY)]

pitiful /ˈpɪtɪfʊl, -f(ə)l/ *adj.* **1** causing pity. **2** contemptible. **3** *archaic* compassionate. □ **pitifully** *adv.* **pitifulness** *n.*

pitiless /ˈpɪtɪlɪs/ *adj.* showing no pity (*the pitiless heat of the desert*). □ **pitilessly** *adv.* **pitilessness** *n.*

pitman /ˈpɪtmən/ *n.* **1** (*pl.* **-men**) a collier. **2** *US* (*pl.* **-mans**) a connecting rod in machinery.

pit of the stomach *n.* **1** the floor of the stomach. **2** the depression below the bottom of the breastbone.

piton /ˈpiːtɒn/ *n.* a peg or spike driven into a rock or crack to support a climber or a rope. [French, = eye bolt]

Pitot tube /ˈpiːtəʊ/ *n.* a device consisting of an open-ended right-angled tube used to measure the speed or flow of a fluid. [named after H. *Pitot*, French physicist d. 1771]

pitpan /ˈpɪtpan/ *n.* a Central American boat made from a tree trunk. [Miskito]

pit pony *n. Brit. hist.* a pony kept underground for haulage in coal mines.

pit prop *n.* a balk of wood used to support the roof of a coal mine.

pit-saw *n.* a large saw for use in a saw-pit.

pit stop *n. Motor Racing* a stop at a pit for servicing and refuelling.

pitta[1] /ˈpɪtə/ *n.* (also **pita**) a flat hollow unleavened bread which can be split and filled with salad etc. [modern Greek, = a cake]

pitta[2] /ˈpɪtə/ *n.* a brightly coloured passerine bird with a strong bill and short tail, of the Old World genus *Pitta* and family Pittidae. [Telegu *pitta* '(young) bird']

pittance /ˈpɪt(ə)ns/ *n.* **1** a scanty or meagre allowance, remuneration, etc. (*paid him a mere pittance*). **2** a small number or amount. **3** *hist.* a pious bequest to a religious house for extra food etc. [Middle English via Old French *pitance* and medieval Latin *pi(e)tantia* from Latin *pietas* PITY]

pitter-patter var. of PIT-A-PAT.

pittosporum /pɪˈtɒsp(ə)rəm/ *n.* any evergreen shrub of the genus *Pittosporum*, chiefly native to Australasia, with small often fragrant flowers. [Greek *pitta* PITCH[2] + *sporos* 'seed']

pituitary /prˈtjuːɪt(ə)ri/ *n.* & *adj.* ● *n.* (*pl.* **-ies**) (also **pituitary gland** or **pituitary body**) a small ductless gland at the base of the brain secreting various hormones essential for growth and other bodily functions. ● *adj.* of or relating to this gland. [Latin *pituitarius* 'secreting phlegm' from *pituita* 'phlegm']

pit viper *n.* a viper of the subfamily Crotalinae of America and Asia, having sensory pits on the head which can detect prey by heat, e.g. the rattlesnake.

pity /ˈpɪti/ *n. & v.* ● *n.* (*pl.* **-ies**) **1** sorrow and compassion aroused by another's condition (*felt pity for the child*). **2** something to be regretted; grounds for regret (*what a pity!*; *the pity of it is that he didn't mean it*). ● *v.tr.* (**-ies, -ied**) feel (often contemptuous) pity for (*they are to be pitied*; *I pity you if you think that*). □ **for pity's sake** an exclamation of urgent supplication, anger, etc. **more's the pity** so much the worse. **take pity on** feel or act compassionately towards. □ **pitying** *adj.* **pityingly** *adv.* [Middle English via Old French *pité* from Latin *pietas* (as PIETY)]

pityriasis /pɪtɪˈrʌɪəsɪs/ *n. Med.* any of a group of skin diseases characterized by the shedding of fine flaky scales. [modern Latin from Greek *pituriasis*, from *pituron* 'bran']

più /pju:/ *adv. Mus.* more (*più piano*). [Italian]

pivot /ˈpɪvət/ *n. & v.* ● *n.* **1** a short shaft or pin on which something turns or oscillates. **2** a crucial or essential person, point, etc., in a scheme or enterprise. **3** *Mil.* the man or men about whom a body of troops wheels. ● *v.* (**pivoted, pivoting**) **1** *intr.* turn on or as if on a pivot. **2** *intr.* (foll. by *on, upon*) hinge on; depend on. **3** *tr.* provide with or attach by a pivot. □ **pivotable** *adj.* **pivotability** /-ˈbɪlɪti/ *n.* **pivotal** *adj.* [French, of uncertain origin]

pix[1] /pɪks/ *n.pl. colloq.* pictures, esp. photographs. [abbreviation: cf. PIC]

pix[2] var. of PYX.

pixel /ˈpɪks(ə)l, -sɛl/ *n. Electronics* any of the minute areas of uniform illumination of which an image on a display screen is composed. [abbreviation of *picture element*: cf. PIX[1]]

pixelate /ˈpɪksəleɪt/ *v.tr. Electronics* display as or divide into pixels. □ **pixelation** /-ˈleɪʃ(ə)n/ *n.*

pixie /ˈpɪksi/ *n.* (also **pixy**) (*pl.* **-ies**) a being like a fairy; an elf. [17th c.: origin unknown]

pixie hat *n.* (also **pixie hood**) a child's hat with a pointed crown.

pixilated /ˈpɪksɪleɪtɪd/ *adj.* (also **pixillated**) **1** bewildered; crazy. **2** drunk. [variant of *pixie-led* (as PIXIE, LED)]

pizazz /pɪˈzaz/ *n.* (also **pizzazz, pzazz,** etc.) *slang* verve, energy, liveliness, sparkle.

pizza /ˈpi:tsə/ *n.* a flat round base of dough baked with a topping of tomatoes, cheese, onions, etc. [Italian, = pie]

pizzeria /pi:tsəˈri:ə/ *n.* a place where pizzas are made or sold; a pizza restaurant. [Italian (as PIZZA)]

pizzicato /pɪtsɪˈkɑ:təʊ/ *adv., adj., & n. Mus.* ● *adv.* plucking the strings of a violin etc. with the finger. ● *adj.* (of a note, passage, etc.) performed pizzicato. ● *n.* (*pl.* **pizzicatos** or **pizzicati** /-ti/) a note, passage, etc. played pizzicato. [Italian, past part. of *pizzicare* 'twitch', via *pizzare* from *pizza* 'edge']

pizzle /ˈpɪz(ə)l/ *n.* esp. *Austral.* the penis of an animal, esp. a bull, formerly used as a whip. [Low German *pesel*, diminutive of Middle Low German *pēse*, Middle Dutch *pēze*]

pk. *abbr.* **1** park. **2** peak. **3** peck(s).

pl. *abbr.* **1** place. **2** plate. **3** esp. *Mil.* platoon. **4** plural.

PLA *abbr.* (in the UK) Port of London Authority.

placable /ˈplakəb(ə)l/ *adj.* easily placated; mild; forgiving. □ **placability** /-ˈbɪlɪti/ *n.* **placably** *adv.* [Middle English from Old French *placable* or Latin *placabilis*, from *placare* 'appease']

placard /ˈplakɑ:d/ *n. & v.* ● *n.* a printed or handwritten poster esp. for advertising. ● *v.tr.* /also plaˈkɑ:d/ **1** set up placards on (a wall etc.). **2** advertise by placards. **3** display (a poster etc.) as a placard. [Middle English via Old French *placquart*, from *plaquier* 'to plaster', from Middle Dutch *placken*]

placate /pləˈkeɪt, ˈplakeɪt, ˈpleɪ-/ *v.tr.* pacify; conciliate. □ **placatingly** *adv.* **placation** /pləˈkeɪʃ(ə)n/ *n.* **placatory** /pləˈkeɪt(ə)ri/ *adj.* [Latin *placare placat-*]

place /pleɪs/ *n. & v.* ● *n.* **1 a** a particular portion of space. **b** a portion of space occupied by a person or thing (*it has changed its place*). **c** a proper or natural position (*he is out of his place*; *take your places*). **2** a city, town, village, etc. (*was born in this place*). **3** a residence; a dwelling (*has a place in the country*; *come round to my place*). **4 a** a group of houses in a town etc., esp. a square. **b** a country house with its surroundings. **5** a person's rank or status (*know their place*; *a place in history*). **6** a space, esp. a seat, for a person (*two places in the coach*). **7** a building or area for a specific purpose (*place of worship*; *bathing place*). **8 a** a point reached in a book etc. (*lost my place*). **b** a passage in a book. **9** a particular spot on a surface, esp. of the skin (*a sore place on his wrist*). **10 a** employment or office, esp. government employment (*lost his place at the Ministry*). **b** the duties or entitlements of office etc. (*is his place to hire staff*). **11** a position as a member of a team, a student in a college, etc. **12 a** *Brit.* any of the first three or sometimes four positions in a race, esp. other than the winner (*backed it for a place*). **b** *US* the second position, esp. in a horse race. **13** the position of a figure in a series indicated in decimal or similar notation (*calculated to 50 decimal places*). ● *v.tr.* **1** put (a thing etc.) in a particular place or state; arrange. **2** identify, classify, or remember correctly (*cannot place him*). **3** assign to a particular place; locate. **4 a** appoint (a person, esp. a member of the clergy) to a post. **b** find a situation, living, etc. for. **c** (usu. foll. by *with*) consign to a person's care etc. (*placed her with her aunt*). **5** assign rank, importance, or worth to (*place him among the best teachers*). **6 a** dispose of (goods) to a customer. **b** make (an order for goods etc.). **7** (often foll. by *in, on,* etc.) have (confidence etc.). **8** invest (money). **9** *Brit.* state the position of (any of the first three or sometimes four runners) in a race. **10** *tr.* (as **placed** *adj.*) **a** esp. *Brit.* among the first three or sometimes four in a race. **b** *US* second in a race. **11** *Football* get (a goal) by a place-kick. □ **all over the place** in disorder; chaotic. **give place to 1** make room for. **2** yield precedence to. **3** be succeeded by. **go places** *colloq.* be successful. **in place 1** in the right position; suitable. **2** *US* not moving; on the spot (*running in place*). **in place of** in exchange for; instead of. **in places** at some places or in some parts, but not others. **keep a person in his** or **her place** suppress a person's aspirations or pretensions. **out of place 1** in the wrong position. **2** unsuitable. **put oneself in another's place** imagine oneself in another's position. **put a person in his** or **her place** deflate or humiliate a person. **take place** occur. **take one's place** go to one's correct position, be seated, etc. **take the place of** be substituted for; replace. □ **placeless** *adj.* **placement** *n.* [Middle English from Old French via Latin *platea* from Greek *plateia* (*hodos*) 'broad (way)']

place-bet *n.* **1** *Brit.* a bet on a horse to come first, second, third, or sometimes fourth in a race. **2** *US* a bet on a horse to come second.

placebo /pləˈsi:bəʊ/ *n.* (*pl.* **-os**) **1 a** a pill, medicine, etc. prescribed for psychological reasons but having no physiological effect. **b** a blank sample used as a control in testing new drugs etc. **2** something that is said or done to calm or humour a person but does not address the cause of his or her anxiety. **3** *RC Ch.* the opening antiphon of the vespers for the dead. [Latin, = I shall be acceptable or pleasing (first word of Ps. 116:9 in the Vulgate) from *placēre* 'please']

placebo effect *n.* a beneficial (or adverse) effect produced by a placebo and not due to any property of the placebo itself.

place brick *n.* an imperfectly burnt brick from the windward side of the kiln.

place card *n.* a card marking a person's place at a table etc.

place in the sun *n.* a favourable situation, position, etc.

place-kick *n. Football* a kick made when the ball is previously placed on the ground. □ **place-kicker** *n.*

placeman /ˈpleɪsman/ *n.* (*pl.* **-men**) a person appointed to a position chiefly to implement the political policies of a higher authority.

place mat *n.* a small mat on a table underneath a person's plate.

place name *n.* the name of a town, village, hill, field, lake, etc.

placenta /pləˈsɛntə/ *n.* (*pl.* **placentae** /-tiː/ or **placentas**) **1** a flattened circular organ in the uterus of pregnant eutherian mammals, nourishing and maintaining the foetus through the umbilical cord and expelled after birth. **2** (in flowers) part of the ovary wall carrying the ovules. □ **placental** *adj.* [Latin from Greek *plakous -ountos* 'flat cake', from the root of *plax plakos* 'flat plate']

placer /ˈpleɪsə/ *n.* a deposit of sand, gravel, etc., in the bed of a stream etc., containing valuable minerals in particles. [Latin American Spanish, related to *placel* 'sandbank' from *plaza* PLACE]

place setting *n.* a set of plates, cutlery, etc. for one person at a meal.

placet /ˈpleɪsɛt/ *n. Brit.* an affirmative vote in a Church or university assembly. [Latin, = it pleases]

placid /ˈplasɪd/ *adj.* **1** (of a person) not easily aroused or disturbed; peaceful. **2** mild; calm; serene. □ **placidity** /pləˈsɪdɪti/ *n.* **placidly** *adv.* **placidness** *n.* [French *placide* or Latin *placidus* from *placēre* 'please']

placing /ˈpleɪsɪŋ/ *n.* **1** the fact or condition of being placed, esp. of being ranked in a race or of being found a situation. **2** an instance of being placed.

placket /ˈplakɪt/ *n.* **1** an opening or slit in a garment, for fastenings or access to a pocket. **2** the flap of fabric under this. [variant of PLACARD in an obsolete sense 'garment worn under an open coat or gown']

placoid /ˈplakɔɪd/ *adj.* & *n.* ● *adj.* **1** (of a fish scale) toothlike, with a flat base and a spiny backward projection, as in sharks and rays (cf. CTENOID). **2** (of a fish) covered with these scales. ● *n.* a placoid fish. [Greek *plax plakos* 'flat plate']

plafond /plaˈfɔ̃(d), French plafɔ̃/ *n.* **1 a** an ornately decorated ceiling. **b** a painting or decoration on a ceiling. **2** an early form of contract bridge. [French, from *plat* 'flat' + *fond* 'bottom']

plagal /ˈpleɪg(ə)l/ *adj. Mus.* (of a Church mode) containing notes between the dominant and its octave (cf. AUTHENTIC *adj.* 2). [medieval Latin *plagalis*, from *plaga* 'plagal mode', via Latin *plagius* from medieval Greek *plagios* (in classical Greek = oblique) from Greek *plagos* 'side']

plagal cadence *n.* (also **plagal close**) *Mus.* a cadence in which the chord of the subdominant immediately precedes that of the tonic.

plage /plɑːʒ/ *n.* **1** *Astron.* an unusually bright region on the sun. **2** a sea beach, esp. at a fashionable resort. [French, = beach]

plagiarism /ˈpleɪdʒərɪz(ə)m/ *n.* **1** the act or an instance of plagiarizing. **2** something plagiarized. □ **plagiarist** *n.* **plagiaristic** /-ˈrɪstɪk/ *adj.*

plagiarize /ˈpleɪdʒərʌɪz/ *v.tr.* (also **-ise**) (also *absol.*) **1** take and use (the thoughts, writings, inventions, etc. of another person) as one's own. **2** pass off the thoughts etc. of (another person) as one's own. □ **plagiarizer** *n.* [Latin *plagiarius* 'kidnapper' from *plagium* 'a kidnapping', from Greek *plagion*]

plagio- /ˈpleɪdʒɪəʊ, ˈplagɪəʊ/ *comb. form* oblique. [Greek *plagios* 'oblique' from *plagos* 'side']

plagioclase /ˈpleɪdʒɪəkleɪz/ *n.* a series of feldspar minerals forming glassy crystals. [PLAGIO- + Greek *klasis* 'cleavage']

plague /pleɪg/ *n.* & *v.* ● *n.* **1 a** (prec. by *the*) a contagious bacterial disease characterized by fever and delirium, with the formation of buboes (**bubonic plague**) and sometimes infection of the lungs (**pneumonic plague**). **b** any severe or fatal contagious disease spreading rapidly over a wide area. **2** (foll. by *of*) an unusual infestation of a pest etc. (*a plague of frogs*). **3 a** great trouble. **b** an affliction, esp. as regarded as divine punishment. **4** *colloq.* a nuisance. **5** (in *int.*) *joc.* or *archaic* a curse etc. (*a plague on it!*). ● *v.tr.* (**plagues**, **plagued**, **plaguing**) **1** afflict, torment (*plagued by war*). **2** *colloq.* pester or harass continually. □ **plaguesome** *adj.* [Middle English from Latin *plaga* 'stroke, wound', probably from Greek *plaga*, *plēgē*]

plaice /pleɪs/ *n.* (*pl.* same) **1** a European flatfish, *Pleuronectes platessa*, having a brown back with orange spots and a white underside, much used for food. **2** (in full **American plaice**) a N. Atlantic fish, *Hippoglossoides platessoides*. [Middle English via Old French *plaïz* from Late Latin *platessa*, apparently from Greek *platus* 'broad']

plaid /plad/ *n.* **1** (often *attrib.*) chequered or tartan, esp. woollen, twilled cloth (*a plaid skirt*). **2** a long piece of plaid worn over the shoulder as part of Scottish Highland dress. □ **plaided** *adj.* [Gaelic *plaide*, of unknown origin]

plain[1] /pleɪn/ *adj.*, *adv.*, & *n.* ● *adj.* **1** clear; evident (*is plain to see*). **2** readily understood; simple (*in plain words*). **3 a** (of food, sewing, decoration, etc.) uncomplicated; not elaborate; unembellished; simple. **b** without a decorative pattern. **4** (esp. of a woman or girl) not beautiful or pretty; ugly. **5** outspoken; straightforward. **6** (of manners, dress, etc.) unsophisticated; homely (*a plain man*). **7** (of drawings etc.) not coloured (*penny plain, twopence coloured*). **8** not in code. **9** (of a knitting stitch) made by putting the needle through the front of the stitch from left to right (opp. PURL[1] *adj.*). ● *adv.* **1** clearly; unequivocally (*to speak plain, I don't approve*). **2** simply (*that is plain stupid*). ● *n.* a level tract of esp. treeless country. □ **be plain with** speak bluntly to. □ **plainly** *adv.* **plainness** /ˈpleɪnnɪs/ *n.* [Middle English via Old French *plain* (*adj.* & *n.*) from Latin *planus* (*adj.*), *planum* (*n.*)]

plain[2] /pleɪn/ *v.intr. archaic* or *poet.* **1** mourn. **2** complain. **3** make a plaintive sound. [Middle English via Old French *plaindre* (stem *plaign-*) from Latin *plangere planct-* 'lament']

plain card *n.* neither a trump nor a court card.

plainchant /ˈpleɪntʃɑːnt/ *n.* = PLAINSONG.

plain chocolate *n. Brit.* dark chocolate without added milk.

plain clothes *n.* & *adj.* ● *n.pl.* ordinary clothes worn esp. as a disguise by police officers etc. ● *attrib.adj.* (**plain-clothes**) wearing plain clothes (*plain-clothes policeman*).

plain cook *n. Brit.* a person competent in unelaborate English cooking.

plain dealing *n.* candour; straightforwardness.

plain flour *n.* flour not containing a raising agent.

plain sailing *n.* **1** sailing a straightforward course. **2** an uncomplicated situation or course of action.

plainsman /ˈpleɪnzmən/ *n.* (*pl.* **-men**) a person who lives on a plain, esp. in N. America.

plainsong /ˈpleɪnsɒŋ/ *n.* unaccompanied church music sung in unison in medieval modes and in free rhythm corresponding to the accentuation of the words (cf. GREGORIAN CHANT).

plain-spoken *adj.* outspoken; blunt.

plain suit *n. Cards* a suit that is not trumps.

plaint /pleɪnt/ *n.* **1** *Brit. Law* an accusation; a charge. **2** *literary* or *archaic* a complaint; a lamentation. [Middle English via Old French *plainte*, fem. past part. of *plaindre*, and Old French *plaint* from Latin *planctus* (as PLAIN[2])]

plain text *n.* a text not in cipher or code.

plaintiff /ˈpleɪntɪf/ *n. Law* a person who brings a case against another into court (opp. DEFENDANT). [Middle English from Old French *plaintif* (*adj.*) (as PLAINTIVE)]

plain time *n. Brit.* time not paid for at overtime rates.

plaintive /ˈpleɪntɪv/ *adj.* **1** expressing sorrow; mournful. **2** mournful-sounding. □ **plaintively** *adv.* **plaintiveness** *n.* [Middle English from Old French (*plaintif*, *-ive*), from *plainte* (as PLAINT)]

plain weaving *n.* weaving with the weft alternately over and under the warp.

plait /plat/ *n.* & *v.* ● *n.* **1** a length of hair, straw, etc., in three or more interlaced strands. **2** = PLEAT *n.* ● *v.tr.* **1** form (hair etc.) into a plait. **2** make (a belt, mat, etc.) by plaiting. [Middle English from Old French *pleit* 'a fold', ultimately from Latin *plicare* 'to fold']

plan /plan/ *n.* & *v.* ● *n.* **1 a** a formulated and esp. detailed method by which a thing is to be done; a design or scheme. **b** an intention or proposed proceeding (*my plan was to distract them*; *plan of campaign*). **2** a drawing or diagram made by projection on a horizontal plane, esp. showing a building or one floor of a building (cf. ELEVATION 2a). **3** a fairly large-scale map of a town or district. **4 a** a table etc. indicating times, places, etc. of intended proceedings. **b** a diagram of an arrangement (*prepared the seating plan*). **5** an imaginary plane perpendicular to the line of vision and containing the objects shown in a picture. ● *v.* (**planned**, **planning**) **1** *tr.* (often foll. by *that* + clause or *to* + infin.) arrange (a procedure etc.) beforehand; form a plan (*planned to catch the evening ferry*). **2** *tr.* **a** design (a building, new town, etc.). **b** make a plan of (an existing building, an area, etc.). **3** *tr.* (as **planned** *adj.*) in accordance with a plan (*his planned arrival*; *planned parenthood*). **4** *intr.* make plans. □ **plan on** *colloq.* aim at doing or having; intend. □ **planning** *n.* [French from earlier *plant*, from Italian *pianta* 'plan of building': cf. PLANT]

planar /ˈpleɪnə/ *adj. Math.* of, relating to, or in the form of a plane.

planarian /pləˈnɛːrɪən/ *n.* any flatworm of the division Tricladida, usu. living in fresh water. [modern Latin genus name *Planaria*, fem. of Latin *planarius* 'lying flat']

planchet /ˈplan(t)ʃɪt/ *n.* a plain metal disc from which a coin is made. [diminutive of *planch* 'slab of metal' from Old French *planche*: see PLANK]

planchette /plɑːnˈʃɛt/ *n.* a small usu. heart-shaped board on castors with a pencil that is supposedly caused to write spirit messages when a person's fingers rest lightly on it. [French, diminutive of *planche* PLANK]

Planck's constant /plaŋks/ *n.* (also **Planck constant**) a fundamental constant, equal to the energy of quanta of electromagnetic radiation divided by its frequency, with a value of 6.626×10^{-34} joules. [named after M. *Planck*, German physicist d. 1947]

plane[1] /pleɪn/ *n.*, *adj.*, & *v.* ● *n.* **1 a** a flat surface on which a straight line joining any two points on it would wholly lie. **b** an imaginary flat surface through or joining etc. material objects. **2** a level surface. **3** = AEROPLANE. **4** a flat surface producing lift by the action of air or water over and under it (usu. in *comb.*: *hydroplane*). **5** (often foll. by *of*) a level of attainment, thought, knowledge, etc. **6** a flat thin object such as a table top. ● *adj.* **1** (of a surface etc.) perfectly level. **2** (of an angle, figure, etc.) lying in a plane. ● *v.intr.* **1** (often foll. by *down*) travel or glide in an aeroplane. **2** (of a speedboat etc.) skim over water. **3** soar. [Latin *planum* 'flat surface', neut. of *planus* PLAIN[1] (differentiated from PLAIN[1] in 17th c.): the adj. suggested by French *plan*, *plane*]

plane[2] /pleɪn/ *n.* & *v.* ● *n.* **1** a tool consisting of a wooden or metal block with a projecting steel blade, used to smooth a wooden surface by paring shavings from it. **2** a similar tool for smoothing metal. ● *v.tr.* **1** smooth (wood, metal, etc.) with a plane. **2** (often foll. by *away*, *down*) pare (irregularities) with a plane. **3** *archaic* level (*plane the way*). [Middle English from Old French variant of *plaine* via Late Latin *plana* from Latin *planus* PLAIN[1]]

plane[3] /pleɪn/ *n.* (in full **plane tree**) any tree of the genus *Platanus* often growing to great heights, with maple-like leaves and bark which peels in uneven patches (see also LONDON PLANE). [Middle English from Old French via Latin *platanus* from Greek *platanos*, from *platus* 'broad']

plane chart *n.* a chart on which meridians and parallels of latitude are represented by equidistant straight lines, used in plane sailing.

plane polarization *n.* (also **-isation**) a process restricting the vibrations of electromagnetic radiation, esp. light, to one direction.

planer /ˈpleɪnə/ *n.* = PLANE[2] *n.* 1.

plane sailing *n.* **1** the practice of determining a ship's position on the theory that it is moving on a plane. **2** = PLAIN SAILING.

planet /ˈplanɪt/ *n.* **1 a** a celestial body moving in an elliptical orbit round a star. **b** (prec. by *the*) the earth. **2** esp. *Astrol.* & *hist.* a celestial body distinguished from the fixed stars by having an apparent motion of its own (including the moon and sun), esp. with reference to its supposed influence on people and events. □ **planetology** /-ˈtɒlədʒi/ *n.* [Middle English via Old French *planete* and Late Latin *planeta*, *planetes* from Greek *planētēs* 'wanderer, planet', from *planaomai* 'wander']

plane-table *n.* a surveying instrument used for direct plotting in the field, with a circular drawing board and pivoted alidade.

planetarium /planɪˈtɛːrɪəm/ *n.* (*pl.* **planetariums** or **planetaria** /-rɪə/) **1** a domed building in which images of stars, planets, constellations, etc. are projected for public entertainment or education. **2** the device used for such projection. **3** = ORRERY. [modern Latin (as PLANET)]

planetary /ˈplanɪt(ə)ri/ *adj.* **1** of or like planets (*planetary influence*). **2** terrestrial; mundane. **3** wandering; erratic. [Late Latin *planetarius* (as PLANET)]

planetary nebula *n.* a ring-shaped nebula formed by an expanding shell of gas round a star.

planetesimal /planɪˈtɛsɪm(ə)l/ *n.* any of a vast number of minute planets or planetary bodies. [PLANET, on the pattern of *infinitesimal*]

planetesimal hypothesis *n.* the theory that planets were formed by the accretion of planetesimals in a cold state.

planetoid /ˈplanɪtɔɪd/ *n.* = ASTEROID.

plangent /ˈplan(d)ʒ(ə)nt/ *adj.* **1** (of a sound) loud and reverberating. **2** (of a sound) plaintive; sad. □ **plangency** *n.* **plangently** *adv.* [Latin *plangere plangent-* 'lament']

planimeter /pləˈnɪmɪtə/ *n.* an instrument for mechanically measuring the area of a plane figure. □ **planimetric** /-ˈmɛtrɪk/ *adj.* **planimetrical** /-ˈmɛtrɪk(ə)l/ *adj.* **planimetry** *n.* [French *planimètre* from Latin *planus* 'level']

planish /ˈplanɪʃ/ *v.tr.* flatten (sheet metal, coining-metal, etc.) with a smooth-faced hammer or between rollers. □ **planisher** *n.* [Middle English from Old French *planir* 'to smooth', from *plain* PLANE[1] *adj.*]

planisphere /ˈplanɪsfɪə/ *n.* a map formed by the projection of a sphere or part of a sphere on a plane, esp. an adjustable circular star map that shows the appearance of the heavens at a specific time and place. □ **planispheric** /-ˈsfɛrɪk/ *adj.* [Middle English from medieval Latin *planisphaerium* (as PLANE[1], SPHERE): influenced by French *planisphère*]

plank /plaŋk/ *n.* & *v.* ● *n.* **1** a long flat piece of timber used esp. in building, flooring, etc. **2** an item of a political or other programme (cf. PLATFORM 6). ● *v.tr.* **1** provide, cover, or floor, with planks. **2** (usu. foll. by *down*; also *absol.*) esp. *US colloq.* **a** put (a thing, person, etc.) down roughly or violently. **b** pay (money) on the spot or abruptly (*planked down $5*). □ **walk the plank** *hist.* (of a pirate's captive etc.) be made to walk blindfold along a plank over the side of a ship to one's death in the sea. [Middle English via Old Northern

French *planke*, Old French *planche* from Late Latin *planca* 'board', from *plancus* 'flat-footed']

plank bed *n.* a bed of boards without a mattress, esp. in prison.

planking /'plaŋkɪŋ/ *n.* planks as flooring etc.

plankton /'plaŋ(k)t(ə)n, -tɒn/ *n.* the small and microscopic organisms drifting or floating in the sea or fresh water (cf. NEKTON). □ **planktonic** /-'tɒnɪk/ *adj.* [German from Greek *plagktos* 'wandering', from *plazomai* 'wander']

planned economy *n.* an economy in which production, prices, incomes, etc. are determined centrally by government.

planner /'planə/ *n.* **1** a person who controls or plans the development of new towns, designs buildings, etc. **2** a person who makes plans. **3** a list, table, etc., with information helpful in planning.

planning permission *n. Brit.* formal permission for building development etc., esp. from a local authority.

plano- /'pleɪnəʊ/ *comb. form* level, flat. [Latin *planus* 'flat']

planoconcave /pleɪnəʊ'kɒnkeɪv/ *adj.* (of a lens etc.) with one surface plane and the other concave.

planoconvex /pleɪnəʊ'kɒnvɛks/ *adj.* (of a lens etc.) with one surface plane and the other convex.

planographic /pleɪnə'grafɪk/ *adj.* relating to or produced by a process in which printing is done from a plane surface. □ **planography** /plə'nɒgrəfi/ *n.*

planometer /plə'nɒmɪtə/ *n.* a flat plate used as a gauge for plane surfaces in metalwork.

plant /plɑːnt/ *n.* & *v.* ● *n.* **1 a** any living organism of the kingdom Plantae, usu. containing chlorophyll enabling it to live wholly on inorganic substances and lacking specialized sense organs and the power of voluntary movement. **b** a small organism of this kind, as distinguished from a shrub or tree. **2 a** machinery, fixtures, etc., used in industrial processes. **b** a factory. **3** *colloq.* **a** something, esp. incriminating or compromising, positioned or concealed so as to be discovered later. **b** a person stationed as a spy or source of information. ● *v.tr.* **1** place (a seed, bulb, or growing thing) in the ground so that it may take root and flourish. **2** (often foll. by *in*, *on*, etc.) **a** put or fix in position. **b** *refl.* take up a position (*planted myself by the door*). **c** place (a bomb) in a building etc. **3** deposit (young fish, spawn, oysters, etc.) in a river or lake. **4** station (a person etc.), esp. as a spy or source of information. **5** cause (an idea etc.) to be established, esp. in another person's mind. **6** deliver (a blow, kiss, etc.) with a deliberate aim. **7** *colloq.* position or conceal (something incriminating or compromising) for later discovery. **8 a** settle or people (a colony etc.). **b** found or establish (a city, community, etc.). **9** bury. □ **plant out** transfer (a plant) from a pot or frame to the open ground; set out (seedlings) at intervals. □ **plantable** *adj.* **plantlet** *n.* **plantlike** *adj.* [Old English *plante* from Latin *planta* 'sprout, slip, cutting', later influenced by French *plante*]

Plantagenet /plan'tadʒɪnɪt/ *adj.* & *n.* ● *adj.* of or relating to the kings of England from Henry II to Richard III. ● *n.* any of these kings. [= sprig of broom (Latin *planta genista*) worn as a distinctive mark, the origin of their surname]

plantain[1] /'plantɪn, -teɪn/ *n.* any low-growing plant of the genus *Plantago*, with usu. broad flat leaves forming a rosette on the ground, and seeds used as food for birds and as a mild laxative. [Middle English via Old French from Latin *plantago -ginis*, from *planta* 'sole of the foot' (from its broad prostrate leaves)]

plantain[2] /'plantɪn, -teɪn/ *n.* **1** a plant, *Musa paradisiaca*, related to the banana and widely grown in warm countries for its fruit. **2** the starchy fruit of this, containing less sugar than a dessert banana and chiefly used in cooking. [earlier *platan* from Spanish *plá(n)tano* 'plane tree', probably assimilated from Galibi *palatana* etc.]

plantain lily *n.* = HOSTA.

plantar /'plantə/ *adj.* of or relating to the sole of the foot. [Latin *plantaris* from *planta* 'sole']

plantation /plan'teɪʃ(ə)n, plɑːn-/ *n.* **1** an estate on which cotton, tobacco, etc. is cultivated, esp. in former colonies, formerly by slave labour. **2** an area planted with trees etc. **3** *hist.* a colony; colonization. [Middle English from Old French *plantation* or Latin *plantatio* (as PLANT)]

plantation song *n.* a song of the kind formerly sung by blacks on American plantations.

planter /'plɑːntə/ *n.* **1** a person who cultivates the soil. **2** the manager or occupier of a coffee, cotton, tobacco, etc. plantation. **3** a large container for decorative plants. **4** a machine for planting seeds etc. (*potato-planter*).

plantigrade /'plantɪgreɪd/ *adj.* & *n.* ● *adj.* (of an animal) walking on the soles of its feet. ● *n.* a plantigrade animal, e.g. humans or bears (cf. DIGITIGRADE). [French from modern Latin *plantigradus*, from Latin *planta* 'sole' + *-gradus* '-walking']

plant-louse *n.* a small insect that infests plants, esp. an aphis.

plantsman /'plɑːntsmən/ *n.* (*pl.* **-men**; *fem.* **plantswoman**, *pl.* **-women**) an expert in garden plants and gardening.

plaque /plak, plɑːk/ *n.* **1** an ornamental tablet of metal, porcelain, etc., esp. affixed to a building in commemoration. **2** a deposit on teeth where bacteria proliferate. **3** *Med.* **a** a patch or eruption of skin etc. as a result of damage. **b** a fibrous lesion in atherosclerosis. **4** a small badge of rank in an honorary order. □ **plaquette** /pla'kɛt/ *n.* [French from Dutch *plak* 'tablet', from *plakken* 'to stick']

plash[1] /plaʃ/ *n.* & *v.* ● *n.* **1** a splash; a plunge. **2 a** a marshy pool. **b** a puddle. ● *v.* **1** *tr.* & *intr.* splash. **2** *tr.* strike the surface of (water). □ **plashy** *adj.* [Old English *plæsc*, probably imitative]

plash[2] /plaʃ/ *v.tr.* esp. *Brit.* **1** bend down and interweave (branches, twigs, etc.) to form a hedge. **2** make or renew (a hedge) in this way. [Middle English from Old French *pla(i)ssier*, ultimately from Latin *plectere* 'plait': cf. PLEACH]

plasma /'plazmə/ *n.* (also **plasm** /'plaz(ə)m/) **1 a** the colourless fluid part of blood, lymph, or milk, in which corpuscles or fat-globules are suspended. **b** this taken from donated blood for administering in transfusions. **2** = PROTOPLASM. **3** a gas of positive ions and free electrons with an approximately equal positive and negative charge. **4** a green variety of quartz used in mosaic and for other decorative purposes. □ **plasmatic** /-'matɪk/ *adj.* **plasmic** *adj.* [Late Latin, = mould, from Greek *plasma -atos* from *plassō* 'to shape']

plasmid /'plazmɪd/ *n. Biol.* a genetic structure in a cell that can replicate independently of the chromosomes, esp. a circular DNA strand in a bacterium or protozoan. [PLASMA + -ID[2]]

plasmodesma /plazmə(ʊ)'dɛzmə/ *n.* (*pl.* **plasmodesmata** /-mətə/) a narrow thread of cytoplasm that passes through cell walls and affords communication between plant cells. [PLASMA + Greek *desma* 'bond, fetter']

plasmodium /plaz'məʊdɪəm/ *n.* (*pl.* **plasmodia** /-dɪə/) **1** any parasitic protozoan of the genus *Plasmodium*, including those causing malaria in man. **2** a form within the life cycle of various micro-organisms including slime moulds, usu. consisting of a mass of naked protoplasm containing many nuclei. □ **plasmodial** *adj.* [modern Latin, from PLASMA + *-odium*: see -ODE[1]]

plasmolyse /'plazməlʌɪz/ *v.intr.* & *tr.* (*US* **plasmolyze**) undergo or subject to plasmolysis.

plasmolysis /plaz'mɒlɪsɪs/ *n.* contraction of the protoplast of a plant cell as a result of loss of water from the cell. [modern Latin (as PLASMA, -LYSIS)]

plasteel /'plasti:l/ *n.* (in science fiction) an ultra-strong non-metallic material. [PLASTIC + STEEL]

plaster /'plɑ:stə/ *n.* & *v.* ● *n.* **1** a soft pliable mixture esp. of lime putty with sand or Portland cement etc. for spreading on walls, ceilings, etc., to form a smooth hard surface when dried. **2** *Brit.* = STICKING PLASTER. **3** = PLASTER OF PARIS. **4** *hist.* a curative or protective substance spread on a bandage etc. and applied to the body (*mustard plaster*). ● *v.tr.* **1** cover (a wall etc.) with plaster or a similar substance. **2** (often foll. by *with*) coat thickly or to excess; bedaub (*plastered the bread with jam*; *the wall was plastered with slogans*). **3** stick or apply (a thing) thickly like plaster (*plastered glue all over it*). **4** (often foll. by *down*) make (esp. hair) smooth with water, cream, etc.; fix flat. **5** (as **plastered** *adj.*) *slang* drunk. **6** apply a medical plaster or plaster cast to. **7** *slang* bomb or shell heavily. □ **plasterer** *n.* **plastery** *adj.* [Old English via medieval Latin *plastrum* and Latin *emplastrum* from Greek *emplastron*, later reinforced by Old French *plastre* and French *plastrer*]

plasterboard /'plɑ:stəbɔ:d/ *n.* two boards with a filling of plaster used to form or line the inner walls of houses etc.

plaster cast *n.* **1** a bandage dipped in plaster of Paris, applied to a broken limb etc., and left to set. **2** a statue or mould made of plaster.

plaster of Paris *n.* fine white plaster made of gypsum and used for making plaster casts etc.

plaster saint *n.* *iron.* a person regarded as being without moral faults or human frailty.

plasterwork /'plɑ:stəwə:k/ *n.* work done in plaster, esp. the plaster-covered surface of a wall or decorative plaster surfaces.

plastic /'plastɪk/ *n.* & *adj.* ● *n.* **1** any of a number of synthetic polymeric substances that can be given any required shape. **2** (*attrib.*) **a** made of plastic (*plastic bag*). **b** artificial, insincere. **3** *colloq.* = PLASTIC MONEY. ● *adj.* **1** capable of being moulded; pliant; supple. **2** moulding or giving form to clay, wax, etc. **3** *Biol.* exhibiting an adaptability to environmental changes. **4** (esp. in philosophy) formative, creative. □ **plastically** *adv.* **plasticity** /-'stɪsɪti/ *n.* **plasticize** /-sʌɪz/ *v.tr.* (also **-ise**). **plasticization** /-sʌɪ'zeɪʃ(ə)n/ *n.* **plasticizer** /-sʌɪzə/ *n.* **plasticky** *adj.* [French *plastique* or Latin *plasticus* from Greek *plastikos*, from *plassō* 'mould']

plastic arts *n.pl.* art forms involving modelling or moulding, e.g. sculpture and ceramics, or art involving the representation of solid objects with three-dimensional effects.

plastic bomb *n.* a bomb containing plastic explosive.

plastic bullet *n.* a bullet made of PVC or another plastic material.

plastic explosive *n.* a putty-like explosive capable of being moulded by hand.

plasticine /'plastɪsi:n/ *n. propr.* a soft plastic material used, esp. by children, for modelling. [PLASTIC + -INE[4]]

plastic money *n. colloq.* credit cards or other types of plastic card that can be used instead of money.

plastic surgery *n.* the process of reconstructing or repairing parts of the body by the transfer of tissue, either in the treatment of injury or for cosmetic reasons. □ **plastic surgeon** *n.*

plastic wood *n.* a mouldable material which hardens to resemble wood, used for filling crevices etc.

plastid /'plastɪd/ *n.* any small organelle in the cytoplasm of a plant cell, containing pigment or food. [German, from Greek *plastos* 'shaped']

plastron /'plastrən/ *n.* **1 a** a fencer's leather-covered breastplate. **b** a lancer's breast-covering of facings material. **2 a** an ornamental front on a woman's bodice. **b** a man's starched shirt-front. **3 a** the ventral part of the shell of a tortoise or turtle. **b** the corresponding part in other animals. **4** *hist.* a steel breastplate. □ **plastral** *adj.* [French from Italian *piastrone*, augmentative of *piastra* 'breastplate', from Latin *emplastrum* PLASTER]

-plasty /plasti/ *comb. form* forming nouns meaning the moulding, grafting, or formation of esp. a part of the body (*angioplasty*; *rhinoplasty*).

plat[1] /plat/ *n. US* **1** a plot of land. **2** a plan of an area of land. [Middle English: collateral form of PLOT]

plat[2] /plat/ *n.* & *v.* ● *n.* = PLAIT *n.* 1. ● *v.tr.* (**platted**, **platting**) = PLAIT *v.*

platan /'plat(ə)n/ *n.* = PLANE[3]. [Middle English from Latin *platanus*: see PLANE[3]]

plat du jour /,plɑ: du: 'ʒʊə, French pla dy ʒur/ *n.* (*pl.* ***plats du jour*** *pronunc.* same) a dish specially featured on a day's menu. [French, = dish of the day]

plate /pleɪt/ *n.* & *v.* ● *n.* **1 a** a shallow vessel, usu. circular and of earthenware or china, from which food is eaten or served. **b** the contents of this (*ate a plate of sandwiches*). **2** a similar vessel usu. of metal or wood, used esp. for making a collection in a church etc. **3** *US* a main course of a meal, served on one plate. **4** *Austral.* & *NZ* a contribution of cakes, sandwiches, etc., to a social gathering. **5** (*collect.*) **a** utensils of silver, gold, or other metal. **b** objects of plated metal. **6 a** a piece of metal with a name or inscription for affixing to a door, container, etc. **b** = NUMBER PLATE. **7** an illustration on special paper in a book. **8** a thin sheet of metal, glass, etc., coated with a sensitive film for photography. **9** a flat thin usu. rigid sheet of metal etc. with an even surface and uniform thickness, often as part of a mechanism. **10 a** a smooth piece of metal etc. for engraving. **b** an impression made from this. **11 a** a silver or gold cup as a prize for a horse race etc. **b** a race with this as a prize. **12 a** a thin piece of plastic material, moulded to the shape of the mouth and gums, to which artificial teeth or another orthodontic appliance are attached. **b** *colloq.* a complete denture or orthodontic appliance. **13** *Geol.* each of several rigid sheets of rock thought to form the earth's outer crust. **14** *Biol.* a thin flat organic structure or formation. **15** a light shoe for a racehorse. **16** a stereotype, electrotype, or plastic cast of a page of composed movable types, or a metal or plastic copy of filmset matter, from which sheets are printed. **17** *Baseball* a flat piece of whitened rubber marking the station of a batter or pitcher. **18** *US* the anode of a thermionic valve. **19** a horizontal timber laid along the top of a wall to support the ends of joists or rafters (*window plate*). ● *v.tr.* **1** apply a thin coat esp. of silver, gold, or tin to (another metal). **2** cover (esp. a ship) with plates of metal, esp. for protection. **3** make a plate of (type etc.) for printing. □ **on a plate** *colloq.* available with little trouble to the recipient. **on one's plate** esp. *Brit.* for one to deal with or consider. □ **plateful** *n.* (*pl.* **-fuls**). **plateless** *adj.* **plater** *n.* [Middle English via Old French from medieval Latin *plata* 'plate armour', from *platus* (*adj.*), ultimately from Greek *platus* 'flat']

plate armour *n.* armour of metal plates, for a man, ship, etc.

plateau /'platəʊ/ *n.* & *v.* ● *n.* (*pl.* **plateaux** /-təʊz/ or **plateaus**) **1** an area of fairly level high ground. **2** a state of little variation after an increase. ● *v.intr.* (**plateaus**, **plateaued**) (often foll. by *out*) reach a level or stable state after an increase. [French from Old French *platel*, diminutive of *plat* 'flat surface']

plate glass *n.* thick fine-quality glass for shop windows etc., originally cast in plates.

platelayer /'pleɪtleɪə/ *n. Brit.* a person employed in fixing and repairing railway rails.

platelet /'pleɪtlɪt/ *n.* a small colourless disc-shaped cell fragment without a nucleus, found in large numbers in blood and involved in clotting. Also called *thrombocyte*.

platemaker /'pleɪtmeɪkə/ *n.* a person or machine that makes printing plates.

platen /'plat(ə)n/ *n.* **1** a plate in a printing press which presses the paper against the type. **2** a cylindrical roller in a typewriter against which the paper is held. [Old French *platine* 'a flat piece' from *plat* 'flat']

plate rack *n. Brit.* a rack in which plates are stored or placed to drain.

plateresque /platəˈrɛsk/ *adj.* richly ornamented in a style suggesting silverware. [Spanish *plateresco* via *platero* 'silversmith' from *plata* 'silver']

plate tectonics *n.pl.* (usu. treated as *sing.*) a theory of the earth's surface based on the interaction of rigid lithospheric plates which move slowly on the underlying mantle.

plate tracery *n. Archit.* tracery with perforations in otherwise continuous stone.

platform /ˈplatfɔːm/ *n.* **1** a raised level surface; a natural or artificial terrace. **2** a raised surface from which a speaker addresses an audience. **3** a raised elongated structure along the side of a track in a railway station. **4** the floor area at the entrance to a bus. **5** a thick sole of a shoe. **6** the declared policy of a political party. [French *plateforme* 'ground plan', from *plate* 'flat' + *forme* FORM]

platform ticket *n. Brit.* a ticket allowing a non-traveller access to a station platform.

■ **Usage** The term *platform ticket* is becoming increasingly uncommon in the UK, as at most stations platforms are freely accessible to people not holding tickets for travel.

plating /ˈpleɪtɪŋ/ *n.* **1** a coating of gold, silver, etc. **2** racing for plates.

platinic /pləˈtɪnɪk/ *adj.* of or containing (esp. tetravalent) platinum.

platinize /ˈplatɪnʌɪz/ *v.tr.* (also **-ise**) coat with platinum. □ **platinization** /-ˈzeɪʃ(ə)n/ *n.*

platinoid /ˈplatɪnɔɪd/ *n.* an alloy of copper, zinc, nickel, and tungsten.

platinum /ˈplatɪnəm/ *n. Chem.* a ductile malleable silvery-white metallic element occurring naturally in nickel and copper ores, unaffected by simple acids and fusible only at a very high temperature, used in making jewellery and laboratory apparatus (symbol **Pt**). [earlier *platina* from Spanish, diminutive of *plata* 'silver']

platinum-black *n.* platinum in powder form like lampblack.

platinum blonde *adj. & n.* (also **platinum blond**) ● *adj.* silvery-blond. ● *n.* a person with silvery-blond hair.

platinum disc *n.* the highest of a series of awards given to a recording artist or group for sales of a record etc. exceeding a specified high figure (cf. GOLD DISC).

platinum metal *n.* any metallic element found with and resembling platinum, e.g. osmium, iridium, and palladium.

platitude /ˈplatɪtjuːd/ *n.* **1** a trite or commonplace remark, esp. one solemnly delivered. **2** the use of platitudes; dullness, insipidity. □ **platitudinize** /-ˈtjuːdɪnʌɪz/ *v.intr.* (also **-ise**). **platitudinous** /-ˈtjuːdɪnəs/ *adj.* [French from *plat* 'flat', on the pattern of *multitude, multitudinous*, etc.]

Platonic /pləˈtɒnɪk/ *adj.* **1** of or associated with the Greek philosopher Plato (d. 347 BC) or his ideas. **2** (**platonic**) (of love or friendship) purely spiritual, not sexual. **3** (**platonic**) confined to words or theory; not leading to action; harmless. □ **Platonically** *adv.* [Latin *Platonicus* from Greek *Platōnikos*, from *Platōn* 'Plato']

Platonic solid *n.* (also **Platonic body**) any of the five regular solids (tetrahedron, cube, octahedron, dodecahedron, icosahedron).

Platonism /ˈpleɪt(ə)nɪz(ə)m/ *n.* the philosophy of Plato or his followers. □ **Platonist** *n.*

platoon /pləˈtuːn/ *n.* **1** *Mil.* a subdivision of a company, a tactical unit commanded by a lieutenant and usu. divided into three sections. **2** a group of persons acting together. [French *peloton* 'small ball', diminutive of *pelote*: see PELLET, -OON]

platteland /ˈplatəland/ *n. S.Afr.* remote country districts. □ **plattelander** *n.* [Afrikaans, = flat land]

platter /ˈplatə/ *n.* **1** a large flat dish or plate, esp. for food. **2** *slang* a gramophone record. **3** the rotating metal disc of a record player turntable. **4** *Computing* a rigid disk used to store data magnetically. □ **on a platter** = *on a plate* (see PLATE). [Middle English & Anglo-French *plater* from Anglo-French *plat* PLATE]

platy- /ˈplati/ *comb. form* broad, flat. [Greek *platu-* from *platus* 'broad, flat']

platyhelminth /platɪˈhɛlmɪnθ/ *n.* = FLATWORM. [modern Latin *Platyhelminthes* (*n.pl.*), from PLATY- + Greek *helminth* 'worm']

platypus /ˈplatɪpəs/ *n.* (in full **duck-billed platypus**) (*pl.* **platypuses**) an Australian aquatic egg-laying mammal, *Ornithorhynchus anatinus*, having a soft pliable bill shaped like a duck's, webbed feet, and sleek grey fur. Also called *duckbill*. [modern Latin from Greek *platupous* 'flat-footed', from *platus* 'flat' + *pous* 'foot']

platyrrhine /ˈplatɪrʌɪn/ *adj. & n.* ● *adj.* (of primates) having nostrils far apart and directed forwards or sideways, as in New World monkeys (cf. CATARRHINE). ● *n.* such an animal. [PLATY- + Greek *rhis rhin-* 'nose']

plaudit /ˈplɔːdɪt/ *n.* (usu. in *pl.*) **1** a round of applause. **2** an emphatic expression of approval. [shortened from Latin *plaudite*, imperative pl. of *plaudere plaus-* 'applaud', said by Roman actors at the end of a play]

plausible /ˈplɔːzɪb(ə)l/ *adj.* **1** (of an argument, statement, etc.) seeming reasonable or probable. **2** (of a person) persuasive but deceptive. □ **plausibility** /-ˈbɪlɪti/ *n.* **plausibly** *adv.* [Latin *plausibilis* (as PLAUDIT)]

play /pleɪ/ *v. & n.* ● *v.* **1** *intr.* (often foll. by *with*) occupy or amuse oneself pleasantly with some recreation, game, exercise, etc. **2** *intr.* (foll. by *with*) act light-heartedly or flippantly (with feelings etc.). **3 a** *tr.* perform on or be able to perform on (a musical instrument). **b** *tr.* perform (a piece of music etc.). **c** *tr.* cause (a record, record player, etc.) to produce sounds. **d** *intr.* (of a record, record player, etc.) produce sounds. **4 a** *intr.* (foll. by *in*) perform a role in (a drama etc.). **b** *tr.* perform (a drama or role) on stage, or in a film or broadcast. **c** *tr.* give a dramatic performance at (a particular theatre or place). **5** *tr.* act in real life the part of (*play truant; play the fool*). **6** *tr.* (foll. by *on*) perform (a trick or joke etc.) on (a person). **7** *tr.* (foll. by *for*) regard (a person) as (something specified) (*played me for a fool*). **8** *intr. colloq.* participate, cooperate; do what is wanted (*they won't play*). **9** *intr.* gamble. **10** *tr.* gamble on. **11** *tr.* **a** (also *absol.*) take part in (a game or recreation). **b** compete with (another player or team) in a game. **c** occupy (a specified position) in a team for a game. **d** (foll. by *in, on, at*, etc.) assign (a player) to a position. **12** *tr.* move (a piece) or display (a playing card) in one's turn in a game. **13** *tr.* (also *absol.*) strike (a ball etc.) or execute (a stroke) in a game. **14** *intr.* move about in a lively or unrestrained manner. **15** *intr.* (often foll. by *on*) **a** touch gently. **b** emit light, water, etc. (*fountains gently playing*). **16** *tr.* allow (a fish) to exhaust itself pulling against a line. **17** *intr.* (often foll. by *at*) **a** engage in a half-hearted way (in an activity). **b** pretend to be. **18** *intr.* (of a cricket ground etc.) be conducive to play as specified (*the pitch is playing fast*). **19** *intr.* act or behave (as specified) (*play fair*). **20** *tr.* (foll. by *in, out*, etc.) accompany (a person) with music (*were played out with bagpipes*). ● *n.* **1** recreation, amusement, esp. as the spontaneous activity of children and young animals. **2 a** the playing of a game. **b** the action or manner of this. **c** the status of the ball etc. in a game as being available to be played according to the rules (*in play; out of play*). **3** a dramatic piece for the stage etc. **4** activity or operation (*brought into play*). **5 a** freedom of movement. **b** space or scope for this. **6** brisk, light, or fitful movement. **7** gambling. **8** an action or manoeuvre, esp. in or as in a game. □ **at play** engaged in recreation. **in play** for amusement; not seriously. **make play** act effectively. **make a play for** *colloq.* make a conspicuous attempt to acquire. **make play with** use ostentatiously. **play about** (or **around**) behave irresponsibly. **play along** pretend to cooperate. **play back** play (sounds recently recorded), esp. to monitor recording quality etc. **play ball** see BALL[1]. **play**

by ear 1 perform (music) without having seen a score of it. **2** (also **play it by ear**) proceed instinctively or step by step according to results and circumstances. **play one's cards close to one's chest** see CHEST. **play one's cards right** (or **well**) make good use of opportunities; act shrewdly. **play down** minimize the importance of. **play ducks and drakes with** see DUCK[1]. **played out** exhausted of energy or usefulness. **play false** act, or treat a (person), deceitfully or treacherously. **play fast and loose** act unreliably; ignore one's obligations. **play the field** see FIELD. **play for time** seek to gain time by delaying. **play the game** see GAME[1]. **play God** see GOD. **play havoc with** see HAVOC. **play hell with** see HELL. **play hookey** see HOOKEY. **play into a person's hands** act so as unwittingly to give a person an advantage. **play it cool** *colloq.* **1** affect indifference. **2** be relaxed or unemotional. **play the man** = *be a man* (see MAN). **play the market** speculate in stocks etc. **play off** (usu. foll. by *against*) **1** oppose (one person against another), esp. for one's own advantage. **2** play an extra match to decide a draw or tie. **play on 1** continue to play. **2** take advantage of (a person's feelings etc.). **play oneself in** *Brit.* become accustomed to the prevailing conditions in a game etc. **play on words** a pun. **play safe** (or **for safety**) avoid risks. **play to the gallery** see GALLERY. **play up 1** *Brit.* **a** behave mischievously. **b** cause trouble; be irritating (*my rheumatism is playing up again*). **c** obstruct or annoy in this way (*played the teacher up*). **2** emphasize, make the most of. **3** *Brit.* put all one's energy into a game. **play up to** flatter, esp. to win favour. **play with fire** take foolish risks. □ **playable** *adj.* **playability** /-'bɪlɪti/ *n.* [Old English *plega* (*n.*), *pleg(i)an* (*v.*), originally = (to) exercise]

playa /'plʌɪə/ *n.* a flat dried-up area, esp. a desert basin from which water evaporates quickly. [Spanish, = beach, from Late Latin *plagia*]

play-act /'pleɪakt/ *v.* **1** *intr.* act in a play. **2** *intr.* behave affectedly or insincerely. **3** *tr.* act (a scene, part, etc.). □ **play-acting** *n.* **play-actor** *n.*

playback /'pleɪbak/ *n.* the playing back of a sound or sounds; an instance of this.

playbill /'pleɪbɪl/ *n.* **1** a poster announcing a theatrical performance. **2** *US* a theatre programme.

playboy /'pleɪbɔɪ/ *n.* an irresponsible pleasure-seeking man, esp. a wealthy one.

player /'pleɪə/ *n.* **1** a person taking part in a sport or game. **2** a person playing a musical instrument (often in *comb.* : *flute-player*). **3** a person who plays a part on the stage; an actor. **4** any device for playing records, compact discs, cassettes, etc.[Old English *plegere* (as PLAY)]

player-manager *n.* a person who both plays in a team and manages it.

player-piano *n.* a piano fitted with an apparatus enabling it to be played automatically.

playfellow /'pleɪfɛləʊ/ *n.* a playmate.

playful /'pleɪfʊl, -f(ə)l/ *adj.* **1** fond of or inclined to play. **2** done in fun; humorous, jocular. □ **playfully** *adv.* **playfulness** *n.*

playgoer /'pleɪgəʊə/ *n.* a person who goes often to the theatre.

playground /'pleɪgraʊnd/ *n.* an outdoor area for children to play on.

playgroup /'pleɪgru:p/ *n. Brit.* a group of pre-school children who play regularly together at a particular place under supervision.

playhouse /'pleɪhaʊs/ *n.* **1** a theatre. **2** a toy house for children to play in.

playing card *n.* each of a set of usu. 52 oblong pieces of card or other material with an identical pattern on one side and different values represented by numbers and symbols on the other, used to play various games.

playing field *n.* a field used for outdoor team games.

playlet /'pleɪlɪt/ *n.* a short play or dramatic piece.

playlist /'pleɪlɪst/ *n.* & *v.* ● *n.* a list of pieces to be played, esp. of musical recordings chosen to be broadcast on a radio show. ● *v.tr.* place on a playlist.

playmaker /'pleɪmeɪkə/ *n.* a player in a team game who leads attacks or brings other players in the same side into a position to score.

playmate /'pleɪmeɪt/ *n.* **1** a child's companion in play. **2** a lover.

play-off *n.* a match played to decide a draw or tie.

playpen /'pleɪpɛn/ *n.* a portable enclosure for young children to play in.

play-reading *n.* **1** the activity of reading through a play. **2** an instance of this.

playroom /'pleɪru:m, -rʊm/ *n.* a room set aside for children to play in.

play school *n.* a nursery school or kindergarten.

playsuit /'pleɪsu:t, -sju:t/ *n.* a garment for a young child.

plaything /'pleɪθɪŋ/ *n.* **1** a toy or other thing to play with. **2** a person treated as a toy.

playtime /'pleɪtʌɪm/ *n.* time for play or recreation.

playwright /'pleɪrʌɪt/ *n.* a person who writes plays.

playwriting /'pleɪrʌɪtɪŋ/ *n.* the activity or process of writing plays.

plaza /'plɑ:zə/ *n.* a market place or open square (esp. in a Spanish town). [Spanish, = place]

plc *abbr.* (also **PLC**) *Brit.* Public Limited Company.

plea /pli:/ *n.* **1** an earnest appeal or entreaty. **2** *Law* a formal statement by or on behalf of a defendant. **3** an argument or excuse. [Middle English & Anglo-French *ple, plai*, Old French *plait, plaid* 'agreement, discussion' from Latin *placitum* 'a decree', neut. past part. of *placēre* 'to please']

plea bargaining *n.* orig. *US* an arrangement between prosecutor and defendant whereby the defendant pleads guilty to a lesser charge in the expectation of leniency. □ **plea bargain** *n.* & *v.intr.*

pleach /pli:tʃ/ *v.tr.* entwine or interlace (esp. branches to form a hedge). [Middle English *pleche* from Old French (as PLASH[2])]

plead /pli:d/ *v.* (*past* and *past part.* **pleaded** or esp. *N. Amer., Sc., & dial.* **pled** /plɛd/) **1** *intr.* (foll. by *with*) make an earnest appeal to. **2** *intr. Law* address a law court as an advocate on behalf of a party. **3** *tr.* maintain (a cause) esp. in a law court. **4** *tr. Law* declare to be one's state as regards guilt in or responsibility for a crime (*plead guilty*; *plead insanity*). **5** *tr.* offer or allege as an excuse (*pleaded forgetfulness*). **6** *intr.* make an appeal or entreaty. □ **pleadable** *adj.* **pleader** *n.* **pleadingly** *adv.* [Middle English from Anglo-French *pleder*, Old French *plaidier* (as PLEA)]

pleading /'pli:dɪŋ/ *n.* (usu. in *pl.*) a formal statement of the cause of an action or defence.

plea of tender *n. Law* a plea that the defendant has always been ready to satisfy the plaintiff's claim and now brings the sum into court.

pleasance /'plɛz(ə)ns/ *n.* a secluded enclosure or part of a garden, esp. one attached to a large house. [Middle English from Old French *plaisance* (as PLEASANT)]

pleasant /'plɛz(ə)nt/ *adj.* (**pleasanter**, **pleasantest**) pleasing to the mind, feelings, or senses. □ **pleasantly** *adv.* **pleasantness** *n.* [Middle English from Old French *plaisant* (as PLEASE)]

pleasantry /'plɛz(ə)ntri/ *n.* (*pl.* **-ies**) **1** (usu. in *pl.*) a courteous or polite remark, esp. made in casual conversation. **2** (esp. in *pl.*) an amusing remark. **3** jocularity. [French *plaisanterie* (as PLEASANT)]

please /pli:z/ *v.* **1** *tr.* (also *absol.*) be agreeable to; make glad; give pleasure to (*the gift will please them*; *anxious to please*). **2** *tr.* (in *passive*) **a** (foll. by *to* + infin.) be glad or willing to (*am pleased to help*). **b** (often foll. by *about, at, with*) derive pleasure or satisfaction (from). **3** *tr.* (prec. by *it* as subject; usu. foll. by *to* + infin.) be the inclination or wish of (*it did not please them to attend*). **4** *intr.* think fit; have the will or desire (*take as many as you please*). **5** *tr.* (short for **may it please you**) used in polite requests (*come in, please*). □ **(as) pleased as Punch** see PUNCH[4]. **if you please** if you are willing, esp. *iron.* to indicate unreasonableness (*then, if you please, we had to pay*). **please oneself** do as one likes. □ **pleased** *adj.* **pleasing** *adj.* **pleasingly** *adv.* [Middle English *plaise* via Old French *plaisir* from Latin *placēre*]

pleasurable /ˈplɛʒ(ə)rəb(ə)l/ *adj.* causing pleasure; agreeable. □ **pleasurableness** *n.* **pleasurably** *adv.* [PLEASURE + -ABLE, on the pattern of *comfortable*]

pleasure /ˈplɛʒə/ *n.* & *v.* ● *n.* **1** a feeling of satisfaction or joy. **2** enjoyment. **3** a source of pleasure or gratification (*painting was my chief pleasure; it is a pleasure to talk to them*). **4** *formal* a person's will or desire (*what is your pleasure?*). **5** sensual gratification or enjoyment (*a life of pleasure*). **6** (*attrib.*) done or used for pleasure (*pleasure boat; pleasure trip*). ● *v.* **1** *tr.* give (esp. sexual) pleasure to. **2** *intr.* (often foll. by *in*) take pleasure. □ **take pleasure in** like doing. **with pleasure** gladly. [Middle English & Old French *plesir*, *plaisir* PLEASE, used as a noun]

pleat /pliːt/ *n.* & *v.* ● *n.* a fold or crease, esp. a flattened fold in cloth doubled upon itself. ● *v.tr.* make a pleat or pleats in. [Middle English, variant of PLAIT]

pleb /plɛb/ *n. colloq.* usu. *derog.* = PLEBEIAN *n.* 2. □ **plebby** *adj.* [abbreviation of PLEBEIAN]

plebeian /plɪˈbiːən/ *n.* & *adj.* ● *n.* **1** a commoner, esp. in ancient Rome. **2** a working-class person, esp. an uncultured one. ● *adj.* **1** of low birth; of the common people. **2** uncultured. **3** coarse, ignoble. □ **plebeianism** *n.* [Latin *plebeius* from *plebs plebis* 'the common people']

plebiscite /ˈplɛbɪsʌɪt, -sɪt/ *n.* **1** the direct vote of all the electors of a state etc. on an important public question, e.g. a change in the constitution. **2** the public expression of a community's opinion, with or without binding force. **3** *Rom.Hist.* a law enacted by the plebeians' assembly. □ **plebiscitary** /-ˈbɪsɪt(ə)ri/ *adj.* [French *plébiscite* from Latin *plebiscitum*, from *plebs plebis* 'the common people' + *scitum* 'decree' from *sciscere* 'vote for']

plectrum /ˈplɛktrəm/ *n.* (*pl.* **plectrums** or **plectra** /-trə/) **1** a thin flat piece of plastic or horn etc. held in the hand and used to pluck a string, esp. of a guitar. **2** the corresponding mechanical part of a harpsichord etc. [Latin from Greek *plēktron*, from *plēssō* 'strike']

pled see PLEAD.

pledge /plɛdʒ/ *n.* & *v.* ● *n.* **1** a solemn promise or undertaking. **2** a thing given as security for the fulfilment of a contract, the payment of a debt, etc., and liable to forfeiture in the event of failure. **3** a thing put in pawn. **4 a** the promise of a donation to charity. **b** such a donation. **5** a thing given as a token of love, favour, or something to come. **6** the drinking of a person's health; a toast. **7** a solemn undertaking to abstain from alcohol (*sign the pledge*). **8** the state of being pledged (*goods lying in pledge*). ● *v.tr.* **1 a** deposit as security. **b** pawn. **2** promise solemnly by the pledge of (one's honour, word, etc.). **3** (often *refl.*) bind by a solemn promise. **4** drink to the health of. □ **pledge one's troth** see TROTH. □ **pledgeable** *adj.* **pledger** *n.* **pledgor** *n. Law.* [Middle English *plege* via Old French *plege* from Late Latin *plebium*, from *plebire* 'assure']

pledgee /plɛˈdʒiː/ *n.* a person to whom a pledge is given.

pledget /ˈplɛdʒɪt/ *n.* a small wad of lint etc. [16th c.: origin unknown]

pleiad /ˈplʌɪəd/ *n.* a brilliant group of (usu. seven) persons or things. [named after PLEIADES]

Pleiades /ˈplʌɪədiːz/ *n.pl.* a cluster of stars in the constellation Taurus. Also called *the Seven Sisters*. [Middle English via Latin *Pleïas* from Greek *Plēias -ados*, each of the seven mythical daughters of Atlas and Pleione]

plein-air /pleɪnˈɛː, French plɛnɛr/ *adj.* (of a painting) representing an outdoor scene and executed with a spontaneous technique. [French *en plein air* 'in the open air']

pleiotropy /plʌɪˈɒtrəpi/ *n. Biol.* the production by a single gene of two or more apparently unrelated effects. □ **pleiotropic** /-ˈtrəʊpɪk, -ˈtrɒpɪk/ *adj.* **pleiotropism** *n.* [Greek *pleiōn* 'more' + *tropē* 'turning']

Pleistocene /ˈplʌɪstəsiːn/ *adj.* & *n. Geol.* ● *adj.* of or relating to the first epoch of the Quaternary period marked by great fluctuations in temperature with glacial periods followed by interglacial periods. Cf. Appendix X. ● *n.* this epoch or system. [Greek *pleistos* 'most' + *kainos* 'new']

plenary /ˈpliːnəri/ *adj.* **1** entire, unqualified, absolute (*plenary indulgence*). **2** (of an assembly) to be attended by all members. [Late Latin *plenarius* from *plenus* 'full']

plenipotentiary /ˌplɛnɪpəˈtɛnʃ(ə)ri/ *n.* & *adj.* ● *n.* (*pl.* **-ies**) a person (esp. a diplomat) invested with the full power of independent action. ● *adj.* **1** having this power. **2** (of power) absolute. [medieval Latin *plenipotentiarius*, from *plenus* 'full' + *potentia* 'power']

plenitude /ˈplɛnɪtjuːd/ *n. literary* **1** fullness, completeness. **2** abundance. [Middle English via Old French from Late Latin *plenitudo*, from *plenus* 'full']

plenteous /ˈplɛntɪəs/ *adj. poet.* plentiful. □ **plenteously** *adv.* **plenteousness** *n.* [Middle English from Old French *plentivous*, via *plentif -ive* from *plenté* PLENTY: cf. *bounteous*]

plentiful /ˈplɛntɪfʊl, -f(ə)l/ *adj.* abundant, copious. □ **plentifully** *adv.* **plentifulness** *n.*

plenty /ˈplɛnti/ *n., adj., & adv.* ● *n.* (often foll. by *of*) a great or sufficient quantity or number (*we have plenty; plenty of time*). ● *adj. colloq.* existing in an ample quantity. ● *adv. colloq.* fully, entirely (*it is plenty large enough*). [Middle English *plenteth*, *plente* via Old French *plentet* from Latin *plenitas -tatis*, from *plenus* 'full']

plenum /ˈpliːnəm/ *n.* **1** a full assembly of people or a committee etc. **2** *Physics* space filled with matter. [Latin, neut. of *plenus* 'full']

pleochroic /pliːəˈkrəʊɪk/ *adj.* (of a crystal etc.) showing different colours when viewed in different directions. □ **pleochroism** *n.* [Greek *pleiōn* 'more' + *-khroos* from *khrōs* 'colour']

pleomorphism /pliːəˈmɔːfɪz(ə)m/ *n.* the occurrence of more than one distinct form, e.g. of a crystalline substance, tumour, virus, organism (esp. at different stages of the life cycle), etc. □ **pleomorphic** *adj.* [Greek *pleiōn* 'more' + *morphē* 'form']

pleonasm /ˈpliːənaz(ə)m/ *n.* the use of more words than are needed to give the sense (e.g. *see with one's eyes.*) □ **pleonastic** /-ˈnastɪk/ *adj.* **pleonastically** /-ˈnastɪk(ə)li/ *adv.* [Late Latin *pleonasmus* from Greek *pleonasmos*, from *pleonazō* 'be superfluous']

plesiosaurus /pliːsɪəˈsɔːrəs, pliːz-/ *n.* (also **plesiosaur** /ˈpliːsɪəsɔː, ˈpliːz-/) any of a group of large extinct marine reptiles with a broad flat body, large paddle-like limbs, and often a long flexible neck. [modern Latin, from Greek *plēsios* 'near' + *sauros* 'lizard']

plessor var. of PLEXOR.

plethora /ˈplɛθ(ə)rə/ *n.* **1** an oversupply, glut, or excess. **2** *Med.* **a** an abnormal excess of red corpuscles in the blood. **b** an excess of any body fluid. □ **plethoric** /also plɪˈθɒrɪk/ *adj.* **plethorically** /plɪˈθɒrɪk(ə)li/ *adv.* [Late Latin from Greek *plēthōrē*, from *plēthō* 'be full']

pleura[1] /ˈplʊərə/ *n.* (*pl.* **pleurae** /-riː/) **1** each of a pair of serous membranes lining the thorax and enveloping the lungs in mammals. **2** either of the lateral extensions of the body wall in arthropods. □ **pleural** *adj.* [medieval Latin from Greek, = side of the body, rib]

pleura[2] *pl.* of PLEURON.

pleurisy /ˈplʊərɪsi/ *n.* inflammation of the pleurae, marked by pain in the chest or side, fever, etc. □ **pleuritic** /-ˈrɪtɪk/ *adj.* [Middle English via Old French *pleurisie*, Late Latin *pleurisis* 'pleurisy' and Latin *pleuritis* from Greek (as PLEURA[1])]

pleuro- /ˈplʊərəʊ/ *comb. form* **1** denoting the pleura. **2** denoting the side.

pleuron /ˈplʊərɒn/ *n.* (*pl.* **pleura** /-rə/) = PLEURA[1] 2. [Greek, = side of the body, rib]

pleuropneumonia /ˌpluərəʊnjuːˈməʊnɪə/ *n.* pneumonia complicated with pleurisy.

plexiglas /ˈplɛksɪglɑːs/ *n. propr.* = PERSPEX. [formed as PLEXOR + GLASS]

plexor /ˈplɛksə/ *n.* (also **plessor** /ˈplɛsə/) *Med.* a small hammer used to test reflexes and in percussing. [formed irregularly from Greek *plēxis* 'percussion' + -OR[1]]

plexus /ˈplɛksəs/ *n.* (*pl.* same or **plexuses**) **1** *Anat.* a network of nerves or vessels in an animal body (*gastric plexus*). **2** any network or weblike formation. □ **plexiform** *adj.* [Latin from *plectere plex-* 'plait']

pliable /ˈplʌɪəb(ə)l/ *adj.* **1** bending easily; supple. **2** yielding, compliant. □ **pliability** /-ˈbɪlɪti/ *n.* **pliableness** *n.* **pliably** *adv.* [French from *plier* 'bend': see PLY[1]]

pliant /ˈplʌɪənt/ *adj.* = PLIABLE 1. □ **pliancy** *n.* **pliantly** *adv.* [Middle English from Old French (as PLIABLE)]

plicate /ˈplʌɪkət, ˈplʌɪkeɪt/ *adj. Biol. & Geol.* folded, crumpled, corrugated. □ **plicated** /plɪˈkeɪtɪd/ *adj.* [Latin *plicatus*, past part. of *plicare* 'fold']

plication /plɪˈkeɪʃ(ə)n, plʌɪ-/ *n.* **1** the act of folding. **2** a fold; a folded condition. [Middle English from medieval Latin *plicatio* or Latin *plicare* 'fold', on the pattern of *complication*]

plié /ˈpliːeɪ/ *n.* (*pl.* **pliés**) *Ballet* a bending of the knees with the feet on the ground. [French, past part. of *plier* 'bend': see PLY[1]]

pliers /ˈplʌɪəz/ *n.pl.* pincers with parallel flat usu. serrated surfaces for holding small objects, bending wire, etc. [dialect *ply* 'bend' from French *plier*: see PLY[1]]

plight[1] /plʌɪt/ *n.* a condition or state, esp. an unfortunate one. [Middle English & Anglo-French *plit* = Old French *pleit* 'fold': see PLAIT: *-gh-* by confusion with PLIGHT[2]]

plight[2] /plʌɪt/ *v. & n. archaic* ● *v.tr.* **1** pledge or promise solemnly (one's faith, loyalty, etc.). **2** (foll. by *to*) engage, esp. in marriage. ● *n.* an engagement or act of pledging. □ **plight one's troth** see TROTH. [Old English *pliht* 'danger', from Germanic]

plimsoll /ˈplɪms(ə)l/ *n.* (also **plimsole**) *Brit.* a rubber-soled canvas sports shoe. [probably from the resemblance of the side of the sole to a PLIMSOLL LINE]

Plimsoll line /ˈplɪms(ə)l/ *n.* (also **Plimsoll mark**) a marking on a ship's side showing the limit of legal submersion under various conditions. [named after S. *Plimsoll*, English politician d. 1898, promoter of the Merchant Shipping Act of 1876]

plinth /plɪnθ/ *n.* **1** *Archit.* the lower square slab at the base of a column. **2** a base supporting a vase or statue etc. [French *plinthe* or Latin *plinthus* from Greek *plinthos* 'tile, brick, squared stone']

Pliocene /ˈplʌɪə(ʊ)siːn/ *adj. & n. Geol.* ● *adj.* of or relating to the last epoch of the Tertiary period with evidence of the extinction of many mammals, and the development of hominids. Cf. Appendix X. ● *n.* this epoch or system. [Greek *pleiōn* 'more' + *kainos* 'new']

plissé /ˈpliːseɪ/ *adj. & n.* ● *adj.* (of cloth etc.) treated so as to cause permanent puckering. ● *n.* material treated in this way. [French, past part. of *plisser* 'pleat']

PLO *abbr.* Palestine Liberation Organization.

plod /plɒd/ *v. & n.* ● *v.* (**plodded**, **plodding**) **1** *intr.* (often foll. by *along*, *on*, etc.) walk doggedly or laboriously; trudge. **2** *intr.* (often foll. by *at*) work slowly and steadily. **3** *tr.* tread or make (one's way) laboriously. ● *n.* the act or a spell of plodding. □ **plodder** *n.* **ploddingly** *adv.* [16th c.: probably imitative]

-ploid /plɔɪd/ *comb. form Biol.* forming adjectives denoting the number of sets of chromosomes in a cell (*diploid*; *polyploid*). [on the pattern of HAPLOID]

ploidy /ˈplɔɪdi/ *n.* the number of sets of chromosomes in a cell. [on the pattern of DIPLOIDY, POLYPLOIDY, etc.]

plonk[1] /plɒŋk/ *v. & n.* ● *v.tr.* **1** set down hurriedly or clumsily. **2** (usu. foll. by *down*) set down firmly. ● *n.* **1** an act of plonking. **2** a heavy thud. [imitative]

plonk[2] /plɒŋk/ *n. Brit. colloq.* cheap or inferior wine. [originally Australian: probably a corruption of *blanc* in French *vin blanc* 'white wine']

plonker /ˈplɒŋkə/ *n. coarse slang* **1** *derog.* a foolish or inept person. **2** the penis.

plop /plɒp/ *n., v., & adv.* ● *n.* **1** a sound as of a smooth object dropping into water without a splash. **2** an act of falling with this sound. ● *v.intr.* (**plopped**, **plopping**) *& tr.* fall or drop with a plop. ● *adv.* with a plop. [19th c.: imitative]

plosion /ˈpləʊʒ(ə)n/ *n. Phonet.* the sudden release of air in the pronunciation of a plosive. [EXPLOSION]

plosive /ˈpləʊsɪv, -z-/ *adj. & n. Phonet.* ● *adj.* denoting a consonant that is produced by stopping the airflow using the lips, teeth, or palate, followed by a sudden release of air. ● *n.* a plosive speech sound. [EXPLOSIVE]

plot /plɒt/ *n. & v.* ● *n.* **1** a defined and usu. small piece of ground. **2** the interrelationship of the main events in a play, novel, film, etc. **3** a conspiracy or secret plan, esp. to achieve an unlawful end. **4** esp. *US* a diagram, chart, or map. **5** a graph showing the relation between two variables. ● *v.tr.* (**plotted**, **plotting**) **1** make a plan or map of (an existing object, a place or thing to be laid out, constructed, etc.). **2** (also *absol.*) plan or contrive secretly (a crime, conspiracy, etc.). **3** mark (a point or course etc.) on a chart or diagram. **4 a** mark out or allocate (points) on a graph. **b** make (a curve etc.) by marking out a number of points. **5** devise or plan the plot of (a play, novel, film, etc.). □ **plotless** *adj.* **plotlessness** *n.* **plotter** *n.* [Old English and from Old French *complot* 'secret plan': both of unknown origin]

plough /plaʊ/ *n. & v.* (esp. *N. Amer.* **plow**) ● *n.* **1** an implement with a cutting blade fixed in a frame drawn by a tractor or by horses, for cutting furrows in the soil and turning it up. **2** an implement resembling this and having a comparable function (*snowplough*). **3** ploughed land. **4** (**the Plough**) the constellation Ursa Major or its seven bright stars. ● *v.* **1** *tr.* (also *absol.*) turn up (the earth) with a plough, esp. before sowing. **2** *tr.* (foll. by *out*, *up*, *down*, etc.) turn or extract (roots, weeds, etc.) with a plough. **3** *tr.* furrow or scratch (a surface) as if with a plough. **4** *tr.* produce (a furrow or line) in this way. **5** *intr.* (foll. by *through*) advance laboriously, esp. through work, a book, etc. **6** *intr.* (foll. by *through*, *into*) travel or be propelled clumsily or violently. **7** *intr. & tr. Brit. colloq.* fail (in an examination). □ **plough back 1** plough (grass etc.) into the soil to enrich it. **2** reinvest (profits) in the business producing them. **plough under** bury in the soil by ploughing. **put one's hand to the plough** undertake a task (Luke 9:62). □ **ploughable** *adj.* **plougher** *n.* [Old English *plōh* from Old Norse *plógr*, from Germanic]

ploughland /ˈplaʊland/ *n.* (*N. Amer* **plowland**) land that is ploughed for growing crops.

ploughman /ˈplaʊmən/ *n.* (*N. Amer* **plowman**) (*pl.* **-men**) a person who uses a plough.

ploughman's lunch *n. Brit.* a meal of bread and usu. cheese with pickle or salad.

ploughman's spikenard *n.* a composite fragrant plant, *Inula conyzae*, with purplish-yellow flower heads.

Plough Monday *n.* the first Monday after the Epiphany. [from the custom of dragging a plough through the streets to mark the beginning of the ploughing season]

ploughshare /ˈplaʊʃɛː/ *n.* (*N. Amer.* **plowshare**) the cutting blade of a plough. [Middle English, from PLOUGH + Old English *scaer*, *scear* 'ploughshare', related to SHEAR]

plover /ˈplʌvə/ *n.* any short-billed gregarious bird of the family Charadriidae, esp. of the genus *Charadrius*, often found by water. [Middle English & Anglo-French from Old French *plo(u)vier*, ultimately from Latin *pluvia* 'rain']

plow *N. Amer.* var. of PLOUGH.

ploy /plɔɪ/ *n.* a stratagem; a cunning manoeuvre to gain an advantage. [originally Scots, 17th c.: origin unknown]

PLP *abbr.* (in the UK) Parliamentary Labour Party.

PLR *abbr.* (in the UK) Public Lending Right.

pluck /plʌk/ *v. & n.* ● *v.* **1** *tr.* (often foll. by *out, off*, etc.) remove by picking or pulling out or away. **2** *tr.* strip (a bird) of feathers. **3** *tr.* pull at, twitch. **4** *intr.* (foll. by *at*) tug or snatch at. **5** *tr.* sound (the string of a musical instrument) with the finger or a plectrum etc. **6** *tr.* plunder. **7** *tr.* swindle. ● *n.* **1** courage, spirit. **2** an act of plucking; a twitch. **3** the heart, liver, and lungs of an animal as food. ▫ **pluck up** summon up (one's courage, spirits, etc.). ▫ **plucker** *n.* **pluckless** *adj.* [Old English *ploccian, pluccian*, from Germanic]

plucky /ˈplʌki/ *adj.* (**pluckier**, **pluckiest**) brave, spirited. ▫ **pluckily** *adv.* **pluckiness** *n.*

plug /plʌg/ *n. & v.* ● *n.* **1** a piece of solid material fitting tightly into a hole, used to fill a gap or cavity or act as a wedge or stopper. **2 a** a device of metal pins in an insulated casing fitting into holes in a socket for making an electrical connection, esp. between an appliance and the mains. **b** *colloq.* an electric socket. **3** = SPARK PLUG. **4** *colloq.* a piece of (often free) publicity for an idea, product, etc. **5** a mass of solidified lava filling the neck of a volcano. **6** a cake or stick of tobacco; a piece of this for chewing. **7** = FIREPLUG. ● *v.* (**plugged**, **plugging**) **1** *tr.* (often foll. by *up*) stop (a hole etc.) with a plug. **2** *tr. slang* shoot or hit (a person etc.). **3** *tr. colloq.* seek to popularize (an idea, product, etc.) by constant recommendation. **4** *intr.* (often foll. by *at*) *colloq.* work steadily away (at). ▫ **plug in** connect electrically by inserting a plug in a socket. ▫ **plugger** *n.* [Middle Dutch & Middle Low German *plugge*, of unknown origin]

plughole /ˈplʌghəʊl/ *n.* a hole at the lowest point of a bath, basin, sink, etc., which can be stopped with a plug.

plug-in *attrib.adj.* able to be connected by means of a plug.

plug-ugly *n. & adj. US slang* ● *n.* (*pl.* **-ies**) a thug or ruffian. ● *adj.* villainous-looking.

plum /plʌm/ *n. & adj.* ● *n.* **1 a** an oval fleshy fruit, usu. purple or reddish when ripe, with sweet pulp and a flattish pointed stone. **b** (also **plum tree**) any deciduous tree of the genus *Prunus* (rose family), esp. *P. domestica*, which bears this fruit. **c** the wood of such a tree. **2** a reddish-purple colour. **3** a dried grape or raisin used in cooking (*plum pudding*). **4** the best of a collection; something especially prized (often *attrib.*: *a plum job*). ● *adj.* of a reddish-purple colour. ▫ **a plum in one's mouth** a rich-sounding voice or affected accent. [Old English *plūme* via medieval Latin *pruna* from Latin *prunum*]

plumage /ˈplu:mɪdʒ/ *n.* a bird's feathers. ▫ **plumaged** *adj.* (usu. in *comb.*). [Middle English from Old French (as PLUME)]

plumassier /plu:məˈsɪə/ *n.* a person who trades or works in ornamental feathers. [French from *plumasse*, augmentative of *plume* PLUME]

plumb[1] /plʌm/ *n., adv., adj., & v.* ● *n.* a ball of lead or other heavy material, esp. one attached to the end of a line for finding the depth of water or determining the vertical on an upright surface. ● *adv.* **1** exactly (*plumb in the centre*). **2** vertically. **3** *N. Amer. slang* quite, utterly (*plumb crazy*). ● *adj.* **1** vertical. **2** downright, sheer (*plumb nonsense*). **3** *Cricket* (of the wicket) level, true. ● *v.tr.* **1 a** measure the depth of (water) with a plumb. **b** determine (a depth). **2** test (an upright surface) to determine the vertical. **3** reach or experience in extremes (*plumb the depths of fear*). **4** learn in detail the facts about (a matter). ▫ **out of plumb** not vertical. [Middle English, probably ultimately from Latin *plumbum* 'lead', assimilated to Old French *plomb* 'lead']

plumb[2] /plʌm/ *v.* **1** *tr.* provide (a building or room etc.) with plumbing. **2** *tr.* (often foll. by *in*) fit as part of a plumbing system. **3** *intr.* work as a plumber. [back-formation from PLUMBER]

plumbago /plʌmˈbeɪgəʊ/ *n.* (*pl.* **-os**) **1** = GRAPHITE. **2** any plant of the genus *Plumbago*, with grey or blue flowers; also called LEADWORT. [Latin, from *plumbum* LEAD[2]]

plumbeous /ˈplʌmbɪəs/ *adj.* **1** of or like lead. **2** lead-glazed. [Latin *plumbeus* from *plumbum* LEAD[2]]

plumber /ˈplʌmə/ *n.* a person who fits and repairs the apparatus of a water supply, heating, etc. [Middle English *plummer* etc. via Old French *plommier* from Latin *plumbarius*, from *plumbum* LEAD[2]]

plumber's snake see SNAKE *n.* 4.

plumbic /ˈplʌmbɪk/ *adj.* **1** *Chem.* containing lead esp. in its tetravalent form. **2** *Med.* due to the presence of lead. [Latin *plumbum* LEAD[2]]

plumbing /ˈplʌmɪŋ/ *n.* **1** the system or apparatus of water supply, heating, etc., in a building. **2** the work of a plumber. **3** *colloq.* lavatory installations.

plumbism /ˈplʌmbɪz(ə)m/ *n. Med.* = LEAD POISONING.

plumbless /ˈplʌmlɪs/ *adj. literary* (of a depth of water etc.) that cannot be plumbed.

plumb line *n.* a line with a plumb attached.

plumbous /ˈplʌmbəs/ *n. Chem.* containing lead in its divalent form.

plumb rule *n.* a mason's plumb line attached to a board.

plum cake *n.* esp. *Brit.* a cake containing raisins, currants, etc.

plum duff *n. Brit.* a plain flour pudding with raisins or currants.

plume /plu:m/ *n. & v.* ● *n.* **1** a feather, esp. a large one used for ornament. **2** an ornament of feathers etc. attached to a helmet or hat or worn in the hair. **3** something resembling this (*a plume of smoke*). **4** *Zool.* a feather-like part or formation. ● *v.* **1** *tr.* decorate or provide with a plume or plumes. **2** *refl.* (foll. by *on, upon*) pride (oneself on esp. something trivial). **3** *tr.* (of a bird) preen (itself or its feathers). ▫ **plumeless** *adj.* **plumelike** *adj.* **plumery** *n.* [Middle English via Old French from Latin *pluma* 'down']

plume moth *n.* a small moth of the family Pterophoridae, with long legs and narrow divided feathery wings.

plummet /ˈplʌmɪt/ *n. & v.* ● *n.* **1** a plumb or plumb line. **2** a sounding line. **3** a weight attached to a fishing line to keep the float upright. ● *v.intr.* (**plummeted**, **plummeting**) fall or plunge rapidly. [Middle English from Old French *plommet*, diminutive of *plomb* (as PLUMB[1])]

plummy /ˈplʌmi/ *adj.* (**plummier**, **plummiest**) **1** abounding or rich in plums. **2** *colloq.* (of a voice) sounding affectedly rich or deep in tone. **3** *colloq.* good, desirable.

plumose /plu:ˈməʊs, ˈplu:məʊs/ *adj.* **1** feathered. **2** feather-like. [Latin *plumosus* (as PLUME)]

plump[1] /plʌmp/ *adj. & v.* ● *adj.* (esp. of a person or animal or part of the body) having a full rounded shape; fleshy; filled out. ● *v.tr. & intr.* (often foll. by *up, out*) make or become plump; fatten. ▫ **plumpish** *adj.* **plumply** *adv.* **plumpness** *n.* **plumpy** *adj.* [Middle English *plompe* from Middle Dutch *plomp* 'blunt', Middle Low German *plump, plomp* 'shapeless' etc.]

plump[2] /plʌmp/ *v., n., adv., & adj.* ● *v.* **1** *intr. & tr.* (often foll. by *down*) drop or fall abruptly (*plumped down on the chair; plumped it on the floor*). **2** *intr.* (foll. by *for*) decide definitely in favour of (one of two or more possibilities). **3** *tr.* (often foll. by *out*) utter abruptly; blurt out. ● *n.* an abrupt plunge; a heavy fall. ● *adv. colloq.* **1** with a sudden or heavy fall. **2** directly, bluntly (*I told him plump*). ● *adj. colloq.* direct, unqualified (*answered with a plump 'no'*). [Middle English from Middle Low German *plumpen*, Middle Dutch *plompen*: originally imitative]

plum pudding *n.* a rich boiled suet pudding with raisins, currants, spices, etc.

plumule /ˈplu:mju:l/ *n.* **1** the rudimentary shoot or stem of an embryo plant. **2** a down feather on a young bird. ▫ **plumulaceous** /plu:mjʊˈleɪʃəs/ *adj.* (in sense 2).

plumular /'plu:mjʊlə/ *adj.* (in sense 1). [French *plumule* or Latin *plumula*, diminutive of *pluma* 'down']

plumy /'plu:mi/ *adj.* (**plumier**, **plumiest**) **1** plumelike, feathery. **2** adorned with plumes.

plunder /'plʌndə/ *v. & n.* ● *v.tr.* **1** rob (a place or person) or steal (goods), esp. systematically or as in war. **2** steal from (another's writings etc.). ● *n.* **1** the violent or dishonest acquisition of property. **2** property acquired by plundering. **3** *colloq.* profit, gain. □ **plunderer** *n.* [Low German *plündern*, literally 'rob of household goods' from Middle High German *plunder* 'clothing etc.']

plunge /plʌn(d)ʒ/ *v. & n.* ● *v.* **1** (usu. foll. by *in, into*) **a** *tr.* thrust forcefully or abruptly. **b** *intr.* dive; propel oneself forcibly. **c** *intr. & tr.* enter or cause to enter a certain condition or embark on a certain course abruptly or impetuously (*they plunged into a lively discussion*; *the room was plunged into darkness*). **2** *tr.* immerse completely. **3** *intr.* **a** move suddenly and dramatically downward. **b** (foll. by *down, into*, etc.) move with a rush (*plunged down the stairs*). **c** diminish rapidly (*share prices have plunged*). **4** *intr.* (of a horse) start violently forward. **5** *intr.* (of a ship) pitch. **6** *intr. colloq.* gamble heavily; run into debt. ● *n.* a plunging action or movement; a dive. □ **take the plunge** *colloq.* commit oneself to a (usu. risky) course of action. [Middle English from Old French *plungier*, ultimately from Latin *plumbum* 'plummet']

plunger /'plʌn(d)ʒə/ *n.* **1** a part of a mechanism that works with a plunging or thrusting movement. **2** a rubber cup on a handle for clearing blocked pipes by a plunging and sucking action. **3** *colloq.* a reckless gambler.

plunging neckline *n.* (also **plunge neckline**) a low-cut neckline.

plunk /plʌŋk/ *n. & v.* ● *n.* **1** the sound made by the sharply plucked string of a stringed instrument. **2** *US* a heavy blow. **3** *US* = PLONK[1] *n.* ● *v.* **1** *intr. & tr.* sound or cause to sound with a plunk. **2** *tr. US* hit abruptly. **3** *tr. US* = PLONK[1] *v.* [imitative]

pluperfect /plu:'pə:fɪkt/ *adj. & n. Gram.* ● *adj.* (of a tense) denoting an action completed prior to some past point of time specified or implied, formed in English by *had* and the past participle, as: *he had gone by then.* ● *n.* the pluperfect tense. [modern Latin *plusperfectum* from Latin *plus quam perfectum* 'more than perfect']

plural /'plʊər(ə)l/ *adj. & n.* ● *adj.* **1** more than one in number. **2** *Gram.* (of a word or form) denoting more than one, or (in languages with dual number) more than two. ● *n. Gram.* **1** a plural word or form. **2** the plural number. □ **plurally** *adv.* [Middle English via Old French *plurel* from Latin *pluralis*, from *plus pluris* 'more']

pluralism /'plʊər(ə)lɪz(ə)m/ *n.* **1** holding more than one office, esp. an ecclesiastical office or benefice, at a time. **2 a** a political theory or system of power-sharing among a number of political parties. **b** a theory or system of devolution and autonomy for individual bodies in preference to monolithic state control. **c** a form of society in which the members of minority groups maintain their independent cultural traditions. **3** *Philos.* a theory or system that recognizes more than one ultimate principle (cf. MONISM 2). □ **pluralist** *n.* **pluralistic** /-'lɪstɪk/ *adj.* **pluralistically** /-'lɪstɪk(ə)li/ *adv.*

plurality /plʊə'ralɪti/ *n.* (*pl.* **-ies**) **1** the state of being plural. **2** = PLURALISM 1. **3** a large or the greater number. **4** *US* **a** the number of votes cast for a candidate who receives more than any other but does not receive an absolute majority. **b** the number by which this exceeds the number of votes cast for the candidate placed second. [Middle English via Old French *pluralité* from Late Latin *pluralitas* (as PLURAL)]

pluralize /'plʊər(ə)lʌɪz/ *v.* (also **-ise**) **1** *tr. & intr.* make or become plural. **2** *tr.* express in the plural. **3** *intr.* hold more than one ecclesiastical office or benefice. □ **pluralization** /-'zeɪʃ(ə)n/ *n.*

pluri- /'plʊəri/ *comb. form* several. [Latin *plus pluris* 'more', *plures* 'several']

plus /plʌs/ *prep., adj., n., & conj.* ● *prep.* **1** *Math.* with the addition of (*3 plus 4 equals 7*) (symbol +). **2** (of temperature) above zero (*plus 2° C*). **3** *colloq.* with; having gained; newly possessing (*returned plus a new car*). ● *adj.* **1** (after a number) at least (*fifteen plus*). **2** (after a grade etc.) rather better than (*beta plus*). **3** *Math.* positive. **4** having a positive electrical charge. **5** (*attrib.*) additional, extra (*plus business*). ● *n.* **1** = PLUS SIGN. **2** *Math.* an additional or positive quantity. **3** an advantage (*experience is a definite plus*). ● *conj. colloq. disp.* also; and furthermore (*they arrived late, plus they were hungry*). [Latin, = more]

■ **Usage** The use of *plus* as a conjunction, as in *They arrived late, plus they wanted a meal*, is considered incorrect by some people.

plus ça change /ply sa ʃɑ̃ʒ/ *int.* expressing the fundamental immutability of human nature, institutions, etc. [French, abbreviation of *plus ça change, plus c'est la même chose* 'the more it changes, the more it stays the same']

plus fours *n.* long wide men's knickerbockers usu. worn for golf etc. [20th c.: so named because the overhang at the knee requires an extra four inches of material]

plush /plʌʃ/ *n. & adj.* ● *n.* cloth of silk or cotton etc., with a long soft nap. ● *adj.* **1** made of plush. **2** *colloq.* plushy. □ **plushly** *adv.* **plushness** *n.* [obsolete French *pluche*, contraction from *peluche*, from Old French *peluchier* via Italian *peluzzo*, diminutive of *pelo*, from Latin *pilus* 'hair']

plushy /'plʌʃi/ *adj.* (**plushier**, **plushiest**) *colloq.* stylish, luxurious. □ **plushiness** *n.*

plus sign *n.* the symbol +, indicating addition or a positive value.

plutarchy /'plu:tɑ:ki/ *n.* (*pl.* **-ies**) plutocracy. [Greek *ploutos* 'wealth' + *-arkhia* '-rule']

Pluto /'plu:təʊ/ *n.* a small planet, for most of its orbit the outermost planet of the solar system. [Latin from Greek *Ploutōn*, the god of the underworld]

plutocracy /plu:'tɒkrəsi/ *n.* (*pl.* **-ies**) **1 a** government by the wealthy. **b** a state governed in this way. **2** a wealthy elite or ruling class. □ **plutocratic** /plu:tə'kratɪk/ *adj.* **plutocratically** /plu:tə'kratɪk(ə)li/ *adv.* [Greek *ploutokratia*, from *ploutos* 'wealth' + -CRACY]

plutocrat /'plu:təkrat/ *n.* esp. *derog.* or *joc.* **1** a member of a plutocracy or wealthy elite. **2** a wealthy and influential person.

pluton /'plu:t(ə)n/ *n. Geol.* a body of plutonic rock. [back-formation from PLUTONIC]

Plutonian /plu:'təʊnɪən/ *adj.* **1** infernal. **2** of the infernal regions. [Latin *Plutonius* from Greek *Ploutōnios* (as PLUTO)]

plutonic /plu:'tɒnɪk/ *adj.* **1** *Geol.* (of rock) formed as igneous rock by solidification below the surface of the earth. **2** (**Plutonic**) = PLUTONIAN. [formed as PLUTONIAN]

plutonium /plu:'təʊnɪəm/ *n. Chem.* a dense silvery radioactive metallic transuranic element of the actinide series, used in some nuclear reactors and weapons (symbol **Pu**). [PLUTO, on the pattern of NEPTUNIUM, being the next planet beyond Neptune]

pluvial /'plu:vɪəl/ *adj. & n.* ● *adj.* **1** of rain; rainy. **2** *Geol.* caused by rain. ● *n.* a period of prolonged rainfall. □ **pluvious** *adj.* (in sense 1). [Latin *pluvialis* from *pluvia* 'rain']

pluviometer /plu:vɪ'ɒmɪtə/ *n.* a rain gauge. □ **pluviometric** /-ə'mɛtrɪk/ *adj.* **pluviometrical** /-ə'mɛtrɪk(ə)l/ *adj.* **pluviometrically** /-ə'mɛtrɪk(ə)li/ *adv.* [Latin *pluvia* 'rain' + -METER]

ply[1] /plʌɪ/ *n.* (*pl.* **-ies**) **1** a thickness or layer of certain materials, esp. wood or cloth (*three-ply*). **2** a strand of yarn or rope etc. [Middle English via French *pli*, from *plier*, *pleier*, from Latin *plicare* 'to fold']

ply[2] /plʌɪ/ *v.* (**-ies**, **-ied**) **1** *tr.* use or wield vigorously (a tool, weapon, etc.). **2** *tr.* work steadily at (one's business or trade). **3** *tr.* (foll. by *with*) **a** supply (a person) continuously (with food, drink, etc.). **b** approach repeatedly (with questions, demands, etc.). **4 a** *intr.* (often foll. by *between*) (of a vehicle etc.) travel regularly (to and fro between two points). **b** *tr.* work (a route) in this way. **5** *intr.* (of a taxi driver, boatman, etc.) attend regularly for custom (*ply for trade*). **6** *intr. Naut.* sail to windward. [Middle English *plye*, from APPLY]

Plymouth Brethren /ˈplɪməθ/ *n.pl.* a strict Calvinistic religious body formed at Plymouth in Devon *c.*1830, having no formal creed and no official order of ministers.

plywood /ˈplʌɪwʊd/ *n.* a strong thin board consisting of two or more layers glued and pressed together with the direction of the grain alternating.

PM *abbr.* **1** Prime Minister. **2** post-mortem. **3** Provost Marshal.

Pm *symb. Chem.* the element promethium.

p.m. *abbr.* after noon. [Latin *post meridiem*]

PMG *abbr.* **1** Paymaster General. **2** Postmaster General.

PMS *abbr. Med.* premenstrual syndrome.

PMT *abbr.* esp. *Brit.* premenstrual tension.

PNdB *abbr.* perceived noise decibel(s).

pneumatic /njuːˈmatɪk/ *adj.* **1** of or relating to air or wind. **2** containing or operated by compressed air. **3** connected with or containing air cavities esp. in the bones of birds or in fish. □ **pneumatically** *adv.* **pneumaticity** /njuːməˈtɪsɪti/ *n.* [French *pneumatique* or Latin *pneumaticus* from Greek *pneumatikos*, via *pneuma* 'wind' from *pneō* 'breathe']

pneumatic drill *n.* a drill driven by compressed air, for breaking up a hard surface.

pneumatics /njuːˈmatɪks/ *n.* the science of the mechanical properties of gases.

pneumatic trough *n.* a shallow container used in laboratories to collect gases in jars over the surface of water or mercury.

pneumato- /ˈnjuːmətəʊ/ *comb. form* denoting: **1** air. **2** breath. **3** spirit. [Greek from *pneuma* (as PNEUMATIC)]

pneumatology /njuːməˈtɒlədʒi/ *n.* **1** the branch of theology concerned with the Holy Ghost and other spiritual concepts. **2** *archaic* psychology. □ **pneumatological** /-təˈlɒdʒɪk(ə)l/ *adj.*

pneumatophore /ˈnjuːmətəfɔː/ *n.* **1** the air-filled float of some colonial hydrozoa, e.g. the Portuguese man-of-war. **2** an aerial root specialized for gaseous exchange found in various swamp plants, e.g. mangroves.

pneumo- /ˈnjuːməʊ/ *comb. form* denoting the lungs. [abbreviation of *pneumono-* from Greek *pneumōn* 'lung']

pneumococcus /njuːmə(ʊ)ˈkɒkəs/ *n.* (*pl.* **pneumococci** /-ˈkɒk(s)ʌɪ, -ˈkɒk(s)iː/) *Med.* a paired bacterium, *Streptococcus pneumoniae*, associated with pneumonia and sometimes meningitis.

pneumoconiosis /ˌnjuːmə(ʊ)kəʊnɪˈəʊsɪs/ *n.* a lung disease caused by inhalation of dust or small particles. [PNEUMO- + Greek *konis* 'dust']

pneumocystis carinii pneumonia /njuːmə(ʊ)ˌsɪstɪs kəˈrʌmɪʌɪ/ *n.* = PCP 2.

pneumogastric /njuːməʊˈgastrɪk/ *adj.* of or relating to the lungs and stomach.

pneumonectomy /njuːmə(ʊ)ˈnɛktəmi/ *n.* (*pl.* **-ies**) the surgical removal of a lung or part of a lung.

pneumonia /njuːˈməʊnɪə/ *n.* a bacterial inflammation of one lung (**single pneumonia**) or both lungs (**double pneumonia**) causing the air sacs to fill with pus and become solid. □ **pneumonic** /njuːˈmɒnɪk/ *adj.* [Latin from Greek, from *pneumōn* 'lung']

pneumonic plague see PLAGUE *n.* 1a.

pneumonitis /njuːməˈnʌɪtɪs/ *n.* inflammation of the lungs usu. caused by a virus.

pneumothorax /njuːməʊˈθɔːraks/ *n.* the presence of air or gas in the cavity between the lungs and the chest wall.

PNG *abbr.* Papua New Guinea.

PO *abbr.* **1** Post Office. **2** postal order. **3** Petty Officer. **4** Pilot Officer.

Po *symb. Chem.* the element polonium.

po /pəʊ/ *n.* (*pl.* **pos**) *Brit. colloq.* a chamber pot.

POA *abbr.* (in the UK) Prison Officers' Association.

poach[1] /pəʊtʃ/ *v.tr.* **1** cook (an egg) without its shell in or over boiling water. **2** cook (fish etc.) by simmering in a small amount of liquid. □ **poacher** *n.* [Middle English from Old French *pochier* (originally = enclose in a bag), from *poche* POKE[2]]

poach[2] /pəʊtʃ/ *v.* **1** *tr.* (also *absol.*) catch (game or fish) illegally. **2** *intr.* (often foll. by *on*) trespass or encroach (on another's property, ideas, etc.). **3** *tr.* appropriate illicitly or unfairly (a person, thing, idea, etc.). **4** *tr. Tennis* etc. take (a shot) in one's partner's portion of the court. **5 a** *tr.* trample or cut up (turf) with hoofs. **b** *intr.* (of land) become sodden by being trampled. □ **poacher** *n.* [earlier *poche*, perhaps from French *pocher* 'put in a pocket' (as POACH[1])]

pochard /ˈpəʊtʃəd, ˈpɒ-, -kəd/ *n.* (*pl.* same or **pochards**) any duck of the genus *Aythya*, esp. *A. ferina*, the male of which has a bright reddish-brown head and neck and a grey breast. [16th c.: origin unknown]

pochette /pɒˈʃɛt/ *n.* a woman's envelope-shaped handbag. [French, diminutive of *poche* 'pocket': see POKE[2]]

pock /pɒk/ *n.* = POCKMARK. □ **pocked** *adj.* **pocky** *adj.* [Old English *poc*, from Germanic]

pocket /ˈpɒkɪt/ *n.* & *v.* ● *n.* **1** a small bag sewn into or on clothing, for carrying small articles. **2** a pouchlike compartment in a suitcase, car door, etc. **3** one's financial resources (*it is beyond my pocket*). **4** an isolated group or area (*a few pockets of resistance remain*). **5** a cavity in a rock or stratum, usu. filled with ore (esp. gold) or water. **6** a pouch at the corner or on the side of a billiard or snooker table into which balls are driven. **7** = AIR POCKET 2. **8** (*attrib.*) **a** of a suitable size and shape for carrying in a pocket. **b** smaller than the usual size. ● *v.tr.* (**pocketed**, **pocketing**) **1** put into one's pocket. **2** appropriate, esp. dishonestly. **3** confine as in a pocket. **4** submit to (an injury or affront). **5** conceal or suppress (one's feelings). **6** *Billiards* etc. drive (a ball) into a pocket. □ **in pocket 1** having gained in a transaction. **2** (of money) available. **in a person's pocket 1** under a person's control. **2** close to or intimate with a person. **out of pocket** having lost in a transaction. **put one's hand in one's pocket** spend or provide money. □ **pocketable** *adj.* **pocketless** *adj.* **pockety** *adj.* (in sense 5 of *n.*). [Middle English from Anglo-French *poket(e)*, diminutive of *poke* POKE[2]]

pocket battleship *n. hist.* a warship armoured and equipped like, but smaller than, a battleship.

pocketbook /ˈpɒkɪtbʊk/ *n.* **1** a notebook. **2** a booklike case for papers or money carried in a pocket. **3** *US* a purse or handbag. **4** *N. Amer.* a paperback or other small book.

pocket borough *n. Brit. hist.* a borough in which the election of political representatives was controlled by one person or family.

pocketful /ˈpɒkɪtfʊl/ *n.* (*pl.* **-fuls**) as much as a pocket will hold.

pocket gopher *n.* = GOPHER[1] 1.

pocket knife *n.* a knife with a folding blade or blades, for carrying in the pocket.

pocket money *n.* **1** money for minor expenses. **2** *Brit.* an allowance of money made to a child.

pockmark /ˈpɒkmɑːk/*n.* **1** a small pus-filled spot on the skin, esp. caused by chickenpox or smallpox. **2** a mark resembling this. □ **pock-marked** *adj.*

poco /ˈpəʊkəʊ/ *adv. Mus.* a little; rather (*poco adagio*). [Italian]

pod[1] /pɒd/ *n.* & *v.* ● *n.* **1** a long seed vessel esp. of a leguminous plant, e.g. a pea. **2** the cocoon of a silkworm. **3** the case surrounding locust eggs. **4** a narrow-necked eel-net. **5** a compartment suspended under an aircraft for equipment etc. ● *v.* (**podded, podding**) **1** *intr.* bear or form pods. **2** *tr.* remove (peas etc.) from pods. □ **in pod** *colloq.* pregnant. [back-formation from dialect *podware, podder* 'field crops', of unknown origin]

pod[2] /pɒd/ *n.* a small herd or school of marine animals, esp. whales. [19th c., originally US: origin unknown]

podagra /pə'dagrə, 'pɒdəgrə/ *n. Med.* gout of the foot, esp. the big toe. □ **podagral** *adj.* **podagric** *adj.* **podagrous** *adj.* [Latin, from Greek *pous podos* 'foot' + *agra* 'seizure']

podgy /'pɒdʒi/ *adj.* (**podgier, podgiest**) *Brit.* **1** (of a person) short and fat. **2** (of a face etc.) plump, fleshy. □ **podginess** *n.* [19th c.: from *podge* 'a short fat person', of unknown origin]

podiatry /pə(ʊ)'dʌɪətri/ *n.* = CHIROPODY. □ **podiatrist** *n.* [Greek *pous podos* 'foot' + *iatros* 'physician']

podium /'pəʊdɪəm/ *n.* (*pl.* **podiums** or **podia** /-dɪə/) **1** a continuous projecting base or pedestal round a room or house etc. **2** a raised platform round the arena of an amphitheatre. **3** a platform or rostrum. [Latin from Greek *podion*, diminutive of *pous pod-* 'foot']

podzol /'pɒdzɒl/ *n.* (also **podsol** /-sɒl/) an infertile acidic soil with minerals leached from its surface layers into a lower stratum. □ **podzolize** *v.tr. & intr.* (also **-ise**). [Russian, from *pod* 'under', *zola* 'ashes']

poem /'pəʊɪm/ *n.* **1** a metrical composition, usu. concerned with feeling or imaginative description. **2** an elevated composition in verse or prose. **3** something with poetic qualities (*a poem in stone*). [French *poème* or Latin *poema* from Greek *pōēma* = *poiēma*, from *poieō* 'make']

poesy /'pəʊɪzi, -si/ *n. archaic* **1** poetry. **2** the art or composition of poetry. [Middle English from Old French *poesie*, ultimately via Latin *poesis* from Greek *poēsis* = *poiēsis* 'making, poetry' (as POEM)]

poet /'pəʊɪt/ *n.* (*fem.* **poetess** /-tɪs/) **1** a writer of poems. **2** a person possessing high powers of imagination or expression etc. [Middle English via Old French *poete* and Latin *poeta* from Greek *poētēs* = *poiētēs* 'maker, poet' (as POEM)]

poetaster /pəʊɪ'tastə/ *n.* a paltry or inferior poet. [modern Latin (as POET): see -ASTER]

poetic /pəʊ'ɛtɪk/ *adj.* (also **poetical** /-tɪk(ə)l/) **1 a** of or like poetry or poets. **b** written in verse. **2** elevated or sublime in expression. □ **poetically** *adv.* [French *poétique* via Latin *poeticus* from Greek *poētikos* (as POET)]

poeticize /pəʊ'ɛtɪsʌɪz/ *v.tr.* (also **-ise**) make (a theme) poetic.

poetic justice *n.* well-deserved unforeseen retribution or reward.

poetic licence *n.* a writer's or artist's transgression of established rules for effect.

poetics /pəʊ'ɛtɪks/ *n.* **1** the art of writing poetry. **2** the study of poetry and its techniques.

poetize /'pəʊɪtʌɪz/ *v.* (also **-ise**) **1** *intr.* play the poet. **2** *intr.* compose poetry. **3** *tr.* treat poetically. **4** *tr.* celebrate in poetry. [French *poétiser* (as POET)]

Poet Laureate *n.* (*pl.* **Poets Laureate**) (in the UK) a poet appointed to write poems for state occasions.

poetry /'pəʊɪtri/ *n.* **1** the art or work of a poet. **2** poems collectively. **3** a poetic or tenderly pleasing quality. **4** anything likened to poetry in respect of its beauty, soulfulness, etc. [Middle English via medieval Latin *poetria* from Latin *poeta* POET, probably on the pattern of *geometry*]

Poets' Corner *n.* part of Westminster Abbey where several poets are buried or commemorated.

po-faced /pəʊ'feɪst/ *adj. Brit.* **1** solemn-faced, humourless. **2** smug. [20th c.: perhaps from PO, influenced by *poker-faced*]

pogo /'pəʊgəʊ/ *n.* (*pl.* **-os**) (also **pogo stick**) a toy consisting of a spring-loaded stick with rests for the feet, for springing about on. [20th c.: origin uncertain]

pogrom /'pɒgrəm, -grɒm, pə'grɒm/ *n.* an organized massacre (originally of Jews in Russia). [Russian, = devastation, from *gromit'* 'destroy']

poignant /'pɔɪnjənt/ *adj.* **1** painfully sharp to the emotions or senses; deeply moving. **2** arousing sympathy. **3** sharp or pungent in taste or smell. **4** pleasantly piquant. □ **poignance** *n.* **poignancy** *n.* **poignantly** *adv.* [Middle English from Old French, pres. part. of *poindre* 'prick', from Latin *pungere*]

poikilotherm /'pɔɪkɪlə,θəːm/ *n.* an organism that regulates its body temperature by behavioural means, such as basking or burrowing; a cold-blooded organism (cf. HOMEOTHERM). □ **poikilothermal** /-'θəːm(ə)l/ *adj.* **poikilothermia** /-'θəːmɪə/ *n.* **poikilothermic** /-'θəːmɪk/ *adj.* **poikilothermy** *n.* [Greek *poikilos* 'multicoloured, changeable' + *thermē* 'heat']

poilu /pwɑː'luː, French pwaly/ *n. hist.* a French private soldier, esp. as a nickname. [French, literally 'hairy' from *poil* 'hair']

poinciana /pɔɪnsɪ'ɑːnə/ *n.* any tropical tree of the former genus *Poinciana* (now *Caesalpinia* or *Delonix*), with bright showy red flowers. [modern Latin, from the name of M. de *Poinci*, 17th-c. governor in the West Indies + fem. suffix *-ana*]

poind /pɔɪnd, pɪnd/ *v. & n. Sc.* ● *v.tr.* distrain upon; impound. ● *n.* **1** an act of poinding. **2** an animal or chattel poinded. [Middle English from Old English *pyndan* 'impound']

poinsettia /pɔɪn'sɛtɪə/ *n.* a shrub, *Euphorbia pulcherrima*, with large showy scarlet or pink bracts surrounding small yellow flowers. [modern Latin, named after J. R. *Poinsett*, American diplomat d. 1851]

point /pɔɪnt/ *n. & v.* ● *n.* **1** the sharp or tapered end of a tool, weapon, pencil, etc. **2** a tip or extreme end. **3** that which in geometry has position but not magnitude, e.g. the intersection of two lines. **4** a particular place or position (*Bombay and points east*; *point of contact*). **5 a** a precise or particular moment (*at the point of death*). **b** the critical or decisive moment (*when it came to the point, he refused*). **6** a very small mark on a surface. **7 a** a dot or other punctuation mark, esp. = FULL STOP 1. **b** a dot or small stroke used in Semitic languages to indicate vowels or distinguish consonants. **8** = DECIMAL POINT. **9** a stage or degree in progress or increase (*abrupt to the point of rudeness*; *at that point we gave up*). **10** a level of temperature at which a change of state occurs (*freezing point*). **11** a single item; a detail or particular (*we differ on these points*). **12 a** a unit of scoring in games or of measuring value etc. **b** an advantage or success in less quantifiable contexts such as an argument or discussion. **c** a unit of weight (2 mg) for diamonds. **d** a unit (of varying value) in quoting the price of stocks etc. **13 a** (usu. prec. by *the*) the significant or essential thing; what is actually intended or under discussion (*that was the point of the question*). **b** (usu. with *neg.* or *interrog.*; often foll. by *in*) sense or purpose; advantage or value (*saw no point in staying*). **c** (usu. prec. by *the*) a salient feature of a story, joke, remark, etc. (*don't see the point*). **14** a distinctive feature or characteristic (*it has its points*; *tact is not his good point*). **15** pungency, effectiveness (*their comments lacked point*). **16 a** each of 32 directions marked at equal distances round a compass. **b** the corresponding direction towards the horizon. **17** (usu. in *pl.*) *Brit.* a junction of two railway lines, with a pair of linked tapering rails that can be moved laterally to allow a train to pass from one line to the other. **18** *Brit.* = POWER POINT. **19** (in *pl.*) the pair of electrical contacts acting as a circuit breaker in the ignition system of an internal combustion engine. **20** *Cricket* **a** a fielder on the off side near the batsman. **b** this position. **21** the tip of the toe in ballet. **22** a promontory. **23** the prong of a deer's antler. **24** (usu. in *pl.*) the extremities of a dog, horse, etc. **25** *Printing* a unit of measurement for type bodies (in the UK and US 0.351 mm, in Europe 0.376 mm). **26** *Hunting* **a** a spot to which a straight run is made. **b** such a run. **27** *Heraldry* any of nine particular positions on a shield used for specifying the position of charges etc. **28** an area of contrasting colour in the fur of certain cats. **29** *Boxing* the tip of the chin as a spot for a knockout blow. **30** *Mil.* a small leading party of an advanced guard. **31** *hist.* a tagged lace for lacing a bodice, attaching a hose to a doublet, etc. **32** *Naut.* a short piece of cord at the lower edge of a sail for tying up a reef. **33** the act or position of a dog in pointing. ● *v.* **1** (usu. foll. by *to, at*) **a** *tr.* direct or aim (a finger, weapon, etc.). **b** *intr.* direct attention in a certain direction (*pointed to the house across the road*). **2** *intr.* (foll. by *at, towards*) **a** aim or be directed to. **b** tend towards. **3** *intr.* (foll. by *to*) indicate; be evidence of (*it all points to murder*). **4** *tr.* give point or force to (words or actions). **5** *tr.* fill in or repair the joints of (brickwork) with smoothly finished mortor or cement. **6** *tr.* **a** punctuate. **b** insert points in (written Hebrew etc.). **c** mark (Psalms etc.) with signs for chanting. **7** *tr.* sharpen (a pencil, tool, etc.). **8** *tr.* (also *absol.*) (of a dog) indicate the presence of (game) by acting as pointer. □ **at all points** in every part or respect. **at the point of** (often foll. by verbal noun) on the verge of; about to do (the action specified). **beside the point** irrelevant or irrelevantly. **case in point** an instance that is relevant or (prec. by *the*) under consideration. **have a point** be correct or effective in one's contention. **in point** apposite, relevant. **in point of fact** see FACT. **make** (or **prove) a** (or **one's) point** establish a proposition; prove one's contention. **make a point of** (often foll. by verbal noun) insist on; treat or regard as essential. **on** (or **upon) the point of** (foll. by verbal noun) about to do (the action specified). **point out** (often foll. by *that* + clause) indicate, show; draw attention to. **point up** emphasize; show as important. **score points off** get the better of in an argument etc. **take a person's point** esp. *Brit.* concede that a person has made a valid contention. **to the point** relevant or relevantly. **up to a point** to some extent but not completely. **win on points** *Boxing* win by scoring more points, not by a knockout. [Middle English via Old French *point, pointer* from Latin *punctum*, from *pungere punct-* 'prick']

point-blank *adj. & adv.* ● *adj.* **1 a** (of a shot) aimed or fired horizontally at a range very close to the target. **b** (of a distance or range) very close. **2** (of a remark, question, etc.) blunt, direct. ● *adv.* **1** at very close range. **2** directly, bluntly. [probably from POINT + BLANK = white spot in the centre of a target]

point duty *n. Brit.* the duty of a police officer or traffic warden stationed at a crossroad or other point to control traffic.

pointed /ˈpɔɪntɪd/ *adj.* **1** sharpened or tapering to a point. **2** (of a remark etc.) having point; penetrating, cutting. **3** emphasized; made evident. □ **pointedly** *adv.* **pointedness** *n.*

pointer /ˈpɔɪntə/ *n.* **1** a thing that points, e.g. the index hand of a gauge etc. **2** a rod for pointing to features on a map, chart, etc. **3** *colloq.* a hint, clue, or indication. **4 a** a dog of a breed that on scenting game stands rigid looking towards it. **b** this breed. **5** (in *pl.*) two stars in Ursa Major in line with the pole star.

pointillism /ˈpwantɪlɪz(ə)m/ *n. Art* a technique of Impressionist painting using tiny dots of various pure colours, which become blended in the viewer's eye. □ **pointillist** *n. & adj.* **pointillistic** /-ˈlɪstɪk/ *adj.* [French *pointillisme* from *pointiller* 'mark with dots']

pointing /ˈpɔɪntɪŋ/ *n.* **1** cement or mortar filling the joints of brickwork. **2** facing produced by this. **3** the process of producing this.

point lace *n.* thread lace made wholly with a needle.

pointless /ˈpɔɪntlɪs/ *adj.* **1** without a point. **2** lacking force, purpose, or meaning. **3** (in games) without a point scored. □ **pointlessly** *adv.* **pointlessness** *n.*

point of honour *n.* an action or circumstance that affects one's reputation or conscience.

point of no return *n.* a point in a journey or enterprise at which it becomes essential or more practical to continue to the end.

point of order *n.* a query in a debate etc. as to whether correct procedure is being followed.

point of sale *n.* (hyphenated when *attrib.*) the place at which goods are retailed.

point of view *n.* **1** a position from which a thing is viewed. **2** a particular way of considering a matter.

pointsman /ˈpɔɪntsmən/ *n.* (*pl.* **-men**) *Brit.* **1** a person in charge of railway points. **2** a police officer or traffic warden on point duty.

point-to-point *n.* a steeplechase over a marked course for horses used regularly in hunting. □ **point-to-pointer** *n.* **point-to-pointing** *n.*

pointy /ˈpɔɪnti/ *adj.* (**pointier**, **pointiest**) having a noticeably sharp end; pointed.

poise[1] /pɔɪz/ *n. & v.* ● *n.* **1** composure or self-possession of manner. **2** equilibrium; a stable state. **3** carriage (of the head etc.). ● *v.* **1** *tr.* balance; hold suspended or supported. **2** *tr.* carry (one's head etc. in a specified way). **3** *intr.* be balanced; hover in the air etc. [Middle English from Old French *pois, peis, peser*, ultimately via Latin *pensum* 'weight' from *pendere pens-* 'weigh']

poise[2] /pɔɪz/ *n. Physics* a unit of dynamic viscosity, such that a tangential force of one dyne per square centimetre causes a velocity change one centimetre per second between two parallel planes separated by one centimetre in a liquid. [named after J. L. M. *Poiseuille*, French physician d. 1869]

poised /pɔɪzd/ *adj.* **1** composed, self-assured. **2** (often foll. by *for*, or *to* + infin.) ready for action.

poison /ˈpɔɪz(ə)n/ *n. & v.* ● *n.* **1** a substance that when introduced into or absorbed by a living organism causes death or injury, esp. one that kills by rapid action even in a small quantity. **2** a harmful influence or principle etc. **3** *Physics & Chem.* a substance that interferes with the normal progress of a nuclear reaction, chain reaction, catalytic reaction, etc. ● *v.tr.* **1** administer poison to (a person or animal). **2** kill or injure or infect with poison. **3** infect (air, water, etc.) with poison. **4** (esp. as **poisoned** *adj.*) treat (a weapon) with poison. **5** corrupt or pervert (a person or mind). **6** spoil or destroy (a person's pleasure etc.). **7** render (land etc.) foul and unfit for its purpose by a noxious application etc. □ **poisoner** *n.* **poisonous** *adj.* **poisonously** *adv.* [Middle English from Old French *poison, poisonner* (as POTION)]

poisoned chalice *n.* an assignment, award, honour, etc. which is likely to prove a disadvantage or source of problems to the recipient.

poison gas *n.* = GAS *n.* 4.

poison ivy *n.* a N. American climbing plant, *Rhus radicans*, secreting an irritant oil from its leaves.

poison oak *n.* either of two N. American shrubs, *Rhus toxicodendron* and *R. diversilobia*, related to poison ivy and having similar properties.

poison pen letter *n.* an anonymous libellous or abusive letter.

poison pill *n.* **1** a pill containing esp. fast-acting poison. **2** *Finance* any of various ploys used by a company threatened with an unwelcome takeover bid to make itself unattractive to the bidder.

Poisson distribution /ˈpwasɒn/ *n. Statistics* a discrete frequency distribution which gives the probability of events occurring in a fixed time. [named after S. D. *Poisson*, French mathematician d. 1840]

poke[1] /pəʊk/ *v. & n.* ● *v.* **1** (foll. by *in, up, down*, etc.) **a** *tr.* thrust or push with the hand, point of a stick, etc. **b** *intr.* be thrust forward. **2** *intr.* (foll. by *at* etc.) make thrusts with a stick etc. **3** *tr.* thrust the end of a finger etc. against. **4** *tr.* (foll. by *in*) produce (a hole etc. in a thing) by poking. **5** *tr.* thrust forward, esp. obtrusively. **6** *tr.* stir (a fire) with a poker. **7** *intr.* **a** (often foll. by *about, around*) move or act desultorily; potter. **b** (foll. by *about, into*) pry; search casually. **8** *tr. coarse slang* have sexual intercourse with. **9** *tr.* (foll. by *up*) *colloq.* confine (esp. oneself) in a poky place. ● *n.* **1** the act or an instance of poking. **2** a thrust or nudge. **3** a device fastened on cattle etc. to prevent them breaking through fences. **4 a** a projecting brim or front of a woman's bonnet or hat. **b** (in full **poke-bonnet**) a bonnet having this. □ **poke fun at** ridicule, tease. **poke one's nose into** *colloq.* pry or intrude into (esp. a person's affairs). [Middle English from Middle Dutch and Middle Low German *poken*, of unknown origin]

poke[2] /pəʊk/ *n. dial.* a bag or sack. □ **buy a pig in a poke** see PIG. [Middle English from Old Northern French *poke, poque* = Old French *poche*: cf. POUCH]

poker[1] /ˈpəʊkə/ *n.* a metal rod with a handle, for stirring an open fire.

poker[2] /ˈpəʊkə/ *n.* a card game in which bluff is used as players bet on the value of their hands. [19th c.: origin unknown: cf. German *pochen* 'to brag', *Pochspiel* 'bragging game']

poker dice *n.* dice with card designs from nine to ace instead of spots.

poker-face *n.* **1** the impassive countenance appropriate to a poker player. **2** a person with this. □ **poker-faced** *adj.*

pokerwork /ˈpəʊkəwəːk/ *n. Brit.* **1** the technique of burning designs on white wood etc. with a heated metal rod. **2** a design made in this way.

pokeweed /ˈpəʊkwiːd/ *n.* a tall hardy American plant, *Phytolacca americana*, with spikes of cream flowers and purple berries that yield emetics and purgatives. [Algonquian *poke* + WEED]

pokey /ˈpəʊki/ *n.* (usu. prec. by *the*) esp. *US slang* prison. [perhaps from POKY]

poky /ˈpəʊki/ *adj.* (**pokier, pokiest**) **1** (of a room etc.) small and cramped. **2** *US* annoyingly slow. □ **pokily** *adv.* **pokiness** *n.* [POKE[1] (in colloq. sense 'confine') + -Y[1]]

polack /ˈpəʊlak/ *n. N. Amer. slang offens.* a person of Polish origin. [French *Polaque* and German *Polack* from Polish *Polak*]

polar /ˈpəʊlə/ *adj.* **1 a** of or near a pole of the earth or a celestial body, or of the celestial sphere. **b** (of a species or variety) living in the north polar region. **2** having magnetic polarity. **3 a** (of a molecule) having a positive charge at one end and a negative charge at the other. **b** (of a compound) having electric charges. **4** *Geom.* of or relating to a pole. **5** directly opposite in character or tendency. □ **polarly** *adv.* [French *polaire* or modern Latin *polaris* (in medieval Latin = heavenly): see POLE[2]]

polar bear *n.* a white bear, *Thalarctos maritimus*, of the Arctic regions.

polar body *n.* a small cell produced from an oocyte during the formation of an ovum, which does not develop further.

polar coordinate *n.* either of a pair of coordinates describing the position of a point in a plane, the first being the length of the straight line connecting the point to the origin, and the second the angle made by this line with a fixed line.

polar curve *n.* a curve related in a particular way to a given curve and to a fixed point called a pole.

polar distance *n.* the angular distance of a point on a sphere from the nearest pole.

polari- /ˈpəʊləri/ *comb. form* polar. [modern Latin *polaris* (as POLE[2])]

polarimeter /pəʊləˈrɪmɪtə/ *n.* an instrument used to measure the polarization of light or the effect of a substance on the rotation of the plane of polarized light. □ **polarimetric** /-ˈmɛtrɪk/ *adj.* **polarimetry** *n.*

Polaris /pə(ʊ)ˈlɑːrɪs/ *n.* **1** = POLE STAR 1. **2** a type of submarine-launched ballistic missile. [medieval Latin: see POLAR]

polariscope /pə(ʊ)ˈlarɪskəʊp/ *n.* = POLARIMETER. □ **polariscopic** /-ˈskɒpɪk/ *adj.*

polarity /pə(ʊ)ˈlarɪti/ *n.* (*pl.* **-ies**) **1** the tendency of a lodestone, magnetized bar, etc., to point with its extremities to the magnetic poles of the earth. **2** the condition of having two poles with contrary qualities. **3** the state of having two opposite tendencies, opinions, etc. **4** the electrical condition of a body (positive or negative). **5** a magnetic attraction towards an object or person.

polarize /ˈpəʊlərʌɪz/ *v.* (also **-ise**) **1** *tr.* restrict the vibrations of (a transverse wave, esp. light) to one direction. **2** *tr.* give magnetic or electric polarity to (a substance or body). **3** *tr.* reduce the voltage of (an electric cell) by the action of electrolysis products. **4** *tr. & intr.* divide into two groups of opposing opinion etc. □ **polarizable** *adj.* **polarization** /-ˈzeɪʃ(ə)n/ *n.* **polarizer** *n.*

polarography /pəʊləˈrɒgrəfi/ *n. Chem.* chemical analysis of a substance by electrolysing it at successively higher voltages and measuring the resulting current. □ **polarographic** /-əˈgrafɪk/ *adj.*

Polaroid /ˈpəʊlərɔɪd/ *n. propr.* **1** material in thin plastic sheets that produces a high degree of plane polarization in light passing through it. **2 a** a type of camera with internal processing that produces a finished print rapidly after each exposure. **b** a photograph taken with such a camera. **3** (in *pl.*) sunglasses with lenses made from Polaroid. [POLARI- + -OID]

polar star *n.* = POLE STAR.

polder /ˈpəʊldə/ *n.* a piece of low-lying land reclaimed from the sea or a river, esp. in the Netherlands. [Middle Dutch *polre*, Dutch *polder*]

Pole /pəʊl/ *n.* **1** a native or national of Poland. **2** a person of Polish descent. [German from Polish *Polanie*, literally 'field-dwellers', from *pole* 'field']

pole[1] /pəʊl/ *n. & v.* ● *n.* **1** a long slender rounded piece of wood or metal, esp. with the end placed in the ground as a support etc. **2** a wooden shaft fitted to the front of a vehicle and attached to the yokes or collars of the draught animals. **3** *Athletics* a long slender flexible rod of wood, fibreglass, etc. used by a competitor in pole-vaulting. **4** esp. *US* a simple fishing rod. **5** *hist.* = PERCH[1] 3. ● *v.tr.* **1** provide with a pole or poles. **2** (usu. foll. by *off*) push off (a punt etc.) with a pole. □ **under bare poles** *Naut.* with no sail set. **up the pole** *Brit. slang* **1** crazy, eccentric. **2** in difficulty. [Old English *pāl*, ultimately from Latin *palus* 'stake']

pole[2] /pəʊl/ *n.* **1** (in full **north pole, south pole**) **a** each of the two points in the celestial sphere about which the stars appear to revolve. **b** each of the extremities of the axis of rotation of the earth or another body. **c** see MAGNETIC POLE. **2** each of the two opposite points on the surface of a magnet at which magnetic forces are strongest. **3** each of two terminals (positive and negative) of an electric cell or battery etc. **4** each of two opposed principles or ideas. **5** *Geom.* each of two points in which the axis of a circle cuts the surface of a sphere. **6** *Geom.* a fixed point to which others are referred. **7** *Biol.* an extremity of the main axis of any spherical or oval organ. □ **be poles apart** differ greatly, esp. in nature or opinion. □ **poleward** *adj.* **polewards** *adj. & adv.* [Middle English via Latin *polus* from Greek *polos* 'pivot, axis, sky']

■ **Usage** In sense 1, the spelling is *North Pole* and *South Pole* (capitals) when used as geographical designations.

pole-axe /ˈpəʊlaks/ *n. & v.* (*US* **poleax**) ● *n.* **1** *hist.* = BATTLEAXE 1. **2** a butcher's axe. ● *v.tr.* hit or kill with or as if with a pole-axe. [Middle English *pol(l)ax, -ex* from Middle Dutch *pol(l)aex*, Middle Low German *pol(l)exe* (as POLL[1], AXE)]

polecat /ˈpəʊlkat/ *n.* **1** *Brit.* a small European brownish-black fetid flesh-eating mammal, *Mustela putorius*, of the weasel family. **2** *US* a skunk. [*pole* (unexplained) + CAT[1]]

polemic /pəˈlɛmɪk/ *n. & adj.* ● *n.* **1** (also in *pl.*) a controversial discussion. **2** *Polit.* a verbal or written attack, esp. on a political opponent. **3** (in *pl.*; also treated as *sing.*) the art of controversial discussion, esp. in theology. ● *adj.* (also **polemical**) involving dispute; controversial. □ **polemically** *adv.* **polemicist** /-sɪst/ *n.* **polemicize** *v.intr.* (also **-ise**). **polemize** /ˈpɒlɪmʌɪz/

v.intr. (also **-ise**). [medieval Latin *polemicus* from Greek *polemikos*, from *polemos* 'war']

polenta /pə(ʊ)'lɛntə/ *n.* porridge made of maize meal etc. [Italian from Latin, = pearl barley]

pole position *n.* the most favourable position at the start of a motor race (originally next to the inside boundary fence).

pole star *n.* **1** *Astron.* a star in Ursa Minor now about 1° distant from the celestial North Pole. **2 a** a thing or principle serving as a guide. **b** a centre of attraction.

pole vault *n. & v.* ● *n.* the athletic sport of vaulting over a high bar with the aid of a long flexible pole held in the hands and giving extra spring. ● *v.intr.* (**pole-vault**) take part in this sport. □ **pole-vaulter** *n.*

police /pə'li:s/ *n. & v.* ● *n.* **1** (usu. prec. by *the*; usu. treated as *pl.*) the civil force of a state, responsible for maintaining public order. **2** (treated as *pl.*) the members of a police force (*several hundred police*). **3** (usu. treated as *pl.*) a force with similar functions of enforcing regulations (*military police*; *railway police*). ● *v.tr.* **1** control (a country or area) by means of police. **2** provide with police. **3** keep order in; control; monitor. [French from medieval Latin *politia* POLICY[1]]

police constable see CONSTABLE.

police dog *n.* a dog, esp. an Alsatian, used in police work.

police force *n.* the body of police of a country, district, or town.

police informer *n.* a person who gives police information about crimes and offenders.

policeman /pə'li:smən/ *n.* (*pl.* **-men**) a male member of a police force.

police officer *n.* a policeman or policewoman.

police state *n.* a totalitarian state controlled by political police supervising the citizens' activities.

police station *n.* the office of a local police force.

policewoman /pə'li:swʊmən/ *n.* (*pl.* **-women**) a female member of a police force.

policy[1] /'pɒlɪsi/ *n.* (*pl.* **-ies**) **1** a course or principle of action adopted or proposed by a government, party, business, or individual etc. **2** prudent conduct; sagacity. [Middle English via Old French *policie* and Latin *politia* from Greek *politeia* 'citizenship', via *politēs* 'citizen' from *polis* 'city']

■ **Usage** See Usage Note at POLITY.

policy[2] /'pɒlɪsi/ *n.* (*pl.* **-ies**) **1** a contract of insurance. **2** a document containing this. [French *police* 'bill of lading, contract of insurance' from Provençal *poliss(i)a*, probably from medieval Latin *apodissa*, *apodixa* via Latin *apodixis* from Greek *apodeixis* 'evidence, proof' (as APO-, *deiknumi* 'show')]

policyholder /'pɒlɪsɪ,həʊldə/ *n.* a person or body holding an insurance policy.

polio /'pəʊlɪəʊ/ *n.* = POLIOMYELITIS. [abbreviation]

poliomyelitis /,pəʊlɪəʊmʌɪə'lʌɪtɪs, ,pɒlɪəʊ-/ *n. Med.* an infectious viral disease that affects the central nervous system and which can cause temporary or permanent paralysis. [modern Latin, from Greek *polios* 'grey' + *muelos* 'marrow']

Polish /'pəʊlɪʃ/ *adj. & n.* ● *adj.* **1** of or relating to Poland. **2** of the Poles or their language. ● *n.* the language of Poland.

polish /'pɒlɪʃ/ *v. & n.* ● *v.* **1** *tr. & intr.* make or become smooth or glossy by rubbing. **2** *tr.* (esp. as **polished** *adj.*) refine or improve; add finishing touches to. ● *n.* **1** a substance used for polishing. **2** smoothness or glossiness produced by friction. **3** the act or an instance of polishing. **4** refinement or elegance of manner, conduct, etc. □ **polish off** finish (esp. food) quickly. **polish up** revise or improve (a skill etc.). □ **polishable** *adj.* **polisher** *n.* [Middle English via Old French *polir* from Latin *polire polit-*]

Polish notation *n. Math.* a system of formula notation without brackets and punctuation.

politburo /'pɒlɪt,bjʊərəʊ/ *n.* (*pl.* **-os**) the principal policy-making committee of a Communist party, esp. in the former USSR. [Russian *politbyuro* from *politícheskoe byuró* 'political bureau']

polite /pə'lʌɪt/ *adj.* (**politer**, **politest**) **1** having good manners; courteous. **2** cultivated, cultured. **3** refined, elegant (*polite letters*). □ **politely** *adv.* **politeness** *n.* [Latin *politus* (as POLISH)]

politesse /pɒlɪ'tɛs/ *n.* formal politeness. [French from Italian *politezza*, *pulitezza*, from *pulito* 'polite']

politic /'pɒlɪtɪk/ *adj. & v.* ● *adj.* **1** (of an action) judicious, expedient. **2** (of a person) prudent, sagacious. **3** political (now only in *body politic*). ● *v.intr.* (**politicked**, **politicking**) engage in politics. □ **politicly** *adv.* [Middle English via Old French *politique* and Latin *politicus* from Greek *politikos*, via *politēs* 'citizen' from *polis* 'city']

political /pə'lɪtɪk(ə)l/ *adj.* **1 a** of or concerning the state or its government, or public affairs generally. **b** of, relating to, or engaged in politics. **c** belonging to or forming part of a civil administration. **2** having an organized form of society or government. **3** taking or belonging to a side in politics or in controversial matters. **4** relating to or affecting interests of status or authority in an organization rather than matters of principle (*a political decision*). □ **politically** *adv.* [Latin *politicus* (as POLITIC)]

political asylum *n.* protection given by a state to a political refugee from another country.

political correctness *n.* the avoidance of forms of expression or action that exclude, marginalize, or insult certain racial or cultural groups.

political economist *n.* a student of or expert in political economy.

political economy *n.* the study of the economic aspects of government.

political geography *n.* that dealing with boundaries and the possessions of states.

politically correct *adj.* (also **politically incorrect**) exhibiting (or failing to exhibit) political correctness.

political prisoner *n.* a person imprisoned for political beliefs or actions.

political science *n.* the study of the state and systems of government. □ **political scientist** *n.*

politician /pɒlɪ'tɪʃ(ə)n/ *n.* **1** a person engaged in or concerned with politics, esp. as a practitioner. **2** esp. *Brit.* a person skilled in politics. **3** *US derog.* **a** a person with self-interested political concerns. **b** a person who strives for power by manipulation.

politicize /pə'lɪtɪsʌɪz/ *v.* (also **-ise**) **1** *tr.* **a** give a political character to. **b** make politically aware. **2** *intr.* engage in or talk politics. □ **politicization** /-'zeɪʃ(ə)n/ *n.*

politico /pə'lɪtɪkəʊ/ *n.* (*pl.* **-os**) *colloq.* a politician or political enthusiast. [Spanish or Italian (as POLITIC)]

politico- /pə'lɪtɪkəʊ/ *comb. form* **1** politically. **2** political and (*politico-social*). [Greek *politikos*: see POLITIC]

politics /'pɒlɪtɪks/ *n.pl.* **1** (treated as *sing.* or *pl.*) **a** the art and science of government. **b** public life and affairs as involving authority and government. **2** (usu. treated as *pl.*) **a** a particular set of ideas, principles, or commitments in politics (*what are their politics?*). **b** activities concerned with the acquisition or exercise of authority or government. **c** an organizational process or principle affecting authority, status, etc. (*the politics of the decision*).

polity /'pɒlɪti/ *n.* (*pl.* **-ies**) **1** a form or process of civil government or constitution. **2** an organized society; a state as a political entity. [Latin *politia* from Greek *politeia*, via *politēs* 'citizen' from *polis* 'city']

■ **Usage** This word is sometimes confused with *policy*. It means neither 'policy' nor 'politics'.

polka /'pɒlkə, 'pəʊlkə/ *n. & v.* ● *n.* **1** a lively dance of Bohemian origin in duple time. **2** the music for this. ● *v.intr.* (**polkas**, **polkaed** /-kəd/ or **polka'd**, **polkaing**

/-kəŋ/) dance the polka. [French and German from Czech *půlka* 'half-step', from *půl* 'half']

polka dot *n.* a round dot as one of many forming a regular pattern on a textile fabric etc.

poll[1] /pəʊl/ *n.* & *v.* ● *n.* **1 a** the process of voting at an election. **b** the counting of votes at an election. **c** the result of voting. **d** the number of votes recorded (*a heavy poll*). **e** (usu. in *pl.*) a place where votes are cast. **2** = GALLUP POLL. **3 a** *Sc.* & *dial.* a human head. **b** the part of this on which hair grows (*flaxen poll*). **4** a hornless animal, esp. one of a breed of hornless cattle. ● *v.* **1** *tr.* **a** take the vote or votes of. **b** (in *passive*) have one's vote taken. **c** (of a candidate) receive (so many votes). **d** give (a vote). **2** *tr.* record the opinion of (a person or group) in an opinion poll. **3** *intr.* give one's vote. **4** *tr.* cut off the top of (a tree or plant), esp. make a pollard of. **5** *tr.* (esp. as **polled** *adj.*) cut the horns off (cattle). **6** *tr. Computing* check the status of (a computer system) at intervals. □ **pollee** /pəʊ'li:/ *n.* (in sense 2 of *n.*). [Middle English, perhaps from Low German or Dutch]

poll[2] /pɒl/ *n.* a tame parrot (*Pretty poll!*). [*Poll*, a conventional name for a parrot, alteration of *Moll*, a familiar form of *Mary*]

pollack /'pɒlək/ *n.* (also **pollock**) (*pl.* same or **-s**) a European marine fish, *Pollachius pollachius*, with a characteristic protruding lower jaw, used for food. [earlier (Scots) *podlock*: origin unknown]

pollan /'pɒlən/ *n.* a form of freshwater whitefish found in Irish lakes. [perhaps from Irish *poll* 'deep water']

pollard /'pɒləd/ *n.* & *v.* ● *n.* **1** an animal that has lost or cast its horns; an ox, sheep, or goat of a hornless breed. **2** a tree whose branches have been cut off to encourage the growth of new young branches, esp. a riverside willow. **3 a** the bran sifted from flour. **b** a fine bran containing some flour. ● *v.tr.* make (a tree) a pollard. [POLL[1] + -ARD]

pollen /'pɒlən/ *n.* the fine dustlike grains discharged from the male part of a flower, each containing a gamete that can fertilize the female ovule. □ **pollenless** *adj.* [Latin *pollen pollinis* 'fine flour, dust']

pollen analysis *n.* = PALYNOLOGY.

pollen count *n.* an index of the amount of pollen in the air, published esp. for the benefit of those allergic to it.

pollex /'pɒlɛks/ *n.* (*pl.* **pollices** /-lɪsi:z/) the innermost digit of a forelimb, usu. the thumb in primates. [Latin, = thumb or big toe]

pollie var. of POLLY[2].

pollinate /'pɒlɪneɪt/ *v.tr.* (also *absol.*) sprinkle (a stigma) with pollen to fertilize the flower. □ **pollination** /-'neɪʃ(ə)n/ *n.* **pollinator** *n.*

polling /'pəʊlɪŋ/ *n.* the registering or casting of votes.

polling booth *n.* a compartment in which a voter stands to mark a ballot paper.

polling day *n.* the day of a local or general election.

polling station *n.* a building, often a school, where voting takes place during an election.

pollinic /pə'lɪnɪk/ *adj.* of or relating to pollen.

polliniferous /pɒlɪ'nɪf(ə)rəs/ *adj.* bearing or producing pollen.

polliwog /'pɒlɪwɒg/ *n.* (also **pollywog**) *US dial.* a tadpole. [earlier *polwigge*, *polwygle* from POLL[1] + WIGGLE]

pollock var. of POLLACK.

poll parrot *n.* a user of conventional or clichéd phrases and arguments.

pollster /'pəʊlstə/ *n.* a person who conducts or analyses opinion polls.

poll tax *n. hist.* **1** a tax levied on every adult. **2** = COMMUNITY CHARGE.

pollute /pə'lu:t/ *v.tr.* **1** contaminate or defile (the environment). **2** make foul or filthy. **3** destroy the purity or sanctity of. □ **pollutant** *adj.* & *n.* **polluter** *n.* **pollution** *n.* [Middle English from Latin *polluere pollut-*]

polly[1] /'pɒli/ *n.* (*pl.* **-ies**) *Brit. colloq.* a bottle or glass of Apollinaris water. [abbreviation]

polly[2] /'pɒli/ *n.* (also **pollie**) (*pl.* **-ies**) *Austral.* a politician. [abbreviation]

Pollyanna /pɒlɪ'anə/ *n.* a cheerful optimist; an excessively cheerful person. □ **Pollyannaish** *adj.* **Pollyannaism** *n.* [a character in a novel (1913) by E. Porter]

pollywog var. of POLLIWOG.

polo /'pəʊləʊ/ *n.* a game of Eastern origin resembling hockey, played on horseback with a long-handled mallet. [Tibetan *pholo*, literally 'ball game']

polonaise /pɒlə'neɪz/ *n.* & *adj.* ● *n.* **1** a dance of Polish origin in triple time. **2** the music for this. **3** *hist.* a woman's dress consisting of a bodice and a skirt open from the waist downwards to show an underskirt. ● *adj.* cooked in a Polish style. [French, fem. of *polonais* 'Polish', from medieval Latin *Polonia* 'Poland']

polo neck *n.* (hyphenated when *attrib.*) *Brit.* **1** a high round turned-over collar. **2** a pullover with this.

polonium /pə'ləʊnɪəm/ *n. Chem.* a rare radioactive metallic element, occurring naturally in uranium ores (symbol **Po**). [French and modern Latin from medieval Latin *Polonia* 'Poland' (the native country of Marie Curie, its co-discoverer) + -IUM]

polony /pə'ləʊni/ *n.* (*pl.* **-ies**) *Brit.* = BOLOGNA SAUSAGE. [apparently alteration of *Bologna*]

polo shirt *n.* a short-sleeved casual shirt with a collar and only partly buttoned down the front.

polo stick *n.* a mallet for playing polo.

poltergeist /'pɒltəgʌɪst/ *n.* a noisy mischievous ghost, esp. one manifesting itself by moving physical objects. [German, from *poltern* 'create a disturbance' + *Geist* GHOST]

poltroon /pɒl'tru:n/ *n.* a spiritless coward. □ **poltroonery** *n.* [French *poltron* from Italian *poltrone*, perhaps from *poltro* 'sluggard']

poly /'pɒli/ *n.* (*pl.* **polys**) *Brit. colloq.* polytechnic. [abbreviation]

poly- /'pɒli/ *comb. form* **1** denoting many or much. **2** *Chem.* denoting the presence of many radicals etc. of a particular kind in a molecule (*polysaccharide*; *polystyrene*). [Greek *polu-* from *polus* 'much', *polloi* 'many']

polyadelphous /,pɒlɪə'dɛlfəs/ *adj. Bot.* having numerous stamens grouped into three or more bundles.

polyamide /pɒlɪ'eɪmʌɪd, -'am-/ *n. Chem.* any of a class of condensation polymers produced from the interaction of an amino group of one molecule and a carboxylic acid group of another, and which includes many synthetic fibres such as nylon.

polyandry /'pɒlɪandri/ *n.* **1** polygamy in which a woman has more than one husband. **2** *Bot.* the state of having numerous stamens. □ **polyandrous** /-'andrəs/ *adj.* [POLY- + *andry* from Greek *anēr andros* 'male']

polyanthus /pɒlɪ'anθəs/ *n.* (*pl.* **polyanthuses**) a flower cultivated from hybridized primulas. [modern Latin (as POLY- + Greek *anthos* 'flower')]

polycarbonate /pɒlɪ'kɑ:bəneɪt/ *n.* any of a class of polymers in which the units are linked through a carbonate group, mainly used as moulding materials.

polychaete /'pɒlɪki:t/ *n.* any aquatic annelid worm of the class Polychaeta, including lugworms and ragworms, having numerous bristles on the fleshy lobes of each body segment. □ **polychaetan** /-'ki:t(ə)n/ *adj.* **polychaetous** /-'ki:təs/ *adj.*

polychlorinated biphenyl see PCB.

polychromatic /,pɒlɪkrə(ʊ)'matɪk/ *adj.* **1** many-coloured. **2** (of radiation) containing more than one wavelength. □ **polychromatism** /-'krəʊmətɪz(ə)m/ *n.*

polychrome /'pɒlɪkrəʊm/ *adj.* & *n.* ● *adj.* painted, printed, or decorated in many colours. ● *n.* **1** a work of art in several colours, esp. a coloured statue. **2** varied colouring. □ **polychromic** /-'krəʊmɪk/ *adj.* **polychromous** /-'krəʊməs/ *adj.* [French from Greek *polukhrōmos* (as POLY-, *khrōma* 'colour')]

polychromy /ˈpɒlɪkrəʊmi/ *n.* the art of painting in several colours, esp. as applied to ancient pottery, architecture, etc. [French *polychromie* (as POLYCHROME)]

polyclinic /pɒlɪˈklɪnɪk/ *n.* a clinic devoted to various diseases; a general hospital.

polycotton /ˈpɒlɪkɒt(ə)n/ *n.* fabric made from a mixture of cotton and polyester fibre.

polycrystalline /pɒlɪˈkrɪstəlʌɪn/ *adj.* (of a solid substance) consisting of many crystalline parts at various orientations, e.g. a metal casting.

polycyclic /pɒlɪˈsʌɪklɪk, -ˈsɪk-/ *adj. Chem.* having more than one ring of atoms in the molecule.

polydactyl /pɒlɪˈdaktɪl/ *adj.* (of a person or animal) having more than five fingers or toes on one (or on each) hand or foot.

polyester /pɒlɪˈɛstə/ *n.* **1** any of a group of condensation polymers used to form synthetic fibres such as Terylene or to make resins. **2** a fabric made from such a polymer.

polyethene /pɒlɪˈɛθiːn, ˈpɒlɪθiːn/ *n. Chem.* = POLYTHENE.

polyethylene /pɒlɪˈɛθɪliːn/ *n. Chem.* = POLYTHENE.

polygamous /pəˈlɪgəməs/ *adj.* **1** having more than one wife or husband at the same time. **2** having more than one mate. **3** *Bot.* bearing some flowers with stamens only, some with pistils only, some with both, on the same or different plants. □ **polygamic** /-ˈgamɪk/ *adj.* **polygamist** *n.* **polygamously** *adv.* **polygamy** *n.* [Greek *polugamos* (as POLY-, *-gamos* 'marrying')]

polygene /ˈpɒlɪdʒiːn/ *n. Biol.* each of a group of independent genes that collectively affect a characteristic.

polygenesis /pɒlɪˈdʒɛnɪsɪs/ *n.* the (usu. postulated) origination of a race or species from several independent stocks. □ **polygenetic** /-dʒɪˈnɛtɪk/ *adj.*

polygeny /pəˈlɪdʒ(ə)ni/ *n.* the theory that humankind originated from several independent pairs of ancestors. □ **polygenism** *n.* **polygenist** *n.*

polyglot /ˈpɒlɪglɒt/ *adj.* & *n.* ● *adj.* **1** of many languages. **2** (of a person) speaking or writing several languages. **3** (of a book, esp. the Bible) with the text translated into several languages. ● *n.* **1** a polyglot person. **2** a polyglot book, esp. a Bible. □ **polyglottal** /-ˈglɒt(ə)l/ *adj.* **polyglottic** /-ˈglɒtɪk/ *adj.* **polyglottism** *n.* [French *polyglotte* from Greek *poluglōttos* (as POLY-, *glōtta* 'tongue')]

polygon /ˈpɒlɪg(ə)n/ *n.* a plane figure with many (usu. a minimum of three) sides and angles. □ **polygonal** /pəˈlɪg(ə)n(ə)l/ *adj.* [Late Latin *polygonum* from Greek *polugōnon* (neut. adj.) (as POLY- + *-gōnos* 'angled')]

polygon of forces *n.* a polygon that represents by the length and direction of its sides all the forces acting on a body or point.

polygonum /pəˈlɪg(ə)nəm/ *n.* any plant of the genus *Polygonum*, with small bell-shaped flowers and jointed stems. Also called KNOTGRASS, KNOTWEED. [modern Latin from Greek *polugonon* (as POLY-, *gonu* 'knee, joint', from the plant's swollen joints)]

polygraph /ˈpɒlɪgrɑːf/ *n.* a machine designed to detect and record changes in physiological characteristics (e.g. rates of pulse and breathing), used esp. as a lie detector.

polygyny /pəˈlɪdʒɪni/ *n.* polygamy in which a man has more than one wife. □ **polygynous** /pəˈlɪdʒɪnəs/ *adj.* [POLY- + *gyny* from Greek *gunē* 'woman']

polyhedron /pɒlɪˈhiːdrən, -ˈhɛd-/ *n.* (*pl.* **polyhedra** /-drə/ or **polyhedrons**) a solid figure with many (usu. more than six) faces. □ **polyhedral** *adj.* **polyhedric** *adj.* [Greek *poluedron*, neut. of *poluedros* (as POLY-, *hedra* 'base')]

polyhistor /pɒlɪˈhɪstə/ *n.* = POLYMATH. [Greek *poluistōr* 'very learned' (as POLY-, *histōr* 'wise man')]

polymath /ˈpɒlɪmaθ/ *n.* a person of much or varied learning; a great scholar. □ **polymathic** /pɒlɪˈmaθɪk/ *adj.* **polymathy** /pəˈlɪməθi/ *n.* [Greek *polumathēs* (as POLY-, *math-* stem of *manthanō* 'learn')]

polymer /ˈpɒlɪmə/ *n.* a compound composed of one or more large molecules that are formed from repeated units of smaller molecules. □ **polymeric** /-ˈmɛrɪk/ *adj.* **polymerism** *n.* **polymerize** *v.intr.* & *tr.* (also **-ise**). **polymerization** /-ˈzeɪʃ(ə)n/ *n.* [German from Greek *polumeros* 'having many parts' (as POLY-, *meros* 'share')]

polymerase /ˈpɒlɪməreɪz, pəˈlɪməreɪz/ *n. Biochem.* any enzyme which catalyses the formation of a polymer, esp. of DNA or RNA.

polymerous /pəˈlɪm(ə)rəs/ *adj. Biol.* having many parts.

polymorphism /pɒlɪˈmɔːfɪz(ə)m/ *n.* the occurrence of something in several different forms. □ **polymorphic** *adj.* **polymorphous** *adj.*

Polynesian /pɒlɪˈniːzj(ə)n, -ʒ(ə)n/ *adj.* & *n.* ● *adj.* of or relating to Polynesia, a group of Pacific islands including New Zealand, Hawaii, Samoa, etc. ● *n.* **1 a** a native of Polynesia. **b** a person of Polynesian descent. **2** the Polynesian languages as a group, including Maori, Hawaiian, and Samoan. [as POLY- + Greek *nēsos* 'island']

polyneuritis /ˌpɒlɪnjʊəˈrʌɪtɪs/ *n. Med.* any disorder that affects many of the peripheral nerves. □ **polyneuritic** /-ˈrɪtɪk/ *adj.*

polynomial /pɒlɪˈnəʊmɪəl/ *n.* & *adj. Math.* ● *n.* an expression of more than two algebraic terms, esp. the sum of several terms that contain different powers of the same variable(s). ● *adj.* of or being a polynomial. [POLY-, on the pattern of *multinomial*]

polynya /pə(ʊ)ˈlɪnjə/ *n.* a stretch of open water surrounded by ice, esp. in the Arctic seas. [Russian, from *pole* 'field']

polyp /ˈpɒlɪp/ *n.* **1** *Zool.* an individual coelenterate. **2** *Med.* a small usu. benign growth protruding from a mucous membrane. [French *polype* (as POLYPUS)]

polypary /ˈpɒlɪp(ə)ri/ *n.* (*pl.* **-ies**) the common stem or support of a colony of polyps. [modern Latin *polyparium* (as POLYPUS)]

polypeptide /pɒlɪˈpɛptʌɪd/ *n. Biochem.* a peptide formed by the combination of about ten or more amino acids. [German *Polypeptid* (as POLY-, PEPTONE)]

polyphagous /pəˈlɪfəgəs/ *adj. Zool.* able to feed on various kinds of food.

polyphase /ˈpɒlɪfeɪz/ *adj. Electr.* (of a device or circuit) designed to supply or use simultaneously several alternating currents of the same voltage but with different phases.

polyphone /ˈpɒlɪfəʊn/ *n. Philol.* a symbol or letter that represents several different sounds.

polyphonic /pɒlɪˈfɒnɪk/ *adj.* **1** *Mus.* (of vocal music etc.) in two or more relatively independent parts; contrapuntal. **2** *Philol.* (of a letter etc.) representing more than one sound. □ **polyphonically** *adv.* [Greek *poluphōnos* (as POLY-, *phōnē* 'voice, sound')]

polyphony /pəˈlɪf(ə)ni/ *n.* (*pl.* **-ies**) **1** *Mus.* **a** polyphonic style in musical composition; counterpoint. **b** a composition written in this style. **2** *Philol.* the symbolization of different vocal sounds by the same letter or character. □ **polyphonous** *adj.*

polyphosphate /pɒlɪˈfɒsfeɪt/ *n.* any of various complex phosphates, used esp. in detergents or as food additives.

polyphyletic /ˌpɒlɪfʌɪˈlɛtɪk/ *adj. Biol.* (of a group of organisms) derived from more than one common evolutionary ancestor or ancestral group.

polypi *pl.* of POLYPUS.

polyploid /ˈpɒlɪplɔɪd/ *n.* & *adj. Biol.* ● *n.* a nucleus or organism that contains more than two sets of chromosomes. ● *adj.* of or being a polyploid. □ **polyploidy** *n.* [German (as POLY-, -PLOID)]

polypod /ˈpɒlɪpɒd/ *adj. Zool.* having many feet or footlike appendages. [French *polypode* (*adj.*) from Greek (as POLYPUS)]

polypody /ˈpɒlɪpəʊdi/ *n.* (*pl.* **-ies**) any fern of the genus *Polypodium*, usu. found in woods growing on trees, walls, and stones. [Middle English via Latin *polypodium* from Greek *polupodion* (as POLYPUS)]

polypoid /ˈpɒlɪpɔɪd/ *adj.* of or like a polyp. □ **polypous** /-pəs/ *adj.*

polypropene /pɒlɪ'prəʊpi:n/ *n.* = POLYPROPYLENE.

polypropylene /pɒlɪ'prəʊpɪli:n/ *n. Chem.* any of various polymers of propylene including thermoplastic materials used for films, fibres, or moulding materials. Also called POLYPROPENE.

polypus /'pɒlɪpəs/ *n.* (*pl.* **polypi** /-pʌɪ/ or **polypuses**) *Med.* = POLYP 2. [Middle English via Latin from Greek *pōlupos*, *polupous* 'cuttlefish, polyp' (as POLY-, *pous podos* 'foot')]

polysaccharide /pɒlɪ'sakərʌɪd/ *n.* any carbohydrate whose molecules consist of long chains of monosaccharides.

polysemy /'pɒlɪsi:mi, pə'lɪsɪmi/ *n. Philol.* the existence of many meanings (of a word etc.). □ **polysemic** /-'si:mɪk/ *adj.* **polysemous** /-'si:məs/ *adj.* [POLY- + Greek *sēma* 'sign']

polystyrene /pɒlɪ'stʌɪri:n/ *n.* a polymer of styrene, esp. a thermoplastic polymer often expanded with a gas to produce a lightweight rigid white substance used for insulation and in packaging.

polysyllabic /,pɒlɪsɪ'labɪk/ *adj.* **1** (of a word) having many syllables. **2** characterized by the use of words of many syllables. □ **polysyllabically** *adv.*

polysyllable /'pɒlɪsɪləb(ə)l/ *n.* a polysyllabic word.

polytechnic /pɒlɪ'tɛknɪk/ *n.* & *adj.* ● *n.* an institution of higher education offering courses in many (esp. vocational) subjects at degree level or below. ● *adj.* dealing with or devoted to various vocational or technical subjects. [French *polytechnique* from Greek *polutekhnos* (as POLY-, + *tekhnē* 'art')]

■ **Usage** In 1989 British polytechnics gained autonomy from their local education authorities and in 1992 were able to call themselves universities.

polytetrafluoroethylene /,pɒlɪtɛtrəflʊərəʊ'ɛθɪli:n/ *n. Chem.* a tough translucent polymer resistant to chemical action and with a low coefficient of friction, used for seals and bearings, to coat non-stick cooking utensils, etc. (abbr.: **PTFE**). Cf. TEFLON. [POLY- + TETRA- + FLUORO- + ETHYLENE]

polytheism /'pɒlɪθi:ɪz(ə)m/ *n.* the belief in or worship of more than one god. □ **polytheist** *n.* **polytheistic** /-'ɪstɪk/ *adj.* [French *polythéisme* from Greek *polutheos* 'of many gods' (as POLY-, *theos* 'god')]

polythene /'pɒlɪθi:n/ *n.* esp. *Brit.* a tough light plastic, a thermoplastic polymer of ethylene, usu. translucent and flexible or opaque and rigid, used for packaging and insulating materials. Also called POLYETHYLENE, POLYETHENE.

polytonality /,pɒlɪtə(ʊ)'nalɪti/ *n. Mus.* the simultaneous use of two or more keys in a composition. □ **polytonal** /-'təʊn(ə)l/ *adj.*

polyunsaturate /,pɒlɪʌn'satʃʊreɪt, -'satjʊreɪt/ *n.* a polyunsaturated fat or fatty acid.

polyunsaturated /,pɒlɪʌn'satʃʊreɪtɪd, -'satjʊreɪtɪd/ *adj. Chem.* (of a compound, esp. a fat or oil molecule) containing several double or triple bonds and therefore capable of further reaction.

polyurethane /pɒlɪ'jʊərɪθeɪn/ *n.* any polymer containing the urethane group, used in adhesives, paints, plastics, rubbers, foams, etc.

polyvalent /pɒlɪ'veɪl(ə)nt/ *adj. Chem.* having a valency of more than two, or several valencies. □ **polyvalence** *n.*

polyvinyl acetate /pɒlɪ'vʌɪnɪl, -(ə)l/ *n. Chem.* a soft plastic polymer used in paints and adhesives (abbr.: **PVA**).

polyvinyl chloride /pɒlɪ'vʌɪnɪl, -(ə)l/ *n.* a tough transparent solid polymer of vinyl chloride, easily coloured and used for a wide variety of products including pipes, flooring, etc. (abbr.: **PVC**).

polyzoan /pɒlɪ'zəʊən/ *n.* = BRYOZOAN.

Pom /pɒm/ *n.* **1** a Pomeranian dog. **2** *Austral.* & *NZ slang offens.* = POMMY. [abbreviation]

pomace /'pʌmɪs/ *n.* **1** the mass of crushed apples in cider-making before or after the juice is pressed out. **2** the refuse of fish etc. after the oil has been extracted, generally used as a fertilizer. [Middle English via medieval Latin *pomacium* 'cider' from Latin *pomum* 'apple']

pomade /pə'meɪd, -mɑ:d/ *n.* & *v.* ● *n.* scented dressing for the hair and the skin of the head. ● *v.tr.* dress with pomade. [French *pommade* from Italian *pomata* via medieval Latin from Latin *pomum* 'apple' (from which it was originally made)]

pomander /pə'mandə, 'pɒməndə/ *n.* **1** a ball of mixed aromatic substances placed in a cupboard etc. or *hist.* carried in a box, bag, etc. as a supposed protection against infection. **2** a (usu. spherical) container for this. **3** a spiced orange etc. similarly used. [earlier *pom(e)amber* via Anglo-French from Old French *pome d'embre* from medieval Latin *pomum de ambra* 'apple of ambergris']

pomatum /pə(ʊ)'meɪtəm/ *n.* & *v.tr.* = POMADE. [modern Latin from Latin *pomum* 'apple']

pome /pəʊm/ *n.* a firm-fleshed fruit in which the carpels from the central core enclose the seeds, e.g. the apple, pear, and quince. □ **pomiferous** /pə'mɪf(ə)rəs/ *adj.* [Middle English from Old French, ultimately from *poma*, pl. of Latin *pomum* 'fruit, apple']

pomegranate /'pɒmɪgranɪt/ *n.* **1 a** an orange-sized fruit with a tough golden-orange outer skin containing many seeds in a red pulp. **b** the tree bearing this fruit, *Punica granatum*, native to N. Africa and W. Asia. **2** an ornamental representation of a pomegranate. [Middle English from Old French *pome grenate* (as POME, Latin *granatum* 'having many seeds' from *granum* 'seed')]

pomelo /'pɒmələʊ, 'pʌm-/ *n.* (*pl.* **-os**) **1** = SHADDOCK. **2** = GRAPEFRUIT. [19th c.: origin unknown]

Pomeranian /pɒmə'reɪnɪən/ *n.* **1** a small dog with long silky hair, a pointed muzzle, and pricked ears. **2** this breed. [*Pomerania* in Germany and Poland]

pomfret /'pɒmfrɪt/ *n.* **1** any of various fish of the family Stromateidae of the Indian and Pacific Oceans. **2** a dark-coloured deep-bodied marine fish, *Brama brama*, used as food. [apparently from Portuguese *pampo*]

pomfret-cake /'pɒmfrɪt, 'pʌm-/ *n.* (also **Pontefract-cake** /'pɒntɪfrakt/) *Brit.* a small round flat liquorice sweet originally made at Pontefract (earlier *Pomfret*) in Yorkshire.

pomiculture /'pəʊmɪkʌltʃə/ *n.* fruit-growing. [Latin *pomum* 'fruit' + CULTURE]

pommel /'pʌm(ə)l/ *n.* & *v.* ● *n.* **1** a knob, esp. at the end of a sword-hilt. **2** the upward projecting front part of a saddle. ● *v.tr.* (**pommelled**, **pommelling**; *US* **pommeled**, **pommeling**) = PUMMEL. [Middle English via Old French *pomel* from a Romanic diminutive from Latin *pomum* 'fruit, apple']

pommel horse *n.* a vaulting horse fitted with a pair of curved handgrips.

Pommy /'pɒmi/ *n.* (also **Pommie**) (*pl.* **-ies**) *Austral.* & *NZ slang offens.* a British person, esp. a recent immigrant. [20th c.: origin uncertain]

pomology /pə(ʊ)'mɒlədʒi/ *n.* the science of fruit-growing. □ **pomological** /-mə'lɒdʒɪk(ə)l/ *adj.* **pomologist** *n.* [Latin *pomum* 'fruit' + -LOGY]

pomp /pɒmp/ *n.* **1** a splendid display; splendour. **2** (often in *pl.*) vain glory (*the pomps and vanities of this wicked world*). [Middle English via Old French *pompe* and Latin *pompa* from Greek *pompē* 'procession, pomp', from *pempō* 'send']

pompadour /'pɒmpədʊə/ *n.* a woman's hairstyle with the hair in a high turned-back roll round the face. [named after the Marquise de *Pompadour*, the mistress of Louis XV of France, d. 1764]

pompano /'pɒmpənəʊ/ *n.* (*pl.* **-os**) any of various fish of the family Carangidae or Stromateidae of the Atlantic and Pacific Oceans, used as food. [Spanish *pámpano*]

pom-pom /'pɒmpɒm/ *n.* an automatic quick-firing gun esp. on a ship. [imitative]

pompon /'pɒmpɒn/ *n.* (also **pompom**) **1** an ornamental ball or bobble made of wool, silk, or ribbons, usu. worn on women's or children's hats or clothing. **2** the round tuft on a soldier's cap, the front of a shako, etc. **3** (often *attrib.*) a dahlia or chrysanthemum with small tightly-clustered petals. [French, of unknown origin]

pompous /ˈpɒmpəs/ *adj.* **1** self-important, affectedly grand or solemn. **2** (of language) pretentious; unduly grand in style. **3** *archaic* magnificent; splendid. □ **pomposity** /pɒmˈpɒsɪti/ *n.* (*pl.* **-ies**). **pompously** *adv.* **pompousness** *n.* [Middle English via Old French *pompeux* from Late Latin *pomposus* (as POMP)]

'pon /pɒn/ *prep. archaic* = UPON. [abbreviation]

ponce /pɒns/ *n.* & *v. Brit. slang* ● *n.* **1** a man who lives off a prostitute's earnings; a pimp. **2** *offens.* a homosexual; an effeminate man. ● *v.intr.* act as a ponce. □ **ponce about** move about effeminately or ineffectually. □ **poncey** *adj.* (also **poncy**) (in sense 2 of *n.*). [perhaps from POUNCE[1]]

poncho /ˈpɒn(t)ʃəʊ/ *n.* (*pl.* **-os**) **1** a S. American cloak made of a blanket-like piece of cloth with a slit in the middle for the head. **2** a garment in this style. [Latin American Spanish, from Araucanian (a Chilean language)]

pond /pɒnd/ *n.* & *v.* ● *n.* **1** a fairly small body of still water formed naturally or by hollowing or embanking. **2** (prec. by *the*) *joc.* the sea, esp. the Atlantic ocean. ● *v.* **1** *tr.* hold back, dam up (a stream etc.). **2** *intr.* form a pond. [Middle English variant of POUND[3]]

ponder /ˈpɒndə/ *v.* **1** *tr.* weigh mentally; think over; consider. **2** *intr.* (usu. foll. by *on*, *over*) think; muse. [Middle English via Old French *ponderer* from Latin *ponderare*, from *pondus -eris* 'weight']

ponderable /ˈpɒnd(ə)rəb(ə)l/ *adj. literary* having appreciable weight or significance. □ **ponderability** /-ˈbɪlɪti/ *n.* [Late Latin *ponderabilis* (as PONDER)]

ponderation /pɒndəˈreɪʃ(ə)n/ *n. literary* the act or an instance of weighing, balancing, or considering. [Latin *ponderatio* (as PONDER)]

ponderosa /pɒndəˈrəʊzə, -sə/ *n. US* **1** a N. American pine tree, *Pinus ponderosa*. **2** the timber of this tree. [modern Latin, fem. of Latin *ponderosus*: see PONDEROUS]

ponderous /ˈpɒnd(ə)rəs/ *adj.* **1** heavy; unwieldy. **2** laborious. **3** (of style etc.) dull; tedious. □ **ponderosity** /-ˈrɒsɪti/ *n.* **ponderously** *adv.* **ponderousness** *n.* [Middle English from Latin *ponderosus*, from *pondus -eris* 'weight']

pond life *n.* animals (esp. invertebrates) that live in ponds.

pond-skater *n.* a predatory heteropterous bug of the family Gerridae, which runs on water supported by the surface tension.

pond snail *n.* a freshwater snail inhabiting ponds, esp. one of the genus *Limnaea*.

pondweed /ˈpɒndwiːd/ *n.* any of various aquatic plants, esp. of the genus *Potamogeton*, growing in still or running water.

pone[1] /pəʊn/ *n. US* **1** unleavened maize bread, esp. as made by N. American Indians. **2** a fine light bread made with milk, eggs, etc. **3** a cake or loaf of this. [Algonquian, = bread]

pone[2] /pəʊni/ *n.* the dealer's opponent in two-handed card games. [Latin, 2nd sing. imperative of *ponere* 'place']

pong /pɒŋ/ *n.* & *v. Brit. colloq.* ● *n.* an unpleasant smell. ● *v.intr.* stink. □ **pongy** /ˈpɒŋi/ *adj.* (**pongier**, **pongiest**). [20th c.: origin unknown]

pongal /ˈpɒŋg(ə)l/ *n.* **1** the Tamil New Year festival at which new rice is cooked. **2** a dish of cooked rice. [Tamil *poṅkal* 'boiling']

pongee /pʌnˈdʒiː, pɒn-/ *n.* **1** a soft usu. unbleached type of Chinese silk fabric. **2** an imitation of this in cotton etc. [Chinese *běnjī* literally 'own loom' or *běnzhī* literally 'home-woven']

pongid /ˈpɒn(d)ʒɪd/ *n.* & *adj.* ● *n.* any ape of the family Pongidae, including gorillas, chimpanzees, and orang-utans. ● *adj.* of or relating to this family. [modern Latin *Pongidae* from the genus name *Pongo*: see PONGO]

pongo /ˈpɒŋgəʊ/ *n.* (*pl.* **-os**) **1** an orang-utan. **2** *Naut. slang* a soldier. **3** *Austral.* & *NZ slang offens.* an Englishman. [originally used of African apes: from Congolese *mpongo*]

poniard /ˈpɒnjəd/ *n. literary* a small slim dagger. [French *poignard* via Old French *poignal* and medieval Latin *pugnale* from Latin *pugnus* 'fist']

pons /pɒnz/ *n.* (*pl.* **pontes** /ˈpɒntiːz/) *Anat.* (in full **pons Varolii**) /vəˈrəʊlɪʌɪ/ the part of the brainstem that links the medulla oblongata and the thalamus. [Latin, = bridge: *Varolii* after C. *Varoli*, Italian anatomist d. 1575]

pons asinorum /asɪˈnɔːrəm/ *n.* any difficult proposition, originally a rule of geometry from Euclid. [Latin, literally 'bridge of asses']

pont /pɒnt/ *n. S.Afr.* a flat-bottomed ferry boat. [Dutch]

Pontefract-cake var. of POMFRET-CAKE.

pontes *pl.* of PONS.

pontifex /ˈpɒntɪfɛks/ *n.* (*pl.* **pontifices** /pɒnˈtɪfɪsiːz/) **1** = PONTIFF. **2** *Rom. Antiq.* a member of the principal college of priests in Rome. [Latin *pontifex -ficis*, from *pons pontis* 'bridge' + *-fex* from *facere* 'make']

Pontifex Maximus /ˈmaksɪməs/ *n.* (in ancient Rome) the head of the college of pontifices.

pontiff /ˈpɒntɪf/ *n.* (in full **sovereign** or **supreme pontiff**) *RC Ch.* the Pope. [French *pontife* (as PONTIFEX)]

pontifical /pɒnˈtɪfɪk(ə)l/ *adj.* & *n.* ● *adj.* **1** *RC Ch.* of or befitting a pontiff; papal. **2** pompously dogmatic; with an attitude of infallibility. ● *n. RC Ch.* **1** an office-book of the Western Church containing rites to be performed by the Pope or bishops. **2** (in *pl.*) the vestments and insignia of a bishop, cardinal, or abbot. □ **pontifically** *adv.* [Middle English from French *pontifical* or Latin *pontificalis* (as PONTIFEX)]

pontifical Mass *n.* a High Mass, usu. celebrated by a cardinal, bishop, etc.

pontificate *v.* & *n.* ● *v.intr.* /pɒnˈtɪfɪkeɪt/ **1 a** play the pontiff; pretend to be infallible. **b** be pompously dogmatic. **2** *RC Ch.* officiate as bishop, esp. at Mass. ● *n.* /pɒnˈtɪfɪkət/ **1** the office of pontifex, bishop, or pope. **2** the period of this. [Latin *pontificatus* (as PONTIFEX)]

pontifices *pl.* of PONTIFEX.

pontoon[1] /pɒnˈtuːn/ *n. Brit.* **1** a card game in which players try to acquire cards with a face value totalling 21 and no more. **2** = NATURAL *n.* 4a. [probably corruption of *vingt-un*, obsolete variant of VINGT-ET-UN]

pontoon[2] /pɒnˈtuːn/ *n.* & *v.* ● *n.* **1** a flat-bottomed boat. **2 a** each of several boats, hollow metal cylinders, etc., used to support a temporary bridge. **b** (also **pontoon bridge**) such a bridge. **3** = CAISSON 1, 2. ● *v.tr.* cross (a river) by means of pontoons. [French *ponton* from Latin *ponto -onis*, from *pons pontis* 'bridge']

pony /ˈpəʊni/ *n.* (*pl.* **-ies**) **1** a horse of any small breed. **2** a small drinking glass. **3** (in *pl.*) *slang* racehorses. **4** *Brit. slang* £25. [probably from French *poulenet*, diminutive of *poulain* 'foal']

ponytail /ˈpəʊnɪteɪl/ *n.* a hairstyle in which the hair is drawn back and tied, causing it to hang down like a pony's tail.

pony-trekking *n. Brit.* the activity of travelling across country on a pony for pleasure. □ **pony-trekker** *n.*

poo var. of POOH.

pooch /puːtʃ/ *n. colloq.* a dog. [20th c.: origin unknown]

poodle /ˈpuːd(ə)l/ *n.* & *v.* ● *n.* **1 a** a dog of a breed with a curly coat that is usually clipped. **b** this breed. **2** *Brit.* a lackey or servile follower. ● *v.intr. colloq.* move or travel in a leisurely manner. [German *Pudel*(*hund*) from Low German *pud*(*d*)*eln* 'splash in water': cf. PUDDLE]

poof[1] /pʊf, puːf/ *n.* (also **pouf**, **poove** /puːv/) *Brit. slang offens.* **1** an effeminate man. **2** a male homosexual. □ **poofy** /ˈpʊfi/ *adj.* [19th c.: cf. PUFF in sense 'braggart']

poof[2] /pʊf/ *int.* expressing contemptuous rejection or announcing a sudden disappearance. [imitative]

poofter /ˈpʊftə, ˈpu:-/ *n. Brit. slang offens.* = POOF[1]. [extension of POOF[1]]

pooh /pu:/ *int. & n.* (also **poo**) ● *int.* **1** expressing impatience or contempt. **2** expressing disgust at a bad smell. ● *n. slang* (a child's word for) excrement. [imitative]

Pooh-Bah /pu:ˈbɑ:/ *n.* (also **pooh-bah**) **1** a holder of many offices at once. **2** a pompous self-important person. [a character in W. S. Gilbert's *The Mikado* (1885)]

pooh-pooh /ˈpu:pu:, pu:ˈpu:/ *v.tr.* express contempt for; ridicule; dismiss (an idea etc.) scornfully. [reduplication of POOH]

pooja var. of PUJA.

pooka /ˈpu:kə/ *n. Ir.* a hobgoblin. [Irish *púca*]

pool[1] /pu:l/ *n. & v.* ● *n.* **1** a small body of still water, usu. of natural formation. **2** a small shallow body of any liquid. **3** = SWIMMING POOL. **4** a deep place in a river. ● *v.intr.* **1** (of water etc.) form a pool. **2** (of blood) accumulate in parts of the venous system. [Old English *pōl*, from West Germanic]

pool[2] /pu:l/ *n. & v.* ● *n.* **1 a** (often *attrib.*) a common supply of persons, vehicles, commodities, etc. for sharing by a group of people (*a typing pool*; *a pool car*). **b** a group of persons sharing duties etc. **2 a** the collective amount of players' stakes in gambling etc. **b** a receptacle for this. **3 a** a joint commercial venture, esp. an arrangement between competing parties to fix prices and share business to eliminate competition. **b** the common funding for this. **4 a** *N. Amer.* a game on a billiard table with usu. 16 balls. **b** *Brit.* a game on a billiard table in which each player has a ball of a different colour with which he or she tries to pocket the others in fixed order, the winner taking all of the stakes. **5** a group of contestants who compete against each other in a tournament for the right to advance to the next round. ● *v.tr.* **1** put (resources etc.) into a common fund. **2** share (things) in common. **3** (of transport or organizations etc.) share (traffic, receipts). **4** *Austral. slang* **a** involve (a person) in a scheme etc., often by deception. **b** implicate, inform on. □ **the pools** *Brit.* = FOOTBALL POOL. [originally = a game of cards in which there is a pool (sense 2 a): French *poule* 'stake, kitty': associated with POOL[1]]

pool hall *n.* a hall for playing pool.

pool room *n. US* **1** a betting shop. **2** a place for playing pool.

poolside /ˈpu:lsʌɪd/ *n.* the side of a swimming pool (often *attrib.*: *poolside bar*).

poon /pu:n/ *n.* any large Indo-Malayan evergreen tree of the genus *Calophyllum*. [Sinhalese *pūna*]

poon oil *n.* an oil from the seeds of the poon tree, used in medicine and for lamps.

poop[1] /pu:p/ *n. & v.* ● *n.* **1** the stern of a ship. **2** (also **poop deck**) the aftermost and highest deck of a ship. ● *v.tr.* **1** (of a wave) break over the stern of (a ship). **2** (of a ship) receive (a wave) over the stern. [Middle English from Old French *pupe*, *pope*, ultimately from Latin *puppis*]

poop[2] /pu:p/ *v.tr.* (esp. as **pooped** *adj.*) *US colloq.* exhaust; tire out. [20th c.: origin unknown]

poop[3] /pu:p/ *n. & v.* ● *n.* **1** a short blast made in a hollow tube; a toot. **2** *slang* an act of breaking wind or defecating. ● *v.intr. slang* break wind; defecate. [imitative]

poop[4] /pu:p/ *n.* esp. *N. Amer. slang* up-to-date or inside information. [20th c.: origin unknown]

poop[5] /pu:p/ *n. colloq.* a stupid or ineffectual person. [perhaps abbreviation of NINCOMPOOP]

pooper scooper /ˈpu:pə/ *n.* (also **poop scoop**) *colloq.* an implement for clearing up (esp. dog) excrement. [POOP[3]]

poor /pʊə/ *adj.* **1** lacking adequate money or means to live comfortably. **2** (foll. by *in*) deficient in (a possession or quality) (*the poor in spirit*). **3 a** scanty, inadequate (*a poor crop*). **b** less good than is usual or expected (*poor visibility*; *is a poor driver*; *in poor health*). **c** paltry; inferior (*poor condition*; *came a poor third*). **4 a** deserving pity or sympathy; unfortunate (*you poor thing*). **b** with reference to a dead person (*as my poor father used to say*). **5** spiritless; despicable (*is a poor creature*). **6** often *iron.* or *joc.* humble; insignificant (*in my poor opinion*). □ **poor man's** an inferior or cheaper substitute for. **take a poor view of** regard with disfavour or pessimism. [Middle English & Old French *pov(e)re*, *poure* from Latin *pauper*]

poor box *n.* a collection box, esp. in church, for the relief of the poor.

poorhouse /ˈpʊəhaʊs/ *n. hist.* = WORKHOUSE 1.

poor law *n. hist.* a law relating to the support of paupers.

poorly /ˈpʊəli/ *adv. & adj.* ● *adv.* **1** scantily; defectively. **2** with no great success. **3** meanly; contemptibly. ● *predic.adj.* esp. *Brit.* unwell.

poor man's weather-glass *n.* the pimpernel. [from its closing its flowers before rain]

poorness /ˈpʊənɪs/ *n.* **1** defectiveness. **2** the lack of some good quality or constituent.

poor rate *n. hist.* a rate or assessment for relief or support of the poor.

poor relation *n.* an inferior or subordinate member of a family or any other group.

poor-spirited *adj.* timid; cowardly.

poor white *n.* esp. *US offens.* a member of a group of white people regarded as socially inferior.

pootle /ˈpu:t(ə)l/ *v.intr. colloq.* = POODLE *v.* [blend of POODLE *v.* and TOOTLE *v.*]

poove var. of POOF[1].

POP *abbr. Brit.* Post Office Preferred (size of envelopes etc.).

pop[1] /pɒp/ *n., v., & adv.* ● *n.* **1** a sudden sharp explosive sound as of a cork when drawn. **2** *colloq.* an effervescent sweet drink. ● *v.* (**popped**, **popping**) **1** *intr. & tr.* make or cause to make a pop. **2** *intr. & tr.* (foll. by *in*, *out*, *up*, *down*, etc.) go, move, come, or put unexpectedly or in a quick or hasty manner (*pop out to the shops*; *pop in for a visit*; *pop it on your head*). **3 a** *intr. & tr.* burst, making a popping sound. **b** *tr.* heat (popcorn etc.) until it pops. **4** *intr.* (often foll. by *at*) *colloq.* fire a gun (at birds etc.). **5** *tr. Brit. slang* pawn. **6** *tr. slang* take or inject (a drug etc.). **7** *intr.* (often foll. by *up*) (of a cricket ball) rise sharply off the pitch. ● *adv.* with the sound of a pop (*heard it go pop*). □ **in pop** *Brit. slang* in pawn. **pop off** *colloq.* **1** die. **2** quietly slip away (cf. sense 2 of *v.*). **pop the question** *colloq.* propose marriage. [Middle English: imitative]

pop[2] /pɒp/ *adj. & n. colloq.* ● *adj.* (usu. *attrib.*) **1** in a popular or modern style. **2** of, performing, or relating to pop music (*pop concert*; *pop group*). ● *n.* **1** (in full **pop music**) commercial popular music, esp. that since the 1950s. **2** a pop record or song (*top of the pops*). [abbreviation]

pop[3] /pɒp/ *n.* esp. *US colloq.* father. [abbreviation of POPPA]

pop. *abbr.* population.

popadom (also **popadam**) var. of POPPADOM.

pop art *n.* art based on modern popular culture and the mass media, esp. as a critical comment on traditional fine art values.

popcorn /ˈpɒpkɔ:n/ *n.* **1** maize which bursts open when heated. **2** these kernels when popped.

pop culture *n.* commercial culture based on popular taste.

pope[1] /pəʊp/ *n.* **1** (as title usu. **Pope**) the Bishop of Rome as head of the Roman Catholic Church. **2** the head of the Coptic Church, the patriarch of Alexandria. **3** = RUFF[2] 1. □ **popedom** *n.* **popeless** *adj.* [Old English via ecclesiastical Latin *pāpa* 'bishop, pope' from ecclesiastical Greek *papas* = Greek *pappas* 'father': cf. PAPA]

pope[2] /pəʊp/ *n.* a parish priest of the Orthodox Church in Russia etc. [Russian *pop* via Old Church Slavonic *popŭ* and West Germanic from ecclesiastical Greek (as POPE[1])]

Popemobile /ˈpəʊpməbiːl/ *n.* a bulletproof vehicle with a raised viewing area, used by the Pope on official visits.

popery /ˈpəʊp(ə)ri/ *n. derog.* **1** the papal system. **2 a** the Roman Catholic Church. **b** the doctrines and ceremonies associated with Roman Catholicism.

pope's eye *n.* **1** a lymphatic gland surrounded with fat in the middle of a sheep's leg. **2** *Sc.* a cut of steak.

pop-eyed /pɒpˈʌɪd/ *adj. colloq.* **1** having bulging eyes. **2** wide-eyed (with surprise etc.).

pop festival *n.* a festival at which popular music etc. is performed.

popgun /ˈpɒpgʌn/ *n.* **1** a child's toy gun which shoots a pellet etc. by the compression of air with a piston. **2** *derog.* an inefficient firearm.

popinjay /ˈpɒpɪndʒeɪ/ *n.* **1** a fop, a conceited person, a coxcomb. **2 a** *archaic* a parrot. **b** *hist.* a figure of a parrot on a pole as a mark to shoot at. [Middle English from Anglo-French *papeiaye*, Old French *papingay* etc. via Spanish *papagayo* from Arabic *babaġā*: assimilated to JAY]

popish /ˈpəʊpɪʃ/ *adj. derog.* Roman Catholic. □ **popishly** *adv.*

poplar /ˈpɒplə/ *n.* **1** any tree of the genus *Populus*, typically tall and fast growing. **2** *N. Amer.* = TULIP TREE. [Middle English via Anglo-French *popler*, Old French *poplier*, from *pople*, from Latin *populus*]

poplin /ˈpɒplɪn/ *n.* a plain-woven fabric usu. of cotton, with a corded surface. [obsolete French *papeline*, perhaps from Italian *papalina* (fem.) PAPAL, from the papal town Avignon where it was made]

popliteal /pɒˈplɪtɪəl, pɒplɪˈtiːəl/ *adj.* of the hollow at the back of the knee. [modern Latin *popliteus* from Latin *poples -itis* 'this hollow']

pop music see POP[2] *n.* 1.

poppa /ˈpɒpə/ *n. US colloq.* father (esp. as a child's word). [variant of PAPA]

poppadom /ˈpɒpədəm/ *n.* (also **poppadam**, **popadom**, **popadam**) (in Indian cookery) a thin, crisp, spiced bread eaten with curry etc. [Tamil *pappaḍam*]

popper /ˈpɒpə/ *n.* **1** *Brit. colloq.* a press stud. **2** a person or thing that pops. **3** *colloq.* a small vial of amyl nitrite used for inhalation.

poppet /ˈpɒpɪt/ *n.* **1** *Brit. colloq.* (esp. as a term of endearment) a small or dainty person. **2** the head of a lathe. **3** a small square piece of wood fitted inside the gunwale or washstrake of a boat. [Middle English *popet(te)*, ultimately from Latin *pup(p)a*: cf. PUPPET]

poppet-head *n. Brit.* the frame at the top of a mine shaft, supporting pulleys for the ropes used in hoisting.

poppet-valve *n. Engin.* a mushroom-shaped valve, lifted bodily from its seat rather than hinged.

popping crease /ˈpɒpɪŋ/ *n. Cricket* a line four feet in front of and parallel to the wicket, within which the batsman must keep the bat or one foot grounded to avoid the risk of being stumped. [POP[1], perhaps in obsolete sense 'strike']

popple /ˈpɒp(ə)l/ *v. & n.* ● *v.intr.* (of water) tumble about, toss to and fro. ● *n.* the act or an instance of rolling, tossing, or rippling of water. □ **popply** *adj.* [Middle English, probably from Middle Dutch *popelen* 'murmur, quiver', of imitative origin]

poppy[1] /ˈpɒpi/ *n.* (*pl.* **-ies**) any plant of the genus *Papaver*, with showy flowers, milky sap and rounded seed-capsules, esp. the red-flowered corn poppy, *P. rhoeas*, and the opium poppy. □ **poppied** *adj.* [Old English *popig*, *papæg*, etc. via medieval Latin *papauum* from Latin *papaver*]

poppy[2] /ˈpɒpi/ *adj.* (of music, a group, etc.) having a sound characteristic of pop music. [POP[2] *n.* + -Y[1]]

poppycock /ˈpɒpɪkɒk/ *n. slang* nonsense. [Dutch dialect *pappekak*, from *pap* 'soft' + *kak* 'dung']

Poppy Day *n. Brit.* = REMEMBRANCE SUNDAY.

poppy-head *n.* **1** the seed capsule of the poppy. **2** an ornamental top on the end of a church pew.

pop-shop *n. Brit. slang* a pawnbroker's shop.

Popsicle /ˈpɒpsɪk(ə)l/ *n.* esp. *N. Amer. propr.* an ice lolly. [fanciful name]

popsy /ˈpɒpsi/ *n.* (also **popsie**) (*pl.* **-ies**) esp. *Brit. colloq.* (usu. as a term of endearment) a young woman. [shortening of POPPET]

populace /ˈpɒpjʊləs/ *n.* **1** the common people. **2** *derog.* the rabble. [French from Italian *popolaccio*, from *popolo* 'people' + pejorative suffix *-accio*]

popular /ˈpɒpjʊlə/ *adj.* **1** liked or admired by many people or by a specified group (*popular teachers*; *a popular hero*). **2 a** of or carried on by the general public (*popular meetings*). **b** prevalent among the general public (*popular discontent*). **3** adapted to the understanding, taste, or means of the people (*popular science*; *popular medicine*). □ **popularism** *n.* **popularity** /-ˈlarɪti/ *n.* **popularly** *adv.* [Middle English from Anglo-French *populer*, Old French *populeir* or Latin *popularis*, from *populus* 'people']

popular front *n.* a party or coalition representing left-wing elements.

popularize /ˈpɒpjʊlərʌɪz/ *v.tr.* (also **-ise**) **1** make popular. **2** cause (a person, principle, etc.) to be generally known or liked. **3** present (a technical subject, specialized vocabulary, etc.) in a popular or readily understandable form. □ **popularization** /-ˈzeɪʃ(ə)n/ *n.* **popularizer** *n.*

popular music *n.* music appealing to a wide public.

populate /ˈpɒpjʊleɪt/ *v.tr.* **1** inhabit; form the population of (a town, country, etc.). **2** supply with inhabitants; people (*a densely populated district*). [medieval Latin *populare populat-* (as PEOPLE)]

population /pɒpjʊˈleɪʃ(ə)n/ *n.* **1 a** the inhabitants of a place, country, etc. referred to collectively. **b** any specified group within this (*the Irish population of Liverpool*). **2** the total number of any of these (*a population of eight million*; *the seal population*). **3** the act or process of supplying with inhabitants (*the population of forest areas*). **4** *Statistics* any finite or infinite collection of items under consideration. [Late Latin *populatio* (as PEOPLE)]

population explosion *n.* a sudden large increase of population.

populist /ˈpɒpjʊlɪst/ *n. & adj.* ● *n.* **1** a member or adherent of a political party seeking support mainly from the ordinary people. **2** a person who holds, or who is concerned with, the views of ordinary people. ● *adj.* of or relating to a populist or populist ideology. □ **populism** *n.* **populistic** /-ˈlɪstɪk/ *adj.* [Latin *populus* 'people']

populous /ˈpɒpjʊləs/ *adj.* thickly inhabited. □ **populously** *adv.* **populousness** *n.* [Middle English from Late Latin *populosus* (as PEOPLE)]

pop-up *attrib.adj.* **1** (of a toaster etc.) operating so as to move the object (toast when ready etc.) quickly upwards. **2** (of a book, greetings card, etc.) containing three-dimensional figures, illustrations, etc., that rise up when the page is turned. **3** *Computing* (of a menu) able to be superimposed on the screen being worked on and suppressed rapidly.

porbeagle /ˈpɔːbiːg(ə)l/ *n.* a large shark, *Lamna nasus*, having a pointed snout. [18th-c. Cornish dialect, perhaps from *porth* 'harbour, cove' + *bugel* 'shepherd']

porcelain /ˈpɔːs(ə)lɪn/ *n.* **1** a hard vitrified translucent ceramic. **2** objects made of this. □ **porcellaneous** /pɔːsɪˈleɪnɪəs/ *adj.* **porcellanous** /pɔːˈsɛlənəs/ *adj.* [French *porcelaine*, from Italian *porcellana* 'cowrie shell', hence 'chinaware']

porcelain clay *n.* kaolin.

porch /pɔːtʃ/ *n.* **1** a covered shelter for the entrance of a building. **2** *N. Amer.* a veranda. **3** (**the Porch**) *Philos.* = STOA 2. □ **porched** *adj.* **porchless** *adj.* [Middle English via Old French *porche* from Latin *porticus* (translation of Greek *stoa*) from *porta* 'passage']

porcine /ˈpɔːsʌɪn/ *adj.* of or like pigs. [French *porcin* or from Latin *porcinus* from *porcus* 'pig']

porcupine /ˈpɔːkjʊpʌɪn/ *n.* **1** any rodent of the family Hystricidae native to Africa, Asia, and SE Europe, or the family Erethizontidae native to America, having defensive spines or quills. **2** (*attrib.*) denoting any of various animals or other organisms with spines. [Middle English via Old French *porc espin* from Provençal *porc espi(n)*, ultimately from Latin *porcus* 'pig' + *spina* 'thorn']

porcupine fish *n.* a marine fish, *Diodon hystrix*, covered with sharp spines and often distending itself into a spherical shape.

pore[1] /pɔː/ *n.* esp. *Biol.* a minute opening in a surface through which gases, liquids, or fine solids may pass. [Middle English from Old French via Latin *porus* from Greek *poros* 'passage, pore']

pore[2] /pɔː/ *v.intr.* (foll. by *over*) **1** be absorbed in studying (a book etc.). **2** meditate on, think intently about (a subject). [Middle English, perhaps related to PEER[1]]

porgy /ˈpɔːgi/ *n.* (*pl.* **-ies**) *N. Amer.* any of various sparid fishes used as food, chiefly of W. Atlantic coastal waters, esp. one of the genus *Calamus*. [Spanish & Portuguese *pargo*]

poriferan /pəˈrɪf(ə)rən/ *n.* & *adj.* ● *n.* any aquatic invertebrate of the phylum Porifera, which comprises the sponges. ● *adj.* of or relating to this phylum. [modern Latin *Porifera*, from Latin *porus* PORE[1] + *-fer* 'bearing']

pork /pɔːk/ *n.* **1** the (esp. unsalted) flesh of a pig, used as food. **2** *US slang* = PORK BARREL. [Middle English *porc* via Old French from Latin *porcus* 'pig']

pork barrel *n.* (hyphenated when *attrib.*) *N. Amer. colloq.* **1** a source of government funds for projects designed to win votes (*disapproved of pork-barrel funding*). **2** the funds themselves. □ **pork-barrelling** *n.*

pork butcher *n.* a person who slaughters pigs for sale, or who sells pork rather than other meats.

porker /ˈpɔːkə/ *n.* **1** a pig raised for food. **2** a young fattened pig.

porkling /ˈpɔːklɪŋ/ *n.* a young or small pig.

pork pie *n.* a pie of minced pork etc. eaten cold.

pork-pie hat *n.* a hat with a flat crown and a brim turned up all round.

pork scratchings see SCRATCHINGS.

porky[1] /ˈpɔːki/ *adj.* & *n.* ● *adj.* (**porkier**, **porkiest**) **1** *colloq.* fleshy, fat. **2** of or like pork. ● *n.* (*pl.* **porkies**) (also **porky-pie**) *Brit. rhyming slang* a lie.

porky[2] /ˈpɔːki/ *n.* (*pl.* **-ies**) *US colloq.* a porcupine. [abbreviation]

porn /pɔːn/ *n.* & *adj.* (also **porno** /ˈpɔːnəʊ/) *colloq.* ● *n.* pornography. ● *attrib.adj.* pornographic. [abbreviation]

pornography /pɔːˈnɒgrəfi/ *n.* **1** the explicit description or exhibition of sexual activity in literature, films, etc., intended to stimulate erotic rather than aesthetic or emotional feelings. **2** literature etc. characterized by this. □ **pornographer** *n.* **pornographic** /-nəˈgrafɪk/ *adj.* **pornographically** /-nəˈgrafɪk(ə)li/ *adv.* [Greek *pornographos* 'writing of harlots', from *pornē* 'prostitute' + *graphō* 'write']

porous /ˈpɔːrəs/ *adj.* **1** full of pores. **2** letting through air, water, etc. **3** (of an argument, security system, etc.) leaky, admitting infiltration. □ **porosity** /pɔːˈrɒsɪti/ *n.* **porously** *adv.* **porousness** *n.* [Middle English via Old French *poreux* and medieval Latin *porosus* from Latin *porus* PORE[1]]

porphyria /pɔːˈfɪrɪə/ *n.* any of a group of genetic disorders involving abnormal metabolism of porphyrin pigments and their excretion in the urine. [from PORPHYRIN + -IA[1]]

porphyrin /ˈpɔːfɪrɪn/ *n.* *Biochem.* any of a class of pigments whose molecules contain a flat ring of four linked heterocyclic rings, occurring widely in nature esp. as derivatives containing metal atoms, e.g. haem and chlorophyll. [Greek *porphura* 'purple' + -IN]

porphyry /ˈpɔːfɪri/ *n.* (*pl.* **-ies**) **1** a hard rock quarried in ancient Egypt, composed of crystals of white or red feldspar in a red matrix. **2** *Geol.* an igneous rock with large crystals scattered in a matrix of much smaller crystals. □ **porphyritic** /-ˈrɪtɪk/ *adj.* [Middle English, ultimately via medieval Latin *porphyreum* from Greek *porphuritēs*, from *porphura* 'purple']

porpoise /ˈpɔːpəs, -pɔɪs/ *n.* any of various small toothed whales of the family Phocaenidae, esp. of the genus *Phocaena*, with a low triangular dorsal fin and a blunt rounded snout. [Middle English *porpays* etc. from Old French *po(u)rpois* etc., ultimately from Latin *porcus* 'pig' + *piscis* 'fish']

porridge /ˈpɒrɪdʒ/ *n.* **1** a dish consisting of oatmeal or another meal or cereal boiled in water or milk. **2** *Brit. slang* imprisonment. □ **porridgy** *adj.* [16th c.: alteration of POTTAGE]

porringer /ˈpɒrɪn(d)ʒə/ *n.* a small bowl, often with a handle, for soup, stew, etc. [earlier *pottinger* from Old French *potager*, from *potage* (see POTTAGE): *-n-* as in *messenger* etc.]

port[1] /pɔːt/ *n.* **1** a harbour. **2** a place of refuge. **3** a town or place possessing a harbour where ships load or unload, esp. one where customs officers are stationed. [Old English from Latin *portus*, readopted in Middle English from Old French]

port[2] /pɔːt/ *n.* (in full **port wine**) a strong, sweet, dark red (occasionally brown or white) fortified wine of Portugal. [shortened form of *Oporto*, city in Portugal from which port is shipped]

port[3] /pɔːt/ *n.* & *v.* ● *n.* the left-hand side (looking forward) of a ship, boat, or aircraft (cf. STARBOARD). ● *v.tr.* (also *absol.*) turn (the helm) to port. [probably originally the side turned towards PORT[1]]

port[4] /pɔːt/ *n.* **1 a** an opening in the side of a ship for entrance, loading, etc. **b** a porthole. **2** an aperture for the passage of steam, water, etc. **3** *Electr.* a socket or aperture in an electronic circuit, esp. in a computer network, where connections can be made with peripheral equipment or disks etc. inserted. **4** an aperture in a wall etc. for a gun to be fired through. **5** esp. *Sc.* a gate or gateway, esp. of a walled town. [Middle English & Old French *porte* from Latin *porta*]

port[5] /pɔːt/ *v.* & *n.* ● *v.tr. Mil.* carry (a rifle, or other weapon) diagonally across and close to the body with the barrel etc. near the left shoulder (esp. *port arms!*). ● *n.* **1** *Mil.* this position. **2** esp. *literary* a person's carriage or bearing. [Middle English from Old French *port*, ultimately from Latin *portare* 'carry']

port[6] /pɔːt/ *n. Austral. colloq.* **1** a suitcase or travelling bag. **2** a bag of a specified kind, e.g. a shopping bag etc. [abbreviation of PORTMANTEAU]

port[7] /pɔːt/ *v.tr. Computing* transfer (software) from one system to another. [probably from PORT[5], influenced by PORT[4] *n.* 3]

portable /ˈpɔːtəb(ə)l/ *adj.* & *n.* ● *adj.* **1** easily movable, convenient for carrying (*portable TV*; *portable computer*). **2** (of a right, privilege, etc.) capable of being transferred or adapted in altered circumstances (*portable pension*). ● *n.* a portable object, e.g. a radio, typewriter, etc. (*decided to buy a portable*). □ **portability** /pɔːtəˈbɪlɪti/ *n.* **portableness** *n.* **portably** *adv.* [Middle English via Old French *portable* or Late Latin *portabilis* from Latin *portare* 'carry']

portage /ˈpɔːtɪdʒ/ *n.* & *v.* ● *n.* **1** the carrying of boats or goods between two navigable waters. **2** a place at which this is necessary. **3 a** the act or an instance of carrying or transporting. **b** the cost of this. ● *v.tr.* convey (a boat or goods) between navigable waters. [Middle English from Old French, from *porter*: see PORT[5]]

Portakabin /ˈpɔːtəkabɪn/ *n. Brit. propr.* a portable room or building designed for quick assembly. [PORTABLE + CABIN]

portal[1] /ˈpɔːt(ə)l/ *n.* a doorway or gate etc., esp. a large and elaborate one. [Middle English via Old French from medieval Latin *portale* (neut. adj.): see PORTAL[2]]

portal² /ˈpɔːt(ə)l/ *adj.* of or relating to the transverse fissure of the liver, through which pass blood vessels etc. [modern Latin *portalis* from Latin *porta* 'gate']

portal vein *n.* a vein conveying blood to the liver from the spleen, stomach, pancreas, and intestines.

portamento /pɔːtəˈmentəʊ/ *n.* (*pl.* **-os** or **portamenti** /-ti/) *Mus.* **1** the act or an instance of gliding from one note to another in singing, playing the violin, etc. **2** piano playing in a manner intermediate between legato and staccato. [Italian, = carrying]

portative /ˈpɔːtətɪv/ *adj.* **1** serving to carry or support. **2** *Mus. hist.* (esp. of a small pipe organ) portable. [Middle English from Old French *portatif*, apparently alteration of *portatil*, via medieval Latin *portatilis* from Latin *portare* 'carry']

portcullis /pɔːtˈkʌlɪs/ *n.* **1** a strong heavy grating sliding up and down in vertical grooves, lowered to block a gateway in a fortress etc. **2** (**Portcullis**) *Heraldry* one of the four pursuivants of the English College of Arms, with this as a badge. ▫ **portcullised** *adj.* [Middle English from Old French *porte coleïce* 'sliding door', from *porte* 'door' (from Latin *porta*) + *col(e)ïce*, fem. of *couleïs* 'sliding', ultimately from Latin *colare* 'filter']

Porte /pɔːt/ *n.* (in full **the Sublime** or **Ottoman Porte**) *hist.* the Ottoman court at Constantinople. [French (*la Sublime Porte* = the exalted gate), translation of Turkish title of the central office of the Ottoman government]

porte cochère /pɔːt kəʊˈʃɛː, kɒ-/ *n.* **1** a porch large enough for vehicles to pass through, usu. into a courtyard. **2** *US* a roofed structure extending from the entrance of a building over a place where vehicles stop to discharge passengers. [French, from *porte* PORT⁴ + *cochère* (fem. adj.) from *coche* COACH]

portend /pɔːˈtend/ *v.tr.* **1** foreshadow as an omen. **2** give warning of. [Middle English from Latin *portendere portent-*, from *por-* PRO-¹ + *tendere* 'stretch']

portent /ˈpɔːtent, -t(ə)nt/ *n.* **1** an omen, a sign of something to come, esp. something momentous or calamitous. **2** a prodigy; a marvellous thing. [Latin *portentum* (as PORTEND)]

portentous /pɔːˈtentəs/ *adj.* **1** like or serving as a portent. **2** pompously solemn. ▫ **portentously** *adv.* **portentousness** *n.*

■ **Usage** The spelling *portentious* (due to the influence of *pretentious*) is wrong.

porter¹ /ˈpɔːtə/ *n.* **1 a** a person employed to carry luggage etc., esp. a railway, airport, or hotel employee. **b** a hospital employee who moves equipment, trolleys, etc. **2** a dark brown bitter beer brewed from charred or browned malt (apparently originally made esp. for porters). **3** *US* a sleeping car attendant. [Middle English via Old French *port(e)our* from medieval Latin *portator -oris*, from *portare* 'carry']

porter² /ˈpɔːtə/ *n. Brit.* a gatekeeper or doorkeeper, esp. of a large building. [Middle English & Anglo-French, Old French *portier* from Late Latin *portarius*, from *porta* 'door']

porterage /ˈpɔːt(ə)rɪdʒ/ *n.* **1** the work of carrying luggage etc. **2** a charge for this. [PORTER¹ + -AGE]

porterhouse /ˈpɔːtəhaʊs/ *n.* esp. *N. Amer. hist.* **1** a house at which porter and other drinks were retailed. **2** a house where steaks, chops, etc. were served.

porterhouse steak *n.* a thick steak cut from the thick end of a sirloin.

porter's knot see KNOT¹ *n.* 9.

portfire /ˈpɔːtfʌɪə/ *n.* a device for firing rockets, igniting explosives in mining, etc. [partial Anglicization of French *porte-feu*, from *porter* 'carry' + *feu* 'fire']

portfolio /pɔːtˈfəʊlɪəʊ/ *n.* (*pl.* **-os**) **1** a case for keeping loose sheets of paper, drawings, etc. **2** a range of investments held by a person, a company, etc. **3** the office of a Minister of State (cf. MINISTER WITHOUT PORTFOLIO). **4** samples of an artist's work. [Italian *portafogli*, from *portare* 'carry' + *foglio* 'leaf' from Latin *folium*]

porthole /ˈpɔːthəʊl/ *n.* **1** an (esp. glazed) aperture in a ship's or aircraft's side for the admission of light. **2** *hist.* an aperture for pointing a cannon through.

portico /ˈpɔːtɪkəʊ/ *n.* (*pl.* **-oes** or **-os**) a colonnade; a roof supported by columns at regular intervals usu. attached as a porch to a building. [Italian from Latin *porticus* PORCH]

portière /pɔːtɪˈɛː/ *n.* a curtain hung over a door or doorway. [French from *porte* 'door', from Latin *porta*]

portion /ˈpɔːʃ(ə)n/ *n.* & *v.* ● *n.* **1** a part or share. **2** the amount of food allotted to one person. **3** a specified or limited quantity. **4** one's destiny or lot. **5** a dowry. ● *v.tr.* **1** divide (a thing) into portions. **2** (foll. by *out*) distribute. **3** give a dowry to. **4** (foll. by *to*) assign (a thing) to (a person). ▫ **portionless** *adj.* (in sense 5 of *n.*). [Middle English via Old French *porcion portion* from Latin *portio -onis*]

Portland cement /ˈpɔːtlənd/ *n.* a cement manufactured from chalk and clay which when hard resembles Portland stone in colour.

Portland stone /ˈpɔːtlənd/ *n.* a limestone from the Isle of Portland in Dorset, used in building.

portly /ˈpɔːtli/ *adj.* (**portlier**, **portliest**) **1** corpulent; stout. **2** *archaic* of a stately appearance. ▫ **portliness** *n.* [PORT⁵ (in the sense 'bearing') + -LY¹]

portmanteau /pɔːtˈmantəʊ/ *n.* (*pl.* **portmanteaus** or **portmanteaux** /-əʊz/) a travelling bag for clothes etc., esp. of leather and opening into two equal parts. [French *portmanteau*, from *porter* 'carry' (from Latin *portare*) + *manteau* MANTLE]

portmanteau word *n.* a word blending the sounds and combining the meanings of two others, e.g. *motel*, *Oxbridge*.

port of call *n.* a place where a ship, person, etc. stops on a journey.

Port of London Authority *n.* the corporate body controlling the London harbour and docks.

portolan /ˈpɔːtəlan/ *n.* (also **portolano** /pɔːtəˈlɑːnəʊ/) (*pl.* **portolans** or **portolanos**) *hist.* a book of sailing directions with charts, descriptions of harbours, etc. [Italian *portolano* from *porto* PORT¹]

portrait /ˈpɔːtrɪt/ *n.* **1** a representation of a person or animal, esp. of the face, made by drawing, painting, photography, etc. **2** a verbal picture; a graphic description. **3** a person etc. resembling or typifying another (*is the portrait of his father*). **4** (in graphic design etc.) a format in which the height of an illustration etc. is greater than the width (cf. LANDSCAPE *n.* 3). [French, past part. of Old French *portraire* PORTRAY]

portraitist /ˈpɔːtrɪtɪst/ *n.* a person who takes or paints portraits.

portraiture /ˈpɔːtrɪtʃə/ *n.* **1** the art of painting or taking portraits. **2** graphic description. **3** a portrait. [Middle English from Old French (as PORTRAIT)]

portray /pɔːˈtreɪ/ *v.tr.* **1** make a likeness of. **2** describe graphically; depict in words. ▫ **portrayable** *adj.* **portrayal** *n.* **portrayer** *n.* [Middle English from Old French *portraire*, from *por-* = PRO-¹ + *traire* 'draw' from Latin *trahere*]

Port Salut /pɔː səˈluː/ *n.* a pale mild type of cheese. [after the Trappist monastery in France where it was first produced]

port tack see TACK¹ 4.

Portuguese /pɔːtjʊˈɡiːz, pɔːtʃʊˈɡiːz/ *n.* & *adj.* ● *n.* (*pl.* same) **1 a** a native or national of Portugal. **b** a person of Portuguese descent. **2** the language of Portugal. ● *adj.* of or relating to Portugal or its people or language. [Portuguese *portuguez* from medieval Latin *portugalensis*]

Portuguese man-of-war *n.* a dangerous tropical or subtropical marine hydrozoan of the genus *Physalia* with a large crest and a poisonous sting.

port watch see WATCH *n.* 3b.

port wine see PORT[2].

POS *abbr.* point-of-sale.

pose[1] /pəʊz/ *v. & n.* ● *v.* **1** *intr.* assume a certain attitude of body, esp. when being photographed or being painted for a portrait. **2** *intr.* (foll. by *as*) set oneself up as or pretend to be (another person etc.) (*posing as a celebrity*). **3** *intr.* behave affectedly in order to impress others. **4** *tr.* put forward or present (a question etc.). **5** *tr.* place (an artist's model etc.) in a certain attitude or position. ● *n.* **1** an attitude of body or mind. **2** an attitude or pretence, esp. one assumed for effect (*his generosity is a mere pose*). [French *poser* (*v.*), *pose* (*n.*) from Late Latin *pausare* PAUSE: some senses by confusion with Latin *ponere* 'place' (cf. COMPOSE)]

pose[2] /pəʊz/ *v.tr.* puzzle (a person) with a question or problem. [obsolete *appose* from Old French *aposer*, variant of *oposer* OPPOSE]

poser /'pəʊzə/ *n.* **1** = POSEUR. **2** a puzzling question or problem.

poseur /pəʊ'zɜː/ *n.* (*fem.* **poseuse** /pəʊ'zɜːz/) a person who poses for effect or behaves affectedly. [French, from *poser* POSE[1]]

posey /'pəʊzi/ *adj. colloq.* affected, pretentious. [POSE[1] + -Y[1]]

posh /pɒʃ/ *adj. & adv. colloq.* ● *adj.* **1** smart; stylish. **2** esp. *Brit.* of or associated with the upper classes (*spoke with a posh accent*). ● *adv.* esp. *Brit.* in a stylish or upper-class way (*talk posh*; *act posh*). □ **posh up** esp. *Brit.* smarten up. □ **poshly** *adv.* **poshness** *n.* [20th c.: perhaps from slang *posh* 'a dandy': *port out starboard home* (referring to the more comfortable accommodation on ships to and from the East) is a later association and not the true origin]

posit /'pɒzɪt/ *v. & n.* ● *v.tr.* (**posited**, **positing**) **1** assume as a fact, postulate. **2** put in place or position. ● *n. Philos.* a statement which is made on the assumption that it will prove valid. [Latin *ponere posit-* 'place']

position /pə'zɪʃ(ə)n/ *n. & v.* ● *n.* **1** a place occupied by a person or thing. **2** the way in which a thing or its parts are placed or arranged (*sitting in an uncomfortable position*). **3** the proper place (*in position*). **4** the state of being advantageously placed (*jockeying for position*). **5** a person's mental attitude; a way of looking at a question (*changed their position on nuclear disarmament*). **6** a person's situation in relation to others (*puts one in an awkward position*). **7** rank or status; high social standing. **8** paid employment; a job. **9** a place where troops etc. are posted for strategic purposes (*the position was stormed*). **10** the configuration of chessmen etc. during a game. **11** a specific pose in ballet etc. (*hold first position*). **12** *Logic* **a** a proposition. **b** a statement of a proposition. ● *v.tr.* place in position. □ **in a position to** enabled by circumstances, resources, information, etc. to (do, state, etc.). □ **positional** *adj.* **positionally** *adv.* **positioner** *n.* [Middle English from Old French *position* or Latin *positio -onis* (as POSIT)]

position paper *n.* (in business etc.) a written report of attitude or intentions.

position vector *n. Math.* a vector which determines the position of a point.

positive /'pɒzɪtɪv/ *adj. & n.* ● *adj.* **1** formally or explicitly stated; definite, unquestionable (*positive proof*). **2** (of a person) convinced or confident in his or her opinion (*positive that I was not there*). **3** **a** absolute; not relative. **b** *Gram.* (of an adjective or adverb) expressing a simple quality without comparison (cf. COMPARATIVE *adj.* 4, SUPERLATIVE *adj.* 2). **4** *colloq.* downright; complete (*it would be a positive miracle*). **5** constructive; directional (*positive criticism*; *positive thinking*). **6** marked by the presence rather than absence of qualities or *Med.* symptoms (*a positive reaction to the plan*; *the test was positive*). **7** esp. *Philos.* dealing only with matters of fact; practical (cf. POSITIVISM 1). **8** tending in a direction naturally or arbitrarily taken as that of increase or progress (*clockwise rotation is positive*). **9** greater than zero (*positive and negative integers*) (opp. NEGATIVE *adj.* 6). **10** *Electr.* of, containing, or producing the kind of electrical charge produced by rubbing glass with silk; an absence of electrons. **11** (of a photographic image) showing lights and shades or colours true to the original (cf. NEGATIVE *n.* 2a). ● *n.* a positive adjective, photograph, quantity, etc. □ **positively** *adv.* **positiveness** *n.* **positivity** /pɒzɪ'tɪvɪti/ *n.* [Middle English from Old French *positif -ive* or Latin *positivus* (as POSIT)]

positive discrimination *n. Brit.* the practice of making distinctions in favour of groups considered to be underprivileged.

positive feedback *n.* **1** *Electronics* the return of part of an output signal to the input, tending to increase the amplification etc. **2** esp. *Biol.* the enhancing or amplification of an effect by its own influence on the process which gives rise to it. **3** a constructive response to an experiment, questionnaire, etc.

positive geotropism *n.* the tendency of roots to grow towards the centre of the earth.

positive pole *n.* the north-seeking pole.

positive prescription see PRESCRIPTION 3.

positive ray *n. Physics* a canal ray.

positive sign *n.* = PLUS SIGN.

positive vetting *n. Brit.* an exhaustive inquiry into the background and character of a candidate for a post in the Civil Service that involves access to secret material.

positivism /'pɒzɪtɪvɪz(ə)m/ *n. Philos.* **1** **a** the philosophical system of Auguste Comte (d. 1857), recognizing only non-metaphysical facts and observable phenomena, and rejecting metaphysics and theism. **b** a religious system founded on this. **2** = LOGICAL POSITIVISM. □ **positivist** *n. & adj.* **positivistic** /-'vɪstɪk/ *adj.* **positivistically** /-'vɪstɪk(ə)li/ *adv.* [French *positivisme* (as POSITIVE)]

positron /'pɒzɪtrɒn/ *n. Physics* a subatomic particle with a positive charge equal to the negative charge of an electron and having the same mass as an electron. [POSITIVE + -TRON]

posology /pə'sɒlədʒi/ *n.* the study of the dosage of medicines. □ **posological** /pɒsə'lɒdʒɪk(ə)l/ *adj.* [French *posologie* from Greek *posos* 'how much']

posse /'pɒsi/ *n.* **1** a strong force or company or assemblage. **2** (in full **posse comitatus** /kɒmɪ'teɪtəs/) **a** a body of constables, law-enforcers, etc. **b** esp. *US* a body of men summoned by a sheriff etc. to enforce the law. **3** *slang* a gang of black (esp. Jamaican) youths involved in usu. drug-related crime. [medieval Latin, = power, from Latin *posse* 'be able': *comitatus* = of the county]

possess /pə'zɛs/ *v.tr.* **1** hold as property; own. **2** have as a faculty, quality, etc. (*they possess a special value for us*). **3** (also *refl.*; foll. by *in*) maintain (oneself, one's soul, etc.) in a specified state (*possess oneself in patience*). **4** **a** (of a demon etc.) occupy; have power over (a person etc.) (*possessed by the Devil*). **b** (of an emotion, infatuation, etc.) dominate, be an obsession of (*possessed by fear*). **5** have sexual intercourse with (esp. a woman). □ **be possessed of** own, have. **possess oneself of** take or get for one's own. **what possessed you?** an expression of incredulity. □ **possessor** *n.* **possessory** *adj.* [Old French *possesser* from Latin *possidēre possess-*, from *potis* 'able' + *sedēre* 'sit']

possession /pə'zɛʃ(ə)n/ *n.* **1** the act or state of possessing or being possessed. **2** the thing possessed. **3** the act or state of actual holding or occupancy. **4** *Law* power or control similar to lawful ownership but which may exist separately from it (*prosecuted for possession of narcotic drugs*). **5** (in *pl.*) property, wealth, subject territory, etc. **6** *Football* etc. temporary control of the ball by a particular player. □ **in possession** **1** (of a person) possessing. **2** (of a thing) possessed. **in possession of** **1** having in one's possession. **2** maintaining control over (*in possession of one's wits*). **in the possession of** held or owned by. **take possession** (often foll. by *of*) become the owner or possessor (of a thing). □ **possessionless** *adj.* [Middle English from Old French *possession* or Latin *possessio -onis* (as POSSESS)]

possession order *n. Brit.* an order made by a court directing that possession of a property be given to the owner.

possessive /pəˈzɛsɪv/ *adj. & n.* ● *adj.* **1** showing a desire to possess or retain what one already owns. **2** showing jealous and domineering tendencies towards another person. **3** *Gram.* indicating possession. ● *n.* (in full **possessive case**) *Gram.* the case of nouns and pronouns expressing possession. □ **possessively** *adv.* **possessiveness** *n.* [Latin *possessivus* (as POSSESS), translation of Greek *ktētikē* (*ptōsis* 'case')]

possessive pronoun *n.* each of the pronouns indicating possession (*my*, *your*, *his*, *their*, etc.) or the corresponding absolute forms (*mine*, *yours*, *his*, *theirs*, etc.).

posset /ˈpɒsɪt/ *n. hist.* a drink made of hot milk curdled with ale, wine, etc., often flavoured with spices, formerly used as a remedy for colds etc. [Middle English *poshote*: origin unknown]

possibility /pɒsɪˈbɪlɪti/ *n.* (*pl.* **-ies**) **1** the state or fact of being possible, or an occurrence of this (*outside the range of possibility*; *saw no possibility of going away*). **2** a thing that may exist or happen (*there are three possibilities*). **3** (usu. in *pl.*) the capability of being used, improved, etc.; the potential of an object or situation (esp. *have possibilities*). [Middle English from Old French *possibilité* or Late Latin *possibilitas -tatis* (as POSSIBLE)]

possible /ˈpɒsɪb(ə)l/ *adj. & n.* ● *adj.* **1** capable of existing or happening; that may be managed, achieved, etc. (*came as early as possible*; *did as much as possible*). **2** that is likely to happen etc. (*few thought their victory possible*). **3** acceptable; potential (*a possible way of doing it*). ● *n.* **1** a possible candidate, member of a team, etc. **2** (prec. by *the*) whatever is likely, manageable, etc. **3** the highest possible score, esp. in shooting etc. [Middle English from Old French *possible* or Latin *possibilis*, from *posse* 'be able']

possibly /ˈpɒsɪbli/ *adv.* **1** perhaps. **2** in accordance with possibility (*cannot possibly refuse*).

possum /ˈpɒsəm/ *n.* **1** *colloq.* = OPOSSUM 1. **2** *Austral.* a phalanger resembling an American opossum. □ **play possum 1** pretend to be asleep or unconscious when threatened. **2** feign ignorance. [abbreviation]

post[1] /pəʊst/ *n. & v.* ● *n.* **1** a long stout piece of timber or metal set upright in the ground etc.: **a** to support something, esp. in building. **b** to mark a position, boundary, etc. **c** to carry notices. **2** a pole etc. marking the start or finish of a race. ● *v.tr.* **1** (often foll. by *up*) **a** attach (a paper etc.) in a prominent place; stick up (*post no bills*). **b** announce or advertise by placard or in a published text. **2** publish the name of (a ship etc.) as overdue or missing. **3** placard (a wall etc.) with bills etc. **4** *N. Amer.* achieve (a score in a game etc.). [Old English from Latin *postis*: reinforced in Middle English also from Old French, Middle Low German, Middle Dutch]

post[2] /pəʊst/ *n., v., & adv.* ● *n.* **1** *Brit.* the official conveyance of parcels, letters, etc. (*send it by post*). **2** *Brit.* a single collection, dispatch, or delivery of these; the letters etc. dispatched (*has the post arrived yet?*). **3** *Brit.* a place where letters etc. are dealt with; a post office or postbox (*take it to the post*). **4** *hist.* **a** one of a series of couriers who carried mail on horseback between fixed stages. **b** a letter-carrier; a mail cart. ● *v.* **1** *tr.* put (a letter etc.) in the post. **2** *tr.* (esp. as **posted** *adj.*) (*US* often foll. by *up*) supply a person with information (*keep me posted*). **3** *tr.* **a** enter (an item) in a ledger. **b** (often foll. by *up*) complete (a ledger) in this way. **c** carry (an entry) from an auxiliary book to a more formal one, or from one account to another. **4** *intr.* **a** travel with haste, hurry. **b** *hist.* travel with relays of horses. ● *adv. archaic* or *hist.* express; with haste. [French *poste* (fem.) from Italian *posta*, ultimately from Latin *ponere posit-* 'place']

post[3] /pəʊst/ *n. & v.* ● *n.* **1** a place where a soldier is stationed or which he or she patrols. **2** a place of duty. **3 a** a position taken up by a body of soldiers. **b** a force occupying this. **c** a fort. **4** a situation, paid employment. **5** = TRADING POST. **6** *Naut. hist.* a commission as an officer in command of a vessel of 20 guns or more. ● *v.tr.* **1** place or station (soldiers, an employee, etc.). **2** appoint to a post or command. [French *poste* (masc.) from Italian *posto* via Romanic from Latin *ponere posit-* 'place']

post- /pəʊst/ *prefix* after in time or order. [from or suggested by Latin *post* (adv. & prep.)]

postage /ˈpəʊstɪdʒ/ *n.* the amount charged for sending a letter etc. by post, usu. prepaid in the form of a stamp (*£25 including postage and packing*).

postage meter *n. N. Amer.* a franking machine.

postage stamp *n.* an official stamp affixed to or imprinted on a letter etc. indicating the amount of postage paid.

postal /ˈpəʊst(ə)l/ *adj. & n.* ● *adj.* **1** of the post. **2** esp. *Brit.* by post (*postal vote*). ● *n. US* a postcard. □ **postally** *adv.* [French (*poste* POST[2])]

postal card *n. US* = POSTCARD.

postal code *n.* = POSTCODE.

postal meter *n.* a franking machine.

postal note *n. Austral. & NZ* = POSTAL ORDER.

postal order *n. Brit.* a money order issued by the Post Office, payable to a specified person.

Postal Union *n.* a union of the governments of various countries for the regulation of international postage.

postbag /ˈpəʊs(t)bag/ *n. Brit.* = MAILBAG.

postbox /ˈpəʊs(t)bɒks/ *n. Brit.* a public box in which mail is posted for subsequent collection and delivery.

postcard /ˈpəʊs(t)kɑːd/ *n.* a card, often with a photograph, cartoon, etc. on one side, for sending a short message by post without an envelope.

post-chaise /ˈpəʊs(t)ʃeɪz/ *n. hist.* a travelling carriage hired from stage to stage or drawn by horses hired in this manner.

post-classical /pəʊs(t)ˈklasɪk(ə)l/ *adj.* (esp. of Greek and Roman literature) later than the classical period.

postcode /ˈpəʊs(t)kəʊd/ *n. Brit.* a group of figures or letters and figures which are added to a postal address to assist sorting.

post-coital /pəʊs(t)ˈkəʊɪt(ə)l/ *adj.* occurring or existing after sexual intercourse. □ **post-coitally** *adv.*

post-date *v. & n.* ● *v.tr.* /pəʊs(t)ˈdeɪt/ affix or assign a date later than the actual one to (a document, event, etc.). ● *n.* /ˈpəʊs(t)deɪt/ such a date.

postdoctoral /pəʊs(t)ˈdɒkt(ə)r(ə)l/ *adj.* of or relating to research undertaken after the completion of doctoral research.

post-entry /ˈpəʊstentri/ *n.* (*pl.* **-ies**) a late or subsequent entry, esp. in a race or in bookkeeping.

poster /ˈpəʊstə/ *n.* **1** a placard in a public place. **2** a large printed picture. **3** a billposter.

poste restante /pəʊst ˈrɛst(ə)nt/ *n. Brit.* **1** a direction on a letter to indicate that it should be kept at a specified post office until collected by the addressee. **2** the service department in a post office keeping such letters. [French, = letter(s) remaining]

posterior /pɒˈstɪərɪə/ *adj. & n.* ● *adj.* **1** later; coming after in series, order, or time. **2** situated at the back. ● *n.* the buttocks. □ **posteriority** /pɒˌstɪərɪˈɒrɪti/ *n.* **posteriorly** *adv.* [Latin, comparative of *posterus* 'following', from *post* 'after']

posterity /pɒˈstɛrɪti/ *n.* **1** all succeeding generations. **2** the descendants of a person. [Middle English via Old French *posterité* from Latin *posteritas -tatis*, from *posterus*: see POSTERIOR]

postern /ˈpɒst(ə)n, ˈpəʊst-/ *n.* **1** a back door. **2** a side way or entrance. [Middle English via Old French *posterne*, *posterle*, from Late Latin *posterula*, diminutive of *posterus*: see POSTERIOR]

poster paint *n.* a gummy opaque paint.

post exchange *n. US Mil.* a shop at a military camp etc.

post-feminist /pəʊst'fɛmɪnɪst/ *adj. & n.* ● *adj.* of or relating to the ideas, attitudes, etc., which ignore or reject feminist ideas of the 1960s and subsequent decades. ● *n.* a person holding such ideas and attitudes. ▫ **post-feminism** *n.*

postfix *n. & v.* ● *n.* /'pəʊs(t)fɪks/ a suffix. ● *v.tr.* /pəʊs(t)'fɪks/ append (letters) at the end of a word.

post-free *adj. & adv. Brit.* carried by post free of charge or with the postage prepaid.

postglacial /pəʊs(t)'gleɪʃ(ə)l, -sɪəl/ *adj. & n.* ● *adj.* formed or occurring after a glacial period. ● *n.* a postglacial period or deposit.

postgrad *adj. & n. colloq.* = POSTGRADUATE. [abbreviation]

postgraduate /pəʊs(t)'gradjʊət/ *adj. & n.* ● *adj.* **1** (of a course of study) carried on after taking a first degree. **2** of or relating to students following this course of study (*postgraduate accommodation*). ● *n.* a postgraduate student.

post-haste *adv.* with great speed. [POST[2]]

post-horn *n. hist.* a valveless horn formerly used to announce the arrival of the post.

posthumous /'pɒstjʊməs/ *adj.* **1** occurring after death. **2** (of a child) born after the death of its father. **3** (of a book etc.) published after the author's death. ▫ **posthumously** *adv.* [Latin *postumus* 'last' (superlative from *post* 'after'): in Late Latin *posth-* by association with *humus* 'ground']

postiche /pɒ'sti:ʃ/ *n.* a coil of false hair, worn as an adornment. [French, = false, from Italian *posticcio*]

postie /'pəʊsti/ *n. Brit. colloq.* a postman or postwoman. [abbreviation]

postil /'pɒstɪl/ *n. hist.* **1** a marginal note or comment, esp. on a text of Scripture. **2** a commentary. [Middle English via Old French *postille* from medieval Latin *postilla*, of uncertain origin]

postilion /pɒ'stɪlɪən/ *n.* (also **postillion**) the rider on the near (left-hand side) horse drawing a coach etc. when there is no coachman. [French *postillon* from Italian *postiglione* 'post-boy', from *posta* POST[2]]

post-Impressionism /pəʊstɪm'preʃ(ə)nɪz(ə)m/ *n.* artistic aims and methods developed from, or as a reaction against, Impressionism and intending to express the individual artist's conception of the objects represented rather than the general observer's view. ▫ **post-Impressionist** *n. & adj.*

post-industrial /pəʊstɪn'dʌstrɪəl/ *adj.* relating to or characteristic of a society or economy which no longer relies on heavy industry.

postliminy /pəʊs(t)'lɪmɪni/ *n.* **1** (in international law) the restoration to their former status of persons and things taken in war. **2** (in Roman law) the right of a banished person or captive to resume civic privileges on return from exile. [Latin *postliminium* (as POST-, *limen liminis* 'threshold')]

postlude /'pəʊs(t)lu:d/ *n. Mus.* a concluding voluntary. [POST-, after PRELUDE]

postman /'pəʊs(t)mən/ *n.* (*pl.* **-men**) a man who is employed to deliver and collect letters etc.

postman's knock *n. Brit.* a game in which imaginary letters are delivered in exchange for kisses.

postmark /'pəʊs(t)mɑ:k/ *n. & v.* ● *n.* an official mark stamped on a letter, esp. one giving the place, date, etc. of dispatch or arrival, and serving to cancel the stamp. ● *v.tr.* mark (an envelope etc.) with this.

postmaster /'pəʊs(t)mɑ:stə/ *n.* a man in charge of a post office.

postmaster general *n.* the head of a country's postal service (abolished in the UK as an office in 1969).

post-mill *n.* a windmill pivoted on a post and turning to catch the wind.

post-millennial /pəʊs(t)mɪ'lɛnɪəl/ *adj.* following the millennium.

post-millennialism /pəʊs(t)mɪ'lɛnɪəlɪz(ə)m/ *n.* the doctrine that a second Advent will follow the millennium. ▫ **post-millennialist** *n.*

postmistress /'pəʊs(t)mɪstrɪs/ *n.* a woman in charge of a post office.

postmodern /pəʊs(t)'mɒd(ə)n/ *adj.* (in literature, architecture, the arts, etc.) denoting a movement reacting against modern tendencies, esp. by drawing attention to former conventions. ▫ **postmodernism** *n.* **postmodernist** *n. & adj.* **postmodernity** /-'də:nɪti/ *n.*

post-mortem /pəʊs(t)'mɔ:təm/ *n., adv., & adj.* ● *n.* **1** (in full **post-mortem examination**) an examination made after death, esp. to determine its cause. **2** a discussion analysing the course and result of a game, election, etc. ● *adv. & adj.* after death. [Latin]

post-natal /pəʊs(t)'neɪt(ə)l/ *adj.* characteristic of or relating to the period after childbirth. ▫ **post-natally** *adv.*

post-natal depression *n.* depression suffered by a mother following childbirth.

post-nuptial /pəʊs(t)'nʌpʃ(ə)l/ *adj.* after marriage.

post-obit /pəʊst'əʊbɪt, -'ɒbɪt/ *n. & adj.* ● *n. Brit.* a bond given to a lender by a borrower securing a sum for payment on the death of another person from whom the borrower expects to inherit. ● *adj.* taking effect after death. [Latin *post obitum*, from *post* 'after' + *obitus* 'decease' from *obire* 'die']

Post Office *n.* **1** the public department or corporation responsible for postal services and (in some countries) telecommunications. **2** (**post office**) **a** a room or building where postal business is carried on. **b** *US* = POSTMAN'S KNOCK.

post office box *n.* a numbered place in a post office where letters are kept until called for.

post-operative /pəʊst'ɒp(ə)rətɪv/ *adj.* of the period following a surgical operation.

post-paid *adj. & adv.* on which postage has been paid.

post-partum /pəʊs(t)'pɑ:təm/ *adj.* following parturition. [Latin *post partum* 'after childbirth' (as POST[1], PARTURIENT)]

postpone /pəʊs(t)'pəʊn, pə'spəʊn/ *v.tr.* cause or arrange (an event etc.) to take place at a later time. ▫ **postponable** *adj.* **postponement** *n.* **postponer** *n.* [Latin *postponere* (as POST-, *ponere posit-* 'place')]

postposition /pəʊs(t)pə'zɪʃ(ə)n/ *n. Gram.* **1** a word or particle, esp. an enclitic, placed after the word it modifies, e.g. *-ward* in *homeward* and *at* in *the books we looked at*. **2** the use of a postposition. ▫ **postpositional** *adj. & n.* **postpositive** /pəʊs(t)'pɒzɪtɪv/ *adj. & n.* **postpositively** /-'pɒzɪtɪvli/ *adv.* [Late Latin *postpositio* (as POSTPONE)]

postprandial /pəʊs(t)'prandɪəl/ *adj. formal* or *joc.* after dinner or lunch. [POST- + Latin *prandium* 'a meal']

post-production /pəʊstprə'dʌkʃ(ə)n/ *n.* work done on a film, broadcast, etc. after filming or recording has taken place (usu. *attrib.*: *post-production costs*).

post room *n. Brit.* the department of a company that deals with incoming and outgoing mail.

postscript /'pəʊs(t)skrɪpt/ *n.* **1** an additional paragraph or remark, usu. at the end of a letter after the signature and introduced by 'PS'. **2** any additional information, action, etc. [Latin *postscriptum*, neut. past part. of *postscribere* (as POST-, *scribere* 'write')]

post-structuralism /pəʊs(t)'strʌktʃ(ə)r(ə)lɪz(ə)m/ *n.* an extension and critique of structuralism, esp. as used in critical textual analysis. ▫ **post-structuralist** *n. & adj.*

post-tax /pəʊs(t)'taks/ *attrib.adj. Brit.* (of income) after the deduction of taxes.

post town *n. Brit.* a town with a post office, esp. one that is not a sub-office of another.

post-traumatic stress disorder /pəʊs(t)trɔ:matɪk, -traʊ-/ *n. Med.* a condition of persistent mental and emotional stress occurring after injury or severe psychological shock.

postulant /ˈpɒstjʊl(ə)nt/ *n.* a candidate, esp. for admission into a religious order. [French *postulant* or Latin *postulans -antis* (as POSTULATE)]

postulate *v.* & *n.* ● *v.tr.* /ˈpɒstjʊleɪt/ **1** (often foll. by *that* + clause) assume as a necessary condition, esp. as a basis for reasoning; take for granted. **2** claim. **3** (in ecclesiastical law) nominate or elect to a higher rank. ● *n.* /ˈpɒstjʊlət/ **1** a thing postulated. **2** a fundamental prerequisite or condition. **3** *Math.* an assumption used as a basis for mathematical reasoning. □ **postulation** /pɒstjʊˈleɪʃ(ə)n/ *n.* [Latin *postulare postulat-* 'demand']

postulator /ˈpɒstjʊleɪtə/ *n.* **1** a person who postulates. **2** *RC Ch.* a person who presents a case for canonization or beatification.

posture /ˈpɒstʃə/ *n.* & *v.* ● *n.* **1** the relative position of parts, esp. of the body (*in a reclining posture*). **2** carriage or bearing (*improved by good posture and balance*). **3** a mental or spiritual attitude or condition. **4** the condition or state (of affairs etc.) (*in more diplomatic postures*). ● *v.* **1** *intr.* assume a mental or physical attitude, esp. for effect (*inclined to strut and posture*). **2** *tr.* pose (a person). □ **postural** *adj.* **posturer** *n.* [French via Italian *postura* from Latin *positura*, from *ponere posit-* 'place']

post-war /pəʊs(t)ˈwɔː, ˈpəʊs(t)-/ *adj.* occurring or existing after a war (esp. the most recent major war).

postwoman /ˈpəʊs(t)wʊmən/ *n.* (*pl.* **-women**) a woman who is employed to deliver and collect letters etc.

posy /ˈpəʊzi/ *n.* (*pl.* **-ies**) **1** a small bunch of flowers. **2** *archaic* a short motto, line of verse, etc., inscribed within a ring. [alteration of POESY]

posy ring *n.* a ring engraved with a motto etc.

pot[1] /pɒt/ *n.* & *v.* ● *n.* **1 a** a vessel, usu. rounded, of ceramic ware or metal or glass for holding liquids or solids or for cooking in. **b** such a vessel designed to hold a particular substance (*coffee pot*; *teapot*) **2 a** = FLOWERPOT. **b** = CHIMNEY POT. **c** = LOBSTER POT. **d** = CHAMBER POT, POTTY[2]. **3** a drinking vessel of pewter etc. **4** the contents of a pot (*ate a whole pot of jam*). **5** the total amount of the bet in a game etc. **6** *colloq.* a large sum (*pots of money*). **7** *slang* a vessel given as a prize in an athletic contest, esp. a silver cup. **8** = POT BELLY 1. ● *v.tr.* (**potted**, **potting**) **1** place in a pot. **2** (usu. as **potted** *adj.*) preserve in a sealed pot (*potted shrimps*). **3** *Brit.* sit (a young child) on a chamber pot. **4** *Brit.* pocket (a ball) in billiards etc. **5** shoot at, hit, or kill (an animal) with a pot-shot. **6** seize or secure. **7** (esp. as **potted** *adj.*) *Brit.* abridge or epitomize (*in a potted version*; *potted wisdom*). □ **go to pot** *colloq.* deteriorate; be ruined. **pot of gold** an imaginary reward; an ideal; a jackpot. □ **potful** *n.* (*pl.* **-fuls**). [Old English *pott*, corresponding to Old Frisian, Middle Dutch, Middle Low German *pot*, from popular Latin]

pot[2] /pɒt/ *n. slang* marijuana. [probably from Mexican Spanish *potiguaya*]

pot[3] /pɒt/ *n.* & *v. Austral.* & *NZ* ● *n.* a dropped goal in rugby. ● *v.tr.* (**potted**, **potting**) score (a dropped goal). [perhaps from POT-SHOT]

potable /ˈpəʊtəb(ə)l/ *adj.* drinkable. □ **potability** /-ˈbɪlɪti/ *n.* [French *potable* or Late Latin *potabilis* from Latin *potare* 'drink']

potage /pɒˈtɑːʒ/ *n.* thick soup. [French (as POTTAGE)]

potager /ˈpɒtədʒə/ *n.* a kitchen garden. [French]

potamic /pəˈtamɪk/ *adj.* of rivers. □ **potamology** /pɒtəˈmɒlɪdʒi/ *n.* [Greek *potamos* 'river']

potash /ˈpɒtaʃ/ *n.* an alkaline potassium compound, usu. potassium carbonate or hydroxide. [17th-c. *pot-ashes* from Dutch *pot-asschen* (as POT[1], ASH[1]): originally obtained by leaching vegetable ashes and evaporating the solution in iron pots]

potassium /pəˈtasɪəm/ *n. Chem.* a soft silver-white metallic element occurring naturally in sea water and various minerals, an essential element for living organisms, and forming many useful compounds used industrially (symbol K). □ **potassic** *adj.* [POTASH + -IUM]

potassium-argon dating *n. Geol.* a method of dating rocks from the relative proportions of radioactive potassium-40 and its decay produce, argon-40.

potassium carbonate *n.* a hygroscopic white crystalline solid, alkaline in solution, with many industrial applications. Chem. formula: K_2CO_3.

potassium chloride *n.* a white crystalline solid used as a fertilizer and in photographic processing. Chem. formula: KC1.

potassium cyanide *n.* a highly toxic solid that releases poisonous hydrogen cyanide gas when hydrolysed. Chem. formula: KCN.

potassium iodide *n.* a white crystalline solid used as an additive in table salt to prevent iodine deficiency. Chem. formula: KI.

potassium permanganate *n.* a purple crystalline solid that is used in solution as an oxidizing agent and disinfectant. Chem. formula: $KMnO_4$.

potation /pə(ʊ)ˈteɪʃ(ə)n/ *n. formal* or *joc.* **1** a drink. **2** the act or an instance of drinking. **3** (usu. in *pl.*) the act or an instance of tippling. □ **potatory** /ˈpəʊtət(ə)ri, pə(ʊ)ˈteɪt(ə)ri/ *adj.* [Middle English via Old French *potation* or Latin *potatio* from *potare* 'drink']

potato /pəˈteɪtəʊ/ *n.* (*pl.* **-oes**) **1** a starchy plant tuber that is cooked and used for food. **2** the plant, *Solanum tuberosum*, bearing this. **3** *Brit. colloq.* a hole in (esp. the heel of) a sock or stocking. [Spanish *patata*, variant of Taino *batata* SWEET POTATO]

potato chip *n.* = CHIP *n.* 3.

potato crisp see CRISP *n.*

pot-au-feu /pɒtəʊˈfə, French pɔtofø/ *n.* (*pl.* same) **1** French soup of usu. boiled beef and vegetables cooked in a large pot. **2** the broth from this. [French, = pot on the fire]

pot belly *n.* (*pl.* **-ies**) **1** a protruding stomach. **2** a person with this. **3** a small bulbous stove. □ **pot-bellied** *adj.*

potboiler /ˈpɒtbɔɪlə/ *n.* **1** a work of literature or art done merely to make the writer or artist a living. **2** a writer or artist who does this.

pot-bound *adj.* (of a plant) having roots which fill the flowerpot, leaving no room to expand.

potch /pɒtʃ/ *n.* an opal of inferior quality. [19th c.: origin unknown]

pot cheese *n. US* cottage cheese.

poteen /pɒˈtiːn/ *n.* (also **potheen** /-ˈtʃiːn/) *Ir.* alcohol made illicitly, usu. from potatoes. [Irish *poitín*, diminutive of *pota* POT[1]]

potent[1] /ˈpəʊt(ə)nt/ *adj.* **1** powerful; strong. **2** (of a reason) cogent; forceful. **3** (of a male) capable of sexual erection or orgasm. **4** *literary* mighty. □ **potence** *n.* **potency** *n.* **potently** *adv.* [Latin *potens -entis*, pres. part. of *posse* 'be able']

potent[2] /ˈpəʊt(ə)nt/ *adj.* & *n. Heraldry* ● *adj.* **1** with a crutch-head shape. **2** (of a fur) formed by a series of such shapes. ● *n.* this fur. [Middle English via Old French *potence* 'crutch' from Latin *potentia* 'power' (as POTENT[1])]

potentate /ˈpəʊt(ə)nteɪt/ *n.* a monarch or ruler. [Middle English from Old French *potentat* or Latin *potentatus* 'dominion' (as POTENT[2])]

potential /pə(ʊ)ˈtɛnʃ(ə)l/ *adj.* & *n.* ● *adj.* capable of coming into being or action; latent. ● *n.* **1** the capacity for use or development; possibility (*achieved its highest potential*). **2** usable resources. **3** *Physics* the quantity determining the energy of mass in a gravitational field or of charge in an electric field. □ **potentiality** /-ʃɪˈalɪti/ *n.* **potentialize** *v.tr.* (also **-ise**). **potentially** *adv.* [Middle English via Old French *potencial* or Late Latin *potentialis* from *potentia* (as POTENT[1])]

potential barrier *n.* a region of high potential impeding the movement of particles etc.

potential difference *n.* the difference of electric potential between two points.

potential energy *n.* a body's ability to do work by virtue of its position relative to others, stresses within itself, electric charge, etc.

potentiate /pə(ʊ)'tɛnʃɪeɪt/ *v.tr.* **1** make more powerful, esp. increase the effectiveness of (a drug). **2** make possible. [POTENT[1], on the pattern of SUBSTANTIATE]

potentilla /pəʊt(ə)n'tɪlə/ *n.* any plant or shrub of the genus *Potentilla*; a cinquefoil. [medieval Latin, diminutive of Latin *potens* POTENT[1]]

potentiometer /pə(ʊ),tɛnʃɪ'ɒmɪtə/ *n.* an instrument for measuring or adjusting small electrical potentials. □ **potentiometric** /-ʃɪə'mɛtrɪk/ *adj.* **potentiometry** /-ʃɪ'ɒmɪtri/ *n.*

pothead /'pɒthɛd/ *n. slang* a person who smokes pot. [POT[2]]

potheen var. of POTEEN.

pother /'pɒðə/ *n. & v. literary* ● *n.* a noise; commotion; fuss. ● *v.* **1** *tr.* fluster, worry. **2** *intr.* make a fuss. [16th c.: origin unknown]

pot-herb *n.* any herb grown for culinary use.

pothole /'pɒthəʊl/ *n. & v.* ● *n.* **1** a deep hole or system of caves and underground river beds formed by the erosion of rock esp. by the action of water. **2** a deep hole in the ground or a river bed. **3** a hole in a road surface caused by wear or subsidence. ● *v.intr. Brit.* explore potholes. □ **potholer** *n.* **potholing** *n.* [*pot* 'pit' (perhaps from Scandinavian) + HOLE]

pot-hook *n.* **1** a hook over a hearth for hanging a pot etc. on, or for lifting a hot pot. **2** a curved stroke in handwriting, esp. as made in learning to write.

pot-hunter *n.* **1** a person who hunts for game at random. **2** a person who takes part in a contest merely for the sake of the prize.

potion /'pəʊʃ(ə)n/ *n.* a liquid medicine, drug, poison, etc. [Middle English via Old French from Latin *potio -onis*, from *potus* 'having drunk']

potlatch /'pɒtlatʃ/ *n.* (among certain N. American Indians) a ceremonial giving away or destruction of property to display wealth. [Chinook from Nootka *patlatsh* 'gift']

potluck /'pɒtlʌk, pɒt'lʌk/ *n.* (also **pot luck**) whatever is available.

potoroo /pɒtə'ru:/ *n.* a rat kangaroo, esp. of the genus *Potorus*. [Aboriginal, probably Dharuk *badaru*]

pot pie *n.* a pie of meat etc. or fruit with a crust baked in a pot.

pot plant *n. Brit.* a plant grown in a flowerpot.

pot-pourri /pəʊ'pʊəri, -'ri:, pɒt'pʊəri/ *n.* (*pl.* **pot-pourris**) **1** a mixture of dried petals and spices used to perfume a room etc. **2** a musical or literary medley. [earlier = a stew made of different kinds of meat: French, = rotten pot]

potrero /pɒ'trɛ:rəʊ/ *n.* (*pl.* **-os**) **1** (in the south-western US and S. America) a paddock or pasture for horses or cattle. **2** (in the south-western US) a narrow steep-sided plateau. [Spanish from *potro* 'colt, pony']

pot roast *n. & v.* ● *n.* a piece of meat cooked slowly in a covered dish. ● *v.tr.* (**pot-roast**) cook (a piece of meat) in this way.

potsherd /'pɒt-ʃə:d/ *n.* a broken piece of ceramic material, esp. one found on an archaeological site.

pot-shot *n.* **1** a random shot. **2** a shot aimed at an animal etc. within easy reach. **3** a shot at a game bird etc. merely to provide a meal.

pottage /'pɒtɪdʒ/ *n. archaic* soup, stew. [Middle English from Old French *potage* (as POT[1])]

potter[1] /'pɒtə/ *v.* (*US* **putter** /'pʌtə/) **1** *intr.* **a** (often foll. by *about, around*) work or occupy oneself in a desultory but pleasant manner (*likes pottering about in the garden*). **b** (often foll. by *at, in*) dabble in a subject or occupation. **2** *intr. Brit.* go slowly, dawdle, loiter (*pottered up to the pub*). **3** *tr.* (foll. by *away*) fritter away (one's time etc.). □ **potterer** *n.* [frequentative of dialect *pote* 'push', from Old English *potian*]

potter[2] /'pɒtə/ *n.* a maker of ceramic vessels. [Old English *pottere* (as POT[1])]

potter's field *n.* a burial place for paupers, strangers, etc. (after Matt. 27:7).

potter's wheel *n.* a horizontal revolving disc to carry clay for making pots.

pottery /'pɒt(ə)ri/ *n.* (*pl.* **-ies**) **1** vessels etc. made of fired clay. **2** a potter's work. **3** a potter's workshop. □ **the Potteries** a district in N. Staffordshire, where the English pottery industry is centred. [Middle English from Old French *poterie*, from *potier* POTTER[2]]

potting shed /'pɒtɪŋ/ *n.* a building in which plants are potted and tools etc. are stored.

pottle /'pɒt(ə)l/ *n.* **1** *Brit.* a small punnet or carton for strawberries etc. **2** *archaic* **a** a measure for liquids; a half gallon. **b** a pot etc. containing this. [Middle English from Old French *potel* (as POT[1])]

potto /'pɒtəʊ/ *n.* (*pl.* **-os**) a W. African lemur-like mammal, *Perodicticus potto*. [perhaps from Guinea dialect]

Pott's fracture /pɒts/ *n.* a fracture of the lower end of the fibula, usu. with dislocation of the ankle. [P. *Pott*, English surgeon d. 1788]

potty[1] /'pɒti/ *adj.* (**pottier**, **pottiest**) *Brit. colloq.* **1** foolish or crazy. **2** (usu. foll. by *little*) insignificant, trivial (*a potty little place*). □ **pottiness** *n.* [19th c.: origin unknown]

potty[2] /'pɒti/ *n.* (*pl.* **-ies**) *colloq.* a chamber pot, esp. for a child.

potty-train *v.tr.* train (a small child) to use a potty.

pot-valiant *adj.* courageous because of drunkenness. □ **pot-valour** *n.*

pouch /paʊtʃ/ *n. & v.* ● *n.* **1** a small bag or detachable outside pocket. **2** a baggy area of skin underneath the eyes etc. **3** **a** a pocket-like receptacle in which marsupials carry their young during lactation. **b** any of several similar structures in various animals, e.g. in the cheeks of rodents. **4** a soldier's leather ammunition bag. **5** a lockable bag for mail or dispatches. **6** *Bot.* a bag-like cavity, esp. the seed vessel, in a plant. ● *v.tr.* **1** put or make into a pouch. **2** take possession of; pocket. **3** make (part of a dress etc.) hang like a pouch. □ **pouched** *adj.* **pouchy** *adj.* [Middle English from Old Northern French *pouche*: cf. POKE[2]]

pouf var. of POOF[1], POUFFE.

pouffe /pu:f/ *n.* (also **pouf**) a large firm cushion used as a low seat or footstool. [French *pouf*; ultimately imitative]

poulard /pu:'lɑ:d/ *n.* a domestic hen that has been spayed and fattened for eating. [French *poularde* from *poule* 'hen']

poult[1] /pəʊlt/ *n.* a young domestic fowl, turkey, pheasant, etc. [Middle English, contraction from PULLET]

poult[2] /pu:lt, pɒlt/ *n.* (in full **poult-de-soie** /pu:də'swɑ:/) a fine corded silk or taffeta, usu. coloured. [French, of unknown origin]

poulterer /'pəʊlt(ə)rə/ *n. Brit.* a dealer in poultry and usu. game. [Middle English *poulter* from Old French *pouletier* (as PULLET)]

poultice /'pəʊltɪs/ *n. & v.* ● *n.* a soft medicated and usu. heated mass applied to the body and kept in place with muslin etc., for relieving soreness and inflammation. ● *v.tr.* apply a poultice to. [originally *pultes* (pl.) from Latin *puls pultis* 'pottage, pap', etc.]

poultry /'pəʊltri/ *n.* domestic fowls (ducks, geese, turkeys, chickens, etc.), esp. as a source of food. [Middle English from Old French *pouletrie* (as POULTERER)]

pounce[1] /paʊns/ *v. & n.* ● *v.intr.* **1** spring or swoop, esp. as in capturing prey. **2** (often foll. by *on, upon*) **a** make a sudden attack. **b** seize eagerly upon an object, remark, etc. (*pounced on what we said*). ● *n.* **1** the act or an instance of pouncing. **2** the claw or talon of a bird of prey. □ **pouncer** *n.* [perhaps from PUNCHEON[1]]

pounce[2] /paʊns/ *n. & v.* ● *n.* **1** a fine powder formerly used to prevent ink from spreading on unglazed paper. **2** powdered charcoal etc. dusted over a perforated pattern to transfer the design to the object beneath. ● *v.tr.* **1** dust with pounce. **2** transfer (a design etc.) by use of pounce. **3** smooth (paper etc.) with pounce or pumice. □ **pouncer** *n.* [French *ponce, poncer* from Latin *pumex* PUMICE]

pouncet-box /'paʊnsɪt/ *n. archaic* a small box with a perforated lid for perfumes etc. [16th c.: perhaps originally erroneously from *pounced* (= perforated) *box*]

pound[1] /paʊnd/ *n.* **1** a unit of weight equal to 16 oz avoirdupois (0.4536 kg), or 12 oz troy (0.3732 kg). **2** (in full **pound sterling**) (*pl.* same or **pounds**) the chief monetary unit of the UK and several other countries. [Old English *pund*, ultimately from Latin *pondo*, a Roman pound weight of 12 ounces]

pound[2] /paʊnd/ *v.* **1** *tr.* **a** crush or beat with repeated heavy blows. **b** thump or pummel, esp. with the fists. **c** grind to a powder or pulp. **2** *intr.* (foll. by *at, on*) deliver heavy blows or gunfire. **3** *intr.* (foll. by *along* etc.) make one's way heavily or clumsily. **4** *intr.* (of the heart) beat heavily. □ **pound out** produce with or as if with heavy blows. □ **pounder** *n.* [Old English *pūnian*, related to Dutch *puin*, Low German *pün* 'rubbish']

pound[3] /paʊnd/ *n. & v.* ● *n.* **1** an enclosure where stray animals or officially removed vehicles are kept until redeemed. **2** a place of confinement. ● *v.tr.* enclose (cattle etc.) in a pound. [Old English, of uncertain origin]

poundage /'paʊndɪdʒ/ *n.* **1** *Brit.* a commission or fee of so much per pound sterling or weight. **2** *Brit.* a percentage of the total earnings of a business, paid as wages. **3** a person's weight, esp. that which is regarded as excess.

poundal /'paʊnd(ə)l/ *n. Physics* a unit of force equal to the force required to give a mass of one pound an acceleration of one foot per second per second. [POUND[1] + *-al*, perhaps suggested by *quintal*]

pound cake *n.* a rich cake containing a pound (or equal weights) of each chief ingredient.

pound coin *n.* a coin worth one pound sterling.

pounder /'paʊndə/ *n.* (usu. in *comb.*) **1** a thing or person weighing a specified number of pounds (*a five-pounder*). **2** a gun carrying a shell of a specified number of pounds. **3** a thing worth, or a person possessing, so many pounds sterling.

pound lock *n.* a lock with two gates to confine water and often a side reservoir to maintain the water level. [POUND[3], in the sense 'body of still water, pond']

pound of flesh *n.* any legitimate but crippling demand. [with allusion to Shakespeare's *Merchant of Venice*]

pound Scots *n. hist.* 1s. 8d.

pound sign *n.* the sign £, representing a pound.

pound sterling see POUND[1] 2.

pour /pɔː/ *v.* **1** *intr. & tr.* (usu. foll. by *down, out, over,* etc.) flow or cause to flow esp. downwards in a stream or shower. **2** *tr.* dispense (a drink, e.g. tea) by pouring. **3** *intr.* (of rain, or prec. by *it* as subject) fall heavily. **4** *intr.* (usu. foll. by *in, out,* etc.) come or go in profusion or rapid succession (*the crowd poured out; letters poured in; poems poured from her fertile mind*). **5** *tr.* discharge or send freely (*poured forth arrows*). **6** *tr.* (often foll. by *out*) utter at length or in a rush (*poured out their story*). □ **it never rains but it pours** misfortunes rarely come singly. **pour cold water on** see COLD. **pour oil on the waters** (or **on troubled waters**) calm a disagreement or disturbance, esp. with conciliatory words. **pour scorn on** see SCORN. □ **pourable** *adj.* **pourer** *n.* [Middle English: origin unknown]

pourboire /pʊə'bwɑː, French purbwar/ *n.* a gratuity or tip. [French, = *pour boire* (money) for drinking]

poussin /'puːsã/ *n.* a young chicken bred for eating. [French]

pout[1] /paʊt/ *v. & n.* ● *v.* **1** *intr.* **a** push the lips forward as an expression of displeasure or sulking. **b** (of the lips) be pushed forward. **2** *tr.* push (the lips) forward in pouting. ● *n.* **1** such an action or expression. **2** (**the pouts**) a fit of sulking. □ **poutingly** *adv.* **pouty** *adj.* [Middle English, perhaps from an Old English word meaning 'be inflated': cf. POUT[2]]

pout[2] /paʊt/ *n.* **1** = BIB[1] 3. **2** = EELPOUT. [Old English *-puta* in *ǣlepūta* 'eelpout', from West Germanic]

pouter /'paʊtə/ *n.* **1** a person who pouts. **2** a kind of pigeon able to inflate its crop considerably.

poverty /'pɒvəti/ *n.* **1** the state of being poor; want of the necessities of life. **2** (often foll. by *of, in*) scarcity or lack. **3** inferiority, poorness, meanness. **4** *Eccl.* renunciation of the right to individual ownership of property. [Middle English via Old French *poverte, poverté* from Latin *paupertas -tatis*, from *pauper* 'poor']

poverty line *n.* the minimum income level needed to secure the necessities of life.

poverty-stricken *adj.* extremely poor.

poverty trap *n. Brit.* a situation in which an increase of income incurs a loss of state benefits, making real improvement impossible.

POW *abbr.* prisoner of war.

pow /paʊ/ *int.* expressing the sound of a blow or explosion. [imitative]

powder /'paʊdə/ *n. & v.* ● *n.* **1** a substance in the form of fine dry particles. **2** a medicine or cosmetic in this form. **3** = GUNPOWDER 1. ● *v.tr.* **1** **a** apply powder to (*powder one's nose*). **b** sprinkle or decorate with or as with powder. **2** (esp. as **powdered** *adj.*) reduce to a fine powder (*powdered milk*). □ **keep one's powder dry** be cautious and alert. **take a powder** *slang* depart quickly. □ **powdery** *adj.* [Middle English via Old French *poudre* from Latin *pulvis pulveris* 'dust']

powder blue *n. & adj.* ● *n.* pale blue. ● *adj.* (hyphenated when *attrib.*) of this colour.

powder flask *n. hist.* a small case for carrying gunpowder.

powder keg *n.* **1** a barrel of gunpowder. **2** a dangerous or volatile situation.

powder metallurgy *n.* the production of metals as fine powders which can be pressed and sintered to form objects.

powder monkey *n. hist.* a boy employed on board ship to carry powder to the guns.

powder puff *n.* a soft pad for applying powder to the skin, esp. the face.

powder room *n.* a women's cloakroom or lavatory in a public building.

powder snow *n.* loose dry snow on a ski run etc.

power /'paʊə/ *n. & v.* ● *n.* **1** the ability to do or act (*will do all in my power; has the power to change colour*). **2** a particular faculty of body or mind (*lost the power of speech; powers of persuasion*). **3** **a** government, influence, or authority. **b** political or social ascendancy or control (*the party in power; black power*). **4** authorization; delegated authority (*power of attorney; police powers*). **5** (often foll. by *over*) personal ascendancy. **6** an influential person, group, or organization (*the press is a power in the land*). **7** **a** military strength. **b** a state having international influence, esp. based on military strength (*the leading powers*). **8** vigour, energy. **9** an active property or function (*has a high heating power*). **10** *colloq.* a large number or amount (*has done me a power of good*). **11** the capacity for exerting mechanical force or doing work (*horsepower*). **12** mechanical or electrical energy as distinct from hand-labour (often *attrib.*: *power tools; power steering*). **13** **a** a public supply of (esp. electrical) energy. **b** a particular source or form of energy (*hydroelectric power*). **14** a mechanical force applied e.g. by means of a lever. **15** *Physics* the rate of energy output. **16** *Math.* the product obtained when a number is multiplied by itself a certain number of times (*2 to the power of 3 = 8*). **17** the magnifying capacity of a lens. **18** **a** a deity. **b** (in *pl.*) the sixth order of the ninefold celestial hierarchy (see ORDER *n.* 19). ● *v.tr.* **1** supply with mechanical or electrical energy. **2** (foll. by *up, down*) increase or decrease the power supplied to (a device); switch on or off. □ **in the power of** under the control of. **more power to your elbow!** *Brit.* an expression of encouragement or approval. **power**

behind the throne a person who asserts authority or influence without having formal status. **the powers that be** those in authority (after Rom. 13:1). □ **powered** *adj.* (also in *comb.*). [Middle English & Anglo-French *poer* etc., Old French *poeir*, ultimately from Latin *posse* 'be able']

power-assisted *adj.* (esp. of steering and brakes in a motor vehicle) employing an inanimate source of power to assist manual operation.

power base *n.* a source of authority or support.

power block *n.* a group of nations constituting an international political force.

powerboat /'paʊəbəʊt/ *n.* a powerful motor boat.

power-broker *n.* esp. *N. Amer.* a person who exerts influence or affects the equilibrium of political power by intrigue. □ **power-broking** *n. & adj.*

power cut *n.* a temporary withdrawal or failure of an electric power supply.

power-dive *n. & v.* ● *n.* a steep dive of an aircraft with the engines providing thrust. ● *v.intr.* perform a power-dive.

powerful /'paʊəfʊl, -f(ə)l/ *adj.* **1** having much power or strength. **2** politically or socially influential. **3** having a strong emotional effect (*powerful drama*). □ **powerfully** *adv.* **powerfulness** *n.*

powerhouse /'paʊəhaʊs/ *n.* **1** = POWER STATION. **2** a person or thing of great energy.

powerless /'paʊəlɪs/ *adj.* **1** without power or strength. **2** (often foll. by *to* + infin.) wholly unable (*powerless to help*). □ **powerlessly** *adv.* **powerlessness** *n.*

power line *n.* a conductor supplying electrical power, esp. one supported by pylons or poles.

power of attorney *n.* the authority to act for another person in legal or financial matters.

power pack *n.* **1** a unit for supplying power. **2** the equipment for converting an alternating current (from the mains) to a direct current at a different (usu. lower) voltage.

power plant *n.* an apparatus or an installation which provides power for industry, a machine, etc.

power play *n.* **1** tactics involving the concentration of players at a particular point. **2** similar tactics in business, politics, etc., involving a concentration of resources, effort, etc. **3** *Ice Hockey* play involving a formation of players adopted when the opponents are one or more players down.

power point *n. Brit.* a socket in a wall etc. for connecting an electrical device to the mains.

power politics *n.pl.* (treated as *sing.* or *pl.*) political action based on power or influence.

power-sharing *n.* a policy agreed between parties or within a coalition to share responsibility for decision-making and political action.

power shovel *n.* = MECHANICAL EXCAVATOR.

power station *n.* a building where electrical power is generated for distribution.

power stroke *n.* the stroke of an internal-combustion engine, in which the piston is moved downward by the expansion of gases.

power tool *n.* an electrically powered tool.

power train *n. Mech.* **1** the mechanism that transmits the drive from the engine of a vehicle to its axle. **2** this together with the engine and axle.

powwow /'paʊwaʊ/ *n. & v.* ● *n.* a conference or meeting for discussion (originally among N. American Indians). ● *v.intr.* hold a powwow. [Algonquian *powah*, *powwaw* 'magician' (literally 'he dreams')]

pox /pɒks/ *n.* **1** any virus disease producing a rash of pimples that become pus-filled and leave pockmarks on healing. **2** *colloq.* = SYPHILIS. **3** a plant disease that causes pocklike spots. □ **a pox on** *archaic* an exclamation of anger or impatience with (a person). [alteration of spelling of *pocks*, pl. of POCK]

poxy /'pɒksi/ *adj.* (**poxier**, **poxiest**) esp. *Brit.* **1** infected by pox. **2** *slang* of poor quality; worthless.

Pozidriv /'pɒzɪdrʌɪv/ *n. propr.* a type of cross-head screwdriver.

pozzolana /pɒtsə'lɑːnə/ *n.* (also **puzzolana**) a volcanic ash used for mortar or hydraulic cement. [Italian, from *pozz(u)olano* '(earth) of *Pozzuoli*', a town near Naples]

pp *abbr.* pianissimo.

pp. *abbr.* pages.

p.p. *abbr.* (also **pp**) *per pro.*

■ **Usage** See Usage Note at PER PRO.

PPARC *abbr.* (in the UK) Particle Physics and Astronomy Research Council.

PPE *abbr. Brit.* philosophy, politics, and economics (as a degree course at Oxford University).

p.p.m. *abbr.* parts per million.

PPS *abbr.* **1** *Brit.* Parliamentary Private Secretary. **2** additional postscript.

PR *abbr.* **1** public relations. **2** proportional representation. **3** *US* Puerto Rico.

Pr *symb. Chem.* the element praseodymium.

pr. *abbr.* pair.

PRA *abbr.* (in the UK) President of the Royal Academy.

praam var. of PRAM².

practicable /'praktɪkəb(ə)l/ *adj.* **1** that can be done or used. **2** possible in practice. □ **practicability** /-'bɪlɪti/ *n.* **practicableness** *n.* **practicably** *adv.* [French *praticable* from *pratiquer* 'put into practice' (as PRACTICAL)]

practical /'praktɪk(ə)l/ *adj. & n.* ● *adj.* **1** of or concerned with practice or use rather than theory. **2** suited to use or action; designed mainly to fulfil a function (*practical shoes*). **3** (of a person) **a** inclined to action rather than speculation; able to make things function well. **b** skilled at manual tasks. **4 a** that is such in effect, though not nominally (*for all practical purposes*). **b** virtual (*in practical control*). **5** feasible, realistic; concerned with what is actually possible (*practical politics*; *practical solutions*). ● *n. Brit.* a practical examination or lesson. □ **practicality** /-'kalɪti/ *n.* (*pl.* **-ies**). **practicalness** *n.* [earlier *practic*, via obsolete French *practique* or Late Latin *practicus* from Greek *praktikos*, from *prassō* 'do, act']

practical joke *n.* a humorous trick played on a person. □ **practical joker** *n.*

practically /'praktɪk(ə)li/ *adv.* **1** virtually, almost (*practically nothing*). **2** in a practical way.

practice /'praktɪs/ *n. & v.* ● *n.* **1** habitual action or performance (*the practice of teaching*; *makes a practice of saving*). **2** a habit or custom (*has been my regular practice*). **3 a** repeated exercise in an activity requiring the development of skill (*to sing well needs much practice*). **b** a session of this (*they had a short practice*). **4** action or execution as opposed to theory. **5** the professional work or business of a doctor, lawyer, etc. (*has a practice in town*). **6** an established method of legal procedure. **7** procedure generally, esp. of a specified kind (*bad practice*). ● *v.tr. & intr. US* var. of PRACTISE. □ **in practice 1** when actually applied; in reality. **2** skilful because of recent exercise in a particular pursuit. **out of practice** lacking a former skill from lack of recent practice. **put into practice** actually apply (an idea, method, etc.). [Middle English from PRACTISE, on the pattern of *advice*, *device*]

practician /prak'tɪʃ(ə)n/ *n.* a worker; a practitioner. [obsolete French *practicien* from *practique*, via medieval Latin *practica* from Greek *praktikē*, fem. of *praktikos*: see PRACTICAL]

practise /'praktɪs/ *v.* (*US* **practice**) **1** *tr.* perform habitually; carry out in action (*practise the same method*; *practise what you preach*). **2** *tr.* & (foll. by *in*, *on*) *intr.* do repeatedly as an exercise to improve a skill; exercise oneself in or on (an activity requiring skill) (*had to practise in the art of speaking*; *practise your reading*). **3** *tr.* (as **practised** *adj.*) experienced, expert (*a practised liar*; *with a practised hand*). **4** *tr.* **a** pursue or be engaged in (a profession, religion, etc.). **b** (as **practising** *adj.*) currently active or engaged in (a profession or activity) (*a practising Christian*; *a practising lawyer*). **5** *intr.* (foll. by *on*, *upon*) take advantage of; impose upon. **6** *intr. archaic* scheme, contrive (*when first we practise to deceive*). ▫ **practiser** *n.* [Middle English from Old French *pra(c)tiser* or medieval Latin *practizare*, alteration of *practicare* (as PRACTICAL)]

practitioner /prak'tɪʃ(ə)nə/ *n.* a person practising a profession, esp. medicine (*general practitioner*). [obsolete *practitian* = PRACTICIAN]

prae- /priː/ *prefix* = PRE- (esp. in words regarded as Latin or relating to Roman antiquity). [Latin: see PRE-]

praecipe /'priːsɪpi/ *n.* **1** a writ demanding action or an explanation of non-action. **2** an order requesting a writ. [Latin (the first word of the writ), imperative of *praecipere* 'enjoin': see PRECEPT]

praecocial var. of PRECOCIAL.

praedial var. of PREDIAL.

praemunire /priːmjuː'nɪəri/ *n. hist.* a writ charging a sheriff to summon a person accused of asserting or maintaining papal jurisdiction in England. [medieval Latin, = forewarn, for Latin *praemonēre* (as PRAE-, *monēre* 'warn'): the words *praemunire facias* 'that you warn' (a person to appear) occur in the writ]

praenomen /priː'nəʊmen/ *n.* an ancient Roman's first or personal name (e.g. *Marcus* Tullius Cicero). [Latin, from *prae* 'before' + *nomen* 'name']

praepostor /prɪ'pɒstə/ *n.* (also **prepostor**) *Brit.* (at some public schools) a prefect or monitor. [*praepositor*, alteration of Latin *praepositus*, past part. of *praeponere* 'set over' (as PRAE-, *ponere posit-* 'place')]

praesidium var. of PRESIDIUM.

praetor /'priːtə, -tɔː/ *n.* (*US* also **pretor**) *Rom.Hist.* each of two ancient Roman magistrates ranking below consul. ▫ **praetorial** /-'tɔːrɪəl/ *adj.* **praetorship** *n.* [Middle English from French *préteur* or Latin *praetor* (perhaps as PRAE-, *ire it-* 'go')]

praetorian /priː'tɔːrɪən/ *adj.* & *n.* (*US* also **pretorian**) *Rom.Hist.* ● *adj.* of or having the powers of a praetor. ● *n.* a man of praetorian rank. [Middle English from Latin *praetorianus* (as PRAETOR)]

praetorian guard *n.* the bodyguard of the Roman emperor.

pragmatic /prag'matɪk/ *adj.* **1** dealing with matters with regard to their practical requirements or consequences. **2** treating the facts of history with reference to their practical lessons. **3** *hist.* of or relating to the affairs of a state. **4** (also **pragmatical**) **a** concerning pragmatism. **b** meddlesome. **c** dogmatic. ▫ **pragmaticality** /-'kalɪti/ *n.* **pragmatically** *adv.* [Late Latin *pragmaticus* from Greek *pragmatikos*, from *pragma -matos* 'deed']

pragmatics /prag'matɪks/ *n.pl.* (usu. treated as *sing.*) the branch of linguistics dealing with language in use.

pragmatic sanction *n. hist.* an imperial or royal ordinance issued as a fundamental law, esp. regarding a question of royal succession.

pragmatism /'pragmətɪz(ə)m/ *n.* **1** a pragmatic attitude or procedure. **2** a philosophy that evaluates assertions solely by their practical consequences and bearing on human interests. ▫ **pragmatist** *n.* **pragmatistic** /-'tɪstɪk/ *adj.* [Greek *pragma*: see PRAGMATIC]

pragmatize /'pragmətʌɪz/ *v.tr.* (also **-ise**) **1** represent as real. **2** rationalize (a myth).

prahu var. of PROA.

prairie /'prɛːri/ *n.* a large area of usu. treeless grassland esp. in N. America. [French from Old French *praerie*, ultimately from Latin *pratum* 'meadow']

prairie chicken *n.* (also **prairie hen**) a N. American grouse, *Tympanuchus cupido*.

prairie dog *n.* any N. American rodent of the genus *Cynomys*, living in burrows and making a barking sound.

prairie oyster *n.* a seasoned raw egg, often served in spirits and swallowed in one as a cure for a hangover.

prairie schooner *n. US* a covered wagon used by the 19th-c. pioneers in crossing the N. American prairies.

prairie wolf *n.* = COYOTE.

praise /preɪz/ *v.* & *n.* ● *v.tr.* **1** express warm approval or admiration of. **2** glorify (God) in words. ● *n.* the act or an instance of praising; commendation (*won high praise*; *were loud in their praises*). ▫ **praise be!** an exclamation of pious gratitude. **sing the praises of** commend (a person) highly. ▫ **praiseful** *adj.* **praiser** *n.* [Middle English from Old French *preisier* 'price, prize, praise', via Late Latin *pretiare* from Latin *pretium* 'price': cf. PRIZE[1]]

praiseworthy /'preɪzwəːði/ *adj.* worthy of praise; commendable. ▫ **praiseworthily** *adv.* **praiseworthiness** *n.*

Prakrit /'prɑːkrɪt/ *n.* any of the (esp. ancient or medieval) vernacular dialects of North and Central India existing alongside or derived from Sanskrit. [Sanskrit *prākṛta* 'unrefined, natural': cf. SANSKRIT]

praline /'prɑːliːn/ *n.* a smooth sweet substance made by boiling nuts in sugar and used esp. as a filling for chocolates. [French, named after Marshal de Plessis-*Praslin*, French soldier d. 1675, whose cook invented it]

pralltriller /'praltrɪlə/ *n.* a musical ornament consisting of one rapid alternation of the written note with the note immediately above it. [German, from *prallen* 'rebound' + *Triller* TRILL]

pram[1] /pram/ *n. Brit.* a four-wheeled carriage for a baby, pushed by a person on foot. [abbreviation of PERAMBULATOR]

pram[2] /prɑːm, pram/ *n.* (also **praam**) **1** a flat-bottomed gunboat or Baltic cargo boat. **2** a ship's dinghy. [Middle Dutch *prame*, *praem*, Middle Low German *prāme*, perhaps from Czech *prám*]

prana /'prɑːnə/ *n.* **1** (in Hinduism) breath as a life-giving force. **2** the breath; breathing. [Sanskrit]

prance /prɑːns/ *v.* & *n.* ● *v.intr.* **1** (of a horse) raise the forelegs and spring from the hind legs. **2** (often foll. by *about*) walk or behave in an elated or arrogant manner. ● *n.* **1** the act of prancing. **2** a prancing movement. ▫ **prancer** *n.* [Middle English: origin unknown]

prandial /'prandɪəl/ *adj. formal* or *joc.* of or relating to dinner or lunch. [Latin *prandium* 'meal']

prang /praŋ/ *v.* & *n. Brit. slang* ● *v.tr.* **1** crash or damage (an aircraft or vehicle). **2** bomb (a target) successfully. ● *n.* the act or an instance of pranging. [imitative]

prank /praŋk/ *n.* a practical joke; a piece of mischief. ▫ **prankish** *adj.* **pranksome** *adj.* [16th c.: origin unknown]

prankster /'praŋkstə/ *n.* a person fond of playing pranks.

prase /preɪz/ *n.* a translucent leek-green type of quartz. [French via Latin *prasius* from Greek *prasios* 'leek-green', from *prason* 'leek']

praseodymium /preɪzɪə'dɪmɪəm/ *n. Chem.* a soft silvery metallic element of the lanthanide series, occurring naturally in various minerals and used in catalyst mixtures (symbol **Pr**). [German *Praseodym*, from Greek *prasios* (see PRASE, from its green salts) + German *Didym* DIDYMIUM]

prat /prat/ *n. slang* **1** *Brit.* a silly or foolish person. **2** the buttocks. [16th-c. slang (in sense 2): origin unknown]

prate /preɪt/ *v.* & *n.* ● *v.* **1** *intr.* chatter; talk too much. **2** *intr.* talk foolishly or irrelevantly. **3** *tr.* tell or say in a prating manner. ● *n.* prating; idle talk. ▫ **prater** *n.* **prating** *adj.* [Middle English from Middle Dutch, Middle Low German *praten*, probably imitative]

pratfall /'pratfɔːl/ *n. US slang* **1** a fall on the buttocks. **2** a humiliating failure.

pratie /'preɪti/ *n.* esp. *Ir.* a potato. [corruption]

pratincole /'pratɪŋkəʊl/ *n.* a fork-tailed insectivorous plover-like bird of the genus *Glareola*, living near water. [modern Latin *pratincola*, from Latin *pratum* 'meadow' + *incola* 'inhabitant']

pratique /'pratiːk/ *n.* a licence to have dealings with a port, granted to a ship after quarantine or on showing a clean bill of health. [French, = practice, intercourse, via Italian *pratica* from medieval Latin *practica*: see PRACTICIAN]

prattle /ˈprat(ə)l/ *v. & n.* ● *v.intr. & tr.* chatter or say in a childish or inconsequential way. ● *n.* **1** childish chatter. **2** inconsequential talk. ▫ **prattler** *n.* **prattling** *adj.* [Middle Low German *pratelen* (as PRATE)]

prau var. of PROA.

prawn /prɔːn/ *n. & v.* ● *n.* any of various marine crustaceans, resembling a shrimp but usu. larger. ● *v.intr.* fish for prawns. ▫ **come the raw prawn** see RAW. [Middle English *pra(y)ne*, of unknown origin]

praxis /ˈpraksɪs/ *n.* **1** accepted practice or custom. **2** the practising of an art or skill. [medieval Latin from Greek, = doing, from *prassō* 'do']

pray /preɪ/ *v.* (often foll. by *for* or *to* + infin. or *that* + clause) **1** *intr.* (often foll. by *to*) say prayers (to God etc.); make devout supplication. **2 a** *tr.* entreat, beseech. **b** *tr. & intr.* ask earnestly (*prayed to be released*). **3** *tr.* (as *imper.*) *formal* or *joc.* please (*pray tell me*). [Middle English from Old French *preier* via Late Latin *precare* from Latin *precari* 'entreat']

prayer[1] /prɛː/ *n.* **1 a** a solemn request or thanksgiving to God or an object of worship (*say a prayer*). **b** a formula or form of words used in praying (*the Lord's prayer*). **c** the act of praying (*be at prayer*). **d** a religious service consisting largely of prayers (*morning prayers*). **2 a** an entreaty to a person. **b** a thing entreated or prayed for. ▫ **not have a prayer** *N. Amer. colloq.* have no chance (of success etc.). ▫ **prayerless** *adj.* [Middle English from Old French *preiere*, ultimately via Latin *precarius* 'obtained by entreaty' from *prex precis* 'prayer']

prayer[2] /preɪə/ *n.* a person who prays.

prayer book *n.* a book containing the forms of prayer in regular use, esp. the Book of Common Prayer.

prayerful /ˈprɛːfʊl, -f(ə)l/ *adj.* **1** (of a person) given to praying; devout. **2** (of speech, actions, etc.) characterized by or expressive of prayer. ▫ **prayerfully** *adv.* **prayerfulness** *n.*

prayer mat *n.* a small carpet used by Muslims when praying.

prayer shawl *n.* = TALLITH.

prayer wheel *n.* a revolving cylindrical box inscribed with or containing prayers, used esp. by Tibetan Buddhists.

praying mantis see MANTIS.

pre- /priː, prɪ/ *prefix* before (in time, place, order, degree, or importance) (*pre-Christmas*). [from or suggested by Latin *prae-*, from *prae* (adv. & prep.)]

preach /priːtʃ/ *v.* **1 a** *intr.* deliver a sermon or religious address. **b** *tr.* deliver (a sermon); proclaim or expound (the Gospel etc.). **2** *intr.* give moral advice in an obtrusive way. **3** *tr.* advocate or inculcate (a quality or practice etc.). ▫ **preach to the converted** commend an opinion to a person or persons already in agreement. ▫ **preachable** *adj.* [Middle English via Old French *prechier* from Latin *praedicare* 'proclaim', in ecclesiastical Latin 'preach' (as PRAE-, *dicare* 'declare')]

preacher /ˈpriːtʃə/ *n.* a person who preaches, esp. a minister of religion. [Middle English via Anglo-French *prech(o)ur*, Old French *prech(e)or* from ecclesiastical Latin *praedicator* (as PREACH)]

preachify /ˈpriːtʃɪfʌɪ/ *v.intr.* (**-ies, -ied**) *colloq.* preach or moralize tediously.

preachment /ˈpriːtʃm(ə)nt/ *n.* usu. *derog.* preaching, sermonizing.

preachy /ˈpriːtʃi/ *adj.* (**preachier, preachiest**) *colloq.* inclined to preach or moralize. ▫ **preachiness** *n.*

pre-adolescent /ˌpriːadəˈlɛs(ə)nt/ *adj. & n.* ● *adj.* **1** (of a child) having nearly reached adolescence. **2** of or relating to the two or three years preceding adolescence. ● *n.* a pre-adolescent child. ▫ **pre-adolescence** *n.*

preamble /priːˈamb(ə)l, ˈpriː-/ *n.* **1** a preliminary statement or introduction. **2** the introductory part of a statute or deed etc. ▫ **preambular** /-ˈambjʊlə/ *adj.* [Middle English via Old French *preambule* and medieval Latin *praeambulum* from Late Latin *praeambulus* 'going before' (as PRE-, AMBLE)]

preamp /ˈpriːamp/ *n.* = PREAMPLIFIER. [abbreviation]

preamplifier /priːˈamplɪfʌɪə/ *n.* an electronic device that amplifies a very weak signal (e.g. from a microphone or pick-up) and transmits it to a main amplifier. ▫ **preamplified** *adj.*

pre-arrange /priːəˈreɪn(d)ʒ/ *v.tr.* arrange beforehand. ▫ **pre-arrangement** *n.*

preatomic /priːəˈtɒmɪk/ *adj.* existing or occurring before the use of atomic energy.

Preb. *abbr.* Prebendary.

prebend /ˈprɛb(ə)nd/ *n.* **1** = PREBENDARY 1. **2** *hist.* the stipend of a canon or member of chapter. **3** *hist.* a portion of land or tithe from which this is drawn. [Middle English via Old French *prebende* from Late Latin *praebenda* 'pension', neut. pl. gerundive of Latin *praebēre* 'grant', from *prae* 'forth' + *habēre* 'hold']

prebendal /prɪˈbɛnd(ə)l/ *adj.* of or relating to a prebend or a prebendary.

prebendary /ˈprɛb(ə)nd(ə)ri/ *n.* (*pl.* **-ies**) **1** an honorary canon. **2** *hist.* the holder of a prebend. ▫ **prebendaryship** *n.* [Middle English from medieval Latin *praebendarius* (as PREBEND)]

pre-book /priːˈbʊk/ *v.tr.* book in advance. ▫ **pre-bookable** *adj.*

Precambrian /priːˈkambrɪən/ *adj. & n. Geol.* ● *adj.* of or relating to the earliest era of geological time from the formation of the earth to the first forms of life. Cf. Appendix X. ● *n.* this era.

precancerous /priːˈkans(ə)rəs/ *adj.* tending to develop into cancer.

precarious /prɪˈkɛːrɪəs/ *adj.* **1** uncertain; dependent on chance (*makes a precarious living*). **2** insecure, perilous (*precarious health*). ▫ **precariously** *adv.* **precariousness** *n.* [Latin *precarius*: see PRAYER[1]]

pre-cast /priːˈkɑːst/ *adj.* (of concrete) cast in its final shape before positioning.

precative /ˈprɛkətɪv/ *adj.* (of a word or form) expressing a wish or request. [Late Latin *precativus* from *precari* 'pray']

precaution /prɪˈkɔːʃ(ə)n/ *n.* **1** an action taken beforehand to avoid risk or ensure a good result. **2** (in *pl.*) *colloq.* the use of contraceptives. ▫ **precautionary** *adj.* [French *précaution* via Late Latin *praecautio -onis* from Latin *praecavēre* (as PRAE-, *cavēre caut-* 'beware of')]

precede /prɪˈsiːd/ *v.tr.* **1 a** come or go before in time, order, importance, etc. (*preceding generations*; *the preceding paragraph*; *sons of barons precede baronets*). **b** walk etc. in front of (*preceded by our guide*). **2** (foll. by *by*) cause to be preceded (*must precede this measure by milder ones*). [Old French *preceder* from Latin *praecedere* (as PRAE-, *cedere cess-* 'go')]

precedence /ˈprɛsɪd(ə)ns, ˈpriː-, prɪˈsiːd(ə)ns/ *n.* (also **precedency** /-(ə)nsi/) **1** priority in time, order, or importance, etc. **2** the right of preceding others on formal occasions. ▫ **take precedence** (often foll. by *over*, *of*) have priority (over).

precedent *n. & adj.* ● *n.* /ˈprɛsɪd(ə)nt/ a previous case or legal decision etc. taken as a guide for subsequent cases or as a justification. ● *adj.* /prɪˈsiːd(ə)nt, ˈprɛsɪ-/ preceding in time, order, importance, etc. ▫ **precedently** /ˈpriːsɪd(ə)ntli, ˈprɛsɪ-/ *adv.* [Middle English from Old French (*n. & adj.*) (as PRECEDE)]

precedented /ˈprɛsɪdɛntɪd/ *adj.* having or supported by a precedent.

precent /prɪˈsɛnt/ *v.* **1** *intr.* act as a precentor. **2** *tr.* lead the singing of (a psalm etc.). [back-formation from PRECENTOR]

precentor /prɪˈsɛntə/ *n.* **1** a person who leads the singing or (in a synagogue) the prayers of a congregation. **2** a minor canon who administers the musical life of a cathedral. ▫ **precentorship** *n.* [French *précenteur* or Latin *praecentor* from *praecinere* (as PRAE-, *canere* 'sing')]

precept /ˈpriːsɛpt/ *n.* **1** a command; a rule of conduct. **2** moral instruction (*example is better than precept*). **3 a** a writ or warrant. **b** *Brit.* an order for collection or payment of money under a local rate. □ **preceptive** /prɪˈsɛptɪv/ *adj.* [Middle English from Latin *praeceptum*, neut. past part. of *praecipere praecept-* 'warn, instruct' (as PRAE-, *capere* 'take')]

preceptor /prɪˈsɛptə/ *n.* (*fem.* **preceptress** /-trɪs/) a teacher or instructor. □ **preceptorial** /priːsɛpˈtɔːrɪəl/ *adj.* **preceptorship** *n.* [Latin *praeceptor* (as PRECEPT)]

precession /prɪˈsɛʃ(ə)n/ *n.* the slow movement of the axis of a spinning body around another axis. □ **precessional** *adj.* [Late Latin *praecessio* (as PRECEDE)]

precession of the equinoxes *n.* **1** the slow retrograde motion of equinoctial points along the ecliptic. **2** the resulting earlier occurrence of equinoxes in each successive sideral year.

pre-Christian /priːˈkrɪstʃ(ə)n, -tɪən/ *adj.* before Christ or the advent of Christianity.

precinct /ˈpriːsɪŋ(k)t/ *n.* **1** an enclosed or clearly defined area, e.g. around a cathedral, college, etc. **2** a specially designated area in a town, esp. with the exclusion of traffic (*shopping precinct*). **3** (in *pl.*) **a** the surrounding area or environs. **b** the boundaries. **4** *US* **a** a subdivision of a county, city, etc., for police or electoral purposes. **b** *colloq.* the police station of such a subdivision. **c** (in *pl.*) a neighbourhood. [Middle English from medieval Latin *praecinctum*, neut. past part. of *praecingere* 'encircle' (as PRAE-, *cingere* 'gird')]

preciosity /prɛʃɪˈɒsɪti/ *n.* over-refinement in art or language, esp. in the choice of words. [Old French *préciosité* from Latin *pretiositas*, from *pretiosus* (as PRECIOUS)]

precious /ˈprɛʃəs/ *adj.* & *adv.* ● *adj.* **1** of great value or worth. **2** beloved; much prized (*precious memories*). **3** affectedly refined, esp. in language or manner. **4** *colloq.* often *iron.* **a** considerable (*a precious lot you know about it*). **b** expressing contempt or disdain (*you can keep your precious flowers*). ● *adv. colloq.* extremely, very (*tried precious hard*; *had precious little left*). □ **preciously** *adv.* **preciousness** *n.* [Middle English via Old French *precios* from Latin *pretiosus*, from *pretium* 'price']

precious metals *n.pl.* gold, silver, and platinum.

precious stone *n.* a piece of mineral having great value and visual appeal, esp. as used in jewellery.

precipice /ˈprɛsɪpɪs/ *n.* **1** a vertical or steep face of a rock, cliff, mountain, etc. **2** a dangerous situation. [French *précipice* or Latin *praecipitium* 'falling headlong, precipice' (as PRECIPITOUS)]

precipitant /prɪˈsɪpɪt(ə)nt/ *adj.* & *n.* ● *adj.* = PRECIPITATE *adj.* ● *n. Chem.* a substance that causes another substance to precipitate. □ **precipitance** *n.* **precipitancy** *n.* [obsolete French *précipitant*, pres. part. of *précipiter* (as PRECIPITATE)]

precipitate *v.*, *adj.*, & *n.* ● *v.tr.* /prɪˈsɪpɪteɪt/ **1** hasten the occurrence of; cause to occur prematurely. **2** (foll. by *into*) send rapidly into a certain state or condition (*were precipitated into war*). **3** throw down headlong. **4** *Chem.* cause (a substance) to be deposited in solid form from a solution. **5** *Physics* **a** cause (dust etc.) to be deposited from the air on a surface. **b** condense (vapour) into drops and so deposit it. ● *adj.* /prɪˈsɪpɪtət/ **1** headlong; violently hurried (*precipitate departure*). **2** (of a person or act) hasty, rash, inconsiderate. ● *n.* /prɪˈsɪpɪtət, -teɪt/ **1** *Chem.* a substance precipitated from a solution. **2** *Physics* moisture condensed from vapour by cooling and depositing, e.g. rain or dew. □ **precipitable** /prɪˈsɪpɪtəb(ə)l/ *adj.* **precipitability** /prɪˌsɪpɪtəˈbɪlɪti/ *n.* **precipitately** /prɪˈsɪpɪtətli/ *adv.* **precipitateness** /prɪˈsɪpɪtətnɪs/ *n.* **precipitator** /prɪˈsɪpɪteɪtə/ *n.* [Latin *praecipitare praecipitat-* from *praeceps praecipitis* 'headlong' (as PRAE-, *caput* 'head')]

precipitation /prɪˌsɪpɪˈteɪʃ(ə)n/ *n.* **1** the act of precipitating or the process of being precipitated. **2** rash haste. **3 a** rain or snow etc. falling to the ground. **b** a quantity of this. [French *précipitation* or Latin *praecipitatio* (as PRECIPITATE)]

precipitous /prɪˈsɪpɪtəs/ *adj.* **1 a** of or like a precipice. **b** dangerously steep. **2** = PRECIPITATE *adj.* □ **precipitously** *adv.* **precipitousness** *n.* [obsolete French *précipiteux* from Latin *praeceps* (as PRECIPITATE)]

précis /ˈpreɪsi/ *n.* & *v.* ● *n.* (*pl.* same /-siːz/) a summary or abstract, esp. of a text or speech. ● *v.tr.* (**précises** /-siːz/; **précised** /-siːd/; **précising** /-siːɪŋ/) make a précis of. [French, = PRECISE (used as a noun)]

precise /prɪˈsʌɪs/ *adj.* **1 a** accurately expressed; exact in statement (*precise description*; *to be precise, ...*). **b** exact in measurement, value, etc. (*a precise quote for installation*). **2** punctilious; scrupulous in being exact, observing rules, etc. **3** identical, same (*at that precise moment*). □ **preciseness** *n.* [French *précis -ise* from Latin *praecidere praecis-* 'cut short' (as PRAE-, *caedere* 'cut')]

precisely /prɪˈsʌɪsli/ *adv.* **1** in a precise manner; exactly. **2** (as a reply) quite so; as you say.

precisian /prɪˈsɪʒ(ə)n/ *n.* a person who is rigidly precise or punctilious, esp. in religious observance. □ **precisianism** *n.*

precision /prɪˈsɪʒ(ə)n/ *n.* **1** the condition of being precise; accuracy. **2** the degree of refinement in measurement etc. **3** (*attrib.*) marked by or adapted for precision (*precision instruments*; *precision timing*). □ **precisionism** *n.* **precisionist** *n.* & *adj.* [French *précision* or Latin *praecisio* (as PRECISE)]

preclassical /priːˈklasɪk(ə)l/ *adj.* before a period regarded as classical, esp. in music and literature.

preclinical /priːˈklɪnɪk(ə)l/ *adj.* **1** of or relating to the first, chiefly theoretical, stage of a medical education. **2** (of a stage in a disease) before symptoms can be identified.

preclude /prɪˈkluːd/ *v.tr.* **1** (foll. by *from*) prevent, exclude (*precluded from taking part*). **2** make impossible; remove (*so as to preclude all doubt*). □ **preclusion** /-ˈkluːʒ(ə)n/ *n.* **preclusive** /-ˈkluːsɪv/ *adj.* [Latin *praecludere praeclus-* (as PRAE-, *claudere* 'shut')]

precocial /prɪˈkəʊʃ(ə)l/ *adj.* & *n.* (also **praecocial**) ● *adj.* (of a bird) having young that can feed themselves as soon as they are hatched. ● *n.* a precocial bird (cf. ALTRICIAL).

precocious /prɪˈkəʊʃəs/ *adj.* **1** often *derog.* (of a person, esp. a child) prematurely developed in some faculty or characteristic. **2** (of an action etc.) indicating such development. **3** (of a plant) flowering or fruiting early. □ **precociously** *adv.* **precociousness** *n.* **precocity** /-ˈkɒsɪti/ *n.* [Latin *praecox -cocis* from *praecoquere* 'ripen fully' (as PRAE-, *coquere* 'cook')]

precognition /priːkɒɡˈnɪʃ(ə)n/ *n.* **1** (supposed) foreknowledge, esp. of a supernatural kind. **2** *Sc.* the preliminary examination of witnesses etc., esp. to decide whether there is ground for a trial. □ **precognitive** /-ˈkɒɡnɪtɪv/ *adj.* [Late Latin *praecognitio* (as PRE-, COGNITION)]

pre-coital /priːˈkəʊɪt(ə)l/ *adj.* preceding sexual intercourse. □ **pre-coitally** *adv.*

pre-Columbian /priːkəˈlʌmbɪən/ *adj.* before the arrival in America of Columbus.

preconceive /priːkənˈsiːv/ *v.tr.* form (an idea or opinion etc.) beforehand.

preconception /priːkənˈsɛpʃ(ə)n/ *n.* **1** a preconceived idea. **2** a prejudice.

preconcert /priːkənˈsəːt/ *v.tr.* arrange or organize beforehand.

precondition /priːkənˈdɪʃ(ə)n/ *n.* & *v.* ● *n.* a prior condition, that must be fulfilled before other things can be done. ● *v.tr.* bring into a required condition beforehand.

preconize /ˈpriːkənʌɪz/ *v.tr.* (also **-ise**) **1** proclaim or commend publicly. **2** summon by name. **3** *RC Ch.* (of the Pope) approve publicly the appointment of (a bishop). □ **preconization** /-ˈzeɪʃ(ə)n/ *n.* [Middle English via medieval Latin *praeconizare* from Latin *praeco -onis* 'herald']

preconscious /priːˈkɒnʃəs/ *adj. & n. Psychol.* ● *adj.* **1** preceding consciousness. **2** of or associated with a part of the mind below the level of immediate conscious awareness, from which memories and emotions can be recalled. ● *n.* this part of the mind. □ **preconsciousness** *n.*

pre-cook /priːˈkʊk/ *v.tr.* cook in advance.

pre-cool /priːˈkuːl/ *v.tr.* cool in advance.

precordial /priːˈkɔːdɪəl/ *adj.* in front of or about the heart.

precostal /priːˈkɒst(ə)l/ *adj.* in front of the ribs.

precursor /prɪˈkɜːsə/ *n.* **1 a** a forerunner. **b** a person who precedes in office etc. **2** a harbinger. **3** a substance from which another is formed by decay or chemical reaction etc. [Latin *praecursor* from *praecurrere praecurs-* (as PRAE-, *currere* 'run')]

precursory /prɪˈkɜːs(ə)ri/ *adj.* (also **precursive** /-sɪv/) **1** preliminary, introductory. **2** (foll. by *of*) serving as a harbinger of. [Latin *praecursorius* (as PRECURSOR)]

pre-cut /priːˈkʌt/ *v.tr.* (**-cutting**; *past* and *past part.* **-cut**) cut in advance.

predacious /prɪˈdeɪʃəs/ *adj.* (also **predaceous**) **1** (of an animal) predatory. **2** relating to such animals (*predacious instincts*). □ **predaciousness** *n.* **predacity** /-ˈdæsɪti/ *n.* [Latin *praeda* 'booty': cf. *audacious*]

pre-date /priːˈdeɪt/ *v.tr.* exist or occur at a date earlier than.

predation /prɪˈdeɪʃ(ə)n/ *n.* **1** (usu. in *pl.*) = DEPREDATION. **2** *Zool.* the natural preying of one animal on others. [Latin *praedatio -onis* 'taking of booty' from *praeda* 'booty']

predator /ˈprɛdətə/ *n.* **1** an animal naturally preying on others. **2** a rapacious, exploitative person, state, etc. [Latin *praedator* 'plunderer', via *praedari* 'seize as plunder' from *praeda* 'booty']

predatory /ˈprɛdət(ə)ri/ *adj.* **1** (of an animal) preying naturally upon others. **2** (of a nation, state, or individual) exploitative; rapacious. □ **predatorily** *adv.* **predatoriness** *n.* [Latin *praedatorius* (as PREDATOR)]

predecease /priːdɪˈsiːs/ *v. & n.* ● *v.tr.* die earlier than (another person). ● *n.* a death preceding that of another.

predecessor /ˈpriːdɪsɛsə/ *n.* **1** a former holder of an office or position with respect to a later holder (*my immediate predecessor*). **2** an ancestor. **3** a thing to which another has succeeded (*the new plan will share the fate of its predecessor*). [Middle English via Old French *predecesseur* from Late Latin *praedecessor* (as PRAE-, *decessor* 'retiring officer', as DECEASE)]

pre-decimal /priːˈdɛsɪm(ə)l/ *adj.* of or relating to a time before the introduction of a decimal system, esp. of coinage.

predella /prɪˈdɛlə/ *n.* **1** an altar step, or raised shelf at the back of an altar. **2** a painting or sculpture on this, or any picture forming an appendage to a larger one esp. beneath an altarpiece. [Italian, = stool]

predestinarian /prɪˌdɛstɪˈnɛːrɪən/ *n. & adj.* ● *n.* a person who believes in predestination. ● *adj.* of or relating to predestination.

predestinate *v. & adj.* ● *v.tr.* /priːˈdɛstɪneɪt/ = PREDESTINE. ● *adj.* /priːˈdɛstɪnət/ predestined. [Middle English from ecclesiastical Latin *praedestinare praedestinat-* (as PRAE-, *destinare* 'establish')]

predestination /priːˌdɛstɪˈneɪʃ(ə)n/ *n. Theol.* (as a belief or doctrine) the divine foreordaining of all that will happen, esp. with regard to the salvation of some and not others. [Middle English from ecclesiastical Latin *praedestinatio* (as PREDESTINATE)]

predestine /priːˈdɛstɪn/ *v.tr.* **1** determine beforehand. **2** ordain in advance by divine will or as if by fate. [Middle English from Old French *predestiner* or ecclesiastical Latin *praedestinare* PREDESTINATE *v.*]

predetermine /priːdɪˈtɜːmɪn/ *v.tr.* **1** determine or decree beforehand. **2** predestine. □ **predeterminable** *adj.* **predeterminate** /-nət/ *adj.* **predetermination** /-ˈneɪʃ(ə)n/ *n.* [Late Latin *praedeterminare* (as PRAE-, DETERMINE)]

predeterminer /priːdɪˈtɜːmɪnə/ *n. Gram.* a word or phrase that occurs before a determiner, generally quantifying the noun group, e.g. *both, all, a lot of.*

predial /ˈpriːdɪəl/ *adj. & n.* (also **praedial**) *hist.* ● *adj.* **1 a** of land or farms. **b** rural, agrarian. **c** (of a slave, tenant, etc.) attached to farms or the land. **2** (of a tithe) consisting of agricultural produce. ● *n.* a predial slave. [medieval Latin *praedialis* from Latin *praedium* 'farm']

predicable /ˈprɛdɪkəb(ə)l/ *adj. & n.* ● *adj.* that may be predicated or affirmed. ● *n.* **1** a predicable thing. **2** (in *pl.*) *Logic* the five classes to which predicates belong: genus, species, difference, property, and accident. □ **predicability** /-ˈbɪlɪti/ *n.* [medieval Latin *praedicabilis* 'that may be affirmed' (as PREDICATE)]

predicament /prɪˈdɪkəm(ə)nt/ *n.* **1** a difficult, unpleasant, or embarrassing situation. **2** *Philos.* a category in (esp. Aristotelian) logic. [Middle English (in sense 2) from Late Latin *praedicamentum* 'thing predicated': see PREDICATE]

predicant /ˈprɛdɪk(ə)nt/ *adj. & n.* ● *adj. hist.* (of a religious order, esp. the Dominicans) engaged in preaching. ● *n.* **1** *hist.* a predicant person, esp. a Dominican friar. **2** *S.Afr.* = PREDIKANT. [Latin *praedicans*, part. of *praedicare* (as PREDICATE)]

predicate *v. & n.* ● *v.tr.* /ˈprɛdɪkeɪt/ **1** assert (something) about the subject of a proposition. **2** (foll. by *on*) found or base (a statement etc.) on. ● *n.* /ˈprɛdɪkət/ **1** *Gram.* what is said about the subject of a sentence etc. (e.g. *went home* in *John went home*). **2** *Logic* **a** what is predicated. **b** what is affirmed or denied of the subject by means of the copula (e.g. *mortal* in *all men are mortal*). □ **predication** /-ˈkeɪʃ(ə)n/ *n.* [Latin *praedicare praedicat-* 'proclaim' (as PRAE-, *dicare* 'declare')]

predicative /prɪˈdɪkətɪv/ *adj.* **1** *Gram.* (of an adjective or noun) forming or contained in the predicate, as *old* in *the dog is old* (but not in *the old dog*) and *house* in *there is a large house* (opp. ATTRIBUTIVE). **2** that predicates. □ **predicatively** *adv.* [Latin *praedicativus* (as PREDICATE)]

predict /prɪˈdɪkt/ *v.tr.* (often foll. by *that* + clause) make a statement about the future; foretell, prophesy. □ **predictive** *adj.* **predictively** *adv.* **predictor** *n.* [Latin *praedicere praedict-* (as PRAE-, *dicere* 'say')]

predictable /prɪˈdɪktəb(ə)l/ *adj.* **1** that can be predicted or is to be expected. **2** (of a person) likely to behave in a way that is easy to predict. □ **predictability** /-ˈbɪlɪti/ *n.* **predictably** *adv.*

prediction /prɪˈdɪkʃ(ə)n/ *n.* **1** the art of predicting or the process of being predicted. **2** a thing predicted; a forecast. [Latin *praedictio -onis* (as PREDICT)]

predigest /priːdɪˈdʒɛst, -dʌɪ-/ *v.tr.* **1** render (food) easily digestible before being eaten. **2** make (reading matter) easier to read or understand. □ **predigestion** /-ˈdʒɛstʃ(ə)n/ *n.*

predikant /prɛdɪˈkant, Dutch ˌpreɪdiːˈkɑːnt/ *n. S.Afr.* a minister of the Dutch Reformed Church. [Dutch (as PREDICANT)]

predilection /priːdɪˈlɛkʃ(ə)n/ *n.* (often foll. by *for*) a preference or special liking. [French *prédilection*, ultimately from Latin *praediligere praedilect-* 'prefer' (as PRAE-, *diligere* 'select': see DILIGENT)]

predispose /priːdɪˈspəʊz/ *v.tr.* **1** influence favourably in advance. **2** (foll. by *to*, or *to* + infin.) render liable or inclined beforehand. □ **predisposition** /-pəˈzɪʃ(ə)n/ *n.*

prednisone /ˈprɛdnɪzəʊn/ *n.* a synthetic drug similar to cortisone, used to relieve rheumatic and allergic conditions and to treat leukaemia. [perhaps from *pregnant* + *diene* + *cortisone*]

predominant /prɪˈdɒmɪnənt/ *adj.* **1** predominating. **2** being the strongest or main element. □ **predominance** *n.* **predominantly** *adv.*

predominate /prɪˈdɒmɪneɪt/ *v.intr.* **1** (foll. by *over*) have or exert control. **2** be superior. **3** be the strongest or main element; preponderate (*a garden in which dahlias predominate*). [medieval Latin *praedominari* (as PRAE-, DOMINATE)]

predominately /prɪˈdɒmɪnətli/ *adv.* = PREDOMINANTLY (see PREDOMINANT). [rare *predominate* (*adj.*) = PREDOMINANT]

predoom /priːˈduːm/ *v.tr.* doom beforehand.

predorsal /priːˈdɔːs(ə)l/ *adj.* in front of the dorsal region.

predynastic /ˌpriːdɪˈnastɪk, -dʌɪ-/ *adj.* of or relating to a period before the normally recognized dynasties (esp. of ancient Egypt).

pre-echo /priːˈɛkəʊ/ *n.* (*pl.* **-oes**) **1** a faint copy heard just before an actual sound in a recording, caused by the accidental transfer of signals. **2** a foreshadowing.

pre-eclampsia /priːɪˈklam(p)sɪə/ *n.* a condition of pregnancy characterized by high blood pressure and other symptoms associated with eclampsia. □ **pre-eclamptic** *adj.* & *n.*

pre-elect /priːɪˈlɛkt/ *v.tr.* elect beforehand.

pre-election /priːɪˈlɛkʃ(ə)n/ *n.* & *adj.* ● *n.* an election held beforehand. ● *attrib.adj.* done, given, or existing, before an election.

pre-embryo /priːˈɛmbrɪəʊ/ *n. Med.* a human embryo in the first fourteen days after fertilization. □ **pre-embryonic** /-ˈɒnɪk/ *adj.*

pre-eminent /priːˈɛmɪnənt/ *adj.* **1** excelling others. **2** outstanding; distinguished in some quality. □ **pre-eminence** *n.* **pre-eminently** *adv.* [Middle English from Latin *praeeminens* (as PRAE-, EMINENT)]

pre-empt /priːˈɛm(p)t/ *v.* **1** *tr.* **a** forestall. **b** acquire or appropriate in advance. **2** *tr.* obtain by pre-emption. **3** *tr. US* take for oneself (esp. public land) so as to have the right of pre-emption. **4** *intr. Bridge* make a pre-emptive bid. □ **pre-emptor** *n.* [back-formation from PRE-EMPTION]

■ **Usage** *Pre-empt* is sometimes used to mean 'prevent', but this is considered incorrect in standard English.

pre-emption /priːˈɛm(p)ʃ(ə)n/ *n.* **1 a** the purchase or appropriation by one person or party before the opportunity is offered to others. **b** the right to purchase (esp. *N. Amer.* & *Austral. hist.* public land) in this way. **2** prior appropriation or acquisition. **3** *Mil.* the action or strategy of making a pre-emptive attack. [medieval Latin *praeemptio* (as PRAE-, *emere empt-* 'buy')]

pre-emptive /priːˈɛm(p)tɪv/ *adj.* **1** pre-empting; serving to pre-empt. **2** (of military action) intended to prevent attack by disabling the enemy (*a pre-emptive strike*). **3** *Bridge* (of a bid) intended to be high enough to discourage further bidding.

preen /priːn/ *v.tr.* & *refl.* **1** (of a bird) tidy (the feathers or itself) with its beak. **2** (of a person) smarten or admire (oneself, one's hair, clothes, etc.). **3** (often foll. by *on*) congratulate or pride (oneself). □ **preener** *n.* [Middle English, apparently variant of earlier *prune*, ultimately as PRO-[1], Latin *ungere* 'anoint': associated with Scots & dialect *preen* 'pierce, pin', from the 'pricking' action of the bird's beak]

pre-engage /priːɪnˈgeɪdʒ, -ɛn-/ *v.tr.* engage beforehand. □ **pre-engagement** *n.*

preen gland *n.* a gland situated at the base of a bird's tail and producing oil used in preening.

pre-establish /priːɪˈstablɪʃ, priːɛ-/ *v.tr.* establish beforehand.

pre-exist /priːɪgˈzɪst, -ɛg-/ *v.intr.* & *tr.* **1** exist at an earlier time. **2** *tr.* exist earlier than. □ **pre-existence** *n.* **pre-existent** *adj.*

pref. *abbr.* **1** preface. **2 a** preference. **b** preferred.

prefab /ˈpriːfab/ *n. colloq.* a prefabricated building (often *attrib.*: *prefab houses*). [abbreviation]

prefabricate /priːˈfabrɪkeɪt/ *v.tr.* **1** manufacture sections of (a building etc.) prior to their assembly on a site. **2** produce in an artificially standardized way. □ **prefabrication** /-ˈkeɪʃ(ə)n/ *n.*

preface /ˈprɛfəs/ *n.* & *v.* ● *n.* **1** an introduction to a book stating its subject, scope, etc. **2** the preliminary part of a speech. **3** *Eccl.* the introduction to the central part of the Eucharistic service. ● *v.tr.* **1** (foll. by *with*) introduce or begin (a speech or event) (*prefaced my remarks with a warning*). **2** provide (a book etc.) with a preface. **3** (of an event etc.) lead up to (another). □ **prefatorial** /-ˈtɔːrɪəl/ *adj.* **prefatory** /-t(ə)ri/ *adj.* [Middle English via Old French from medieval Latin *praefatia*, for Latin *praefatio* from *praefari* (as PRAE-, *fari* 'speak')]

prefect /ˈpriːfɛkt/ *n.* **1 a** a chief officer, magistrate, or governor. **b** the chief administrative officer of a department in France. **2** esp. *Brit.* a senior pupil in a school etc. authorized to enforce discipline. **3** *Rom.Hist.* a senior magistrate or military commander. □ **prefectoral** /-ˈfɛkt(ə)r(ə)l/ *adj.* **prefectorial** /-ˈtɔːrɪəl/ *adj.* [Middle English via Old French from Latin *praefectus*, past part. of *praeficere* 'set in authority over' (as PRAE-, *facere* 'make')]

prefecture /ˈpriːfɛktjʊə/ *n.* **1** a district under the government of a prefect. **2 a** a prefect's office or tenure. **b** the official residence of a prefect. □ **prefectural** /prɪˈfɛktʃ(ə)r(ə)l/ *adj.* [French *préfecture* or Latin *praefectura* (as PREFECT)]

prefer /prɪˈfəː/ *v.tr.* (**preferred**, **preferring**) **1** (often foll. by *to*, or *to* + infin.) choose rather; like better (*would prefer to stay*; *prefers coffee to tea*). **2** submit (information, an accusation, etc.) for consideration. **3** promote or advance (a person). [Middle English via Old French *preferer* from Latin *praeferre* (as PRAE-, *ferre lat-* 'bear')]

preferable /ˈprɛf(ə)rəb(ə)l/ *adj.* **1** to be preferred. **2** (often foll. by *to*) more desirable. □ **preferability** /-ˈbɪlɪti/ *n.* **preferably** *adv.*

■ **Usage** *Preferable to* means 'more desirable than', and should, therefore, be intensified by *far*, *greatly*, or *much*, rather than *more*, e.g. *Travelling by train is far/greatly/much preferable to driving.*

preference /ˈprɛf(ə)r(ə)ns/ *n.* **1** the act or an instance of preferring or being preferred. **2** a preferred thing. **3 a** the favouring of one person etc. before others. **b** *Commerce* the favouring of one country by admitting its products at a lower import duty. **4** *Law* a prior right, esp. to the payment of debts. □ **in preference to** as a thing preferred over (another). [French *préférence* from medieval Latin *praeferentia* (as PREFER)]

preference share *n.* (*US* **preferred share**) a share whose entitlement to dividend takes priority over that of an ordinary share.

preference stock *n. Brit.* (also *US* **preferred stock**) stock whose entitlement to dividend takes priority over that of ordinary stock.

preferential /prɛfəˈrɛnʃ(ə)l/ *adj.* **1** of or involving preference (*preferential treatment*). **2** giving or receiving a favour. **3** *Commerce* (of a tariff etc.) favouring particular countries. **4** (of voting) in which the voter puts candidates in order of preference. □ **preferentially** *adv.* [PREFERENCE, on the pattern of *differential*]

preferment /prɪˈfəːm(ə)nt/ *n.* promotion to office.

preferred share *US* var. of PREFERENCE SHARE.

preferred stock *US* var. of PREFERENCE STOCK.

prefigure /priːˈfɪgə/ *v.tr.* **1** represent beforehand by a figure or type. **2** imagine beforehand. □ **prefiguration** /-ˈreɪʃ(ə)n/ *n.* **prefigurative** /-rətɪv/ *adj.* **prefigurement** *n.* [Middle English from ecclesiastical Latin *praefigurare* (as PRAE-, FIGURE)]

prefix /ˈpriːfɪks/ *n.* & *v.* ● *n.* **1** a verbal element placed at the beginning of a word to adjust or qualify its meaning (e.g. *ex-*, *non-*, *re-*) or (in some languages) as an inflectional formative. **2** a title placed before a name (e.g. *Mr*). ● *v.tr.* (often foll. by *to*) **1** add as an introduction. **2** join (a word or element) as a prefix.

□ **prefixation** /-'seɪʃ(ə)n/ *n.* **prefixion** /-'fɪkʃ(ə)n/ *n.* [earlier as verb: Middle English from Old French *prefixer* (as PRE-, FIX): the noun from Latin *praefixum*]

pre-flight /'priːflʌɪt/ *attrib.adj.* occurring or provided before an aircraft flight.

preform /priː'fɔːm/ *v.tr.* form beforehand. □ **preformation** /-'meɪʃ(ə)n/ *n.*

preformative /priː'fɔːmətɪv/ *adj. & n.* ● *adj.* **1** forming beforehand. **2** prefixed as the formative element of a word. ● *n.* a preformative syllable or letter.

prefrontal /priː'frʌnt(ə)l/ *adj.* **1** in front of the frontal bone of the skull. **2** in the forepart of the frontal lobe of the brain.

preglacial /priː'gleɪʃ(ə)l, -sɪəl/ *adj.* before a glacial period.

pregnable /'prɛgnəb(ə)l/ *adj.* able to be captured etc.; not impregnable. [Middle English from Old French *prenable* 'takable': see IMPREGNABLE[1]]

pregnancy /'prɛgnənsi/ *n.* (*pl.* **-ies**) the condition or an instance of being pregnant.

pregnant /'prɛgnənt/ *adj.* **1** (of a woman or female animal) having a child or young developing in the uterus. **2** full of meaning; significant or suggestive (*a pregnant pause*). **3** (esp. of a person's mind) imaginative, inventive. **4** (foll. by *with*) plentifully provided (*pregnant with danger*). □ **pregnantly** *adv.* (in sense 2). [Middle English from French *prégnant* or Latin *praegnans -antis*, earlier *praegnas* (probably as PRAE-, (*g*)*nasci* 'be born')]

pregnant construction *n. Gram.* one in which more is implied than the words express (e.g. *not have a chance* implying *of success* etc.).

preheat /priː'hiːt/ *v.tr.* heat beforehand.

prehensile /prɪ'hɛnsʌɪl/ *adj. Zool.* (of a tail or limb) capable of grasping. □ **prehensility** /-'sɪlɪti/ *n.* [French *préhensile* from Latin *prehendere prehens-* (as PRE-, *hendere* 'grasp')]

prehension /prɪ'hɛnʃ(ə)n/ *n.* **1** grasping, seizing. **2** mental apprehension. [Latin *prehensio* (as PREHENSILE)]

prehistoric /priːhɪ'stɒrɪk/ *adj.* **1** of or relating to the period before written records. **2** *colloq.* utterly out of date. □ **prehistorian** /-'stɔːrɪən/ *n.* **prehistorically** *adv.* **prehistory** /-'hɪst(ə)ri/ *n.* [French *préhistorique* (as PRE-, HISTORIC)]

pre-human /priː'hjuːmən/ *adj.* existing before the time of man.

pre-ignition /priːɪg'nɪʃ(ə)n/ *n.* the premature firing of the explosive mixture in an internal-combustion engine.

pre-industrial /priːɪn'dʌstrɪəl/ *adj.* of or relating to the time before industrialization.

prejudge /priː'dʒʌdʒ/ *v.tr.* **1** form a premature judgement on (a person, issue, etc.). **2** pass judgement on (a person) before a trial or proper inquiry. □ **prejudgement** *n.* **prejudication** /-ˌdʒuːdɪ'keɪʃ(ə)n/ *n.*

prejudice /'prɛdʒʊdɪs/ *n. & v.* ● *n.* **1 a** a preconceived opinion. **b** (foll. by *against*, *in favour of*) bias or partiality. **2** harm or injury that results or may result from some action or judgement (*to the prejudice of*). ● *v.tr.* **1** impair the validity or force of (a right, claim, statement, etc.). **2 a** (often as **prejudiced** *adj.*) cause (a person) to have a prejudice. **b** (as **prejudiced** *adj.*) not impartial; bigoted. □ **without prejudice** (often foll. by *to*) without detriment (to any existing right or claim). [Middle English via Old French from Latin *praejudicium* (as PRAE-, *judicium* 'judgement')]

prejudicial /prɛdʒʊ'dɪʃ(ə)l/ *adj.* causing prejudice; detrimental. □ **prejudicially** *adv.* [Middle English from Old French *prejudiciel* (as PREJUDICE)]

prelacy /'prɛləsi/ *n.* (*pl.* **-ies**) **1** Church government by prelates. **2** (prec. by *the*) prelates collectively. **3** the office or rank of prelate. [Middle English via Anglo-French *prelacie* from medieval Latin *prelatia* (as PRELATE)]

prelapsarian /priːlap'sɛːrɪən/ *adj.* before the Fall of Man; innocent.

prelate /'prɛlət/ *n.* **1** a high ecclesiastical dignitary, e.g. a bishop. **2** *hist.* an abbot or prior. □ **prelatic** /prɪ'latɪk/ *adj.* **prelatical** /prɪ'latɪk(ə)l/ *adj.* [Middle English via Old French *prelat* from medieval Latin *praelatus*, past part. of *praeferre*: see PREFER]

prelature /'prɛlətjʊə/ *n.* **1** the office of prelate. **2** (prec. by *the*) prelates collectively. [French *prélature* from medieval Latin *praelatura* (as PRELATE)]

prelim /'priːlɪm, prɪ'lɪm/ *n. colloq.* **1** a preliminary examination, esp. at a university. **2** (in *pl.*) the pages preceding the text of a book. [abbreviation]

preliminary /prɪ'lɪmɪn(ə)ri/ *adj., n., & adv.* ● *adj.* introductory, preparatory. ● *n.* (*pl.* **-ies**) (usu. in *pl.*) **1** a preliminary action or arrangement (*dispense with the preliminaries*). **2** a preliminary trial or contest. **3** (in *pl.*) = PRELIM 2. ● *adv.* (foll. by *to*) preparatory to; in advance of (*was completed preliminary to the main event*). □ **preliminarily** *adv.* [modern Latin *praeliminaris* or French *préliminaire* (as PRE-, Latin *limen liminis* 'threshold')]

pre-linguistic /priːlɪŋ'gwɪstɪk/ *adj.* existing or occurring before the development of language or the acquisition of speech.

preliterate /priː'lɪt(ə)rət/ *adj.* of or relating to a society or culture that has not developed the use of writing.

prelude /'prɛljuːd/ *n. & v.* ● *n.* (often foll. by *to*) **1** an action, event, or situation serving as an introduction. **2** the introductory part of a poem etc. **3 a** an introductory piece of music, often preceding a fugue or forming the first piece of a suite or beginning an act of an opera. **b** a short piece of music of a similar type, esp. for the piano. ● *v.tr.* **1** serve as a prelude to. **2** introduce with a prelude. □ **preludial** /prɪ'ljuːdɪəl/ *adj.* [French *prélude* or medieval Latin *praeludium* from Latin *praeludere praelus-* (as PRAE-, *ludere* 'play')]

premarital /priː'marɪt(ə)l/ *adj.* existing or (esp. of sexual relations) occurring before marriage. □ **premaritally** *adv.*

premature /'prɛmətjʊə/ *adj.* **1 a** occurring or done before the usual or proper time; too early (*a premature decision*). **b** too hasty (*must not be premature*). **2** (of a baby) born (esp. three or more weeks) before the end of the full term of gestation. □ **prematurely** *adv.* **prematureness** *n.* **prematurity** /-'tjʊərɪti/ *n.* [Latin *praematurus* 'very early' (as PRAE-, MATURE)]

premaxillary /priːmak'sɪləri/ *adj.* in front of the upper jaw.

pre-med /priː'mɛd/ *n. colloq.* **1** = PRE-MEDICATION. **2** (**premed**) a premedical course or student. [abbreviation]

premedical /priː'mɛdɪk(ə)l/ *adj.* of or relating to study in preparation for a course in medicine.

pre-medication /ˌpriːmɛdɪ'keɪʃ(ə)n/ *n.* medication to prepare for an operation or other treatment.

premeditate /priː'mɛdɪteɪt/ *v.tr.* think out or plan (an action) beforehand (*premeditated murder*). □ **premeditation** /-'teɪʃ(ə)n/ *n.* [Latin *praemeditari* (as PRAE-, MEDITATE)]

premenstrual /priː'mɛnstrʊəl/ *adj.* of, occurring, or experienced, before menstruation (*premenstrual tension*). □ **premenstrually** *adv.*

premenstrual syndrome *n.* any of a complex of symptoms (including tension, fluid retention, etc.) experienced by some women in the days immediately before menstruation (abbr. PMS).

premier /'prɛmɪə, 'priː-/ *n. & adj.* ● *n.* (usu. **Premier**) a prime minister or other head of government. ● *adj.* **1** first in importance, order, or time. **2** of earliest creation (*premier earl*). □ **premiership** *n.* [Middle English from Old French = first, from Latin (as PRIMARY)]

premiere /'prɛmɪɛː/ *n. & v.* (also **première**) ● *n.* the first performance or showing of a play or film. ● *v.tr.* give a premiere of. [French, fem. of *premier* (*adj.*) (as PREMIER)]

premillennial /priːmɪ'lɛnɪəl/ *adj.* existing or occurring before the millennium, esp. with reference to the prophesied second coming of Christ. □ **premillennialism** *n.* **premillennialist** *n.*

premise *n.* & *v.* ● *n.* /ˈprɛmɪs/ **1** *Logic* = PREMISS. **2** (in *pl.*) **a** a house or building with its grounds and appurtenances. **b** *Law* houses, lands, or tenements previously specified in a document etc. ● *v.tr.* /prɪˈmʌɪz/ **1 a** say or write by way of introduction. **b** assume from a premiss. **2** (foll. by *on*) base on (*justice premised on fundamental equality*). □ **on the premises** in the building etc. concerned. [Middle English via Old French *premisse* and medieval Latin *praemissa* (*propositio*) '(proposition) set in front' from Latin *praemittere praemiss-* (as PRAE-, *mittere* 'send')]

premiss /ˈprɛmɪs/ *n. Brit. Logic* a previous statement from which another is inferred. [variant of PREMISE]

premium /ˈpriːmɪəm/ *n.* (*pl.* **premiums**) **1** an amount to be paid for a contract of insurance. **2 a** a sum added to interest, wages, etc.; a bonus. **b** a sum added to ordinary charges. **3** a reward or prize. **4** (*attrib.*) (of a commodity) of best quality and therefore more expensive. □ **at a premium 1** above the usual or nominal price. **2** scarce and in demand. **put a premium on 1** provide or act as an incentive to. **2** attach special value to. [Latin *praemium* 'booty, reward' (as PRAE-, *emere* 'buy, take')]

Premium Bond *n.* (also **Premium Savings Bond**) *Brit.* a government security without interest but with a draw for cash prizes.

premolar /priːˈməʊlə/ *adj.* & *n.* ● *adj.* in front of a molar tooth. ● *n.* (in an adult human) each of eight teeth situated in pairs between each of the four canine teeth and each first molar.

premonition /prɛməˈnɪʃ(ə)n, priː-/ *n.* a forewarning; a presentiment. □ **premonitor** /prɪˈmɒnɪtə/ *n.* **premonitory** /prɪˈmɒnɪt(ə)ri/ *adj.* [French *prémonition* or Late Latin *praemonitio* from Latin *praemonēre praemonit-* (as PRAE-, *monēre* 'warn')]

Premonstratensian /ˌpriːmɒnstrəˈtɛnsɪən/ *adj.* & *n. hist.* ● *adj.* of or relating to an order of regular canons founded at Prémontré in France in 1120, or of the corresponding order of nuns. ● *n.* a member of either of these orders. [medieval Latin *Praemonstratensis* from *Praemonstratus* (literally 'foreshown'), the Latin name of the abbey of Prémontré, so called because the site was prophetically pointed out by the order's founder, St Norbert]

premorse /priːˈmɔːs/ *adj. Bot.* & *Zool.* with the end abruptly terminated. [Latin *praemordēre praemors-* 'bite off' (as PRAE-, *mordēre* 'bite')]

prenatal /priːˈneɪt(ə)l/ *adj.* of or concerning the period before birth. □ **prenatally** *adv.*

prentice /ˈprɛntɪs/ *n.* & *v. archaic* ● *n.* = APPRENTICE. ● *v.tr.* (as **prenticed** *adj.*) apprenticed. □ **prenticeship** *n.* [Middle English, from APPRENTICE]

prentice hand *n.* an inexperienced hand.

prenuptial /priːˈnʌpʃ(ə)l/ *adj.* existing or occurring before marriage.

preoccupation /prɪˌɒkjʊˈpeɪʃ(ə)n/ *n.* **1** the state of being preoccupied. **2** a thing that engrosses the mind. [French *préoccupation* or Latin *praeoccupatio* (as PREOCCUPY)]

preoccupy /priːˈɒkjʊpʌɪ/ *v.tr.* (**-ies**, **-ied**) **1** (of a thought etc.) dominate or engross the mind of (a person) to the exclusion of other thoughts. **2** (as **preoccupied** *adj.*) otherwise engrossed; mentally distracted. **3** occupy beforehand. [PRE- + OCCUPY, suggested by Latin *praeoccupare* 'seize beforehand']

preocular /priːˈɒkjʊlə/ *adj.* in front of the eye.

preordain /priːɔːˈdeɪn/ *v.tr.* ordain or determine beforehand.

pre-owned /priːˈəʊnd/ *adj.* esp. *US* second-hand.

prep[1] /prɛp/ *n.* & *adj.* ● *n. colloq.* **1** *Brit.* **a** school work done outside lessons, esp. in an independent school. **b** a period when this is done. **2** *US* a student in a preparatory school. ● *attrib.adj. Brit.* **1** relating to work set as prep or the time allocated for this (*prep book*; *prep period*). **2** relating to education in a preparatory school (*prep department*). [abbreviation of PREPARATION]

prep[2] /prep/ *v.* (**prepped**, **prepping**) *colloq.* **1** *tr. N. Amer.* prepare, make ready or suitable. **2** *intr. US* prepare oneself for an event. [abbreviation of PREPARE]

prep. *abbr.* preposition.

pre-pack /priːˈpak/ *v.tr.* (also **pre-package** /-ˈpakɪdʒ/) pack (goods) on the site of production or before retail.

prepaid *past* and *past part.* of PREPAY.

preparation /prɛpəˈreɪʃ(ə)n/ *n.* **1** the act or an instance of preparing; the process of being prepared. **2** (often in *pl.*) something done to make ready. **3** a specially prepared substance, esp. a food or medicine. **4** work done by school pupils to prepare for a lesson. **5** *Mus.* the sounding of the discordant note in a chord in the preceding chord where it is not discordant, lessening the effect of the discord. [Middle English via Old French from Latin *praeparatio -onis* (as PREPARE)]

preparative /prɪˈparətɪv/ *adj.* & *n.* ● *adj.* preparatory. ● *n.* **1** *Mil.* & *Naut.* a signal on a drum, bugle, etc., as an order to make ready. **2** a preparatory act. □ **preparatively** *adv.* [Middle English via Old French *preparatif -ive* from medieval Latin *praeparativus* (as PREPARE)]

preparatory /prɪˈparət(ə)ri/ *adj.* & *adv.* ● *adj.* **1** (often foll. by *to*) serving to prepare; introductory. **2** *Brit.* = PREP[1] *adj.* 2. ● *adv.* (often foll. by *to*) in a preparatory manner (*was packing preparatory to departure*). □ **preparatorily** *adv.* [Middle English from Late Latin *praeparatorius* (as PREPARE)]

preparatory school *n.* a usu. private school preparing pupils *Brit.* for esp. a public school, or *US* for college or university.

prepare /prɪˈpɛː/ *v.* **1** *tr.* make or get ready for use, consideration, etc. **2** *tr.* make ready or assemble (food, a meal, etc.) for eating. **3 a** *tr.* make (a person or oneself) ready or disposed in some way (*prepares students for university*; *prepared them for a shock*). **b** *intr.* put oneself or things in readiness, get ready (*prepare to jump*). **4** *tr.* make (a chemical product etc.) by a regular process; manufacture. **5** *tr. Mus.* lead up to (a discord). □ **be prepared 1** (usu. foll. by *for*) be ready or disposed (*was prepared for a legal battle*). **2** (foll. by *to*) be willing to. □ **preparer** *n.* [Middle English from French *préparer* or Latin *praeparare* (as PRAE-, *parare* 'make ready')]

■ **Usage** The use of *be prepared* in the sense 'be willing' was criticized in the past by some authorities, but it is now established usage.

preparedness /prɪˈpɛːrɪdnɪs/ *n.* a state of readiness, esp. for war.

prepay /priːˈpeɪ/ *v.tr.* (*past* and *past part.* **prepaid**) **1** pay (a charge) in advance. **2** pay postage on (a letter or parcel etc.) before posting. □ **prepayable** *adj.* **prepayment** *n.*

prepense /prɪˈpɛns/ *adj.* (usu. placed after noun) esp. *Law* deliberate, intentional (*malice prepense*). □ **prepensely** *adv.* [earlier *prepensed*, past part. of obsolete *prepense*, alteration of earlier *purpense* from Anglo-French & Old French *purpenser* (as PUR-, *penser* 'think'): see PENSIVE]

pre-plan /priːˈplan/ *v.tr.* (**pre-planned**, **pre-planning**) plan in advance.

preponderant /prɪˈpɒnd(ə)r(ə)nt/ *adj.* surpassing in influence, power, number, or importance; predominant, preponderating. □ **preponderance** *n.* **preponderantly** *adv.*

preponderate /prɪˈpɒndəreɪt/ *v.intr.* (often foll. by *over*) **1 a** be greater in influence, quantity, or number. **b** predominate. **2 a** be of greater importance. **b** weigh more. [Latin *praeponderare* (as PRAE-, PONDER)]

prepone /priːˈpəʊn/ *v.tr.* bring forward to an earlier date or time. [PRE- + POSTPONE]

prepose /priːˈpəʊz/ *v.tr. Linguistics* place in front; preface, prefix. [French *préposer* (as PREPOSITION)]

preposition /prɛpəˈzɪʃ(ə)n/ *n. Gram.* a word governing (and usu. preceding) a noun or pronoun and expressing a relation to another word or element, as in: 'the man *on* the platform', 'came *after* dinner', 'what did you do it *for*?'. ▫ **prepositional** *adj.* **prepositionally** *adv.* [Middle English from Latin *praepositio*, from *praeponere praeposit-* (as PRAE-, *ponere* 'place')]

prepositive /priːˈpɒzɪtɪv/ *adj. Gram.* (of a word, particle, etc.) that should be placed before or prefixed. [Late Latin *praepositivus* (as PREPOSITION)]

prepossess /priːpəˈzɛs/ *v.tr.* **1** (usu. in *passive*) (of an idea, feeling, etc.) take possession of (a person); imbue. **2 a** prejudice (usu. favourably and spontaneously). **b** (as **prepossessing** *adj.*) attractive, appealing. ▫ **prepossession** /-ˈzɛʃ(ə)n/ *n.*

preposterous /prɪˈpɒst(ə)rəs/ *adj.* **1** utterly absurd; outrageous. **2** contrary to nature, reason, or common sense. ▫ **preposterously** *adv.* **preposterousness** *n.* [Latin *praeposterus* 'reversed, absurd' (as PRAE-, *posterus* 'coming after')]

prepostor var. of PRAEPOSTOR.

prepotent /prɪˈpəʊt(ə)nt/ *adj.* **1** greater than others in power, influence, etc. **2** *Biol.* **a** having a greater power of fertilization. **b** dominant in transmitting hereditary qualities. ▫ **prepotence** *n.* **prepotency** *n.* [Middle English from Latin *praepotens -entis*, part. of *praeposse* (as PRAE-, *posse* 'be able')]

preppy /ˈprɛpi/ *n. & adj.* (also **preppie**) *N. Amer. colloq.* ● *n.* (*pl.* **-ies**) a person attending an expensive private school or who looks like such a person (with short hair, blazer, etc.). ● *adj.* (**preppier**, **preppiest**) **1** like a preppy. **2** neat and fashionable. [PREP SCHOOL + -Y²]

pre-prandial /priːˈprandɪəl/ *adj. formal* or *joc.* before dinner or lunch. [PRE- + Latin *prandium* 'a meal']

pre-preference /priːˈprɛf(ə)r(ə)ns/ *adj. Brit.* (of shares, claims, etc.) ranking before preference shares etc.

pre-print /ˈpriːprɪnt/ *n.* a printed document issued in advance of general publication.

pre-process /priːˈprəʊsɛs/ *v.tr.* subject to a preliminary processing.

pre-processor /priːˈprəʊsɛsə/ *n.* a computer program that modifies data to conform with the input requirements of another program.

pre-production /priːprəˈdʌkʃ(ə)n/ *n.* work done on a film, broadcast, etc. before production begins (usu. *attrib.*: *pre-production discussions*).

pre-program /priːˈprəʊgram/ *v.tr.* (**-programmed**, **-programming**) program (a computer etc.) beforehand.

prep school /prɛp/ *n.* = PREPARATORY SCHOOL. [abbreviation of PREPARATORY]

pre-pubescent /priːpjʊˈbɛs(ə)nt/ *adj. & n.* ● *adj.* (also **pre-pubertal** /-ˈbəːt(ə)l/) **1** occurring prior to puberty. **2** that has not yet reached puberty. ● *n.* a pre-pubescent boy or girl.

pre-publication /ˌpriːpʌblɪˈkeɪʃ(ə)n/ *adj. & n.* ● *attrib.adj.* produced or occurring before publication. ● *n.* publication in advance or beforehand.

prepuce /ˈpriːpjuːs/ *n.* **1** = FORESKIN. **2** the fold of skin surrounding the clitoris. ▫ **preputial** /priːˈpjuːʃ(ə)l/ *adj.* [Middle English from Latin *praeputium*]

pre-qualify /priːˈkwɒlɪfʌɪ/ *v.intr.* qualify in advance, esp. in advance of a sporting event.

prequel /ˈpriːkw(ə)l/ *n.* a story, film, etc., whose events or concerns precede those of an existing work. [PRE- + SEQUEL]

Pre-Raphaelite /priːˈrafəlʌɪt/ *n. & adj.* ● *n.* a member of a group of English 19th-c. artists, including Holman Hunt, Millais, and D. G. Rossetti, emulating the work of Italian artists from before the time of Raphael. ● *adj.* **1** of or relating to the Pre-Raphaelites. **2** (**pre-Raphaelite**) (esp. of a woman) like a type painted by a Pre-Raphaelite (e.g. with long thick curly auburn hair). ▫ **Pre-Raphaelitism** *n.*

Pre-Raphaelite Brotherhood *n.* the chosen name of the Pre-Raphaelites.

pre-record /priːrɪˈkɔːd/ *v.tr.* (esp. as **pre-recorded** *adj.*) record (esp. material for broadcasting) in advance.

prerequisite /priːˈrɛkwɪzɪt/ *adj. & n.* ● *adj.* required as a precondition. ● *n.* a prerequisite thing.

■ **Usage** See Usage Note at PERQUISITE.

prerogative /prɪˈrɒgətɪv/ *n.* **1** a right or privilege exclusive to an individual or class. **2** (in full **royal prerogative**) *Brit.* the right of the sovereign, theoretically subject to no restriction. [Middle English via Old French *prerogative* or Latin *praerogativa* 'privilege' (originally to vote first) from *praerogativus* 'asked first' (as PRAE-, *rogare* 'ask')]

Pres. *abbr.* President.

presage /ˈprɛsɪdʒ/ *n. & v.* ● *n.* **1** an omen or portent. **2** a presentiment or foreboding. ● *v.tr.* /also prɪˈseɪdʒ/ **1** portend, foreshadow. **2** give warning of (an event etc.) by natural means. **3** (of a person) predict or have a presentiment of. ▫ **presageful** /prɪˈseɪdʒfʊl, -f(ə)l/ *adj.* **presager** *n.* [Middle English via French *présage*, *présager* from Latin *praesagium*, from *praesagire* 'forebode' (as PRAE-, *sagire* 'perceive keenly')]

presbyopia /prɛzbɪˈəʊpɪə/ *n.* long-sightedness caused by loss of elasticity of the eye lens, occurring esp. in middle and old age. ▫ **presbyopic** /-ˈɒpɪk/ *adj.* [modern Latin, from Greek *presbus* 'old man' + *ōps ōpos* 'eye']

presbyter /ˈprɛzbɪtə/ *n.* **1** an elder in the early Christian Church. **2** (in the Episcopal Church) a minister of the second order; a priest. **3** (in the Presbyterian Church) an elder. ▫ **presbyteral** /-ˈbɪt(ə)r(ə)l/ *adj.* **presbyterate** /-ˈbɪt(ə)rət/ *n.* **presbyterial** /-ˈtɪərɪəl/ *adj.* **presbytership** *n.* [ecclesiastical Latin from Greek *presbuteros* 'elder', comparative of *presbus* 'old']

Presbyterian /prɛzbɪˈtɪərɪən/ *adj. & n.* ● *adj.* (of a Church) governed by elders all of equal rank, esp. with reference to the national Church of Scotland. ● *n.* **1** a member of a Presbyterian Church. **2** an adherent of the Presbyterian system. ▫ **Presbyterianism** *n.* [ecclesiastical Latin *presbyterium* (as PRESBYTERY)]

presbytery /ˈprɛzbɪt(ə)ri/ *n.* (*pl.* **-ies**) **1** the eastern part of a chancel beyond the choir; the sanctuary. **2 a** a body of presbyters, esp. a court next above a Kirk-session. **b** a district represented by this. **3** the house of a Roman Catholic priest. [Middle English from Old French *presbiterie* via ecclesiastical Latin from Greek *presbuterion* (as PRESBYTER)]

pre-school /ˈpriːskuːl, priːˈskuːl/ *adj.* of or relating to the time before a child is old enough to go to school. ▫ **pre-schooler** /-ˈskuːlə/ *n.*

prescient /ˈprɛsɪənt/ *adj.* having foreknowledge or foresight. ▫ **prescience** *n.* **presciently** *adv.* [Latin *praescire praescient-* 'know beforehand' (as PRAE-, *scire* 'know')]

prescind /prɪˈsɪnd/ *v.* **1** *tr.* (foll. by *from*) cut off (a part from a whole), esp. prematurely or abruptly. **2** *intr.* (foll. by *from*) leave out of consideration. [Latin *praescindere* (as PRAE-, *scindere* 'cut')]

prescribe /prɪˈskrʌɪb/ *v.* **1** *tr.* **a** advise the use of (a medicine etc.), esp. by an authorized prescription. **b** recommend, esp. as a benefit (*prescribed a change of scenery*). **2** *tr.* lay down or impose authoritatively. **3** *intr.* (foll. by *to, for*) assert a prescriptive right or claim. ▫ **prescriber** *n.* [Latin *praescribere praescript-* 'direct in writing' (as PRAE-, *scribere* 'write')]

■ **Usage** *Prescribe*, meaning 'advise, recommend, impose authoritatively', is sometimes confused with *proscribe*, meaning 'to forbid'. Note the difference in sense between *prescribed drugs* and *proscribed drugs*.

prescript /ˈpriːskrɪpt/ *n.* an ordinance, law, or command. [Latin *praescriptum*, neut. past part. of *praescribere*: see PRESCRIBE]

prescription /prɪˈskrɪpʃ(ə)n/ *n.* **1** the act or an instance of prescribing. **2 a** a doctor's (usu. written) instruction for the composition and use of a medicine. **b** a medicine prescribed. **3** (in full **positive prescription**) uninterrupted use or possession from time immemorial or for the period fixed by law as giving a title or right. **4 a** an ancient custom viewed as authoritative. **b** a claim founded on long use. [Middle English via Old French from Latin *praescriptio -onis* (as PRESCRIBE)]

prescriptive /prɪˈskrɪptɪv/ *adj.* **1** prescribing. **2** *Linguistics* concerned with or laying down rules of usage (opp. DESCRIPTIVE 3). **3** based on prescription (*prescriptive right*). **4** prescribed by custom. □ **prescriptively** *adv.* **prescriptiveness** *n.* **prescriptivism** *n.* **prescriptivist** *n. & adj.* [Late Latin *praescriptivus* (as PRESCRIBE)]

pre-season /priːˈsiːz(ə)n/ *n.* the period before a season (esp. a sporting season) begins (usu. *attrib.*: *pre-season friendlies*).

pre-select /priːsɪˈlɛkt/ *v.tr.* select in advance. □ **pre-selection** *n.*

pre-selective /priːsɪˈlɛktɪv/ *adj.* that can be selected or set in advance.

pre-selector /priːsɪˈlɛktə/ *n.* any of various devices for selecting a mechanical or electrical operation in advance of its execution, e.g. of a gear change in a motor vehicle.

presence /ˈprɛz(ə)ns/ *n.* **1** the state or condition of being present (*your presence is requested*). **2** a place where a person is (*was admitted to their presence*). **3 a** a person's appearance or bearing, esp. when imposing (*an august presence*). **b** a person's force of personality (esp. *have presence*). **4** a person or thing that is present (*the royal presence*; *there was a presence in the room*). **5** representation for reasons of political influence (*maintained a presence*). □ **in the presence of** in front of; observed by. [Middle English via Old French from Latin *praesentia* (as PRESENT[1])]

presence chamber *n.* a room in which a monarch or other distinguished person receives visitors.

presence of mind *n.* calmness and self-command in sudden difficulty etc.

present[1] /ˈprɛz(ə)nt/ *adj. & n.* ● *adj.* **1** (usu. *predic.*) being in the place in question (*was present at the trial*). **2 a** now existing, occurring, or being such (*the present Duke*; *during the present season*). **b** now being considered or discussed etc. (*in the present case*). **3** *Gram.* expressing an action etc. now going on or habitually performed (*present participle*; *present tense*). ● *n.* (prec. by *the*) **1** the time now passing (*no time like the present*). **2** *Gram.* the present tense. □ **at present** now. **by these presents** *Law* by this document (*know all men by these presents*). **for the present 1** just now. **2** as far as the present is concerned. **present company excepted** excluding those who are here now. [Middle English via Old French from Latin *praesens -entis*, part. of *praeesse* 'be at hand' (as PRAE-, *esse* 'be')]

present[2] /prɪˈzɛnt/ *v. & n.* ● *v.tr.* **1** introduce, offer, or exhibit, esp. for public attention or consideration. **2 a** (with a thing as object, foll. by *to*) offer, award, or give as a gift (to a person), esp. formally or ceremonially. **b** (with a person as object, foll. by *with*) make available to; cause to have (*presented them with a new car*; *that presents us with a problem*). **3 a** (of a company, producer, etc.) put (a form of entertainment) before the public. **b** (of a performer, compère, etc.) introduce or put before an audience . **4** introduce (a person) formally (*may I present my fiancé?*; *was presented at court*). **5** offer, give (compliments etc.) (*may I present my card*; *present my regards to your family*). **6 a** (of a circumstance) reveal (some quality etc.) (*this presents some difficulty*). **b** exhibit (an appearance etc.) (*presented a rough exterior*). **7** (of an idea etc.) offer or suggest itself. **8** deliver (a cheque, bill, etc.) for acceptance or payment. **9 a** (usu. foll. by *at*) aim (a weapon). **b** hold out (a weapon) in a position for aiming. **10** (*refl.* or *absol.*) *Med.* **a** (of an illness etc.) manifest itself. **b** (of a patient) come forward for or undergo initial medical examination. **11** (*absol.*) *Med.* (of a part of a foetus) be directed toward the cervix at the time of delivery. **12** (foll. by *to*) *Law* bring formally under notice, submit (an offence, complaint, etc.). **13** (foll. by *to*) *Eccl.* recommend (a clergyman) to a bishop for institution to a benefice. ● *n.* the position of presenting arms in salute. □ **present arms** hold a rifle etc. vertically in front of the body as a salute. **present oneself 1** appear. **2** come forward for examination etc. □ **presenter** *n.* (esp. in sense 3b of *v.*). [Middle English via Old French *presenter* from Latin *praesentare* (as PRESENT[1])]

present[3] /ˈprɛz(ə)nt/ *n.* a gift; a thing given or presented. □ **make a present of** give as a gift. [Middle English from Old French (as PRESENT[1]), originally in the phrase *mettre une chose en present à quelqu'un* 'put a thing into the presence of a person']

presentable /prɪˈzɛntəb(ə)l/ *adj.* **1** of good appearance; fit to be presented to other people. **2** fit for presentation. □ **presentability** /-ˈbɪlɪti/ *n.* **presentableness** *n.* **presentably** *adv.*

presentation /prɛz(ə)nˈteɪʃ(ə)n/ *n.* **1 a** the act or an instance of presenting; the process of being presented. **b** a thing presented. **2** the manner or quality of presenting. **3** a demonstration or display of materials, information, etc.; a lecture. **4** an exhibition or theatrical performance. **5** a formal introduction. **6** the position of the foetus in relation to the cervix at the time of delivery. □ **presentational** *adj.* **presentationally** *adv.* [Middle English via Old French from Late Latin *praesentatio -onis* (as PRESENT[2])]

presentationism /prɛz(ə)nˈteɪʃ(ə)nɪz(ə)m/ *n. Philos.* the doctrine that in perception the mind has immediate cognition of the object. □ **presentationist** *n.*

presentative /prɪˈzɛntətɪv/ *adj.* **1** *Philos.* subject to direct cognition. **2** *hist.* (of a benefice) to which a patron has the right of presentation. [Middle English, probably from medieval Latin (as PRESENTATION)]

present-day *attrib.adj.* of this time; modern.

presentee /prɛz(ə)nˈtiː/ *n.* **1** the recipient of a present. **2** a person presented. [Middle English from Anglo-French (as PRESENT[2])]

presentient /prɪˈsɛnʃ(ə)nt, -ˈzɛn-/ *adj.* (often foll. by *of*) having a presentiment. [Latin *praesentiens* (as PRAE-, SENTIENT)]

presentiment /prɪˈzɛntɪm(ə)nt, -ˈsɛn-/ *n.* a vague expectation; a foreboding (esp. of misfortune). [obsolete French *présentiment* (as PRE-, SENTIMENT)]

presently /ˈprɛz(ə)ntli/ *adv.* **1** soon; after a short time. **2** esp. *N. Amer.* & *Sc.* at the present time; now.

presentment /prɪˈzɛntm(ə)nt/ *n.* the act of presenting information, esp. a statement on oath by a jury of a fact known to them. [Middle English from Old French *presentement* (as PRESENT[2])]

preservation /prɛzəˈveɪʃ(ə)n/ *n.* **1** the act of preserving or process of being preserved. **2** a state of being well or badly preserved (*in an excellent state of preservation*). [Middle English via Old French from medieval Latin *praeservatio -onis* (as PRESERVE)]

preservationist /prɛzəˈveɪʃ(ə)nɪst/ *n.* a supporter or advocate of preservation, esp. of antiquities and historic buildings.

preservative /prɪˈzəːvətɪv/ *n. & adj.* ● *n.* a substance for preserving perishable foodstuffs, wood, etc. ● *adj.* tending to preserve. [Middle English via Old French *preservatif -ive* from medieval Latin *praeservativus -um* (as PRESERVE)]

preserve /prɪˈzəːv/ *v. & n.* ● *v.tr.* **1 a** keep safe or free from harm, decay, etc. **b** keep alive (a name, memory, etc.). **2** maintain (a thing) in its existing state. **3** retain (a quality or condition). **4 a** treat or refrigerate (food) to prevent decomposition or fermentation. **b** prepare (fruit) by boiling it with sugar, for long-term storage. **5** keep (game, a river, etc.) undisturbed for private use. ● *n.* (in *sing.* or *pl.*) **1** preserved fruit; jam. **2** a place where game or fish etc. are preserved. **3** a sphere or area of activity regarded as a person's own. □ **preservable** *adj.* **preserver** *n.* [Middle English via Old French *preserver* from Late Latin *praeservare* (as PRAE-, *servare* 'keep')]

pre-set /priːˈsɛt/ *v.tr.* (**-setting**; *past* and *past part.* **-set**) **1** set or fix (a device) in advance of its operation. **2** settle or decide beforehand.

pre-shrunk /priːˈʃrʌŋk/ *adj.* (of a fabric or garment) treated so that it shrinks during manufacture and not in use.

preside /prɪˈzʌɪd/ *v.intr.* **1** (often foll. by *at, over*) be in a position of authority, esp. as the chairperson or president of a meeting. **2 a** exercise control or authority. **b** (foll. by *at*) *colloq.* play an instrument in company (*presided at the piano*). [French *présider* from Latin *praesidēre* (as PRAE-, *sedēre* 'sit')]

presidency /ˈprɛzɪd(ə)nsi/ *n.* (*pl.* **-ies**) **1** the office of president. **2** the period of this. [Spanish & Portuguese *presidencia*, Italian *presidenza*, from medieval Latin *praesidentia* (as PRESIDE)]

president /ˈprɛzɪd(ə)nt/ *n.* **1** the elected head of a republican state. **2** the head of a society or council etc. **3** the head of certain colleges. **4** *N. Amer.* **a** the head of a university. **b** the head of a company, etc. **5** a person in charge of a meeting, council, etc. □ **presidential** /-ˈdɛnʃ(ə)l/ *adj.* **presidentially** /-ˈdɛnʃ(ə)li/ *adv.* **presidentship** *n.* [Middle English via Old French from Latin (as PRESIDE)]

president-elect *n.* (*pl.* **presidents-elect**) a president who has been elected but has not yet taken up office.

presidium /prɪˈsɪdɪʌm, -ˈzɪ-/ *n.* (also **praesidium**) a standing executive committee in a Communist country, esp. in the former USSR. [Russian *prezidium* from Latin *praesidium* 'protection' etc. (as PRESIDE)]

presocratic /priːsəˈkratɪk/ *adj.* (of philosophy) of the time before Socrates.

press[1] /prɛs/ *v.* & *n.* ● *v.* **1** *tr.* apply steady force to (a thing in contact) (*press a switch*; *pressed the two surfaces together*). **2** *tr.* **a** compress or apply pressure to a thing to flatten, shape, or smooth it, as by ironing (*got the curtains pressed*). **b** squeeze (a fruit etc.) to extract its juice. **c** manufacture (a gramophone record etc.) by moulding under pressure. **3** *tr.* (foll. by *out of, from,* etc.) squeeze (juice etc.). **4** *tr.* embrace or caress by squeezing (*pressed my hand*). **5** *intr.* (foll. by *on, against,* etc.) exert pressure. **6** *intr.* be urgent; demand immediate action (*time was pressing*). **7** *intr.* (foll. by *for*) make an insistent demand. **8** *intr.* (foll. by *up, round,* etc.) form a crowd. **9** *intr.* (foll. by *on, forward,* etc.) hasten insistently. **10** *tr.* (often in *passive*) (of an enemy etc.) bear heavily on. **11** *tr.* (often foll. by *for,* or *to* + infin.) urge or entreat (*pressed me to stay*; *pressed me for an answer*). **12** *tr.* (foll. by *on, upon*) **a** put forward or urge (an opinion, claim, or course of action). **b** insist on the acceptance of (an offer, a gift, etc.). **13** *tr.* insist on (*did not press the point*). **14** *intr.* (foll. by *on*) produce a strong mental or moral impression; oppress; weigh heavily. **15** *intr. Golf* try too hard for a long shot etc. and so strike the ball imperfectly. ● *n.* **1** the act or an instance of pressing (*give it a slight press*). **2 a** a device for compressing, flattening, shaping, extracting juice, etc. (*trouser press*; *flower press*; *wine press*). **b** a frame for preserving the shape of a racket when not in use. **c** a machine that applies pressure to a workpiece by means of a tool, in order to punch shapes, bend it, etc. **3** = PRINTING PRESS. **4** (prec. by *the*) **a** the art or practice of printing. **b** newspapers, journalists, etc., generally or collectively (*read it in the press*; *pursued by the press*). **5** a notice or piece of publicity in newspapers etc. (*got a good press*). **6** (**Press**) **a** a printing house or establishment. **b** a publishing company (*Athlone Press*). **7 a** crowding. **b** a crowd (of people etc.). **8** the pressure of affairs. **9** esp. *Ir.* & *Sc.* a large usu. shelved cupboard for clothes, books, etc., esp. in a recess. □ **at** (or **in**) **press** (or **the press**) being printed. **be pressed for** have barely enough (time etc.). **go** (or **send**) **to press** go or send to be printed. **press the button 1** set machinery in motion. **2** *colloq.* initiate an action or train of events, esp. nuclear war. **press (the) flesh** esp. *US* shake hands. [Middle English via Old French *presser*, *presse* from Latin *pressare*, frequentative of *premere press-*]

press[2] /prɛs/ *v.* & *n.* ● *v.tr.* **1** *hist.* force to serve in the army or navy. **2** bring into use as a makeshift (*was pressed into service*). ● *n. hist.* compulsory enlistment esp. in the navy. [alteration, by association with PRESS[1], of obsolete *prest* 'pay given on enlistment, enlistment by such payment': via Old French *prest* 'loan, advance pay', from *prester*, from Latin *praestare* 'furnish, provide' (as PRAE-, *stare* 'stand')]

press agent *n.* a person employed to attend to advertising and press publicity.

press box *n.* a reporters' enclosure esp. at a sports event.

press-button *n.* & *attrib.adj. Brit.* = PUSH-BUTTON.

press conference *n.* an interview given to journalists to make an announcement or answer questions.

press cutting *n.* a cutting taken from a newspaper etc.

pressed steel *n.* steel moulded under pressure.

press gallery *n.* a gallery for reporters esp. in a legislative assembly.

press-gang *n.* & *v.* ● *n.* **1** *hist.* a body of men employed to press men into service in the army or navy. **2** any group using similar coercive methods. ● *v.tr.* force into service.

pressie var. of PREZZIE.

pressing /ˈprɛsɪŋ/ *adj.* & *n.* ● *adj.* **1** urgent (*pressing business*). **2 a** urging strongly (*a pressing invitation*). **b** persistent, importunate (*since you are so pressing*). ● *n.* **1** a thing made by pressing, esp. a gramophone record. **2** a series of these made at one time. **3** the act or an instance of pressing a thing, esp. a gramophone record, grapes, etc. (*all at one pressing*). □ **pressingly** *adv.*

pressman /ˈprɛsmən/ *n.* (*pl.* **-men**) **1** a journalist. **2** an operator of a printing press.

pressmark /ˈprɛsmɑːk/ *n. Brit.* a library shelf mark showing the location of a book etc.

press-on *adj.* (of a material) that can be pressed or ironed on to something.

press release *n.* an official statement issued to newspapers for information.

press stud *n. Brit.* a small fastening device engaged by pressing its two halves together.

press-up *n. Brit.* an exercise in which the prone body is raised from the legs or trunk upwards by pressing down on the hands to straighten the arms.

pressure /ˈprɛʃə/ *n.* & *v.* ● *n.* **1 a** the exertion of continuous force on or against a body by another in contact with it. **b** the force exerted. **c** the amount of this (expressed by the force on a unit area) (*atmospheric pressure*). **2** urgency; the need to meet a deadline etc. (*work under pressure*). **3** affliction or difficulty (*under financial pressure*). **4** constraining influence (*if pressure is brought to bear*). ● *v.tr.* **1** apply (esp. psychological or moral) pressure to. **2** (often foll. by *into*) persuade; coerce (*was pressured into attending*). [Middle English from Latin *pressura* (as PRESS[1])]

pressure cooker *n.* an airtight pan for cooking quickly under steam pressure. □ **pressure-cook** *v.tr.*

pressure gauge *n.* a gauge showing the pressure of steam etc.

pressure group *n.* a group or association formed to promote a particular interest or cause by influencing public policy.

pressure point *n.* **1** a point where an artery can be pressed against a bone to inhibit bleeding. **2** a point on the skin sensitive to pressure. **3** a target for political pressure or influence.

pressure suit *n.* an inflatable suit for flying at a high altitude.

pressurize /ˈprɛʃərʌɪz/ *v.tr.* (also **-ise**) **1** (esp. as **pressurized** *adj.*) maintain normal atmospheric pressure in (an aircraft cabin etc.) at a high altitude. **2** raise to a high pressure. **3** pressure (a person). □ **pressurization** /-ˈzeɪʃ(ə)n/ *n.*

pressurized-water reactor *n.* a nuclear reactor in which the coolant is water at high pressure.

presswork /ˈprɛswəːk/ *n.* **1 a** the pressing or drawing of metal into a shaped hollow die. **b** a piece of metal shaped by such means. **2 a** the work and management of a printing press. **b** work turned out from a press, esp. with regard to its quality.

Prestel /ˈprɛstɛl/ *n. propr.* (in the UK) the computerized visual information system operated by British Telecom. [a blend of PRESS[1] + TELECOMMUNICATION]

prestidigitator /prɛstɪˈdɪdʒɪteɪtə/ *n. formal* a conjuror. □ **prestidigitation** /-ˈteɪʃ(ə)n/ *n.* [French *prestidigitateur*, from *preste* 'nimble' (as PRESTO) + Latin *digitus* 'finger']

prestige /prɛˈstiːʒ, -ˈstiːdʒ/ *n.* **1** respect, reputation, or influence derived from achievements, power, associations, etc. **2** (*attrib.*) having or conferring prestige. □ **prestigeful** *adj.* [French, = illusion, glamour, from Late Latin *praestigium* (as PRESTIGIOUS)]

prestigious /prɛˈstɪdʒəs/ *adj.* having or showing prestige. □ **prestigiously** *adv.* **prestigiousness** *n.* [originally = deceptive, via Latin *praestigiosus* from *praestigiae* 'juggler's tricks']

prestissimo /prɛˈstɪsɪməʊ/ *adv. & n. Mus.* ● *adv.* in a very quick tempo. ● *n.* (*pl.* **-os**) a movement or passage played in this way. [Italian, superlative (as PRESTO)]

presto /ˈprɛstəʊ/ *adv., adj., n., & int.* ● *adv. & adj. Mus.* in quick tempo. ● *n.* (*pl.* **-os**) *Mus.* a presto passage or movement. ● *int.* = HEY PRESTO! [Italian, via Late Latin *praestus* from Latin *praesto* ready]

prestressed /priːˈstrɛst/ *adj.* strengthened by stressing in advance, esp. of concrete by means of stretched rods or wires put in during manufacture.

presumably /prɪˈzjuːməbli/ *adv.* as may reasonably be presumed.

presume /prɪˈzjuːm/ *v.* **1** *tr.* (often foll. by *that* + clause) suppose to be true; take for granted. **2** *tr.* (often foll. by *to* + infin.) **a** take the liberty; be impudent enough (*presumed to question their authority*). **b** dare, venture (*may I presume to ask?*). **3** *intr.* be presumptuous; take liberties. **4** *intr.* (foll. by *on, upon*) take advantage of or make unscrupulous use of (a person's good nature etc.). □ **presumable** *adj.* **presumedly** *adv.* [Middle English via Old French *presumer* from Latin *praesumere praesumpt-* 'anticipate, venture' (as PRAE-, *sumere* 'take')]

presuming /prɪˈzjuːmɪŋ/ *adj.* presumptuous. □ **presumingly** *adv.* **presumingness** *n.*

presumption /prɪˈzʌm(p)ʃ(ə)n/ *n.* **1** arrogance; presumptuous behaviour. **2 a** the act of presuming a thing to be true. **b** a thing that is or may be presumed to be true. **3** a ground for presuming (*a strong presumption against their being guilty*). **4** *Law* an inference from known facts. [Middle English via Old French *presumpcion* from Latin *praesumptio -onis* (as PRESUME)]

presumptive /prɪˈzʌm(p)tɪv/ *adj.* giving grounds for presumption (*presumptive evidence*). □ **presumptively** *adv.* [French *présomptif -ive* from Late Latin *praesumptivus* (as PRESUME)]

presumptuous /prɪˈzʌm(p)tʃʊəs/ *adj.* unduly or overbearingly confident and presuming. □ **presumptuously** *adv.* **presumptuousness** *n.* [Middle English via Old French *presumptueux* from Late Latin *praesumptuosus, -tiosus* (as PRESUME)]

presuppose /priːsəˈpəʊz/ *v.tr.* (often foll. by *that* + clause) **1** assume beforehand. **2** require as a precondition; imply. [Middle English from Old French *presupposer*, after medieval Latin *praesupponere* (as PRE-, SUPPOSE)]

presupposition /ˌpriːsʌpəˈzɪʃ(ə)n/ *n.* **1** the act or an instance of presupposing. **2** a thing assumed beforehand as the basis of argument etc. [medieval Latin *praesuppositio* (as PRAE-, *supponere* as SUPPOSE)]

pre-tax /ˈpriːtaks/ *attrib.adj.* (of income or profits) before the deduction of taxes.

pre-teen /priːˈtiːn/ *adj.* of or relating to a child just under the age of thirteen.

pretence /prɪˈtɛns/ *n.* (*US* **pretense**) **1** pretending, make-believe. **2 a** a pretext or excuse (*on the slightest pretence*). **b** a false show of intentions or motives (*under the pretence of friendship; under false pretences*). **3** (foll. by *to*) a claim, esp. a false or ambitious one (*has no pretence to any great talent*). **4 a** affectation, display. **b** pretentiousness, ostentation (*stripped of all pretence*). [Middle English from Anglo-French *pretense*, ultimately from medieval Latin *pretensus* 'pretended' (as PRETEND)]

pretend /prɪˈtɛnd/ *v. & adj.* ● *v.* **1** *tr.* (often foll. by *to* + infin. or *that* + clause) claim or assert falsely so as to deceive (*pretend knowledge; pretended that they were foreigners*). **2** *tr.* imagine to oneself in play (*pretended to be monsters; pretended it was night*). **3** *tr.* **a** profess, esp. falsely or extravagantly (*does not pretend to be a scholar*). **b** (as **pretended** *adj.*) falsely claim to be such (*a pretended friend*). **4** *intr.* (foll. by *to*) **a** lay claim to (a right or title etc.). **b** profess to have (a quality etc.). ● *adj. colloq.* pretended; in pretence (*pretend money*). [Middle English from French *prétendre* or from Latin (as PRAE-, *tendere tent-*, later *tens-* 'stretch')]

pretender /prɪˈtɛndə/ *n.* **1** a person who claims a throne or title etc. **2** a person who pretends.

pretense *US* var. of PRETENCE.

pretension /prɪˈtɛnʃ(ə)n/ *n.* **1** (often foll. by *to*) **a** an assertion of a claim. **b** a justifiable claim (*has no pretensions to the name; has some pretensions to be included*). **2** pretentiousness. [medieval Latin *praetensio, -tio* (as PRETEND)]

pretentious /prɪˈtɛnʃəs/ *adj.* **1** making an excessive claim to great merit or importance. **2** ostentatious. □ **pretentiously** *adv.* **pretentiousness** *n.* [French *prétentieux* (as PRETENSION)]

preter- /ˈpriːtə/ *comb. form* more than. [Latin *praeter* (*adv. & prep.*), = past, beyond]

preterite /ˈprɛt(ə)rɪt/ *adj. & n.* (*US* also **preterit**) *Gram.* ● *adj.* expressing a past action or state. ● *n.* a preterite tense or form. [Middle English from Old French *preterite* or Latin *praeteritus*, past part. of *praeterire* 'pass' (as PRETER-, *ire it-* 'go')]

pre-term /priːˈtəːm/ *adj. & adv.* born or occurring prematurely.

pretermit /priːtəˈmɪt/ *v.tr.* (**pretermitted, pretermitting**) *formal* **1** omit to mention (a fact etc.). **2** omit to do or perform; neglect. **3** leave off (a custom or continuous action) for a time. □ **pretermission** /-ˈmɪʃ(ə)n/ *n.* [Latin *praetermittere* (as PRETER-, *mittere miss-* 'let go')]

preternatural /priːtəˈnatʃ(ə)r(ə)l/ *adj.* outside the ordinary course of nature; supernatural. □ **preternaturalism** *n.* **preternaturally** *adv.*

pretext /ˈpriːtɛkst/ *n.* **1** an ostensible or alleged reason or intention. **2** an excuse offered. □ **on** (or **under**) **the pretext** (foll. by *of*, or *that* + clause) professing as one's object or intention. [Latin *praetextus* 'outward display' from *praetexere praetext-* (as PRAE-, *texere* 'weave')]

pretor *US* var. of PRAETOR.

pretorian *US* var. of PRAETORIAN.

pretreat /priːˈtriːt/ *v.tr.* treat beforehand. □ **pretreatment** *n.*

prettify /ˈprɪtɪfʌɪ/ *v.tr.* (**-ies, -ied**) make (a thing or person) pretty esp. in an affected way. □ **prettification** /-fɪˈkeɪʃ(ə)n/ *n.* **prettifier** *n.*

pretty /ˈprɪti/ *adj., adv., n., & v.* ● *adj.* (**prettier, prettiest**) **1** attractive in a delicate way without being truly beautiful or handsome (*a pretty child; a pretty dress; a pretty tune*). **2** pleasing; fine or good of its kind (*a pretty wit*). **3** *colloq. iron.* considerable, fine (*a pretty penny; a pretty mess you have made*). ● *adv. colloq.* fairly, moderately; considerably (*am pretty well; find it pretty difficult*). ● *n.* (*pl.* **-ies**) a pretty person (esp. as a form of address to a child). ● *v.tr.* (**-ies, -ied**) (often foll. by *up*) make pretty or attractive. □ **pretty much** (or **nearly** or **well**) *colloq.* almost; very nearly. **sitting**

pretty *colloq.* in a favourable or advantageous position. □ **prettily** *adv.* **prettiness** *n.* **prettyish** *adj.* **prettyism** *n.* [Old English *prættig*, from West Germanic]

pretty-pretty *adj. Brit.* too pretty.

pretzel /ˈprɛts(ə)l/ *n.* a crisp knot-shaped or stick-shaped salted biscuit. [German]

prevail /prɪˈveɪl/ *v.intr.* **1** (often foll. by *against, over*) be victorious or gain mastery. **2** be the more usual or predominant. **3** exist or occur in general use or experience; be current. **4** (foll. by *on, upon*) persuade. □ **prevailingly** *adv.* [Middle English from Latin *praevalēre* (as PRAE-, *valēre* 'have power'), influenced by AVAIL]

prevailing wind *n.* the wind that most frequently occurs at a place.

prevalent /ˈprɛv(ə)l(ə)nt/ *adj.* **1** generally existing or occurring. **2** predominant. □ **prevalence** *n.* **prevalently** *adv.* [as PREVAIL]

prevaricate /prɪˈvarɪkeɪt/ *v.intr.* **1** speak or act evasively or misleadingly. **2** quibble, equivocate. □ **prevarication** /-ˈkeɪʃ(ə)n/ *n.* **prevaricator** *n.* [Latin *praevaricari* 'walk crookedly, practise collusion', in ecclesiastical Latin 'transgress' (as PRAE-, *varicari* 'straddle' from *varus* 'bent, knock-kneed')]

■ **Usage** *Prevaricate* is often confused with *procrastinate*, which means 'to defer or put off an action'.

prevenient /prɪˈviːnɪənt/ *adj. formal* preceding something else. [Latin *praeveniens*, pres. part. of *praevenire* (as PREVENT)]

prevent /prɪˈvɛnt/ *v.tr.* **1** (often foll. by *from* + verbal noun) stop from happening or doing something; hinder; make impossible (*the weather prevented me from going*). **2** *archaic* go or arrive before, precede. □ **preventable** *adj.* (also **preventible**). **preventability** /-təˈbɪlɪti/ *n.* (also **preventibility**). **preventer** *n.* **prevention** *n.* [Middle English = anticipate, from Latin *praevenire praevent-* 'come before, hinder' (as PRAE-, *venire* 'come')]

■ **Usage** The use of *prevent* in sense 1 without *from*, as in *prevented me going*, is informal. An acceptable alternative is *prevented my going*.

preventative /prɪˈvɛntətɪv/ *adj.* & *n.* = PREVENTIVE. □ **preventatively** *adv.*

preventive /prɪˈvɛntɪv/ *adj.* & *n.* ● *adj.* serving to prevent, esp. preventing disease, breakdown, etc. (*preventive medicine*; *preventive maintenance*). ● *n.* a preventive agent, measure, drug, etc. □ **preventively** *adv.*

preventive detention *n.* the imprisonment of a criminal for corrective training etc.

preview /ˈpriːvjuː/ *n.* & *v.* ● *n.* **1** the act of seeing in advance. **2 a** the showing of a film, play, exhibition, etc., before the official opening. **b** (*N. Amer.* also **prevue**) a film trailer. ● *v.tr.* see or show in advance.

previous /ˈpriːvɪəs/ *adj.* & *adv.* ● *adj.* **1** coming before in time or order (*previous afternoon*; *previous attempts*). **2** *colloq.* done or acting hastily. ● *adv.* (foll. by *to*) before (*had called previous to writing*). □ **previously** *adv.* **previousness** *n.* [Latin *praevius* (as PRAE-, *via* 'way')]

previous question *n. Parl.* a motion concerning the vote on a main question.

previse /prɪˈvʌɪz/ *v.tr. literary* foresee or forecast (an event etc.). □ **prevision** /-ˈvɪʒ(ə)n/ *n.* **previsional** /-ˈvɪʒ(ə)n(ə)l/ *adj.* [Latin *praevidēre praevis-* (as PRAE-, *vidēre* 'see')]

prevue *N. Amer.* var. of PREVIEW *n.* 2b.

pre-war /priːˈwɔː/ *adj.* existing, occurring, or built before a war (esp. the most recent major war).

■ **Usage** *Pre-war* should not be used as an adverb, e.g. *Pre-war, my father used to smoke. Before the war* is preferable.

pre-wash /priːˈwɒʃ/ *n.* & *adj.* ● *n.* a preliminary wash, esp. as performed in an automatic washing machine. ● *v.tr.* give a preliminary wash to, esp. before putting on sale.

prex /prɛks/ *n. US slang* a president, esp. the president of a college. [alteration of abbreviation of PRESIDENT]

prexy /ˈprɛksi/ *n.* (*pl.* **-ies**) *US slang* = PREX. [PREX + -Y[2]]

prey /preɪ/ *n.* & *v.* ● *n.* **1** an animal that is hunted or killed by another for food. **2** (often foll. by *to*) a person or thing that is influenced by or vulnerable to (something undesirable) (*became a prey to morbid fears*). **3** *Bibl.* or *archaic* plunder, booty, etc. ● *v.intr.* (foll. by *on, upon*) **1** seek or take as prey. **2** make a victim of. **3** (of a disease, emotion, etc.) exert a harmful influence (*fear preyed on his mind*). □ **preyer** *n.* [Middle English via Old French *preie* from Latin *praeda* 'booty']

prezzie /ˈprɛzi/ *n.* (also **pressie**) *Brit. colloq.* a present or gift. [abbreviation]

priapic /prʌɪˈapɪk/ *adj.* phallic. [*Priapos* (as PRIAPISM) + -IC]

priapism /ˈprʌɪəpɪz(ə)m/ *n.* **1** lewdness, licentiousness. **2** *Med.* persistent erection of the penis. [French *priapisme* via Late Latin *priapismus* and Greek *priapismos* from *priapizō* 'be lewd', from *Priapos*, the name of the god of procreation]

price /prʌɪs/ *n.* & *v.* ● *n.* **1 a** the amount of money or goods for which a thing is bought or sold. **b** value or worth (*a pearl of great price*; *beyond price*). **2** what is or must be given, done, sacrificed, etc., to obtain or achieve something. **3** the odds in betting (*starting price*). ● *v.tr.* **1** fix or find the price of (a thing for sale). **2** estimate the value of. □ **above** (or **beyond** or **without) price** so valuable that no price can be stated. **at any price** no matter what the cost, sacrifice, etc. (*peace at any price*). **at a price** at a high cost. **price on a person's head** a reward for a person's capture or death. **price oneself out of the market** lose to one's competitors by charging more than customers are willing to pay. **set a price on** declare the price of. **what price ...?** (often foll. by verbal noun) *colloq.* **1** what is the chance of ...? (*what price your finishing the course?*). **2** *iron.* the expected or much boasted ... proves disappointing (*what price your friendship now?*). □ **priced** *adj.* (also in *comb.*). **pricer** *n.* [the noun Middle English via Old French *pris* from Latin *pretium*: the verb a variant of *prise* = PRIZE[1]: cf. PRAISE]

price-fixing *n.* the maintaining of prices at a certain level by agreement between competing sellers.

priceless /ˈprʌɪslɪs/ *adj.* **1** invaluable; beyond price. **2** *colloq.* very amusing or absurd. □ **pricelessly** *adv.* **pricelessness** *n.*

price list *n.* a list of current prices of items on sale.

price ring *n.* a group of traders acting illegally to control certain prices.

price-sensitive *adj.* **1** (of a product) whose sales are greatly influenced by its price. **2** (of information) that would affect prices if it were made public.

price tag *n.* **1** the label on an item showing its price. **2** the cost of an enterprise or undertaking.

price war *n.* fierce competition among traders cutting prices.

pricey /ˈprʌɪsi/ *adj.* (also **pricy**) (**pricier**, **priciest**) *colloq.* expensive. □ **priciness** *n.*

prick /prɪk/ *v.* & *n.* ● *v.* **1** *tr.* pierce slightly; make a small hole in. **2** *tr.* (foll. by *off, out*) mark (esp. a pattern) with small holes or dots. **3** *tr.* trouble mentally (*my conscience is pricking me*). **4** *intr.* feel a pricking sensation. **5** *intr.* (foll. by *at, into*, etc.) make a thrust as if to prick. **6** *tr.* (foll. by *in, off, out*) plant (seedlings etc.) in small holes pricked in the earth. **7** *tr. Brit. archaic* mark off (a name in a list, esp. to select a sheriff) by pricking. **8** *tr. archaic* spur or urge on (a horse etc.). ● *n.* **1** the act or an instance of pricking. **2** a small hole or mark made by pricking. **3** a pain caused as by pricking. **4** a mental pain (*felt the pricks of conscience*). **5** *coarse slang* **a** the penis. **b** *derog.* (as a term of contempt) a man. **6** *archaic* a goad for oxen. □ **kick against the pricks** persist in futile resistance.

prick up one's ears 1 (of a dog etc.) make the ears erect when on the alert. 2 (of a person) become suddenly attentive. □ **pricker** *n.* [Old English *prician* (*v.*), *pricca* (*n.*)]

pricket /'prɪkɪt/ *n.* 1 a male fallow deer in its second year, having straight unbranched horns. 2 a spike for holding a candle. [Middle English from Anglo-Latin *prikettus -um*, diminutive of PRICK]

prickle /'prɪk(ə)l/ *n.* & *v.* ● *n.* 1 **a** a small thorn. **b** *Bot.* a thornlike process developed from the epidermis of a plant. 2 a hard-pointed spine of a hedgehog etc. 3 a prickling sensation. ● *v.* 1 *tr.* & *intr.* affect or be affected with a sensation as of pricking. 2 *intr.* react defensively or aggressively to a situation. [Old English *pricel* PRICK: the verb partly a diminutive of PRICK]

prickly /'prɪkli/ *adj.* (**pricklier**, **prickliest**) 1 (esp. in the names of plants and animals) having prickles. 2 (of a person) ready to take offence. 3 tingling. □ **prickliness** *n.*

prickly heat *n.* an itchy inflammation of the skin, causing a tingling sensation and common in hot countries.

prickly pear *n.* 1 any cactus of the genus *Opuntia*, native to arid regions of America, bearing barbed bristles and large pear-shaped prickly fruits. 2 its fruit.

prickly poppy *n.* a tropical poppy, *Argemone mexicana*, with prickly leaves and yellow flowers.

pricy var. of PRICEY.

pride /prʌɪd/ *n.* & *v.* ● *n.* 1 **a** a feeling of elation or satisfaction at achievements or qualities or possessions etc. that do one credit. **b** (prec. by *the*; foll. by *of*) the object of this feeling (*the pride of the museum's collection*). 2 a high or overbearing opinion of one's worth or importance. 3 (in full **proper pride**) a proper sense of what befits one's position; self-respect. 4 a group or company (of animals, esp. lions). 5 esp. *literary* the best condition; the prime. ● *v.refl.* (foll. by *on*, *upon*) be proud of. □ **my, his**, etc. **pride and joy** a thing of which one is very proud. **take pride** (or **a pride**) **in** 1 be proud of. 2 maintain in good condition or appearance. □ **prideful** *adj.* **pridefully** *adv.* **prideless** *adj.* [Old English *prȳtu*, *prȳte*, *prȳde* from *prūd* PROUD]

pride of place *n.* the most important or prominent position.

pride of the morning *n.* a mist or shower at sunrise, supposedly indicating a fine day to come.

prie-dieu /pri:'djə:/ *n.* (*pl.* **prie-dieux** *pronunc.* same) a kneeling-desk for prayer. [French, = pray God]

priest /pri:st/ *n.* & *v.* ● *n.* 1 an ordained minister of the Roman Catholic or Orthodox Church, or of the Anglican Church (above a deacon and below a bishop), authorized to perform certain rites and administer certain sacraments. 2 an official minister of a non-Christian religion. ● *v.tr.* make (a person) a priest; ordain. □ **priestless** *adj.* **priestlike** *adj.* **priestling** *n.* [Old English *prēost*, ultimately from ecclesiastical Latin *presbyter*: see PRESBYTER]

priestcraft /'pri:s(t)krɑ:ft/ *n.* usu. *derog.* the work and influence of priests.

priestess /'pri:stɪs/ *n.* a female priest of a non-Christian religion.

priesthood /'pri:sthʊd/ *n.* (usu. prec. by *the*) 1 the office or position of priest. 2 priests in general.

priest-in-charge *n.* (*pl.* **priests-in-charge**) a minister in charge of a parish which for the time being lacks an incumbent priest.

priestly /'pri:stli/ *adj.* of or associated with priests. □ **priestliness** *n.* [Old English *prēostlic* (as PRIEST)]

priest's hole *n. hist.* a hiding place for a Roman Catholic priest during times of religious persecution.

prig /prɪg/ *n.* a self-righteously correct or moralistic person. □ **priggery** *n.* **priggish** *adj.* **priggishly** *adv.* **priggishness** *n.* [16th-c. slang, = tinker, hence 'an unpleasant person': origin unknown]

prim /prɪm/ *adj.* & *v.* ● *adj.* (**primmer**, **primmest**) 1 (of a person or manner) stiffly formal and precise. 2 (of a woman or girl) demure. 3 prudish. ● *v.tr.* (**primmed**, **primming**) 1 form (the face, lips, etc.) into a prim expression. 2 make prim. □ **primly** *adv.* **primness** *n.* [18th c.: probably via Old French *prin prime* 'excellent' from Latin *primus* 'first']

prima ballerina /ˌpri:mə balə'ri:nə/ *n.* (*pl.* **prima ballerinas**) the chief female dancer in a ballet or ballet company. [Italian]

primacy /'prʌɪməsi/ *n.* (*pl.* **-ies**) 1 pre-eminence. 2 the office of a primate. [Middle English from Old French *primatie* or medieval Latin *primatia* (as PRIMATE)]

prima donna /pri:mə 'dɒnə/ *n.* (*pl.* **prima donnas**) 1 the chief female singer in an opera or opera company. 2 a temperamentally self-important person. □ **prima donna-ish** *adj.* [Italian]

primaeval var. of PRIMEVAL.

prima facie /prʌɪmə 'feɪʃi:/ *adv.* & *adj.* ● *adv.* at first sight; from a first impression (*seems prima facie to be guilty*). ● *adj.* (of evidence) based on the first impression (*can see a prima facie reason for it*). [Middle English from Latin, fem. ablative of *primus* 'first', *facies* FACE]

primal /'prʌɪm(ə)l/ *adj.* 1 primitive, primeval. 2 chief, fundamental. □ **primally** *adv.* [medieval Latin *primalis* from Latin *primus* 'first']

primary /'prʌɪm(ə)ri/ *adj.* & *n.* ● *adj.* 1 **a** of the first importance; chief (*that is our primary concern*). **b** fundamental, basic. 2 earliest, original; first in a series. 3 of the first rank in a series; not derived (*the primary meaning of a word*). 4 (of a battery or cell) generating electricity by irreversible chemical reaction. 5 (of education) for young children, esp. below the age of 11. 6 (**Primary**) *Geol.* of the lowest series of strata. 7 *Biol.* belonging to the first stage of development. 8 (of an industry or source of production) concerned with obtaining or using raw materials. 9 *Gram.* (of a tense in Latin and Greek) present, future, perfect, or future perfect (cf. HISTORIC 2). ● *n.* (*pl.* **-ies**) 1 a thing that is primary. 2 (in full **primary election**) (in the US) a preliminary election to appoint delegates to a party conference or to select the candidates for a principal (esp. presidential) election. 3 *Astron.* **a** the body orbited by a satellite etc. **b** = PRIMARY PLANET. 4 (**Primary**) *Geol.* the Primary period. 5 = PRIMARY FEATHER. 6 = PRIMARY COIL. □ **primarily** /'prʌɪm(ə)rɪli, -'mɛrɪli/ *adv.* [Middle English from Latin *primarius*, from *primus* 'first']

primary coil *n.* a coil to which current is supplied in a transformer.

primary colour *n.* any of the colours red, green, and blue, or (for pigments) red, blue, and yellow, from which all other colours can be obtained by mixing.

primary feather *n.* a large flight feather of a bird's wing.

primary planet *n.* a planet that directly orbits the sun (cf. SECONDARY PLANET).

primary school *n.* a school where young children are taught, esp. below the age of 11.

primate /'prʌɪmeɪt/ *n.* 1 any animal of the order Primates, the highest order of mammals, including tarsiers, lemurs, apes, monkeys, and humans. 2 /also 'prʌɪmət/ an archbishop. □ **primatial** /-'meɪʃ(ə)l/ *adj.* [Middle English via Old French *primat* from Latin *primas -atis* 'of the first rank', from *primus* 'first', in medieval Latin = primate]

Primate of All England *n.* the Archbishop of Canterbury.

Primate of England *n.* the Archbishop of York.

primatology /prʌɪmə'tɒlədʒi/ *n.* the branch of zoology that deals with primates. □ **primatological** /-tə'lɒdʒɪk(ə)l/ *adj.* **primatologist** *n.*

primavera /pri:mə'vɛrə/ *n.* 1 a Central American tree, *Cybistax donnellsmithii*, bearing yellow blooms. 2 the hard light-coloured timber from this. [Spanish, = spring (the season), from Latin *primus* 'first' + *ver* SPRING]

prime[1] /prʌɪm/ *adj.* & *n.* ● *adj.* **1** chief, most important (*the prime agent; the prime motive*). **2** (esp. of cattle and provisions) first-rate, excellent. **3** primary, fundamental. **4** *Math.* **a** (of a number) divisible only by itself and unity (e.g. 2, 3, 5, 7, 11). **b** (of numbers) having no common factor but unity. ● *n.* **1** the state of the highest perfection of something (*in the prime of life*). **2** (prec. by *the*; foll. by *of*) the best part. **3** the beginning or first age of anything. **4** *Eccl.* **a** the office of the second canonical hour of prayer, originally said at the first hour of the day (i.e. 6 a.m.). **b** *archaic* this time. **5** a prime number. **6** *Printing* a symbol (′) added to a letter etc. as a distinguishing mark, or to a figure as a symbol for minutes or feet. **7** the first of eight parrying positions in fencing. □ **primeness** *n.* [the noun Old English *prīm* from Latin *prima* (*hora*) 'first (hour)', & Middle French from Old French *prime*: the adjective Middle English via Old French from Latin *primus* 'first']

prime[2] /prʌɪm/ *v.tr.* **1** prepare (a thing) for use or action. **2** prepare (a gun) for firing or (an explosive) for detonation. **3 a** pour a liquid into (a pump) to prepare it for working. **b** inject petrol into (the cylinder or carburettor of an internal-combustion engine). **4** prepare (wood etc.) for painting by applying a substance that prevents paint from being absorbed. **5** equip (a person) with information etc. **6** ply (a person) with food or drink in preparation for something. [16th c.: origin unknown]

prime cost *n.* the direct cost of a commodity in terms of materials, labour, etc.

prime meridian *n.* **1** the meridian from which longitude is reckoned, esp. that passing through Greenwich. **2** the corresponding line on a map.

prime minister *n.* the head of an elected government; the principal minister of a sovereign or state.

prime mover *n.* **1** an initial natural or mechanical source of motive power. **2** the author of a fruitful idea.

primer[1] /ˈprʌɪmə/ *n.* **1** a substance used to prime wood etc. **2** a cap, cylinder, etc., used to ignite the powder of a cartridge etc.

primer[2] /ˈprʌɪmə/ *n.* **1** an elementary textbook for teaching children to read. **2** an introductory book. [Middle English from Anglo-French via medieval Latin *primarius -arium* from Latin *primus* 'first']

prime rate *n.* the lowest rate at which money can be borrowed commercially.

prime time *n.* the time at which a radio or television audience is expected to be at its highest (hyphenated when *attrib.*: *prime-time viewing*).

primeval /prʌɪˈmiːv(ə)l/ *adj.* (also **primaeval**) **1** of or relating to the first age of the world. **2** ancient, primitive. □ **primevally** *adv.* [Latin *primaevus*, from *primus* 'first' + *aevum* 'age']

prime vertical *n.* the great circle of the heavens passing through the zenith and the E. and W. points of the horizon.

primigravida /priːmɪˈgravɪdə, prʌɪm-/ *n.* (*pl.* **primigravidae** /-diː/) a woman who is pregnant for the first time. [modern Latin, fem., from Latin *primus* 'first' + *gravidus* 'pregnant': see GRAVID]

priming[1] /ˈprʌɪmɪŋ/ *n.* **1** a mixture used by painters for a preparatory coat. **2** a preparation of sugar added to beer. **3 a** gunpowder placed in the pan of a firearm. **b** a train of powder connecting the fuse with the charge in blasting etc.

priming[2] /ˈprʌɪmɪŋ/ *n.* an acceleration of the tides taking place from the neap to the spring tides. [from the verb *prime* (from PRIME[1]) + -ING[1]]

primipara /prʌɪˈmɪp(ə)rə/ *n.* (*pl.* **primiparae** /-riː/) *Med.* a woman who is giving birth for the first time. □ **primiparous** *adj.* [modern Latin, fem., from *primus* 'first' + *-parus* from *parere* 'bring forth']

primitive /ˈprɪmɪtɪv/ *adj.* & *n.* ● *adj.* **1** early, ancient; at an early stage of civilization (*primitive man*). **2** undeveloped, crude, simple (*primitive methods*). **3** original, primary. **4** *Gram.* & *Philol.* (of words or language) radical; not derivative. **5** *Math.* (of a line, figure, etc.) from which another is derived, from which some construction begins, etc. **6** (of a colour) primary. **7** *Geol.* of the earliest period. **8** *Biol.* appearing in the earliest or a very early stage of growth or evolution. ● *n.* **1 a** a painter of the period before the Renaissance. **b** a modern imitator of such. **c** an untutored painter with a direct naive style. **d** a picture by such a painter. **2** a primitive word, line, etc. □ **primitively** *adv.* **primitiveness** *n.* [Middle English from Old French *primitif -ive* or Latin *primitivus* 'first of its kind', via *primitus* 'in the first place' from *primus* 'first']

Primitive Church *n.* (prec. by *the*) the Christian Church in its earliest times.

primitivism /ˈprɪmɪtɪvɪz(ə)m/ *n.* **1** primitive behaviour. **2** belief in the superiority of what is primitive. **3** the practice of primitive art. □ **primitivist** *n.* & *adj.*

primo /ˈpriːməʊ/ *n.* (*pl.* **-os**) *Mus.* the leading or upper part in a duet etc. [Italian, = first]

primogenitor /prʌɪmə(ʊ)ˈdʒɛnɪtə/ *n.* **1** the earliest ancestor of a people etc. **2** an ancestor. [variant of *progenitor*, suggested by PRIMOGENITURE]

primogeniture /prʌɪmə(ʊ)ˈdʒɛnɪtʃə/ *n.* **1** the fact or condition of being the first-born child. **2** (in full **right of primogeniture**) the right of succession belonging to the first-born, esp. the feudal rule by which the whole real estate of an intestate passes to the eldest son. □ **primogenital** *adj.* **primogenitary** *adj.* [medieval Latin *primogenitura*, from Latin *primo* 'first' + *genitura* from *gignere genit-* 'beget']

primordial /prʌɪˈmɔːdɪəl/ *adj.* **1** existing at or from the beginning, primeval. **2** original, fundamental. □ **primordiality** /-ˈalɪti/ *n.* **primordially** *adv.* [Middle English from Late Latin *primordialis* (as PRIMORDIUM)]

primordium /prʌɪˈmɔːdɪəm/ *n.* (*pl.* **primordia** /-dɪə/) *Biol.* an organ or tissue in the early stages of development. [Latin, neut. of *primordius* 'original', from *primus* 'first' + *ordiri* 'begin']

primp /prɪmp/ *v.tr.* **1** make (the hair, one's clothes, etc.) tidy. **2** *refl.* make (oneself) smart. [dialect variant of PRIM]

primrose /ˈprɪmrəʊz/ *n.* & *adj.* ● *n.* **1** any plant of the genus *Primula*, esp. *P. vulgaris*, bearing pale yellow flowers. **2** (in full **primrose yellow**) a pale yellow colour. ● *adj.* (in full **primrose yellow**; hyphenated when *attrib.*) pale yellow. [Middle English *primerose*, corresponding to Old French *primerose* and medieval Latin *prima rosa*, literally 'first rose': reason for the name unknown]

primrose path *n.* the pursuit of pleasure, esp. with disastrous consequences (with reference to Shakespeare's *Hamlet* I. iii. 50).

primula /ˈprɪmjʊlə/ *n.* any plant of the genus *Primula*, bearing primrose-like flowers in a wide variety of colours during the spring, including primroses, cowslips, and polyanthuses. [medieval Latin, fem. of *primulus*, diminutive of *primus* 'first']

primum mobile /prʌɪməm ˈməʊbɪli, priːməm/ *n.* **1** the central or most important source of motion or action. **2** *Astron.* in the medieval version of the Ptolemaic system, an outer sphere supposed to move round the earth in 24 hours carrying the inner spheres with it. [medieval Latin, = first moving thing]

Primus /ˈprʌɪməs/ *n. Brit. propr.* a brand of portable stove burning vaporized oil for cooking etc. [Latin (as PRIMUS)]

primus /ˈprʌɪməs/ *n.* the presiding bishop of the Scottish Episcopal Church. [Latin, = first]

primus inter pares /ˌpriːməs ɪntə ˈpɑːriːz, ˌprʌɪməs/ *n.* a first among equals; the senior or representative member of a group. [Latin]

prince /prɪns/ *n.* (as a title usu. **Prince**) **1** a male member of a royal family other than a reigning king. **2** (in full **prince of the blood**) a son or grandson of a British monarch. **3** a ruler of a small state, actually or nominally subject to a king or emperor. **4** (as an English rendering of foreign titles) a noble usu. ranking next below a duke. **5** (as a courtesy title in some connections) a duke, marquess, or earl. **6** (often foll. by *of*) the chief or greatest (*the prince of novelists*). □ **princedom** *n.* **princelike** *adj.* **princeship** *n.* [Middle English via Old French from Latin *princeps principis* 'first, chief, sovereign', from *primus* 'first' + *capere* 'take']

Prince Charming *n.* an idealized young hero or lover.

prince consort *n.* **1** the husband of a reigning female sovereign who is himself a prince. **2** the title conferred on him.

princeling /'prɪnslɪŋ/ *n.* **1** a young prince. **2** the ruler of a small principality or domain.

princely /'prɪnsli/ *adj.* (**princelier, princeliest**) **1 a** of or worthy of a prince. **b** held by a prince. **2** sumptuous, generous, splendid. □ **princeliness** *n.*

Prince of Darkness *n.* Satan.

Prince of Peace *n.* Christ.

prince of the blood see PRINCE 2.

Prince of Wales *n.* the heir apparent to the British throne, the eldest son of the sovereign.

Prince Regent *n.* a prince who acts as regent, esp. George (afterwards IV) as regent 1811–20.

prince royal *n.* the eldest son of a reigning monarch.

prince's feather *n.* a tall plant, *Amaranthus hypochondriacus*, with feathery spikes of small red flowers.

prince's metal *n.* a brasslike alloy of copper and zinc.

princess /prɪn'sɛs/ *n.* (as a title usu. **Princess** /'prɪnsɛs/) **1** the wife of a prince. **2** a female member of a royal family other than a reigning queen. **3** (in full **princess of the blood**) a daughter or granddaughter of a British monarch. **4** a pre-eminent woman or thing personified as a woman. [Middle English from Old French *princesse* (as PRINCE)]

Princess Regent *n.* **1** a princess who acts as regent. **2** the wife of a Prince Regent.

Princess Royal *n.* the eldest daughter of a reigning monarch, esp. as a title conferred by the British monarch.

principal /'prɪnsɪp(ə)l/ *adj. & n.* ● *adj.* **1** (usu. *attrib.*) first in rank or importance; chief (*the principal town of the district*). **2** main, leading (*a principal cause of my success*). **3** (of money) constituting the original sum invested or lent. ● *n.* **1** a head, ruler, or superior. **2** the head of some schools, colleges, and universities. **3** the leading performer in a concert, play, etc. **4** a capital sum as distinguished from interest or income. **5** a person for whom another acts as agent etc. **6** (in the UK) a civil servant of the grade below Secretary. **7** the person actually responsible for a crime. **8** a person for whom another is surety. **9** *hist.* each of the combatants in a duel. **10 a** a main rafter supporting purlins. **b** a main girder. **11** an organ stop sounding an octave above the diapason. **12** *Mus.* the leading player in each section of an orchestra. □ **principalship** *n.* [Middle English via Old French from Latin *principalis* 'first, original' (as PRINCE)]

principal boy *n.* (also **principal girl**) *Brit.* an actress who takes the leading male (or female) part in a pantomime.

principal clause *n. Gram.* a clause to which another clause is subordinate.

principal in the first degree *n.* a person directly responsible for a crime as its actual perpetrator.

principal in the second degree *n.* a person directly responsible for a crime as aiding in its perpetration.

principality /prɪnsɪ'palɪti/ *n.* (*pl.* **-ies**) **1** a state ruled by a prince. **2** the government of a prince. **3** (in *pl.*) the fifth order of the ninefold celestial hierarchy (see ORDER *n.* 19). **4** (**the Principality**) *Brit.* Wales. [Middle English via Old French *principalité* from Late Latin *principalitas -tatis* (as PRINCIPAL)]

principally /'prɪnsɪp(ə)li/ *adv.* for the most part; chiefly.

principal parts *n.pl. Gram.* the parts of a verb from which all other parts can be deduced.

principate /'prɪnsɪpət/ *n. Rom.Hist.* **1** the rule of the early emperors during which some republican forms were retained. **2** this period. [Middle English from Old French *principat* or Latin *principatus* 'first place' (as PRINCE)]

principle /'prɪnsɪp(ə)l/ *n.* **1** a fundamental truth or law as the basis of reasoning or action (*arguing from first principles; moral principles*). **2 a** a personal code of conduct (*a person of high principle*). **b** (in *pl.*) such rules of conduct (*has no principles*). **3** a general law in physics etc. (*the uncertainty principle*). **4** a law of nature forming the basis for the construction or working of a machine etc. **5** a fundamental source; a primary element (*held water to be the first principle of all things*). **6** *Chem.* a constituent of a substance, esp. one giving rise to some quality etc. □ **in principle** as regards fundamentals but not necessarily in detail. **on principle** on the basis of a moral attitude (*I refuse on principle*). [Middle English via Old French *principe* from Latin *principium* 'source' (in pl.) 'foundations' (as PRINCE)]

principled /'prɪnsɪp(ə)ld/ *adj.* based on or having (esp. praiseworthy) principles of behaviour.

prink /prɪŋk/ *v.* **1** *tr.* (usu. *refl.*) **a** make (oneself etc.) smart. **b** (foll. by *up*) smarten (oneself) up. **c** (of a bird) preen. **2** *intr.* dress oneself up. [16th c.: probably from *prank* 'dress, adorn', related to Middle Low German *prank* 'pomp', Dutch *pronk* 'finery']

print /prɪnt/ *n. & v.* ● *n.* **1** an indentation or mark on a surface left by the pressure of a thing in contact with it (*fingerprint; footprint*). **2 a** printed lettering or writing (*large print*). **b** words in printed form. **c** a printed publication, esp. a newspaper. **d** the quantity of a book etc. printed at one time. **e** the state of being printed. **3** a picture or design printed from a block or plate. **4** *Photog.* a picture produced on paper from a negative. **5** a printed cotton fabric. ● *v.tr.* **1 a** produce or reproduce (a book, picture, etc.) by applying inked types, blocks, or plates, to paper, vellum, etc. **b** (of an author, publisher, or editor) cause (a book or manuscript etc.) to be produced or reproduced in this way. **2** express or publish in print. **3 a** (often foll. by *on, in*) impress or stamp (a mark or figure on a surface). **b** (often foll. by *with*) impress or stamp (a soft surface, e.g. of butter or wax, with a seal, die, etc.). **4** (often *absol.*) write (words or letters) without joining, in imitation of typography. **5** (often foll. by *off, out*) *Photog.* produce (a picture) by the transmission of light through a negative. **6** (usu. foll. by *out*) (of a computer etc.) produce output in printed form. **7** mark (a textile fabric) with a decorative design in colours. **8** (foll. by *on*) impress (an idea, scene, etc. on the mind or memory). **9** transfer (a coloured or plain design) from paper etc. to the unglazed or glazed surface of ceramic ware. □ **appear in print** have one's work published. **in print 1** (of a book etc.) available from the publisher. **2** in printed form. **out of print** no longer available from the publisher. □ **printable** *adj.* **printability** /-tə'bɪlɪti/ *n.* **printless** *adj.* (in sense 1 of *n.*). [Middle English via Old French *priente, preinte*, fem. past part. of *preindre* 'press', from Latin *premere*]

printed circuit *n.* an electric circuit with thin strips of conductor on a flat insulating sheet, usu. made by a process like printing.

printer /'prɪntə/ *n.* **1** a person who prints books, magazines, advertising matter, etc. **2** the owner of a printing business. **3** a device that prints, esp. as part of a computer system.

printer's devil *n. hist.* an errand-boy in a printing office.

printer's mark *n.* a device used as a printer's trade mark.

printer's pie *n.* = PIE[3] *n.* 1

printery /ˈprɪnt(ə)ri/ *n.* (*pl.* **-ies**) *US* a printer's office or works.

printhead /ˈprɪnthɛd/ *n.* the component in a printer (see PRINTER 3) that assembles and prints the characters on the paper.

printing /ˈprɪntɪŋ/ *n.* **1** the production of printed books etc. **2** a single impression of a book. **3** printed letters or writing imitating them.

printing press *n.* a machine for printing from types or plates etc.

printmaker /ˈprɪntmeɪkə/ *n.* a person who makes prints. □ **printmaking** *n.*

printout /ˈprɪntaʊt/ *n.* **1** output in printed form. **2** an instance of this.

printworks /ˈprɪntwəːks/ *n.pl.* a factory where fabrics are printed.

prion[1] /ˈprʌɪən/ *n.* a small saw-billed petrel of the genus *Pachyptila*, of southern seas. [modern Latin (former genus name) from Greek *priōn* 'a saw']

prion[2] /ˈpriːɒn/ *n. Biol.* a protein particle associated with and believed to be the cause of encephalopathies such as scrapie, BSE, kuru, and Creutzfeldt–Jakob disease. [by rearrangement from '*pro*teinaceous *in*fectious particle']

prior /ˈprʌɪə/ *adj., adv., & n.* ● *adj.* **1** earlier. **2** (often foll. by *to*) coming before in time, order, or importance. ● *adv.* (foll. by *to*) before (*decided prior to their arrival*). ● *n.* (*fem.* **prioress** /-rɪs/) **1** the superior officer of a religious house or order. **2** (in an abbey) the officer next under the abbot (or abbess). □ **priorate** /-rət/ *n.* **priorship** *n.* [Latin, = former, elder, comparative of Old Latin *pri* = Latin *prae* 'before']

priority /prʌɪˈɒrɪti/ *n.* (*pl.* **-ies**) **1** the fact or condition of being earlier or antecedent. **2** precedence in rank etc. **3** an interest having prior claim to consideration. □ **prioritize** *v.tr.* (also **-ise**). **prioritization** /-tʌɪˈzeɪʃ(ə)n/ *n.* [Middle English via Old French *priorité* and medieval Latin *prioritas -tatis* from Latin *prior* (as PRIOR)]

priory /ˈprʌɪəri/ *n.* (*pl.* **-ies**) a monastery governed by a prior or a nunnery governed by a prioress. [Middle English from Anglo-French *priorie*, medieval Latin *prioria* (as PRIOR)]

prise /prʌɪz/ *v. & n.* (*US* **prize**) ● *v.tr.* **1** (usu. foll. by *up*, *open*, etc.) force open or out by leverage (*prised up the lid; prised the box open*). **2** move or remove with difficulty (*could not be prised from his vantage point*). ● *n.* leverage, purchase. [Middle English & Old French *prise* 'levering instrument' (as PRIZE[1])]

prism /ˈprɪz(ə)m/ *n.* **1** a solid geometric figure whose two ends are similar, equal, and parallel rectilinear figures, and whose sides are parallelograms. **2** a transparent body in this form, usu. triangular with refracting surfaces at an acute angle with each other, which separates white light into a spectrum of colours. □ **prismal** /ˈprɪzm(ə)l/ *adj.* [Late Latin *prisma* from Greek *prisma prismatos* 'thing sawn', from *prizō* 'to saw']

prismatic /prɪzˈmatɪk/ *adj.* **1** of, like, or using a prism. **2 a** (of colours) distributed by or as if by a transparent prism. **b** (of light) displayed in the form of a spectrum. □ **prismatically** *adv.* [French *prismatique* from Greek *prisma* (as PRISM)]

prismoid /ˈprɪzmɔɪd/ *n.* a body like a prism, with similar but unequal parallel polygonal ends. □ **prismoidal** /-ˈmɔɪd(ə)l/ *adj.*

prison /ˈprɪz(ə)n/ *n. & v.* ● *n.* **1** a place in which a person is kept in captivity, esp. a building to which persons are legally committed while awaiting trial or for punishment; a jail. **2** custody, confinement (*in prison*). ● *v.tr.* (**prisoned**, **prisoning**) *poet.* put in prison. [Middle English via Old French *prisun*, *-on* from Latin *prensio -onis*, via *prehensio* from *prehendere prehens-* 'lay hold of']

prison-breaking *n.* escape from prison.

prison camp *n.* a camp for prisoners of war or of state.

prisoner /ˈprɪz(ə)nə/ *n.* **1** a person kept in prison. **2** (in full **prisoner at the bar**) a person in custody on a criminal charge and on trial. **3** a person or thing confined by illness, another's grasp, etc. **4** = PRISONER OF WAR. □ **take prisoner** seize and hold as a prisoner. [Middle English from Anglo-French *prisoner*, Old French *prisonier* (as PRISON)]

prisoner of conscience *n.* a person imprisoned by a state for holding political or religious views it does not tolerate.

prisoner of state *n.* (also **state prisoner**) a person confined for political reasons.

prisoner of war *n.* a person who is captured in war (hyphenated when *attrib.*: *prisoner-of-war camp*).

prisoner's base *n.* a game played by two parties of children, each occupying a distinct base or home.

prissy /ˈprɪsi/ *adj.* (**prissier**, **prissiest**) prim, prudish. □ **prissily** *adv.* **prissiness** *n.* [perhaps from PRIM + SISSY]

pristine /ˈprɪstiːn, -stʌɪn/ *adj.* **1** in its original condition; unspoilt. **2** *disp.* spotless; fresh as if new. **3** ancient, primitive. [Latin *pristinus* 'former']

■ **Usage** The use of *pristine* in sense 2 is considered incorrect by some people.

prithee /ˈprɪðiː/ *int. archaic* pray, please. [= *I pray thee*]

privacy /ˈprɪvəsi, ˈprʌɪ-/ *n.* **1 a** the state of being private and undisturbed. **b** a person's right to this. **2** freedom from intrusion or public attention. **3** avoidance of publicity.

private /ˈprʌɪvət/ *adj. & n.* ● *adj.* **1** belonging to an individual; one's own; personal (*private property*). **2** confidential; not to be disclosed to others (*private talks*). **3** kept or removed from public knowledge or observation. **4 a** not open to the public. **b** for an individual's exclusive use (*private room*). **5** (of a place) secluded; affording privacy. **6** (of a person) not holding public office or an official position. **7** (of education or *Brit.* medical treatment) conducted outside the state system, at the individual's expense. ● *n.* **1** a private soldier. **2** (in *pl.*) *colloq.* the genitals. □ **in private** privately; in private company or life. □ **privately** *adv.* [Middle English from Latin *privatus* 'withdrawn from public life', originally past part. of *privare* 'bereave, deprive']

private bill *n.* a legislative bill affecting an individual or corporation only.

private company *n. Brit.* a company with restricted membership and no issue of shares.

private detective *n.* a usu. freelance detective carrying out investigations for a private employer.

private enterprise *n.* **1** a business or businesses not under state control. **2** individual initiative.

privateer /prʌɪvəˈtɪə/ *n.* **1** an armed vessel owned and officered by private individuals holding a government commission and authorized for war service. **2 a** a commander of such a vessel. **b** (in *pl.*) its crew. □ **privateering** *n.* [PRIVATE, on the pattern of *volunteer*]

privateersman /prʌɪvəˈtɪəzmən/ *n.* (*pl.* **-men**) = PRIVATEER 2.

private eye *n. colloq.* a private detective.

private first class *n. US* a soldier ranking above an ordinary private but below a corporal.

private hotel *n.* a hotel not obliged to take all comers.

private house *n.* the dwelling house of a private person, as distinct from a shop, office, or public building.

private law *n.* a law relating to individual persons and private property.

private life *n.* life as a private person, not as an official, public performer, etc.

private means *n.pl.* income from investments etc., apart from earned income.

private member *n.* a member of a legislative body not holding a government office.

private member's bill *n. Brit.* a bill introduced by a private member, not part of government legislation.

private parts *n.pl.* the genitals.

private patient *n. Brit.* a patient treated by a doctor other than under the National Health Service.

private practice *n.* **1** *Brit.* medical practice that is not part of the National Health Service. **2** *US* the work of a doctor, lawyer, etc. who is self-employed.

private press *n.* a printing establishment operated by a private person or group not primarily for profit and usu. on a small scale.

private school *n.* **1** *Brit.* a school supported wholly by the payment of fees. **2** *US* a school not supported mainly by the State.

private secretary *n.* a secretary dealing with the personal and confidential concerns of a businessman or businesswoman.

private sector *n.* the part of the economy not under direct state control.

private soldier *n.* an ordinary soldier other than the officers (and *US* other than recruits).

private view *n.* the viewing of an exhibition (esp. of paintings) before it is open to the public.

private war *n.* **1** a feud between persons or families disregarding the law of murder etc. **2** hostilities against members of another state without the sanction of one's own government.

private wrong *n.* an offence against an individual but not against society as a whole.

privation /prʌɪˈveɪʃ(ə)n/ *n.* **1** lack of the comforts or necessities of life (*suffered many privations*). **2** (often foll. by *of*) loss or absence (of a quality). [Middle English from Latin *privatio* (as PRIVATE)]

privative /ˈprɪvətɪv/ *adj.* **1** consisting in or marked by the loss or removal or absence of some quality or attribute. **2** (of a term) denoting the privation or absence of a quality etc. **3** *Gram.* (of a particle etc.) expressing privation, as Greek *a-* = 'not'. [French *privatif -ive* or Latin *privativus* (as PRIVATION)]

privatize /ˈprʌɪvətʌɪz/ *v.tr.* (also **-ise**) make private, esp. assign (a business etc.) to private as distinct from state control or ownership; denationalize. □ **privatization** /-ˈzeɪʃ(ə)n/ *n.* **privatizer** *n.*

privet /ˈprɪvɪt/ *n.* any partly evergreen shrub of the genus *Ligustrum*, bearing small white flowers and black berries, and much used for hedges. [16th c.: origin unknown]

privilege /ˈprɪvɪlɪdʒ/ *n.* & *v.* ● *n.* **1 a** a right, advantage, or immunity, belonging to a person, class, or office. **b** the freedom of members of a legislative assembly when speaking at its meetings. **2** a special benefit or honour (*it is a privilege to meet you*). **3** a monopoly or patent granted to an individual, corporation, etc. **4** *US Stock Exch.* an option. ● *v.tr.* **1** invest with a privilege. **2** (foll. by *to* + infin.) allow (a person) as a privilege (to do something). **3** (often foll. by *from*) exempt (a person from a liability etc.). □ **privileged** *adj.* [Middle English via Old French *privilege* from Latin *privilegium* 'bill or law affecting an individual', from *privus* 'private' + *lex legis* 'law']

privity /ˈprɪvɪti/ *n.* (*pl.* **-ies**) **1** *Law* a relation between two parties that is recognized by law, e.g. that of blood, lease, or service. **2** (often foll. by *to*) the state of being privy (to plans etc.). [Middle English via Old French *priveté* and medieval Latin *privitas -tatis* from Latin *privus* 'private']

privy /ˈprɪvi/ *adj.* & *n.* ● *adj.* **1** (foll. by *to*) sharing in the secret of (a person's plans etc.). **2** *archaic* hidden, secret. ● *n.* (*pl.* **-ies**) **1** *US* or *archaic* a lavatory, esp. an outside one. **2** *Law* a person having a part or interest in any action, matter, or thing. □ **privily** *adv.* [Middle English via Old French *privé* from Latin *privatus* PRIVATE]

Privy Council *n.* **1** a body of advisers appointed by a sovereign or a Governor-General (now chiefly on an honorary basis and including present and former government ministers etc.). **2** usu. *hist.* a sovereign's or Governor-General's private counsellors.

privy counsellor *n.* (also **privy councillor**) a private adviser, esp. a member of a Privy Council.

privy purse *n. Brit.* **1** an allowance from the public revenue for the monarch's private expenses. **2** the keeper of this.

privy seal *n.* (in the UK) a seal formerly affixed to documents that are afterwards to pass the Great Seal or that do not require it.

prize[1] /prʌɪz/ *n.* & *v.* ● *n.* **1** something that can be won in a competition or lottery etc. **2** a reward given as a symbol of victory or superiority. **3** something striven for or worth striving for (*missed all the great prizes of life*). **4** (*attrib.*) **a** to which a prize is awarded (*a prize bull*; *a prize poem*). **b** supremely excellent or outstanding of its kind. ● *v.tr.* value highly (*a much prized possession*). [the noun Middle English, variant of PRICE: the verb Middle English from Old French *pris-*, stem of *preisier* PRAISE]

prize[2] /prʌɪz/ *n.* & *v.* ● *n.* **1** a ship or property captured in naval warfare. **2** a find or windfall. ● *v.tr.* make a prize of. [Middle English via Old French *prise* 'taking, booty', fem. past part. of *prendre*, from Latin *prehendere prehens-* 'seize': later identified with PRIZE[1]]

prize[3] *US* var. of PRISE.

prize court *n.* a department of an admiralty court concerned with prizes.

prizefight /ˈprʌɪzfʌɪt/ *n.* a boxing match fought for prize money. □ **prizefighter** *n.* **prizefighting** *n.*

prize-giving *n. Brit.* an award of prizes, esp. formally at a school etc.

prizeman /ˈprʌɪzmən/ *n.* (*pl.* **-men**) a winner of a prize, esp. a specified academic one.

prize money *n.* money offered as a prize.

prize ring *n.* **1** an enclosed area (now usu. a square) for prizefighting. **2** the practice of prizefighting.

prizewinner /ˈprʌɪzwɪnə/ *n.* a winner of a prize. □ **prizewinning** *adj.*

PRO *abbr.* **1** Public Record Office. **2** public relations officer.

pro[1] /prəʊ/ *n.* & *adj. colloq.* ● *n.* (*pl.* **-os**) **1** a professional. **2** a prostitute. ● *adj.* professional. [abbreviation]

pro[2] /prəʊ/ *adj.*, *n.*, *prep.*, & *adv.* ● *adj.* (of an argument or reason) for; in favour. ● *n.* (*pl.* **-os**) a reason or argument for or in favour. ● *prep.* & *adv.* in favour of (cf. CON[2]). [Latin, = for, on behalf of]

pro-[1] /prəʊ/ *prefix* **1** favouring or supporting (*pro-government*). **2** acting as a substitute or deputy for (*proconsul*). **3** forwards (*produce*). **4** forwards and downwards (*prostrate*). **5** onwards (*proceed*; *progress*). **6** in front of (*protect*). [Latin *pro* 'in front (of), for, on behalf of, instead of, on account of']

pro-[2] /prəʊ/ *prefix* before in time, place, order, etc. (*problem*; *proboscis*; *prophet*). [Greek *pro* 'before']

proa /ˈprəʊə/ *n.* (also **prau**, **prahu** /ˈprɑːuː/) a Malay boat, esp. with a large triangular sail and a canoe-like outrigger. [Malay *prāū*, *prāhū*]

proactive /prəʊˈaktɪv/ *adj.* **1** (of a person, policy, etc.) creating or controlling a situation by taking the initiative. **2** *Psychol.* of or relating to mental conditioning or a habit etc. which has been learnt. □ **proaction** /-ˈakʃ(ə)n/ *n.* **proactively** *adv.* **proactivity** /-ˈtɪvɪti/ *n.* [PRO-[2], on the pattern of REACTIVE]

pro-am /prəʊˈam/ *adj.* & *n.* ● *adj.* involving professionals and amateurs. ● *n.* a pro-am event.

prob /prɒb/ *n.* a problem. [abbreviation]

probabilistic /prɒbəbəˈlɪstɪk/ *adj.* relating to probability; involving chance variation.

probability /prɒbəˈbɪlɪti/ *n.* (*pl.* **-ies**) **1** the state or condition of being probable. **2** the likelihood of something happening. **3** a probable or most probable event (*the probability is that they will come*). **4** *Math.* the extent to which an event is likely to occur, measured by the ratio of the favourable cases to the whole number of cases possible. □ **in all probability** most probably. [French *probabilité* or Latin *probabilitas* (as PROBABLE)]

probable /ˈprɒbəb(ə)l/ *adj. & n.* ● *adj.* (often foll. by *that* + clause) that may be expected to happen or prove true; likely (*the probable explanation*; *it is probable that they forgot*). ● *n.* a probable candidate, member of a team, etc. □ **probably** *adv.* [Middle English via Old French from Latin *probabilis*, from *probare* PROVE]

proband /ˈprəʊbənd/ *n.* a person forming the starting point for the genetic study of a family etc. [Latin *probandus*, gerundive of *probare* 'test']

probang /ˈprəʊbaŋ/ *n. Surgery* a strip of flexible material with a sponge etc. at the end, used to remove an object from the throat or apply medication to it. [17th c. (named *provang* by its inventor): origin unknown, perhaps alteration suggested by *probe*]

probate /ˈprəʊbeɪt/ *n. & v.* ● *n.* **1** the official proving of a will. **2** a verified copy of a will with a certificate as handed to the executors. ● *v.tr. N. Amer.* establish the validity of (a will). [Middle English from Latin *probatum*, neut. past part. of *probare* PROVE]

probation /prəˈbeɪʃ(ə)n/ *n.* **1** *Law* a system of supervising and monitoring the behaviour of (esp. young) offenders. **2** a process or period of testing the character or abilities of a person in a certain role, esp. of a new employee. **3** a moral trial or discipline. □ **on probation** undergoing probation, esp. legal supervision. □ **probational** *adj.* **probationary** *adj.* [Middle English from Old French *probation* or Latin *probatio* (as PROVE)]

probationer /prəˈbeɪʃ(ə)nə/ *n.* **1** a person on probation, e.g. a newly appointed nurse, teacher, etc. **2** an offender on probation. □ **probationership** *n.*

probation officer *n.* an official supervising offenders on probation.

probative /ˈprəʊbətɪv/ *adj.* affording proof; evidential. [Latin *probativus* (as PROVE)]

probe /prəʊb/ *n. & v.* ● *n.* **1** a penetrating investigation. **2** any small device, esp. an electrode, for measuring, testing, etc. **3** a blunt-ended surgical instrument usu. of metal for exploring a wound etc. **4** (in full **space probe**) an unmanned exploratory spacecraft transmitting information about its environment. ● *v.tr.* **1** examine or enquire into closely. **2** explore (a wound or part of the body) with a probe. **3** penetrate with a sharp instrument. □ **probeable** *adj.* **prober** *n.* **probingly** *adv.* [Late Latin *proba* 'proof', in medieval Latin = examination, from Latin *probare* 'test']

probit /ˈprɒbɪt/ *n. Statistics* a unit of probability based on deviation from the mean of a standard distribution. [*prob*ability un*it*]

probity /ˈprəʊbɪti, ˈprɒb-/ *n.* uprightness, honesty. [French *probité* or Latin *probitas* from *probus* 'good']

problem /ˈprɒbləm/ *n.* **1** a doubtful or difficult matter requiring a solution (*how to prevent it is a problem*; *the problem of ventilation*). **2** something hard to understand or accomplish or deal with. **3** (*attrib.*) **a** causing problems; difficult to deal with (*problem child*). **b** in which a social or other problem is treated (*problem page*). **4 a** *Physics* & *Math.* an inquiry starting from given conditions to investigate or demonstrate a fact, result, or law. **b** *Geom.* a proposition in which something has to be constructed (cf. THEOREM 1). **5 a** (in various games, esp. chess) an arrangement of men, cards, etc., in which the solver has to achieve a specified result. **b** a puzzle or question for solution. □ **that's your, his,** etc., **problem** said to disclaim responsibility or involvement. [Middle English via Old French *probleme* or Latin *problema* from Greek *problēma -matos*, from *proballō* (as PRO-², *ballō* 'throw')]

problematic /prɒbləˈmatɪk/ *adj.* (also **problematical**) **1** attended by difficulty. **2** doubtful or questionable. **3** *Logic* enunciating or supporting what is possible but not necessarily true. □ **problematically** *adv.* [French *problématique* or Late Latin *problematicus* from Greek *problēmatikos* (as PROBLEM)]

problematize /ˈprɒbləmətʌɪz/ *v.tr.* (also **-ise**) make into or regard as a problem requiring a solution. □ **problematization** /-ˈzeɪʃ(ə)n/ *n.* [PROBLEMATIC + -IZE]

pro bono /prəʊ ˈbəʊnəʊ/ *attrib.adj. US Law* **1** (of legal work) undertaken without charge for a client on low income. **2** (of a lawyer) undertaking such work. [Latin *pro bono publico* 'for the public good']

proboscidean /prɒbəˈsɪdɪən/ *adj. & n.* (also **proboscidian**) ● *adj.* **1** having a proboscis. **2** of or like a proboscis. **3** of the mammalian order Proboscidea, including elephants and their extinct relatives. ● *n.* a mammal of this order. [modern Latin *Proboscidea* (as PROBOSCIS)]

proboscis /prə(ʊ)ˈbɒsɪs/ *n.* (*pl.* **probosces** /-ˈbɒsiːz/, **-scides** /-sɪdiːz/, **-scises**) **1** the long flexible trunk or snout of some mammals, e.g. an elephant or tapir. **2** the elongated mouthparts of some insects. **3** the sucking organ in some worms. **4** *joc.* the human nose. □ **proboscidiferous** /-sɪˈdɪf(ə)rəs/ *adj.* **proboscidiform** /-ˈsɪdɪfɔːm/ *adj.* [Latin *proboscis -cidis* from Greek *proboskis*, from *proboskō* (as PRO-², *boskō* 'feed')]

proboscis monkey *n.* a monkey, *Nasalis larvatus*, native to Borneo, the male of which has a large pendulous nose.

procaine /ˈprəʊkeɪn/ *n.* (also **procain**) a synthetic compound used as a local anaesthetic, esp. in dentistry. [PRO-¹ + COCAINE]

procaryote var. of PROKARYOTE.

procedure /prəˈsiːdʒə/ *n.* **1** a way of proceeding, esp. a mode of conducting business or a legal action. **2** a mode of performing a task. **3** a series of actions conducted in a certain order or manner. **4** a proceeding. **5** *Computing* = SUBROUTINE. □ **procedural** *adj.* **procedurally** *adv.* [French *procédure* (as PROCEED)]

proceed /prəˈsiːd/ *v.intr.* **1** (often foll. by *to*) go forward or on further; make one's way. **2** (often foll. by *with*, or *to* + infin.) continue; go on with an activity (*proceeded with their work*; *proceeded to tell the whole story*). **3** (of an action) be carried on or continued (*the case will now proceed*). **4** adopt a course of action (*how shall we proceed?*). **5** go on to say. **6** (foll. by *against*) start a lawsuit (against a person). **7** (often foll. by *from*) come forth or originate (*shouts proceeded from the bedroom*). **8** (foll. by *to*) *Brit.* advance to a higher rank, university degree, etc. [Middle English via Old French *proceder* from Latin *procedere process-* (as PRO-¹, *cedere* 'go')]

proceeding /prəˈsiːdɪŋ/ *n.* **1** an action or piece of conduct (*a high-handed proceeding*). **2** (in *pl.*) (in full **legal proceedings**) an action at law; a lawsuit. **3** (in *pl.*) a published report of discussions or a conference.

proceeds /ˈprəʊsiːdz/ *n.pl.* money produced by a transaction or other undertaking. [pl. of obsolete noun *proceed* from PROCEED]

process¹ /ˈprəʊsɛs/ *n. & v.* ● *n.* **1** a course of action or a procedure, esp. a series of stages in manufacture or some other operation. **2 a** the progress or course of something (*in process of construction*). **b** the course of becoming, happening, etc. (*regeneration is in process*). **3** a natural or involuntary operation or series of changes (*the process of growing old*). **4** an action at law; a summons or writ. **5** *Anat.*, *Zool.*, & *Bot.* a natural appendage or outgrowth on an organism. ● *v.tr.* **1** handle or deal with by a particular process. **2** treat (food, esp. to prevent decay) (*processed cheese*). **3** *Computing* operate on (data) by means of a program. □ **in process of time** as time goes on. □ **processable** *adj.* [Middle English via Old French *proces* from Latin *processus* (as PROCEED)]

process² /prəˈsɛs/ *v.intr.* walk in procession. [back-formation from PROCESSION]

procession /prəˈsɛʃ(ə)n/ *n.* **1** a number of people or vehicles etc. moving forward in orderly succession, esp. at a ceremony, demonstration, or festivity. **2** the movement of such a group (*go in procession*). **3** a race in which no competitor is able to overtake another. **4** *Theol.* the emanation of the Holy Spirit. □ **processionist** *n.* [Middle English via Old French from Latin *processio -onis* (as PROCEED)]

processional /prə'sɛʃ(ə)n(ə)l/ *adj. & n.* ● *adj.* **1** of or relating to processions. **2** used, carried, or sung in processions. ● *n. Eccl.* an office-book of processional hymns etc. [medieval Latin *processionalis* (*adj.*), *-ale* (*n.*) (as PROCESSION)]

processor /'prəʊsɛsə/ *n.* a machine that processes things, esp.: **1** = CENTRAL PROCESSOR. **2** = FOOD PROCESSOR.

process server *n.* a sheriff's officer who serves writs.

procès-verbal /ˌprɒseɪvəː'bɑːl/ *n.* (*pl.* **procès-verbaux** /-'bəʊ/) a written report of proceedings; minutes. [French]

pro-choice /prəʊ'tʃɔɪs/ *adj.* favouring the right of a woman to choose to have an abortion.

prochronism /'prəʊkrənɪz(ə)m/ *n.* the action of referring an event etc. to an earlier date than the true one. [PRO-[2] + Greek *khronos* 'time']

proclaim /prə'kleɪm/ *v.tr.* **1** (often foll. by *that* + clause) announce or declare publicly or officially. **2** declare (a person) to be (a king, traitor, etc.). **3** reveal as being (*an accent that proclaims you a Scot*). □ **proclaimer** *n.* **proclamation** /prɒklə'meɪʃ(ə)n/ *n.* **proclamatory** /-'klamət(ə)ri/ *adj.* [Middle English *proclame* from Latin *proclamare* 'cry out' (as PRO-[1], CLAIM)]

proclitic /prə(ʊ)'klɪtɪk/ *adj. & n. Gram.* ● *adj.* (of a monosyllable) closely attached in pronunciation to a following word and having itself no accent. ● *n.* such a word, e.g. *at* in *at home*. □ **proclitically** *adv.* [modern Latin *procliticus* (from Greek *proklinō* 'lean forward'), on the pattern of Late Latin *encliticus*: see ENCLITIC]

proclivity /prə'klɪvɪti/ *n.* (*pl.* **-ies**) a tendency or inclination. [Latin *proclivitas* from *proclivis* 'inclined' (as PRO-[1], *clivus* 'slope')]

proconsul /prəʊ'kɒns(ə)l/ *n.* **1** *Rom.Hist.* a governor of a province, in the later republic usu. an ex-consul. **2** a governor of a modern colony etc. **3** a deputy consul. □ **proconsular** /-sjʊlə/ *adj.* **proconsulate** /-sjʊlət/ *n.* **proconsulship** *n.* [Middle English from Latin, earlier *pro consule* '(one acting) for the consul']

procrastinate /prə(ʊ)'krastɪneɪt/ *v.intr.* defer action; be dilatory. □ **procrastination** /-'neɪʃ(ə)n/ *n.* **procrastinative** /-nətɪv/ *adj.* **procrastinator** *n.* **procrastinatory** *adj.* [Latin *procrastinare procrastinat-* (as PRO-[1], *crastinus* 'of tomorrow' from *cras* 'tomorrow')]

■ **Usage** See Usage Note at PREVARICATE.

procreate /'prəʊkrɪeɪt/ *v.tr.* (often *absol.*) bring (offspring) into existence by the natural process of reproduction. □ **procreant** /'prəʊkrɪənt/ *adj.* **procreation** /-'eɪʃ(ə)n/ *n.* **procreative** *adj.* **procreator** *n.* [Latin *procreare procreat-* (as PRO-[1], *creare* 'create')]

Procrustean /prə(ʊ)'krʌstɪən/ *adj.* seeking to enforce uniformity by forceful or ruthless methods. [Greek *Prokroustēs*, literally 'stretcher', from *prokrouō* 'beat out': the name of a legendary robber who fitted victims to a bed by stretching them or cutting off parts of them]

proctology /prɒk'tɒlədʒi/ *n.* the branch of medicine concerned with the anus and rectum. □ **proctological** /-tə'lɒdʒɪk(ə)l/ *adj.* **proctologist** *n.* [Greek *prōktos* 'anus' + -LOGY]

proctor /'prɒktə/ *n.* **1** *Brit.* an officer (usu. one of two) at certain universities, appointed annually and having mainly disciplinary functions. **2** *US* a supervisor of students in an examination etc. **3** *Law* a person managing causes in a court (now chiefly ecclesiastical) that administers civil or canon law. **4** a representative of the clergy in the Church of England convocation. □ **proctorial** /-'tɔːrɪəl/ *adj.* **proctorship** *n.* [Middle English, syncopation of PROCURATOR]

proctoscope /'prɒktəskəʊp/ *n.* a medical instrument for inspecting the rectum. [Greek *prōktos* 'anus' + -SCOPE]

procumbent /prə(ʊ)'kʌmb(ə)nt/ *adj.* **1** lying on the face; prostrate. **2** *Bot.* growing along the ground. [Latin *procumbere* 'fall forwards' (as PRO-[1], *cumbere* 'lay oneself')]

procuration /prɒkjʊ'reɪʃ(ə)n/ *n.* **1** *formal* the action of procuring, obtaining, or bringing about. **2** the function or an authorized action of an attorney. [Middle English from Old French *procuration* or Latin *procuratio* (as PROCURE)]

procurator /'prɒkjʊreɪtə/ *n.* **1** an agent or proxy, esp. one who has power of attorney. **2** *Rom.Hist.* a treasury officer in an imperial province. □ **procuratorial** /-rə'tɔːrɪəl/ *adj.* **procuratorship** *n.* [Middle English from Old French *procurateur* or Latin *procurator* 'administrator, finance agent' (as PROCURE)]

procurator fiscal *n.* (in Scotland) a local coroner and public prosecutor.

procure /prə'kjʊə/ *v.tr.* **1** obtain, esp. by care or effort; acquire (*managed to procure a copy*). **2** bring about (*procured their dismissal*). **3** (also *absol.*) obtain (women) for prostitution. □ **procurable** *adj.* **procural** *n.* **procurement** *n.* [Middle English via Old French *procurer* from Latin *procurare* 'take care of, manage' (as PRO-[1], *curare* 'see to')]

procurer /prə'kjʊərə/ *n.* (*fem.* **procuress** /-rɪs/) a person who obtains women for prostitution. [Middle English via Anglo-French *procurour*, Old French *procureur* from Latin *procurator*: see PROCURATOR]

Prod /prɒd/ *n.* (also **Proddy**, **Proddie** /'prɒdi/) *slang offens.* (esp. in Ireland) a Protestant.

prod /prɒd/ *v. & n.* ● *v.* (**prodded**, **prodding**) **1** *tr.* poke with the finger or a pointed object. **2** *tr.* stimulate or goad to action. **3** *intr.* (foll. by *at*) make a prodding motion. ● *n.* **1** a poke or thrust. **2** a stimulus to action. **3** a pointed instrument. □ **prodder** *n.* [16th c.: perhaps imitative]

prodigal /'prɒdɪg(ə)l/ *adj. & n.* ● *adj.* **1** recklessly wasteful. **2** (foll. by *of*) lavish. ● *n.* **1** a prodigal person. **2** (in full **prodigal son**) a repentant wastrel, returned wanderer, etc. (after Luke 15:11–32). □ **prodigality** /-'galɪti/ *n.* **prodigally** *adv.* [medieval Latin *prodigalis* from Latin *prodigus* 'lavish']

prodigious /prə'dɪdʒəs/ *adj.* **1** marvellous or amazing. **2** enormous. **3** abnormal. □ **prodigiously** *adv.* **prodigiousness** *n.* [Latin *prodigiosus* (as PRODIGY)]

prodigy /'prɒdɪdʒi/ *n.* (*pl.* **-ies**) **1** a person endowed with exceptional qualities or abilities, esp. a precocious child. **2** a marvellous thing, esp. one out of the ordinary course of nature. **3** (foll. by *of*) a wonderful example (of a quality). [Latin *prodigium* 'portent']

prodrome /'prəʊdrəʊm, 'prɒdrəʊm/ *n. Med.* a premonitory symptom. □ **prodromal** /'prɒdrəʊm(ə)l, prə'drəʊm(ə)l/ *adj.* **prodromic** /prə'drɒmɪk/ *adj.* [French via modern Latin from Greek *prodromos* 'precursor' (as PRO-[2], *dromos* 'running')]

produce *v. & n.* ● *v.tr.* /prə'djuːs/ **1** bring forward for consideration, inspection, or use (*will produce evidence*). **2** manufacture (goods) from raw materials etc. **3** bear or yield (offspring, fruit, a harvest, etc.). **4** bring into existence. **5** cause or bring about (a reaction, sensation, etc.). **6** *Geom.* extend or continue (a line). **7 a** bring (a play, book, etc.) before the public. **b** supervise the making of (a film, broadcast, record, etc.) (cf. DIRECT *v.* 6). ● *n.* /'prɒdjuːs/ **1 a** what is produced, esp. agricultural and natural products collectively (*dairy produce*). **b** an amount of this. **2** (often foll. by *of*) a result (of labour, efforts, etc.). **3** a yield, esp. in the assay of ore. □ **producible** /prə'djuːsɪb(ə)l/ *adj.* **producibility** /prəˌdjuːsɪ'bɪlɪti/ *n.* [Middle English from Latin *producere* (as PRO-[1], *ducere duct-* 'lead')]

producer /prə'djuːsə/ *n.* **1 a** *Econ.* a person who produces goods or commodities. **b** a person or thing which produces something or someone. **2** a person generally responsible for the production of a film or play (apart from the direction of the acting) or of a broadcast programme, record, etc.

producer gas *n.* a combustible gas formed by passing air, or air and steam, through red-hot carbon.

product /ˈprɒdʌkt/ *n.* **1** a thing or substance produced by natural process or manufacture. **2** a result (*the product of their labours*). **3** *Math.* a quantity obtained by multiplying quantities together. [Middle English from Latin *productum*, neut. past part. of *producere* PRODUCE]

production /prəˈdʌkʃ(ə)n/ *n.* **1** the act or an instance of producing; the process of being produced. **2** the process of being manufactured, esp. in large quantities (*go into production*). **3** a total yield. **4 a** the process or administrative management of making a film, play, record, etc. **b** a film, play, record, etc., produced. □ **productional** *adj.* [Middle English via Old French from Latin *productio -onis* (as PRODUCT)]

production line *n.* a systematized sequence of mechanical or manual operations involved in producing a commodity.

productive /prəˈdʌktɪv/ *adj.* **1** of or engaged in the production of goods. **2** producing much (*productive soil*; *a productive writer*). **3** *Econ.* producing commodities of exchangeable value (*productive labour*). **4** (foll. by *of*) producing or giving rise to (*productive of great annoyance*). **5** *Philol.* (of a word-element) frequently used in forming new words. □ **productively** *adv.* **productiveness** *n.* [French *productif -ive* or Late Latin *productivus* (as PRODUCT)]

productivity /prɒdʌkˈtɪvɪti/ *n.* **1** the capacity to produce; the state of being productive. **2** the effectiveness of productive effort, esp. in industry. **3** production per unit of effort.

proem /ˈprəʊɪm/ *n.* **1** a preface or preamble to a book or speech. **2** a beginning or prelude. □ **proemial** /-ˈiːmɪəl/ *adj.* [Middle English via Old French *proeme* or Latin *prooemium* from Greek *prooimion* 'prelude' (as PRO-[2], *oimē* 'song')]

Prof. *abbr.* Professor.

prof /prɒf/ *n. colloq.* a professor. [abbreviation]

profane /prəˈfeɪn/ *adj.* & *v.* ● *adj.* **1** not belonging to what is sacred or biblical; secular. **2 a** irreverent, blasphemous. **b** (of language) blasphemous or obscene. **3** (of a rite etc.) heathen. **4** not initiated into religious rites or any esoteric knowledge. ● *v.tr.* **1** treat (a sacred thing) with irreverence or disregard. **2** violate or sully (what is entitled to respect). □ **profanation** /prɒfəˈneɪʃ(ə)n/ *n.* **profanely** *adv.* **profaneness** *n.* **profaner** *n.* [Middle English *prophane* via Old French *prophane* or medieval Latin *prophanus* from Latin *profanus* 'before (i.e. outside) the temple, not sacred' (as PRO-[1], *fanum* 'temple')]

profanity /prəˈfanɪti/ *n.* (*pl.* **-ies**) **1** a profane act. **2 a** profane language; blasphemy. **b** an oath, a swear word. [Late Latin *profanitas* (as PROFANE)]

profess /prəˈfɛs/ *v.* **1** *tr.* claim openly to have (a quality or feeling). **2** *tr.* (foll. by *to* + infin.) pretend. **3** *tr.* (often foll. by *that* + clause; also *refl.*) declare (*profess ignorance*; *professed herself satisfied*). **4** *tr.* affirm one's faith in or allegiance to. **5** *tr.* receive into a religious order under vows. **6** *tr.* have as one's profession or business. **7 a** *tr.* teach (a subject) as a professor. **b** *intr.* perform the duties of a professor. [Middle English from Latin *profitēri profess-* 'declare publicly' (as PRO-[1], *fatēri* 'confess')]

professed /prəˈfɛst/ *adj.* **1** self-acknowledged (*a professed Christian*). **2** alleged, ostensible. **3** claiming to be duly qualified. **4** (of a monk or nun) having taken the vows of a religious order. □ **professedly** /-sɪdli/ *adv.* (in senses 1, 2).

profession /prəˈfɛʃ(ə)n/ *n.* **1** a vocation or calling, esp. one that involves some branch of advanced learning or science (*the medical profession*). **2** a body of people engaged in a profession. **3** a declaration or avowal. **4** a declaration of belief in a religion. **5 a** the declaration or vows made on entering a religious order. **b** the ceremony or fact of being professed in a religious order. □ **the oldest profession** *colloq.* or *joc.* prostitution. □ **professionless** *adj.* [Middle English via Old French from Latin *professio -onis* (as PROFESS)]

professional /prəˈfɛʃ(ə)n(ə)l/ *adj.* & *n.* ● *adj.* **1** of or belonging to or connected with a profession. **2 a** having or showing the skill of a professional; competent. **b** worthy of a professional (*professional conduct*). **3** engaged in a specified activity as one's main paid occupation (cf. AMATEUR *adj.* 1a) (*a professional boxer*). **4** *derog.* engaged in a specified habitual activity regarded with disfavour (*a professional agitator*). ● *n.* a professional person. □ **professionally** *adv.*

professional foul *n. Brit.* a deliberate foul in football etc., esp. to prevent an opponent from scoring.

professionalism /prəˈfɛʃ(ə)n(ə)lɪz(ə)m/ *n.* the qualities or typical features of a profession or of professionals, esp. competence, skill, etc.

professionalize /prəˈfɛʃ(ə)n(ə)lʌɪz/ *v.tr.* (also **-ise**) make (an occupation, activity, etc.) professional. □ **professionalization** /-ˈzeɪʃ(ə)n/ *n.*

professor /prəˈfɛsə/ *n.* **1 a** (often as a title) a university academic of the highest rank; the holder of a university chair. **b** *US* a university teacher. **2** a person who professes a religion. □ **professorate** *n.* **professorial** /prɒfɪˈsɔːrɪəl/ *adj.* **professorially** /prɒfɪˈsɔːrɪəli/ *adv.* **professoriate** /prɒfɪˈsɔːrɪət/ *n.* **professorship** *n.* [Middle English from Old French *professeur* or Latin *professor* (as PROFESS)]

proffer /ˈprɒfə/ *v.* & *n.* ● *v.tr.* (esp. as **proffered** *adj.*) offer (a gift, services, a hand, etc.). ● *n. literary* an offer or proposal. [Middle English from Anglo-French & Old French *proffrir* (as PRO-[1], *offrir* OFFER)]

proficient /prəˈfɪʃ(ə)nt/ *adj.* & *n.* ● *adj.* (often foll. by *in*, *at*) adept, expert. ● *n.* a person who is proficient. □ **proficiency** /-si/ *n.* **proficiently** *adv.* [Latin *proficiens proficient-* (as PROFIT)]

profile /ˈprəʊfʌɪl/ *n.* & *v.* ● *n.* **1 a** an outline (esp. of a human face) as seen from one side. **b** a representation of this. **2** a short biographical or character sketch. **3** *Statistics* a representation by a graph or chart of information (esp. on certain characteristics) recorded in a quantified form. **4** a characteristic personal manner or attitude. **5** a vertical cross-section of a structure. **6** a flat outline piece of scenery on stage. ● *v.tr.* **1** represent in profile. **2** give a profile to. □ **in profile** as seen from one side. **keep a low profile** remain inconspicuous. □ **profiler** *n.* **profilist** *n.* [obsolete Italian *profilo*, *profilare* (as PRO-[1], *filare* 'spin', formerly 'draw a line' from Latin *filare*, from *filum* 'thread')]

profit /ˈprɒfɪt/ *n.* & *v.* ● *n.* **1** an advantage or benefit. **2** financial gain; excess of returns over outlay. ● *v.* (**profited**, **profiting**) **1** *tr.* (also *absol.*) be beneficial to. **2** *intr.* obtain an advantage or benefit (*profited by the experience*). □ **at a profit** with financial gain. □ **profitless** *adj.* [Middle English via Old French from Latin *profectus* 'progress, profit', from *proficere profect-* 'advance' (as PRO-[1], *facere* 'do')]

profitable /ˈprɒfɪtəb(ə)l/ *adj.* **1** yielding profit; lucrative. **2** beneficial; useful. □ **profitability** /-ˈbɪlɪti/ *n.* **profitableness** *n.* **profitably** *adv.* [Middle English from Old French (as PROFIT)]

profit and loss account *n.* an account to which incomes and gains are credited and expenses and losses debited, so as to show the net profit or loss over a given period.

profiteer /prɒfɪˈtɪə/ *v.* & *n.* ● *v.intr.* make or seek to make excessive profits, esp. illegally or in black market conditions. ● *n.* a person who profiteers.

profiterole /prəˈfɪtərəʊl/ *n.* a small hollow case of choux pastry usu. filled with cream and covered with chocolate sauce. [French, diminutive of *profit* PROFIT]

profit margin *n.* the profit remaining in a business after costs have been deducted.

profit-sharing *n.* the sharing of profits esp. between employer and employees.

profit-taking *n.* the sale of shares etc. at a time when profit will accrue.

profligate /ˈprɒflɪɡət/ *adj. & n.* ● *adj.* **1** licentious; dissolute. **2** recklessly extravagant. ● *n.* a profligate person. □ **profligacy** /-ɡəsi/ *n.* **profligately** *adv.* [Latin *profligatus* 'dissolute', past part. of *profligare* 'overthrow, ruin' (as PRO-[1], *fligere* 'strike down')]

pro forma /prəʊ ˈfɔːmə/ *adv., adj., & n.* ● *adv. & adj.* as or being a matter of form. ● *n.* (in full **pro forma invoice**) an invoice sent in advance of goods supplied. [Latin]

profound /prəˈfaʊnd/ *adj. & n.* ● *adj.* (**profounder**, **profoundest**) **1 a** having or showing great knowledge or insight (*a profound treatise*). **b** demanding deep study or thought (*profound doctrines*). **2** (of a state or quality) deep, intense, unqualified (*a profound sleep*; *profound indifference*). **3** at or extending to a great depth (*profound crevasses*). **4** (of a sigh) deep-drawn. **5** (of a disease) deep-seated. ● *n.* (prec. by *the*) *poet.* the vast depth (of the ocean, soul, etc.). □ **profoundly** *adv.* **profoundness** *n.* **profundity** /prəˈfʌndɪti/ *n.* (*pl.* **-ies**). [Middle English via Anglo-French & Old French *profund*, *profond* from Latin *profundus* 'deep' (as PRO-[1], *fundus* 'bottom')]

profuse /prəˈfjuːs/ *adj.* **1** (often foll. by *in*) lavish; extravagant (*was profuse in her generosity*). **2** (of a thing) exuberantly plentiful; abundant (*profuse bleeding*; *a profuse variety*). □ **profusely** *adv.* **profuseness** *n.* **profusion** /prəˈfjuːʒ(ə)n/ *n.* [Middle English from Latin *profusus*, past part. of *profundere profus-* (as PRO-[1], *fundere fus-* 'pour')]

prog /prɒɡ/ *n. slang* a television or radio programme. [abbreviation]

progenitive /prə(ʊ)ˈdʒɛnɪtɪv/ *adj.* capable of or connected with the production of offspring.

progenitor /prə(ʊ)ˈdʒɛnɪtə/ *n.* **1** the ancestor of a person, animal, or plant. **2** a political or intellectual predecessor. **3** the origin of a copy. □ **progenitorial** /-ˈtɔːrɪəl/ *adj.* **progenitorship** *n.* [Middle English via Old French *progeniteur* from Latin *progenitor -oris*, from *progignere progenit-* (as PRO-[1], *gignere* 'beget')]

progeniture /prə(ʊ)ˈdʒɛnɪtʃə/ *n.* **1** the act or an instance of procreation. **2** young, offspring.

progeny /ˈprɒdʒ(ə)ni/ *n.* **1** the offspring of a person or other organism. **2** a descendant or descendants. **3** an outcome or issue. [Middle English via Old French *progenie* from Latin *progenies*, from *progignere* (as PROGENITOR)]

progesterone /prə(ʊ)ˈdʒɛstərəʊn/ *n.* a steroid hormone released by the corpus luteum which stimulates the preparation of the uterus for pregnancy (see also PROGESTOGEN). [*progest*in (as PRO-[2], GESTATION) + luteo*sterone* from CORPUS LUTEUM + STEROL]

progestogen /prə(ʊ)ˈdʒɛstədʒ(ə)n/ *n.* **1** any of a group of steroid hormones (including progesterone) that maintain pregnancy and prevent further ovulation during it. **2** a similar hormone produced synthetically.

proglottid /prəʊˈɡlɒtɪd/ *n.* (also **proglottis** /-tɪs/) (*pl.* **proglottids** or **proglottides** /-diːz/) each segment in the strobila of a tapeworm that contains a complete reproductive system. [modern Latin from Greek *proglōssis* (as PRO-[2], *glōssis* from *glōssa*, *glōtta* 'tongue'), from its shape]

prognathous /prɒɡˈneɪθəs, ˈprɒɡnəθəs/ *adj.* **1** having a projecting jaw. **2** (of a jaw) projecting. □ **prognathic** /prɒɡˈnaθɪk/ *adj.* **prognathism** *n.* [PRO-[2] + Greek *gnathos* 'jaw']

prognosis /prɒɡˈnəʊsɪs/ *n.* (*pl.* **prognoses** /-siːz/) **1** a forecast; a prognostication. **2** a forecast of the course of a disease. [Late Latin from Greek *prognōsis* (as PRO-[2], *gignōskō* 'know')]

prognostic /prɒɡˈnɒstɪk/ *n. & adj.* ● *n.* **1** (often foll. by *of*) an advance indication or omen, esp. of the course of a disease etc. **2** a prediction; a forecast. ● *adj.* foretelling; predictive (*prognostic of a good result*). □ **prognostically** *adv.* [Middle English via Old French *pronostique* and Latin *prognosticum* from Greek *prognōstikon*, neut. of *prognōstikos* (as PROGNOSIS)]

prognosticate /prɒɡˈnɒstɪkeɪt/ *v.tr.* **1** (often foll. by *that* + clause) foretell; foresee; prophesy. **2** (of a thing) betoken; indicate (future events etc.). □ **prognosticable** /-kəb(ə)l/ *adj.* **prognostication** /-ˈkeɪʃ(ə)n/ *n.* **prognosticative** /-kətɪv/ *adj.* **prognosticator** *n.* **prognosticatory** *adj.* [medieval Latin *prognosticare* (as PROGNOSTIC)]

programme /ˈprəʊɡram/ *n. & v.* (*US & Austral.* **program**) ● *n.* **1** a usu. printed list of a series of events, performers, etc. at a public function etc. **2** a radio or television broadcast. **3** a plan of future events (*the programme is dinner and an early night*). **4** a course or series of studies, lectures, etc.; a syllabus. **5** (usu. **program**) a series of coded instructions to control the operation of a computer or other machine. ● *v.tr.* (**programmed**, **programming**) **1** make a programme or definite plan of. **2** (usu. **program**) **a** provide (a computer etc.) with coded instructions for the automatic performance of a particular task. **b** train to behave in a predetermined way. □ **programmable** *adj.* **programmability** /-ˈbɪlɪti/ *n.* **programmatic** /-ɡrəˈmatɪk/ *adj.* **programmatically** /-ɡrəˈmatɪk(ə)li/ *adv.* **programmer** *n.* [Late Latin *programma* from Greek *programma -atos*, from *prographō* 'write publicly' (as PRO-[2], *graphō* 'write'): spelling influenced by French *programme*]

programme music *n.* a piece of music intended to tell a story, evoke images, etc.

progress *n. & v.* ● *n.* /ˈprəʊɡrɛs/ **1** forward or onward movement towards a destination. **2** advance or development towards completion, betterment, etc.; improvement (*has made little progress this term*; *the progress of civilization*). **3** *Brit. archaic* a state journey or official tour, esp. by royalty. ● *v.* /prəˈɡrɛs/ **1** *intr.* move or be moved forward or onward; continue (*the argument is progressing*). **2** *intr.* advance or develop towards completion, improvement, etc. (*science progresses*). **3** *tr.* cause (work etc.) to make regular progress. □ **in progress** in the course of developing; going on. [Middle English from Latin *progressus* from *progredi* (as PRO-[1], *gradi* 'walk': the verb readopted from US after becoming obsolete in British use in the 17th c.]

progress-chaser *n. Brit.* a person employed to check the regular progress of manufacturing work.

progression /prəˈɡrɛʃ(ə)n/ *n.* **1** the act or an instance of progressing (*a mode of progression*). **2** a succession; a series. **3** *Math.* **a** = ARITHMETIC PROGRESSION. **b** = GEOMETRIC PROGRESSION. **c** = HARMONIC PROGRESSION. **4** *Mus.* passing from one note or chord to another. □ **progressional** *adj.* [Middle English from Old French *progression* or Latin *progressio* (as PROGRESS)]

progressionist /prəˈɡrɛʃ(ə)nɪst/ *n.* **1** an advocate of or believer in esp. political or social progress. **2** a person who believes in the theory of gradual progression to higher forms of life.

progressive /prəˈɡrɛsɪv/ *adj. & n.* ● *adj.* **1** moving forward (*progressive motion*). **2** proceeding step by step; cumulative (*progressive drug use*). **3 a** (of a political party, government, etc.) favouring or implementing rapid progress or social reform. **b** modern; efficient (*this is a progressive company*). **4** (of disease, violence, etc.) increasing in severity or extent. **5** (of taxation) at rates increasing with the sum taxed. **6** (of a card game, dance, etc.) with periodic changes of partners. **7** *Gram.* (of an aspect) expressing an action in progress, e.g. *am writing*, *was writing*. **8** (of education) informal and without strict discipline, stressing individual needs. ● *n.* (also **Progressive**) an advocate of progressive political policies or social reform. □ **progressively** *adv.* **progressiveness** *n.* **progressivism** *n.* **progressivist** *n. & adj.* [French *progressif -ive* or medieval Latin *progressivus* (as PROGRESS)]

progress report *n.* an account of progress made.

pro hac vice /ˌprəʊ hɑːk ˈvʌɪsi/ *adv.* for this occasion (only). [Latin]

prohibit /prə(ʊ)ˈhɪbɪt/ *v.tr.* (**prohibited**, **prohibiting**) (often foll. by *from* + verbal noun) **1** formally forbid, esp. by authority. **2** prevent; make impossible (*his accident prohibits him from playing football*). □ **prohibiter** *n.* **prohibitor** *n.* **prohibitory** *adj.* [Middle English from Latin *prohibēre* (as PRO-[1], *habēre* 'hold')]

prohibited degrees *n.pl.* = FORBIDDEN DEGREES.

prohibition /prəʊhɪˈbɪʃ(ə)n, prəʊɪ-/ *n.* **1** the act or an instance of forbidding; a state of being forbidden. **2** *Law* **a** an edict or order that forbids. **b** *Brit.* a writ from a superior court forbidding an inferior court from proceeding in a suit deemed to be beyond its cognizance. **3** (usu. **Prohibition**) the prevention by law of the manufacture and sale of alcohol, esp. in the US (1920–33). □ **prohibitionary** *adj.* **prohibitionist** *n.* [Middle English from Old French *prohibition* or Latin *prohibitio* (as PROHIBIT)]

prohibitive /prə(ʊ)ˈhɪbɪtɪv/ *adj.* **1** prohibiting. **2** (of prices, taxes, etc.) so high as to prevent purchase, use, abuse, etc. (*published at a prohibitive price*). □ **prohibitively** *adv.* **prohibitiveness** *n.* [French *prohibitif -ive* or Latin *prohibitivus* (as PROHIBIT)]

project *n.* & *v.* ● *n.* /ˈprɒdʒɛkt/ **1** a plan; a scheme. **2** a planned undertaking. **3** a usu. long-term task undertaken by a student to be submitted for assessment. ● *v.* /prəˈdʒɛkt/ **1** *tr.* plan or contrive (a course of action, scheme, etc.). **2** *intr.* protrude; jut out. **3** *tr.* throw; cast; impel (*projected the stone into the water*). **4** *tr.* extrapolate (results etc.) to a future time; forecast (*I project that we shall produce two million next year*). **5** *tr.* cause (light, shadow, images, etc.) to fall on a surface, screen, etc. **6** *tr.* cause (a sound, esp. the voice) to be heard at a distance. **7** *tr.* (often *refl.* or *absol.*) express or promote (oneself or a positive image) forcefully or effectively. **8** *tr. Geom.* **a** draw straight lines from a centre or parallel lines through every point of (a given figure) to produce a corresponding figure on a surface or a line by intersecting it. **b** draw (such lines). **c** produce (such a corresponding figure). **9** *tr.* make a projection of (the earth, sky, etc.). **10** *tr. Psychol.* **a** (also *absol.*) attribute (an emotion etc.) to an external object or person, esp. unconsciously. **b** (*refl.*) project (oneself) into another's feelings, the future, etc. [Middle English from Latin *projectum*, neut. past part. of *projicere* (as PRO-[1], *jacĕre* 'throw')]

projectile /prə(ʊ)ˈdʒɛktʌɪl, -tɪl/ *n.* & *adj.* ● *n.* **1** a missile, esp. fired by a rocket. **2** a bullet, shell, etc. fired from a gun. **3** any object thrown as a weapon. ● *adj.* **1** capable of being projected by force, esp. from a gun. **2** projecting or impelling. [modern Latin *projectilis* (*adj.*), *-ile* (*n.*) (as PROJECT)]

projection /prəˈdʒɛkʃ(ə)n/ *n.* **1** the act or an instance of projecting; the process of being projected. **2** a thing that projects or obtrudes. **3** the presentation of an image etc. on a surface or screen. **4 a** a forecast or estimate based on present trends (*a projection of next year's profits*). **b** this process. **5 a** a mental image or preoccupation viewed as an objective reality. **b** the unconscious transfer of one's own impressions or feelings to external objects or persons. **6** *Geom.* the act or an instance of projecting a figure. **7** the representation on a plane surface of any part of the surface of the earth or a celestial sphere (*Mercator projection*). □ **projectionist** *n.* (in sense 3). [Latin *projectio* (as PROJECT)]

projective /prəˈdʒɛktɪv/ *adj.* **1** *Geom.* **a** relating to or derived by projection. **b** (of a property of a figure) unchanged by projection. **2** *Psychol.* mentally projecting or projected (*a projective imagination*). □ **projectively** *adv.*

projective geometry *n.* the study of the projective properties of geometric figures.

projector /prəˈdʒɛktə/ *n.* **1 a** an apparatus containing a source of light and a system of lenses for projecting slides or film on to a screen. **b** an apparatus for projecting rays of light. **2** a person who forms or promotes a project. **3** *archaic* a promoter of speculative companies.

prokaryote /prəʊˈkarɪəʊt, -ɒt/ *n.* (also **procaryote**) a single-celled organism which has neither a distinct nucleus with a membrane nor other specialized organelles, e.g. a bacterium, a blue-green alga (cf. EUKARYOTE). □ **prokaryotic** /-ˈɒtɪk/ *adj.* [PRO-[2] + KARYO- + *-ote* as in ZYGOTE]

prolactin /prəʊˈlaktɪn/ *n.* a hormone released from the anterior pituitary gland that stimulates milk production after childbirth. [PRO-[1] + LACTATION]

prolapse *n.* & *v.* ● *n.* /ˈprəʊlaps, prəˈlaps/ (also **prolapsus** /-ˈlapsəs/) **1** the forward or downward displacement of a part or organ. **2** the prolapsed part or organ, esp. the womb or rectum. ● *v.intr.* /prəʊˈlaps/ undergo prolapse. [Latin *prolabi prolaps-* (as PRO-[1], *labi* 'slip')]

prolate /ˈprəʊleɪt/ *adj.* **1** *Geom.* (of a spheroid) lengthened in the direction of a polar diameter (cf. OBLATE[2]). **2** growing or extending in width. **3** widely spread. **4** *Gram.* = PROLATIVE. □ **prolately** *adv.* [Latin *prolatus*, past part. of *proferre* 'prolong' (as PRO-[1], *ferre* 'carry')]

prolative /prə(ʊ)ˈleɪtɪv/ *adj. Gram.* serving to continue or complete a predication, e.g. *go* (prolative infinitive) in *you may go*.

prole /prəʊl/ *adj.* & *n. derog. colloq.* ● *adj.* proletarian. ● *n.* a proletarian. [abbreviation]

proleg /ˈprəʊlɛg/ *n.* a fleshy abdominal limb of a caterpillar or similar insect larva. [PRO-[1] + LEG]

prolegomenon /prəʊlɪˈgɒmɪnən/ *n.* (*pl.* **prolegomena**) (usu. in *pl.*) an introduction or preface to a book etc., esp. when critical or discursive. □ **prolegomenary** *adj.* **prolegomenous** *adj.* [Latin from Greek, neut. passive pres. part. of *prolegō* (as PRO-[2], *legō* 'say')]

prolepsis /prəʊˈlɛpsɪs, -ˈliːpsɪs/ *n.* (*pl.* **prolepses** /-siːz/) **1** *Rhet.* the anticipation and answering of possible objections in rhetorical speech. **2** anticipation. **3** the representation of a thing as existing before it actually does or did so, as in *he was a dead man when he entered*. **4** *Gram.* the anticipatory use of adjectives, as in *paint the town red*. □ **proleptic** *adj.* [Late Latin from Greek *prolēpsis*, from *prolambanō* 'anticipate' (as PRO-[2], *lambanō* 'take')]

proletarian /prəʊlɪˈtɛːrɪən/ *adj.* & *n.* ● *adj.* of or concerning the proletariat. ● *n.* a member of the proletariat. □ **proletarianism** *n.* **proletarianize** *v.tr.* (also **-ise**). [Latin *proletarius*, a person who served the State not with property but with offspring (*proles*)]

proletariat /prəʊlɪˈtɛːrɪət/ *n.* (also **proletariate**) **1 a** *Econ.* wage earners collectively, esp. those without capital and dependent on selling their labour. **b** esp. *derog.* the lowest class of the community, esp. when considered as uncultured. **2** *Rom.Hist.* the lowest class of citizens. [French *prolétariat* (as PROLETARIAN)]

pro-life /prəʊˈlʌɪf/ *adj.* in favour of preserving life, esp. in opposing abortion.

proliferate /prəˈlɪfəreɪt/ *v.* **1** *intr.* reproduce; increase rapidly in numbers; grow by multiplication. **2** *tr.* produce (cells etc.) rapidly. □ **proliferation** /-ˈreɪʃ(ə)n/ *n.* **proliferative** /-rətɪv/ *adj.* **proliferator** *n.* [back-formation from *proliferation* from French *prolifération*, from *prolifère* (as PROLIFEROUS)]

proliferous /prəˈlɪf(ə)rəs/ *adj.* **1** (of a plant) producing many leaf or flower buds; growing luxuriantly. **2** growing or multiplying by budding. **3** spreading by proliferation. [Latin *proles* 'offspring' + -FEROUS]

prolific /prəˈlɪfɪk/ *adj.* **1** producing many offspring or much output. **2** (often foll. by *of*) abundantly productive. **3** (often foll. by *in*) abounding, copious. □ **prolificacy** *n.* **prolifically** *adv.* **prolificness** *n.* [medieval Latin *prolificus* (as PROLIFEROUS)]

proline /ˈprəʊliːn/ *n. Biochem.* an amino acid with a cyclic molecule, present in many proteins, esp. collagen. [contraction of chemical name *pyrrolidine-2-carboxylic acid*]

prolix /ˈprəʊlɪks, prəˈlɪks/ *adj.* (of speech, writing, etc.) lengthy; tedious. □ **prolixity** /-ˈlɪksɪti/ *n.* **prolixly** *adv.* [Middle English from Old French *prolixe* or Latin *prolixus* 'poured forth, extended' (as PRO-[1], *liquēre* 'be liquid')]

prolocutor /'prəʊləkjuːtə, 'prɒl-, prə(ʊ)'lɒkjʊtə/ *n.* **1** *Eccl.* the chairperson esp. of the lower house of convocation of either province of the Church of England. **2** a spokesman. □ **prolocutorship** *n.* [Middle English from Latin, from *proloqui prolocut-* (as PRO-[1], *loqui* 'speak')]

Prolog /'prəʊlɒg/ *n.* (also **PROLOG**) *Computing* a high-level programming language first devised for artificial intelligence applications. [*programming* (see PROGRAMME) + LOGIC]

prologize /'prəʊlɒgʌɪz/ *v.intr.* (also **prologuize**, **-ise**) write or speak a prologue. [medieval Latin *prologizare* from Greek *prologizō* 'speak a prologue' (as PROLOGUE)]

prologue /'prəʊlɒg/ *n.* & *v.* ● *n.* **1 a** a preliminary speech, poem, etc., esp. introducing a play (cf. EPILOGUE 3). **b** the actor speaking the prologue. **2** (usu. foll. by *to*) any act or event serving as an introduction. ● *v.tr.* (**prologues**, **prologued**, **prologuing**) introduce with or provide with a prologue. [Middle English *prolog* via Old French *prologue* and Latin *prologus* from Greek *prologos* (as PRO-[2], *logos* 'speech')]

prolong /prə'lɒŋ/ *v.tr.* **1** extend (an action, condition, etc.) in time or space. **2** lengthen the pronunciation of (a syllable etc.). **3** (as **prolonged** *adj.*) lengthy, esp. tediously so. □ **prolongation** /prəʊlɒŋ'geɪʃ(ə)n/ *n.* **prolongedly** /-ɪdli/ *adv.* **prolonger** *n.* [Middle English from Old French *prolonger* & from Late Latin *prolongare* (as PRO-[1], *longus* 'long')]

prolusion /prə'l(j)uːʒ(ə)n/ *n. formal* **1** a preliminary essay or article. **2** a first attempt. □ **prolusory** /-s(ə)ri/ *adj.* [Latin *prolusio* from *proludere prolus-* 'practise beforehand' (as PRO-[2], *ludere lus-* 'play')]

prom /prɒm/ *n. colloq.* **1** *Brit.* = PROMENADE *n.* 1a. **2** *Brit.* = PROMENADE CONCERT. **3** *US* = PROMENADE *n.* 3. [abbreviation]

promenade /prɒmə'nɑːd, -'neɪd, 'prɒm-/ *n.* & *v.* ● *n.* **1 a** *Brit.* a paved public walk along the seafront at a resort. **b** any paved public walk. **2** a walk, or sometimes a ride or drive, taken esp. for display, leisure, etc. **3** *US* a school or university ball or dance, esp. for one class. **4** a march of dancers in country dancing etc. ● *v.* **1** *intr.* make a promenade. **2** *tr.* lead (a person etc.) about a place esp. for display. **3** *tr.* make a promenade through (a place). [French, from *se promener* 'walk', refl. of *promener* 'take for a walk']

promenade concert *n.* esp. *Brit.* a concert of usu. classical music at which the audience, or part of it, can stand, sit on the floor, or move about.

promenade deck *n.* an upper deck on a passenger ship where passengers may promenade.

promenader /prɒmə'nɑːdə/ *n.* **1** a person who promenades. **2** *Brit.* a person who attends a promenade concert, esp. regularly.

promethazine /prə(ʊ)'mɛθəziːn/ *n.* an antihistamine drug used to treat allergies, motion sickness, etc. [PROPYL + di*meth*ylamine + phenothi*azine*]

Promethean /prə'miːθɪən/ *adj.* daring or inventive like Prometheus, who in Greek myth was punished for stealing fire from the gods and giving it to the human race along with other skills.

promethium /prə'miːθɪəm/ *n. Chem.* a radioactive metallic element of the lanthanide series occurring in nuclear-waste material (symbol **Pm**). [*Prometheus*: see PROMETHEAN]

prominence /'prɒmɪnəns/ *n.* (also **prominency**) **1** the state of being prominent. **2** a prominent thing, esp. a jutting outcrop, mountain, etc. **3** *Astron.* a stream of incandescent gas projecting above the sun's chromosphere. [obsolete French from Latin *prominentia* 'jutting out' (as PROMINENT)]

prominent /'prɒmɪnənt/ *adj.* & *n.* ● *adj.* **1** jutting out; projecting. **2** conspicuous. **3** distinguished; important. ● *n.* (in full **prominent moth**) a moth of the family Notodontidae, with tufted forewings and larvae with humped backs. □ **prominently** *adv.* [Latin *prominēre* 'jut out': cf. EMINENT]

prominenti /prɒmɪ'nɛnti, Italian promi'nɛnti/ *n.pl.* distinguished or eminent people. [Italian, from *prominente* 'prominent']

promiscuous /prə'mɪskjʊəs/ *adj.* **1 a** (of a person) having frequent and diverse sexual relationships, esp. transient ones. **b** (of sexual relationships) of this kind. **2** of mixed and indiscriminate composition or kinds; indiscriminate (*promiscuous hospitality*). **3** *colloq.* carelessly irregular; casual. □ **promiscuity** /prɒmɪ'skjuːɪti/ *n.* **promiscuously** *adv.* **promiscuousness** *n.* [Latin *promiscuus* (as PRO-[1], *miscēre* 'mix')]

promise /'prɒmɪs/ *n.* & *v.* ● *n.* **1** an assurance that one will or will not undertake a certain action, behaviour, etc. (*a promise of help*; *gave a promise to be generous*). **2** a sign or signs of future achievements, good results, etc. (*a writer of great promise*). ● *v.tr.* **1** (usu. foll. by *to* + infin., or *that* + clause; also *absol.*) make (a person) a promise, esp. to do, give, or procure (a thing) (*I promise you a fair hearing*; *they promise not to be late*; *promised that he would be there*; *cannot positively promise*). **2 a** afford expectations of (*the discussions promise future problems*; *promises to be a good cook*). **b** (foll. by *to* + infin.) seem likely to (*is promising to rain*). **3** *colloq.* assure, confirm (*I promise you, it will not be easy*). **4** (usu. in *passive*) *archaic* betroth (*she is promised to another*). □ **promise oneself** look forward to (a pleasant time etc.). **promise well** (or **ill** etc.) hold out good (or bad etc.) prospects. □ **promisee** /-'siː/ *n.* esp. *Law.* **promiser** *n.* **promisor** *n.* esp. *Law.* [Middle English from Latin *promissum*, neut. past part. of *promittere* 'put forth, promise' (as PRO-[1], *mittere* 'send')]

promised land *n.* (prec. by *the*) **1** *Bibl.* Canaan (Gen. 12:7 etc.). **2 a** any place where happiness is expected, esp. heaven. **b** any coveted situation (*a promised land of economic freedom*).

promising /'prɒmɪsɪŋ/ *adj.* likely to turn out well; hopeful; full of promise (*a promising start*). □ **promisingly** *adv.*

promissory /'prɒmɪs(ə)ri/ *adj.* **1** conveying or implying a promise. **2** (often foll. by *of*) full of promise. [medieval Latin *promissorius* from Latin *promissor* (as PROMISE)]

promissory note *n.* a signed document containing a written promise to pay a stated sum to a specified person or the bearer at a specified date or on demand.

prommer /'prɒmə/ *n. colloq.* a person who attends a promenade concert.

promo /'prəʊməʊ/ *n.* & *adj. colloq.* ● *n.* (*pl.* **-os**) **1** publicity, advertising. **2** a trailer for a television programme. ● *adj.* promotional. [abbreviation]

promontory /'prɒm(ə)nt(ə)ri/ *n.* (*pl.* **-ies**) **1** a point of high land jutting out into the sea etc.; a headland. **2** *Anat.* a prominence or protuberance in the body. [medieval Latin *promontorium*, alteration (influenced by *mons montis* 'mountain') from Latin *promunturium* (perhaps from PRO-[1], *mons*)]

promote /prə'məʊt/ *v.tr.* **1** (often foll. by *to*) **a** advance or raise (a person) to a higher office, rank, etc. (*was promoted to captain*). **b** transfer (a sports team) to a higher division of a league etc. **2** help forward; encourage; support actively (a cause, process, desired result, etc.) (*promoted women's suffrage*). **3** publicize and sell (a product). **4** attempt to ensure the passing of (a private Act of Parliament). **5** *Chess* raise (a pawn) to the rank of queen etc. when it reaches the opponent's end of the board. □ **promotable** *adj.* **promotability** /-'bɪlɪti/ *n.* **promotion** /-'məʊʃ(ə)n/ *n.* **promotional** /-'məʊʃ(ə)n(ə)l/ *adj.* **promotive** *adj.* [Middle English from Latin *promovēre promot-* (as PRO-[1], *movēre* 'move')]

promoter /prə'məʊtə/ *n.* **1** a person who promotes. **2** a person who finances, organizes, etc. a sporting event, theatrical production, etc. **3** (in full **company promoter**) a person who promotes the formation of a joint-stock company. **4** *Chem.* an additive that increases the activity of a catalyst. [earlier *promotour*, via Anglo-French from medieval Latin *promotor* (as PROMOTE)]

prompt /prɒm(p)t/ *adj., adv., v., & n.* ● *adj.* **1 a** acting with alacrity; ready. **b** made, done, etc. readily or at once (*a prompt reply*). **2 a** (of a payment) made forthwith. **b** (of goods) for immediate delivery and payment. ● *adv. Brit.* punctually (*at six o'clock prompt*). ● *v.tr.* **1** (usu. foll. by *to*, or *to* + infin.) incite; urge (*prompted them to action*). **2 a** (also *absol.*) supply a forgotten word, sentence, etc., to (an actor, reciter, etc.). **b** assist (a hesitating speaker) with a suggestion. **3** give rise to; inspire (a feeling, thought, action, etc.). ● *n.* **1 a** an act of prompting. **b** something spoken said to help the memory of an actor etc. **c** = PROMPTER 2. **d** *Computing* an indication or sign on a VDU screen to show that the system is waiting for input. **2** the time limit for the payment of an account, stated on a promot-note □ **prompting** *n.* **promptitude** *n.* **promptly** *adv.* **promptness** *n.* [Middle English from Old French *prompt* or Latin *promptus*, past part. of *promere prompt-* 'produce' (as PRO-[1], *emere* 'take')]

prompt book *n.* a copy of a play for a prompter's use.

prompt box *n.* a box in front of the footlights beneath the stage where the prompter sits.

prompter /ˈprɒm(p)tə/ *n.* **1** a person who prompts. **2** *Theatr.* a person seated out of sight of the audience who prompts the actors.

prompt-note *n.* a note sent to a customer as a reminder of payment due.

prompt side *n.* the side of the stage where the prompter sits, usu. to the actor's left in the UK but to the actor's right in the US.

promulgate /ˈprɒm(ə)lgeɪt/ *v.tr.* **1** make known to the public; disseminate; promote (a cause etc.). **2** proclaim (a decree, news, etc.). □ **promulgation** /-ˈgeɪʃ(ə)n/ *n.* **promulgator** *n.* [Latin *promulgare* (as PRO-[1], *mulgēre* 'milk, cause to come forth')]

promulge /prəˈmʌldʒ/ *v.tr. archaic* = PROMULGATE. [PROMULGATE]

pronaos /prəʊˈneɪɒs/ *n.* (*pl.* **pronaoi** /-ˈneɪɔɪ/) *Gk Antiq.* the space in front of the body of a temple, enclosed by a portico and projecting side walls. [Latin from Greek *pronaos* 'hall of a temple' (as PRO-[2], NAOS)]

pronate /ˈprəʊneɪt/ *v.tr.* put (the hand, forearm, etc.) into a prone position (with the palm etc. downwards) (cf. SUPINATE). □ **pronation** /-ˈneɪʃ(ə)n/ *n.* [back-formation from *pronation* (as PRONE)]

pronator /prəʊˈneɪtə/ *n. Anat.* any muscle producing or assisting in pronation.

prone /prəʊn/ *adj.* **1 a** lying face downwards (cf. SUPINE *adj.* 1). **b** lying flat; prostrate. **c** having the front part downwards, esp. the palm of the hand. **2** (usu. foll. by *to*, or *to* + infin.) disposed or liable, esp. to a bad action, condition, etc. (*is prone to bite his nails*). **3** (usu. in *comb.*) more than usually likely to suffer (*accident-prone*). **4** *archaic* with a downward slope or direction. □ **pronely** *adv.* **proneness** /ˈprəʊnnɪs/ *n.* [Middle English from Latin *pronus*, from *pro* 'forwards']

■ **Usage** *Prone* in sense 2 means the same as *liable*, but is usually used with a person as its subject.

proneur /prəʊˈnəː, French prɔnœr/ *n.* a person who extols; a flatterer. [French *prôneur*, via *prôner* 'eulogize' from *prône*, a place in church where addresses were delivered]

prong /prɒŋ/ *n. & v.* ● *n.* each of two or more projecting pointed parts at the end of a fork etc. ● *v.tr.* **1** pierce or stab with a fork. **2** turn up (soil) with a fork. □ **pronged** *adj.* (also in *comb.*). [Middle English (also *prang*), perhaps related to Middle Low German *prange* 'pinching instrument']

pronghorn /ˈprɒŋhɔːn/ *n.* (also **prong-horned antelope**) a N. American deerlike ruminant, *Antilocapra americana*, the male of which has horns with forward-pointing prongs.

pronominal /prəʊˈnɒmɪn(ə)l/ *adj.* of, relating to, or serving as, a pronoun. □ **pronominalize** *v.tr.* (also **-ise**). **pronominally** *adv.* [Late Latin *pronominalis* from Latin *pronomen* (as PRO-[1], *nomen, nominis* 'noun')]

pronoun /ˈprəʊnaʊn/ *n.* a word used instead of and to indicate a noun already mentioned or known, esp. to avoid repetition (e.g. *we, their, this, ourselves*). [PRO-[1], + NOUN, suggested by French *pronom*, Latin *pronomen* (as PRO-[1], *nomen* 'name')]

pronounce /prəˈnaʊns/ *v.* **1** *tr.* (also *absol.*) utter or speak (words, sounds, etc.) in a certain way. **2** *tr.* **a** utter or deliver (a judgement, sentence, curse, etc.) formally or solemnly. **b** proclaim or announce officially (*I pronounce you man and wife*). **3** *tr.* state or declare, as being one's opinion (*the apples were pronounced excellent*). **4** *intr.* (usu. foll. by *on, for, against, in favour of*) pass judgement; give one's opinion (*pronounced for the defendant*). □ **pronounceable** /-səb(ə)l/ *adj.* **pronounceability** /-səˈbɪlɪti/ *n.* **pronouncement** *n.* **pronouncer** *n.* [Middle English via Old French *pronuncier* from Latin *pronuntiare* (as PRO-[1], *nuntiare* 'announce' from *nuntius* 'messenger')]

pronounced /prəˈnaʊnst/ *adj.* **1** (of a word, sound, etc.) uttered. **2** strongly marked; decided (*a pronounced flavour*; *a pronounced limp*). □ **pronouncedly** /-ˈnaʊnsɪdli/ *adv.*

pronto /ˈprɒntəʊ/ *adv. colloq.* promptly, quickly. [Spanish from Latin (as PROMPT)]

pronunciation /prənʌnsɪˈeɪʃ(ə)n/ *n.* **1** the way in which a word is pronounced, esp. with reference to a standard. **2** the act or an instance of pronouncing. **3** a person's way of pronouncing words etc. [Middle English from Old French *prononciation* or Latin *pronuntiatio* (as PRONOUNCE)]

■ **Usage** *Pronunciation* is often pronounced with the sound /naʊns/ (rhyming with *bounce*) instead of /nʌns/ (rhyming with *dunce*) in the second syllable, as if it were spelt like *pronounce*. This should be avoided.

pro-nuncio /prəʊˈnʌnsɪəʊ, -ʃɪəʊ/ *n.* (*pl.* **-os**) a papal ambassador to a country which does not accord the Pope's ambassador automatic precedence. [PRO-[1] + NUNCIO]

proof /pruːf/ *n., adj., & v.* ● *n.* **1** facts, evidence, argument, etc. establishing or helping to establish a fact (*proof of their honesty*; *no proof that he was there*). **2** *Law* the spoken or written evidence in a trial. **3** a demonstration or act of proving (*not capable of proof*; *in proof of my assertion*). **4** a test or trial (*put them to the proof*; *the proof of the pudding is in the eating*). **5** the standard of strength of distilled alcoholic liquors. **6** *Printing* a trial impression taken from type or film, used for making corrections before final printing. **7** the stages in the resolution of a mathematical or philosophical problem. **8** each of a limited number of impressions from an engraved plate before the ordinary issue is printed and usu. (in full **proof before letters**) before an inscription or signature is added. **9** a photographic print made for selection etc. **10** *Sc. Law* a trial before a judge instead of by a jury. **11** any of various preliminary impressions of coins struck as specimens. ● *adj.* **1** impervious to penetration, ill effects, etc. (*proof against the severest weather*; *his soul is proof against corruption*). **2** (*in comb.*) able to withstand damage or destruction by a specified agent (*soundproof*; *childproof*). **3** being of proof alcoholic strength. **4** (of armour) of tried strength. ● *v.tr.* **1** make (something) proof, esp. make (fabric) waterproof. **2** make a proof of (a printed work, engraving, etc.). □ **above proof** (of alcohol) having a stronger than standard strength. □ **proofless** *adj.* [Middle English *prōf prōve*, earlier *prēf* etc., via Old French *proeve, prueve* and Late Latin *proba* from Latin *probare* (see PROVE): the adjective and sometimes the verb formed apparently by ellipsis from the phrase *of proof* = proved to be impenetrable]

proof-plane *n.* a small flat conductor on an insulating handle for measuring the electrification of a body.

proof positive *n.* absolutely certain proof.

proof-read *v.tr.* (*past* and *past part.* **-read** /-rɛd/) read (printer's proofs) and mark any errors. □ **proof-reader** *n.* **proof-reading** *n.*

proof-sheet *n.* a sheet of printer's proof.

proof spirit *n.* a mixture of alcohol and water having proof strength.

prop[1] /prɒp/ *n.* & *v.* ● *n.* **1** a rigid support, esp. one not an integral part of the thing supported. **2** a person who supplies support, assistance, comfort, etc. **3** (in full **prop forward**) *Rugby* a forward at either end of the front row of a scrum. **4** esp. *Austral.* a horse's action of propping. ● *v.* (**propped**, **propping**) **1** *tr.* (often foll. by *against*, *up*, etc.) support with or as if with a prop (*propped him against the wall*; *propped it up with a brick*). **2** *intr.* esp. *Austral.* (of a horse etc.) come to a dead stop with the forelegs rigid. [Middle English, probably from Middle Dutch *proppe*]

prop[2] /prɒp/ *n. Theatr. colloq.* **1** = PROPERTY 3. **2** (in *pl.*) a property man or mistress. [abbreviation]

prop[3] /prɒp/ *n. colloq.* an aircraft propeller. [abbreviation]

prop. *abbr.* **1** proprietor. **2** proposition.

propaedeutic /prəʊpiːˈdjuːtɪk/ *adj.* & *n.* ● *adj.* serving as an introduction to higher study; introductory. ● *n.* (esp. in *pl.*) preliminary learning; a propaedeutic subject, study, etc. □ **propaedeutical** *adj.* [PRO-[2] + Greek *paideutikos* 'of teaching', suggested by Greek *propaideuō* 'teach beforehand']

propaganda /prɒpəˈgandə/ *n.* **1 a** an organized programme of publicity, selected information, etc., used to propagate a doctrine, practice, etc. **b** usu. *derog.* the information, doctrines, etc., propagated in this way, esp. regarded as misleading or dishonest. **2** (**Propaganda**) *RC Ch.* a committee of cardinals responsible for foreign missions. [Italian from modern Latin *congregatio de propaganda fide* 'congregation for propagation of the faith']

propagandist /prɒpəˈgandɪst/ *n.* & *adj.* ● *n.* a member or agent of a propaganda organization; a person who spreads propaganda. ● *adj.* consisting of or spreading propaganda. □ **propagandism** *n.* **propagandistic** /-ˈdɪstɪk/ *adj.* **propagandistically** /-ˈdɪstɪk(ə)li/ *adv.* **propagandize** *v.intr.* & *tr.* (also **-ise**).

propagate /ˈprɒpəgeɪt/ *v.tr.* **1 a** breed specimens of (a plant, animal, etc.) by natural processes from the parent stock. **b** (*refl.* or *absol.*) (of a plant, animal, etc.) reproduce itself. **2** disseminate; spread (a statement, belief, theory, etc.). **3** hand down (a quality etc.) from one generation to another. **4** extend the operation of; transmit (a vibration, earthquake, etc.). □ **propagation** /-ˈgeɪʃ(ə)n/ *n.* **propagative** *adj.* [Latin *propagare propagat-* 'multiply plants from layers', from *propago* (as PRO-[1], *pangere* 'fix, layer')]

propagator /ˈprɒpəgeɪtə/ *n.* **1** a person or thing that propagates. **2** a small box that can be heated, used for germinating seeds or raising seedlings.

propane /ˈprəʊpeɪn/ *n.* a gaseous hydrocarbon of the alkane series used as bottled fuel. Chem. formula: C_3H_8. [PROPIONIC ACID + -ANE[2]]

propanoic acid /prəʊpəˈnəʊɪk/ *n. Chem.* = PROPIONIC ACID. □ **propanoate** /prəˈpanəʊeɪt/ *n.* [PROPANE + -IC]

propanone /ˈprəʊpənəʊn/ *n. Chem.* = ACETONE. [PROPANE + -ONE]

propel /prəˈpɛl/ *v.tr.* (**propelled**, **propelling**) **1** drive or push forward. **2** urge on; encourage. [Middle English, = expel, from Latin *propellere* (as PRO-[1], *pellere puls-* 'drive')]

propellant /prəˈpɛl(ə)nt/ *n.* & *adj.* ● *n.* **1** a thing that propels. **2** an inert compressed fluid in which the active contents of an aerosol are dispersed. **3** an explosive that fires bullets etc. from a firearm. **4** a substance used as a reagent in a rocket engine etc. to provide thrust. ● *adj.* = PROPELLENT.

propellent /prəˈpɛl(ə)nt/ *adj.* propelling; capable of driving or pushing forward.

propeller /prəˈpɛlə/ *n.* **1** a person or thing that propels. **2** a revolving shaft with blades, esp. for propelling a ship or aircraft (cf. *screw propeller*).

propeller shaft *n. Brit.* a shaft transmitting power from an engine to a propeller or to the driven wheels of a motor vehicle.

propeller turbine *n.* = TURBOPROP.

propelling pencil *n. Brit.* a pencil with a replaceable lead moved upward by twisting the outer case.

propene /ˈprəʊpiːn/ *n. Chem.* = PROPYLENE. [PROPANE + ALKENE]

propensity /prəˈpɛnsɪti/ *n.* (*pl.* **-ies**) an inclination or tendency (*has a propensity for wandering*). [*propense* from Latin *propensus* 'inclined', past part. of *propendēre* (as PRO-[1], *pendēre* 'hang')]

proper /ˈprɒpə/ *adj.*, *adv.*, & *n.* ● *adj.* **1 a** accurate, correct (*in the proper sense of the word*; *gave him the proper amount*). **b** fit, suitable, right (*at the proper time*; *do it the proper way*). **2** decent; respectable, esp. excessively so (*not quite proper*). **3** (usu. foll. by *to*) belonging or relating exclusively or distinctively (*with the respect proper to them*). **4** (usu. placed after noun) strictly so called; real; genuine (*this is the crypt, not the cathedral proper*). **5** esp. *Brit. colloq.* thorough; complete (*had a proper row about it*). **6** *Eccl.* (of a psalm, lesson, prayer, etc.) appointed for a particular day, occasion, or season. **7** (usu. placed after noun) *Heraldry* in the natural, not conventional, colours (*a peacock proper*). **8** *archaic* (of a person) handsome; comely. **9** (usu. with possessive pronoun) *archaic* own (*with my proper eyes*). ● *adv. Brit. dial.* or *colloq.* **1** completely; very (*felt proper daft*). **2** (with reference to speech) in a genteel manner (*learn to talk proper*). ● *n. Eccl.* the part of a service that varies with the season or feast. □ **properness** *n.* [Middle English via Old French *propre* from Latin *proprius* 'one's own, special']

proper fraction *n.* a fraction that is less than unity, with the numerator less than the denominator.

properly /ˈprɒp(ə)li/ *adv.* **1** fittingly; suitably (*do it properly*). **2** accurately; correctly (*properly speaking*). **3** rightly (*he very properly refused*). **4** with decency; respectably (*behave properly*). **5** esp. *Brit. colloq.* thoroughly (*they were properly ashamed*).

proper motion *n. Astron.* the part of the apparent motion of a fixed star etc. that is due to its actual movement in space relative to the sun.

proper name *n.* (also **proper noun**) *Gram.* a name used for an individual person, place, animal, country, title, etc., and spelt with a capital letter, e.g. Jane, London, Everest.

proper pride see PRIDE *n.* 3.

propertied /ˈprɒpətɪd/ *adj.* having property, esp. land.

property /ˈprɒpəti/ *n.* (*pl.* **-ies**) **1 a** something owned; a possession, esp. a house, land, etc. **b** *Law* the right to possession, use, etc. **c** possessions collectively, esp. real estate (*has money in property*). **2** an attribute, quality, or characteristic (*has the property of dissolving grease*). **3** a movable object used on a theatre stage, in a film, etc. **4** *Logic* a quality common to a whole class but not necessary to distinguish it from others. [Middle English via Anglo-French from Old French *propriété*, from Latin *proprietas -tatis* (as PROPER)]

property man *n.* (*fem.* **property mistress**) a man (or woman) in charge of theatrical properties.

property qualification *n.* a qualification for office, or for the exercise of a right, based on the possession of property.

property tax *n.* a tax levied directly on property.

prop forward see PROP[1] *n.* 3.

prophase /ˈprəʊfeɪz/ *n. Biol.* the phase in cell division in which chromosomes contract and each becomes visible as two chromatids. [PRO-[2] + PHASE]

prophecy /ˈprɒfɪsi/ *n.* (*pl.* **-ies**) **1 a** a prophetic utterance, esp. biblical. **b** a prediction of future events (*a prophecy of massive inflation*). **2** the faculty, function, or practice of prophesying (*the gift of prophecy*). [Middle

English via Old French *profecie* and Late Latin *prophetia* from Greek *prophēteia* (as PROPHET)]

prophesy /ˈprɒfɪsʌɪ/ *v.* (**-ies**, **-ied**) **1** *tr.* (usu. foll. by *that, who*, etc.) foretell (an event etc.). **2** *intr.* speak as a prophet; foretell future events. **3** *intr. archaic* expound the Scriptures. □ **prophesier** /-sʌɪə/ *n.* [Middle English from Old French *profecier* (as PROPHECY)]

prophet /ˈprɒfɪt/ *n.* (*fem.* **prophetess** /-tɪs/) **1** a teacher or interpreter of the supposed will of God, esp. any of the Old Testament or Hebrew prophets. **2 a** a person who foretells events. **b** a person who advocates and speaks innovatively for a cause (*a prophet of the new order*). **3** (**the Prophet**) **a** Muhammad. **b** Joseph Smith, founder of the Mormons, or one of his successors. **4** (**the Prophets**) **a** the prophetic writings of the Old Testament. **b** one of the three canonical divisions of the Hebrew Bible (cf. LAW *n.* 12b, WRITING 4). **5** *colloq.* a tipster. □ **prophethood** *n.* **prophetism** *n.* [Middle English via Old French *prophete* and Latin *propheta, prophetes* from Greek *prophētēs* 'spokesman' (as PRO-[2], *phētēs* 'speaker' from *phēmi* 'speak')]

prophetic /prəˈfɛtɪk/ *adj.* **1** (often foll. by *of*) containing a prediction; predicting. **2** of or concerning a prophet. □ **prophetical** *adj.* **prophetically** *adv.* [French *prophétique* or Late Latin *propheticus* from Greek *prophētikos* (as PROPHET)]

prophylactic /prɒfɪˈlaktɪk/ *adj. & n.* ● *adj.* tending to prevent disease. ● *n.* **1** a preventive medicine or course of action. **2** esp. *N. Amer.* a condom. [French *prophylactique* from Greek *prophulaktikos*, from *prophulassō* (as PRO-[2], *phulassō* 'guard')]

prophylaxis /prɒfɪˈlaksɪs/ *n.* preventive treatment against disease. [modern Latin, from PRO-[2] + Greek *phulaxis* 'act of guarding']

propinquity /prəˈpɪŋkwɪti/ *n.* **1** nearness in space; proximity. **2** close kinship. **3** similarity. [Middle English from Old French *propinquité* or Latin *propinquitas*, via *propinquus* 'near' from *prope* 'near to']

propionic acid /prəʊpɪˈɒnɪk/ *n.* a colourless sharp-smelling liquid carboxylic acid used for inhibiting the growth of mould in bread (also called *propanoic acid*). Chem. formula: C_2H_5COOH. □ **propionate** /ˈprəʊpɪəneɪt/ *n.* [French *propionique* (as PRO-[2] + Greek *piōn* 'fat'), as being the first member of the fatty acid series to form fats]

propitiate /prəˈpɪʃɪeɪt/ *v.tr.* appease (an offended person etc.). □ **propitiator** *n.* [Latin *propitiare* (as PROPITIOUS)]

propitiation /prəpɪʃɪˈeɪʃ(ə)n/ *n.* **1** appeasement. **2** *Bibl.* atonement, esp. Christ's. **3** *archaic* a gift etc. meant to propitiate. [Middle English from Late Latin *propitiatio* (as PROPITIATE)]

propitiatory /prəˈpɪʃɪət(ə)ri/ *adj.* serving or intended to propitiate (*a propitiatory smile*). □ **propitiatorily** *adv.* [Middle English from Late Latin *propitiatorius* (as PROPITIATE)]

propitious /prəˈpɪʃəs/ *adj.* **1** (of an omen etc.) favourable. **2** (often foll. by *for, to*) (of the weather, an occasion, etc.) suitable. **3** well disposed (*the fates were propitious*). □ **propitiously** *adv.* **propitiousness** *n.* [Middle English from Old French *propicieus* or Latin *propitius*]

prop-jet *n.* a turboprop.

propolis /ˈprɒp(ə)lɪs/ *n.* a red or brown resinous substance collected by bees from buds for use in constructing hives. [Latin from Greek *propolis* 'suburb, bee-glue', from PRO-[2] + *polis* 'city']

proponent /prəˈpəʊnənt/ *n. & adj.* ● *n.* a person advocating a motion, theory, or proposal. ● *adj.* proposing or advocating a theory etc. [Latin *proponere* (as PROPOUND)]

proportion /prəˈpɔːʃ(ə)n/ *n. & v.* ● *n.* **1 a** a comparative part or share (*a large proportion of the profits*). **b** a comparative ratio (*the proportion of births to deaths*). **2** the correct or pleasing relation of things or parts of a thing (*the house has fine proportions; exaggerated out of all proportion*). **3** (in *pl.*) dimensions; size (*large proportions*). **4** *Math.* **a** an equality of ratios between two pairs of quantities, e.g. 3:5 and 9:15. **b** a set of such quantities. **c** *Math.* = RULE OF THREE. See also DIRECT PROPORTION, INVERSE PROPORTION. ● *v.tr.* (usu. foll. by *to*) make (a thing etc.) proportionate (*must proportion the punishment to the crime*). □ **in proportion 1** by the same factor. **2** without exaggerating (importance etc.) (*must get the facts in proportion*). □ **proportioned** *adj.* (also in *comb.*). **proportionless** *adj.* **proportionment** *n.* [Middle English from Old French *proportion* or Latin *proportio* (as PRO-[1], PORTION)]

■ **Usage** *Proportion* as a noun means 'comparative share or part' (see sense 1); it should not be used as a mere synonym for *part*.

---

proportionable /prəˈpɔːʃ(ə)nəb(ə)l/ *adj.* = PROPORTIONAL. □ **proportionably** *adv.*

proportional /prəˈpɔːʃ(ə)n(ə)l/ *adj. & n.* ● *adj.* in due proportion; comparable (*a proportional increase in the expense; resentment proportional to his injuries*). ● *n.* *Math.* each of the terms of a proportion. □ **proportionality** /-ˈnalɪti/ *n.* **proportionally** *adv.*

proportionalist /prəˈpɔːʃ(ə)n(ə)lɪst/ *n.* an advocate of proportional representation.

proportional representation *n.* an electoral system in which all parties gain seats in proportion to the number of votes cast for them.

proportionate /prəˈpɔːʃ(ə)nət/ *adj.* = PROPORTIONAL. □ **proportionately** *adv.*

proposal /prəˈpəʊz(ə)l/ *n.* **1 a** the act or an instance of proposing something. **b** a course of action etc. so proposed (*the proposal was never carried out*). **2** an offer of marriage.

propose /prəˈpəʊz/ *v.* **1** *tr.* (also *absol.*) put forward for consideration or as a plan. **2** *tr.* (usu. foll. by *to* + infin., or verbal noun) intend; purpose (*propose to open a restaurant*). **3** *intr.* (usu. foll. by *to*) offer oneself in marriage. **4** *tr.* nominate (a person) as a member of a society, for an office, etc. **5** *tr.* offer (a person's health, a person, etc.) as a subject for a toast. □ **proposer** *n.* [Middle English via Old French *proposer* from Latin *proponere* (as PROPOUND)]

proposition /prɒpəˈzɪʃ(ə)n/ *n. & v.* ● *n.* **1** a statement or assertion. **2** a scheme proposed; a proposal. **3** *Logic* a statement consisting of subject and predicate that is subject to proof or disproof. **4** *colloq.* a problem, opponent, prospect, etc. that is to be dealt with (*a difficult proposition*). **5** *Math.* a formal statement of a theorem or problem, often including the demonstration. **6 a** an enterprise etc. with regard to its likelihood of commercial etc. success. **b** a person regarded similarly. **7** *colloq.* a sexual proposal. ● *v.tr. colloq.* make a proposal (esp. of sexual intercourse) to. □ **not a proposition** unlikely to succeed. □ **propositional** *adj.* [Middle English from Old French *proposition* or Latin *propositio* (as PROPOUND)]

propound /prəˈpaʊnd/ *v.tr.* **1** offer for consideration; propose. **2** *Law* produce (a will etc.) before the proper authority so as to establish its legality. □ **propounder** *n.* [earlier *propoune, propone* from Latin *proponere* (as PRO-[1], *ponere posit-* 'place'): cf. *compound, expound*]

proprietary /prəˈprʌɪət(ə)ri/ *adj.* **1 a** of, holding, or concerning property (*the proprietary classes*). **b** of or relating to a proprietor (*proprietary rights*). **2** held in private ownership. **3** (of a product, esp. a drug or medicine) marketed under and protected by a registered trade name. [Late Latin *proprietarius* (as PROPERTY)]

proprietary name *n.* (also **proprietary term**) a name of a product etc. registered by its owner as a trade mark and not usable by another without permission.

proprietor /prəˈprʌɪətə/ *n.* (*fem.* **proprietress** /-trɪs/) **1** a holder of property. **2** the owner of a business etc. □ **proprietorial** /-ˈtɔːrɪəl/ *adj.* **proprietorially** /-ˈtɔːrɪəli/ *adv.* **proprietorship** *n.*

propriety /prəˈprʌɪəti/ *n.* (*pl.* **-ies**) **1** fitness; rightness (*doubt the propriety of refusing him*). **2** correctness of behaviour or morals (*highest standards of propriety*). **3**

(in *pl.*) the details or rules of correct conduct (*must observe the proprieties*). [Middle English, = ownership, peculiarity, from Old French *propriētē* PROPERTY]

proprioceptive /ˌprəʊprɪə(ʊ)ˈsɛptɪv/ *adj.* relating to stimuli produced and perceived within an organism, esp. relating to the position and movement of the body. [Latin *proprius* 'own' + RECEPTIVE]

proptosis /prɒpˈtəʊsɪs/ *n. Med.* protrusion or displacement, esp. of an eye. [Late Latin from Greek *proptōsis* (as PRO-², *piptō* 'fall')]

propulsion /prəˈpʌlʃ(ə)n/ *n.* **1** the act or an instance of driving or pushing forward. **2** *archaic* an impelling influence; an impulse. ▫ **propulsive** /-ˈpʌlsɪv/ *adj.* [medieval Latin *propulsio* from Latin *propellere* (as PROPEL)]

propyl /ˈprəʊpʌɪl, -pɪl/ *n.* (usu. *attrib.*) *Chem.* the monovalent radical of propane, C_3H_7–. [PROPIONIC ACID + -YL]

propyla *pl.* of PROPYLON.

propylaeum /prɒpɪˈliːəm/ *n.* (*pl.* **propylaea** /-ˈliːə/) **1** the entrance to a temple. **2** (**the Propylaeum**) the entrance to the Acropolis at Athens. [Latin from Greek *propulaion* (as PRO-², *pulē* 'gate')]

propylene /ˈprəʊpɪliːn/ *n. Chem.* a gaseous hydrocarbon of the alkene series used in the manufacture of chemicals. Chem. formula: C_3H_6.

propylon /ˈprɒpɪlɒn/ *n.* (*pl.* **propylons** or **propyla** /-lə/) = PROPYLAEUM. [Latin from Greek *propulon* (as PRO-², *pulē* 'gate')]

pro rata /prəʊ ˈrɑːtə, ˈreɪtə/ *adj.* & *adv.* ● *adj.* proportional. ● *adv.* proportionally. [Latin, = according to the rate]

prorate /prəʊˈreɪt, ˈprəʊ-/ *v.tr.* allocate or distribute pro rata. ▫ **proration** *n.*

prorogue /prə(ʊ)ˈrəʊg/ *v.* (**prorogues**, **prorogued**, **proroguing**) **1** *tr.* discontinue the meetings of (a parliament etc.) without dissolving it. **2** *intr.* (of a parliament etc.) be prorogued. ▫ **prorogation** /-rəˈgeɪʃ(ə)n/ *n.* [Middle English *proroge* via Old French *proroger*, *-guer* from Latin *prorogare* 'prolong' (as PRO-¹, *rogare* 'ask')]

pros- /prɒs/ *prefix* **1** to, towards. **2** in addition. [Greek from *pros* (prep.)]

prosaic /prə(ʊ)ˈzeɪɪk/ *adj.* **1** like prose, lacking poetic beauty. **2** unromantic; dull; commonplace (*took a prosaic view of life*). ▫ **prosaically** *adv.* **prosaicness** *n.* [French *prosaïque* or Late Latin *prosaicus* (as PROSE)]

prosaist /ˈprəʊzeɪɪst/ *n.* **1** a prose-writer. **2** a prosaic person. ▫ **prosaism** *n.* [French *prosaïste* from Latin *prosa* PROSE]

pros and cons *n.pl.* reasons or considerations for and against a proposition etc.

proscenium /prə(ʊ)ˈsiːnɪəm/ *n.* (*pl.* **prosceniums** or **proscenia** /-nɪə/) **1** the part of the stage in front of the drop or curtain, usu. with the enclosing arch. **2** the stage of an ancient theatre. [Latin from Greek *proskēnion* (as PRO-², *skēnē* 'stage')]

prosciutto /prəʊˈʃuːtəʊ/ *n.* Italian ham, esp. raw and eaten as an hors d'oeuvre. [Italian]

proscribe /prə(ʊ)ˈskrʌɪb/ *v.tr.* **1** forbid, esp. by law (*proscribed drugs*). **2** reject or denounce (a practice etc.) as unwanted or dangerous. **3** esp. *hist.* outlaw (a person). ▫ **proscription** /-ˈskrɪpʃ(ə)n/ *n.* **proscriptive** /-ˈskrɪptɪv/ *adj.* [Latin *proscribere* (as PRO-¹, *scribere script-* 'write')]

■ **Usage** See Usage Note at PRESCRIBE.

prose /prəʊz/ *n.* & *v.* ● *n.* **1** the ordinary form of the written or spoken language (opp. POETRY 2, VERSE *n.* 1a) (also *attrib.*: *Milton's prose works*). **2** a passage of prose, esp. for translation into a foreign language. **3 a** dull or commonplace speech, writing, etc. **b** an instance of this. **4** a plain matter-of-fact quality (*the prose of existence*). **5** *Eccl.* = SEQUENCE 8. ● *v.* **1** *intr.* (usu. foll. by *about*, *away*, etc.) talk tediously (*was prosing away about his dog*). **2** *tr.* turn (a poem etc.) into prose. ▫ **proser** *n.* [Middle English via Old French from Latin *prosa* (*oratio*) 'straightforward (discourse)', fem. of *prosus*, earlier *prorsus* 'direct']

prosector /prə(ʊ)ˈsɛktə/ *n.* esp. *hist.* a person who dissects dead bodies in preparation for an anatomical lecture etc. [Late Latin = anatomist, from *prosecare prosect-* (as PRO-¹, *secare* 'cut'), perhaps influenced by French *prosecteur*]

prosecute /ˈprɒsɪkjuːt/ *v.tr.* **1** (also *absol.*) **a** institute legal proceedings against (a person). **b** institute legal proceedings with reference to (a claim, crime, action, etc.) (*right to prosecute his own action*). **2** follow up, pursue (an inquiry, studies, etc.). **3** carry on (a trade, pursuit, etc.). ▫ **prosecutable** *adj.* [Middle English from Latin *prosequi prosecut-* (as PRO-¹, *sequi* 'follow')]

prosecution /prɒsɪˈkjuːʃ(ə)n/ *n.* **1 a** the institution and carrying on of a criminal charge in a court. **b** the carrying on of legal proceedings against a person. **c** the prosecuting party in a court case (*the prosecution denied this*). **2** the act or an instance of prosecuting (*met her in the prosecution of his hobby*). [Old French *prosecution* or Late Latin *prosecutio* (as PROSECUTE)]

prosecutor /ˈprɒsɪkjuːtə/ *n.* (*fem.* **prosecutrix** /-trɪks/) a person who prosecutes, esp. in a criminal court. ▫ **prosecutorial** /-ˈtɔːrɪəl/ *adj.*

prose idyll *n.* a short description in prose of a picturesque, esp. rustic, incident, character, etc.

proselyte /ˈprɒsɪlʌɪt/ *n.* & *v.* ● *n.* **1** a person converted, esp. recently, from one opinion, creed, party, etc., to another. **2** a Gentile convert to Judaism. ● *v.tr. US* = PROSELYTIZE. ▫ **proselytism** /-lɪtɪz(ə)m/ *n.* [Middle English via Late Latin *proselytus* from Greek *prosēluthos* 'stranger, convert' (as PROS-, *ēluth-*, stem of *erkhomai* 'come')]

proselytize /ˈprɒsɪlɪtʌɪz/ *v.tr.* (also **-ise**) (also *absol.*) convert (a person or people) from one belief etc. to another, esp. habitually. ▫ **proselytizer** *n.*

prosencephalon /prɒsɛnˈsɛfəlɒn, -ˈkɛf-/ *n. Anat.* = FOREBRAIN. [Greek *prosō* 'forwards' + ENCEPHALON]

prosenchyma /prɒˈsɛŋkɪmə/ *n.* a plant tissue of elongated cells with interpenetrating tapering ends, occurring esp. in vascular tissue. ▫ **prosenchymal** *adj.* **prosenchymatous** /-ˈkɪmətəs/ *adj.* [Greek *pros* 'toward' + *egkhuma* 'infusion', on the pattern of *parenchyma*]

prose poem *n.* (also **prose poetry**) a piece of imaginative poetic writing in prose.

prosify /ˈprəʊzɪfʌɪ/ *v.* (**-ies**, **-ied**) **1** *tr.* turn into prose. **2** *tr.* make prosaic. **3** *intr.* write prose.

prosimian /prəʊˈsɪmɪən/ *n.* & *adj. Zool.* ● *n.* a primitive primate of the suborder Prosimii, which includes lemurs, lorises, galagos, and tarsiers. ● *adj.* of or relating to this suborder. [PRO-² + SIMIAN]

prosit /ˈprəʊzɪt/ *int.* an expression used in drinking a person's health etc. [German from Latin, = may it benefit]

prosody /ˈprɒsədi/ *n.* **1** the theory and practice of versification; the laws of metre. **2** the study of speech rhythms. ▫ **prosodic** /prəˈsɒdɪk/ *adj.* **prosodist** *n.* [Middle English via Latin *prosodia* 'accent' from Greek *prosōidia* (as PROS-, ODE)]

prosopography /prɒsə(ʊ)ˈpɒgrəfi/ *n.* (*pl.* **-ies**) **1** a description of a person's appearance, personality, social and family connections, career, etc. **2** the study of such descriptions, esp. in Roman history. ▫ **prosopographer** *n.* **prosopographic** /-pəˈgrafɪk/ *adj.* **prosopographical** /-pəˈgrafɪk(ə)l/ *adj.* [modern Latin *prosopographia* (as Greek *prosōpon* 'face, person', -GRAPHY)]

prosopopoeia /prɒsəpəˈpiːə/ *n.* the rhetorical introduction of a pretended speaker or the personification of an abstract thing. [Latin from Greek *prosōpopoiia*, from *prosōpon* 'person' + *poieō* 'make']

prospect *n.* & *v.* ● *n.* /ˈprɒspɛkt/ **1 a** (often in *pl.*) an expectation, esp. of success in a career etc. (*his prospects were brilliant*; *offers a gloomy prospect*; *no prospect of success*). **b** something one has to look forward to (*don't relish the prospect of meeting him*). **2**

an extensive view of landscape etc. (*a striking prospect*). **3** a mental picture (*a new prospect in his mind*). **4** a possible or probable customer, subscriber, etc. **5 a** a place likely to yield mineral deposits. **b** a sample of ore for testing. **c** the resulting yield. ● *v.* /prəˈspɛkt/ **1** *intr.* (usu. foll. by *for*) **a** explore a region for gold etc. **b** look out for or search for something. **2** *tr.* **a** explore (a region) for gold etc. **b** work (a mine) experimentally. **c** (of a mine) promise (a specified yield). □ **prospect well** (or **ill** etc.) (of a mine) promise well (or ill etc.). □ **prospectless** *adj.* **prospector** /prəˈspɛktə/ *n.* [Middle English from Latin *prospectus*: see PROSPECTUS]

prospective /prəˈspɛktɪv/ *adj.* **1** concerned with or applying to the future (*implies a prospective obligation*) (cf. RETROSPECTIVE *adj.* 1). **2** some day to be; expected; future (*prospective bridegroom*). □ **prospectively** *adv.* **prospectiveness** *n.* [obsolete French *prospectif -ive* or Late Latin *prospectivus* (as PROSPECTUS)]

prospectus /prəˈspɛktəs/ *n.* (*pl.* **prospectuses**) a printed document advertising or describing a school, commercial enterprise, forthcoming book, etc. [Latin, = prospect, from *prospicere* (as PRO-[1], *specere* 'to look')]

prosper /ˈprɒspə/ *v.* **1** *intr.* succeed; thrive (*nothing he touches prospers*). **2** *tr.* make successful (*Heaven prosper him*). [Middle English from Old French *prosperer* or Latin *prosperare* (as PROSPEROUS)]

prosperity /prɒˈspɛrɪti/ *n.* a state of being prosperous; wealth or success.

prosperous /ˈprɒsp(ə)rəs/ *adj.* **1** successful; rich (*a prosperous merchant*). **2** flourishing; thriving (*a prosperous enterprise*). **3** auspicious (*a prosperous wind*). □ **prosperously** *adv.* **prosperousness** *n.* [Middle English via obsolete French *prospereus* from Latin *prosper(us)*]

prostaglandin /prɒstəˈglandɪn/ *n. Biochem.* any of a group of cyclic fatty acids with varying hormone-like effects in mammals, including the promotion of uterine contractions. [German (as PROSTATE + GLAND[1] + -IN)]

prostate /ˈprɒsteɪt/ *n.* (in full **prostate gland**) a gland surrounding the neck of the bladder in male mammals and releasing a fluid forming part of the semen. □ **prostatic** /-ˈstatɪk/ *adj.* [French via modern Latin *prostata* from Greek *prostatēs* 'one that stands before' (as PRO-[2], *statos* 'standing')]

prosthesis /ˈprɒsθɪsɪs, -ˈθiːsɪs/ *n.* (*pl.* **prostheses** /-siːz/) **1 a** an artificial part supplied to remedy a deficiency, e.g. a false breast, leg, tooth, etc. **b** the branch of surgery supplying and fitting prostheses. **2** *Gram.* the addition of a letter or syllable at the beginning of a word, e.g. *be-* in *beloved*. □ **prosthetic** /-ˈθɛtɪk/ *adj.* **prosthetically** /-ˈθɛtɪk(ə)li/ *adv.* [Late Latin from Greek *prosthesis* from *prostithēmi* (as PROS-, *tithēmi* 'place')]

prosthetics /prɒsˈθɛtɪks/ *n.pl.* (usu. treated as *sing.*) = PROSTHESIS 1b.

prostitute /ˈprɒstɪtjuːt/ *n.* & *v.* ● *n.* **1 a** a woman or girl who engages in sexual activity for payment. **b** (usu. **male prostitute**) a man or boy who engages in sexual activity, esp. with homosexual men, for payment. **2** a person who debases himself or herself for personal gain. ● *v.tr.* **1** (esp. *refl.*) make a prostitute of (esp. oneself). **2 a** misuse (one's talents, skills, etc.) for money. **b** offer (oneself, one's honour, etc.) for unworthy ends, esp. for money. □ **prostitution** /-ˈtjuːʃ(ə)n/ *n.* **prostitutor** *n.* [Latin *prostituere prostitut-* 'offer for sale' (as PRO-[1], *statuere* 'set up, place')]

prostrate *adj.* & *v.* ● *adj.* /ˈprɒstreɪt/ **1 a** lying face downwards, esp. in submission. **b** lying horizontally. **2** overcome, esp. by grief, exhaustion, etc. (*prostrate with self-pity*). **3** *Bot.* growing along the ground. ● *v.tr.* /prɒˈstreɪt/ **1** lay (a person etc.) flat on the ground. **2** (*refl.*) throw (oneself) down in submission etc. **3** (of fatigue, illness, etc.) overcome; reduce to extreme physical weakness. □ **prostration** /prɒˈstreɪʃ(ə)n/ *n.* [Middle English from Latin *prostratus*, past part. of *prosternere* (as PRO-[1], *sternere strat-* 'lay flat')]

prostyle /ˈprəʊstʌɪl/ *n.* & *adj.* ● *n.* a portico with not more than four columns. ● *adj.* (of a building) having such a portico. [Latin *prostylos* 'having pillars in front' (as PRO-[2], STYLE)]

prosy /ˈprəʊzi/ *adj.* (**prosier**, **prosiest**) tedious; commonplace; dull (*prosy talk*). □ **prosily** *adv.* **prosiness** *n.*

Prot. *abbr.* **1** Protectorate. **2** Protestant.

protactinium /prəʊtakˈtɪnɪəm/ *n. Chem.* a radioactive metallic element whose chief isotope yields actinium by decay (symbol **Pa**). [German (as PROTO-, ACTINIUM)]

protagonist /prəˈtag(ə)nɪst/ *n.* **1** the chief person in a drama, story, etc. **2** the leading person in a contest etc.; a principal performer. **3** (usu. foll. by *of*, *for*) *disp.* an advocate or champion of a cause, course of action, etc. (*a protagonist of women's rights*). [Greek *prōtagōnistēs* (as PROTO-, *agōnistēs* 'actor')]

■ **Usage** The use of *protagonist* in sense 3 to mean 'a champion or advocate of a cause' is considered incorrect in standard English. The word contains the Greek prefix *proto-* meaning 'first', not the prefix *pro-* meaning 'in favour of'.

protamine /ˈprəʊtəmiːn/ *n.* any of a group of simple proteins found combined with nucleic acids, esp. in fish sperm. [PROTO- + AMINE]

protasis /ˈprɒtəsɪs/ *n.* (*pl.* **protases** /-siːz/) the clause expressing the condition in a conditional sentence. □ **protatic** /-ˈtatɪk/ *adj.* [Latin, from Greek *protasis* 'proposition' (as PRO-[2], *teinō* 'stretch')]

protea /ˈprəʊtɪə/ *n.* any shrub of the genus *Protea* native to S. Africa, with conelike flower heads. [modern Latin from PROTEUS, with reference to the many species]

protean /ˈprəʊtɪən, prəʊˈtiːən/ *adj.* **1** variable, taking many forms. **2** (of an artist, writer, etc.) versatile. [from PROTEUS]

protease /ˈprəʊtɪeɪz/ *n.* any enzyme able to hydrolyse proteins and peptides; a proteolytic enzyme. [PROTEIN + -ASE]

protect /prəˈtɛkt/ *v.tr.* **1** (often foll. by *from*, *against*) keep (a person, thing, etc.) safe; defend; guard (*goggles protected her eyes from dust*; *guards protected the queen*). **2** *Econ.* shield (home industry) from competition by imposing import duties on foreign goods. **3** *Brit.* provide funds to meet (a bill, draft, etc.). **4** provide (machinery etc.) with appliances to prevent injury from it. [Latin *protegere protect-* (as PRO-[1], *tegere* 'cover')]

protection /prəˈtɛkʃ(ə)n/ *n.* **1 a** the act or an instance of protecting. **b** the state of being protected; defence (*affords protection against the weather*). **c** a thing, person, or animal that provides protection (*bought a dog as protection*). **2** (also **protectionism** /-nɪz(ə)m/) *Econ.* the theory or practice of protecting home industries. **3** *colloq.* **a** immunity from molestation obtained by payment to gangsters etc. under threat of violence. **b** (in full **protection money**) the money so paid, esp. on a regular basis. **4** = SAFE CONDUCT. **5** *archaic* the keeping of a woman as a mistress. □ **protectionist** *n.* [Middle English from Old French *protection* or Late Latin *protectio* (as PROTECT)]

protective /prəˈtɛktɪv/ *adj.* & *n.* ● *adj.* **1** protecting; intended or intending to protect. **2** (of food) protecting against deficiency diseases. ● *n. Brit.* something that protects, esp. a condom. □ **protectively** *adv.* **protectiveness** *n.*

protective clothing *n.* clothing worn to shield the body from dangerous substances or a hostile environment.

protective colouring *n.* colouring disguising or camouflaging a plant or animal.

protective custody *n.* the detention of a person for his or her own protection.

protector /prəˈtɛktə/ *n.* (*fem.* **protectress** /-trɪs/) **1 a** a person who protects. **b** a guardian or patron. **2** (usu. **Protector**) *hist.* a regent in charge of a kingdom during the minority, absence, etc. of the sovereign. **3** (often in *comb.*) a thing or device that protects (*chest protector*). **4** (**Protector**) (in full **Lord Protector of the**

Commonwealth) *hist.* the title of Oliver Cromwell 1653–8 and his son Richard Cromwell 1658–9. □ **protectoral** *adj.* **protectorship** *n.* [Middle English via Old French *protecteur* from Late Latin *protector* (as PROTECT)]

protectorate /prəˈtɛkt(ə)rət/ *n.* **1 a** a state that is controlled and protected by another. **b** such a relation of one state to another. **2** (usu. **Protectorate**) *hist.* **a** the office of the protector of a kingdom or state. **b** the period of this, esp. in England under the Cromwells 1653–9.

protégé /ˈprɒtɪʒeɪ, -tɛʒeɪ, ˈprəʊ-/ *n.* (*fem.* **protégée** *pronunc.* same) a person under the protection, patronage, tutelage, etc. of another. [French, past part. of *protéger*, from Latin *protegere* PROTECT]

protein /ˈprəʊtiːn/ *n.* **1** any of a class of nitrogenous organic compounds having large compact or fibrous molecules composed of one or more chains of amino acids and forming an essential part of all living organisms. **2** such substances collectively, esp. as a dietary component. □ **proteinaceous** /-ˈneɪʃəs/ *adj.* **proteinic** /-ˈtiːnɪk/ *adj.* **proteinous** /-ˈtiːnəs, -ˈtiːnəs/ *adj.* [French *protéine*, German *Protein* from Greek *prōteios* 'primary']

pro tem /prəʊ ˈtɛm/ *adj.* & *adv. colloq.* = PRO TEMPORE. [abbreviation]

pro tempore /prəʊ ˈtɛmpəri/ *adj.* & *adv.* for the time being. [Latin]

proteolysis /prəʊtɪˈɒlɪsɪs/ *n.* the splitting of proteins or peptides by the action of enzymes esp. during the process of digestion. □ **proteolytic** /-əˈlɪtɪk/ *adj.* [modern Latin, from PROTEIN + -LYSIS]

Proterozoic /prəʊt(ə)rəˈzəʊɪk/ *adj.* & *n. Geol.* ● *adj.* of or relating to the later part of the Precambrian era, characterized by the oldest forms of life (cf. ARCHAEAN). ● *n.* this era. [Greek *proteros* 'former' + *zōē* 'life', *zōos* 'living']

protest *n.* & *v.* ● *n.* /ˈprəʊtɛst/ **1** a statement of dissent or disapproval; a remonstrance (*made a protest*). **2** (often *attrib.*) a usu. public demonstration of objection to government etc. policy (*marched in protest*; *protest demonstration*). **3** a solemn declaration. **4** *Law* a written declaration, usu. by a notary public, that a bill has been presented and payment or acceptance refused. ● *v.* /prəˈtɛst/ **1** *intr.* (usu. foll. by *against*, *at*, *about*, etc.) make a protest against an action, proposal, etc. **2** *tr.* (often foll. by *that* + clause; also *absol.*) affirm (one's innocence etc.) solemnly, esp. in reply to an accusation etc. **3** *tr. Law* write or obtain a protest in regard to (a bill). **4** *tr. N. Amer.* object to (a decision etc.). □ **under protest** unwillingly. □ **protester** *n.* **protestingly** *adv.* **protestor** *n.* [Middle English via Old French *protest* (*n.*), *protester* (*v.*), from Latin *protestari* (as PRO-[1], *testari* 'assert' from *testis* 'witness')]

Protestant /ˈprɒtɪst(ə)nt/ *n.* & *adj.* ● *n.* **1** a member or follower of any of the western Christian Churches that are separate from the Roman Catholic Church in accordance with the principles of the Reformation. **2** (**protestant**) /also prəˈtɛst(ə)nt/ a protesting person. ● *adj.* **1** of or relating to any of the Protestant Churches or their members etc. **2** (**protestant**) /also prəˈtɛst(ə)nt/ protesting. □ **Protestantism** *n.* **Protestantize** *v.tr.* & *intr.* (also **-ise**). [modern Latin *protestans*, part. of Latin *protestari* (see PROTEST)]

protestation /prɒtɪˈsteɪʃ(ə)n/ *n.* **1** a strong affirmation. **2** a protest. [Middle English from Old French *protestation* or Late Latin *protestatio* (as PROTESTANT)]

Proteus /ˈprəʊtɪəs, -tjuːs/ *n.* **1** a changing or inconstant person or thing. **2** (**proteus**) **a** a bacterium of the genus *Proteus*, found in the intestines of animals and in the soil. **b** = OLM. [Latin from Greek *Prōteus*, a sea-god able to take various forms at will]

prothalamium /prəʊθəˈleɪmɪəm/ *n.* (also **prothalamion** /-mɪən/) (*pl.* **prothalamia** /-mɪə/) a song or poem to celebrate a forthcoming wedding. [title of a poem by Spenser, on the pattern of *epithalamium*]

prothallium /prəʊˈθalɪəm/ *n.* (*pl.* **prothallia** /-lɪə/) = PROTHALLUS. [modern Latin, from PRO-[2] + Greek *thallion*, diminutive of *thallos*: see PROTHALLUS]

prothallus /prəʊˈθaləs/ *n.* (*pl.* **prothalli** /-lʌɪ, -liː/) *Bot.* the gametophyte of certain plants, esp. of a fern. [modern Latin, from PRO-[2] + Greek *thallos* 'green shoot']

prothesis /ˈprɒθɪsɪs/ *n.* (*pl.* **protheses** /-siːz/) **1** *Eccl.* (esp. in the Orthodox Church) **a** the placing of the Eucharistic elements on the credence table. **b** a credence table. **c** the part of a church where this stands. **2** *Gram.* = PROSTHESIS 2. □ **prothetic** /prəˈθɛtɪk/ *adj.* [Greek from *protithēmi* (as PRO-[2], *tithēmi* 'place')]

prothonotary var. of PROTONOTARY.

prothonotary warbler *n.* a N. American wood warbler, *Protonotarius citrea*.

protist /ˈprəʊtɪst/ *n.* any primitive organism of the kingdom Protista, with both plant and animal characteristics, including protozoans and simple algae and fungi. □ **protistology** /-ˈtɒlədʒi/ *n.* [modern Latin *Protista* from Greek *prōtista*, neut. pl. superl. of *prōtos* 'first']

protium /ˈprəʊtɪəm/ *n.* the ordinary isotope of hydrogen as distinct from heavy hydrogen (cf. DEUTERIUM, TRITIUM). [modern Latin, from PROTO- + -IUM]

proto- /ˈprəʊtəʊ/ *comb. form* **1** original, primitive (*proto-Germanic*; *proto-Slavic*). **2** first, original (*protomartyr*; *protophyte*). [Greek *prōto-* from *prōtos* 'first']

protocol /ˈprəʊtəkɒl/ *n.* & *v.* ● *n.* **1 a** official, esp. diplomatic, formality and etiquette observed on state occasions etc. **b** the rules, formalities, etc. of any procedure, group, etc. **2** the original draft of a diplomatic document, esp. of the terms of a treaty agreed to in conference and signed by the parties. **3** a formal statement of a transaction. **4** the official formulae at the beginning and end of a charter, papal bull, etc. **5** *US* a record of experimental observations etc. **6** a set of rules governing the exchange or transmission of data electronically between devices. ● *v.* (**protocolled**, **protocolling**) **1** *intr.* draw up a protocol or protocols. **2** *tr.* record in a protocol. [originally Scots *prothocoll*, via Old French *prothocole* and medieval Latin *protocollum* from Greek *protokollon* 'first page, flyleaf' (as PROTO-, *kolla* 'glue')]

protomartyr /prəʊtəʊˈmɑːtə/ *n.* the first martyr in any cause, esp. the first Christian martyr St Stephen.

proton /ˈprəʊtɒn/ *n. Physics* a stable subatomic particle occurring in all atomic nuclei, with a positive electric charge equal in magnitude to that of an electron. □ **protonic** /prə(ʊ)ˈtɒnɪk/ *adj.* [Greek, neut. of *prōtos* 'first']

protonotary /prəʊtəˈnəʊt(ə)ri, prəˈtɒnət(ə)ri/ *n.* (also **prothonotary** /prəʊθ-, prəˈθɒnə-/) (*pl.* **-ies**) a chief clerk in some law courts, originally in the Byzantine court. [medieval Latin *protonotarius* from late Greek *protonotarios* (as PROTO-, NOTARY)]

Protonotary Apostolic *n.* (also **Protonotary Apostolical**) a member of the college of prelates who register papal acts, direct the canonization of saints, etc.

protopectin /prəʊtəˈpɛktɪn/ *n.* = PECTOSE.

protophyte /ˈprəʊtəfʌɪt/ *n.* a unicellular plant bearing gametes.

protoplasm /ˈprəʊtə(ʊ)plaz(ə)m/ *n. Biol.* the material comprising the living part of a cell, consisting of a nucleus embedded in membrane-enclosed cytoplasm. □ **protoplasmal** /-ˈplazm(ə)l/ *adj.* **protoplasmatic** /-ˈmatɪk/ *adj.* **protoplasmic** /-ˈplazmɪk/ *adj.* [Greek *protoplasma* (as PROTO-, PLASMA)]

protoplast /ˈprəʊtəplast/ *n. Biol.* the protoplasm of one cell, esp. a living plant or bacterial cell whose cell wall has been removed. □ **protoplastic** /-ˈplastɪk/ *adj.* [French *protoplaste* or Late Latin *protoplastus* from Greek *protoplastos* (as PROTO-, *plassō* 'mould')]

prototherian /prəʊtə(ʊ)ˈθɪərɪən/ *n.* & *adj.* ● *n.* any mammal of the subclass Prototheria, including monotremes. ● *adj.* of or relating to this subclass. [PROTO- + Greek *thēr* 'wild beast']

prototype /'prəʊtətʌɪp/ *n.* & *v.* ● *n.* **1** an original thing or person of which or whom copies, imitations, improved forms, representations, etc. are made. **2** a trial model or preliminary version of a vehicle, machine, etc. ● *v.tr.* make a prototype of (a product). □ **prototypal** *adj.* **prototypic** /-'tɪpɪk/ *adj.* **prototypical** /-'tɪpɪk(ə)l/ *adj.* **prototypically** /-'tɪpɪk(ə)li/ *adv.* [French *prototype* or Late Latin *prototypus* from Greek *prototupos* (as PROTO-, TYPE)]

protozoan /prəʊtə'zəʊən/ *n.* & *adj.* ● *n.* (also **protozoon** /-'zəʊɒn/) (*pl.* **protozoa** /-'zəʊə/ or **protozoans**) a usu. unicellular and microscopic organism of the phylum or subkingdom Protozoa, e.g. an amoeba or a ciliate. ● *adj.* (also **protozoic** /-'zəʊɪk/) of or relating to this group of organisms. □ **protozoal** *adj.* [modern Latin (as PROTO-, Greek *zōion* 'animal')]

protract /prə'trakt/ *v.tr.* **1** prolong or lengthen in space or esp. time (*protracted their stay for some weeks*). **2** draw (a plan of ground etc.) to scale. □ **protractedly** *adv.* **protractedness** *n.* [Latin *protrahere protract-* (as PRO-[1], *trahere* 'draw')]

protractile /prə'traktʌɪl, -tɪl/ *adj.* (of a part of the body etc.) capable of being protruded or extended.

protraction /prə'trakʃ(ə)n/ *n.* **1** the act or an instance of protracting; the state of being protracted. **2** a drawing to scale. **3** the action of a protractor muscle. [French *protraction* or Late Latin *protractio* (as PROTRACT)]

protractor /prə'traktə/ *n.* **1** an instrument for measuring angles, usu. in the form of a graduated semicircle. **2** a muscle serving to extend a limb etc.

protrude /prə'tru:d/ *v.* **1** *intr.* extend beyond or above a surface; project. **2** *tr.* thrust or cause to thrust out. □ **protrudent** *adj.* **protrusible** *adj.* **protrusion** /-ʒ(ə)n/ *n.* **protrusive** *adj.* [Latin *protrudere* (as PRO-[1], *trudere trus-* 'thrust')]

protrusile /prə'tru:sʌɪl/ *adj.* (of a limb etc.) capable of being thrust forward. [PRO-[1] + EXTRUSILE: see EXTRUDE]

protuberant /prə'tju:b(ə)r(ə)nt/ *adj.* bulging out; prominent. □ **protuberance** *n.* [Late Latin *protuberare* (as PRO-[1], *tuber* 'bump')]

proud /praʊd/ *adj.* **1** feeling greatly honoured or pleased (*am proud to know him*; *proud of his friendship*). **2 a** (often foll. by *of*) valuing oneself, one's possessions, etc. highly, or esp. too highly; haughty; arrogant (*proud of his ancient name*). **b** (often in *comb.*) having a proper pride; satisfied (*house-proud*; *proud of a job well done*). **3 a** (of an occasion etc.) justly arousing pride (*a proud day for us*; *a proud sight*). **b** (of an action etc.) showing pride (*a proud wave of the hand*). **4** (of a thing) imposing; splendid. **5** *Brit.* slightly projecting from a surface etc. (*the nail stood proud of the plank*). **6** (of flesh) overgrown round a healing wound. **7** (of water) swollen in flood. □ **do proud** *colloq.* **1** treat (a person) with lavish generosity or honour (*they did us proud on our anniversary*). **2** (*refl.*) act honourably or worthily. □ **proudly** *adv.* **proudness** *n.* [Old English *prūt, prūd* from Old French *prud, prod,* oblique case of *pruz* etc. 'valiant', ultimately via Late Latin *prode* from Latin *prodesse* 'be of value' (as PRO-[1], *esse* 'be')]

proud-hearted *adj.* haughty; arrogant.

Prov. *abbr.* **1** Proverbs (Old Testament). **2** Province.

prove /pru:v/ *v.* (*past part.* **proved** or **proven** /'pru:v(ə)n, 'prəʊ-/) **1** *tr.* (often foll. by *that* + clause) demonstrate the truth of by evidence or argument. **2** *intr.* **a** (usu. foll. by *to* + infin.) be found (*it proved to be untrue*). **b** emerge incontrovertibly as (*will prove the winner*). **3** *tr. Math.* test the accuracy of (a calculation). **4** *tr.* establish the genuineness and validity of (a will). **5** *intr.* (of dough) rise in bread-making. **6** *tr.* = PROOF 6. **7** *tr.* subject (a gun etc.) to a testing process. **8** *tr. archaic* test the qualities of; try. □ **not proven** (in Scottish Law) a verdict that there is insufficient evidence to establish guilt or innocence. **prove oneself** show one's abilities, courage, etc. □ **provable** *adj.* **provability** /-'bɪlɪti/ *n.* **provably** *adv.* [Middle English via Old French *prover* from Latin *probare* 'test, approve, demonstrate', from *probus* 'good']

■ **Usage** The use of *proven* as the past participle is uncommon except in certain expressions, such as *of proven ability*. It is, however, standard in Scots and American English.

provenance /'prɒv(ə)nəns/ *n.* **1** the place of origin or earliest known history, esp. of a work of art, manuscript, etc. **2** origin. [French from *provenir* from Latin *provenire* (as PRO-[1], *venire* 'come')]

Provençal /prɒvɒn:'sɑ:l, -vɒ̃-, -'sal/ *adj.* & *n.* ● *adj.* of or concerning the language, inhabitants, landscape, etc. of Provence, a former province of SE France. ● *n.* **1** a native of Provence. **2** the language of Provence. [French (as PROVINCIAL, from *provincia* 'province' as Latin colloq. name for southern Gaul under Roman rule)]

provender /'prɒvɪndə/ *n.* **1** animal fodder. **2** *joc.* food for human beings. [Middle English from Old French *provendre, provende,* ultimately from Latin *praebenda* (see PREBEND)]

provenience /prə'vi:nɪəns/ *n. US* = PROVENANCE. [Latin *provenire* (as PROVENANCE)]

proverb /'prɒvə:b/ *n.* **1** a short pithy saying in general use, held to embody a general truth. **2** a person or thing that is notorious (*he is a proverb for inaccuracy*). **3** (**Proverbs** or **Book of Proverbs**) a didactic poetic Old Testament book of maxims attributed to Solomon and others. [Middle English from Old French *proverbe* or Latin *proverbium* (as PRO-[1], *verbum* 'word')]

proverbial /prə'və:bɪəl/ *adj.* **1** (esp. of a specific characteristic etc.) as well known as a proverb; famous, notorious (*his proverbial honesty*). **2** of or referred to in a proverb; familiar as a proverb or catchphrase or as a stock character (*the proverbial ill wind*). □ **proverbiality** /-bɪ'alɪti/ *n.* **proverbially** *adv.* [Middle English from Latin *proverbialis* (as PROVERB)]

provide /prə'vʌɪd/ *v.* **1** *tr.* supply; furnish (*provided them with food*; *provided food for them*; *provided a chance for escape*). **2** *intr.* **a** (usu. foll. by *for, against*) make due preparation (*provided for any eventuality*; *provided against invasion*). **b** (usu. foll. by *for*) prepare for the maintenance of a person etc. **3** *tr.* (also *refl.*) equip with necessities (*they had to provide themselves*). **4** *tr.* (usu. foll. by *that*) stipulate in a will, statute, etc. **5** *tr.* (usu. foll. by *to*) *Eccl. hist.* **a** appoint (an incumbent) to a benefice. **b** (of the Pope) appoint (a successor) to a benefice not yet vacant. [Middle English from Latin *providēre* (as PRO-[1], *vidēre vis-* 'see')]

provided /prə'vʌɪdɪd/ *adj.* & *conj.* ● *adj.* supplied, furnished. ● *conj.* (often foll. by *that*) on the condition or understanding (that).

providence /'prɒvɪd(ə)ns/ *n.* **1** the protective care of God or nature. **2** (**Providence**) God in this aspect. **3** timely care or preparation; foresight; thrift. [Middle English from Old French *providence* or Latin *providentia* (as PROVIDE)]

provident /'prɒvɪd(ə)nt/ *adj.* having or showing foresight; thrifty. □ **providently** *adv.* [Middle English from Latin (as PROVIDE)]

providential /prɒvɪ'dɛnʃ(ə)l/ *adj.* **1** of or by divine foresight or interposition. **2** opportune, lucky. □ **providentially** *adv.* [PROVIDENCE + -IAL, on the pattern of *evidential* etc.]

Provident Society *n. Brit.* = FRIENDLY SOCIETY.

provider /prə'vʌɪdə/ *n.* **1** a person or thing that provides. **2** the breadwinner of a family etc.

providing /prə'vʌɪdɪŋ/ *conj.* = PROVIDED *conj.*

Provie /'prəʊvi, 'prɒvi/ *n. colloq.* = PROVO. [abbreviation of *Provisional*]

province /'prɒvɪns/ *n.* **1** a principal administrative division of a country etc. **2** (**the Province**) *Brit.* Northern Ireland. **3** (**the provinces**) the whole of a country outside the capital or *US* other major cities, esp. regarded as uncultured, unsophisticated, etc. **4** a sphere of action; business (*outside my province as a* *teacher*). **5** a branch of learning etc. (*in the province of aesthetics*). **6** *Eccl.* a district under an archbishop or a metropolitan. **7** *Rom.Hist.* a territory outside Italy under a Roman governor. [Middle English via Old French from Latin *provincia* 'charge, province']

provincial /prəˈvɪnʃ(ə)l/ *adj. & n.* ● *adj.* **1 a** of or concerning a province. **b** of or concerning the provinces. **2** unsophisticated or uncultured in manner, speech, opinion, etc. ● *n.* **1** an inhabitant of a province or the provinces. **2** an unsophisticated or uncultured person. **3** *Eccl.* the head or chief of a province or of a religious order in a province. □ **provinciality** /-ʃɪˈalɪti/ *n.* **provincialize** *v.tr.* (also **-ise**). **provincially** *adv.* [Middle English via Old French from Latin *provincialis* (as PROVINCE)]

provincialism /prəˈvɪnʃ(ə)lɪz(ə)m/ *n.* **1** provincial manners, fashion, mode of thought, etc., esp. regarded as restricting or narrow. **2** a word or phrase peculiar to a provincial region. **3** concern for one's local area rather than one's country. □ **provincialist** *n.*

provision /prəˈvɪʒ(ə)n/ *n. & v.* ● *n.* **1 a** the act or an instance of providing (*made no provision for his future*). **b** something provided (*a provision of bread*). **2** (in *pl.*) food, drink, etc., esp. for an expedition. **3 a** a legal or formal statement providing for something. **b** a clause of this. **4** *Eccl. hist.* an appointment to a benefice not yet vacant (cf. PROVIDE 5). ● *v.tr.* supply (an expedition etc.) with provisions. □ **provisioner** *n.* **provisionless** *adj.* **provisionment** *n.* [Middle English via Old French from Latin *provisio -onis* (as PROVIDE)]

provisional /prəˈvɪʒ(ə)n(ə)l/ *adj. & n.* ● *adj.* **1** providing for immediate needs only; temporary. **2** (**Provisional**) designating the unofficial wing of the IRA established in 1969, advocating terrorism. ● *n.* (**Provisional**) a member of the Provisional wing of the IRA. □ **provisionality** /-ˈnalɪti/ *n.* **provisionally** *adv.* **provisionalness** *n.*

proviso /prəˈvʌɪzəʊ/ *n.* (*pl.* **-os**) **1** a stipulation. **2** a clause of stipulation or limitation in a document. [Latin, neut. ablative past part. of *providēre* PROVIDE, in the medieval Latin phrase *proviso quod* 'it being provided that']

provisor /prəˈvʌɪzə/ *n. Eccl.* **1** a deputy of a bishop or archbishop. **2** *hist.* the holder of a provision (see PROVISION *n.* 4). [Middle English via Anglo-French *provisour* from Latin *provisor -oris* (as PROVIDE)]

provisory /prəˈvʌɪz(ə)ri/ *adj.* **1** conditional; having a proviso. **2** making provision (*provisory care*). □ **provisorily** *adv.* [French *provisoire* or medieval Latin *provisorius* (as PROVISOR)]

Provo /ˈprəʊvəʊ/ *n.* (*pl.* **-os**) *colloq.* a member of the Provisional IRA. [abbreviation]

provocation /prɒvəˈkeɪʃ(ə)n/ *n.* **1** the act or an instance of provoking; a state of being provoked (*did it under severe provocation*). **2** a cause of annoyance. **3** *Law* an action, insult, etc. held to be likely to provoke physical retaliation. [Middle English from Old French *provocation* or Latin *provocatio* (as PROVOKE)]

provocative /prəˈvɒkətɪv/ *adj. & n.* ● *adj.* **1** (usu. foll. by *of*) tending to provoke, esp. anger or sexual desire. **2** intentionally annoying. ● *n.* a provocative thing. □ **provocatively** *adv.* **provocativeness** *n.* [Middle English via obsolete French *provocatif -ive* from Late Latin *provocativus* (as PROVOKE)]

provoke /prəˈvəʊk/ *v.tr.* **1 a** incite to anger (*insolence will only provoke him*). **b** (often foll. by *to*, *to* + infin., or *into*) rouse or incite (*provoked him to fury*; *provoked her into retaliating*). **c** (as **provoking** *adj.*) exasperating; irritating. **2** call forth; instigate (indignation, an inquiry, a storm, etc.). **3** tempt; allure. **4** cause, give rise to (*will provoke fermentation*). □ **provokable** *adj.* **provoker** *n.* **provokingly** *adv.* [Middle English via Old French *provoquer* from Latin *provocare* (as PRO-[1], *vocare* 'call')]

provost /ˈprɒvəst/ *n.* **1** *Brit.* the head of some colleges esp. at Oxford or Cambridge. **2** *Eccl.* **a** the head of a chapter in a cathedral. **b** *hist.* the head of a religious community. **3** *Sc.* the head of a municipal corporation or burgh. **4** the Protestant minister of the principal church of a town etc. in Germany etc. **5** *US* a high administrative officer in a university. **6** = PROVOST MARSHAL. □ **provostship** *n.* [Old English *profost*, reinforced in Middle English by Anglo-French *provost*, *prevost* from medieval Latin *propositus*, for *praepositus*: see PRAEPOSTOR]

provost guard *n. US* a body of soldiers under a provost marshal.

provost marshal *n.* **1** the head of military police in camp or on active service. **2** the master-at-arms of a ship in which a court-martial is held.

prow /praʊ/ *n.* **1** the forepart or bow of a ship adjoining the stern. **2** a pointed or projecting front part. [French *proue* from Provençal *proa* or Italian dialect *prua* via Latin *prora* from Greek *prōira*]

prowess /ˈpraʊɪs/ *n.* **1** skill; expertise. **2** valour; gallantry. [Middle English from Old French *proesce*, from *prou* 'valiant']

prowl /praʊl/ *v. & n.* ● *v.* **1** *tr.* roam (a place) in search or as if in search of prey, plunder, etc. **2** *intr.* (often foll. by *about*, *around*) move about like a hunter. ● *n.* the act or an instance of prowling. □ **on the prowl** moving about secretively or rapaciously. □ **prowler** *n.* [Middle English *prolle*, of unknown origin]

prowl car *n. US* a police squad car.

prox. *abbr.* proximo.

prox. acc. *abbr. proxime accessit.*

proxemics /prɒkˈsiːmɪks/ *n.* the study of socially conditioned spatial factors in ordinary human relations. [PROXIMITY + *-emics*: cf. *phonemics*]

proximal /ˈprɒksɪm(ə)l/ *adj.* situated nearer to the centre of the body or towards the point of attachment (opp. DISTAL). □ **proximally** *adv.* [Latin *proximus* 'nearest']

proximate /ˈprɒksɪmət/ *adj.* **1** nearest or next before or after (in place, order, time, causation, thought process, etc.). **2** approximate. □ **proximately** *adv.* [Latin *proximatus*, past part. of *proximare* 'draw near' (as PROXIMAL)]

proxime accessit /ˌprɒksɪmɪ akˈsɛsɪt/ *n.* **1** second place in an examination etc. **2** a person gaining this. [Latin, = came very near]

proximity /prɒkˈsɪmɪti/ *n.* nearness in space, time, etc. (*sat in close proximity to them*). [Middle English from French *proximité* or Latin *proximitas* (as PROXIMAL)]

proximity fuse *n.* an electronic detonator causing a projectile to explode within a predetermined distance of its target.

proximity of blood *n.* kinship.

proximo /ˈprɒksɪməʊ/ *adj. Commerce* of next month (*the third proximo*). [Latin *proximo mense* 'in the next month']

proxy /ˈprɒksi/ *n.* (*pl.* **-ies**) (also *attrib.*) **1** the authorization given to a substitute or deputy (*a proxy vote*; *was married by proxy*). **2** a person authorized to act as a substitute etc. **3 a** a document giving the power to act as a proxy, esp. in voting. **b** a vote given by this. [Middle English from obsolete *procuracy*, from medieval Latin *procuratia* (as PROCURATION)]

PRS *abbr.* **1** (in the UK) President of the Royal Society. **2** Performing Rights Society.

prude /pruːd/ *n.* a person having or affecting an attitude of extreme propriety or modesty esp. in sexual matters. □ **prudery** *n.* (*pl.* **-ies**). **prudish** *adj.* **prudishly** *adv.* **prudishness** *n.* [French, back-formation from *prudefemme*, fem. of *prud'homme* 'good man and true', from *prou* 'worthy']

prudent /ˈpruːd(ə)nt/ *adj.* **1** (of a person or conduct) careful to avoid undesired consequences; circumspect. **2** discreet. □ **prudence** *n.* **prudently** *adv.* [Middle English from Old French *prudent* or Latin *prudens* = *providens* PROVIDENT]

prudential /prʊˈdɛnʃ(ə)l/ *adj. & n.* ● *adj.* of, involving, or marked by prudence (*prudential motives*). ● *n.* (in *pl.*)

1 prudential considerations or matters. **2** *US* minor administrative or financial matters. ▫ **prudentialism** *n.* **prudentialist** *n.* **prudentially** *adv.* [PRUDENT + -IAL, on the pattern of *evidential* etc.]

pruinose /ˈpruːɪnəʊs/ *adj.* esp. *Bot.* covered with white powdery granules; frosted in appearance. [Latin *pruinosus* from *pruina* 'hoar frost']

prune[1] /pruːn/ *n.* **1** a plum preserved by drying and having a black, wrinkled appearance. **2** *colloq.* a silly or disliked person. [Middle English from Old French, ultimately via Latin *prunum* from Greek *prou(m)non* 'plum']

prune[2] /pruːn/ *v.* & *n.* ● *v.tr.* **1 a** (often foll. by *down*) trim (a tree etc.) by cutting away dead or overgrown branches etc. **b** (usu. foll. by *off, away*) lop (branches etc.) from a tree. **2** reduce (costs etc.) (*must try to prune expenses*). **3 a** (often foll. by *of*) clear (a book etc.) of superfluities. **b** remove (superfluities). ● *n.* an instance of pruning. ▫ **pruner** *n.* [Middle English *prouyne* from Old French *pro(o)ignier*, ultimately from Latin *rotundus* ROUND]

prunella[1] /prʊˈnɛlə/ *n.* any plant of the genus *Prunella*, esp. *P. vulgaris*, bearing pink, purple, or white flower spikes, and formerly thought to cure quinsy. Also called SELF-HEAL. [modern Latin, = quinsy: earlier *brunella*, a disease causing a brown coating on the tongue (diminutive of medieval Latin *brunus* 'brown')]

prunella[2] /prʊˈnɛlə/ *n.* a strong silk or worsted fabric used formerly for barristers' gowns, the uppers of women's shoes, etc. [perhaps from French *prunelle*, of uncertain origin]

pruning hook *n.* a long-handled hooked cutting tool used for pruning.

prurient /ˈprʊərɪənt/ *adj.* **1** having an unhealthy obsession with sexual matters. **2** encouraging such an obsession. ▫ **prurience** *n.* **pruriency** *n.* **pruriently** *adv.* [Latin *prurire* 'itch, be wanton']

prurigo /prʊəˈrʌɪɡəʊ/ *n.* a skin disease marked by severe itching. ▫ **pruriginous** /prʊəˈrɪdʒɪnəs/ *adj.* [Latin *prurigo -ginis* from *prurire* 'to itch']

pruritus /prʊəˈrʌɪtəs/ *n.* severe itching of the skin. ▫ **pruritic** /-ˈrɪtɪk/ *adj.* [Latin, = itching (as PRURIGO)]

Prussian /ˈprʌʃ(ə)n/ *adj.* & *n.* ● *adj.* of or relating to Prussia, a former German state, or the militaristic tradition associated with it. ● *n.* a native of Prussia.

Prussian blue *n.* & *adj.* ● *n.* a deep blue pigment, ferric ferrocyanide, used in painting and dyeing. ● *adj.* (hyphenated when *attrib.*) of this colour.

prussic acid *n.* hydrocyanic acid. [French *prussique* from *Prusse* 'Prussia']

pry[1] /prʌɪ/ *v.intr.* (**pries, pried**) **1** (usu. foll. by *into*) enquire impertinently (into a person's private affairs etc.). **2** (usu. foll. by *into, about*, etc.) look or peer inquisitively. ▫ **prying** *adj.* **pryingly** *adv.* [Middle English *prie*, of unknown origin]

pry[2] /prʌɪ/ *v.tr.* (**pries, pried**) (often foll. by *out of, open*, etc.) *N. Amer.* = PRISE. [PRISE, taken as *pries*, 3rd sing. present]

PS *abbr.* **1** Police Sergeant. **2** postscript. **3** private secretary. **4** prompt side.

Ps. *abbr.* (*pl.* **Pss.**) Psalm, Psalms (Old Testament).

psalm /sɑːm/ *n.* **1** *Bibl.* **a** (also **Psalm**) any of the sacred songs contained in the Book of Psalms, esp. when set for metrical chanting in a service. **b** (**the Psalms** or **the Book of Psalms**) the book of the Old Testament containing the Psalms. **2** a sacred song or hymn. ▫ **psalmic** *adj.* [Old English *(p)sealm* via Late Latin *psalmus* from Greek *psalmos* 'song sung to a harp', from *psallō* 'pluck']

psalm-book *n.* a book containing psalms, esp. with metrical settings for worship.

psalmist /ˈsɑːmɪst/ *n.* **1** the author or composer of a psalm. **2** (**the Psalmist**) David or the author of any of the Psalms. [Late Latin *psalmista* (as PSALM)]

psalmody /ˈsɑːmədi, ˈsalm-/ *n.* **1** the practice or art of singing psalms, hymns, etc., esp. in public worship. **2 a** the arrangement of psalms for singing. **b** the psalms so arranged. ▫ **psalmodic** /salˈmɒdɪk/ *adj.* **psalmodist** *n.* **psalmodize** *v.intr.* (also **-ise**). [Middle English via Late Latin *psalmodia* from Greek *psalmōidia* 'singing to a harp' (as PSALM, *ōidē* 'song')]

psalter /ˈsɔːltə, ˈsɒl-/ *n.* (also **Psalter**) **1 a** the Book of Psalms. **b** a version of this (*the English Psalter*; *Prayer-Book Psalter*). **2** a copy of the Psalms, esp. for liturgical use. [Old English *(p)saltere*, reinforced in Middle English by Anglo-French *sauter*, Old French *sautier*, via Late Latin *psalterium* from Greek *psaltērion*, a stringed instrument (in ecclesiastical Latin and Greek = Book of Psalms), from *psallō* 'pluck']

psalterium /sɔːlˈtɪərɪəm, sɒl-/ *n.* = OMASUM. [Latin (see PSALTER): named from the many folds of tissue inside it]

psaltery /ˈsɔːlt(ə)ri, ˈsɒl-/ *n.* (*pl.* **-ies**) an ancient and medieval instrument like a dulcimer but played by plucking the strings with the fingers or a plectrum. [Middle English via Old French *sauterie* etc. from Latin (as PSALTER)]

PSBR *abbr. Brit.* public sector borrowing requirement.

psephology /sɛˈfɒlədʒi, sɪ-/ *n.* the statistical study of elections, voting, etc. ▫ **psephological** /-fəˈlɒdʒɪk(ə)l/ *adj.* **psephologically** /-fəˈlɒdʒɪk(ə)li/ *adv.* **psephologist** *n.* [Greek *psēphos* 'pebble, vote' + -LOGY]

pseud /sjuːd/ *adj.* & *n. colloq.* ● *adj.* intellectually or socially pretentious; not genuine. ● *n.* such a person; a poseur. [abbreviation of PSEUDO]

pseud- var. of PSEUDO-.

pseudepigrapha /sjuːdɪˈpɪɡrəfə/ *n.pl.* **1** Jewish writings ascribed to various biblical patriarchs and prophets etc. but written *c.*200 BC–AD 200. **2** spurious writings. ▫ **pseudepigraphal** *adj.* **pseudepigraphic** /-ˈɡrafɪk/ *adj.* **pseudepigraphical** /-ˈɡrafɪk(ə)l/ *adj.* [neut. pl. of Greek *pseudepigraphos* 'with false title' (as PSEUDO-, EPIGRAPH)]

pseudo /ˈsjuːdəʊ/ *adj.* & *n.* ● *adj.* **1** sham; spurious. **2** insincere. ● *n.* (*pl.* **-os**) a pretentious or insincere person. [see PSEUDO-]

pseudo- /ˈsjuːdəʊ/ *comb. form* (also **pseud-** before a vowel) **1** supposed or purporting to be but not really so; false; not genuine (*pseudo-intellectual*; *pseudepigrapha*). **2** resembling or imitating (often in technical applications) (*pseudo-language*; *pseudo-acid*). [Greek, from *pseudēs* 'false', *pseudos* 'falsehood']

pseudocarp /ˈsjuːdə(ʊ)kɑːp/ *n.* a fruit formed from parts other than the ovary, e.g. the strawberry or fig. [PSEUDO- + Greek *karpos* 'fruit']

pseudomorph /ˈsjuːdə(ʊ)mɔːf/ *n.* **1** a crystal etc. consisting of one mineral with the form proper to another. **2** a false form. ▫ **pseudomorphic** /-ˈmɔːfɪk/ *adj.* **pseudomorphism** /-ˈmɔːfɪz(ə)m/ *n.* **pseudomorphous** /-ˈmɔːfəs/ *adj.* [PSEUDO- + Greek *morphē* 'form']

pseudonym /ˈsjuːdənɪm/ *n.* a fictitious name, esp. one assumed by an author. [French *pseudonyme* from Greek *pseudōnymos* (as PSEUDO-, *-ōnumos* from *onoma* 'name')]

pseudonymous /sjuːˈdɒnɪməs/ *adj.* writing or written under a false name. ▫ **pseudonymity** /-ˈnɪmɪti/ *n.* **pseudonymously** *adv.*

pseudopod /ˈsjuːdə(ʊ)pɒd/ *n.* = PSEUDOPODIUM. [modern Latin (as PSEUDOPODIUM)]

pseudopodium /sjuːdə(ʊ)ˈpəʊdɪəm/ *n.* (*pl.* **pseudopodia** /-dɪə/) (in amoeboid cells) a temporary protrusion of the cell surface for movement, feeding, etc. [modern Latin (as PSEUDO-, PODIUM)]

pseudo-science /ˈsjuːdəʊˌsʌɪəns/ *n.* a pretended or spurious science; a collection of beliefs mistakenly regarded as based on scientific method. ▫ **pseudo-scientific** /-ˈtɪfɪk/ *adj.*

pshaw /pʃɔː, ʃɔː/ *int. archaic* an expression of contempt or impatience. [imitative]

psi /psʌɪ, sʌɪ/ *n.* **1** the twenty-third letter of the Greek alphabet (Ψ, ψ). **2** supposed parapsychological faculties, phenomena, etc. regarded collectively. [Greek]

p.s.i. *abbr.* pounds per square inch.

psilocybin /sʌɪlə'sʌɪbɪn/ *n.* a hallucinogenic alkaloid found in toadstools of the genus *Psilocybe.* [modern Latin genus name *Psilocybe*, from Greek *psilos* 'bald' + *kubē* 'head']

psilosis /sʌɪ'ləʊsɪs/ *n.* = SPRUE². [Greek *psilōsis* from *psilos* 'bare']

psittacine /'sɪtəkʌɪn, 'sɪtəsʌɪn/ *adj.* of or relating to parrots; parrot-like. [Latin *psittacinus* from *psittacus*, from Greek *psittakos* 'parrot']

psittacism /'sɪtəsɪz(ə)m/ *n. formal* the mechanical repetition of received ideas or images; the repetition of words or phrases parrot-fashion.

psittacosis /sɪtə'kəʊsɪs/ *n.* a contagious disease of birds, caused by chlamydiae and transmissible (esp. from parrots) to human beings as a form of pneumonia. [from Latin *psittacus* 'parrot' + -OSIS]

psoas /'səʊas/ *n.* either of two muscles used in flexing the hip joint. [Greek, accusative pl. of *psoa*, taken as sing.]

psoriasis /sɒ'rʌɪəsɪs/ *n.* a skin disease marked by red scaly patches. □ **psoriatic** /sɔːrɪ'atɪk/ *adj.* [modern Latin from Greek *psōriasis*, via *psōriaō* 'have an itch' from *psōra* 'itch']

psst /p(ə)st/ *int.* (also **pst**) a whispered exclamation seeking to attract a person's attention surreptitiously. [imitative]

PST *abbr.* Pacific Standard Time.

PSV *abbr. Brit.* public service vehicle.

psych /sʌɪk/ *v.* (also **psyche**) *colloq.* **1** *tr.* (usu. foll. by *up*; often *refl.*) prepare (oneself or another person) mentally for an ordeal etc. **2** *tr.* **a** (usu. foll. by *out*) analyse (a person's motivation etc.) for one's own advantage (*can't psych him out*). **b** subject to psychoanalysis. **3** *tr.* (often foll. by *out*) influence a person psychologically, esp. negatively; intimidate, frighten. **4** *intr. Bridge* make a psychic bid. □ **psych out** break down mentally; become confused or deranged. [abbreviation]

psyche¹ /'sʌɪki/ *n.* **1** the soul; the spirit. **2** the mind. [Latin from Greek *psukhē* 'breath, life, soul']

psyche² var. of PSYCH.

psychedelia /sʌɪkɪ'diːlɪə/ *n.pl.* **1** psychedelic articles, esp. posters, paintings, etc. **2** psychedelic drugs.

psychedelic /sʌɪkɪ'delɪk, -'diːlɪk/ *adj.* & *n.* ● *adj.* **1 a** expanding the mind's awareness etc., esp. through the use of hallucinogenic drugs. **b** (of an experience) hallucinatory; bizarre. **c** (of a drug) producing hallucinations. **2** *colloq.* **a** producing an effect resembling that of a psychedelic drug; having vivid colours or designs etc. **b** (of colours, patterns, etc.) bright, bold, and often abstract. ● *n.* a hallucinogenic drug. □ **psychedelically** *adv.* [formed irregularly from Greek (as PSYCHE¹, *dēlos* 'clear, manifest')]

psychiatric nurse *n.* a nurse dealing with mentally ill patients.

psychiatric patient *n.* a patient suffering from mental illness.

psychiatry /sʌɪ'kʌɪətri/ *n.* the study and treatment of mental disease. □ **psychiatric** /-kɪ'atrɪk/ *adj.* **psychiatrical** /-kɪ'atrɪk(ə)l/ *adj.* **psychiatrically** /-kɪ'atrɪk(ə)li/ *adv.* **psychiatrist** *n.* [as PSYCHE¹ + *iatreia* 'healing' from *iatros* 'healer']

psychic /'sʌɪkɪk/ *adj.* & *n.* ● *adj.* **1 a** (of a person) considered to have occult powers, such as telepathy, clairvoyance, etc. **b** (of a faculty, phenomenon, etc.) inexplicable by natural laws. **2** of the soul or mind. **3** *Bridge* (of a bid) that deliberately misrepresents the bidder's hand. ● *n.* **1** a person considered to have psychic powers; a medium. **2** *Bridge* a psychic bid. **3** (in *pl.*) the study of psychic phenomena. □ **psychism** /-ɪz(ə)m/ *n.* **psychicist** /-ɪsɪst/ *n.* [Greek *psukhikos* (as PSYCHE¹)]

psychical /'sʌɪkɪk(ə)l/ *adj.* **1** concerning psychic phenomena or faculties (*psychical research*). **2** of the soul or mind. □ **psychically** *adv.*

psycho /'sʌɪkəʊ/ *n.* & *adj. colloq.* ● *n.* (*pl.* **-os**) a psychopath. ● *adj.* psychopathic. [abbreviation]

psycho- /'sʌɪkəʊ/ *comb. form* relating to the mind or psychology. [Greek *psukho-* (as PSYCHE¹)]

psychoactive /sʌɪkəʊ'aktɪv/ *adj.* affecting the mind.

psychoanalysis /ˌsʌɪkəʊə'nalɪsɪs/ *n.* a therapeutic method of treating mental disorders by investigating the interaction of conscious and unconscious elements in the mind and bringing repressed fears and conflicts into the conscious mind. □ **psychoanalyse** /-'an(ə)lʌɪz/ *v.tr.* (*US* **-analyze**). **psychoanalyst** /-'an(ə)lɪst/ *n.* **psychoanalytic** /-anə'lɪtɪk/ *adj.* **psychoanalytical** /-anə'lɪtɪk(ə)l/ *adj.* **psychoanalytically** /-anə'lɪtɪk(ə)li/ *adv.*

psychobabble /'sʌɪkəʊbab(ə)l/ *n. US colloq. derog.* jargon used in popular psychology.

psychobiology /ˌsʌɪkəʊbʌɪ'ɒlədʒi/ *n.* the branch of science that deals with the biological basis of behaviour and mental phenomena. □ **psychobiological** /-'lɒdʒɪk(ə)l/ *adj.* **psychobiologist** *n.*

psychodrama /'sʌɪkəʊdrɑːmə/ *n.* **1** a form of psychotherapy in which patients act out events from their past. **2** a play or film etc. in which psychological elements are the main interest.

psychodynamics /ˌsʌɪkəʊdʌɪ'namɪks/ *n.pl.* (treated as *sing.*) the study of the activity of and the interrelation between the various parts of an individual's personality or psyche. □ **psychodynamic** *adj.* **psychodynamically** *adv.*

psychogenesis /sʌɪkə(ʊ)'dʒenɪsɪs/ *n.* the study of the origin and development of the mind.

psychographics /sʌɪkə(ʊ)'grafɪks/ *n.pl.* (usu. treated as *sing.*) the study and classification of people according to their attitudes, aspirations, etc., esp. in market research. □ **psychographic** *adj.*

psychokinesis /ˌsʌɪkəʊkɪ'niːsɪs, -kʌɪ-/ *n.* the movement of objects supposedly by mental effort without the action of physical forces.

psycholinguistics /ˌsʌɪkəʊlɪŋ'gwɪstɪks/ *n.pl.* (treated as *sing.*) the study of the psychological aspects of language and language-learning. □ **psycholinguist** /-'lɪŋgwɪst/ *n.* **psycholinguistic** *adj.*

psychological /sʌɪkə'lɒdʒɪk(ə)l/ *adj.* **1** of, relating to, or arising in the mind. **2** of or relating to psychology. **3** *colloq.* (of an ailment etc.) having a basis in the mind; imaginary (*her cold is psychological*). □ **psychologically** *adv.*

psychological block *n.* = MENTAL BLOCK.

psychological moment *n.* the most appropriate time for achieving a particular effect or purpose.

psychological warfare *n.* a campaign directed at reducing an opponent's morale.

psychology /sʌɪ'kɒlədʒi/ *n.* (*pl.* **-ies**) **1** the scientific study of the human mind and its functions, esp. those affecting behaviour in a given context. **2** a treatise on or theory of this. **3 a** the mental characteristics or attitude of a person or group. **b** the mental factors governing a situation or activity (*the psychology of crime*). □ **psychologist** *n.* **psychologize** *v.tr.* & *intr.* (also **-ise**). [modern Latin *psychologia* (as PSYCHO-, -LOGY)]

psychometrics /sʌɪkə(ʊ)'metrɪks/ *n.pl.* (treated as *sing.*) the science of measuring mental capacities and processes.

psychometry /sʌɪ'kɒmɪtri/ *n.* **1** the supposed divination of facts about events, people, etc., from inanimate objects associated with them. **2** the measurement of mental abilities. □ **psychometric** /-kə'metrɪk/ *adj.* **psychometrically** /-kə'metrɪk(ə)li/ *adv.* **psychometrist** *n.*

psychomotor /sʌɪkəʊ'məʊtə/ *adj.* of or relating to the origination of movement in conscious mental activity.

psychoneurosis /ˌsʌɪkəʊnjʊə'rəʊsɪs/ *n.* neurosis, esp. with the indirect expression of emotions.

psychopath /'sʌɪkəpaθ/ *n.* **1** a person suffering from chronic mental disorder esp. with abnormal or violent social behaviour. **2** a mentally or emotionally unstable person. □ **psychopathic** /-ˈpaθɪk/ *adj.* **psychopathically** /-ˈpaθɪk(ə)li/ *adv.*

psychopathology /ˌsʌɪkəʊpəˈθɒlədʒi/ *n.* **1** the scientific study of mental disorders. **2** a mentally or behaviourally disordered state. □ **psychopathological** /-paθəˈlɒdʒɪk(ə)l/ *adj.*

psychopathy /sʌɪˈkɒpəθi/ *n.* psychopathic or psychologically abnormal behaviour.

psychophysics /sʌɪkə(ʊ)ˈfɪzɪks/ *n.* the science of the relation between the mind and the body. □ **psychophysical** *adj.*

psychophysiology /ˌsʌɪkəʊfɪzɪˈɒlədʒi/ *n.* the branch of physiology dealing with mental phenomena. □ **psychophysiological** /-zɪəˈlɒdʒɪk(ə)l/ *adj.*

psychosexual /sʌɪkə(ʊ)ˈsɛksjʊəl, -ʃʊəl/ *adj.* of or involving the psychological aspects of the sexual impulse. □ **psychosexually** *adv.*

psychosis /sʌɪˈkəʊsɪs/ *n.* (*pl.* **psychoses** /-siːz/) a severe mental derangement, esp. when resulting in delusions and loss of contact with external reality. [Greek *psukhōsis* from *psukhoō* 'give life to' (as PSYCHE[1])]

psychosocial /sʌɪkəʊˈsəʊʃ(ə)l/ *adj.* of or involving the influence of social factors or human interactive behaviour. □ **psychosocially** *adv.*

psychosomatic /ˌsʌɪkə(ʊ)səˈmatɪk/ *adj.* **1** (of an illness etc.) caused or aggravated by mental conflict, stress, etc. **2** of the mind and body together. □ **psychosomatically** *adv.*

psychosurgery /sʌɪkə(ʊ)ˈsəːdʒ(ə)ri/ *n.* brain surgery as a means of treating mental disorder. □ **psychosurgical** *adj.*

psychotherapy /sʌɪkə(ʊ)ˈθɛrəpi/ *n.* the treatment of mental disorder by psychological means. □ **psychotherapeutic** /-ˈpjuːtɪk/ *adj.* **psychotherapist** *n.*

psychotic /sʌɪˈkɒtɪk/ *adj.* & *n.* ● *adj.* of or characterized by a psychosis. ● *n.* a person suffering from a psychosis. □ **psychotically** *adv.*

psychotropic /sʌɪkə(ʊ)ˈtrəʊpɪk, -ˈtrɒp-/ *n.* (of a drug) acting on the mind.

psychrometer /sʌɪˈkrɒmɪtə/ *n.* a thermometer consisting of a dry bulb and a wet bulb for measuring atmospheric humidity. [Greek *psukhros* 'cold' + -METER]

PT *abbr.* physical training.

Pt *symb. Chem.* the element platinum.

pt. *abbr.* **1** part. **2** pint. **3** point. **4** port.

PTA *abbr.* **1** parent-teacher association. **2** Passenger Transport Authority.

ptarmigan /ˈtɑːmɪg(ə)n/ *n.* any of various grouselike northern game birds of the genus *Lagopus*, with feathered legs and feet, and plumage that usually changes to white in winter, esp. *L. mutus* of mountainous and Arctic regions. [Gaelic *tàrmachan*: *p*- suggested by Greek words in *pt*-]

PT boat *n. US* a motor torpedo boat. [*P*atrol *T*orpedo]

Pte. *abbr.* Private (soldier).

pteridology /tɛrɪˈdɒlədʒi/ *n.* the study of ferns. □ **pteridological** /-dəˈlɒdʒɪk(ə)l/ *adj.* **pteridologist** *n.* [Greek *pteris -idos* 'fern' + -LOGY]

pteridophyte /ˈtɛrɪdəfʌɪt/ *n.* any flowerless plant of the division Pteridophyta, including ferns, clubmosses, and horsetails. [Greek *pteris -idos* 'fern' + *phuton* 'plant']

ptero- /ˈtɛrəʊ/ *comb. form* wing. [Greek *pteron* 'wing']

pterodactyl /tɛrəˈdaktɪl/ *n.* a pterosaur, esp. one of the genus *Pterodactylus*, with teeth and a long slender head, neck, and tail.

pteropod /ˈtɛrəpɒd/ *n.* a marine gastropod with the middle part of its foot expanded into a pair of winglike lobes. [PTERO- + Greek *pous podos* 'foot']

pterosaur /ˈtɛrəsɔː/ *n.* any of a group of extinct flying reptiles with large bat-like wings, including pterodactyls. [PTERO- + Greek *saura* 'lizard']

pteroylglutamic acid /ˌtɛrəʊʌɪlgluˈtamɪk, -rəʊɪl-/ *n.* = FOLIC ACID. [*pteroic* acid (a precursor: ultimately from Greek *pteron* 'wing', with reference to insect pigments) + -YL + GLUTAMIC ACID]

pterygoid process /ˈtɛrɪgɔɪd/ *n.* each of a pair of processes from the sphenoid bone in the skull. [Greek *pterux -ugos* 'wing']

PTFE *abbr.* polytetrafluoroethylene.

PTO *abbr.* please turn over.

Ptolemaic /tɒləˈmeɪɪk/ *adj. hist.* **1** of or relating to Ptolemy, a 2nd-c. Alexandrian astronomer, or his theories. **2** of or relating to the Ptolemies, Macedonian rulers of Egypt from the death of Alexander the Great (323 BC) to the death of Cleopatra (30 BC). [Latin *Ptolemaeus* from Greek *Ptolemaios*]

Ptolemaic system *n. hist.* the theory that the earth is the stationary centre of the Universe (cf. COPERNICAN SYSTEM).

ptomaine /ˈtəʊmeɪn/ *n.* any of various amine compounds of unpleasant taste and odour found in putrefying animal and vegetable matter, associated with and formerly thought to cause food poisoning. [French *ptomaïne* from Italian *ptomaina*, formed irregularly from Greek *ptōma* 'corpse']

ptosis /ˈtəʊsɪs/ *n.* a drooping of the upper eyelid due to paralysis etc. □ **ptotic** /ˈtəʊtɪk/ *adj.* [Greek *ptōsis* from *piptō* 'fall']

PTSD *abbr.* post-traumatic stress disorder.

Pty. *abbr. Austral., NZ, & S.Afr.* proprietary.

ptyalin /ˈtʌɪəlɪn/ *n. Biochem.* a form of amylase found in the saliva of humans and some other animals. [Greek *ptualon* 'spittle']

Pu *symb. Chem.* the element plutonium.

pub[1] /pʌb/ *n.* **1** *Brit.* a public house. **2** *Austral.* a hotel. [abbreviation]

pub[2] /pʌb/ *n.* & *v.* (also **pub.**) ● *n.* publication. ● *v.tr.* (**pubbed**, **pubbing**; *past part.* also **pub**) publish. [abbreviation]

pub crawl *n.* esp. *Brit. colloq.* a drinking tour of several pubs.

puberty /ˈpjuːbəti/ *n.* the period during which adolescents reach sexual maturity and become capable of reproduction. □ **pubertal** *adj.* [Middle English from French *puberté* or Latin *pubertas*, from *puber* 'adult']

pubes[1] /ˈpjuːbiːz, pjuːbz/ *n.* (*pl.* same) **1** the lower part of the abdomen at the front of the pelvis, covered with hair from puberty. **2** *colloq.* the pubic hair. [Latin]

pubes[2] *pl.* of PUBIS.

pubescence /pjʊˈbɛs(ə)ns/ *n.* **1** the time when puberty begins. **2** *Bot.* soft down on the leaves and stems of plants. **3** *Zool.* soft down on various parts of animals, esp. insects. □ **pubescent** *adj.* [French *pubescence* or medieval Latin *pubescentia* from Latin *pubescere* 'reach puberty']

pubic /ˈpjuːbɪk/ *adj.* of or relating to the pubes or pubis.

pubis /ˈpjuːbɪs/ *n.* (*pl.* **pubes** /-biːz/) either of a pair of bones forming the two sides of the pelvis. [Latin *os pubis* 'bone of the pubes']

public /ˈpʌblɪk/ *adj.* & *n.* ● *adj.* **1** of or concerning the people as a whole (*a public holiday*; *the public interest*). **2** open to or shared by all the people (*public baths*; *public library*; *public meeting*). **3** done or existing openly (*made his views public*; *a public protest*). **4** (of a service, funds, etc.) provided by or concerning local or central government (*public money*; *public records*; *public expenditure*). **5 a** of or involved in the affairs of the community, esp. in government or entertainment (*a distinguished public career*; *public figures*). **b** of or relating to a person in his or her capacity as a public figure (*had a likeable public face*). **6** *Brit.* of, for, or acting for, a university (*public examination*). ● *n.* **1** (treated as *sing.* or *pl.*) the community in general, or members of the community. **2** a section of the community having a particular interest or in some special connection (*the reading public*; *my public demands my loyalty*). **3** *Brit. colloq.* **a** = PUBLIC BAR. **b** = PUBLIC HOUSE. □ **go public 1** become a public company. **2** make one's intentions plain; come out into the open.

in public openly, publicly. **in the public domain** belonging to the public as a whole, esp. not subject to copyright. **in the public eye** famous or notorious. □ **publicly** *adv.* [Middle English from Old French *public* or Latin *publicus*, from *pubes* 'adult']

public act *n.* an act of legislation affecting the public as a whole.

public address system *n.* loudspeakers, microphones, amplifiers, etc., used in addressing large audiences.

publican /ˈpʌblɪk(ə)n/ *n.* **1 a** *Brit.* the keeper of a public house. **b** *Austral.* the keeper of a hotel. **2** *Rom.Hist.* & *Bibl.* a tax collector or tax farmer. [Middle English via Old French *publicain* from Latin *publicanus*, from *publicum* 'public revenue' (as PUBLIC)]

public analyst *n.* a member of a body that analyses foodstuffs for toxic substances etc.

publication /pʌblɪˈkeɪʃ(ə)n/ *n.* **1 a** the preparation and issuing of a book, newspaper, engraving, music, etc. to the public. **b** a book etc. so issued. **2** the act or an instance of making something publicly known. [Middle English via Old French from Latin *publicatio -onis* (as PUBLISH)]

public bar *n. Brit.* the least expensive bar in a public house.

public bill *n.* a bill of legislation affecting the public as a whole.

public company *n. Brit.* a company that sells shares to all buyers on the open market.

public enemy *n.* a notorious wanted criminal.

public figure *n.* a famous person.

public health *n.* services intended to protect the health of the public, esp. the provision of adequate sanitation, drainage, etc. by government.

public house *n.* **1** *Brit.* an inn providing alcoholic drinks for consumption on the premises. **2** an inn.

publicist /ˈpʌblɪsɪst/ *n.* **1** a publicity agent or public relations officer. **2** a journalist, esp. concerned with current affairs. **3** *archaic* a writer or other person skilled in international law. □ **publicistic** /-ˈsɪstɪk/ *adj.* [French *publiciste* from Latin (*jus*) *publicum* 'public law']

publicity /pʌbˈlɪsɪti/ *n.* **1 a** the professional exploitation of a product, company, person, etc., by advertising or popularizing. **b** material or information used for this. **2** public exposure; notoriety. [French *publicité* (as PUBLIC)]

publicity agent *n.* a person employed to produce or heighten public exposure.

publicize /ˈpʌblɪsʌɪz/ *v.tr.* (also **-ise**) advertise; make publicly known.

public law *n.* **1** the law of relations between individuals and the State. **2** = PUBLIC ACT.

public lending right *n.* (in the UK) the right of authors to payment when their books etc. are lent by public libraries.

public libel *n. Law* a published libel.

public nuisance *n.* **1** an illegal act against the public generally. **2** *colloq.* an obnoxious person.

public opinion *n.* views, esp. moral, prevalent among the general public.

public orator see ORATOR 2.

public ownership *n.* state ownership of the means of production, distribution, and exchange.

public prosecutor *n.* a law officer conducting criminal proceedings on behalf of the state or in the public interest.

public purse *n.* the national treasury.

Public Record Office *n.* (in the UK) an institution keeping official archives for public inspection.

public relations *n.pl.* the professional maintenance of a favourable public image, esp. by a company, famous person, etc.

public relations officer *n.* a person employed by a company etc. to promote a favourable public image.

public school *n.* **1** (in England and Wales) a private fee-paying secondary school, esp. for boarders. **2** (in Scotland, N. America, etc.) a non-fee-paying school.

public sector *n.* that part of an economy, industry, etc., that is controlled by the State.

public servant *n.* a State official.

public spirit *n.* a willingness to engage in community action. □ **public-spirited** *adj.* **public-spiritedly** *adj.* **public-spiritedness** *adj.*

public transport *n.* buses, trains, etc., charging set fares and running on fixed routes, esp. when state-owned.

public utility *n.* an organization supplying water, gas, etc. to the community.

public works *n.pl.* building operations etc. done by or for the State on behalf of the community.

public wrong *n.* an offence against society as a whole.

publish /ˈpʌblɪʃ/ *v.tr.* **1** (also *absol.*) (of an author, publisher, etc.) prepare and issue (a book, newspaper, engraving, etc.) for public sale. **2** make generally known. **3** announce (an edict etc.) formally; read (marriage banns). **4** *Law* communicate (a libel etc.) to a third party. **5** (esp. as **published** *adj.*) publish the works of (a particular writer or composer) (*she was already a published poet at the age of twenty*). □ **publishable** *adj.* [Middle English *puplise* etc., via Old French *puplier*, *publier* from Latin *publicare* (as PUBLIC)]

publisher /ˈpʌblɪʃə/ *n.* **1** a person or esp. a company that produces and distributes copies of a book, newspaper, etc. for sale. **2** *N. Amer.* a newspaper proprietor. **3** a person or thing that publishes.

puce /pjuːs/ *n.* & *adj.* ● *n.* a dark red or purple-brown colour. ● *adj.* of this colour. [French, = flea(-colour), from Latin *pulex -icis*]

puck[1] /pʌk/ *n.* a rubber disc used as a ball in ice hockey. [19th c.: origin unknown]

puck[2] /pʌk/ *n.* **1** a mischievous or evil sprite. **2** a mischievous child. □ **puckish** *adj.* **puckishly** *adv.* **puckishness** *n.* **pucklike** *adj.* [Old English *pūca*: cf. Welsh *pwca*, Irish *púca*]

pucka var. of PUKKA.

pucker /ˈpʌkə/ *v.* & *n.* ● *v.tr.* & *intr.* (often foll. by *up*) gather or cause to gather into wrinkles, folds, or bulges (*puckered her eyebrows*; *this seam is puckered up*). ● *n.* such a wrinkle, bulge, fold, etc. □ **puckery** *adj.* [probably frequentative, formed as POKE[2], POCKET (cf. PURSE)]

pud /pʊd/ *n. Brit. colloq.* = PUDDING. [abbreviation]

pudding /ˈpʊdɪŋ/ *n.* **1 a** any of various sweet cooked dishes (*plum pudding*; *rice pudding*). **b** a savoury dish containing flour, suet, etc. (*Yorkshire pudding*; *steak and kidney pudding*). **c** *Brit.* the sweet course of a meal. **d** the intestines of a pig etc. stuffed with oatmeal, spices, blood, etc. (*black pudding*). **e** *US* a cold dessert with a soft or creamy consistency. **2** *colloq.* a fat, dumpy, or stupid person. **3** (*Naut.* **puddening** /ˈpʊd(ə)nɪŋ/) *Brit.* a pad or tow binding to prevent chafing etc. □ **in the pudding club** *Brit. slang* pregnant. □ **puddingy** *adj.* [Middle English *poding* from Old French *boudin* 'black pudding', ultimately from Latin *botellus* 'sausage': see BOWEL]

pudding basin *n.* a basin in which puddings are made and often steamed.

pudding cloth *n.* a cloth used for tying up some puddings for boiling.

pudding face *n. Brit. colloq.* a large fat face.

pudding-head *n. colloq.* a stupid person.

pudding-stone *n.* a conglomerate rock consisting of rounded pebbles in a siliceous matrix.

puddle /ˈpʌd(ə)l/ *n.* & *v.* ● *n.* **1** a small pool, esp. of rainwater on a road etc. **2** clay and sand mixed with water and used as a watertight covering for embankments etc. **3** a circular patch of disturbed water made by the blade of an oar at each stroke. ● *v.* **1** *tr.* **a** knead (clay and sand) into puddle. **b** line (a canal etc.)

with puddle. **2** *intr.* make puddle from clay etc. **3** *tr.* stir (molten iron) to produce wrought iron by expelling carbon. **4** *intr.* **a** dabble or wallow in mud or shallow water. **b** busy oneself in an untidy way. **5** *tr.* make (water etc.) muddy. **6** *tr.* work (mixed water and clay) to separate gold or opal. □ **puddler** *n.* **puddly** *adj.* [Middle English *podel, puddel,* diminutive of Old English *pudd* 'ditch']

pudency /'pju:d(ə)nsi/ *n. literary* modesty; shame. [Late Latin *pudentia* (as PUDENDUM)]

pudendum /pjʊ'dɛndəm/ *n.* (*pl.* **pudenda** /-də/) (usu. in *pl.*) the genitals, esp. of a woman. □ **pudendal** *adj.* **pudic** /'pju:dɪk/ *adj.* [Latin *pudenda* (*membra* 'parts'), neut. pl. of gerundive of *pudēre* 'be ashamed']

pudgy /'pʌdʒi/ *adj.* (**pudgier, pudgiest**) *colloq.* (esp. of a person) plump, thickset. □ **pudge** *n.* **pudgily** *adv.* **pudginess** *n.* [cf. PODGY]

pueblo /'pwɛbləʊ/ *n. & adj.* ● *n.* (*pl.* **-os**) **1** a town or village in Spain or Spanish America, esp. a N. American Indian settlement. **2** (**Pueblo**) a member of a N. American Indian people living in pueblos esp. in New Mexico and Arizona. ● *adj.* of or relating to the Pueblos or their culture. [Spanish, = people, from Latin *populus*]

puerile /'pjʊərʌɪl/ *adj.* **1** trivial, childish, immature. **2** of or like a child. □ **puerilely** *adv.* **puerility** /-'rɪlɪti/ *n.* (*pl.* **-ies**). [French *puéril* or Latin *puerilis* from *puer* 'boy']

puerperal /pju:'ə:p(ə)r(ə)l/ *adj.* of or caused by childbirth. [Latin *puerperus,* from *puer* 'child' + *-parus* 'bearing']

puerperal fever *n.* fever following childbirth and caused by uterine infection.

Puerto Rican /pwə:tə(ʊ) 'ri:k(ə)n/ *n. & adj.* ● *n.* **1** a native of Puerto Rico, an island of the Greater Antilles. **2** a person of Puerto Rican descent. ● *adj.* of or relating to Puerto Rico or its inhabitants.

puff /pʌf/ *n. & v.* ● *n.* **1 a** a short quick light blast of breath or wind. **b** the sound of this; a similar sound. **c** a small quantity of vapour, smoke, etc., emitted in one blast (*went up in a puff of smoke*). **2** a cake etc. containing jam, cream, etc., and made of light esp. puff pastry. **3** a gathered mass of material in a dress etc. (*puff sleeve*). **4** a rolled protuberant mass of hair. **5 a** an extravagantly enthusiastic review of a book etc., esp. in a newspaper. **b** *Brit.* an advertisement for goods etc., esp. in a newspaper. **6** = POWDER PUFF. **7** *N. Amer.* an eiderdown. **8** *Brit. colloq.* one's life (*in all my puff*). ● *v.* **1** *intr.* emit a puff of air or breath; blow with short blasts. **2** *intr.* (usu. foll. by *away, out,* etc.) (of a person smoking, a steam engine, etc.) emit or move with puffs (*puffing away at his cigar; a train puffed out of the station*). **3** *tr.* (usu. in *passive*; often foll. by *out*) put out of breath (*arrived somewhat puffed; completely puffed him out*). **4** *intr.* breathe hard; pant. **5** *tr.* utter pantingly (*'No more,' he puffed*). **6** *intr. & tr.* (usu. foll. by *up, out*) become or cause to become inflated; swell (*his eye was inflamed and puffed up; puffed up the balloon*). **7** *tr.* (usu. foll. by *out, up, away*) blow or emit (dust, smoke, a light object, etc.) with a puff. **8** *tr.* smoke (a pipe etc.) in puffs. **9** *tr.* (usu. as **puffed up** *adj.*) elate; make proud or boastful. **10** *tr.* advertise or promote (goods, a book, etc.) with exaggerated or false praise. □ **puff and blow** = sense 4 of *v.* **puff up** = sense 9 of *v.* [Middle English *puf, puffe,* perhaps from Old English, imitative of the sound of breath]

puff-adder *n.* a large venomous African viper, *Bitis arietans,* which inflates the upper part of its body and hisses when excited.

puffball /'pʌfbɔ:l/ *n.* **1** any of various fungi having a ball-shaped spore case. **2** a short full skirt gathered around the hemline to produce a soft puffy shape. **3** a powder puff or an object resembling one.

puffer /'pʌfə/ *n.* **1** a person or thing that puffs. **2** = PUFF-PUFF.

puffer fish *n.* = GLOBE-FISH.

puffery /'pʌf(ə)ri/ *n.* exaggerated praise or commendation. [PUFF *v.* 10 + -ERY]

puffin /'pʌfɪn/ *n.* any of various seabirds of the family Alcidae native to the N. Atlantic and N. Pacific, esp. *Fratercula arctica,* having a large head with a brightly coloured triangular bill, and black and white plumage. [Middle English *poffin, pophyn,* originally denoting a shearwater, apparently from PUFF + -ING[3] with reference to that bird's fat nestlings]

puffin crossing *n.* (in the UK) a pedestrian crossing with traffic lights operated as long as pedestrians are detected on the crossing by infra-red detectors and mats. [from *p*edestrian *u*ser *f*riendly *in*telligent, respelt after the bird name]

puff pastry *n.* light flaky pastry.

puff-puff *n. Brit.* a childish word for a steam engine or train.

puffy /'pʌfi/ *adj.* (**puffier, puffiest**) **1** swollen, esp. of the face etc. **2** fat. **3** gusty. **4** short-winded; puffed out. □ **puffily** *adv.* **puffiness** *n.*

pug[1] /pʌg/ *n.* **1** (in full **pug-dog**) **a** a dwarf breed of dog like a bulldog with a broad flat nose and deeply wrinkled face. **b** a dog of this breed. **2** a fox. **3** a small geometrid moth of the genus *Eupithecia* or a related genus. □ **puggish** *adj.* **puggy** *adj.* [16th c.: perhaps from Low German or Dutch]

pug[2] /pʌg/ *n. & v.* ● *n.* loam or clay mixed and prepared for making bricks, pottery, etc. ● *v.tr.* (**pugged, pugging**) **1** prepare (clay) thus. **2** pack (esp. the space under the floor to deaden sound) with pug, sawdust, etc. □ **pugging** *n.* [19th c.: origin unknown]

pug[3] /pʌg/ *n. slang* a boxer. [abbreviation of PUGILIST]

pug[4] /pʌg/ *n. & v.* ● *n.* the footprint of an animal. ● *v.tr.* (**pugged, pugging**) track by pugs. [Hindi *pag* 'footprint']

pug-dog see PUG[1] 1.

puggaree /'pʌg(ə)ri:/ *n.* **1** an Indian turban. **2** a thin muslin scarf tied round a sun-helmet etc. and shielding the neck. [Hindi *pagṛī* 'turban']

pugilist /'pju:dʒɪlɪst/ *n.* a boxer, esp. a professional. □ **pugilism** *n.* **pugilistic** /-'lɪstɪk/ *adj.* [Latin *pugil* 'boxer']

pug-mill *n.* a mill for preparing pug. [PUG[2]]

pugnacious /pʌg'neɪʃəs/ *adj.* quarrelsome; disposed to fight. □ **pugnaciously** *adv.* **pugnaciousness** *n.* **pugnacity** /-'nasɪti/ *n.* [Latin *pugnax -acis,* via *pugnare* 'fight' from *pugnus* 'fist']

pug-nose *n.* a short squat or snub nose. □ **pug-nosed** *adj.*

puisne /'pju:ni/ *adj. Brit. Law* denoting a judge of a superior court inferior in rank to chief justices. [Old French, from *puis* (from Latin *postea* 'afterwards') + *né* 'born' from Latin *natus*: cf. PUNY]

puissance /'pju:ɪs(ə)ns, 'pwi:-, 'pwɪ-/ *n.* **1** /also 'pwi:sɒ̃s/ a test of a horse's ability to jump large obstacles in showjumping. **2** *archaic* great power, might, or influence. [Middle English (in sense 2) from Old French (as PUISSANT)]

puissant /'pju:ɪs(ə)nt, 'pwi:-, 'pwɪ-/ *adj. literary* or *archaic* having great power or influence; mighty. □ **puissantly** *adv.* [Middle English via Old French from Latin *posse* 'be able': cf. POTENT[1]]

puja /'pu:dʒə/ *n.* (also **pooja**) a Hindu rite of worship; an offering. [Sanskrit]

puke /pju:k/ *v. & n. slang* ● *v.tr. & intr.* vomit. ● *n.* vomit. □ **pukey** *adj.* [16th c.: probably imitative]

pukeko /'pu:kɛkəʊ/ *n.* (*pl.* **-os**) *NZ* a purple gallinule, *Porphyrio porphyrio.* [Maori]

pukka /'pʌkə/ *adj.* (also **pukkah, pucka**) *Anglo-Ind.* **1** genuine. **2** of good quality; reliable (*did a pukka job*). **3** of full weight. [Hindi *pakkā* 'cooked, ripe, substantial']

pulchritude /'pʌlkrɪtju:d/ *n. literary* beauty. □ **pulchritudinous** /-'tju:dɪnəs/ *adj.* [Middle English from Latin *pulchritudo -dinis*, from *pulcher -chri* 'beautiful']

pule /pjuːl/ *v.intr. literary* cry querulously or weakly; whine, whimper. [Middle English, probably imitative: cf. French *piauler*]

Pulitzer Prize /ˈpʊlɪtsə, ˈpjuː-/ *n.* each of 13 annual awards for achievements in American journalism, literature, and music. [established by J. *Pulitzer*, American newspaper publisher d. 1911]

pull /pʊl/ *v. & n.* ● *v.* **1** *tr.* exert force on (a thing) tending to move it towards oneself or the origin of the force (*stop pulling my hair*). **2** *tr.* cause to move in this way (*pulled it nearer; pulled me into the room*). **3** *intr.* exert a pulling force (*the horse pulls well; the engine will not pull*). **4** *tr.* extract (a cork or tooth) by pulling. **5** *tr.* damage (a muscle etc.) by abnormal strain. **6 a** *tr.* move (a boat) by pulling on the oars. **b** *intr.* (of a boat etc.) be caused to move, esp. in a specified direction. **7** *intr.* (often foll. by *up*) proceed with effort (up a hill etc.). **8** *tr.* (foll. by *on*) bring out (a weapon) for use against (a person). **9 a** *tr.* check the speed of (a horse), esp. so as to make it lose the race. **b** *intr.* (of a horse) strain against the bit. **10** *tr.* attract or secure (custom or support). **11** *tr. Brit.* draw (liquor) from a barrel etc. **12** *intr.* (foll. by *at*) tear or pluck at. **13** *intr.* (often foll. by *on, at*) inhale deeply; draw or suck (on a pipe etc.). **14** *tr.* (often foll. by *up*) remove (a plant) by the root. **15** *tr.* **a** *Cricket* play (the ball) round to the leg side from the off. **b** *Golf & Baseball* strike (the ball) widely to the left (or, of a left-handed player, the right). **16** *tr.* print (a proof etc.). **17** *tr. colloq.* achieve or accomplish (esp. something illicit). **18** *tr. slang* succeed in attracting sexually; pick up (a sexual partner). ● *n.* **1** the act of pulling. **2** the force exerted by this. **3** a means of exerting influence; an advantage. **4** something that attracts or draws attention. **5** a deep draught of liquor. **6** a prolonged effort, e.g. in going up a hill. **7** a handle etc. for applying a pull. **8** a spell of rowing. **9** a printer's rough proof. **10** *Cricket & Golf* a pulling stroke. **11** a suck at a cigarette. □ **pull about 1** treat roughly. **2** pull from side to side. **pull all the stops out** exert extreme effort. **pull apart** (or **to pieces**) = *take to pieces* (see PIECE). **pull back** retreat or cause to retreat. **pull down 1** demolish (esp. a building). **2** humiliate. **3** *colloq.* earn (a sum of money) as wages etc. **pull a face** esp. *Brit.* assume a distinctive or specified (e.g. sad or angry) expression. **pull a fast one** see FAST[1]. **pull in 1** (of a bus, train, etc.) arrive to take passengers. **2** (of a vehicle) move to the side of or off the road. **3** earn or acquire. **4** *colloq.* arrest. **5** rein in, hold in, check. **pull a person's leg** deceive a person playfully. **pull off 1** remove by pulling. **2** succeed in achieving or winning. **pull oneself together** recover control of oneself. **pull the other one** *Brit. colloq.* expressing disbelief (with reference to *pull a person's leg*). **pull out 1** take out by pulling. **2** depart. **3** withdraw from an undertaking. **4** (of a bus, train, etc.) leave with its passengers. **5** (of a vehicle) move out from the side of the road, or from its normal position to overtake. **pull over** (of a vehicle) pull in. **pull the plug** (often foll. by *on*) *colloq.* put an end to an enterprise etc.; destroy; cut off (supplies etc.). **pull one's punches** avoid using one's full force. **pull rank** take unfair advantage of one's seniority. **pull round** esp. *Brit.* recover or cause to recover from an illness. **pull strings** exert (esp. clandestine) influence. **pull the strings** be the real actuator of what another does. **pull through 1** get through an illness, a dangerous situation, or a difficult undertaking. **2** enable (a person) to do this. **pull together** work in harmony. **pull up 1** stop or cause to stop moving. **2** pull out of the ground. **3** reprimand. **4** check oneself. **pull one's weight** do one's fair share of work. **pull wires** esp. *US* = *pull strings*. □ **puller** *n.* [Old English (*ā*)*pullian*, perhaps related to Low German *pūlen*, Middle Dutch *polen* 'to shell']

pull-back *n.* **1** a retarding influence. **2** a withdrawal of troops.

pull-down *adj. & n.* ● *attrib.adj.* that may be, or is designed to be, pulled down. ● *n.* a thing that may be pulled down or which pulls something down.

pullet /ˈpʊlɪt/ *n.* a young hen, esp. one less than one year old. [Middle English from Old French *poulet*, diminutive of *poule*, ultimately from fem. of Latin *pullus* 'chicken']

pulley /ˈpʊli/ *n. & v.* ● *n.* (*pl.* **-eys**) **1** a grooved wheel or set of wheels for a cord etc. to pass over, set in a block and used for changing the direction of a force. **2** a wheel or drum fixed on a shaft and turned by a belt, used esp. to increase speed or power. ● *v.tr.* (**-eys, -eyed**) **1** hoist or work with a pulley. **2** provide with a pulley. [Middle English from Old French *polie*, probably ultimately from a medieval Greek diminutive of *polos* POLE[2]]

pull-in *n. Brit.* a roadside café or other stopping place.

Pullman /ˈpʊlmən/ *n.* (*pl.* **Pullmans**) **1** a railway carriage or motor coach affording special comfort. **2** a sleeping car. **3** a train consisting of Pullman carriages. [named after G. M. *Pullman*, American designer d. 1897]

pull-off *adj. & n.* ● *attrib.adj.* that may be, or is designed to be, pulled off. ● *n.* **1** an act of pulling something off. **2** a lay-by.

pull-on *adj. & n.* ● *attrib.adj.* designating a garment without fasteners that is pulled on. ● *n.* such a garment.

pull-out *n.* **1** something that can be pulled out, esp. a section of a magazine. **2** the act of pulling out; a withdrawal, esp. from military involvement.

pullover /ˈpʊləʊvə/ *n.* a knitted garment put on over the head and covering the top half of the body.

pullulate /ˈpʌljʊleɪt/ *v.intr.* **1** (of a seed, shoot, etc.) bud, sprout, germinate. **2** (esp. of an animal) swarm, throng; breed prolifically. **3** develop; spring up; come to life. **4** (foll. by *with*) abound. □ **pullulant** *adj.* **pullulation** /-ˈleɪʃ(ə)n/ *n.* [Latin *pullulare* 'sprout' from *pullulus*, diminutive of *pullus* 'young of an animal']

pull-up *n.* **1** an exercise involving raising oneself with one's arms by pulling up against a horizontal bar etc. fixed above one's head. **2** a place for pulling up or stopping, esp. in a motor vehicle. **3** the act of pulling up; a sudden stop.

pulmonary /ˈpʌlmən(ə)ri/ *adj.* **1** of or relating to the lungs. **2** having lungs or lunglike organs. **3** affected with or susceptible to lung disease. □ **pulmonate** /-nət/ *adj.* [Latin *pulmonarius* from *pulmo -onis* 'lung']

pulmonary artery *n.* the artery conveying blood from the heart to the lungs.

pulmonary tuberculosis *n.* a form of tuberculosis caused by inhaling the tubercle bacillus into the lungs.

pulmonary vein *n.* the vein carrying oxygenated blood from the lungs to the heart.

pulmonic /pʌlˈmɒnɪk/ *adj.* = PULMONARY 1. [French *pulmonique* or via modern Latin *pulmonicus* from Latin *pulmo* (as PULMONARY)]

pulp /pʌlp/ *n. & v.* ● *n.* **1** the soft fleshy part of fruit etc. **2** any soft thick wet mass. **3** a soft shapeless mass derived from rags, wood, etc., used in papermaking. **4** (often *attrib.*) popular or sensational writing often regarded as of poor quality (originally printed on rough paper) (*pulp fiction*). **5** vascular tissue filling the interior cavity and root canals of a tooth. **6** *Mining* pulverized ore mixed with water. ● *v.* **1** *tr.* reduce to pulp. **2** *tr.* withdraw (a publication) from the market, usu. recycling the paper. **3** *tr.* remove pulp from. **4** *intr.* become pulp. □ **pulper** *n.* **pulpy** *adj.* **pulpiness** *n.* [Latin *pulpa*]

pulpit /ˈpʊlpɪt/ *n.* **1** a raised enclosed platform in a church etc. from which the preacher delivers a sermon. **2** (prec. by *the*) preachers or preaching collectively. **3 a** a standing place on the bowsprit of a fishing vessel etc. **b** a railed-in area at the bow (or stern) of a yacht etc. [Middle English from Latin *pulpitum* 'scaffold, platform']

pulpwood /ˈpʌlpwʊd/ *n.* timber suitable for making pulp.

pulque /ˈpʊlkeɪ, ˈpʊlki/ *n.* a Mexican fermented drink made from the sap of the maguey. [Latin American Spanish, from Nahuatl *puliúhki* 'decomposed']

pulque brandy *n.* a strong intoxicant made from pulque.

pulsar /ˈpʌlsɑː/ *n. Astron.* a celestial object, thought to be a rapidly rotating neutron star, emitting regular pulses of radio waves and other electromagnetic radiation. [*puls*ating *star*, on the pattern of *quasar*]

pulsate /pʌlˈseɪt, ˈpʌlseɪt/ *v.intr.* **1** expand and contract rhythmically; throb. **2** vibrate, quiver, thrill. □ **pulsation** /-ˈseɪʃ(ə)n/ *n.* **pulsator** /-ˈseɪtə/ *n.* **pulsatory** /ˈpʌlsət(ə)ri/ *adj.* [Latin *pulsare*, frequentative of *pellere puls-* 'drive, beat']

pulsatile /ˈpʌlsətʌɪl/ *adj.* **1** of or having the property of pulsation. **2** (of a musical instrument) played by percussion. [medieval Latin *pulsatilis* (as PULSATE)]

pulsatilla /pʌlsəˈtɪlə/ *n.* any plant of the genus *Pulsatilla*, esp. the pasque flower. [modern Latin, diminutive of *pulsatus* 'beaten about', because it quivers in the wind]

pulse[1] /pʌls/ *n. & v.* ● *n.* **1 a** a rhythmical throbbing of the arteries as blood is propelled through them, esp. as felt in the wrists, temples, etc. **b** each successive beat of the arteries or heart. **2** a throb or thrill of life or emotion. **3** a general feeling or opinion (*tried to read the pulse of the nation*). **4** a single vibration of sound, electric current, light, etc., esp. as a signal. **5** a musical beat. **6** any regular or recurrent rhythm, e.g. of the stroke of oars. ● *v.intr.* **1** pulsate. **2** (foll. by *out*, *in*, etc.) transmit etc. by rhythmical beats. □ **pulseless** *adj.* [Middle English via Old French *pous* from Latin *pulsus*, from *pellere puls-* 'drive, beat']

pulse[2] /pʌls/ *n.* (treated as *sing.* or *pl.*) **1** the edible seeds of various leguminous plants, e.g. chickpeas, lentils, beans, etc. **2** the plant or plants producing this. [Middle English via Old French *pols* from Latin *puls pultis* 'porridge of meal or pulse']

pulse code *n.* the coding of information using pulses.

pulse code modulation *n.* a pulse modulation technique of representing a signal by a sequence of binary codes.

pulse modulation *n.* a type of modulation in which pulses are varied to represent a signal.

pulsimeter /pʌlˈsɪmɪtə/ *n.* an instrument for measuring the rate or force of a pulse.

pulverize /ˈpʌlvərʌɪz/ *v.* (also **-ise**) **1** *tr.* reduce to fine particles. **2** *tr. & intr.* crumble to dust. **3** *colloq. tr.* **a** demolish. **b** defeat utterly. □ **pulverizable** *adj.* **pulverization** /-ˈzeɪʃ(ə)n/ *n.* **pulverizator** *n.* **pulverizer** *n.* [Middle English from Late Latin *pulverizare*, from *pulvis pulveris* 'dust']

pulverulent /pʌlˈvɛrʊl(ə)nt/ *adj.* **1** consisting of fine particles; powdery. **2** likely to crumble. [Latin *pulverulentus* (as PULVERIZE)]

puma /ˈpjuːmə/ *n.* a wild American cat, *Felis concolor*, usu. with a tawny or greyish coat. Also called COUGAR, PANTHER, *mountain lion*. [Spanish from Quechua]

pumice /ˈpʌmɪs/ *n. & v.* ● *n.* (in full **pumice stone**) **1** a light porous volcanic rock often used as an abrasive in cleaning or polishing substances. **2** a piece of this used for removing hard skin etc. ● *v.tr.* rub or clean with a pumice. □ **pumiceous** /pjuːˈmɪʃəs/ *adj.* [Middle English via Old French *pomis* from Latin *pumex pumicis* (dialect *pom-*): cf. POUNCE[2]]

pummel /ˈpʌm(ə)l/ *v.tr.* (**pummelled**, **pummelling**; *US* **pummeled**, **pummeling**) strike repeatedly esp. with the fist. [alteration of POMMEL]

pump[1] /pʌmp/ *n. & v.* ● *n.* **1** a machine, usu. with rotary action or the reciprocal action of a piston, for raising or moving liquids, compressing gases, inflating tyres, etc. **2** an instance of pumping; a stroke of a pump. ● *v.* **1** *tr.* (often foll. by *in*, *out*, *into*, *up*, etc.) raise or remove (liquid, gas, etc.) with a pump. **2** *tr.* (often foll. by *up*) fill (a tyre etc.) with air. **3** *tr.* remove (water etc.) with a pump. **4** *intr.* work a pump. **5** *tr.* (often foll. by *out*) cause to move, pour forth, etc., as if by pumping. **6** *tr.* try to elicit information from (a person) by persistent questioning. **7** *tr.* **a** move vigorously up and down. **b** shake (a person's hand) effusively. □ **pump iron** *colloq.* exercise with weights. [Middle English *pumpe, pompe* (originally *nautical*): probably imitative]

pump[2] /pʌmp/ *n.* **1** a plimsoll. **2** a light shoe for dancing etc. **3** *N. Amer.* a court shoe. [16th c.: origin unknown]

pump-action *attrib.adj.* designating a repeating firearm activated by a horizontally operating slide action.

pump-brake *n.* the handle of a pump, esp. with a transverse bar for several people to work at.

pumpernickel /ˈpʊmpənɪk(ə)l, ˈpʌm-/ *n.* German wholemeal rye bread. [German, earlier = lout, bumpkin, of uncertain origin]

pump-handle *v.tr. colloq.* shake (a person's hand) effusively.

pumpkin /ˈpʌm(p)kɪn/ *n.* **1** any of various plants of the genus *Cucurbita*, esp. *C. maxima*, with large lobed leaves and tendrils. **2** the large rounded yellow fruit of this with a thick rind and edible flesh. [alteration of earlier *pompon*, *pumpion* from obsolete French *po(m)pon* via Latin *pepo -onis* from Greek *pepōn* 'large melon': see PEPO]

pump-priming *n.* **1** the introduction of fluid etc. into a pump to prepare it for working. **2** esp. *US* the stimulation of commerce etc. by investment.

pump room *n.* **1** a room where fuel pumps etc. are stored or controlled. **2** a room at a spa etc. where medicinal water is dispensed.

pun[1] /pʌn/ *n. & v.* ● *n.* the humorous use of a word to suggest different meanings, or of words of the same sound and different meanings. ● *v.intr.* (**punned**, **punning**) (foll. by *on*) make a pun or puns with (words). □ **punningly** *adv.* [17th c.: perhaps from obsolete *pundigrion*, perhaps a fanciful alteration of PUNCTILIO]

pun[2] /pʌn/ *v.tr.* (**punned**, **punning**) *Brit.* consolidate (earth or rubble) by pounding or ramming. □ **punner** *n.* [dialect variant of POUND[2]]

puna /ˈpuːnə/ *n.* **1** a high plateau in the Peruvian Andes. **2** = MOUNTAIN SICKNESS. [Quechua, in sense 1]

punch[1] /pʌn(t)ʃ/ *v. & n.* ● *v.tr.* **1** strike bluntly, esp. with a closed fist. **2** prod or poke with a blunt object. **3 a** pierce a hole in (metal, paper, a ticket, etc.) as or with a punch. **b** pierce (a hole) by punching. **4** *N. Amer.* drive (cattle) by prodding with a stick etc. ● *n.* **1** a blow with a fist. **2** the ability to deliver this. **3** *colloq.* vigour, momentum; effective force. □ **puncher** *n.* [Middle English, variant of POUNCE[1]]

punch[2] /pʌn(t)ʃ/ *n.* **1** a device or machine for punching holes in materials (e.g. paper, leather, metal, plaster). **2** a tool or machine for impressing a design or stamping a die on a material. [perhaps an abbreviation of PUNCHEON[1], or from PUNCH[1]]

punch[3] /pʌn(t)ʃ/ *n.* a drink of wine or spirits mixed with water, fruit juices, spices, etc., and usu. served hot. [probably from Sanskrit *pañca* 'five, five kinds of' (as the drink properly had five ingredients)]

punch[4] /pʌn(t)ʃ/ *n.* **1** (**Punch**) a grotesque humpbacked figure in a puppet show called *Punch and Judy*. **2** (in full **Suffolk punch**) a short-legged thickset draught horse. □ **(as) pleased as Punch** showing great pleasure. [abbreviation of PUNCHINELLO]

punchbag /ˈpʌn(t)ʃbag/ *n. Brit.* a stuffed bag suspended at a height for boxers etc. to practise punching.

punchball /ˈpʌn(t)ʃbɔːl/ *n.* **1** *Brit.* a stuffed or inflated ball suspended or mounted on a stand, used for punching practice by boxers etc. **2** *US* a ball game in which a rubber ball is punched with the fist or head.

punchbowl /ˈpʌn(t)ʃbəʊl/ *n.* **1** a bowl in which punch is mixed. **2** a deep round hollow in a hill.

punchcard /ˈpʌn(t)ʃkɑːd/ *n.* (also **punched card**) a card perforated according to a code, for conveying instructions or data to a data processor etc.

punch-drunk *adj.* stupefied from or as though from a series of heavy blows.

puncheon[1] /ˈpʌn(t)ʃ(ə)n/ *n.* **1** a short post, esp. one supporting a roof in a coal mine. **2** = PUNCH². [Middle English from Old French *poinson, po(i)nchon*, ultimately from Latin *pungere punct-* 'prick']

puncheon[2] /ˈpʌn(t)ʃ(ə)n/ *n. hist.* a large cask for liquids etc. holding from 72 to 120 gallons. [Middle English from Old French *poinson, po(i)nchon*, of unknown origin (probably not the same as in PUNCHEON¹)]

Punchinello /pʌn(t)ʃɪˈnɛləʊ/ *n.* (*pl.* **-os**) **1** the chief character in a traditional Italian puppet show. **2** a short stout person of comical appearance. [Neapolitan dialect *Polecenella*, Italian *Pulcinella*, perhaps diminutive of *pollecena* 'young turkey-cock with a hooked beak' from *pulcino* 'chicken', ultimately from Latin *pullus*]

punching bag *n. US* = PUNCHBAG.

punchline /ˈpʌn(t)ʃlʌɪn/ *n.* words giving the point of a joke or story.

punch tape *n.* (also **punched tape**) a paper tape perforated according to a code, for conveying instructions or data to a data processor etc.

punch-up *n. Brit. colloq.* a fist fight; a brawl.

punchy /ˈpʌn(t)ʃi/ *adj.* (**punchier**, **punchiest**) having punch or vigour; forceful. □ **punchily** *adv.* **punchiness** *n.*

puncta *pl.* of PUNCTUM.

punctate /ˈpʌŋ(k)teɪt/ *adj. Biol.* marked or studded with points, dots, spots, etc. □ **punctation** /-ˈteɪʃ(ə)n/ *n.* [Latin *punctum* (as POINT)]

punctilio /pʌŋ(k)ˈtɪlɪəʊ/ *n.* (*pl.* **-os**) **1** a delicate point of ceremony or honour. **2** the etiquette of such points. **3** petty formality. [Italian *puntiglio* & Spanish *puntillo*, diminutive of *punto* POINT]

punctilious /pʌŋ(k)ˈtɪlɪəs/ *adj.* **1** attentive to formality or etiquette. **2** precise in behaviour. □ **punctiliously** *adv.* **punctiliousness** *n.* [French *pointilleux* from *pointille*, from Italian (as PUNCTILIO)]

punctual /ˈpʌŋ(k)tʃʊəl, -tjʊəl/ *adj.* observing the appointed time; neither early nor late. □ **punctuality** /-ˈalɪti/ *n.* **punctually** *adv.* [Middle English via medieval Latin *punctualis* from Latin *punctum* POINT]

punctuate /ˈpʌŋ(k)tʃʊeɪt, -tjʊ-/ *v.tr.* **1** insert punctuation marks in. **2** interrupt at intervals (*punctuated his tale with heavy sighs*). [medieval Latin *punctuare punctuat-* (as PUNCTUAL)]

punctuation /pʌŋ(k)tʃʊˈeɪʃ(ə)n, -tjʊ-/ *n.* **1** the system or arrangement of marks used to punctuate a written passage. **2** the practice or skill of punctuating. [medieval Latin *punctuatio* (as PUNCTUATE)]

punctuation mark *n.* a mark (e.g. a full stop, comma, etc.) used in writing to separate sentences and phrases etc. and to clarify meaning.

punctum /ˈpʌŋ(k)təm/ *n.* (*pl.* **puncta** /-tə/) *Biol.* a speck, dot, spot of colour, etc., or an elevation or depression on a surface. [Latin, = POINT]

puncture /ˈpʌŋ(k)tʃə/ *n.* & *v.* ● *n.* **1** a prick or pricking, esp. the accidental piercing of a pneumatic tyre. **2** a hole made in this way. ● *v.* **1** *tr.* make a puncture in. **2** *intr.* undergo puncture. **3** *tr.* prick or pierce. **4** *tr.* deflate (pomposity etc.); debunk. [Middle English from Latin *punctura*, from *pungere punct-* 'prick']

pundit /ˈpʌndɪt/ *n.* **1** (also **pandit**) a Hindu learned in Sanskrit and in the philosophy, religion, and jurisprudence of India. **2** often *iron.* a learned expert or teacher. □ **punditry** *n.* [Hindustani *paṇḍit* from Sanskrit *paṇḍita* 'learned']

pungent /ˈpʌn(d)ʒ(ə)nt/ *adj.* **1** having a sharp or strong taste or smell, esp. so as to produce a pricking sensation. **2** (of remarks) penetrating, biting, caustic. **3** mentally stimulating. **4** *Biol.* having a sharp point. □ **pungency** *n.* **pungently** *adv.* [Latin *pungent-*, pres. part. of *pungere* 'prick']

Punic /ˈpjuːnɪk/ *adj.* & *n.* ● *adj.* of or relating to ancient Carthage in N. Africa or its language. ● *n.* the language of Carthage, related to Phoenician. [Latin *Punicus*, *Poenicus* from *Poenus*, from Greek *Phoinix* 'Phoenician']

Punic faith *n.* treachery. [from the character attributed to the Carthaginians by the Romans]

punish /ˈpʌnɪʃ/ *v.tr.* **1** cause (an offender) to suffer for an offence. **2** inflict a penalty for (an offence). **3** *colloq.* inflict severe blows on (an opponent). **4 a** tax severely; subject to severe treatment. **b** abuse or treat improperly. □ **punishable** *adj.* **punisher** *n.* **punishing** *adj.* (in sense 4a). **punishingly** *adv.* [Middle English via Old French *punir* from Latin *punire* = *poenire*, from *poena* 'penalty']

punishment /ˈpʌnɪʃm(ə)nt/ *n.* **1** the act or an instance of punishing; the condition of being punished. **2** the loss or suffering inflicted in this. **3** *colloq.* severe treatment or suffering. [Middle English from Anglo-French & Old French *punissement*, from *punir*]

punitive /ˈpjuːnɪtɪv/ *adj.* (also **punitory** /-t(ə)ri/) **1** inflicting or intended to inflict punishment. **2** (of taxation etc.) extremely severe. □ **punitively** *adv.* [French *punitif -ive* or medieval Latin *punitivus* (as PUNISHMENT)]

punitive damages *n.pl. Law* = VINDICTIVE DAMAGES.

Punjabi /pʌnˈdʒɑːbi, pʊn-/ *n.* & *adj.* ● *n.* (*pl.* **Punjabis**) **1 a** *hist.* a native of the Punjab in India, now divided between India and Pakistan. **b** a native of the state of Punjab in India or the province Punjab in Pakistan. **2** the language spoken in these areas. ● *adj.* of or relating to these areas, their inhabitants, or their language. [Hindi *pañjābī*]

punk /pʌŋk/ *n.* & *adj.* ● *n.* **1 a** a worthless person or thing (often as a general term of abuse). **b** nonsense. **2 a** (in full **punk rock**) a loud fast-moving form of rock music with crude and aggressive effects. **b** (in full **punk rocker**) a devotee of this. **3** *N. Amer.* a hoodlum or ruffian. **4** *US* a passive male homosexual. **5** *US* an inexperienced young person; a novice. **6** soft crumbly wood that has been attacked by fungus, used as tinder. ● *adj.* **1** worthless, rotten. **2** denoting punk rock and its associations. □ **punkish** *adj.* **punky** *adj.* [17th c.: origin unknown, perhaps related to SPUNK]

punkah /ˈpʌŋkə, -kɑː/ *n.* **1** (in India) a fan usu. made from the leaf of the palmyra. **2** a large swinging cloth fan on a frame worked by a cord or electrically. [Hindi *pankhā* 'fan' from Sanskrit *pakṣaka*, from *pakṣa* 'wing']

punnet /ˈpʌnɪt/ *n. Brit.* a small light basket or container for fruit or vegetables. [19th c.: perhaps diminutive of dialect *pun* POUND¹]

punster /ˈpʌnstə/ *n.* a person who makes puns, esp. habitually.

punt[1] /pʌnt/ *n.* & *v.* ● *n.* a long narrow flat-bottomed boat, square at both ends, used mainly for pleasure on rivers and propelled using a long pole. ● *v.* **1** *tr.* propel (a punt) with a pole. **2** *intr.* & *tr.* travel or convey in a punt. □ **punter** *n.* [Middle English via Middle Low German *punte, punto* & Middle Dutch *ponte* 'ferry boat' from Latin *ponto*, a Gaulish transport vessel]

punt[2] /pʌnt/ *v.* & *n.* ● *v.tr.* kick (a ball, esp. in rugby and American football) after it has dropped from the hands and before it reaches the ground. ● *n.* such a kick. □ **punter** *n.* [probably from dialect *punt* 'push forcibly': cf. BUNT³]

punt[3] /pʌnt/ *v.* & *n.* ● *v.intr.* **1** (in some card games) lay a stake against the bank. **2** *Brit. colloq.* **a** bet on a horse etc. **b** speculate in shares etc. ● *n.* **1** esp. *Brit.* a bet. **2** a point in faro. [French *ponter* from *ponte* 'player against the bank', from Spanish *punto* POINT]

punt[4] /pʊnt/ *n.* the chief monetary unit of the Republic of Ireland. [Irish, = pound]

punter /ˈpʌntə/ *n.* **1** *Brit.* a person who gambles or lays a bet. **2** *Brit.* **a** *colloq.* a customer or client; a member of an audience; a member of the general public. **b** *slang* a prostitute's client. **3** a point in faro.

puny /ˈpjuːni/ *adj.* (**punier**, **puniest**) **1** undersized. **2** weak, feeble. **3** petty. □ **punily** *adv.* **puniness** *n.* [phonetic spelling of PUISNE]

pup /pʌp/ *n.* & *v.* ● *n.* **1** a young dog. **2** a young wolf, rat, seal, etc. **3** esp. *Brit.* an unpleasant or arrogant young man. ● *v.tr.* (**pupped**, **pupping**) (also *absol.*) (of a bitch etc.) bring forth (young). □ **in pup** (of a bitch) pregnant. **sell a person a pup** *Brit.* swindle a person, esp. by selling something worthless. [back-formation from PUPPY, as if a diminutive ending in -Y[2]]

pupa /'pju:pə/ *n.* (*pl.* **pupae** /-pi:/) an inactive immature form of an insect, being the resting stage between larva and adult, e.g. a chrysalis. □ **pupal** *adj.* [modern Latin from Latin *pupa* 'girl, doll']

pupate /pju:'peɪt/ *v.intr.* become a pupa. □ **pupation** *n.*

pupil[1] /'pju:pɪl, -p(ə)l/ *n.* **1** a person who is taught by another, esp. a schoolchild or student in relation to a teacher. **2** *Law* a trainee barrister. □ **pupillary** *adj.* (also **pupilary**). [Middle English, originally = orphan, ward, from Old French *pupille* or Latin *pupillus*, *-illa*, diminutive of *pupus* 'boy', *pupa* 'girl']

pupil[2] /'pju:pɪl, -p(ə)l/ *n.* the dark circular opening in the centre of the iris of the eye, varying in size to regulate the passage of light to the retina. □ **pupillar** *adj.* (also **pupilar**). **pupillary** *adj.* (also **pupilary**). [Old French *pupille* or Latin *pupilla*, diminutive of *pūpa* 'doll' (as PUPIL[1]): so called from the tiny reflected images visible in the eye]

pupillage /'pju:pɪlɪdʒ/ *n.* (also **pupilage**) **1** the condition of being a pupil or student. **2** *Law* apprenticeship to a member of the Bar, qualifying a barrister to practise independently.

pupiparous /pju:'pɪp(ə)rəs/ *adj.* (of an insect) bringing forth young which are already ready to pupate. [modern Latin *pupipara*, neut. pl. of *pupiparus* (as PUPA, *parere* 'bring forth')]

puppet /'pʌpɪt/ *n.* **1** a small figure representing a human being or animal and moved by various means as entertainment. **2** a person whose actions are controlled by another. □ **puppetry** *n.* [later form of POPPET]

puppeteer /pʌpɪ'tɪə/ *n.* **1** a person who works puppets. **2** a person who manipulates others. □ **puppeteering** *n.*

puppet state *n.* a country that is nominally independent but actually under the control of another power.

puppy /'pʌpi/ *n.* (*pl.* **-ies**) **1** a young dog. **2** *colloq.* a conceited or arrogant young man. □ **puppyhood** *n.* **puppyish** *adj.* [Middle English, perhaps via Old French *po(u)pee* 'doll, plaything, toy' from Romanic (as POPPET)]

puppy fat *n.* temporary fatness of a child or adolescent.

puppy love *n.* = CALF LOVE.

pur- /pə:/ *prefix* = PRO-[1] (*purchase*; *pursue*). [Anglo-French via Old French *por-*, *pur-*, *pour-* from Latin *por-*, *pro-*]

Purana /pʊ'rɑ:nə/ *n.* any of a class of Sanskrit sacred writings on Hindu mythology, folklore, etc. □ **Puranic** *adj.* [Sanskrit *purāṇa* 'ancient legend, ancient' from *purā* 'formerly']

Purbeck marble /'pə:bɛk/ *n.* (also **Purbeck stone**) a hard usu. polished limestone from Purbeck in Dorset, used in pillars, effigies, etc.

purblind /'pə:blʌɪnd/ *adj.* **1** partly blind; dim-sighted. **2** obtuse, dim-witted. □ **purblindness** *n.* [originally = completely blind: Middle English *pur(e) blind* from PURE, originally in the sense 'utterly', with assimilation to PUR-]

purchase /'pə:tʃɪs/ *v.* & *n.* ● *v.tr.* **1** acquire by payment; buy. **2** obtain or achieve at some cost. **3** *Naut.* haul up (an anchor etc.) by means of a pulley, lever, etc. ● *n.* **1** the act or an instance of buying. **2** something bought. **3** *Law* the acquisition of property by one's personal action and not by inheritance. **4 a** a firm hold on a thing to move it or to prevent it from slipping; leverage. **b** a device or tackle for moving heavy objects. **5** the annual rent or return from land. □ **purchasable** *adj.* **purchaser** *n.* [Middle English from Anglo-French *purchacer*, Old French *pourchacier* 'seek to obtain' (as PUR-, CHASE[1])]

purchase tax *n.* *Brit.* *hist.* a tax on goods bought, levied at higher rates for non-essential or luxury goods.

purchasing power *n.* **1** a person's financial ability to make purchases. **2** the amount that a sum of money etc. can purchase.

purdah /'pə:də/ *n.* **1** a system in certain Muslim and Hindu societies of screening women from men or strangers by means of a veil or curtain. **2** a curtain in a house, used for this purpose. [Urdu & Persian *pardah* 'veil, curtain']

pure /pjʊə/ *adj.* **1** unmixed, unadulterated (*pure white*; *pure alcohol*). **2** of unmixed origin or descent (*pure-blooded*). **3** chaste. **4** morally or sexually undefiled; not corrupt. **5** guiltless. **6** sincere. **7** mere, simple, nothing but, sheer (*it was pure malice*). **8** (of a sound) not discordant, perfectly in tune. **9** (of a subject of study) dealing with abstract concepts and not practical application. **10 a** (of a vowel) not joined with another in a diphthong. **b** (of a consonant) not accompanied by another. □ **pureness** *n.* [Middle English via Old French *pur* 'pure' from Latin *purus*]

pure-bred *adj.* & *n.* ● *adj.* (of an animal) bred from parents of the same breed or variety; of unmixed ancestry. ● *n.* such an animal.

purée /'pjʊəreɪ/ *n.* & *v.* ● *n.* a pulp of vegetables or fruit etc. reduced to a smooth cream. ● *v.tr.* (**purées**, **puréed**) make a purée of. [French, from *purer* 'purify']

purely /'pjʊəli/ *adv.* **1** in a pure manner. **2** merely, solely, exclusively.

pure mathematics see MATHEMATICS 1.

pure science *n.* a science depending on deductions from demonstrated truths (e.g. mathematics or logic), or one studied without regard to practical applications.

purfle /'pə:f(ə)l/ *n.* & *v.* ● *n.* **1** an ornamental border, esp. on a violin etc. **2** *archaic* the ornamental or embroidered edge of a garment. ● *v.tr.* **1** decorate with a purfle. **2** (often foll. by *with*) ornament (the edge of a building). **3** beautify. □ **purfling** *n.* [Middle English from Old French *porfil*, *porfiler*, ultimately from Latin *filum* 'thread']

purgation /pə:'geɪʃ(ə)n/ *n.* **1** purification. **2** purging of the bowels. **3** spiritual cleansing, esp. (*RC Ch.*) of a soul in purgatory. **4** *hist.* the action of clearing oneself of accusation or suspicion by an oath or ordeal. [Middle English from Old French *purgation* or Latin *purgatio* (as PURGE)]

purgative /'pə:gətɪv/ *adj.* & *n.* ● *adj.* **1** serving to purify. **2** strongly laxative. ● *n.* **1** a purgative thing. **2** a laxative. [Middle English from Old French *purgatif -ive* or Late Latin *purgativus* (as PURGE)]

purgatory /'pə:gət(ə)ri/ *n.* & *adj.* ● *n.* (*pl.* **-ies**) **1** the condition or supposed place of spiritual cleansing, esp. (*RC Ch.*) of those who die in the grace of God but have to expiate venial sins etc. **2** a place or state of temporary suffering or expiation. ● *adj.* purifying. □ **purgatorial** /-'tɔ:rɪəl/ *adj.* [Middle English via Anglo-French *purgatorie*, Old French *-oire* from medieval Latin *purgatorium*, neut. of Late Latin *purgatorius* (as PURGE)]

purge /pə:dʒ/ *v.* & *n.* ● *v.tr.* **1** (often foll. by *of*, *from*) make physically or spiritually clean. **2** remove by a cleansing process. **3** rid (an organization, party, etc.) of persons regarded as undesirable. **4 a** empty (the bowels). **b** administer a laxative to empty the bowels of. **5** *Law* atone for or wipe out (an offence, esp. contempt of court). ● *n.* **1** the act or an instance of purging. **2** a purgative. □ **purger** *n.* [Middle English via Old French *purg(i)er* from Latin *purgare* 'purify', from *purus* 'pure']

purify /'pjʊərɪfʌɪ/ *v.tr.* (**-ies**, **-ied**) **1** (often foll. by *of*, *from*) cleanse or make pure. **2** make ceremonially clean. **3** clear of extraneous elements. □ **purification** /-fɪ'keɪʃ(ə)n/ *n.* **purificatory** /-fɪ'keɪt(ə)ri/ *adj.* **purifier** *n.* [Middle English via Old French *purifier* from Latin *purificare* (as PURE)]

Purim /'pʊərɪm, pʊ'ri:m/ *n.* a Jewish spring festival commemorating the defeat of Haman's plot to massacre the Jews (Esth. 9). [Hebrew, pl. of *pūr*, perhaps = LOT *n.* 2]

purine /ˈpjʊəriːn/ *n.* **1** *Chem.* a cyclic organic nitrogenous base forming uric acid on oxidation. **2** any of a group of compounds with a similar structure, including the nucleotide constituents adenine and guanine. [German *Purin*, from Latin *purus* 'pure' + *uricum* 'uric acid' + *-in* -INE[4]]

purist /ˈpjʊərɪst/ *n.* a stickler for or advocate of scrupulous purity, esp. in language or art. ▫ **purism** *n.* **puristic** /-ˈrɪstɪk/ *adj.* [French *puriste* from *pur* PURE]

puritan /ˈpjʊərɪt(ə)n/ *n.* & *adj.* ● *n.* **1** (**Puritan**) *hist.* a member of a group of English Protestants who regarded the Reformation of the Church under Elizabeth as incomplete and sought to simplify and regulate forms of worship. **2** a purist member of any party. **3** a person practising or affecting extreme strictness in religion or morals. ● *adj.* **1** (usu. **Puritan**) *hist.* of or relating to the Puritans. **2** scrupulous and austere in religion or morals. ▫ **puritanism** *n.* (also **Puritanism**). [Late Latin *puritas* (as PURITY) on the pattern of earlier *Catharan* (as CATHAR)]

puritanical /pjʊərɪˈtanɪk(ə)l/ *adj.* often *derog.* practising or affecting strict religious or moral behaviour. ▫ **puritanically** *adv.*

purity /ˈpjʊərɪti/ *n.* **1** pureness, cleanness. **2** freedom from physical contamination or moral pollution. [Middle English from Old French *pureté*, with assimilation to Late Latin *puritas -tatis* from Latin *purus* 'pure']

purl[1] /pəːl/ *adj.*, *n.*, & *v.* ● *adj.* (of a knitting stitch) made by putting the needle through the front of the stitch from right to left (opp. PLAIN[1] *adj.* 9). ● *n.* **1** a cord of twisted gold or silver wire for bordering. **2** a chain of minute loops; a picot. **3** the ornamental edges of lace, ribbon, etc. ● *v.tr.* (also *absol.*) knit with a purl stitch. [originally *pyrle*, *pirle* from Scots *pirl* 'twist': the knitting sense may be from a different word]

purl[2] /pəːl/ *v.* & *n.* ● *v.intr.* (of a brook etc.) flow with a swirling motion and babbling sound. ● *n.* this motion or sound. [16th c.: probably imitative: cf. Norwegian *purla* 'bubble up']

purler /ˈpəːlə/ *n.* *Brit. colloq.* a headlong fall. [*purl* 'upset', related to PURL[1]]

purlieu /ˈpəːljuː/ *n.* (*pl.* **purlieus**) **1** a person's bounds or limits. **2** a person's usual haunts. **3** *Brit. hist.* a tract on the border of a forest, esp. one earlier included in it and still partly subject to forest laws. **4** (in *pl.*) the outskirts; an outlying region. [Middle English *purlew*, probably alteration (suggested by French *lieu* 'place') of Anglo-French *purale(e)*, Old French *pourallee* 'a going round to settle the boundaries', from *po(u)raler* 'traverse']

purlin /ˈpəːlɪn/ *n.* a horizontal beam along the length of a roof, resting on principals and supporting the common rafters or boards. [Middle English: origin uncertain]

purloin /pəːˈlɔɪn/ *v.tr.* *literary* or *joc.* steal, pilfer. ▫ **purloiner** *n.* [Middle English from Anglo-French *purloigner* 'put away, do away with' (as PUR-, *loign* 'far' from Latin *longe*)]

purple /ˈpəːp(ə)l/ *n.*, *adj.*, & *v.* ● *n.* **1** a colour intermediate between red and blue. **2** (in full **Tyrian purple**) a crimson dye obtained from some molluscs. **3** a purple robe, esp. as the dress of an emperor or senior magistrate. **4** the scarlet official dress of a cardinal. **5** (prec. by *the*) a position of rank, authority, or privilege. ● *adj.* of a purple colour. ● *v.tr.* & *intr.* make or become purple. ▫ **born in the purple 1** born into a reigning family. **2** belonging to the most privileged class. ▫ **purpleness** *n.* **purplish** *adj.* **purply** *adj.* [Old English, alteration of *purpure purpuran* from Latin *purpura* (as PURPURA)]

purple emperor *n.* a large butterfly, *Apatura iris*, with purple wings.

purple heart *n.* **1** *Brit. colloq.* a heart-shaped stimulant tablet, esp. of amphetamine. **2** (**Purple Heart**) (in the US) a decoration for those wounded in action.

purple passage *n.* an ornate or elaborate passage in a literary composition.

purple patch *n.* **1** = PURPLE PASSAGE. **2** *colloq.* a period of success or good fortune.

purple prose *n.* prose that is too elaborate or ornate.

purport *v.* & *n.* ● *v.tr.* /pəˈpɔːt/ **1** profess; be intended to seem (*purports to be the royal seal*). **2** (often foll. by *that* + clause) (of a document or speech) have as its meaning; state. ● *n.* /ˈpəːpɔːt/ **1** the ostensible meaning of something. **2** the sense or tenor (of a document or statement). ▫ **purportedly** /pəˈpɔːtɪdli/ *adv.* [Middle English via Anglo-French & Old French *purport*, *porport*, from *purporter*, from medieval Latin *proportare* (as PRO-[1], *portare* 'carry')]

purpose /ˈpəːpəs/ *n.* & *v.* ● *n.* **1** an object to be attained; a thing intended. **2** the intention to act. **3** resolution, determination. ● *v.tr.* have as one's purpose; design, intend. ▫ **on purpose** intentionally. **to no purpose** with no result or effect. **to the purpose 1** relevant. **2** useful. [Middle English via Old French *porpos*, *purpos* from Latin *proponere* (as PROPOUND)]

purpose-built *adj.* *Brit.* built or made for a specific purpose.

purposeful /ˈpəːpəsfʊl, -f(ə)l/ *adj.* **1** having or indicating purpose. **2** intentional. **3** resolute. ▫ **purposefully** *adv.* **purposefulness** *n.*

purposeless /ˈpəːpəslɪs/ *adj.* having no aim or plan. ▫ **purposelessly** *adv.* **purposelessness** *n.*

purposely /ˈpəːpəsli/ *adv.* on purpose; intentionally.

purpose-made *adj.* esp. *Brit.* made for a specific purpose.

purposive /ˈpəːpəsɪv/ *adj.* **1** having or serving a purpose. **2** done with a purpose. **3** (of a person or conduct) having purpose or resolution; purposeful. ▫ **purposively** *adv.* **purposiveness** *n.*

purpura /ˈpəːpjʊrə/ *n.* *Med.* a rash of purple spots on the skin caused by internal bleeding from small blood vessels. ▫ **purpuric** /-ˈpjʊərɪk/ *adj.* [Latin from Greek *porphura* 'purple']

purpure /ˈpəːpjʊə/ *n.* & *adj.* *Heraldry* purple. [Old English *purpure* & Old French *purpre* from Latin *purpura* (as PURPURA)]

purpurin /ˈpəːpjʊrɪn/ *n.* a red colouring matter occurring naturally in madder roots, or manufactured synthetically.

purr /pəː/ *v.* & *n.* ● *v.* **1** *intr.* (of a cat) make a low vibratory sound expressing contentment. **2** *intr.* (of machinery etc.) make a similar sound. **3** *intr.* (of a person) express pleasure by making low contented sounds. **4** *tr.* utter or express (words or pleasure) in a contented or seductive way. ● *n.* a purring sound. [imitative]

purse /pəːs/ *n.* & *v.* ● *n.* **1** a small pouch of leather etc. for carrying money on the person. **2** *N. Amer.* a handbag. **3** a receptacle resembling a purse in form or purpose. **4** money, funds. **5** a sum collected as a present or given as a prize in a contest. ● *v.* **1** *tr.* (often foll. by *up*) pucker or contract (the lips). **2** *intr.* become contracted and wrinkled. ▫ **hold the purse strings** have control of expenditure. [Old English *purs* via medieval Latin *bursa*, *byrsa* 'purse' from Greek *bursa* 'hide, leather']

purser /ˈpəːsə/ *n.* an officer on a ship who keeps the accounts, esp. the head steward in a passenger vessel.

purse seine *n.* a fishing net or seine which may be drawn into the shape of a bag, used for catching shoal fish (hyphenated when *attrib.*: *purse-seine vessels*). ▫ **purse-seiner** *n.*

purslane /ˈpəːslən/ *n.* any of various plants of the genus *Portulaca*, esp. *P. oleracea*, with green or golden leaves, used as a herb and salad vegetable. [Middle English from Old French *porcelaine* (cf. PORCELAIN), alteration of Latin *porcil(l)aca*, *portulaca*]

pursuance /pəˈsjuːəns/ *n.* (foll. by *of*) the carrying out or observance (of a plan, idea, etc.).

pursuant /pə'sju:ənt/ *adj. & adv.* ● *adj.* pursuing. ● *adv.* (foll. by *to*) conforming to or in accordance with. ◻ **pursuantly** *adv.* [Middle English, = prosecuting, from Old French *po(u)rsuiant*, part. of *po(u)rsu(iv)ir* (as PURSUE), assimilated to Anglo-French *pursuer* and PURSUE]

pursue /pə'sju:/ *v.* (**pursues**, **pursued**, **pursuing**) **1** *tr.* follow with intent to overtake or capture or do harm to. **2** *tr.* continue or proceed along (a route or course of action). **3** *tr.* follow or engage in (study or other activity). **4** *tr.* proceed in compliance with (a plan etc.). **5** *tr.* seek after, aim at. **6** *tr.* continue to investigate or discuss (a topic). **7** *tr.* seek the attention or acquaintance of (a person) persistently. **8** *tr.* (of misfortune etc.) persistently assail. **9** *tr.* persistently attend, stick to. **10** *intr.* go in pursuit. ◻ **pursuable** *adj.* **pursuer** *n.* [Middle English from Anglo-French *pursiwer*, *-suer* = Old French *porsivre* etc., ultimately from Latin *prosequi* 'follow after']

pursuit /pə'sju:t/ *n.* **1** the act or an instance of pursuing. **2** an occupation or activity pursued. ◻ **in pursuit of** pursuing. [Middle English from Old French *poursuite* (as PUR-, SUIT)]

pursuivant /'pə:sɪv(ə)nt/ *n.* **1** *Brit.* an officer of the College of Arms ranking below a herald. **2** *archaic* a follower or attendant. [Middle English from Old French *pursivant*, pres. part. of *pursivre* (as PURSUE)]

pursy /'pə:si/ *adj.* **1** short-winded; puffy. **2** corpulent. ◻ **pursiness** *n.* [Middle English, earlier *pursive*, via Anglo-French *porsif* from Old French *polsif*, via *polser* 'breathe with difficulty' from Latin *pulsare* (as PULSATE)]

purulent /'pjʊərʊl(ə)nt/ *adj.* **1** consisting of or containing pus. **2** discharging pus. ◻ **purulence** *n.* **purulency** *n.* **purulently** *adv.* [French *purulent* or Latin *purulentus* (as PUS)]

purvey /pə'veɪ/ *v.* **1** *tr.* provide or supply (articles of food) as one's business. **2** *intr.* (often foll. by *for*) **a** make provision. **b** act as supplier. ◻ **purveyor** *n.* [Middle English via Anglo-French *purveier*, Old French *porveiir* from Latin *providēre* PROVIDE]

purveyance /pə'veɪəns/ *n.* **1** the act of purveying. **2** *Brit. hist.* the right of the sovereign to provisions etc. at a fixed price. [Middle English via Old French *porveance* from Latin *providentia* PROVIDENCE]

purview /'pə:vju:/ *n.* **1** the scope or range of a document, scheme, etc. **2** the range of physical or mental vision. [Middle English from Anglo-French *purveü*, Old French *porveü*, past part. of *porveiir* (as PURVEY)]

pus /pʌs/ *n.* a thick yellowish or greenish liquid produced from infected tissue, consisting of dead bacteria and white blood cells with tissue debris and serum. [Latin *pus puris*]

push /pʊʃ/ *v. & n.* ● *v.* **1** *tr.* exert a force on (a thing) to move it away from oneself or from the origin of the force. **2** *tr.* cause to move in this direction. **3** *intr.* exert such a force (*do not push against the door*). **4** *intr. & tr.* **a** thrust forward or upward. **b** project or cause to project (*pushes out new roots*; *the cape pushes out into the sea*). **5** *intr.* move forward by force or persistence. **6** *tr.* make (one's way) by pushing. **7** *intr.* exert oneself, esp. to surpass others. **8** *tr.* (often foll. by *to*, *into*, or *to* + infin.) urge or impel. **9** *tr.* tax the abilities or tolerance of; press (a person) hard. **10** *tr.* pursue (a claim etc.). **11** *tr.* promote the use or sale or adoption of, e.g. by advertising. **12** *intr.* (foll. by *for*) demand persistently (*pushed hard for reform*). **13** *tr. colloq.* sell (a drug) illegally. ● *n.* **1** the act or an instance of pushing; a shove or thrust. **2** the force exerted in this. **3** a vigorous effort. **4** a military attack in force. **5** enterprise; determination to succeed. **6** the use of influence to advance a person. **7** the pressure of affairs. **8** a crisis. ◻ **be pushed for** *colloq.* have very little of (esp. time). **get the push** *Brit. colloq.* be dismissed or sent away. **give a person the push** *Brit. colloq.* dismiss or send away a person. **push about** *colloq.* = *push around*. **push along** (often in *imper.*) *Brit. colloq.* depart, leave. **push around** *colloq.* **1** move (a person) roughly from place to place. **2** bully. **push one's luck 1** take undue risks. **2** act presumptuously. **push off 1** push with an oar etc. to get a boat out into a river etc. **2** (often in *imper.*) *colloq.* go away. **push through** get (a scheme, proposal, etc.) completed or accepted quickly. **when push comes to shove** *colloq.* when action must be taken; when a decision must be made. [Middle English via Old French *pousser*, *pou(l)ser* from Latin *pulsare* (as PULSATE)]

push-bike *n. Brit. colloq.* a bicycle worked by pedals.

push-button *n.* **1** a button to be pushed esp. to operate an electrical device. **2** (*attrib.*) operated in this way.

pushcart /'pʊʃkɑ:t/ *n.* a handcart or barrow.

pushchair /'pʊʃtʃɛ:/ *n. Brit.* a folding chair on wheels, in which a child can be pushed along.

pusher /'pʊʃə/ *n.* **1** *colloq.* an illegal seller of drugs. **2** *colloq.* a pushing or pushy person. **3** a child's utensil for pushing food onto a spoon etc.

pushful /'pʊʃfʊl, -f(ə)l/ *adj.* pushy; arrogantly self-assertive. ◻ **pushfully** *adv.*

pushing /'pʊʃɪŋ/ *adj.* **1** pushy; aggressively ambitious. **2** *colloq.* having nearly reached (a specified age).

pushover /'pʊʃəʊvə/ *n. colloq.* **1** something that is easily done. **2** a person who can easily be overcome, persuaded, etc.

push-pull *adj.* **1** operated by pushing and pulling. **2** *Electronics* consisting of two valves etc. operated alternately.

pushrod /'pʊʃrɒd/ *n.* a rod operated by cams, that opens and closes the valves in an internal-combustion engine.

push-start *n. & v.* ● *n.* the starting of a motor vehicle by pushing it to turn the engine. ● *v.tr.* start (a vehicle) in this way.

Pushtu /'pʌʃtu:/ *n. & adj.* = PASHTO. [Persian *puštū*]

push-up *n.* = PRESS-UP.

pushy /'pʊʃi/ *adj.* (**pushier**, **pushiest**) *colloq.* **1** excessively or unpleasantly self-assertive. **2** selfishly determined to succeed. ◻ **pushily** *adv.* **pushiness** *n.*

pusillanimous /pju:sɪ'lanɪməs/ *adj.* lacking courage; timid. ◻ **pusillanimity** /-lə'nɪmɪti/ *n.* **pusillanimously** *adv.* [ecclesiastical Latin *pusillanimis*, from *pusillus* 'very small' + *animus* 'mind']

puss /pʊs/ *n. colloq.* **1** a cat (esp. as a form of address). **2** a playful or coquettish girl. **3** *Brit.* a hare. [probably from Middle Low German *pūs*, Dutch *poes*, of unknown origin]

puss moth *n.* a large European moth, *Cerura vinula*. [from its fluffy body]

pussy /'pʊsi/ *n.* (*pl.* **-ies**) **1** (also **pussy cat**) *colloq.* a cat. **2** *coarse slang* **a** the vulva. **b** *offens.* women considered generally.

pussyfoot /'pʊsɪfʊt/ *v.intr.* **1** move stealthily or warily. **2** act cautiously or non-committally. ◻ **pussyfooter** *n.*

pussy willow *n.* any of various willows with soft fluffy catkins appearing before the leaves.

pustulate *v. & adj.* ● *v.tr. & intr.* /'pʌstjʊleɪt/ form into pustules. ● *adj.* /'pʌstjʊlət/ of or relating to a pustule or pustules. ◻ **pustulation** /-'leɪʃ(ə)n/ *n.* [Late Latin *pustulare* from *pustula* PUSTULE]

pustule /'pʌstju:l/ *n.* a pimple containing pus. ◻ **pustular** *adj.* **pustulous** *adj.* [Middle English from Old French *pustule* or Latin *pustula*]

put[1] /pʊt/ *v. & n.* ● *v.* (**putting**; *past* and *past part.* **put**) **1** *tr.* move to or cause to be in a specified place or position (*put it in your pocket*; *put the children to bed*; *put your signature here*). **2** *tr.* bring into a specified condition, relation, or state (*puts me in great difficulty*; *an accident put the car out of action*). **3** *tr.* **a** (often foll. by *on*) impose or assign (*put a tax on beer*; *where do you put the blame?*). **b** (foll. by *on*, *to*) impose or enforce the existence of (*put a veto on it*; *put a stop to it*). **4** *tr.* **a** cause (a person) to go or be, habitually or temporarily (*put them at their ease*; *put them on the right track*). **b** *refl.* imagine (oneself) in a specified situation (*put* *yourself in my shoes*). **5** *tr.* (foll. by *for*) substitute (one thing for another). **6** *tr.* express (a thought or idea) in a specified way (*to put it mildly*). **7** *tr.* (foll. by *at*) estimate (an amount etc. at a specified amount) (*put the cost at £50*). **8** *tr.* (foll. by *into*) express or translate in (words, or another language). **9** *tr.* (foll. by *into*) invest (money in an asset, e.g. land). **10** *tr.* (foll. by *on*) stake (money) on (a horse etc.). **11** *tr.* (foll. by *to*) apply or devote to a use or purpose (*put it to good use*). **12** *tr.* (foll. by *to*) submit for consideration or attention (*let me put it to you another way*; *shall now put it to a vote*). **13** *tr.* (foll. by *to*) subject (a person) to (death, suffering, etc.). **14** *tr.* throw (esp. a shot or weight) as an athletic sport or exercise. **15** *tr.* (foll. by *to*) couple (an animal) with (another of the opposite sex) for breeding. **16** *intr.* (foll. by *back*, *off*, *out*, etc.) (of a ship etc.) proceed or follow a course in a specified direction. **17** *intr.* (foll. by *in*, *out of*) *US* (of a river) flow in a specified direction. ● *n.* **1** a throw of the shot or weight. **2** *Stock Exch.* the option of selling stock at a fixed price at a given date. □ **not know where to put oneself** feel deeply embarrassed. **put about 1** spread (information, rumour, etc.). **2** *Naut.* turn round; put (a ship) on the opposite tack. **3** esp. *Sc.* & *N.Engl.* trouble, distress. **put across 1** make acceptable or effective. **2** express in an understandable way. **put away 1** put (a thing) back in the place where it is normally kept. **2** lay (money etc.) aside for future use. **3 a** confine or imprison. **b** commit to a home or mental institution. **4** *colloq.* consume (food and drink), esp. in large quantities. **5** put (an old or sick animal) to death. **put back 1** restore to its proper or former place. **2** change (a planned event) to a later date or time. **3** move back the hands of (a clock or watch). **4** check the advance of. **put a bold** etc. **face on it** see FACE. **put the boot in** see BOOT[1]. **put by** lay (money etc.) aside for future use. **put down 1** suppress by force or authority. **2** *colloq.* snub or humiliate. **3** record or enter in writing. **4** enter the name of (a person) on a list, esp. as a member or subscriber. **5** (foll. by *as*, *for*) account or reckon. **6** (foll. by *to*) attribute (*put it down to bad planning*). **7** put (an old or sick animal) to death. **8** preserve or store (eggs etc.) for future use. **9** pay (a specified sum) as a deposit. **10** put (a baby) to bed. **11** land (an aircraft). **12** stop to let (passengers) get off. **put an end to** see END. **put one's finger on** see FINGER. **put the finger on** see FINGER. **put one's foot down** see FOOT. **put one's foot in it** see FOOT. **put forth 1** (of a plant) send out (buds or leaves). **2** *formal* submit or put into circulation. **put forward 1** suggest or propose. **2** advance the hands of (a clock or watch). **3** (often *refl.*) put into a prominent position; draw attention to. **put one's hands on** = *lay one's hands on* (see LAY[1]). **put in 1 a** enter or submit (a claim etc.). **b** (foll. by *for*) submit a claim for (a specified thing). **2** (foll. by *for*) be a candidate for (an appointment, election, etc.). **3** spend (time). **4** perform (a spell of work) as part of a whole. **5** interpose (a remark, blow, etc.). **put a person in mind of** see MIND. **put it across** *colloq.* get the better of, deceive (a person). **put it to a person** (often foll. by *that* + clause) challenge a person to deny. **put one's mind to** see MIND. **put off 1 a** postpone. **b** postpone an engagement with (a person). **2** (often foll. by *with*) evade (a person) with an excuse etc. **3** hinder or dissuade. **4** *Brit.* offend, disconcert; cause (a person) to lose interest in something. **put on 1** clothe oneself with. **2** cause (an electrical device, light, etc.) to function. **3** cause (transport) to be available. **4** stage (a play, show, etc.). **5** advance the hands of (a clock or watch). **6 a** pretend to be affected by (an emotion). **b** assume, take on (a character or appearance). **c** (**put it on**) exaggerate one's feelings etc. **7** increase one's weight by (a specified amount). **8** send (a cricketer) on to bowl. **9** (foll. by *to*) make aware of or put in touch with (*put us on to their new accountant*). **put one across** (or **over**) (foll. by *on*) *colloq.* get the better of; trick. **put out 1 a** (often as **put out** *adj.*) disconcert or annoy. **b** (often *refl.*) inconvenience (*don't put yourself out*). **2** extinguish (a fire or light). **3** cause (a batsman or side) to be out. **4** dislocate (a joint). **5** exert (strength etc.). **6** lend (money) at interest. **7** allocate (work) to be done off the premises. **8** blind (a person's eyes). **put over 1** make acceptable or effective. **2** express in an understandable way. **3** *US* postpone. **4** (often foll. by *on*) *US* achieve by deceit. **put the screws on** see SCREW. **put a sock in it** see SOCK[1]. **put store by** see STORE. **put through 1** carry out or complete (a task or transaction). **2** (often foll. by *to*) connect (a person) by telephone to another. **put to bed** see BED. **put to flight** see FLIGHT[2]. **put together 1** assemble (a whole) from parts. **2** combine (parts) to form a whole. **put two and two together** see TWO. **put under** render unconscious by anaesthetic etc. **put up 1** build or erect. **2 a** raise (a hand) to answer or ask a question). **b** raise (one's hands) to indicate surrender. **3** esp. *Brit.* increase (a price etc.). **4** take or provide with accommodation (*friends put me up for the night*). **5** engage in (a fight, struggle, etc.) as a form of resistance. **6** present (a proposal). **7 a** present oneself for election. **b** propose for election. **8** provide (money) as a backer in an enterprise. **9** display (a notice). **10** publish (banns). **11** offer for sale or competition. **12** cause (game) to rise from cover. **13** put (a sword) back in its sheath. **put upon** (usu. in *passive*; hyphenated when *attrib.*) *colloq.* make unfair or excessive demands on; take advantage of (a person) (*was sorely put upon*). **put up or shut up** *colloq.* defend or justify oneself or remain silent. **put a person up to 1** inform or instruct a person about. **2** (usu. foll. by verbal noun) instigate a person in (*put them up to stealing the money*). **put up with** endure, tolerate; submit to. **put the wind up** see WIND[1]. **put a person wise** see WISE[1]. **put words into a person's mouth** see MOUTH. □ **putter** *n.* [Middle English from an unrecorded Old English word, of unknown origin]

put[2] var. of PUTT.

putative /ˈpjuːtətɪv/ *adj.* reputed, supposed (*his putative father*). □ **putatively** *adv.* [Middle English via Old French *putatif -ive* or Late Latin *putativus* from Latin *putare* 'think']

put-down *n. colloq.* a snub or humiliating criticism.

put-in *n.* the act of putting the ball into a scrum in rugby.

putlog /ˈpʌtlɒg/ *n.* (also **putlock** /-lɒk/) a short horizontal timber projecting from a wall, on which scaffold floorboards rest. [17th c.: origin uncertain]

put-on *n. colloq.* a deception or hoax.

put-put /ˈpʌtpʌt/ *n.* & *v.* ● *n.* the rapid intermittent sound of a small petrol engine. ● *v.intr.* (**put-putted**, **put-putting**) make this sound. [imitative]

putrefy /ˈpjuːtrɪfʌɪ/ *v.* (**-ies**, **-ied**) **1** *intr.* & *tr.* become or make putrid; go bad. **2** *intr.* fester, suppurate. **3** *intr.* become morally corrupt. □ **putrefacient** /-ˈfeɪʃ(ə)nt/ *adj.* **putrefaction** /-ˈfakʃ(ə)n/ *n.* **putrefactive** /-ˈfaktɪv/ *adj.* [Middle English from Latin *putrefacere*, from *puter putris* 'rotten']

putrescent /pjuːˈtrɛs(ə)nt/ *adj.* **1** in the process of rotting. **2** of or accompanying this process. □ **putrescence** *n.* [Latin *putrescere*, inceptive of *putrēre* (as PUTRID)]

putrid /ˈpjuːtrɪd/ *adj.* **1** decomposed, rotten. **2** foul, noxious. **3** corrupt. **4** *slang* of poor quality; contemptible; very unpleasant. □ **putridity** /-ˈtrɪdɪti/ *n.* **putridly** *adv.* **putridness** *n.* [Latin *putridus*, via *putrēre* 'to rot' from *puter putris* 'rotten']

putsch /pʊtʃ/ *n.* an attempt at political revolution; a violent uprising. [Swiss German, = thrust, blow]

putt /pʌt/ *v.* & *n.* (also **put**) ● *v.tr.* (**putted**, **putting**) strike (a golf ball) gently to direct it into or nearer to a hole on a putting green. ● *n.* a putting stroke. [differentiated from PUT[1]]

puttee /ˈpʌti/ *n.* **1** a long strip of cloth wound spirally round the leg from ankle to knee for protection and support. **2** *US* a leather legging. [Hindi *paṭṭī* 'band, bandage']

putter[1] /ˈpʌtə/ *n.* **1** a golf club used in putting. **2** a golfer who putts.

putter[2] /ˈpʌtə/ *n.* & *v.* = PUT-PUT. [imitative]

putter[3] *US* var. of POTTER[1].

putting green *n.* (in golf) the smooth area of grass round a hole.

putto /ˈpʊtəʊ/ *n.* (*pl.* **putti** /-ti/) a representation of a naked child (esp. a cherub or a cupid) in (esp. Renaissance) art. [Italian, = boy, from Latin *putus*]

putty /ˈpʌti/ *n.* & *v.* ● *n.* (*pl.* **-ies**) **1** a cement made from whiting and raw linseed oil, used for fixing panes of glass, filling holes in woodwork, etc. **2** a fine white mortar of lime and water, used in pointing brickwork, etc. **3** a polishing powder usu. made from tin oxide, used in jewellery work. ● *v.tr.* (**-ies, -ied**) cover, fix, join, or fill up with putty. □ **be putty in a person's hands** be subservient to, or easily influenced by, a person. [French *potée*, literally 'potful']

put-up *adj.* (usu. in phr. **put-up job**) fraudulently presented or devised.

put-you-up *n. Brit.* a makeshift or temporary bed; a camp bed.

puy /pwiː/ *n.* a small extinct volcanic cone, esp. in the Auvergne, France. [French, = hill, from Latin *podium*: see PODIUM]

puzzle /ˈpʌz(ə)l/ *n.* & *v.* ● *n.* **1** a difficult or confusing problem; an enigma. **2** a problem or toy designed to test knowledge or ingenuity. ● *v.* **1** *tr.* confound or disconcert mentally. **2** *intr.* (usu. foll. by *over* etc.) be perplexed (about). **3** *tr.* (usu. as **puzzling** *adj.*) require much thought to comprehend (*a puzzling situation*). **4** *tr.* (foll. by *out*) solve or understand by hard thought. □ **puzzlement** *n.* **puzzlingly** *adv.* [16th c.: origin unknown]

puzzler /ˈpʌzlə/ *n.* a difficult question or problem.

puzzolana var. of POZZOLANA.

PVA *abbr.* polyvinyl acetate.

PVC *abbr.* polyvinyl chloride.

PVS *abbr. Med.* **1** persistent vegetative state. **2** post-viral (fatigue) syndrome (= ME 2).

Pvt. *abbr.* **1** private. **2** *US* private soldier.

PW *abbr.* policewoman.

p.w. *abbr.* per week.

PWA *n.* (*pl.* **PWAs**) esp. *US* person with Aids. [abbreviation]

PWR *abbr.* pressurized-water reactor.

PX *abbr. US* post exchange.

pyaemia /pʌɪˈiːmɪə/ *n.* (*US* **pyemia**) blood poisoning caused by the spread of pus-forming bacteria in the bloodstream from a source of infection. □ **pyaemic** *adj.* [modern Latin, from Greek *puon* 'pus' + *haima* 'blood']

pycnic var. of PYKNIC.

pye-dog /ˈpʌɪdɒg/ *n.* (also **pie-dog, pi-dog**) a vagrant mongrel, esp. in Asia. [Anglo-Indian *pye, paë*, Hindi *pāhī* 'outsider' + DOG]

pyelitis /pʌɪəˈlʌɪtɪs/ *n.* inflammation of the renal pelvis. [Greek *puelos* 'trough, basin' + -ITIS]

pyemia *US* var. of PYAEMIA.

pygmy /ˈpɪgmi/ *n.* (also **pigmy**) (*pl.* **-ies**) **1** a member of a dwarf people of equatorial Africa and parts of SE Asia. **2** a very small person, animal, or thing. **3** an insignificant person. **4** (*attrib.*) **a** of or relating to pygmies. **b** (of a person, animal, etc.) dwarf. □ **pygmaean** /-ˈmiːən/ *adj.* **pygmean** /-ˈmiːən/ *adj.* [Middle English via Latin *pygmaeus* from Greek *pugmaios* 'dwarf', from *pugmē* 'the length from elbow to knuckles, fist']

pygmy chimpanzee see CHIMPANZEE.

pygmy hippopotamus see HIPPOPOTAMUS 2.

pyjamas /pəˈdʒɑːməz/ *n.pl.* (*US* **pajamas**) **1** a suit of loose trousers and jacket for sleeping in. **2** loose trousers tied round the waist, worn by both sexes in some Asian countries. **3** (**pyjama**) (*attrib.*) designating parts of a suit of pyjamas (*pyjama jacket; pyjama trousers*). [Urdu and Persian, from *pay* 'leg' + *jāma* 'clothing']

pyknic /ˈpɪknɪk/ *adj.* & *n.* (also **pycnic**) *Anthropol.* ● *adj.* characterized by a thick neck, large abdomen, and relatively short limbs. ● *n.* a person of this bodily type. [Greek *puknos* 'thick']

pylon /ˈpʌɪlən, -ɒn/ *n.* **1** a tall structure erected as a support (esp. for electric power cables) or boundary or decoration. **2** a gateway, esp. of an ancient Egyptian temple. **3** a structure marking a path for aircraft. **4** a structure on the wing of an aircraft supporting an engine or weapon. [Greek *pulōn* from *pulē* 'gate']

pylorus /pʌɪˈlɔːrəs/ *n.* (*pl.* **pylori** /-rʌɪ/) *Anat.* the opening from the stomach into the duodenum. □ **pyloric** /-ˈlɒrɪk/ *adj.* [Late Latin from Greek *pulōros, pulouros* 'gatekeeper', from *pulē* 'gate' + *ouros* 'warder']

pyorrhoea /pʌɪəˈriːə/ *n.* (*US* **pyorrhea**) **1** a disease of periodontal tissue causing shrinkage of the gums and loosening of the teeth. **2** any discharge of pus. [Greek *puo-* (from *puon* 'pus') + *rhoia* 'flux' from *rheō* 'flow']

pyracantha /pʌɪrəˈkanθə/ *n.* any evergreen thorny shrub of the genus *Pyracantha*, having white flowers and bright red or yellow berries. [Latin from Greek *purakantha*, the name of an unidentified plant, from *pur* 'fire' + *akantha* 'thorn']

pyralid /pʌɪˈralɪd, -ˈreɪl-/ *n.* & *adj.* ● *n.* a small moth of the family Pyralidae. ● *adj.* of or relating to this family. [modern Latin from Greek *puralis*, a mythical fly said to live in fire, from *pur* 'fire']

pyramid /ˈpɪrəmɪd/ *n.* **1** a monumental structure, usu. of stone, with a square base and sloping sides meeting centrally at an apex, esp. an ancient Egyptian royal tomb. **2** a polyhedron or solid figure of this type with a base of three or more sides. **3** a pyramid-shaped thing or pile of things. **4** (in *pl.*) a game played on a billiard table with (usu. fifteen) coloured balls and a cue ball. □ **pyramidal** /-ˈramɪd(ə)l/ *adj.* **pyramidally** /-ˈramɪd(ə)li/ *adv.* **pyramidic** /-ˈmɪdɪk/ *adj.* (also **pyramidical** /-ˈmɪdɪk(ə)l/). **pyramidically** /-ˈmɪdɪk(ə)li/ *adv.* [Middle English via Latin *pyramis* from Greek *puramis -idos*]

pyramid selling *n.* a system of selling goods in which agency rights are sold to an increasing number of distributors at successively lower levels.

pyre /pʌɪə/ *n.* a heap of combustible material, esp. a funeral pile for burning a corpse. [Latin *pyra* from Greek *pura*, from *pur* 'fire']

pyrethrin /pʌɪˈriːθrɪn/ *n.* any of a class of compounds found in pyrethrum flowers and used in the manufacture of insecticides.

pyrethroid /pʌɪˈriːθrɔɪd/ *n. Chem.* any of a group of substances similar to pyrethrins in structure and properties.

pyrethrum /pʌɪˈriːθrəm/ *n.* **1** any of several aromatic plants of the genus *Tanacetum* (daisy family), esp. *T. coccineum*. **2** an insecticide made from the dried flowers of these plants, esp. *Tanacetum cinerariifolium*. [Latin former genus name from Greek *purethron* 'feverfew']

pyretic /pʌɪˈrɛtɪk, pɪ-/ *adj.* of, for, or producing fever. [modern Latin *pyreticus* from Greek *puretos* 'fever']

Pyrex /ˈpʌɪrɛks/ *n. propr.* a hard heat-resistant type of glass, often used for ovenware. [invented word]

pyrexia /pʌɪˈrɛksɪə, pɪ-/ *n. Med.* = FEVER *n.* 1a. □ **pyrexial** *adj.* **pyrexic** *adj.* **pyrexical** *adj.* [modern Latin from Greek *purexis*, via *puressō* 'be feverish' from *pur* 'fire']

pyridine /ˈpɪrɪdiːn/ *n. Chem.* a colourless volatile odorous liquid, originally obtained from coal tar, used as a solvent and in chemical manufacture. Chem. formula: C_5H_5N. [Greek *pur* 'fire' + -IDE + -INE[4]]

pyridoxine /pɪrɪˈdɒksɪn, -iːn/ *n.* a vitamin of the B complex found in yeast, and important in the body's use of unsaturated fatty acids. Also called *vitamin* B_6. [PYRIDINE + OX- + -INE[4]]

pyrimidine /pɪˈrɪmɪdiːn/ *n.* **1** *Chem.* a cyclic organic nitrogenous base. Chem. formula: $C_4H_4N_2$. **2** any of a group of compounds with similar structure, including the nucleotide constituents uracil, thymine, and cytosine. [German *Pyrimidin* from *Pyridin* (as PYRIDINE, IMIDE)]

pyrite /ˈpʌɪrʌɪt/ *n.* = PYRITES. [French *pyrite* or Latin (as PYRITES)]

pyrites /pʌɪˈrʌɪtiːz/ *n.* (in full **iron pyrites**) a yellow lustrous form of iron disulphide. □ **pyritic** /-ˈrɪtɪk/ *adj.* **pyritiferous** /-rɪˈtɪf(ə)rəs/ *adj.* **pyritize** /ˈpʌɪrɪtʌɪz/ *v.tr.* (also **-ise**). **pyritous** /ˈpʌɪrɪtəs/ *adj.* [Latin from Greek *puritēs* 'of fire', from *pur* 'fire']

pyro /ˈpʌɪrəʊ/ *n. colloq.* = PYROGALLIC ACID.

pyro- /ˈpʌɪrəʊ/ *comb. form* **1** denoting fire. **2** *Chem.* denoting a new substance formed from another by elimination of water (*pyrophosphate*). **3** *Mineral.* denoting a mineral etc. showing some property or change under the action of heat, or having a fiery red or yellow colour. [Greek *puro-* from *pur* 'fire']

pyroclastic /pʌɪrə(ʊ)ˈklastɪk/ *adj.* of or formed from fragments of rock from a volcanic eruption. □ **pyroclast** *n.*

pyroclastic flow *n. Geol.* a dense mass of very hot ash, lava fragments, and gases ejected explosively from a volcano and often flowing at great speed.

pyroelectric /ˌpʌɪrəʊɪˈlɛktrɪk/ *adj.* having the property of becoming electrically charged when heated. □ **pyroelectricity** /-ˈtrɪsɪti/ *n.*

pyrogallic acid /pʌɪrə(ʊ)ˈgalɪk/ *n.* a weak acid used as a developer in photography, etc.

pyrogallol /pʌɪrə(ʊ)ˈgalɒl/ *n.* = PYROGALLIC ACID.

pyrogenic /pʌɪrə(ʊ)ˈdʒɛnɪk/ *adj.* (also **pyrogenous** /pʌɪˈrɒdʒɪnəs/) **1 a** producing heat, esp. in the body. **b** producing fever. **2** produced by combustion or volcanic processes.

pyrography /pʌɪˈrɒgrəfi/ *n.* = POKERWORK 1.

pyrolyse /ˈpʌɪrəlʌɪz/ *v.tr.* (*US* **pyrolyze**) decompose by pyrolysis. [PYROLYSIS, on the pattern of *analyse*]

pyrolysis /pʌɪˈrɒlɪsɪs/ *n.* chemical decomposition brought about by heat. □ **pyrolytic** /pʌɪrəˈlɪtɪk/ *adj.*

pyromania /pʌɪrə(ʊ)ˈmeɪnɪə/ *n.* an obsessive desire to set fire to things. □ **pyromaniac** *n.*

pyrometer /pʌɪˈrɒmɪtə/ *n.* an instrument for measuring high temperatures, esp. in furnaces and kilns. □ **pyrometric** /-rəˈmɛtrɪk/ *adj.* **pyrometrically** /-rəˈmɛtrɪk(ə)li/ *adv.* **pyrometry** /-mɪtri/ *n.*

pyrope /ˈpʌɪrəʊp/ *n.* a deep red variety of garnet. [Middle English via Old French *pirope* and Latin *pyropus* from Greek *purōpos* 'gold-bronze', literally 'fiery-eyed', from *pur* 'fire' + *ōps* 'eye']

pyrophoric /pʌɪrə(ʊ)ˈfɒrɪk/ *adj.* (of a substance) liable to ignite spontaneously on exposure to air. [modern Latin *pyrophorus* from Greek *purophoros* 'fire-bearing', from *pur* 'fire' + *pherō* 'bear']

pyrosis /pʌɪˈrəʊsɪs/ *n. Med.* a burning sensation in the lower part of the chest, combined with the return of gastric acid to the mouth. [modern Latin from Greek *purōsis*, via *puroō* 'set on fire' from *pur* 'fire']

pyrotechnic /pʌɪrə(ʊ)ˈtɛknɪk/ *adj.* **1** of or relating to fireworks. **2** (of wit etc.) brilliant or sensational. □ **pyrotechnical** *adj.* **pyrotechnist** *n.* **pyrotechny** /ˈpʌɪrə(ʊ)-/ *n.* [PYRO- + Greek *tekhnē* 'art']

pyrotechnics /pʌɪrə(ʊ)ˈtɛknɪks/ *n.pl.* **1** (treated as *sing.*) the art of making fireworks. **2** a display of fireworks. **3** any brilliant display.

pyroxene /pʌɪˈrɒksiːn/ *n.* any of a group of minerals commonly found as components of igneous rocks, composed of silicates of calcium, magnesium, and iron. [PYRO- + Greek *xenos* 'stranger' (because supposed to be alien to igneous rocks)]

pyroxylin /pʌɪˈrɒksɪlɪn/ *n.* a form of nitrocellulose, soluble in ether and alcohol, used as a basis for lacquers, artificial leather, etc. [French *pyroxyline* (as PYRO-, Greek *xulon* 'wood')]

pyrrhic[1] /ˈpɪrɪk/ *adj.* (of a victory) won at too great a cost to be of use to the victor. [from the name of *Pyrrhus* of Epirus, who defeated the Romans at Asculum in 279 BC, but sustained heavy losses]

pyrrhic[2] /ˈpɪrɪk/ *n. & adj.* ● *n.* a metrical foot of two short or unaccented syllables. ● *adj.* written in or based on pyrrhics. [Latin *pyrrhichius*, from Greek *purrhikhios* (*pous*) 'pyrrhic (foot)', the metre of a song accompanying a war dance, named after *Purrhikhos*, inventor of the dance]

Pyrrhonism /ˈpɪrənɪz(ə)m/ *n.* **1** the philosophy of Pyrrho of Elis (*c.*300 BC), maintaining that certainty of knowledge is unattainable. **2** scepticism; philosophic doubt. □ **Pyrrhonist** *n. & adj.* [Greek *Purrhōn* 'Pyrrho']

pyruvate /pʌɪˈruːveɪt/ *n. Biochem.* any salt or ester of pyruvic acid.

pyruvic acid /pʌɪˈruːvɪk/ *n.* an organic acid occurring as an intermediate in many metabolic pathways. [as PYRO- + Latin *uva* 'grape']

Pythagoras' theorem /pʌɪˈθag(ə)rəs/ *n.* the theorem attributed to Pythagoras (see PYTHAGOREAN) that the square on the hypotenuse of a right-angled triangle is equal to the sum of the squares on the other two sides.

Pythagorean /pʌɪˌθagəˈriːən/ *adj. & n.* ● *adj.* of or relating to the Greek philosopher Pythagoras (6th c. BC) or his philosophy, esp. regarding the transmigration of souls. ● *n.* a follower of Pythagoras.

Pythian /ˈpɪθɪən/ *adj.* of or relating to Delphi (in central Greece) or its ancient oracle of Apollo. [Latin *Pythius* from Greek *Puthios*, from *Puthō*, an older name of Delphi]

python /ˈpʌɪθ(ə)n/ *n.* any non-venomous snake of the family Pythonidae, esp. of the genus *Python*, found throughout the tropics in the Old World, and killing prey by compressing and asphyxiating it. □ **pythonic** /-ˈθɒnɪk/ *adj.* [Latin from Greek *Puthōn*, a huge serpent or monster killed by Apollo]

Pythonesque /pʌɪθəˈnɛsk/ *adj.* after the style of, or resembling the humour of, *Monty Python's Flying Circus*, a popular British television comedy series of the 1970s noted esp. for its absurdist or surrealist humour. [Monty *Python*'s Flying Circus + -ESQUE]

pythoness /ˈpʌɪθənɪs/ *n.* **1** the Pythian priestess. **2** a witch. [Middle English via Old French *phitonise* and medieval Latin *phitonissa* from Late Latin *pythonissa*, fem. of *pytho*, from Greek *puthōn* 'soothsaying demon': cf. PYTHON]

pyuria /pʌɪˈjʊərɪə/ *n. Med.* the presence of pus in the urine. [Greek *puon* 'pus' + -URIA]

pyx /pɪks/ *n.* (also **pix**) **1** *Eccl.* the vessel in which the consecrated bread of the Eucharist is kept. **2** (in the UK) a box at the Royal Mint in which specimen gold and silver coins are deposited to be tested annually. [Middle English from Latin (as PYXIS)]

pyxidium /pɪkˈsɪdɪəm/ *n.* (*pl.* **pyxidia** /-dɪə/) *Bot.* a seed capsule with a top that comes off like the lid of a box. [modern Latin from Greek *puxidion*, diminutive of *puxis*: see PYXIS]

pyxis /ˈpɪksɪs/ *n.* (*pl.* **pyxides** /-ˌdiːz/) **1** a small box or casket. **2** = PYXIDIUM. [Middle English via Latin from Greek *puxis*, from *puxos* BOX[3]]

pzazz var. of PIZAZZ.

Qq

Q[1] /kju:/ *n.* (also **q**) (*pl.* **Qs** or **Q's**) the seventeenth letter of the alphabet.

Q[2] *abbr.* (also **Q.**) **1** Queen, Queen's. **2** question. **3** *Theol.* used to denote the hypothetical source of the passages shared by the gospels of Matthew and Luke, but not found in Mark. [sense 3 probably from German *Quelle* 'source']

Qantas /'kwɒntəs/ *n.* the international airline of Australia. [abbreviation of *Q*ueensland *an*d Northern *T*erritory *A*erial *S*ervices]

QARANC *abbr.* Queen Alexandra's Royal Army Nursing Corps.

QB *abbr.* Queen's Bench.

QC *abbr. Law* Queen's Counsel.

QCD *abbr.* quantum chromodynamics.

QED *abbr. quod erat demonstrandum.*

Q fever /kju:/ *n.* a mild febrile disease caused by rickettsiae. [*Q* = query]

qibla var. of KIBLAH.

Qld. *abbr.* Queensland.

QM *abbr.* quartermaster.

QMG *abbr.* Quartermaster General.

QMS *abbr.* Quartermaster Sergeant.

QPM *abbr.* (in the UK) Queen's Police Medal.

qr. *abbr.* quarter(s).

Q-ship /'kju:ʃɪp/ *n. hist.* an armed and disguised merchant ship used as a decoy or to destroy submarines. [*Q* = query]

QSO *abbr.* quasi-stellar object, quasar.

qt. *abbr.* quart(s).

q.t. *n. colloq.* quiet (esp. in phr. **on the q.t.**). [abbreviation]

qu. *abbr.* **1** query. **2** question.

qua /kweɪ, kwɑ:/ *conj.* in the capacity of; as being (*Napoleon qua general*). [Latin, ablative fem. sing. of *qui* 'who']

quack[1] /kwak/ *n.* & *v.* ● *n.* the harsh sound made by ducks. ● *v.intr.* **1** utter this sound. **2** *colloq.* talk loudly and foolishly. [imitative: cf. Dutch *kwakken*, German *quacken* 'croak, quack']

quack[2] /kwak/ *n.* **1 a** an unqualified practiser of medicine. **b** (*attrib.*) of or characteristic of unskilled medical practice (*quack cure*). **2** *slang* any doctor or medical officer. **3** a charlatan. □ **quackery** *n.* **quackish** *adj.* [abbreviation of *quacksalver* from Dutch (probably from obsolete *quacken* 'prattle' + *salf* SALVE[1])]

quad[1] /kwɒd/ *n. colloq.* a quadrangle. [abbreviation]

quad[2] /kwɒd/ *n. colloq.* = QUADRUPLET 1. [abbreviation]

quad[3] /kwɒd/ *n. Printing* a piece of blank metal type used in spacing. [abbreviation of earlier QUADRAT]

quad[4] /kwɒd/ *n.* & *adj.* ● *n.* quadraphony. ● *adj.* quadraphonic. [abbreviation]

quadragenarian /ˌkwɒdrədʒɪ'nɛ:rɪən/ *n.* & *adj.* ● *n.* a person from 40 to 49 years old. ● *adj.* of this age. [Late Latin *quadragenarius* from *quadrageni*, distributive of *quadraginta* 'forty']

Quadragesima /kwɒdrə'dʒɛsɪmə/ *n.* the first Sunday in Lent. [Late Latin, fem. of Latin *quadragesimus* 'fortieth', from *quadraginta* 'forty', Lent having 40 days]

quadragesimal /kwɒdrə'dʒɛsɪm(ə)l/ *adj.* **1** (of a fast, esp. in Lent) lasting forty days. **2** Lenten.

quadrangle /'kwɒdraŋg(ə)l/ *n.* **1** a four-sided plane figure, esp. a square or rectangle. **2 a** a four-sided court, esp. enclosed by buildings, as in some colleges. **b** such a court with the buildings round it. □ **quadrangular** /-'raŋgjʊlə/ *adj.* [Middle English via Old French from Late Latin *quadrangulum* 'square', neut. of *quadrangulus* (as QUADRI-, ANGLE[1])]

quadrant /'kwɒdr(ə)nt/ *n.* **1** a quarter of a circle's circumference. **2** a plane figure enclosed by two radii of a circle at right angles and the arc cut off by them. **3** a quarter of a sphere or spherical body. **4** any of four parts of a plane divided by two lines at right angles. **5 a** a thing, esp. a graduated strip of metal, shaped like a quarter-circle. **b** an instrument graduated (esp. through an arc of 90°) for taking angular measurements. □ **quadrantal** /-'drant(ə)l/ *adj.* [Middle English from Latin *quadrans -antis* 'quarter', from *quattuor* 'four']

quadraphonic /kwɒdrə'fɒnɪk/ *adj.* (also **quadrophonic**) (of sound reproduction) using four transmission channels. □ **quadraphonically** *adv.* **quadraphonics** *n.pl.* **quadraphony** /-'drɒf(ə)ni/ *n.* [QUADRI- + STEREOPHONIC]

quadrat /'kwɒdrət/ *n. Ecol.* a small square area marked out for study. [variant of QUADRATE]

quadrate *adj.*, *n.*, & *v.* ● *adj.* /'kwɒdrət/ esp. *Anat.* & *Zool.* square or rectangular (*quadrate bone*; *quadrate muscle*). ● *n.* /'kwɒdrət/ **1** a quadrate bone or muscle. **2** a rectangular object. ● *v.* /kwɒ'dreɪt, 'kwɒdreɪt/ **1** *tr.* make square. **2** *intr.* & *tr.* (often foll. by *with*) conform or make conform. [Middle English from Latin *quadrare quadrat-* 'make square', from *quattuor* 'four']

quadratic /kwɒ'dratɪk/ *adj.* & *n. Math.* ● *adj.* **1** involving the second and no higher power of an unknown quantity or variable (*quadratic equation*). **2** square. ● *n.* **1** a quadratic equation. **2** (in *pl.*) the branch of algebra dealing with these. [French *quadratique* or modern Latin *quadraticus* (as QUADRATE)]

quadrature /'kwɒdrətʃə/ *n.* **1** *Math.* the process of constructing a square with an area equal to that of a figure bounded by a curve, e.g. a circle. **2** *Astron.* **a** each of two points at which the moon is 90° from the sun as viewed from earth. **b** the position of a celestial body in relation to another 90° away. [French *quadrature* or Latin *quadratura* (as QUADRATE)]

quadrennial /kwɒ'drɛnɪəl/ *adj.* **1** lasting four years. **2** recurring every four years. □ **quadrennially** *adv.* [as QUADRENNIUM]

quadrennium /kwɒ'drɛnɪəm/ *n.* (*pl.* **quadrenniums** or **quadrennia** /-nɪə/) a period of four years. [Latin *quadriennium* (as QUADRI-, *annus* 'year')]

quadri- /'kwɒdri/ *comb. form* denoting four. [Latin from *quattuor* 'four']

quadric /'kwɒdrɪk/ *adj.* & *n. Geom.* ● *adj.* (of a surface) described by an equation of the second degree. ● *n.* a quadric surface. [Latin *quadra* 'square']

quadriceps /'kwɒdrɪsɛps/ *n. Anat.* a four-headed muscle at the front of the thigh. [modern Latin (as QUADRI-, BICEPS)]

quadrifid /'kwɒdrɪfɪd/ *adj. Bot.* having four divisions or lobes. [Latin *quadrifidus* (as QUADRI-, *findere fid-* 'cleave')]

quadrilateral /kwɒdrɪ'lat(ə)r(ə)l/ *adj.* & *n.* ● *adj.* having four sides. ● *n.* a four-sided figure. [Late Latin *quadrilaterus* (as QUADRI-, *latus lateris* 'side')]

quadrille[1] /kwə'drɪl/ *n.* **1** a square dance containing usu. five figures. **2** the music for this. [French, via

Spanish *cuadrilla* 'troop, company' from *cuadra* 'square', or Italian *quadriglia* from *quadra* 'square']

quadrille[2] /kwə'drɪl/ *n.* a card game for four players with forty cards, fashionable in the 18th c. [French, perhaps via Spanish *cuartillo* from *cuarto* 'fourth', assimilated to QUADRILLE[1]]

quadrillion /kwɒ'drɪljən/ *n.* (*pl.* same or **quadrillions**) a thousand raised to the fifth (or formerly, esp. *Brit.*, the eighth) power (10^{15} and 10^{24} respectively). [French (as QUADRI-, MILLION)]

quadrinomial /kwɒdrɪ'nəʊmɪəl/ *n.* & *adj. Math.* ● *n.* an expression of four algebraic terms. ● *adj.* of or being a quadrinomial. [QUADRI- + Greek *nomos* 'part, portion']

quadripartite /kwɒdrɪ'pɑ:tʌɪt/ *adj.* **1** consisting of four parts. **2** shared by or involving four parties.

quadriplegia /kwɒdrɪ'pli:dʒə/ *n. Med.* paralysis of all four limbs. □ **quadriplegic** *adj.* & *n.* [modern Latin (as QUADRI-, Greek *plēgē* 'blow, strike')]

quadrivalent /kwɒdrɪ'veɪl(ə)nt/ *adj. Chem.* = TETRAVALENT.

quadrivium /kwɒ'drɪvɪəm/ *n. hist.* a medieval university course of arithmetic, geometry, astronomy, and music. [Latin, = the place where four roads meet (as QUADRI-, *via* 'road')]

quadroon /kwɒ'dru:n/ *n.* the offspring of a white person and a mulatto; a person of one-quarter Negro blood. [Spanish *cuarterón* from *cuarto* 'fourth', assimilated to QUADRI-]

quadrophonic var. of QUADRAPHONIC.

quadrumanous /kwɒ'dru:mənəs, kwɒdrʊ'mɑ:nəs/ *adj.* (of primates other than humans) four-handed, i.e. with opposable digits on all four limbs. [modern Latin *quadrumana*, neut. pl. of *quadrumanus* (as QUADRI-, Latin *manus* 'hand')]

quadruped /'kwɒdrʊped/ *n.* & *adj.* ● *n.* a four-footed animal, esp. a four-footed mammal. ● *adj.* four-footed. □ **quadrupedal** /-'pi:d(ə)l, -'ru:pɪd(ə)l/ *adj.* [French *quadrupède* or Latin *quadrupes -pedis* from *quadru-*, variant of QUADRI- + Latin *pes ped-* 'foot']

quadruple /'kwɒdrʊp(ə)l, kwɒ'dru:p(ə)l/ *adj.*, *n.*, & *v.* ● *adj.* **1** fourfold. **2 a** having four parts. **b** involving four participants (*quadruple alliance*). **3** being four times as many or as much. **4** (of time in music) having four beats in a bar. ● *n.* a fourfold number or amount. ● *v.tr.* & *intr.* multiply by four; increase fourfold. □ **quadruply** *adv.* [French from Latin *quadruplus* (as QUADRI-, *-plus* as in *duplus* DUPLE)]

quadruplet /'kwɒdrʊplɪt, kwɒ'dru:plɪt/ *n.* **1** each of four children born at one birth. **2** a set of four things in combination. **3** *Mus.* a group of four notes to be performed in the time of three. [QUADRUPLE, on the pattern of *triplet*]

quadruplicate *adj.* & *v.* ● *adj.* /kwɒ'dru:plɪkət/ **1** fourfold. **2** of which four copies are made. ● *v.tr.* /kwɒ'dru:plɪkeɪt/ **1** multiply by four. **2** make four identical copies of. □ **in quadruplicate** in four identical copies. □ **quadruplication** /-'keɪʃ(ə)n/ *n.* [Latin *quadruplicare* from *quadruplex -plicis* 'fourfold': cf. QUADRUPED, DUPLEX]

quadruplicity /kwɒdrʊ'plɪsɪti/ *n.* the state of being fourfold. [Latin *quadruplex -plicis* (see QUADRUPLICATE), on the pattern of *duplicity*]

quaestor /'kwi:stə/ *n.* either of two ancient Roman magistrates with mainly financial responsibilities. □ **quaestorial** /-'stɔ:rɪəl/ *adj.* **quaestorship** *n.* [Middle English from Latin, from *quaerere quaesit-* 'seek']

quaff /kwɒf, kwɑ:f/ *v. literary* **1** *tr.* & *intr.* drink deeply. **2** *tr.* drain (a cup etc.) in long draughts. □ **quaffable** *adj.* **quaffer** *n.* [16th c.: perhaps from Middle Low German *quassen* 'eat or drink immoderately']

quag /kwag, kwɒg/ *n.* a marshy or boggy place. □ **quaggy** *adj.* [related to dialect verb *quag* = shake: probably imitative]

quagga /'kwagə/ *n.* an extinct zebra formerly native to S. Africa, which was yellowish-brown with stripes on the head, neck, and forebody. [Nama *qua-ha'*]

quagmire /'kwagmʌɪə, 'kwɒg-/ *n.* **1** a soft boggy or marshy area that gives way underfoot. **2** a hazardous or awkward situation. [QUAG + MIRE]

quahog /'kwɔ:hɒg, 'kwɑ:-/ *n.* (also **quahaug** /-hɔ:g/) *US* the edible round clam, *Venus mercenaria*, of the Atlantic coast of N. America. [Narragansett]

quaich /kweɪk, -x/ *n.* (also **quaigh**) *Sc.* a kind of drinking cup, usu. of wood and with two handles. [Gaelic *cuach* 'cup', probably from Latin *caucus*]

quail[1] /kweɪl/ *n.* (*pl.* same or **quails**) any small short-tailed game bird of the genus *Coturnix*, related to the partridge, esp. the migratory *C. coturnix*. [Middle English via Old French *quaille* from medieval Latin *coacula* (probably imitative)]

quail[2] /kweɪl/ *v.intr.* flinch; be apprehensive with fear. [Middle English, of unknown origin]

quaint /kweɪnt/ *adj.* **1** piquantly or attractively unfamiliar or old-fashioned. **2** daintily odd. □ **quaintly** *adv.* **quaintness** *n.* [earlier senses 'wise, cunning': Middle English via Old French *cointe* from Latin *cognitus*, past part. of *cognoscere* 'ascertain']

quake /kweɪk/ *v.* & *n.* ● *v.intr.* **1** shake, tremble. **2** rock to and fro. **3** (of a person) shake or shudder (*was quaking with fear*). ● *n.* **1** *colloq.* an earthquake. **2** an act of quaking. □ **quaky** *adj.* (**quakier**, **quakiest**). [Old English *cwacian*]

Quaker /'kweɪkə/ *n.* & *adj.* ● *n.* a member of the Society of Friends, a Christian movement devoted to peaceful principles and eschewing formal doctrine, sacraments, and ordained ministers. ● *adj.* of or relating to Quakers. □ **Quakerish** *adj.* **Quakerism** *n.* [QUAKE + -ER[1]: originally *derog.*, perhaps from its founder's direction to 'tremble at the name of the Lord', or from fits supposedly suffered when moved by the Spirit]

quaking-grass *n.* any grass of the genus *Briza*, having slender stalks and trembling in the wind. Also called *dodder-grass*.

qualification /ˌkwɒlɪfɪ'keɪʃ(ə)n/ *n.* **1** the act or an instance of qualifying. **2** an accomplishment fitting a person for a position or purpose. **3 a** a circumstance, condition, etc., that modifies or limits (*the statement had many qualifications*). **b** a thing that detracts from completeness or absoluteness (*their relief had one qualification*). **4** a condition that must be fulfilled before a right can be acquired etc. **5** an attribution of a quality (*the qualification of our policy as opportunist is unfair*). □ **qualificatory** /'kwɒlɪfɪkeɪt(ə)ri/ *adj.* [French *qualification* or medieval Latin *qualificatio* (as QUALIFY)]

qualify /'kwɒlɪfʌɪ/ *v.* (**-ies**, **-ied**) **1** *tr.* make competent or fit for a position or purpose. **2** *tr.* make legally entitled. **3** *intr.* (usu. foll. by *for*) (of a person) satisfy the conditions or requirements (for a position, award, competition, etc.). **4** *tr.* add reservations to; modify or make less absolute (a statement or assertion). **5** *tr. Gram.* (of a word, esp. an adjective) attribute a quality to another word, esp. a noun. **6** *tr.* moderate, mitigate; make less severe or extreme. **7** *tr.* alter the strength or flavour of. **8** *tr.* (foll. by *as*) attribute a specified quality to; describe as (*the idea was qualified as absurd*). **9** *tr.* (as **qualifying** *adj.*) serving to determine those that qualify (*qualifying examination*). □ **qualifiable** *adj.* **qualifier** *n.* [French *qualifier* via medieval Latin *qualificare* from Latin *qualis* 'such as']

qualitative /'kwɒlɪtətɪv/ *adj.* concerned with or depending on quality (*led to a qualitative change in society*). □ **qualitatively** *adv.* [Late Latin *qualitativus* (as QUALITY)]

qualitative analysis *n. Chem.* detection of the constituents, as elements, functional groups, etc., present in a substance (cf. QUANTITATIVE ANALYSIS).

quality /'kwɒlɪti/ *n.* (*pl.* **-ies**) **1** the degree of excellence of a thing (*of good quality*; *poor in quality*). **2 a** general excellence (*their work has quality*). **b** (*attrib.*) of high quality (*a quality product*). **3** a distinctive attribute or faculty; a characteristic trait. **4** the relative nature or kind or character of a thing (*is made in three qualities*). **5 a** the distinctive timbre of a voice or sound. **b** *Phonet.*

the distinguishing characteristic or characteristics of a sound. **6** *archaic* high social standing (*people of quality*). **7** *Logic* the property of a proposition's being affirmative or negative. [Middle English via Old French *qualité* from Latin *qualitas -tatis*, from *qualis* 'of what kind']

quality control *n.* a system of maintaining standards in manufactured products by testing a sample of the output against the specification. □ **quality controller** *n.*

quality paper *n.* (also **quality newspaper**) a newspaper considered to be of a high cultural standard.

quality time *n.* time spent productively or profitably, esp. with reference to the limited time working parents can spend with their children.

qualm /kwɑːm, kwɔːm/ *n.* **1** a misgiving; an uneasy doubt esp. about one's own conduct. **2** a scruple of conscience. **3** a momentary faint or sick feeling. □ **qualmish** *adj.* [16th c.: origin uncertain]

quandary /'kwɒnd(ə)ri/ *n.* (*pl.* **-ies**) **1** a state of perplexity. **2** a difficult situation; a practical dilemma. [16th c.: origin uncertain]

quango /'kwaŋgəʊ/ *n.* (*pl.* **-os**) *Brit.* a semi-public body with financial support from and senior appointments made by the government. [abbreviation of *qua*si (or *qua*si-*a*utonomous) *n*on-*g*overnment(al) *o*rganization]

quant /kwɒnt, kwant/ *n.* & *v.* ● *n. Brit.* a punting-pole with a prong at the bottom to prevent it sinking into the mud, as used by Norfolk bargemen etc. ● *v.tr.* (also *absol.*) propel (a boat) with a quant. [Middle English, perhaps via Latin *contus* from Greek *kontos* 'boat-pole']

quanta *pl.* of QUANTUM.

quantal /'kwɒnt(ə)l/ *adj.* **1** composed of discrete units; varying in steps, not continuously. **2** of or relating to a quantum or quantum theory. □ **quantally** *adv.* [Latin *quantus* 'how much']

quantic /'kwɒntɪk/ *n.* *Math.* a rational integral homogeneous function of two or more variables.

quantify /'kwɒntɪfʌɪ/ *v.tr.* (**-ies**, **-ied**) **1** determine the quantity of. **2** measure or express as a quantity. **3** *Logic* define the application of (a term or proposition) by the use of *all*, *some*, etc., e.g. 'for all *x* if *x* is A then *x* is B'. □ **quantifiable** *adj.* **quantifiability** /-ə'bɪlɪti/ *n.* **quantification** /ˌkwɒntɪfɪ'keɪʃ(ə)n/ *n.* **quantifier** *n.* [medieval Latin *quantificare* (as QUANTAL)]

quantitative /'kwɒntɪtətɪv, -teɪtɪv/ *adj.* **1 a** concerned with quantity. **b** measured or measurable by quantity. **2** of or based on the quantity of syllables. □ **quantitatively** *adv.* [medieval Latin *quantitativus* (as QUANTITY)]

quantitative analysis *n. Chem.* measurement of the amounts of the constituents of a substance (cf. QUALITATIVE ANALYSIS).

quantitive /'kwɒntɪtɪv/ *adj.* = QUANTITATIVE. □ **quantitively** *adv.*

quantity /'kwɒntɪti/ *n.* (*pl.* **-ies**) **1** that property of things that is (in principle) measurable. **2** the size or extent or weight or amount or number. **3** a specified or considerable portion or number or amount (*buys in quantity*; *the quantity of heat in a body*). **4** (in *pl.*) large amounts or numbers; an abundance (*quantities of food*; *is found in quantities on the shore*). **5** the length or shortness of vowel sounds or syllables. **6** *Math.* **a** a value, component, etc. that may be expressed in numbers. **b** the figure or symbol representing this. [Middle English via Old French *quantité* from Latin *quantitas -tatis*, from *quantus* 'how much']

quantity mark *n.* a mark put over a vowel etc. to indicate its length.

quantity surveyor *n. Brit.* a person who measures and prices building work.

quantity theory *n.* the hypothesis that prices correspond to changes in the monetary supply.

quantize /'kwɒntʌɪz/ *v.tr.* (also **-ise**) **1** form into quanta. **2** apply quantum mechanics to. □ **quantization** /-'zeɪʃ(ə)n/ *n.*

quantum /'kwɒntəm/ *n.* (*pl.* **quanta** /-tə/) **1** *Physics* **a** a discrete quantity of energy proportional in magnitude to the frequency of the radiation it represents. **b** an analogous discrete amount of any other physical quantity. **2 a** a required or allowed amount. **b** a share or portion. [Latin, neut. of *quantus* 'how much']

quantum chromodynamics /ˌkrəʊməʊdʌɪ'namɪks/ *n.* *Physics* a theory in which the strong interaction between subatomic particles is described in terms of the exchange by quarks of gluons. [CHROMO-[2] 'colour' (see COLOUR *n.* 11), on the pattern of THERMODYNAMICS]

quantum jump *n.* (also **quantum leap**) **1** a sudden large increase or advance. **2** *Physics* an abrupt transition in an atom or molecule from one quantum state to another.

quantum mechanics *n. Physics* a mathematical form of quantum theory dealing with the motion and interaction of (esp. subatomic) particles and incorporating the concept that these particles can also be regarded as waves. □ **quantum-mechanical** *adj.*

quantum number *n. Physics* a number expressing the value of some property of a particle occurring in quanta.

quantum theory *n. Physics* the body of theory based on the concept of quanta of energy.

quaquaversal /kweɪkwə'vəːs(ə)l/ *adj. Geol.* pointing in every direction. [Late Latin *quaquaversus*, from *quaqua* 'wheresoever' + *versus* 'towards']

quarantine /'kwɒr(ə)ntiːn/ *n.* & *v.* ● *n.* **1** isolation imposed on persons or animals that have arrived from elsewhere or been exposed to, and might spread, infectious or contagious disease. **2** the period of this isolation. ● *v.tr.* impose such isolation on; put in quarantine. [Italian *quarantina* 'forty days' from *quaranta* 'forty']

quark[1] /kwɑːk/ *n. Physics* any of a class of unobserved subatomic particles with a fractional electric charge, of which protons, neutrons, and other hadrons are thought to be composed. [invented word, associated with 'Three quarks for Muster Mark' in Joyce's *Finnegans Wake* (1939)]

quark[2] /kwɑːk/ *n.* a type of low-fat curd cheese. [German]

quarrel[1] /'kwɒr(ə)l/ *n.* & *v.* ● *n.* **1** a violent contention or altercation between individuals or with others. **2** a rupture of friendly relations. **3** an occasion of complaint against a person, a person's actions, etc. ● *v.intr.* (**quarrelled**, **quarrelling**; *US* **quarreled**, **quarreling**) **1** (often foll. by *with*) fall out; have a dispute; break off friendly relations. **2** (foll. by *with*) take exception; find fault. □ **quarreller** *n.* [Middle English via Old French *querele* from Latin *querel(l)a* 'complaint', from *queri* 'complain']

quarrel[2] /'kwɒr(ə)l/ *n. hist.* a short heavy square-headed arrow or bolt used in a crossbow or arbalest. [Middle English from Old French *quar(r)el*, ultimately from Late Latin *quadrus* 'square']

quarrelsome /'kwɒr(ə)ls(ə)m/ *adj.* given to or characterized by quarrelling. □ **quarrelsomely** *adv.* **quarrelsomeness** *n.*

quarrian /'kwɒrɪən/ *n.* (also **quarrion**) *Austral.* a cockatiel. [Wiradhuri *guwarraying*]

quarry[1] /'kwɒri/ *n.* & *v.* ● *n.* (*pl.* **-ies**) **1** an excavation made by taking stone etc. for building etc. from its bed. **2** a place from which stone etc. may be extracted. **3** a source of information, knowledge, etc. ● *v.* (**-ies**, **-ied**) **1** *tr.* extract (stone) from a quarry. **2** *tr.* extract (facts etc.) laboriously from books etc. **3** *intr.* laboriously search documents etc. [Middle English via medieval Latin *quare(r)ia* and Old French *quarriere*, from Latin *quadrum* 'square']

quarry[2] /'kwɒri/ *n.* (*pl.* **-ies**) **1** the object of pursuit by a bird of prey, hounds, hunters, etc. **2** an intended victim or prey. [originally = parts of deer placed on the hide and given to hounds: Middle English via Anglo-French from Old French *cuiree*, *couree* (assimilated to *cuir* 'leather' and *curer* 'disembowel'), ultimately from Latin *cor* 'heart']

quarry[3] /ˈkwɒri/ *n.* (*pl.* **-ies**) **1** a diamond-shaped pane of glass as used in lattice windows. **2** (in full **quarry tile**) an unglazed floor-tile. [a later form of QUARREL[2] in the same sense]

quarryman /ˈkwɒrɪmən/ *n.* (*pl.* **-men**) a worker in a quarry.

quart /kwɔːt/ *n.* **1** a liquid measure equal to a quarter of a gallon; two pints. **2** a vessel containing this amount. **3** *US* a dry measure, equivalent to one-thirty-second of a bushel (1.1 litre). **4** /kɑːt/ (also **quarte, carte**) the fourth of eight parrying positions in fencing. □ **a quart into a pint pot** *Brit.* **1** a large amount etc. fitted into a small space. **2** something difficult or impossible to achieve. [Middle English via Old French *quarte* from Latin *quarta*, fem. of *quartus* 'fourth', from *quattuor* 'four']

quartan /ˈkwɔːt(ə)n/ *adj.* (of a fever etc.) recurring every fourth day. [Middle English via Old French *quartaine* from Latin (*febris* 'fever') *quartana*, from *quartus* 'fourth']

quarter /ˈkwɔːtə/ *n.* & *v.* ● *n.* **1** each of four equal parts into which a thing is or might be divided. **2** a period of three months, usu. for which payments become due on the quarter day. **3** a point of time 15 minutes before or after any hour. **4** a school or *US* university term. **5 a** 25 US or Canadian cents. **b** a coin of this denomination. **6** a part of a town, esp. as occupied by a particular class or group (*residential quarter*). **7 a** a point of the compass. **b** a region at such a point. **8** the direction, district, or source of supply etc. (*help from any quarter*; *came from all quarters*). **9** (in *pl.*) **a** lodgings; an abode. **b** *Mil.* the living accommodation of troops etc. **10 a** one-fourth of a lunar month. **b** the moon's position between the first and second (**first quarter**) or third and fourth (**last quarter**) of these. **11 a** each of the four parts into which an animal's or bird's carcass is divided, each including a leg or wing. **b** (in *pl.*) *hist.* the four parts into which a traitor etc. was cut after execution. **c** (in *pl.*) = HINDQUARTERS. **12** mercy offered or granted to an enemy in battle etc. on condition of surrender. **13 a** one-fourth of a pound weight. **b** *Brit.* a grain measure equivalent to 8 bushels. **c** one-fourth of a hundredweight (28 lb or *US* 25 lb). **14 a** each of four divisions on a shield. **b** a charge occupying this, placed in chief. **15** either side of a ship abaft the beam. **16** (in American and Australian football) each of four equal periods into which a match is divided. ● *v.tr.* **1** divide into quarters. **2** *hist.* divide (the body of an executed person) in this way. **3 a** put (troops etc.) into quarters. **b** station or lodge in a specified place. **4** (foll. by *on*) impose (a person) on another as a lodger. **5** cut (a log) into quarters, and these into planks so as to show the grain well. **6** (esp. of a hunting dog or bird of prey) range or traverse (the ground) in every direction. **7** *Heraldry* **a** place or bear (charges or coats of arms) on the four quarters of a shield's surface. **b** add (another's coat) to one's hereditary arms. **c** (foll. by *with*) place in alternate quarters with. **d** divide (a shield) into four or more parts by vertical and horizontal lines. [Middle English via Anglo-French *quarter*, Old French *quartier* from Latin *quartarius* 'fourth part' (of a measure), from *quartus* 'fourth']

quarterage /ˈkwɔːt(ə)rɪdʒ/ *n.* **1** a quarterly payment. **2** a quarter's wages, allowance, pension, etc.

quarterback /ˈkwɔːtəbak/ *n.* a player in American football who directs attacking play.

quarter-binding *n.* the type of bookbinding in which the spine is bound in one material (usu. leather) and the sides in another.

quarter day *n. Brit.* one of four days on which quarterly payments are due, tenancies begin and end, etc.

quarterdeck /ˈkwɔːtədɛk/ *n.* **1** part of a ship's upper deck near the stern, usu. reserved for officers. **2** the officers of a ship or the navy.

quarter-final *n.* a match or round preceding the semi-final.

quarter-hour *n.* (also **quarter of an hour**) **1** a period of 15 minutes. **2** = QUARTER *n.* 3.

quartering /ˈkwɔːt(ə)rɪŋ/ *n.* **1** (in *pl.*) the coats of arms marshalled on a shield to denote the alliances of a family with the heiresses of others. **2** the provision of quarters for soldiers. **3** the act or an instance of dividing, esp. into four equal parts.

quarter-light *n. Brit.* a window in the side of a motor vehicle, closed carriage, etc. other than the main door window.

quarter-line *n. Rugby* a space enclosed by a line across the ground 22 metres from the goal line.

quarterly /ˈkwɔːtəli/ *adj., adv.,* & *n.* ● *adj.* **1** produced or occurring once every quarter of a year. **2** (of a shield) quartered. ● *adv.* **1** once every quarter of a year. **2** in the four, or in two diagonally opposite, quarters of a shield. ● *n.* (*pl.* **-ies**) a quarterly review or magazine.

quartermaster /ˈkwɔːtəmɑːstə/ *n.* **1** a regimental officer in charge of quartering, rations, etc. **2** a naval petty officer in charge of steering, signals, etc.

Quartermaster General *n.* (*pl.* **Quartermaster Generals**) the head of the army department in charge of quartering etc.

quartermaster sergeant *n.* a sergeant assisting an army quartermaster.

quartern /ˈkwɔːt(ə)n/ *n. Brit. archaic* a quarter of a pint. [Middle English, = quarter, via Anglo-French *quartrun*, Old French *quart(e)ron* from QUART 'fourth' or *quartier* QUARTER]

quartern loaf *n.* a four-pound loaf.

quarter note *n.* esp. *N. Amer. Mus.* a crotchet.

quarter-plate *n.* **1** a photographic plate or film 8.3 × 10.8 cm. **2** a photograph reproduced from it.

quarter-pounder *n.* something, esp. a hamburger, that weighs a quarter of a pound.

quarter sessions *n.pl. hist.* (in the UK) a court of limited criminal and civil jurisdiction and of appeal, usu. held quarterly.

quarterstaff /ˈkwɔːtəstɑːf/ *n. hist.* a stout pole 6–8 feet long, formerly used as a weapon.

quarter-tone *n. Mus.* half a semitone.

quartet /kwɔːˈtɛt/ *n.* (also **quartette**) **1** *Mus.* **a** a composition for four voices or instruments. **b** the performers of such a piece. **2** any group of four. [French *quartette* from Italian *quartetto*, via *quarto* 'fourth' from Latin *quartus*]

quartic /ˈkwɔːtɪk/ *adj.* & *n. Math.* ● *adj.* involving the fourth and no higher power of an unknown quantity or variable. ● *n.* a quartic equation. [Latin *quartus* 'fourth']

quartile /ˈkwɔːtʌɪl/ *adj.* & *n.* ● *adj. Astrol.* relating to the aspect of two celestial bodies 90° apart. ● *n.* **1** a quartile aspect. **2** *Statistics* each of three values of a variable dividing a population into four equal groups as regards the value of that variable. [medieval Latin *quartilis* from Latin *quartus* 'fourth']

quarto /ˈkwɔːtəʊ/ *n.* (*pl.* **-os**) *Printing* **1** the size of book or paper given by folding a (usu. specified) sheet of paper twice, commonly 10 in. × 8 in. **2** a book consisting of sheets folded in this way (abbr.: **4to**). [Latin (*in*) *quarto* '(in) the fourth' (of a sheet), ablative of *quartus* 'fourth']

quarto paper *n.* paper folded twice and cut into sheets.

quartz /kwɔːts/ *n.* a mineral form of silica that crystallizes as hexagonal prisms. [German *Quarz* from West Slavonic *kwardy*]

quartz clock *n.* a clock operated by vibrations of an electrically driven quartz crystal.

quartzite /ˈkwɔːtsʌɪt/ *n.* a metamorphic rock consisting mainly of quartz.

quartz lamp *n.* a quartz tube containing mercury vapour and used as a light source.

quartz watch *n.* a watch in which a quartz crystal is employed as in a quartz clock.

quasar /ˈkweɪzɑː, -sɑː/ *n. Astron.* any of a class of starlike celestial objects often associated with intense radio emission and apparently of great size and remoteness. [*quasi*-stell*ar*]

quash /kwɒʃ/ *v.tr.* **1** annul; reject as not valid, esp. by a legal procedure. **2** suppress; crush (a rebellion etc.). [Middle English via Old French *quasser*, *casser* 'annul' from Late Latin *cassare*, from *cassus* 'null, void', or from Latin *cassare*, frequentative of *quatere* 'shake']

quasi /ˈkweɪzʌɪ, -sʌɪ, ˈkwɑːzi/ *adv.* (introducing an exclamation) that is to say; as it were. [Latin, = as if, almost]

quasi- /ˈkweɪzʌɪ, -sʌɪ, ˈkwɑːzi/ *comb. form* **1** seemingly; apparently but not really (*quasi-scientific*). **2** being partly or almost (*quasi-independent*). [Latin *quasi* 'as if, almost']

quassia /ˈkwɒʃə, ˈkwɒʃɪə, ˈkwasɪə/ *n.* **1** an evergreen tree, *Quassia amara*, native to S. America. **2** the wood, bark, or root of this tree, yielding a bitter medicinal tonic and insecticide. [named after G. *Quassi*, 18th-c. Suriname slave, who discovered its medicinal properties]

quatercentenary /kwatəsɛnˈtiːn(ə)ri, -ˈtɛn-, -ˈsɛntɪn-, kweɪtə-/ *n.* & *adj.* ● *n.* (*pl.* **-ies**) **1** a four-hundredth anniversary. **2** a festival marking this. ● *adj.* of this anniversary. [Latin *quater* 'four times' + CENTENARY]

quaternary /kwəˈtəːn(ə)ri/ *adj.* & *n.* ● *adj.* **1** fourth in order or rank etc. **2** (**Quaternary**) *Geol.* of or relating to the most recent period in the Cenozoic era with evidence of many species of present-day plants and animals (cf. PLEISTOCENE, HOLOCENE). Cf. Appendix X. **3** *Chem.* (of an ammonium compound) containing four atoms or groups (other than hydrogen atoms) bonded to a nitrogen atom. ● *n.* (*pl.* **-ies**) **1** a quaternary thing, compound, etc. **2** (**Quaternary**) *Geol.* the Quaternary period or system. [Middle English from Latin *quaternarius* from *quaterni*, distributive of *quattuor* 'four']

quaternion /kwəˈtəːnɪən/ *n.* **1** a set of four. **2** *Math.* a complex number of the form $w + xi + yj + zk$, where w, x, y, z are real numbers and i, j, k are imaginary units that satisfy certain conditions. [Middle English from Late Latin *quaternio -onis* (as QUATERNARY)]

quatorzain /ˈkatəzeɪn/ *n.* a fourteen-line poem; an irregular sonnet. [French *quatorzaine* from *quatorze* 'fourteen', from Latin *quattuordecim*]

quatorze /kəˈtɔːz/ *n.* a set of four aces, kings, queens, or jacks, in one hand at piquet, scoring fourteen. [French: see QUATORZAIN]

quatrain /ˈkwɒtreɪn/ *n.* a stanza of four lines, usu. with alternate rhymes. [French from *quatre* 'four', from Latin *quattuor*]

quatrefoil /ˈkatrəfɔɪl/ *n.* a four-pointed or four-leafed figure, esp. as an ornament in architectural tracery, resembling a flower or cloverleaf. [Middle English from Anglo-French, from *quatre* 'four': see FOIL[2]]

quattrocento /kwatrə(ʊ)ˈtʃɛntəʊ/ *n.* the style of Italian art of the 15th c. □ **quattrocentist** *n.* & *adj.* [Italian, = 400, short for *milquattrocento* '1400', used with reference to the years 1400–99]

quaver /ˈkweɪvə/ *v.* & *n.* ● *v.* **1** *intr.* **a** (esp. of a voice or musical sound) vibrate, shake, tremble. **b** use trills or shakes in singing. **2** *tr.* **a** sing (a note or song) with quavering. **b** (often foll. by *out*) say in a trembling voice. ● *n.* **1** *Mus.* a note having the time value of an eighth of a semibreve or half a crotchet and represented by a large dot with a hooked stem. **2** a trill in singing. **3** a tremble in speech. □ **quaveringly** *adv.* **quavery** *adj.* [Middle English from *quave*, perhaps from an Old English word related to QUAKE]

quay /kiː/ *n.* a solid stationary artificial landing place lying alongside or projecting into water for loading and unloading ships. □ **quayage** *n.* [Middle English *key*(*e*), *kay* via Old French *kay* and Gaulish *caio* from Celtic]

quayside /ˈkiːsʌɪd/ *n.* the land forming or near a quay.

Que. *abbr.* Quebec.

quean /kwiːn/ *n. archaic* an impudent or ill-behaved girl or woman. [Old English *cwene* 'woman': cf. QUEEN]

queasy /ˈkwiːzi/ *adj.* (**-ier**, **-iest**) **1 a** (of a person) feeling nauseous. **b** (of a person's stomach) easily upset; weak of digestion. **2** (of the conscience etc.) overscrupulous, tender. □ **queasily** *adv.* **queasiness** *n.* [Middle English *queysy*, *coisy*, perhaps from Anglo-French & Old French, related to Old French *coisir* 'hurt']

Quebecker /kwɪˈbɛkə/ *n.* (also **Quebecer**) a native or inhabitant of Quebec.

Quechua /ˈkɛtʃwə/ *n.* & *adj.* (also **Quichua** /ˈkɪ-/) ● *n.* (*pl.* same or **Quechuas**) **1** a member of a S. American Indian people of Peru and neighbouring countries. **2** the language of this people. ● *adj.* of or relating to this people or their language. □ **Quechuan** *adj.* [Spanish from Quechua]

queen /kwiːn/ *n.* & *v.* ● *n.* **1** (as a title usu. **Queen**) a female sovereign etc., esp. the hereditary ruler of an independent state. **2** (in full **queen consort**) a king's wife. **3** a woman, country, or thing pre-eminent or supreme in a specified area or of its kind (*tennis queen*; *the queen of roses*). **4** the fertile female among ants, bees, etc. **5** the most powerful piece in chess. **6** a court card with a picture of a queen. **7** *slang offens.* a male homosexual, esp. an effeminate one. **8** (as a title usu. **Queen**) **a** an honoured female, e.g. the Virgin Mary (*Queen of Heaven*). **b** an ancient goddess (*Venus, Queen of love*). **9** a belle or mock sovereign on some occasion (*beauty queen*; *queen of the May*). **10** a person's sweetheart, wife, or mistress. **11** (**the Queen**) the national anthem when there is a female sovereign. ● *v.tr.* **1** make (a woman) queen. **2** *Chess* convert (a pawn) into a queen when it reaches the opponent's side of the board. □ **queen it** play the queen. □ **queendom** *n.* **queenhood** *n.* **queenless** *adj.* **queenlike** *adj.* **queenship** *n.* [Old English *cwēn*, from Germanic; cf. QUEAN]

Queen-Anne *adj.* (usu. *attrib.*) in the style of English architecture, furniture, etc., in or about Queen Anne's time, the early 18th c.

Queen Anne's lace *n. Bot.* = COW-PARSLEY.

queen bee *n.* **1** the fertile female in a hive. **2** the chief or controlling woman in an organization or social group.

queen cake *n.* a small soft cake often with raisins etc.

queen consort see QUEEN *n.* 2.

queen dowager *n.* the widow of a king.

queenie /ˈkwiːni/ *n. slang offens* = QUEEN *n.* 7.

Queen in Council *n. Brit.* the Privy Council as issuing Orders in Council or receiving petitions etc.

queenly /ˈkwiːnli/ *adj.* (**queenlier**, **queenliest**) **1** fit for or appropriate to a queen. **2** majestic; queenlike. □ **queenliness** *n.*

queen mother *n.* the dowager who is mother of the sovereign.

queen of puddings *n.* a pudding made with bread, jam, and meringue.

Queen of the May *n.* = MAY QUEEN.

queen of the meadows *n. Bot.* meadowsweet.

queen post *n.* either of two upright timbers between the tie-beam and principal rafters of a roof-truss.

Queen's Bench *n.* (in the UK) a division of the High Court of Justice.

Queensberry Rules /ˈkwiːnzb(ə)ri/ *n.pl.* the standard rules, esp. of boxing. [named after the 8th Marquess of *Queensberry*, English nobleman d. 1900, who supervised the preparation of boxing laws in 1867]

queen's bishop *n. Chess* the bishop on the queen's side of the board at the start of a game.

Queen's bounty *n. Brit. hist.* = KING'S BOUNTY.

Queen's Champion *n.* (in the UK) = CHAMPION OF ENGLAND.

Queen's colour *n.* (in the UK) a flag carried by a regiment.

Queen's Counsel *n.* (in the UK) counsel to the Crown, taking precedence over other barristers.

Queen's English *n.* the English language as correctly written or spoken in Britain.

Queen's evidence *n. Brit. Law* evidence for the prosecution given by a participant in or accomplice to the crime at issue.

Queen's Guide *n.* (in the UK) a Guide (see GUIDE *n.* 10) who has reached the highest rank of proficiency.

Queen's highway *n. Brit.* a public road, regarded as being under the sovereign's protection.

queen-size *adj.* (also **queen-sized**) of a larger than normal size, usu. smaller than king-size.

queen's knight *n. Chess* the knight on the queen's side of the board at the start of a game.

Queen's Messenger *n.* (in the UK) a courier in the diplomatic service.

queen's pawn *n. Chess* the pawn in front of the queen at the beginning of a game.

Queen's Proctor *n.* (in the UK) an official who has the right to intervene in probate, divorce, and nullity cases when collusion or the suppression of facts is alleged.

queen's rook *n. Chess* the rook on the queen's side of the board at the start of a game.

Queen's Scout *n.* (in the UK) a Scout (see SCOUT[1] *n.* 4) who has reached the highest standard of proficiency.

Queen's Speech *n.* (in the UK) a statement including the Government's proposed measures read by the sovereign at the opening of Parliament.

queen's-ware *n.* cream-coloured Wedgwood.

queer /kwɪə/ *adj., n., & v.* ● *adj.* **1** strange; odd; eccentric. **2** shady; suspect; of questionable character. **3** *Brit.* **a** slightly ill; giddy; faint. **b** *slang* drunk. **4** *slang offens.* (esp. of a man) homosexual. ● *n. slang offens.* a (esp. male) homosexual. ● *v.tr. slang* spoil; put out of order. □ **in Queer Street** *Brit. slang* in a difficulty, in debt or trouble or disrepute. **queer a person's pitch** *Brit.* spoil a person's chances, esp. secretly or maliciously. □ **queerish** *adj.* **queerly** *adv.* **queerness** *n.* [perhaps from German *quer* 'oblique' (as THWART)]

quell /kwɛl/ *v.tr.* **1 a** crush or put down (a rebellion etc.). **b** reduce (rebels etc.) to submission. **2** suppress or alleviate (fear, anger, etc.). □ **queller** *n.* (also in *comb.*). [Old English *cwellan* 'kill', from Germanic]

quench /kwɛn(t)ʃ/ *v.tr.* **1** satisfy (thirst) by drinking. **2** extinguish (a fire or light etc.). **3** cool, esp. with water (heat or a heated thing). **4** esp. *Metallurgy* cool (esp. hot metal) rapidly in cold water, air, oil, etc. **5 a** stifle or suppress (desire etc.). **b** *Physics & Electronics* inhibit or prevent (oscillation, luminescence, etc.) by counteractive means. **6** *Brit. slang* reduce (an opponent) to silence. □ **quenchable** *adj.* **quencher** *n.* **quenchless** *adj.* [Old English *-cwencan* (in *acwencan*), from Germanic]

quenelle /kəˈnɛl/ *n.* a small seasoned ball or roll of pounded fish or meat. [French, of unknown origin]

querist /ˈkwɪərɪst/ *n. literary* a person who asks questions; a questioner. [Latin *quaerere* 'ask']

quern /kwəːn/ *n.* **1** a mill for grinding corn, typically consisting of two stones. **2** a small hand mill for pepper etc. [Old English *cweorn(e)*, from Germanic]

quern-stone *n.* either of the two stones forming a quern.

querulous /ˈkwɛrʊləs, -jʊləs/ *adj.* complaining, peevish. □ **querulously** *adj.* **querulousness** *n.* [Late Latin *querulosus* or Latin *querulus* from *queri* 'complain']

query /ˈkwɪəri/ *n. & v.* ● *n.* (*pl.* **-ies**) **1** a question, esp. expressing doubt or objection. **2** a question mark, or the word *query* spoken or written to question accuracy or as a mark of interrogation. ● *v.* (**-ies, -ied**) **1** *tr.* (often foll. by *whether*, *if*, etc. + clause) ask or enquire. **2** *tr.* call (a thing) in question in speech or writing. **3** *tr.* dispute the accuracy of. **4** *intr.* put a question. [Anglicized form of *quaere* from Latin *quaerere* 'ask', influenced by INQUIRY]

quest /kwɛst/ *n. & v.* ● *n.* **1** a search or the act of seeking. **2** the thing sought, esp. the object of a medieval knight's pursuit. ● *v.* **1** *intr.* (often foll. by *about*) **a** (often foll. by *after*, *for*) go about in search of something. **b** (of a dog etc.) search about for game. **2** *tr. poet.* search for; seek out. □ **in quest of** seeking. □ **quester** *n.* (also **questor**). **questingly** *adv.* [Middle English from Old French *queste*, *quester*, ultimately from Latin *quaerere quaest-* 'seek']

question /ˈkwɛstʃ(ə)n/ *n. & v.* ● *n.* **1** a sentence worded or expressed so as to seek information. **2 a** doubt about or objection to a thing's truth, credibility, advisability, etc. (*allowed it without question*; *is there any question as to its validity?*). **b** the raising of such doubt etc. **3** a matter to be discussed or decided or voted on. **4** a problem requiring an answer or solution. **5** (foll. by *of*) a matter or concern depending on conditions (*it's a question of money*). ● *v.tr.* **1** ask questions of; interrogate. **2** subject (a person) to examination. **3** throw doubt upon; raise objections to. **4** seek information from the study of (phenomena, facts). □ **be a question of time** be certain to happen sooner or later. **beyond all question** undoubtedly. **come into question** be discussed; become of practical importance. **in question** that is being discussed or referred to (*the person in question*). **is not the question** is irrelevant. **no question of** no possibility of (*there's no question of my giving in*). **out of the question** too impracticable etc. to be worth discussing; impossible. **put the question** require supporters and opponents of a proposal to record their votes, divide a meeting. □ **questioner** *n.* **questioningly** *adv.* **questionless** *adj.* [Middle English via Anglo-French *questiun*, Old French *question*, *questionner* from Latin *quaestio -onis*, from *quaerere quaest-* 'seek']

questionable /ˈkwɛstʃ(ə)nəb(ə)l/ *adj.* **1** doubtful as regards truth or quality. **2** not clearly in accordance with honesty, honour, wisdom, etc. □ **questionability** /kwɛstʃ(ə)nəˈbɪlɪti/ *n.* **questionableness** *n.* **questionably** *adv.*

questionary /ˈkwɛstʃ(ə)n(ə)ri/ *n.* (*pl.* **-ies**) *archaic* or *Med.* = QUESTIONNAIRE. [medieval Latin *quaestionarium*, or French (as QUESTIONNAIRE)]

question mark *n.* **1** a punctuation mark (?) indicating a question. **2** a cause for doubt or uncertainty (*there's still a question mark over the plans*).

question master *n. Brit.* a person who presides over a quiz game etc.

questionnaire /kwɛstʃəˈnɛː, kɛstjə-/ *n.* **1** a formulated series of questions, esp. for statistical study. **2** a document containing these. [French, from *questionner* QUESTION + *-aire* -ARY[1]]

question time *n.* (in the House of Commons) a period during parliamentary proceedings when MPs may question ministers.

quetzal /ˈkɛts(ə)l, ˈkwɛt-/ *n.* **1** any of various brilliantly coloured birds of the family Trogonidae, esp. the Central and S. American *Pharomachrus mocinno*, the male of which has long green tail coverts. **2** the chief monetary unit of Guatemala. [Spanish from Nahuatl *quetzalli*, the bird's tail feather]

queue /kjuː/ *n. & v.* ● *n.* **1** a line or sequence of persons, vehicles, etc., awaiting their turn to be attended to or to proceed. **2** a pigtail or plait of hair. **3** *Computing* a list of data items, commands, etc., stored so as to be retrievable in a definite order, usu. the order of insertion. ● *v.* (**queues, queued, queuing** or **queueing**) **1** *intr.* (often foll. by *up*) (of persons etc.) form a queue; take one's place in a queue. **2** *tr.* esp. *Computing* arrange in a queue. [French from Latin *cauda* 'tail']

queue-jump *v.intr. Brit.* push forward out of turn in a queue.

quibble /ˈkwɪb(ə)l/ *n. & v.* ● *n.* **1** a petty objection; a trivial point of criticism. **2** a play on words; a pun. **3** an evasion; an insubstantial argument which relies on an ambiguity etc. ● *v.intr.* use quibbles. □ **quibbler** *n.* **quibbling** *adj.* **quibblingly** *adv.* [diminutive of obsolete *quib*, probably from Latin *quibus*, dative & ablative pl. of *qui* 'who' (familiar from use in legal documents)]

quiche /kiːʃ/ *n.* an open flan or tart with a savoury filling. [French, related to German *Kuchen* 'cake']

Quichua var. of QUECHUA.

quick /kwɪk/ *adj., adv., & n.* ● *adj.* **1** taking only a short time (*a quick worker*). **2** arriving after a short time, prompt (*quick action; quick results*). **3** with only a short interval (*in quick succession*). **4** lively, intelligent. **5** acute, alert (*has a quick ear*). **6** (of a temper) easily roused. **7** *archaic* living, alive (*the quick and the dead*). ● *adv.* **1** quickly; at a rapid rate. **2** (as *int.*) come, go, etc., quickly. ● *n.* **1** the soft flesh below the nails, or the skin, or a sore. **2** the seat of feeling or emotion (*cut to the quick*). □ **be quick** act quickly. **quick with child** *archaic* at a stage of pregnancy when movements of the foetus have been felt. □ **quickly** *adv.* **quickness** *n.* [Old English *cwic(u)* 'alive', from Germanic]

quicken /ˈkwɪk(ə)n/ *v.* **1** *tr. & intr.* make or become quicker; accelerate. **2** *tr.* give life or vigour to; rouse; animate; stimulate. **3** *intr.* **a** (of a woman) reach a stage in pregnancy when movements of the foetus can be felt. **b** (of a foetus) begin to show signs of life. **4** *tr. archaic* kindle; make (a fire) burn brighter. **5** *intr.* come to life.

quick-fire *attrib.adj.* **1** (of repartee etc.) rapid. **2** firing shots in quick succession.

quick fix *n.* a rapid (esp. inadequate) solution to a problem.

quick-freeze *v.tr.* freeze (food) rapidly so as to preserve its natural qualities.

quickie /ˈkwɪki/ *n. & adj. colloq.* ● *n.* **1** a thing done or made quickly or hastily. **2** an alcoholic drink taken quickly. **3** a brief act of sexual intercourse. ● *adj.* made or executed quickly (*quickie divorce; quickie production*).

quicklime /ˈkwɪklʌɪm/ *n.* = LIME[1] *n.* 1.

quick march *n. & int. Mil.* ● *n.* a march in quick time. ● *int.* the command to begin this.

quick one *n. colloq.* an alcoholic drink taken quickly.

quicksand /ˈkwɪksand/ *n.* **1 a** loose wet sand that sucks in anything placed or falling into it. **b** a bed of this. **2** a treacherous thing or situation.

quickset /ˈkwɪksɛt/ *adj. & n. Brit.* ● *adj.* (of a hedge) formed of slips of plants, esp. hawthorn, set in the ground to grow. ● *n.* **1** such slips. **2** a hedge formed in this way.

quicksilver /ˈkwɪksɪlvə/ *n. & v.* ● *n.* **1** liquid mercury. **2** mobility of temperament or mood. ● *v.tr.* coat (mirror glass) with an amalgam of tin.

quickstep /ˈkwɪkstɛp/ *n. & v.* ● *n.* **1** a fast foxtrot. **2** (**quick step**) *Mil.* a step used in quick time. ● *v.intr.* (**-stepped, -stepping**) dance the quickstep.

quick-tempered *adj.* easily angered.

quickthorn /ˈkwɪkθɔːn/ *n.* the hawthorn.

quick time *n. Mil.* marching at about 120 paces per minute.

quick trick *n. Bridge* **1** a trick in the first two rounds of a suit. **2** a card that should win this.

quick-witted *adj.* quick to grasp a situation, make repartee, etc. □ **quick-wittedness** *n.*

quid[1] /kwɪd/ *n.* (*pl.* same) *Brit. slang* one pound sterling. □ **not the full quid** *Austral. slang* mentally deficient. **quids in** *slang* in a position of profit. [probably from *quid* 'the nature of a thing' from Latin *quid* 'what, something']

quid[2] /kwɪd/ *n.* a lump of tobacco for chewing. [dialect variant of CUD]

quiddity /ˈkwɪdɪti/ *n.* (*pl.* **-ies**) **1** *Philos.* the essence of a person or thing; what makes a thing what it is. **2** a quibble; a trivial objection. [medieval Latin *quidditas* from Latin *quid* 'what']

quidnunc /ˈkwɪdnʌŋk/ *n. archaic* a newsmonger, a person given to gossip. [Latin *quid* 'what' + *nunc* 'now']

quid pro quo /kwɪd prəʊ ˈkwəʊ/ *n.* (*pl.* **quid pro quos**) **1** a thing given as compensation. **2** return made (for a gift, favour, etc.). [Latin, = something for something]

quiescent /kwɪˈɛs(ə)nt, kwʌɪ-/ *adj.* **1** motionless, inert. **2** silent, dormant. □ **quiescence** *n.* **quiescency** *n.* **quiescently** *adv.* [Latin *quiescere* from *quies* QUIET]

quiet /ˈkwʌɪət/ *adj., n., & v.* ● *adj.* (**quieter, quietest**) **1** with little or no sound or motion. **2** of gentle or peaceful disposition. **3** (of a colour, piece of clothing, etc.) unobtrusive; not showy. **4** not overt; private; disguised (*quiet resentment*). **5** undisturbed; uninterrupted; free or far from vigorous action (*a quiet time for prayer*). **6** informal; simple (*just a quiet wedding*). **7** enjoyed in quiet (*a quiet smoke*). **8** tranquil; not anxious or remorseful. ● *n.* **1** silence; stillness. **2** an undisturbed state; tranquillity. **3** a state of being free from urgent tasks or agitation (*a time of quiet at work*). **4** a peaceful state of affairs (*there was quiet along the frontier*). ● *v.* **1** *tr.* soothe; make quiet. **2** *intr.* (often foll. by *down*) become quiet or calm. □ **be quiet** (esp. in *imper.*) cease talking etc. **keep quiet 1** refrain from making a noise. **2** (often foll. by *about*) suppress or refrain from disclosing information etc. **on the quiet** *colloq.* unobtrusively; secretly. □ **quietly** *adv.* **quietness** *n.* [Middle English via Anglo-French *quiete* and Old French *quiet(e)*, *quieté* from Latin *quietus*, past part. of *quiescere*: see QUIESCENT]

quieten /ˈkwʌɪət(ə)n/ *v.tr. & intr.* (often foll. by *down*) *Brit.* = QUIET *v.*

quietism /ˈkwʌɪɪtɪz(ə)m/ *n.* **1** a passive attitude towards life, with devotional contemplation and abandonment of the will, as a form of religious mysticism. **2** the principle of non-resistance. □ **quietist** *n. & adj.* **quietistic** /-ˈtɪstɪk/ *adj.* [Italian *quietismo* (as QUIET)]

quietude /ˈkwʌɪɪtjuːd/ *n.* a state of quiet.

quietus /kwʌɪˈiːtəs/ *n.* (*pl.* **quietuses**) **1** discharge or release from life; death; that which brings death. **2** something which quiets or represses; a sedative. [medieval Latin *quietus est* 'he is quit', used as a form of receipt on payment of a debt: see QUIT]

quiff /kwɪf/ *n.* esp. *Brit.* **1** a man's tuft of hair, brushed upward over the forehead. **2** a curl plastered down on the forehead. [19th c.: origin unknown]

quill /kwɪl/ *n. & v.* ● *n.* **1** (in full **quill-feather**) a large feather in a wing or tail. **2** the hollow stem of this. **3** (in full **quill pen**) a pen made of a quill. **4** (usu. in *pl.*) the spines of a porcupine. **5** a musical pipe made of a hollow stem. ● *v.tr.* form into cylindrical quill-like folds; goffer. [Middle English, probably from (Middle) Low German *quiele*]

quill-coverts *n.pl.* the feathers covering the base of quill-feathers.

quilling /ˈkwɪlɪŋ/ *n.* **1** a piece of quilled lace edging etc. **2** *US* the art of making ornamental filigree from tightly rolled columns of paper.

quilt[1] /kwɪlt/ *n. & v.* ● *n.* **1** a bed-covering made of padding enclosed between layers of cloth etc. and kept in place by cross lines of stitching. **2** a bedspread of similar design (*patchwork quilt*). ● *v.tr.* **1** cover or line with padded material. **2** make or join together (pieces of cloth with padding between) after the manner of a quilt. **3** sew up (a coin, letter, etc.) between two layers of a garment etc. **4** compile (a literary work) out of extracts or borrowed ideas. □ **quilter** *n.* **quilting** *n.* [Middle English via Old French *coilte*, *cuilte* from Latin *culcita* 'mattress, cushion']

quilt[2] /kwɪlt/ *v.tr. Austral. slang* thrash; clout. [perhaps from QUILT[1]]

quim /kwɪm/ *n. coarse slang* the female genitals. [18th c.: origin unknown]

quin /kwɪn/ *n.* esp. *Brit. colloq.* a quintuplet. [abbreviation]

quinacrine /ˈkwɪnəkriːn, -krɪn/ *n.* an antimalarial drug derived from acridine. [*quin*ine + *acridine*]

quinary /ˈkwʌɪnəri/ *adj.* **1** of the number five. **2** having five parts. [Latin *quinarius* from *quini*, distributive of *quinque* 'five']

quinate /ˈkwʌɪneɪt/ *adj. Bot.* (of a leaf) having five leaflets. [Latin *quini* (as QUINARY)]

quince /kwɪns/ *n.* **1** a hard acid pear-shaped fruit used as a preserve or flavouring. **2** any shrub or small tree of the genus *Cydonia* (rose family), esp. *C. oblonga*, bearing this fruit. See also JAPANESE QUINCE. [Middle English, originally collective pl. of obsolete *quoyn, coyn*, via Old French *cooin* from Latin *cotoneum*, variant of *cydoneum* (*malum*) '(apple) of *Cydonia*' (now Canea) in Crete]

quincentenary /kwɪnsɛn'ti:n(ə)ri, -'tɛn-, kwɪn'sɛntɪn-/ *n. & adj.* ● *n.* (*pl.* **-ies**) **1** a five-hundredth anniversary. **2** a festival marking this. ● *adj.* of this anniversary. □ **quincentennial** /-'tɛnɪəl/ *adj.* & *n.* [formed irregularly from Latin *quinque* 'five' + CENTENARY]

quincunx /'kwɪnkʌŋks/ *n.* **1** five objects set so that four are at the corners of a square or rectangle and the fifth is at its centre, e.g. the five on dice or cards. **2** this arrangement, esp. in planting trees. □ **quincuncial** /kwɪn'kʌnʃ(ə)l/ *adj.* **quincuncially** /-'kʌnʃ(ə)li/ *adv.* [Latin, = five-twelfths, from *quinque* 'five', *uncia* 'twelfth']

quinella /kwɪ'nɛlə/ *n.* a form of betting in which the better must select the first two place-winners in a race, not necessarily in the correct order. [Latin American Spanish *quiniela*]

quinine /'kwɪni:n, kwɪ'ni:n/ *n.* **1** an alkaloid found esp. in cinchona bark. **2** a bitter toxic drug containing this, formerly used as a tonic and esp. as a remedy for malaria. [*quina* 'cinchona bark' from Spanish *quina*, from Quechua *kina* 'bark']

quinol /'kwɪnɒl/ *n.* = HYDROQUINONE.

quinoline /'kwɪnəli:n/ *n. Chem.* an oily amine obtained from coal tar or by synthesis and used in the preparation of drugs etc.

quinone /'kwɪnəʊn, kwɪ'nəʊn/ *n. Chem.* **1** = BENZOQUINONE. **2** any compound with the same ring structure as benzoquinone.

quinquagenarian /ˌkwɪŋkwədʒɪ'nɛ:rɪən/ *n. & adj.* ● *n.* a person from 50 to 59 years old. ● *adj.* of or relating to this age. [Latin *quinquagenarius* from *quinquageni*, distributive of *quinquaginta* 'fifty']

Quinquagesima /kwɪŋkwə'dʒɛsɪmə/ *n.* (in full **Quinquagesima Sunday**) the Sunday before the beginning of Lent. [medieval Latin, fem. of Latin *quinquagesimus* 'fifty', influenced by QUADRAGESIMA, from its being ten days before the forty penitential days of Lent]

quinque- /'kwɪŋkwi/ *comb. form* five. [Latin from *quinque* 'five']

quinquennial /kwɪŋ'kwɛnɪəl/ *adj.* **1** lasting five years. **2** recurring every five years. □ **quinquennially** *adv.* [Latin *quinquennis* (as QUINQUENNIUM)]

quinquennium /kwɪŋ'kwɛnɪəm/ *n.* (*pl.* **quinquenniums** or **quinquennia** /-nɪə/) a period of five years. [Latin, from *quinque* 'five' + *annus* 'year']

quinquereme /'kwɪŋkwɪri:m/ *n.* an ancient Roman galley probably having five oarsmen to each bank of oars. [Latin *quinqueremis* (as QUINQUE-, *remus* 'oar')]

quinquevalent /kwɪnkwɪ'veɪl(ə)nt/ *adj. Chem.* = PENTAVALENT.

quinsy /'kwɪnzi/ *n.* an inflammation of the throat, esp. an abscess in the region of the tonsils. □ **quinsied** *adj.* [Middle English via Old French *quinencie* and medieval Latin *quinancia* from Greek *kunagkhē*, from *kun-* 'dog' + *agkhō* 'throttle']

quint /kɪnt, kwɪnt/ *n.* **1** a sequence of five cards in the same suit in piquet etc. **2** *N. Amer.* a quintuplet. [French *quinte* from Latin *quinta*, fem. of *quintus* 'fifth' from *quinque* 'five']

quintain /'kwɪntɪn/ *n. hist.* **1** a post set up as a mark in tilting, and often provided with a sandbag to swing round and strike an unsuccessful tilter. **2** the medieval military exercise of tilting at such a mark. [Middle English from Old French *quintaine*, perhaps ultimately via Latin *quintana*, a street in a Roman camp separating the fifth and sixth maniples, from *quintus* (*manipulus*) 'fifth (maniple)']

quintal /'kwɪnt(ə)l/ *n.* **1** a weight of about 100 lb. **2** a hundredweight (112 lb). **3** a weight of 100 kg. [Middle English via Old French *quintal*, medieval Latin *quintale* from Arabic *ḳinṭār*]

quintan /'kwɪnt(ə)n/ *adj.* (of a fever etc.) recurring every fifth day. [Latin *quintana* from *quintus* 'fifth']

quinte /kãt/ *n.* the fifth of eight parrying positions in fencing. [French: see QUINT]

quintessence /kwɪn'tɛs(ə)ns/ *n.* **1** (usu. foll. by *of*) the purest and most perfect, or most typical, form, manifestation, or embodiment of some quality or class. **2** the most essential part of a substance; a refined extract. **3** (in ancient philosophy) a fifth substance (beside the four elements) forming heavenly bodies and pervading all things. □ **quintessential** /kwɪntɪ'sɛnʃ(ə)l/ *adj.* **quintessentially** /kwɪntɪ'sɛnʃ(ə)li/ *adv.* [Middle English (in sense 3) via French from medieval Latin *quinta essentia* 'fifth ESSENCE']

quintet /kwɪn'tɛt/ *n.* (also **quintette**) **1** *Mus.* **a** a composition for five voices or instruments. **b** the performers of such a piece. **2** any group of five. [French *quintette* via Italian *quintetto*, from *quinto* 'fifth', from Latin *quintus*]

quintillion /kwɪn'tɪljən/ *n.* (*pl.* same or **quintillions**) a thousand raised to the sixth (or formerly, esp. *Brit.*, the tenth) power (10^{18} and 10^{30} respectively). □ **quintillionth** *adj. & n.* [Latin *quintus* 'fifth' + MILLION]

quint major *n. Cards* a quint headed by an ace.

quintuple /'kwɪntjʊp(ə)l/ *adj., n., & v.* ● *adj.* **1** fivefold; consisting of five parts. **2** involving five parties. **3** (of time in music) having five beats in a bar. ● *n.* a fivefold number or amount. ● *v.tr. & intr.* multiply by five; increase fivefold. □ **quintuply** *adv.* [French *quintuple* from Latin *quintus* 'fifth', on the patten of QUADRUPLE]

quintuplet /'kwɪntjʊplɪt, kwɪn'tju:plɪt/ *n.* **1** each of five children born at one birth. **2** a set of five things working together. **3** *Mus.* a group of five notes to be performed in the time of three or four. [QUINTUPLE, on the pattern of QUADRUPLET, TRIPLET]

quintuplicate *adj. & v.* ● *adj.* /kwɪn'tju:plɪkət/ **1** fivefold. **2** of which five copies are made. ● *v.tr. & intr.* /kwɪn'tju:plɪkeɪt/ multiply by five. □ **in quintuplicate 1** in five identical copies. **2** in groups of five. [French *quintuple* from Latin *quintus* 'fifth', on the pattern of QUADRUPLICATE]

quip /kwɪp/ *n. & v.* ● *n.* **1** a clever saying; an epigram; a sarcastic remark etc. **2** a quibble; an equivocation. ● *v.intr.* (**quipped**, **quipping**) make quips. □ **quipster** *n.* [perhaps from Latin *quippe* 'forsooth']

quipu /'ki:pu:, 'kwɪ-/ *n.* the ancient Peruvian method of recording information, events, etc. by knotting threads of various colours in different ways. [Quechua, = knot]

quire /kwʌɪə/ *n.* **1** four sheets of paper etc. folded to form eight leaves, as often in medieval manuscripts. **2** any collection of leaves one within another in a manuscript or book. **3** 25 (formerly 24) sheets of paper; one-twentieth of a ream. □ **in quires** unbound; in sheets. [Middle English from Old French *qua(i)er*, ultimately from Latin *quaterni* 'set of four' (as QUATERNARY)]

quirk /kwə:k/ *n.* **1** a peculiarity of behaviour. **2** a trick of fate; a freak. **3** a flourish in writing. **4** (often *attrib.*) *Archit.* a hollow in a moulding. □ **quirkish** *adj.* **quirky** *adj.* (**quirkier**, **quirkiest**). **quirkily** *adv.* **quirkiness** *n.* [16th c.: origin unknown]

quirt /kwə:t/ *n. & v.* ● *n.* a short-handled riding whip with a braided leather lash. ● *v.tr.* strike with this. [Spanish *cuerda* CORD]

quisling /'kwɪzlɪŋ/ *n.* **1** a person cooperating with an occupying enemy; a collaborator or fifth columnist. **2** a traitor. □ **quislingite** *adj. & n.* [from the name of V. *Quisling*, renegade Norwegian Army officer d. 1945]

quit /kwɪt/ *v. & adj.* ● *v.tr.* (**quitting**; *past* and *past part.* **quitted** or **quit**) **1** (also *absol.*) give up; let go; abandon (a task etc.). **2** *N. Amer.* cease; stop (*quit grumbling*). **3** **a** leave or depart from (a place, person, etc.). **b** (*absol.*) (of a tenant) leave occupied premises (esp. *notice to quit*). **4** (*refl.*) acquit; behave (*quit oneself well*).

●*predic.adj.* (foll. by *of*) rid (*glad to be quit of the problem*). □ **quit hold of** loose. [Middle English via Old French *quitte*, *quitter* and medieval Latin *quittus* from Latin *quietus* QUIET]

quitch /kwɪtʃ/ *n.* (in full **quitch-grass**) = COUCH². [Old English *cwice*, perhaps related to QUICK]

quite /kwʌɪt/ *adv.* **1** completely; entirely; wholly; to the utmost extent; in the fullest sense (*I quite agree*). **2** somewhat; rather; to some extent (*she's quite nice*). **3** (often foll. by *so*) said to indicate agreement. □ **quite a** a remarkable or outstanding (person or thing) (*it was quite an event*). **quite another** (or **other**) very different (*that's quite another matter*). **quite a few** *colloq.* a fairly large number of. **quite some** a large amount of (*quite some time*). **quite something** a remarkable thing. [Middle English from obsolete adjective *quite* = QUIT]

quits /kwɪts/ *predic.adj.* on even terms by retaliation or repayment (*then we'll be quits*). □ **call it** (or **cry**) **quits** acknowledge that things are now even; agree not to proceed further in a quarrel etc. [perhaps colloq. abbreviation of medieval Latin *quittus*: see QUIT]

quittance /ˈkwɪt(ə)ns/ *n. archaic* or *poet.* **1** (foll. by *from*) a release. **2** an acknowledgement of payment; a receipt. [Middle English from Old French *quitance*, from *quiter* QUIT]

quitter /ˈkwɪtə/ *n. colloq.* **1** a person who gives up easily. **2** a shirker.

quiver¹ /ˈkwɪvə/ *v.* & *n.* ●*v.* **1** *intr.* tremble or vibrate with a slight rapid motion, esp.: **a** (usu. foll. by *with*) as the result of emotion (*quiver with anger*). **b** (usu. foll. by *in*) as the result of air currents etc. (*quiver in the breeze*). **2** *tr.* (of a bird, esp. a skylark) make (its wings) quiver. ●*n.* a quivering motion or sound. □ **quiveringly** *adv.* **quivery** *adj.* [Middle English from obsolete *quiver* 'nimble': cf. QUAVER]

quiver² /ˈkwɪvə/ *n.* an archer's portable case for holding arrows. □ **have an arrow** (or **shaft**) **left in one's quiver** not be resourceless. [Middle English via Old French *quivre* from West Germanic: related to Old English *cocor*]

quiverful /ˈkwɪvəfʊl, -f(ə)l/ *n.* (*pl.* **-fuls**) **1** as much as a quiver can hold. **2** many children of one parent (Ps. 127:5). [QUIVER²]

qui vive /kiː ˈviːv/ *n.* □ **on the qui vive** on the alert; watching for something to happen. [French, literally '(long) live who?', i.e. 'on whose side are you?', as a sentry's challenge]

quixotic /kwɪkˈsɒtɪk/ *adj.* extravagantly and romantically chivalrous; naively idealistic; impractical. □ **quixotically** *adv.* **quixotism** /ˈkwɪksətɪz(ə)m/ *n.* **quixotry** /ˈkwɪksətri/ *n.* [from the name of Don *Quixote*, hero of Cervantes' romance, from Spanish *quixote* 'thigh armour']

quiz¹ /kwɪz/ *n.* & *v.* ●*n.* (*pl.* **quizzes**) **1** a test of knowledge, esp. between individuals or teams as a form of entertainment. **2** an interrogation, examination, or questionnaire. ●*v.tr.* (**quizzed**, **quizzing**) examine by questioning. [19th-c., originally *US*: origin unknown]

quiz² /kwɪz/ *v.* & *n. Brit. archaic* ●*v.tr.* (**quizzed**, **quizzing**) **1** look curiously at; observe the ways or oddities of; survey through an eyeglass. **2** make sport of; regard with a mocking air. ●*n.* (*pl.* **quizzes**) **1** a hoax; a thing done to burlesque or expose another's oddities. **2 a** an odd or eccentric person; a person of ridiculous appearance. **b** a person given to quizzing. □ **quizzer** *n.* [18th c.: origin unknown]

quizmaster /ˈkwɪzmɑːstə/ *n.* a person who presides over a quiz.

quiz show *n.* a television or radio light-entertainment programme in which people compete in a quiz, often for prizes.

quizzical /ˈkwɪzɪk(ə)l/ *adj.* **1** expressing or done with mild or amused perplexity. **2** strange; comical. □ **quizzicality** /-ˈkalɪti/ *n.* **quizzically** *adv.* **quizzicalness** *n.*

quod /kwɒd/ *n. Brit. slang* prison. [17th c.: origin unknown]

quod erat demonstrandum /kwɒd ˌɛrat dɛmənˈstrandʊm/ (esp. at the conclusion of a proof etc.) which was the thing to be proved (abbr.: **QED**). [Latin]

quodlibet /ˈkwɒdlɪbɛt/ *n.* **1** *hist.* **a** a topic for philosophical or theological discussion. **b** an exercise on this. **2** a light-hearted medley of well-known tunes. □ **quodlibetarian** /-bɪˈtɛːrɪən/ *n.* [Middle English from Latin, from *quod* 'what' + *libet* 'it pleases one']

quod vide /kwɒd ˈviːdeɪ/ which see (in cross-references etc.) (abbr.: **q.v.**). [Latin]

quoin /kɔɪn, kwɔɪn/ *n.* & *v.* ●*n.* **1** an external angle of a building. **2** a stone or brick forming an angle; a cornerstone. **3** *Printing* a wedge used for locking type in a forme. **4** a wedge for raising the level of a gun, keeping the barrel from rolling, etc. ●*v.tr.* secure or raise with quoins. □ **quoining** *n.* [variant of COIN]

quoit /kɔɪt, kwɔɪt/ *n.* & *v.* ●*n.* **1** a heavy flattish sharp-edged iron ring thrown to encircle an iron peg or to land as near as possible to the peg. **2** (in *pl.*) a game consisting of aiming and throwing these. **3** a ring of rope, rubber, etc. for use in a similar game. **4 a** the flat stone of a dolmen. **b** the dolmen itself. ●*v.tr.* fling like a quoit. [Middle English: origin unknown]

quokka /ˈkwɒkə/ *n.* a small Australian short-tailed wallaby, *Setonix brachyurus*. [Nyungar]

quondam /ˈkwɒndəm, -dam/ *attrib.adj.* that once was; sometime; former. [Latin (*adv.*), = formerly]

Quonset /ˈkwɒnsɪt/ *n. US propr.* a prefabricated metal building with a semicylindrical corrugated roof. [named after *Quonset* Point, Rhode Island, where it was first made]

quorate /ˈkwɔːrət, -reɪt/ *adj. Brit.* (of a meeting) attended by a quorum. [QUORUM]

Quorn /kwɔːn/ *n. propr.* a type of textured vegetable protein made from an edible fungus and used as a meat substitute. [the former name of a village (now *Quorndon*) in Leicestershire, incorporated in the name of the original manufacturer]

quorum /ˈkwɔːrəm/ *n.* the fixed minimum number of members that must be present to make the proceedings of an assembly or society valid. [Latin, = of whom (we wish that you be two, three, etc.), in the wording of commissions]

quota /ˈkwəʊtə/ *n.* (*pl.* **quotas**) **1** the share that an individual person or company is bound to contribute to or entitled to receive from a total. **2** a quantity of goods etc. which under official controls must be manufactured, exported, imported, etc. **3** the number of yearly immigrants allowed to enter a country, students allowed to enrol for a course, etc. [medieval Latin *quota* (*pars*) 'how great (a part)', fem. of *quotus*, from *quot* 'how many']

quotable /ˈkwəʊtəb(ə)l/ *adj.* worth, or suitable for, quoting. □ **quotability** /-ˈbɪlɪti/ *n.*

quotation /kwə(ʊ)ˈteɪʃ(ə)n/ *n.* **1** the act or an instance of quoting or being quoted. **2** a passage or remark quoted. **3** a contractor's estimate. **4** *Stock Exch.* an amount stated as the current price of stocks or commodities. **5** *Mus.* a short passage or tune taken from one piece of music to another. [medieval Latin *quotatio* (as QUOTE)]

quotation mark *n.* each of a set of punctuation marks, single (' ') or double (" "), used to mark the beginning and end of a quoted passage, a book title, etc., or words regarded as slang or jargon.

quote /kwəʊt/ *v.* & *n.* ●*v.tr.* **1** cite or appeal to (an author, book, etc.) in confirmation of some view. **2** repeat a statement by (another person) or copy out a passage from (*don't quote me*). **3** (often *absol.*) **a** repeat or copy out (a passage) usu. with an indication that it is borrowed. **b** (foll. by *from*) cite (an author, book, etc.). **4** (foll. by *as*) cite (an author etc.) as proof, evidence, etc. **5 a** enclose (words) in quotation marks. **b** (as *int.*) (in dictation, reading aloud, etc.) indicate the presence of opening quotation marks (*he said, quote, 'I shall stay'*). **6 a** state (the price) of a job to a person (*they quoted £600 for the work*). **b** (often foll. by *at*) state the price of (a commodity, stock, etc.); name (a racehorse) at specified odds (*the securities had not yet been quoted*; *the horse was quoted at 200 to 1*). **7** *Stock Exch.* regularly list the price of. ● *n. colloq.* **1** a passage quoted. **2** a price quoted. **3** (usu. in *pl.*) quotation marks. [earlier = mark with numbers: Middle English from medieval Latin *quotare*, from *quot* 'how many', or as QUOTA]

quoth /kwəʊθ/ *v.tr.* (only in 1st and 3rd person) *archaic* said. [Old English *cwæth*, past of *cwethan* 'say', from Germanic]

quotidian /kwɒ'tɪdɪən, kwəʊ-/ *adj. & n.* ● *adj.* **1** daily; of every day. **2** commonplace, trivial. ● *n.* (in full **quotidian fever**) a fever recurring every day. [Middle English from Old French *cotidien* & Latin *cotidianus*, from *cotidie* 'daily']

quotient /'kwəʊʃ(ə)nt/ *n.* a result obtained by dividing one quantity by another. [Middle English from Latin *quotiens* 'how many times', from *quot* 'how many', by confusion with -ENT]

Quran (also **Qur'an**) var. of KORAN.

q.v. *abbr. quod vide.*

qwerty /'kwɜːti/ *attrib.adj.* (also **QWERTY**) denoting the standard keyboard on English-language typewriters, word processors, etc., with *q, w, e, r, t,* and *y* as the first keys on the top row of letters.

qy. *abbr.* query.

Rr

R[1] /ɑː/ *n.* (also **r**) (*pl.* **Rs** or **R's**) the eighteenth letter of the alphabet. □ **the r months** the months with r in their names (September to April) as the season for oysters.

R[2] *abbr.* (also **R.**) **1** *Regina* (*Elizabeth R*). **2** *Rex.* **3** River. **4** (also ®) registered as a trade mark. **5** *Chess* rook. **6** right. **7** rand. **8** Réaumur. **9** radius. **10** reverse (gear).

R[3] *symb.* **1** roentgen. **2** electrical resistance. **3** (in chemical formulae) an organic radical or group.

r *abbr.* (also **r.**) **1** right. **2** recto. **3** run(s). **4** radius.

RA *abbr.* **1 a** (in the UK) Royal Academy. **b** (in the UK) Royal Academician. **2** (in the UK) Royal Artillery. **3** right ascension.

Ra *symb. Chem.* the element radium.

RAAF *abbr.* Royal Australian Air Force.

rabbet /ˈrabɪt/ *n. & v.* ● *n.* a step-shaped channel etc. cut along the edge or face or projecting angle of a length of wood etc., usu. to receive the edge or tongue of another piece. Also called *rebate.* ● *v.tr.* (**rabbeted, rabbeting**) **1** join or fix with a rabbet. **2** make a rabbet in. [Middle English from Old French *rab(b)at* 'abatement, recess', from *rabattre* REBATE[1]]

rabbet plane *n.* a plane for cutting a groove along an edge.

rabbi /ˈrabʌɪ/ *n.* (*pl.* **rabbis**) **1** a Jewish scholar or teacher, esp. of the law. **2** a person appointed as a Jewish religious leader. □ **rabbinate** /ˈrabɪnət/ *n.* [Old English from ecclesiastical Latin via Greek *rhabbi* from Hebrew *rabbî* 'my master', from *raḇ* 'master' + pronominal suffix]

rabbinical /rəˈbɪnɪk(ə)l/ *adj.* (also **rabbinic**) of or relating to rabbis, or to Jewish law or teaching. □ **rabbinically** *adv.*

rabbit /ˈrabɪt/ *n. & v.* ● *n.* **1 a** any of various burrowing gregarious plant-eating mammals of the family Leporidae, esp. *Oryctolagus cuniculus*, with long ears and a short tail, varying in colour from brown in the wild to black and white, and kept as a pet or for meat. **b** *US* a hare. **c** the fur of the rabbit. **2** *Brit. colloq.* a poor performer in any sport or game. ● *v.intr.* (**rabbited, rabbiting**) **1** hunt rabbits. **2** (often foll. by *on, away*) *Brit. colloq.* talk excessively or pointlessly; chatter (*rabbiting on about his holiday*). □ **rabbity** *adj.* [Middle English, perhaps from Old French (cf. French dialect *rabotte*), perhaps of Low Dutch origin]

rabbit punch *n.* a short chop with the edge of the hand to the nape of the neck.

rabbit warren *n.* an area in which rabbits have their burrows, or are kept for meat etc.

rabble[1] /ˈrab(ə)l/ *n.* **1** a disorderly crowd; a mob. **2** a contemptible or inferior set of people. **3** (prec. by *the*) the lower classes or disorderly section of the populace. [Middle English: origin uncertain]

rabble[2] /ˈrab(ə)l/ *n.* an iron bar with a bent end for stirring molten metal etc. [French *râble* from medieval Latin *rotabulum*, Latin *rutabulum* 'fire-shovel', from *ruere rut-* 'rake up']

rabble-rouser *n.* a person who stirs up the rabble or a crowd of people in agitation for social or political change. □ **rabble-rousing** *adj. & n.*

Rabelaisian /rabəˈleɪzɪən/ *adj. & n.* ● *adj.* **1** of or like Rabelais or his writings. **2** marked by exuberant imagination and language, coarse humour, and satire. ● *n.* an admirer or student of Rabelais. [F. *Rabelais*, French satirist d. 1553]

rabid /ˈrabɪd, ˈreɪ-/ *adj.* **1** furious, violent (*rabid hate*). **2** unreasoning; headstrong; fanatical (*a rabid anarchist*). **3** (esp. of a dog) affected with rabies; mad. **4** of or connected with rabies. □ **rabidity** /rəˈbɪdɪti/ *n.* **rabidly** *adv.* **rabidness** *n.* [Latin *rabidus* from *rabere* 'rave']

rabies /ˈreɪbiːz, -ɪz/ *n.* a contagious and fatal viral disease of dogs and other mammals, transmissible through the saliva to humans etc. and causing madness and convulsions; hydrophobia. [Latin from *rabere* 'rave']

RAC *abbr.* **1** (in the UK) Royal Automobile Club. **2** (in the UK) Royal Armoured Corps.

raccoon /rəˈkuːn/ *n.* (also **racoon**) **1** any greyish-brown furry N. American nocturnal flesh-eating mammal of the genus *Procyon*, with a bushy tail and sharp snout. **2** the fur of the raccoon. [Algonquian dialect]

race[1] /reɪs/ *n. & v.* ● *n.* **1** a contest of speed between runners, horses, vehicles, ships, etc. **2** (in *pl.*) a series of these for horses, dogs, etc. at a fixed time on a regular course. **3** a contest between persons to be first to achieve something. **4 a** a strong or rapid current flowing through a narrow channel in the sea or a river (*a tide race*). **b** the channel of a stream etc. (*a mill-race*). **5** each of two grooved rings in a ball-bearing or roller bearing. **6** *Austral.* a fenced passageway for drafting sheep etc. **7** *Brit.* a passageway along which football players etc. run to enter the field. **8** (in weaving) the channel along which the shuttle moves. **9** *archaic* **a** the course of the sun or moon. **b** the course of life (*has run his race*). ● *v.* **1** *intr.* take part in a race. **2** *tr.* have a race with. **3** *tr.* try to surpass in speed. **4** *intr.* (foll. by *with*) compete in speed with. **5** *tr.* cause (a horse, car, etc.) to race. **6 a** *intr.* move swiftly; go at full or (of an engine, propeller, the pulse, etc.) excessive speed. **b** *tr.* cause (a person or thing) to do this (*raced the bill through the House*). **7** *intr.* (usu. as **racing** *adj.*) follow or take part in horse racing (*a racing man*). □ **not in the race** *Austral. slang* having no chance. [Middle English, = running, from Old Norse *rás*]

race[2] /reɪs/ *n.* **1** each of the major divisions of humankind, having distinct physical characteristics. **2** a tribe, nation, etc., regarded as of a distinct ethnic stock. **3** the fact or concept of division into races (*discrimination based on race*). **4** a genus, species, breed, or variety of animals, plants, or micro-organisms. **5** a group of persons, animals, or plants connected by common descent. **6** any great division of living creatures (*the feathered race*; *the four-footed race*). **7** descent; kindred (*of noble race*; *separate in language and race*). **8** a class of persons etc. with some common feature (*the race of poets*). [French from Italian *razza*, of unknown origin]

race[3] /reɪs/ *n.* a ginger root. [Old French *rais*, *raiz* from Latin *radix radicis* 'root']

racecard /ˈreɪskɑːd/ *n.* a programme of races.

racecourse /ˈreɪskɔːs/ *n.* a ground or track for horse racing.

racegoer /ˈreɪsgəʊə/ *n.* a person who frequents horse races.

racehorse /ˈreɪshɔːs/ *n.* a horse bred or kept for racing.

racemate /ˈrasɪmeɪt/ *n. Chem.* a racemic mixture.

raceme /ˈrasiːm, rəˈsiːm/ *n. Bot.* a flower cluster with the separate flowers attached by short equal stalks at equal distances along a central stem (cf. CYME). [Latin *racemus* 'grape-bunch']

race meeting *n. Brit.* a sporting event consisting of a sequence of horse races at one place.

race memory *n.* a supposedly inherited subconscious memory of events in human history or prehistory.

racemic /rəˈsiːmɪk, rəˈsɛmɪk/ *adj. Chem.* composed of equal numbers of dextrorotatory and laevorotatory molecules of a compound. □ **racemize** /ˈrasɪmʌɪz/ *v.tr.* & *intr.* (also **-ise**). [RACEME + -IC, originally of tartaric acid in grape juice]

racemose /ˈrasɪməʊs/ *adj.* **1** *Bot.* in the form of a raceme. **2** *Anat.* (of a gland etc.) clustered. [Latin *racemosus* (as RACEME)]

racer /ˈreɪsə/ *n.* **1** a horse, yacht, bicycle, etc., of a kind used for racing. **2** a circular horizontal rail along which the carriage or traversing-platform of a heavy gun moves. **3** a person or thing that races.

race relations *n.pl.* relations between members of different races usu. in the same country.

race riot *n.* an outbreak of violence due to racial antagonism.

racetrack /ˈreɪstrak/ *n.* **1** = RACECOURSE. **2** a track for motor racing.

raceway /ˈreɪsweɪ/ *n.* **1** a track or channel along which something runs, esp.: **a** a channel for water. **b** a groove in which ball-bearings run. **c** a pipe or tubing enclosing electrical wires. **2** esp. *US* **a** a track for trotting, pacing, or harness racing. **b** a racecourse. **c** a track for motor racing.

rachis /ˈreɪkɪs/ *n.* (*pl.* **rachides** /-kɪdiːz/) **1** *Bot.* **a** a stem of grass etc. bearing flower stalks at short intervals. **b** the axis of a compound leaf or frond. **2** *Anat.* the vertebral column or the cord from which it develops. **3** *Zool.* the shaft of a feather, esp. the part bearing the barbs. □ **rachidial** /rəˈkɪdɪəl/ *adj.* [modern Latin from Greek *rhakhis* 'spine': the English pl. *-ides* is erroneous]

rachitis /rəˈkʌɪtɪs/ *n.* rickets. □ **rachitic** /-ˈkɪtɪk/ *adj.* [modern Latin from Greek *rhakhitis* (as RACHIS)]

Rachmanism /ˈrakmənɪz(ə)m/ *n. Brit.* the exploitation and intimidation of tenants by unscrupulous landlords. [named after P. *Rachman*, London landlord of the early 1960s]

racial /ˈreɪʃ(ə)l/ *adj.* **1** of or concerning race (*racial diversities*; *racial minority*). **2** on the grounds of or connected with difference in race (*racial discrimination*; *racial tension*). □ **racially** *adv.*

racialism /ˈreɪʃəlɪz(ə)m/ *n.* = RACISM 1. □ **racialist** *n.* & *adj.*

racing car *n.* a motor car built for racing on a prepared track.

racing driver *n.* a driver of racing cars.

racism /ˈreɪsɪz(ə)m/ *n.* **1 a** a belief in the superiority of a particular race; prejudice based on this. **b** antagonism towards, or discrimination against, other races, esp. as a result of this. **2** the theory that human abilities etc. are determined by race. □ **racist** *n.* & *adj.*

rack[1] /rak/ *n.* & *v.* ● *n.* **1 a** a framework usu. with rails, bars, hooks, etc., for holding or storing things. **b** a frame for holding animal fodder. **2** a cogged or toothed bar or rail engaging with a wheel or pinion etc., or using pegs to adjust the position of something. **3** *hist.* an instrument of torture stretching the victim's joints by the turning of rollers to which the wrists and ankles were tied. ● *v.tr.* **1** (of disease or pain) inflict suffering on. **2** *hist.* torture (a person) on the rack. **3** place in or on a rack. **4** shake violently. **5** injure by straining. **6** oppress (tenants) by exacting excessive rent. **7** exhaust (the land) by excessive use. □ **on the rack** suffering intense distress or strain. **rack one's brains** make a great mental effort (*racked my brains for something to say*). **rack up** *N. Amer.* accumulate or achieve (a score etc.). [Middle English *rakke* from Middle Dutch, Middle Low German *rak*, *rek*, probably from *recken* 'stretch']

rack[2] /rak/ *n.* destruction (esp. *rack and ruin*). [variant of WRACK, WRECK]

rack[3] /rak/ *n.* a joint of lamb etc. including the front ribs. [perhaps from RACK[1]]

rack[4] /rak/ *v.tr.* (often foll. by *off*) draw off (wine, beer, etc.) from the lees. [Middle English from Provençal *arracar*, from *raca* 'stems and husks of grapes, dregs']

rack[5] /rak/ *n.* & *v.* ● *n.* driving clouds. ● *v.intr.* (of clouds) be driven before the wind. [Middle English, probably of Scandinavian origin: cf. Norwegian and Swedish dialect *rak* 'wreckage' etc. from *reka* 'drive']

rack[6] /rak/ *n.* & *v.* ● *n.* a horse's gait between a trot and a canter. ● *v.intr.* progress in this way. [16th c.: origin unknown]

rack-and-pinion *attrib.adj.* (esp. of a steering system) using a rack and pinion (see RACK[1] *n.* 2, PINION[2]).

racket[1] /ˈrakɪt/ *n.* (also **racquet**) **1** a bat with a round or oval frame strung with catgut, nylon, etc., used in tennis, squash, etc. **2** (in *pl.*) a ball game for two or four persons played with rackets in a plain four-walled court. **3** a snowshoe resembling a racket. [French *racquette* via Italian *racchetta* from Arabic *rāḥa* 'palm of the hand']

racket[2] /ˈrakɪt/ *n.* & *v.* ● *n.* **1 a** a disturbance; an uproar; a din. **b** social excitement; gaiety. **2** *slang* **a** a scheme for obtaining money or attaining other ends by fraudulent and often violent means. **b** a dodge; a sly game. **3** *colloq.* an activity; a way of life; a line of business (*starting up a new racket*). ● *v.intr.* (**racketed**, **racketing**) (often foll. by *along*, *around*) make a racket, esp. by moving noisily. □ **rackety** *adj.* [16th c.: perhaps imitative]

racketeer /rakɪˈtɪə/ *n.* a person who operates a dishonest business. □ **racketeering** *n.*

racket-tail *n.* a S. American hummingbird, *Loddigesia mirabilis*, with a racket-shaped tail.

rack railway *n.* a railway with a cogged rail between the bearing rails.

rack-rent *n.* & *v.* ● *n.* **1** a high rent, annually equalling the full value of the property to which it relates. **2** an extortionate rent. ● *v.tr.* exact this from (a tenant) or for (land). [RACK[1] *v.* + RENT[1] *n.*]

rack-renter *n.* a tenant paying or a landlord exacting an extortionate rent.

rack-wheel *n.* a cogwheel.

raclette /raˈklɛt/ *n.* a Swiss dish of melted cheese, usu. eaten with potatoes. [French, = small scraper, from the practice of holding the cheese over the heat and scraping it on to a plate as it melts]

racon /ˈreɪkɒn/ *n.* esp. *US* a radar beacon that can be identified and located by its response to a radar signal from a ship etc. [*radar* + *beacon*]

raconteur /rakɒnˈtəː/ *n.* (*fem.* **raconteuse** /-ˈtəːz/) a teller of anecdotes. [French from *raconter* 'relate, recount': see RECOUNT]

racoon var. of RACCOON.

racquet var. of RACKET[1].

racy /ˈreɪsi/ *adj.* (**racier**, **raciest**) **1** lively and vigorous in style. **2** risqué, suggestive. **3** having characteristic qualities in a high degree (*a racy flavour*). □ **racily** *adv.* **raciness** *n.* [RACE[2] + -Y[1]]

rad[1] /rad/ *n.* (*pl.* same) radian. [abbreviation]

rad[2] /rad/ *n. slang* a political radical. [abbreviation]

rad[3] /rad/ *n. Physics* a unit of absorbed dose of ionizing radiation, corresponding to the absorption of 0.01 joule per kilogram of absorbing material. [*r*adiation *a*bsorbed *d*ose]

rad[4] /rad/ *adj. slang* excellent, fantastic, cool. [probably abbreviation of RADICAL]

rad[5] /rad/ *n. colloq.* radiator. [abbreviation]

RADA /ˈrɑːdə/ *abbr.* (in the UK) Royal Academy of Dramatic Art.

radar /ˈreɪdɑː/ *n.* **1** a system for detecting the direction, range, or presence of aircraft, ships, and other (usu. moving) objects, by sending out pulses of high-frequency electromagnetic waves. **2** the apparatus used for this. [*ra*dio *d*etection *a*nd *r*anging]

radar trap *n.* the use of radar to detect vehicles exceeding a speed limit.

RADC *abbr.* (in the UK) Royal Army Dental Corps.

raddle /ˈrad(ə)l/ *n.* & *v.* ● *n.* red ochre (often used to mark sheep). ● *v.tr.* **1** colour with raddle or too much rouge. **2** (as **raddled** *adj.*) worn out; untidy, unkempt. [variant of RUDDLE]

radial /ˈreɪdɪəl/ *adj.* & *n.* ● *adj.* **1** of, concerning, or in rays. **2 a** arranged like rays or radii; having the position or direction of a radius. **b** having spokes or radiating lines. **c** acting or moving along lines diverging from a centre. **3** *Anat.* relating to the radius (*radial artery*). **4** (in full **radial-ply**) (of a vehicle tyre) having the core fabric layers arranged radially at right angles to the circumference and the tread strengthened. ● *n.* **1** *Anat.* the radial nerve or artery. **2** a radial-ply tyre (see sense 4 of *adj.*). □ **radially** *adv.* [medieval Latin *radialis* (as RADIUS)]

radial engine *n.* an engine having cylinders arranged along radii.

radial keratotomy see KERATOTOMY.

radial symmetry *n.* symmetry occurring about any number of lines or planes passing through the centre of an organism etc.

radial velocity *n.* esp. *Astron.* the speed of motion along a radial line, esp. between a star etc. and an observer.

radian /ˈreɪdɪən/ *n. Geom.* a unit of angle, equal to an angle at the centre of a circle the arc of which is equal in length to the radius. [RADIUS + -AN]

radiant /ˈreɪdɪənt/ *adj.* & *n.* ● *adj.* **1** emitting rays of light. **2** (of eyes or looks) beaming with joy or hope or love. **3** (of beauty) splendid or dazzling. **4** (of light) issuing in rays. **5** operating radially. **6** extending radially; radiating. ● *n.* **1** the point or object from which light or heat radiates, esp. in an electric or gas heater. **2** *Astron.* a radiant point. □ **radiance** *n.* **radiancy** *n.* **radiantly** *adv.* [Middle English from Latin *radiare* (as RADIUS)]

radiant heat *n.* heat transmitted by radiation, not by conduction or convection. □ **radiant heater** *n.*

radiant point *n.* **1** a point from which rays or radii proceed. **2** *Astron.* the apparent focal point of a meteor shower.

radiate *v.* & *adj.* ● *v.* /ˈreɪdɪeɪt/ **1** *intr.* **a** emit rays of light, heat, or other electromagnetic waves. **b** (of light or heat) be emitted in rays. **2** *tr.* emit (light, heat, or sound) from a centre. **3** *tr.* transmit or demonstrate (life, love, joy, etc.) (*radiates happiness*). **4** *intr.* & *tr.* diverge or cause to diverge or spread from a centre. **5** *tr.* (as **radiated** *adj.*) with parts arranged in rays. ● *adj.* /ˈreɪdɪət/ having divergent rays or parts radially arranged. □ **radiately** /-ətli/ *adv.* **radiative** /-ətɪv/ *adj.* [Latin *radiare radiat-* (as RADIUS)]

radiation /reɪdɪˈeɪʃ(ə)n/ *n.* **1** the act or an instance of radiating; the process of being radiated. **2** *Physics* **a** the emission of energy as electromagnetic waves or as moving particles. **b** the energy transmitted in this way, esp. invisibly. □ **radiational** *adj.* **radiationally** *adv.* [Latin *radiatio* (as RADIATE)]

radiation chemistry *n.* the study of the chemical effects of radiation on matter.

radiation sickness *n.* sickness caused by exposure to radiation, such as X-rays or gamma rays.

radiation therapy *n.* = RADIOTHERAPY.

radiator /ˈreɪdɪeɪtə/ *n.* **1** a person or thing that radiates. **2 a** a device for heating a room etc., consisting of a metal case through which hot water or steam circulates. **b** a usu. portable oil or electric heater resembling this. **3** an engine-cooling device in a motor vehicle or aircraft with a large surface for cooling circulating water.

radiator grille *n.* a grille at the front of a motor vehicle allowing air to circulate to the radiator.

radical /ˈradɪk(ə)l/ *adj.* & *n.* ● *adj.* **1** of the root or roots; fundamental (*a radical error*). **2** far-reaching; thorough; going to the root (*radical change*). **3 a** advocating thorough reform; holding extreme political views; revolutionary. **b** (of a measure etc.) advanced by or according to principles of this kind. **4** forming the basis; primary (*the radical idea*). **5** *Math.* of the root of a number or quantity. **6** (of surgery etc.) seeking to ensure the removal of all diseased tissue. **7** of the roots of words. **8** *Mus.* belonging to the root of a chord. **9** *Bot.* of, or springing direct from, the root. **10** *hist.* belonging to an extreme section of the Liberal party. **11** *US hist.* seeking extreme anti-South action at the time of the Civil War. **12** *slang* excellent, outstanding, cool. ● *n.* **1** a person holding radical views or belonging to a radical party. **2** *Chem.* **a** a free radical. **b** an element or atom or a group of these normally forming part of a compound and remaining unaltered during the compound's ordinary chemical changes. **3 a** the root of a word. **b** any of the basic set of approximately 214 Chinese characters from which more complex ones are mainly derived. **4** a fundamental principle; a basis. **5** *Math.* **a** a quantity forming or expressed as the root of another. **b** a radical sign. □ **radicalism** *n.* **radicalize** *v.tr.* & *intr.* (also **-ise**). **radicalization** /-ˈzeɪʃ(ə)n/ *n.* **radically** *adv.* **radicalness** *n.* [Middle English via Late Latin *radicalis* from Latin *radix radicis* 'root']

radical chic *n.* **1** the fashionable affectation of radical left-wing views. **2** the dress, lifestyle, etc., associated with this.

radical sign *n.* $\sqrt{}$, $\sqrt[3]{}$, etc., indicating the square, cube, etc., root of the number following.

radicchio /raˈdiːkɪəʊ/ *n.* (*pl.* **-os**) a variety of chicory with dark red leaves. [Italian, = chicory]

radices *pl.* of RADIX.

radicle /ˈradɪk(ə)l/ *n.* **1** the part of a plant embryo that develops into the primary root; a rootlet. **2** a rootlike subdivision of a nerve or vein. □ **radicular** /rəˈdɪkjʊlə/ *adj.* [Latin *radicula* (as RADIX)]

radii *pl.* of RADIUS.

radio /ˈreɪdɪəʊ/ *n.* & *v.* ● *n.* (*pl.* **-os**) **1** (often *attrib.*) **a** the transmission and reception of sound messages etc. by electromagnetic waves of radio frequency (cf. WIRELESS). **b** an apparatus for receiving, broadcasting, or transmitting radio signals. **c** a message sent or received by radio. **2 a** sound broadcasting in general (*prefers the radio*). **b** a broadcasting station or channel (*Radio One*). ● *v.* (**-oes, -oed**) **1** *tr.* **a** send (a message) by radio. **b** send a message to (a person) by radio. **2** *intr.* communicate or broadcast by radio. [short for *radio-telegraphy* etc.]

radio- /ˈreɪdɪəʊ/ *comb. form* **1** denoting radio or broadcasting. **2 a** connected with radioactivity. **b** denoting artificially prepared radioisotopes of elements (*radio-caesium*). **3** connected with rays or radiation. **4** *Anat.* belonging to the radius in conjunction with some other part (*radio-carpal*). [RADIUS + -O-, or from RADIO]

radioactive /ˌreɪdɪəʊˈaktɪv/ *adj.* of or exhibiting radioactivity. □ **radioactively** *adv.*

radioactivity /ˌreɪdɪəʊakˈtɪvɪti/ *n.* **1** the spontaneous disintegration of atomic nuclei, with the emission of usu. penetrating radiation or particles. **2** radioactive substances, or the radiation they emit.

radio-assay /ˌreɪdɪəʊəˈseɪ/ *n.* an analysis of a substance based on radiation from a sample.

radio astronomy *n.* the branch of astronomy concerned with the radio-frequency range of the electromagnetic spectrum.

radiobiology /ˌreɪdɪəʊbʌɪˈɒlədʒi/ *n.* the biology concerned with the effects of radiation on organisms and the application in biology of radiological techniques. □ **radiobiological** /-əˈlɒdʒɪk(ə)l/ *adj.* **radiobiologically** /-əˈlɒdʒɪk(ə)li/ *adv.* **radiobiologist** *n.*

radio cab *n.* (also **radio car**) a cab or car equipped with a two-way radio.

radiocarbon /ˌreɪdɪəʊˈkɑːb(ə)n/ *n.* a radioactive isotope of carbon.

radiocarbon dating *n.* = CARBON DATING.

radio cassette player *n.* a cassette player and radio in one unit.

radiochemistry /ˌreɪdɪəʊ'kemɪstri/ *n.* the chemistry of radioactive materials. □ **radiochemical** *adj.* **radiochemist** *n.*

radio-controlled /ˌreɪdɪəʊkən'trəʊld/ *adj.* (of a model aircraft etc.) controlled from a distance by radio.

radio-element /ˌreɪdɪəʊ'elɪm(ə)nt/ *n.* a natural or artificial radioactive element or isotope.

radio fix *n.* the position of an aircraft, ship, etc., found by radio.

radio frequency *n.* (*pl.* **-ies**) the frequency band of telecommunication, ranging from 10^4-10^{11} or 10^{12} Hz (hyphenated when *attrib.*: *radio-frequency spectrum*).

radio galaxy *n.* a galaxy emitting radiation in the radio-frequency range of the electromagnetic spectrum.

radiogenic /ˌreɪdɪə(ʊ)'dʒenɪk, -'dʒiːn-/ *adj.* **1** produced by radioactivity. **2** suitable for broadcasting by radio. □ **radiogenically** *adv.*

radio-goniometer /ˌreɪdɪəʊgəʊnɪ'ɒmɪtə/ *n.* an instrument for finding direction using radio waves.

radiogram /'reɪdɪə(ʊ)gram/ *n.* **1** *Brit.* a combined radio and record player. **2** a picture obtained by X-rays, gamma rays, etc. **3** a radio-telegram. [RADIO- + -GRAM, GRAMOPHONE]

radiograph /'reɪdɪə(ʊ)grɑːf/ *n.* & *v.* ● *n.* **1** an instrument recording the intensity of radiation. **2** = RADIOGRAM 2. ● *v.tr.* obtain a picture of by X-ray, gamma ray, etc. □ **radiographer** /-'ɒgrəfə/ *n.* **radiographic** /-dɪə'grafɪk/ *adj.* **radiographically** /-dɪə'grafɪk(ə)li/ *adv.* **radiography** /-'ɒgrəfi/ *n.*

radio ham see HAM *n.* 4.

radioimmunology /ˌreɪdɪəʊɪmjʊ'nɒlədʒi/ *n.* the application of radiological techniques in immunology.

radioisotope /ˌreɪdɪəʊ'ʌɪsətəʊp/ *n.* a radioactive isotope. □ **radioisotopic** /-'tɒpɪk/ *adj.* **radioisotopically** /-'tɒpɪk(ə)li/ *adv.*

radiolarian /ˌreɪdɪə(ʊ)'lɛːrɪən/ *n.* any marine protozoan of the superclass Actinopoda, having a siliceous skeleton and radiating pseudopodia. [modern Latin *Radiolaria* former order name, from Latin *radiolus*, diminutive of RADIUS]

radiology /reɪdɪ'ɒlədʒi/ *n.* the scientific study of X-rays and other high-energy radiation, esp. as used in medicine. □ **radiologic** /-ə'lɒdʒɪk/ *adj.* **radiological** /-ə'lɒdʒɪk(ə)l/ *adj.* **radiologist** *n.*

radiometer /reɪdɪ'ɒmɪtə/ *n.* an instrument for measuring the intensity or force of radiation. □ **radiometry** *n.*

radiometric /ˌreɪdɪə(ʊ)'metrɪk/ *adj.* of or relating to the measurement of radioactivity.

radiometric dating *n.* a method of dating geological specimens by determining the relative proportions of the isotopes of a radioactive element present in a sample.

radionics /reɪdɪ'ɒnɪks/ *n.* the study and interpretation of radiation believed to be emitted from substances, esp. as a form of diagnosis. [RADIO- + *-onics*, on the pattern of ELECTRONICS]

radionuclide /ˌreɪdɪəʊ'njuːklʌɪd/ *n.* a radioactive nuclide.

radiopaque /ˌreɪdɪəʊ'peɪk/ *adj.* (also **radio-opaque**) opaque to X-rays or similar radiation. □ **radiopacity** /-'pasɪti/ *n.* [RADIO- + OPAQUE]

radiophonic /ˌreɪdɪə(ʊ)'fɒnɪk/ *adj.* of or relating to synthetic sound, esp. music, produced electronically.

radioscopy /reɪdɪ'ɒskəpi/ *n.* the examination by X-rays etc. of objects opaque to light. □ **radioscopic** /-ə'skɒpɪk/ *adj.*

radiosonde /'reɪdɪəʊsɒnd/ *n.* a miniature radio transmitter broadcasting information about pressure, temperature, etc., from various levels of the atmosphere, carried esp. by balloon. [RADIO- + German *Sonde* 'probe']

radio-telegram /ˌreɪdɪəʊ'telɪgram/ *n.* a telegram sent by radio, usu. from a ship to land.

radio-telegraphy /ˌreɪdɪəʊtɪ'legrəfi/ *n.* telegraphy using radio transmission. □ **radio-telegraph** /-'telɪgrɑːf/ *n.*

radio-telephony /ˌreɪdɪəʊtɪ'lef(ə)ni/ *n.* telephony using radio transmission. □ **radio-telephone** /-'telɪfəʊn/ *n.* **radio-telephonic** /-telɪ'fɒnɪk/ *adj.*

radio telescope *n.* a directional aerial system for collecting and analysing radiation in the radio-frequency range from stars etc.

radiotelex /ˌreɪdɪəʊ'teleks/ *n.* a telex sent usu. from a ship to land.

radiotherapy /ˌreɪdɪə(ʊ)'θerəpi/ *n.* the treatment of cancer and other diseases by X-rays or other forms of radiation. □ **radiotherapeutic** /-'pjuːtɪk/ *adj.* **radiotherapist** *n.*

radish /'radɪʃ/ *n.* **1** a cruciferous plant, *Raphanus sativus*, with a fleshy pungent root. **2** this root, eaten esp. raw in salads etc. [Old English *rædic* from Latin *radix radicis* 'root']

radium /'reɪdɪəm/ *n. Chem.* a radioactive metallic element present in pitchblende and other uranium ores, used esp. in luminous materials and in radiotherapy (symbol **Ra**). [Latin *radius* 'ray']

radium emanation *n.* = RADON.

radium therapy *n.* the treatment of disease by the use of radium.

radius /'reɪdɪəs/ *n.* & *v.* ● *n.* (*pl.* **radii** /-dɪʌɪ/ or **radiuses**) **1** *Math.* **a** a straight line from the centre to the circumference of a circle or sphere. **b** a radial line from the focus to any point of a curve. **c** the length of the radius of a circle etc. **2** a usu. specified distance from a centre in all directions (*within a radius of 20 miles*; *has a large radius of action*). **3 a** the thicker and shorter of the two bones in the human forearm (cf. ULNA). **b** the corresponding bone in a vertebrate's foreleg or a bird's wing. **4** any of the five arm-like structures of a starfish. **5 a** any of a set of lines diverging from a point like the radii of a circle. **b** an object of this kind, e.g. a spoke. **6 a** the outer rim of a composite flower head, e.g. a daisy. **b** a radiating branch of an umbel. ● *v.tr.* (**radiused**, **radiusing**) give a rounded form to (an edge etc.). [Latin, = staff, spoke, ray]

radius vector *n. Math.* a variable line drawn from a fixed point to an orbit or other curve, or to any point as an indication of the latter's position.

radix /'radɪks, 'reɪ-/ *n.* (*pl.* **radices** /-dɪsiːz/) **1** *Math.* a number or symbol used as the basis of a numeration scale (e.g. ten in the decimal system). **2** (usu. foll. by *of*) a source or origin. [Latin, = root]

radome /'reɪdəʊm/ *n.* a dome or other structure, transparent to radio waves, protecting radar equipment, esp. on the outer surface of an aircraft. [*ra*dar + *dome*]

radon /'reɪdɒn/ *n. Chem.* a naturally occurring gaseous radioactive inert element arising from the disintegration of radium, and used in radiotherapy (symbol **Rn**). [RADIUM, on the pattern of *argon* etc.]

radula /'radjʊlə/ *n.* (*pl.* **radulae** /-liː/) a filelike structure in molluscs for scraping off food particles and drawing them into the mouth. □ **radular** *adj.* [Latin, = scraper, from *radere* 'scrape']

RAF /*colloq.* raf/ *abbr.* (in the UK) Royal Air Force.

Rafferty's rules /'rafətɪz/ *n. Austral.* & *NZ colloq.* no rules at all, esp. in boxing. [probably English dialect corruption of *refractory*]

raffia /'rafɪə/ *n.* **1** a palm tree, *Raphia ruffia*, native to Madagascar, having very long leaves. **2** the fibre from its leaves used for making hats, baskets, etc., and for tying plants etc. [Malagasy]

raffinate /'rafɪneɪt/ *n. Chem.* a refined liquid oil produced by solvent extraction of impurities. [French *raffiner* + -ATE[1]]

raffish /'rafɪʃ/ *adj.* **1** disreputable, esp. in an attractive manner; rakish. **2** tawdry. □ **raffishly** *adv.* **raffishness** *n.* [as RAFT[2] + -ISH[1]]

raffle[1] /ˈraf(ə)l/ *n. & v.* ● *n.* a fund-raising lottery with goods as prizes. ● *v.tr.* (often foll. by *off*) dispose of by means of a raffle. [Middle English, a kind of dice game, from Old French *raf(f)le*, of unknown origin]

raffle[2] /ˈraf(ə)l/ *n.* **1** rubbish; refuse. **2** lumber; debris. [Middle English, perhaps from Old French *ne rifle, ne rafle* 'nothing at all']

raft[1] /rɑːft/ *n. & v.* ● *n.* **1** a flat floating structure of timber or other materials for conveying persons or things. **2** a lifeboat or small (often inflatable) boat, esp. for use in emergencies. **3** a floating accumulation of trees, ice, etc. ● *v.* **1** *tr.* transport as or on a raft. **2** *tr.* cross (water) on a raft. **3** *tr.* form into a raft. **4** *intr.* (often foll. by *across*) work a raft (across water etc.). [Middle English from Old Norse *raptr* RAFTER[1] (the earliest use in English)]

raft[2] /rɑːft/ *n. colloq.* **1** a large collection. **2** (foll. by *of*) a crowd. [*raff* 'rubbish', perhaps of Scandinavian origin]

rafter[1] /ˈrɑːftə/ *n.* each of the sloping beams forming the framework of a roof. □ **raftered** *adj.* [Old English *ræfter*, related to RAFT[1]]

rafter[2] /ˈrɑːftə/ *n.* **1** a person who rafts timber. **2** a person who travels by raft.

raftsman /ˈrɑːf(t)smən/ *n.* (*pl.* **-men**) a worker on a raft.

rag[1] /rag/ *n.* **1 a** a torn, frayed, or worn piece of woven material. **b** one of the irregular scraps to which cloth etc. is reduced by wear and tear. **2** (in *pl.*) old or worn clothes. **3** (*collect.*) scraps of cloth used as material for paper, stuffing, etc. **4** *derog.* **a** a newspaper. **b** a flag, handkerchief, curtain, etc. **5** (usu. with *neg.*) the smallest scrap of cloth etc. (*not a rag to cover him*). **6** an odd scrap; an irregular piece. **7** a jagged projection, esp. on metal. □ **in rags 1** much torn. **2** in old torn clothes. [Middle English, probably a back-formation from RAGGED]

rag[2] /rag/ *n. & v.* ● *n. Brit.* **1** a fund-raising programme of stunts, parades, and entertainment organized by students. **2** *colloq.* a prank. **3 a** a rowdy celebration. **b** a noisy disorderly scene. ● *v.* (**ragged**, **ragging**) **1** *tr.* tease; torment; play rough jokes on. **2** *tr.* scold; reprove severely. **3** *intr. Brit.* engage in rough play; be noisy and riotous. [18th c.: origin unknown: cf. BALLYRAG]

rag[3] /rag/ *n.* **1** a large coarse roofing slate. **2** *Brit.* any of various kinds of hard coarse sedimentary stone that break into thick slabs. [Middle English: origin unknown, but associated with RAG[1]]

rag[4] /rag/ *n. Mus.* a ragtime composition or tune. [perhaps from RAGGED: see RAGTIME]

raga /ˈrɑːgə/ *n.* (also **rag** /rɑːg/) (in Indian music) **1** a pattern of notes used as a basis for improvisation. **2** a piece using a particular raga. [Sanskrit, = colour, musical tone]

ragamuffin /ˈragəmʌfɪn/ *n.* **1** a person in ragged dirty clothes, esp. a child. **2** (also **raggamuffin**) **a** an exponent or follower of ragga, typically dressing in ragged clothes. **b** = RAGGA. [probably based on RAG[1]: cf. 14th-c. *ragamoffyn*, the name of a demon]

rag-and-bone man *n. Brit.* an itinerant dealer in old clothes, furniture, etc.

ragbag /ˈragbag/ *n.* **1** a bag in which scraps of fabric etc. are kept for use. **2** (often foll. by *of*) a miscellaneous collection. **3** *slang* a sloppily-dressed woman.

rag bolt *n.* a bolt with barbs to keep it tight when it has been driven in.

rag book *n. Brit.* a children's book made of untearable cloth.

rag doll *n.* a stuffed doll made of cloth.

rage /reɪdʒ/ *n. & v.* ● *n.* **1** fierce or violent anger. **2** a fit of this (*flew into a rage*). **3** the violent action of a natural force (*the rage of the storm*). **4** (foll. by *for*) **a** a vehement desire or passion. **b** a widespread temporary enthusiasm or fashion. **5** *poet.* poetic, prophetic, or martial enthusiasm or ardour. **6** esp. *Austral. & NZ colloq.* a lively party. ● *v.intr.* **1** be full of anger. **2** (often foll. by *at, against*) speak furiously or madly; rave. **3 a** (of wind, battle, fever, etc.) be violent; be at its height; continue unchecked. **b** (as **raging** *adj.*) extreme, very painful (*raging thirst; a raging headache*). **4** *Austral. & NZ colloq.* seek enjoyment; have a good time; revel. □ **all the rage** very popular, fashionable. □ **rager** *n.* (esp. in sense 4 of *v.*). [Middle English from Old French *rager*, ultimately from Latin RABIES]

ragee /ˈrɑːgiː/ *n.* (also **raggee**) a coarse cereal, *Eleusine coracana*, forming a staple food in parts of India etc. [Hindi *rāgī*]

ragga /ˈragə/ *n.* a style of popular music combining elements of reggae and hip hop. [RAGAMUFFIN, from the style of clothing worn by its followers]

raggamuffin var. of RAGAMUFFIN 2.

ragged /ˈragɪd/ *adj.* **1** (of clothes etc.) torn; frayed. **2** rough; shaggy; hanging in tufts. **3** (of a person) in ragged clothes. **4** with a broken or jagged outline or surface. **5** *Printing* (esp. of a right margin) unjustified and so uneven. **6** faulty; imperfect. **7** lacking finish, smoothness, or uniformity (*ragged rhymes*). **8** exhausted (esp. *be run ragged*). □ **raggedly** *adv.* **raggedness** *n.* **raggedy** *adj.* [Middle English from Old Norse *roggvathr* 'tufted']

ragged robin *n.* a pink-flowered campion, *Lychnis flos-cuculi*, with tattered petals. Also called CUCKOO FLOWER.

raggee var. of RAGEE.

raggle-taggle /ˈrag(ə)ltag(ə)l/ *adj.* (also **wraggle-taggle**) ragged; rambling, straggling. [apparently fanciful variant of RAGTAG]

raglan /ˈraglən/ *n.* (often *attrib.*) an overcoat without shoulder seams, the sleeves running up to the neck. [named after Lord *Raglan*, British commander d. 1855]

raglan sleeve *n.* a sleeve which runs up to the neck of a garment.

ragout /raˈguː/ *n. & v.* ● *n.* a highly-seasoned dish of meat cut into small pieces and stewed with vegetables. ● *v.tr.* make a ragout of. [French *ragoût* from *ragoûter* 'revive the taste of']

rag paper *n.* paper made from rags.

ragpicker /ˈragpɪkə/ *n.* esp. *hist.* a collector and seller of rags.

ragstone /ˈragstəʊn/ *n.* = RAG[3] 2.

rags-to-riches *attrib.adj.* denoting a person who starts out poor and ends up rich, or a story describing such a development.

ragtag /ˈragtag/ *n.* (in full **ragtag and bobtail**) *derog.* the rabble or common people. [earlier *tag-rag, tag and rag*, from RAG[1] + TAG[1]]

ragtail /ˈragteɪl/ *adj.* esp. *US* disorganized, ill-assorted, scraggly. [RAG[1] + TAIL[1], perhaps influenced by *ragtag and bobtail*]

ragtime /ˈragtʌɪm/ *n. & adj.* ● *n.* music characterized by a syncopated melodic line and regularly accented accompaniment, evolved by American black musicians in the 1890s and played esp. on the piano. ● *adj. slang* disorderly, disreputable, inferior (*a ragtime army*). [probably from RAG[4]]

rag trade *n. colloq.* the business of designing, making, and selling clothes.

raguly /ˈragjʊli/ *adj. Heraldry* like a row of sawn-off branches. [perhaps from RAGGED, on the pattern of *nebuly*]

ragweed /ˈragwiːd/ *n.* **1** = RAGWORT. **2** *N. Amer.* any plant of the genus *Ambrosia*, with allergenic pollen.

ragworm /ˈragwəːm/ *n.* a carnivorous marine polychaete worm of the family Nereidae, esp. *Nereis diversicolor*, often used for bait. [RAG[1]]

ragwort /ˈragwəːt/ *n.* any yellow-flowered ragged-leaved plant of the genus *Senecio*, esp. *S. jacobaea*, a common weed of pastures that is poisonous to cattle.

rah /rɑː/ *int.* esp. *N. Amer. colloq.* an expression of encouragement, approval, etc. [shortening of HURRAH]

rah-rah /ˈrɑːrɑː/ *adj. US slang* marked by great enthusiasm or excitement. [reduplication of RAH]

rah-rah skirt *n.* a short flounced skirt like that worn by a cheerleader.

rai /rʌɪ/ *n.* a style of music fusing Arabic and Algerian folk elements with Western rock. [Arabic]

raid /reɪd/ *n.* & *v.* ● *n.* **1** a rapid surprise attack, esp.: **a** by troops, aircraft, etc. in warfare. **b** to commit a crime or do harm. **2** a surprise attack by police etc. to arrest suspected persons or seize illicit goods. **3** *Stock Exch.* an attempt to lower prices by the concerted selling of shares. **4** (foll. by *on*, *upon*) a forceful or insistent attempt to make a person or thing provide something. ● *v.tr.* **1** make a raid on (a person, place, or thing). **2** plunder, deplete . □ **raider** *n.* [Middle English, Scots form of Old English *rād* ROAD[1]]

rail[1] /reɪl/ *n.* & *v.* ● *n.* **1** a level or sloping bar or series of bars: **a** used to hang things on. **b** running along the top of a set of banisters. **c** forming part of a fence or barrier as protection against contact, falling over, etc. **2** a steel bar or continuous line of bars laid on the ground, usu. as one of a pair forming a railway track. **3** (often *attrib.*) a railway (*send it by rail*; *rail fares*). **4** (in *pl.*) the inside boundary fence of a racecourse. **5** a horizontal piece in the frame of a panelled door etc. (cf. STILE[2]). ● *v.tr.* **1** furnish with a rail or rails. **2** (usu. foll. by *in*, *off*) enclose with rails (*a small space was railed off*). **3** convey (goods) by rail. □ **off the rails** deranged; astray. **over the rails** over the side of a ship. □ **railage** *n.* **railless** *adj.* [Middle English via Old French *reille* 'iron rod' from Latin *regula* RULE]

rail[2] /reɪl/ *v.intr.* (often foll. by *at*, *against*) complain using abusive language; rant. □ **railer** *n.* **railing** *n.* [Middle English via French *railler* from Provençal *ralhar* 'jest', ultimately from Latin *rugire* 'bellow']

rail[3] /reɪl/ *n.* any bird of the family Rallidae, often inhabiting marshes, esp. the corncrake and water rail. [Middle English via Old Northern French *raille* from Romanic, perhaps imitative]

railcar /ˈreɪlkɑː/ *n.* a railway vehicle consisting of a single powered coach.

railcard /ˈreɪlkɑːd/ *n. Brit.* a pass entitling the holder to reduced rail fares.

rail fence *n.* esp. *US* a fence made of posts and rails.

rail gun *n.* an electromagnetic projectile launcher used esp. as an anti-missile weapon.

railhead /ˈreɪlhɛd/ *n.* **1** the furthest point reached by a railway under construction. **2** the point on a railway at which road transport of goods begins.

railing /ˈreɪlɪŋ/ *n.* **1** (usu. in *pl.*) a fence or barrier made of rails. **2** the material for these.

raillery /ˈreɪləri/ *n.* (*pl.* **-ies**) **1** good-humoured ridicule; rallying. **2** an instance of this. [French *raillerie* (as RAIL[2])]

railman /ˈreɪlmən/ *n.* (*pl.* **-men**) = RAILWAYMAN.

railroad /ˈreɪlrəʊd/ *n.* & *v.* ● *n.* esp. *US* = RAILWAY. ● *v.tr.* **1** (often foll. by *to*, *into*, *through*, etc.) rush or coerce (a person or thing) (*railroaded me into going too*). **2** send (a person) to prison by means of false evidence.

railway /ˈreɪlweɪ/ *n.* **1** a track or set of tracks made of steel rails along which goods trucks and passenger trains run. **2** such a system worked by a single company (*Great Western Railway*). **3** the organization and personnel required for its working. **4** a similar set of tracks for other vehicles etc.

railwayman /ˈreɪlweɪmən/ *n.* (*pl.* **-men**) esp. *Brit.* a railway employee.

railway yard *n.* the area where rolling stock is kept and made up into trains.

raiment /ˈreɪm(ə)nt/ *n. archaic* clothing. [Middle English from obsolete *arrayment* (as ARRAY)]

rain /reɪn/ *n.* & *v.* ● *n.* **1 a** the condensed moisture of the atmosphere falling visibly in separate drops. **b** the fall of such drops. **2** (in *pl.*) **a** (prec. by *the*) the rainy season in tropical countries. **b** rainfalls. **3 a** falling liquid or solid particles or objects. **b** the rainlike descent of these. **c** a large or overwhelming quantity (*a rain of congratulations*). ● *v.* **1** *intr.* (prec. by *it* as subject) rain falls (*it is raining*; *if it rains*). **2 a** *intr.* fall in showers or like rain (*tears rained down their cheeks*; *blows rain upon him*). **b** *tr.* (prec. by *it* as subject) send in large quantities (*it rained blood*; *it is raining invitations*). **3** *tr.* send down like rain; lavishly bestow (*rained benefits on us*; *rained blows upon him*). **4** *intr.* (of the sky, the clouds, etc.) send down rain. □ **rain cats and dogs** see CAT[1]. **rain off** (or *N. Amer.* **out**) (esp. in *passive*) cause (an event etc.) to be terminated or cancelled because of rain. **rain or shine** whether it rains or not. □ **rainless** *adj.* [Old English *regn*, *rēn*, *regnian*, from Germanic]

rainbird /ˈreɪnbəːd/ *n.* a bird said to foretell rain by its cry, esp. the green woodpecker.

rainbow /ˈreɪnbəʊ/ *n.* & *adj.* ● *n.* **1** an arch of colours (conventionally red, orange, yellow, green, blue, indigo, violet) formed in the sky (or across a cataract etc.) opposite the sun by reflection, twofold refraction, and dispersion of the sun's rays in falling rain or in spray or mist. **2** a similar effect formed by the moon's rays. **3** a wide variety of related things (*a rainbow of colours*; *a rainbow of political opinion*). ● *adj.* many-coloured. [Old English *regnboga* (as RAIN, BOW[1])]

rainbow coalition *n.* a political alliance of minority peoples and other disadvantaged groups.

rainbow lorikeet *n.* a small brightly coloured Polynesian parrot, *Trichoglossus haematodus*.

rainbow trout *n.* a large trout, *Oncorhynchus mykiss*, originally of the Pacific coast of N. America.

rain check *n.* esp. *N. Amer.* **1** a ticket given for later use when a sporting fixture or other outdoor event is interrupted or postponed by rain. **2** a promise that an offer will be maintained though deferred. □ **take a rain check on** reserve the right to take up (an offer) at a later date.

rain cloud *n.* a cloud bringing rain.

raincoat /ˈreɪnkəʊt/ *n.* a waterproof or water-resistant coat.

raindrop /ˈreɪndrɒp/ *n.* a single drop of rain. [Old English *regndropa*]

rainfall /ˈreɪnfɔːl/ *n.* **1** a fall of rain. **2** the quantity of rain falling within a given area in a given time.

rainforest /ˈreɪnfɒrɪst/ *n.* luxuriant forest in esp. tropical areas with consistently heavy rainfall.

rain gauge *n.* an instrument measuring rainfall.

rainmaker /ˈreɪnmeɪkə/ *n.* **1** a person who seeks to cause rain to fall, either by magic or by a technique such as seeding. **2** *N. Amer. slang* a person who is highly successful esp. in business. □ **rainmaking** *n.*

rainout /ˈreɪnaʊt/ *n. N. Amer.* the cancellation or premature ending of an event because of rain.

rainproof /ˈreɪnpruːf/ *adj.* (esp. of a building, garment, etc.) resistant to rainwater.

rain shadow *n.* a region shielded from rain by mountains etc.

rainstorm /ˈreɪnstɔːm/ *n.* a storm with heavy rain.

rainswept /ˈreɪnswɛpt/ *adj.* exposed to the rain.

rain-wash *n.* **1** loose material carried away by rain. **2** the movement of this.

rainwater /ˈreɪnwɔːtə/ *n.* water obtained from collected rain, as distinct from a well etc.

rainwear /ˈreɪnwɛː/ *n.* clothes for wearing in the rain.

rain-worm *n.* the common earthworm.

rainy /ˈreɪni/ *adj.* (**rainier**, **rainiest**) **1** (of weather, a climate, day, region, etc.) in or on which rain is falling or much rain usually falls. **2** (of cloud, wind, etc.) laden with or bringing rain. □ **rainily** *adv.* **raininess** *n.* [Old English *rēnig* (as RAIN)]

rainy day *n.* a time of special usu. financial need in the future.

raise /reɪz/ *v.* & *n.* ● *v.tr.* **1** put or take into a higher position. **2** (often foll. by *up*) cause to rise or stand up or be vertical; set upright. **3** increase the amount or value or strength of (*raised their prices*). **4** (often foll. by *up*) construct or build up. **5** levy or collect or bring together (*raise money*; *raise an army*). **6** cause to be heard or considered (*raise a shout*; *raise an objection*). **7**

set going or bring into being; arouse (*raise a protest*; *raise hopes*). **8** rouse from sleep or death, or from a lair. **9** bring up; educate. **10** breed or grow (*raise one's own vegetables*). **11** promote to a higher rank. **12** (foll. by *to*) *Math.* multiply a quantity to a specified power. **13** cause (bread) to rise, esp. with yeast. **14** *Cards* **a** bet more than (another player). **b** increase (a stake). **c** *Bridge* make a bid contracting for more tricks in the same suit as (one's partner); increase (a bid) in this way. **15** abandon or force an enemy to abandon (a siege or blockade). **16** remove (a barrier or embargo). **17** cause (a ghost etc.) to appear (opp. LAY[1] *v.* 6b). **18** *colloq.* find (a person etc. wanted). **19** establish contact with (a person etc.) by radio or telephone. **20** (usu. as **raised** *adj.*) cause (pastry etc.) to stand without support (*a raised pie*). **21** *Naut.* come in sight of (land, a ship, etc.). **22** make a nap on (cloth). **23** extract from the earth. ● *n.* **1** *Cards* an increase in a stake or bid (cf. sense 14 of *v.*). **2** esp. *N. Amer.* an increase in salary. □ **raise Cain** see CAIN. **raise the devil** *colloq.* make a disturbance. **raise a dust** *Brit.* **1** cause turmoil. **2** obscure the truth. **raise one's eyebrows** see EYEBROW. **raise one's eyes** see EYE. **raise from the dead** restore to life. **raise one's glass to** drink the health of. **raise one's hand to** make as if to strike (a person). **raise one's hat** (often foll. by *to*) remove it momentarily as a gesture of courtesy or respect. **raise hell** *colloq.* make a disturbance. **raise a laugh** cause others to laugh. **raise a person's spirits** give him or her new courage or cheerfulness. **raise one's voice** speak, esp. louder. **raise the wind** *Brit.* procure money for a purpose. □ **raisable** *adj.* [Middle English from Old Norse *reisa*, related to REAR[2]]

raised beach *n. Geol.* a former beach now lying above water level owing to changes since its formation.

raisin /ˈreɪz(ə)n/ *n.* a partially dried grape. □ **raisiny** *adj.* [Middle English from Old French, ultimately from Latin *racemus* 'grape-bunch']

raison d'être /reɪzɒ̃ ˈdɛtrə, French rɛzɔ̃ dɛtr/ *n.* (*pl.* ***raisons d'être*** *pronunc.* same) a purpose or reason that accounts for or justifies or originally caused a thing's existence. [French, = reason for being]

raita /rɑːˈiːtə/ *n.* an Indian side dish of chopped cucumber (or other vegetables) and spices in yogurt. [Hindustani *rāytā*]

Raj /rɑː(d)ʒ/ *n.* (prec. by *the*) *hist.* British sovereignty in India. [Hindi *rāj* 'reign']

raja /ˈrɑːdʒə/ *n.* (also **rajah**) *hist.* **1** an Indian king or prince. **2** a petty dignitary or noble in India. **3** a Malay or Javanese chief. [Hindi *rājā* from Sanskrit *rājan* 'king']

raja yoga *n.* a form of yoga intended to achieve control over the mind and emotions. [Sanskrit, from *rājan* 'king' + YOGA]

Rajput /ˈrɑːdʒpʊt/ *n.* (also **Rajpoot**) a member of a Hindu soldier caste claiming Kshatriya descent. [Hindi *rājpūt*, from Sanskrit *rājan* 'king' + *putra* 'son']

rake[1] /reɪk/ *n. & v.* ● *n.* **1 a** an implement consisting of a pole with a crossbar toothed like a comb at the end, or with several tines held together by a crosspiece, for drawing together hay etc. or smoothing loose soil or gravel. **b** a wheeled implement for the same purpose. **2** a similar implement used for other purposes, e.g. by a croupier drawing in money at a gaming table. ● *v.* **1** *tr.* collect or gather or remove with or as with a rake. **2** *tr.* make tidy or smooth with a rake (*raked it level*). **3** *intr.* use a rake. **4** *tr. & intr.* search with or as with a rake, search thoroughly, ransack. **5** *tr.* **a** direct gunfire along (a line) from end to end. **b** sweep with the eyes. **c** (of a window etc.) have a commanding view of. **6** *tr.* scratch or scrape. □ **rake in** *colloq.* amass (profits etc.). **rake up** (or **over**) revive the memory of (past quarrels, grievances, etc.). □ **raker** *n.* [Old English *raca*, *racu*, from Germanic: the verb partly from Old Norse *raka* 'scrape, rake']

rake[2] /reɪk/ *n.* a dissolute man of fashion. □ **rake's progress** a progressive deterioration, esp. through self-indulgence (the title of a series of engravings by Hogarth 1735). [short for archaic *rakehell* in the same sense]

rake[3] /reɪk/ *v. & n.* ● *v.* **1** *tr. & intr.* set or be set at a sloping angle. **2** *intr.* **a** (of a mast or funnel) incline from the perpendicular towards the stern. **b** (of a ship or its bow or stern) project at the upper part of the bow or stern beyond the keel. ● *n.* **1** a raking position or build. **2** the amount by which a thing rakes. **3** the slope of the stage or the auditorium in a theatre. **4** the slope of the back of a seat etc. **5** the angle of the edge or face of a cutting tool. [17th c.: probably related to German *ragen* 'project', of unknown origin]

rake-off *n. colloq.* a commission or share, esp. in a disreputable deal.

raki /rəˈkiː, ˈraki/ *n.* (*pl.* **rakis**) any of various spirits made in E. Europe and the Middle East. [Turkish *raqi*]

rakish[1] /ˈreɪkɪʃ/ *adj.* of or like a rake (see RAKE[2]); dashing, jaunty. □ **rakishly** *adv.* **rakishness** *n.*

rakish[2] /ˈreɪkɪʃ/ *adj.* (of a ship) smart and fast-looking, seemingly built for speed and therefore open to suspicion of piracy. [RAKE[3], associated with RAKE[2]]

raku /ˈrɑːkuː/ *n.* a kind of Japanese lead-glazed earthenware, primarily for use in the tea ceremony. [Japanese, literally 'enjoyment']

rale /rɑːl/ *n.* an abnormal rattling sound heard in the auscultation of unhealthy lungs. [French, from *râler* 'to rattle']

rall. /ral/ *abbr.* rallentando.

rallentando /ralənˈtandəʊ/ *adv., adj., & n. Mus.* ● *adv. & adj.* with a gradual decrease of speed. ● *n.* (*pl.* **-os** or **rallentandi** /-di/) a passage to be performed in this way. [Italian, pres. part. of *rallentare* 'slow down']

ralli car /ˈrali/ *n.* (also **ralli cart**) *hist.* a light two-wheeled horse-drawn vehicle for four persons. [*Ralli*, name of the first purchaser 1885]

rally[1] /ˈrali/ *v. & n.* ● *v.* (**-ies, -ied**) **1** *tr. & intr.* (often foll. by *round*, *behind*, *to*) bring or come together as support or for concentrated action. **2** *tr. & intr.* bring or come together again after a rout or dispersion. **3 a** *tr.* revive (courage etc.) by an effort of will. **b** *tr.* rouse (a person or animal) to fresh energy. **c** *intr.* pull oneself together. **4** *intr.* recover after illness or prostration or fear, regain health or consciousness, revive. **5** *intr.* (of share prices etc.) increase after a fall. ● *n.* (*pl.* **-ies**) **1** an act of reassembling forces or renewing conflict; a reunion for fresh effort. **2** a recovery of energy after or in the middle of exhaustion or illness. **3** a mass meeting of supporters or persons having a common interest. **4** a competition for motor vehicles, usu. over public roads or rough terrain. **5** *Tennis* etc. an extended exchange of strokes between players. □ **rallier** *n.* [French *rallier* (as RE-, ALLY[1])]

rally[2] /ˈrali/ *v.tr.* (**-ies, -ied**) subject to good-humoured ridicule. [French *railler*: see RAIL[2]]

rallycross /ˈralɪkrɒs/ *n. Brit.* a form of motor racing over roads and cross-country.

RAM *abbr.* **1** /ram/ *Computing* random-access memory. **2** (in the UK) Royal Academy of Music.

ram /ram/ *n. & v.* ● *n.* **1** an uncastrated male sheep, a tup. **2** (**the Ram**) the zodiacal sign or constellation Aries. **3** *hist.* **a** = BATTERING RAM. **b** a beak projecting from the bow of a battleship, for piercing the sides of other ships. **c** a battleship with such a beak. **4** the falling weight of a piledriving machine. **5 a** a hydraulic machine for raising water or for lifting. **b** the piston of a hydrostatic press. **c** the plunger of a force-pump. ● *v.tr.* (**rammed, ramming**) **1** force or squeeze into place by pressure. **2** (usu. foll. by *down*, *in*, *into*) beat down or drive in by heavy blows. **3** (of a ship, vehicle, etc.) strike violently, crash against. **4** (foll. by *against*, *at*, *on*, *into*) dash or violently impel. □ **ram home** stress forcefully (an argument, lesson, etc.). □ **rammer** *n.* (in senses 1 and 2 of *v.*). [Old English *ram(m)*, perhaps related to Old Norse *rammr* 'strong']

Ramadan /ˈramədan, raməˈdan/ *n.* (also **Ramadhan** /-zan/) the ninth month of the Muslim year, during which strict fasting is observed from sunrise to sunset. [Arabic *ramaḍān* from *ramaḍa* 'be hot'; reason for name uncertain]

ramal /ˈreɪm(ə)l/ *adj. Bot.* of or proceeding from a branch. [Latin *ramus* 'branch']

Raman effect /ˈrɑːmən/ *n.* the change of frequency in the scattering of radiation in a medium, used in spectroscopic analysis. [named after Sir C. V. *Raman*, Indian physicist d. 1970]

ramble /ˈramb(ə)l/ *v. & n.* ● *v.intr.* **1** walk for pleasure, with or without a definite route. **2** wander in discourse, talk or write disconnectedly. ● *n.* a walk taken for pleasure. [probably from Middle Dutch *rammelen* (of an animal) 'wander about in sexual excitement', frequentative of *rammen* 'copulate with', related to RAM]

rambler /ˈramblə/ *n.* **1** a person who rambles. **2** a straggling or climbing rose (*crimson rambler*).

rambling /ˈramblɪŋ/ *adj.* **1** peripatetic, wandering. **2** disconnected, desultory, incoherent. **3** (of a house, street, etc.) irregularly arranged. **4** (of a plant) straggling, climbing. □ **ramblingly** *adv.*

rambunctious /ramˈbʌŋ(k)ʃəs/ *adj. N. Amer. colloq.* **1** uncontrollably exuberant. **2** unruly. □ **rambunctiously** *adv.* **rambunctiousness** *n.* [19th c.: origin unknown]

rambutan /ramˈbuːt(ə)n/ *n.* **1** a red plum-sized prickly fruit. **2** a Malaysian tree, *Nephelium lappaceum*, that bears this. [Malay *rambūtan* from *rambut* 'hair', in allusion to its spines]

RAMC *abbr.* (in the UK) Royal Army Medical Corps.

ramekin /ˈramɪkɪn, ˈramkɪn/ *n.* **1** (in full **ramekin case** or **dish**) a small dish for baking and serving an individual portion of food. **2** food served in such a dish, esp. a small quantity of cheese baked with breadcrumbs, eggs, etc. [French *ramequin*, of Low German or Dutch origin]

ramie /ˈrami/ *n.* **1** a tall East Asian plant, *Boehmeria nivea*. **2** a strong fibre obtained from this, woven into cloth. [Malay *rāmī*]

ramification /ˌramɪfɪˈkeɪʃ(ə)n/ *n.* **1** the act or an instance of ramifying; the state of being ramified. **2** a subdivision of a complex structure or process comparable to a tree's branches. **3** a consequence, esp. when complex or unwelcome. [French from *ramifier*: see RAMIFY]

ramify /ˈramɪfʌɪ/ *v.* (**-ies, -ied**) **1** *intr.* form branches or subdivisions or offshoots, branch out. **2** *tr.* (usu. in *passive*) cause to branch out; arrange in a branching manner. [French *ramifier* via medieval Latin *ramificare* from Latin *ramus* 'branch']

ramin /raˈmiːn/ *n.* **1** any Malaysian tree of the genus *Gonystylus*, esp. *G. bancanus*. **2** the light-coloured hardwood obtained from this tree. [Malay]

ramjet /ˈramdʒɛt/ *n.* a type of jet engine in which the air drawn in for combustion is compressed solely by the forward motion of the aircraft.

rammer see RAM.

rammy /ˈrami/ *n.* (*pl.* **-ies**) *Sc. slang* a brawl, a fight (esp. between gangs); a quarrel. [perhaps from Scots *rammle* 'row, uproar', variant of RAMBLE]

ramose /ˈraməʊs, ˈreɪ-/ *adj.* branched; branching. [Latin *ramosus* from *ramus* 'branch']

ramp[1] /ramp/ *n. & v.* ● *n.* **1** a slope or inclined plane, esp. for joining two levels of ground, floor, etc. **2** movable stairs for entering or leaving an aircraft. **3** an upward bend in a stair-rail. **4** *Brit.* a transverse ridge in a road to control the speed of vehicles; a speed bump. ● *v.* **1** *tr.* furnish or build with a ramp. **2** *intr.* **a** assume or be in a threatening posture. **b** (often foll. by *about*) storm, rage, rush. **c** *Heraldry* be rampant. **3** *intr. Archit.* (of a wall) ascend or descend to a different level. [Middle English (as verb in heraldic sense) from French *rampe*, from Old French *ramper* 'creep, crawl']

ramp[2] /ramp/ *n. & v. Brit. slang* ● *n.* a swindle or racket, esp. one conducted by the levying of exorbitant prices. ● *v.* **1** *intr.* engage in a ramp. **2** *tr.* subject (a person etc.) to a ramp. [16th c.: origin unknown]

rampage /ramˈpeɪdʒ/ *v. & n.* ● *v.intr.* **1** (often foll. by *about*) rush wildly or violently about. **2** rage, storm. ● *n.* /often ˈram-/ wild or violent behaviour. □ **on the rampage** rampaging. □ **rampageous** *adj.* **rampager** *n.* [17th c., perhaps from RAMP[1]]

rampant /ˈramp(ə)nt/ *adj.* **1** (placed after noun) *Heraldry* (of an animal) standing on its left hind foot with its forepaws in the air (*lion rampant*). **2** unchecked, flourishing excessively (*rampant violence*). **3** violent or extravagant in action or opinion (*rampant theorists*). **4** rank, luxuriant. □ **rampancy** *n.* **rampantly** *adv.* [Middle English from Old French, part. of *ramper*: see RAMP[1]]

rampart /ˈrampɑːt/ *n. & v.* ● *n.* **1 a** a defensive wall with a broad top and usu. a stone parapet. **b** a walkway on top of such a wall. **2** a defence or protection. ● *v.tr.* fortify or protect with or as with a rampart. [French *rempart*, *rempar*, via *remparer* 'fortify' from *emparer* 'take possession of', ultimately from Latin *ante* 'before' + *parare* 'prepare']

rampion /ˈrampɪən/ *n.* **1** a bellflower, *Campanula rapunculus*, with white tuberous roots used as a salad. **2** any of various plants of the genus *Phyteuma*, with clusters of hornlike buds and flowers. [ultimately from medieval Latin *rapuncium*, *rapontium*, probably from Latin *rapum* RAPE[2]]

ram-raid *n.* a robbery in which a shop window is rammed with a vehicle and looted. □ **ram-raider** *n.* **ram-raiding** *n.*

ramrod /ˈramrɒd/ *n.* **1** a rod for ramming down the charge of a muzzle-loading firearm. **2** a thing that is very straight or rigid.

ramshackle /ˈramʃak(ə)l/ *adj.* (usu. of a house or vehicle) tumbledown, rickety. [earlier *ramshackled*, alteration of past part. of obsolete *ransackle* RANSACK]

ram's-horn snail *n.* a herbivorous freshwater snail of the family Planorbidae, having a flat spiral shell.

ramsons /ˈrams(ə)nz/ *n.* (usu. treated as *sing.*) **1** a broadleaved garlic, *Allium ursinum*, with elongate pungent-smelling bulbous roots. **2** the root of this, eaten as a relish. [Old English *hramsan*, pl. of *hramsa* 'wild garlic', later taken as sing.]

RAN *abbr.* Royal Australian Navy.

ran *past* of RUN.

ranch /rɑːn(t)ʃ/ *n. & v.* ● *n.* **1 a** a cattle-breeding establishment, esp. in the western US and Canada. **b** a farm where other animals are bred (*mink ranch*). **2** (in full **ranch house**) *N. Amer.* a single-storey or split-level house. ● *v.intr.* farm on a ranch. [Spanish *rancho* 'group of persons eating together']

rancher /ˈrɑːn(t)ʃə/ *n.* **1** a person who farms on a ranch. **2** *N. Amer.* a modern single-storey house.

ranchero /rɑːnˈtʃɛːrəʊ/ *n.* (*pl.* **-os**) a person who farms or works on a ranch, esp. in Mexico. [Spanish (as RANCH)]

rancid /ˈransɪd/ *adj.* smelling or tasting like rank stale fat. □ **rancidity** /-ˈsɪdɪti/ *n.* **rancidness** *n.* [Latin *rancidus* 'stinking']

rancour /ˈraŋkə/ *n.* (*US* **rancor**) inveterate bitterness, malignant hate, spitefulness. □ **rancorous** *adj.* **rancorously** *adv.* [Middle English via Old French from Late Latin *rancor -oris* (as RANCID)]

rand[1] /rand, rant/ *n.* **1** the chief monetary unit of South Africa and Namibia. **2** *S.Afr.* a ridge of high ground on either side of a river. [Afrikaans, = edge, related to RAND[2]: sense 1 from *the Rand*, goldfield district near Johannesburg]

rand[2] /rand/ *n.* a levelling strip of leather between the heel and sides of a shoe or boot. [Old English from Germanic]

R & B *abbr.* (also **R. & B.**) rhythm and blues.

R & D *abbr.* (also **R. & D.**) research and development.

random /ˈrandəm/ *adj.* **1** made, done, etc., without method or conscious choice (*random selection*). **2**

Statistics **a** with equal chances for each item. **b** given by a random process. **3** (of masonry) with stones of irregular size and shape. □ **at random** without aim or purpose or principle. □ **randomize** *v.tr.* (also **-ise**). **randomization** /-ˈzeɪʃ(ə)n/ *n.* **randomly** *adv.* **randomness** *n.* [Middle English from Old French *randon* 'great speed', from *randir* 'gallop']

random-access *adj. Computing* (of a memory or file) having all parts directly accessible, so that it need not be read sequentially.

random error *n. Statistics* an error in measurement caused by factors which vary from one measurement to another.

R and R *abbr.* (also **R. and R.**) **1** rescue and resuscitation. **2** rest and recreation. **3** rock and roll.

randy /ˈrandi/ *adj.* (**randier**, **randiest**) **1** lustful; eager for sexual gratification. **2** *Sc.* loud-tongued, boisterous, lusty. □ **randily** *adv.* **randiness** *n.* [perhaps via obsolete *rand* from obsolete Dutch *randen, ranten* RANT]

ranee /ˈrɑːniː/ *n.* (also **rani**) *hist.* a raja's wife or widow; a Hindu queen. [Hindi *rānī* = Sanskrit *rājñī*, fem. of *rājan* 'king']

rang *past* of RING[2].

rangatira /raŋgəˈtɪərə/ *n. NZ* a Maori chief or noble. [Maori]

range /reɪn(d)ʒ/ *n. & v.* ● *n.* **1 a** the region between limits of variation, esp. as representing a scope of effective operation (*a voice of astonishing range; the whole range of politics*). **b** such limits. **c** a limited scale or series (*the range of the thermometer readings is about 10 degrees*). **2** the area included in or concerned with something. **3 a** the distance attainable by a gun or projectile (*the enemy are out of range*). **b** the distance between a gun or projectile and its objective. **4** a row, series, line, or tier, esp. of mountains or buildings. **5 a** an open or enclosed area with targets for shooting. **b** a testing ground for military equipment. **6 a** a large cooking stove of which the burners and oven(s) are kept continually hot. **b** *N. Amer* an electric or gas cooker with several burners. **7** the area over which a thing, esp. a plant or animal, is distributed (*gives the ranges of all species*). **8** the distance that can be covered by a vehicle or aircraft without refuelling. **9** the distance between a camera and the subject to be photographed. **10** the extent of time covered by a forecast etc. **11 a** a large area of open land for grazing or hunting. **b** a tract over which one wanders. **12** lie, direction (*the range of the strata is east and west*). ● *v.* **1** *intr.* **a** reach; lie spread out; extend; be found or occur over a specified district; vary between limits (*ages ranging from twenty to sixty*). **b** run in a line (*ranges north and south*). **2** *tr.* (usu. in *passive* or *refl.*) place or arrange in a row or ranks or in a specified situation or order or company (*ranged their troops; ranged themselves with the majority party; trees ranged in ascending order of height*). **3** *intr.* rove, wander (*ranged through the woods; his thoughts range over past, present, and future*). **4** *tr.* traverse in all directions (*ranging the woods*). **5** *Brit. Printing* **a** *tr.* make (type) lie flush at the ends of successive lines. **b** *intr.* (of type) lie flush. **6** *intr.* **a** (often foll. by *with*) be level. **b** (foll. by *with, among*) rank; find one's right place (*ranges with the great writers*). **7** *intr.* **a** (of a gun) send a projectile over a specified distance (*ranges over a mile*). **b** (of a projectile) cover a specified distance. **c** obtain the range of a target by adjustment after firing past it or short of it. [Middle English from Old French *range* 'row, rank', via *ranger* from *rang* RANK[1]]

rangé /rɑ̃ˈʒeɪ, French rɑ̃ʒe/ *adj.* (*fem.* ***rangée***) domesticated, orderly, settled. [French]

rangefinder /ˈreɪn(d)ʒfʌɪndə/ *n.* an instrument for estimating the distance of an object, esp. one to be shot at or photographed.

ranger /ˈreɪn(d)ʒə/ *n.* **1** a keeper of a royal or national park, or of a forest. **2** a member of a body of armed men, esp.: **a** a mounted soldier. **b** *US* a commando. **3** (**Ranger**) *Brit.* a senior Guide. **4** a wanderer. □ **rangership** *n.*

ranging-pole *n.* (also **ranging-rod**) *Surveying* a pole or rod for setting a straight line.

rangy /ˈreɪn(d)ʒi/ *adj.* (**rangier**, **rangiest**) (of a person) tall and slim.

rani var. of RANEE.

rank[1] /raŋk/ *n. & v.* ● *n.* **1 a** a position in a hierarchy, a grade of advancement. **b** a distinct social class, a grade of dignity or achievement (*people of all ranks; in the top rank of performers*). **c** high social position (*persons of rank*). **d** a place in a scale. **2** a row or line. **3** a single line of soldiers drawn up abreast. **4** *Brit.* a place where taxis stand to await customers. **5** order, array. **6** *Chess* a row of squares across the board (cf. FILE[2] *n.* 3). ● *v.* **1** *intr.* have rank or place (*ranks next to the king*). **2** *tr.* classify, give a certain grade to. **3** *tr.* arrange (esp. soldiers) in a rank or ranks. **4** *US* **a** *tr.* take precedence over (a person) in respect to rank. **b** *intr.* have the senior position among the members of a hierarchy etc. □ **break rank** (or **ranks**) fail to remain in line; fail to maintain solidarity. **close ranks** maintain solidarity. **keep rank** remain in line. **the ranks** the common soldiers, i.e. privates and corporals. **rise from the ranks 1** (of a private or a non-commissioned officer) receive a commission. **2** (of a self-made man or woman) advance by one's own exertions. [Old French *ranc, renc*, from Germanic: related to RING[1]]

rank[2] /raŋk/ *adj.* **1** too luxuriant; choked with or apt to produce weeds or excessive foliage. **2 a** foul-smelling, offensive. **b** loathsome, indecent, corrupt. **3** flagrant, virulent, gross, complete, unmistakable, strongly marked (*rank outsider*). □ **rankly** *adv.* **rankness** *n.* [Old English *ranc*, from Germanic]

rank and file *n.* (usu. treated as *pl.*) ordinary undistinguished people (hyphenated when *attrib.*: *rank-and-file members*).

rank correlation *n. Statistics* assessment of the degree of correlation between alternative ways of ranking the members of a set.

ranker /ˈraŋkə/ *n. Brit.* **1** a soldier in the ranks. **2** a commissioned officer who has been in the ranks.

ranking /ˈraŋkɪŋ/ *n. & adj.* ● *n.* ordering by rank; classification. ● *adj. US* having a high rank or position.

rankle /ˈraŋk(ə)l/ *v.intr.* **1** (of envy, disappointment, etc., or their cause) cause persistent annoyance or resentment. **2** *archaic* (of a wound, sore, etc.) fester, continue to be painful. [Middle English (in sense 2) via Old French *rancler*, from *rancle, draoncle* 'festering sore' from medieval Latin *dranculus, dracunculus*, diminutive of *draco* 'serpent']

ransack /ˈransak/ *v.tr.* **1** pillage or plunder (a house, country, etc.). **2** thoroughly search (a place, a receptacle, a person's pockets, one's conscience, etc.). □ **ransacker** *n.* [Middle English from Old Norse *rannsaka*, from *rann* 'house' + *-saka* from *sœkja* 'seek']

ransom /ˈrans(ə)m/ *n. & v.* ● *n.* **1** a sum of money or other payment demanded or paid for the release of a prisoner. **2** the liberation of a prisoner in return for this. ● *v.tr.* **1** buy the freedom or restoration of; redeem. **2** hold to ransom. **3** release for a ransom. [Middle English via Old French *ransoun(er)* from Latin *redemptio -onis* REDEMPTION]

rant /rant/ *v. & n.* ● *v.* **1** *intr.* use bombastic language. **2** *tr. & intr.* declaim, recite theatrically. **3** *intr.* speak vehemently or wildly. **4** *tr. & intr.* preach noisily. ● *n.* **1** a piece of ranting, a tirade. **2** empty turgid talk. □ **rant and rave** express anger noisily and forcefully. □ **ranter** *n.* **rantingly** *n.* [Dutch *ranten* 'rave']

ranunculaceous /rəˌnʌŋkjʊˈleɪʃəs/ *adj.* of or relating to the family Ranunculaceae of flowering plants, including clematis, buttercups, and delphiniums.

ranunculus /rəˈnʌŋkjʊləs/ *n.* (*pl.* **ranunculuses** or **ranunculi** /-lʌɪ, -liː/) any plant of the genus *Ranunculus*, usu. having bowl-shaped flowers with many stamens and carpels, including buttercups and crowfoots. [Latin, originally diminutive of *rana* 'frog']

RAOC *abbr.* (in the UK) Royal Army Ordnance Corps.

rap[1] /rap/ *n. & v.* ● *n.* **1** a smart slight blow. **2** a knock, a sharp tapping sound. **3** *slang* blame, censure, or punishment. **4** *slang* a conversation. **5 a** a rhyming monologue recited rhythmically to pre-recorded music. **b** (in full **rap music**) a style of black popular music with a pronounced beat to which words are recited rather than sung. ● *v.* (**rapped**, **rapping**) **1** *tr.* strike smartly. **2** *intr.* knock; make a sharp tapping sound (*rapped on the table*). **3** *tr.* criticize adversely. **4** *intr. slang* talk. **5** *intr.* perform rap music, talk in the style of rap. □ **beat the rap** *N. Amer.* escape punishment. **rap on** (or **over**) **the knuckles** a reprimand or reproof. **rap out 1** utter (an oath, order, pun, etc.) abruptly or on the spur of the moment. **2** express or reproduce (a rhythm, signal, etc.) by raps. **take the rap** suffer the consequences. □ **rapper** *n.* [Middle English, probably imitative]

rap[2] /rap/ *n.* a small amount, the least bit (*don't care a rap*). [Irish *ropaire* 'robber', used as the name of an Irish counterfeit coin]

rapacious /rəˈpeɪʃəs/ *adj.* grasping, extortionate, predatory. □ **rapaciously** *adv.* **rapaciousness** *n.* **rapacity** /rəˈpasɪti/ *n.* [Latin *rapax -acis* from *rapere* 'snatch']

RAPC *abbr.* (in the UK) Royal Army Pay Corps.

rape[1] /reɪp/ *n. & v.* ● *n.* **1 a** the act of forcing a woman to have sexual intercourse against her will. **b** forcible sodomy. **2** (often foll. by *of*) violent assault, forcible interference, violation. **3** *poet.* carrying off (esp. of a woman) by force. **4** an instance of rape. ● *v.tr.* **1** commit rape on (a person, usu. a woman). **2** violate, assault, pillage. **3** *poet.* carry off by force. □ **raper** *n.* esp. *US* [Middle English via Anglo-French *rap(e)* (*n.*), *raper* (*v.*) from Latin *rapere* 'seize']

rape[2] /reɪp/ *n.* a plant, *Brassica napus*, grown as food for livestock and for its seed, from which oil is made. Also called COLE, COLZA. [Middle English from Latin *rapum*, *rapa* 'turnip']

rape[3] /reɪp/ *n. hist.* (in the UK) any of the six ancient divisions of Sussex. [Old English, variant of *rāp* ROPE, with reference to the fencing-off of land]

rape[4] /reɪp/ *n.* **1** the refuse of grapes after wine-making, used in making vinegar. **2** a vessel used in vinegar-making. [French *râpe*, medieval Latin *raspa*]

rape-cake *n.* rapeseed pressed into a flat shape after the extraction of oil and used as manure or food for livestock.

rape-oil *n.* an oil made from rapeseed and used as a lubricant and in foodstuffs.

rapeseed /ˈreɪpsiːd/ *n.* the seed of the rape plant. [RAPE[2] + SEED]

raphide /ˈreɪfʌɪd/ *n.* a needle-shaped crystal of calcium oxalate formed within the tissues of a plant. [back-formation from *raphides*, pl. of *raphis*, from Greek *rhaphis -idos* 'needle']

rapid /ˈrapɪd/ *adj. & n.* ● *adj.* (**rapider**, **rapidest**) **1** quick, swift. **2** acting or completed in a short time. **3** (of a slope) descending steeply. **4** *Photog.* fast. ● *n.* (usu. in *pl.*) a steep descent in a river bed, with a swift current. □ **rapidity** /rəˈpɪdɪti/ *n.* **rapidly** *adv.* **rapidness** *n.* [Latin *rapidus* from *rapere* 'seize']

rapid eye-movement *n.* a type of jerky movement of the eyes during periods of dreaming.

rapid-fire *attrib.adj.* fired, asked, etc., in quick succession.

rapid transit *adj.* (*attrib.*) denoting high-speed urban transport of passengers.

rapier /ˈreɪpɪə/ *n.* **1** a light slender sword used for thrusting. **2** (*attrib.*) quick, sharp (*rapier wit*). [probably from Dutch *rapier* or Low German *rappir*, from French *rapière*, of unknown origin]

rapine /ˈrapʌɪn, -pɪn/ *n. literary* plundering, robbery. [Middle English from Old French, or via Latin *rapina* from *rapere* 'seize']

rapist /ˈreɪpɪst/ *n.* a person who commits rape.

rapparee /rapəˈriː/ *n. hist.* a 17th-c. Irish irregular soldier or freebooter. [Irish *rapaire* 'short pike']

rappee /raˈpiː/ *n.* a coarse kind of snuff. [French (*tabac*) *râpé* 'rasped (tobacco)']

rappel /raˈpɛl/ *n. & v.intr.* (**rappelled**, **rappelling**) = ABSEIL. [French, = recall, from *rappeler* (as RE-, APPEAL)]

rapport /raˈpɔː/ *n.* **1** relationship or communication, esp. when useful and harmonious (*in rapport with*; *establish a rapport*). **2** communication through a spiritualistic medium. [French from *rapporter* (as RE-, AP-[1], *porter* from Latin *portare* 'carry')]

rapporteur /rapɔːˈtəː/ *n.* a person who prepares an account of the proceedings of a committee etc. for a higher body. [French (as RAPPORT)]

rapprochement /raˈprɒʃmɒ̃/ *n.* the resumption of harmonious relations, esp. between states. [French from *rapprocher* (as RE-, APPROACH)]

rapscallion /rapˈskalɪən/ *n. archaic* or *joc.* a rascal, scamp, or rogue. [earlier *rascallion*, perhaps from RASCAL]

rapt /rapt/ *adj.* **1** fully absorbed or intent, enraptured (*listen with rapt attention*). **2** carried away with joyous feeling or lofty thought. **3** *poet.* carried away bodily. **4** *Austral. colloq.* overjoyed, delighted. □ **raptly** *adv.* **raptness** *n.* [Middle English from Latin *raptus*, past part. of *rapere* 'seize']

raptor /ˈraptə/ *n.* any bird of prey, e.g. an owl, falcon, etc. [Latin, = ravisher, plunderer, from *rapere rapt-* 'seize']

raptorial /rapˈtɔːrɪəl/ *adj. & n.* ● *adj.* (of a bird or animal) adapted for seizing prey; predatory. ● *n.* **1** = RAPTOR. **2** a predatory animal. [Latin *raptor*: see RAPTOR]

rapture /ˈraptʃə/ *n.* **1 a** ecstatic delight, mental transport. **b** (in *pl.*) great pleasure or enthusiasm or the expression of it. **2 a** (**Rapture**) (in some millenarian teaching) the transporting of believers to heaven at the second coming of Christ. **b** *archaic* the act of transporting a person from one place to another. □ **go into** (or **be in**) **raptures** be enthusiastic; talk enthusiastically. □ **rapturous** *adj.* **rapturously** *adv.* **rapturousness** *n.* [obsolete French *rapture* or medieval Latin *raptura* (as RAPT)]

rara avis /rɛːrə ˈeɪvɪs, rɑːrə ˈavɪs/ *n.* (*pl.* ***rarae aves*** /-riː -viːz/) a rarity; a kind of person or thing rarely encountered. [Latin, = rare bird]

rare[1] /rɛː/ *adj.* (**rarer**, **rarest**) **1** seldom done, found, or occurring; uncommon, unusual; few and far between. **2** esp. *Brit.* exceptionally good (*had a rare time*). **3** of less than the usual density, with only loosely packed substance (*the rare atmosphere of the mountain tops*). □ **rareness** *n.* [Middle English from Latin *rarus*]

rare[2] /rɛː/ *adj.* (**rarer**, **rarest**) (of meat) underdone. [variant of obsolete *rear* 'half-cooked' (of eggs), from Old English *hrēr*]

rare bird *n.* = RARA AVIS.

rarebit /ˈrɛːbɪt/ *n.* = WELSH RABBIT. [RARE[1] + BIT[1]]

rare earth *n.* **1** a lanthanide element. **2** an oxide of such an element.

raree-show /ˈrɛːriːʃəʊ/ *n.* **1** a show or spectacle. **2** a show carried about in a box; a peep-show. [apparently = *rare show* as pronounced by Savoyard showmen]

rarefy /ˈrɛːrɪfʌɪ/ *v.* (also **rarify**) (**-ies**, **-ied**) **1** *tr. & intr.* make or become less dense or solid (*rarefied air*). **2** *tr.* purify or refine (a person's nature etc.). **3** *tr.* make (an idea etc.) subtle. □ **rarefaction** /-ˈfakʃ(ə)n/ *n.* **rarefactive** /-ˈfaktɪv/ *adj.* **rarefication** /-fɪˈkeɪʃ(ə)n/ *n.* [Middle English via Old French *rarefier* or medieval Latin *rarificare* from Latin *rarefacere*, from *rarus* 'rare' + *facere* 'make']

rare gas *n.* = NOBLE GAS.

rarely /ˈrɛːli/ *adv.* **1** seldom; not often. **2** in an unusual degree; exceptionally. **3** exceptionally well.

raring /ˈrɛːrɪŋ/ *adj.* (foll. by *to* + infin.) *colloq.* enthusiastic, eager (*raring to go*). [part. of *rare*, dialect variant of ROAR or REAR[2]]

rarity /ˈrɛːrɪti/ *n.* (*pl.* **-ies**) **1** rareness. **2** an uncommon thing, esp. one valued for being rare. [French *rareté* or Latin *raritas* (as RARE[1])]

rascal /ˈrɑːsk(ə)l/ *n.* often *joc.* a dishonest or mischievous person, esp. a child. □ **rascality** /-ˈskalɪti/ *n.* (*pl.* **-ies**). **rascally** *adj.* [Middle English from Old French *rascaille* 'rabble', probably ultimately from Latin *radere ras-* 'scrape']

rase var. of RAZE.

rash[1] /raʃ/ *adj.* reckless, impetuous, hasty; acting or done without due consideration. □ **rashly** *adv.* **rashness** *n.* [Middle English, probably via Old English from Germanic]

rash[2] /raʃ/ *n.* **1** an eruption of the skin in spots or patches. **2** (usu. foll. by *of*) a sudden widespread phenomenon, esp. of something unwelcome (*a rash of strikes*). [18th c.: probably related to Old French *ra(s)che* 'eruptive sores', = Italian *raschia* 'itch']

rasher /ˈraʃə/ *n.* a thin slice of bacon or ham. [16th c.: origin unknown]

rasp /rɑːsp/ *n.* & *v.* ● *n.* **1** a coarse kind of file having separate teeth. **2** a grating noise or utterance. ● *v.* **1** *tr.* **a** scrape with a rasp. **b** scrape roughly. **c** (foll. by *off, away*) remove by scraping. **2 a** *intr.* make a grating sound. **b** *tr.* say gratingly or hoarsely. **3** *tr.* grate upon (a person or a person's feelings), irritate. □ **raspingly** *adv.* **raspy** *adj.* [Middle English from Old French *raspe(r)*, ultimately from West Germanic]

raspberry /ˈrɑːzb(ə)ri/ *n.* & *adj.* ● *n.* (*pl.* **-ies**) **1 a** a bramble, *Rubus idaeus*, having usu. red berries consisting of numerous drupels on a conical receptacle. **b** this berry. **2** the red colour of a raspberry, varying in shade from pink to scarlet. **3** *colloq.* **a** a sound made with the lips expressing dislike, derision, or disapproval (originally *raspberry tart, rhyming slang = fart*). **b** a show of strong disapproval (*got a raspberry from the audience*). ● *adj.* of the colour of a raspberry; red, pink, scarlet. [16th-c. *rasp* (now dialect) from obsolete *raspis*, of unknown origin, + BERRY]

raspberry cane *n.* a raspberry plant.

rasper /ˈrɑːspə/ *n.* **1** a person or thing that rasps. **2** *Hunting* a high difficult fence.

Rasta /ˈrastə/ *n.* & *adj.* *colloq.* = RASTAFARIAN. [abbreviation]

Rastafarian /rastəˈfɑːrɪən, -ˈfɛːrɪən/ *n.* & *adj.* ● *n.* a member of a sect of Jamaican origin regarding blacks as a chosen people and the former Emperor Haile Selassie of Ethiopia (d. 1975) as the Messiah. ● *adj.* of or relating to this sect. □ **Rastafarianism** *n.* [*Ras Tafari*, name by which Haile Selassie was known 1916–30]

raster /ˈrastə/ *n.* a pattern of scanning lines for a cathode ray tube picture. [German, = screen, via Latin *rastrum* 'rake' from *radere ras-* 'scrape']

rasterize /ˈrastərʌɪz/ *v.tr.* (also **-ise**) *Computing* convert (a digitized image) into a form that can be displayed on a cathode ray tube or printed. □ **rasterization** /ˌrastərʌɪˈzeɪʃ(ə)n/ *n.* **rasterizer** *n.*

rat /rat/ *n.* & *v.* ● *n.* **1 a** any of several rodents of the genus *Rattus* (*brown rat*). **b** any similar rodent (*muskrat; water rat*). **2** a deserter from a party, cause, difficult situation, etc.; a turncoat (from the superstition that rats desert a sinking ship). **3** *colloq.* an unpleasant person. **4** a worker who refuses to join a strike, or who blacklegs. **5** (in *pl.*) *slang* an exclamation of contempt, annoyance, etc. ● *v.intr.* (**ratted**, **ratting**) **1** (of a person or dog) hunt or kill rats. **2** *colloq.* desert a cause, party, etc. **3** (foll. by *on*) *colloq.* **a** betray; let down. **b** inform on. [Old English *ræt*, later reinforced by Old French *rat*]

rata /ˈrɑːtə/ *n.* any large tree of the genus *Metrosideros*, esp. *M. robusta* of New Zealand, with crimson flowers and hard red wood. [Maori]

ratable var. of RATEABLE.

ratafia /ratəˈfɪə/ *n.* **1** a liqueur flavoured with almonds or kernels of peach, apricot, or cherry. **2** a kind of biscuit similarly flavoured. [French, perhaps related to TAFIA]

ratan var. of RATTAN.

rataplan /ratəˈplan/ *n.* & *v.* ● *n.* a drumming sound. ● *v.* (**rataplanned**, **rataplanning**) **1** *tr.* play (a tune) on or as on a drum. **2** *intr.* make a rataplan. [French: imitative]

rat-arsed *adj.* *slang* drunk.

ratatat (also **rat-a-tat**) var. of RAT-TAT.

ratatouille /ratəˈtuːi, -ˈtwiː/ *n.* a vegetable dish of onions, courgettes, tomatoes, aubergines, and peppers, fried and stewed in oil. [French dialect]

ratbag /ˈratbag/ *n.* *Brit.* *slang* an unpleasant or disgusting person.

rat-catcher *n.* a person who rids buildings of rats etc.

ratch /ratʃ/ *n.* **1** a ratchet. **2** a ratchet-wheel. [perhaps from German *Ratsche*: cf. RATCHET]

ratchet /ˈratʃɪt/ *n.* & *v.* ● *n.* **1** a set of teeth on the edge of a bar or wheel in which a device engages to ensure motion in one direction only. **2** (in full **ratchet-wheel**) a wheel with a rim so toothed. ● *v.* (**ratcheted**, **ratcheting**) **1** *tr.* **a** provide with a ratchet. **b** make into a ratchet. **2** *tr.* & *intr.* (often foll. by *up*) move as under the control of a ratchet. [French *rochet* 'blunt lance-head, bobbin, ratchet', etc., probably ultimately from Germanic]

rate[1] /reɪt/ *n.* & *v.* ● *n.* **1** a stated numerical proportion between two sets of things (the second usu. expressed as unity), esp. as a measure of amount or degree (*moving at a rate of 50 miles per hour*) or as the basis of calculating an amount or value (*rate of taxation*). **2** a fixed or appropriate charge or cost or value; a measure of this (*postal rates; the rate for the job*). **3** rapidity of movement or change (*travelling at a great rate; prices increasing at a dreadful rate*). **4** class or rank (*first-rate*). **5** *Brit.* **a** a tax levied by local authorities on commercial properties (and, until recently, dwellings) at so much per pound of the assessed value of buildings and land owned or leased (now replaced by the council tax for dwellings). **b** (in *pl.*) the amount payable by this. ● *v.* **1** *tr.* **a** estimate the worth or value of (*I do not rate him very highly; how do you rate your chances of winning?*). **b** assign a fixed value to (a coin or metal) in relation to a monetary standard. **c** assign a value to (work, the power of a machine, etc.). **2** *tr.* consider; regard as (*I rate them among my benefactors*). **3** *intr.* (foll. by *as*) rank or be rated. **4** *tr.* *Brit.* **a** subject to the payment of a local rate. **b** value for the purpose of assessing rates. **5** *tr.* be worthy of, deserve. **6** *tr.* **a** place (a film etc.) in a category relative to its suitability for viewing. **b** *Naut.* place (a sailor) in a specified class (cf. RATING[1] 3). □ **at any rate** in any case, whatever happens. **at this** (or **that**) **rate** if this example is typical or this assumption is true. [Middle English via Old French and medieval Latin *rata* (from Latin *pro rata parte* or *portione* 'according to the proportional share') from *ratus*, past part. of *rēri* 'reckon']

rate[2] /reɪt/ *v.tr.* scold angrily. [Middle English: origin unknown]

rate[3] var. of RET.

rateable /ˈreɪtəb(ə)l/ *adj.* (also **ratable**) **1** *Brit.* esp. *hist.* liable to the levy of rates (see RATE[1] *n.* 5). **2** able to be rated or estimated. □ **rateability** /-ˈbɪlɪti/ *n.* **rateably** *adv.*

rateable value *n.* *Brit.* the value at which a house etc. is assessed for payment of rates.

rate-capping *n.* *Brit.* *hist.* the imposition of an upper limit on the rate leviable by a local authority (see RATE[1] *n.* 5). □ **rate-cap** *v.tr.*

ratel /ˈreɪt(ə)l, ˈrɑː-/ *n.* an African and Indian nocturnal flesh-eating burrowing mammal, *Mellivora capensis*. Also called *honey badger*. [Afrikaans, of unknown origin]

ratepayer /ˈreɪtpeɪə/ *n.* **1** *Brit.* esp. *hist.* a person liable to pay rates (see RATE[1] *n.* 5). **2** *N. Amer.* a customer of a public utility.

rathe /reɪð/ *adj. poet.* coming, blooming, etc., early in the year or day. [Old English *hræth*, *hræd*, from Germanic]

rather /ˈrɑːðə/ *adv.* **1** (often foll. by *than*) by preference; for choice (*would rather not go*; *would rather stay than go*). **2** (usu. foll. by *than*) more truly; as a more likely alternative (*is stupid rather than honest*). **3** more precisely (*a book, or rather, a pamphlet*). **4** slightly; to some extent; somewhat (*became rather drunk*; *I rather think you know him*). **5** /rɑːˈðəː/ *Brit.* (as an emphatic response) indeed, assuredly (*Did you like it? – Rather!*). □ **had rather** *archaic* or *literary* would rather. [Middle English from Old English *hrathor*, comparative of *hræthe* (*adv.*), from *hræth* (*adj.*): see RATHE]

rathe-ripe *adj.* **1** ripening early. **2** precocious.

rathskeller /ˈrɑːtskɛlə/ *n. US* a beer hall or restaurant in a basement. [German (now *Ratskeller*), = (restaurant in) town hall cellar]

ratify /ˈratɪfʌɪ/ *v.tr.* (**-ies**, **-ied**) confirm or accept (an agreement made in one's name) by formal consent, signature, etc. □ **ratifiable** *adj.* **ratification** /-fɪˈkeɪʃ(ə)n/ *n.* **ratifier** *n.* [Middle English via Old French *ratifier* from medieval Latin *ratificare* (as RATE[1])]

rating[1] /ˈreɪtɪŋ/ *n.* **1** the act or an instance of placing in a rank or class or assigning a value to. **2** the estimated standing of a person as regards credit etc. **3** *Naut.* **a** *Brit.* a non-commissioned sailor. **b** a person's position or class on a ship's books. **4** *Brit.* esp. *hist.* an amount fixed as a local rate (cf. RATE[1] *n.* 5). **5** the relative popularity of a broadcast programme as determined by the estimated size of the audience. **6** *Naut.* any of the classes into which racing yachts are distributed by tonnage.

rating[2] /ˈreɪtɪŋ/ *n.* an angry reprimand.

ratio /ˈreɪʃɪəʊ/ *n.* (*pl.* **-os**) the quantitative relation between two similar magnitudes determined by the number of times one contains the other integrally or fractionally (*in the ratio of three to two*; *the ratios 1:5 and 20:100 are the same*). [Latin (as RATE[1])]

ratiocinate /ratɪˈɒsɪneɪt, raʃɪ-/ *v.intr. literary* go through logical processes, reason, esp. using syllogisms. □ **ratiocination** /-ˈneɪʃ(ə)n/ *n.* **ratiocinative** /-nətɪv/ *adj.* **ratiocinator** *n.* [Latin *ratiocinari* (as RATIO)]

ration /ˈraʃ(ə)n/ *n.* & *v.* ● *n.* **1** a fixed official allowance of food, clothing, etc., in a time of shortage. **2** (foll. by *of*) a single portion of provisions, fuel, clothing, etc. **3** (usu. in *pl.*) a fixed daily allowance of food, esp. in the armed forces (and formerly of forage for animals). **4** (in *pl.*) provisions. ● *v.tr.* **1** limit (persons or provisions) to a fixed ration. **2** (usu. foll. by *out*) share out (food etc.) in fixed quantities. □ **given out with the rations** *Mil. slang* awarded without regard to merit. [French via Italian *razione* or Spanish *ración* from Latin *ratio -onis* 'reckoning', RATIO]

rational /ˈraʃ(ə)n(ə)l/ *adj.* **1** of or based on reasoning or reason. **2** sensible, sane, moderate; not foolish or absurd or extreme. **3** endowed with reason, reasoning. **4** rejecting what is unreasonable or cannot be tested by reason in religion or custom. **5** *Math.* (of a quantity or ratio) expressible as a ratio of whole numbers. □ **rationality** /-ˈnalɪti/ *n.* **rationally** *adv.* [Middle English from Latin *rationalis* (as RATION)]

rational dress *n. hist.* a style of dress adopted by some women in the late nineteenth century, including bloomers or knickerbockers.

rationale /raʃəˈnɑːl/ *n.* **1** (often foll. by *for*) the fundamental reason or logical basis of anything. **2** a reasoned exposition; a statement of reasons. [modern Latin, neut. of Latin *rationalis*: see RATIONAL]

rational horizon see HORIZON 1c.

rationalism /ˈraʃ(ə)n(ə)lɪz(ə)m/ *n.* **1** *Philos.* the theory that reason is the foundation of certainty in knowledge (opp. EMPIRICISM, SENSATIONALISM 2). **2** *Theol.* the practice of treating reason as the ultimate authority in religion. **3** a belief in reason rather than religion as a guiding principle in life. □ **rationalist** *n.* **rationalistic** /-ˈlɪstɪk/ *adj.* **rationalistically** /-ˈlɪstɪk(ə)li/ *adv.*

rationalize /ˈraʃ(ə)n(ə)lʌɪz/ *v.* (also **-ise**) **1 a** *tr.* offer or subconsciously adopt a rational but specious explanation of (one's behaviour or attitude). **b** *intr.* explain one's behaviour or attitude in this way. **2** *tr.* make logical and consistent. **3** *tr.* make (a business etc.) more efficient by reorganizing it to reduce or eliminate waste of labour, time, or materials. **4** *tr.* (often foll. by *away*) explain or explain away rationally. **5** *tr. Math.* clear of surds. **6** *intr.* be or act as a rationalist. □ **rationalization** /-ˈzeɪʃ(ə)n/ *n.* **rationalizer** *n.*

ration book *n.* (also **ration card**) a document entitling the holder to a ration.

ratite /ˈratʌɪt/ *adj.* & *n.* ● *adj.* (of a bird) having a keelless breastbone, and unable to fly (opp. CARINATE). ● *n.* a flightless bird, e.g. an ostrich, emu, cassowary, etc. [Latin *ratis* 'raft']

rat kangaroo *n. Austral.* any of various small ratlike marsupials of the family Potoroidae, having kangaroo-like hind limbs for jumping.

ratline /ˈratlɪn/ *n.* (also **ratlin**) (usu. in *pl.*) any of the small lines fastened across a sailing ship's shrouds like ladder rungs. [Middle English: origin unknown]

ratoon /rəˈtuːn/ *n.* & *v.* ● *n.* a new shoot springing from a root of sugar cane etc. after cropping. ● *v.intr.* send up ratoons. [Spanish *retoño* 'sprout']

rat race *n.* a fiercely competitive struggle for position, power, etc.

rat-run *n. colloq.* a route on minor roads used by traffic to avoid congestion at peak periods.

ratsbane /ˈratsbeɪn/ *n. literary* rat-poison.

rat's tail *n.* a thing shaped like a rat's tail, e.g. a tapering cylindrical file.

rat-tail *n.* **1** the grenadier fish. **2** a horse with a hairless tail. **3** such a tail.

rat-tail spoon *n.* (also **rat-tailed spoon**) a spoon with a tail-like moulding from the handle to the back of the bowl.

rattan /rəˈtan/ *n.* (also **ratan**) **1** any Malaysian climbing palm of the genus *Calamus* etc. with long thin jointed pliable stems. **2** a piece of rattan stem used as a walking stick etc. [earlier *rot(t)ang* from Malay *rōtan*, probably from *raut* 'pare']

rat-tat /ratˈtat/ *n.* (also **rat-tat-tat** /rattatˈtat/, **ratatat**, **rat-a-tat** /ratəˈtat/) a rapping sound, esp. of a knocker. [imitative]

ratted /ˈratɪd/ *adj. slang* = RAT-ARSED.

ratter /ˈratə/ *n.* **1** a dog or other animal that hunts rats. **2** *slang* a person who betrays a cause, party, friend, etc.

rattle /ˈrat(ə)l/ *v.* & *n.* ● *v.* **1 a** *intr.* give out a rapid succession of short sharp hard sounds, usu. through being shaken or knocking against something. **b** *tr.* make (a chair, window, crockery, etc.) do this. **c** *intr.* cause such sounds by shaking something (*rattled at the door*). **2 a** *intr.* move with a rattling noise. **b** *intr.* drive a vehicle or ride or run briskly. **c** *tr.* cause to move quickly (*the bill was rattled through Parliament*). **3 a** *tr.* (usu. foll. by *off*) say or recite rapidly. **b** *intr.* (usu. foll. by *on*) talk in a lively thoughtless way. **4** *tr. colloq.* disconcert, alarm, fluster, make nervous, frighten. ● *n.* **1** a rattling sound. **2** an instrument or plaything made to rattle esp. in order to amuse babies or to give an alarm. **3** the set of horny rings in a rattlesnake's tail. **4** a plant with seeds that rattle in their cases when ripe (*red rattle*; *yellow rattle*). **5** uproar, bustle, noisy gaiety, racket. **6 a** a noisy flow of words. **b** empty chatter, trivial talk. **7** *archaic* a lively or thoughtless incessant talker. □ **rattle the sabre** threaten war. □ **rattly** *adj.* [Middle English, probably from Middle Dutch & Low German *ratelen* (imitative)]

rattlebox /ˈrat(ə)lbɒks/ *n.* **1** a rattle consisting of a box with objects inside. **2** a rickety old vehicle etc.

rattler /ˈratlə/ *n.* **1** a thing that rattles, esp. an old or rickety vehicle. **2** *colloq.* a rattlesnake. **3** *Brit. slang* a remarkably good specimen of anything.

rattlesnake /ˈrat(ə)lsneɪk/ *n.* any of various poisonous American snakes of the family Viperidae, esp. of the genus *Crotalus* or *Sistrurus*, with a rattling structure of horny rings in its tail.

rattletrap /'rat(ə)ltrap/ *n. & adj. colloq.* ● *n.* a rickety old vehicle etc. ● *adj.* rickety.

rattling /'ratlɪŋ/ *adj. & adv.* ● *adj.* **1** that rattles. **2** brisk, vigorous (*a rattling pace*). ● *adv.* remarkably (*a rattling good story*).

ratty /'rati/ *adj.* (**rattier**, **rattiest**) **1** relating to or infested with rats. **2** *Brit. colloq.* irritable or angry. **3** *colloq.* wretched, shabby, nasty. □ **rattily** *adv.* **rattiness** *n.*

raucous /'rɔːkəs/ *adj.* harsh-sounding, loud and hoarse. □ **raucously** *adv.* **raucousness** *n.* [Latin *raucus*]

raunchy /'rɔːn(t)ʃi/ *adj.* (**raunchier**, **raunchiest**) *colloq.* **1** coarse, earthy, boisterous; sexually provocative. **2** esp. *US* slovenly, grubby. □ **raunchily** *adv.* **raunchiness** *n.* [20th c.: origin unknown]

ravage /'ravɪdʒ/ *v. & n.* ● *v.tr. & intr.* devastate, plunder. ● *n.* **1** the act or an instance of ravaging; devastation, damage. **2** (usu. in *pl.*; foll. by *of*) destructive effect (*survived the ravages of winter*). □ **ravager** *n.* [French *ravage(r)*, alteration of *ravine* 'rush of water']

rave[1] /reɪv/ *v. & n.* ● *v.* **1** *intr.* talk wildly or furiously in or as in delirium. **2** *intr.* (usu. foll. by *about, of, over*) speak with rapturous admiration; go into raptures. **3** *tr.* bring into a specified state by raving (*raved himself hoarse*). **4** *tr.* utter with ravings (*raved their grief*). **5** *intr.* (of the sea, wind, etc.) howl, roar. **6** *tr. & intr. colloq.* enjoy oneself freely (esp. *rave it up*). ● *n.* **1** (usu. *attrib.*) *colloq.* a highly enthusiastic review of a film, play, etc. (*a rave review*). **2** *Brit. slang* an infatuation. **3** *Brit. colloq.* **a** (also **rave-up**) a lively party. **b** a large often illicit party or event with dancing to loud fast pop music. **4** the sound of the wind etc. raving. [Middle English, probably from Old Northern French *raver*, related to (Middle) Low German *reven* 'be senseless, rave']

rave[2] /reɪv/ *n.* **1** a rail of a cart. **2** (in *pl.*) a permanent or removable framework added to the sides of a cart to increase its capacity. [variant of dialect *rathe* (Middle English, of unknown origin)]

ravel /'rav(ə)l/ *v. & n.* ● *v.* (**ravelled**, **ravelling**; *US* **raveled**, **raveling**) **1** *tr. & intr.* entangle or become entangled or knotted. **2** *tr.* confuse or complicate (a question or problem). **3** *intr.* fray out. **4** *tr.* (often foll. by *out*) disentangle, unravel, distinguish the separate threads or subdivisions of. ● *n.* **1** a tangle or knot. **2** a complication. **3** a frayed or loose end. [probably from Dutch *ravelen* 'tangle, fray out, unweave']

ravelin /'ravlɪn/ *n. hist.* an outwork of fortifications, with two faces forming a salient angle. [French from obsolete Italian *ravellino*, of unknown origin]

ravelling /'rav(ə)lɪŋ/ *n.* a thread from fabric which is frayed or unravelled.

raven[1] /'reɪv(ə)n/ *n. & adj.* ● *n.* a large glossy blue-black crow, *Corvus corax*, feeding chiefly on carrion etc. and having a hoarse cry. ● *adj.* glossy black (*raven tresses*). [Old English *hræfn*, from Germanic]

raven[2] /'rav(ə)n/ *v.* **1** *intr.* **a** plunder. **b** (foll. by *after*) seek prey or booty. **c** (foll. by *about*) go plundering. **d** prowl for prey (*ravening beast*). **2** **a** *tr.* devour voraciously. **b** *intr.* (esp. as **ravening** *adj.*) (occasionally foll. by *for*) have a ravenous appetite. **c** *intr.* (often foll. by *on*) feed voraciously. [Old French *raviner* 'ravage', ultimately from Latin *rapina* RAPINE]

ravenous /'rav(ə)nəs/ *adj.* **1** very hungry, famished. **2** (of hunger, eagerness, etc., or of an animal) voracious. **3** rapacious. □ **ravenously** *adv.* **ravenousness** *n.* [Middle English from Old French *ravineus* (as RAVEN[2])]

raver /'reɪvə/ *n.* **1** *colloq.* **a** an uninhibited pleasure-loving person. **b** a person who goes to raves. **2** a person who raves; a madman or madwoman.

rave-up var. of RAVE[1] *n.* 3a.

ravin /'ravɪn/ *n. poet.* or *literary* **1** robbery, plundering. **2** the seizing and devouring of prey. **3** prey. [Middle English via Old French *ravine* from Latin *rapina* RAPINE]

ravine /rə'viːn/ *n.* a deep narrow gorge or cleft. □ **ravined** *adj.* [French (as RAVIN)]

raving /'reɪvɪŋ/ *n., adj., & adv.* ● *n.* (usu. in *pl.*) wild or delirious talk. ● *adj.* delirious, frenzied. ● *adj. & adv. colloq.* as an intensive (*a raving beauty*; *raving mad*).

ravioli /ravɪ'əʊli/ *n.* small pasta envelopes containing minced meat etc. [Italian]

ravish /'ravɪʃ/ *v.tr.* **1** commit rape on. **2** enrapture; fill with delight. **3** *archaic* **a** carry off (a person or thing) by force. **b** (of death, circumstances, etc.) take from life or from sight. □ **ravisher** *n.* **ravishment** *n.* [Middle English from Old French *ravir*, ultimately from Latin *rapere* 'seize']

ravishing /'ravɪʃɪŋ/ *adj.* entrancing, delightful. □ **ravishingly** *adv.*

raw /rɔː/ *adj. & n.* ● *adj.* **1** (of food) uncooked. **2** in the natural state; not processed or manufactured (*raw sewage*). **3** (of alcoholic spirit) undiluted. **4** (of statistics etc.) not analysed or processed. **5** (of a person) inexperienced, untrained; new to an activity (*raw recruits*). **6** **a** stripped of skin; having the flesh exposed. **b** sensitive to the touch from having the flesh exposed. **c** abnormally sensitive (*touched a raw nerve*). **7** (of the atmosphere, day, etc.) chilly and damp. **8** crude in artistic quality; lacking finish. **9** (of the edge of cloth) without hem or selvedge. **10** (of silk) as reeled from cocoons. **11** (of grain) unmalted. ● *n.* a raw place on a person's or horse's body. □ **come the raw prawn** *Austral. slang* attempt to deceive. **in the raw** **1** in its natural state without mitigation (*life in the raw*). **2** naked. **touch on the raw** upset (a person) on a sensitive matter. □ **rawish** *adj.* **rawly** *adv.* **rawness** *n.* [Old English *hrēaw*, from Germanic]

raw-boned *adj.* gaunt and bony.

raw deal *n.* harsh or unfair treatment.

rawhide /'rɔːhʌɪd/ *n.* **1** untanned hide. **2** a rope or whip of this.

Rawlplug /'rɔːlplʌg/ *n. Brit. propr.* a thin cylinder of fibre or plastic for holding a screw or nail in masonry. [*Rawl*ings, name of the engineers who introduced it]

raw material *n.* that from which the process of manufacture makes products.

raw sienna *n.* a brownish-yellow ferruginous earth used as a pigment.

raw umber *n.* umber in its natural state, dark yellow in colour.

ray[1] /reɪ/ *n. & v.* ● *n.* **1** a single line or narrow beam of light from a small or distant source. **2** a straight line in which radiation travels to a given point. **3** (in *pl.*) radiation of a specified type (*gamma rays*; *X-rays*). **4** a trace or beginning of an enlightening or cheering influence (*a ray of hope*). **5** **a** any of a set of radiating lines or parts or things. **b** any of a set of straight lines passing through one point. **6** the marginal portion of a composite flower, e.g. a daisy. **7** **a** a radial division of a starfish. **b** each of a set of bones etc. supporting a fish's fin. ● *v.* **1** *intr.* (foll. by *forth, out*) (of light, thought, emotion, etc.) issue in or as if in rays. **2** *intr. & tr.* radiate. □ **rayed** *adj.* **rayless** *adj.* **raylet** *n.* [Middle English via Old French *rai* from Latin *radius*: see RADIUS]

ray[2] /reɪ/ *n.* a cartilaginous fish of the order Batiformes, with a broad flat body, winglike pectoral fins and a long slender tail. [Middle English via Old French *raie* from Latin *raia*]

ray[3] /reɪ/ *n.* (also **re**) *Mus.* **1** (in tonic sol-fa) the second note of a major scale. **2** the note D in the fixed-doh system. [Middle English *re* from Latin *resonare*: see GAMUT]

ray gun *n.* (esp. in science fiction) a gun causing injury or damage by the emission of rays.

rayon /'reɪɒn/ *n.* any of various textile fibres or fabrics made from viscose. [arbitrary formation from RAY[1]]

raze /reɪz/ *v.tr.* (also **rase**) **1** completely destroy; tear down (esp. *raze to the ground*). **2** erase; scratch out (esp. in abstract senses). [Middle English *rase* = wound slightly, from Old French *raser* 'shave close', ultimately from Latin *radere ras-* 'scrape']

razor /'reɪzə/ *n. & v.* ● *n.* an instrument with a sharp blade used in cutting hair esp. from the skin. ● *v.tr.* **1** use a razor on. **2** shave; cut down close. [Middle English from Old French *rasor* (as RAZE)]

razorback /'reɪzəbak/ *n.* an animal with a sharp ridged back, esp. a rorqual, or a semi-wild hog of the southern US.

razorbill /'reɪzəbɪl/ *n.* a black and white auk, *Alca torda*, with a deep bill likened to a cut-throat razor.

razor blade *n.* a blade used in a razor, esp. a flat piece of metal with a sharp edge or edges used in a safety razor.

razor cut *n. & v.* ● *n.* a haircut made with a razor. ● *v.tr.* cut (hair) using this method.

razor edge *n.* (also **razor's edge**) **1** a keen edge. **2** a sharp mountain ridge. **3** a critical situation (*found themselves on a razor edge*). **4** a sharp line of division. □ **razor-edged** *adj.*

razor-fish *n.* (*pl.* usu. same) = RAZOR-SHELL.

razor-sharp *adj.* extremely sharp.

razor-shell *n.* any of various bivalve molluscs of the superfamily Solenacea, with a shell like the handle of a cut-throat razor.

razor wire *n.* a type of sharp wire used as a barrier or run along the top of walls etc. to discourage intruders.

razz /raz/ *n. & v. US slang* ● *n.* = RASPBERRY 3. ● *v.tr.* tease, ridicule. [*razzberry*, corruption of RASPBERRY]

razzle-dazzle /'raz(ə)ldaz(ə)l/ *n.* (also **razzle**) *slang* **1 a** glamorous excitement; bustle. **b** a spree. **2** extravagant publicity. [reduplication of DAZZLE]

razzmatazz /razmə'taz/ *n.* (also **razzamatazz** /raz(ə)mə-/) *colloq.* **1** = RAZZLE-DAZZLE. **2** insincere actions; humbug. [probably alteration of RAZZLE-DAZZLE]

Rb *symb. Chem.* the element rubidium.

RC *abbr.* **1** Roman Catholic. **2** Red Cross. **3** reinforced concrete.

RCA *abbr.* **1** (in the UK) Royal College of Art. **2** (in the US) Radio Corporation of America.

RCM *abbr.* (in the UK) Royal College of Music.

RCMP *abbr.* Royal Canadian Mounted Police.

RCN *abbr.* (in the UK) Royal College of Nursing.

RCP *abbr.* (in the UK) Royal College of Physicians.

RCS *abbr.* (in the UK): **1** Royal College of Scientists. **2** Royal College of Surgeons. **3** Royal Corps of Signals.

RCVS *abbr.* (in the UK) Royal College of Veterinary Surgeons.

RD *abbr.* **1** *Brit.* refer to drawer. **2** (in the UK) Royal Naval Reserve Decoration.

Rd. *abbr.* Road (in names).

RDC *abbr. Brit. hist.* Rural District Council.

RDF *abbr.* radio direction-finder.

RDX *abbr.* a high explosive. [*R*esearch *D*epartment explosive]

RE *abbr.* **1** (in the UK) Royal Engineers. **2** religious education.

Re *symb. Chem.* the element rhenium.

re[1] /reɪ, riː/ *prep.* **1** in the matter of (as the first word in a heading, esp. of a legal document). **2** *colloq.* about, concerning. [Latin, ablative of *res* 'thing']

■ **Usage** The use of *re* in sense 2 to mean simply 'about' or 'concerning' is best avoided.

re[2] var. of RAY[3].

re- /riː, rɪ, rɛ/ *prefix* **1** attachable to almost any verb or its derivative, meaning: **a** once more; afresh, anew (*readjust*; *renumber*). **b** back; with return to a previous state (*reassemble*; *reverse*). **2** (also **red-** before a vowel, as in *redolent*) in verbs and verbal derivatives denoting: **a** in return; mutually (*react*; *resemble*). **b** opposition (*repel*; *resist*). **c** behind or after (*relic*; *remain*). **d** retirement or secrecy (*recluse*; *reticence*). **e** off, away, down (*recede*; *relegate*; *repress*). **f** frequentative or intensive force (*redouble*; *refine*; *resplendent*). **g** negative force (*recant*; *reveal*). [Latin *re-*, *red-* 'again, back', etc.]

■ **Usage** In sense 1, a hyphen is normally used when the word begins with *e* (*re-enact*), or to distinguish the compound from a more familiar one-word form (*re-form* = form again).

're *abbr. colloq.* (usu. after pronouns) are (*we're*; *you're*).

reabsorb /riːəb'zɔːb, -'sɔːb/ *v.tr.* absorb again. □ **reabsorption** *n.*

reaccept /riːək'sɛpt/ *v.tr.* accept again. □ **reacceptance** *n.*

reaccustom /riːə'kʌstəm/ *v.tr.* accustom again.

reach /riːtʃ/ *v. & n.* ● *v.* **1** *intr. & tr.* (often foll. by *out*) stretch out; extend. **2** *intr.* stretch out a limb, the hand, etc.; make a reaching motion or effort. **3** *intr.* (often foll. by *for*) make a motion or effort to touch or get hold of, or to attain (*reached for his pipe*). **4** *tr.* get as far as; arrive at (*reached Lincoln at lunchtime*; *your letter reached me today*). **5** *tr.* get to or attain (a specified point) on a scale (*the temperature reached 90°*; *the number of applications reached 100*). **6** *intr.* (foll. by *to*) attain to; be adequate for (*my income will not reach to it*). **7** *tr.* succeed in achieving; attain (*have reached agreement*). **8** *tr.* make contact with the hand etc., or by telephone etc. (*was out all day and could not be reached*). **9** *tr.* (of a broadcast, broadcasting station, etc.) be received by. **10** *tr.* succeed in influencing or having the required effect on (*could not manage to reach their audience*). **11** *tr.* hand, pass (*reach me that book*). **12** *tr.* take with an outstretched hand. **13** *intr. Naut.* sail with the wind abeam or abaft the beam. ● *n.* **1** the extent to which a hand etc. can be reached out, influence exerted, motion carried out, or mental powers used. **2** an act of reaching out. **3** a continuous extent, esp. a stretch of river between two bends, or the part of a canal between locks. **4** *Naut.* a distance traversed in reaching. **5** the number of people who watch a specified television channel or listen to a specified radio station at any time during a specified period. □ **out of reach** not able to be reached or attained. □ **reachable** *adj.* [Old English *rǣcan*, from West Germanic]

reach-me-down *adj. & n. Brit.* ● *adj.* **1** ready-made. **2** second-hand. ● *n.* a reach-me-down thing.

reacquaint /riːə'kweɪnt/ *v.tr. & refl.* (usu. foll. by *with*) make (a person or oneself) acquainted again. □ **reacquaintance** *n.*

reacquire /riːə'kwʌɪə/ *v.tr.* acquire anew. □ **reacquisition** /-ˌakwɪ'zɪʃ(ə)n/ *n.*

react /rɪ'akt/ *v.* **1** *intr.* (foll. by *to*) respond to a stimulus; undergo a change or show behaviour due to some influence (*how did they react to the news?*). **2** *intr.* (often foll. by *against*) be actuated by repulsion to; tend in a reverse or contrary direction. **3** *intr.* (often foll. by *upon*) produce a reciprocal or responsive effect; act upon the agent (*they react upon each other*). **4** *intr.* (foll. by *with*) *Chem. & Physics* (of a substance or particle) be the cause of activity or interaction with another (*nitrous oxide reacts with the metal*). **5** *tr.* (foll. by *with*) *Chem.* cause (a substance) to react with another. **6** *intr. Mil.* make a counter-attack. **7** *intr. Stock Exch.* (of shares) fall after rising. [RE- + ACT, or medieval Latin *reagere react-* (as RE-, Latin *agere* 'do, act')]

reactance /rɪ'akt(ə)ns/ *n. Electr.* a component of impedance in an AC circuit, due to capacitance or inductance or both.

reactant /rɪ'akt(ə)nt/ *n. Chem.* a substance that takes part in, and undergoes change during a reaction.

reaction /rɪ'akʃ(ə)n/ *n.* **1** the act or an instance of reacting; a responsive or reciprocal action. **2 a** a responsive feeling (*what was your reaction to the news?*). **b** an immediate or first impression. **3** the occurrence of a (physical or emotional) condition after a period of its opposite. **4 a** a bodily response to an external stimulus. **b** an adverse response to a drug. **5** a tendency to oppose change or to advocate return to a former system, esp. in politics. **6** the interaction of substances undergoing chemical change. **7** propulsion by emitting a jet of particles etc. in the direction opposite to that of the intended motion. □ **reactionist** *n.* & *adj.* [REACT + -ION, or medieval Latin *reactio* (as RE-, ACTION)]

reactionary /rɪˈakʃ(ə)n(ə)ri/ *adj.* & *n.* ● *adj.* tending to oppose (esp. political) change and advocate return to a former system. ● *n.* (*pl.* **-ies**) a reactionary person.

reactivate /rɪˈaktɪveɪt/ *v.tr.* restore to a state of activity; bring into action again. □ **reactivation** /-ˈveɪʃ(ə)n/ *n.*

reactive /rɪˈaktɪv/ *adj.* **1** showing reaction. **2** reacting rather than taking the initiative. **3** having a tendency to react chemically. **4** of or relating to reactance. □ **reactivity** /-ˈtɪvɪti/ *n.*

reactor /rɪˈaktə/ *n.* **1** a person or thing that reacts. **2** (in full **nuclear reactor**) an apparatus or structure in which a controlled nuclear chain reaction releases energy. **3** *Electr.* a component used to provide reactance, esp. an inductor. **4** an apparatus for the chemical reaction of substances. **5** *Med.* a person who has a reaction to a drug etc.

read /riːd/ *v.* & *n.* ● *v.* (*past* and *past part.* **read** /rɛd/) **1** *tr.* (also *absol.*) reproduce mentally or (often foll. by *aloud, out, off,* etc.) vocally the written or printed words of (a book, author, etc.) by following the symbols with the eyes or by feeling embossed symbols with the fingers. **2** *tr.* convert or be able to convert into the intended words or meaning (written or other symbols or the things expressed in this way). **3** *tr.* interpret mentally. **4** *tr.* deduce or declare an (esp. accurate) interpretation of (*read the expression on my face*). **5** *tr.* (often foll. by *that* + clause) find (a thing) recorded or stated in print etc. (*I read somewhere that you are leaving*). **6** *tr.* interpret (a statement or action) in a certain sense (*my silence is not to be read as consent*). **7** *tr.* (often foll. by *into*) assume as intended or deducible from a writer's words; find (implications) (*you read too much into my letter*). **8** *tr.* bring into a specified state by reading (*read myself to sleep*). **9 a** *tr.* (of a meter or other recording instrument) show (a specified figure etc.) (*the thermometer reads 20°*). **b** inspect and record elsewhere the figure shown on such an instrument (*read the meter*). **10** *intr.* convey meaning in a specified manner when read (*it reads persuasively*). **11** *intr.* sound or affect a hearer or reader as specified when read (*the book reads like a parody*). **12 a** *tr.* esp. *Brit.* study by reading (esp. a subject at university). **b** *intr.* carry out a course of study by reading (*is reading for the Bar*). **13** *tr.* (as **read** /rɛd/ *adj.*) versed in a subject (esp. literature) by reading (*a well-read person; was widely read in law*). **14** *tr.* **a** (of a computer) copy or transfer (data). **b** (foll. by *in, out*) enter or extract (data) in an electronic storage device. **15** *tr.* receive and understand the words of (a person) by radio or telephone (*do you read me?*). **16** *tr.* **a** understand (a person) by interpretation of outward signs etc. **b** interpret (cards, a person's hand, etc.) as a fortune-teller. **c** interpret (the sky) as an astrologer or meteorologist. **17** *tr. Printing* check the correctness of and emend (a proof). **18** *tr.* **a** (of a text) have at a particular place (*reads 'battery' not 'buttery'*). **b** substitute (a word etc.) for an incorrect one (*for 'illitterate' read 'illiterate'*). ● *n.* **1** esp. *Brit.* a spell of reading. **2** *colloq.* a book etc. as regards its readability (*is a really good read*). □ **read between the lines** look for or find hidden meaning (in a document etc.). **read a person like a book** have clear insight into a person's motives etc. **read out 1** read aloud. **2** (often foll. by *of*) *US* expel from a political party etc. **read up** (often foll. by *on*) make a special study of (a subject). [Old English *rǣdan* 'advise, consider, discern', from Germanic]

readable /ˈriːdəb(ə)l/ *adj.* **1** able to be read; legible. **2** interesting or pleasant to read. □ **readability** /-ˈbɪlɪti/ *n.* **readableness** *n.* **readably** *adv.*

readapt /riːəˈdapt/ *v.intr.* & *tr.* become or cause to become adapted anew. □ **readaptation** /riːˌadapˈteɪʃ(ə)n/ *n.*

readdress /riːəˈdrɛs/ *v.tr.* **1** change the address of (a letter or parcel). **2** address (a problem etc.) anew. **3** speak or write to anew.

reader /ˈriːdə/ *n.* **1** a person who reads or is reading. **2** a book of extracts for learning, esp. a language. **3** a device for producing an image that can be read from microfilm etc. **4** (also **Reader**) *Brit.* a university lecturer of the highest grade below professor. **5** a publisher's employee who reports on submitted manuscripts. **6** a printer's proof-corrector. **7** a person appointed to read aloud, esp. parts of a service in a church. **8** a person entitled to use a particular library. □ **readerly** *adj.* [Old English (as READ)]

readership /ˈriːdəʃɪp/ *n.* **1** the readers of a newspaper etc. **2** the number or extent of these. **3** (also **Readership**) *Brit.* the position of Reader.

readily /ˈrɛdɪli/ *adv.* **1** without showing reluctance; willingly. **2** without difficulty.

read-in *n.* the entry of data in an electronic storage device.

reading /ˈriːdɪŋ/ *n.* **1 a** the act or an instance of reading or perusing (*the reading of the will*). **b** matter to be read (*have plenty of reading with me*). **c** the specified quality of this (*it made exciting reading*). **2** (in *comb.*) used for reading (*reading-lamp; reading-room*). **3** literary knowledge (*a person of wide reading*). **4** an entertainment at which a play, poems, etc., are read (*poetry reading*). **5** a figure etc. shown by a meter or other recording instrument. **6** an interpretation or view taken (*what is your reading of the facts?*). **7** an interpretation made (of drama, music, etc.). **8** each of the successive occasions on which a bill must be presented to a legislature for acceptance (see also FIRST READING, SECOND READING, THIRD READING). **9** the version of a text, or the particular wording, conjectured or given by an editor etc. [Old English (as READ)]

reading age *n.* reading ability expressed as the age for which the same ability is calculated as average (*has a reading age of eight*).

readjust /riːəˈdʒʌst/ *v.tr.* adjust again or to a former state. □ **readjustment** *n.*

readmit /riːədˈmɪt/ *v.tr.* (**readmitted**, **readmitting**) admit again. □ **readmission** /-ˈmɪʃ(ə)n/ *n.*

read-only memory *n. Computing* a memory read at high speed but not capable of being changed by program instructions.

readopt /riːəˈdɒpt/ *v.tr.* adopt again. □ **readoption** *n.*

read-out *n.* **1** a record or display of the output from a computer or scientific instrument. **2** the transfer or display of data from a computer etc.

re-advertise /riːˈadvətʌɪz/ *v.tr.* & *intr.* advertise again. □ **re-advertisement** /riːədˈvəːtɪzm(ə)nt/ *n.*

read-write *adj. Computing* capable of reading existing data and accepting alterations or further input (cf. READ-ONLY MEMORY).

ready /ˈrɛdi/ *adj., adv., n.,* & *v.* ● *adj.* (**readier**, **readiest**) (usu. *predic.*) **1** with preparations complete (*dinner is ready*). **2** in an appropriate state (*are you ready to go?*). **3** willing, inclined, or resolved (*he is always ready to complain; I am ready for anything*). **4** within reach; easily secured (*a ready source of income*). **5** fit for immediate use (*was ready to hand*). **6** immediate, unqualified (*found ready acceptance*). **7** prompt, quick, facile (*is always ready with excuses; has a ready wit*). **8** (foll. by *to* + infin.) about to do something (*a bud just ready to burst*). **9** provided beforehand. ● *adv.* esp. *Brit.* **1** beforehand. **2** so as not to require doing when the time comes for use (*the cases are ready packed*). ● *n.* (*pl.* **-ies**) esp. *Brit. slang* **1** (prec. by *the*) = READY MONEY. **2** (in *pl.*) bank notes. ● *v.tr.* (**-ies, -ied**) make ready; prepare. □ **at the ready** ready for action. **make ready** prepare. **ready, steady** (or **get set**), **go** the usual formula for starting a race.

□ **readiness** *n.* [Middle English *rædi(g)*, *re(a)di*, via Old English *rǣde* from Germanic]

ready-made *adj.* (esp. of clothes) made in a standard size, not to measure.

ready-mixed *adj.* (also **ready-mix**) (of concrete, paint, food, etc.) having some or all of the constituents already mixed together.

ready money *n.* **1** actual coin or notes. **2** payment on the spot.

ready reckoner *n.* a book or table listing standard numerical calculations as used esp. in commerce.

ready-to-wear *adj.* (of clothes) made in a standard size, not to measure.

reaffirm /riːəˈfəːm/ *v.tr.* affirm again. □ **reaffirmation** /-ˌafəˈmeɪʃ(ə)n/ *n.*

reafforest /riːəˈfɒrɪst/ *v.tr.* esp. *Brit.* replant (former forest land) with trees. □ **reafforestation** /-ˈsteɪʃ(ə)n/ *n.*

reagency /rɪˈeɪdʒ(ə)nsi/ *n.* reactive power or operation.

reagent /rɪˈeɪdʒ(ə)nt/ *n. Chem.* **1** a substance used to cause a reaction, esp. to detect another substance. **2** a reactive substance or force. [RE- + AGENT: cf. REACT]

real[1] /riːl/ *adj. & adv.* ● *adj.* **1** actually existing as a thing or occurring in fact. **2** genuine; rightly so called; not artificial or merely apparent. **3** *Law* consisting of or relating to immovable property such as land or houses (*real estate*) (cf. PERSONAL PROPERTY). **4** appraised by purchasing power; adjusted for changes in the value of money (*real value*; *income in real terms*). **5** *Philos.* having an absolute and necessary and not merely contingent existence. **6** *Math.* (of a quantity) having no imaginary part (see IMAGINARY 2). **7** *Optics* (of an image etc.) such that light actually passes through it. ● *adv. Sc. & N. Amer. colloq.* really, very. □ **for real** *colloq.* as a serious or actual concern; in earnest. **the real McCoy** see McCOY. **the real thing 1** not illusory, simulated, or inferior. **2** true love, not infatuation. □ **realness** *n.* [Anglo-French = Old French *reel*, Late Latin *realis*, from Latin *res* 'thing']

real[2] /reɪˈɑːl/ *n.* **1** the chief monetary unit of Brazil since 1994. **2** *hist.* a former coin and monetary unit of various Spanish-speaking countries. [Spanish *real* ROYAL, used as a noun]

real ale *n.* esp. *Brit.* beer regarded as brewed in a traditional way, with secondary fermentation in the cask.

realgar /rɪˈalgə/ *n.* a mineral of arsenic sulphide used as a pigment and in fireworks. Also called *red arsenic*. [Middle English via medieval Latin from Arabic *rahj al-ġār* 'dust of the cave']

realign /riːəˈlaɪn/ *v.tr.* **1** align again. **2** regroup in politics etc. □ **realignment** *n.*

realism /ˈrɪəlɪz(ə)m/ *n.* **1** the practice of regarding things in their true nature and dealing with them as they are. **2** fidelity to nature in representation; the showing of life etc. as it is in fact. **3** *Philos.* **a** the doctrine that universals or abstract concepts have an objective existence (opp. NOMINALISM). **b** the belief that matter as an object of perception has real existence. □ **realist** *n.*

realistic /rɪəˈlɪstɪk/ *adj.* **1** regarding things as they are; following a policy of realism. **2** based on facts rather than ideals. □ **realistically** *adv.*

reality /rɪˈalɪti/ *n.* (*pl.* **-ies**) **1** what is real or existent or underlies appearances. **2** (foll. by *of*) the real nature of (a thing). **3** real existence; the state of being real. **4** resemblance to an original (*the model was impressive in its reality*). □ **in reality** in fact. [medieval Latin *realitas* or French *réalité* (as REAL[1])]

realize /ˈrɪəlaɪz/ *v.tr.* (also **-ise**) **1** (often foll. by *that* + clause; also *absol.*) be fully aware of; conceive as real. **2** (also *absol.*) understand clearly. **3** present as real; make realistic; give apparent reality to (*the story was powerfully realized on stage*). **4 a** convert into actuality; achieve (*realized a childhood dream*). **b** *refl.* develop one's own faculties, abilities, etc. **5 a** convert into money. **b** acquire (profit). **c** be sold for (a specified price). **6** *Mus.* reconstruct (a part) in full from a figured bass. □ **realizable** *adj.* **realizability** /-ˈbɪlɪti/ *n.* **realization** /-ˈzeɪʃ(ə)n/ *n.* **realizer** *n.*

real life *n.* **1** that lived by actual people, as distinct from fiction, drama, etc. **2** (**real-life**) (*attrib.*) actual, not fictional (*real-life husband*).

real live *attrib.adj.* often *joc.* actual; not pretended or simulated (*a real live burglar*).

reallocate /riːˈaləkeɪt/ *v.tr.* allocate again or differently. □ **reallocation** /-ˈkeɪʃ(ə)n/ *n.*

reallot /riːəˈlɒt/ *v.tr.* (**reallotted**, **reallotting**) allot again or differently. □ **reallotment** *n.*

really /ˈrɪəli/ *adv.* **1** in reality; in fact. **2** positively, assuredly (*really useful*). **3** (as a strong affirmative) indeed, I assure you. **4** an expression of mild protest or surprise. **5** (in *interrog.*) (expressing disbelief) is that so? (*They're musicians. — Really?*).

realm /rɛlm/ *n.* **1** *formal* esp. *Law* a kingdom. **2** a sphere or domain (*the realm of imagination*). [Middle English via Old French *realme*, *reaume* from Latin *regimen -minis* (see REGIMEN): influenced by Old French *reiel* ROYAL]

real money *n.* **1** current coin or notes; cash. **2** *colloq.* a large sum of money.

realpolitik /reɪˈɑːlpɒlɪtiːk/ *n.* politics based on realities and material needs, rather than on morals or ideals. [German]

real tennis *n. Brit.* the original form of tennis played on an indoor court.

real time *n.* **1** the actual time during which a process or event occurs. **2** (**real-time**) (*attrib.*) *Computing* **a** (of a system) in which input data is processed within milliseconds so that it is available virtually immediately as feedback to the process from which it is coming, e.g. in a missile-guidance or an airline booking system. **b** (of information, an image, etc.) responding virtually immediately to changes in the state of affairs it reflects (*real-time stock-exchange prices*).

realtor /ˈrɪəltə/ *n. N. Amer.* a real-estate agent, esp. (**Realtor** *propr.*) a member of the National Association of Realtors.

realty /ˈrɪəlti/ *n. Law* real estate (opp. PERSONALTY).

ream[1] /riːm/ *n.* **1** twenty quires or 500 (formerly 480) sheets of paper (or a larger number, to allow for waste). **2** (in *pl.*) a large quantity of paper or writing (*wrote reams about it*). [Middle English *rēm*, *rīm* from Old French *raime* etc., ultimately from Arabic *rizma* 'bundle']

ream[2] /riːm/ *v.tr.* **1** widen (a hole in metal etc.) with a borer. **2** *Naut.* open (a seam) for caulking. **3** *US* squeeze the juice from (fruit). □ **reamer** *n.* [18th c.: origin uncertain]

reanimate /riːˈanɪmeɪt/ *v.tr.* **1** restore to life. **2** restore to activity or liveliness. □ **reanimation** /-ˈmeɪʃ(ə)n/ *n.*

reap /riːp/ *v.tr.* **1** cut or gather (a crop, esp. grain) as a harvest. **2** harvest the crop of (a field etc.). **3** receive as the consequence of one's own or others' actions. [Old English *ripan*, *reopan*, of unknown origin]

reaper /ˈriːpə/ *n.* **1** a person who reaps. **2** a machine for reaping. □ **the Reaper** (or **Grim Reaper**) death personified.

reappear /riːəˈpɪə/ *v.intr.* appear again or as previously. □ **reappearance** *n.*

reapply /riːəˈplaɪ/ *v.tr. & intr.* (**-ies**, **-ied**) apply again, esp. submit a further application (for a position etc.). □ **reapplication** /ˌriːaplɪˈkeɪʃ(ə)n/ *n.*

reappoint /riːəˈpɔɪnt/ *v.tr.* appoint again to a position previously held. □ **reappointment** *n.*

reapportion /riːəˈpɔːʃ(ə)n/ *v.tr.* apportion again or differently. □ **reapportionment** *n.*

reappraise /riːəˈpreɪz/ *v.tr.* appraise or assess again. □ **reappraisal** *n.*

rear[1] /rɪə/ *n. & adj.* ● *n.* **1** the back part of anything. **2** the space behind, or position at the back of, anything (*a large house with a terrace at the rear*). **3** the hindmost part of an army or fleet. **4** *colloq.* the buttocks. ● *adj.* at the back. □ **bring up the rear** come last. **in the rear** behind; at the back. **take in the rear** *Mil.* attack from behind. [probably from (*in the*) REARWARD or REARGUARD]

rear[2] /rɪə/ *v.* **1** *tr.* **a** bring up and educate (children). **b** breed and care for (animals). **c** cultivate (crops). **2** *intr.* (of a horse etc.) raise itself on its hind legs. **3** *tr.* **a** set upright. **b** build. **c** hold upwards (*rear one's head*). **4** *intr.* extend to a great height. □ **rearer** *n.* [Old English *rǣran*, from Germanic]

rear admiral *n.* a naval officer ranking below vice admiral.

rear commodore *n.* a yacht club officer below vice commodore.

rearguard /ˈrɪəɡɑːd/ *n.* **1** a body of troops detached to protect the rear, esp. in retreats. **2** a defensive or conservative element in an organization etc. [Old French *rereguarde* (as RETRO-, GUARD)]

rearguard action *n.* **1** *Mil.* an engagement undertaken by a rearguard. **2** a defensive stand in argument etc., esp. when losing.

rear lamp *n.* (also **rear light**) esp. *Brit.* a usu. red light at the rear of a vehicle.

rearm /riːˈɑːm/ *v.tr.* (also *absol.*) arm again, esp. with improved weapons. □ **rearmament** *n.*

rearmost /ˈrɪəməʊst/ *adj.* furthest back.

rearrange /riːəˈreɪn(d)ʒ/ *v.tr.* arrange again in a different way. □ **rearrangement** *n.*

rearrest /riːəˈrɛst/ *v.* & *n.* ● *v.tr.* arrest again. ● *n.* an instance of rearresting or being rearrested.

rear sight *n.* the sight nearest to the stock on a firearm.

rear-view mirror *n.* a mirror fixed inside the windscreen of a motor vehicle enabling the driver to see traffic etc. behind.

rearward /ˈrɪəwəd/ *n., adj.,* & *adv.* ● *n.* (esp. in prepositional phrases) rear (*to the rearward of*; *in the rearward*). ● *adj.* to the rear. ● *adv.* (also **rearwards**) towards the rear. [Anglo-French *rerewarde* = REARGUARD]

rear-wheel drive *n.* drive acting on the rear wheels of a motor vehicle (see DRIVE *n.* 6a).

reascend /riːəˈsɛnd/ *v.tr.* & *intr.* ascend again or to a former position. □ **reascension** *n.*

reason /ˈriːz(ə)n/ *n.* & *v.* ● *n.* **1** a motive, cause, or justification (*has good reasons for doing this*; *there is no reason to be angry*). **2** a fact adduced or serving as this (*I can give you my reasons*). **3** the intellectual faculty by which conclusions are drawn from premisses. **4** sanity (*has lost his reason*). **5** *Logic* a premiss of a syllogism, esp. a minor premiss when given after the conclusion. **6** a faculty transcending the understanding and providing a priori principles; intuition. **7** sense; sensible conduct; what is right or practical or practicable; moderation. ● *v.* **1** *intr.* form or try to reach conclusions by connected thought. **2** *intr.* (foll. by *with*) use an argument (with a person) by way of persuasion. **3** *tr.* (foll. by *that* + clause) conclude or assert in argument. **4** *tr.* (foll. by *why, whether, what* + clause) discuss; ask oneself. **5** *tr.* (foll. by *into, out of*) persuade or move by argument (*I reasoned them out of their fears*). **6** *tr.* (foll. by *out*) think or work out (consequences etc.). **7** *tr.* (often as **reasoned** *adj.*) express in logical or argumentative form. **8** *tr.* embody reason in (an amendment etc.). □ **by reason of** owing to. **in** (or **within**) **reason** within the bounds of sense or moderation. **it stands to reason** (often foll. by *that* + clause) it is evident or logical. **listen to reason** be persuaded to act sensibly. **see reason** acknowledge the force of an argument. **with reason** justifiably. □ **reasoner** *n.* **reasoning** *n.* **reasonless** *adj.* [Middle English from Old French *reisun, res(o)un, raisoner*, ultimately via Latin *ratio -onis* from *rēri rat-* 'consider']

■ **Usage** *The reason* (*why*) ... *is* ... should be followed by *that*, not *because*, e.g. *The reason why I can't stay any longer is that I have an urgent appointment.*

reasonable /ˈriːz(ə)nəb(ə)l/ *adj.* **1** having sound judgement; moderate; ready to listen to reason. **2** in accordance with reason; not absurd. **3 a** within the limits of reason; not greatly less or more than might be expected. **b** inexpensive; not extortionate. **c** tolerable, fair. **4** *archaic* endowed with the faculty of reason. □ **reasonableness** *n.* **reasonably** *adv.* [Middle English from Old French *raisonable* (as REASON), suggested by Latin *rationabilis*]

reassemble /riːəˈsɛmb(ə)l/ *v.intr.* & *tr.* assemble again or into a former state. □ **reassembly** *n.*

reassert /riːəˈsəːt/ *v.tr.* assert again. □ **reassertion** *n.*

reassess /riːəˈsɛs/ *v.tr.* assess again, esp. differently. □ **reassessment** *n.*

reassign /riːəˈsʌɪn/ *v.tr.* assign again or differently. □ **reassignment** *n.*

reassume /riːəˈsjuːm/ *v.tr.* take on oneself or undertake again. □ **reassumption** /-ˈsʌm(p)ʃ(ə)n/ *n.*

reassure /riːəˈʃʊə/ *v.tr.* **1** restore confidence to; dispel the apprehensions of. **2** confirm in an opinion or impression. □ **reassurance** *n.* **reassuring** *adj.* **reassuringly** *adv.*

reattach /riːəˈtatʃ/ *v.tr.* attach again or in a former position. □ **reattachment** *n.*

reattain /riːəˈteɪn/ *v.tr.* attain again. □ **reattainment** *n.*

reattempt /riːəˈtɛm(p)t/ *v.tr.* attempt again, esp. after failure.

Réaumur /ˈreɪə(ʊ)mjʊə/ *adj.* & *n.* ● *adj.* expressed in or related to the scale of temperature at which water freezes at 0° and boils at 80° under standard conditions. ● *n.* (in full **Réaumur's scale**) this scale. [named after R. de *Réaumur*, French physicist d. 1757]

reave /riːv/ *v.* (*past* and *past part.* **reft** /rɛft/) *archaic* **1** *tr.* **a** (foll. by *of*) forcibly deprive of. **b** (foll. by *away, from*) take by force or carry off. **2** *intr.* make raids; plunder; = REIVE. [Old English *rēafian* from Germanic: related to ROB]

reawaken /riːəˈweɪk(ə)n/ *v.tr.* & *intr.* awaken again.

rebadge /riːˈbadʒ/ *v.tr.* relaunch (a product etc.) under a different name, logo, etc.

rebarbative /rɪˈbɑːbətɪv/ *adj. literary* repellent, unattractive. [French *rébarbatif -ive* from *barbe* 'beard']

rebase /riːˈbeɪs/ *v.tr.* establish a new base level for (a price index etc.).

rebate[1] /ˈriːbeɪt/ *n.* & *v.* ● *n.* **1** a partial refund of money paid. **2** a deduction from a sum to be paid; a discount. ● *v.tr.* pay back as a rebate. □ **rebatable** *adj.* [earlier = diminish: Middle English from Old French *rabattre* (as RE-, ABATE)]

rebate[2] /ˈriːbeɪt/ *n.* & *v.tr.* = RABBET. [respelling of RABBET, after REBATE[1]]

rebec /ˈriːbɛk/ *n.* (also **rebeck**) *Mus.* a medieval usu. three-stringed instrument played with a bow. [French *rebec*, variant of Old French *rebebe rubebe*, from Arabic *rabāb*]

rebel *n., adj.,* & *v.* ● *n.* /ˈrɛb(ə)l/ **1** a person who fights against, resists, or refuses allegiance to, the established government. **2** a person or thing that resists authority or control. ● *adj.* /ˈrɛb(ə)l/ (*attrib.*) **1** rebellious. **2** of or concerning rebels. **3** in rebellion. ● *v.intr.* /rɪˈbɛl/ (**rebelled, rebelling**) (usu. foll. by *against*) **1** act as a rebel; revolt. **2** feel or display repugnance. [Middle English via Old French *rebelle, rebeller* from Latin *rebellis* (as RE-, *bellum* 'war')]

rebellion /rɪˈbɛljən/ *n.* **1** open resistance to authority, esp. organized armed resistance to an established government. **2** an instance of this. [Middle English via Old French from Latin *rebellio -onis* (as REBEL)]

rebellious /rɪˈbɛljəs/ *adj.* **1** tending to rebel, insubordinate. **2** in rebellion. **3** defying lawful authority. **4** (of a thing) unmanageable, refractory. □ **rebelliously** *adv.* **rebelliousness** *n.* [Middle English from REBELLION + -OUS, or from earlier *rebellous* + -IOUS]

rebid /ˈriːbɪd/ *v.* & *n.* ● *v.* /also riːˈbɪd/ (**rebidding**; *past* and *past part.* **rebid**) **1** *intr.* bid again. **2** *tr. Cards* bid (a suit) again at a higher level. ● *n.* **1** the act of rebidding. **2** a bid made in this way.

rebind /riːˈbʌɪnd/ *v.tr.* (*past* and *past part.* **rebound**) bind (esp. a book) again or differently.

rebirth /riːˈbəːθ/ *n.* **1** a new incarnation. **2** spiritual enlightenment. **3** a revival (*the rebirth of learning*). □ **reborn** /riːˈbɔːn/ *adj.*

rebirthing /riːˈbəːθɪŋ/ *n.* a treatment for neurosis involving controlled breathing intended to simulate the trauma of being born. □ **rebirther** *n.*

reboot /riːˈbuːt/ *v.* & *n.* *Computing* ● *v.tr.* (often *absol.*) boot up (a system) again. ● *n.* an act or instance of rebooting.

rebore *v.* & *n.* ● *v.tr.* /riːˈbɔː/ make a new boring in, esp. widen the bore of (the cylinder in an internal-combustion engine). ● *n.* /ˈriːbɔː/ **1** the process of doing this. **2** a rebored engine.

rebound[1] *v.* & *n.* ● *v.intr.* /rɪˈbaʊnd/ **1** spring back after action or impact. **2** (foll. by *on*, *upon*) (of an action) have an adverse effect upon (the doer). ● *n.* /ˈriːbaʊnd/ **1** the act or an instance of rebounding; recoil. **2** a reaction after a strong emotion. □ **on the rebound** while still recovering from an emotional shock, esp. rejection by a lover. [Middle English from Old French *rebonder*, *rebondir* (as RE-, BOUND[1])]

rebound[2] *past* and *past part.* of REBIND.

rebounder /riːˈbaʊndə/ *n.* a small circular trampoline used for exercising.

rebroadcast /riːˈbrɔːdkɑːst/ *v.* & *n.* ● *v.tr.* (*past* **rebroadcast** or **rebroadcasted**; *past part.* **rebroadcast**) broadcast again. ● *n.* a repeat broadcast.

rebuff /rɪˈbʌf/ *n.* & *v.* ● *n.* **1** a rejection of a person who makes advances, proffers help or sympathy, shows interest or curiosity, makes a request, etc. **2** a repulse; a snub. ● *v.tr.* give a rebuff to. [obsolete French *rebuffe(r)* from Italian *ribuffo*, *ribuffare*, *rabbuffo*, *rabbuffare* (as RE-, *buffo* 'puff')]

rebuild /riːˈbɪld/ *v.tr.* (*past* and *past part.* **rebuilt**) build again or differently. □ **rebuilder** *n.*

rebuke /rɪˈbjuːk/ *v.* & *n.* ● *v.tr.* reprove sharply; subject to protest or censure. ● *n.* **1** the act of rebuking. **2** the process of being rebuked. **3** a reproof. □ **rebuker** *n.* **rebukingly** *adv.* [Middle English from Anglo-French & Old Northern French *rebuker* (as RE-, Old French *buchier* 'beat', originally 'cut down wood', from *busche* 'log')]

rebury /riːˈbɛri/ *v.tr.* (**-ies**, **-ied**) bury again. □ **reburial** *n.*

rebus /ˈriːbəs/ *n.* (*pl.* **rebuses**) **1** an enigmatic representation of a word (esp. a name), by pictures etc. suggesting its parts. **2** *Heraldry* a device suggesting the name of its bearer. [French *rébus* from Latin *rebus*, ablative pl. of *res* 'thing']

rebut /rɪˈbʌt/ *v.tr.* (**rebutted**, **rebutting**) **1** refute or disprove (evidence or a charge). **2** force or turn back; check. □ **rebutment** *n.* **rebuttable** *adj.* **rebuttal** *n.* [Middle English from Anglo-French *rebuter*, Old French *rebo(u)ter* (as RE-, BUTT[1])]

rebutter /rɪˈbʌtə/ *n.* **1** a refutation. **2** *Law* a defendant's reply to the plaintiff's surrejoinder. [Anglo-French *rebuter* (as REBUT)]

rec /rɛk/ *n. colloq.* recreation ground. [abbreviation]

recalcitrant /rɪˈkalsɪtr(ə)nt/ *adj.* & *n.* ● *adj.* **1** obstinately disobedient. **2** objecting to restraint. ● *n.* a recalcitrant person. □ **recalcitrance** *n.* **recalcitrantly** *adv.* [Latin *recalcitrare* (as RE-, *calcitrare* 'kick out with the heels' from *calx calcis* 'heel')]

recalculate /riːˈkalkjʊleɪt/ *v.tr.* calculate again. □ **recalculation** /-ˈleɪʃ(ə)n/ *n.*

recalescence /riːkəˈlɛs(ə)ns/ *n.* a temporary rise in temperature during cooling of a metal, caused by a change in crystal structure. □ **recalescent** *adj.* [Latin *recalescere* (as RE-, *calescere* 'grow hot')]

recall /rɪˈkɔːl/ *v.* & *n.* ● *v.tr.* **1** summon to return from a place, activity, state of inattention, a digression, etc. **2** recollect, remember. **3** bring back to memory; serve as a reminder of. **4** revoke or annul (an action or decision). **5** cancel or suspend the appointment of (an official sent overseas etc.). **6** revive, resuscitate. **7** take back (a gift). ● *n.* /also ˈriːkɔːl/ **1** the act or an instance of recalling, esp. a summons to come back. **2** the act of remembering. **3** the ability to remember. **4** the possibility of recalling, esp. in the sense of revoking (*beyond recall*). **5** *US* removal of an elected official from office. **6** a request for the return of a faulty product. □ **recallable** *adj.*

recant /rɪˈkant/ *v.* **1** *tr.* withdraw and renounce (a former belief or statement) as erroneous or heretical. **2** *intr.* disavow a former opinion, esp. with a public confession of error. □ **recantation** /ˌriːkanˈteɪʃ(ə)n/ *n.* **recanter** *n.* [Latin *recantare* 'revoke' (as RE-, *cantare* 'sing, chant')]

recap /ˈriːkap/ *v.* & *n. colloq.* ● *v.tr.* & *intr.* (**recapped**, **recapping**) recapitulate. ● *n.* recapitulation. [abbreviation]

recapitalize /riːˈkapɪt(ə)lʌɪz/ *v.tr.* (also **-ise**) capitalize (shares etc.) again. □ **recapitalization** /-ˈzeɪʃ(ə)n/ *n.*

recapitulate /riːkəˈpɪtjʊleɪt/ *v.tr.* **1** go briefly through again; summarize. **2** go over the main points or headings of. □ **recapitulative** /-lətɪv/ *adj.* **recapitulatory** /-lət(ə)ri/ *adj.* [Latin *recapitulare* (as RE-, *capitulum* CHAPTER)]

recapitulation /ˌriːkəpɪtjʊˈleɪʃ(ə)n/ *n.* **1** the act or an instance of recapitulating. **2** *Biol.* the appearance during embryonic development of successive forms resembling those of the organism's evolutionary predecessors. **3** *Mus.* part of a movement, esp. in sonata form, in which themes from the exposition are restated. [Middle English from Old French *recapitulation* or Late Latin *recapitulatio* (as RECAPITULATE)]

recapture /riːˈkaptʃə/ *v.* & *n.* ● *v.tr.* **1** capture again; recover by capture. **2** re-experience (a past emotion etc.). ● *n.* the act or an instance of recapturing.

recast /riːˈkɑːst/ *v.* & *n.* ● *v.tr.* (*past* and *past part.* **recast**) **1** put into a new form. **2** improve the arrangement of. **3** change the cast of (a play etc.). ● *n.* **1** the act or an instance of recasting. **2** a recast form.

recce /ˈrɛki/ *n.* & *v.* esp. *Brit. colloq.* ● *n.* a reconnaissance. ● *v.tr.* & *intr.* (**recced**, **recceing**) reconnoitre. [abbreviation]

recd. *abbr.* received.

recede /rɪˈsiːd/ *v.intr.* **1** go or shrink back or further off. **2** be left at an increasing distance by an observer's motion. **3** slope backwards (*a receding chin*). **4** decline in force or value. **5** (foll. by *from*) withdraw from (an engagement, opinion, etc.). **6** (of a man's hair) cease to grow at the front, sides, etc. [Middle English from Latin *recedere* (as RE-, *cedere cess-* 'go')]

re-cede /riːˈsiːd/ *v.tr.* cede back to a former owner.

receipt /rɪˈsiːt/ *n.* & *v.* ● *n.* **1** the act or an instance of receiving or being received into one's possession (*will pay on receipt of the goods*). **2** a written acknowledgement of this, esp. of the payment of money. **3** (usu. in *pl.*) an amount of money etc. received. **4** *archaic* a recipe. ● *v.tr.* place a written or printed receipt on (a bill). □ **in receipt of** having received. [Middle English *receit(e)* via Anglo-French & Old Northern French *receite*, Old French *reçoite*, *recete* from medieval Latin *recepta*, fem. past part. of Latin *recipere* RECEIVE: *-p-* inserted in imitation of the Latin]

receive /rɪˈsiːv/ *v.tr.* **1** take or accept (something offered or given) into one's hands or possession. **2** acquire; be provided with or given (*have received no news*; *will receive a small fee*). **3** accept delivery of (something sent). **4** have conferred or inflicted on one (*received many honours*; *received a heavy blow on the head*). **5 a** stand the force or weight of. **b** bear up against; encounter with opposition. **6** consent to hear (a confession or oath) or consider (a petition). **7** (also *absol.*) accept or have dealings with (stolen property), knowing of the theft. **8** admit; consent or prove able to hold; provide accommodation for (*received many visitors*). **9** (of a receptacle) be able to hold (a specified amount or contents). **10** greet or welcome, esp. in a specified manner (*how did they receive your offer?*). **11** react to (news, a play, etc.) in a specified way (*novel was warmly received*). **12** entertain as a guest etc. **13** admit to membership of a society, organization, etc. **14** be marked more or less permanently with (an impression etc.). **15** convert (broadcast signals) into sound or pictures. **16** *Tennis* etc. be the player to whom the server serves (the ball etc.). **17** (often as **received** *adj.*) give credit to; accept as authoritative or true (*received opinion*). **18** eat or drink (the Eucharistic bread and wine). □ **be at** (or **on**) **the receiving end** *colloq.* bear the brunt of something unpleasant. □ **receivable** *adj.* [Middle English via Old French *receivre, reçoivre* from Latin *recipere recept-* (as RE-, *capere* 'take')]

received pronunciation *n.* (also **Received Standard**) the form of spoken English based on educated speech in southern England.

receiver /rɪ'siːvə/ *n.* **1** a person or thing that receives. **2** the part of a machine or instrument that receives sound, signals, etc. (esp. the part of a telephone that contains the earpiece). **3** (in full *Brit.* **official receiver**) a person appointed by a court to administer the property of a bankrupt or insane person, or property under litigation. **4** a radio or television receiving apparatus. **5** a person who receives stolen goods. **6** *Chem.* a vessel for collecting the products of distillation, chromatography, etc. **7** *Amer. Football* **a** an offensive player eligible to catch a pass. **b** a defensive player designated to receive a kick-off.

receivership /rɪ'siːvəʃɪp/ *n.* **1** the office of official receiver. **2** (esp. in phr. **in receivership**) the state of being dealt with by a receiver.

receiving order *n. Brit.* an order of a court authorizing a receiver (see RECEIVER 3) to act.

recension /rɪ'sɛnʃ(ə)n/ *n.* **1** the revision of a text. **2** a particular form or version of a text resulting from such revision. [Latin *recensio* from *recensēre* 'revise' (as RE-, *censēre* 'review')]

recent /'riːs(ə)nt/ *adj. & n.* ● *adj.* **1** not long past; that happened, appeared, began to exist, or existed lately or just before the present time. **2** not long established; lately begun; modern. **3** (**Recent**) *Geol.* = HOLOCENE. ● *n.* (**Recent**) *Geol.* = HOLOCENE. □ **recency** *n.* **recently** *adv.* **recentness** *n.* [Latin *recens recentis* or French *récent*]

receptacle /rɪ'sɛptək(ə)l/ *n.* **1** a containing vessel, place, or space. **2** *Bot.* **a** the common base of floral organs. **b** the part of a leaf or thallus in some algae where the reproductive organs are situated. **3** *Zool.* an organ or structure which receives a secretion, eggs, sperm, etc. [Middle English from Old French *receptacle* or Latin *receptaculum* (as RECEPTION)]

reception /rɪ'sɛpʃ(ə)n/ *n.* **1** the act or an instance of receiving or the process of being received, esp. of a person into a place or group. **2** the manner in which a person or thing is received (*got a cool reception*). **3** a social occasion for receiving guests, esp. after a wedding. **4** a formal or ceremonious welcome. **5** a place where guests or clients etc. report on arrival at a hotel, office, etc. **6** **a** the receiving of broadcast signals. **b** the quality of this (*we have excellent reception*). [Middle English from Old French *reception* or Latin *receptio* (as RECEIVE)]

receptionist /rɪ'sɛpʃ(ə)nɪst/ *n.* a person employed in an office or *Brit.* a hotel to receive clients, guests, etc.

reception order *n. Brit.* an order authorizing the entry of a patient into a psychiatric hospital.

reception room *n.* esp. *Brit.* a room available or suitable for receiving company or visitors.

receptive /rɪ'sɛptɪv/ *adj.* **1** able or quick to receive impressions or ideas. **2** concerned with receiving stimuli etc. □ **receptively** *adv.* **receptiveness** *n.* **receptivity** /riːsɛp'tɪvɪti/ *n.* [French *réceptif -ive* or medieval Latin *receptivus* (as RECEPTION)]

receptor /rɪ'sɛptə/ *n.* (often *attrib.*) *Biol.* **1** an organ or cell able to respond to an external stimulus such as light, heat, or a drug, and transmit a signal to a sensory nerve. **2** a region of a tissue or molecule in a cell membrane etc. which responds specifically to a substance e.g. a neurotransmitter or hormone. [Old French *receptour* or Latin *receptor* (as RECEPTIVE)]

recess /rɪ'sɛs, 'riːsɛs/ *n. & v.* ● *n.* **1** a space set back in a wall; a niche. **2** (often in *pl.*) a remote or secret place (*the innermost recesses*). **3** a temporary cessation from work, esp. of Parliament, or *N. Amer.* of a law court or during a school day. **4** *Anat.* a fold or indentation in an organ. **5** *Geog.* a receding part of a mountain chain etc. ● *v.* **1** *tr.* make a recess in. **2** *tr.* place in a recess; set back. **3** *N. Amer.* **a** *intr.* take a recess; adjourn. **b** *tr.* order a temporary cessation from the work of (a court etc.). [Latin *recessus* (as RECEDE)]

recession /rɪ'sɛʃ(ə)n/ *n.* **1** a temporary decline in economic activity or prosperity. **2** a receding or withdrawal from a place or point. **3** a receding part of an object; a recess. □ **recessionary** *adj.* [Latin *recessio* (as RECESS)]

recessional /rɪ'sɛʃ(ə)n(ə)l/ *adj. & n.* ● *adj.* sung while the clergy and choir withdraw after a service. ● *n.* a recessional hymn.

recessive /rɪ'sɛsɪv/ *adj.* **1** tending to recede. **2** *Phonet.* (of an accent) falling near the beginning of a word. **3** *Genetics* (of an inherited characteristic) appearing in offspring only when not masked by a dominant characteristic inherited from one parent. □ **recessively** *adv.* **recessiveness** *n.* [RECESS, on the pattern of *excessive*]

recharge *v. & n.* ● *v.* /riː'tʃɑːdʒ/ **1** *tr.* charge again. **2** *tr.* reload. **3** *intr.* (of a battery etc.) be recharged. ● *n.* /'riːtʃɑːdʒ/ **1** an act or the action of recharging. **2** a renewed or return charge in battle. □ **rechargeable** /riː'tʃɑːdʒəb(ə)l/ *adj.*

recharger /riː'tʃɑːdʒə/ *n.* a device for recharging batteries or battery-powered equipment.

réchauffé /reɪ'ʃəʊfeɪ, French reʃofe/ *n.* **1** a warmed-up dish. **2** a rehash. [French, past part. of *réchauffer* (as RE-, CHAFE)]

recheck *v. & n.* ● *v.tr. & intr.* /riː'tʃɛk/ check again. ● *n.* /'riːtʃɛk/ a second or further check or inspection.

recherché /rə'ʃɛːʃeɪ/ *adj.* **1** carefully sought out; rare or exotic. **2** far-fetched, obscure. [French, past part. of *rechercher* (as RE-, *chercher* 'seek')]

rechristen /riː'krɪs(ə)n/ *v.tr.* **1** christen again. **2** give a new name to.

recidivist /rɪ'sɪdɪvɪst/ *n.* a person who relapses into crime. □ **recidivism** *n.* **recidivistic** /-'vɪstɪk/ *adj.* [French *récidiviste*, from *récidiver*, via medieval Latin *recidivare* from Latin *recidivus*, from *recidere* (as RE-, *cadere* 'fall')]

recipe /'rɛsɪpi/ *n.* **1** a statement of the ingredients and procedure required for preparing a mixture, esp. a culinary dish. **2** an expedient; a device for achieving something. **3** a medical prescription. [2nd sing. imperative (as used in prescriptions) of Latin *recipere* 'take, RECEIVE']

recipient /rɪ'sɪpɪənt/ *n. & adj.* ● *n.* a person who receives something. ● *adj.* **1** receiving. **2** receptive. □ **recipiency** *n.* [French *récipient* from Italian *recipiente* or Latin *recipiens*, from *recipere* RECEIVE]

reciprocal /rɪ'sɪprək(ə)l/ *adj. & n.* ● *adj.* **1** in return (*offered a reciprocal greeting*). **2** mutual (*their feelings are reciprocal*). **3** *Gram.* (of a pronoun) expressing mutual action or relation (as in *each other*). **4** inversely correspondent; complementary (*natural kindness matched by a reciprocal severity*). ● *n. Math.* an expression or function so related to another that their product is unity (*½ is the reciprocal of 2*). □ **reciprocality** /-'kalɪti/ *n.* **reciprocally** *adv.* [Latin *reciprocus*, ultimately from *re-* 'back' + *pro* 'forward']

reciprocate /rɪ'sɪprəkeɪt/ *v.* **1** *tr.* return or requite (affection etc.). **2** *intr.* (foll. by *with*) offer or give something in return (*reciprocated with an invitation to lunch*). **3** *tr.* give and receive mutually; interchange. **4** **a** *intr.* (of a part of a machine) move backwards and forwards. **b** *tr.* cause to do this. □ **reciprocation**

/-ˈkeɪʃ(ə)n/ *n.* **reciprocator** *n.* [Latin *reciprocare reciprocat-* (as RECIPROCAL)]

reciprocating engine *n.* an engine using a piston or pistons moving up and down in cylinders.

reciprocity /rɛsɪˈprɒsɪti/ *n.* **1** the condition of being reciprocal. **2** mutual action. **3** give and take, esp. the interchange of privileges between countries and organizations. [French *réciprocité*, from *réciproque*, from Latin *reciprocus* (as RECIPROCATE)]

recirculate /riːˈsəːkjʊleɪt/ *v.tr. & intr.* circulate again, esp. make available for reuse. □ **recirculation** /-ˈleɪʃ(ə)n/ *n.*

recital /rɪˈsʌɪt(ə)l/ *n.* **1** the act or an instance of reciting or being recited. **2** the performance of a programme of music by a solo instrumentalist or singer or by a small group. **3** (foll. by *of*) a detailed account of (connected things or facts); a narrative. **4** *Law* the part of a legal document that states the facts. □ **recitalist** *n.*

recitation /rɛsɪˈteɪʃ(ə)n/ *n.* **1** the act or an instance of reciting. **2** a thing recited. [Old French *recitation* or Latin *recitatio* (as RECITE)]

recitative /ˌrɛsɪtəˈtiːv/ *n.* **1** musical declamation of the kind usual in the narrative and dialogue parts of opera and oratorio. **2** the words or part given in this form. [Italian *recitativo* (as RECITE)]

recite /rɪˈsʌɪt/ *v.* **1** *tr.* repeat aloud or declaim (a poem or passage) from memory, esp. before an audience. **2** *intr.* give a recitation. **3** *tr.* mention in order; enumerate. □ **reciter** *n.* [Middle English from Old French *reciter* or Latin *recitare* (as RE-, CITE)]

reck /rɛk/ *v.* (only in *neg.* or *interrog.*) *archaic* or *poet.* **1** *intr.* (foll. by *of*) pay heed to; take account of; care about. **2** *tr.* pay heed to. **3** *intr.* (usu. prec. by *it* as subject) be of importance (*it recks little*). [partly from an Old English word related to Old High German *ruohhen*, from Germanic; partly from Old English *reccan*, of unknown origin]

reckless /ˈrɛklɪs/ *adj.* disregarding the consequences or danger etc.; lacking caution; rash. □ **recklessly** *adv.* **recklessness** *n.* [Old English *recceléas* (as RECK)]

reckon /ˈrɛk(ə)n/ *v.* **1** *tr.* count or compute by calculation. **2** *tr.* (foll. by *in*) count in or include in computation. **3** *tr.* (often foll. by *as* or *to be*) consider or regard (*reckon him wise*; *reckon them to be beyond hope*). **4** *tr.* **a** (foll. by *that* + clause) conclude after calculation; be of the considered opinion. **b** (foll. by *to* + infin.) *colloq.* expect (*reckons to finish by Friday*). **c** *colloq.* think, suppose. **5** *intr.* **a** make calculations; add up an account or sum. **b** (foll. by *with*) settle accounts with. **6** *intr.* (foll. by *on*, *upon*) rely on, count on, or base plans on. **7** *intr.* (foll. by *with* or *without*) take (or fail to take) into account. □ **reckon up 1** count up; find the total of. **2** settle accounts. **to be reckoned with** of considerable importance; not to be ignored. [Old English (*ge*)*recenian*, from West Germanic]

reckoner /ˈrɛk(ə)nə/ *n.* = READY RECKONER.

reckoning /ˈrɛk(ə)nɪŋ/ *n.* **1** the act or an instance of counting or calculating. **2** a consideration or opinion. **3** **a** the settlement of an account. **b** an account.

reclaim /rɪˈkleɪm/ *v. & n.* ● *v.tr.* **1** seek the return of (one's property). **2** claim in return or as a rebate etc. **3** bring under cultivation, esp. from a state of being under water. **4** **a** win back or away from vice or error or a waste condition; reform. **b** tame, civilize. ● *n.* the act or an instance of reclaiming; the process of being reclaimed. □ **reclaimable** *adj.* **reclaimer** *n.* **reclamation** /rɛkləˈmeɪʃ(ə)n/ *n.* [Middle English via Old French *reclamer reclaim-* from Latin *reclamare* 'cry out against' (as RE-, *clamare* 'shout')]

reclassify /riːˈklasɪfʌɪ/ *v.tr.* (**-ies**, **-ied**) classify again or differently. □ **reclassification** /-fɪˈkeɪʃ(ə)n/ *n.*

reclinate /ˈrɛklɪneɪt/ *adj. Bot.* bending downwards. [Latin *reclinatus*, past part. of *reclinare* (as RECLINE)]

recline /rɪˈklʌɪn/ *v.* **1** *intr.* assume or be in a horizontal or leaning position, esp. in resting. **2** *tr.* cause to recline or move from the vertical. □ **reclinable** *adj.* [Middle English from Old French *recliner* or Latin *reclinare* 'bend back, recline' (as RE-, *clinare* 'bend')]

recliner /rɪˈklʌɪnə/ *n.* **1** a comfortable chair for reclining in. **2** a person who reclines.

reclothe /riːˈkləʊð/ *v.tr.* clothe again or differently.

recluse /rɪˈkluːs/ *n. & adj.* ● *n.* a person given to or living in seclusion or isolation, esp. as a religious discipline; a hermit. ● *adj.* favouring seclusion; solitary. □ **reclusion** /rɪˈkluːʒ(ə)n/ *n.* **reclusive** *adj.* **reclusiveness** *n.* [Middle English via Old French *reclus recluse*, past part. of *reclure*, from Latin *recludere reclus-* (as RE-, *claudere* 'shut')]

recode /riːˈkəʊd/ *v.tr.* code again or differently.

recognition /rɛkəgˈnɪʃ(ə)n/ *n.* the act or an instance of recognizing or being recognized. □ **recognitory** /rɪˈkɒgnɪt(ə)ri/ *adj.* [Latin *recognitio* (as RECOGNIZE)]

recognizance /rɪˈkɒ(g)nɪz(ə)ns/ *n.* (also **recognisance**) **1** a bond by which a person undertakes before a court or magistrate to observe some condition, e.g. to appear when summoned. **2** a sum pledged as surety for this. [Middle English from Old French *recon(n)issance* (as RE-, COGNIZANCE)]

recognizant /rɪˈkɒgnɪz(ə)nt/ *adj.* (also **recognisant**) (usu. foll. by *of*) **1** showing recognition (of a favour etc.). **2** conscious or showing consciousness (of something).

recognize /ˈrɛkəgnʌɪz/ *v.tr.* (also **-ise**) **1** identify (a person or thing) as already known; know again. **2** realize or discover the nature of. **3** (foll. by *that*) realize or admit. **4** acknowledge the existence, validity, character, or claims of. **5** show appreciation of; reward. **6** (foll. by *as*, *for*) treat or acknowledge. **7** (of a chairperson etc.) allow (a person) to speak in a debate etc. □ **recognizable** *adj.* **recognizability** /-əˈbɪlɪti/ *n.* **recognizably** *adv.* **recognizer** *n.* [Old French *recon(n)iss-*, stem of *reconnaistre*, from Latin *recognoscere recognit-* (as RE-, *cognoscere* 'learn')]

recoil /rɪˈkɔɪl/ *v. & n.* ● *v.intr.* **1** suddenly move or spring back in fear, horror, or disgust. **2** shrink mentally in this way. **3** rebound after an impact. **4** (foll. by *on*, *upon*) have an adverse reactive effect on (the originator). **5** (of a gun) be driven backwards by its discharge. **6** retreat under an enemy's attack. **7** *Physics* (of an atom etc.) move backwards by the conservation of momentum on emission of a particle. ● *n.* /also ˈriːkɔɪl/ **1** the act or an instance of recoiling. **2** the sensation of recoiling. [Middle English from Old French *reculer* (as RE-, Latin *culus* 'buttocks')]

recollect /rɛkəˈlɛkt/ *v.tr.* **1** remember. **2** succeed in remembering; call to mind. [Latin *recolligere recollect-* (as RE-, COLLECT[1])]

re-collect /riːkəˈlɛkt/ *v.tr.* **1** collect again. **2** (*refl.*) recover control of (oneself).

recollection /rɛkəˈlɛkʃ(ə)n/ *n.* **1** the act or power of recollecting. **2** a thing recollected. **3** **a** a person's memory (*to the best of my recollection*). **b** the time over which memory extends (*happened within my recollection*). □ **recollective** *adj.* [French *recollection* or medieval Latin *recollectio* (as RECOLLECT)]

recolonize /riːˈkɒlənʌɪz/ *v.tr.* (also **-ise**) colonize again. □ **recolonization** /-ˈzeɪʃ(ə)n/ *n.*

recolour /riːˈkʌlə/ *v.tr.* (*US* **recolor**) colour again or differently.

recombinant /rɪˈkɒmbɪnənt/ *adj. & n. Biol.* ● *adj.* (of a gene etc.) formed by recombination. ● *n.* a recombinant organism or cell.

recombinant DNA *n.* DNA that has been recombined using constituents from different sources.

recombination /riːˌkɒmbɪˈneɪʃ(ə)n, ˌriːkɒmb-/ *n. Biol.* the rearrangement, esp. by crossing over in chromosomes, of genes to form a combination different from that of the parents.

recombine /riːkəmˈbʌɪn/ *v.tr. & intr.* combine again or differently.

recommence /riːkəˈmɛns/ *v.tr. & intr.* begin again. □ **recommencement** *n.*

recommend /rɛkə'mɛnd/ *v.tr.* **1** suggest as fit for some purpose or use. **2** (often foll. by *that* + clause or *to* + infin.) advise as a course of action etc. (*I recommend that you stay where you are*). **3** (of qualities, conduct, etc.) make acceptable or desirable. **4** (foll. by *to*) *Brit.* commend or entrust (to a person or a person's care). □ **recommendable** *adj.* **recommendation** /-'deɪʃ(ə)n/ *n.* **recommendatory** /-dət(ə)ri/ *adj.* **recommender** *n.* [Middle English (in sense 4) from medieval Latin *recommendare* (as RE-, COMMEND)]

recommission /ri:kə'mɪʃ(ə)n/ *v.tr.* commission again.

recommit /ri:kə'mɪt/ *v.tr.* (**recommitted, recommitting**) **1** commit again. **2** return (a bill etc.) to a committee for further consideration. □ **recommitment** *n.* **recommittal** *n.*

recompense /'rɛkəmpɛns/ *v. & n.* ● *v.tr.* **1** make amends to (a person) or for (a loss etc.). **2** requite; reward or punish (a person or action). ● *n.* **1** a reward; requital. **2** retribution; satisfaction given for an injury. [Middle English via Old French *recompense* (*n.*), *recompenser* (*v.*) from Late Latin *recompensare* (as RE-, COMPENSATE)]

recompose /ri:kəm'pəʊz/ *v.tr.* compose again or differently.

recon /rɪ'kɒn/ *n.* (often *attrib.*) *US slang* military reconnaissance. [abbreviation]

reconcile /'rɛk(ə)nsʌɪl/ *v.tr.* **1** make friendly again after an estrangement. **2** (usu. in *refl.* or *passive*; foll. by *to*) make acquiescent or contentedly submissive to (something disagreeable or unwelcome) (*was reconciled to failure*). **3** settle (a quarrel etc.). **4 a** harmonize; make compatible. **b** show the compatibility of by argument or in practice (*cannot reconcile your views with the facts*). □ **reconcilable** *adj.* **reconcilability** /-ə'bɪlɪti/ *n.* **reconcilement** *n.* **reconciler** *n.* **reconciliation** /-sɪlɪ'eɪʃ(ə)n/ *n.* **reconciliatory** /-kən'sɪlɪət(ə)ri/ *adj.* [Middle English from Old French *reconcilier* or Latin *reconciliare* (as RE-, *conciliare* CONCILIATE)]

recondite /'rɛk(ə)ndʌɪt, rɪ'kɒn-/ *adj.* **1** (of a subject or knowledge) abstruse; out of the way; little known. **2** (of an author or style) dealing in abstruse knowledge or allusions; obscure. □ **reconditely** *adv.* **reconditeness** *n.* [Latin *reconditus* (as RE-, *conditus*, past part. of *condere* 'hide')]

recondition /ri:kən'dɪʃ(ə)n/ *v.tr.* **1** overhaul, refit, renovate. **2** make usable again.

reconfigure /ri:kən'fɪgə/ *v.tr.* configure again or differently. □ **reconfiguration** /-gə'reɪʃ(ə)n/ *n.*

reconfirm /ri:kən'fə:m/ *v.tr.* confirm, establish, or ratify anew. □ **reconfirmation** /-kɒnfə'meɪʃ(ə)n/ *n.*

reconnaissance /rɪ'kɒnɪs(ə)ns/ *n.* **1** a survey of a region, esp. a military examination to locate an enemy or ascertain strategic features. **2** a preliminary survey or inspection. [French (earlier *-oissance*), from the stem of *reconnaître* (as RECONNOITRE)]

reconnect /ri:kə'nɛkt/ *v.tr.* connect again. □ **reconnection** *n.*

reconnoitre /rɛkə'nɔɪtə/ *v. & n.* (*US* **reconnoiter**) ● *v.* **1** *tr.* make a reconnaissance of (an area, enemy position, etc.). **2** *intr.* make a reconnaissance. ● *n.* a reconnaissance. [obsolete French *reconnoître* from Latin *recognoscere* RECOGNIZE]

reconquer /ri:'kɒŋkə/ *v.tr.* conquer again. □ **reconquest** *n.*

reconsecrate /ri:'kɒnsɪkreɪt/ *v.tr.* consecrate (a church etc.) again. □ **reconsecration** /-'kreɪʃ(ə)n/ *n.*

reconsider /ri:kən'sɪdə/ *v.tr. & intr.* consider again, esp. for a possible change of decision. □ **reconsideration** /-'reɪʃ(ə)n/ *n.*

reconsign /ri:kən'sʌɪn/ *v.tr.* consign again or differently. □ **reconsignment** *n.*

reconsolidate /ri:kən'sɒlɪdeɪt/ *v.tr. & intr.* consolidate again. □ **reconsolidation** /-'deɪʃ(ə)n/ *n.*

reconstitute /ri:'kɒnstɪtju:t/ *v.tr.* **1** build up again from parts; reconstruct. **2** reorganize. **3** restore the previous constitution of (dried food etc.) by adding water. □ **reconstitution** /-'tju:ʃ(ə)n/ *n.*

reconstruct /ri:kən'strʌkt/ *v.tr.* **1** build or form again. **2 a** form a mental or visual impression of (past events) by assembling the evidence for them. **b** re-enact (a crime). **3** reorganize. □ **reconstructable** *adj.* (also **reconstructible**). **reconstruction** *n.* **reconstructive** *adj.* **reconstructor** *n.*

reconvene /ri:kən'vi:n/ *v.tr. & intr.* convene again, esp. (of a meeting etc.) after a pause in proceedings.

reconvert /ri:kən'və:t/ *v.tr.* convert back to a former state. □ **reconversion** *n.*

record *n. & v.* ● *n.* /'rɛkɔ:d/ **1 a** a piece of evidence or information constituting an (esp. official) account of something that has occurred, been said, etc. **b** a document preserving this. **2** the state of being set down or preserved in writing or some other permanent form (*is a matter of record*). **3 a** (in full **gramophone record** or *N. Amer.* **phonograph record**) a thin plastic disc carrying recorded sound in grooves on each surface, for reproduction by a record player. **b** a trace made on this or some other medium, e.g. magnetic tape. **4 a** an official report of the proceedings and judgement in a court of justice. **b** a copy of the pleadings etc. constituting a case to be decided by a court (see also COURT OF RECORD). **5** the facts known about a person's past (*has an honourable record of service*). **6** (in full **criminal record**) **a** a list of a person's previous criminal convictions. **b** a history of being convicted for crime (*has a record*). **7** the best performance (esp. in sport) or most remarkable event of its kind on record (often *attrib.*: *a record attempt*). **8** an object serving as a memorial of a person or thing; a portrait. **9** *Computing* a number of related items of information which are handled as a unit. ● *v.tr.* /rɪ'kɔ:d/ **1** set down in writing or some other permanent form for later reference, esp. as an official record. **2** convert (sound, a broadcast, etc.) into permanent form for later reproduction. **3** establish or constitute a historical or other record of. □ **break** (or **beat**) **the record** outdo all previous performances etc. **for the record** as an official statement etc. **go on record** state one's opinion or judgement openly or officially, so that it is recorded. **a matter of record** a thing established as a fact by being recorded. **off the record** as an unofficial or confidential statement etc. **on record** officially recorded; publicly known. **put** (or **get** or **set** etc.) **the record straight** correct a misapprehension. □ **recordable** *adj.* [Middle English via Old French *record* 'remembrance', *recorder* 'to record', from Latin *recordari* 'remember' (as RE-, *cor cordis* 'heart')]

record-breaking *attrib.adj.* that breaks a record (see RECORD *n.* 7).

recorded delivery *n. Brit.* a Post Office service in which the dispatch and receipt of a letter or parcel are recorded.

recorder /rɪ'kɔ:də/ *n.* **1** an apparatus for recording, esp. a tape recorder. **2 a** a keeper of records. **b** a person who makes an official record. **3** (usu. **Recorder**) **a** (in England and Wales) a barrister or solicitor of at least ten years' standing, appointed to serve as a part-time judge. **b** *Brit. hist.* a judge in certain courts. **4** *Mus.* a woodwind instrument like a flute but blown through the end and having a more hollow tone. □ **recordership** *n.* (in sense 3). [Middle English, partly from Anglo-French *recordour*, Old French *recordeur*; partly from RECORD (in obsolete sense 'practise a tune')]

record holder *n.* a person who holds a record (see RECORD *n.* 7).

recording /rɪ'kɔ:dɪŋ/ *n.* **1** the process by which audio or video signals are recorded for later reproduction. **2** material or a programme recorded.

recording angel *n.* an angel that supposedly registers each person's good and bad actions.

recordist /rɪ'kɔ:dɪst/ *n.* esp. *Brit.* a person who records sound.

record player *n.* an apparatus for reproducing sound from gramophone records by means of a turntable and stylus etc.

recount /rɪˈkaʊnt/ *v.tr.* **1** narrate. **2** tell in detail. [Old Northern French & Anglo-French *reconter* (as RE-, COUNT[1])]

re-count *v.* & *n.* ● *v.tr.* /riːˈkaʊnt/ count again. ● *n.* /ˈriːkaʊnt/ a re-counting, esp. of votes in an election.

recoup /rɪˈkuːp/ *v.tr.* **1** recover or regain (a loss). **2** compensate or reimburse for a loss. **3** *Law* deduct or keep back (part of a sum due). □ **recoup oneself** recover a loss. □ **recoupable** *adj.* **recoupment** *n.* [French *recouper* (as RE-, *couper* 'cut')]

recourse /rɪˈkɔːs/ *n.* **1** resorting to a possible source of help. **2** a person or thing resorted to. □ **have recourse to** turn to (a person or thing) for help. **without recourse** a formula used by the endorser of a bill etc. to disclaim responsibility for payment. [Middle English via Old French *recours* from Latin *recursus* (as RE-, COURSE)]

recover /rɪˈkʌvə/ *v.* & *n.* ● *v.* **1** *tr.* regain possession or use or control of; reclaim. **2** *intr.* return to health or consciousness or to a normal state or position (*have recovered from my illness; the country never recovered from the war*). **3** *tr.* obtain or secure (compensation etc.) by legal process. **4** *tr.* retrieve or make up for (a loss, setback, etc.). **5** *refl.* regain composure or consciousness or control of one's limbs. **6** *tr.* retrieve (reusable substances) from industrial waste. ● *n.* the recovery of a normal position in fencing etc. □ **recoverable** *adj.* **recoverability** /-ˈbɪlɪti/ *n.* **recoverer** *n.* [Middle English via Anglo-French *recoverer*, Old French *recovrer* from Latin *recuperare* RECUPERATE]

re-cover /riːˈkʌvə/ *v.tr.* **1** cover again. **2** provide (a chair etc.) with a new cover.

recovery /rɪˈkʌv(ə)ri/ *n.* (*pl.* **-ies**) **1** the act or an instance of recovering; the process of being recovered. **2** *Golf* a stroke bringing the ball out of a bunker etc. [Middle English from Anglo-French *recoverie*, Old French *reco(u)vree* (as RECOVER)]

recreant /ˈrɛkrɪənt/ *adj.* & *n. literary* ● *adj.* **1** craven, cowardly. **2** apostate. ● *n.* **1** a coward. **2** an apostate. □ **recreancy** *n.* **recreantly** *adv.* [Middle English from Old French, part. of *recroire*, from medieval Latin (*se*) *recredere* 'yield in trial by combat' (as RE-, *credere* 'entrust')]

recreate /riːkrɪˈeɪt/ *v.tr.* create over again; reconstruct. □ **re-creation** *n.*

recreation /rɛkrɪˈeɪʃ(ə)n/ *n.* **1** the process or means of refreshing or entertaining oneself. **2** a pleasurable activity. □ **recreational** *adj.* **recreationally** *adv.* **recreative** /ˈrɛkrɪeɪtɪv/ *adj.* [Middle English via Old French from Latin *recreatio -onis*, from *recreare* 'create again, renew']

recreation ground *n. Brit.* public land for games etc.

recriminate /rɪˈkrɪmɪneɪt/ *v.intr.* make mutual or counter accusations. □ **recrimination** /-ˈneɪʃ(ə)n/ *n.* **recriminative** /-nətɪv/ *adj.* **recriminatory** /-nət(ə)ri/ *adj.* [medieval Latin *recriminare* (as RE-, *criminare* 'accuse' from *crimen* CRIME)]

recross /riːˈkrɒs/ *v.tr.* & *intr.* cross or pass over again.

recrudesce /riːkruːˈdɛs, rɛk-/ *v.intr.* (of a disease or difficulty etc.) break out again, esp. after a dormant period. □ **recrudescence** *n.* **recrudescent** *adj.* [back-formation from *recrudescent, -ence*, from Latin *recrudescere* (as RE-, *crudus* 'raw')]

recruit /rɪˈkruːt/ *n.* & *v.* ● *n.* **1** a serviceman or servicewoman newly enlisted and not yet fully trained. **2** a new member of a society or organization. **3** a beginner. ● *v.* **1** *tr.* enlist (a person) as a recruit. **2** *tr.* form (an army etc.) by enlisting recruits. **3** *intr.* get or seek recruits. **4** *tr.* replenish or reinvigorate (numbers, strength, etc.). □ **recruitable** *adj.* **recruiter** *n.* **recruitment** *n.* [earlier = reinforcement: obsolete French dialect *recrute*, ultimately via French *recroître* 'increase again' from Latin *recrescere*]

recrystallize /riːˈkrɪst(ə)lʌɪz/ *v.tr.* & *intr.* (also **-ise**) crystallize again. □ **recrystallization** /-ˈzeɪʃ(ə)n/ *n.*

recta *pl.* of RECTUM.

rectal /ˈrɛkt(ə)l/ *adj.* of or by means of the rectum. □ **rectally** *adv.*

rectangle /ˈrɛktaŋg(ə)l/ *n.* a plane figure with four straight sides and four right angles, esp. one with the adjacent sides unequal. [French *rectangle* or medieval Latin *rectangulum* from Late Latin *rectiangulum*, from Latin *rectus* 'straight' + *angulus* ANGLE[1]]

rectangular /rɛkˈtaŋgjʊlə/ *adj.* **1 a** shaped like a rectangle. **b** having the base or sides or section shaped like a rectangle. **2 a** placed at right angles. **b** having parts or lines placed at right angles. □ **rectangularity** /-ˈlarɪti/ *n.* **rectangularly** *adv.*

rectangular coordinate *n.* (usu. in *pl.*) each of a set of coordinates measured along axes at right angles to one another.

rectangular hyperbola *n.* a hyperbola with rectangular asymptotes.

recti *pl.* of RECTUS.

rectified spirit *n. Chem.* an azeotropic mixture of alcohol (95.6%) and water produced by distillation.

rectifier /ˈrɛktɪfʌɪə/ *n.* **1** a person or thing that rectifies. **2** *Electr.* an electrical device that allows a current to flow preferentially in one direction by converting an alternating current into a direct one.

rectify /ˈrɛktɪfʌɪ/ *v.tr.* (**-ies, -ied**) **1** adjust or make right; correct, amend. **2** purify or refine, esp. by repeated distillation. **3** find a straight line equal in length to (a curve). **4** convert (alternating current) to direct current. □ **rectifiable** *adj.* **rectification** /-fɪˈkeɪʃ(ə)n/ *n.* [Middle English via Old French *rectifier* from medieval Latin *rectificare*, from Latin *rectus* 'right']

rectilinear /rɛktɪˈlɪnɪə/ *adj.* (also **rectilineal** /-nɪəl/) **1** bounded or characterized by straight lines. **2** in or forming a straight line. □ **rectilinearity** /-ˈarɪti/ *n.* **rectilinearly** *adv.* [Late Latin *rectilineus*, from Latin *rectus* 'straight' + *linea* LINE[1]]

rectitude /ˈrɛktɪtjuːd/ *n.* **1** moral uprightness. **2** righteousness. **3** correctness. [Middle English via Old French *rectitude* or Late Latin *rectitudo* from Latin *rectus* 'right']

recto /ˈrɛktəʊ/ *n.* (*pl.* **-os**) **1** the right-hand page of an open book (opp. VERSO 1a). **2** the front of a printed leaf of paper or manuscript (opp. VERSO 1b). [Latin *recto* (*folio*) 'on the right (leaf)']

rector /ˈrɛktə/ *n.* **1 a** (in the Church of England) the incumbent of a parish where all tithes formerly passed to the incumbent (cf. VICAR 1a). **b** (in other Anglican churches) a member of the clergy who has charge of a parish. **2** *RC Ch.* a priest in charge of a church or of a religious institution. **3 a** the head of some schools, universities, and colleges. **b** (in Scotland) an elected representative of students on a university's governing body. □ **rectorate** /-rət/ *n.* **rectorial** /-ˈtɔːrɪəl/ *adj.* **rectorship** *n.* [Middle English from Old French *rectour* or Latin *rector* 'ruler', from *regere rect-* 'rule']

rectory /ˈrɛkt(ə)ri/ *n.* (*pl.* **-ies**) **1** a rector's house. **2** (in the Church of England) a rector's benefice. [Anglo-French & Old French *rectorie* or medieval Latin *rectoria* (as RECTOR)]

rectrix /ˈrɛktrɪks/ *n.* (*pl.* **rectrices** /-rɪsiːz/) a bird's strong tail feather directing flight. [Latin, fem. of *rector* 'ruler': see RECTOR]

rectum /ˈrɛktəm/ *n.* (*pl.* **rectums** or **recta** /-tə/) the final section of the large intestine, terminating at the anus. [Latin *rectum* (*intestinum*) 'straight (intestine)']

rectus /ˈrɛktəs/ *n.* (*pl.* **recti** /-tʌɪ/) *Anat.* a straight muscle. [Latin, = straight]

recumbent /rɪˈkʌmbənt/ *adj.* lying down; reclining. □ **recumbency** *n.* **recumbently** *adv.* [Latin *recumbere* 'recline' (as RE-, *cumbere* 'lie')]

recuperate /rɪˈkuːpəreɪt/ *v.* **1** *intr.* recover from illness, exhaustion, loss, etc. **2** *tr.* regain (health, something lost, etc.). ▫ **recuperable** *adj.* **recuperation** /-'reɪʃ(ə)n/ *n.* **recuperative** /-rətɪv/ *adj.* **recuperator** *n.* [Latin *recuperare recuperat-* 'recover']

■ **Usage** In sense 2, *recover* is preferable to *recuperate.*

recur /rɪ'kə:/ *v.intr.* (**recurred, recurring**) **1** occur again; be repeated. **2** (of a thought, idea, etc.) come back to one's mind. **3** (foll. by *to*) go back in thought or speech. [Latin *recurrere recurs-* (as RE-, *currere* 'run')]

recurrent /rɪ'kʌr(ə)nt/ *adj.* **1** recurring; happening repeatedly. **2** (of a nerve, vein, branch, etc.) turning back so as to reverse direction. ▫ **recurrence** *n.* **recurrently** *adv.*

recurring decimal *n.* a decimal fraction in which the same figures are repeated indefinitely.

recursion /rɪ'kə:ʃ(ə)n/ *n. Math. & Linguistics* **1** the application or use of a recursive procedure or definition. **2** a recursive definition.

recursion formula *n. Math.* an expression giving successive terms of a series etc.

recursive /rɪ'kə:sɪv/ *adj.* **1** characterized by recurrence or repetition. **2 a** *Math. & Linguistics* relating to or involving the repeated application of a rule, definition, or procedure to successive results. **b** *Computing* relating to or involving a program or routine, a part of which requires the application of the whole. ▫ **recursively** *adv.* [Late Latin *recurs-*, past part. stem of *recurrere* RECUR]

recurve /rɪ'kə:v/ *v.tr. & intr.* bend backwards. ▫ **recurvate** /-vət/ *adj.* **recurvature** *n.* [Latin *recurvare recurvat-* (as RE-, *curvare* 'bend')]

recusant /'rɛkjʊz(ə)nt/ *n. & adj.* ● *n.* a person who refuses submission to an authority or compliance with a regulation, esp. *hist.* one who refused to attend services of the Church of England. ● *adj.* of or being a recusant. ▫ **recusance** *n.* **recusancy** *n.* [Latin *recusare* 'refuse']

recycle /ri:'sʌɪk(ə)l/ *v.tr.* return (material) to a previous stage of a cyclic process, esp. convert (waste) to reusable material. ▫ **recyclable** *adj.* **recycler** *n.*

red /rɛd/ *adj. & n.* ● *adj.* (**redder, reddest**) **1** of or near the colour seen at the least-refracted end of the visible spectrum, of shades ranging from that of blood to pink or deep orange. **2** flushed in the face with shame, anger, etc. **3** (of the eyes) bloodshot or red-rimmed with weeping. **4** (of the hair) reddish brown, orange, tawny. **5** involving or having to do with bloodshed, burning, violence, or revolution. **6** *colloq.* communist or socialist. **7** (**Red**) *hist.* Russian, Soviet (*the Red Army*). **8** (of wine) made from dark grapes and coloured by their skins. ● *n.* **1** a red colour or pigment. **2** red clothes or material (*dressed in red*). **3** *colloq.* a communist or socialist. **4 a** a red ball, piece, etc., in a game or sport. **b** the player using such pieces. **5** the debit side of an account (*in the red*). **6** a red light. ▫ **reddish** *adj.* **reddy** *adj.* **redly** *adv.* **redness** *n.* [Old English *rēad*, from Germanic]

redact /rɪ'dakt/ *v.tr.* put into literary form; edit for publication. ▫ **redactor** *n.* [Latin *redigere redact-* (as RE-, *agere* 'bring')]

redaction /rɪ'dakʃ(ə)n/ *n.* **1** preparation for publication. **2** revision, editing, rearrangement. **3** a new edition. ▫ **redactional** *adj.* [French *rédaction* from Late Latin *redactio* (as REDACT)]

red admiral *n.* a butterfly, *Vanessa atalanta*, with red bands on each pair of wings.

redan /rɪ'dan/ *n.* a fieldwork with two faces forming a salient angle. [French from *redent* 'notching' (as RE-, *dent* 'tooth')]

red arsenic *n.* = REALGAR.

red-back *n.* (in full **red-back spider**) a venomous Australian spider of the genus *Latrodectus*.

red bark *n.* a red kind of cinchona.

red biddy *n. Brit. colloq.* a mixture of cheap wine and methylated spirits.

red blood cell see RED CELL.

red-blooded *adj.* virile, vigorous. ▫ **red-bloodedness** *n.*

redbreast /'rɛdbrɛst/ *n.* esp. *Brit. colloq.* a robin.

red-brick *attrib.adj.* (of a British university) founded in the late 19th or early 20th century.

redbud /'rɛdbʌd/ *n.* any American tree of the genus *Cercis*, with pale pink flowers.

redcap /'rɛdkap/ *n.* **1** *Brit. slang* a member of the military police. **2** *N. Amer.* a railway porter.

red card *n. Football* a card shown by the referee to a player being sent off the field.

red carpet *n.* privileged treatment of an eminent visitor.

red cedar *n.* an American juniper, *Juniperus virginiana*.

red cell *n.* (also **red blood cell**) = ERYTHROCYTE.

red cent *n. N. Amer.* **1** the (originally copper) coin of the lowest value. **2** a trivial sum.

redcoat /'rɛdkəʊt/ *n.* **1** *hist.* a British soldier (so called from the scarlet uniform of most regiments). **2** (in the UK) a steward at a Butlin's holiday camp.

red coral see CORAL *n.* 1b.

Red Crescent *n.* an organization like the Red Cross in Muslim countries.

Red Cross *n.* **1** an international organization (originally medical) bringing relief to victims of war or natural disaster. **2** the emblem of this organization.

red cross *n.* **1** St George's cross, the national emblem of England. **2** the Christian side in the Crusades.

redcurrant /rɛd'kʌr(ə)nt/ *n.* **1** a widely cultivated shrub, *Ribes rubrum*. **2** a small red edible berry of this plant.

redd[1] /rɛd/ *v.tr.* (*past* and *past part.* **redd**) *dial.* **1** clear up. **2** arrange, tidy, compose, settle. [Middle English, perhaps from Old English, and related to RID]

redd[2] /rɛd/ *n.* a hollow in a river bed made by a trout or salmon to spawn in. [17th c.: origin unknown]

red deer *n.* a deer, *Cervus elaphus*, with a rich red-brown summer coat turning dull brown in winter.

redden /'rɛd(ə)n/ *v.* **1** *tr. & intr.* make or become red. **2** *intr.* blush.

reddle /'rɛd(ə)l/ *n.* red ochre; ruddle. [variant of RUDDLE]

red duster *n. Brit. Naut. slang* = RED ENSIGN.

red dwarf *n.* an old relatively cool star.

rede /ri:d/ *n. & v. archaic* ● *n.* advice, counsel. ● *v.tr.* **1** advise. **2** read (a riddle or dream). [Old English *rǣd* from Germanic, related to READ (of which the verb is a Middle English variant retained for archaic senses)]

redecorate /ri:'dɛkəreɪt/ *v.tr.* decorate again or differently. ▫ **redecoration** /-'reɪʃ(ə)n/ *n.*

rededicate /ri:'dɛdɪkeɪt/ *v.tr.* dedicate anew. ▫ **rededication** /-'keɪʃ(ə)n/ *n.*

redeem /rɪ'di:m/ *v.tr.* **1** buy back; recover by expenditure of effort or by a stipulated payment. **2** make a single payment to discharge (a regular charge or obligation). **3** convert (tokens or bonds etc.) into goods or cash. **4** (of God or Christ) deliver from sin and damnation. **5** make up for; be a compensating factor in (*has one redeeming feature*). **6** (foll. by *from*) save from (a defect). **7** *refl.* save (oneself) from blame. **8** purchase the freedom of (a person). **9** save (a person's life) by ransom. **10** save or rescue or reclaim. **11** fulfil (a promise). ▫ **redeemable** *adj.* [Middle English from Old French *redimer* or Latin *redimere redempt-* (as RE-, *emere* 'buy')]

redeemer /rɪ'di:mə/ *n.* a person who redeems. ▫ **the Redeemer** Christ.

redefine /ri:dɪ'fʌɪn/ *v.tr.* define again or differently. ▫ **redefinition** /-dɛfɪ'nɪʃ(ə)n/ *n.*

redemption /rɪ'dɛm(p)ʃ(ə)n/ *n.* **1** the act or an instance of redeeming; the process of being redeemed. **2** *Theol.* man's deliverance from sin and damnation. **3** a thing that redeems. ▫ **redemptive** *adj.* [Middle English via Old French from Latin *redemptio* (as REDEEM)]

red ensign *n.* the ensign of the British merchant navy.

redeploy /riːdɪˈplɔɪ/ *v.tr.* send (troops, workers, etc.) to a new place or task. ▫ **redeployment** *n.*

redesign /riːdɪˈzʌɪn/ *v.tr.* design again or differently.

redetermine /riːdɪˈtəːmɪn/ *v.tr.* determine again or differently. ▫ **redetermination** /-ˈneɪʃ(ə)n/ *n.*

redevelop /riːdɪˈvɛləp/ *v.tr.* develop anew (esp. an urban area, with new buildings). ▫ **redeveloper** *n.* **redevelopment** *n.*

red-eye *n.* **1** = RUDD. **2** *US slang* cheap whisky. **3** a red reflection from a person's retina, seen in a flash photograph taken with the flashgun too near the camera lens. **4** (in full **red-eye flight**) *colloq.* an airline flight on which a traveller is unable to get adequate sleep.

red-faced *adj.* embarrassed, ashamed.

redfish /ˈrɛdfɪʃ/ *n.* (*pl.* usu. same) **1** any of various reddish fishes. **2** *Brit.* a male salmon in the spawning season.

red flag *n.* **1** the symbol of socialist revolution. **2** a warning of danger.

red fox *n.* a common fox, *Vulpes vulpes,* of Eurasia and N. America, usu. having a reddish or fawn coat.

red giant *n.* a relatively cool giant star.

red grouse *n.* a subspecies of the willow grouse, native to Britain and familiar as a game bird.

Red Guard *n. hist.* a member of a militant youth movement in China (1966–76).

red gum *n.* **1** a facial rash in young children, esp. during teething. **2 a** a reddish resin. **b** any of various kinds of eucalyptus yielding this.

red-handed *adv.* in or just after the act of committing a crime, doing wrong, etc. (*was caught red-handed*).

red hat *n.* **1** a cardinal's hat. **2** the symbol of a cardinal's office.

redhead /ˈrɛdhɛd/ *n.* a person with red hair.

red-headed *adj.* **1** (of a person) having red hair. **2** (of birds etc.) having a red head.

red heat *n.* **1** the temperature or state of something so hot as to emit red light. **2** great excitement.

red herring *n.* **1** dried smoked herring. **2** a misleading clue or distraction (so called from the practice of using the scent of red herring in training hounds).

red-hot *adj.* **1** heated until red. **2** highly exciting. **3** (of news) fresh; completely new. **4** intensely excited. **5** enraged.

red-hot poker *n.* a cultivated kniphofia, esp. *Kniphofia uvaria,* with the upper flowers in the spike red and the lower ones yellow.

redial /riːˈdʌɪl/ *v.tr.* & *intr.* (**redialled**, **redialling**; *US* **redialed**, **redialing**) dial again.

redid *past* of REDO.

rediffusion /riːdɪˈfjuːʒ(ə)n/ *n. Brit.* the relaying of broadcast programmes esp. by cable from a central receiver.

Red Indian *n.* esp. *Brit. offens.* an American Indian.

redingote /ˈrɛdɪŋgəʊt/ *n.* a woman's long coat with a cutaway front or a contrasting piece on the front. [French from English *riding coat*]

redintegrate /rɛˈdɪntɪgreɪt/ *v.tr.* **1** restore to wholeness or unity. **2** renew or re-establish in a united or perfect state. ▫ **redintegration** /-ˈgreɪʃ(ə)n/ *n.* **redintegrative** /-ˈgrətɪv/ *adj.* [Middle English from Latin *redintegrare* (as RE-, INTEGRATE)]

redirect /riːdʌɪˈrɛkt, -dɪˈrɛkt/ *v.tr.* direct again, esp. change the address of (a letter). ▫ **redirection** *n.*

rediscover /riːdɪˈskʌvə/ *v.tr.* discover again. ▫ **rediscovery** *n.* (*pl.* **-ies**).

redissolve /riːdɪˈzɒlv/ *v.tr.* & *intr.* dissolve again. ▫ **redissolution** /-dɪsəˈluːʃ(ə)n/ *n.*

redistribute /riːdɪˈstrɪbjuːt, riːˈdɪs-/ *v.tr.* distribute again or differently. ▫ **redistribution** /-ˈbjuːʃ(ə)n/ *n.* **redistributive** /-ˈtrɪbjʊtɪv/ *adj.*

▪ **Usage** The second pronunciation given, with the stress on the second syllable, is considered incorrect by some people.

redivide /riːdɪˈvʌɪd/ *v.tr.* divide again or differently. ▫ **redivision** /-ˈvɪʒ(ə)n/ *n.*

redivivus /rɛdɪˈviːvəs/ *adj.* (placed after noun) come back to life. [Latin (as RE-, *vivus* 'living')]

red lead *n.* a red form of lead oxide used as a pigment.

Red Leicester see LEICESTER.

red-letter day *n.* a day that is pleasantly noteworthy or memorable (originally a festival marked in red on the calendar).

red light *n.* **1** a red light used as a signal to stop on a road, railway, etc. **2** a warning or refusal.

red-light district *n.* a district containing many brothels, strip clubs, etc.

red man *n. offens.* = RED INDIAN.

red meat *n.* meat that is red when raw (e.g. beef or lamb).

red mullet *n.* a mullet of the family Mullidae, esp. *Muletus surmuletus* of Europe, valued as food.

redneck /ˈrɛdnɛk/ *n. N. Amer. offens.* a working-class white in the southern US, esp. a politically conservative one.

redo /riːˈduː/ *v.tr.* (*3rd sing. present* **redoes**; *past* **redid**; *past part.* **redone**) **1** do again or differently. **2** redecorate.

redolent /ˈrɛd(ə)l(ə)nt/ *adj.* **1** (foll. by *of, with*) strongly reminiscent or suggestive or mentally associated. **2** fragrant. **3** having a strong smell; odorous. ▫ **redolence** *n.* **redolently** *adv.* [Middle English from Old French *redolent* or Latin *redolēre* (as RE-, *olēre* 'smell')]

red orpiment *n.* = REALGAR.

redouble /riːˈdʌb(ə)l/ *v.* & *n.* ● *v.* **1** *tr.* & *intr.* make or grow greater or more intense or numerous; intensify, increase. **2** *intr. Bridge* double again a bid already doubled by an opponent. ● *n. Bridge* the redoubling of a bid. [French *redoubler* (as RE-, DOUBLE)]

redoubt /rɪˈdaʊt/ *n. Mil.* an outwork or fieldwork usu. square or polygonal and without flanking defences. [French *redoute* via obsolete Italian *ridotta* and medieval Latin *reductus* 'refuge' from the past part. of Latin *reducere* 'withdraw' (see REDUCE): *-b-* suggested by DOUBT (cf. REDOUBTABLE)]

redoubtable /rɪˈdaʊtəb(ə)l/ *adj.* formidable, esp. as an opponent. ▫ **redoubtably** *adv.* [Middle English from Old French *redoutable,* from *redouter* 'to fear' (as RE-, DOUBT)]

redound /rɪˈdaʊnd/ *v.intr.* **1** (foll. by *to*) (of an action etc.) make a great contribution to (one's credit or advantage etc.). **2** (foll. by *upon, on*) come as the final result to; come back or recoil upon. [originally = overflow: Middle English via Old French *redonder* from Latin *redundare* 'surge' (as RE-, *unda* 'wave')]

redox /ˈriːdɒks, ˈrɛdɒks/ *n.* (often *attrib.*) *Chem.* oxidation and reduction. [*red*uction + *ox*idation]

red pepper *n.* the ripe fruit of *Capsicum annuum.*

redpoll /ˈrɛdpəʊl/ *n.* a finch, *Acanthis flammea,* with a red forehead, similar to a linnet.

redraft /riːˈdrɑːft/ *v.tr.* draft (a writing or document) again.

red rag *n.* something that excites a person's rage (so called because red is supposed to provoke bulls).

red rattle *n.* a pink-flowered marsh plant, *Pedicularis palustris.*

redraw /riːˈdrɔː/ *v.tr.* (*past* **redrew**; *past part.* **redrawn**) draw again or differently.

redress /rɪˈdrɛs/ *v.* & *n.* ● *v.tr.* **1** remedy or rectify (a wrong or grievance etc.). **2** readjust; set straight again. ● *n.* **1** reparation for a wrong. **2** (foll. by *of*) the act or process of redressing (a grievance etc.). ▫ **redress the balance** restore equality. ▫ **redressable** *adj.* **redressal** *n.* **redresser** *n.* (also **redressor**). [Middle English from Old French *redresser, redrecier* (as RE-, DRESS): the noun via Anglo-French *redresse, redresce*]

re-dress /riːˈdrɛs/ *v.tr.* & *intr.* dress again or differently.

red roan *adj.* & *n.* ● *adj.* (of an animal's coat) bay or chestnut mixed with white or grey. ● *n.* a red roan animal.

red rose *n.* the emblem of Lancashire or the Lancastrians.

red sandalwood *n.* the red wood from either of two SE Asian trees, *Adenanthera pavonina* and *Pterocarpus santalinus*, used as timber and to produce a red dye.

redshank /ˈrɛdʃaŋk/ *n.* either of two sandpipers, *Tringa totanus* and *T. erythropus*, with bright red legs.

red shift *n.* the displacement of the spectrum to longer wavelengths in the light coming from distant galaxies etc. in recession.

redskin /ˈrɛdskɪn/ *n. colloq. offens.* an American Indian.

red snapper *n.* an edible marine fish of the family Lutjanidae, esp. *Lutjanus campechinus* of the W. Atlantic.

red spider *n.* (also **red spider mite**) = SPIDER MITE.

red squirrel *n.* **1** the common Eurasian squirrel, *Sciurus vulgaris*, with reddish fur. **2** *US* a small N. American squirrel, *Tamiasciurus hudsonicus*.

Red Star *n.* esp. *hist.* the emblem of some Communist countries.

redstart /ˈrɛdstɑːt/ *n.* **1** any red-tailed European songbird of the genus *Phoenicurus*. **2** any of various American warblers of the family Parulidae with orange-red markings. [RED + Old English *steort* 'tail']

red tape *n.* excessive bureaucracy or adherence to formalities, esp. in public business. [from the red or pink tape used to secure official documents]

red tide *n.* a discoloration of the sea caused by an outbreak of toxic red dinoflagellates.

reduce /rɪˈdjuːs/ *v.* **1** *tr. & intr.* make or become smaller or less. **2** *tr.* (foll. by *to*) bring by force or necessity (to some undesirable state or action) (*reduced them to tears*; *were reduced to begging*). **3** *tr.* convert to another (esp. simpler) form (*reduced it to a powder*). **4** *tr.* convert (a fraction) to the form with the lowest terms. **5** *tr.* (foll. by *to*) bring or simplify or adapt by classification or analysis (*the dispute may be reduced to three issues*). **6** *tr.* make lower in status or rank. **7** *tr.* lower the price of. **8** *intr.* lessen one's weight or size. **9** *tr.* weaken (*is in a very reduced state*). **10** *tr.* impoverish. **11** *tr.* subdue; bring back to obedience. **12** *Chem. intr. & tr.* **a** combine or cause to combine with hydrogen. **b** undergo or cause to undergo addition of electrons (opp. OXIDIZE 3). **13** *tr. Chem.* convert (oxide etc.) to metal. **14** *tr.* **a** (in surgery) restore (a dislocated etc. part) to its proper position. **b** remedy (a dislocation etc.) in this way. **15** *tr. Photog.* make (a negative or print) less dense. **16** *tr. Cookery* boil so as to concentrate (a liquid, sauce, etc.). □ **reduce to the ranks** demote (an NCO) to the rank of private. □ **reducer** *n.* **reducible** *adj.* **reducibility** /-ˈbɪlɪti/ *n.* [Middle English in the sense 'restore to original or proper position', from Latin *reducere reduct-* (as RE-, *ducere* 'bring')]

reduced circumstances *n.pl.* poverty after relative prosperity.

reducing agent *n. Chem.* a substance that brings about reduction by becoming oxidized and losing electrons.

reductio ad absurdum /rɪˌdʌktɪəʊ ad abˈsəːdəm/ *n.* a method of proving the falsity of a premiss by showing that the logical consequence is absurd; an instance of this. [Latin, = reduction to the absurd]

reduction /rɪˈdʌkʃ(ə)n/ *n.* **1** the act or an instance of reducing; the process of being reduced. **2** an amount by which prices etc. are reduced. **3** a reduced copy of a picture etc. **4** an arrangement of an orchestral score for piano etc. □ **reductive** *adj.* [Middle English from Old French *reduction* or Latin *reductio* (as REDUCE)]

reductionism /rɪˈdʌkʃ(ə)nɪz(ə)m/ *n.* **1** the tendency to or principle of analysing complex things into simple constituents. **2** often *derog.* the doctrine that a system can be fully understood in terms of its isolated parts, or an idea in terms of simple concepts (cf. HOLISM 1). □ **reductionist** *n. & adj.* **reductionistic** /-ˈnɪstɪk/ *adj.*

redundant /rɪˈdʌnd(ə)nt/ *adj.* **1** superfluous; not needed. **2** that can be omitted without any loss of significance. **3** *Brit.* (of a person) no longer needed at work and therefore unemployed. **4** *Engin.* & *Computing* (of a component) not needed but included in case of failure in another component. □ **redundancy** *n.* (*pl.* **-ies**). **redundantly** *adv.* [Latin *redundare redundant-* (as REDOUND)]

reduplicate /rɪˈdjuːplɪkeɪt/ *v.tr.* **1** make double. **2** repeat. **3** repeat (a letter or syllable or word) exactly or with a slight change (e.g. hurly-burly, see-saw). □ **reduplication** /-ˈkeɪʃ(ə)n/ *n.* **reduplicative** /-kətɪv/ *adj.* [Late Latin *reduplicare* (as RE-, DUPLICATE)]

red valerian see VALERIAN 2.

redwater /ˈrɛdwɔːtə/ *n.* (in full **redwater fever**) a blood disease of cattle characterized by the passing of red or blackish urine, caused esp. by a tick-borne protozoan parasite of the genus *Babesia*.

redwing /ˈrɛdwɪŋ/ *n.* **1** a migratory thrush, *Turdus iliacus*, of N. Europe, with red underwings showing in flight. **2** any of several other red-winged birds, esp. the American red-winged blackbird, *Agelaius phoeniceus*.

redwood /ˈrɛdwʊd/ *n.* **1** a sequoia, esp. the very tall *Sequoia sempervirens*, of the western US. **2** any tree with reddish wood.

reebok var. of RHEBOK.

re-echo /riːˈɛkəʊ/ *v.intr. & tr.* (**-oes**, **-oed**) **1** echo. **2** echo repeatedly; resound.

reed /riːd/ *n. & v.* ● *n.* **1 a** any of various water or marsh plants with a firm stem, esp. of the genus *Phragmites*. **b** a tall straight stalk of this. **2** (*collect.*) reeds growing in a mass or used as material esp. for thatching. **3** *Brit.* wheat straw prepared for thatching. **4** a pipe of reed or straw. **5 a** the vibrating part of the mouthpiece of some wind instruments, e.g. the oboe and clarinet, made of reed or other material and producing the sound. **b** a reed instrument. **c** (in *pl.*) the section of the orchestra playing such instruments. **6** a weaver's comblike implement for separating the threads of the warp and correctly positioning the weft. **7** (in *pl.*) a set of semicylindrical adjacent mouldings like reeds laid together. ● *v.tr.* **1** thatch with reed. **2** make (straw) into reed. **3** fit (a musical instrument) with a reed. **4** decorate with a moulding of reeds. [Old English *hrēod*, from West Germanic]

reed-bed *n.* a bed or growth of reeds.

reedbuck /ˈriːdbʌk/ *n.* an African antelope of the genus *Redunca*, characterized by a whistling call and high bouncing jumps, esp. *R. arundinum* of eastern and southern Africa.

reed bunting *n.* a small brown bird, *Emberiza schoeniclus*, of reed-beds and similar habitats.

reeded /ˈriːdɪd/ *adj. Mus.* (of an instrument) having a vibrating reed.

reeding /ˈriːdɪŋ/ *n. Archit.* a small semicylindrical moulding or ornamentation (cf. REED *n.* 7).

re-edit /riːˈɛdɪt/ *v.tr.* (**-edited**, **-editing**) edit again or differently. □ **re-edition** /-ɪˈdɪʃ(ə)n/ *n.*

reedling /ˈriːdlɪŋ/ *n.* = BEARDED TIT.

reed mace *n.* a tall reedlike water plant, *Typha latifolia*, with straplike leaves and a head of numerous tiny red-brown flowers.

reed-organ *n.* a harmonium etc. with the sound produced by metal reeds.

reed pipe *n.* **1** a wind instrument with sound produced by a reed. **2** an organ pipe with a reed.

reed-stop *n.* a reeded organ stop.

re-educate /riːˈɛdjʊkeɪt/ *v.tr.* educate again, esp. to change a person's views or beliefs. □ **re-education** /-ˈkeɪʃ(ə)n/ *n.*

reed warbler *n.* any bird of the genus *Acrocephalus*, esp. *A. scirpaceus*, frequenting reed-beds.

reedy /ˈriːdi/ *adj.* (**reedier**, **reediest**) **1** full of reeds. **2** like a reed, esp. in weakness or slenderness. **3** (of a voice) like a reed instrument in tone; not full. □ **reediness** *n.*

reef[1] /riːf/ *n.* **1** a ridge of rock or coral etc. at or near the surface of the sea. **2 a** a lode of ore. **b** the bedrock surrounding this. [earlier *riff(e)*, via Middle Dutch, Middle Low German *rif*, *ref*, from Old Norse *rif* RIB]

reef[2] /ri:f/ *n.* & *v. Naut.* ● *n.* each of several strips across a sail, for taking it in or rolling it up to reduce the surface area in a high wind. ● *v.tr.* **1** take in a reef or reefs of (a sail). **2** shorten (a topmast or a bowsprit). [Middle English *riff*, *refe* via Dutch *reef*, *rif* from Old Norse *rif* RIB, in the same sense: cf. REEF[1]]

reefer /'ri:fə/ *n.* **1** *slang* a marijuana cigarette. **2** = REEFING-JACKET. **3 a** a person who reefs. **b** *colloq.* a midshipman. [REEF[2] (in sense 1, = a thing rolled) + -ER[1]]

reefing-jacket *n.* a thick close-fitting double-breasted jacket.

reef knot *n.* a double knot made symmetrically to hold securely and cast off easily.

reefpoint /'ri:fpɔɪnt/ *n.* each of several short pieces of rope attached to a sail to secure it when reefed.

reek /ri:k/ *v.* & *n.* ● *v.intr.* (often foll. by *of*) **1** smell strongly and unpleasantly. **2** have unpleasant or suspicious associations (*this reeks of corruption*). **3** give off smoke or fumes. ● *n.* **1** a foul or stale smell. **2** esp. *Sc.* smoke. **3** vapour; a visible exhalation (esp. from a chimney). □ **reeky** *adj.* [Old English *rēocan* (*v.*), *rēc* (*n.*), from Germanic]

reel /ri:l/ *n.* & *v.* ● *n.* **1** a cylindrical device on which film, tape, etc., or *Brit.* thread, yarn, wire, etc., are wound. **2** a quantity of thread etc. wound on a reel. **3** a device for winding and unwinding a line as required, esp. in fishing. **4** a revolving part in various machines. **5 a** a lively folk or Scottish dance, of two or more couples facing each other. **b** a piece of music for this usu. in duple time. ● *v.* **1** *tr.* wind (thread, a fishing line, etc.) on a reel. **2** *tr.* (foll. by *in*, *up*) draw (fish etc.) in or up by the use of a reel. **3** *intr.* stand or walk or run unsteadily. **4** *intr.* be shaken mentally or physically. **5** *intr.* rock from side to side, or swing violently. **6** *intr.* dance a reel. □ **reel off** say or recite very rapidly and without apparent effort. □ **reeler** *n.* [Old English *hrēol*, of unknown origin]

re-elect /ri:ɪ'lɛkt/ *v.tr.* elect again, esp. to a further term of office. □ **re-election** /-ɪ'lɛkʃ(ə)n/ *n.*

re-eligible /ri:'ɛlɪdʒɪb(ə)l/ *adj.* eligible for re-election to a further term of office.

re-embark /ri:ɪm'bɑ:k, -ɛm-/ *v.intr.* & *tr.* go or put on board ship again. □ **re-embarkation** /-'keɪʃ(ə)n/ *n.*

re-emerge /ri:ɪ'mə:dʒ/ *v.intr.* emerge again; come back out. □ **re-emergence** *n.* **re-emergent** *adj.*

re-emphasize /ri:'ɛmfəsʌɪz/ *v.tr.* (also **-ise**) place renewed emphasis on. □ **re-emphasis** /-'ɛmfəsɪs/ *n.*

re-employ /ri:ɪm'plɔɪ, -ɛm-/ *v.tr.* employ again. □ **re-employment** *n.*

re-enact /ri:ɪ'nakt, -ɛ'nakt/ *v.tr.* act out (a past event). □ **re-enactment** *n.*

re-enlist /ri:ɪn'lɪst, -ɛn-/ *v.intr.* enlist again, esp. in the armed services. □ **re-enlister** *n.*

re-enter /rɪ'ɛntə/ *v.tr.* & *intr.* enter again; go back in. □ **re-entrance** /-'ɛntr(ə)ns/ *n.*

re-entrant /rɪ'ɛntr(ə)nt/ *adj.* & *n.* ● *adj.* **1** (of an angle, esp. in fortification) pointing inwards (opp. SALIENT *adj.* 2). **2** *Geom.* reflex. ● *n.* a re-entrant angle.

re-entry /rɪ'ɛntri/ *n.* (*pl.* **-ies**) **1** the act of entering again, esp. (of a spacecraft, missile, etc.) re-entering the earth's atmosphere. **2** *Law* an act of retaking or repossession.

re-equip /ri:ɪ'kwɪp/ *v.tr.* & *intr.* (**-equipped**, **-equipping**) provide or be provided with new equipment.

re-erect /ri:ɪ'rɛkt/ *v.tr.* erect again. □ **re-erection** /-ɪ'rɛkʃ(ə)n/ *n.*

re-establish /ri:ɪ'stablɪʃ, ri:ɛ-/ *v.tr.* establish again or anew. □ **re-establishment** *n.*

re-evaluate /ri:ɪ'valjʊeɪt/ *v.tr.* evaluate again or differently. □ **re-evaluation** /-'eɪʃ(ə)n/ *n.*

reeve[1] /ri:v/ *n.* **1** *hist.* **a** the chief magistrate of a town or district. **b** an official supervising a landowner's estate. **c** any of various minor local officials. **2** *Canad.* the president of a village or town council. [Old English *(ge)rēfa*, *girǣfa*]

reeve[2] /ri:v/ *v.tr.* (*past* **rove** /rəʊv/ or **reeved**) *Naut.* **1** (usu. foll. by *through*) thread (a rope or rod etc.) through a ring or other aperture. **2** pass a rope through (a block etc.). **3** fasten (a rope or block) in this way. [probably from Dutch *rēven* REEF[2]]

reeve[3] /ri:v/ *n.* a female ruff (see RUFF[1] 4). [17th c.: origin unknown]

re-examine /ri:ɪg'zamɪn, -ɛg-/ *v.tr.* examine again or further (esp. a witness after cross-examination). □ **re-examination** /-'neɪʃ(ə)n/ *n.*

re-export *v.* & *n.* ● *v.tr.* /ri:ɪk'spɔ:t, -ɛk-/ export again (esp. imported goods after further processing or manufacture). ● *n.* /ri:'ɛkspɔ:t/ **1** the process of re-exporting. **2** something re-exported. □ **re-exportation** /-'teɪʃ(ə)n/ *n.* **re-exporter** /ri:ɪk'spɔ:tə, -ɛk-/ *n.*

ref /rɛf/ *n. colloq.* a referee in sports. [abbreviation]

ref. *abbr.* **1** reference. **2** refer to.

reface /ri:'feɪs/ *v.tr.* put a new facing on (a building).

refashion /ri:'faʃ(ə)n/ *v.tr.* fashion again or differently.

refection /rɪ'fɛkʃ(ə)n/ *n. literary* **1** refreshment by food or drink (*we took refection*). **2** a light meal. [Middle English via Old French from Latin *refectio -onis*, from *reficere* (as REFECTORY)]

refectory /rɪ'fɛkt(ə)ri/ *n.* (*pl.* **-ies**) a room used for communal meals, esp. in a monastery or college. [Late Latin *refectorium* from Latin *reficere* 'refresh' (as RE-, *facere* 'make')]

refectory table *n.* a long narrow table.

refer /rɪ'fə:/ *v.* (**referred**, **referring**) (usu. foll. by *to*) **1** *tr.* trace or ascribe (to a person or thing as a cause or source) (*referred their success to their popularity*). **2** *tr.* consider as belonging (to a certain date or place or class). **3** *tr.* send on or direct (a person, or a question for decision) (*the matter was referred to arbitration*; *referred him to her previous answer*). **4** *intr.* make an appeal or have recourse to (some authority or source of information) (*referred to his notes*). **5** *tr.* send or direct (a person) to a medical specialist etc. **6** *tr.* (foll. by *back to*) send (a proposal etc.) back to (a lower body, court, etc.). **7** *intr.* (foll. by *to*) (of a person speaking) make an allusion or direct the hearer's attention (*decided not to refer to our other problems*). **8** *intr.* (foll. by *to*) (of a statement etc.) have a particular relation or be directed to (*this paragraph refers to the events of last year*). **9** *tr.* (foll. by *to*) interpret (a statement) as being directed to (a particular context etc.). **10** *tr.* fail (a candidate in an examination). □ **refer to drawer** *Brit.* a banker's note suspending payment of a cheque. □ **referable** /rɪ'fə:rəb(ə)l, 'rɛf(ə)r-/ *adj.* **referrer** *n.* [Middle English via Old French *referer* from Latin *referre* 'carry back' (as RE-, *ferre* 'bring')]

referee /rɛfə'ri:/ *n.* & *v.* ● *n.* **1** an umpire esp. in football or boxing. **2** a person whose opinion or judgement is sought in some connection, or who is referred to for a decision in a dispute etc. **3** a person willing to testify to the character of an applicant for employment etc. ● *v.* (**referees**, **refereed**) **1** *intr.* act as referee. **2** *tr.* be the referee of (a game etc.).

reference /'rɛf(ə)r(ə)ns/ *n.* & *v.* ● *n.* **1** the referring of a matter for decision or settlement or consideration to some authority. **2** the scope given to this authority. **3** (foll. by *to*) **a** a relation or respect or correspondence (*success seems to have little reference to merit*). **b** an allusion (*made no reference to our problems*). **c** a direction to a book etc. (or a passage in it) where information may be found. **d** a book or passage so cited. **4 a** the act of looking up a passage etc. or looking in a book for information. **b** the act of referring to a person etc. for information. **5 a** a written testimonial supporting an applicant for employment etc. **b** a person giving this. ● *v.tr.* provide (a book etc.) with references to authorities. □ **with** (or **in**) **reference to** regarding; as regards; about. **without reference to** not taking account of. □ **referential** /-'rɛnʃ(ə)l/ *adj.* **referentiality** /-rɛnʃɪ'alɪti/ *n.*

reference book *n.* a book intended to be consulted for information on individual matters rather than read continuously.

reference library *n.* a library in which the books are for consultation not loan.

referendum /rɛfəˈrɛndəm/ *n.* (*pl.* **referendums** or **referenda** /-də/) **1** the process of referring a political question to the electorate for a direct decision by general vote. **2** a vote taken by referendum. [Latin, gerund or neut. gerundive of *referre*: see REFER]

referent /ˈrɛf(ə)r(ə)nt/ *n.* the idea or thing that a word etc. symbolizes. [Latin *referent-*, pres. part. stem of *referre*: see REFER]

referral /rɪˈfəːr(ə)l/ *n.* the referring of an individual to an expert or specialist for advice, esp. the directing of a patient by a GP to a medical specialist.

referred pain *n.* pain felt in a part of the body other than its actual source.

refill *v.* & *n.* ● *v.tr.* /riːˈfɪl/ **1** fill again. **2** provide a new filling for. ● *n.* /ˈriːfɪl/ **1** a new filling. **2** the material for this. □ **refillable** /-ˈfɪləb(ə)l/ *adj.*

refinance /riːˈfʌɪnans/ *v.tr.* finance again; provide with further capital.

refine /rɪˈfʌɪn/ *v.* **1** *tr.* free from impurities or defects; purify, clarify. **2** *tr.* & *intr.* make or become more polished or elegant or cultured. **3** *tr.* & *intr.* make or become more subtle or delicate in thought, feelings, etc. □ **refinable** *adj.* [RE- + FINE[1] *v.*, influenced by French *raffiner*]

refined /rɪˈfʌɪnd/ *adj.* characterized by polish or elegance or subtlety.

refinement /rɪˈfʌɪnm(ə)nt/ *n.* **1** the act of refining or the process of being refined. **2** fineness of feeling or taste. **3** polish or elegance in behaviour or manner. **4** an added development or improvement (*a car with several refinements*). **5** a piece of subtle reasoning. **6** a fine distinction. **7** a subtle or ingenious example or display (*all the refinements of reasoning*). [REFINE + -MENT, influenced by French *raffinement*]

refiner /rɪˈfʌɪnə/ *n.* a person or company whose business is to refine crude oil, metal, sugar, etc.

refinery /rɪˈfʌɪn(ə)ri/ *n.* (*pl.* **-ies**) a place where oil etc. is refined.

refinish /riːˈfɪnɪʃ/ *v.tr.* apply a new finish to (a surface).

refit *v.* & *n.* ● *v.tr.* & *intr.* /riːˈfɪt/ (**refitted**, **refitting**) make or become fit or serviceable again (esp. of a ship undergoing renewal and repairs). ● *n.* /ˈriːfɪt/ the act or an instance of refitting; the process of being refitted. □ **refitment** *n.*

reflag /riːˈflag/ *v.tr.* (**reflagged**, **reflagging**) change the national registration of (a ship).

reflate /riːˈfleɪt/ *v.tr.* cause reflation of (a currency or economy etc.). [RE-, on the pattern of *inflate, deflate*]

reflation /riːˈfleɪʃ(ə)n/ *n.* the inflation of a financial system to restore its previous condition after deflation. □ **reflationary** *adj.* [RE-, on the pattern of *inflation, deflation*]

reflect /rɪˈflɛkt/ *v.* **1** *tr.* **a** (of a surface or body) throw back (heat, light, sound, etc.). **b** cause to rebound (*reflected light*). **2** *tr.* (of a mirror) show an image of; reproduce to the eye or mind. **3** *tr.* correspond in appearance or effect to; have as a cause or source (*their behaviour reflects a wish to succeed*). **4** *tr.* **a** (of an action, result, etc.) show or bring (credit, discredit, etc.). **b** (*absol.*; usu. foll. by *on, upon*) bring discredit on. **5 a** *intr.* (often foll. by *on, upon*) meditate on; think about. **b** *tr.* (foll. by *that, how*, etc. + clause) consider; remind oneself. **6** *intr.* (usu. foll. by *upon, on*) make disparaging remarks. [Middle English from Old French *reflecter* or Latin *reflectere* (as RE-, *flectere flex-* 'bend')]

reflectance /rɪˈflɛkt(ə)ns/ *n.* *Physics* a measure of the proportion of light or other radiation falling on a surface and then being reflected or scattered.

reflecting telescope *n.* = REFLECTOR 2a.

reflection /rɪˈflɛkʃ(ə)n/ *n.* (also *Brit.* **reflexion**) **1** the act or an instance of reflecting; the process of being reflected. **2 a** reflected light, heat, or colour. **b** a reflected image. **3** reconsideration (*on reflection*). **4** (often foll. by *on*) discredit or a thing bringing discredit. **5** (often foll. by *on, upon*) an idea arising in the mind; a comment or apophthegm. □ **angle of reflection** *Physics* the angle made by a reflected ray with a perpendicular to the reflecting surface. [Middle English from Old French *reflexion* or Late Latin *reflexio* (as REFLECT), with assimilation to *reflect*]

reflective /rɪˈflɛktɪv/ *adj.* **1** (of a surface etc.) giving a reflection or image. **2** (of mental faculties) concerned in reflection or thought. **3** (of a person or mood etc.) thoughtful; given to meditation. □ **reflectively** *adv.* **reflectiveness** *n.*

reflectivity /riːflɛkˈtɪvɪti/ *n.* *Physics* the property of reflecting light or radiation, esp. reflectance as measured independently of the thickness of a material.

reflector /rɪˈflɛktə/ *n.* **1** a piece of glass or metal etc. for reflecting light in a required direction, e.g. a red one on the back of a motor vehicle or bicycle. **2 a** a telescope etc. using a mirror to produce images. **b** the mirror itself.

reflet /rəˈfleɪ/ *n.* lustre or iridescence, esp. on pottery. [French from Italian *riflesso* 'reflection, REFLEX']

reflex /ˈriːflɛks/ *adj.* & *n.* ● *adj.* **1** (of an action) independent of the will, as an automatic response to the stimulation of a nerve (e.g. a sneeze). **2** (of an angle) exceeding 180°. **3** bent backwards. **4** (of light) reflected. **5** (of a thought etc.) introspective; directed back upon itself or its own operations. **6** (of an effect or influence) reactive; coming back upon its author or source. ● *n.* **1** a reflex action. **2** a sign or secondary manifestation (*law is a reflex of public opinion*). **3** reflected light or a reflected image. **4** a word formed by development from an earlier stage of a language. □ **reflexly** *adv.* [Latin *reflexus* (as REFLECT)]

reflex arc *n.* *Anat.* the sequence of nerves involved in a reflex action.

reflex camera *n.* a camera with a ground-glass focusing screen on which the image is formed by a combination of lens and mirror, enabling the scene to be correctly composed and focused.

reflexible /rɪˈflɛksɪb(ə)l/ *adj.* capable of being reflected. □ **reflexibility** /-ˈbɪlɪti/ *n.*

reflexion *Brit.* var. of REFLECTION.

reflexive /rɪˈflɛksɪv/ *adj.* & *n.* *Gram.* ● *adj.* **1** (of a word or form) referring back to the subject of a sentence (esp. of a pronoun, e.g. *myself*). **2** (of a verb) having a reflexive pronoun as its object (as in *to wash oneself*). ● *n.* a reflexive word or form, esp. a pronoun. □ **reflexively** *adv.* **reflexiveness** *n.* **reflexivity** /-ˈsɪvɪti/ *n.*

reflexology /riːflɛkˈsɒlədʒi/ *n.* **1** a system of massage through reflex points on the feet, hands, and head, used to relieve tension and treat illness. **2** *Psychol.* the scientific study of reflexes. □ **reflexologist** *n.*

refloat /riːˈfləʊt/ *v.tr.* set (a stranded ship) afloat again.

refluent /ˈrɛflʊənt/ *adj.* flowing back (*refluent tide*). □ **refluence** *n.* [Middle English from Latin *refluere* (as RE-, *fluere* 'flow')]

reflux /ˈriːflʌks/ *n.* & *v.* ● *n.* **1** a backward flow. **2** *Chem.* a method of boiling a liquid so that any vapour is liquefied and returned to the boiler. ● *v.tr.* & *intr.* *Chem.* boil or be boiled under reflux.

refocus /riːˈfəʊkəs/ *v.tr.* (**refocused**, **refocusing** or **refocussed**, **refocussing**) focus again or adjust the focus of.

reforest /riːˈfɒrɪst/ *v.tr.* = REAFFOREST. □ **reforestation** /-ˈsteɪʃ(ə)n/ *n.*

reforge /riːˈfɔːdʒ/ *v.tr.* forge again or differently.

reform /rɪˈfɔːm/ *v.* & *n.* ● *v.* **1** *tr.* & *intr.* make or become better by the removal of faults and errors. **2** *tr.* abolish or cure (an abuse or malpractice). **3** *tr.* *US* correct (a legal document). **4** *tr.* *Chem.* convert (a straight-chain hydrocarbon) by catalytic reaction to a branched molecular form for use as petrol. ● *n.* **1** the removal of faults or abuses, esp. of a moral or political or social kind. **2** an improvement made or suggested. □ **reformable** *adj.* [Middle English from Old French *reformer* or Latin *reformare* (as RE-, FORM)]

re-form /riːˈfɔːm/ *v.tr. & intr.* form again.

reformat /riːˈfɔːmat/ *v.tr.* (**reformatted, reformatting**) revise or represent in another format; format again.

reformation /rɛfəˈmeɪʃ(ə)n/ *n.* **1** the act of reforming or process of being reformed, esp. a radical change for the better in political or religious or social affairs. **2** (**the Reformation**) *hist.* a 16th-c. movement for the reform of abuses in the Roman Church ending in the establishment of the Reformed and Protestant Churches. □ **Reformational** *adj.* [Middle English from Old French *reformation* or Latin *reformatio* (as REFORM)]

re-formation /riːfɔːˈmeɪʃ(ə)n/ *n.* the process or an instance of forming or being formed again.

reformative /rɪˈfɔːmətɪv/ *adj.* tending or intended to produce reform. [Old French *reformatif -ive* or medieval Latin *reformativus* (as REFORM)]

reformatory /rɪˈfɔːmət(ə)ri/ *n. & adj.* ● *n.* (*pl.* **-ies**) *N. Amer. & hist.* = REFORM SCHOOL. ● *adj.* reformative.

Reformed Church *n.* a Church that has accepted the principles of the Reformation, esp. a Calvinist Church (as distinct from Lutheran).

reformer /rɪˈfɔːmə/ *n.* a person who advocates or brings about (esp. political or social) reform.

reformism /rɪˈfɔːmɪz(ə)m/ *n.* a policy of reform rather than abolition or revolution. □ **reformist** *n.*

Reform Judaism *n.* a simplified and rationalized form of Judaism.

reform school *n.* an institution to which young offenders are sent to be reformed.

reformulate /riːˈfɔːmjʊleɪt/ *v.tr.* formulate again or differently. □ **reformulation** /-ˈleɪʃ(ə)n/ *n.*

refract /rɪˈfrakt/ *v.tr.* **1** (of water, air, glass, etc.) deflect (a ray of light etc.) at a certain angle when it enters obliquely from another medium. **2** determine the refractive condition of (the eye). [Latin *refringere refract-* (as RE-, *frangere* 'break')]

refraction /rɪˈfrakʃ(ə)n/ *n.* the process by which or the extent to which light is refracted. □ **angle of refraction** the angle made by a refracted ray with the perpendicular to the refracting surface. [French *réfraction* or Late Latin *refractio* (as REFRACT)]

refractive /rɪˈfraktɪv/ *adj.* of or involving refraction.

refractive index *n.* the ratio of the velocity of light in a vacuum to its velocity in a specified medium.

refractometer /riːfrakˈtɒmɪtə/ *n.* an instrument for measuring a refractive index. □ **refractometric** /-təˈmɛtrɪk/ *adj.* **refractometry** *n.*

refractor /rɪˈfraktə/ *n.* **1** a refracting medium or lens. **2** a telescope using a lens to produce an image.

refractory /rɪˈfrakt(ə)ri/ *adj. & n.* ● *adj.* **1** stubborn, unmanageable, rebellious. **2 a** (of a wound, disease, etc.) not yielding to treatment. **b** (of a person etc.) resistant to infection. **3** (of a substance) hard to fuse or work. ● *n.* (*pl.* **-ies**) a substance especially resistant to heat, corrosion, etc. □ **refractorily** *adv.* **refractoriness** *n.* [alteration of obsolete *refractary* from Latin *refractarius* (as REFRACT)]

refrain[1] /rɪˈfreɪn/ *v.intr.* (foll. by *from*) avoid doing (an action); forbear, desist (*refrain from smoking*). □ **refrainment** *n.* [Middle English via Old French *refrener* from Latin *refrenare* (as RE-, *frenum* 'bridle')]

refrain[2] /rɪˈfreɪn/ *n.* **1** a recurring phrase or number of lines, esp. at the ends of stanzas. **2** the music accompanying this. [Middle English from Old French *refrain* (earlier *refrait*), ultimately from Latin *refringere* (as RE-, *frangere* 'break'), because the refrain 'broke' the sequence]

refrangible /rɪˈfran(d)ʒɪb(ə)l/ *adj.* that can be refracted. □ **refrangibility** /-ˈbɪlɪti/ *n.* [modern Latin *refrangibilis* from *refrangere* = Latin *refringere*: see REFRACT]

refreeze /riːˈfriːz/ *v.tr. & intr.* (*past* **refroze**; *past part.* **refrozen**) freeze again.

refresh /rɪˈfrɛʃ/ *v.tr.* **1 a** (of food, rest, amusement, etc.) give fresh spirit or vigour to. **b** (esp. *refl.*) revive with food, rest, etc. (*refreshed myself with a short sleep*). **2** revive or stimulate (the memory), esp. by consulting the source of one's information. **3** make cool. [Middle English from Old French *refreschi(e)r*, from *fres fresche* FRESH]

refresher /rɪˈfrɛʃə/ *n.* **1** something that refreshes, esp. a drink. **2** *Brit. Law* an extra fee payable to counsel in a prolonged case.

refresher course *n.* a course reviewing or updating previous studies.

refreshing /rɪˈfrɛʃɪŋ/ *adj.* **1** serving to refresh. **2** welcome or stimulating because sincere or untypical (*refreshing innocence*). □ **refreshingly** *adv.*

refreshment /rɪˈfrɛʃm(ə)nt/ *n.* **1** the act of refreshing or the process of being refreshed in mind or body. **2** (usu. in *pl.*) food or drink that refreshes. **3** something that refreshes or stimulates the mind. [Middle English from Old French *refreschement* (as REFRESH)]

refrigerant /rɪˈfrɪdʒ(ə)r(ə)nt/ *n. & adj.* ● *n.* **1** a substance used for refrigeration. **2** *Med.* a substance that cools or allays fever. ● *adj.* cooling. [French *réfrigérant* or Latin *refrigerant-* (as REFRIGERATE)]

refrigerate /rɪˈfrɪdʒəreɪt/ *v.* **1** *tr. & intr.* make or become cool or cold. **2** *tr.* subject (food etc.) to cold in order to freeze or preserve it. □ **refrigeration** /-ˈreɪʃ(ə)n/ *n.* **refrigerative** /-rətɪv/ *adj.* [Latin *refrigerare* (as RE-, *frigus frigoris* 'cold')]

refrigerator /rɪˈfrɪdʒəreɪtə/ *n.* a cabinet or room in which food etc. is kept cold.

refrigeratory /rɪˈfrɪdʒ(ə)rət(ə)ri/ *adj. & n.* ● *adj.* serving to cool. ● *n.* (*pl.* **-ies**) *hist.* a cold-water vessel attached to a still for condensing vapour. [modern Latin *refrigeratorium* (*n.*), Latin *refrigeratorius* (*adj.*) (as REFRIGERATE)]

refringent /rɪˈfrɪn(d)ʒ(ə)nt/ *adj.* *Physics* refracting. □ **refringence** *n.* **refringency** *n.* [Latin *refringere*: see REFRACT]

refroze *past* of REFREEZE.

refrozen *past part.* of REFREEZE.

reft *past* and *past part.* of REAVE.

refuel /riːˈfjʊəl, -ˈfjuːəl/ *v.* (**refuelled, refuelling**; *US* **refueled, refueling**) **1** *intr.* replenish a fuel supply. **2** *tr.* supply with more fuel.

refuge /ˈrɛfjuːdʒ/ *n.* **1** a shelter from pursuit or danger or trouble. **2** a person or place etc. offering this. **3** a person, thing, or course resorted to in difficulties. **4** a traffic island. [Middle English via Old French from Latin *refugium* (as RE-, *fugere* 'flee')]

refugee /rɛfjʊˈdʒiː/ *n.* a person taking refuge, esp. in a foreign country from war or persecution or natural disaster. [French *réfugié*, past part. of (*se*) *réfugier* (as REFUGE)]

refugium /rɪˈfjuːdʒɪəm/ *n.* (*pl.* **refugia** /-dʒɪə/) *Biol.* an area in which a population of organisms can survive through a period of unfavourable conditions, esp. glaciation. [Latin, = place of refuge]

refulgent /rɪˈfʌldʒ(ə)nt/ *adj. literary* shining; gloriously bright. □ **refulgence** *n.* **refulgently** *adv.* [Latin *refulgēre* (as RE-, *fulgēre* 'shine')]

refund *v. & n.* ● *v.tr.* /rɪˈfʌnd/ (also *absol.*) **1** pay back (money or expenses). **2** reimburse (a person). ● *n.* /ˈriːfʌnd/ **1** an act of refunding. **2** a sum refunded; a repayment. □ **refundable** /rɪˈfʌndəb(ə)l/ *adj.* [originally = pour back: Middle English from Old French *refonder* or Latin *refundere* (as RE-, *fundere* 'pour'), later associated with FUND]

re-fund /riːˈfʌnd/ *v.tr.* fund (a debt etc.) again.

refurbish /riːˈfəːbɪʃ/ *v.tr.* **1** brighten up. **2** restore and redecorate. □ **refurbishment** *n.*

refurnish /riːˈfəːnɪʃ/ *v.tr.* furnish again or differently.

refusal /rɪˈfjuːz(ə)l/ *n.* **1** the act or an instance of refusing; the state of being refused. **2** (in full **first refusal**) the right or privilege of deciding to take or leave a thing before it is offered to others.

refuse[1] /rɪˈfjuːz/ *v.tr.* **1** withhold acceptance of or consent to (*refuse an offer*; *refuse orders*). **2** (often foll. by *to* + infin.; also *absol.*) indicate unwillingness (*I refuse to go*; *the car refuses to start*; *I refuse!*). **3** (often with double object) not grant (a request) made by (a person) (*refused me a day off*; *I could not refuse them*). **4** (also *absol.*) (of a horse) be unwilling to jump (a fence etc.). □ **refuser** *n.* [Middle English from Old French *refuser*, probably ultimately from Latin *recusare* (see RECUSANT), influenced by *refutare* REFUTE]

refuse[2] /ˈrɛfjuːs/ *n.* items rejected as worthless; waste. [Middle English, perhaps from Old French *refusé*, past part. of *refuser* (as REFUSE[1])]

re-fuse /riːˈfjuːz/ *v.tr.* fuse again; provide with a new fuse.

refusenik /rɪˈfjuːznɪk/ *n.* **1** *hist.* a Jew in the former Soviet Union who was refused permission to emigrate to Israel. **2** a person who refuses to follow orders or obey the law, esp. as a protest. [REFUSE[1] + -NIK]

refute /rɪˈfjuːt/ *v.tr.* **1** prove the falsity or error of (a statement etc. or the person advancing it). **2** rebut or repel by argument. **3** *disp.* deny or contradict (without argument). □ **refutable** *adj.* **refutal** *n.* **refutation** /rɛfjʊˈteɪʃ(ə)n/ *n.* **refuter** *n.* [Latin *refutare* (as RE-: cf. CONFUTE)]

■ **Usage** The use of *refute* in sense 3 is considered incorrect by some people. It is often confused in this sense with *repudiate*.

reg /rɛdʒ/ *n. Brit. colloq.* = REGISTRATION MARK. [abbreviation]

regain /rɪˈgeɪn/ *v.tr.* obtain possession or use of after loss (*regain consciousness*). [French *regagner* (as RE-, GAIN)]

regal /ˈriːg(ə)l/ *adj.* **1** royal; of or by a monarch or monarchs. **2** fit for a monarch; magnificent. □ **regally** *adv.* [Middle English from Old French *regal* or Latin *regalis*, from *rex regis* 'king']

regale /rɪˈgeɪl/ *v.tr.* **1** entertain lavishly with feasting. **2** (foll. by *with*) entertain or divert with (talk etc.). **3** (of beauty, flowers, etc.) give delight to. □ **regalement** *n.* [French *régaler* (as RE-, Old French *gale* 'pleasure')]

regalia /rɪˈgeɪlɪə/ *n.pl.* **1** the insignia of royalty used at coronations. **2** the insignia of an order or of civic dignity. [medieval Latin, = royal privileges, from Latin, neut. pl. of *regalis* REGAL]

■ **Usage** Note that *regalia* is a plural noun with no singular form in English.

regalism /ˈriːg(ə)lɪz(ə)m/ *n.* the doctrine of a sovereign's ecclesiastical supremacy.

regality /rɪˈgalɪti/ *n.* (*pl.* **-ies**) **1** the state of being a king or queen. **2** an attribute of sovereign power. **3** a royal privilege. [Middle English from Old French *regalité* or medieval Latin *regalitas* (as REGAL)]

regard /rɪˈgɑːd/ *v. & n.* ● *v.tr.* **1** give heed to; take into account; let one's course be affected by. **2** look upon or contemplate mentally in a specified way (*I regard them kindly*; *I regard it as an insult*). **3** gaze on steadily (usu. in a specified way) (*regarded them suspiciously*). **4** (of a thing) have relation to; have some connection with. ● *n.* **1** (foll. by *to, for*) attention or care. **2** (foll. by *for*) esteem; kindly feeling; respectful opinion. **3** a gaze; a steady or significant look. **4** a respect; a point attended to (*in this regard*). **5** (in *pl.*) an expression of friendliness in a letter etc.; compliments (*sent my best regards*). □ **as regards** about, concerning; in respect of. **in** (or **with**) **regard to** as concerns; in respect of. [Middle English from Old French *regard*, from *regarder* (as RE-, *garder* GUARD)]

regardant /rɪˈgɑːd(ə)nt/ *adj. Heraldry* looking backwards. [Anglo-French & Old French (as REGARD)]

regardful /rɪˈgɑːdfʊl, -f(ə)l/ *adj.* (foll. by *of*) mindful of; paying attention to.

regarding /rɪˈgɑːdɪŋ/ *prep.* about, concerning; in respect of.

regardless /rɪˈgɑːdlɪs/ *adj. & adv.* ● *adj.* (foll. by *of*) without regard or consideration for (*regardless of the expense*). ● *adv.* without paying attention (*carried on regardless*). □ **regardlessly** *adv.* **regardlessness** *n.*

regather /riːˈgaðə/ *v.tr. & intr.* **1** gather or collect again. **2** meet again.

regatta /rɪˈgatə/ *n.* a sporting event consisting of a series of boat or yacht races. [Italian (Venetian), = a fight, a contest]

regd. *abbr.* registered.

regelate /riːdʒɪˈleɪt/ *v.intr.* freeze again (esp. of pieces of ice etc. frozen together after temporary thawing of the surfaces). □ **regelation** /-ˈleɪʃ(ə)n/ *n.* [RE- + Latin *gelare* 'freeze']

regency /ˈriːdʒ(ə)nsi/ *n.* (*pl.* **-ies**) **1** the office of regent. **2** a commission acting as regent. **3 a** the period of office of a regent or regency commission. **b** (**Regency**) a particular period of a regency, esp. (in Britain) from 1811 to 1820, and (in France) from 1715 to 1723 (often *attrib.*: *Regency costume*). [Middle English from medieval Latin *regentia* (as REGENT)]

regenerate *v. & adj.* ● *v.* /rɪˈdʒɛnəreɪt/ **1** *tr. & intr.* bring or come into renewed existence; generate again. **2** *tr.* improve the moral condition of. **3** *tr.* impart new and more vigorous life to (a person or institution etc.). **4** *intr.* reform oneself. **5** *tr.* invest with a new and higher spiritual nature. **6** *intr. & tr. Biol.* regrow or cause (new tissue) to regrow to replace lost or injured tissue. **7** *tr. & intr. Chem.* restore or be restored to an initial state of reaction or process. ● *adj.* /rɪˈdʒɛn(ə)rət/ **1** spiritually born again. **2** reformed. □ **regeneration** /-ˈreɪʃ(ə)n/ *n.* **regenerative** /-rətɪv/ *adj.* **regeneratively** /-rətɪvli/ *adv.* **regenerator** *n.* [Latin *regenerare* (as RE-, GENERATE)]

regent /ˈriːdʒ(ə)nt/ *n. & adj.* ● *n.* **1** a person appointed to administer a state because the monarch is a minor or is absent or incapacitated. **2** *US* a member of the governing body of a state university. ● *adj.* (placed after noun) acting as regent (*Prince Regent*). [Middle English from Old French *regent* or Latin *regere* 'rule']

regent-bird *n.* an Australian bower bird, *Sericulus chrysocephalus*.

regerminate /riːˈdʒəːmɪneɪt/ *v.tr. & intr.* germinate again. □ **regermination** /-ˈneɪʃ(ə)n/ *n.*

reggae /ˈrɛgeɪ/ *n.* a W. Indian style of music with a strongly accented subsidiary beat. [West Indian]

regicide /ˈrɛdʒɪsʌɪd/ *n.* **1** a person who kills or takes part in killing a king. **2** the act of killing a king. □ **regicidal** /-ˈsʌɪd(ə)l/ *adj.* [Latin *rex regis* 'king' + -CIDE]

regild /riːˈgɪld/ *v.tr.* gild again, esp. to renew faded or worn gilding.

regime /reɪˈʒiːm/ *n.* (also **régime**) **1 a** a method or system of government. **b** *derog.* a particular government. **2** a prevailing order or system of things. **3** the conditions under which a scientific or industrial process occurs. **4** a (medical) regimen. [French *régime* (as REGIMEN)]

regimen /ˈrɛdʒɪmən/ *n.* **1** esp. *Med.* a prescribed course of exercise, way of life, and diet. **2** *archaic* a system of government. [Latin from *regere* 'rule']

regiment *n. & v.* ● *n.* /ˈrɛdʒɪm(ə)nt/ **1 a** a permanent unit of an army usu. commanded by a colonel and divided into several companies or troops or batteries and often into two battalions. **b** an operational unit of artillery etc. **2** (usu. foll. by *of*) a large array or number. **3** *archaic* rule, government. ● *v.tr.* /ˈrɛdʒɪmɛnt/ **1** organize (esp. oppressively) in groups or according to a system. **2** form into a regiment or regiments. □ **regimentation** /-ˈteɪʃ(ə)n/ *n.* [Middle English (in sense 3) via Old French from Late Latin *regimentum* (as REGIMEN)]

regimental /rɛdʒɪˈmɛnt(ə)l/ *adj. & n.* ● *adj.* of or relating to a regiment. ● *n.* (in *pl.*) military uniform, esp. of a particular regiment. □ **regimentally** *adv.*

regimental colour *n.* = QUEEN'S COLOUR.

regimental sergeant major see SERGEANT MAJOR 1.

Regina /rɪˈdʒʌɪnə/ *n.* the reigning queen (following a name or in the titles of lawsuits, e.g. *Regina v. Jones* the Crown versus Jones). [Latin, = queen]

region /ˈriːdʒ(ə)n/ *n.* **1** an area of land, or division of the earth's surface, having definable boundaries or characteristics (*a mountainous region*; *the region between London and the coast*). **2** an administrative district esp. in Scotland. **3** a part of the body round or near some organ etc. (*the lumbar region*). **4** a sphere or realm (*the region of metaphysics*). **5 a** a separate part of the world or universe. **b** a layer of the atmosphere or the sea according to its height or depth. □ **in the region of** approximately. □ **regional** *adj.* **regionalism** *n.* **regionalist** *n. & adj.* **regionalize** *v.tr.* (also **-ise**). **regionally** *adv.* [Middle English via Old French from Latin *regio -onis* 'direction, district', from *regere* 'direct']

regisseur /reɪʒɪˈsəː/ *n.* the director of a theatrical production, esp. a ballet. [French *régisseur* 'stage manager']

register /ˈrɛdʒɪstə/ *n. & v.* ● *n.* **1** an official list e.g. of births, marriages, and deaths, of shipping, of professionally qualified persons, or of qualified voters in a constituency. **2** a book in which items are recorded for reference. **3** a device recording speed, force, etc. **4** (in electronic devices) a location in a store of data, used for a specific purpose and with quick access time. **5 a** the compass of a voice or instrument. **b** a part of this compass (*lower register*). **6** an adjustable plate for widening or narrowing an opening and regulating a draught, esp. in a fire-grate. **7 a** a set of organ pipes. **b** a sliding device controlling this. **8** = CASH REGISTER. **9** *Linguistics* each of several forms of a language (colloquial, formal, literary, etc.) usually used in particular circumstances. **10** *Printing* the exact correspondence of the position of printed matter on the two sides of a leaf. **11** *Printing* & *Photog.* the correspondence of the position of colour-components in a printed positive. ● *v.* **1** *tr.* set down (a name, fact, etc.) formally; record in writing. **2** *tr.* make a mental note of; notice. **3** *tr.* enter or cause to be entered in a particular register. **4** *tr.* entrust (a letter etc.) to a post office for transmission by registered post. **5** *intr. & refl.* put one's name on a register, esp. as an eligible voter or as a guest in a register kept by a hotel etc. **6** *tr.* (of an instrument) record automatically; indicate. **7 a** *tr.* express (an emotion) facially or by gesture (*registered surprise*). **b** *intr.* (of an emotion) show in a person's face or gestures. **8** *intr.* make an impression on a person's mind (*did not register at all*). **9** *intr. & tr. Printing* correspond or cause to correspond exactly in position. □ **registrable** *adj.* [Middle English & Old French *regestre*, *registre* or medieval Latin *regestrum*, *registrum*, alteration of *regestum*, from Late Latin *regesta* 'things recorded' (as RE-, Latin *gerere gest-* 'carry')]

registered nurse *n.* a nurse with a State certificate of competence.

registered post *n. Brit.* a postal procedure with special precautions for safety and for compensation in case of loss.

register office *n. Brit.* a State office where civil marriages are conducted and births, marriages, and deaths are recorded with the issue of certificates.

■ **Usage** *Register office* is the official name, although *registry office* is often heard in colloquial usage.

register ton see TON[1] 5b.

registrar /ˈrɛdʒɪstrɑː, rɛdʒɪˈstrɑː/ *n.* **1** an official responsible for keeping a register or official records. **2** *Brit.* the chief administrative officer in a university. **3** a middle-ranking hospital doctor undergoing training as a specialist. **4** (in the UK) the judicial and administrative officer of the High Court etc. □ **registrarship** *n.* [medieval Latin *registrarius* from *registrum* REGISTER]

Registrar General *n.* a government official responsible for holding a population census.

registrary /ˈrɛdʒɪstrəri/ *n.* (*pl.* **-ies**) the registrar of Cambridge University.

registration /rɛdʒɪˈstreɪʃ(ə)n/ *n.* the act or an instance of registering; the process of being registered. [obsolete French *régistration* or medieval Latin *registratio* (as REGISTRAR)]

registration document *n. Brit.* a document stating the registered keeper of a motor vehicle.

■ **Usage** The official name is *vehicle registration document*.

registration mark *n.* (also **registration number**) a combination of letters and figures identifying a motor vehicle etc.

registry /ˈrɛdʒɪstri/ *n.* (*pl.* **-ies**) **1** a place or office where registers or records are kept. **2** registration. [obsolete *registery* from medieval Latin *registerium* (as REGISTER)]

registry office *n.* = REGISTER OFFICE.

■ **Usage** See Usage Note at REGISTER OFFICE.

Regius professor /ˈriːdʒɪəs/ *n.* (in the UK) the holder of a chair founded by a sovereign (esp. one at Oxford or Cambridge instituted by Henry VIII) or filled by Crown appointment. [Latin *regius* 'royal', from *rex regis* 'king']

reglaze /riːˈgleɪz/ *v.tr.* glaze (a window etc.) again.

reglet /ˈrɛglɪt/ *n.* **1** *Archit.* a narrow strip separating mouldings. **2** *Printing* a thin strip of wood or metal separating type. [French *réglet*, diminutive of *règle* (as RULE)]

regnal /ˈrɛgn(ə)l/ *adj.* of a reign. [Anglo-Latin *regnalis* (as REIGN)]

regnal year *n.* a year reckoned from the date or anniversary of a sovereign's accession.

regnant /ˈrɛgnənt/ *adj.* **1** (often *predic.*) reigning (*Queen regnant*). **2** (of things, qualities, etc.) predominant, prevalent. [Latin *regnare* REIGN]

rego /ˈrɛdʒəʊ/ *n.* (often *attrib.*) *Austral. slang* motor vehicle registration.

regolith /ˈrɛg(ə)lɪθ/ *n. Geol.* unconsolidated solid material covering the bedrock of a planet. [erroneously from Greek *rhēgos* 'rug, blanket' + -LITH]

regorge /riːˈgɔːdʒ/ *v.* **1** *tr.* bring up or expel again after swallowing. **2** *intr.* gush or flow back from a pit, channel, etc. [French *regorger*, or RE- + GORGE]

regrade /riːˈgreɪd/ *v.tr.* grade again or differently.

regress *v. & n.* ● *v.* /rɪˈgrɛs/ **1** *intr.* move backwards, esp. (in abstract senses) return to a former state. **2** *intr. & tr. Psychol.* return or cause to return mentally to a former stage of life, esp. through hypnosis or mental illness. ● *n.* /ˈriːgrɛs/ **1** the act or an instance of going back. **2** reasoning from effect to cause. [Middle English (as *n.*) from Latin *regressus*, from *regredi regress-* (as RE-, *gradi* 'step, walk')]

regression /rɪˈgrɛʃ(ə)n/ *n.* **1** a backward movement, esp. a return to a former state. **2** a relapse or reversion. **3** *Psychol.* a return to an earlier stage of development, esp. through hypnosis or mental illness. **4** *Statistics* a measure of the relation between the mean value of one variable (e.g. output) and corresponding values of other variables (e.g. time and cost). [Latin *regressio* (as REGRESS)]

regressive /rɪˈgrɛsɪv/ *adj.* **1** regressing; characterized by regression. **2** (of a tax) proportionally greater on lower incomes. □ **regressively** *adv.* **regressiveness** *n.*

regret /rɪˈgrɛt/ *v. & n.* ● *v.tr.* (**regretted**, **regretting**) (often foll. by *that* + clause) **1** feel or express sorrow or repentance or distress over (an action or loss etc.) (*I regret that I forgot*; *regretted your absence*). **2** (often foll. by *to* + infin. or *that* + clause) acknowledge with sorrow or remorse (*I regret to say that you are wrong*; *regretted he would not be attending*). ● *n.* **1** a feeling of sorrow, repentance, disappointment, etc., over an action or loss etc. **2** (often in *pl.*) an (esp. polite or formal) expression of disappointment or sorrow at an occurrence, inability to comply, etc. (*refused with many regrets*; *heard with regret of her death*). □ **give** (or **send**) **one's regrets** formally decline an invitation. [Middle English from Old French *regreter* 'bewail']

regretful /rɪ'grɛtfʊl, -f(ə)l/ *adj.* feeling or showing regret. □ **regretfully** *adv.* **regretfulness** *n.*

■ **Usage** *Regretfully* should be used only when 'in a regretful manner' is meant, e.g. *She shook her head regretfully*, and not where *regrettably* is meant, e.g. *Regrettably, he cannot be here tonight*.

regrettable /rɪ'grɛtəb(ə)l/ *adj.* (of events or conduct) undesirable, unwelcome; deserving censure. □ **regrettably** *adv.*

■ **Usage** See Usage Note at REGRETFUL.

regroup /ri:'gru:p/ *v.tr. & intr.* group or arrange again or differently. □ **regroupment** *n.*

regrow /ri:'grəʊ/ *v.intr. & tr.* (*past* **-grew**, *past part.* **-grown**) grow again, esp. after an interval. □ **regrowth** *n.*

Regt. *abbr.* Regiment.

regulable /'rɛgjʊləb(ə)l/ *adj.* able to be regulated.

regular /'rɛgjʊlə/ *adj. & n.* ● *adj.* **1** conforming to a rule or principle; systematic. **2** (of a structure or arrangement) harmonious, symmetrical (*regular features*). **3** acting or done or recurring uniformly or calculably in time or manner; habitual, constant, orderly. **4** conforming to a standard of etiquette or procedure; correct; according to convention. **5** properly constituted or qualified; not defective or amateur; pursuing an occupation as one's main pursuit (*cooks as well as a regular cook*; *has no regular profession*). **6** *Gram.* (of a noun, verb, etc.) following the normal type of inflection. **7** *colloq.* complete, thorough, absolute (*a regular hero*). **8** *Geom.* **a** (of a figure) having all sides and all angles equal. **b** (of a solid) bounded by a number of equal figures. **9** *Eccl.* (placed before or after noun) **a** bound by religious rule. **b** belonging to a religious or monastic order (*canon regular*). **10** (of forces or troops etc.) relating to or constituting a permanent professional body (*regular soldiers*; *regular police force*). **11** (of a person) defecating or menstruating at predictable times. **12** *Bot.* (of a flower) having radial symmetry. ● *n.* **1** a regular soldier. **2** *colloq.* a regular customer, visitor, etc. **3** *Eccl.* one of the regular clergy. □ **keep regular hours** do the same thing, esp. going to bed and getting up, at the same time each day. □ **regularity** /-'larɪti/ *n.* **regularize** *v.tr.* (also **-ise**). **regularization** /-'zeɪʃ(ə)n/ *n.* **regularly** *adv.* [Middle English *reguler*, *regular* via Old French *reguler* from Latin *regularis*, from *regula* RULE]

regular octahedron *n.* an octahedron contained by equal and equilateral triangles.

regulate /'rɛgjʊleɪt/ *v.tr.* **1** control by rule. **2** subject to restrictions. **3** adapt to requirements. **4** alter the speed of (a machine or clock) so that it may work accurately. □ **regulative** /-lətɪv/ *adj.* **regulator** *n.* **regulatory** /-lət(ə)ri/ *adj.* [Late Latin *regulare regulat-* from Latin *regula* RULE]

regulation /rɛgjʊ'leɪʃ(ə)n/ *n.* **1** the act or an instance of regulating; the process of being regulated. **2** a prescribed rule; an authoritative direction. **3** (*attrib.*) **a** in accordance with regulations; of the correct type etc. (*the regulation speed*; *a regulation tie*). **b** *colloq.* usual (*the regulation soup*).

regulo /'rɛgjʊləʊ/ *n.* (usu. foll. by a numeral) *Brit.* each of the numbers of a scale denoting temperature in a gas oven (*cook at regulo 6*). [*Regulo*, proprietary term for a thermostatic gas oven control]

regulus /'rɛgjʊləs/ *n.* (*pl.* **reguluses** or **reguli** /-lʌɪ, -li:/) *Chem.* **1** the purer or metallic part of a mineral that separates by sinking on reduction. **2** an impure metallic product formed during the smelting of various ores. □ **reguline** /-lʌɪn/ *adj.* [Latin, diminutive of *rex regis* 'king': originally of a metallic form of antimony, so called because of its readiness to combine with gold]

regurgitate /rɪ'gə:dʒɪteɪt/ *v.* **1** *tr.* bring (swallowed food) up again to the mouth. **2** *tr.* cast or pour out again (*required by the exam to regurgitate facts*). **3** *intr.* be brought up again; gush back. □ **regurgitation** /-'teɪʃ(ə)n/ *n.* [medieval Latin *regurgitare* (as RE-, Latin *gurges gurgitis* 'whirlpool')]

rehab /'ri:hab/ *n. colloq.* rehabilitation. [abbreviation]

rehabilitate /ri:hə'bɪlɪteɪt/ *v.tr.* **1** restore to effectiveness or normal life by training etc., esp. after imprisonment or illness. **2** restore to former privileges or reputation or a proper condition. □ **rehabilitation** /-'teɪʃ(ə)n/ *n.* **rehabilitative** /-tətɪv/ *adj.* [medieval Latin *rehabilitare* (as RE-, HABILITATE)]

rehandle /ri:'hand(ə)l/ *v.tr.* **1** handle again. **2** give a new form or arrangement to.

rehang /ri:'haŋ/ *v.tr.* (*past* and *past part.* **rehung**) hang (esp. a picture or a curtain) again or differently.

rehash *v. & n.* ● *v.tr.* /ri:'haʃ/ put (old material) into a new form without significant change or improvement. ● *n.* /'ri:haʃ/ **1** material rehashed. **2** the act or an instance of rehashing.

rehear /ri:'hɪə/ *v.tr.* (*past* and *past part.* **reheard** /ri:'hə:d/) hear again.

rehearsal /rɪ'hə:s(ə)l/ *n.* **1** the act or an instance of rehearsing. **2** a trial performance or practice of a play, recital, etc.

rehearse /rɪ'hə:s/ *v.* **1** *tr.* practise (a play, recital, etc.) for later public performance. **2** *intr.* hold a rehearsal. **3** *tr.* train (a person) by rehearsal. **4** *tr.* recite or say over. **5** *tr.* give a list of; enumerate. □ **rehearser** *n.* [Middle English from Anglo-French *rehearser*, Old French *reherc(i)er* (perhaps as RE- + *hercer* 'to harrow' from *herse* 'harrow'): see HEARSE]

reheat *v. & n.* ● *v.tr.* /ri:'hi:t/ heat again. ● *n.* /'ri:hi:t/ the process of using the hot exhaust to burn extra fuel in a jet engine and produce extra power. □ **reheater** /-'hi:tə/ *n.*

reheel /ri:'hi:l/ *v.tr.* fit (a shoe etc.) with a new heel.

rehoboam /ri:hə'bəʊəm, ri:ə-/ *n.* a wine bottle of about six times the standard size. [*Rehoboam*, the name of a king of Israel (1 Kings 11–14)]

rehome /ri:'həʊm/ *v.tr.* find a new home for (a pet).

rehouse /ri:'haʊz/ *v.tr.* provide with new housing.

rehung *past* and *past part.* of REHANG.

rehydrate /ri:hʌɪ'dreɪt/ *v.* **1** *intr.* absorb water again after dehydration. **2** *tr.* add water to (esp. food) again to restore to a palatable state. □ **rehydratable** *adj.* **rehydration** /-'dreɪʃ(ə)n/ *n.*

Reich /rʌɪk, -x/ *n.* the former German State, esp. the Third Reich. [German, = empire]

■ **Usage** Only *Third Reich* is normal historical terminology.

Reichstag /'rʌɪxstɑ:g/ *n. hist.* **1** the main legislature of the German state under the Second and Third Reichs. **2** the building in which this met. [German]

reify /'ri:ɪfʌɪ, 'reɪɪ-/ *v.tr.* (**-ies**, **-ied**) convert (a person, abstraction, etc.) mentally into a thing; materialize. □ **reification** /-fɪ'keɪʃ(ə)n/ *n.* **reificatory** /-fɪ'keɪt(ə)ri/ *adj.* [Latin *res* 'thing' + -FY]

reign /reɪn/ *v. & n.* ● *v.intr.* **1** hold royal office; be king or queen. **2** have power or predominance; prevail; hold sway (*confusion reigns*). **3** (as **reigning** *adj.*) (of a winner, champion, etc.) currently holding the title etc. ● *n.* **1** sovereignty, rule. **2** the period during which a sovereign rules. [Middle English from Old French *reigne* 'kingdom', *reignier* 'reign', ultimately from Latin *rex, regis* 'king']

reignite /ri:ɪg'nʌɪt/ *v.tr. & intr.* ignite again.

reign of terror *n.* a period of remorseless repression or bloodshed, esp. a period of the French Revolution 1793–4.

Reilly var. of RILEY.

reimburse /ri:ɪm'bə:s/ *v.tr.* **1** repay (a person who has expended money). **2** repay (a person's expenses). □ **reimbursable** *adj.* **reimbursement** *n.* [RE- + obsolete *imburse* 'put in a purse' from medieval Latin *imbursare* (as IM-, PURSE)]

reimport *v.* & *n.* ● *v.tr.* /riːɪm'pɔːt/ import (goods processed from exported materials). ● *n.* /riː'ɪmpɔːt/ **1** the act or an instance of reimporting. **2** a reimported item. □ **reimportation** /-'teɪʃ(ə)n/ *n.*

reimpose /riːɪm'pəʊz/ *v.tr.* impose again, esp. after a lapse. □ **reimposition** /-pə'zɪʃ(ə)n/ *n.*

rein /reɪn/ *n.* & *v.* ● *n.* (in *sing.* or *pl.*) **1** a long narrow strap with each end attached to the bit, used to guide or check a horse etc. in riding or driving. **2** a similar device used to restrain a young child. **3** a means of control or guidance; a curb; a restraint. ● *v.tr.* **1** check or manage with reins. **2** (foll. by *up*, *back*) pull up or back with reins. **3** (foll. by *in*) hold in as with reins; restrain. **4** govern, restrain, control. □ **draw rein** *Brit.* **1** stop one's horse. **2** pull up. **3** abandon an effort. **give free rein to** remove constraints from; allow full scope to. **keep a tight rein on** allow little freedom to. □ **reinless** *adj.* [Middle English from Old French *rene*, *reigne*, earlier *resne*, ultimately from Latin *retinēre* RETAIN]

reincarnation /ˌriːɪnkɑː'neɪʃ(ə)n/ *n.* (in some beliefs) the rebirth of a soul in a new body. □ **reincarnate** /-'kɑːneɪt/ *v.tr.* **reincarnate** /-'kɑːnət/ *adj.*

reincorporate /riːɪn'kɔːpəreɪt/ *v.tr.* incorporate afresh. □ **reincorporation** /-'reɪʃ(ə)n/ *n.*

reindeer /'reɪndɪə/ *n.* (*pl.* same or **reindeers**) a subarctic deer, *Rangifer tarandus*, both sexes of which have large antlers, domesticated in northern Eurasia for drawing sledges and as a source of milk, flesh, and hide. Cf. CARIBOU. [Middle English from Old Norse *hreindýri*, from *hreinn* 'reindeer' + *dýr* DEER]

reindeer moss *n.* an Arctic lichen, *Cladonia rangiferina*, growing in clumps and providing the chief winter food of reindeer.

reindustrialize /riːɪn'dʌstrɪəlʌɪz/ *v.tr.* & *intr.* (also **-ise**) modernize or develop industrially. □ **reindustrialization** /-'zeɪʃ(ə)n/ *n.*

reinfect /riːɪn'fɛkt/ *v.tr.* infect again. □ **reinfection** /riːɪn'fɛkʃ(ə)n/ *n.*

reinforce /riːɪn'fɔːs/ *v.tr.* strengthen or support, esp. with additional personnel or material or by an increase of numbers or quantity or size etc. □ **reinforcer** *n.* [earlier *renforce* from French *renforcer*]

reinforced concrete *n.* concrete with metal bars or wire etc. embedded to increase its tensile strength.

reinforcement /riːɪn'fɔːsm(ə)nt/ *n.* **1** the act or an instance of reinforcing; the process of being reinforced. **2** a thing that reinforces. **3** (in *pl.*) reinforcing personnel or equipment etc.

reinsert /riːɪn'səːt/ *v.tr.* insert again. □ **reinsertion** /-'səːʃ(ə)n/ *n.*

reinstate /riːɪn'steɪt/ *v.tr.* **1** replace in a former position. **2** restore (a person etc.) to former privileges. □ **reinstatement** *n.*

reinsure /riːɪn'ʃʊə/ *v.tr.* & *intr.* insure again (esp. of an insurer securing himself by transferring some or all of the risk to another insurer). □ **reinsurance** *n.* **reinsurer** *n.*

reintegrate /riː'ɪntɪgreɪt/ *v.tr.* **1** = REDINTEGRATE. **2** integrate back into society. □ **reintegration** /-'greɪʃ(ə)n/ *n.*

reinter /riːɪn'təː/ *v.tr.* inter (a corpse) again. □ **reinterment** *n.*

reinterpret /riːɪn'təːprɪt/ *v.tr.* (**reinterpreted**, **reinterpreting**) interpret again or differently. □ **reinterpretation** /-'teɪʃ(ə)n/ *n.*

reintroduce /ˌriːɪntrə'djuːs/ *v.tr.* introduce again. □ **reintroduction** /-'dʌkʃ(ə)n/ *n.*

reinvent /riːɪn'vɛnt/ *v.tr.* invent again. □ **reinvention** /-'vɛnʃ(ə)n/ *n.*

reinvest /riːɪn'vɛst/ *v.tr.* invest again (esp. money in other property etc.). □ **reinvestment** *n.*

reinvigorate /riːɪn'vɪgəreɪt/ *v.tr.* impart fresh vigour to. □ **reinvigoration** /-'reɪʃ(ə)n/ *n.*

reissue /riː'ɪʃ(j)uː, -'ɪsjuː/ *v.* & *n.* ● *v.tr.* (**reissues**, **reissued**, **reissuing**) issue again or in a different form. ● *n.* a new issue, esp. of a record or previously published book.

reiterate /riː'ɪtəreɪt/ *v.tr.* say or do again or repeatedly. □ **reiteration** /-'reɪʃ(ə)n/ *n.* **reiterative** /-rətɪv/ *adj.* [Latin *reiterare* (as RE-, ITERATE)]

reive /riːv/ *v.intr.* esp. *Sc.* make raids; plunder. □ **reiver** *n.* [variant of REAVE]

reject *v.* & *n.* ● *v.tr.* /rɪ'dʒɛkt/ **1** put aside or send back as not to be used or done or complied with etc. **2** refuse to accept or believe in. **3** rebuff or snub (a person). **4** (of a body or digestive system) cast up again; vomit, evacuate. **5** *Med.* show an immune response to (a transplanted organ or tissue) so that it fails to survive. ● *n.* /'riːdʒɛkt/ a thing or person rejected as unfit or below standard. □ **rejectable** /rɪ'dʒɛktəb(ə)l/ *adj.* **rejection** /rɪ'dʒɛkʃ(ə)n/ *n.* **rejective** *adj.* **rejector** *n.* [Middle English from Latin *rejicere reject-* (as RE-, *jacere* 'throw')]

rejectionist /rɪ'dʒɛkʃ(ə)nɪst/ *n.* a person who rejects a proposed policy etc., esp. an Arab who refuses to accept a negotiated peace with Israel (often *attrib.*: *rejectionist groups*).

rejig /riː'dʒɪg/ *v.tr.* (**rejigged**, **rejigging**) esp. *Brit.* **1** re-equip (a factory etc.) for a new kind of work. **2** rearrange.

rejoice /rɪ'dʒɔɪs/ *v.* **1** *intr.* feel great joy. **2** *intr.* (foll. by *that* + clause or *to* + infin.) be glad. **3** *intr.* (foll. by *in*, *at*) take delight. **4** *intr.* celebrate some event. **5** *tr.* cause joy to. □ **rejoicer** *n.* **rejoicingly** *adv.* [Middle English from Old French *rejoir rejoiss-* (as RE-, JOY)]

rejoin[1] /riː'dʒɔɪn/ *v.* **1** *tr.* & *intr.* join together again; reunite. **2** *tr.* join (a companion etc.) again.

rejoin[2] /rɪ'dʒɔɪn/ *v.* **1** *tr.* say in answer; retort. **2** *intr.* *Law* reply to a charge or pleading in a lawsuit. [Middle English from Old French *rejoindre rejoign-* (as RE-, JOIN)]

rejoinder /rɪ'dʒɔɪndə/ *n.* **1** what is said in reply. **2** a retort. **3** *Law* a reply by rejoining. [Anglo-French *rejoinder* (unrecorded: as REJOIN[2])]

rejuvenate /rɪ'dʒuːvɪneɪt/ *v.tr.* make young or as if young again. □ **rejuvenation** /-'neɪʃ(ə)n/ *n.* **rejuvenator** *n.* [RE- + Latin *juvenis* 'young']

rejuvenesce /rɪˌdʒuːvɪ'nɛs/ *v.* **1** *intr.* become young again; regain vitality. **2** *Biol.* **a** *intr.* (of cells) change to a more active form. **b** *tr.* change (cells) into a more active form. □ **rejuvenescent** *adj.* **rejuvenescence** *n.* [Late Latin *rejuvenescere* (as RE-, Latin *juvenis* 'young')]

rekey /riː'kiː/ *v.tr.* esp. *Computing* re-enter (text or other data) using a keyboard.

rekindle /riː'kɪnd(ə)l/ *v.tr.* & *intr.* kindle again.

-rel /r(ə)l/ *suffix* with diminutive or derogatory force (*cockerel*; *scoundrel*). [from or after Old French *-erel(le)*]

relabel /riː'leɪb(ə)l/ *v.tr.* (**relabelled**, **relabelling**; *US* **relabeled**, **relabeling**) label (esp. a commodity) again or differently.

relaid *past* and *past part.* of RELAY[2].

relapse /rɪ'laps/ *v.* & *n.* ● *v.intr.* (usu. foll. by *into*) fall back or sink again (into a worse state after an improvement). ● *n.* /also 'riː-/ the act or an instance of relapsing, esp. a deterioration in a patient's condition after a partial recovery. □ **relapser** *n.* [Latin *relabi relaps-* (as RE-, *labi* 'slip')]

relapsing fever *n.* an infectious disease marked by recurrent fever, caused by spirochaetes of the genus *Borrelia*.

relate /rɪ'leɪt/ *v.* **1** *tr.* narrate or recount (incidents, a story, etc.). **2** *tr.* (in *passive*; often foll. by *to*) be connected by blood or marriage. **3** *tr.* (usu. foll. by *to*, *with*) bring into relation (with one another); establish a connection between (*cannot relate your opinion to my own experience*). **4** *intr.* (foll. by *to*) have reference to; concern (*see only what relates to themselves*). **5** *intr.* (foll. by *to*) bring oneself into relation to; associate with.

□ **relatable** *adj.* [Latin *referre relat-* 'bring back': see REFER]

related /rɪˈleɪtɪd/ *adj.* connected, esp. by blood or marriage. □ **relatedness** *n.*

relater /rɪˈleɪtə/ *n.* (also **relator**) a person who relates something, esp. a story; a narrator.

relation /rɪˈleɪʃ(ə)n/ *n.* **1 a** the way in which one person or thing is related to another. **b** the existence or effect of a connection, correspondence, contrast, or feeling prevailing between persons or things, esp. when qualified in some way (*bears no relation to the facts*; *enjoyed good relations for many years*). **2** a relative; a kinsman or kinswoman. **3** (in *pl.*) **a** (foll. by *with*) dealings (with others). **b** sexual intercourse. **4** = RELATIONSHIP. **5 a** narration (*his relation of the events*). **b** a narrative. **6** *Law* the laying of an information (see INFORMATION 2). □ **in relation to** as regards. [Middle English from Old French *relation* or Latin *relatio* (as RELATE)]

relational /rɪˈleɪʃ(ə)n(ə)l/ *adj.* **1** of, belonging to, or characterized by relation. **2** having relation. □ **relationally** *adv.*

relational database *n. Computing* a database structured to recognize the relation of stored items of information.

relationship /rɪˈleɪʃ(ə)nʃɪp/ *n.* **1** the fact or state of being related. **2 a** a connection or association (*enjoyed a good working relationship*). **b** an emotional (esp. sexual) association between two people. **3** a condition or character due to being related. **4** kinship.

relative /ˈrɛlətɪv/ *adj.* & *n.* ● *adj.* **1** considered or having significance in relation to something else; not absolute (*they live in relative comfort*; *truth is relative*). **2** (foll. by *to*) proportionate to (something else); in proportion to (*growth is relative to input*; *low energy content relative to its bulk*). **3** (foll. by *to*) in comparison with; compared with (*wage levels were low relative to the rest of the South-East*). **4 a** comparative; compared one with another (*their relative advantages*). **b** (foll. by *to*) in relation to (*move slowly relative to each other*). **5** (usu. foll. by *to*) having reference; relating, relevant (*the facts relative to the issue*; *need more relative proof*). **6** having mutual relations; corresponding in some way; related to each other. **7** *Gram.* **a** (of a word, esp. a pronoun) referring to an expressed or implied antecedent and attaching a subordinate clause to it, e.g. *which, who*. **b** (of a clause) attached to an antecedent by a relative word. **8** *Mus.* (of major and minor keys) having the same key signature. **9** (of a service rank) corresponding in grade to another in a different service. ● *n.* **1** a person connected by blood or marriage. **2** a species related to another by common origin (*the apes, man's closest relatives*). **3** *Gram.* a relative word, esp. a pronoun. **4** *Philos.* a relative thing or term. □ **relatival** /-ˈtʌɪv(ə)l/ *adj.* (in sense 3 of *n.*). **relatively** *adv.* [Middle English from Old French *relatif -ive* or Late Latin *relativus* 'having reference or relation' (as RELATE)]

relative atomic mass *n.* the ratio of the average mass of one atom of an element to one-twelfth of the mass of an atom of carbon-12. Also called *atomic weight*.

relative density *n. Chem.* the ratio of the density of a substance to the density of a standard, usu. water for a liquid or solid, and air for a gas.

relative humidity *n.* the proportion of moisture to the value for saturation at the same temperature.

relative molecular mass *n.* the ratio of the average mass of one molecule of an element or compound to one-twelfth of the mass of an atom of carbon-12. Also called *molecular weight*.

relativism /ˈrɛlətɪvɪz(ə)m/ *n.* the doctrine that knowledge, truth, morality, etc., are relative and not absolute. □ **relativist** *n.*

relativistic /rɛlətɪˈvɪstɪk/ *adj. Physics* (of phenomena etc.) accurately described only by the theory of relativity. □ **relativistically** *adv.*

relativity /rɛləˈtɪvɪti/ *n.* **1** the fact or state of being relative. **2** *Physics* **a** (**special theory of relativity**) a theory based on the principle that all motion is relative and that light has constant velocity, regarding space-time as a four-dimensional continuum, and modifying previous conceptions of geometry. **b** (**general theory of relativity**) a theory extending this to gravitation and accelerated motion.

relator /rɪˈleɪtə/ *n.* **1** var. of RELATER. **2** *Law* a person who makes a relation (see RELATION 6). [Latin (as RELATE)]

relaunch *v.* & *n.* ● *v.tr.* /riːˈlɔːn(t)ʃ/ launch again. ● *n.* /ˈriːlɔːn(t)ʃ/ an instance of relaunching something, esp. a business or product.

relax /rɪˈlaks/ *v.* **1** *tr.* & *intr.* make or become less stiff or rigid or tense. **2** *tr.* & *intr.* make or become less formal or strict (*rules were relaxed*). **3** *tr.* reduce or abate (one's attention, efforts, etc.). **4** *intr.* cease work or effort. **5** *tr.* (as **relaxed** *adj.*) at ease; unperturbed. □ **relaxedly** *adv.* **relaxedness** *n.* **relaxer** *n.* [Middle English from Latin *relaxare* (as RE-, LAX)]

relaxant /rɪˈlaks(ə)nt/ *n.* & *adj.* ● *n.* a drug etc. that relaxes and reduces tension. ● *adj.* causing relaxation.

relaxation /riːlakˈseɪʃ(ə)n/ *n.* **1** the act of relaxing or state of being relaxed. **2** recreation or rest, esp. after a period of work. **3** a partial remission or relaxing of a penalty, duty, etc. **4** a lessening of severity, precision, etc. **5** *Physics* the restoration of equilibrium following disturbance. [Latin *relaxatio* (as RELAX)]

relaxing /rɪˈlaksɪŋ/ *adj.* conducive to relaxation (*a relaxing atmosphere*; *a relaxing holiday*).

relay[1] /ˈriːleɪ/ *n.* & *v.* ● *n.* **1** a fresh set of people or horses substituted for tired ones. **2** a gang of workers, supply of material, etc., deployed on the same basis (*operated in relays*). **3** = RELAY RACE. **4** a device activating changes in an electric circuit etc. in response to other changes affecting itself. **5 a** a device to receive, reinforce, and transmit a telegraph message, broadcast programme, etc. **b** a relayed message or transmission. ● *v.tr.* /also rɪˈleɪ/ **1** receive (a message, broadcast, etc.) and transmit it to others. **2 a** arrange in relays. **b** provide with or replace by relays. [Middle English from Old French *relai* (*n.*), *relayer* (*v.*) (as RE-, *laier*, ultimately from Latin *laxare*): cf. RELAX]

relay[2] /riːˈleɪ/ *v.tr.* (*past* and *past part.* **relaid**) lay again or differently.

relay race *n.* a race between teams of which each member in turn covers part of the distance.

relearn /riːˈləːn/ *v.tr.* (*past* and *past part.* **relearned** or **relearnt**) learn again.

release /rɪˈliːs/ *v.* & *n.* ● *v.tr.* **1** (often foll. by *from*) set free; liberate, unfasten. **2** allow to move from a fixed position. **3 a** make (information, a recording, etc.) publicly or generally available. **b** issue (a film etc.) for general exhibition. **4** *Law* **a** remit (a debt). **b** surrender (a right). **c** make over (property or money) to another. ● *n.* **1** deliverance or liberation from a restriction, duty, or difficulty. **2** a handle or catch that releases part of a mechanism. **3** a document or item of information made available for publication (*press release*). **4 a** a film or record etc. that is released. **b** the act or an instance of releasing or the process of being released in this way. **5** *Law* **a** the act of releasing (property, money, or a right) to another. **b** a document effecting this. □ **releasable** *adj.* **releasee** /-ˈsiː/ *n.* (in sense 4 of *v.*). **releaser** *n.* **releasor** *n.* (in sense 4 of *v.*). [Middle English from Old French *reles* (*n.*), *relesser*, *relaiss(i)er* (*v.*) from Latin *relaxare*: see RELAX]

relegate /ˈrɛlɪɡeɪt/ *v.tr.* **1** consign or dismiss to an inferior or less important position; demote. **2** transfer (a sports team) to a lower division of a league etc. **3** banish or send into exile. **4** (foll. by *to*) **a** transfer (a matter) for decision or implementation. **b** refer (a person) for information. □ **relegable** *adj.* **relegation** /-ˈɡeɪʃ(ə)n/ *n.* [Latin *relegare relegat-* (as RE-, *legare* 'send')]

relent /rɪˈlɛnt/ *v.intr.* **1** abandon a harsh intention. **2** yield to compassion. **3** relax one's severity; become less stern. [Middle English from medieval Latin (as RE- + Latin *lentāre* 'bend') from *lentus* 'flexible']

relentless /rɪˈlɛntlɪs/ *adj.* **1** unrelenting; insistent and uncompromising. **2** continuous; oppressively constant (*the pressure was relentless*). ▫ **relentlessly** *adv.* **relentlessness** *n.*

relet *v. & n.* esp. *Brit.* ● *v.tr.* /riːˈlɛt/ (**-letting**; *past* and *past part.* **-let**) let (a property) for a further period or to a new tenant. ● *n.* /ˈriːlɛt/ a relet property.

relevant /ˈrɛlɪv(ə)nt/ *adj.* (often foll. by *to*) bearing on or having reference to the matter in hand. ▫ **relevance** *n.* **relevancy** *n.* **relevantly** *adv.* [medieval Latin *relevans*, part. of Latin *relevare* 'raise up, RELIEVE']

reliable /rɪˈlʌɪəb(ə)l/ *adj.* **1** that may be relied on. **2** of sound and consistent character or quality. ▫ **reliability** /-ˈbɪlɪti/ *n.* **reliableness** *n.* **reliably** *adv.*

reliance /rɪˈlʌɪəns/ *n.* **1** (foll. by *in*, *on*) trust, confidence (*put full reliance in you*). **2** a thing relied upon. ▫ **reliant** *adj.*

relic /ˈrɛlɪk/ *n.* **1** an object interesting because of its age or association. **2** a part of a deceased holy person's body or belongings kept as an object of reverence. **3** a surviving custom or belief etc. from a past age. **4** a memento or souvenir. **5** (in *pl.*) what has survived destruction or wasting or use. **6** (in *pl.*) the dead body or remains of a person. [Middle English *relike*, *relique*, etc. via Old French *relique* from Latin *reliquiae*: see RELIQUIAE]

relict /ˈrɛlɪkt/ *n.* **1 a** a geological or other object surviving in its primitive form. **b** an animal or plant known to have existed in the same form in previous geological ages. **2** (foll. by *of*) *archaic* a widow. [Latin *relinquere relict-* 'leave behind' (as RE-, *linquere* 'leave'): sense 2 via Old French *relicte* from Latin *relicta*]

relief /rɪˈliːf/ *n.* **1 a** the alleviation of or deliverance from pain, distress, anxiety, etc. **b** the feeling accompanying such deliverance. **2** a feature etc. that diversifies monotony or relaxes tension. **3** assistance (esp. financial) given to those in special need or difficulty (*rent relief*). **4 a** the replacing of a person or persons on duty by another or others. **b** a person or persons replacing others in this way. **5** (usu. *attrib.*) *Brit.* a thing supplementing another in some service, esp. an extra vehicle providing public transport at peak times. **6 a** a method of moulding or carving or stamping in which the design stands out from the surface, with projections proportioned and more (**high relief**) or less (**low relief**) closely approximating to those of the objects depicted (cf. ROUND *n.* 9). **b** a piece of sculpture etc. in relief. **c** a representation of relief given by an arrangement of line or colour or shading. **7** vividness, distinctness (*brings the facts out in sharp relief*). **8** (foll. by *of*) the reinforcement (esp. the raising of a siege) of a place. **9** esp. *Law* the redress of a hardship or grievance. ▫ **on relief** esp. *N. Amer.* receiving State assistance because of need. [Middle English from Anglo-French *relef*, Old French *relief* (in sense 6 French *relief* from Italian *rilievo*), from *relever*: see RELIEVE]

relief map *n.* **1** a map indicating hills and valleys by shading etc. rather than by contour lines alone. **2** a map-model showing elevations and depressions, usu. on an exaggerated relative scale.

relief printing *n.* = LETTERPRESS 2.

relief road *n. Brit.* a road taking traffic around a congested (esp. urban) area.

relieve /rɪˈliːv/ *v.tr.* **1** bring or provide aid or assistance to. **2** alleviate or reduce (pain, suffering, etc.). **3** mitigate the tedium or monotony of. **4** bring military support for (a besieged place). **5** release (a person) from a duty by acting as or providing a substitute. **6** (foll. by *of*) take (a burden or responsibility) away from (a person). **7** bring into relief; cause to appear solid or detached. ▫ **relieve one's feelings** use strong language or vigorous behaviour when annoyed. **relieve oneself** urinate or defecate. ▫ **relievable** *adj.* **reliever** *n.* [Middle English via Old French *relever* from Latin *relevare* (as RE-, *levis* 'light')]

relieved /rɪˈliːvd/ *predic.adj.* freed from anxiety or distress (*am very relieved to hear it*). ▫ **relievedly** *adv.*

relievo /rɪˈliːvəʊ/ *n.* (also **rilievo** /rɪˈljeɪvəʊ/) (*pl.* **-os**) = RELIEF 6. [Italian *rilievo*]

relight /riːˈlʌɪt/ *v.tr.* (*past* and *past part.* **relighted** or **relit** /-ˈlɪt/) light (a fire etc.) again.

religio- /rɪˈlɪdʒɪəʊ/ *comb. form* **1** religion. **2** religious.

religion /rɪˈlɪdʒ(ə)n/ *n.* **1** the belief in a superhuman controlling power, esp. in a personal God or gods entitled to obedience and worship. **2** the expression of this in worship. **3** a particular system of faith and worship. **4** life under monastic vows (*the way of religion*). **5** a thing that one is devoted to (*football is their religion*). ▫ **religionless** *adj.* [Middle English via Anglo-French *religiun*, Old French *religion* from Latin *religio -onis* 'obligation, bond, reverence']

religionism /rɪˈlɪdʒ(ə)nɪz(ə)m/ *n.* excessive religious zeal. ▫ **religionist** *n.*

religiose /rɪˈlɪdʒɪəʊs/ *adj.* excessively religious. [Latin *religiosus* (as RELIGIOUS)]

religiosity /rɪˌlɪdʒɪˈɒsɪti/ *n.* the condition of being religious or religiose. [Middle English from Latin *religiositas* (as RELIGIOUS)]

religious /rɪˈlɪdʒəs/ *adj. & n.* ● *adj.* **1** devoted to religion; pious, devout. **2** of or concerned with religion. **3** of or belonging to a monastic order. **4** scrupulous, conscientious (*a religious attention to detail*). ● *n.* (*pl.* same) a person bound by monastic vows. ▫ **religiously** *adv.* **religiousness** *n.* [Middle English via Anglo-French *religius*, Old French *religious* from Latin *religiosus* (as RELIGION)]

reline /riːˈlʌɪn/ *v.tr.* renew the lining of (a garment, boiler, etc.).

relinquish /rɪˈlɪŋkwɪʃ/ *v.tr.* **1** surrender or resign (a right or possession). **2** give up or cease from (a habit, plan, belief, etc.). **3** relax hold of (an object held). ▫ **relinquishment** *n.* [Middle English via Old French *relinquir* from Latin *relinquere* (as RE-, *linquere* 'leave')]

reliquary /ˈrɛlɪkwəri/ *n.* (*pl.* **-ies**) a receptacle for esp. holy relics. [French *reliquaire* (as RELIC)]

reliquiae /rɪˈlɪkwiiː/ *n.pl.* **1** remains. **2** *Geol.* fossil remains of animals or plants. [Latin from *reliquus* 'remaining' (as RE- + *linquere liq-* 'leave')]

relish /ˈrɛlɪʃ/ *n. & v.* ● *n.* **1** (often foll. by *for*) **a** great liking or enjoyment. **b** keen or pleasurable longing (*had no relish for travelling*). **2 a** an appetizing flavour. **b** an attractive quality (*fishing loses its relish in winter*). **3** a condiment eaten with plainer food to add flavour, esp. a piquant sauce, pickle, etc. **4** (foll. by *of*) a distinctive taste or tinge. ● *v.tr.* **1 a** get pleasure out of; enjoy greatly. **b** look forward to; anticipate with pleasure (*did not relish what lay before her*). **2** add relish to. ▫ **relishable** *adj.* [alteration (with assimilation to -ISH²) of obsolete *reles* from Old French *reles*, *relais* 'remainder' from *relaisser*: see RELEASE]

relive /riːˈlɪv/ *v.tr.* live (an experience etc.) over again, esp. in the imagination.

reload /riːˈləʊd/ *v.tr.* (also *absol.*) load (esp. a gun) again.

relocate /riːlə(ʊ)ˈkeɪt/ *v.* **1** *tr.* locate in a new place. **2** *tr. & intr.* move to a new place (esp. to live or work). ▫ **relocation** /-ˈkeɪʃən/ *n.*

reluctant /rɪˈlʌkt(ə)nt/ *adj.* (often foll. by *to* + infin.) unwilling or disinclined (*most reluctant to agree*). ▫ **reluctance** *n.* **reluctantly** *adv.* [Latin *reluctari* (as RE-, *luctari* 'struggle')]

rely /rɪˈlʌɪ/ *v.intr.* (**-ies**, **-ied**) (foll. by *on*, *upon*) **1** depend on with confidence or assurance (*am relying on your judgement*). **2** be dependent on (*relies on her for everything*). [earlier senses 'rally, be a vassal of': Middle English via Old French *relier* 'bind together' from Latin *religare* (as RE-, *ligare* 'bind')]

REM *abbr.* rapid eye-movement.

rem /rɛm/ *n.* (*pl.* same or **rems**) a unit of effective absorbed dose of ionizing radiation in human tissue, equivalent to one roentgen of X-rays. [*r*oentgen *e*quivalent *m*an]

remade *past* and *past part.* of REMAKE.

remain /rɪˈmeɪn/ *v.intr.* **1** be left over after others or other parts have been removed or used or dealt with. **2** be in the same place or condition during further time; continue to exist or stay; be left behind (*remained at home*). **3** (foll. by compl.) continue to be (*remained calm*; *remains President*). [Middle English from Old French *remain*-, stressed stem of *remanoir*, or from Old French *remaindre*, ultimately from Latin *remanēre* (as RE-, *manēre* 'stay')]

remainder /rɪˈmeɪndə/ *n.* & *v.* ● *n.* **1** a part remaining or left over. **2** remaining persons or things. **3** a number left after division or subtraction. **4** the copies of a book left unsold when demand has fallen. **5** *Law* an interest in an estate that becomes effective in possession only when a prior interest (devised at the same time) ends. ● *v.tr.* dispose of (a remainder of books) at a reduced price. [Middle English (in sense 5) from Anglo-French, = Old French *remaindre*: see REMAIN]

remains /rɪˈmeɪnz/ *n.pl.* **1** what remains after other parts have been removed or used etc. **2** relics of antiquity, esp. of buildings (*Roman remains*). **3** a person's body after death. **4** an author's (esp. unpublished) works left after death.

remake *v.* & *n.* ● *v.tr.* /riːˈmeɪk/ (*past* and *past part.* **remade**) make again or differently. ● *n.* /ˈriːmeɪk/ a thing that has been remade, esp. a cinema film.

reman /riːˈman/ *v.tr.* (**remanned**, **remanning**) **1** equip (a fleet etc.) with new personnel. **2** *poet.* make courageous again.

remand /rɪˈmɑːnd/ *v.* & *n.* ● *v.tr.* return (a prisoner) to custody, esp. to allow further inquiries to be made. ● *n.* a recommittal to custody. □ **on remand** in custody pending trial. [Middle English from Late Latin *remandare* (as RE-, *mandare* 'commit')]

remand centre *n.* (in the UK) an institution to which accused persons are remanded pending trial.

remanent /ˈrɛmənənt/ *adj.* **1** remaining, residual. **2** (of magnetism) remaining after the magnetizing field has been removed. □ **remanence** *n.* [Middle English from Latin *remanēre* REMAIN]

remark /rɪˈmɑːk/ *v.* & *n.* ● *v.* **1** *tr.* (often foll. by *that* + clause) **a** say by way of comment. **b** take notice of; regard with attention. **2** *intr.* (usu. foll. by *on*, *upon*) make a comment. ● *n.* **1** a written or spoken comment; anything said. **2 a** the act of noticing or observing (*worthy of remark*). **b** the act of commenting (*let it pass without remark*). [French *remarque*, *remarquer* (as RE-, MARK[1])]

remarkable /rɪˈmɑːkəb(ə)l/ *adj.* **1** worthy of notice; exceptional, extraordinary. **2** striking, conspicuous. □ **remarkableness** *n.* **remarkably** *adv.* [French *remarquable* (as REMARK)]

remarry /riːˈmari/ *v.intr.* & *tr.* (**-ies**, **-ied**) marry again. □ **remarriage** *n.*

remaster /riːˈmɑːstə/ *v.tr.* make a new master of (a recording), esp. to improve the sound quality.

rematch /ˈriːmatʃ/ *n.* a return match or game.

REME /ˈriːmiː/ *abbr.* (in the UK) Royal Electrical and Mechanical Engineers.

remeasure /riːˈmɛʒə/ *v.tr.* measure again. □ **remeasurement** *n.*

remedial /rɪˈmiːdɪəl/ *adj.* **1** affording or intended as a remedy (*remedial therapy*). **2** (of teaching) for slow or backward children. □ **remedially** *adv.* [Late Latin *remedialis* from Latin *remedium* (as REMEDY)]

remedy /ˈrɛmɪdi/ *n.* & *v.* ● *n.* (*pl.* **-ies**) (often foll. by *for*, *against*) **1** a medicine or treatment (for a disease etc.). **2** a means of counteracting or removing anything undesirable. **3** redress; legal or other reparation. **4** the margin within which coins as minted may differ from the standard fineness and weight. ● *v.tr.* (**-ies**, **-ied**) rectify; make good. □ **remediable** /rɪˈmiːdɪəb(ə)l/ *adj.* [Middle English from Anglo-French *remedie*, Old French *remede* or Latin *remedium* (as RE-, *mederi* 'heal')]

remember /rɪˈmɛmbə/ *v.tr.* **1** keep in the memory; not forget. **2** (also *absol.*) **a** bring back into one's thoughts, call to mind (knowledge or experience etc.). **b** (often foll. by *to* + infin. or *that* + clause) have in mind (a duty, commitment, etc.) (*will you remember to lock the door?*). **3** think of or acknowledge (a person) in some connection, esp. in making a gift etc. **4** (foll. by *to*) convey greetings from (one person) to (another) (*remember me to your mother*). **5** mention (in prayer). □ **remember oneself** recover one's manners or intentions after a lapse. □ **rememberer** *n.* [Middle English via Old French *remembrer* from Late Latin *rememorari* (as RE-, Latin *memor* 'mindful')]

remembrance /rɪˈmɛmbr(ə)ns/ *n.* **1** the act of remembering or process of being remembered. **2** a memory or recollection. **3** a keepsake or souvenir. **4** (in *pl.*) greetings conveyed through a third person. [Middle English from Old French (as REMEMBER)]

Remembrance Day *n.* **1** = REMEMBRANCE SUNDAY. **2** *hist.* Armistice Day.

Remembrance Sunday *n.* (in the UK) the Sunday nearest 11 Nov., when those who were killed in the First and Second World Wars and later conflicts are commemorated.

remex /ˈriːmɛks/ *n.* (*pl.* **remiges** /ˈrɛmɪdʒiːz/) a primary or secondary feather in a bird's wing. [Latin, = rower, from *remus* 'oar']

remind /rɪˈmʌɪnd/ *v.tr.* **1** (foll. by *of*) cause (a person) to think of. **2** (usu. foll. by *to* + infin. or *that* + clause) cause (a person) to remember a commitment etc. (*remind them to pay their subscriptions*).

reminder /rɪˈmʌɪndə/ *n.* **1 a** a thing that reminds, esp. a letter or bill. **b** a means of reminding (*leave it here as a reminder*). **2** (often foll. by *of*) a memento or souvenir.

remindful /rɪˈmʌɪn(d)fʊl, -f(ə)l/ *adj.* (often foll. by *of*) acting as a reminder; reviving the memory.

reminisce /rɛmɪˈnɪs/ *v.intr.* (often foll. by *about*) indulge in reminiscence. □ **reminiscer** *n.* [back-formation from REMINISCENCE]

reminiscence /rɛmɪˈnɪs(ə)ns/ *n.* **1** the act of remembering things past; the recovery of knowledge by mental effort. **2 a** a past fact or experience that is remembered. **b** the process of narrating this. **3** (in *pl.*) a collection in literary form of incidents and experiences that a person remembers. **4** *Philos.* (esp. in Platonism) the theory of the recovery of things known to the soul in previous existences. **5** a characteristic of one thing reminding or suggestive of another. □ **reminiscential** /-ˈsɛnʃ(ə)l/ *adj.* [Late Latin *reminiscentia* from Latin *reminisci* 'remember']

reminiscent /rɛmɪˈnɪs(ə)nt/ *adj.* **1** (foll. by *of*) tending to remind one of or suggest. **2** concerned with reminiscence. **3** (of a person) given to reminiscing. □ **reminiscently** *adv.*

remise /rɪˈmiːz/ *v.* & *n.* ● *v.intr.* **1** *Law* surrender or make over (a right or property). **2** *Fencing* make a remise. ● *n.* *Fencing* a second thrust made after the first has failed. [French from *remis*, *remise*, past part. of *remettre* 'put back': cf. REMIT]

remiss /rɪˈmɪs/ *adj.* careless of duty; lax, negligent. □ **remissly** *adv.* **remissness** *n.* [Middle English from Latin *remissus*, past part. of *remittere* 'slacken': see REMIT]

remissible /rɪˈmɪsɪb(ə)l/ *adj.* that may be remitted. [French *rémissible* or Late Latin *remissibilis* (as REMIT)]

remission /rɪˈmɪʃ(ə)n/ *n.* **1** *Brit.* the reduction of a prison sentence on account of good behaviour. **2** the remitting of a debt or penalty etc. **3** a diminution of force, effect, or degree (esp. of disease or pain). **4** (often foll. by *of*) forgiveness (of sins etc.). □ **remissive** *adj.* [Middle English from Old French *remission* or Latin *remissio* (as REMIT)]

remit *v.* & *n.* ● *v.* /rɪˈmɪt/ (**remitted**, **remitting**) **1** *tr.* cancel or refrain from exacting or inflicting (a debt or punishment etc.). **2** *intr. & tr.* abate or slacken; cease or cease from partly or entirely. **3** *tr.* send (money etc.) in payment. **4** *tr.* cause to be conveyed by post. **5** *tr.* **a** (foll. by *to*) refer (a matter for decision etc.) to some authority. **b** *Law* send back (a case) to a lower court. **6** *tr.* **a** (often foll. by *to*) postpone or defer. **b** (foll. by *in, into*) send or put back into a previous state. **7** *tr. Theol.* (usu. of God) pardon (sins etc.). ● *n.* /ˈriːmɪt, rɪˈmɪt/ **1** the terms of reference of a committee etc. **2** an item remitted for consideration. □ **remittable** /rɪˈmɪtəb(ə)l/ *adj.* **remittal** /rɪˈmɪt(ə)l/ *n.* **remittee** /rɪmɪˈtiː/ *n.* **remitter** /rɪˈmɪtə/ *n.* [Middle English from Latin *remittere remiss-* (as RE-, *mittere* 'send')]

remittance /rɪˈmɪt(ə)ns/ *n.* **1** money sent, esp. by post, for goods or services or as an allowance. **2** the act of sending money.

remittance man *n. hist.* an emigrant subsisting on remittances from home.

remittent /rɪˈmɪt(ə)nt/ *adj.* (of a fever) that abates at intervals. [Latin *remittere* (as REMIT)]

remix *v. & n.* ● *v.tr.* /riːˈmɪks/ mix again. ● *n.* /ˈriːmɪks/ a sound recording that has been remixed to produce a new version (see MIX *v.* 8). □ **remixer** *n.*

remnant /ˈrɛmnənt/ *n.* **1** a small remaining quantity. **2** a piece of cloth etc. left when the greater part has been used or sold. **3** (foll. by *of*) a surviving trace (*a remnant of empire*). [Middle English (earlier *remenant*) from Old French *remenant*, from *remenoir* REMAIN]

remodel /riːˈmɒd(ə)l/ *v.tr.* (**remodelled**, **remodelling**; *US* **remodeled**, **remodeling**) **1** model again or differently. **2** reconstruct.

remodify /riːˈmɒdɪfʌɪ/ *v.tr.* (**-ies**, **-ied**) modify again. □ **remodification** /-fɪˈkeɪʃ(ə)n/ *n.*

remold *US* var. of REMOULD.

remonetize /riːˈmʌnɪtʌɪz/ *v.tr.* (also **-ise**) restore (a metal etc.) to its former position as legal tender. □ **remonetization** /-ˈzeɪʃ(ə)n/ *n.*

remonstrance /rɪˈmɒnstr(ə)ns/ *n.* **1** the act or an instance of remonstrating. **2** an expostulation or protest. [Middle English from obsolete French *remonstrance* or medieval Latin *remonstrantia* (as REMONSTRATE)]

remonstrate /ˈrɛmənstreɪt/ *v.* **1** *intr.* (foll. by *with*) make a protest; argue forcibly (*remonstrated with them over the delays*). **2** *tr.* (often foll. by *that* + clause) urge protestingly. □ **remonstrant** /rɪˈmɒnstr(ə)nt/ *adj.* **remonstration** /-ˈstreɪʃ(ə)n/ *n.* **remonstrative** /rɪˈmɒnstrətɪv/ *adj.* **remonstrator** *n.* [medieval Latin *remonstrare* (as RE-, *monstrare* 'show')]

remontant /rɪˈmɒnt(ə)nt/ *adj. & n.* ● *adj.* (esp. of a rose) blooming more than once a year. ● *n.* a remontant rose etc.. [French from *remonter* REMOUNT]

remora /ˈrɛmərə/ *n. Zool.* any of various slender marine fish of the family Echeneidae, which attach themselves by modified sucker-like dorsal fins to larger fish and to ships. [Latin, = hindrance (as RE-, *mora* 'delay', from the former belief that the fish slowed ships down)]

remorse /rɪˈmɔːs/ *n.* **1** deep regret for a wrong committed. **2** compunction; a compassionate reluctance to inflict pain (esp. in *without remorse*). [Middle English via Old French *remors* and medieval Latin *remorsus* from Latin *remordēre remors-* 'vex' (as RE-, *mordēre* 'bite')]

remorseful /rɪˈmɔːsfʊl, -f(ə)l/ *adj.* filled with repentance. □ **remorsefully** *adv.*

remorseless /rɪˈmɔːslɪs/ *adj.* without compassion or compunction. □ **remorselessly** *adv.* **remorselessness** *n.*

remortgage /riːˈmɔːgɪdʒ/ *v. & n.* ● *v.tr.* (also *absol.*) mortgage again; revise the terms of an existing mortgage on (a property). ● *n.* a different or altered mortgage.

remote /rɪˈməʊt/ *adj.* (**remoter**, **remotest**) **1** far away in place or time. **2** out of the way; situated away from the main centres of population, society, etc. **3** distantly related (*a remote ancestor*). **4** slight, faint (esp. in *not the remotest chance, idea*, etc.). **5** (of a person) aloof; not friendly. **6** (foll. by *from*) widely different; separate by nature (*ideas remote from the subject*). □ **remotely** *adv.* **remoteness** *n.* [Middle English from Latin *remotus* (as REMOVE)]

remote control *n.* **1** control of a machine or apparatus from a distance by means of signals transmitted from a radio or electronic device. **2** such a device. □ **remote-controlled** *adj.*

remote sensing *n.* the scanning of the earth by satellite or high-flying aircraft in order to obtain information about it.

remould *v. & n.* (*US* **remold**) ● *v.tr.* /riːˈməʊld/ **1** mould again; refashion. **2** *Brit.* re-form the tread of (a tyre). ● *n.* /ˈriːməʊld/ a remoulded tyre.

remount *v. & n.* ● *v.* /riːˈmaʊnt/ **1 a** *tr.* mount (a horse etc.) again. **b** *intr.* get on horseback again. **2** *tr.* get on to or ascend (a ladder, hill, etc.) again. **3** *tr.* provide (a person) with a fresh horse etc. **4** *tr.* put (a picture etc.) on a fresh mount. ● *n.* /ˈriːmaʊnt/ **1** a fresh horse for a rider. **2** a supply of fresh horses for a regiment.

removal /rɪˈmuːv(ə)l/ *n.* **1** the act or an instance of removing; the process of being removed. **2** esp. *Brit.* the transfer of furniture and other contents on moving house. **3** *Ir.* the taking of a body to a church for the funeral.

remove /rɪˈmuːv/ *v. & n.* ● *v.* **1** *tr.* take off or away from the place or position occupied; detach (*remove the top carefully*). **2** *tr.* **a** move or take to another place; change the situation of (*will you remove the tea things?*). **b** get rid of; eliminate (*will remove all doubts*). **3** *tr.* cause to be no longer present or available; take away (*all privileges were removed*). **4** *tr.* (often foll. by *from*) dismiss (from office). **5** *tr. colloq.* kill, assassinate. **6** *tr.* (in *passive*; foll. by *from*) distant or remote in condition (*the country is not far removed from anarchy*). **7** *tr.* (as **removed** *adj.*) (esp. of cousins) separated by a specified number of steps of descent (*a first cousin twice removed* = a grandchild of a first cousin). **8** *formal* **a** *intr.* (usu. foll. by *from, to*) change one's home or place of residence. **b** *tr.* conduct the removal of. ● *n.* **1** a degree of remoteness; a distance. **2** a stage in a gradation; a degree (*is several removes from what I expected*). **3** a form or division in some British schools. □ **removable** *adj.* **removability** /-ˈbɪlɪti/ *n.* **remover** *n.* (esp. in sense 8b of *v.*). [Middle English via Old French *removeir* from Latin *removēre remot-* (as RE-, *movēre* 'move')]

remunerate /rɪˈmjuːnəreɪt/ *v.tr.* **1** reward; pay for services rendered. **2** serve as or provide recompense for (toil etc.) or to (a person). □ **remuneration** /-ˈreɪʃ(ə)n/ *n.* **remunerative** /-rətɪv/ *adj.* [Latin *remunerari* (as RE-, *munus muneris* 'gift')]

Renaissance /rɪˈneɪs(ə)ns, -ɒ̃s/ *n.* **1** the revival of art and literature under the influence of classical models in the 14th–16th c. **2** the period of this. **3** the culture and style of art, architecture, etc. developed during this era. **4** (**renaissance**) any similar revival. [French *renaissance* (as RE-, French *naissance* 'birth' from Latin *nascentia*, or French *naître naiss-* 'be born' from Romanic: cf. NASCENT)]

Renaissance man *n.* a person with many talents or pursuits, esp. in the humanities.

renal /ˈriːn(ə)l/ *adj.* of or concerning the kidneys. [French *rénal* via Late Latin *renalis* from Latin *renes* 'kidneys']

rename /riːˈneɪm/ *v.tr.* name again; give a new name to.

renascence /rɪˈnas(ə)ns/ *n.* **1** rebirth; renewal. **2** = RENAISSANCE. [RENASCENT]

renascent /rɪˈnas(ə)nt/ *adj.* springing up anew; being reborn or renewed. [Latin *renasci* (as RE-, *nasci* 'be born')]

renationalize /riːˈnaʃ(ə)n(ə)lʌɪz/ *v.tr.* (also **-ise**) take (a privatized industry) back into state control. □ **renationalization** /-ˈzeɪʃ(ə)n/ *n.*

rencontre /rɛnˈkɒntə/ *n. archaic* = RENCOUNTER *n.*. [French (as RENCOUNTER)]

rencounter /rɛnˈkaʊntə/ *n. & v.* ● *n.* **1** an encounter; a chance meeting. **2** a battle, skirmish, or duel. ● *v.tr.* encounter; meet by chance. [French *rencontre(r)* (as RE-, ENCOUNTER)]

rend /rɛnd/ *v.* (*past* and *past part.* **rent** /rɛnt/) *archaic* or *literary* **1** *tr.* (foll. by *off, from, away*, etc.; also *absol.*) tear or wrench forcibly. **2** *tr. & intr.* split or divide in pieces or into factions (*a country rent by civil war*). **3** *tr.* cause emotional pain to (the heart etc.). □ **rend the air** sound piercingly. **rend one's garments** (or **hair**) display extreme grief or rage. [Old English *rendan*, related to Middle Low German *rende*]

render /ˈrɛndə/ *v.tr.* **1** cause to be or become; make (*rendered us helpless*). **2** give or pay (money, service, etc.), esp. in return or as a thing due (*render thanks*; *rendered good for evil*). **3** (often foll. by *to*) **a** give (assistance) (*rendered aid to the injured man*). **b** show (obedience etc.). **c** do (a service etc.). **4** submit; send in; present (an account, reason, etc.). **5 a** represent or portray artistically, musically, etc. **b** act (a role); represent (a character, idea, etc.) (*the dramatist's conception was well rendered*). **c** *Mus.* perform; execute. **6** translate (*rendered the poem into French*). **7** (often foll. by *down*) melt down (fat etc.), esp. to clarify; extract by melting. **8** cover (stone or brick) with a coat of plaster. **9** *literary* **a** give back; hand over; deliver, give up, surrender (*render unto Caesar the things that are Caesar's*). **b** show (obedience). □ **renderer** *n.* [Middle English from Old French *rendre*, ultimately from Latin *reddere reddit-* (as RE-, *dare* 'give')]

rendering /ˈrɛnd(ə)rɪŋ/ *n.* **1 a** the act or an instance of performing music, drama, etc.; an interpretation or performance (*an excellent rendering of the part*). **b** a translation. **2 a** the act or an instance of plastering stone, brick, etc. **b** this coating. **3** *literary* the act or an instance of giving, yielding, or surrendering.

rendezvous /ˈrɒndɪvuː, -deɪvuː/ *n. & v.* ● *n.* (*pl.* same /-vuːz/) **1** an agreed or regular meeting place. **2** a meeting by arrangement. **3** a place appointed for assembling troops, ships, etc. **4** a pre-arranged meeting between spacecraft in space. ● *v.intr.* (**rendezvouses** /-vuːz/; **rendezvoused** /-vuːd/; **rendezvousing** /-vuːɪŋ/) meet at a rendezvous. [French *rendez-vous* 'present yourselves' from *rendre*: see RENDER]

rendition /rɛnˈdɪʃ(ə)n/ *n.* (often foll. by *of*) **1** an interpretation or rendering of a dramatic role, piece of music, etc. **2** a visual representation. [obsolete French from *rendre* RENDER]

rendzina /rɛn(d)ˈziːnə/ *n.* a fertile lime-rich soil with dark humus above a pale soft calcareous layer, typical of grassland on chalk or limestone. [Russian from Polish *rędzina*]

renegade /ˈrɛnɪgeɪd/ *n., adj., & v.* ● *n.* **1 a** a person who deserts a party or principles; a rebel. **b** a person who changes allegiance. **2** *archaic* an apostate; a person who abandons one religion for another. ● *adj.* **1** traitorous, rebellious. **2** of changed allegiance. ● *v.intr.* be a renegade. [Spanish *renegado* from medieval Latin *renegatus* (as RE-, Latin *negare* 'deny')]

renegado /rɛnɪˈgeɪdəʊ/ *n.* (*pl.* **-oes**) *archaic* = RENEGADE *n.* [Spanish (as RENEGADE)]

renege /rɪˈniːg, rɪˈneɪg/ *v.* (also **renegue**) **1** *intr.* **a** go back on one's word; change one's mind; recant. **b** (foll. by *on*) go back on (a promise or undertaking or contract). **2** *tr.* deny, renounce, abandon (a person, faith, etc.). **3** *intr. Cards* revoke. □ **reneger** *n.* **reneguer** *n.* [medieval Latin *renegare* (as RE-, Latin *negare* 'deny')]

renegotiate /riːnɪˈgəʊʃɪeɪt/ *v.tr.* (also *absol.*) negotiate again or on different terms. □ **renegotiable** *adj.* **renegotiation** /-ˈeɪʃ(ə)n/ *n.*

renew /rɪˈnjuː/ *v.tr.* **1** revive; regenerate; make new again; restore to the original state. **2** reinforce; resupply; replace. **3** repeat or re-establish, resume after an interruption (*renewed our acquaintance*; *a renewed attack*). **4** get, begin, make, say, give, etc. anew. **5** (also *absol.*) grant or be granted a continuation of or continued validity of (a licence, subscription, lease, etc.). **6** recover (one's youth, strength, etc.). □ **renewable** *adj. & n.* **renewability** /-əˈbɪlɪti/ *n.* **renewal** *n.* **renewer** *n.*

reniform /ˈriːnɪfɔːm/ *adj.* esp. *Med.* kidney-shaped. [Latin *ren* 'kidney' + -FORM]

rennet /ˈrɛnɪt/ *n.* **1** curdled milk found in the stomach of an unweaned calf, containing rennin and used in curdling milk for cheese, junket, etc. **2** a preparation containing rennin made from the stomach membrane of a calf or from certain fungi, used for the same purpose. [Middle English, probably from an Old English word related to RUN]

rennin /ˈrɛnɪn/ *n. Biochem.* an enzyme secreted into the stomach of unweaned mammals causing the clotting of milk. [RENNET + -IN]

renominate /riːˈnɒmɪneɪt/ *v.tr.* nominate for a further term of office. □ **renomination** /-ˈneɪʃ(ə)n/ *n.*

renounce /rɪˈnaʊns/ *v.* **1** *tr.* consent formally to abandon; surrender; give up (a claim, right, possession, etc.). **2** *tr.* repudiate; refuse to recognize any longer (*renouncing their father's authority*). **3** *tr.* **a** decline further association or disclaim relationship with (*renounced my former friends*). **b** withdraw from; discontinue; forsake. **4** *intr. Law* refuse or resign a right or position esp. as an heir or trustee. **5** *intr. Cards* follow with a card of another suit when having no card of the suit led (cf. REVOKE *v.* 2). □ **renounce the world** abandon society or material affairs. □ **renounceable** *adj.* **renouncement** *n.* **renouncer** *n.* [Middle English via Old French *renoncer* from Latin *renuntiare* (as RE-, *nuntiare* 'announce')]

renovate /ˈrɛnəveɪt/ *v.tr.* **1** restore to good condition; repair. **2** make new again. □ **renovation** /-ˈveɪʃ(ə)n/ *n.* **renovator** *n.* [Latin *renovare* (as RE-, *novus* 'new')]

renown /rɪˈnaʊn/ *n.* fame; high distinction; celebrity (*a city of great renown*). [Middle English from Anglo-French *ren(o)un*, Old French *renon*, *renom*, from *renomer* 'make famous' (as RE-, Latin *nominare* NOMINATE)]

renowned /rɪˈnaʊnd/ *adj.* famous; celebrated.

rent[1] /rɛnt/ *n. & v.* ● *n.* **1** a tenant's periodical payment to an owner or landlord for the use of land or premises. **2** payment for the use of a service, equipment, etc. ● *v.* **1** *tr.* (often foll. by *from*) take, occupy, or use at a rent (*rented a cottage from the local farmer*). **2** *tr.* (often foll. by *out*) let or hire (a thing) for rent. **3** *intr.* (foll. by *at*, *for*) esp. *N. Amer.* be let or hired out at a specified rate (*the land rents at £100 per month*). □ **for rent** *N. Amer.* available to be rented. [Middle English via Old French *rente* from Romanic (as RENDER)]

rent[2] /rɛnt/ *n.* **1** a large tear in a garment etc. **2** an opening in clouds etc. **3** a cleft, fissure, or gorge. [obsolete *rent*, variant of REND]

rent[3] *past* and *past part.* of REND.

rent-a- *comb.form* often *joc.* denoting availability for hire (*rent-a-van*; *rent-a-crowd*).

rentable /ˈrɛntəb(ə)l/ *adj.* **1** available or suitable for renting. **2** giving an adequate ratio of profit to capital. □ **rentability** /-ˈbɪlɪti/ *n.*

rental /ˈrɛnt(ə)l/ *n.* **1** the amount paid or received as rent. **2** the act of renting. **3** *N. Amer.* a rented house etc. [Middle English from Anglo-French *rental* or Anglo-Latin *rentale* (as RENT[1])]

rental library *n. US* a library which rents books for a fee.

rent boy *n. Brit.* a young male prostitute.

renter /ˈrɛntə/ *n.* **1** a person who rents. **2** *Cinematog.* (in the UK) a person who distributes cinema films. **3** *Brit. slang* a male prostitute.

rent-free *adj. & adv.* with exemption from rent.

rentier /ˈrɒntɪeɪ/ *n.* a person living on dividends from property, investments, etc. [French from *rente* 'dividend']

rent roll *n.* the register of a landlord's lands etc. with the rents due from them; the sum of one's income from rent.

renumber /riːˈnʌmbə/ *v.tr.* change the number or numbers given or allocated to.

renunciation /rɪnʌnsɪˈeɪʃ(ə)n/ *n.* **1** the act or an instance of renouncing or giving up. **2** self-denial. **3** a document expressing renunciation. □ **renunciant** /rɪˈnʌnsɪənt/ *n.* & *adj.* **renunciative** /rɪˈnʌnsɪətɪv/ *adj.* **renunciatory** /rɪˈnʌnʃət(ə)ri/ *adj.* [Middle English from Old French *renonciation* or Late Latin *renuntiatio* (as RENOUNCE)]

renvoi /ˈrɒnvwɑː/ *n. Law* the act or an instance of referring a case, dispute, etc. to a different jurisdiction. [French from *renvoyer* 'send back']

reoccupy /riːˈɒkjʊpʌɪ/ *v.tr.* (**-ies**, **-ied**) occupy again. □ **reoccupation** /-ˈpeɪʃ(ə)n/ *n.*

reoccur /riːəˈkəː/ *v.intr.* (**reoccurred**, **reoccurring**) occur again or habitually. □ **reoccurrence** /-ˈkʌr(ə)ns/ *n.*

reoffend /riːəˈfɛnd/ *v.intr.* offend again; commit a further offence.

reopen /riːˈəʊp(ə)n/ *v.tr.* & *intr.* open again.

reorder /riːˈɔːdə/ *v.* & *n.* ● *v.tr.* order again. ● *n.* a renewed or repeated order for goods.

reorganize /riːˈɔːg(ə)nʌɪz/ *v.tr.* (also **-ise**) organize differently. □ **reorganization** /-ˈzeɪʃ(ə)n/ *n.* **reorganizer** *n.*

reorient /riːˈɔːrɪɛnt, -ˈɒr-/ *v.tr.* **1** give a new direction to (ideas etc.); redirect (a thing). **2** help (a person) find his or her bearings again. **3** change the outlook of (a person). **4** (refl., often foll. by *to*) adjust oneself to or come to terms with something.

reorientate /riːˈɔːrɪənteɪt, -ˈɒr-/ *v.tr.* = REORIENT. □ **reorientation** /-ˈteɪʃ(ə)n/ *n.*

Rep. *abbr. US Polit.* **1** a Representative in Congress. **2** a Republican.

rep[1] /rɛp/ *n.* & *v. colloq.* ● *n.* a representative, esp. a commercial traveller. ● *v.intr.* (**repped**, **repping**) act as a representative for a company, product, etc. [abbreviation]

rep[2] /rɛp/ *n. colloq.* **1** repertory. **2** a repertory theatre or company. [abbreviation]

rep[3] /rɛp/ *n.* (also **repp**) a textile fabric with a corded surface, used in curtains and upholstery. [French *reps*, of unknown origin]

rep[4] /rɛp/ *n. US slang* reputation. [abbreviation]

repack /riːˈpak/ *v.tr.* pack again.

repackage /riːˈpakɪdʒ/ *v.tr.* **1** package again or differently. **2** present in a new form. □ **repackaging** *n.*

repaginate /riːˈpadʒɪneɪt/ *v.tr.* paginate again; renumber the pages of. □ **repagination** /-ˈneɪʃ(ə)n/ *n.*

repaid *past* and *past part.* of REPAY.

repaint *v.* & *n.* ● *v.tr.* /riːˈpeɪnt/ **1** paint again or differently. **2** restore the paint or colouring of. ● *n.* /ˈriːpeɪnt/ **1** the act of repainting. **2** a repainted thing, esp. a golf ball.

repair[1] /rɪˈpɛː/ *v.* & *n.* ● *v.tr.* **1** restore to good condition after damage or wear. **2** renovate or mend by replacing or fixing parts or by compensating for loss or exhaustion. **3** set right or make amends for (loss, wrong, error, etc.). ● *n.* **1** the act or an instance of restoring to sound condition (*in need of repair*; *closed during repair*). **2** the result of this (*the repair is hardly visible*). **3** good or relative condition for working or using (*must be kept in repair*; *in good repair*). □ **repairable** *adj.* **repairer** *n.* [Middle English via Old French *reparer* from Latin *reparare* (as RE-, *parare* 'make ready')]

repair[2] /rɪˈpɛː/ *v.* & *n.* ● *v.intr.* (foll. by *to*) resort; have recourse; go often or in great numbers or for a specific purpose (*repaired to Spain*). ● *n. archaic* **1** resort (*have repair to*). **2** a place of frequent resort. **3** popularity (*a place of great repair*). [Middle English via Old French *repaire(r)* from Late Latin *repatriare* REPATRIATE]

repairman /rɪˈpɛːmən/ *n.* (*pl.* **-men**) a man who repairs machinery etc.

repand /rɪˈpand/ *adj. Bot.* with an undulating margin; wavy. [Latin *repandus* (as RE-, *pandus* 'bent')]

repaper /riːˈpeɪpə/ *v.tr.* paper (a wall etc.) again.

reparable /ˈrɛp(ə)rəb(ə)l/ *adj.* (of a loss etc.) that can be made good. [French from Latin *reparabilis* (as REPAIR[1])]

reparation /rɛpəˈreɪʃ(ə)n/ *n.* **1** the act or an instance of making amends. **2 a** compensation. **b** (esp. in *pl.*) compensation for war damage paid by the defeated state. **3** the act or an instance of repairing or being repaired. □ **reparative** /ˈrɛp(ə)rətɪv, rɪˈparətɪv/ *adj.* [Middle English via Old French from Late Latin *reparatio -onis* (as REPAIR[1])]

repartee /rɛpɑːˈtiː/ *n.* **1** the practice or faculty of making witty retorts; sharpness or wit in quick reply. **2 a** a witty retort. **b** witty retorts collectively. [French *repartie*, fem. past part. of *repartir* 'start again, reply promptly' (as RE-, *partir* PART)]

repartition /riːpɑːˈtɪʃ(ə)n/ *v.tr.* partition again.

repass /riːˈpɑːs/ *v.tr.* & *intr.* pass again, esp. on the way back. [Middle English from Old French *repasser*]

repast /rɪˈpɑːst/ *n.* esp. *formal* **1** a meal, esp. of a specified kind (*a light repast*). **2** food and drink supplied for or eaten at a meal. [Middle English via Old French *repaistre* from Late Latin *repascere repast-* 'feed']

repat /ˈriːpat, riːˈpat/ *n. Brit. colloq.* **1** a repatriate. **2** repatriation. [abbreviation]

repatriate /riːˈpatrɪeɪt, -ˈpeɪ-/ *v.* & *n.* ● *v.* **1** *tr.* restore (a person) to his or her native land. **2** *intr.* return to one's own native land. ● *n.* a person who has been repatriated. □ **repatriation** /-ˈeɪʃ(ə)n/ *n.* [Late Latin *repatriare* (as RE-, Latin *patria* 'native land')]

repay /riːˈpeɪ, rɪ-/ *v.* (*past* and *past part.* **repaid**) **1** *tr.* pay back (money). **2** *tr.* return (a blow, visit, etc.). **3** *tr.* make repayment to (a person). **4** *tr.* make return for; requite (a service, action, etc.) (*must repay their kindness*; *the book repays close study*). **5** *tr.* (often foll. by *for*) give in recompense. **6** *intr.* make repayment. □ **repayable** *adj.* **repayment** *n.* [Old French *repaier* (as RE-, PAY[1])]

repeal /rɪˈpiːl/ *v.* & *n.* ● *v.tr.* revoke, rescind, or annul (a law, an Act of Parliament, etc.). ● *n.* the act or an instance of repealing. □ **repealable** *adj.* [Middle English from Anglo-French *repeler*, Old French *rapeler* (as RE-, APPEAL)]

repeat /rɪˈpiːt/ *v.* & *n.* ● *v.* **1** *tr.* say or do over again. **2** *tr.* recite, rehearse, or reproduce (something from memory) (*repeated a poem*). **3** *tr.* say or report (something heard). **4** *tr.* imitate (an action etc.). **5** *intr.* recur; appear again, perhaps several times (*a repeating pattern*). **6** *tr.* used for emphasis (*am not, repeat not, going*). **7** *intr.* (of food) be tasted intermittently for some time after being swallowed as a result of belching or indigestion. **8** *intr.* (of a watch etc.) strike the last quarter etc. over again when required. **9** *intr.* (of a firearm) fire several shots without reloading. **10** *intr. US* illegally vote more than once in an election. ● *n.* **1 a** the act or an instance of repeating. **b** a thing repeated (often *attrib.*: *repeat prescription*). **2** a repeated broadcast. **3** *Mus.* **a** a passage intended to be repeated. **b** a mark indicating this. **4** a pattern repeated in wallpaper etc. **5** *Commerce* **a** a consignment similar to a previous one. **b** an order given for this; a reorder. □ **repeat itself** recur in the same form. **repeat oneself** say or do the same thing over again. □ **repeatable** *adj.* **repeatability** /-ˈbɪlɪti/ *n.* **repeatedly** *adv.* [Middle English via Old French *repeter* from Latin *repetere* (as RE-, *petere* 'seek')]

repeater /rɪˈpiːtə/ *n.* **1** a person or thing that repeats. **2** a firearm which fires several shots without reloading. **3** a watch or clock which repeats its last strike when required. **4** a device for the automatic retransmission or amplification of an electrically transmitted message. **5** a railway signal lamp indicating the state of another that is invisible.

repeating decimal *n.* a recurring decimal.

repêchage /ˈrɛpəʃɑːʒ/ *n.* (in rowing etc.) an extra contest in which the runners-up in the eliminating heats compete for a place in the final. [French *repêcher* 'fish out, rescue']

repel /rɪˈpɛl/ *v.tr.* (**repelled**, **repelling**) **1** drive back; ward off; repulse (*repel an assailant*). **2** refuse to accept or admit (an argument etc.). **3** be repulsive or distasteful to. **4** resist mixing with or admitting (*oil repels water; surface repels moisture*). **5** (often *absol.*) (of a magnetic pole) push away from itself (*like poles repel*). □ **repeller** *n.* [Middle English from Latin *repellere* (as RE-, *pellere puls-* 'drive')]

repellent /rɪˈpɛl(ə)nt/ *adj.* & *n.* ● *adj.* **1** that repels. **2** disgusting, repulsive. ● *n.* a substance that repels esp. insects etc. □ **repellence** *n.* **repellency** *n.* **repellently** *adv.* [Latin *repellere* (as REPEL)]

repent[1] /rɪˈpɛnt/ *v.* **1** *intr.* (often foll. by *of*) feel deep sorrow about one's actions etc. **2** *tr.* (also *absol.*) wish one had not done, regret (one's wrong, omission, etc.); resolve not to continue (a wrongdoing etc.). **3** *refl.* (often foll. by *of*) *archaic* feel regret or penitence about (*now I repent me*). □ **repentance** *n.* **repentant** *adj.* **repenter** *n.* [Middle English from Old French *repentir* (as RE-, *pentir*, ultimately from Latin *paenitēre*)]

repent[2] /ˈriːp(ə)nt/ *adj. Bot.* creeping, esp. growing along the ground or just under the surface. [Latin *repere* 'creep']

repeople /riːˈpiːp(ə)l/ *v.tr.* repopulate.

repercussion /riːpəˈkʌʃ(ə)n/ *n.* **1** (often foll. by *of*) an indirect effect or reaction following an event or action (*consider the repercussions of moving*). **2** the recoil after impact. **3** an echo or reverberation. □ **repercussive** /-ˈkʌsɪv/ *adj.* [Middle English from Old French *repercussion* or Latin *repercussio* (as RE-, PERCUSSION)]

repertoire /ˈrɛpətwɑː/ *n.* **1** a stock of pieces etc. that a company or a performer knows or is prepared to give. **2** a stock of regularly performed pieces, regularly used techniques, etc. (*went through his repertoire of excuses*). [French *répertoire* from Late Latin (as REPERTORY)]

repertory /ˈrɛpət(ə)ri/ *n.* (*pl.* **-ies**) **1** = REPERTOIRE. **2** the theatrical performance of various plays for short periods by one company. **3 a** a repertory company. **b** repertory theatres regarded collectively. **4** a store or collection, esp. of information, instances, etc. [Late Latin *repertorium* from Latin *reperire repert-* 'find']

repertory company *n.* a theatrical company that performs plays from a repertoire.

repetend /ˈrɛpɪtɛnd, rɛpɪˈtɛnd/ *n.* **1** the recurring figures of a decimal. **2** the recurring word or phrase; a refrain. [Latin *repetendum* (as REPEAT)]

répétiteur /rɛˌpɛtɪˈtəː/ *n.* **1** a tutor or coach of musicians, esp. opera singers. **2** a person who supervises ballet rehearsals etc. [French]

repetition /rɛpɪˈtɪʃ(ə)n/ *n.* **1 a** the act or an instance of repeating or being repeated. **b** the thing repeated. **2** a copy or replica. **3** a piece to be learnt by heart. **4** the ability of a musical instrument to repeat a note quickly. □ **repetitional** *adj.* **repetitionary** *adj.* [French *répétition* or Latin *repetitio* (as REPEAT)]

repetitious /rɛpɪˈtɪʃəs/ *adj.* characterized by repetition, esp. when unnecessary or tiresome. □ **repetitiously** *adv.* **repetitiousness** *n.*

repetitive /rɪˈpɛtɪtɪv/ *adj.* = REPETITIOUS. □ **repetitively** *adv.* **repetitiveness** *n.*

repetitive strain injury *n.* injury arising from the prolonged use of particular muscles, esp. during keyboarding.

rephrase /riːˈfreɪz/ *v.tr.* express in an alternative way.

repine /rɪˈpʌɪn/ *v.intr.* (often foll. by *at, against, for*) *literary* fret; be discontented. [RE- + PINE[2], on the pattern of *repent*]

repique /rɪˈpiːk/ *n.* & *v.* ● *n.* (in piquet) the winning of 30 points on cards alone before beginning to play. ● *v.* (**repiques**, **repiqued**, **repiquing**) **1** *intr.* score repique. **2** *tr.* score repique against (another person). [French *repic* (as RE-, PIQUE[2])]

replace /rɪˈpleɪs/ *v.tr.* **1** put back in place. **2** take the place of; succeed; be substituted for. **3** find or provide a substitute for; renew. **4** (often foll. by *with, by*) fill up the place of. **5** (in *passive*, often foll. by *by*) be succeeded or have one's place filled by another; be superseded. □ **replaceable** *adj.* **replacer** *n.*

replacement /rɪˈpleɪsm(ə)nt/ *n.* **1** the act or an instance of replacing or being replaced. **2** a person or thing that takes the place of another.

replan /riːˈplan/ *v.tr.* (**replanned**, **replanning**) plan again or differently.

replant /riːˈplɑːnt/ *v.tr.* **1** transfer (a plant etc.) to a larger pot, a new site, etc. **2** plant (ground) again; provide with new plants.

replay *v.* & *n.* ● *v.tr.* /riːˈpleɪ/ play (a match, recording, etc.) again. ● *n.* /ˈriːpleɪ/ the act or an instance of replaying a match, a recording, or a recorded incident in a game etc.

replenish /rɪˈplɛnɪʃ/ *v.tr.* **1** (often foll. by *with*) fill up again. **2** renew (a supply etc.). **3** (as **replenished** *adj.*) filled; fully stored or stocked; full. □ **replenisher** *n.* **replenishment** *n.* [Middle English from Old French *replenir* (as RE-, *plenir* from *plein* 'full', from Latin *plenus*)]

replete /rɪˈpliːt/ *adj.* (often foll. by *with*) **1** filled or well-supplied with. **2** stuffed; gorged; sated. □ **repleteness** *n.* **repletion** *n.* [Middle English from Old French *replet replete* or Latin *repletus*, past part. of *replēre* (as RE-, *plēre plet-* 'fill')]

replevin /rɪˈplɛvɪn/ *n. Law* **1** the provisional restoration or recovery of distrained goods pending the outcome of trial and judgement. **2** a writ granting this. **3** the action arising from this process. [Middle English via Anglo-French from Old French *replevir* (as REPLEVY)]

replevy /rɪˈplɛvi/ *v.tr.* (**-ies**, **-ied**) *Law* recover by replevin. [Old French *replevir* 'recover' (as RE-, *plevir*) from Germanic, related to PLEDGE]

replica /ˈrɛplɪkə/ *n.* **1** a duplicate of a work made by the original artist. **2** a facsimile, an exact copy. **3** a copy or model, esp. on a smaller scale. [Italian, from *replicare* REPLY]

replicate *v., adj.,* & *n.* ● *v.tr.* /ˈrɛplɪkeɪt/ **1** repeat (an experiment etc.). **2** make a replica of. **3** fold back. ● *adj.* /ˈrɛplɪkət/ *Bot.* folded back on itself. ● *n.* /ˈrɛplɪkət/ *Mus.* a tone one or more octaves above or below the given tone. □ **replicable** /ˈrɛplɪkəb(ə)l/ *adj.* (in sense 1 of *v.*). **replicability** /ˌrɛplɪkəˈbɪlɪti/ *n.* (in sense 1 of *v.*). **replicative** /ˈrɛplɪkətɪv/ *adj.* **replicator** /ˈrɛplɪkeɪtə/ *n.* (esp. in sense 2 of *v.*). [Latin *replicare* (as RE-, *plicare* 'fold')]

replication /rɛplɪˈkeɪʃ(ə)n/ *n.* **1** a reply or response, esp. a reply to an answer. **2** *Law* the plaintiff's reply to the defendant's plea. **3 a** the act or an instance of copying. **b** a copy. **c** the process by which genetic material or a living organism gives rise to a copy of itself. [Middle English via Old French *replicacion* from Latin *replicatio -onis* (as REPLICATE)]

reply /rɪˈplʌɪ/ *v.* & *n.* ● *v.* (**-ies**, **-ied**) **1** *intr.* (often foll. by *to*) make an answer, respond in word or action. **2** *tr.* say in answer (*he replied, 'Please yourself'*). ● *n.* (*pl.* **-ies**) **1** the act of replying (*what did they say in reply?*). **2** what is replied; a response. **3** *Law* = REPLICATION 2. □ **replier** *n.* [Middle English via Old French *replier* from Latin (as REPLICATE)]

reply coupon *n.* a coupon exchangeable for stamps in any country for prepaying the reply to a letter.

reply-paid *adj.* **1** (of an envelope etc.) for which the addressee undertakes to pay postage. **2** *hist.* (of a telegram) with the cost of a reply prepaid by the sender.

repoint /riːˈpɔɪnt/ *v.tr.* point (esp. brickwork) again.

repolish /riːˈpɒlɪʃ/ *v.tr.* polish again.

repopulate /riːˈpɒpjʊleɪt/ *v.tr.* populate again or increase the population of. □ **repopulation** /-ˈleɪʃ(ə)n/ *n.*

report /rɪˈpɔːt/ *v.* & *n.* ● *v.* **1** *tr.* **a** bring back or give an account of. **b** state as fact or news, narrate or describe or repeat, esp. as an eyewitness or hearer etc. **c** relate as spoken by another. **2** *tr.* make an official or formal statement about. **3** *tr.* (often foll. by *to*) name or specify (an offender or offence) (*shall report you for insubordination*; *reported them to the police*). **4** *intr.* (often foll. by *to*) present oneself as having returned or arrived (*report to the manager on arrival*). **5** *tr.* (also *absol.*) take down word for word or summarize or write a description of for publication. **6** *intr.* **a** make, draw up, or send in a report. **b** (usu. foll. by *on*) investigate as a journalist; act as a reporter. **7** *intr.* (foll. by *to*) be responsible to (a superior, supervisor, etc.) (*reports directly to the managing director*). **8** *tr. Parl.* (of a committee chairman) announce that the committee has dealt with (a bill). **9** *intr.* (often foll. by *of*) give a report to convey that one is adversely or favourably impressed (*reports well of the prospects*). ● *n.* **1** an account given or opinion formally expressed after investigation or consideration. **2** a description, summary, or reproduction of an event, speech, or law case, esp. for newspaper publication or broadcast. **3** common talk; rumour. **4** the way a person or thing is spoken of (*I hear a good report of you*). **5** a periodical statement on (esp. a school pupil's) work, conduct, etc. **6** the sound of an explosion. □ **report back** deliver a report to the person, organization, etc. for whom one acts etc. **report progress** state what has been done so far. □ **reportable** *adj.* **reportedly** *adv.* [Middle English via Old French *reporter* from Latin *reportare* (as RE-, *portare* 'bring')]

reportage /rɛpɔːˈtɑːʒ, rɪˈpɔːtɪdʒ/ *n.* **1** the describing of events, esp. the reporting of news etc. for the press and for broadcasting. **2** the typical style of this. **3** factual presentation in a book etc. [REPORT, influenced by French]

reported speech *n.* the speaker's words with the changes of person, tense, etc. usual in reports, e.g. *he said that he would go* (opp. DIRECT SPEECH). Also called *indirect speech*.

reporter /rɪˈpɔːtə/ *n.* **1** a person employed to report news etc. for newspapers or broadcasts. **2** a person who reports.

reportorial /rɛpɔːˈtɔːrɪəl/ *adj. US* of or characteristic of newspaper reporters. □ **reportorially** *adv.* [REPORTER, on the pattern of *editorial*]

report stage *n.* (in the UK) the debate on a bill in the House of Commons or House of Lords after it is reported.

repose[1] /rɪˈpəʊz/ *n.* & *v.* ● *n.* **1** the cessation of activity or excitement or toil. **2** sleep. **3** a peaceful or quiescent state; stillness; tranquillity. **4** *Art* a restful effect; harmonious combination. **5** composure or ease of manner. ● *v.* **1** *intr.* & *refl.* lie down in rest (*reposed on a sofa*). **2** *tr.* (often foll. by *on*) lay (one's head etc.) to rest (on a pillow etc.). **3** *intr.* (often foll. by *in, on*) lie, be lying or laid, esp. in sleep or death. **4** *tr.* give rest to; refresh with rest. **5** *intr.* (foll. by *on, upon*) be supported or based on. **6** *intr.* (foll. by *on*) (of memory etc.) dwell on. □ **reposal** *n.* **reposeful** *adj.* **reposefully** *adv.* **reposefulness** *n.* [Middle English via Old French *repos(er)* from Late Latin *repausare* (as RE-, *pausare* PAUSE)]

repose[2] /rɪˈpəʊz/ *v.tr.* (foll. by *in*) place (trust etc.) in. □ **reposal** *n.* [earlier = replace, restore: RE- + POSE[1] suggested by Latin *reponere reposit-* 'replace' etc.]

reposition /riːpəˈzɪʃ(ə)n/ *v.* **1** *tr.* move or place in a different position. **2** *intr.* adjust or alter one's position.

repository /rɪˈpɒzɪt(ə)ri/ *n.* (*pl.* **-ies**) **1** a place where things are stored or may be found, esp. a warehouse or museum. **2** a receptacle. **3** (often foll. by *of*) **a** a book, person, etc. regarded as a store of information etc. **b** the recipient of confidences or secrets. [obsolete French *repositoire* or Latin *repositorium* (as REPOSE[2])]

repossess /riːpəˈzɛs/ *v.tr.* regain possession of (esp. property or goods on which repayment of a debt is in arrears). □ **repossession** /-ˈzɛʃ(ə)n/ *n.* **repossessor** *n.*

repot /riːˈpɒt/ *v.tr.* (**repotted**, **repotting**) put (a plant) in another, esp. larger, pot.

repoussé /rəˈpuːseɪ/ *adj.* & *n.* ● *adj.* hammered into relief from the reverse side. ● *n.* ornamental metalwork fashioned in this way. [French, past part. of *repousser* (as RE-, *pousser* PUSH)]

repp var. of REP[3].

repped /rɛpt/ *adj.* having a surface like rep.

repr. *abbr.* **1** represent, represented, etc. **2** reprint, reprinted.

reprehend /rɛprɪˈhɛnd/ *v.tr.* rebuke; blame; find fault with. □ **reprehension** *n.* [Middle English from Latin *reprehendere* (as RE-, *prehendere* 'seize')]

reprehensible /rɛprɪˈhɛnsɪb(ə)l/ *adj.* deserving censure or rebuke; blameworthy. □ **reprehensibility** /-ˈbɪlɪti/ *n.* **reprehensibly** *adv.* [Late Latin *reprehensibilis* (as REPREHEND)]

represent /rɛprɪˈzɛnt/ *v.tr.* **1** stand for or correspond to (*the comment does not represent all our views*). **2** (often in *passive*) be a specimen or example of; exemplify (*all types of people were represented in the audience*). **3** act as an embodiment of; symbolize (*the sovereign represents the majesty of the state*; *numbers are represented by letters*). **4** call up in the mind by description or portrayal or imagination; place a likeness of before the mind or senses. **5** serve or be meant as a likeness of. **6** **a** state by way of expostulation or persuasion (*represented the rashness of it*). **b** (foll. by *to*) try to bring (the facts influencing conduct) home to (*represented the risks to his client*). **7** (often foll. by *as, to be*) describe or depict as; declare or make out (*represented them as martyrs*; *not what you represent it to be*). **8** (foll. by *that* + clause) allege. **9** show, or play the part of, on stage. **10** fill the place of; be a substitute or deputy for; be entitled to act or speak for (*the Queen was represented by the Duke of Edinburgh*). **11** be elected as a Member of Parliament, member of a legislature, etc., by (*represents a rural constituency*). □ **representable** *adj.* **representability** /-ˈbɪlɪti/ *n.* [Middle English from Old French *representer* or from Latin *repraesentare* (as RE-, PRESENT[2])]

re-present /riːprɪˈzɛnt/ *v.tr.* present (esp. a cheque) again. □ **re-presentation** /-ˈteɪʃ(ə)n/ *n.*

representation /ˌrɛprɪzɛnˈteɪʃ(ə)n/ *n.* **1** the act or an instance of representing or being represented. **2** an image, likeness, or reproduction of a thing, e.g. a painting or drawing. **3** (esp. in *pl.*) a statement made by way of allegation or to convey opinion. [Middle English from Old French *representation* or Latin *repraesentatio* (as REPRESENT)]

representational /ˌrɛprɪzɛnˈteɪʃ(ə)n(ə)l/ *adj.* of representation. □ **representationalism** *n.* **representationalist** *adj.* & *n.*

representational art *n.* art seeking to portray the physical appearance of a subject.

representationism /ˌrɛprɪzɛnˈteɪʃ(ə)nɪz(ə)m/ *n.* the doctrine that perceived objects are only a representation of real external objects. □ **representationist** *n.*

representative /rɛprɪˈzɛntətɪv/ *adj.* & *n.* ● *adj.* **1** typical of a class or category. **2** containing typical specimens of all or many classes (*a representative sample*). **3** **a** consisting of elected deputies etc. **b** based on the representation of a nation etc. by such deputies (*representative government*). **4** (foll. by *of*) serving as a portrayal or symbol of (*representative of their attitude to work*). **5** that presents or can present ideas to the mind (*imagination is a representative faculty*). **6** (of art) representational. ● *n.* **1** (foll. by *of*) a sample, specimen, or typical embodiment or analogue of. **2** **a** the agent of a person or society. **b** a commercial traveller. **3** a delegate; a substitute. **4** a deputy in a representative assembly. □ **representatively** *adv.* **representativeness** *n.* [Middle English from Old French *representatif -ive* or medieval Latin *repraesentativus* (as REPRESENT)]

repress /rɪˈprɛs/ *v.tr.* **1** **a** check; restrain; keep under; quell. **b** suppress; prevent from sounding, rioting, or bursting out. **2** **a** suppress or control (thoughts, desires, etc.) in oneself or another. **b** *Psychol.* actively exclude (an unwelcome thought) from conscious awareness. **3** (usu. as **repressed** *adj.*) subject (a person) to the suppression of his or her thoughts or impulses. □ **represser** *n.* **repressible** *adj.* **repression** /-ˈprɛʃ(ə)n/ *n.* **repressive** *adj.* **repressively** *adv.* **repressiveness** *n.* [Middle English from Latin *reprimere* (as RE-, *premere* PRESS[1])]

repressor /rɪˈprɛsə/ *n. Biochem.* a substance which acts on an operon to inhibit enzyme synthesis.

reprice /riːˈprʌɪs/ *v.tr.* price again or differently.

reprieve /rɪˈpriːv/ *v. & n.* ● *v.tr.* **1 a** relieve or rescue from impending punishment. **b** remit, commute, or postpone the execution of (a condemned person). **2** give respite to. ● *n.* **1 a** the act or an instance of reprieving or being reprieved. **b** a warrant for this. **2** respite; a respite or temporary escape. [Middle English as past part. *repryed* from Anglo-French & Old French *repris*, past part. of *reprendre* (as RE-, *prendre* from Latin *prehendere* 'take'): 16th-c. *-v-* unexplained]

reprimand /ˈrɛprɪmɑːnd/ *n. & v.* ● *n.* (often foll. by *for*) an official or sharp rebuke (for a fault etc.). ● *v.tr.* administer this to. [French *réprimande* via Spanish *reprimenda* from Latin *reprimenda*, neut. pl. gerundive of *reprimere* REPRESS]

reprint *v. & n.* ● *v.tr.* /riːˈprɪnt/ print again. ● *n.* /ˈriːprɪnt/ **1** the act or an instance of reprinting a book etc. **2 a** a book etc. reprinted. **b** an offprint. **3** the quantity reprinted. □ **reprinter** *n.*

reprisal /rɪˈprʌɪz(ə)l/ *n.* **1** an act of retaliation. **2** *hist.* the forcible seizure of a foreign subject or his or her goods as an act of retaliation. [Middle English (in sense 2) via Anglo-French *reprisaille* from medieval Latin *reprisalia*, from *repraehensalia* (as REPREHEND)]

reprise /rɪˈpriːz/ *n. & v.* ● *n.* **1** a repeated passage in music. **2** a repeated item in a musical programme. ● *v.tr.* repeat (a performance, song, etc.); restage, rewrite. [French, fem. past part. of *reprendre* (see REPRIEVE)]

repro /ˈriːprəʊ/ *n.* (*pl.* **-os**) (often *attrib.*) *colloq.* a reproduction or copy. [abbreviation]

reproach /rɪˈprəʊtʃ/ *v. & n.* ● *v.tr.* **1** express disapproval to (a person) for a fault etc. **2** scold; rebuke; censure. **3** *archaic* rebuke (an offence). ● *n.* **1** a rebuke or censure (*heaped reproaches on them*). **2** (often foll. by *to*) a thing that brings disgrace or discredit (*their behaviour is a reproach to us all*). **3** a disgraced or discredited state (*live in reproach and ignominy*). **4** (in *pl.*) *RC Ch.* a set of antiphons and responses for Good Friday representing the reproaches of Christ to his people. □ **above** (or **beyond**) **reproach** perfect. □ **reproachable** *adj.* **reproacher** *n.* **reproachingly** *adv.* [Middle English via Old French *reproche* (*n.*), *reprocher* (*v.*) from Romanic (as RE-, Latin *prope* 'near')]

reproachful /rɪˈprəʊtʃfʊl, -f(ə)l/ *adj.* full of or expressing reproach. □ **reproachfully** *adv.* **reproachfulness** *n.*

reprobate /ˈrɛprəbeɪt/ *n., adj., & v.* ● *n.* **1** an unprincipled person; a person of highly immoral character. **2** a person who is condemned by God. ● *adj.* **1** immoral. **2** hardened in sin. ● *v.tr.* **1** express or feel disapproval of; censure. **2** (of God) condemn; exclude from salvation. □ **reprobation** /-ˈbeɪʃ(ə)n/ *n.* [Middle English from Latin *reprobare reprobat-* 'disapprove' (as RE-, *probare* 'approve')]

reprocess /riːˈprəʊsɛs/ *v.tr.* process again or differently.

reproduce /riːprəˈdjuːs/ *v.* **1** *tr.* produce a copy or representation of. **2** *tr.* cause to be seen or heard etc. again (*tried to reproduce the sound exactly*). **3** *intr.* produce further members of the same species by natural means. **4** *refl.* produce offspring (*reproduced itself several times*). **5** *intr.* give a specified quality or result when copied (*reproduces badly in black and white*). **6** *tr. Biol.* form afresh (a lost part etc. of the body). □ **reproducer** *n.* **reproducible** *adj.* **reproducibility** /-ˈbɪlɪti/ *n.* **reproducibly** *adv.*

reproduction /riːprəˈdʌkʃ(ə)n/ *n.* **1** the act or an instance of reproducing. **2** a copy of a work of art, esp. a print or photograph of a painting. **3** (*attrib.*) (of furniture etc.) made in imitation of a certain style or of an earlier period. **4** the quality of reproduced sound. □ **reproductive** *adj.* **reproductively** *adv.* **reproductiveness** *n.*

reprogram /riːˈprəʊgram/ *v.tr.* (also **reprogramme**) (**reprogrammed**, **reprogramming**) program (esp. a computer) again or differently. □ **reprogrammable** *adj.*

reprographics /riːprəˈgrafɪks/ *n.pl.* (usu. treated as *sing.*) = REPROGRAPHY.

reprography /rɪˈprɒgrəfi/ *n.* the science and practice of copying documents by photography, xerography, etc. □ **reprographer** *n.* **reprographic** /riːprəˈgrafɪk/ *adj.* **reprographically** /riːprəˈgrafɪk(ə)li/ *adv.* [REPRODUCE + -GRAPHY]

reproof[1] /rɪˈpruːf/ *n.* **1** blame (*a glance of reproof*). **2** a rebuke; words expressing blame. [Middle English from Old French *reprove*, from *reprover* REPROVE]

reproof[2] /riːˈpruːf/ *v.tr.* **1** *Brit.* render (a coat etc.) waterproof again. **2** make a fresh proof of (printed matter etc.).

reprove /rɪˈpruːv/ *v.tr.* rebuke (a person, a person's conduct, etc.). □ **reprovable** *adj.* **reprover** *n.* **reprovingly** *adv.* [Middle English via Old French *reprover* from Late Latin *reprobare* 'disapprove': see REPROBATE]

reptile /ˈrɛptʌɪl/ *n. & adj.* ● *n.* **1** any cold-blooded scaly animal of the class Reptilia, including snakes, lizards, crocodiles, turtles, tortoises, etc. **2** a mean, grovelling, or repulsive person. ● *adj.* **1** (of an animal) creeping. **2** mean, grovelling, repulsive. □ **reptilian** /-ˈtɪlɪən/ *adj. & n.* [Middle English via Late Latin *reptilis* from Latin *repere rept-* 'crawl']

republic /rɪˈpʌblɪk/ *n.* **1** a state in which supreme power is held by the people or their elected representatives or by an elected or nominated president, not by a monarch etc. **2** a society with equality between its members (*the literary republic*). [French *république* from Latin *respublica*, from *res* 'concern' + *publicus* PUBLIC]

republican /rɪˈpʌblɪk(ə)n/ *adj. & n.* ● *adj.* **1** of or constituted as a republic. **2** characteristic of a republic. **3** advocating or supporting republican government. ● *n.* **1** a person advocating or supporting republican government. **2** (**Republican**) (in the US) a member or supporter of the Republican Party. **3** (also **Republican**) an advocate of a united Ireland. □ **republicanism** *n.*

Republican Party *n.* one of the two main US political parties, favouring a lesser degree of central power (cf. DEMOCRATIC PARTY).

Republic Day *n.* the day on which the foundation of a republic is commemorated; (in India) 26 Jan.

republish /riːˈpʌblɪʃ/ *v.tr.* (also *absol.*) publish again or in a new edition etc. □ **republication** /-ˈkeɪʃ(ə)n/ *n.*

repudiate /rɪˈpjuːdɪeɪt/ *v.tr.* **1 a** disown; disavow; reject. **b** refuse dealings with. **c** deny. **2** refuse to recognize or obey (authority or a treaty). **3** refuse to discharge (an obligation or debt). **4** (esp. of the ancients or non-Christians) divorce (one's wife). □ **repudiation** /-ˈeɪʃ(ə)n/ *n.* **repudiator** *n.* [Latin *repudiare* from *repudium* 'divorce']

■ **Usage** See Usage Note at REFUTE.

repugnance /rɪˈpʌgnəns/ *n.* (also **repugnancy** /-ənsi/) **1** (usu. foll. by *to, against*) antipathy; aversion. **2** (usu. foll. by *of, between, to, with*) inconsistency or incompatibility of ideas, statements, etc. [Middle English (in sense 2) from French *répugnance* or Latin *repugnantia*, from *repugnare* 'oppose' (as RE-, *pugnare* 'fight')]

repugnant /rɪˈpʌgnənt/ *adj.* **1** (often foll. by *to*) extremely distasteful. **2** (often foll. by *to*) contradictory. **3** (often foll. by *with*) incompatible. **4** *poet.* refractory; resisting. □ **repugnantly** *adv.* [Middle English from French *répugnant* or Latin (as REPUGNANCE)]

repulse /rɪˈpʌls/ *v.* & *n.* ● *v.tr.* **1** drive back (an attack or attacking enemy) by force of arms. **2 a** rebuff (friendly advances or their maker). **b** refuse (a request or offer or its maker). **3** be repulsive to, repel. **4** foil in controversy. ● *n.* **1** the act or an instance of repulsing or being repulsed. **2** a rebuff. [Latin *repellere repuls-* 'drive back' (as REPEL)]

repulsion /rɪˈpʌlʃ(ə)n/ *n.* **1** aversion; disgust. **2** esp. *Physics* the force by which bodies tend to repel each other or increase their mutual distance (opp. ATTRACTION). [Late Latin *repulsio* (as REPEL)]

repulsive /rɪˈpʌlsɪv/ *adj.* **1** causing aversion or loathing; loathsome, disgusting. **2** *Physics* exerting repulsion. **3** *archaic* (of behaviour etc.) cold, unsympathetic. ▫ **repulsively** *adv.* **repulsiveness** *n.* [French *répulsif -ive*, or from REPULSE]

repurchase /riːˈpəːtʃɪs/ *v.* & *n.* ● *v.tr.* purchase again. ● *n.* the act or an instance of purchasing again.

repurify /riːˈpjʊərɪfʌɪ/ *v.tr.* (**-ies, -ied**) purify again. ▫ **repurification** /-fɪˈkeɪʃ(ə)n/ *n.*

reputable /ˈrɛpjʊtəb(ə)l/ *adj.* of good repute; respectable. ▫ **reputably** *adv.* [obsolete French, or from medieval Latin *reputabilis* (as REPUTE)]

reputation /rɛpjʊˈteɪʃ(ə)n/ *n.* **1** what is generally said or believed about a person's or thing's character or standing (*has a reputation for dishonesty*). **2** the state of being well thought of; distinction; respectability (*an international reputation in her field*). **3** (foll. by *of*, *for* + verbal noun) credit, fame, or notoriety (*has the reputation of driving hard bargains*). [Middle English from Latin *reputatio* (as REPUTE)]

repute /rɪˈpjuːt/ *n.* & *v.* ● *n.* reputation (*known by repute*). ● *v.tr.* **1** (as **reputed** *adj.*) (often foll. by *to* + infin.) be generally considered or reckoned (*is reputed to be the best*). **2** (as **reputed** *adj.*) passing as being, but probably not being (*his reputed father*). ▫ **reputedly** *adv.* [Middle English from Old French *reputer* or Latin *reputare* (as RE-, *putare* 'think')]

request /rɪˈkwɛst/ *n.* & *v.* ● *n.* **1** the act or an instance of asking for something; a petition (*came at his request*). **2** a thing asked for. **3** the state of being sought after; demand (*in great request*). **4 a** a letter etc. asking for a particular record etc. to be played on a radio programme, often with a personal message. **b** the record etc. played in response to such a letter etc. ● *v.tr.* **1** ask to be given or allowed or favoured with (*request a hearing*; *requests your presence*). **2** (foll. by *to* + infin.) ask a person to do something (*requested her to answer*). **3** (foll. by *that* + clause) ask that. ▫ **by** (or **on**) **request** in response to an expressed wish. ▫ **requester** *n.* [Middle English from Old French *requeste* (*n.*), *requester* (*v.*), ultimately from Latin *requaerere* (as REQUIRE)]

request programme *n.* a radio etc. programme composed of items requested by the audience.

request stop *n. Brit.* a stop at which a bus halts only on a passenger's request.

requiem /ˈrɛkwɪəm, -ɪɛm/ *n.* **1** (**Requiem**) (also *attrib.*) esp. *RC Ch.* a Mass for the repose of the souls of the dead. **2** *Mus.* a musical setting for this. **3** (often foll. by *for*) a memorial (*his book was a fitting requiem*). [Middle English, from the accusative of Latin *requies* 'rest', the initial word of the Mass]

requiem shark *n.* a shark of the family Carcharinidae, which includes some large voracious sharks such as tiger sharks and whaler sharks. [from obsolete French *requiem*, variant of *requin* 'shark', influenced by REQUIEM]

requiescat /rɛkwɪˈɛskat/ *n.* a wish or prayer for the repose of a dead person. [Latin, = may he or she rest (in peace)]

require /rɪˈkwʌɪə/ *v.tr.* **1** need; depend on for success or fulfilment (*the work requires much patience*). **2** lay down as an imperative (*did all that was required by law*). **3** command; instruct (a person etc.). **4** order; insist on (an action or measure). **5** (often foll. by *of*, *from*, or *that* + clause) demand (of or from a person) as a right. **6** wish to have (*is there anything else you require?*). ▫ **requirer** *n.* **requirement** *n.* [Middle English from Old French *requere*, ultimately from Latin *requirere* (as RE-, *quaerere* 'seek')]

requisite /ˈrɛkwɪzɪt/ *adj.* & *n.* ● *adj.* required by circumstances; necessary to success etc. ● *n.* (often foll. by *for*) a thing needed (for some purpose). ▫ **requisitely** *adv.* [Middle English from Latin *requisitus*, past part. of *requirere* (as REQUIRE)]

requisition /rɛkwɪˈzɪʃ(ə)n/ *n.* & *v.* ● *n.* **1** an official order laying claim to the use of property or materials. **2** a formal written demand that some duty should be performed. **3** being called or put into service. ● *v.tr.* demand the use or supply of, esp. by requisition order. ▫ **under** (or **in**) **requisition** being used or applied. ▫ **requisitioner** *n.* **requisitionist** *n.* [French *réquisition* or Latin *requisitio* (as REQUIRE)]

requite /rɪˈkwʌɪt/ *v.tr.* **1** make return for (a service). **2** (often foll. by *with*) reward or avenge (a favour or injury). **3** (often foll. by *for*) make return to (a person). **4** (often foll. by *for*, *with*) repay with good or evil (*requite like for like*; *requite hate with love*). ▫ **requital** *n.* [RE- + *quite*, variant of QUIT]

reran *past* of RERUN.

reread *v.* & *n.* ● *v.tr.* /riːˈriːd/ (*past* and *past part.* **reread** /-ˈrɛd/) read again. ● *n.* /ˈriːriːd/ an instance of reading again. ▫ **re-readable** *adj.*

re-record /riːrɪˈkɔːd/ *v.tr.* record again.

reredos /ˈrɪədɒs/ *n. Eccl.* an ornamental screen covering the wall at the back of an altar. [Middle English via Anglo-French from Old French *areredos*, from *arere* 'behind' + *dos* 'back': cf. ARREARS]

re-release /riːrɪˈliːs/ *v.* & *n.* ● *v.tr.* release (a record, film, etc.) again. ● *n.* a re-released record, film, etc.

re-roof /riːˈruːf/ *v.tr.* provide (a building etc.) with a new roof.

re-route /riːˈruːt/ *v.tr.* (**-routeing** or **-routing**) send or carry by a different route.

rerun *v.* & *n.* ● *v.tr.* /riːˈrʌn/ (**rerunning**; *past* **reran**; *past part.* **rerun**) run (a race, film, etc.) again. ● *n.* /ˈriːrʌn/ **1** the act or an instance of rerunning. **2** a film, television programme, etc. shown again.

resale /riːˈseɪl/ *n.* the sale of a thing previously bought. ▫ **resaleable** *adj.* (also **resalable**).

resale price maintenance *n. Brit.* a manufacturer's practice of setting a minimum resale price for goods.

resat *past* and *past part.* of RESIT.

reschedule /riːˈʃɛdjuːl, -ˈskɛd-/ *v.tr.* alter the schedule of; replan.

rescind /rɪˈsɪnd/ *v.tr.* abrogate, revoke, cancel. ▫ **rescindable** *adj.* **rescission** /-ˈsɪʒ(ə)n/ *n.* [Latin *rescindere resciss-* (as RE-, *scindere* 'cut')]

rescript /ˈriːskrɪpt/ *n.* **1** *Rom.Hist.* an emperor's written reply to an appeal for guidance, esp. on a legal point. **2** *RC Ch.* the Pope's decision on a question of doctrine or papal law. **3** an official edict or announcement. **4 a** the act or an instance of rewriting. **b** the thing rewritten. [Latin *rescriptum*, neut. past part. of *rescribere rescript-* (as RE-, *scribere* 'write')]

rescue /ˈrɛskjuː/ *v.* & *n.* ● *v.tr.* (**rescues, rescued, rescuing**) **1** (often foll. by *from*) save or set free or bring away from attack, custody, danger, or harm. **2** *Law* **a** unlawfully liberate (a person). **b** forcibly recover (property). ● *n.* the act or an instance of rescuing or being rescued; deliverance. ▫ **rescuable** *adj.* **rescuer** *n.* [Middle English *rescowe* via Old French *rescoure* from Romanic, formed as RE- + Latin *excutere* 'shake out, discard' (as EX-[1], *quatere* 'shake')]

rescue bid *n. Bridge* a bid made to get one's partner out of a difficult situation.

reseal /riːˈsiːl/ *v.tr.* seal again. ▫ **resealable** *adj.*

research /rɪˈsəːtʃ, ˈriːsəːtʃ/ *n.* & *v.* ● *n.* **1 a** the systematic investigation into and study of materials, sources, etc., in order to establish facts and reach new conclusions. **b** (usu. in *pl.*) an endeavour to discover new or collate old facts etc. by the scientific study of a subject or by a course of critical investigation. **2** (*attrib.*) engaged in or intended for research (*research assistant*). ● *v.* **1** *tr.* do research into (a subject) or for (a book etc.). **2** *intr.* make researches. ◻ **researchable** *adj.* **researcher** *n.* [obsolete French *recerche* (as RE-, SEARCH)]

■ **Usage** The second pronunciation given, with the stress on the first syllable, is considered incorrect in standard British English by some people, especially when used for the noun.

research and development *n.* (in industry etc.) work directed towards the innovation, introduction, and improvement of products and processes.

reseat /riːˈsiːt/ *v.tr.* **1** (also *refl.*) seat (oneself, a person, etc.) again. **2** provide with a fresh seat or seats. **3** realign or repair in order to fit (a tap, nail, etc.) into its former correct position.

resect /rɪˈsɛkt/ *v.tr. Surgery* **1** cut out part of (a lung etc.). **2** pare down (bone, cartilage, etc.). ◻ **resection** *n.* **resectional** *adj.* **resectionist** *n.* [Latin *resecare resect-* (as RE-, *secare* 'cut')]

reseda /ˈrɛsɪdə, rɪˈsiːdə/ *n.* & *adj.* ● *n.* **1** any plant of the genus *Reseda*, with sweet-scented flowers, e.g. a mignonette. **2** /also ˈrɛz-/ the pale green colour of mignonette flowers. ● *adj.* pale green. [Latin, perhaps from imperative of *resedare* 'assuage', with reference to its supposed curative powers]

reseed /riːˈsiːd/ *v.tr.* sow (an area of land) with seed again, esp. grass seed.

reselect /riːsɪˈlɛkt/ *v.tr.* select again or differently. ◻ **reselection** *n.*

resell /riːˈsɛl/ *v.tr.* (*past* and *past part.* **resold**) sell (an object etc.) after buying it. ◻ **reseller** *n.*

resemblance /rɪˈzɛmbl(ə)ns/ *n.* (often foll. by *to*, *between*, *of*) a likeness or similarity. ◻ **resemblant** *adj.* [Middle English from Anglo-French (as RESEMBLE)]

resemble /rɪˈzɛmb(ə)l/ *v.tr.* be like; have a similarity to, or features in common with, or the same appearance as. ◻ **resembler** *n.* [Middle English from Old French *resembler* (as RE-, *sembler* from Latin *similare*, from *similis* 'like')]

resent /rɪˈzɛnt/ *v.tr.* show or feel indignation at; be aggrieved by (a circumstance, action, or person) (*we resent being patronized*). [obsolete French *resentir* (as RE-, Latin *sentire* 'feel')]

resentful /rɪˈzɛntfʊl, -f(ə)l/ *adj.* feeling resentment. ◻ **resentfully** *adv.* **resentfulness** *n.*

resentment /rɪˈzɛntm(ə)nt/ *n.* (often foll. by *at*, *of*) indignant or bitter feelings; anger. [Italian *risentimento* or French *ressentiment* (as RESENT)]

reserpine /rɪˈsəːpiːn/ *n.* an alkaloid obtained from plants of the genus *Rauwolfia*, used as a tranquillizer and in the treatment of hypertension. [German *Reserpin*, from modern Latin species name *Rauwolfia serpentina* (named after L. *Rauwolf*, German botanist d. 1596)]

reservation /rɛzəˈveɪʃ(ə)n/ *n.* **1** the act or an instance of reserving or being reserved. **2** a booking (of a room, berth, seat, etc.). **3** the thing booked, e.g. a room in a hotel. **4** an express or tacit limitation or exception to an agreement etc. (*had reservations about the plan*). **5** (in full **central reservation**) *Brit.* a strip of land between the carriageways of a road. **6** an area of land reserved for occupation by N. American Indians, Australian Aboriginals, etc. **7 a** a right or interest retained in an estate being conveyed. **b** the clause reserving this. **8** *Eccl.* **a** the practice of retaining for some purpose a portion of the Eucharistic elements (esp. the bread) after celebration. **b** *RC Ch.* the power of absolution reserved to a superior. **c** *RC Ch.* the right reserved to the Pope of nomination to a vacant benefice. [Middle English from Old French *reservation* or Late Latin *reservatio* (as RESERVE)]

reserve /rɪˈzəːv/ *v.* & *n.* ● *v.tr.* **1** postpone, put aside, keep back for a later occasion or special use. **2** order to be specially retained or allocated for a particular person or at a particular time. **3** retain or secure, esp. by formal or legal stipulation (*reserve the right to*). **4** postpone delivery of (judgement etc.) (*reserved my comments until the end*). ● *n.* **1** a thing reserved for future use; an extra stock or amount (*a great reserve of strength*; *huge energy reserves*). **2** a limitation, qualification, or exception attached to something (*accept your offer without reserve*). **3 a** self-restraint; reticence; lack of cordiality (*difficult to overcome his reserve*). **b** (in artistic or literary expression) absence from exaggeration or ill-proportioned effects. **4** *Brit.* a company's profit added to capital. **5** (in *sing.* or *pl.*) assets kept readily available as cash or at a central bank, or as gold or foreign exchange (*reserve currency*). **6** (in *sing.* or *pl.*) **a** troops withheld from action to reinforce or protect others. **b** forces in addition to the regular army, navy, air force, etc., but available in an emergency. **7** a member of the military reserve. **8 a** an extra player chosen to be a possible substitute in a team. **b** (in *pl.*: prec. by *the*) the second-choice team. **9** a place reserved for special use, esp.: **a** as a habitat for a native people (*Indian reserve*). **b** for wildlife (*nature reserve*). **10** the intentional suppression of the truth (*exercised a certain amount of reserve*). **11** (in the decoration of ceramics or textiles) an area which still has the original colour of the material or the colour of the background. ◻ **in reserve** unused and available if required. **with all** (or **all proper**) **reserve** without endorsing. ◻ **reservable** *adj.* **reserver** *n.* [Middle English via Old French *reserver* from Latin *reservare* (as RE-, *servare* 'keep')]

re-serve /riːˈsəːv, ˈriːsəːv/ *v.tr.* & *intr.* serve again.

reserved /rɪˈzəːvd/ *adj.* **1** reticent; slow to reveal emotion or opinions; uncommunicative. **2 a** set apart, destined for some use or fate. **b** (often foll. by *for*, *to*) left by fate for; falling first or only to. ◻ **reservedly** /-vɪdli/ *adv.* **reservedness** *n.*

reserved occupation *n. Brit.* an occupation from which a person will not be taken for military service.

reserve grade *n. Austral.* a second-grade team.

reserve price *n.* the lowest acceptable price stipulated for an item sold at an auction.

reservist /rɪˈzəːvɪst/ *n.* a member of the reserve forces.

reservoir /ˈrɛzəvwɑː/ *n.* **1** a large natural or artificial lake used as a source of water supply. **2 a** any natural or artificial receptacle esp. for or of fluid. **b** a place where fluid etc. collects. **3** a part of a machine etc. holding fluid. **4** (usu. foll. by *of*) a reserve or supply, esp. of information. [French *réservoir* from *réserver* RESERVE]

reset /riːˈsɛt/ *v.tr.* (**resetting**; *past* and *past part.* **reset**) set (a broken bone, gems, a mechanical device, etc.) again or differently. ◻ **resettable** *adj.* **resettability** /-ˈbɪlɪti/ *n.*

resettle /riːˈsɛt(ə)l/ *v.tr.* & *intr.* settle again in a new or former place. ◻ **resettlement** *n.*

reshape /riːˈʃeɪp/ *v.tr.* shape or form again or differently.

reshuffle *v.* & *n.* ● *v.tr.* /riːˈʃʌf(ə)l/ **1** shuffle (cards) again. **2** interchange the posts of (government ministers etc.). ● *n.* /ˈriːʃʌf(ə)l/ the act or an instance of reshuffling.

reside /rɪˈzʌɪd/ *v.intr.* **1** (often foll. by *at*, *in*, *abroad*, etc.) (of a person) have one's home, dwell permanently. **2** (of power, a right, etc.) rest or be vested in. **3** (of an incumbent official) be in residence. **4** (foll. by *in*) (of a quality) be present or inherent in. [Middle English, probably a back-formation from RESIDENT influenced by French *résider* or Latin *residēre* (as RE-, *sedēre* 'sit')]

residence /ˈrɛzɪd(ə)ns/ *n.* **1** the act or an instance of residing. **2 a** the place where a person resides; an abode. **b** the official house of a government minister etc. **c** a mansion (*their London residence is impressive*). ◻ **in residence** living in or occupying a specified place, esp. for the performance of duties or work. [Middle English via Old French *residence* or medieval Latin *residentia* from Latin *residēre*: see RESIDE]

residency /ˈrɛzɪd(ə)nsi/ *n.* (*pl.* **-ies**) **1** = RESIDENCE 1, 2a. **2** *N. Amer.* a period of specialized medical training; the position of a resident. **3** *hist.* **a** the official residence of the Governor-General's representative or other government agent at the court of an Indian state. **b** the territory supervised by this official. **4** *Brit.* a musician's regular engagement at a club etc. **5** a group or organization of intelligence agents in a foreign country.

resident /ˈrɛzɪd(ə)nt/ *n. & adj.* ● *n.* **1** (often foll. by *of*) **a** a permanent inhabitant (of a town or neighbourhood). **b** a bird belonging to a species that does not migrate. **2 a** *Brit.* a guest in a hotel etc. staying overnight. **b** *US* a person who boards at a boarding school. **3** *hist.* a British government agent in any semi-independent state, esp. the Governor-General's agent at the court of an Indian state. **4** *N. Amer.* a medical graduate engaged in specialized practice under supervision in a hospital. **5** an intelligence agent in a foreign country. ● *adj.* **1** residing; in residence. **2 a** having quarters on the premises of one's work etc. (*resident housekeeper*; *resident doctor*). **b** working regularly in a particular place. **3** located; inherent (*powers of feeling are resident in the nerves*). **4** (of birds etc.) non-migratory. ▫ **residentship** *n.* (in sense 3 of *n.*). [Middle English from Old French or Latin: see RESIDE]

residential /rɛzɪˈdɛnʃ(ə)l/ *adj.* **1** suitable for or occupied by private houses (*residential area*). **2** used as a residence (*residential hotel*). **3** based on or connected with residence (*the residential qualification for voters*; *a residential course of study*). ▫ **residentially** *adv.*

residentiary /rɛzɪˈdɛnʃ(ə)ri/ *adj. & n.* ● *adj.* of, subject to, or requiring, official residence. ● *n.* (*pl.* **-ies**) an ecclesiastic who must officially reside in a place. [medieval Latin *residentiarius* (as RESIDENCE)]

residua *pl.* of RESIDUUM.

residual /rɪˈzɪdjʊəl/ *adj. & n.* ● *adj.* **1** remaining; left as a residue or residuum. **2** *Math.* resulting from subtraction. **3** (in calculation) still unaccounted for or not eliminated. ● *n.* **1** a quantity left over or *Math.* resulting from subtraction. **2** an error in calculation not accounted for or eliminated. ▫ **residually** *adv.*

residuary /rɪˈzɪdjʊəri/ *adj.* **1** of the residue of an estate (*residuary bequest*). **2** of or being a residuum; residual; still remaining.

residue /ˈrɛzɪdjuː/ *n.* **1** what is left over or remains; a remainder; the rest. **2** *Law* what remains of an estate after the payment of charges, debts, and bequests. **3** esp. *Chem.* a residuum. [Middle English via Old French *residu* from Latin *residuum*: see RESIDUUM]

residuum /rɪˈzɪdjʊəm/ *n.* (*pl.* **residua** /-djʊə/) **1** *Chem.* a substance left after combustion or evaporation. **2** a remainder or residue. [Latin, neut. of *residuus* 'remaining', from *residēre*: see RESIDE]

resign /rɪˈzʌɪn/ *v.* **1** *intr.* **a** (often foll. by *from*) give up office, one's employment, etc. (*resigned from the Home Office*). **b** (often foll. by *as*) retire (*resigned as chief executive*). **2** *tr.* (often foll. by *to, into*) give up (office, one's employment, etc.); surrender; hand over (a right, charge, task, etc.). **3** *tr.* give up (hope etc.). **4** *refl.* (usu. foll. by *to*) **a** reconcile (oneself, one's mind, etc.) to the inevitable (*have resigned myself to the idea*). **b** surrender (oneself to another's guidance). **5** *intr. Chess* etc. discontinue play and admit defeat. ▫ **resigner** *n.* [Middle English via Old French *resigner* from Latin *resignare* 'unseal, cancel' (as RE-, *signare* 'sign, seal')]

re-sign /riːˈsʌɪn/ *v.tr. & intr.* sign again.

resignal /riːˈsɪgn(ə)l/ *v.tr.* (**resignalled**, **resignalling**; *US* **resignaled**, **resignaling**) resupply with railway signals.

resignation /rɛzɪgˈneɪʃ(ə)n/ *n.* **1** the act or an instance of resigning, esp. from one's job or office. **2** the document etc. conveying this intention. **3** the state of being resigned; the uncomplaining endurance of a sorrow or difficulty. [Middle English via Old French from medieval Latin *resignatio* (as RESIGN)]

resigned /rɪˈzʌɪnd/ *adj.* (often foll. by *to*) having resigned oneself; submissive, acquiescent. ▫ **resignedly** /-nɪdli/ *adv.* **resignedness** *n.*

resile /rɪˈzʌɪl/ *v.intr.* **1** (of something stretched or compressed) recoil to resume a former size and shape; spring back. **2** have or show resilience or recuperative power. **3** (usu. foll. by *from*) withdraw from a course of action. [obsolete French *resilir* or Latin *resilire* (as RE-, *salire* 'jump')]

resilient /rɪˈzɪlɪənt/ *adj.* **1** (of a substance etc.) recoiling; springing back; resuming its original shape after bending, stretching, compression, etc. **2** (of a person) readily recovering from shock, depression, etc.; buoyant. ▫ **resilience** *n.* **resiliency** *n.* **resiliently** *adv.* [Latin *resiliens resilient-* (as RESILE)]

resin /ˈrɛzɪn/ *n. & v.* ● *n.* **1** an adhesive inflammable substance insoluble in water, secreted by some plants, and often extracted by incision, esp. from fir and pine (cf. GUM[1] *n.* 1a). **2** (in full **synthetic resin**) a solid or liquid organic compound made by polymerization etc. and used in plastics etc. ● *v.tr.* (**resined**, **resining**) rub or treat with resin. ▫ **resinate** /-nət/ *n.* **resinate** /-neɪt/ *v.tr.* **resinoid** *adj. & n.* **resinous** *adj.* [Middle English *resyn, rosyn*, from Latin *resina* & medieval Latin *rosina, rosinum*]

resist /rɪˈzɪst/ *v. & n.* ● *v.* **1** *tr.* withstand the action or effect of; repel. **2** *tr.* stop the course or progress of; prevent from reaching, penetrating, etc. **3** *tr.* abstain from (pleasure, temptation, etc.). **4** *tr.* strive against; try to impede; refuse to comply with (*resist arrest*). **5** *intr.* offer opposition; refuse to comply. ● *n.* a protective coating of a resistant substance, applied esp. to parts of calico that are not to take dye or to parts of pottery that are not to take glaze or lustre. ▫ **cannot** (or **could not** etc.) **resist 1** (foll. by verbal noun) feel strongly inclined to (*cannot resist teasing me about it*). **2** is certain to be amused, attracted, etc., by (*can't resist children's clothes*). ▫ **resistant** *adj.* **resister** *n.* **resistible** *adj.* **resistibility** /-ˈbɪlɪti/ *n.* [Middle English from Old French *resister* or Latin *resistere* (as RE-, *sistere* 'stop', reduplication of *stare* 'stand')]

resistance /rɪˈzɪst(ə)ns/ *n.* **1** the act or an instance of resisting; refusal to comply. **2** the power of resisting (*showed resistance to wear and tear*). **3 a** *Biol.* the ability to withstand adverse conditions. **b** *Med. & Biol.* lack of sensitivity to a drug, insecticide, etc., esp. owing to continued exposure or genetic change. **4** the impeding, slowing, or stopping effect exerted by one material thing on another. **5** *Physics* **a** the property of hindering the conduction of electricity, heat, etc. **b** the measure of this in a body (symbol **R**). **6** a resistor. **7** (in full **resistance movement**) a secret organization resisting authority, esp. in an occupied country. [Middle English via French *résistance*, *résistence* from Late Latin *resistentia* (as RESIST)]

resistive /rɪˈzɪstɪv/ *adj.* **1** able to resist. **2** *Electr.* of or concerning resistance.

resistivity /rɪzɪˈstɪvɪti/ *n. Electr.* a measure of the resisting power of a specified material to the flow of an electric current.

resistless /rɪˈzɪs(t)lɪs/ *adj. archaic poet.* **1** irresistible; relentless. **2** unresisting. ▫ **resistlessly** *adv.*

resistor /rɪˈzɪstə/ *n. Electr.* a device having resistance to the passage of an electrical current.

resit *v. & n. Brit.* ● *v.tr.* /riːˈsɪt/ (**resitting**; *past* and *past part.* **resat**) sit (an examination) again after failing. ● *n.* /ˈriːsɪt/ **1** the act or an instance of resitting an examination. **2** an examination held specifically to enable candidates to resit.

resite /riːˈsʌɪt/ *v.tr.* place on another site; relocate.

resize /riːˈsʌɪz/ *v.tr.* alter the size of.

reskill /riːˈskɪl/ *v.tr.* teach, or equip with, new skills.

resold *past* and *past part.* of RESELL.

resoluble /rɪˈzɒljʊb(ə)l/ *adj.* **1** that can be resolved. **2** (foll. by *into*) analysable. [French *résoluble* or Latin *resolubilis* (as RESOLVE, on the pattern of *soluble*)]

re-soluble /riːˈsɒljʊb(ə)l/ *adj.* that can be dissolved again.

resolute /ˈrɛzəluːt/ *adj.* (of a person or a person's mind or action) determined; decided; firm of purpose; not vacillating. □ **resolutely** *adv.* **resoluteness** *n.* [Latin *resolutus*, past part. of *resolvere* (see RESOLVE)]

resolution /rɛzəˈluːʃ(ə)n/ *n.* **1** a resolute temper or character; boldness and firmness of purpose. **2** a thing resolved on; an intention (*New Year's resolutions*). **3 a** a formal expression of opinion or intention by a legislative body or public meeting. **b** the formulation of this (*passed a resolution*). **4** (usu. foll. by *of*) the act or an instance of solving doubt or a problem or question (*towards a resolution of the difficulty*). **5 a** esp. *Chem.* separation into components; decomposition. **b** the replacing of a single force etc. by two or more jointly equivalent to it. **6** (foll. by *into*) analysis; conversion into another form. **7** *Mus.* the act or an instance of causing discord to pass into concord. **8** *Physics* etc. **a** the smallest interval measurable by a scientific (esp. optical) instrument; the resolving power. **b** the degree of detail visible in a photographic or television image. **9** *Med.* the disappearance of inflammation etc. without suppuration. **10** *Prosody* the substitution of two short syllables for one long. [Middle English from Latin *resolutio* (as RESOLVE)]

resolutive /ˈrɛzəluːtɪv/ *adj. Med.* having the power or ability to dissolve. [medieval Latin *resolutivus* (as RESOLVE)]

resolutive condition *n. Law* a condition whose fulfilment terminates a contract etc.

resolve /rɪˈzɒlv/ *v. & n.* ● *v.* **1** *intr.* make up one's mind; decide firmly (*resolve to do better*). **2** *tr.* (of circumstances etc.) cause (a person) to do this (*events resolved him to leave*). **3** *tr.* (foll. by *that* + clause) (of an assembly or meeting) pass a resolution by vote (*the committee resolved that immediate action should be taken*). **4** *intr. & tr.* (often foll. by *into*) separate or cause to separate into constituent parts; disintegrate; analyse; dissolve. **5** *tr.* (of optical or photographic equipment) separate or distinguish between closely adjacent objects. **6** *tr. & intr.* (foll. by *into*) convert or be converted. **7** *tr. & intr.* (foll. by *into*) reduce by mental analysis into. **8** *tr.* solve; explain; clear up; settle (doubt, argument, etc.). **9** *tr. & intr. Mus.* convert or be converted into concord. **10** *tr. Med.* remove (inflammation etc.) without suppuration. **11** *tr. Prosody* replace (a long syllable) by two short syllables. **12** *tr. Mech.* replace (a force etc.) by two or more jointly equivalent to it. ● *n.* **1 a** a firm mental decision or intention; a resolution (*made a resolve not to go*). **b** *US* a formal resolution by a legislative body or public meeting. **2** resoluteness; steadfastness. □ **resolvable** *adj.* **resolvability** /-ˈbɪlɪti/ *n.* **resolver** *n.* [Middle English from Latin *resolvere resolut-* (as RE-, SOLVE)]

resolved /rɪˈzɒlvd/ *adj.* resolute, determined. □ **resolvedly** /-vɪdli/ *adv.* **resolvedness** *n.*

resolvent /rɪˈzɒlv(ə)nt/ *adj. & n.* esp. *Med.* ● *adj.* (of a drug, application, substance, etc.) effecting the resolution of a tumour etc. ● *n.* such a drug etc.

resolving power *n.* an instrument's ability to distinguish very small or very close objects.

resonance /ˈrɛz(ə)nəns/ *n.* **1** the reinforcement or prolongation of sound by reflection or synchronous vibration. **2** *Mech.* a condition in which an object or system is subjected to an oscillating force having a frequency close to its own natural frequency. **3** *Chem.* the property of a molecule having a structure best represented by two or more forms rather than a single structural formula. **4** *Physics* a short-lived subatomic particle that is an excited state of a more stable particle. [Old French from Latin *resonantia* 'echo' (as RESONANT)]

resonant /ˈrɛz(ə)nənt/ *adj.* **1** (of sound) echoing, resounding; continuing to sound; reinforced or prolonged by reflection or synchronous vibration. **2** (of a body, room, etc.) tending to reinforce or prolong sounds esp. by synchronous vibration. **3** (often foll. by *with*) (of a place) resounding. **4** of or relating to resonance. □ **resonantly** *adv.* [French *résonnant* or Latin *resonare resonant-* (as RE-, *sonare* 'sound')]

resonate /ˈrɛz(ə)neɪt/ *v.intr.* produce or show resonance; resound. [Latin *resonare resonat-* (as RESONANT)]

resonator /ˈrɛz(ə)neɪtə/ *n. Mus.* **1** an instrument responding to a single note and used for detecting it in combinations. **2** an appliance for giving resonance to sound or other vibrations.

resorb /rɪˈsɔːb/ *v.tr.* absorb again. □ **resorbence** *n.* **resorbent** *adj.* [Latin *resorbēre resorpt-* (as RE-, *sorbēre* 'absorb')]

resorcin /rɪˈzɔːsɪn/ *n.* = RESORCINOL. [RESIN + ORCIN]

resorcinol /rɪˈzɔːsɪnɒl/ *n. Chem.* a crystalline organic compound usu. made by synthesis and used in the production of dyes, drugs, resins, etc.

resorption /rɪˈzɔːpʃ(ə)n, -ˈsɔːp-/ *n.* **1** the act or an instance of resorbing; the state of being resorbed. **2** *Physiol.* the breaking down and absorption of tissue within the body. □ **resorptive** /-tɪv/ *adj.* [RESORB, on the pattern of *absorption*]

resort /rɪˈzɔːt/ *n. & v.* ● *n.* **1** a place frequented esp. for holidays or for a specified purpose or quality (*seaside resort*; *health resort*). **2 a** a thing to which one has recourse; an expedient or measure (*a taxi was our best resort*). **b** (foll. by *to*) recourse to; use of (*without resort to violence*). **3** a tendency to frequent or be frequented (*places of great resort*). ● *v.intr.* **1** (foll. by *to*) turn to as an expedient (*resorted to threats*). **2** (foll. by *to*) go often or in large numbers to. □ **in the** (or **as a**) **last resort** when all else has failed. □ **resorter** *n.* [Middle English from Old French *resortir* (as RE-, *sortir* 'come or go out')]

re-sort /riːˈsɔːt/ *v.tr.* sort again or differently.

resound /rɪˈzaʊnd/ *v.* **1** *intr.* (often foll. by *with*) (of a place) ring or echo (*the hall resounded with laughter*). **2** *intr.* (of a voice, instrument, sound, etc.) produce echoes; go on sounding; fill a place with sound. **3** *intr.* **a** (of fame, a reputation, etc.) be much talked of. **b** (foll. by *through*) produce a sensation (*the scandal resounded through Europe*). **4** *tr.* (often foll. by *of*) proclaim or repeat loudly (the praises) of a person or thing (*resounded the praises of Greece*). **5** *tr.* (of a place) re-echo (a sound). [Middle English from RE- + SOUND[1] *v.*, suggested by Old French *resoner* or Latin *resonare*: see RESONANT]

resounding /rɪˈzaʊndɪŋ/ *adj.* **1** in senses of RESOUND. **2** unmistakable; emphatic (*was a resounding success*). □ **resoundingly** *adv.*

resource /rɪˈsɔːs, rɪˈzɔːs/ *n. & v.* ● *n.* **1** an expedient or device (*escape was their only resource*). **2** (usu. in *pl.*) **a** the means available to achieve an end, fulfil a function, etc. **b** a stock or supply that can be drawn on. **c** *N. Amer.* available assets. **3** (in *pl.*) a country's collective wealth or means of defence. **4** a leisure occupation (*reading is a great resource*). **5 a** (often in *pl.*) skill in devising expedients (*a person of great resource*). **b** practical ingenuity; quick wit (*full of resource*). **6** *archaic* the possibility of aid (*lost without resource*). ● *v.tr.* provide with resources. □ **one's own resources** one's own abilities, ingenuity, etc. □ **resourceful** *adj.* **resourcefully** *adv.* **resourcefulness** *n.* **resourceless** *adj.* **resourcelessness** *n.* [French *ressource, ressourse*, fem. past part. of Old French dialect *resourdre* (as RE-, Latin *surgere* 'rise')]

respect /rɪˈspɛkt/ *n. & v.* ● *n.* **1** deferential esteem felt or shown towards a person or quality. **2 a** (foll. by *of, for*) heed or regard. **b** (foll. by *to*) attention to or consideration of (*without respect to the results*). **3** an aspect, detail, particular, etc. (*correct except in this one respect*). **4** reference, relation (*a morality that has no respect to religion*). **5** (in *pl.*) a person's polite messages or attentions (*give my respects to your mother*). ● *v.tr.* **1** regard with deference, esteem, or honour. **2 a** avoid interfering with, harming, degrading, insulting, injuring, or interrupting. **b** treat with consideration. **c** refrain from offending, corrupting, or tempting (a person, a person's feelings, etc.). □ **in respect of** (or **with respect to**) as concerns; with reference to. **in respect that** because. **with** (or **with all due**) **respect** a mollifying formula preceding an expression of disagreement with another's views. □ **respecter** *n.* [Middle English from Old French *respect* or Latin *respectus*, from *respicere* (as RE-, *specere* 'look at'), or from *respectare*, frequentative of *respicere*]

respectability /rɪˌspɛktəˈbɪlɪti/ *n.* **1** the state of being respectable. **2** those who are respectable.

respectable /rɪˈspɛktəb(ə)l/ *adj.* **1** deserving respect. **2 a** of fair social standing. **b** having the qualities necessary for such standing. **3** honest and decent in conduct etc. **4** of some merit or importance. **5** tolerable, passable, fairly good or competent (*a respectable try*). **6** (of activities, clothes, etc.) presentable; befitting a respectable person. **7** reasonably good in condition or appearance. **8** appreciable in number, size, amount, etc. **9** primly conventional. □ **respectably** *adv.*

respectful /rɪˈspɛk(t)fʊl, -f(ə)l/ *adj.* showing deference (*stood at a respectful distance*). □ **respectfully** *adv.* **respectfulness** *n.*

respecting /rɪˈspɛktɪŋ/ *prep.* with reference or regard to; concerning.

respective /rɪˈspɛktɪv/ *adj.* concerning or appropriate to each of several individually; proper to each (*go to your respective places*). [French *respectif -ive* from medieval Latin *respectivus* (as RESPECT)]

respectively /rɪˈspɛktɪvli/ *adv.* for each separately or in turn, and in the order mentioned (*she and I gave £10 and £1 respectively*).

respell /riːˈspɛl/ *v.tr.* (*past* and *past part.* **respelt** or **respelled**) spell again or differently, esp. phonetically.

respirable /ˈrɛsp(ə)rəb(ə)l, rɪˈspʌɪ-/ *adj.* (of air, gas, etc.) able or fit to be breathed. [French *respirable* or Late Latin *respirabilis* (as RESPIRE)]

respirate /ˈrɛspɪreɪt/ *v.tr.* subject to artificial respiration. [back-formation from RESPIRATION]

respiration /rɛspɪˈreɪʃ(ə)n/ *n.* **1 a** the act or an instance of breathing. **b** a single inspiration or expiration; a breath. **2** *Biol.* in living organisms, the process involving the production of energy and release of carbon dioxide from the oxidation of complex organic substances. [Middle English from French *respiration* or Latin *respiratio* (as RESPIRE)]

respirator /ˈrɛspɪreɪtə/ *n.* **1** an apparatus worn over the face to prevent poison gas, cold air, dust particles, etc., from being inhaled. **2** *Med.* an apparatus for maintaining artificial respiration.

respire /rɪˈspʌɪə/ *v.* **1** *intr.* breathe air. **2** *intr.* inhale and exhale air. **3** *intr.* (of a plant) carry out respiration. **4** *tr.* breathe (air etc.). **5** *intr.* breathe again; take a breath. **6** *intr.* get rest or respite; recover hope or spirit. □ **respiratory** /rɪˈspɪrət(ə)ri, ˈrɛsp(ə)rət(ə)ri/ *adj.* [Middle English from Old French *respirer* or from Latin *respirare* (as RE-, *spirare* 'breathe')]

respite /ˈrɛspʌɪt, -spɪt/ *n.* & *v.* ● *n.* **1** an interval of rest or relief. **2** a delay permitted before the discharge of an obligation or the suffering of a penalty. ● *v.tr.* **1** grant respite to; reprieve (a condemned person). **2** postpone the execution or exaction of (a sentence, obligation, etc.). **3** give temporary relief from (pain or care) or to (a sufferer). [Middle English via Old French *respit* from Latin *respectus* RESPECT]

resplendent /rɪˈsplɛnd(ə)nt/ *adj.* brilliant; dazzlingly or gloriously bright. □ **resplendence** *n.* **resplendency** *n.* **resplendently** *adv.* [Middle English from Latin *resplendēre* (as RE-, *splendēre* 'glitter')]

respond /rɪˈspɒnd/ *v.* & *n.* ● *v.* **1** *intr.* answer, give a reply. **2** *intr.* act or behave in an answering or corresponding manner. **3** *intr.* (usu. foll. by *to*) show sensitiveness to by behaviour or change (*does not respond to kindness*). **4** *intr.* (of a congregation) make answers to a priest etc. **5** *intr. Bridge* make a bid on the basis of a partner's preceding bid. **6** *tr.* say (something) in answer. ● *n.* **1** *Archit.* a half-pillar or half-pier attached to a wall to support an arch, esp. at the end of an arcade. **2** *Eccl.* a responsory; a response to a versicle. □ **respondence** *n.* **respondency** *n.* **responder** *n.* [Middle English from Old French *respondre* 'answer', ultimately from Latin *respondēre respons-* (as RE-, *spondēre* 'pledge')]

respondent /rɪˈspɒnd(ə)nt/ *n.* & *adj.* ● *n.* **1** a defendant, esp. in an appeal or divorce case. **2** a person who makes an answer or defends an argument etc. ● *adj.* **1** making answer. **2** (foll. by *to*) responsive. **3** in the position of defendant.

response /rɪˈspɒns/ *n.* **1** an answer given in word or act; a reply. **2** a feeling, movement, change, etc., caused by a stimulus or influence. **3** (often in *pl.*) *Eccl.* any part of the liturgy said or sung in answer to the priest; a responsory. **4** *Bridge* a bid made in responding. [Middle English from Old French *respons(e)* or Latin *responsum*, neut. past part. of *respondēre* RESPOND]

responsibility /rɪˌspɒnsɪˈbɪlɪti/ *n.* (*pl.* **-ies**) **1 a** (often foll. by *for*, *of*) the state or fact of being responsible (*refuses all responsibility for it; will take the responsibility of doing it*). **b** authority; the ability to act independently and make decisions (*a job with more responsibility*). **2** the person or thing for which one is responsible (*the food is my responsibility*). □ **on one's own responsibility** without authorization.

responsible /rɪˈspɒnsɪb(ə)l/ *adj.* **1** (often foll. by *to*, *for*) liable to be called to account (to a person or for a thing). **2** morally accountable for one's actions; capable of rational conduct. **3** of good credit, position, or repute; respectable; evidently trustworthy. **4** (often foll. by *for*) being the primary cause (*a short circuit was responsible for the power failure*). **5** (of a ruler or government) not autocratic. **6** involving responsibility (*a responsible job*). □ **responsibleness** *n.* **responsibly** *adv.* [obsolete French from Latin *respondēre*: see RESPOND]

responsive /rɪˈspɒnsɪv/ *adj.* **1** (often foll. by *to*) responding readily (to some influence). **2** sympathetic; impressionable. **3 a** answering. **b** by way of answer. **4** (of a liturgy etc.) using responses. □ **responsively** *adv.* **responsiveness** *n.* [French *responsif -ive* or Late Latin *responsivus* (as RESPOND)]

responsorial /rɪspɒnˈsɔːrɪəl/ *adj.* relating to or involving (liturgical) responses.

responsory /rɪˈspɒns(ə)ri/ *n.* (*pl.* **-ies**) an anthem said or sung by a soloist and choir after a lesson. [Middle English from Late Latin *responsorium* (as RESPOND)]

respray *v.* & *n.* ● *v.tr.* /riːˈspreɪ/ spray again (esp. to change the colour of the paint on a vehicle). ● *n.* /ˈriːspreɪ/ the act or an instance of respraying.

rest[1] /rɛst/ *v.* & *n.* ● *v.* **1** *intr.* cease, abstain, or be relieved from exertion, action, movement, or employment; be tranquil. **2** *intr.* be still or asleep, esp. to refresh oneself or recover strength. **3** *tr.* give relief or repose to; allow to rest (*a chair to rest my legs*). **4** *intr.* (foll. by *on*, *upon*, *against*) lie on; be supported by; be spread out on; be propped against. **5** *intr.* (foll. by *on*, *upon*) depend, be based, or rely on. **6** *intr.* (foll. by *on*, *upon*) (of a look) alight or be steadily directed on. **7** *tr.* (foll. by *on*, *upon*) place for support or foundation. **8** *intr.* (of a problem or subject) be left without further investigation or discussion (*let the matter rest*). **9** *intr.* **a** lie in death. **b** (foll. by *in*) lie buried in (a churchyard etc.). **10** *tr.* (as **rested** *adj.*) refreshed or reinvigorated by resting. **11** *intr. US* conclude the calling of witnesses in a law case (*the prosecution rests*). **12** *intr.* (of land) lie fallow. **13** *intr.* (foll. by *in*) repose trust in (*am content to rest in God*). ● *n.* **1** repose or sleep, esp. in bed at night (*get a good night's rest*). **2** freedom from or the cessation of exertion, worry, activity, etc. (*give the subject a rest*). **3** a period of resting (*take a 15-minute rest*). **4** a support or prop for holding or steadying something. **5** *Mus.* **a** an interval of silence of a specified duration. **b** the sign denoting this. **6** a place of resting or abiding, esp. a lodging place or shelter provided for sailors, taxi drivers, etc. **7** a pause in elocution. **8** a caesura in verse. ▫ **at rest** not moving; not agitated or troubled; dead. **be resting** *Brit. euphem.* (of an actor) be out of work. **rest one's case** conclude one's argument etc. **rest** (or **God rest**) **his** (or **her**) **soul** may God grant his (or her) soul repose. **rest on one's laurels** see LAUREL. **rest on one's oars** see OAR. **rest up** *US* rest oneself thoroughly. **set at rest** settle or relieve (a question, a person's mind, etc.). [Old English *ræst*, *rest* (*n.*), *ræstan*, *restan* (*v.*)]

rest² /rɛst/ *n.* & *v.* ● *n.* (prec. by *the*) **1** the remaining part or parts; the others; the remainder of some quantity or number (*finish what you can and leave the rest*). **2** *Brit. Econ.* the reserve fund, esp. of the Bank of England. **3** *hist.* a rally in tennis. ● *v.intr.* **1** remain in a specified state (*rest assured*). **2** (foll. by *with*) be left in the hands or charge of (*the final arrangements rest with you*). ▫ **and all the rest** (or **the rest of it**) and all else that might be mentioned; et cetera. **for the rest** as regards anything else. [Middle English via Old French *reste* (*n.*), *rester* (*v.*) from Latin *restare* (as RE-, *stare* 'stand')]

restage /riːˈsteɪdʒ/ *v.tr.* stage (a play etc.) again or differently.

restart *v.* & *n.* ● *v.tr.* & *intr.* /riːˈstɑːt/ begin again. ● *n.* /ˈriːstɑːt/ a new beginning.

restate /riːˈsteɪt/ *v.tr.* express again or differently, esp. more clearly or convincingly. ▫ **restatement** *n.*

restaurant /ˈrɛst(ə)rɒnt, -r(ə)nt, -rɒ̃/ *n.* public premises where meals or refreshments may be had. [French from *restaurer* RESTORE]

restaurant car *n. Brit.* a dining car on a train.

restaurateur /rɛst(ə)rəˈtəː, ˌrɛstɒr-/ *n.* a restaurant-keeper. [French, from *restaurer* 'restor' + *-ateur* -ATOR]

▪ **Usage** The word *restaurateur* is frequently misspelt *restauranteur* under the influence of the word *restaurant.*

rest-cure *n.* a rest usu. of some weeks as a medical treatment.

rest day *n.* **1** a day spent in rest. **2** = *day of rest*.

restful /ˈrɛs(t)fʊl, -f(ə)l/ *adj.* **1** favourable to quiet or repose. **2** free from disturbing influences. **3** soothing. ▫ **restfully** *adv.* **restfulness** *n.*

rest-harrow /ˈrɛstharəʊ/ *n.* any tough-rooted plant of the genus *Ononis*, native to Europe and the Mediterranean. [obsolete *rest* (v.) = ARREST (in sense 'stop') + HARROW]

rest home *n.* a place where old or frail people can be cared for.

rest house *n.* (in the Indian subcontinent, S.E. Asia, and Africa) a house for travellers to rest in.

resting place *n.* a place provided or used for resting.

restitution /rɛstɪˈtjuːʃ(ə)n/ *n.* **1** (often foll. by *of*) the act or an instance of restoring a thing to its proper owner. **2** reparation for an injury (esp. *make restitution*). **3** esp. *Theol.* the restoration of a thing to its original state. **4** the resumption of an original shape or position because of elasticity. ▫ **restitutive** /ˈrɛstɪtjuːtɪv/ *adj.* [Middle English from Old French *restitution* or Latin *restitutio*, from *restituere restitut-* 'restore' (as RE-, *statuere* 'establish')]

restive /ˈrɛstɪv/ *adj.* **1** fidgety; restless. **2** (of a horse) refusing to advance, stubbornly standing still or moving backwards or sideways; refractory. **3** (of a person) unmanageable; rejecting control. ▫ **restively** *adv.* **restiveness** *n.* [Middle English via Old French *restif -ive* from Romanic (as REST²)]

restless /ˈrɛs(t)lɪs/ *adj.* **1** finding or affording no rest. **2** uneasy; agitated. **3** constantly in motion, fidgeting, etc. ▫ **restlessly** *adv.* **restlessness** *n.* [Old English *restlēas* (as REST¹, -LESS)]

rest mass *n. Physics* the mass of a body when at rest.

restock /riːˈstɒk/ *v.tr.* (also *absol.*) stock again or differently.

restoration /rɛstəˈreɪʃ(ə)n/ *n.* **1** the act or an instance of restoring or being restored. **2** a model or drawing representing the supposed original form of an extinct animal, ruined building, etc. **3 a** the re-establishment of a monarch etc. **b** the period of this. **4** (**Restoration**) *hist.* **a** (prec. by *the*) the re-establishment of Charles II as King of England in 1660. **b** (often *attrib.*) the literary period following this (*Restoration comedy*). [17th-c. alteration (influenced by RESTORE) of Middle English *restauration* from Old French *restauration* or Late Latin *restauratio* (as RESTORE)]

restorationism /rɛstəˈreɪʃ(ə)nɪz(ə)m/ *n.* (also **Restorationism**) **1** a charismatic Christian movement seeking to restore the beliefs and practices of the early Church. **2** the doctrine and practices of this movement. ▫ **restorationist** *n.* & *adj.*

restorative /rɪˈstɒrətɪv/ *adj.* & *n.* ● *adj.* tending to restore health or strength. ● *n.* a restorative medicine, food, etc. (*needs a restorative*). ▫ **restoratively** *adv.* [Middle English variant of obsolete *restaurative* from Old French *restauratif -ive* (as RESTORE)]

restore /rɪˈstɔː/ *v.tr.* **1** bring back or attempt to bring back to the original state by rebuilding, repairing, repainting, emending, etc. **2** bring back to health etc.; cure. **3** give back to the original owner etc.; make restitution of. **4** reinstate; bring back to dignity or right. **5** replace; put back; bring back to a former condition. **6** make a representation of the supposed original state of (a ruin, extinct animal, etc.). **7** reinstate by conjecture (missing words in a text, missing pieces, etc.). ▫ **restorable** *adj.* **restorer** *n.* [Middle English via Old French *restorer* from Latin *restaurare*]

restrain /rɪˈstreɪn/ *v.tr.* **1** (often *refl.*, usu. foll. by *from*) check or hold in; keep in check or under control or within bounds. **2** repress; keep down. **3** confine; imprison. ▫ **restrainable** *adj.* **restrainer** *n.* [Middle English via Old French *restrei(g)n-*, stem of *restreindre*, from Latin *restringere restrict-* (as RE-, *stringere* 'tie')]

re-strain /riːˈstreɪn/ *v.tr.* strain again.

restrainedly /rɪˈstreɪnɪdli/ *adv.* with self-restraint.

restraint /rɪˈstreɪnt/ *n.* **1** the act or an instance of restraining or being restrained. **2** a stoppage; a check; a controlling agency or influence. **3 a** self-control; avoidance of excess or exaggeration. **b** austerity of literary expression. **4** reserve of manner. **5** confinement, esp. because of insanity. **6** something which restrains or holds in check; bondage, shackles. ▫ **in restraint of** in order to restrain. [Middle English from Old French *restreinte*, fem. past part. of *restreindre*: see RESTRAIN]

restraint of trade *n.* action seeking to interfere with free-market conditions.

restrict /rɪˈstrɪkt/ *v.tr.* (often foll. by *to*, *within*) **1** confine, bound, limit (*restricted parking*; *restricted them to five days a week*). **2** subject to limitation. **3** withhold from general circulation or disclosure. ▫ **restrictedly** *adv.* **restrictedness** *n.* [Latin *restringere*: see RESTRAIN]

restricted area *n.* **1** *Brit.* an area in which there is a special speed limit for vehicles. **2** *US* an area which military personnel, unauthorized people, etc., are not allowed to enter.

restriction /rɪˈstrɪkʃ(ə)n/ *n.* **1** the act or an instance of restricting; the state of being restricted. **2** a thing that restricts. **3** a limitation placed on action. ▫ **restrictionist** *adj.* & *n.* [Middle English from Old French *restriction* or Latin *restrictio* (as RESTRICT)]

restriction enzyme *n. Biochem.* an enzyme which divides DNA at or near a specific sequence of bases.

restrictive /rɪˈstrɪktɪv/ *adj.* imposing restrictions. ▫ **restrictively** *adv.* **restrictiveness** *n.* [Middle English from Old French *restrictif -ive* or medieval Latin *restrictivus* (as RESTRICT)]

restrictive clause *n. Gram.* a relative clause, usu. without surrounding commas.

restrictive practice *n. Brit.* an agreement to limit competition or output in industry.

restring /riːˈstrɪŋ/ *v.tr.* (*past* and *past part.* **restrung**) **1** fit (a musical instrument) with new strings. **2** thread (beads etc.) on a new string.

restroom /ˈrɛstruːm, -rʊm/ *n.* esp. *US* a public lavatory in a factory, shop, etc.

restructure /riːˈstrʌktʃə/ *v.tr.* give a new structure to; rebuild; rearrange.

restudy /riːˈstʌdi/ *v.tr.* (**-ies**, **-ied**) study again.

restyle *v.* & *n.* ● *v.tr.* /riːˈstʌɪl/ **1** reshape; remake in a new style. **2** give a new designation to (a person or thing). ● *n.* /ˈriːstʌɪl/ an instance of restyling; a new style.

resubmit /riːsəbˈmɪt/ *v.tr.* submit (a plan, application, etc.) again.

result /rɪˈzʌlt/ *n.* & *v.* ● *n.* **1** a consequence, issue, or outcome of something. **2** a satisfactory outcome; a favourable result (*gets results*). **3** a quantity, formula, etc., obtained by calculation. **4** (in *pl.*) a list of scores or winners etc. in an examination or sporting event. ● *v.intr.* **1** (often foll. by *from*) arise as the actual consequence or follow as a logical consequence (from conditions, causes, etc.). **2** (often foll. by *in*) have a specified end or outcome (*resulted in a large profit*). □ **without result** in vain; fruitless. □ **resultless** *adj.* [Middle English via medieval Latin *resultare* from Latin (as RE-, *saltare*, frequentative of *salire* 'jump')]

resultant /rɪˈzʌlt(ə)nt/ *adj.* & *n.* ● *adj.* resulting, esp. as the total outcome of more or less opposed forces. ● *n.* *Math.* a force etc. equivalent to two or more acting in different directions at the same point.

resume /rɪˈzjuːm/ *v.* & *n.* ● *v.* **1** *tr.* & *intr.* begin again or continue after an interruption. **2** *tr.* & *intr.* begin to speak, work, or use again; recommence. **3** *tr.* get back; take back; recover; reoccupy (*resume one's seat*). ● *n.* = RÉSUMÉ. □ **resumable** *adj.* [Middle English from Old French *resumer* or Latin *resumere resumpt-* (as RE-, *sumere* 'take')]

résumé /ˈrɛzjʊmeɪ/ *n.* (also **resumé**) **1** a summary. **2** *N. Amer.* a curriculum vitae. [French, past part. of *résumer* (as RESUME)]

resumption /rɪˈzʌm(p)ʃ(ə)n/ *n.* the act or an instance of resuming (*ready for the resumption of negotiations*). □ **resumptive** *adj.* [Middle English from Old French *resumption* or Late Latin *resumptio* (as RESUME)]

resupinate /rɪˈsuːpɪneɪt, -ˈsjuː-/ *adj.* (of a leaf etc.) upside down. [Latin *resupinatus*, past part. of *resupinare* 'bend back': see SUPINE]

resupply /riːsəˈplʌɪ/ *v.* & *n.* ● *v.* (**-ies**, **-ied**) **1** *tr.* supply again; provide with a fresh supply. **2** *intr.* take on or acquire a fresh supply. ● *n.* the act or resupplying something or being resupplied.

resurface /riːˈsəːfɪs/ *v.* **1** *tr.* lay a new surface on (a road etc.). **2** *intr.* rise or arise again; turn up again.

resurgent /rɪˈsəːdʒ(ə)nt/ *adj.* **1** rising or arising again. **2** tending to rise again. □ **resurgence** *n.* [Latin *resurgere resurrect-* (as RE-, *surgere* 'rise')]

resurrect /rɛzəˈrɛkt/ *v.* **1** *tr.* *colloq.* revive the practice, use, or memory of. **2** *tr.* take from the grave; exhume. **3** *tr.* dig up. **4** *tr.* & *intr.* raise or rise from the dead. [back-formation from RESURRECTION]

resurrection /rɛzəˈrɛkʃ(ə)n/ *n.* **1** the act or an instance of rising from the dead. **2** (**Resurrection**) **a** Christ's rising from the dead. **b** the rising of the dead at the Last Judgement. **3** a revival after disuse, inactivity, or decay. **4** exhumation. **5** the unearthing of a lost or forgotten thing; restoration to vogue or memory. □ **resurrectional** *adj.* [Middle English via Old French from Late Latin *resurrectio -onis* (as RESURGENT)]

resurrection plant *n.* any of various plants, including clubmosses of the genus *Selaginella* and the Rose of Jericho, unfolding when moistened after being dried.

resurvey *v.* & *n.* ● *v.tr.* /riːsəˈveɪ/ survey again; reconsider. ● *n.* /riːˈsəːveɪ/ the act or an instance of resurveying.

resuscitate /rɪˈsʌsɪteɪt/ *v.tr.* & *intr.* **1** revive from unconsciousness or apparent death. **2** return or restore to vogue, vigour, or vividness. □ **resuscitation** /-ˈteɪʃ(ə)n/ *n.* **resuscitative** *adj.* **resuscitator** *n.* [Latin *resuscitare* (as RE-, *suscitare* 'raise')]

ret /rɛt/ *v.* (also **rate** /reɪt/) (**retted**, **retting**) **1** *tr.* soften (flax, hemp, etc.) by soaking or by exposure to moisture. **2** *intr.* (often as **retted** *adj.*) (of hay etc.) be spoilt by wet or rot. [Middle English, related to ROT]

ret. *abbr.* retired; returned.

retable /rɪˈteɪb(ə)l/ *n.* **1** a frame enclosing decorated panels above the back of an altar. **2** a shelf. [French *rétable, retable* via Spanish *retablo* from medieval Latin *retrotabulum* 'rear table' (as RETRO-, TABLE)]

retail /ˈriːteɪl/ *n.*, *adj.*, *adv.*, & *v.* ● *n.* the sale of goods in relatively small quantities to the public, and usu. not for resale (cf. WHOLESALE). ● *adj.* & *adv.* by retail; at a retail price (*do you buy wholesale or retail?*). ● *v.* /also rɪˈteɪl/ **1** *tr.* sell (goods) in retail trade. **2** *intr.* (often foll. by *at*, *for*) (of goods) be sold in this way (esp. for a specified price) (*retails at £4.95*). **3** *tr.* recount; relate details of. □ **retailer** *n.* [Middle English from Old French *retaille* 'a piece cut off' from *retaillier* (as RE-, TAIL[2])]

retail price index *n.* an index of the variation in the prices of retail goods.

retain /rɪˈteɪn/ *v.tr.* **1 a** keep possession of; not lose; continue to have, practise, or recognize. **b** not abolish, discard, or alter. **2** keep in one's memory. **3** keep in place; hold fixed. **4** secure the services of (a person, esp. a barrister) with a preliminary payment. □ **retainable** *adj.* **retainability** /-ˈbɪlɪti/ *n.* **retainment** *n.* [Middle English via Anglo-French *retei(g)n-* from the stem of Old French *retenir*, ultimately from Latin *retinēre retent-* (as RE-, *tenēre* 'hold')]

retainer /rɪˈteɪnə/ *n.* **1** a person or thing that retains. **2** esp. *Law* a fee for retaining a barrister etc. **3 a** *hist.* a dependant or follower of a person of rank. **b** *joc.* an old and faithful friend or servant (esp. *old retainer*). **4** *Brit.* a reduced rent paid to retain accommodation during a period of non-occupancy. **5** *Dentistry* a structure cemented to a tooth to keep a bridge in place.

retaining fee *n.* a fee paid to secure a person, service, etc.

retaining wall *n.* a wall supporting and confining a mass of earth or water.

retake *v.* & *n.* ● *v.tr.* /riːˈteɪk/ (*past* **retook**; *past part.* **retaken**) **1** take again. **2** recapture. ● *n.* /ˈriːteɪk/ **1 a** the act or an instance of retaking. **b** a thing retaken, e.g. an examination. **2 a** the act or an instance of filming a scene or recording music etc. again. **b** the scene or recording obtained in this way.

retaliate /rɪˈtalɪeɪt/ *v.* **1** *intr.* repay an injury, insult, etc., in kind; attack in return; make reprisals. **2** *tr.* **a** (usu. foll. by *upon*) cast (an accusation) back upon a person. **b** repay (an injury or insult) in kind. □ **retaliation** /-ˈeɪʃ(ə)n/ *n.* **retaliative** /-ˈtaljətɪv/ *adj.* **retaliator** *n.* **retaliatory** /-ˈtaljət(ə)ri/ *adj.* [Latin *retaliare* (as RE-, *talis* 'such')]

retard /rɪˈtɑːd/ *v.* & *n.* ● *v.tr.* **1** make slow or late. **2** delay the progress, development, arrival, or accomplishment of. ● *n.* **1** retardation. **2** /ˈriːtɑːd/ *US slang offens.* a mentally retarded person. □ **in retard** *Brit.* delayed, in the rear. □ **retardant** *adj.* & *n.* **retardation** /riːtɑːˈdeɪʃ(ə)n/ *n.* **retardative** *adj.* **retardatory** *adj.* **retarder** *n.* **retardment** *n.* [French *retarder* from Latin *retardare* (as RE-, *tardus* 'slow')]

retardate /rɪˈtɑːdeɪt/ *adj.* & *n.* *N. Amer.* ● *adj.* mentally retarded. ● *n.* a mentally retarded person. [Latin *retardare*: see RETARD]

retarded /rɪˈtɑːdɪd/ *adj.* backward in mental or physical development.

retch /rɛtʃ/ *v.* & *n.* ● *v.intr.* make a motion of vomiting, esp. involuntarily and without effect. ● *n.* such a motion or the sound of it. [variant of (now dialect) *reach*, from Old English *hrǣcan* 'spit', Old Norse *hrǣkja* from Germanic, of imitative origin]

retd. *abbr.* **1** retired. **2** returned.

rete /ˈriːtiː/ *n.* (*pl.* **retia** /-tɪə, -ʃɪə/) *Anat.* an elaborate network or plexus of blood vessels or nerve cells. [Latin *rete* 'net']

reteach /riːˈtiːtʃ/ *v.tr.* (*past* and *past part.* **retaught**) teach again or differently.

retell /riːˈtɛl/ *v.tr.* (*past* and *past part.* **retold**) tell again or in a different version.

retention /rɪˈtɛnʃ(ə)n/ *n.* **1 a** the act or an instance of retaining; the state of being retained. **b** the ability to retain things experienced or learnt; memory. **2** *Med.* the failure to evacuate urine or another secretion. [Middle English from Old French *retention* or Latin *retentio* (as RETAIN)]

retentive /rɪˈtɛntɪv/ *adj.* **1** (often foll. by *of*) tending to retain (moisture etc.). **2** (of memory or a person) not forgetful. **3** *Surgery* (of a ligature etc.) serving to keep something in place. □ **retentively** *adv.* **retentiveness** *n.* [Middle English from Old French *retentif -ive* or medieval Latin *retentivus* (as RETAIN)]

retexture /riːˈtɛkstʃə/ *v.tr.* treat (material, a garment, etc.) so as to restore its original texture.

rethink *v.* & *n.* ● *v.tr.* /riːˈθɪŋk/ (*past* and *past part.* **rethought**) think about (something) again, esp. with a view to making changes. ● *n.* /ˈriːθɪŋk/ a reassessment; a period of rethinking.

retia *pl.* of RETE.

retiarius /rɛtɪˈɑːrɪəs, -ˈɛːrɪəs/ *n.* (*pl.* **retiarii** /-rɪʌɪ, -rɪiː/) *Rom.Hist.* a Roman gladiator using a net to trap his opponent. [Latin, from *rete* 'net']

reticence /ˈrɛtɪs(ə)ns/ *n.* **1** the avoidance of saying all one knows or feels, or of saying more than is necessary; reserve in speech. **2** a disposition to silence; taciturnity. **3** the act or an instance of holding back some fact. □ **reticent** *adj.* **reticently** *adv.* [Latin *reticentia* from *reticēre* (as RE-, *tacēre* 'be silent')]

reticle /ˈrɛtɪk(ə)l/ *n.* a network of fine threads or lines in the focal plane of an optical instrument to help accurate observation. [Latin *reticulum*: see RETICULUM]

reticula *pl.* of RETICULUM.

reticulate *v.* & *adj.* ● *v.tr.* & *intr.* /rɪˈtɪkjʊleɪt/ **1** divide or be divided in fact or appearance into a network. **2** arrange or be arranged in small squares or with intersecting lines. ● *adj.* /rɪˈtɪkjʊlət/ reticulated. □ **reticulately** /rɪˈtɪkjʊlətli/ *adv.* **reticulation** /-ˈleɪʃ(ə)n/ *n.* [Latin *reticulatus* 'reticulated' (as RETICULUM)]

reticule /ˈrɛtɪkjuːl/ *n.* **1** = RETICLE. **2** esp. *hist.* a woman's netted or other bag, esp. with a drawstring, carried or worn to serve the purpose of a pocket. [French *réticule* from Latin (as RETICULUM)]

reticulum /rɪˈtɪkjʊləm/ *n.* (*pl.* **reticula** /-lə/) **1** a netlike structure; a fine network, esp. of membranes etc. in living organisms. **2** a ruminant's second stomach. □ **reticular** *adj.* **reticulose** *adj.* [Latin, diminutive of *rete* 'net']

retie /riːˈtʌɪ/ *v.tr.* (**retying**) tie again.

retiform /ˈriːtɪfɔːm, ˈrɛti-/ *adj.* netlike, reticulated. [Latin *rete* 'net' + -FORM]

re-time /riːˈtʌɪm/ *v.tr.* esp. *Railways* set a new or different time for; reschedule.

retina /ˈrɛtɪnə/ *n.* (*pl.* **retinas**, **retinae** /-niː/) a layer at the back of the eyeball sensitive to light, and triggering nerve impulses via the optic nerve to the brain where the visual image is formed. □ **retinal** *adj.* [Middle English via medieval Latin from Latin *rete* 'net']

retinitis /rɛtɪˈnʌɪtɪs/ *n.* inflammation of the retina.

retinol /ˈrɛtɪnɒl/ *n.* a vitamin found in green and yellow vegetables, egg yolk, and fish-liver oil, essential for growth and vision in dim light. Also called *vitamin A*. [RETINA + -OL[1]]

retinue /ˈrɛtɪnjuː/ *n.* a body of attendants accompanying an important person. [Middle English from Old French *retenue*, fem. past part. of *retenir* RETAIN]

retiral /rɪˈtʌɪr(ə)l/ *n.* esp. *Sc.* retirement from office etc.

retire /rɪˈtʌɪə/ *v.* **1 a** *intr.* leave office or employment, esp. because of age (*retire from the army*; *retire on a pension*). **b** *tr.* cause (a person) to retire from work. **2** *intr.* withdraw; go away; retreat. **3** *intr.* seek seclusion or shelter. **4** *intr.* go to bed. **5** *tr.* withdraw (troops). **6 a** *intr.* & *tr.* *Cricket* (of a batsman) voluntarily end or be compelled to suspend one's innings (*retired hurt*). **b** *tr.* *Baseball* put out (a batter); cause (a side) to end a turn at bat. **7** *tr.* *Econ.* withdraw (a bill or note) from circulation or currency. □ **retire from the world** become a recluse. **retire into oneself** become uncommunicative or unsociable. □ **retirer** *n.* [French *retirer* (as RE-, *tirer* 'draw')]

retired /rɪˈtʌɪəd/ *adj.* **1 a** having retired from employment (*a retired teacher*). **b** relating to a retired person (*received retired pay*). **2** withdrawn from society or observation; secluded (*lives a retired life*). □ **retiredness** *n. archaic.*

retirement /rɪˈtʌɪəm(ə)nt/ *n.* **1 a** the act or an instance of retiring. **b** the condition of having retired. **2 a** seclusion or privacy. **b** a secluded place.

retirement age *n.* the age at which most people normally retire from work.

retirement home *n.* **1** a house, flat, etc. to which a person moves in old age. **2** an institution for elderly people needing care.

retirement pension *n. Brit.* a pension paid by the state to retired people above a certain age.

retiring /rɪˈtʌɪərɪŋ/ *adj.* shy; fond of seclusion. □ **retiringly** *adv.*

retiring age *n. Brit.* = RETIREMENT AGE.

retitle /riːˈtʌɪt(ə)l/ *v.tr.* give a different title to.

retold *past* and *past part.* of RETELL.

retook *past* of RETAKE.

retool /riːˈtuːl/ *v.tr.* equip (a factory etc.) with new tools.

retort[1] /rɪˈtɔːt/ *n.* & *v.* ● *n.* **1** an incisive or witty or angry reply. **2** the turning of a charge or argument against its originator. **3** a retaliation. ● *v.* **1 a** *tr.* say by way of a retort. **b** *intr.* make a retort. **2** *tr.* repay (an insult or attack) in kind. **3** *tr.* (often foll. by *on*, *upon*) return (mischief, a charge, sarcasm, etc.) to its originator. **4** *tr.* (often foll. by *against*) make (an argument) tell against its user. **5** *tr.* (as **retorted** *adj.*) recurved; twisted or bent backwards. [Latin *retorquēre retort-* (as RE-, *torquēre* 'twist')]

retort[2] /rɪˈtɔːt/ *n.* & *v.* ● *n.* **1** a container, usu. of glass, with a long recurved neck used in distilling liquids. **2** a large receptacle or furnace for heating mercury for purification, coal to generate gas, or iron and carbon to make steel. ● *v.tr.* purify (mercury) by heating in a retort. [French *retorte* from medieval Latin *retorta*, fem. past part. of *retorquēre*: see RETORT[1]]

retortion /rɪˈtɔːʃ(ə)n/ *n.* **1** the act or an instance of bending back; the condition of being bent back. **2** (in international law) retaliation by a state on the subjects of another. [RETORT[1], perhaps on the pattern of *contortion*]

retouch /riːˈtʌtʃ/ *v.* & *n.* ● *v.tr.* improve or repair (a composition, picture, photographic negative or print, etc.) by fresh touches or alterations. ● *n.* the act or an instance of retouching. □ **retoucher** *n.* [probably from French *retoucher* (as RE-, TOUCH)]

retrace /rɪˈtreɪs/ *v.tr.* **1** go back over (one's steps etc.). **2** trace back to a source or beginning. **3** recall the course of in one's memory. [French *retracer* (as RE-, TRACE[1])]

retract /rɪˈtrakt/ *v.* **1** *tr.* (also *absol.*) withdraw or revoke (a statement or undertaking). **2 a** *tr.* & *intr.* (esp. with reference to part of the body) draw or be drawn back or in. **b** *tr.* draw (an undercarriage etc.) into the body of an aircraft. □ **retractable** *adj.* **retraction** *n.* **retractive** *adj.* [Latin *retrahere* or (in sense 1) *retractare* (as RE-, *trahere tract-* 'draw')]

retractile /rɪˈtraktʌɪl/ *adj.* capable of being retracted. □ **retractility** /-ˈtɪlɪti/ *n.* [RETRACT, on the pattern of *contractile*]

retractor /rɪˈtraktə/ *n.* **1** a muscle used for retracting. **2** a device for retracting.

retrain /riːˈtreɪn/ *v.tr.* & *intr.* train again or further, esp. for new work.

retral /ˈriːtr(ə)l/ *adj. Biol.* hinder, posterior; at the back. [RETRO- + -AL]

retranslate /riːtransˈleɪt, -trɑːns-, -nz-/ *v.tr.* translate again, esp. translate (a translation) back into the original language. □ **retranslation** *n.*

retransmit /riːtranzˈmɪt, -trɑːnz-, -ns-/ *v.tr.* (**retransmitted**, **retransmitting**) transmit (esp. radio signals or broadcast programmes) back again or to a further distance. □ **retransmission** /-ˈmɪʃ(ə)n/ *n.*

retread *v. & n.* ● *v.tr.* /riːˈtrɛd/ **1** (*past* **retrod**; *past part.* **retrodden**) tread (a path etc.) again. **2** (*past* and *past part.* **retreaded**) put a fresh tread on (a tyre). ● *n.* /ˈriːtrɛd/ **1** a retreaded tyre. **2** a person recalled to service or retrained for new work. **3** a thing or person superficially altered but essentially the same as a predecessor.

retreat /rɪˈtriːt/ *v. & n.* ● *v.* **1 a** *intr.* (esp. of military forces) go back, retire; relinquish a position. **b** *tr.* cause to retreat; move back. **2** *intr.* (esp. of features) recede; slope back. ● *n.* **1 a** the act or an instance of retreating. **b** *Mil.* a signal for this. **2** withdrawal into privacy or security. **3** a place of shelter or seclusion. **4** a period of seclusion for prayer and meditation. **5** *Mil.* **a** a bugle call at sunset. **b** a flag-lowering ceremony including this. **6** an establishment for the care of the elderly, the mentally ill, etc. [Middle English via Old French *retret* (*n.*), *retraiter* (*v.*) from Latin *retrahere*: see RETRACT]

retrench /rɪˈtrɛn(t)ʃ/ *v.* **1 a** *tr.* reduce the amount of (costs). **b** *intr.* cut down expenses; introduce economies. **2** *tr.* shorten or abridge. **3** *tr.* esp. *Austral.* make (an employee) redundant; sack. □ **retrenchment** *n.* [obsolete French *retrencher* (as RE-, TRENCH)]

retrial /riːˈtrʌɪəl/ *n.* a second or further (judicial) trial.

retribution /rɛtrɪˈbjuːʃ(ə)n/ *n.* requital usu. for evil done; vengeance. □ **retributive** /rɪˈtrɪbjʊtɪv/ *adj.* **retributory** /rɪˈtrɪbjʊt(ə)ri/ *adj.* [Middle English from Late Latin *retributio* (as RE-, *tribuere tribut-* 'assign')]

retrieve /rɪˈtriːv/ *v. & n.* ● *v.tr.* **1 a** regain possession of. **b** recover by investigation or effort of memory. **2 a** restore to knowledge or recall to mind. **b** obtain (information stored in a computer etc.). **3** (of a dog) find and bring in (killed or wounded game etc.). **4** (foll. by *from*) recover or rescue (esp. from a bad state). **5** restore to a flourishing state; revive. **6** repair or set right (a loss or error etc.) (*managed to retrieve the situation*). ● *n.* the possibility of recovery (*beyond retrieve*). □ **retrievability** /-ˈbɪlɪti/ *n.* **retrievable** *adj.* **retrieval** *n.* [Middle English from Old French *retroeve-*, stressed stem of *retrover* (as RE-, *trover* 'find')]

retriever /rɪˈtriːvə/ *n.* **1 a** a dog of a breed used for retrieving game. **b** this breed. **2** a person who retrieves something.

retro /ˈrɛtrəʊ/ *n. & adj.* ● *n.* (*pl.* **-os**) **1** a thing imitating something from the past. **2** a nostalgic style or fashion in dress, music, etc. ● *adj.* imitative of a style or fashion from the past. [French *rétro*, abbreviation of *rétrograde*]

retro- /ˈrɛtrəʊ/ *comb. form* **1** denoting action back or in return (*retroact*; *retroflex*). **2** *Anat. & Med.* denoting location behind. [Latin *retro* 'backwards']

retroact /rɛtrəʊˈakt/ *v.intr.* **1** operate in a backward direction. **2** have a retrospective effect. **3** react. □ **retroaction** *n.*

retroactive /rɛtrəʊˈaktɪv/ *adj.* (esp. of legislation) having retrospective effect. □ **retroactively** *adv.* **retroactivity** /-ˈtɪvɪti/ *n.*

retrocede /rɛtrə(ʊ)ˈsiːd/ *v.* **1** *intr.* move back; recede. **2** *tr.* cede back again. □ **retrocedence** *n.* **retrocedent** *adj.* **retrocession** /-ˈsɛʃ(ə)n/ *n.* **retrocessive** /-ˈsɛsɪv/ *adj.* [Latin *retrocedere* (as RETRO-, *cedere cess-* 'go')]

retrochoir /ˈrɛtrəʊkwʌɪə/ *n.* the part of a cathedral or large church behind the high altar. [medieval Latin *retrochorus* (as RETRO-, CHOIR)]

retrod *past* of RETREAD 1.

retrodden *past part.* of RETREAD 1.

retrofit /ˈrɛtrəʊfɪt/ *v.tr.* (**-fitted**, **-fitting**) modify (machinery, vehicles, etc.) to incorporate changes and developments introduced after manufacture. [RETROACTIVE + REFIT]

retroflex /ˈrɛtrə(ʊ)flɛks/ *adj.* (also **retroflexed**) **1** *Anat., Med., & Bot.* turned backwards. **2** *Phonet.* pronounced with the tip of the tongue curled up towards the hard palate. □ **retroflexion** /-ˈflɛkʃ(ə)n/ *n.* [Latin *retroflectere retroflex-* (as RETRO-, *flectere* 'bend')]

retrogradation /ˌrɛtrəʊgrəˈdeɪʃ(ə)n/ *n. Astron.* **1** the apparent backward motion of an outer planet, from east to west, when it is overtaken in its orbit by the earth. **2** the orbiting of a celestial body in a reverse direction to normal. [Late Latin *retrogradatio* (as RETRO-, GRADATION)]

retrograde /ˈrɛtrəgreɪd/ *adj., n., & v.* ● *adj.* **1** directed backwards; retreating. **2** reverting esp. to an inferior state; declining. **3** inverse, reversed (*in retrograde order*). **4** *Astron.* in or showing retrogradation. ● *n.* a degenerate person. ● *v.intr.* **1** move backwards; recede, retire. **2** decline, revert. **3** *Astron.* show retrogradation. □ **retrogradely** *adv.* [Middle English from Latin *retrogradus* (as RETRO-, *gradus* 'step', *gradi* 'walk')]

retrogress /rɛtrə(ʊ)ˈgrɛs/ *v.intr.* **1** go back; move backwards. **2** deteriorate. □ **retrogressive** *adj.* [RETRO-, on the pattern of PROGRESS *v.*]

retrogression /rɛtrə(ʊ)ˈgrɛʃ(ə)n/ *n.* **1** backward or reversed movement. **2** a return to a less advanced state; a reversal of development; a decline or deterioration. **3** *Astron.* = RETROGRADATION. □ **retrogressive** /-sɪv/ *adj.* [RETRO-, on the pattern of *progression*]

retroject /rɛtrə(ʊ)ˈdʒɛkt/ *v.tr.* throw back (usu. opp. PROJECT). [RETRO-, on the pattern of PROJECT *v.*]

retro-rocket /ˈrɛtrəʊrɒkɪt/ *n.* an auxiliary rocket for slowing down a spacecraft etc., e.g. when re-entering the earth's atmosphere.

retrorse /rɪˈtrɔːs/ *adj. Biol.* turned back or down. □ **retrorsely** *adv.* [Latin *retrorsus* = *retroversus* (as RETRO-, *versus*, past part. of *vertere* 'turn')]

retrospect /ˈrɛtrəspɛkt/ *n.* **1** (foll. by *to*) regard or reference to precedent or authority, or to previous conditions. **2** a survey of past time or events. □ **in retrospect 1** when looked back on. **2** when looking back; with hindsight. [RETRO-, on the pattern of PROSPECT *n.*]

retrospection /rɛtrə(ʊ)ˈspɛkʃ(ə)n/ *n.* **1** the action of looking back, esp. into the past. **2** an indulgence or engagement in retrospect. [probably from verb *retrospect* (as RETROSPECT)]

retrospective /rɛtrə(ʊ)ˈspɛktɪv/ *adj. & n.* ● *adj.* **1** looking back on or dealing with the past. **2** (of an exhibition, recital, etc.) showing an artist's development over his or her lifetime. **3** esp. *Brit.* (of a statute etc.) applying to the past as well as the future; retroactive. **4** (of a view) lying to the rear. ● *n.* a retrospective exhibition, recital, etc. □ **retrospectively** *adv.*

retrosternal /rɛtrə(ʊ)ˈstəːn(ə)l/ *adj. Anat. & Med.* behind the breastbone.

retroussé /rəˈtruːseɪ/ *adj.* (of the nose) turned up at the tip. [French, past part. of *retrousser* 'tuck up' (as RE-, TRUSS)]

retrovert /ˈrɛtrəvəːt/ *v.tr.* **1** turn backwards. **2** (as **retroverted** *adj.*) *Med.* (of the womb) having a backward inclination. □ **retroversion** /-ˈvəːʃ(ə)n/ *n.* [Late Latin *retrovertere* (as RETRO-, *vertere vers-* 'turn')]

retrovirus /ˈrɛtrəʊvʌɪrəs/ *n. Biol.* any of a group of RNA viruses which insert a DNA copy of their genome into the host cell in order to replicate, e.g. HIV. [modern Latin, from the initial letters of *reverse transcriptase* + -O- + VIRUS]

retry /riːˈtrʌɪ/ *v.tr.* (**-ies**, **-ied**) try (a defendant or lawsuit) a second or further time.

retsina /rɛtˈsiːnə/ *n.* a Greek white or rosé wine flavoured with resin. [modern Greek]

retune /riːˈtjuːn/ *v.tr.* **1** tune (a musical instrument) again or differently. **2** tune (a radio etc.) to a different frequency.

returf /riːˈtəːf/ *v.tr. Brit.* provide with new turf.

return /rɪˈtəːn/ *v.* & *n.* ● *v.* **1** *intr.* come or go back. **2** *tr.* bring, put, or send back to the person or place etc. where originally belonging or obtained (*returned the fish to the river; have you returned my scissors?*). **3** *tr.* pay back or reciprocate; give in response (*decided not to return the compliment*). **4** *tr.* yield (a profit). **5** *tr.* say in reply; retort. **6** *tr.* (in cricket, tennis, etc.) hit or send (the ball) back after receiving it. **7** *tr.* state or mention or describe officially, esp. in answer to a writ or formal demand. **8** *tr. Brit.* (of an electorate) elect as an MP, government, etc. **9** *tr. Cards* **a** lead (a suit) previously led or bid by a partner. **b** lead (a suit or card) after taking a trick. **10** *tr. Archit.* continue (a wall etc.) in a changed direction, esp. at right angles. ● *n.* **1** the act or an instance of coming or going back. **2 a** the act or an instance of giving or sending or putting or paying back. **b** a thing given or sent back. **3** (in full **return ticket**) esp. *Brit.* a ticket for a journey to a place and back to the starting point. **4** (in *sing.* or *pl.*) **a** the proceeds or profit of an undertaking. **b** the acquisition of these. **5** a formal report or statement compiled or submitted by order (*an income tax return*). **6** (in full **return match** or **game**) a second match etc. between the same opponents. **7** *Electr.* a conductor bringing a current back to its source. **8** *Brit.* a sheriff's report on a writ. **9** esp. *Brit.* **a** a person's election as an MP etc. **b** a returning officer's announcement of this. **10** *Archit.* a part receding from the line of the front, e.g. the side of a house or of a window opening. **11 a** (in full **carriage return key**) a key pressed to return the carriage of an electric typewriter to a fixed position. **b** (in full **return key**) a key pressed on a computer keyboard to simulate this. □ **by return (of post)** *Brit.* by the next available post in the return direction. **in return** as an exchange or reciprocal action. **many happy returns (of the day)** a greeting on a birthday. **return thanks** *Brit.* express thanks esp. in a grace at meals or in response to a toast or condolence. □ **returnable** *adj.* **returner** *n.* **returnless** *adj.* [Middle English from Old French *returner* (as RE-, TURN)]

return crease *n. Cricket* each of two lines joining the popping crease and bowling crease at right angles to the bowling crease and extending beyond it.

returnee /rɪtəːˈniː/ *n.* **1** a person who returns home from abroad, esp. after war service. **2** a person who returns to work, esp. after bringing up a family.

returning officer *n. Brit.* an official conducting an election in a constituency and announcing the results.

retuse /rɪˈtjuːs/ *adj.* esp. *Bot.* having a broad end with a central depression. [Latin *retundere retus-* (as RE-, *tundere* 'beat')]

retying *pres. part.* of RETIE.

retype /riːˈtʌɪp/ *v.tr.* type again, esp. to correct errors.

reunify /riːˈjuːnɪfʌɪ/ *v.tr.* (**-ies**, **-ied**) restore (esp. separated territories) to a political unity. □ **reunification** /-fɪˈkeɪʃ(ə)n/ *n.*

reunion /riːˈjuːnjən, -ɪən/ *n.* **1 a** the act or an instance of reuniting. **b** the condition of being reunited. **2** a social gathering esp. of people formerly associated. [French *réunion* or Anglo-Latin *reunio* from Latin *reunire* 'unite' (as RE-, UNION)]

reunite /riːjʊˈnʌɪt/ *v.tr.* & *intr.* bring or come back together.

reupholster /riːʌpˈhəʊlstə, -ˈhɒl-/ *v.tr.* upholster anew. □ **reupholstery** *n.*

reuse *v.* & *n.* ● *v.tr.* /riːˈjuːz/ use again or more than once. ● *n.* /riːˈjuːs/ a second or further use. □ **reusable** /-ˈjuːzəb(ə)l/ *adj.*

reutilize /riːˈjuːtɪlʌɪz/ *v.tr.* (also **-ise**) utilize again or for a different purpose. □ **reutilization** /-ˈzeɪʃ(ə)n/ *n.*

Rev. *abbr.* **1** Reverend. **2** Revelation (New Testament).

rev /rɛv/ *n.* & *v. colloq.* ● *n.* (in *pl.*) the number of revolutions of an engine per minute (*running at 3,000 revs*). ● *v.* (**revved**, **revving**) **1** *intr.* (of an engine) revolve; turn over. **2** *tr.* (also *absol.*; often foll. by *up*) cause (an engine) to run quickly. [abbreviation]

revaccinate /riːˈvaksɪneɪt/ *v.tr.* vaccinate again. □ **revaccination** /-ˈneɪʃ(ə)n/ *n.*

revalue /riːˈvaljuː/ *v.tr.* (**revalues**, **revalued**, **revaluing**) *Econ.* give a different value to, esp. give a higher value to (a currency) in relation to other currencies or gold (opp. DEVALUE). □ **revaluation** /-ˈeɪʃ(ə)n/ *n.*

revamp /riːˈvamp/ *v.tr.* **1** renovate, revise, improve. **2** patch up. [RE- + VAMP[1]]

revanchism /rɪˈvan(t)ʃɪz(ə)m/ *n. Polit.* a policy of seeking to retaliate, esp. to recover lost territory. □ **revanchist** *n.* & *adj.* [French *revanche* (as REVENGE)]

revarnish /riːˈvɑːnɪʃ/ *v.tr.* varnish again.

rev counter *n.* = REVOLUTION COUNTER.

Revd *abbr.* Reverend.

reveal[1] /rɪˈviːl/ *v.tr.* **1** display or show; allow to appear. **2** (often as **revealing** *adj.*) disclose, divulge, betray (*revealed his plans; a revealing remark*). **3** *tr.* (in *refl.* or *passive*) come to sight or knowledge. **4** *Relig.* (esp. of God) make known by inspiration or supernatural means. □ **revealable** *adj.* **revealer** *n.* **revealingly** *adv.* [Middle English from Old French *reveler* or Latin *revelare* (as RE-, *velum* 'veil')]

reveal[2] /rɪˈviːl/ *n.* an internal side surface of an opening or recess, esp. of a doorway or window aperture. [obsolete *revale* 'to lower', via Old French *revaler* from *avaler* (as RE-, VAIL)]

revealed religion *n.* a religion based on revelation (opp. NATURAL RELIGION).

revegetate /riːˈvɛdʒɪteɪt/ *v.tr.* produce a new growth of vegetation on (disturbed or barren ground). □ **revegetation** /-ˈteɪʃ(ə)n/ *n.*

reveille /rɪˈvali/ *n.* a military waking-signal sounded in the morning on a bugle or drums etc. [French *réveillez*, imperative pl. of *réveiller* 'awaken' (as RE-, *veiller* from Latin *vigilare* 'keep watch')]

revel /ˈrɛv(ə)l/ *v.* & *n.* ● *v.* (**revelled**, **revelling**; *US* **reveled**, **reveling**) **1** *intr.* have a good time; be extravagantly festive. **2** *intr.* (foll. by *in*) take keen delight in. **3** *tr.* (foll. by *away*) throw away (money or time) in revelry. ● *n.* (in *sing.* or *pl.*) the act or an instance of revelling. □ **reveller** *n.* **revelry** *n.* (*pl.* **-ies**). [Middle English via Old French *reveler* 'riot' from Latin *rebellare* REBEL *v.*]

revelation /rɛvəˈleɪʃ(ə)n/ *n.* **1 a** the act or an instance of revealing, esp. the supposed disclosure of knowledge to humankind by a divine or supernatural agency. **b** knowledge disclosed in this way. **2** a striking disclosure (*it was a revelation to me*). **3** (**Revelation** or *colloq.* **Revelations**) (in full **the Revelation of St John the Divine**) the last book of the New Testament, recounting a divine revelation of the future to St John. □ **revelational** *adj.* [Middle English from Old French *revelation* or Late Latin *revelatio* (as REVEAL[1])]

revelationist /rɛvəˈleɪʃ(ə)nɪst/ *n.* a believer in divine revelation.

revelatory /rɛvəˈleɪt(ə)ri, ˈrɛv(ə)lət(ə)ri/ *adj.* serving to reveal, esp. something significant. [Latin *revelare*: see REVEAL[1]]

revenant /ˈrɛv(ə)nənt/ *n.* a person who has returned, esp. supposedly from the dead. [French, pres. part. of *revenir*: see REVENUE]

revenge /rɪˈvɛn(d)ʒ/ *n.* & *v.* ● *n.* **1** retaliation for an offence or injury. **2** an act of retaliation. **3** the desire for this; a vindictive feeling. **4** (in games) a chance to win after an earlier defeat. ● *v.* **1** *tr.* (*refl.* or in *passive*; often foll. by *on*, *upon*) inflict retaliation for an offence. **2** *tr.* inflict retaliation for (an offence). **3** *tr.* inflict retaliation on behalf of (a person). **4** *intr.* take vengeance. □ **revenger** *n.* [Middle English via Old

French *revenger, revencher* from Late Latin *revindicare* (as RE-, *vindicare* 'lay claim to')]

■ **Usage** The verb *revenge* is usually used in the passive or as a reflexive verb, often followed by *on* or *upon*, e.g. *He intended to be revenged upon them all*; *They revenged themselves on their creditors* (see sense 1 above). *Avenge* is also, but less commonly, used in these constructions. Like *avenge, revenge* can mean 'inflict retaliation for (an offence) or on behalf of (a person)', but it is less common than *avenge* in these senses (see senses 2 and 3 above). See also Usage Note at AVENGE.

revengeful /rɪ'vɛn(d)ʒfʊl, -f(ə)l/ *adj.* eager for revenge. □ **revengefully** *adv.* **revengefulness** *n.*

revenue /'rɛvənju:/ *n.* **1 a** income, esp. of a large amount, from any source. **b** (in *pl.*) items constituting this. **2** a state's annual income from which public expenses are met. **3** the department of the civil service collecting this. [Middle English from Old French *revenu(e)*, past part. of *revenir*, from Latin *revenire* 'return' (as RE-, *venire* 'come')]

revenue tax *n.* a tax imposed to raise revenue, rather than to affect trade.

reverb /'ri:və:b, rɪ'və:b/ *n. Mus. colloq.* **1** reverberation. **2** a device to produce this. [abbreviation]

reverberate /rɪ'və:bəreɪt/ *v.* **1 a** *intr.* (of sound, light, or heat) be returned or echoed or reflected repeatedly. **b** *tr.* return (a sound etc.) in this way. **2** *intr.* **a** (of a story, rumour, etc.) be heard much or repeatedly. **b** (of an event) have continuing effects. □ **reverberant** *adj.* **reverberantly** *adv.* **reverberation** /-'reɪʃ(ə)n/ *n.* **reverberative** /-rətɪv/ *adj.* **reverberator** *n.* **reverberatory** /-rət(ə)ri/ *adj.* [Latin *reverberare* (as RE-, *verberare* 'to lash' from *verbera* (pl.) 'scourge')]

reverberatory furnace *n.* (also **reverberating furnace**) a furnace constructed to throw heat back on to the substance exposed to it.

revere /rɪ'vɪə/ *v.tr.* hold in deep and usu. affectionate or religious respect; venerate. [French *révérer* or Latin *reverēri* (as RE-, *verēri* 'fear')]

reverence /'rɛv(ə)r(ə)ns/ *n. & v.* ● *n.* **1 a** the act of revering or the state of being revered (*hold in reverence; feel reverence for*). **b** the capacity for revering (*lacks reverence*). **2** *archaic* a gesture showing that one reveres; a bow or curtsy. **3** (**Reverence**) a title used of or to some members of the clergy. ● *v.tr.* regard or treat with reverence. [Middle English via Old French from Latin *reverentia* (as REVERE)]

reverend /'rɛv(ə)r(ə)nd/ *adj. & n.* ● *adj.* (esp. as the title of a clergyman) deserving reverence. ● *n. colloq.* a clergyman. [Middle English from Old French *reverend* or Latin *reverendus*, gerundive of *reverēri*: see REVERE]

■ **Usage** Note the difference between *reverend* 'deserving reverence' and *reverent* 'showing reverence'.

Reverend Mother *n.* the title of the Mother Superior of a convent.

reverent /'rɛv(ə)r(ə)nt/ *adj.* feeling or showing reverence. □ **reverently** *adv.* [Middle English from Latin *reverens* (as REVERE)]

■ **Usage** See Usage Note at REVEREND.

reverential /rɛvə'rɛnʃ(ə)l/ *n.* of the nature of, due to, or characterized by reverence. □ **reverentially** *adv.* [medieval Latin *reverentialis* (as REVERE)]

reverie /'rɛv(ə)ri/ *n.* **1** a fit of abstracted musing (*was lost in a reverie*). **2** *archaic* a fantastic notion or theory; a delusion. **3** *Mus.* an instrumental piece suggesting a dreamy or musing state. [obsolete French *resverie* from Old French *reverie* 'rejoicing, revelry', from *rever* 'be delirious', of unknown origin]

revers /rɪ'vɪə/ *n.* (*pl.* same /-'vɪəz/) **1** the turned-back edge of a garment revealing the undersurface. **2** the material on this surface. [French, = REVERSE]

reverse /rɪ'və:s/ *v., adj., & n.* ● *v.* **1** *tr.* turn the other way round or up or inside out. **2** *tr.* change to the opposite character or effect (*reversed the decision*). **3** *intr. & tr.* travel or cause to travel backwards. **4** *tr.* make (an engine etc.) work in a contrary direction. **5** *tr.* revoke or annul (a decree, act, etc.). **6** *intr.* (of a dancer, esp. in a waltz) revolve in the opposite direction. ● *adj.* **1** placed or turned in an opposite direction or position. **2** opposite or contrary in character or order; inverted. ● *n.* **1** the opposite or contrary (*the reverse is the case; is the reverse of the truth*). **2** the contrary of the usual manner. **3** an occurrence of misfortune; a disaster, esp. a defeat in battle (*suffered a reverse*). **4** reverse gear or motion. **5** the reverse side of something. **6 a** the side of a coin or medal etc. bearing the secondary design. **b** this design (cf. OBVERSE 1). **7** the verso of a leaf of a book etc. □ **reverse arms** hold a rifle with the butt upwards. **reverse the charges** make the recipient of a telephone call responsible for payment. □ **reversal** *n.* **reversely** *adv.* **reverser** *n.* **reversible** *adj.* **reversibility** /-'bɪlɪti/ *n.* **reversibly** *adv.* [Middle English via Old French *revers* (*n.*), *reverser* (*v.*) from Latin *revertere revers-* (as RE-, *vertere* 'turn')]

■ **Usage** *Reversal* is the noun corresponding to the verb *reverse*, e.g. *The reversal of the decision*, while *reversion* is the noun corresponding to the verb *revert*, e.g. *The reversion of the building to its original use*.

reverse-charge *adj. Brit.* (of a telephone call) for which the recipient pays.

reverse engineering *n.* the reproduction of another manufacturer's product following detailed examination of its construction or composition.

reverse fault *n. Geol.* an oblique fault in which the rock strata above the fault are displaced upwards in relation to those below it.

reverse gear *n.* a gear used to make a vehicle etc. travel backwards.

reverse Polish notation see POLISH NOTATION.

reverse take-over *n.* the take-over of a public company by a smaller esp. private one.

reversing light *n. Brit.* a white light at the rear of a vehicle operated when the vehicle is in reverse gear.

reversion /rɪ'və:ʃ(ə)n/ *n.* **1** a return to a previous state, habit, etc. **2 a** the legal right (esp. of the original owner, or his or her heirs) to possess or succeed to property on the death of the present possessor. **b** property to which a person has such a right. **3** *Biol.* a return to ancestral type. **4** a sum payable on a person's death, esp. by way of life insurance. □ **reversional** *adj.* **reversionary** *adj.* [Middle English from Old French *reversion* or Latin *reversio* (as REVERSE)]

■ **Usage** See Usage Note at REVERSE.

revert /rɪ'və:t/ *v.* **1** *intr.* (foll. by *to*) return to a former state, practice, opinion, etc. **2** *intr.* (of property, an office, etc.) return by reversion. **3** *intr.* fall back into a wild state. **4** *tr.* turn (one's eyes or steps) back. □ **reverter** *n.* (in sense 2). [Middle English from Old French *revertir* or Latin *revertere* (as REVERSE)]

revertible /rɪ'və:tɪb(ə)l/ *adj.* (of property) subject to reversion.

revet /rɪ'vɛt/ *v.tr.* (**revetted, revetting**) face (a rampart, wall, etc.) with masonry, esp. in fortification. [French *revêtir* via Old French *revestir* from Late Latin *revestire* (as RE-, *vestire* 'clothe' from *vestis*)]

revetment /rɪ'vɛtm(ə)nt/ *n.* (esp. in fortification) a retaining wall or facing of masonry etc. [French *revêtement* (as REVET)]

review /rɪ'vju:/ *n. & v.* ● *n.* **1** a general survey or assessment of a subject or thing. **2** a retrospect or survey of the past. **3** revision or reconsideration (*is under review*). **4** a display and formal inspection of troops etc. **5** a published account or criticism of a book, play, etc. **6** a periodical publication with critical articles on current events, the arts, etc. **7** a second view. **8** a facility for playing a tape recording during a fast rewind. ● *v.tr.* **1** survey or look back on. **2** reconsider or revise. **3** hold a review of (troops etc.). **4** write a review of (a book, play, etc.). **5** view again.

□ **reviewable** *adj.* **reviewal** *n.* **reviewer** *n.* [obsolete French *reveue* from *revoir* (as RE-, *voir* 'see')]

revile /rɪ'vʌɪl/ *v.* **1** *tr.* abuse; criticize abusively. **2** *intr.* talk abusively; rail. □ **revilement** *n.* **reviler** *n.* **reviling** *n.* [Middle English from Old French *reviler* (as RE-, VILE)]

revise /rɪ'vʌɪz/ *v.* & *n.* ● *v.tr.* **1** examine or re-examine and improve or amend (esp. written or printed matter). **2** consider and alter (an opinion etc.). **3** (also *absol.*) *Brit.* read again (work learnt or done) to improve one's knowledge, esp. for an examination. ● *n. Printing* a proof-sheet including corrections made in an earlier proof. □ **revisable** *adj.* **revisal** *n.* **reviser** *n.* **revisory** *adj.* [French *réviser* 'look at', or Latin *revisere* (as RE-, *visere*, intensive of *vidēre vis-* 'see')]

Revised Standard Version *n.* a revision of the American Standard Version of the Bible (which was based on the Revised Version), published in 1946–57.

Revised Version *n.* a revision of the Authorized Version of the Bible, published in 1881–95.

revision /rɪ'vɪʒ(ə)n/ *n.* **1** the act or an instance of revising; the process of being revised. **2** a revised edition or form. □ **revisionary** *adj.* [Old French *revision* or Late Latin *revisio* (as REVISE)]

revisionism /rɪ'vɪʒ(ə)nɪz(ə)m/ *n.* often *derog.* **1** a policy of revision or modification, esp. of Marxism on evolutionary socialist (rather than revolutionary) or pluralist principles. **2** the theory or practice of revising one's attitude to a previously accepted situation or point of view. □ **revisionist** *n.* & *adj.*

revisit /riː'vɪzɪt/ *v.tr.* (**revisited**, **revisiting**) visit again.

revitalize /riː'vʌɪt(ə)lʌɪz/ *v.tr.* (also **-ise**) imbue with new life and vitality. □ **revitalization** /-'zeɪʃ(ə)n/ *n.*

revival /rɪ'vʌɪv(ə)l/ *n.* **1** the act or an instance of reviving; the process of being revived. **2** a new production of an old play etc. **3** a revived use of an old practice, custom, etc. **4 a** a reawakening of religious fervour. **b** a series of evangelistic meetings to promote this. **5** restoration to bodily or mental vigour or to life or consciousness.

revivalism /rɪ'vʌɪv(ə)lɪz(ə)m/ *n.* **1** belief in or the promotion of a revival of religious fervour. **2** a tendency or desire to revive a former custom or practice. □ **revivalist** *n.* & *adj.* **revivalistic** /-'lɪstɪk/ *adj.*

revive /rɪ'vʌɪv/ *v.intr.* & *tr.* **1** come or bring back to consciousness or life or strength. **2** come or bring back to existence, use, notice, etc. □ **revivable** *adj.* [Middle English from Old French *revivre* or Late Latin *revivere* (as RE-, Latin *vivere* 'live')]

reviver /rɪ'vʌɪvə/ *n.* **1** a person or thing that revives. **2** esp. *Brit. colloq.* a stimulating drink. **3** a preparation used for restoring a faded colour, lustre, etc.

revivify /rɪ'vɪvɪfʌɪ/ *v.tr.* (**-ies**, **-ied**) restore to animation, activity, vigour, or life. □ **revivification** /-fɪ'keɪʃ(ə)n/ *n.* [French *revivifier* or Late Latin *revivificare* (as RE-, VIVIFY)]

revoke /rɪ'vəʊk/ *v.* & *n.* ● *v.* **1** *tr.* rescind, withdraw, or cancel (a decree or promise etc.). **2** *intr. Cards* fail to follow suit when able to do so. ● *n. Cards* the act of revoking. □ **revocable** /'rɛvəkəb(ə)l/ *adj.* **revocability** /rɛvəkə'bɪlɪti/ *n.* **revocation** /rɛvə'keɪʃ(ə)n/ *n.* **revocatory** /'rɛvəkət(ə)ri/ *adj.* **revoker** *n.* [Middle English from Old French *revoquer* or Latin *revocare* (as RE-, *vocare* 'call')]

revolt /rɪ'vəʊlt/ *v.* & *n.* ● *v.* **1** *intr.* **a** rise in rebellion. **b** (as **revolted** *adj.*) having revolted. **2 a** *tr.* (often in *passive*) affect with loathing; nauseate (*was revolted by the thought of it*). **b** *intr.* (often foll. by *at*, *against*) feel strong disgust. ● *n.* **1** an act of rebelling. **2** a state of insurrection (*in revolt*). **3** a sense of loathing. **4** a mood of protest or defiance. [French *révolter* from Italian *rivoltare*, ultimately from Latin *revolvere* (as REVOLVE)]

revolting /rɪ'vəʊltɪŋ/ *adj.* disgusting, horrible. □ **revoltingly** *adv.*

revolute /'rɛvəluːt/ *adj. Bot.* etc. having a rolled-back edge. [Latin *revolutus*, past part. of *revolvere*: see REVOLVE]

revolution /rɛvə'luːʃ(ə)n/ *n.* **1 a** the forcible overthrow of a government or social order, in favour of a new system. **b** (in Marxism) the replacement of one ruling class by another; the class struggle which is expected to lead to political change and the triumph of communism. **2** any fundamental change or reversal of conditions. **3** the act or an instance of revolving. **4 a** motion in orbit or a circular course or round an axis or centre; rotation. **b** the single completion of an orbit or rotation. **c** the time taken for this. **5** a cyclic recurrence. □ **revolutionism** *n.* **revolutionist** *n.* [Middle English from Old French *revolution* or Late Latin *revolutio* (as REVOLVE)]

revolutionary /rɛvə'luːʃ(ə)n(ə)ri/ *adj.* & *n.* ● *adj.* **1** involving great and often violent change or innovation. **2** of or causing political revolution. **3** (**Revolutionary**) of or relating to a particular revolution, esp. the War of American Independence. ● *n.* (*pl.* **-ies**) an instigator or supporter of political revolution.

revolution counter *n.* a device for indicating the number or rate of revolutions of an engine etc.

revolutionize /rɛvə'luːʃ(ə)nʌɪz/ *v.tr.* (also **-ise**) introduce fundamental change to.

revolve /rɪ'vɒlv/ *v.* **1** *intr.* & *tr.* turn or cause to turn round, esp. on an axis; rotate. **2** *intr.* move in a circular orbit. **3** *tr.* ponder (a problem etc.) in the mind. **4** *intr.* (foll. by *around*) have as its chief concern; be centred upon (*his life revolves around his job*). [Middle English from Latin *revolvere* (as RE-, *volvere* 'roll')]

revolver /rɪ'vɒlvə/ *n.* a pistol with revolving chambers enabling several shots to be fired without reloading.

revolving credit *n.* credit that is automatically renewed as debts are paid off.

revolving door *n.* a door with usu. four partitions turning round a central axis.

revue /rɪ'vjuː/ *n.* a theatrical entertainment of a series of short usu. satirical sketches and songs. [French, = REVIEW *n.*]

revulsion /rɪ'vʌlʃ(ə)n/ *n.* **1** abhorrence; a sense of loathing. **2** a sudden violent change of feeling. **3** a sudden reaction in taste, fortune, trade, etc. **4** *Med.* counterirritation; the treatment of one disordered organ etc. by acting upon another. [French *revulsion* or Latin *revulsio* (as RE-, *vellere vuls-* 'pull')]

revulsive /rɪ'vʌlsɪv/ *adj.* & *n. Med.* ● *adj.* producing revulsion. ● *n.* a revulsive substance.

reward /rɪ'wɔːd/ *n.* & *v.* ● *n.* **1 a** a return or recompense for service or merit. **b** requital for good or evil; retribution. **2** a sum offered for the detection of a criminal, the restoration of lost property, etc. ● *v.tr.* give a reward to (a person) or for (a service etc.). □ **rewardless** *adj.* [Middle English from Anglo-French, Old Northern French *reward* = Old French *reguard* REGARD]

rewarding /rɪ'wɔːdɪŋ/ *adj.* (of an activity etc.) well worth doing; providing satisfaction. □ **rewardingly** *adv.*

rewarewa /'reɪwəreɪwə/ *n.* a tall red-flowered tree, *Knightia excelsa*, of New Zealand. [Maori]

rewash /riː'wɒʃ/ *v.tr.* wash again.

reweigh /riː'weɪ/ *v.tr.* weigh again.

rewind *v.* & *n.* ● *v.tr.* /riː'wʌɪnd/ (*past* and *past part.* **rewound**) wind (a film or tape etc.) back to the beginning. ● *n.* /'riːwʌɪnd/ **1** a mechanism for rewinding film, tape, etc. **2** the action or process of rewinding film, tape, etc. □ **rewinder** *n.*

rewire /riː'wʌɪə/ *v.tr.* provide (a building etc.) with new wiring. □ **rewirable** *adj.*

reword /riː'wəːd/ *v.tr.* change the wording of.

rework /riː'wəːk/ *v.tr.* revise; refashion, remake. □ **reworking** *n.*

rewound *past* and *past part.* of REWIND.

rewrap /riː'rap/ *v.tr.* (**rewrapped**, **rewrapping**) wrap again or differently.

rewrite *v.* & *n.* ● *v.tr.* /riːˈrʌɪt/ (*past* **rewrote**; *past part.* **rewritten**) write again or differently. ● *n.* /ˈriːrʌɪt/ **1** the act or an instance of rewriting. **2** a thing rewritten.

Rex /rɛks/ *n.* the reigning king (following a name or in the titles of lawsuits, e.g. *Rex v. Jones* the Crown versus Jones). [Latin]

Rexine /ˈrɛksiːn/ *n. Brit. propr.* an artificial leather used in upholstery, bookbinding, etc. [20th c.: origin unknown]

Reynard /ˈrɛnɑːd, ˈreɪ-/ *n.* a fox (esp. as a proper name in stories). [Middle English from Old French *Renart*, the name of a fox in the medieval fable *Roman de Renart*]

Reynolds number /ˈrɛn(ə)ldz/ *n. Physics* a quantity indicating the degree of turbulence of flow around an object, in a pipe, etc. [named after O. *Reynolds*, English physicist d. 1912]

Rf *symb. Chem.* the element rutherfordium.

r.f. *abbr.* radio frequency.

RFA *abbr.* (in the UK) Royal Fleet Auxiliary.

RFC *abbr.* **1** Rugby Football Club. **2** *hist.* Royal Flying Corps.

RGS *abbr.* Royal Geographical Society.

Rh *symb.* **1** *Chem.* the element rhodium. **2** *Med.* rhesus (factor).

r.h. *abbr.* right hand.

RHA *abbr.* (in the UK) Royal Horse Artillery.

rhabdomancy /ˈrabdəmansi/ *n.* the use of a divining rod, esp. for discovering subterranean water or mineral ore. [Greek *rhabdomanteia* from *rhabdos* 'rod': see -MANCY]

Rhadamanthine /radəˈmanθʌɪn/ *adj.* stern and incorruptible in judgement. [Latin *Rhadamanthus* from Greek *Rhadamanthos*, the name of a judge in the underworld]

Rhaeto-Romance /ˌriːtə(ʊ)rəʊˈmans/ *adj.* & *n.* (also **Rhaeto-Romanic** /-ˈmanɪk/) ● *adj.* of or in any of the Romance dialects of SE Switzerland and Tyrol, esp. Romansh and Ladin. ● *n.* any of these dialects. [Latin *Rhaetus* 'of Rhaetia', a Roman province in the Alps + ROMANCE]

rhapsode /ˈrapsəʊd/ *n. Gk Hist.* a usu. professional reciter of epic poems, esp. of Homer. [Greek *rhapsōidos*, from *rhaptō* 'stitch' + *ōidē* 'song, ODE']

rhapsodist /ˈrapsədɪst/ *n.* **1** a person who rhapsodizes. **2** *Gk Hist.* = RHAPSODE.

rhapsodize /ˈrapsədʌɪz/ *v.intr.* (also **-ise**) write rhapsodies or talk in a rhapsodic manner.

rhapsody /ˈrapsədi/ *n.* (*pl.* **-ies**) **1** an enthusiastic, ecstatic, or extravagant utterance or composition. **2** *Mus.* a piece of music in one extended movement, usu. emotional in character. **3** *Gk Hist.* an epic poem, or part of it, of a length for one recitation. □ **rhapsodic** /rapˈsɒdɪk/ *adj.* **rhapsodical** /rapˈsɒdɪk(ə)l/ *adj.* (in senses 1, 2). [Latin *rhapsodia* from Greek *rhapsōidia* (as RHAPSODE)]

rhatany /ˈratəni/ *n.* (*pl.* **-ies**) **1** a. S. American shrub, *Krameria trianda*, from which an astringent root extract is obtained. **2** the root of this. [modern Latin *rhatania* via Portuguese *ratanha*, Spanish *ratania* from Quechua *rataña*]

rhea /ˈriːə/ *n.* any of several S. American flightless birds of the family Rheidae, like but smaller than an ostrich. [modern Latin genus name from Latin and Greek *Rhea*, the name of the mother of Zeus]

rhebok /ˈriːbɒk/ *n.* (also **reebok**) a small southern African antelope, *Pelea capreolus*, with a long slender neck and short straight horns. [Dutch *reebok* 'roebuck']

Rhenish /ˈrɛnɪʃ/ *adj.* & *n.* ● *adj.* of the Rhine and the regions adjoining it. ● *n.* wine from this area. [Middle English *rynis*, *rynisch* etc. via Anglo-French *reneis*, Old French *r(a)inois* from Latin *Rhenanus*, from *Rhenus* 'Rhine']

rhenium /ˈriːnɪəm/ *n. Chem.* a rare metallic element of the manganese group, occurring naturally in molybdenum ores and used in the manufacture of superconducting alloys (symbol **Re**). [modern Latin from Latin *Rhenus* 'Rhine']

rheology /rɪˈɒlədʒi/ *n.* the science dealing with the flow and deformation of matter. □ **rheological** /-əˈlɒdʒɪk(ə)l/ *adj.* **rheologist** *n.* [Greek *rheos* 'stream' + -LOGY]

rheostat /ˈriːəstat/ *n. Electr.* an instrument used to control a current by varying the resistance. □ **rheostatic** /-ˈstatɪk/ *adj.* [Greek *rheos* 'stream' + -STAT]

rhesus /ˈriːsəs/ *n.* (in full **rhesus monkey**) a small catarrhine monkey, *Macaca mulatta*, common in N. India. [modern Latin, arbitrary use of Latin *Rhesus* from Greek *Rhēsos*, the name of a mythical king of Thrace]

rhesus baby *n.* an infant with a haemolytic disorder caused by the incompatibility of its own rhesus-positive blood with its mother's rhesus-negative blood.

rhesus factor *n.* an antigen occurring on the red blood cells of most humans and some other primates (as in the rhesus monkey, in which it was first observed).

rhesus-negative *adj.* lacking the rhesus factor.

rhesus-positive *adj.* having the rhesus factor.

rhetor /ˈriːtə/ *n.* **1** an ancient Greek or Roman teacher or professor of rhetoric. **2** usu. *derog.* an orator. [Middle English via Late Latin *rethor* and Latin *rhetor* from Greek *rhētōr*]

rhetoric /ˈrɛtərɪk/ *n.* **1** the art of effective or persuasive speaking or writing. **2** language designed to persuade or impress (often with an implication of insincerity or exaggeration etc.). [Middle English via Old French *rethorique* and Latin *rhetorica*, *-ice* from Greek *rhētorikē* (*tekhnē*) '(art) of rhetoric' (as RHETOR)]

rhetorical /rɪˈtɒrɪk(ə)l/ *adj.* **1** expressed with a view to persuasive or impressive effect; artificial or extravagant in language. **2** of the nature of rhetoric. **3 a** of or relating to the art of rhetoric. **b** given to rhetoric; oratorical. □ **rhetorically** *adv.* [Middle English via Latin *rhetoricus* from Greek *rhētorikos* (as RHETOR)]

rhetorical question *n.* a question asked not for information but to produce an effect, e.g. *who cares?* for *nobody cares*.

rhetorician /rɛtəˈrɪʃ(ə)n/ *n.* **1** an orator. **2** a teacher of rhetoric. **3** a rhetorical speaker or writer. [Middle English from Old French *rethoricien* (as RHETORICAL)]

rheum /ruːm/ *n.* a watery discharge from a mucous membrane, esp. of the eyes or nose. □ **rheumy** *adj.* [Middle English from Old French *reume*, ultimately via Greek *rheuma -atos* 'stream' from *rheō* 'flow']

rheumatic /rʊˈmatɪk/ *adj.* & *n.* ● *adj.* **1** of, relating to, or suffering from rheumatism. **2** producing or produced by rheumatism. ● *n.* a person suffering from rheumatism. □ **rheumatically** *adv.* **rheumaticky** *adj. colloq.* [Middle English via Old French *reumatique* or Latin *rheumaticus* from Greek *rheumatikos* (as RHEUM)]

rheumatic fever *n.* a non-infectious fever with inflammation and pain in the joints.

rheumatics /rʊˈmatɪks/ *n.pl.* (usu. treated as *sing.*; often prec. by *the*) *colloq.* rheumatism.

rheumatism /ˈruːmətɪz(ə)m/ *n.* any disease marked by inflammation and pain in the joints, muscles, or fibrous tissue, esp. rheumatoid arthritis. [French *rhumatisme* or Latin *rheumatismus* from Greek *rheumatismos*, via *rheumatizō* 'to snuffle' from *rheuma* 'stream']

rheumatoid /ˈruːmətɔɪd/ *adj.* having the character of rheumatism.

rheumatoid arthritis *n.* a chronic progressive disease causing inflammation and stiffening of the joints.

rheumatology /ruːməˈtɒlədʒi/ *n.* the study of rheumatic diseases. □ **rheumatological** /-təˈlɒdʒɪk(ə)l/ *adj.* **rheumatologist** *n.*

RHG *abbr.* (in the UK) Royal Horse Guards.

rhinal /ˈrʌɪn(ə)l/ *adj. Anat.* of a nostril or the nose. [Greek *rhis rhin-*: see RHINO-]

rhinestone /ˈrʌɪnstəʊn/ *n.* an imitation diamond. [*Rhine*, a river and region in Germany + STONE]

rhinitis /rʌɪˈnʌɪtɪs, rɪ-/ *n.* inflammation of the mucous membrane of the nose. [Greek *rhis rhinos* 'nose']

rhino /ˈrʌɪnəʊ/ *n.* (*pl.* **-os** or same) *colloq.* a rhinoceros. [abbreviation]

rhino- /ˈrʌɪnəʊ/ *comb. form Anat.* the nose. [Greek *rhis rhinos* 'nostril, nose']

rhinoceros /rʌɪˈnɒs(ə)rəs/ *n.* (*pl.* same or **rhinoceroses**) any of various large thick-skinned plant-eating ungulates of the family Rhinocerotidae of Africa and S. Asia, with one horn or in some cases two horns on the nose and plated or folded skin. □ **rhinocerotic** /rʌɪˌnɒsəˈrɒtɪk/ *adj.* [Middle English via Latin from Greek *rhinokerōs* (as RHINO-, *keras* 'horn')]

rhinoceros beetle *n.* a very large horned scarabaeid beetle of the subfamily Dynastinae.

rhinoceros bird *n.* = OX-PECKER.

rhinoceros horn *n.* a mass of keratinized fibres, reputed to have medicinal or aphrodisiac powers.

rhinopharyngeal /ˌrʌɪnəʊfəˈrɪn(d)ʒɪəl, -far(ə)nˈdʒiːəl/ *adj.* of or relating to the nose and pharynx.

rhinoplasty /ˈrʌɪnə(ʊ)plasti/ *n.* plastic surgery performed on the nose. □ **rhinoplastic** *adj.*

rhizo- /ˈrʌɪzəʊ/ *comb. form Bot.* a root. [Greek *rhiza* 'root']

rhizobium /rʌɪˈzəʊbɪəm/ *n.* a nitrogen-fixing soil bacterium of the genus *Rhizobium*, found esp. in the root nodules of leguminous plants. [modern Latin genus name, from RHIZO- + Greek *bios* 'life' + -IUM]

rhizocarp /ˈrʌɪzə(ʊ)kɑːp/ *n.* a plant with a perennial root but stems that wither. [RHIZO- + Greek *karpos* 'fruit']

rhizoid /ˈrʌɪzɔɪd/ *adj. & n. Bot.* ● *adj.* rootlike. ● *n.* a root-hair or filament in mosses, ferns, etc.

rhizome /ˈrʌɪzəʊm/ *n.* an underground rootlike stem bearing both roots and shoots. [Greek *rhizōma* from *rhizoō* 'take root' (as RHIZO-)]

rhizopod /ˈrʌɪzə(ʊ)pɒd/ *n.* any protozoan of the class Rhizopoda, having extensible pseudopodia, e.g. an amoeba. [modern Latin *Rhizopoda*, from RHIZO- + Greek *pous podos* 'foot']

rho /rəʊ/ *n.* the seventeenth letter of the Greek alphabet (Ρ, ρ). [Greek]

rhodamine /ˈrəʊdəmiːn/ *n. Chem.* any of various red synthetic dyes used to colour textiles. [RHODO- + AMINE]

Rhode Island Red /rəʊd/ *n.* an originally American breed of reddish-black domestic fowl. [*Rhode Island*, a state in the north-eastern US]

Rhodes Scholarship /rəʊdz/ *n.* any of several scholarships awarded annually and tenable at Oxford University by students from certain Commonwealth countries, South Africa, the United States, and Germany. □ **Rhodes Scholar** *n.* [named after Cecil *Rhodes*, British statesman (d. 1902), who founded them]

rhodium /ˈrəʊdɪəm/ *n. Chem.* a hard white metallic element of the platinum group, occurring naturally in platinum ores and used in making alloys and plating jewellery (symbol **Rh**). [Greek *rhodon* 'rose' (from the colour of the solution of its salts)]

rhodo- /ˈrəʊdəʊ/ *comb. form* esp. *Mineral. & Chem.* rose-coloured. [Greek *rhodon* 'rose']

rhodochrosite /rəʊdə(ʊ)ˈkrəʊsʌɪt/ *n.* a mineral form of manganese carbonate occurring in rose-red crystals. [Greek *rhodokhrous* 'rose-coloured']

rhododendron /rəʊdəˈdɛndr(ə)n/ *n.* a shrub of the genus *Rhododendron*, esp. an evergreen one, with large clusters of bell-shaped flowers. [Latin, = oleander, from Greek (as RHODO-, *dendron* 'tree')]

rhodopsin /rə(ʊ)ˈdɒpsɪn/ *n.* = VISUAL PURPLE. [Greek *rhodon* 'rose' + *opsis* 'sight']

rhodora /rə(ʊ)ˈdɔːrə/ *n.* a N. American pink-flowered shrub, *Rhododendron canadense.* [modern Latin *Rhodora* former genus name, from a Latin plant-name, from Greek *rhodon* 'rose']

rhomb /rɒm(b)/ *n.* = RHOMBUS. □ **rhombic** *adj.* [French *rhombe* or Latin *rhombus*]

rhombencephalon /rɒmbɛnˈsɛf(ə)lɒn, -ˈkɛf-/ *n. Anat.* = HINDBRAIN. [RHOMB + ENCEPHALON]

rhombi *pl.* of RHOMBUS.

rhombohedron /rɒmbə(ʊ)ˈhiːdr(ə)n, -ˈhɛd-/ *n.* (*pl.* **rhombohedra** /-drə/ or **rhombohedrons**) **1** a solid bounded by six equal rhombuses. **2** a crystal in this form. □ **rhombohedral** *adj.* [RHOMBUS, on the pattern of *polyhedron* etc.]

rhomboid /ˈrɒmbɔɪd/ *adj. & n.* ● *adj.* (also **rhomboidal** /-ˈbɔɪd(ə)l/) having or nearly having the shape of a rhombus. ● *n.* a quadrilateral of which only the opposite sides and angles are equal. [French *rhomboïde* or Late Latin *rhomboides* from Greek *rhomboeidēs* (as RHOMB)]

rhomboideus /rɒmˈbɔɪdɪəs/ *n.* (*pl.* **rhomboidei** /-dɪʌɪ/) *Anat.* a muscle connecting the shoulder blade to the vertebrae. [modern Latin *rhomboideus* RHOMBOID]

rhombus /ˈrɒmbəs/ *n.* (*pl.* **rhombuses** or **rhombi** /-bʌɪ/) *Geom.* a parallelogram with oblique angles and equal sides. [Latin from Greek *rhombos*]

rhotic /ˈrəʊtɪk/ *adj.* of or relating to a dialect or variety of English in which *r* is pronounced before a consonant (as in *hard*) and at the ends of words (as in *far*). [Greek *rhot-*, stem of RHO + -IC]

RHS *abbr.* **1** Royal Historical Society. **2** Royal Horticultural Society. **3** Royal Humane Society.

rhubarb /ˈruːbɑːb/ *n.* **1 a** any of various plants of the genus *Rheum*, esp. *R. rhaponticum*, producing long fleshy dark red leaf-stalks used cooked as food. **b** the leaf-stalks of this. **2 a** a root of a Chinese and Tibetan plant of the genus *Rheum*. **b** a purgative made from this. **3** *Brit.* **a** *colloq.* a murmurous conversation or noise, esp. the repetition of the word 'rhubarb' by crowd actors. **b** *slang* nonsense; worthless stuff. **4** *US slang* a heated dispute. [Middle English from Old French *r(e)ubarbe*, shortening of medieval Latin *r(h)eubarbarum*, alteration (by association with Greek *rhēon* 'rhubarb') of *rhabarbarum* 'foreign rhubarb', ultimately from Greek *rha* (also meaning 'rhubarb') + *barbaros* 'foreign']

rhumb /rʌm/ *n. Naut.* **1** any of the 32 points of the compass. **2** the angle between two successive compass points. **3** (in full **rhumb-line**) **a** a line cutting all meridians at the same angle. **b** the line followed by a ship sailing in a fixed direction. [French *rumb*, probably from Dutch *ruim* 'room', associated with Latin *rhombus*: see RHOMBUS]

rhumba var. of RUMBA.

rhyme /rʌɪm/ *n. & v.* (also *archaic* **rime**) ● *n.* **1** identity of sound between words or the endings of words, esp. in verse. **2** (in *sing.* or *pl.*) verse having rhymes. **3 a** the use of rhyme. **b** a poem having rhymes. **4** a word providing a rhyme. ● *v.* **1** *intr.* **a** (of words or lines) produce a rhyme. **b** (foll. by *with*) act as a rhyme (with another). **2** *intr.* make or write rhymes; versify. **3** *tr.* put or make (a story etc.) into rhyme. **4** *tr.* (foll. by *with*) treat (a word) as rhyming with another. □ **without rhyme or reason** lacking discernible sense or logic. □ **rhymeless** *adj.* **rhymer** *n.* **rhymist** *n.* [Middle English *rime* via Old French *rime*, and medieval Latin *rithmus*, *rythmus* from Latin, from Greek *rhuthmos* RHYTHM]

rhymester /ˈrʌɪmstə/ *n.* a writer of (esp. simple) rhymes.

rhyming slang *n.* (esp. Cockney) slang that replaces words by rhyming words or phrases, e.g. *stairs* by *apples and pears*, often with the rhyming element omitted (as in TITFER).

rhyolite /ˈrʌɪəlʌɪt/ *n.* a fine-grained volcanic rock of granitic composition. [German *Rhyolit*, from Greek *rhuax* 'lava-stream' + *lithos* 'stone']

rhythm /ˈrɪð(ə)m/ *n.* **1** a measured flow of words and phrases in verse or prose determined by various relations of long and short or accented and unaccented syllables. **2 a** the aspect of musical composition concerned with periodical accent and the duration of notes. **b** a particular type of pattern formed by this (*samba rhythm*). **3** *Physiol.* movement with a regular succession of strong and weak elements. **4** a regularly recurring pattern of events or actions. **5** a sense of rhythm. **6** *Art* a harmonious correlation of parts. □ **rhythmless** *adj.* [French *rhythme* or Latin *rhythmus* from Greek *rhuthmos*, related to *rheō* 'flow']

rhythm and blues *n.* popular music with a blues theme and a strong rhythm.

rhythmic /ˈrɪðmɪk/ *adj.* (also **rhythmical**) **1** relating to or characterized by rhythm. **2** regularly occurring. □ **rhythmically** *adv.* [French *rhythmique* or Latin *rhythmicus* (as RHYTHM)]

rhythmic gymnastics *n.pl.* (also treated as *sing.*) a form of gymnastics emphasing dancelike rhythmic routines, often with ribbons, hoops, etc.

rhythmicity /rɪðˈmɪsɪti/ *n.* **1** rhythmical quality or character. **2** the capacity for maintaining a rhythm.

rhythm method *n.* birth control by avoiding sexual intercourse when ovulation is likely to occur.

rhythm section *n.* the part of a dance band or jazz band mainly supplying rhythm, usu. consisting of piano or guitar etc., bass, and drums.

RI *abbr.* **1** King and Emperor. **2** Queen and Empress. **3** *US* Rhode Island (also in official postal use). **4** Royal Institute or Institution. [sense 1 from Latin *rex et imperator*: sense 2 from Latin *regina et imperatrix*]

RIA *abbr.* Royal Irish Academy.

ria /ˈriːə/ *n. Geog.* a long narrow inlet formed by the partial submergence of a river valley. [Spanish *ría* 'estuary']

rial /ˈriːɑːl/ *n.* (also **riyal**) the chief monetary unit of Iran, equal to 100 dinars. [Persian, via Arabic *riyal* from Spanish *real* ROYAL]

rib /rɪb/ *n. & v.* ● *n.* **1** each of the curved bones articulated in pairs to the spine and protecting the thoracic cavity and its organs. **2** a joint of meat from this part of an animal. **3** a ridge or long raised piece often of stronger or thicker material across a surface or through a structure serving to support or strengthen it. **4** any of a ship's transverse curved timbers forming the framework of the hull. **5** *Knitting* a combination of plain and purl stitches producing a ribbed somewhat elastic fabric. **6** each of the hinged rods supporting the fabric of an umbrella. **7** a vein of a leaf or an insect's wing. **8** *Aeron.* a structural member in an aerofoil. ● *v.tr.* (**ribbed**, **ribbing**) **1** provide with ribs; act as the ribs of. **2** *colloq.* make fun of; tease. **3** mark with ridges. **4** plough with spaces between the furrows. □ **ribless** *adj.* [Old English *rib*, *ribb*, from Germanic]

RIBA *abbr.* Royal Institute of British Architects.

ribald /ˈrɪb(ə)ld/ *adj. & n.* ● *adj.* (of language or its user) coarsely or disrespectfully humorous; scurrilous. ● *n.* a user of ribald language. [Middle English (earlier sense 'low-born retainer') via Old French *ribau(l)d*, from *riber* 'pursue licentious pleasures', from Germanic]

ribaldry /ˈrɪb(ə)ldri/ *n.* ribald talk or behaviour.

riband /ˈrɪb(ə)nd/ *n.* a ribbon. [Middle English from Old French *riban*, probably from a Germanic compound of BAND[1]]

ribbed /rɪbd/ *adj.* having ribs or riblike markings.

ribbing /ˈrɪbɪŋ/ *n.* **1** ribs or a riblike structure, esp. a band of knitting in rib. **2** *colloq.* the act or an instance of teasing.

ribbon /ˈrɪb(ə)n/ *n.* **1 a** a narrow strip or band of fabric, used esp. for trimming or decoration. **b** material in this form. **2** a ribbon of a special colour etc. worn to indicate some honour or membership of a sports team etc. **3** a long narrow strip of anything, e.g. impregnated material forming the inking agent in a typewriter. **4** (in *pl.*) ragged strips (*torn to ribbons*). □ **ribboned** *adj.* [variant of RIBAND]

ribbon development *n. Brit.* the building of houses along a main road, usu. one leading out of a town or village.

ribbonfish /ˈrɪb(ə)nfɪʃ/ *n.* (*pl.* usu. same) any of various long slender fishes with a flattened body, esp. of the families Trachipteridae and Regalecidae.

ribbon worm *n.* a nemertean.

ribcage /ˈrɪbkeɪdʒ/ *n.* the wall of bones formed by the ribs round the chest.

riboflavin /rʌɪbə(ʊ)ˈfleɪvɪn/ *n.* (also **riboflavine** /-viːn/) a vitamin of the B complex, found in liver, milk, and eggs, essential for energy production. Also called *vitamin* B_2. [RIBOSE + Latin *flavus* 'yellow']

ribonucleic acid /ˌrʌɪbənjuːˈkleɪɪk, -ˈkliːɪk/ *n.* a nucleic acid yielding ribose on hydrolysis, present in living cells, esp. in ribosomes where it is involved in protein synthesis (abbr.: **RNA**). [RIBOSE + NUCLEIC ACID]

ribose /ˈrʌɪbəʊz, -s/ *n.* a sugar found in many nucleosides and in several vitamins and enzymes. [German, alteration of *Arabinose*, a related sugar]

ribosome /ˈrʌɪbəsəʊm/ *n. Biochem.* each of the minute particles consisting of RNA and associated proteins found in the cytoplasm of living cells, concerned with the synthesis of proteins. □ **ribosomal** *adj.* [RIBONUCLEIC ACID + -SOME[3]]

rib-tickler *n.* something amusing; a joke.

ribwort /ˈrɪbwəːt/ *n.* a kind of plantain (see PLANTAIN[1]) with long narrow ribbed leaves.

Ricardian /rɪˈkɑːdɪən/ *adj. & n.* ● *adj.* **1** of or relating to the time of any of three kings of England, Richard I, II, and III. **2** of or holding the view that Richard III (reigned 1483–5) was unjustly misrepresented by later writers. ● *n.* a supporter of Richard III. [medieval Latin *Ricardus* 'Richard' + -IAN]

rice /rʌɪs/ *n. & v.* ● *n.* **1** a swamp grass, *Oryza sativa*, cultivated in marshes, esp. in Asia. **2** the grains of this, used as cereal food. ● *v.tr. US* sieve (cooked potatoes etc.) into thin strings. □ **ricer** *n.* [Middle English *rys* via Old French *ris* from Italian *riso*, ultimately from Greek *oruza*, of oriental origin]

rice-bowl *n.* an area producing much rice.

rice-paper *n.* edible paper made from the pith of an oriental tree and used for painting and in cookery.

ricercar /riːtʃəˈkɑː, ˈriːtʃəkɑː/ *n.* (also **ricercare** /-ˈkɑːreɪ/) an elaborate contrapuntal instrumental composition in fugal or canonic style, esp. of the 16th–18th c. [Italian, = seek out]

rich /rɪtʃ/ *adj.* **1** having much wealth. **2** (often foll. by *in*, *with*) splendid, costly, elaborate (*rich tapestries*; *rich with lace*). **3** valuable (*rich offerings*). **4** copious, abundant, ample (*a rich harvest*; *a rich supply of ideas*). **5** (often foll. by *in*, *with*) (of soil or a region etc.) abounding in natural resources or means of production; fertile (*rich in nutrients*; *rich with vines*). **6** (of food or diet) containing much fat or spice etc. **7** (of the mixture in an internal-combustion engine) containing a high proportion of fuel. **8** (of colour or sound or smell) mellow and deep, strong and full. **9 a** (of an incident or assertion etc.) highly amusing or ludicrous; outrageous. **b** (of humour) earthy. □ **richen** *v.intr. & tr.* **richness** *n.* [Old English *rīce* via Germanic from Celtic, related to Latin *rex* 'king': reinforced in Middle English from Old French *riche* 'rich, powerful', of Germanic origin]

riches /ˈrɪtʃɪz/ *n.pl.* abundant means; valuable possessions. [Middle English *richesse* from Old French *richeise*, from *riche* RICH, taken as pl.]

richly /ˈrɪtʃli/ *adv.* **1** in a rich way. **2** fully, thoroughly (*richly deserves success*).

Richter scale /ˈrɪktə/ *n.* a logarithmic scale of 0 to 10 for representing the strength of an earthquake. [named after C. F. *Richter*, American seismologist d. 1985]

ricin /ˈrʌɪsɪn, ˈrɪsɪn/ *n.* a toxic substance obtained from castor oil beans and causing gastroenteritis, jaundice, and heart failure. [modern Latin *Ricinus communis*, the castor oil plant]

rick[1] /rɪk/ *n. & v.* ● *n.* a stack of hay, corn, etc., built into a regular shape and usu. thatched. ● *v.tr.* form into a rick or ricks. [Old English *hrēac*, of unknown origin]

rick[2] /rɪk/ *n. & v. Brit.* (also **wrick**) ● *n.* a slight sprain or strain. ● *v.tr.* sprain or strain slightly. [Middle English *wricke* from Middle Low German *wricken* 'move about, sprain']

rickets /'rɪkɪts/ *n.* (treated as *sing.* or *pl.*) a disease of children with softening of the bones (esp. the spine) and bow-legs, caused by a deficiency of vitamin D. [17th c.: origin uncertain, but associated by medical writers with Greek *rhakhitis* RACHITIS]

rickettsia /rɪ'kɛtsɪə/ *n.* a parasitic micro-organism of the genus *Rickettsia* causing typhus and other febrile diseases. □ **rickettsial** *adj.* [modern Latin, named after H. T. *Ricketts*, American pathologist d. 1910]

rickety /'rɪkɪti/ *adj.* **1 a** insecure or shaky in construction; likely to collapse. **b** feeble. **2 a** suffering from rickets. **b** resembling or of the nature of rickets. □ **ricketiness** *n.* [RICKETS + -Y[1]]

rickey /'rɪki/ *n.* (*pl.* **-eys**) a drink of spirit (esp. gin), lime juice, etc. [19th c.: probably from the surname *Rickey*]

rickrack var. of RICRAC.

rickshaw /'rɪkʃɔː/ *n.* (also **ricksha** /-ʃə/) a light two-wheeled hooded vehicle drawn by one or more persons. [abbreviation of *jinricksha, jinrikshaw* from Japanese *jinrikisha*, from *jin* 'person' + *riki* 'power' + *sha* 'vehicle']

ricochet /'rɪkəʃeɪ, -ʃɛt/ *n. & v.* ● *n.* **1** the action of a projectile, esp. a shell or bullet, in rebounding off a surface. **2** a hit made after this. ● *v.intr.* (**ricocheted** /-ʃeɪd/; **ricocheting** /-ʃeɪɪŋ/ or **ricochetted** /-ʃɛtɪd/; **ricochetting** /-ʃɛtɪŋ/) (of a projectile) rebound one or more times from a surface. [French, of unknown origin]

ricotta /rɪ'kɒtə/ *n.* a soft Italian cheese. [Italian, = recooked, from Latin *recoquere* (as RE-, *coquere* 'cook')]

ricrac /'rɪkrak/ *n.* (also **rickrack**) a zigzag braided trimming for garments. [reduplication of RACK[1]]

RICS *abbr.* Royal Institution of Chartered Surveyors.

rictus /'rɪktəs/ *n.* **1** *Anat. & Zool.* the expanse or gape of a mouth or beak. **2** a fixed grimace or grin. □ **rictal** *adj.* [Latin, = open mouth, from *ringi rict-* 'to gape']

rid /rɪd/ *v.tr.* (**ridding**; *past* and *past part.* **rid** or *archaic* **ridded**) (foll. by *of*) make (a person or place) free of something unwanted. □ **be** (or **get**) **rid of** be freed or relieved of (something unwanted); dispose of. [earlier = clear (land etc.): Middle English from Old Norse *rythja*]

riddance /'rɪd(ə)ns/ *n.* the act of getting rid of something. □ **good riddance** welcome relief from an unwanted person or thing.

ridden *past part.* of RIDE.

riddle[1] /'rɪd(ə)l/ *n. & v.* ● *n.* **1** a question or statement testing ingenuity in divining its answer or meaning. **2** a puzzling fact or thing or person. ● *v.* **1** *intr.* speak in or propound riddles. **2** *tr.* solve or explain (a riddle). □ **riddler** *n.* [Old English *rǣdels, rǣdelse* 'opinion, riddle', related to READ]

riddle[2] /'rɪd(ə)l/ *v. & n.* ● *v.tr.* (usu. foll. by *with*) **1** make many holes in, esp. with gunshot. **2** (in *passive*) fill; spread through; permeate (*was riddled with errors*). **3** pass through a riddle. ● *n.* a coarse sieve. [Old English *hriddel*, earlier *hrīder*: cf. *hrīdrian* 'sift']

riddling /'rɪdlɪŋ/ *adj.* expressed in riddles; puzzling. □ **riddlingly** *adv.*

ride /rʌɪd/ *v. & n.* ● *v.* (*past* **rode** /rəʊd/; *past part.* **ridden** /'rɪd(ə)n/) **1** *tr.* travel or be carried on (a bicycle etc.) or esp. *N. Amer.* in (a vehicle). **2** *intr.* (often foll. by *on, in*) travel or be conveyed (on a bicycle or in a vehicle). **3** *tr.* sit on and control or be carried by (a horse etc.). **4** *intr.* (often foll. by *on*) be carried (on a horse etc.). **5** *tr.* be carried or supported by (*the ship rides the waves*). **6** *tr.* **a** traverse on horseback etc., ride over or through (*ride 50 miles; rode the prairie*). **b** compete or take part in on horseback etc. (*rode a good race*). **7** *intr.* **a** lie at anchor; float buoyantly. **b** (of the moon) seem to float. **8** *intr.* (foll. by *in, on*) rest in or on while moving. **9** *tr.* yield to (a blow) so as to reduce its impact. **10** *tr.* give a ride to; cause to ride (*rode the child on his back*). **11** *tr.* (of a rider) cause (a horse etc.) to move forward (*rode their horses at the fence*). **12** *tr.* **a** (in *passive*; foll. by *by, with*) be oppressed or dominated by; be infested with (*was ridden with guilt*). **b** (in *comb.* as **ridden** *adj.*) infested or afflicted (*a rat-ridden cellar*). **13** *intr.* (of a thing normally level or even) project or overlap. **14** *tr. coarse slang* mount (a female) in copulation. **15** *tr. US* annoy or seek to annoy. ● *n.* **1** an act or period of travel in a vehicle. **2** a spell of riding on a horse, bicycle, person's back, etc. **3** *Brit.* a path (esp. through woods) for riding on. **4** the quality of sensations when riding (*gives a bumpy ride*). **5** a roundabout, roller-coaster, etc., ridden at an amusement park or fairground. □ **let a thing ride** leave it alone; let it take its natural course. **ride again** reappear, esp. unexpectedly and reinvigorated. **ride down** overtake or trample on horseback. **ride for a fall** act recklessly risking defeat or failure. **ride herd on** see HERD. **ride high** be elated or successful. **ride out** come safely through (a storm etc., or a danger or difficulty). **ride roughshod over** see ROUGHSHOD. **ride shotgun** esp. *N. Amer.* **1** travel as a guard in the seat next to the driver of a vehicle. **2** ride in the passenger seat of a vehicle. **3** act as a protector. **ride to hounds** see HOUND. **ride up** (of a garment, carpet, etc.) work or move out of its proper position. **take for a ride** *colloq.* hoax or deceive. □ **rideable** *adj.* (also **ridable**). [Old English *rīdan*]

ride-off *n.* (in a riding competition) a round held to resolve a tie or determine qualifiers for a later stage.

ride-on *attrib.adj.* (esp. of a lawnmower) on which one rides while operating it.

rider /'rʌɪdə/ *n.* **1** a person who rides (esp. a horse). **2 a** an additional clause amending or supplementing a document. **b** *Brit. Parl.* an addition or amendment to a bill at its third reading. **c** a corollary. **d** *Brit.* a recommendation etc. added to a judicial verdict. **3** a piece in a machine etc. that surmounts or bridges or works on or over others. **4** (in *pl.*) an additional set of timbers or iron plates strengthening a ship's frame. □ **riderless** *adj.* [Old English *rīdere* (as RIDE)]

ridge /rɪdʒ/ *n. & v.* ● *n.* **1** the line of the junction of two surfaces sloping upwards towards each other (*the ridge of a roof*). **2** a long narrow hilltop, mountain range, or watershed. **3** any narrow elevation across a surface. **4** *Meteorol.* an elongated region of high barometric pressure. **5** a raised strip of arable land, usu. one of a set separated by furrows. **6** a raised hotbed for melons etc. ● *v.* **1** *tr.* mark with ridges. **2** *tr.* break up (land) into ridges. **3** *tr.* plant (cucumbers etc.) in ridges. **4** *tr. & intr.* gather into ridges. □ **ridgy** *adj.* [Old English *hrycg*, from Germanic]

ridge piece *n.* (also **ridge tree**) a beam along the ridge of a roof.

ridge pole *n.* **1** the horizontal pole of a long tent. **2** = RIDGE PIECE.

ridge tile *n.* a tile used in making a roof-ridge.

ridgeway /'rɪdʒweɪ/ *n.* a road or track along a ridge.

ridicule /'rɪdɪkjuːl/ *n. & v.* ● *n.* derision or mockery. ● *v.tr.* make fun of; subject to ridicule; laugh at. [French, or from Latin *ridiculum*, neut. of *ridiculus* 'laughable', from *ridēre* 'laugh']

ridiculous /rɪ'dɪkjʊləs/ *adj.* **1** deserving or inviting ridicule. **2** unreasonable, absurd. □ **ridiculously** *adv.* **ridiculousness** *n.* [Latin *ridiculosus* (as RIDICULE)]

riding[1] /'rʌɪdɪŋ/ *n.* **1** in senses of RIDE *v.* **2** the practice or skill of riders of horses. **3** = RIDE *n.* 3.

riding[2] /'rʌɪdɪŋ/ *n.* **1** each of three former administrative divisions (**East Riding, North Riding, West Riding**) of Yorkshire. **2** an electoral division of Canada. [Old English *thriding* (unrecorded) from Old Norse *thrithjungr* 'third part', from *thrithi* THIRD: *th*- was lost owing to the preceding *-t* or *-th* of *east* etc.]

riding habit see HABIT *n.* 6b.

riding light *n.* (also **riding lamp**) a light shown by a ship at anchor.

riding school *n.* an establishment teaching skills in horsemanship.

Riesling /'ri:zlɪŋ, -slɪŋ/ *n.* **1** a kind of dry white wine produced in Germany, Austria, and elsewhere. **2** the variety of grape from which this is produced. [German]

rife /rʌɪf/ *predic.adj.* **1** of common occurrence; widespread. **2** (foll. by *with*) abounding in; teeming with. □ **rifeness** *n.* [Old English *rȳfe*, probably from Old Norse *rífr* 'acceptable', from *reifa* 'enrich', *reifr* 'cheerful']

riff /rɪf/ *n. & v.* ● *n.* a short repeated phrase in jazz etc. ● *v.intr.* play riffs. [20th c.: abbreviation of RIFFLE *n.*]

riffle /'rɪf(ə)l/ *v. & n.* ● *v.* **1** *tr.* **a** turn (pages) in quick succession. **b** shuffle (playing cards) esp. by flexing and combining the two halves of a pack. **2** *intr.* (often foll. by *through*) leaf quickly (through pages). ● *n.* **1** the act or an instance of riffling. **2** (in gold-washing) a groove or slat set in a trough or sluice to catch gold particles. **3** *N. Amer.* **a** a shallow part of a stream where the water flows brokenly. **b** a patch of waves or ripples on water. [perhaps a variant of RUFFLE]

riff-raff /'rɪfraf/ *n.* (often prec. by *the*) rabble; disreputable or undesirable persons. [Middle English *riff and raff* from Old French *rif et raf*: cf. RAFFLE[2]]

rifle[1] /'rʌɪf(ə)l/ *n. & v.* ● *n.* **1** a gun with a long rifled barrel, esp. one fired from shoulder level. **2** (in *pl.*) riflemen. ● *v.tr.* make spiral grooves in (a gun or its barrel or bore) to make a bullet spin. [Old French *rifler* 'graze, scratch', from Germanic]

rifle[2] /'rʌɪf(ə)l/ *v.* **1** *intr.* (foll. by *through*) search through. **2** *tr.* search and rob, esp. of all that can be found. **3** *tr.* carry off as booty. [Middle English via Old French *rifler* 'graze, scratch, plunder' from Old Dutch *riffelen*]

rifle bird *n.* any bird of paradise of the genus *Ptiloris*, with mainly velvety-black plumage.

rifleman /'rʌɪf(ə)lmən/ *n.* (*pl.* **-men**) **1** a soldier armed with a rifle. **2** a small yellow and green New Zealand bird, *Acanthisitta chloris*.

rifle range *n.* a place for rifle practice.

rifle shot *n.* **1** the distance coverable by a shot from a rifle. **2** a shot fired with a rifle.

rifling /'rʌɪflɪŋ/ *n.* the arrangement of grooves on the inside of a gun's barrel.

rift /rɪft/ *n. & v.* ● *n.* **1 a** a crack or split in an object. **b** an opening in a cloud etc. **2** a cleft or fissure in earth or rock. **3** a disagreement; a breach in friendly relations. ● *v.tr.* tear or burst apart. □ **riftless** *adj.* [Middle English, of Scandinavian origin]

rift valley *n.* a steep-sided valley formed by subsidence of the earth's crust between nearly parallel faults.

rig[1] /rɪg/ *v. & n.* ● *v.tr.* (**rigged**, **rigging**) **1 a** provide (a sailing ship) with sails, rigging, etc. **b** prepare ready for sailing. **2** (often foll. by *out*, *up*) fit with clothes or other equipment. **3** (foll. by *up*) set up hastily or as a makeshift. **4** assemble and adjust the parts of (an aircraft). ● *n.* **1** the arrangement of masts, sails, rigging, etc., of a sailing ship. **2** equipment for a special purpose, e.g. a radio transmitter or fishing tackle. **3** = OIL RIG, DRILLING RIG. **4** a person's or thing's look as determined by clothing, equipment, etc., esp. uniform. **5** esp. *N. Amer. & Austral.* a lorry or truck; a semi-trailer. □ **in full rig** *colloq.* smartly or ceremonially dressed. □ **rigged** *adj.* (also in *comb.*). [Middle English, perhaps of Scandinavian origin: cf. Norwegian *rigga* 'bind or wrap up']

rig[2] /rɪg/ *v. & n.* ● *v.tr.* (**rigged**, **rigging**) manage or conduct fraudulently (*they rigged the election*). ● *n.* **1** a trick or dodge. **2** a way of swindling. □ **rig the market** cause an artificial rise or fall in prices. □ **rigger** *n.* [18th c.: origin unknown]

rigadoon /rɪgə'du:n/ *n.* **1** a lively dance in duple or quadruple time for two persons. **2** the music for this. [French *rigodon*, *rigaudon*, perhaps named after its inventor, said to be a dancing master called *Rigaud*]

rigger /'rɪgə/ *n.* **1 a** a person who rigs or who arranges rigging. **b** a person who erects and maintains scaffolding, lifting tackle, etc. **2** *Rowing* = OUTRIGGER 5a. **3** a ship rigged in a specified way. **4** a worker on an oil rig.

rigging /'rɪgɪŋ/ *n.* **1** a ship's spars, ropes, etc., supporting and controlling the sails. **2** the ropes and wires supporting the structure of an airship or biplane.

right /rʌɪt/ *adj., n., v., adv., & int.* (opp. LEFT[1]) ● *adj.* **1** (of conduct etc.) just, morally or socially correct (*it is only right to tell you*; *I want to do the right thing*). **2** true, correct; not mistaken (*the right time*; *you were right about the weather*). **3** less wrong or not wrong (*which is the right way to town?*). **4** more or most suitable or preferable (*the right person for the job*; *along the right lines*). **5** in a sound or normal condition; physically or mentally healthy; satisfactory (*the engine doesn't sound right*). **6 a** on or towards the side of the human body which corresponds to the position of east if one regards oneself as facing north. **b** on or towards that part of an object which is analogous to a person's right side or (with opposite sense) which is nearer to a spectator's right hand. **7** esp. *Brit. colloq.* or *archaic* real; properly so called (*made a right mess of it*; *a right royal welcome*). **8** (also **Right**) *Polit.* of the Right. ● *n.* **1** that which is morally or socially correct or just; fair treatment (often in *pl.*: *the rights and wrongs of the case*). **2** (often foll. by *to*, or *to* + infin.) a justification or fair claim (*has no right to speak like that*). **3** a thing one may legally or morally claim; the state of being entitled to a privilege or immunity or authority to act (*a right of reply*; *human rights*). **4** the right-hand part or region or direction. **5** *Boxing* **a** the right hand. **b** a blow with this. **6** (often **Right**) *Polit.* **a** a group or section favouring conservatism (originally the more conservative section of a continental legislature, seated on the president's right). **b** such conservatives collectively. **7** the side of a stage which is to the right of a person facing the audience. **8** (esp. in marching) the right foot. **9** the right wing of an army. ● *v.tr.* **1** (often *refl.*) restore to a proper or straight or vertical position. **2 a** correct (mistakes etc.); set in order. **b** avenge (a wrong or a wronged person); make reparation for or to. **c** vindicate, justify, rehabilitate. ● *adv.* **1** straight (*go right on*). **2** *colloq.* immediately; without delay (*I'll be right back*; *do it right now*). **3 a** (foll. by *to*, *round*, *through*, etc.) all the way (*sank right to the bottom*; *ran right round the block*). **b** (foll. by *off*, *out*, etc.) completely (*came right off its hinges*; *am right out of butter*). **4** exactly, quite (*right in the middle*). **5** justly, properly, correctly, truly, satisfactorily (*did not act right*; *not holding it right*; *if I remember right*). **6** on or to the right side. **7** *archaic* very; to the full (*am right glad to hear it*; *dined right royally*). ● *int. colloq.* expressing agreement or assent. □ **as right as rain** perfectly sound and healthy. **at right angles** placed to form a right angle. **by right** (or **rights**) if right were done. **do right by** act dutifully towards (a person). **in one's own right** through one's own position or effort etc. **in the right** having justice or truth on one's side. **in one's right mind** sane; competent to think and act. **of** (or **as of**) **right** having legal or moral etc. entitlement. **put** (or **set**) **right 1** restore to order, health, etc. **2** correct the mistaken impression etc. of (a person). **put** (or **set**) **to rights** make correct or well ordered. **right and left** (or **right, left, and centre**) on all sides. **right away** (or **off**) immediately. **right oh!** (or **ho!**) = RIGHTO. **right on!** *slang* an expression of strong approval or encouragement (cf. RIGHT-ON). **a right one** *Brit. colloq.* a silly or foolish person. **right you are!** *colloq.* an exclamation of assent. **she's** (or **she'll be**) **right** *Austral. colloq.* that will be all right. **too right** *colloq.* an expression of agreement. **within one's rights** not exceeding one's authority or entitlement. □ **rightable** *adj.* **righter** *n.* **rightish** *adj.* **rightless** *adj.* **rightlessness** *n.* **rightness** *n.* [Old English *riht* (adj.), *rihtan* (v.), *rihte* (adv.)]

right about *n.* (also **right about-face** or *Brit.* **right about-turn**) **1** esp. *Mil.* a right turn continued to face the rear. **2** a reversal of policy. **3** a hasty retreat.

right angle *n.* an angle of 90°, as formed by dividing a circle into quarters. ◻ **right-angled** *adj.*

right arm *n.* one's most reliable helper.

right ascension *n. Astron.* longitude measured along the celestial equator.

right-back *n.* (in football, hockey, etc.) a back who plays primarily on the right of the pitch.

right bank *n.* the bank of a river on the right facing downstream.

right bower see BOWER[3].

righten /ˈrʌɪt(ə)n/ *v.tr.* make right or correct.

righteous /ˈrʌɪtʃəs/ *adj.* (of a person or conduct) morally right; virtuous, law-abiding. ◻ **righteously** *adv.* **righteousness** *n.* [Old English *rihtwīs* (as RIGHT *n.* + -WISE or RIGHT *adj.* + WISE[2]), assimilated to *bounteous* etc.]

right field *n. Baseball* the part of the outfield to the right of the batter when facing the pitcher.

right-footed *adj.* **1** using the right foot by preference as more serviceable than the left. **2** (of a kick etc.) done or made with the right foot.

rightful /ˈrʌɪtfʊl, -f(ə)l/ *adj.* **1 a** (of a person) legitimately entitled to (a position etc.) (*the rightful heir*). **b** (of status or property etc.) that one is entitled to. **2** (of an action etc.) equitable, fair. ◻ **rightfully** *adv.* **rightfulness** *n.* [Old English *rihtful* (as RIGHT *n.*)]

right-hand *adj.* **1** on or towards the right side of a person or thing (*right-hand drive*). **2** done with the right hand (*right-hand blow*). **3** (of a screw) = RIGHT-HANDED 4b.

right hand *n.* **1** = RIGHT-HAND MAN. **2** the most important position next to a person (*stand at the President's right hand*).

right-handed *adj.* **1** using the right hand by preference as more serviceable than the left. **2** (of a tool etc.) made to be used with the right hand. **3** (of a blow) struck with the right hand. **4 a** turning to the right; towards the right. **b** (of a screw) advanced by turning to the right (clockwise). ◻ **right-handedly** *adv.* **right-handedness** *n.*

right-hander *n.* **1** a right-handed person. **2** a right-handed blow.

right-hand man *n.* an indispensable or chief assistant.

Right Honourable *n. Brit.* a title given to certain high officials, e.g. Privy Counsellors.

rightism /ˈrʌɪtɪz(ə)m/ *n. Polit.* the principles or policy of the right. ◻ **rightist** *n. & adj.*

rightly /ˈrʌɪtli/ *adv.* justly, properly, correctly, justifiably.

right-minded *adj.* having sound views and principles.

rightmost /ˈrʌɪtməʊst/ *adj.* furthest to the right.

righto /ˈrʌɪtəʊ, rʌɪtˈəʊ/ *int.* (also **righty-ho** /rʌɪtɪˈhəʊ/) *Brit. colloq.* expressing agreement or assent.

right of abode *n. Brit.* a person's right to take up residence or remain resident in a country.

right of common see COMMON *n.* 4.

right of primogeniture see PRIMOGENITURE 2.

right of search *n.* a belligerent's right to stop a neutral vessel and search it for prohibited goods.

right of user *n. Law* **1** a right to use. **2** a presumptive right arising from the user.

right of visitation *n.* (also **right of visit**) the right to conduct a visitation of a vessel, not including the right of search.

right of way *n.* **1** a right established by usage to pass over another's ground. **2** a path subject to such a right. **3** the right of one vehicle or ship etc. to proceed before another.

right-on *adj. slang* excellent; fashionable; politically correct (cf. *right on*).

Right Reverend *n.* the title of a bishop.

right side *n.* the better or desirable, or usable side of something, esp. fabric. ◻ **on the right side of 1** in favour with (a person). **2** somewhat less than (a specified age). **right side out** with the right side outwards; not inside out.

right sphere *n.* the sphere of the apparent heavens at a place where there is a right angle between the equator and the horizon.

right-thinking *adj.* = RIGHT-MINDED.

right-to-life *adj.* = PRO-LIFE.

right turn *n.* a turn that brings one's front to face as one's right side did before; a turn or turning to the right.

rightward /ˈrʌɪtwəd/ *adv. & adj.* ● *adv.* (also **rightwards** /-wədz/) towards the right. ● *adj.* going towards or facing the right.

right whale *n.* any large-headed whale of the family Balaenidae, rich in whalebone and easily captured.

right-wing *adj.* **1** conservative; reactionary. **2** of or relating to the right wing in football etc.

right wing *n.* **1** the conservative section of a political party or system. **2** the right side of a football etc. team on the field. ◻ **right-winger** *n.*

righty-ho var. of RIGHTO.

rigid /ˈrɪdʒɪd/ *adj. & n.* ● *adj.* **1** not flexible; that cannot be bent (*a rigid frame*). **2** (of a person, conduct, etc.) inflexible, unbending, strict, harsh, punctilious (*a rigid disciplinarian*; *rigid economy*). ● *n.* a lorry or truck which is not articulated. ◻ **rigidity** /-ˈdʒɪdɪti/ *n.* **rigidly** *adv.* **rigidness** *n.* [French *rigide* or Latin *rigidus*, from *rigēre* 'be stiff']

rigidify /rɪˈdʒɪdɪfʌɪ/ *v.tr. & intr.* (**-ies**, **-ied**) make or become rigid.

rigmarole /ˈrɪgmərəʊl/ *n.* **1** a lengthy and complicated procedure. **2 a** a rambling or meaningless account or tale. **b** such talk. [originally *ragman roll* = a catalogue, of unknown origin]

rigor[1] /ˈrɪgɔː, ˈrʌɪgɔː, -gə/ *n. Med.* **1** a sudden feeling of cold with shivering accompanied by a rise in temperature, preceding a fever etc. **2** rigidity of the body caused by shock or poisoning etc. [Middle English from Latin, from *rigēre* 'be stiff']

rigor[2] *US* var. of RIGOUR.

rigor mortis /rɪgə ˈmɔːtɪs/ *n.* stiffening of the body after death. [Latin, = stiffness of death]

rigorous /ˈrɪg(ə)rəs/ *adj.* **1** characterized by or showing rigour; strict, severe. **2** strictly exact or accurate. **3** (of the weather) cold, severe. ◻ **rigorously** *adv.* **rigorousness** *n.* [Old French *rigorous* or Late Latin *rigorosus* (as RIGOR[1])]

rigour /ˈrɪgə/ *n.* (*US* **rigor**) **1 a** severity, strictness, harshness. **b** (in *pl.*) harsh measures or conditions. **c** (often in *pl.*) severity of weather or climate; extremity of cold. **2** logical exactitude. **3** strict enforcement of rules etc. (*the utmost rigour of the law*). **4** austerity of life; puritanical discipline. [Middle English via Old French *rigour* from Latin *rigor* (as RIGOR[1])]

rig-out *n. Brit. colloq.* an outfit of clothes.

Rig-Veda /rɪgˈveɪdə, -ˈviːdə/ *n.* the oldest and principal of the Hindu Vedas (see VEDA). [Sanskrit *ṛigvēda*, from *ṛic* 'praise' + *vēda* VEDA]

rile /rʌɪl/ *v.tr.* **1** *colloq.* anger, irritate. **2** *US* make (water) turbulent or muddy. [variant of ROIL]

Riley /ˈrʌɪli/ *n.* (also **Reilly**) ◻ **the life of Riley** *colloq.* a carefree existence. [20th c.: origin unknown]

rilievo var. of RELIEVO.

rill /rɪl/ *n.* **1** a small stream. **2** a shallow channel cut in the surface of soil or rocks by running water. **3** var. of RILLE. [Low German *ril*, *rille*]

rille /rɪl/ *n.* (also **rill**) *Astron.* a cleft or narrow valley on the moon's surface. [German (as RILL)]

rim /rɪm/ *n. & v.* ● *n.* **1 a** a raised edge or border. **b** a margin or verge, esp. of something circular. **2** the part of a pair of spectacles surrounding the lenses. **3** the outer edge of a wheel, on which the tyre is fitted. **4** a boundary line (*the rim of the horizon*). ● *v.tr.* (**rimmed**, **rimming**) **1 a** provide with a rim. **b** be a rim for or to. **2** edge, border. ◻ **rimless** *adj.* **rimmed** *adj.* (also in *comb.*). [Old English *rima* 'edge': cf. Old Norse *rimi* 'ridge' (the only known cognate)]

rim-brake *n.* a brake acting on the rim of a wheel.

rime[1] /rʌɪm/ *n.* & *v.* ● *n.* **1** frost, esp. formed from cloud or fog. **2** *poet.* hoar frost. ● *v.tr.* cover with rime. [Old English *hrīm*]

rime[2] *archaic* var. of RHYME.

rimose /'rʌɪməʊs, rʌɪ'məʊs, -z/ *adj.* (also **rimous** /-məs/) esp. *Bot.* full of chinks or fissures. [Latin *rimosus* from *rima* 'chink']

rimu /'ri:mu:/ *n.* *NZ* **1** a softwood tree, *Dacrydium cupressinum*, native to New Zealand. **2** its light brown streaked wood, used for furniture and interior fittings. [Maori]

rimy /'rʌɪmi/ *adj.* (**rimier**, **rimiest**) frosty; covered with frost.

rind /rʌɪnd/ *n.* & *v.* ● *n.* **1** the tough outer layer or covering of fruit and vegetables, cheese, bacon, etc. **2** the bark of a tree or plant. ● *v.tr.* strip the bark from. □ **rinded** *adj.* (also in *comb.*). **rindless** *adj.* [Old English *rind(e)*]

rinderpest /'rɪndəpɛst/ *n.* a virulent infectious viral disease of ruminants (esp. cattle). [German, from *Rinder* 'cattle' + *Pest* PEST]

ring[1] /rɪŋ/ *n.* & *v.* ● *n.* **1** a circular band, usu. of precious metal, worn on a finger as an ornament or a token of marriage or betrothal. **2** a circular band of any material. **3** the rim of a cylindrical or circular object, or a line or band round it. **4** a mark or part having the form of a circular band (*had rings round his eyes*; *smoke rings*). **5** = ANNUAL RING. **6 a** an enclosure for a circus performance, betting at races, the showing of cattle, etc. **b** (prec. by *the*) bookmakers collectively. **c** a roped enclosure for boxing or wrestling. **7 a** a group of people or things arranged in a circle. **b** such an arrangement. **8** a combination of traders, bookmakers, spies, politicians, etc. acting together usu. illicitly for the control of operations or profit. **9** a circular or spiral course. **10** = GAS RING. **11** *Astron.* **a** a thin band or disc of particles etc. round a planet. **b** a halo round the moon. **12** *Archaeol.* a circular prehistoric earthwork, usu. consisting of a bank and ditch. **13** *Chem.* a group of atoms each bonded to two others in a closed sequence. **14** *Math.* a set of elements with two binary operations, addition and multiplication, the second being distributive over the first and associative. ● *v.tr.* **1** make or draw a circle round. **2** (often foll. by *round*, *about*, *in*) encircle or hem in (game or cattle). **3** put a ring on (a bird etc.) or through the nose of (a pig, bull, etc.). **4** cut (fruit, vegetables, etc.) into rings. □ **run** (or **make**) **rings round** *colloq.* outclass or outwit (another person). □ **ringed** *adj.* (also in *comb.*). **ringless** *adj.* [Old English *hring*, from Germanic]

ring[2] /rɪŋ/ *v.* & *n.* ● *v.* (*past* **rang** /raŋ/; *past part.* **rung** /rʌŋ/) **1** *intr.* (often foll. by *out* etc.) give a clear resonant or vibrating sound of or as of a bell (*a shot rang out*; *a ringing laugh*; *the telephone rang*). **2** *tr.* **a** make (esp. a bell) ring. **b** (*absol.*) call for service or attention by ringing a bell (*you rang, madam?*). **3** *tr.* (also *absol.*; often foll. by *up*) esp. *Brit.* call by telephone (*will ring you on Monday*; *did you ring?*). **4** *intr.* (usu. foll. by *with*, *to*) (of a place) resound or be permeated with a sound, or an attribute, e.g. fame (*the theatre rang with applause*). **5** *intr.* (of the ears) be filled with a sensation of ringing. **6** *tr.* **a** sound (a peal etc.) on bells. **b** (of a bell) sound (the hour etc.). **7** *tr.* (foll. by *in*, *out*) usher in or out with bell-ringing (*ring in the May*; *rang out the Old Year*). **8** *intr.* (of sentiments etc.) convey a specified impression (*words rang hollow*). ● *n.* **1** a ringing sound or tone. **2 a** the act of ringing a bell. **b** the sound caused by this. **3** *colloq.* a telephone call (*give me a ring*). **4** a specified feeling conveyed by an utterance (*had a melancholy ring*). **5** a set of esp. church bells. □ **ring back** make a return telephone call to (a person who has telephoned earlier). **ring a bell** see BELL[1]. **ring the changes (on)** see CHANGE. **ring down** (or **up**) **the curtain 1** *Theatr.* cause the curtain to be lowered or raised. **2** (foll. by *on*) mark the end or the beginning of (an enterprise etc.). **ring in 1** *Brit.* report or make contact by telephone. **2** *Austral.* & *NZ slang* substitute fraudulently. **ring in one's ears** (or **heart** etc.) linger in the memory. **ring off** *Brit.* end a telephone call by replacing the receiver. **ring round** telephone several people. **ring true** (or **false**) convey an impression of truth or falsehood. **ring up 1** *Brit.* call by telephone. **2** record (an amount etc.) on a cash register. □ **ringed** *adj.* (also in *comb.*). **ringer** *n.* **ringing** *adj.* **ringingly** *adv.* [Old English *hringan*]

ringbark /'rɪŋbɑ:k/ *v.tr.* cut a ring in the bark of (a tree) to kill it, or to check rapid growth and thereby improve fruit production.

ring-binder *n.* a loose-leaf binder with ring-shaped clasps that can be opened to pass through holes in the paper.

ringbolt /'rɪŋbəʊlt/ *n.* a bolt with a ring attached for fitting a rope to etc.

ring circuit *n.* an electrical circuit serving a number of power points with one fuse in the supply to the circuit.

ring-dove *n.* **1** the wood pigeon. **2** the collared dove.

ringed plover *n.* either of two small plovers, *Charadrius hiaticula* and *C. dubius*.

ringer /'rɪŋə/ *n.* *slang* **1 a** esp. *US* an athlete or horse entered in a competition by fraudulent means, esp. as a substitute. **b** a person's or thing's double, esp. an impostor. **2** *Austral.* **a** the fastest shearer in a shed. **b** a stockman or station hand. **3** a person who rings, esp. a bell-ringer. □ **be a ringer** (or **dead ringer) for** resemble (a person) exactly. [RING[2] + -ER[1]]

ringette /rɪŋ'ɛt/ *n.* *Canad.* a game resembling ice hockey, played (esp. by women and girls) with a straight stick and a rubber ring.

ring-fence *n.* & *v.* ● *n.* **1** a fence completely enclosing a piece of land. **2** an effective barrier. ● *v.tr.* **1** enclose with a ring-fence. **2 a** guard securely. **b** *Finance* protect or guarantee (funds).

ring finger *n.* the finger next to the little finger, esp. of the left hand, on which the wedding ring is usu. worn.

ringhals var. of RINKHALS.

ringing tone *n.* a sound heard by a telephone caller when the number dialled is being rung.

ringleader /'rɪŋli:də/ *n.* a leading instigator in an illicit or illegal activity.

ringlet /'rɪŋlɪt/ *n.* **1** a lock of hair hanging in a corkscrew-shaped curl. **2** a butterfly, *Aphantopus hyperantus*, with spots on its wings. □ **ringletted** *adj.* (*US* **ringleted**). **ringlety** *adj.*

ring main *n.* *Brit.* **1** an electrical supply serving a series of consumers and returning to the original source, so that each consumer has an alternative path in the event of a failure. **2** = RING CIRCUIT.

ringmaster /'rɪŋmɑ:stə/ *n.* the person directing a circus performance.

ring-neck *n.* any of various ring-necked birds esp. a type of pheasant, *Phasianus colchicus*, with a white neck ring.

ring-necked *adj.* *Zool.* having a band or bands of colour round the neck.

ring ouzel *n.* a thrush, *Turdus torquatus*, with a white crescent across its breast.

ring-pull *n.* a ring on a tin for pulling to break its seal.

ring road *n.* esp. *Brit.* a bypass encircling a town.

ringside /'rɪŋsʌɪd/ *n.* the area immediately beside a boxing ring or circus ring etc. (often *attrib.*: *a ringside seat*; *a ringside view*). □ **ringsider** *n.*

ringster /'rɪŋstə/ *n.* a person who participates in a political or commercial ring (see RING[1] *n.* 8).

ringtail /'rɪŋteɪl/ *n.* **1** a ring-tailed opossum, lemur, or phalanger. **2** a golden eagle up to its third year. **3** a female hen harrier.

ring-tailed *adj.* **1** (of monkeys, lemurs, raccoons, etc.) having a tail ringed in alternate colours. **2** with the tail curled at the end.

ringworm /ˈrɪŋwəːm/ *n.* any of various fungal infections of the skin causing circular inflamed patches, esp. on the scalp.

rink /rɪŋk/ *n.* **1** an area of natural or artificial ice for skating or the game of curling etc. **2** an enclosed area for roller skating. **3** a building containing either of these. **4** *Bowls* a strip of the green used for playing a match. **5** a team in bowls or curling. [Middle English (originally Scots), = jousting-ground: perhaps originally from Old French *renc* RANK[1]]

rinkhals /ˈrɪŋkhals/ *n.* (also **ringhals** /ˈrɪŋhals/) a large venomous spitting cobra, *Hemachatus hemachatus*, of southern Africa, with one or two white rings across the neck. [Afrikaans *rinkhals*, from *ring* RING[1] + *hals* 'neck']

rinse /rɪns/ *v.* & *n.* ● *v.tr.* (often foll. by *through, out*) **1** wash with clean water. **2** apply liquid to. **3** wash lightly. **4** put (clothes etc.) through clean water to remove soap or detergent. **5** (foll. by *out, away*) clear (impurities) by rinsing. ● *n.* **1** the act or an instance of rinsing (*give it a rinse*). **2** a solution for cleansing the mouth. **3** a dye for the temporary tinting of hair (*a blue rinse*). □ **rinser** *n.* [Middle English from Old French *rincer, raincier*, of unknown origin]

Rioja /rɪˈɒhə/ *n.* wine produced in Rioja, a district in northern Spain.

riot /ˈrʌɪət/ *n.* & *v.* ● *n.* **1 a** a disturbance of the peace by a crowd; an occurrence of public disorder. **b** (*attrib.*) involved in suppressing riots (*riot police; riot shield*). **2** uncontrolled revelry; noisy behaviour. **3** (foll. by *of*) a lavish display or enjoyment (*a riot of emotion; a riot of colour and sound*). **4** *colloq.* a very amusing thing or person. ● *v.intr.* **1** make or engage in a riot. **2** live wantonly; revel. □ **read the riot act** put a firm stop to insubordination etc.; give a severe warning (from the name of a former act partly read out to disperse rioters). **run riot 1** throw off all restraint. **2** (of plants) grow or spread uncontrolled. □ **rioter** *n.* [Middle English from Old French *riote, rioter, rihoter*, of unknown origin]

riot gear *n.* protective clothing, helmets, etc., worn by police or prison officers in situations of violence or potential violence.

riotous /ˈrʌɪətəs/ *adj.* **1** marked by or involving rioting. **2** characterized by wanton conduct. **3** wildly profuse. □ **riotously** *adv.* **riotousness** *n.* [Middle English from Old French (as RIOT)]

RIP *abbr.* may he or she or they rest in peace. [Latin *requiescat* (pl. *requiescant*) *in pace*]

rip[1] /rɪp/ *v.* & *n.* ● *v.* (**ripped, ripping**) **1** *tr.* tear or cut (a thing) quickly or forcibly away or apart (*ripped out the lining; ripped the book up*). **2** *tr.* **a** make (a hole etc.) by ripping. **b** make a long tear or cut in. **3** *intr.* come violently apart; split. **4** *intr.* rush along. ● *n.* **1** a long tear or cut. **2** an act of ripping. □ **let rip** *colloq.* **1** act or proceed without restraint. **2** speak violently. **3** not check the speed of or interfere with (a person or thing). **rip into** attack (a person) verbally. **rip off** *colloq.* defraud, steal. [Middle English: origin unknown]

rip[2] /rɪp/ *n.* a stretch of rough water in the sea or in a river, caused by the meeting of currents. [18th c.: perhaps related to RIP[1]]

rip[3] /rɪp/ *n.* **1** a dissolute person. **2** a rascal. **3** a worthless horse. [perhaps from *rep*, abbreviation of REPROBATE]

riparian /rʌɪˈpɛːrɪən/ *adj.* & *n.* esp. *Law* ● *adj.* of or on a river bank (*riparian rights*). ● *n.* an owner of property on a river bank. [Latin *riparius* from *ripa* 'bank']

ripcord /ˈrɪpkɔːd/ *n.* a cord for releasing a parachute from its pack.

rip current *n.* an intermittent strong surface current flowing from the seashore. [RIP[2]]

ripe /rʌɪp/ *adj.* **1** (of grain, fruit, cheese, etc.) ready to be reaped or picked or eaten. **2** mature; fully developed (*ripe in judgement; a ripe beauty*). **3** (of a person's age) advanced. **4** (often foll. by *for*) fit or ready (*when the time is ripe; land ripe for development*). **5** (of the complexion etc.) red and full like ripe fruit. □ **ripely** *adv.* **ripeness** *n.* [Old English *rīpe*, from West Germanic]

ripen /ˈrʌɪp(ə)n/ *v.tr.* & *intr.* make or become ripe.

ripieno /rɪpɪˈeɪnəʊ/ *n.* (*pl.* **-os** or **ripieni** /-ni/) *Mus.* a body of accompanying instruments in baroque concerto music. [Italian (as RE-, *pieno* 'full')]

rip-off *n. colloq.* **1** a fraud or swindle. **2** financial exploitation.

riposte /rɪˈpɒst/ *n.* & *v.* ● *n.* **1** a quick sharp reply or retort. **2** a quick return thrust in fencing. ● *v.intr.* deliver a riposte. [French *ri(s)poste, ri(s)poster* from Italian *risposta* RESPONSE]

ripper /ˈrɪpə/ *n.* **1** a person or thing that rips. **2** a murderer who rips or mutilates victims' bodies.

ripping /ˈrɪpɪŋ/ *adj. Brit. archaic colloq.* splendid, excellent (*a ripping good yarn*). □ **rippingly** *adv.*

ripple[1] /ˈrɪp(ə)l/ *n.* & *v.* ● *n.* **1** a ruffling of the water's surface, a small wave or series of waves. **2** a gentle lively sound that rises and falls, e.g. of laughter or applause. **3** a wavy appearance in hair, material, etc. **4** *Electr.* a slight variation in the strength of a current etc. **5** ice cream with added syrup giving a coloured ripple effect (*raspberry ripple*). **6** *US* a riffle in a stream. ● *v.* **1 a** *intr.* form ripples; flow in ripples. **b** *tr.* cause to do this. **2** *intr.* show or sound like ripples. □ **ripplet** *n.* **ripply** *adj.* [17th c.: origin unknown]

ripple[2] /ˈrɪp(ə)l/ *n.* & *v.* ● *n.* a toothed implement used to remove seeds from flax. ● *v.tr.* treat with a ripple. [Middle English, corresponding to Middle Dutch & Middle Low German *repel(en)*, Old High German *riffila, rifilōn*]

ripple mark *n.* a ridge or ridged surface left on sand, mud, or rock by the action of water or wind.

riprap /ˈrɪprap/ *n. US* a collection of loose stone as a foundation for a structure. [reduplication of RAP[1]]

rip-roaring /ˈrɪprɔːrɪŋ/ *adj.* **1** wildly noisy or boisterous. **2** excellent, first-rate. □ **rip-roaringly** *adv.*

ripsaw /ˈrɪpsɔː/ *n.* a coarse saw for sawing wood along the grain.

ripsnorter /ˈrɪpsnɔːtə/ *n. colloq.* an energetic, remarkable, or excellent person or thing. □ **ripsnorting** *adj.* **ripsnortingly** *adv.*

ripstop /ˈrɪpstɒp/ *adj.* & *n.* ● *attrib.adj.* (of fabric, clothing, etc.) woven so that a tear will not spread. ● *n.* ripstop fabric. [RIP[1] + STOP]

rip tide *n.* **1** = RIP CURRENT. **2** = RIP[2]. **3** a state of conflicting psychological forces.

RISC /rɪsk/ *n.* **1** a computer designed to perform a limited set of operations at high speed. **2** computing using this kind of computer. [acronym, from *r*educed *i*nstruction *s*et *c*omputer (or computing)]

rise /rʌɪz/ *v.* & *n.* ● *v.intr.* (*past* **rose** /rəʊz/; *past part.* **risen** /ˈrɪz(ə)n/) **1** move from a lower position to a higher one; come or go up. **2** grow, project, expand, or incline upwards; become higher. **3** (of the sun, moon, or stars) appear above the horizon. **4 a** get up from lying or sitting or kneeling (*rose to their feet; rose from the table*). **b** get out of bed, esp. in the morning (*do you rise early?*). **5** recover a standing or vertical position; become erect (*rose to my full height*). **6** esp. *Brit.* (of a meeting etc.) cease to sit for business; adjourn (*Parliament rises next week; the court will rise*). **7** reach a higher position or level or amount (*the flood has risen; prices are rising*). **8** develop greater intensity, strength, volume, or pitch (*the colour rose in her cheeks; the wind is rising; their voices rose with excitement*). **9** make progress; reach a higher social position (*rose from the ranks*). **10 a** come to the surface of liquid (*bubbles rose from the bottom; waited for the fish to rise*). **b** (of a person) react to provocation (*rise to the bait*). **11** become or be visible above the surroundings etc., stand prominently (*mountains rose to our right*). **12 a** (of buildings etc.) undergo construction from the foundations (*office blocks were rising all around*). **b** (of a tree etc.) grow to a (usu. specified) height. **13** come to life again (*rise from the ashes*; *risen from the dead*). **14** (of dough) swell by the action of yeast etc. **15** (often foll. by *up*) cease to be quiet or submissive; rebel (*rose up against the despot*). **16** originate; have as its source (*the river rises in the mountains*). **17** (of wind) start to blow. **18** (of a person's spirits) become cheerful. **19** (of a barometer) show a higher atmospheric pressure. **20** (of a horse) rear (*rose on its hind legs*). **21** (of a bump, blister, etc.) form. **22** (of the stomach) become nauseated (esp. in phr. **one's gorge rises at**). ● *n.* **1** an act or manner or amount of rising. **2** an upward slope or hill or movement (*a rise in the road*; *the house stood on a rise*; *the rise and fall of the waves*). **3** an increase in sound or pitch. **4 a** an increase in amount, extent, etc. (*a rise in unemployment*). **b** *Brit.* an increase in salary, wages, etc. **5** an increase in status or power. **6** social, commercial, or political advancement; upward progress. **7** the movement of a fish to the surface, to take a fly or bait. **8** origin. **9 a** the vertical height of a step, arch, incline, etc. **b** = RISER 2. □ **get** (or **take**) **a rise out of** *colloq.* provoke an emotional reaction from (a person), esp. by teasing. **on the rise** on the increase. **rise above 1** be superior to (petty feelings etc.). **2** show dignity or strength in the face of (difficulty, poor conditions, etc.). **rise and shine** (usu. as *imper.*) *colloq.* get out of bed smartly; wake up. **rise in the world** attain a higher social position. **rise to** develop powers equal to (an occasion). **rise with the sun** (or **lark**) get up early in the morning. [Old English *rīsan*, from Germanic]

riser /ˈrʌɪzə/ *n.* **1** a person who rises esp. from bed (*an early riser*). **2** a vertical section between the treads of a staircase. **3** a vertical pipe for the flow of liquid or gas. **4** a low platform on a stage, in a studio, etc.

rishi /ˈrɪʃi/ *n.* (*pl.* **rishis**) a Hindu sage or saint. [Sanskrit *ṛṣi*]

risible /ˈrɪzɪb(ə)l/ *adj.* **1** laughable, ludicrous. **2** inclined to laugh. **3** *Anat.* relating to laughter (*risible nerves*). □ **risibility** /-ˈbɪlɪti/ *n.* **risibly** *adv.* [Late Latin *risibilis* from Latin *ridēre ris-* 'to laugh']

rising /ˈrʌɪzɪŋ/ *adj.* & *n.* ● *adj.* **1** going up; getting higher. **2** increasing (*rising costs*). **3** advancing to maturity or high standing (*the rising generation*; *a rising young lawyer*). **4** *Brit.* approaching a specified age (*the rising fives*). **5** (of ground) sloping upwards. ● *n.* a revolt or insurrection.

rising damp *n. Brit.* moisture absorbed from the ground into a wall.

risk /rɪsk/ *n.* & *v.* ● *n.* **1** a chance or possibility of danger, loss, injury, or other adverse consequences (*a health risk*; *a risk of fire*). **2** a person or thing causing a risk or regarded in relation to risk (*is a poor risk*). ● *v.tr.* **1** expose to risk. **2** accept the chance of (*could not risk getting wet*). **3** venture on. □ **at risk** exposed to danger. **at one's (own) risk** accepting responsibility, agreeing to make no claims. **at the risk of** with the possibility of (an adverse consequence). **put at risk** expose to danger. **risk one's neck** put one's own life in danger. **run a** (or **the**) **risk** (often foll. by *of*) expose oneself to danger or loss etc. **take** (or **run**) **a risk** chance the possibility of danger etc. [French *risque*, *risquer* from Italian *risco* 'danger', *riscare* 'run into danger']

risk capital *n.* money put up for speculative business investment.

risky /ˈrɪski/ *adj.* (**riskier**, **riskiest**) **1** involving risk. **2** = RISQUÉ. □ **riskily** *adv.* **riskiness** *n.*

Risorgimento /rɪˌsɔːdʒɪˈmɛntəʊ/ *n. hist.* a movement for the unification and independence of Italy (achieved in 1870). [Italian, = resurrection]

risotto /rɪˈzɒtəʊ/ *n.* (*pl.* **-os**) an Italian dish of rice cooked in stock with meat, onions, etc. [Italian, from *riso* 'rice']

risqué /ˈriːskeɪ, ˈrɪskeɪ, rɪˈskeɪ/ *adj.* (of a story etc.) slightly indecent or liable to shock. [French, past part. of *risquer* RISK]

rissole /ˈrɪsəʊl/ *n.* a compressed mixture of meat and spices, coated in breadcrumbs and fried. [French from Old French *ruissole*, *roussole*, ultimately via Late Latin *russeolus* 'reddish' from Latin *russus* 'red']

rit. /rɪt/ *abbr. Mus.* ritardando.

ritardando /rɪtɑːˈdandəʊ/ *adv.*, *adj.*, & *n.* (*pl.* **-os** or **ritardandi** /-di/) *Mus.* = RALLENTANDO. [Italian]

rite /rʌɪt/ *n.* **1** a religious or solemn observance or act (*burial rites*). **2** an action or procedure required or usual in this. **3** a body of customary observances characteristic of a Church or a part of it (*the Latin rite*). □ **riteless** *adj.* [Middle English from Old French *rit*, *rite* or Latin *ritus* (esp. religious) 'usage']

ritenuto /rɪtəˈnuːtəʊ/ *adv.* & *n. Mus.* ● *adv.* with immediate reduction of speed. ● *n.* (*pl.* **-os**) a passage played in this way. [Italian]

rite of passage *n.* (often in *pl.*) a ritual or event marking a stage of a person's advance through life, e.g. marriage.

ritornello /rɪtɔːˈnɛləʊ/ *n. Mus.* (*pl.* **-os** or **ritornelli** /-li/) a short instrumental refrain, interlude, etc., in a vocal work. [Italian, diminutive of *ritorno* RETURN]

ritual /ˈrɪtʃʊəl/ *n.* & *adj.* ● *n.* **1** a prescribed order of performing rites. **2** a procedure regularly followed. ● *adj.* of or done as a ritual or rites (*ritual murder*). □ **ritualize** *v.tr.* & *intr.* (also **-ise**). **ritualization** /-ˈzeɪʃ(ə)n/ *n.* (also **-isation**). **ritually** *adv.* [Latin *ritualis* (as RITE)]

ritualism /ˈrɪtʃʊəlɪz(ə)m/ *n.* the regular or excessive practice of ritual. □ **ritualist** *n.* **ritualistic** /-ˈlɪstɪk/ *adj.* **ritualistically** /-ˈlɪstɪk(ə)li/ *adv.*

ritzy /ˈrɪtsi/ *adj.* (**ritzier**, **ritziest**) *colloq.* **1** high-class, luxurious. **2** ostentatiously smart. □ **ritzily** *adv.* **ritziness** *n.* [*Ritz*, the name of luxury hotels from C. Ritz, Swiss hotel-owner d. 1918]

rival /ˈrʌɪv(ə)l/ *n.* & *v.* ● *n.* **1** a person competing with another for the same objective. **2** a person or thing that equals another in quality. **3** (*attrib.*) being a rival or rivals (*a rival firm*). ● *v.tr.* (**rivalled**, **rivalling**; *US* **rivaled**, **rivaling**) **1** be the rival of or comparable to. **2** seem or claim to be as good as. [Latin *rivalis*, originally = using the same stream, from *rivus* 'stream']

rivalry /ˈrʌɪv(ə)lri/ *n.* (*pl.* **-ies**) the state or an instance of being rivals; competition.

rive /rʌɪv/ *v.* (*past* **rived**; *past part.* **riven** /ˈrɪv(ə)n/) *archaic* or *poet.* **1** *tr.* split or tear apart violently. **2 a** *tr.* split (wood or stone). **b** *intr.* be split. [Middle English from Old Norse *rífa*]

river /ˈrɪvə/ *n.* **1** a copious natural stream of water flowing in a channel to the sea or a lake etc. **2** a copious flow (*a river of lava*; *rivers of blood*). **3** (*attrib.*) (in the names of animals, plants, etc.) living in or associated with rivers. □ **sell down the river** *colloq.* betray or let down. □ **rivered** *adj.* (also in *comb.*). **riverless** *adj.* [Middle English from Anglo-French *river*, *rivere*, Old French *riviere* 'river, river bank', ultimately via Latin *riparius* from *ripa* 'bank']

river blindness *n.* a tropical skin disease transmitted by the bite of blackflies and caused by the parasitic threadworm *Onchocerca volvulus*, the larvae of which can migrate into the eye and cause blindness. Also called ONCHOCERCIASIS.

riverboat /ˈrɪvəbəʊt/ *n.* a boat designed for use on rivers.

river capture *n. Brit.* the diversion of the upper headwaters of a mountain stream into a more powerful one.

riverine /ˈrɪvərʌɪn/ *adj.* of or on a river or river bank; riparian.

riverside /ˈrɪvəsʌɪd/ *n.* the ground along a river bank.

rivet /ˈrɪvɪt/ *n.* & *v.* ● *n.* a nail or bolt for holding together metal plates etc., its headless end being beaten out or pressed down when in place. ● *v.tr.* (**riveted**, **riveting**) **1 a** join or fasten with rivets. **b** beat out or press down the end of (a nail or bolt). **c** fix; make immovable. **2 a** (foll. by *on*, *upon*) direct intently (one's eyes or attention etc.). **b** (esp. as **riveting** *adj.*) engross (a person or the attention). □ **riveter** *n.* [Middle English from Old French, from *river* 'clench', of unknown origin]

riviera /rɪvɪˈɛːrə/ *n.* a coastal region with a subtropical climate, vegetation, etc., esp. that of SE France and NW Italy. [Italian, = seashore]

rivière /rɪvɪˈɛː/ *n.* a gem necklace, esp. of more than one string. [French, = RIVER]

rivulet /ˈrɪvjʊlɪt/ *n.* a small stream. [obsolete *riveret* from French, diminutive of *rivière* RIVER, perhaps suggested by Italian *rivoletto*, diminutive of *rivolo*, diminutive of *rivo*, from Latin *rivus* 'stream']

riyal var. of RIAL.

RL *abbr.* Rugby League.

rly. *abbr.* railway.

RM *abbr.* **1** (in the UK) Royal Marines. **2** Resident Magistrate. **3** (in the UK) Royal Mail.

rm. *abbr.* room.

RMA *abbr.* Royal Military Academy.

r.m.s. *abbr. Math.* root-mean-square.

RMT *abbr.* National Union of Rail, Maritime, and Transport Workers.

RN *abbr.* **1** (in the UK) Royal Navy. **2** Registered Nurse.

Rn *symb. Chem.* the element radon.

RNA *abbr.* ribonucleic acid.

RNAS *abbr.* (in the UK) Royal Naval Air Service (or Station).

RNLI *abbr.* (in the UK) Royal National Lifeboat Institution.

RNZAF *abbr.* Royal New Zealand Air Force.

RNZN *abbr.* Royal New Zealand Navy.

roach[1] /rəʊtʃ/ *n.* (*pl.* same) a small freshwater fish, esp. *Rutilus rutilus*, allied to the carp. [Middle English from Old French *roc(h)e*, of unknown origin]

roach[2] /rəʊtʃ/ *n.* **1** *N. Amer. colloq.* a cockroach. **2** *slang* the butt of a marijuana cigarette. [abbreviation]

roach[3] /rəʊtʃ/ *n. Naut.* **1 a** a curved part of a fore-and-aft sail extending beyond a straight line between its corners, esp. on the leech side. **b** the breadth of this. **2** an upward curve in the foot of a square sail. [18th c.: origin unknown]

road[1] /rəʊd/ *n.* **1 a** a path or way with a specially prepared surface, used by vehicles, pedestrians, etc. **b** the part of this used by vehicles (*don't step in the road*). **2** esp. *Brit.* one's way or route (*our road took us through unexplored territory*). **3** an underground passage in a mine. **4** *US* a railway. **5** (usu. in *pl.*) a partly sheltered piece of water near the shore in which ships can ride at anchor. □ **by road** using transport along roads. **get out of the** (or **my** etc.) **road** *colloq.* cease to obstruct a person. **in the** (or **my** etc.) **road** *colloq.* obstructing a person or thing. **one for the road** *colloq.* a final (esp. alcoholic) drink before departure. **on the road** travelling, esp. as a firm's representative, itinerant performer, or vagrant. **the road to** the way of getting to or achieving (*the road to London*; *the road to ruin*). **take the road** set out. □ **roadless** *adj.* [Old English *rād* from *rīdan* RIDE]

road[2] /rəʊd/ *v.tr.* (also *absol.*) (of a dog) follow up (a game bird) by the scent of its trail. [19th c.: origin unknown]

roadbed /ˈrəʊdbɛd/ *n.* **1** the foundation structure of a railway. **2** the material laid down to form a road. **3** *US* the part of a road on which vehicles travel.

roadblock /ˈrəʊdblɒk/ *n.* a barrier or barricade on a road, esp. one set up by the authorities to stop and examine traffic.

road fund *n. Brit. hist.* a fund for the construction and maintenance of roads and bridges.

road fund licence *n. Brit.* a disc displayed on a vehicle certifying payment of road tax.

road hog *n. colloq.* a reckless or inconsiderate road user, esp. a motorist.

road-holding *n.* the capacity of a moving vehicle to remain stable when cornering at high speeds etc.

roadhouse /ˈrəʊdhaʊs/ *n.* an inn or club on a major road.

road hump *n.* = SLEEPING POLICEMAN.

roadie /ˈrəʊdi/ *n. colloq.* an assistant employed by a touring band of musicians to erect and maintain equipment.

road kill *n.* esp. *N. Amer.* **1** the killing of an animal by a road vehicle. **2** an animal that has been so killed.

roadman /ˈrəʊdmən/ *n.* (*pl.* **-men**) *Brit.* a man employed to repair or maintain roads.

road manager *n.* the organizer and supervisor of a musicians' tour.

road map *n.* a map showing the roads of a country or area.

road metal *n. Brit.* broken stone used in road-making or for railway ballast.

road-pricing *n.* the practice of charging motorists to use busy roads at certain times.

roadroller /ˈrəʊdrəʊlə/ *n.* a motor vehicle with a heavy roller, used in road-making.

roadrunner /ˈrəʊdrʌnə/ *n.* a fast-running bird of Mexican and US deserts, *Geococcyx californianus*, related to the cuckoo.

road sense *n. Brit.* a person's capacity for safe behaviour on the road, esp. in traffic.

roadshow /ˈrəʊdʃəʊ/ *n.* **1 a** a performance given by a touring company, esp. a group of pop musicians. **b** a company giving such performances. **2** a radio or television programme done on location, esp. a series of programmes each from a different venue. **3** a touring political or advertising campaign.

roadside /ˈrəʊdsʌɪd/ *n.* the strip of land beside a road (often *attrib.*: *roadside café*).

road sign *n.* a sign giving information or instructions to road users.

roadstead /ˈrəʊdstɛd/ *n.* = ROAD[1] 5. [ROAD[1] + *stead* in obsolete sense 'place']

roadster /ˈrəʊdstə/ *n.* **1** an open two-seater motor car. **2** a bicycle or (formerly) a horse for use on the road.

road sweeper *n.* a person who sweeps roads for a living.

road tax *n. Brit.* a periodic tax payable on road vehicles.

road test *n.* & *v.* ● *n.* a test of the performance of a vehicle on the road. ● *v.tr.* (**road-test**) test (a vehicle) on the road.

road train *n.* esp. *Austral.* a large lorry pulling one or more trailers.

roadway /ˈrəʊdweɪ/ *n.* **1** a road. **2** = ROAD[1] 1b. **3** the part of a bridge or railway used for traffic.

roadwork /ˈrəʊdwəːk/ *n.* **1** (in *pl.*) *Brit.* the construction or repair of roads, or other work involving digging up a road surface. **2** athletic exercise or training involving running on roads.

roadworthy /ˈrəʊdwəːði/ *adj.* fit to be used on the road. □ **roadworthiness** *n.*

roam /rəʊm/ *v.* & *n.* ● *v.* **1** *intr.* ramble, wander. **2** *tr.* travel unsystematically over, through, or about. ● *n.* an act of roaming; a ramble. □ **roamer** *n.* [Middle English: origin unknown]

roan[1] /rəʊn/ *adj.* & *n.* ● *adj.* (of an animal, esp. a horse or cow) having a coat of which the prevailing colour is thickly interspersed with hairs of another colour, esp. bay or sorrel or chestnut mixed with white or grey. ● *n.* a roan animal. [Old French, of unknown origin]

roan[2] /rəʊn/ *n.* soft sheepskin leather used in bookbinding as a substitute for morocco. [Middle English, perhaps from *Roan*, old name of *Rouen* in N. France]

roar /rɔː/ *n.* & *v.* ● *n.* **1** a loud deep hoarse sound, as made by a lion, a person in pain or rage or excitement, thunder, a loud engine, etc. **2** a loud laugh. ● *v.* **1** *intr.* **a** utter or make a roar. **b** utter loud laughter. **c** (of a horse) make a loud noise in breathing as a symptom of disease. **2** *intr.* travel in a vehicle at high speed, esp. with the engine roaring. **3** *tr.* (often foll. by *out*) say, sing, or utter (words, an oath, etc.) in a loud tone. □ **roarer** *n.* [Old English *rārian*, of imitative origin]

roaring /ˈrɔːrɪŋ/ *adj.* in senses of ROAR *v.* □ **roaring drunk** *colloq.* very drunk and noisy. **roaring success** *colloq.* a great success. **roaring trade** (or **business**) *colloq.* very brisk trade or business. □ **roaringly** *adv.*

roaring forties *n.pl.* stormy ocean tracts between latitudes 40° and 50° S.

roaring twenties *n.pl. colloq.* the decade of the 1920s (with reference to its post-war buoyancy).

roast /rəʊst/ *v., adj., & n.* ● *v.* **1** *tr.* **a** cook (food, esp. meat) in an oven or by exposure to open heat. **b** heat (coffee beans) before grinding. **2** *tr.* heat (the ore of metal) in a furnace. **3** *tr.* **a** expose (a torture victim) to fire or great heat. **b** *tr. & refl.* expose (oneself or part of oneself) to warmth. **4** *tr.* criticize severely, denounce. **5** *intr.* undergo roasting. ● *attrib.adj.* (of meat or a potato, chestnut, etc.) roasted. ● *n.* **1 a** roast meat. **b** a dish of this. **c** a piece of meat for roasting. **2** the process of roasting. **3** *US* a party where roasted food is eaten. [Middle English from Old French *rost, rostir*, from Germanic]

roaster /ˈrəʊstə/ *n.* **1** a person or thing that roasts. **2 a** an oven or dish for roasting food in. **b** an ore-roasting furnace. **c** a coffee-roasting apparatus. **3** something fit for roasting, e.g. a fowl, a potato, etc.

roasting /ˈrəʊstɪŋ/ *adj. & n.* ● *adj.* very hot and dry. ● *n.* **1** in senses of ROAST *v.* **2** a severe criticism or denunciation.

rob /rɒb/ *v.tr.* (**robbed, robbing**) (often foll. by *of*) **1** take unlawfully from, esp. by force or threat of force (*robbed the safe*; *robbed her of her jewels*). **2** deprive of what is due or normal (*was robbed of my sleep*). **3** (*absol.*) commit robbery. □ **rob Peter to pay Paul** take away from one to give to another, discharge one debt by incurring another. [Middle English from Old French *rob(b)er*, from Germanic: related to REAVE]

robber /ˈrɒbə/ *n.* a person who commits robbery. [Middle English from Anglo-French & Old French (as ROB)]

robber baron *n.* **1** *hist.* a plundering feudal lord. **2** an unscrupulous plutocrat.

robbery /ˈrɒb(ə)ri/ *n.* (*pl.* **-ies**) **1 a** the act or process of robbing, esp. with force or threat of force. **b** an instance of this. **2** excessive financial demand or cost (*set us back £20 — it was sheer robbery*). [Middle English from Old French *roberie* (as ROB)]

robe /rəʊb/ *n. & v.* ● *n.* **1** a long loose outer garment. **2** esp. *N. Amer.* a dressing gown. **3** a baby's outer garment esp. at a christening. **4** (often in *pl.*) a long outer garment worn as an indication of the wearer's rank, office, profession, etc.; a gown or vestment. **5** *N. Amer.* a blanket or wrap of fur. ● *v.* **1** *tr.* clothe (a person) in a robe; dress. **2** *intr.* put on one's robes or vestments. [Middle English via Old French from Germanic (as ROB, originally in the sense 'booty')]

robin /ˈrɒbɪn/ *n.* **1** (also **robin redbreast**) a small brown European bird, *Erithacus rubecula*, the adult of which has a red throat and breast. **2** *N. Amer.* a red-breasted thrush, *Turdus migratorius.* **3** a bird similar in appearance etc. to either of these. □ **Robin Hood** (with reference to the legend of the medieval forest outlaw) a person who acts illegally or unfavourably towards the rich for the benefit of the poor. [Middle English from Old French, familiar variant of the name *Robert*]

robinia /rəˈbɪnɪə/ *n.* any N. American tree or shrub of the genus *Robinia*, e.g. a locust tree or false acacia. [modern Latin, named after J. *Robin*, 17th-c. French gardener]

roborant /ˈrəʊb(ə)r(ə)nt, ˈrɒb-/ *adj. & n. Med.* ● *adj.* strengthening. ● *n.* a strengthening drug. [Latin *roborare* from *robur -oris* 'strength']

robot /ˈrəʊbɒt/ *n.* **1** a machine with a human appearance or functioning like a human. **2** a machine capable of carrying out a complex series of actions automatically. **3** a person who works mechanically and efficiently but insensitively. **4** *S.Afr.* an automatic traffic signal. □ **robotic** /-ˈbɒtɪk/ *adj.* **robotically** /-ˈbɒtɪk(ə)li/ *adv.* **robotize** *v.tr.* (also **-ise**). **robotization** /-ˈzeɪʃ(ə)n/ *n.* (also **-isation**). [Czech (used in K. Čapek's play *R.U.R.* (*Rossum's Universal Robots*), 1920), from *robota* 'forced labour']

robotics /rəʊˈbɒtɪks/ *n.pl.* (usu. treated as *sing.*) the study of robots; the art or science of their design and operation.

robust /rə(ʊ)ˈbʌst/ *adj.* (**robuster, robustest**) **1** (of a person, animal, or thing) strong and sturdy, esp. in physique or construction. **2** (of exercise, discipline, etc.) vigorous, requiring strength. **3** (of intellect or mental attitude) straightforward, not given to nor confused by subtleties. **4** (of a statement, reply, etc.) bold, firm, unyielding. **5** (of wine etc.) full-bodied. □ **robustly** *adv.* **robustness** *n.* [French *robuste* or Latin *robustus* 'firm and hard' from *robus, robur* 'oak, strength']

robusta /rə(ʊ)ˈbʌstə/ *n.* **1** coffee or coffee beans from a widely grown African species of coffee plant, *Coffea canephora* (formerly *robusta*). **2** the plant itself (cf. ARABICA). [modern Latin, from Latin *robustus* 'robust']

ROC *abbr.* (in the UK) Royal Observer Corps.

roc /rɒk/ *n.* a gigantic bird of Eastern legend. [Spanish *rocho*, ultimately from Arabic *ruḵ*]

rocaille /rə(ʊ)ˈkʌɪ/ *n.* **1** an 18th-c. style of ornamentation based on rock and shell motifs. **2** a rococo style. [French from *roc* (as ROCK[1])]

rocambole /ˈrɒk(ə)mbəʊl/ *n.* an allium, *Allium scorodoprasum*, with a garlic-like bulb used for seasoning. [French from German *Rockenbolle*]

roche moutonnée /rɒʃ muːˈtɒneɪ/ *n. Geol.* a small bare outcrop of rock shaped by glacial erosion. [French, = fleecy rock]

rochet /ˈrɒtʃɪt/ *n.* a vestment resembling a surplice, used chiefly by bishops and abbots. [Middle English from Old French, diminutive of a Germanic word related to Old High German *roch* 'coat']

rock[1] /rɒk/ *n.* **1 a** the hard material of the earth's crust, exposed on the surface or underlying the soil. **b** a similar material on other planets. **2** *Geol.* any natural material, hard or soft (e.g. clay), consisting of one or more minerals. **3 a** a mass of rock projecting and forming a hill, cliff, reef, etc. **b** (**the Rock**) Gibraltar. **4** a large detached stone. **5** *US* a stone of any size. **6** a firm and dependable support or protection. **7** a source of danger or destruction. **8** *Brit.* a kind of hard confectionery usu. made in cylindrical peppermint-flavoured sticks. **9** (in *pl.*) *US slang* money. **10** *slang* a precious stone, esp. a diamond. **11** *slang* a solid form of cocaine. **12** (in *pl.*) *coarse slang* the testicles. □ **between a rock and a hard place** *N. Amer.* in a dilemma. **get one's rocks off** *coarse slang* **1** have a sexual orgasm. **2** obtain enjoyment. **on the rocks** *colloq.* **1** short of money. **2** (esp. of a marriage) in danger of breaking up. **3** (of a drink) served undiluted with ice cubes. □ **rockless** *adj.* **rocklet** *n.* **rocklike** *adj.* [Middle English from Old French *ro(c)que, roche*, medieval Latin *rocca*, of unknown origin]

rock[2] /rɒk/ *v. & n.* ● *v.* **1** *tr.* move gently to and fro in or as if in a cradle; set or maintain such motion (*rock him to sleep*; *the ship was rocked by the waves*). **2** *intr.* be or continue in such motion (*sat rocking in his chair*; *the ship was rocking on the waves*). **3 a** *intr.* sway from side to side; shake, oscillate, reel (*the house rocks*). **b** *tr.* cause to do this (*an earthquake rocked the house*). **4** *tr.* distress, perturb. **5** *intr.* dance to or play rock music. ● *n.* **1** a rocking movement (*gave the chair a rock*). **2** a spell of rocking (*had a rock in his chair*). **3 a** = ROCK AND ROLL. **b** any of a variety of types of modern popular music with a rocking or swinging beat, derived from rock and roll. □ **rock the boat** *colloq.* disturb the equilibrium of a situation. [Old English *roccian*, probably from Germanic]

rockabilly /ˈrɒkəbɪli/ *n.* a type of popular music combining elements of rock and roll and hill-billy music. [blend of *rock and roll* and *hill-billy*]

rock and roll *n.* (also **rock 'n' roll**) a type of popular dance music originating in the 1950s, characterized by a heavy beat and simple melodies, often with a blues element. □ **rock and roller** *n.*

rock-bed *n.* a base of rock or a rocky bottom.

rock-bottom *adj. & n.* ● *adj.* (of prices etc.) the very lowest. ● *n.* the very lowest level.

rock-bound *adj.* (of a coast) rocky and inaccessible.

rockburst /'rɒkbə:st/ *n.* a sudden rupture or collapse of highly stressed rock in a mine.

rock cake *n.* esp. *Brit.* a small currant cake with a hard rough surface.

rock candy *n. N. Amer.* = ROCK[1] *n.* 8.

rock-climbing *n.* the sport of climbing rock faces, esp. with the aid of ropes etc. □ **rock-climber** *n.*

rock cress *n.* = ARABIS.

rock crystal *n.* transparent colourless quartz usu. in hexagonal prisms.

rock-dove *n.* a wild dove, *Columba livia*, frequenting rocks, supposed ancestor of the domestic pigeon.

rocker /'rɒkə/ *n.* **1** a person or thing that rocks. **2** a curved bar or similar support, on which something can rock. **3** a rocking chair. **4 a** *Brit.* a devotee of rock music, characteristically associated with leather clothing and motorcycles. **b** a rock musician. **5** a skate with a highly curved blade. **6** a switch constructed on a pivot mechanism operating between the 'on' and 'off' positions. **7** any rocking device forming part of a mechanism. □ **off one's rocker** *slang* crazy.

rockery /'rɒk(ə)ri/ *n.* (*pl.* **-ies**) a heaped arrangement of rough stones with soil between them for growing rock plants on.

rocket[1] /'rɒkɪt/ *n. & v.* ● *n.* **1** a cylindrical projectile that can be propelled to a great height or distance by combustion of its contents, used esp. as a firework or signal. **2** an engine using a similar principle but not dependent on air intake for its operation. **3** a rocket-propelled missile, spacecraft, etc. **4** *Brit. colloq.* a severe reprimand. ● *v.* (**rocketed**, **rocketing**) **1** *tr.* bombard with rockets. **2** *intr.* **a** move rapidly upwards or away. **b** increase rapidly (*prices rocketed*). [French *roquette* from Italian *rochetto*, diminutive of *rocca* ROCK[2], with reference to its cylindrical shape]

rocket[2] /'rɒkɪt/ *n.* **1** (also **sweet rocket**) any of various fast-growing plants, esp. of the genus *Hesperis* or *Sisymbrium*. **2** a variety of the cruciferous annual plant *Eruca vesicaria* grown for salad; also called *roquette*, *arugula*. [French *roquette* via Italian *rochetta*, *ruchetta*, diminutive of *ruca*, from Latin *eruca* 'downy-stemmed plant']

rocketeer /rɒkɪ'tɪə/ *n.* **1** a person who discharges rocket-propelled missiles. **2** a person who works with space rockets; a rocket enthusiast.

rocketry /'rɒkɪtri/ *n.* the science or practice of rocket propulsion.

rock face *n.* a vertical surface of natural rock.

rockfall /'rɒkfɔ:l/ *n.* **1** a descent of loose rocks. **2** a mass of fallen rock.

rockfish /'rɒkfɪʃ/ *n.* (*pl.* usu. same) a rock-frequenting goby, bass, wrasse, catfish, etc.

rock garden *n.* an artificial mound or bank of earth and stones planted with rock plants etc.; a garden in which rockeries are the chief feature.

rockhopper /'rɒkhɒpə/ *n.* a small penguin, *Eudyptes crestatus*, of the Antarctic and New Zealand, with a crest of feathers on the forehead.

rocking chair *n.* a chair mounted on rockers or springs for gently rocking in.

rocking horse *n.* a model of a horse on rockers or springs for a child to rock on.

rocking-stone *n.* a poised boulder easily rocked; a logan-stone.

rockling /'rɒklɪŋ/ *n.* any of various small marine fish of the cod family, esp. of the genus *Ciliata* and *Rhinomenus*, found in pools among rocks.

rock 'n' roll var. of ROCK AND ROLL.

rock-pigeon *n.* = ROCK-DOVE.

rock pipit *n.* a species of pipit, *Anthus spinoletta*, frequenting rocky shores.

rock plant *n.* any plant growing on or among rocks.

rock pool *n.* a pool of water among rocks.

rock python *n.* any large snake of the family Boidae, esp. the African python *Python sebae*.

rock rabbit *n.* any of several species of hyrax.

rock rose *n.* any plant of the genus *Cistus*, *Helianthemum*, etc., with roselike flowers.

rock salmon *n.* **1** any of several fishes, esp. *Brit.* (as a commercial name) the catfish and dogfish. **2** *US* an amberjack.

rock salt *n.* common salt as a solid mineral.

rock-shaft *n.* a shaft that oscillates about an axis without making complete revolutions.

rock-solid *adj.* very solid or firm.

rockumentary /rɒkjʊ'mɛnt(ə)ri/ *n.* a documentary about rock music and musicians. [ROCK[2] + DOCUMENTARY]

rock-wool *n.* inorganic material made into matted fibre esp. for insulation or soundproofing.

rocky[1] /'rɒki/ *adj. & n.* ● *adj.* (**rockier**, **rockiest**) **1** of or like rock. **2** full of or abounding in rock or rocks (*a rocky shore*). ● *n.* (**the Rockies**) the Rocky Mountains in western N. America. □ **rockiness** *n.* [ROCK[1]]

rocky[2] /'rɒki/ *adj.* (**rockier**, **rockiest**) *colloq.* unsteady, tottering. □ **rockily** *adv.* **rockiness** *n.* [ROCK[2]]

Rocky Mountain goat see MOUNTAIN GOAT 2.

Rocky Mountain spotted fever see SPOTTED FEVER 3.

rococo /rə'kəʊkəʊ/ *adj. & n.* ● *adj.* **1** of a late baroque style of decoration prevalent in 18th-c. continental Europe, with asymmetrical patterns involving scrollwork, shell motifs, etc. **2** (of literature, music, architecture, and the decorative arts) highly ornamented, florid. ● *n.* the rococo style. [French, jocular alteration of ROCAILLE]

rod /rɒd/ *n.* **1** a slender straight bar esp. of wood or metal. **2** this as a symbol of office. **3 a** a stick or bundle of twigs used in caning or flogging. **b** (prec. by *the*) the use of this. **4 a** = FISHING ROD. **b** an angler using a rod. **5 a** a slender straight round stick growing as a shoot on a tree. **b** this when cut. **6** esp. *Brit. hist.* (as a measure) a perch or square perch (see PERCH[1] 3). **7** *US slang* = HOT ROD. **8** *US slang* a pistol or revolver. **9** *Anat.* any of numerous rod-shaped structures in the eye, detecting dim light. □ **make a rod for one's own back** *Brit.* act in a way that will bring one trouble later. □ **rodless** *adj.* **rodlet** *n.* **rodlike** *adj.* [Old English *rodd*, probably related to Old Norse *rudda* 'club']

rode[1] *past* of RIDE.

rode[2] /rəʊd/ *v.intr.* **1** (of wildfowl) fly landwards in the evening. **2** (of woodcock) fly in the evening during the breeding season. [18th c.: origin unknown]

rodent /'rəʊd(ə)nt/ *n. & adj.* ● *n.* a mammal of the order Rodentia, with strong incisors and no canine teeth, e.g. rat, mouse, squirrel, beaver, porcupine. ● *adj.* **1** of the order Rodentia. **2** gnawing (esp. *Med.* of slow-growing ulcers). □ **rodential** /-'dɛnʃ(ə)l/ *adj.* [Latin *rodere ros-* 'gnaw']

rodenticide /rə'dɛntɪsʌɪd/ *n.* a poison used to kill rodents.

rodent officer *n. Brit.* an official dealing with rodent pests.

rodeo /'rəʊdɪəʊ, rə'deɪəʊ/ *n.* (*pl.* **-os**) **1** an exhibition or entertainment involving cowboys' skills in handling animals. **2** an exhibition of other skills, e.g. in motorcycling. **3 a** a round-up of cattle on a ranch for branding etc. **b** an enclosure for this. [Spanish from *rodear* 'go round', ultimately from Latin *rotare* ROTATE[1]]

rodham /'rɒdəm/ *n.* a raised bank in the Fen district of E. Anglia, formed on the bed of a dry river course. [20th c.: origin uncertain]

rodomontade /,rɒdə(ʊ)mɒn'teɪd/ *n., adj., & v.* ● *n.* **1** boastful or bragging talk or behaviour. **2** an instance of this. ●*adj.* boastful or bragging. ●*v.intr.* brag, talk boastfully. [French from obsolete Italian *rodomontada*, from French *rodomont* & Italian *rodomonte*, from the name of a boastful character in the medieval *Orlando* epics]

roe[1] /rəʊ/ *n.* **1** (also **hard roe**) the mass of eggs in a female fish's ovary. **2** (also **soft roe**) the milt of a male fish. □ **roed** *adj.* (also in *comb.*). [Middle English *row(e)*, *rough*, from Middle Low German, Middle Dutch *roge(n)*]

roe[2] /rəʊ/ *n.* (*pl.* same or **roes**) (also **roe-deer**) a small European and Asian deer, *Capreolus capreolus*. [Old English *rā(ha)*]

roebuck /'rəʊbʌk/ *n.* a male roe-deer.

roentgen /'rʌntjən; 'rə:nt-, 'rɒnt-/ *n.* (also **röntgen**) a unit of ionizing radiation, the amount producing one electrostatic unit of positive or negative ionic charge in one cubic centimetre of air under standard conditions. [named after W. C. *Röntgen*, German physicist (d. 1923), discoverer of X-rays]

roentgenography /rʌntjə'nɒgrəfi, rə:nt-, rɒnt-/ *n.* photography using X-rays.

roentgenology /rʌntjə'nɒlədʒi, rə:nt-, rɒnt-/ *n.* = RADIOLOGY.

roentgen rays *n.pl. hist.* X-rays.

roe-stone *n.* oolite.

rogation /rə(ʊ)'geɪʃ(ə)n/ *n.* (usu. in *pl.*) *Eccl.* a solemn supplication consisting of the litany of the saints chanted on the three days before Ascension Day. □ **rogational** *adj.* [Middle English from Latin *rogatio*, from *rogare* 'ask']

Rogation Days *n.pl.* the three days before Ascension Day.

Rogation Sunday *n.* the Sunday preceding the Rogation Days.

Rogationtide /rə(ʊ)'geɪʃ(ə)ntʌɪd/ *n.* the period of the Rogation Days.

roger /'rɒdʒə/ *int. & v.* ●*int.* **1** your message has been received and understood (used in radio communication etc.). **2** *slang* I agree. ●*v. Brit. coarse slang* **1** *intr.* have sexual intercourse. **2** *tr.* have sexual intercourse with (a woman). [the name *Roger*, code for *R*]

rogue /rəʊg/ *n. & v.* ●*n.* **1** a dishonest or unprincipled person. **2** *joc.* a mischievous person, esp. a child. **3** (usu. *attrib.*) **a** a wild animal driven away or living apart from the herd and of fierce temper (*rogue elephant*). **b** a stray, irresponsible, or undisciplined person or thing (*rogue trader*). **4** an inferior or defective specimen among many acceptable ones. ●*v.tr.* remove inferior or defective specimens from. [16th-c.: origin uncertain]

roguery /'rəʊg(ə)ri/ *n.* (*pl.* **-ies**) conduct or an action characteristic of rogues.

rogues' gallery *n.* a collection of photographs of known criminals etc., used for identification of suspects.

roguish /'rəʊgɪʃ/ *adj.* **1** playfully mischievous. **2** characteristic of rogues. □ **roguishly** *adv.* **roguishness** *n.*

roil /rɔɪl/ *v.tr.* **1** make (a liquid) turbid by agitating it. **2** *US* = RILE 1. [perhaps via Old French *ruiler* 'mix mortar' from Late Latin *regulare* 'regulate']

roister /'rɔɪstə/ *v.intr.* (esp. as **roistering** *adj.*) revel noisily; be uproarious. □ **roisterer** *n.* **roistering** *n.* **roisterous** *adj.* [obsolete *roister* 'roisterer' from French *rustre* 'ruffian', variant of *ruste*, from Latin *rusticus* RUSTIC]

Roland /'rəʊlənd/ *n.* □ **a Roland for an Oliver 1** an effective retort. **2** a well-balanced combat or exchange. [name of the legendary nephew of Charlemagne celebrated with his comrade Oliver in the *Chanson de Roland*]

role /rəʊl/ *n.* (also **rôle**) **1** an actor's part in a play, film, etc. **2** a person's or thing's characteristic or expected function (*the role of the tape recorder in language-learning*). [French *rôle* and obsolete French *roule, rolle*, = ROLL *n.*]

role model *n.* a person looked to by others as an example in a particular role or situation.

role-playing *n.* (also **role-play**) an exercise or game in which participants act the part of another character, used in psychotherapy, language-teaching, etc. □ **role-play** *v.intr. & tr.*

role reversal *n.* the assumption of a role which is the reverse of that normally performed.

roll /rəʊl/ *v. & n.* ●*v.* **1 a** *intr.* move or go in some direction by turning over and over on an axis (*the ball rolled under the table*; *a barrel started rolling*). **b** *tr.* cause to do this (*rolled the barrel into the cellar*). **2** *tr.* make revolve between two surfaces (*rolled the clay between his palms*). **3 a** *intr.* (foll. by *along*, *by*, etc.) move or advance on or (of time etc.) as if on wheels etc. (*the bus rolled past*; *the pram rolled off the pavement*; *the years rolled by*). **b** *tr.* cause to do this (*rolled the tea trolley into the kitchen*). **c** *intr.* (of a person) be conveyed in a vehicle (*the farmer rolled by on his tractor*). **4 a** *tr.* turn over and over on itself to form a more or less cylindrical or spherical shape (*rolled a newspaper*). **b** *tr.* make by forming material into a cylinder or ball (*rolled a cigarette*; *rolled a huge snowball*). **c** *tr.* accumulate into a mass (*rolled the dough into a ball*). **d** *intr.* (foll. by *into*) make a specified shape of itself (*the hedgehog rolled into a ball*). **5** *tr.* flatten or form by passing a roller etc. over or by passing between rollers (*roll the lawn*; *roll pastry*; *roll thin foil*). **6** *intr. & tr.* change or cause to change direction by rotatory movement (*his eyes rolled*; *he rolled his eyes*). **7** *intr.* **a** wallow, turn about in a fluid or a loose medium (*the dog rolled in the dust*). **b** (of a horse etc.) lie on its back and kick about, esp. so as to dislodge its rider. **8** *intr.* **a** (of a moving ship, aircraft, or vehicle) sway to and fro on an axis parallel to the direction of motion. **b** walk with an unsteady swaying gait (*they rolled out of the pub*). **9 a** *intr.* undulate, show or go with an undulating surface or motion (*rolling hills*; *rolling mist*; *the waves roll in*). **b** *tr.* carry or propel with such motion (*the river rolls its waters to the sea*). **10 a** *intr.* (of machinery) start functioning or moving (*the cameras rolled*; *the train began to roll*). **b** *tr.* cause (machinery) to do this. **11 a** *tr.* display (credits for a film or television programme) moving as if on a roller up the screen. **b** *intr.* (of credits) be displayed in this way. **12** *intr. & tr.* sound or utter with a vibratory or trilling effect (*words rolled off his tongue*; *thunder rolled in the distance*; *he rolls his* rs). **13** *N. Amer. slang* **a** *tr.* overturn (a car etc.). **b** *intr.* (of a car etc.) overturn. **14** *tr. US* throw (dice). **15** *tr. slang* rob (esp. a helpless victim). ●*n.* **1** a rolling motion or gait; undulation (*the roll of the hills*). **2 a** a spell of rolling (*a roll in the mud*). **b** a gymnastic exercise in which the body is rolled into a tucked position and turned in a forward or backward circle. **c** (esp. **a roll in the hay**) *colloq.* an act of sexual intercourse or erotic fondling. **3** the continuous rhythmic sound of thunder or a drum. **4** *Aeron.* a complete revolution of an aircraft about its longitudinal axis. **5 a** a cylinder formed by turning flexible material over and over on itself without folding (*a roll of carpet*; *a roll of wallpaper*). **b** a filled cake or pastry of similar form (*fig roll*; *sausage roll*). **6 a** a small portion of bread individually baked. **b** this with a specified filling (*ham roll*). **7** a more or less cylindrical or semicylindrical straight or curved mass of something (*rolls of fat*; *a roll of hair*). **8 a** an official list or register (*the electoral roll*). **b** the total numbers on this (*the schools' rolls have fallen*). **c** a document, esp. an official record, in scroll form. **9** a cylinder or roller, esp. to shape metal in a rolling mill. **10** *Archit.* **a** a moulding of convex section. **b** a spiral scroll of an Ionic capital. **11** *US* & *Austral.* money, esp. as banknotes rolled together. □ **be rolling** *colloq.* be very rich. **be rolling in** *colloq.* have plenty of (esp. money). **on a roll** *N. Amer. slang* experiencing a bout of success or progress; engaged in a period of intense activity. **roll back** *N. Amer.* cause (esp. prices) to decrease. **rolled into one** combined in one person or thing. **roll in**

arrive in great numbers or quantity. **rolling drunk** swaying or staggering from drunkenness. **roll of honour** a list of those honoured, esp. the dead in war. **roll on 1** put on or apply by rolling. **2** (in *imper.*) *colloq.* (of a time, in eager expectation) come quickly (*roll on Friday!*). **roll over 1** send (a person) sprawling or rolling. **2** *Econ.* finance the repayment of (maturing stock etc.) by an issue of new stock. **roll up 1** *colloq.* arrive in a vehicle; appear on the scene. **2** make into or form a roll. **3** *Mil.* drive the flank of (an enemy line) back and round so that the line is shortened or surrounded. **roll up one's sleeves** see SLEEVE. **strike off the rolls** debar (esp. a solicitor) from practising after dishonesty etc. ▫ **rollable** *adj.* [Middle English via Old French *rol(l)er*, *rouler*, *ro(u)lle* from Latin *rotulus*, diminutive of *rota* 'wheel']

rollaway /ˈrəʊləweɪ/ *adj. US* (of a bed etc.) that can be removed on wheels or castors.

roll-back *n.* a reduction (esp. in price).

roll bar *n.* an overhead metal bar strengthening the frame of a vehicle (esp. in racing) and protecting the occupants if the vehicle overturns.

roll-call *n.* a process of calling out a list of names to establish who is present.

rolled gold *n.* gold in the form of a thin coating applied to a baser metal by rolling.

rolled oats *n.pl.* oats that have been husked and crushed.

roller /ˈrəʊlə/ *n.* **1 a** a hard revolving cylinder for smoothing the ground, spreading ink or paint, crushing or stamping, rolling cloth around, hanging a towel on, etc., used alone or as a rotating part of a machine. **b** a cylinder for diminishing friction when moving a heavy object. **2** a small cylinder on which hair is rolled for setting. **3** a long swelling wave. **4** (also **roller bandage**) a long surgical bandage rolled up for convenient application. **5** a kind of tumbler pigeon. **6 a** a brilliantly plumaged bird of the family Coraciidae, with characteristic tumbling display-flight. **b** a breed of canary with a trilling song.

rollerball /ˈrəʊləbɔːl/ *n.* a ballpoint pen using thinner ink than other ballpoints.

roller bearing *n.* a bearing like a ball-bearing but with small cylinders instead of balls.

Rollerblade /ˈrəʊləbleɪd/ *n.* & *v.* ● *n. propr.* each of a pair of boots fitted with small wheels, one behind the other, underneath, for roller skating in the manner of ice-skating. ● *v.intr.* (**rollerblade**) skate using such boots. ▫ **rollerblader** *n.*

roller blind *n.* a blind over a window etc., fitted on a roller.

roller coaster *n.*, *adj.*, & *v.* ● *n.* a switchback at a fair etc. ● *attrib.adj.* (**roller-coaster**) that goes up and down, or changes, suddenly and repeatedly. ● *v.intr.* (**roller-coaster**) (also **roller-coast**) go up and down or change in this way.

roller skate *n.* & *v.* ● *n.* each of a pair of metal frames with small wheels, fitted to shoes for gliding across a hard surface. ● *v.intr.* move on roller skates. ▫ **roller skater** *n.*

roller towel *n.* a towel with the ends joined, hung on a roller.

rollick /ˈrɒlɪk/ *v.* & *n.* ● *v.intr.* (esp. as **rollicking** *adj.*) be jovial or exuberant, indulge in high spirits, revel. ● *n.* **1** exuberant gaiety. **2** a spree or escapade. [19th-c., probably dialect: perhaps from ROMP + FROLIC]

rolling barrage *n.* = CREEPING BARRAGE.

rolling mill *n.* a machine or factory for rolling metal into shape.

rolling pin *n.* a cylinder for rolling out pastry, dough, etc.

rolling stock *n.* **1** the locomotives, carriages, or other vehicles, used on a railway. **2** *US* the road vehicles of a company.

rolling stone *n.* a person who is unwilling to settle for long in one place.

rolling strike *n.* industrial action through a series of limited strikes by consecutive groups.

rollmop /ˈrəʊlmɒp/ *n.* a rolled uncooked pickled herring fillet. [German *Rollmops*]

roll-neck *n.* & *adj.* ● *n.* **1** a high loosely turned-over neck. **2** a sweater etc. having this. ● *attrib.adj.* having a roll-neck.

roll-on *adj.* & *n.* ● *attrib.adj.* (of deodorant etc.) applied by means of a rotating ball in the neck of the container. ● *n. Brit.* a light elastic corset.

roll-on roll-off *adj. Brit.* (usu. *attrib.*) (of a ship, a method of transport, etc.) in which vehicles are driven directly on at the start of the voyage and off at the end of it.

roll-out *n.* **1 a** the official wheeling out of a new aircraft or spacecraft. **b** the official launch of a new product. **2** the part of a landing during which an aircraft travels along the runway losing speed.

roll-over *n.* **1** *Econ.* the extension or transfer of a debt or other financial relationship. **2** *colloq.* the overturning of a vehicle etc.

roll-top desk *n.* a desk with a flexible cover sliding in curved grooves.

roll-up *n.* (also **roll-your-own**) *Brit.* a hand-rolled cigarette.

roly-poly /ˌrəʊlɪˈpəʊli/ *n.* & *adj.* ● *n.* (*pl.* **-ies**) **1** (also **roly-poly pudding**) *Brit.* a pudding made of a sheet of suet pastry covered with jam etc., formed into a roll, and steamed or baked. **2** *US* a tumbler toy. **3** *Austral.* a bushy plant, esp. *Salsola kali*, that breaks off and is rolled by the wind. ● *adj.* (usu. of a child) podgy, plump. [probably formed on ROLL]

ROM /rɒm/ *n. Computing* read-only memory. [abbreviation]

Rom /rɒm/ *n.* (*pl.* **Roma** /ˈrɒmə/) a male gypsy. [Romany, = man, husband]

Rom. *abbr.* Romans (New Testament).

rom. *abbr.* roman (type).

Romaic /rə(ʊ)ˈmeɪɪk/ *n.* & *adj.* ● *n.* the vernacular language of modern Greece. ● *adj.* of or relating to this language. [Greek *Rhōmaikos* 'Roman' (used esp. of the Eastern Empire)]

romaine /rə(ʊ)ˈmeɪn/ *n. N. Amer.* a cos lettuce. [French, fem. of *romain* (as ROMAN)]

romaji /ˈrəʊmədʒi/ *n.* a system of romanized spelling used to transliterate Japanese. [Japanese]

Roman /ˈrəʊmən/ *adj.* & *n.* ● *adj.* **1 a** of ancient Rome or its territory or people. **b** *archaic* of its language. **2** of medieval or modern Rome. **3** of papal Rome, esp. = ROMAN CATHOLIC. **4** of a kind ascribed to the early Romans (*Roman honesty*; *Roman virtue*). **5** surviving from a period of ancient Roman rule (*Roman road*). **6** (**roman**) (of type) of a plain upright kind used in ordinary print. **7** (of the alphabet etc.) based on the ancient Roman system with letters A–Z. ● *n.* **1 a** a citizen of the ancient Roman Republic or Empire. **b** a soldier of the Roman Empire. **2** a citizen of modern Rome. **3** = ROMAN CATHOLIC. **4** (**roman**) roman type. **5** (in *pl.*) the Christians of ancient Rome. [Middle English via Old French *Romain* (*n.* & *adj.*) from Latin *Romanus*, from *Roma* 'Rome']

roman-à-clef /rəʊˌmɑːnɑːˈkleɪ, French rɔmɑ̃akle/ *n.* (*pl.* ***romans-à-clef*** *pronunc.* same) a novel in which real persons or events appear with invented names. [French, = novel with a key]

Roman candle *n.* a firework discharging a series of flaming coloured balls and sparks.

Roman Catholic *adj.* & *n.* ● *adj.* of the part of the Christian Church acknowledging the Pope as its head. ● *n.* a member of this Church. ▫ **Roman Catholicism** *n.* [17th-c. translation of Latin (*Ecclesia*) *Romana Catholica* (*et Apostolica*) 'Catholic (and Apostolic) (Church) of Rome', apparently originally as a conciliatory term in place of the earlier *Roman*, *Romanist*, or *Romish*, which had aquired derogatory overtones: see ROMAN, CATHOLIC]

romance /rə(ʊ)'mans, 'rəʊmans/ *n., adj., & v.* ● *n.* **1** an atmosphere or tendency characterized by a sense of remoteness from or idealization of everyday life. **2 a** a prevailing sense of wonder or mystery surrounding the mutual attraction in a love affair. **b** sentimental or idealized love. **c** a love affair. **3 a** a literary genre with romantic love or highly imaginative unrealistic episodes forming the central theme. **b** a work of this genre. **4** a medieval tale, usu. in verse, of some hero of chivalry, of the kind common in the Romance languages. **5 a** exaggeration or picturesque falsehood. **b** an instance of this. **6** (**Romance**) the languages descended from Latin regarded collectively. **7** *Mus.* a short informal piece. ● *adj.* (**Romance**) of any of the languages descended from Latin (French, Italian, Spanish, etc.). ● *v.* **1** *intr.* exaggerate or distort the truth, esp. fantastically. **2** *tr.* **a** court, woo. **b** seek the attention or custom of, esp. by flattery. [Middle English from Old French *romanz, -ans, -ance,* ultimately from Latin *Romanicus* ROMANIC]

romancer /rəʊ'mansə/ *n.* **1** a writer of romances, esp. in the medieval period. **2** a liar who resorts to fantasy.

Roman Empire *n. hist.* that established by Augustus in 27 BC and divided by Theodosius in AD 395 into the Western or Latin and Eastern or Greek Empire.

Romanesque /rəʊmə'nɛsk/ *n. & adj.* ● *n.* a style of architecture prevalent in Europe *c.*900–1200, with massive vaulting and round arches (cf. NORMAN *adj.* 2). ● *adj.* of or relating to the Romanesque style of architecture. [French from *roman* ROMANCE]

roman-fleuve /rəʊmɑːn'fləːv, French rɔmɑ̃flœv/ *n.* (*pl.* ***romans-fleuves*** *pronunc.* same) **1** a novel featuring the leisurely description of the lives of members of a family etc. **2** a sequence of self-contained novels. [French, = river novel]

Roman holiday *n.* enjoyment derived from others' discomfiture.

Romanian /rə(ʊ)'meɪnɪən, rʊ-/ *n. & adj.* (also **Rumanian, Roumanian** /ruː-/) ● *n.* **1 a** a native or national of Romania in E. Europe. **b** a person of Romanian descent. **2** the language of Romania. ● *adj.* of or relating to Romania or its people or language.

Romanic /rə(ʊ)'manɪk/ *n. & adj.* ● *n.* = ROMANCE *n.* 6. ● *adj.* **1 a** of or relating to Romance. **b** Romance-speaking. **2** descended from the ancient Romans or inheriting aspects of their social or political life. [Latin *Romanicus* (as ROMAN)]

Romanism /'rəʊmənɪz(ə)m/ *n.* Roman Catholicism.

Romanist /'rəʊmənɪst/ *n.* **1** a student of Roman history or law or of the Romance languages. **2 a** a supporter of Roman Catholicism. **b** a Roman Catholic. **3** any of several 16th-c. Dutch and Flemish painters influenced by Italian Renaissance art. [modern Latin *Romanista* (as ROMAN)]

romanize /'rəʊmənʌɪz/ *v.tr.* (also **-ise**) **1** make Roman or Roman Catholic in character. **2** put into the Roman alphabet or into roman type. □ **romanization** /-'zeɪʃ(ə)n/ *n.*

Roman law *n.* the law-code developed by the ancient Romans and forming the basis of many modern codes.

Roman nose *n.* one with a high bridge; an aquiline nose.

Roman numeral *n.* any of the Roman letters representing numbers: I = 1, V = 5, X = 10, L = 50, C = 100, D = 500, M = 1,000.

Romano /rə(ʊ)'mɑːnəʊ/ *n.* a strong-tasting hard cheese, originally made in Italy . [Italian,= ROMAN]

Romano- /rə(ʊ)'mɑːnəʊ/ *comb. form* Roman; Roman and (*Romano-British*).

Romansh /rə(ʊ)'manʃ, -'mɑːnʃ/ *n. & adj.* (also **Rumansh** /rʊ-/) ● *n.* the Rhaeto-Romanic dialects, esp. as spoken in the Swiss canton of Grisons. ● *adj.* of these dialects. [Romansh *Ruman(t)sch, Roman(t)sch* from medieval Latin *romanice* (*adv.*) (as ROMANCE)]

romantic /rə(ʊ)'mantɪk/ *adj. & n.* ● *adj.* **1** of, characterized by, or suggestive of an idealized, sentimental, or fantastic view of reality; remote from experience (*a romantic picture*; *a romantic setting*). **2** inclined towards or suggestive of romance in love (*a romantic woman*; *a romantic evening*; *romantic words*). **3** (of a person) imaginative, visionary, idealistic. **4 a** (of style in art, music, etc.) concerned more with feeling and emotion than with form and aesthetic qualities; preferring grandeur or picturesqueness to finish and proportion. **b** (also **Romantic**) of or relating to the 18th–19th-c. romantic movement or style in the European arts. **5** (of a project etc.) unpractical, fantastic. ● *n.* **1** a romantic person. **2** a romanticist. □ **romantically** *adv.* [*romant* 'tale of chivalry' from Old French, from *romanz* ROMANCE]

romanticism /rə(ʊ)'mantɪsɪz(ə)m/ *n.* (also **Romanticism**) adherence to a romantic style in art, music, etc.

romanticist /rə(ʊ)'mantɪsɪst/ *n.* (also **Romanticist**) a writer or artist of the romantic school.

romanticize /rə(ʊ)'mantɪsʌɪz/ *v.* (also **-ise**) **1** *tr.* **a** make or render romantic or unreal (*a romanticized account of war*). **b** describe or portray in a romantic fashion. **2** *intr.* indulge in romantic thoughts or actions. □ **romanticization** /-'zeɪʃ(ə)n/ *n.*

Romany /'rɒməni, 'rəʊ-/ *n. & adj.* ● *n.* (*pl.* **-ies**) **1** a gypsy. **2** the Indo-European language of the gypsies. ● *adj.* of or relating to gypsies or their language. [Romany *Romani*, fem. and pl. of *Romano* (*adj.*), from ROM]

Romeo /'rəʊmɪəʊ/ *n.* (*pl.* **-os**) a passionate male lover or seducer. [the hero of Shakespeare's *Romeo and Juliet*]

romer /'rəʊmə/ *n.* a small piece of card, plastic, etc., marked with graduations for measuring grid references on a map. [named after C. *Romer*, its British inventor d. 1951]

Romish /'rəʊmɪʃ/ *adj.* usu. *derog.* Roman Catholic.

romneya /'rɒmnɪə/ *n.* any shrubby poppy of the genus *Romneya*, bearing showy white flowers. [named after T. *Romney* Robinson, Irish astronomer d. 1882]

romp /rɒmp/ *v. & n.* ● *v.intr.* **1** play about roughly and energetically. **2** (foll. by *along, past,* etc.) *colloq.* proceed without effort. ● *n.* **1** a spell of romping or boisterous play. **2** *Sport* an easy victory. □ **romp in** (or **home**) *colloq.* finish as the easy winner. □ **rompy** *adj.* (**rompier, rompiest**). [perhaps variant of RAMP[1]]

romper /'rɒmpə/ *n.* (usu. in *pl.*) (also **romper suit**) a young child's one-piece garment covering legs and trunk.

rondavel /rɒn'dɑːv(ə)l/ *n. S.Afr.* **1** a round tribal hut usu. with a thatched conical roof. **2** a similar building, esp. as a holiday cottage, or as an outbuilding on a farm etc. [Afrikaans *rondawel*]

ronde /rɒnd/ *n.* **1** a dance in which the dancers move in a circle. **2** a course of talk, activity, etc. [French, fem. of *rond* ROUND *adj.*]

rondeau /'rɒndəʊ/ *n.* (*pl.* **rondeaux** *pronunc.* same or /-əʊz/) a poem of ten or thirteen lines with only two rhymes throughout and with the opening words used twice as a refrain. [French, earlier *rondel*: see RONDEL]

rondel /'rɒnd(ə)l/ *n.* a rondeau, esp. one of special form. [Middle English from Old French, from *rond* ROUND: cf. ROUNDEL]

rondo /'rɒndəʊ/ *n.* (*pl.* **-os**) *Mus.* a form with a recurring leading theme, often found in the final movement of a sonata or concerto etc. [Italian from French *rondeau*: see RONDEAU]

rone /rəʊn/ *n. Sc.* a gutter for carrying off rain from a roof. [16th cent.: origin unknown]

ronin /'rəʊnɪn/ *n.* (*pl.* same or **ronins**) **1** *hist.* (in feudal Japan) a lordless wandering samurai; an outlaw. **2** a Japanese student retaking a university examination. [Japanese]

röntgen etc. var. of ROENTGEN etc.

roo /ruː/ *n.* (also **'roo**) *Austral. colloq.* a kangaroo. [abbreviation]

rood /ruːd/ *n.* **1** a crucifix, esp. one raised on a screen or beam at the entrance to the chancel. **2** a quarter of an acre. [Old English *rōd*]

rood-loft *n.* a gallery on top of a rood-screen.

rood-screen *n.* a wooden or stone carved screen separating nave and chancel.

roof /ruːf/ *n.* & *v.* ● *n.* (*pl.* **roofs** or *disp.* **rooves** /ruːvz/) **1 a** the upper covering of a building, usu. supported by its walls. **b** the top of a covered vehicle. **c** the top inner surface of an oven, refrigerator, etc. **2** the overhead rock in a cave or mine etc. **3** *poet.* the branches or the sky etc. overhead. **4** (of prices etc.) the upper limit or ceiling. ● *v.tr.* **1** (often foll. by *in*, *over*) cover with or as with a roof. **2** be the roof of. □ **go through the roof** *colloq.* (of prices etc.) reach extreme or unexpected heights. **hit** (or **go through** or **raise**) **the roof** *colloq.* become very angry. **a roof over one's head** somewhere to live. **under one roof** in the same building. **under a person's roof** in a person's house (esp. with reference to hospitality). □ **roofed** *adj.* (also in *comb.*). **roofless** *adj.* [Old English *hrōf*]

roofage /ˈruːfɪdʒ/ *n.* the expanse of a roof or roofs.

roofer /ˈruːfə/ *n.* a person who constructs or repairs roofs.

roof garden *n.* a garden on the flat roof of a building.

roofing /ˈruːfɪŋ/ *n.* **1** material for constructing a roof. **2** the process of constructing a roof or roofs.

roof light *n.* **1** a window panel built into a roof. **2 a** a flashing warning light on the top of a police car etc. **b** an interior light on the ceiling of a motor vehicle.

roof of the mouth *n.* the palate.

roof-rack *n.* a framework for carrying luggage etc. on the roof of a vehicle.

roofscape /ˈruːfskeɪp/ *n.* a scene or view of roofs.

rooftop /ˈruːftɒp/ *n.* **1** the outer surface of a roof (often *attrib.*: *rooftop terrace*). **2** (esp. in *pl.*) the level of a roof. □ **shout it from the rooftops** make a thing embarrassingly public.

roof-tree *n.* the ridge piece of a roof.

rooibos /ˈrɔɪbɒs/ *n. S.Afr.* **1** an evergreen shrub of the genus *Aspalathus*, with leaves used to make tea. **2** a shrub or small tree, *Combretum apiculatum*, with spikes of scented yellow flowers. [Afrikaans, = red bush]

rooinek /ˈrɔɪnɛk/ *n. S.Afr. slang offens.* a British or English-speaking South African. [Afrikaans, = red-neck]

rook[1] /rʊk/ *n.* & *v.* ● *n.* **1** a black European and Asiatic bird, *Corvus frugilegus*, of the crow family, nesting in colonies in treetops. **2** *slang* a sharper, esp. at dice or cards; a person who lives off inexperienced gamblers etc. ● *v.tr. slang* **1** charge (a customer) extortionately. **2** win money from (a person) at cards etc., esp. by swindling. [Old English *hrōc*]

rook[2] /rʊk/ *n.* a chess piece with its top in the shape of a battlement. [Middle English from Old French *roc(k)*, ultimately from Arabic *rukk*, original sense uncertain]

rookery /ˈrʊk(ə)ri/ *n.* (*pl.* **-ies**) **1 a** a colony of rooks. **b** a clump of trees having rooks' nests. **2** a colony of seabirds (esp. penguins) or seals.

rookie /ˈrʊki/ *n. slang* **1** a new recruit, esp. in the army or police. **2** *N. Amer.* a member of a sports team in his or her first full season. [corruption of *recruit*, influenced by ROOK[1]]

room /ruːm, rʊm/ *n.* & *v.* ● *n.* **1 a** space that is or might be occupied by something; capaciousness or ability to accommodate contents (*it takes up too much room*; *there is plenty of room*; *we have no room here for idlers*). **b** space in or on (*houseroom*; *shelf room*). **2 a** a part of a building enclosed by walls or partitions, floor and ceiling. **b** (in *pl.*) a set of these occupied by a person or family; apartments or lodgings. **c** persons present in a room (*the room fell silent*). **3** (in *comb.*) a room or area for a specified purpose (*auction room*). **4** (foll. by *for*, or *to* + infin.) opportunity or scope (*room to improve things*; *no room for dispute*). ● *v.intr.* (often foll. by *with*) esp. *N. Amer.* have a room or rooms; lodge, board. □ **make room** (often foll. by *for*) clear a space (for a person or thing) by removal of others; make way, yield place. **not** (or **no**) **room to swing a cat** a very confined space. □ **-roomed** *adj.* (in *comb.*). **roomful** *n.* (*pl.* **-fuls**). [Old English *rūm*, from Germanic]

roomer /ˈruːmə, ˈrʊmə/ *n. N. Amer.* a lodger occupying a room or rooms without board.

roomette /ruːˈmɛt, rʊ-/ *n. N. Amer.* **1** a private single compartment in a sleeping car. **2** a small bedroom for letting.

roomie /ˈruːmi, ˈrʊmi/ *n. N. Amer. colloq.* a room-mate.

rooming house *n.* a lodging house.

room-mate *n.* (*US* usu. **roommate**) a person occupying the same room as another.

room service *n.* (in a hotel etc.) service of food or drink taken to a guest's room.

roomy /ˈruːmi, ˈrʊmi/ *adj.* (**roomier**, **roomiest**) having much room, spacious. □ **roomily** *adv.* **roominess** *n.*

roost[1] /ruːst/ *n.* & *v.* ● *n.* **1** a branch or other support on which a bird perches, esp. a place where birds regularly settle to sleep. **2** a place offering temporary sleeping accommodation. ● *v.* **1** *intr.* **a** (of a bird) settle for rest or sleep. **b** (of a person) stay for the night. **2** *tr.* provide with a sleeping place. □ **come home to roost** (of a scheme etc.) recoil unfavourably upon the originator. [Old English *hrōst*]

roost[2] /ruːst/ *n.* a tidal race in the Orkneys and Shetlands. [Old Norse *röst*]

rooster /ˈruːstə/ *n.* esp. *N. Amer.*, *Austral.*, etc. a domestic cock.

root[1] /ruːt/ *n.* & *v.* ● *n.* **1 a** the part of a plant normally below the ground, attaching it to the earth and conveying nourishment to it from the soil. **b** (in *pl.*) such a part divided into branches or fibres. **c** the corresponding organ of an epiphyte; the part attaching ivy to its support. **d** the permanent underground stock of a plant. **e** any small plant with a root for transplanting. **2 a** any plant, e.g. a turnip or carrot, with an edible root. **b** (also **root vegetable**) such a root. **3** (in *pl.*) social, ethnic, or cultural origins, esp. as the reasons for one's long-standing emotional attachment to a place, community, etc. **4 a** the embedded part of a bodily organ or structure, e.g. hair, tooth, nail, etc. **b** the part of a thing attaching it to a greater or more fundamental whole. **c** (in *pl.*) the base of a mountain etc. **5 a** the basic cause, source, or origin (*love of money is the root of all evil*; *has its roots in the distant past*). **b** (*attrib.*) (of an idea etc.) from which the rest originated. **6** the basis of something, its means of continuance or growth (*has its root(s) in selfishness*; *has no root in the nature of things*). **7** the essential substance or nature of something (*get to the root of things*). **8** *Math.* **a** a number or quantity that when multiplied by itself a usu. specified number of times gives a specified number or quantity (*the cube root of eight is two*). **b** a square root. **c** a value of an unknown quantity satisfying a given equation. **9** *Philol.* any ultimate unanalysable element of language; a basis, not necessarily surviving as a word in itself, on which words are made by the addition of prefixes or suffixes or by other modification. **10** *Mus.* the fundamental note of a chord. **11** *Bibl.* a scion, an offshoot (*there shall be a root of Jesse*). **12** *Austral.* & *NZ coarse slang* **a** an act of sexual intercourse. **b** a (usu. female) sexual partner. ● *v.* **1 a** *intr.* take root or grow roots. **b** *tr.* cause to do this (*take care to root the cuttings firmly*). **2** *tr.* **a** fix firmly; establish (*fear rooted him to the spot*). **b** (as **rooted** *adj.*) firmly established (*her affection was deeply rooted*; *rooted objection to*). **3** *tr.* (usu. foll. by *out*, *up*) drag or dig up by the roots. **4** *tr. Austral.* & *NZ coarse slang* **a** have sexual intercourse with. **b** exhaust, frustrate. □ **pull up by the roots 1** uproot. **2** eradicate, destroy. **put down roots 1** begin to draw nourishment from the soil. **2** become settled or established. **root and branch** thorough(ly), radical(ly). **root out** find and get rid of. **strike at the root** (or **roots**) **of** set about destroying.

strike (or **take**) **root** **1** begin to grow and draw nourishment from the soil. **2** become fixed or established. □ **rootage** *n.* **rootedness** *n.* **rootless** *adj.* **rootlet** *n.* **rootlike** *adj.* **rooty** *adj.* [Old English *rōt* from Old Norse *rót*, related to WORT & Latin *radix*: see RADIX]

root[2] /ru:t/ *v.* **1 a** *intr.* (of an animal, esp. a pig) turn up the ground with the snout, beak, etc., in search of food. **b** *tr.* (foll. by *up*) turn up (the ground) by rooting. **2 a** *intr.* (foll. by *around*, *in*, etc.) rummage. **b** *tr.* (foll. by *out* or *up*) find or extract by rummaging. **3** *intr.* (foll. by *for*) orig. *US slang* encourage by applause or support. □ **rooter** *n.* (in sense 3). [earlier *wroot*, from Old English *wrōtan* & Old Norse *róta*: related to Old English *wrōt* 'snout']

root beer *n. N. Amer.* an effervescent soft drink made from an extract of roots.

root canal *n. Dentistry* **1** the pulp-filled cavity in the root of a tooth. **2** *US* a procedure to replace infected pulp with an inert material.

rootle /'ru:t(ə)l/ *v.intr. & tr. Brit.* = ROOT[2] 1, 2. [ROOT[2]]

root-mean-square *n. Math.* the square root of the arithmetic mean of the squares of a set of values.

root sign *n. Math.* = RADICAL SIGN.

rootstock /'ru:tstɒk/ *n.* **1** a rhizome. **2** a plant into which a graft is inserted. **3** a primary form from which offshoots have arisen.

rootsy /'ru:tsi/ *adj. colloq.* (of music) uncommercialized, full-blooded, esp. showing traditional origins.

root vegetable see ROOT[1] *n.* 2b.

rooves see ROOF.

rope /rəʊp/ *n. & v.* ● *n.* **1 a** stout cord made by twisting together strands of hemp, sisal, flax, cotton, nylon, wire, or similar material. **b** a piece of this. **c** *US* a lasso. **2** (foll. by *of*) a quantity of onions, ova, or pearls strung together. **3** (in *pl.*, prec. by *the*) **a** the conditions in some sphere of action (*know the ropes*; *show a person the ropes*). **b** the ropes enclosing a boxing or wrestling ring or cricket ground. **4** (prec. by *the*) **a** a halter for hanging a person. **b** execution by hanging. ● *v.* **1** *tr.* fasten, secure, or catch with rope. **2** *tr.* (usu. foll. by *off*, *in*) enclose (a space) with rope. **3** *Mountaineering* **a** *tr.* connect (a party) with a rope; attach (a person) to a rope. **b** (*absol.*) put on a rope. **c** *intr.* (foll. by *down*, *up*) climb down or up using a rope. □ **give a person plenty of rope** (or **enough rope to hang himself** or **herself**) give a person enough freedom of action to bring about his or her own downfall. **on the rope** *Mountaineering* roped together. **on the ropes 1** *Boxing* forced against the ropes by the opponent's attack. **2** near defeat. **rope in** persuade to take part. **rope into** persuade to take part in (*was roped into doing the washing-up*). **rope of sand** delusive security. [Old English *rāp*, from Germanic]

ropeable /'rəʊpəb(ə)l/ *adj.* (also **ropable**) **1** capable of being roped. **2** *Austral. & NZ slang* angry.

rope ladder *n.* two long ropes connected by short crosspieces, used as a ladder.

ropemanship /'rəʊpmənʃɪp/ *n.* skill in rope-walking or climbing with ropes.

rope-moulding *n.* a moulding cut spirally in imitation of rope-strands.

rope's end *n. hist.* a short piece of rope used to flog (formerly, esp. a sailor) with.

rope-walk *n. hist.* a long piece of ground where ropes are made.

rope-walker *n.* a performer on a tightrope. □ **rope-walking** *n.*

ropeway /'rəʊpweɪ/ *n.* a cable railway.

rope-yard *n.* a rope-making establishment.

rope-yarn *n.* **1** material obtained by unpicking rope-strands, or used for making them. **2** a piece of this. **3** a mere trifle.

roping /'rəʊpɪŋ/ *n.* a set or arrangement of ropes.

ropy /'rəʊpi/ *adj.* (also **ropey**) (**ropier**, **ropiest**) **1** *Brit. colloq.* poor in quality. **2** (of wine, bread, etc.) forming viscous or gelatinous threads. **3** like a rope. □ **ropily** *adv.* **ropiness** *n.*

roque /rəʊk/ *n. US* croquet played on a hard court surrounded by a bank. [alteration of form of ROQUET]

Roquefort /'rɒkfɔ:/ *n. propr.* **1** a soft blue cheese made from ewes' milk. **2** a salad dressing made of this. [*Roquefort*, a village in S. France]

roquet /'rəʊkeɪ, -ki/ *v. & n. Croquet* ● *v.* (**roqueted**, **roqueting**) **1** *tr.* **a** cause one's ball to strike (another ball). **b** (of a ball) strike (another). **2** *intr.* strike another ball thus. ● *n.* an instance of roqueting. [apparently arbitrary alteration of CROQUET *v.*, originally used in the same sense]

roquette /rɒ'kɛt/ *n.* = ROCKET[2] 2. [French]

ro-ro /'rəʊrəʊ/ *adj. Brit.* roll-on roll-off. [abbreviation]

rorqual /'rɔ:kw(ə)l/ *n.* any baleen whale of the family Balaenopteridae, with a pleated throat and small dorsal fin, esp. the fin whale. [French from Norwegian *røyrkval*, from Old Norse *reythr* the specific name + *hvalr* WHALE[1]]

Rorschach test /'rɔ:ʃɑ:k/ *n. Psychol.* a type of personality test in which a standard set of ink-blots is presented one by one to the subject, who is asked to describe what they suggest or resemble. [named after H. *Rorschach*, Swiss psychiatrist d. 1922]

rort /rɔ:t/ *n. Austral. slang* **1** a trick, a fraud; a dishonest practice. **2** a wild party. [back-formation from RORTY]

rorty /'rɔ:ti/ *adj.* (**rortier**, **rortiest**) *Brit. slang* **1** splendid; boisterous, rowdy (*had a rorty time*). **2** coarse, earthy. [19th c.: origin unknown]

rosace /'rəʊzeɪs/ *n.* **1** a rose window. **2** a rose-shaped ornament or design. [French from Latin *rosaceus*: see ROSACEOUS]

rosaceous /rəʊ'zeɪʃəs/ *adj. Bot.* of the large plant family Rosaceae, which includes the rose, apple, plum, blackberry, hawthorn, etc. [Latin *rosaceus* from *rosa* 'rose']

rosaline /'rəʊzəli:n/ *n.* a variety of fine needlepoint or pillow lace. [probably French]

rosaniline /rəʊ'zanɪli:n, -lɪn, -lʌɪn/ *n.* **1 a** an organic base derived from aniline. **b** a red dye obtained from this. **2** fuchsine. [ROSE[1] + ANILINE]

rosarian /rəʊ'zɛ:rɪən/ *n.* a person who cultivates roses, esp. professionally. [Latin *rosarium* 'rose garden, ROSARY']

rosarium /rəʊ'zɛ:rɪəm/ *n.* a rose garden. [Latin (as ROSARY)]

rosary /'rəʊz(ə)ri/ *n.* (*pl.* **-ies**) **1** *RC Ch.* **a** a form of devotion in which five (or fifteen) decades of Hail Marys are repeated, each decade preceded by an Our Father and followed by a Glory Be. **b** a string of 55 (or 165) beads for keeping count in this. **c** a book containing this devotion. **2** a similar form of bead-string used in other religions. **3** a rose garden or rose bed. [Middle English from Latin *rosarium* 'rose garden', neut. of *rosarius* (as ROSE[1])]

roscoe /'rɒskəʊ/ *n. US slang* a gun, esp. a pistol or revolver. [the name *Roscoe*]

rose[1] /rəʊz/ *n., adj., & v.* ● *n.* **1** any prickly bush or shrub of the genus *Rosa* (family Rosaceae), bearing usu. fragrant flowers generally of a red, pink, yellow, or white colour. **2** this flower. **3** any flowering plant resembling this (*Christmas rose*; *rock rose*). **4 a** a light crimson colour, pink. **b** (usu. in *pl.*) a rosy complexion (*roses in her cheeks*). **5 a** a representation of the flower in heraldry or decoration (esp. as the national emblem of England). **b** a rose-shaped design, e.g. on a compass card or on the soundhole of a lute etc. **6** the sprinkling-nozzle of a watering can or hose. **7** a circular mounting on a ceiling through which the wiring of an electric light passes. **8 a** a rose diamond. **b** a rose window. **9** (in *pl.*) used in various phrases to express favourable circumstances, ease, success, etc. (*roses all the way*; *everything's roses*). **10** an excellent person or thing, esp. a beautiful woman (*English rose*; *rose between two* *thorns*). ● *adj.* = ROSE-COLOURED 1. ● *v.tr.* (esp. as **rosed** *adj.*) *literary* make rosy (*the rosed Alps*). ◻ **under the rose** in confidence; under pledge of secrecy. ◻ **roseless** *adj.* **roselike** *adj.* [Old English *rōse* from Latin *rosa*, reinforced in Middle English from Old French]

rose[2] *past* of RISE.

rosé /ˈrəʊzeɪ/ *n.* any light pink wine, coloured by only brief contact with red grape skins. [French, = pink]

rose-apple *n.* **1** a tropical tree of the genus *Syzygium*, cultivated for its foliage and fragrant fruit. **2** this fruit.

roseate /ˈrəʊzɪət/ *adj.* **1** = ROSE-COLOURED 1, 2. **2** having a partly pink plumage (*roseate spoonbill*; *roseate tern*). [Latin *roseus* 'rosy' (as ROSE[1])]

rosebay /ˈrəʊzbeɪ/ *n.* **1 a** the oleander. **b** a N. American azalea. **2** (in full **rosebay willowherb**) a tall willowherb, *Chamerion angustifolium*, with pink flowers; also called FIREWEED.

rosebowl /ˈrəʊzbəʊl/ *n.* a bowl for displaying cut roses.

rosebud /ˈrəʊzbʌd/ *n.* **1** a bud of a rose. **2** *Brit.* a pretty young woman.

rose bush *n.* a rose plant.

rose-chafer *n.* a green or copper-coloured beetle, *Cetonia aurata*, frequenting roses.

rose colour *n.* the colour of a pale red rose; warm pink.

rose-coloured *adj.* **1** of a warm pink colour. **2** optimistic, sanguine, cheerful (*takes rose-coloured views*). ◻ **see through rose-coloured** (or **-tinted**) **spectacles** regard (circumstances etc.) with unfounded favour or optimism.

rose comb *n.* a flat fleshy comb of a fowl.

rose-cut *adj.* cut as a rose diamond.

rose diamond *n.* a hemispherical diamond with the curved part cut in triangular facets.

rose-engine *n.* an appendage to a lathe for engraving curved patterns.

rose-fish *n.* (*pl.* usu. same) a bright red food fish, *Sebastes marinus*, of the N. Atlantic.

rose geranium *n.* a pink-flowered sweet-scented pelargonium, *Pelargonium graveolus*.

rose-hip *n.* = HIP[2].

rose leaf *n.* **1** a petal of a rose. **2** a leaf of a rose.

rosella /rə(ʊ)ˈzɛlə/ *n.* **1** any brightly coloured Australian parakeet of the genus *Platycercus*. **2** *Austral.* an easily-shorn sheep. [corruption of *Rosehill*, NSW, where the bird was first found]

rose madder *n.* a pale pink pigment.

rosemaling /ˈrəʊsəmɑːlɪŋ, -mɔːlɪŋ, -zə-/ *n.* the art of painting wooden furniture etc. with flower motifs. [Norwegian, = rose painting]

rose-mallow *n.* = HIBISCUS.

rosemary /ˈrəʊzm(ə)ri/ *n.* an evergreen fragrant shrub, *Rosmarinus officinalis*, with leaves used as a culinary herb, in perfumery, etc., and taken as an emblem of remembrance. [Middle English, earlier *rosmarine*, ultimately from Latin *ros marinus*, from *ros* 'dew' + *marinus* MARINE, with assimilation to ROSE[1] and *Mary* name of the Virgin]

rose nail *n.* a nail with a head shaped like a rose diamond.

rose of Jericho *n.* a resurrection plant, *Anastatica hierochuntica*.

rose of Sharon *n.* **1** a species of hypericum, *Hypericum calycinum*, with dense foliage and golden-yellow flowers; also called AARON'S BEARD. **2** *Bibl.* a flowering plant of unknown identity.

roseola /rə(ʊ)ˈziːələ/ *n. Med.* **1** a rosy rash occurring in measles, typhoid, syphilis, and other diseases. **2** *archaic* = RUBELLA. ◻ **roseolar** *adj.* **roseolous** *adj.* [modern variant of RUBEOLA from Latin *roseus* 'rose-coloured']

rose pink *n.* & *adj.* ● *n.* = ROSE COLOUR. ● *adj.* (hyphenated when *attrib.*) = ROSE-COLOURED 1.

rose-point *n.* a point lace with a design of roses.

rose quartz *n.* a translucent pink variety of quartz.

rose red *adj.* & *n.* ● *adj.* (hyphenated when *attrib.*) red like a rose, rose-coloured. ● *n.* this colour.

rose-root *n.* a yellow-flowered plant, *Rhodiola rosea*, with roots smelling like a rose when dried or bruised.

rosery /ˈrəʊzəri/ *n.* (*pl.* **-ies**) a rose garden.

rose-tinted *adj.* = ROSE-COLOURED.

rose tree *n.* a rose plant, esp. a standard rose.

Rosetta Stone /rə(ʊ)ˈzɛtə/ *n.* a key to previously unattainable understanding. [a stone found near *Rosetta* in Egypt, with a trilingual inscription of the 2nd c. BC in hieroglyphic and demotic Egyptian, and Greek, important in the deciphering of hieroglyphs]

rosette /rə(ʊ)ˈzɛt/ *n.* **1** a rose-shaped ornament made usu. of ribbon and worn esp. as a supporter's badge, or as an award or the symbol of an award in a competition, esp. by a prizewinning animal. **2** *Archit.* **a** a carved or moulded ornament resembling or representing a rose. **b** a rose window. **3** an object or symbol or arrangement of parts resembling a rose. **4** *Biol.* **a** a roselike cluster of parts. **b** markings resembling a rose. **5** a rose diamond. ◻ **rosetted** *adj.* [French, diminutive of *rose* ROSE[1]]

rose water *n.* perfume made from roses.

rose window *n.* a circular window, usu. with roselike or spokelike tracery.

rosewood /ˈrəʊzwʊd/ *n.* **1** any of several fragrant close-grained woods used in making furniture. **2** a tree yielding such wood, esp. a tropical leguminous tree of the genus *Dalbergia*.

Rosh Hashana /rɒʃ həˈʃɑːnə/ *n.* (also **Rosh Hashanah**) the Jewish New Year. [Hebrew, = beginning (literally 'head') of the year]

Roshi /ˈrəʊʃi/ *n.* (*pl.* **Roshis**) the spiritual leader of a community of Zen Buddhist monks. [Japanese]

Rosicrucian /rəʊzɪˈkruːʃ(ə)n/ *n.* & *adj.* ● *n.* **1** *hist.* a member of a 17th–18th-c. society devoted to the study of metaphysical and mystical lore (said to have been founded in 1484 by Christian Rosenkreuz). **2** a member of any of several later organizations deriving from this. ● *adj.* of or relating to the Rosicrucians. ◻ **Rosicrucianism** *n.* [modern Latin *rosa crucis* (or *crux*), as Latinization of German *Rosenkreuz*]

rosin /ˈrɒzɪn/ *n.* & *v.* ● *n.* resin, esp. the solid residue after distillation of oil of turpentine from crude turpentine. ● *v.tr.* (**rosined**, **rosining**) **1** rub (esp. the bow of a violin etc.) with rosin. **2** smear or seal up with rosin. ◻ **rosiny** *adj.* [Middle English, alteration of RESIN]

rosolio /rə(ʊ)ˈzəʊlɪəʊ/ *n.* (also **rosoglio**) (*pl.* **-os**) a sweet cordial of spirits, sugar, and flavouring. [Italian, from modern Latin *ros solis* 'dew of the sun']

RoSPA /ˈrɒspə/ *abbr.* (in the UK) Royal Society for the Prevention of Accidents.

roster /ˈrɒstə, ˈrəʊst-/ *n.* & *v.* ● *n.* **1** a list or plan showing turns of duty or leave for individuals or groups esp. of a military force. **2** a list usu. of names, esp. *N. Amer.* of sports players available for team selection. ● *v.tr.* place on a roster. [Dutch *rooster* 'list', originally 'gridiron', from *roosten* ROAST, with reference to its parallel lines]

rostra *pl.* of ROSTRUM.

rostral /ˈrɒstr(ə)l/ *adj.* **1** *Zool.* & *Bot.* of or on the rostrum. **2** *Anat.* **a** nearer the hypophysial area in the early embryo. **b** nearer the region of the nose and mouth in post-embryonic life. **3** (of a column etc.) adorned with the beaks of ancient war-galleys or with representations of these. ◻ **rostrally** *adv.*

rostrated /rɒˈstreɪtɪd/ *adj.* **1** *Zool.* & *Bot.* having or ending in a rostrum. **2** = ROSTRAL 3. [Latin *rostratus* (as ROSTRUM)]

rostrum /ˈrɒstrəm/ *n.* (*pl.* **rostra** /-strə/ or **rostrums**) **1 a** a platform for public speaking. **b** a conductor's platform facing the orchestra. **c** a similar platform for other purposes, e.g. for supporting a film or television camera. **2** *Zool.* & *Bot.* a beak, stiff snout, or beaklike part, esp. of an insect or arachnid. **3** *Rom. Antiq.* the beak of a war-galley. ◻ (all in sense 2) **rostrate** /-strət/ *adj.* **rostriferous** /-ˈstrɪf(ə)rəs/ *adj.* **rostriform** *adj.*

[Latin, = beak, from *rodere ros-* 'gnaw': originally *rostra* (pl., in sense 1a) in the Roman forum adorned with beaks of captured galleys]

rosy /'rəʊzi/ *adj.* (**rosier**, **rosiest**) **1 a** coloured like a pink or red rose (*rosy lips, rosy sky*). **b** pink as an indication of health or youth (*rosy cheeks*). **2** optimistic, hopeful, cheerful (*a rosy future*; *a rosy attitude to life*). □ **rosily** *adv.* **rosiness** *n.*

rot /rɒt/ *v., n., & int.* ● *v.* (**rotted**, **rotting**) **1** *intr.* **a** (of animal or vegetable matter) lose its original form by the chemical action of bacteria, fungi, etc.; decay. **b** (foll. by *off, away*) crumble or drop from a stem etc. through decomposition. **2** *intr.* **a** (of society, institutions, etc.) gradually perish from lack of vigour or use. **b** (of a prisoner etc.) waste away (*left to rot in prison*); (of a person) languish. **3** *tr.* cause to rot, make rotten. **4** *tr. Brit. slang* tease, abuse, denigrate. **5** *intr. Brit. slang* joke. ● *n.* **1** the process or state of rotting. **2** *colloq.* nonsense; an absurd or foolish statement, argument, or proposal. **3** *Brit.* a sudden series of (usu. unaccountable) failures; a rapid decline in standards etc. (*a rot set in*; *we must try to stop the rot*). **4** (often prec. by *the*) necrosis of the liver in sheep, caused by infestation with liver-flukes. ● *int. colloq.* expressing incredulity or ridicule. [Old English *rotian* (*v.*): the noun Middle English, perhaps from Scandinavian: cf. Icelandic, Norwegian *rot*]

rota /'rəʊtə/ *n.* **1** esp. *Brit.* a list of persons acting, or duties to be done, in rotation; a roster. **2** (**Rota**) *RC Ch.* the supreme ecclesiastical and secular court. [Latin, = wheel]

Rotarian /rəʊ'tɛːrɪən/ *n. & adj.* ● *n.* a member of Rotary. ● *adj.* of Rotary. [ROTARY + -AN]

rotary /'rəʊt(ə)ri/ *adj. & n.* ● *adj.* acting by rotation (*rotary drill*; *rotary pump*). ● *n.* (*pl.* **-ies**) **1** a rotary machine. **2** *N. Amer.* a traffic roundabout. **3** (**Rotary**) (in full **Rotary International**) a worldwide charitable society of businessmen and professional men, originally named from members entertaining in rotation. [medieval Latin *rotarius* (as ROTA)]

Rotary club *n.* a local branch of Rotary.

rotary-wing *attrib.adj.* (of an aircraft) deriving lift from rotary aerofoils.

rotate[1] /rə(ʊ)'teɪt/ *v.* **1** *intr. & tr.* move round an axis or centre, revolve. **2 a** *tr.* take or arrange in rotation. **b** *intr.* act or take place in rotation (*the chairmanship will rotate*). □ **rotatable** *adj.* **rotative** /'rəʊtətɪv/ *adj.* **rotatory** /'rəʊtət(ə)ri, -'teɪt(ə)ri/ *adj.* [Latin *rotare* from *rota* 'wheel']

rotate[2] /'rəʊteɪt/ *adj. Bot.* wheel-shaped. [Latin *rota* 'wheel']

rotation /rə(ʊ)'teɪʃ(ə)n/ *n.* **1** the act or an instance of rotating or being rotated. **2** a recurrence; a recurrent series or period; a regular succession of various members of a group in office etc. **3** a system of growing different crops in regular order to avoid exhausting the soil. □ **rotational** *adj.* **rotationally** *adv.* [Latin *rotatio*]

rotator /rə(ʊ)'teɪtə/ *n.* **1** a machine or device for causing something to rotate. **2** *Anat.* a muscle that rotates a limb etc. **3** a revolving apparatus or part. [Latin (as ROTATE[1])]

Rotavator /'rəʊtəveɪtə/ *n.* (also **Rotovator**) *Brit. propr.* a machine with a rotating blade for breaking up or tilling the soil. □ **rotavate** *v.tr.* [ROTARY + CULTIVATOR]

rote /rəʊt/ *n.* (usu. prec. by *by*) mechanical or habitual repetition (with reference to acquiring knowledge). [Middle English: origin unknown]

rote learning *n.* learning by rote.

rotenone /'rəʊtənəʊn/ *n.* a toxic crystalline substance obtained from the roots of derris and other plants, used as an insecticide. [Japanese *rotenon* from *roten* 'derris']

rot-gut *n. slang* cheap harmful alcoholic liquor.

rotifer /'rəʊtɪfə/ *n.* any minute aquatic animal of the phylum Rotifera, with a characteristic wheel-like ciliated organ used in swimming and feeding. [modern Latin *rotiferus*, from Latin *rota* 'wheel' + *-fer* 'bearing']

rotisserie /rə(ʊ)'tɪs(ə)ri/ *n.* **1** a restaurant etc. where meat is roasted or barbecued. **2** a cooking appliance with a rotating spit for roasting and barbecuing meat. [French *rôtisserie* from *rostir* ROAST]

rotogravure /rəʊtəgrə'vjʊə/ *n.* **1** a printing system using a rotary press with intaglio cylinders, usu. running at high speed. **2** a sheet etc. printed with this system, esp. *N. Amer.* the colour magazine of a Sunday newspaper. [German *Rotogravur* (name of a company) assimilated to PHOTOGRAVURE]

rotor /'rəʊtə/ *n.* **1** a rotary part of a machine, esp. in the distributor of an internal-combustion engine. **2** a set of radiating aerofoils round a hub on a helicopter, providing lift when rotated. [formed irregularly from ROTATOR]

rototill /'rəʊtətɪl/ *v.tr. N. Amer.* = ROTAVATE (see ROTAVATOR).

Rotovator var. of ROTAVATOR.

rotten /'rɒt(ə)n/ *adj.* (**rottener**, **rottenest**) **1** rotting or rotted; falling to pieces or liable to break or tear from age or use. **2** morally, socially, or politically corrupt. **3** *colloq.* **a** disagreeable, unpleasant (*had a rotten time*). **b** (of a plan etc.) ill-advised, unsatisfactory (*a rotten idea*). **c** disagreeably ill (*feel rotten today*). □ **rottenly** *adv.* **rottenness** /'rɒt(ə)nnɪs/ *n.* [Middle English from Old Norse *rotinn*: related to ROT, RET]

rotten apple *n. colloq.* a bad or esp. a morally corrupt person in a group etc.

rotten borough *n. hist.* (before 1832) an English borough able to elect an MP though having very few voters.

rotten-stone *n.* decomposed siliceous limestone used as a powder for polishing metals.

rotter /'rɒtə/ *n.* esp. *Brit. colloq.* an objectionable, unpleasant, or reprehensible person. [ROT]

Rottweiler /'rɒtvʌɪlə, -wʌɪlə/ *n.* **1** a large powerful dog of a tall black and tan breed. **2** this breed. [German, from *Rottweil* in SW Germany]

rotund /rə(ʊ)'tʌnd/ *adj.* **1 a** circular, round. **b** (of a person) large and plump, podgy. **2** (of speech, literary style, etc.) sonorous, grandiloquent. □ **rotundity** *n.* **rotundly** *adv.* [Latin *rotundus* from *rotare* ROTATE[1]]

rotunda /rə(ʊ)'tʌndə/ *n.* **1** a building with a circular ground plan, esp. one with a dome. **2** a circular hall or room. [earlier *rotonda* from Italian *rotonda* (*camera*) 'round (chamber)', fem. of *rotondo* 'round' (as ROTUND)]

rouble /'ruːb(ə)l/ *n.* (also **ruble**) the chief monetary unit of Russia and some other former republics of the USSR. [French from Russian *rubl'*]

roué /'ruːeɪ/ *n.* a debauchee, esp. an elderly one; a rake. [French, past part. of *rouer* 'break on wheel', = one deserving this]

rouge /ruːʒ/ *n. & v.* ● *n.* **1** a red powder or cream used for colouring the cheeks. **2** powdered ferric oxide etc. as a polishing agent esp. for metal. ● *v.* **1** *tr.* colour with rouge. **2** *intr.* **a** apply rouge to one's cheeks. **b** become red, blush. [French, = red, from Latin *rubeus*, related to RED]

rouge-et-noir /ruːʒeɪ'nwɑː/ *n.* a gambling game using a table with red and black marks, on which players place stakes. [French, = red and black]

rough /rʌf/ *adj., adv., n., & v.* ● *adj.* **1 a** having an uneven or irregular surface, not smooth or level or polished. **b** *Tennis* etc. applied to the face of a racket on which the loops formed from the stringing process project (opp. SMOOTH *adj.* 1b). **2** (of ground, country, etc.) having many bumps, obstacles, etc. **3 a** hairy, shaggy. **b** (of cloth) coarse in texture. **4 a** (of a person or behaviour) not mild or quiet or gentle; boisterous, unrestrained (*rough manners*; *rough play*). **b** (of language etc.) coarse, indelicate. **c** (of wine etc.) sharp or harsh in taste. **5** (of the sea, weather, etc.) violent, stormy. **6** disorderly, riotous (*a rough part of town*). **7** harsh, insensitive, inconsiderate (*rough words*; *rough treatment*). **8 a** unpleasant, severe, demanding (*had a rough time*). **b** *Brit.* unfortunate, unreasonable, undeserved (*had rough luck*). **c** (foll. by *on*) hard or unfair towards. **9** lacking finish, elaboration, comfort, etc. (*rough lodgings*; *a rough welcome*). **10** incomplete, rudimentary (*a rough attempt*; *a rough makeshift*). **11 a** inexact, approximate, preliminary (*a rough estimate*; *a rough sketch*). **b** (of stationery etc.) for use in writing rough notes etc. **12** *colloq.* **a** ill, unwell (*am feeling rough*). **b** depressed, dejected. ● *adv.* in a rough manner (*the land should be ploughed rough*; *play rough*). ● *n.* **1** (usu. prec. by *the*) a hard part or aspect of life; hardship (*take the rough with the smooth*). **2** rough ground (*over rough and smooth*). **3** esp. *Brit.* a rough or violent person (*met a bunch of roughs*). **4** *Golf* rough ground off the fairway between tee and green. **5** an unfinished or provisional or natural state (*have written it in rough*; *shaped from the rough*). **6** (prec. by *the*) esp. *Brit.* the general way or tendency (*is true in the rough*). ● *v.tr.* **1** (foll. by *up*) ruffle (feathers, hair, etc.) by rubbing in the wrong direction. **2 a** (foll. by *out*) shape or plan roughly. **b** (foll. by *in*) sketch roughly. **3** give the first shaping to (a gun, lens, etc.). □ **bit of rough** *slang* a (usu. male) sexual partner whose toughness or lack of sophistication is a source of attraction. **the rough edge** (or **side**) **of one's tongue** severe or harsh words. **rough it** do without basic comforts. **rough up** *colloq.* treat (a person) with violence; attack violently. **sleep rough** *Brit.* sleep outdoors, or not in a proper bed. □ **roughness** *n.* [Old English *rūh*, from West Germanic]

roughage /ˈrʌfɪdʒ/ *n.* **1** fibrous indigestible material in vegetable foodstuffs which aids the passage of food etc. through the gut. **2** coarse fodder. [ROUGH + -AGE 3]

rough-and-ready *adj.* rough or crude but effective; not elaborate or over-particular.

rough-and-tumble *adj.* & *n.* ● *adj.* irregular, scrambling, disorderly. ● *n.* a haphazard fight; a scuffle.

rough breathing see BREATHING 2.

roughcast /ˈrʌfkɑːst/ *n.*, *adj.*, & *v.* ● *n.* plaster of lime and gravel, used on outside walls. ● *adj.* **1** (of a wall etc.) coated with roughcast. **2** (of a plan etc.) roughly formed, preliminary. ● *v.tr.* (*past* and *past part.* **-cast**) **1** coat (a wall) with roughcast. **2** prepare (a plan, essay, etc.) in outline.

rough coat *n.* a first coat of plaster applied to a surface.

rough copy *n.* **1** a first or original draft. **2** a copy of a picture etc. showing only the essential features.

rough deal *n.* hard or unfair treatment.

rough diamond *n.* **1** an uncut diamond. **2** a person of good nature but rough manners.

rough-dry *v.tr.* (**-dries, -dried**) dry (clothes) without ironing.

roughen /ˈrʌf(ə)n/ *v.tr.* & *intr.* make or become rough.

rough-handle *v.tr.* treat or handle roughly.

rough-hew *v.tr.* (*past part.* **-hewed** or **-hewn**) shape out roughly; give crude form to.

rough-hewn *adj.* **1** formed or shaped out roughly. **2** uncouth, unrefined.

rough hound *n.* a dogfish, esp. the lesser spotted dogfish, *Scyliorhinus canicula.*

rough house *n.* & *v. slang* ● *n.* a disturbance or row; boisterous play. ● *v.* (**rough-house**) **1** *tr.* handle (a person) roughly. **2** *intr.* make a disturbance; act violently.

roughie /ˈrʌfi/ *n. slang* **1** *Brit. dial.* & *Austral.* a rough; a hooligan. **2** *Austral.* **a** an outsider in a horse race etc. **b** an unfair or unreasonable act. See also ROUGHY.

roughish /ˈrʌfɪʃ/ *adj.* somewhat rough.

rough justice *n.* **1** treatment that is approximately fair. **2** treatment that is not at all fair.

roughly /ˈrʌfli/ *adv.* **1** in a rough manner. **2** approximately (*roughly 20 people attended*). □ **roughly speaking** in an approximate sense (*it is, roughly speaking, a square*).

roughneck /ˈrʌfnɛk/ *n. colloq.* **1** a rough or rowdy person. **2** a worker on an oil rig.

rough passage *n.* **1** a crossing over rough sea. **2** a difficult time or experience.

rough ride *n.* a difficult time or experience.

rough-rider *n.* a person who breaks in or can ride unbroken horses.

roughshod /ˈrʌfʃɒd/ *adj.* (of a horse) having shoes with nail heads projecting to prevent slipping. □ **ride roughshod over** treat inconsiderately or arrogantly.

rough stuff *n. colloq.* boisterous or violent behaviour.

rough tongue *n.* a habit of rudeness in speaking.

rough trade *n. slang* a tough or sadistic element among male homosexuals.

rough work *n.* **1** preliminary or provisional work. **2** *colloq.* violence. **3** a task requiring the use of force.

roughy /ˈrʌfi/ *n.* (also **roughie**) (*pl.* **-ies**) esp. *Austral.* either of two rough-scaled fishes, the tommy ruff, *Arripis georgianus*, or a small reef fish, *Trachichthys australis.* [perhaps from ROUGH or RUFF[2]]

roulade /rʊˈlɑːd/ *n.* **1** a dish cooked or served in the shape of a roll, esp. a rolled piece of meat or sponge with a filling. **2** a florid passage of runs etc. in solo vocal music, usu. sung to one syllable. [French from *rouler* 'to roll']

rouleau /ˈruːləʊ, rʊˈləʊ/ *n.* (*pl.* **rouleaux** or **rouleaus** /-əʊz/) **1** a cylindrical packet of coins. **2** a coil or roll of ribbon etc., esp. as trimming. [French from *rôle* ROLL *n.*]

roulette /rʊˈlɛt/ *n.* **1** a gambling game using a table in which a ball is dropped on to a revolving wheel with numbered compartments, players betting on the number at which the ball comes to rest. **2** *Math.* a curve generated by a point on a curve rolling on another. **3 a** a revolving toothed wheel used in engraving. **b** a similar wheel for making perforations between postage stamps in a sheet. □ **rouletted** *adj.* (in sense 3b). [French, diminutive of *rouelle*, from Late Latin *rotella*, diminutive of Latin *rota* 'wheel']

Roumanian var. of ROMANIAN.

round /raʊnd/ *adj.*, *n.*, *adv.*, *prep.*, & *v.* ● *adj.* **1** shaped like or approximately like a circle, sphere, or cylinder; having a convex or circular outline or surface; curved, not angular. **2** done with or involving circular motion. **3 a** entire, continuous, complete (*a round dozen*); fully expressed or developed; all together, not broken or defective or scanty. **b** (of a sum of money) considerable. **4** genuine, candid, outspoken; (of a statement etc.) categorical, unmistakable. **5** (usu. *attrib.*) (of a number) expressed for convenience or as an estimate in fewer significant numerals or with a fraction removed (*spent £297.32, or in round figures £300*). **6 a** (of a style) flowing. **b** (of a voice) not harsh. **7** *Phonet.* (of a vowel) pronounced with rounded lips. ● *n.* **1** a round object or form. **2 a** a revolving motion, a circular or recurring course (*the earth in its yearly round*). **b** a regular recurring series of activities or functions (*one's daily round*; *a continuous round of pleasure*). **c** a recurring succession or series of meetings for discussion etc. (*a new round of talks on disarmament*). **3 a** esp. *Brit.* a fixed route on which things are regularly delivered (*milk round*). **b** (often in *pl.*) a route or sequence by which people or things are regularly supervised or inspected (*a watchman's round*; *a doctor's rounds*). **4** an allowance of something distributed or measured out, esp.: **a** a single provision of drinks etc. to each member of a group. **b** ammunition to fire one shot; the act of firing this. **5 a** *Brit.* a slice across a loaf of bread. **b** *Brit.* a sandwich made from whole slices of bread. **c** a thick disc of beef cut from the haunch as a joint. **6** each of a set or series, a sequence of actions by each member of a group in turn, esp.: **a** one spell of play in a game etc. **b** one stage in a competition. **7** *Golf* the playing of all the holes in a course once. **8** *Archery* a fixed number of arrows shot from a fixed distance. **9** (**the round**) a form of sculpture in which the figure stands clear of any ground (cf. RELIEF 6a). **10** *Mus.* a canon for three or more unaccompanied voices singing at the same pitch or in octaves. **11** (in *pl.*) *Mil.* **a** a watch that goes round inspecting sentries. **b** a circuit made by this. **12** a rung of a ladder. **13** (foll. by *of*) the circumference, bounds, or extent of (*in all the round of Nature*). ● *adv.* esp. *Brit.*

1 with circular motion (*wheels go round*). **2** with return to the starting point or an earlier state (*summer soon comes round*). **3 a** with rotation, or change to an opposite position (*he turned round to look*). **b** with change to an opposite opinion etc. (*they were angry but I soon won them round*). **4** to, at, or affecting all or many points of a circumference or an area or the members of a company etc. (*tea was then handed round*; *may I look round?*). **5** in every direction from a centre or within a radius (*spread destruction round*; *everyone for a mile round*). **6** by a circuitous way (*will you jump over or go round?*; *go a long way round*). **7 a** to a person's house etc. (*ask him round*; *will be round soon*). **b** to a more prominent or convenient position (*brought the car round*). **8** measuring a (specified distance) in girth. ● *prep.* esp. *Brit.* **1** so as to encircle or enclose (*tour round the world*; *has a blanket round him*). **2** at or to points on the circumference of (*sat round the table*). **3** with successive visits to (*hawks them round the cafés*). **4** in various directions from or with regard to (*towns round Birmingham*; *shells bursting round them*). **5** having as an axis of revolution or as a central point (*turns round its centre of gravity*; *write a book round an event*). **6 a** so as to double or pass in a curved course (*go round the corner*). **b** having passed in this way (*be round the corner*). **c** in the position that would result from this (*find them round the corner*). **7** so as to come close from various sides but not into contact. ● *v.* **1 a** *tr.* give a round shape to. **b** *intr.* assume a round shape. **2** *tr.* double or pass round (a corner, cape, etc.). **3** *tr.* express (a number) in a less exact but more convenient form (also foll. by *down* when the number is decreased and *up* when it is increased). **4** *tr. Phonet.* pronounce (a vowel) with rounded lips. □ **go the round** (or **rounds**) (of news etc.) be passed on from person to person. **in the round 1** with all features shown; all things considered. **2** *Theatr.* with the audience round at least three sides of the stage. **3** (of sculpture) with all sides shown; not in relief. **make the round of** go round. **make** (or **go**) **one's rounds** take a customary route for inspection etc. **round about 1** in a ring (about); all round; on all sides (of). **2** with a change to an opposite position. **3** approximately (*cost round about £50*). **round and round** several times round. **round the bend** see BEND[1]. **round down** see sense 3 of *v.* **round off 1** bring to a complete or symmetrical or well-ordered state. **2** smooth out; blunt the corners or angles of. **round on a person** make a sudden verbal attack on or unexpected retort to a person. **round out 1** = *round off* 1. **2** provide more detail about. **round peg in a square hole** = *square peg in a round hole* (see PEG). **round the twist** see TWIST. **round up** collect or bring together, esp. by going round (see also sense 3 of *v.*). □ **roundish** *adj.* **roundness** *n.* [Middle English from Old French *ro(u)nd-*, stem of *ro(o)nt*, *reont*, from Latin *rotundus* ROTUND]

roundabout /ˈraʊndəbaʊt/ *n. & adj.* ● *n.* **1** *Brit.* a road junction at which traffic moves in one direction round a central island. **2** *Brit.* **a** a large revolving device in a playground, for children to ride on. **b** = MERRY-GO-ROUND 1. ● *adj.* circuitous, circumlocutory, indirect.

round-arm *adj. Cricket* (of bowling) performed with an outward horizontal swing of the arm.

round brackets *n.pl. Brit.* brackets of the form ( ).

round dance *n.* **1** a dance in which couples move in circles round the ballroom. **2** a dance in which the dancers form one large circle.

roundel /ˈraʊnd(ə)l/ *n.* **1 a** a small disc, esp. a decorative medallion. **b** *Heraldry* any of various circular charges. **2** a circular identifying mark painted on military aircraft, esp. the red, white, and blue of the RAF. **3** a poem of eleven lines in three stanzas. [Middle English from Old French *rondel(le)* (as ROUND)]

roundelay /ˈraʊndəleɪ/ *n.* a short simple song with a refrain. [French *rondelet* (as RONDEL), with assimilation to LAY[3] or *virelay*, a medieval song or lyric poem]

rounder /ˈraʊndə/ *n.* **1** (in *pl.*; treated as *sing.*) a game with a bat and ball in which players after hitting the ball run through a round of bases. **2** a complete run of a player through all the bases as a unit of scoring in rounders.

Roundhead /ˈraʊndhɛd/ *n. hist.* a member of the Parliamentary party in the English Civil War. [from their custom of wearing the hair cut short]

roundhouse /ˈraʊndhaʊs/ *n.* **1** a repair shed for railway locomotives, built round a turntable. **2** *slang* a blow given with a wide sweep of the arm. **3** *hist.* a prison; a place of detention. **4** *Naut.* a cabin or set of cabins on the after part of the quarterdeck, esp. on a sailing ship.

roundhouse kick *n.* (esp. in karate) a kick made with a wide sweep of the leg and rotation of the body.

roundly /ˈraʊn(d)li/ *adv.* **1** bluntly, in plain language, severely (*was roundly criticized*; *told them roundly that he refused*). **2** in a thoroughgoing manner (*go roundly to work*). **3** in a circular way (*swells out roundly*).

round robin *n.* **1** a petition esp. with signatures written in a circle to conceal the order of writing. **2** *N. Amer.* a tournament in which each competitor plays in turn against every other.

round-shouldered *adj.* with shoulders bent forward so that the back is rounded.

roundsman /ˈraʊn(d)zmən/ *n.* (*pl.* **-men**) **1** *Brit.* a trader's employee going round delivering and taking orders. **2** *US* a police officer in charge of a patrol. **3** *Austral.* a journalist covering a specified subject (*political roundsman*).

Round Table *n.* **1** an international charitable association which holds discussions, debates, etc., and undertakes community service. **2** (**round table**) an assembly for discussion, esp. at a conference (often *attrib.*: *round-table talks*). [alluding to the one at which King Arthur and his knights sat so that none should have precedence]

round-the-clock *attrib.adj.* lasting or covering all day and (usu.) all night (*round-the-clock care*). Cf. *round the clock* (CLOCK[1]).

round trip *n.* a trip to one or more places and back again (esp. by a circular route).

round-up *n.* **1** a systematic rounding up of people or things. **2** a summary; a résumé of facts or events.

roundworm /ˈraʊn(d)wəːm/ *n.* a nematode worm, esp. a parasitic one.

roup[1] /raʊp/ *n. & v. Sc. & N.Engl.* ● *n.* an auction. ● *v.tr.* sell by auction. [Middle English = to shout, roar, croak, of Scandinavian origin]

roup[2] /ruːp/ *n.* an infectious poultry disease, esp. of the respiratory tract. □ **roupy** *adj.* [as ROUP[1]]

rouse /raʊz/ *v.* **1 a** *tr.* (often foll. by *from*, *out of*) bring out of sleep, wake. **b** *intr.* (often foll. by *up*) cease to sleep, wake up. **2** (often foll. by *up*) **a** *tr.* stir up, make active or excited, startle out of inactivity or confidence or carelessness (*roused them from their complacency*; *was roused to protest*). **b** *intr.* become active. **3** *tr.* provoke to anger (*is terrible when roused*). **4** *tr.* evoke (feelings). **5** *tr.* (usu. foll. by *in*, *out*, *up*) *Naut.* haul vigorously. **6** *tr.* startle (game) from a lair or cover. **7** *tr.* stir (liquid, esp. beer while brewing). □ **rouse oneself** overcome one's indolence. □ **rousable** *adj.* **rouser** *n.* [originally as a hawking and hunting term, so probably from Anglo-French: origin unknown]

rouseabout /ˈraʊzəbaʊt/ *n. Austral. & NZ* an unskilled labourer or odd jobber, esp. on a farm.

rousing /ˈraʊzɪŋ/ *adj.* **1** exciting, stirring (*a rousing cheer*; *a rousing song*). **2** (of a fire) blazing strongly. □ **rousingly** *adv.*

roust /raʊst/ *v.tr.* **1** (often foll. by *up*, *out*) **a** rouse, stir up. **b** root out. **2** *N. Amer. slang* jostle, harass, rough up. □ **roust around** rummage. [perhaps alteration of ROUSE]

roustabout /ˈraʊstəbaʊt/ *n.* **1** a labourer on an oil rig. **2** an unskilled or casual labourer. **3** *US* **a** a dock labourer or deckhand. **b** a circus labourer. **4** *Austral.* = ROUSEABOUT.

rout[1] /raʊt/ *n. & v.* ● *n.* **1 a** a disorderly retreat of defeated troops. **b** a decisive defeat. **2 a** an assemblage or company, esp. of revellers or rioters. **b** *Law* an assemblage of three or more persons who have made a move towards committing an illegal act. **3** riot, tumult, disturbance, clamour, fuss. **4** *Brit. archaic* a large evening party or reception. ● *v.tr.* cause to retreat in disorder; defeat. □ **put to rout** put to flight, defeat utterly. [Middle English from Anglo-French *rute*, Old French *route*, ultimately from Latin *ruptus* 'broken']

rout[2] /raʊt/ *v.* **1** *intr. & tr.* = ROOT[2]. **2** *tr.* cut a groove, or any pattern not extending to the edges, in (a wooden or metal surface). □ **rout out** force or fetch out of bed or from a house or hiding place. [variant of ROOT[2]]

route /ruːt/ *n. & v.* ● *n.* **1** a way or course taken (esp. regularly) in getting from a starting point to a destination. **2** *N. Amer.* a round travelled in delivering, selling, or collecting goods. **3** /also raʊt/ *Mil. archaic* marching orders. ● *v.tr.* (**routeing** or **routing**) send or forward or direct to be sent by a particular route. [Middle English from Old French *r(o)ute* 'road', ultimately from Latin *ruptus* 'broken']

route man *n. N. Amer.* = ROUNDSMAN 1.

route march *n.* a training march for troops.

router /ˈraʊtə/ *n.* a type of plane with two handles or esp. a power tool used in routing.

routine /ruːˈtiːn/ *n., adj., & v.* ● *n.* **1** a regular course or procedure, an unvarying performance of certain acts. **2** a set sequence in a performance, esp. a dance, comedy act, etc. **3** *Computing* a sequence of instructions for performing a task. ● *adj.* **1** performed as part of a routine (*routine duties*). **2** of a customary or standard kind. ● *v.tr.* organize according to a routine. □ **routinely** *adv.* [French (as ROUTE)]

routinism /ruːˈtiːnɪz(ə)m/ *n.* the prevalence of routine. □ **routinist** *n. & adj.*

routinize /ruːˈtiːnʌɪz/ *v.tr.* (also **-ise**) subject to a routine; make into a matter of routine. □ **routinization** /-ˈzeɪʃ(ə)n/ *n.*

roux /ruː/ *n.* (*pl.* same) a mixture of fat (esp. butter) and flour used in making sauces etc. [French, = browned (butter): see RUSSET]

rove[1] /rəʊv/ *v. & n.* ● *v.* **1** *intr.* wander without a settled destination, roam, ramble. **2** *intr.* (of eyes) look in changing directions. **3** *tr.* wander over or through. ● *n.* an act of roving (*on the rove*). [originally a term in archery = shoot at a casual mark with the range not determined: Middle English perhaps from dialect *rave* 'stray', probably of Scandinavian origin]

rove[2] *past* of REEVE[2].

rove[3] /rəʊv/ *n. & v.* ● *n.* a sliver of cotton, wool, etc., drawn out and slightly twisted. ● *v.tr.* form into roves. [18th c.: origin unknown]

rove[4] /rəʊv/ *n.* a small metal plate or ring for a rivet to pass through and be clenched over, esp. in boat-building. [Old Norse *ró*, with parasitic *v*]

rove beetle *n.* any long-bodied beetle of the family Staphylinidae, usu. found in decaying animal and vegetable matter. [ROVE[1]]

rover[1] /ˈrəʊvə/ *n.* **1** a roving person; a wanderer. **2** *Croquet* **a** a ball that has passed all the hoops but not pegged out. **b** a player whose ball is a rover. **3** *Archery* **a** a mark chosen at undetermined range. **b** a mark for long-distance shooting. **4** *Amer. Football* a defensive linebacker assigned to move around in anticipation of opponents' play. **5** (**Rover**) *Brit.* a senior Scout (now called *Venture Scout*).

rover[2] /ˈrəʊvə/ *n.* a sea robber, a pirate. [Middle English from Middle Low German, Middle Dutch *rōver*, from *rōven* 'rob': related to REAVE]

rover[3] /ˈrəʊvə/ *n.* a person or machine that makes roves of fibre.

rover ticket *n.* a ticket permitting unlimited bus or railway travel in an area for a specified period.

roving commission *n. Brit.* authority given to a person or persons conducting an inquiry to travel as may be necessary.

roving eye *n.* (esp. in a man) a tendency to flirt or to be fickle sexually.

row[1] /rəʊ/ *n.* **1** a number of persons or things in a more or less straight line. **2** a line of seats across a theatre etc. (*in the front row*). **3** a street with a continuous line of houses along one or each side. **4** a line of plants in a field or garden. **5** a horizontal line of entries in a table etc. □ **a hard row to hoe** a difficult task. **in a row 1** forming a row. **2** *colloq.* in succession (*two Sundays in a row*). [Old English *rāw*, from Germanic]

row[2] /rəʊ/ *v. & n.* ● *v.* **1** *tr.* propel (a boat) with oars. **2** *tr.* convey (a passenger) in a boat in this way. **3** *intr.* propel a boat in this way. **4** *tr.* make (a stroke) or achieve (a rate of striking) in rowing. **5** *tr.* compete in (a race) by rowing. **6** *tr.* row a race with. ● *n.* **1** a spell of rowing. **2** an excursion in a rowing boat. □ **row down** overtake in a rowing, esp. bumping, race. **row out** exhaust by rowing (*the crew were completely rowed out at the finish*). **row over** complete the course of a boat race with little effort, owing to the absence or inferiority of competitors. □ **rower** *n.* [Old English *rōwan* from Germanic: related to RUDDER, Latin *remus* 'oar']

row[3] /raʊ/ *n. & v. colloq.* ● *n.* **1** esp. *Brit.* a loud noise or commotion. **2** a fierce quarrel or dispute. **3** *Brit.* **a** a severe reprimand. **b** the condition of being reprimanded (*shall get into a row*). ● *v.* **1** *intr.* make or engage in a row. **2** *tr. Brit.* reprimand. □ **make** (or **kick up**) **a row 1** esp. *Brit.* make a noise or commotion. **2** make a vigorous protest. [18th-c. slang: origin unknown]

rowan /ˈrəʊən, ˈraʊən/ *n.* **1** (also **rowan tree**) **a** *Brit.* the mountain ash, *Sorbus aucuparia*. **b** *US* a similar tree, *Sorbus americana*, native to America. **2** (in full **rowan-berry**) the scarlet berry of either of these trees. [Scandinavian, corresponding to Norwegian *rogn*, *raun*, Icelandic *reynir*]

rowboat /ˈrəʊbəʊt/ *n. N. Amer.* = ROWING BOAT.

rowdy /ˈraʊdi/ *adj. & n.* ● *adj.* (**rowdier**, **rowdiest**) noisy and disorderly. ● *n.* (*pl.* **-ies**) a rowdy person. □ **rowdily** *adv.* **rowdiness** *n.* **rowdyism** *n.* [19th-c. US, originally = lawless backwoodsman: origin unknown]

rowel /ˈraʊ(ə)l/ *n. & v.* ● *n.* **1** a spiked revolving disc at the end of a spur. **2** *hist.* a circular piece of leather etc. with a hole in the centre inserted between a horse's skin and flesh to discharge an exudate. ● *v.tr.* (**rowelled**, **rowelling**; *US* **roweled**, **roweling**) **1** urge with a rowel. **2** *hist.* insert a rowel in. [Middle English via Old French *roel(e)* from Late Latin *rotella*, diminutive of Latin *rota* 'wheel']

rowen /ˈraʊən/ *n.* (in *sing.* or *pl.*) *US* a second growth of grass, an aftermath. [Middle English from Old French *regain* (as RE-, GAIN)]

row house *n. N. Amer.* a terrace house.

rowing boat *n. Brit.* a small boat propelled by oars.

rowing machine *n.* a device for exercising the muscles used in rowing.

rowlock /ˈrɒlək, ˈrʌlək/ *n.* a device on a boat's gunwale, esp. a pair of thole-pins, serving as a fulcrum for an oar and keeping it in place. [alteration of earlier OARLOCK, influenced by ROW[2]]

Rowton house /ˈraʊt(ə)n/ *n. Brit. hist.* a type of cheap lodging house for poor single men, providing accommodation of a decent standard. [named after Lord *Rowton*, English social reformer d. 1903]

royal /ˈrɔɪəl/ *adj. & n.* ● *adj.* **1** of or suited to or worthy of a king or queen. **2** in the service or under the patronage of a king or queen. **3** belonging to the king or queen (*the royal hands*; *the royal anger*). **4** of the family of a king or queen. **5** majestic, stately, splendid. **6** on a great scale, of exceptional size or quality, first-rate (*gave us royal entertainment*; *in royal spirits*; *had a royal time*). ● *n.* **1** *colloq.* a member of the royal family. **2** a royal sail or mast. **3** a royal stag. **4** a size of paper, about 620 × 500 mm (25 × 20 in.). **5** (**the Royals**) (in the UK) the Royal Marines. □ **royal road to** way of attaining without trouble. □ **royally** *adv.* [Middle English via Old French *roial* from Latin *regalis* REGAL]

Royal Air Force *n.* the British air force.

royal assent *n.* assent of the sovereign to a bill passed by Parliament.

royal blue *n.* & *adj.* ● *n.* a deep vivid blue. ● *adj.* (hyphenated when *attrib.*) of this colour.

Royal British Legion *n.* (in the UK) an association of ex-servicemen (and now women) formed in 1921.

royal burgh *n. hist.* (in Scotland) a burgh holding a charter from the Crown.

Royal Commission *n.* (in the UK) **1** a commission of inquiry appointed by the Crown at the instance of the Government. **2** a committee so appointed.

royal duke *n.* a duke who is also a royal prince.

Royal Engineers *n.pl.* the engineering branch of the British army.

royal family *n.* the family to which a sovereign belongs.

royal fern *n.* a fern, *Osmunda regalis*, with huge spreading fronds.

royal flush *n.* a straight poker flush headed by an ace.

royal icing *n.* esp. *Brit.* a hard white icing made from icing sugar and egg whites.

Royal Institution *n.* a British society founded in 1799 for the diffusion of scientific knowledge.

royalist /ˈrɔɪəlɪst/ *n.* **1 a** a supporter of monarchy. **b** *hist.* a supporter of the King against Parliament in the English Civil War. **2** *US* a reactionary, esp. a reactionary business tycoon. □ **royalism** *n.*

royal jelly *n.* a substance secreted by honey bee workers and fed by them to future queen bees.

Royal Marine *n.* a British marine (see MARINE *n.* 2a).

royal mast *n.* a mast above a topgallant mast.

Royal Navy *n.* the British navy.

royal oak *n.* a sprig of oak worn on 29 May to commemorate the restoration of Charles II (1660), who hid in an oak after the battle of Worcester (1651).

royal plural *n.* = ROYAL 'WE'.

royal prerogative see PREROGATIVE 2.

royal sail *n.* a sail above a topgallant sail.

Royal Society *n.* (in full **Royal Society of London**) a society founded in 1662 to promote scientific discussion.

royal stag *n. Brit.* a stag with a head of 12 or more points.

royal standard *n.* a banner bearing royal heraldic arms.

royal tennis *n.* real tennis.

royalty /ˈrɔɪəlti/ *n.* (*pl.* **-ies**) **1** the office or dignity or power of a king or queen, sovereignty. **2 a** royal persons. **b** a member of a royal family. **3** a sum paid to a patentee for the use of a patent or to an author etc. for each copy of a book etc. sold or for each public performance of a work. **4 a** a royal right (now esp. over minerals) granted by the sovereign to an individual or corporation. **b** a payment made by a producer of minerals, oil, or natural gas to the owner of the site or of the mineral rights over it. [Middle English from Old French *roialté* (as ROYAL)]

Royal Victorian Chain *n.* (in the UK) an order founded by Edward VII in 1902 and conferred by the sovereign on special occasions.

Royal Victorian Order *n.* (in the UK) an order founded by Queen Victoria in 1896 and conferred usu. for great service rendered to the sovereign.

royal warrant *n.* a warrant authorizing a tradesperson to supply goods to a specified royal person.

royal 'we' *n.* the use of 'we' instead of 'I' by a single person (as traditionally by a sovereign).

rozzer /ˈrɒzə/ *n. Brit. slang* a police officer. [19th c.: origin unknown]

RP *abbr.* received pronunciation.

RPG *abbr.* **1** *Computing* report program generator, a high-level commercial programming language. **2** rocket-propelled grenade. **3** role-playing game.

RPI *abbr.* retail price index.

r.p.m. *abbr.* **1** revolutions per minute. **2** resale price maintenance.

RPO *abbr.* Royal Philharmonic Orchestra.

rpt *abbr.* repeat.

RR *abbr. US* **1** railroad. **2** rural route.

RS *abbr.* **1** (in the UK) Royal Society. **2** *US Linguistics* Received Standard. **3** (in the UK) Royal Scots.

Rs. *abbr.* rupee(s).

RSA *abbr.* **1** (in the UK) Royal Society of Arts. **2** Royal Scottish Academy; Royal Scottish Academician. **3** Republic of South Africa.

RSC *abbr.* **1** (in the UK) Royal Shakespeare Company. **2** (in the UK) Royal Society of Chemistry.

RSE *abbr.* Royal Society of Edinburgh.

RSFSR *abbr. hist.* Russian Soviet Federative Socialist Republic.

RSI *abbr.* repetitive strain injury.

RSJ *abbr.* rolled steel joist.

RSM *abbr. Brit.* Regimental Sergeant Major.

RSPB *abbr.* (in the UK) Royal Society for the Protection of Birds.

RSPCA *abbr.* (in the UK) Royal Society for the Prevention of Cruelty to Animals.

RSV *abbr.* Revised Standard Version (of the Bible).

RSVP *abbr.* (in an invitation etc.) please answer. [French *répondez s'il vous plaît*]

RT *abbr.* **1** radio-telegraphy. **2** radio-telephony.

rt. *abbr.* right.

Rt. Hon. *abbr. Brit.* Right Honourable.

Rt. Revd. *abbr.* (also **Rt. Rev.**) Right Reverend.

RU *abbr.* Rugby Union.

Ru *symb. Chem.* the element ruthenium.

rub[1] /rʌb/ *v.* & *n.* ● *v.* (**rubbed**, **rubbing**) **1** *tr.* move one's hand or another object with firm pressure over the surface of. **2** *tr.* (usu. foll. by *against*, *in*, *on*, *over*) apply (one's hand etc.) in this way. **3** *tr.* clean or polish or make dry or bare by rubbing. **4** *tr.* (often foll. by *over*) apply (polish, ointment, etc.) by rubbing. **5** *tr.* (foll. by *in*, *into*, *through*) use rubbing to make (a substance) go into or through something. **6** *tr.* (often foll. by *together*) move or slide (objects) against each other. **7** *intr.* (foll. by *against*, *on*) move with contact or friction. **8** *tr.* chafe or make sore by rubbing. **9** *intr.* (of cloth, skin, etc.) become frayed or worn or sore or bare with friction. **10** *tr.* reproduce the design of (a sepulchral brass or a stone) by rubbing paper laid on it with heelball or coloured chalk etc. **11** *tr.* (foll. by *to*) reduce to powder etc. by rubbing. **12** *intr. Bowls* (of a bowl) be slowed or diverted by the unevenness of the ground. ● *n.* **1** a spell or an instance of rubbing (*give it a rub*). **2 a** an impediment or difficulty (*there's the rub*). **b** *Bowls* an inequality of the ground impeding or diverting a bowl; the diversion or hindering of a bowl by this. □ **rub along** *Brit. colloq.* cope or manage without undue difficulty. **rub down** dry or smooth or clean by rubbing. **rub elbows with** *US* = *rub shoulders with*. **rub one's hands** rub one's hands together usu. in sign of keen satisfaction, or for warmth. **rub it in** (or **rub a person's nose in it**) emphasize or repeat an embarrassing fact etc. **rub noses** rub one's nose against another's in greeting. **rub off 1** (usu. foll. by *on*) be transferred by contact, be transmitted (*some of his attitudes have rubbed off on me*). **2** remove by rubbing. **rub on** *Brit. colloq.* = *rub along*. **rub out 1** erase with a rubber. **2** esp. *N. Amer. slang* kill, eliminate. **rub shoulders with** associate or come into contact with (another person). **rub up 1** polish (a tarnished object). **2** *Brit.* brush up (a subject or one's memory). **3** mix (pigment etc.) into paste by rubbing. **rub** (or *Brit.* **rub up**) **the wrong way** irritate or repel as by stroking a cat against the lie of its fur. [Middle English *rubben*, perhaps from Low German *rubben*, of unknown origin]

rub² /rʌb/ *n.* = RUBBER². [abbreviation]

rubato /rʊˈbɑːtəʊ/ *n. & adj. Mus.* ● *n.* (*pl.* **-os** or **rubati** /-ti/) the temporary disregarding of strict tempo. ● *adj.* performed with a flexible tempo. [Italian, = robbed]

rubber¹ /ˈrʌbə/ *n.* **1** a tough elastic polymeric substance made from the latex of plants or synthetically. **2** esp. *Brit.* a piece of this or another substance for erasing pencil or ink marks. **3** *colloq.* a condom. **4** (in *pl.*) *US* galoshes. **5** a person who rubs; a masseur or masseuse. **6 a** an implement used for rubbing. **b** part of a machine operating by rubbing. □ **rubbery** *adj.* **rubberiness** *n.* [RUB¹ + -ER¹, from its early use to rub out pencil marks]

rubber² /ˈrʌbə/ *n.* **1** a match of three or five successive games between the same sides or persons at whist, bridge, cricket, tennis, etc. **2** (prec. by *the*) **a** the act of winning a majority of games in a rubber. **b** a deciding game when scores are level. [origin unknown: used as a term in bowls from *c.*1600]

rubber band *n.* a loop of rubber for holding papers etc. together.

rubber bullet *n.* a baton round made of rubber.

rubberize /ˈrʌbərʌɪz/ *v.tr.* (also **-ise**) treat or coat with rubber.

rubberneck /ˈrʌbənɛk/ *n. & v. colloq.* ● *n.* a person, esp a tourist, who cranes and stares inquisitively or stupidly. ● *v.intr.* act in this way.

rubber plant *n.* **1** an evergreen plant, *Ficus elastica*, with dark green shiny leaves, often cultivated as a house plant. **2** (also **rubber tree**) any of various tropical trees yielding latex, esp. *Hevea brasiliensis*.

rubber solution *n.* a liquid drying to a rubber-like material, used esp. as an adhesive in mending rubber articles.

rubber stamp *n. & v.* ● *n.* **1** a device for inking and imprinting on a surface. **2 a** a person who mechanically copies or agrees to others' actions. **b** an indication of such agreement. ● *v.tr.* (**rubber-stamp**) approve automatically without proper consideration.

rubbing /ˈrʌbɪŋ/ *n.* **1** in senses of RUB¹ *v.* **2** an impression or copy made by rubbing (see RUB¹ *v.* 10).

rubbish /ˈrʌbɪʃ/ *n. & v.* ● *n.* esp. *Brit.* **1** waste material; debris, refuse, litter. **2** worthless material or articles; junk. **3** (often as *int.*) absurd ideas or suggestions; nonsense. ● *v.tr. Brit. colloq.* **1** criticize severely. **2** reject as worthless. □ **rubbishy** *adj.* [Middle English from Anglo-French *rubbous* etc., perhaps related to RUBBLE]

rubble /ˈrʌb(ə)l/ *n.* **1** waste or rough fragments of stone or brick etc. **2** pieces of undressed stone used, esp. as filling, for walls. **3** *Geol.* loose angular stones etc. as the covering of some rocks. **4** water-worn stones. □ **rubbly** *adj.* [Middle English *robyl*, *rubel*, of uncertain origin: perhaps related to Old French *robe* 'spoils']

rub-down *n.* an instance of rubbing down.

rube /ruːb/ *n. N. Amer. colloq.* a country bumpkin. [abbreviation of the name *Reuben*]

rubella /rʊˈbɛlə/ *n. Med.* an acute infectious virus disease with a red rash; German measles. [modern Latin, neut. pl. of Latin *rubellus* 'reddish']

rubellite /ˈruːbəlʌɪt/ *n.* a red variety of tourmaline. [Latin *rubellus* 'reddish']

rubeola /rʊˈbiːələ/ *n. Med.* measles. [medieval Latin from Latin *rubeus* 'red']

Rubicon /ˈruːbɪk(ə)n, -ɒn/ *n.* **1** a boundary which once crossed signifies irrevocable commitment; a point of no return. **2** (**rubicon**) the act of winning a game in piquet before an opponent has scored 100. [the ancient name of a stream forming the boundary of Julius Caesar's province and crossed by him in 49 BC as the start of a war with Pompey]

rubicund /ˈruːbɪk(ə)nd/ *adj.* (of a face, complexion, or person in these respects) ruddy, high-coloured. □ **rubicundity** /-ˈkʌndɪti/ *n.* [French *rubicond* or Latin *rubicundus*, from *rubēre* 'be red']

rubidium /rʊˈbɪdɪəm/ *n. Chem.* a soft silvery element occurring naturally in various minerals and as the radioactive isotope rubidium-87 (symbol **Rb**). [Latin *rubidus* 'red' (with reference to its spectral lines)]

rubiginous /rʊˈbɪdʒɪnəs/ *adj. formal* rust-coloured. [Latin *rubigo- inis* 'rust']

Rubik's cube /ˈruːbɪks/ *n. propr.* a puzzle in which the aim is to restore the faces of a composite cube to single colours by rotating layers of constituent smaller cubes. [named after E. *Rubik* (b. 1944), its Hungarian inventor]

ruble var. of ROUBLE.

rub of the green *n.* (also **rub on the green**) *Golf* an accidental interference with the course or position of a ball.

rubric /ˈruːbrɪk/ *n.* **1** a direction for the conduct of divine service inserted in a liturgical book. **2** a heading or passage in red or special lettering. **3** explanatory words. **4** an established custom. □ **rubrical** *adj.* [Middle English from Old French *rubrique*, *rubrice* or Latin *rubrica* (*terra*) 'red (earth or ochre)' as writing material, related to *rubeus* 'red']

rubricate /ˈruːbrɪkeɪt/ *v.tr.* **1** mark with red; print or write in red. **2** provide with rubrics. □ **rubrication** /-ˈkeɪʃ(ə)n/ *n.* **rubricator** *n.* [Latin *rubricare* from *rubrica*: see RUBRIC]

rub-up *n.* the act or an instance of rubbing up.

ruby /ˈruːbi/ *n., adj., & v.* ● *n.* (*pl.* **-ies**) **1** a rare precious stone consisting of corundum with a colour varying from deep crimson or purple to pale rose. **2** a glowing purplish-red colour. ● *adj.* of this colour. ● *v.tr.* (**-ies**, **-ied**) dye or tinge with a ruby colour. [Middle English via Old French *rubi* from medieval Latin *rubinus* (*lapis*) 'red (stone)', related to Latin *rubeus* 'red']

ruby glass *n.* glass coloured with oxides of copper, iron, lead, tin, etc.

ruby-tail *n.* a wasp, *Chrysis ignita*, with a ruby-coloured hinder part.

ruby wedding *n.* the fortieth anniversary of a wedding.

RUC *abbr.* Royal Ulster Constabulary.

ruche /ruːʃ/ *n.* a frill or gathering of lace etc. as a trimming. □ **ruched** *adj.* **ruching** *n.* [French from medieval Latin *rusca* 'tree-bark', of Celtic origin]

ruck¹ /rʌk/ *n. & v.* ● *n.* **1** (prec. by *the*) the main body of competitors not likely to overtake the leaders. **2** an undistinguished crowd of persons or things. **3** *Rugby* a loose scrum with the ball on the ground. **4** *Austral. Rules* a group of three players who follow the play without fixed positions. ● *v.intr. Rugby* & *Austral. Rules* participate in a ruck. [Middle English, = stack of fuel, heap, rick: apparently Scandinavian, corresponding to Norwegian *ruka* in the same senses]

ruck² /rʌk/ *v. & n.* ● *v.tr. & intr.* (often foll. by *up*) make or become creased or wrinkled. ● *n.* a crease or wrinkle. [Old Norse *hrukka*]

ruckle /ˈrʌk(ə)l/ *v. & n. Brit.* = RUCK².

rucksack /ˈrʌksak, ˈrʊk-/ *n.* a bag slung by straps from both shoulders and resting on the back. [German, from *rucken* (dialect variant of *Rücken* 'back') + *Sack* SACK¹]

ruckus /ˈrʌkəs/ *n.* esp. *N. Amer.* a row or commotion. [19th c.: perhaps related to RUCTION, RUMPUS]

ruction /ˈrʌkʃ(ə)n/ *n. colloq.* **1** a disturbance or tumult. **2** (in *pl.*) unpleasant arguments or reactions. [19th c.: origin unknown]

rudaceous /rʊˈdeɪʃəs/ *adj.* (of rock) composed of fragments of relatively large size. [Latin *rudus* 'rubble']

rudbeckia /rʌdˈbɛkɪə, ruːd-/ *n.* a garden plant of the genus *Rudbeckia* (daisy family), native to N. America. [modern Latin, named after O. *Rudbeck*, Swedish botanist d. 1740]

rudd /rʌd/ *n.* (*pl.* same) a freshwater fish, *Scardinius erythrophthalmus*, resembling a roach and having red fins. [apparently related to *rud* 'red colour' from Old English *rudu*, related to RED]

rudder /ˈrʌdə/ *n.* **1 a** a flat piece hinged vertically to the stern of a ship for steering. **b** a vertical aerofoil pivoted from the tailplane of an aircraft, for controlling its horizontal movement. **2** a guiding principle etc.

□ **rudderless** *adj.* [Old English *rōther* from West Germanic *rōthra-*, from the stem of ROW[2]]

ruddle /'rʌd(ə)l/ *n. & v.* ● *n.* a red ochre, esp. of a kind used for marking sheep. ● *v.tr.* mark or colour with or as with ruddle. [related to obsolete *rud*: see RUDD]

ruddock /'rʌdək/ *n. dial.* the robin redbreast. [Old English *rudduc* (as RUDDLE)]

ruddy /'rʌdi/ *adj. & v.* ● *adj.* (**ruddier**, **ruddiest**) **1 a** (of a person or complexion) freshly or healthily red. **b** (of health, youth, etc.) marked by this. **2** reddish. **3** *Brit. colloq.* bloody, damnable. ● *v.tr. & intr.* (**-ies**, **-ied**) make or grow ruddy. □ **ruddily** *adv.* **ruddiness** *n.* [Old English *rudig* (as RUDD)]

ruddy duck *n.* an American duck, *Oxyura jamaicensis*, naturalized in Britain etc., the male of which has deep red-brown plumage.

rude /ru:d/ *adj.* **1** (of a person, remark, etc.) impolite or offensive. **2** roughly made or done; lacking subtlety or accuracy (*a rude plough*). **3 a** primitive or unsophisticated (*rude simplicity*). **b** *archaic* uneducated. **4** abrupt, sudden, startling, violent (*a rude awakening*; *a rude reminder*). **5** *colloq.* indecent, lewd (*a rude joke*). **6** esp. *Brit.* vigorous or hearty (*rude health*). □ **be rude to** speak impolitely to; insult. □ **rudely** *adv.* **rudeness** *n.* **rudery** *n.* **rudish** *adj.* [Middle English via Old French from Latin *rudis* 'unwrought']

ruderal /'ru:d(ə)r(ə)l/ *adj. & n.* ● *adj.* (of a plant) growing on or in rubbish or rubble. ● *n.* a ruderal plant. [modern Latin *ruderalis* from Latin *rudera*, pl. of *rudus* 'rubble']

rudiment /'ru:dɪm(ə)nt/ *n.* **1** (in *pl.*) the elements or first principles of a subject. **2** (in *pl.*) an imperfect beginning of something undeveloped or yet to develop. **3** *Biol.* an undeveloped or immature part or organ, esp. a structure in an embryo or larva which will develop into an organ, limb, etc. [French *rudiment* or Latin *rudimentum* (as RUDE, on the pattern of *elementum* ELEMENT)]

rudimentary /ru:dɪ'mɛnt(ə)ri/ *adj.* **1** involving basic principles; fundamental. **2** incompletely developed; vestigial. □ **rudimentarily** /-'mɛnt(ə)rɪli/ *adv.* **rudimentariness** /-'mɛnt(ə)rɪnɪs/ *n.*

rue[1] /ru:/ *v. & n.* ● *v.tr.* (**rues**, **rued**, **rueing** or **ruing**) repent of; bitterly feel the consequences of; wish to be undone or non-existent (esp. *rue the day*). ● *n. archaic* **1** repentance; dejection at some occurrence. **2** compassion or pity. [Old English *hrēow*, *hrēowan*]

rue[2] /ru:/ *n.* a perennial evergreen shrub, *Ruta graveolens*, with bitter strong-scented leaves formerly used in medicine. [Middle English from Old French via Latin *ruta* from Greek *rhutē*]

rueful /'ru:fʊl, -f(ə)l/ *adj.* expressing sorrow or regret in a genuine or humorous way. □ **ruefully** *adv.* **ruefulness** *n.* [Middle English, from RUE[1]]

rufescent /rʊ'fɛs(ə)nt/ *adj. Zool.* etc. reddish. □ **rufescence** *n.* [Latin *rufescere* from *rufus* 'reddish']

ruff[1] /rʌf/ *n.* **1** a projecting starched frill worn round the neck esp. in the 16th c. **2** a projecting or conspicuously coloured ring of feathers or hair round a bird's or animal's neck. **3** a domestic pigeon like a jacobin. **4** (*fem.* **reeve** /ri:v/) a wading bird, *Philomachus pugnax*, of which the male has a ruff and ear-tufts in the breeding season. □ **rufflike** *adj.* [perhaps from *ruff* = ROUGH]

ruff[2] /rʌf/ *n.* any of various rough-scaled fishes, esp.: **1** (usu. **ruffe**) a perch-like European freshwater fish, *Gymnocephalus cernua*. **2** esp. *Austral.* (in full **tommy ruff**) an Australian marine food fish, *Arripis georgianus*, related to the Australian salmon; also called ROUGHY. [Middle English, probably from ROUGH]

ruff[3] /rʌf/ *v. & n.* ● *v.intr. & tr.* trump at cards. ● *n.* an act of ruffing. [originally the name of a card game: from Old French *roffle*, *rouffle*, = Italian *ronfa* (perhaps alteration of *trionfo* TRUMP[1])]

ruffe see RUFF[2] 1.

ruffian /'rʌfɪən/ *n.* a violent lawless person. □ **ruffianism** *n.* **ruffianly** *adv.* [French *ruf(f)ian* from Italian *ruffiano*, perhaps from dialect *rofia* 'scurf']

ruffle /'rʌf(ə)l/ *v. & n.* ● *v.* **1** *tr.* disturb the smoothness or tranquillity of. **2** *tr.* upset the calmness of (a person). **3** *tr.* gather (lace etc.) into a ruffle. **4** *tr.* (often foll. by *up*) (of a bird) erect (its feathers) in anger, display, etc. **5** *intr.* undergo ruffling. **6** *intr.* lose smoothness or calmness. ● *n.* **1** an ornamental gathered or goffered frill of lace etc. worn at the opening of a garment esp. round the wrist, breast, or neck. **2** perturbation, bustle. **3** a rippling effect on water. **4** the ruff of a bird etc. (see RUFF[1] 2). **5** *Mil.* a vibrating drum beat. [Middle English: origin unknown]

rufous /'ru:fəs/ *adj.* (esp. of animals) reddish brown. [Latin *rufus* 'red, reddish']

rug /rʌg/ *n.* **1** a floor-mat of shaggy material or thick pile. **2** esp. *Brit.* a thick woollen coverlet or wrap. □ **pull the rug from under** deprive of support; weaken, unsettle. [probably from Scandinavian: cf. Norwegian dialect *rugga* 'coverlet', Swedish *rugg* 'ruffled hair': related to RAG[1]]

rugby /'rʌgbi/ *n.* (also **Rugby**) (in full **rugby football**) a team game played with an oval ball that may be kicked, carried, and passed from hand to hand. [*Rugby* School in the midlands of England, where it was first played]

Rugby League *n.* partly professional rugby with teams of 13.

Rugby Union *n.* amateur rugby with teams of 15.

rugged /'rʌgɪd/ *adj.* **1** (of ground or terrain) having a rough uneven surface. **2** (of features) strongly marked; irregular in outline. **3 a** unpolished; lacking gentleness or refinement (*rugged grandeur*). **b** harsh in sound. **c** austere, unbending (*rugged honesty*). **d** involving hardship (*a rugged life*). **4** (esp. of a machine) robust, sturdy. □ **ruggedly** *adv.* **ruggedness** *n.* [Middle English, probably from Scandinavian: cf. RUG, and Swedish *rugga* 'roughen']

ruggedized /'rʌgɪdʌɪzd/ *adj.* esp. *US* (of a piece of equipment etc.) made hard-wearing or shock-resistant. □ **ruggedization** /-'zeɪʃ(ə)n/ *n.*

rugger /'rʌgə/ *n. Brit. colloq.* rugby.

rugosa /ru:'gəʊzə/ *n.* a Japanese rose, *Rosa rugosa*, which has dark green wrinkled leaves and deep pink flowers. [Latin, fem. of *rugosus* (see RUGOSE) used as specific epithet]

rugose /'ru:gəʊs, rʊ'gəʊs/ *adj.* esp. *Biol.* wrinkled, corrugated. □ **rugosely** *adv.* **rugosity** /-'gɒsɪti/ *n.* [Latin *rugosus* from *ruga* 'wrinkle']

ruin /'ru:ɪn/ *n. & v.* ● *n.* **1** a destroyed or wrecked state. **2** a person's or thing's downfall or elimination (*the ruin of my hopes*). **3 a** the complete loss of one's property or position (*bring to ruin*). **b** a person who has suffered ruin. **4** (in *sing.* or *pl.*) the remains of a building etc. that has suffered ruin (*an old ruin*; *ancient ruins*). **5** a cause of ruin (*will be the ruin of us*). ● *v.* **1** *tr.* **a** bring to ruin (*your extravagance has ruined me*). **b** utterly impair or wreck (*the rain ruined my hat*). **2** *tr.* (esp. as **ruined** *adj.*) reduce to ruins. **3** *intr. poet.* fall headlong or with a crash. □ **in ruins 1** in a state of ruin. **2** completely wrecked (*their hopes were in ruins*). [Middle English via Old French *ruine* from Latin *ruina*, from *ruere* 'to fall']

ruination /ru:ɪ'neɪʃ(ə)n/ *n.* **1** the act of bringing to ruin. **2** the act of ruining or the state of being ruined. [obsolete *ruinate* (as RUIN)]

ruinous /'ru:ɪnəs/ *adj.* **1** bringing ruin; disastrous (*at ruinous expense*). **2** in ruins; dilapidated. □ **ruinously** *adv.* **ruinousness** *n.* [Middle English from Latin *ruinosus* (as RUIN)]

rule /ru:l/ *n. & v.* ● *n.* **1** a principle to which an action conforms or is required to conform. **2** a prevailing custom or standard; the normal state of things. **3** government or dominion (*under British rule*; *the rule of law*). **4** a graduated straight measure used in carpentry etc.; a ruler. **5** *Printing* **a** a thin strip of metal for separating headings, columns, etc. **b** a thin line or dash.

6 a code of discipline of a religious order. **7** *Law* an order made by a judge or court with reference to a particular case only. **8** (**Rules**) *Austral.* = AUSTRALIAN RULES. ● *v.* **1** *tr.* exercise decisive influence over; keep under control. **2** *tr.* & (often foll. by *over*) *intr.* have sovereign control of (*rules over a vast kingdom*). **3** *tr.* (often foll. by *that* + clause) pronounce authoritatively (*was ruled out of order*). **4** *tr.* **a** make parallel lines across (paper). **b** make (a straight line) with a ruler etc. **5** *intr.* (of prices or goods etc. in regard to price or quality etc.) have a specified general level; be for the most part (*the market ruled high*). **6** *tr.* (in *passive*; foll. by *by*) consent to follow (advice etc.); be guided by. □ **as a rule** usually; more often than not. **by rule** in a regulation manner; mechanically. **rule in** pronounce as included. **rule out** exclude; pronounce irrelevant or ineligible. **rule the roost** be in control. **run the rule over** *Brit.* examine cursorily for correctness or adequacy. □ **ruleless** *adj.* [Middle English via Old French *reule, reuler* from Late Latin *regulare*, from Latin *regula* 'straight stick']

Rule 43 *n.* (in the UK) a prison regulation whereby offenders can be isolated or segregated for their own protection.

rule of the road *n.* the custom or law regulating which side of the road is to be taken by vehicles (also riders or ships) meeting or passing each other.

rule of three *n.* a method of finding a number in the same ratio to one given as exists between two others given.

rule of thumb *n.* a rule for general guidance, based on experience or practice rather than theory.

ruler /'ru:lə/ *n.* **1** a person exercising government or dominion. **2** a straight usu. graduated strip or cylinder of wood, metal, etc., used to draw lines or measure distance. □ **rulership** *n.*

ruling /'ru:lɪŋ/ *n.* & *adj.* ● *n.* an authoritative decision or announcement. ● *adj.* dominant, prevailing; currently in force (*ruling prices*).

ruling passion *n.* a motive that habitually directs one's actions.

rum[1] /rʌm/ *n.* **1** a spirit distilled from sugar cane residues or molasses. **2** *N. Amer.* intoxicating liquor. [17th c.: perhaps abbreviation of contemporary forms *rumbullion, rumbustion*, of unknown origin]

rum[2] /rʌm/ *adj.* (**rummer, rummest**) *Brit. colloq.* odd, strange, queer. □ **rum go** (or **start**) *colloq.* a surprising occurrence or unforeseen turn of affairs. □ **rumly** *adv.* **rumness** *n.* [18th-c.: origin unknown]

Rumanian var. of ROMANIAN.

Rumansh var. of ROMANSH.

rumba /'rʌmbə/ *n.* & *v.* (also **rhumba**) ● *n.* **1** a dance originating among Cuban blacks. **2 a** a ballroom dance imitative of this. **b** the music for it. ● *v.intr.* (**rumbas, rumbaed** /-bəd/ or **rumba'd, rumbaing** /-bə(r)ɪŋ/) dance the rumba. [Latin American Spanish]

rum baba see BABA.

rumble /'rʌmb(ə)l/ *v.* & *n.* ● *v.* **1** *intr.* make a continuous deep resonant sound as of distant thunder. **2** *intr.* (foll. by *along, by, past*, etc.) (of a person or vehicle) move with a rumbling noise. **3** *tr.* (often foll. by *out*) utter or say with a rumbling sound. **4** *tr. Brit. slang* find out about (esp. something illicit), discover the misbehaviour of (a person). ● *n.* **1** a rumbling sound. **2** *N. Amer. slang* a street fight between gangs. □ **rumbler** *n.* [Middle English *romble*, probably from Middle Dutch *rommelen, rummelen* (imitative)]

rumble seat *n. N. Amer.* an uncovered folding seat in the rear of a motor car.

rumble strip *n.* a series of raised strips across a road or along its edge to make vehicles vibrate, warning drivers of speed restrictions or of the edge of the road.

rumblings /'rʌmblɪŋz/ *n.pl.* early indications of some state of things or incipient change (*rumblings of discontent*).

rumbustious /rʌm'bʌstʃəs, -tɪəs/ *adj.* esp. *Brit. colloq.* boisterous, noisy, uproarious. □ **rumbustiously** *adv.* **rumbustiousness** *n.* [probably a variant of *robustious* 'boisterous, ROBUST']

rum butter *n.* a rich sweet hard sauce made with rum, butter, and sugar.

rumen /'ru:mɛn/ *n.* (*pl.* **rumens** or **rumina** /-mɪnə/) the first stomach of a ruminant, in which food, esp. cellulose, is partly digested by bacteria. [Latin *rumen ruminis* 'throat']

ruminant /'ru:mɪnənt/ *n.* & *adj.* ● *n.* an animal that chews the cud regurgitated from its rumen. ● *adj.* **1** of or belonging to ruminants. **2** contemplative; given to or engaged in meditation. [Latin *ruminari ruminant-* (as RUMEN)]

ruminate /'ru:mɪneɪt/ *v.* **1** *tr.* & (foll. by *over, on*, etc.) *intr.* meditate, ponder. **2** *intr.* (of ruminants) chew the cud. □ **rumination** /-'neɪʃ(ə)n/ *n.* **ruminative** /-nətɪv/ *adj.* **ruminatively** /-nətɪvli/ *adv.* **ruminator** *n.*

rummage /'rʌmɪdʒ/ *v.* & *n.* ● *v.* **1** *tr.* & (foll. by *in, through, among*) *intr.* search, esp. untidily and unsystematically. **2** *tr.* (foll. by *out, up*) find among other things. **3** *tr.* (foll. by *about*) disarrange; make untidy in searching. ● *n.* **1** an instance of rummaging. **2** things found by rummaging; a miscellaneous accumulation. □ **rummager** *n.* [earlier as noun in obsolete sense 'arranging of casks etc. in a hold': Old French *arrumage* from *arrumer* 'stow' (as AD-, *run* 'ship's hold' from Middle Dutch *ruim* ROOM)]

rummage sale *n.* esp. *N. Amer.* a jumble sale.

rummer /'rʌmə/ *n.* a large drinking glass. [related to Dutch *roemer*, Low German *römer* from *roemen* 'praise, boast']

rummy[1] /'rʌmi/ *n.* a card game played usu. with two packs, in which the players try to form sets and sequences of cards. [20th c.: origin unknown]

rummy[2] /'rʌmi/ *adj.* (**-ier, -iest**) *Brit. colloq.* = RUM[2].

rumour /'ru:mə/ *n.* & *v.* (*US* **rumor**) ● *n.* **1** general talk or hearsay of doubtful accuracy. **2** (often foll. by *of*, or *that* + clause) a current but unverified statement or assertion (*heard a rumour that you are leaving*). ● *v.tr.* (usu. in *passive*) report by way of rumour (*it is rumoured that you are leaving*; *you are rumoured to be leaving*). [Middle English via Old French *rumur, rumor* from Latin *rumor -oris* 'noise']

rumour-monger *n.* (*US* **rumormonger**) a spreader of rumours. □ **rumour-mongering** *n.*

rump /rʌmp/ *n.* **1** the hind part of a mammal, esp. the buttocks. **2 a** a small or contemptible remnant. **b** (**the Rump**) *hist.* the remnant of the English Long Parliament 1648–53 or after its restoration in 1659. □ **rumpless** *adj.* [Middle English, probably from Scandinavian]

rumple /'rʌmp(ə)l/ *v.tr.* & *intr.* make or become creased or ruffled. □ **rumply** *adj.* [obsolete noun *rumple* from Middle Dutch *rompel*, from *rompe* 'wrinkle']

rump steak *n.* a cut of beef from the rump.

rumpus /'rʌmpəs/ *n.* (*pl.* **rumpuses**) *colloq.* a disturbance, brawl, row, or uproar. [18th c.: probably fanciful]

rumpus room *n. N. Amer., Austral., & NZ* a room usu. in the basement of a house for games and play.

run /rʌn/ *v.* & *n.* ● *v.* (**running**; *past* **ran** /ran/; *past part.* **run**) **1** *intr.* go with quick steps on alternate feet, never having both or all feet on the ground at the same time. **2** *intr.* flee, abscond. **3** *intr.* go or travel hurriedly, briefly, etc. **4** *intr.* **a** advance by or as by rolling or on wheels, or smoothly or easily. **b** be in action or operation (*left the engine running*). **5** *intr.* be current or operative; have duration (*the lease runs for 99 years*). **6** *intr.* (of a bus, train, etc.) travel or be travelling on its route (*the train is running late*). **7** *intr.* (of a play, exhibition, etc.) be staged or presented (*is now running at the Apollo*). **8** *intr.* extend; have a course or order or tendency (*the road runs by the coast*; *prices are running* *high*). **9 a** *intr.* compete in a race. **b** *intr.* finish a race in a specified position. **c** *tr.* compete in (a race). **10** *intr.* (often foll. by *for*) seek election (*ran for president*). **11 a** *intr.* (of a liquid etc.) flow, drip profusely. **b** *tr.* flow with. **c** *intr.* (foll. by *with*) flow or be wet; drip (*his face ran with sweat*). **12** *tr.* **a** cause (water etc.) to flow. **b** fill (a bath) with water. **13** *intr.* spread or pass rapidly (*a shiver ran down my spine*). **14** *intr. Cricket* (of a batsman) run from one wicket to the other in scoring a run. **15** *tr.* traverse or make one's way through or over (a course, race, or distance). **16** *tr.* perform (an errand). **17** *tr.* publish (an article etc.) in a newspaper or magazine. **18 a** *tr.* cause (a machine or vehicle etc.) to operate. **b** *intr.* (of a mechanism or component etc.) move or work freely. **19** *tr.* direct or manage (a business etc.). **20** *tr.* own and drive (a vehicle) regularly. **21** *tr.* take (a person) for a journey in a vehicle (*shall I run you to the shops?*). **22** *tr.* cause to run or go in a specified way (*ran the car into a tree*). **23** *tr.* enter (a horse etc.) for a race. **24** *tr.* smuggle (guns etc.). **25** *tr.* chase or hunt. **26** *tr.* allow (an account) to accumulate for a time before paying. **27** *intr. Naut.* (of a ship etc.) go straight and fast. **28** *intr.* (of salmon) go upriver from the sea. **29** *intr.* (of a colour in a fabric) spread from the dyed parts. **30 a** *intr.* (of a thought, the eye, the memory, etc.) pass in a transitory or cursory way (*ideas ran through my mind*). **b** *tr.* cause (one's eye) to look cursorily (*ran my eye down the page*). **31** *intr.* (of hosiery) ladder. **32** *intr.* (of a candle) gutter. **33** *intr.* (of an orifice, esp. the eyes or nose) exude liquid matter. **34** *tr.* sew (fabric) loosely or hastily with running stitches. **35** *tr.* turn (cattle etc.) out to graze. ● *n.* **1** an act or spell of running. **2** a short trip or excursion, esp. for pleasure. **3** a distance travelled. **4** a general tendency of development or movement. **5** a rapid motion. **6** a regular route. **7** a continuous or long stretch or spell or course (*a metre's run of wiring*; *had a run of bad luck*). **8** (often foll. by *on*) **a** a high general demand (for a commodity, currency, etc.) (*a run on the dollar*). **b** a sudden demand for repayment by a large number of customers (of a bank). **9** a quantity produced in one period of production (*a print run*). **10** a general or average type or class (*not typical of the general run*). **11 a** *Cricket* a point scored by the batsmen each running to the other's wicket, or an equivalent point awarded for some other reason. **b** *Baseball* a point scored usu. by the batter returning to the plate after touching the other bases. **12** (foll. by *of*) free use of or access to (*had the run of the house*). **13 a** an animal's regular track. **b** an enclosure for fowls, rabbits, etc. **c** a range of pasture. **14** a ladder in hosiery. **15** *Mus.* a rapid scale passage. **16** a class or line of goods. **17** a batch or drove of animals born or reared together. **18** a shoal of fish in motion. **19** a trough for water to run in. **20** *US* a small stream or brook. **21 a** a single journey, esp. by an aircraft. **b** (of an aircraft) a flight on a straight and even course at a constant speed before or while dropping bombs. **c** an offensive military operation. □ **at a** (or **the**) **run** running. **on the run 1** escaping, running away. **2** hurrying about from place to place. **run about 1** bustle; hurry from one person or place to another. **2** (esp. of children) play or wander without restraint. **run across 1** happen to meet. **2** (foll. by *to*) make a brief journey or a flying visit (to a place). **run after 1** pursue with attentions; seek the society of. **2** give much time to (a pursuit etc.). **3** pursue at a run. **run against 1** *archaic* happen to meet. **2** compete against, esp. in a political contest. **run along** *colloq.* depart. **run around 1** *Brit.* take from place to place by car etc. **2** deceive or evade repeatedly. **3** (often foll. by *with*) *colloq.* engage in sexual relations (esp. casually or illicitly). **run at** attack by charging or rushing. **run away 1** get away by running; flee, abscond. **2** elope. **3** (of a horse) bolt. **run away with 1** carry off (a person, stolen property, etc.). **2** win (a prize) easily. **3** accept (a notion) hastily. **4** (of expense etc.) consume (money etc.). **5** (of a horse) bolt with (a rider, a carriage or its occupants). **6** leave home to have a relationship with. **7** deprive of self-control or common sense (*let his ideas run away with him*). **run a blockade** see BLOCKADE. **run down 1** knock down or collide with. **2** reduce the strength or numbers of (resources). **3** (of an unwound clock etc.) stop. **4** (of a person or a person's health) become feeble from overwork or undernourishment. **5** discover after a search. **6** disparage. **run dry** cease to flow, be exhausted. **run for it** seek safety by fleeing. **a run** (or **a good run**) **for one's money 1** vigorous competition. **2** pleasure derived from an activity. **3** return for outlay or effort. **run foul** (*N. Amer.* also **afoul**) **of 1** *Naut.* collide or become entangled with (another vessel etc.). **2** act contrary to; go against (*ran foul of their code of practice*). **run the gauntlet** see GAUNTLET[2]. **run a person hard** (or **close**) press a person severely in a race or competition, or in comparative merit. **run high 1** (of the sea) have a strong current with a high tide. **2** (of feelings) be strong. **run in 1** *Brit.* run (a new engine or vehicle) carefully in the early stages. **2** *colloq.* arrest. **3** (of a combatant) rush to close quarters. **4** incur (a debt). **run in the family** (of a trait) be common in the members of a family. **run into 1** collide with. **2** encounter. **3** reach as many as (a specified figure). **4** fall into (a practice, absurdity, etc.). **5** be continuous or coalesce with. **run into the ground** *colloq.* bring (a person) to exhaustion etc. **run it fine** see FINE[1]. **run its course** follow its natural progress; be left to itself. **run low** (or **short**) become depleted, have too little (*our tea ran low*; *we ran short of sugar*). **run off 1** flee. **2** produce (copies etc.) on a machine. **3** decide (a race or other contest) after a series of heats or in the event of a tie. **4** flow or cause to flow away. **5** write or recite fluently. **6** digress suddenly. **run off one's feet** *Brit.* very busy. **run on 1** (of written characters) be joined together. **2** continue in operation. **3** elapse. **4** speak volubly. **5** talk incessantly. **6** *Printing* continue on the same line as the preceding matter. **run out 1** come to an end; become used up. **2** (foll. by *of*) exhaust one's stock of. **3** *Cricket* put down the wicket of (a batsman who is running). **4** escape from a container. **5** (of rope) pass out; be paid out. **6** jut out. **7** *Brit.* come out of a contest in a specified position etc. or complete a required score etc. (*they ran out worthy winners*). **8** complete (a race). **9** advance (a gun etc.) so as to project. **10** exhaust oneself by running. **run out on** *colloq.* desert (a person). **run over 1** overflow. **2** study or repeat quickly. **3** (of a vehicle or its driver) pass over, knock down or crush. **4** touch (the keys of a piano etc.) in quick succession. **5** (often foll. by *to*) go quickly by a brief journey or for a flying visit. **run ragged** exhaust (a person). **run rings round** see RING[1]. **run riot** see RIOT. **run a** (or **the**) **risk** see RISK. **the runs** *colloq.* diarrhoea. **run the show** *colloq.* dominate in an undertaking etc. **run a temperature** be feverish. **run through 1** examine or rehearse briefly. **2** peruse. **3** deal successively with. **4** consume (an estate etc.) by reckless or quick spending. **5** pass through by running. **6** pervade. **7** pierce with a sword etc. **8** draw a line through (written words). **run to 1** have the money or ability for. **2** reach (an amount or number). **3** (of a person) show a tendency to (*runs to fat*). **4 a** be enough for (some expense or undertaking). **b** have the resources or capacity for. **5** fall into (ruin). **run to earth** (or **to ground**) **1** *Hunting* chase to its lair. **2** discover after a long search. **run to meet** anticipate (one's troubles etc.). **run to seed** see SEED. **run up 1** accumulate (a debt etc.) quickly. **2** build or make hurriedly. **3** raise (a flag). **4** grow quickly. **5** rise in price. **6** (foll. by *to*) amount to. **7** force (a rival bidder) to bid higher. **8** add up (a column of figures). **9** (foll. by *to*) go quickly by a brief journey or for a flying visit. **run up against** meet with (a difficulty or difficulties). **run upon** (of a person's thoughts etc.) be engrossed by; dwell upon. **run wild** grow or stray unchecked or undisciplined or untrained. □ **runnable** *adj.* [Old English *rinnan*]

runabout /ˈrʌnəbaʊt/ *n.* a light car, aircraft, or (esp. *US*) motor boat.

run-around *n.* (esp. in phr. **give a person the run-around**) deceit or evasion.

runaway /ˈrʌnəweɪ/ *n.* **1** a fugitive. **2** an animal or vehicle that is running out of control. **3** (*attrib.*) **a** that is running away or out of control (*runaway inflation; had a runaway success*). **b** done or performed after running away (*a runaway wedding*).

runcible spoon /ˈrʌnsɪb(ə)l/ *n.* a fork curved like a spoon, with three broad prongs, one edged. [nonsense word used by E. Lear, English humorist (d. 1888), perhaps suggested by *rouncival*, a large variety of pea]

runcinate /ˈrʌnsɪnət/ *adj. Bot.* (of a leaf) saw-toothed, with lobes pointing towards the base. [modern Latin *runcinatus* from Latin *runcina* PLANE[2] (formerly taken to mean 'saw')]

rundown *n. & adj.* ● *n.* /ˈrʌndaʊn/ **1** a reduction in numbers. **2** a detailed analysis. ● *adj.* /rʌnˈdaʊn/ (**run-down**) **1** decayed after prosperity. **2** enfeebled through overwork etc.

rune /ruːn/ *n.* **1** any of the letters of the earliest Germanic alphabet used by Scandinavians and Anglo-Saxons from about the 3rd c. and formed by modifying Roman or Greek characters to suit carving. **2** a similar mark of mysterious or magic significance. **3** a Finnish poem or a division of it. □ **runic** *adj.* [Old Norse *rún* (only in pl. *rúnar*) 'magic sign', related to Old English *rūn*]

rune-staff *n.* **1** a magic wand inscribed with runes. **2** a runic calendar.

rung[1] /rʌŋ/ *n.* **1** each of the horizontal supports of a ladder. **2** a strengthening crosspiece in the structure of a chair etc. □ **runged** *adj.* **rungless** *adj.* [Old English *hrung*]

rung[2] *past part.* of RING[2].

run-in *n.* **1** the approach to an action or event. **2** *colloq.* a quarrel.

runlet /ˈrʌnlɪt/ *n.* a small stream.

runnel /ˈrʌn(ə)l/ *n.* **1** a brook or rill. **2** a gutter. [later form (assimilated to RUN) of *rinel* from Old English *rynel* (as RUN)]

runner /ˈrʌnə/ *n.* **1** a person, horse, etc., that runs, esp. in a race. **2 a** a creeping plant stem that can take root. **b** a twining plant. **3** a rod or groove or blade on which a thing slides. **4** a sliding ring on a rod etc. **5** a messenger, scout, collector, or agent for a bank etc.; a tout. **6** *hist.* a police officer. **7** a running bird. **8 a** *slang* a smuggler of a specified kind (*drug runner*). **b** = BLOCKADE-RUNNER. **9** a revolving millstone. **10** *Naut.* a rope in a single block with one end round a tackle-block and the other having a hook. **11** (in full **runner bean**) **a** a twining bean plant, *Phaseolus coccineus*, with red flowers and long green seed pods; also called *scarlet runner*. **b** the bean from this. **12** each of the long pieces on the underside of a sledge etc. that forms the contact in sliding. **13** a roller for moving a heavy article. **14** a long narrow ornamental cloth or rug. □ **do a runner** *Brit. slang* leave hastily; abscond.

runner-up *n.* (*pl.* **runners-up** or **runner-ups**) the competitor or team taking second place.

running /ˈrʌnɪŋ/ *n. & adj.* ● *n.* **1 a** the action of a runner. **b** the sport of racing on foot. **2** the way a race etc. proceeds. ● *adj.* **1** continuing on an essentially continuous basis though changing in detail (*a running battle*). **2** consecutive; one after another (*three days running*). **3** done with a run (*a running jump*). □ **in** (or **out of**) **the running** (of a competitor) with a good (or poor) chance of winning. **make** (or **take up**) **the running** take the lead; set the pace. **take a running jump** (esp. as *int.*) *colloq.* go away.

running account *n. Brit.* a current account.

running back *n. Amer. Football* a back whose main task is to run carrying the ball.

running-board *n.* a footboard on either side of a vehicle.

running commentary *n.* an oral description of events as they occur.

running fire *n.* successive shots from a line of troops etc.

running gear *n.* **1** the moving parts of a machine, esp. the wheels, steering, and suspension of a vehicle. **2** the rope and tackle used in handling a boat.

running hand *n.* writing in which the pen etc. is not lifted after each letter.

running head *n.* (also **running headline**) a heading printed at the top of a number of consecutive pages of a book etc.

running knot *n.* a knot that slips along the rope etc. and changes the size of a noose.

running light *n.* **1** = NAVIGATION LIGHT. **2** each of a small set of lights on a motor vehicle that remain illuminated while the vehicle is running.

running mate *n.* esp. *US* **1** a candidate for a secondary position in an election. **2** a horse entered in a race in order to set the pace for another horse from the same stable which is intended to win.

running repairs *n.pl.* minor or temporary repairs etc. to machinery while in use.

running rope *n.* a rope that is freely movable through a pulley etc.

running sore *n.* a suppurating sore.

running stitch *n.* **1** a line of small non-overlapping stitches for gathering etc. **2** one of these stitches.

running water *n.* water flowing in a stream or from a tap etc.

runny /ˈrʌni/ *adj.* (**runnier**, **runniest**) **1** tending to run or flow. **2** excessively fluid.

run-off *n.* **1** an additional competition, election, race, etc., after a tie or inconclusive result. **2** an amount of rainfall that is carried off an area by streams and rivers. **3** *NZ* a separate area of land where young animals etc. are kept.

run-of-the-mill *adj.* ordinary, undistinguished.

run-out *n. Cricket* the dismissal of a batsman by being run out.

runt /rʌnt/ *n.* **1** a small pig or other animal, esp. the smallest in a litter. **2** a weakling; an undersized person. **3** a large domestic pigeon. **4** a small ox or cow, esp. of various Scottish Highland or Welsh breeds. □ **runty** *adj.* [16th c.: origin unknown]

run-through *n.* **1** a rehearsal. **2** a brief survey.

run-up *n.* **1** (often foll. by *to*) the period preceding an important event. **2** *Golf* a low approach shot.

runway /ˈrʌnweɪ/ *n.* **1** a specially prepared surface along which aircraft take off and land. **2** a trail to an animals' watering place. **3** an incline down which logs are slid. **4** a raised gangway in a theatre, fashion show, etc.

rupee /ruːˈpiː/ *n.* the chief monetary unit of India, Pakistan, Sri Lanka, Nepal, Mauritius, and the Seychelles. [Hindustani *rūpiyah* from Sanskrit *rūpya* 'wrought silver']

rupestrian /ruːˈpɛstrɪən/ *adj.* (of art) done on rock or cave walls. [modern (botanical) Latin *rupestris* 'found on rocks', from Latin *rupes* 'rock']

rupiah /ruːˈpiːə/ *n.* the chief monetary unit of Indonesia. [as RUPEE]

rupture /ˈrʌptʃə/ *n. & v.* ● *n.* **1** the act or an instance of breaking; a breach. **2** a breach of harmonious relations; a disagreement and parting. **3** *Med.* an abdominal hernia. ● *v.* **1** *tr.* break or burst (a cell or membrane etc.). **2** *tr.* sever (a connection). **3** *intr.* undergo a rupture. **4** *tr. & intr.* affect with or suffer a hernia. □ **rupturable** *adj.* [Middle English from Old French *rupture* or Latin *ruptura*, from *rumpere rupt-* 'break']

rural /ˈrʊər(ə)l/ *adj.* in, of, or suggesting the country (opp. URBAN); pastoral or agricultural (*in rural seclusion; a rural constituency*). □ **ruralism** *n.* **ruralist** *n.* **rurality** /-ˈralɪti/ *n.* **ruralize** *v.* (also **-ise**). **ruralization** /-lʌɪˈzeɪʃ(ə)n/ *n.* **rurally** *adv.* [Middle English from Old French *rural* or Late Latin *ruralis*, from *rus ruris* 'the country']

rural dean see DEAN[1] 1b.

rural district *n. Brit. hist.* a group of country parishes governed by an elected council.

Ruritanian /rʊərɪˈteɪnɪən/ *adj.* relating to or characteristic of romantic adventure or its setting. [*Ruritania*, an imaginary setting in SE Europe in the novels of Anthony Hope (d. 1933)]

rusa /ˈruːsə/ *n.* a large Indonesian deer, *Cervus timorensis*. [modern Latin former genus name, from Malay]

ruse /ruːz/ *n.* a stratagem or trick. [Middle English from Old French, from *ruser* 'drive back', perhaps ultimately from Latin *rursus* 'backwards': cf. RUSH[1]]

rush[1] /rʌʃ/ *v. & n.* ● *v.* **1** *intr.* go, move, or act precipitately or with great speed. **2** *tr.* move or transport with great haste (*was rushed to hospital*). **3** *intr.* (foll. by *at*) **a** move suddenly and quickly towards. **b** begin impetuously. **4** *tr.* perform or deal with hurriedly (*don't rush your dinner*; *the bill was rushed through Parliament*). **5** *tr.* force (a person) to act hastily. **6** *tr.* attack or capture by sudden assault. **7** *tr. Amer. Football* charge in order to hinder (esp. the quarterback). **8** *tr. Brit. slang* overcharge (a customer). **9** *tr. US* pay attentions to (a person), esp. when recruiting for a fraternity or sorority. **10** *tr.* pass (an obstacle) with a rapid dash. **11** *intr.* flow, fall, spread, or roll impetuously or fast (*felt the blood rush to my face*; *the river rushes past*). ● *n.* **1 a** an act of rushing; a violent advance or attack. **b** a sudden flow or flood. **2** a period of great activity. **3** (*attrib.*) done with great haste or speed (*a rush job*). **4** a sudden migration of large numbers. **5** (foll. by *on, for*) a sudden strong demand for a commodity. **6** (in *pl.*) *colloq.* the first prints of a film after a period of shooting. **7** *Football, Rugby, etc.* **a** a combined dash by one or several players with the ball. **b** *Amer. Football* an act of charging at usu. the quarterback. □ **rush one's fences** *Brit.* act with undue haste. □ **rusher** *n.* **rushingly** *adv.* [Middle English from Anglo-French *russher*, = Old French *ruser*, *russer*: see RUSE]

rush[2] /rʌʃ/ *n.* **1 a** any marsh or waterside plant of the family Juncaceae, with naked slender tapering pith-filled stems (properly leaves) formerly used for strewing floors and still used for making chair-bottoms and plaiting baskets etc. **b** a stem of this. **c** (*collect.*) rushes as a material. **2** *archaic* a thing of no value (*not worth a rush*). □ **rushlike** *adv.* **rushy** *adj.* [Old English *rysc*, *rysce*, corresponding to Middle Low German, Middle High German *rusch*]

rush candle *n.* a candle made by dipping the pith of a rush in tallow.

rush hour *n.* (often hyphenated when *attrib.*) time(s) each day when traffic is at its heaviest.

rushlight /ˈrʌʃlʌɪt/ *n.* a rush candle.

rusk /rʌsk/ *n.* a slice of bread rebaked usu. as a light biscuit, esp. as food for babies. [Spanish or Portuguese *rosca* 'twist, coil, roll of bread']

russet /ˈrʌsɪt/ *adj. & n.* ● *adj.* **1** reddish brown. **2** *archaic* rustic, homely, simple. ● *n.* **1** a reddish-brown colour. **2** a kind of rough-skinned russet-coloured apple. **3** *hist.* a coarse homespun reddish-brown or grey cloth used for simple clothing. □ **russety** *adj.* [Middle English via Anglo-French from Old French *rosset*, *rousset*, diminutive of *roux* 'red', via Provençal *ros*, Italian *rosso* from Latin *russus* 'red']

Russia leather /ˈrʌʃə/ *n.* a durable bookbinding leather from skins impregnated with birch-bark oil. [*Russia* in E. Europe]

Russian /ˈrʌʃ(ə)n/ *n. & adj.* ● *n.* **1 a** a native or national of Russia or the former Soviet Union. **b** a person of Russian descent. **2** the language of Russia and the official language of the former Soviet Union. ● *adj.* **1** of or relating to Russia. **2** of or in Russian. □ **Russianize** *v.tr.* (also **-ise**). **Russianization** /-nʌɪˈzeɪʃ(ə)n/ *n.* **Russianness** /ˈrʌʃ(ə)nnɪs/ *n.* [medieval Latin *Russianus*]

Russian boot *n.* a boot that loosely encloses the calf.

Russian olive *n.* = OLEASTER.

Russian roulette *n.* **1** an act of daring in which one (usu. with others in turn) squeezes the trigger of a revolver held to one's head with one chamber loaded, having first spun the chamber. **2** a potentially dangerous enterprise.

Russian salad *n. Brit.* a salad of mixed diced vegetables with mayonnaise.

Russify /ˈrʌsɪfʌɪ/ *v.tr.* (**-ies**, **-ied**) make Russian in character. □ **Russification** /-fɪˈkeɪʃ(ə)n/ *n.*

Russki /ˈrʌski/ *n.* (also **Russky**) (*pl.* **Russkis** or **-ies**) *slang offens.* a Russian; *hist.* (loosely) a Soviet citizen. [from Russian *russkiĭ* RUSSIAN, suggested by Russian surnames ending in *-skiĭ*]

Russo- /ˈrʌsəʊ/ *comb. form* Russian; Russian and.

Russophile /ˈrʌsəʊfʌɪl/ *n.* a person who is fond of Russia or the Russians.

rust /rʌst/ *n. & v.* ● *n.* **1 a** a reddish- or yellowish-brown coating formed on iron or steel by oxidation, esp. as a result of moisture. **b** a similar coating on other metals. **2 a** any of various plant diseases with rust-coloured spots caused by fungi of the class Urediniomycetes or genus *Albugo*. **b** the fungus causing this. **3** an impaired state due to disuse or inactivity. **4** a reddish-brown or brownish-red colour. ● *v.* **1** *tr. & intr.* affect or be affected with rust; undergo oxidation. **2** *intr.* (of bracken etc.) become rust-coloured. **3** *intr.* (of a plant) be attacked by rust. **4** *intr.* lose quality or efficiency by disuse or inactivity. □ **rustless** *adj.* [Old English *rūst*, from Germanic]

rust belt *n. colloq.* an area of once profitable industry, esp. in the American Midwest and north-eastern states.

rustic /ˈrʌstɪk/ *adj. & n.* ● *adj.* **1** having the characteristics of or associations with the country or country life. **2** unsophisticated, simple, unrefined. **3** of rude or country workmanship. **4** made of untrimmed branches or rough timber (*a rustic bench*). **5** (of lettering) freely formed. **6** *Archit.* with rough-hewn or roughened surface or with sunk joints. **7** *archaic* rural. ● *n.* a person from or living in the country, esp. a simple unsophisticated one. □ **rustically** *adv.* **rusticity** /-ˈstɪsɪti/ *n.* [Middle English from Latin *rusticus*, from *rus* 'the country']

rusticate /ˈrʌstɪkeɪt/ *v.* **1** *tr. Brit.* send down (a student) temporarily from university. **2** *intr.* retire to or live in the country. **3** *tr.* make rural. **4** *tr.* mark (masonry) with sunk joints or a roughened surface. □ **rustication** /-ˈkeɪʃ(ə)n/ *n.* [Latin *rusticari* 'live in the country' (as RUSTIC)]

rustle /ˈrʌs(ə)l/ *v. & n.* ● *v.* **1** *intr. & tr.* make or cause to make a gentle sound as of dry leaves blown in a breeze. **2** *intr.* (often foll. by *along* etc.) move with a rustling sound. **3** *tr.* (also *absol.*) steal (cattle, horses, or sheep). **4** *intr. US colloq.* move or act quickly or energetically. ● *n.* a rustling sound or movement. □ **rustle up** *colloq.* produce quickly when needed. □ **rustler** *n.* (esp. in sense 3 of *v.*). [Middle English *rustel* etc. (imitative): cf. obsolete Flemish *ruysselen*, Dutch *ritselen*]

rustproof /ˈrʌs(t)pruːf/ *adj. & v.* ● *adj.* (of a metal) not susceptible to corrosion by rust. ● *v.tr.* make rustproof.

rustre /ˈrʌstə/ *n. Heraldry* a lozenge with a round hole. [French]

rusty /ˈrʌsti/ *adj.* (**rustier**, **rustiest**) **1** rusted or affected by rust. **2** stiff with age or disuse. **3** (of knowledge etc.) faded or impaired by neglect (*my French is a bit rusty*). **4** rust-coloured. **5** (of black clothes) discoloured by age. **6 a** of antiquated appearance. **b** antiquated or behind the times. **7** (of a voice) croaking or creaking. □ **rustily** *adv.* **rustiness** *n.* [Old English *rūstig* (as RUST)]

rut[1] /rʌt/ *n. & v.* ● *n.* **1** a deep track made by the passage of wheels. **2** an established (esp. tedious) mode of practice or procedure. ● *v.tr.* (**rutted**, **rutting**) mark with ruts. □ **in a rut** following a fixed (esp. tedious or dreary) pattern of behaviour that is difficult to change. □ **rutty** *adj.* [probably from Old French *rote* (as ROUTE)]

rut² /rʌt/ *n.* & *v.* ● *n.* the periodic sexual excitement of a male deer, goat, sheep, etc. ● *v.intr.* (**rutted**, **rutting**) be affected with rut. □ **ruttish** *adj.* [Middle English via Old French *rut*, *ruit* from Latin *rugitus*, from *rugire* 'roar']

rutabaga /ruːtəˈbeɪgə/ *n.* a swede. [Swedish dialect *rotabagge*]

ruthenium /rʊˈθiːnɪəm/ *n. Chem.* a rare hard white metallic transition element, occurring naturally in platinum ores, and used as a chemical catalyst and in certain alloys (symbol **Ru**). [medieval Latin *Ruthenia* Russia (from its discovery in ores from the Urals)]

rutherfordium /rʌðəˈfɔːdɪəm/ *n. Chem.* a name variously proposed for the artificial radioactive elements of atomic number 104 and 106 (symbol **Rf**). [named after E. *Rutherford*, New Zealand-born physicist d. 1937]

ruthless /ˈruːθlɪs/ *adj.* having no pity or compassion. □ **ruthlessly** *adv.* **ruthlessness** *n.* [Middle English, from *ruth* 'compassion', from RUE¹]

rutile /ˈruːtɪl, ˈruːtʌɪl/ *n.* a mineral form of titanium dioxide. [French *rutile* or German *Rutil* from Latin *rutilus* 'reddish']

RV *abbr.* **1** Revised Version (of the Bible). **2** *US* recreational vehicle (esp. denoting a motorized caravan).

Ry. *abbr.* Railway.

-ry /ri/ var. of -ERY. [shortened from -ERY, or by analogy]

rye /rʌɪ/ *n.* **1 a** a cereal plant, *Secale cereale*, with spikes bearing florets which yield wheatlike grains. **b** the grain of this used for bread and fodder. **2** (in full **rye whisky**) whisky distilled from fermented rye. [Old English *ryge*, from Germanic]

ryegrass /ˈrʌɪgrɑːs/ *n.* any forage or lawn grass of the genus *Lolium*, esp. *L. perenne*. [obsolete *ray-grass*, of unknown origin]

ryokan /rɪˈəʊkan/ *n.* a traditional Japanese inn. [Japanese]

ryot /ˈrʌɪət/ *n.* an Indian peasant. [Urdu *raʿīyat* from Arabic *raʿīya* 'flock, subjects', from *raʿā* 'to pasture']

Ss

S[1] /ɛs/ *n.* (also **s**) (*pl.* **Ss** or **S's**) **1** the nineteenth letter of the alphabet. **2** an S-shaped object or curve.

S[2] *abbr.* (also **S.**) **1** Saint. **2** South, Southern.

S[3] *symb.* **1** *Chem.* the element sulphur. **2** siemens.

s *abbr.* (also **s.**) **1** second(s). **2** shilling(s). **3** singular. **4** son. **5** succeeded. **6** *Chem.* solid. [sense 2 originally from Latin *solidus*: see SOLIDUS]

's /s, z after a vowel sound or voiced consonant/ *abbr. colloq.* **1** is, has (*he's arrived*; *it's raining*; *John's late*). **2** us (*let's*). **3** does (*what's he say?*).

's- /s, z before a voiced consonant/ *prefix archaic* (esp. in oaths) God's (*'sblood*; *'strewth*). [abbreviation]

-s[1] /s, z after a vowel sound or voiced consonant/ *suffix* denoting the plurals of nouns (cf. -ES[1]). [Old English pl. ending *-as*]

-s[2] /s, z after a vowel sound or voiced consonant/ *suffix* forming the 3rd person sing. present of verbs (cf. -ES[2]). [Old English dialect, probably from Old English 2nd person sing. present ending *-es*, *-as*]

-s[3] /s, z after a vowel sound or voiced consonant/ *suffix* **1** forming adverbs (*afterwards*; *besides*). **2** forming possessive pronouns (*hers*; *ours*). [formed as -'s[1]]

-s[4] /s, z after a vowel sound or voiced consonant/ *suffix* forming nicknames or pet names (*Fats*; *ducks*). [suggested by -s[1]]

-s' /s; z after a vowel sound or voiced consonant/ *suffix* denoting the possessive case of plural nouns and sometimes of singular nouns ending in *s* (*the boys' shoes*; *Charles' book*). [as -'s[1]]

-'s[1] /s, z after a vowel sound or voiced consonant, ɪz after a sibilant/ *suffix* denoting the possessive case of singular nouns and of plural nouns not ending in *-s* (*John's book*; *the book's cover*; *the children's shoes*; *Mr Jones's dog*). [Old English genitive sing. ending]

-'s[2] /s, z after a vowel sound or voiced consonant, ɪz after a sibilant/ *suffix* denoting the plural of a letter or symbol (*S's*; *8's*). [as -s[1]]

SA *abbr.* **1** Salvation Army. **2** sex appeal. **3 a** South Africa. **b** South America. **c** South Australia. **4** *hist. Sturmabteilung* (the paramilitary force of the Nazi party).

sab /sab/ *n.* & *v. slang* ● *n.* a hunt saboteur. ● *v.tr.* (**sabbed**, **sabbing**) disrupt (a hunt). [abbreviation of SABOTEUR]

sabadilla /sabəˈdɪlə/ *n.* **1** a Mexican plant, *Schoenocaulon officinale*, with seeds yielding veratrine. **2** a preparation of these seeds, used in medicine and agriculture. [Spanish *cebadilla*, diminutive of *cebada* 'barley']

Sabaoth /ˈsabeɪɒθ, saˈbeɪɒθ/ *n.pl. Bibl.* heavenly hosts (see HOST[1] 2) (*Lord of Sabaoth*). [Middle English from Late Latin via Greek *Sabaōth* from Hebrew *ṣᵉḇāʾōṯ* pl. of *ṣāḇâ* 'host' (of heaven)]

Sabbatarian /sabəˈtɛːrɪən/ *n.* & *adj.* ● *n.* **1** a strict sabbath-keeping Jew. **2** a Christian who favours observing Sunday strictly as the sabbath. **3** a Christian who observes Saturday as the sabbath. ● *adj.* relating to or holding the tenets of Sabbatarians. □ **Sabbatarianism** *n.* [Late Latin *sabbatarius* from Latin *sabbatum*: see SABBATH]

sabbath /ˈsabəθ/ *n.* **1** (in full **sabbath day**) a day of rest and religious observance kept by Jews on Saturday. **2** Sunday as a day of Christian religious observance and abstinence from work and play. **3** (in full **witches' sabbath**) a supposed general midnight meeting of witches with the Devil. [Old English *sabat*, Latin *sabbatum*, & Old French *sabbat*, via Greek *sabbaton* from Hebrew *šabbāṯ*, from *šāḇaṯ* 'to rest']

sabbatical /səˈbatɪk(ə)l/ *adj.* & *n.* ● *adj.* **1** of or appropriate to the sabbath. **2** (of leave) granted at intervals to a university teacher for study or travel, originally every seventh year. ● *n.* a period of sabbatical leave. □ **sabbatically** *adv.* [Late Latin *sabbaticus* from Greek *sabbatikos* 'of the sabbath']

sabbatical year *n.* **1** *Bibl.* every seventh year, prescribed by the Mosaic law to be observed as a 'sabbath', during which the land was allowed to rest. **2** a year's sabbatical leave.

saber *US* var. of SABRE.

Sabian /ˈseɪbɪən/ *adj.* & *n.* ● *adj.* of a sect classed in the Koran with Muslims, Jews, and Christians, as believers in the true God. ● *n.* a member of this sect. [Arabic *ṣābi'*]

sabicu /sabɪˈkuː/ *n.* **1** a W. Indian tree, *Lysiloma latisiliqua*, grown for timber. **2** the mahogany-like wood of this tree. [Cuban Spanish *sabicú*]

Sabine /ˈsabʌɪn/ *adj.* & *n.* ● *adj.* of or relating to a people of the central Apennines in ancient Italy. ● *n.* a member of this people. [Latin *Sabinus*]

Sabin vaccine /ˈseɪbɪn/ *n.* an oral vaccine giving immunity against poliomyelitis. [named after A. B. *Sabin*, US virologist b. 1906]

sable[1] /ˈseɪb(ə)l/ *n.* **1 a** a small brown-furred flesh-eating mammal, *Martes zibellina*, of N. Europe and parts of N. Asia, related to the marten. **b** its skin or fur. **2** a fine paintbrush made of sable fur. [Middle English via Old French from medieval Latin *sabelum*, from Slavonic]

sable[2] /ˈseɪb(ə)l/ *n.* & *adj.* ● *n.* **1** esp. *poet.* black. **2** (in *pl.*) mourning garments. **3** (in full **sable antelope**) a large African antelope, *Hippotragus niger*, with long curved horns, the male of which has a black coat with a white belly. ● *adj.* **1** (usu. placed after noun) *Heraldry* black. **2** esp. *poet.* dark, gloomy. □ **sabled** *adj.* **sably** *adv.* [Middle English from Old French (in Heraldry): generally taken to be identical with SABLE[1], although sable fur is dark brown]

sabot /ˈsabəʊ/ *n.* **1** a kind of simple shoe hollowed out from a block of wood. **2** a wooden-soled shoe. **3** *Austral.* a small snub-nosed yacht. □ **saboted** /ˈsabəʊd/ *adj.* [French, blend of *savate* 'shoe' + *botte* 'boot']

sabotage /ˈsabətɑːʒ/ *n.* & *v.* ● *n.* deliberate damage to productive capacity, esp. as a political act. ● *v.tr.* **1** commit sabotage on. **2** destroy, spoil; make useless (*sabotaged my plans*). [French from *saboter* 'make a noise with sabots, bungle, wilfully destroy': see SABOT]

saboteur /sabəˈtəː/ *n.* a person who commits sabotage. [French]

sabra /ˈsabrə/ *n.* an Israeli born in Israel. [modern Hebrew *sābrāh* 'opuntia fruit' (opuntias are common in coastal regions of Israel)]

sabre /ˈseɪbə/ *n.* & *v.* (*US* **saber**) ● *n.* **1** a cavalry sword with a curved blade. **2** a cavalry soldier and horse. **3** a light fencing-sword with a tapering blade. ● *v.tr.* cut down or wound with a sabre. [French, earlier *sable*, via German *Sabel*, *Säbel*, *Schabel* from Polish *szabla* or Hungarian *szablya*]

sabre-cut *n.* **1** a blow with a sabre. **2** a wound made or a scar left by this.

sabre-rattling *n.* a display or threat of military force.

sabre saw *n.* a portable electric jigsaw.

sabretache /ˈsabətaʃ/ *n.* a flat satchel on long straps worn by some cavalry officers from the left of the waist-belt. [French from German *Säbeltasche* (as SABRE, *Tasche* 'pocket')]

sabre-toothed tiger *n.* (also **sabre-toothed cat**) an extinct mammal of the cat family with long curved upper canine teeth, esp. one of the genus *Smilodon* of the Pleistocene epoch in America.

sabreur /saˈbrəː/ *n.* a user of the sabre, esp. a cavalryman. [French from *sabrer* SABRE *v.*]

sabrewing /ˈseɪbəwɪŋ/ *n.* a S. American hummingbird of the genus *Campylopterus*, with long curved wings.

SAC *abbr.* Senior Aircraftman.

sac /sak/ *n.* **1** a bag-like cavity, enclosed by a membrane, in an animal or plant. **2** the distended membrane surrounding a hernia, cyst, tumour, etc. [French *sac* or Latin *saccus* SACK[1]]

saccade /saˈkɑːd/ *n.* a brief rapid movement of the eye between fixation points. □ **saccadic** /saˈkadɪk/ *adj.* [French, = violent pull, from Old French *saquer*, *sachier* 'to pull']

saccate /ˈsakeɪt/ *adj. Bot.* **1** dilated into a bag. **2** contained in a sac.

saccharide /ˈsakərʌɪd/ *n. Chem.* = SUGAR *n.* 2. [modern Latin *saccharum* 'sugar' + -IDE]

saccharimeter /sakəˈrɪmɪtə/ *n.* a polarimeter for measuring the sugar content of a solution. [French *saccharimètre* (as SACCHARIDE)]

saccharin /ˈsakərɪn/ *n.* a very sweet substance used as a non-fattening substitute for sugar. [German (as SACCHARIDE) + -IN]

saccharine /ˈsakərʌɪn, -ɪn, -iːn/ *adj.* **1** sugary. **2** of, containing, or like sugar. **3** unpleasantly over-polite, sentimental, etc.

saccharo- /ˈsakərəʊ/ *comb. form* sugar; sugar and. [Greek *sakkharon* 'sugar']

saccharometer /sakəˈrɒmɪtə/ *n.* a hydrometer for estimating the sugar content of a solution.

saccharose /ˈsakərəʊz, -s/ *n. Chem.* sucrose. [modern Latin *saccharum* 'sugar' + -OSE[2]]

sacciform /ˈsaksɪfɔːm/ *adj.* sac-shaped. [Latin *saccus* 'sac' + -FORM]

saccule /ˈsakjuːl/ *n.* a small sac or cyst. □ **saccular** *adj.* [Latin *sacculus* (as SAC)]

sacerdotal /sasəˈdəʊt(ə)l, sakə-/ *adj.* **1** of priests or the priestly office; priestly. **2** (of a doctrine etc.) ascribing sacrificial functions and supernatural powers to ordained priests; claiming excessive authority for the priesthood. □ **sacerdotalism** *n.* **sacerdotalist** *n.* **sacerdotally** *adv.* [Middle English from Old French *sacerdotal* or Latin *sacerdotalis*, from *sacerdos -dotis* 'priest']

sachem /ˈseɪtʃəm, ˈsatʃəm/ *n.* **1** the supreme chief of some American Indian tribes. **2** *N. Amer. colloq.* a leader (*political sachem; mafia sachem*). [Narragansett, = SAGAMORE]

sachet /ˈsaʃeɪ/ *n.* **1** esp. *Brit.* a small usu. sealed and airtight bag or packet. **2** a small scented bag. **3 a** dry perfume for laying among clothes etc. **b** a packet of this. [French, diminutive of *sac*, from Latin *saccus* SACK[1]]

sack[1] /sak/ *n.* & *v.* ● *n.* **1 a** a large strong bag, usu. made of hessian, paper, or plastic, for storing or conveying goods. **b** (usu. foll. by *of*) this with its contents (*a sack of potatoes*). **c** a quantity contained in a sack. **2** (prec. by *the*) *colloq.* dismissal from employment. **3** (prec. by *the*) *N. Amer. slang* bed. **4 a** a woman's short loose dress with a sacklike appearance. **b** *archaic* or *hist.* a woman's loose gown, or a silk train attached to the shoulders of this. **5** a man's or woman's loose-hanging coat not shaped to the back. ● *v.tr.* **1** put into a sack or sacks. **2** *colloq.* dismiss from employment. □ **hit the sack** *colloq.* go to bed. □ **sackable** *adj.* **sackful** *n.* (*pl.* **-fuls**). **sacklike** *adj.* [Old English *sacc* via Latin *saccus* from Greek *sakkos*, of Semitic origin]

sack[2] /sak/ *v.* & *n.* ● *v.tr.* **1** plunder and destroy (a captured town etc.). **2** steal valuables from (a place). ● *n.* the sacking of a captured place. [originally as noun, from French *sac* in the phrase *mettre à sac* 'put to sack', from Italian *sacco* SACK[1]]

sack[3] /sak/ *n. hist.* a white wine formerly imported into Britain from Spain and the Canaries (*sherry sack*). [16th-c. *wyne seck*, from French *vin sec* 'dry wine']

sackbut /ˈsakbʌt/ *n.* an early form of trombone. [French *saquebute*, earlier *saqueboute* 'hook for pulling a man off a horse' from *saquer* 'pull' + *boute* (as BUTT[1])]

sackcloth /ˈsakklɒθ/ *n.* **1** a coarse fabric of flax or hemp. **2** clothing made of this, formerly worn as a penance or in mourning (esp. *sackcloth and ashes*).

sacking /ˈsakɪŋ/ *n.* material for making sacks; sackcloth.

sack race *n.* a race between competitors in sacks up to the waist or neck.

sacra *pl.* of SACRUM.

sacral /ˈseɪkr(ə)l, ˈsak-/ *adj.* **1** *Anat.* of or relating to the sacrum. **2** *Anthropol.* of or for sacred rites.

sacrament /ˈsakrəm(ə)nt/ *n.* **1** a religious ceremony or act of the Christian Churches regarded as an outward and visible sign of inward and spiritual grace: applied by the Eastern, pre-Reformation Western, and Roman Catholic Churches to the seven rites of baptism, confirmation, the Eucharist, penance, extreme unction, ordination, and matrimony, but restricted by most Protestants to baptism and the Eucharist. **2** a thing of mysterious and sacred significance; a sacred influence, symbol, etc. **3** (also **Blessed** or **Holy Sacrament**) (prec. by *the*) **a** the Eucharist. **b** the consecrated elements, esp. the bread or Host. **4** an oath or solemn engagement taken. [Middle English via Old French *sacrement* from Latin *sacramentum* 'solemn oath' etc., via *sacrare* 'hallow' from *sacer* SACRED, used in Christian Latin as translation of Greek *mustērion* MYSTERY[1]]

sacramental /sakrəˈmɛnt(ə)l/ *adj.* & *n.* ● *adj.* **1** of or of the nature of a sacrament or the sacrament. **2** (of a doctrine etc.) attaching great importance to the sacraments. ● *n.* an observance analogous to but not reckoned among the sacraments, e.g. the use of holy water or the sign of the cross. □ **sacramentalism** *n.* **sacramentalist** *n.* **sacramentality** /-ˈtalɪti/ *n.* **sacramentally** *adv.* [Middle English from French *sacramental* or Late Latin *sacramentalis* (as SACRAMENT)]

sacrarium /səˈkrɛːrɪəm/ *n.* (*pl.* **sacraria** /-rɪə/) **1** the sanctuary of a church. **2** *RC Ch.* a piscina. **3** *Rom. Antiq.* a shrine; the room (in a house) containing the penates. [Latin, from *sacer sacri* 'holy']

sacred /ˈseɪkrɪd/ *adj.* **1 a** (often foll. by *to*) exclusively dedicated or appropriated (to a god or to some religious purpose). **b** made holy by religious association. **c** connected with religion; used for a religious purpose (*sacred music*). **2 a** safeguarded or required by religion, reverence, or tradition. **b** sacrosanct. **3** (of writings etc.) embodying the laws or doctrines of a religion. □ **sacredly** *adv.* **sacredness** *n.* [Middle English, past part. of obsolete *sacre* 'consecrate', via Old French *sacrer* from Latin *sacrare*, from *sacer sacri* 'holy']

Sacred College *n. RC Ch.* the body of cardinals.

sacred cow *n. colloq.* an idea or institution unreasonably held to be above criticism (with reference to the Hindus' respect for the cow as a holy animal).

Sacred Heart *n. RC Ch.* **1** the heart of Christ as an object of devotion. **2** an image representing this.

sacred ibis *n.* an ibis, *Threskiornis aethiopicus*, native to Africa and Madagascar, venerated by the ancient Egyptians.

sacred number *n.* a number associated with religious symbolism, e.g. 7.

sacrifice /ˈsakrɪfʌɪs/ *n.* & *v.* ● *n.* **1 a** the act of giving up something valued for the sake of something else more important or worthy. **b** a thing given up in this way. **c** the loss entailed in this. **2 a** the slaughter of an animal or person or the surrender of a possession as an offering to a deity. **b** an animal, person, or thing offered in this way. **3** an act of prayer, thanksgiving, or penitence as propitiation. **4** *Theol.* **a** Christ's offering of himself in the Crucifixion. **b** the Eucharist as either a propitiatory offering of the body and blood of Christ or an act of thanksgiving. **5** (in games) a loss incurred deliberately to avoid a greater loss or to obtain a compensating advantage. ● *v.* **1** *tr.* give up (a thing) as a sacrifice. **2** *tr.* (foll. by *to*) devote or give over to. **3** *tr.* (also *absol.*) offer or kill as a sacrifice. □ **sacrificial** /-ˈfɪʃ(ə)l/ *adj.* **sacrificially** /-ˈfɪʃ(ə)li/ *adv.* [Middle English via Old French from Latin *sacrificium*, from *sacrificus* (as SACRED)]

sacrificial anode *n.* a metal anode that is used up in protecting another metal against corrosion (cf. CATHODIC PROTECTION).

sacrilege /ˈsakrɪlɪdʒ/ *n.* the violation or misuse of what is regarded as sacred. □ **sacrilegious** /-ˈlɪdʒəs/ *adj.* **sacrilegiously** /-ˈlɪdʒəsli/ *adv.* [Middle English via Old French from Latin *sacrilegium*, from *sacrilegus* 'stealer of sacred things', from *sacer sacri* 'sacred' + *legere* 'take possession of']

sacring /ˈseɪkrɪŋ/ *n. archaic* **1** the consecration of the Eucharistic elements. **2** the ordination and consecration of a bishop, sovereign, etc. [Middle English from obsolete *sacre*: see SACRED]

sacring bell *n.* a bell rung at the elevation of the elements in the Eucharist.

sacristan /ˈsakrɪstən/ *n.* **1** a person in charge of a sacristy and its contents. **2** *archaic* the sexton of a parish church. [Middle English from medieval Latin *sacristanus* (as SACRED)]

sacristy /ˈsakrɪsti/ *n.* (*pl.* **-ies**) a room in a church, where the vestments, sacred vessels, etc., are kept and the celebrant can prepare for a service. [French *sacristie*, Italian *sacrestia* or medieval Latin *sacristia* (as SACRED)]

sacro- /ˈseɪkrəʊ, ˈsakrəʊ-/ *comb. form* denoting the sacrum (*sacro-iliac*).

sacroiliac /seɪkrəʊˈɪlɪak, sak-/ *adj. Anat.* relating to the sacrum and the ilium, esp. designating the rigid joint between them at the back of the pelvis.

sacrosanct /ˈsakrə(ʊ)saŋ(k)t, ˈseɪkrə(ʊ)-/ *adj.* (of a person, place, law, etc.) most sacred; inviolable. □ **sacrosanctity** /-ˈsaŋktɪti/ *n.* [Latin *sacrosanctus*, from *sacro*, ablative of *sacrum* 'sacred rite' (see SACRED) + *sanctus* (as SAINT)]

sacrum /ˈseɪkrəm, ˈsak-/ *n.* (*pl.* **sacra** /-krə/ or **sacrums**) *Anat.* a triangular bone formed from fused vertebrae and situated between the two hip bones of the pelvis. [Latin *os sacrum*, translation of Greek *hieron osteon* 'sacred bone' (from the belief that the soul resides in it)]

SACW *abbr.* Senior Aircraftwoman.

SAD *abbr.* seasonal affective disorder.

sad /sad/ *adj.* (**sadder**, **saddest**) **1** unhappy; feeling sorrow or regret. **2** causing or suggesting sorrow (*a sad story*). **3** regrettable. **4** shameful, deplorable (*is in a sad state*). **5** (of a colour) dull, neutral-tinted. **6** (of dough etc.) heavy, having failed to rise. **7** *slang* contemptible, pathetic, unfashionable. □ **saddish** *adj.* **sadly** *adv.* **sadness** *n.* [Old English *sæd* from Germanic: related to Latin *satis*]

sadden /ˈsad(ə)n/ *v.tr. & intr.* make or become sad.

saddle /ˈsad(ə)l/ *n. & v.* ● *n.* **1** a seat of leather etc., usu. raised at the front and rear, fastened on a horse etc. for riding. **2** a seat for the rider of a bicycle etc. **3** a joint of meat consisting of the two loins. **4** a ridge rising to a summit at each end. **5** the part of a draught horse's harness to which the shafts are attached. **6** a part of an animal's back resembling a saddle in shape or marking. **7** the rear part of a male fowl's back. **8** a support for a cable or wire on top of a suspension bridge, pier, or telegraph pole. **9** a fireclay bar for supporting ceramic ware in a kiln. ● *v.tr.* **1** put a saddle on (a horse etc.). **2** **a** (foll. by *with*) burden (a person) with a task, responsibility, etc. **b** (foll. by *on*, *upon*) impose (a burden) on a person. **3** (of a trainer) enter (a horse) for a race. □ **in the saddle 1** mounted. **2** in office or control. □ **saddleless** *adj.* [Old English *sadol*, *sadul*, from Germanic]

saddleback /ˈsad(ə)lbak/ *n.* **1** *Archit.* a roof of a tower with two opposite gables. **2** a hill with a concave upper outline. **3** a black pig with a white stripe across the back. **4** any of various birds with a saddle-like marking esp. a New Zealand bird, *Creadion carunculatus*. □ **saddlebacked** *adj.*

saddlebag /ˈsad(ə)lbag/ *n.* **1** each of a pair of bags laid across a horse etc. behind the saddle. **2** a bag attached behind the saddle of a bicycle or motorcycle.

saddle bow *n.* the arched front or rear of a saddle.

saddle-cloth *n.* a cloth laid on a horse's back under the saddle.

saddle-horse *n.* a horse for riding.

saddler /ˈsadlə/ *n.* a maker of or dealer in saddles and other equipment for horses.

saddlery /ˈsadləri/ *n.* (*pl.* **-ies**) **1** the saddles and other equipment of a saddler. **2** a saddler's business or premises.

saddle-sore *adj.* chafed by riding on a saddle.

saddle stitch *n. & v.* ● *n.* a stitch of thread or a wire staple passed through the centre of a magazine or booklet. ● *v.tr.* (**saddle-stitch**) sew with this stitch.

saddle tree *n.* **1** the frame of a saddle. **2** a tulip tree (with saddle-shaped leaves).

Sadducee /ˈsadjʊsiː/ *n.* a member of a Jewish sect or party of the time of Christ that denied the resurrection of the dead, the existence of spirits, and the obligation of the traditional oral law (cf. PHARISEE, ESSENE). □ **Sadducean** /-ˈsiːən/ *adj.* [Old English *sadducēas* via Late Latin *Sadducaeus* and Greek *Saddoukaios* from Hebrew *ṣᵉḏûqî*, probably = descendant of Zadok (2 Sam. 8:17)]

sadhu /ˈsɑːduː/ *n.* (in India) a holy man, sage, or ascetic. [Sanskrit, = holy man]

sad-iron *n.* a solid flat iron.

sadism /ˈseɪdɪz(ə)m/ *n.* **1** a form of sexual perversion characterized by the enjoyment of inflicting pain or suffering on others (cf. MASOCHISM 1). **2** *colloq.* the enjoyment of cruelty to others. □ **sadist** *n.* **sadistic** /səˈdɪstɪk/ *adj.* **sadistically** /səˈdɪstɪk(ə)li/ *adv.* [French *sadisme*, named after the Count or 'Marquis' de *Sade*, French writer d. 1814]

sadomasochism /seɪdəʊˈmasəkɪz(ə)m/ *n.* the combination of sadism and masochism in one person. □ **sadomasochist** *n.* **sadomasochistic** /-ˈkɪstɪk/ *adj.*

sad sack *n. US colloq.* a very inept person.

sae *abbr. Brit.* stamped addressed envelope.

safari /səˈfɑːri/ *n.* (*pl.* **safaris**) **1** a hunting or scientific expedition, esp. in E. Africa (*go on safari*). **2** a sightseeing trip to see African animals in their natural habitat. [Swahili from Arabic *safara* 'to travel']

safari park *n.* an enclosed area where lions etc. are kept in relatively open spaces for public viewing from vehicles driven through.

safari suit *n.* a lightweight suit usu. with short sleeves and four pleated pockets in the jacket.

safe /seɪf/ *adj. & n.* ● *adj.* **1 a** free of danger or injury. **b** (often foll. by *from*) out of or not exposed to danger (*safe from their enemies*). **2** affording security or not involving danger or risk (*put it in a safe place*). **3** reliable, certain; that can be reckoned on (*a safe catch*; *a safe method*; *is safe to win*). **4** prevented from escaping or doing harm (*have got him safe*). **5** (also **safe and sound**) uninjured; with no harm done. **6** cautious and unenterprising; consistently moderate. ● *n.* **1** a strong lockable cabinet etc. for valuables. **2** = MEAT SAFE. □ **on the safe side** with a margin of security against risks. □ **safely** *adv.* **safeness** *n.* [Middle English via Anglo-French *saf*, Old French *sauf* from Latin *salvus* 'uninjured': the noun originally *save*, from SAVE[1]]

safe bet *n.* a bet that is certain to succeed.

safe-breaker *n.* (also **safe-blower** or *US* **safe-cracker**) a person who breaks open and robs safes.

safe conduct *n.* **1** a privilege of immunity from arrest or harm, esp. on a particular occasion. **2** a document securing this.

safe deposit *n.* a strongroom or safe for the safe keeping of valuables, usu. within a bank, hotel, etc. (also *attrib.*: *safe deposit box*).

safeguard /ˈseɪfgɑːd/ *n.* & *v.* ● *n.* **1** a proviso, stipulation, quality, or circumstance, that tends to prevent something undesirable. **2** a safe conduct. ● *v.tr.* guard or protect (rights etc.) by a precaution or stipulation. [Middle English from Anglo-French *salve garde*, Old French *sauve garde* (as SAFE, GUARD)]

safe house *n.* a place of refuge or rendezvous for spies, criminals, etc.

safe keeping *n.* preservation in a safe place.

safe light *n.* *Photog.* a filtered light for use in a darkroom.

safe period *n.* the time during and near the menstrual period when conception is least likely.

safe seat *n.* a seat in Parliament etc. that is usually won with a large margin by a particular party.

safe sex *n.* sexual activity in which precautions are taken to reduce the risk of spreading sexually transmitted diseases, esp. Aids.

safety /ˈseɪfti/ *n.* (*pl.* **-ies**) **1** the condition of being safe; freedom from danger or risks. **2** (*attrib.*) **a** designating any of various devices for preventing injury from machinery (*safety bar*; *safety lock*). **b** designating items of protective clothing (*safety helmet*). **3** *Amer. Football* a defensive back who plays in a deep position. □ **safety first** a motto advising caution. [Middle English *sauvete* via Old French *sauveté* from medieval Latin *salvitas -tatis*, from Latin *salvus* (as SAFE)]

safety belt *n.* **1** = SEAT BELT. **2** a belt or strap securing a person to prevent injury.

safety catch *n.* a contrivance for locking a gun trigger or preventing the accidental operation of machinery.

safety curtain *n.* a fireproof curtain that can be lowered to cut off the auditorium in a theatre from the stage.

safety factor *n.* **1** the ratio of a material's strength to an expected strain. **2** a margin of security against risks.

safety film *n.* a cinematographic film on a slow-burning or non-flammable base.

safety fuse *n.* **1** a fuse (see FUSE[2] *n.* 1) containing a slow-burning composition for firing detonators from a distance. **2** *Electr.* a protective fuse (see FUSE[1] *n.*).

safety glass *n.* glass that will not splinter when broken.

safety harness *n.* a system of belts or restraints to hold a person to prevent falling or injury.

safety lamp *n.* a miner's lamp so protected as not to ignite firedamp.

safety match *n.* a match igniting only on a specially prepared surface.

safety net *n.* **1** a net placed to catch an acrobat etc. in case of a fall. **2** a safeguard against possible hardship or adversity.

safety pin *n.* a pin with a point that is bent back to the head and is held in a guard when closed.

safety razor *n.* a razor with a guard to reduce the risk of cutting the skin.

safety valve *n.* **1** (in a steam boiler) a valve opening automatically to relieve excessive pressure. **2** a means of giving harmless vent to excitement etc.

safety zone *n.* *US* an area of a road marked off for pedestrians etc. to wait safely.

safflower /ˈsaflaʊə/ *n.* **1** an orange-flowered thistle-like plant, *Carthamus tinctorius*, whose seeds yield an edible oil. **2 a** its dried petals. **b** a red dye made from these, used in rouge etc. [Dutch *saffloer* or German *Safflor* via Old French *saffleur* from obsolete Italian *saffiore* from Arabic *aṣfar*]

saffron /ˈsafr(ə)n/ *n.* & *adj.* ● *n.* **1** an orange-yellow flavouring and food colouring made from the dried stigmas of the crocus, *Crocus sativus*. **2** the orange-yellow colour of this. **3** = MEADOW SAFFRON. ● *adj.* of an orange-yellow colour. □ **saffrony** *adj.* [Middle English via Old French *safran* from Arabic *zaʻfarān*]

safranine /ˈsafrəniːn/ *n.* (also **safranin** /-nɪn/) any of a large group of mainly red dyes used in biological staining etc. [originally of dye from saffron: French *safranine* (as SAFFRON)]

sag /sag/ *v.* & *n.* ● *v.intr.* (**sagged**, **sagging**) **1** sink or subside under weight or pressure, esp. unevenly. **2** have a downward bulge or curve in the middle. **3** fall in price. **4** (of a ship) drift from its course, esp. to leeward. ● *n.* **1 a** the amount that a rope etc. sags. **b** the distance from the middle of its curve to a straight line between its supports. **2** a sinking condition; subsidence. **3** a fall in price. **4** *Naut.* a tendency to leeward. □ **saggy** *adj.* [Middle English from Middle Low German *sacken*, Dutch *zakken* subside]

saga /ˈsɑːgə/ *n.* **1** a long story of heroic achievement, esp. a medieval Icelandic or Norwegian prose narrative. **2** a series of connected books giving the history of a family etc. **3** a long involved story. [Old Norse, = narrative, related to SAW[3]]

sagacious /səˈgeɪʃəs/ *adj.* **1** mentally penetrating; gifted with discernment; having practical wisdom. **2** acute-minded, shrewd. **3** (of a saying, plan, etc.) showing wisdom. **4** (of an animal) exceptionally intelligent; seeming to reason or deliberate. □ **sagaciously** *adv.* **sagacity** /səˈgasɪti/ *n.* [Latin *sagax sagacis*]

sagamore /ˈsagəmɔː/ *n.* = SACHEM 1. [Algonquian]

sage[1] /seɪdʒ/ *n.* **1** an aromatic herb, *Salvia officinalis*, with dull greyish-green leaves. **2** its leaves used in cookery. □ **sagy** *adj.* [Middle English via Old French *sauge* from Latin *salvia* 'healing plant', from *salvus* 'safe']

sage[2] /seɪdʒ/ *n.* & *adj.* ● *n.* **1** often *iron.* a profoundly wise man. **2** any of the ancients traditionally regarded as the wisest of their time. ● *adj.* **1** profoundly wise, esp. from experience. **2** of or indicating profound wisdom. **3** often *iron.* wise-looking; solemn-faced. □ **sagely** *adv.* **sageness** *n.* **sageship** *n.* [Middle English from Old French, ultimately from Latin *sapere* 'be wise']

sage and onion *n.* (in full **sage and onion stuffing**) a stuffing used with poultry, pork, etc.

sagebrush /ˈseɪdʒbrʌʃ/ *n.* **1** an area covered by shrubby aromatic plants of the genus *Artemisia*, esp. *A. tridentata*, found in some semi-arid regions of western N. America. **2** this plant.

sage Derby *n.* (also **sage Derby cheese**) a cheese made with an infusion of sage which flavours and mottles it.

sage green *n.* & *adj.* ● *n.* the colour of sage leaves. ● *adj.* (hyphenated when *attrib.*) of this colour.

sage grouse *n.* a large grouse, *Centrocercus urophasianus*, of western N. America, noted for the male's courtship display.

sage tea *n.* a medicinal infusion of sage leaves.

saggar /ˈsagə/ *n.* (also **sagger**) a protective fireclay box enclosing ceramic ware while it is being fired. [probably a contraction of SAFEGUARD]

sagittal /ˈsadʒɪt(ə)l, səˈdʒɪ-/ *adj.* *Anat.* **1** of or relating to the suture on top of the skull between the parietal bones. **2** of or in a plane parallel to this suture, esp. that dividing the body into left and right halves. [French from medieval Latin *sagittalis*, from *sagitta* 'arrow']

Sagittarius /sadʒɪˈtɛːrɪəs/ *n.* **1** *Astron.* a large constellation (the Archer), said to represent a centaur carrying a bow and arrow, and in which the centre of the Galaxy is situated. **2** *Astrol.* **a** the ninth sign of the zodiac, which the sun enters about 22 Nov. **b** a person born when the sun is in this sign. □ **Sagittarian** *adj.* & *n.* [Middle English from Latin, = archer, from *sagitta* 'arrow']

sagittate /ˈsadʒɪteɪt/ *adj. Bot. & Zool.* shaped like an arrowhead.

sago /ˈseɪɡəʊ/ *n.* (*pl.* **-os**) **1** a kind of starch, made from the powdered pith of the sago palm and used in puddings etc. **2** (in full **sago palm**) any of several tropical palms and cycads, esp. *Cycas circinalis* and *Metroxylon sagu*, from which sago is made. [Malay *sāgū* (originally through Portuguese)]

saguaro /səˈɡwɑːrəʊ/ *n.* (also **sahuaro** /səˈwɑːrəʊ/) (*pl.* **-os**) a giant cactus, *Carnegiea gigantea*, of the SW United States and Mexico. [Mexican Spanish]

sahib /ˈsɑː(h)ɪb, sɑːb/ *n.* **1** (in India) a polite form of address, often placed after a person's name or title. **2** a gentleman (*pukka sahib*). [Urdu from Arabic *ṣāḥīb* 'friend, lord']

said *past* and *past part.* of SAY.

saiga /ˈseɪɡə, ˈsʌɪɡə/ *n.* an antelope, *Saiga tartarica*, of the Asian steppes, having a distinctive inflated snout. [Russian]

sail /seɪl/ *n. & v.* ● *n.* **1** a piece of material (originally canvas, now usu. nylon etc.) extended on rigging to catch the wind and propel a boat or ship. **2** a ship's sails collectively. **3 a** a voyage or excursion in a sailing ship. **b** a voyage of specified duration. **4** a ship, esp. as discerned from its sails. **5** (*collect.*) ships in a squadron or company (*a fleet of twenty sail*). **6** (in *pl.*) *Brit. Naut.* **a** *slang* a maker or repairer of sails. **b** *hist.* a chief petty officer in charge of rigging. **7** a wind-catching apparatus, usu. a set of boards, attached to the arm of a windmill. **8 a** the dorsal fin of a sailfish. **b** the tentacle of a nautilus. **c** the float of a Portuguese man-of-war. ● *v.* **1** *intr.* travel on water by the use of sails or engine power. **2** *tr.* **a** navigate (a ship etc.). **b** travel on (a sea). **3** *tr.* set (a toy boat) afloat. **4** *intr.* glide or move smoothly or in a stately manner. **5** *intr.* (often foll. by *through*) *colloq.* succeed easily (*sailed through the exams*). □ **sail close to** (or **near**) **the wind 1** sail as nearly against the wind as possible. **2** come close to indecency or dishonesty; risk overstepping the mark. **sail into** *colloq.* attack physically or verbally with force. **take in sail 1** furl the sail or sails of a vessel. **2** moderate one's ambitions. **under sail** with sails set. □ **sailable** *adj.* **sailed** *adj.* (also in *comb.*). **sailless** *adj.* [Old English *segel*, from Germanic]

sail-arm *n.* the arm of a windmill.

sailboard /ˈseɪlbɔːd/ *n.* a board with a mast and sail, used in windsurfing. □ **sailboarder** *n.* **sailboarding** *n.*

sailboat /ˈseɪlbəʊt/ *n. US* = SAILING BOAT.

sailcloth /ˈseɪlklɒθ/ *n.* **1** canvas or other material for sails. **2** a canvas-like dress material.

sailer /ˈseɪlə/ *n.* a ship of specified sailing-power (*a good sailer*).

sailfish /ˈseɪlfɪʃ/ *n.* (*pl.* usu. same) **1** any large marine game fish of the genus *Istiophorus*, with a tall dorsal fin and a spearlike snout. **2** a basking shark.

sail-fluke *n.* = MEGRIM².

sailing boat *n.* esp. *Brit.* a boat driven by sails.

sailing master *n.* an officer navigating a ship, esp. *Brit.* a yacht.

sailing orders *n.pl.* instructions to a captain regarding departure, destination, etc.

sailing ship *n.* = SAILING BOAT.

sailmaker /ˈseɪlmeɪkə/ *n.* a person who makes, repairs, or alters sails. □ **sailmaking** *n.*

sailor /ˈseɪlə/ *n.* **1** a member of the crew of a ship or boat, esp. one below the rank of officer. **2** a person considered as liable or not liable to seasickness (*a good sailor*). □ **sailoring** *n.* **sailorless** *adj.* **sailorly** *adj.* [variant of SAILER]

sailor hat *n.* **1** a straw hat with a straight narrow brim and flat top. **2** a hat with a turned-up brim in imitation of a sailor's, worn by women and children.

sailor suit *n.* a suit like that of an ordinary seaman, worn esp. by small boys.

sailplane /ˈseɪlpleɪn/ *n.* a glider designed for sustained flight.

sainfoin /ˈseɪnfɔɪn, ˈsan-/ *n.* a pink-flowered leguminous plant, *Onobrychis viciifolia*, grown for fodder. [obsolete French *saintfoin* from modern Latin *sanum foenum* 'wholesome hay' (because of its medicinal properties)]

saint /seɪnt, before a name usu. s(ə)nt/ *n. & v.* ● *n.* (*abbr.* **St** or **S**; *pl.* **Sts** or **SS**) **1** a holy or (in some Churches) a canonized person regarded as having a place in heaven. **2** (**Saint** or **St**) the title of a saint or archangel, hence used in the names of churches etc. (*St Paul's*), sometimes without reference to a saint (*St Cross*; *St Saviour's*), or (often with the loss of the apostrophe) in the names of places. (*St Andrews*; *St Albans*). **3** a very virtuous person; a person of great real or affected holiness (*would try the patience of a saint*). **4** a member of the company of heaven (*with all the angels and saints*). **5** (*Bibl.*, *archaic*, and used by Puritans, Mormons, etc.) one of God's chosen people; a member of the Christian Church or one's own branch of it. ● *v.tr.* **1** canonize; admit to the calendar of saints. **2** call or regard as a saint. **3** (as **sainted** *adj.*) sacred; of a saintly life; worthy to be regarded as a saint. □ **my sainted aunt** see AUNT. □ **saintdom** *n.* **sainthood** *n.* **saintlike** *adj.* **saintling** *n.* **saintship** *n.* [Middle English via Old French *seint*, *saint* from Latin *sanctus* 'holy', past part. of *sancire* 'consecrate']

St Andrew's cross /ˈandruːz/ *n.* an X-shaped cross.

St Anthony cross /ˈantəni/ *n.* (also **St Anthony's cross** /ˈantənɪz/) a T-shaped cross.

St Anthony's fire /ˈantənɪz/ *n.* erysipelas or ergotism.

St Bernard /ˈbəːnəd/ *n.* (in full **St Bernard dog**) **1** a very large dog of a breed originally kept to rescue travellers by the monks of the Hospice on the Great St Bernard pass in the Alps. **2** this breed.

St Elmo's fire /ˈɛlməʊz/ *n.* a corposant. [from its being regarded as a sign of protection from St Elmo, the patron saint of sailors]

St George's cross /ˈdʒɔːdʒɪz/ *n.* a +-shaped cross, red on a white background.

St John's wort /dʒɒnz/ *n.* any yellow-flowered plant of the genus *Hypericum*, esp. *H. androsaemum*. [so named because some species come into flower near the feast day of St John the Baptist (24 June)]

St Leger /ˈlɛdʒə/ *n.* a horse race at Doncaster in England for three-year-olds. [named after Col. B. *St Leger* (d. 1789), who founded the race in 1776]

St Luke's summer /luːks/ *n. Brit.* a period of fine weather expected about 18 Oct. (the saint's feast day).

saintly /ˈseɪntli/ *adj.* (**saintlier**, **saintliest**) very holy or virtuous. □ **saintliness** *n.*

St Martin's summer /ˈmɑːtɪnz/ *n. Brit.* a period of fine weather expected about 11 Nov. (the feast day of St Martin of Tours).

saintpaulia /s(ə)ntˈpɔːlɪə/ *n.* = AFRICAN VIOLET. [named after Baron W. von *Saint Paul*, German soldier d. 1910, its discoverer]

saint's day *n.* a Church festival in memory of a saint.

St Vitus's dance /ˈvʌɪtəsɪz/ *n.* = SYDENHAM'S CHOREA. [so named because a visit to the saint's shrine was believed to alleviate the disease]

saith /sɛθ/ *archaic 3rd sing. present* of SAY.

saithe /seɪθ/ *n.* a codlike edible fish, *Pollachius virens*, with skin that soils fingers like wet coal. Also called *coalfish*, *coley*. [Old Norse *seithr*]

sake¹ /seɪk/ *n.* □ **for Christ's** (or **God's** or **goodness'** or **heaven's** or **Pete's** etc.) **sake** an expression of urgency, impatience, supplication, anger, etc. **for old times' sake** in memory of former times. **for the sake of** (or **for a person's sake**) **1** out of consideration for; in the interest of; because of; owing to (*for my own sake as well as yours*). **2** in order to please, honour, get, or keep (*for the sake of uniformity*). [Old English *sacu* 'contention, charge, fault, sake', from Germanic]

sake² /ˈsɑːki, ˈsakeɪ/ *n.* a Japanese alcoholic drink made from rice. [Japanese]

saker /ˈseɪkə/ *n.* **1** a large Eurasian falcon, *Falco cherrug*, used in falconry. **2** *hist.* an old form of cannon.

[Middle English via Old French *sacre* (in both senses) from Arabic *ṣaḳr*]

saki /ˈsɑːki/ *n.* (*pl.* **sakis**) any monkey of the genus *Pithecia* or *Chiropotes*, native to S. America, having coarse fur and a long non-prehensile tail. [French, from Tupi *çahy*]

Sakta /ˈʃɑːktə/ *n.* a member of a Hindu sect worshipping the Sakti. [Sanskrit *śākta*, relating to power or to the SAKTI]

Sakti /ˈʃakti/ *n.* (also **sakti**) (in Hinduism) the female principle, esp. when personified as the wife of a god. [Sanskrit *śakti* 'power, divine energy']

sal /sɑːl/ *n.* a N. Indian tree, *Shorea robusta*, yielding teaklike timber and dammar resin. [Hindi *sāl*]

salaam /səˈlɑːm/ *n.* & *v.* ● *n.* **1** the oriental salutation 'Peace'. **2** an obeisance, with or without the salutation, often consisting of a low bow of the head and body with the right palm on the forehead. **3** (in *pl.*) respectful compliments. ● *v.* **1** *tr.* make a salaam to (a person). **2** *intr.* make a salaam. [Arabic *salām*]

salable var. of SALEABLE.

salacious /səˈleɪʃəs/ *adj.* **1** lustful; lecherous. **2** (of writings, pictures, talk, etc.) tending to cause sexual desire. ▫ **salaciously** *adv.* **salaciousness** *n.* **salacity** /səˈlasɪti/ *n.* [Latin *salax salacis* from *salire* 'leap']

salad /ˈsaləd/ *n.* **1** a cold dish of various mixtures of raw or cooked vegetables or herbs, usu. seasoned with oil, vinegar, etc. **2** a vegetable or herb suitable for eating raw. [Middle English via Old French *salade* from Provençal *salada*, ultimately from Latin *sal* 'salt']

salad cream *n. Brit.* creamy salad dressing.

salad days *n.pl.* a period of youthful inexperience.

salad dressing *n.* a mixture of oil, vinegar, etc., used with salad.

salade var. of SALLET.

salamander /ˈsaləmandə/ *n.* **1** *Zool.* any tailed newtlike amphibian of the order Urodela, esp. the genus *Salamandra*, once thought able to endure fire. **2** a mythical lizard-like creature credited with this property. **3** *US dial.* = GOPHER[1] 1. **4** an elemental spirit living in fire. **5** a red-hot iron used for lighting pipes, gunpowder, etc. **6** a metal plate heated and placed over food to brown it. ▫ **salamandrian** /-ˈmandrɪən/ *adj.* **salamandrine** /-ˈmandrɪn/ *adj.* **salamandroid** /-ˈmandrɔɪd/ *adj.* & *n.* (in sense 1). [Middle English via Old French *salamandre* and Latin *salamandra* from Greek *salamandra*]

salami /səˈlɑːmi/ *n.* (*pl.* **salamis**) a highly-seasoned originally Italian sausage often flavoured with garlic. [Italian, pl. of *salame*, from a Late Latin word meaning 'to salt']

sal ammoniac /sal əˈməʊnɪak/ *n.* ammonium chloride, a white crystalline salt. [Latin *sal ammoniacus* 'salt of Ammon': see AMMONIACAL]

salariat /səˈlɛːrɪət/ *n.* the salaried class. [French from *salaire* (see SALARY), on the pattern of *prolétariat*]

salary /ˈsaləri/ *n.* & *v.* ● *n.* (*pl.* **-ies**) a fixed regular payment, usu. monthly or quarterly, made by an employer to an employee, esp. a professional or white-collar worker (cf. WAGE *n.* 1). ● *v.tr.* (**-ies**, **-ied**) (usu. as **salaried** *adj.*) pay a salary to. [Middle English via Anglo-French *salarie*, Old French *salaire* from Latin *salarium*, originally a soldier's salt-money, from *sal* 'salt']

salaryman /ˈsalərɪman/ *n.* (*pl.* **salarymen**) (in Japan) a white-collar worker.

salbutamol /salˈbjuːtəmɒl/ *n. Pharm.* a drug used esp. as a bronchodilator to treat asthma. Cf. VENTOLIN. [from SALICYLIC ACID + BUTYL + AMINE + -OL[1]]

salchow /ˈsalkəʊ/ *n.* a jump in figure skating from the backward inside edge of one skate to the backward outside edge of the other, with a full turn in the air. [named after U. *Salchow*, Swedish skater d. 1949]

sale /seɪl/ *n.* **1** the exchange of a commodity for money etc.; an act or instance of selling. **2** the amount sold (*the sales were enormous*). **3** the rapid disposal of goods at reduced prices for a period esp. at the end of a season etc. **4 a** an event at which goods are sold. **b** a public auction. ▫ **on** (or **for** or **up for**) **sale** offered for purchase. [Old English *sala* from Old Norse]

saleable /ˈseɪləb(ə)l/ *adj.* (also **salable**) fit to be sold; finding purchasers. ▫ **saleability** /-ˈbɪlɪti/ *n.*

sale of work *n. Brit.* an event where goods made by parishioners etc. are sold for charity.

sale or return *n.* (often hyphenated when *attrib.*) *Brit.* an arrangement by which a purchaser takes a quantity of goods with the right of returning surplus goods without payment.

salep /ˈsaləp/ *n.* a starchy preparation of the dried tubers of various orchids, used in cookery and formerly medicinally. [French via Turkish *sālep* from Arabic (*ḳuṣa-'l-*) *ta'lab* 'fox, fox's testicles', the name of an orchid]

saleratus /saləˈreɪtəs/ *n. US* an ingredient of baking powder consisting mainly of potassium or sodium bicarbonate. [modern Latin *sal aeratus* 'aerated salt']

sale ring *n. Brit.* a circle of buyers at an auction.

saleroom /ˈseɪlruːm, -rʊm/ *n.* esp. *Brit.* a room in which items are sold at auction.

sales clerk *n. N. Amer.* a salesman or saleswoman in a shop.

sales department *n.* the section of a firm concerned with selling as opposed to manufacturing or dispatching goods.

sales engineer *n.* a salesperson with technical knowledge of the goods and their market.

salesgirl /ˈseɪlzgəːl/ *n.* a saleswoman.

Salesian /səˈliːzj(ə)n, -liːʒ(ə)n/ *n.* & *adj.* ● *n.* a member of an educational religious order within the Roman Catholic Church. ● *adj.* of or relating to this order. [from the name of the order's founder, St François de *Sales*, French RC bishop d. 1622]

saleslady /ˈseɪlzleɪdi/ *n.* (*pl.* **-ies**) a saleswoman.

salesman /ˈseɪlzmən/ *n.* (*pl.* **-men**; *fem.* **saleswoman**, *pl.* **-women**) **1** a person employed to sell goods in a shop, or as an agent between the producer and retailer. **2** *US* a commercial traveller.

salesmanship /ˈseɪlzmənʃɪp/ *n.* **1** skill in selling. **2** the techniques used in selling.

salesperson /ˈseɪlzpəːs(ə)n/ *n.* (*pl.* **-persons** or **people**) a salesman or saleswoman (used as a neutral alternative).

sales resistance *n.* the opposition or apathy of a prospective customer etc. to be overcome by salesmanship.

salesroom /ˈseɪlzruːm, -rʊm/ *n. US* = SALEROOM.

sales talk *n.* persuasive talk to promote the sale of goods or the acceptance of an idea etc.

sales tax *n.* a tax on sales or on the receipts from sales.

saleswoman see SALESMAN.

Salian /ˈseɪlɪən/ *adj.* & *n.* ● *adj.* of or relating to the Salii, a 4th-c. Frankish people living near the River Ijssel, from which the Merovingians were descended. ● *n.* a member of this people. [Late Latin *Salii*]

Salic /ˈsalɪk, ˈseɪ-/ *adj.* = SALIAN *adj.* [French *Salique* or medieval Latin *Salicus* from *Salii* (as SALIAN)]

salicet /ˈsalɪsɛt/ *n.* an organ stop like a salicional but one octave higher. [as SALICIONAL]

salicin /ˈsalɪsɪn/ *n.* (also **salicine** /-siːn/) a bitter crystalline glucoside with analgesic properties, obtained from poplar and willow bark. [French *salicine* from Latin *salix -icis* 'willow']

salicional /səˈlɪʃ(ə)n(ə)l/ *n.* an organ stop with a soft reedy tone like that of a willow-pipe. [German, from Latin *salix -icis* 'willow']

Salic law *n. hist.* **1** a law excluding females from dynastic succession, esp. as the alleged fundamental law of the French monarchy. **2** a Frankish law-book extant in Merovingian and Carolingian times.

salicylic acid /salɪˈsɪlɪk/ *n.* a bitter chemical used as a fungicide and in the manufacture of aspirin and dyestuffs. □ **salicylate** /sə'lɪsɪleɪt/ *n.* [*salicyl*, its radical, from French *salicyle* (as SALICIN)]

salient /'seɪlɪənt/ *adj.* & *n.* ● *adj.* **1** jutting out; prominent; conspicuous, most noticeable. **2** (of an angle, esp. in fortification) pointing outwards (opp. RE-ENTRANT *adj.* 1). **3** *Heraldry* (of a lion etc.) standing on its hind legs with the forepaws raised. **4** *archaic* **a** leaping or dancing. **b** (of water etc.) jetting forth. ● *n.* **1** a salient angle or part of a work in fortification. **2** an outward bulge in a line of military attack or defence. □ **salience** *n.* **saliency** *n.* **saliently** *adv.* [Latin *salire* 'leap']

salientian /seɪlɪ'ɛnʃɪən, -'ɛnt-/ *adj.* & *n.* = ANURAN. [modern Latin *Salientia* (as SALIENT)]

salient point *n.* **1** an important or significant point. **2** *archaic* the initial stage, origin, or first beginning.

saliferous /sə'lɪf(ə)rəs/ *adj. Geol.* (of rock etc.) containing much salt. [Latin *sal* 'salt' + -FEROUS]

salina /sə'lʌɪnə/ *n.* **1** a salt lake, spring, or marsh. **2** a salt pan or salt works. [Spanish from medieval Latin, = salt pit (as SALINE)]

saline /'seɪlʌɪn/ *adj.* & *n.* ● *adj.* **1** (of natural waters, springs, etc.) impregnated with or containing salt or salts. **2** (of food or drink etc.) tasting of salt. **3** of chemical salts. **4** of the nature of a salt. **5** *Med.* containing a salt or salts of alkaline metals or magnesium, esp. sodium chloride. ● *n.* **1** = SALINA. **2** a solution of salt in water. **3** a saline substance, esp. = PHYSIOLOGICAL SALINE. □ **salinity** /sə'lɪnɪti/ *n.* **salinization** /salɪnʌɪ'zeɪʃ(ə)n/ *n.* (also **-isation**). **salinometer** /salɪ'nɒmɪtə/ *n.* [Middle English from Latin *sal* 'salt']

saliva /sə'lʌɪvə/ *n.* liquid secreted into the mouth by glands to provide lubrication, facilitate chewing and swallowing, and aid digestion. □ **salivary** /sə'lʌɪ-, 'salɪ-/ *adj.* [Middle English from Latin]

salivate /'salɪveɪt/ *v.* **1** *intr.* secrete or discharge saliva esp. in excess or in greedy anticipation. **2** *tr.* produce an unusual secretion of saliva in (a person) usu. with mercury. □ **salivation** /salɪ'veɪʃ(ə)n/ *n.* [Latin *salivare* (as SALIVA)]

saliva test *n.* a scientific test requiring a saliva sample.

Salk vaccine /sɔːlk/ *n.* a vaccine developed against polio. [named after J. E. *Salk*, American scientist b. 1914]

sallee var. of SALLY[3].

sallet /'salɪt/ *n.* (also **salade** /sə'lɑːd/) *hist.* a light helmet with an outward-curving rear part. [French *salade*, ultimately via Latin *caelare* 'engrave' from *caelum* 'chisel']

sallow[1] /'saləʊ/ *adj.* & *v.* ● *adj.* (**sallower**, **sallowest**) (of the skin or complexion, or of a person) of a sickly yellow or pale brown. ● *v.tr.* & *intr.* make or become sallow. □ **sallowish** *adj.* **sallowness** *n.* [Old English *salo* 'dusky', from Germanic]

sallow[2] /'saləʊ/ *n.* **1** a willow tree, esp. one of a low-growing or shrubby kind. **2** the wood or a shoot of this. □ **sallowy** *adj.* [Old English *salh salg-* from Germanic: related to Old High German *salaha*, Old Norse *selja*, Latin *salix*]

Sally /'sali/ *n. Brit.* (*pl.* **-ies**) *colloq.* **1** (usu. prec. by *the*) the Salvation Army. **2** a member of this. [abbreviation]

sally[1] /'sali/ *n.* & *v.* (*pl.* **-ies**) ● *n.* **1** a sudden charge from a fortification upon its besiegers; a sortie. **2** a going forth; an excursion. **3** a witticism; a piece of banter; a lively remark esp. by way of attack upon a person or thing or of a diversion in argument. **4** a sudden start into activity; an outburst. **5** *archaic* an escapade. ● *v.intr.* (**-ies**, **-ied**) **1** (usu. foll. by *out*, *forth*) go for a walk, set out on a journey etc. **2** (usu. foll. by *out*) make a military sally. **3** *archaic* issue or come out suddenly. [French *saillie*, fem. past part. of *saillir* 'issue', via Old French *salir* from Latin *salire* 'leap']

sally[2] /'sali/ *n. Brit.* (*pl.* **-ies**) **1** the part of a bell rope prepared with inwoven wool for holding. **2** **a** the first movement of a bell when set for ringing. **b** the bell's position when set. [perhaps from SALLY[1] in sense 'leaping motion']

sally[3] /'sali/ *n.* (also **sallee**) (*pl.* **-ies** or **-ees**) *Austral.* any of several eucalypts and acacias resembling the willow. [dialect variant of SALLOW[2]]

sally-hole *n.* the hole through which the bell rope passes.

Sally Lunn /salɪ 'lʌn/ *n.* a sweet light teacake, properly served hot. [perhaps from the name of a woman selling them at Bath *c.*1800]

sally-port *n.* an opening in a fortification for making a sally from.

salmagundi /salmə'gʌndi/ *n.* (*pl.* **salmagundis**) **1** a dish of chopped meat, anchovies, eggs, onions, etc., and seasoning. **2** a general mixture; a miscellaneous collection of articles, subjects, qualities, etc. [French *salmigondis*, of unknown origin]

salmanazar /salmə'neɪzə/ *n.* a wine bottle of about 12 times the standard size. [named after *Shalmaneser*, King of Assyria (2 Kings 17-18)]

salmi /'salmi/ *n.* (*pl.* **salmis**) a ragout or casserole esp. of partly roasted game birds. [French, abbreviation formed as SALMAGUNDI]

salmon /'samən/ *n.* & *adj.* ● *n.* (*pl.* same or (esp. of types) **salmons**) **1** a migratory fish of the family Salmonidae, esp. of the genus *Salmo*, much prized for its pink flesh. **2** any of various similar but unrelated fishes, including: **a** *Austral.* & *NZ* (in full **Australian salmon**) a large green and silver marine fish, *Arripis trutta*. **b** *US* an American sea trout of the genus *Cynoscion*. **3** salmon pink. ● *adj.* salmon pink. □ **salmonoid** *adj.* & *n.* (in sense 1 of *n.*). **salmony** *adj.* [Middle English via Anglo-French *sa(u)moun*, Old French *saumon* from Latin *salmo -onis*]

salmonella /salmə'nɛlə/ *n.* (*pl.* **salmonellae** /-liː/) **1** any bacterium of the genus *Salmonella*, esp. any of various serotypes causing food poisoning. **2** food poisoning caused by infection with salmonellae. □ **salmonellosis** /-'ləʊsɪs/ *n.* [modern Latin, named after D. E. *Salmon*, American veterinary surgeon d. 1914]

salmonid /'salmənɪd, sal'mɒnɪd/ *adj.* & *n.* ● *adj.* of or relating to the family Salmonidae, which includes salmon and trout. ● *n.* a fish of this family.

salmon-ladder *n.* (also **salmon-leap**) a series of steps or other arrangement incorporated in a dam to allow salmon to pass upstream.

salmon pink *n.* & *adj.* ● *n.* the colour of salmon flesh. ● *adj.* (hyphenated when *attrib.*) of this colour.

salmon trout *n.* **1** = SEA TROUT 1. **2** any of various similar fishes, e.g. the Australian salmon, the N. American lake trout.

salon /'salɒn/ *n.* **1** the reception room of a large, esp. French or continental, house. **2** a room or establishment where a hairdresser, beautician, etc., conducts trade. **3** **a** *hist.* a meeting of eminent people in the reception room of a (esp. Parisian) lady of fashion. **b** *US* a meeting of esp. intellectuals at the invitation of usu. a celebrity or socialite. **4** (**Salon**) an annual exhibition in Paris of the work of living artists. [French: see SALOON]

salon music *n.* light music for the drawing room etc.

saloon /sə'luːn/ *n.* **1** esp. *Brit.* **a** a large room or hall, esp. in a hotel or public building. **b** a public room or gallery for a specified purpose (*billiard saloon*; *shooting saloon*). **2** (in full **saloon car**) *Brit.* a motor car with a closed body, boot, and no partition behind the driver. **3** a public room on a ship. **4** *US colloq.* or *joc.* a drinking bar. **5** (in full **saloon bar**) *Brit.* the more comfortable bar in a public house. **6** (in full **saloon car**) *Brit.* a luxurious railway carriage serving as a lounge etc. [French *salon* from Italian *salone*, augmentative of *sala* 'hall']

saloon deck *n.* a deck for passengers using the saloon.

saloon-keeper *n. US* a publican or bartender.

saloon pistol *n.* (also **saloon rifle**) *Brit.* a pistol or rifle adapted for short-range practice in a shooting saloon.

salopettes /salə'pɛts/ *n.pl.* trousers with a high waist and shoulder straps, worn esp. for skiing. [French *salopette* + *-s* by analogy with *trousers* etc.]

Salopian /sə'ləʊpɪən/ *n. & adj.* ● *n.* a native or inhabitant of Shropshire. ● *adj.* of or relating to Shropshire. [Anglo-French *Salopesberia* via Middle English from Old English *Scrobbesbyrig* 'Shrewsbury']

salpiglossis /salpɪ'glɒsɪs/ *n.* any plant of the genus *Salpiglossis* (nightshade family), cultivated for its funnel-shaped flowers. [modern Latin, formed irregularly from Greek *salpigx* 'trumpet' + *glōssa* 'tongue']

salping- /'salpɪŋ/ *comb. form Med.* denoting the Fallopian tubes. [Greek *salpigx salpiggos*, literally 'trumpet']

salpingectomy /salpɪŋ'dʒɛktəmi/ *n.* (*pl.* **-ies**) the surgical removal of the Fallopian tubes.

salpingitis /salpɪn'dʒʌɪtɪs/ *n. Med.* inflammation of the Fallopian tubes.

salsa /'salsə/ *n.* **1** a kind of dance music of Latin American origin, incorporating jazz and rock elements. **2** a dance performed to this music. **3** (esp. in Latin American cookery) a usu. spicy sauce, esp. one served with meat. [Spanish (as SAUCE)]

salsify /'salsɪfi/ *n.* (*pl.* **-ies**) **1** a European plant, *Tragopogon porrifolius*, with long cylindrical fleshy roots. **2** this root used as a vegetable. [French *salsifis* from obsolete Italian *salsefica*, of unknown origin]

SALT /sɔːlt, sɒlt/ *abbr.* Strategic Arms Limitation Talks (or Treaty).

salt /sɔːlt, sɒlt/ *n., adj., & v.* ● *n.* **1** (also **common salt**) sodium chloride; the substance that gives sea water its characteristic taste, obtained in crystalline form by mining from strata consisting of it or by the evaporation of sea water, and used for seasoning or preserving food, or for other purposes. **2** a chemical compound formed from the reaction of an acid with a base, with all or part of the hydrogen of the acid replaced by a metal or metal-like radical. **3** sting; piquancy; pungency; wit (*added salt to the conversation*). **4** (in *sing.* or *pl.*) **a** a substance resembling salt in taste, form, etc. (*bath salts*; *Epsom salts*; *smelling salts*). **b** (esp. in *pl.*) this type of substance used as a laxative. **5** (in full **salt marsh**) a marsh, esp. one flooded by the tide, often used as a pasture or for collecting water for salt-making. **6** (also **old salt**) an experienced sailor. **7** (in *pl.*) an exceptional rush of sea water upriver. ● *adj.* **1** impregnated with, containing, or tasting of salt; cured or preserved or seasoned with salt. **2** (of a plant) growing in the sea or in salt marshes. **3** (of tears etc.) bitter. **4** (of wit) pungent. ● *v.tr.* **1** cure or preserve with salt or brine. **2** season with salt. **3** make (a narrative etc.) piquant. **4** sprinkle (the ground etc.) with salt esp. in order to melt snow etc. **5** treat with a solution of salt or mixture of salts. **6** (as **salted** *adj.*) (of a horse or person) hardened or proof against diseases etc. caused by the climate or by special conditions. □ **eat salt with** *Brit.* be a guest of. **in salt** sprinkled with salt or immersed in brine as a preservative. **not made of salt** not disconcerted by wet weather. **put salt on the tail of** capture (with reference to jocular directions given to children for catching a bird). **salt an account** *slang* set an extremely high or low price for articles. **salt away** (or **down**) *slang* put (money etc.) by. **salt the books** *slang* show receipts as larger than they really have been. **salt a mine** *slang* introduce extraneous ore, material, etc., to make the source seem rich. **the salt of the earth** a person or people of great worthiness, reliability, honesty, etc.; those whose qualities are exemplary (Matt. 5:13). **take with a pinch** (or **grain**) **of salt** regard as exaggerated; be incredulous about; believe only part of. **worth one's salt** efficient, capable. □ **saltish** *adj.* **saltless** *adj.* **saltly** *adv.* **saltness** *n.* [Old English *s(e)alt s(e)altan* from Germanic: related to Latin *sal*]

salt-and-pepper *adj.* (of materials etc. and esp. of hair) with light and dark colours mixed together.

saltarello /saltə'rɛləʊ/ *n.* (*pl.* **-os** or **saltarelli** /-li/) an Italian and Spanish dance for one couple, with sudden skips. [Italian *salterello*, Spanish *saltarelo*, related to Italian *saltare* and Spanish *saltar* 'leap, dance', from Latin *saltare* (as SALTATION)]

saltation /sal'teɪʃ(ə)n, sɔː-, sɒ-/ *n.* **1** the act or an instance of leaping or dancing; a jump. **2** a sudden transition, esp. *Biol.* an abrupt evolutionary change. □ **saltatory** /'saltət(ə)ri, 'sɔː-, 'sɒ-/ *adj.* **saltatorial** /saltə'tɔːrɪəl, sɔː-, sɒ-/ *adj.* [Latin *saltatio* from *saltare*, frequentative of *salire salt-* 'leap']

saltbush /'sɔːltbʊʃ, 'sɒ-/ *n.* = ORACHE.

salt-cat *n.* a mass of salt mixed with gravel, urine, etc., to attract pigeons and keep them at home.

salt cellar *n.* **1** a small container for holding salt and *Brit.* for sprinkling salt on food. **2** *colloq.* an unusually deep hollow above the collarbone, esp. found in women. [SALT + obsolete *saler* from Anglo-French via Old French *salier* 'salt-box' from Latin (as SALARY), assimilated to CELLAR]

salt dome *n.* a mass of salt forced up into sedimentary rocks.

salter /'sɔːltə, 'sɒ-/ *n.* **1** a manufacturer or dealer in salt. **2** a workman at a salt works. **3** a person who salts fish etc. **4** = DRY-SALTER. [Old English *sealtere* (as SALT)]

saltern /'sɔːltən, 'sɒ-/ *n.* **1** a salt works. **2** a set of pools for the natural evaporation of sea water. [Old English *sealtærn* (as SALT, *ærn* 'building')]

salt fish *n. W.Ind.* preserved cod.

salt-glaze *n. & v.* ● *n.* a hard stoneware glaze produced by throwing salt into a hot kiln containing the ware. ● *v.tr.* apply salt-glaze to.

salt grass *n. US* grass growing in salt meadows or in alkaline regions.

salt horse *n. Naut. slang* **1** salt beef. **2** *Brit.* a naval officer with general duties.

saltigrade /'saltɪgreɪd, 'sɔː-, 'sɒ-/ *adj. & n. Zool.* ● *adj.* (of arthropods) moving by leaping or jumping. ● *n.* a saltigrade arthropod, e.g. a spider, sand-hopper, etc. [modern Latin *Saltigradae* from Latin *saltus* 'leap' (from *salire salt-* 'to leap') + *-gradus* 'walking']

salting /'sɔːltɪŋ, 'sɒ-/ *n.* **1** in senses of SALT *v.* **2** (esp. in *pl.*) *Brit. Geol.* a salt marsh; a marsh overflowed by the sea.

saltire /'saltʌɪə, 'sɔː-/ *n. Heraldry* an ordinary formed by a bend and a bend sinister crossing like a St Andrew's cross. □ **in saltire** arranged in this way. □ **saltirewise** *adv.* [Middle English via Old French *sau(l)toir* etc. 'stirrup-cord, stile, saltire', from medieval Latin *saltatorium* (as SALTATION)]

salt lake *n.* a lake of salt water.

salt lick *n.* **1** a place where animals go to lick salt from the ground. **2** a block of this salt.

salt marsh see SALT *n.* 5.

salt meadow *n.* a meadow subject to flooding with salt water.

salt mine *n.* a mine yielding rock salt.

salt pan *n.* a vessel, or a depression near the sea, used for getting salt by evaporation.

saltpetre /sɔːlt'piːtə, sɒ-/ *n.* (*US* **saltpeter**) potassium nitrate, a white crystalline salty substance used in preserving meat and as a constituent of gunpowder. [Middle English via Old French *salpetre* from medieval Latin *salpetra*, probably for *sal petrae* (unrecorded) 'salt of rock' (i.e. found as an incrustation): assimilated to SALT]

salt shaker *n. N. Amer.* a container of salt for sprinkling on food.

salt spoon *n.* a small spoon usu. with a short handle and a roundish deep bowl for taking table salt.

saltus /'saltəs/ *n. literary* a sudden transition; a breach of continuity. [Latin, = leap]

salt water *n. & adj.* ● *n.* **1** sea water. **2** *slang* tears. ● *attrib.adj.* (**salt-water**) of or living in the sea.

salt well *n.* a bored well yielding brine.

salt works *n.pl.* a place where salt is produced.

saltwort /ˈsɔːltwəːt, ˈsɒ-/ *n.* any salt marsh plant of the genus *Salsola*, rich in alkali; glasswort.

salty /ˈsɔːlti, ˈsɒ-/ *adj.* **(saltier, saltiest) 1** tasting of, containing, or preserved with salt. **2** (of humour etc.) racy, risqué. **3** *slang* tough or aggressive. □ **saltiness** *n.*

salubrious /səˈluːbrɪəs/ *adj.* **1** health-giving; healthy. **2** (of surroundings etc.) pleasant; agreeable. □ **salubriously** *adv.* **salubriousness** *n.* **salubrity** *n.* [Latin *salubris* from *salus* 'health']

saluki /səˈluːki/ *n.* (*pl.* **salukis) 1** a tall swift slender dog of a silky-coated breed with large drooping ears and fringed feet. **2** this breed. [Arabic *salūkī*]

salutary /ˈsaljʊt(ə)ri/ *adj.* **1** producing good effects; beneficial. **2** *archaic* health-giving. [Middle English from French *salutaire* or Latin *salutaris*, from *salus -utis* 'health']

salutation /saljʊˈteɪʃ(ə)n/ *n.* **1** a sign or expression of greeting or recognition of another's arrival or departure. **2** (usu. in *pl.*) words spoken or written to enquire about another's health or well-being. □ **salutational** *adj.* [Middle English from Old French *salutation* or Latin *salutatio* (as SALUTE)]

salutatory /səˈljuːtət(ə)ri/ *adj.* & *n.* ● *adj.* of salutation. ● *n.* (*pl.* **-ies**) *US* an oration, esp. as given by a member of a graduating class, often the second-ranking member. □ **salutatorian** /-ˈtɔːrɪən/ *n.* (in sense of n.). [Latin *salutatorius* (as SALUTE)]

salute /səˈluːt, səˈljuːt/ *n.* & *v.* ● *n.* **1** a gesture of respect, homage, or courteous recognition, esp. made to or by a person when arriving or departing. **2 a** *Mil.* & *Naut.* a prescribed or specified movement of the hand or of weapons or flags as a sign of respect or recognition. **b** (prec. by *the*) the attitude taken by an individual soldier, sailor, police officer, etc., in saluting. **3** the discharge of a gun or guns as a formal or ceremonial sign of respect or celebration. **4** *Fencing* the formal performance of certain guards etc. by fencers before engaging. ● *v.* **1 a** *tr.* make a salute to. **b** *intr.* (often foll. by *to*) perform a salute. **2** *tr.* greet; make a salutation to. **3** *tr.* (foll. by *with*) receive or greet with (a smile etc.). **4** *tr. archaic* hail as (king etc.). □ **take the salute 1** (of the highest officer present) acknowledge it by gesture as meant for him. **2** receive ceremonial salutes by members of a procession. □ **saluter** *n.* [Middle English from Latin *salutare*, from *salus -utis* 'health, welfare, greeting']

Salvadorean /salvəˈdɔːrɪən/ *adj.* & *n.* ● *adj.* of or relating to El Salvador, a republic in Central America. ● *n.* a native or national of El Salvador.

salvage /ˈsalvɪdʒ/ *n.* & *v.* ● *n.* **1** the rescue of a ship, its cargo, or other property, from loss at sea, destruction by fire, etc. **2** the property etc. saved in this way. **3 a** the saving and utilization of waste paper, scrap material, etc. **b** the materials salvaged. **4** payment made or due to a person who has saved a ship or its cargo. ● *v.tr.* **1** save from a wreck, fire, etc. **2** retrieve or preserve (something favourable) in adverse circumstances (*tried to salvage some dignity*). □ **salvageable** *adj.* **salvager** *n.* [French via medieval Latin *salvagium* from Latin *salvare* SAVE[1]]

salvation /salˈveɪʃ(ə)n/ *n.* **1** the act of saving or being saved; preservation from loss, calamity, etc. **2** *Theol.* deliverance from sin and its consequences and admission to heaven, brought about by Christ. **3** a religious conversion. **4** a person or thing that saves (*was the salvation of*). □ **salvationism** *n.* **salvationist** *n.* (both nouns esp. with reference to the Salvation Army). [Middle English via Old French *sauvacion*, *salvacion* from ecclesiastical Latin *salvatio -onis*, from *salvare* SAVE[1], translation of Greek *sōtēria*]

Salvation Army *n.* a worldwide evangelical organization on quasi-military lines for the revival of Christianity and helping the poor.

salve[1] /salv/ *n.* & *v.* ● *n.* **1** a healing ointment. **2** (often foll. by *for*) a thing that is soothing or consoling for wounded feelings, an uneasy conscience, etc. **3** *archaic* a thing that explains away a discrepancy or palliates a fault. ● *v.tr.* **1** soothe (pride, self-love, conscience, etc.). **2** *archaic* anoint (a wound etc.). **3** *archaic* smooth over, make good, vindicate, harmonize, etc. [Old English *s(e)alf(e)*, *s(e)alfian* from Germanic; senses 1 and 3 of the verb partly from Latin *salvare* SAVE[1]]

salve[2] /salv/ *v.tr.* **1** save (a ship or its cargo) from loss at sea. **2** save (property) from fire. □ **salvable** *adj.* [back-formation from SALVAGE]

salver /ˈsalvə/ *n.* a tray usu. of gold, silver, brass, or electroplate, on which drinks, letters, etc., are offered. [French *salve* 'tray for presenting food to the king', from Spanish *salva* 'assaying of food' from *salvar* SAVE[1]: associated with *platter*]

Salve Regina /ˌsalveɪ rəˈdʒiːnə/ *n.* **1** a Roman Catholic hymn or prayer said or sung after compline and after the Divine Office from Trinity Sunday to Advent. **2** the music for this. [from the opening words *salve regina* 'hail (holy) queen']

salvia /ˈsalvɪə/ *n.* any plant of the genus *Salvia*, esp. *S. splendens* with scarlet flowers. [Latin, = SAGE[1]]

Salvo /ˈsalvəʊ/ *n.* (*pl.* **-os**) *Austral. slang* a member of the Salvation Army. [abbreviation]

salvo[1] /ˈsalvəʊ/ *n.* (*pl.* **-oes** or **-os**) **1** the simultaneous firing of artillery or other guns esp. as a salute, or in a sea-fight. **2** a number of bombs released from aircraft at the same moment. **3** a round of applause. [earlier *salve* from French, from Italian *salva* 'salutation' (as SAVE[1])]

salvo[2] /ˈsalvəʊ/ *n.* (*pl.* **-os**) **1** a saving clause; a reservation (*with an express salvo of their rights*). **2** a tacit reservation. **3** a quibbling evasion; a bad excuse. **4** an expedient for saving reputation or soothing pride or conscience. [Latin, ablative of *salvus* SAFE as used in *salvo jure* 'without prejudice to the rights of' (a person)]

sal volatile /sal vəˈlatɪli/ *n.* ammonium carbonate, esp. in the form of a scented solution in alcohol used as smelling salts. [modern Latin, = volatile salt]

salvor /ˈsalvə, ˈsalvɔː/ *n.* a person or ship making or assisting in salvage. [SALVE[2]]

SAM *abbr.* surface-to-air missile.

Sam. *abbr.* Samuel (Old Testament).

samadhi /səˈmɑːdi/ *n.* *Buddhism* & *Hinduism* **1** a state of concentration induced by meditation. **2** a state into which a perfected holy man is said to pass at his apparent death. [Sanskrit *samādhi* 'contemplation']

samara /ˈsamərə, səˈmɑːrə/ *n.* *Bot.* a winged seed from the sycamore, ash, etc. [modern Latin from Latin, = elm seed]

Samaritan /səˈmarɪt(ə)n/ *n.* & *adj.* ● *n.* **1** (in full **good Samaritan**) a charitable or helpful person (with reference to Luke 10:33 etc.). **2** (in the UK) a member of an organization which counsels people in distress by telephone or face to face. **3** a native or inhabitant of Samaria, a region west of the Jordan. **4** the language of the people of Samaria. **5** an adherent of the Samaritan religious system, accepting only the Samaritan Pentateuch. ● *adj.* of or relating to Samaria or the Samaritans. □ **Samaritanism** *n.* [Late Latin *Samaritanus* from Greek *Samareitēs*, from *Samareia* 'Samaria']

Samaritan Pentateuch *n.* a recension used by Samaritans of which the MSS are in archaic characters.

samarium /səˈmɛːrɪəm/ *n.* *Chem.* a hard silvery metallic element of the lanthanide series, occurring naturally in monazite etc. and used in making ferromagnetic alloys (symbol **Sm**). [*samarskite*, the mineral in which its spectrum was first observed, from *Samarski* the name of a 19th-c. Russian official]

samba /ˈsambə/ *n.* & *v.* ● *n.* **1** a Brazilian dance of African origin. **2** a ballroom dance imitative of this. **3** the music for this. ● *v.intr.* (**sambas**, **sambaed** /-bəd/ or **samba'd**, **sambaing** /-bə(r)ɪŋ/) dance the samba. [Portuguese, of African origin]

sambar /ˈsambə/ *n.* (also **sambur**) a large deer, *Cervus unicolor*, of S. Asia. [Hindi *s̱ā(m)bar*]

Sambo /ˈsambəʊ/ *n.* (*pl.* **-os** or **-oes**) **1** *slang offens.* a black person. **2** (**sambo**) *hist.* a person of mixed race esp. of Negro and Indian or Negro and European blood. [Spanish *zambo*, perhaps = *zambo* 'bandy-legged'; sense 1 perhaps a different word from a W. African word meaning 'uncle']

Sam Browne /sam 'braʊn/ *n.* (in full **Sam Browne belt**) an army officer's belt and the strap supporting it. [named after Sir *Sam*uel J. *Browne*, British military commander d. 1901]

same /seɪm/ *adj., pron., & adv.* ● *adj.* **1** (often prec. by *the*) identical; not different; unchanged (*everyone was looking in the same direction*; *the same car was used in another crime*; *saying the same thing over and over*). **2** unvarying, uniform, monotonous (*the same old story*). **3** (usu. prec. by *this, these, that, those*) (of a person or thing) previously alluded to; just mentioned; aforesaid (*this same man was later my husband*). ● *pron.* (prec. by *the*) **1** the same person or thing (*the others asked for the same*). **2** *Law* or *archaic* the person or thing just mentioned (*detected the youth breaking in and apprehended the same*). ● *adv.* (usu. prec. by *the*) similarly; in the same way (*we all feel the same*; *I want to go, the same as you do*). See Usage Note. □ **all** (or **just**) **the same 1** emphatically the same. **2** in spite of changed conditions, adverse circumstances, etc. (*but you should offer, all the same*). **at the same time 1** simultaneously. **2** notwithstanding; in spite of circumstances etc. **be all** (or **just**) **the same to** an expression of indifference or impartiality (*it's all the same to me what we do*). **by the same token** see TOKEN. **same here** *colloq.* the same applies to me. **the same to you!** may you do, have, find, etc., the same thing; likewise. **the very same** emphatically the same. □ **sameness** *n.* [Middle English from Old Norse *sami, sama*, with Germanic cognates]

■ **Usage** The use of (*the*) *same* as an adverb, as exemplified by *I want to go*, (*the*) *same as you do* and *he worked his way through university*, (*the*) *same as I did*, is considered non-standard by some people. It can be avoided by using *in the same way as* or *just as*.

samey /'seɪmi/ *adj.* (**samier, samiest**) *Brit. colloq.* lacking in variety; monotonous. □ **sameyness** *n.*

samfu /'samfu:/ *n.* a suit consisting of a jacket and trousers, worn by Chinese women and sometimes men. [Cantonese]

Samhain /saʊn, 'saʊn, 'sawɪn/ *n. Brit.* 1 Nov., celebrated by the ancient Celts as a festival marking the beginning of winter and their new year. [Irish]

Samian /'seɪmɪən/ *n. & adj.* ● *n.* a native or inhabitant of Samos, an island in the Aegean Sea. ● *adj.* of or relating to Samos. [Latin *Samius* from Greek *Samios* 'Samos']

Samian ware *n.* fine red pottery from various parts of the Roman Empire, esp. Gaulish pottery often found on Roman sites in Britain.

samisen /'samɪsɛn/ *n.* a long three-stringed Japanese guitar, played with a plectrum. [Japanese from Chinese *san-hsien*, from *san* 'three' + *hsien* 'string']

samite /'samʌɪt, seɪ-/ *n. hist.* a rich medieval dress fabric of silk occasionally interwoven with gold. [Middle English via Old French *samit* and medieval Latin *examitum* from medieval Greek *hexamiton*, from Greek *hexa-* 'six' + *mitos* 'thread']

samizdat /'samɪzdat, samɪz'dat/ *n.* **1** the clandestine copying and distribution of literature, esp. in the former Communist countries of eastern Europe. **2** literature so produced. [Russian, = self-publishing house]

Samnite /'samnʌɪt/ *n. & adj.* ● *n.* **1** a member of a people of ancient Italy often at war with republican Rome. **2** the language of this people. ● *adj.* of this people or their language. [Middle English from Latin *Samnites* (pl.), related to *Sabinus* SABINE]

Samoan /sə'məʊən/ *n. & adj.* ● *n.* **1** a native of Samoa, a group of islands in the Pacific. **2** the language of the Samoans. ● *adj.* of or relating to Samoa or its people or language.

samosa /sə'məʊsə/ *n.* a triangular pastry fried in ghee or oil, containing spiced vegetables or meat. [Hindustani]

samovar /'saməvɑ:, samə'vɑ:/ *n.* a Russian tea urn, with an internal heating device to keep the water at boiling point. [Russian, = self-boiler]

Samoyed /'saməjɛd/ *n.* **1** a member of a people of northern Siberia. **2** the language of this people. **3** (also **samoyed**) **a** a dog of a white Arctic breed. **b** this breed. [Russian *samoed*]

Samoyedic /samə'jɛdɪk/ *n. & adj.* ● *n.* the language of the Samoyeds. ● *adj.* of or relating to the Samoyeds.

samp /samp/ *n. US* **1** coarsely ground maize. **2** porridge made of this. [Algonquian *nasamp* 'softened by water']

sampan /'sampan/ *n.* a small boat, usu. with a stern-oar or stern-oars, used in the Far East. [Chinese *san-ban*, from *san* 'three' + *ban* 'board']

samphire /'samfʌɪə/ *n.* **1** an umbelliferous maritime rock plant, *Crithmum maritimum*, with aromatic fleshy leaves used in pickles. **2** a glasswort of the genus *Salicornia*. [earlier *samp(i)ere* from French (*herbe de*) *Saint Pierre* 'St Peter('s herb)']

sample /'sɑ:mp(ə)l/ *n. & v.* ● *n.* **1** (also *attrib.*) a small part or quantity intended to show what the whole is like. **2** a small amount of fabric, food, or other commodity, esp. given to a prospective customer. **3** a specimen, esp. one taken for scientific testing or analysis. **4** an illustrative or typical example. **5** *Electronics* a sound created by sampling. ● *v.tr.* **1** take or give samples of. **2** try the qualities of. **3** get a representative experience of. [Middle English from Anglo-French *assample*, Old French *essample* EXAMPLE]

sample bag *n. Austral.* an (originally free) bag of advertisers' samples.

sampler[1] /'sɑ:mplə/ *n.* a piece of embroidery worked in various stitches as a specimen of proficiency (often displayed on a wall etc.). [Old French *essamplaire* (as EXEMPLAR)]

sampler[2] /'sɑ:mplə/ *n.* **1** a person who samples. **2** an electronic device for sampling music and sound. **3** *US* a collection of representative items etc.

sampling /'sɑ:mplɪŋ/ *n.* **1** the taking of a sample or samples. **2** *Mus.* the technique of digitally encoding sound and reusing it as part of a composition or recording.

sampling error *n.* error in a statistical analysis etc. arising from unrepresentativeness of the sample taken.

sampling frame *n. Statistics* a list of the items, people, etc., forming a population from which a sample is taken.

samsara /səm'sɑ:rə/ *n. Hinduism* the endless cycle of death and rebirth to which life in the material world is bound. □ **samsaric** *adj.* [Sanskrit *saṃsāra* 'a wandering through']

samskara /səm'skɑ:rə/ *n. Hinduism* **1** a purificatory ceremony or rite marking an event in one's life. **2** a mental impression, instinct, or memory. [Sanskrit *saṃskāra* 'a making perfect, preparation']

Samson /'sams(ə)n/ *n.* a person of great strength or resembling Samson in some respect. [Late Latin via Greek *Sampsōn* from Hebrew *šimšôn* (Judg. 13–16)]

Samson post *n.* (also **Samson's post**) **1** a strong pillar passing through the hold of a ship or between decks. **2** a post in a whaleboat to which a harpoon rope is attached.

samurai /'samʊrʌɪ, -jʊrʌɪ/ *n.* (*pl.* same) **1** a Japanese army officer. **2** *hist.* a member of a military caste in feudal Japan. [Japanese]

san /san/ *n.* = SANATORIUM 2. [abbreviation]

sanative /'sanətɪv/ *adj.* **1** healing; curative. **2** of or tending to physical or moral health. [Middle English from Old French *sanatif* or Late Latin *sanativus*, from Latin *sanare* 'cure']

sanatorium /sanə'tɔ:rɪəm/ *n.* (*pl.* **sanatoriums** or **sanatoria** /-rɪə/) **1** an establishment for the treatment of invalids, esp. of convalescents and the chronically sick. **2** *Brit.* a room or building for sick people in a school etc. [modern Latin (as SANATIVE)]

sanctify /ˈsaŋ(k)tɪfʌɪ/ *v.tr.* **(-ies, -ied) 1** consecrate; set apart or observe as holy. **2** purify or free from sin. **3** make legitimate or binding by religious sanction; justify; give the colour of morality or innocence to. **4** make productive of or conducive to holiness. ▫ **sanctification** /-fɪˈkeɪʃ(ə)n/ *n.* **sanctifier** *n.* [Middle English via Old French *saintifier* from ecclesiastical Latin *sanctificare*, from Latin *sanctus* 'holy']

sanctimonious /saŋ(k)tɪˈməʊnɪəs/ *adj.* making a show of sanctity or piety. ▫ **sanctimoniously** *adv.* **sanctimoniousness** *n.* **sanctimony** /ˈsaŋ(k)tɪməni/ *n.* [Latin *sanctimonia* 'sanctity' (as SAINT)]

sanction /ˈsaŋ(k)ʃ(ə)n/ *n.* & *v.* ● *n.* **1** approval or encouragement given to an action etc. by custom or tradition; express permission. **2** confirmation or ratification of a law etc. **3 a** a penalty for disobeying a law or rule, or a reward for obeying it. **b** a clause containing this. **4** *Ethics* a consideration operating to enforce obedience to any rule of conduct. **5** (esp. in *pl.*) military or esp. economic action by a state to coerce another to conform to an international agreement or norms of conduct. **6** *Law hist.* a law or decree. ● *v.tr.* **1** authorize, countenance, or agree to (an action etc.). **2** ratify; attach a penalty or reward to; make binding. ▫ **sanctionable** *adj.* [French from Latin *sanctio -onis*, from *sancire sanct-* 'make sacred']

sanctitude /ˈsaŋ(k)tɪtjuːd/ *n. archaic* saintliness. [Middle English from Latin *sanctitudo* (as SAINT)]

sanctity /ˈsaŋ(k)tɪti/ *n.* (*pl.* **-ies**) **1** holiness of life; saintliness. **2** sacredness; the state of being hallowed. **3** inviolability. **4** (in *pl.*) sacred obligations, feelings, etc. [Middle English from Old French *sain(c)tité* or Latin *sanctitas* (as SAINT)]

sanctuary /ˈsaŋ(k)tjʊəri/ *n.* (*pl.* **-ies**) **1** a holy place; a church, temple, etc. **2 a** the inmost recess or holiest part of a temple etc. **b** the part of the chancel containing the high altar. **3** a place where birds, wild animals, etc., breed and are protected. **4** a place of refuge, esp. for political refugees. **5 a** immunity from arrest. **b** the right to offer this. **6** *hist.* a sacred place where a fugitive from the law or a debtor was secured by medieval Church law against arrest or violence. ▫ **take sanctuary** resort to a place of refuge. [Middle English via Anglo-French *sanctuarie*, Old French *sanctuaire* from Latin *sanctuarium* (as SAINT)]

sanctum /ˈsaŋ(k)təm/ *n.* (*pl.* **sanctums**) **1** a holy place. **2** *colloq.* a person's private room, study, or den. [Latin, neut. of *sanctus* 'holy', past part. of *sancire* 'consecrate']

sanctum sanctorum /saŋ(k)təm saŋ(k)ˈtɔːrəm/ *n.* (*pl.* **sancta sanctorum** or **sanctum sanctorums**) **1** the holy of holies in the Jewish temple. **2** *colloq.* = SANCTUM 2. [Latin, as SANCTUM + *sanctorum* genitive pl. of *sanctus* 'holy', translating Hebrew *kōdeš hakkodāšîm* 'holy of holies']

sanctus /ˈsaŋ(k)təs/ *n.* (also **Sanctus**) **1** the prayer or hymn beginning 'Holy, holy, holy' said or sung at the end of the Eucharistic preface. **2** the music for this. [Middle English from Latin, = holy]

sanctus bell *n.* a handbell or the bell in the turret at the junction of the nave and the chancel, rung at the sanctus or at the elevation of the Eucharist.

sand /sand/ *n.* & *v.* ● *n.* **1** a loose granular substance resulting from the wearing down of esp. siliceous rocks and found on the seashore, river beds, deserts, etc. **2** (in *pl.*) grains of sand. **3** (in *pl.*) an expanse or tracts of sand. **4** a light yellow-brown colour like that of sand. **5** (in *pl.*) a sandbank. **6** *US colloq.* firmness of purpose; grit. ● *v.tr.* **1** smooth or polish with sand or sandpaper, or a mechanical sander. **2** sprinkle or overlay with, or bury under, sand. **3** adulterate (sugar etc.) with sand. ▫ **the sands are running out** the allotted time is nearly at an end. ▫ **sandlike** *adj.* [Old English *sand*, from Germanic]

sandal[1] /ˈsand(ə)l/ *n.* & *v.* ● *n.* **1** a light shoe with an openwork upper or no upper, attached to the foot usu. by straps. **2** a strap for fastening a low shoe, passing over the instep or around the ankle. ● *v.tr.* (**sandalled**, **sandalling**; *US* **sandaled**, **sandaling**) **1** (esp. as **sandalled** *adj.*) put sandals on (a person, his feet). **2** fasten or provide (a shoe) with a sandal. [Middle English via Latin *sandalium* from Greek *sandalion*, diminutive of *sandalon* 'wooden shoe', probably of Asiatic origin]

sandal[2] /ˈsand(ə)l/ *n.* = SANDALWOOD. [Middle English from medieval Latin *sandalum*, ultimately from Sanskrit *candana*]

sandal tree *n.* any tree yielding sandalwood, esp. the white sandalwood.

sandalwood /ˈsand(ə)lwʊd/ *n.* **1 a** the scented wood of a tree of the genus *Santalum*, esp. (in full **white sandalwood**) *S. Album*. **b** a perfume or incense derived from this. **2** any tree yielding a similar wood (cf. RED SANDALWOOD).

sandalwood oil *n.* a yellow aromatic oil made from the white sandalwood.

sandarac /ˈsandərak/ *n.* (also **sandarach**) **1** the gummy resin of a N. African conifer, *Tetraclinis articulata*, used in making varnish. **2** = REALGAR. [Latin *sandaraca* from Greek *sandarakē*, of Asiatic origin]

sandbag /ˈsan(d)bag/ *n.* & *v.* ● *n.* a bag filled with sand for use: **1** (in fortification) for making temporary defences or for the protection of a building etc. against blast and splinters or flood waters. **2** as ballast esp. for a boat or balloon. **3** as a weapon to inflict a heavy blow without leaving a mark. **4** to stop a draught from a window or door. ● *v.* (**-bagged**, **-bagging**) **1** *tr.* barricade or defend. **2** *tr.* place sandbags against (a window, chink, etc.). **3** *tr.* fell with a blow from a sandbag. **4** *tr. N. Amer.* coerce by harsh means. **5** *intr. Sport* deliberately underperform in a race or competition to gain an unfair advantage. ▫ **sandbagger** *n.*

sandbank /ˈsan(d)baŋk/ *n.* a deposit of sand forming a shallow place in the sea or a river.

sandbar /ˈsan(d)bɑː/ *n.* a sandbank at the mouth of a river or *US* on the coast.

sand-bath *n.* a vessel of heated sand to provide uniform heating.

sand-bed *n.* a stratum of sand.

sandblast /ˈsan(d)blɑːst/ *v.* & *n.* ● *v.tr.* roughen, treat, or clean with a jet of sand driven by compressed air or steam. ● *n.* this jet. ▫ **sandblaster** *n.*

sandbox /ˈsan(d)bɒks/ *n.* **1** a box of sand on a locomotive for sprinkling slippery rails. **2** *Golf* a container for sand used in teeing. **3** a sandpit enclosed in a box. **4** *hist.* a device for sprinkling sand to dry ink.

sandboy /ˈsan(d)bɔɪ/ *n.* ▫ **happy as a sandboy** extremely happy or carefree. [probably = a boy hawking sand for sale]

sandcastle /ˈsan(d)kɑːs(ə)l/ *n.* a shape like a castle made in sand, usu. by a child on the seashore.

sand cloud *n.* driving sand in a simoom.

sand-crack *n.* **1** a fissure in a horse's hoof. **2** a crack in the human foot from walking on hot sand. **3** a crack in brick due to imperfect mixing.

sand dollar *n.* any flat asymmetrical sea urchin of the order Clypeasteroida.

sand dune *n.* a mound or ridge of sand formed by the wind.

sand eel *n.* any eel-like fish of the family Ammodytidae or Hypotychidae: also called LAUNCE.

sander /ˈsandə/ *n.* a power tool for smoothing surfaces.

sanderling /ˈsandəlɪŋ/ *n.* a small wading bird, *Calidris alba*, of the sandpiper family. [perhaps from Old English (as SAND + *yrthling* 'ploughman', also the name of a bird)]

sanders /ˈsɑːndəz, ˈsan-/ *n.* (also **saunders** /ˈsɔː-/) the red sandalwood, *Pterocarpus santalinus*. [Middle English from Old French *sandre*, variant of *sandle* SANDAL[2]]

sand flea *n.* **1** = CHIGGER 1. **2** = SAND-HOPPER.

sandfly /ˈsan(d)flʌɪ/ *n.* (*pl.* **-flies**) **1** any biting blackfly of the genus *Simulium*. **2** any tropical biting fly of the genus *Phlebotomus*, transmitting the disease leishmaniasis.

sand-glass *n.* = HOURGLASS 1.

sand-groper *n. Austral.* **1** a gold rush pioneer. **2** *joc.* a Western Australian.

sandgrouse /ˈsan(d)graʊs/ *n.* a seed-eating ground bird of the family Pteroclididae, related to pigeons and found in arid regions of the Old World.

sandhi /ˈsandi/ *n. Gram.* the process whereby the form of a word changes as a result of its position in an utterance (e.g. the change from *a* to *an* before a vowel). [Sanskrit *saṃdhi* 'putting together']

sandhill /ˈsandhɪl/ *n.* = SAND DUNE.

sandhog /ˈsandhɒg/ *n. US* a person who works underwater laying foundations, constructing tunnels, etc.

sand-hopper *n.* any of various small jumping crustaceans of the order Amphipoda, burrowing on the seashore.

sandiver /ˈsandɪvə/ *n.* liquid scum formed in glass-making. [Middle English, apparently from French *suin de verre* 'exhalation of glass', from *suer* 'to sweat' + *verre* 'glass']

sandlot /ˈsan(d)lɒt/ *n. US* a piece of unoccupied sandy land used for children's games.

sandman /ˈsan(d)man/ *n.* the personification of tiredness causing children's eyes to smart towards bedtime.

sand martin *n.* a swallow-like bird, *Riparia riparia*, nesting in the side of a sandy bank etc.

sandpaper /ˈsan(d)peɪpə/ *n. & v.* ● *n.* paper with sand or another abrasive stuck to it for smoothing or polishing. ● *v.tr.* smooth with sandpaper.

sandpiper /ˈsan(d)pʌɪpə/ *n.* any of various wading birds of the family Scolopacidae, frequenting moorland and coastal areas.

sandpit /ˈsan(d)pɪt/ *n. Brit.* a hollow partly filled with sand, usu. for children to play in.

sand-shoe *n.* a shoe with a canvas, rubber, hemp, etc., sole for use on sand.

sand-skipper *n.* = SAND-HOPPER.

sandsoap /ˈsan(d)səʊp/ *n.* heavy-duty gritty soap.

sand spurrey see SPURREY.

sandstock /ˈsan(d)stɒk/ *n.* brick made with sand dusted on the surface.

sandstone /ˈsan(d)stəʊn/ *n.* **1** any clastic rock containing particles visible to the naked eye. **2** a sedimentary rock of consolidated sand commonly red, yellow, brown, grey, or white.

sandstorm /ˈsan(d)stɔːm/ *n.* a desert storm of wind with clouds of sand.

sandwich /ˈsanwɪdʒ, -wɪtʃ/ *n. & v.* ● *n.* **1** two or more slices of usu. buttered bread with a filling of meat, cheese, etc., between them. **2** *Brit.* a cake of two or more layers with jam or cream between (*bake a sponge sandwich*). ● *v.tr.* **1** put (a thing, statement, etc.) between two of another character. **2** squeeze in between others (*sat sandwiched in the middle*). [named after the 4th Earl of *Sandwich*, English nobleman d. 1792, said to have eaten food in this form so as not to leave the gaming table]

sandwich-board *n.* one of two advertisement boards carried by a sandwich-man.

sandwich course *n. Brit.* a course of training with alternate periods of practical experience and theoretical instruction.

sandwich-man *n.* (*pl.* **-men**) a man who walks the streets with sandwich-boards hanging before and behind.

Sandwich tern *n.* a crested tern, *Sterna sandvicensis*, of both Old and New Worlds. [*Sandwich*, town in Kent]

sandwort /ˈsandwəːt/ *n.* any low-growing plant of the genus *Arenaria* (pink family), usu. bearing small white flowers.

sandy /ˈsandi/ *adj.* (**sandier**, **sandiest**) **1** having the texture of sand. **2** having much sand. **3 a** (of hair) yellowish red. **b** (of a person) having sandy hair. □ **sandiness** *n.* **sandyish** *adj.* [Old English *sandig* (as SAND)]

sand yacht *n.* a boat on wheels propelled along a beach by wind.

sandy blight *n. Austral.* conjunctivitis with sandlike grains in the eye.

sane /seɪn/ *adj.* **1** of sound mind; not mad. **2** (of views etc.) moderate; sensible. □ **sanely** *adv.* **saneness** *n.* [Latin *sanus* 'healthy']

Sanforized /ˈsanfərʌɪzd/ *adj.* (also **-ised**) *propr.* (of cotton or other fabrics) pre-shrunk by a special process. [L. Cluett *Sandford* (d. 1968), US inventor of the process + -IZE]

sang *past* of SING.

sangar /ˈsaŋgə/ *n.* (also **sanga**) a stone breastwork round a hollow. [Pashto *sangar*]

sangaree /saŋgəˈriː/ *n.* a cold drink of wine diluted and spiced. [Spanish *sangría* SANGRIA]

sang-froid /sɒŋˈfrwɑː/ *n.* composure, coolness, etc., in danger or under agitating circumstances. [French, = cold blood]

sangrail /saŋˈgreɪl/ *n.* = GRAIL. [Middle English from Old French *saint graal* (as SAINT, GRAIL)]

sangria /saŋˈgriːə/ *n.* a Spanish drink of red wine with lemonade, fruit, etc. [Spanish, = bleeding: cf. SANGAREE]

sanguinary /ˈsaŋgwɪn(ə)ri/ *adj.* **1** accompanied by or delighting in bloodshed. **2** bloody; bloodthirsty. **3** (of laws) inflicting death freely. □ **sanguinarily** *adv.* **sanguinariness** *n.* [Latin *sanguinarius* from *sanguis -inis* 'blood']

sanguine /ˈsaŋgwɪn/ *adj. & n.* ● *adj.* **1** optimistic; confident. **2** (of the complexion) florid; bright; ruddy. **3** *hist.* relating to the predominance of blood over the other bodily humours, characterized by a ruddy complexion and a courageous, amorous disposition (cf. HUMOUR *n.* 5). **4** *Heraldry* or *literary* blood red. **5** *archaic* bloody; bloodthirsty. ● *n.* **1** a blood red colour. **2** a crayon of chalk coloured red or flesh with iron oxide. □ **sanguinely** *adv.* **sanguineness** *n.* (both in sense 1 of *n.*). [Middle English via Old French *sanguin -ine* 'blood red' from Latin *sanguineus* (as SANGUINARY)]

sanguineous /saŋˈgwɪnɪəs/ *adj.* **1** sanguinary. **2** *Med.* of or relating to blood. **3** blood red. **4** full-blooded; plethoric. [Latin *sanguineus* (as SANGUINE)]

Sanhedrin /ˈsanɪdrɪn, sanˈhiːdrɪn, sanˈhɛdrɪn/ *n.* (also **Sanhedrim** /-rɪm/) the highest court of justice and the supreme council in ancient Jerusalem with 71 members. [late Hebrew *sanhedrîn* from Greek *sunedrion* (as SYN-, *hedra* 'seat')]

sanicle /ˈsanɪk(ə)l/ *n.* any umbelliferous plant of the genus *Sanicula*, esp. *S. europaea*, formerly believed to have healing properties. [Middle English, ultimately from medieval Latin *sanicula*, perhaps from Latin *sanus* 'healthy']

sanify /ˈsanɪfʌɪ/ *v.tr.* (**-ies**, **-ied**) make healthy; improve the sanitary state of. [Latin *sanus* 'healthy']

sanitarium /sanɪˈtɛːrɪəm/ *n.* (*pl.* **sanitariums** or **sanitaria** /-rɪə/) *US* = SANATORIUM. [pseudo-Latin from Latin *sanitas* 'health']

sanitary /ˈsanɪt(ə)ri/ *adj.* **1** of the conditions that affect health, esp. with regard to dirt and infection. **2** hygienic; free from or designed to kill germs, infection, etc. □ **sanitarian** /-ˈtɛːrɪən/ *n. & adj.* **sanitarily** *adv.* **sanitariness** *n.* [French *sanitaire* from Latin *sanitas*: see SANITY]

sanitary engineer *n.* a person dealing with systems needed to maintain public health.

sanitary towel *n.* (*N. Amer.* **sanitary napkin**) an absorbent pad used during menstruation.

sanitary ware *n.* porcelain for lavatories etc.

sanitation /sanɪˈteɪʃ(ə)n/ *n.* **1** sanitary conditions. **2** the maintenance or improving of these. **3** the disposal of sewage and refuse from houses etc. □ **sanitate**

/ˈsanɪteɪt/ *v.tr. & intr.* **sanitationist** *n.* [formed irregularly from SANITARY]

sanitize /ˈsanɪtʌɪz/ *v.tr.* (also **-ise**) **1** make sanitary; disinfect. **2** *US colloq.* render (information etc.) more acceptable by removing improper or disturbing material. □ **sanitization** /-ˈzeɪʃ(ə)n/ *n.* **sanitizer** *n.*

sanity /ˈsanɪti/ *n.* **1 a** the state of being sane. **b** mental health. **2** the tendency to avoid extreme views. [Middle English from Latin *sanitas* (as SANE)]

sank *past* of SINK.

sannyasi /sənˈjɑːsi/ *n.* (also **sanyasi**) (*pl.* same) a Hindu religious mendicant. [Sanskrit *saṃnyāsī* nominative sing. of *saṃnyāsin* 'laying aside, ascetic', from *saṃ* 'together', *ni* 'down', *as* 'throw']

sans /sanz/ *prep. archaic* or *joc.* without. [Middle English from Old French *san(z)*, *sen(s)*, ultimately from Latin *sine*, influenced by Latin *absentia* 'in the absence of']

sans-culotte /sanzkjʊˈlɒt/ *n.* **1** *hist.* a lower-class Parisian republican in the French Revolution. **2** an extreme republican or revolutionary. □ **sans-culottism** *n.* [French, literally 'without knee-breeches']

Sanskrit /ˈsanskrɪt/ *n. & adj.* ● *n.* the ancient and sacred language of the Hindus in India. ● *adj.* of or relating to this language. □ **Sanskritic** /-ˈskrɪtɪk/ *adj.* **Sanskritist** *n.* [Sanskrit *saṃskṛta* 'composed, elaborated', from *saṃ* 'together' + *kṛ* 'make' + past part. ending *-ta*]

sans serif /san ˈserɪf/ *n. & adj.* (also **sanserif**) *Printing* ● *n.* a form of type without serifs. ● *adj.* without serifs. [apparently from SANS + SERIF]

Santa Claus /ˈsantə klɔːz/ *n.* (also *colloq.* **Santa**) a person said to bring children presents on the night before Christmas. [originally US from Dutch dialect *Sante Klaas* 'St Nicholas']

santolina /santəˈliːnə/ *n.* any aromatic shrub of the genus *Santolina*, with finely divided leaves and small usu. yellow flowers. [modern Latin, variant of SANTONICA]

santonica /sanˈtɒnɪkə/ *n.* **1** a shrubby wormwood plant, *Artemisia cina*, yielding santonin. **2** the dried flower heads of this used as an anthelmintic. [Latin from *Santones*, the name of an Aquitanian tribe]

santonin /ˈsantənɪn/ *n.* a toxic drug extracted from santonica and other plants of the genus *Artemisia*, used as an anthelmintic. [SANTONICA + -IN]

sanyasi var. of SANNYASI.

sap[1] /sap/ *n. & v.* ● *n.* **1** the vital juice circulating in plants. **2** vigour; vitality. **3** = SAPWOOD. **4** *US slang* a bludgeon (originally one made from a sapling). ● *v.tr.* (**sapped, sapping**) **1** drain or dry (wood) of sap. **2** remove the sapwood from (a log). **3** *US slang* hit with a sap. □ **sapful** *adj.* **sapless** *adj.* [Old English *sæp*, probably from Germanic]

sap[2] /sap/ *n. & v.* ● *n.* **1** a tunnel or trench to conceal assailants' approach to a fortified place; a covered siege-trench. **2** an insidious or slow undermining of a belief, resolution, etc. ● *v.* (**sapped, sapping**) **1** *intr.* **a** dig a sap or saps. **b** approach by a sap. **2** *tr.* undermine; make insecure by removing the foundations. **3** *tr.* weaken or destroy insidiously (*his confidence has been sapped*). [ultimately from Italian *zappa* 'spade, spadework', in part through French *sappe sap(p)er*, probably of Arabic origin]

sap[3] /sap/ *n. slang* a foolish person. [abbreviation of *sapskull*, from SAP[1] = sapwood + SKULL]

sapanwood var. of SAPPANWOOD.

sapele /səˈpiːli/ *n.* **1** any of several large W. African hardwood trees of the genus *Entandrophragma*. **2** the reddish-brown mahogany-like timber of these trees. [West African name]

sap green *n. & adj.* ● *n.* **1** the green pigment made from buckthorn berries. **2** the colour of this. ● *adj.* (hyphenated when *attrib.*) of this green colour.

sapid /ˈsapɪd/ *adj. literary* **1** having (esp. an agreeable) flavour; savoury; palatable; not insipid. **2** *literary* (of talk, writing, etc.) not vapid or uninteresting. □ **sapidity** /səˈpɪdɪti/ *n.* [Latin *sapidus* from *sapere* 'taste']

sapient /ˈseɪpɪənt/ *adj. literary* **1** wise. **2** aping wisdom; of fancied sagacity. □ **sapience** *n.* **sapiently** *adv.* [Middle English from Old French or Latin part. stem of *sapere* 'be wise']

sapiential /seɪpɪˈenʃ(ə)l/ *adj. literary* of or relating to wisdom. [Middle English from French *sapiential* or ecclesiastical Latin *sapientialis*, from Latin *sapientia* 'wisdom']

sapling /ˈsaplɪŋ/ *n.* **1** a young tree. **2** a youth. **3** a greyhound in its first year.

sapodilla /sapəˈdɪlə/ *n.* a large evergreen tropical American tree, *Manilkara zapota*, with edible fruit and durable wood, and sap from which chicle is obtained. [Spanish *zapotillo*, diminutive of *zapote*, from Nahuatl *tzápotl*]

sapodilla plum *n.* the fruit of the sapodilla tree.

saponaceous /sapəˈneɪʃəs/ *adj.* **1** of, like, or containing soap; soapy. **2** *joc.* unctuous; flattering. [modern Latin *saponaceus* from Latin *sapo -onis* 'soap']

saponify /səˈpɒnɪfʌɪ/ *v.* (**-ies, -ied**) **1** *tr.* turn (fat or oil) into soap by reaction with an alkali. **2** *tr.* convert (an ester) to an acid and alcohol. **3** *intr.* become saponified. □ **saponifiable** *adj.* **saponification** /-fɪˈkeɪʃ(ə)n/ *n.* [French *saponifier* (as SAPONACEOUS)]

saponin /ˈsapənɪn/ *n.* any of a group of plant glycosides, esp. those derived from the bark of the soapbark tree *Quillaja saponaria*, that foam when shaken with water and are used in detergents and fire extinguishers. [French *saponine* from Latin *sapo -onis* 'soap']

sapor /ˈseɪpɔː, -pə/ *n.* **1** a quality perceptible by taste, e.g. sweetness. **2** the distinctive taste of a substance. **3** the sensation of taste. [Middle English from Latin *sapere* 'taste']

sappanwood /ˈsapənwʊd/ *n.* (also **sapanwood**) the heartwood of an E. Indian tree, *Caesalpinia sappan*, formerly used as a source of red dye. [Dutch *sapan* from Malay *sapang*, of S. Indian origin]

sapper /ˈsapə/ *n.* **1** a person who digs saps. **2** *Brit.* a soldier of the Royal Engineers (esp. as the official term for a private). **3** *US* a military engineer who lays or detects and disarms mines.

Sapphic /ˈsafɪk/ *adj. & n.* ● *adj.* **1** of or relating to Sappho, poetess of Lesbos *c.*600 BC, or her poetry. **2** lesbian. ● *n.* (in *pl.*) (**sapphics**) verse in a metre associated with Sappho. [French *sa(p)phique* via Latin *Sapphicus* from Greek *Sapphikos*, from *Sapphō*]

sapphire /ˈsafʌɪə/ *n. & adj.* ● *n.* **1** a transparent blue precious stone consisting of corundum. **2** precious transparent corundum of any colour. **3** = SAPPHIRE BLUE *n.* **4** a hummingbird with bright blue colouring. ● *adj.* = SAPPHIRE BLUE *adj.* □ **sapphirine** /ˈsafɪrʌɪn/ *adj.* [Middle English via Old French *safir* and Latin *sapphirus* from Greek *sappheiros*, probably = lapis lazuli]

sapphire blue *n. & adj.* ● *n.* a bright blue colour. ● *adj.* (hyphenated when *attrib.*) of this colour.

sapphire wedding *n.* a 45th wedding anniversary.

sappy /ˈsapi/ *adj.* (**sappier, sappiest**) **1** full of sap. **2** young and vigorous. **3** *N. Amer. colloq.* over-sentimental; mawkish. □ **sappily** *adv.* **sappiness** *n.*

sapro- /ˈsaprəʊ/ *comb. form Biol.* rotten, putrefying. [Greek *sapros* 'putrid']

saprogenic /saprəˈdʒenɪk/ *adj.* causing or produced by putrefaction.

saprophagous /saˈprɒfəgəs/ *adj.* feeding on decaying matter.

saprophile /ˈsaprə(ʊ)fʌɪl/ *n.* a bacterium inhabiting putrid matter. □ **saprophilous** /-ˈprɒfɪləs/ *adj.*

saprophyte /ˈsaprə(ʊ)fʌɪt/ *n.* any plant or micro-organism living on dead or decayed organic matter. □ **saprophytic** /-ˈfɪtɪk/ *adj.*

sapsucker /ˈsapsʌkə/ *n.* a small American woodpecker of the genus *Sphyrapicus*, which pecks holes in trees and visits them for sap and insects.

sapwood /ˈsapwʊd/ *n.* the soft outer layers of recently formed wood between the heartwood and the bark.

saraband /ˈsarəband/ *n.* **1** a stately old Spanish dance. **2** music for or the rhythm of this, usu. in triple time and often with a long note on the second beat of the bar. [French *sarabande* from Spanish & Italian *zarabanda*]

Saracen /ˈsarəs(ə)n/ *n. & adj. hist.* ● *n.* **1** an Arab or Muslim at the time of the Crusades. **2** a nomad of the Syrian and Arabian desert. ● *adj.* of the Saracens. □ **Saracenic** /sarəˈsɛnɪk/ *adj.* [Middle English via Old French *sar(r)azin, sar(r)acin* and Late Latin *Saracenus* from late Greek *Sarakēnos*, perhaps from Arabic *šarkī* 'eastern']

Saracen corn *n. Brit. archaic* buckwheat.

Saracen's head *n.* the head of a Saracen or Turk as a heraldic charge or inn-sign.

sarangi /səˈraŋgi, sɑːˈrʌŋgi/ *n.* (*pl.* **sarangis**) an Indian stringed instrument played with a bow. [Hindi *sāraṅgī*]

sarape var. of SERAPE.

sarcasm /ˈsɑːkaz(ə)m/ *n.* **1** the use of bitter or wounding, esp. ironic, remarks; language consisting of such remarks (*suffered from constant sarcasm about his work*). **2** such a remark. □ **sarcastic** /sɑːˈkastɪk/ *adj.* **sarcastically** /sɑːˈkastɪk(ə)li/ *adv.* [French *sarcasme* or Late Latin *sarcasmus* from late Greek *sarkasmos*, from Greek *sarkazō* 'tear flesh', in late Greek 'gnash the teeth, speak bitterly', from *sarx sarkos* 'flesh']

sarcenet var. of SARSENET.

sarcoma /sɑːˈkəʊmə/ *n.* (*pl.* **sarcomas** or **sarcomata** /-mətə/) a malignant tumour of connective or other non-epithelial tissue. □ **sarcomatosis** /-ˈtəʊsɪs/ *n.* **sarcomatous** *adj.* [modern Latin from Greek *sarkōma*, via *sarkoō* 'become fleshy' from *sarx sarkos* 'flesh']

sarcophagus /sɑːˈkɒfəgəs/ *n.* (*pl.* **sarcophagi** /-gʌɪ, -dʒʌɪ/) a stone coffin, esp. one adorned with a sculpture or inscription. [Latin from Greek *sarkophagos* 'flesh-consuming' (as SARCOMA, *-phagos* '-eating')]

sarcoplasm /ˈsɑːkə(ʊ)plaz(ə)m/ *n. Anat.* the cytoplasm of striated muscle cells. [Greek *sarx sarkos* 'flesh' + PLASMA]

sarcous /ˈsɑːkəs/ *adj.* consisting of flesh or muscle. [Greek *sarx sarkos* 'flesh']

Sard /sɑːd/ *adj. & n.* = SARDINIAN.

sard /sɑːd/ *n.* a yellow or orange-red cornelian. [Middle English via French *sarde* or Latin *sarda* = Late Latin *sardius* from Greek *sardios*, probably from *Sardō* 'Sardinia']

sardar var. of SIRDAR.

sardelle /sɑːˈdɛl/ *n.* a sardine, anchovy, or other small fish similarly prepared for eating. [Italian *sardella*, diminutive of *sarda*, from Latin (as SARDINE[1])]

sardine[1] /sɑːˈdiːn/ *n.* a young pilchard or similar young or small herring-like marine fish. □ **like sardines** crowded close together (as sardines are in tins). [Middle English via Old French *sardine* = Italian *sardina*, via Latin, from *sarda* from Greek, perhaps from *Sardō* 'Sardinia']

sardine[2] /ˈsɑːdʌɪn/ *n.* = SARDIUS. [Middle English via Late Latin *sardinus* from Greek *sardinos*, variant of *sardios* SARD (Rev. 4:3)]

Sardinian /sɑːˈdɪnɪən/ *n. & adj.* ● *n.* **1** a native or inhabitant of Sardinia, a Mediterranean island now administratively part of Italy. **2** the Romance language of Sardinia. ● *adj.* of or relating to Sardinia or its people or language.

sardius /ˈsɑːdɪəs/ *n.* a red precious stone mentioned in the Bible (e.g. Exod. 28:17) and in classical writings. [Middle English via Late Latin from Greek *sardios* 'sard']

sardonic /sɑːˈdɒnɪk/ *adj.* **1** grimly jocular. **2** (of laughter etc.) bitterly mocking or cynical. □ **sardonically** *adv.* **sardonicism** /-sɪz(ə)m/ *n.* [French *sardonique*, earlier *sardonien*, via Latin *sardonius* from Greek *sardonios* 'of Sardinia', alteration of *sardanios*, a Homeric epithet of bitter or scornful laughter]

sardonyx /ˈsɑːdənɪks/ *n.* onyx in which white layers alternate with sard. [Middle English via Latin from Greek *sardonux* (probably as SARD, ONYX)]

saree var. of SARI.

sargasso /sɑːˈgasəʊ/ *n.* (also **sargassum**) any seaweed of the genus *Sargassum*, with berry-like air-vessels, found floating in island-like masses, esp. in the Sargasso Sea of the N. Atlantic. Also called GULFWEED. [Portuguese *sargaço*, of unknown origin]

sarge /sɑːdʒ/ *n. slang* sergeant. [abbreviation]

sari /ˈsɑːri/ *n.* (also **saree**) (*pl.* **saris** or **sarees**) a length of cotton or silk draped round the body, traditionally worn as a main garment by Indian women. [Hindi *sār(h)ī*]

sarin /ˈsɑːrɪn/ *n.* an organic phosphorus compound used as a nerve gas. [German]

sark /sɑːk/ *n. Sc. & N.Engl.* a shirt or chemise. [Middle English *serk* from Old Norse *serkr*, from Germanic]

sarking /ˈsɑːkɪŋ/ *n.* orig. *Sc.* & *N.Engl.* boarding between the rafters and the roof. [SARK + -ING[1]]

sarky /ˈsɑːki/ *adj.* (**sarkier**, **sarkiest**) *Brit. slang* sarcastic. □ **sarkily** *adv.* **sarkiness** *n.* [abbreviation]

sarmentose /ˈsɑːməntəʊs, sɑːmənˈtəʊs, -z/ *adj.* (also **sarmentous** /-ˈmɛntəs/) *Bot.* having long thin trailing shoots. [Latin *sarmentosus*, via *sarmenta* (pl.) 'twigs, brushwood' from *sarpere* 'to prune']

sarnie /ˈsɑːniː/ *n. Brit. colloq.* a sandwich. [abbreviation]

sarong /səˈrɒŋ/ *n.* **1** a Malay and Javanese garment consisting of a long strip of (often striped) cloth worn by both sexes tucked round the waist or under the armpits. **2** a woman's garment resembling this. [Malay, literally 'sheath']

saros /ˈsɛːrɒs/ *n. Astron.* a period of about 18 years between repetitions of eclipses. [Greek from Babylonian *šār(u)* '3,600 (years)': the sense apparently based on a misinterpretation of *šāru* as approximately 18.5 years]

sarrusophone /səˈrʌsəfəʊn/ *n.* a metal wind instrument played with a double reed like an oboe. [named after *Sarrus*, 19th-c. French bandmaster, who invented it]

sarsaparilla /sɑːs(ə)pəˈrɪlə/ *n.* **1** a preparation of the dried roots of various plants, esp. smilax, used to flavour some drinks and medicines and formerly as a tonic. **2** any of the plants yielding this. [Spanish *zarzaparilla*, from *zarza* 'bramble', probably + a diminutive of *parra* 'vine']

sarsen /ˈsɑːs(ə)n/ *n. Geol.* a silicified sandstone boulder as found on the chalk downs of southern England. [probably variant of SARACEN]

sarsenet /ˈsɑːsnɪt/ *n.* (also **sarcenet**) a fine soft silk material used esp. for linings. [Middle English from Anglo-French *sarzinett*, perhaps a diminutive of *sarzin* SARACEN, suggested by Old French *drap sarrasinois* 'Saracen cloth']

sartorial /sɑːˈtɔːrɪəl/ *adj.* **1** of or relating to a tailor or tailoring. **2** of or relating to clothes, esp. in respect of their elegance, neatness, etc. □ **sartorially** *adv.* [Latin *sartor* 'tailor' from *sarcire sart-* 'to patch']

sartorius /sɑːˈtɔːrɪəs/ *n. Anat.* the long narrow muscle running across the front of each thigh. [modern Latin from Latin *sartor* 'tailor' (the muscle being used in adopting a tailor's cross-legged posture)]

Sarum use /ˈsɛːrəm/ *n. Eccl.* the order of divine service used in the diocese of Salisbury before the Reformation. [medieval Latin *Sarum* 'Salisbury', perhaps from *Sarisburia*, Latinized form of Old English *Searobyrg*]

SAS *abbr.* (in the UK) Special Air Service.

s.a.s.e. *abbr.* (also **SASE**) *US* self-addressed stamped envelope.

sash[1] /saʃ/ *n.* a long strip or loop of cloth worn over one shoulder or round the waist, usu. as part of a uniform or insignia. □ **sashed** *adj.* [earlier *shash*, from Arabic *šāš* 'muslin, turban']

sash² /saʃ/ *n.* **1** a frame holding the glass in a window, esp. a sash window. **2** the glazed sliding light of a glasshouse or garden frame. ◻ **sashed** *adj.* [*sashes*, corruption of CHASSIS, mistaken for pl.]

sashay /sa'ʃeɪ/ *v.intr.* esp. *N. Amer. colloq.* walk or move ostentatiously, casually, or diagonally. [corruption of CHASSÉ]

sash cord *n.* a strong cord attaching the sash weights of a sash window to a sash.

sashimi /'saʃɪmi/ *n.* a Japanese dish of bite-sized pieces of raw fish eaten with soy sauce and horseradish paste. [Japanese]

sash tool *n.* a glazier's or painter's brush for work on sash windows.

sash weight *n.* (on a sash window) a weight attached to each end of a sash to balance it at any height.

sash window *n.* a window with one or two sashes of which one or either can be slid vertically over the other to make an opening.

sasin /'sasɪn/ *n.* = BLACKBUCK. [Nepali]

sasine /'seɪsɪn/ *n. Sc. Law* **1** the possession of feudal property. **2** an act or document granting this. [variant of SEISIN]

Sask. *abbr.* Saskatchewan.

Sasquatch /'saskwatʃ, -wɒtʃ/ *n.* = BIGFOOT. [Salishan]

sass /sas/ *n.* & *v. N. Amer. colloq.* ● *n.* impudence, cheek. ● *v.tr.* be impudent to, cheek. [variant of SAUCE]

sassaby var. of TSESSEBI.

sassafras /'sasəfras/ *n.* **1** a small tree, *Sassafras albidum*, native to N. America, with aromatic leaves and bark. **2** a preparation of oil extracted from the leaves, or from its bark, used medicinally or in perfumery. [Spanish *sasafrás* or Portuguese *sassafraz*, of unknown origin]

Sassanian /sa'seɪnɪən/ *n.* & *adj.* (also **Sassanid** /'sasənɪd/) ● *n.* a member of a Persian dynasty ruling 224–651. ● *adj.* of or relating to this dynasty. [from *Sasan*, the name of the founder of the dynasty]

Sassenach /'sasənax, -nak/ *n.* & *adj. Sc.* & *Ir.* usu. *derog.* ● *n.* an English person. ● *adj.* English. [Gaelic *Sasunnoch*, Irish *Sasanach* from Latin *Saxones* 'Saxons']

sassy /'sasi/ *adj.* (**sassier**, **sassiest**) esp. *N. Amer. colloq.* = SAUCY. ◻ **sassily** *adv.* **sassiness** *n.* [variant of SAUCY]

sastrugi /sa'stru:gi/ *n.pl.* wavelike irregularities on the surface of hard polar snow, caused by winds. [Russian *zastrugi* 'small ridges']

SAT *abbr.* standard assessment task.

Sat. *abbr.* Saturday.

sat *past* and *past part.* of SIT.

Satan /'seɪt(ə)n/ *n.* the Devil; Lucifer. [Old English via Late Latin and Greek from Hebrew *śāṭān*, literally 'adversary', from *śaṭan* 'oppose, plot against']

satanic /sə'tanɪk/ *adj.* **1** of, like, or befitting Satan. **2** diabolical, hellish. ◻ **satanically** *adv.*

Satanism /'seɪt(ə)nɪz(ə)m/ *n.* **1** the worship of Satan, with a travesty of Christian forms. **2** the pursuit of evil for its own sake; deliberate wickedness. ◻ **Satanist** *n.* **Satanize** *v.tr.* (also **-ise**).

Satanology /seɪtə'nɒlədʒi/ *n.* **1** beliefs concerning the Devil. **2** a history or collection of these.

satay /'sateɪ/ *n.* (also **satai**, **saté**) an Indonesian and Malaysian dish consisting of small pieces of meat grilled on a skewer and usu. served with spiced sauce. [Malay *satai sate*, Indonesian *sate*]

SATB *abbr. Mus.* soprano, alto, tenor, and bass (as a combination of voices).

satchel /'satʃ(ə)l/ *n.* a small bag usu. of leather and hung from the shoulder with a strap, for carrying books etc. esp. to and from school. [Middle English via Old French *sachel* from Latin *saccellus* (as SACK¹)]

sate /seɪt/ *v.tr.* **1** gratify (desire, or a desirous person) to the full. **2** cloy, surfeit, weary with over-abundance (*sated with pleasure*). ◻ **sateless** *adj. poet.* [probably dialect *sade* from Old English *sadian* (related to SAD), assimilated to SATIATE]

sateen /sa'ti:n/ *n.* cotton fabric woven like satin with a glossy surface. [*satin*, on the pattern of *velveteen*]

satellite /'satəlʌɪt/ *n.* & *adj.* ● *n.* **1** a celestial body orbiting the earth or another planet. **2** an artificial body placed in orbit round the earth or another planet. **3** a follower; a hanger-on. **4** an underling; a member of an important person's staff or retinue. **5** (in full **satellite state**) a small country etc. nominally independent but controlled by or dependent on another. ● *adj.* **1** transmitted by satellite (*satellite communications*; *satellite television*). **2** on the periphery (*satellite estates of London*). ◻ **satellitic** /-'lɪtɪk/ *adj.* **satellitism** *n.* [French *satellite* or Latin *satelles satellitis* 'attendant']

satellite dish *n.* a concave dish-shaped aerial for receiving broadcasting signals transmitted by satellite.

satellite town *n.* a small town economically or otherwise dependent on a nearby larger town.

sati var. of SUTTEE.

satiate /'seɪʃɪeɪt/ *adj.* & *v.* ● *adj. archaic* satiated. ● *v.tr.* = SATE. ◻ **satiable** /-ʃəb(ə)l/ *adj. archaic.* **satiation** /-'eɪʃ(ə)n/ *n.* [Latin *satiatus*, past part. of *satiare*, from *satis* 'enough']

satiety /sə'tʌɪɪti/ *n.* **1** the state of being glutted or satiated. **2** the feeling of having too much of something. **3** (foll. by *of*) a cloyed dislike of. ◻ **to satiety** to an extent beyond what is desired. [obsolete French *sacieté* from Latin *satietas -tatis*, from *satis* 'enough']

satin /'satɪn/ *n.*, *adj.*, & *v.* ● *n.* a fabric of silk or various man-made fibres, with a glossy surface on one side produced by a twill weave with the weft-threads almost hidden. ● *adj.* smooth as satin. ● *v.tr.* (**satined**, **satining**) give a glossy surface to (paper). ◻ **satinized** *adj.* (also **-ised**). **satiny** *adj.* [Middle English via Old French from Arabic *zaytūnī* 'of Tsinkiang', a town in China]

satinette /satɪ'nɛt, 'satɪnɪt/ *n.* (also **satinet**) a satin-like fabric made partly or wholly of cotton or synthetic fibre.

satin finish *n.* **1** a polish given to silver etc. with a metallic brush. **2** any effect resembling satin in texture produced on materials in various ways.

satinflower /'satɪnflaʊə/ *n.* any plant whose flowers have a satiny sheen, e.g. greater stitchwort, *Stellaria holostea*.

satin paper *n.* fine glossy writing paper.

satin spar *n.* a fibrous variety of gypsum.

satin stitch *n.* a long straight embroidery stitch, giving the appearance of satin.

satinwood /'satɪnwʊd/ *n.* **1 a** (in full **Ceylon** or **Sri Lanka satinwood**) a tree, *Chloroxylon swietenia*, native to central and southern India and Sri Lanka. **b** (in full **West Indian** or **Jamaican satinwood**) a tree, *Fagara flava*, native to the West Indies, Bermuda, and southern Florida. **2** the yellow glossy timber of either of these trees.

satire /'satʌɪə/ *n.* **1** the use of ridicule, irony, sarcasm, etc., to expose folly or vice or to lampoon an individual. **2** a work or composition in prose or verse using satire. **3** this branch of literature. **4** a thing that brings ridicule upon something else. **5** *Rom. Antiq.* a poetic medley, esp. a poem ridiculing prevalent vices or follies. [French *satire* or Latin *satira*, later form of *satura* 'medley']

satiric /sə'tɪrɪk/ *adj.* **1** of satire or satires. **2** containing satire (*wrote a satiric review*). **3** writing satire (*a satiric poet*). [French *satirique* or Late Latin *satiricus* (as SATIRE)]

satirical /sə'tɪrɪk(ə)l/ *adj.* **1** = SATIRIC. **2** given to the use of satire in speech or writing or to cynical observation of others; sarcastic; humorously critical. ◻ **satirically** *adv.*

satirist /'satɪrɪst/ *n.* **1** a writer of satires. **2** a satirical person.

satirize /'satɪrʌɪz/ *v.tr.* (also **-ise**) **1** assail or ridicule with satire. **2** write a satire upon. **3** describe satirically.

□ **satirization** /-ˈzeɪʃ(ə)n/ *n.* [French *satiriser* (as SATIRE)]

satisfaction /satɪsˈfakʃ(ə)n/ *n.* **1** the act or an instance of satisfying; the state of being satisfied (*heard this with great satisfaction*). **2** a thing that satisfies desire or gratifies feeling (*is a great satisfaction to me*). **3** a thing that settles an obligation or pays a debt. **4 a** (foll. by *for*) atonement; compensation (*demanded satisfaction*). **b** *Theol.* Christ's atonement for the sins of mankind. □ **to one's satisfaction** so that one is satisfied. [Middle English via Old French from Latin *satisfactio -onis* (as SATISFY)]

satisfactory /satɪsˈfakt(ə)ri/ *adj.* **1** adequate; causing or giving satisfaction (*was a satisfactory pupil*). **2** satisfying expectations or needs; leaving no room for complaint (*a satisfactory result*). □ **satisfactorily** *adv.* **satisfactoriness** *n.* [French *satisfactoire* or medieval Latin *satisfactorius* (as SATISFY)]

satisfy /ˈsatɪsfʌɪ/ *v.* (**-ies, -ied**) **1** *tr.* **a** meet the expectations or desires of; comply with (a demand). **b** be accepted by (a person, his taste) as adequate; be equal to (a preconception etc.). **2** *tr.* put an end to (an appetite or want) by supplying what was required. **3** *tr.* rid (a person) of an appetite or want in a similar way. **4** *intr.* give satisfaction; leave nothing to be desired. **5** *tr.* pay (a debt or creditor). **6** *tr.* adequately meet, fulfil, or comply with (conditions, obligations, etc.) (*has satisfied all the legal conditions*). **7** *tr.* (often foll. by *of, that*) provide with adequate information or proof, convince (*satisfied the others that they were right; satisfy the court of their innocence*). **8** *tr. Math.* (of a quantity) make (an equation) true. **9** *tr.* (in *passive*) **a** (foll. by *with*) contented or pleased with. **b** (foll. by *to*) demand no more than or consider it enough to do. □ **satisfy the examiners** *Brit.* reach the standard required to pass an examination. **satisfy oneself** (often foll. by *that* + clause) be certain in one's own mind. □ **satisfiable** *adj.* **satisfiability** /-əˈbɪlɪti/ *n.* **satisfiedly** *adv.* **satisfying** *adj.* **satisfyingly** *adv.* [Middle English via Old French *satisfier* from Latin *satisfacere satisfact-*, from *satis* 'enough']

satnav /ˈsatnav/ *n.* esp. *Naut.* **1** navigation assisted by information from satellites. **2** a navigation system capable of receiving such information. [acronym from *sat*ellite *nav*igation]

satori /səˈtɔːri/ *n. Buddhism* sudden enlightenment. [Japanese, = awakening]

satrap /ˈsatrap/ *n.* **1** a provincial governor in the ancient Persian empire. **2** a subordinate ruler, colonial governor, etc. [Middle English from Old French *satrape* or Latin *satrapa* via Greek *satrapēs* from Old Persian *xšathra-pāvan* 'country-protector']

satrapy /ˈsatrəpi/ *n.* (*pl.* **-ies**) a province ruled over by a satrap.

satsuma /satˈsuːmə/ *n.* **1** a variety of tangerine originally grown in Japan. **2** /also ˈsatsʊmə, -sjʊ-/ (**Satsuma**) (in full **Satsuma ware**) cream-coloured Japanese pottery. [*Satsuma*, a province in Japan]

saturate /ˈsatʃʊreɪt, -tjʊreɪt/ *v.tr.* **1** fill with moisture; soak thoroughly. **2** (often foll. by *with*) fill to capacity. **3** cause (a substance, solution, vapour, metal, or air) to absorb, hold, or combine with the greatest possible amount of another substance, or of moisture, magnetism, electricity, etc. **4** supply (a market) beyond the point at which the demand for a product is satisfied. **5** (foll. by *with, in*) imbue with or steep in (learning, tradition, prejudice, etc.). **6** overwhelm (enemy defences, a target area, etc.) by concentrated bombing. **7** (as **saturated** *adj.*) **a** (of colour) full; rich; free from an admixture of white. **b** *Chem.* (of fat molecules) containing the greatest possible number of hydrogen atoms and no carbon–carbon double bonds. □ **saturate** /-rət/ *adj. literary.* **saturable** /-rəb(ə)l/ *adj.* **saturant** /-r(ə)nt/ *n. & adj.* [Latin *saturare* from *satur* 'full']

saturation /satʃʊˈreɪʃ(ə)n, -tjʊ-/ *n.* the act or an instance of saturating; the state of being saturated.

saturation bombing *n. Mil.* intensive aerial bombing.

saturation point *n.* the stage beyond which no more can be absorbed or accepted.

Saturday /ˈsatədeɪ, -di/ *n. & adv.* ● *n.* the seventh day of the week, following Friday. ● *adv. colloq.* **1** on Saturday. **2** (**Saturdays**) on Saturdays; each Saturday. [Old English *Sætern(es) dæg*, translation of Latin *Saturni dies* 'day of Saturn']

Saturn /ˈsat(ə)n/ *n.* the sixth planet from the sun, circled by a system of broad flat rings, and the most distant of the five planets known in the ancient world. [Latin *Saturnus*, the name of the Roman god of agriculture (identified with Kronos, father of Zeus), perhaps from Etruscan]

saturnalia /satəˈneɪlɪə/ *n.* (*pl.* same or **saturnalias**) **1** (usu. **Saturnalia**) *Rom.Hist.* the festival of Saturn in December, characterized by unrestrained merrymaking for all, the predecessor of Christmas. **2** (treated as *sing.* or *pl.*) a scene of wild revelry or tumult; an orgy. □ **saturnalian** *adj.* [Latin, neut. pl. of *Saturnalis* (as SATURN)]

Saturnian /səˈtəːnɪən/ *adj.* **1** of or relating to the planet Saturn. **2** = SATURNINE 1.

saturnic /səˈtəːnɪk/ *adj. Med. archaic* affected with lead poisoning. □ **saturnism** /ˈsatənɪz(ə)m/ [SATURN]

saturniid /səˈtəːnɪɪd/ *n.* any large moth of the family Saturniidae, including emperor moths. [modern Latin]

saturnine /ˈsatənʌɪn/ *adj.* **1 a** of a sluggish gloomy temperament. **b** (of looks etc.) dark and brooding. **2** *archaic* **a** of the metal lead. **b** *Med.* of or affected by lead poisoning. □ **saturninely** *adv.* [Middle English via Old French *saturnin* from medieval Latin *Saturninus* 'of Saturn' (identified with lead by the alchemists and associated with slowness and gloom by astrologers]

satyagraha /sʌˈtjɑːɡrəhɑː/ *n.* **1** *hist.* a policy of passive resistance to British rule in India, advocated by Gandhi. **2** passive resistance as a policy. [Sanskrit, from *satya* 'truth' + *āgraha* 'obstinacy']

satyr /ˈsatə/ *n.* **1** (in Greek mythology) one of a class of Greek woodland gods with a horse's ears and tail, or (in Roman representations) with a goat's ears, tail, legs, and budding horns. **2** a lustful or sensual man. **3** = SATYRID. [Middle English via Old French *satyre* or Latin *satyrus* from Greek *saturos*]

satyriasis /satɪˈrʌɪəsɪs/ *n. Med.* excessive sexual desire in men. [Late Latin from Greek *saturiasis* (as SATYR)]

satyric /səˈtɪrɪk/ *adj.* (in Greek mythology) of or relating to satyrs. [Latin *satyricus* from Greek *saturikos* (as SATYR)]

satyric drama *n.* a kind of ancient Greek comic play with a chorus of satyrs.

satyrid /səˈtɪrɪd/ *n.* any butterfly of the family Satyridae, often brown with small eye-spots on the wings. [modern Latin *Satyridae* from Latin *Satyrus* (as SATYR), used as a genus name]

sauce /sɔːs/ *n. & v.* ● *n.* **1** a liquid or semi-solid accompaniment to food, often of a specified flavour etc.; the liquid constituent of a dish (*mint sauce; tomato sauce; chicken in a lemon sauce*). **2** something adding piquancy or excitement. **3** esp. *Brit. colloq.* impudence, impertinence, cheek. **4** *N. Amer.* stewed fruit esp. apples, eaten as dessert or used as a garnish. ● *v.tr.* **1** *colloq.* be impudent to; cheek. **2** *archaic* **a** season with sauce or condiments. **b** add excitement to. □ **(what is) sauce for the goose (is sauce for the gander)** what is appropriate in one case (by implication appropriate in others). □ **sauceless** *adj.* [Middle English from Old French, ultimately from Latin *salsus*, via *salere sals-* 'to salt' from *sal* 'salt']

sauce-boat *n.* a kind of jug or dish used for serving sauces etc.

saucepan /ˈsɔːspən/ *n.* a usu. metal cooking pan, usu. round with a lid and a long handle at the side, used for boiling, stewing, etc., on top of a cooker. □ **saucepanful** *n.* (*pl.* **-fuls**).

saucer /ˈsɔːsə/ *n.* **1** a shallow circular dish used for standing a cup on and to catch drips. **2** any similar dish used to stand a plant pot etc. on. □ **saucerful** *n.* (*pl.* **-fuls**). **saucerless** *adj.* [Middle English, = condiment-dish, from Old French *saussier(e)* 'sauce-boat', probably from Late Latin *salsarium* (as SAUCE)]

sauce tartare *n.* = TARTARE SAUCE.

saucy /ˈsɔːsi/ *adj.* (**saucier**, **sauciest**) **1** impudent, cheeky. **2** *colloq.* smart-looking (*a saucy hat*). **3** *colloq.* smutty, suggestive. □ **saucily** *adv.* **sauciness** *n.* [earlier sense 'savoury', from SAUCE]

Saudi /ˈsaʊdi, ˈsɔːdi/ *n. & adj.* (also **Saudi Arabian**) ● *n.* (*pl.* **Saudis**) **1 a** a native or national of Saudi Arabia. **b** a person of Saudi descent. **2** a member of the dynasty founded by King Saud. ● *adj.* of or relating to Saudi Arabia or the Saudi dynasty. [from the name of A. Ibn-*Saud*, Arabic king d. 1953]

sauerkraut /ˈsaʊəkraʊt/ *n.* a German dish of chopped pickled cabbage. [German, from *sauer* SOUR + *Kraut* 'vegetable']

sauger /ˈsɔːgə/ *n. US* a small N. American pikeperch, *Stizostedion canadense*. [19th c.: origin unknown]

sauna /ˈsɔːnə/ *n.* **1** a special room heated to a high temperature to clean and refresh the body. **2** a period spent in such a room. [Finnish]

saunders var. of SANDERS.

saunter /ˈsɔːntə/ *v. & n.* ● *v.intr.* **1** walk slowly; amble, stroll. **2** proceed without hurry or effort. ● *n.* **1** a leisurely ramble. **2** a slow gait. □ **saunterer** *n.* [Middle English, = muse: origin unknown]

saurian /ˈsɔːrɪən/ *adj.* of or like a lizard. [modern Latin *Sauria* from Greek *saura* 'lizard']

saurischian /sɔːˈrɪskɪən, -ˈrɪʃɪən/ *adj. & n.* ● *adj.* of or relating to the order Saurischia of dinosaurs with a pelvic structure like that of lizards. ● *n.* a dinosaur of this order. [modern Latin *Saurischia*, from Greek *sauros* 'lizard' + *iskhion* 'hip joint']

sauropod /ˈsɔːrəpɒd/ *n.* any of a group of large plant-eating dinosaurs with a long neck and tail, small head, and massive limbs. [Greek *saura* 'lizard' + *pous pod-* 'foot']

saury /ˈsɔːri/ *n.* (*pl.* **-ies**) a long-beaked marine fish, *Scomberesox saurus*, of temperate waters. [perhaps via Late Latin from Greek *sauros* 'horse mackerel']

sausage /ˈsɒsɪdʒ/ *n.* **1** a short length of minced pork, beef, or other meat seasoned and often mixed with other ingredients, encased in a cylindrical skin, sold to be cooked before eating. **2 a** minced pork, beef, or other meat seasoned and preserved and encased in a cylindrical skin, sold mainly to be eaten cold in slices or as a spread. **b** a length of this. **3** a sausage-shaped object. □ **not a sausage** *Brit. colloq.* nothing at all. [Middle English via Old Northern French *saussiche* and medieval Latin *salsicia* from Latin *salsus*: see SAUCE]

sausage dog *n. Brit. colloq.* a dachshund.

sausage machine *n.* **1** a sausage-making machine. **2** *Brit.* a relentlessly uniform process.

sausage meat *n.* minced meat used in sausages or as a stuffing etc.

sausage roll *n. Brit.* sausage meat enclosed in a pastry roll and baked.

sauté /ˈsəʊteɪ/ *adj., n., & v.* ● *adj.* (esp. of potatoes etc.) quickly fried in a little hot fat. ● *n.* food cooked in this way. ● *v.tr.* (**sautéd** or **sautéed**) cook in this way. [French, past part. of *sauter* 'jump']

Sauternes /sə(ʊ)ˈtɜːn/ *n.* a sweet white wine from Sauternes in the Bordeaux region of France.

savage /ˈsævɪdʒ/ *adj., n., & v.* ● *adj.* **1** fierce; cruel (*savage persecution*; *a savage blow*). **2** wild; primitive (*savage tribes*; *a savage animal*). **3** *archaic* (of scenery etc.) uncultivated (*a savage scene*). **4** *colloq.* angry; bad-tempered (*in a savage mood*). **5** *Heraldry* (of the human figure) naked. ● *n.* **1** *archaic offens.* a member of a primitive tribe. **2** a cruel or barbarous person. ● *v.tr.* **1** (esp. of a dog, wolf, etc.) attack and bite or trample. **2** (of a critic etc.) attack fiercely. □ **savagedom** *n.* **savagely** *adv.* **savageness** *n.* **savagery** *n.* (*pl.* **-ies**). [Middle English via Old French *sauvage* 'wild' from Latin *silvaticus*, from *silva* 'a wood']

savannah /səˈvænə/ *n.* (also **savanna**) a grassy plain in tropical and subtropical regions, with few or no trees. [Spanish *zavana*, perhaps of Carib origin]

savant /ˈsæv(ə)nt/ *n.* (*fem.* **savante** /ˈsæv(ə)nt or French savɑ̃t/) a learned person, esp. a distinguished scientist etc. [French, part. of *savoir* 'know' (as SAPIENT)]

savate /səˈvɑːt/ *n.* a form of boxing in which feet and fists are used. [French, originally a kind of shoe: cf. SABOT]

save[1] /seɪv/ *v. & n.* ● *v.* **1** *tr.* (often foll. by *from*) rescue, preserve, protect, or deliver from danger, harm, discredit, etc. (*saved my life*; *saved me from drowning*). **2** *tr.* (often foll. by *up*) keep for future use; reserve; refrain from spending (*saved up £150 for a new bike*; *likes to save plastic bags*). **3** *tr.* (often *refl.*) **a** relieve (another person or oneself) from spending (money, time, trouble, etc.) (*saved myself £50*; *a word processor saves time*). **b** obviate the need or likelihood of (*soaking saves scrubbing*; *will save me a lot of bother*). **4** *tr.* preserve from damnation; convert (*saved her soul*). **5** *tr. & refl.* husband or preserve (one's strength, health, etc.) (*saving himself for the last lap*; *save your energy*). **6** *intr.* (often foll. by *up*) save money for future use. **7** *tr.* **a** avoid losing (a game, match, etc.). **b** prevent an opponent from scoring (a goal etc.). **c** stop (a ball etc.) from entering the goal. ● *n.* **1** *Football* etc. the act of preventing an opponent's scoring etc. **2** *Bridge* a sacrifice-bid to prevent unnecessary losses. □ **save appearances** present a prosperous, respectable, etc. appearance. **save-as-you-earn** *Brit.* a method of saving by regular deduction from earnings at source. **save one's breath** not waste time speaking to no effect. **save oneself the trouble** (or **bother**) avoid useless or pointless effort. **save face** see FACE. **save a person's face** see FACE. **save the situation** (or **day**) find or provide a solution to difficulty or disaster. **save one's skin** (or **neck** or **bacon**) avoid loss, injury, or death; escape from danger. **save the tide** get in and out of port etc. while the tide lasts. □ **savable** *adj.* (also **saveable**). [Middle English via Anglo-French *sa(u)ver*, Old French *salver*, *sauver* from Late Latin *salvare*, from Latin *salvus* SAFE]

save[2] /seɪv/ *prep. & conj. archaic* or *poet.* ● *prep.* except; but (*all save him*). ● *conj.* (often foll. by *for*) unless; but; except (*happy save for one want*; *is well save that he has a cold*). [Middle English via Old French *sauf sauve* from Latin *salvo*, *salva*, ablative sing. of *salvus* SAFE]

save-all *n.* **1** a device to prevent waste. **2** *hist.* a pan with a spike for burning up candle-ends.

saveloy /ˈsævəlɔɪ/ *n. Brit.* a seasoned red pork sausage, dried and smoked, and sold ready to eat. [corruption of French *cervelas*, *-at*, from Italian *cervellata*: cf. CERVELAT]

saver /ˈseɪvə/ *n.* **1** a person who saves esp. money. **2** (often in *comb.*) a device for economical use (of time etc.) (*found the short cut a time-saver*). **3** (often *attrib.*) a cheap, esp. off-peak fare. **4** *Racing slang* a hedging bet.

savin /ˈsævɪn/ *n.* (also **savine**) **1** a bushy juniper, *Juniperus sabina*, usu. spreading horizontally, and yielding oil formerly used in the treatment of amenorrhoea. **2** *US* = RED CEDAR. [Old English from Old French *savine*, from Latin *sabina* (*herba*) 'Sabine (herb)']

saving /ˈseɪvɪŋ/ *adj., n., & prep.* ● *adj.* (often in *comb.*) making economical use of (*labour-saving*). ● *n.* **1** anything that is saved. **2** an economy (*a saving in expenses*). **3** (usu. in *pl.*) money saved. ● *prep.* **1** with the exception of; except (*all saving that one*). **2** without offence to (*saving your presence*). [Middle English from SAVE[1]: the preposition probably from SAVE[2] on the pattern of *touching*]

saving clause *n. Law* a clause containing a stipulation of exemption etc.

saving grace *n.* **1** the redeeming grace of God. **2** a redeeming quality or characteristic.

savings account *n.* a deposit account.

savings and loan *n.* (in the US) a cooperative association which accepts savings at interest and lends money to savers for house or other purchases (also *attrib.*: *savings and loan bailout*).

savings bank *n.* a bank receiving small deposits at interest and returning the profits to the depositors.

savings certificate *n. Brit.* an interest-bearing document issued by the Government for the benefit of savers.

saviour /'seɪvjə/ *n.* (*US* **savior**) **1** a person who saves or delivers from danger, harm, etc. (*the saviour of the nation*). **2** (**Saviour**) (prec. by *the, our*) Christ. [Middle English via Old French *sauvëour* and ecclesiastical Latin *salvator -oris* (translation of Greek *sōtēr*) from Late Latin *salvare* SAVE[1]]

savoir faire /savwɑː 'fɛː/ *n.* the ability to act suitably in any situation; tact. [French, = know how to do]

savor *US* var. of SAVOUR.

savory[1] /'seɪv(ə)ri/ *n.* (*pl.* **-ies**) any herb of the genus *Satureja*, esp. *S. hortensis* and *S. montana*, used esp. in cookery. [Middle English *saverey*, perhaps via Old English *sætherie* from Latin *satureia*]

savory[2] *US* var. of SAVOURY.

savour /'seɪvə/ *n. & v.* (*US* **savor**) ● *n.* **1** a characteristic taste, flavour, relish, etc. **2** a quality suggestive of or containing a small amount of another. **3** *archaic* a characteristic smell. ● *v.* **1** *tr.* **a** appreciate and enjoy the taste of (food). **b** enjoy or appreciate (an experience etc.). **2** *intr.* (foll. by *of*) **a** suggest by taste, smell, etc. (*savours of mushrooms*). **b** imply or suggest a specified quality (*savours of impertinence*). □ **savourless** *adj.* [Middle English via Old French from Latin *sapor -oris*, from *sapere* 'to taste']

savoury /'seɪv(ə)ri/ *adj. & n.* (*US* **savory**) ● *adj.* **1** (of food) salty or piquant, not sweet (*a savoury omelette*). **2** having an appetizing taste or smell. **3** pleasant; acceptable. ● *n.* (*pl.* **-ies**) *Brit.* a savoury dish, esp. one served as an appetizer or at the end of dinner. □ **savourily** *adv.* **savouriness** *n.* [Middle English from Old French *savouré* past part. of *savourer* (as SAVOUR)]

savoy /sə'vɔɪ/ *n.* a hardy variety of cabbage with wrinkled leaves. [*Savoy*, a region in SE France]

Savoyard /sə'vɔɪɑːd, savɔɪ'ɑːd/ *n. & adj.* ● *n.* a native of Savoy in SE France. ● *adj.* of or relating to Savoy or its people. [French from *Savoie* 'Savoy']

savvy /'savi/ *v., n., & adj. slang* ● *v.intr. & tr.* (**-ies, -ied**) know. ● *n.* knowingness; shrewdness; understanding. ● *adj.* (**savvier, savviest**) *US* knowing; wise. [originally black & Pidgin English imitating Spanish *sabe usted* 'you know']

saw[1] /sɔː/ *n. & v.* ● *n.* **1 a** a hand tool having a toothed blade used to cut esp. wood with a to-and-fro movement. **b** any of several mechanical power-driven devices with a toothed rotating disc or moving band, for cutting. **2** *Zool.* etc. a serrated organ or part. ● *v.* (*past part.* **sawn** /sɔːn/ or **sawed**) **1** *tr.* **a** cut (wood etc.) with a saw. **b** make (logs etc.) with a saw. **2** *intr.* use a saw. **3 a** *intr.* move to and fro with a motion as of a saw or person sawing (*sawing away on his violin*). **b** *tr.* divide (the air etc.) with gesticulations. □ **sawlike** *adj.* [Old English *saga*, from Germanic]

saw[2] *past* of SEE[1].

saw[3] /sɔː/ *n.* a proverb; a maxim (*that's just an old saw*). [Old English *sagu* from Germanic: related to SAY, SAGA]

sawbench /'sɔːbɛn(t)ʃ/ *n.* a circular saw with a bench to support the material and advance it to the saw.

sawbill /'sɔːbɪl/ *n.* a merganser.

sawbones /'sɔːbəʊnz/ *n. slang* a doctor or surgeon.

sawbuck /'sɔːbʌk/ *n. US* **1** a sawhorse. **2** *slang* a $10 note.

saw-doctor *n.* a machine for giving a saw a serrated edge.

sawdust /'sɔːdʌst/ *n.* powdery particles of wood produced in sawing.

saw-edged *adj.* with a jagged edge like a saw.

sawed-off *US* var. of SAWN-OFF.

sawfish /'sɔːfɪʃ/ *n.* (*pl.* usu. same) any large marine fish of the family Pristidae, with a toothed flat snout used as a weapon.

sawfly /'sɔːflʌɪ/ *n.* (*pl.* **-flies**) any insect of the superfamily Tenthredinoidea, with a serrated ovipositor, the larvae of which are injurious to plants.

saw frame *n.* a frame in which a saw blade is held taut.

saw-gate *n.* = SAW FRAME.

saw-gin *n. Brit.* = COTTON GIN.

sawgrass /'sɔːgrɑːs/ *n.* esp. *US* a sedge of the genus *Cladium*, with sharp-edged leaves.

sawhorse /'sɔːhɔːs/ *n.* a rack supporting wood for sawing.

sawmill /'sɔːmɪl/ *n.* a factory in which wood is sawn mechanically into planks or boards.

sawn *past part.* of SAW[1].

sawn-off *adj.* (*US* **sawed-off**) **1** (of a gun) having a specially shortened barrel to make handling easier and to give a wider field of fire. **2** *colloq.* (of a person) short.

saw-pit *n.* a pit in which the lower of two men working a pit-saw stands.

saw-set *n.* a tool for wrenching saw-teeth in alternate directions to allow the saw to work freely.

sawtooth /'sɔːtuːθ/ *adj.* **1** (also **sawtoothed** /-tuːθt/) (esp. of a roof, wave, etc.) shaped like the teeth of a saw with one steep and one slanting side. **2** (of a waveform) showing a slow linear rise and rapid linear fall.

saw-wort *n.* a plant of the daisy family, *Serratula tinctoria*, yielding a yellow dye from its serrated leaves.

sawyer /'sɔːjə/ *n.* **1** a person who saws timber professionally. **2** *US* an uprooted tree held fast by one end in a river. **3** *NZ* a large wingless horned grasshopper whose larvae bore in wood. [Middle English, earlier *sawer*, from SAW[1]]

sax[1] /saks/ *n. colloq.* **1** a saxophone. **2** a saxophone-player. □ **saxist** *n.* [abbreviation]

sax[2] /saks/ *n.* (also **zax** /zaks/) a slater's chopper, with a point for making nail holes. [Old English *seax* 'knife', from Germanic]

saxatile /'saksətʌɪl, -tɪl/ *adj.* living or growing on or among rocks. [French *saxatile* or Latin *saxatilis*, from *saxum* 'rock']

saxboard /'saksbɔːd/ *n.* the uppermost strake of an open boat. [probably from SAX[2] + BOARD: cf. Old Norse use of *sax* = gunwale near the prow]

saxe /saks/ *n. & adj.* = SAXE BLUE. [French, = Saxony, the source of a dye of this colour]

saxe blue *n. & adj.* ● *n.* a lightish blue colour with a greyish tinge. ● *adj.* (hyphenated when *attrib.*) of this colour.

saxhorn /'sakshɔːn/ *n.* any of a series of different-sized brass wind instruments with valves and a funnel-shaped mouthpiece, used mainly in military and brass bands. [*Sax*, name of its Belgian inventors, + HORN]

saxicoline /sak'sɪk(ə)lʌɪn/ *adj.* (also **saxicolous**) *Biol.* = SAXATILE. [modern Latin *saxicolus*, from *saxum* 'rock' + *colere* 'inhabit']

saxifrage /'saksɪfreɪdʒ/ *n.* any plant of the genus *Saxifraga*, growing on rocky or stony ground and usu. bearing small white, yellow, or red flowers. [Middle English from Old French *saxifrage* or Late Latin *saxifraga* (*herba*), from Latin *saxum* 'rock' + *frangere* 'break']

Saxon /'saks(ə)n/ *n. & adj.* ● *n.* **1** *hist.* **a** a member of a Germanic people that conquered parts of England in 5th–6th c. **b** (usu. **Old Saxon**) the language of the Saxons. **2** = ANGLO-SAXON. **3** a native of modern Saxony in Germany. **4** the Germanic (as opposed to Latin or Romance) elements of English. ● *adj.* **1** *hist.* of or concerning the Saxons. **2** belonging to or originating from the Saxon language or Old English. **3** of or concerning modern Saxony or Saxons. □ **Saxondom** *n.* **Saxonism** *n.* **Saxonist** *n.* **Saxonize** /-nʌɪz/ *v.tr. & intr.* (also **-ise**). [Middle English via Old French and Late

Latin *Saxo -onis* from Greek *Saxones* (pl.), from West Germanic: related to Old English *Seaxan, Seaxe* (pl.)]

Saxon architecture *n.* the form of Romanesque architecture preceding the Norman in England.

Saxon blue *n.* a solution of indigo in sulphuric acid as a dye.

saxony /ˈsaks(ə)ni/ *n.* **1** a fine kind of wool. **2** cloth made from this. [*Saxony*, a region in Germany, from Late Latin *Saxonia* (as SAXON)]

saxophone /ˈsaksəfəʊn/ *n.* **1** a metal woodwind reed instrument in several sizes and registers, used esp. in jazz and dance music. **2** a saxophone-player. □ **saxophonic** /-ˈfɒnɪk/ *adj.* **saxophonist** /-ˈsɒf(ə)nɪst, -səfəʊnɪst/ *n.* [*Sax* (as SAXHORN) + -PHONE]

say /seɪ/ *v.* & *n.* ● *v.* (*3rd sing. present* **says** /sɛz/; *past* and *past part.* **said** /sɛd/) **1** *tr.* (often foll. by *that* + clause) **a** utter (specified words) in a speaking voice; remark (*said 'Damn!'; said that he was satisfied*). **b** put into words; express (*that was well said; cannot say what I feel*). **2** *tr.* (often foll. by *that* + clause) **a** state; promise or prophesy (*says that there will be war*). **b** have specified wording; indicate (*says here that he was killed; the clock says ten to six*). **3** *tr.* (in *passive*; usu. foll. by *to* + infin.) be asserted or described (*is said to be 93 years old*). **4** *tr.* (foll. by *to* + infin.) *colloq.* tell a person to do something (*he said to bring the car*). **5** *tr.* convey (information) (*spoke for an hour but said little*). **6** *tr.* put forward as an argument or excuse (*much to be said in favour of it; what have you to say for yourself?*). **7** *tr.* (often *absol.*) form and give an opinion or decision as to (*who did it I cannot say; do say which you prefer*). **8** *tr.* select, assume, or take as an example or (a specified number etc.) as near enough (*shall we say this one?; paid, say, £20*). **9** *tr.* **a** speak the words of (prayers, Mass, a grace, etc.). **b** repeat (a lesson etc.); recite (*can't say his tables*). **10** *tr. Art* etc. convey (inner meaning or intention) (*what is the director saying in this film?*). **11** *intr.* **a** speak; talk. **b** (in *imper.*) *poet.* tell me (*what is your name, say!*). **12** *tr.* (as **the said** *adj.*) *Law* or *joc.* the previously mentioned (*the said witness*). **13** *intr.* (as *int.*) *N. Amer.* an exclamation of surprise, to attract attention, etc. ● *n.* **1 a** an opportunity for stating one's opinion etc. (*let him have his say*). **b** a stated opinion. **2** a share in a decision etc. (*had no say in the matter*). □ **how say you?** *Law* how do you find? (addressed to the jury requesting its verdict). **I** etc. **cannot** (or **could not**) **say** I etc. do not know. **I'll say** *colloq.* yes indeed. **I say!** *Brit.* an exclamation expressing surprise, drawing attention, etc. **it is said** the rumour is that. **not to say** and indeed; or possibly even (*his language was rude not to say offensive*). **said he** (or **I** etc.) esp. *Brit. colloq.* or *poet.* he etc. said. **say for oneself** say by way of conversation, oratory, etc. **say much** (or **something**) **for** indicate the high quality of. **say no** refuse or disagree. **say out** express fully or candidly. **says I** (or **he** etc.) esp. *Brit. colloq.* I, he, etc., said (used in reporting conversation). **say something** make a short speech. **says you!** *colloq.* I disagree. **say when** *colloq.* indicate when enough drink or food has been given. **say the word 1** indicate that you agree or give permission. **2** give the order etc. **say yes** agree. **that is to say 1** in other words, more explicitly. **2** or at least. **they say** it is rumoured. **to say nothing of** = *not to mention* (see MENTION). **what do** (or **would**) **you say to ...?** would you like ...? **when all is said and done** after all, in the long run. **you can say that again!** (or **you said it!**) *colloq.* I agree emphatically. **you don't say so** *colloq.* an expression of amazement or disbelief. □ **sayable** *adj.* **sayer** *n.* [Old English *secgan*, from Germanic]

SAYE *abbr. Brit.* save-as-you-earn.

saying /ˈseɪɪŋ/ *n.* **1** the act or an instance of saying. **2** a maxim, proverb, adage, etc. □ **as the saying goes** (or **is**) an expression used in introducing a proverb, cliché, etc. **go without saying** be too well known or obvious to need mention. **there is no saying** it is impossible to know.

say-so *n.* **1** the power of decision. **2** mere assertion (*cannot proceed merely on his say-so*).

Sb *symb. Chem.* the element antimony. [Latin *stibium*]

S-bend *n.* an S-shaped bend in a road, pipe, etc.

SBN *abbr.* Standard Book Number (cf. ISBN).

S. by E. *abbr.* South by East.

S. by W. *abbr.* South by West.

SC *abbr.* **1** *US* South Carolina (also in official postal use). **2** special constable.

Sc *symb. Chem.* the element scandium.

sc. *abbr.* scilicet; to wit, that is to say, namely (*he asserted that he had met him* (*sc. the defendant*) *on that evening*).

s.c. *abbr. Printing* small capitals.

scab /skab/ *n.* & *v.* ● *n.* **1** a dry rough protective crust over a cut, sore, etc., formed in healing. **2** (often *attrib.*) *colloq. derog.* a person who refuses to strike or join a trade union, or who tries to break a strike by working; a blackleg. **3** the mange or a similar skin disease esp. in animals. **4** a fungous plant disease causing scablike roughness. **5** a dislikeable person. ● *v.intr.* (**scabbed**, **scabbing**) **1** act as a scab. **2** (of a wound etc.) form a scab; heal over. □ **scabbed** *adj.* **scabby** *adj.* (**scabbier**, **scabbiest**). **scabbiness** *n.* **scablike** *adj.* [Middle English from Old Norse *skabb*, related to Old English *sceabb*]

scabbard /ˈskabəd/ *n.* **1** a sheath for a sword, bayonet, etc. **2** *US* a sheath for a revolver etc. [Middle English *sca(u)berc* etc. from Anglo-French, probably from Frankish]

scabbard-fish *n.* (*pl.* usu. same) an elongated marine fish of the family Trichiuridae, esp. the edible silvery-white *Lepidopus caudatus*.

scabies /ˈskeɪbiːz/ *n.* a contagious skin disease with severe itching and red papules, caused by the itch mite. [Middle English from Latin, from *scabere* 'to scratch']

scabious /ˈskeɪbɪəs/ *n.* & *adj.* ● *n.* any plant of the genus *Scabiosa*, *Knautia*, etc., with pink, white, or esp. blue pincushion-shaped flowers. ● *adj.* affected with mange; scabby. [Middle English from medieval Latin *scabiosa* (*herba*) formerly regarded as a cure for skin disease: see SCABIES]

scabrous /ˈskeɪbrəs, ˈskabrəs/ *adj.* **1** having a rough surface; bearing short stiff hairs, scales, etc.; scurfy. **2** (of a subject, situation, etc.) requiring tactful treatment; hard to handle with decency. **3 a** indecent, salacious. **b** behaving licentiously. □ **scabrously** *adv.* **scabrousness** *n.* [French *scabreux* or Late Latin *scabrosus*, from Latin *scaber* 'rough']

■ **Usage** Note that *scabrous* does not mean 'scathing', 'scurrilous', or 'abusive'.

scad /skad/ *n.* any fish of the family Carangidae native to tropical and subtropical seas, usu. having an elongated body and very large spiky scales, esp. the horse mackerel *Trachurus trachurus*. [17th c.: origin unknown]

scads /skadz/ *n.pl. US colloq.* large quantities. [19th c.: origin unknown]

scaffold /ˈskafəʊld, -f(ə)ld/ *n.* & *v.* ● *n.* **1 a** *hist.* a raised wooden platform used for the execution of criminals. **b** a similar platform used for drying tobacco etc. **2** = SCAFFOLDING 1a. **3** (prec. by *the*) death by execution. ● *v.tr.* attach scaffolding to (a building). □ **scaffolder** *n.* [Middle English via Anglo-French from Old French *(e)schaffaut*, earlier *escadafaut*: cf. CATAFALQUE]

scaffolding /ˈskafəʊldɪŋ, -f(ə)ld-/ *n.* **1 a** a temporary structure formed of poles, planks, etc., erected by workmen and used by them while building or repairing a house etc. **b** materials used for this. **2** a temporary conceptual framework used for constructing theories etc.

scag var. of SKAG.

scagliola /skalˈjəʊlə/ *n.* imitation stone or plaster mixed with glue. [Italian *scagliuola*, diminutive of *scaglia* SCALE[1]]

scalable /ˈskeɪləb(ə)l/ *adj.* **1** capable of being scaled or climbed. **2** *Computing* able to be used or produced at different ranges of size, capability, etc. □ **scalability** /-ˈbɪlɪti/ *n.*

scalar /ˈskeɪlə/ *adj.* & *n. Math.* & *Physics* ● *adj.* (of a quantity) having only magnitude, not direction. ● *n.* a scalar quantity (cf. VECTOR *n.* 1). [Latin *scalaris* from *scala* 'ladder'; see SCALE[3]]

scalawag var. of SCALLYWAG.

scald[1] /skɔːld/ *v.* & *n.* ● *v.tr.* **1** burn (the skin etc.) with hot liquid or steam. **2** heat (esp. milk) to near boiling point. **3** (usu. foll. by *out*) clean (a pan etc.) by rinsing with boiling water. **4** treat (poultry etc.) with boiling water to remove feathers etc. **5** (as **scalding** *adj.*) produce an effect or sensation like that of scalding (*scalding tears*; *scalding truths*). ● *n.* **1** a burn etc. caused by scalding. **2** a disease of fruit marked by browning etc., caused esp. by air pollution etc. □ **like a scalded cat** moving unusually fast. [Middle English via Anglo-French, Old Northern French *escalder*, Old French *eschalder* from Late Latin *excaldare* (as EX-[1], Latin *calidus* 'hot')]

scald[2] var. of SKALD.

scale[1] /skeɪl/ *n.* & *v.* ● *n.* **1** each of the small thin bony or horny overlapping plates protecting the skin of fish and reptiles. **2** something resembling a fish scale, esp.: **a** a pod or husk. **b** a flake of skin; a scab. **c** a rudimentary leaf, feather, or bract. **d** each of the structures covering the wings of butterflies and moths. **e** *Bot.* a layer of a bulb. **3 a** a flake formed on the surface of rusty iron. **b** a thick white deposit formed in a kettle, boiler, etc. by the action of heat on water. **4** plaque formed on teeth. ● *v.* **1** *tr.* remove scale or scales from (fish, nuts, iron, etc.). **2** *tr.* remove plaque from (teeth) by scraping. **3** *intr.* **a** (of skin, metal, etc.) form, come off in, or drop, scales. **b** (usu. foll. by *off*) (of scales) come off. □ **scales fall from a person's eyes** a person is no longer deceived (cf. Acts 9:18). □ **scaled** *adj.* (also in *comb.*). **scaleless** /ˈskeɪllɪs/ *adj.* **scaler** *n.* [Middle English via Old French *escale* from Germanic: related to SCALE[2]]

scale[2] /skeɪl/ *n.* & *v.* ● *n.* **1 a** (often in *pl.*) a weighing machine or device (*bathroom scales*). **b** (also **scale-pan**) each of the dishes on a simple scale balance. **2** (**the Scales**) the zodiacal sign or constellation Libra. ● *v.tr.* (of something weighed) show (a specified weight) in the scales. □ **throw into the scale** cause to be a factor in a contest, debate, etc. **tip** (or **turn**) **the scales 1** (usu. foll. by *at*) outweigh the opposite scale-pan (at a specified weight); weigh. **2** (of a motive, circumstance, etc.) be decisive. [Middle English via Old Norse *skál* 'bowl' from Germanic]

scale[3] /skeɪl/ *n.* & *v.* ● *n.* **1** a series of degrees; a graded classification system (*pay fees according to a prescribed scale*; *high on the social scale*; *seven points on the Richter scale*). **2 a** (often *attrib.*) *Geog.* & *Archit.* a ratio of size in a map, model, picture, etc. (*on a scale of one centimetre to the kilometre*; *a scale model*). **b** relative dimensions or degree (*generosity on a grand scale*). **3** *Mus.* an arrangement of the notes in any system of music in ascending or descending order of pitch (*chromatic scale*; *major scale*). **4 a** a set of marks on a line used in measuring, reducing, enlarging, etc. **b** a rule determining the distances between these. **c** a piece of metal, apparatus, etc. on which these are marked. **5** (in full **scale of notation**) *Math.* the ratio between units in a numerical system (*decimal scale*). ● *v.* **1** *tr.* **a** (also *absol.*) climb (a wall, height, etc.) esp. with a ladder. **b** climb (the social scale, heights of ambition, etc.). **2** *tr.* represent in proportional dimensions; reduce to a common scale. **3** *intr.* (of quantities etc.) have a common scale; be commensurable. □ **in scale** (of drawing etc.) in proportion to the surroundings etc. **play** (or **sing**) **scales** *Mus.* perform the notes of a scale as an exercise for the fingers or voice. **scale down** make smaller in proportion; reduce in size. **scale up** make larger in proportion; increase in size. **to scale** with a uniform reduction or enlargement. □ **scaler** *n.* [the noun Middle English, in the sense 'ladder', from Latin *scala*: the verb Middle English via Old French *escaler* or medieval Latin *scalare* from Latin *scala* 'ladder, staircase', related to *scandere* 'climb']

scale armour *n. hist.* armour formed of metal scales attached to leather etc.

scale-board *n.* very thin wood used for the back of a mirror, picture, etc.

scale-bug *n.* = SCALE INSECT.

scale-fern *n.* any of various spleenworts, esp. *Asplenium ceterach.*

scale insect *n.* a homopterous bug of the family Coccidae, clinging to plants and secreting a shieldlike scale as covering.

scale-leaf *n.* a modified leaf resembling a scale.

scale-moss *n.* a type of liverwort with scalelike leaves.

scalene /ˈskeɪliːn/ *adj.* & *n.* ● *adj.* (esp. of a triangle) having sides unequal in length. ● *n.* **1** (in full **scalene muscle**) = SCALENUS. **2** a scalene triangle. [Late Latin *scalenus* from Greek *skalēnos* 'unequal', related to *skolios* 'bent']

scalene cone *n.* (also **scalene cylinder**) a cone (or cylinder) with the axis not perpendicular to the base.

scalenus /skəˈliːnəs/ *n.* (*pl.* **scaleni** /-nʌɪ/) any of several muscles extending from the neck to the first and second ribs. [modern Latin: see SCALENE]

scale of notation see SCALE[3] *n.* 5.

scale-winged *adj.* lepidopterous.

scale work *n.* work, ornament, etc., consisting of an overlapping arrangement.

scaling-ladder *n. hist.* a ladder used to climb esp. fortress walls, esp. to break a siege.

scallawag var. of SCALLYWAG.

scallion /ˈskalɪən/ *n.* a shallot or spring onion; any long-necked onion with a small bulb. [Middle English from Anglo-French *scal(o)un* = Old French *escalo(i)gne*, ultimately from Latin *Ascalonia* (*caepa*) '(onion) of *Ascalon*', a port in ancient Palestine]

scallop /ˈskɒləp, ˈskaləp/ *n.* & *v.* (also **scollop** /ˈskɒl-/) ● *n.* **1** any of various bivalve molluscs of the family Pectinidae, esp. of the genus *Chlamys* or *Pecten*, used as food. **2** (in full **scallop shell**) **a** a single valve from the shell of a scallop, with grooves and ridges radiating from the middle of the hinge and edged with small rounded lobes, often used for cooking or serving food. **b** *hist.* a representation of this shell worn as a pilgrim's badge. **3** (in *pl.*) an ornamental edging cut in material in imitation of the edge of a scallop shell. **4** a small pan or dish shaped like a scallop shell and used for baking or serving food. **5** = ESCALOPE. ● *v.tr.* (**scalloped, scalloping**) **1 a** ornament (an edge or material) with scallops or scalloping. **b** cut or shape in the form of a scallop. **2** cook in a scallop. □ **scalloper** *n.* **scalloping** *n.* (in sense 3 of *n.*). [Middle English from Old French *escalope*, probably from Germanic]

scallywag /ˈskalɪwag/ *n.* (also **scalawag, scallawag** /ˈskalə-/) a scamp; a rascal. [19th-c. US slang: origin unknown]

scalp /skalp/ *n.* & *v.* ● *n.* **1** the skin covering the top of the head, with the hair etc. attached. **2 a** *hist.* the scalp of an enemy cut or torn away as a trophy by an American Indian. **b** a trophy or symbol of triumph, conquest, etc. **3** *Sc.* a bare rock projecting above water etc. ● *v.tr.* **1** *hist.* take the scalp of (an enemy). **2** criticize savagely. **3** *US* defeat; humiliate. **4** *N. Amer. colloq.* resell (shares, tickets, etc.) at a high or quick profit. □ **scalpless** *adj.* [Middle English, probably of Scandinavian origin]

scalpel /ˈskalp(ə)l/ *n.* a surgeon's small sharp knife shaped for holding like a pen. [French *scalpel* or Latin *scalpellum*, diminutive of *scalprum* 'chisel', from *scalpere* 'scratch']

scalper /ˈskalpə/ *n.* **1** a person or thing that scalps (esp. in sense 4 of SCALP *v.*). **2** (also **scauper, scorper** /ˈskɔːpə/) an engraver's tool for hollowing out woodcut or linocut designs. [SCALP + -ER[1]: sense 2 also from Latin *scalper* 'cutting tool', from *scalpere* 'carve']

scaly /'skeɪli/ *adj.* (**scalier**, **scaliest**) covered in or having many scales or flakes. ▫ **scaliness** *n.*

scam /skam/ *n. & v.* ● *n. US slang* **1** a trick or swindle; a fraud. **2** a story or rumour. ● *v.* (**scammed**, **scamming**) **1** *intr.* commit fraud. **2** *tr.* swindle. ▫ **scammer** *n.* [20th c.: origin unknown]

scammony /'skaməni/ *n.* (*pl.* **-ies**) an Asian plant, *Convolvulus scammonia*, bearing white or pink flowers, the dried roots of which are used as a purgative. [Middle English via Old French *scamonee, escamonie* or Latin *scammonia* from Greek *skammōnia*]

scamp[1] /skamp/ *n. colloq.* a rascal; a rogue. ▫ **scampish** *adj.* [*scamp* 'rob on highway', probably via Middle Dutch *schampen* 'decamp' from Old French *esc(h)amper* (as EX-[1], Latin *campus* 'field')]

scamp[2] /skamp/ *v.tr.* do (work etc.) in a perfunctory or inadequate way. [perhaps formed as SCAMP[1]: cf. SKIMP]

scamper /'skampə/ *v. & n.* ● *v.intr.* (usu. foll. by *about, through*) run and skip impulsively or playfully. ● *n.* the act or an instance of scampering. [earlier = run away, decamp: probably as SCAMP[1]]

scampi /'skampi/ *n.pl.* **1** Norway lobsters. **2** (often treated as *sing.*) a dish of these, usu. fried. [Italian]

scan /skan/ *v. & n.* ● *v.* (**scanned**, **scanning**) **1** *tr.* look at intently or quickly (*scanned the horizon*; *scanned the speech for errors*). **2** *intr.* (of a verse etc.) be metrically correct; be capable of being recited etc. metrically (*this line doesn't scan*). **3** *tr.* **a** examine all parts of (a surface etc.) to detect radioactivity etc. **b** cause (a particular region) to be traversed by a radar etc. beam. **4** *tr.* resolve (a picture) into its elements of light and shade in a pre-arranged pattern for the purposes esp. of television transmission. **5** *tr.* test the metre of (a line of verse etc.) by reading with the emphasis on its rhythm, or by examining the number of feet etc. **6** *tr.* **a** make a scan of (the body or part of it). **b** examine (a patient etc.) with a scanner. ● *n.* **1** the act or an instance of scanning. **2** an image obtained by scanning or with a scanner. ▫ **scannable** *adj.* [Middle English from Latin *scandere* 'climb': in Late Latin = scan (verses), with allusion to the raising of one's foot in marking rhythm]

scandal /'skand(ə)l/ *n.* **1 a** a thing or a person causing general public outrage or indignation. **b** the outrage etc. so caused, esp. as a subject of common talk. **c** malicious gossip or backbiting. **2** *Law* a public affront, esp. an irrelevant abusive statement in court. ▫ **scandalous** *adj.* **scandalously** *adv.* **scandalousness** *n.* [earlier = an obstacle to faith, discredit to religion from the bad behaviour of a religious person: Middle English via Old French *scandale* and ecclesiastical Latin *scandalum* from Greek *skandalon* 'snare, stumbling block']

scandalize /'skand(ə)lʌɪz/ *v.tr.* (also **-ise**) offend the moral feelings, sensibilities, etc. of; shock. [Middle English in the sense 'make a scandal of', via French *scandaliser* or ecclesiastical Latin *scandaliso* from Greek *skandalizō* (as SCANDAL)]

scandalmonger /'skand(ə)lmʌŋgə/ *n.* a person who spreads malicious scandal.

scandal sheet *n. derog.* a newspaper etc. giving prominence to esp. malicious gossip.

Scandinavian /skandɪ'neɪvɪən/ *n. & adj.* ● *n.* **1 a** a native or inhabitant of Scandinavia (Denmark, Norway, Sweden, and Iceland). **b** a person of Scandinavian descent. **2** the family of languages of Scandinavia. ● *adj.* of or relating to Scandinavia or its people or languages. [Latin *Scandinavia*]

scandium /'skandɪəm/ *n. Chem.* a rare soft silver-white metallic element occurring naturally in lanthanide ores (symbol **Sc**). [modern Latin from *Scandia*, contraction of *Scandinavia* (source of the minerals containing it)]

scannable see SCAN.

scanner /'skanə/ *n.* **1** a device for scanning, systematically examining, reading, or monitoring something. **2** a machine for measuring the intensity of radiation, ultrasound reflections, etc., from the body as a diagnostic aid. **3** a person who scans or examines critically. **4** a person who scans verse.

scanning electron microscope *n.* an electron microscope in which the surface of a specimen is scanned by a beam of electrons which are reflected to form an image (abbr.: **SEM**).

scansion /'skanʃ(ə)n/ *n.* **1** the metrical scanning of verse. **2** the way a verse etc. scans. [Latin *scansio* from *scandere scans-* 'climb': cf. SCAN]

scant /skant/ *adj. & v.* ● *adj.* barely sufficient; deficient (*with scant regard for the truth*; *scant of breath*). ● *v.tr. archaic* provide (a supply, material, a person, etc.) grudgingly; skimp; stint. ▫ **scantly** *adv.* **scantness** *n.* [Middle English from Old Norse *skamt*, neut. of *skammr* 'short']

scantling /'skantlɪŋ/ *n.* **1 a** a timber beam of small cross-section. **b** a size to which a stone or timber is to be cut. **2** a set of standard dimensions for parts of a structure, esp. in shipbuilding. **3** (usu. foll. by *of*) *archaic* **a** a specimen or sample. **b** one's necessary supply; a modicum or small amount. [alteration suggested by -LING[1] from obsolete *scantlon*, from Old French *escantillon* 'sample']

scanty /'skanti/ *adj.* (**scantier**, **scantiest**) **1** of small extent or amount. **2** meagre; barely sufficient. ▫ **scantily** *adv.* **scantiness** *n.* [obsolete *scant* 'scanty supply' from Old Norse *skamt* neut. adj.: see SCANT]

scape /skeɪp/ *n.* **1** a long flower stalk coming directly from the root. **2** the base of an insect's antenna. [Latin *scapus* from Greek *skapos*, related to SCEPTRE]

-scape /skeɪp/ *comb. form* forming nouns denoting a view or a representation of a view (*moonscape*; *seascape*). [on the pattern of LANDSCAPE]

scapegoat /'skeɪpgəʊt/ *n. & v.* ● *n.* **1** a person bearing the blame for the sins, shortcomings, etc. of others, esp. as an expedient. **2** *Bibl.* a goat sent into the wilderness after the Jewish chief priest had symbolically laid the sins of the people upon it (Lev. 16). ● *v.tr.* make a scapegoat of. ▫ **scapegoater** *n.* [*scape* (archaic, = escape) + GOAT, = the goat that escapes]

scapegrace /'skeɪpgreɪs/ *n.* a rascal; a scamp, esp. a young person or child. [literally, a person who escapes the grace of God: from *scape* (as SCAPEGOAT) + GRACE]

scaphoid /'skafɔɪd/ *adj. & n. Anat.* = NAVICULAR. [modern Latin *scaphoides* from Greek *skaphoeidēs*, from *skaphos* 'boat']

scapula /'skapjʊlə/ *n.* (*pl.* **scapulae** /-liː/ or **scapulas**) the shoulder blade. [Late Latin, sing. of Latin *scapulae*]

scapular /'skapjʊlə/ *adj. & n.* ● *adj.* of or relating to the shoulder or shoulder blade. ● *n.* **1 a** a monastic short cloak covering the shoulders. **b** a symbol of affiliation to an ecclesiastical order, consisting of two strips of cloth hanging down the breast and back and joined across the shoulders. **2** a bandage for or over the shoulders. **3** a scapular feather. [the adj. from SCAPULA: the noun from Late Latin *scapulare* (as SCAPULA)]

scapular feather *n.* a feather covering the shoulder, growing above where the wing joins the body.

scapulary /'skapjʊləri/ *n.* (*pl.* **-ies**) **1** = SCAPULAR *n.* 1. **2** = SCAPULAR *n.* 3. [Middle English via Old French *eschapeloyre* from medieval Latin *scapelorium*, *scapularium* (as SCAPULA)]

scar[1] /skɑː/ *n. & v.* ● *n.* **1** a usu. permanent mark on the skin left after the healing of a wound, burn, or sore. **2** the lasting effect of grief etc. on a person's character or disposition. **3** a mark left by damage etc. (*the table bore many scars*). **4** a mark left at the point of separation of a leaf etc. from a plant. ● *v.* (**scarred**, **scarring**) **1** *tr.* (esp. as **scarred** *adj.*) mark with a scar or scars (*was scarred for life*). **2** *intr.* heal over; form a scar. **3** *tr.* form a scar on. ▫ **scarless** *adj.* [Middle English via Old French *eschar(r)e* and Late Latin *eschara* from Greek *eskhara* 'scab']

scar[2] /skɑː/ *n.* (also **scaur** /skɔː/) a steep craggy outcrop of a mountain or cliff. [Middle English from Old Norse *sker* 'low reef in the sea']

scarab /ˈskarəb/ *n.* **1 a** a large dung-beetle, *Scarabaeus sacer*, regarded as sacred in ancient Egypt. **b** = SCARABAEID. **2** an ancient Egyptian gem cut in the form of a beetle and engraved with symbols on its flat side, used as a signet etc. [Latin *scarabaeus* from Greek *skarabeios*]

scarabaeid /skarəˈbiːɪd/ *n.* any beetle of the family Scarabaeidae, including the dung-beetle, cockchafer, etc. [modern Latin *Scarabaeidae* (as SCARAB)]

scaramouch /ˈskarəmaʊtʃ, -muːtʃ/ *n. archaic* a boastful coward; a braggart. [Italian *Scaramuccia*, the name of a stock character in Italian farce, from *scaramuccia* = SKIRMISH, influenced by French form *Scaramouche*]

scarce /skɛːs/ *adj. & adv.* ● *adj.* **1** (usu. *predic.*) (esp. of food, money, etc.) insufficient for the demand; scanty. **2** hard to find; rare. ● *adv. archaic* or *literary* scarcely. □ **make oneself scarce** *colloq.* keep out of the way; surreptitiously disappear. □ **scarceness** *n.* [Middle English via Anglo-French & Old Northern French *(e)scars*, Old French *eschars* from Latin *excerpere*: see EXCERPT]

scarcely /ˈskɛːsli/ *adv.* **1** barely; only just (*I scarcely know him*). **2** surely not (*he can scarcely have said so*). **3** a mild, apologetic, or ironical substitute for 'not' (*I scarcely expected to be insulted*).

scarcity /ˈskɛːsɪti/ *n.* (*pl.* **-ies**) (often foll. by *of*) a lack or inadequacy, esp. of food.

scare /skɛː/ *v. & n.* ● *v.* **1** *tr.* frighten, esp. suddenly (*his expression scared us*). **2** *tr.* (as **scared** *adj.*) (usu. foll. by *of*, or *to* + infin.) frightened; terrified (*scared of his own shadow*). **3** *tr.* (usu. foll. by *away*, *off*, *up*, etc.) drive away by frightening. **4** *intr.* become scared (*they don't scare easily*). ● *n.* **1** a sudden attack of fright (*gave me a scare*). **2** a general, esp. baseless, fear of war, invasion, epidemic, etc. (*a measles scare*). **3** a financial panic causing share-selling etc. □ **scare up** (or **out**) esp. *N. Amer.* **1** frighten (game etc.) out of cover. **2** *colloq.* manage to find; discover (*see if we can scare up a meal*). □ **scarer** *n.* [Middle English *skerre* from Old Norse *skirra* 'frighten', from *skjarr* 'timid']

scarecrow /ˈskɛːkrəʊ/ *n.* **1** an object resembling a human figure dressed in old clothes and set up in a field to scare birds away. **2** *colloq.* a badly dressed, grotesque-looking, or very thin person. **3** *archaic* an object of baseless fear.

scaredy-cat /ˈskɛːdɪkat/ *n. colloq.* a timid person.

scaremonger /ˈskɛːmʌŋgə/ *n.* a person who spreads frightening reports or rumours. □ **scaremongering** *n.*

scarf[1] /skɑːf/ *n.* (*pl.* **scarves** /skɑːvz/ or **scarfs**) a square, triangular, or esp. long narrow strip of material worn round the neck, over the shoulders, or tied round the head (of a woman), for warmth or ornament. □ **scarfed** *adj.* [probably an alteration of *scarp* (influenced by SCARF[2]) from Old Northern French *escarpe* = Old French *escherpe* 'sash']

scarf[2] /skɑːf/ *v. & n.* ● *v.tr.* **1** join the ends of (pieces of esp. timber, metal, or leather) by bevelling or notching them to fit and then bolting, brazing, or sewing them together. **2** cut the blubber of (a whale). ● *n.* **1** a joint made by scarfing. **2** a cut on a whale made by scarfing. [Middle English (earlier as noun), probably via Old French from Old Norse]

scarf[3] /skɑːf/ *v.tr.* (often foll. by *down*) *N. Amer. colloq.* eat or drink greedily. [variant of SCOFF[2]]

scarf pin *n. Brit.* an ornamental pin for fastening a scarf.

scarf ring *n. Brit.* an ornamental ring through which the ends or corners of a scarf are threaded and held in position.

scarf-skin *n.* the outermost layer of the skin constantly scaling off, esp. that at the base of the nails.

scarifier /ˈskarɪfʌɪə, ˈskɛːrɪ-/ *n.* **1** an implement for cutting and removing debris from the turf of a lawn. **2** a spiked road-breaking machine. **3** esp. *Austral.* a machine with prongs for loosening soil without turning it. [SCARIFY[1]]

scarify[1] /ˈskarɪfʌɪ, ˈskɛːrɪ-/ *v.tr.* (**-ies**, **-ied**) **1 a** make superficial incisions in. **b** cut off skin from. **2** hurt by severe criticism etc. **3** cut and remove (debris from a lawn) with a scarifier. **4** esp. *Austral.* loosen (soil) with a scarifier. □ **scarification** /-fɪˈkeɪʃ(ə)n/ *n.* [Middle English from Old French *scarifier* via Late Latin *scarificare* and Latin *scarifare* from Greek *skariphaomai*, from *skariphos* 'stylus']

scarify[2] /ˈskɛːrɪfʌɪ/ *v.tr. & intr.* (**-ies**, **-ied**) *colloq.* scare; terrify. [formed irregularly from SCARE *v.* + -I- + -FY, perhaps on the pattern of TERRIFY]

scarious /ˈskɛːrɪəs/ *adj.* (of a part of a plant etc.) having a dry membranous appearance; thin and brittle. [French *scarieux* or modern Latin *scariosus*]

scarlatina /skɑːləˈtiːnə/ *n.* = SCARLET FEVER. [modern Latin from Italian *scarlattina* (*febbre* 'fever'), diminutive of *scarlatto* SCARLET]

scarlet /ˈskɑːlɪt/ *n. & adj.* ● *n.* **1** a brilliant red colour tinged with orange. **2** clothes or material of this colour (*dressed in scarlet*). ● *adj.* of a scarlet colour. [Middle English from Old French *escarlate*: ultimate origin unknown]

scarlet fever *n.* an infectious bacterial disease affecting esp. children, and causing fever and a scarlet rash.

scarlet hat *n. RC Ch.* a cardinal's hat as a symbol of rank.

scarlet pimpernel *n.* a small annual wild plant, *Anagallis arvensis*, with small esp. scarlet flowers closing in rainy or cloudy weather: also called POOR MAN'S WEATHER-GLASS.

scarlet rash *n.* = ROSEOLA 1.

scarlet runner *n.* esp. *Brit.* **1** a runner bean. **2** a scarlet-flowered climber bearing this bean.

scarlet woman *n. derog.* a notoriously promiscuous woman, a prostitute.

scaroid /ˈskarɔɪd, ˈskɛː-/ *n. & adj.* ● *n.* any colourful marine fish of the family Scaridae, native to tropical and temperate seas, including the scarus. ● *adj.* of or relating to this family.

scarp /skɑːp/ *n. & v.* ● *n.* **1** the inner wall or slope of a ditch in a fortification (cf. COUNTERSCARP). **2** a steep slope. ● *v.tr.* **1** make (a slope) perpendicular or steep. **2** provide (a ditch) with a steep scarp and counterscarp. **3** (as **scarped** *adj.*) (of a hillside etc.) steep; precipitous. [Italian *scarpa*]

scarper /ˈskɑːpə/ *v.intr. Brit. slang* run away; escape. [probably from Italian *scappare* 'escape', influenced by rhyming slang *Scapa Flow* 'go']

Scart /skɑːt/ *n.* (also **SCART**) (usu. *attrib.*) a 24-pin socket used to connect video equipment (*Scart socket*; *Scart connector*). [acronym from *S*yndicat des *C*onstructeurs des *A*ppareils *R*adiorécepteurs et *T*éléviseurs, the designers]

scarus /ˈskɛːrəs/ *n.* any fish of the genus *Scarus*, with brightly coloured scales, and teeth fused to form a parrot-like beak used for eating coral. Also called PARROTFISH. [Latin from Greek *skaros*]

scarves *pl.* of SCARF[1].

scary /ˈskɛːri/ *adj.* (**scarier**, **scariest**) *colloq.* scaring, frightening. □ **scarily** *adv.* **scariness** *n.*

scat[1] /skat/ *v. & int. colloq.* ● *v.intr.* (**scatted**, **scatting**) depart quickly. ● *int.* go! [perhaps abbreviation of SCATTER]

scat[2] /skat/ *n. & v.* ● *n.* improvised jazz singing using sounds imitating instruments, instead of words (cf. VOCALESE). ● *v.intr.* (**scatted**, **scatting**) sing scat. [probably imitative]

scat[3] /skat/ *n.* **1** excrement. **2** the droppings of an animal, esp a carnivore. [Greek *skōr skatos* 'dung']

scathe /skeɪð/ *v. & n.* ● *v.tr.* **1** *poet.* injure esp. by blasting or withering. **2** (as **scathing** *adj.*) witheringly scornful (*scathing sarcasm*). **3** (with *neg.*) do the least harm to (*shall not be scathed*) (cf. UNSCATHED). ● *n.* (usu. with *neg.*) *archaic* harm; injury (*without scathe*). □ **scatheless** *predic.adj.* **scathingly** *adv.* [the verb Middle English from Old Norse *skatha* = Old English *sceathian*: the noun Old English from Old Norse *skathi* = Old English *sceatha* 'malefactor, injury', from Germanic]

scatology /ska'tɒlədʒi/ *n.* **1 a** a morbid interest in excrement. **b** a preoccupation with obscene literature, esp. that concerned with the excretory functions. **c** such literature. **2** the study of fossilized dung. **3** the study of excrement for esp. diagnosis. □ **scatological** /-tə'lɒdʒɪk(ə)l/ *adj.* [Greek *skōr skatos* 'dung' + -LOGY]

scatophagous /ska'tɒfəgəs/ *adj.* feeding on dung. [as SCATOLOGY + Greek *-phagos* '-eating']

scatter /'skatə/ *v.* & *n.* ● *v.* **1** *tr.* **a** throw here and there; strew (*scattered gravel on the road*). **b** cover by scattering (*scattered the road with gravel*). **2** *tr.* & *intr.* **a** move or cause to move in flight etc.; disperse (*scattered to safety at the sound*). **b** disperse or cause (hopes, clouds, etc.) to disperse. **3** *tr.* (as **scattered** *adj.*) not clustered together; wide apart; sporadic (*scattered villages*). **4** *tr. Physics* deflect or diffuse (light, particles, etc.). **5 a** *intr.* (of esp. a shotgun) fire a charge of shot diffusely. **b** *tr.* fire (a charge) in this way. ● *n.* **1** the act or an instance of scattering. **2** a small amount scattered. **3** the extent of distribution of esp. shot. □ **scatterer** *n.* [Middle English, probably a variant of SHATTER]

scatterbrain /'skatəbreɪn/ *n.* a person given to silly or disorganized thought with lack of concentration. □ **scatterbrained** *adj.*

scatter cushion *n.* (also **scatter rug** etc.) any of a number of small cushions, rugs, etc., placed here and there for effect.

scatter diagram *n.* (also **scatter plot**) *Statistics* a graph in which the values of two variables are plotted along two axes, the pattern of the resulting points revealing any correlation present.

scatter-gun *n.* & *adj.* esp. *N. Amer.* ● *n.* a shot gun. ● *adj.* = SCATTERSHOT.

scattershot /'skatəʃɒt/ *adj.* esp. *N. Amer.* random, haphazard.

scatty /'skati/ *adj.* (**scattier**, **scattiest**) *Brit. colloq.* scatterbrained; disorganized. □ **scattily** *adv.* **scattiness** *n.* [abbreviation]

scaup /skɔːp/ *n.* any diving duck of the genus *Aythya*. [*scaup*, Scots variant of *scalp* 'mussel-bed', which it frequents (probably related to SCALP)]

scauper var. of SCALPER 2.

scaur var. of SCAR².

scavenge /'skavɪn(d)ʒ/ *v.* & *n.* ● *v.* **1** *tr.* & *intr.* (usu. foll. by *for*) search for and collect (discarded items). **2** *intr.* (foll. by *on*) (of an animal or bird) feed on (carrion). **3** *tr.* remove unwanted products from (an internal-combustion engine cylinder etc.). ● *n.* the action or process of scavenging. [back-formation from SCAVENGER]

scavenger /'skavɪn(d)ʒə/ *n.* **1** a person who seeks and collects discarded items. **2** an animal feeding on carrion, refuse, etc. **3** *Brit. archaic* a person employed to clean the streets etc. □ **scavengery** *n.* [Middle English *scavager* from Anglo-French *scawager* from *scawage*, via Old Northern French *escauwer* 'inspect' from Flemish *scauwen*, related to SHOW: for *-n-* cf. MESSENGER]

scazon /'skeɪz(ə)n, 'ska-/ *n. Prosody* a modification of the iambic trimeter, in which a spondee or trochee takes the place of the final iambus. [Latin from Greek *skazōn*, from *skazō* 'limp']

Sc.D. *abbr.* Doctor of Science. [Latin *scientiae doctor*]

SCE *abbr.* Scottish Certificate of Education.

scena /'ʃeɪnɑː, Italian 'ʃɛːna/ *n. Mus.* **1** a scene or part of an opera. **2** an elaborate dramatic solo usu. including recitative. [Italian from Latin: see SCENE]

scenario /sɪ'nɑːrɪəʊ/ *n.* (*pl.* **-os**) **1** an outline of the plot of a play, film, opera, etc., with details of the scenes, situations, etc. **2** a postulated sequence of imagined (usu. future) events (*in a different scenario, suppose the pressure had built up and eroded the seal*). □ **scenarist** *n.* (in sense 1). [Italian from Latin *scena*: see SCENE]

■ **Usage** The use of *scenario* in sense 2 is valid when a detailed sequence of events that might come about under certain conditions is denoted. It should not be used in standard English as a loose synonym for 'situation' or 'scene', as in *it was an unpleasant scenario.*

scend /sɛnd/ *n.* & *v. Naut.* ● *n.* **1** the impulse given by a wave or waves (*scend of the sea*). **2** a plunge of a vessel. ● *v.intr.* (of a vessel) plunge or pitch owing to the impulse of a wave. [alteration of SEND or DESCEND]

scene /siːn/ *n.* **1** a place in which events in real life, drama, or fiction occur; the locality of an event etc. (*the scene was set in India*; *the scene of the disaster*). **2 a** an incident in real life, fiction, etc. (*distressing scenes occurred*). **b** a description or representation of an incident etc. (*scenes of clerical life*). **3** a public incident displaying emotion, temper, etc., esp. when embarrassing to others (*made a scene in the restaurant*). **4 a** a continuous portion of a play in a fixed setting and usu. without a change of personnel; a subdivision of an act. **b** a similar section of a film, book, etc. **5 a** any of the pieces of scenery used in a play. **b** these collectively. **6** a landscape or a view (*a desolate scene*). **7** *colloq.* **a** an area of action or interest (*not my scene*). **b** a way of life; a milieu (*well known on the jazz scene*). **8** *archaic* the stage of a theatre. □ **behind the scenes 1** *Theatr.* among the actors, scenery, etc. off stage. **2** unknown to the public; secretly. **behind-the-scenes** (*attrib.*) secret, using secret information (*a behind-the-scenes investigation*). **change of scene** a move to different surroundings esp. through travel. **come on** (or *colloq.* **hit** or *US* **make**) **the scene** arrive; appear. **quit the scene** die; leave. **set the scene 1** describe the location of events. **2** give preliminary information. [Latin *scena* from Greek *skēnē* 'tent, stage']

scene-dock *n.* a space for storing scenery near the stage.

scenery /'siːn(ə)ri/ *n.* **1** the general appearance of the natural features of a landscape, esp. when picturesque. **2** *Theatr.* the painted representations of landscape, rooms, etc., used as the background in a play etc. □ **change of scenery** = *change of scene* (see SCENE). [earlier *scenary* from Italian SCENARIO: assimilated to -ERY]

scene-shifter *n.* esp. *Brit.* a person who moves scenery in a theatre. □ **scene shifting** *n.*

scenic /'siːnɪk/ *adj.* **1 a** picturesque; impressive or beautiful (*took the scenic route*). **b** of or concerning natural scenery (*flatness is the main scenic feature*). **2** (of a picture etc.) representing an incident. **3** *Theatr.* of or on the stage (*scenic performances*). □ **scenically** *adv.* [Latin *scenicus* from Greek *skēnikos* 'of the stage' (as SCENE)]

scenic railway *n.* **1** a miniature railway running through artificial scenery at funfairs etc. **2** *Brit.* = BIG DIPPER 1.

scenography /siː'nɒgrəfi/ *n.* **1** the painting or design of theatrical scenery. **2** *Art* the representation of objects in perspective. □ **scenographer** *n.* [French *scénographie* or Latin *scenographia* from Greek *skēnographia* 'scene-painting', from *skēnē* (see SCENE)]

scent /sɛnt/ *n.* & *v.* ● *n.* **1** a distinctive, esp. pleasant, smell (*the scent of spring flowers*). **2 a** a scent trail left by an animal perceptible to hounds etc. **b** clues etc. that can be followed like a scent trail (*lost the scent in Paris*). **c** the power of detecting or distinguishing smells etc. or of discovering things (*some dogs have little scent*; *the scent for talent*). **3** *Brit.* = PERFUME 2. **4** a trail laid in a paperchase. ● *v.* **1** *tr.* **a** discern by scent (*the dog scented game*). **b** sense the presence of; detect (*scent treachery*).

2 *tr.* make fragrant or foul-smelling. **3** *tr.* (as **scented** *adj.*) having esp. a pleasant smell (*scented soap*). **4** *tr.* apply the sense of smell to (*scented the air*). ▫ **on the scent** in possession of a useful clue in an investigation. **put** (or **throw**) **off the scent** deceive by false clues etc. **scent out** discover by smelling or searching. ▫ **scentless** *adj.* [Middle English *sent* via Old French *sentir* 'perceive, smell' from Latin *sentire*: the *-c-* (added in 17th c.) is unexplained]

scent-bag *n.* a bag of aniseed etc. used to lay a trail in drag-hunting.

scent gland *n.* (also **scent organ**) a gland in some animals secreting musk, civet, etc.

scepter *US* var. of SCEPTRE.

sceptic /ˈskɛptɪk/ *n.* & *adj.* (*US* **skeptic**) ● *n.* **1** a person inclined to doubt all accepted opinions; a cynic. **2** a person who doubts the truth of Christianity and other religions. **3** *hist.* a person who accepts the philosophy of Pyrrhonism. ● *adj.* = SCEPTICAL. ▫ **scepticism** /-sɪz(ə)m/ *n.* [French *sceptique* or Latin *scepticus* from Greek *skeptikos*, from *skepsis* 'inquiry, doubt']

sceptical /ˈskɛptɪk(ə)l/ *adj.* (*US* **skeptical**) **1** inclined to question the truth or soundness of accepted ideas, facts, etc.; critical; incredulous. **2** *Philos.* of or accepting the philosophy of Pyrrhonism, denying the possibility of knowledge. ▫ **sceptically** *adv.*

sceptre /ˈsɛptə/ *n.* (*US* **scepter**) **1** a staff borne esp. at a coronation as a symbol of sovereignty. **2** royal or imperial authority. ▫ **sceptred** *adj.* [Middle English via Old French (*s*)*ceptre* and Latin *sceptrum* from Greek *skēptron*, from *skēptō* 'lean on']

sch. *abbr.* **1** scholar. **2** school. **3** schooner.

schadenfreude /ˈʃɑːd(ə)nfrɔɪdə, German ʃɑːdənfrɔydə/ *n.* the malicious enjoyment of another's misfortunes. [German, from *Schaden* 'harm' + *Freude* 'joy']

schappe /ʃap, ˈʃapə/ *n.* fabric or yarn made from waste silk. [German, = waste silk]

schedule /ˈʃɛdjuːl, ˈskɛd-/ *n.* & *v.* ● *n.* **1 a** a list or plan of intended events, times, etc.; a timetable. **b** a plan of work (*not on my schedule for next week*). **2** any list, form, classification, or tabular statement, e.g. a list of rates or prices, a tabulated inventory, etc. **3** (with reference to the British income tax system) any of the forms (named 'A', 'B', etc.) issued for completion and relating to the various classes into which taxable income is divided. ● *v.tr.* **1** include in a schedule. **2** make a schedule of. **3** *Brit.* include (a building) in a list for preservation or protection. ▫ **according to** (or **on**) **schedule** as planned; on time. **behind schedule** behind time. ▫ **schedular** *adj.* **scheduler** *n.* [Middle English via Old French *cedule* from Late Latin *schedula* 'slip of paper', diminutive of *scheda* from Greek *skhedē* 'papyrus leaf']

scheduled flight *n.* (also **scheduled service** etc.) a public flight, service, etc., according to a regular timetable.

scheduled territories *n.pl. hist.* = STERLING AREA.

scheelite /ˈʃiːlʌɪt/ *n. Mineral.* calcium tungstate in its mineral crystalline form. [named after K. W. *Scheele*, Swedish chemist d. 1786]

schema /ˈskiːmə/ *n.* (*pl.* **schemata** /-mətə/ or **schemas**) **1** a synopsis, outline, or diagram. **2** a proposed arrangement. **3** *Logic* a syllogistic figure. **4** (in Kantian philosophy) a conception of what is common to all members of a class; a general type or essential form. [Greek *skhēma -atos* 'form, figure']

schematic /skiːˈmatɪk, skɪ-/ *adj.* & *n.* ● *adj.* **1** of or concerning a scheme or schema. **2** representing objects by symbols etc. ● *n.* a schematic diagram, esp. of an electronic circuit. ▫ **schematically** *adv.*

schematism /ˈskiːmətɪz(ə)m/ *n.* a schematic arrangement or presentation. [modern Latin *schematismus* from Greek *skhēmatismos* (as SCHEMATIZE)]

schematize /ˈskiːmətʌɪz/ *v.tr.* (also **-ise**) **1** put in a schematic form; arrange. **2** represent by a scheme or schema. ▫ **schematization** /-ˈzeɪʃ(ə)n/ *n.*

scheme /skiːm/ *n.* & *v.* ● *n.* **1 a** a systematic plan or arrangement for work, action, etc. **b** a proposed or operational systematic arrangement (*a colour scheme*). **2** an artful or deceitful plot. **3** a timetable, outline, syllabus, etc. ● *v.* **1** *intr.* (often foll. by *for*, or *to* + infin.) plan esp. secretly or deceitfully; intrigue. **2** *tr.* plan to bring about, esp. artfully or deceitfully (*schemed their downfall*). ▫ **schemer** *n.* [Latin *schema* from Greek (as SCHEMA)]

scheming /ˈskiːmɪŋ/ *adj.* & *n.* ● *adj.* artful, cunning, or deceitful. ● *n.* plots; intrigues. ▫ **schemingly** *adv.*

schemozzle var. of SHEMOZZLE.

scherzando /skɛːtˈsandəʊ/ *adv.*, *adj.*, & *n. Mus.* ● *adv.* & *adj.* in a playful manner. ● *n.* (*pl.* **-os** or **scherzandi** /-di/) a passage played in this way. [Italian, gerund of *scherzare* 'to jest' (as SCHERZO)]

scherzo /ˈskɛːtsəʊ/ *n.* (*pl.* **-os** or **scherzi** /-tsi/) *Mus.* a vigorous, light, or playful composition, usu. as a movement in a symphony, sonata, etc. [Italian, literally 'jest']

schilling /ˈʃɪlɪŋ/ *n.* **1** the chief monetary unit of Austria. **2** a coin of this value. [German (as SHILLING)]

schipperke /ˈskɪpəki, ˈʃɪp-, -kə/ *n.* **1** a small black tailless dog of a breed with a ruff of fur round its neck. **2** this breed. [Dutch dialect, = little boatman, from its use as a watchdog on barges]

schism /ˈsɪz(ə)m, ˈskɪz(ə)m/ *n.* **1 a** the division of a group into opposing sections or parties. **b** any of the sections so formed. **2 a** the separation of a Church into two Churches or the secession of a group owing to doctrinal, disciplinary, etc., differences. **b** the offence of causing or promoting such a separation. [Middle English via Old French *s*(*c*)*isme* and ecclesiastical Latin *schisma* from Greek *skhisma -atos* 'cleft', from *skhizō* 'to split']

schismatic /sɪzˈmatɪk, skɪz-/ *adj.* & *n.* (also **schismatical**) ● *adj.* **1** of, concerning, or inclining to, schism. **2** *Eccl.* guilty of the offence of schism. ● *n.* **1** a holder of schismatic opinions. **2** a member of a schismatic faction or a seceded branch of a Church. ▫ **schismatically** *adv.* [Middle English via Old French *scismatique* and ecclesiastical Latin *schismaticus* from ecclesiastical Greek *skhismatikos* (as SCHISM)]

schist /ʃɪst/ *n.* a foliated metamorphic rock composed of layers of different minerals and splitting into thin irregular plates. ▫ **schistose** *adj.* [French *schiste* via Latin *schistos* from Greek *skhistos* 'split' (as SCHISM)]

schistosome /ˈʃɪstə(ʊ)səʊm/ *n.* a parasitic tropical flatworm of the genus *Schistosoma*, carried by freshwater snails and infesting the blood vessels of birds and mammals, causing bilharzia in humans. Also called *blood fluke*. [Greek *skhistos* 'divided' (as SCHISM) + *sōma* 'body']

schistosomiasis /ʃɪstə(ʊ)səˈmʌɪəsɪs/ *n.* = BILHARZIA 1. [modern Latin genus name *Schistosoma* (as SCHISTOSOME)]

schizanthus /skɪtˈsanθəs/ *n.* any plant of the genus *Schizanthus*, with showy flowers in various colours, and finely divided leaves. [modern Latin, from Greek *skhizō* 'to split' + *anthos* 'flower']

schizo /ˈskɪtsəʊ/ *adj.* & *n. colloq. offens.* ● *adj.* schizophrenic. ● *n.* (*pl.* **-os**) a schizophrenic. [abbreviation]

schizocarp /ˈskɪtsə(ʊ)kɑːp/ *n. Bot.* a dry fruit that splits into single-seeded parts when ripe. ▫ **schizocarpic** /-ˈkɑːpɪk/ *adj.* **schizocarpous** /-ˈkɑːpəs/ *adj.* [Greek *skhizō* 'to split' + *karpos* 'fruit']

schizoid /ˈskɪtsɔɪd, skɪdz-/ *adj.* & *n.* ● *adj.* **1** (of a person or personality etc.) tending to or resembling schizophrenia or a schizophrenic, but usu. without delusions. **2** having inconsistent or contradictory elements (*a schizoid musical arrangement*). ● *n.* a schizoid person.

schizophrenia /skɪtsə(ʊ)'fri:nɪə/ *n.* **1** a mental disease marked by a breakdown in the relation between thoughts, feelings, and actions, frequently accompanied by delusions and retreat from social life. **2** *colloq.* a mentality or approach characterized by inconsistent or contradictory elements (*political schizophrenia*). □ **schizophrenic** /-'frɛnɪk, -'fri:nɪk/ *adj. & n.* [modern Latin, from Greek *skhizō* 'to split' + *phrēn* 'mind']

schizothymia /skɪtsə(ʊ)'θʌɪmɪə/ *n. Psychol.* an introvert condition with a tendency to schizophrenia. □ **schizothymic** *adj.* [modern Latin (as SCHIZOPHRENIA + Greek *thumos* 'temper')]

schlemiel /ʃlə'mi:l/ *n. US colloq.* a foolish or unlucky person. [Yiddish *shlemiel*]

schlep /ʃlɛp/ *v. & n.* (also **schlepp**) *colloq.* ● *v.* (**schlepped, schlepping**) **1** *tr.* carry, drag. **2** *intr.* go or work tediously or effortfully. ● *n. US* **1** a tedious journey; a trek. **2** an inept or stupid person. [Yiddish *shlepn* from German *schleppen* 'drag']

schlieren /'ʃlɪərən/ *n.* **1** a visually discernible area or stratum of different density in a transparent medium. **2** *Geol.* an irregular streak of mineral in igneous rock. [German, pl. of *Schliere* 'streak']

schlock /ʃlɒk/ *n. N. Amer. colloq.* inferior goods; trash. [Yiddish *shlak* 'an apoplectic stroke', *schlog* 'wretch, untidy person, apoplectic stroke']

schlump /ʃlʊmp/ *n.* esp. *US slang* a slow or slovenly person; a slob, a fool. [apparently related to Yiddish *shlumperdik* 'dowdy' and German *Schlumpe* 'slattern']

schmaltz /ʃmɔ:lts, ʃmalts/ *n.* esp. *US colloq.* sentimentality, esp. in music, drama, etc. □ **schmaltzy** *adj.* (**schmaltzier, schmaltziest**). [Yiddish from German *Schmalz* 'dripping, lard']

schmuck /ʃmʌk/ *n.* esp. *US slang* a foolish or contemptible person. [Yiddish *shmok* 'penis']

schnapps /ʃnaps/ *n.* any of various strong spirits resembling genever gin. [German, = dram of liquor, from Low German & Dutch *snaps* 'mouthful' (as SNAP)]

schnauzer /'ʃnaʊtsə/ *n.* **1** a dog of a German breed with a close wiry coat and heavy whiskers round the muzzle. **2** this breed. [German from *Schnauze* 'muzzle, SNOUT']

schnitzel /'ʃnɪtz(ə)l/ *n.* an escalope of veal. [German, = slice]

schnorkel var. of SNORKEL.

schnorrer /'ʃnɒrə, 'ʃnɔ:rə/ *n.* esp. *US slang* a beggar or scrounger; a layabout. [Yiddish from German *Schnurrer*]

scholar /'skɒlə/ *n.* **1** a learned person, esp. in language, literature, etc.; an academic. **2** *Brit.* the holder of a scholarship. **3 a** a person with specified academic ability (*is a poor scholar*). **b** a person who learns (*am a scholar of life*). **4** *archaic colloq.* a person able to read and write. **5** *archaic* a schoolboy or schoolgirl. □ **scholarly** *adj.* **scholarliness** *n.* [Middle English via Old English *scol(i)ere* & Old French *escol(i)er* from Late Latin *scholaris*, from Latin *schola* SCHOOL[1]]

scholarship /'skɒləʃɪp/ *n.* **1 a** academic achievement; learning of a high level. **b** the methods and standards characteristic of a good scholar (*shows great scholarship*). **2** a payment from the funds of a school, university, local government, etc., to maintain a student in full-time education, awarded on the basis of scholarly achievement.

scholar's mate see MATE[2].

scholastic /skə'lastɪk/ *adj. & n.* ● *adj.* **1** of or concerning universities, schools, education, teachers, etc. **2** pedantic; formal (*shows scholastic precision*). **3** *Philos. hist.* of, resembling, or concerning the schoolmen, esp. in dealing with logical subtleties. ● *n.* **1** *Philos. hist.* a schoolman. **2** *hist.* a theologian of scholastic tendencies. **3** *RC Ch.* a member of any of several religious orders, who is between the novitiate and the priesthood. □ **scholastically** *adv.* **scholasticism** /-sɪz(ə)m/ *n.* [Latin *scholasticus* from Greek *skholastikos* 'studious', via *skholazō* 'be at leisure, devote one's leisure to study' from *skholē*: see SCHOOL[1]]

scholiast /'skəʊlɪast/ *n. hist.* an ancient or medieval scholar, esp. a grammarian, who annotated ancient literary texts. □ **scholiastic** /-'astɪk/ *adj.* [medieval Greek *skholiastēs* from *skholiazō* 'write scholia': see SCHOLIUM]

scholium /'skəʊlɪəm/ *n.* (*pl.* **scholia** /-lɪə/) a marginal note or explanatory comment, esp. by an ancient grammarian on a classical text. [modern Latin from Greek *skholion*, from *skholē*: see SCHOOL[1]]

school[1] /sku:l/ *n. & v.* ● *n.* **1 a** an institution for educating or giving instruction, esp. *Brit.* for children under 19 years, or *N. Amer.* for any level of instruction including college or university. **b** (*attrib.*) associated with or for use in school (*a school bag*; *school dinners*). **2 a** the buildings used by such an institution. **b** the pupils, staff, etc. of a school. **c** the time during which teaching is done, or the teaching itself (*no school today*). **3 a** a branch of study with separate examinations at a university; a department or faculty (*the history school*). **b** *Brit.* the hall in which university examinations are held. **c** (in *pl.*) *Brit.* such examinations. **4 a** the disciples, imitators, or followers of a philosopher, artist, etc. (*the school of Epicurus*). **b** a group of artists etc. whose works share distinctive characteristics. **c** a group of people sharing a cause, principle, method, etc. (*school of thought*). **5** *Brit.* a group of gamblers or of persons drinking together (*a poker school*). **6** *colloq.* instructive or disciplinary circumstances, occupation, etc. (*the school of adversity*; *learnt in a hard school*). **7** *hist.* a medieval lecture room. **8** *Mus.* (usu. foll. by *of*) a handbook or book of instruction (*school of counterpoint*). **9** (in *pl.*; prec. by *the*) *hist.* medieval universities, their teachers, disputations, etc. ● *v.tr.* **1** send to school; provide for the education of. **2** (often foll. by *to*) discipline; train; control. **3** (as **schooled** *adj.*) (foll. by *in*) educated or trained (*schooled in humility*). □ **at** (*US* **in**) **school** attending lessons etc. **go to school 1** begin one's education. **2** attend lessons. **leave school** finish one's education. **of the old school** according to former and esp. better tradition (*a gentleman of the old school*). **school of hard knocks** experience gained from adversity. [Old English *scōl, scolu*, ultimately via Latin *schola* 'school' from Greek *skholē* 'leisure, disputation, philosophy, lecture-place', reinforced in Middle English by Old French *escole*]

school[2] /sku:l/ *n. & v.* ● *n.* (often foll. by *of*) a shoal of fish, porpoises, whales, etc. ● *v.intr.* form schools. [Middle English via Middle Low German, Middle Dutch *schōle* from West Germanic: related to Old English *scolu* 'troop']

schoolable /'sku:ləb(ə)l/ *adj.* liable by age etc. to compulsory education.

school age *n.* the age range in which children normally attend school (often hyphenated when *attrib.*: *school-age children*).

school board *n. N. Amer.* or *hist.* a board or authority for local education.

schoolboy /'sku:lbɔɪ/ *n.* a boy attending school.

schoolchild /'sku:ltʃʌɪld/ *n.* (*pl.* **-children**) a child attending school.

schooldays /'sku:ldeɪz/ *n.* the time of being at school, esp. in retrospect.

schoolfellow /'sku:lfɛləʊ/ *n.* a past or esp. present member of the same school.

schoolgirl /'sku:lgə:l/ *n.* a girl attending school.

schoolhouse /'sku:lhaʊs/ *n. Brit.* **1** a building used as a school, esp. in a village. **2** a dwelling house adjoining a school.

schoolie /'sku:li/ *n. Austral. slang & dial.* a schoolteacher.

schooling /'sku:lɪŋ/ *n.* **1** education, esp. at school. **2** training or discipline, esp. of an animal.

school inspector *n.* (in the UK) a government official reporting on the efficiency, teaching standards, etc. of schools.

school leaver *n. Brit.* a teenager who is about to leave or has just left school.

school-leaving age *n. Brit.* the minimum age at which a child may cease attending school.

schoolman /ˈsku:lmən/ *n.* (*pl.* **-men**) **1** *hist.* a teacher in a medieval European university. **2** *RC Ch. hist.* a theologian seeking to deal with religious doctrines by the rules of Aristotelian logic. **3** *US* a male teacher.

school-marm /ˈsku:lmɑ:m/*n.* (also **school-ma'm**) esp. *colloq.* a schoolmistress.

school-marmish *adj.* esp. *US colloq.* prim and fussy.

schoolmaster /ˈsku:lmɑ:stə/ *n.* a head or assistant male teacher. □ **schoolmasterly** *adj.*

schoolmastering /ˈsku:lmɑ:st(ə)rɪŋ/ *n.* teaching as a profession.

schoolmate /ˈsku:lmeɪt/ *n.* = SCHOOLFELLOW.

schoolmistress /ˈsku:lmɪstrɪs/ *n.* a head or assistant female teacher.

schoolmistressy /ˈsku:lmɪstrɪsi/ *adj. colloq.* prim and fussy.

schoolroom /ˈsku:lru:m, -rʊm/ *n.* a room used for lessons in a school or in the large private home of a wealthy family.

school-ship *n.* a training ship.

schoolteacher /ˈsku:lti:tʃə/ *n.* a person who teaches in a school. □ **schoolteaching** *n.*

school time *n.* **1** lesson time at school or at home. **2** schooldays.

school year *n.* = ACADEMIC YEAR.

schooner /ˈsku:nə/ *n.* **1** a fore-and-aft rigged ship with two or more masts, the foremast being smaller than the other masts. **2 a** *Brit.* a measure or glass for esp. sherry. **b** *US* & *Austral.* a tall beer glass. **3** *US hist.* = PRAIRIE SCHOONER. [18th c.: origin uncertain]

schorl /ʃɔ:l/ *n.* black tourmaline. [German *Schörl*, of unknown origin]

schottische /ʃɒˈti:ʃ, ˈʃɒtɪʃ/ *n.* **1** a kind of slow polka. **2** the music for this. [German *der schottische Tanz* 'the Scottish dance']

Schottky effect /ˈʃɒtki/ *n. Electronics* the increase in thermionic emission from a solid surface due to the presence of an external electric field. [named after W. *Schottky*, German physicist d. 1976]

Schrödinger equation /ˈʃrə:dɪŋə, ˈʃrəʊ-/ *n. Physics* a differential equation used in quantum mechanics for the wave function of a particle. [named after E. *Schrödinger*, Austrian physicist d. 1961]

schuss /ʃʊs/ *n.* & *v.* ● *n.* a straight downhill run on skis. ● *v.intr.* make a schuss. [German, literally 'shot']

schwa /ʃwɑ:/ *n.* (also **sheva** /ʃəˈvɑ:/) *Phonet.* **1** an indistinct unstressed vowel sound (as in *a* moment *a*go). **2** the symbol /ə/ representing this in the International Phonetic Alphabet. [German from Hebrew *šᵉwā*, apparently from *šaw'* 'emptiness']

sciagraphy /sʌɪˈagrəfi/ *n.* (also **skiagraphy** /skʌɪ-/) the art of shading in drawing etc. □ **sciagram** /ˈsʌɪəgram/ *n.* **sciagraph** /ˈsʌɪəgrɑ:f/ *n.* & *v.tr.* **sciagraphic** /sʌɪəˈgrafɪk/ *adj.* [French *sciagraphie* via Latin *sciagraphia* from Greek *skiagraphia*, from *skia* 'shadow']

sciamachy /sʌɪˈaməki/ *n.* (also **skiamachy** /skʌɪ-/) *formal* **1** fighting with shadows. **2** imaginary or futile combat. [Greek *skiamakhia* (as SCIAGRAPHY, *-makhia* '-fighting')]

sciatic /sʌɪˈatɪk/ *adj.* **1** of the hip. **2** of or affecting the sciatic nerve. **3** suffering from or liable to sciatica. □ **sciatically** *adv.* [French *sciatique* via Late Latin *sciaticus* and Latin *ischiadicus* from Greek *iskhiadikos* 'subject to sciatica', from *iskhion* 'hip joint']

sciatica /sʌɪˈatɪkə/ *n.* neuralgia of the hip and thigh; a pain in the sciatic nerve. [Middle English from Late Latin *sciatica* (*passio* 'affliction'), fem. of *sciaticus*: see SCIATIC]

sciatic nerve *n.* the largest nerve in the human body, running from the pelvis to the thigh.

science /ˈsʌɪəns/ *n.* **1** a branch of knowledge conducted on objective principles involving the systematized observation of and experiment with phenomena, esp. concerned with the material and functions of the physical universe (see also NATURAL SCIENCE). **2 a** systematic and formulated knowledge, esp. of a specified type or on a specified subject (*political science*). **b** the pursuit or principles of this. **3** an organized body of knowledge on a subject (*the science of philology*). **4** skilful technique rather than strength or natural ability. **5** *archaic* knowledge of any kind. [Middle English via Old French from Latin *scientia*, from *scire* 'know']

science fiction *n.* fiction based on imagined future scientific or technological advances, major social or environmental changes, etc., frequently portraying space or time travel, life on other planets, etc.

science park *n.* an area devoted to scientific research or the development of science-based industries.

scienter /sʌɪˈɛntə/ *adv. Law* intentionally; knowingly. [Latin from *scire* know]

sciential /sʌɪˈɛnʃ(ə)l/ *adj.* concerning or having knowledge. [Late Latin *scientialis* (as SCIENCE)]

scientific /sʌɪənˈtɪfɪk/ *adj.* **1 a** (of an investigation etc.) according to rules laid down in exact science for performing observations and testing the soundness of conclusions. **b** systematic, accurate. **2** used in, engaged in, or relating to (esp. natural) science (*scientific discoveries*; *scientific terminology*). **3** assisted by expert knowledge. □ **scientifically** *adv.* [French *scientifique* or Late Latin *scientificus* (as SCIENCE)]

scientism /ˈsʌɪəntɪz(ə)m/ *n.* **1 a** a method or doctrine regarded as characteristic of scientists. **b** the use or practice of this. **2** often *derog.* an excessive belief in or application of scientific method. □ **scientistic** /-ˈtɪstɪk/ *adj.*

scientist /ˈsʌɪəntɪst/ *n.* **1** a person with expert knowledge of a (usu. physical or natural) science. **2** a person using scientific methods.

Scientology /sʌɪənˈtɒlədʒi/ *n. propr.* a religious system based on self-improvement and promotion through grades of esp. self-knowledge. □ **Scientologist** *n.* [Latin *scientia* 'knowledge' + -LOGY]

sci-fi /ˈsʌɪfʌɪ/ *n.* (often *attrib.*) *colloq.* science fiction. [abbreviation: cf. HI-FI]

scilicet /ˈsʌɪlɪsɛt, ˈski:lɪkɛt/ *adv.* to wit; that is to say; namely (introducing a word to be supplied or an explanation of an ambiguity). [Middle English from Latin, = *scire licet* 'one is permitted to know']

scilla /ˈsɪlə/ *n.* any plant of the genus *Scilla* (lily family), related to the bluebell, usu. bearing small blue star-shaped or bell-shaped flowers and having long glossy straplike leaves. [Latin from Greek *skilla*]

Scillonian /sɪˈləʊnɪən/ *adj.* & *n.* ● *adj.* of or relating to the Scilly Isles off the coast of Cornwall. ● *n.* a native of the Scilly Isles. [*Scilly*, perhaps on the pattern of *Devonian*]

scimitar /ˈsɪmɪtə/ *n.* an oriental curved sword usu. broadening towards the point. [French *cimeterre*, Italian *scimitarra*, etc., of unknown origin]

scintigram /ˈsɪntɪgram/ *n.* an image of an internal part of the body, produced by scintigraphy.

scintigraphy /sɪnˈtɪgrəfi/ *n.* the use of a radioisotope and a scintillation counter to obtain an image or record of a bodily organ etc. [SCINTILLATION + -GRAPHY]

scintilla /sɪnˈtɪlə/ *n.* **1** a trace. **2** a spark. [Latin]

scintillate /ˈsɪntɪleɪt/ *v.intr.* **1** (esp. as **scintillating** *adj.*) talk cleverly or wittily; be brilliant. **2** sparkle; twinkle; emit sparks. **3** *Physics* fluoresce momentarily when struck by a charged particle etc. □ **scintillant** *adj.* **scintillatingly** *adv.* [Latin *scintillare* (as SCINTILLA)]

scintillation /sɪntɪˈleɪʃ(ə)n/ *n.* **1** the process or state of scintillating. **2** the twinkling of a star. **3** a flash produced in a material by an ionizing particle etc.

scintillation counter *n.* a device for detecting and recording scintillation.

scintiscan /ˈsɪntɪskan/ *n.* an image or other record showing the distribution of radioactive traces in parts of the body, used in the detection and diagnosis of various diseases. [SCINTILLATION + SCAN]

sciolist /ˈsʌɪəlɪst/ *n.* a superficial pretender to knowledge. □ **sciolism** /-ˈlɪz(ə)m/ *n.* **sciolistic** /-ˈlɪstɪk/ *adj.* [Late Latin *sciolus*, diminutive of Latin *scius* 'knowing', from *scire* 'know']

scion /ˈsʌɪən/ *n.* **1** (*US* also **cion**) a shoot of a plant etc., esp. one cut for grafting or planting. **2** a descendant; a younger member of (esp. a noble) family. [Middle English from Old French *ciun, cion, sion* 'shoot, twig', of unknown origin]

scire facias /sʌɪriː ˈfeɪʃɪas/ *n. Law* a writ to enforce or annul a judgement, patent, etc. [Latin, = let (him) know]

scirocco var. of SIROCCO.

scirrhus /ˈsɪrəs, ˈskɪ-/ *n.* (*pl.* **scirrhi** /-rʌɪ/) a carcinoma which is hard to the touch. □ **scirrhoid** *adj.* **scirrhosity** /sɪˈrɒsɪti/ *n.* **scirrhous** *adj.* [modern Latin from Greek *skir(r)os*, from *skiros* 'hard']

scissel /ˈsɪs(ə)l/ *n.* waste clippings etc. of metal produced during coin manufacture. [French *cisaille* from *cisailler* 'clip with shears']

scissile /ˈsɪsʌɪl, -sɪl/ *adj.* able to be cut or divided. [Latin *scissilis* from *scindere sciss-* 'to cut']

scission /ˈsɪʃ(ə)n/ *n.* **1** the act or an instance of cutting; the state of being cut. **2** a division or split. [Middle English from Old French *scission* or Late Latin *scissio* (as SCISSILE)]

scissor /ˈsɪzə/ *v.tr.* **1** (usu. foll. by *off, up, into*, etc.) cut with scissors. **2** (usu. foll. by *out*) clip out (a newspaper cutting etc.).

scissor-bill *n.* = SKIMMER 4.

scissor-bird *n.* (also **scissor-tail**) a fork-tailed flycatcher, *Tyrannus forficatus.*

scissors /ˈsɪzəz/ *n.pl.* **1** (also **pair of scissors** *sing.*) an instrument for cutting fabric, paper, hair, etc., having two pivoted blades with finger and thumb holes in the handles, operating by closing on the material to be cut. **2** (treated as *sing.*) **a** a method of high jump with a forward and backward movement of the legs. **b** a hold in wrestling in which the opponent's body or esp. head is gripped between the legs. □ **scissorwise** *adv.* [Middle English *sisoures* via Old French *cisoires* from Late Latin *cisoria*, pl. of *cisorium* 'cutting instrument' (as CHISEL): associated with Latin *scindere sciss-* 'to cut']

scissors and paste *n.* (usu. hyphenated when *attrib.*) = CUT-AND-PASTE.

sciurine /ˈsʌɪjʊərɪn, -rʌɪn/ *adj.* **1** of or relating to the family Sciuridae, including squirrels and chipmunks. **2** squirrel-like. □ **sciuroid** *adj.* [Latin *sciurus* from Greek *skiouros* 'squirrel', from *skia* 'shadow' + *oura* 'tail']

sclera /ˈsklɪərə/ *n.* the white of the eye; a white membrane coating the eyeball. □ **scleral** *adj.* **sclerotomy** /-ˈrɒtəmi/ *n.* (*pl.* **-ies**). [modern Latin, from fem. of Greek *sklēros* 'hard']

sclerenchyma /sklɪəˈrɛŋkɪmə, sklə-/ *n.* the woody tissue found in a plant, formed from lignified cells and usu. providing support. [modern Latin, from Greek *sklēros* 'hard' + *egkhuma* 'infusion', on the pattern of *parenchyma*]

sclerite /ˈsklɪərʌɪt, ˈsklɛ-/ *n. Zool.* a component section of an exoskeleton, esp. each of the plates forming the skeleton of an arthropod. [Greek *sklēros* 'hard']

scleritis /sklɪəˈrʌɪtɪs, sklə-/ *n. Med.* inflammation of the sclera of the eye.

scleroderma /sklɪərəˈdəːmə/ *n. Med.* a chronic hardening of the skin and connective tissue. [Greek *sklēros* 'hard' + *derma* 'skin']

scleroid /ˈsklɪərɔɪd, ˈsklɛ-/ *adj. Bot. & Zool.* having a hard texture; hardened. [Greek *sklēros* 'hard']

scleroma /sklɪəˈrəʊmə, sklə-/ *n.* (*pl.* **scleromata** /-mətə/) an abnormal patch of hardened skin or mucous membrane. [modern Latin from Greek *sklērōma* (as SCLEROSIS)]

sclerometer /sklɪəˈrɒmɪtə, sklə-/ *n.* an instrument for determining the hardness of materials. [Greek *sklēros* 'hard' + -METER]

sclerophyll /ˈsklɪərəfɪl, ˈsklɛ-/ *n.* any woody plant with leathery leaves retaining water. □ **sclerophyllous** /-ˈrɒfɪləs/ *adj.* [Greek *sklēros* 'hard' + *phullon* 'leaf']

scleroprotein /sklɪərəʊˈprəʊtiːn, sklɛ-/ *n. Biochem.* any insoluble structural protein, e.g. keratin. [Greek *sklēros* 'hard' + PROTEIN]

sclerosed /sklɪəˈrəʊst, sklə-, ˈsklɪə-/ *adj.* affected by sclerosis.

sclerosis /sklɪəˈrəʊsɪs, sklə-/ *n.* **1** an abnormal hardening of body tissue (see also ARTERIOSCLEROSIS, ATHEROSCLEROSIS). **2** (in full **multiple sclerosis**) a chronic and often progressive disease of the nervous system resulting in symptoms such as numbness, severe fatigue, and impairment of muscular coordination. Also called *disseminated sclerosis.* **3** *Bot.* the hardening of a cell wall with lignified matter. [Middle English via medieval Latin from Greek *sklērōsis*, from *sklēroō* 'harden']

sclerotic /sklɪəˈrɒtɪk, sklə-/ *adj. & n.* ● *adj.* **1** of or having sclerosis. **2** of or relating to the sclera. ● *n.* = SCLERA. □ **sclerotitis** /-rəˈtʌɪtɪs/ *n.* [medieval Latin *sclerotica* (as SCLEROSIS)]

sclerous /ˈsklɪərəs/ *adj. Physiol.* hardened; bony. [Greek *sklēros* 'hard']

SCM *abbr.* (in the UK) **1** State Certified Midwife. **2** Student Christian Movement.

scoff[1] /skɒf/ *v. & n.* ● *v.intr.* (usu. foll. by *at*) speak derisively, esp. of serious subjects; mock; be scornful. ● *n.* **1** mocking words; a taunt. **2** an object of ridicule. □ **scoffer** *n.* **scoffingly** *adv.* [perhaps from Scandinavian: cf. early modern Danish *skuf, skof* 'jest, mockery']

scoff[2] /skɒf/ *v. & n.* esp. *Brit. colloq.* ● *v.tr. & intr.* eat greedily. ● *n.* food; a meal. [the noun from Afrikaans *schoff*, representing Dutch *schoft* 'quarter of a day' (hence, a meal): the verb originally a variant of dialect *scaff*, associated with the noun]

scold /skəʊld/ *v. & n.* ● *v.* **1** *tr.* rebuke or chide (esp. a child). **2** *intr.* find fault noisily; complain; rail. ● *n. archaic* a nagging or grumbling woman. □ **scolder** *n.* **scolding** *n.* [Middle English (earlier as noun), probably from Old Norse *skáld* SKALD]

scolex /ˈskəʊlɛks/ *n.* (*pl.* **scoleces** /-ˈliːsiːz/ or **scolices** /-lɪsiːz/) the anterior end of a tapeworm, bearing suckers and hooks for attachment. [modern Latin from Greek *skōlēx* 'worm']

scoliosis /skɒlɪˈəʊsɪs, skəʊ-/ *n.* abnormal lateral curvature of the spine. □ **scoliotic** /-ˈɒtɪk/ *adj.* [modern Latin from Greek, from *skolios* 'bent']

scollop var. of SCALLOP.

scolopendrium /skɒlə(ʊ)ˈpɛndrɪəm/ *n.* the hart's tongue fern. [modern Latin from Greek *skolopendrion*, from *skolopendra* 'millipede' (because of the supposed resemblance)]

scombroid /ˈskɒmbrɔɪd/ *n. & adj.* ● *n.* any marine fish of the family Scombridae, including mackerels, tunas, and bonitos, or of the superfamily Scombroidea. ● *adj.* of or relating to this family or superfamily. □ **scombrid** *n.* [Latin from Greek *skombros*]

sconce[1] /skɒns/ *n.* **1** a flat candlestick with a handle. **2** a bracket candlestick to hang on a wall. [Middle English via Old French *esconse* 'lantern' or medieval Latin *sconsa* from Latin *absconsa* (*laterna*) 'dark (lantern)', from *abscondere* 'hide': see ABSCOND]

sconce[2] /skɒns/ *n.* **1** a small fort or earthwork usu. defending a ford, pass, etc. **2** *archaic* a shelter or screen. [Dutch *schans* 'brushwood' from Middle High German *schanze*]

scone /skɒn, skəʊn/ *n.* a small sweet or savoury cake of flour, fat, and milk, baked for a short time in an oven. [originally Scots, perhaps from Middle Dutch *schoon*(*broot*), Middle Low German *schon*(*brot*) 'fine (bread)']

scoop /sku:p/ *n.* & *v.* ● *n.* **1** any of various objects resembling a spoon, esp.: **a** a short-handled deep shovel used for transferring grain, sugar, coal, coins, etc. **b** a large long-handled ladle used for transferring liquids. **c** the excavating part of a digging machine etc. **d** *Med.* a long-handled spoonlike instrument used for scraping parts of the body etc. **e** an instrument used for serving portions of mashed potato, ice cream, etc. **2** a quantity taken up by a scoop. **3** a movement of or resembling scooping. **4** a piece of news published by a newspaper etc. in advance of its rivals. **5** a large profit made quickly or by anticipating one's competitors. **6** *Mus.* a singer's exaggerated portamento. **7** a scooped-out hollow etc. ● *v.tr.* **1** (usu. foll. by *out*) hollow out with or as if with a scoop. **2** (usu. foll. by *up*) lift with or as if with a scoop. **3** forestall (a rival newspaper, reporter, etc.) with a scoop. **4** secure (a large profit etc.) esp. suddenly. □ **scooper** *n.* **scoopful** *n.* (*pl.* **-fuls**). [Middle English from Middle Dutch, Middle Low German *schōpe* 'bucket' etc.: related to SHAPE]

scoop neck *n.* the rounded low-cut neck of a garment.

scoop-net *n.* a net used for sweeping a river bottom, or for catching bait.

scoot /sku:t/ *v.* & *n.* *colloq.* ● *v.intr.* run or dart away, esp. quickly. ● *n.* the act or an instance of scooting. [18th-c. US (earlier *scout*): origin unknown]

scooter /'sku:tə/ *n.* & *v.* ● *n.* **1** a child's toy consisting of a footboard mounted on two wheels and a steering column with handles, propelled by resting one foot on the footboard and pushing the other against the ground. **2** (in full **motor scooter**) a light two-wheeled open motor vehicle with a shieldlike protective front. **3** *N. Amer.* a sailboat able to travel on either water or ice. ● *v.intr.* travel or ride on a scooter. □ **scooterist** *n.*

scopa /'skəʊpə/ *n.* (*pl.* **scopae** /-pi:/) a small brushlike tuft of hairs, esp. on the leg of a bee for collecting pollen. [sing. of Latin *scopae* = twigs, broom]

scope[1] /skəʊp/ *n.* **1 a** the extent to which it is possible to range (*this is beyond the scope of our research*). **b** the sweep or reach of mental activity, observation, or outlook (*an intellect limited in its scope*). **c** space or freedom to act (*doesn't leave us much scope*). **2** *Naut.* the length of cable extended when a ship rides at anchor. **3** *archaic* a purpose, end, or intention. [Italian *scopo* 'aim' from Greek *skopos* 'target', from *skeptomai* 'look at']

scope[2] /skəʊp/ *n.* *colloq.* a telescope, microscope, or other device ending in *-scope*. [abbreviation]

-scope /skəʊp/ *comb. form* forming nouns denoting: **1** a device looked at or through (*kaleidoscope*; *telescope*). **2** an instrument for observing or showing (*gyroscope*; *oscilloscope*). □ **-scopic** /'skɒpɪk/ *comb. form* forming adjectives. [from or suggested by modern Latin *-scopium* from Greek *skopeō* 'look at']

scopolamine /skə'pɒləmi:n/ *n.* = HYOSCINE. [*Scopolia*, genus name of the plants yielding it, from the name of G. A. *Scopoli*, Italian naturalist d. 1788 + AMINE]

scopula /'skɒpjʊlə/ *n.* (*pl.* **scopulae** /-li:/) any of various small brushlike structures, esp. on the legs of spiders. [Late Latin, diminutive of Latin *scopa*: see SCOPA]

-scopy /skəpi/ *comb. form* indicating viewing or observation, usu. with an instrument ending in *-scope* (*microscopy*).

scorbutic /skɔ:'bju:tɪk/ *adj.* & *n.* ● *adj.* relating to, resembling, or affected with scurvy. ● *n.* a person affected with scurvy. □ **scorbutically** *adv.* [modern Latin *scorbuticus* from medieval Latin *scorbutus* 'scurvy', perhaps from Middle Low German *schorbūk*, from *schoren* 'break' + *būk* 'belly']

scorch /skɔ:tʃ/ *v.* & *n.* ● *v.* **1** *tr.* **a** burn the surface of with flame or heat so as to discolour, parch, injure, or hurt. **b** affect with the sensation of burning. **2** *intr.* become discoloured etc. with heat. **3** *tr.* (as **scorching** *adj.*) *colloq.* **a** (of the weather) very hot. **b** (of criticism etc.) stringent; harsh. **4** *intr. colloq.* (of a motorist etc.) go at excessive speed. ● *n.* **1** a mark made by scorching. **2** *colloq.* a spell of fast driving etc. □ **scorchingly** *adv.* [Middle English, perhaps related to Old Norse *skorpna* 'be shrivelled']

scorched earth policy *n.* the burning of crops etc. and the removing or destroying of anything that might be of use to an enemy force occupying a country.

scorcher /'skɔ:tʃə/ *n.* **1** a person or thing that scorches. **2** a very hot day. **3** *Brit. colloq.* a fine specimen.

score /skɔ:/ *n.* & *v.* ● *n.* **1 a** the number of points, goals, runs, etc., made by a player, side, etc., in some games. **b** the total number of points etc. at the end of a game (*the score was 5–0*). **c** the act of gaining esp. a goal (*a superb score there!*). **2** (*pl.* same or **scores**) twenty or a set of twenty. **3** (in *pl.*) a great many (*scores of people arrived*). **4 a** a reason or motive (*rejected on the score of absurdity*). **b** topic, subject (*no worries on that score*). **5** *Mus.* **a** a usu. printed copy of a composition showing all the vocal and instrumental parts arranged one below the other. **b** the music composed for a film or play, esp. for a musical. **6** *colloq.* **a** a piece of good fortune. **b** the act or an instance of scoring off another person. **7** *colloq.* the state of affairs; the present situation (*asked what the score was*). **8** a notch, line, etc. cut or scratched into a surface. **9 a** an amount due for payment. **b** a running account kept by marks against a customer's name. **10** *Naut.* a groove in a block or deadeye to hold a rope. ● *v.* **1** *tr.* **a** win or gain (a goal, run, points, success, etc.) (*scored a century*). **b** count for a score of (points in a game etc.) (*a bull's-eye scores most points*). **c** allot a score to (a competitor etc.). **d** make a record of (a point etc.). **2** *intr.* **a** make a score in a game (*failed to score*). **b** keep the tally of points, runs, etc. in a game. **3** *tr.* mark with notches, incisions, lines, etc.; slash; furrow (*scored his name on the desk*). **4** *intr.* secure an advantage by luck, cunning, etc. (*that is where he scores*). **5** *tr. Mus.* **a** orchestrate (a piece of music). **b** (usu. foll. by *for*) arrange for an instrument or instruments. **c** write the music for (a film, musical, etc.). **d** write out in a score. **6** *tr.* **a** (usu. foll. by *up*) mark (a total owed etc.) in a score (see sense 9b of *n.*). **b** (usu. foll. by *against*, *to*) enter (an item of debt to a customer). **7** *intr. slang* **a** obtain drugs illegally. **b** (of a man) make a sexual conquest. **8** *tr.* (usu. foll. by *against*, *to*) mentally record (an offence etc.). **9** *tr. N. Amer.* criticize (a person) severely. □ **keep score** (or **the score**) register the score as it is made. **know the score** *colloq.* be aware of the essential facts. **on the score of** *Brit.* for the reason that; because of. **on that score** so far as that is concerned. **pay** (or **settle**) **a** (or **the**) **score 1** requite an obligation. **2** avenge an injury. **score off** (or **score points off**) *Brit. colloq.* humiliate, esp. verbally in repartee etc. **score out** draw a line through (words etc.). **score points** outdo another person; make a more favourable impression. **score under** underline. □ **scoreless** *adj.* **scorer** *n.* **scoring** *n.* *Mus.* [the noun from Old English (sense 5 from the line or bar drawn through all staves): the verb partly from Old Norse *skora* from *skor* 'notch, tally, twenty', from Germanic: related to SHEAR]

scoreboard /'skɔ:bɔ:d/ *n.* a large board for publicly displaying the score in a game or match.

scorebook /'skɔ:bʊk/ *n.* (also **scorecard** or **score sheet**) a book etc. prepared for entering esp. cricket scores in.

score draw *n.* a draw in football in which goals are scored.

scoreline /'skɔ:lʌɪn/ *n.* the number of points, goals, etc. scored in a match; the score; the result. [originally the line in a newspaper etc. giving the score in a sports contest]

scoria /'skɔ:rɪə/ *n.* (*pl.* **scoriae** /-rɪi:/) **1** cellular lava, or fragments of it. **2** the slag or dross of metals. □ **scoriaceous** /-'eɪʃəs/ *adj.* [Latin from Greek *skōria* 'refuse', from *skōr* 'dung']

scorify /'skɔ:rɪfʌɪ/ *v.tr.* (**-ies**, **-ied**) **1** reduce to dross. **2** assay (precious metal) by treating a portion of its ore fused with lead and borax. □ **scorification** /-frˈkeɪʃ(ə)n/ *n.* **scorifier** *n.*

scorn /skɔːn/ *n.* & *v.* ● *n.* **1** disdain, contempt, derision. **2** an object of contempt etc. (*the scorn of all onlookers*). ● *v.tr.* **1** hold in contempt or disdain. **2** (often foll. by *to* + infin.) abstain from or refuse to do as unworthy (*scorns lying*; *scorns to lie*). □ **pour scorn on** express contempt or disdain for. **think scorn of** *Brit. archaic* despise. □ **scorner** *n.* [Middle English from Old French *esc(h)arn(ir)*, ultimately from Germanic: cf. Old Saxon *skern* MOCKERY]

scornful /ˈskɔːnfʊl, -f(ə)l/ *adj.* (often foll. by *of*) full of scorn; contemptuous. □ **scornfully** *adv.* **scornfulness** *n.*

scorper var. of SCALPER 2.

Scorpio /ˈskɔːpɪəʊ/ *n.* (*pl.* **-os**) **1** (usu. **Scorpius** /-pɪəs/) *Astron.* a large constellation (the Scorpion), said to represent the scorpion which killed Orion. **2** *Astrol.* **a** the eighth sign of the zodiac, which the sun enters about 23 Oct. **b** a person born when the sun is in this sign. □ **Scorpian** *adj.* & *n.* [Middle English from Latin (as SCORPION)]

scorpioid /ˈskɔːpɪɔɪd/ *adj.* & *n.* ● *adj.* **1** *Zool.* of, relating to, or resembling a scorpion; of the scorpion order. **2** *Bot.* (of an inflorescence) curled up at the end, and uncurling as the flowers develop. ● *n.* this type of inflorescence. [Greek *skorpioeidēs* (as SCORPIO)]

scorpion /ˈskɔːpɪən/ *n.* **1** an arachnid of the order Scorpiones, with lobster-like pincers and a jointed tail that can be bent over to inflict a poisoned sting on prey held in its pincers. **2** (in full **false scorpion**) a similar arachnid of the order Pseudoscorpiones, smaller and without a tail. **3** (**the Scorpion**) the zodiacal sign Scorpio or the constellation Scorpius. **4** (in *pl.*) a whip with metal points (in allusion to 1 Kings 12:11). [Middle English via Old French from Latin *scorpio -onis*, via *scorpius* from Greek *skorpios*]

scorpion fish *n.* any of various marine fish of the family Scorpaenidae, with venomous spines on the head and gills.

scorpion fly *n.* any insect of the order Mecoptera, esp. of the genus *Panorpa*, the males of which have a swollen abdomen curved upwards like a scorpion's sting.

scorpion grass *n.* = FORGET-ME-NOT.

Scorpius see SCORPIO 1.

scorzonera /skɔːzə(ʊ)ˈnɪərə/ *n.* **1** a plant of the daisy family, *Scorzonera hispanica*, with long tapering purple-brown roots. **2** the root used as a vegetable. [Italian from *scorzone* 'venomous snake' (against whose venom the plant may have been regarded as an antidote), ultimately from medieval Latin *curtio*]

Scot /skɒt/ *n.* **1 a** a native of Scotland. **b** a person of Scottish descent. **2** *hist.* a member of a Gaelic people that migrated from Ireland to Scotland around the late 5th c. [Old English *Scottas* (pl.) from Late Latin *Scottus*]

■ **Usage** See Usage Note at SCOTCHMAN.

scot /skɒt/ *n. hist.* a payment corresponding to a modern tax, rate, etc. □ **pay scot and lot** share the financial burdens of a borough etc. (and so be allowed to vote). [Middle English from Old Norse *skot* & from Old French *escot*, of Germanic origin: cf. SHOT[3]]

Scotch /skɒtʃ/ *adj.* & *n.* ● *adj.* var. of SCOTTISH or SCOTS. ● *n.* **1** var. of SCOTTISH or SCOTS. **2** Scotch whisky. [contraction of SCOTTISH]

■ **Usage** The use of *Scotch* as an alternative to *Scottish* or *Scots* is generally regarded as offensive or old-fashioned by Scottish people. It should be avoided except in sense 2 above (to mean 'Scotch whisky') and in the special compounds (*Scotch broth* etc.) listed below.

scotch[1] /skɒtʃ/ *v.* & *n.* ● *v.tr.* **1** put an end to; frustrate (*injury scotched his attempt*). **2** *archaic* **a** wound without killing; slightly disable. **b** make incisions in; score. ● *n.* **1** *archaic* a slash. **2** a line on the ground for hopscotch. [Middle English: origin unknown]

scotch[2] /skɒtʃ/ *n.* & *v.* ● *n.* a wedge or block placed against a wheel etc. to prevent its slipping. ● *v.tr.* hold back (a wheel, barrel, etc.) with a scotch. [17th c.: perhaps = *scatch* 'stilt' from Old French *escache*]

Scotch broth *n.* a soup made from beef or mutton with pearl barley etc.

Scotch cap *n.* = BONNET *n.* 1b.

Scotch catch *n. Mus.* a short note on the beat followed by a long one.

Scotch egg *n.* a hard-boiled egg enclosed in sausage meat and fried.

Scotch fir *n.* = SCOTS PINE.

Scotch kale *n.* a variety of kale with purplish leaves.

Scotchman /ˈskɒtʃmən/ *n.* (*pl.* **-men**; *fem.* **Scotchwoman**, *pl.* **-women**) = SCOTSMAN.

■ **Usage** Like *Scotch*, *Scotchman* and *Scotchwoman* are old-fashioned and may be regarded as offensive by Scottish people. *Scot*, *Scotsman*, or *Scotswoman* should be used instead.

Scotch mist *n.* **1** a thick drizzly mist common in the Highlands. **2** *Brit.* a retort made to a person implying that he or she has imagined or failed to understand something.

Scotch pebble *n.* agate, jasper, cairngorm, etc., found in Scotland.

Scotch snap *n.* = SCOTCH CATCH.

Scotch tape *n.* esp. *US propr.* adhesive transparent tape.

Scotch whisky *n.* whisky distilled in Scotland, esp. from malted barley.

scoter /ˈskəʊtə/ *n.* (*pl.* same or **scoters**) a large marine duck of the genus *Melanitta*. [17th c.: origin unknown]

scot-free *adv.* unharmed; unpunished.

scotia /ˈskəʊʃə/ *n.* a concave moulding, esp. at the base of a column. [Latin from Greek *skotia*, from *skotos* 'darkness', with reference to the shadow produced]

Scoticism var. of SCOTTICISM.

Scoticize var. of SCOTTICIZE.

Scotland Yard /skɒtlənd ˈjɑːd/ *n.* **1** the headquarters of the London Metropolitan Police. **2** its Criminal Investigation Department. [Great and New *Scotland Yard*, streets where it was successively situated until 1967]

scotoma /skɒˈtəʊmə, skə(ʊ)-/ *n.* (*pl.* **scotomata** /-mətə/ or **scotomas**) a partial loss of vision or blind spot in an otherwise normal visual field. [Late Latin from Greek *skotōma*, via *skotoō* 'darken' from *skotos* 'darkness']

Scots /skɒts/ *adj.* & *n.* esp. *Sc.* ● *adj.* **1** = SCOTTISH *adj.* **2** in the dialect, accent, etc., of (esp. Lowlands) Scotland. ● *n.* **1** = SCOTTISH *n.* **2** the form of English spoken in (esp. Lowlands) Scotland. [Middle English, originally *Scottis*, northern variant of SCOTTISH]

Scots fir *n.* = SCOTS PINE.

Scotsman /ˈskɒtsmən/ *n.* (*pl.* **-men**; *fem.* **Scotswoman**, *pl.* **-women**) **1** a native of Scotland. **2** a person of Scottish descent.

Scots pine *n.* a pine tree, *Pinus sylvestris*, native to Europe and much planted for timber and other products. Also called *Scots fir*, *Scotch fir*.

Scotticism /ˈskɒtɪsɪz(ə)m/ *n.* (also **Scoticism**) a Scottish phrase, word, or idiom. [Late Latin *Scot(t)icus*]

Scotticize /ˈskɒtɪsʌɪz/ *v.* (also **Scoticize**, **-ise**) **1** *tr.* imbue with or model on Scottish ways etc. **2** *intr.* imitate the Scottish in idiom or habits.

Scottie /ˈskɒti/ *n. colloq.* **1** (also **Scottie dog**) a Scottish terrier. **2** a Scot.

Scottish /ˈskɒtɪʃ/ *adj.* & *n.* ● *adj.* of or relating to Scotland or its inhabitants. ● *n.* (prec. by *the*; treated as *pl.*) the people of Scotland. See also SCOTS. □ **Scottishness** *n.*

Scottish terrier *n.* **1** a small terrier of a rough-haired short-legged breed. **2** this breed.

scoundrel /ˈskaʊndr(ə)l/ *n.* an unscrupulous villain; a rogue. □ **scoundreldom** *n.* **scoundrelism** *n.* **scoundrelly** *adj.* [16th c.: origin unknown]

scour[1] /ˈskaʊə/ *v. & n.* ● *v.tr.* **1 a** cleanse or brighten (esp. metal) by rubbing, esp. with soap, chemicals, sand, etc. **b** (usu. foll. by *away, off,* etc.) clear (rust, stains, reputation, etc.) by rubbing, hard work, etc. (*scoured the slur from his name*). **2** clear out (a pipe, channel, etc.) by flushing through with or by the natural action of water. **3** *hist.* purge (the bowels) drastically. ● *n.* **1** the act or an instance of scouring; the state of being scoured, esp. by a swift water current (*the scour of the tide*). **2** diarrhoea in farm animals, esp. cattle and pigs. **3** a substance used for scouring. □ **scourer** *n.* [Middle English via Middle Dutch, Middle Low German *schūren* and French *escurer* from Late Latin *excurare* 'clean (off)' (as EX-[1], CURE)]

scour[2] /ˈskaʊə/ *v.* **1** *tr.* hasten over (an area etc.) searching thoroughly (*scoured the streets for him; scoured the pages of the newspaper*). **2** *intr.* range hastily esp. in search or pursuit. [Middle English: origin unknown]

scourge /skəːdʒ/ *n. & v.* ● *n.* **1** a whip used for punishment, esp. of people. **2** a person or thing seen or regarded as an agent of punishment, esp. on a large scale (*the scourge of famine; Genghis Khan, the scourge of Asia*). ● *v.tr.* **1** whip. **2** punish; afflict; oppress. □ **scourger** *n.* [Middle English from Old French *escorge* (*n.*), *escorgier* (*v.*) (ultimately as EX-[1], Latin *corrigia* 'thong, whip')]

scouring pad *n.* a pad of abrasive material for cleaning kitchenware etc.

scouring powder *n.* an abrasive powder for cleaning kitchenware etc.

scouring-rush *n.* any of various horsetails, esp. *Equisetum hyemale*, with a rough siliceous coating used for polishing wood etc.

Scouse /skaʊs/ *n. & adj. colloq.* ● *n.* **1** the dialect of Liverpool. **2** (also **Scouser** /ˈskaʊsə/) a native of Liverpool. **3** (**scouse**) = LOBSCOUSE. ● *adj.* of or relating to Liverpool. [abbreviation of LOBSCOUSE]

scout[1] /skaʊt/ *n. & v.* ● *n.* **1** a person, esp. a soldier, sent out to get information about the enemy's position, strength, etc. **2** the act of seeking (esp. military) information (*on the scout*). **3** = TALENT SCOUT. **4** (**Scout**) a member of the Scout Association, an international youth organization (originally for boys) intended to develop character esp. by open-air activities. **5** a domestic worker at a college, esp. at Oxford University. **6** *archaic colloq.* a person; a fellow. **7** a ship or aircraft designed for reconnoitring, esp. a small fast aircraft. ● *v.* **1** *intr.* act as a scout. **2** *intr.* (foll. by *about, around, for*) make a search. **3** *tr.* (often foll. by *out*) *colloq.* explore to get information about (territory etc.). □ **scouter** *n.* **scouting** *n.* [Middle English from Old French *escouter* 'listen', earlier *ascolter*, ultimately from Latin *auscultare*]

scout[2] /skaʊt/ *v.tr.* reject (an idea etc.) with scorn. [Scandinavian: cf. Old Norse *skúta, skúti* 'taunt']

Scouter /ˈskaʊtə/ *n.* an adult leader in the Scout Association.

Scoutmaster /ˈskaʊtmɑːstə/ *n.* a person in charge of a group of Scouts.

scow /skaʊ/ *n.* esp. *US* a flat-bottomed boat used as a lighter etc. [Dutch *schouw* 'ferry boat']

scowl /skaʊl/ *n. & v.* ● *n.* a severe frown producing a sullen, bad-tempered, or threatening look on a person's face. ● *v.intr.* make a scowl. □ **scowler** *n.* [Middle English, probably from Scandinavian: cf. Danish *skule* 'look down or sidelong']

SCPS *abbr.* (in the UK) Society of Civil and Public Servants.

SCR *abbr. Brit.* Senior Common (or Combination) Room.

scr. *abbr.* scruple(s) (of weight).

scrabble /ˈskrab(ə)l/ *v. & n.* ● *v.intr.* (often foll. by *about, at*) scratch or grope to find or collect or hold on to something. ● *n.* **1** an act of scrabbling. **2** (**Scrabble**) *propr.* a game in which players build up words from letter-blocks on a board. [Middle Dutch *schrabbelen*, frequentative of *schrabben* SCRAPE]

Scrabbler /ˈskrablə/ *n. colloq.* a person who plays Scrabble.

scrag /skrag/ *n. & v.* esp. *Brit.* ● *n.* **1** (also **scrag-end**) the inferior end of a neck of mutton. **2** a skinny person or animal. **3** *colloq.* a person's neck. ● *v.tr.* (**scragged, scragging**) *slang* **1** strangle, hang. **2** seize roughly by the neck. **3** handle roughly; beat up. [perhaps alteration of dialect *crag* 'neck', related to Middle Dutch *crāghe*, Middle Low German *krage*]

scraggly /ˈskragli/ *adj.* sparse and irregular.

scraggy /ˈskragi/ *adj.* (**scraggier, scraggiest**) thin and bony. □ **scraggily** *adv.* **scragginess** *n.*

scram /skram/ *v.intr.* (**scrammed, scramming**) (esp. in *imper.*) *colloq.* go away. [20th c.: perhaps from SCRAMBLE]

scramble /ˈskramb(ə)l/ *v. & n.* ● *v.* **1** *intr.* make one's way over rough ground, rocks, etc., by clambering, crawling, etc. **2** *intr.* (foll. by *for, at*) struggle with competitors (for a thing or share of it). **3** *intr.* move with difficulty, hastily, or awkwardly. **4** *tr.* **a** mix together indiscriminately. **b** jumble or muddle. **5** *tr.* cook (eggs) by heating them when broken and well mixed with butter, milk, etc. **6** *tr.* change the speech frequency of (a broadcast transmission or telephone conversation) so as to make it unintelligible without a corresponding decoding device. **7** *tr. colloq.* execute (an action etc.) awkwardly and inefficiently. **8** *intr.* (of fighter aircraft or their pilots) take off quickly in an emergency or for action. ● *n.* **1** an act of scrambling. **2** a difficult climb or walk. **3** (foll. by *for*) an eager struggle or competition. **4** *Brit.* a motorcycle race over rough ground. **5** an emergency take-off by fighter aircraft. [16th c. (imitative): cf. dialect synonyms *scamble, cramble*]

scrambled egg *n.* **1** a dish of eggs cooked by scrambling. **2** *colloq.* or *joc.* gold braid on a military officer's cap.

scrambler /ˈskramblə/ *n.* **1** a device for scrambling telephone conversations. **2** a motorcycle for racing on rough ground. **3** a plant with long slender stems supported by other plants.

scran /skran/ *n. slang* **1** food, eatables, or (esp. *Naut.*) rations. **2** remains of food; scraps. □ **bad scran** *Ir.* bad luck. [18th c.: origin unknown]

scrap[1] /skrap/ *n. & v.* ● *n.* **1** a small detached piece; a fragment or remnant. **2** rubbish or waste material. **3** an extract or cutting from something written or printed. **4** discarded metal for reprocessing (often *attrib.*: *scrap metal*). **5** (with *neg.*) the smallest piece or amount (*not a scrap of food left*). **6** (in *pl.*) **a** odds and ends. **b** bits of uneaten food. **7** (in *sing.* or *pl.*) a residuum of melted fat or of fish with the oil expressed. ● *v.tr.* (**scrapped, scrapping**) discard as useless. [Middle English from Old Norse *skrap*, related to *skrapa* SCRAPE]

scrap[2] /skrap/ *n. & v. colloq.* ● *n.* a fight or rough quarrel, esp. a spontaneous one. ● *v.tr.* (**scrapped, scrapping**) (often foll. by *with*) have a scrap. □ **scrapper** *n.* [perhaps from SCRAPE]

scrapbook /ˈskrapbʊk/ *n.* a book of blank pages for sticking cuttings, drawings, etc., in.

scrape /skreɪp/ *v. & n.* ● *v.* **1** *tr.* **a** move a hard or sharp edge across (a surface), esp. to make something smooth. **b** apply (a hard or sharp edge) in this way. **2** *tr.* (foll. by *away, off,* etc.) remove (a stain, projection, etc.) by scraping. **3** *tr.* **a** rub (a surface) harshly against another. **b** scratch or damage by scraping. **4** *tr.* (often foll. by *out*) make (a hollow) by scraping. **5 a** *tr.* draw or move with a sound of, or resembling, scraping. **b** *intr.* emit or produce such a sound. **c** *tr.* produce such a sound from. **6** *intr.* (often foll. by *along, by, through,* etc.) move or pass along while almost touching close or surrounding features, obstacles, etc. (*the car scraped through the narrow lane*). **7** *tr.* just manage to achieve (a living, an examination pass, etc.). **8** *intr.* (often foll. by *by, through*) **a** barely manage. **b** pass an examination etc. with difficulty. **9** *tr.* (foll. by *together, up*) contrive to bring or provide; amass with difficulty. **10** *intr.* be economical. **11** *intr.* draw back a foot in making a clumsy bow. **12** *tr.* clear (a ship's bottom) of barnacles etc. **13** *tr.* completely clear (a plate) of food. **14** *tr.* (foll. by *back*) *Brit.* draw (the hair) tightly back off the forehead. ● *n.* **1** the act or sound of scraping. **2** a scraped place (on the skin etc.). **3** *Brit.* a thinly applied layer of butter etc. on bread. **4** the scraping of a foot in bowing. **5** *colloq.* an awkward predicament, esp. resulting from an escapade. □ **scrape acquaintance with** contrive to get to know (a person). **scrape the barrel** *colloq.* be reduced to one's last resources. [Middle English from Old Norse *skrapa* or Middle Dutch *schrapen*]

scraper /ˈskreɪpə/ *n.* a device used for scraping, esp. for removing dirt or paint from a surface.

scraperboard /ˈskreɪpəbɔːd/ *n. Brit.* cardboard or board with a blackened surface which can be scraped off for making white-line drawings.

scrap heap *n.* **1** a pile of scrap materials. **2** a state of uselessness (esp. in phr. **on the scrap heap**).

scrapie /ˈskreɪpi/ *n.* a disease of sheep involving the central nervous system, characterized by lack of coordination causing affected animals to rub against trees etc. for support, and thought to be caused by a virus-like agent such as a prion.

scraping /ˈskreɪpɪŋ/ *n.* **1** in senses of SCRAPE. **2** (esp. in *pl.*) a fragment produced by scraping off, up, or together.

scrap merchant *n.* a dealer in scrap.

scrappy /ˈskrapi/ *adj.* (**scrappier**, **scrappiest**) **1** consisting of scraps. **2** incomplete; carelessly arranged or put together. □ **scrappily** *adv.* **scrappiness** *n.*

scrapyard /ˈskrapjɑːd/ *n.* a place where (esp. metal) scrap is collected.

scratch /skratʃ/ *v., n., & adj.* ● *v.* **1** *tr.* score or mark the surface of with a sharp or pointed object. **2** *tr.* **a** make a long narrow superficial wound in (the skin). **b** cause (a person or part of the body) to be scratched (*scratched himself on the table*). **3** *tr.* (also *absol.*) scrape without marking, esp. with the hand to relieve itching (*stood there scratching*). **4** *tr.* make or form by scratching. **5** *tr.* scribble; write hurriedly or awkwardly (*scratched a quick reply; scratched a large A*). **6** *tr.* (foll. by *together, up*, etc.) obtain (a thing) by scratching or with difficulty. **7** *tr.* (foll. by *out, off, through*) cancel or strike (out) with a pencil etc. **8** *tr.* (also *absol.*) withdraw (a competitor, candidate, etc.) from a race or competition. **9** *intr.* (often foll. by *about, around*, etc.) **a** scratch the ground etc. in search. **b** look around haphazardly (*they were scratching about for evidence*). ● *n.* **1** a mark or wound made by scratching. **2** a sound of scratching. **3** a spell of scratching oneself (*had a scratch*). **4** *colloq.* a superficial wound. **5 a** a line from which competitors in a race (esp. those not receiving a handicap) start. **b** *Golf* a handicap of zero. **6** (in *pl.*) a disease of horses in which the pastern appears scratched. **7** *slang* money. **8** a technique, used esp. in rap music, of stopping a record by hand and moving it back and forth to make a scratching sound. ● *attrib.adj.* **1** collected by chance. **2** collected or made from whatever is available; heterogeneous (*a scratch crew*). **3** with no handicap given (*a scratch race*). □ **from scratch 1** from the beginning. **2** without help or advantage. **scratch along** make a living etc. with difficulty. **scratch one's head** be perplexed. **scratch my back and I will scratch yours 1** do me a favour and I will return it. **2** used in reference to mutual aid or flattery. **scratch the surface 1** gain a superficial insight (into a problem, matter, etc.). **2** investigate further (*scratch the surface and you'll find corruption*). **up to scratch** up to the required standard. □ **scratcher** *n.* [Middle English, probably from synonymous Middle English *scrat* and *cratch*, both of uncertain origin: cf. Middle Low German *kratsen*, Old High German *krazzōn*]

scratchings /ˈskratʃɪŋz/ *n.pl.* (in full **pork scratchings**) crisp pieces of pork fat left after rendering lard, sold in packets as a snack.

scratch pad *n.* **1** esp. *N. Amer.* a pad of paper for scribbling. **2** *Computing* a small fast memory for the temporary storage of data.

scratch video *n.* a video made by mixing together short clips, esp. with a synchronized soundtrack.

scratchy /ˈskratʃi/ *adj.* (**scratchier**, **scratchiest**) **1** tending to make scratches or a scratching noise. **2** (esp. of a garment) tending to cause itchiness. **3** (of a drawing etc.) done in scratches or carelessly. □ **scratchily** *adv.* **scratchiness** *n.*

scrawl /skrɔːl/ *v. & n.* ● *v.* **1** *tr. & intr.* write in a hurried untidy way. **2** *tr.* (foll. by *out*) cross out by scrawling over. ● *n.* **1** a piece of hurried writing. **2** a scrawled note. □ **scrawly** *adj.* [perhaps from obsolete *scrawl* 'sprawl', alteration of CRAWL]

scrawny /ˈskrɔːni/ *adj.* (**scrawnier**, **scrawniest**) lean, scraggy. □ **scrawniness** *n.* [variant of dialect *scranny*: cf. archaic *scrannel* (of sound) 'weak, feeble']

scream /skriːm/ *n. & v.* ● *n.* **1** a loud high-pitched piercing cry expressing fear, pain, extreme fright, etc. **2** a similar sound, e.g. of sirens. **3** *colloq.* an irresistibly funny occurrence or person. ● *v.* **1** *intr.* emit a scream. **2** *tr.* speak or sing (words etc.) in a screaming tone. **3** *intr.* **a** move with a shrill sound like a scream (*a train screamed past*). **b** make a noise like a scream. **4** *intr.* laugh uncontrollably. **5** *intr.* be blatantly obvious or conspicuous. **6** *intr. colloq.* turn informer. [Old English or Middle Dutch]

screamer /ˈskriːmə/ *n.* **1** a person or thing that screams. **2** any S. American goose-like bird of the family Anhimidae, frequenting marshland and having a characteristic shrill cry. **3** *colloq.* a tale that raises screams of laughter. **4** *US colloq.* a sensational headline.

screamingly /ˈskriːmɪŋli/ *adv.* **1** extremely (*screamingly funny*). **2** blatantly (*screamingly obvious*).

scree /skriː/ *n.* (in *sing.* or *pl.*) **1** small loose stones. **2** a mountain slope covered with these. [probably a back-formation from *screes* (pl.), ultimately from Old Norse *skritha* 'landslip', related to *skrítha* 'glide']

screech /skriːtʃ/ *n. & v.* ● *n.* a harsh high-pitched scream. ● *v.tr. & intr.* utter with or make a screech. □ **screecher** *n.* **screechy** *adj.* (**screechier**, **screechiest**). [16th-c. variant of Middle English *scritch* (imitative)]

screech owl *n.* an owl with a screeching rather than a hooting call, esp. the barn owl or a small American owl, *Otus asio*.

screed /skriːd/ *n.* **1** a long usu. tiresome piece of writing or speech. **2 a** a strip of plaster or other material placed on a surface as a guide to thickness. **b** a levelled layer of material (e.g. cement) applied to a floor or other surface. □ **screeding** *n.* (in sense 2b). [Middle English, probably a variant of SHRED]

screen /skriːn/ *n. & v.* ● *n.* **1** a fixed or movable upright partition for separating, concealing, or sheltering from draughts or excessive heat or light. **2** a thing used as a shelter, esp. from observation. **3 a** a measure adopted for concealment. **b** the protection afforded by this (*under the screen of night*). **4 a** a blank usu. white or silver surface on which a photographic image is projected. **b** (prec. by *the*) the cinema industry. **5** the surface of a cathode ray tube or similar electronic device, esp. of a television, VDU, etc., on which images appear. **6** = SIGHT-SCREEN. **7** = WINDSCREEN. **8** a frame with fine wire netting to keep out flies, mosquitoes, etc. **9** *Physics* a body intercepting light, heat, electric or magnetic induction, etc., in a physical apparatus. **10** *Photog.* a piece of ground glass in a camera for focusing. **11** a large sieve or riddle, esp. for sorting grain, coal, etc., into sizes. **12** a system of checking for the presence or absence of a disease, ability, attribute, etc. **13** *Printing* a transparent finely ruled plate or film used in half-tone reproduction. **14** *Mil.* a body of troops, ships, etc., detached to warn of the presence of an enemy force. ● *v.tr.* **1** (often foll. by *from*) **a** afford shelter to; hide partly or completely. **b** protect from detection, censure, etc. **2** (foll. by *off*) shut off or hide behind a screen. **3 a** show (a film etc.) on a screen. **b** broadcast (a television programme). **4** prevent from causing, or protect from, electrical interference. **5 a** test (a person or group) for the presence or absence of a disease. **b** check on (a person) for the presence or absence of a quality, esp. reliability or loyalty. **6** pass (grain, coal, etc.) through a screen. □ **screenable** *adj.* **screener** *n.* **screening** *n.* [Middle English from Old Northern French *escren, escran*: cf. Old High German *skrank* 'barrier']

screenings /'skri:nɪŋz/ *n.pl.* refuse separated by sifting.

screenplay /'skri:npleɪ/ *n.* the script of a film, with acting instructions, scene directions, etc.

screen printing *n.* a process like stencilling with ink forced through a prepared sheet of fine material (originally silk). □ **screen print** *n.* **screen-print** *v.tr.* (usu. as **screen-printed** *adj.*).

screen saver *n. Computing* a program which, after a set time, replaces an unchanging screen display with a moving image to prevent damage to the phosphor.

screen test *n.* an audition for a part in a cinema film.

screenwriter /'skri:nrʌɪtə/ *n.* a person who writes a screenplay. □ **screenwriting** *n.*

screw /skru:/ *n. & v.* ● *n.* **1** a thin cylinder or cone with a spiral ridge or thread running round the outside (**male screw**) or the inside (**female screw**). **2** (in full **woodscrew** /'wʊdskru:/) a metal male screw with a slotted head and a sharp point for fastening things, esp. in carpentry, by being rotated to form a thread in wood etc. **3** (in full **screw-bolt**) a metal male screw with a blunt end on which a nut is threaded to bolt things together. **4** a wooden or metal straight screw used to exert pressure. **5** (in *sing.* or *pl.*) an instrument of torture acting in this way. **6** (in full **screw propeller**) a form of propeller with twisted blades acting like a screw on the water or air. **7** one turn of a screw. **8** (foll. by *of*) *Brit.* a small twisted-up paper (of tobacco etc.). **9** *Brit.* (in billiards etc.) an oblique curling motion of the ball. **10** *slang offens.* a prison warder. **11** *Brit. slang* an amount of salary or wages. **12** *coarse slang* **a** an act of sexual intercourse. **b** a partner in this. **13** *Brit. slang* a mean or miserly person. **14** *Brit. slang* a worn-out horse. ● *v.* **1** *tr.* fasten or tighten with a screw or screws. **2** *tr.* turn (a screw). **3** *intr.* twist or turn round like a screw. **4** *tr.* **a** put psychological etc. pressure on to achieve an end. **b** oppress. **5** *tr.* **a** (foll. by *out of*) extort (consent, money, etc.) from (a person). **b** swindle. **6** *tr.* (also *absol.*) *coarse slang* have sexual intercourse with. **7** *Brit.* **a** *intr.* (esp. of a billiard ball) take a curling course; swerve. **b** *tr.* cause (esp. a billiard ball) to swerve. **8** *tr.* = *screw up*. □ **have one's head screwed on the right way** *colloq.* have common sense. **have a screw loose** *colloq.* be slightly crazy. **put the screws on** (also *absol.*) *colloq.* exert pressure on (a person), esp. to extort something or to intimidate. **screw around** *coarse slang* be sexually promiscuous. **screw up 1** contract or contort (one's face etc.). **2** contract and crush into a tight mass (a piece of paper etc.). **3** summon up (one's courage etc.). **4** *slang* **a** bungle or mismanage. **b** spoil or ruin (an event, opportunity, etc.). **5** *slang* upset; disturb mentally. □ **screwable** *adj.* **screwer** *n.* [Middle English via Old French *escroue* 'female screw, nut', from Latin *scrofa* 'sow']

screwball /'skru:bɔ:l/ *n. & adj. N. Amer.* ● *n.* **1** *Baseball* a ball pitched with reverse spin against the natural curve. **2** *slang* a crazy or eccentric person. ● *adj. slang* crazy.

screw cap *n.* = SCREW TOP.

screw-coupling *n.* a female screw with threads at both ends for joining lengths of pipes or rods.

screwdriver /'skru:drʌɪvə/ *n.* **1** a tool with a shaped tip to fit into the head of a screw to turn it. **2** a cocktail made from vodka and orange juice.

screwed /skru:d/ *adj.* **1** twisted. **2** *slang* **a** ruined; rendered ineffective. **b** drunk.

screw eye *n.* a screw with a loop for passing cord etc. through instead of a slotted head.

screw gear *n.* an endless screw with a cogwheel or pinion.

screw hook *n.* a hook to hang things on, with a screw point for fastening it.

screw-jack *n.* a vehicle jack (see JACK[1] *n.* 1) worked by a screw device.

screw pine *n.* = PANDANUS 1.

screw-plate *n.* a steel plate with threaded holes for making male screws.

screw propeller see SCREW *n.* 6.

screw-tap *n.* a tool for making female screws.

screw top *n.* (hyphenated when *attrib.*) a cap or lid that can be screwed on to a bottle, jar, etc.

screw-up *n. slang* a bungle, muddle, or mess.

screw valve *n.* a stopcock opened and shut by a screw.

screwy /'skru:i/ *adj.* (**screwier, screwiest**) *slang* **1** crazy or eccentric. **2** absurd. □ **screwiness** *n.*

scribble[1] /'skrɪb(ə)l/ *v. & n.* ● *v.* **1** *tr. & intr.* write carelessly or hurriedly. **2** *intr.* often *derog.* be an author or writer. **3** *intr. & tr.* draw carelessly or meaninglessly. ● *n.* **1** a scrawl. **2** a hasty note etc. **3** careless handwriting. □ **scribbler** *n.* **scribbly** *adj.* [Middle English from medieval Latin *scribillare*, diminutive of Latin *scribere* 'write']

scribble[2] /'skrɪb(ə)l/ *v.tr.* card (wool, cotton, etc.) coarsely. [probably from Low German: cf. German *schrubbeln* (in the same sense), frequentative of Low German *schrubben*: see SCRUB[1]]

scribe /skrʌɪb/ *n. & v.* ● *n.* **1** a person who writes out documents, esp. *hist.* an ancient or medieval copyist of manuscripts. **2** *Jewish Hist.* an ancient Jewish record-keeper or, later, a professional theologian and jurist. **3** (in full **scribe-awl**) a pointed instrument for making marks on wood, bricks, etc., to guide a saw, or in signwriting. **4** *N. Amer. colloq.* a writer, esp. a journalist. ● *v.tr.* mark (wood etc.) with a scribe (see sense 3 of *n.*). □ **scribal** *adj.* [the noun Middle English from Latin *scriba*, from *scribere* 'write': the verb perhaps from DESCRIBE]

scriber /'skrʌɪbə/ *n.* = SCRIBE *n.* 3.

scrim /skrɪm/ *n.* open-weave fabric for lining or upholstery etc. [18th c.: origin unknown]

scrimmage /'skrɪmɪdʒ/ *n. & v.* ● *n.* **1** a rough or confused struggle; a brawl. **2** *Amer. Football* a sequence of play beginning with the placing of the ball on the ground with its longest axis at right angles to the goal line. ● *v.* **1** *intr.* engage in a scrimmage. **2** *tr. Amer. Football* put (the ball) into a scrimmage. □ **scrimmager** *n.* [variant of SKIRMISH]

scrimp /skrɪmp/ *v.* **1** *intr.* be sparing or parsimonious. **2** *tr.* use sparingly. □ **scrimpy** *adj.* [17th c., originally Scots: perhaps related to SHRIMP]

scrimshander /'skrɪmʃandə/ *v. & n.* ● *v.tr.* (also *absol.*) = SCRIMSHAW. ● *n.* a person who scrimshaws.

scrimshank /'skrɪmʃaŋk/ *v.intr. Brit. slang* esp. *Mil.* shirk duty. □ **scrimshanker** *n.* [19th c.: origin unknown]

scrimshaw /'skrɪmʃɔ:/ *v. & n.* ● *v.tr.* (also *absol.*) adorn (shells, ivory, etc.) with carved or coloured designs (as sailors' pastime at sea). ● *n.* work or a piece of work of this kind. [19th c.: perhaps from a surname]

scrip /skrɪp/ *n.* **1** a provisional certificate of money subscribed to a bank or company etc. entitling the holder to a formal certificate and dividends. **2** (*collect.*) such certificates. **3** an extra share or shares instead of a dividend. [abbreviation of *subscription receipt*]

script /skrɪpt/ *n. & v.* ● *n.* **1** handwriting as distinct from print; written characters. **2** type imitating handwriting. **3** an alphabet or system of writing (*the Russian script*). **4** the text of a play, film, or broadcast. **5** an examinee's set of written answers. **6** *Law* an original document as distinct from a copy. ● *v.tr.* write a script for (a film etc.). [Middle English, = thing written, via Old French *escri(p)t* from Latin *scriptum*, neut. past part. of *scribere* 'write']

scriptorium /skrɪp'tɔːrɪəm/ *n.* (*pl.* **scriptoria** /-rɪə/ or **scriptoriums**) a room set apart for writing, esp. in a monastery. □ **scriptorial** *adj.* [medieval Latin (as SCRIPT)]

scriptural /'skrɪptʃ(ə)r(ə)l/ *adj.* **1** of or relating to a scripture, esp. the Bible. **2** having the authority of a scripture. □ **scripturally** *adv.* [Late Latin *scripturalis* from Latin *scriptura*: see SCRIPTURE]

scripture /'skrɪptʃə/ *n.* **1** sacred writings. **2** (**Scripture** or **the Scriptures**) **a** the Bible as a collection of sacred writings in Christianity. **b** the sacred writings of any other religion. [Middle English from Latin *scriptura*, past part. stem of *scribere* 'write']

scriptwriter /'skrɪptrʌɪtə/ *n.* a person who writes a script for a film, broadcast, etc. □ **scriptwriting** *n.*

scrivener /'skrɪv(ə)nə/ *n. hist.* **1** a copyist or drafter of documents. **2** a notary. **3** a broker. **4** a moneylender. [Middle English from obsolete *scrivein* from Old French *escrivein*, ultimately from Latin (as SCRIBE)]

scrobiculate /skrə'bɪkjʊlət/ *adj. Bot. & Zool.* pitted, furrowed. [Latin *scrobiculus* from *scrobis* 'trench']

scrod /skrɒd/ *n. N. Amer.* a young cod or haddock, esp. as food. [19th c.: origin unknown]

scrofula /'skrɒfjʊlə/ *n. archaic* a disease with glandular swellings, probably a form of tuberculosis. Also called KING'S EVIL. □ **scrofulous** *adj.* [Middle English from medieval Latin (sing.), from Late Latin *scrofulae* (pl.) 'scrofulous swelling', diminutive of Latin *scrofa* 'a sow']

scroll /skrəʊl/ *n. & v.* ● *n.* **1** a roll of parchment or paper esp. with writing on it. **2** a book in the ancient roll form. **3** an ornamental design or carving imitating a roll of parchment. ● *v.* **1** *tr.* (often foll. by *down, up*) move (a display on a VDU screen) in order to view new material. **2** *tr.* inscribe in or like a scroll. **3** *intr.* curl up like paper. □ **scroller** *n.* (in sense 1 of *v.*). [Middle English *scrowle*, alteration of *rowle* ROLL, perhaps influenced by *scrow* (in the same sense), from ESCROW]

scroll bar *n.* a long thin section at the edge of a computer display by which material can be scrolled using a mouse.

scrolled /skrəʊld/ *adj.* having a scroll ornament.

scroll saw *n.* a saw for cutting along curved lines in ornamental work.

scrollwork /'skrəʊlwəːk/ *n.* decoration of spiral lines, esp. as cut by a scroll saw.

Scrooge /skruːdʒ/ *n.* a mean or miserly person. [a character in Dickens's *A Christmas Carol*]

scrotum /'skrəʊtəm/ *n.* (*pl.* **scrota** /-tə/ or **scrotums**) a pouch of skin containing the testicles. □ **scrotal** *adj.* [Latin]

scrounge /skraʊn(d)ʒ/ *v. & n. colloq.* ● *v.* **1** *tr.* (also *absol.*) obtain (things) illicitly or by cadging. **2** *intr.* search about to find something at no cost. ● *n.* an act of scrounging. □ **on the scrounge** *Brit.* engaged in scrounging. □ **scrounger** *n.* [variant of dialect *scrunge* 'steal']

scrub[1] /skrʌb/ *v. & n.* ● *v.* (**scrubbed, scrubbing**) **1** *tr.* rub hard so as to clean, esp. with a hard brush. **2** *intr.* use a brush in this way. **3** *intr.* (often foll. by *up*) (of a surgeon etc.) thoroughly clean the hands and arms by scrubbing, before operating. **4** *tr. colloq.* scrap or cancel (a plan, order, etc.). **5** *tr.* use water to remove impurities from (gas etc.). **6 a** *intr.* (of tyres) scrape on the road surface, esp. when cornering. **b** *tr.* (foll. by *off*) reduce speed by allowing the tyres to scrape the road. ● *n.* the act or an instance of scrubbing; the process of being scrubbed. □ **scrub round** *Brit. colloq.* circumvent, avoid. [Middle English, probably from Middle Low German, Middle Dutch *schrobben, schrubben*]

scrub[2] /skrʌb/ *n.* **1 a** vegetation consisting mainly of brushwood or stunted forest growth. **b** an area of land covered with this. **2** *N. Amer.* an animal of inferior breed or physique (often *attrib.*: *scrub horse*). **3** a small or dwarf variety (often *attrib.*: *scrub pine*). **4** *US Sport colloq.* a team or player not of the first class. □ **scrubby** *adj.* [Middle English, variant of SHRUB[1]]

scrubber /'skrʌbə/ *n.* **1** an apparatus using water or a solution for purifying gases etc. **2** *Brit. slang offens.* a sexually promiscuous woman.

scrubbing-brush *n.* (*N. Amer.* **scrub-brush**) a hard brush for scrubbing floors.

scrubland /'skrʌblənd/ *n.* land consisting of scrub vegetation.

scrub turkey *n.* a megapode.

scrub typhus *n.* a rickettsial disease transmitted to humans by mites.

scruff[1] /skrʌf/ *n.* the back of the neck as used to grasp and lift or drag an animal or person by (esp. *scruff of the neck*). [alteration of *scuff*, perhaps from Old Norse *skoft* 'hair']

scruff[2] /skrʌf/ *n. Brit. colloq.* an untidy or scruffy person. [originally = SCURF, later 'worthless thing', or back-formation from SCRUFFY]

scruffy /'skrʌfi/ *adj.* (**scruffier, scruffiest**) *colloq.* shabby, slovenly, untidy. □ **scruffily** *adv.* **scruffiness** *n.* [*scruff* (variant of SCURF) + -Y[1]]

scrum /skrʌm/ *n. & v.* ● *n.* **1** *Rugby* an arrangement of the forwards of each team in two opposing groups, each with arms interlocked and heads down, with the ball thrown in between them to restart play. **2** *Brit. colloq.* a disorderly crowd. ● *v.intr.* **1** (often foll. by *down*) *Rugby* form a scrum. **2** *colloq.* jostle, crowd. [abbreviation of SCRUMMAGE]

scrum-half *n. Rugby* a half-back who puts the ball into the scrum.

scrummage /'skrʌmɪdʒ/ *n. & v. Rugby* ● *n.* = SCRUM *n.* 1. ● *v.intr.* = SCRUM *v.* 1. □ **scrummager** *n.* [as SCRIMMAGE]

scrump /skrʌmp/ *v.tr. Brit. colloq.* steal (fruit) from an orchard or garden. [cf. SCRUMPY]

scrumple /'skrʌmp(ə)l/ *v.tr. Brit.* crumple, wrinkle. [variant of CRUMPLE]

scrumptious /'skrʌm(p)ʃəs/ *adj. colloq.* **1** delicious. **2** pleasing, delightful. □ **scrumptiously** *adv.* **scrumptiousness** *n.* [19th c.: origin unknown]

scrumpy /'skrʌmpi/ *n. Brit. colloq.* rough cider, esp. as made in the West Country of England. [dialect *scrump* 'small apple']

scrunch /skrʌn(t)ʃ/ *v. & n.* ● *v.* **1** *tr. & intr.* (usu. foll. by *up*) make or become crushed or crumpled. **2** *intr. & tr.* make or cause to make a crunching sound. **3** *tr.* style (hair) by squeezing or crushing in the hands to give a tousled look. ● *n.* the act or an instance of scrunching. [variant of CRUNCH]

scrunch-dry *v.tr.* dry (hair) while scrunching it.

scrunchy /'skrʌn(t)ʃi/ *n.* (*pl.* **-ies**) (also **scrunchie**) a circular band of fabric-covered elastic used for fastening the hair.

scruple /'skruːp(ə)l/ *n. & v.* ● *n.* **1** (in *sing.* or *pl.*) **a** regard to the morality or propriety of an action. **b** a feeling of doubt or hesitation caused by this. **2** *hist.* an apothecaries' weight of 20 grains. **3** *archaic* a very small quantity. ● *v.intr.* **1** (foll. by *to* + infin.; usu. with *neg.*) be reluctant because of scruples (*did not scruple to stop their allowance*). **2** feel or be influenced by scruples. [French *scrupule* or Latin *scrupulus*, from *scrupus* 'rough pebble, anxiety']

scrupulous /'skruːpjʊləs/ *adj.* **1** conscientious or thorough even in small matters. **2** careful to avoid doing wrong. **3** punctilious; over-attentive to details. □ **scrupulosity** /-'lɒsɪti/ *n.* **scrupulously** *adv.* **scrupulousness** *n.* [Middle English from French *scrupuleux* or Latin *scrupulosus* (as SCRUPLE)]

scrutineer /skruːtɪ'nɪə/ *n.* a person who scrutinizes or examines something, esp. *Brit.* the conduct and result of a ballot.

scrutinize /'skruːtɪnʌɪz/ *v.tr.* (also **-ise**) look closely at; examine with close scrutiny. □ **scrutinization** /-'zeɪʃ(ə)n/ *n.* **scrutinizer** *n.*

scrutiny /ˈskru:tɪni/ *n.* (*pl.* **-ies**) **1** a critical gaze. **2** a close investigation or examination of details. **3** an official examination of ballot papers to check their validity or accuracy of counting. [Middle English from Latin *scrutinium*, via *scrutari* 'search' (originally 'sort rubbish') from *scruta* 'rubbish']

scry /skrʌɪ/ *v.intr.* (**-ies**, **-ied**) divine by crystal-gazing. □ **scryer** *n.* [shortening of DESCRY]

scuba /ˈsku:bə, ˈskju:bə/ *n.* (*pl.* **scubas**) an aqualung. [acronym from *s*elf-*c*ontained *u*nderwater *b*reathing *a*pparatus]

scuba-diving /ˈsku:bədʌɪvɪŋ, ˈskju:-/ *n.* swimming underwater using a scuba, esp. as a sport. □ **scuba-dive** *v.intr.* **scuba-diver** *n.*

scud /skʌd/ *v. & n.* ● *v.intr.* (**scudded**, **scudding**) **1** fly or run straight, fast, and lightly; skim along. **2** *Naut.* run before the wind. ● *n.* **1** a spell of scudding. **2** a scudding motion. **3** vapoury driving clouds. **4** a driving shower; a gust. **5** wind-blown spray. **6** (usu. **Scud**) a type of long-range surface-to-surface guided missile originally developed in the former USSR. [perhaps alteration of SCUT, as if to race like a hare]

scuff /skʌf/ *v. & n.* ● *v.* **1** *tr.* graze or brush against. **2** *tr.* mark or wear down (shoes) in this way. **3** *intr.* walk with dragging feet; shuffle. ● *n.* a mark made by scuffing. [imitative]

scuffle /ˈskʌf(ə)l/ *n. & v.* ● *n.* a confused struggle or disorderly fight at close quarters. ● *v.intr.* engage in a scuffle. [probably of Scandinavian origin: cf. Swedish *skuffa* 'to push', related to SHOVE]

sculduggery var. of SKULDUGGERY.

scull /skʌl/ *n. & v.* ● *n.* **1** either of a pair of small oars used by a single rower. **2** an oar placed over the stern of a boat to propel it, usu. by a twisting motion. **3** a small boat propelled with a scull or a pair of sculls. **4** (in *pl.*) a race between boats with single pairs of oars. ● *v.tr.* propel (a boat) with sculls. [Middle English: origin unknown]

sculler /ˈskʌlə/ *n.* **1** a user of sculls. **2** a boat intended for sculling.

scullery /ˈskʌl(ə)ri/ *n.* (*pl.* **-ies**) a small kitchen or room at the back of a house for washing dishes etc. [Middle English via Anglo-French *squillerie*, Old French *escuelerie*, from *escuele* 'dish' from Latin *scutella* 'salver', diminutive of *scutra* 'wooden platter']

scullion /ˈskʌlɪən/ *n. archaic* **1** a cook's boy. **2** a person who washes dishes etc. [Middle English: origin unknown but perhaps influenced by *scullery*]

sculpin /ˈskʌlpɪn/ *n.* any of numerous fish of the family Cottidae, native to non-tropical regions, having large spiny heads. [perhaps from obsolete *scorpene*, via Latin *scorpaena* from Greek *skorpaina*, a kind of fish]

sculpt /skʌlpt/ *v.tr. & intr.* (also **sculp**) sculpture. [French *sculpter* from *sculpteur* SCULPTOR: now regarded as a back-formation from SCULPTOR or SCULPTURE]

sculptor /ˈskʌlptə/ *n.* (*fem.* **sculptress** /-trɪs/) an artist who makes sculptures. [Latin (as SCULPTURE)]

sculpture /ˈskʌlptʃə/ *n. & v.* ● *n.* **1** the art of making forms, often representational, in the round or in relief by chiselling stone, carving wood, modelling clay, casting metal, etc. **2** a work or works of sculpture. **3** *Zool.* & *Bot.* raised or sunken markings on a shell etc. ● *v.* **1** *tr.* represent in or adorn with sculpture. **2** *intr.* practise sculpture. □ **sculptural** *adj.* **sculpturally** *adv.* **sculpturesque** *adj.* [Middle English from Latin *sculptura*, from *sculpere sculpt-* 'carve']

scum /skʌm/ *n. & v.* ● *n.* **1** a layer of dirt, froth, or impurities etc. forming at the top of liquid, esp. in boiling or fermentation. **2** (foll. by *of*) the most worthless part of something. **3** *colloq.* a worthless person or group. ● *v.* (**scummed**, **scumming**) **1** *tr.* remove scum from; skim. **2** *tr.* be or form a scum on. **3** *intr.* (of a liquid) develop scum. □ **scummy** *adj.* (**scummier**, **scummiest**). [Middle English via Middle Low German, Middle Dutch *schūm* from Germanic]

scumbag /ˈskʌmbag/ *n. slang* a contemptible or disgusting person.

scumble /ˈskʌmb(ə)l/ *v. & n.* ● *v.tr.* **1** modify (a painting) by applying a thin opaque coat of paint to give a softer or duller effect. **2** modify (a drawing) similarly with light pencilling etc. ● *n.* **1** material used in scumbling. **2** the effect produced by scumbling. [perhaps frequentative of SCUM *v.*]

scuncheon /ˈskʌn(t)ʃ(ə)n/ *n.* the inside face of a door jamb, window frame, etc. [Middle English from Old French *escoinson* (as EX-[1], COIN)]

scunge /skʌn(d)ʒ/ *n. Austral.* & *NZ colloq.* **1** dirt, scum. **2** a dirty or disagreeable person. □ **scungy** *adj.* (**scungier**, **scungiest**). [perhaps from English dialect *scrunge* 'steal': cf. SCROUNGE]

scunner /ˈskʌnə/ *v. & n. Sc.* ● *v.intr.* feel disgust or nausea. ● *n.* **1** a strong dislike (esp. *take a scunner at* or *against*). **2** an object of loathing. [Middle English: origin uncertain]

scupper[1] /ˈskʌpə/ *n.* a hole in a ship's side to carry off water from the deck. [Middle English (perhaps from Anglo-French) via Old French *escopir* from Romanic *skuppire* (unrecorded) 'to spit': originally imitative]

scupper[2] /ˈskʌpə/ *v.tr. Brit. slang* **1** sink (a ship or its crew). **2** defeat or ruin (a plan etc.). **3** kill. [19th c.: origin unknown]

scurf /skə:f/ *n.* **1** flakes on the surface of the skin, cast off as fresh skin develops below, esp. those of the head; dandruff. **2** any scaly matter on a surface. □ **scurfy** *adj.* [Old English, probably from Old Norse & earlier Old English *sceorf*, related to *sceorfan* 'gnaw', *sceorfian* 'cut to shreds']

scurrilous /ˈskʌrɪləs/ *adj.* **1** (of a person or language) grossly or indecently abusive. **2** given to or expressed with low humour. □ **scurrility** /-ˈrɪlɪti/ *n.* (*pl.* **-ies**). **scurrilously** *adv.* **scurrilousness** *n.* [French *scurrile* or Latin *scurrilus*, from *scurra* 'buffoon']

scurry /ˈskʌri/ *v. & n.* ● *v.intr.* (**-ies**, **-ied**) run or move hurriedly, esp. with short quick steps; scamper. ● *n.* (*pl.* **-ies**) **1** the act or sound of scurrying. **2** bustle, haste. **3** a flurry of rain or snow. [abbreviation of *hurry-scurry*, reduplication of HURRY]

scurvy /ˈskə:vi/ *n. & adj.* ● *n.* a disease caused by a deficiency of vitamin C, characterized by swollen bleeding gums and the opening of previously healed wounds, esp. formerly affecting sailors. ● *adj.* (**scurvier**, **scurviest**) *archaic* dishonourable, contemptible. □ **scurvied** *adj.* **scurvily** *adv.* [SCURF + -Y[1]: noun sense by association with French *scorbut* (cf. SCORBUTIC)]

scurvy grass *n.* any cresslike seaside plant of the genus *Cochlearia*, originally taken as a cure for scurvy.

scut /skʌt/ *n.* a short tail, esp. of a hare, rabbit, or deer. [Middle English: origin unknown: cf. obsolete *scut* 'short, shorten']

scuta *pl.* of SCUTUM.

scutage /ˈskju:tɪdʒ/ *n. hist.* money paid by a feudal landowner instead of personal service. [Middle English via medieval Latin *scutagium* from Latin *scutum* 'shield']

scutch /skʌtʃ/ *v.tr.* dress (fibrous material, esp. retted flax) by beating. □ **scutcher** *n.* [Old French *escoucher*, dialect variant of *escousser*, ultimately from Latin *excutere excuss-* (as EX-[1], *quatere* 'shake')]

scutcheon /ˈskʌtʃ(ə)n/ *n.* **1** = ESCUTCHEON. **2** an ornamented brass etc. plate round or over a keyhole. **3** a plate for a name or inscription. [Middle English from ESCUTCHEON]

scute /skju:t/ *n. Zool.* = SCUTUM. [Latin (as SCUTUM)]

scutellum /skjʊˈtɛləm/ *n.* (*pl.* **scutella** /-lə/) *Bot.* & *Zool.* a scale, plate, or any shieldlike formation on a plant, insect, bird, etc., esp. one of the horny scales on a bird's foot. □ **scutellate** /ˈskju:tələt/ *adj.* **scutellation** /skju:təˈleɪʃ(ə)n/ *n.* [modern Latin diminutive of Latin *scutum* 'shield']

scutter /ˈskʌtə/ *v. & n.* esp. *Brit.* ● *v.intr. colloq.* scurry. ● *n.* the act or an instance of scuttering. [perhaps alteration of SCUTTLE²]

scuttle¹ /ˈskʌt(ə)l/ *n.* **1** a receptacle for carrying and holding a small supply of coal. **2** *Brit.* the part of a motor car body between the windscreen and the bonnet. [Middle English via Old Norse *skutill*, Old High German *scuzzila* from Latin *scutella* 'dish']

scuttle² /ˈskʌt(ə)l/ *v. & n.* ● *v.intr.* **1** scurry; hurry along. **2** run away; flee from danger or difficulty. ● *n.* **1** a hurried gait. **2** a precipitate flight or departure. [cf. dialect *scuddle*, frequentative of SCUD]

scuttle³ /ˈskʌt(ə)l/ *n. & v.* ● *n.* a hole with a lid in a ship's deck or side. ● *v.tr.* let water into (a ship) to sink it, esp. by opening the seacocks. [Middle English, perhaps via obsolete French *escoutille* from Spanish *escotilla* 'hatchway', diminutive of *escota* 'the cutting out of cloth']

scuttlebutt /ˈskʌt(ə)lbʌt/ *n.* **1** a water-butt on the deck of a ship, for drinking from. **2** *colloq.* rumour, gossip.

scutum /ˈskjuːtəm/ *n.* (*pl.* **scuta** /-tə/) each of the shieldlike plates or scales forming the bony covering of a crocodile, sturgeon, turtle, armadillo, etc. □ **scutal** *adj.* **scutate** *adj.* [Latin, = oblong shield]

scuzzy /ˈskʌzi/ *adj. slang* abhorrent or disgusting. □ **scuzz** *n.* [probably an abbreviation of DISGUSTING]

Scylla and Charybdis /ˌsɪlə(r) (ə)nd kəˈrɪbdɪs/ *n.pl.* two dangers such that avoidance of one increases the risk from the other. [the names of a sea monster and whirlpool in Greek mythology]

scyphozoan /sʌɪfəˈzəʊən, skʌɪf-, skɪf-/ *n. & adj.* ● *n.* any marine jellyfish of the class Scyphozoa, with tentacles bearing stinging cells. ● *adj.* of or relating to this class. [as SCYPHUS + Greek *zōion* 'animal']

scyphus /ˈsʌɪfəs/ *n.* (*pl.* **scyphi** /-fʌɪ/) **1** *Gk Antiq.* a footless drinking cup with two handles below the level of the rim. **2** *Bot.* a cup-shaped part as in a narcissus flower or in lichens. □ **scyphose** *adj.* [modern Latin from Greek *skuphos*]

scythe /sʌɪð/ *n. & v.* ● *n.* a mowing and reaping implement with a long curved blade swung over the ground by a long pole with two short handles projecting from it. ● *v.tr.* cut with a scythe. [Old English *sīthe*, from Germanic]

Scythian /ˈsɪðɪən, ˈsɪθ-/ *adj. & n.* ● *adj.* of or relating to ancient Scythia, a region north of the black Sea. ● *n.* **1** an inhabitant of Scythia. **2** the language of this region. [Latin *Scythia* from Greek *Skuthia* 'Scythia']

SD *abbr. US* South Dakota (in official postal use).

S.Dak. *abbr.* South Dakota.

SDI *abbr.* strategic defence initiative.

SDLP *abbr.* (in N. Ireland) Social Democratic and Labour Party.

SDP *abbr. hist.* (in the UK) Social Democratic Party.

SDR *abbr.* special drawing right (from the International Monetary Fund).

SE *abbr.* **1** south-east. **2** south-eastern.

Se *symb. Chem.* the element selenium.

se- /sə, sɪ/ *prefix* apart, without (*seclude*; *secure*). [Latin from Old Latin *se* (*prep. & adv.*)]

sea /siː/ *n.* **1** the expanse of salt water that covers most of the earth's surface and surrounds its land masses. **2** any part of this as opposed to land or fresh water. **3** a particular (usu. named) tract of salt water partly or wholly enclosed by land (*the North Sea*; *the Dead Sea*). **4** a large inland lake (*the Caspian Sea*). **5** the waves of the sea, esp. with reference to their local motion or state (*a choppy sea*). **6** (foll. by *of*) a vast quantity or expanse (*a sea of troubles*; *a sea of faces*). **7** (*attrib.*) living or used in, on, or near the sea (often prefixed to the name of a marine animal, plant, etc., having a superficial resemblance to what it is named after) (*sea lettuce*). □ **at sea 1** in a ship on the sea. **2** (also **all at sea**) perplexed, confused. **by sea** in a ship or ships. **go to sea** become a sailor. **on the sea 1** in a ship at sea. **2** situated on the coast. **put** (or **put out**) **to sea** leave land or port. [Old English *sǣ*, from Germanic]

sea anchor *n.* a device such as a heavy bag dragged in the water to retard the drifting of a ship.

sea anemone *n.* any of various coelenterates of the order Actiniaria having a polypoid body bearing a ring of tentacles around the mouth.

sea-angel *n.* an angelfish.

sea bass see BASS² 3.

seabed /ˈsiːbɛd/ *n.* the ground under the sea; the ocean floor.

seabird /ˈsiːbəːd/ *n.* a bird frequenting the sea or the land near the sea.

seaboard /ˈsiːbɔːd/ *n.* **1** the seashore or coastal region. **2** the line of a coast.

seaborgium /siːˈbɔːgɪəm/ *n. Chem.* (a name proposed for) the artificial radioactive element of atomic number 106 (symbol **Sg**). [named after G. *Seaborg*, US physicist b. 1912]

seaborne /ˈsiːbɔːn/ *adj.* transported by sea.

sea bream see BREAM¹ 2.

sea breeze *n.* a breeze blowing towards the land from the sea, esp. during the day (cf. LAND BREEZE).

sea buckthorn *n.* a maritime shrub, *Hippophae rhamnoides*, with orange berries.

sea change *n.* a notable or unexpected transformation (with reference to Shakespeare's *Tempest* I. ii. 403).

sea-chest *n.* a sailor's storage-chest.

sea coal *n. archaic* mineral coal, as distinct from charcoal etc.

seacock /ˈsiːkɒk/ *n.* a valve below a ship's waterline for letting water in or out.

sea cow *n.* a sirenian, esp. a manatee.

sea cucumber *n.* a holothurian, esp. a *bêche-de-mer*.

sea dog *n.* an old or experienced sailor.

sea eagle *n.* any fish-eating eagle esp. of the genus *Haliaeetus*.

sea-ear *n.* = ORMER.

sea elephant *n.* = ELEPHANT SEAL.

sea fan *n.* any colonial coral of the order Gorgonacea supported by a fanlike horny skeleton.

seafarer /ˈsiːfɛːrə/ *n.* **1** a sailor. **2** a traveller by sea.

seafaring /ˈsiːfɛːrɪŋ/ *adj. & n.* travelling by sea, esp. regularly.

seafood /ˈsiːfuːd/ *n.* edible sea fish or shellfish.

seafront /ˈsiːfrʌnt/ *n.* the part of a coastal town etc. directly facing the sea.

sea-girt *adj. literary* surrounded by sea.

seagoing /ˈsiːgəʊɪŋ/ *adj.* **1** (of ships) fit for crossing the sea. **2** (of a person) seafaring.

sea gooseberry *n.* any ctenophore (coelenterate) with an ovoid body bearing numerous cilia.

sea green *n. & adj.* ● *n.* a bluish green (as of the sea). ● *adj.* (hyphenated when *attrib.*) of this colour.

seagull /ˈsiːgʌl/ *n.* = GULL¹.

sea hare *n.* any sea slug of the order Anaspidea, esp. of the genus *Aplysia*, having an internal shell and long extensions from its foot.

sea holly *n.* a spiny-leaved blue-flowered evergreen plant, *Eryngium maritimum*.

sea horse *n.* **1** any of various small upright marine fish of the family Syngnathidae, esp. *Hippocampus hippocampus*, having a body suggestive of the head and neck of a horse. **2** a mythical creature with a horse's head and fish's tail.

sea-island cotton *n.* a fine-quality long-stapled cotton grown on islands off the southern US.

seajack /ˈsiːdʒak/ *v. & n.* ● *v.tr.* hijack at sea. ● *n.* an act of seajacking. □ **seajacker** *n.*

seakale /ˈsiːkeɪl/ *n.* a cruciferous maritime plant, *Crambe maritima*, having coarsely toothed leaves and used as a vegetable.

seakale beet *n.* = CHARD.

seal¹ /siːl/ *n. & v.* ● *n.* **1** a piece of wax, lead, paper, etc., with a stamped design, attached to a document as a guarantee of authenticity. **2** a similar material attached to a receptacle, envelope, etc., affording security by having to be broken to allow access to the contents. **3** an engraved piece of metal, gemstone, etc., for stamping a design on a seal. **4 a** a substance or device used to close an aperture or act as a fastening. **b** an amount of water standing in the trap of a drain to prevent foul air from rising. **5** an act, gesture, or event regarded as a confirmation or guarantee (*gave her seal of approval to the venture*). **6** a significant or prophetic mark (*has the seal of death in his face*). **7** a decorative adhesive stamp. **8** esp. *Eccl.* a vow of secrecy; an obligation to silence. ● *v.tr.* **1** close securely or hermetically. **2** stamp or fasten with a seal. **3** fix a seal to. **4** certify as correct with a seal or stamp. **5** (often foll. by *up*) confine or fasten securely. **6** settle or decide (*their fate is sealed*). **7** (foll. by *off*) put barriers round (an area) to prevent entry and exit, esp. as a security measure. **8** apply a non-porous coating to (a surface) to make it impervious. □ **one's lips are sealed** one is obliged to keep a secret. **set one's seal to** (or **on**) authorize or confirm. □ **sealable** *adj.* [Middle English via Anglo-French *seal*, Old French *seel* from Latin *sigillum*, diminutive of *signum* SIGN]

seal[2] /si:l/ *n. & v.* ● *n.* any fish-eating amphibious sea mammal of the family Phocidae or Otariidae, with flippers and webbed feet. ● *v.intr.* hunt for seals. [Old English *seolh seol-*, from Germanic]

sealant /ˈsi:lənt/ *n.* material for sealing, esp. to make something airtight or watertight.

sea lavender *n.* any maritime plant of the genus *Limonium*, with small brightly coloured funnel-shaped flowers.

sealed-beam *attrib.adj.* designating a vehicle headlamp with a sealed unit consisting of the light source, reflector, and lens.

sealed book *n.* = CLOSED BOOK.

sealed orders *n.pl.* orders for procedure not to be opened before a specified time.

sea legs *n.pl.* the ability to keep one's balance and avoid seasickness when at sea.

sealer[1] /ˈsi:lə/ *n.* **1** a device or substance used for making esp. a hermetic or an impervious seal. **2** (in full **sealer jar**) *Canad.* a jar designed to preserve fruit etc.

sealer[2] /ˈsi:lə/ *n.* a ship or person engaged in hunting seals.

sealery /ˈsi:ləri/ *n.* (*pl.* **-ies**) a place for hunting seals.

sea level *n.* the mean level of the sea's surface, used in reckoning the height of hills etc. and as a barometric standard.

sea lily *n.* any sessile echinoderm of the class Crinoidea, with long jointed stalks and feather-like arms for trapping food.

sealing wax *n.* a mixture of shellac and rosin with turpentine and pigment, softened by heating and used to make seals.

sea lion *n.* any large, eared seal of the Pacific, esp. of the genus *Zalophus* or *Otaria*.

sea loch *n.* = LOCH 2.

Sea Lord *n.* (in the UK) either of two senior naval officers (**First Sea Lord**, **Second Sea Lord**) serving originally as members of the Admiralty Board (now of the Ministry of Defence).

sealpoint /ˈsi:lpɔɪnt/ *n.* **1** a dark brown marking on the fur of one type of Siamese cat. **2** such a cat. [SEAL[2]]

seal ring *n.* a finger ring with a seal.

sealskin /ˈsi:lskɪn/ *n.* **1** the skin or prepared fur of a seal. **2** (often *attrib.*) a garment made from this.

seals of office *n.pl.* (in the UK) seals (see SEAL[1] *n.* 3) held during tenure, esp. by the Lord Chancellor or a Secretary of State, and symbolizing the office held.

Sealyham /ˈsi:lɪəm/ *n.* (in full **Sealyham terrier**) **1** a terrier of a wire-haired short-legged breed. **2** this breed. [*Sealyham*, a village in SW Wales, where the dog was first bred]

seam /si:m/ *n. & v.* ● *n.* **1** a line where two edges join, esp. of two pieces of cloth etc. turned back and stitched together, or of boards fitted edge to edge. **2** a fissure between parallel edges. **3** a wrinkle or scar. **4** a stratum of coal etc. ● *v.tr.* **1** join with a seam. **2** (esp. as **seamed** *adj.*) mark or score with or as with a seam. □ **bursting at the seams** full to overflowing. □ **seamer** *n.* [Old English *sēam*, from Germanic]

seaman /ˈsi:mən/ *n.* (*pl.* **-men**) **1** a sailor, esp. one below the rank of officer. **2** a person regarded in terms of skill in navigation (*a poor seaman*). □ **seamanlike** *adj.* **seamanly** *adj.* [Old English *sǣman* (as SEA, MAN)]

seamanship /ˈsi:mənʃɪp/ *n.* skill in managing a ship or boat.

seam bowler *n.* *Cricket* a bowler who makes the ball deviate by bouncing off its seam.

sea mile *n.* a unit of length varying between approx. 2,014 yards (1,842 metres) at the equator and 2,035 yards (1,861 metres) at the pole.

seamless /ˈsi:mlɪs/ *adj.* **1** without a seam or seams. **2** uninterrupted, smooth. □ **seamlessly** *adv.* (in sense 2).

sea mouse *n.* any marine annelid worm of the genus *Aphrodite*, with a broad iridescent body.

seamstress /ˈsi:mstrɪs/ *n.* (also **sempstress**) a woman who sews, esp. professionally; a needlewoman. [Old English *sēamestre*, fem. from *sēamere* 'tailor', formed as SEAM + -STER + -ESS[1]]

seamy /ˈsi:mi/ *adj.* (**seamier**, **seamiest**) **1** marked with or showing seams. **2** sordid, disreputable (esp. *the seamy side*). □ **seaminess** *n.*

Seanad /ˈʃanəð, -d/ *n.* the upper House of Parliament in the Republic of Ireland. [Irish, = senate]

seance /ˈseɪɑ:ns, -ɒ̃s, -ɒns/ *n.* (also **séance**) a meeting at which spiritualists attempt to make contact with the dead. [French *séance* via Old French *seoir* from Latin *sedēre* 'sit']

sea onion *n.* = SQUILL 2.

sea otter *n.* a marine otter, *Enhydra lutris*, of N. Pacific coasts, noted for using a stone balanced on its abdomen to crack open bivalve molluscs.

sea pen *n.* a colonial hydroid of the order Pennatulacea, resembling a quill pen.

sea pink *n.* a maritime plant, *Armeria maritima*, with bright pink flowers. Also called THRIFT.

seaplane /ˈsi:pleɪn/ *n.* an aircraft designed to take off from and land and float on water.

seaport /ˈsi:pɔ:t/ *n.* a town with a harbour for seagoing ships.

sea purse *n.* = MERMAID'S PURSE.

SEAQ *abbr.* (in the UK) Stock Exchange Automated Quotations (computerized access to share information).

seaquake /ˈsi:kweɪk/ *n.* an earthquake under the sea.

sear /sɪə/ *v. & adj.* ● *v.tr.* **1 a** scorch, esp. with a hot iron; cauterize, brand. **b** (as **searing** *adj.*) scorching, burning (*searing pain*). **2** cause (esp. emotional) pain or great anguish to. **3** brown (meat) quickly at a high temperature so that it will retain its juices in cooking. **4** make (one's conscience, feelings, etc.) no longer sensitive. **5** *archaic* blast, wither. ● *adj.* (also **sere**) *literary* (esp. of a plant etc.) withered, dried up. [Old English *sēar* (*adj.*), *sēarian* (*v.*), from Germanic]

search /sə:tʃ/ *v. & n.* ● *v.* **1** *tr.* look through or go over thoroughly to find something. **2** *tr.* examine or feel over (a person) to find anything concealed. **3** *tr.* **a** probe or penetrate into. **b** examine or question (one's mind, conscience, etc.) thoroughly. **4** *intr.* (often foll. by *for*) make a search or investigation. **5** *intr.* (as **searching** *adj.*) (of an examination) thorough; leaving no loopholes. **6** *tr.* (foll. by *out*) look probingly for; seek out. ● *n.* **1** an act of searching. **2** an investigation. □ **in search of** trying to find. **search me!** *colloq.* I do not know. □ **searchable** *adj.* **searcher** *n.* **searchingly** *adv.* [Middle English via Anglo-French *sercher*, Old French *cerchier* from Late Latin *circare* 'go round' (as CIRCUS)]

search engine *n.* *Computing* a program for the retrieval of data, files, etc. from a database or network.

searchlight /ˈsəːtʃlʌɪt/ *n.* **1** a powerful outdoor electric light with a concentrated beam that can be turned in any direction. **2** the light or beam from this.

search party *n.* a group of people organized to look for a lost person or thing.

search warrant *n.* an official authorization to enter and search a building.

sea room *n.* clear space at sea for a ship to turn or manoeuvre in.

sea salt *n.* salt produced by evaporating sea water.

seascape /ˈsiːskeɪp/ *n.* a picture or view of the sea.

Sea Scout *n.* (esp. in the UK) a member of the maritime branch of the Scout Association.

sea serpent *n.* **1** an enormous legendary serpent-like sea monster. **2** = SEA SNAKE 1.

sea shanty see SHANTY[2].

seashell /ˈsiːʃɛl/ *n.* the shell of a salt-water mollusc.

seashore /ˈsiːʃɔː/ *n.* **1** land close to or bordering on the sea. **2** *Law* the area between high and low water marks.

seasick /ˈsiːsɪk/ *adj.* suffering from sickness or nausea from the motion of a ship at sea. ▫ **seasickness** *n.*

seaside /ˈsiːsʌɪd/ *n.* (often *attrib.*) the sea coast, esp. as a holiday resort.

sea slug *n.* a shell-less marine gastropod mollusc, esp. of the order Nudibranchia, with external gills.

sea snail *n.* **1** a small slimy fish of the family Cyclopteridae, with a ventral sucker, esp. *Liparis liparis* of the NE Atlantic. **2** any spiral-shelled marine mollusc, e.g. a whelk.

sea snake *n.* **1** a venomous tropical marine snake of the family Hydrophidae. **2** = SEA SERPENT 1.

season /ˈsiːz(ə)n/ *n. & v.* ● *n.* **1** each of the four divisions of the year (spring, summer, autumn, and winter) associated with a type of weather and a stage of vegetation. **2** a time of year characterized by climatic or other features (*the dry season*). **3 a** the time of year when a plant is mature or flowering etc. **b** the time of year when an animal breeds or is hunted. **4** a proper or suitable time. **5** a time when something is plentiful or active or in vogue. **6** (usu. prec. by *the*) = HIGH SEASON. **7** the time of year regularly devoted to an activity (*the football season*). **8** the time of year dedicated to social life generally (*went up to London for the season*). **9** a period of indefinite or varying length. **10** *Brit. colloq.* = SEASON TICKET. ● *v.* **1** *tr.* flavour (food) with salt, herbs, etc. **2** *tr.* enhance with wit, excitement, etc. **3** *tr.* temper or moderate. **4** *tr. & intr.* **a** make or become suitable or in the desired condition, esp. by exposure to the air or weather; mature. **b** make or become experienced or accustomed (*seasoned soldiers*). ▫ **in season 1** (of foodstuff) available in plenty and in good condition. **2** (of an animal) on heat. **3** timely. [Middle English via Old French *seson* from Latin *satio -onis* (in Romanic sense 'seed-time') from *serere sat-* 'to sow']

seasonable /ˈsiːz(ə)nəb(ə)l/ *adj.* **1** (of weather) suitable to or usual in the season (*the rain was seasonable if unwelcome*). **2** coming at the right time, opportune; meeting the needs of the occasion (*seasonable advice*). ▫ **seasonableness** *n.* **seasonably** *adv.*

▪ **Usage** *Seasonable*, meaning 'suitable; opportune', should not be confused with the (more common) word *seasonal* meaning, 'of or relating to the seasons'.

seasonal /ˈsiːz(ə)n(ə)l/ *adj.* of or relating to the seasons of the year or some other temporal cycle; characteristic of or dependent on a particular season; varying with season (*seasonal changes; seasonal work*). ▫ **seasonality** /-ˈnalɪti/ *n.* **seasonally** *adv.*

▪ **Usage** See Usage Note at SEASONABLE.

seasonal affective disorder *n.* a depressive state associated with late autumn and winter and thought to be caused by a lack of light.

seasoning /ˈsiːz(ə)nɪŋ/ *n.* condiments added to food.

season ticket *n.* a ticket entitling the holder to any number of journeys, admittances, etc., in a given period.

sea squirt *n.* any marine tunicate of the class Ascidiacea, having a bag-like body with orifices through which water flows into and out of a central pharynx.

seat /siːt/ *n. & v.* ● *n.* **1** a thing made or used for sitting on; a chair, stool, saddle, etc. **2** the buttocks. **3** the part of the trousers etc. covering the buttocks. **4** the part of a chair etc. on which the sitter's weight directly rests. **5** the part of a thing on which it rests; the base. **6** a place for one person in a theatre, vehicle, etc. **7** the occupation of a seat. **8** esp. *Brit.* **a** the right to occupy a seat, esp. as a Member of the House of Commons. **b** a member's constituency. **9** the part of a machine that supports or guides another part. **10** a site or location of something specified (*a seat of learning; the seat of the emotions*). **11** a country mansion, esp. with large grounds. **12** the manner of sitting on a horse etc. ● *v.tr.* **1** cause to sit. **2 a** provide sitting accommodation for (*the cinema seats 500*). **b** provide with seats. **3** (as **seated** *adj.*) sitting. **4** put or fit in position. ▫ **be seated** sit down. **by the seat of one's pants** *colloq.* by instinct rather than logic or knowledge. **take a** (or **one's**) **seat** sit down. ▫ **seatless** *adj.* [Middle English from Old Norse *sæti* (= Old English *gesete* from Germanic)]

seat belt *n.* a belt securing a person in the seat of a motor vehicle or aircraft.

-seater /ˈsiːtə/ *comb. form* denoting a vehicle, sofa, building, etc. with a specified number of seats (*a 16-seater bus*).

seating /ˈsiːtɪŋ/ *n.* **1** seats collectively. **2** sitting accommodation.

SEATO /ˈsiːtəʊ/ *abbr.* South-East Asia Treaty Organization.

sea trout *n.* **1** a large silvery fish of a migratory race of the trout, *Salmo trutta*; also called SALMON TROUT. **2** *US* an unrelated marine fish of the genus *Cynoscion*.

sea urchin *n.* a small marine echinoderm of the class Echinoidea, with a spherical or flattened spiny shell.

sea wall *n.* a wall or embankment erected to prevent encroachment by the sea.

seaward /ˈsiːwəd/ *adv., adj., & n.* ● *adv.* (also **seawards**) towards the sea. ● *adj.* going or facing towards the sea. ● *n.* such a direction or position.

sea wasp *n.* an Indo-Pacific jellyfish of the order Cubomedusae, with a dangerous sting.

sea water *n.* water in or taken from the sea.

seaway /ˈsiːweɪ/ *n.* **1** an inland waterway open to seagoing ships. **2** a ship's progress. **3** a ship's path across the sea.

seaweed /ˈsiːwiːd/ *n.* any large alga growing in the sea or on rocks below the high water mark; such plants collectively.

seaworthy /ˈsiːwəːði/ *adj.* (esp. of a ship) fit to put to sea. ▫ **seaworthiness** *n.*

sebaceous /sɪˈbeɪʃəs/ *adj.* fatty; of or relating to tallow or fat. [Latin *sebaceus* from *sebum* 'tallow']

sebaceous gland *n.* (also **sebaceous follicle** or **sebaceous duct**) a gland etc. secreting or conveying oily matter to lubricate the skin and hair.

seborrhoea /sɛbəˈriːə/ *n.* (*US* **seborrhea**) *Med.* excessive discharge of sebum from the sebaceous glands. ▫ **seborrhoeic** *adj.* [SEBUM + *-rrhoea* from Greek *rhoia* 'flux, flow']

sebum /ˈsiːbəm/ *n.* the oily secretion of the sebaceous glands. [modern Latin from Latin *sebum* 'grease']

Sec. *abbr.* secretary.

sec[1] /sɛk/ *abbr.* secant.

sec[2] /sɛk/ *n. colloq.* (in phrs.) a second (of time). [abbreviation]

sec[3] /sɛk/ *adj.* (of wine) dry. [French from Latin *siccus*]

sec. *abbr.* second(s).

secant /ˈsiːk(ə)nt, ˈsɛk-/ *adj. & n. Math.* ● *adj.* cutting (*secant line*). ● *n.* **1** a line cutting a curve at one or more points. **2** the ratio of the hypotenuse to the shorter side adjacent to an acute angle (in a right-angled triangle) (abbr.: **sec**). [French *sécant(e)* from Latin *secare secant-* 'to cut']

secateurs /sɛkəˈtəːz, ˈsɛkətəːz/ *n.pl.* esp. *Brit.* a pair of pruning clippers for use with one hand. [French *sécateur* 'cutter', formed irregularly from Latin *secare* 'to cut']

secco /ˈsɛko/ *n.* the technique of painting on dry plaster with pigments mixed in water. [Italian, = dry, from Latin *siccus*]

secede /sɪˈsiːd/ *v.intr.* (usu. foll. by *from*) withdraw formally from membership of a political federation or a religious body. □ **seceder** *n.* [Latin *secedere secess-* (as SE-, *cedere* 'go')]

secession /sɪˈsɛʃ(ə)n/ *n.* **1** the act or an instance of seceding. **2** (**Secession**) *hist.* the withdrawal of eleven southern states from the US Union in 1860, leading to the Civil War. □ **secessional** *adj.* **secessionism** *n.* **secessionist** *n.* [French *sécession* or Latin *secessio* (as SECEDE)]

seclude /sɪˈkluːd/ *v.tr.* (also *refl.*) **1** keep (a person or place) retired or away from company. **2** (esp. as **secluded** *adj.*) hide or screen from view. [Middle English from Latin *secludere seclus-* (as SE-, *claudere* 'shut')]

seclusion /sɪˈkluːʒ(ə)n/ *n.* **1** a secluded state; retirement, privacy. **2** a secluded place. □ **seclusionist** *n.* **seclusive** /-sɪv/ *adj.* [medieval Latin *seclusio* (as SECLUDE)]

second[1] /ˈsɛk(ə)nd/ *n., adj., & v.* ● *n.* **1** the position in a sequence corresponding to that of the number 2 in the sequence 1–2. **2** something occupying this position. **3** the second person etc. in a race or competition. **4** *Mus.* **a** an interval or chord spanning two consecutive notes in the diatonic scale (e.g. C to D). **b** a note separated from another by this interval. **5** = SECOND GEAR. **6** another person or thing in addition to one previously mentioned or considered (*the policeman was then joined by a second*). **7** (in *pl.*) **a** goods of a second or inferior quality. **b** coarse flour, or bread made from it. **8** (in *pl.*) *colloq.* **a** a second helping of food at a meal. **b** the second course of a meal. **9** an attendant assisting a combatant in a duel, boxing match, etc. **10** esp. *Brit.* **a** a place in the second class of an examination. **b** a person having this. ● *adj.* **1** that is the second; next after first. **2** additional, further; other besides one previously mentioned or considered (*ate a second cake*). **3** subordinate in position or importance etc.; inferior. **4** *Mus.* performing a lower or subordinate part (*second violins*). **5** such as to be comparable to; closely reminiscent of (*a second Callas*). ● *v.tr.* **1** supplement, support; back up. **2** formally support or endorse (a nomination or resolution etc., or its proposer). □ **at second hand** by hearsay, not direct observation etc. **in the second place** as a second consideration etc. **second to none** surpassed by no other. □ **seconder** *n.* (esp. in sense 2 of *v.*). [Middle English via Old French from Latin *secundus*, from *sequi* 'follow']

second[2] /ˈsɛk(ə)nd/ *n.* **1** a sixtieth of a minute of time (symbol s or ″), which as the SI unit of time is defined in terms of the natural periodicity of the radiation of a caesium-133 atom. **2** *colloq.* a very short time (*wait a second*). **3** a sixtieth of a minute of angular distance (symbol ″). [French from medieval Latin *secunda (minuta)* 'secondary (minute)', being the result of dividing by sixty for a second time]

second[3] /sɪˈkɒnd/ *v.tr. Brit.* transfer (a military officer or other official or worker) temporarily to other employment or to another position. □ **secondee** /-ˈdiː/ *n.* **secondment** *n.* [French *en second* 'in the second rank' (of officers)]

second advent *n.* = SECOND COMING.

secondary /ˈsɛk(ə)nd(ə)ri/ *adj. & n.* ● *adj.* **1** coming after or next below what is primary. **2** derived from or depending on or supplementing what is primary. **3** (of education, a school, etc.) for those who have had primary education, usu. from 11 to 18 years. **4** *Electr.* **a** (of a cell or battery) having a reversible chemical reaction and therefore able to store energy. **b** denoting a device using electromagnetic induction, esp. a transformer. ● *n.* (*pl.* **-ies**) **1** a secondary thing. **2** a secondary device or current. □ **secondarily** *adv.* **secondariness** *n.* [Middle English from Latin *secundarius* (as SECOND[1])]

secondary colour *n.* a colour resulting from the mixing of two primary colours.

secondary feather *n.* a feather growing from the second joint of a bird's wing.

secondary picketing *n. Brit.* the picketing of premises of a firm not otherwise involved in the dispute in question.

secondary planet *n.* a satellite of a planet (cf. PRIMARY PLANET).

secondary rainbow *n.* an additional arch with the colours in reverse order sometimes seen inside or outside a rainbow by twofold reflection and twofold refraction.

secondary sexual characteristics *n.pl.* physical characteristics developed at puberty.

second ballot *n.* a deciding ballot between candidates coming first (without an absolute majority) and second in a previous ballot.

second-best *adj. & n.* ● *adj.* next after best. ● *n.* a less adequate or desirable alternative.

second cause *n. Logic* a cause that is itself caused.

second chamber *n.* the upper house of a bicameral parliament.

second childhood *n.* a person's dotage.

second-class *adj. & adv.* ● *adj.* **1** of or belonging to or travelling by the second class. **2** inferior in quality, status, etc. (*second-class citizens*). ● *adv.* by second class (*travelled second-class*).

second class *n.* **1** a set of persons or things grouped together as second-best. **2** the second-best accommodation in a train, ship, etc. **3 a** (in the UK) the class of mail not given priority in handling. **b** (in N. America) a class of mail for the handling of newspapers and periodicals. **4 a** the second highest division in a list of examination results. **b** a place in this.

second coming *n. Theol.* the future return of Christ to earth.

second cousin see COUSIN.

second-degree *adj. Med.* denoting burns that cause blistering but not permanent scars.

seconde /səˈkɒ̃d/ *n. Fencing* the second of eight parrying positions. [French, fem. of *second* SECOND[1]]

second fiddle see FIDDLE.

second floor *n.* **1** *Brit.* the floor two levels above the ground floor. **2** *N. Amer.* the floor above the ground floor.

second gear *n.* the second (and next to lowest) in a sequence of gears.

second-generation *adj.* denoting the offspring of a first generation, esp. of immigrants.

second-guess *v.tr. colloq.* **1** anticipate or predict by guesswork. **2** judge or criticize with hindsight.

second-hand *adj. & adv.* ● *adj.* **1 a** (of goods) having had a previous owner; not new. **b** (of a shop etc.) where such goods can be bought. **2** (of information etc.) accepted on another's authority and not from original investigation. ● *adv.* **1** on a second-hand basis. **2** at second hand; not directly.

second hand *n.* an extra hand in some watches and clocks, recording seconds.

second honeymoon *n.* a holiday like a honeymoon, taken by a couple after some years of marriage.

second in command *n.* the officer next in rank to the commanding or chief officer.

second intention *n. Med.* the healing of a wound by granulation.

second intentions *n.pl. Logic* one's secondary conceptions (e.g. difference, identity, species).

second lieutenant *n.* an army officer next below lieutenant or *US* first lieutenant.

secondly /ˈsɛk(ə)ndli/ *adv.* **1** furthermore; in the second place. **2** as a second item.

second name *n. Brit.* a surname.

second nature *n.* (often foll. by *to*) an acquired tendency that has become instinctive (*is second nature to him*).

secondo /sɪˈkɒndəʊ/ *n.* (*pl.* **secondi** /-di/) *Mus.* the second or lower part in a duet etc. [Italian]

second officer *n.* an assistant mate on a merchant ship.

second person see PERSON 3.

second-rate *adj.* of mediocre quality; inferior. □ **second rater** *n.*

second reading *n.* a second presentation of a bill to a legislative assembly, in the UK to approve its general principles and in the US to debate committee reports.

Second Reich *n.* the German Empire 1871–1918.

second self *n.* a close friend or associate.

second sight *n.* the supposed power of being able to perceive future or distant events. □ **second-sighted** *adj.*

second string *n.* **1** an alternative course of action, means of livelihood, etc., invoked if the main one is unsuccessful. **2** *US* a reserve, esp. for a sports team.

second teeth *n.pl.* the teeth that replace the milk teeth in a mammal.

second thoughts *n.pl.* a new opinion or resolution reached after further consideration.

second wind *n.* **1** recovery of the power of normal breathing during exercise after initial breathlessness. **2** renewed energy to continue an effort.

secrecy /ˈsiːkrɪsi/ *n.* **1** the keeping of secrets as a fact, habit, or faculty. **2** a state in which all information is withheld (*was done in great secrecy*). □ **sworn to secrecy** having promised to keep a secret. [Middle English, SECRET *adj.*, probably on the pattern of *privacy*]

secret /ˈsiːkrɪt/ *adj. & n.* ● *adj.* **1** kept or meant to be kept private, unknown, or hidden from all or all but a few. **2** acting or operating secretly. **3** fond of, prone to, or able to preserve secrecy. **4** (of a place) hidden, completely secluded. ● *n.* **1** a thing kept or meant to be kept secret. **2** a thing known only to a few. **3** a mystery. **4** a valid but not commonly known or recognized method of achieving or maintaining something (*what's their secret?*; *correct breathing is the secret of good health*). **5** *RC Ch.* a prayer concluding the offertory of the Mass. □ **in secret** secretly. **in** (or **in on**) **the secret** among the number of those who know the secret. **keep a secret** not reveal information given in confidence. □ **secretly** *adv.* [Middle English from Old French from Latin *secretus* (*adj.*) 'separate, set apart' from *secernere secret-* (as SE-, *cernere* 'sift')]

secret agent *n.* a spy acting for a country.

secretaire /sɛkrɪˈtɛː/ *n.* an escritoire. [French (as SECRETARY)]

secretariat /sɛkrɪˈtɛːrɪət/ *n.* **1** a permanent administrative office or department, esp. a governmental one. **2** its members or premises. **3** the office of secretary. [French *secrétariat* from medieval Latin *secretariatus* (as SECRETARY)]

secretary /ˈsɛkrɪt(ə)ri/ *n.* (*pl.* **-ies**) **1** a person employed by an individual or in an office etc. to assist with correspondence, keep records, make appointments, etc. **2** an official appointed by a society etc. to conduct its correspondence, keep its records, organize its affairs, etc. **3** (in some organizations) the chief executive. **4** (in the UK) the principal assistant of a government minister, ambassador, etc. □ **secretarial** /-ˈtɛːrɪəl/ *adj.* **secretaryship** *n.* [earlier = a person entrusted with a secret: Middle English from Late Latin *secretarius* (as SECRET)]

secretary bird *n.* a long-legged snake-eating African bird, *Sagittarius serpentarius*, with a crest likened to a quill pen stuck over a writer's ear.

Secretary-General *n.* (*pl.* **Secretary-Generals**) the principal administrator of an organization.

Secretary of State *n.* **1** (in the UK) the head of a major government department. **2** (in the US) the chief government official responsible for foreign affairs.

secret ballot *n.* a ballot in which votes are cast in secret.

secrete[1] /sɪˈkriːt/ *v.tr. Biol.* (of a cell, organ, etc.) produce by secretion. □ **secretor** *n.* **secretory** *adj.* [back-formation from SECRETION]

secrete[2] /sɪˈkriːt/ *v.tr.* conceal; put into hiding. [obsolete verb *secret* from SECRET]

secretion /sɪˈkriːʃ(ə)n/ *n.* **1** *Biol.* **a** a process by which substances are produced and discharged from a cell, gland, or organ for a function in the organism or for excretion. **b** the secreted substance. **2** the act or an instance of concealing (*the secretion of stolen goods*). [French *sécrétion* or Latin *secretio* 'separation' (as SECRET)]

secretive /ˈsiːkrɪtɪv/ *adj.* inclined to make or keep secrets; uncommunicative. □ **secretively** *adv.* **secretiveness** *n.* [back-formation from *secretiveness*, suggested by French *secrétivité* (as SECRET)]

secret police *n.* a police force operating in secret for political purposes.

secret service *n.* **1** a government department concerned with espionage. **2** (**Secret Service**) (in the US) a branch of the Treasury Department dealing with counterfeiting and providing protection for the President etc.

secret society *n.* a society whose members are sworn to secrecy about it.

sect /sɛkt/ *n.* **1 a** a body of people subscribing to religious doctrines different from those of others within the same religion; a group deviating from orthodox tradition, often regarded as heretical. **b** usu. *derog.* a body separated from an established Church; a nonconformist Church. **c** a party or faction in a religious body. **d** a religious denomination. **2** the followers of a particular philosopher or philosophy, or school of thought in politics etc. [Middle English from Old French *secte* or Latin *secta*, from the stem of *sequi secut-* 'follow']

sect. *abbr.* section.

sectarian /sɛkˈtɛːrɪən/ *adj. & n.* ● *adj.* **1** of or concerning a sect. **2** bigoted or narrow-minded in following the doctrines of one's sect. ● *n.* **1** a member of a sect. **2** a bigot. □ **sectarianism** *n.* **sectarianize** *v.tr.* (also **-ise**). [SECTARY]

sectary /ˈsɛktəri/ *n.* (*pl.* **-ies**) a member of a religious or political sect. [medieval Latin *sectarius* 'adherent' (as SECT)]

section /ˈsɛkʃ(ə)n/ *n. & v.* ● *n.* **1** a part cut off or separated from something. **2** each of the parts into which a thing is divided (actually or conceptually) or divisible or out of which a structure can be fitted together. **3** a distinct group or subdivision of a larger body of people (*the wind section of an orchestra*). **4** a subdivision of a book, document, statute, etc. **5 a** *N. Amer.* one square mile of land. **b** esp. *US* a particular district of a town (*residential section*). **6** a subdivision of an army platoon. **7** esp. *Surgery* a separation by cutting. **8** *Biol.* a thin slice of tissue etc., cut off for microscopic examination. **9 a** the cutting of a solid by or along a plane. **b** the resulting figure or the area of this. **10** a representation of the internal structure of something as if cut across along a vertical or horizontal plane. **11** *Biol.* a group, esp. a subgenus. ● *v.tr.* **1** arrange in or divide into sections. **2** (esp. as **sectioned** *adj.*) *Brit.* cause (a person) to be compulsorily committed to a psychiatric hospital in accordance with a section of a mental health act. **3** *Biol.* cut into thin slices for microscopic examination. [French *section* or Latin *sectio*, from *secare sect-* 'cut']

sectional /ˈsɛkʃ(ə)n(ə)l/ *adj. & n.* ● *adj.* **1 a** relating to a section, esp. of a community. **b** partisan. **2** made in sections. **3** local rather than general. ● *n.* a sofa or other comfortable seating made up in sections for separate or combined use. □ **sectionalism** *n.* **sectionalist** *n. & adj.* **sectionalize** *v.tr.* (also **-ise**). **sectionally** *adv.*

section-mark *n.* the sign (§) used as a reference mark to indicate the start of a section of a book etc.

sector /ˈsɛktə/ *n.* **1** a distinct part or branch of an enterprise, or of society, the economy, etc. **2** *Mil.* a subdivision of an area for military operations, controlled by one commander or headquarters. **3** the plane figure enclosed by two radii of a circle, ellipse, etc., and the arc between them. **4** a mathematical instrument consisting of two arms hinged at one end and marked with sines, tangents, etc., for making diagrams etc. □ **sectoral** *adj.* [Late Latin, technical use of Latin *sector* 'cutter' (as SECTION)]

sectorial /sɛkˈtɔːrɪəl/ *adj.* **1** of or like a sector or sectors. **2** = CARNASSIAL.

secular /ˈsɛkjʊlə/ *adj. & n.* ● *adj.* **1** concerned with the affairs of this world; not spiritual or sacred. **2** (of education etc.) not concerned with religion or religious belief. **3 a** not ecclesiastical or monastic. **b** (of clergy) not bound by a religious rule. **4** occurring once in an age or century. **5 a** lasting for or occurring over an indefinitely long time. **b** *Astron.* of or designating slow changes in the motion of the sun or planets. ● *n.* a secular priest. □ **secularism** *n.* **secularist** *n.* **secularity** /-ˈlarɪti/ *n.* **secularize** *v.tr.* (also **-ise**). **secularization** /-ˈzeɪʃ(ə)n/ *n.* **secularly** *adv.* [Middle English (in senses 1–3 via Old French *seculer*) from Latin *saecularis*, from *saeculum* 'generation, age', in ecclesiastical Latin = the world (as opposed to the Church)]

secund /sɪˈkʌnd/ *adj. Bot.* arranged on one side only (as the flowers of lily of the valley). □ **secundly** *adv.* [Latin *secundus* (as SECOND[1])]

secure /sɪˈkjʊə/ *adj. & v.* ● *adj.* **1** untroubled by danger or fear. **2** safe against attack; impregnable. **3** reliable; certain not to fail (*the plan is secure*). **4** fixed or fastened so as not to give way or get loose or be lost (*made the door secure*). **5 a** (foll. by *of*) certain to achieve (*secure of victory*). **b** (foll. by *against, from*) safe, protected (*secure against attack*). **6** (of a prison etc.) difficult to escape from. **7** (of a person) not a risk to security; trustworthy. ● *v.tr.* **1** make secure or safe; fortify. **2** fasten, close, or confine securely. **3** succeed in obtaining or achieving (*have secured front seats*). **4** guarantee against loss (*a loan secured by property*). **5** compress (a blood vessel) to prevent bleeding. □ **secure arms** *Mil.* hold a rifle with the muzzle downward and the lock in the armpit to guard it from rain. □ **securable** *adj.* **securely** *adv.* **securement** *n.* [Latin *securus* (as SE-, *cura* 'care')]

securitize /sɪˈkjʊərɪtʌɪz/ *v.tr.* (also **-ise**) (often in *passive*) convert (an asset) into securities, usu. in order to raise cash. □ **securitization** /-ˈzeɪʃ(ə)n/ *n.*

security /sɪˈkjʊərɪti/ *n.* (*pl.* **-ies**) **1** a secure condition or feeling. **2** a thing that guards or guarantees. **3 a** the safety of a state, company, etc., against espionage, theft, or other danger. **b** an organization for ensuring this. **4** a thing deposited or pledged as a guarantee of the fulfilment of an undertaking or the payment of a loan, to be forfeited in case of default. **5** (often in *pl.*) a certificate attesting credit or the ownership of stock, bonds, etc. □ **on security of** using as a guarantee. [Middle English from Old French *securité* or Latin *securitas* (as SECURE)]

security blanket *n.* **1** *Brit.* an official sanction on information in the interest of security. **2** a blanket or other familiar object given as a comfort to a child.

Security Council *n.* a permanent body of the United Nations seeking to maintain peace and security.

security guard *n.* a person employed to protect the security of buildings, vehicles, etc.

security risk *n.* a person, situation, etc. posing a possible threat to security.

sedan /sɪˈdan/ *n.* **1** (in full **sedan chair**) an enclosed chair for conveying one person, carried between horizontal poles by two porters, common in the 17th–18th c. **2** *N. Amer.* an enclosed motor car for four or more people. [perhaps alteration of an Italian dialect word, ultimately via Latin *sella* 'saddle' from *sedēre* 'sit']

sedate[1] /sɪˈdeɪt/ *adj.* tranquil and dignified; equable, serious. □ **sedately** *adv.* **sedateness** *n.* [Latin *sedatus*, past part. of *sedare* 'settle', from *sedēre* 'sit']

sedate[2] /sɪˈdeɪt/ *v.tr.* put under sedation. [back-formation from SEDATION]

sedation /sɪˈdeɪʃ(ə)n/ *n.* a state of rest or sleep esp. produced by a sedative drug. [French *sédation* or Latin *sedatio* (as SEDATE[1])]

sedative /ˈsɛdətɪv/ *n. & adj.* ● *n.* a drug, influence, etc., that tends to calm or soothe. ● *adj.* calming, soothing; inducing sleep. [Middle English from Old French *sedatif* or medieval Latin *sedativus* (as SEDATE[1])]

sedentary /ˈsɛd(ə)nt(ə)ri/ *adj.* **1** sitting (*a sedentary posture*). **2** (of work etc.) characterized by much sitting and little physical exercise. **3** (of a person) spending much time seated. **4** *Zool.* **a** inhabiting the same locality throughout life; not migratory. **b** confined to one spot; sessile. □ **sedentarily** *adv.* **sedentariness** *n.* [French *sédentaire* or Latin *sedentarius*, from *sedēre* 'sit']

Seder /ˈseɪdə/ *n.* a Jewish ritual service and ceremonial dinner for the first night or first two nights of the Passover. [Hebrew *sēḏer* 'order, procedure']

sederunt /sɪˈdɪərənt, -ˈdɛː-/ *n. Sc.* a sitting of an ecclesiastical assembly or other body. [Latin, = (the following persons) sat, from *sedēre* 'sit']

sedge /sɛdʒ/ *n.* **1** any grasslike plant of the genus *Carex* with triangular stems, usu. growing in wet areas. **2** an expanse of this plant. □ **sedgy** *adj.* [Old English *secg*, from Germanic]

sedge warbler *n.* a small streaked warbler, *Acrocephalus schoenobaenus*, often found around marshes and reed-beds.

sedile /sɪˈdʌɪli/ *n.* (*pl.* **sedilia** /-ˈdɪlɪə/) (usu. in *pl.*) *Eccl.* each of usu. three stone seats for priests in the south wall of a chancel, often canopied and decorated. [Latin, = seat, from *sedēre* 'sit']

sediment /ˈsɛdɪm(ə)nt/ *n. & v.* ● *n.* **1** matter that settles to the bottom of a liquid; dregs. **2** *Geol.* matter that is carried by water or wind and deposited on the surface of the land, and may in time become consolidated into rock. ● *v.tr.* (as **sedimented** *adj.*) **1 a** *Geol.* deposited as sediment. **b** deep-rooted, long-established (*sedimented radicalism*). **2** (of beer) having a sediment. □ **sedimentary** /-ˈmɛnt(ə)ri/ *adj.* **sedimentation** /-ˈteɪʃ(ə)n/ *n.* [French *sédiment* or Latin *sedimentum* (as SEDILE)]

sedition /sɪˈdɪʃ(ə)n/ *n.* **1** conduct or speech inciting to rebellion or a breach of public order. **2** agitation against the authority of a state. □ **seditious** *adj.* **seditiously** *adv.* [Middle English from Old French *sedition* or Latin *seditio*, from *sed-* = SE- + *ire it-* 'go']

seduce /sɪˈdjuːs/ *v.tr.* **1** tempt or entice into sexual activity. **2 a** tempt, lure (*seduced by the smell of coffee*). **b** (often foll. by *into*) lead astray (*seduced into a life of crime*). **c** (often as **seduced** *adj.*) beguiled (*seduced by outward appearances*). □ **seducer** *n.* **seducible** *adj.* [Latin *seducere seduct-* (as SE-, *ducere* 'lead')]

seduction /sɪˈdʌkʃ(ə)n/ *n.* **1** the act or an instance of seducing; the process of being seduced. **2** something that tempts or allures. [French *séduction* or Latin *seductio* (as SEDUCE)]

seductive /sɪˈdʌktɪv/ *adj.* tending to seduce; alluring, enticing. □ **seductively** *adv.* **seductiveness** *n.* [SEDUCTION, on the pattern of *inductive* etc.]

seductress /sɪˈdʌktrɪs/ *n.* a female seducer. [obsolete *seductor* 'male seducer' (as SEDUCE)]

sedulous /ˈsɛdjʊləs/ *adj.* **1** persevering, diligent, assiduous. **2** (of an action etc.) deliberately and consciously continued; painstaking. □ **sedulity**

/sɪˈdjuːlɪti/ *n.* **sedulously** *adv.* **sedulousness** *n.* [Latin *sedulus* 'zealous']

sedum /ˈsiːdəm/ *n.* any plant of the genus *Sedum*, with fleshy leaves and star-shaped yellow, pink, or white flowers, e.g. stonecrop. [Latin, = houseleek]

see[1] /siː/ *v.* (*past* **saw** /sɔː/; *past part.* **seen** /siːn/) **1** *tr.* discern by use of the eyes; observe; look at (*can you see that spider?*; *saw him fall over*). **2** *intr.* have or use the power of discerning objects with the eyes (*sees best at night*). **3** *tr.* discern mentally; understand (*I see what you mean*; *could not see the joke*). **4** *tr.* watch; be a spectator of (a film, game, etc.). **5** *tr.* ascertain or establish by inquiry or research or reflection (*I will see if the door is open*). **6** *tr.* consider; deduce from observation (*I see that you are a brave man*). **7** *tr.* contemplate; foresee mentally (*we saw that no good would come of it*; *can see myself doing this job indefinitely*). **8** *tr.* look at for information (usu. in *imper.* as a direction in or to a book: *see page 15*). **9** *tr.* meet or be near and recognize (*I saw your mother in town*). **10** *tr.* **a** meet socially (*sees her sister most weeks*). **b** meet regularly as a boyfriend or girlfriend; court (*is still seeing that man*). **11** *tr.* give an interview to (*the doctor will see you now*). **12** *tr.* visit to consult (*went to see the doctor*). **13** *tr.* find out or learn, esp. from a visual source (*I see the match has been cancelled*). **14** *intr.* reflect; consider further; wait until one knows more (*we shall have to see*). **15** *tr.* interpret or have an opinion of (*I see things differently now*). **16** *tr.* experience; have presented to one's attention (*I never thought I would see this day*). **17** *tr.* recognize as acceptable; foresee (*do you see your daughter marrying this man?*). **18** *tr.* observe without interfering (*stood by and saw them squander my money*). **19** *tr.* find attractive (*can't think what she sees in him*). **20** *intr.* (usu. foll. by *to*, or *that* + infin.) make provision for; ensure; attend to (*shall see to your request immediately*; *see that he gets home safely*) (cf. *see to it*). **21** *tr.* escort or conduct (to a place etc.) (*saw them home*). **22** *tr.* be a witness of (an event etc.) (*see the New Year in*). **23** *tr.* supervise (an action etc.) (*will stay and see the doors locked*). **24** *tr.* **a** (in gambling, esp. poker) equal (a bet). **b** equal the bet of (a player), esp. to see the player's cards. □ **as far as I can see** to the best of my understanding or belief. **as I see it** in my opinion. **do you see?** do you understand? **has seen better days** has declined from former prosperity, good condition, etc. **I'll be seeing you** *colloq.* an expression on parting. **I see** I understand (referring to an explanation etc.). **let me see** an appeal for time to think before speaking etc. **see about** attend to. **see after 1** take care of. **2** = *see about.* **see the back of** *Brit. colloq.* be rid of (an unwanted person or thing). **see a person damned first** *Brit. colloq.* refuse categorically and with hostility to do what a person wants. **see eye to eye** see EYE. **see fit** see FIT[1]. **see here!** calling attention, expressing a protest, etc. **see into** investigate. **see life** gain experience of the world, often by enjoying oneself. **see the light 1** realize one's mistakes etc. **2** suddenly see the way to proceed. **3** undergo religious conversion. **see the light of day** (usu. with *neg.*) come into existence. **see off 1** be present at the departure of (a person) (*saw them off at Heathrow*). **2** *Brit. colloq.* ward off, get the better of (*managed to see off an investigation into their working methods*). **see out 1** accompany out of a building etc. **2** *Brit.* finish (a project etc.) completely. **3** *Brit.* remain awake, alive, etc., until the end of (a period). **4** *Brit.* last longer than; outlive. **see over** inspect; tour and examine. **see reason** see REASON. **see red** become suddenly enraged. **see a person right** *Brit. colloq.* make sure that a person is rewarded, safe, etc. **see service** see SERVICE[1]. **see stars** *colloq.* see lights before one's eyes as a result of a blow on the head. **see things** have hallucinations or false imaginings. **see through 1** not be deceived by; detect the true nature of. **2** penetrate visually. **see a person through** support a person during a difficult time. **see a thing through** persist with it until it is completed. **see to it** (foll. by *that* + clause) ensure (*see to it that I am not disturbed*) (cf. sense 20 of *v.*). **see one's way clear to** feel able or entitled to. **see the world** see WORLD. **see you** (or **see you later**) *colloq.* an expression on parting. **we shall see 1** let us await the outcome. **2** a formula for declining to act at once. **will see about it** a formula for declining to act at once. **you see 1** you understand. **2** you will understand when I explain. □ **seeable** *adj.* [Old English *sēon*, from Germanic]

see[2] /siː/ *n.* **1** the area under the authority of a bishop or archbishop, a diocese (*the see of Norwich*). **2** the office or jurisdiction of a bishop or archbishop (*fill a vacant see*). [Middle English from Anglo-French *se(d)*, ultimately via Latin *sedes* 'seat' from *sedēre* 'sit']

seed /siːd/ *n.* & *v.* ● *n.* **1 a** a flowering plant's unit of reproduction (esp. in the form of grain) capable of developing into another such plant. **b** seeds collectively, esp. as collected for sowing (*is full of seed*; *to be kept for seed*). **2 a** semen. **b** milt. **3** (foll. by *of*) the beginning or initial germ of development (*seeds of doubt*). **4** *archaic* offspring, progeny, descendants (*the seed of Abraham*). **5** *Sport* a seeded player. **6** a small seedlike container for the application of radium etc. **7** a seed crystal. ● *v.* **1** *tr.* **a** place seeds in. **b** sprinkle with or as with seed. **2** *intr.* sow seeds. **3** *intr.* produce or drop seed. **4** *tr.* remove seeds from (fruit etc.). **5** *tr.* place a crystal or crystalline substance in (a solution etc.) to cause crystallization or condensation (esp. in a cloud to produce rain). **6** *tr. Sport* **a** assign to (a strong competitor in a knockout competition) a position in an ordered list so that strong competitors do not meet each other in early rounds (*is seeded seventh*). **b** arrange (the order of play) in this way. **7** *intr.* go to seed. □ **go** (or **run**) **to seed 1** cease flowering as seed develops. **2** become degenerate, unkempt, ineffective, etc. **raise up seed** *archaic* beget children. □ **seedless** *adj.* [Old English *sǣd* from Germanic: related to SOW[1]]

seedbed /ˈsiːdbed/ *n.* **1** a bed of fine soil in which to sow seeds. **2** a place of development.

seed cake *n.* cake containing whole seeds esp. of caraway as flavouring.

seed-coat *n.* the outer integument of a seed.

seedcorn /ˈsiːdkɔːn/ *n.* **1** good-quality corn kept for seed. **2** *Brit.* assets reused for future profit or benefit.

seed crystal *n.* a crystal used to initiate crystallization.

seed-eater *n.* a bird (esp. a finch) living mainly on seeds.

seeder /ˈsiːdə/ *n.* **1** a person or thing that seeds. **2** a machine for sowing seed, esp. a drill. **3** an apparatus for seeding raisins etc. **4** *Brit.* a spawning fish.

seed-fish *n.* (*pl.* usu. same) a fish that is ready to spawn.

seed-head *n.* a flower head in seed.

seed-leaf *n.* a cotyledon.

seedling /ˈsiːdlɪŋ/ *n.* a young plant, esp. one raised from seed and not from a cutting etc.

seed-lip *n.* esp. *Brit.* a basket for seed used in sowing by hand.

seed money *n.* money allocated to initiate a project.

seedpearl /ˈsiːdpəːl/ *n.* a very small pearl.

seed-plot *n.* a place of development.

seed potato *n.* a potato kept for seed.

seedsman /ˈsiːdzmən/ *n.* (*pl.* **-men**) a dealer in seeds.

seed-time *n.* the sowing season.

seed vessel *n.* a pericarp.

seedy /ˈsiːdi/ *adj.* (**seedier**, **seediest**) **1** full of seed. **2** going to seed. **3** shabby-looking, in worn clothes. **4** *colloq.* unwell. □ **seedily** *adv.* **seediness** *n.*

seeing /ˈsiːɪŋ/ *conj.* & *n.* ● *conj.* (usu. foll. by *that* + clause) considering that, inasmuch as, because (*seeing that you do not know it yourself*). ● *n. Astron.* the quality of observed images as determined by atmospheric conditions.

seek /siːk/ *v.* (*past* and *past part.* **sought** /sɔːt/) **1 a** *tr.* make a search or inquiry for. **b** *intr.* (foll. by *for, after*) make a search or inquiry. **2** *tr.* **a** try or want to find or get. **b** ask for; request (*sought help from him*; *seeks my* *aid*). **3** *tr.* (foll. by *to* + infin.) endeavour or try. **4** *tr.* make for or resort to (a place or person, for advice, health, etc.) (*sought his bed*; *sought a fortune-teller*; *sought the shore*). **5** *tr. archaic* aim at, attempt. **6** *intr.* (foll. by *to*) *archaic* resort. □ **seek dead** *Brit.* an order to a retriever to find killed game. **seek out 1** search for and find. **2** single out for companionship, etc. **to seek** (or **much to seek** or **far to seek**) esp. *Brit.* deficient, lacking, or not yet found (*the reason is not far to seek*; *an efficient leader is yet to seek*). □ **seeker** *n.* (also in *comb.*). [Old English *sēcan*, from Germanic]

seel /si:l/ *v.tr. archaic* close (a person's eyes). [Middle English from French *ciller*, *siller*, or medieval Latin *ciliare* from Latin *cilium* 'eyelid']

seem /si:m/ *v.intr.* **1** give the impression or sensation of being (*seems ridiculous*; *seems certain to win*). **2** (foll. by *to* + infin.) appear or be perceived or ascertained (*he seems to be breathing*; *they seem to have left*). □ **can't seem to** *colloq.* seem unable to. **do not seem to** *colloq.* somehow do not (*I do not seem to like him*). **it seems** (or **would seem**) (often foll. by *that* + clause) it appears to be true or the fact (in a hesitant, guarded, or ironical statement). [originally = suit, befit, be appropriate: Middle English from Old Norse *sœma* 'honour', from *sœmr* 'fitting']

seeming[1] /'si:mɪŋ/ *adj.* **1** apparent but perhaps not real (*with seeming sincerity*). **2** apparent only; ostensible (usu. in *comb.*: *seeming-virtuous*). □ **seemingly** *adv.*

seeming[2] /'si:mɪŋ/ *n. literary* **1** appearance, aspect. **2** deceptive appearance.

seemly /'si:mli/ *adj.* (**seemlier**, **seemliest**) conforming to propriety or good taste; decorous, suitable. □ **seemliness** *n.* [Middle English from Old Norse *sœmiligr* (as SEEM)]

seen *past part.* of SEE[1].

See of Rome *n.* the papacy, the Holy See.

seep /si:p/ *v.* & *n.* ● *v.intr.* ooze out; percolate slowly. ● *n. US* a place where petroleum etc. oozes slowly out of the ground. [perhaps a dialect form of Old English *sipian* 'to soak']

seepage /'si:pɪdʒ/ *n.* **1** the act of seeping. **2** the quantity that seeps out.

seer[1] /'si:ə, sɪə/ *n.* **1** a person who sees. **2** a prophet; a person who sees visions; a person of supposed supernatural insight esp. as regards the future. [Middle English from SEE[1]]

seer[2] /sɪə/ *n.* (in the Indian subcontinent) a varying unit of weight (about one kilogram) or liquid measure (about one litre). [Hindi *ser*]

seersucker /'sɪəsʌkə/ *n.* material of linen, cotton, etc., with a puckered surface. [Persian *šir o šakar*, literally 'milk and sugar']

see-saw /'si:sɔ:/ *n.*, *v.*, *adj.*, & *adv.* ● *n.* **1 a** a device consisting of a long plank balanced on a central support for children to sit on at each end and move up and down by pushing the ground with their feet. **b** a game played on this. **2** an up-and-down or to-and-fro motion. **3** a contest in which the advantage repeatedly changes from one side to the other. ● *v.intr.* **1** play on a see-saw. **2** move up and down as on a see-saw. **3** vacillate in policy, emotion, etc. ● *adj.* & *adv.* with up-and-down or backward-and-forward motion (*see-saw motion*). □ **go see-saw** vacillate or alternate. [reduplication of SAW[1]]

seethe /si:ð/ *v.* **1** *intr.* boil, bubble over. **2** *intr.* be very agitated, esp. with anger (*seething with discontent*; *I was seething inwardly*). **3** *tr.* & *intr. archaic* cook by boiling. □ **seethingly** *adv.* [Old English *sēothan*, from Germanic]

see-through /'si:θru:/*adj.* (esp. of clothing) translucent.

segment /'sɛgm(ə)nt/ *n.* & *v.* ● *n.* **1** each of several parts into which a thing is or can be divided or marked off. **2** *Geom.* a part of a figure cut off by a line or plane intersecting it, esp.: **a** the part of a circle enclosed between an arc and a chord. **b** the part of a line included between two points. **c** the part of a sphere cut off by any plane not passing through the centre. **3** the smallest distinct part of a spoken utterance. **4** *Zool.* each of the series of similar anatomical units of which the body and limbs are composed in various animals, often visible, e.g. as the rings along an earthworm. ● *v.* /usu. -'mɛnt/ **1** *intr.* & *tr.* divide into segments. **2** *intr. Biol.* (of a cell) undergo cleavage or divide into many cells. □ **segmental** /-'mɛnt(ə)l/ *adj.* **segmentalize** /-'mɛnt(ə)lʌɪz/ *v.tr.* (also **-ise**). **segmentalization** /-ˌmɛnt(ə)lʌɪ'zeɪʃ(ə)n/ *n.* **segmentally** /-'mɛnt(ə)li/ *adv.* **segmentary** *adj.* **segmentation** /-'teɪʃ(ə)n/ *n.* [Latin *segmentum* from *secare* 'cut']

sego /'si:gəʊ/ *n.* (*pl.* **-os**) (in full **sego lily**) a N. American plant, *Calochortus nuttallii*, with green and white bell-shaped flowers. [Paiute (an American Indian language of the south-western US)]

segregate[1] /'sɛgrɪgeɪt/ *v.* **1** *tr.* put apart from the rest; isolate. **2** *tr.* enforce racial segregation on (persons) or in (a community etc.). **3** *intr.* separate from a mass and collect together. **4** *intr. Biol.* (of alleles) be transmitted independently of each other. □ **segregable** /-gəb(ə)l/ *adj.* **segregative** *adj.* [Latin *segregare* (as SE-, *grex gregis* 'flock')]

segregate[2] /'sɛgrɪgət/ *adj.* **1** *Zool.* simple or solitary, not compound. **2** *archaic* set apart, separate. [Latin *segregatus*, past part. of *segregare* (as SEGREGATE[1])]

segregation /sɛgrɪ'geɪʃ(ə)n/ *n.* **1** enforced separation of racial groups in a community etc. **2** the act or an instance of segregating; the state of being segregated. □ **segregational** *adj.* **segregationist** *n.* & *adj.* [Late Latin *segregatio* (as SEGREGATE[1])]

segue /'sɛgweɪ/ *v.* & *n.* esp. *Mus.* ● *v.intr.* (**segues**, **segued**, **seguing**) (usu. foll. by *into*) go on without a pause. ● *n.* an uninterrupted transition from one song or melody to another. [Italian, = follows]

seguidilla /sɛgɪ'di:ljə/ *n.* **1** a Spanish dance in triple time. **2** the music for this. [Spanish, via *seguida* 'following' from *seguir* 'follow']

Sehnsucht /'zemzu:xt, German 'ze:nzʊxt/ *n.* yearning, wistful longing. [German]

sei see SEI WHALE.

seicento /seɪ'tʃɛntəʊ/ *n.* the style of Italian art and literature of the 17th c. □ **seicentist** *n.* **seicentoist** *n.* [Italian, = 600, shortened from *mille seicento* '1600', used with reference to the years 1600–99]

seiche /seɪʃ/ *n.* a fluctuation in the water level of a lake etc., esp. as caused by changes in atmospheric pressure. [Swiss French]

Seidlitz powder /'sɛdlɪts/ *n.* (*US* **Seidlitz powders**) a laxative medicine of two powders mixed separately with water and then poured together to effervesce. [named with reference to the mineral water of *Seidlitz* in Bohemia]

seif /si:f, seɪf/ *n.* (in full **seif dune**) a sand dune in the form of a long narrow ridge. [Arabic *saif* 'sword' (from its shape)]

seigneur /seɪ'njə:/ *n.* (also **seignior** /'seɪnjə/) a feudal lord; the lord of a manor. □ **seigneurial** *adj.* **seigniorial** /-'njɔ:rɪəl/ *adj.* [Middle English via Old French *seigneur*, *seignor* from Latin SENIOR]

seigniorage /'seɪnjərɪdʒ/ *n.* (also **seignorage**) **1 a** a profit made by issuing currency, esp. by issuing coins rated above their intrinsic value. **b** *hist.* the Crown's right to a percentage on bullion brought to a mint for coining. **2** *hist.* something claimed by a sovereign or feudal superior as a prerogative. [Middle English from Old French *seignorage*, *seigneurage* (as SEIGNEUR)]

seigniory /'seɪnjəri/ *n.* (*pl.* **-ies**) **1** lordship, sovereign authority. **2** (also **seigneury**) a seigneur's domain. [Middle English from Old French *seignorie* (as SEIGNEUR)]

seine /seɪn/ *n.* & *v.* ● *n.* (also **seine-net**) a fishing net for encircling fish, with floats at the top and weights at the bottom edge, and usu. hauled ashore. ● *v.intr.* & *tr.* fish or catch with a seine. □ **seiner** *n.* [Old English *segne* from West Germanic via Latin *sagena* from Greek sagēnē; reinforced in Middle English by Old French saïne]

seise var. of SEIZE 9.

seisin /'si:zın/ *n.* (also **seizin**) *Law* **1** possession of land by freehold. **2** the act of taking such possession. **3** what is so held. [Middle English from Anglo-French *sesine*, Old French *seisine, saisine* (as SEIZE)]

seismic /'sʌızmık/ *adj.* **1** of or relating to an earthquake or earthquakes or other vibrations of the earth and its crust. **2** relating to or involving vibrations of the earth produced artificially by explosions. **3** of enormous proportions or effect (*seismic revolutionary events*). □ **seismal** *adj.* **seismical** *adj.* **seismically** *adv.* [Greek *seismos* 'earthquake' from *seiō* 'shake']

seismicity /sʌız'mısıti/ *n.* seismic activity; esp. the frequency of earthquakes per unit area in a region.

seismic survey *n.* a survey for oil and gas, employing seismic methods.

seismo- /'sʌızməʊ/ *comb. form* earthquake. [Greek *seismos*]

seismogram /'sʌızmə(ʊ)gram/ *n.* a record given by a seismograph.

seismograph /'sʌızmə(ʊ)grɑ:f/ *n.* an instrument that records the force, direction, etc., of earthquakes. □ **seismographic** /-'grafık/ *adj.* **seismographical** /-'grafık(ə)l/ *adj.*

seismology /sʌız'mɒlədʒi/ *n.* the scientific study and recording of earthquakes and related phenomena. □ **seismological** /-mə'lɒdʒık(ə)l/ *adj.* **seismologically** /-mə'lɒdʒık(ə)li/ *adv.* **seismologist** *n.*

sei whale /seı/ *n.* a small rorqual, *Balaenoptera borealis*. [Norwegian *sejhval*]

seize /si:z/ *v.* **1** *tr.* take hold of forcibly or suddenly. **2** *tr.* take possession of forcibly (*seized the fortress; seized power*). **3** *tr.* take possession of (contraband goods, documents, etc.) by warrant or legal right, confiscate, impound. **4** *tr.* affect suddenly (*panic seized us; was seized by apoplexy; was seized with remorse*). **5** *tr.* take advantage of (an opportunity). **6** *tr.* comprehend quickly or clearly. **7** *intr.* (usu. foll. by *on, upon*) **a** take hold forcibly or suddenly. **b** take advantage eagerly (*seized on a pretext*). **8** *intr.* (usu. foll. by *up*) **a** (of a moving part in a machine) become stuck or jammed from undue heat, friction, etc. **b** (of part of the body etc.) become stiff. **9** *tr.* (also **seise**) (usu. foll. by *of*) *Law* put in possession of. **10** *tr. Naut.* fasten or attach by binding with turns of yarn etc. □ **seized** (or **seised**) **of 1** possessing legally. **2** aware or informed of. □ **seizable** *adj.* **seizer** *n.* [Middle English from Old French *seizir, saisir* 'give seisin', from Frankish via Latin *sacire* from Germanic]

seizin var. of SEISIN.

seizing /'si:zıŋ/ *n. Naut.* a cord or cords used for seizing (see SEIZE 10).

seizure /'si:ʒə/ *n.* **1** the act or an instance of seizing; the state of being seized. **2** a sudden fit or attack of apoplexy etc., a stroke.

sejant /'si:dʒ(ə)nt/ *adj.* (placed after noun) *Heraldry* (of an animal) sitting upright on its haunches. [properly *seiant* from Old French, variant of *seant* 'sitting' via *seoir* from Latin *sedēre* 'sit']

Sekt /zɛkt/ *n.* a German sparkling white wine. [German]

selachian /sı'leıkıən/ *n. & adj.* ● *n.* any fish of the subclass Selachii, including sharks and dogfish. ● *adj.* of or relating to this subclass. [modern Latin *Selachii* from Greek *selakhos* 'shark']

seladang /sə'lɑ:daŋ/ *n.* a Malayan gaur. [Malay]

selah /'si:lə, -lɑ:/ *int.* occurring frequently at the end of a verse in Psalms and Habakkuk, probably as a musical direction. [Hebrew *se·lāh*]

seldom /'sɛldəm/ *adv. & adj.* ● *adv.* rarely, not often. ● *adj.* rare, uncommon. [Old English *seldan*, from Germanic]

select /sı'lɛkt/ *v. & adj.* ● *v.tr.* choose, esp. as the best or most suitable. ● *adj.* **1** chosen for excellence or suitability; choice. **2** (of a society etc.) exclusive, cautious in admitting members. □ **selectable** *adj.* **selectness** *n.* [Latin *seligere select-* (as SE-, *legere* 'choose')]

select committee *n.* a small parliamentary committee appointed for a special purpose.

selectee /sılɛk'ti:/ *n. US* a conscript.

selection /sı'lɛkʃ(ə)n/ *n.* **1** the act or an instance of selecting; the state of being selected. **2** a selected person or thing. **3** things from which a choice may be made. **4** *Biol.* the process in which environmental and genetic influences determine which types of organism thrive better than others, regarded as a factor in evolution. □ **selectional** *adj.* **selectionally** *adv.* [Latin *selectio* (as SELECT)]

selective /sı'lɛktıv/ *adj.* **1** using or characterized by selection. **2** able to select, esp. (of a radio receiver) able to respond to a chosen frequency without interference from others. **3** (of the memory etc.) selecting what is convenient. □ **selectively** *adv.* **selectiveness** *n.* **selectivity** /sılɛk'tıvıti, sɛl-, si:l-/ *n.*

selective service *n. US hist.* service in the armed forces under conscription.

selector /sı'lɛktə/ *n.* **1** a person who selects, esp. one who selects a representative team in a sport. **2** a device that selects, esp. a device in a vehicle that selects the required gear.

selenite /'sɛlınʌıt/ *n.* a form of gypsum occurring as transparent crystals or thin plates. □ **selenitic** /-'nıtık/ *adj.* [Latin *selenites* from Greek *selēnitēs lithos* 'moonstone', from *selēnē* 'moon', *lithos* 'stone']

selenium /sı'li:nıəm/ *n. Chem.* a non-metallic element occurring naturally in various metallic sulphide ores and characterized by the variation of its electrical resistivity with intensity of illumination (symbol Se). □ **selenate** /'sɛlıneıt/ *n.* **selenic** /sı'li:nık/ *adj.* **selenious** *adj.* [modern Latin, from Greek *selēnē* 'moon' + -IUM]

selenium cell *n.* a piece of selenium used as a photoelectric device.

seleno- /sı'li:nəʊ/ *comb. form* moon. [Greek *selēnē* 'moon']

selenography /sɛlı'nɒgrəfi, si:-/ *n.* the study or mapping of the moon. □ **selenographer** *n.* **selenographic** /-nə'grafık/ *adj.*

selenology /sɛlı'nɒlədʒi, si:-/ *n.* the scientific study of the moon. □ **selenologist** *n.*

self /sɛlf/ *n., adj., & v.* ● *n.* (*pl.* **selves** /sɛlvz/) **1** a person's or thing's own individuality or essence (*showed his true self*). **2** a person or thing as the object of introspection or reflexive action (*the consciousness of self*). **3 a** one's own interests or pleasure (*cares for nothing but self*). **b** concentration on these (*self is a bad guide to happiness*). **4** *Commerce* or *colloq.* myself, yourself, himself, etc. (*cheque drawn to self; ticket admitting self and friend*). **5** used in phrs. equivalent to *myself, yourself, himself*, etc. (*his very self; your good selves*). **6** (*pl.* **selfs**) a flower of uniform colour, or of the natural wild colour. ● *adj.* **1** of the same colour as the rest or throughout. **2** (of a flower) of the natural wild colour. **3** (of colour) uniform, the same throughout. ● *v.tr.* (usu. in *passive*) *Bot.* self-fertilize. □ **one's better self** one's nobler impulses. **one's former** (or **old**) **self** oneself as one formerly was. [Old English from Germanic]

self- /sɛlf/ *comb. form* expressing reflexive action: **1** of or directed towards oneself or itself (*self-respect; self-cleaning*). **2** by oneself or itself, esp. without external agency (*self-evident*). **3** on, in, for, or relating to oneself or itself (*self-absorbed; self-confident*).

self-abandon /sɛlfə'band(ə)n/ *n.* (also **self-abandonment**) the abandonment of oneself, esp. to passion or an impulse. □ **self-abandoned** *adj.*

self-abasement /sɛlfə'beısm(ə)nt/ *n.* the abasement or humiliation of oneself; cringing.

self-abhorrence /sɛlfəb'hɒr(ə)ns/ *n.* the abhorrence of oneself; self-hatred.

self-abnegation /sɛlf,abnɪ'geɪʃ(ə)n/ *n.* = SELF-DENIAL.

self-absorption /sɛlfəb'zɔ:pʃ(ə)n, -'sɔ:p-/ *n.* **1** absorption in oneself. **2** *Physics* the absorption, by a body, of radiation emitted within it. □ **self-absorbed** /-'zɔ:bd/ *adj.*

self-abuse /sɛlfə'bju:s/ *n.* **1** the reviling or abuse of oneself. **2** masturbation.

self-accusation /sɛlf,akju:'zeɪʃ(ə)n/ *n.* the accusing of oneself. □ **self-accusatory** /-ə'kju:zət(ə)ri/ *adj.*

self-acting /sɛlf 'aktɪŋ/ *adj.* acting without external influence or control; automatic. □ **self-action** /-'akʃ(ə)n/ *n.* **self-activity** /-ak'tɪvɪti/ *n.*

self-addressed /sɛlfə'drɛst/ *adj.* (of an envelope etc.) having one's own address on for return communication.

self-adhesive /sɛlfəd'hi:sɪv/ *adj.* (of an envelope, label, etc.) adhesive, esp. without being moistened.

self-adjusting /sɛlfə'dʒʌstɪŋ/ *adj.* (of machinery etc.) adjusting itself. □ **self-adjustment** *n.*

self-admiration /sɛlf,admə'reɪʃ(ə)n/ *n.* the admiration of oneself; pride; conceit.

self-advancement /sɛlfəd'vɑ:nsm(ə)nt/ *n.* the advancement of oneself or one's own interests.

self-advertisement /sɛlfəd'və:tɪzm(ə)nt/ *n.* the advertising or promotion of oneself. □ **self-advertiser** /-'advətʌɪzə/ *n.*

self-affirmation /sɛlf,afə'meɪʃ(ə)n/ *n. Psychol.* the recognition and assertion of the existence of the conscious self.

self-aggrandizement /sɛlfə'grandɪzm(ə)nt/ *n.* (also **-isement**) the act or process of trying to make oneself more powerful or seemingly more important. □ **self-aggrandizing** /-'grandʌɪzɪŋ/ *adj.*

self-analysis /sɛlfə'nalɪsɪs/ *n. Psychol.* the analysis of oneself, one's motives, character, etc. □ **self-analysing** /-'an(ə)lʌɪzɪŋ/ *adj.*

self-appointed /sɛlfə'pɔɪntɪd/ *adj.* designated so by oneself, not authorized by another (*a self-appointed guardian*).

self-appreciation /,sɛlfəpri:ʃɪ'eɪʃ(ə)n, -sɪ-/ *n.* a good opinion of oneself; conceit.

self-approbation /sɛlf,aprə'beɪʃ(ə)n/ *n.* approval of oneself; self-appreciation.

self-approval /sɛlfə'pru:v(ə)l/ *n.* = SELF-APPRECIATION.

self-assembly /sɛlfə'sɛmbli/ *n.* (often *attrib.*) the construction of furniture etc. from materials sold in kit form.

self-assertion /sɛlfə'sə:ʃ(ə)n/ *n.* the aggressive promotion of oneself, one's views, etc. □ **self-asserting** *adj.* **self-assertive** *adj.* **self-assertiveness** *n.*

self-assurance /sɛlfə'ʃʊər(ə)ns/ *n.* confidence in one's own abilities etc. □ **self-assured** *adj.* **self-assuredly** *adv.*

self-aware /sɛlfə'wɛ:/ *adj.* conscious of one's character, feelings, motives, etc. □ **self-awareness** *n.*

self-begotten /sɛlfbɪ'gɒt(ə)n/ *adj.* produced by oneself or itself; not made externally.

self-betrayal /sɛlfbɪ'treɪəl/ *n.* **1** the betrayal of oneself. **2** the inadvertent revelation of one's true thoughts etc.

self-binder /sɛlf 'bʌɪndə/ *n.* a reaping machine with an automatic mechanism for binding the sheaves.

self-born /sɛlf 'bɔ:n/ *adj.* produced by itself or oneself; not made externally.

self-build /sɛlf 'bɪld/ *n.* (often *attrib.*) the building of homes by their future owners (*self-build cooperative*). □ **self-builder** *n.*

self-catering /sɛlf 'keɪt(ə)rɪŋ/ *adj.* & *n. Brit.* ● *adj.* (esp. of a holiday or holiday premises) providing rented accommodation with cooking facilities but without food. ● *n.* the activity of catering for oneself in rented temporary or holiday accommodation.

self-censorship /sɛlf 'sɛnsəʃɪp/ *n.* the censoring of oneself.

self-centred /sɛlf 'sɛntəd/ *adj.* preoccupied with one's own personality or affairs; selfish. □ **self-centredly** *adv.* **self-centredness** *n.*

self-certify /sɛlf 'sə:tɪfʌɪ/ *v.tr. Brit.* **1** attest to in writing (a thing concerning oneself, esp. one's financial standing). **2** (as **self-certified** *adj.*) acquired as a result of such attestation (*self-certified loan*). □ **self-certification** /-fɪ'keɪʃ(ə)n/ *n.*

self-cleaning /sɛlf 'kli:nɪŋ/ *adj.* (esp. of an oven) cleaning itself when heated etc.

self-closing /sɛlf 'kləʊzɪŋ/ *adj.* (of a door etc.) closing automatically.

self-cocking /sɛlf 'kɒkɪŋ/ *adj.* (of a gun) with the hammer raised by the trigger, not by hand.

self-collected /sɛlfkə'lɛktɪd/ *adj.* composed, serene, self-assured.

self-coloured /sɛlf 'kʌləd/ *adj.* (*US* **self-colored**) **1 a** having the same colour throughout. **b** (of material) natural; undyed. **2 a** (of a flower) of uniform colour. **b** having its colour unchanged by cultivation or hybridization.

self-command /sɛlfkə'mɑ:nd/ *n.* = SELF-CONTROL.

self-communion /sɛlfkə'mju:njən/ *n.* meditation upon one's own character, conduct, etc.

self-conceit /sɛlfkən'si:t/ *n.* = SELF-SATISFACTION. □ **self-conceited** *adj.*

self-condemnation /sɛlf,kɒndɛm'neɪʃ(ə)n/ *n.* **1** the blaming of oneself. **2** the inadvertent revelation of one's own sin, crime, etc. □ **self-condemned** /-kən'dɛmd/ *adj.*

self-confessed /sɛlfkən'fɛst/ *adj.* openly admitting oneself to be (*a self-confessed thief*).

self-confidence /sɛlf 'kɒnfɪd(ə)ns/ *n.* = SELF-ASSURANCE. □ **self-confident** *adj.* **self-confidently** *adv.*

self-congratulation /,sɛlfkəngratjʊ'leɪʃ(ə)n/ *n.* = SELF-SATISFACTION. □ **self-congratulatory** /-kən'gratʊlət(ə)ri/ *adj.*

self-conquest /sɛlf 'kɒŋkwɛst/ *n.* the overcoming of one's worst characteristics etc.

self-conscious /sɛlf 'kɒnʃəs/ *adj.* **1** unduly aware of one's appearance or actions through embarrassment or shyness. **2** *Philos.* having knowledge of one's own existence; self-contemplating. □ **self-consciously** *adv.* **self-consciousness** *n.*

self-consistent /sɛlfkən'sɪst(ə)nt/ *adj.* (of parts of the same whole etc.) consistent; not conflicting. □ **self-consistency** *n.*

self-constituted /sɛlf 'kɒnstɪtju:tɪd/ *adj.* (of a person, group, etc.) assuming a function without authorization or right; self-appointed.

self-contained /sɛlfkən'teɪnd/ *adj.* **1** (of a person) uncommunicative; independent. **2** *Brit.* (esp. of living accommodation) complete in itself. □ **self-containment** *n.*

self-contempt /sɛlfkən'tɛm(p)t/ *n.* contempt for oneself. □ **self-contemptuous** *adj.*

self-content /sɛlfkən'tɛnt/ *n.* satisfaction with oneself, one's life, achievements, etc. □ **self-contented** *adj.*

self-contradiction /sɛlf,kɒntrə'dɪkʃ(ə)n/ *n.* internal inconsistency. □ **self-contradictory** *adj.*

self-control /sɛlfkən'trəʊl/ *n.* the power of controlling one's external reactions, emotions, etc. □ **self-controlled** *adj.*

self-convicted /sɛlfkən'vɪktɪd/ *adj.* = *self-condemned* (see SELF-CONDEMNATION).

self-correcting /sɛlfkə'rɛktɪŋ/ *adj.* correcting itself without external help.

self-created /sɛlfkrɪ'eɪtɪd/ *adj.* created by oneself or itself. □ **self-creation** /-'eɪʃ(ə)n/ *n.*

self-critical /sɛlf 'krɪtɪk(ə)l/ *adj.* critical of oneself, one's abilities, etc. □ **self-criticism** /-sɪz(ə)m/ *n.*

self-deception /sɛlfdɪ'sɛpʃ(ə)n/ *n.* deceiving oneself esp. concerning one's true feelings etc. □ **self-deceit** /-dɪ'si:t/ *n.* **self-deceiver** /-dɪ'si:və/ *n.* **self-deceiving** /-dɪ'si:vɪŋ/ *adj.* **self-deceptive** *adj.*

self-defeating /sɛlfdɪ'fi:tɪŋ/ *adj.* (of an attempt, action, etc.) doomed to failure because of internal inconsistencies etc.

self-defence /sɛlfdɪ'fɛns/ *n.* **1** a defence of oneself, one's rights or position (*hit him in self-defence*). **2** an instance of aggression in such defence (*it was self-defence*). □ **the noble art of self-defence** boxing. □ **self-defensive** *adj.*

self-delight /sɛlfdɪˈlʌɪt/ *n.* delight in oneself or one's existence.

self-delusion /sɛlfdɪˈluːʒ(ə)n, -ˈljuːʒ(ə)n/ *n.* the act or an instance of deluding oneself.

self-denial /sɛlfdɪˈnʌɪəl/ *n.* the denial of one's own interests, needs, etc.; self-sacrifice. □ **self-denying** *adj.*

self-denying ordinance *n. Brit. hist.* a resolution of the Long Parliament 1645 depriving Members of Parliament of civil and military office.

self-dependence /sɛlfdɪˈpɛnd(ə)ns/ *adj.* dependence only on oneself or itself; independence. □ **self-dependent** *adj.*

self-deprecation /sɛlfˌdɛprɪˈkeɪʃ(ə)n/ *n.* the act of disparaging or belittling oneself. □ **self-deprecating** /-ˈdɛprɪkeɪtɪŋ/ *adj.* **self-deprecatingly** /-ˈdɛprɪkeɪtɪŋli/ *adv.* **self-deprecatory** *adj.*

■ **Usage** See Usage Note at DEPRECATE.

self-depreciation /ˌsɛlfdɪpriːʃɪˈeɪʃ(ə)n/ *n.* = SELF-DEPRECATION. □ **self-depreciatory** /-ˈpriːʃ(ɪ)ət(ə)ri/ *adj.*

■ **Usage** See Usage Note at DEPRECATE.

self-despair /sɛlfdɪˈspɛː/ *n.* despair with oneself.

self-destroying /sɛlfdɪˈstrɔɪɪŋ/ *adj.* destroying oneself or itself.

self-destruct /sɛlfdɪˈstrʌkt/ *v.* & *adj.* orig. *N. Amer.* ● *v.intr.* (of a spacecraft, bomb, etc.) explode or disintegrate automatically, esp. when pre-set to do so. ● *attrib.adj.* enabling a thing to self-destruct (*a self-destruct device*).

self-destruction /sɛlfdɪˈstrʌkʃ(ə)n/ *n.* **1** the process or an act of destroying oneself or itself. **2** orig. *N. Amer.* the process or an act of self-destructing. □ **self-destructive** *adj.* **self-destructively** *adv.*

self-determination /ˌsɛlfdɪtəːmɪˈneɪʃ(ə)n/ *n.* **1** a nation's right to determine its own allegiance, government, etc. **2** the ability to act with free will, as opposed to fatalism etc. □ **self-determined** /-ˈtəːmɪnd/ *adj.* **self-determining** /-ˈtəːmɪnɪŋ/ *adj.*

self-development /sɛlfdɪˈvɛləpm(ə)nt/ *n.* the development of oneself, one's abilities, etc.

self-devotion /sɛlfdɪˈvəʊʃ(ə)n/ *n.* the devotion of oneself to a person or cause.

self-discipline /sɛlf ˈdɪsɪplɪn/ *n.* the act of or ability to apply oneself, control one's feelings, etc.; self-control. □ **self-disciplined** *adj.*

self-discovery /sɛlfdɪˈskʌv(ə)ri/ *n.* the process of acquiring insight into oneself, one's character, desires, etc.

self-disgust /sɛlfdɪsˈgʌst/ *n.* disgust with oneself.

self-doubt /sɛlf ˈdaʊt/ *n.* lack of confidence in oneself, one's abilities, etc.

self-drive /sɛlf ˈdrʌɪv/ *adj. Brit.* (of a hired vehicle) driven by the hirer.

self-educated /sɛlf ˈɛdjʊkeɪtɪd/ *adj.* educated by oneself by reading etc., without formal instruction. □ **self-education** /-ˈkeɪʃ(ə)n/ *n.*

self-effacing /sɛlfɪˈfeɪsɪŋ/ *adj.* retiring; modest; timid. □ **self-effacement** *n.* **self-effacingly** *adv.*

self-elective /sɛlfɪˈlɛktɪv/ *adj. Brit.* (of a committee etc.) proceeding esp. by co-opting members etc.

self-employed /sɛlfɪmˈplɔɪd/ *adj.* working for oneself, as a freelance or owner of a business etc.; not employed by an employer. □ **self-employment** *n.*

self-esteem /sɛlfɪˈstiːm/ *n.* a good opinion of oneself.

self-evident /sɛlf ˈɛvɪd(ə)nt/ *adj.* obvious; without the need of evidence or further explanation. □ **self-evidence** *n.* **self-evidently** *adv.*

self-examination /ˌsɛlfɪgzamɪˈneɪʃ(ə)n/ *n.* **1** the study of one's own conduct, reasons, etc. **2** the examining of one's body for signs of illness etc.

self-executing /sɛlf ˈɛksɪkjuːtɪŋ/ *adj. Law* (of a law, legal clause, etc.) not needing legislation etc. to be enforced; automatic.

self-existent /sɛlfɪgˈzɪst(ə)nt/ *adj.* existing without prior cause; independent.

self-explanatory /sɛlfɪkˈsplanət(ə)ri/ *adj.* easily understood; not needing explanation.

self-expression /sɛlfɪkˈsprɛʃ(ə)n/ *n.* the expression of one's feelings, thoughts, etc., esp. in writing, painting, music, etc. □ **self-expressive** *adj.*

self-faced /sɛlf ˈfeɪst/ *adj.* (of stone) unhewn; undressed.

self-feeder /sɛlf ˈfiːdə/ *n.* **1** a furnace, machine, etc., that renews its own fuel or material automatically. **2** a device for supplying food to farm animals automatically. □ **self-feeding** *adj.*

self-fertile /sɛlf ˈfəːtʌɪl/ *adj.* (of a plant etc.) self-fertilizing. □ **self-fertility** /-ˈtɪlɪti/ *n.*

self-fertilization /sɛlfˌfəːtɪlʌɪˈzeɪʃ(ə)n/ *n.* (also **-isation**) the fertilization of plants and some invertebrate animals by their own pollen or sperm, not that of another. □ **self-fertilized** /-ˈfəːtɪlʌɪzd/ *adj.* **self-fertilizing** /-ˈfəːtɪlʌɪzɪŋ/ *adj.*

self-financing /sɛlf ˈfʌɪnansɪŋ/ *adj.* that finances itself, esp. (of a project or undertaking) that pays for its own implementation or continuation. □ **self-financed** *adj.*

self-flagellation /ˌsɛlfflad͡ʒəˈleɪʃ(ə)n/ *n.* **1** the flagellation of oneself, esp. as a form of religious discipline. **2** excessive self-criticism.

self-flattery /sɛlf ˈflat(ə)ri/ *n.* = SELF-APPRECIATION. □ **self-flattering** *adj.*

self-forgetful /sɛlffəˈgɛtfʊl, -f(ə)l/ *adj.* unselfish. □ **self-forgetfulness** *n.*

self-fulfilling /sɛlffʊlˈfɪlɪŋ/ *adj.* (of a prophecy, forecast, etc.) bound to come true as a result of actions brought about by its being made.

self-fulfilment /sɛlffʊlˈfɪlm(ə)nt/ *n.* (*US* **-fulfillment**) the fulfilment of one's own hopes and ambitions.

self-generating /sɛlf ˈd͡ʒɛnəreɪtɪŋ/ *adj.* generated by itself or oneself, not externally.

self-glorification /sɛlfˌglɔːrɪfɪˈkeɪʃ(ə)n/ *n.* the proclamation of oneself, one's abilities, etc.; boasting.

self-governing /sɛlf ˈgʌv(ə)nɪŋ/ *adj.* **1** (of a British hospital or school) having opted out of local authority control. **2** (esp. of a former colony etc.) administering its own affairs.

self-government /sɛlf ˈgʌv(ə)nm(ə)nt/ *n.* **1** (esp. of a former colony etc.) government by its own people. **2** = SELF-CONTROL. □ **self-governed** *adj.*

self-hate /sɛlf ˈheɪt/ *n.* = SELF-HATRED.

self-hatred /sɛlf ˈheɪtrɪd/ *n.* hatred of oneself, esp. of one's actual self when contrasted with one's imagined self.

self-heal /ˈsɛlfhiːl/ *n.* any of several plants, esp. *Prunella vulgaris*, believed to have healing properties.

self-help /sɛlf ˈhɛlp/ *n.* (often *attrib.*) **1** the theory that individuals should provide for their own support and improvement in society. **2** the act or faculty of providing for or improving oneself (*self-help groups*).

selfhood /ˈsɛlfhʊd/ *n.* personality, separate and conscious existence.

self-image /sɛlf ˈɪmɪd͡ʒ/ *n.* one's own idea or picture of oneself, esp. in relation to others.

self-immolation /ˌsɛlfɪməˈleɪʃ(ə)n/ *n.* the offering of oneself as a sacrifice.

self-importance /sɛlfɪmˈpɔːt(ə)ns/ *n.* a high opinion of oneself; pompousness. □ **self-important** *adj.* **self-importantly** *adv.*

self-imposed /sɛlfɪmˈpəʊzd/ *adj.* (of a task or condition etc.) imposed on and by oneself, not externally (*self-imposed exile*).

self-improvement /sɛlfɪmˈpruːvm(ə)nt/ *n.* the improvement of one's own position or disposition by one's own efforts.

self-induced /sɛlfɪnˈdjuːst/ *adj.* **1** induced by oneself or itself. **2** *Electr.* produced by self-induction.

self-inductance /sɛlfɪnˈdʌkt(ə)ns/ *n. Electr.* the property of an electric circuit that causes an electromotive force to be generated in it by a change in the current flowing through it (cf. MUTUAL INDUCTANCE).

self-induction /sɛlfɪnˈdʌkʃ(ə)n/ *n. Electr.* the production of an electromotive force in a circuit when the current in that circuit is varied. □ **self-inductive** *adj.*

self-indulgent /sɛlfɪnˈdʌldʒ(ə)nt/ *adj.* **1** indulging or tending to indulge oneself in pleasure, idleness, etc. **2** (of a work of art etc.) lacking economy and control. □ **self-indulgence** *n.* **self-indulgently** *adv.*

self-inflicted /sɛlfɪnˈflɪktɪd/ *adj.* (esp. of a wound, damage, etc.) inflicted by and on oneself, not externally.

self-interest /sɛlf ˈɪnt(ə)rɪst/ *n.* one's personal interest or advantage. □ **self-interested** *adj.*

self-involved /sɛlfɪnˈvɒlvd/ *adj.* wrapped up in oneself or one's own thoughts. □ **self-involvement** *n.*

selfish /ˈsɛlfɪʃ/ *adj.* **1** deficient in consideration for others; concerned chiefly with one's own personal profit or pleasure; actuated by self-interest. **2** (of a motive etc.) appealing to self-interest. □ **selfishly** *adv.* **selfishness** *n.*

self-justification /sɛlˌdʒʌstɪfɪˈkeɪʃ(ə)n/ *n.* the justification or excusing of oneself, one's actions, etc. □ **self-justifying** /-ˈdʒʌstɪfʌɪɪŋ/ *adj.*

self-knowledge /sɛlf ˈnɒlɪdʒ/ *n.* the understanding of oneself, one's motives, etc.

selfless /ˈsɛlflɪs/ *adj.* disregarding oneself or one's own interests; unselfish. □ **selflessly** *adv.* **selflessness** *n.*

self-loading /sɛlf ˈləʊdɪŋ/ *adj.* (esp. of a gun) loading itself. □ **self-loader** *n.*

self-locking /sɛlf ˈlɒkɪŋ/ *adj.* locking itself.

self-love /sɛlf ˈlʌv/ *n.* **1** selfishness; self-indulgence. **2** *Philos.* regard for one's own well-being and happiness.

self-made /sɛlf ˈmeɪd/ *adj.* **1** successful or rich by one's own effort. **2** made by oneself.

self-mastery /sɛlf ˈmɑːst(ə)ri/ *n.* = SELF-CONTROL.

selfmate /ˈsɛlfmeɪt/ *n. Chess* checkmate in which a player forces the opponent to achieve checkmate.

self-mocking /sɛlf ˈmɒkɪŋ/ *adj.* mocking oneself or itself.

self-motion /sɛlf ˈməʊʃ(ə)n/ *n.* motion caused by oneself or itself, not externally. □ **self-moving** /-ˈmuːvɪŋ/ *adj.*

self-motivated /sɛlf ˈməʊtɪveɪtɪd/ *adj.* acting on one's own initiative without external pressure. □ **self-motivation** /-ˈveɪʃ(ə)n/ *n.*

self-murder /sɛlf ˈməːdə/ *n.* = SUICIDE. □ **self-murderer** *n.*

self-mutilation /ˌsɛlfmjuːtɪˈleɪʃ(ə)n/ *n.* the mutilation of oneself.

self-neglect /sɛlfnɪˈglɛkt/ *n.* neglect of oneself.

selfness /ˈsɛlfnɪs/ *n.* **1** individuality, personality, essence. **2** selfishness or self-regard.

self-opinionated /sɛlfəˈpɪnjəneɪtɪd/ *adj.* **1** stubbornly adhering to one's own opinions. **2** arrogant. □ **self-opinion** *n.*

self-parody /sɛlf ˈparədi/ *n.* the act or an instance of parodying oneself. □ **self-parodying** *adj.*

self-perpetuating /sɛlfpəˈpɛtʃʊeɪtɪŋ, -tjʊeɪt-/ *adj.* perpetuating itself or oneself without external agency. □ **self-perpetuation** /-ˈeɪʃ(ə)n/ *n.*

self-pity /sɛlf ˈpɪti/ *n.* extreme sorrow for one's own troubles etc. □ **self-pitying** *adj.* **self-pityingly** *adv.*

self-pollination /sɛlˌpɒlɪˈneɪʃ(ə)n/ *n.* the pollination of a flower by pollen from the same plant. □ **self-pollinated** *adj.* **self-pollinating** *adj.* **self-pollinator** *n.*

self-portrait /sɛlf ˈpɔːtrɪt/ *n.* a portrait or description of an artist, writer, etc., by himself or herself.

self-possessed /sɛlfpəˈzɛst/ *adj.* habitually exercising self-control; composed. □ **self-possession** /-ˈzɛʃ(ə)n/ *n.*

self-praise /sɛlf ˈpreɪz/ *n.* boasting; self-glorification.

self-preservation /sɛlˌprɛzəˈveɪʃ(ə)n/ *n.* **1** the preservation of one's own life, safety, etc. **2** this as a basic instinct of human beings and animals.

self-proclaimed /sɛlfprəˈkleɪmd/ *adj.* proclaimed by oneself or itself to be such.

self-propagating /sɛlf ˈprɒpəgeɪtɪŋ/ *adj.* (esp. of a plant) able to propagate itself.

self-propelled /sɛlfprəˈpɛld/ *adj.* (esp. of a motor vehicle etc.) moving or able to move without external propulsion. □ **self-propelling** *adj.*

self-protection /sɛlfprəˈtɛkʃ(ə)n/ *n.* protecting oneself or itself. □ **self-protective** *adj.*

self-raising /sɛlf ˈreɪzɪŋ/ *adj. Brit.* (of flour) having a raising agent already added.

self-realization /sɛlfˌrɪəlʌɪˈzeɪʃ(ə)n/ *n.* (also **-isation**) **1** the development of one's faculties, abilities, etc. **2** this as an ethical principle.

self-recording /sɛlfrɪˈkɔːdɪŋ/ *adj.* (of a scientific instrument etc.) automatically recording its measurements.

self-referential /sɛlˌrɛfəˈrɛnʃ(ə)l/ *adj.* characterized by or making reference to oneself or itself. □ **self-referentiality** /-ʃɪˈalɪti/ *n.*

self-regard /sɛlfrɪˈgɑːd/ *n.* **1** a proper regard for oneself. **2 a** selfishness. **b** conceit. □ **self-regarding** *adj.*

self-registering /sɛlf ˈrɛdʒɪst(ə)rɪŋ/ *adj.* (of a scientific instrument etc.) automatically registering its measurements.

self-regulating /sɛlf ˈrɛgjʊleɪtɪŋ/ *adj.* regulating oneself or itself without intervention. □ **self-regulation** /-ˈleɪʃ(ə)n/ *n.* **self-regulatory** /-lət(ə)ri/ *adj.*

self-reliance /sɛlfrɪˈlʌɪəns/ *n.* reliance on one's own resources etc.; independence. □ **self-reliant** *adj.* **self-reliantly** *adv.*

self-renewal /sɛlfrɪˈnjuːəl/ *n.* the act or process of renewing oneself or itself.

self-renunciation /ˌsɛlfrɪnʌnsɪˈeɪʃ(ə)n/ *n.* **1** = SELF-SACRIFICE. **2** unselfishness.

self-reproach /sɛlfrɪˈprəʊtʃ/ *n.* reproach or blame directed at oneself. □ **self-reproachful** *adj.*

self-respect /sɛlfrɪˈspɛkt/ *n.* respect for oneself, a feeling that one is behaving with honour, dignity, etc. □ **self-respecting** *adj.*

self-restraint /sɛlfrɪˈstreɪnt/ *n.* = SELF-CONTROL. □ **self-restrained** *adj.*

self-revealing /sɛlfrɪˈviːlɪŋ/ *adj.* revealing one's character, motives, etc., esp. inadvertently. □ **self-revelation** /-rɛvəˈleɪʃ(ə)n/ *n.*

self-righteous /sɛlf ˈrʌɪtʃəs/ *adj.* excessively conscious of or insistent on one's rectitude, correctness, etc. □ **self-righteously** *adv.* **self-righteousness** *n.*

self-righting /sɛlf ˈrʌɪtɪŋ/ *adj.* (of a boat) righting itself when capsized.

self-rising /sɛlf ˈrʌɪzɪŋ/ *adj. US* = SELF-RAISING.

self-rule /sɛlf ˈruːl/ *n.* = SELF-GOVERNMENT 1.

self-sacrifice /sɛlf ˈsakrɪfʌɪs/ *n.* the negation of one's own interests, wishes, etc., in favour of those of others. □ **self-sacrificing** *adj.*

selfsame /ˈsɛlfseɪm/ *attrib.adj.* (prec. by *the*) the very same (*the selfsame village*).

self-satisfaction /ˌsɛlfsatɪsˈfakʃ(ə)n/ *n.* excessive and unwarranted satisfaction with oneself, one's achievements, etc.; complacency. □ **self-satisfied** /-ˈsatɪsfʌɪd/ *adj.*

self-sealing /sɛlf ˈsiːlɪŋ/ *adj.* **1** (of a pneumatic tyre, fuel tank, etc.) automatically able to seal small punctures. **2** (of an envelope) self-adhesive.

self-seed /sɛlf ˈsiːd/ *v.intr.* (of a plant) propagate itself by seed. □ **self-seeder** *n.* **self-seeding** *adj.*

self-seeking /sɛlf ˈsiːkɪŋ/ *adj.* & *n.* ● *adj.* seeking one's own welfare before that of others. ● *n.* the activity of doing this. □ **self-seeker** *n.*

self-selection /sɛlfsɪˈlɛkʃ(ə)n/ *n.* the act of selecting oneself or itself. □ **self-selecting** *adj.*

self-service /sɛlf ˈsəːvɪs/ *adj.* & *n.* ● *adj.* (often *attrib.*) **1** (of a shop, restaurant, garage, etc.) where customers serve themselves and pay at a checkout counter etc. **2** (of a machine) serving goods after the insertion of coins. ● *n. colloq.* a self-service store, garage, etc.

self-serving /sɛlf ˈsəːvɪŋ/ *adj.* & *n.* = SELF-SEEKING.

self-slaughter /sɛlf ˈslɔːtə/ *n.* = SUICIDE *n.* 1a.

self-sown /sɛlf ˈsəʊn/ *adj.* grown from seed scattered naturally.

self-starter /sɛlf ˈstɑːtə/ *n.* **1** an electric appliance for starting a motor vehicle engine without the use of a crank. **2** an ambitious person who needs no external motivation.

self-sterile /sɛlf ˈstɛrʌɪl/ *adj. Biol.* not self-fertilizing. □ **self-sterility** /-stəˈrɪlɪti/ *n.*

self-styled /sɛlf ˈstʌɪld/ *adj.* called so by oneself; would-be; pretended (*a self-styled artist*).

self-sufficient /sɛlfsəˈfɪʃ(ə)nt/ *adj.* **1 a** needing nothing; independent. **b** (of a person, nation, etc.) able to supply one's needs for a commodity, esp. food, from one's own resources. **2** content with one's own opinion; arrogant. □ **self-sufficiency** *n.* **self-sufficiently** *adv.* **self-sufficing** /-səˈfʌɪsɪŋ/ *adj.*

self-suggestion /sɛlfsəˈdʒɛstʃ(ə)n/ *n.* = AUTO-SUGGESTION.

self-supporting /sɛlfsəˈpɔːtɪŋ/ *adj.* **1** capable of maintaining oneself or itself financially. **2** staying up or standing without external aid. □ **self-support** *n.*

self-surrender /sɛlfsəˈrɛndə/ *n.* the surrender of oneself or one's will etc. to an influence, emotion, or other person.

self-sustaining /sɛlfsəˈsteɪnɪŋ/ *adj.* sustaining oneself or itself. □ **self-sustained** *adj.*

self-tapping /sɛlf ˈtapɪŋ/ *adj.* (of a screw) able to cut its own thread.

self-taught /sɛlf ˈtɔːt/ *adj.* educated or trained by oneself, not externally.

self-torture /sɛlf ˈtɔːtʃə/ *n.* the inflicting of pain, esp. mental, on oneself.

self-understanding /ˌsɛlfʌndəˈstandɪŋ/ *n.* **1** the act or an instance of comprehending one's actions and reactions. **2** sympathetic tolerance or awareness of oneself.

self-willed /sɛlf ˈwɪld/ *adj.* obstinately pursuing one's own wishes. □ **self-will** *n.*

self-winding /sɛlf ˈwʌɪndɪŋ/ *adj.* (of a watch etc.) having an automatic winding apparatus.

self-worth /sɛlf ˈwəːθ/ *n.* = SELF-ESTEEM.

Seljuk /ˈsɛldʒuːk/ *n. & adj.* ● *n.* a member of any of the Turkish dynasties (11th–13th c.) of central and western Asia preceding Ottoman rule. ● *adj.* of or relating to the Seljuks. □ **Seljukian** /-ˈdʒuːkɪən/ *adj. & n.* [Turkish *seljūq* (the name of their reputed ancestor)]

sell /sɛl/ *v. & n.* ● *v.* (*past* and *past part.* **sold** /səʊld/) **1** *tr.* make over or dispose of in exchange for money. **2** *tr.* keep a stock of for sale or be a dealer in (*do you sell candles?*). **3 a** *intr.* (of goods) be purchased (*will never sell; these are selling well*). **b** *tr.* (of a publication or recording) attain sales of (a specified number of copies) (*the book has sold 10,000 copies*). **4** *intr.* (foll. by *at, for*) have a specified price (*sells at £5*). **5** *tr.* **a** betray for money or other reward (*sell one's country*). **b** offer dishonourably for money or other reward; make a matter of corrupt bargaining (*sell justice; sell one's honour*). **6** *tr.* **a** advertise or publish the merits of. **b** give (a person) information on the value of something, inspire with a desire to buy or acquire or agree to something. **7** *tr.* cause to be sold (*the author's name alone will sell many copies*). **8** *tr.* esp. *Brit. slang* disappoint by not keeping an engagement etc., by failing in some way, or by trickery (*sold again!*). ● *n. colloq.* **1** a manner of selling (*soft sell*). **2** a deception or disappointment. □ **sell a person a bill of goods** *N. Amer.* see BILL OF GOODS. **sell down the river** see RIVER. **sell the** (or **a**) **dummy** see DUMMY. **sell one's life dear** (or **dearly**) do great injury before being killed. **sell off** sell the remainder of (goods) at reduced prices. **sell oneself 1** promote one's own abilities. **2 a** offer one's services dishonourably for money or other reward. **b** be a prostitute. **sell out 1 a** (often foll. by *of*) sell all one's stock of a commodity (*the shop sold out of bread; wanted to buy some milk but the shop had sold out*). **b** (of a commodity) be completely or all sold (*tickets are quickly selling out*). **c** (of a performance etc.) sell all its tickets (*the Christmas pantomime always sells out before December*). **d** (also *absol.*) dispose of the whole of (one's property, shares, etc.) by sale. **2 a** (often foll. by *to*) abandon one's principles, honourable aims, etc. for personal gain. **b** betray (a person etc.). **sell the pass** see PASS[2]. **sell a person a pup** see PUP. **sell short** disparage, underestimate. **sell up** *Brit.* **1** sell one's business, house, etc. **2** sell the goods of (a debtor). **sold on** *colloq.* enthusiastic about. □ **sellable** *adj.* [Old English *sellan*, from Germanic]

sell-by date *n. Brit.* **1** the latest recommended date of sale marked on the packaging of perishable food etc. **2** (often in phr. **past his, her, its,** etc. **sell-by date**) the time after which a commodity is not saleable, or a person or thing is no longer attractive or fit for an activity (*the bus was well past its sell-by date; has Ibsen reached his sell-by date?*).

seller /ˈsɛlə/ *n.* **1** a person who sells. **2** a commodity that sells well or badly. □ **seller's** (or **sellers'**) **market** an economic position in which goods are scarce and expensive.

selling point *n.* an advantageous feature.

selling race *n.* a horse race after which the winning horse must be auctioned.

sell-off *n.* (often foll. by *of*) **1** the privatization of a state company by a sale of shares. **2** esp. *US Stock Exch.* a sale or disposal of bonds, shares, etc., usu. causing a fall in price. **3** a sale, esp. to dispose of property.

Sellotape /ˈsɛlə(ʊ)teɪp/ *n. & v. Brit.* ● *n. propr.* adhesive usu. transparent cellulose or plastic tape. ● *v.tr.* (**sellotape**) fix with Sellotape. [CELLULOSE + TAPE]

sell-out *n.* **1** a commercial success, esp. the selling of all tickets for a show. **2** a betrayal.

seltzer /ˈsɛltzə/ *n.* (in full **seltzer water**) **1** medicinal mineral water from Nieder-Selters in Germany. **2** an artificial substitute for this; soda water. [German *Selterser* 'from *Selters*']

selvedge /ˈsɛlvɪdʒ/ *n.* (also **selvage**) **1 a** an edging that prevents cloth from unravelling (either an edge along the warp or a specially woven edging). **b** a border of different material or finish intended to be removed or hidden. **2** *Geol.* an alteration zone at the edge of a rock mass. **3** the edge-plate of a lock with an opening for the bolt. [Middle English from SELF + EDGE, on the pattern of Dutch *selfegghe*]

selves *pl.* of SELF.

SEM *abbr.* scanning electron microscope.

semanteme /sɪˈmantiːm/ *n. Linguistics* a fundamental element expressing an image or idea. [French *sémantème* (as SEMANTIC)]

semantic /sɪˈmantɪk/ *adj.* relating to meaning in language; relating to the connotations of words. □ **semantically** *adv.* [French *sémantique* from Greek *sēmantikos* 'significant', via *sēmainō* 'signify' from *sēma* 'sign']

semantics /sɪˈmantɪks/ *n.pl.* (usu. treated as *sing.*) the branch of linguistics concerned with meaning. □ **semantician** /-ˈtɪʃ(ə)n/ *n.* **semanticist** /-tɪsɪst/ *n.*

semaphore /ˈsɛməfɔː/ *n. & v.* ● *n.* **1** *Mil.* etc. a system of sending messages by holding the arms or two flags in certain positions according to an alphabetic code. **2** a signalling apparatus consisting of a post with a movable arm or arms, lanterns, etc., for use (esp. on railways) by day or night. ● *v.intr. & tr.* signal or send by semaphore. □ **semaphoric** /-ˈfɒrɪk/ *adj.* **semaphorically** /-ˈfɒrɪk(ə)li/ *adv.* [French *sémaphore*, formed irregularly from Greek *sēma* 'sign' + *-phoros* -PHORE]

semasiology /sɪˌmeɪzɪˈɒlədʒi/ *n.* semantics. □ **semasiological** /-əˈlɒdʒɪk(ə)l/ *adj.* [German *Semasiologie* from Greek *sēmasia* 'meaning', from *sēmainō* 'signify']

sematic /sɪˈmatɪk/ *adj. Zool.* (of colouring, markings, etc.) significant; serving to warn off enemies or attract attention. [Greek *sēma sēmatos* 'sign']

semblable /ˈsɛmbləb(ə)l/ *n.* & *adj.* ● *n.* a counterpart or equal. ● *adj. archaic* having the semblance of something, seeming. [Middle English from Old French (as SEMBLANCE)]

semblance /ˈsɛmbləns/ *n.* **1** the outward or superficial appearance of something (*put on a semblance of anger*). **2** resemblance. [Middle English via Old French, from *sembler*, from Latin *similare, simulare* SIMULATE]

semé /ˈsɛmi, sɛmeɪ/ *adj.* (also **semée**) *Heraldry* covered with small bearings of indefinite number (e.g. stars, fleurs-de-lis) arranged all over the field. [French, past part. of *semer* 'to sow']

semeiology var. of SEMIOLOGY.

semeiotics var. of SEMIOTICS.

sememe /ˈsɛmiːm, ˈsiːm-/ *n. Linguistics* the unit of meaning carried by a morpheme. [as SEMANTIC + -EME]

semen /ˈsiːmən/ *n.* the reproductive fluid of male animals, containing spermatozoa in suspension. [Middle English from Latin *semen seminis* 'seed', from *serere* 'to sow']

semester /sɪˈmɛstə/ *n.* a half-year course or term in (esp. German and US) universities. [German from Latin *semestris* 'six-monthly', from *sex* 'six' + *mensis* 'month']

semi /ˈsɛmi/ *n.* (*pl.* **semis**) *colloq.* **1** *Brit.* a semi-detached house. **2** a semi-final. **3** *N. Amer.* & *Austral.* a semi-trailer. [abbreviation]

semi- /ˈsɛmi/ *prefix* **1** half (*semicircle*). **2** partly; in some degree or particular (*semi-official; semi-detached*). **3** almost (*a semi-smile*). **4** occurring or appearing twice in a specified period (*semi-annual*). [French, Italian, etc. or Latin, corresponding to Greek HEMI-, Sanskrit *sāmi*]

semi-annual /sɛmɪˈanjʊəl/ *adj.* occurring, published, etc., twice a year. ◻ **semi-annually** *adv.*

semiaquatic /ˌsɛmɪəˈkwatɪk/ *adj.* **1** (of an animal) living partly on land and partly in water. **2** (of a plant) growing in very wet ground.

semi-automatic /ˌsɛmɪɔːtəˈmatɪk/ *adj.* **1** partially automatic. **2** (of a firearm) having a mechanism for continuous loading but not for continuous firing.

semi-autonomous /ˌsɛmɪɔːˈtɒnəməs/ *adj.* **1** partly self-governing. **2** acting to some degree independently or having the partial freedom to do so.

semi-basement /sɛmɪˈbeɪsm(ə)nt/ *n.* a storey partly below ground level.

semi-bold /sɛmɪˈbəʊld/ *adj. Printing* printed in a type darker than normal but not as dark as bold.

semibreve /ˈsɛmɪbriːv/ *n.* esp. *Brit. Mus.* the longest note now in common use, having the time value of two minims or four crotchets, and represented by a ring with no stem.

semicircle /ˈsɛmɪsəːk(ə)l/ *n.* **1** half of a circle or of its circumference. **2** a set of objects ranged in, or an object forming, a semicircle. [Latin *semicirculus* (as SEMI-, CIRCLE)]

semicircular /sɛmɪˈsəːkjʊlə/ *adj.* **1** forming or shaped like a semicircle. **2** arranged as or in a semicircle. [Late Latin *semicircularis* (as SEMICIRCLE)]

semicircular canal *n.* each of three fluid-filled channels in the ear giving information to the brain to help maintain balance.

semi-civilized /sɛmɪˈsɪvɪlʌɪzd/ *adj.* partially civilized.

semicolon /sɛmɪˈkəʊlən, -ˈkəʊlɒn/ *n.* a punctuation mark (;) of intermediate value between a comma and full stop.

semiconducting /ˌsɛmɪkənˈdʌktɪŋ/ *adj.* having the properties of a semiconductor.

semiconductor /ˌsɛmɪkənˈdʌktə/ *n.* a solid substance that is a non-conductor when pure or at a low temperature but has a conductivity between that of insulators and that of most metals when containing a suitable impurity or at a higher temperature and is used in integrated circuits, transistors, diodes, etc.

semi-conscious /sɛmɪˈkɒnʃəs/ *adj.* partially conscious.

semicylinder /sɛmɪˈsɪlɪndə/ *n.* half of a cylinder cut longitudinally. ◻ **semicylindrical** /-ˈlɪndrɪk(ə)l/ *adj.*

semi-darkness /sɛmɪˈdɑːknɪs/ *adj.* (esp. in phr. **in the semi-darkness**) partial darkness.

semidemisemiquaver /ˌsɛmɪdɛmɪˈsɛmɪkweɪvə/ *n.* esp. *Brit. Mus.* = HEMIDEMISEMIQUAVER. [SEMI- + DEMISEMIQUAVER]

semi-deponent /ˌsɛmɪdɪˈpəʊnənt/ *adj. Gram.* (of a Latin verb) having active forms in present tenses and passive forms with active sense in perfect tenses.

semi-derelict /sɛmɪˈdɛrəlɪkt/ *adj.* in a partially derelict state.

semi-detached /ˌsɛmɪdɪˈtatʃt/ *adj.* & *n.* ● *adj.* (of a house) joined to another by a party wall on one side only. ● *n. Brit.* a semi-detached house.

semidiameter /ˌsɛmɪdʌɪˈamɪtə/ *n.* half of a diameter. [Late Latin (as SEMI-, DIAMETER)]

semi-documentary /ˌsɛmɪdɒkjʊˈmɛnt(ə)ri/ *adj.* & *n.* ● *adj.* (of a film) having a factual background and a fictitious story. ● *n.* (*pl.* **-ies**) a semi-documentary film.

semi-dome /ˈsɛmɪdəʊm/ *n.* **1** a half-dome formed by vertical section. **2** a part of a structure more or less resembling a dome.

semi-double /sɛmɪˈdʌb(ə)l/ *adj.* (of a flower) intermediate between single and double in having only the outer stamens converted to petals.

semi-final /sɛmɪˈfʌɪn(ə)l/ *n.* a match or round immediately preceding the final. ◻ **semi-finalist** *n.*

semi-finished /sɛmɪˈfɪnɪʃt/ *adj.* prepared for the final stage of manufacture.

semi-fitted /sɛmɪˈfɪtɪd/ *adj.* (of a garment) shaped to the body but not closely fitted.

semi-fluid /sɛmɪˈfluːɪd/ *adj.* & *n.* ● *adj.* of a consistency between solid and liquid. ● *n.* a semi-fluid substance.

semi-independent /ˌsɛmɪɪndɪˈpɛnd(ə)nt/ *adj.* **1 a** partially independent of control or authority. **b** partially self-governing. **2** partially independent of financial support from public funds.

semi-infinite /sɛmɪˈɪnfɪnɪt/ *adj. Math.* limited in one direction and stretching to infinity in the other.

semi-invalid /sɛmɪˈɪnvəliːd, -lɪd/ *n.* a partially disabled or somewhat infirm person.

semi-liquid /sɛmɪˈlɪkwɪd/ *adj.* & *n.* = SEMI-FLUID.

semi-literate /sɛmɪˈlɪt(ə)rət/ *adj.* **1** unable to read or write with ease or fluency; poorly educated. **2** *derog.* having little interest in literature. **3** *derog.* (of a text) displaying a lack of literacy on the part of the author. ◻ **semi-literacy** *n.*

semi-lunar /sɛmɪˈluːnə/ *adj.* shaped like a half-moon or crescent. [modern Latin *semilunaris* (as SEMI-, LUNAR)]

semi-lunar bone *n.* a bone of this shape in the carpus.

semi-lunar cartilage *n.* a cartilage of this shape in the knee.

semi-lunar valve *n.* a valve of this shape in the heart.

semi-metal /ˈsɛmɪmɛt(ə)l/ *n.* a substance with some of the properties of metals. [modern Latin *semimetallum* (as SEMI-, METAL)]

semi-monthly /sɛmɪˈmʌnθli/ *adj.* & *adv.* ● *adj.* occurring, published, etc., twice a month. ● *adv.* twice a month.

seminal /ˈsɛmɪn(ə)l/ *adj.* **1 a** of or relating to semen. **b** of or relating to the seeds of plants. **2 a** (of ideas etc.) providing the basis for future development. **b** (of a person, literary work, etc.) central to the understanding of a subject; influential. ◻ **seminally** *adv.* [Middle English from Old French *seminal* or Latin *seminalis* (as SEMEN)]

seminal fluid *n.* semen.

seminar /ˈsɛmɪnɑː/ *n.* **1** a small class at a university etc. for discussion and research. **2** a short intensive course of study. **3** a conference of specialists. [German (as SEMINARY)]

seminary /ˈsɛmɪn(ə)ri/ *n.* (*pl.* **-ies**) **1** a training college for priests, rabbis, etc. **2** a place of education or development. ◻ **seminarian** /-ˈnɛːrɪən/ *n.* **seminarist** *n.* [Middle English from Latin *seminarium* 'seed-plot', neut. of *seminarius* (*adj.*) (as SEMEN)]

seminiferous /sɛmɪˈnɪf(ə)rəs/ *adj.* **1** bearing seed. **2** conveying semen. [Latin *semin-* (from SEMEN) + -FEROUS]

semi-official /ˌsɛmɪəˈfɪʃ(ə)l/ *adj.* **1** partly official. **2** (of communications to newspapers etc.) made by an official with the stipulation that the source should not be revealed. □ **semi-officially** *adv.*

semiology /siːmɪˈɒlədʒi, sɛmɪ-/ *n.* (also **semeiology**) = SEMIOTICS. □ **semiological** /-əˈlɒdʒɪk(ə)l/ *adj.* **semiologist** *n.* [Greek *sēmeion* 'sign' from *sēma* 'mark']

semi-opaque /sɛmɪə(ʊ)ˈpeɪk/ *adj.* partially transparent.

semiotics /siːmɪˈɒtɪks, sɛm-/ *n.* (also **semeiotics**) **1** the study of signs and symbols in various fields, esp. language. **2** *Med.* symptomatology. □ **semiotic** *adj.* **semiotical** *adj.* **semiotically** *adv.* **semiotician** /-ˈtɪʃ(ə)n/ *n.* [Greek *sēmeiōtikos* 'of signs' (as SEMIOLOGY)]

semipalmated /ˌsɛmɪpalˈmeɪtɪd/ *adj. Zool.* having toes etc. webbed for part of their length. [SEMI- + Latin *palmatus* PALMATE]

semi-permanent /sɛmɪˈpəːm(ə)nənt/ *adj.* rather less than permanent.

semi-permeable /sɛmɪˈpəːmɪəb(ə)l/ *adj.* (of a membrane etc.) selectively permeable, esp. allowing passage of a solvent but not of certain solutes.

semi-plume /ˈsɛmɪpluːm/ *n.* a feather with a firm stem and a downy web.

semi-precious /sɛmɪˈprɛʃəs/ *adj.* (of a gem) less valuable than a precious stone.

semi-pro /sɛmɪˈprəʊ/ *adj. & n.* (*pl.* **-os**) *US colloq.* = SEMI-PROFESSIONAL.

semi-professional /ˌsɛmɪprəˈfɛʃ(ə)n(ə)l/ *adj. & n.* ● *adj.* **1** receiving payment for an activity but not relying on it for a living. **2** involving semi-professionals. ● *n.* a semi-professional musician, sportsman, etc.

semiquaver /ˈsɛmɪkweɪvə/ *n.* esp. *Brit. Mus.* a note having the time value of half a quaver and represented by a large dot with a two-hooked stem. Also called SIXTEENTH NOTE.

semi-retired /ˌsɛmɪrɪˈtʌɪəd/ *adj.* having partially retired from employment or an occupation. □ **semi-retirement** *n.*

semi-rigid /sɛmɪˈrɪdʒɪd/ *adj.* (of an airship) having a stiffened keel attached to a flexible gas container.

semi-skilled /sɛmɪˈskɪld/ *adj.* (of work or a worker) having or needing some training but less than for a skilled worker.

semi-skimmed /sɛmɪˈskɪmd/ *adj.* (of milk) from which some cream has been skimmed.

semi-smile /ˈsɛmɪsmʌɪl/ *n.* an expression that is not quite a smile.

semi-solid /sɛmɪˈsɒlɪd/ *adj.* viscous, semi-fluid.

semi-sweet /sɛmɪˈswiːt/ *adj.* (of biscuits etc.) slightly sweetened.

semi-synthetic /ˌsɛmɪsɪnˈθɛtɪk/ *adj. Chem.* (of a substance) that is prepared synthetically but derives from a naturally occurring material.

Semite /ˈsiːmʌɪt, ˈsɛm-/ *n.* a member of any of the peoples supposed to be descended from Shem, son of Noah (Gen. 10:21 ff.), including esp. the Jews, Arabs, Assyrians, Babylonians, and Phoenicians. □ **Semitism** /ˈsɛmɪtɪz(ə)m/ *n.* **Semitist** /ˈsɛmɪtɪst/ *n.* **Semitize** /ˈsɛmɪtʌɪz/ *v.tr.* (also **-ise**). **Semitization** /ˌsɛmɪtʌɪˈzeɪʃ(ə)n/ *n.* [modern Latin *Semita* via Late Latin from Greek *Sēm* 'Shem']

Semitic /sɪˈmɪtɪk/ *adj.* **1** of or relating to the Semites, esp. the Jews. **2** of or relating to the languages of the family including Hebrew and Arabic. [modern Latin *Semiticus* (as SEMITE)]

semitone /ˈsɛmɪtəʊn/ *n. Mus.* the smallest interval used in classical European music; half a tone.

semi-trailer /ˈsɛmɪtreɪlə/ *n.* a trailer having wheels at the back but supported at the front by a towing vehicle.

semi-transparent /ˌsɛmɪtransˈpar(ə)nt, -trɑː-, -ˈspɛː-/ *adj.* partially or imperfectly transparent.

semi-tropics /sɛmɪˈtrɒpɪks/ *n.pl.* = SUBTROPICS. □ **semi-tropical** *adj.*

semivowel /ˈsɛmɪvaʊ(ə)l/ *n.* **1** a sound intermediate between a vowel and a consonant (e.g. *w*, *y*). **2** a letter representing this. [after Latin *semivocalis*]

semi-weekly /sɛmɪˈwiːkli/ *adj. & adv.* ● *adj.* occurring, published, etc., twice a week. ● *adv.* twice a week.

semmit /ˈsɛmɪt/ *n. Sc.* an undershirt. [Middle English: origin unknown]

semolina /sɛməˈliːnə/ *n.* **1** the hard grains left after the milling of flour, used in puddings etc. and in pasta. **2** a pudding etc. made of this. [Italian *semolino*, diminutive of *semola* 'bran', from Latin *simila* 'flour']

sempervivum /sɛmpəˈvʌɪvəm/ *n.* a succulent plant of the genus *Sempervivum*, esp. the houseleek. [modern Latin genus name, from Latin *semper* 'always' + *vivus* 'living']

sempiternal /sɛmpɪˈtəːn(ə)l/ *adj. literary* eternal, everlasting. □ **sempiternally** *adv.* **sempiternity** *n.* [Middle English via Old French *sempiternel* and Late Latin *sempiternalis* from Latin *sempiternus*, from *semper* 'always' + *aeternus* 'eternal']

semplice /ˈsɛmplɪtʃeɪ, -tʃi, Italian ˈsemplitʃe/ *adv. Mus.* in a simple style of performance. [Italian, = SIMPLE]

sempre /ˈsɛmpreɪ, -ri, Italian ˈsempre/ *adv. Mus.* throughout, always (*sempre forte*). [Italian]

sempstress var. of SEAMSTRESS.

Semtex /ˈsɛmtɛks/ *n.* a very pliable, odourless plastic explosive. [probably from *Semtín*, a village in the Czech Republic near the place of production + *ex*plosive]

SEN *abbr.* (in the UK) State Enrolled Nurse.

Sen. *abbr.* **1** Senior. **2** *US* **a** Senator. **b** Senate.

senarius /sɪˈnɛːrɪəs/ *n.* (*pl.* **senarii** /-rɪiː, -rɪʌɪ/) *Prosody* a verse of six feet, esp. an iambic trimeter. [Latin: see SENARY]

senary /ˈsiːnəri, ˈsɛn-/ *adj.* of six, by sixes. [Latin *senarius* from *seni*, distributive of *sex* 'six']

senate /ˈsɛnɪt/ *n.* (often **Senate**) **1** a legislative body, esp. the smaller upper assembly in the US, France, and other countries, in states of the US, etc. **2** the governing body of a university or (in the US) of a university or college. **3** *Rom.Hist.* the State council of the republic and empire sharing legislative power with the popular assemblies, administration with the magistrates, and judicial power with the knights. [Middle English via Old French *senat* from Latin *senatus*, from *senex* 'old man']

senator /ˈsɛnətə/ *n.* **1** a member of a senate. **2** (in Scotland) a Lord of Session. □ **senatorial** /-ˈtɔːrɪəl/ *adj.* **senatorship** *n.* [Middle English via Old French *senateur* from Latin *senator -oris* (as SENATE)]

send /sɛnd/ *v.* (*past* and *past part.* **sent** /sɛnt/) **1** *tr.* **a** order or cause to go or be conveyed (*send a message to headquarters*; *sent me a book*; *sends goods all over the world*). **b** propel; cause to move (*send a bullet*; *sent him flying*). **c** cause to go or become (*send into raptures*; *send to sleep*). **d** dismiss with or without force (*sent her away*; *sent him about his business*). **2** *intr.* send a message or letter (*he sent to warn me*). **3** *tr.* (of God, providence, etc.) grant or bestow or inflict; bring about; cause to be (*send rain*; *send a judgement*; *send her victorious!*). **4** *tr. slang* affect emotionally, put into ecstasy. □ **send away for** send a order to a dealer for (goods). **send down** *Brit.* **1** rusticate or expel from a university. **2** sentence to imprisonment. **3** *Cricket* bowl (a ball or an over). **send for 1** summon. **2** order by post. **send in 1** cause to go in. **2** submit (an entry etc.) for a competition etc. **send off 1** get (a letter, parcel, etc.) dispatched. **2** attend the departure of (a person) as a sign of respect etc. **3** *Sport* (of a referee) order (a player) to leave the field and take no further part in the game. **send off for** = *send away for*. **send on** transmit to a further destination or in advance of one's own arrival. **send a person to Coventry** see COVENTRY. **send up 1** cause to go up. **2** transmit to a higher authority. **3** *colloq.* satirize or ridicule, esp. by mimicking. **4** *US* sentence to imprisonment. **send word**

send information. □ **sendable** *adj.* **sender** *n.* [Old English *sendan*, from Germanic]

sendal /ˈsɛnd(ə)l/ *n. hist.* **1** a thin rich silk material. **2** a garment of this. [Middle English from Old French *cendal*, ultimately from Greek *sindōn*]

send-off *n.* a demonstration of goodwill etc. at the departure of a person, the start of a project, etc.

send-up *n. colloq.* a satire or parody.

senecio /səˈniːsɪəʊ, -ʃɪəʊ/ *n.* (*pl.* **-os**) any plant of the genus *Senecio* (daisy family), including many cultivated species as well as groundsel and ragwort. [Latin *senecio* 'old man, groundsel', with reference to the hairy fruits]

senesce /sɪˈnɛs/ *v.intr.* grow old. □ **senescence** *n.* **senescent** *adj.* [Latin *senescere* from *senex* 'old']

seneschal /ˈsɛnɪʃ(ə)l/ *n.* **1** *hist.* the steward or major-domo of a medieval great house. **2** a judge in Sark. [Middle English via Old French and medieval Latin *seniscalus* from Germanic words meaning 'old' and 'servant']

senhor /sɛnˈjɔː/ *n.* a title used of or to a Portuguese or Brazilian man. [Portuguese from Latin *senior*: see SENIOR]

senhora /sɛnˈjɔːrə/ *n.* a title used of or to a Portuguese woman or a Brazilian married woman. [Portuguese, fem. of SENHOR]

senhorita /sɛnjəˈriːtə/ *n.* a title used of or to a young Brazilian esp. unmarried woman. [Portuguese, diminutive of SENHORA]

senile /ˈsiːnʌɪl/ *adj. & n.* ● *adj.* **1** of or characteristic of old age (*senile apathy*; *senile decay*). **2** having the weaknesses or diseases of old age. ● *n.* a senile person. □ **senility** /sɪˈnɪlɪti/ *n.* [French *sénile* or Latin *senilis*, from *senex* 'old man']

senile dementia *n.* a severe form of mental deterioration in old age, characterized by loss of memory and control of bodily functions.

senior /ˈsiːnɪə, ˈsiːnjə/ *adj. & n.* ● *adj.* **1** (often foll. by *to*) more or most advanced in age or standing. **2** of high or highest position. **3** (placed after a person's name) senior to another of the same name. **4** *Brit.* (of a school) having pupils in an older age range (cf. JUNIOR *adj.* 5). **5** *US* of the final year at a university, high school, etc. ● *n.* **1** a person of advanced age or comparatively long service etc. **2** one's elder, or one's superior in length of service, membership, etc. (*is my senior*). **3** a senior student. □ **seniority** /siːnɪˈɒrɪti/ *n.* [Middle English from Latin, = older, older man, comparative of *senex senis* 'old man, old']

senior aircraftman *n.* (*fem.* **senior aircraftwoman**) the rank above leading aircraftman in the RAF.

senior citizen *n.* an elderly person, esp. an old-age pensioner.

senior college *n. N. Amer.* a college in which the last two years' work for a bachelor's degree is done.

senior common room *n.* (also **senior combination room**) *Brit.* a room for use by senior members of a college.

senior high school *n. N. Amer.* a secondary school comprising usu. the three highest grades.

senior management *n.* **1** the highest level of management in an organization, immediately below the board of directors. **2** the managers at this level (cf. MIDDLE MANAGEMENT, JUNIOR MANAGEMENT).

senior nursing officer *n. Brit.* the person in charge of nursing services in a hospital.

senior officer *n.* an officer to whom a junior is responsible.

senior partner *n.* the head of a firm.

senior registrar *n.* a hospital doctor undergoing specialist training, one grade below that of consultant.

senior service *n. Brit.* the Royal Navy as opposed to the Army.

senior tutor *n. Brit.* a college tutor in charge of the teaching arrangements.

senna /ˈsɛnə/ *n.* **1** a cassia tree. **2** a laxative prepared from the dried pods of this. [medieval Latin *sena* from Arabic *sanā*]

sennet /ˈsɛnɪt/ *n. hist.* a signal call on a trumpet or cornet (in the stage directions of Elizabethan plays). [perhaps a variant of SIGNET]

sennight /ˈsɛnʌɪt/ *n. archaic* a week. [Old English *seofon nihta* 'seven nights']

sennit /ˈsɛnɪt/ *n.* **1** *hist.* plaited straw, palm leaves, etc., used for making hats. **2** = SINNET. [variant of SINNET]

señor /sɛnˈjɔː/ *n.* (*pl.* **señores** /-rɪz/) a title used of or to a Spanish-speaking man. [Spanish from Latin *senior*: see SENIOR]

señora /sɛnˈjɔːrə/ *n.* a title used of or to a Spanish-speaking married woman. [Spanish, fem. of SEÑOR]

señorita /sɛnjəˈriːtə/ *n.* a title used of or to a young Spanish-speaking esp. unmarried woman. [Spanish, diminutive of SEÑORA]

Senr. *abbr.* Senior.

sensate /ˈsɛnseɪt, -sət/ *adj.* perceived by the senses. [Late Latin *sensatus* 'having senses' (as SENSE)]

sensation /sɛnˈseɪʃ(ə)n/ *n.* **1** the consciousness of perceiving or seeming to perceive some state or condition of one's body or its parts or of the senses; an instance of such consciousness (*lost all sensation in my left arm*; *the sensation of falling*; *a burning sensation in his leg*). **2** an awareness or impression (*created the sensation of time passing*; *a sensation of being watched*). **3 a** a stirring of emotions or intense interest esp. among a large group of people (*the news caused a sensation*). **b** a person, event, etc., causing such interest. **c** the sensational use of printed material. [medieval Latin *sensatio* from Latin *sensus* SENSE]

sensational /sɛnˈseɪʃ(ə)n(ə)l/ *adj.* **1** causing or intended to cause great public excitement etc. **2** of or causing sensation. □ **sensationalize** *v.tr.* (also **-ise**). **sensationally** *adv.*

sensationalism /sɛnˈseɪʃ(ə)n(ə)lɪz(ə)m/ *n.* **1** the use of or interest in the sensational in literature, political agitation, etc. **2** *Philos.* the theory that ideas are derived solely from sensation (opp. RATIONALISM 1). □ **sensationalist** *n. & adj.* **sensationalistic** /-ˈlɪstɪk/ *adj.*

sense /sɛns/ *n. & v.* ● *n.* **1 a** any of the special bodily faculties by which sensation is roused (*has keen senses*; *has a dull sense of smell*). **b** sensitiveness of all or any of these. **2** the ability to perceive or feel or to be conscious of the presence or properties of things. **3** (foll. by *of*) consciousness (*sense of having done well*; *sense of one's own importance*). **4** (often foll. by *of*) **a** quick or accurate appreciation, understanding, or instinct regarding a specified matter (*sense of the ridiculous*; *road sense*; *the moral sense*). **b** the habit of basing one's conduct on such instinct. **5** practical wisdom or judgement, common sense; conformity to these (*has plenty of sense*; *what is the sense of talking like that?*; *has more sense than to do that*). **6 a** a meaning; the way in which a word etc. is to be understood (*the sense of the word is clear*; *I mean that in the literal sense*). **b** intelligibility or coherence or possession of a meaning. **7** the prevailing opinion among a number of people (*take the sense of the meeting*). **8** (in *pl.*) a person's sanity or normal state of mind. **9** *Math.* etc. **a** a direction of movement. **b** that which distinguishes a pair of entities which differ only in that each is the reverse of the other. ● *v.tr.* **1** perceive by a sense or senses. **2** be vaguely aware of. **3** realize. **4** (of a machine etc.) detect. **5** *US* understand. □ **bring a person to his** or **her senses 1** cure a person of folly. **2** restore a person to consciousness. **come to one's senses 1** regain consciousness. **2** become sensible after acting foolishly. **in a** (or **one**) **sense** if the statement is understood in a particular way (*what you say is true in a sense*). **in one's senses** sane. **make sense** be intelligible or practicable. **make sense of** show or find the meaning of. **out of one's senses** in or into a state of madness (*is out of her senses*; *frightened him out of his* *senses*). **take leave of one's senses** go mad. **under a sense of wrong** feeling wronged. [Middle English from Latin *sensus* 'faculty of feeling, thought, meaning', from *sentire sens-* 'feel']

sense datum *n. Philos.* an element of experience received through the senses.

senseless /'sɛnslɪs/ *adj.* **1** unconscious. **2** wildly foolish. **3** without meaning or purpose. **4** incapable of sensation. □ **senselessly** *adv.* **senselessness** *n.*

sense of direction *n.* the ability to know without guidance the direction in which one is or should be moving.

sense of humour see HUMOUR *n.* 2.

sense organ *n.* a bodily organ conveying (esp. external) stimuli to the sensory system.

sensibility /sɛnsɪ'bɪlɪti/ *n.* (*pl.* **-ies**) **1 a** openness to emotional impressions, susceptibility, sensitiveness (*sensibility to kindness*). **b** *archaic* an exceptional or excessive degree of this (*sense and sensibility*). **2 a** (in *pl.*) emotional capacities or feelings (*was limited in his sensibilities*). **b** (in *sing.* or *pl.*) a person's moral, emotional, or aesthetic ideas or standards (*offended the sensibilities of believers*). **3** sensitivity to sensory stimuli (*sensibility in the retina*). [Middle English from Late Latin *sensibilitas* (as SENSIBLE)]

■ **Usage** *Sensibility* should not be used in standard English as a noun corresponding to sense 1 of *sensible*, i.e. it does not mean 'possession of common sense, reasonableness'. The correct noun to use is *sensibleness*; alternatively, a phrase such as *good sense* can be used.

sensible /'sɛnsɪb(ə)l/ *adj.* **1** having or showing wisdom or common sense; reasonable, judicious (*a sensible person; a sensible compromise*). **2 a** perceptible by the senses (*sensible phenomena*). **b** great enough to be perceived; appreciable (*a sensible difference*). **3** (of clothing etc.) practical and functional. **4** (foll. by *of*) aware; not unmindful (*was sensible of his peril*). □ **sensibleness** *n.* **sensibly** *adv.* [Middle English from Old French *sensible* or Latin *sensibilis* (as SENSE)]

■ **Usage** See Usage Note at SENSIBILITY.

sensible horizon see HORIZON 1b.

sensitive /'sɛnsɪtɪv/ *adj.* & *n.* ● *adj.* **1** (often foll. by *to*) very open to or acutely affected by external stimuli or mental impressions; having sensibility. **2** (of a person) easily offended or emotionally hurt. **3** (often foll. by *to*) (of an instrument etc.) responsive to or recording slight changes. **4** (often foll. by *to*) **a** (of photographic materials) prepared so as to respond (esp. rapidly) to the action of light. **b** (of any material) readily affected by or responsive to external action. **5** (of a topic etc.) subject to restriction of discussion to prevent embarrassment, ensure security, etc. **6** (of a market) liable to quick changes of price. ● *n.* a person who is sensitive (esp. to supposed occult influences). □ **sensitively** *adv.* **sensitiveness** *n.* [Middle English, = sensory, from Old French *sensitif -ive* or medieval Latin *sensitivus*, formed irregularly from Latin *sentire sens-* 'feel']

sensitive plant *n.* **1** a plant whose leaves curve downwards and leaflets fold together when touched, esp. *Mimosa pudica*. **2** a sensitive person.

sensitivity /sɛnsɪ'tɪvɪti/ *n.* (*pl.* **-ies**) **1** the quality or degree of being sensitive. **2** (in *pl.*) fine differences of feeling, attitude, or reaction.

sensitize /'sɛnsɪtʌɪz/ *v.tr.* (also **-ise**) **1** make sensitive. **2** *Photog.* make sensitive to light. **3** make (an organism etc.) abnormally sensitive to a foreign substance. □ **sensitization** /-'zeɪʃ(ə)n/ *n.* **sensitizer** *n.*

sensitometer /sɛnsɪ'tɒmɪtə/ *n. Photog.* a device for measuring sensitivity to light.

sensor /'sɛnsə/ *n.* a device which detects or measures a physical property and records, indicates, or otherwise responds to it. [SENSORY, on the pattern of MOTOR]

sensorium /sɛn'sɔːrɪəm/ *n.* (*pl.* **sensoria** /-rɪə/ or **sensoriums**) **1** the seat of sensation, the brain, brain and spinal cord, or grey matter of these. **2** *Biol.* the whole sensory apparatus including the nerve system. □ **sensorial** *adj.* **sensorially** *adv.* [Late Latin from Latin *sentire sens-* 'feel']

sensory /'sɛns(ə)ri/ *adj.* of sensation or the senses. □ **sensorily** *adv.* [as SENSORIUM]

sensual /'sɛnsjʊəl, -ʃʊəl/ *adj.* **1 a** of or depending on the senses only and not on the intellect or spirit; carnal, fleshly (*sensual pleasures*). **b** given to the pursuit of sensual pleasures or the gratification of the appetites; self-indulgent sexually or in regard to food and drink; voluptuous, licentious. **c** indicative of a sensual nature (*sensual lips*). **2** of sense or sensation, sensory. **3** *Philos.* of, according to, or holding the doctrine of, sensationalism. □ **sensualism** *n.* **sensualist** *n.* **sensualize** *v.tr.* (also **-ise**). **sensually** *adv.* [Middle English from Late Latin *sensualis* (as SENSE)]

■ **Usage** *Sensual* is sometimes confused with *sensuous*. While *sensual* is used to describe things that are gratifying to the body, and has sexual overtones, *sensuous* is used to mean 'affecting or appealing to the senses' in an aesthetic sense, without the pejorative implications of *sensual*.

sensuality /sɛnsjʊ'alɪti, sɛnʃʊ-/ *n.* gratification of the senses, self-indulgence. [Middle English via French *sensualité* from Late Latin *sensualitas* (as SENSUAL)]

sensum /'sɛnsəm/ *n.* (*pl.* **sensa** /-sə/) *Philos.* a sense datum. [modern Latin, neut. past part. of Latin *sentire* 'feel']

sensuous /'sɛnsjʊəs, 'sɛnʃʊəs/ *adj.* of or derived from or affecting the senses, esp. aesthetically rather than sensually. □ **sensuously** *adv.* **sensuousness** *n.* [Latin *sensus* 'sense']

■ **Usage** See Usage Note at SENSUAL.

sensu stricto /sɛnsuː 'strɪktəʊ/ *adv.* strictly speaking, in the narrow sense. [Latin, = in the restricted sense]

sent *past* and *past part.* of SEND.

sentence /'sɛnt(ə)ns/ *n.* & *v.* ● *n.* **1 a** a set of words complete in itself as the expression of a thought, containing or implying a subject and predicate, and conveying a statement, question, exclamation, or command. **b** a piece of writing or speech between two full stops or equivalent pauses, often including several grammatical sentences (e.g. *I went; he came*). **2 a** a decision of a law court, esp. the punishment allotted to a person convicted in a criminal trial. **b** the declaration of this. **3** *Logic* a series of signs or symbols expressing a proposition in an artificial or logical language. ● *v.tr.* **1** declare the sentence of (a convicted criminal etc.). **2** (foll. by *to*) declare (such a person) to be condemned to a specified punishment. □ **under sentence of** having been condemned to (*under sentence of death*). [originally = way of thinking, opinion: Middle English via Old French from Latin *sententia* 'opinion', from *sentire* 'feel, be of the opinion']

sentential /sɛn'tɛnʃ(ə)l/ *adj. Gram.* & *Logic* of a sentence. [Latin *sententialis* (as SENTENCE)]

sententious /sɛn'tɛnʃəs/ *adj.* **1** (of a person) fond of pompous moralizing. **2** (of a style) affectedly formal. **3** aphoristic, pithy, given to the use of maxims, affecting a concise impressive style. □ **sententiously** *adv.* **sententiousness** *n.* [Latin *sententiosus* (as SENTENCE)]

sentient /'sɛnʃ(ə)nt/ *adj.* having the power of perception by the senses. □ **sentience** *n.* **sentiency** *n.* **sentiently** *adv.* [Latin *sentire* 'feel']

sentiment /'sɛntɪm(ə)nt/ *n.* **1** the sum of what one feels on some subject; an opinion or part of view. **2** an opinion or feeling as distinguished from the words meant to convey it; an emotional feeling conveyed in literature, art, etc. (*the sentiment is good though the words are injudicious*). **3 a** emotional or tender feelings collectively, esp. mawkish tenderness. **b** the display of this. **4** a mental feeling (*the sentiment of pity*). **5** *archaic* the expression of a view or desire esp. as formulated for a toast (*concluded his speech with a sentiment*). [Middle

English via Old French *sentement* and medieval Latin *sentimentum* from Latin *sentire* 'feel']

sentimental /sɛntɪ'mɛnt(ə)l/ *adj.* **1** of or characterized by sentiment. **2** showing or affected by emotion rather than reason. **3** appealing to sentiment. □ **sentimentalism** *n.* **sentimentalist** *n.* **sentimentality** /-'talɪti/ *n.* **sentimentalize** *v.intr.* & *tr.* (also **-ise**). **sentimentalization** /-lʌɪ'zeɪʃ(ə)n/ *n.* **sentimentally** *adv.*

sentimental value *n.* the value of a thing to a particular person because of its associations.

sentinel /'sɛntɪn(ə)l/ *n.* & *v.* ● *n.* a sentry or lookout. ● *v.tr.* (**sentinelled**, **sentinelling**; *US* **sentineled**, **sentineling**) **1** station sentinels at or in. **2** *poet.* keep guard over or in. [French *sentinelle* from Italian *sentinella*, of unknown origin]

sentry /'sɛntri/ *n.* (*pl.* **-ies**) a soldier etc. stationed to keep guard. [perhaps from obsolete *centrinel*, variant of SENTINEL]

sentry box *n.* a wooden cabin intended to shelter a standing sentry.

sentry-go *n. Brit.* the duty of pacing up and down as a sentry.

sepal /'sɛp(ə)l, 'si:/ *n. Bot.* each of the divisions or leaves of the calyx. [French *sépale*, modern Latin *sepalum*, from Greek *skepē* 'covering' influenced by French *pétale* 'petal']

separable /'sɛp(ə)rəb(ə)l/ *adj.* **1** able to be separated. **2** *Gram.* (of a prefix, or a verb in respect of a prefix) written as a separate word in some collocations. □ **separability** /-'bɪlɪti/ *n.* **separableness** *n.* **separably** *adv.* [French *séparable* or Latin *separabilis* (as SEPARATE)]

separate *adj., n., & v.* ● *adj.* /'sɛp(ə)rət/ (often foll. by *from*) forming a unit that is or may be regarded as apart or by itself; physically disconnected, distinct, or individual (*living in separate rooms*; *the two questions are essentially separate*). ● *n.* /'sɛp(ə)rət/ **1** (in *pl.*) separate articles of clothing suitable for wearing together in various combinations. **2** an offprint. ● *v.* /'sɛpəreɪt/ **1** *tr.* make separate, sever, disunite. **2** *tr.* prevent union or contact of. **3** *intr.* go different ways, disperse. **4** *intr.* cease to live together as a married couple. **5** *intr.* (foll. by *from*) secede. **6** *tr.* **a** divide or sort (milk, ore, fruit, light, etc.) into constituent parts or sizes. **b** (often foll. by *out*) extract or remove (an ingredient, waste product, etc.) by such a process for use or rejection. **7** *tr. US* discharge, dismiss. □ **separately** *adv.* **separateness** *n.* **separative** /-rətɪv/ *adj.* **separatory** /-rət(ə)ri/ *adj.* [Latin *separare separat-* (as SE-, *parare* 'make ready')]

separation /sɛpə'reɪʃ(ə)n/ *n.* **1** the act or an instance of separating; the state of being separated. **2** (in full **judicial separation** or **legal separation**) an arrangement by which a husband and wife remain married but live apart. **3** any of three or more monochrome reproductions of a coloured picture which can combine to reproduce the full colour of the original. [Middle English via Old French from Latin *separatio -onis* (as SEPARATE)]

separation order *n.* an order of court for judicial separation.

separatist /'sɛp(ə)rətɪst/ *n.* a person who favours separation, esp. for political or ecclesiastical independence (opp. UNIONIST 2). □ **separatism** *n.*

separator /'sɛpəreɪtə/ *n.* a machine for separating, e.g. cream from milk.

Sephardi /sɪ'fɑ:di/ *n.* (*pl.* **Sephardim** /-dɪm/) a Jew of Spanish or Portuguese descent (cf. ASHKENAZI). □ **Sephardic** *adj.* [modern Hebrew, from *sᵉpārad*, a country mentioned in Obad. 20 and taken to be Spain]

sepia /'si:pɪə/ *n.* & *adj.* ● *n.* **1** a dark reddish-brown colour. **2 a** a brown pigment prepared from a black fluid secreted by cuttlefish, used in monochrome drawing and in watercolours. **b** a brown tint used in photography. **3** a drawing done in sepia. **4** the fluid secreted by cuttlefish. ● *adj.* of a dark reddish-brown colour. [Latin from Greek *sēpia* 'cuttlefish']

sepoy /'si:pɔɪ/ *n. hist.* a native Indian soldier under European, esp. British, discipline. [Urdu & Persian *sipāhī* 'soldier' from *sipāh* 'army']

seppuku /sɛ'pu:ku:/ *n.* hara-kiri. [Japanese, from *setsu* 'to cut' + *fuku* 'abdomen']

sepsis /'sɛpsɪs/ *n.* **1** the state of being septic. **2** blood poisoning. [modern Latin from Greek *sēpsis*, from *sēpō* 'make rotten']

Sept. *abbr.* **1** September. **2** Septuagint.

sept /sɛpt/ *n.* a clan, esp. in Ireland. [probably alteration of SECT]

sept- var. of SEPTI-.

septa *pl.* of SEPTUM.

septal[1] /'sɛpt(ə)l/ *adj.* **1** of a septum or septa. **2** *Archaeol.* (of a stone or slab) separating compartments in a burial chamber. [SEPTUM]

septal[2] /'sɛpt(ə)l/ *adj.* of a sept or septs.

septate /'sɛpteɪt/ *adj. Bot., Zool., & Anat.* having a septum or septa; partitioned. □ **septation** /-'teɪʃ(ə)n/ *n.*

septcentenary /sɛp(t)sɛn'ti:n(ə)ri, -'tɛn-, sɛpt'sɛntɪn-/ *n.* & *adj.* ● *n.* (*pl.* **-ies**) **1** a seven-hundredth anniversary. **2** a festival marking this. ● *adj.* of or concerning a septcentenary.

September /sɛp'tɛmbə/ *n.* the ninth month of the year. [Middle English from Latin *September*, from *septem* 'seven': originally the seventh month of the Roman year]

septenarius /sɛptɪ'nɛ:rɪəs/ *n.* (*pl.* **septenarii** /-rɪʌɪ/) *Prosody* a verse of seven feet, esp. a trochaic or iambic tetrameter catalectic. [Latin from *septeni*, distributive of *septem* 'seven']

septenary /'sɛptɪn(ə)ri, -'ti:n(ə)ri/ *adj.* & *n.* ● *adj.* of seven, by sevens, on the basis of seven. ● *n.* (*pl.* **-ies**) **1** a group or set of seven (esp. years). **2** a septenarius. [Latin *septenarius* (as SEPTENARIUS)]

septenate /'sɛptɪnət, -eɪt/ *adj. Bot.* **1** growing in sevens. **2** having seven divisions. [Latin *septeni* (as SEPTENARIUS)]

septennial /sɛp'tɛnɪəl/ *adj.* **1** lasting for seven years. **2** recurring every seven years. [Late Latin *septennis*, from Latin *septem* 'seven' + *annus* 'year']

septennium /sɛp'tɛnɪəm/ *n.* (*pl.* **septenniums** or **septennia** /-nɪə/) a period of seven years.

septet /sɛp'tɛt/ *n.* (also **septette**) **1** *Mus.* **a** a composition for seven performers. **b** the performers of such a composition. **2** any group of seven. [German *Septett* from Latin *septem* 'seven']

septfoil /'sɛtfɔɪl/ *n.* **1** a seven-lobed ornamental figure. **2** *archaic* tormentil. [Late Latin *septifolium*, on the pattern of CINQUEFOIL, TREFOIL]

septi- /'sɛpti/ *comb. form* (also **sept-** before a vowel) seven. [Latin from *septem* 'seven']

septic /'sɛptɪk/ *adj.* contaminated with bacteria from a festering wound etc., putrefying. □ **septically** *adv.* **septicity** /-'tɪsɪti/ *n.* [Latin *septicus* from Greek *sēptikos*, from *sēpō* 'make rotten']

septicaemia /sɛptɪ'si:mɪə/ *n.* (*US* **septicemia**) blood poisoning. □ **septicaemic** *adj.* [modern Latin, from Greek *sēptikos* + *haima* 'blood']

septic tank *n.* a usu. underground tank in which the organic matter in sewage is decomposed through bacterial activity.

septillion /sɛp'tɪljən/ *n.* (*pl.* same) a thousand raised to the eighth (or formerly, esp. *Brit.*, the fourteenth) power (10^{24} and 10^{42} respectively). [French from *sept* 'seven', on the pattern of *billion* etc.]

septimal /'sɛptɪm(ə)l/ *adj.* of the number seven. [Latin *septimus* 'seventh' from *septem* 'seven']

septime /'sɛptɪm, -ti:m/ *n. Fencing* the seventh of the eight parrying positions. [Latin *septimus* (as SEPTIMAL)]

septivalent /sɛptɪ'veɪl(ə)nt/ *adj.* (also **septavalent**) *Chem.* = HEPTAVALENT.

septuagenarian /ˌsɛptjʊədʒɪ'nɛ:rɪən/ *n.* & *adj.* ● *n.* a person from 70 to 79 years old. ● *adj.* of this age. [Latin *septuagenarius* from *septuageni*, distributive of *septuaginta* 'seventy']

Septuagesima /ˌsɛptjʊəˈdʒɛsɪmə/ *n.* (in full **Septuagesima Sunday**) the Sunday before Sexagesima. [Middle English from Latin, = seventieth (day), formed as SEPTUAGINT, perhaps named loosely as preceding Sexagesima and QUINQUAGESIMA, or with reference to the period of 70 days from Septuagesima to the Saturday after Easter]

Septuagint /ˈsɛptjʊədʒɪnt/ *n.* a Greek version of the Old Testament including the Apocrypha, said to have been made about 270 BC by about 70 translators. [Latin *septuaginta* 'seventy']

septum /ˈsɛptəm/ *n.* (*pl.* **septa** /-tə/) *Anat.*, *Bot.*, & *Zool.* a partition such as that between the nostrils or the chambers of a poppy-fruit or of a shell. [Latin *s(a)eptum*, via *saepire saept-* 'enclose' from *saepes* 'hedge']

septuple /ˈsɛptjʊp(ə)l, sɛpˈtjuːp(ə)l/ *adj.*, *n.*, & *v.* ● *adj.* **1** sevenfold, having seven parts. **2** being seven times as many or as much. ● *n.* a sevenfold number or amount. ● *v.tr.* & *intr.* multiply by seven. [Late Latin *septuplus* from Latin *septem* 'seven']

septuplet /ˈsɛptjʊplɪt, -ˈtjuːplɪt/ *n.* **1** each of seven children born at one birth. **2** *Mus.* a group of seven notes to be played in the time of four or six. [as SEPTUPLE, on the pattern of TRIPLET etc.]

sepulchral /sɪˈpʌlkr(ə)l/ *adj.* **1** of a tomb or interment (*sepulchral mound*; *sepulchral customs*). **2** suggestive of the tomb, funereal, gloomy, dismal (*sepulchral look*). □ **sepulchrally** *adv.* [French *sépulchral* or Latin *sepulchralis* (as SEPULCHRE)]

sepulchre /ˈsɛp(ə)lkə/ *n.* & *v.* (*US* **sepulcher**) ● *n.* a tomb esp. cut in rock or built of stone or brick, a burial vault or cave. ● *v.tr.* **1** lay in a sepulchre. **2** serve as a sepulchre for. [Middle English via Old French from Latin *sepulc(h)rum*, from *sepelire sepult-* 'bury']

sepulture /ˈsɛp(ə)ltʃə/ *n. literary* the act or an instance of burying or putting in the grave. [Middle English via Old French from Latin *sepultura* (as SEPULCHRE)]

seq. *abbr.* (*pl.* **seqq.**) the following. [Latin *sequens*, pres. part. of *sequi* 'follow']

sequacious /sɪˈkweɪʃəs/ *adj.* **1** (of reasoning or a reasoner) not inconsequent, coherent. **2** *archaic* inclined to follow, lacking independence or originality, servile. □ **sequaciously** *adv.* **sequacity** /sɪˈkwasɪti/ *n.* [Latin *sequax* from *sequi* 'follow']

sequel /ˈsiːkw(ə)l/ *n.* **1** what follows (esp. as a result). **2** a novel, film, etc., that continues the story of an earlier one. □ **in the sequel** *Brit.* as things developed afterwards. [Middle English from Old French *sequelle* or Latin *sequel(l)a*, from *sequi* 'follow']

sequela /sɪˈkwiːlə/ *n.* (*pl.* **sequelae** /-liː/) *Med.* (esp. in *pl.*) a morbid condition or symptom following a disease. [Latin from *sequi* 'follow']

sequence /ˈsiːkw(ə)ns/ *n.* & *v.* ● *n.* **1** succession, coming after or next. **2** order of succession (*shall follow the sequence of events*; *give the facts in historical sequence*). **3** a set of things belonging next to one another on some principle of order; a series without gaps. **4** a part of a film dealing with one scene or topic. **5** a set of poems on one theme. **6** a set of three or more playing cards next to one another in value. **7** *Mus.* repetition of a phrase or melody at a higher or lower pitch. **8** *Eccl.* a hymn said or sung after the Gradual or Alleluia that precedes the Gospel. **9** succession without implication of causality (opp. CONSEQUENCE 1). ● *v.tr.* **1** arrange in a definite order. **2** *Biochem.* ascertain the sequence of monomers in (esp. a polypeptide or nucleic acid). [Middle English via Late Latin *sequentia* from Latin *sequens*, pres. part. of *sequi* 'follow']

sequence of tenses *n. Gram.* the dependence of the tense of a subordinate verb on the tense of the principal verb, according to certain rules (e.g. *I think you* are, *thought you* were, *wrong*).

sequencer /ˈsiːkw(ə)nsə/ *n.* **1** *Mus.* a programmable electronic device for storing sequences of musical notes, chords, rhythms, etc. and transmitting them when required to an electronic musical instrument. **2** an apparatus for performing or initiating operations in the correct sequence, esp. one forming part of the control system of a computer. **3** *Biochem.* an apparatus for determining the sequence of monomers in a biological polymer.

sequent /ˈsiːkw(ə)nt/ *adj.* **1** following as a sequence or consequence. **2** consecutive. □ **sequently** *adv.* [Old French *sequent* or Latin *sequens* (as SEQUENCE)]

sequential /sɪˈkwɛnʃ(ə)l/ *adj.* **1** forming a sequence, consequence, or sequela. **2** esp. *Computing* performed or used in sequence. □ **sequentiality** /-ʃɪˈalɪti/ *n.* **sequentially** *adv.* [SEQUENCE, on the pattern of CONSEQUENTIAL]

sequester /sɪˈkwɛstə/ *v.tr.* **1** (esp. as **sequestered** *adj.*) seclude, isolate, set apart (*sequester oneself from the world*; *a sequestered life*; *a sequestered cottage*). **2** = SEQUESTRATE. **3** *Chem.* bind (a metal ion) so that it cannot react. [Middle English via Old French *sequestrer* or Late Latin *sequestrare* 'commit for safe keeping' from Latin *sequester* 'trustee']

sequestrate /sɪˈkwɛstreɪt, ˈsiːkwɪs-/ *v.tr.* **1** confiscate, appropriate. **2** *Law* take temporary possession of (a debtor's estate etc.). **3** *Eccl.* apply (the income of a benefice) to clearing the incumbent's debts or accumulating a fund for the next incumbent. □ **sequestrable** *adj.* **sequestration** /siːkwɪˈstreɪʃ(ə)n/ *n.* **sequestrator** /ˈsiːkwɪstreɪtə/ *n.* [Late Latin *sequestrare* (as SEQUESTER)]

sequestrum /sɪˈkwɛstrəm/ *n.* (*pl.* **sequestra** /-trə/) a piece of dead bone or other tissue detached from the surrounding parts. □ **sequestral** *adj.* **sequestrotomy** /siːkwɪˈstrɒtəmi/ *n.* (*pl.* **-ies**). [modern Latin, neut. of Latin *sequester* 'standing apart']

sequin /ˈsiːkwɪn/ *n.* **1** a circular spangle for attaching to clothing as an ornament. **2** *hist.* a Venetian gold coin. □ **sequinned** *adj.* (also **sequined**). [French, via Italian *zecchino*, from *zecca* 'a mint' from Arabic *sikka* 'a die']

sequoia /sɪˈkwɔɪə/ *n.* either of two Californian evergreen coniferous trees of very great height and girth, *Sequoia sempervirens* and (in full **giant sequoia**) *Sequoiadendron giganteum* (also called *big tree*). [modern Latin genus name, from *Sequoiah*, the name of a Cherokee]

sera *pl.* of SERUM.

serac /ˈsɛrak, sɛˈrak/ *n.* a pinnacle or ridge of ice on the surface of a glacier where crevasses intersect. [Swiss French *sérac*, originally the name of a compact white cheese]

seraglio /sɛˈrɑːlɪəʊ, sɪ-/ *n.* (*pl.* **-os**) **1** a harem. **2** *hist.* a Turkish palace, esp. that of the Sultan with government offices etc. at Constantinople. [Italian *serraglio* via Turkish from Persian *sarāy* 'palace': cf. SERAI]

serai /səˈrʌɪ/ *n.* a caravanserai. [Turkish from Persian (as SERAGLIO)]

serang /səˈraŋ/ *n. Anglo-Ind.* a native head of a Lascar crew. [Persian and Urdu *sar-hang* 'commander', from *sar* 'head' + *hang* 'authority']

serape /sɛˈrɑːpeɪ/ *n.* (also **sarape** /sa-/, **zarape** /za-/) a shawl or blanket worn as a cloak by Spanish Americans. [Mexican Spanish]

seraph /ˈsɛrəf/ *n.* (*pl.* **seraphim** /-fɪm/ or **seraphs**) an angelic being, one of the highest order of the ninefold celestial hierarchy gifted esp. with love and associated with light, ardour, and purity (see ORDER *n.* 19). [back-formation from *seraphim* (pl.) via Late Latin and Greek from Hebrew *śᵉrāpīm* (cf. CHERUB)]

seraphic /səˈrafɪk/ *adj.* **1** of or like the seraphim. **2** ecstatically adoring, fervent, or serene. □ **seraphically** *adv.* [medieval Latin *seraphicus* from Late Latin (as SERAPH)]

seraskier /sɛrəˈskɪə/ *n. hist.* the Turkish commander-in-chief and minister of war. [Turkish from Persian *sar'askar* 'head of army']

Serb /sɜːb/ *n.* & *adj.* ● *n.* **1** a native of Serbia, part of former Yugoslavia. **2** a person of Serbian descent. ● *adj.* = SERBIAN. [Serbian *Srb*]

Serbian /ˈsɜːbɪən/ *n.* & *adj.* ● *n.* **1** the dialect of the Serbs (cf. SERBO-CROAT). **2** = SERB. ● *adj.* of or relating to the Serbs or their dialect.

Serbo- /ˈsɜːbəʊ/ *comb. form* Serbian.

Serbo-Croat /sɜːbəʊˈkrəʊat/ *n.* & *adj.* (also **Serbo-Croatian** /-krəʊˈeɪʃ(ə)n/) ● *n.* the main official language of former Yugoslavia, combining Serbian and Croatian dialects. ● *adj.* of or relating to this language.

SERC *abbr. hist.* (in the UK) Science and Engineering Research Council.

sere[1] var. of SEAR *adj.*

sere[2] /sɪə/ *n. Ecol.* a natural succession of plant (or animal) communities, esp. a full series from uncolonized habitat to the appropriate climax vegetation (cf. SUCCESSION 3). [Latin *serere* 'join in a SERIES']

serein /səˈreɪn, French sərɛ̃/ *n.* a fine rain falling in tropical climates from a cloudless sky. [French from Old French *serain*, ultimately via Latin *serum* 'evening' from *serus* 'late']

serenade /sɛrəˈneɪd/ *n.* & *v.* ● *n.* **1** a piece of music sung or played at night, esp. by a lover under his lady's window, or suitable for this. **2** = SERENATA. ● *v.tr.* sing or play a serenade to. □ **serenader** *n.* [French *sérénade* from Italian *serenata*, from *sereno* SERENE]

serenata /sɛrəˈnɑːtə/ *n. Mus.* **1** a cantata with a pastoral subject. **2** a simple form of suite for orchestra or wind band. [Italian (as SERENADE)]

serendipity /sɛr(ə)nˈdɪpɪti/ *n.* the faculty of making happy and unexpected discoveries by accident. □ **serendipitous** *adj.* **serendipitously** *adv.* [coined by Horace Walpole (1754) after *The Three Princes of Serendip* (now Sri Lanka), a fairy tale]

serene /sɪˈriːn/ *adj.* & *n.* ● *adj.* (**serener**, **serenest**) **1** placid, tranquil, unperturbed. **2 a** (of the sky, the air, etc.) clear and calm. **b** (of the sea etc.) unruffled. ● *n. poet.* a serene expanse of sky, sea, etc. □ **all serene** *Brit. slang* all right. □ **serenely** *adv.* **sereneness** *n.* [Latin *serenus*]

Serene Highness *n.* a title used in addressing and referring to members of some European royal families (*His Serene Highness*; *Their Serene Highnesses*; *Your Serene Highness*).

serenity /sɪˈrɛnɪti/ *n.* (*pl.* **-ies**) **1** tranquillity, being serene. **2** (**Serenity**) a title used in addressing and referring to a reigning prince or similar dignitary (*Your Serenity*). [French *sérénité* or Latin *serenitas* (as SERENE)]

serf /sɜːf/ *n.* **1** *hist.* a labourer not allowed to leave the land on which he worked, a villein. **2** an oppressed person, a drudge. □ **serfage** *n.* **serfdom** *n.* **serfhood** *n.* [Old French from Latin *servus* 'slave']

serge /sɜːdʒ/ *n.* a durable twilled worsted etc. fabric. [Middle English from Old French *sarge*, *serge*, ultimately via Latin *serica* (*lana* 'wool') from *seres*: see SILK]

sergeant /ˈsɑːdʒ(ə)nt/ *n.* **1** a non-commissioned Army or Air Force officer ranking above corporal. **2** a police officer ranking below (*Brit.*) inspector or (*US*) lieutenant. □ **sergeancy** *n.* (*pl.* **-ies**). **sergeantship** *n.* [Middle English via Old French *sergent* from Latin *serviens -entis* 'servant', from *servire* SERVE]

Sergeant Baker *n. Austral.* a large brightly coloured marine fish, *Aulopus purpurissatus*.

sergeant-fish *n.* (*pl.* usu. same) a marine fish, *Rachycentron canadum*, with lateral stripes suggesting a chevron.

sergeant major *n. Mil.* **1** (in full **regimental sergeant major**) *Brit.* a warrant officer assisting the adjutant of a regiment or battalion. **2** *US* the highest-ranking non-commissioned officer.

Sergt. *abbr.* Sergeant.

serial /ˈsɪərɪəl/ *n.* & *adj.* ● *n.* **1** a story, play, or film which is published, broadcast, or shown in regular instalments. **2** a periodical. ● *adj.* **1** of or in or forming a series. **2** (of a story etc.) in the form of a serial. **3** *Mus.* using transformations of a fixed series of notes (see SERIES 8). **4** (of a publication) appearing in successive parts published usu. at regular intervals; periodical. □ **seriality** /-ɪˈalɪti/ *n.* **serially** *adv.* [SERIES + -AL]

serialist /ˈsɪərɪəlɪst/ *n.* a composer or advocate of serial music. □ **serialism** *n.*

serialize /ˈsɪərɪəlʌɪz/ *v.tr.* (also **-ise**) **1** publish or produce in instalments. **2** arrange in a series. **3** *Mus.* compose according to a serial technique. □ **serialization** /-ˈzeɪʃ(ə)n/ *n.*

serial killer *n.* a person who commits a sequence of murders with no apparent motive.

serial number *n.* a number showing the position of an item in a series.

serial rights *n.pl.* the right to publish a story or book as a serial.

seriate *adj.* & *v.* ● *adj.* /ˈsɪərɪət/ in the form of a series; in orderly sequence. ● *v.tr.* /ˈsɪərɪeɪt/ arrange in a seriate manner. □ **seriation** /-ˈeɪʃ(ə)n/ *n.*

seriatim /sɪərɪˈeɪtɪm, sɛr-/ *adv.* point by point; taking one subject etc. after another in regular order (*consider seriatim*). [medieval Latin from Latin *series*, on the pattern of LITERATIM etc.]

Seric /ˈsɪərɪk/ *adj. archaic* Chinese. [Latin *sericus*; see SILK]

sericeous /sɪˈrɪʃɪəs/ *adj. Bot.* & *Zool.* covered with silky hairs. [Late Latin *sericeus* 'silken']

sericulture /ˈsɛrɪkʌltʃə/ *n.* **1** silkworm-breeding. **2** the production of raw silk. □ **sericultural** /-ˈkʌltʃ(ə)r(ə)l/ *adj.* **sericulturist** /-ˈkʌltʃərɪst/ *n.* [French *sériciculture* from Late Latin *sericum*: see SILK, CULTURE]

seriema /sɛrɪˈiːmə/ *n.* (also **cariama** /karɪˈɑːmə/) *Zool.* any S. American bird of the family Cariamidae, having a long neck and legs and a crest above the bill. [modern Latin from Tupi *siriema* etc. 'crested']

series /ˈsɪəriːz, -rɪz/ *n.* (*pl.* same) **1** a number of things of which each is similar to the preceding or in which each successive pair are similarly related; a sequence, succession, order, row, or set. **2** a set of successive games between the same teams. **3** a set of programmes with the same actors etc. or on related subjects but each complete in itself. **4** a set of lectures by the same speaker or on the same subject. **5 a** a set of successive issues of a periodical, of articles on one subject or by one writer, etc., esp. when numbered separately from a preceding or following set (*second series*). **b** a set of independent books in a common format or under a common title or supervised by a common general editor. **6** a set of stamps, coins, etc., of different denominations but issued at one time, in one reign, etc. **7** *Geol.* **a** a set of strata with a common characteristic. **b** the rocks deposited during a specific epoch. **8** *Mus.* an arrangement of the twelve notes of the chromatic scale as a basis for serial music. **9** *Electr.* **a** a set of circuits or components arranged so that the current passes through each successively. **b** a set of batteries etc. having the positive electrode of each connected with the negative electrode of the next. **10** *Chem.* a set of elements with common properties or of compounds related in composition or structure. **11** *Math.* a set of quantities constituting a progression or having the several values determined by a common relation. □ **in series 1** in ordered succession. **2** *Electr.* (of a set of circuits or components) arranged so that the current passes through each successively. [Latin, = row, chain, from *serere* 'join, connect']

serif /ˈsɛrɪf/ *n.* a slight projection finishing off a stroke of a letter as in T contrasted with T (cf. SANS SERIF). □ **seriffed** *adj.* [perhaps from Dutch *schreef* 'dash, line', from Germanic]

serigraphy /sɛˈrɪɡrəfi/ *n.* the art or process of printing designs by means of a silk screen. □ **serigraph**

/ˈsɛrɪɡrɑːf/ *n.* **serigrapher** *n.* [formed irregularly from Latin *sericum* SILK]

serin /ˈsɛrɪn/ *n.* any small yellow Mediterranean finch of the genus *Serinus*, esp. the wild canary *S. serinus*. [French, originally = canary, of uncertain origin]

serine /ˈsɪəriːn, ˈsɛr-/ *n. Biochem.* a hydrophilic amino acid present in proteins. [Latin *sericum* 'silk' + -INE[4]]

serinette /sɛrɪˈnɛt/ *n.* a small barrel organ used for teaching cage birds to sing. [French (as SERIN)]

seringa /səˈrɪŋɡə/ *n.* **1** = SYRINGA. **2** (in Brazil) the rubber tree, *Hevea brasiliensis*. [French (as SYRINGA)]

serio-comic /ˌsɪərɪəʊˈkɒmɪk/ *adj.* combining the serious and the comic, jocular in intention but simulating seriousness or vice versa. □ **serio-comically** *adv.*

serious /ˈsɪərɪəs/ *adj.* **1** thoughtful, earnest, sober, sedate, responsible, not reckless or given to trifling (*has a serious air*; *a serious young person*). **2** important, demanding consideration (*this is a serious matter*). **3** not slight or negligible (*a serious injury*; *a serious offence*). **4** sincere, in earnest, not ironical or joking (*are you serious?*). **5** (of music and literature) not merely for amusement (opp. LIGHT[2] 5a). **6** not perfunctory (*serious thought*). **7** not to be trifled with (*a serious opponent*). **8** concerned with religion or ethics (*serious subjects*). **9** *colloq.* (of price or value) high; (of an amount of money) large. □ **seriousness** *n.* [Middle English via Old French *serieux* or Late Latin *seriosus* from Latin *serius*]

seriously /ˈsɪərɪəsli/ *adv.* **1** in a serious manner (esp. introducing a sentence, implying that irony etc. is now to cease). **2** to a serious extent. **3** *colloq.* very, really (*seriously rich*).

serjeant /ˈsɑːdʒ(ə)nt/ *n. Brit.* **1** (in full **serjeant-at-law**, *pl.* **serjeants-at-law**) *hist.* a barrister of the highest rank. **2** (in official lists) a sergeant in the Army. □ **serjeantship** *n.* [variant of SERGEANT]

serjeant-at-arms *n.* (*pl.* **serjeants-at-arms**) *Brit.* an official of a court or city or parliament, with ceremonial duties.

sermon /ˈsəːmən/ *n.* **1** a spoken or written discourse on a religious or moral subject, esp. a discourse based on a text or passage of Scripture and delivered in a service by way of religious instruction or exhortation. **2** a piece of admonition or reproof, a lecture. **3** a moral reflection suggested by natural objects etc. (*sermons in stones*). [Middle English via Anglo-French *sermun*, Old French *sermon* from Latin *sermo -onis* 'discourse, talk']

sermonette /səːməˈnɛt/ *n.* a short sermon.

sermonize /ˈsəːmənʌɪz/ *v.* (also **-ise**) **1** *tr.* deliver a moral lecture to. **2** *intr.* deliver a moral lecture. □ **sermonizer** *n.*

Sermon on the Mount *n.* the discourse of Christ recorded in Matt. 5–7.

serology /sɪəˈrɒlədʒi/ *n.* the scientific study of blood sera and their effects. □ **serological** /-rəˈlɒdʒɪk(ə)l/ *adj.* **serologist** *n.*

seronegative /ˌsɪərəʊˈnɛɡətɪv/ *adj. Med.* giving a negative result in a test of blood serum e.g. for presence of a virus.

seropositive /ˌsɪərəʊˈpɒzɪtɪv/ *adj. Med.* giving a positive result in a test of blood serum e.g. for presence of a virus.

serosa /sɪˈrəʊsə/ *n.* a serous membrane. [modern Latin, fem. of medieval Latin *serosus* SEROUS]

serotine /ˈsɛrətʌɪn/ *n.* (in full **serotine bat**) a chestnut-coloured European bat, *Eptesicus serotinus*. [French *sérotine* from Latin *serotinus* 'late, of the evening', from *serus* 'late']

serotonin /sɛrəˈtəʊnɪn/ *n. Biol.* a compound present in blood platelets and serum, which constricts the blood vessels and acts as a neurotransmitter. [SERUM + TONIC + -IN]

serous /ˈsɪərəs/ *adj.* of or like or producing serum; watery. □ **serosity** /-ˈrɒsɪti/ *n.* [French *séreux* or medieval Latin *serosus* (as SERUM)]

serous gland *n.* (also **serous membrane**) a gland or membrane with a serous secretion.

serow /ˈsɛrəʊ/ *n.* either of two thick-coated goat-antelopes, *Capriconus sumatrensis* of mountains in S. and E. Asia, and *C. crispus* of Taiwan and Japan. [Lepcha (Sikkim) *sā-ro*]

serpent /ˈsəːp(ə)nt/ *n.* **1** usu. *literary* a scaly limbless reptile; a snake. **2** a sly or treacherous person, esp. one who exploits a position of trust to betray it. **3** *Mus.* an old bass wind instrument made from leather-covered wood, roughly in the form of an S. **4** (**the Serpent**) *Bibl.* Satan (see Gen. 3, Rev. 20). [Middle English via Old French from Latin *serpens -entis*, part. of *serpere* 'creep']

serpentine /ˈsəːp(ə)ntʌɪn/ *adj., n., & v.* ● *adj.* **1** of or like a serpent. **2** coiling, tortuous, sinuous, meandering, writhing (*the serpentine windings of the stream*). **3** cunning, subtle, treacherous. ● *n.* **1** a soft rock mainly of hydrated magnesium silicate, usu. dark green and sometimes mottled or spotted like a serpent's skin, taking a high polish and used as a decorative material. **2** *Skating* a figure of three circles in a line. ● *v.intr.* move sinuously, meander. [Middle English via Old French *serpentin* from Late Latin *serpentinus* (as SERPENT)]

serpentine verse *n.* a metrical line beginning and ending with the same word.

serpiginous /səːˈpɪdʒɪnəs/ *adj.* **1** like a serpent; winding, tortuous. **2** *Med.* (of a skin lesion) having a wavy margin. [medieval Latin *serpigo -ginis* 'ringworm' from Latin *serpere* 'creep']

SERPS /səːps/ *abbr.* (in the UK) State earnings-related pension scheme.

serpula /ˈsəːpjʊlə/ *n.* (*pl.* **serpulae** /-liː/) any of various marine worms of the family Serpulidae, living in intricately twisted shell-like tubes. [Late Latin, = small serpent, from Latin *serpere* 'creep']

serra /ˈsɛrə/ *n.* (*pl.* **serrae** /-riː/) a serrated organ, structure, or edge. [Latin, = 'saw']

serradilla /sɛrəˈdɪlə/ *n.* (*pl.* **serradillas**) a Mediterranean clover, *Ornithopus sativus*, grown as fodder. [Portuguese, diminutive of *serrado* 'serrated']

serranid /səˈranɪd, ˈsɛrə-/ *n. & adj.* ● *n.* any marine fish of the family Serranidae, comprising heavy predatory fishes such as sea basses and groupers. ● *adj.* of or relating to this family. [modern Latin *Serranus* (genus name) from Latin *serra* 'saw']

serrate *v. & adj.* ● *v.tr.* /sɛˈreɪt/ (usu. as **serrated** *adj.*) provide with a sawlike edge. ● *adj.* /ˈsɛreɪt/ esp. *Anat., Bot., & Zool.* notched like a saw. □ **serration** *n.* [Late Latin *serrare serrat-* from Latin *serra* 'saw']

serried /ˈsɛrɪd/ *adj.* (of ranks of soldiers, rows of trees, etc.) pressed together; without gaps; close. [past part. of *serry* 'press close', probably from French *serré*, past part. of *serrer* 'close', ultimately from Latin *sera* 'lock', or past part. of obsolete *serr* from Old French *serrer*]

serrulate /ˈsɛrjʊleɪt/ *adj.* esp. *Anat., Bot., & Zool.* finely serrate; with a series of small notches. □ **serrulation** /-ˈleɪʃ(ə)n/ *n.* [modern Latin *serrulatus* from Latin *serrula*, diminutive of *serra* 'saw']

serum /ˈsɪərəm/ *n.* (*pl.* **sera** /-rə/ or **serums**) **1 a** the amber-coloured protein-rich liquid in which blood cells are suspended and which separates out when blood coagulates. **b** whey. **2** *Med.* the blood serum of an animal used esp. to provide immunity to a pathogen or toxin by inoculation or as a diagnostic agent. **3** a watery fluid in animal bodies. [Latin, = whey]

serum sickness *n.* a reaction to an injection of serum, characterized by skin eruption, fever, etc.

serval /ˈsəːv(ə)l/ *n.* a tawny black-spotted long-legged African cat, *Felis serval*. [French from Portuguese *cerval* 'deerlike', via *cervo* 'deer' from Latin *cervus*]

servant /ˈsəːv(ə)nt/ *n.* **1** a person who has undertaken (usu. in return for stipulated pay) to carry out the orders of an individual or corporate employer, esp. a person employed in a house on domestic duties or as a personal attendant. **2** a devoted follower, a person willing to serve another (*a servant of Jesus Christ*). [Middle English from Old French (as SERVE)]

serve /sə:v/ *v.* & *n.* ● *v.* **1** *tr.* do a service for (a person, community, etc.). **2** *tr.* (also *absol.*) be a servant to. **3** *intr.* carry out duties (*served on six committees*). **4** *intr.* **a** (foll. by *in*) be employed in (an organization, esp. the armed forces, or a place, esp. a foreign country) (*served in the air force*). **b** be a member of the armed forces. **5 a** *tr.* be useful to or serviceable for; meet the needs of; do what is required for (*serve a purpose*; *one packet serves him for a week*). **b** *intr.* meet requirements; perform a function (*a sofa serving as a bed*). **c** *intr.* (foll. by *to* + infin.) avail, suffice (*his attempt served only to postpone the inevitable*; *it serves to show the folly of such action*). **6** *tr.* **a** go through a due period of (office, apprenticeship, a prison sentence, etc.). **b** go through (a due period) of imprisonment etc. **7** *tr.* set out or present (food) for those about to eat it (*asparagus served with butter*; *dinner was then served*). **8** *intr.* (in full **serve at table**) act as a waiter. **9** *tr.* **a** attend to (a customer in a shop). **b** (foll. by *with*) supply with (goods) (*was serving a customer with apples*; *served the town with gas*). **10** *tr.* treat or act towards (a person) in a specified way (*has served me shamefully*; *you may serve me as you will*). **11** *tr.* **a** (often foll. by *on*) deliver (a writ etc.) to the person concerned in a legally formal manner (*served a warrant on him*). **b** (foll. by *with*) deliver a writ etc. to (a person) in this way (*served her with a summons*). **12** *tr. Tennis* etc. **a** (also *absol.*) deliver (a ball etc.) to begin or resume play. **b** produce (a fault etc.) in doing this. **13** *tr. Mil.* keep (a gun, battery, etc.) firing. **14** *tr.* (of an animal, esp. a stallion etc. hired for the purpose) copulate with (a female). **15** *tr. Brit.* distribute (*served the ammunition out*; *served the rations round*). **16** *tr.* render obedience to (a deity etc.). **17** *Eccl.* **a** *intr.* act as a server. **b** *tr.* act as a server at (a service). **18** *intr.* (of a tide) be suitable for a ship to leave harbour etc. **19** *tr. Naut.* bind (a rope etc.) with thin cord to strengthen it. **20** *tr. archaic* play (a trick etc.) on. ● *n.* **1** *Tennis* etc. **a** the act or an instance of serving. **b** a manner of serving. **c** a person's turn to serve. **2** *Austral. slang* a reprimand. □ **it will serve** it will be adequate. **serve one's needs** (or **need**) be adequate. **serve out** *Brit. archaic colloq.* retaliate on (*he'll serve you out for saying that*). **serve the purpose of** take the place of, be used as. **serve a person right** be a person's deserved punishment or misfortune. **serve** (or esp. *US* **serve out**) **one's time 1** hold office for the normal period. **2** (also **serve time**) undergo imprisonment, apprenticeship, etc. **serve one's** (or **the**) **turn** be adequate. **serve up** offer for acceptance. [Middle English via Old French *servir* from Latin *servire*, from *servus* 'slave']

server /'sə:və/ *n.* **1** a person who serves or attends to the requirements of another. **2** (in tennis etc.) the player who serves the ball. **3** *Eccl.* a person assisting the celebrant at a service, esp. the Eucharist. **4** *Computing* **a** a program which manages shared access to a centralized resource or service in a network. **b** a device on which such a program is run. **5** (in *pl.*) a spoon and fork for serving food, esp. salad.

servery /'sə:v(ə)ri/ *n.* (*pl.* **-ies**) *Brit.* a room from which meals etc. are served and in which utensils are kept.

service[1] /'sə:vɪs/ *n.* & *v.* ● *n.* **1** the act of helping or doing work for another or for a community etc. **2** work done in this way. **3** assistance or benefit given to someone. **4 a** *Brit.* the provision or system of supplying a public need, e.g. transport, or (often in *pl.*) the supply of water, gas, electricity, telephone, etc. **b** (in *pl.*) = SERVICE AREA 1. **5 a** the fact or status of being a servant. **b** employment or a position as a servant. **6** a state or period of employment doing work for an individual or organization (*resigned after 15 years' service*). **7 a** a public or Crown department or organization employing officials working for the State (*civil service*; *secret service*). **b** employment in this. **8** (in *pl.*) the armed forces. **9** (*attrib.*) of the kind issued to the armed forces (*a service revolver*). **10 a** a ceremony of worship according to prescribed forms. **b** a form of liturgy for this. **11 a** the provision of what is necessary for the installation and maintenance of a machine etc. or operation. **b** a periodic routine maintenance of a motor vehicle etc. **12** assistance or advice given to customers after the sale of goods. **13 a** the act or process of serving food, drinks, etc. **b** an extra charge nominally made for this. **14** a set of dishes, plates, etc., used for serving meals (*a dinner service*). **15** *Tennis* etc. **a** the act or an instance of serving. **b** a person's turn to serve. **c** the manner or quality of serving. **d** (in full **service game**) a game in which a particular player serves. ● *v.tr.* **1** provide service or services for, esp. maintain. **2** maintain or repair (a car, machine, etc.). **3** pay interest on (a debt). **4** supply with a service. **5 a** (of a male animal) copulate with (a female animal). **b** *coarse slang* (of a man) have sexual intercourse with (a woman). □ **at a person's service** ready to serve or assist a person. **be of service** be available to assist. **in service 1** employed as a servant. **2** available for use. **on active service** serving in the armed forces in wartime. **out of service** not available for use. **see service 1** have experience of service, esp. in the armed forces. **2** (of a thing) be much used. **take service with** *Brit.* become a servant to. [Middle English via Old French *service* or Latin *servitium* from *servus* 'slave']

service[2] /'sə:vɪs/ *n.* **1** (in full **service tree**) a southern European tree of the rose family, *Sorbus domestica*, with toothed leaves, cream-coloured flowers, and small round or pear-shaped fruit eaten when overripe. **2** (in full **wild service tree**) a related small Eurasian tree, *Sorbus torminalis*, with lobed leaves and bitter fruit. [earlier *serves*, pl. of obsolete *serve*, via Old English *syrfe* from Germanic, ultimately from Latin *sorbus*]

serviceable /'sə:vɪsəb(ə)l/ *adj.* **1** useful or usable. **2** able to render service. **3** durable; capable of withstanding difficult conditions. **4** suited for ordinary use rather than ornament. □ **serviceability** /-'bɪlɪti/ *n.* **serviceableness** *n.* **serviceably** *adv.* [Middle English from Old French *servisable* (as SERVICE[1])]

service area *n.* **1** an area beside a major road for the supply of petrol, refreshments, etc. **2** the area served by a broadcasting station.

service-berry *n.* **1** the fruit of the service tree. **2 a** any American shrub of the genus *Amelanchier* (rose family). **b** the edible fruit of this.

service book *n.* a book of authorized forms of worship of a Church.

service bus *n.* (also **service car**) *Austral.* & *NZ* a motor coach.

service charge *n.* an additional charge for service in a restaurant, hotel, etc.

service dress *n. Brit.* ordinary military etc. uniform.

service flat *n.* a flat in which domestic service and sometimes meals are provided by the management.

service game see SERVICE[1] *n.* 15.

service industry *n.* one providing services not goods.

service line *n.* (in tennis etc.) a line marking the limit of the area into which the ball must be served.

serviceman /'sə:vɪsmən/ *n.* (*pl.* **-men**) **1** a man serving in the armed forces. **2** a man providing service or maintenance.

service road *n.* a road parallel to a main road, serving houses, shops, etc.

service station *n.* an establishment beside a road selling petrol and oil etc. to motorists and often able to carry out maintenance.

service tree see SERVICE[2].

servicewoman /'sə:vɪswʊmən/ *n.* (*pl.* **-women**) a woman serving in the armed forces.

serviette /sə:vɪ'ɛt/ *n.* esp. *Brit.* a napkin for use at table. [Middle English from Old French, from *servir* SERVE]

servile /'sə:vʌɪl/ *adj.* **1** of or being or like a slave or slaves. **2** slavish, fawning; completely dependent. □ **servilely** *adv.* **servility** /-'vɪlɪti/ *n.* [Middle English from Latin *servilis*, from *servus* 'slave']

serving /'sə:vɪŋ/ *n.* a quantity of food served to one person.

servitor /ˈsəːvɪtə/ *n.* **1** *archaic* **a** a servant. **b** an attendant. **2** *hist.* an Oxford undergraduate performing menial duties in exchange for assistance from college funds. □ **servitorship** *n.* [Middle English via Old French from Late Latin (as SERVE)]

servitude /ˈsəːvɪtjuːd/ *n.* **1** slavery. **2** subjection (esp. involuntary); bondage. **3** *Law* the subjection of property to an easement. [Middle English via Old French from Latin *servitudo -inis*, from *servus* 'slave']

servo /ˈsəːvəʊ/ *n.* (*pl.* **-os**) **1** (in full **servo-mechanism**) a powered mechanism producing motion or forces at a higher level of energy than the input level, e.g. in the brakes and steering of large motor vehicles, esp. where feedback is employed to make the control automatic. **2** (in full **servo-motor**) the motive element in a servo-mechanism. **3** (in *comb.*) of or involving a servo-mechanism (*servo-assisted*). [Latin *servus* 'slave']

sesame /ˈsɛsəmi/ *n.* **1** an African herbaceous plant, *Sesamum orientale*, with seeds used as food and yielding an edible oil. **2** its seeds. □ **open sesame** a means of acquiring or achieving what is normally unattainable (from the magic words used in the *Arabian Nights' Entertainments*). [Latin *sesamum* from Greek *sēsamon, sēsamē*]

sesamoid /ˈsɛsəmɔɪd/ *adj.* & *n.* ● *adj.* shaped like a sesame seed; nodular (esp. of small independent bones developed in tendons passing over an angular structure such as the kneecap and the navicular bone). ● *n.* a sesamoid bone.

sesqui- /ˈsɛskwi/ *comb. form* **1** denoting one and a half. **2** *Chem.* (of a compound) in which there are three equivalents of a named element or radical to two others (*sesquioxide*). [Latin (as SEMI-, *-que* 'and')]

sesquicentenary /ˌsɛskwɪsɛnˈtiːn(ə)ri, -ˈtɛn-, sɛskwɪˈsɛntɪn-/ *n.* (*pl.* **-ies**) a one-hundred-and-fiftieth anniversary.

sesquicentennial /ˌsɛskwɪsɛnˈtɛnɪəl/ *n.* & *adj.* ● *n.* = SESQUICENTENARY. ● *adj.* of or relating to a sesquicentennial.

sesquipedalian /ˌsɛskwɪpɪˈdeɪlɪən/ *adj.* **1** (of a word etc.) polysyllabic, long. **2** characterized by long words; long-winded. [Latin *sesquipedalis* = a foot and a half long, from SESQUI- + *pes pedis-* 'foot']

sess var. of CESS[1].

sessile /ˈsɛsʌɪl, ˈsɛsɪl/ *adj.* **1** *Bot.* & *Zool.* (of a flower, leaf, eye, etc.) attached directly by its base without a stalk or peduncle. **2 a** (of an animal, e.g. a barnacle) fixed in one spot. **b** immobile. [Latin *sessilis* from *sedēre sess-* 'sit']

sessile oak *n.* = DURMAST.

session /ˈsɛʃ(ə)n/ *n.* **1** the process of assembly of a deliberative or judicial body to conduct its business. **2** a single meeting for this purpose. **3** a period during which such meetings are regularly held. **4 a** an academic year. **b** the period during which a school etc. has classes. **5 a** a period devoted to an activity (*poker session*; *recording session*). **b** *colloq.* a period of heavy or sustained drinking. **6** the governing body of a Presbyterian Church. □ **in session** assembled for business; not on vacation. □ **sessional** *adj.* [Middle English from Old French *session* or Latin *sessio -onis* (as SESSILE)]

sesterce /ˈsɛstəːs/ *n.* (also **sestertius** /sɛˈstəːʃəs/) (*pl.* **sesterces** /ˈsɛstəˌsiːz/ or **sestertii** /-ˈstəːʃiː/) an ancient Roman coin and monetary unit equal to one-quarter of a denarius. [Latin *sestertius* (*nummus* 'coin') = 2½, from *semis* 'half' + *tertius* 'a third']

sestet /sɛsˈtɛt/ *n.* **1** the last six lines of a sonnet. **2** a sextet. [Italian *sestetto* from *sesto*, from Latin *sextus* 'a sixth']

sestina /sɛˈstiːnə/ *n.* a form of rhymed or unrhymed poem with six stanzas of six lines and a final triplet, all stanzas having the same six words at the line-ends in six different sequences. [Italian (as SESTET)]

set[1] /sɛt/ *v.* (**setting**; *past* and *past part.* **set**) **1** *tr.* put, lay, or stand (a thing) in a certain position or location (*set it on the table*; *set it upright*). **2** *tr.* (foll. by *to*) apply (one thing) to (another) (*set pen to paper*). **3** *tr.* **a** fix ready or in position. **b** dispose suitably for use, action, or display. **4** *tr.* **a** adjust the hands of (a clock or watch) to show the right time. **b** adjust (an alarm clock) to sound at the required time. **5** *tr.* **a** fix, arrange, or mount. **b** insert (a jewel) in a ring, framework, etc. **6** *tr.* make (a device) ready to operate. **7** *tr.* lay (a table) for a meal. **8** *tr.* arrange (the hair) while damp so that it dries in the required style. **9** *tr.* (foll. by *with*) ornament or provide (a surface, esp. a precious item) (*gold set with gems*). **10** *tr.* bring by placing or arranging or other means into a specified state; cause to be (*set things in motion*; *set it on fire*). **11** *intr.* & *tr.* harden or solidify (*the jelly is set*; *the cement has set*). **12** *intr.* (of the sun, moon, etc.) appear to move towards and below the earth's horizon (as the earth rotates). **13** *tr.* represent (a story, play, scene, etc.) as happening in a certain time or place. **14** *tr.* **a** (foll. by *to* + infin.) cause or instruct (a person) to perform a specified activity (*set them to work*). **b** (foll. by pres. part.) start (a person or thing) doing something (*set him chatting*; *set the ball rolling*). **15** *tr.* present or impose as work to be done or a matter to be dealt with (*set them an essay*). **16** *tr.* exhibit as a type or model (*set a good example*). **17** *tr.* initiate; take the lead in (*set the fashion*; *set the pace*). **18** *tr.* establish (a record etc.). **19** *tr.* determine or decide (*the itinerary is set*). **20** *tr.* appoint or establish (*set them in authority*). **21** *tr.* join, attach, or fasten. **22** *tr.* **a** put parts of (a broken or dislocated bone, limb, etc.) into the correct position for healing. **b** deal with (a fracture or dislocation) in this way. **23** *tr.* (in full **set to music**) provide (words etc.) with music for singing. **24** *tr.* (often foll. by *up*) *Printing* **a** arrange or produce (type or film etc.) as required. **b** arrange the type or film etc. for (a book etc.). **25** *intr.* (of a tide, current, etc.) have a certain motion or direction. **26** *intr.* (of a face) assume a hard expression. **27** *tr.* **a** cause (a hen) to sit on eggs. **b** place (eggs) for a hen to sit on. **28** *tr.* put (a seed, plant, etc.) in the ground to grow. **29** *tr.* give the teeth of (a saw) an alternate outward inclination. **30** *tr.* esp. *US* start (a fire). **31** *intr.* (of eyes etc.) become motionless. **32** *intr.* feel or show a certain tendency (*opinion is setting against it*). **33** *intr.* **a** (of blossom) form into fruit. **b** (of fruit) develop from blossom. **c** (of a tree) develop fruit. **34** *intr.* (in full **set to partner**) (of a dancer) take a position facing one's partner. **35** *intr.* (of a hunting dog) take a rigid attitude indicating the presence of game. **36** *intr. dial.* or *slang* sit. □ **set about 1** begin or take steps towards. **2** *Brit. colloq.* attack. **set against 1** consider or reckon (a person or thing) as a counterpoise or compensation for (another). **2** cause (a person or persons) to oppose (a person or thing). **set apart** separate, reserve, differentiate. **set aside** see ASIDE. **set back 1** place further back in place or time. **2** impede or reverse the progress of. **3** *colloq.* cost (a person) a specified amount. **set by** *archaic* or *US* save for future use. **set down 1** record in writing. **2** allow to alight from a vehicle. **3** (foll. by *to*) attribute to. **4** (foll. by *as*) explain or describe to oneself as. **set eyes on** see EYE. **set one's face against** see FACE. **set foot on** (or **in**) see FOOT. **set forth 1** begin a journey. **2** make known; expound. **set forward** begin to advance. **set free** release. **set one's hand to** see HAND. **set one's heart** (or **hopes**) **on** want or hope for eagerly. **set in 1** (of weather, a condition, etc.) begin (and seem likely to continue), become established. **2** insert (esp. a sleeve etc. into a garment). **set little by** consider to be of little value. **set a person's mind at rest** see MIND. **set much by** consider to be of much value. **set off 1** begin a journey. **2** detonate (a bomb etc.). **3** initiate, stimulate. **4** cause (a person) to start laughing, talking, etc. **5** serve as an adornment or foil to; enhance. **6** (foll. by *against*) use as a compensating item. **set on** (or **upon**) **1** attack violently. **2** cause or urge to attack. **set out 1** begin a journey. **2** (foll. by *to* + infin.) aim or intend. **3** demonstrate, arrange, or exhibit. **4** mark out. **5** declare. **set sail 1** hoist the sails. **2** begin a voyage. **set the**

scene see SCENE. **set the stage** see STAGE. **set store by** (or **on**) see STORE. **set one's teeth 1** clench them. **2** summon one's resolve. **set to** begin doing something vigorously, esp. fighting, arguing, or eating. **set up 1** place in position or view. **2** organize or start (a business etc.). **3** establish in some capacity. **4** supply the needs of. **5** begin making (a loud sound). **6** cause or make arrangements for (a condition or situation). **7** prepare (a task etc. for another). **8** restore or enhance the health of (a person). **9** establish (a record). **10** propound (a theory). **11** *colloq.* cause (a person) to incriminate himself or herself or to look foolish; frame (a person). **set oneself up as** make pretensions to being. [Old English *settan*, from Germanic]

set[2] /sɛt/ *n.* **1** a number of things or persons that belong together or resemble one another or are usually found together. **2** a collection or group. **3** a section of society consorting together or having similar interests etc. **4** a collection of implements, vessels, etc., regarded collectively and needed for a specified purpose (*cricket set*; *teaset*; *a set of teeth*). **5** a piece of electric or electronic apparatus, esp. a radio or television receiver. **6** (in tennis, darts, etc.) a group of games counting as a unit towards a match for the player or side that wins a defined number or proportion of the games. **7** *Math. & Logic* a collection of distinct entities, individually specified or satisfying specified conditions, forming a unit. **8** a group of pupils or students having the same average ability. **9 a** a slip, shoot, bulb, etc., for planting. **b** a young fruit just set. **10 a** a habitual posture or conformation; the way the head etc. is carried or a dress etc. flows. **b** (also **dead set**) a setter's pointing in the presence of game. **11** the way, drift, or tendency (of a current, public opinion, state of mind, etc.) (*the set of public feeling is against it*). **12** the way in which a machine, device, etc., is set or adjusted. **13** esp. *Austral. & NZ colloq.* a grudge. **14 a** the alternate outward deflection of the teeth of a saw. **b** the amount of this. **15** the last coat of plaster on a wall. **16** *Printing* **a** the amount of spacing in type controlling the distance between letters. **b** the width of a piece of type. **17** a warp or bend or displacement caused by continued pressure or a continued position. **18** a setting, including stage furniture etc., for a play or film etc. **19** a sequence of songs or pieces performed in jazz or popular music. **20** the setting of the hair when damp. **21** var. of SETT 1. **22** var. of SETT 2. **23** a predisposition or expectation influencing a response. **24** a number of people making up a square dance. □ **make a dead set at** *Brit.* **1** make a determined attack on. **2** seek to win the affections of. [sense 1 (and related senses) via Old French *sette* from Latin *secta* SECT: other senses from SET[1]]

set[3] /sɛt/ *adj.* **1** in senses of SET[1]. **2** prescribed or determined in advance. **3** fixed, unchanging, unmoving. **4** (of a phrase or speech etc.) having invariable or predetermined wording; not extempore. **5** prepared for action. **6** (foll. by *on*, *upon*) determined to acquire or achieve etc. **7** (of a book etc.) specified for reading in preparation for an examination. [past part. of SET[1]]

seta /ˈsiːtə/ *n.* (*pl.* **setae** /-tiː/) *Bot. & Zool.* a stiff hair or bristle. □ **setaceous** /-ˈteɪʃəs/ *adj.* [Latin, = bristle]

set-aside *n.* **1** the action of setting something aside for a special purpose. **2** the policy of taking land out of production to reduce crop surpluses (often *attrib.*: *set-aside land*).

setback /ˈsɛtbak/ *n.* **1** a reversal or arrest of progress. **2** a relapse.

se-tenant /siːˈtɛnənt, French sətənɑ̃/ *adj. Philately* (of stamps, esp. of different designs) joined together side by side as when printed. [French, = holding together]

set fair *adj. Brit.* (of the weather) fine without a sign of breaking.

SETI *abbr.* search for extraterrestrial intelligence.

setiferous /sɪˈtɪf(ə)rəs/ *adj.* (also **setigerous** /sɪˈtɪdʒ(ə)rəs/) *Biol.* having bristles. [Latin *seta* 'bristle', *setiger* 'bristly' + -FEROUS, -GEROUS]

set menu *n.* a limited menu of a set number of courses.

set-off *n.* **1** a thing set off against another. **2** a thing of which the amount or effect may be deducted from that of another or opposite tendency. **3** a counterpoise. **4** a counter-claim. **5** a thing that embellishes; an adornment to something. **6** *Printing* = OFFSET 7.

seton /ˈsiːt(ə)n/ *n. Surgery* a skein of cotton etc. passed below the skin and left with the ends protruding to promote drainage etc. [Middle English from medieval Latin *seto*, *seta* 'silk', apparently from Latin *seta* 'bristle']

setose /ˈsiːtəʊs, -z/ *adj. Biol.* bristly. [Latin *seta* 'bristle']

set phrase *n.* an invariable or usual arrangement of words.

set piece *n.* **1** a formal or elaborate arrangement, esp. in art or literature (hyphenated when *attrib.*: *set-piece occasions*). **2** a pre-arranged movement in a team game at a free-kick, scrum, etc. **3** an arrangement of fireworks composing a picture or design.

set point *n. Tennis* etc. **1** the state of a game when one side needs only one more point to win the set. **2** this point.

set screw *n.* a screw for adjusting or clamping parts of a machine.

set scrum *n. Rugby* a scrum ordered by the referee.

set square *n.* a right-angled triangular plate for drawing lines, esp. at 90°, 45°, 60°, or 30°.

Setswana var. of TSWANA *n.* 3.

sett /sɛt/ *n.* (also **set**) **1** a badger's burrow. **2** a granite paving block.

settee /sɛˈtiː/ *n.* a seat (usu. upholstered), with a back and usu. arms, for more than one person. [18th c.: perhaps a fanciful variant of SETTLE[2]]

setter /ˈsɛtə/ *n.* **1 a** a dog of a large long-haired breed trained to stand rigid when scenting game (see SET[1] 35). **b** this breed. **2** a person or thing that sets.

set theory *n.* the branch of mathematics which deals with the properties of sets (without regard to the nature of their individual constituents).

setting /ˈsɛtɪŋ/ *n.* **1** the position or manner in which a thing is set. **2** the immediate surroundings (of a house etc.). **3** the surroundings of any object regarded as its framework; the environment of a thing. **4** the place and time, scenery, etc., of a story, drama, etc. **5** a frame in which a jewel is set. **6** the music to which words of a poem, song, etc., are set. **7** a set of cutlery and other accessories for one person at a table. **8** the way in which or level at which a machine is set to operate.

setting lotion *n.* lotion used to prepare the hair for being set.

settle[1] /ˈsɛt(ə)l/ *v.* **1** *tr. & intr.* (often foll. by *down*) establish or become established in a more or less permanent abode or way of life. **2** *intr. & tr.* (often foll. by *down*) **a** cease or cause to cease from wandering, disturbance, movement, etc. **b** adopt a regular or secure style of life. **c** (foll. by *to*) apply oneself (to work, an activity, a way of life, etc.) (*settled down to writing letters*). **3 a** *intr.* sit or come down to stay for some time. **b** *tr.* cause to do this. **4** *tr. & intr.* bring to or attain fixity, certainty, composure, or quietness. **5** *tr.* determine or decide or agree upon (*shall we settle a date?*). **6** *tr.* **a** resolve (a dispute etc.). **b** deal with (a matter) finally. **7** *tr.* terminate (a lawsuit) by mutual agreement. **8** *intr.* **a** (foll. by *for*) accept or agree to (esp. an alternative not one's first choice). **b** (foll. by *on*) decide on. **9** *tr.* (also *absol.*) pay (a debt, an account, etc.). **10** *intr.* (as **settled** *adj.*) not likely to change for a time (*settled weather*). **11** *tr.* **a** aid the digestion of (food). **b** remedy the disordered state of (nerves, the stomach, etc.). **12** *tr.* **a** colonize. **b** establish colonists in. **13** *intr.* subside; fall to the bottom or on to a surface (*the foundations have settled*; *wait till the sediment settles*; *the dust will settle*). **14** *intr.* (of a ship) begin to sink. **15** *tr.* get rid of the obstruction of (a person) by argument or conflict or killing. □ **settle one's affairs** make any necessary arrangements (e.g. write a will) when death is near. **settle a person's hash** see HASH[1]. **settle in** become established in a place. **settle up 1** (also *absol.*) pay (an account, debt, etc.). **2** finally arrange (a matter). **settle with 1** pay all or part of an amount due to (a creditor). **2** get revenge on. □ **settleable** *adj.* [Old English *setlan* (as SETTLE[2]), from Germanic]

settle[2] /'sɛt(ə)l/ *n.* a bench with a high back and arms and often with a box fitted below the seat. [Old English *setl* 'a place to sit', from Germanic]

settlement /'sɛt(ə)lm(ə)nt/ *n.* **1** the act or an instance of settling; the process of being settled. **2 a** the colonization of a region. **b** a place or area occupied by settlers. **c** a small village. **3 a** a political or financial etc. agreement. **b** an arrangement ending a dispute. **4 a** the terms on which property is given to a person. **b** a deed stating these. **c** the amount of property given. **d** = MARRIAGE SETTLEMENT. **5** the process of settling an account. **6** subsidence of a wall, house, soil, etc.

settler /'sɛtlə/ *n.* a person who goes to settle in a new country or place; an early colonist.

settling day *n.* (in the UK) the fortnightly pay day on the Stock Exchange.

settlor /'sɛtlə/ *n. Law* a person who makes a settlement esp. of a property.

set-to *n.* (*pl.* **-tos**) *colloq.* a fight or argument.

set-up *n.* **1 a** the way in which something is organized or arranged. **b** an organization or arrangement. **2** *colloq.* a conspiracy or trick whereby a person is caused to incriminate himself or herself or to look foolish, or a criminal is caught red-handed.

seven /'sɛv(ə)n/ *n. & adj.* ● *n.* **1** one more than six, or three less than ten; the sum of four units and three units. **2** a symbol for this (7, vii, VII). **3** a size etc. denoted by seven. **4** a set or team of seven individuals. **5** the time of seven o'clock. **6** a playing card with seven pips. ● *adj.* that amount to seven. □ **the seven wonders of the world** see WONDER. [Old English *seofon*, from Germanic]

seven deadly sins *n.pl.* (prec. by *the*) the sins of pride, covetousness, lust, anger, gluttony, envy, and sloth.

sevenfold /'sɛv(ə)nfəʊld/ *adj. & adv.* **1** seven times as much or as many. **2** consisting of seven parts.

seven seas *n.pl.* (prec. by *the*) the oceans of the world: the Arctic, Antarctic, N. Pacific, S. Pacific, N. Atlantic, S. Atlantic, and Indian Oceans.

Seven Sisters *n.pl.* (prec. by *the*) = PLEIADES.

seventeen /sɛv(ə)n'tiːn, 'sɛv(ə)ntiːn/ *n. & adj.* ● *n.* **1** one more than sixteen, or seven more than ten. **2** a symbol for this (17, xvii, XVII). **3** a size etc. denoted by seventeen. ● *adj.* that amount to seventeen. □ **seventeenth** *adj. & n.* [Old English *seofontīene*]

seventh /'sɛv(ə)nθ/ *n. & adj.* ● *n.* **1** the position in a sequence corresponding to the number 7 in the sequence 1–7. **2** something occupying this position. **3** one of seven equal parts of a thing. **4** *Mus.* **a** an interval or chord spanning seven consecutive notes in the diatonic scale (e.g. C to B). **b** a note separated from another by this interval. ● *adj.* that is the seventh. □ **in seventh heaven** see HEAVEN. □ **seventhly** *adv.*

Seventh-Day Adventist *n.* a member of a strict protestant sect preaching the imminent return of Christ to earth, and observing the sabbath on Saturday.

seventy /'sɛv(ə)nti/ *n. & adj.* ● *n.* (*pl.* **-ies**) **1** the product of seven and ten. **2** a symbol for this (70, lxx, LXX). **3** (in *pl.*) the numbers from 70 to 79, esp. the years of a century or of a person's life. ● *adj.* that amount to seventy. □ **seventy-first, -second**, etc. the ordinal numbers between seventieth and eightieth. **seventy-one, -two**, etc. the cardinal numbers between seventy and eighty. □ **seventieth** *adj. & n.* **seventyfold** *adj. & adv.* [Old English *-seofontig*]

seventy-eight *n. hist.* a gramophone record played at 78 r.p.m.

seven year itch *n.* a supposed tendency to infidelity after seven years of marriage.

sever /'sɛvə/ *v.* **1** *tr. & intr.* (often foll. by *from*) divide, break, or make separate, esp. by cutting. **2** *tr. & intr.* break off or away; separate, part, divide (*severed our friendship*). **3** *tr.* end the employment contract of (a person). □ **severable** *adj.* [Middle English from Anglo-French *severer*, Old French *sevrer*, ultimately from Latin *separare* SEPARATE *v.*]

several /'sɛv(ə)r(ə)l/ *det., pron., & adj.* ● *det. & pron.* more than two but not many (*several things*; *several people*; *several of them were present*; *she offered him one but he took several*). ● *adj.* **1** separate or respective; distinct (*all went their several ways*). **2** *Law* applied or regarded separately (opp. JOINT *adj.* 1). □ **severally** *adv.* [Middle English from Anglo-French, via Anglo-Latin *separalis* from Latin *separ* SEPARATE *adj.*]

severalty /'sɛv(ə)r(ə)lti/ *n.* **1** separateness. **2** the individual or unshared tenure of an estate etc. (esp. *in severalty*). [Middle English from Anglo-French *severalte* (as SEVERAL)]

severance /'sɛv(ə)r(ə)ns/ *n.* **1** the act or an instance of severing. **2** a severed state.

severance pay *n.* an amount paid to an employee on the early termination of a contract.

severe /sɪ'vɪə/ *adj.* **1** rigorous, strict, and harsh in attitude or treatment (*a severe critic*; *severe discipline*). **2** serious, critical (*a severe shortage*). **3** vehement or forceful (*a severe storm*). **4** extreme (in an unpleasant quality) (*a severe winter*; *severe cold*). **5** arduous or exacting; making great demands on energy, skill, etc. (*severe competition*). **6** unadorned; plain in style (*severe dress*). □ **severely** *adv.* **severity** /-'vɛrɪti/ *n.* [French *sévère* or Latin *severus*]

severy /'sɛvəri/ *n.* (*pl.* **-ies**) *Archit.* a space or compartment in a vaulted ceiling. [Middle English from Old French *civoire* (as CIBORIUM)]

Seville orange /'sɛvɪl/ *n.* a bitter orange used for marmalade. [*Seville*, a city and province in Spain]

Sèvres /'seɪvrə/ *n.* fine porcelain, often with elaborate decoration, made at Sèvres in the suburbs of Paris.

sew /səʊ/ *v.tr.* (*past part.* **sewn** /səʊn/ or **sewed**) **1** (also *absol.*) fasten, join, etc., by making stitches with a needle and thread or a sewing machine. **2** make (a garment etc.) by sewing. **3** (often foll. by *on*, *in*, etc.) attach by sewing (*shall I sew on your buttons?*). □ **sew up 1** join or enclose by sewing. **2** (esp. in *passive*) *colloq.* bring to a desired conclusion or condition; complete satisfactorily; ensure the favourable outcome of (a thing). □ **sewer** *n.* [Old English *si(o)wan*]

sewage /'suːɪdʒ, 'sjuː-/ *n.* waste matter, esp. excrement, conveyed in sewers.

sewage farm *n.* (also **sewage works**) a place where sewage is treated, esp. to produce manure.

sewen var. of SEWIN.

sewer /'suːə, 'sjuːə/ *n.* a conduit, usu. underground, for carrying off drainage water and sewage. [Middle English from Anglo-French *sever(e)*, Old Northern French *se(u)wiere* 'channel to carry off the overflow from a fish pond', ultimately from Latin *ex-* 'out of' + *aqua* 'water']

sewerage /'suːərɪdʒ, 'sjuː-/ *n.* **1** a system of or drainage by sewers. **2** *US* = SEWAGE.

sewer rat *n.* the common brown rat.

sewin /'sjuːɪn/ *n.* (also **sewen**) a salmon trout of Welsh etc. rivers. [16th c.: origin unknown]

sewing /'səʊɪŋ/ *n.* material or work to be sewn.

sewing machine *n.* a machine for sewing or stitching.

sewn *past part.* of SEW.

sex /sɛks/ *n., adj., & v.* ● *n.* **1** either of the main divisions (male and female) into which living things are placed on the basis of their reproductive functions. **2** the fact of belonging to one of these. **3** males or females collectively. **4** sexual instincts, desires, etc., or their manifestation. **5** *colloq.* sexual intercourse. ● *adj.* **1** of or relating to sex (*sex education*). **2** arising from a difference or consciousness of sex (*sex antagonism*; *sex urge*). ● *v.tr.* **1** determine the sex of. **2** (as **sexed** *adj.*) **a**

having a sexual appetite (*highly sexed*). **b** having sexual characteristics. □ **sexer** *n.* [Middle English from Old French *sexe* or Latin *sexus*]

sex act *n.* (usu. prec. by *the*) the (or an) act of sexual intercourse.

sexagenarian /ˌsɛksədʒɪ'nɛ:rɪən/ *n.* & *adj.* ● *n.* a person from 60 to 69 years old. ● *adj.* of this age. [Latin *sexagenarius* from *sexageni*, distributive of *sexaginta* 'sixty']

Sexagesima /sɛksə'dʒɛsɪmə/ *n.* the Sunday before Quinquagesima. [Middle English from ecclesiastical Latin, = sixtieth (day), probably named loosely as preceding QUINQUAGESIMA]

sexagesimal /sɛksə'dʒɛsɪm(ə)l/ *adj.* & *n.* ● *adj.* **1** of sixtieths. **2** of sixty. **3** reckoning or reckoned by sixtieths. ● *n.* (in full **sexagesimal fraction**) a fraction with a denominator equal to a power of 60 as in the divisions of the degree and hour. □ **sexagesimally** *adv.* [Latin *sexagesimus* (as SEXAGESIMA)]

sex appeal *n.* sexual attractiveness.

sexcentenary /sɛk(s)sɛn'ti:n(ə)ri, -'tɛn-, sɛk(s)'sɛntɪn-/ *n.* & *adj.* ● *n.* (*pl.* **-ies**) **1** a six-hundredth anniversary. **2** a celebration of this. ● *adj.* **1** of or relating to a sexcentenary. **2** occurring every six hundred years.

sex change *n.* an apparent change of sex by surgical means and hormone treatment.

sex chromosome *n.* a chromosome concerned in determining the sex of an organism, usu. one of two kinds (in mammals the X and Y chromosomes).

sexennial /sɛk'sɛnɪəl/ *adj.* **1** lasting six years. **2** recurring every six years. [SEXI- + Latin *annus* 'year']

sexfoil /'sɛksfɔɪl/ *n.* a six-lobed ornamental figure. [SEXI-, on the pattern of CINQUEFOIL, TREFOIL]

sex hormone *n.* a hormone affecting sexual development or behaviour.

sexi- /'sɛksi/ *comb. form* (also **sex-** before a vowel) six. [Latin *sex* 'six']

sexism /'sɛksɪz(ə)m/ *n.* prejudice or discrimination, esp. against women, on the grounds of sex. □ **sexist** *adj.* & *n.*

sexivalent /sɛksɪ'veɪl(ə)nt/ *adj.* (also **sexvalent**) *Chem.* = HEXAVALENT.

sex kitten *n. colloq.* a young woman who asserts her sex appeal.

sexless /'sɛkslɪs/ *adj.* **1** *Biol.* neither male nor female. **2** lacking in sexual desire or attractiveness. □ **sexlessly** *adv.* **sexlessness** *n.*

sex life *n.* a person's activity related to sexual instincts.

sex-linked *adj. Genetics* carried on or by a sex chromosome.

sex maniac *n. colloq.* a person needing or seeking excessive gratification of the sexual instincts.

sex object *n.* a person regarded mainly in terms of sexual attractiveness.

sex offender *n.* a person who commits a sexual crime.

sexology /sɛk'sɒlədʒi/ *n.* the study of sexual life or relationships, esp. in human beings. □ **sexological** /-ə'lɒdʒɪk(ə)l/ *adj.* **sexologist** *n.*

sexpartite /sɛks'pɑ:tʌɪt/ *adj.* divided into six parts.

sexploitation /sɛksplɔɪ'teɪʃ(ə)n/ *n. colloq.* the exploitation of sex, esp. commercially.

sexpot /'sɛkspɒt/ *n. colloq.* a sexy person (esp. a woman).

sex-starved *adj.* lacking sexual gratification.

sex symbol *n.* a person widely noted for sex appeal.

sext /sɛkst/ *n. Eccl.* the office of the fourth canonical hour of prayer, originally said at the sixth hour of the day (i.e. noon). [Middle English from Latin *sexta hora* 'sixth hour', from *sextus* 'sixth']

sextant /'sɛkst(ə)nt/ *n.* an instrument with a graduated arc of 60° used in navigation and surveying for measuring the angular distance of objects by means of mirrors. [Latin *sextans -ntis* 'sixth part' from *sextus* 'sixth']

sextet /sɛks'tɛt/ *n.* (also **sextette**) **1** *Mus.* a composition for six voices or instruments. **2** the performers of such a piece. **3** any group of six. [alteration of SESTET suggested by Latin *sex* 'six']

sextillion /sɛks'tɪljən/ *n.* (*pl.* same or **sextillions**) a thousand raised to the seventh (or formerly, esp. *Brit.*, the twelfth) power (10^{21} and 10^{36} respectively) (cf. BILLION *n.* 1, 2). □ **sextillionth** *adj.* & *n.* [French from Latin *sex* 'six', on the pattern of *septillion* etc.]

sextodecimo /sɛkstəʊ'dɛsɪməʊ/ *n.* (*pl.* **-os**) **1** a size of book in which each leaf is one-sixteenth the size of a printing-sheet. **2** a book of this size. [Latin *sextus decimus* '16th' (as QUARTO)]

sexton /'sɛkst(ə)n/ *n.* a person who looks after a church and churchyard, often acting as bell-ringer and gravedigger. [Middle English *segerstane* etc., via Anglo-French, Old French *segerstein*, *secrestein* from medieval Latin *sacristanus* SACRISTAN]

sexton beetle *n.* any beetle of the genus *Nicrophorus*, burying carrion to serve as a nidus for its eggs.

sextuple /'sɛkstjʊp(ə)l, sɛks'tju:p(ə)l/ *adj.*, *n.*, & *v.* ● *adj.* **1** sixfold. **2** having six parts. **3** being six times as many or much. ● *n.* a sixfold number or amount. ● *v.tr.* & *intr.* multiply by six; increase sixfold. □ **sextuply** *adv.* [medieval Latin *sextuplus*, formed irregularly from Latin *sex* 'six', on the pattern of Late Latin *quintuplus* QUINTUPLE]

sextuplet /'sɛkstjʊplɪt, -'tju:plɪt/ *n.* **1** each of six children born at one birth. **2** *Mus.* a group of six notes to be played in the time of four. [SEXTUPLE, on the pattern of *triplet* etc.]

sexual /'sɛksjʊəl, -ʃʊəl/ *adj.* **1** of or relating to sex, or to the sexes or the relations between them. **2** *Bot.* (of classification) based on the distinction of sexes in plants. **3** *Biol.* having a sex. □ **sexuality** /-'alɪti/ *n.* **sexually** *adv.* [Late Latin *sexualis* (as SEX)]

sexual intercourse *n.* physical contact between individuals involving sexual stimulation of the genitals, esp. the insertion of a man's erect penis into a woman's vagina, usu. followed by the ejaculation of semen.

sexvalent var. of SEXIVALENT.

sexy /'sɛksi/ *adj.* (**sexier**, **sexiest**) **1** sexually attractive or stimulating. **2** sexually aroused. **3** concerned with sex. **4** *colloq.* (of a project etc.) exciting, appealing, trendy. □ **sexily** *adv.* **sexiness** *n.*

sez /sɛz/ *slang* says (*sez you*). [phonetic representation]

SF *abbr.* science fiction.

sf *abbr. Mus.* sforzando.

SFA *abbr.* Scottish Football Association.

sforzando /sfɔ:'tsandəʊ/ *adj.*, *adv.*, & *n.* (also **sforzato** /-'tsɑ:təʊ/) *Mus.* ● *adj.* & *adv.* with sudden emphasis. ● *n.* (*pl.* **-os** or **sforzandi** /-di/) **1** a note or group of notes especially emphasized. **2** an increase in emphasis and loudness. [Italian, verbal noun and past part. of *sforzare* 'use force']

sfumato /sfʊ'mɑ:təʊ, Italian sfu'ma:to/ *adj.* & *n. Art* ● *adj.* with indistinct outlines. ● *n.* the technique of allowing tones and colours to shade gradually into one another. [Italian, past part. of *sfumare* 'shade off', from *s-* = EX-[1] + *fumare* 'to smoke']

sfz *abbr. Mus.* sforzando.

SG *abbr.* **1** *US* senior grade. **2** *Law* Solicitor-General. **3** specific gravity.

sgd. *abbr.* signed.

SGML *abbr. Computing* Standard Generalized Mark-up Language, a form of generic coding used for producing printed material in electronic form.

sgraffito /sgra'fi:təʊ/ *n.* (*pl.* **sgraffiti** /-ti/) a form of decoration made by scratching through wet plaster on a wall or through slip on ceramic ware, showing a different-coloured undersurface. [Italian, past part. of *sgraffire* 'scratch', from *s-* = EX-[1] + *graffio* 'scratch']

Sgt. *abbr.* Sergeant.

sh /ʃ/ *int.* calling for silence. [variant of HUSH]

sh. *abbr. Brit. hist.* shilling(s).

shabby /'ʃabi/ *adj.* (**shabbier**, **shabbiest**) **1** in bad repair or condition; faded and worn, dingy, dilapidated. **2** dressed in old or worn clothes. **3** of poor quality. **4**

contemptible, dishonourable (*a shabby trick*). □ **shabbily** *adv.* **shabbiness** *n.* **shabbyish** *adj.* [*shab* 'scab', from Old English *sceabb* from Old Norse, related to SCAB]

shabrack /ˈʃabrak/ *n. hist.* a cavalry saddle-cloth. [German *Schabracke* of E. European origin: cf. Russian *shabrak*]

shack /ʃak/ *n. & v.* ● *n.* a roughly built hut or cabin. ● *v.intr.* (foll. by *up*) *slang* cohabit, esp. as lovers. [perhaps from Mexican *jacal*, Nahuatl *xacatli* 'wooden hut']

shackle /ˈʃak(ə)l/ *n. & v.* ● *n.* **1** a metal loop or link, closed by a bolt, to connect chains etc. **2** a fetter enclosing the ankle or wrist. **3** (usu. in *pl.*) a restraint or impediment. ● *v.tr.* fetter, impede, restrain. [Old English *sc(e)acul* 'fetter', corresponding to Low German *shäkel* 'link, coupling', Old Norse *skökull* 'wagon-pole', from Germanic]

shackle-bolt *n.* **1** a bolt for closing a shackle. **2** a bolt with a shackle at its end.

shad /ʃad/ *n.* (*pl.* same or **shads**) any deep-bodied edible marine fish of the genus *Alosa*, spawning in fresh water. [Old English *sceadd*, of unknown origin]

shaddock /ˈʃadək/ *n.* **1** the largest citrus fruit, with a thick yellow skin and bitter pulp. Also called POMELO. **2** the tree, *Citrus grandis*, bearing these. [named after Capt. *Shaddock*, who introduced it to the W. Indies in the 17th c.]

shade /ʃeɪd/ *n. & v.* ● *n.* **1** comparative darkness (and usu. coolness) caused by shelter from direct light and heat. **2** a place or area sheltered from the sun. **3** a darker part of a picture etc. **4** a colour, esp. with regard to its depth or as distinguished from one nearly like it. **5** a slight amount (*am a shade better today*). **6** a translucent cover for a lamp etc. **7** a screen excluding or moderating light. **8** an eye-shield. **9** (in *pl.*) orig. *US colloq.* sunglasses. **10** a slightly differing variety (*all shades of opinion*). **11** *literary* **a** a ghost. **b** (in *pl.*) Hades. **12** (in *pl.*; foll. by *of*) suggesting reminiscence or unfavourable comparison (*shades of Dr Johnson!*). ● *v.* **1** *tr.* screen from light. **2** *tr.* cover, moderate, or exclude the light of. **3** *tr.* darken, esp. with parallel pencil lines, to represent shadow etc. **4** *intr. & tr.* (often foll. by *away, off, into*) pass or change by degrees. □ **put in the shade** appear or be very superior to (a person or thing). □ **shadeless** *adj.* [Old English *sc(e)adu*, from Germanic]

shading /ˈʃeɪdɪŋ/ *n.* **1** the representation of light and shade, e.g. by pencilled lines, on a map or drawing. **2** the graduation of tones from light to dark to create a sense of depth.

shadoof /ʃəˈduːf/ *n.* a pole with a bucket and counterpoise used esp. in Egypt for raising water. [Egyptian Arabic *šādūf*]

shadow /ˈʃadəʊ/ *n. & v.* ● *n.* **1** shade or a patch of shade. **2** a dark figure projected by a body intercepting rays of light, often regarded as an appendage. **3** an inseparable attendant or companion. **4** a person secretly following another. **5** the slightest trace (*not the shadow of a doubt*). **6** a weak or insubstantial remnant or thing (*a shadow of his former self*). **7** (*attrib.*) *Brit.* denoting members of a political party in opposition holding responsibilities parallel to those of the government (*shadow Home Secretary*; *shadow Cabinet*). **8** the shaded part of a picture. **9** a substance used to colour the eyelids. **10** gloom or sadness. ● *v.tr.* **1** cast a shadow over. **2** secretly follow and watch the movements of. **3** accompany (a person) at work either as training or to obtain insight into a profession. □ **shadower** *n.* **shadowless** *adj.* [representing Old English *scead(u)we*, oblique case of *sceadu* SHADE]

shadow-boxing *n.* boxing against an imaginary opponent as a form of training.

shadowgraph /ˈʃadəʊɡrɑːf/ *n.* **1** an image or photograph made by means of X-rays; = RADIOGRAM 2. **2** a picture formed by a shadow cast on a lighted surface. **3** an image formed by light refracted differently by different densities of a fluid.

shadow theatre *n.* a display for an audience, in which shadows are watched on a translucent screen, projected from the puppets behind.

shadowy /ˈʃadəʊi/ *adj.* **1** like or having a shadow. **2** full of shadows. **3** vague, indistinct. □ **shadowiness** *n.*

shady /ˈʃeɪdi/ *adj.* (**shadier**, **shadiest**) **1** giving shade. **2** situated in shade. **3** (of a person or behaviour) disreputable; of doubtful honesty. □ **shadily** *adv.* **shadiness** *n.*

shaft /ʃɑːft/ *n. & v.* ● *n.* **1 a** an arrow or spear. **b** the long slender stem of these. **2** a remark intended to hurt or provoke (*a shaft of malice*; *shafts of wit*). **3** (foll. by *of*) **a** a ray (of light). **b** a bolt (of lightning). **4** the stem or handle of a tool, implement, etc. **5** a column, esp. between the base and capital. **6** a long narrow space, usu. vertical, for access to a mine, a lift in a building, for ventilation, etc. **7** a long and narrow part supporting or connecting or driving a part or parts of greater thickness etc. **8** each of the pair of poles between which a horse is harnessed to a vehicle. **9** the central stem of a feather. **10** *Mech.* a large axle or revolving bar transferring force by belts or cogs. **11** *slang* a penis. **12** *N. Amer. colloq.* harsh or unfair treatment. ● *v.tr.* **1** fit (a weapon, tool, or arrowhead) with a shaft. **2** *N. Amer. colloq.* treat unfairly. [Old English *scæft*, *sceaft*, from Germanic]

shafting /ˈʃɑːftɪŋ/ *n. Mech.* **1** a system of connected shafts for transmitting motion. **2** material from which shafts are cut.

shag[1] /ʃaɡ/ *n.* **1 a** a rough growth or mass of hair etc. **b** (*attrib.*) (of a carpet) with a long rough pile. **c** (*attrib.*) (of a pile) long and rough. **2** a coarse kind of cut tobacco. **3** a cormorant, esp. *Phalacrocorax aristotelis* of Europe and N. Africa, with greenish-black plumage and a curly crest. [Old English *sceacga*, related to Old Norse *skegg* 'beard', Old English *sceaga* 'coppice']

shag[2] /ʃaɡ/ *v. & n. Brit. coarse slang* ● *v.tr.* (**shagged**, **shagging**) **1** have sexual intercourse with. **2** (usu. in *passive*; often foll. by *out*) exhaust; tire out. ● *n.* an act of sexual intercourse. □ **shagger** *n.* (in sense 1 of *v.*; often as a term of abuse). [18th c.: origin unknown]

shaggy /ˈʃaɡi/ *adj.* (**shaggier**, **shaggiest**) **1** hairy, rough-haired. **2** unkempt. **3** (of the hair) coarse and abundant. **4** *Biol.* having a hairlike covering. □ **shaggy-dog story** a long rambling story amusing only by its being inconsequential. □ **shaggily** *adv.* **shagginess** *n.*

shagreen /ʃaˈɡriːn/ *n.* **1** a kind of untanned leather with a rough granulated surface. **2** a sharkskin rough with natural papillae, used for rasping and polishing. [variant of CHAGRIN in the sense 'rough skin']

shah /ʃɑː/ *n. hist.* a title of the former monarch of Iran. □ **shahdom** *n.* [Persian *šāh* from Old Persian *kšāyṯiya* 'king']

shaikh var. of SHEIKH.

shake /ʃeɪk/ *v. & n.* ● *v.* (*past* **shook** /ʃʊk/; *past part.* **shaken** /ˈʃeɪk(ə)n/) **1** *tr. & intr.* move forcefully or quickly up and down or to and fro. **2 a** *intr.* tremble or vibrate markedly. **b** *tr.* cause to do this. **3** *tr.* **a** agitate or shock. **b** *colloq.* upset the composure of. **4** *tr.* weaken or impair; make less convincing or firm or courageous (*shook his confidence*). **5** *intr.* (of a voice, note, etc.) make tremulous or rapidly alternating sounds; trill (*his voice shook with emotion*). **6** *tr.* brandish; make a threatening gesture with (one's fist, a stick, etc.). **7** *intr. colloq.* shake hands (*they shook on the deal*). **8** *tr.* esp. *US colloq.* = *shake off*. ● *n.* **1** the act or an instance of shaking; the process of being shaken. **2** a jerk or shock. **3** (in *pl.*; prec. by *the*) a fit of or tendency to trembling or shivering. **4** *Mus.* a trill. **5** = MILK SHAKE. □ **in two shakes (of a lamb's** or **dog's tail)** very quickly. **no great shakes** *colloq.* not very good or significant. **shake a person by the hand** = *shake hands*. **shake down 1** settle or cause to fall by shaking. **2** settle down. **3** become established; get into harmony with circumstances, surroundings, etc. **4** *N. Amer. slang* extort money from. **shake the dust off one's feet** depart indignantly or disdainfully. **shake hands** (often foll. by *with*) clasp right hands at meeting or parting, in reconciliation or congratulation, or over a concluded bargain. **shake one's head** turn one's head from side to side in refusal, denial, disapproval, or concern. **shake in one's shoes** tremble with apprehension. **shake a leg** *colloq.* **1** begin dancing. **2** make a start. **shake off 1** get rid of (something unwanted). **2** manage to evade (a person who is following or pestering one). **shake out 1** empty by shaking. **2** spread or open (a sail, flag, etc.) by shaking. **3** shed (personnel) as a result of reorganization. **shake up 1** mix (ingredients) by shaking. **2** restore to shape by shaking. **3** disturb or make uncomfortable. **4** rouse from lethargy, apathy, conventionality, etc. □ **shakeable** *adj.* (also **shakable**). [Old English *sc(e)acan*, from Germanic]

shakedown /'ʃeɪkdaʊn/ *n.* **1** a makeshift bed. **2** a period or process of adjustment or change. **3** esp. *US slang* a swindle; a piece of extortion. **4** (*attrib.*) *colloq.* denoting a voyage, flight, etc., to test a new ship, aircraft, etc., and its crew.

shaken *past part.* of SHAKE.

shake-out *n.* an upheaval or reorganization, esp. in a business and involving streamlining, closures, redundancies, etc.

shaker /'ʃeɪkə/ *n.* **1** a person or thing that shakes. **2** a container for shaking together the ingredients of cocktails etc. **3** (**Shaker**; *fem.* **Shakeress**) a member of an American religious sect living simply, in celibate mixed communities. □ **Shakerism** *n.* (in sense 3). [Middle English, from SHAKE: sense 3 from religious dances]

Shakespearean /ʃeɪk'spɪərɪən/ *adj.* & *n.* (also **Shakespearian**) ● *adj.* **1** of or relating to William Shakespeare, English dramatist d. 1616. **2** in the style of Shakespeare. ● *n.* a student of Shakespeare's works etc.

shake-up *n.* an upheaval or drastic reorganization.

shako /'ʃeɪkəʊ, 'ʃakəʊ/ *n.* (*pl.* **-os**) a cylindrical peaked military hat with a plume. [French *schako* via Hungarian *csákó* (*süveg*) 'peaked (cap)', from *csák* 'peak', from German *Zacken* 'spike']

shakuhachi /ʃakʊ'hatʃi/ *n.* (*pl.* **shakuhachis**) a Japanese bamboo flute. [Japanese, from *shaku*, a measure of length + *hachi* 'eight' (tenths)]

shaky /'ʃeɪki/ *adj.* (**shakier**, **shakiest**) **1** unsteady; apt to shake; trembling. **2** unsound, infirm (*a shaky hand*). **3** unreliable, wavering (*a shaky promise*; *got off to a shaky start*). □ **shakily** *adv.* **shakiness** *n.*

shale /ʃeɪl/ *n.* soft finely stratified rock that splits easily, consisting of consolidated mud or clay. □ **shaly** *adj.* [probably via German *Schale* from Old English *sc(e)alu*, related to Old Norse *skál* (see SCALE[2])]

shale oil *n.* oil obtained from bituminous shale.

shall /ʃal, ʃ(ə)l/ *v.aux.* (*3rd sing. present* **shall**; *archaic 2nd sing. present* **shalt** /ʃalt/; *past* **should** /ʃʊd, ʃəd/) (foll. by infin. without *to*, or *absol.*; present and past only in use) **1** (in the 1st person) expressing the future tense (*I shall return soon*) or (with *shall* stressed) emphatic intention (*I shall have a party*). **2** (in the 2nd and 3rd persons) expressing a strong assertion or command rather than a wish (cf. WILL[1]) (*you shall not catch me again*; *they shall go to the party*). **3** expressing a command or duty (*thou shalt not steal*; *they shall obey*). **4** (in 2nd-person questions) expressing an enquiry, esp. to avoid the form of a request (cf. WILL[1]) (*shall you go to France?*). □ **shall I?** do you want me to? [Old English *sceal*, from Germanic]

■ **Usage** There is considerable confusion about when to use *shall* and *will*. The traditional rule in standard British English is that *shall* is used for the first person singular and plural (*I* and *we*) to form the future tense, while *will* is used for the second and third persons (*you, he, she, it, they*), e.g. *I shall be late*; *She will not be there*. In informal usage, *I will* and *we will* are quite often used for the future tense, e.g. *We will try to help*, but this is unacceptable to some people. Conversely, *shall* is also used with *you* in polite questions (see sense 4 above), and this is quite acceptable.

When expressing a strong assertion or command the traditional rule is that *will* is used with the first person singular and plural, and *shall* for the second and third persons, e.g. *I will not tolerate this*; *You shall go to school*; *Competitors shall arrive by 8 a.m.* In practice, however, *shall* is often used for the first person singular and plural in emphatic contexts (e.g. *I shall have a new car*), and *will* for the second and third persons (e.g. *You will go to bed early*). These usages are now fully acceptable.

shallot /ʃə'lɒt/ *n.* an onion-like plant, *Allium ascalonicum*, with a cluster of small bulbs. [*eschalot* from French *eschalotte*, alteration of Old French *eschaloigne*: see SCALLION]

shallow /'ʃaləʊ/ *adj.*, *n.*, & *v.* ● *adj.* **1** of little depth. **2** superficial, trivial (*a shallow mind*). ● *n.* (often in *pl.*) a shallow place. ● *v.intr.* & *tr.* become or make shallow. □ **shallowly** *adv.* **shallowness** *n.* [Middle English, probably related to *schald*, Old English *sceald* SHOAL[2]]

shalom /ʃə'lɒm/ *n.* & *int.* a Jewish salutation at meeting or parting. [Hebrew *šālôm* 'peace']

shalt *archaic 2nd person sing.* of SHALL.

sham /ʃam/ *v.*, *n.*, & *adj.* ● *v.* (**shammed**, **shamming**) **1** *intr.* feign, pretend. **2** *tr.* **a** pretend to be. **b** simulate (*is shamming sleep*). ● *n.* **1** imposture, pretence. **2** a person or thing pretending or pretended to be what he or she or it is not. ● *adj.* pretended, counterfeit. □ **shammer** *n.* [perhaps northern dialect variant of SHAME]

shaman /'ʃamən, 'ʃeɪm-/ *n.* a person regarded as having access to the world of good and evil spirits, esp. among some peoples of northern Asia and North America. □ **shamanic** /ʃə'manɪk/ *adj.* **shamanism** *n.* **shamanist** *n.* & *adj.* **shamanistic** /-'nɪstɪk/ *adj.* [German *Schamane* & Russian *shaman* from Tungus *samán*]

shamateur /'ʃamətə, -tjʊə/ *n.* *Brit.* *derog.* a sports player who makes money from sporting activities though classed as an amateur. □ **shamateurism** *n.* [SHAM + AMATEUR]

shamble /'ʃamb(ə)l/ *v.* & *n.* ● *v.intr.* walk or run with a shuffling or awkward gait. ● *n.* a shambling gait. [probably from dialect *shamble* 'ungainly', perhaps from *shamble legs* with reference to straddling trestles: see SHAMBLES]

shambles /'ʃamb(ə)lz/ *n.pl.* (usu. treated as *sing.*) **1** *colloq.* a mess or muddle (*the room was a shambles*). **2** a butcher's slaughterhouse. **3** a scene of carnage. [pl. of *shamble* 'stool, stall' from Old English *sc(e)amul* via West Germanic from Latin *scamellum*, diminutive of *scamnum* 'bench']

shambolic /ʃam'bɒlɪk/ *adj.* *Brit.* *colloq.* chaotic, unorganized. [SHAMBLES, probably influened by SYMBOLIC]

shame /ʃeɪm/ *n.* & *v.* ● *n.* **1** a feeling of distress or humiliation caused by consciousness of the guilt or folly of oneself or an associate. **2** a capacity for experiencing this feeling, esp. as imposing a restraint on behaviour (*has no sense of shame*). **3** a state of disgrace, discredit, or intense regret. **4 a** a person or thing that brings disgrace etc. **b** a thing or action that is wrong or regrettable. ● *v.tr.* **1** bring shame on; make ashamed; put to shame. **2** (foll. by *into*, *out of*) force by shame (*was shamed into confessing*). □ **for shame!** a reproof to a person for not showing shame. **put to shame** disgrace or humiliate by revealing superior qualities etc. **shame on you!** you should be ashamed. **what a shame!** how unfortunate! [Old English *sc(e)amu*]

shamefaced /ʃeɪm'feɪst, 'ʃeɪm-/ *adj.* **1** showing shame. **2** bashful, diffident. □ **shamefacedly** /also -sɪdli/ *adv.* **shamefacedness** *n.* [16th-c. alteration of *shamefast*, by assimilation to FACE]

shameful /'ʃeɪmfʊl, -f(ə)l/ *adj.* **1** that causes or is worthy of shame. **2** disgraceful, scandalous.

□ **shamefully** *adv.* **shamefulness** *n.* [Old English *sc(e)amful* (as SHAME, -FUL)]

shameless /'ʃeɪmlɪs/ *adj.* **1** having or showing no sense of shame. **2** impudent. □ **shamelessly** *adv.* **shamelessness** *n.* [Old English *sc(e)amlēas* (as SHAME, -LESS)]

shammy /'ʃami/ *n.* (*pl.* **-ies**) (in full **shammy leather**) *colloq.* = CHAMOIS 2. [representing corrupted pronunciation]

shampoo /ʃam'pu:/ *n.* & *v.* ● *n.* **1** liquid or cream used to lather and wash the hair. **2** a similar substance for washing a car or carpet etc. **3** an act or instance of washing with shampoo. ● *v.tr.* (**shampoos, shampooed**) wash with shampoo. [Hindustani *chhāmpo*, imperative of *chhāmpnā* 'to press']

shamrock /'ʃamrɒk/ *n.* any of various plants with trifoliate leaves, esp. *Trifolium minus*, *T. repens*, or *Medicago lupulina*, used as the national emblem of Ireland. [Irish *seamróg* 'trefoil' (diminutive of *seamar* 'clover') + *og* 'young']

shamus /'ʃeɪməs/ *n. US slang* a detective. [20th c.: origin uncertain]

shandy /'ʃandi/ *n.* (*pl.* **-ies**) a drink of beer mixed with lemonade or ginger beer. [19th c.: origin unknown]

shanghai /ʃaŋ'hʌɪ/ *v.* & *n.* ● *v.tr.* (**shanghais, shanghaied, shanghaiing**) **1** force (a person) to be a sailor on a ship by using drugs or other trickery. **2** *colloq.* put into detention or an awkward situation by trickery. **3** *Austral.* & *NZ* shoot with a catapult. ● *n.* (*pl.* **shanghais**) *Austral.* & *NZ* a catapult. [*Shanghai*, a major seaport in China]

Shangri-La /ʃaŋgrɪ'lɑ:/ *n.* an imaginary paradise on earth. [the name of a hidden Tibetan valley in J. Hilton's *Lost Horizon* (1933)]

shank /ʃaŋk/ *n.* **1 a** the leg. **b** the lower part of the leg; the leg from knee to ankle. **c** the shin bone. **2 a** the lower part of an animal's foreleg. **b** *archaic* part of an animal's hind leg as a cut of meat. **c** *US* = SHIN *n.* 2. **3** a shaft or stem. **4 a** the long narrow part of a tool etc. joining the handle to the working end. **b** the stem of a key, spoon, anchor, etc. **c** the straight part of a nail or fish-hook. **5** the narrow middle of the sole of a shoe. □ **shanked** *adj.* (also in *comb.*). [Old English *sceanca*, from West Germanic]

shanks's pony *n.* (also **shanks's mare**) one's own legs as a means of conveyance.

shanny /'ʃani/ *n.* (*pl.* **-ies**) a long-bodied olive-green European marine fish, *Blennius pholis*. [19th c.: origin unknown: cf. 18th-c. *shan*]

shan't /ʃɑ:nt/ *contr.* shall not.

shantung /ʃan'tʌŋ/ *n.* soft undressed Chinese silk, usu. undyed. [*Shantung*, Chinese province, where it was originally made]

shanty[1] /'ʃanti/ *n.* (*pl.* **-ies**) **1** a hut or cabin. **2** a crudely built shack. [19th c., originally North American: perhaps from Canadian French *chantier* 'lumberjack's cabin, logging camp']

shanty[2] /'ʃanti/ *n.* (also **chanty**) (*pl.* **-ies**) (in full **sea shanty**) a song with alternating solo and chorus, of a kind originally sung by sailors while hauling ropes etc. [probably French *chantez*, imperative pl. of *chanter* 'sing': see CHANT]

shanty town *n.* a poor or depressed area of a town, consisting of shanties.

SHAPE /ʃeɪp/ *abbr.* Supreme Headquarters Allied Powers Europe.

shape /ʃeɪp/ *n.* & *v.* ● *n.* **1** the total effect produced by the outlines of a thing. **2** the external form or appearance of a person or thing. **3** a specific form or guise. **4** a description or sort or way (*not on offer in any shape or form*). **5** a definite or proper arrangement (*must get our ideas into shape*). **6 a** condition, as qualified in some way (*in good shape*; *in poor shape*). **b** (when unqualified) good condition (*back in shape*). **7** a person or thing as seen, esp. indistinctly or in the imagination (*a shape emerged from the mist*). **8** a mould or pattern. **9** *Brit.* a jelly etc. shaped in a mould. **10** a piece of material, paper, etc., made or cut in a particular form. ● *v.* **1** *tr.* give a certain shape or form to; fashion, create. **2** *tr.* (foll. by *to*) adapt or make conform. **3** *intr.* give signs of a future shape or development. **4** *tr.* frame mentally; imagine. **5** *intr.* assume or develop into a shape. **6** *tr.* direct (one's life, course, etc.). □ **lick** (or **knock**) **into shape** make presentable or efficient. **shape up 1** take a (specified) form. **2** show promise; make good progress. **shape up well** be promising. □ **shapable** *adj.* (also **shapeable**). **shaped** *adj.* (also in *comb.*). **shaper** *n.* [Old English *gesceap* 'creation', from Germanic]

shapeless /'ʃeɪplɪs/ *adj.* lacking definite or attractive shape. □ **shapelessly** *adv.* **shapelessness** *n.*

shapely /'ʃeɪpli/ *adj.* (**shapelier, shapeliest**) **1** well formed or proportioned. **2** of elegant or pleasing shape or appearance. □ **shapeliness** *n.*

shard /ʃɑ:d/ *n.* **1** a broken piece of pottery or glass etc. **2** = POTSHERD. **3** a fragment of volcanic rock. **4** the wing-case of a beetle. [Old English *sceard*: sense 4 from *shard-borne* (Shakespeare) = born in a shard (dialect, = cow-dung), wrongly taken as 'borne on shards']

share[1] /ʃɛ:/ *n.* & *v.* ● *n.* **1** a portion that a person receives from or gives to a common amount. **2 a** a part contributed by an individual to an enterprise or commitment. **b** a part received by an individual from this (*got a large share of the credit*). **3** part-proprietorship of property held by joint owners, esp. any of the equal parts into which a company's capital is divided entitling its owner to a proportion of the profits. ● *v.* **1** *tr.* get or have or give a share of. **2** *tr.* use or benefit from jointly with others. **3** *tr.* have in common (*I share your opinion*). **4** *intr.* have a share; be a sharer (*shall I share with you?*). **5** *intr.* (foll. by *in*) participate. **6** *tr.* (often foll. by *out*) *Brit.* **a** divide and distribute. **b** give away part of. □ **share and share alike** make an equal division. □ **shareable** *adj.* (also **sharable**). **sharer** *n.* [Old English *scearu* 'division' from Germanic: related to SHEAR]

share[2] /ʃɛ:/ *n.* = PLOUGHSHARE. [Old English *scear*, *scær*, from Germanic]

sharecropper /'ʃɛ:krɒpə/ *n.* esp. *US* a tenant farmer who gives a part of each crop as rent. □ **sharecrop** *v.tr.* & *intr.* (**-cropped, -cropping**).

share-farmer *n. Austral.* & *NZ* a tenant farmer who receives a share of the profits from the owner.

shareholder /'ʃɛ:həʊldə/ *n.* an owner of shares in a company. □ **shareholding** *n.*

share-out *n.* an act of sharing out; a distribution.

shareware /'ʃɛ:wɛ:/ *n. Computing* software that is available free of charge and often distributed informally for evaluation, after which a fee is requested for continued use.

sharia /ʃə'ri:ə/ *n.* the Muslim code of religious law. [Arabic *šarī'a*]

sharif /ʃə'ri:f/ *n.* (also **shereef, sherif**) **1** a descendant of Muhammad through his daughter Fatima, entitled to wear a green turban or veil. **2** a Muslim leader. [Arabic *šarīf* 'noble' from *šarafa* 'be exalted']

shark[1] /ʃɑ:k/ *n.* any of various large usu. voracious marine fish with a long body, cartilaginous skeleton, and prominent dorsal fin. [Middle English: origin unknown]

shark[2] /ʃɑ:k/ *n. colloq.* a person who unscrupulously exploits or swindles others. [16th c.: originally perhaps from German *Schurke* 'worthless rogue': influenced by SHARK[1]]

sharkskin /'ʃɑ:kskɪn/ *n.* **1** the rough scaly skin of a shark. **2** a smooth slightly lustrous fabric.

sharon fruit /'ʃɛ:r(ə)n, 'ʃar(ə)n/ *n.* a persimmon, esp. of an orange variety grown in Israel. [*Sharon*, a plain in Israel]

sharp /ʃɑ:p/ *adj., n., adv.,* & *v.* ● *adj.* **1** having an edge or point able to cut or pierce. **2** tapering to a point or edge. **3** abrupt, steep, angular (*a sharp fall*; *a sharp* *turn*). **4** well defined, clean-cut. **5 a** severe or intense (*has a sharp temper*). **b** (of food or its flavour) pungent, acid. **c** keen (*a sharp appetite*). **d** (of a frost) severe, hard. **6** (of a voice or sound) shrill and piercing. **7** (of sand etc.) composed of angular grains. **8** (of words, temper, a person, etc.) harsh or acrimonious (*had a sharp tongue*). **9** (of a person) acute; quick to perceive or comprehend. **10** *derog.* quick to take advantage; artful, unscrupulous, dishonest. **11** vigorous or brisk. **12** *Mus.* **a** above the normal pitch. **b** (of a key) having a sharp or sharps in the signature. **c** (as **C sharp, F sharp**, etc.), a semitone higher than C, F, etc. **13** *colloq.* stylish or flashy with regard to dress. ● *n.* **1** *Mus.* **a** a note raised a semitone above natural pitch. **b** the sign (♯) indicating this. **2** *colloq.* a swindler or cheat. **3** a fine sewing-needle. ● *adv.* **1** punctually (*at nine o'clock sharp*). **2** suddenly, abruptly, promptly (*pulled up sharp*). **3** at a sharp angle. **4** *Mus.* above the true pitch (*sings sharp*). ● *v.* **1** *intr. archaic* cheat or swindle at cards etc. **2** *tr. US Mus.* make sharp. ▫ **sharply** *adv.* **sharpness** *n.* [Old English *sc(e)arp*, from Germanic]

sharpen /ˈʃɑːp(ə)n/ *v.tr. & intr.* make or become sharp. ▫ **sharpener** *n.*

sharp end *n.* **1** *Brit. joc.* the bow of a ship. **2** *colloq.* the scene of direct action or decision.

sharper /ˈʃɑːpə/ *n.* a swindler, esp. at cards.

sharp-featured *adj.* (of a person) having well-defined facial features.

sharpish /ˈʃɑːpɪʃ/ *adj. & adv. colloq.* ● *adj.* fairly sharp. ● *adv.* **1** fairly sharply. **2** quite quickly.

sharp practice *n.* dishonest or barely honest dealings.

sharp-set *adj.* **1** set with a sharp edge. **2** hungry.

sharpshooter /ˈʃɑːpʃuːtə/ *n.* a skilled marksman. ▫ **sharpshooting** *n. & adj.*

sharp-tongued *adj.* harsh or cutting in speech; abrasive.

sharp-witted *adj.* keenly perceptive or intelligent. ▫ **sharp-wittedly** *adv.* **sharp-wittedness** *n.*

shashlik /ˈʃaʃlɪk/ *n.* (in Asia and E. Europe) a kebab of mutton and garnishings. [Russian *shashlyk*, ultimately from Turkish *şiş* 'spit, skewer': cf. SHISH KEBAB]

Shasta daisy /ˈʃastə/ *n.* a European plant, *Leucanthemum maximum*, with large daisy-like flowers. [Mount *Shasta* in California]

Shastra /ˈʃɑːstrə/ *n.* (often in *pl.*) any of the sacred writings of the Hindus. [Sanskrit *śāstra*]

shat *past* and *past part.* of SHIT.

shatter /ˈʃatə/ *v.* **1** *tr. & intr.* break suddenly in pieces. **2** *tr.* severely damage or utterly destroy (*shattered hopes*). **3** *tr.* greatly upset or discompose. **4** *tr.* (usu. as **shattered** *adj.*) *colloq.* exhaust. ▫ **shatterer** *n.* **shattering** *adj.* **shatteringly** *adv.* **shatter-proof** *adj.* [Middle English, related to SCATTER]

shave /ʃeɪv/ *v. & n.* ● *v.tr.* (*past part.* **shaved** or (as *adj.*) **shaven**) **1** remove (bristles or hair) from the face etc. with a razor. **2** (also *absol.*) remove bristles or hair with a razor from the face etc. of (a person) or from (a part of the body). **3 a** reduce by a small amount. **b** take (a small amount) away from. **4** cut thin slices from the surface of (wood etc.) to shape it. **5** pass close to without touching; miss narrowly. ● *n.* **1** an act of shaving or the process of being shaved. **2** a close approach without contact. **3** a narrow miss or escape; = CLOSE SHAVE. **4** a tool for shaving wood etc. [Old English *sc(e)afan* (sense 4 of noun from Old English *sceafa*), from Germanic]

shaveling /ˈʃeɪvlɪŋ/ *n. archaic* **1** a shaven person. **2** a monk, friar, or priest.

shaven see SHAVE.

shaver /ˈʃeɪvə/ *n.* **1** a person or thing that shaves. **2** an electric razor. **3** *colloq.* a young lad.

Shavian /ˈʃeɪvɪən/ *adj. & n.* ● *adj.* of or in the manner of G. B. Shaw, Irish-born dramatist d. 1950, or his ideas. ● *n.* an admirer of Shaw. [*Shavius*, Latinized form of *Shaw*]

shaving /ˈʃeɪvɪŋ/ *n.* **1** a thin strip cut off the surface of wood etc. **2** (*attrib.*) used in shaving the face (*shaving-cream*).

Shavuoth /ʃəˈvuːəs, ʃɑːvʊˈɒt/ *n.* (also **Shavuot**) the Jewish Pentecost. [Hebrew *šāḇûʻôṯ*, = weeks, with reference to the weeks between Passover and Pentecost]

shaw /ʃɔː/ *n.* esp. *Brit.* the stalks and leaves of potatoes, turnips, etc. [perhaps = SHOW *n.*]

shawl /ʃɔːl/ *n.* a piece of fabric, usu. rectangular and often folded into a triangle, worn over the shoulders or head or wrapped round a baby. ▫ **shawled** *adj.* [Urdu from Persian *šāl*, probably from *Shāliāt*, a town in India]

shawl collar *n.* a rolled collar extended down the front of a garment without lapel notches.

shawm /ʃɔːm/ *n. Mus.* a medieval double-reed wind instrument with a sharp penetrating tone. [Middle English from Old French *chalemie*, *chalemel*, *chalemeaus* (pl.), ultimately via Latin *calamus* from Greek *kalamos* 'reed']

shchi /ʃtʃiː/ *n.* a Russian cabbage soup. [Russian]

she /ʃiː/ *pron. & n.* ● *pron.* (*obj.* **her**; *poss.* **her**; *pl.* **they**) **1** the woman or girl or female animal previously named or in question. **2** a thing regarded as female, e.g. a vehicle or ship. **3** *Austral.* & *NZ colloq.* it; the state of affairs (*she'll be right*). ● *n.* **1** a female; a woman. **2** (in *comb.*) female (*she-goat*). [Middle English *scæ*, *sche*, etc., probably a phonetic development of Old English fem. personal pronoun *heō*, accusative *hīe*]

s/he *pron.* a written representation of 'he or she' used to indicate both sexes.

shea /ʃiː, ˈʃiːə/ *n.* a W. African tree, *Vitellaria paradoxa*, bearing nuts containing a large amount of fat. [from a West African name]

shea-butter *n.* a butter made from the fat of the shea nut.

sheading /ˈʃiːdɪŋ/ *n.* each of the six administrative divisions of the Isle of Man. [SHED[1] + -ING[1]]

sheaf /ʃiːf/ *n. & v.* ● *n.* (*pl.* **sheaves** /ʃiːvz/) a group of things held lengthways together, esp. a bundle of cornstalks tied after reaping, or a collection of papers. ● *v.tr.* make into sheaves. [Old English *scēaf* from Germanic (as SHOVE)]

shealing var. of SHIELING.

shear /ʃɪə/ *v. & n.* ● *v.* (*past* **sheared**, *archaic* **shore** /ʃɔː/; *past part.* **shorn** /ʃɔːn/ or **sheared**) **1** *tr.* clip the wool off (a sheep etc.). **2** *tr.* remove or take off by cutting. **3** *tr.* cut with scissors or shears etc. **4** *tr.* (foll. by *of*) **a** strip bare. **b** deprive. **5** *tr. & intr.* (often foll. by *off*) distort or be distorted, or break, from a structural strain. ● *n.* **1** *Mech.* & *Geol.* a strain produced by pressure in the structure of a substance, when its layers are laterally shifted in relation to each other. **2** (in *pl.*) (also **pair of shears** *sing.*) a large clipping or cutting instrument shaped like scissors for use in gardens etc. ▫ **shearer** *n.* [Old English *sceran*, from Germanic]

shearling /ˈʃɪəlɪŋ/ *n.* **1** a sheep that has been shorn once. **2** wool from a shearling.

shearwater /ˈʃɪəwɔːtə/ *n.* **1** any long-winged seabird of the family Procellariidae, related to petrels, often flying low over the surface of the water. **2** = SKIMMER 4.

sheath /ʃiːθ/ *n.* (*pl.* **sheaths** /ʃiːðz, ʃiːθs/) **1** a close-fitting cover, esp. for the blade of a knife or sword. **2** a condom. **3** *Bot.*, *Anat.*, & *Zool.* an enclosing case or tissue. **4** the protective covering round an electric cable. **5** a woman's close-fitting dress. ▫ **sheathless** *adj.* [Old English *scǣth*, *scēath*]

sheathe /ʃiːð/ *v.tr.* **1** put into a sheath. **2** encase; protect with a sheath. [Middle English, from SHEATH]

sheathing /ˈʃiːðɪŋ/ *n.* a protective casing or covering.

sheath knife *n.* a dagger-like knife carried in a sheath.

sheave[1] /ʃiːv/ *v.tr.* make into sheaves.

sheave[2] /ʃiːv/ *n.* a grooved wheel in a pulley-block etc., for a rope to run on. [Middle English, ultimately from Germanic]

sheaves *pl.* of SHEAF.

shebang /ʃɪ'bæŋ/ *n. N. Amer. slang* **1** a matter or affair (esp. *the whole shebang*). **2** a shed or hut. [19th c.: origin unknown]

shebeen /ʃɪ'bi:n/ *n.* (esp. in Ireland, Scotland, and S. Africa) an unlicensed house selling alcoholic liquor. [Anglo-Irish *síbín* from *séibe* 'mugful']

shed[1] /ʃɛd/ *n. & v.* ● *n.* **1** a one-storeyed structure usu. of wood for storage or shelter for animals etc., or as a workshop. **2** a large roofed structure often with one side or more sides open, for storing or maintaining machinery, vehicles, etc. (*bicycle shed*). **3** *Austral. & NZ* an open-sided building for shearing sheep or milking cattle. ● *v.tr.* (**shedded, shedding**) (usu. in *passive*) park (rolling stock, buses, etc.) in a depot. [apparently a variant of SHADE]

shed[2] /ʃɛd/ *v.tr.* (**shedding**; *past* and *past part.* **shed**) **1** let or cause to fall off (*trees shed their leaves*). **2** take off (clothes). **3** reduce (an electrical power load) by disconnection etc. **4** cause to fall or flow (*shed blood*; *shed tears*). **5** disperse, diffuse, radiate (*shed light*). **6** (of a business) reduce its number of (jobs or employees) through redundancy, natural wastage, etc. □ **shed light on** see LIGHT[1]. [Old English *sc(e)adan*, from Germanic]

she'd /ʃi:d, ʃɪd/ *contr.* **1** she had. **2** she would.

shedder /'ʃɛdə/ *n.* **1** a person or thing that sheds. **2** a female salmon after spawning.

she-devil *n.* a malicious or spiteful woman.

shedhand /'ʃɛdhand/ *n. Austral. & NZ* an unskilled assistant in a shearing shed.

sheen /ʃi:n/ *n.* **1** a gloss or lustre on a surface. **2** radiance, brightness. □ **sheeny** *adj.* [obsolete *sheen* 'beautiful, resplendent' from Old English *scēne*: sense assimilated to SHINE]

sheep /ʃi:p/ *n.* (*pl.* same) **1** any ruminant mammal of the genus *Ovis* with a thick woolly coat, esp. kept in flocks for its wool or meat, and proverbial for its timidity. **2** a bashful, defenceless, or easily-led person. **3** (usu. in *pl.*) **a** a member of a minister's congregation. **b** a parishioner. □ **separate the sheep from the goats** divide into superior and inferior groups (cf. Matt. 25:33). □ **sheeplike** *adj.* [Old English *scēp, scǣp, scēap*]

sheep-dip *n.* **1** a preparation for cleansing sheep of vermin or preserving their wool. **2** the place where sheep are dipped in this.

sheepdog /'ʃi:pdɒg/ *n.* **1** a dog trained to guard and herd sheep. **2** a dog of various breeds suitable for this.

sheepfold /'ʃi:pfəʊld/ *n.* an enclosure for penning sheep.

sheepish /'ʃi:pɪʃ/ *adj.* **1** bashful, shy, reticent. **2** embarrassed through shame. □ **sheepishly** *adv.* **sheepishness** *n.*

sheep-run *n.* an extensive sheepwalk, esp. in Australia.

sheep's-bit *n.* a plant, *Jasione montana*, resembling a scabious.

sheepshank /'ʃi:pʃaŋk/ *n.* a knot used to shorten a rope temporarily.

sheepskin /'ʃi:pskɪn/ *n.* **1** a garment or rug of sheep's skin with the wool on. **2** leather from a sheep's skin used in bookbinding.

sheepwalk /'ʃi:pwɔ:k/ *n. Brit.* a tract of land on which sheep are pastured.

sheer[1] /ʃɪə/ *adj. & adv.* ● *adj.* **1** no more or less than; mere, unqualified, absolute (*sheer luck*; *sheer determination*). **2** (of a cliff or ascent etc.) perpendicular; very steep. **3** (of a textile) very thin; diaphanous. ● *adv.* **1** directly, outright. **2** perpendicularly. □ **sheerly** *adv.* **sheerness** *n.* [Middle English *schere*, probably via dialect *shire* 'pure, clear' from Old English *scīr*, from Germanic]

sheer[2] /ʃɪə/ *v. & n.* ● *v.intr.* **1** esp. *Naut.* swerve or change course. **2** (foll. by *away, off*) go away, esp. from a person or topic one dislikes or fears. ● *n. Naut.* a deviation from a course. [perhaps from Middle Low German *scheren* = SHEAR *v.*]

sheer[3] /ʃɪə/ *n.* the upward slope of a ship's lines towards the bow and stern. [probably from SHEAR *n.*]

sheerlegs /'ʃɪəlɛgz/ *n.pl.* (treated as *sing.*) a hoisting apparatus made from poles joined at or near the top and separated at the bottom for masting ships, installing engines, etc. [*sheer* (variant of SHEAR *n.*) + LEG]

sheet[1] /ʃi:t/ *n. & v.* ● *n.* **1** a large rectangular piece of cotton or other fabric, used esp. in pairs as inner bedclothes. **2 a** a broad usu. thin flat piece of material (e.g. paper or metal). **b** (*attrib.*) made in sheets (*sheet steel*). **3** a wide continuous surface or expanse of water, ice, flame, falling rain, etc. **4** a set of unseparated postage stamps. **5** *derog.* a newspaper, esp. a disreputable one. **6** a complete piece of paper of the size in which it was made, for printing and folding as part of a book. ● *v.* **1** *tr.* provide or cover with sheets. **2** *tr.* form into sheets. **3** *intr.* (of rain etc.) fall in sheets. [Old English *scēte, scīete*, from Germanic]

sheet[2] /ʃi:t/ *n.* **1** a rope or chain attached to the lower corner of a sail for securing or controlling it. **2** (in *pl.*) the space at the bow or stern of an open boat. [Middle English from Old English *scēata*, Old Norse *skaut* (as SHEET[1])]

sheet anchor *n.* **1** a second anchor for use in emergencies. **2** a person or thing depended on in the last resort.

sheet bend *n.* a method of temporarily fastening one rope through the loop of another.

sheeting /'ʃi:tɪŋ/ *n.* material for making bed linen.

sheet lightning *n.* lightning with its brightness diffused by reflection in clouds etc.

sheet metal *n.* metal formed into thin sheets by rolling, hammering, etc.

sheet music *n.* **1** printed music, as opposed to performed or recorded music and books about music. **2** music published in single or interleaved sheets, not bound.

sheikh /ʃeɪk, ʃi:k/ *n.* (also **shaikh, sheik**) **1** a chief or head of an Arab tribe, family, or village. **2** a Muslim leader. □ **sheikhdom** *n.* [ultimately from Arabic *šayḵ* 'old man, sheikh', from *šāḵa* 'be or grow old']

sheila /'ʃi:lə/ *n. Austral. & NZ slang* a girl or young woman. [originally *shaler* (of unknown origin): assimilated to the name *Sheila*]

shekel /'ʃɛk(ə)l/ *n.* **1** the chief monetary unit of modern Israel. **2** *hist.* a silver coin and unit of weight used in ancient Israel and the Middle East. **3** (in *pl.*) *colloq.* money; riches. [Hebrew *šeḳel* from *šāḳal* 'weigh']

shelduck /'ʃɛldʌk/ *n.* (*pl.* same or **shelducks**; *masc.* **sheldrake**, *pl.* same or **sheldrakes**) any large bright-plumaged gooselike duck of the genus *Tadorna*, esp. *T. tadorna* of Eurasian and N. African coasts. [Middle English, probably from dialect *sheld* 'pied' (related to Middle Dutch *schillede* 'variegated') + DUCK[1], DRAKE]

shelf[1] /ʃɛlf/ *n.* (*pl.* **shelves** /ʃɛlvz/) **1 a** a thin flat piece of wood or metal etc. projecting from a wall, or as part of a unit, used to support books etc. **b** the flat bottom surface of a recess in a wall etc. used similarly. **2 a** a projecting horizontal ledge in a cliff face etc. **b** a reef or sandbank under water. **c** = CONTINENTAL SHELF. □ **on the shelf 1** (of a woman) past the age when she might expect to be married. **2** (esp. of a retired person) no longer active or of use. □ **shelfful** *n.* (*pl.* **-fuls**). **shelf-like** *adj.* [Middle English from (Middle) Low Germsn *schelf*, related to Old English *scylfe* 'partition', *scylf* 'crag']

shelf[2] /ʃɛlf/ *n. & v. Austral. slang* ● *n.* (*pl.* **shelfs**) an informer. ● *v.tr.* inform upon. [from SHELF[1]]

shelf-life *n.* (*pl.* **-lives**) the length of time for which a stored item of food etc. remains usable.

shelf mark *n.* a notation on a book showing its place in a library.

shelf room *n.* available space on a shelf.

shell /ʃɛl/ *n. & v.* ● *n.* **1 a** the hard outer case of many marine molluscs (*cockleshell*). **b** the esp. hard but fragile outer covering of a bird's, reptile's, etc. egg. **c** the usu. hard outer case of a nut-kernel, seed, etc. **d** the carapace of a tortoise, turtle, etc. **e** the wing-case or pupa-case of many insects etc. **2 a** an explosive projectile or bomb for use in a big gun or mortar. **b** a hollow metal or paper case used as a container for fireworks, explosives, cartridges, etc. **c** *US* a cartridge. **3** a mere semblance or outer form without substance. **4** any of several things resembling a shell in being an outer case, esp.: **a** a light racing boat. **b** a hollow pastry case. **c** the metal framework of a vehicle body etc. **d** the walls of an unfinished or gutted building, ship, etc. **e** an inner or roughly made coffin. **f** a building shaped like a conch. **g** the handguard of a sword. **5** a group of electrons in an atom with almost equal energy. **6** *Computing* = SHELL PROGRAM. ● *v.* **1** *tr.* remove the shell or pod from. **2** *tr.* bombard (a town, troops, etc.) with shells. **3** *tr.* provide or cover with a shell or shells. **4** *intr.* (usu. foll. by *off*) (of metal etc.) come off in scales. **5** *intr.* (of a seed etc.) be released from a shell. □ **come out of one's shell** cease to be shy; become communicative. **shell out** (also *absol.*) *colloq.* **1** pay (money). **2** hand over (a required sum). □ **shelled** *adj.* **shell-less** *adj.* **shell-like** *adj.* **shellproof** *adj.* (in sense 2a of *n.*). **shelly** *adj.* [Old English *sc(i)ell* from Germanic: related to SCALE[1]]

she'll /ʃiːl, ʃɪl/ *contr.* she will; she shall.

shellac /ʃəˈlak/ *n.* & *v.* ● *n.* lac resin in thin flakes, used for making varnish (cf. LAC[1]). ● *v.tr.* (**shellacked, shellacking**) **1** varnish with shellac. **2** *US slang* defeat or thrash soundly. [SHELL + LAC[1], translation of French *laque en écailles* 'lac in thin plates']

shellback /ˈʃɛlbak/ *n. slang* an old sailor.

shell-bit *n.* a gouge-shaped boring bit.

shell company *n.* a company quoted on the Stock Exchange, although not trading, and used to make takeover bids etc.

shell egg *n.* an egg still in its shell, not dried etc.

shellfire /ˈʃɛlfʌɪə/ *n.* the firing of shells, esp. repeatedly.

shellfish /ˈʃɛlfɪʃ/ *n.* (*pl.* same) **1** an aquatic shelled mollusc, e.g. an oyster, winkle, etc. **2** a crustacean, e.g. a crab, shrimp, etc.

shell game *n. N. Amer.* **1** = THIMBLERIG. **2** (esp. in phr. **play a shell game**) *colloq.* a confidence trick; a deception.

shell-heap *n. hist.* a kitchen midden.

shell-jacket *n.* an army officer's tight-fitting undress jacket reaching to the waist.

shell-lime *n.* fine-quality lime produced by burning seashells.

shell-money *n.* shells used as a medium of exchange, e.g. wampum.

shell-mound *n.* = SHELL-HEAP.

shell-out *n.* **1** the act of shelling out. **2** a game of snooker etc. played by three or more people.

shell pink *n.* & *adj..* ● *n.* a delicate pale pink. ● *adj.* (hyphenated when *attrib.*) of this colour.

shell program *n. Computing* a program which provides an interface between the user and the operating system.

shell-shock *n.* a nervous breakdown or other psychological disturbance resulting from exposure to battle. □ **shell-shocked** *adj.*

shell suit *n.* a tracksuit with a soft lining and a weatherproof nylon outer 'shell', used for leisure wear.

shell-work *n.* ornamentation consisting of shells cemented on to wood etc.

Shelta /ˈʃɛltə/ *n.* an ancient secret language used by Irish tinkers, gypsies, etc. and based largely on altered Irish or Gaelic words. [19th c.: origin unknown]

shelter /ˈʃɛltə/ *n.* & *v.* ● *n.* **1** anything serving as a shield or protection from danger, bad weather, etc. **2 a** a place of refuge provided esp. for the homeless etc. **b** *N. Amer.* an animal sanctuary. **3** a shielded condition; protection (*took shelter under a tree*). ● *v.* **1** *tr.* act or serve as shelter to; protect; conceal; defend (*sheltered them from the storm*; *had a sheltered upbringing*). **2** *intr.* & *refl.* find refuge; take cover (*sheltered under a tree*; *sheltered themselves behind the wall*). □ **shelterer** *n.* **shelterless** *adj.* [16th c.: perhaps via obsolete *sheltron* 'phalanx' from Old English *scieldtruma* (as SHIELD, *truma* 'troop')]

shelter belt *n.* a line of trees etc. planted to protect crops from the wind.

sheltered accommodation *n.* accommodation for the elderly or handicapped in which people live in private independent units but with access to some shared facilities and a warden, doctor, etc.

sheltie /ˈʃɛlti/ *n.* (also **shelty**) (*pl.* **-ies**) a Shetland pony or sheepdog. [probably representing Old Norse *Hjalti* 'Shetlander', as pronounced in Orkney]

shelve[1] /ʃɛlv/ *v.tr.* **1 a** abandon or defer (a plan etc.). **b** remove (a person) from active work etc. **2** put (books etc.) on a shelf. **3** fit (a cupboard etc.) with shelves. □ **shelver** *n.* **shelving** *n.* [*shelves*, pl. of SHELF[1]]

shelve[2] /ʃɛlv/ *v.intr.* (of ground etc.) slope in a specified direction (*land shelved away to the horizon*). [perhaps via *shelvy* 'having underwater reefs' from *shelve* 'a ledge', from SHELVE[1]]

shelves *pl.* of SHELF[1].

shemozzle /ʃɪˈmɒz(ə)l/ *n.* (also **schemozzle**) *slang* **1** a brawl or commotion. **2** a muddle. [Yiddish, suggested by Late Hebrew *šel-lō'-mazzāl* 'of no luck']

shenanigan /ʃɪˈnanɪg(ə)n/ *n.* (esp. in *pl.*) *colloq.* **1** high-spirited behaviour; nonsense. **2** trickery; dubious manoeuvres. [19th c.: origin unknown]

Sheol /ˈʃiːəʊl, ˈʃiːɒl/ *n.* the Hebrew underworld abode of the dead. [Hebrew *šᵉ'ôl*]

shepherd /ˈʃɛpəd/ *n.* & *v.* ● *n.* **1** (*fem.* **shepherdess** /ˈʃɛpədɪs, ʃɛpəˈdɛs/) a person employed to tend sheep, esp. at pasture. **2** a member of the clergy etc. who cares for and guides a congregation. ● *v.tr.* **1 a** tend (sheep etc.) as a shepherd. **b** guide (followers etc.). **2** marshal or drive (a crowd etc.) like sheep. [Old English *scēaphierde* (as SHEEP, HERD)]

shepherd dog *n.* a sheepdog.

shepherd's crook *n.* a staff with a hook at one end used by shepherds.

shepherd's needle *n.* a white-flowered umbelliferous plant, *Scandix pecten-veneris*, with spiny fruit, common as a weed of cornfields.

shepherd's pie *n.* a dish of minced meat under a layer of mashed potato.

shepherd's plaid *n.* **1** a small black and white check pattern. **2** woollen cloth with this pattern.

shepherd's purse *n.* a white-flowered cruciferous plant, *Capsella bursa-pastoris*, with triangular or cordate pods, common as a weed.

sherardize /ˈʃɛrədʌɪz/ *v.tr.* (also **-ise**) coat (iron or steel) with zinc by heating in contact with zinc dust. [from the name of *Sherard* Cowper-Coles, English inventor d. 1936]

Sheraton /ˈʃɛrət(ə)n/ *n.* (often *attrib.*) a style of furniture introduced in England *c.*1790, with delicate and graceful forms. [from the name of T. *Sheraton*, English furniture-maker d. 1806]

sherbet /ˈʃəːbət/ *n.* **1 a** *Brit.* a flavoured sweet effervescent powder or drink. **b** *N. Amer.* a water ice. **2** a cooling drink of sweet diluted fruit juices esp. in Arab countries. **3** *Austral. joc.* beer. [Turkish *şerbet*, Persian *šerbet* from Arabic *šarba* 'drink', from *šariba* 'to drink': cf. SHRUB[2], SYRUP]

sherd /ʃəːd/ *n.* = POTSHERD. [variant of SHARD]

shereef (also **sherif**) var. of SHARIF.

sheriff /ˈʃɛrɪf/ *n.* **1** *Brit.* **a** (also **High Sheriff**) the chief executive officer of the Crown in a county, administering justice etc. **b** an honorary officer elected annually in some towns. **2** *US* an elected officer in a county, responsible for keeping the peace. □ **sheriffalty** *n.* (*pl.* **-ies**). **sheriffdom** *n.* **sheriffhood** *n.* **sheriffship** *n.* [Old English *scīr-gerēfa* (as SHIRE, REEVE[1])]

sheriff court *n. Sc.* a county court.

sheriff-depute *n. Sc.* the chief judge of a county or district.

Sherpa /ˈʃɜːpə/ *n.* (*pl.* same or **Sherpas**) a member of a Himalayan people living on the borders of Nepal and Tibet renowned for their skill in mountaineering. [native name]

sherry /ˈʃɛri/ *n.* (*pl.* **-ies**) **1** a fortified wine originally from southern Spain. **2** a glass of this. [earlier *sherris* from Spanish (*vino de*) *Xeres* (now Jerez de la Frontera) in Andalusia]

sherry cobbler see COBBLER 2.

sherry glass *n.* a small wineglass used for sherry.

she's /ʃiːz, ʃɪz/ *contr.* **1** she is. **2** she has.

Shetlander /ˈʃɛtləndə/ *n.* a native of the Shetland Islands, NNE of the mainland of Scotland.

Shetland lace /ˈʃɛtlənd/ *n.* openwork woollen trimming.

Shetland pony /ˈʃɛtlənd/ *n.* **1** a pony of a small hardy rough-coated breed. **2** this breed.

Shetland sheepdog /ˈʃɛtlənd/ *n.* **1** a small dog of a collie-like breed. **2** this breed.

Shetland wool /ˈʃɛtlənd/ *n.* a fine loosely twisted wool from Shetland sheep.

sheva var. of SCHWA.

shew *archaic* var. of SHOW.

shewbread /ˈʃəʊbrɛd/ *n.* twelve loaves that were displayed in a Jewish temple and renewed each sabbath.

Shia /ˈʃɪə/ *n. & adj.* (also **Shi'a**) ● *n.* (*pl.* same or **Shias**) **1** one of the two main branches of Islam, esp. in Iran, that rejects the first three Sunni caliphs and regards Ali, the fourth caliph, as Muhammad's first successor (cf. SUNNI). **2** a Shi'ite. ● *adj.* of or relating to Shia. [Arabic *šīʿa* 'party' (of Ali, Muhammad's cousin and son-in-law)]

shiatsu /ʃɪˈatsuː/ *n.* a kind of therapy of Japanese origin, in which pressure is applied with the thumbs, palms, etc. to certain points of the body. [Japanese, = finger pressure]

shibboleth /ˈʃɪbəlɛθ/ *n.* a custom, doctrine, phrase, etc., distinguishing a particular class or group of people. [Middle English from Hebrew *šibbōleṯ* 'ear of corn', used as a test of nationality for its difficult pronunciation (Judg. 12:6)]

shicer /ˈʃʌɪsə/ *n. Austral.* **1** *Mining* an unproductive claim or mine. **2** *slang* **a** a swindler, welsher, or cheat. **b** a worthless thing; a failure. [German *Scheisser* 'contemptible person']

shicker /ˈʃɪkə/ *adj.* (also **shickered** /ˈʃɪkəd/) *Austral. & NZ slang* drunk. [Yiddish *shiker* from Hebrew *šikkôr*, from *šākar* 'be drunk']

shied *past* and *past part.* of SHY².

shield /ʃiːld/ *n. & v.* ● *n.* **1** **a** esp. *hist.* a piece of armour of esp. metal, carried on the arm or in the hand to deflect blows from the head or body. **b** a thing serving to protect (*insurance is a shield against disaster*). **2** a thing resembling a shield, esp.: **a** a trophy in the form of a shield. **b** a protective plate or screen in machinery etc. **c** a shieldlike part of an animal, esp. a shell. **d** a similar part of a plant. **e** *Geol.* a large rigid area of the earth's crust, usu. of Precambrian rock, which has been unaffected by later orogenic episodes. **f** *US* a police officer's shield-shaped badge. **3** *Heraldry* a stylized representation of a shield used for displaying a coat of arms etc. ● *v.tr.* protect or screen, esp. from blame or lawful punishment. □ **shieldless** *adj.* [Old English *sc(i)eld* from a Germanic word probably meaning 'board']

shield bug *n.* a broad flat hemipteran bug, esp. of the family Pentatomidae.

shield fern *n.* **1** any common fern of the genus *Polystichum*, with shield-shaped indusia. **2** = BUCKLER 2.

shield volcano *n. Geol.* a broad domed volcano with gently sloping sides.

shieling /ˈʃiːlɪŋ/ *n.* (also **shealing**) *Sc.* **1** a roughly constructed hut originally esp. for pastoral use. **2** pasture for cattle. [Scots *shiel* 'hut': of unknown origin]

shift /ʃɪft/ *v. & n.* ● *v.* **1** *intr. & tr.* change or move or cause to change or move from one position to another. **2** *tr. Brit.* remove, esp. with effort (*washing won't shift the stains*). **3** *Brit. slang* **a** *intr.* hurry (*we'll have to shift!*). **b** *tr.* consume (food or drink) hastily or in bulk. **c** *tr. colloq.* sell, esp. quickly, in large quantities, or dishonestly. **4** *intr.* contrive or manage as best one can. **5** *N. Amer.* **a** *tr.* change (gear) in a vehicle. **b** *intr.* change gear. **6** *intr.* (of cargo) get shaken out of place. **7** *intr. archaic* be evasive or indirect. ● *n.* **1** **a** the act or an instance of shifting. **b** the substitution of one thing for another; a rotation. **2** **a** a relay of workers (*the night shift*). **b** the time for which they work (*an eight-hour shift*). **3** **a** a device, stratagem, or expedient. **b** a dodge, trick, or evasion. **4** **a** a woman's straight unwaisted dress. **b** *archaic* a loose-fitting undergarment. **5** a displacement of spectral lines (see also RED SHIFT). **6** (also **sound shift**) a systematic change in pronunciation as a language evolves. **7** a key on a keyboard used to switch between lower and upper case etc. **8** *Bridge* **a** a change of suit in bidding. **b** *US* a change of suit in play. **9** the positioning of successive rows of bricks so that their ends do not coincide. **10** *N. Amer.* **a** a gear lever in a motor vehicle. **b** a mechanism for this. □ **make shift** manage or contrive; get along somehow (*made shift without it*). **shift for oneself** rely on one's own efforts. **shift one's ground** take up a new position in an argument etc. **shift off** get rid of (responsibility etc.) to another. □ **shiftable** *adj.* **shifter** *n.* [Old English *sciftan* 'arrange, divide', etc., from Germanic]

shiftless /ˈʃɪftlɪs/ *adj.* lacking resourcefulness; lazy; inefficient. □ **shiftlessly** *adv.* **shiftlessness** *n.*

shift work *n.* work comprising a relay of periods of duty.

shifty /ˈʃɪfti/ *adj.* (**shiftier**, **shiftiest**) *colloq.* not straightforward; evasive; deceitful. □ **shiftily** *adv.* **shiftiness** *n.*

shigella /ʃɪˈgɛlə/ *n.* any bacterium of the genus *Shigella*, some of which cause dysentery. [modern Latin, from the name of K. *Shiga*, Japanese bacteriologist d. 1957 + diminutive suffix]

shih-tzu /ʃiːˈtsuː/ *n.* **1** a dog of a breed with long silky erect hair and short legs. **2** this breed. [Chinese *shizi* 'lion']

shiitake /ʃɪˈtɑːkeɪ, ʃiː-/ *n.* (in full **shiitake mushroom**) an edible mushroom, *Lentinus edodes*, cultivated in Japan and China on oak logs etc. [Japanese, from *shii* a kind of oak and *take* 'mushroom']

Shi'ite /ˈʃiːʌɪt/ *n. & adj.* (also **Shiite**) ● *n.* an adherent of the Shia branch of Islam. ● *adj.* of or relating to Shia. □ **Shi'ism** /ˈʃiːɪz(ə)m/ *n.* (also **Shiism**).

shikar /ʃɪˈkɑː/ *n. Anglo-Ind.* hunting. [Urdu from Persian *šikār*]

shiksa /ˈʃɪksə/ *n. offens.* (used by Jews) a gentile girl or woman. [Yiddish *shikse* from Hebrew *šiqṣâ*, from *sheqeṣ* 'detested thing' + fem. suffix *-â*]

shill /ʃɪl/ *n. N. Amer.* a person employed to decoy or entice others into buying, gambling, etc. [probably from earlier *shillaber*, of unknown origin]

shillelagh /ʃɪˈleɪlə, -li/ *n.* a thick stick of blackthorn or oak used in Ireland esp. as a weapon. [*Shillelagh* in Co. Wicklow, Ireland]

shilling /ˈʃɪlɪŋ/ *n.* **1** *hist.* a former British coin and monetary unit equal to one-twentieth of a pound or twelve pence. **2** a monetary unit in Kenya, Tanzania, and Uganda. □ **take the King's** (or **Queen's**) **shilling** *Brit. hist.* enlist as a soldier (formerly a soldier was paid a shilling on enlisting). [Old English *scilling*, from Germanic]

shilling-mark *n. hist.* = SOLIDUS 1.

shilly-shally /ˈʃɪlɪʃali/ *v., adj., & n.* ● *v.intr.* (**-ies, -ied**) hesitate to act or choose; be undecided; vacillate. ● *adj.* vacillating. ● *n.* indecision; vacillation. □ **shilly-**

shallyer *n.* (also **-shallier**). [originally *shill I, shall I,* reduplication of *shall I?*]

shim /ʃɪm/ *n. & v.* ● *n.* a thin strip of material used in machinery etc. to make parts fit. ● *v.tr.* (**shimmed, shimming**) fit or fill up with a shim. [18th c.: origin unknown]

shimmer /ˈʃɪmə/ *v. & n.* ● *v.intr.* shine with a tremulous or faint diffused light. ● *n.* such a light. ▫ **shimmeringly** *adv.* **shimmery** *adj.* [Old English *scymrian* from Germanic: related to SHINE]

shimmy /ˈʃɪmi/ *n. & v.* ● *n.* (*pl.* **-ies**) **1** *hist.* a kind of ragtime dance in which the whole body is shaken. **2** *archaic colloq.* = CHEMISE. **3** an abnormal vibration of esp. the front wheels of a motor vehicle. ● *v.intr.* (**-ies, -ied**) **1 a** *hist.* dance a shimmy. **b** move in a similar manner. **2** shake or vibrate abnormally. [20th c.: origin uncertain]

shin /ʃɪn/ *n. & v.* ● *n.* **1** the front of the leg below the knee. **2** a cut of beef from the lower part of the animal's leg. ● *v.tr. &* (usu. foll. by *up, down*) *intr.* (**shinned, shinning**) climb quickly by clinging with the arms and legs. [Old English *sinu*]

shin bone *n.* = TIBIA.

shindig /ˈʃɪndɪg/ *n. colloq.* **1** a festive, esp. noisy, party. **2** = SHINDY 1. [probably from SHINDY]

shindy /ˈʃɪndi/ *n.* (*pl.* **-ies**) *colloq.* **1** a brawl, disturbance, or noise (*kicked up a shindy*). **2** = SHINDIG 1. [perhaps alteration of SHINTY]

shine /ʃʌɪn/ *v. & n.* ● *v.* (*past* and *past part.* **shone** /ʃɒn/ or **shined**) **1** *intr.* emit or reflect light; be bright; glow (*the lamp was shining*; *his face shone with gratitude*). **2** *intr.* (of the sun, a star, etc.) not be obscured by clouds etc.; be visible. **3** *tr.* cause (a lamp etc.) to shine. **4** *tr.* (*past* and *past part.* **shined**) make bright; polish (*shined his shoes*). **5** *intr.* be brilliant in some respect; excel (*does not shine in conversation*; *is a shining example*). ● *n.* **1** light; brightness, esp. reflected. **2** a high polish; lustre. **3** *US* the act or an instance of shining esp. shoes. ▫ **shine up to** *US* seek to ingratiate oneself with. **take the shine out of 1** spoil the brilliance or newness of. **2** throw into the shade by surpassing. **take a shine to** *colloq.* take a fancy to; like. ▫ **shiningly** *adv.* [Old English *scīnan*, from Germanic]

shiner /ˈʃʌɪnə/ *n.* **1** a thing that shines. **2** *colloq.* a black eye. **3** *US* any of various small silvery freshwater fish, esp. of the genus *Notropis*. **4** (usu. in *pl.*) *slang* **a** *archaic* money. **b** a jewel.

shingle[1] /ˈʃɪŋg(ə)l/ *n.* (in *sing.* or *pl.*) small rounded pebbles, esp. on a seashore. ▫ **shingly** *adj.* [Middle English: origin uncertain]

shingle[2] /ˈʃɪŋg(ə)l/ *n. & v.* ● *n.* **1** a rectangular wooden tile used on roofs, spires, or esp. walls. **2** *archaic* **a** shingled hair. **b** the act of shingling hair. **3** *N. Amer.* a small signboard, esp. of a doctor, lawyer, etc. ● *v.tr.* **1** roof or clad with shingles. **2** *archaic* **a** cut (a woman's hair) short. **b** cut the hair of (a person or head) in this way. [Middle English, apparently from Latin *scindula*, earlier *scandula* 'a split piece of wood']

shingles /ˈʃɪŋg(ə)lz/ *n.pl.* (usu. treated as *sing.*) an acute painful inflammation of the nerve ganglia, with a skin eruption often forming a girdle around the middle of the body, caused by the same virus as chicken-pox. Also called *herpes zoster*. [Middle English via medieval Latin *cingulus* from Latin *cingulum* 'girdle', from *cingere* 'gird']

shin-guard *n.* = SHIN-PAD.

shinny /ˈʃɪni/ *v.intr.* (**-ies, -ied**) (usu. foll. by *up, down*) *N. Amer. colloq.* shin (up or down a tree etc.).

shin-pad *n.* a protective pad for the shins, worn when playing football etc.

Shinto /ˈʃɪntəʊ/ *n.* a religion incorporating the worship of ancestors and nature spirits, until 1945 the state religion of Japan. ▫ **Shintoism** *n.* **Shintoist** *n.* [Japanese from Chinese *shen dao* 'way of the gods']

shinty /ˈʃɪnti/ *n.* (*pl.* **-ies**) *Brit.* **1** a game like hockey played with a ball and curved sticks, and taller goalposts. **2** a stick or ball used in shinty. [earlier *shinny*, apparently from the cry used in the game *shin ye, shin you, shin t' ye*, of unknown origin]

shiny /ˈʃʌɪni/ *adj.* (**shinier, shiniest**) **1** having a shine; glistening; polished; bright. **2** (of clothing, esp. the seat of trousers etc.) having the nap worn off. ▫ **shinily** *adv.* **shininess** *n.* [SHINE]

ship /ʃɪp/ *n. & v.* ● *n.* **1 a** any large seagoing vessel (cf. BOAT *n.* 2). **b** a sailing vessel with a bowsprit and three, four, or five square-rigged masts. **2** *US* an aircraft. **3** a spaceship. **4** *colloq.* a boat, esp. a racing boat. ● *v.* (**shipped, shipping**) **1** *tr.* put, take, or send away (goods, passengers, sailors, etc.) on board ship. **2** *tr.* **a** take in (water) over the side of a ship, boat, etc. **b** take (oars) from the rowlocks and lay them inside a boat. **c** fix (a rudder etc.) in its place on a ship etc. **d** step (a mast). **3** *intr.* **a** take ship; embark. **b** (of a sailor) take service on a ship (*shipped for Africa*). **4** *tr.* deliver (goods) to a forwarding agent for conveyance. ▫ **ship off 1** send or transport by ship. **2** *colloq.* send (a person) away. **ship a sea** *Brit.* be flooded by a wave. **take ship** embark. **when a person's ship comes home** (or **in**) when a person's fortune is made. ▫ **shipless** *adj.* **shippable** *adj.* [Old English *scip*, *scipian*, from Germanic]

-ship /ʃɪp/ *suffix* forming nouns denoting: **1** a quality or condition (*friendship*; *hardship*). **2** status, office, or honour (*authorship*; *lordship*). **3** a tenure of office (*chairmanship*). **4** a skill in a certain capacity (*workmanship*). **5** the collective individuals of a group (*membership*). [Old English *-scipe* etc., from Germanic]

shipboard /ˈʃɪpbɔːd/ *n.* (usu. *attrib.*) used or occurring on board a ship (*a shipboard romance*). ▫ **on shipboard** on board ship.

ship-breaker *n.* a contractor who breaks up old ships.

shipbroker /ˈʃɪpbrəʊkə/ *n.* an agent in shipping goods and insuring ships.

shipbuilder /ˈʃɪpbɪldə/ *n.* a person, company, etc., that constructs ships. ▫ **shipbuilding** *n.*

ship burial *n. Archaeol.* burial in a wooden ship under a mound.

ship canal *n.* a canal large enough for ships to pass inland.

ship chandler *n.* (also **ship's chandler**) a dealer in cordage, canvas, etc.

ship-fever *n.* typhus.

shiplap /ˈʃɪplap/ *v. & n.* ● *v.tr.* fit (boards) together for cladding etc. so that each overlaps the one below. ● *n.* such cladding.

shipload /ˈʃɪpləʊd/ *n.* a quantity of goods forming a cargo.

shipmaster /ˈʃɪpmɑːstə/ *n.* a ship's captain.

shipmate /ˈʃɪpmeɪt/ *n.* a fellow member of a ship's crew.

shipment /ˈʃɪpm(ə)nt/ *n.* **1** an amount of goods shipped; a consignment. **2** the act or an instance of shipping goods etc.

ship money *n. hist.* a tax raised to provide ships for the navy in the 17th c.

ship of the desert *n.* the camel.

ship of the line *n. hist.* a ship of sufficient size for the front line of battle.

shipowner /ˈʃɪpəʊnə/ *n.* a person owning a ship or ships or shares in ships.

shipper /ˈʃɪpə/ *n.* a person or company that sends or receives goods by ship, or *US* by land or air. [Old English *scipere* (as SHIP)]

shipping /ˈʃɪpɪŋ/ *n.* **1** the act or an instance of shipping goods etc. **2** ships, esp. the ships of a country, port, etc.

shipping agent *n.* a person acting for a ship or ships at a port etc.

shipping-articles *n.pl.* = SHIP'S ARTICLES.

shipping-bill *n. Brit.* a manifest of goods shipped.

shipping-master *n. Brit.* an official presiding at the signing of ship's articles, paying off of seamen, etc.

shipping-office *n.* the office of a shipping agent or shipping master.

ship-rigged *adj.* square-rigged.

ship's articles *n.pl.* the terms on which seamen take service on a ship.

ship's biscuit *n. hist.* a hard coarse kind of biscuit kept and eaten on board ship.

ship's boat *n.* a small boat carried on board a ship.

ship's chandler var. of SHIP CHANDLER.

ship's company *n.* a ship's crew.

ship's corporal see CORPORAL[1] 2.

shipshape /'ʃɪpʃeɪp/ *adv. & predic.adj.* in good order; trim and neat.

ship's husband *n.* an agent appointed by the owners to see to the provisioning of a ship in port.

ship's papers *n.pl.* documents establishing the ownership, nationality, nature of the cargo, etc., of a ship.

ship-to-shore *adj. & n.* ● *adj.* from a ship to land. ● *n.* a radio-telephone for such use.

shipway /'ʃɪpweɪ/ *n.* a slope on which a ship is built and down which it slides to be launched.

shipworm /'ʃɪpwə:m/ *n.* = TEREDO.

shipwreck /'ʃɪprɛk/ *n. & v.* ● *n.* **1 a** the destruction of a ship by a storm, foundering, etc. **b** a ship so destroyed. **2** (often foll. by *of*) the destruction of hopes, dreams, etc. ● *v.* **1** *tr.* inflict shipwreck on (a ship, a person's hopes, etc.). **2** *intr.* suffer shipwreck.

shipwright /'ʃɪprʌɪt/ *n.* **1** a shipbuilder. **2** a ship's carpenter.

shipyard /'ʃɪpjɑ:d/ *n.* a place where ships are built, repaired, etc.

shiralee /'ʃɪrəli:/ *n. Austral.* a tramp's swag or bundle. [19th c.: origin unknown]

shire /'ʃʌɪə/ *n. Brit.* **1** a county. **2** **(the Shires)** **a** a group of English counties with names ending or formerly ending in *-shire*, extending NE from Hampshire and Devon. **b** the midland counties of England. **c** the fox-hunting district of mainly Leicestershire and Northamptonshire. **3** *Austral.* a rural area with its own elected council. [Old English *scīr*, Old High German *scīra* 'care, official charge': origin unknown]

-shire /ʃə, ʃɪə/ *suffix* forming the names of counties (*Derbyshire*; *Hampshire*).

shire county *n.* (in the UK) a non-metropolitan county (in existence since 1974).

shire-horse *n.* a heavy powerful type of draught horse bred chiefly in the midland counties of England.

shirk /ʃə:k/ *v. & n.* ● *v.tr.* (also *absol.*) shrink from; avoid; get out of (duty, work, responsibility, fighting, etc.). ● *n.* a person who shirks. □ **shirker** *n.* [obsolete *shirk* 'sponger', perhaps from German *Schurke* 'scoundrel']

shirr /ʃə:/ *n. & v.* ● *n.* **1** two or more rows of esp. elastic gathered threads in a garment etc. forming smocking. **2** elastic webbing. ● *v.tr.* **1** gather (material) with parallel threads. **2** *US* bake (eggs) without shells. □ **shirring** *n.* [19th c.: origin unknown]

shirt /ʃə:t/ *n.* **1** a man's upper-body garment of cotton etc., having a collar, sleeves, and esp. buttons down the front, and often worn under a jacket or sweater. **2** a similar garment worn by a woman; a blouse. **3** = NIGHTSHIRT. □ **keep one's shirt on** *colloq.* keep one's temper. **lose one's shirt** *colloq.* lose all one's possessions. **put one's shirt on** *Brit. colloq.* bet all one has on; be sure of. **the shirt off one's back** *colloq.* one's last remaining possessions. □ **shirted** *adj.* **shirting** *n.* **shirtless** *adj.* [Old English *scyrte*, corresponding to Old Norse *skyrta* (cf. SKIRT), from Germanic: related to SHORT]

shirt blouse *n.* = SHIRT 2.

shirt-dress *n.* = SHIRTWAISTER.

shirt-front *n.* the breast of a shirt, esp. of a stiffened evening shirt.

shirtsleeve /'ʃə:tsli:v/ *n.* (usu. in *pl.*) the sleeve of a shirt. □ **in shirtsleeves** wearing a shirt with no jacket etc. over it.

shirt-tail *n.* the lower curved part of a shirt below the waist.

shirtwaist /'ʃə:tweɪst/ *n.* esp. *US* a woman's blouse resembling a shirt.

shirtwaister /'ʃə:tweɪstə, -'weɪstə/ *n.* a woman's dress with a bodice like a shirt. [SHIRT, WAIST]

shirty /'ʃə:ti/ *adj.* **(shirtier, shirtiest)** *Brit. colloq.* angry; annoyed. □ **shirtily** *adv.* **shirtiness** *n.*

shish kebab /ʃɪʃ kɪ'bab/ *n.* a dish of pieces of marinated meat and vegetables cooked and served on skewers. [Turkish *şiş kebabı*, from *şiş* 'skewer', KEBAB 'roast meat']

shit /ʃɪt/ *v., n., & int. coarse slang* ● *v.intr. & tr.* **(shitting**; *past* and *past part.* **shitted** or **shit** or **shat** /ʃat/) expel faeces from the body or cause (faeces etc.) to be expelled. ● *n.* **1** faeces. **2** an act of defecating. **3** a contemptible or worthless person or thing. **4** rubbish; nonsense. **5** an intoxicating drug, esp. cannabis. ● *int.* an exclamation of disgust, anger, etc. □ **in the shit** in trouble; in a difficult situation. **not give a shit** not care at all. **up shit creek** in a predicament. [Old English *scitte* (*n.*), from Germanic]

shitbag /ʃɪtbag/ *n.* (also **shithead** /-hɛd/) *coarse slang* a contemptible or worthless person.

shite /ʃʌɪt/ *n. & int. coarse slang* = SHIT *n. & int.*

shithouse /'ʃɪthaʊs/ *n. coarse slang* **1** a lavatory. **2** a contemptible place.

shitless /'ʃɪtlɪs/ *predic.adj. coarse slang* □ **be scared shitless** be extremely frightened.

shit-scared *predic.adj. coarse slang* terrified.

shitty /'ʃɪti/ *adj.* **(shittier, shittiest)** *coarse slang* **1** disgusting, contemptible. **2** covered with excrement.

Shiva var. of SIVA.

shivaree esp. *US* var. of CHARIVARI.

shiver[1] /'ʃɪvə/ *v. & n.* ● *v.intr.* **1** tremble with cold, fear, etc. **2** suffer a quick trembling movement of the body; shudder. ● *n.* **1** a momentary shivering movement. **2** (in *pl.*; prec. by *the*) an attack of shivering, esp. from fear or horror (*got the shivers in the dark*). □ **shiverer** *n.* **shiveringly** *adv.* **shivery** *adj.* [Middle English *chivere*, perhaps from *chavele* 'chatter' (as JOWL[1])]

shiver[2] /'ʃɪvə/ *n. & v.* ● *n.* (esp. in *pl.*) each of the small pieces into which esp. glass is shattered when broken; a splinter. ● *v.tr. & intr.* break into shivers. □ **shiver my timbers** a reputed piratical curse. [Middle English *scifre*, related to Old High German *scivaro* 'splinter', from Germanic]

shivoo /ʃɪ'vu:/ *n. Austral. colloq.* a party or celebration. [19th c. from earlier *shiveau*, of unknown origin]

shoal[1] /ʃəʊl/ *n. & v.* ● *n.* **1** a great number of fish swimming together (cf. SCHOOL[2]). **2** esp. *Brit.* a multitude; a crowd (*shoals of letters*). ● *v.intr.* (of fish) form shoals. [probably readoption of Middle Dutch *schōle* SCHOOL[2]]

shoal[2] /ʃəʊl/ *n., v., & adj.* ● *n.* **1 a** an area of shallow water. **b** a submerged sandbank visible at low water. **2** (esp. in *pl.*) hidden danger or difficulty. ● *v.* **1** *intr.* (of water) get shallower. **2** *tr.* (of a ship etc.) move into a shallower part of (water). ● *adj. archaic* or *Sc. & N. Amer. dial.* (of water) shallow. □ **shoaly** *adj.* [Old English *sceald* from Germanic: related to SHALLOW]

shoat /ʃəʊt/ *n. US* a young pig, esp. newly weaned. [Middle English, of unknown origin: cf. West Flemish *schote*]

shock[1] /ʃɒk/ *n. & v.* ● *n.* **1** a violent collision, impact, tremor, etc. **2** a sudden and disturbing effect on the emotions, physical reactions, etc. (*the news was a great shock*). **3** an acute state of prostration following a wound, pain, etc., esp. when much blood is lost (*in shock*). **4** = ELECTRIC SHOCK. **5** a disturbance causing instability in an organization, monetary system, etc. **6** esp. *N. Amer.* = SHOCK ABSORBER. ● *v.* **1** *tr.* **a** affect with shock; horrify; outrage; disgust; sadden. **b** (*absol.*) cause shock. **2** *tr.* (esp. in *passive*) affect with an electric or pathological shock. **3** *intr.* experience shock (*I don't shock easily*). **4** *intr. archaic* collide violently. □ **shockable** *adj.* **shockability** /-ˈbɪlɪti/ *n.* [French *choc*, *choquer*, of unknown origin]

shock² /ʃɒk/ *n.* & *v.* ● *n.* a group of usu. twelve corn-sheaves stood up with their heads together in a field. ● *v.tr.* arrange (corn) in shocks. [Middle English, perhaps from Old English]

shock³ /ʃɒk/ *n.* (usu. foll. by *of*) an unkempt or shaggy mass of hair. [cf. obsolete *shock(-dog)*, earlier *shough*, 'shaggy-haired poodle']

shock absorber *n.* a device on a vehicle etc. for absorbing shocks, vibrations, etc.

shock-brigade *n.* a body of esp. voluntary workers in the former USSR engaged in an especially arduous task.

shock cord *n.* **1** heavy elasticated cord designed to absorb shock. **2** a length of this.

shocker /ˈʃɒkə/ *n. colloq.* **1** a shocking, horrifying, unacceptable, etc. person or thing. **2** *hist.* a sordid or sensational novel etc. **3** *Brit.* a shock absorber.

shocking /ˈʃɒkɪŋ/ *adj.* & *adv.* ● *adj.* **1** causing indignation or disgust. **2** *Brit. colloq.* very bad (*shocking weather*). ● *adv. colloq.* shockingly; extremely (*shocking bad manners*). □ **shockingly** *adv.* **shockingness** *n.*

shocking pink *adj.* & *n.* ● *n.* a vibrant shade of pink. ● *adj.* of this colour.

shockproof /ˈʃɒkpruːf/ *adj.* resistant to the effects of (esp. physical) shock.

shock stall *n.* excessive strain produced by air resistance on an aircraft approaching the speed of sound.

shock tactics *n.pl.* **1** sudden and violent action. **2** *Mil.* a massed cavalry charge.

shock therapy *n.* (also **shock treatment**) *Psychol.* a method of treating depressive patients by electric shock or drugs inducing coma and convulsions.

shock troops *n.pl.* troops specially trained for assault.

shock wave *n.* a sharp change of pressure in a narrow region travelling through air etc. caused by explosion or by a body moving faster than sound.

shock-workers *n.pl.* = SHOCK-BRIGADE.

shod *past* and *past part.* of SHOE.

shoddy /ˈʃɒdi/ *adj.* & *n.* ● *adj.* (**shoddier**, **shoddiest**) **1** trashy; shabby; poorly made. **2** counterfeit. ● *n.* (*pl.* **-ies**) **1 a** an inferior cloth made partly from the shredded fibre of old woollen cloth. **b** such fibre. **2** any thing of shoddy quality. □ **shoddily** *adv.* **shoddiness** *n.* [19th c.: originally dialect, origin unknown]

shoe /ʃuː/ *n.* & *v.* ● *n.* **1** either of a pair of protective foot-coverings of leather, plastic, etc., having a sturdy sole and not reaching above the ankle. **2** a metal rim nailed to the hoof of a horse etc.; a horseshoe. **3** anything resembling a shoe in shape or use, esp.: **a** a drag for a wheel. **b** = BRAKE SHOE. **c** a socket. **d** a ferrule, esp. on a sledge-runner. **e** a step (for a mast). **f** a box from which cards are dealt in casinos at baccarat etc. ● *v.tr.* (**shoes**, **shoeing**; *past* and *past part.* **shod** /ʃɒd/) **1** fit (esp. a horse etc.) with a shoe or shoes. **2** protect (the end of a pole etc.) with a metal shoe. **3** (as **shod** *adj.*) (in *comb.*) having shoes etc. of a specified kind (*dry-shod*; *roughshod*). □ **be in a person's shoes** be in his or her situation, difficulty, etc. **dead men's shoes** property or a position etc. coveted by a prospective successor. **if the shoe fits** *N. Amer.* = *if the cap fits* (see CAP). **where the shoe pinches** where one's difficulty or trouble is. □ **shoeless** *adj.* [Old English *scōh*, *scōg(e)an*, from Germanic]

shoebill /ˈʃuːbɪl/ *n.* (also **shoe-billed stork**) = WHALE-HEADED STORK.

shoeblack /ˈʃuːblak/ *n.* esp. *Brit.* a person who cleans the shoes of passers-by for payment.

shoebox /ˈʃuːbɒks/ *n.* **1** a box for packing shoes. **2** *colloq.* a very small space or dwelling.

shoe-buckle *n.* a buckle worn as ornament or as a fastening on a shoe.

shoehorn /ˈʃuːhɔːn/ *n.* & *v.* ● *n.* a curved piece of horn, metal, etc., for easing the heel into a shoe. ● *v.tr.* force into an inadequate space.

shoelace /ˈʃuːleɪs/ *n.* a cord for lacing up shoes.

shoe leather *n.* leather for shoes, esp. for the soles when worn through by walking.

shoemaker /ˈʃuːmeɪkə/ *n.* a maker of boots and shoes. □ **shoemaking** *n.*

shoeshine /ˈʃuːʃʌɪn/ *n.* esp. *N. Amer.* a polish given to shoes.

shoestring /ˈʃuːstrɪŋ/ *n.* **1** a shoelace. **2** *colloq.* a small esp. inadequate amount of money (*living on a shoestring*). **3** (*attrib.*) barely adequate; precarious (*a shoestring majority*).

shoe-tree *n.* a shaped block for keeping a shoe in shape when not worn.

shofar /ˈʃəʊfə/ *n.* (*pl.* **shofroth** /ˈʃəʊfrəʊt/) a ram's-horn trumpet used by Jews in religious ceremonies and as an ancient battle-signal. [Hebrew *šôpār*, pl. *šôpārôṯ*]

shogun /ˈʃəʊgʊn/ *n. hist.* any of a succession of hereditary commanders-in-chief in feudal Japan whose regime dominated Japanese polity from 1192–1867. □ **shogunate** /-nət/ *n.* [Japanese, from Chinese *jiang jun* 'general']

shone *past* and *past part.* of SHINE.

shonky /ˈʃɒŋki/ *adj.* & *n. Austral. slang* ● *adj.* (**shonkier**, **shonkiest**) unreliable, dishonest. ● *n.* (also **shonk**) a person engaged in shady business activities. [perhaps English dialect *shonk* 'smart']

shoo /ʃuː/ *int.* & *v.* ● *int.* an exclamation used to frighten away birds, children, etc. ● *v.* (**shoos**, **shooed**) **1** *intr.* utter the word 'shoo'. **2** *tr.* (usu. foll. by *away*) drive (birds etc.) away by shooing. [imitative]

shoo-in *n. N. Amer.* something easy or certain to succeed.

shook¹ /ʃʊk/ *past* of SHAKE. ● *predic.adj. colloq.* **1** (foll. by *up*) emotionally or physically disturbed; upset. **2** (foll. by *on*) *Austral.* & *NZ* keen on; enthusiastic about (*not too shook on the English climate*).

shook² /ʃʊk/ *n. US* a set of staves and headings for a cask, ready for fitting together. [18th c.: origin unknown]

shoot /ʃuːt/ *v.*, *n.*, & *int.* ● *v.* (*past* and *past part.* **shot** /ʃɒt/) **1** *tr.* **a** cause (a gun, bow, etc.) to fire. **b** discharge (a bullet, arrow, etc.) from a gun, bow, etc. **c** kill or wound (a person, animal, etc.) with a bullet, arrow, etc. from a gun, bow, etc. **2** *intr.* discharge a gun etc., esp. in a specified way (*shoots well*). **3** *tr.* send out, discharge, propel, etc., esp. violently or swiftly (*shot out the contents*; *shot a glance at his neighbour*). **4** *intr.* (often foll. by *out*, *along*, *forth*, etc.) come or go swiftly or vigorously. **5** *intr.* **a** (of a plant etc.) put forth buds etc. **b** (of a bud etc.) appear. **6** *intr.* **a** hunt game etc. with a gun. **b** (usu. foll. by *over*) shoot game over an estate etc. **7** *tr.* shoot game in or on (coverts, an estate, etc.). **8** *tr.* film or photograph (a scene, film, etc.). **9** esp. *Football* **a** *intr.* take a shot at the goal. **b** *tr.* score (a goal). **10** *tr.* (of a boat) sweep swiftly down or under (a bridge, rapids, falls, etc.). **11** *tr.* move (a door bolt) to fasten or unfasten a door etc. **12** *tr.* let (rubbish, a load, etc.) fall or slide from a container, lorry, etc. **13** *intr.* **a** (usu. foll. by *through*, *up*, etc.) (of a pain) pass with a stabbing sensation. **b** (of part of the body) be intermittently painful. **14** *intr.* (often foll. by *out*) project abruptly (*the mountain shoots out against the sky*). **15** *tr.* (often foll. by *up*) *slang* inject esp. oneself with (a drug). **16** *tr. N. Amer. colloq.* **a** play a game of (craps, pool, etc.). **b** throw (a die or dice). **17** *tr. Golf colloq.* make (a specified score) for a round or hole. **18** *tr. colloq.* pass (traffic lights at red). **19** *tr.* plane (the edge of a board) accurately. **20** *intr. Cricket* (of a ball) dart along the ground after pitching. **21** *intr.* (in *imper.*) used to demand a reply, information, etc. (*I'm listening, shoot!*). ● *n.* **1** the act or an instance of shooting. **2 a** a young branch or sucker. **b** the new growth of a plant. **3** *Brit.* **a** a hunting party, expedition, etc. **b** land shot over for game. **4** = CHUTE¹. **5** a rapid in a stream. ● *int.*

N. Amer. slang euphem. an exclamation of disgust, anger, etc. (see SHIT). ◻ **shoot ahead** come quickly to the front of competitors etc. **shoot one's bolt** see BOLT[1]. **shoot down 1** kill (a person) by shooting. **2** cause (an aircraft, its pilot, etc.) to crash by shooting. **3** argue effectively against (a person, argument, etc.). **shoot it out** *slang* engage in a decisive gun battle. **shoot a line** *Brit. slang* talk pretentiously. **shoot one's mouth off** *slang* talk too much or indiscreetly. **shoot through** *Austral. & NZ slang* depart; escape, abscond. **shoot up 1** grow rapidly, esp. (of a person) grow taller. **2** rise suddenly. **3** terrorize (a district) by indiscriminate shooting. **4** *slang* = sense 15 of *v.* **the whole shoot** *Brit.* = *the whole shooting match* (see SHOOTING). ◻ **shootable** *adj.* [Old English *scēotan* from Germanic: related to SHEET[1], SHOT[1], SHUT]

shooter /'ʃu:tə/ *n.* **1** a person or thing that shoots. **2 a** (in *comb.*) a gun or other device for shooting (*pea-shooter*; *six-shooter*). **b** *slang* a pistol etc. **3** a player who shoots or is able to shoot a goal in football, netball, etc. **4** *Cricket* a ball that shoots. **5** a person who throws a die or dice.

shooting /'ʃu:tɪŋ/ *n. & adj.* ● *n.* **1** the act or an instance of shooting. **2 a** the right of shooting over an area of land. **b** an estate etc. rented to shoot over. ● *adj.* moving, growing, etc. quickly (*a shooting pain in the arm*). ◻ **the whole shooting match** *colloq.* everything.

shooting box *n. Brit.* a lodge used by sportsmen in the shooting season.

shooting brake *n.* (also **shooting break**) *Brit.* an estate car.

shooting coat *n.* (also **shooting jacket**) a coat designed to be worn when shooting game.

shooting gallery *n.* a place used for shooting at targets with rifles etc.

shooting iron *n.* esp. *US colloq.* a firearm.

shooting range *n.* a ground with butts for rifle practice.

shooting star *n.* a small meteor moving rapidly and burning up on entering the earth's atmosphere.

shooting stick *n.* a walking stick with a handle that unfolds to form a seat.

shooting war *n.* a war in which there is shooting (opp. COLD WAR, WAR OF NERVES, etc.).

shoot-out *n. colloq.* **1** a decisive gun battle. **2** (in full **penalty shoot-out**) *Football* a tie-breaker decided by each side taking a specified number of penalty shots.

shop /ʃɒp/ *n. & v.* ● *n.* **1** a building, room, etc., for the retail sale of goods or services (*chemist's shop*; *betting shop*). **2** *colloq.* an act of going shopping (*our big weekly shop*). **3** a place in which manufacture or repairing is done; a workshop (*engineering shop*). **4** a profession, trade, business, etc., esp. as a subject of conversation (*talk shop*). **5** *colloq.* an institution, establishment, place of business, etc. ● *v.* (**shopped**, **shopping**) **1** *intr.* **a** go to a shop or shops to buy goods. **b** *US* = WINDOW-SHOP. **2** *tr.* esp. *Brit. slang* inform against (a criminal etc.). ◻ **all over the shop** *Brit. colloq.* **1** in disorder (*scattered all over the shop*). **2** in every place (*looked for it all over the shop*). **3** wildly (*hitting out all over the shop*). **set up shop** establish oneself in business etc. **shop around** look for the best bargain. ◻ **shopless** *adj.* **shoppy** *adj.* [Middle English via Anglo-French & Old French *eschoppe* 'booth' from Middle Low German *schoppe*, Old High German *scopf* 'porch']

shopaholic /ʃɒpə'hɒlɪk/ *n. colloq.* a compulsive shopper. [blend of SHOP + ALCOHOLIC]

shop assistant *n. Brit.* a person who serves customers in a shop.

shop-bought *adj.* bought in a shop as opposed to being home-made.

shop boy see SHOP GIRL.

shopfitter /'ʃɒpfɪtə/ *n.* a person who job is fitting shops with counters, shelves, etc. ◻ **shopfitting** *n.*

shop floor *n.* (hyphenated when *attrib.*) *Brit.* **1** workers in a factory etc. as distinct from management. **2** their area or place of work.

shopfront /'ʃɒpfrʌnt/ *n.* the façade of a shop.

shop girl *n.* (also **shop boy**) an assistant in a shop.

shopkeeper /'ʃɒpki:pə/ *n.* the owner and manager of a shop. ◻ **shopkeeping** *n.*

shoplifter /'ʃɒplɪftə/ *n.* a person who steals goods while appearing to shop. ◻ **shoplift** *v.tr.* (also *absol.*). **shoplifting** *n.*

shopman /'ʃɒpmən/ *n.* (*pl.* **-men**) **1** *Brit.* a shopkeeper or shop assistant. **2** a workman in a repair shop.

shopper /'ʃɒpə/ *n.* **1** a person who makes purchases in a shop. **2** *Brit.* a shopping bag or trolley. **3** a small-wheeled bicycle with a basket. **4** *Brit. slang* an informer.

shopping /'ʃɒpɪŋ/ *n.* **1** (often *attrib.*) the purchase of goods etc. (*shopping expedition*). **2** goods purchased (*put the shopping on the table*).

shopping cart see CART *n.* 4.

shopping centre *n.* an area or complex of shops, with associated facilities.

shop-soiled *adj. Brit.* **1** (of an article) soiled or faded by display in a shop. **2** (of a person, idea, etc.) grubby; tarnished; no longer fresh or new.

shop steward *n.* a person elected by workers in a factory etc. to represent them in dealings with management.

shop talk *n.* talk about one's occupation or business.

shopwalker /'ʃɒpwɔ:kə/ *n. Brit.* an attendant in a large shop who directs customers, supervises assistants, etc.

shop window *n.* **1** a display window in a shop. **2** an opportunity for displaying skills, talents, etc.

shopworker /'ʃɒpwə:kə/ *n.* a person who works in a shop.

shopworn /'ʃɒpwɔ:n/ *adj.* esp. *US* = SHOP-SOILED.

shoran /'ʃɔ:ran, 'ʃɒran/ *n.* a system of aircraft navigation using the return of two radar signals by two ground stations. [*sho*rt *ra*nge *n*avigation]

shore[1] /ʃɔ:/ *n.* **1** the land that adjoins the sea or a large body of water. **2** (usu. in *pl.*) a country; a sea coast (*often visits these shores*; *on a distant shore*). **3** *Law* land between ordinary high and low water marks. ◻ **in shore** on the water near or nearer to the shore (cf. INSHORE). **on shore** ashore. ◻ **shoreless** *adj.* **shoreward** *adj. & adv.* **shorewards** *adv.* [Middle English from Middle Dutch, Middle Low German *schōre*, perhaps related to SHEAR]

shore[2] /ʃɔ:/ *n. & v.* ● *n.* a prop or beam set obliquely against a ship, wall, tree, etc., as a support. ● *v.tr.* (often foll. by *up*) support with or as if with a shore or shores; hold up. ◻ **shoring** *n.* [Middle English from Middle Dutch, Middle Low German *schore* 'prop', of unknown origin]

shore[3] see SHEAR.

shore-based *adj.* operating from a base on shore.

shorebird /'ʃɔ:bə:d/ *n.* a bird which frequents the shore, esp. *N. Amer.* a wader of the order Charadriiformes.

shore leave *n. Naut.* **1** permission to go ashore. **2** a period of time ashore.

shoreline /'ʃɔ:lʌɪn/ *n.* the line along which a stretch of water, esp. a sea or lake, meets the shore.

shoreweed /'ʃɔ:wi:d/ *n.* a stoloniferous plant, *Littorella uniflora*, growing in shallow water.

shorn *past part.* of SHEAR.

short /ʃɔ:t/ *adj., adv., n., & v.* ● *adj.* **1 a** measuring little; not long from end to end (*a short distance*). **b** not long in duration (*a short time ago*; *had a short life*). **c** seeming less than the stated amount (*a few short years of happiness*). **2** of small height; not tall (*a short square tower*; *was shorter than average*). **3 a** (usu. foll. by *of*, (*colloq.*) *on*) having a partial or total lack; deficient; scanty (*short of spoons*; *is rather short on sense*). **b** not far-reaching; acting or being near at hand (*within short range*). **4 a** concise; brief (*kept his speech short*). **b** curt; uncivil (*was short with her*). **5** (of the memory) unable to remember distant events. **6** *Phonet.* & *Prosody* of a vowel or syllable: **a** having the lesser of the two recognized durations. **b** (of a vowel) categorized as short with regard to quality and length (cf. LONG[1] *adj.* 8). **7 a** (of pastry) crumbling; not holding together. **b** (of clay) having poor plasticity. **8** esp. *Stock Exch.* **a** (of stocks, a stockbroker, crops, etc.) sold or selling when the amount is not in hand, with reliance on getting the deficit in time for delivery. **b** (of a bill of exchange) maturing at an early date. **9** *Cricket* **a** (of a ball) pitching relatively near the bowler. **b** (of a fielding position) relatively near the batsman. **10** *Brit.* (of a drink of spirits) undiluted (see also SHORT DRINK). ● *adv.* **1** before the natural or expected time or place; abruptly (*pulled up short; cut short the celebrations*). **2** rudely; uncivilly (*spoke to him short*). ● *n.* **1** *Brit. colloq.* = SHORT DRINK. **2** a short circuit. **3** a short film. **4** *Stock Exch.* **a** a person who sells short. **b** (in *pl.*) short-dated stocks. **5** (in *pl.*) a mixture of bran and coarse flour. ● *v.tr.* & *intr.* (often foll. by *out*) short-circuit. □ **be caught** (or *Brit.* **taken**) **short 1** be put at a disadvantage. **2** *Brit. colloq.* urgently need to urinate or defecate. **bring up** (or **pull up**) **short** check or pause abruptly. **come short** be inadequate or disappointing. **come short of** fail to reach or amount to. **for short** as a short name (*Tom for short*). **get** (or **have**) **by the short and curlies** *colloq.* be in complete control of (a person). **go short** (often foll. by *of*) not have enough. **in short** to use few words; briefly. **in short order** *US* immediately, rapidly. **in the short run** over a short period of time. **in short supply** scarce. **in the short term** = *in the short run.* **make short work of** accomplish, dispose of, destroy, consume, etc. quickly. **short and sweet** esp. *iron.* brief and pleasant. **short for** an abbreviation for (*'Bob' is short for 'Robert'*). **short of 1** see sense 3a of *adj.* **2** less than (*nothing short of a miracle*). **3** distant from; before reaching (*two miles short of home*). **4** without going so far as; except (*did everything short of destroying it*). **short of breath** panting, short-winded. **short on** *colloq.* see sense 3a of *adj.* □ **shortish** *adj.* **shortness** *n.* [Old English *sceort* from Germanic: related to SHIRT, SKIRT]

shortage /ˈʃɔːtɪdʒ/ *n.* (often foll. by *of*) a deficiency; an amount lacking (*a shortage of 100 tons*).

short-arm *adj.* (of a blow etc.) delivered with the arm not fully extended.

short back and sides *n. Brit.* a haircut in which the hair is cut short at the back and the sides.

shortbread /ˈʃɔːtbrɛd/ *n.* a crisp rich crumbly type of biscuit made with butter, flour, and sugar.

shortcake /ˈʃɔːtkeɪk/ *n.* **1** = SHORTBREAD. **2** a cake made of short pastry and filled with fruit and cream.

short change *n.* & *v.* ● *n.* insufficient money given as change. ● *v.tr.* (**short-change**) rob or cheat by giving short change.

short circuit *n.* & *v.* ● *n.* an electric circuit through small resistance, esp. instead of the resistance of a normal circuit. ● *v.* (**short-circuit**) **1** *intr.* & *tr.* cause a short circuit; cause a short circuit in. **2** *tr.* shorten or avoid (a journey, work, etc.) by taking a more direct route etc.

shortcoming /ˈʃɔːtkʌmɪŋ/ *n.* failure to come up to a standard; a defect.

short commons *n.pl. Brit.* insufficient food.

shortcrust /ˈʃɔːtkrʌst/ *n.* (in full **shortcrust pastry**) *Brit.* a type of crumbly pastry made with flour, fat, and a little water.

short cut *n.* **1** a route shortening the distance travelled. **2** a quick way of accomplishing something.

short date *n.* an early date for the maturing of a bill etc.

short-dated *adj.* due for early payment or redemption.

short-day *adj.* (of a plant) needing the period of light each day to fall below some limit to cause flowering.

short division *n. Math.* division in which the quotient is written directly without being worked out in writing.

short drink *n. Brit.* a strong alcoholic drink served in small measures.

short-eared owl *n.* a migratory owl, *Asio flammeus*, frequenting open country and often hunting by day.

shorten /ˈʃɔːt(ə)n/ *v.* **1** *intr.* & *tr.* become or make shorter or short; curtail. **2** *tr. Naut.* reduce the amount of (sail spread). **3** *intr.* & *tr.* (with reference to gambling odds, prices, etc.) become or make shorter; decrease.

shortening /ˈʃɔːt(ə)nɪŋ/ *n.* fat used for making pastry, esp. for making short pastry.

shortfall /ˈʃɔːtfɔːl/ *n.* a shortage or deficit.

short fuse *n. colloq.* a quick temper.

short game *n. Golf* approaching and putting.

shorthair /ˈʃɔːthɛː/ *n.* **1** a breed of short-haired cat. **2** a cat of a short-haired breed.

shorthand /ˈʃɔːthand/ *n.* **1** (often *attrib.*) a method of rapid writing in abbreviations and symbols esp. for taking dictation. **2** an abbreviated or symbolic mode of expression.

short-handed *adj.* undermanned or understaffed.

shorthand typist *n. Brit.* a typist qualified to take and transcribe shorthand.

short haul *n.* **1** the transport of goods over a short distance (hyphenated when *attrib. short-haul routes*). **2** a short-term effort.

short head *n.* & *v. Brit. Racing* ● *n.* a distance less than the length of a horse's head. ● *v.tr.* (**short-head**) beat by a short head.

shorthold /ˈʃɔːthəʊld/ *adj.* (of a tenancy or lease) whereby a tenant agrees to rent a property for a short fixed term, at the end of which the landlord may recover it.

shorthorn /ˈʃɔːthɔːn/ *n.* **1** an animal of a breed of cattle with short horns. **2** this breed.

short hundredweight see HUNDREDWEIGHT 3.

shortie var. of SHORTY.

short leet *n.* & *v.* esp. *Sc.* = SHORTLIST.

shortlist /ˈʃɔːtlɪst/ *n.* & *v.* ● *n.* a list of selected candidates from which a final choice is made. ● *v.tr.* put on a shortlist.

short-lived *adj.* ephemeral; not long-lasting.

shortly /ˈʃɔːtli/ *adv.* **1** (often foll. by *before, after*) before long; soon (*will arrive shortly; arrived shortly after him*). **2** in a few words; briefly. **3** curtly. [Old English *scortlice* (as SHORT, -LY[2])]

short mark *n.* = BREVE 2.

short measure *n.* less than the professed amount.

short metre *n. Prosody* a hymn stanza of four lines with 6, 6, 8, and 6 syllables.

short notice *n.* a small, esp. insufficient, length of warning time.

short odds *n.pl.* nearly equal stakes or chances in betting.

short order *n. N. Amer.* an order for quickly cooked food (hyphenated when *attrib.*: *short-order chef*).

short-pitched *adj. Cricket* (of a ball) pitching relatively near the bowler.

short-range *adj.* **1** having a short range. **2** relating to a fairly immediate future time (*short-range possibilities*).

short rib *n. Brit.* = FLOATING RIB.

shorts /ʃɔːts/ *n.pl.* **1** trousers reaching only to the knees or higher. **2** *US* underpants.

short score *n. Mus.* a score in which the parts are condensed on to a small number of staves.

short shrift *n.* **1** curt treatment. **2** *archaic* little time between condemnation and execution or punishment.

short sight *n.* the inability to focus except on comparatively near objects.

short-sighted *adj.* **1** having short sight. **2** lacking imagination or foresight. □ **short-sightedly** *adv.* **short-sightedness** *n.*

short-sleeved *adj.* with sleeves not reaching below the elbow.

short-staffed *adj.* having insufficient staff.

shortstop /ˈʃɔːtstɒp/ *n.* a baseball fielder between second and third base.

short story *n.* a story with a fully developed theme but shorter than a novel.

short suit *n. Cards* a suit of which a player has fewer than four cards.

short temper *n.* a tendency to lose one's temper quickly. □ **short-tempered** *adj.*

short-term *adj.* occurring in or relating to a short period of time.

short-termism *n.* concentration on short-term projects etc. for immediate profit at the expense of long-term security.

short time *n.* the condition of working fewer than the regular hours per day or days per week.

short title *n.* an abbreviated form of a title of a book etc.

short ton see TON[1] 2.

short view *n.* a consideration of the present only, not the future.

short waist *n.* **1** a high or shallow waist of a dress. **2** a short upper body.

short wave *n.* a radio wave of frequency greater than 3 MHz.

short weight *n.* weight less than it is alleged to be.

short whist *n.* whist with ten or five points to a game.

short wind *n.* breathing power that is quickly exhausted.

short-winded *adj.* **1** having short wind. **2** incapable of sustained effort.

shorty /ˈʃɔːti/ *n.* (also **shortie**) (*pl.* **-ies**) *colloq.* **1** a person shorter than average. **2** a short garment, esp. a nightdress or raincoat.

shot[1] /ʃɒt/ *n.* **1** the act or an instance of firing a gun, cannon, etc. (*several shots were heard*). **2** an attempt to hit by shooting or throwing etc. (*took a shot at him*). **3 a** a single non-explosive missile for a cannon, gun, etc. **b** (*pl.* same or **shots**) a small lead pellet used in quantity in a single charge or cartridge in a shotgun. **c** (treated as *pl.*) these collectively. **4 a** a photograph. **b** a film sequence photographed continuously by one camera. **5 a** a stroke; a kick in a ball game. **b** a kick etc. made with the aim of scoring. **c** *colloq.* an attempt to guess or do something (*let him have a shot at it*). **6** *colloq.* a person having a specified skill with a gun etc. (*is not a good shot*). **7** a heavy ball thrown by a shot-putter. **8** the launch of a space rocket (*a moonshot*). **9** the range, reach, or distance to or at which a thing will carry or act (*out of earshot*). **10** a remark aimed at a person. **11** *colloq.* **a** a drink of esp. spirits. **b** an injection of a drug, vaccine, etc. (*has had his shots*). □ **like a shot** *colloq.* without hesitation; willingly. **make a bad shot** guess wrong. **not a shot in one's** (or **the**) **locker** *Brit.* **1** no money left. **2** not a chance left. **shot across the bows** see BOW[3]. **shot in the arm** *colloq.* **1** stimulus or encouragement. **2** *Brit.* an alcoholic drink. **shot in the dark** a mere guess. □ **shotproof** *adj.* [Old English *sc(e)ot, gesc(e)ot*, from Germanic]

shot[2] /ʃɒt/ *past* and *past part.* of SHOOT. ● *adj.* **1** (of coloured material) woven so as to show different colours at different angles. **2** *colloq.* **a** exhausted; finished; ruined. **b** drunk. **3** (of a board-edge) accurately planed. □ **be** (or **get**) **shot of** *Brit. slang* be (or get) rid of. **shot through** permeated or suffused. [past part. of SHOOT]

shot[3] /ʃɒt/ *n. Brit. colloq.* a reckoning, a bill, esp. at an inn etc. (*paid his shot*). [Middle English, = SHOT[1]: cf. Old English *scēotan* 'shoot, pay, contribute', and SCOT]

shot-blasting *n.* the cleaning of metal etc. by the impact of a stream of shot. □ **shot-blast** *v.tr.*

shot-firer *n.* a person who fires a blasting-charge in a mine etc.

shotgun /ˈʃɒtgʌn/ *n.* a smooth-bore gun for firing small shot at short range.

shotgun marriage *n.* (also **shotgun wedding**) *colloq.* an enforced or hurried wedding, esp. because of the bride's pregnancy.

shot-put *n.* an athletic contest in which a shot is thrown a great distance. □ **shot-putter** *n.*

shotten herring /ˈʃɒt(ə)n/ *n.* **1** a herring that has spawned. **2** *archaic* a weakened or dispirited person. [Middle English, archaic past part. of SHOOT]

shot-tower *n. hist.* a tower in which shot was made from molten lead poured through sieves at the top and falling into water at the bottom.

should /ʃʊd/ *v.aux.* (*3rd sing.* **should**) *past* of SHALL, used esp.: **1** in reported speech, esp. with the reported element in the 1st person (*I said I should be home by evening*). **2 a** to express a duty, obligation, or likelihood; = OUGHT[1] (*I should tell you*; *you should have been more careful*; *they should have arrived by now*). **b** (in the 1st person) to express a tentative suggestion (*I should like to say something*). **3 a** expressing the conditional mood in the 1st person (cf. WOULD) (*I should have been killed if I had gone*). **b** forming a conditional protasis or indefinite clause (*if you should see him*; *should they arrive, tell them where to go*). **4** expressing purpose = MAY, MIGHT[1] (*in order that we should not worry*).

■ **Usage** *Should* and *would* are used in reported speech (see sense 1 above), and in forming the conditional mood (see sense 3a above). As with *shall* and *will*, there is much confusion as to when to use *should* and *would*. The traditional rule in standard British English is that *should* is used for the first person singular and plural (*I* and *we*), and *would* with the second and third persons (*you, he, she, it, they*). Examples are *I said I should be late*; *you said you would be late* (reported speech); *I should have given it to her if I had seen her*; *they would have laughed if they had seen us* (conditional). However, *would* is now more often used with *I* and *we* than *should*, i.e. *I said I would be late*; *I would have given it to her if I had seen her*, in order to avoid the sense of obligation or duty implied by *should* (see sense 2a above).

In senses 2a, 3b, and 4 *should* and not *would* is used with all the persons.

shoulder /ˈʃəʊldə/ *n.* & *v.* ● *n.* **1 a** the part of the body at which the arm, foreleg, or wing is attached. **b** (in full **shoulder joint**) the end of the upper arm joining with the collarbone and blade-bone. **c** either of the two projections below the neck from which the arms hang. **2** the upper foreleg and shoulder blade of a pig, lamb, etc. when butchered. **3** (often in *pl.*) **a** the upper part of the back and arms. **b** this part of the body regarded as capable of bearing a burden or blame, providing comfort, etc. (*needs a shoulder to cry on*). **4** a strip of land next to a metalled road (*pulled over on to the shoulder*). **5** a part of a garment covering the shoulder. **6** a part of anything resembling a shoulder in form or function, as in a bottle, mountain, tool, etc. ● *v.* **1 a** *tr.* push with the shoulder; jostle. **b** *intr.* make one's way by jostling (*shouldered through the crowd*). **2** *tr.* take (a burden etc.) on one's shoulders (*shouldered the family's problems*). □ **put** (or **set**) **one's shoulder to the wheel** set to work vigorously. **shoulder arms** hold a rifle with the barrel against the shoulder and the butt in the hand. **shoulder to shoulder 1** side by side. **2** with closed ranks or united effort. □ **shouldered** *adj.* (also in *comb.*). [Old English *sculdor*, from West Germanic]

shoulder bag *n.* a bag, esp. a woman's handbag, that can be hung from the shoulder.

shoulder-belt *n.* a bandolier or other strap passing over one shoulder and under the opposite arm.

shoulder blade *n. Anat.* either of the large flat bones of the upper back; the scapula.

shoulder-high *adj.* & *adv.* up to or as high as the shoulders.

shoulder holster *n.* a gun holster worn in the armpit.

shoulder joint see SHOULDER *n.* 1b.

shoulder-knot *n.* a knot of ribbon, metal, lace, etc. worn as part of a ceremonial dress.

shoulder-length *adj.* (of hair etc.) reaching to the shoulders.

shoulder loop *n. US* the shoulder strap of an army, air force, or marines officer.

shoulder mark *n. US* the shoulder strap of a naval officer.

shoulder note *n. Printing* a marginal note at the top of a page.

shoulder-of-mutton sail *n.* = LEG-OF-MUTTON SAIL.

shoulder pad *n.* a pad sewn into a garment to bulk out the shoulder.

shoulder strap *n.* **1** a strip of cloth going over the shoulder from front to back of a garment. **2** a strap suspending a bag etc. from the shoulder. **3** a strip of cloth from shoulder to collar on a military uniform bearing a symbol of rank etc. **4** a similar strip on a raincoat.

shouldn't /ˈʃʊd(ə)nt/ *contr.* should not.

shout /ʃaʊt/ *v. & n.* ● *v.* **1** *intr.* make a loud cry or vocal sound; speak loudly (*shouted for attention*). **2** *tr.* say or express loudly; call out (*shouted that the coast was clear*). **3** *tr.* (also *absol.*) *Austral. & NZ colloq.* treat (another person) to drinks etc. ● *n.* **1** a loud cry expressing joy etc. or calling attention. **2** *Brit. colloq.* one's turn to order and pay for a round of drinks etc. (*your shout, I think*). □ **all over bar** (or **but) the shouting** *colloq.* the contest is virtually decided. **shout at** speak loudly to etc. **shout down** reduce to silence by shouting. **shout for** call for by shouting. □ **shouter** *n.* [Middle English, perhaps related to SHOOT: cf. Old Norse *skúta* 'a taunt', SCOUT[2]]

shout-up *n. Brit. colloq.* a noisy argument.

shove /ʃʌv/ *v. & n.* ● *v.* **1** *tr.* (also *absol.*) push vigorously; move by hard or rough pushing (*shoved him out of the way*). **2** *intr.* (usu. foll. by *along, past, through*, etc.) make one's way by pushing (*shoved through the crowd*). **3** *tr. colloq.* put somewhere (*shoved it in the drawer*). ● *n.* an act of shoving or of prompting a person into action. □ **shove off 1** start from the shore in a boat. **2** *slang* depart; go away (*told him to shove off*). [Old English *scūfan*, from Germanic]

shove-halfpenny *n.* a form of shovelboard played with coins etc. on a table esp. in licensed premises.

shovel /ˈʃʌv(ə)l/ *n. & v.* ● *n.* **1 a** a spadelike tool for shifting quantities of coal, earth, etc., esp. having the sides curved upwards. **b** the amount contained in a shovel; a shovelful. **2** a machine or part of a machine having a similar form or function. ● *v.tr.* (**shovelled, shovelling**; *US* **shoveled, shoveling**) **1** shift or clear (coal etc.) with or as if with a shovel. **2** *colloq.* move (esp. food) in large quantities or roughly (*shovelled peas into his mouth*). □ **shovelful** *n.* (*pl.* **-fuls**). [Old English *scofl* from Germanic: related to SHOVE]

shovelboard /ˈʃʌv(ə)lbɔːd/ *n. Brit.* a game played esp. on a ship's deck by pushing discs with the hand or with a long-handled shovel over a marked surface. [earlier *shoveboard*, from SHOVE + BOARD]

shovel hat *n.* a broad-brimmed hat esp. worn by some clergymen.

shovelhead /ˈʃʌv(ə)lhɛd/ *n.* = BONNETHEAD.

shoveller /ˈʃʌv(ə)lə/ *n.* (*US* **shoveler**) **1** a person or thing that shovels. **2** (usu. **shoveler**) a duck, *Anas clypeata*, with a broad shovel-like beak. [SHOVEL: sense 2 earlier *shovelard* (see -ARD), perhaps influenced by *mallard*]

show /ʃəʊ/ *v. & n.* ● *v.* (*past part.* **shown** /ʃəʊn/ or **showed**) **1** *intr. & tr.* be, or allow or cause to be, visible; manifest; appear (*the buds are beginning to show; white shows the dirt*). **2** *tr.* (often foll. by *to*) offer, exhibit, or produce (a thing) for scrutiny etc. (*show your tickets please; showed him my poems*). **3** *tr.* (often foll. by *to, towards*) demonstrate (kindness, rudeness, etc.) to a person (*showed respect towards him; showed him no mercy*). **4** *intr.* (of feelings etc.) be manifest (*his dislike shows*). **5** *tr.* **a** point out; prove (*has shown it to be false; showed that he knew the answer*). **b** (usu. foll. by *how to* + infin.) cause (a person) to understand or be capable of doing (*showed them how to knit*). **6** *tr.* (*refl.*) **a** exhibit oneself as being (*showed herself a generous host*). **b** (foll. by *to be*) exhibit oneself to be (*showed herself to be fair*). **7** *tr. & intr.* (with reference to a film) be presented or cause to be presented. **8** *tr.* exhibit (a picture, animal, flower, etc.) in a show. **9** *tr.* (often foll. by *in, out, up*, etc.) conduct or lead (*showed them to their rooms*). **10** *intr.* = *show up* 3 (*waited but he didn't show*). **11** *intr. N. Amer.* finish third or in the first three in a race. ● *n.* **1** the act or an instance of showing; the state of being shown. **2 a** a spectacle, display, exhibition, etc. (*a fine show of blossom*). **b** a collection of things etc. shown for public entertainment or in competition (*dog show; flower show*). **3 a** a play etc., esp. a musical. **b** a light entertainment programme on television etc. **c** any public entertainment or performance. **4 a** an outward appearance, semblance, or display (*made a show of agreeing; a show of strength*). **b** empty appearance; mere display (*did it for show; that's all show*). **5** *colloq.* an undertaking, business, etc. (*sold the whole show*). **6** esp. *Brit. colloq.* an opportunity of acting, defending oneself, etc. (*gave him a fair show; made a good show of it*). **7** *Med.* a discharge of blood etc. from the vagina at the onset of childbirth. □ **give the show** (or **whole show**) **away** demonstrate the inadequacies or reveal the truth. **good** (or **bad** or **poor**) **show!** esp. *Brit. colloq.* **1** that was well (or badly) done. **2** that was lucky (or unlucky). **nothing to show for** no visible result of (effort etc.). **on show** being exhibited. **show one's cards** = *show one's hand*. **show cause** *Law* allege with justification. **show a person** etc. **a clean pair of heels** *colloq.* retreat speedily from a person etc.; run away. **show one's colours** make one's opinion clear. **show a person the door** dismiss or eject a person. **show one's face** make an appearance; let oneself be seen. **show fight** be persistent or belligerent. **show the flag** see FLAG[1]. **show forth** *archaic* exhibit; expound. **show one's hand 1** disclose one's plans. **2** reveal one's cards. **show in** see sense 9 of *v.* **show a leg** *Brit. colloq.* **1** get out of bed. **2** make one's appearance. **show off 1** display to advantage. **2** *colloq.* act pretentiously; display one's wealth, knowledge, etc. **show oneself 1** be seen in public. **2** see sense 6 of *v.* **show out** see sense 9 of *v.* **show round** (*US* **around**) take (a person) to places of interest; act as guide for (a person) in a building etc. **show one's teeth** *Brit.* reveal one's strength; be aggressive. **show through 1** be visible through a covering. **2** (of real feelings etc.) be revealed inadvertently. **show up 1** make or be conspicuous or clearly visible. **2** expose (a fraud, impostor, inferiority, etc.). **3** *colloq.* appear; be present; arrive. **4** *colloq.* embarrass or humiliate (*don't show me up by wearing jeans*). **show the way 1** indicate what has to be done etc. by attempting it first. **2** show others which way to go etc. **show the white feather** *Brit.* appear cowardly (see also WHITE FEATHER). **show willing** display a willingness to help etc. [Old English *scēawian*, from West Germanic]

showband /ˈʃəʊband/ *n.* **1** a jazz band which performs with verve and theatrical extravagance. **2** a band which plays cover versions of popular songs.

showbiz /ˈʃəʊbɪz/ *n. colloq.* = SHOW BUSINESS.

showboat /ˈʃəʊbəʊt/ *n. US* a river steamer on which theatrical performances are given.

show business *n. colloq.* the theatrical profession.

showcard /ˈʃəʊkɑːd/ *n.* a card used for advertising.

showcase /ˈʃəʊkeɪs/ *n. & v.* ● *n.* **1** a glass case used for exhibiting goods etc. **2** a place or medium for presenting something (esp. attractively) to general attention. ● *v.tr.* display in or as if in a showcase.

showdown /ˈʃəʊdaʊn/ *n.* **1** a final test or confrontation; a decisive situation. **2** the laying down face up of the players' cards in poker.

shower /ˈʃaʊə/ *n. & v.* ● *n.* **1** a brief fall of esp. rain, hail, sleet, or snow. **2 a** a brisk flurry of arrows, bullets, dust, stones, sparks, etc. **b** a flurry of gifts, letters, honours, praise, etc. **3** (in full **shower-bath**) **a** a cubicle, bath, etc. in which one stands under a spray of water. **b** the apparatus etc. used for this. **c** the act of bathing in a shower. **4** a group of particles produced by a cosmic-ray particle in the earth's atmosphere. **5** *N. Amer.* a party for giving presents to a prospective bride, etc. **6** *Brit. slang* a contemptible or unpleasant person or group of people. ● *v.* **1** *tr.* discharge (water, missiles, etc.) in a shower. **2** *intr.* use a shower-bath. **3** *tr.* (usu. foll. by *on, upon*) lavishly bestow (gifts etc.). **4** *intr.* descend or come in a shower (*it showered on and off all day*). ◻ **showery** *adj.* [Old English *scūr*, from Germanic]

showerproof /ˈʃaʊəpruːf/ *adj. & v.* ● *adj.* resistant to light rain. ● *v.tr.* make showerproof.

showgirl /ˈʃəʊɡəːl/ *n.* an actress who sings and dances in musicals, variety shows, etc.

showground /ˈʃəʊɡraʊnd/ *n.* an area of land on which a show takes place.

show house *n.* (also **show home**) *Brit.* a furnished and decorated house on a new estate shown to prospective buyers.

showing /ˈʃəʊɪŋ/ *n.* **1** the act or an instance of showing. **2** a usu. specified quality of performance (*made a poor showing*). **3** the presentation of a case; evidence (*on present showing it must be true*). [Old English *scēawung* (as SHOW)]

showjumping /ˈʃəʊdʒʌmpɪŋ/ *n.* the sport of riding horses over a course of fences and other obstacles, with penalty points for errors. ◻ **showjump** *v.intr.* **showjumper** *n.*

showman /ˈʃəʊmən/ *n.* (*pl.* **-men**) **1** the proprietor or manager of a circus etc. **2** a person skilled in self-advertisement or publicity. ◻ **showmanship** *n.*

shown *past part.* of SHOW.

show-off *n. colloq.* a person who shows off.

show of force *n.* a demonstration of one's readiness to use force.

show of hands *n.* raised hands indicating a vote for or against, usu. without being counted.

showpiece /ˈʃəʊpiːs/ *n.* **1** an item of work presented for exhibition or display. **2** an outstanding example or specimen.

showplace /ˈʃəʊpleɪs/ *n.* a house etc. that tourists go to see.

showroom /ˈʃəʊruːm, -rʊm/ *n.* a room in a factory, office building, etc. used to display goods for sale.

show-stopper *n. colloq.* a performance receiving prolonged applause. ◻ **show-stopping** *adj.*

show trial *n.* esp. *hist.* a judicial trial designed by the state to terrorize or impress the public.

show-window *n.* a window for exhibiting goods etc.

showy /ˈʃəʊi/ *adj.* (**showier**, **showiest**) **1** brilliant; gaudy, esp. vulgarly so. **2** striking. ◻ **showily** *adv.* **showiness** *n.*

s.h.p. *abbr.* shaft horsepower.

shrank *past* of SHRINK.

shrapnel /ˈʃrapn(ə)l/ *n.* **1** fragments of a bomb etc. thrown out by an explosion. **2** a shell containing bullets or pieces of metal timed to burst short of impact. [named after Gen. H. *Shrapnel*, British soldier d. 1842, inventor of the shell]

shred /ʃrɛd/ *n. & v.* ● *n.* **1** a scrap, fragment, or strip of esp. cloth, paper, etc. **2** the least amount, remnant (*not a shred of evidence*). ● *v.tr.* (**shredded**, **shredding**) tear or cut into shreds. ◻ **tear to shreds** completely refute (an argument etc.). [Old English *scrēad* 'piece cut off', *scrēadian* 'trim, prune', from West Germanic: related to SHROUD]

shredder /ˈʃrɛdə/ *n.* **1** a machine used to reduce documents to shreds. **2** any device used for shredding.

shrew /ʃruː/ *n.* **1** any small usu. insect-eating mouselike mammal of the family Soricidae, with a long pointed snout. **2** a bad-tempered or scolding woman. ◻ **shrewish** *adj.* (in sense 2). **shrewishly** *adv.* **shrewishness** *n.* [Old English *scrēawa*, *scrǣwa* 'shrew-mouse': related to Old High German *scrawaz* 'dwarf', Middle High German *schrawaz* etc. 'devil']

shrewd /ʃruːd/ *adj.* **1 a** showing astute powers of judgement; clever and judicious (*a shrewd observer*; *made a shrewd guess*). **b** (of a face etc.) shrewd-looking. **2** *archaic* **a** (of pain, cold, etc.) sharp, biting. **b** (of a blow, thrust, etc.) severe, hard. **c** mischievous; malicious. ◻ **shrewdly** *adv.* **shrewdness** *n.* [Middle English, = malignant, from SHREW in the sense 'evil person or thing', or past part. of obsolete *shrew* 'to curse', from SHREW]

shriek /ʃriːk/ *v. & n.* ● *v.* **1** *intr.* **a** utter a shrill screeching sound or words, esp. in pain or terror. **b** (foll. by *of*) provide a clear or blatant indication of. **2** *tr.* **a** utter (sounds or words) by shrieking (*shrieked his name*). **b** indicate clearly or blatantly. ● *n.* a high-pitched piercing cry or sound; a scream. ◻ **shriek out** say in shrill tones. **shriek with laughter** laugh uncontrollably. ◻ **shrieker** *n.* [imitative: cf. dialect *screak*, Old Norse *skrækja*, and SCREECH]

shrieval /ˈʃriːv(ə)l/ *adj.* of or relating to a sheriff. [*shrieve*, obsolete variant of SHERIFF]

shrievalty /ˈʃriːv(ə)lti/ *n.* (*pl.* **-ies**) **1** a sheriff's office or jurisdiction. **2** the tenure of this. [as SHRIEVAL + *-alty* as in *mayoralty* etc.]

shrift /ʃrɪft/ *n. archaic* **1** confession to a priest. **2** confession and absolution. [Old English *scrift* (verbal noun) from SHRIVE]

shrike /ʃrʌɪk/ *n.* any bird of the family Laniidae, with a strong hooked and toothed bill, that impales its prey of small birds and insects on thorns. Also called BUTCHER-BIRD. [perhaps related to Old English *scric* 'thrush', Middle Low German *schrīk* 'corncrake' (imitative)]

shrill /ʃrɪl/ *adj. & v.* ● *adj.* **1** piercing and high-pitched in sound. **2** *derog.* (esp. of a protester) sharp, unrestrained, unreasoning. ● *v.* **1** *intr.* (of a cry etc.) sound shrilly. **2** *tr.* (of a person etc.) utter or send out (a song, complaint, etc.) shrilly. ◻ **shrillness** *n.* **shrilly** *adv.* [Middle English, related to Low German *schrell* 'sharp in tone or taste', from Germanic]

shrimp /ʃrɪmp/ *n. & v.* ● *n.* **1** (*pl.* same or **shrimps**) any of various small (esp. marine) edible crustaceans, with ten legs, grey-green when alive and pink when cooked. **2** *colloq.* a very small slight person. ● *v.intr.* go catching shrimps. ◻ **shrimper** *n.* [Middle English, probably related to Middle Low German *schrempen* 'to wrinkle', Middle High German *schrimpfen* 'to contract', and SCRIMP]

shrimp plant *n.* an evergreen shrub, *Justicia brandegeana*, bearing small white flowers in clusters of pinkish-brown bracts.

shrine /ʃrʌɪn/ *n. & v.* ● *n.* **1** esp. *RC Ch.* **a** a chapel, church, altar, etc., sacred to a saint, holy person, relic, etc. **b** the tomb of a saint etc. **c** a casket esp. containing sacred relics; a reliquary. **d** a niche containing a holy statue etc. **2** a place associated with or containing memorabilia of a particular person, event, etc. **3** a Shinto place of worship. ● *v.tr. poet.* enshrine. [Old English *scrīn* from Germanic, from Latin *scrinium* 'case for books' etc.]

shrink /ʃrɪŋk/ *v. & n.* ● *v.* (*past* **shrank** /ʃraŋk/; *past part.* **shrunk** /ʃrʌŋk/ or (esp. as *adj.*) **shrunken** /ˈʃrʌŋk(ə)n/) **1** *tr. & intr.* make or become smaller; contract, esp. by the action of moisture, heat, or cold. **2** *intr.* (usu. foll. by *from*) **a** retire; recoil; flinch; cower (*shrank from her touch*). **b** be averse from doing (*shrinks from meeting them*). **3** *intr.* (as **shrunken** *adj.*) (esp. of a face, person, etc.) having grown smaller esp. because of age, illness, etc. ● *n.* **1** the act or an instance of shrinking; shrinkage. **2** *slang* a psychiatrist (from 'head-shrinker'). ◻ **shrink into oneself** become withdrawn. **shrink on** slip (a metal tyre etc.) on while expanded with heat and allow to tighten. ◻ **shrinkable** *adj.* **shrinker** *n.* **shrinkingly** *adv.* **shrink-proof** *adj.*

[Old English *scrincan*, corresponding to Swedish *skrynka* 'to wrinkle']

shrinkage /'ʃrɪŋkɪdʒ/ *n.* **1 a** the process or fact of shrinking. **b** the degree or amount of shrinking. **2** an allowance made for the reduction in takings due to wastage, theft, etc.

shrinking violet *n.* an exaggeratedly shy person.

shrink-resistant *adj.* (of textiles etc.) resistant to shrinkage when wet etc.

shrink-wrap *v.tr.* (**-wrapped**, **-wrapping**) enclose (an article) in (esp. transparent) film that shrinks tightly on to it.

shrive /ʃraɪv/ *v.tr.* (*past* **shrove** /ʃrəʊv/; *past part.* **shriven** /'ʃrɪv(ə)n/) *Eccl. archaic* **1** (of a priest) hear the confession of, assign penance to, and absolve. **2** (*refl.*) (of a penitent) submit oneself to a priest for confession etc. [Old English *scrīfan* 'impose as penance', via West Germanic from Latin *scribere* 'write']

shrivel /'ʃrɪv(ə)l/ *v.tr. & intr.* (**shrivelled**, **shrivelling**; *US* **shriveled**, **shriveling**) contract or wither into a wrinkled, folded, rolled-up, contorted, or dried-up state. [perhaps from Old Norse: cf. Swedish dialect *skryvla* 'to wrinkle']

shriven *past part.* of SHRIVE.

shroud /ʃraʊd/ *n. & v.* ● *n.* **1** a sheetlike garment for wrapping a corpse for burial. **2** anything that conceals like a shroud (*wrapped in a shroud of mystery*). **3** (in *pl.*) *Naut.* a set of ropes forming part of the standing rigging and supporting the mast or topmast. ● *v.tr.* **1** clothe (a body) for burial. **2** cover, conceal, or disguise (*hills shrouded in mist*). □ **shroudless** *adj.* [Old English *scrūd* from Germanic: related to SHRED]

shroud-laid *adj.* (of a rope) having four strands laid right-handed on a core.

shrove *past* of SHRIVE.

Shrovetide /'ʃrəʊvtaɪd/ *n.* Shrove Tuesday and the two days preceding it when it was formerly customary to be shriven. [Middle English *shrove*, formed irregularly as past part. of SHRIVE]

Shrove Tuesday /ʃrəʊv/ *n.* the day before Ash Wednesday.

shrub[1] /ʃrʌb/ *n.* a woody plant smaller than a tree and having a very short stem with branches near the ground. □ **shrubby** *adj.* [Old English *scrubb*, *scrybb* 'shrubbery': cf. North Frisian *skrobb* 'brushwood', West Flemish *schrobbe* 'vetch', Norwegian *skrubba* 'dwarf cornel', and SCRUB[2]]

shrub[2] /ʃrʌb/ *n.* a cordial made of sweetened fruit juice and spirits, esp. rum. [Arabic *šurb*, *šarāb* from *šariba* 'to drink': cf. SHERBET, SYRUP]

shrubbery /'ʃrʌb(ə)ri/ *n.* (*pl.* **-ies**) an area planted with shrubs.

shrug /ʃrʌg/ *v. & n.* ● *v.* (**shrugged**, **shrugging**) **1** *intr.* slightly and momentarily raise the shoulders to express indifference, ignorance, helplessness, contempt, etc. **2** *tr.* **a** raise (the shoulders) in this way. **b** shrug the shoulders to express (indifference etc.) (*shrugged his consent*). ● *n.* the act or an instance of shrugging. □ **shrug off** dismiss as unimportant etc. by or as if by shrugging. [Middle English: origin unknown]

shrunk (also **shrunken**) *past part.* of SHRINK.

shtick /ʃtɪk/ *n. slang* a theatrical routine, gimmick, etc. [Yiddish from German *Stück* 'piece']

shtook /ʃtʊk/ *n. slang* trouble (esp. in phr. **in shtook**). [20th c.: origin unknown]

shubunkin /ʃʊ'bʌŋkɪn/ *n.* a breed of ornamental goldfish with black spots and red patches and long fins and tail. [Japanese]

shuck /ʃʌk/ *n. & v. US* ● *n.* **1** a husk or pod. **2** the shell of an oyster or clam. **3** (in *pl.*) *colloq.* an expression of contempt or regret or self-deprecation in response to praise. ● *v.tr.* **1** remove the shucks of; shell. **2** (often foll. by *off*) remove, throw or strip off (clothes etc.). □ **shucker** *n.* [17th c.: origin unknown]

shudder /'ʃʌdə/ *v. & n.* ● *v.intr.* **1** shiver esp. convulsively from fear, cold, repugnance, etc. **2** feel strong repugnance etc. (*shudder to think what might happen*). **3** (of a machine etc.) vibrate or quiver. ● *n.* **1** the act or an instance of shuddering. **2** (in *pl.*; prec. by *the*) *colloq.* a state of shuddering. □ **shudderingly** *adv.* **shuddery** *adj.* [Middle English *shod(d)er* from Middle Dutch *schūderen*, Middle Low German *schōderen*, from Germanic]

shuffle /'ʃʌf(ə)l/ *v. & n.* ● *v.* **1** *tr. & intr.* move with a scraping, sliding, or dragging motion (*shuffles along*; *shuffling his feet*). **2** *tr.* **a** (also *absol.*) rearrange (a pack of cards) by sliding them over each other quickly. **b** rearrange; intermingle; confuse (*shuffled the documents*). **3** *tr.* (usu. foll. by *on*, *off*, *into*) assume or remove (clothes, a burden, etc.) esp. clumsily or evasively (*shuffled on his clothes*; *shuffled off responsibility*). **4** *intr.* **a** equivocate; prevaricate. **b** continually shift one's position; fidget. **5** *intr.* (foll. by *out of*) escape evasively (*shuffled out of the blame*). ● *n.* **1** a shuffling movement. **2** the act or an instance of shuffling cards. **3** a general change of relative positions. **4** a piece of equivocation; sharp practice. **5** a quick scraping movement of the feet in dancing (see also DOUBLE SHUFFLE). □ **shuffle the cards** change policy etc. □ **shuffler** *n.* [perhaps from Low German *schuffeln* 'walk clumsily', from Germanic: related to SHOVE]

shuffle-board *n. N. Amer.* = SHOVELBOARD.

shufti /'ʃʊfti/ *n.* (*pl.* **shuftis**) *Brit. colloq.* a look or glimpse. [Arabic *šaffa* 'try to see']

shul /ʃuːl/ *n.* a synagogue. [Yiddish from German *Schule* 'school']

shun /ʃʌn/ *v.tr.* (**shunned**, **shunning**) avoid; keep clear of (*shuns human company*). [Old English *scunian*, of unknown origin]

shunt /ʃʌnt/ *v. & n.* ● *v.* **1** *intr. & tr.* diverge or cause (a train) to be diverted esp. on to a siding. **2** *tr. Electr.* provide (a current) with a shunt. **3** *tr.* **a** postpone or evade. **b** divert (a decision etc.) on to another person etc. ● *n.* **1** the act or an instance of shunting on to a siding. **2** *Electr.* a conductor joining two points of a circuit, through which more or less of a current may be diverted. **3** *Surgery* **a** an alternative path for the circulation of the blood. **b** the construction of such a route. **4** *Brit. slang* a motor accident, esp. a collision of vehicles travelling one close behind another. □ **shunter** *n.* [Middle English, perhaps from SHUN]

shush /ʃʊʃ, ʃʌʃ/ *int., v., & n.* ● *int.* = HUSH *int.* ● *v.* **1** *intr.* **a** call for silence by saying *shush*. **b** be silent (*they shushed at once*). **2** *tr.* make or attempt to make silent. ● *n. colloq.* **1** silence. **2** an utterance of 'shush'. [imitative]

shut /ʃʌt/ *v.* (**shutting**; *past* and *past part.* **shut**) **1** *tr.* **a** move (a door, window, lid, lips, etc.) into position so as to block an aperture (*shut the lid*). **b** close or seal (a room, window, box, eye, mouth, etc.) by moving a door etc. (*shut the box*). **2** *intr.* become or be capable of being closed or sealed (*the door shut with a bang*; *the lid shuts automatically*). **3** *intr. & tr.* esp. *Brit.* become or make (a shop, business, etc.) closed for trade (*the shops shut at five*; *shuts his shop at five*). **4** *tr.* bring (a book, hand, telescope, etc.) into a folded-up or contracted state. **5** *tr.* (usu. foll. by *in*, *out*) keep (a person, sound, etc.) in or out of a room etc. by shutting a door etc. (*shut out the noise*; *shut them in*). **6** *tr.* (usu. foll. by *in*) catch (a finger, dress, etc.) by shutting something on it (*shut her finger in the door*). **7** *tr.* bar access to (a place etc.) (*this entrance is shut*). □ **be** (or **get**) **shut of** *slang* be (or get) rid of (*were glad to get shut of him*). **shut the door on** refuse to consider; make impossible. **shut down 1** stop (a factory, nuclear reactor, etc.) from operating. **2** (of a factory etc.) stop operating. **3** push or pull (a window sash etc.) down into a closed position. **shut one's eyes** (or **ears** or **heart** or **mind**) **to** pretend not, or refuse, to see (or hear or feel sympathy for or think about). **shut in** (of hills, houses, etc.) encircle, prevent access etc. to or escape from (*were shut in by the sea on three sides*) (see also sense 5). **shut off 1 a** stop the flow of (water, gas, etc.) by shutting a valve. **b** switch off (a machine etc.). **2** separate from society etc. **shut out 1** exclude (a person, light, etc.) from a place, situation, etc. **2** screen (landscape etc.) from view. **3** prevent (a possibility etc.). **4** block (a painful memory etc.) from the mind. **5** *N. Amer.* prevent (an opponent) from scoring (see also sense 5). **shut to 1** close (a door etc.). **2** (of a door etc.) close as far as it will go. **shut up 1** close all doors and windows of (a house etc.); bolt and bar. **2** imprison (a person). **3** close (a box etc.) securely. **4** *colloq.* reduce to silence by rebuke etc. **5** put (a thing) away in a box etc. **6** (esp. in *imper.*) *colloq.* stop talking. **shut up shop 1** close a business, shop, etc. **2** cease business etc. permanently. **shut your face** (or **head** or **mouth** or **trap**)! *slang* an impolite request to stop talking. [Old English *scyttan* from West Germanic: related to SHOOT]

shutdown /ˈʃʌtdaʊn/ *n.* the closure of a factory etc.

shut-eye *n. colloq.* sleep.

shut-off *n.* **1** something used for stopping an operation. **2** a cessation of flow, supply, or activity.

shutout /ˈʃʌtaʊt/ *n. N. Amer.* the act of preventing an opponent from scoring.

shut-out bid *n. Bridge* a pre-emptive bid.

shutter /ˈʃʌtə/ *n.* & *v.* ● *n.* **1** a person or thing that shuts. **2 a** each of a pair or set of panels fixed inside or outside a window for security or privacy or to keep the light in or out. **b** a structure of slats on rollers used for the same purpose. **3** a device that exposes the film in a photographic camera. **4** *Mus.* the blind of a swell-box in an organ used for controlling the sound level. ● *v.tr.* **1** put up the shutters of. **2** provide with shutters. □ **put up the shutters 1** cease business for the day. **2** cease business etc. permanently. □ **shutterless** *adj.*

shuttering /ˈʃʌt(ə)rɪŋ/ *n.* **1** a temporary structure usu. of wood, used to hold concrete during setting. **2** material for making shutters.

shuttle /ˈʃʌt(ə)l/ *n.* & *v.* ● *n.* **1 a** a bobbin with two pointed ends used for carrying the weft-thread across between the warp-threads in weaving. **b** a bobbin carrying the lower thread in a sewing machine. **2** a train, bus, etc., going to and fro over a short route continuously. **3** = SHUTTLECOCK. **4** = SPACE SHUTTLE. ● *v.* **1** *intr.* & *tr.* move or cause to move to and fro like a shuttle. **2** *intr.* travel in a shuttle. [Old English *scytel* 'dart' from Germanic: related to SHOOT]

shuttle armature *n. Electr.* an armature with a single coil wound on an elongated iron bobbin.

shuttlecock /ˈʃʌt(ə)lkɒk/ *n.* **1** a cork with a ring of feathers, or a similar device of plastic, struck between players in badminton and in battledore and shuttlecock. **2** a thing passed repeatedly back and forth. [SHUTTLE + COCK[1], probably from the flying motion]

shuttle diplomacy *n.* negotiations conducted by a mediator who travels successively to several countries.

shuttle service *n.* a train or bus etc. service operating to and fro over a short route.

shy[1] /ʃʌɪ/ *adj.*, *v.*, & *n.* ● *adj.* (**shyer**, **shyest**) **1 a** diffident or uneasy in company; timid. **b** (of an animal, bird, etc.) easily startled; timid. **2** (foll. by *of*) avoiding; chary of (*shy of his aunt*; *shy of going to meetings*). **3** (in *comb.*) showing fear of or distaste for (*gun-shy*; *work-shy*). **4** (often foll. by *of*, *on*) *colloq.* having lost; short of (*I'm shy three quid*; *shy of the price of admission*). ● *v.intr.* (**shies**, **shied**) **1** (usu. foll. by *at*) (esp. of a horse) start suddenly aside (at an object, noise, etc.) in fright. **2** (usu. foll. by *away from*, *at*) avoid accepting or becoming involved in (a proposal etc.) in alarm. ● *n.* a sudden startled movement, esp. of a horse. □ **shyer** *n.* **shyly** *adv.* **shyness** *n.* [Old English *sceoh*, from Germanic]

shy[2] /ʃʌɪ/ *v.* & *n.* ● *v.tr.* (**shies**, **shied**) (also *absol.*) fling or throw (a stone etc.). ● *n.* (*pl.* **shies**) the act or an instance of shying. □ **have a shy at** *colloq.* **1** try to hit with a stone etc. **2** make an attempt at. **3** jeer at. □ **shyer** *n.* [18th c.: origin unknown]

Shylock /ˈʃʌɪlɒk/ *n.* a hard-hearted moneylender; a miser. [a character in Shakespeare's *Merchant of Venice*]

shyster /ˈʃʌɪstə/ *n.* esp. *N. Amer. colloq.* a person, esp. a lawyer, who uses unscrupulous methods. [19th c.: origin uncertain]

SI *abbr.* **1** (Order of the) Star of India. **2** the international system of units of measurement (French *Système International*).

Si *symb. Chem.* the element silicon.

si /siː/ *n. Mus.* = TE. [French from Italian, perhaps from the initials of *Sancte Iohannes*: see GAMUT]

sial /ˈsʌɪəl/ *n. Geol.* **1** the upper layer of the earth's crust, comprising the continental masses. **2** the material of this, relatively light rock rich in silica and alumina. [SILICA + ALUMINA]

sialogogue /ˈsʌɪələgɒg/ *n.* & *adj.* ● *n.* a medicine inducing the flow of saliva. ● *adj.* inducing such a flow. [French, from Greek *sialon* 'saliva' + *agōgos* 'leading']

siamang /ˈsʌɪəmaŋ, ˈsiːə-/ *n.* a large black gibbon, *Hylobates syndactylus*, native to Sumatra and the Malay peninsula. [Malay]

Siamese /sʌɪəˈmiːz/ *n.* & *adj.* ● *n.* (*pl.* same) **1 a** a native of Siam (now Thailand) in SE Asia. **b** the language of Siam. **2** (in full **Siamese cat**) **a** a cat of a lightly-built short-haired breed characterized by slanting blue eyes and usu. pale fur with points of brown, blue, etc. **b** this breed. ● *adj.* of or concerning Siam, its people, or language.

Siamese fighting fish see FIGHTING FISH.

Siamese twins *n.pl.* **1** twins joined at any part of the body and sometimes sharing organs etc. **2** any closely associated pair.

sib /sɪb/ *n.* & *adj.* ● *n.* **1** esp. *Genetics* a brother or sister; a sibling. **2** a blood relative. **3** a group of people recognized by an individual as his or her kindred. ● *adj.* (usu. foll. by *to*) esp. *Sc.* related; akin. [Old English *sib(b)*]

Siberian /sʌɪˈbɪərɪən/ *n.* & *adj.* ● *n.* **1** a native of Siberia in the north-eastern part of the Russian Federation. **2** a person of Siberian descent. ● *adj.* of or relating to Siberia.

sibilant /ˈsɪbɪl(ə)nt/ *adj.* & *n.* ● *adj.* **1** (of a letter or set of letters) sounded with a hiss, e.g. *s*, *sh*. **2** hissing (*a sibilant whisper*). ● *n.* a sibilant letter or letters. □ **sibilance** *n.* **sibilancy** *n.* [Latin *sibilare sibilant-* 'hiss']

sibilate /ˈsɪbɪleɪt/ *v.tr.* & *intr.* pronounce with or utter a hissing sound. □ **sibilation** /-ˈleɪʃ(ə)n/ *n.*

sibling /ˈsɪblɪŋ/ *n.* each of two or more children having one or both parents in common. [SIB + -LING[1]]

sibship /ˈsɪbʃɪp/ *n.* **1** the state of belonging to a sib or the same sib. **2** a group of children having the same two parents.

sibyl /ˈsɪbɪl/ *n.* **1** any of certain women in ancient times supposed to utter the oracles and prophecies of a god. **2** a prophetess, fortune-teller, or witch. [Middle English via Old French *Sibile* or medieval Latin *Sibilla* and Latin *Sibylla* from Greek *Sibulla*]

sibylline /ˈsɪbɪlʌɪn/ *adj.* **1** of or from a sibyl. **2** oracular; prophetic. [Latin *Sibyllinus* (as SIBYL)]

Sibylline books *n.pl.* a collection of oracles belonging to the ancient Roman State and used for guidance by magistrates etc.

sic /sɪk/ *adv.* (usu. in brackets) used, spelt, etc., as written (confirming, or calling attention to, the form of quoted or copied words). [Latin, = so, thus]

■ **Usage** The word *sic* is placed in brackets after a word that appears odd or erroneous to show that the word is quoted exactly as it stands in the original, e.g. *They say they will take measures to insure* (sic) *compliance.*

siccative /ˈsɪkətɪv/ *n.* & *adj.* ● *n.* a substance causing drying, esp. mixed with oil paint etc. for quick drying. ● *adj.* having such properties. [Late Latin *siccativus* from *siccare* 'to dry']

sice[1] /sʌɪs/ *n.* the six on dice. [Middle English via Old French *sis* from Latin *sex* 'six']

sice[2] var. of SYCE.

Sicilian /sɪˈsɪlɪən/ *n. & adj.* ● *n.* **1** a native of Sicily, an island off the S. coast of Italy. **2** a person of Sicilian descent. ● *adj.* of or relating to Sicily. [Latin *Sicilia* 'Sicily']

siciliano /sɪˌtʃɪlɪˈɑːnəʊ/ *n.* (*pl.* **-os**) (also **siciliana** /-nə/; *pl.* **-as**) a dance, song, or instrumental piece in 6/8 or 12/8 time, often in a minor key, and evoking a pastoral mood. [Italian, = Sicilian]

sick[1] /sɪk/ *adj., n., & v.* ● *adj.* **1** (often in *comb.*) esp. *Brit.* vomiting or tending to vomit (*feels sick*; *was sick after the meal*; *seasick*). **2** ill; affected by illness (*has been off sick for a week*; *a sick man*). **3 a** (often foll. by *at*) esp. mentally perturbed; disordered (*the product of a sick mind*; *sick at heart*). **b** (often foll. by *for*, or in *comb.*) pining; longing (*sick for a sight of home*; *lovesick*). **4** (often foll. by *of*) *colloq.* **a** disgusted; surfeited (*sick of chocolates*). **b** angry, esp. because of surfeit (*am sick of being teased*). **5** *colloq.* (of humour etc.) jeering at misfortune, illness, death, etc.; morbid (*sick joke*). **6** (of a ship) needing repair (esp. of a specified kind) (*paint-sick*). ● *n. Brit. colloq.* vomit. ● *v.tr.* (usu. foll. by *up*) *Brit. colloq.* vomit (*sicked up his dinner*). □ **go sick** report oneself as ill. **look sick** *colloq.* be unimpressive or embarrassed. **sick at** (or **to**) **one's stomach** *US* vomiting or tending to vomit. **take sick** *colloq.* be taken ill. □ **sickish** *adj.* [Old English *sēoc*, from Germanic]

■ **Usage** In British English, the predicative use of the adjective *sick* in sense 2, to mean 'ill', as in *He had to cancel his holiday because he was sick*, is still considered non-standard by some people, although it is standard in American English. The exception to this is its use in the phrase *off sick* ('away on sick leave') which is acceptable in British English. See also Usage Note at ILL.

sick[2] /sɪk/ *v.tr.* (usu. in *imper.*) (esp. to a dog) set upon, attack. [19th c., dialect variant of SEEK]

sickbay /ˈsɪkbeɪ/ *n.* **1** part of a ship used as a hospital. **2** any room etc. for sick people.

sickbed /ˈsɪkbɛd/ *n.* **1** an invalid's bed. **2** the state of being an invalid.

sick benefit *n.* = SICKNESS BENEFIT.

sick building syndrome *n.* a high incidence of illness in office workers, attributed to the immediate working surroundings.

sick call *n.* **1** a visit by a doctor to a sick person etc. **2** *Mil.* a summons for sick men to attend.

sicken /ˈsɪk(ə)n/ *v.* **1** *tr.* affect with loathing or disgust. **2** *intr.* **a** (often foll. by *for*) *Brit.* show symptoms of illness (*is sickening for measles*). **b** (often foll. by *at*, or *to* + infin.) feel nausea or disgust (*he sickened at the sight*). **3** *tr.* (as **sickening** *adj.*) **a** loathsome, disgusting. **b** *colloq.* very annoying. □ **sickeningly** *adv.*

sickener /ˈsɪk(ə)nə/ *n.* **1** something causing nausea, disgust, or severe disappointment. **2** a red toadstool of the genus *Russula*, esp. the poisonous *R. emetica*.

sick flag *n.* a yellow flag indicating disease at a quarantine station or on ship.

sick headache *n.* = MIGRAINE.

sickie /ˈsɪki/ *n. Austral. & NZ colloq.* a period of sick leave, esp. taken with insufficient medical reason.

sickle /ˈsɪk(ə)l/ *n.* **1** a short-handled farming tool with a semicircular blade, used for cutting corn, lopping, or trimming. **2** anything sickle-shaped, esp. the crescent moon. [Old English *sicol*, *sicel* from Latin *secula*, from *secare* 'to cut']

sick leave *n.* leave of absence granted because of illness.

sickle-bill *n.* a bird with a long narrow curved bill, esp. any hummingbird of the genus *Eutoxeres*.

sickle-cell anaemia *n.* (*US* **sickle-cell anemia**) a severe hereditary form of anaemia, affecting mainly blacks, in which a mutated form of haemoglobin distorts the red blood cells into a crescent shape at low oxygen levels.

sickle-feather *n.* each of the long middle feathers of a cock's tail.

sick list *n.* a list of the sick, esp. in a regiment, ship, etc.

sickly /ˈsɪkli/ *adj.* (**sicklier**, **sickliest**) **1 a** of weak health; apt to be ill. **b** (of a person's complexion, look, etc.) languid, faint, or pale, suggesting sickness (*a sickly smile*). **c** (of light or colour) faint, pale, feeble. **2** causing ill health (*a sickly climate*). **3** (of a book etc.) sentimental or mawkish. **4** inducing or connected with nausea (*a sickly taste*). **5** (of a colour etc.) of an unpleasant shade inducing nausea (*a sickly green*). □ **sickliness** *n.* [Middle English, probably suggested by Old Norse *sjukligr* (as SICK[1])]

sick-making *adj. colloq.* sickening.

sickness /ˈsɪknɪs/ *n.* **1** the state of being ill; disease. **2** a specified disease (*sleeping sickness*). **3** vomiting or a tendency to vomit. [Old English *sēocnesse* (as SICK[1], -NESS)]

sickness benefit *n.* (in the UK) benefit paid by the State for sickness interrupting paid employment.

sick nurse *n.* = NURSE[1] *n.* 1.

sicko /ˈsɪkəʊ/ *n.* (*pl.* **-os**) *N. Amer. slang* a mentally ill or perverted person.

sick pay *n.* pay given to an employee etc. on sick leave.

sickroom /ˈsɪkruːm, -rʊm/ *n.* **1** a room occupied by a sick person. **2** a room adapted for sick people.

sidalcea /sɪˈdalsɪə/ *n.* any mallow-like plant of the genus *Sidalcea*, bearing racemes of white, pink, or purple flowers. [modern Latin, from *Sida* + *Alcea*, names of related genera]

side /sʌɪd/ *n. & v.* ● *n.* **1 a** each of the more or less flat surfaces bounding an object (*a cube has six sides*; *this side up*). **b** a more or less vertical inner or outer plane or surface (*the side of a house*; *a mountainside*). **c** such a vertical lateral surface or plane as distinct from the top or bottom, front or back, or ends (*at the side of the house*). **2 a** the half of a person or animal that is on the right or the left, esp. of the torso (*has a pain in his right side*). **b** the left or right half or a specified part of a thing, area, building, etc. (*put the box on that side*). **c** (often in *comb.*) a position next to a person or thing (*graveside*; *seaside*; *stood at my side*). **d** a specified direction relating to a person or thing (*on the north side of*; *came from all sides*). **e** half of a butchered carcass (*a side of bacon*). **3 a** either surface of a thing regarded as having two surfaces. **b** the amount of writing needed to fill one side of a sheet of paper (*write three sides*). **4** any of several aspects of a question, character, etc. (*many sides to his character*; *look on the bright side*). **5 a** each of two sets of opponents in war, politics, games, etc. (*the side that bats first*; *much to be said on both sides*). **b** a cause or philosophical position etc. regarded as being in conflict with another (*on the side of right*). **6 a** a part or region near the edge and remote from the centre (*at the side of the room*; also *attrib.*: *side door*). **b** (*attrib.*) a subordinate, peripheral, or detached part (*a side road*; *a side table*). **7 a** each of the bounding lines of a plane rectilinear figure (*a hexagon has six sides*). **b** each of two quantities stated to be equal in an equation. **8** a position nearer or farther than, or right or left of, a given dividing line (*on this side of the Alps*; *on the other side of the road*). **9** a line of hereditary descent through the father or the mother. **10** (in full **side spin**) *Brit.* a spinning motion given to a billiard ball etc. by hitting it on one side, not centrally. **11** *Brit. slang* boastfulness; swagger (*has no side about him*). **12** *Brit. colloq.* a television channel, considered as one of two or more available channels (*shall we try another side?*). ● *v.intr.* (usu. foll. by *with*) take part or be on the same side as a disputant etc. (*sided with his father*). □ **by the side of 1** close to. **2** compared with. **from side to side 1** right across. **2** alternately each way from a central line. **let the side down** *Brit.* fail one's colleagues, esp. by frustrating their efforts or embarrassing them. **on one**

side **1** not in the main or central position. **2** aside (*took him on one side to explain*). **on the ... side** fairly, somewhat (qualifying an adjective: *on the high side*). **on the side 1** as a sideline; in addition to one's regular work etc. **2** secretly or illicitly. **3** *N. Amer.* as a side dish. **on this side of the grave** in life. **side by side** standing close together, esp. for mutual support. **take sides** support one or other cause etc. □ **sideless** *adj.* [Old English *sīde*, from Germanic]

side arms *n.pl.* weapons worn at the side, e.g. swords, bayonets, or pistols.

side band *n.* a range of frequencies near the carrier frequency of a radio wave, within which modulated frequences fall.

side-bet *n.* a bet between opponents, esp. in card games, over and above the ordinary stakes.

sideboard /ˈsʌɪdbɔːd/ *n.* **1** a table or esp. a flat-topped cupboard at the side of a dining room for supporting and containing dishes, table linen, decanters, etc. **2** (usu. in *pl.*) *Brit. colloq.* hair grown by a man down each side of his face; side-whisker.

side-bone *n.* either of the small forked bones under the wings of poultry.

sideburn /ˈsʌɪdbəːn/ *n.* (usu. in *pl.*) = SIDEBOARD 2. [originally *burnside*, from the name of General *Burnside* d. 1881, who affected this style]

sidecar /ˈsʌɪdkɑː/ *n.* **1** a small car for a passenger or passengers attached to the side of a motorcycle. **2** a cocktail of orange liqueur, lemon juice, and brandy. **3** *hist.* a jaunting car.

side chain *n. Chem.* a group of atoms attached to the main part of a molecule.

side chapel *n.* a chapel in the aisle or at the side of a church.

sided /ˈsʌɪdɪd/ *adj.* **1** having sides. **2** (in *comb.*) having a specified side or number of sides (*flat-sided*; *three-sided*). □ **-sidedly** *adv.* **sidedness** *n.* (also in *comb.*).

side dish *n.* an extra dish subsidiary to the main course.

side door *n.* **1** a door in or at the side of a building. **2** an indirect means of access.

side drum *n.* a small double-headed drum in a jazz or military band or in an orchestra (originally hung at the drummer's side).

side effect *n.* a secondary, usu. undesirable, effect.

side glance *n.* a sideways or brief glance.

sidehill /ˈsʌɪdhɪl/ *n. US* a hillside.

side issue *n.* a point that distracts attention from what is important.

sidekick /ˈsʌɪdkɪk/ *n. colloq.* a close associate.

sidelamp /ˈsʌɪdlamp/ *n.* a lamp placed at the side of something, esp. on a motor vehicle.

sidelight /ˈsʌɪdlʌɪt/ *n.* **1** a light from the side. **2** incidental information etc. **3** *Brit.* a light at the side of the front of a motor vehicle to warn of its presence. **4** *Naut.* the red port or green starboard light on a ship under way.

sideline /ˈsʌɪdlʌɪn/ *n. & v.* ● *n.* **1** an activity done in addition to one's main work etc. **2** (usu. in *pl.*) **a** a line bounding the side of a hockey pitch, tennis court, etc. **b** the space next to these where spectators etc. sit. ● *v.tr. US* remove (a player) from a team through injury, suspension, etc. □ **on** (or **from**) **the sidelines** in (or from) a position removed from the main action.

sidelong /ˈsʌɪdlɒŋ/ *adj. & adv.* ● *adj.* inclining to one side; oblique (*a sidelong glance*). ● *adv.* obliquely (*moved sidelong*). [earlier *sideling* (as SIDE, -LING[2]): see -LONG]

side note *n.* a marginal note.

side-on *adv. & adj.* ● *adv.* from the side. ● *adj.* **1** from or towards one side. **2** (of a collision) involving the side of a vehicle.

side plate *n.* a plate of approximately 15-20 cm diameter, used for bread etc.

sidereal /sʌɪˈdɪərɪəl/ *adj.* of or concerning the constellations or fixed stars. [Latin *sidereus* from *sidus sideris* 'star']

sidereal clock *n.* a clock showing sidereal time.

sidereal day *n.* the time between successive meridional transits of a star or esp. of the first point of Aries, about four minutes shorter than the solar day.

sidereal time *n.* time measured by the apparent diurnal motion of the stars.

sidereal year *n.* a year longer than the solar year by 20 minutes 23 seconds because of precession.

siderite /ˈsʌɪdərʌɪt, ˈsɪd-/ *n.* **1** a mineral form of ferrous carbonate. **2** a meteorite consisting mainly of nickel and iron. [Greek *sidēros* 'iron']

sidero- /ˈsɪdərəʊ, ˈsʌɪ-/ *comb. form* **1** of or relating to iron. **2** of or relating to the stars. [sense 1 from Greek *sidēros* 'iron'; sense 2 from Latin *sider- sidus* 'star']

side road *n.* a minor or subsidiary road, esp. joining or diverging from a main road.

siderostat /ˈsɪd(ə)rə(ʊ)stat/ *n.* an instrument used for keeping the image of a celestial body in a fixed position. [Latin *sidus sideris* 'star', on the pattern of *heliostat*]

side-saddle *n. & adv.* ● *n.* a saddle for a woman rider who rides with both feet on the same side of the horse. ● *adv.* sitting in this position on a horse.

side salad *n.* a salad served as a side dish.

side seat *n. Brit.* a seat in a vehicle etc. in which the occupant has his or her back to the side of the vehicle.

sideshow /ˈsʌɪdʃəʊ/ *n.* **1** a small show or stall in an exhibition, fair, etc. **2** a minor incident or issue.

side-slip *n. & v.* ● *n.* **1** a skid. **2** *Aeron.* a sideways movement, esp. downwards towards the inside of a turn. ● *v.intr.* **1** skid. **2** *Aeron.* move in a side-slip.

sidesman /ˈsʌɪdzmən/ *n.* (*pl.* **-men**) *Brit.* a churchwarden's assistant, who shows worshippers to their seats, takes the collection, etc.

side spin see SIDE *n.* 10.

side-splitting *adj.* causing violent laughter.

sidestep /ˈsʌɪdstɛp/ *n. & v.* ● *n.* a step taken sideways. ● *v.tr.* (**-stepped**, **-stepping**) **1** esp. *Football* avoid (esp. a tackle) by stepping sideways. **2** evade. □ **sidestepper** *n.*

side street *n.* a minor or subsidiary street.

sidestroke /ˈsʌɪdstrəʊk/ *n.* **1** a stroke towards or from a side. **2** an incidental action. **3** a swimming stroke in which the swimmer lies on his or her side.

sideswipe /ˈsʌɪdswʌɪp/ *n. & v.* ● *n.* **1** a glancing blow along the side. **2** an incidental critical remark. ● *v.tr.* hit with or as if with a sideswipe.

side table *n.* a table placed at the side of a room or apart from the main table.

sidetrack /ˈsʌɪdtrak/ *n. & v.* ● *n.* a railway siding. ● *v.tr.* **1** turn into a siding; shunt. **2 a** postpone, evade, or divert treatment or consideration of. **b** divert (a person) from considering etc.

side trip *n.* a minor excursion during a voyage or trip; a detour.

side valve *n.* a valve in a vehicle engine, operated from the side of the cylinder.

side view *n.* **1** a view obtained sideways. **2** a profile.

sidewalk /ˈsʌɪdwɔːk/ *n. N. Amer.* a pedestrian path at the side of a road; a pavement.

sideward /ˈsʌɪdwəd/ *adj. & adv.* ● *adj.* = SIDEWAYS. ● *adv.* (also **sidewards** /-wədz/) = SIDEWAYS.

sideways /ˈsʌɪdweɪz/ *adv. & adj.* ● *adv.* **1** to or from a side (*moved sideways*). **2** with one side facing forward (*sat sideways on the bus*). ● *adj.* **1** to or from a side (*a sideways movement*). **2** unconventional, unorthodox (*a sideways look at recent events*). □ **sidewise** *adv. & adj.*

side-wheeler *n. US* a steamer with paddle wheels.

side-whiskers *n.pl.* whiskers growing on the cheeks.

side wind *n.* **1** wind from the side. **2** an indirect agency or influence.

sidewinder[1] /'sʌɪdwʌɪndə/ *n.* a N. American desert rattlesnake, *Crotalus cerastes*, that moves sideways by throwing its body into S-shaped curves.

sidewinder[2] /'sʌɪdwɪndə/ *n. N. Amer.* a sideways blow.

siding /'sʌɪdɪŋ/ *n.* **1** a short track at the side of and opening on to a railway line, used for shunting trains. **2** *N. Amer.* cladding material for the outside of a building.

sidle /'sʌɪd(ə)l/ *v. & n.* ● *v.intr.* (usu. foll. by *along*, *up*) walk in a timid, furtive, stealthy, or cringing manner. ● *n.* the act or an instance of sidling. [back-formation from *sideling*, SIDELONG]

SIDS *abbr.* sudden infant death syndrome; = COT DEATH.

siege /si:dʒ/ *n.* **1 a** a military operation in which an attacking force seeks to compel the surrender of a fortified place by surrounding it and cutting off supplies etc. **b** a similar operation by police etc. to force the surrender of an armed person. **c** the period during which a siege lasts. **2** a persistent attack or campaign of persuasion. □ **lay siege to** esp. *Mil.* conduct the siege of. **raise the siege of** abandon or cause the abandonment of an attempt to take (a place) by siege. [Middle English from Old French *sege* 'seat', from *assegier* BESIEGE]

siege gun *n.* a heavy gun used in sieges.

siege-train *n.* artillery and other equipment for a siege, with vehicles etc.

siemens /'si:mənz/ *n.* (*pl.* same) *Electr.* the SI unit of conductance, equal to one reciprocal ohm (abbr.: **S**). [named after W. von *Siemens*, German electrical engineer, d. 1892]

sienna /sɪ'ɛnə/ *n.* **1** a kind of ferruginous earth used as a pigment in paint. **2** its colour of yellowish brown (**raw sienna**) or reddish brown (**burnt sienna**). [Italian (*terra di*) *Sienna* '(earth of) Siena', a city and province in Tuscany]

sierra /sɪ'ɛrə, sɪ'ɛ:rə/ *n.* a long jagged mountain chain, esp. in Spain, Spanish America, or the western US. [Spanish, from Latin *serra* 'saw']

siesta /sɪ'ɛstə/ *n.* an afternoon sleep or rest esp. in hot countries. [Spanish, from Latin *sexta* (*hora*) 'sixth hour']

sieve /sɪv/ *n. & v.* ● *n.* a utensil having a perforated or meshed bottom for separating solids or coarse material from liquids or fine particles, or for reducing a soft solid to a fine pulp. ● *v.tr.* **1** put through or sift with a sieve. **2** examine (evidence etc.) to select or separate. □ **head like a sieve** *colloq.* a memory that retains little. □ **sievelike** *adj.* [Old English *sife*, from West Germanic]

sievert /'si:vət/ *n.* an SI unit of dosage of ionizing radiation, defined as that which delivers a joule of energy per kilogram of recipient mass. [named after R. M. *Sievert*, Swedish radiologist b. 1896]

sifaka /sɪ'fakə/ *n.* a long-tailed arboreal lemur of the genus *Propithecus*, of Madagascar, with white to blackish-brown fur. [Malagasy]

siffleur /si:'flə:r, French siflœ:r/ *n.* (*fem.* ***siffleuse*** /-'flə:z, French -fløz/) *Brit.* a professional whistler. [French from *siffler* 'to whistle']

sift /sɪft/ *v.* **1** *tr.* sieve (material), esp. to separate finer and coarser parts. **2** *tr.* (usu. foll. by *from*, *out*) separate (finer or coarser parts) from material. **3** *tr.* sprinkle (esp. sugar) from a perforated container. **4** *tr.* examine (evidence, facts, etc.) in order to assess authenticity etc. **5** *intr.* (of snow, light, etc.) fall as if from a sieve. □ **sift through** examine by sifting. □ **sifter** *n.* (also in *comb.*). [Old English *siftan*, from West Germanic]

Sig. *abbr.* Signor.

sigh /sʌɪ/ *v. & n.* ● *v.* **1** *intr.* emit a long deep audible breath expressive of sadness, weariness, longing, relief, etc. **2** *intr.* (foll. by *for*) yearn for (a lost person or thing). **3** *tr.* utter or express with sighs (*'Never!' he sighed*). **4** *intr.* (of the wind etc.) make a sound like sighing. ● *n.* **1** the act or an instance of sighing. **2** a sound made in sighing (*a sigh of relief*). [Middle English *sihen* etc., probably a back-formation from *sihte*, past of *sīhen*, from Old English *sīcan*]

sight /sʌɪt/ *n. & v.* ● *n.* **1 a** the faculty of seeing with the eyes (*lost his sight*). **b** the act or an instance of seeing; the state of being seen. **2** a thing seen; a display, show, or spectacle (*not a pretty sight*; *a beautiful sight*). **3** a way of looking at or considering a thing (*in my sight he can do no wrong*). **4** a range of space within which a person etc. can see or an object be seen (*he's out of sight*; *they are just coming into sight*). **5** (usu. in *pl.*) noteworthy features of a town, area, etc. (*went to see the sights*). **6 a** a device on a gun or optical instrument used for assisting the precise aim or observation. **b** the aim or observation so gained (*got a sight of him*). **7** *colloq.* a person or thing having a ridiculous, repulsive, or dishevelled appearance (*looked a perfect sight*). **8** *colloq.* a great quantity (*will cost a sight of money*; *is a sight better than he was*). ● *v.tr.* **1** get sight of, esp. by approaching (*they sighted land*). **2** observe the presence of (esp. aircraft, animals, etc.) (*sighted buffalo*). **3** take observations of (a star etc.) with an instrument. **4 a** provide (a gun, quadrant, etc.) with sights. **b** adjust the sight of (a gun etc.). **c** aim (a gun etc.) with sights. □ **at first sight** on first glimpse or impression. **at** (or **on**) **sight** as soon as a person or a thing has been seen (*plays music at sight*; *liked him on sight*). **catch** (or **lose**) **sight of** begin (or cease) to see or be aware of. **get a sight of** manage to see; glimpse. **have lost sight of** no longer know the whereabouts of. **in sight 1** visible. **2** near at hand (*salvation is in sight*). **in** (or **within**) **sight of** so as to see or be seen from. **lower one's sights** become less ambitious. **out of my sight!** go at once! **out of sight 1** not visible. **2** *colloq.* excellent; delightful. **out of sight out of mind** we forget those who are absent. **put out of sight** hide, ignore. **set one's sights on** aim at (*set her sights on a directorship*). **sight for sore eyes** (or *Brit.* **sight for the gods**) a welcome person or thing, esp. a visitor. □ **sighter** *n.* [Old English (*ge*)*sihth*]

sighted /'sʌɪtɪd/ *adj.* **1** capable of seeing; not blind. **2** (in *comb.*) having a specified kind of sight (*long-sighted*).

sight-glass *n.* a transparent device for observing the interior of apparatus etc.

sighting shot *n.* an experimental shot to guide gunners in adjusting their sights.

sightless /'sʌɪtlɪs/ *adj.* **1** blind. **2** *poet.* invisible. □ **sightlessly** *adv.* **sightlessness** *n.*

sight line *n.* a hypothetical line from a person's eye to what is seen.

sightly /'sʌɪtli/ *adj.* attractive to the sight; not unsightly. □ **sightliness** *n.*

sight-read *v.tr.* (*past* and *past part.* **-read** /-rɛd/) (also *absol.*) read and perform (music) at sight. □ **sight-reader** *n.*

sight-screen *n. Cricket* a large usu. movable white screen placed near the boundary in line with the wicket to help the batsman see the ball.

sightseer /'sʌɪtsi:ə/ *n.* a person who visits places of interest; a tourist. □ **sightsee** *v.intr. & tr.* **sightseeing** *n.*

sight-sing *v.tr. & intr.* sing (music) at sight.

sight unseen *adv.* without previous inspection.

sightworthy /'sʌɪtwə:ði/ *adj.* worth seeing.

sigillate /'sɪdʒɪlət/ *adj.* **1** (of pottery) having impressed patterns. **2** *Bot.* having seal-like marks. [Latin *sigillatus* from *sigillum* 'seal', diminutive of *signum* 'sign']

siglum /sɪgləm/ *n.* (*pl.* **sigla** /-lə/) a letter (esp. an initial) or other symbol used to denote a word in a book, esp. to refer to a particular text. [Late Latin *sigla* (pl.), perhaps from *singula*, neut. pl. of *singulus* 'single']

sigma /'sɪgmə/ *n.* the eighteenth letter of the Greek alphabet (Σ, σ, or, when final, ς; also, in uncial form, C, c). [Latin from Greek]

sigmate /'sɪgmət/ *adj.* **1** sigma-shaped. **2** S-shaped.

sigmoid /'sɪgmɔɪd/ *adj. & n.* ● *adj.* **1** curved like the uncial sigma (C); crescent-shaped. **2** S-shaped. ● *n.* (in full **sigmoid flexure**) *Anat.* the curved part of the intestine between the colon and the rectum. [Greek *sigmoeidēs* (as SIGMA)]

sigmoidoscopy /sɪgmɔɪ'dɒskəpi/ *n.* (*pl.* **-ies**) an examination of the lower intestine by means of a flexible tube inserted through the anus. □ **sigmoidoscope** /sɪg'mɔɪdəskəʊp/ *n.*

sign /sʌɪn/ *n.* & *v.* ● *n.* **1 a** a thing indicating or suggesting a quality or state etc.; a thing perceived as indicating a future state or occurrence (*violence is a sign of weakness*; *shows all the signs of decay*). **b** a miracle evidencing supernatural power; a portent (*did signs and wonders*). **2 a** a mark, symbol, or device used to represent something or to distinguish the thing on which it is put (*marked the jar with a sign*). **b** a technical symbol used in algebra, music, etc. (*a minus sign*; *a repeat sign*). **3 a** a gesture or action used to convey information, an order, request, etc. (*gave him a sign to leave*; *conversed by signs*). **b** a gesture used in a system of sign language. **c** = SIGN LANGUAGE. **4** a publicly displayed board etc. giving information; a signboard or signpost. **5** an objective indication of a disease, usu. specified (*Babinski's sign*) (cf. SYMPTOM 1). **6** a password (*advanced and gave the sign*). **7** each of the twelve divisions of the zodiac, named from the constellations formerly situated in them (*the sign of Cancer*). **8** *US* the trail of a wild animal. **9** *Math.* etc. the positiveness or negativeness of a quantity. ● *v.* **1** *tr.* **a** (also *absol.*) write (one's name, initials, etc.) on a document etc. indicating that one has authorized it. **b** write one's name etc. on (a document) as authorization. **2** *intr.* & *tr.* **a** communicate by gesture (*signed to me to come*; *signed their assent*). **b** communicate in a sign language. **3** *tr.* & *intr.* engage or be engaged by signing a contract etc. (see also *sign on*, *sign up*). **4** *tr.* mark with a sign (esp. with the sign of the cross in baptism). □ **make no sign** seem unconscious; not protest. **sign away** convey (one's right, property, etc.) by signing a deed etc. **sign for** acknowledge receipt of by signing. **sign in 1** sign a register on arrival in a hotel etc. **2** authorize the admittance of (a person) by signing a register. **sign off 1** end work, broadcasting, a letter, etc., esp. by writing or speaking one's name. **2 a** end a period of employment, contract, etc. **b** end the period of employment or contract of (a person). **3** *Brit.* register to stop receiving unemployment benefit after finding work. **4** *Bridge* indicate by a conventional bid that one is seeking to end the bidding. **sign on 1** agree to a contract, employment, etc. **2** begin work, broadcasting, etc., esp. by writing or announcing one's name. **3** employ (a person). **4** *Brit.* register as unemployed. **sign out 1** sign a register on leaving a hotel etc. **2** authorize the release or record the departure of (a person or thing) by signing a register. **sign up 1** engage or employ (a person). **2** enlist in the armed forces. **3 a** commit (another person or oneself) by signing etc. (*signed you up for dinner*). **b** enrol (*signed up for evening classes*). □ **signable** *adj.* **signer** *n.* [Middle English via Old French *signe*, *signer* from Latin *signum*, *signare*]

signage /ˈsʌɪnɪdʒ/ *n.* signs collectively, esp. commercial or public display signs.

signal[1] /ˈsɪgn(ə)l/ *n.* & *v.* ● *n.* **1 a** a usu. pre-arranged sign conveying information, guidance, etc. esp. at a distance (*waved as a signal to begin*). **b** a message made up of such signs (*signals made with flags*). **2** an immediate occasion for, or cause, of movement, action, etc. (*the uprising was a signal for repression*). **3** *Electr.* **a** an electrical impulse or impulses or radio waves transmitted or received. **b** a sequence of these. **4** a light, semaphore, etc., on a railway giving instructions or warnings to train drivers etc. **5** *Bridge* a pre-arranged mode of bidding or play to convey information to one's partner. ● *v.* (**signalled**, **signalling**; *US* **signaled**, **signaling**) **1** *intr.* make signals. **2** *tr.* **a** (often foll. by *to* + infin.) make signals to; direct. **b** transmit (an order, information, etc.) by signal; announce (*signalled her agreement*; *signalled that the town had been taken*). □ **signaller** *n.* [Middle English from Old French, via Romanic & medieval Latin *signale*, neut. of Late Latin *signalis*, from Latin *signum* SIGN]

signal[2] /ˈsɪgn(ə)l/ *adj.* remarkably good or bad; noteworthy (*a signal victory*). □ **signally** *adv.* [French *signalé* from Italian past part. *segnalato* 'distinguished', from *segnale* SIGNAL[1]]

signal-book *n.* a list of signals arranged for sending esp. naval and military messages.

signal box *n. Brit.* a building beside a railway track from which signals, points, etc., are controlled.

signalize /ˈsɪgn(ə)lʌɪz/ *v.tr.* (also **-ise**) **1** make noteworthy or remarkable. **2** lend distinction or lustre to. **3** indicate.

signalman /ˈsɪgn(ə)lmən/ *n.* (*pl.* **-men**) **1** a railway employee responsible for operating signals and points. **2** a person who displays or receives naval etc. signals.

signal of distress *n.* esp. *Naut.* an appeal for help, esp. from a ship by firing guns.

signal-to-noise ratio *n.* the ratio of the strength of an electrical or other signal carrying information to that of unwanted interference, usu. expressed in decibels.

signal tower *n. US* = SIGNAL BOX.

signary /ˈsɪgnəri/ *n.* (*pl.* **-ies**) a list of signs constituting the syllabic or alphabetic symbols of a language. [Latin *signum* SIGN + -ARY[1], on the pattern of *syllabary*]

signatory /ˈsɪgnət(ə)ri/ *n.* & *adj.* ● *n.* (*pl.* **-ies**) a party or esp. a state that has signed an agreement or esp. a treaty. ● *adj.* having signed such an agreement etc. [Latin *signatorius* 'of sealing' from *signare signat-* 'to sign, mark']

signature /ˈsɪgnətʃə/ *n.* **1 a** a person's name, initials, or mark used in signing a letter, document, etc. **b** the act of signing a document etc. **2** a distinctive pattern or characteristic by which something can be identified. **3** *Mus.* **a** = KEY SIGNATURE. **b** = TIME SIGNATURE. **4** *Printing* **a** a letter or figure placed at the foot of one or more pages of each sheet of a book as a guide for binding. **b** such a sheet after folding. **5** *US* directions given to a patient as part of a medical prescription. [medieval Latin *signatura* (in Late Latin = marking of sheep), as SIGNATORY]

signature dish *n.* a speciality dish created by and associated with a particular chef.

signature tune *n.* esp. *Brit.* a distinctive tune used to introduce a particular programme or performer on television or radio.

signboard /ˈsʌɪnbɔːd/ *n.* a board with a name or symbol etc. displayed outside a shop or hotel etc.

signee /sʌɪˈniː/ *n.* a person who has signed a contract, register, etc.

signet /ˈsɪgnɪt/ *n.* **1** a seal used instead of or with a signature as authentication. **2** (prec. by *the*) the royal seal formerly used for special purposes in England and Scotland, and in Scotland later as the seal of the Court of Session. [Middle English from Old French *signet* or medieval Latin *signetum* (as SIGN)]

signet ring *n.* a ring with a seal set in it.

significance /sɪgˈnɪfɪk(ə)ns/ *n.* **1** importance; noteworthiness (*his opinion is of no significance*). **2** a concealed or real meaning (*what is the significance of his statement?*). **3** the state of being significant. **4** *Statistics* the extent to which a result deviates from that expected to arise simply from random variation or errors in sampling. [Old French *significance* or Latin *significantia* (as SIGNIFY)]

significant /sɪgˈnɪfɪk(ə)nt/ *adj.* **1** having a meaning; indicative. **2** having an unstated or secret meaning; suggestive (*refused it with a significant gesture*). **3** noteworthy; important; consequential (*a significant figure in history*). **4** *Statistics* of or relating to significance; departing from the null hypothesis. □ **significantly** *adv.* [Latin *significare*: see SIGNIFY]

significant figure *n. Math.* a digit conveying information about a number containing it, and not a zero used simply to fill vacant space at the beginning or end.

signification /ˌsɪgnɪfɪˈkeɪʃ(ə)n/ *n.* **1** the act of signifying. **2** (usu. foll. by *of*) exact meaning or sense, esp. of a word or phrase. [Middle English via Old French from Latin *significatio -onis* (as SIGNIFY)]

significative /sɪɡˈnɪfɪkətɪv/ *adj.* **1** (esp. of a symbol etc.) signifying. **2** having a meaning. **3** (usu. foll. by *of*) serving as a sign or evidence. [Middle English from Old French *significatif -ive* or Late Latin *significativus* (as SIGNIFY)]

signify /ˈsɪɡnɪfʌɪ/ *v.* (**-ies, -ied**) **1** *tr.* be a sign or indication of (*a yawn signifies boredom*). **2** *tr.* mean; have as its meaning (*'Dr' signifies 'doctor'*). **3** *tr.* communicate; make known (*signified their agreement*). **4** *intr.* be of importance; matter (*it signifies little*). □ **signifier** *n.* [Middle English via Old French *signifier* from Latin *significare* (as SIGN)]

signing /ˈsʌɪnɪŋ/ *n. Brit.* a person who has recently signed a contract, esp. to join a professional sports team.

sign language *n.* a system of communication by visual gestures, used esp. by the deaf.

sign-off *n. Bridge* a conventional bid made to indicate that the bidder wishes to end bidding.

sign of the cross *n.* a Christian sign made in blessing or prayer, by tracing a cross from the forehead to the chest and to each shoulder, or in the air.

sign of the times *n.* a portent etc. showing a likely trend.

signor /ˈsiːnjɔː/ *n.* (*pl.* **signori** /-ˈnjɔːriː/) **1** a title or form of address used of or to an Italian-speaking man, corresponding to Mr or sir. **2** an Italian man. [Italian from Latin *senior*: see SENIOR]

signora /siːnˈjɔːrə/ *n.* **1** a title or form of address used of or to an Italian-speaking married woman, corresponding to Mrs or madam. **2** a married Italian woman. [Italian, fem. of SIGNOR]

signorina /siːnjəˈriːnə/ *n.* **1** a title or form of address used of or to an Italian-speaking unmarried woman. **2** an Italian unmarried woman. [Italian, diminutive of SIGNORA]

signory /ˈsiːnjəri/ *n.* (*pl.* **-ies**) **1** = SEIGNIORY. **2** *hist.* the governing body of a medieval Italian republic. [Middle English from Old French *s(e)ignorie* (as SEIGNEUR)]

signpost /ˈsʌɪnpəʊst/ *n.* & *v.* ● *n.* **1** a sign indicating the direction to and sometimes also the distance from various places, esp. a post with arms at a road junction. **2** a means of guidance; an indication. ● *v.tr.* **1** provide with a signpost or signposts. **2** esp. *Brit.* indicate (a course of action, direction, etc.).

signwriter /ˈsʌɪnrʌɪtə/ *n.* (also **sign-painter**) a person who paints signboards etc. □ **signwriting** *n.*

sika /ˈsiːkə/ *n.* a forest-dwelling deer, *Cervus nippon*, native to Japan and SE Asia and naturalized in Britain and elsewhere. [Japanese *shika*]

Sikh /siːk/ *n.* & *adj.* ● *n.* a member of an Indian monotheistic sect founded in the 16th c. ● *adj.* of or relating to Sikhs or Sikhism. [Punjabi, Hindi, from Sanskrit *śisya* 'disciple']

Sikhism /ˈsiːkɪz(ə)m, ˈsɪk-/ *n.* the religious tenets of the Sikhs.

silage /ˈsʌɪlɪdʒ/ *n.* & *v.* ● *n.* **1** storage in a silo. **2** green fodder preserved by pressure in a silo. ● *v.tr.* put into a silo. [alteration of ENSILAGE, influenced by *silo*]

sild /sɪld/ *n.* a small immature herring, esp. one caught in N. European seas. [Danish & Norwegian]

silence /ˈsʌɪləns/ *n.* & *v.* ● *n.* **1** absence of sound. **2** abstinence from speech or noise. **3** the avoidance of mentioning a thing, betraying a secret, etc. **4** oblivion; the state of not being mentioned. ● *v.tr.* **1** make silent, esp. by coercion or superior argument. **2** (usu. as **silenced** *adj.*) fit (a gun, exhaust system, etc.) with a silencer. □ **in silence** without speech or other sound. **reduce** (or **put**) **to silence** refute in argument. [Middle English via Old French from Latin *silentium* (as SILENT)]

silencer /ˈsʌɪlənsə/ *n.* any of various devices for reducing the noise emitted by a gun or *Brit.* the exhaust of a motor vehicle.

silent /ˈsʌɪlənt/ *adj.* **1** not speaking; not uttering or making or accompanied by any sound. **2** (of a letter) written but not pronounced, e.g. *b* in *doubt*. **3** (of a film) without a synchronized soundtrack. **4** (of a person) taciturn; speaking little. **5** saying or recording nothing on some subject (*the records are silent on the incident*). **6** (of spirits) unflavoured. □ **silently** *adv.* [Latin *silēre silent-* 'be silent']

silent majority *n.* those of moderate opinions who rarely assert them.

silent partner *n. N. Amer.* = SLEEPING PARTNER.

silenus /sʌɪˈliːnəs/ *n.* (*pl.* **sileni** /-nʌɪ/) (in Greek mythology) a bearded old man like a satyr, sometimes with the tail and legs of a horse. [Latin from Greek *seilēnos*]

silex /ˈsʌɪlɛks/ *n.* silica, esp. quartz or flint. [Latin (as SILICA)]

silhouette /sɪlʊˈɛt/ *n.* & *v.* ● *n.* **1** a representation of a person or thing showing the outline only, usu. done in solid black on white or cut from paper. **2** the dark shadow or outline of a person or thing against a lighter background. ● *v.tr.* represent or (usu. in *passive*) show in silhouette. □ **in silhouette** seen or placed in outline. [named, for an obscure reason, after Étienne de *Silhouette*, French author and politician d. 1767]

silica /ˈsɪlɪkə/ *n.* silicon dioxide, occurring as quartz etc. and as a principal constituent of sandstone and other rocks. □ **siliceous** /-ˈlɪʃəs/ *adj.* (also **silicious**). [Latin *silex -icis* 'flint', on the pattern of *alumina* etc.]

silica gel *n.* hydrated silica in a hard granular hygroscopic form used as a desiccant.

silicate /ˈsɪlɪkeɪt, -kət/ *n.* any of the many insoluble compounds of a metal combined with silicon and oxygen, occurring widely in the rocks of the earth's crust.

silicic /sɪˈlɪsɪk/ *adj. Chem.* of silica or silicon.

silicify /sɪˈlɪsɪfʌɪ/ *v.tr.* (**-ies, -ied**) convert into or impregnate with silica. □ **silicification** /-sɪfɪˈkeɪʃ(ə)n/ *n.*

silicon /ˈsɪlɪk(ə)n/ *n. Chem.* a metalloid element occurring widely in silica and silicates, and used in the manufacture of glass (symbol **Si**). [Latin *silex -icis* 'flint' (on the pattern of *carbon*, *boron*), alteration of earlier *silicium*]

silicon carbide *n.* = CARBORUNDUM.

silicon chip *n.* a silicon microchip.

silicone /ˈsɪlɪkəʊn/ *n.* & *v.* ● *n.* any of the many polymeric organic compounds of silicon and oxygen with high resistance to cold, heat, water, and the passage of electricity. ● *v.tr.* treat with silicone.

Silicon Valley *n.* an area with a high concentration of electronics industries.

silicosis /sɪlɪˈkəʊsɪs/ *n.* lung fibrosis caused by the inhalation of dust containing silica. □ **silicotic** /-ˈkɒtɪk/ *adj.*

siliqua /ˈsɪlɪkwə/ *n.* (also **silique** /sɪˈliːk/) (*pl.* **siliquae** /-kwiː/ or **siliques** /sɪˈliːks/) the long narrow seed pod of a cruciferous plant. □ **siliquose** /-kwəʊs/ *adj.* **siliquous** /-kwəs/ *adj.* [Latin, = pod]

silk /sɪlk/ *n.* **1** a fine strong soft lustrous fibre produced by silkworms in making cocoons. **2** a similar fibre spun by some spiders etc. **3 a** thread or cloth made from silk fibre. **b** a fine soft thread (*embroidery silk*). **4** (in *pl.*) kinds of silk cloth or garments made from it, esp. as worn by a jockey in a horse-owner's colours. **5** *Brit. colloq.* Queen's (or King's) Counsel, as having the right to wear a silk gown. **6** (*attrib.*) made of silk (*silk blouse*). **7** the silky styles of the female maize-flower. □ **take silk** *Brit.* become a Queen's (or King's) Counsel. □ **silklike** *adj.* [Old English *sioloc*, *seolec* from Late Latin *sericum*, neut. of Latin *sericus*, ultimately from Greek *Sēres*, the name given to the inhabitants of the Far Eastern countries from which silk first came to Europe]

silk cotton *n.* kapok or a similar substance.

silken /ˈsɪlk(ə)n/ *adj.* **1** made of silk. **2** wearing silk. **3** soft or lustrous as silk. **4** (of a person's manner etc.) suave or insinuating. [Old English *seolcen* (as SILK)]

silk-fowl *n.* a breed of fowl with a silky plumage.

silk-gland *n.* a gland secreting the substance produced as silk.

silk hat *n.* a tall cylindrical hat covered with silk plush.

silk moth *n.* any of various large moths of the families Bombycidae and Saturniidae, whose caterpillars spin a protective silken cocoon, esp. the adult of the silkworm.

silk screen *n.* & *v.* ● *n.* a screen of fine mesh used in screen printing. ● *v.tr.* (**silk-screen**) print, decorate, or reproduce using a silk screen.

silkworm /ˈsɪlkwəːm/ *n.* the caterpillar of the moth *Bombyx mori*, which spins a cocoon of silk and is bred commercially for this. [Old English *seolcwyrm* (as SILK, WORM)]

silky /ˈsɪlki/ *adj.* (**silkier**, **silkiest**) **1** like silk in smoothness, softness, fineness, or lustre. **2** (of a person's manner etc.) suave, insinuating. □ **silkily** *adv.* **silkiness** *n.*

sill /sɪl/ *n.* (also (esp. *Building*) **cill**) **1** a shelf or slab of stone, wood, or metal at the foot of a window or doorway. **2** a horizontal timber at the bottom of a dock or lock entrance, against which the gates close. **3** *Geol.* a tabular sheet of igneous rock intruded between other rocks and parallel with their planar structure. [Old English *syll*, *sylle*]

sillabub var. of SYLLABUB.

sillimanite /ˈsɪlɪmənʌɪt/ *n.* an aluminium silicate occurring in orthorhombic crystals or fibrous masses. [named after B. *Silliman*, American chemist d. 1864]

silly /ˈsɪli/ *adj.* & *n.* ● *adj.* (**sillier**, **silliest**) **1** lacking sense; foolish, imprudent, unwise. **2** weak-minded. **3** *Cricket* (of a fielder or position) very close to the batsman (*silly mid-off*). **4** *archaic* innocent, simple, helpless. ● *n.* (*pl.* **-ies**) *colloq.* a foolish person. □ **sillily** *adv.* **silliness** *n.* [later form of Middle English *sely* (dialect *seely*) 'happy', representing Old English *sǣlig* (recorded in *unsǣlig* 'unhappy'), from Germanic]

silly billy *n. colloq.* a foolish person.

silly season *n.* high summer as the season when newspapers often publish trivial material for lack of important news.

silo /ˈsʌɪləʊ/ *n.* & *v.* ● *n.* (*pl.* **-os**) **1** a pit or airtight structure in which green crops are pressed and kept for fodder, undergoing fermentation. **2** a pit or tower for the storage of grain, cement, etc. **3** an underground chamber in which a guided missile is kept ready for firing. ● *v.tr.* (**-oes**, **-oed**) make silage of. [Spanish, via Latin *sirus* from Greek *siros* 'corn-pit']

silt /sɪlt/ *n.* & *v.* ● *n.* sediment deposited by water in a channel, harbour, etc. ● *v.tr.* & *intr.* (often foll. by *up*) choke or be choked with silt. □ **siltation** /-ˈteɪʃ(ə)n/ *n.* **silty** *adj.* [Middle English, perhaps related to Danish, Norwegian *sylt*, Old Low German *sulta*, Old High German *sulza* 'salt marsh': related to SALT]

siltstone /ˈsɪltstəʊn/ *n.* rock of consolidated silt.

Silurian /sʌɪˈljʊərɪən, sɪ-/ *adj.* & *n. Geol.* ● *adj.* of or relating to the third period of the Palaeozoic era with evidence of the first fish and land plants, and the formation of mountains and new land areas. Cf. Appendix X. ● *n.* this period or system. [Latin *Silures*, a people of ancient SE Wales]

silva var. of SYLVA.

silvan var. of SYLVAN.

silver /ˈsɪlvə/ *n.*, *adj.*, & *v.* ● *n. Chem.* **1** a greyish-white lustrous malleable ductile precious metallic element, occurring naturally as the element and in mineral form, and used chiefly with an admixture of harder metals for coin, plate, and ornaments, as a subordinate monetary medium, and in compounds for photography etc. (symbol Ag). **2** the colour of silver. **3** silver or cupro-nickel coins. **4** esp. *Sc.* money. **5** silver vessels or implements, esp. cutlery. **6** household cutlery of any material. **7** = SILVER MEDAL. ● *adj.* **1** made wholly or chiefly of silver. **2** coloured like silver. ● *v.* **1** *tr.* coat or plate with silver. **2** *tr.* provide (mirror glass) with a backing of tin amalgam etc. **3** *tr.* (of the moon or a white light) give a silvery appearance to. **4 a** *tr.* turn (the hair) grey or white. **b** *intr.* (of the hair) turn grey or white. [Old English *seolfor*, from Germanic]

silver age *n.* a period regarded as inferior to a golden age, e.g. that of post-classical Latin literature in the early Imperial period.

silver band *n. Brit.* a band playing silver-plated instruments.

silver birch *n.* a common birch, *Betula alba*, with silver-coloured bark.

silver fern *n.* **1** a New Zealand tree fern, *Cyathea dealbata*. **2** a stylized silver fern leaf as an emblem of New Zealand.

silver fir *n.* any fir of the genus *Abies*, with the undersides of its leaves coloured silver.

silverfish /ˈsɪlvəfɪʃ/ *n.* (*pl.* usu. same) **1** any small silvery wingless insect of the order Thysanura, esp. *Lepisma saccharina* in houses and other buildings. **2** a silver-coloured fish, esp. a colourless variety of goldfish.

silver fox *n.* **1** an American red fox at a time when its fur is black with white tips. **2** its fur.

silver gilt *n.* **1** gilded silver. **2** an imitation gilding of yellow lacquer over silver leaf.

silver grey *n.* & *adj.* ● *n.* a lustrous grey. ● *adj.* (hyphenated when *attrib.*) of this colour.

silver jubilee *n.* **1** the 25th anniversary of a sovereign's accession. **2** any other 25th anniversary.

silver Latin *n.* literary Latin of the early Imperial period.

silver-leaf *n.* a fungal disease of fruit trees.

silver lining *n.* a consolation or hopeful feature in misfortune.

silver medal *n.* a silver-coloured medal, usu. awarded as second prize.

silvern /ˈsɪlv(ə)n/ *adj. archaic* or *poet.* = SILVER *adj.* [Old English *seolfren*, *silfren* (as SILVER)]

silver nitrate *n.* a colourless solid, soluble in water, formerly used in photography. Chem. formula: $AgNO_3$.

silver paper *n.* **1** esp. *Brit.* aluminium or occasionally tin foil. **2** a fine white tissue paper for wrapping silver.

silver plate *n.* vessels, spoons, etc., of copper etc. plated with silver.

silver salmon *n.* = COHO.

silver sand *n. Brit.* a fine pure sand used in gardening.

silver screen *n.* (usu. prec. by *the*) motion pictures collectively.

silverside /ˈsɪlvəsʌɪd/ *n.* **1** *Brit.* the upper side of a round of beef from the outside of the leg. **2** (also **silversides**) a small fish of the mainly marine family Atherinidae, with a silver line along the side.

silversmith /ˈsɪlvəsmɪθ/ *n.* a worker in silver; a manufacturer of silver articles. □ **silversmithing** *n.*

silver solder *n.* solder containing silver.

silver spoon *n.* a sign of future prosperity.

silver standard *n.* a system by which the value of a currency is defined in terms of silver, for which the currency may be exchanged.

silver thaw *n.* the formation of a glassy coating of ice on the ground or an exposed surface by freezing rain or the refreezing of thawed ice.

silver tongue *n.* eloquence.

silverware /ˈsɪlvəwɛː/ *n.* articles made of or coated with silver.

silver wedding *n.* the 25th anniversary of a wedding.

silverweed /ˈsɪlvəwiːd/ *n.* a plant with silvery leaves, esp. a potentilla, *Potentilla anserina*, with silver-coloured leaves.

silvery /ˈsɪlv(ə)ri/ *adj.* **1** like silver in colour or appearance. **2** having a clear gentle ringing sound. **3** (of the hair) white and lustrous. □ **silveriness** *n.*

silviculture /ˈsɪlvɪkʌltʃə/ *n.* (also **sylviculture**) the growing and tending of trees as a branch of forestry. □ **silvicultural** /-ˈkʌltʃ(ə)r(ə)l/ *adj.* **silviculturist** /-ˈkʌltʃərɪst/ *n.* [French, from Latin *silva* 'a wood' + French *culture* CULTURE]

sima /ˈsʌɪmə/ *n. Geol.* **1** the lower layer of the earth's crust, underlying both the oceans and continental masses. **2** the material of this, relatively heavy basic rock rich in silica and magnesia. [SILICA + MAGNESIA]

simian /ˈsɪmɪən/ *adj. & n.* ● *adj.* **1** of or concerning the anthropoid apes. **2** like an ape or monkey (*a simian walk*). ● *n.* an ape or monkey. [Latin *simia* 'ape', perhaps via Latin *simus* from Greek *simos* 'flat-nosed']

similar /ˈsɪmɪlə/ *adj. & n.* ● *adj.* **1** (often foll. by *to*) like, alike; of the same kind, nature, or amount; having a resemblance (*your house is similar to mine*; *we have similar tastes*). **2** *Geom.* shaped alike. ● *n.* a person or thing similar to another; a counterpart. □ **similarity** /-ˈlarɪti/ *n.* (*pl.* **-ies**). **similarly** *adv.* [French *similaire* or medieval Latin *similaris* from Latin *similis* 'like']

■ **Usage** In sense 1, similar should be followed by *to*, not *as*. The following are non-standard: *I have had similar problems as yourself*; *You've come up with similar suggestions as we have.* They can be reworded as follows: *I have had problems similar to yours*; *You've come up with suggestions similar to ours.*

simile /ˈsɪmɪli/ *n.* **1** a figure of speech involving the comparison of one thing with another of a different kind, as an illustration or ornament (e.g. *as brave as a lion*). **2** the use of such comparison. [Middle English from Latin, neut. of *similis* 'like']

similitude /sɪˈmɪlɪtjuːd/ *n.* **1** the likeness, guise, or outward appearance of a thing or person. **2** a comparison or the expression of a comparison. **3** *archaic* a counterpart or facsimile. [Middle English from Old French *similitude* or Latin *similitudo* (as SIMILE)]

simmer /ˈsɪmə/ *v. & n.* ● *v.* **1** *intr. & tr.* be or keep bubbling or boiling gently. **2** *intr.* be in a state of suppressed anger or excitement. ● *n.* a simmering condition. □ **simmer down** become calm or less agitated. [alteration of Middle English (now dialect) *simper*, perhaps imitative]

simnel cake /ˈsɪmn(ə)l/ *n. Brit.* a rich fruit cake, usu. with a marzipan layer and decoration, eaten esp. at Easter or during Lent. [Middle English from Old French *simenel*, ultimately from Latin *simila* or Greek *semidalis* 'fine flour']

simon-pure /sʌɪmənˈpjʊə/ *adj.* real, genuine. [(*the real*) *Simon Pure*, a character in Centlivre's *Bold Stroke for a Wife* (1717), who for part of the play is impersonated by another character]

simony /ˈsʌɪməni, ˈsɪm-/ *n.* the buying or selling of ecclesiastical privileges, e.g. pardons or benefices. □ **simoniac** /-ˈməʊnɪak/ *adj. & n.* **simoniacal** /-ˈnʌɪək(ə)l/ *adj.* [Middle English via Old French *simonie* from Late Latin *simonia*, from *Simon* Magus (Acts 8:18)]

simoom /sɪˈmuːm/ *n.* (also **simoon** /-muːn/) a hot dry dust-laden wind blowing at intervals esp. in the Arabian desert. [Arabic *samūm* from *samma* 'to poison']

simp /sɪmp/ *n. US colloq.* a simpleton. [abbreviation]

simpatico /sɪmˈpatɪkəʊ/ *adj.* congenial, likeable. [Italian & Spanish (as SYMPATHY)]

simper /ˈsɪmpə/ *v. & n.* ● *v.* **1** *intr.* smile in a silly or affected way. **2** *tr.* express by or with simpering. ● *n.* a silly or affected smile. □ **simperingly** *adv.* [16th c., of unkown origin: cf. Dutch and Scandinavian *semper*, *simper*, German *zimp(f)er* 'elegant, delicate']

simple /ˈsɪmp(ə)l/ *adj. & n.* ● *adj.* (**simpler**, **simplest**) **1** easily understood or done; presenting no difficulty (*a simple explanation*; *a simple task*). **2** not complicated or elaborate; without luxury or sophistication. **3** not compound; consisting of or involving only one element or operation etc. **4** absolute, unqualified, straightforward (*the simple truth*; *a simple majority*). **5** foolish or ignorant; gullible, feeble-minded (*am not so simple as to agree to that*). **6** plain in appearance or manner; unsophisticated, ingenuous, artless. **7** of low rank; humble, insignificant (*simple people*). **8** *Bot.* **a** consisting of one part. **b** (of fruit) formed from one pistil. ● *n. archaic* **1** a herb used medicinally. **2** a medicine made from it. □ **simpleness** *n.* [Middle English via Old French from Latin *simplus*]

simple eye *n.* an eye of an insect etc. having only one lens. Also called OCELLUS; cf. COMPOUND EYE.

simple fracture *n.* a fracture of the bone only, without a skin wound.

simple harmonic motion see HARMONIC MOTION.

simple interest *n.* interest payable on a capital sum only (cf. COMPOUND INTEREST).

simple interval *n. Mus.* an interval of one octave or less.

simple machine *n.* any of the basic mechanical devices for applying a force (e.g. an inclined plane, wedge, or lever).

simple-minded *adj.* **1** feeble-minded; foolish. **2** unsophisticated; ingenuous. □ **simple-mindedly** *adv.* **simple-mindedness** *n.*

simple sentence *n.* a sentence with a single subject and predicate.

Simple Simon *n.* a foolish person (from the nursery-rhyme character).

simple time *n. Mus.* a tempo with two, three, or four beats in a bar.

simpleton /ˈsɪmp(ə)lt(ə)n/ *n.* a foolish, gullible, or half-witted person. [SIMPLE, on the pattern of surnames from place names in *-ton*]

simplex /ˈsɪmplɛks/ *adj. & n.* ● *adj.* **1** simple; not compounded. **2** *Computing* (of a communication system, computer circuit, etc.) allowing transmission of signals in one direction only (opp. DUPLEX *adj.* 3). ● *n.* a simple or uncompounded thing, esp. a word. [Latin, = single, variant of *simplus* 'simple']

simplicity /sɪmˈplɪsɪti/ *n.* the fact or condition of being simple. □ **be simplicity itself** be extremely easy. [Old French *simplicité* or Latin *simplicitas* (as SIMPLEX)]

simplify /ˈsɪmplɪfʌɪ/ *v.tr.* (**-ies**, **-ied**) make simple; make easy or easier to do or understand. □ **simplification** /-fɪˈkeɪʃ(ə)n/ *n.* [French *simplifier* from medieval Latin *simplificare* (as SIMPLE)]

simplism /ˈsɪmplɪz(ə)m/ *n.* **1** affected simplicity. **2** the unjustifiable simplification of a problem etc.

simplistic /sɪmˈplɪstɪk/ *adj.* **1** excessively or affectedly simple. **2** oversimplified so as to conceal or distort difficulties. □ **simplistically** *adv.*

simply /ˈsɪmpli/ *adv.* **1** in a simple manner. **2** absolutely; without doubt (*simply astonishing*). **3** merely (*was simply trying to please*).

simulacrum /sɪmjʊˈleɪkrəm/ *n.* (*pl.* **simulacra** /-krə/) **1** an image of something. **2 a** a shadowy likeness; a deceptive substitute. **b** mere pretence. [Latin (as SIMULATE)]

simulate /ˈsɪmjʊleɪt/ *v.tr.* **1 a** pretend to have or feel (an attribute or feeling). **b** pretend to be. **2** imitate or counterfeit. **3 a** imitate the conditions of (a situation etc.), e.g. for training. **b** produce a computer model of (a process). **4** (as **simulated** *adj.*) made to resemble the real thing but not genuinely such (*simulated fur*). **5** (of a word) take or have an altered form suggested by (a word wrongly taken to be its source, e.g. *amuck*). □ **simulation** /-ˈleɪʃ(ə)n/ *n.* **simulative** /-lətɪv/ *adj.* [Latin *simulare* from *similis* 'like']

simulator /ˈsɪmjʊleɪtə/ *n.* **1** a person or thing that simulates. **2** a device designed to simulate the operations of a complex system, used esp. in training (*flight simulator*).

simulcast /ˈsɪm(ə)lkɑːst/ *n.* simultaneous transmission of the same programme on radio and television. [SIMULTANEOUS + BROADCAST]

simultaneous /sɪm(ə)lˈteɪmɪəs/ *adj.* (often foll. by *with*) occurring or operating at the same time. □ **simultaneity** /-təˈneɪɪti/ *n.* **simultaneously** *adv.* **simultaneousness** *n.* [medieval Latin *simultaneus* from Latin *simul* 'at the same time', probably influenced by *instantaneus* etc.]

simultaneous equations *n.pl.* equations involving two or more unknowns that are to have the same values in each equation.

simurg /sɪˈmə:g/ *n.* a monstrous bird of Persian myth, with the power of reasoning and speech. [Persian *sīmurġ*, from Pahlavi *sīn* 'eagle' + *murġ* 'bird']

sin[1] /sɪn/ *n. & v.* ● *n.* **1 a** the breaking of divine or moral law, esp. by a conscious act. **b** such an act. **2** an offence against good taste or propriety etc. ● *v.* (**sinned, sinning**) **1** *intr.* commit a sin. **2** *intr.* (foll. by *against*) offend. **3** *tr. archaic* commit (a sin). □ **as sin** *colloq.* extremely (*ugly as sin*). **for one's sins** esp. *Brit. joc.* as a judgement on one for something or other. **like sin** *colloq.* vehemently or forcefully. **live in sin** *colloq.* live together without being married. □ **sinless** *adj.* **sinlessly** *adv.* **sinlessness** *n.* [Old English *syn(n)*]

sin[2] /sʌɪn/ *abbr.* sine.

Sinaitic /sʌɪneɪˈɪtɪk/ *adj.* of or relating to Mount Sinai or of the Sinai peninsula. [variant of *Sinaic*, from *Sinai*, from Hebrew *sīnay*, with *t* added for euphony]

Sinanthropus /sɪˈnanθrəpəs/ *n.* a fossil hominid now usu. classed as *Homo erectus*. [modern Latin former genus name, as SINO- 'Chinese' (remains having been found near Beijing) + Greek *anthrōpos* 'man']

sin bin *n. colloq.* **1** *Ice Hockey* a penalty box. **2** *Brit.* a place set aside for offenders of various kinds.

since /sɪns/ *prep., conj., & adv.* ● *prep.* throughout, or at a point in, the period between (a specified time, event, etc.) and the time present or being considered (*must have happened since yesterday*; *has been going on since June*; *the greatest composer since Beethoven*). ● *conj.* **1** during or in the time after (*what have you been doing since we met?*; *has not spoken since the dog died*). **2** for the reason that, because; inasmuch as (*since you are drunk I will drive you home*). **3** (*ellipt.*) as being (*a more useful, since better designed, tool*). ● *adv.* **1** from that time or event until now or the time being considered (*have not seen them since*; *had been healthy ever since*; *has since been cut down*). **2** ago (*happened many years since*). [Middle English, reduced form of obsolete *sithence*, or from dialect *sin* (from *sithen* 'then, thereupon, afterwards') from Old English *siththon*]

sincere /sɪnˈsɪə/ *adj.* (**sincerer, sincerest**) **1** free from pretence or deceit; the same in reality as in appearance. **2** genuine, honest, frank. □ **sincereness** *n.* **sincerity** /-ˈsɛrɪti/ *n.* [Latin *sincerus* 'clean, pure']

sincerely /sɪnˈsɪəli/ *adv.* in a sincere manner. □ **yours sincerely** a formula for ending a usu. informal letter.

sinciput /ˈsɪnsɪpʌt/ *n. Anat.* the front of the skull from the forehead to the crown. □ **sincipital** /-ˈsɪpɪt(ə)l/ *adj.* [Latin, from *semi-* 'half' + *caput* 'head']

sine /sʌɪn/ *n. Math.* **1** the trigonometric function that is equal to the ratio of the side opposite a given angle (in a right-angled triangle) to the hypotenuse. **2** a function of the line drawn from one end of an arc perpendicularly to the radius through the other. [Latin *sinus* 'curve, fold of a toga', used in medieval Latin as translation of Arabic *jayb* 'bosom, sine']

sinecure /ˈsʌɪnɪkjʊə, ˈsɪn-/ *n.* a position that requires little or no work but usu. yields profit or honour. □ **sinecurism** *n.* **sinecurist** *n.* [Latin *sine cura* 'without care']

sine curve *n.* (also **sine wave**) a curve representing periodic oscillations of constant amplitude as given by a sine function: also called SINUSOID.

sine die /sʌɪni ˈdʌɪi:, sɪneɪ ˈdi:eɪ/ *adv.* (of business etc. adjourned indefinitely) with no appointed date. [Latin, = without day]

sine qua non /ˌsʌɪni kweɪ ˈnɒn, ˌsɪneɪ kwɑ: ˈnəʊn/ *n.* an indispensable condition or qualification. [Latin, = without which not]

sinew /ˈsɪnju:/ *n. & v.* ● *n.* **1** tough fibrous tissue uniting muscle to bone; a tendon. **2** (in *pl.*) muscles; bodily strength; wiriness. **3** (in *pl.*) that which forms the strength or framework of a plan, city, organization, etc. ● *v.tr. poet.* serve as the sinews of; sustain; hold together. □ **sinewless** *adj.* **sinewy** *adj.* [Old English *sin(e)we*, from Germanic]

sinews of war *n.pl.* money.

sinfonia /sɪnfəˈni:ə, sɪnˈfəʊnɪə/ *n. Mus.* **1** a symphony. **2** (in baroque music) an orchestral piece used as an introduction to an opera, cantata, or suite. **3** (**Sinfonia**; usu. in names) a small symphony orchestra. [Italian, = SYMPHONY]

sinfonietta /ˌsɪnfəʊnɪˈɛtə/ *n. Mus.* **1** a short or simple symphony. **2** (**Sinfonietta**; usu. in names) a small symphony orchestra. [Italian, diminutive of SINFONIA]

sinful /ˈsɪnfʊl, -f(ə)l/ *adj.* **1** (of a person) committing sin, esp. habitually. **2 a** (of an act) involving or characterized by sin. **b** *colloq.* reprehensible. □ **sinfully** *adv.* **sinfulness** *n.* [Old English *synfull* (as SIN[1], -FUL)]

sing /sɪŋ/ *v. & n.* ● *v.* (*past* **sang** /saŋ/; *past part.* **sung** /sʌŋ/) **1** *intr.* utter musical sounds with the voice, esp. words with a set tune. **2** *tr.* utter or produce by singing (*sing another song*). **3** *intr.* (of the wind, a kettle, etc.) make melodious, humming, buzzing, or whistling sounds. **4** *intr.* (of the ears) be affected as with a buzzing sound. **5** *tr.* bring to a specified state by singing (*sang the child to sleep*). **6** *tr.* (foll. by *in, out*) usher (esp. the new or old year) in or out with singing. **7** *intr. slang* turn informer; confess. **8** *intr. archaic* compose poetry. **9** *tr.* & (foll. by *of*) *intr.* celebrate in verse. ● *n.* **1** an act or spell of singing. **2** *US* a meeting for amateur singing. □ **sing along** sing in accompaniment to a song or piece of music. **sing out** call out loudly; shout. **sing the praises of** see PRAISE. **sing up** sing more loudly. □ **singable** *adj.* **singer** *n.* **singingly** *adv.* [Old English *singan*, from Germanic]

■ **Usage** The use of *sung* instead of *sang* for the past tense as in *She sung three songs* is non-standard.

sing. *abbr.* singular.

singalong /ˈsɪŋəlɒŋ/ *n.* **1** a tune etc. to which one can sing in accompaniment (also *attrib.*: *a singalong chorus*). **2** an occasion of community singing (also *attrib.*: *a singalong evening*).

singe /sɪn(d)ʒ/ *v. & n.* ● *v.* (**singeing**) **1** *tr. & intr.* burn superficially or lightly. **2** *tr.* burn the bristles or down off (the carcass of a pig or fowl) to prepare it for cooking. **3** *tr.* burn off the tips of (the hair) in hairdressing. ● *n.* a superficial burn. □ **singe one's wings** suffer harm esp. in a risky attempt. [Old English *sencgan*, from West Germanic]

singer-songwriter *n.* a person who sings and writes songs, esp. professionally.

Singh /sɪŋ/ *n.* **1** a title adopted by the warrior castes of northern India. **2** a surname adopted by male Sikhs. [Punjabi *siṅgh* 'lion' from Sanskrit *siṃha* 'lion']

Singhalese var. of SINHALESE.

singing hinny *n.* a currant cake baked on a griddle.

singing saw *n.* = MUSICAL SAW.

single /ˈsɪŋg(ə)l/ *adj., n., & v.* ● *adj.* **1** one only, not double or multiple. **2** united or undivided. **3 a** designed or suitable for one person (*single room*). **b** used or done by one person etc. or one set or pair. **4** one by itself; not one of several (*a single tree*). **5** regarded separately (*every single thing*). **6** not married; not involved in a sexual relationship. **7** *Brit.* (of a ticket) valid for an outward journey only, not for the return. **8** (with *neg.* or *interrog.*) even one; not to speak of more (*did not see a single person*). **9** (of a flower) having only one circle of petals. **10** lonely, unaided. **11** *archaic* free from duplicity, sincere, consistent, guileless, ingenuous. ● *n.* **1** a single thing, or item in a series. **2** *Brit.* a single ticket. **3** a short record with one piece of music etc. on each side. **4 a** *Cricket* a hit for one run. **b** *Baseball* a one-base hit. **5** (usu. *in pl.*) a game with one player on each side. **6** an unmarried person (*young singles*). **7** *US colloq.* a one-dollar note. ● *v.tr.* (foll. by *out* and often by *for, as*) select from a group as worthy of special attention, praise, etc. (*singled out for praise*; *singled out as the finest*). □ **singleness** *n.* **singly** *adv.* [Middle

English via Old French from Latin *singulus*, related to *simplus* SIMPLE]

single acrostic *n.* an acrostic using the first letter only of each line.

single-acting *adj.* (of an engine etc.) having pressure applied only to one side of the piston.

single-breasted *adj.* (of a jacket etc.) having only one set of buttons and buttonholes, not overlapping.

single combat *n.* a duel.

single cream *n. Brit.* thin cream with a relatively low fat content.

single cut *adj.* (of a file) with grooves cut in one direction only, not crossing.

single-decker *n.* esp. *Brit.* a bus having only one deck.

single entry *n.* a system of bookkeeping in which each transaction is entered in one account only.

single file *n. & adv.* ● *n.* a line of people or things arranged one behind another. ● *adv.* one behind another.

single-handed *adv. & adj.* ● *adv.* **1** without help from another. **2** with one hand. ● *adj.* **1** done etc. single-handed. **2** for one hand. □ **single-handedly** *adv.*

single-lens reflex *adj.* denoting a reflex camera in which a single lens serves the film and the viewfinder.

single-line *attrib.adj.* with movement of traffic in only one direction at a time.

single market *n.* an association of countries trading without restrictions, esp. in the European Union.

single-minded *adj.* having or intent on only one purpose. □ **single-mindedly** *adv.* **single-mindedness** *n.*

single parent *n.* a person bringing up a child or children without a partner.

singles bar *n.* a bar for single people seeking company.

single-seater *n.* a vehicle with one seat.

single stick *n.* **1** a basket-hilted stick of about a sword's length. **2** one-handed fencing with this.

singlet /'sɪŋglɪt/ *n.* **1** esp. *Brit.* a garment worn under or instead of a shirt; a vest. **2** a single unresolvable line in a spectrum. [originally, a man's short jacket: SINGLE + -ET[1], on the pattern of *doublet*, the garment being unlined]

singleton /'sɪŋg(ə)lt(ə)n/ *n.* **1** one card only of a suit, esp. as dealt to a player. **2 a** a single person or thing. **b** an only child. **3** a single child or animal born, not a twin etc. [SINGLE, on the pattern of *simpleton*]

singletree /'sɪŋg(ə)ltriː/ *n. US* = SWINGLETREE.

sing-song *adj., n., & v.* ● *adj.* uttered with a monotonous rhythm or cadence. ● *n.* **1** a sing-song manner. **2** *Brit.* an informal gathering for singing. ● *v.intr. & tr.* (*past* and *past part.* **sing-songed**) speak or recite in a sing-song manner.

singular /'sɪŋgjʊlə/ *adj. & n.* ● *adj.* **1** unique; much beyond the average; extraordinary. **2** eccentric or strange. **3** *Gram.* (of a word or form) denoting or referring to a single person or thing. **4** *Math.* possessing unique properties. **5** single, individual. ● *n. Gram.* **1** a singular word or form. **2** the singular number. □ **singularly** *adv.* [Middle English via Old French *singuler* from Latin *singularis* (as SINGLE)]

singularity /sɪŋgjʊ'larɪti/ *n.* (*pl.* **-ies**) **1** the state or condition of being singular. **2** an odd trait or peculiarity. **3** *Physics & Math.* a point at which a function takes an infinite value, esp. in space-time when matter is infinitely dense as at the centre of a black hole. [Middle English via Old French *singularité* from Late Latin *singularitas* (as SINGULAR)]

singularize /'sɪŋgjʊlərʌɪz/ *v.tr.* (also **-ise**) **1** distinguish, individualize. **2** make singular. □ **singularization** /-'zeɪʃ(ə)n/ *n.*

sinh /ʃʌɪn, sɪntʃ, sʌɪ'neɪtʃ/ *abbr. Math.* hyperbolic sine. [*sine* + *h*yperbolic]

Sinhalese /sɪnhə'liːz, sɪnə-/ *n. & adj.* (also **Singhalese** /sɪŋ-/) ● *n.* (*pl.* same) **1** a member of a people originally from N. India and now forming the majority of the population of Sri Lanka. **2** an Indic language spoken by this people. ● *adj.* of or relating to this people or language. [Sanskrit *siṅhalam* 'Sri Lanka' (Ceylon) + -ESE]

sinister /'sɪnɪstə/ *adj.* **1** suggestive of evil; looking malignant or villainous. **2** wicked or criminal (*a sinister motive*). **3** of evil omen. **4** *Heraldry* of or on the left-hand side of a shield etc. (i.e. to the observer's right). **5** *archaic* left-hand. □ **sinisterly** *adv.* **sinisterness** *n.* [Middle English from Old French *sinistre* or Latin *sinister* 'left']

sinistral /'sɪnɪstr(ə)l/ *adj.* **1** left-handed. **2** of or on the left. **3** (of a flatfish) with the left side uppermost. **4** (of a spiral shell) with whorls rising to the left and not (as usually) to the right. □ **sinistrality** /-'tralɪti/ *n.* **sinistrally** *adv.*

sinistrorse /'sɪnɪstrɔːs/ *adj.* rising towards the left, esp. of the spiral stem of a plant. [Latin *sinistrorsus*, from *sinister* 'left' + *vorsus*, past part. of *vertere* 'turn']

sink /sɪŋk/ *v. & n.* ● *v.* (*past* **sank** /saŋk/ or **sunk** /sʌŋk/; *past part.* **sunk** or as *adj.* **sunken**) **1** *intr.* fall or come slowly downwards. **2** *intr.* disappear below the horizon (*the sun is sinking*). **3** *intr.* **a** go or penetrate below the surface esp. of a liquid. **b** (of a ship) go to the bottom of the sea etc. **4** *intr.* settle down comfortably (*sank into a chair*). **5** *intr.* **a** gradually lose strength or value or quality etc.; decline (*my heart sank*). **b** (of the voice) descend in pitch or volume. **c** (of a sick person) approach death. **6** *tr.* send (a ship) to the bottom of the sea etc. **7** *tr.* cause or allow to sink or penetrate (*sank its teeth into my leg*). **8** *tr.* cause the failure of (a plan etc.) or the discomfiture of (a person). **9** *tr.* dig (a well) or bore (a shaft). **10** *tr.* engrave (a die) or inlay (a design). **11** *tr.* **a** invest (money) (*sunk a large sum into the business*). **b** lose (money) by investment. **12** *tr.* **a** cause (a ball) to enter a pocket in billiards, a hole at golf, etc. **b** achieve this by (a stroke). **13** *tr.* overlook or forget; keep in the background (*sank their differences*). **14** *intr.* (of a price etc.) become lower. **15** *intr.* (of a storm or river) subside. **16** *intr.* (of ground) slope down, or reach a lower level by subsidence. **17** *intr.* (foll. by *on, upon*) (of darkness) descend (on a place). **18** *tr.* lower the level of. **19** *tr.* (usu. in *passive*; foll. by *in*) absorb; hold the attention of (*be sunk in thought*). ● *n.* **1** a fixed basin with a water supply and outflow pipe. **2** a place where foul liquid collects. **3** a place of vice or corruption. **4** a pool or marsh in which a river's water disappears by evaporation or percolation. **5** *Physics* a body or process used to absorb or dissipate heat. **6** (in full **sink-hole**) *Geol.* a cavity in limestone etc. into which a stream etc. disappears. □ **sink in 1** penetrate or make its way in. **2** become gradually comprehended (*paused to let the words sink in*). **sink or swim** even at the risk of complete failure (*determined to try, sink or swim*). □ **sinkable** *adj.* **sinkage** *n.* [Old English *sincan*, from Germanic]

■ **Usage** In the past tense either *sank* or *sunk* is acceptable in standard English, as in *It sank* or *sunk its teeth into her hand.*

sinker /'sɪŋkə/ *n.* **1** a weight used to sink a fishing line or sounding line. **2** *US* a doughnut. **3** *Baseball* a ball which drops markedly after being pitched or hit.

sinking feeling *n.* a bodily sensation, esp. in the abdomen, caused by hunger or apprehension.

sinking fund *n.* money set aside for the gradual repayment of a debt.

sinner /'sɪnə/ *n.* a person who sins, esp. habitually.

sinnet /'sɪnɪt/ *n.* (also **sennit**) *Naut.* braided cordage in flat or round or square form, made from 3 to 9 cords. [17th c.: origin unknown]

Sinn Fein /ʃɪn 'feɪn/ *n.* a political movement and party seeking a united republican Ireland, now linked to the IRA. □ **Sinn Feiner** *n.* [Irish *sinn féin* 'we ourselves']

Sino- /'sʌɪnəʊ/ *comb. form* Chinese; Chinese and (*Sino-British*). [Greek *Sinai* 'the Chinese']

sinologue /'sʌɪnəlɒg, 'sɪ-/ *n.* an expert in sinology. [French (as SINO- + Greek *-logos* 'speaking')]

sinology /sʌɪˈnɒlədʒi, sɪ-/ *n.* the study of Chinese language, history, customs, etc. ◻ **sinological** /-nəˈlɒdʒɪk(ə)l/ *adj.* **sinologist** *n.*

sinter /ˈsɪntə/ *n.* & *v.* ● *n.* **1** a siliceous or calcareous rock formed by deposition from springs. **2** a substance formed by sintering. ● *v.intr.* & *tr.* coalesce or cause to coalesce from powder into solid by heating. [German, = English *sinder* CINDER]

sinuate /ˈsɪnjʊət/ *adj.* esp. *Bot.* wavy-edged; with distinct inward and outward bends along the edge. [Latin *sinuatus*, past part. of *sinuare* 'bend']

sinuosity /sɪnjʊˈɒsɪti/ *n.* (*pl.* **-ies**) **1** the state of being sinuous. **2** a bend, esp. in a stream or road. [French *sinuosité* or medieval Latin *sinuositas* (as SINUOUS)]

sinuous /ˈsɪnjʊəs/ *adj.* with many curves; tortuous, undulating. ◻ **sinuously** *adv.* **sinuousness** *n.* [French *sinueux* or Latin *sinuosus* (as SINUS)]

sinus /ˈsʌɪnəs/ *n.* **1** a cavity of bone or tissue, esp. in the skull connecting with the nostrils. **2** *Med.* a fistula, esp. to a deep abscess. **3** *Bot.* the curve between the lobes of a leaf. [Latin, = bosom, recess]

sinusitis /sʌɪnəˈsʌɪtɪs/ *n.* inflammation of a nasal sinus.

sinusoid /ˈsʌɪnəsɔɪd/ *n.* **1** a curve having the form of a sine wave. **2** a small irregularly-shaped blood vessel, esp. found in the liver. ◻ **sinusoidal** /-ˈsɔɪd(ə)l/ *adj.* **sinusoidally** /-ˈsɔɪd(ə)li/ *adv.* [French *sinusoïde* from Latin *sinus*: see SINUS]

Sion var. of ZION.

-sion /ʃ(ə)n, ʒ(ə)n/ *suffix* forming nouns (see -ION) from Latin participial stems in *-s-* (*mansion*; *mission*; *persuasion*).

Sioux /suː/ *n.* & *adj.* ● *n.* (*pl.* same) **1** a member of a group of N. American Indian peoples chiefly inhabiting the upper Mississippi and Missouri river basins. **2** the language of these peoples. ● *adj.* of or relating to these peoples or language. ◻ **Siouan** /ˈsuːən/ *adj.* & *n.* [N. American French from *Nadouessioux* from Ojibwa (Ottawa dialect) *nātowēssiwak*, with French pl. ending *-x* replacing Ojibwa pl. ending *-ak*]

sip /sɪp/ *v.* & *n.* ● *v.tr.* & *intr.* (**sipped**, **sipping**) drink in one or more small amounts or by spoonfuls. ● *n.* **1** a small mouthful of liquid (*a sip of brandy*). **2** the act of taking this. ◻ **sipper** *n.* [Middle English: perhaps a modification of SUP[1]]

sipe /sʌɪp/ *n.* a groove or channel in the tread of a tyre to improve its grip. [dialect *sipe* 'to ooze' from Old English *sīpian*, Middle Low German *sīpen*, of unknown origin]

siphon var. of SYPHON.

siphonophore /sʌɪˈfɒnəfɔː/ *n.* any usu. translucent marine hydrozoan of the order Siphonophora, e.g. the Portuguese man-of-war. [Greek *siphōno-* (as SYPHON, -PHORE)]

sippet /ˈsɪpɪt/ *n.* **1** a small piece of bread etc. soaked in liquid. **2** a piece of toast or fried bread as a garnish. **3** a fragment. [apparently diminutive of SOP]

sir /səː/ *n.* **1** a polite or respectful form of address or mode of reference to a man. **2** (**Sir**) a titular prefix to the forename of a knight or baronet. [Middle English, reduced form of SIRE]

sirdar /ˈsəːdɑː/ *n.* (also **sardar** *pronunc.* same) **1** (esp. in the Indian subcontinent) a person of high political or military rank; a leader. **2** a Sikh. [Urdu *sardār*, from Persian *sar* 'head' + *dār* 'possessor']

sire /sʌɪə/ *n.* & *v.* ● *n.* **1** the male parent of an animal, esp. a stallion kept for breeding. **2** *archaic* a respectful form of address, now esp. to a king. **3** *archaic poet.* a father or male ancestor. ● *v.tr.* (esp. of an animal) beget. [Middle English from Old French, ultimately from Latin *senior*: see SENIOR]

siren /ˈsʌɪr(ə)n/ *n.* **1 a** a device for making a loud prolonged signal or warning sound, esp. by revolving a perforated disc over a jet of compressed air or steam. **b** the sound made by this. **2** (in Greek mythology) each of a number of women or winged creatures whose singing lured unwary sailors on to rocks. **3** a sweet singer. **4 a** a dangerously fascinating woman; a temptress. **b** a tempting pursuit etc. **5** (*attrib.*) irresistibly tempting. **6** an eel-shaped tailed amphibian of the family Sirenidae. [Middle English via Old French *sereine*, *sirene* from Late Latin *Sirena*, fem. of Latin *siren*, from Greek *Seirēn*]

sirenian /sʌɪˈriːnɪən/ *adj.* & *n.* ● *adj.* of the order Sirenia of large aquatic plant-eating mammals, e.g. the manatee and dugong. ● *n.* any mammal of this order. [modern Latin *Sirenia* (as SIREN)]

siren suit *n.* a one-piece garment for the whole body, easily put on or taken off, originally for use in air-raid shelters.

sirloin /ˈsəːlɔɪn/ *n.* the upper and choicer part of a loin of beef. [Old French (as SUR-[1], LOIN)]

sirocco /sɪˈrɒkəʊ/ *n.* (also **scirocco**) (*pl.* **-os**) a hot, oppressive, often dusty or rainy wind blowing from N. Africa across the Mediterranean to southern Europe. [French from Italian *scirocco*, ultimately from Arabic *Šarūḳ* 'east wind']

sirrah /ˈsɪrə/ *n.* *archaic* = SIR (as a form of address). [probably from Middle English *sirě* SIR]

sirree /sɪˈriː/ *int.* *US colloq.* as an emphatic, esp. after *yes* or *no*. [SIR + emphatic suffix]

sirup *US* var. of SYRUP.

SIS *abbr.* (in the UK) Secret Intelligence Service.

sis /sɪs/ *n.* *colloq.* a sister. [abbreviation]

sisal /ˈsʌɪs(ə)l/ *n.* **1** a Mexican plant, *Agave sisalana*, with large fleshy leaves. **2** the fibre made from this plant, used for cordage, ropes, etc. [*Sisal*, a port in Yucatán, Mexico]

siskin /ˈsɪskɪn/ *n.* a dark-streaked yellowish-green songbird, *Carduelis spinus*, allied to the goldfinch. [Middle Dutch *siseken* diminutive, related to Middle Low German *sīsek*, Middle High German *zīse*, *zīsec*, of Slavonic origin]

sissy /ˈsɪsi/ *n.* & *adj.* (also **cissy**) *colloq.* ● *n.* (*pl.* **-ies**) an effeminate or cowardly person. ● *adj.* (**sissier**, **sissiest**) effeminate; cowardly. ◻ **sissified** *adj.* **sissiness** *n.* **sissyish** *adj.* [SIS + -Y[2]]

sister /ˈsɪstə/ *n.* **1** a woman or girl in relation to sons and other daughters of her parents. **2 a** (often as a form of address) a close female friend or associate. **b** a female fellow member of a trade union, class, sect, or the human race. **c** a fellow feminist. **3** *Brit.* a senior female nurse. **4** a member of a female religious order. **5** (often *attrib.*) of the same type or design or origin etc. (*sister ship*; *prose, the younger sister of verse*). ◻ **sisterless** *adj.* **sisterly** *adj.* **sisterliness** *n.* [Middle English *sister* (from Old Norse), *suster* etc. (representing Old English *sweoster*, from Germanic)]

sister city *n.* a city that is twinned with another.

sister german see GERMAN 1.

sisterhood /ˈsɪstəhʊd/ *n.* **1** the relationship between sisters. **2 a** a society or association of women, esp. when bound by monastic vows or devoting themselves to religious or charitable work or the feminist cause. **b** its members collectively. **3** community of feeling and mutual support between women.

sister-in-law *n.* (*pl.* **sisters-in-law**) **1** the sister of one's wife or husband. **2** the wife of one's brother. **3** the wife of one's brother-in-law.

Sister of Mercy *n.* a member of an educational or charitable order of women, esp. that founded in Dublin in 1827.

sister uterine see UTERINE 2.

Sistine /ˈsɪstiːn, -tʌɪn/ *adj.* of any of the Popes called Sixtus, esp. Sixtus IV. [Italian *Sistino* from *Sisto* 'Sixtus']

Sistine Chapel *n.* a chapel in the Vatican, with frescoes by Michelangelo and other painters.

sistrum /ˈsɪstrəm/ *n.* (*pl.* **sistra** /-trə/) a jingling metal instrument used by the ancient Egyptians esp. in the worship of Isis. [Middle English via Latin from Greek *seistron*, from *seiō* 'shake']

Sisyphean /sɪsɪˈfiːən/ *adj.* (of toil) endless and fruitless like that of Sisyphus in Greek mythology (whose task in Hades was to push uphill a stone that at once rolled down again).

sit /sɪt/ *v. & n.* ● *v.* (**sitting**; *past* and *past part.* **sat** /sat/) **1** *intr.* adopt or be in a position in which the body is supported more or less upright by the buttocks resting on the ground or a raised seat etc., with the thighs usu. horizontal. **2** *tr.* cause to sit; place in a sitting position. **3** *intr.* **a** (of a bird) perch. **b** (of an animal) rest with the hind legs bent and the body close to the ground. **4** *intr.* (of a bird) remain on its nest to hatch its eggs. **5** *intr.* **a** be engaged in an occupation in which the sitting position is usual. **b** (of a committee, legislative body, etc.) be engaged in business. **c** (of an individual) be entitled to hold some office or position (*sat as a magistrate*). **6** *intr.* (usu. foll. by *for*) pose, usu. in a sitting position (for a portrait). **7** *intr.* (foll. by *for*) be a Member of Parliament for (a constituency). **8** *tr.* & (foll. by *for*) *intr. Brit.* take (an examination). **9** *intr.* be in a more or less permanent position or condition (esp. of inactivity or being out of use or out of place). **10** *intr.* (of clothes etc.) fit or hang in a certain way. **11** *tr.* keep or have one's seat on (a horse etc.). **12** *intr.* act as a babysitter. **13** *intr.* (often foll. by *before*) (of an army) take a position outside a city etc. to besiege it. ● *n.* the way clothing sits on a person. □ **make a person sit up** *colloq.* surprise or interest a person. **sit at a person's feet** be a person's pupil. **sit back** relax one's efforts. **sit by** look on without interfering. **sit down 1** sit after standing. **2** cause to sit. **3** (foll. by *under*) *Brit.* submit tamely to (an insult etc.). **sit heavy on the stomach** take a long time to be digested. **sit in 1** occupy a place as a protest. **2** (foll. by *for*) take the place of. **3** (foll. by *on*) be present as a guest or observer at (a meeting etc.). **sit in judgement** assume the right of judging others; be censorious. **sit loosely on** not be very binding. **sit on 1** be a member of (a committee etc.). **2** hold a session or inquiry concerning. **3** *colloq.* delay action about (*the government has been sitting on the report*). **4** *colloq.* repress or rebuke or snub (*felt rather sat on*). **sit on the fence** see FENCE. **sit on one's hands 1** take no action. **2** refuse to applaud. **sit out 1** take no part in (a dance etc.). **2** stay till the end of (esp. an ordeal). **3** sit outdoors. **4** outstay (other visitors). **sit tight** *colloq.* **1** remain firmly in one's place. **2** not be shaken off or move away or yield to distractions. **sit up 1** rise from a lying to a sitting position. **2** sit firmly upright. **3** go to bed later than the usual time. **4** *colloq.* become interested or aroused etc. **sit up and take notice** *colloq.* have one's interest aroused, esp. suddenly. **sit well** have a good seat in riding. **sit well on** suit or fit. [Old English *sittan*, from Germanic]

sitar /ˈsɪtɑː, sɪˈtɑː/ *n.* a long-necked Indian lute with movable frets. □ **sitarist** /sɪˈtɑːrɪst/ *n.* [Hindi *sitār*]

sitatunga /sɪtəˈtʌŋgə/ *n.* a medium-sized brown or greyish antelope, *Tragelaphus spekii*, of swamps in central and E. Africa, with splayed hoofs and, in the male, spiral horns. [Swahili]

sitcom /ˈsɪtkɒm/ *n. colloq.* a situation comedy. [abbreviation]

sit-down *adj. & n.* ● *adj.* **1** (of a meal) eaten sitting at a table. **2** (of a protest etc.) in which demonstrators occupy their workplace or sit down on the ground in a public place. ● *n.* **1** a period of sitting. **2** a sit-down protest etc.

site /sʌɪt/ *n. & v.* ● *n.* **1** the ground chosen or used for a town or building. **2** a place where some activity is or has been conducted (*camping site*; *launching site*). ● *v.tr.* **1** locate or place. **2** provide with a site. [Middle English from Anglo-French *site* or Latin *situs* 'local position']

sit-in *n.* a protest involving sitting in.

Sitka /ˈsɪtkə/ *n.* (in full **Sitka spruce**) a fast-growing spruce, *Picea sitchensis*, native to N. America and yielding timber. [*Sitka*, a town in Alaska]

sitrep /ˈsɪtrɛp/ *n.* a report on the current military situation in an area. [*sit*uation *rep*ort]

sits vac /sɪts ˈvak/ *n.pl. Brit. colloq.* situations vacant. [abbreviation]

sitter /ˈsɪtə/ *n.* **1** a person who sits, esp. for a portrait. **2** = BABYSITTER (see BABYSIT). **3** *colloq.* **a** an easy catch or shot. **b** an easy task. **4** a sitting hen.

sitting /ˈsɪtɪŋ/ *n. & adj.* ● *n.* **1** a continuous period of being seated, esp. engaged in an activity (*finished the book in one sitting*). **2** a time during which an assembly is engaged in business. **3** a session in which a meal is served (*dinner will be served in two sittings*). **4** *Brit. Law* = TERM 5c. **5** a clutch of eggs. ● *adj.* **1** having sat down. **2** (of an animal or bird) not running or flying. **3** (of a hen) engaged in hatching. **4** (of an MP) current. □ **sitting pretty** see PRETTY.

sitting duck *n.* (also **sitting target**) *colloq.* a vulnerable person or thing.

sitting room *n.* **1** esp. *Brit.* a room in a house for relaxed sitting in. **2** space enough to accommodate seated persons.

sitting tenant *n. Brit.* a tenant already in occupation of premises, esp. when there is a change of owner.

situate *v. & adj.* ● *v.tr.* /ˈsɪtjʊeɪt/ (usu. in *passive*) **1** put in a certain position or circumstances (*is situated at the top of a hill*; *how are you situated at the moment?*). **2** establish or indicate the place of; put in a context. ● *adj.* /ˈsɪtjʊət/ *Law* or *archaic* situated. [medieval Latin *situare situat-* from Latin *situs* 'site']

situation /sɪtjʊˈeɪʃ(ə)n/ *n.* **1** a place and its surroundings (*the house stands in a fine situation*). **2** a set of circumstances; a position in which one finds oneself; a state of affairs (*came out of a difficult situation with credit*). **3** an employee's position or job. **4** a critical point or complication in a drama. □ **situations vacant** (or **wanted**) esp. *Brit.* headings of lists of employment offered and sought. □ **situational** *adj.* **situationally** *adv.* [Middle English from French *situation* or medieval Latin *situatio* (as SITUATE)]

■ **Usage** In sense 2, *situation* can be preceded by an adjective as shown above. The substitution of an attributive noun should be avoided where possible since the result is usually ugly (e.g. *the rainforest situation*) and often tautologous (e.g. *in a crisis situation*: a crisis is in itself a situation). These can be reworded as *the situation regarding the rainforests* and *in a situation of crisis*.

situation comedy *n.* a comedy, esp. as part of a television or radio series, in which the humour derives from the situations the characters are placed in.

situationism /sɪtjʊˈeɪʃ(ə)nɪz(ə)m/ *n.* the theory that human behaviour is determined by surrounding circumstances rather than by personal qualities. □ **situationist** *n. & adj.*

sit-up *n.* a physical exercise in which a person sits up from a supine position without using the arms for leverage.

sit-upon *n. Brit. colloq.* the buttocks.

sitz-bath /ˈsɪtsbɑːθ/ *n.* a hip bath. [partial translation of German *Sitzbad*, from *sitzen* 'sit' + *Bad* 'bath']

Siva /ˈsiːvə, ˈʃiːvə/ *n.* (also **Shiva** /ˈʃiːvə/) a Hindu deity associated with the powers of reproduction and dissolution, regarded by some as the supreme being and by others as a member of the triad. □ **Sivaism** *n.* **Sivaite** *n. & adj.* [Sanskrit *Śiva*, literally 'the auspicious one']

six /sɪks/ *n. & adj.* ● *n.* **1** one more than five, or four less than ten; the product of two units and three units. **2** a symbol for this (6, vi, VI). **3** a size etc. denoted by six. **4** a set or team of six individuals. **5** *Cricket* a hit scoring six runs by clearing the boundary without bouncing. **6** the time of six o'clock. **7** a card etc. with six pips. ● *adj.* that amount to six. □ **at sixes and sevens** in confusion or disagreement. **knock for six** *Brit. colloq.* utterly surprise or overcome (a person). **six of one and half a dozen of the other** a situation of little real difference between the alternatives. [Old English *siex* etc., from Germanic]

sixain /'sɪkseɪn/ *n.* a six-line stanza. [French from *six* 'six']

Six Counties *n.pl.* the counties of N. Ireland.

sixer /'sɪksə/ *n.* **1** *Brit.* the leader of a group of six Brownies or Cubs. **2** *Cricket* a hit for six runs.

sixfold /'sɪksfəʊld/ *adj. & adv.* **1** six times as much or as many. **2** consisting of six parts.

six-gun *n.* = SIX-SHOOTER.

six-pack *n.* a pack of six cans of beer held together with a plastic fastener.

sixpence /'sɪksp(ə)ns/ *n. Brit.* **1** the sum of six pence, esp. before decimalization. **2** *hist.* a coin worth six old pence (2½ p). □ **on a sixpence 1** within a small area or short distance. **2** quickly and with ease.

sixpenny /'sɪkspəni/ *adj. Brit.* costing or worth six pence, esp. before decimalization.

six-shooter *n.* a revolver with six chambers.

sixte /sɪkst/ *n. Fencing* the sixth of the eight parrying positions. [French, from Latin *sextus* 'sixth']

sixteen /sɪks'tiːn, 'sɪkstiːn/ *n. & adj.* ● *n.* **1** one more than fifteen, or six more than ten. **2** a symbol for this (16, xvi, XVI). **3** a size etc. denoted by sixteen. ● *adj.* that amount to sixteen. □ **sixteenth** *adj. & n.* [Old English *siextiene* (as SIX, -TEEN)]

sixteenmo /sɪks'tiːnməʊ/ *n.* (*pl.* **-os**) = SEXTODECIMO. [English reading of the symbol 16mo]

sixteenth note *n.* esp. *N. Amer. Mus.* = SEMIQUAVER.

sixth /sɪksθ/ *n. & adj.* ● *n.* **1** the position in a sequence corresponding to that of the number 6 in the sequence 1-6. **2** something occupying this position. **3** any of six equal parts of a thing. **4** *Mus.* **a** an interval or chord spanning six consecutive notes in the diatonic scale (e.g. C to A). **b** a note separated from another by this interval. ● *adj.* that is the sixth. □ **sixthly** *adv.*

sixth form *n. Brit.* a form in a secondary school for pupils over 16.

sixth-form college *n. Brit.* a college for pupils over 16.

sixth-former *n. Brit.* a pupil in the sixth form.

sixth sense *n.* **1** a supposed faculty giving intuitive or extrasensory knowledge. **2** such knowledge.

Sixtine /'sɪkstiːn, -taɪn/ *adj.* = SISTINE. [modern Latin *Sixtinus* from *Sixtus*]

sixty /'sɪksti/ *n. & adj.* ● *n.* (*pl.* **-ies**) **1** the product of six and ten. **2** a symbol for this (60, lx, LX). **3** (in *pl.*) the numbers from 60 to 69, esp. the years of a century or of a person's life. **4** a set of sixty persons or things. ● *adj.* that amount to sixty. □ **sixty-first, -second**, etc. the ordinal numbers between sixtieth and seventieth. **sixty-one, -two**, etc. the cardinal numbers between sixty and seventy. □ **sixtieth** *adj. & n.* **sixtyfold** *adj. & adv.* [Old English *siextig* (as SIX, -TY²)]

sixty-fourmo /sɪkstɪ'fɔːməʊ/ *n.* (*pl.* **-os**) **1** a size of book in which each leaf is one-sixty-fourth the size of a printing-sheet. **2** a book of this size (on the pattern of DUODECIMO etc.).

sixty-fourth note *n.* esp. *N. Amer. Mus.* = HEMIDEMISEMIQUAVER.

sixty-four thousand dollar question *n.* (also **sixty-four dollar question**) a difficult and crucial question (from the top prize in a broadcast quiz show).

sizable var. of SIZEABLE.

sizar /'sʌɪzə/ *n.* an undergraduate at Cambridge or at Trinity College, Dublin, receiving financial help from the college and formerly having certain menial duties. □ **sizarship** *n.* [SIZE¹ = ration]

size¹ /sʌɪz/ *n. & v.* ● *n.* **1** the relative bigness or extent of a thing, dimensions, magnitude (*is of vast size*; *size matters less than quality*). **2** each of the classes, usu. numbered, into which things otherwise similar, esp. garments, are divided according to size (*is made in several sizes*; *takes size 7 in gloves*; *is three sizes too big*). ● *v.tr.* sort or group in sizes or according to size. □ **of a size** having the same size. **of some size** fairly large. **the size of** as big as. **the size of it** *colloq.* a true account of the matter (*that is the size of it*). **size up 1** estimate the size of. **2** *colloq.* form a judgement of. **what size?** how big? □ **sized** *adj.* (also in *comb.*). **sizer** *n.* [Middle English from Old French *sise*, from *assise* ASSIZE, or from ASSIZE (the earliest sense)]

size² /sʌɪz/ *n. & v.* ● *n.* a gelatinous solution used in glazing paper, stiffening textiles, preparing plastered walls for decoration, etc. ● *v.tr.* glaze or stiffen or treat with size. [Middle English, perhaps = SIZE¹]

sizeable /'sʌɪzəb(ə)l/ *adj.* (also **sizable**) large or fairly large. □ **sizeably** *adv.*

size-stick *n.* a shoemaker's measure for taking the length of a foot.

sizzle /'sɪz(ə)l/ *v. & n.* ● *v.* **1 a** *intr.* make a sputtering or hissing sound when or as if frying. **b** *tr.* fry or burn. **2** *intr. colloq.* **a** be in a state of great heat or excitement (*Britain sizzled in the heatwave*; *articles sizzling with the news*). **b** be salacious. ● *n.* **1** a sizzling sound. **2** *colloq.* a state of great heat or excitement. □ **sizzler** *n.* **sizzling** *adj. & adv.* (*sizzling hot*). [imitative]

SJ *abbr.* Society of Jesus.

SJAA *abbr.* (in the UK) St John Ambulance Association.

SJAB *abbr.* (in the UK) St John Ambulance Brigade.

sjambok /'ʃambɒk/ *n. & v.* ● *n.* (in S. Africa) a long stiff whip, originally made of rhinoceros hide. ● *v.tr.* flog with a sjambok. [Afrikaans, via Malay *samboq*, *chambok* from Urdu *chābuk*]

SJC *abbr.* (in the US) Supreme Judicial Court.

ska /skɑː/ *n.* a style of fast popular music with a strong offbeat, originating in Jamaica. [20th c.: origin unknown]

skag /skag/ *n.* (also **scag**) esp. *US slang* **1** a cigarette; a cigarette stub. **2** heroin. [20th c.: origin unknown]

skald /skɔːld, skald/ *n.* (also **scald**) (in ancient Scandinavia) a composer and reciter of poems honouring heroes and their deeds. □ **skaldic** *adj.* [Old Norse *skáld*, of unknown origin]

skat /skɑːt/ *n.* a three-handed card game with bidding. [German, via Italian *scarto* 'a discard' from *scartare* 'discard']

skate¹ /skeɪt/ *n. & v.* ● *n.* **1** each of a pair of steel blades (or of boots with blades attached) for gliding on ice. **2** = ROLLER SKATE *n.* **3** a device on which a heavy object moves. ● *v.* **1 a** *intr.* move on skates. **b** *tr.* perform (a specified figure) on skates. **2** *intr.* (foll. by *over*) refer fleetingly to, disregard. □ **get one's skates on** *Brit. colloq.* make haste. **skate on thin ice** *colloq.* behave rashly, risk danger, esp. by dealing with a subject needing tactful treatment. □ **skater** *n.* [originally *scates* (pl.) from Dutch *schaats* (sing.), from Old Northern French *escace*, Old French *eschasse* 'stilt']

skate² /skeɪt/ *n.* (*pl.* same or **skates**) any cartilaginous marine fish of the family Rajidae, esp. *Raja batis*, a large flat rhomboidal fish used as food. [Middle English from Old Norse *skata*]

skate³ /skeɪt/ *n. slang* a contemptible, mean, or dishonest person (esp. in *cheapskate*). [19th c.: origin uncertain]

skateboard /'skeɪtbɔːd/ *n. & v.* ● *n.* a short narrow board mounted on two wheeled trucks, used for riding on while standing, and propelled by one foot pushing occasionally against the ground. ● *v.intr.* ride on a skateboard. □ **skateboarder** *n.*

skatepark /'skeɪtpɑːk/ *n.* a park with ramps etc. for skateboarding.

skating rink *n.* **1** a piece of ice artificially made, or a floor used, for skating. **2** a building containing this.

skean /skiːn, 'skiːən/ *n. hist.* a Gaelic dagger formerly used in Ireland and Scotland. [Gaelic *sgian* 'knife']

skean-dhu /skiːn 'duː, skiːən-/ *n.* a dagger worn in the stocking as part of Highland dress. [Gaelic *dubh* 'black']

sked /skɛd/ *n. & v.* esp. *N. Amer. colloq.* ● *n.* = SCHEDULE. ● *v.tr.* (**skedded, skedding**) = SCHEDULE. [abbreviation]

skedaddle /skɪˈdad(ə)l/ *v. & n. colloq.* ● *v.intr.* run away, depart quickly, flee. ● *n.* a hurried departure or flight. [19th c.: origin unknown]

skeet /skiːt/ *n.* a shooting sport in which a clay target is thrown from a trap to simulate the flight of a bird. [Old Norse *skjóta* SHOOT]

skeeter[1] /ˈskiːtə/ *n.* esp. *N. Amer. & Austral. colloq. & dial.* a mosquito. [abbreviation]

skeeter[2] var. of SKITTER.

skeg /skɛg/ *n.* **1** a fin underneath the rear of a surfboard. **2** the after part of a vessel's keel or a projection from it. [Old Norse *skeg* 'beard', perhaps via Dutch *scheg(ge)*]

skein /skeɪn/ *n.* **1** a loosely-coiled bundle of yarn or thread. **2** a flock of wild geese etc. in flight. **3** a tangle or confusion. [Middle English from Old French *escaigne*, of unknown origin]

skeletal /ˈskɛlɪt(ə)l, skəˈliːt(ə)l/ *adj.* **1** of, forming, or resembling a skeleton. **2** very thin, emaciated. **3** consisting of only a bare outline or minimum. ◻ **skeletally** *adv.*

skeletal muscle *n.* = STRIATED MUSCLE.

skeleton /ˈskɛlɪt(ə)n/ *n.* **1 a** a hard internal or external framework of bones, cartilage, shell, woody fibre, etc., supporting or containing the body of an animal or plant. **b** the dried bones of a human being or other animal fastened together in the same relative positions as in life. **2** the supporting framework or structure or essential part of a thing. **3** a very thin or emaciated person or animal. **4** the remaining part of anything after its life or usefulness is gone. **5** an outline sketch, an epitome or abstract. **6** (*attrib.*) having only the essential or minimum number of persons, parts, etc. (*skeleton plan*; *skeleton staff*). ◻ **skeletonize** *v.tr.* (also **-ise**). [modern Latin from Greek, neut. of *skeletos* 'dried-up' from *skellō* 'dry up']

skeleton in the cupboard *n.* (*US* **skeleton in the closet**) a discreditable or embarrassing fact kept secret.

skeleton key *n.* a key designed to fit many locks by having the interior of the bit hollowed.

skelf /skɛlf/ *n. Sc.* **1** a splinter, a sliver. **2** *colloq.* a person who is a nuisance. [Middle English, probably from or as SHELF[1] (the earliest sense)]

skep /skɛp/ *n.* **1 a** a wooden or wicker basket of any of various forms. **b** the quantity contained in this. **2** a straw or wicker beehive. [Middle English from Old Norse *skeppa*]

skeptic *US* var. of SCEPTIC.

skeptical *US* var. of SCEPTICAL.

skepticism *US* var. of SCEPTICISM (see SCEPTIC).

skerrick /ˈskɛrɪk/ *n.* (usu. with *neg.*) esp. *Austral. colloq.* the smallest bit (*not a skerrick left*). [northern English dialect; origin uncertain]

skerry /ˈskɛri/ *n.* (*pl.* **-ies**) *Sc.* a reef or rocky island. [Orkney dialect from Old Norse *sker*: cf. SCAR[2]]

sketch /skɛtʃ/ *n. & v.* ● *n.* **1** a rough, slight, merely outlined, or unfinished drawing or painting, often made to assist in making a more finished picture. **2** a brief account without many details conveying a general idea of something; a rough draft or general outline. **3** a very short usu. humorous play or performance, often limited to one scene in a revue, comedy programme, etc. **4** a short descriptive piece of writing. **5** a musical composition of a single movement. **6** *colloq.* a comical person or thing. ● *v.* **1** *tr.* make or give a sketch of. **2** *intr.* draw sketches esp. of landscape (*went out sketching*). **3** *tr.* (often foll. by *in*, *out*) indicate briefly or in outline. ◻ **sketcher** *n.* [Dutch *schets* or German *Skizze* from Italian *schizzo*, from *schizzare* 'make a sketch', ultimately from Greek *skhēdios* 'extempore']

sketchbook /ˈskɛtʃbʊk/ *n.* (also **sketch-block**, **sketch pad**) a pad of drawing paper for doing sketches on.

sketch map *n.* a roughly drawn map with few details.

sketchy /ˈskɛtʃi/ *adj.* (**sketchier**, **sketchiest**) **1** giving only a slight or rough outline, like a sketch. **2** *colloq.* unsubstantial or imperfect, esp. through haste. ◻ **sketchily** *adv.* **sketchiness** *n.*

skeuomorph /ˈskjuːə(ʊ)mɔːf/ *n.* **1** an object or feature copying the design of a similar artefact in another material. **2** an ornamental design resulting from the nature of the material used or the method of working it. ◻ **skeuomorphic** /-ˈmɔːfɪk/ *adj.* [Greek *skeuos* 'vessel, implement' + *morphē* 'form']

skew /skjuː/ *adj., n., & v.* ● *adj.* **1** oblique, slanting, set askew. **2** *Math.* **a** lying in three dimensions (*skew curve*). **b** (of lines) not coplanar. **c** (of a statistical distribution) not symmetrical. ● *n.* **1** a slant. **2** *Statistics* skewness. ● *v.* **1** *tr.* make skew. **2** *tr.* distort. **3** *intr.* move obliquely. **4** *intr.* twist. ◻ **on the skew** askew. ◻ **skewness** *n.* [Old Northern French *eskiu(w)er* = Old French *eschiver* ESCHEW]

skew arch *n.* (also **skew bridge**) an arch (or bridge) with the line of the arch not at right angles to the abutment.

skewback /ˈskjuːbak/ *n.* the sloping face of the abutment on which an extremity of an arch rests.

skewbald /ˈskjuːbɔːld/ *adj. & n.* ● *adj.* (of an animal) with irregular patches of white and another colour (properly not black) (cf. PIEBALD *adj.* 1). ● *n.* a skewbald animal, esp. a horse. [Middle English *skued* (origin uncertain), on the pattern of PIEBALD]

skew chisel *n.* a chisel with an oblique edge.

skewer /ˈskjuːə/ *n. & v.* ● *n.* a long pin designed for holding meat etc. compactly together, or the pieces of meat etc. of a kebab, while cooking. ● *v.tr.* **1** fasten together or pierce with or as with a skewer. **2** esp. *N. Amer.* criticize sharply. [Middle English: origin unknown]

skew gear *n.* a gear consisting of two cogwheels having non-parallel, non-intersecting axes.

skew-whiff /skjuːˈwɪf/ *adj. & adv. Brit. colloq.* askew.

ski /skiː/ *n. & v.* ● *n.* (*pl.* **skis**) **1** each of a pair of long narrow pieces of wood etc., usu. pointed and turned up at the front, fastened under the feet for travelling over snow. **2** a similar device under a vehicle or aircraft. **3** = WATER-SKI. **4** (*attrib.*) for wear when skiing (*ski boots*). ● *v.* (**skis**, **skied** /skiːd/; **skiing** or **ski-ing**) **1** *intr.* travel on skis. **2** *tr.* ski at (a place). ◻ **skiable** *adj.* [Norwegian from Old Norse *skíth* 'billet, snowshoe']

skiagraphy var. of SCIAGRAPHY.

skiamachy var. of SCIAMACHY.

ski-bob *n. & v.* ● *n.* a machine like a bicycle with skis instead of wheels. ● *v.intr.* (**-bobbed**, **-bobbing**) ride a ski-bob. ◻ **ski-bobber** *n.*

skid /skɪd/ *v. & n.* ● *v.* (**skidded**, **skidding**) **1** *intr.* (of a vehicle, a wheel, or a driver) slide on slippery ground, esp. sideways or obliquely. **2** *tr.* cause (a vehicle etc.) to skid. **3** *intr.* slip, slide. **4** *intr. colloq.* fail or decline or err. **5** *tr.* support or move or protect or check with a skid. ● *n.* **1** the act or an instance of skidding. **2** a piece of wood etc. serving as a support, ship's fender, inclined plane, etc. **3** a braking device, esp. a wooden or metal shoe preventing a wheel from revolving or used as a drag. **4** a runner beneath an aircraft for use when landing. ◻ **hit the skids** *colloq.* enter a rapid decline or deterioration. **on the skids** *colloq.* **1** about to be discarded or defeated. **2** ready for launching. **put the skids under** *colloq.* **1** hasten the downfall or failure of. **2** cause to hasten. [17th c., origin unknown: perhaps related to Old Norse *skíth* (see SKI)]

skid-lid *n. Brit. slang* a crash helmet.

skidoo /skɪˈduː/ *v.intr.* (also **skiddoo**) (**-oos**, **-ooed**) *N. Amer. slang* go away; depart. [perhaps from SKEDADDLE]

skid-pan *n. Brit.* **1** a slippery surface prepared for vehicle-drivers to practise control of skidding. **2** a braking device.

skid road *n. N. Amer.* **1** a road for hauling logs along. **2** *colloq.* a part of a town frequented by loggers or vagrants.

skid row *n. N. Amer. colloq.* a part of a town frequented by vagrants, alcoholics, etc.

skier[1] /ˈskiːə/ *n.* a person who skis.

skier[2] var. of SKYER.

skiff /skɪf/ *n.* a light rowing boat or sculling boat. [French *esquif* from Italian *schifo*, related to SHIP]

skiffle /ˈskɪf(ə)l/ *n.* **1** *Brit.* a kind of folk music with a blues or jazz flavour, popular in the 1950s and played by a small group, mainly with a rhythmic accompaniment to a singing guitarist or banjoist, often incorporating improvised instruments such as washboard, jug, etc. **2** *US* a style of 1920s and 30s jazz deriving from blues, ragtime, and folk music, and using improvised as well as conventional instruments. [perhaps imitative]

ski-joring /ˈskiːdʒɔːrɪŋ, ʃiːˈjəːrɪŋ/ *n.* a winter sport in which a skier is towed by a horse or vehicle. ▫ **ski-jorer** *n.* [Norwegian *skikjøring* (as SKI, *kjøre* 'drive')]

ski jump *n.* **1** a steep slope levelling off before a sharp drop to allow a skier to leap through the air. **2** a jump made from this. ▫ **ski jumper** *n.* **ski jumping** *n.*

skilful /ˈskɪlfʊl, -f(ə)l/ *adj.* (*US* **skillful**) (often foll. by *at*, *in*) having or showing skill; practised, expert, adroit, ingenious. ▫ **skilfully** *adv.* **skilfulness** *n.*

ski lift *n.* a device for carrying skiers up a slope, usu. on seats hung from an overhead cable.

skill /skɪl/ *n.* (often foll. by *in*) expertness, practised ability, facility in an action; dexterity or tact. ▫ **skill-less** *adj.* (*archaic* **skilless**). [Middle English from Old Norse *skil* 'distinction']

skilled /skɪld/ *adj.* **1** (often foll. by *in*) having or showing skill; skilful. **2** (of a worker) highly trained or experienced. **3** (of work) requiring skill or special training.

skillet /ˈskɪlɪt/ *n.* **1** *Brit.* a small metal cooking pot with a long handle and usu. legs. **2** *N. Amer.* a frying pan. [Middle English, perhaps via Old French *escuelete*, diminutive of *escuele* 'platter', from Late Latin *scutella*]

skillful *US* var. of SKILFUL.

skilly /ˈskɪli/ *n. Brit.* **1** a thin broth or soup or gruel (usu. of oatmeal and water flavoured with meat). **2** an insipid beverage; tea or coffee. [abbreviation from *skilligalee*, probably fanciful]

skim /skɪm/ *v.* & *n.* ● *v.* (**skimmed**, **skimming**) **1** *tr.* **a** take scum or cream or a floating layer from the surface of (a liquid). **b** take (cream etc.) from the surface of a liquid. **2** *tr.* **a** keep touching lightly or nearly touching (a surface) in passing over. **b** deal with or treat (a subject) superficially. **3** *intr.* **a** (often foll. by *over*, *along*) go lightly over a surface, glide along in the air. **b** (foll. by *over*) = sense 2b of *v.* **4 a** *tr.* read superficially, look over cursorily, gather the salient facts contained in. **b** *intr.* (usu. foll. by *through*) read or look over cursorily. **5** *tr. US slang* conceal or divert (income) to avoid paying tax. ● *n.* **1** the act or an instance of skimming. **2** a thin covering on a liquid (*skim of ice*). ▫ **skim the cream off** take the best part of. [Middle English, back-formation from SKIMMER]

skimmer /ˈskɪmə/ *n.* **1** a device for skimming liquids. **2** a person who skims. **3** a flat hat, esp. a broad-brimmed straw hat. **4** any long-winged seabird of the genus *Rynchops* that feeds by skimming over water with its knifelike lower mandible immersed. **5** a hydroplane, hydrofoil, hovercraft, or other vessel that has little or no displacement at speed. **6** *US* a sheath-like dress. [Middle English from Old French *escumoir*, via *escumer* from *escume* SCUM]

skimmia /ˈskɪmɪə/ *n.* any evergreen shrub of the genus *Skimmia*, native to E. Asia, with red berries. [modern Latin from Japanese]

skim milk *n.* (also **skimmed milk**) milk from which the cream has been skimmed.

skimp /skɪmp/ *v.*, *adj.*, & *n.* ● *v.* **1** *tr.* (often foll. by *in*) supply (a person etc.) meagrely with food, money, etc. **2** *tr.* use a meagre or insufficient amount of, stint (material, expenses, etc.). **3** *tr.* do hastily or carelessly. **4** *intr.* be parsimonious. ● *adj.* scanty. ● *n. colloq.* a small or scanty thing, esp. a skimpy garment. [18th c.: origin unknown: cf. SCAMP[2], SCRIMP]

skimpy /ˈskɪmpi/ *adj.* (**skimpier**, **skimpiest**) meagre; not ample or sufficient. ▫ **skimpily** *adv.* **skimpiness** *n.*

skin /skɪn/ *n.* & *v.* ● *n.* **1** the flexible continuous covering of a human or other animal body. **2 a** the skin of a flayed animal with or without the hair etc. **b** a material prepared from skins esp. of smaller animals (opp. HIDE[2] *n.* 1). **3** a person's skin with reference to its colour or complexion (*has a fair skin*). **4** an outer layer or covering, esp. the coating of a plant, fruit, or sausage. **5** a film like skin on the surface of a liquid etc. **6** a container for liquid, made of an animal's whole skin. **7 a** the planking or plating of a ship or boat, inside or outside the ribs. **b** the outer covering of any craft or vehicle, esp. an aircraft or spacecraft. **8** *Brit. slang* a skinhead. **9** *US Cards* a game in which each player has one card which he or she bets will not be the first to be matched by a card dealt from the pack. **10** = GOLD-BEATER'S SKIN. **11** a duplicating stencil. ● *v.* (**skinned**, **skinning**) **1** *tr.* **a** remove the skin from. **b** graze (a part of the body). **2** (often foll. by *over*) **a** *tr.* cover (a sore etc.) with or as with skin. **b** *intr.* (of a wound etc.) become covered with new skin. **3** *tr. slang* fleece or swindle. ▫ **be skin and bone** be very thin. **by** (or **with**) **the skin of one's teeth** by a very narrow margin. **change one's skin** undergo an impossible change of character etc. **get under a person's skin** *colloq.* interest or annoy a person intensely. **have a thick** (or **thin**) **skin** be insensitive (or sensitive) to criticism etc. **no skin off one's nose** *colloq.* a matter of indifference or even benefit to one. **to the skin** through all one's clothing (*soaked to the skin*). **with a whole skin** unwounded. ▫ **skinless** *adj.* **skinlike** *adj.* **skinned** *adj.* (also in *comb.*). [Old English *scin(n)* from Old Norse *skinn*]

skincare /ˈskɪnkɛː/ *n.* care of the skin by using cosmetics.

skin-deep *adj.* & *adv.* ● *adj.* (of a wound, or of an emotion, an impression, a quality, etc.) superficial, not deep or lasting. ● *adv.* superficially, slightly.

skin diver *n.* a person who swims underwater without a diving suit, usu. in deep water with an aqualung and flippers. ▫ **skin diving** *n.*

skin effect *n. Electr.* the tendency of a high-frequency alternating current to flow through the outer layer only of a conductor.

skin-flick *n. slang* an explicitly pornographic film.

skinflint /ˈskɪnflɪnt/ *n.* a miserly person.

skin-food *n.* a cosmetic intended to improve the condition of the skin.

skin friction *n.* friction at the surface of a solid and a fluid in relative motion.

skinful /ˈskɪnfʊl, -f(ə)l/ *n.* (*pl.* **-fuls**) *Brit. colloq.* enough alcoholic liquor to make one drunk.

skin game *n. US slang* a rigged gambling game; a swindle.

skin graft *n.* **1** the surgical transplanting of skin. **2** a piece of skin transferred in this way.

skinhead /ˈskɪnhɛd/ *n.* **1** a person, esp. a youth, characterized by close-cropped hair and heavy boots, esp. one of an aggressive gang. **2** *US* a recruit in the Marines.

skink /skɪŋk/ *n.* a smooth-bodied lizard of the family Scincidae, with the limbs short or even absent. [French *scinc* or Latin *scincus* from Greek *skigkos*]

skinner /ˈskɪnə/ *n.* **1** a person who skins animals or prepares skins. **2** a dealer in skins, a furrier. **3** *Austral. Racing slang* a result very profitable to bookmakers.

skinny /ˈskɪni/ *adj.* (**skinnier**, **skinniest**) **1** thin or emaciated. **2** (of clothing) tight-fitting. **3** made of or like skin. ▫ **skinniness** *n.*

skinny-dipping *n.* esp. *N. Amer. colloq.* bathing in the nude.

skint /skɪnt/ *adj. Brit. colloq.* having no money left. [= *skinned*, past part. of SKIN]

skin test *n.* a test to determine whether an immune reaction is elicited when a substance is applied to or injected into the skin.

skintight /skɪn'tʌɪt/ *adj.* (of a garment) very close-fitting.

skip[1] /skɪp/ *v. & n.* ● *v.* (**skipped**, **skipping**) **1** *intr.* **a** move along lightly, esp. by taking two steps with each foot in turn. **b** jump lightly from the ground, esp. so as to clear a skipping rope. **c** jump about, gambol, caper, frisk. **2** *intr.* (often foll. by *from, off, to*) move quickly from one point, subject, or occupation to another; be desultory. **3** *tr.* (also *absol.*) omit in dealing with a series or in reading (*skip every tenth row*). **4** *tr. colloq.* not participate in. **5** *tr. colloq.* depart quickly from; leave hurriedly. **6** *intr.* (often foll. by *out, off*) *colloq.* make off, disappear. **7** *tr.* make (a stone) ricochet on the surface of water. ● *n.* **1** a skipping movement or action. **2** *Computing* the action of passing over part of a sequence of data or instructions. **3** *N. Amer. colloq.* a person who defaults or absconds. □ **skip it** *slang* **1** abandon a topic etc. **2** make off, disappear. [Middle English, probably from Scandinavian]

skip[2] /skɪp/ *n.* **1** *Brit.* a large container for builders' refuse etc. **2** a cage, bucket, etc., in which men or materials are lowered and raised in mines and quarries. **3** = SKEP 1. [variant of SKEP]

skip[3] /skɪp/ *n. & v.* ● *n.* the captain or director of a side at bowls or curling. ● *v.tr.* (**skipped**, **skipping**) be the skip of. [abbreviation of SKIPPER[1]]

skipjack /'skɪpdʒak/ *n.* **1** (in full **skipjack tuna**) a small striped Pacific tuna, *Katsuwonus pelamis*, used as food. **2** a click beetle. **3** a kind of sailing boat used off the east coast of the US. [SKIP[1] + JACK[1]]

ski-plane *n.* an aeroplane having its undercarriage fitted with skis for landing on snow or ice.

ski pole *n.* either of two light metal rods held by a skier to assist propulsion and balance.

skipper[1] /'skɪpə/ *n. & v.* ● *n.* **1** a sea captain, esp. the master of a small trading or fishing vessel. **2** the captain of an aircraft. **3** the captain of a side in a game or sport. ● *v.tr.* act as captain of. [Middle English from Middle Dutch, Middle Low German *schipper*, from *schip* SHIP]

skipper[2] /'skɪpə/ *n.* **1** a person who skips. **2** any brown thick-bodied butterfly of the family Hesperiidae.

skippet /'skɪpɪt/ *n.* a small round wooden box to enclose and protect a seal attached to a document. [Middle English: origin unknown]

skipping rope *n.* (*N. Amer.* **skip-rope**) a length of rope revolved over the head and under the feet while jumping as a game or exercise.

skip zone *n.* the annular region round a broadcasting station where neither direct nor reflected waves are received.

skirl /skə:l/ *n. & v.* ● *n.* the shrill sound characteristic of bagpipes. ● *v.intr.* make a skirl. [probably Scandinavian: ultimately imitative]

skirmish /'skə:mɪʃ/ *n. & v.* ● *n.* **1** a piece of irregular or unpremeditated fighting, esp. between small or outlying parts of armies or fleets; a slight engagement. **2** a short argument or contest of wit etc. ● *v.intr.* engage in a skirmish. □ **skirmisher** *n.* [Middle English via Old French *eskirmir, escremir* from Frankish]

skirr /skə:/ *v.intr.* move rapidly esp. with a whirring sound. [perhaps related to SCOUR[1] or SCOUR[2]]

skirret /'skɪrɪt/ *n.* a perennial umbelliferous plant, *Sium sisarum*, formerly cultivated in Europe for its edible root. [Middle English *skirwhit(e)*, perhaps formed as SHEER[1], WHITE]

skirt /skə:t/ *n. & v.* ● *n.* **1** a woman's outer garment hanging from the waist. **2** the part of a coat, dress, etc. that hangs below the waist. **3** a hanging part round the base of a hovercraft. **4** (in *sing.* or *pl.*) an edge, border, or extreme part. **5** (also *Brit.* **bit of skirt**) *slang offens.* a woman regarded as an object of sexual desire. **6** (in full **skirt of beef** etc.) **a** the diaphragm and other membranes as food. **b** *Brit.* a cut of meat from the lower flank. **7** a flap of a saddle. **8** a surface that conceals or protects the wheels or underside of a vehicle or aircraft. ● *v.* **1** *tr.* go along or round or past the edge of. **2** *tr.* be situated along. **3** *tr.* avoid dealing with (an issue etc.). **4** *intr.* (foll. by *along*) go along the coast, a wall, etc. □ **skirted** *adj.* (also in *comb.*). **skirtless** *adj.* [Middle English from Old Norse *skyrta* 'shirt', corresponding to Old English *scyrte*: see SHIRT]

skirting /'skə:tɪŋ/ *n.* (in full **skirting board**) *Brit.* a narrow board etc. running along the base of an interior wall.

ski run *n.* a slope prepared for skiing.

ski stick *n.* = SKI POLE.

skit[1] /skɪt/ *n.* (often foll. by *on*) a light, usu. short, piece of satire or burlesque. [related to *skit* 'move lightly and rapidly', perhaps from Old Norse (cf. *skjóta* SHOOT)]

skit[2] /skɪt/ *n. Brit. colloq.* **1** a large number, a crowd. **2** (in *pl.*) heaps, lots. [20th c.: origin unknown]

skite /skʌɪt/ *v. & n.* ● *v.intr. Austral. & NZ colloq.* boast, brag. ● *n.* **1** *Austral. & NZ colloq.* **a** a boaster. **b** boasting; boastfulness. **2** *Sc.* a drinking bout; a spree (*on the skite*). [Scots & northern English dialect, = a person regarded with contempt: cf. BLATHERSKITE]

skitter /'skɪtə/ *v.intr.* (also **skeeter** /'ski:tə/) **1 a** (usu. foll. by *along, across*) move lightly or hastily. **b** (usu. foll. by *about, off*) hurry about, dart off. **2** fish by drawing bait jerkily across the surface of the water. [apparently frequentative of dialect *skite*, perhaps formed as SKIT[1]]

skittery /'skɪt(ə)ri/ *adj.* skittish, restless.

skittish /'skɪtɪʃ/ *adj.* **1** lively, playful. **2** (of a horse etc.) nervous, inclined to shy, fidgety. □ **skittishly** *adv.* **skittishness** *n.* [Middle English, perhaps formed as SKIT[1]]

skittle /skɪt(ə)l/ *n. & v.* ● *n.* **1** a pin used in the game of skittles. **2** (in *pl.*; usu. treated as *sing.*) **a** a game played with usu. nine wooden pins set up at the end of an alley to be bowled down usu. with wooden balls or a wooden disc. **b** (in full **table skittles**) a game played with similar pins set up on a board to be knocked down by swinging a suspended ball. **c** *Brit. colloq.* chess not played seriously. ● *v.tr.* (often foll. by *out*) *Cricket* get (batsmen) out in rapid succession. [17th c. (also *kittle-pins*): origin unknown]

skive /skʌɪv/ *v. & n.* ● *v.* **1** *tr.* split or pare (hides, leather, etc.). **2** *intr. Brit. colloq.* **a** evade a duty, shirk. **b** (often foll. by *off*) avoid work by absenting oneself, play truant. ● *n. colloq.* **1** an instance of shirking. **2** an easy option. □ **skiver** *n.* [Old Norse *skífa*, related to Middle English *schīve* 'slice']

skivvy /'skɪvi/ *n. & v.* ● *n.* (*pl.* **-ies**) **1 a** *Brit. colloq. derog.* a female domestic servant. **b** a person doing work considered menial or poorly paid. **2 a** *US & Austral.* a thin high-necked long-sleeved garment. **b** (in *pl.*) *N. Amer.* underwear of vest and underpants. ● *v.intr.* (**-ies**, **-ied**) *colloq.* work as a skivvy. [20th c.: origin unknown]

skol /skɒl, skəʊl/ *n.* (also ***skoal***) used as a toast in drinking. [Danish *skaal*, Swedish *skål*, from Old Norse *skál* 'bowl']

skua /'skju:ə/ *n.* any large brownish predatory seabird of the family Stercorariidae which pursues other birds and makes them disgorge the fish they have caught. Cf. JAEGER. [modern Latin from Faroese *skúgvur*, Old Norse *skúfr*]

skulduggery /skʌl'dʌg(ə)ri/ *n.* (also **sculduggery**, **skullduggery**) trickery; unscrupulous behaviour. [earlier *sculduddery*, originally Scots = unchastity (18th c.: origin unknown)]

skulk /skʌlk/ *v. & n.* ● *v.intr.* **1** move stealthily, lurk, or keep oneself concealed, esp. in a cowardly or sinister way. **2** stay or sneak away in time of danger. **3** *Brit.* shirk duty. ● *n.* **1** a person who skulks. **2** a company of foxes. □ **skulker** *n.* [Middle English from Scandinavian:

cf. Norwegian *skulka* lurk, Danish *skulke*, Swedish *skolka* 'shirk']

skull /skʌl/ *n.* **1** the bony case of the brain of a vertebrate. **2 a** the part of the skeleton corresponding to the head. **b** this with the skin and soft internal parts removed. **c** a representation of this. **3** the head as the seat of intelligence. □ **out of one's skull** *slang* **1** out of one's mind, crazy. **2** very drunk. □ **skulled** *adj.* (also in *comb.*). [Middle English *scolle*: origin unknown]

skull and crossbones *n.pl.* a representation of a skull with two thigh bones crossed below it as an emblem of piracy or death.

skullcap /'skʌlkap/ *n.* **1** a small close-fitting peakless cap. **2** the top part of the skull. **3** any plant of the genus *Scutellaria*, having a helmet-shaped calyx after flowering.

skull session *n. US slang* a discussion or conference.

skunk /skʌŋk/ *n. & v.* ● *n.* **1 a** any of various cat-sized flesh-eating mammals of the family Mustelidae, esp. *Mephitis mephitis* having a distinctive black and white striped fur and able to emit a powerful stench from a liquid secreted by its anal glands as a defence. **b** its fur. **2** *colloq.* a thoroughly contemptible person. ● *v.tr.* **1** *N. Amer. slang* defeat soundly. **2** fail to pay (a bill etc.). [Algonquian]

skunk-bear *n. US* = GLUTTON 3.

skunk-cabbage *n. US* a herbaceous plant, *Lysichiton americanum*, with an offensive-smelling spathe.

sky /skʌɪ/ *n. & v.* ● *n.* (*pl.* **skies**) (in *sing.* or *pl.*) **1** the region of the atmosphere and outer space seen from the earth. **2** the weather or climate evidenced by this. ● *v.tr.* (**skies**, **skied**) **1** *Cricket* etc. hit (a ball) high into the air. **2** hang (a picture) high on a wall. □ **the sky is the limit** there is practically no limit. **to the skies** very highly; without reserve (*praised to the skies*). **under the open sky** out of doors. □ **skyey** *adj.* **skyless** *adj.* [Middle English *ski(es)* 'cloud(s)' from Old Norse *ský*]

sky blue *n. & adj.* ● *n.* a bright clear blue. ● *adj.* (hyphenated when *attrib.*) of this colour.

sky-blue pink *n. & adj.* ● *n.* an imaginary colour. ● *adj.* of this colour.

sky-clad *adj.* naked (esp. in connection with modern pagan ritual). [probably translation of Sanskrit *Digāmbara*, denoting a Jain sect]

sky cloth *n. Theatr.* a backcloth painted or coloured to represent the sky.

skydiving /'skʌɪdʌɪvɪŋ/ *n.* the sport of performing acrobatic manoeuvres under free fall with a parachute. □ **skydive** *v.intr.* **skydiver** *n.*

skyer /'skʌɪə/ *n.* (also **skier**) *Cricket* a high hit.

Skye terrier /skʌɪ/ *n.* a small long-haired slate-coloured or fawn-coloured variety of Scottish terrier. [*Skye*, an island of the Inner Hebrides]

sky-high *adv. & adj.* as if reaching the sky, very high.

skyjack /'skʌɪdʒak/ *v. & n. slang* ● *v.tr.* hijack (an aircraft). ● *n.* an act of skyjacking. □ **skyjacker** *n.* [SKY + HIJACK]

skylark /'skʌɪlɑːk/ *n. & v.* ● *n.* a lark, *Alauda arvensis* of Eurasia and N. Africa, that sings while hovering in flight. ● *v.intr.* play tricks or practical jokes, indulge in horseplay, frolic. [SKY + LARK[1]: the verb with pun on LARK[2]]

skylight /'skʌɪlʌɪt/ *n.* a window set in the plane of a roof or ceiling.

skyline /'skʌɪlʌɪn/ *n.* the outline of hills, buildings, etc., defined against the sky; the visible horizon.

sky pilot *n. slang* a clergyman.

skyrocket /'skʌɪrɒkɪt/ *n. & v.* ● *n.* a rocket exploding high in the air. ● *v.intr.* (**-rocketed**, **-rocketing**) (esp. of prices etc.) rise very steeply or rapidly.

skysail /'skʌɪseɪl, -s(ə)l/ *n.* a light sail above the royal in a square-rigged ship.

skyscape /'skʌɪskeɪp/ *n.* **1** a picture chiefly representing the sky. **2** a view of the sky.

skyscraper /'skʌɪskreɪpə/ *n.* a very tall building of many storeys.

sky-shouting *n. Brit.* the sending of messages from an aircraft to the ground by means of a loudspeaker.

sky-sign *n.* an advertisement on the roof of a building.

skywalk /'skʌɪwɔːk/ *n.* = SKYWAY 3.

skyward /'skʌɪwəd/ *adv. & adj.* ● *adv.* (also **skywards**) towards the sky. ● *adj.* moving skyward.

skywatch /'skʌɪwɒtʃ/ *n.* the activity of watching the sky for aircraft etc.

sky wave *n.* a radio wave reflected from the ionosphere.

skyway /'skʌɪweɪ/ *n.* **1** a route used by aircraft. **2** the sky as a medium of transport. **3** a covered overhead walkway between buildings.

sky-writing *n.* legible smoke-trails made by an aeroplane esp. for advertising.

slab /slab/ *n. & v.* ● *n.* **1** a flat broad fairly thick usu. square or rectangular piece of solid material, esp. stone. **2** a large flat piece of cake, chocolate, etc. **3** (of timber) an outer piece sawn from a log. **4** *Brit.* a mortuary table. ● *v.tr.* (**slabbed**, **slabbing**) remove slabs from (a log or tree) to prepare it for sawing into planks. [Middle English: origin unknown]

slack[1] /slak/ *adj., n., v., & adv.* ● *adj.* **1** not taut; not held tensely (*slack rope*; *slack muscles*). **2** inactive or sluggish. **3** negligent or remiss. **4** (of tide etc.) neither ebbing nor flowing. **5** (of trade or business or a market) with little happening. **6** *Phonet.* = LAX 3. **7** relaxed, languid. ● *n.* **1** the slack part of a rope (*haul in the slack*). **2** a slack time in trade etc. **3** *colloq.* a spell of inactivity or laziness. **4** (in *pl.*) full-length loosely-cut trousers for informal wear. ● *v.* **1 a** *tr. & intr.* slacken. **b** *tr.* loosen (rope etc.). **2** *intr. Brit. colloq.* take a rest; be lazy; shirk. **3** *tr.* slake (lime). ● *adv.* **1** slackly. **2** slowly or insufficiently (*dry slack*; *bake slack*). □ **slack off 1** loosen. **2** lose or cause to lose vigour. **slack up** reduce the speed of a train etc. before stopping. **take up the slack** use up a surplus or make up a deficiency; avoid an undesirable lull. □ **slackly** *adv.* **slackness** *n.* [Old English *slæc*, from Germanic]

slack[2] /slak/ *n.* coal dust or small pieces of coal. [Middle English, probably from Low German or Dutch]

slacken /'slak(ə)n/ *v.tr. & intr.* make or become slack. □ **slacken off** = *slack off* (see SLACK[1]).

slacker /'slakə/ *n.* a shirker; an indolent person.

slack lime *n.* slaked lime.

slack suit *n. US* casual clothes of slacks and a matching jacket or shirt.

slack water *n.* a time near the turn of the tide, esp. at low tide.

slag /slag/ *n. & v.* ● *n.* **1** vitreous refuse left after ore has been smelted, dross separated in a fused state in the reduction of ore, clinkers. **2** volcanic scoria. **3** *Brit. slang offens.* **a** a prostitute or promiscuous woman. **b** a worthless or insignificant person. ● *v.* (**slagged**, **slagging**) **1** *intr.* **a** form slag. **b** cohere into a mass like slag. **2** *tr.* (often foll. by *off*) *Brit. slang* criticize, insult. □ **slaggy** *adj.* (**slaggier**, **slaggiest**). [Middle Low German *slagge*, perhaps from *slagen* 'strike', with reference to fragments formed by hammering]

slag heap *n.* a hill of refuse from a mine etc.

slag-wool *n.* = MINERAL WOOL.

slain *past part.* of SLAY[1].

slainte /'slɑːntʃə, Gaelic slaŋə/ *int.* a Gaelic toast: good health! [Gaelic *sláinte*, literally 'health']

slake /sleɪk/ *v.tr.* **1** assuage or satisfy (thirst, revenge, etc.). **2** disintegrate (quicklime) by chemical combination with water. [Old English *slacian* from *slæc* SLACK[1]]

slaked lime see LIME[1] *n.* 2.

slalom /'slɑːləm/ *n.* **1** a ski race down a zigzag course defined by artificial obstacles. **2** an obstacle race in canoes or cars or on skateboards or water-skis. [Norwegian, literally 'sloping track']

slam[1] /slam/ *v. & n.* ● *v.* (**slammed**, **slamming**) **1** *tr. & intr.* shut forcefully and loudly. **2** *tr.* put down (an object) with a similar sound. **3** *intr.* move violently (*he* *slammed out of the room*). **4** *tr. & intr.* put or come into action suddenly or forcefully (*slam the brakes on*). **5** *tr. slang* criticize severely. **6** *tr. slang* hit. **7** *tr. slang* gain an easy victory over. ● *n.* **1** a sound of or as of a slammed door. **2** the shutting of a door etc. with a loud bang. **3** (usu. prec. by *the*) *N. Amer. slang* prison. [probably from Scandinavian: cf. Old Norse *slam(b)ra*]

slam² /slam/ *n. Cards* the winning of every trick in a game. [originally the name of a card game: perhaps from obsolete *slampant* 'trickery']

slambang /slam'baŋ/ *adv. & adj.* ● *adv.* with the sound of a slam. ● *adj. colloq.* impressive, exciting, or energetic.

slam dunk *n.* (also **slamdunk**) *Basketball* a play in which a player jumps and thrusts the ball forcefully down into the basket.

slammer /'slamə/ *n.* (usu. prec. by *the*) *slang* prison.

slander /'slɑːndə/ *n. & v.* ● *n.* **1** a malicious, false, and injurious statement spoken about a person. **2** the uttering of such statements; calumny. **3** *Law* false oral defamation (cf. LIBEL *n.* 1). ● *v.tr.* utter slander about; defame falsely. □ **slanderer** *n.* **slanderous** *adj.* **slanderously** *adv.* [Middle English *sclaundre* via Anglo-French *esclaundre*, Old French *esclandre*, alteration of *escandle*, from Late Latin *scandalum*: see SCANDAL]

slang /slaŋ/ *n. & v.* ● *n.* words, phrases, and uses that are regarded as very informal and are often restricted to special contexts or are peculiar to a specified profession, class, etc. (*racing slang*; *schoolboy slang*). ● *v.* **1** *tr.* use abusive language to. **2** *intr.* use such language. [18th-c.: origin unknown]

slanging match *n. Brit.* a prolonged exchange of insults.

slangy /'slaŋi/ *adj.* (**slangier**, **slangiest**) **1** of the character of slang. **2** fond of using slang. □ **slangily** *adv.* **slanginess** *n.*

slant /slɑːnt/ *v., n., & adj.* ● *v.* **1** *intr.* slope; diverge from a line; lie or go obliquely to a vertical or horizontal line. **2** *tr.* cause to do this. **3** *tr.* (often as **slanted** *adj.*) present (information) from a particular angle esp. in a biased or unfair way. ● *n.* **1** a slope; an oblique position. **2** a way of regarding a thing; a point of view, esp. a biased one. ● *adj.* sloping, oblique. □ **on a** (or **the**) **slant** aslant. [aphetic form of ASLANT: the verb related to Middle English *slent* from Old Norse *sletta* 'dash, throw']

slant-eyed *adj.* having slanting eyes.

slant height *n.* the height of a cone from the vertex to the periphery of the base.

slantwise /'slɑːntwʌɪz/ *adv.* aslant.

slap /slap/ *v., n., & adv.* ● *v.* (**slapped**, **slapping**) **1** *tr. & intr.* strike with the palm of the hand or a flat object, or so as to make a similar noise. **2** *tr.* lay forcefully (*slapped the money on the table*; *slapped a writ on the offender*). **3** *tr.* put hastily or carelessly (*slap some paint on the walls*). **4** *tr.* (often foll. by *down*) *colloq.* reprimand or snub. ● *n.* **1** a blow with the palm of the hand or a flat object. **2** a slapping sound. ● *adv.* **1** with the suddenness or effectiveness or true aim of a blow; suddenly, fully, directly (*ran slap into him*; *hit me slap in the eye*). **2** = SLAP BANG. □ **slap on the back** *n.* congratulations. ● *v.tr.* congratulate. [Low German *slapp* (imitative)]

slap and tickle *n. Brit. colloq.* light-hearted amorous amusement.

slap bang *adv.* **1** exactly, precisely (*slap bang in the middle of the town*). **2** violently, noisily, headlong. **3** conspicuously, prominently.

slapdash /'slapdaʃ/ *adj. & adv.* ● *adj.* hasty and careless. ● *adv.* in a slapdash manner.

slap-happy *adj. colloq.* **1** cheerfully casual or flippant. **2** punch-drunk.

slaphead /'slaphɛd/ *n. slang derog.* a person with very short hair or very little hair.

slap in the face *n.* a rebuff or affront.

slapjack /'slapdʒak/ *n. N. Amer.* a kind of pancake cooked on a griddle. [SLAP + JACK¹]

slapper /'slapə/ *n. Brit. slang offens.* a promiscuous woman.

slapstick /'slapstɪk/ *n.* **1** boisterous knockabout comedy. **2** a flexible divided lath used by a clown. [SLAP + STICK¹]

slap-up *attrib.adj.* esp. *Brit. colloq.* excellent, lavish; done regardless of expense (*slap-up meal*).

slash /slaʃ/ *v. & n.* ● *v.* **1** *intr.* make a sweeping or random cut or cuts with a knife, sword, whip, etc. **2** *tr.* make such a cut or cuts at. **3** *tr.* make a long narrow gash or gashes in. **4** *tr.* reduce (prices etc.) drastically. **5** *tr.* censure vigorously. **6** *tr.* make (one's way) by slashing. **7** *tr.* **a** lash (a person etc.) with a whip. **b** crack (a whip). ● *n.* **1** **a** a slashing cut or stroke. **b** a wound or slit made by this. **2** an oblique stroke; a solidus. **3** *Brit. slang* an act of urinating. **4** *N. Amer.* debris resulting from the felling or destruction of trees. [Middle English, perhaps from Old French *esclachier* 'break in pieces']

slash-and-burn *adj.* (of cultivation) in which vegetation is cut down, allowed to dry, and then burned off before seeds are planted.

slashed /slaʃt/ *adj.* (of a sleeve etc.) having slits to show a lining or puffing of other material.

slasher /'slaʃə/ *n.* **1** a person or thing that slashes. **2** (in full **slasher film**, **slasher movie**) a film depicting violent assault with a knife etc.

slashing /'slaʃɪŋ/ *adj.* vigorously incisive or effective.

slat /slat/ *n.* a thin narrow piece of wood or plastic or metal, esp. used in an overlapping series as in a fence or venetian blind. [Middle English *s(c)lat* via Old French *esclat* 'splinter' etc., from *esclater* 'split', from Romanic]

slate /sleɪt/ *n., v., & adj.* ● *n.* **1** a fine-grained grey, green, or bluish-purple metamorphic rock easily split into flat smooth plates. **2** a piece of such a plate used as roofing-material. **3** a piece of such a plate used for writing on, usu. framed in wood. **4** a bluish-grey colour. **5** *N. Amer.* a list of nominees for office etc. ● *v.tr.* **1** cover with slates esp. as roofing. **2** *Brit. colloq.* criticize severely; scold. **3** *N. Amer.* make arrangements for (an event etc.). **4** *N. Amer.* propose or nominate for office etc. ● *adj.* made of slate. □ **on the slate** *Brit.* recorded as a debt to be paid. **wipe the slate clean** forgive or cancel the record of past offences. □ **slating** *n.* **slaty** *adj.* [Middle English *s(c)late* from Old French *esclate*, fem. form of *esclat* SLAT]

slate blue *n. & adj.* ● *n.* a shade of blue occurring in slate. ● *adj.* (hyphenated when *attrib.*) of this colour.

slate colour *n. & adj.* ● *n.* a dark bluish or greenish grey. ● *adj.* (hyphenated when *attrib.*) of this colour. □ **slate-coloured** *adj.*

slate grey *n. & adj.* ● *n.* a shade of grey occurring in slate. ● *adj.* (hyphenated when *attrib.*) of this colour.

slate-pencil *n.* a small rod of soft slate used for writing on slate.

slater /'sleɪtə/ *n.* **1** a person who slates roofs etc. **2** a woodlouse or similar crustacean.

slather /'slaðə/ *n. & v.* ● *n.* **1** (usu. in *pl.*) *US colloq.* a large amount. **2** (often **open slather**) *Austral. & NZ slang* unrestricted scope for action. ● *v.tr. N. Amer. colloq.* **1** spread thickly. **2** squander. [19th c.: origin unknown]

slatted /'slatɪd/ *adj.* having slats.

slattern /'slat(ə)n/ *n.* a slovenly woman. □ **slatternly** *adj.* **slatternliness** *n.* [17th c.: related to *slattering* 'slovenly', from dialect *slatter* 'to spill, slop, waste', frequentative of *slat* 'strike', of unknown origin]

slaughter /'slɔːtə/ *n. & v.* ● *n.* **1** the killing of an animal or animals. **2** the killing of many persons or animals at once or continuously; carnage, massacre. ● *v.tr.* **1** kill (people) in a ruthless manner or on a great scale. **2** kill (animals) esp. in large numbers. **3** *colloq.* defeat utterly. □ **slaughterer** *n.* **slaughterous** *adj.* [Middle English *slahter*, ultimately from Old Norse *slátr* 'butcher's meat', related to SLAY[1]]

slaughterhouse /'slɔ:təhaʊs/ *n.* **1** a place for the slaughter of animals as food. **2** a place of carnage.

Slav /slɑ:v/ *n. & adj.* ● *n.* a member of a group of peoples in central and eastern Europe speaking Slavonic languages. ● *adj.* **1** of or relating to the Slavs. **2** = SLAVONIC *adj.* 1. □ **Slavism** *n.* [Middle English *Sclave* from medieval Latin *Sclavus*, late Greek *Sklabos*, later also from medieval Latin *Slavus*]

slave /sleɪv/ *n. & v.* ● *n.* **1** a person who is the legal property of another or others and is bound to absolute obedience; a human chattel. **2** a drudge; a person working very hard. **3** (foll. by *of, to*) a helpless victim of some dominating influence (*slave of fashion*; *slave to duty*). **4** a machine, or part of one, directly controlled by another. ● *v.* **1** *intr.* (often foll. by *at, over*) work very hard. **2** *tr.* (foll. by *to*) subject (a device) to control by another. [Middle English from Old French *esclave* = medieval Latin *sclavus, sclava* 'Slavonic (captive)': see SLAV]

slave-bangle *n.* a bangle of gold, glass, etc., worn by a woman usu. above the elbow.

slave-born *adj.* born in slavery; born of slave parents.

slave-bracelet *n.* = SLAVE-BANGLE.

slave-driver *n.* **1** an overseer of slaves at work. **2** a person who works others hard, esp. excessively so. □ **slave-drive** *v.tr.* (*past* **-drove**; *past part.* **-driven**).

slave labour *n.* forced labour.

slaver[1] /'sleɪvə/ *n. hist.* a ship or person engaged in the slave trade.

slaver[2] /'slavə, 'sleɪvə/ *n. & v.* ● *n.* **1** saliva running from the mouth. **2 a** fulsome or servile flattery. **b** drivel, nonsense. ● *v.intr.* **1** let saliva run from the mouth; dribble. **2** (foll. by *over*) show excessive sentimentality over, or desire for. [Middle English, probably from Low German or Dutch: cf. SLOBBER]

slavery /'sleɪv(ə)ri/ *n.* **1** the condition of a slave. **2** exhausting labour; drudgery. **3** the custom of having slaves.

slave ship *n. hist.* a ship transporting slaves, esp. from Africa.

Slave State *n. hist.* any of the southern states of the US in which slavery was legal before the Civil War.

slave trade *n. hist.* the procuring, transporting, and selling of human beings, esp. African blacks, as slaves. □ **slave trader** *n.*

slavey /'sleɪvi/ *n.* (*pl.* **-eys**) *Brit. colloq.* a maidservant, esp. a hard-worked one.

Slavic /'slɑ:vɪk/ *adj. & n.* = SLAVONIC.

slavish /'sleɪvɪʃ/ *adj.* **1** of, like, or as of slaves. **2** showing no attempt at originality or development. **3** abject, servile, base. □ **slavishly** *adv.* **slavishness** *n.*

Slavonic /slə'vɒnɪk/ *adj. & n.* ● *adj.* **1** of or relating to the group of Indo-European languages including Russian, Polish, and Czech. **2** of or relating to the Slavs. ● *n.* the Slavonic language group. [medieval Latin *S(c)lavonicus*, via *S(c)lavonia* 'country of Slavs' from *Sclavus* SLAV]

slaw /slɔ:/ *n. N. Amer.* coleslaw. [Dutch *sla*, shortened from *salade* SALAD]

slay[1] /sleɪ/ *v.tr.* (*past* **slew** /slu:/; *past part.* **slain** /sleɪn/) **1** *literary* or *N. Amer.* kill. **2** *colloq.* overwhelm with delight; convulse with laughter. □ **slayer** *n.* [Old English *slēan*, from Germanic]

slay[2] var. of SLEY.

SLBM *abbr.* submarine-launched ballistic missile.

SLD *abbr.* (in the UK) Social and Liberal Democrats (formed in 1988 from a majority of the membership of the Liberal Party and the SDP and officially replaced by *Liberal Democrats* in 1989).

sleaze /sli:z/ *n. & v. colloq.* ● *n.* **1** sleaziness; sleazy material or conditions. **2** a person of low moral standards. ● *v.intr.* move in a sleazy fashion. [back-formation from SLEAZY]

sleazeball /'sli:zbɔ:l/ *n.* (also **sleazebag** /'sli:zbag/) *slang* a sordid or despicable person.

sleazy /'sli:zi/ *adj.* (**sleazier**, **sleaziest**) **1** squalid, tawdry, sordid. **2** slatternly. **3** (of textiles etc.) flimsy. □ **sleazily** *adv.* **sleaziness** *n.* [17th c.: origin unknown]

sled /slɛd/ *n. & v. N. Amer.* ● *n.* = SLEDGE[1] *n.* ● *v.intr. & tr.* (**sledded**, **sledding**) = SLEDGE[1] *v.* [Middle Low German *sledde*, related to SLIDE]

sledge[1] /slɛdʒ/ *n. & v.* ● *n.* **1** a vehicle on runners for conveying loads or passengers esp. over snow, drawn by horses, dogs, or reindeer, or pushed or pulled by one or more persons. **2** *Brit.* a toboggan. ● *v.intr. & tr.* ride or convey on a sledge. [Middle Dutch *sleedse*, related to SLED]

sledge[2] /slɛdʒ/ *n.* = SLEDGEHAMMER 1.

sledgehammer /'slɛdʒhamə/ *n.* **1** a large heavy hammer used to break stone etc. **2** (*attrib.*) heavy or powerful (*a sledgehammer blow*). [Old English *slecg* (related to SLAY[1]) + HAMMER]

sledging /'slɛdʒɪŋ/ *n. Cricket slang* the heaping of insults on an opposing player in order to break his or her concentration. [*sledge* 'use a sledgehammer on']

sleek /sli:k/ *adj. & v.* ● *adj.* **1** (of hair, fur, or skin, or of an animal or person with such hair etc.) smooth and glossy. **2** looking well-fed and comfortable. **3** ingratiating. **4** (of a thing) smooth and polished. ● *v.tr.* make sleek, esp. by stroking or pressing down. □ **sleekly** *adv.* **sleekness** *n.* **sleeky** *adj.* [later variant of SLICK]

sleep /sli:p/ *n. & v.* ● *n.* **1** a condition of body and mind such as that which normally recurs for several hours every night, in which the nervous system is inactive, the eyes closed, the postural muscles relaxed, and consciousness practically suspended. **2** a period of sleep (*shall try to get a sleep*). **3** a state like sleep, such as rest, quiet, or death. **4** the prolonged inert condition of hibernating animals. **5** a substance found in the corners of the eyes after sleep. ● *v.* (*past* and *past part.* **slept** /slɛpt/) **1** *intr.* **a** be in a state of sleep. **b** fall asleep. **2** *intr.* (foll. by *at, in*, etc.) spend the night. **3** *tr.* provide sleeping accommodation for (*the house sleeps six*). **4** *intr.* (foll. by *with, together*) have sexual intercourse, esp. in bed. **5** *intr.* (foll. by *on, over*) not decide (a question) until the next day. **6** *intr.* (foll. by *through*) fail to be woken by. **7** *intr.* be inactive or dormant. **8** *intr.* be dead; lie in the grave. **9** *tr.* **a** (foll. by *off*) remedy by sleeping (*slept off his hangover*). **b** (foll. by *away*) spend in sleeping (*sleep the hours away*). **10** *intr.* (of a top) spin so steadily as to seem motionless. □ **get to sleep** manage to fall asleep. **go to sleep 1** enter a state of sleep. **2** (of a limb) become numbed by pressure. **in one's sleep** while asleep. **let sleeping dogs lie** avoid stirring up trouble. **put to sleep 1** anaesthetize. **2** *euphem.* kill (an animal) painlessly. **sleep around** *colloq.* be sexually promiscuous. **sleep in 1** remain asleep later than usual in the morning. **2** sleep by night at one's place of work. **sleep like a log** (or **top**) sleep soundly. **the sleep of the just** sound sleep. **sleep out** sleep by night out of doors, or not at one's place of work. [Old English *slēp*, *slǣp* (*n.*), *slēpan*, *slǣpan* (*v.*), from Germanic]

sleeper /'sli:pə/ *n.* **1** a person or animal that sleeps. **2** a wooden or concrete beam laid horizontally as a support, esp. *Brit.* for railway track. **3 a** a sleeping car. **b** a berth in this. **4** *Brit.* a ring worn in a pierced ear to keep the hole from closing. **5** a thing that is suddenly successful after being undistinguished. **6** a sleeping suit. **7** a spy or saboteur etc. who remains inactive while establishing a secure position.

sleeping bag *n.* a lined or padded bag to sleep in, esp. when camping etc.

Sleeping Beauty *n.* a fairy tale heroine who slept for 100 years.

sleeping car *n.* (also *Brit.* **sleeping carriage**) a railway coach provided with beds or berths.

sleeping draught *n. Brit.* a drink to induce sleep.

sleeping partner *n. Brit.* a partner not sharing in the actual work of a firm.
sleeping pill *n.* a pill to induce sleep.
sleeping policeman *n. Brit.* a ramp etc. in the road intended to cause traffic to reduce speed.
sleeping sickness *n.* any of several tropical diseases with extreme lethargy caused by a trypanosome transmitted by a tsetse-fly bite.
sleeping suit *n. Brit.* a young child's one-piece garment, worn esp. as nightwear.
sleep-learning *n.* learning by hearing while asleep.
sleepless /'sli:plɪs/ *adj.* **1** characterized by lack of sleep (*a sleepless night*). **2** unable to sleep. **3** continually active or moving. □ **sleeplessly** *adv.* **sleeplessness** *n.*
sleep-out *n. Austral.* & *NZ* a veranda, porch, or outbuilding providing sleeping accommodation.
sleepover /'sli:pəʊvə/ *n.* & *adj.* ● *n.* an occasion of spending the night away from home. ● *adj.* involving or relating to spending the night away from home.
sleepwalk /'sli:pwɔ:k/ *v.intr.* walk or perform other actions while asleep. □ **sleepwalker** *n.*
sleepy /'sli:pi/ *adj.* (**sleepier**, **sleepiest**) **1** drowsy; ready for sleep; about to fall asleep. **2** lacking activity or bustle (*a sleepy little town*). **3** habitually indolent, unobservant, etc. □ **sleepily** *adv.* **sleepiness** *n.*
sleepyhead /'sli:pɪhɛd/ *n.* (esp. as a form of address) a sleepy or inattentive person.
sleepy sickness *n. Brit.* encephalitis lethargica, an infection of the brain with drowsiness and sometimes a coma.
sleet /sli:t/ *n.* & *v.* ● *n.* **1** a mixture of snow and rain falling together. **2** hail or snow melting as it falls. **3** *US* a thin coating of ice. ● *v.intr.* (prec. by *it* as subject) sleet falls (*it is sleeting*; *if it sleets*). □ **sleety** *adj.* [Middle English probably from Old English: related to Middle Low German *slōten* (pl.) 'hail', Middle High German *slōz(e)*, from Germanic]
sleeve /sli:v/ *n.* **1** the part of a garment that wholly or partly covers an arm. **2** the cover of a gramophone record. **3** a tube enclosing a rod or smaller tube. **4 a** a windsock. **b** a drogue towed by an aircraft. □ **roll up one's sleeves** prepare to fight or work. **up one's sleeve** concealed but ready for use; in reserve. □ **sleeved** *adj.* (also in *comb.*). **sleeveless** *adj.* [Old English *slēfe, slīefe, slȳf*]
sleeve board *n.* a small ironing board for pressing sleeves.
sleeve-coupling *n.* a tube for connecting shafts or pipes.
sleeve link *n. Brit.* a cuff link.
sleeve note *n. Brit.* a descriptive note on a record sleeve.
sleeve-nut *n.* a long nut with right-hand and left-hand screw-threads for drawing together pipes or shafts conversely threaded.
sleeve-valve *n.* a valve in the form of a cylinder with a sliding movement.
sleeving /'sli:vɪŋ/ *n. Brit.* tubular covering for electric cable etc.
sleigh /sleɪ/ *n.* & *v.* ● *n.* a sledge, esp. one for riding on, rather than conveying loads, and drawn by horses or reindeer. ● *v.intr.* travel on a sleigh. [originally US, from Dutch *slee*, related to SLED]
sleigh bell *n.* any of a number of tinkling bells attached to the harness of a sleigh-horse etc.
sleight /slʌɪt/ *n. archaic* **1** a deceptive trick or device or movement. **2** dexterity. **3** cunning. [Middle English *sleghth* from Old Norse *slœgth*, from *slœgr* SLY]
sleight of hand *n.* **1** dexterity esp. in conjuring or fencing. **2** a display of dexterity, esp. a conjuring trick.
slender /'slɛndə/ *adj.* (**slenderer**, **slenderest**) **1 a** of small girth or breadth (*a slender pillar*). **b** gracefully thin (*a slender waist*). **2** relatively small or scanty; slight, meagre, inadequate (*slender hopes*; *slender resources*). □ **slenderly** *adv.* **slenderness** *n.* [Middle English: origin unknown]
slenderize /'slɛndərʌɪz/ *v.* (also **-ise**) **1** *tr.* **a** make (a thing) slender. **b** make (one's figure) appear slender. **2** *intr.* make oneself slender; slim.
slender loris see LORIS.
slept *past* and *past part.* of SLEEP.
sleuth /slu:θ/ *n.* & *v. colloq.* ● *n.* a detective. ● *v.* **1** *intr.* act as a detective. **2** *tr.* investigate. [originally in *sleuth-hound*: Middle English *sleuth* 'track, trail' from Old Norse *slóth*: cf. SLOT[2]]
sleuth-hound *n.* **1** a bloodhound. **2** *colloq.* a detective, an investigator.
S level *n.* (in the UK except Scotland) a GCE examination usu. taken together with an A level, and having a more advanced syllabus. [abbreviation of *special* or (formerly) *scholarship level*]
slew[1] /slu:/ *v.* & *n.* (also **slue**) ● *v.tr.* & *intr.* (often foll. by *round*) turn or swing forcibly or with effort out of the forward or ordinary position. ● *n.* such a change of position. [18th-c., nautical: origin unknown]
slew[2] *past* of SLAY[1].
slew[3] /slu:/ *n.* esp. *N. Amer. colloq.* a large number or quantity. [Irish *sluagh*]
sley /sleɪ/ *n.* (also **slay**) a weaver's reed. [Old English *slege*, related to SLAY[1]]
slice /slʌɪs/ *n.* & *v.* ● *n.* **1** a thin broad piece or wedge cut off or out esp. from meat or bread or a cake, pie, or large fruit. **2** a share; a part taken or allotted or gained (*a slice of territory*; *a slice of the profits*). **3** a kitchen utensil with a broad flat often perforated blade for serving fish, cake, etc. **4** *Golf, Tennis*, etc. a slicing stroke. ● *v.* **1** *tr.* (often foll. by *up*) cut into slices. **2** *tr.* (foll. by *off*) cut (a piece) off. **3** *intr.* (foll. by *into*, *through*) cut with or like a knife. **4** *tr.* (also *absol.*) **a** *Golf* strike (the ball) so that it deviates away from the striker. **b** (in other sports) propel (the ball) forward at an angle. **5** *tr.* go through (air etc.) with a cutting motion. □ **sliceable** *adj.* **slicer** *n.* (also in *comb.*). [Middle English via Old French *esclice*, *esclicier* splinter from Frankish *slītjan*: related to SLIT]
slice of life *n.* a realistic representation of everyday experience.
slick /slɪk/ *adj.*, *n.*, & *v.* ● *adj.* **1 a** (of a person or action) skilful or efficient; dexterous (*gave a slick performance*). **b** superficially or pretentiously smooth and dexterous. **c** glib. **2 a** sleek, smooth. **b** slippery. ● *n.* **1** a smooth patch of oil etc., esp. on the sea. **2** *Motor Racing* a smooth tyre. **3** *US* a glossy magazine. **4** *US slang* a slick person. ● *v.tr.* **1** make sleek or smart. **2** (usu. foll. by *down*) flatten (one's hair etc.). □ **slickly** *adv.* **slickness** *n.* [Middle English *slike(n)*, probably from Old English: cf. SLEEK]
slicker /'slɪkə/ *n. N. Amer.* **1** *colloq.* **a** a plausible rogue. **b** = CITY SLICKER[1]. **2** a raincoat of smooth material.
slide /slʌɪd/ *v.* & *n.* ● *v.* (*past* and *past part.* **slid** /slɪd/) **1 a** *intr.* move along a smooth surface with continuous contact on the same part of the thing moving (cf. ROLL *v.* 1a). **b** *tr.* cause to do this (*slide the drawer into place*). **2** *intr.* move quietly; glide; go smoothly along. **3** *intr.* pass gradually or imperceptibly. **4** *intr.* glide over ice on one or both feet without skates (under gravity or with momentum got by running). **5** *intr.* (foll. by *over*) barely touch upon (a delicate subject etc.). **6** *intr.* & *tr.* (often foll. by *into*) move or cause to move quietly or unobtrusively (*slid his hand into mine*). **7** *intr.* take its own course (*let it slide*). ● *n.* **1 a** the act or an instance of sliding. **b** a rapid decline. **2** an inclined plane down which children, goods, etc., slide; a chute. **3 a** a track made by or for sliding, esp. on ice. **b** a slope prepared with snow or ice for tobogganing. **4** a part of a machine or instrument that slides, esp. a slide-valve. **5 a** a thing slid into place, esp. a piece of glass holding an object for a microscope. **b** a mounted transparency usu. placed in a projector for viewing on a screen. **6** *Brit.* = HAIRSLIDE. **7** a part or parts of a machine on or between which a sliding part works. □ **let things slide** be negligent; allow deterioration. □ **slidable** *adj.* **slidably** *adv.* **slider** *n.* [Old English *slīdan*]

slide fastener *n. US* a zip fastener.

slide rule *n.* a ruler with a sliding central strip, graduated logarithmically for making rapid calculations, esp. multiplication and division.

slide-valve *n.* a sliding piece that opens and closes an aperture by sliding across it.

slideway /ˈslʌɪdweɪ/ *n.* = SLIDE *n.* 7.

sliding door *n.* a door drawn across an aperture on a slide, not turning on hinges.

sliding keel *n. Brit. Naut.* a centreboard.

sliding roof *n.* a part of a roof (esp. in a motor car) made able to slide and so form an aperture.

sliding scale *n.* a scale of fees, taxes, wages, etc., that varies as a whole in accordance with variation of some standard.

sliding seat *n.* a seat able to slide to and fro on runners etc., esp. in a racing boat to adjust the length of a stroke.

slight /slʌɪt/ *adj., v., & n.* ● *adj.* **1 a** inconsiderable; of little significance (*has a slight cold; the damage is very slight*). **b** barely perceptible (*a slight smell of gas*). **c** not much or great or thorough; inadequate, scanty (*a conclusion based on very slight observation; paid him slight attention*). **2** slender, frail-looking (*saw a slight figure approaching; supported by a slight framework*). **3** (in *superl.*, with *neg.* or *interrog.*) any whatever (*paid not the slightest attention*). ● *v.tr.* **1** treat or speak of (a person etc.) as not worth attention; fail in courtesy or respect towards; markedly neglect. **2** *hist.* make militarily useless; raze (a fortification etc.). ● *n.* a marked piece of neglect; a failure to show due respect. □ **put a slight upon** = sense 1 of *v.* □ **slightingly** *adv.* **slightish** *adj.* **slightly** *adv.* **slightness** *n.* [originally = smooth, sleek: Middle English *slyght, sleght* from Old Norse *sléttr* 'level, smooth', from Germanic]

slily var. of SLYLY (see SLY).

slim /slɪm/ *adj., v., & n.* ● *adj.* (**slimmer**, **slimmest**) **1 a** of small girth or thickness; of long narrow shape. **b** gracefully thin; slenderly built. **c** not fat or overweight. **2** small, insufficient (*a slim chance of success*). **3** clever, artful, crafty, unscrupulous. **4** reduced to an economical or efficient size, level, etc. ● *v.* (**slimmed**, **slimming**) **1** *intr. Brit.* make oneself slimmer by dieting, exercise, etc. **2** *tr.* make slim or slimmer. ● *n.* **1** a course of slimming. **2** (in full **slim disease**) (esp. in African use) Aids. □ **slimly** *adv.* **slimmer** *n.* **slimming** *n. & adj.* **slimness** *n.* [Low German or Dutch from Germanic]

slime /slʌɪm/ *n. & v.* ● *n.* thick slippery mud or a substance of similar consistency, e.g. liquid bitumen or a mucus exuded by fish etc. ● *v.tr.* cover with slime. [Old English *slīm* from Germanic: related to Latin *limus* 'mud', Greek *limnē* 'marsh']

slime mould *n.* a spore-bearing micro-organism secreting slime, esp. a myxomycete.

slimline /ˈslɪmlʌɪn/ *adj.* **1** of slender design. **2** (of a drink etc.) not fattening.

slimy /ˈslʌɪmi/ *adj.* (**slimier**, **slimiest**) **1** of the consistency of slime. **2** covered, smeared with, or full of slime. **3** *colloq.* disgustingly dishonest, meek, or flattering. **4** slippery; hard to hold. □ **slimily** *adv.* **sliminess** *n.*

sling[1] /slɪŋ/ *n. & v.* ● *n.* **1** a strap, belt, etc., used to support or raise a hanging weight, e.g. a rifle, a ship's boat, or goods being transferred. **2** a bandage looped round the neck to support an injured arm. **3** a strap or string used with the hand to give impetus to a small missile, esp. a stone. **4** a pouch or frame supported by a strap round the neck or shoulders for carrying a young child. **5** *Austral. slang* a tip or bribe. ● *v.tr.* (*past* and *past part.* **slung** /slʌŋ/) **1** (also *absol.*) hurl (a stone etc.) from a sling. **2** *colloq.* throw. **3** suspend with a sling; allow to swing suspended; arrange so as to be supported from above; hoist or transfer with a sling. □ **sling one's hook** see HOOK. **sling off at** *Austral.* & *NZ slang* disparage; mock; make fun of. [Middle English, probably from Old Norse verb *slyngva*]

sling[2] /slɪŋ/ *n.* a sweetened drink of spirits (esp. gin) and water. [18th c.: origin unknown]

sling-back *n.* **1** a shoe held in place by a strap above the heel. **2** (in full **sling-back chair**) a chair with a fabric seat suspended from a rigid frame.

sling-bag *n. Brit.* a bag with a long strap which may be hung from the shoulder.

slinger /ˈslɪŋə/ *n.* a person who slings, esp. the user of a sling.

slingshot /ˈslɪŋʃɒt/ *n. US* a catapult.

slink[1] /slɪŋk/ *v.intr.* (*past* and *past part.* **slunk** /slʌŋk/) (often foll. by *off, away, by*) move in a stealthy or guilty or sneaking manner. [Old English *slincan* 'crawl']

slink[2] /slɪŋk/ *v. & n.* ● *v.tr.* (also *absol.*) (of an animal) produce (young) prematurely. ● *n.* **1** an animal, esp. a calf, so born. **2** its flesh. [apparently from SLINK[1]]

slinky /ˈslɪŋki/ *adj.* (**slinkier**, **slinkiest**) **1** stealthy. **2** (of a garment) close-fitting and flowing; sinuous. **3** gracefully slender. □ **slinkily** *adv.* **slinkiness** *n.*

slip[1] /slɪp/ *v. & n.* ● *v.* (**slipped**, **slipping**) **1** *intr.* slide unintentionally esp. for a short distance; lose one's footing or balance or place by unintended sliding. **2** *intr.* go or move with a sliding motion (*as the door closes the catch slips into place; slipped into her nightdress*). **3** *intr.* escape restraint or capture by being slippery or hard to hold or by not being grasped (*the eel slipped through his fingers*). **4** *intr.* make one's or its way unobserved or quietly or quickly (*just slip across to the baker's; errors will slip in*). **5** *intr.* **a** make a careless or casual mistake. **b** fall below the normal standard; deteriorate, lapse. **6** *tr.* insert or transfer stealthily or casually or with a sliding motion (*slipped a coin into his hand; slipped the papers into his pocket*). **7** *tr.* **a** release from restraint (*slipped the greyhounds from the leash*). **b** detach (an anchor) from a ship. **c** *Brit.* detach (a carriage) from a moving train. **d** release (the clutch of a motor vehicle) for a moment. **e** (of an animal) produce (young) prematurely. **8** *tr.* move (a stitch) to the other needle without knitting it. **9** *tr.* (foll. by *on, off*) pull (a garment) hastily on or off. **10** *tr.* escape from; give the slip to (*the dog slipped its collar; point slipped my mind*). ● *n.* **1** the act or an instance of slipping. **2** an accidental or slight mistake. **3** a loose covering or garment, esp. a petticoat or pillowcase. **4 a** a reduction in the movement of a pulley etc. due to slipping of the belt. **b** a reduction in the distance travelled by a ship or aircraft arising from the nature of the medium in which its propeller revolves. **5** (in *sing.* or *pl.*) **a** an artificial slope of stone etc. on which boats are landed. **b** an inclined structure on which ships are built or repaired. **6** *Cricket* **a** a player stationed for fielding any ball glancing off the bat to the off side. **b** (in *sing.* or *pl.*) the position of such a fielder (*caught in the slips; caught at slip*). **7** a leash to slip dogs. □ **give a person the slip** escape from or evade him or her. **let slip 1** release accidentally or deliberately, esp. from a leash. **2** miss (an opportunity). **3** utter inadvertently. **let slip through one's fingers 1** lose hold of. **2** miss the opportunity of having. **slip away** depart without leave-taking etc. **slip off** depart without leave-taking etc. **slip something over on** *colloq.* outwit. **slip up** *colloq.* make a mistake. **there's many a slip 'twixt cup and lip** nothing is certain till it has happened. [Middle English, probably from Middle Low German *slippen*: cf. SLIPPERY]

slip[2] /slɪp/ *n.* **1 a** a small piece of paper, esp. for writing on. **b** a long narrow strip of thin wood, paper, etc. **c** a printer's proof on such paper; a galley proof. **2** a cutting taken from a plant for grafting or planting; a scion. □ **slip of a** small and slim (*a slip of a girl*). [Middle English, probably from Middle Dutch, Middle Low German *slippe* 'cut, strip', etc.]

slip[3] /slɪp/ *n.* clay in a creamy mixture with water, used mainly for decorating earthenware. [Old English *slipa, slyppe* 'slime': cf. COWSLIP]

slip-carriage *n. Brit.* a railway carriage on an express for detaching at a station where the rest of the train does not stop.

slip case *n.* a close-fitting case for a book etc.

slip casting *n.* the manufacture of ceramic ware by allowing slip to solidify in a mould. [SLIP³]

slip-coach *n. Brit.* = SLIP-CARRIAGE.

slip cover *n.* **1** a detachable cover for a chair, sofa, etc., esp. when out of use; a loose cover. **2** a jacket or slip case for a book.

slip form *n.* a mould in which a structure of uniform cross-section is cast by filling it with concrete and continually moving and refilling it.

slip-hook *n.* a hook with a contrivance for releasing it readily when necessary.

slip-knot *n.* **1** a knot that can be undone by a pull. **2** a running knot.

slip of the pen *n.* (also **slip of the tongue**) a small mistake in which something is written (or said) unintentionally.

slip-on *adj. & n.* ● *adj.* (of shoes or clothes) that can be easily slipped on and off. ● *n.* a slip-on shoe or garment.

slipover /ˈslɪpəʊvə/ *n. & adj.* ● *n.* a pullover, usu. without sleeves. ● *adj.* (**slip-over**) (of a garment) to be slipped over the head.

slippage /ˈslɪpɪdʒ/ *n.* **1** the act or an instance of slipping. **2 a** a decline, esp. in popularity or value. **b** failure to meet a deadline or fulfil a promise; delay.

slipped disc *n.* a cartilaginous disc between vertebrae that has become displaced, pinching the spinal nerve and causing lumbar pain.

slipper /ˈslɪpə/ *n. & v.* ● *n.* **1** a light loose comfortable indoor shoe. **2** a light slip-on shoe for dancing etc. ● *v.tr.* beat or strike with a slipper. □ **slippered** *adj.*

slipper bath *n. Brit.* a bath shaped like a slipper, with a covered end.

slipper sock *n.* a thick sock, usu. with a leather sole, for use as a slipper.

slipperwort /ˈslɪpəwəːt/ *n.* calceolaria.

slippery /ˈslɪp(ə)ri/ *adj.* **1** difficult to hold firmly because of smoothness, wetness, sliminess, or elusive motion. **2** (of a surface) difficult to stand on, causing slips by its smoothness or muddiness. **3** unreliable, unscrupulous, shifty. **4** (of a subject) requiring tactful handling. □ **slipperily** *adv.* **slipperiness** *n.* [dialect *slipper* from Old English *slipor*: probably coined by Coverdale (1535) to translate Luther's *schlipfferig*, from Middle High German *slipferig*: ultimately from Germanic]

slippery elm *n.* **1** the N. American red elm, *Ulmus fulva*. **2** the medicinal inner bark of this.

slippery slope *n.* a course leading to disaster.

slippy /ˈslɪpi/ *adj.* (**slippier**, **slippiest**) *colloq.* slippery. □ **look** (or **be**) **slippy** *Brit.* look sharp; make haste. □ **slippiness** *n.*

slip ring *n.* a ring for sliding contact in a dynamo or electric motor.

slip road *n. Brit.* a road for entering or leaving a motorway etc.

slip-rope *n. Naut.* a rope with both ends on board so that casting loose either end frees the ship from its moorings.

slip sheet *n. Printing* a sheet of paper placed between newly printed sheets to prevent set-off or smudging.

slipshod /ˈslɪpʃɒd/ *adj.* **1** (of speech or writing, a speaker or writer, a method of work, etc.) careless, unsystematic; loose in arrangement. **2** slovenly. **3** having shoes down at heel.

slip stitch *n. & v.* ● *n.* **1** a loose stitch joining layers of fabric and not visible externally. **2** a stitch moved to the other needle without being knitted. ● *v.tr.* (**slip-stitch**) sew with slip stitches.

slipstream /ˈslɪpstriːm/ *n. & v.* ● *n.* **1** a current of air or water driven back by a revolving propeller or a moving vehicle. **2** an assisting force regarded as drawing something along with or behind something else. ● *v.tr.* **1** follow closely behind (another vehicle). **2** pass after travelling in another's slipstream.

slip-up *n. colloq.* a mistake, a blunder.

slipware /ˈslɪpwɛː/ *n.* pottery decorated with slip (see SLIP³).

slipway /ˈslɪpweɪ/ *n.* a slip for building ships or landing boats.

slit /slɪt/ *n. & v.* ● *n.* **1** a long straight narrow incision. **2** a long narrow opening comparable to a cut. ● *v.tr.* (**slitting**; *past* and *past part.* **slit**) **1** make a slit in; cut or tear lengthwise. **2** cut into strips. □ **slitted** *adj.* **slitter** *n.* [Middle English *slitte*, related to Old English *slītan*, from Germanic]

slit-eyed *adj.* having long narrow eyes.

slither /ˈslɪðə/ *v. & n.* ● *v.intr.* slide unsteadily; go with an irregular slipping motion. ● *n.* an instance of slithering. □ **slithery** *adj.* [Middle English variant of *slidder* (now dialect) from Old English *slid(e)rian*, frequentative from *slid-*, weak grade of *slīdan* SLIDE]

slit pocket *n.* a pocket with a vertical opening giving access to the pocket or to a garment beneath.

slit trench *n.* a narrow trench for a soldier or a weapon.

slitty /ˈslɪti/ *adj.* (**slittier**, **slittiest**) usu. *derog.* (of the eyes) long and narrow.

sliver /ˈslɪvə, ˈslʌɪ-/ *n. & v.* ● *n.* **1** a long thin piece cut or split off. **2** a piece of wood torn from a tree or from timber. **3** a splinter, esp. from an exploded shell. **4** a strip of loose textile fibres after carding. ● *v.tr. & intr.* **1** break off as a sliver. **2** break up into slivers. **3** form into slivers. [Middle English, related to *slive* 'cleave' (now dialect) from Old English]

slivovitz /ˈslɪvəvɪts/ *n.* a plum brandy made esp. in the former Yugoslavia and Romania. [Serbo-Croat *šljivovica* from *šljiva* 'plum']

Sloane /sləʊn/ *n.* (in full **Sloane Ranger**) *Brit. slang* a fashionable and conventional upper-class young person, usu. a woman, living esp. in London. □ **Sloaney** *adj.* [*Sloane* Square, London + Lone *Ranger*, a cowboy hero]

slob /slɒb/ *n.* **1** *colloq.* a stupid, careless, coarse, or fat person. **2** *Ir.* muddy land. □ **slobbish** *adj.* [Irish *slab* 'mud' from English *slab* 'ooze, sludge', probably from Scandinavian]

slobber /ˈslɒbə/ *v. & n.* ● *v.intr.* **1** slaver. **2** (foll. by *over*) show excessive sentiment. ● *n.* saliva running from the mouth; slaver. □ **slobbery** *adj.* [Middle English, = Dutch *slobbern*, of imitative origin]

sloe /sləʊ/ *n.* **1** = BLACKTHORN 1. **2** the small bluish-black fruit of this, with a sharp sour taste. [Old English *slā(h)*, from Germanic]

sloe-eyed *adj.* **1** having bluish-black eyes. **2** slant-eyed.

sloe gin *n.* a liqueur of sloes steeped in gin.

slog /slɒg/ *v. & n.* ● *v.* (**slogged**, **slogging**) **1** *intr. & tr.* hit hard and usu. wildly, esp. in boxing or cricket. **2** *intr.* (often foll. by *away*, *on*) walk or work doggedly. ● *n.* **1** a hard random hit. **2 a** hard steady work or walking. **b** a spell of this. □ **slogger** *n.* [19th c.: origin unknown: cf. SLUG²]

slogan /ˈsləʊg(ə)n/ *n.* **1** a short catchy phrase used in advertising etc. **2** a party cry; a watchword or motto. **3** *hist.* a Scottish Highland war cry. [Gaelic *sluagh-ghairm*, from *sluagh* 'army' + *gairm* 'shout']

sloop /sluːp/ *n.* **1** a small one-masted fore-and-aft rigged vessel with mainsail and jib. **2** (in full **sloop of war**) *Brit. hist.* a small warship with guns on the upper deck only. [Dutch *sloep(e)*, of unknown origin]

sloop-rigged *adj.* rigged like a sloop.

sloosh /sluːʃ/ *n. & v. Brit. colloq.* ● *n.* a pouring or pouring sound of water. ● *v.intr.* **1** flow with a rush. **2** make a heavy splashing or rushing noise. [imitative]

sloot /sluːt/ *n.* (also **sluit** /sluːt, ˈsluːɪt/) *S.Afr.* a deep gully formed by heavy rain. [Afrikaans from Dutch *sloot* 'ditch']

slop¹ /slɒp/ *v. & n.* ● *v.* (**slopped**, **slopping**) **1** (often foll. by *over*) **a** *intr.* spill or flow over the edge of a vessel. **b** *tr.* allow to do this. **2** *tr.* make (the floor, clothes, etc.)

wet or messy by slopping, spill or splash liquid on. **3** *intr.* (usu. foll. by *over*) gush; be effusive or maudlin. ● *n.* **1** a quantity of liquid spilled or splashed. **2** weakly sentimental language. **3** (in *pl.*) waste liquid, esp. dirty water or the waste contents of kitchen, bedroom, or prison vessels. **4** (in *sing.* or *pl.*) unappetizing weak liquid food. **5** *Naut.* a choppy sea. □ **slop about** esp. *Brit.* move about in a slovenly manner. **slop out** esp. *Brit.* carry slops out (in prison etc.). [originally = a mudhole: probably related to Old English *slyppe*: cf. COWSLIP]

slop[2] /slɒp/ *n.* **1** a workman's loose outer garment. **2** (in *pl.*) esp. *Brit.* ready-made or cheap clothing. **3** (in *pl.*) clothes and bedding supplied to sailors in the navy. **4** (in *pl.*) *archaic* wide baggy trousers esp. as worn by sailors. [Middle English: cf. Old English *oferslop* 'surplice', from Germanic]

slop basin *n. Brit.* a basin for the dregs of cups at table.

slop bucket *n.* a bucket for removing bedroom or kitchen slops.

slope /sləʊp/ *n.* & *v.* ● *n.* **1** an inclined position or direction; a state in which one end or side is at a higher level than another; a position in a line neither parallel nor perpendicular to level ground or to a line serving as a standard. **2** a piece of rising or falling ground. **3 a** a difference in level between the two ends or sides of a thing (*a slope of 5 metres*). **b** the rate at which this increases with distance etc. **4** a place for skiing on the side of a hill or mountain. **5** (prec. by *the*) the position of a rifle when sloped. ● *v.* **1** *intr.* have or take a slope; slant esp. up or down; lie or tend obliquely, esp. to ground level. **2** *tr.* place or arrange or make in or at a slope. □ **slope arms** place one's rifle in a sloping position against one's shoulder. **slope off** *colloq.* go away, esp. to evade work etc. [shortening of ASLOPE]

sloppy /'slɒpi/ *adj.* (**sloppier**, **sloppiest**) **1 a** (of the ground) wet with rain; full of puddles. **b** (of food etc.) watery and disagreeable. **c** (of a floor, table, etc.) wet with slops, having water etc. spilt on it. **2** unsystematic; careless, not thorough. **3** (of a garment) ill-fitting or untidy. **4** (of sentiment or talk) weakly emotional, maudlin. **5** *colloq.* (of the sea) choppy. □ **sloppily** *adv.* **sloppiness** *n.*

slosh /slɒʃ/ *v.* & *n.* ● *v.* **1** *intr.* (often foll. by *about*) splash or flounder about; move with a splashing sound. **2** *tr. Brit. slang* hit esp. heavily. **3** *tr. colloq.* **a** pour (liquid) clumsily. **b** pour liquid on. ● *n.* **1** slush. **2 a** an instance of splashing. **b** the sound of this. **3** *Brit. slang* a heavy blow. **4** a quantity of liquid. [variant of SLUSH]

sloshed /slɒʃt/ *adj. slang* drunk.

sloshy /'slɒʃi/ *adj.* (**sloshier**, **sloshiest**) **1** slushy. **2** sloppy, sentimental.

slot[1] /slɒt/ *n.* & *v.* ● *n.* **1** a slit or other aperture in a machine etc. for something (esp. a coin) to be inserted. **2** a slit, groove, channel, or long aperture into which something fits or in which something works. **3** an allotted place in an arrangement or scheme, esp. in a broadcasting schedule. ● *v.* (**slotted**, **slotting**) **1** *tr.* & *intr.* place or be placed into or as if into a slot. **2** *tr.* provide with a slot or slots. [Middle English, = hollow of the breast, from Old French *esclot*, of unknown origin]

slot[2] /slɒt/ *n.* **1** the track of a deer etc., esp. as shown by footprints. **2** a deer's foot. [Old French *esclot* 'hoof-print of a horse', probably from Old Norse *slóth* 'trail': cf. SLEUTH]

sloth /sləʊθ/ *n.* **1** laziness or indolence; reluctance to make an effort. **2** any slow-moving nocturnal mammal of the family Bradypodidae or Megalonychidae of S. America, having long limbs and hooked claws for hanging upside down from branches of trees. [Middle English, from SLOW + -TH[2]]

sloth bear *n.* a large-lipped black shaggy bear, *Melursus ursinus*, of India.

slothful /'sləʊθfʊl, -f(ə)l/ *adj.* lazy; characterized by sloth. □ **slothfully** *adv.* **slothfulness** *n.*

slot machine *n.* a machine worked by the insertion of a coin, esp.: **1** *Brit.* one for automatic retail of small articles. **2** *Brit.* one allowing a spell of play at a pin-table etc. **3** *US* = FRUIT MACHINE.

slouch /slaʊtʃ/ *v.* & *n.* ● *v.* **1** *intr.* stand or move or sit in a drooping ungainly fashion. **2** *tr.* bend one side of the brim of (a hat) downwards (opp. COCK[1] *v.* 3). **3** *intr.* droop; hang down loosely. ● *n.* **1** a slouching posture or movement; a stoop. **2** a downward bend of a hat-brim. **3** *colloq.* an incompetent or slovenly worker, operator, or performance (*he's no slouch*). □ **slouchy** *adj.* [16th c.:origin unknown]

slouch hat *n.* a hat with a wide flexible brim.

slough[1] /slaʊ/ *n.* a swamp; a miry place; a quagmire. □ **sloughy** *adj.* [Old English *slōh*, *slō(g)*]

slough[2] /slʌf/ *n.* & *v.* ● *n.* **1** a part that an animal casts or moults, esp. a snake's cast skin. **2** dead tissue that drops off from living flesh etc. **3** a habit etc. that has been abandoned. ● *v.* **1** *tr.* cast off as a slough. **2** *intr.* (often foll. by *off*) drop off as a slough. **3** *intr.* cast off a slough. **4** *intr.* (often foll. by *away, down*) (of soil, rock, etc.) collapse or slide into a hole or depression. □ **sloughy** *adj.* [Middle English, perhaps related to Low German *slu(we)* 'husk']

Slough of Despond /slaʊ/ *n.* a state of hopeless depression (with reference to Bunyan's *Pilgrim's Progress*). [SLOUGH[1]]

Slovak /'sləʊvak/ *n.* & *adj.* ● *n.* **1** a member of a Slavonic people inhabiting Slovakia in central Europe, formerly part of Czechoslovakia and now an independent republic. **2** the West Slavonic language of this people. ● *adj.* of or relating to the Slovaks or their language. [Slovak etc. *Slovák*, related to SLOVENE]

sloven /'slʌv(ə)n/ *n.* a person who is habitually untidy or careless. [Middle English, perhaps from Flemish *sloef* 'dirty' or Dutch *slof* 'careless']

Slovene /'sləʊviːn, sləʊ'viːn/ *n.* & *adj.* (also **Slovenian** /-'viːnɪən/) ● *n.* **1** a member of a Slavonic people inhabiting Slovenia in south-east central Europe, formerly part of Yugoslavia. **2** the language of this people. ● *adj.* of or relating to Slovenia, its people, or its language. [German *Slowene* from Slovene etc. *Slovenec*, from a Slavonic root shared with SLOVAK, perhaps related to *slovo* 'word']

slovenly /'slʌv(ə)nli/ *adj.* & *adv.* ● *adj.* careless and untidy; unmethodical. ● *adv.* in a slovenly manner. □ **slovenliness** *n.*

slow /sləʊ/ *adj., adv.,* & *v.* ● *adj.* **1 a** taking a relatively long time to do a thing or cover a distance (also foll. by *of*: *slow of speech*). **b** not quick; acting or moving or done without speed. **2** gradual; obtained over a length of time (*slow growth*). **3** not producing, allowing, or conducive to speed (*in the slow lane*). **4** (of a clock etc.) showing a time earlier than is the case. **5** (of a person) not understanding readily; not learning easily. **6** dull; uninteresting; tedious. **7** slack or sluggish (*business is slow*). **8** (of a fire or oven) giving little heat. **9** *Photog.* **a** (of a film) needing long exposure. **b** (of a lens) having a small aperture. **10 a** reluctant; tardy (*not slow to defend himself*). **b** not hasty or easily moved (*slow to take offence*). **11** (of a cricket pitch, tennis court, putting green, etc.) on which the ball bounces or runs slowly. ● *adv.* **1** at a slow pace; slowly (see Usage Note). **2** (in *comb.*) (*slow-moving traffic*). ● *v.* (usu. foll. by *down, up*) **1** *intr.* & *tr.* reduce one's speed or the speed of (a vehicle etc.). **2** *intr.* reduce one's pace of life; live or work less actively or intensely. □ **slow and sure** of the attitude that haste is risky. **slow but sure** achieving the required result eventually. □ **slowish** *adj.* **slowly** *adv.* **slowness** *n.* [Old English *slāw*, from Germanic]

■ **Usage** The use of *slow* as an adverb is chiefly confined to compounds such as *slow-acting*, *slow-burning*, *slow-moving*. It is also established in the expression *go slow* and the noun *go-slow*. In sentences such as *he drives too slow* and *go as slow as you can*, *slowly* is preferable in formal contexts. Compare *fast* which is fully acceptable as an adverb in standard English.

slowcoach /'sləʊkəʊtʃ/ *n. Brit.* **1** a slow or lazy person. **2** a dull-witted person. **3** a person behind the times in opinions etc.

slow cooker *n.* a large electric pot used for cooking stews etc. very slowly.

slowdown /'sləʊdaʊn/ *n.* the action of slowing down; a go-slow.

slow handclap *n.* slow clapping by an audience as a sign of displeasure or boredom.

slow loris see LORIS.

slow march *n.* the marching time adopted by troops in a funeral procession etc.

slow match *n.* a slow-burning match for lighting explosives etc.

slow motion *n.* **1** the operation or speed of a film using slower projection or more rapid exposure so that actions etc. appear much slower than usual. **2** the simulation of this in real action.

slow neutron *n.* a neutron with low kinetic energy esp. after moderation (cf. FAST NEUTRON).

slowpoke /'sləʊpəʊk/ *n. N. Amer. colloq.* = SLOWCOACH.

slow puncture *n.* esp. *Brit.* a puncture causing only slow deflation of the tyre.

slow reactor *n. Physics* a nuclear reactor using mainly slow neutrons (cf. FAST REACTOR).

slow track *n.* a route, course, method, etc., which results in slow progress (*at school he was assigned to the slow track*).

slow virus *n.* a virus or virus-like organism that multiplies slowly in the host organism and has a long incubation period.

slow-worm /'sləʊwəːm/ *n.* a small European legless lizard, *Anguis fragilis*, giving birth to live young. Also called BLINDWORM. [Old English *slā-wyrm*: first element of uncertain origin, assimilated to SLOW]

SLR *abbr.* **1** *Photog.* single-lens reflex. **2** self-loading rifle.

slub[1] /slʌb/ *n. & adj.* ● *n.* **1** a lump or thick place in yarn or thread. **2** fabric woven from thread etc. with slubs. ● *adj.* (of material etc.) with an irregular appearance caused by uneven thickness of the warp. [19th c.: origin unknown]

slub[2] /slʌb/ *n. & v.* ● *n.* wool slightly twisted in preparation for spinning. ● *v.tr.* (**slubbed**, **slubbing**) twist (wool) in this way. [19th c.: origin unknown]

sludge /slʌdʒ/ *n.* **1** thick greasy mud. **2** muddy or slushy sediment. **3** sewage. **4** *Mech.* an accumulation of dirty oil, esp. in the sump of an internal-combustion engine. **5** *Geol.* sea ice newly formed in small pieces. **6** (usu. *attrib.*) a muddy colour (*sludge green*). ▫ **sludgy** *adj.* [17th c., origin uncertain: cf. SLUSH]

slue var. of SLEW[1].

slug[1] /slʌg/ *n. & v.* ● *n.* **1** a small shell-less mollusc of the class Gastropoda often destructive to plants. **2 a** a bullet esp. of irregular shape. **b** a missile for an airgun. **3** *Printing* **a** a metal bar used in spacing. **b** a line of type in Linotype printing. **4** orig. *US* a tot of usu. liquor. **5** a unit of mass, given an acceleration of 1 foot per second per second by a force of 1 lb. **6** a roundish lump of metal. **7** a thick piece or lump of something; a (large) portion. ● *v.tr.* (**slugged**, **slugging**) drink in large draughts; swig. [Middle English *slugg(e)* 'sluggard', probably from Scandinavian]

slug[2] /slʌg/ *v. & n.* esp. *N. Amer.* ● *v.tr.* (**slugged**, **slugging**) strike with a hard blow. ● *n.* a hard blow. ▫ **slug it out 1** fight it out. **2** endure; stick it out. ▫ **slugger** *n.* [19th c., origin unknown: cf. SLOG]

slugabed /'slʌgəbɛd/ *n. archaic* a lazy person who lies late in bed. [*slug* (*v.*) (see SLUGGARD) + ABED]

sluggard /'slʌgəd/ *n.* a lazy sluggish person. ▫ **sluggardly** *adj.* **sluggardliness** *n.* [Middle English from *slug* 'be slothful' (probably from Scandinavian: cf. SLUG[1]) + -ARD]

sluggish /'slʌgɪʃ/ *adj.* inert; inactive; slow-moving; torpid; indolent (*a sluggish circulation*; *a sluggish stream*). ▫ **sluggishly** *adv.* **sluggishness** *n.* [Middle English from SLUG[1] or *slug* (*v.*): see SLUGGARD]

slug pellet *n.* a pellet containing a substance poisonous to slugs.

sluice /sluːs/ *n. & v.* ● *n.* **1** (also **sluice-gate**, **sluice-valve**) a sliding gate or other contrivance for controlling the volume or flow of water. **2** (also **sluice-way**) an artificial water channel esp. for washing ore. **3** a place for rinsing. **4** the act or an instance of rinsing. **5** the water above or below or issuing through a floodgate. ● *v.* **1** *tr.* provide or wash with a sluice or sluices. **2** *tr.* rinse, pour or throw water freely upon. **3** *tr.* (foll. by *out*, *away*) wash out or away with a flow of water. **4** *tr.* flood with water from a sluice. **5** *intr.* (of water) rush out from a sluice, or as if from a sluice. [Middle English from Old French *escluse*, ultimately from Latin *excludere* EXCLUDE]

sluit var. of SLOOT.

slum /slʌm/ *n. & v.* ● *n.* **1** an overcrowded and squalid backstreet, district, etc., usu. in a city and inhabited by very poor people. **2** a house or building unfit for human habitation. ● *v.intr.* (**slummed**, **slumming**) **1** live in slumlike conditions. **2** go about the slums through curiosity, to examine the condition of the inhabitants, or for charitable purposes. ▫ **slum it** *colloq.* put up with conditions less comfortable than usual. ▫ **slummy** *adj.* (**slummier**, **slummiest**). **slumminess** *n.* [19th c.: originally slang]

slumber /'slʌmbə/ *v. & n. poet. literary* ● *v.intr.* **1** sleep, esp. in a specified manner. **2** be idle, drowsy, or inactive. ● *n.* a sleep, esp. of a specified kind (*fell into a fitful slumber*). ▫ **slumber away** spend (time) in slumber. ▫ **slumberer** *n.* **slumberous** *adj.* **slumbrous** *adj.* [Middle English *slūmere* etc. via *slūmen* (*v.*) or *slūme* (*n.*) from Old English *slūma*: *-b-* as in *number*]

slumberwear /'slʌmbəwɛː/ *n.* nightclothes.

slumgullion /slʌm'gʌljən/ *n. N. Amer. slang* sludge, esp. watery stew.

slump /slʌmp/ *n. & v.* ● *n.* **1** a sudden severe or prolonged fall in prices or values of commodities or securities. **2** a sharp or sudden decline in trade or business, usu. bringing widespread unemployment. **3** a lessening of interest or commitment in a subject or undertaking. ● *v.intr.* **1** undergo a slump; fail; fall in price. **2** sit or fall heavily or limply (*slumped into a chair*). **3** lean or subside. [17th c., originally 'sink in a bog': imitative]

slung *past* and *past part.* of SLING[1].

slung shot *n.* a metal ball attached by a thong etc. to the wrist and used esp. by criminals as a weapon.

slunk *past* and *past part.* of SLINK[1].

slur /sləː/ *v. & n.* ● *v.* (**slurred**, **slurring**) **1** *tr. & intr.* pronounce or write indistinctly so that the sounds or letters run into one another. **2** *tr. Mus.* **a** perform (a group of two or more notes) legato. **b** mark (notes) with a slur. **3** *tr. archaic* or *US* put a slur on (a person or a person's character); make insinuations against. **4** *tr.* (usu. foll. by *over*) pass over (a fact, fault, etc.) lightly; conceal or minimize. ● *n.* **1** an imputation of wrongdoing; blame; stigma (*a slur on my reputation*). **2** the act or an instance of slurring in pronunciation, singing, or writing. **3** *Mus.* a curved line to show that two or more notes are to be sung to one syllable or played or sung legato. [17th c.: origin unknown]

slurp /sləːp/ *v. & n.* ● *v.tr.* eat or drink noisily. ● *n.* the sound of this; a slurping gulp. [Dutch *slurpen*, *slorpen*]

slurry /'slʌri/ *n.* (*pl.* **-ies**) **1** a semi-liquid mixture of fine particles and water; thin mud. **2** thin liquid cement. **3** a fluid form of manure. **4** a residue of water and particles of coal left at pithead washing plants. [Middle English, related to dialect *slur* 'thin mud', of unknown origin]

slush /slʌʃ/ *n. & v.* ● *n.* **1** watery mud or thawing snow. **2** silly sentiment. ● *v.intr.* squelch, splash; make a squelching or splashing sound. [17th c., also *sludge* and *slutch*: origin unknown]

slush fund *n.* reserve funding esp. as used for political bribery.

slushy /ˈslʌʃi/ *adj.* (**slushier**, **slushiest**) **1** like slush; watery. **2** *colloq.* sentimental; mawkish. □ **slushiness** *n.*

slut /slʌt/ *n. offens.* a slovenly or promiscuous woman. □ **sluttish** *adj.* **sluttishness** *n.* [Middle English: origin unknown]

sly /slʌɪ/ *adj.* (**slyer**, **slyest**) **1** cunning; crafty; wily. **2 a** (of a person) practising secrecy or stealth. **b** (of an action etc.) done etc. in secret. **3** hypocritical; ironical. **4** knowing; arch; bantering; insinuating. **5** *Austral.* & *NZ slang* (esp. of liquor) illicit. □ **on the sly** privately; covertly; without publicity (*smuggled some through on the sly*). □ **slyly** *adv.* (also **slily**). **slyness** *n.* [Middle English *sleh* etc. from Old Norse *slœgr* 'cunning', originally 'able to strike' from *slóg-*, past stem of *slá* 'strike': cf. SLEIGHT]

slyboots /ˈslʌɪbuːts/ *n. colloq.* a sly person.

sly dog *n. colloq.* a person who is discreet about mistakes or pleasures.

slype /slʌɪp/ *n.* a covered way or passage between a cathedral etc. transept and the chapter house or deanery. [perhaps a variant of *slipe* 'a long narrow piece of ground', = SLIP[2] 1]

SM *abbr.* **1** sadomasochism. **2** Sergeant Major.

Sm *symb. Chem.* the element samarium.

smack[1] /smak/ *n., v., & adv.* ● *n.* **1** a sharp slap or blow esp. with the palm of the hand or a flat object. **2** a hard hit at cricket etc. **3** a loud kiss (*gave her a hearty smack*). **4** a loud sharp sound (*heard the smack as it hit the floor*). ● *v.* **1** *tr.* strike with the open hand etc. **2** *tr.* part (one's lips) noisily in eager anticipation or enjoyment of food or another delight. **3** *tr.* crack (a whip). **4** *tr.* & *intr.* move, hit, etc., with a smack. ● *adv. colloq.* **1** with a smack. **2** suddenly; directly; violently (*landed smack on my desk*). **3** exactly (*hit it smack in the centre*). □ **have a smack at** *colloq.* make an attempt at or attack on. **a smack in the eye** (or **face**) *colloq.* a rebuff; a setback. [Middle Dutch *smack(en)*, of imitative origin]

smack[2] /smak/ *v. & n.* (foll. by *of*) ● *v.intr.* **1** have a flavour of; taste of (*smacked of garlic*). **2** suggest the presence or effects of (*it smacks of nepotism*). ● *n.* **1** a flavour; a taste that suggests the presence of something. **2** (in a person's character etc.) a barely discernible quality (*just a smack of superciliousness*). **3** (in food etc.) a very small amount (*add a smack of ginger*). [Old English *smæc*]

smack[3] /smak/ *n.* a single-masted sailing boat for coasting or fishing. [Dutch *smak* from earlier *smacke*: ultimate origin unknown]

smack[4] /smak/ *n. slang* a hard drug, esp. heroin, sold or used illegally. [probably alteration of Yiddish *schmeck* 'sniff']

smack-dab *adv.* esp. *N. Amer.* = SMACK[1] *adv.* 3.

smacker /ˈsmakə/ *n. colloq.* **1** a loud kiss. **2** a resounding blow. **3 a** *Brit. slang* £1. **b** *N. Amer.* $1.

small /smɔːl/ *adj., n., & adv.* ● *adj.* **1** not large or big. **2** slender; thin. **3** not great in importance, amount, number, strength, or power. **4** not much; trifling (*a small token*; *paid small attention*). **5** insignificant; unimportant (*a small matter*; *from small beginnings*). **6** consisting of small particles (*small gravel*; *small shot*). **7** doing something on a small scale (*a small farmer*). **8** socially undistinguished; poor or humble. **9** petty; mean; ungenerous; paltry (*a small spiteful nature*). **10** young; not fully grown or developed (*a small child*). ● *n.* **1** the slenderest part of something (esp. in phr. **small of the back**). **2** (in *pl.*) *Brit. colloq.* small items of laundry, esp. underwear. ● *adv.* into small pieces (*chop it small*). □ **feel** (or **look**) **small** be humiliated; appear mean or humiliated. **in a small way** unambitiously; on a small scale. **no small** considerable; a good deal of (*no small excitement about it*). **small potatoes** an insignificant person or thing. **small profits and quick returns** the policy of a cheap shop etc. relying on large trade. **small wonder** not very surprising. □ **smallish** *adj.* **smallness** *n.* [Old English *smæl*, from Germanic]

small arms *n.pl.* portable firearms, esp. rifles, pistols, light machine-guns, sub-machine guns, etc.

small beer *n.* **1** esp. *Brit.* a trifling matter; something unimportant. **2** weak beer.

small-bore *adj.* (of a firearm) with a narrow bore, in international and Olympic shooting usu. .22 inch calibre (5.6 millimetre bore).

small bower see BOWER[2].

small calorie see CALORIE 1.

small capital *n.* a capital letter which is of the same dimensions as the lower-case letters in the same typeface minus ascenders and descenders, as THIS.

small change *n.* **1** money in the form of coins as opposed to notes. **2** trivial remarks.

small circle *n.* a circle on the surface of a sphere whose plane does not pass through the sphere's centre.

small claims court *n.* a local tribunal in which claims for small amounts can be heard and decided quickly and cheaply without legal representation.

small craft *n.* a general term for small boats and fishing vessels.

small fry *n.pl.* **1** young children or the young of various species. **2** small or insignificant things or people.

smallgoods /ˈsmɔːlgʊdz/ *n.pl. Austral.* delicatessen meats.

smallholder /ˈsmɔːlhəʊldə/ *n. Brit.* a person who farms a smallholding.

smallholding /ˈsmɔːlhəʊldɪŋ/ *n. Brit.* an agricultural holding smaller than a farm.

small hours *n.pl.* the early hours of the morning after midnight.

small intestine *n.* the duodenum, jejunum, and ileum collectively.

small letter *n.* (in printed material) a lower-case letter.

small mercy *n.* a minor concession, benefit, etc. (*be grateful for small mercies*).

small-minded /smɔːlˈmʌɪndɪd/ *adj.* petty; of rigid opinions or narrow outlook. □ **small-mindedly** *adv.* **small-mindedness** *n.*

smallpox /ˈsmɔːlpɒks/ *n.* an acute contagious viral disease, with fever and pustules usu. leaving permanent scars, effectively eradicated through vaccination by 1979. Also called *variola*.

small print *n.* **1** printed matter in small type. **2** inconspicuous and usu. unfavourable limitations etc. in a contract.

small-scale *adj.* made or occurring in small amounts or to a lesser degree.

small slam *n. Bridge* the winning of 12 tricks.

small-sword *n.* a light tapering thrusting-sword, esp. *hist.* for duelling.

small talk *n.* light social conversation.

small-time *attrib.adj. colloq.* unimportant or petty. □ **small-timer** *n.*

small-town *attrib.adj.* relating to or characteristic of a small town; unsophisticated; provincial.

smalt /smɔːlt, smɒlt/ *n.* **1** glass coloured blue with cobalt. **2** a pigment made by pulverizing this. [French from Italian *smalto*, from Germanic: related to SMELT[1]]

smarm /smɑːm/ *v. & n. Brit. colloq.* ● *v.* **1** *tr.* (often foll. by *down*) smooth, plaster down (hair etc.) usu. with cream or oil. **2** *intr.* be ingratiating. ● *n.* obsequiousness. [originally dialect (also *smalm*), of uncertain origin]

smarmy /ˈsmɑːmi/ *adj.* (**smarmier**, **smarmiest**) esp. *Brit. colloq.* ingratiating; flattering; obsequious. □ **smarmily** *adv.* **smarminess** *n.*

smart /smɑːt/ *adj., v., n., & adv.* ● *adj.* **1 a** clever; ingenious; quick-witted (*a smart talker*; *gave a smart answer*). **b** keen in bargaining; quick to take advantage. **c** (of transactions etc.) unscrupulous to the point of dishonesty. **2** well-groomed; neat; bright and fresh in appearance (*a smart suit*). **3** in good repair; showing bright colours, new paint, etc. (*a smart red bicycle*). **4** stylish; fashionable; prominent in society (*in all the* *smart restaurants*; *the smart set*). **5** quick; brisk (*set a smart pace*). **6** painfully severe; sharp; vigorous (*a smart blow*). ● *v.intr.* **1** (of a person or a part of the body) feel or give acute pain or distress (*my eye smarts*; *smarting from the insult*). **2** (of an insult, grievance, etc.) rankle. **3** (foll. by *for*) suffer the consequences of (*you will smart for this*). ● *n.* a bodily or mental sharp pain; a stinging sensation. ● *adv.* smartly; in a smart manner. □ **look smart** esp. *Brit.* make haste. □ **smartingly** *adv.* **smartish** *adj.* & *adv. Brit.* **smartly** *adv.* **smartness** *n.* [Old English *smeart, smeortan*]

smart alec /ˈalɪk/ *n.* (also **smart aleck**, **smart alick**) *colloq.* a person displaying ostentatious or smug cleverness. □ **smart-alecky** *adj.* [SMART + *Alec*, diminutive of the name *Alexander*]

smart-arse *n.* (*US* **smart-ass**) *slang* = SMART ALEC.

smart card *n.* a plastic card with a built-in microprocessor, esp. as a credit or other bank card for the instant transfer of funds etc.

smarten /ˈsmɑːt(ə)n/ *v.tr.* & *intr.* (usu. foll. by *up*) make or become smart or smarter.

smart money *n.* **1** money paid or exacted as a penalty or compensation. **2** money invested by persons with expert knowledge.

smarty /ˈsmɑːti/ *n.* (*pl.* **-ies**) *colloq.* **1** a know-all; a smart alec. **2** a smartly-dressed person; a member of a smart set. [SMART]

smarty-pants *n.pl.* (also *Brit.* **smarty-boots**) = SMARTY 1.

smash /smaʃ/ *v., n., & adv.* ● *v.* **1** *tr.* & *intr.* (often foll. by *up*) **a** break into pieces; shatter. **b** bring or come to sudden or complete destruction, defeat, or disaster. **2** *tr.* (foll. by *into, through*) (of a vehicle etc.) move with great force and impact. **3** *tr.* & *intr.* (foll. by *in*) break in with a crushing blow (*smashed in the window*). **4** *tr.* (in tennis, squash, etc.) hit (a ball etc.) with great force, esp. downwards (*smashed it back over the net*). **5** *intr. colloq.* (of a business etc.) go bankrupt; come to grief. **6** *tr.* (as **smashed** *adj.*) *slang* intoxicated. ● *n.* **1** the act or an instance of smashing; a violent fall, collision, or disaster. **2** the sound of this. **3** (in full **smash hit**) a very successful play, song, performer, etc. **4** a stroke in tennis, squash, etc., in which the ball is hit esp. downwards with great force. **5** a violent blow with a fist etc. **6** *colloq.* bankruptcy; a series of commercial failures. **7** a mixture of spirits (usu. brandy) with flavoured water and ice. ● *adv.* with a smash (*fell smash on the floor*). □ **go to smash** *colloq.* be ruined etc. [18th c., probably imitative, suggested by *smack, smite* and *bash, mash*, etc.]

smash-and-grab *adj.* (of a robbery etc.) in which the thief smashes a shop window and seizes goods.

smasher /ˈsmaʃə/ *n.* **1** *Brit. colloq.* a very beautiful or pleasing person or thing. **2** a person or thing that smashes.

smashing /ˈsmaʃɪŋ/ *adj.* esp. *Brit. colloq.* superlative; excellent; wonderful; beautiful. □ **smashingly** *adv.*

smash-up *n. colloq.* a violent collision; a complete smash.

smatter /ˈsmatə/ *n.* (also **smattering**) a slight superficial knowledge of a language or subject. □ **smatterer** *n.* [Middle English *smatter* 'talk ignorantly, prate': origin unknown]

smear /smɪə/ *v. & n.* ● *v.tr.* **1** daub or mark with a greasy or sticky substance or with something that stains. **2** blot; smudge; obscure the outline of (writing, artwork, etc.). **3** defame the character of; slander; attempt to or succeed in discrediting (a person or his name) publicly. ● *n.* **1** the act or an instance of smearing. **2** *Med.* **a** material smeared on a microscopic slide etc. for examination. **b** a specimen of this. □ **smearer** *n.* **smeary** *adj.* [Old English *smierwan*, from Germanic]

smear campaign *n.* a planned effort to slander and so discredit a public figure.

smear test *n.* = CERVICAL SMEAR.

smectic /ˈsmɛktɪk/ *adj. & n.* ● *adj.* designating or involving a state of a liquid crystal in which the molecules are oriented in parallel and arranged in well-defined planes (cf. NEMATIC). ● *n.* a smectic substance. [Latin *smecticus*, Greek *smēktikos* 'cleansing' (from the soaplike consistency)]

smegma /ˈsmɛɡmə/ *n.* a sebaceous secretion in the folds of the skin, esp. of the foreskin. □ **smegmatic** /-ˈmatɪk/ *adj.* [Latin from Greek *smēgma -atos* 'soap', from *smēkhō* 'cleanse']

smell /smɛl/ *n. & v.* ● *n.* **1** the faculty of perceiving odours or scents (*has a fine sense of smell*). **2** the quality in substances that is perceived by this (*the smell of thyme*; *this rose has no smell*). **3** an unpleasant odour. **4** the act of inhaling to ascertain smell. ● *v.* (*past* and *past part.* **smelt** /smɛlt/ or **smelled**) **1** *tr.* perceive the smell of; examine by smell (*thought I could smell gas*). **2** *intr.* emit odour. **3** *intr.* seem by smell to be (*this milk smells sour*). **4** *intr.* (foll. by *of*) **a** be redolent of (*smells of fish*). **b** be suggestive of (*smells of dishonesty*). **5** *intr.* have a strong or unpleasant odour. **6** *tr.* perceive as if by smell; detect, discern, suspect (*smell a bargain*; *smell blood*). **7** *intr.* have or use a sense of smell. **8** *intr.* (foll. by *about*) sniff or search about. **9** *intr.* (foll. by *at*) inhale the smell of. □ **smell out 1** detect by small; find out by investigation. **2** (of a dog etc.) hunt out by smell. **smell a rat** begin to suspect trickery etc. □ **smellable** *adj.* **smeller** *n.* **smell-less** *adj.* [Middle English *smel(le)*, probably from Old English]

smelling bottle *n.* a small bottle of smelling salts.

smelling salts *n.pl.* ammonium carbonate mixed with scent to be sniffed as a restorative in faintness etc.

smelly /ˈsmɛli/ *adj.* (**smellier**, **smelliest**) having a strong or unpleasant smell. □ **smelliness** *n.*

smelt[1] /smɛlt/ *v.tr.* **1** extract metal from (ore) by melting. **2** extract (metal) from ore by melting. □ **smelter** *n.* **smeltery** *n.* (*pl.* **-ies**). [Middle Dutch, Middle Low German *smelten*, related to MELT]

smelt[2] *past* and *past part.* of SMELL.

smelt[3] /smɛlt/ *n.* (*pl.* same or **smelts**) any small green and silver fish of the genus *Osmerus* etc. allied to salmon and used as food. [Old English, of uncertain origin: cf. SMOLT]

smew /smjuː/ *n.* a small merganser, *Mergus albellus*. [17th c., obscurely related to Dutch *smient* 'wigeon', German *Schmeiente* etc. 'small wild duck']

smidgen /ˈsmɪdʒɪn/ *n.* (also **smidgeon**, **smidgin**) *colloq.* a small bit or amount. [perhaps from *smitch* in the same sense: cf. dialect *smitch* woodsmoke]

smilax /ˈsmʌɪlaks/ *n.* **1** any climbing shrub of the genus *Smilax*, the roots of some species of which yield sarsaparilla. **2** a climbing kind of asparagus, *Myrsiphyllum asparagoides*, used decoratively by florists. [Latin from Greek, = bindweed]

smile /smʌɪl/ *v. & n.* ● *v.* **1** *intr.* relax the features into a pleased or kind or gently sceptical expression or a forced imitation of these, usu. with the lips parted and the corners of the mouth turned up. **2** *tr.* express by smiling (*smiled their consent*). **3** *tr.* give (a smile) of a specified kind (*smiled a sardonic smile*). **4** *intr.* (foll. by *on, upon*) adopt a favourable attitude towards; encourage (*fortune smiled on me*). **5** *intr.* have a bright or favourable aspect (*the smiling countryside*). **6** *tr.* (foll. by *away*) drive (a person's anger etc.) away (*smiled their tears away*). **7** *intr.* (foll. by *at*) **a** ridicule or show indifference to; show indulgent amusement towards (*smiled at my feeble attempts*). **b** favour; smile on. **8** *tr.* (foll. by *into, out of*) bring (a person) into or out of a specified mood etc. by smiling (*smiled them into agreement*). ● *n.* **1** the act or an instance of smiling. **2** a smiling expression or aspect. □ **come up smiling** *colloq.* recover from adversity and cheerfully face what is to come. □ **smileless** *adj.* **smiler** *n.* **smiley** *adj.* **smilingly** *adv.* [Middle English, perhaps from Scandinavian: related to SMIRK]

smirch /sməːtʃ/ *v. & n.* ● *v.tr.* mark, soil, or smear (a thing, a person's reputation, etc.). ● *n.* **1** a spot or stain.

2 a blot (on one's character etc.). [Middle English: origin unknown]

smirk /smə:k/ *n.* & *v.* ● *n.* an affected, conceited, or silly smile. ● *v.intr.* put on or wear a smirk. □ **smirker** *n.* **smirkingly** *adv.* **smirky** *adj.* **smirkily** *adv.* [Old English *sme(a)rcian*]

smit /smɪt/ *archaic past part.* of SMITE.

smite /smʌɪt/ *v.* & *n.* ● *v.* (*past* **smote** /sməʊt/; *past part.* **smitten** /ˈsmɪt(ə)n/) esp. *archaic* or *literary* **1** *tr.* strike or hit. **2** *tr.* chastise; defeat. **3** *tr.* (in *passive*) **a** have a sudden strong effect on (*was smitten by his conscience*). **b** infatuate, fascinate (*was smitten by her beauty*). **4** *intr.* (foll. by *on, upon*) come forcibly or abruptly upon. ● *n.* a blow or stroke. □ **smiter** *n.* [Old English *smītan* 'smear', from Germanic]

smith /smɪθ/ *n.* & *v.* ● *n.* (esp. in *comb.*) **1** a worker in metal (*goldsmith*; *tinsmith*). **2** a person who forges iron; a blacksmith. **3** a craftsman (*wordsmith*). ● *v.tr.* make or treat by forging. [Old English from Germanic]

smithereens /smɪðəˈri:nz/ *n.pl.* (also **smithers** /ˈsmɪðəz/) small fragments (*smash into smithereens*). [probably from Irish *smidirín*]

smithery /ˈsmɪθ(ə)ri/ *n.* (*pl.* **-ies**) **1** a smith's work. **2** (esp. in naval dockyards) a smithy.

smithy /ˈsmɪði/ *n.* (*pl.* **-ies**) a blacksmith's workshop; a forge. [Middle English from Old Norse *smithja*]

smitten *past part.* of SMITE.

smock /smɒk/ *n.* & *v.* ● *n.* **1** a loose shirtlike garment with the upper part closely gathered in smocking. **2** (also **smock-frock**) a loose overall, esp. *hist.* a field-labourer's outer linen garment. ● *v.tr.* adorn with smocking. [Old English *smoc*, probably related to Old English *smūgan* 'creep', Old Norse *smjúga* 'put on a garment']

smocking /ˈsmɒkɪŋ/ *n.* an ornamental effect on cloth made by gathering the material tightly into pleats, often with stitches in a honeycomb pattern.

smog /smɒg/ *n.* fog intensified by atmospheric pollutants esp. smoke. □ **smoggy** *adj.* (**smoggier**, **smoggiest**). [portmanteau word]

smoke /sməʊk/ *n.* & *v.* ● *n.* **1** a visible suspension of carbon etc. in air, emitted from a burning substance. **2** an act or period of smoking tobacco (*had a quiet smoke*). **3** *colloq.* a cigarette or cigar (*got a smoke?*). **4** (**the Smoke**) *Brit.* & *Austral. colloq.* a big city, esp. London. ● *v.* **1** *intr.* **a** emit smoke or visible vapour (*the smoking ruins*). **b** (of a lamp etc.) burn badly with the emission of smoke. **c** (of a chimney or fire) discharge smoke into the room. **2** **a** *intr.* inhale and exhale the smoke of a cigarette or cigar or pipe. **b** *intr.* do this habitually. **c** *tr.* use (a cigarette etc.) in this way. **3** *tr.* cure or darken by the action of smoke (*smoked salmon*). **4** *tr.* **a** rid of insects etc. by the action of smoke. **b** subdue (insects, esp. bees) in this way. **5** *tr. archaic* make fun of. **6** *tr.* bring (oneself) into a specified state by smoking. □ **go up in smoke** *colloq.* **1** be destroyed by fire. **2** (of a plan etc.) come to nothing. **no smoke without fire** rumours are not entirely baseless. **smoke out** **1** drive out by means of smoke. **2** drive out of hiding or secrecy etc. □ **smokable** *adj.* (also **smokeable**). [Old English *smoca*, from weak grade of the stem of *smēocan* 'emit smoke']

smoke-ball *n.* **1** a puffball. **2** a projectile filled with material emitting dense smoke, used to conceal military operations etc.

smoke bomb *n.* a bomb that emits dense smoke on exploding.

smoke box *n.* a chamber in a steam engine or boiler between the flues and the funnel or chimney stack.

smoke bush *n.* = SMOKE PLANT.

smoked glass *n.* glass darkened by exposure to smoke.

smoke-dried *adj.* cured in smoke.

smoke-free *adj.* **1** free from smoke. **2** where smoking is not permitted.

smoke-ho var. of SMOKO.

smokeless /ˈsməʊklɪs/ *adj.* having or producing little or no smoke.

smokeless zone *n. Brit.* a district in which it is illegal to create smoke and where only smokeless fuel may be used.

smoke plant *n.* any ornamental shrub of the genus *Cotinus*, with a feathery smokelike inflorescence.

smoker /ˈsməʊkə/ *n.* **1** a person or thing that smokes, esp. a person who habitually smokes tobacco. **2** a compartment on a train, in which smoking is allowed. **3** esp. *US* an informal social gathering of men. **4** a device for stupefying bees.

smoke ring *n.* smoke from a cigarette etc. exhaled in the shape of a ring.

smoke-room *n. Brit.* = SMOKING ROOM.

smoker's cough *n.* a persistent cough caused by excessive smoking.

smokescreen /ˈsməʊkskri:n/ *n.* **1** a cloud of smoke diffused to conceal (esp. military) operations. **2** a device or ruse for disguising one's activities.

smokestack /ˈsməʊkstak/ *n.* **1** a chimney or funnel for discharging the smoke of a locomotive or steamer. **2** a tall chimney.

smoke-stone *n.* cairngorm.

smoke tree *n.* = SMOKE PLANT.

smoke-tunnel *n.* a form of wind tunnel using smoke filaments to show the motion of air.

smoking gun *n.* (also **smoking pistol**) a piece of incontrovertible incriminating evidence.

smoking jacket *n.* a jacket, often of velvet, formerly worn by men while smoking.

smoking room *n.* a room in a hotel or house, kept for smoking in.

smoko /ˈsməʊkəʊ/ *n.* (also **smoke-ho**) (*pl.* **-os**) *Austral.* & *NZ colloq.* **1** a stoppage of work for a rest and a smoke. **2** a tea break.

smoky /ˈsməʊki/ *adj.* (**smokier**, **smokiest**) **1** emitting, veiled or filled with, or obscured by, smoke (*smoky fire*; *smoky room*). **2** stained with or coloured like smoke (*smoky glass*). **3** having the taste or flavour of smoked food (*smoky bacon*). □ **smokily** *adv.* **smokiness** *n.*

smolder *US* var. of SMOULDER.

smolt /sməʊlt/ *n.* a young salmon migrating to the sea for the first time. [Middle English (originally Scots & northern English): origin unknown: cf. SMELT[3]]

smooch /smu:tʃ/ *n.* & *v. colloq.* ● *n.* **1** *Brit.* a period of slow dancing close together. **2** a spell of kissing and caressing; a kiss. ● *v.intr.* engage in a smooch. □ **smoocher** *n.* **smoochy** *adj.* (**smoochier**, **smoochiest**). [dialect *smouch*, imitative]

smoodge /smu:dʒ/ *v.intr.* (also **smooge**) *Austral.* & *NZ* **1** behave in a fawning or ingratiating manner. **2** behave amorously. [probably variant of dialect *smudge* 'kiss, sidle up to, beg in a sneaking way']

smooth /smu:ð/ *adj.*, *v.*, *n.*, & *adv.* ● *adj.* **1** **a** having a relatively even and regular surface; free from perceptible projections, lumps, indentations, and roughness. **b** *Tennis* etc. applied to the face of a racket with a smooth surface, the projecting loops from the stringing process being on the reverse side (opp. ROUGH *adj.* 1b). **2** not wrinkled, pitted, scored, or hairy (*smooth skin*). **3** that can be traversed without check. **4** (of liquids) of even consistency; without lumps (*mix to a smooth paste*). **5** (of the sea etc.) without waves or undulations. **6** (of a journey, passage, progress, etc.) untroubled by difficulties or adverse conditions. **7** having an easy flow or correct rhythm (*smooth breathing*; *a smooth metre*). **8** **a** not harsh in sound or taste. **b** (of wine etc.) not astringent. **9** (of a person, his or her manner, etc.) suave, conciliatory, flattering, unruffled, or polite (*a smooth talker*; *he's very smooth*). **10** (of movement etc.) not suddenly varying; not jerky. ● *v.* (also **smoothe**) **1** *tr.* & *intr.* (often foll. by *out*, *down*) make or become smooth. **2** (often foll. by *out*, *down, over, away*) **a** *tr.* reduce or get rid of (differences, faults, difficulties, etc.) in fact or appearance. **b** *intr.* (of difficulties etc.) diminish; become less obtrusive (*it will all smooth over*). **3** *tr.* modify (a graph, curve, etc.) so as to lessen irregularities. **4** *tr.* free from impediments or discomfort (*smooth the way; smooth the declining years*). ● *n.* **1** a smoothing touch or stroke (*gave his hair a smooth*). **2** the easy part of life (*take the rough with the smooth*). ● *adv.* smoothly (*the course of true love never did run smooth*). □ **in smooth water** having passed obstacles or difficulties. □ **smoothable** *adj.* **smoother** *n.* **smoothish** *adj.* **smoothly** *adv.* **smoothness** *n.* [Old English *smōth*]

smooth-bore *n.* (often *attrib.*) a gun with an unrifled barrel.

smooth-faced *adj.* **1** hypocritically friendly. **2** having smooth facial skin; clean-shaven.

smooth hound *n.* a small shark of shallow water, of the genus *Mustelus.*

smoothie /'smu:ði/ *n. colloq.* **1** a person who is smooth (see SMOOTH *adj.* 9). **2** esp. *US, Austral,,* & *NZ* a thick smooth drink of fresh fruit puréed with milk, yogurt, or ice cream. [SMOOTH]

smoothing iron *n. hist.* a flat iron.

smoothing plane *n.* a small plane for finishing the planing of wood.

smooth muscle *n.* a muscle without striations, usu. occurring in hollow organs and performing involuntary functions.

smooth talk *n.* & *v. colloq.* ● *n.* bland specious language. ● *v.tr.* (**smooth-talk**) address or persuade with this.

smooth-tongued *adj.* insincerely flattering.

smorgasbord /'smɔ:gəsbɔ:d/ *n.* **1** open sandwiches served with delicacies as hors d'oeuvres or a buffet. **2** = BUFFET[1] 2. **3** a medley; a miscellany; a variety. [Swedish, from *smörgås* '(slice of) bread and butter' (from *smör* 'butter' + *gås* 'goose, lump of butter') + *bord* 'table']

smorzando /smɔ:'tsandəʊ/ *adj., adv.,* & *n. Mus.* ● *adj.* & *adv.* dying away. ● *n.* (*pl.* **-os** or **smorzandi** /-di/) a smorzando passage. [Italian, gerund of *smorzare* 'extinguish']

smote *past* of SMITE.

smother /'smʌðə/ *v.* & *n.* ● *v.* **1** *tr.* suffocate; stifle; kill by stopping the breath of or excluding air from. **2** *tr.* (foll. by *with*) overwhelm with (kisses, gifts, kindness, etc.) (*smothered with affection*). **3** *tr.* (foll. by *in, with*) cover entirely in or with (*chicken smothered in mayonnaise*). **4** *tr.* extinguish or deaden (a fire or flame) by covering it or heaping it with ashes etc. **5** *intr.* **a** die of suffocation. **b** have difficulty breathing. **6** *tr.* (often foll. by *up*) suppress or conceal; keep from notice or publicity. **7** *tr. US* defeat rapidly or utterly. **8** *tr.* cook in a covered vessel. ● *n.* **1** a cloud of dust or smoke. **2** obscurity caused by this. [Middle English *smorther* from the stem of Old English *smorian* 'suffocate']

smothered mate *n. Chess* checkmate in which the king, having no vacant square to move to, is checkmated by a knight.

smothery /'smʌð(ə)ri/ *adj.* tending to smother; stifling.

smoulder /'sməʊldə/ *v.* & *n.* (*US* **smolder**) ● *v.intr.* **1** burn slowly with smoke but without a flame; slowly burn internally or invisibly. **2** (of emotions etc.) exist in a suppressed or concealed state. **3** (of a person) show silent or suppressed anger, hatred, etc. ● *n.* a smouldering or slow-burning fire. □ **smoulderingly** *adv.* [Middle English, related to Low German *smöln,* Middle Dutch *smölen*]

smriti /'smrɪti/ *n.* Hindu traditional teachings on religion etc. [Sanskrit *smṛti* 'remembrance']

smudge[1] /smʌdʒ/ *n.* & *v.* ● *n.* **1** a blurred or smeared line or mark; a blot; a smear of dirt. **2** a stain or blot on a person's character etc. ● *v.* **1** *tr.* make a smudge on. **2** *intr.* become smeared or blurred (*smudges easily*). **3** *tr.* smear or blur the lines of (writing, drawing, etc.) (*smudge the outline*). **4** *tr.* defile, sully, stain, or disgrace (a person's name, character, etc.). □ **smudgeless** *adj.* [Middle English: origin unknown]

smudge[2] /smʌdʒ/ *n. N. Amer.* an outdoor fire with dense smoke made to keep off insects, protect plants against frost, etc. [*smudge* 'cure (herring) by smoking' (16th c.: origin unknown)]

smudge pot *n.* a container holding burning material that produces a smudge (see SMUDGE[2]).

smudgy /'smʌdʒi/ *adj.* (**smudgier, smudgiest**) **1** smudged. **2** likely to produce smudges. □ **smudgily** *adv.* **smudginess** *n.*

smug /smʌg/ *adj.* (**smugger, smuggest**) self-satisfied; complacent. □ **smugly** *adv.* **smugness** *n.* [originally 'neat': from Low German *smuk* 'pretty']

smuggle /'smʌg(ə)l/ *v.tr.* **1** (also *absol.*) import or export (goods) illegally, esp. without payment of customs duties. **2** (foll. by *in, out*) convey secretly. **3** (foll. by *away*) put into concealment. □ **smuggler** *n.* **smuggling** *n.* [Low German *smukkeln smuggelen*]

smut /smʌt/ *n.* & *v.* ● *n.* **1** a small flake of soot etc. **2** a spot or smudge made by this. **3** obscene or lascivious talk, pictures, or stories. **4** **a** a fungal disease of cereals in which parts of the ear change to black powder. **b** any fungus of the order Ustilaginales causing this. ● *v.* (**smutted, smutting**) **1** *tr.* mark with smuts. **2** *tr.* infect (a plant) with smut. **3** *intr.* (of a plant) contract smut. □ **smutty** *adj.* (**smuttier, smuttiest**) (esp. in sense 3 of *n.*). **smuttily** *adv.* **smuttiness** *n.* [related to Low German *smutt,* Middle High German *smutz(en)* etc.: cf. Old English *smitt(ian)* 'smear', and SMUDGE[1]]

smut-ball *n.* grain affected by smut.

smut-mill *n.* a machine for freeing grain from smut.

Sn *symb. Chem.* the element tin. [Late Latin *stannum*]

snack /snak/ *n.* & *v.* ● *n.* **1** a light, casual, or hurried meal. **2** a small amount of food eaten between meals. **3** *Austral. slang* something easy to accomplish. ● *v.intr.* (often foll. by *on*) eat a snack. [originally a snap or bite: Middle English, from Middle Dutch *snac(k),* from *snacken* 'to bite', variant of *snappen*]

snack bar *n.* a place where snacks are sold.

snaffle /'snaf(ə)l/ *n.* & *v.* ● *n.* (in full **snaffle-bit**) (on a bridle) a simple bit without a curb and usu. with a single rein. ● *v.tr.* **1** put a snaffle on. **2** *colloq.* steal; seize; appropriate. [probably from Low German or Dutch: cf. Middle Low German, Middle Dutch *snavel* 'beak, mouth']

snafu /sna'fu:, 'snafu:/ *adj.* & *n. slang* ● *adj.* in utter confusion or chaos. ● *n.* this state. [acronym for 'situation *n*ormal: *a*ll *f*ouled (or *f*ucked) *u*p']

snag[1] /snag/ *n.* & *v.* ● *n.* **1** an unexpected or hidden obstacle or drawback. **2** a jagged or projecting point or broken stump. **3** a tear in material etc. **4** a short tine of an antler. ● *v.tr.* (**snagged, snagging**) **1** catch or tear on a snag. **2** clear (land, a waterway, a tree trunk, etc.) of snags. **3** *N. Amer.* catch or obtain by quick action. □ **snagged** *adj.* **snaggy** *adj.* [probably from Scandinavian: cf. Norwegian dialect *snag(e)* 'sharp point']

snag[2] /snag/ *n.* (usu. in *pl.*) *Austral. slang* a sausage. [20th c.: origin unknown]

snaggle-tooth /'snag(ə)l/ *n.* (*pl.* **snaggle-teeth**) an irregular or projecting tooth. □ **snaggle-toothed** *adj.* [SNAG[1] + -LE[2]]

snail /sneɪl/ *n.* any slow-moving gastropod mollusc with a spiral shell able to enclose the whole body. □ **snail-like** *adj.* [Old English *snæg(e)l,* from Germanic]

snail mail *n. slang* **1** the ordinary postal system as opposed to the electronic mail system. **2** correspondence sent using this.

snail's pace *n.* a very slow movement.

snake /sneɪk/ *n.* & *v.* ● *n.* **1** **a** any long limbless reptile of the suborder Ophidia, including boas, pythons, and poisonous forms such as cobras and vipers. **b** a limbless lizard or amphibian. **2** (also **snake in the grass**) a treacherous person or secret enemy. **3** (prec. by *the*) a system of interconnected exchange rates for the EC currencies. **4** (in full **plumber's snake**) a long flexible wire for clearing obstacles in piping. ● *v.intr.* move or twist like a snake. □ **snakelike** *adj.* [Old English *snaca*]

snake bird *n.* an anhinga or darter, *Anhinga anhinga*.

snake charmer *n.* a person appearing to make snakes move by music etc.

snake oil *n. colloq.* a quack medicine.

snake-pit *n.* **1** a pit containing snakes. **2** a scene of vicious behaviour.

snakeroot /ˈsneɪkruːt/ *n.* any of various N. American plants with roots reputed to contain an antidote to snake's poison, e.g. *Aristolochia serpentaria*.

snakes and ladders *n.pl.* a game with counters moved along a board with advances up 'ladders' or returns down 'snakes' depicted on the board.

snake's head *n.* a bulbous plant, *Fritillaria meleagris*, with bell-shaped pendent flowers.

snakeskin /ˈsneɪkskɪn/ *n. & adj.* ● *n.* the skin of a snake. ● *adj.* made of or resembling snakeskin.

snaky /ˈsneɪki/ *adj.* **1** of or like a snake. **2** winding; sinuous. **3** showing coldness, ingratitude, venom, or guile. **4** infested with or composed of snakes. **5** *Austral. slang* angry; irritable. □ **snakily** *adv.* **snakiness** *n.*

snap /snap/ *v., n., adv., & adj.* ● *v.* (**snapped**, **snapping**) **1** *intr. & tr.* break suddenly or with a snap. **2** *intr. & tr.* emit or cause to emit a sudden sharp sound or crack. **3** *intr. & tr.* open or close with a snapping sound (*the bag snapped shut*). **4 a** *intr.* (often foll. by *at*) speak irritably or spitefully (to a person) (*did not mean to snap at you*). **b** *tr.* say irritably or spitefully. **5** *intr.* (often foll. by *at*) (esp. of a dog etc.) make a sudden audible bite. **6** *tr. & intr.* move quickly (*snap into action*). **7** *tr.* take a snapshot of. **8** *tr. Amer. Football* put (the ball) into play on the ground by a quick backward movement. ● *n.* **1** an act or sound of snapping. **2** a crisp biscuit or cake (*brandy snap*; *ginger snap*). **3** a snapshot. **4** (in full **cold snap**) a sudden brief spell of cold weather. **5** *Brit.* **a** a card game in which players call 'snap' when two similar cards are exposed. **b** (as *int.*) on noticing the (often unexpected) similarity of two things. **6** crispness of style; fresh vigour or liveliness in action; zest; dash; spring. **7** *N. Amer. slang* an easy task (*it was a snap*). ● *adv.* with the sound of a snap (*heard it go snap*). ● *adj.* done or taken on the spur of the moment, unexpectedly, or without notice (*snap decision*). □ **snap at** accept (bait, a chance, etc.) eagerly (see also senses 4a and 5 of *v.*). **snap off** break off or bite off. **snap off a person's head** address a person angrily or rudely. **snap one's fingers 1** make an audible fillip, esp. in rhythm to music etc. **2** (often foll. by *at*) defy; show contempt for. **snap out** say irritably. **snap out of** *colloq.* get rid of (a mood, habit, etc.) by a sudden effort. **snap up 1** accept (an offer, a bargain) quickly or eagerly. **2** pick up or catch hastily or smartly. **3** interrupt (another person) before he or she has finished speaking. □ **snappable** *adj.* **snappingly** *adv.* [probably from Middle Dutch or Middle Low German *snappen* 'seize': partly imitative]

snap bean *n. US* a bean grown for its pods which are broken into pieces and eaten.

snap-bolt *n.* a bolt which locks automatically when a door or window closes.

snap-brim *adj.* (of a hat) with a brim that can be turned up and down at opposite sides.

snapdragon /ˈsnapdrag(ə)n/ *n.* a plant, *Antirrhinum majus*, with an irregular flower which gapes like a mouth when a bee lands on the lower part.

snap-fastener *n.* = PRESS STUD.

snap-hook *n.* (also **snap-link**) a hook or link with a spring allowing the entrance but barring the escape of a cord, link, etc.

snap-lock *n.* = SNAP-BOLT.

snapper /ˈsnapə/ *n.* **1** a person or thing that snaps. **2 a** any of several edible marine fish of the family Lutjanidae, usu. reddish in colour with a triangular head profile. **b** *Austral.* a sparid fish, *Chrysophrys auratus*, used as food. **3** a snapping turtle. **4** *US* a cracker (as a toy).

snapping turtle *n.* any large American freshwater turtle of the family Chelydridae which seizes prey with a snap of its jaws.

snappish /ˈsnapɪʃ/ *adj.* **1** (of a person's manner or a remark) curt; ill-tempered; sharp. **2** (of a dog etc.) inclined to snap. □ **snappishly** *adv.* **snappishness** *n.*

snappy /ˈsnapi/ *adj.* (**snappier**, **snappiest**) *colloq.* **1** brisk; full of zest. **2** neat and elegant (*a snappy dresser*). **3** snappish. □ **make it snappy** be quick about it. □ **snappily** *adv.* **snappiness** *n.*

snapshot /ˈsnapʃɒt/ *n.* a casual photograph taken quickly with a small hand camera.

snare /snɛː/ *n. & v.* ● *n.* **1** a trap for catching birds or animals, esp. with a noose of wire or cord. **2** a thing that acts as a temptation. **3** a device for tempting an enemy etc. to expose himself or herself to danger, failure, loss, capture, defeat, etc. **4** (in *sing.* or *pl.*) *Mus.* twisted strings of gut, hide, or wire stretched across the lower head of a side drum to produce a rattling sound. **5** (in full **snare drum**) a drum fitted with snares. **6** *Surgery* a wire loop for extracting polyps etc. ● *v.tr.* **1** catch (a bird etc.) in a snare. **2** ensnare; lure or trap (a person) with a snare. □ **snarer** *n.* (also in *comb.*). [Old English *sneare* from Old Norse *snara*: senses 4 & 5 probably from Middle Low German or Middle Dutch]

snark /snɑːk/ *n.* a fabulous animal, originally the subject of a nonsense poem. [*The Hunting of the Snark* (1876) by Lewis Carroll]

snarl[1] /snɑːl/ *v. & n.* ● *v.* **1** *intr.* (of a dog) make an angry growl with bared teeth. **2** *intr.* (of a person) speak cynically; make bad-tempered complaints or criticisms. **3** *tr.* (often foll. by *out*) **a** utter in a snarling tone. **b** express (discontent etc.) by snarling. ● *n.* the act or sound of snarling. □ **snarler** *n.* **snarlingly** *adv.* **snarly** *adj.* (**snarlier**, **snarliest**). [earlier *snar*, from (Middle) Low German, Middle High German *snarren*]

snarl[2] /snɑːl/ *v. & n.* ● *v.* **1** *tr.* (often foll. by *up*) twist; entangle; confuse and hamper the movement of (traffic etc.). **2** *intr.* (often foll. by *up*) become entangled, congested, or confused. **3** *tr.* adorn the exterior of (a narrow metal vessel) with raised work. ● *n.* a knot or tangle. [Middle English from *snare* (*n.* & *v.*): sense 3 perhaps from the noun in a dialect sense 'knot in wood']

snarling iron /ˈsnɑːlɪŋ/ *n.* an implement used for snarling metal.

snarl-up *n. colloq.* a traffic jam; a muddle; a mistake.

snatch /snatʃ/ *v. & n.* ● *v.tr.* **1** seize quickly, eagerly, or unexpectedly, esp. with outstretched hands. **2** steal (a wallet, handbag, etc.). **3** secure with difficulty (*snatched an hour's rest*). **4** (foll. by *away, from*) take away or from, esp. suddenly (*snatched away my hand*). **5** (foll. by *from*) rescue narrowly (*snatched from the jaws of death*). **6** (foll. by *at*) **a** try to seize by stretching or grasping suddenly. **b** take (an offer etc.) eagerly. ● *n.* **1** an act of snatching (*made a snatch at it*). **2** a fragment of a song or talk etc. (*caught a snatch of their conversation*). **3** orig. *US colloq.* a kidnapping. **4** (prec. by *the*) (in weightlifting) the rapid raising of a weight from the floor to above the head in one movement. **5** a short spell of activity etc. □ **in** (or **by**) **snatches** in fits and starts. □ **snatcher** *n.* (esp. in sense 3 of *n.*). **snatchy** *adj.* [Middle English *snecchen*, *sna(c)che*, perhaps related to SNACK]

snatch squad *n.* a group of police officers, soldiers, etc., detailed to seize troublemakers in a crowd.

snavel /ˈsnav(ə)l/ *v.tr.* (also **snavle**, **snavvle**) *Austral. slang* catch; take; steal. [English dialect (as SNAFFLE)]

snazzy /ˈsnazi/ *adj.* (**snazzier**, **snazziest**) *colloq.* smart or attractive esp. in an ostentatious way. □ **snazzily** *adv.* **snazziness** *n.* [20th c.: origin unknown]

sneak /sniːk/ *v., n., & adj.* ● *v.* (*past* and *past part.* **sneaked** or *colloq.* **snuck** /snʌk/) **1** *intr. & tr.* (foll. by *in, out, past, away,* etc.) go or convey furtively; slink. **2** *tr. colloq.* steal unobserved; make off with. **3** *intr. Brit.*

school slang tell tales; turn informer. **4** *intr.* (as **sneaking** *adj.*) **a** furtive; undisclosed (*have a sneaking affection for him*). **b** persistent in one's mind; nagging (*a sneaking feeling that it is not right*). ● *n.* **1** a mean-spirited cowardly underhand person. **2** *Brit. school slang* a tell-tale. ● *adj.* acting or done without warning; secret (*a sneak attack*). □ **sneakingly** *adv.* [16th c., probably dialect: perhaps related to Middle English *snike*, Old English *snīcan* 'creep']

■ **Usage** The form *snuck* for the past or past participle should not be used in formal contexts. It arose in American English in the 19th century and remains non-standard in both American and British English.

sneaker /ˈsniːkə/ *n.* esp. *N. Amer.* each of a pair of soft-soled canvas etc. shoes.

sneak thief *n.* a thief who steals without breaking in; a pickpocket.

sneaky /ˈsniːki/ *adj.* (**sneakier**, **sneakiest**) given to or characterized by sneaking; furtive, mean. □ **sneakily** *adv.* **sneakiness** *n.*

sneck /snɛk/ *n.* & *v. Sc.* & *N.Engl.* ● *n.* a latch. ● *v.tr.* latch (a door etc.); close or fasten with a sneck. [Middle English, related to SNATCH]

sneer /snɪə/ *n.* & *v.* ● *n.* a derisive smile or remark. ● *v.* **1** *intr.* (often foll. by *at*) smile derisively. **2** *tr.* say sneeringly. **3** *intr.* (often foll. by *at*) speak derisively, esp. covertly or ironically (*sneered at his attempts*). □ **sneerer** *n.* **sneering** *adj.* **sneeringly** *adv.* [Middle English, perhaps from Old English *fnaeran* 'to snort']

sneeze /sniːz/ *n.* & *v.* ● *n.* **1** a sudden involuntary expulsion of air from the nose and mouth caused by irritation of the nostrils. **2** the sound of this. ● *v.intr.* make a sneeze. □ **not to be sneezed at** *colloq.* not to be underrated; considerable; notable. □ **sneezer** *n.* **sneezy** *adj.* [Middle English *snese*, apparently alteration of obsolete *fnese* from Old English *-fnēsan*, Old Norse *fnýsa*, replacing earlier and less expressive *nese*]

sneezewort /ˈsniːzwəːt/ *n.* a kind of yarrow, *Achillea ptarmica*, whose dried leaves are used to induce sneezing.

Snell's law /snɛlz/ *n. Physics* the law that the ratio of the sines of the angles of incidence and refraction of a wave are constant when it passes between two given media. [named after W. *Snell*, Dutch mathematician d. 1626]

snib /snɪb/ *v.* & *n.* esp. *Sc.* & *Ir.* ● *v.tr.* (**snibbed**, **snibbing**) bolt, fasten, or lock (a door etc.). ● *n.* a lock, catch, or fastening for a door or window. [19th c.: origin uncertain]

snick /snɪk/ *v.* & *n.* ● *v.tr.* **1** cut a small notch in. **2** make a small incision in. **3** *Cricket* deflect (the ball) slightly with the bat. ● *n.* **1** a small notch or cut. **2** *Cricket* a slight deflection of the ball by the bat. [17th c.: probably from *snick-a-snee* 'fight with knives']

snicker /ˈsnɪkə/ *v.* & *n.* ● *v.intr.* **1** = SNIGGER *v.* **2** whinny, neigh. ● *n.* **1** = SNIGGER *n.* **2** a whinny; a neigh. □ **snickeringly** *adv.* [imitative]

snide /snʌɪd/ *adj.* & *n.* ● *adj.* **1** sneering; slyly derogatory; insinuating. **2** counterfeit; bogus. **3** *US* mean; underhand. ● *n.* a snide person or remark. □ **snidely** *adv.* **snideness** *n.* [19th-c. colloq.: origin unknown]

sniff /snɪf/ *v.* & *n.* ● *v.* **1** *intr.* draw up air audibly through the nose to stop it running or to detect a smell or as an expression of contempt. **2** *tr.* (often foll. by *up*) draw in (a scent, drug, liquid, or air) through the nose. **3** *tr.* draw in the scent of (food, drink, flowers, etc.) through the nose. ● *n.* **1** an act or sound of sniffing. **2** the amount of air etc. sniffed up. □ **sniff at 1** try the smell of; show interest in. **2** show contempt for or discontent with. **sniff out** detect; discover by investigation. □ **sniffingly** *adv.* [Middle English, imitative]

sniffer /snɪfə/ *n.* **1** a person who sniffs, esp. one who sniffs a drug or toxic substances (often in *comb.*: *glue-sniffer*). **2** *slang* the nose. **3** *colloq.* any device for detecting gas, radiation, etc.

sniffer dog *n. colloq.* a dog trained to sniff out drugs or explosives.

sniffle /ˈsnɪf(ə)l/ *v.* & *n.* ● *v.intr.* sniff slightly or repeatedly. ● *n.* **1** the act of sniffling. **2** (in *sing.* or *pl.*) a cold in the head causing a running nose and sniffling. □ **sniffler** *n.* **sniffly** *adj.* [imitative: cf. SNIVEL]

sniffy /ˈsnɪfi/ *adj.* (**sniffier**, **sniffiest**) *colloq.* **1** inclined to sniff. **2** disdainful; contemptuous. □ **sniffily** *adv.* **sniffiness** *n.*

snifter /ˈsnɪftə/ *n.* **1** *colloq.* a small drink of alcohol. **2** esp. *N. Amer.* a balloon glass for brandy. [dialect *snift* 'sniff', perhaps from Scandinavian: imitative]

snifter-valve *n.* a valve in a steam engine to allow air in or out.

snig /snɪg/ *v.tr.* (**snigged**, **snigging**) *Austral.* & *NZ* drag with a jerk. [English dialect: origin unknown]

snigger /ˈsnɪgə/ *n.* & *v.* ● *n.* a half-suppressed secretive laugh. ● *v.intr.* utter such a laugh. □ **sniggerer** *n.* **sniggeringly** *adv.* [variant of SNICKER]

sniggery /ˈsnɪgəri/ *adj. colloq.* liable to cause sniggers, or characterized by sniggering.

snigging chain *n.* a chain used to move logs.

sniggle /ˈsnɪg(ə)l/ *v.intr.* fish (for eels) by pushing bait into a hole. [Middle English *snig* 'small eel', of unknown origin]

snip /snɪp/ *v.* & *n.* ● *v.tr.* (**snipped**, **snipping**) (also *absol.*) cut (cloth, a hole, etc.) with scissors or shears, esp. in small quick strokes. ● *n.* **1** an act of snipping. **2** a piece of material etc. snipped off. **3** *colloq.* **a** something easily achieved. **b** *Brit.* a bargain; something cheaply acquired. **4** (in *pl.*) hand shears for metal cutting. □ **snip at** make snipping strokes at. □ **snipping** *n.* [Low German & Dutch *snippen*: imitative]

snipe /snʌɪp/ *n.* & *v.* ● *n.* (*pl.* same or **snipes**) any of various wading birds, esp. of the genus *Gallinago*, with a long straight bill and frequenting marshes. ● *v.* **1** *intr.* fire shots from hiding, usu. at long range. **2** *tr.* kill by sniping. **3** *intr.* (foll. by *at*) make a sly critical attack. **4** *intr.* go snipe-shooting. □ **sniper** *n.* [Middle English, probably from Scandinavian: cf. Icelandic *mýrisnípa*, & Middle Dutch, Middle Low German *snippe*, Old High German *snepfa*]

snipe eel *n.* any eel of the family Nemichthyidae, having a long slender snout.

snipe fish *n.* any marine fish of the family Macrorhamphosidae, with a long slender snout.

snippet /ˈsnɪpɪt/ *n.* **1** a small piece cut off. **2** (usu. in *pl.*; often foll. by *of*) **a** a scrap or fragment of information, knowledge, etc. **b** a short extract from a book, newspaper, etc. □ **snippety** *adj.*

snippy /ˈsnɪpi/ *adj.* (**snippier**, **snippiest**) *colloq.* fault-finding, snappish, sharp. □ **snippily** *adv.* **snippiness** *n.*

snit /snɪt/ *n. N. Amer.* a rage; a sulk (esp. in phr. **in a snit**). [20th c.: origin unknown]

snitch /snɪtʃ/ *v.* & *n. slang* ● *v.* **1** *tr.* steal. **2** *intr.* (often foll. by *on*) inform on a person. ● *n.* an informer. [17th c.: origin unknown]

snivel /ˈsnɪv(ə)l/ *v.* & *n.* ● *v.intr.* (**snivelled**, **snivelling**; *US* **sniveled**, **sniveling**) **1** weep with sniffling. **2** run at the nose; make a repeated sniffing sound. **3** show weak or tearful sentiment. ● *n.* **1** running mucus. **2** hypocritical talk; cant. □ **sniveller** *n.* **snivelling** *adj.* **snivellingly** *adv.* [Middle English, related to Old English *snyflung*, *snofl* 'mucus': cf. SNUFFLE]

snob /snɒb/ *n.* **1 a** a person with an exaggerated respect for social position or wealth and who despises people considered socially inferior. **b** a person who seeks to cultivate people considered socially superior. **c** (*attrib.*) related to or characteristic of these attitudes. **2** a person who despises others whose (usu. specified) tastes or attainments are considered inferior (*an intellectual snob*; *a wine snob*). □ **snobbery** *n.* (*pl.* **-ies**). **snobbish** *adj.* **snobbishly** *adv.* **snobbishness** *n.* **snobby** *adj.*

(**snobbier**, **snobbiest**). [18th c. (now dialect) 'cobbler': origin unknown]

SNOBOL /ˈsnəʊbɒl/ *n. Computing* a high-level programming language used esp. in manipulating textual data. [partial acronym, from *s*tring-*o*riented sym*bo*lic *l*anguage, on the pattern of COBOL]

snoek /snuːk/ *n. S.Afr.* a barracouta. [Afrikaans from Dutch, = PIKE[1], from Middle Low German *snōk*, probably related to SNACK]

snog /snɒg/ *v. & n. Brit. slang* ● *v.intr. & tr.* (**snogged**, **snogging**) kiss and caress. ● *n.* a spell of snogging. □ **snogger** *n.* [20th c.: origin unknown]

snood /snuːd/ *n.* **1** an ornamental hairnet usu. worn at the back of the head. **2** a ring of woollen etc. material worn as a hood. **3** a short line attaching a hook to a main line in sea fishing. **4** *hist.* a ribbon or band worn by unmarried women in Scotland to confine their hair. [Old English *snōd*]

snook[1] /snuːk/ *n.* esp. *Brit. slang* a contemptuous gesture with the thumb to the nose and the fingers spread out. □ **cock a snook** (often foll. by *at*) **1** make this gesture. **2** register one's contempt (for a person, establishment, etc.). [18th c.: origin unknown]

snook[2] /snuːk/ *n.* a marine fish, *Centropomus undecimalis*, used as food. [Dutch *snoek*: see SNOEK]

snooker /ˈsnuːkə/ *n. & v.* ● *n.* **1** a game played with cues on a rectangular baize-covered table in which the players use a cue ball (white) to pocket the other balls (15 red and 6 coloured) in a set order. **2** a position in this game in which a direct shot at a permitted ball is impossible. ● *v.tr.* **1** (also *refl.*) subject (oneself or another player) to a snooker. **2** (esp. as **snookered** *adj.*) *colloq.* defeat; thwart. [19th c.: origin unknown]

snoop /snuːp/ *v. & n. colloq.* ● *v.intr.* **1** pry into matters one need not be concerned with. **2** (often foll. by *about*, *around*) investigate in order to find out transgressions of the law etc. ● *n.* **1** an act of snooping. **2** a person who snoops; a detective. □ **snooper** *n.* **snoopy** *adj.* [Dutch *snœpen* 'eat on the sly']

snooperscope /ˈsnuːpəskəʊp/ *n.* a device which converts infra-red radiation into a visible image, esp. used for seeing in the dark.

snoot /snuːt/ *n. colloq.* the nose. [variant of SNOUT]

snooty /ˈsnuːti/ *adj.* (**snootier**, **snootiest**) *colloq.* supercilious; conceited. □ **snootily** *adv.* **snootiness** *n.* [from SNOOT; cf. SNOTTY]

snooze /snuːz/ *n. & v. colloq.* ● *n.* a short sleep, esp. in the daytime. ● *v.intr.* take a snooze. □ **snoozer** *n.* **snoozy** *adj.* (**snoozier**, **snooziest**). [18th-c. slang: origin unknown]

snore /snɔː/ *n. & v.* ● *n.* a snorting or grunting sound in breathing during sleep. ● *v.intr.* make this sound. □ **snore away** pass (time) sleeping or snoring. □ **snorer** *n.* [Middle English, probably imitative: cf. SNORT]

snorkel /ˈsnɔːk(ə)l/ *n. & v.* (also **schnorkel** /ˈʃnɔː-/) ● *n.* **1** a breathing tube for an underwater swimmer. **2** a device for supplying air to a submerged submarine. **3** (**Snorkel**) *propr.* a type of hydraulically elevated platform for fire-fighting. ● *v.intr.* (**snorkelled**, **snorkelling**; *US* **snorkeled**, **snorkeling**) use a snorkel. □ **snorkeller** *n.* [German *Schnorchel*]

snort /snɔːt/ *n. & v.* ● *n.* **1** an explosive sound made by the sudden forcing of breath through the nose, esp. expressing indignation or incredulity. **2** a similar sound made by an engine etc. **3** *colloq.* a small drink of liquor. **4** *slang* an inhaled dose of a (usu. illegal) powdered drug. ● *v.* **1** *intr.* make a snort. **2** *intr.* (of an engine etc.) make a sound resembling this. **3** *tr.* (also *absol.*) *slang* inhale (a usu. illegal narcotic drug, esp. cocaine or heroin). **4** *tr.* express (defiance etc.) by snorting. □ **snort out** express (words, emotions, etc.) by snorting. [Middle English, probably imitative: cf. SNORE]

snorter /ˈsnɔːtə/ *n. Brit. colloq.* **1** something very impressive or difficult. **2** something vigorous or violent.

snot /snɒt/ *n. slang* **1** nasal mucus. **2** a term of contempt for a person. [probably from Middle Dutch, Middle Low German *snotte*, Middle High German *snuz*, related to SNOUT]

snot-rag *n. slang* a handkerchief.

snotty /ˈsnɒti/ *adj.* (**snottier**, **snottiest**) *slang* **1** running or foul with nasal mucus. **2** contemptible. **3** supercilious, conceited. □ **snottily** *adv.* **snottiness** *n.*

snout /snaʊt/ *n.* **1** the projecting nose and mouth of an animal. **2** *derog.* a person's nose. **3** the pointed front of a thing; a nozzle. **4** *Brit. slang* tobacco or a cigarette. **5** *slang* an informer. □ **snouted** *adj.* (also in *comb.*). **snouty** *adj.* [Middle English from Middle Dutch, Middle Low German *snūt*]

snout-beetle *n.* a weevil.

snow /snəʊ/ *n. & v.* ● *n.* **1** atmospheric water vapour frozen into ice crystals and falling to earth in light white flakes. **2** a fall of this, or a layer of it on the ground. **3 a** a thing resembling snow in whiteness or texture etc. **b** a frozen vapour resembling snow (*carbon dioxide snow*). **4** a mass of flickering white spots on a television or radar screen, caused by interference or a poor signal. **5** *slang* cocaine. **6** a dessert or other dish resembling snow. ● *v.* **1** *intr.* (prec. by *it* as subject) snow falls (*it is snowing*; *if it snows*). **2** *tr.* (foll. by *in*, *over*, *up*, etc.) confine or block with large quantities of snow. **3** *tr. & intr.* sprinkle or scatter or fall as or like snow. **4** *intr.* come in large numbers or quantities. **5** *tr. US slang* deceive or charm with plausible words. □ **be snowed under** be overwhelmed, esp. with work. □ **snowless** *adj.* **snowlike** *adj.* [Old English *snāw*, from Germanic]

snowball /ˈsnəʊbɔːl/ *n. & v.* ● *n.* **1** snow pressed together into a ball, esp. for throwing in play. **2** anything that grows or increases rapidly like a snowball rolled on snow. ● *v.* **1** *intr. & tr.* throw or pelt with snowballs. **2** *intr.* increase rapidly.

snowball tree *n.* a guelder rose.

snowberry /ˈsnəʊb(ə)ri/ *n.* (*pl.* **-ies**) any of various shrubs with white berries, esp. the ornamental *Symphoricarpos albus*.

snow-blind *adj.* temporarily blinded by the glare of light reflected by large expanses of snow. □ **snow-blindness** *n.*

snow-blink *n.* the reflection in the sky of snow or ice fields.

snowblower /ˈsnəʊbləʊə/ *n.* a machine that clears snow by blowing it to the side of the road etc.

snowboard /ˈsnəʊbɔːd/ *n.* a wide ski used for sliding downhill on snow. □ **snowboarder** *n.* **snowboarding** *n.*

snow boot *n. Brit.* an overboot of rubber and cloth.

snowbound /ˈsnəʊbaʊnd/ *adj.* prevented by snow from going out or travelling.

snow-broth *n.* melted or melting snow.

snow bunting *n.* a mainly white bunting, *Plectrophenax nivalis*.

snowcap /ˈsnəʊkap/ *n.* **1** the tip of a mountain when covered with snow. **2** a white-crowned hummingbird, *Microchera albocoronata*, native to Central America. □ **snow-capped** *adj.*

snowdrift /ˈsnəʊdrɪft/ *n.* a bank of snow heaped up by the action of the wind.

snowdrop /ˈsnəʊdrɒp/ *n.* a bulbous plant, *Galanthus nivalis*, with white drooping flowers in the early spring.

snowfall /ˈsnəʊfɔːl/ *n.* **1** a fall of snow. **2** *Meteorol.* the amount of snow that falls on one occasion or on a given area within a given time.

snowfield /ˈsnəʊfiːld/ *n.* a permanent wide expanse of snow in mountainous or polar regions.

snowflake /ˈsnəʊfleɪk/ *n.* **1** a flake of snow, esp. a feathery ice crystal, often displaying delicate sixfold symmetry. **2 a** any bulbous plant of the genus *Leucojum*, with snowdrop-like flowers. **b** the white flower of this plant.

snow goose *n.* a white Arctic goose, *Anser caerulescens*, with black-tipped wings.

snow-ice *n.* opaque white ice formed from melted snow.

snow leopard *n.* = OUNCE[2].

snowline /ˈsnəʊlʌɪn/ *n.* the level above which snow never melts entirely.

snowmaking /ˈsnəʊmeɪkɪŋ/ *n.* the production of artificial snow (often *attrib.*: *snowmaking machine*).

snowman /ˈsnəʊman/ *n.* (*pl.* **-men**) a figure resembling a man, made of compressed snow.

snowmobile /ˈsnəʊməbiːl/ *n.* a motor vehicle, esp. with runners or caterpillar tracks, for travelling over snow.

snow owl *n. US* = SNOWY OWL.

snow partridge *n.* a mainly white partridge, *Lerwa lerwa*.

snow pea *n.* esp. *N. Amer.* = MANGETOUT.

snowplough /ˈsnəʊplaʊ/ *n.* (*US* **snowplow**) **1** a device, or a vehicle equipped with one, for clearing roads of thick snow. **2** *Skiing* an act of turning the points of the skis inwards to slow down.

snowscape /ˈsnəʊskeɪp/ *n.* **1** a snowy landscape. **2** a picture of this.

snowshoe /ˈsnəʊʃuː/ *n.* & *v.* ● *n.* a flat device like a racket attached to a boot for walking on snow without sinking in. ● *v.intr.* travel on snowshoes. ◻ **snowshoer** *n.*

snowshoe hare *n.* (also **snowshoe rabbit**) a N. American hare, *Lepus americanus*, with large hind feet and a white coat in winter.

snow-slip *n. Brit.* an avalanche.

snowstorm /ˈsnəʊstɔːm/ *n.* a heavy fall of snow, esp. with a high wind.

snow white *n.* & *adj.* ● *n.* a pure white colour. ● *adj.* (hyphenated when *attrib.*) of this colour.

snowy /ˈsnəʊi/ *adj.* (**snowier**, **snowiest**) **1 a** of or like snow. **b** pure white. **2** (of the weather etc.) with much snow. ◻ **snowily** *adv.* **snowiness** *n.*

snowy owl *n.* a large white owl, *Nyctea scandiaca*, native to the Arctic.

SNP *abbr.* Scottish National Party.

Snr. *abbr.* Senior.

snub /snʌb/ *v.*, *n.*, & *adj.* ● *v.tr.* (**snubbed**, **snubbing**) **1** rebuff or humiliate with sharp words or a marked lack of cordiality. **2** check the movement of (a boat, horse, etc.), esp. by a rope wound round a post etc. ● *n.* an act of snubbing; a rebuff. ● *adj.* short and blunt in shape. ◻ **snubber** *n.* **snubbingly** *adv.* [Middle English from Old Norse *snubba* 'chide, check the growth of']

snub nose *n.* a short turned-up nose. ◻ **sub-nosed** *adj.*

snuck *colloq. past* and *past part.* of SNEAK.

snuff[1] /snʌf/ *n.* & *v.* ● *n.* the charred part of a candle-wick. ● *v.tr.* trim the snuff from (a candle). ◻ **snuff it** *Brit. slang* die. **snuff out 1** extinguish, put out (a candle etc.). **2** *slang* kill; put an end to. [Middle English *snoffe, snuffe*: origin unknown]

snuff[2] /snʌf/ *n.* & *v.* ● *n.* powdered tobacco or medicine taken by sniffing it up the nostrils. ● *v.intr.* take snuff. ◻ **up to snuff** *colloq.* **1** *Brit.* knowing; not easily deceived. **2** up to standard. [Dutch *snuf* (*tabak* 'tobacco') from Middle Dutch *snuffen* 'snuffle']

snuffbox /ˈsnʌfbɒks/ *n.* a small usu. ornamental box for holding snuff.

snuff-coloured *adj.* of a dark yellowish-brown colour.

snuffer /ˈsnʌfə/ *n.* **1** a small hollow cone with a handle used to extinguish a candle. **2** (in *pl.*) an implement like scissors used to extinguish a candle or trim its wick.

snuffle /ˈsnʌf(ə)l/ *v.* & *n.* ● *v.* **1** *intr.* make sniffing sounds. **2 a** *intr.* speak nasally, whiningly, or like one with a cold. **b** *tr.* (often foll. by *out*) say in this way. **3** *intr.* breathe noisily as through a partially blocked nose. **4** *intr.* sniff. ● *n.* **1** a snuffling sound or tone. **2** (in *pl.*) a partial blockage of the nose causing snuffling. **3** a sniff. ◻ **snuffler** *n.* **snuffly** *adj.* [probably from Low German & Dutch *snuffelen* (as SNUFF[2]): cf. SNIVEL]

snuff movie *n.* (also **snuff video** etc.) *slang* a pornographic film depicting an actual murder.

snuffy[1] /ˈsnʌfi/ *adj.* (**snuffier**, **snuffiest**) **1** annoyed. **2** irritable. **3** supercilious or contemptuous. [SNUFF[1] + -Y[1]]

snuffy[2] /ˈsnʌfi/ *adj.* like snuff in colour or substance. [SNUFF[2] + -Y[2]]

snug /snʌg/ *adj.* & *n.* ● *adj.* (**snugger**, **snuggest**) **1 a** cosy, comfortable, sheltered; well enclosed or placed or arranged. **b** cosily protected from the weather or cold. **2** (of an income etc.) allowing comfort and comparative ease. ● *n. Brit.* a small room in a pub or inn. ◻ **snugly** *adv.* **snugness** *n.* [16th c. (originally nautical): probably of Low German or Dutch origin]

snuggery /ˈsnʌg(ə)ri/ *n.* (*pl.* **-ies**) *Brit.* **1** a snug place, esp. a person's private room or den. **2** = SNUG *n.*

snuggle /ˈsnʌg(ə)l/ *v.intr.* & *tr.* (usu. foll. by *down*, *up*, *together*) settle or draw into a warm comfortable position. [SNUG + -LE[4]]

So. *abbr.* South.

so[1] /səʊ/ *adv.* & *conj.* ● *adv.* **1** (often foll. by *that* + clause) to such an extent, or to the extent implied (*why are you so angry?*; *do stop complaining so*; *they were so pleased that they gave us a bonus*). **2** (with *neg.*; often foll. by *as* + clause) to the extent to which ... is or does etc., or to the extent implied (*was not so late as I expected*; *am not so eager as you*). **3** (foll. by *that* or *as* + clause) to the degree or in the manner implied (*so expensive that few can afford it*; *so small as to be invisible*; *am not so foolish as to agree to that*). **4** (adding emphasis) to that extent; in that or a similar manner (*I want to leave and so does she*; *you said it was good, and so it is*). **5** to a great or notable degree (*I am so glad*). **6** (with verbs of state) in the way described (*am not very fond of it but may become so*). **7** (with verb of saying or thinking etc.) as previously mentioned or described (*I think so*; *so he said*; *so I should hope*). ● *conj.* (often foll. by *that* + clause) **1** with the result that (*there was none left, so we had to go without*). **2** in order that (*came home early so that I could see you*). **3** and then; as the next step (*so then the car broke down*; *and so to bed*). **4 a** (introducing a question) then; after that (*so what did you tell them?*). **b** (*absol.*) = *so what?* ◻ **and so on** (or **forth**) **1** and others of the same kind. **2** and in other similar ways. **so as** (foll. by *to* + infin.) in order to (*did it so as to get it finished*). **so be it** an expression of acceptance or resignation. **so far** see FAR. **so far as** see FAR. **so far so good** see FAR. **so long!** *colloq.* goodbye till we meet again. **so long as** see LONG[1]. **so much 1** a certain amount (of). **2** a great deal of (*is so much nonsense*). **3** (with *neg.*) **a** less than; to a lesser extent (*not so much forgotten as ignored*). **b** not even (*didn't give me so much as a penny*). **so much for** that is all that need be done or said about. **so so** *adj.* (usu. *predic.*) indifferent; not very good. ● *adv.* indifferently; only moderately well. **so to say** (or **speak**) an expression of reserve or apology for an exaggeration or neologism etc. **so what?** *colloq.* why should that be considered significant? [Old English *swā* etc.]

so[2] var. of SOH.

-so /səʊ/ *comb. form* = -SOEVER.

soak /səʊk/ *v.* & *n.* ● *v.* **1** *tr.* & *intr.* make or become thoroughly wet through saturation with or in liquid. **2** *tr.* (of rain etc.) drench. **3** *tr.* (foll. by *in*, *up*) **a** absorb (liquid). **b** acquire (knowledge etc.) copiously. **4** *refl.* (often foll. by *in*) steep (oneself) in a subject of study etc. **5** *intr.* (foll. by *in*, *into*, *through*) (of liquid) make its way or penetrate by saturation. **6** *tr. colloq.* extract money from by an extortionate charge, taxation, etc. (*soak the rich*). **7** *intr. colloq.* drink persistently; booze. **8** *tr.* (as **soaked** *adj.*) very drunk. ● *n.* **1** the act of soaking or the state of being soaked. **2** a drinking bout. **3** *colloq.* a hard drinker. ◻ **soakage** *n.* **soaker** *n.* [Old English *socian*, related to *soc* 'sucking at the breast', *sūcan* SUCK]

soakaway /ˈsəʊkəweɪ/ *n. Brit.* an arrangement for disposing of waste water by letting it percolate through the soil.

soaking /ˈsəʊkɪŋ/ *adj.* & *n.* ● *adj.* (in full **soaking wet**) very wet; wet through. ● *n.* the act of soaking; an instance of being soaked.

so-and-so /ˈsəʊənsəʊ/ *n.* (*pl.* **so-and-sos**) **1** a particular person or thing not needing to be specified (*told me to* *do so-and-so*). **2** *colloq.* a person disliked or regarded with disfavour (*the so-and-so left me behind*).

soap /səʊp/ *n.* & *v.* ● *n.* **1** a cleansing agent that is a compound of fatty acid with soda or potash or (**insoluble soap**) with another metallic oxide, of which the soluble kinds when rubbed in water yield a lather used in washing. **2** *colloq.* = SOAP OPERA. ● *v.tr.* **1** apply soap to. **2** scrub or rub with soap. ◻ **soapless** *adj.* [Old English *sāpe*, from West Germanic]

soapbark /ˈsəʊpbɑːk/ *n.* **1** a tree bark containing saponin. **2** a tree that yields such bark, esp. *Quillaja saponaria*, of Chile.

soapberry /ˈsəʊpbɛri/ *n.* (*pl.* **-ies**) a tree or shrub with fruits containing saponin, esp. one of the genus *Sapindus* of tropical America and Asia.

soapbox /ˈsəʊpbɒks/ *n.* **1** a box for holding soap. **2** a makeshift stand for a public speaker.

soap flakes *n.pl.* soap in the form of thin flakes, for washing clothes etc.

soap opera *n.* a broadcast drama, usu. serialized in many episodes, dealing with esp. domestic themes (so called because originally sponsored in the US by soap manufacturers).

soap powder *n.* powdered soap esp. with additives.

soapstone /ˈsəʊpstəʊn/ *n.* steatite.

soapsuds /ˈsəʊpsʌdz/ *n.pl.* = SUDS 1.

soapwort /ˈsəʊpwəːt/ *n.* a European plant, *Saponaria officinalis*, with pink or white flowers, and leaves yielding a soapy substance.

soapy /ˈsəʊpi/ *adj.* (**soapier**, **soapiest**) **1** of or like soap. **2** containing or smeared with soap. **3** (of a person or manner) unctuous or flattering. ◻ **soapily** *adv.* **soapiness** *n.*

soar /sɔː/ *v.intr.* **1** fly or rise high. **2** reach a high level or standard (*prices soared*). **3** maintain height in the air without flapping the wings or using power. ◻ **soarer** *n.* **soaringly** *adv.* [Middle English from Old French *essorer*, ultimately from Latin (as EX-[1], *aura* 'breeze')]

sob /sɒb/ *v.* & *n.* ● *v.* (**sobbed**, **sobbing**) **1** *intr.* **a** draw breath in convulsive gasps when weeping or from distress, physical exhaustion, etc. **b** weep in this way. **2** *tr.* (usu. foll. by *out*) utter with sobs. **3** *tr.* bring (oneself) to a specified state by sobbing (*sobbed themselves to sleep*). ● *n.* a convulsive drawing of breath, esp. in weeping. ◻ **sobbingly** *adv.* [Middle English *sobbe* (probably imitative)]

sober /ˈsəʊbə/ *adj.* & *v.* ● *adj.* (**soberer**, **soberest**) **1** not under the influence of alcohol. **2** not given to excessive drinking of alcohol. **3** moderate, well-balanced, tranquil, sedate. **4** not fanciful or exaggerated (*the sober truth*). **5** (of a colour etc.) quiet and inconspicuous. ● *v.tr.* & *intr.* (often foll. by *down*, *up*) make or become sober or less wild, reckless, enthusiastic, visionary, etc. (*a sobering thought*). ◻ **sober as a judge** completely sober. ◻ **soberingly** *adv.* **soberly** *adv.* [Middle English via Old French *sobre* from Latin *sobrius*]

sobriety /səˈbrʌɪəti/ *n.* the state of being sober. [Middle English from Old French *sobrieté* or Latin *sobrietas* (as SOBER)]

sobriquet /ˈsəʊbrɪkeɪ/ *n.* (also **soubriquet** /ˈsuː-/) **1** a nickname. **2** an assumed name. [French, originally = 'tap under the chin', of unknown origin]

sob sister *n.* *colloq.* **1** a female journalist writing sentimental reports or answering readers' problems. **2** an actress who plays sentimental roles.

sob story *n.* *colloq.* a story or explanation appealing mainly to the emotions.

sob-stuff *n.* *colloq.* sentimental talk or writing.

Soc. *abbr.* **1** Socialist. **2** Society.

soca /ˈsəʊkə/ *n.* a kind of calypso music with elements of soul, originally from Trinidad. [SOUL + CALYPSO]

socage /ˈsɒkɪdʒ/ *n.* (also **soccage**) *hist.* a feudal tenure of land involving payment of rent or other non-military service to a superior. [Middle English via Anglo-French *socage*, from *soc*, from Old English *sōcn* SOKE]

so-called *adj.* commonly designated or known as, often incorrectly.

soccer /ˈsɒkə/ *n.* Association football. [Assoc. + -ER[3]]

sociable /ˈsəʊʃəb(ə)l/ *adj.* & *n.* ● *adj.* **1** fitted for or liking the society of other people; ready and willing to talk and act with others. **2** (of a person's manner or behaviour etc.) friendly. **3** (of a meeting etc.) marked by friendliness, not stiff or formal. ● *n.* **1** an open carriage with facing side seats. **2** esp. *Brit.* an S-shaped couch for two occupants partly facing each other. **3** *US* a social. ◻ **sociability** /-ˈbɪlɪti/ *n.* **sociableness** *n.* **sociably** *adv.* [French *sociable* or Latin *sociabilis*, via *sociare* 'to unite' from *socius* 'companion']

social /ˈsəʊʃ(ə)l/ *adj.* & *n.* ● *adj.* **1** of or relating to society or its organization. **2** concerned with the mutual relations of human beings or of classes of human beings. **3** living in organized communities; unfitted for a solitary life (*man is a social animal*). **4 a** needing companionship; gregarious, interdependent. **b** cooperative; practising the division of labour. **5** existing only as a member of a compound organism. **6 a** (of insects) living together in organized communities. **b** (of animals or birds) breeding or nesting near each other in communities. **7** (of plants) growing thickly together and monopolizing the ground they grow on. ● *n.* a social gathering, esp. one organized by a club, congregation, etc. ◻ **sociality** /səʊʃɪˈalɪti/ *n.* **socially** *adv.* [French *social* or Latin *socialis* 'allied', from *socius* 'friend']

social anthropology *n.* the comparative study of peoples through their culture and kinship systems.

social climber *n.* *derog.* a person anxious to gain a higher social status.

social conscience *n.* a sense of responsibility or concern for the problems and injustices of society.

social contract *n.* (also **social compact**) an agreement to cooperate for social benefits, e.g. by sacrificing some individual freedom for state protection.

social credit *n.* the economic theory that the profits of industry should be distributed to the general public.

social democracy *n.* a socialist system achieved by democratic means. ◻ **social democrat** *n.*

social engineering *n.* the use of sociological principles in approaching social problems.

socialism /ˈsəʊʃəlɪz(ə)m/ *n.* **1** a political and economic theory of social organization which advocates that the community as a whole should own and control the means of production, distribution, and exchange. **2** policy or practice based on this theory. ◻ **socialist** *n.* & *adj.* **socialistic** /-ˈlɪstɪk/ *adj.* **socialistically** /-ˈlɪstɪkəli/ *adv.* [French *socialisme* (as SOCIAL)]

socialite /ˈsəʊʃəlʌɪt/ *n.* a person prominent in fashionable society.

socialize /ˈsəʊʃəlʌɪz/ *v.* (also **-ise**) **1** *intr.* act in a sociable manner; mix socially with others. **2** *tr.* make social. **3** *tr.* organize on socialistic principles. ◻ **socialization** /-ˈzeɪʃ(ə)n/ *n.*

socialized medicine /ˈsəʊʃəlʌɪzd/ *n.* *US* often *derog.* the provision of medical services for all from public funds.

social order *n.* the network of human relationships in society.

social realism *n.* the realistic depiction of social conditions or political views in art.

social science *n.* **1** the scientific study of human society and social relationships. **2** a branch of this (e.g. politics or economics). ◻ **social scientist** *n.*

social secretary *n.* a person who makes arrangements for the social activities of a person or organization.

social security *n.* State assistance to those lacking in economic security and welfare, e.g. the aged and *Brit.* the unemployed.

social service *n.* **1** philanthropic activity. **2** (in *pl.*) services provided by the state for the community, esp. education, health, and housing.

social war *n.* a war fought between allies.

social work *n.* work of benefit to those in need of help or welfare, esp. done by specially trained personnel. □ **social worker** *n.*

society /sə'sʌɪti/ *n.* (*pl.* **-ies**) **1** the sum of human conditions and activity regarded as a whole functioning interdependently. **2** a social community (*all societies must have firm laws*). **3 a** a social mode of life. **b** the customs and organization of an ordered community. **4** *Ecol.* a plant or animal community. **5 a** the socially advantaged or prominent members of a community (*society would not approve*). **b** this, or a part of it, qualified in some way (*is not done in polite society*). **6** participation in hospitality; other people's homes or company (*avoids society*). **7** companionship, company (*avoids the society of such people*). **8** an association of persons united by a common aim or interest or principle (*formed a music society*). □ **societal** *adj.* (esp. in sense 1). **societally** *adv.* [French *société* from Latin *societas -tatis*, from *socius* 'companion']

Society of Friends see QUAKER.

Society of Jesus see JESUIT.

socio- /'səʊsɪəʊ, 'səʊʃɪəʊ/ *comb. form* **1** of society (and). **2** of or relating to sociology (and). [Latin *socius* 'companion']

sociobiology /ˌsəʊsɪəʊbʌɪ'ɒlədʒi, ˌsəʊʃɪəʊ-/ *n.* the scientific study of the biological aspects of social behaviour in animals and humans. □ **sociobiological** /-bʌɪə'lɒdʒɪk(ə)l/ *adj.* **sociobiologically** /-bʌɪə'lɒdʒɪk(ə)li/ *adv.* **sociobiologist** *n.*

sociocultural /ˌsəʊsɪəʊ'kʌltʃ(ə)r(ə)l, ˌsəʊʃɪəʊ-/ *adj.* combining social and cultural factors. □ **socioculturally** *adv.*

socio-economic /ˌsəʊsɪəʊiːkə'nɒmɪk, ˌsəʊʃɪəʊ-/ *adj.* relating to or concerned with the interaction of social and economic factors. □ **socio-economically** *adv.*

sociolinguistic /ˌsəʊsɪəʊlɪŋ'gwɪstɪk, ˌsəʊʃɪəʊ-/ *adj.* relating to or concerned with language in its social aspects. □ **sociolinguist** *n.* **sociolinguistically** *adv.*

sociolinguistics /ˌsəʊsɪəʊlɪŋ'gwɪstɪks, ˌsəʊʃɪəʊ-/ *n.* the study of language in relation to social factors.

sociology /səʊsɪ'ɒlədʒi, səʊʃɪ-/ *n.* **1** the study of the development, structure, and functioning of human society. **2** the study of social problems. □ **sociological** /-ə'lɒdʒɪk(ə)l/ *adj.* **sociologically** /-ə'lɒdʒɪk(ə)li/ *adv.* **sociologist** *n.* [French *sociologie* (as SOCIO-, -LOGY)]

sociometry /səʊsɪ'ɒmɪtri, səʊʃɪ-/ *n.* the study of relationships within a group of people. □ **sociometric** /-ə'mɛtrɪk/ *adj.* **sociometrically** /-ə'mɛtrɪk(ə)li/ *adv.* **sociometrist** *n.*

socio-political /ˌsəʊsɪəʊpə'lɪtɪk(ə)l, ˌsəʊʃɪəʊ-/ *adj.* combining social and political factors.

sock[1] /sɒk/ *n.* (*pl.* **socks** or *Commerce* **sox** /sɒks/) **1** a short knitted covering for the foot, usu. not reaching the knee. **2** a removable inner sole put into a shoe for warmth etc. **3** an ancient Greek or Roman comic actor's light shoe. **4** comic drama. □ **knock** (or **blow**) **one's socks off** astound, amaze. **pull one's socks up** *colloq.* make an effort to improve. **put a sock in it** *colloq.* be quiet. [Old English *socc* via Latin *soccus* 'comic actor's shoe, light low-heeled slipper', from Greek *sukkhos*]

sock[2] /sɒk/ *v.* & *n.* *colloq.* ● *v.tr.* hit (esp. a person) forcefully. ● *n.* **1** a hard blow. **2** *US* the power to deliver a blow. □ **sock it to** attack or address (a person) vigorously. [17th c.: origin unknown]

socket /'sɒkɪt/ *n.* & *v.* ● *n.* **1** a natural or artificial hollow for something to fit into or stand firm or revolve in. **2** *Electr.* a device receiving a plug, light bulb, etc., to make a connection. **3** *Golf* the part of an iron club into which the shaft is fitted. ● *v.tr.* (**socketed**, **socketing**) **1** place in or fit with a socket. **2** *Brit. Golf* hit (a ball) with the socket of a club. [Middle English from Anglo-French, diminutive of Old French *soc* 'ploughshare', probably of Celtic origin]

sockeye /'sɒkʌɪ/ *n.* a blue-backed salmon of Alaska etc., *Oncorhynchus nerka*. [N. American Indian *sukai* 'fish of fishes']

socle /'səʊk(ə)l, 'sɒk-/ *n.* *Archit.* a plain low block or plinth serving as a support for a column, urn, statue, etc., or as the foundation of a wall. [French from Italian *zoccolo*, originally 'wooden shoe', from Latin *socculus*, from *soccus* SOCK[1]]

Socratic /sə'kratɪk/ *adj.* & *n.* ● *adj.* of or relating to the Greek philosopher Socrates (d. 399 BC) or his philosophy, esp. the method associated with him of seeking the truth by a series of questions and answers. ● *n.* a follower of Socrates. □ **Socratically** *adv.* [Latin *Socraticus* from Greek *Sōkratikos*, from *Sōkratēs*]

Socratic elenchus *n.* an attempted refutation of an opponent's position by short question and answer.

Socratic irony *n.* a pose of ignorance assumed in order to entice others into making statements that can then be challenged.

sod[1] /sɒd/ *n.* & *v.* ● *n.* **1** turf or a piece of turf. **2** the surface of the ground. ● *v.tr.* (**sodded**, **sodding**) cover (the ground) with sods. □ **under the sod** in the grave. [Middle English from Middle Dutch, Middle Low German *sode*, of unknown origin]

sod[2] /sɒd/ *n.* & *v.* esp. *Brit. coarse slang* ● *n.* **1** an unpleasant or awkward person or thing. **2** a person of a specified kind; a fellow (*the lucky sod*). ● *v.tr.* (**sodded**, **sodding**) **1** (often *absol.* or as *int.*) an exclamation of annoyance (*sod them, I don't care!*). **2** (as **sodding** *adj.*) a general term of contempt. □ **sod off** go away. [abbreviation of SODOMITE]

soda /'səʊdə/ *n.* **1** any of various compounds of sodium in common use (*washing soda*; *caustic soda*). **2** (in full **soda water**) water made effervescent by impregnation with carbon dioxide under pressure and used alone or with spirits etc. as a drink (originally made with sodium bicarbonate). **3** esp. *US* a sweet effervescent drink. [originally obtained from the ashes of glasswort etc.: medieval Latin, perhaps from *sodanum* 'glasswort' (used as a remedy for headaches) via *soda* 'headache' from Arabic *ṣudā'*, from *ṣada'a* 'split']

soda bread *n.* bread leavened with baking soda.

soda fountain *n.* esp. *US* **1** a device supplying soda water or soft drinks. **2** a shop or counter featuring this, selling soft drinks, ice cream, etc.

soda lime *n.* a mixture of calcium oxide and sodium hydroxide.

sodality /səʊ'dalɪti/ *n.* (*pl.* **-ies**) a confraternity or association, esp. a Roman Catholic religious guild or brotherhood. [French *sodalité* or Latin *sodalitas*, from *sodalis* 'comrade']

soda syphon *n.* a bottle from which carbonated water is dispensed by allowing the gas pressure to force it out.

soda water see SODA 2.

sodden /'sɒd(ə)n/ *adj.* & *v.* ● *adj.* **1** saturated with liquid; soaked through. **2** rendered dazed or dull etc. with drunkenness. **3** (of bread etc.) doughy; heavy and moist. ● *v.intr.* & *tr.* become or make sodden. □ **soddenly** *adv.* **soddenness** /'sɒd(ə)nnɪs/ *n.* [archaic past part. of SEETHE]

sodium /'səʊdɪəm/ *n.* *Chem.* a soft silver-white reactive metallic element, occurring naturally in soda, salt, etc., that is important in industry and is an essential element in living organisms (symbol Na). □ **sodic** *adj.* [SODA + -IUM]

sodium bicarbonate *n.* a soluble white powder used in fire extinguishers and effervescent drinks and as a raising agent in baking (also called *baking soda*). Chem. formula: $NaHCO_3$.

sodium carbonate *n.* a white powder with many commercial applications including the manufacture of soap and glass (also called *washing soda*). Chem. formula: Na_2CO_3.

sodium chloride *n.* a colourless crystalline compound occurring naturally in sea water and halite; common salt. Chem. formula: NaCl.

sodium hydroxide *n.* a deliquescent compound which is strongly alkaline and used in the manufacture of soap and paper (also called *caustic soda*). Chem. formula: NaOH.

sodium nitrate *n.* a white powdery compound used mainly in the manufacture of fertilizers. Chem. formula: $NaNO_3$.

sodium-vapour lamp *n.* (also **sodium lamp**) a lamp using an electrical discharge in sodium vapour and giving a yellow light.

Sodom /ˈsɒdəm/ *n.* a wicked or depraved place. [*Sodom*, a city in ancient Palestine, destroyed for its wickedness (Gen. 18–19)]

sodomite /ˈsɒdəmʌɪt/ *n.* a person who practises sodomy. [Middle English via Old French and Late Latin *Sodomita* from Greek *Sodomitēs* 'inhabitant of Sodom', from *Sodoma* 'Sodom']

sodomy /ˈsɒdəmi/ *n.* = BUGGERY. □ **sodomize** *v.tr.* (also **-ise**). [Middle English via medieval Latin *sodomia* from Late Latin *peccatum Sodomiticum* 'sin of Sodom': see SODOM]

Sod's Law *n.* = MURPHY'S LAW.

soever /səʊˈɛvə/ *adv. literary* of any kind; to any extent (*how great soever it may be*).

-soever /səʊˈɛvə/ *comb. form* (added to relative pronouns, adverbs, and adjectives) of any kind; to any extent (*whatsoever*; *howsoever*).

sofa /ˈsəʊfə/ *n.* a long upholstered seat with a back and arms, for two or more people. [French, ultimately from Arabic *ṣuffa*]

sofa bed *n.* a sofa that can be converted into a bed, for usu. occasional use.

soffit /ˈsɒfɪt/ *n.* the undersurface of an arch, a balcony, overhanging eaves, etc. [French *soffite* or Italian *soffitta*, *-itto*, ultimately from Latin *suffixus* (as SUFFIX)]

S. of S. *abbr.* Song of Songs (Old Testament).

soft /sɒft/ *adj.*, *adv.*, & *n.* ● *adj.* **1** (of a substance, material, etc.) lacking hardness or firmness; yielding to pressure; easily cut. **2** (of cloth etc.) having a smooth surface or texture; not rough or coarse. **3** (of air etc.) mellow, mild, balmy; not noticeably cold or hot. **4** (of water) free from mineral salts and therefore good for lathering. **5** (of a light or colour etc.) not brilliant or glaring. **6** (of a voice or sounds) gentle and pleasing. **7** *Phonet.* **a** (of a consonant) sibilant or palatal (as *c* in *ice*, *g* in *age*). **b** voiced or unaspirated. **8** (of an outline etc.) not sharply defined. **9** (of an action or manner etc.) gentle, conciliatory, complimentary; amorous. **10** (of the heart or feelings etc.) compassionate, sympathetic. **11** (of a person's character or attitude etc.) feeble, lenient, silly, sentimental. **12** *colloq.* (of a job etc.) easy. **13** (of drugs) mild; not likely to cause addiction. **14** (of radiation) having little penetrating power. **15** (also **soft-core**) (of pornography) suggestive or erotic but not explicit. **16** *Stock Exch.* (of currency, prices, etc.) likely to fall in value. **17** *Polit.* moderate; willing to compromise (*the soft left*). **18** peaceful (*soft slumbers*). **19** *Brit.* (of the weather etc.) rainy or moist or thawing. ● *adv.* softly (*play soft*). ● *n.* a silly weak person. □ **be soft on** *colloq.* **1** be lenient towards. **2** be infatuated with. **have a soft spot for** be fond of or affectionate towards (a person). □ **softish** *adj.* **softness** *n.* [Old English *sōfte* 'agreeable', earlier *sēfte*, from West Germanic]

softa /ˈsɒftə/ *n.* a Muslim student of sacred law and theology. [Turkish from Persian *sūḵta* 'burnt, afire']

soft answer *n.* a good-tempered answer to abuse or an accusation.

softball /ˈsɒf(t)bɔːl/ *n.* **1** a ball like a baseball but larger. **2** a modified form of baseball using this.

soft-boiled *adj.* (of an egg) lightly boiled leaving the yolk soft or liquid.

soft-centred *adj.* **1** (of a sweet) having a soft filling or centre. **2** (of a person) soft-hearted, sentimental.

soft coal *n.* bituminous coal.

soft detergent *n.* a biodegradable detergent.

soft drink *n.* a non-alcoholic drink.

soften /ˈsɒf(ə)n/ *v.* **1** *tr.* & *intr.* make or become soft or softer. **2** *tr.* (often foll. by *up*) **a** reduce the strength of (defences) by bombing or some other preliminary attack. **b** reduce the resistance of (a person). □ **softener** *n.*

softening of the brain *n.* a morbid degeneration of the brain, esp. in old age.

soft focus *n. Photog.* the slight deliberate blurring of a picture.

soft fruit *n. Brit.* small stoneless fruit (strawberry, currant, etc.).

soft furnishings *n.pl. Brit.* curtains, rugs, etc.

soft goods *n.pl. Brit.* textiles.

soft-headed *adj.* feeble-minded. □ **soft-headedness** *n.*

soft-hearted *adj.* tender, compassionate; easily moved. □ **soft-heartedness** *n.*

softie /ˈsɒfti/ *n.* (also **softy**) (*pl.* **-ies**) *colloq.* a weak or silly or soft-hearted person.

soft landing *n.* a landing by a spacecraft without its suffering major damage. □ **soft-land** *v.tr.* & *intr.*

softly /ˈsɒftli/ *adv.* in a soft, gentle, or quiet manner.

softly-softly *attrib.adj.* (of an approach or strategy) cautious; discreet and cunning.

soft option *n.* the easier alternative.

soft palate *n.* the rear part of the palate.

soft-paste *adj.* denoting an 'artificial' porcelain containing glassy materials and fired at a comparatively low temperature.

soft pedal *n.* & *v.* ● *n.* a pedal on a piano that makes the tone softer. ● *v.tr.* & (often foll. on *on*) *intr.* (**soft-pedal**) (**-pedalled**, **pedalling**; *US* **-pedaled**, **pedaling**) **1** refrain from emphasizing; be restrained (about). **2** *Mus.* play with the soft pedal down.

soft roe see ROE[1] 2.

soft sell *n.* & *v.* ● *n.* restrained or subtly persuasive salesmanship. ● *v.tr.* (**soft-sell**) (*past* and *past part.*, **-sold**) sell by this method.

soft soap *n.* & *v.* ● *n.* **1** a semi-fluid soap, esp. one made with potassium not sodium salts. **2** *colloq.* persuasive flattery. ● *v.tr.* (**soft-soap**) *colloq.* persuade (a person) with flattery.

soft-spoken *adj.* speaking with a gentle voice.

soft sugar *n. Brit.* granulated or powdered sugar.

soft tack *n. Brit.* bread or other good food (opp. HARD TACK).

soft target *n.* a relatively vulnerable or unprotected target, esp. for military or terrorist attack.

soft tissues *n.pl.* tissues of the body that are not bony or cartilaginous.

soft-top *n.* **1** a motor vehicle roof that is soft and can be folded back. **2** a vehicle having such a roof.

soft touch *n. slang* = EASY TOUCH.

software /ˈsɒf(t)wɛː/ *n.* the programs and other operating information used by a computer (opp. HARDWARE 3).

soft wicket *n. Cricket* a wicket with moist or sodden turf.

softwood /ˈsɒf(t)wʊd/ *n.* the wood of pine, spruce, or other conifers, easily sawn.

softy var. of SOFTIE.

SOGAT /ˈsəʊgat/ *abbr. hist.* (in the UK) Society of Graphical and Allied Trades (from 1982 officially called SOGAT 82, and from 1991 incorporated in the GPMU).

soggy /ˈsɒgi/ *adj.* (**soggier**, **soggiest**) sodden, saturated, dank. □ **soggily** *adv.* **sogginess** *n.* [dialect *sog* a swamp]

soh /səʊ/ *n.* (also **so**, **sol** /sɒl/) *Mus.* **1** (in tonic sol-fa) the fifth note of a major scale. **2** the note G in the fixed-doh system. [(variant of) Middle English *sol* from Latin *solve*: see GAMUT]

soi-disant /swɑːdiːˈzɒ̃, French swadizɑ̃/ *adj.* self-styled or pretended. [French, from *soi* 'oneself' + *disant* 'saying']

soigné /ˈswɑːnjeɪ, French swaɲe/ *adj.* (*fem.* ***soignée*** *pronunc.* same) carefully finished or arranged; well-groomed. [past part. of French *soigner* 'take care of' from *soin* 'care']

soil[1] /sɔɪl/ *n.* **1** the upper layer of earth in which plants grow, consisting of disintegrated rock usu. with an admixture of organic remains (*alluvial soil; rich soil*). **2** ground belonging to a nation; territory (*on British soil*). □ **soil-less** *adj.* **soily** *adj.* [Middle English from Anglo-French, perhaps from Latin *solium* 'seat', by association with Latin *solum* 'ground']

soil[2] /sɔɪl/ *v. & n.* ● *v.tr.* **1** make dirty; smear or stain with dirt (*soiled linen*). **2** tarnish, defile; bring discredit to (*would not soil my hands with it*). ● *n.* **1** a dirty mark; a stain, smear, or defilement. **2** filth; refuse matter. [Middle English from Old French *suiller*, *soiller*, etc., ultimately from Latin *sucula*, diminutive of *sus* 'pig']

soil[3] /sɔɪl/ *v.tr.* feed (cattle) on fresh-cut green fodder (originally for purging). [perhaps from SOIL[2]]

soil mechanics *n.pl.* (usu treated as *sing.*) the study of the properties of soil as affecting its use in civil engineering.

soil pipe *n.* a sewage or waste water pipe.

soil science *n.* pedology.

soirée /'swɑːreɪ/ *n.* an evening party, usu. in a private house, for conversation or music. [French from *soir* 'evening']

soixante-neuf /swasɒ̃'nəːf/ *n. slang* sexual activity between two people involving mutual oral stimulation of the genitals. [French, = sixty-nine, from the position of the couple]

sojourn /'sɒdʒ(ə)n, -dʒəːn, 'sʌd-/ *n. & v.* ● *n.* a temporary stay. ● *v.intr.* stay temporarily. □ **sojourner** *n.* [Middle English from Old French *sojorn* etc., from Late Latin SUB- + *diurnum* 'day']

soke /səʊk/ *n. Brit. hist.* **1** a right of local jurisdiction. **2** a district under a particular jurisdiction and administration. [Middle English via Anglo-Latin *sōca* from Old English *sōcn* 'prosecution', from Germanic]

Sol /sɒl/ *n.* (in Roman mythology) the sun, esp. as a personification. [Middle English from Latin]

sol[1] var. of SOH.

sol[2] /sɒl/ *n. Chem.* a fluid colloidal suspension of a solid in a liquid. [abbreviation of SOLUTION]

sola[1] /'səʊlə/ *n.* a pithy-stemmed E. Indian swamp plant, *Aeschynomene indica.* [Urdu & Bengali *solā*, Hindi *sholā*]

sola[2] *fem.* of SOLUS.

solace /'sɒləs/ *n. & v.* ● *n.* comfort in distress, disappointment, or tedium. ● *v.tr.* give solace to. □ **solace oneself with** find compensation or relief in. [Middle English via Old French *solas* from Latin *solatium*, from *solari* CONSOLE[1]]

solan /'səʊlən/ *n.* (in full **solan goose**) a gannet, *Sula bassana*. [probably from Old Norse *súla* 'gannet' + *önd*, *and-* 'duck']

solanaceous /sɒlə'neɪʃəs/ *adj.* of or relating to the plant family Solanaceae, including potatoes, nightshades, and tobacco. [modern Latin *solanaceae* from Latin *sōlānum* 'nightshade']

solar /'səʊlə/ *adj. & n.* ● *adj.* of, relating to, or reckoned by the sun (*solar eclipse*; *solar time*). ● *n. Brit.* **1** a solarium. **2** an upper chamber in a medieval house. [Middle English from Latin *solaris*, from *sol* 'sun']

solar battery *n.* (also **solar cell**) a device converting solar radiation into electricity.

solar constant *n.* the rate at which energy reaches the earth's surface from the sun, usually taken to be 1,388 watts per square metre.

solar day *n.* the interval between successive meridian transits of the sun at a place.

solar eclipse *n.* an eclipse in which the sun is obscured by the moon.

solar energy *n.* **1** radiant energy emitted by the sun. **2** = SOLAR POWER.

solarium /sə'lɛːrɪəm/ *n.* (*pl.* **solariums** or **solaria** /-rɪə/) a room equipped with sunlamps or fitted with extensive areas of glass for exposure to the sun. [Latin, = sundial, sunning-place (as SOLAR)]

solarize /'səʊlərʌɪz/ *v.intr. & tr.* (also **-ise**) *Photog.* undergo or cause to undergo change in the relative darkness of parts of an image by long exposure. □ **solarization** /-'zeɪʃ(ə)n/ *n.*

solar month *n.* one-twelfth of the solar year.

solar myth *n.* a myth ascribing the sun's course or attributes to a god or hero.

solar panel *n.* a panel designed to absorb the sun's rays as a source of energy for operating electricity or heating.

solar plexus *n.* a complex of radiating nerves at the pit of the stomach.

solar power *n.* power obtained by harnessing the energy of the sun's rays.

solar system *n.* the sun and the celestial bodies whose motion it governs.

solar wind *n.* the continuous flow of charged particles from the sun.

solar year *n.* the time taken for the earth to travel once round the sun, equal to 365 days, 5 hours, 48 minutes, and 46 seconds.

solatium /sə'leɪʃɪəm/ *n.* (*pl.* **solatia** /-ʃɪə/) a thing given as a compensation or consolation. [Latin, = SOLACE]

sola topi *n.* an Indian sun-helmet made from the pith of the sola.

sold *past* and *past part.* of SELL.

soldanella /sɒldə'nɛlə/ *n.* any dwarf Alpine plant of the genus *Soldanella*, having bell-shaped flowers with fringed petals. [modern Latin from Italian]

solder /'səʊldə, 'sɒldə/ *n. & v.* ● *n.* **1** a fusible alloy used to join less fusible metals or wires etc. **2** a cementing or joining agency. ● *v.tr.* join with solder. □ **solderable** *n.* **solderer** *n.* [Middle English via Old French *soudure*, from *souder*, from Latin *solidare* 'fasten', from *solidus* SOLID]

soldering iron /'səʊldərɪŋ, 'sɒl-/ *n.* a tool used for applying solder.

soldier /'səʊldʒə/ *n. & v.* ● *n.* **1** a person serving in or having served in an army. **2** (in full **common soldier**) a private or NCO in an army. **3** a military commander of specified ability (*a great soldier*). **4** (in full **soldier ant**) a wingless ant or termite with a large head and jaws for fighting in defence of its colony. **5** (in full **soldier beetle**) a carnivorous beetle of the family Cantharidae, with soft reddish wing-cases. **6** *colloq.* a finger of bread for dipping into a soft-boiled egg. ● *v.intr.* serve as a soldier (*was off soldiering*). □ **soldier on** *colloq.* persevere doggedly. □ **soldierly** *adj.* **soldiership** *n.* [Middle English *souder* etc. via Old French *soudier*, *soldier*, from *soulde* '(soldier's) pay', from Latin *solidus*: see SOLIDUS]

soldier of Christ *n.* an active or proselytizing Christian.

soldier of fortune *n.* an adventurous person ready to take service under any state or person; a mercenary.

soldiery /'səʊldʒ(ə)ri/ *n.* (*pl.* **-ies**) **1** soldiers, esp. of a specified character. **2** a group of soldiers.

sole[1] /səʊl/ *n. & v.* ● *n.* **1** the undersurface of the foot. **2** the part of a shoe, sock, etc., corresponding to this (esp. excluding the heel). **3** the lower surface or base of an implement, e.g. a plough, golf club head, etc. **4** the floor of a ship's cabin. ● *v.tr.* provide (a shoe etc.) with a sole; replace the sole of. □ **-soled** *adj.* (in *comb.*). [Middle English from Old French, ultimately via Latin *solea* 'sandal, sill' from *solum* 'bottom, pavement, sole': perhaps already in use in Old English]

sole[2] /səʊl/ *n.* any flatfish of the family Soleidae, esp. *Solea solea* used as food. [Middle English via Old French from Provençal *sola*, ultimately from Latin *solea* (as SOLE[1], named from its shape)]

sole[3] /səʊl/ *adj.* **1** (*attrib.*) one and only; single, exclusive (*the sole reason*; *has the sole right*). **2** *archaic* or *Law* (esp. of a woman) unmarried. **3** *archaic* alone, unaccompanied. □ **solely** *adv.* [Middle English via Old French *soule* from Latin *sola*, fem. of *solus* 'alone']

solecism /ˈsɒlɪsɪz(ə)m/ *n.* **1** a mistake of grammar or idiom; a blunder in the manner of speaking or writing. **2** a piece of bad manners or incorrect behaviour. □ **solecist** *n.* **solecistic** /-ˈsɪstɪk/ *adj.* [French *solécisme* or Latin *soloecismus* from Greek *soloikismos*, from *soloikos* 'speaking incorrectly']

solemn /ˈsɒləm/ *adj.* **1** serious and dignified (*a solemn occasion*). **2** formal; accompanied by ceremony (*a solemn oath*). **3** mysteriously impressive. **4** (of a person) serious or cheerless in manner (*looks rather solemn*). **5** full of importance; weighty (*a solemn warning*). **6** grave, sober, deliberate; slow in movement or action (*a solemn promise; solemn music*). □ **solemnly** *adv.* **solemness** *n.* [Middle English via Old French *solemne* from Latin *sol(l)emnis* 'customary, celebrated at a fixed date', from *sollus* 'entire']

solemnity /səˈlɛmnɪti/ *n.* (*pl.* **-ies**) **1** the state of being solemn; a solemn character or feeling; solemn behaviour. **2** a rite or celebration; a piece of ceremony. [Middle English via Old French *solem(p)nité* from Latin *sollemnitas -tatis* (as SOLEMN)]

solemnize /ˈsɒləmnʌɪz/ *v.tr.* (also **-ise**) **1** duly perform (a ceremony esp. of marriage). **2** celebrate (a festival etc.). **3** make solemn. □ **solemnization** /-ˈzeɪʃ(ə)n/ *n.* [Middle English via Old French *solem(p)niser* from medieval Latin *solemnizare* (as SOLEMN)]

Solemn Mass *n.* = HIGH MASS.

solenoid /ˈsɒlənɔɪd, ˈsəʊl-/ *n.* a cylindrical coil of wire acting as a magnet when carrying electric current. □ **solenoidal** /-ˈnɔɪd(ə)l/ *adj.* [French *solénoïde* from Greek *sōlēn* 'channel, pipe' + -OID]

sole-plate *n.* the bedplate of an engine etc.

sol-fa /ˈsɒlfɑː/ *n.* & *v.* ● *n.* = SOLMIZATION (cf. TONIC SOL-FA). ● *v.tr.* & *intr.* (**-fas**, **-faed**) sing using the sol-fa syllables. [SOL¹ + FA]

solfatara /sɒlfəˈtɑːrə/ *n.* a volcanic vent emitting only sulphurous and other vapours. [name of a volcano near Naples, from Italian *solfo* 'sulphur']

solfeggio /sɒlˈfɛdʒɪəʊ/ *n.* (*pl.* **solfeggi** /-dʒi/) *Mus.* **1** an exercise in singing using sol-fa syllables. **2** solmization. [Italian (as SOL-FA)]

soli *pl.* of SOLO.

solicit /səˈlɪsɪt/ *v.* (**solicited**, **soliciting**) **1** *tr.* & (foll. by *for*) *intr.* ask repeatedly or earnestly for or seek or invite (business etc.). **2** *tr.* (often foll. by *for*) make a request or petition to (a person). **3** *tr.* (also *absol.*) accost (a person) and offer one's services as a prostitute. □ **solicitation** /-ˈteɪʃ(ə)n/ *n.* [Middle English via Old French *solliciter* from Latin *sollicitare* 'agitate', via *sollicitus* 'anxious' from *sollus* 'entire' + *citus*, past part. of *ciēre* 'set in motion']

solicitor /səˈlɪsɪtə/ *n.* **1** *Brit.* a member of the legal profession qualified to deal with conveyancing, draw up wills, etc. advise clients and instruct barristers, and represent clients in the lower courts. **2** a person who solicits. **3** *US* a canvasser. **4** *US* the chief law officer of a city etc. [Middle English from Old French *solliciteur* (as SOLICIT)]

Solicitor-General *n.* (*pl.* **Solicitors-General**) **1** (in the UK) the Crown law officer below the Attorney-General or (in Scotland) below the Lord Advocate. **2** (in the US) the law officer below the Attorney-General.

solicitous /səˈlɪsɪtəs/ *adj.* **1** (often foll. by *of*, *about*, etc.) showing interest or concern. **2** (foll. by *to* + infin.) eager, anxious. □ **solicitously** *adv.* **solicitousness** *n.* [Latin *sollicitus* (as SOLICIT)]

solicitude /səˈlɪsɪtjuːd/ *n.* **1** the state of being solicitous; solicitous behaviour. **2** anxiety or concern. [Middle English via Old French *sollicitude* from Latin *sollicitudo* (as SOLICITOUS)]

solid /ˈsɒlɪd/ *adj., n., & adv.* ● *adj.* (**solider**, **solidest**) **1** firm and stable in shape; not liquid or fluid (*solid food; water becomes solid at 0°C*). **2** of such material throughout, not hollow or containing cavities (*a solid sphere*). **3** of the same substance throughout (*solid silver*). **4** of strong material or construction or build, not flimsy or slender etc. **5 a** having three dimensions. **b** concerned with solids (*solid geometry*). **6 a** sound and reliable; genuine (*solid arguments*). **b** staunch and dependable (*a solid Tory*). **7** sound but without any special flair etc. (*a solid piece of work*). **8** financially sound. **9** (of time) uninterrupted, continuous (*spend four solid hours on it*). **10 a** unanimous, undivided (*support has been pretty solid so far*). **b** (foll. by *for*) united in favour of. **11** (of printing) without spaces between the lines etc. **12** (of a tyre) without a central air space. **13** (foll. by *with*) *US colloq.* on good terms. **14** *Austral.* & *NZ colloq.* severe, unreasonable. ● *n.* **1** a solid substance or body. **2** (in *pl.*) solid food. **3** *Geom.* a body or magnitude having three dimensions. ● *adv.* so as to become solid; solidly (*jammed solid; set solid*). □ **solidly** *adv.* **solidness** *n.* [Middle English via Old French *solide* from Latin *solidus*, related to *salvus* 'safe', *sollus* 'entire']

solid angle *n.* an angle formed by planes etc. meeting at a point.

solidarity /sɒlɪˈdarɪti/ *n.* **1** unity or agreement of feeling or action, esp. among individuals with a common interest. **2** mutual dependence. [French *solidarité*, ultimately from *solide* SOLID]

solid colour *n.* colour covering the whole of an object, without a pattern etc.

solid-drawn *adj.* (of a tube etc.) pressed or drawn out from a solid bar of metal.

solidi *pl.* of SOLIDUS.

solidify /səˈlɪdɪfʌɪ/ *v.tr.* & *intr.* (**-ies**, **-ied**) make or become solid. □ **solidification** /-fɪˈkeɪʃ(ə)n/ *n.* **solidifier** *n.*

solidity /səˈlɪdɪti/ *n.* the state of being solid; firmness.

solid solution *n.* solid material containing one substance uniformly distributed in another.

solid state *n.* & *adj.* ● *n.* the state of matter that retains its boundaries without support. ● *adj.* (**solid-state**) using the electronics properties of solids (e.g. a semiconductor) to replace those of valves.

solidus /ˈsɒlɪdəs/ *n.* (*pl.* **solidi** /-dʌɪ/) **1** esp. *Brit.* an oblique stroke (/) used in writing fractions ($^3/_4$), to separate other figures and letters, or to denote alternatives (*and/or*) and ratios (*miles/day*). **2** (in full **solidus curve**) a curve in a graph of the temperature and composition of a mixture, below which the substance is entirely solid. **3** *hist.* a gold coin of the later Roman Empire. [Middle English (in sense 3) from Latin: see SOLID]

solifluction /sɒlɪˈflʌkʃ(ə)n, səʊlɪ-/ *n.* the gradual movement of wet soil etc. down a slope. [Latin *solum* 'soil' + *fluctio* 'flowing' from *fluere fluct-* 'flow']

soliloquy /səˈlɪləkwi/ *n.* (*pl.* **-ies**) **1** the act of talking when alone or regardless of any hearers, esp. in drama. **2** part of a play involving this. □ **soliloquist** *n.* **soliloquize** *v.intr.* (also **-ise**). [Late Latin *soliloquium*, from Latin *solus* 'alone' + *loqui* 'speak']

soliped /ˈsɒlɪpɛd/ *adj.* & *n.* ● *adj.* (of an animal) solid-hoofed. ● *n.* a solid-hoofed animal. [French *solipède* or modern Latin *solipes -pedis* from Latin *solidipes*, from *solidus* 'solid' + *pes* 'foot']

solipsism /ˈsɒlɪpsɪz(ə)m/ *n. Philos.* the view that the self is all that exists or can be known. □ **solipsist** *n.* **solipsistic** /-ˈsɪstɪk/ *adj.* **solipsistically** /-ˈsɪstɪk(ə)li/ *adv.* [Latin *solus* 'alone' + *ipse* 'self']

solitaire /ˈsɒlɪtɛː, sɒlɪˈtɛː/ *n.* **1** a diamond or other gem set by itself. **2** a ring having a single gem. **3** a game for one player played by removing pegs etc. one at a time from a board by jumping others over them until only one is left. **4** *N. Amer.* = PATIENCE 4. **5** either of two extinct flightless birds related to the dodo and formerly found in the Mascarene Islands. **6** any American thrush of the genus *Myadestes*. [French from Latin *solitarius* (as SOLITARY)]

solitary /ˈsɒlɪt(ə)ri/ *adj. & n.* ● *adj.* **1** living alone; not gregarious; without companions; lonely (*a solitary existence*). **2** (of a place) secluded or unfrequented. **3** single or sole (*a solitary instance*). **4** (of an insect) not living in communities. **5** *Bot.* growing singly, not in a cluster. ● *n.* (*pl.* **-ies**) **1** a recluse or hermit. **2** *colloq.* = SOLITARY CONFINEMENT. □ **solitarily** *adv.* **solitariness** *n.* [Middle English from Latin *solitarius*, from *solus* 'alone']

solitary confinement *n.* isolation of a prisoner in a separate cell as a punishment.

solitude /ˈsɒlɪtjuːd/ *n.* **1** the state of being solitary. **2** a lonely place. [Middle English from Old French *solitude* or Latin *solitudo*, from *solus* 'alone']

solmization /sɒlmɪˈzeɪʃ(ə)n/ *n.* (also **-isation**) *Mus.* a system of associating each note of a scale with a particular syllable, now usu. *doh ray me fah soh lah te*, with doh as C in the fixed-doh system and as the keynote in the movable-doh or tonic sol-fa system. □ **solmizate** /ˈsɒlmɪzeɪt/ *v.intr. & tr.* [French *solmisation* (as SOL[1], MI)]

solo /ˈsəʊləʊ/ *n., v., & adv.* ● *n.* (*pl.* **-os**) **1** (*pl.* **-os** or **soli** /-liː/) **a** a vocal or instrumental piece or passage, or a dance, performed by one person with or without accompaniment. **b** (*attrib.*) performed or performing as a solo (*solo passage*; *solo violin*). **2 a** an unaccompanied flight by a pilot in an aircraft. **b** anything done by one person unaccompanied. **c** (*attrib.*) unaccompanied, alone. **3** (in full **solo whist**) **a** a card game like whist in which one player may oppose the others. **b** a declaration or the act of playing to win five tricks at this. ● *v.* (**-oes, -oed**) **1** *intr.* perform a solo, esp. a solo flight or musical solo. **2** *tr.* perform or achieve as a solo. ● *adv.* unaccompanied, alone (*flew solo for the first time*). [Italian from Latin *solus* 'alone']

solo climbing *n.* the sport of climbing alone unaided by ropes etc. and without assistance from other people. □ **solo climber** *n.*

soloist /ˈsəʊləʊɪst/ *n.* a performer of a solo, esp. in music.

Solomon /ˈsɒləmən/ *n.* a very wise person. □ **Solomonic** /sɒləˈmɒnɪk/ *adj.* [*Solomon*, King of Israel in the 10th c. BC, famed for his wisdom]

Solomon's seal *n.* **1** a figure like the Star of David. **2** any plant of the genus *Polygonatum* (lily family), with arching stems and drooping green and white flowers.

solo stop *n.* an organ stop especially suitable for imitating a solo performance on another instrument.

solo whist see SOLO *n.* 3.

solstice /ˈsɒlstɪs/ *n.* **1** either of the two times in the year when the sun reaches its highest or lowest point in the sky at noon, marked by the longest and shortest days. Cf. SUMMER SOLSTICE, WINTER SOLSTICE. **2** the point in the ecliptic reached by the sun at a solstice. □ **solstitial** /sɒlˈstɪʃ(ə)l/ *adj.* [Middle English via Old French from Latin *solstitium*, from *sol* 'sun' + *sistere stit-* 'make stand']

solubilize /ˈsɒljʊbɪlʌɪz/ *v.tr.* (also **-ise**) make soluble or more soluble. □ **solubilization** /-ˈzeɪʃ(ə)n/ *n.*

soluble /ˈsɒljʊb(ə)l/ *adj.* **1** that can be dissolved, esp. in water. **2** that can be solved. □ **solubility** /-ˈbɪlɪti/ *n.* [Middle English via Old French from Late Latin *solubilis* (as SOLVE)]

soluble glass *n.* = WATER-GLASS 1.

solus /ˈsəʊləs/ *predic.adj.* (*fem.* **sola** /-lə/) (esp. in a stage direction) alone, unaccompanied. [Latin]

solute /ˈsɒljuːt, sɒˈljuːt/ *n.* a dissolved substance. [Latin *solutum*, neut. of *solutus*: see SOLVE]

solution /səˈluːʃ(ə)n/ *n.* **1** the act or a means of solving a problem or difficulty. **2 a** the conversion of a solid or gas into a liquid by mixture with a liquid solvent. **b** the state resulting from this (*held in solution*). **3** the act of dissolving or the state of being dissolved. **4** the act of separating or breaking. **5** = RUBBER SOLUTION. [Middle English via Old French from Latin *solutio -onis* (as SOLVE)]

solution set *n. Math.* the set of all the solutions of an equation or condition.

Solutrean /səˈluːtrɪən/ *adj. & n.* (also **Solutrian**) *Archaeol.* ● *adj.* of or relating to an upper palaeolithic culture in W. Europe, following the Aurignacian and dated to *c.*21,000–18,000 years ago. ● *n.* this culture. [*Solutré* in eastern France, where remains of it were found]

solvate /sɒlˈveɪt/ *v.intr. & tr.* enter or cause to enter into combination with a solvent. □ **solvation** /-ˈveɪʃ(ə)n/ *n.*

solve /sɒlv/ *v.tr.* find an answer to, or a means of removing or effectively dealing with (a problem or difficulty). □ **solvable** *adj.* **solver** *n.* [Middle English, = loosen, from Latin *solvere solut-* 'unfasten, release']

solvent /ˈsɒlv(ə)nt/ *adj. & n.* ● *adj.* **1** able to dissolve or form a solution with something. **2** having enough money to meet one's liabilities. ● *n.* **1** a solvent liquid etc. **2** a dissolving or weakening agent. □ **solvency** *n.* (in sense of *adj.*).

solvent abuse *n.* the use of volatile organic solvents as intoxicants by inhalation, e.g. glue-sniffing.

Som. *abbr.* Somerset.

soma[1] /ˈsəʊmə/ *n.* **1** the body as distinct from the soul. **2** the body of an organism as distinct from its reproductive cells. [Greek *sōma -atos* 'body']

soma[2] /ˈsəʊmə/ *n.* **1** an intoxicating drink used in Vedic ritual. **2** a plant yielding this. [Sanskrit *sōma*]

Somali /səˈmɑːli/ *n. & adj.* ● *n.* **1** (*pl.* same or **Somalis**) a member of a Hamitic Muslim people of Somalia in NE Africa. **2** the Cushitic language of this people. ● *adj.* of or relating to this people or language. □ **Somalian** *adj. & n.* [native name]

somatic /səˈmatɪk/ *adj.* of or relating to the body, esp. as distinct from the mind. □ **somatically** *adv.* [Greek *sōmatikos* (as SOMA[1])]

somatic cell *n.* any cell of a living organism except the reproductive cells.

somato- /ˈsəʊmətəʊ/ *comb. form* the human body. [Greek *sōma -atos* 'body']

somatogenic /ˌsəʊmətə(ʊ)ˈdʒɛnɪk/ *adj.* originating in the somatic cells.

somatology /səʊməˈtɒlədʒi/ *n.* the science of living bodies physically considered.

somatotonic /ˌsəʊmətə(ʊ)ˈtɒnɪk/ *adj.* having an extrovert and aggressive temperament, thought to be associated esp. with a mesomorphic physique.

somatotrophin /ˌsəʊmətə(ʊ)ˈtrəʊfɪn/ *n.* a growth hormone secreted by the pituitary gland. [as SOMATO-, TROPHIC]

somatotype /ˈsəʊmətə(ʊ)tʌɪp/ *n.* physique expressed in relation to various extreme types.

sombre /ˈsɒmbə/ *adj.* (also *US* **somber**) **1** dark, gloomy (*a sombre sky*). **2** oppressively solemn or sober. **3** dismal, foreboding (*a sombre prospect*). □ **sombrely** *adv.* **sombreness** *n.* [French *sombre* from Old French *sombre* (*n.*), ultimately from Latin SUB- + *umbra* 'shade']

sombrero /sɒmˈbrɛːrəʊ/ *n.* (*pl.* **-os**) a broad-brimmed felt or straw hat worn esp. in Mexico and the south western US. [Spanish, from *sombra* 'shade' (as SOMBRE)]

some /sʌm, s(ə)m/ *det., pron., & adv.* ● *det.* **1** an unspecified amount or number of (*some water*; *some apples*; *some of them*). **2** that is unknown or unnamed (*will return some day*; *some fool has locked the door*; *to some extent*). **3** denoting an approximate number (*waited some twenty minutes*). **4** a considerable amount or number of (*went to some trouble*). **5** (usu. stressed) **a** at least a small amount of (*do have some consideration*). **b** such to a certain extent (*that is some help*). **c** *colloq.* notably such (*I call that some story*). ● *pron.* some people or things, some number or amount (*I have some already*; *would you like some more?*). ● *adv. colloq.* to some extent (*we talked some*; *do it some more*). □ **and then some** *slang* and plenty more than that. **some few** see FEW. [Old English *sum*, from Germanic]

-some[1] /səm/ *suffix* forming adjectives meaning: **1** adapted to; productive of (*cuddlesome*; *fearsome*). **2** characterized by being (*fulsome*; *lithesome*). **3** apt to (*tiresome*; *meddlesome*). [Old English *-sum*]

-some[2] /səm/ *suffix* forming nouns from numerals, meaning 'a group of (so many)' (*foursome*). [Old English *sum* SOME, used after numerals in genitive pl.]

-some[3] /səʊm/ *comb. form* denoting a portion of a body, esp. of a cell (*chromosome*; *ribosome*). [Greek *sōma* 'body']

somebody /'sʌmbədi/ *pron. & n.* ● *pron.* some person. ● *n.* (*pl.* **-ies**) a person of importance (*is really somebody now*).

some day *adv.* (also **someday**) at some time in the future.

somehow /'sʌmhaʊ/ *adv.* **1** for some reason or other (*somehow I never liked them*). **2** in some unspecified or unknown way (*he somehow dropped behind*). **3** no matter how (*must get it finished somehow*).

someone /'sʌmwʌn/ *n. & pron.* = SOMEBODY.

someplace /'sʌmpleɪs/ *adv. N. Amer. colloq.* = SOMEWHERE.

somersault /'sʌməsɒlt, -sɔːlt/ *n. & v.* (also **summersault**) ● *n.* an acrobatic movement in which a person turns head over heels in the air or on the ground and lands on the feet. ● *v.intr.* perform a somersault. [Old French *sombresault*, alteration of *sobresault*, ultimately from Latin *supra* 'above' + *saltus* 'leap' from *salire* 'to leap']

something /'sʌmθɪŋ/ *n., pron., & adv.* ● *n. & pron.* **1 a** some unspecified or unknown thing (*have something to tell you*; *something has happened*). **b** (in full **something or other**) as a substitute for an unknown or forgotten description (*a student of something or other*). **2** a known or understood but unexpressed quantity, quality, or extent (*there is something about it I do not like*; *is something of a fool*). **3** *colloq.* an important or notable person or thing (*the party was quite something*). ● *adv. archaic* in some degree. □ **or something** or some unspecified alternative possibility (*must have run away or something*). **see something of** encounter (a person) briefly or occasionally. **something else 1** something different. **2** *colloq.* something exceptional. **something like 1** an amount in the region of (*left something like a million pounds*). **2** somewhat like (*shaped something like a cigar*). **3** *colloq.* impressive; a fine specimen of. **something of** to some extent; in some sense (*is something of an expert*). [Old English *sum thing* (as SOME, THING)]

sometime /'sʌmtʌɪm/ *adv. & adj.* ● *adv.* **1** at some unspecified time. **2** *archaic* formerly. ● *attrib.adj.* former (*the sometime mayor*).

sometimes /'sʌmtʌɪmz/ *adv.* at some times; occasionally.

somewhat /'sʌmwɒt/ *adv., n., & pron.* ● *adv.* to some extent (*behaviour that was somewhat strange*; *answered somewhat hastily*). ● *n. & pron. archaic* something (*loses somewhat of its force*). □ **more than somewhat** *colloq.* very (*was more than somewhat perplexed*).

somewhen /'sʌmwɛn/ *adv. colloq.* at some time.

somewhere /'sʌmwɛː/ *adv. & pron.* ● *adv.* in or to some place. ● *pron.* some unspecified place. □ **get somewhere** *colloq.* achieve success. **somewhere about** approximately.

somite /'səʊmʌɪt/ *n.* = METAMERE. □ **somitic** /səʊ'mɪtɪk/ *adj.* [Greek *sōma* 'body' + -ITE[1]]

sommelier /'sɒm(ə)ljeɪ, sə'mɛljeɪ/ *n.* a wine waiter. [French, = butler, from *somme* 'a pack' (as SUMPTER)]

somnambulism /sɒm'nambjʊlɪz(ə)m/ *n.* **1** sleepwalking. **2** a condition of the brain inducing this. □ **somnambulant** *adj.* **somnambulantly** *adv.* **somnambulist** *n.* **somnambulistic** /-'lɪstɪk/ *adj.* **somnambulistically** /-'lɪstɪk(ə)li/ *adv.* [Latin *somnus* 'sleep' + *ambulare* 'to walk']

somniferous /sɒm'nɪf(ə)rəs/ *adj.* inducing sleep; soporific. [Latin *somnifer* from *somnium* 'dream']

somnolent /'sɒmnəl(ə)nt/ *adj.* **1** sleepy, drowsy. **2** inducing drowsiness. **3** *Med.* in a state between sleeping and waking. □ **somnolence** *n.* **somnolency** *n.* **somnolently** *adv.* [Middle English from Old French *sompnolent* or Latin *somnolentus*, from *somnus* 'sleep']

son /sʌn/ *n.* **1** a boy or man in relation to either or both of his parents. **2 a** a male descendant. **b** (foll. by *of*) a male member of a family, nation, etc. **3** a person regarded as inheriting an occupation, quality, etc., or associated with a particular attribute (*sons of freedom*; *sons of the soil*). **4** (in full **my son**) a form of address esp. to a boy. **5** (**the Son**) (in Christian belief) the second person of the Trinity. □ **sonless** *adj.* **sonship** *n.* [Old English *sunu*, from Germanic]

sonant /'səʊnənt/ *adj. & n. Phonet.* ● *adj.* (of a sound) voiced and syllabic. ● *n.* a voiced sound forming a syllable, a vowel, or any of the consonants *l*, *m*, *n* pronounced as a syllable. □ **sonancy** *n.* [Latin *sonare sonant-* 'to sound']

sonar /'səʊnɑː/ *n.* **1** a system for the underwater detection of objects by reflected or emitted sound. **2** an apparatus for this. [*so*und *na*vigation and *r*anging, on the pattern of *radar*]

sonata /sə'nɑːtə/ *n.* a composition for one instrument or two (one usu. being a piano accompaniment), usu. in several movements with one (esp. the first) or more in sonata form. [Italian, = sounded (originally as distinct from 'sung'): fem. past part. of *sonare* 'sound']

sonata form *n.* a type of composition in three sections (exposition, development, and recapitulation) in which two themes (or subjects) are explored according to set key relationships.

sonatina /sɒnə'tiːnə/ *n.* a simple or short sonata. [Italian, diminutive of SONATA]

sonde /sɒnd/ *n.* a device sent up to obtain information about atmospheric conditions, esp. = RADIOSONDE. [French, = sounding (line)]

sone /səʊn/ *n.* a unit of subjective loudness, equal to 40 phons. [Latin *sonus* 'a sound']

son et lumière /sɒn eɪ 'luːmjɛː, French sɔ̃n e lymjɛr/ *n.* an entertainment by night at a historic monument, building, etc., using lighting effects and recorded sound to give a dramatic narrative of its history. [French, = sound and light]

song /sɒŋ/ *n.* **1** a short poem or other set of words set to music or meant to be sung. **2** singing or vocal music (*burst into song*). **3** a musical composition suggestive of a song. **4** the usu. repeated musical call of some birds or insects. **5** a short poem in rhymed stanzas. **6** *archaic* poetry or verse. □ **for a song** *colloq.* very cheaply. **on song** *Brit. colloq.* performing exceptionally well. □ **songless** *adj.* [Old English *sang*, from Germanic (as SING)]

song and dance *n. colloq.* a fuss or commotion.

songbird /'sɒŋbəːd/ *n.* **1** a bird with a musical call. **2** *Zool.* a perching bird of the group Oscines, possessing a syrinx.

songbook /'sɒŋbʊk/ *n.* a collection of songs with music.

song cycle *n.* a set of musically linked songs on a romantic theme.

Song of Songs *n.* (also **Song of Solomon**) a poetic Old Testament book traditionally attributed to Solomon.

songsmith /'sɒŋsmɪθ/ *n.* a writer of songs.

song sparrow *n.* a N. American sparrow-like bird, *Melospiza melodia*, of the bunting family, with a characteristic musical song.

songster /'sɒŋstə/ *n.* (*fem.* **songstress** /-strɪs/) **1** a singer, esp. a fluent and skilful one. **2** a songbird. **3** a poet. **4** *US* a songbook. [Old English *sangestre* (as SONG, -STER)]

song thrush *n.* a thrush, *Turdus philomelos*, of Europe and W. Asia, with a song partly mimicked from other birds.

songwriter /'sɒŋrʌɪtə/ *n.* a writer of songs or the music for them. □ **songwriting** *n.*

sonic /ˈsɒnɪk/ *adj.* of or relating to or using sound or sound waves. ▫ **sonically** *adv.* [Latin *sonus* 'sound']

sonic barrier *n.* = SOUND BARRIER.

sonic boom *n.* (also **sonic bang**) a loud explosive noise caused by the shock wave from an aircraft when it passes the speed of sound.

sonic mine *n.* a mine exploded by the sound of a passing ship.

son-in-law *n.* (*pl.* **sons-in-law**) the husband of one's daughter.

sonnet /ˈsɒnɪt/ *n.* & *v.* ● *n.* a poem of 14 lines using any of a number of formal rhyme schemes, in English usu. having ten syllables per line. ● *v.* (**sonneted**, **sonneting**) **1** *intr.* write sonnets. **2** *tr.* address sonnets to. [French *sonnet* or Italian *sonetto*, diminutive of *suono* SOUND[1]]

sonneteer /sɒnɪˈtɪə/ *n.* usu. *derog.* a writer of sonnets.

sonny /ˈsʌni/ *n. colloq.* a familiar form of address to a young boy.

sonobuoy /ˈsəʊnəbɔɪ/ *n.* a buoy for detecting underwater sounds and transmitting them by radio. [Latin *sonus* 'sound' + BUOY]

son of a bitch *n.* (*pl.* **sons of bitches**) *slang* a general term of contempt or abuse.

son of a gun *n.* (*pl.* **sons of guns**) *colloq.* a jocular or affectionate form of address or reference.

sonogram /ˈsəʊnəgram/ *n.* **1** a graph representing a sound, showing the distribution of energy at different frequencies. **2** esp. *Med.* a visual image produced from an ultrasound examination. ▫ **sonograph** *n.* [Latin *sonus* 'sound' + -GRAM]

sonometer /səˈnɒmɪtə/ *n.* **1** an instrument for measuring the vibration frequency of a string etc. **2** an audiometer. [Latin *sonus* 'sound' + -METER]

sonorous /ˈsɒn(ə)rəs, səˈnɔːrəs/ *adj.* **1** having a loud, full, or deep sound; resonant. **2** (of a speech, style, etc.) imposing, grand. ▫ **sonority** /səˈnɒrɪti/ *n.* (*pl.* **-ies**). **sonorously** *adv.* **sonorousness** *n.* [Latin *sonorus* from *sonor* 'sound']

sonsy /ˈsɒnsi/ *adj.* (also **sonsie**) (**sonsier**, **sonsiest**) *Sc.* **1** plump, buxom. **2** of a cheerful disposition. **3** bringing good fortune. [ultimately via Irish & Gaelic *sonas* 'good fortune' from *sona* 'fortunate']

sook /suːk, sʊk/ *n.* esp. *Austral.* & *NZ colloq.* **1** *derog.* a timid bashful person; a coward or sissy. **2** a hand-reared calf. [English dialect *suck*, used to call a calf]

sool /suːl/ *v.tr.* esp. *Austral.* & *NZ* **1** (of a dog) attack or worry (an animal). **2** (often foll. by *on*) urge or goad. ▫ **sooler** *n.* [variant of 17th-c. (now dialect) *sowl* 'seize by the ears', of unknown origin]

soon /suːn/ *adv.* **1** after a short interval of time (*shall soon know the result*). **2** relatively early (*must you go so soon?*). **3** (prec. by *how*) early (with relative rather than distinctive sense) (*how soon will it be ready?*). **4** readily or willingly (in expressing choice or preference: *which would you sooner do?*; *would as soon stay behind*). ▫ **as** (or **so**) **soon as** (implying a causal or temporal connection) at the moment that; not later than; as early as (*came as soon as I heard about it*; *disappears as soon as it's time to pay*). **no sooner ... than** at the very moment that (*we no sooner arrived than the rain stopped*; *no sooner had I gone out then it began to rain*). **sooner or later** at some future time; eventually. ▫ **soonish** *adv.* [Old English *sōna*, from West Germanic]

▪ **Usage** *No sooner* should be followed by *than* as shown above, and not by *when*.

soot /sʊt/ *n.* & *v.* ● *n.* a black carbonaceous substance rising in fine flakes in the smoke of wood, coal, oil, etc., and deposited on the sides of a chimney etc. ● *v.tr.* cover with soot. [Old English *sōt*, from Germanic]

sooth /suːθ/ *n. archaic* truth, fact. ▫ **in sooth** really, truly. [Old English *sōth* (originally *adj.*, = true), from Germanic]

soothe /suːð/ *v.tr.* **1** calm (a person or feelings). **2** soften or mitigate (pain). **3** *archaic* flatter or humour. ▫ **soother** *n.* **soothing** *adj.* **soothingly** *adv.* [Old English *sōthian* 'verify' from *sōth* 'true': see SOOTH]

soothsayer /ˈsuːθseɪə/ *n.* a diviner or seer. [Middle English, = a person who says the truth: see SOOTH]

sooty /ˈsʊti/ *adj.* (**sootier**, **sootiest**) **1** covered with or full of soot. **2** (esp. of an animal or bird) black or brownish black. ▫ **sootily** *adv.* **sootiness** *n.*

sop /sɒp/ *n.* & *v.* ● *n.* **1** a thing given or done to pacify or bribe. **2** a piece of bread etc. dipped in gravy etc. ● *v.* (**sopped**, **sopping**) **1** *intr.* be drenched (*came home sopping*; *sopping wet clothes*). **2** *tr.* (foll. by *up*) absorb (liquid) in a towel etc. **3** *tr.* wet thoroughly; soak. [Old English *sopp*, corresponding to Middle Low German *soppe*, Old High German *sopfa* 'bread and milk', probably from a weak grade of the base of Old English *sūpan*: see SUP[1]]

sophism /ˈsɒfɪz(ə)m/ *n.* a false argument, esp. one intended to deceive. [Middle English from Old French *sophime* via Latin from Greek *sophisma* 'clever device', via *sophizomai* 'become wise' from *sophos* 'wise']

sophist /ˈsɒfɪst/ *n.* **1** a person who reasons with clever but fallacious arguments. **2** *Gk Antiq.* a paid teacher of philosophy and rhetoric, esp. one associated with moral scepticism and specious reasoning. ▫ **sophistic** /-ˈfɪstɪk/ *adj.* **sophistical** /səˈfɪstɪk(ə)l/ *adj.* **sophistically** /səˈfɪstɪk(ə)li/ *adv.* [Latin *sophistes* from Greek *sophistēs*, from *sophizomai*: see SOPHISM]

sophisticate *v.*, *adj.*, & *n.* ● *v.* /səˈfɪstɪkeɪt/ **1** *tr.* make (a person etc.) educated, cultured, or refined. **2** *tr.* make (equipment or techniques etc.) highly developed or complex. **3** *tr.* **a** involve (a subject) in sophistry. **b** mislead (a person) by sophistry. **4** *tr.* deprive (a person or thing) of its natural simplicity, make artificial by worldly experience etc. **5** *tr.* tamper with (a text etc.) for purposes of argument etc. **6** *tr.* adulterate (wine etc.). **7** *intr.* use sophistry. ● *adj.* /səˈfɪstɪkət/ sophisticated. ● *n.* /səˈfɪstɪkət/ a sophisticated person. ▫ **sophistication** /-ˈkeɪʃ(ə)n/ *n.* [medieval Latin *sophisticare* 'tamper with' from *sophisticus* (as SOPHISM)]

sophisticated /səˈfɪstɪkeɪtɪd/ *adj.* **1 a** (of a person) cultured and refined; discriminating in taste and judgement. **b** appealing to sophisticated people or sophisticated taste. **2** (of a thing, idea, etc.) highly developed and complex. ▫ **sophisticatedly** *adv.*

sophistry /ˈsɒfɪstri/ *n.* (*pl.* **-ies**) **1** the use of sophisms. **2** a sophism.

sophomore /ˈsɒfəmɔː/ *n. N. Amer.* a second-year university or high school student. ▫ **sophomoric** /-ˈmɒrɪk/ *adj.* [earlier *sophumer* from *sophum*, obsolete variant of SOPHISM]

Sophy /ˈsəʊfi/ *n.* (*pl.* **-ies**) *hist.* a ruler of Persia in the 16th–17th c. [Persian *ṣafī* surname of the dynasty, from Arabic *ṣafī-ud-dīn* 'pure of religion', title of the founder's ancestor]

soporific /sɒpəˈrɪfɪk/ *adj.* & *n.* ● *adj.* tending to produce sleep. ● *n.* a soporific drug or influence. ▫ **soporiferous** *adj.* **soporifically** *adv.* [Latin *sopor* 'sleep' + -FIC]

sopping /ˈsɒpɪŋ/ *adj.* (also **sopping wet**) soaked with liquid; wet through. [pres. part. of SOP *v.*]

soppy /ˈsɒpi/ *adj.* (**soppier**, **soppiest**) **1** *Brit. colloq.* **a** silly or foolish in a feeble or self-indulgent way. **b** mawkishly sentimental. **2** (foll. by *on*) *Brit. colloq.* foolishly infatuated with. **3** soaked with water. ▫ **soppily** *adv.* **soppiness** *n.* [SOP + -Y[1]]

sopranino /sɒprəˈniːnəʊ/ *n.* (*pl.* **-os**) *Mus.* an instrument higher than soprano, esp. a recorder or saxophone. [Italian, diminutive of SOPRANO]

soprano /səˈprɑːnəʊ/ *n.* (*pl.* **-os**) **1 a** the highest singing voice. **b** a female or boy singer with this voice. **c** a part written for it. **2 a** an instrument of a high or the highest pitch in its family. **b** the player of such an instrument. [Italian from *sopra* 'above', from Latin *supra*]

soprano clef *n.* an obsolete clef placing middle C on the lowest line of the staff.

soprano recorder *n. N. Amer.* = DESCANT RECORDER.

sora /ˈsɔːrə, ˈsəʊrə/ *n.* (in full **sora rail**) a bird, *Porzana carolina*, frequenting the marshes of N. and S. Carolina etc. in the autumn and used as food. [probably a native name]

sorb /sɔːb/ *n.* **1** = SERVICE TREE. **2** (in full **sorb-apple**) the fruit of this. [French *sorbe* or Latin *sorbus* 'service tree', *sorbum* 'service-berry']

sorbefacient /sɔːbɪˈfeɪʃ(ə)nt/ *adj.* & *n. Med.* ● *adj.* causing absorption. ● *n.* a sorbefacient drug etc. [Latin *sorbēre* 'suck in' + -FACIENT]

sorbet /ˈsɔːbeɪ, -bɪt/ *n.* **1** a water ice. **2** sherbet. [French via Italian *sorbetto* from Turkish *şerbet*, from Arabic *šarba* 'to drink': cf. SHERBET]

sorbitol /ˈsɔːbɪtɒl/ *n.* a sweet-tasting crystalline alcohol found in some fruit, used in industry and as a food additive. [SORB + -ITE[1] + -OL[1]]

Sorbo /ˈsɔːbəʊ/ *n.* (in full **Sorbo rubber**) *Brit. propr.* a spongy rubber. [ABSORB + -O]

sorcerer /ˈsɔːs(ə)rə/ *n.* (*fem.* **sorceress** /-rɪs/) a person who claims to use magic powers; a magician or wizard. □ **sorcerous** *adj.* **sorcery** *n.* (*pl.* **-ies**). [obsolete *sorcer* from Old French *sorcier*, ultimately from Latin *sors sortis* 'lot']

sordid /ˈsɔːdɪd/ *adj.* **1** dirty or squalid. **2** ignoble, mean, or mercenary. **3** mean or niggardly. **4** dull-coloured. □ **sordidly** *adv.* **sordidness** *n.* [French *sordide* or Latin *sordidus*, from *sordēre* 'be dirty']

sordino /sɔːˈdiːnəʊ/ *n.* (*pl.* **sordini** /-ni/) *Mus.* a mute for a bowed or wind instrument. [Italian from *sordo* 'mute', from Latin *surdus*]

sore /sɔː/ *adj., n., & adv.* ● *adj.* **1** (of a part of the body) painful from injury or disease (*has a sore arm*). **2** (of a person) suffering pain. **3** (often foll. by *about, at*) aggrieved or vexed. **4** *archaic* grievous or severe (*in sore need*). ● *n.* **1** a raw or tender place on the body. **2** a source of distress or annoyance (*reopen old sores*). ● *adv. archaic* grievously, severely. □ **soreness** *n.* [Old English *sār* (*n.* & *adj.*), *sāre* (*adv.*), from Germanic]

sorehead /ˈsɔːhɛd/ *n. N. Amer. colloq.* a touchy or disgruntled person.

sorel /ˈsɒr(ə)l/ *n. Brit.* a male fallow deer in its third year. [variant of SORREL[2]]

sorely /ˈsɔːli/ *adv.* **1** extremely, badly (*am sorely tempted*; *sorely in need of repair*). **2** severely (*am sorely vexed*). [Old English *sārlīce* (as SORE, -LY[2])]

sore point *n.* a subject causing distress or annoyance.

sore throat *n.* an inflammation of the lining membrane at the back of the mouth etc.

sorghum /ˈsɔːgəm/ *n.* any tropical cereal grass of the genus *Sorghum*, e.g. durra. [modern Latin from Italian *sorgo*, perhaps from unrecorded Romanic *syricum* (*gramen*) 'Syrian (grass)']

sori *pl.* of SORUS.

soroptimist /səˈrɒptɪmɪst/ *n.* a member of an international association of clubs for professional and business women. [Latin *soror* 'sister' + OPTIMIST (as OPTIMISM)]

sorority /səˈrɒrɪti/ *n.* (*pl.* **-ies**) *N. Amer.* a female students' society in a university or college. [medieval Latin *sororitas* or Latin *soror* 'sister', on the pattern of *fraternity*]

sorosis /səˈrəʊsɪs/ *n.* (*pl.* **soroses** /-siːz/) *Bot.* a fleshy compound fruit, e.g. a pineapple or mulberry. [modern Latin from Greek *sōros* 'heap']

sorption /ˈsɔːpʃ(ə)n/ *n.* absorption or adsorption happening jointly or separately. [back-formation from *absorption, adsorption*]

sorrel[1] /ˈsɒr(ə)l/ *n.* **1** any acid-leaved plant of the dock family, esp. *Rumex acetosa*, used in salads and for flavouring. **2** any of various plants with acid leaves (*wood sorrel*). [Middle English from Old French *surele, sorele*, from Germanic]

sorrel[2] /ˈsɒr(ə)l/ *adj.* & *n.* ● *adj.* of a light reddish-brown colour. ● *n.* **1** this colour. **2** a sorrel animal, esp. a horse. **3** *Brit.* a sorel. [Middle English via Old French *sorel*, from *sor* 'yellowish', from Frankish]

sorrow /ˈsɒrəʊ/ *n.* & *v.* ● *n.* **1** mental distress caused by loss or disappointment etc. **2** a cause of sorrow. **3** lamentation. ● *v.intr.* **1** feel sorrow. **2** mourn. □ **sorrower** *n.* **sorrowing** *adj.* [Old English *sorh, sorg*]

sorrowful /ˈsɒrə(ʊ)fʊl, -f(ə)l/ *adj.* **1** feeling or showing sorrow. **2** distressing, lamentable. □ **sorrowfully** *adv.* **sorrowfulness** *n.* [Old English *sorhful* (as SORROW, -FUL)]

sorry /ˈsɒri/ *adj.* (**sorrier, sorriest**) **1** (*predic.*) pained or regretful or penitent (*were sorry for what they had done*; *am sorry that you have to go*). **2** (*predic.*; foll. by *for*) feeling pity or sympathy for (a person). **3** as an expression of apology. **4** wretched; in a poor state (*a sorry sight*). □ **sorry for oneself** dejected. □ **sorrily** *adv.* **sorriness** *n.* [Old English *sārig*, from West Germanic (as SORE, -Y[2])]

sort /sɔːt/ *n.* & *v.* ● *n.* **1** a group of things etc. with common attributes; a class or kind. **2** (foll. by *of*) roughly of the kind specified (*is some sort of doctor*). **3** *colloq.* a person of a specified character or kind (*a good sort*). **4** *Printing* a letter or piece in a fount of type. **5** *Computing* the arrangement of data in a prescribed sequence. **6** *archaic* a manner or way. ● *v.tr.* **1** (often foll. by *out, over*) arrange systematically or according to type, class, etc. **2** = *sort out* 3, 4. □ **after a sort** after a fashion. **in some sort** to a certain extent. **of a sort** (or **of sorts**) *colloq.* not fully deserving the name (*a holiday of sorts*). **out of sorts 1** slightly unwell. **2** in low spirits; irritable. **sort of** *colloq.* as it were; to some extent (*I sort of expected it*). **sort out 1** separate into sorts. **2** select (things of one or more sorts) from a miscellaneous group. **3** disentangle or put into order. **4 a** resolve (a problem or difficulty). **b** solve the problems of (a person). **5** *colloq.* deal with or reprimand (a person). □ **sortable** *adj.* **sorter** *n.* **sorting** *n.* [Middle English from Old French *sorte*, ultimately from Latin *sors sortis* 'lot, condition']

■ **Usage** See Usage Note at KIND[1].

sortie /ˈsɔːtiː/ *n.* & *v.* ● *n.* **1** a sally, esp. from a besieged garrison. **2** an operational flight by a single military aircraft. ● *v.intr.* (**sorties, sortied, sortieing**) make a sortie; sally. [French, fem. past part. of *sortir* 'go out']

sortilege /ˈsɔːtɪlɪdʒ/ *n.* divination by lots. [Middle English via Old French from medieval Latin *sortilegium* 'sorcery', from Latin *sortilegus* 'sorcerer' (as SORT, *legere* 'choose')]

sorting office *n.* an office in which mail is sorted according to its destination.

sort-out *n.* an act of sorting out or putting something in order.

sorus /ˈsɔːrəs/ *n.* (*pl.* **sori** /-rʌɪ/) *Bot.* a heap or cluster, esp. of spore cases on the undersurface of a fern leaf, or in a fungus or lichen. [modern Latin from Greek *sōros* 'heap']

SOS *n.* (*pl.* **SOSs**) **1** an international code-signal of extreme distress, used esp. by ships at sea. **2** an urgent appeal for help. **3** *Brit.* a message broadcast to an untraceable person in an emergency. [chosen as being easily transmitted and recognized in Morse code; by folk etymology an abbreviation of *save our souls*]

sostenuto /sɒstəˈnuːtəʊ/ *adv., adj., & n. Mus.* ● *adv.* & *adj.* in a sustained or prolonged manner. ● *n.* (*pl.* **-os**) a passage to be played in this way. [Italian, past part. of *sostenere* SUSTAIN]

sot /sɒt/ *n.* & *v.* ● *n.* a habitual drunkard. ● *v.intr.* (**sotted, sotting**) tipple. □ **sottish** *adj.* [Old English *sott* and Old French *sot* 'foolish', from medieval Latin *sottus*, of unknown origin]

soteriology /sə(ʊ)ˌtɪərɪˈɒlədʒi, sɒ-/ *n. Theol.* the doctrine of salvation. □ **soteriological** /-rɪəˈlɒdʒɪk(ə)l/ *adj.* [Greek *sōtēria* 'salvation' + -LOGY]

Sothic /ˈsəʊθɪk, ˈsɒθ-/ *adj.* of or relating to the dog-star, esp. with reference to the ancient Egyptian year fixed by its heliacal rising. [Greek *Sōthis*, from the Egyptian name of the dog-star]

sotto voce /sɒtəʊ 'vəʊtʃi, Italian sotto 'votʃe/ *adv.* in an undertone or aside. [Italian *sotto* 'under' + *voce* 'voice']

sou /suː/ *n.* **1** *hist.* a former French coin of low value. **2** (usu. with *neg.*) *colloq.* a very small amount of money (*hasn't a sou*). [French, originally pl. *sous*, via Old French *sout* from Latin SOLIDUS]

soubrette /suː'brɛt/ *n.* **1** a pert maidservant or similar female character in a comedy. **2** an actress taking this part. [French from Provençal *soubreto*, fem. of *soubret* 'coy' from *sobrar*, from Latin *superare* 'be above']

soubriquet var. of SOBRIQUET.

souchong /'suːʃɒŋ/ *n.* a fine black kind of China tea. [Chinese *xiao* 'small' + *zhong* 'sort']

souffle /'suːf(ə)l/ *n. Med.* a low murmur heard in the auscultation of various organs etc. [French from *souffler* 'to blow', from Latin *sufflare*]

soufflé /'suːfleɪ/ *n. & adj.* ● *n.* **1** a light spongy dish usu. made with flavoured egg yolks added to stiffly beaten whites of eggs and baked (*cheese soufflé*). **2** any of various light sweet or savoury dishes made with beaten egg whites. ● *adj.* **1** light and frothy or spongy (*omelette soufflé*). **2** (of ceramics) decorated with small spots. [French, past part. of *souffler* (as SOUFFLE)]

sough /saʊ, sʌf/ *v. & n.* ● *v.intr.* make a moaning, whistling, or rushing sound, as of the wind in trees etc. ● *n.* this sound. [Old English *swōgan* 'resound']

sought *past* and *past part.* of SEEK.

sought after *adj.* (hyphenated when *attrib.*) much in demand; generally desired or courted.

souk /suːk/ *n.* (also **suk**, **sukh**, **suq**) an Arab market or market place; a bazaar. [Arabic *sūḳ*]

soul /səʊl/ *n.* **1** the spiritual or immaterial part of a human being or animal, often regarded as immortal. **2** the moral, emotional, or intellectual nature of a person. **3** the personification or pattern of something (*the very soul of discretion*). **4** an individual (*not a soul in sight*). **5 a** a person regarded with familiarity or pity etc. (*the poor soul was utterly confused*). **b** a person regarded as embodying moral or intellectual qualities (*left that to meaner souls*). **6** a person regarded as the animating or essential part of something (*the life and soul of the party*). **7** emotional or intellectual energy or intensity, esp. as revealed in a work of art (*pictures that lack soul*). **8** = SOUL MUSIC. □ **the soul of honour** a person incapable of dishonourable conduct. **upon my soul** an exclamation of surprise. □ **-souled** *adj.* (in *comb.*). [Old English *sāwol, sāwel, sāwl*, from Germanic]

soul-destroying *adj.* (of an activity etc.) deadeningly monotonous.

soul food *n.* the traditional food of American blacks.

soulful /'səʊlfʊl, -f(ə)l/ *adj.* **1** having or expressing or evoking deep feeling. **2** *colloq.* over-emotional. □ **soulfully** *adv.* **soulfulness** *n.*

soulless /'səʊllɪs/ *adj.* **1** lacking sensitivity or noble qualities. **2** having no soul. **3** undistinguished or uninteresting. □ **soullessly** *adv.* **soullessness** *n.*

soulmate /'səʊlmeɪt/ *n.* a person ideally suited to another.

soul music *n.* a kind of music incorporating elements of rhythm and blues and gospel music, popularized by American blacks.

soul-searching *n. & adj.* ● *n.* the examination of one's emotions and motives. ● *adj.* characterized by such examination.

sound[1] /saʊnd/ *n. & v.* ● *n.* **1** a sensation caused in the ear by the vibration of the surrounding air or other medium. **2 a** vibrations causing this sensation. **b** similar vibrations whether audible or not. **3** what is or may be heard. **4** an idea or impression conveyed by words (*don't like the sound of that*). **5** mere words (*sound and fury*). **6** (in full **musical sound**) sound produced by continuous and regular vibrations (cf. NOISE *n.* 3). **7** any of a series of articulate utterances (*vowel and consonant sounds*). **8** music, speech, etc., accompanying a film or other visual presentation. **9** (often *attrib.*) broadcasting by radio as distinct from television. ● *v.* **1** *intr. & tr.* emit or cause to emit sound. **2** *tr.* utter or pronounce (*sound a note of alarm*). **3** *intr.* convey an impression when heard (*you sound worried*). **4** *tr.* give an audible signal for (an alarm etc.). **5** *tr.* test (the lungs etc.) by noting the sound produced. **6** *tr.* cause to resound; make known (*sound their praises*). □ **sound off** talk loudly or express one's opinions forcefully. □ **soundless** *adj.* **soundlessly** *adv.* **soundlessness** *n.* [Middle English via Anglo-French *soun*, Old French *son* (nouns), Anglo-French *suner*, Old French *soner* (verbs) from Latin *sonus*]

sound[2] /saʊnd/ *adj. & adv.* ● *adj.* **1** healthy; not diseased or injured. **2** (of an opinion or policy etc.) correct, orthodox, well-founded, judicious. **3** financially secure (*a sound investment*). **4** undisturbed; tending to sleep deeply and unbrokenly (*sound sleep; a sound sleeper*). **5** severe, hard (*a sound blow*). ● *adv.* soundly (*sound asleep*). □ **soundly** *adv.* **soundness** *n.* [Middle English *sund, isund* from Old English *gesund*, from West Germanic]

sound[3] /saʊnd/ *v. & n.* ● *v.tr. & intr.* **1** *tr.* test the depth or quality of the bottom of (the sea or a river etc.). **2** *tr.* (often foll. by *out*) inquire (esp. cautiously or discreetly) into the opinions or feelings of (a person). **3** *tr.* find the depth of water in (a ship's hold). **4** *tr.* get records of temperature, humidity, pressure, etc. from (the upper atmosphere). **5** *tr.* examine (a person's bladder etc.) with a probe. **6** *intr.* (of a whale or fish) dive to the bottom. ● *n.* a surgeon's probe. □ **sounder** *n.* [Middle English from Old French *sonder*, ultimately from Latin SUB- + *unda* 'wave']

sound[4] /saʊnd/ *n.* **1 a** a narrow passage of water connecting two seas or a sea with a lake etc. **b** an arm of the sea. **2** a fish's swim-bladder. [Old English *sund*, = Old Norse *sund* 'swimming, strait', from Germanic: related to SWIM]

soundalike /'saʊndəlʌɪk/ *n.* a person or thing closely resembling another in sound.

sound barrier *n.* the high resistance of air to aircraft etc. moving at speeds near that of sound.

sound bite *n.* a short extract from a recorded interview, chosen for its pungency or appropriateness.

soundboard /'saʊn(d)bɔːd/ *n.* a thin sheet of wood over which the strings of a piano etc. pass to increase the sound produced.

soundbox /'saʊn(d)bɒks/ *n.* the hollow chamber providing resonance and forming the body of a stringed musical instrument.

sound card *n.* a device which can be slotted into a computer to allow the use of audio components for multimedia applications.

soundcheck /'saʊn(d)tʃɛk/ *n.* a test of sound equipment before a musical performance or recording to check that the desired sound is being produced.

sound effect *n.* a sound other than speech or music made artificially for use in a play, film, etc.

sound engineer *n.* an engineer dealing with acoustics etc., for a broadcast, musical performance, etc.

soundhole /'saʊndhəʊl/ *n.* an aperture in the belly of some stringed instruments.

sounding[1] /'saʊndɪŋ/ *n.* **1 a** the action or process of measuring the depth of water, now usu. by means of echo. **b** an instance of this (*took a sounding*). **2** (in *pl.*) **a** a region close to the shore of the right depth for sounding. **b** *Naut.* measurements taken by sounding. **c** cautious investigation (*made soundings as to his suitability*). **3 a** the determination of any physical property at a depth in the sea or at a height in the atmosphere. **b** an instance of this.

sounding[2] /'saʊndɪŋ/ *adj.* **1** giving forth (esp. loud or resonant) sound (*sounding brass*). **2** emptily boastful, resonant, or imposing (*sounding promises*).

sounding-balloon *n.* a balloon used to obtain information about the upper atmosphere (see SOUND[3] *v.* 4).

sounding board *n.* **1** a canopy over a pulpit etc. to direct sound towards the congregation. **2** = SOUNDBOARD. **3 a** a means of causing opinions etc. to be more widely known (*used his students as a sounding board*). **b** a person etc. used as a trial audience.

sounding line *n.* a line used in sounding the depth of water.

sounding rod *n.* a rod used in finding the depth of water in a ship's hold (see SOUND[3] *v.* 1).

sound post *n.* a small prop between the belly and back of some stringed instruments.

soundproof /ˈsaʊn(d)pruːf/ *adj. & v.* ● *adj.* impervious to sound. ● *v.tr.* make soundproof.

sound shift see SHIFT *n.* 6.

sound spectrograph *n.* an instrument for analysing sound into its frequency components.

sound system *n.* a set of equipment for the reproduction of sound.

soundtrack /ˈsaʊn(d)trak/ *n.* **1** the recorded sound element of a film. **2** this recorded on the edge of a film in optical or magnetic form.

sound wave *n.* a wave of compression and rarefaction, by which sound is propagated in an elastic medium, e.g. air.

soup /suːp/ *n. & v.* ● *n.* **1** a usu. savoury liquid dish made by boiling meat, fish, or vegetables etc. in stock or water. **2** *US slang* nitroglycerine or gelignite, esp. for safe-breaking. **3** *slang* the chemicals in which film is developed. **4** *colloq.* fog; thick cloud. ● *v.tr.* (foll. by *up*) (usu. as **souped-up** *adj.*) *colloq.* **1** increase the power and efficiency of (an engine). **2** increase the power or impact of (writing, music, etc.). ▫ **in the soup** *colloq.* in difficulties. [French *soupe* 'sop, broth', from Late Latin *suppa*, from Germanic]

soup and fish *n. colloq.* men's evening dress.

soupçon /ˈsuːpsɒn/ *n.* a very small quantity; a dash. [French via Old French *sou(s)peçon* from medieval Latin *suspectio -onis*: see SUSPICION]

soup kitchen *n.* a place dispensing soup etc. to the poor.

soup plate *n.* a deep wide-rimmed plate for serving soup.

soup spoon *n.* a large spoon with a round bowl for drinking soup.

soupy /ˈsuːpi/ *adj.* (**soupier, soupiest**) **1** of or resembling soup. **2** *colloq.* sentimental; mawkish. ▫ **soupily** *adv.* **soupiness** *n.*

sour /saʊə/ *adj., n., & v.* ● *adj.* **1** having an acid taste like lemon or vinegar, esp. because of unripeness (*sour apples*). **2 a** (of food, esp. milk or bread) bad because of fermentation. **b** smelling or tasting rancid or unpleasant. **3** (of a person, temper, etc.) harsh; morose; bitter. **4** (of a thing) unpleasant; distasteful. **5** (of the soil) deficient in lime and usually dank. ● *n.* **1** *N. Amer.* an alcoholic drink with lemon juice or lime juice (*whisky sour*). **2** an acid solution used in bleaching etc. ● *v.tr. & intr.* make or become sour (*soured the cream; soured by misfortune*). ▫ **go** (or **turn**) **sour 1** (of food etc.) become sour. **2** turn out badly (*the job went sour on him*). **3** lose one's keenness. ▫ **sourish** *adj.* **sourly** *adv.* **sourness** *n.* [Old English *sūr*, from Germanic]

source /sɔːs/ *n. & v.* ● *n.* **1** a spring or fountain from which a stream issues (*the sources of the Nile*). **2** a place, person, or thing from which something originates (*the source of all our troubles*). **3** a person or document etc. providing evidence (*reliable sources of information; historical source material*). **4 a** a body emitting radiation etc. **b** *Physics* a place from which a fluid or current flows. **c** *Electronics* a part of a transistor from which carriers flow into the interelectrode channel. ● *v.tr.* obtain (esp. components) from a specified source. ▫ **at source** at the point of origin or issue. [Middle English via Old French *sors, sourse*, past part. of *sourdre* 'rise', from Latin *surgere*]

sourcebook /ˈsɔːsbʊk/ *n.* a collection of documentary sources for the study of a subject.

source-criticism *n.* the evaluation of different, esp. successive, literary or historical sources.

sour cream *n.* cream deliberately fermented by adding bacteria.

sourdough /ˈsaʊədəʊ/ *n. N. Amer.* **1** a leaven for making bread etc., consisting of fermenting dough, originally that left over from a previous baking. **2** bread made from this. **3** an experienced prospector in Alaska etc.; an old timer. [dialect, = leaven, in allusion to piece of sour dough for raising bread baked in winter]

sour grapes *n.pl.* resentful disparagement of something one cannot personally acquire.

sour mash *n. US* a mash for brewing or distilling which is made acid to promote fermentation.

sourpuss /ˈsaʊəpʊs/ *n. colloq.* a sour-tempered person. [SOUR + PUSS = face]

soursop /ˈsaʊəsɒp/ *n.* **1** a W. Indian evergreen tree, *Annona muricata*. **2** the large succulent fruit of this tree.

sous- /suː(z)/ *prefix* (in words adopted from French) subordinate, under (*sous-chef*). [French]

sousaphone /ˈsuːzəfəʊn/ *n.* a large brass bass wind instrument encircling the player's body. ▫ **sousaphonist** /-ˈzɒf(ə)nɪst/ *n.* [named after J. P. *Sousa*, American bandmaster d. 1932, on the pattern of *saxophone*]

souse /saʊs/ *v. & n.* ● *v.* **1** *tr.* put (gherkins, fish, etc.) in pickle. **2** *tr. & intr.* plunge into liquid. **3** *tr.* (as **soused** *adj.*) *colloq.* drunk. **4** *tr.* (usu. foll. by *in*) soak (a thing) in liquid. **5** *tr.* (usu. foll. by *over*) throw (liquid) over a thing. ● *n.* **1 a** pickle made with salt. **b** *US* food, esp. a pig's head etc., in pickle. **2** a dip, plunge, or drenching in water. **3** *colloq.* **a** a drinking bout. **b** a drunkard. [Middle English via Old French *sous, souz* 'pickle' from Old Saxon *sultia*, Old High German *sulza* 'brine', from Germanic: related to SALT]

souslik /ˈsuːslɪk/ *n.* (also **suslik** /ˈsʌs-/) a Eurasian ground squirrel of the genus *Spermophilus*, esp. *S. citellus* of SE Europe. [Russian]

soutache /suːˈtaʃ/ *n.* a narrow flat ornamental braid used to trim garments. [French from Hungarian *sujtás*]

soutane /suːˈtɑːn/ *n. RC Ch.* a cassock worn by a priest. [French from Italian *sottana*, via *sotto* 'under' from Latin *subtus*]

souteneur /suːtəˈnəː, French sutənœr/ *n.* a pimp. [French, = protector]

souter /ˈsuːtə/ *n. Sc. & N.Engl.* a shoemaker; a cobbler. [Old English *sūtere* from Latin *sutor*, from *suere sut-* 'sew']

souterrain /ˈsuːtəreɪn/ *n.* esp. *Archaeol.* an underground chamber or passage. [French, from *sous* 'under' + *terre* 'earth']

south /saʊθ/ *n., adj., adv., & v.* ● *n.* **1** the point of the horizon 90° clockwise from east. **2** the compass point corresponding to this. **3** the direction in which this lies. **4** (usu. **the South**) **a** the part of the world or a country or a town lying to the south. **b** the southern states of the US. **5** *Bridge* a player occupying the position designated 'south'. ● *adj.* **1** towards, at, near, or facing the south (*a south wall; south country*). **2** coming from the south (*south wind*). ● *adv.* **1** towards, at, or near the south (*they travelled south*). **2** (foll. by *of*) further south than. ● *v.intr.* **1** move towards the south. **2** (of a celestial body) cross the meridian. ▫ **south by east** (or **west**) between south and south-south-east (or south-south-west). **to the south** (often foll. by *of*) in a southerly direction. [Old English *sūth*]

South African *adj. & n.* ● *adj.* of or relating to the republic of South Africa. ● *n.* **1** a native or national of South Africa. **2** a person of South African descent.

South American *adj. & n.* ● *adj.* of or relating to South America. ● *n.* a native or citizen of South America.

southbound /ˈsaʊθbaʊnd/ *adj.* travelling or leading southwards.

Southdown /ˈsaʊθdaʊn/ *n.* **1** a sheep of a breed raised esp. for mutton, originally on the South Downs of Hampshire and Sussex. **2** this breed.

South-East *n.* the part of a country or town lying to the south-east.

south-east *n., adj., & adv.* ● *n.* **1** the point of the horizon midway between south and east. **2** the compass point corresponding to this. **3** the direction in which this lies. ● *adj.* of, towards, or coming from the south-east. ● *adv.* towards, at, or near the south-east.

southeaster /saʊθˈiːstə/ *n.* a south-east wind.

south-easterly *adj. & adv.* = SOUTH-EAST.

south-eastern *adj.* lying on the south-east side.

south-eastward *adj. & adv.* (also **south-eastwards**) towards the south-east.

souther /ˈsaʊθə/ *n.* a south wind.

southerly /ˈsʌðəli/ *adj., adv., & n.* ● *adj. & adv.* **1** in a southern position or direction. **2** (of a wind) blowing from the south. ● *n.* (*pl.* **-ies**) a southerly wind.

southern /ˈsʌð(ə)n/ *adj.* esp. *Geog.* **1** of or in the south; inhabiting the south. **2** lying or directed towards the south (*at the southern end*). □ **southernmost** *adj.* [Old English *sūtherne* (as SOUTH, -ERN)]

Southern Cone *n.* the region of South America comprising the countries of Brazil, Paraguay, Uruguay, and Argentina.

Southern Cross *n.* a small but prominent constellation of the southern hemisphere, in the shape of a cross.

southerner /ˈsʌð(ə)nə/ *n.* a native or inhabitant of the south.

southern hemisphere *n.* the half of the earth below the equator.

southern lights *n.pl.* the aurora australis.

Southern Ocean *n.* the expanse of ocean surrounding Antarctica.

Southern States *n.pl.* the states in the south, esp. the south-east, of the US.

southernwood /ˈsʌð(ə)nwʊd/ *n.* a bushy kind of wormwood, *Artemisia abrotanum*. Also called *lad's love*.

southing /ˈsaʊθɪŋ/ *n.* **1** a southern movement. **2** *Naut.* the distance travelled or measured southward. **3** *Astron.* the angular distance of a star etc. south of the celestial equator.

southpaw /ˈsaʊθpɔː/ *n. & adj. colloq.* ● *n.* a left-handed person, esp. in boxing. ● *adj.* left-handed.

south pole see POLE² 1.

South Sea *n.* the southern Pacific Ocean.

South Sea Bubble *n. hist.* a scheme for trading in the southern hemisphere to repay the British national debt, which started and collapsed in 1720.

south-south-east *n.* the point or direction midway between south and south-east.

south-south-west *n.* the point or direction midway between south and south-west.

southward /ˈsaʊθwəd/ *adj., adv., & n.* ● *adj. & adv.* (also **southwards**) towards the south. ● *n.* a southward direction or region.

■ **Usage** In nautical use *southward* is often pronounced /ˈsʌðəd/.

South-West *n.* the part of a country or town lying to the south-west.

south-west *n., adj., & adv.* ● *n.* **1** the point of the horizon midway between south and west. **2** the compass point corresponding to this. **3** the direction in which this lies. ● *adj.* of, towards, or coming from the south-west. ● *adv.* towards, at, or near the south-west.

southwester /saʊθˈwɛstə/ *n.* a south-west wind.

south-westerly *adj. & adv.* = SOUTH-WEST.

south-western *adj.* lying on the south-west side.

south-westward *adj. & adv.* (also **south-westwards**) towards the south west.

south wind *n.* a wind blowing from the south.

souvenir /suːvəˈnɪə/ *n. & v.* ● *n.* (often foll. by *of*) a memento of an occasion, place, etc. ● *v.tr. Brit. slang* take as a souvenir; pilfer, steal. [French from *souvenir* 'remember', from Latin *subvenire* 'occur to the mind' (as SUB-, *venire* 'come')]

souvlaki /suːˈvlɑːki/ *n.* (*pl.* **souvlakia** /-kɪə/ or **souvlakis**) a Greek dish of pieces of meat grilled on a skewer. [modern Greek]

sou'wester /saʊˈwɛstə/ *n.* **1** = SOUTHWESTER. **2** a waterproof hat with a broad flap covering the neck.

sov /sɒv/ *n. Brit. colloq.* a sovereign, esp. *hist.* = SOVEREIGN *n.* 2. [abbreviation]

sovereign /ˈsɒvrɪn/ *n. & adj.* ● *n.* **1** a supreme ruler, esp. a monarch. **2** *Brit. hist.* a gold coin nominally worth £1. ● *adj.* **1 a** supreme (*sovereign power*). **b** unmitigated (*sovereign contempt*). **2** excellent; effective (*a sovereign remedy*). **3** possessing sovereign power (*a sovereign state*). **4** royal (*our sovereign lord*). □ **sovereignly** *adv.* [Middle English via Old French *so(u)verain* from Latin: *-g-* by association with *reign*]

sovereign good *n.* (prec. by *the*) the greatest good, esp. for a state, its people, etc.

sovereign pontiff see PONTIFF.

sovereignty /ˈsɒvrɪnti/ *n.* (*pl.* **-ies**) **1** supremacy. **2** self-government. **3** a self-governing state.

soviet /ˈsəʊvɪət, ˈsɒv-/ *n. & adj. hist.* ● *n.* **1** an elected local, district, or national council in the former USSR. **2** (**Soviet**) a citizen of the former USSR. **3** *hist.* a revolutionary council of workers, peasants, etc., in Russia before 1917. ● *adj.* (usu. **Soviet**) of or concerning the former Soviet Union. □ **Sovietize** *v.tr.* (also **-ise**). **Sovietization** /-tʌɪˈzeɪʃ(ə)n/ *n.* [Russian *sovet* 'council']

sovietologist /səʊvɪəˈtɒlədʒɪst, sɒ-/ *n.* a person who studies the former Soviet Union.

sow[1] /səʊ/ *v.tr.* (*past* **sowed** /səʊd/; *past part.* **sown** /səʊn/ or **sowed**) **1** (also *absol.*) **a** scatter or put (seed) on or in the earth. **b** (often foll. by *with*) plant (a field etc.) with seed. **2** initiate; arouse (*sowed doubt in her mind*). **3** (foll. by *with*) cover thickly with. □ **sow the seed** (or **seeds**) **of** first give rise to; implant (an idea etc.). □ **sower** *n.* **sowing** *n.* [Old English *sāwan*, from Germanic]

sow[2] /saʊ/ *n.* **1 a** a female adult pig, esp. after farrowing. **b** a female guinea pig. **c** the female of some other species. **2 a** the main trough through which molten iron runs into side-channels to form pigs. **b** a large block of iron so formed. **3** (in full **sow bug**) esp. *US* a woodlouse. [Old English *sugu*]

sowback /ˈsaʊbak/ *n.* a low ridge of sand etc.

sowbread /ˈsaʊbrɛd/ *n.* a tuberous plant, *Cyclamen hederifolium*, with solitary nodding flowers.

Sowetan /səˈwɛt(ə)n, -ˈweɪt(ə)n/ *n. & adj.* ● *n.* a native or inhabitant of Soweto, a group of black African townships outside Johannesburg, South Africa. ● *adj.* of Soweto or its people. [*Soweto* (acronym from South Western Townships) + -AN]

sown *past part.* of sow¹.

sowthistle /ˈsaʊθɪs(ə)l/ *n.* any plant of the genus *Sonchus* with thistle-like leaves and milky juice.

sox *Commerce pl.* of SOCK¹.

soy /sɔɪ/ *n.* **1** (also **soy sauce**) a sauce made in Japan and China with fermented soya beans. **2** = SOYA 1. [Japanese *shō-yu* from Chinese *shi-you*, from *shi* 'salted beans' + *you* 'oil']

soya /ˈsɔɪə/ *n.* **1 a** a leguminous plant, *Glycine max*, originally of SE Asia, cultivated for its seeds. **b** (in full **soya bean**) the seed of this, used as a replacement for animal protein in certain foods, and as flour, oil, tofu, soy sauce, etc.. **2** (also **soya sauce**) = SOY 1. [Dutch *soja* from Malay *soi* (as SOY)]

soybean /ˈsɔɪbiːn/ *n.* = SOYA 1.

sozzled /ˈsɒz(ə)ld/ *adj. colloq.* very drunk. [past part. of dialect *sozzle* 'mix sloppily' (probably imitative)]

SP *abbr.* starting price.

spa /spɑː/ *n.* **1** a curative mineral spring. **2** a place or resort with this. [*Spa*, a town and resort in Belgium]

space /speɪs/ *n. & v.* ● *n.* **1 a** a continuous unlimited area or expanse which may or may not contain objects etc. **b** an interval between one, two, or three-dimensional points or objects (*a space of 10 metres*). **c** an empty area; room (*clear a space in the corner*; *occupies too much space*). **d** any of a limited number of places for a person or thing (*no spaces left at the table*). **2** a large unoccupied region (*the wide open spaces*). **3 a** (also **outer space**) the physical universe beyond the earth's atmosphere. **b** the near-vacuum extending between the planets and stars, containing small amounts of gas and dust. **4** an interval of time (*in the space of an hour*). **5** the amount of paper used in writing etc. (*hadn't the space to discuss it*). **6 a** a slot in a newspaper or between television or radio programmes for advertising (*he sells space*). **b** (in full **commercial space**) an area rented or sold as business premises. **7 a** a blank between printed, typed, or written words, etc. **b** *Printing* a piece of metal providing this. **8** *Mus.* each of the blanks between the lines of a staff. **9** freedom to think, be oneself, etc. (*need my own space*). ● *v.tr.* **1** set or arrange at intervals. **2** put spaces between (esp. words, letters, lines, etc. in printing, typing, or writing). **3** (as **spaced** *adj.*) (often foll. by *out*) *slang* in a state of euphoria or disorientation, esp. from taking drugs. □ **space out** spread out with more or wider spaces or intervals between. □ **spacer** *n.* **spacing** *n.* (esp. in sense 2 of *v.*). [Middle English via Old French *espace* from Latin *spatium*]

space age *n.* & *adj.* ● *n.* the era when the exploration of space has become possible. ● *attrib.adj.* (**space-age**) very modern.

space bar *n.* a long key on a typewriter or computer keyboard for making a space between words etc.

space blanket *n.* a light metal-coated sheet designed to retain heat.

space capsule *n.* a small spacecraft.

spacecraft /ˈspeɪskrɑːft/ *n.* a vehicle used for travelling in space.

space flight *n.* **1** a journey through space. **2** = SPACE TRAVEL.

Space Invaders *n. propr.* a computer game in which a player shoots at alien spaceships.

spaceman /ˈspeɪsman/ *n.* (*pl.* **-men**; *fem.* **spacewoman**, *pl.* **-women**) a person who travels in space.

space probe *n.* see PROBE *n.* 4.

space rocket *n.* a rocket travelling through space, or used to launch a spacecraft.

space-saving *adj.* **1** occupying little space. **2** that saves space.

spaceship /ˈspeɪsʃɪp/ *n.* a spacecraft, esp. one controlled by its crew.

space shuttle *n.* a rocket for repeated use, esp. between the earth and a space station.

space station *n.* an artificial satellite used as a base for operations in space.

spacesuit /ˈspeɪssuːt, -sjuːt/ *n.* a garment designed to allow an astronaut to survive in space.

space-time *n.* (also **space-time continuum**) the fusion of the concepts of space and time, esp. as a four-dimensional continuum.

space travel *n.* travel through outer space. □ **space traveller** *n.*

space vehicle *n.* = SPACECRAFT.

space walk *n.* any physical activity by an astronaut in space outside a spacecraft.

spacewoman see SPACEMAN.

spacey /ˈspeɪsi/ *adj.* (also **spacy**) (**spacier**, **spaciest**) **1** large, roomy. **2** esp. *N. Amer. slang* out of touch with reality, spaced out.

spacial var. of SPATIAL.

spacious /ˈspeɪʃəs/ *adj.* having ample space; covering a large area; roomy. □ **spaciously** *adv.* **spaciousness** *n.* [Middle English from Old French *spacios* or Latin *spatiosus* (as SPACE)]

spade[1] /speɪd/ *n.* & *v.* ● *n.* **1** a tool used for digging or cutting the ground etc., with a sharp-edged metal blade and a long handle. **2** a tool of a similar shape for various purposes, e.g. for removing the blubber from a whale. **3** anything resembling a spade. ● *v.tr.* dig over (ground) with a spade. □ **call a spade a spade** speak plainly or bluntly. □ **spadeful** *n.* (*pl.* **-fuls**). [Old English *spadu*, *spada*]

spade[2] /speɪd/ *n.* **1 a** a playing card of a suit denoted by black inverted heart-shaped figures with small stalks. **b** (in *pl.*) this suit. **2** *slang offens.* a black person. □ **in spades** *slang* to a high degree, with great force. [Italian *spade*, pl. of *spada* 'sword', via Latin *spatha* from Greek *spathē*, related to SPADE[1]: associated with the shape of a pointed spade]

spade beard *n.* an oblong-shaped beard.

spade foot *n.* a square spadelike enlargement at the end of a chair leg.

spade guinea *n. hist.* a guinea of George III's reign with a spade-shaped shield on the reverse.

spadework /ˈspeɪdwəːk/ *n.* hard or routine preparatory work.

spadille /spəˈdɪl/ *n. Cards* **1** the ace of spades in ombre and quadrille. **2** the highest trump, esp. the ace of spades. [French from Spanish *espadilla*, diminutive of *espada* 'sword' (as SPADE[2])]

spadix /ˈspeɪdɪks/ *n.* (*pl.* **spadices** /-siːz/) *Bot.* a spike of flowers closely arranged round a fleshy axis and usu. enclosed in a spathe. □ **spadiceous** /-ˈdɪʃəs/ *adj.* [Latin from Greek, = palm branch]

spae /speɪ/ *v.intr.* & *tr. Sc.* foretell; prophesy. [Middle English from Old Norse *spá*]

spaewife /ˈspeɪwʌɪf/ *n. Sc.* a female fortune-teller or witch.

spaghetti /spəˈɡɛti/ *n.* pasta made in solid strings, between macaroni and vermicelli in thickness. [Italian, pl. of diminutive of *spago* 'string']

spaghetti Bolognese /bɒləˈneɪz/ *n.* spaghetti served with a sauce of minced beef, tomato, onion, etc. [*Bolognese* Italian, = of Bologna]

spaghetti junction *n. Brit. colloq.* a multi-level road junction, esp. on a motorway.

spaghetti western *n. colloq.* a western film made by Italians, esp. cheaply.

spahi /ˈspɑːhiː/ *n. hist.* **1** a member of the Turkish irregular cavalry. **2** a member of the Algerian cavalry in French service. [Turkish *sipāhī* (as SEPOY)]

spake /speɪk/ *archaic past* of SPEAK.

spall /spɔːl/ *n.* & *v.* ● *n.* a splinter or chip, esp. of rock. ● *v.intr.* & *tr.* break up or cause (ore) to break up in preparation for sorting. [Middle English (also *spale*): origin unknown]

spallation /spɔːˈleɪʃ(ə)n/ *n. Physics* the break-up of a bombarded nucleus into several parts.

spalpeen /spalˈpiːn/ *n. Ir.* **1** a rascal; a villain. **2** a youngster. [Irish *spailpín*, of unknown origin]

spam /spam/ *n. propr.* a tinned meat product made mainly from ham. [*sp*iced h*am*]

span[1] /span/ *n.* & *v.* ● *n.* **1** the full extent from end to end in space or time (*the span of a bridge*; *the whole span of history*). **2** each arch or part of a bridge between piers or supports. **3** the maximum lateral extent of an aeroplane, its wing, a bird's wing, etc. **4 a** the maximum distance between the tips of the thumb and little finger. **b** this as a measurement, equal to 9 inches. **5** a short distance or time (*our life is but a span*). ● *v.* (**spanned**, **spanning**) **1** *tr.* **a** (of a bridge, arch, etc.) stretch from side to side of; extend across (*the bridge spanned the river*). **b** (of a builder etc.) bridge (a river etc.). **2** *tr.* extend across (space or a period of time etc.). **3** *tr.* measure or cover the extent of (a thing) with one's hand with the fingers stretched (*spanned a tenth on the piano*). **4** *intr. US* move in distinct stretches like the span-worm. [Old English *span(n)* or Old French *espan*]

span[2] /span/ *n.* **1** *Naut.* a rope with both ends fastened to take purchase in a loop. **2** *N. Amer.* a matched pair of horses, mules, etc. **3** *S.Afr.* a team of two or more pairs of oxen. [Low German & Dutch *span* from *spannen* 'unite']

span[3] see SPICK AND SPAN.

span[4] *past* of SPIN.

Spandex /'spandɛks/ *n. propr.* a type of polyurethane fabric. [arbitrary formation from EXPAND]

spandrel /'spandrɪl/ *n. Archit.* **1** the almost triangular space between one side of the outer curve of an arch, a wall, and the ceiling or framework. **2** the space between the shoulders of adjoining arches and the ceiling or moulding above. [perhaps from Anglo-French *spaund(e)re*, or from *espaundre* EXPAND]

spandrel wall *n.* a wall built on the curve of an arch, filling in the spandrel.

spang /spaŋ/ *adv. US colloq.* exactly; completely (*spang in the middle*). [19th c.: origin unknown]

spangle /'spaŋg(ə)l/ *n. & v.* ● *n.* **1** a small thin piece of glittering material, esp. used in quantity to ornament a dress etc.; a sequin. **2** a small sparkling object. **3** (in full **spangle gall**) a spongy excrescence on oak leaves. ● *v.tr.* (esp. as **spangled** *adj.*) cover with or as with spangles (*star-spangled*; *spangled costume*). □ **spangly** /-ŋgli/ *adj.* [Middle English from *spang*, via Middle Dutch *spange*, Old High German *spanga*, Old Norse *spöng* 'brooch' from Germanic]

Spaniard /'spanjəd/ *n.* **1 a** a native or national of Spain in southern Europe. **b** a person of Spanish descent. **2** *NZ* a spear grass. [Middle English from Old French *Espaignart*, from *Espaigne* 'Spain']

spaniel /'spanj(ə)l/ *n.* **1 a** a dog of any of various breeds with a long silky coat and drooping ears. **b** any of these breeds. **2** an obsequious or fawning person. [Middle English from Old French *espaigneul* 'Spanish' (dog) via Romanic from Latin *Hispania* 'Spain']

Spanish /'spanɪʃ/ *adj. & n.* ● *adj.* of or relating to Spain, its people, or its language. ● *n.* **1** the language of Spain and Spanish America. **2** (prec. by *the*; treated as *pl.*) the people of Spain. □ **Spanishness** *n.* [Middle English from *Spain*, with shortening of the first element]

Spanish America *n.* those parts of America originally settled by Spaniards, including Central and South America and part of the West Indies.

Spanish Armada *n. hist.* the Spanish war fleet sent against England in 1588.

Spanish bayonet *n.* a yucca, *Yucca aloifolia*, with stiff sharp-pointed leaves.

Spanish chestnut *n.* = CHESTNUT *n.* 1a.

Spanish fly *n.* **1** a bright green beetle, *Lytta vesicatoria*. **2** a toxic preparation of the dried bodies of these beetles, formerly used to raise blisters, and supposedly aphrodisiac. Also called *cantharides*.

Spanish guitar *n.* the standard six-stringed acoustic guitar, used esp. for classical and folk music.

Spanish ibex *n.* (also **Spanish goat**) an ibex, *Capra pyrenaica*, inhabiting the Pyrenees.

Spanish mackerel *n.* any of various large Atlantic game fishes allied to the mackerel, esp. *Scomberomorphus maculatus*.

Spanish Main *n. hist.* the NW coast of South America between the Orinoco river and Panama, and adjoining parts of the Caribbean Sea.

Spanish moss *n.* a tropical American plant, *Tillandsia usneoides*, an epiphytic bromeliad which grows as silvery festoons on trees.

Spanish omelette *n.* an omelette containing chopped vegetables (esp. potatoes) and often not folded.

Spanish onion *n.* a large mild-flavoured onion.

Spanish windlass *n.* a device for tightening a rope etc. using a stick as a lever.

spank /spaŋk/ *v. & n.* ● *v.* **1** *tr.* slap esp. on the buttocks with the open hand, a slipper, etc. **2** *intr.* (of a horse etc.) move briskly, esp. between a trot and a gallop. ● *n.* a slap esp. with the open hand on the buttocks. [perhaps imitative]

spanker /'spaŋkə/ *n.* **1** a person or thing that spanks. **2** *Naut.* a fore-and-aft sail set on the after side of the mizzen-mast. **3** a fast horse. **4** *colloq.* a person or thing of notable size or quality.

spanking /'spaŋkɪŋ/ *adj., adv., & n.* ● *adj.* **1** (esp. of a horse) moving quickly; lively; brisk (*at a spanking trot*). **2** *colloq.* striking; excellent. ● *adv. colloq.* very, exceedingly (*spanking clean*). ● *n.* the act or an instance of slapping, esp. on the buttocks as a punishment for children.

spanner /'spanə/ *n.* **1** esp. *Brit.* an instrument for turning or gripping a nut on a screw etc. (cf. WRENCH *n.* 2). **2** the cross-brace of a bridge etc. □ **spanner in the works** *Brit.* a drawback or impediment. [German *spannen* 'draw tight': see SPAN[2]]

span roof *n.* a roof with two inclined sides (cf. PENTHOUSE 2, LEAN-TO).

spansule /'spansjuːl/ *n. Pharm. propr.* a capsule which when swallowed releases one or more drugs over a set period. [SPAN[1] + CAPSULE]

span-worm *n. US* the caterpillar of the geometer moth.

spar[1] /spɑː/ *n.* **1** a stout pole esp. used for the mast, yard, etc., of a ship. **2** the main longitudinal beam of an aeroplane wing. [Middle English *sparre*, *sperre* from Old French *esparre* or Old Norse *sperra* or direct from Germanic: cf. Middle Dutch, Middle Low German *sparre*, Old Saxon, Old High German *sparro*]

spar[2] /spɑː/ *v. & n.* ● *v.intr.* (**sparred**, **sparring**) **1** (often foll. by *at*) make the motions of boxing without landing heavy blows. **2** engage in argument (*they are always sparring*). **3** (of a gamecock) fight with the feet or spurs. ● *n.* **1 a** a sparring motion. **b** a boxing match. **2** a cockfight. **3** an argument or dispute. [Old English *sperran*, *spyrran*, of unknown origin: cf. Old Norse *sperrask* 'kick out']

spar[3] /spɑː/ *n.* any crystalline, easily cleavable, and non-lustrous mineral, e.g. calcite or fluorspar. □ **sparry** *adj.* [Middle Low German, related to Old English *spæren* 'of plaster', *spærstān* 'gypsum']

sparable /'sparəb(ə)l/ *n.* a headless nail used for the soles and heels of shoes. [contraction of *sparrow-bill*, also used in this sense]

sparaxis /spə'raksɪs/ *n.* any S. African plant of the genus *Sparaxis* (iris family), with showy flowers and jagged spathes. [modern Latin from Greek, = laceration, from *sparassō* 'tear']

spar-buoy *n.* a buoy made of a spar with one end moored so that the other stands up.

spar-deck *n.* the light upper deck of a vessel.

spare /spɛː/ *adj., n., & v.* ● *adj.* **1 a** not required for ordinary use; extra (*have no spare cash*). **b** reserved for emergency or occasional use (*slept in the spare room*). **c** *colloq.* not wanted or used by others (*a spare seat in the front row*). **2** lean; thin. **3** scanty; frugal; not copious (*a spare diet*; *a spare prose style*). ● *n.* **1** a spare part; a duplicate. **2** (in tenpin bowling) the knocking-down of all the pins with the first two balls. ● *v.* **1** *tr.* afford to give or do without; dispense with (*cannot spare him just now*; *can spare you a couple*). **2** *tr.* **a** abstain from killing, hurting, wounding, etc. (*spared his feelings*; *spared her life*). **b** abstain from inflicting or causing; relieve from (*spare me this talk*; *spare my blushes*). **3** *tr.* be frugal or grudging of (*no expense spared*). **4** *intr.* *archaic* be frugal. □ **go spare** *Brit. colloq.* **1** become extremely angry or distraught. **2** be unwanted by others. **not spare oneself** exert one's utmost efforts. **to spare** left over; additional (*an hour to spare*). □ **sparely** *adv.* **spareness** *n.* **sparer** *n.* [Old English *spær*, *sparian*, from Germanic]

spare part *n.* a duplicate part to replace a lost or damaged part of a machine etc.

spare rib *n.* (usu. in *pl.*) closely trimmed ribs of esp. pork. [probably from Middle Low German *ribbesper* (by transposition of the syllables), and associated with SPARE]

spare time *n. & adj.* ● *n.* time which is not taken up by one's usual activities; leisure time. ● *attrib.adj.* (**spare-time**) relating to such time (*spare-time activity*).

spare tyre *n.* **1** an extra tyre carried in a motor vehicle for emergencies. **2** *colloq.* a roll of fat round the waist.

sparge /spɑːdʒ/ *v.tr.* moisten by sprinkling, esp. in brewing. □ **sparger** *n.* [apparently from Latin *spargere* 'sprinkle']

sparid /'sparɪd, 'speərɪd/ *n. & adj.* ● *n.* any deep-bodied marine fish of the family Sparidae, with long spiny dorsal fins, e.g. a sea bream, a porgy. ● *adj.* of or relating to this family. [modern Latin *Sparoides*, via Latin *sparus* from Greek *sparos* 'sea bream']

sparing /'speːrɪŋ/ *adj.* **1** inclined to save; economical. **2** restrained; limited. □ **sparingly** *adv.* **sparingness** *n.*

spark[1] /spɑːk/ *n. & v.* ● *n.* **1** a fiery particle thrown off from a fire, or alight in ashes, or produced by a flint, match, etc. **2** (often foll. by *of*) a particle of a quality etc. (*not a spark of life*; *a spark of interest*). **3** *Electr.* **a** a light produced by a sudden disruptive discharge through the air etc. **b** such a discharge serving to ignite the explosive mixture in an internal-combustion engine. **4 a** a flash of wit etc. **b** anything causing interest, excitement, etc. **5** a small bright object or point, e.g. in a gem. **6** (**Sparks**) a nickname for a radio operator or an electrician. ● *v.* **1** *intr.* emit sparks of fire or electricity. **2** *tr.* (often foll. by *off*) stir into activity; initiate (a process) suddenly. **3** *intr. Electr.* produce sparks at the point where a circuit is interrupted. □ **sparkless** *adj.* **sparky** *adj.* [Middle English from Old English *spærca, spearca*]

spark[2] /spɑːk/ *n. & v. archaic* ● *n.* **1** a lively young fellow. **2** a gallant; a beau. ● *v.intr.* play the gallant. □ **sparkish** *adj.* [probably a figurative use of SPARK[1]]

spark chamber *n.* an apparatus designed to show ionizing particles.

spark-gap *n.* the space between electric terminals where sparks occur.

sparking plug *n. Brit.* = SPARK PLUG.

sparkle /'spɑːk(ə)l/ *v. & n.* ● *v.intr.* **1 a** emit or seem to emit sparks; glitter; glisten (*her eyes sparkled*). **b** be witty; scintillate (*sparkling repartee*). **2** (usu. as **sparkling** *adj.*) (of wine etc.) effervesce (cf. STILL[1] *adj.* 4). ● *n.* a gleam, spark. □ **sparklingly** *adv.* **sparkly** *adj.* [Middle English, from SPARK[1] + -LE[4]]

sparkler /'spɑːklə/ *n.* **1** a person or thing that sparkles. **2** a hand-held sparkling firework. **3** *colloq.* a diamond or other gem.

spark plug *n.* (also **sparking plug**) a device for firing the explosive mixture in an internal-combustion engine.

sparling /'spɑːlɪŋ/ *n.* a European smelt, *Osmerus eperlanus*. [Middle English from Old French *esperlinge*, of Germanic origin]

sparring partner *n.* **1** a boxer employed to engage in sparring with another as training. **2** a person with whom one enjoys arguing.

sparrow /'sparəʊ/ *n.* **1** any small finchlike Old World bird of the family Ploceidae, with brown and grey plumage, esp. (in full **house sparrow**) *Passer domesticus*. **2** a bird resembling these in size or colour, esp. a New World bird of the bunting family (*hedge sparrow*; *song sparrow*). [Old English *spearwa*, from Germanic]

sparrow-grass /'sparəʊgrɑːs/*n.* *dial.* or *colloq.* asparagus.

sparrowhawk /'sparəʊhɔːk/ *n.* a small hawk, *Accipiter nisus*, preying on small birds.

sparse /spɑːs/ *adj.* thinly dispersed or scattered; not dense (*sparse population*; *sparse greying hair*). □ **sparsely** *adv.* **sparseness** *n.* **sparsity** *n.* [Latin *sparsus*, past part. of *spargere* 'scatter']

Spartan /'spɑːt(ə)n/ *adj. & n.* ● *adj.* **1** of or relating to Sparta in ancient Greece. **2 a** possessing the qualities of courage, endurance, stern frugality, etc., associated with Sparta. **b** (of a regime, conditions, etc.) lacking comfort; austere. ● *n.* a citizen of Sparta. [Middle English via Latin *Spartanus*, from *Sparta*, from Greek *Spartē, -tē*]

spartina /spɑː'tʌɪnə, -'tiːnə/ *n.* any grass of the genus *Spartina*, with rhizomatous roots and growing in wet or marshy ground. [Greek *spartinē* 'rope']

spasm /'spaz(ə)m/ *n.* **1** a sudden involuntary muscular contraction. **2** a sudden convulsive movement or emotion etc. (*a spasm of coughing*). **3** (usu. foll. by *of*) *colloq.* a brief spell of an activity. [Middle English via Old French *spasme* or Latin *spasmus* from Greek *spasmos, spasma*, from *spaō* 'pull']

spasmodic /spaz'mɒdɪk/ *adj.* **1** of, caused by, or subject to, a spasm or spasms (*a spasmodic jerk*; *spasmodic asthma*). **2** occurring or done by fits and starts (*spasmodic efforts*). □ **spasmodically** *adv.* [modern Latin *spasmodicus* from Greek *spasmōdēs* (as SPASM)]

spastic /'spastɪk/ *adj. & n.* ● *adj.* **1** often *offens.* suffering from cerebral palsy with spasm of the muscles. **2** *slang offens.* weak, feeble, incompetent. **3** spasmodic. ● *n.* **1** often *offens.* a person suffering from cerebral palsy. **2** *slang offens.* a stupid or incompetent person. □ **spastically** *adv.* **spasticity** /-'tɪsɪti/ *n.* [Latin *spasticus* from Greek *spastikos* 'pulling', from *spaō* 'pull']

■ **Usage** The use of the word *spastic* in the medical sense may be considered offensive as a result of its use as an offensive slang term. To avoid offence, the term *cerebral palsy* can be used, e.g. *She suffers from cerebral palsy* rather than *She is a spastic*.

spat[1] *past* and *past part.* of SPIT[1].

spat[2] /spat/ *n.* **1** (usu. in *pl.*) *hist.* a short cloth gaiter protecting the shoe from mud etc. **2** a cover for the upper part of an aircraft wheel. [abbreviation of SPATTERDASH]

spat[3] /spat/ *n. & v.* orig. *US* esp. *dial*, & *colloq.* ● *n.* a petty quarrel. ● *v.intr.* (**spatted**, **spatting**) quarrel pettily. [probably imitative]

spat[4] /spat/ *n. & v.* ● *n.* the spawn of shellfish, esp. the oyster. ● *v.* (**spatted**, **spatting**) **1** *intr.* (of an oyster) spawn. **2** *tr.* shed (spawn). [Anglo-French, of unknown origin]

spatchcock /'spatʃkɒk/ *n. & v.* ● *n.* a chicken or esp. game bird split open and grilled. ● *v.tr.* **1** treat (poultry) in this way. **2** esp. *Brit. colloq.* insert or interpolate (a phrase, sentence, story, etc.) esp. incongruously. [originally in Irish use, explained by Grose (1785) as from *dispatch-cock*, but cf. SPITCHCOCK]

spate /speɪt/ *n.* **1** *Brit.* a river flood (*the river is in spate*). **2** a large or excessive amount (*a spate of enquiries*). [Middle English, Scots & northern English: origin unknown]

spathe /speɪð/ *n. Bot.* a large bract or pair of bracts enveloping a spadix or flower cluster. □ **spathaceous** /spə'ðeɪʃəs/ *adj.* [Latin from Greek *spathē* 'broad blade' etc.]

spathic /'spaθɪk/ *adj.* (of a mineral) like spar (see SPAR[3]), esp. in cleavage. □ **spathose** *adj.* [*spath* 'spar' from German *Spath*]

spathic iron ore *n.* = SIDERITE 1.

spatial /'speɪʃ(ə)l/ *adj.* (also **spacial**) of or concerning space (*spatial extent*). □ **spatiality** /-ʃɪ'alɪti/ *n.* **spatialize** *v.tr.* (also **-ise**). **spatially** *adv.* [Latin *spatium* 'space']

spatio-temporal /ˌspeɪʃɪəʊ'tɛmp(ə)r(ə)l/ *adj. Physics & Philos.* belonging to both space and time or to space-time. □ **spatio-temporally** *adv.* [formed as SPATIAL + TEMPORAL[1]]

Spätlese /'ʃpɛtleɪzə/ *n.* (*pl.* **Spätleses** or ***Spätlesen*** /German ʃpɛtleːzən/) a white, esp. German, wine made from grapes harvested late in the season. [German, from *spät*, 'late' + *Lese* 'picking, vintage']

spatter /'spatə/ *v. & n.* ● *v.* **1** *tr.* **a** (often foll. by *with*) splash (a person etc.) (*spattered him with mud*). **b** scatter or splash (liquid, mud, etc.) here and there. **2** *intr.* (of rain etc.) fall here and there (*glass spattered down*). **3** *tr.* slander (a person's honour etc.). ● *n.* **1** (usu. foll. by *of*) a splash (*a spatter of mud*). **2** a quick pattering sound. [frequentative from base also found in Dutch, Low German *spatten* 'burst, spout']

spatterdash /'spatədaʃ/ *n.* **1** (usu. in *pl.*) *hist.* a long gaiter or other legging to protect the stockings etc. from mud etc., esp. when riding. **2** *US* = ROUGHCAST *n.*

spatula /'spatjʊlə/ *n.* a tool or implement with a broad, flat, blunt, often flexible blade, used for spreading, stirring, scraping, mixing (paints), etc. [Latin, variant of *spathula*, diminutive of *spatha* SPATHE]

spatulate /'spatjʊlət/ *adj.* **1** spatula-shaped. **2** (esp. of a leaf) having a broad rounded end.

spavin /'spavɪn/ *n.* a disease of a horse's hock with a hard bony swelling or excrescence. □ **spavined** *adj.* [Middle English from Old French *espavin*, variant of *esparvain*, from Germanic]

spawn /spɔːn/ *v.* & *n.* ● *v.* **1 a** *tr.* (also *absol.*) (of a fish, frog, mollusc, or crustacean) release or deposit (eggs). **b** *intr.* be produced as eggs or young. **2** *tr. derog.* (of people) produce (offspring). **3** *tr.* produce or generate, esp. in large numbers. ● *n.* **1** the eggs of fish, frogs, etc. **2** *derog.* human or other offspring. **3** the mycelium of a fungus, esp. of a cultivated mushroom. □ **spawner** *n.* [Middle English from Anglo-French *espaundre* 'shed roe', Old French *espandre* EXPAND]

spay /speɪ/ *v.tr.* sterilize (a female animal) by removing the ovaries. [Middle English via Anglo-French *espeier*, Old French *espeer* 'cut with a sword', from *espee* 'sword', from Latin *spatha*: see SPATHE]

SPCK *abbr.* Society for Promoting Christian Knowledge.

speak /spiːk/ *v.* (*past* **spoke** /spəʊk/; *past part.* **spoken** /'spəʊk(ə)n/) **1** *intr.* make articulate verbal utterances in an ordinary (not singing) voice. **2** *tr.* **a** utter (words). **b** make known or communicate (one's opinion, the truth, etc.) in this way (*never speaks sense*). **3** *intr.* **a** (foll. by *to, with*) hold a conversation (*spoke to him for an hour*; *spoke with them about their work*). **b** (foll. by *of*) mention in writing etc. (*speaks of it in his novel*). **c** (foll. by *for*) articulate the feelings of (another person etc.) in speech or writing (*speaks for our generation*). **4** *intr.* (foll. by *to*) **a** address; converse with (a person etc.). **b** speak in confirmation of or with reference to (*spoke to the resolution*; *can speak to his innocence*). **c** *colloq.* reprove (*spoke to them about their lateness*). **5** *intr.* make a speech before an audience etc. (*spoke for an hour on the topic*; *has a good speaking voice*). **6** *tr.* use or be able to use (a specified language) (*cannot speak French*). **7** *intr.* (of a gun, a musical instrument, etc.) make a sound. **8** *intr.* (usu. foll. by *to*) *poet.* communicate feeling etc., affect, touch (*the sunset spoke to her*). **9** *intr.* (of a hound) bark. **10** *intr.* (foll. by *with*) hail and hold communication with (a ship). **11** *tr. archaic* **a** (of conduct etc.) show (a person) to be (*his conduct speaks him generous*). **b** be evidence of (*the loud laugh speaks the vacant mind*). □ **not** (or **nothing**) **to speak of** not (or nothing) worth mentioning; practically not (or nothing). **speak for itself** need no supporting evidence. **speak for oneself 1** give one's own opinions. **2** not presume to speak for others. **speak one's mind** speak bluntly or frankly. **speak out** speak loudly or freely; give one's opinion. **speak up** = *speak out*. **speak volumes** (of a fact etc.) be very significant. **speak volumes** (or **well** etc.) **for 1** be abundant evidence of. **2** place in a favourable light. □ **speakable** *adj.* [Old English *sprecan*, later *specan*]

speakeasy /'spiːkiːzi/ *n.* (*pl.* **-ies**) *US hist. slang* an illicit liquor shop or drinking club during Prohibition.

speaker /'spiːkə/ *n.* **1** a person who speaks, esp. in public. **2** a person who speaks a specified language (esp. in *comb.*: *a French-speaker*). **3** (**Speaker**) the presiding officer in a legislative assembly, esp. the House of Commons. **4** = LOUDSPEAKER. □ **speakership** *n.*

speakerphone /'spiːkəfəʊn/ *n. N. Amer.* a telephone which does not need to be held in the hand.

speaking /'spiːkɪŋ/ *n.* & *adj.* ● *n.* the act or an instance of uttering words etc. ● *adj.* **1** that speaks; capable of articulate speech. **2** (of a portrait) lifelike; true to its subject (*a speaking likeness*). **3** (in *comb.*) speaking or capable of speaking a specified foreign language (*French-speaking*). **4** with a reference or from a point of view specified (*roughly speaking*; *professionally speaking*). □ **on speaking terms** (foll. by *with*) **1** slightly acquainted. **2** on friendly terms.

speaking acquaintance *n.* **1** a person one knows slightly. **2** this degree of familiarity.

speaking clock *n. Brit.* a telephone service giving the correct time in recorded speech.

speaking-trumpet *n. hist.* an instrument for making the voice carry.

speaking-tube *n.* a tube for conveying the voice from one room, building, etc., to another.

spear /spɪə/ *n.* & *v.* ● *n.* **1** a thrusting or throwing weapon with a pointed usu. steel tip and a long shaft. **2** a similar barbed instrument used for catching fish etc. **3** *archaic* a spearman. **4** a plant shoot, esp. a pointed stem of asparagus or broccoli. ● *v.tr.* pierce or strike with or as if with a spear (*speared an olive*). [Old English *spere*]

speargun /'spɪəgʌn/ *n.* a gun used to propel a spear in underwater fishing.

spearhead /'spɪəhɛd/ *n.* & *v.* ● *n.* **1** the point of a spear. **2** an individual or group chosen to lead a thrust or attack. ● *v.tr.* act as the spearhead of (an attack etc.).

spearman /'spɪəmən/ *n.* (*pl.* **-men**) *archaic* a person, esp. a soldier, who uses a spear.

spearmint /'spɪəmɪnt/ *n.* a common garden mint, *Mentha spicata*, used in cookery and to flavour chewing gum.

spear side *n.* the male side or members of a family etc. (opp. DISTAFF SIDE).

spearwort /'spɪəwəːt/ *n.* an aquatic plant, *Ranunculus lingua*, with thick hollow stems, long narrow spear-shaped leaves, and yellow flowers.

spec[1] /spɛk/ *n. colloq.* a commercial speculation or venture. □ **on spec** in the hope of success; as a gamble, on the off chance. [abbreviation of SPECULATION]

spec[2] /spɛk/ *n. colloq.* a detailed working description; a specification. [abbreviation of SPECIFICATION]

special /'spɛʃ(ə)l/ *adj.* & *n.* ● *adj.* **1 a** particularly good; exceptional; out of the ordinary (*bought them a special present*; *today is a special day*; *took special trouble*). **b** peculiar; specific; not general (*lacks the special qualities required*; *the word has a special sense*). **2** for a particular purpose (*sent on a special assignment*). **3** in which a person specializes (*statistics is his special field*). **4** relating to or denoting education for children with particular needs, e.g. the handicapped. ● *n.* a special person or thing, e.g. a special constable, train, examination, edition of a newspaper, dish on a menu, etc. □ **specially** *adv.* **specialness** *n.* [Middle English from Old French *especial* ESPECIAL or Latin *specialis* (as SPECIES)]

special area *n. Brit.* a district for which special economic provision is made in legislation.

Special Branch *n.* (in the UK) a police department dealing with political security.

special case *n.* **1** a written statement of fact presented by litigants to a court. **2** an exceptional or unusual case.

special constable *n. Brit.* an officer sworn in for occasional duty, to assist the police, esp. in times of emergency etc.

special correspondent *n. Brit.* a journalist writing for a newspaper on special events or a special area of interest.

special delivery *n.* **1** (in the UK) guaranteed delivery of a letter within the UK the day after posting. **2** (in the US) delivery of mail by a special messenger.

special drawing rights *n.pl.* the right to purchase extra foreign currency from the International Monetary Fund.

special edition *n.* an extra edition of a newspaper including later news than the ordinary edition.

special effects *n.pl.* scenic illusions created for films and television by props, camera-work, computer graphics, etc.

special intention *n. RC Ch.* a special aim or purpose for which a Mass is celebrated, prayers are said, etc.

specialist /ˈspɛʃ(ə)lɪst/ *n.* (usu. foll. by *in*) **1** a person who is trained in a particular branch of a profession, esp. medicine (*a specialist in dermatology*). **2** a person who specially or exclusively studies a subject or a particular branch of a subject (opp. GENERALIST). □ **specialism** /-lɪz(ə)m/ *n.* **specialistic** /-ˈlɪstɪk/ *adj.*

speciality /spɛʃɪˈalɪti/ *n.* (*pl.* **-ies**) **1** a special pursuit, product, operation, etc., to which a company or a person gives special attention. **2** a special feature, characteristic, or skill. [Middle English from Old French *especialité* or Late Latin *specialitas* (as SPECIAL)]

specialize /ˈspɛʃ(ə)lʌɪz/ *v.* (also **-ise**) **1** *intr.* (often foll. by *in*) **a** be or become a specialist (*specializes in optics*). **b** devote oneself to an area of interest, skill, etc. (*specializes in insulting people*). **2** *Biol.* **a** *tr.* (esp. in *passive*) adapt or set apart (an organ etc.) for a particular purpose. **b** *intr.* (of an organ etc.) become adapted etc. in this way. **3** *tr.* make specific or individual. **4** *tr.* modify or limit (an idea, statement, etc.). □ **specialization** /-ˈzeɪʃ(ə)n/ *n.* [French *spécialiser* (as SPECIAL)]

special jury *n. hist.* a jury with members of a particular social standing (cf. COMMON JURY).

special licence *n. Brit.* a marriage licence allowing immediate marriage without banns, or at an unusual time or place.

special pleading *n.* **1** *Law* pleading with reference to new facts in a case. **2** (in general use) a specious or unfair argument favouring the speaker's point of view.

special providence *n.* a particular instance of God's providence.

special school *n.* (in the UK) a school catering for children with special educational needs, resulting from a disability or learning difficulty.

specialty /ˈspɛʃ(ə)lti/ *n.* (*pl.* **-ies**) **1** esp. *N. Amer.* = SPECIALITY. **2** *Law* an instrument under seal; a sealed contract. [Middle English from Old French *(e)specialté* (as SPECIAL)]

■ **Usage** In standard British English *specialty* is used only in sense 2 above.

special verdict *n. Law* a verdict stating the facts as proved but leaving the court to draw conclusions from them.

speciation /spiːʃɪˈeɪʃ(ə)n, spiːs-/ *n. Biol.* the formation of new species in the course of evolution. □ **speciate** /ˈspiː-/ *v.intr.* [SPECIES + -ATION]

specie /ˈspiːʃiː, ˈspiːʃi/ *n.* coin money as opposed to paper money. [Latin, ablative of SPECIES in the phrase *in specie* 'in the actual form']

species /ˈspiːʃiːz, -ʃɪz, ˈspiːs-/ *n.* (*pl.* same) **1** a class of things having some common characteristics. **2** *Biol.* a group of living organisms consisting of related similar individuals capable of exchanging genes or interbreeding, classified as a taxonomic rank below a genus and denoted by a Latin binomial. **3** a kind or sort. **4** *Logic* a group subordinate to a genus and containing individuals agreeing in some common attribute(s) and called by a common name. **5** *Law* a form or shape given to materials. **6** *Eccl.* the visible form of each of the elements of consecrated bread and wine in the Eucharist. [Latin, = appearance, kind, beauty, from *specere* 'to look']

speciesism /ˈspiːʃiːzɪz(ə)m, ˈspiːs-/ *n.* an assumption of human superiority leading to the exploitation of animals. □ **speciesist** *adj. & n.* [SPECIES + -ISM on the pattern of *racism*]

specific /spəˈsɪfɪk/ *adj. & n.* ● *adj.* **1** clearly defined; definite (*has no specific name*; *told me so in specific terms*). **2** relating to a particular subject; peculiar (*a style specific to that*). **3 a** of or concerning a species (*the specific name for a plant*). **b** possessing, or concerned with, the properties that characterize a species (*the specific forms of animals*). **4** (of a duty or a tax) assessed by quantity or amount, not by the value of goods. ● *n.* **1** *archaic* a medicine or remedy specifically effective for a disease or part of the body. **2** a specific aspect or factor (*shall we discuss specifics?*). □ **specifically** *adv.* **specificity** /-ˈfɪsɪti/ *n.* **specificness** *n.* [Late Latin *specificus* (as SPECIES)]

specification /ˌspɛsɪfɪˈkeɪʃ(ə)n/ *n.* **1** the act or an instance of specifying; the state of being specified. **2 a** (esp. in *pl.*) a detailed description of the construction, workmanship, materials, etc., of work done or to be done, prepared by an architect, engineer, etc. **b** a specified standard of workmanship, materials, etc., to be achieved (*built to a high specification*). **3** a description by an applicant for a patent of the construction and use of his invention. **4** *Law* the conversion of materials into a new product not held to be the property of the owner of the materials. [medieval Latin *specificatio* (as SPECIFY)]

specific cause *n.* the cause of a particular form of a disease.

specific difference *n.* a factor that differentiates a species.

specific disease *n.* a disease caused by one identifiable agent.

specific gravity *n.* = RELATIVE DENSITY.

specific heat capacity *n.* the heat required to raise the temperature of the unit mass of a given substance by a given amount (usu. one degree).

specific medicine *n.* a medicine having a distinct effect in curing a certain disease.

specific performance *n. Law* the performance of a contractual duty, as ordered in cases where damages would not be adequate remedy.

specify /ˈspɛsɪfʌɪ/ *v.tr.* (**-ies**, **-ied**) **1** (also *absol.*) name or mention expressly (*specified the type he needed*). **2** (usu. foll. by *that* + clause) name as a condition (*specified that he must be paid at once*). **3** include in specifications (*a French window was not specified*). □ **specifiable** *adj.* **specifier** *n.* [Middle English from Old French *specifier* or Late Latin *specificare* (as SPECIFIC)]

specimen /ˈspɛsɪmɪn/ *n.* **1** an individual or part taken as an example of a class or whole, esp. when used for investigation or scientific examination (*specimens of copper ore*; *a specimen of your handwriting*). **2** *Med.* a sample of urine for testing. **3** *colloq.* a person or animal of a specified sort (*a fine specimen*). [Latin from *specere* 'to look']

specious /ˈspiːʃəs/ *adj.* **1** superficially plausible but actually wrong (*a specious argument*). **2** misleadingly attractive in appearance. □ **speciosity** /-ʃɪˈɒsɪti/ *n.* **speciously** *adv.* **speciousness** *n.* [Middle English, = beautiful, from Latin *speciosus* (as SPECIES)]

speck /spɛk/ *n. & v.* ● *n.* **1** a small spot, dot, or stain. **2** (foll. by *of*) a particle (*speck of dirt*). **3** a rotten spot in fruit. ● *v.tr.* (esp. as **specked** *adj.*) mark with specks. □ **speckless** *adj.* [Old English *specca*: cf. SPECKLE]

speckle /ˈspɛk(ə)l/ *n. & v.* ● *n.* a small spot, mark, or stain, esp. in quantity on the skin, a bird's egg, etc. ● *v.tr.* (esp. as **speckled** *adj.*) mark with speckles or patches. [Middle English from Middle Dutch *spekkel*]

specs /spɛks/ *n.pl. colloq.* a pair of spectacles. [abbreviation]

spectacle /ˈspɛktək(ə)l/ *n.* **1** a public show, ceremony, etc. **2** anything attracting public attention (*a charming spectacle*; *a disgusting spectacle*). □ **make a spectacle of oneself** make oneself an object of ridicule. [Middle English via Old French from Latin *spectaculum*, from *spectare*, frequentative of *specere* 'to look']

spectacled /ˈspɛktək(ə)ld/ *adj.* **1** wearing spectacles. **2** (of an animal) having markings resembling spectacles.

spectacled bear *n.* a S. American bear, *Tremarctos ornatus*, with white markings around the eyes.

spectacled cobra *n.* an Asian cobra, *Naja naja*, with a spectacle-like marking on the hood.

spectacles /ˈspɛktək(ə)lz/ *n.pl.* (*US* usu. *joc.*) a pair of lenses in a frame resting on the nose and ears, used to correct defective eyesight or protect the eyes.

spectacular /spɛkˈtakjʊlə/ *adj. & n.* ● *adj.* **1** of or like a public show; striking, amazing, lavish. **2** strikingly large or obvious (*a spectacular increase in output*). ● *n.* an event intended to be spectacular, esp. a musical film or play. □ **spectacularly** *adv.* [SPECTACLE, on the pattern of *oracular* etc.]

spectate /spɛkˈteɪt/ *v.intr.* be a spectator, esp. at a sporting event. [back-formation from SPECTATOR]

■ **Usage** Some people consider that *spectate* should be restricted to informal use; in most contexts *watch* is preferable.

spectator /spɛkˈteɪtə/ *n.* a person who looks on at a show, game, incident, etc. □ **spectatorial** /-təˈtɔːrɪəl/ *adj.* [French *spectateur* or Latin *spectator*, from *spectare*: see SPECTACLE]

spectator sport *n.* a sport providing popular entertainment for spectators.

spectra *pl.* of SPECTRUM.

spectral /ˈspɛktr(ə)l/ *adj.* **1 a** of or relating to spectres or ghosts. **b** ghostlike. **2** of or concerning spectra or the spectrum (*spectral colours*). □ **spectrally** *adv.*

spectral analysis *n.* **1** chemical analysis using a spectroscope. **2** analysis of light, sound, etc. into a spectrum.

spectre /ˈspɛktə/ *n.* (*US* **specter**) **1** a ghost. **2** a haunting presentiment or preoccupation (*the spectre of war*). **3** (usu. in *comb.*) used in the names of some animals because of their thinness, transparency, etc. [French *spectre* or Latin *spectrum*: see SPECTRUM]

spectro- /ˈspɛktrəʊ/ *comb. form* a spectrum.

spectrochemistry /spɛktrə(ʊ)ˈkɛmɪstri/ *n.* chemistry based on the study of the spectra of substances.

spectrogram /ˈspɛktrə(ʊ)gram/ *n.* a record obtained with a spectrograph.

spectrograph /ˈspɛktrə(ʊ)grɑːf/ *n.* an apparatus for photographing or otherwise recording spectra. □ **spectrographic** /-ˈgrafɪk/ *adj.* **spectrographically** /-ˈgrafɪk(ə)li/ *adv.* **spectrography** /spɛkˈtrɒgrəfi/ *n.*

spectroheliograph /spɛktrəʊˈhiːlɪəgrɑːf/ *n.* an instrument for taking photographs of the sun in light of one wavelength only.

spectrohelioscope /spɛktrəʊˈhiːlɪəskəʊp/ *n.* a device similar to a spectroheliograph, for visual observation.

spectrometer /spɛkˈtrɒmɪtə/ *n.* an instrument used for the measurement of observed spectra. □ **spectrometric** /spɛktrəˈmɛtrɪk/ *adj.* **spectrometry** *n.* [German *Spektrometer* or French *spectromètre* (as SPECTRO-, -METER)]

spectrophotometer /ˌspɛktrə(ʊ)fəʊˈtɒmɪtə/ *n.* an instrument for measuring the intensity of light in various parts of the spectrum, esp. as transmitted or emitted by a substance or solution at a particular wavelength. □ **spectrophotometric** /-təˈmɛtrɪk/ *adj.* **spectrophotometry** *n.*

spectroscope /ˈspɛktrəskəʊp/ *n.* an instrument for producing and recording spectra for examination. □ **spectroscopic** /-ˈskɒpɪk/ *adj.* **spectroscopical** /-ˈskɒpɪk(ə)l/ *adj.* **spectroscopist** /-ˈtrɒskəpɪst/ *n.* **spectroscopy** /-ˈtrɒskəpi/ *n.* [German *Spektroskop* or French *spectroscope* (as SPECTRO-, -SCOPE)]

spectrum /ˈspɛktrəm/ *n.* (*pl.* **spectra** /-trə/) **1** a band of colours, as seen in a rainbow etc., produced by separation of the components of light by their different degrees of refraction according to wavelength. **2** the entire range of wavelengths of electromagnetic radiation. **3 a** an image or distribution of components of any electromagnetic radiation arranged in a progressive series according to wavelength. **b** this as characteristic of a body or substance when emitting or absorbing radiation. **4** a similar image or distribution of components of sound, particles, etc., arranged according to frequency, charge, energy, etc. **5** the entire range or a wide range of anything arranged by degree or quality etc. **6** (in full **ocular spectrum**) an after-image. [Latin, = image, apparition, from *specere* 'to look']

spectrum analyser *n.* a device for analysing oscillation, esp. sound, into its separate components.

spectrum analysis *n.* = SPECTRAL ANALYSIS.

specula *pl.* of SPECULUM.

specular /ˈspɛkjʊlə/ *adj.* **1** of or having the nature of a speculum. **2** reflecting. [Latin *specularis* (as SPECULUM)]

specular iron ore *n.* lustrous haematite.

speculate /ˈspɛkjʊleɪt/ *v.* **1** *intr.* (usu. foll. by *on, upon, about*) form a theory or conjecture, esp. without a firm factual basis; meditate (*speculated on their prospects*). **2** *tr.* (foll. by *that, how*, etc. + clause) conjecture, consider (*speculated how he might achieve it*). **3** *intr.* **a** invest in stocks etc. in the hope of gain but with the possibility of loss. **b** gamble recklessly. □ **speculator** *n.* [Latin *speculari* 'spy out, observe', via *specula* 'watchtower' from *specere* 'look']

speculation /spɛkjʊˈleɪʃ(ə)n/ *n.* **1** the act or an instance of speculating; a theory or conjecture (*made no speculation as to her age*; *is given to speculation*). **2 a** a speculative investment or enterprise (*bought it as a speculation*). **b** the practice of business speculating. **3** a game in which trump cards are bought or sold. [Middle English from Old French *speculation* or Late Latin *speculatio* (as SPECULATE)]

speculative /ˈspɛkjʊlətɪv/ *adj.* **1** of, based on, engaged in, or inclined to speculation. **2** (of a business investment) involving the risk of loss (*a speculative builder*). □ **speculatively** *adv.* **speculativeness** *n.* [Middle English from Old French *speculatif -ive* or Late Latin *speculativus* (as SPECULATE)]

speculum /ˈspɛkjʊləm/ *n.* (*pl.* **specula** /-lə/) **1** *Surgery* an instrument for dilating the cavities of the human body for inspection. **2** a mirror, usu. of polished metal, esp. (formerly) in a reflecting telescope. **3** a lustrous coloured area on the wing of some birds, esp. ducks. [Latin, = mirror, from *specere* 'to look']

speculum-metal *n.* an alloy of copper and tin used in mirrors, esp. formerly in telescopes.

sped *past* and *past part.* of SPEED.

speech /spiːtʃ/ *n.* **1** the faculty or act of speaking. **2** a usu. formal address or discourse delivered to an audience or assembly. **3** a manner of speaking (*a man of blunt speech*). **4** a remark (*after this speech he was silent*). **5** the language of a nation, region, group, etc. **6** *Mus.* the act of sounding in an organ pipe etc. □ **speechful** *adj.* [Old English *sprǣc*, later *spēc*, from West Germanic: related to SPEAK]

speech day *n. Brit.* an annual prize-giving day in many schools, usu. marked by speeches etc.

speechify /ˈspiːtʃɪfʌɪ/ *v.intr.* (**-ies, -ied**) *joc.* or *derog.* make esp. boring or long speeches. □ **speechification** /-fɪˈkeɪʃ(ə)n/ *n.* **speechifier** *n.*

speechless /ˈspiːtʃlɪs/ *adj.* **1** temporarily unable to speak because of emotion etc. (*speechless with rage*). **2** dumb. □ **speechlessly** *adv.* **speechlessness** *n.* [Old English *spǣclēas* (as SPEECH, -LESS)]

speech-reading *n.* lip-reading.

speech therapy *n.* treatment to improve defective speech. □ **speech therapist** *n.*

speech-writer *n.* a person employed to write speeches for a politician etc. to deliver.

speed /spiːd/ *n. & v.* ● *n.* **1** rapidity of movement (*with all speed*; *at full speed*). **2** a rate of progress or motion over a distance in time (*attains a high speed*). **3 a** each of the possible gear ratios of a bicycle. **b** esp. *US* or *archaic* such a gear in a motor vehicle. **4** *Photog.* **a** the sensitivity of film to light. **b** the light-gathering power or f-number of a lens. **c** the duration of an exposure. **5** *slang* an amphetamine drug, esp. methamphetamine. **6** *archaic* success, prosperity (*send me good speed*). ● *v.* (*past* and *past part.* **sped** /spɛd/) **1** *intr.* go fast (*sped down the street*). **2** (*past* and *past part.* **speeded**) **a** *intr.*

(of a motorist etc.) travel at an illegal or dangerous speed. **b** *tr.* regulate the speed of (an engine etc.). **c** *tr.* cause (an engine etc.) to go at a fixed speed. **3** *tr.* send fast or on its way (*speed an arrow from the bow*). **4** *intr. & tr. archaic* be or make prosperous or successful (*how have you sped?*; *God speed you!*). □ **at speed** moving quickly. **speed up** move or work at greater speed. □ **speeder** *n.* [Old English *spēd*, *spēdan*, from Germanic]

speedball /ˈspiːdbɔːl/ *n.* **1** *slang* a mixture of cocaine with heroin or morphine. **2** *US* a ball game resembling soccer but in which the ball may be handled.

speedboat /ˈspiːdbəʊt/ *n.* a motor boat designed for high speed.

speed bump *n.* (also *Brit.* **speed hump**) a transverse ridge in the road to control the speed of vehicles.

speed limit *n.* the maximum speed at which a road vehicle, boat, etc., may legally travel in a particular area etc.

speed merchant *n. colloq.* a motorist who enjoys driving fast.

speedo /ˈspiːdəʊ/ *n.* (*pl.* **-os**) *Brit. colloq.* = SPEEDOMETER. [abbreviation]

speedometer /spiːˈdɒmɪtə/ *n.* an instrument on a motor vehicle etc. indicating its speed to the driver. [SPEED + METER[1]]

speed-up *n.* an increase in the speed or rate of working.

speedway /ˈspiːdweɪ/ *n.* **1 a** motorcycle racing. **b** a stadium or track used for this. **2** *N. Amer.* **a** a road or track used for motor car racing. **b** a highway for fast motor traffic.

speedwell /ˈspiːdwɛl/ *n.* any small small herbaceous plant of the genus *Veronica*, with tiny blue or pink flowers. [apparently from SPEED + WELL[1]]

speedy /ˈspiːdi/ *adj.* (**speedier**, **speediest**) **1** moving quickly; rapid. **2** done without delay; prompt (*a speedy answer*). □ **speedily** *adv.* **speediness** *n.*

speiss /spʌɪs/ *n.* a compound of arsenic, iron, etc., formed in smelting certain lead ores. [German *Speise* 'food, amalgam']

speleology /spiːlɪˈɒlədʒi, spɛl-/ *n.* **1** the scientific study of caves. **2** the exploration of caves. □ **speleological** /-əˈlɒdʒɪk(ə)l/ *adj.* **speleologist** *n.* [French *spéléologie*, via Latin *spelaeum* from Greek *spēlaion* 'cave']

spell[1] /spɛl/ *v.tr.* (*past* and *past part.* **spelled** or esp. *Brit.* **spelt**) **1** (also *absol.*) write or name the letters that form (a word etc.) in correct sequence (*spell 'exaggerate'*; *cannot spell properly*). **2 a** (of letters) make up or form (a word etc.). **b** (of circumstances, a scheme, etc.) result in; involve (*spell ruin*). □ **spell out 1** make out (words, writing, etc.) letter by letter. **2** explain in detail (*spelled out what the change would mean*). □ **spellable** *adj.* [Middle English from Old French *espel(l)er*, from Frankish (as SPELL[2])]

spell[2] /spɛl/ *n.* **1** a form of words used as a magical charm or incantation. **2** an attraction or fascination exercised by a person, activity, quality, etc. □ **under a spell** mastered by or as if by a spell. [Old English *spel(l)*, from Germanic]

spell[3] /spɛl/ *n. & v.* ● *n.* **1** a short or fairly short period (*a cold spell in April*). **2** a turn of work (*did a spell of woodwork*). **3** *Austral.* a period of rest from work. ● *v.* **1** *tr.* **a** relieve or take the place of (a person) in work etc. **b** allow to rest briefly. **2** *intr. Austral.* take a brief rest. [earlier as verb: later form of dialect *spele* 'take the place of' from Old English *spelian*, of unknown origin]

spell[4] /spɛl/ *n.* a splinter of wood etc. [perhaps from obsolete *speld*]

spellbind /ˈspɛlbʌɪnd/ *v.tr.* (*past* and *past part.* **spellbound**) **1** bind with or as if with a spell; entrance. **2** (as **spellbound** *adj.*) entranced, fascinated, esp. by a speaker, activity, quality, etc. □ **spellbinder** *n.* **spellbindingly** *adv.*

spell-check *n. & v. Computing* ● *n.* a check of the spelling in a file of text using a spelling checker. ● *v.tr.* check the spelling in (a text) using a spelling checker.

spell-checker *n.* = SPELLING CHECKER.

speller /ˈspɛlə/ *n.* **1** a person who spells esp. in a specified way (*is a poor speller*). **2** a book on spelling.

spellican var. of SPILLIKIN.

spelling /ˈspɛlɪŋ/ *n.* **1** the process or activity of writing or naming the letters of a word etc. **2** the way a word is spelled. **3** the ability to spell (*his spelling is weak*).

spelling-bee *n.* a spelling competition.

spelling checker *n.* a computer program which checks the spelling of words in files of text, usually by comparison with a stored list of words.

spelt[1] *past* and *past part.* of SPELL[1].

spelt[2] /spɛlt/ *n.* a kind of wheat, *Triticum spelta*, formerly cultivated but now displaced by more modern varieties. [Old English from Old Saxon *spelta* (Old High German *spelza*); readopted in Middle English from Middle Low German, Middle Dutch *spelte*]

spelter /ˈspɛltə/ *n.* commercial crude smelted zinc. [corresponding to Old French *espeautre*, Middle Dutch *speauter*, German *Spialter*: related to PEWTER]

spelunker /spɪˈlʌŋkə/ *n. N. Amer.* a person who explores caves, esp. as a hobby. □ **spelunking** *n.* [obsolete *spelunk* 'cave' from Latin *spelunca*]

spence /spɛns/ *n. archaic* a buttery or larder. [Middle English via Old French *despense* from Latin *dispensa*, fem. past part. of *dispendere*: see DISPENSE]

spencer[1] /ˈspɛnsə/ *n.* **1** a short close-fitting jacket. **2** a woman's thin usu. woollen under-bodice worn for extra warmth in winter. [probably named after the 2nd Earl *Spencer*, English politician d. 1834]

spencer[2] /ˈspɛnsə/ *n. Naut.* a trysail. [perhaps named after K. *Spencer* (early 19th c.)]

spend /spɛnd/ *v. & n.* ● *v.tr.* (*past* and *past part.* **spent** /spɛnt/) **1** (usu. foll. by *on*) **a** (also *absol.*) pay out (money) in making a purchase etc. (*spent £5 on a new pen*). **b** pay out (money) for a particular person's benefit or for the improvement of a thing (*had to spend £200 on the car*). **2 a** use or consume (time or energy) (*shall spend no more effort*; *how do you spend your Sundays?*). **b** (also *refl.*) use up; exhaust; wear out (*their ammunition was all spent*; *his anger was soon spent*; *spent herself campaigning for justice*). **3** *tr.* (as **spent** *adj.*) having lost its original force or strength; exhausted (*the storm is spent*; *spent bullets*). ● *n.* **1** the action or an act of spending money. **2** an amount spent, expenditure. □ **spend a penny** *Brit. colloq.* urinate or defecate (with reference to the coin-operated locks of public lavatories). □ **spendable** *adj.* **spender** *n.* [Old English *spendan* from Latin *expendere* (see EXPEND): in Middle English perhaps also from obsolete *dispend* via Old French *despendre* 'expend' from Latin *dispendere*: see DISPENSE]

spending money *n.* pocket money.

spendthrift /ˈspɛn(d)θrɪft/ *n. & adj.* ● *n.* an extravagant person; a prodigal. ● *adj.* extravagant; prodigal.

Spenserian /spɛnˈsɪərɪən/ *adj.* of, relating to, or in the style of Edmund Spenser, English poet d. 1599.

Spenserian stanza *n.* the stanza used by Spenser in the *Faerie Queene*, with eight iambic pentameters and an alexandrine, rhyming ababbcbcc.

spent *past* and *past part.* of SPEND.

spent tan see TAN[1] *n.* 4.

sperm /spəːm/ *n.* (*pl.* same or **sperms**) **1** = SPERMATOZOON. **2** the male reproductive fluid containing spermatozoa; semen. **3** = SPERM WHALE. **4** = SPERMACETI. **5** = SPERM OIL. [Middle English via Late Latin *sperma* from Greek *sperma -atos* 'seed', from *speirō* 'sow']

spermaceti /spəːməˈsiːti, -ˈsɛti/ *n.* a white waxy substance produced by the sperm whale to aid buoyancy, and used in the manufacture of candles, ointments, etc. □ **spermacetic** *adj.* [Middle English from medieval Latin, from Late Latin *sperma* 'sperm' + *ceti*, genitive of *cetus* from Greek *kētos* 'whale', from the belief that it was whale-spawn]

spermatic /spəːˈmatɪk/ *adj.* of or relating to sperm or semen. [Late Latin *spermaticus* from Greek *spermatikos* (as SPERM)]

spermatic cord *n. Anat.* a bundle of nerves, ducts, and blood vessels passing to the testicles.

spermatid /ˈspəːmətɪd/ *n. Biol.* an immature male sex cell formed from a spermatocyte, which may develop into a spermatozoon. □ **spermatidal** /-ˈtʌɪd(ə)l/ *adj.*

spermato- /ˈspəːmətəʊ, spəˈmatəʊ/ *comb. form Biol.* a sperm or seed.

spermatocyte /ˈspəːmətə(ʊ)sʌɪt, spəˈmat-/ *n.* a cell produced from a spermatogonium and which may divide by meiosis into spermatids.

spermatogenesis /spəːmətə(ʊ)ˈdʒɛnɪsɪs, spəˌmat-/ *n.* the production or development of mature spermatozoa. □ **spermatogenetic** /-dʒɪˈnɛtɪk/ *adj.*

spermatogonium /spəːmətə(ʊ)ˈgəʊnɪəm, spəˌmat-/ *n.* (*pl.* **spermatogonia** /-nɪə/) a cell produced at an early stage in the formation of spermatozoa, from which spermatocytes develop. [SPERM + modern Latin *gonium* from Greek *gonos* 'offspring, seed']

spermatophore /ˈspəːmətə(ʊ)fɔː, spəˈmat-/ *n.* an albuminous capsule containing spermatozoa found in various invertebrates. □ **spermatophoric** /-ˈfɔːrɪk/ *adj.*

spermatophyte /ˈspəːmətə(ʊ)fʌɪt, spəˈmat-/ *n.* any seed-bearing plant.

spermatozoid /spəːmətə(ʊ)ˈzəʊɪd, spəˌmat-/ *n.* the mature motile male sex cell of some plants.

spermatozoon /spəːmətə(ʊ)ˈzəʊɒn, spəˌmat-/ *n.* (*pl.* **spermatozoa** /-ˈzəʊə/) the mature motile male sex cell in animals. □ **spermatozoal** *adj.* **spermatozoan** *adj.* [SPERM + Greek *zōion* 'animal']

sperm bank *n.* a supply of semen stored for use in artificial insemination.

sperm count *n.* the number of spermatozoa in one ejaculation or a measured amount of semen.

spermicide /ˈspəːmɪsʌɪd/ *n.* a substance able to kill spermatozoa. □ **spermicidal** /-ˈsʌɪd(ə)l/ *adj.*

spermo- /ˈspəːməʊ/ *comb. form* = SPERMATO-.

sperm oil *n.* an oil obtained from the head of a sperm whale and used as a lubricant.

sperm whale *n.* a large whale, *Physeter macrocephalus*, hunted for the spermaceti and sperm oil contained in its bulbous head, and for the ambergris found in its intestines: also called CACHALOT. [abbreviation of SPERMACETI]

spew /spjuː/ *v.* (also **spue**) **1** *tr. & intr.* (often foll. by *up*) vomit. **2** (often foll. by *out*) **a** *tr.* expel (contents) rapidly and forcibly. **b** *intr.* (of contents) be expelled in this way. □ **spewer** *n.* [Old English *spīwan*, *spēowan*, from Germanic]

SPF *abbr.* sun protection factor (indicating the effectiveness of protective creams etc.).

sp. gr. *abbr.* specific gravity.

sphagnum /ˈsfagnəm/ *n.* (*pl.* **sphagna** /-nə/) (in full **sphagnum moss**) any moss of the genus *Sphagnum*, growing in bogs and peat, and used as packing esp. for plants, as fertilizer, etc. [modern Latin from Greek *sphagnos*, the name of a moss]

sphalerite /ˈsfalərʌɪt/ *n.* = BLENDE. [Greek *sphaleros* 'deceptive': cf. BLENDE]

spheno- /ˈsfiːnəʊ/ *comb. form Anat.* the sphenoid bone. [Greek from *sphēn* 'wedge']

sphenoid /ˈsfiːnɔɪd/ *adj. & n.* ● *adj.* **1** wedge-shaped. **2** *Anat.* of or relating to the sphenoid bone. ● *n.* (in full **sphenoid bone**) a compound bone forming the base of the cranium behind the eyes. □ **sphenoidal** /-ˈnɔɪd(ə)l/ *adj.* [modern Latin *sphenoides* from Greek *sphēnoeidēs*, from *sphēn* 'wedge']

sphere /sfɪə/ *n. & v.* ● *n.* **1** a solid figure, or its surface, with every point on its surface equidistant from its centre. **2** an object having this shape; a ball or globe. **3 a** any celestial body. **b** a globe representing the earth. **c** *poet.* the heavens; the sky. **d** the sky perceived as a vault upon or in which celestial bodies are represented as lying. **e** *hist.* each of a series of revolving concentrically arranged spherical shells in which celestial bodies were formerly thought to be set in a fixed relationship. **4 a** a field of action, influence, or existence (*have done much within their own sphere*). **b** a (usu. specified) stratum of society or social class (*moves in quite another sphere*). ● *v.tr. archaic* or *poet.* **1** enclose in or as in a sphere. **2** form into a sphere. □ **music** (or **harmony**) **of the spheres** the natural harmonic tones supposedly produced by the movement of the celestial spheres (see sense 3e of *n.*) or the bodies fixed in them. □ **spheral** *adj.* [Middle English *sper(e)* via Old French *espere* and Late Latin *sphera*, Latin *sphaera*, from Greek *sphaira* 'ball']

-sphere /sfɪə/ *comb. form* **1** having the form of a sphere (*bathysphere*). **2** a region round the earth (*atmosphere*).

sphere of influence *n.* the claimed or recognized area of a state's interests, an individual's control, etc.

spheric /ˈsfɛrɪk/ *adj.* = SPHERICAL. □ **sphericity** /-ˈrɪsɪti/ *n.*

spherical /ˈsfɛrɪk(ə)l/ *adj.* **1** shaped like a sphere; globular. **2 a** of or relating to the properties of spheres (*spherical geometry*). **b** formed inside or on the surface of a sphere (*spherical triangle*). □ **spherically** *adv.* [Late Latin *sphaericus* from Greek *sphairikos* (as SPHERE)]

spherical aberration *n.* a loss of definition in the image arising from the surface geometry of a spherical mirror or lens.

spherical angle *n.* an angle formed by the intersection of two great circles of a sphere.

spheroid /ˈsfɪərɔɪd/ *n.* **1** a spherelike but not perfectly spherical body. **2** a solid generated by a half-revolution of an ellipse about its major axis (**prolate spheroid**) or minor axis (**oblate spheroid**). □ **spheroidal** /sfɪəˈrɔɪd(ə)l/ *adj.* **spheroidicity** /-ˈdɪsɪti/ *n.*

spherometer /sfɪəˈrɒmɪtə/ *n.* an instrument for finding the radius of a sphere and for the exact measurement of the thickness of small bodies. [French *sphéromètre* (as SPHERE, -METER)]

spherule /ˈsfɛrjuːl/ *n.* a small sphere. □ **spherular** *adj.* [Late Latin *sphaerula*, diminutive of Latin *sphaera* (as SPHERE)]

spherulite /ˈsfɛrjʊlʌɪt/ *n.* a vitreous globule as a constituent of volcanic rocks. □ **spherulitic** /-ˈlɪtɪk/ *adj.*

sphincter /ˈsfɪŋktə/ *n. Anat.* a ring of muscle surrounding and serving to guard or close an opening or tube, esp. the anus. □ **sphincteral** *adj.* **sphincteric** /-ˈtɛrɪk/ *adj.* [Latin from Greek *sphigktēr*, from *sphiggō* 'bind tight']

sphingid /ˈsfɪndʒɪd/ *n.* a hawkmoth (family Sphingidae). [as SPHINX + -ID[3]]

sphinx /sfɪŋks/ *n.* **1** (**Sphinx**) (in Greek mythology) the winged monster of Thebes, having a woman's head and a lion's body, whose riddle Oedipus guessed and who consequently killed herself. **2** *Antiq.* **a** any of several ancient Egyptian stone figures having a lion's body and a human or animal head. **b** (**the Sphinx**) the huge sphinx near the Pyramids at Giza. **3** an enigmatic or inscrutable person. **4** *US* a hawkmoth, esp. of the genus *Sphinx*. **5** a baboon, esp. the mandrill, *Mandrillus sphinx*. [Latin from Greek *Sphigx*, apparently from *sphiggō* 'draw tight']

sphygmo- /ˈsfɪgməʊ/ *comb. form Physiol.* a pulse or pulsation. [Greek *sphugmo-* from *sphugmos* 'pulse', from *sphuzō* 'to throb']

sphygmogram /ˈsfɪgmə(ʊ)gram/ *n.* a record produced by a sphygmograph.

sphygmograph /ˈsfɪgmə(ʊ)grɑːf/ *n.* an instrument for showing the character of a pulse in a series of curves. □ **sphygmographic** /-ˈgrafɪk/ *adj.* **sphygmographically** /-ˈgrafɪk(ə)li/ *adv.* **sphygmography** /-ˈmɒgrəfi/ *n.*

sphygmology /sfɪgˈmɒlədʒi/ *n.* the scientific study of the pulse. □ **sphygmological** /-məˈlɒdʒɪk(ə)l/ *adj.*

sphygmomanometer /ˌsfɪgməʊməˈnɒmɪtə/ *n.* an instrument for measuring blood pressure. □ **sphygmomanometric** /-nəˈmɛtrɪk/ *adj.*

spic[1] /spɪk/ *n. US slang offens.* **1** a Spanish-speaking person from Central or S. America or the Caribbean, esp. a Mexican. **2** the Spanish language spoken by such a person. [abbreviation of *spiggoty*, of uncertain origin: perhaps alteration of *speak the* in 'no speak the English']

spic[2] see SPICK AND SPAN.

spica /ˈspʌɪkə/ *n.* **1** *Bot.* a spike or spikelike form. **2** *Surgery* a spiral bandage with reversed turns, suggesting an ear of corn. □ **spicate** /-keɪt, -kət/ *adj.* **spicated** /-ˈkeɪtɪd/ *adj.* [Latin, = spike, ear of corn, related to *spina* SPINE: in sense 2 influenced by Greek *stakhus*]

spiccato /spɪˈkɑːtəʊ/ *n., adj., & adv. Mus.* ● *n.* a style of staccato playing on stringed instruments involving bouncing the bow on the strings. ● *adj.* performed or to be performed in this style. ● *adv.* in this style. [Italian, = detailed, distinct]

spice /spʌɪs/ *n. & v.* ● *n.* **1** an aromatic or pungent vegetable substance used to flavour food, e.g. cloves, pepper, or mace. **2** spices collectively (*a dealer in spice*). **3 a** an interesting or piquant quality. **b** (foll. by *of*) a slight flavour or suggestion (*a spice of malice*). ● *v.tr.* **1** flavour with spice. **2** add an interesting or piquant quality to (*a book spiced with humour*). [Middle English via Old French *espice(r)* from Latin *species* 'specific kind': in Late Latin pl. = merchandise]

spicebush /ˈspʌɪsbʊʃ/ *n.* an aromatic shrub, *Lindera benzoin* (laurel family), native to America.

spicey var. of SPICY.

spick and span /spɪk (ə)nd ˈspan/ *adj.* (also **spic and span**) **1** neat and clean. **2** smart and new. [16th-c. *spick and span new*, emphatic extension of Middle English *span new* from Old Norse *spán-nýr*, from *spánn* 'chip' + *nýr* 'new']

spicule /ˈspɪkjuːl/ *n.* **1** any small sharp-pointed body. **2** *Zool.* a small hard calcareous or siliceous body, esp. in the framework of a sponge. **3** *Bot.* a small or secondary spike. **4** *Astron.* a spikelike prominence, esp. one appearing as a jet of gas in the sun's corona. □ **spicular** *adj.* **spiculate** /-lət/ *adj.* [modern Latin *spicula*, *spiculum*, diminutives of SPICA]

spicy /ˈspʌɪsi/ *adj.* (also **spicey**) (**spicier**, **spiciest**) **1** of, flavoured with, or fragrant with spice. **2 a** piquant, pungent. **b** sensational or improper (*a spicy story*). □ **spicily** *adv.* **spiciness** *n.*

spider /ˈspʌɪdə/ *n. & v.* ● *n.* **1 a** any eight-legged arthropod of the order Araneae with a round unsegmented body, many of which spin webs for the capture of insects as food. **b** any of various similar or related arachnids, e.g. a red spider. **2** any object comparable to a spider, esp. as having numerous or prominent legs or radiating spokes. **3** *Brit.* a radiating series of elastic ties used to hold a load in place on a vehicle etc. ● *v.intr.* **1** move in a scuttling manner suggestive of a spider (*fingers spidered across the map*). **2** cause to move or appear in this way. **3** (as **spidering** *adj.*) spiderlike in form, manner, or movement (*spidering streets*). □ **spiderish** *adj.* [Old English *spīthra* (as SPIN)]

spider crab *n.* any of various crabs of the family Majidae with a pear-shaped body and long thin legs.

spiderman /ˈspʌɪdəman/ *n.* (*pl.* **-men**) *Brit. colloq.* a person who works at great heights in building construction.

spider mite *n.* (in full **red spider mite**) a plant-feeding mite of the family Tetranychidae, esp. *Tetranychus urticae*, a serious garden and hothouse pest (also called *red spider*).

spider monkey *n.* any S. American monkey of the genera *Ateles* and *Brachyteles*, with long limbs and a prehensile tail.

spider plant *n.* a southern African plant, *Chlorophytum comosum* (lily family), with long narrow striped leaves, often grown as a house plant.

spiderwort /ˈspʌɪdəwəːt/ *n.* any plant of the genus *Tradescantia*, esp. *T. virginiana*, having flowers with long hairy stamens.

spidery /ˈspʌɪd(ə)ri/ *adj.* elongated and thin (*spidery handwriting*).

spiegeleisen /ˈspiːg(ə)lʌɪz(ə)n/ *n.* an alloy of iron and manganese, used in steel-making. [German, from *Spiegel* 'mirror' + *Eisen* 'iron']

spiel /ʃpiːl, spiːl/ *n. & v. slang* ● *n.* a glib speech or story, esp. a salesman's patter. ● *v.* **1** *intr.* speak glibly; hold forth. **2** *tr.* reel off (patter etc.). [German, = play, game]

spieler /ˈʃpiːlə, ˈspiːlə/ *n. slang* **1** esp. *US* a person who spiels. **2** *Austral.* & *NZ* a gambler; a swindler. [German (as SPIEL)]

spiff /spɪf/ *v.tr.* (foll. by *up*) *N. Amer. colloq.* make attractive or smart. [perhaps from dialect *spiff* 'well-dressed']

spiffing /ˈspɪfɪŋ/ *adj. Brit. archaic slang* **1** excellent. **2** smart, handsome. [19th c.: origin unknown]

spiffy /ˈspɪfi/ *adj.* (**spiffier**, **spiffiest**) esp. *N. Amer. colloq.* = SPIFFING. □ **spiffily** *adv.*

spiflicate /ˈspɪflɪkeɪt/ *v.tr.* (also **spifflicate**) esp. *joc.* **1** destroy. **2** beat (in a fight etc.). [18th c.: fanciful]

spignel /ˈspɪgn(ə)l/ *n.* an aromatic white-flowered umbelliferous mountain plant, *Meum athamanticum*. Also called *baldmoney*, *meu*. [perhaps from Middle English plant-name *spigurnel*, from medieval Latin *spigurnellus*, of unknown origin]

spigot /ˈspɪgət/ *n.* **1** a small peg or plug, esp. for insertion into the vent of a cask. **2 a** *US* a tap. **b** a device for controlling the flow of liquid in a tap. **3** the plain end of a section of a pipe fitting into the socket of the next one. [Middle English, perhaps via Provençal *espigou(n)* from Latin *spiculum*, diminutive of *spicum* = SPICA]

spike[1] /spʌɪk/ *n. & v.* ● *n.* **1 a** a sharp point. **b** a pointed piece of metal, esp. the top of an iron railing etc. **2 a** any of several metal points set into the sole of a running shoe to prevent slipping. **b** (in *pl.*) a pair of running shoes with spikes. **3 a** *Brit.* a pointed metal rod standing on a base and used for filing news items etc. esp. when rejected for publication. **b** a similar spike used for bills etc. **4** a large stout nail esp. as used for railways. **5** *slang* a hypodermic needle. **6** *Brit. slang* a doss-house. **7** *Electronics* a pulse of very short duration in which a rapid increase in voltage is followed by a rapid decrease. ● *v.tr.* **1 a** fasten or provide with spikes. **b** fix on or pierce with spikes. **2** (of a newspaper editor etc.) reject (a story) by filing it on a spike. **3** *colloq.* **a** lace (a drink) with alcohol, a drug, etc. **b** contaminate (a substance) with something added. **4** make useless, put an end to or thwart (an idea etc.). **5** *hist.* plug up the vent of (a gun) with a spike. □ **spike a person's guns** spoil his or her plans. [Middle English, perhaps from Middle Low German, Middle Dutch *spiker*, related to SPOKE[1]]

spike[2] /spʌɪk/ *n. Bot.* a flower cluster formed of many flower heads attached closely on a long stem. [Middle English, = ear of corn, from Latin SPICA]

spike heel *n.* a high tapering heel of a shoe.

spikelet /ˈspʌɪklɪt/ *n.* a small spike; esp. the basic unit of a grass flower, with two bracts at the base. [SPIKE[2] + -LET]

spikenard /ˈspʌɪknɑːd/ *n.* **1 a** *hist.* a costly perfumed ointment much valued in ancient times. **b** the plant from whose rhizome this was prepared, probably the Himalayan *Nardostachys grandiflora*. **2** *hist.* = NARD 1. **3** a plant resembling spikenard in fragrance (*ploughman's spikenard*). [Middle English, ultimately from medieval Latin *spica nardi* (as SPIKE[2], NARD), translating Greek *nardostakhus*]

spiky /ˈspʌɪki/ *adj.* (**spikier**, **spikiest**) **1** like a spike; having many spikes. **2** *colloq.* easily offended; prickly. □ **spikily** *adv.* **spikiness** *n.*

spile /spʌɪl/ *n.* & *v.* ● *n.* **1** a wooden peg or spigot. **2** a large timber or pile for driving into the ground. **3** *N. Amer.* a small spout for tapping the sap from a sugar maple etc. ● *v.tr.* broach (a cask etc.) with a spike in order to draw off liquid. [Middle Dutch, Middle Low German, = wooden peg etc.: in sense 2 apparently an alteration of PILE[2]]

spill[1] /spɪl/ *v.* & *n.* ● *v.* (*past* and *past part.* **spilt** or **spilled**) **1** *intr.* & *tr.* fall or run or cause (a liquid, powder, etc.) to fall or run out of a vessel, esp. unintentionally. **2 a** *tr.* & *intr.* throw (a person etc.) from a vehicle, saddle, etc. **b** *intr.* (esp. of a crowd) tumble out quickly from a place etc. (*the fans spilled into the street*). **3** *tr. slang* disclose (information etc.). **4** *tr. Naut.* **a** empty (a sail) of wind. **b** lose (wind) from a sail. ● *n.* **1 a** the act or an instance of spilling or being spilt. **b** a quantity spilt. **2** a tumble or fall, esp. from a horse etc. (*had a nasty spill*). **3** *Austral.* the vacating of all or several posts of a parliamentary party to allow reorganization. □ **spill the beans** *colloq.* divulge information etc., esp. unintentionally or indiscreetly. **spill blood** be guilty of bloodshed. **spill the blood of** kill or injure (a person). **spill over 1** overflow. **2** (of a surplus population) be forced to move (cf. OVERSPILL 2). □ **spillage** /-ɪdʒ/ *n.* **spiller** *n.* [Old English *spillan* 'kill', related to Old English *spildan* 'destroy': origin unknown]

spill[2] /spɪl/ *n.* a thin strip of wood, folded or twisted paper, etc., used for lighting a fire, candles, a pipe, etc. [Middle English, related to SPILE]

spillikin /ˈspɪlɪkɪn/ *n.* (also **spellican** /ˈspɛlɪk(ə)n/) **1** a splinter of wood, bone, etc. **2** (in *pl.*) a game in which a heap of spillikins is to be removed one at a time without moving the others. [SPILL[2] + -KIN]

spillover /ˈspɪləʊvə/ *n.* **1 a** the process or an instance of spilling over. **b** a thing that spills over. **2** a consequence, repercussion, or by-product.

spillway /ˈspɪlweɪ/ *n.* a passage for surplus water from a dam.

spilt *past* and *past part.* of SPILL[1].

spilth /spɪlθ/ *n.* **1** material that is spilled. **2** the act or an instance of spilling. **3** an excess or surplus.

spin /spɪn/ *v.* & *n.* ● *v.* (**spinning**; *past* **spun** /spʌn/ or **span** /span/; *past part.* **spun**) **1** *intr.* & *tr.* turn or cause (a person or thing) to turn or whirl round quickly. **2** *tr.* (also *absol.*) **a** draw out and twist (wool, cotton, etc.) into threads. **b** make (yarn) in this way. **c** make a similar type of thread from (a synthetic substance etc.). **3** *tr.* (of a spider, silkworm, etc.) make (a web, gossamer, a cocoon, etc.) by extruding a fine viscous thread. **4** *tr.* tell or write (a story, essay, article, etc.) (*spins a good tale*). **5** *tr.* impart spin to (a ball). **6** *intr.* (of a person's head etc.) be dizzy through excitement, astonishment, etc. **7** *tr.* shape (metal) in a mould on a lathe etc. **8** *intr.* esp. *Cricket* (of a ball) move through the air with spin. **9** *tr.* (as **spun** *adj.*) converted into threads (*spun glass*; *spun gold*; *spun sugar*). **10** *tr.* fish in (a stream, pool, etc.) with a spinner. **11** *tr.* toss (a coin). **12** *tr.* = *spin-dry* (see SPIN-DRYER). ● *n.* **1** a spinning motion; a whirl. **2** an aircraft's diving descent combined with rotation. **3 a** a revolving motion through the air, esp. in a rifle bullet or in a billiard, tennis, or table tennis ball struck aslant. **b** *Cricket* a twisting motion given to the ball in bowling. **4** *colloq.* a brief drive in a motor vehicle, aeroplane, etc., esp. for pleasure. **5** *Physics* the intrinsic angular momentum of a subatomic particle. **6** *Austral.* & *NZ slang* a piece of good or bad luck. **7** esp. *US Polit.* a bias in information to give a favourable impression. □ **spin off** throw off by centrifugal force in spinning. **spin out 1** prolong (a discussion etc.). **2** make (a story, money, etc.) last as long as possible. **3** spend or consume (time, one's life, etc., by discussion or in an occupation etc.). **4** *US* (esp. of a driver or car) lose or go out of control, esp. in a skid. **5** *Cricket* dismiss (a batsman or side) by spin bowling. **spin a yarn** orig. *Naut.* tell a story. [Old English *spinnan*]

spina bifida /spʌɪnə ˈbɪfɪdə/ *n.* a congenital defect of the spine, in which part of the spinal cord and its meninges are exposed through a gap in the backbone. [modern Latin (as SPINE, BIFID)]

spinach /ˈspɪnɪdʒ, -ɪtʃ/ *n.* **1** a green garden vegetable, *Spinacia oleracea*, with succulent leaves. **2** the leaves of this plant used as food. □ **spinachy** *adj.* [probably Middle Dutch *spinaetse*, *spinag(i)e*, via Old French *espinage*, *espinache*, medieval Latin *spinac(h)ia* etc., and Arabic *ʼisfānāḵ* from Persian *ispānāḵ*: perhaps assimilated to Latin *spina* SPINE, with reference to its prickly seeds]

spinach beet *n.* a variety of beetroot cultivated for its edible leaves.

spinal /ˈspʌɪn(ə)l/ *adj.* of or relating to the spine (*spinal curvature*; *spinal disease*). □ **spinally** *adv.* [Late Latin *spinalis* (as SPINE)]

spinal canal *n.* a cavity through the vertebrae containing the spinal cord.

spinal column *n.* the spine.

spinal cord *n.* a cylindrical structure of the central nervous system enclosed in the spine, connecting all parts of the body with the brain.

spin bowler *n. Cricket* an expert at bowling with spin.

spindle /ˈspɪnd(ə)l/ *n.* & *v.* ● *n.* **1 a** a pin in a spinning wheel used for twisting and winding the thread. **b** a small bar with tapered ends used for the same purpose in hand-spinning. **c** a pin bearing the bobbin of a spinning machine. **2** a pin or axis that revolves or on which something revolves. **3** *US* = SPIKE[1] *n.* 3a. **4** a turned piece of wood used as a banister, chair leg, etc. **5** *Biol.* a spindle-shaped mass of microtubules formed when a cell divides. **6** a varying measure of length for yarn. **7** a slender person or thing. ● *v.intr.* have, or grow into, a long slender form. [Old English *spinel* (as SPIN)]

spindle-berry *n.* the fruit of the spindle tree.

spindle-shanks *n.pl.* **1** long thin legs. **2** (treated as *sing.*) a person with such legs. □ **spindle-shanked** *adj.*

spindle-shaped *adj.* having a circular cross-section and tapering towards each end.

spindle side *n.* = DISTAFF SIDE.

spindle tree *n.* any shrub or small tree of the genus *Euonymus*, esp. *E. europaeus* with greenish-white flowers, pink or red berries, and hard wood used for spindles.

spindly /ˈspɪndli/ *adj.* (**spindlier**, **spindliest**) long or tall and thin; thin and weak.

spin doctor *n. colloq.* a political spokesperson employed to give a favourable interpretation of events to the media.

spindrift /ˈspɪndrɪft/ *n.* spray blown along the surface of the sea. [Scots variant of *spoondrift*, from *spoon* 'run before wind or sea' + DRIFT]

spin-dryer *n.* (also **spin-drier**) a machine for drying wet clothes etc. centrifugally in a revolving drum. □ **spin-dry** *v.*

spine /spʌɪn/ *n.* **1** a series of vertebrae extending from the skull to the small of the back, enclosing the spinal cord and providing support for the thorax and abdomen; the backbone. **2** *Zool.* & *Bot.* any hard pointed process or structure. **3** a sharp ridge or projection, esp. of a mountain range or slope. **4** a central feature, main support, or source of strength. **5** the part of a book's jacket or cover that encloses the inner edges of the pages and usu. faces outwards on a shelf. □ **spined** *adj.* [Middle English from Old French *espine* or Latin *spina* 'thorn, backbone']

spine-chiller *n.* a frightening story, film, etc. □ **spine-chilling** *adj.*

spinel /spɪˈnɛl, ˈspɪn(ə)l/ *n.* **1** any of a group of hard crystalline minerals of various colours, consisting chiefly of oxides of magnesium and aluminium. **2** any substance of similar composition or properties. [French *spinelle* from Italian *spinella*, diminutive of *spina*: see SPINE]

spineless /ˈspʌɪnlɪs/ *adj.* **1 a** having no spine; invertebrate. **b** (of an animal or plant) having no spines. **2** (of a person) lacking energy or resolution; weak and purposeless. □ **spinelessly** *adv.* **spinelessness** *n.*

spinel ruby *n.* a deep red variety of spinel used as a gem.

spinet /spɪˈnɛt, ˈspɪnɪt/ *n.* **1** *hist.* a small harpsichord with oblique strings. **2** *US* a type of small upright piano. [obsolete French *espinette* from Italian *spinetta* 'virginal, spinet', diminutive of *spina* 'thorn' etc. (as SPINE), with reference to the plucked strings]

spinifex /ˈspɪnɪfɛks/ *n.* any Australian grass of the genus *Spinifex*, with coarse, spiny leaves. [modern Latin, from Latin *spina* SPINE + *-fex* 'maker' from *facere* 'make']

spinnaker /ˈspɪnəkə/ *n.* a large triangular sail carried opposite the mainsail of a racing yacht running before the wind. [fanciful from *Sphinx*, the name of the yacht first using it, perhaps influenced by *spanker*]

spinner /ˈspɪnə/ *n.* **1** a person or thing that spins. **2** *Cricket* **a** a spin bowler. **b** a spun ball. **3** a spin-dryer. **4 a** a real or artificial fly for esp. trout-fishing. **b** revolving bait. **5** a manufacturer or merchant engaged in (esp. cotton-) spinning. **6** = SPINNERET 1. **7** *archaic* a spider.

spinneret /ˈspɪnərɛt/ *n.* **1** the spinning-organ in a spider, silkworm, etc. **2** a device for forming filaments of synthetic fibre.

spinney /ˈspɪni/ *n.* (*pl.* **-eys**) *Brit.* a small wood; a thicket. [Old French *espinei* from Latin *spinetum* 'thicket', from *spina* 'thorn']

spinning /ˈspɪnɪŋ/ *n.* the act or an instance of spinning.

spinning jenny *n. hist.* a machine for spinning with more than one spindle at a time.

spinning machine *n.* a machine that spins fibres continuously.

spinning mule see MULE[1] 4.

spinning top *n.* = TOP[2].

spinning wheel *n.* a household machine for spinning yarn or thread with a spindle driven by a wheel attached to a crank or treadle.

spin-off *n.* an incidental result or results esp. as a side benefit from industrial technology.

spinose /ˈspʌɪnəʊs, spʌɪˈnəʊs/ *adj.* (also **spinous** /-nəs/) esp. *Bot.* & *Zool.* having spines, spiny.

Spinozism /spɪˈnəʊzɪz(ə)m/ *n. Philos.* the doctrine of Spinoza that there is one infinite substance of which extension and thought are attributes and human beings are changing forms. □ **Spinozist** *n.* **Spinozistic** /-ˈzɪstɪk/ *adj.* [B. de *Spinoza*, Dutch philosopher d. 1677]

spinster /ˈspɪnstə/ *n.* **1** an unmarried woman. **2** a woman, esp. elderly, thought unlikely to marry. □ **spinsterhood** *n.* **spinsterish** *adj.* **spinsterishness** *n.* [Middle English, originally = woman who spins]

spinthariscope /spɪnˈθarɪskəʊp/ *n.* an instrument with a fluorescent screen showing the incidence of alpha particles by flashes. [formed irregularly from Greek *spintharis* 'spark' + -SCOPE]

spinule /ˈspɪnjuːl/ *n. Bot.* & *Zool.* a small spine. □ **spinulose** *adj.* **spinulous** *adj.* [Latin *spinula*, diminutive of *spina* SPINE]

spiny /ˈspʌɪni/ *adj.* (**spinier**, **spiniest**) **1** full of spines; prickly. **2** perplexing, troublesome, thorny. □ **spininess** *n.*

spiny anteater *n.* = ECHIDNA.

spiny lobster *n.* any of various large edible crustaceans of the family Palinuridae, esp. *Palinuris vulgaris*, with a spiny shell and no large anterior claws.

spiracle /ˈspʌɪrək(ə)l/ *n.* (also **spiraculum** /ˌspaɪəˈrakjʊləm/) (*pl.* **spiracles** or **spiracula** /-lə/) an external respiratory opening in insects, whales, and some fish. □ **spiracular** /-ˈrakjʊlə/ *adj.* [Latin *spiraculum* from *spirare* 'breathe']

spiraea /spʌɪˈriːə/ *n.* (*US* **spirea**) any shrub of the genus *Spiraea* (rose family), with clusters of small white or pink flowers. [Latin from Greek *speiraia*, from *speira* 'a coil']

spiral /ˈspʌɪr(ə)l/ *adj., n., & v.* ● *adj.* **1** winding about a centre in an enlarging or decreasing continuous circular motion, either on a flat plane or rising in a cone; coiled. **2** winding continuously along or as if along a cylinder, like the thread of a screw. ● *n.* **1** a plane or three-dimensional spiral curve. **2** a spiral spring. **3** a spiral formation in a shell etc. **4** a spiral galaxy. **5** a progressive rise or fall of prices, wages, etc., each responding to an upward or downward stimulus provided by the other (*a spiral of rising prices and wages*). ● *v.* (**spiralled**, **spiralling**; *US* **spiraled**, **spiraling**) **1** *intr.* move in a spiral course, esp. upwards or downwards. **2** *tr.* make spiral. **3** *intr.* esp. *Econ.* (of prices, wages, etc.) rise or fall, esp. rapidly (cf. sense 5 of *n.*). □ **spirality** /-ˈralɪti/ *n.* **spirally** *adv.* [French *spiral* or medieval Latin *spiralis* (as SPIRE[2])]

spiral balance *n.* a device for measuring weight by the torsion of a spiral spring.

spiral galaxy *n.* a galaxy in which the matter is concentrated mainly in one or more spiral arms.

spiral staircase *n.* a staircase rising in a spiral round a central axis.

spirant /ˈspʌɪr(ə)nt/ *adj.* & *n. Phonet.* ● *adj.* (of a consonant) uttered with a continuous expulsion of breath, esp. fricative. ● *n.* such a consonant. [Latin *spirare spirant-* 'breathe']

spire[1] /spʌɪə/ *n.* & *v.* ● *n.* **1** a tapering conical or pyramidal structure built esp. on a church tower (cf. STEEPLE). **2** the continuation of a tree trunk above the point where branching begins. **3** any tapering thing, e.g. the spike of a flower. ● *v.tr.* provide with a spire. □ **spiry** /ˈspʌɪri/ *adj.* [Old English *spīr*]

spire[2] /spʌɪə/ *n.* **1 a** a spiral; a coil. **b** a single twist of this. **2** the upper part of a spiral shell. [French via Latin *spira* from Greek *speira* 'a coil']

spirea *US* var. of SPIRAEA.

spirillum /spʌɪˈrɪləm/ *n.* (*pl.* **spirilla** /-lə/) any bacterium with a rigid spiral structure, esp. one of the genus *Spirillum*. [modern Latin, irregular diminutive of Latin *spira* SPIRE[2]]

spirit /ˈspɪrɪt/ *n.* & *v.* ● *n.* **1 a** the vital animating essence of a person or animal (*was sadly broken in spirit*). **b** the intelligent non-physical part of a person; the soul. **2 a** a rational or intelligent being without a material body. **b** a supernatural being such as a ghost, fairy, etc. (*haunted by spirits*). **3** a prevailing mental or moral condition or attitude; a mood; a tendency (*public spirit*; *took it in the wrong spirit*). **4** (usu. in *pl.*) esp. *Brit.* strong distilled liquor, e.g. brandy, whisky, gin, rum. **5** (*US* esp. in *pl.*) **a** a distilled liquid essence (*spirit of hartshorn*). **b** a distilled alcohol (*methylated spirit*). **c** a solution of a volatile principle in alcohol; a tincture (*spirit of ammonia*). **6 a** a person's mental or moral nature or qualities, usu. specified (*has an unbending spirit*). **b** a person viewed as possessing these (*is an ardent spirit*). **c** (in full **high spirit**) courage, energy, vivacity, dash (*played with spirit*; *infused him with spirit*). **7** the real meaning as opposed to lip-service or verbal expression (*the spirit of the law*). **8** *archaic* an immaterial principle thought to govern vital phenomena (*animal spirits*). ● *v.tr.* (**spirited**, **spiriting**) (usu. foll. by *away*, *off*, etc.) convey rapidly and secretly by or as if by spirits. □ **in** (or **in the**) **spirit** inwardly; sensed psychologically as giving support though not present physically (*shall be with you in spirit*). **the spirit moves a person** he or she feels inclined (to do something) (originally in Quaker use). **spirit up** animate or cheer (a person). [Middle English via Anglo-French *(e)spirit*, Old French *esp(e)rit* from Latin *spiritus* 'breath, spirit', from *spirare* 'breathe']

spirit duplicator *n.* a duplicator using an alcoholic solution to reproduce copies from a master sheet.

spirited /ˈspɪrɪtɪd/ *adj.* **1** full of spirit; animated, lively, brisk, or courageous (*a spirited attack*; *a spirited translation*). **2** having a spirit or spirits of a specified kind (*high-spirited*; *mean-spirited*). □ **spiritedly** *adv.* **spiritedness** *n.*

spirit gum *n.* a quick-drying solution of gum used esp. for attaching false hair.

spirit lamp *n.* a lamp burning methylated or other volatile spirits instead of oil.

spiritless /ˈspɪrɪtlɪs/ *adj.* lacking courage, vigour, or vivacity. □ **spiritlessly** *adv.* **spiritlessness** *n.*

spirit level *n.* a device consisting of a sealed glass tube nearly filled with alcohol or other liquid, containing an air bubble whose position is used to test horizontality.

spirit of hartshorn see HARTSHORN 2.

spirit of wine *n.* (also **spirits of wine**) *archaic* purified alcohol.

spiritous /ˈspɪrɪtəs/ *adj.* = SPIRITUOUS.

spirits of salt *n. archaic* hydrochloric acid.

spiritual /ˈspɪrɪtʃʊəl, -tjʊəl/ *adj. & n.* ● *adj.* **1** of or concerning the spirit as opposed to matter. **2** concerned with sacred or religious things; holy; divine; inspired (*the spiritual life*; *spiritual songs*). **3** (of the mind etc.) refined, sensitive; not concerned with the material. **4** (of a relationship etc.) concerned with the soul or spirit etc., not with external reality (*his spiritual home*). ● *n.* = NEGRO SPIRITUAL. □ **spirituality** /-ˈalɪti/ *n.* **spiritually** *adv.* **spiritualness** *n.* [Middle English via Old French *spirituel* from Latin *spiritualis* (as SPIRIT)]

spiritual courts *n.pl.* ecclesiastical courts.

spiritualism /ˈspɪrɪtʃʊəlɪz(ə)m, -tjʊəl-/ *n.* **1 a** the belief that the spirits of the dead can communicate with the living, esp. through mediums. **b** the practice of this. **2** *Philos.* the doctrine that the spirit exists as distinct from matter, or that spirit is the only reality (cf. MATERIALISM 2). □ **spiritualist** *n.* **spiritualistic** /-ˈlɪstɪk/ *adj.*

spiritualize /ˈspɪrɪtʃʊəlʌɪz, -tjʊəl-/ *v.tr.* (also **-ise**) **1** make (a person or a person's character, thoughts, etc.) spiritual; elevate. **2** attach a spiritual as opposed to a literal meaning to. □ **spiritualization** /-ˈzeɪʃ(ə)n/ *n.*

spirituel /ˌspɪrɪtjʊˈɛl/ *adj.* (also **spirituelle**) (of the mind) refined and yet spirited; witty. [French *spirituel*, fem. *-elle* (as SPIRITUAL)]

spirituous /ˈspɪrɪtjʊəs/ *adj.* **1** containing much alcohol. **2** distilled, as whisky, rum, etc. (*spirituous liquor*). [Latin *spiritus* 'spirit', or French *spiritueux*]

spiro-[1] /ˈspʌɪrəʊ/ *comb. form* a coil. [Latin *spira*, Greek *speira* 'a coil']

spiro-[2] /ˈspʌɪrəʊ/ *comb. form* breath. [formed irregularly from Latin *spirare* 'breathe']

spirochaete /ˈspʌɪrə(ʊ)kiːt/ *n.* (*US* **spirochete**) any flexible spirally twisted bacterium of the order Spirochaetales, esp. one that causes syphilis. [SPIRO-[1] + Greek *khaitē* 'long hair']

spirograph /ˈspʌɪrəgrɑːf/ *n.* an instrument for recording breathing movements. □ **spirographic** /-ˈgrafɪk/ *adj.* **spirographically** /-ˈgrafɪk(ə)li/ *adv.*

spirogyra /spʌɪrəˈdʒʌɪrə/ *n.* any filamentous freshwater alga of the genus *Spirogyra*, with cells containing spiral bands of chlorophyll. [modern Latin, from SPIRO-[1] + Greek *guros gura* 'round']

spirometer /spʌɪˈrɒmɪtə/ *n.* an instrument for measuring the air capacity of the lungs.

spirt var. of SPURT.

spit[1] /spɪt/ *v. & n.* ● *v.* (**spitting**; *past* and *past part.* **spat** /spat/ or **spit**) **1** *intr.* **a** eject saliva from the mouth. **b** do this as a sign of hatred or contempt (*spat at him*). **2** *tr.* (usu. foll. by *out*) **a** eject (saliva, blood, food, etc.) from the mouth (*spat the meat out*). **b** utter (oaths, threats, etc.) vehemently (*'Damn you!' he spat*). **3** *intr.* (of a fire, pen, pan, etc.) send out sparks, ink, hot fat, etc. **4** *intr.* (of rain) fall lightly (*it's only spitting*). **5** *intr.* (esp. of a cat) make a spitting or hissing noise in anger or hostility. ● *n.* **1** spittle. **2** the act or an instance of spitting. **3** the foamy liquid secretion of some insects used to protect their young (*cuckoo spit*). □ **the spit** (or **very spit**) **of** *colloq.* the exact double of (cf. SPITTING IMAGE). **spit chips** *Austral. slang* be angry or frustrated. **spit it out** *colloq.* say what is on one's mind. **spit up** *US* (esp. of a baby) vomit. □ **spitter** *n.* [Old English *spittan*, of imitative origin]

spit[2] /spɪt/ *n. & v.* ● *n.* **1** a slender rod on which meat is skewered before being roasted on a fire etc.; a skewer. **2 a** a small point of land projecting into the sea. **b** a long narrow underwater bank. ● *v.tr.* (**spitted**, **spitting**) **1** thrust a spit through (meat etc.). **2** pierce or transfix with a sword etc. □ **spitty** *adj.* [Old English *spitu*, from West Germanic]

spit[3] /spɪt/ *n.* (*pl.* same or **spits**) a spade-depth of earth (*dig it two spit deep*). [Middle Dutch & Middle Low German, = Old English *spittan* 'dig with spade', probably related to SPIT[2]]

spit and polish *n.* **1** the cleaning and polishing duties of a soldier etc. **2** exaggerated neatness and smartness.

spitball /ˈspɪtbɔːl/ *n. & v.* ● *n. N. Amer.* **1** a ball of chewed paper etc. used as a missile. **2** a baseball moistened illegally by the pitcher to affect its flight. ● *v.intr.* throw out suggestions for discussion. □ **spitballer** *n.*

spitchcock /ˈspɪtʃkɒk/ *n. & v.* ● *n.* an eel split and grilled or fried. ● *v.tr.* prepare (an eel, fish, bird, etc.) in this way. [16th c.: origin unknown: cf. SPATCHCOCK]

spite /spʌɪt/ *n. & v.* ● *n.* **1** ill will or malice towards a person (*did it from spite*). **2** a grudge. ● *v.tr.* thwart, mortify, annoy (*does it to spite me*). □ **in spite of** notwithstanding. **in spite of oneself** etc. though one would rather have done otherwise. [Middle English from Old French *despit* DESPITE]

spiteful /ˈspʌɪtfʊl, -f(ə)l/ *adj.* motivated by spite; malevolent. □ **spitefully** *adv.* **spitefulness** *n.*

spitfire /ˈspɪtfʌɪə/ *n.* a person of fiery temper.

spit-roast *v.tr.* cook on a spit.

spitting cobra *n.* the African black-necked cobra, *Naja nigricollis*, that ejects venom by spitting, not striking.

spitting distance *n.* a very short distance.

spitting image *n.* (foll. by *of*) *colloq.* the exact double of (another person or thing).

spittle /ˈspɪt(ə)l/ *n.* saliva, esp. as ejected from the mouth. □ **spittly** *adj.* [alteration of Middle English (now dialect) *spattle* from Old English *spātl*, from *spǣtan* 'to spit', influenced by SPIT[1]]

spittoon /spɪˈtuːn/ *n.* a metal or earthenware pot with esp. a funnel-shaped top, used for spitting into.

spitz /spɪts/ *n.* **1** a small type of dog with a pointed muzzle, esp. a Pomeranian. **2** this breed. [German *Spitz(hund)*, from *spitz* 'pointed' + *Hund* 'dog']

spiv /spɪv/ *n. Brit. colloq.* a man, often characterized by flashy dress, who makes a living by illicit or unscrupulous dealings. □ **spivvish** *adj.* **spivvy** *adj.* [20th c.: origin uncertain, perhaps related to SPIFFY]

splake /spleɪk/ *n.* a hybrid trout of N. American lakes. [*speckled* (*trout*) + *lake* (*trout*)]

splanchnic /ˈsplaŋknɪk/ *adj.* of or relating to the viscera; intestinal. [modern Latin *splanchnicus* from Greek *splagkhnikos*, from *splagkhna* 'entrails']

splash /splaʃ/ *v. & n.* ● *v.* **1** *intr. & tr.* spatter or cause (liquid) to spatter in small drops. **2** *tr.* cause (a person) to be spattered with liquid etc. (*splashed them with mud*). **3** *intr.* **a** (of a person) cause liquid to spatter (*was splashing about in the bath*). **b** (usu. foll. by *across*, *along*, etc.) move while spattering liquid etc. (*splashed across the carpet in his boots*). **c** step, fall, or plunge etc. into a liquid etc. so as to cause a splash (*splashed into the sea*). **4** *tr.* display (news) prominently. **5** *tr.* decorate with scattered colour. **6** *tr.* spend (money) ostentatiously. ● *n.* **1** the act or an instance of splashing. **2 a** a quantity of liquid splashed. **b** the resulting noise (*heard a splash*). **3** a spot of dirt etc. splashed on to a thing. **4** a prominent news feature etc. **5** a daub or patch of colour, esp. on an animal's coat. **6** *colloq.* a small quantity of liquid, esp. of soda water etc. to dilute spirits. □ **make a splash** attract much attention, esp. by extravagance. **splash down** (esp. of a spacecraft) land on water. **splash out** *Brit. colloq.* spend money freely. □ **splashy** *adj.* (**splashier**, **splashiest**). [alteration of PLASH[1]]

splashback /ˈsplaʃbak/ *n.* a panel behind a sink etc. to protect the wall from splashes.

splashdown /ˈsplaʃdaʊn/ *n.* the alighting of a spacecraft on the sea.

splat[1] /splat/ *n.* a flat piece of thin wood in the centre of a chair back. [*splat* 'split up', related to SPLIT]

splat[2] /splat/ *n., adv., & v. colloq.* ● *n.* a sharp cracking or slapping sound (*hit the wall with a splat*). ● *adv.* with a splat (*fell splat on his head*). ● *v.intr. & tr.* (**splatted**, **splatting**) fall or hit with a splat. [abbreviation of SPLATTER]

splatter /ˈsplatə/ *v. & n.* ● *v.* **1** *tr.* (often foll. by *with*) make wet or dirty by splashing. **2** *v.tr. & intr.* splash, esp. with a continuous noisy action. **3** *tr.* (often foll. by *over*) publicize or spread (news etc.) (*the story was splattered over the front page*). ● *n.* **1** a noisy splashing sound. **2** a rough patch of colour etc., esp. splashed on a surface. [imitative]

splay /spleɪ/ *v., n., & adj.* ● *v.* **1** *tr.* (usu. foll. by *out*) spread (the elbows, feet, etc.) out. **2** *intr.* (of an aperture or its sides) diverge in shape or position. **3** *tr.* construct (a window, doorway, aperture, etc.) so that it diverges or is wider at one side of the wall than at the other. ● *n.* a surface making an oblique angle with another, e.g. the splayed side of a window or embrasure. ● *adj.* **1** wide and flat. **2** turned outward. [Middle English, from DISPLAY]

splay-foot *n.* a broad flat foot turned outward. □ **splay-footed** *adj.*

spleen /spliːn/ *n.* **1** an abdominal organ involved in the production and removal of blood cells in most vertebrates and forming part of the immune system. **2** lowness of spirits; moroseness, ill temper, spite (from the earlier belief that the spleen was the seat of such feelings) (*a fit of spleen*; *vented their spleen*). □ **spleenful** *adj.* **spleeny** *adj.* [Middle English via Old French *esplen* and Latin *splen* from Greek *splēn*]

spleenwort /ˈspliːnwəːt/ *n.* any fern of the genus *Asplenium*, formerly used as a remedy for disorders of the spleen.

splen- /spliːn/ *comb. form Anat.* the spleen. [Greek (as SPLEEN)]

splendent /ˈsplɛnd(ə)nt/ *adj. formal* **1** shining; lustrous. **2** illustrious. [Middle English from Latin *splendēre* 'to shine']

splendid /ˈsplɛndɪd/ *adj.* **1** magnificent, gorgeous, brilliant, sumptuous (*a splendid palace*; *a splendid achievement*). **2** dignified; impressive (*splendid isolation*). **3** excellent; fine (*a splendid chance*). □ **splendidly** *adv.* **splendidness** *n.* [French *splendide* or Latin *splendidus* (as SPLENDENT)]

splendiferous /splɛnˈdɪf(ə)rəs/ *adj. colloq.* or *joc.* splendid. □ **splendiferously** *adv.* **splendiferousness** *n.* [formed irregularly from SPLENDOUR]

splendour /ˈsplɛndə/ *n.* (*US* **splendor**) **1** great or dazzling brightness. **2** magnificence; grandeur. [Middle English from Anglo-French *splendeur* or Latin *splendor* (as SPLENDENT)]

splenectomy /splɪˈnɛktəmi/ *n.* (*pl.* **-ies**) the surgical removal of the spleen.

splenetic /splɪˈnɛtɪk/ *adj. & n.* ● *adj.* **1** ill-tempered; peevish. **2** of or concerning the spleen. ● *n.* a splenetic person. □ **splenetically** *adv.* [Late Latin *spleneticus* (as SPLEEN)]

splenic /ˈsplɛnɪk, ˈspliːnɪk/ *adj.* of or in the spleen. □ **splenoid** /ˈspliːnɔɪd/ *adj.* [French *splénique* or Latin *splenicus* from Greek *splēnikos* (as SPLEEN)]

splenic fever *n.* anthrax.

splenitis /splɪˈnʌɪtɪs/ *n.* inflammation of the spleen.

splenius /ˈspliːnɪəs/ *n.* (*pl.* **splenii** /-nɪʌɪ/) *Anat.* either section of muscle on each side of the neck and back serving to draw back the head. □ **splenial** *adj.* [modern Latin from Greek *splēnion* 'bandage']

splenology /spliːˈnɒlədʒi/ *n.* the scientific study of the spleen.

splenomegaly /spliːnə(ʊ)ˈmɛg(ə)li/ *n.* a pathological enlargement of the spleen. [SPLEN- + *megaly* (as MEGALO-)]

splenotomy /spliːˈnɒtəmi/ *n.* (*pl.* **-ies**) a surgical incision into or dissection of the spleen.

splice /splʌɪs/ *v. & n.* ● *v.tr.* **1** join the ends of (ropes) by interweaving strands. **2** join (pieces of timber, magnetic tape, film, etc.) in an overlapping position. **3** (esp. as **spliced** *adj.*) *colloq.* join in marriage. ● *n.* a joint consisting of two ropes, pieces of wood, film, etc., made by splicing, e.g. the handle and blade of a cricket bat. □ **splice the main brace** *Naut. hist.* issue an extra tot of rum. □ **splicer** *n.* [probably from Middle Dutch *splissen*, of uncertain origin]

spliff /splɪf/ *n.* (also **splif**) *slang* a cannabis cigarette. [20th c.: origin unknown]

spline /splʌɪn/ *n. & v.* ● *n.* **1** a rectangular key fitting into grooves in the hub and shaft of a wheel and allowing longitudinal play. **2** a slat. **3** a flexible wood or rubber strip used esp. in drawing large curves. ● *v.tr.* fit with a spline (see sense 1 of *n.*). [originally E. Anglian dialect, perhaps related to SPLINTER]

splint /splɪnt/ *n. & v.* ● *n.* **1 a** a strip of rigid material used for holding a broken bone etc. when set. **b** a rigid or flexible strip of esp. wood used in basketwork etc. **2** a tumour or bony excrescence on the inside of a horse's leg. **3** a thin strip of wood etc. used to light a fire, pipe, etc. **4** = SPLINT-BONE 1. ● *v.tr.* secure (a broken limb etc.) with a splint or splints. [Middle English *splent(e)* from Middle Dutch *splinte* or Middle Low German *splinte*, *splente* 'metal plate or pin', related to SPLINTER]

splint-bone *n.* **1** either of two small bones in a horse's foreleg lying behind and close to the cannon-bone. **2** the human fibula.

splint-coal *n.* hard bituminous laminated coal burning with great heat.

splinter /ˈsplɪntə/ *v. & n.* ● *v.tr. & intr.* break into fragments. ● *n.* a small thin sharp-edged piece broken off from wood, stone, etc. □ **splintery** *adj.* [Middle English from Middle Dutch (= Low German) *splinter*, *splenter*, related to SPLINT]

splinter-bar *n. Brit.* a crossbar in a horse-drawn vehicle to which traces are attached; a swingletree.

splinter group *n.* (also **splinter party**) a group or party that has broken away from a larger one.

splinter-proof *adj.* capable of withstanding splinters e.g. from bursting shells or bombs.

split /splɪt/ *v. & n.* ● *v.* (**splitting**; *past* and *past part.* **split**) **1 a** *intr. & tr.* break or cause to break forcibly into parts, esp. into halves or along the grain. **b** *intr. & tr.* (often foll. by *up*) divide into parts (*split into groups*; *split up the site into sections*). **c** *tr.* (also *absol.*) *slang* divide (money) between usu. accomplices (*split the money between them*). **2** *tr. & intr.* (often foll. by *off*, *away*) remove or be removed by breaking, separating, or dividing (*split the top off the bottle*; *split away from the main group*). **3** *intr. & tr.* **a** (usu. foll. by *up*) *colloq.* separate, esp. through discord (*split up after ten years*). **b** (foll. by *with*) *colloq.* quarrel or cease association with (another person etc.). **c** (often as **split** *adj.*) (usu. foll. by *on*, *over*) separate or divide as a result of opposing views (*the government is split over Europe*). **4** *tr.* cause the fission of (an atom). **5** *intr. & tr. slang* leave, esp. suddenly. **6** *intr.* (usu. foll. by *on*) *Brit. slang* betray secrets; inform (*split on them to the police*). **7** *intr.* **a** (as **splitting** *adj.*) (esp. of a headache) very painful; acute. **b** (of the head) suffer great pain from a headache, noise, etc. **8** *intr.* (of a ship) be wrecked. ● *n.* **1** the act or an instance of splitting; the state of being split. **2** a fissure, vent, crack, cleft, etc. **3** a separation into parties; a schism. **4** (in *pl.*) the athletic feat of leaping in the air or sitting down with the legs at right angles to the body in front and behind, or at the sides with the trunk facing forwards. **5** a split osier etc. used for parts of basketwork. **6** each strip of steel, cane, etc., of the reed in a loom. **7** a single thickness of split hide. **8** the turning up of two cards of equal value in faro, so that the stakes are divided. **9 a** half a bottle of mineral water. **b** half a glass of liquor. **10** *slang* a division of money, esp. the proceeds of crime. □ **split the difference** take the average of two proposed amounts. **split hairs** make small and insignificant distinctions. **split one's sides** be convulsed with laughter. **split the ticket** (or **one's vote**) *US* vote for candidates of more than one party. **split the vote** *Brit.* (of a candidate or minority party) attract votes from another so that both are defeated by a third. □ **splitter** *n.* [originally nautical, from Middle Dutch *splitten*, related to *spletten*, *splīten*, Middle High German *splīzen*]

split end *n.* **1** (usu. in *pl.*) a hair which has split at the end from dryness etc. **2** *Amer. Football* a player at the end of and some distance from a line of players in formation.

split gear *n.* a gear made in halves for removal from a shaft.

split infinitive *n.* a phrase consisting of an infinitive with an adverb etc. inserted between *to* and the verb, e.g. *seems to really like it*.

■ **Usage** It is often said that an infinitive should never be split. However, this is an artificial rule and can produce clumsy or ambiguous sentences. In many cases a split infinitive sounds more natural than its avoidance, e.g. *What is it like to actually live in France?* On other occasions, it is better to place the adverb before or after the infinitive, e.g. *He wanted to completely give up his business* reads better as *He wanted to give up his business completely*.

split-level *adj.* (of a building) having a room or rooms a fraction of a storey higher than other parts.

split pea *n.* a pea dried and split in half for cooking.

split personality *n.* the alteration or dissociation of personality occurring in some mental illnesses, esp. schizophrenia and hysteria.

split pin *n.* a metal cotter pin passed through a hole and held in place by its gaping split end.

split pulley *n.* a pulley made in halves for removal from a shaft.

split ring *n.* a small steel ring with two spiral turns, such as a keyring.

split-screen *n.* a screen on which two or more separate images are displayed.

split second *n.* & *adj.* ● *n.* a very brief moment of time. ● *attrib.adj.* (**split-second**) **1** very rapid. **2** (of timing) very precise.

split shift *n.* a shift comprising two or more separate periods of duty.

split shot *n.* (also **split stroke**) *Croquet* a stroke driving two touching balls in different directions.

split wheel *n.* a wheel made in halves for removal from a shaft.

splodge /splɒdʒ/ *n.* & *v.* *colloq.* ● *n.* a daub, blot, or smear. ● *v.tr.* make a large, esp. irregular, spot or patch on. □ **splodgy** *adj.* [imitative, or alteration of SPLOTCH]

splosh /splɒʃ/ *v.* & *n.* *colloq.* ● *v.tr.* & *intr.* move with a splashing sound. ● *n.* **1** a splashing sound. **2** a splash of water etc. **3** *slang* money. [imitative]

splotch /splɒtʃ/ *n.* & *v.tr.* = SPLODGE. □ **splotchy** *adj.* [perhaps from SPOT + obsolete *plotch* BLOTCH]

splurge /spləːdʒ/ *n.* & *v.* *colloq.* ● *n.* **1** an ostentatious display or effort. **2** an instance of sudden great extravagance. ● *v.intr.* & *tr.* **1** (usu. foll. by *on*) spend (effort or esp. large sums of money) (*splurged the lot on a holiday*). **2** splash heavily. [19th-c. US: probably imitative]

splutter /ˈsplʌtə/ *v.* & *n.* ● *v.* **1** *intr.* **a** speak in a hurried, vehement, or choking manner. **b** emit particles from the mouth, sparks, hot oil, etc., with spitting sounds. **2** *tr.* **a** speak or utter (words, threats, a language, etc.) rapidly or incoherently. **b** emit (food, sparks, hot oil, etc.) with a spitting sound. ● *n.* spluttering speech or sound. □ **splutterer** *n.* **splutteringly** *adv.* [SPUTTER by association with *splash*]

Spode /spəʊd/ *n. propr.* a type of fine pottery or porcelain. [named after J. *Spode*, English maker of china d. 1827]

spoil /spɔɪl/ *v.* & *n.* ● *v.* (*past* and *past part.* **spoilt** (esp. *Brit.*) or **spoiled**) **1** *tr.* **a** damage; diminish the value of (*was spoilt by the rain; will spoil all the fun*). **b** reduce a person's enjoyment etc. of (*the news spoiled his dinner*). **2** *tr.* injure the character of (esp. a child, pet, etc.) by excessive indulgence. **3** *intr.* **a** (of food) go bad, decay; become unfit for eating. **b** (usu. in *neg.*) (of a joke, secret, etc.) become stale through long keeping. **4** *tr.* render (a ballot paper) invalid by improper marking. **5** *tr.* (foll. by *of*) *archaic* or *literary* plunder or deprive (a person of a thing) by force or stealth (*spoiled him of all his possessions*). ● *n.* **1** (usu. in *pl.*) **a** plunder taken from an enemy in war, or seized by force. **b** esp. *joc.* profit or advantages gained by succeeding to public office, high position, etc. **2** earth etc. thrown up in excavating, dredging, etc. □ **be spoiling for** aggressively seek (a fight etc.). **spoilt for choice** *Brit.* having so many choices that it is difficult to choose. [Middle English via Old French *espoillier*, *espoille* from Latin *spoliare*, from *spolium* 'spoil, plunder', or from DESPOIL]

spoilage /ˈspɔɪlɪdʒ/ *n.* **1** paper spoilt in printing. **2** the spoiling of food etc. by decay.

spoiler /ˈspɔɪlə/ *n.* **1** a person or thing that spoils something. **2 a** a device on an aircraft to retard its speed by interrupting the airflow. **b** a similar device on a vehicle to improve its road-holding at speed. **3** an electronic device for preventing unauthorized copying of sound recordings by means of a disruptive signal inaudible on the original. **4** a news item or new product used to divert attention from another.

spoilsman /ˈspɔɪlzmən/ *n.* (*pl.* **-men**) *US* esp. *Polit.* **1** an advocate of the spoils system. **2** a person who seeks to profit by it.

spoilsport /ˈspɔɪlspɔːt/ *n.* a person who spoils others' pleasure or enjoyment.

spoils system *n.* *US* the practice of a successful political party giving public office to its supporters.

spoilt *past* and *past part.* of SPOIL.

spoke[1] /spəʊk/ *n.* & *v.* ● *n.* **1** each of the bars running from the hub to the rim of a wheel. **2** a rung of a ladder. **3** each radial handle of the wheel of a ship etc. ● *v.tr.* **1** provide with spokes. **2** obstruct (a wheel etc.) by thrusting a spoke in. □ **put a spoke in a person's wheel** *Brit.* thwart or hinder a person. □ **spoked** *adj.* **spokewise** *adv.* [Old English *spāca*, from West Germanic]

spoke[2] *past* of SPEAK.

spoken /ˈspəʊk(ə)n/ *past part.* of SPEAK. ● *adj.* (in *comb.*) speaking in a specified way (*smooth-spoken; well-spoken*). □ **spoken for** claimed, requisitioned (*this seat is spoken for*).

spokeshave /ˈspəʊkʃeɪv/ *n.* a blade set transversely between two handles, used for shaping spokes and other esp. curved work where an ordinary plane is not suitable.

spokesman /ˈspəʊksmən/ *n.* (*pl.* **-men**; *fem.* **spokeswoman**, *pl.* **-women**) **1** a person who speaks on behalf of others, esp. in the course of public relations. **2** a person deputed to express the views of a group etc. [formed irregularly from SPOKE[2], on the pattern of *craftsman* etc.]

spokesperson /ˈspəʊkspəːs(ə)n/ *n.* (*pl.* **-persons** or **-people**) a spokesman or spokeswoman.

spoliation /spəʊlɪˈeɪʃ(ə)n/ *n.* **1 a** plunder or pillage, esp. of neutral vessels in war. **b** extortion. **2** *Eccl.* the taking of the fruits of a benefice under a pretended title etc. **3** *Law* the destruction, mutilation, or alteration, of a document to prevent its being used as evidence. □ **spoliator** /ˈspəʊ-/ *n.* **spoliatory** /ˈspəʊlɪət(ə)ri/ *adj.* [Middle English from Latin *spoliatio* (as SPOIL)]

spondaic /spɒn'deɪɪk/ *adj. Prosody* **1** of or concerning spondees. **2** (of a hexameter) having a spondee as a fifth foot. [French *spondaïque* or Late Latin *spondaicus* = Late Latin *spondiacus* from Greek *spondeiakos* (as SPONDEE)]

spondee /'spɒndi:/ *n. Prosody* a foot consisting of two long (or stressed) syllables. [Middle English via Old French *spondee* or Latin *spondeus* from Greek *spondeios* (*pous* 'foot'), from *spondē* 'libation', as being characteristic of music accompanying libations]

spondulicks /spɒn'dju:lɪks/ *n.pl. slang* money. [19th c.: origin unknown]

spondylitis /spɒndɪ'lʌɪtɪs/ *n.* inflammation of the vertebrae. [Latin *spondylus* 'vertebra' (from Greek *spondulos*) + -ITIS]

sponge /spʌn(d)ʒ/ *n. & v.* ● *n.* **1** any sessile aquatic animal of the phylum Porifera, with a porous bag-like body structure and a rigid or elastic internal skeleton. **2 a** the skeleton of a sponge, esp. the soft light elastic absorbent kind used in bathing, cleansing surfaces, etc. **b** a piece of porous rubber or plastic etc. used similarly. **c** a piece of sponge or similar material (esp. one impregnated with spermicide) inserted in the vagina as a contraceptive. **3** a thing of spongelike absorbency or consistency, e.g. a sponge pudding, cake, porous metal, etc. (*lemon sponge*). **4** = SPONGER. **5** *colloq.* a person who drinks heavily. **6** cleansing with or as with a sponge (*had a quick sponge this morning*). ● *v.* (**sponging** or **spongeing**) **1** *tr.* wipe or cleanse with a sponge. **2** *tr.* (also *absol.*; often foll. by *down*, *over*) sluice water over (the body, a car, etc.). **3** *tr.* (often foll. by *out*, *away*, etc.) wipe off or efface (writing, a memory, etc.) with or as with a sponge. **4** *tr.* (often foll. by *up*) absorb with or as with a sponge. **5** *intr.* (often foll. by *on*, *off*) live as a parasite; be meanly dependent upon (another person). **6** *tr.* obtain (drink etc.) by sponging. **7** *intr.* gather sponges. **8** *tr.* apply paint with a sponge to (walls, furniture, etc.). □ **spongeable** *adj.* **spongelike** *adj.* **spongiform** *adj.* (esp. in senses 1, 2a of *n.*). [Old English via Latin *spongia* from Greek *spoggia*, *spoggos*]

sponge bag *n. Brit.* a waterproof bag for toilet articles.

sponge bath *n. US* = BLANKET BATH.

sponge cake *n.* a very light cake with a spongelike consistency.

sponge cloth *n.* **1** soft, lightly-woven cloth with a slightly wrinkled surface. **2** a thin spongy material used for cleaning.

sponge pudding *n. Brit.* a steamed or baked pudding of fat, flour, and eggs with a usu. specified flavour.

sponger /'spʌn(d)ʒə/ *n.* a person who contrives to live at another's expense.

sponge rubber *n.* liquid rubber latex processed into a spongelike substance.

sponge tree *n.* a spiny tropical acacia, *Acacia farnesiana*, with globose heads of fragrant yellow flowers yielding a perfume: also called OPOPANAX.

spongy /'spʌn(d)ʒi/ *adj.* (**spongier**, **spongiest**) **1** like a sponge, esp. in being porous, compressible, elastic, or absorbent. **2** (of metal) finely divided and loosely coherent. □ **spongily** *adv.* **sponginess** *n.*

sponsion /'spɒnʃ(ə)n/ *n.* **1** being a surety for another. **2** a pledge or promise made on behalf of the State by an agent not authorized to do so. [Latin *sponsio* from *spondēre spons-* 'promise solemnly']

sponson /'spɒns(ə)n/ *n.* **1** a projection from the side of a warship or tank to enable a gun to be trained forward and aft. **2** a short subsidiary wing to stabilize a seaplane. **3** a triangular platform supporting the wheel on a paddle steamer. [19th c.: origin unknown]

sponsor /'spɒnsə/ *n. & v.* ● *n.* **1** a person who supports an activity done for charity by pledging money in advance. **2 a** a person or organization that promotes or supports an artistic or sporting activity etc. **b** esp. *US* a business organization that promotes a broadcast programme in return for advertising time. **3** an organization lending support to an election candidate. **4** a person who introduces a proposal for legislation. **5 a** a godparent at baptism. **b** esp. *RC Ch.* a person who presents a candidate for confirmation. **6** a person who makes himself or herself responsible for another. ● *v.tr.* be a sponsor for. □ **sponsorial** /spɒn'sɔ:rɪəl/ *adj.* **sponsorship** *n.* [Latin (as SPONSION)]

spontaneous /spɒn'teɪnɪəs/ *adj.* **1** acting or done or occurring without external cause. **2** voluntary, without external incitement (*made a spontaneous offer of his services*). **3** *Biol.* (of structural changes in plants and muscular activity esp. in young animals) instinctive, automatic, prompted by no motive. **4** (of bodily movement, literary style, etc.) gracefully natural and unconstrained. **5** (of sudden movement etc.) involuntary, not due to conscious volition. **6** growing naturally without cultivation. □ **spontaneity** /spɒntə'ni:ɪti, -'neɪɪti/ *n.* **spontaneously** *adv.* **spontaneousness** *n.* [Late Latin *spontaneus* from *sponte* 'of one's own accord']

spontaneous combustion *n.* the ignition of a mineral or vegetable substance (e.g. a heap of rags soaked with oil, a mass of wet coal) from heat engendered within itself, usu. by rapid oxidation.

spontaneous generation *n. hist.* the supposed production of living from non-living matter as inferred from the appearance of life (due in fact to bacteria etc.) in some infusions; abiogenesis.

spontaneous suggestion *n.* suggestion from association of ideas without conscious volition.

spoof /spu:f/ *n. & v. colloq.* ● *n.* **1** a parody. **2** a hoax or swindle. ● *v.tr.* **1** parody. **2** hoax, swindle. □ **spoofer** *n.* **spoofery** *n.* [coined by A. Roberts, English comedian d. 1933]

spook /spu:k/ *n. & v.* ● *n.* **1** *colloq.* a ghost. **2** *US slang* a spy. ● *v. N. Amer. slang* **1** *tr.* frighten, unnerve, alarm. **2** *intr.* take fright, become alarmed. [Dutch, = Middle Low German *spōk*, of unknown origin]

spooky /'spu:ki/ *adj.* (**spookier**, **spookiest**) **1** *colloq.* ghostly, eerie. **2** *N. Amer. slang* nervous; easily frightened. **3** *US slang* of spies or espionage. □ **spookily** *adv.* **spookiness** *n.*

spool /spu:l/ *n. & v.* ● *n.* **1 a** a reel for winding magnetic tape, photographic film, etc., on. **b** a reel for winding yarn, thread, or wire on. **c** a quantity of tape, yarn, etc., wound on a spool. **2** the revolving cylinder of an angler's reel. ● *v.tr.* wind on a spool. [Middle English from Old French *espole* or from Middle Low German *spōle*, Middle Dutch *spoele*, Old High German *spuolo*, of unknown origin]

spoon /spu:n/ *n. & v.* ● *n.* **1 a** a utensil consisting of an oval or round bowl and a handle for conveying food (esp. liquid) to the mouth, for stirring, etc. **b** a spoonful, esp. of sugar. **c** (in *pl.*) *Mus.* a pair of spoons held in the hand and beaten together rhythmically. **2** a spoon-shaped thing, esp.: **a** (in full **spoon-bait**) a bright revolving piece of metal used as a lure in fishing. **b** an oar with a broad curved blade. **3** *colloq.* **a** a silly or demonstratively fond lover. **b** a simpleton. ● *v.* **1** *tr.* (often foll. by *up*, *out*) take (liquid etc.) with a spoon. **2** *tr.* hit (a ball) feebly upwards. **3** *colloq.* **a** *intr.* behave in an amorous way, esp. foolishly. **b** *tr. archaic* woo in a silly or sentimental way. **4** *intr.* fish with a spoon-bait. □ **born with a silver spoon in one's mouth** born in affluence. □ **spooner** *n.* (in sense 3 of *v.*). **spoonful** *n.* (*pl.* **-fuls**). [Old English *spōn* 'chip of wood', from Germanic]

spoonbill /'spu:nbɪl/ *n.* **1** any large mainly white wading bird of the family Threskiornithidae, related to ibisis, having a bill with a very broad flat tip. **2** a shoveler duck.

spoon-bread *n. US* soft maize bread.

spoonerism /'spu:nərɪz(ə)m/ *n.* a transposition, usu. accidental, of the initial letters etc. of two or more words, e.g. *you have hissed the mystery lectures*. [Revd W. A. *Spooner*, English scholar d. 1930, reputed to make such errors in speaking]

spoon-feed *v.tr.* (*past* and *past part.* **-fed**) **1** feed (a baby etc.) with a spoon. **2** provide help, information, etc., to (a person etc.) without requiring any effort on the recipient's part.

spoony /'spuːni/ *adj. & n. colloq. archaic* ● *adj.* (**spoonier, spooniest**) **1** (often foll. by *on*) sentimental, amorous. **2** foolish, silly. ● *n.* (*pl.* **-ies**) a simpleton. □ **spoonily** *adv.* **spooniness** *n.*

spoor /spʊə, spɔː/ *n. & v.* ● *n.* the track or scent of an animal. ● *v.tr. & intr.* follow by the spoor. □ **spoorer** *n.* [Afrikaans from Middle Dutch *spo(o)r*, from Germanic]

sporadic /spə'radɪk/ *adj.* occurring only here and there or occasionally; separate; scattered. □ **sporadically** *adv.* [medieval Latin *sporadicus* from Greek *sporadikos*, from *sporas -ados* 'scattered': related to *speirō* 'to sow']

sporangium /spə'ran(d)ʒɪəm/ *n.* (*pl.* **sporangia** /-dʒɪə/) *Bot.* a receptacle in which spores are formed. □ **sporangial** *adj.* [modern Latin, from Greek *spora* SPORE + *aggeion* 'vessel']

spore /spɔː/ *n.* **1** a specialized reproductive cell of many plants and micro-organisms. **2** these collectively. [modern Latin *spora* from Greek *spora* 'sowing, seed', from *speirō* 'sow']

sporo- /'spɒrəʊ, 'spɔːrəʊ/ *comb. form Biol.* a spore. [Greek *spora* (as SPORE)]

sporocyst /'spɒrəsɪst, 'spɔːrə-/ *n.* an intermediate stage in the life cycle of various parasites.

sporogenesis /spɒrə(ʊ)'dʒɛnɪsɪs, spɔːrə-/ *n.* the process of spore formation.

sporogenous /spə'rɒdʒɪnəs/ *adj.* producing spores.

sporogony /spə'rɒgəni/ *n.* the process of spore formation, esp. in some protozoans (e.g. the malaria parasite).

sporophore /'spɒrəfɔː, 'spɔːr-/ *n.* a spore-bearing structure esp. in a fungus.

sporophyte /'spɒrəfʌɪt, 'spɔː-/ *n.* the asexual form of a plant that has alternation of generations between this and the gamete-producing form (gametophyte). □ **sporophytic** /-'fɪtɪk/ *adj.* **sporophytically** /-'fɪtɪk(ə)li/ *adv.*

sporozoite /spɔːrə(ʊ)'zəʊʌɪt, spɒ-/ *n. Biol. & Med.* a small motile stage in the life cycle of some protozoans (e.g. the malaria parasite), usually produced inside a host. [SPORO- + Greek *zōion* 'animal' + -ITE[1]]

sporran /'spɒr(ə)n/ *n.* a pouch, usu. of leather or sealskin covered with fur etc., worn by a Highlander in front of the kilt. [Gaelic *sporan* from medieval Latin *bursa* PURSE]

sport /spɔːt/ *n. & v.* ● *n.* **1 a** a game or competitive activity, esp. an outdoor one involving physical exertion, e.g. cricket, football, racing, hunting. **b** such activities collectively (*the world of sport*). **2** (in *pl.*) *Brit.* **a** a meeting for competing in sports, esp. athletics (*school sports*). **b** athletics. **3** amusement, diversion, fun. **4** *colloq.* **a** a fair or generous person. **b** a person behaving in a specified way, esp. regarding games, rules, etc. (*a bad sport at tennis*). **c** *Austral. & US* a form of address, esp. between males. **d** *US* a playboy. **5** *Biol.* an animal or plant showing abnormal or striking variation from the parent type. **6** a plaything or butt (*was the sport of Fortune*). ● *v.* **1** *intr.* divert oneself, take part in a pastime. **2** *tr.* wear, exhibit, or produce, esp. ostentatiously (*sported a gold tiepin*). **3** *intr. Biol.* become or produce a sport. □ **have good sport** *Brit.* be successful in shooting, fishing, etc. **in sport** jestingly. **make sport of** make fun of, ridicule. □ **sporter** *n.* [Middle English, from DISPORT]

sporting /'spɔːtɪŋ/ *adj.* **1** interested in sport (*a sporting man*). **2** sportsmanlike, generous (*a sporting offer*). **3** concerned with sport (*a sporting dog; sporting news*). □ **sportingly** *adv.*

sporting chance *n.* some possibility of success.

sportive /'spɔːtɪv/ *adj.* playful. □ **sportively** *adv.* **sportiveness** *n.*

sport of kings *n.* (prec. by *the*) horse racing (less often war, hunting, or surfing).

sports car *n.* a usu. open, low-built fast car.

sportscast /'spɔːtskɑːst/ *n. N. Amer.* a broadcast of a sports event or information about sport. □ **sportscaster** *n.*

sports coat *n.* (also **sports jacket**) a man's jacket for informal wear.

sports ground *n.* a piece of land used for sports.

sportsman /'spɔːtsmən/ *n.* (*pl.* **-men**; *fem.* **sportswoman**, *pl.* **-women**) **1** a person who takes part in much sport, esp. professionally. **2** a person who behaves fairly and generously. □ **sportsmanlike** *adj.* **sportsmanly** *adj.* **sportsmanship** *n.*

sportsperson /'spɔːtspəːs(ə)n/ *n.* (*pl.* **-persons** or **-people**) a sportsman or sportswoman.

sportswear /'spɔːtswɛː/ *n.* clothes worn for sport or for casual outdoor use.

sports writer *n.* a person who writes (esp. as a journalist) on sports.

sporty /'spɔːti/ *adj.* (**sportier, sportiest**) *colloq.* **1 a** fond of sport. **b** (esp. of clothes) suitable for wearing for sport or for casual outdoor use. **2** rakish, showy. □ **sportily** *adv.* **sportiness** *n.*

sporule /'spɒrjuːl, -ruːl/ *n. Biol.* a small spore. □ **sporular** *adj.* [French *sporule* or modern Latin *sporula* (as SPORE)]

spot /spɒt/ *n. & v.* ● *n.* **1 a** a small part of the surface of a thing distinguished by colour, texture, etc., usu. round or less elongated than a streak or stripe (*a blue tie with pink spots*). **b** a small mark or stain. **c** a pimple. **d** a small circle or other shape used in various numbers to distinguish faces of dice, playing cards in a suit, etc. **e** a moral blemish or stain (*without a spot on his reputation*). **2 a** a particular place; a definite locality (*dropped it on this precise spot; the spot where William III landed*). **b** a place used for a particular activity (often in *comb.*: *nightspot*). **c** (in full **penalty spot**) (prec. by *the*) *Football* the place from which a penalty kick is taken. **3** a particular part of one's body or aspect of one's character. **4 a** *colloq.* one's (esp. regular) position in an organization, programme of events, etc. **b** a place or position in a performance or show (*did the spot before the interval*). **5** *Brit.* **a** *colloq.* a small quantity of anything (*a spot of lunch; a spot of trouble*). **b** a drop (*a spot of rain*). **c** *colloq.* a drink. **6** = SPOTLIGHT *n.* 1, 2. **7** (usu. *attrib.*) money paid or goods delivered immediately after a sale (*spot cash; spot silver*). **8** *Billiards* etc. **a** a small round black patch to mark the position where a ball is placed at certain times. **b** (in full **spot-ball**) the white ball distinguished from the other by two black spots. ● *v.* (**spotted, spotting**) **1** *tr.* **a** *colloq.* single out beforehand (the winner of a race etc.). **b** *colloq.* recognize the identity, nationality, etc., of (*spotted him at once as the murderer*). **c** watch for and take note of (trains, talent, etc.). **d** *colloq.* catch sight of. **e** *Mil.* locate (an enemy's position), esp. from the air. **2 a** *tr. & intr.* mark or become marked with spots. **b** *tr.* stain, soil (a person's character etc.). **3** *intr.* make spots, rain slightly (*it was spotting with rain*). **4** *tr. Billiards* place (a ball) on a spot. □ **hit the spot** *colloq.* be exactly what is required. **in a spot** (or **in a tight** etc. **spot**) *colloq.* in difficulty. **on the spot 1** at the scene of an action or event. **2** *colloq.* in a position such that response or action is required. **3** without delay or change of place, then and there. **4** (of a person) wide awake, equal to the situation, in good form at a game etc. **put on the spot** *colloq.* force to make a difficult decision, answer an awkward question, etc. **running on the spot** *Brit.* raising the feet alternately as in running but without moving forwards or backwards. [Middle English, perhaps from Middle Dutch *spotte*, Low German *spot*, Old Norse *spotti* 'small piece']

spot check *n. & v.* ● *n.* a test made on the spot or on a randomly-selected subject. ● *v.tr.* (**spot-check**) subject to a spot check.

spot height *n.* **1** the altitude of a point. **2** a figure on a map showing this.

spotlamp /'spɒtlamp/ *n.* = SPOTLIGHT *n.* 2.

spotless /ˈspɒtlɪs/ *adj.* immaculate; absolutely clean or pure. □ **spotlessly** *adv.* **spotlessness** *n.*

spotlight /ˈspɒtlʌɪt/ *n.* & *v.* ● *n.* **1** a beam of light directed on a small area, esp. on a particular part of a theatre stage or of the road in front of a vehicle. **2** a lamp projecting this. **3** full attention or publicity. ● *v.tr.* (*past* and *past part.* **-lighted** or **-lit**) **1** direct a spotlight on. **2** make conspicuous, draw attention to.

spot on *adj.* & *adv. Brit. colloq.* ● *adj.* precise; on target. ● *adv.* precisely.

spotted /ˈspɒtɪd/ *adj.* marked or decorated with spots. □ **spottedness** *n.*

spotted dick *n. Brit.* a suet pudding containing currants.

spotted dog *n.* **1** a Dalmatian dog. **2** *Brit.* = SPOTTED DICK.

spotted fever *n.* **1** cerebrospinal meningitis. **2** typhus. **3** (in full **Rocky Mountain spotted fever**) a rickettsial disease transmitted by ticks.

spotter /ˈspɒtə/ *n.* **1** (often in *comb.*) a person who spots people or things (*train-spotter*). **2** an aviator or aircraft employed in locating enemy positions etc.

spotty /ˈspɒti/ *adj.* (**spottier, spottiest**) **1** marked with spots. **2** patchy, irregular. □ **spottily** *adv.* **spottiness** *n.*

spot-weld *v.tr.* join (two metal surfaces) by welding at discrete points. □ **spot weld** *n.* **spot-welder** *n.* **spot-welding** *n.*

spousal /ˈspaʊz(ə)l/ *adj.* esp. *N. Amer. Law* of or relating to marriage or to a husband or wife.

spouse /spaʊz, -s/ *n.* a husband or wife. [Middle English *spūs(e)* from Old French *sp(o)us* (masc.), *sp(o)use* (fem.), variants of *espous(e)* from Latin *sponsus sponsa*, past part. of *spondēre* 'betroth']

spout /spaʊt/ *n.* & *v.* ● *n.* **1 a** a projecting tube or lip through which a liquid etc. is poured from a teapot, kettle, jug, etc., or issues from a fountain, pump, etc. **b** a sloping trough down which a thing may be shot into a receptacle. **c** *hist.* a lift serving a pawnbroker's storeroom. **2** a jet or column of liquid, grain, etc. **3** (in full **spout-hole**) a whale's blowhole (see BLOWHOLE 1). ● *v.tr.* & *intr.* **1** discharge or issue forcibly in a jet. **2** utter (verses etc.) or speak in a declamatory manner, speechify. □ **up the spout** *Brit. slang* **1** useless, ruined, hopeless. **2** pawned. **3** pregnant. □ **spouter** *n.* **spoutless** *adj.* [Middle English from Middle Dutch *spouten*, originally imitative]

SPQR *abbr.* **1** *hist.* the Senate and people of Rome. **2** small profits and quick returns. [sense 1 from Latin *Senatus Populusque Romanus*]

Spr. *abbr.* (in the UK) Sapper.

spraddle /ˈsprad(ə)l/ *v.intr.* & *tr.* esp. *dial.* & *N. Amer.* straddle, splay. [probably a dialect form related to SPREAD]

sprag /sprag/ *n.* **1** a thick piece of wood or similar device used as a brake. **2** a prop in a coal mine. [19th c.: origin unknown]

sprain /spreɪn/ *v.* & *n.* ● *v.tr.* wrench (an ankle, wrist, etc.) violently so as to cause pain and swelling but not dislocation. ● *n.* **1** such a wrench. **2** the resulting inflammation and swelling. [17th c.: origin unknown]

spraint /spreɪnt/ *n.* (also in *pl.*) otter droppings. [Old French *espreintes* from *espaindre* 'squeeze out', related to EXPRESS[1]]

sprang *past* of SPRING.

sprat /sprat/ *n.* & *v.* ● *n.* **1** a small European herring-like fish, *Sprattus sprattus*, much used as food. **2** a similar fish, e.g. a sand eel or a young herring. ● *v.intr.* (**spratted, spratting**) fish for sprats. □ **spratting** *n.* [Old English *sprot*]

sprauncy /ˈsprɔːnsi/ *adj.* (**sprauncier, sprauncier**) *Brit. slang* smart or showy. [20th c.: perhaps related to dialect *sprouncey* 'cheerful']

sprawl /sprɔːl/ *v.* & *n.* ● *v.* **1 a** *intr.* sit or lie or fall with limbs flung out or in an ungainly way. **b** *tr.* spread (one's limbs) in this way. **2** *intr.* (of handwriting, a plant, a town, etc.) be of irregular or straggling form. ● *n.* **1** a sprawling movement or attitude. **2** a straggling group or mass. **3** the straggling expansion of an urban or industrial area. □ **sprawlingly** *adv.* [Old English *spreawlian*]

spray[1] /spreɪ/ *n.* & *v.* ● *n.* **1** water or other liquid flying in small drops from the force of the wind, the dashing of waves, or the action of an atomizer etc. **2** a liquid preparation to be applied in this form with an atomizer etc., esp. for medical purposes. **3** an instrument or apparatus for such application. ● *v.tr.* (also *absol.*) **1** throw (liquid) in the form of spray. **2** sprinkle (an object) with small drops or particles, esp. (a plant) with an insecticide. **3** (*absol.*) (of a male animal, esp. a cat) mark its environment with the smell of its urine, as an attraction to females. □ **sprayable** *adj.* **sprayer** *n.* [earlier *spry*, perhaps related to Middle Dutch *spra(e)yen*, Middle High German *sprœjen* 'sprinkle']

spray[2] /spreɪ/ *n.* **1** a sprig of flowers or leaves, or a branch of a tree with branchlets or flowers, esp. a slender or graceful one. **2** a bunch of flowers decoratively arranged. **3** an ornament in a similar form (*a spray of diamonds*). □ **sprayey** /ˈspreɪi/ *adj.* [Middle English from Old English *(e)sprei*, recorded in personal and place names]

spray-dry *v.tr.* (**-dries, -dried**) dry (milk etc.) by spraying into hot air etc.

spray-gun *n.* a gunlike device for spraying paint etc.

spray-paint *v.tr.* paint (a surface) by means of a spray.

spread /sprɛd/ *v.* & *n.* ● *v.* (*past* and *past part.* **spread**) **1** *tr.* (often foll. by *out*) **a** open or extend the surface of. **b** cause to cover a larger surface (*spread butter on bread*). **c** display to the eye or the mind (*the view was spread out before us*). **2** *intr.* (often foll. by *out*) have a wide or specified or increasing extent (*on every side spread a vast desert*; *spreading trees*). **3** *intr.* & *tr.* become or make widely known, felt, etc. (*rumours are spreading*; *spread a little happiness*). **4** *tr.* **a** cover the surface of (*spread the wall with paint*; *a meadow spread with daisies*). **b** lay (a table). ● *n.* **1** the act or an instance of spreading. **2** capability of expanding (*has a large spread*). **3** diffusion (*spread of learning*). **4** breadth, compass (*arches of equal spread*). **5** an aircraft's wingspan. **6** increased bodily girth (*middle-aged spread*). **7** the difference between two rates, prices, etc. **8** *colloq.* an elaborate meal. **9** a sweet or savoury paste for spreading on bread etc. **10** a bedspread. **11** printed matter spread across two facing pages or across more than one column. **12** *US* a ranch with extensive land. □ **spread oneself** be lavish or discursive. **spread one's wings** see WING. □ **spreadable** *adj.* **spreader** *n.* [Old English *-sprǣdan*, from West Germanic]

spread eagle *n., v., & adj.* ● *n.* **1** a representation of an eagle with legs and wings extended as an emblem. **2** *hist.* a person secured with arms and legs spread out, esp. to be flogged. ● *v.tr.* (**spreadeagle**; usu. as **spreadeagled** *adj.*) **1** place (a person) with arms and legs spread out, esp. to be flogged. **2** defeat utterly. ● *adj.* (**spread-eagle**) *US* **1** bombastic. **2** spreadeagled.

spreadsheet /ˈsprɛdʃiːt/ *n.* a computer program allowing manipulation and flexible retrieval of esp. tabulated numerical data.

Sprechgesang /ˈʃprɛxgəzaŋ, German ˈʃprɛçgəzaŋ/ *n. Mus.* a style of dramatic vocalization between speech and song. [German, literally 'speech song']

Sprechstimme /ˈʃprɛxʃtɪmə, German ˈʃprɛçʃtɪmə/ *n. Mus.* **1** the kind of voice used in *Sprechgesang*. **2** = SPRECHGESANG. [German, literally 'speech voice']

spree /spriː/ *n.* & *v. colloq.* ● *n.* **1** a lively extravagant outing (*shopping spree*). **2** a bout of fun or drinking etc. ● *v.intr.* (**sprees, spreed**) have a spree. □ **on the spree** engaged in a spree. [18th c.: origin unknown]

sprig[1] /sprɪg/ *n.* & *v.* ● *n.* **1** a small branch or shoot. **2** an ornament resembling this, esp. on fabric. **3** usu. *derog.* a youth or young man (*a sprig of the nobility*). ● *v.tr.* (**sprigged, sprigging**) **1** ornament with sprigs (*a dress of sprigged muslin*). **2** (usu. as **sprigging** *n.*) decorate (ceramic ware) with ornaments in applied relief. □ **spriggy** *adj.* [Middle English, from or related to Low German *sprick*]

sprig[2] /sprɪg/ *n.* a small tapering headless tack. [Middle English: origin unknown]

sprightly /'sprʌɪtli/ *adj.* (also **spritely**) (**-lier**, **-liest**) vivacious, lively, brisk. □ **sprightliness** *n.* [*spright*, variant of SPRITE + -LY[1]]

spring /sprɪŋ/ *v.* & *n.* ● *v.* (*past* **sprang** /spraŋ/ or *US* **sprung** /sprʌŋ/; *past part.* **sprung**) **1** *intr.* jump; move rapidly or suddenly (*sprang from his seat*; *sprang through the gap*; *sprang to their assistance*). **2** *intr.* move rapidly as from a constrained position or by the action of a spring (*the branch sprang back*; *the door sprang to*). **3** *intr.* (usu. foll. by *from*) originate or arise (*springs from an old family*; *their actions spring from a false conviction*). **4** *intr.* (usu. foll. by *up*) come into being; appear, esp. suddenly (*a breeze sprang up*; *the belief has sprung up*). **5** *tr.* cause to act suddenly, esp. by means of a spring (*spring a trap*). **6** *tr.* (often foll. by *on*) produce or develop or make known suddenly or unexpectedly (*has sprung a new theory*; *loves to spring surprises*). **7** *tr. slang* contrive the escape or release of. **8** *tr.* rouse (game) from earth or covert. **9 a** *intr.* become warped or split. **b** *tr.* split, crack (wood or a wooden implement). **10** *tr.* (usu. as **sprung** *adj.*) provide (a motor vehicle etc.) with springs. **11 a** *tr. colloq.* spend (money). **b** *intr.* (usu. foll. by *for*) *N. Amer.* & *Austral. slang* pay for a treat. **12** *tr.* cause (a mine) to explode. ● *n.* **1** a jump (*took a spring*; *rose with a spring*). **2** a backward movement from a constrained position; a recoil, e.g. of a bow. **3** elasticity; ability to spring back strongly (*a mattress with plenty of spring*). **4** a resilient device usu. of bent or coiled metal used esp. to drive clockwork or for cushioning in furniture or vehicles. **5 a** the season in which vegetation begins to appear, the first season of the year, in the northern hemisphere from March to May and in the southern hemisphere from September to November. **b** *Astron.* the period from the vernal equinox to the summer solstice. **c** (often foll. by *of*) the early stage of life etc. **d** = SPRING TIDE. **6** a place where water, oil, etc., wells up from the earth; the basin or flow so formed (*hot springs*; *mineral springs*). **7** the motive for or origin of an action, custom, etc. (*the springs of human action*). **8** *slang* an escape or release from prison. **9** the upward curve of a beam etc. from a horizontal line. **10** the splitting or yielding of a plank etc. under strain. □ **spring a leak** develop a leak (orig. *Naut.*, from timbers springing out of position). □ **springless** *adj.* **springlet** *n.* **springlike** *adj.* [Old English *springan*, from Germanic]

■ **Usage** The use of *sprung* instead of *sprang* for the past tense, as in *I sprung out of bed*, is non-standard in British English, but acceptable along with *sprang* in American English.

spring balance *n.* a balance that measures weight by the tension of a spring.

spring bed *n.* a bed with a spring mattress.

springboard /'sprɪŋbɔːd/ *n.* **1** a springy board giving impetus in leaping, diving, etc. **2** a source of impetus in any activity. **3** *N. Amer.* & *Austral.* a platform inserted in the side of a tree, on which a lumberjack stands to chop at some height from the ground.

springbok /'sprɪŋbɒk/ *n.* **1** a southern African gazelle, *Antidorcas marsupialis*, with the ability to run with high springing jumps. **2** (**Springbok**) a South African, esp. one who has played for South Africa in international sporting competitions. [Afrikaans, from Dutch *springen* SPRING + *bok* 'antelope']

spring chicken *n.* **1** a young fowl for eating (originally available only in spring). **2** (esp. with *neg.*) a young person (*she's no spring chicken*).

spring-clean *n.* & *v.* ● *n. Brit.* a thorough cleaning of a house or room, esp. in spring. ● *v.tr.* clean (a house or room) in this way.

springe /sprɪn(d)ʒ/ *n.* a noose or snare for catching small game. [Middle English, related to SPRING]

spring equinox *n.* the equinox in spring, on about 20 March in the northern hemisphere and 22 Sept. in the southern hemisphere; in *Astron.* the equinox in March. Also called *vernal equinox*.

springer /'sprɪŋə/ *n.* **1** a person or thing that springs. **2 a** a small spaniel of a breed used to spring game. **b** this breed. **3** *Archit.* **a** the part of an arch where the curve begins. **b** the lowest stone of this. **c** the bottom stone of the coping of a gable. **d** a rib of a groined roof or vault. **4** a springbok.

spring fever *n.* a restless or lethargic feeling sometimes associated with spring.

spring greens *n.pl.* the leaves of young cabbage plants of a variety that does not develop a heart.

spring-loaded *adj.* containing a compressed or stretched spring pressing one part against another.

spring mattress *n.* a mattress containing or consisting of springs.

spring onion *n. Brit.* an onion taken from the ground before the bulb has formed, and eaten raw in salad.

spring roll *n.* a Chinese snack consisting of a pancake filled with vegetables etc. and fried.

springtail /'sprɪŋteɪl/ *n.* any wingless insect of the order Collembola, leaping by means of a springlike caudal part.

springtide /'sprɪŋtʌɪd/ *n. poet.* = SPRINGTIME.

spring tide *n.* a tide just after new and full moon when there is the greatest difference between high and low water.

springtime /'sprɪŋtʌɪm/ *n.* **1** the season of spring. **2** a time compared to this.

spring water *n.* water from a spring, as opposed to river water or rainwater.

springy /'sprɪŋi/ *adj.* (**springier**, **springiest**) **1** springing back quickly when squeezed or stretched; elastic. **2** (of movements) as of a springy substance. □ **springily** *adv.* **springiness** *n.*

sprinkle /'sprɪŋk(ə)l/ *v.* & *n.* ● *v.tr.* **1** scatter (liquid, ashes, crumbs, etc.) in small drops or particles. **2** (often foll. by *with*) subject (the ground or an object) to sprinkling with liquid etc. **3** (of liquid etc.) fall on in this way. **4** distribute in small amounts. ● *n.* (usu. foll. by *of*) **1** a light shower. **2** = SPRINKLING. [Middle English, perhaps from Middle Dutch *sprenkelen*]

sprinkler /'sprɪŋklə/ *n.* a person or thing that sprinkles, esp. a device for sprinkling water on a lawn or for extinguishing fires.

sprinkling /'sprɪŋklɪŋ/ *n.* (usu. foll. by *of*) a small thinly distributed number or amount.

sprint /sprɪnt/ *v.* & *n.* ● *v.* **1** *intr.* run a short distance at full speed. **2** *tr.* run (a specified distance) in this way. ● *n.* **1 a** such a run. **b** *Sport* a running race over a distance of 400 metres or less. **2** a similar short spell of maximum effort in cycling, swimming, motor racing, etc. [Old Norse *sprinta* (unrecorded), of unknown origin]

sprinter /'sprɪntə/ *n.* **1** an athlete who specializes in short distance races. **2** a vehicle, esp. a train, designed for rapid travel over short distances.

sprit /sprɪt/ *n.* a small spar reaching diagonally from the mast to the upper outer corner of the sail. [Old English *sprēot* 'pole', related to SPROUT]

sprite /sprʌɪt/ *n.* an elf, fairy, or goblin. [Middle English from *sprit*, variant of SPIRIT]

spritely var. of SPRIGHTLY.

spritsail /'sprɪts(ə)l, 'sprɪtseɪl/ *n.* **1** a sail extended by a sprit. **2** *hist.* a sail extended by a yard set under the bowsprit.

spritz /sprɪts/ *v.* & *n. N. Amer.* ● *v.tr.* sprinkle, squirt, or spray. ● *n.* the act or an instance of spritzing. [German *spritzen* 'to squirt']

spritzer /'sprɪtsə/ *n.* a mixture of wine and soda water. [German *Spritzer* 'a splash']

sprocket /'sprɒkɪt/ *n.* **1** each of several teeth on a wheel engaging with links of a chain, e.g. on a bicycle, or with holes in film or tape or paper. **2** (also **sprocket-wheel**) a wheel with sprockets. [16th c.: origin unknown]

sprog /sprɒg/ *n. Brit. slang* a child; a baby. [originally services' slang, = new recruit: perhaps from obsolete *sprag* 'lively young man', of unknown origin]

sprout /spraʊt/ *v. & n.* ●*v.* **1** *tr.* put forth, produce (shoots, hair, etc.) (*has sprouted a moustache*). **2** *intr.* begin to grow, put forth shoots. **3** *intr.* spring up, grow to a height. ●*n.* **1** a shoot of a plant. **2** = BRUSSELS SPROUT. [Old English from West Germanic]

spruce[1] /spru:s/ *adj. & v.* ●*adj.* neat in dress and appearance; trim, smart. ●*v.tr. & intr.* (also *refl.*; usu. foll. by *up*) make or become smart. □ **sprucely** *adv.* **spruceness** *n.* [perhaps from SPRUCE[2] in obsolete sense 'Prussian', in the collocation *spruce (leather) jerkin*]

spruce[2] /spru:s/ *n.* **1** any coniferous tree of the genus *Picea*, with dense foliage growing in a distinctive conical shape. **2** the wood of this tree used as timber. [alteration of obsolete *Pruce* 'Prussia': cf. PRUSSIAN]

spruce[3] /spru:s/ *v. Brit. slang* **1** *tr.* deceive. **2** *intr.* lie, practise deception. **3** *intr.* evade a duty, malinger. □ **sprucer** *n.* [20th c.: origin unknown]

spruce beer *n.* a fermented beverage using spruce twigs and needles as flavouring.

sprue[1] /spru:/ *n.* **1** a channel through which metal or plastic is poured into a mould. **2** a piece of metal or plastic which has filled a sprue and solidified there. [19th c.: origin unknown]

sprue[2] /spru:/ *n.* a tropical disease with ulceration of the mucous membrane of the mouth and chronic enteritis. [Dutch *spruw* THRUSH[2], perhaps related to Flemish *spruwen* 'sprinkle']

spruik /spru:k/ *v.intr. Austral. & NZ slang* speak in public, esp. as a showman. □ **spruiker** *n.* [20th c.: origin unknown]

spruit /spreɪt/ *n. S.Afr.* a small watercourse, usu. dry except during the rainy season. [Dutch, related to SPROUT]

sprung see SPRING.

sprung rhythm *n.* a poetic metre approximating to speech, each foot having one stressed syllable followed by a varying number of unstressed.

spry /sprʌɪ/ *adj.* (**spryer**, **spryest**) active, lively. □ **spryly** *adv.* **spryness** *n.* [18th c., dialect & US: origin unknown]

spud /spʌd/ *n. & v.* ●*n.* **1** *slang* a potato. **2** a small narrow spade for cutting the roots of weeds etc. ●*v.tr.* (**spudded**, **spudding**) **1** (foll. by *up*, *out*) remove (weeds) with a spud. **2** (also *absol.*; often foll. by *in*) make the initial drilling for (an oil well). [Middle English: origin unknown]

spud-bashing *n. Brit. slang* a lengthy spell of peeling potatoes.

spue var. of SPEW.

spumante /spu:'manti/ *n.* an Italian sparkling white wine (cf. ASTI). [Italian, = sparkling]

spume /spju:m/ *n. & v.intr.* froth, foam. □ **spumous** *adj.* **spumy** *adj.* [Middle English from Old French *(e)spume* or Latin *spuma*]

spumoni /spu:'məʊni/ *n. N. Amer.* a kind of ice-cream dessert with different colours and flavours, often in layers. [Italian *spumone* from *spuma* SPUME]

spun *past* and *past part.* of SPIN.

spunk /spʌŋk/ *n.* **1** touchwood. **2** *colloq.* courage, mettle, spirit. **3** *Brit. coarse slang* semen. **4** *Austral. slang* a sexually attractive person. [16th c.: origin uncertain]

spunky /'spʌŋki/ *adj.* (**spunkier**, **spunkiest**) **1** *colloq.* brave, spirited. **2** *Austral. slang* sexually attractive. □ **spunkily** *adv.*

spun silk *n.* a cheap material made of short-fibred and waste silk.

spun yarn *n. Naut.* a line formed of rope-yarns twisted together.

spur /spə:/ *n. & v.* ●*n.* **1** a device with a small spike or a spiked wheel worn on a rider's heel for urging a horse forward. **2** a stimulus or incentive. **3** a spur-shaped thing, esp.: **a** a projection from a mountain or mountain range. **b** a branch road or railway. **c** a hard projection on a cock's leg. **d** a steel point fastened to the leg of a gamecock. **e** a climbing-iron. **f** a small support for ceramic ware in a kiln. **4** *Bot.* **a** a slender hollow projection from part of a flower. **b** a short fruit-bearing shoot. ●*v.* (**spurred**, **spurring**) **1** *tr.* prick (a horse) with spurs. **2** *tr.* **a** (often foll. by *on*) incite (a person) (*spurred him on to greater efforts*; *spurred her to try again*). **b** stimulate (interest etc.). **3** *intr.* (often foll. by *on*, *forward*) ride a horse hard. **4** *tr.* (esp. as **spurred** *adj.*) provide (a person, boots, a gamecock) with spurs. □ **on the spur of the moment** on a momentary impulse; impromptu. **put** (or **set**) **spurs to 1** spur (a horse). **2** stimulate (resolution etc.). □ **spurless** *adj.* **spurred** *adj.* (esp. in senses 1, 3d, 4a of *n.*). [Old English *spora*, *spura* from Germanic: related to SPURN]

spurge /spə:dʒ/ *n.* any plant of the genus *Euphorbia*, exuding an acrid milky juice once used medicinally as a purgative. [Middle English via Old French *espurge*, from *espurgier*, from Latin *expurgare* (as EX-[1], PURGE)]

spur-gear *n.* = SPUR-WHEEL.

spurge laurel *n.* a low-growing shrub, *Daphne laureola*, with glossy leaves and small greenish flowers.

spurious /'spjʊərɪəs/ *adj.* **1** not genuine, not being what it purports to be, not proceeding from the pretended source (*a spurious excuse*). **2** having an outward similarity of form or function only. **3** (of offspring) illegitimate. □ **spuriously** *adv.* **spuriousness** *n.* [Latin *spurius* 'false']

spurn /spə:n/ *v. & n.* ●*v.tr.* **1** reject with disdain; treat with contempt. **2** repel or thrust back with one's foot. ●*n.* an act of spurning. □ **spurner** *n.* [Old English *spurnan*, *spornan*: related to SPUR]

spurrey /'spʌri/ *n.* (also **spurry**) (*pl.* **-eys** or **-ies**) a slender plant of the genus *Spergula* or *Spergularia*, of the pink family, esp. (**corn spurrey**) *Spergula arvensis*, a white-flowered cornfield weed and (**sand spurrey**) *Spergularia rubra*, a pink-flowered plant of sandy soil. [Dutch *spurrie*, probably related to medieval Latin *spergula*]

spurrier /'spʌrɪə, 'spə:r-/ *n.* a spur-maker.

spur royal *n. hist.* a 15-shilling coin of James I bearing a spurlike sun with rays.

spurt /spə:t/ *v. & n.* ●*v.* **1** (also **spirt**) **a** *intr.* gush out in a jet or stream. **b** *tr.* cause (liquid etc.) to do this. **2** *intr.* make a sudden effort. ●*n.* **1** (also **spirt**) a sudden gushing out, a jet. **2** a short sudden effort or increase of pace esp. in racing. [16th c.: origin unknown]

spur-wheel *n.* a cogwheel with radial teeth.

sputnik /'spʊtnɪk, 'spʌt-/ *n.* each of a series of Russian artificial satellites launched from 1957. [Russian, = fellow-traveller]

sputter /'spʌtə/ *v. & n.* ●*v.* **1** *intr.* emit spitting sounds, esp. when being heated. **2** *intr.* (often foll. by *at*) speak in a hurried or vehement fashion. **3** *tr.* emit with a spitting sound. **4** *tr.* speak or utter (words, threats, a language, etc.) rapidly or incoherently. **5** *tr. Physics* deposit (metal) by using fast ions etc. to eject particles of it from a target. ●*n.* a sputtering sound, esp. sputtering speech. □ **sputterer** *n.* [Dutch *sputteren* (imitative)]

sputum /'spju:təm/ *n.* (*pl.* **sputa** /-tə/) **1** saliva, spittle. **2** a mixture of saliva and mucus expectorated from the respiratory tract, usu. a sign of disease. [Latin, neut. past part. of *spuere* 'spit']

spy /spʌɪ/ *n. & v.* ●*n.* (*pl.* **spies**) **1** a person who secretly collects and reports information on the activities, movements, etc., of an enemy, competitor, etc. **2** a person who keeps watch on others, esp. furtively. ●*v.* (**spies**, **spied**) **1** *tr.* discern or make out, esp. by careful observation (*spied a house in the distance*). **2** *intr.* (often foll. by *on*) act as a spy, keep a close and secret watch. **3** *intr.* (often foll. by *into*) pry. □ **spy out** explore or discover, esp. secretly. [Middle English from Old French *espie* 'espying', *espier* 'espy', from Germanic]

spyglass /'spʌɪglɑːs/ *n.* a small telescope.

spyhole /'spʌɪhəʊl/ *n. Brit.* a peephole.

spymaster /'spʌɪmɑːstə/ *n. colloq.* the head of an organization of spies.

sq. *abbr.* square.

SQL *abbr. Computing* structured query language.

Sqn. Ldr. *abbr.* Squadron Leader.

squab /skwɒb/ *n. & adj.* ● *n.* **1** a short fat person. **2** a very young bird, esp. an unfledged pigeon. **3 a** a stuffed cushion. **b** *Brit.* the padded back or side of a car-seat. **4** a sofa or ottoman. ● *adj.* short and fat, squat. [17th c.: origin unknown: cf. obsolete *quab* 'shapeless thing', Swedish dialect *sqvabba* 'fat woman']

squabble /'skwɒb(ə)l/ *n. & v.* ● *n.* a petty or noisy quarrel. ● *v.intr.* engage in a squabble. □ **squabbler** *n.* [probably imitative: cf. Swedish dialect *sqvabbel* 'a dispute']

squabby /'skwɒbi/ *adj.* (**squabbier**, **squabbiest**) short and fat; squat.

squab-chick *n.* an unfledged bird.

squab pie *n. Brit.* **1** pigeon pie. **2** a pie of mutton, pork, onions, and apples.

squacco /'skwakəʊ/ *n.* (in full **squacco heron**) a small crested buff and white heron, *Ardeola ralloides*, of S. Europe and parts of Africa. [Italian dialect *sguacco*]

squad /skwɒd/ *n.* **1** a small group of people sharing a task etc. **2** *Mil.* a small number of men assembled for drill etc. **3** *Sport* a group of players forming a team. **4 a** (often in *comb.*) a specialized unit within a police force (*drug squad*). **b** = FLYING SQUAD. **5** a group or class of people of a specified kind (*the awkward squad*). [French *escouade*, variant of *escadre*, from Italian *squadra* SQUARE]

squad car *n.* a police car having a radio link with headquarters.

squaddie /'skwɒdi/ *n.* (also **squaddy**) (*pl.* **-ies**) *Brit. Mil. slang* **1** a recruit. **2** a private.

squadron /'skwɒdrən/ *n.* **1** an organized body of persons. **2** a principal division of a cavalry regiment or armoured formation, consisting of two troops. **3 a** a detachment of warships employed on a particular duty. **b** a division of a naval fleet under the command of a flag-officer. **4** a unit of the Royal Air Force with 10 to 18 aircraft. [Italian *squadrone* (as SQUAD)]

squadron leader *n.* the commander of a squadron of the Royal Air Force, the officer next below wing commander.

squail /skweɪl/ *n.* **1** (in *pl.*) a game with small wooden discs propelled across a table or board. **2** each of these discs. [19th c.: origin unknown: cf. dialect *kayles* 'skittles']

squail-board *n.* a board used in the game of squails.

squalid /'skwɒlɪd/ *adj.* **1** filthy, repulsively dirty. **2** mean or poor in appearance. **3** wretched, sordid. □ **squalidity** /-'lɪdɪti/ *n.* **squalidly** *adv.* **squalidness** *n.* [Latin *squalidus* from *squalēre* 'be rough or dirty']

squall /skwɔːl/ *n. & v.* ● *n.* **1** a sudden or violent gust or storm of wind, esp. with rain or snow or sleet. **2** a discordant cry; a scream (esp. of a baby). **3** (esp. in *pl.*) trouble, difficulty. ● *v.* **1** *intr.* utter a squall; scream, cry out violently as in fear or pain. **2** *tr.* utter in a screaming or discordant voice. □ **squally** *adj.* [probably from SQUEAL, influenced by BAWL]

squall line *n. Meteorol.* a narrow band of high winds along a cold front.

squalor /'skwɒlə/ *n.* the state of being filthy or squalid. [Latin, as SQUALID]

squama /'skweɪmə/ *n.* (*pl.* **squamae** /-miː/) **1** *Zool. & Bot.* a scale on an animal or plant. **2** *Anat.* a thin scalelike plate of bone. □ **squamate** /-mət, -meɪt/ *adj.* **squamose** *adj.* **squamous** *adj.* **squamule** *n.* [Latin *squama*]

squander /'skwɒndə/ *v.tr.* **1** spend (money, time, etc.) wastefully. **2** dissipate (a fortune etc.) wastefully. □ **squanderer** *n.* [16th c.: origin unknown]

square /skwɛː/ *n., adj., adv., & v.* ● *n.* **1** an equilateral rectangle. **2 a** an object of this shape or approximately this shape. **b** a small square area on a game-board. **c** a square scarf. **d** *Brit.* an academic cap with a stiff square top; a mortarboard. **3 a** an open (usu. four-sided) area surrounded by buildings, esp. one planted with trees etc. and surrounded by houses. **b** an open area at the meeting of streets. **c** *Cricket* a closer-cut area at the centre of a ground, any strip of which may be prepared as a wicket. **d** an area within barracks etc. for drill. **e** *US* a block of buildings bounded by four streets. **4** the product of a number multiplied by itself (*81 is the square of 9*). **5** an L-shaped or T-shaped instrument for obtaining or testing right angles. **6** *slang* a conventional or old-fashioned person, one ignorant of or opposed to current trends. **7** a square arrangement of letters, figures, etc. **8** a body of infantry drawn up in rectangular form. **9** a unit of 100 sq. ft as a measure of flooring etc. **10** *N. Amer. colloq.* a square meal (*three squares a day*). ● *adj.* **1** having the shape of a square. **2** having or in the form of a right angle (*table with square corners*). **3** angular and not round; of square section (*has a square jaw*). **4** designating a unit of measure equal to the area of a square whose side is one of the unit specified (*square metre*). **5** (often foll. by *with*) esp. *Brit.* **a** level, parallel. **b** on a proper footing; even, quits. **6 a** (usu. foll. by *to*) at right angles. **b** *Cricket* on a line through the stumps at right angles to the wicket. **7** having the breadth more nearly equal to the length or height than is usual (*a man of square frame*). **8** properly arranged; in good order, settled (*get things square*). **9** (also **all square**) **a** not in debt, with no money owed. **b** having equal scores, esp. *Golf* having won the same number of holes as one's opponent. **c** (of scores) equal. **10** fair and honest (*his dealings are not always quite square*). **11** uncompromising, direct, thorough (*was met with a square refusal*). **12** *slang* conventional or old-fashioned, unsophisticated, conservative (cf. sense 6 of *n.*). **13** *Mus.* (of rhythm) simple, straightforward. ● *adv.* **1** squarely (*sat square on his seat*). **2** fairly, honestly (*play square*). ● *v.* **1** *tr.* make square or rectangular, give a rectangular cross-section to (timber etc.). **2** *tr.* multiply (a number) by itself (*3 squared is 9*). **3** *tr. & intr.* (usu. foll. by *to, with*) adjust; make or be suitable or consistent; reconcile (*the results do not square with your conclusions*). **4** *tr.* mark out in squares. **5** *tr.* settle or pay (a bill etc.). **6** *tr.* place (one's shoulders etc.) squarely facing forwards. **7** *tr. colloq.* **a** pay or bribe. **b** secure the acquiescence etc. of (a person) in this way. **8** *tr.* (also *absol.*) make the scores of (a match etc.) all square. **9** *intr.* assume the attitude of a boxer. **10** *tr. Naut.* **a** lay (yards) at right angles with the keel making them at the same time horizontal. **b** get (deadeyes) horizontal. **c** get (ratlines) horizontal and parallel to one another. □ **back to square one** *colloq.* back to the starting point with no progress made. **get square with** pay or compound with (a creditor). **on the square** *adj.* **1** *colloq.* honest, fair. **2** having membership of the Freemasons. ● *adv. colloq.* honestly, fairly (*can be trusted to act on the square*). **out of square** not at right angles. **square accounts with** see ACCOUNT. **square away** *US* tidy up. **square the circle 1** construct a square equal in area to a given circle (a problem incapable of a purely geometrical solution). **2** do what is impossible. **square off 1** *US* assume the attitude of a boxer. **2** *Austral.* placate or conciliate. **3** mark out in squares. **square peg in a round hole** see PEG. **square up** settle an account etc. **square up to 1** move towards (a person) in a fighting attitude. **2** face and tackle (a difficulty etc.) resolutely. □ **squarely** *adv.* **squareness** *n.* **squarer** *n.* **squarish** *adj.* [Middle English from Old French *esquare, esquarré, esquarrer*, ultimately from EX-[1] + Latin *quadra* 'square']

square-bashing *n. Brit. Mil. slang* drill on a barrack square.

square brackets *n.pl.* brackets of the form [ ].

square-built *adj.* comparatively broad; broadly-built.

square dance *n.* a dance with usu. four couples facing inwards from four sides.

square deal *n.* a fair bargain, fair treatment.

squared paper *n. Brit.* paper marked out in squares, esp. for plotting graphs.

square-eyed *adj. joc.* affected by or given to excessive viewing of television.

square leg *n. Cricket* **1** the fielding position at some distance on the batsman's leg side and nearly opposite the stumps. **2** a fielder in this position.

square meal *n.* a substantial and satisfying meal.

square measure *n.* measure expressed in square units.

Square Mile *n.* (prec. by *the*) *Brit.* the City, the financial district of London.

square number *n.* the square of an integer e.g. 1, 4, 9, 16, 25, etc.

square perch *n.* 30¼ sq. yards.

square piano *n.* an early type of piano, small and oblong in shape.

square-rigged *adj.* (of a vessel) with the principal sails at right angles to the length of the ship and extended by horizontal yards slung to the mast by the middle (opp. FORE-AND-AFT RIGGED).

square root *n.* the number that multiplied by itself gives a specified number (*3 is the square root of 9*).

square sail *n.* a four-cornered sail extended on a yard slung to the mast by the middle.

square-shouldered *adj.* with broad and not sloping shoulders (cf. ROUND-SHOULDERED).

square-toed *adj.* **1** (of shoes or boots) having square toes. **2** wearing such shoes or boots. **3** formal, prim.

square wave *n. Physics* a wave with periodic sudden alternations between only two values of quantity.

squarrose /'skwarəʊs, 'skwɒ-, -'rəʊs/ *adj. Bot. & Zool.* rough with scalelike projections. [Latin *squarrosus* 'scurfy, scabby']

squash[1] /skwɒʃ/ *v. & n.* ● *v.* **1** *tr.* crush or squeeze flat or into pulp. **2** *intr.* (often foll. by *into*) make one's way by squeezing. **3** *tr.* pack tight, crowd. **4** *tr.* **a** silence (a person) with a crushing retort etc. **b** dismiss (a proposal etc.). **c** quash (a rebellion). ● *n.* **1** a crowd; a crowded assembly. **2** a sound of or as of something being squashed, or of a soft body falling. **3** *Brit.* a concentrated drink made of crushed fruit etc., diluted or to be diluted with water. **4** (in full **squash rackets**) a game played with rackets and a small fairly soft ball against the walls of a closed court. **5** a squashed thing or mass. □ **squashy** *adj.* (**squashier**, **squashiest**). **squashily** *adv.* **squashiness** *n.* [alteration of QUASH]

squash[2] /skwɒʃ/ *n.* (*pl.* same or **squashes**) **1** any of various trailing gourd plants of the genus *Cucurbita* having pumpkin-like fruits, esp. *C. maxima*, *C. moschata*, and *C. pepo*. **2** the fruit of these cooked and eaten as a vegetable. [obsolete *(i)squoutersquash* from Narragansett *asquutasquash*, from *asq* 'uncooked' + *squash* 'green']

squash bug *n.* a N. American hemipteran bug, *Anasa tristis*, which is a pest of squashes, pumpkins, and melons.

squash tennis *n. US* a game similar to squash, played with a tennis ball.

squat /skwɒt/ *v., adj., & n.* ● *v.* (**squatted**, **squatting**) **1** *intr.* **a** crouch with the hams resting on the backs of the heels. **b** sit on the ground etc. with the knees drawn up and the heels close to or touching the hams. **2** *tr.* put (a person) into a squatting position. **3** *intr. colloq.* sit down. **4** **a** *intr.* act as a squatter. **b** *tr.* occupy (a building) as a squatter. **5** *intr.* (of an animal) crouch close to the ground. ● *adj.* (**squatter**, **squattest**) **1** (of a person etc.) short and thick, dumpy. **2** in a squatting posture. ● *n.* **1** a squatting posture. **2** **a** a place occupied by a squatter or squatters. **b** being a squatter. **3** *N. Amer. slang* = DIDDLY-SQUAT. □ **squatly** *adv.* **squatness** *n.* [Middle English from Old French *esquatir* 'flatten', from *es-* EX-[1] + *quatir* 'press down, crouch', ultimately from Latin *coactus*, past part. of *cogere* 'compel': see COGENT]

squatter /'skwɒtə/ *n.* **1** a person who takes unauthorized possession of unoccupied premises. **2** *Austral.* **a** a sheep farmer esp. on a large scale. **b** *hist.* a person who gets the right of pasturage from the government on easy terms. **3** a person who settles on new esp. public land without title. **4** a person who squats.

squat thrust *n.* an exercise in which the legs are thrust backwards starting from a squatting position with the hands on the floor.

squaw /skwɔː/ *n. offens.* a N. American Indian woman or wife. [Narragansett *squaws*, Massachusetts Algonquian *squa* 'woman']

squawk /skwɔːk/ *n. & v.* ● *n.* **1** a loud harsh cry esp. of a bird. **2** a complaint. ● *v.tr. & intr.* utter with or make a squawk. □ **squawker** *n.* [imitative]

squawk-box *n. colloq.* a loudspeaker or intercom.

squaw-man *n. offens.* a white or black man married to a N. American Indian woman.

squaw winter *n.* (in N. America) a brief wintry spell before an Indian summer.

squeak /skwiːk/ *n. & v.* ● *n.* **1** **a** a short shrill cry as of a mouse. **b** a slight high-pitched sound as of an unoiled hinge. **2** (also **narrow squeak**) a narrow escape, a success barely attained. ● *v.* **1** *intr.* make a squeak. **2** *tr.* utter (words) shrilly. **3** *intr.* (foll. by *by*, *through*) *colloq.* pass narrowly. **4** *intr. slang* turn informer. [Middle English, imitative: cf. SQUEAL, SHRIEK, and Swedish *skväka* 'croak']

squeaker /'skwiːkə/ *n.* **1** a person or thing that squeaks. **2** a young bird, esp. a pigeon. **3** esp. *N. Amer.* a game, election, etc. won by a narrow margin.

squeaky /'skwiːki/ *adj.* (**squeakier**, **squeakiest**) making a squeaking sound. □ **squeakily** *adv.* **squeakiness** *n.*

squeaky clean *adj.* **1** completely clean. **2** above criticism; beyond reproach.

squeal /skwiːl/ *n. & v.* ● *n.* a prolonged shrill sound, esp. a cry of a child or a pig. ● *v.* **1** *intr.* make a squeal. **2** *tr.* utter (words) with a squeal. **3** *intr. slang* turn informer. **4** *intr. slang* protest loudly or excitedly. □ **squealer** *n.* [Middle English, imitative]

squeamish /'skwiːmɪʃ/ *adj.* **1** easily nauseated or disgusted. **2** fastidious or overscrupulous in questions of propriety, honesty, etc. □ **squeamishly** *adv.* **squeamishness** *n.* [Middle English variant of *squeamous* (now dialect), from Anglo-French *escoymos*, of unknown origin]

squeegee /'skwiːdʒiː/ *n. & v.* ● *n.* **1** a rubber-edged implement set on a handle and used for cleaning windows etc. **2** a small similar instrument or roller used in photography. ● *v.tr.* (**squeegees**, **squeegeed**) clean or scrape with a squeegee. [*squeege*, strengthened form of SQUEEZE]

squeeze /skwiːz/ *v. & n.* ● *v.* **1** *tr.* **a** exert pressure on from opposite or all sides, esp. in order to extract moisture or reduce size. **b** compress with one's hand or between two bodies. **c** reduce the size of or alter the shape of by squeezing. **2** *tr.* (often foll. by *out*) extract (moisture) by squeezing. **3** **a** *tr.* force (a person or thing) into or through a small or narrow space. **b** *intr.* make one's way by squeezing. **c** *tr.* make (one's way) by squeezing. **4** *tr.* **a** harass by exactions; extort money etc. from. **b** constrain; bring pressure to bear on. **c** (usu. foll. by *out of*) obtain (money etc.) by extortion, entreaty, etc. **d** *Bridge* subject (a player) to a squeeze. **5** *tr.* press (a person's hand) with one's own as a sign of sympathy, affection, etc. **6** *tr.* (often foll. by *out*) produce with effort (*squeezed out a tear*). ● *n.* **1** an instance of squeezing; the state of being squeezed. **2** a close embrace. **3** a crowd or crowded state; a crush. **4** a small quantity produced by squeezing (*a squeeze of lemon*). **5** a sum of money extorted or exacted, esp. an illicit commission. **6** *Econ.* a restriction on borrowing, investment, etc., in a financial crisis. **7** an impression of a coin etc. taken by pressing damp paper, wax, etc., against it. **8** (in full **squeeze play**) **a** *Bridge* leading winning cards until an opponent is forced to discard an important card. **b** *Baseball* hitting a ball short to the infield to enable a runner on third base to start for home as soon as the ball is pitched. □ **put the squeeze on** *colloq.* coerce or pressure (a person). □ **squeezable** *adj.* **squeezer** *n.* [earlier *squise*, intensive of obsolete *queise*, of unknown origin]

squeeze bottle *n.* a flexible container whose contents are extracted by squeezing it.

squeeze-box *n. colloq.* an accordion or concertina.

squeezy /ˈskwiːzi/ *adj.* **1** (esp. of a bottle) flexible and able to be squeezed to force out the contents. **2** suggestive of squeezing, esp. tight, confined, restricted.

squelch /skwɛltʃ/ *v.* & *n.* ● *v.* **1** *intr.* **a** make a sucking sound as of treading in thick mud. **b** move with a squelching sound. **2** *tr.* **a** disconcert, silence. **b** stamp on, crush flat, put an end to. ● *n.* **1** an instance of squelching. **2** (in full **squelch circuit**) *Radio* a circuit that suppresses the output of a receiver if the signal strength falls below a certain level. □ **squelcher** *n.* **squelchy** *adj.* [imitative]

squib /skwɪb/ *n.* & *v.* ● *n.* **1** a small firework burning with a hissing sound and usu. with a final explosion. **2** a short satirical composition, a lampoon. ● *v.* (**squibbed**, **squibbing**) **1** *tr. Amer. Football* kick (the ball) a comparatively short distance on a kick-off; execute (a kick) in this way. **2** *archaic* **a** *intr.* write lampoons. **b** *tr.* lampoon. [16th c.: origin unknown: perhaps imitative]

squid /skwɪd/ *n.* & *v.* ● *n.* **1** any elongated fast-swimming cephalopod mollusc of the order Teuthoidea, with eight arms and two long tentacles, esp. a common edible one of the genus *Loligo*. **2** artificial bait for fish imitating a squid in form. ● *v.intr.* (**squidded**, **squidding**) fish with squid as bait. [16th c.: origin unknown]

squidgy /ˈskwɪdʒi/ *adj.* (**squidgier**, **squidgiest**) *colloq.* squashy, soggy. [imitative]

squiffed /skwɪft/ *adj. slang* = SQUIFFY.

squiffy /ˈskwɪfi/ *adj.* (**squiffier**, **squiffiest**) esp. *Brit. slang* slightly drunk. [19th c.: origin unknown]

squiggle /ˈskwɪɡ(ə)l/ *n.* & *v.* ● *n.* a short curly line, esp. in handwriting or doodling. ● *v.* **1** *tr.* write in a squiggly manner; scrawl. **2** *intr.* wriggle, squirm. □ **squiggly** *adj.* [imitative]

squill /skwɪl/ *n.* **1** **a** a bulbous plant of the genus *Scilla* (hyacinth family), typically with star-shaped blue flowers. **b** (in full **striped squill**) the related plant *Puschkinia scilloides*. **2** **a** a white-flowered Mediterranean plant, *Drimia maritima* (hyacinth family). Also called *sea onion*. **b** an extract of the bulb of this, used in cough mixtures and other medicines. **3** a crustacean of the genus *Squilla* with spiny front legs like a mantis. [Middle English via Latin *squilla*, *scilla* from Greek *skilla*]

squinch[1] /skwɪn(t)ʃ/ *n.* a straight or arched structure across an interior angle of a square tower to carry a superstructure, e.g. a dome. [variant of obsolete *scunch*, abbreviation of SCUNCHEON]

squinch[2] /skwɪn(t)ʃ/ *v.* esp. *US* **1** (usu. foll. by *up*) **a** *tr.* screw up one's eyes, face, etc. **b** *intr.* (of the eyes etc.) screw up, squint. **2** *intr.* & *tr.* (often foll. by *up*, *down*) squeeze or squash compactly. [perhaps a blend of SQUEEZE *v.* + PINCH *v.*]

squint /skwɪnt/ *v.*, *n.*, & *adj.* ● *v.* **1** *intr.* have the eyes turned in different directions, have a squint. **2** *intr.* (often foll. by *at*) look obliquely or with half-closed eyes. **3** *tr.* close (one's eyes) quickly, hold (one's eyes) half-shut. ● *n.* **1** = STRABISMUS. **2** a stealthy or sidelong glance. **3** *colloq.* a glance or look (*had a squint at it*). **4** an oblique opening through the wall of a church affording a view of the altar. **5** a leaning or inclination towards a particular object or aim. ● *adj.* **1** squinting. **2** looking different ways. □ **squinter** *n.* **squinty** *adj.* [ASQUINT: the adjective perhaps from *squint-eyed* from obsolete adverb *squint*, from ASQUINT]

squint-eyed *adj.* **1** squinting. **2** malignant, ill-willed.

squire /skwʌɪə/ *n.* & *v.* ● *n.* **1** a country gentleman, esp. the chief landowner in a country district. **2** *hist.* a knight's attendant. **3** *Brit. colloq.* a jocular form of address to a man. **4** *US* a local magistrate or judge in some rural districts. **5** *Austral.* = COCKNEY *n.* 2. ● *v.tr.* (of a man) attend upon or escort (a woman). □ **squiredom** *n.* **squirehood** *n.* **squirelet** *n.* **squireling** *n.* **squirely** *adj.* **squireship** *n.* [Middle English from Old French *esquier* ESQUIRE]

squirearch /ˈskwʌɪərɑːk/ *n.* a member of the squirearchy. □ **squirearchical** /-ˈrɑːkɪk(ə)l/ *adj.* (also **squirarchical**). [back-formation from SQUIREARCHY, on the pattern of MONARCH]

squirearchy /ˈskwʌɪərɑːki/ *n.* (also **squirarchy**) (*pl.* **-ies**) landowners collectively, esp. as a class having political or social influence; a class or body of squires. [SQUIRE, on the pattern of HIERARCHY etc.]

squireen /skwʌɪəˈriːn/ *n. Brit.* the owner of a small landed property esp. in Ireland. [SQUIRE + diminutive suffix from Irish *-ín*]

squirl /skwəːl/ *n. colloq.* a flourish or twirl, esp. in handwriting. [perhaps from SQUIGGLE + TWIRL or WHIRL]

squirm /skwəːm/ *v.* & *n.* ● *v.intr.* **1** wriggle, writhe. **2** show or feel embarrassment or discomfiture. ● *n.* a squirming movement. □ **squirmer** *n.* **squirmy** *adj.* (**squirmier**, **squirmiest**). [imitative, probably associated with WORM]

squirrel /ˈskwɪr(ə)l/ *n.* & *v.* ● *n.* **1** any rodent of the family Sciuridae, often living in trees, with a bushy tail arching over its back (*grey squirrel*; *red squirrel*). **2** the fur of this animal. **3** a person who hoards objects, food, etc. ● *v.* (**squirrelled**, **squirrelling**; *US* **squirreled**, **squirreling**) **1** *tr.* (often foll. by *away*) hoard (objects, food, time, etc.) (*squirrelled it away in the cupboard*). **2** *intr.* (often foll. by *around*) bustle about. [Middle English from Anglo-French *esquirel*, Old French *esquireul*, ultimately via Latin *sciurus* from Greek *skiouros*, from *skia* 'shade' + *oura* 'tail']

squirrel cage *n.* **1** a small cage containing a revolving cylinder like a treadmill, on which a captive squirrel may exercise. **2** a form of rotor used in small electric motors, resembling the cylinder of a squirrel cage. **3** a monotonous or repetitive way of life.

squirrel grass *n.* (also **squirrel-tail grass**) a grass, *Hordeum jubatum*, with bushy spikelets.

squirrelly /ˈskwɪr(ə)li/ *adj.* **1** like a squirrel. **2** **a** inclined to bustle about. **b** (of a person) unpredictable, nervous, demented.

squirrel-monkey *n.* a small yellow-haired monkey, *Saimiri sciureus*, native to S. America.

squirt /skwəːt/ *v.* & *n.* ● *v.* **1** *tr.* eject (liquid or powder) in a jet as from a syringe. **2** *intr.* (of liquid or powder) be discharged in this way. **3** *tr.* splash with liquid or powder ejected by squirting. ● *n.* **1** **a** a jet of water etc. **b** a small quantity produced by squirting. **2** a syringe. **3** *colloq.* an insignificant but presumptuous person. □ **squirter** *n.* [Middle English, imitative]

squirt gun *n.* a water pistol.

squish /skwɪʃ/ *n.* & *v.* ● *n.* a slight squelching sound. ● *v.* **1** *intr.* move with a squish. **2** *tr. colloq.* squash, squeeze. □ **squishy** *adj.* (**squishier**, **squishiest**). [imitative]

squit /skwɪt/ *n. Brit.* **1** *slang* a small or insignificant person. **2** *dial.* nonsense. **3** (**the squits**) *dial.* & *colloq.* diarrhoea. [perhaps related to dialect *squirt* 'insignificant person', and *squit* 'to squirt']

squitch /skwɪtʃ/ *n.* couch grass. [alteration of QUITCH]

squitters /ˈskwɪtəz/ *n.pl. dial.* & *colloq.* diarrhoea. [perhaps f. dialect *squit* 'to squirt']

squiz /skwɪz/ *n. Austral.* & *NZ slang* a look or glance. [probably from QUIZ[2]]

SR *abbr. hist.* Southern Railway.

Sr *symb. Chem.* the element strontium.

Sr. *abbr.* **1** Senior. **2** Señor. **3** Signor. **4** *Eccl.* Sister.

sr *abbr.* steradian(s).

Sri Lankan /ʃrɪ ˈlaŋk(ə)n, srɪ-/ *n.* & *adj.* ● *n.* **1** a native or national of Sri Lanka (formerly Ceylon), an island in the Indian Ocean. **2** a person of Sri Lankan descent. ● *adj.* of or relating to Sri Lanka or its people.

SRN *abbr.* (in the UK) State Registered Nurse.

SRO *abbr.* **1** standing room only. **2** *Finance* self-regulatory organization. **3** Statutory Rules and Orders.

SS *abbr.* **1** Saints. **2** steamship. **3** *hist.* Nazi special police force. [sense 3 from German *SchutzStaffel*]

SSAFA *abbr.* (in the UK) Soldiers', Sailors', and Airmen's Families Association.

SSC *abbr.* **1** (in Scotland) Solicitor in the Supreme Court. **2** Superconducting Super Collider.

SSE *abbr.* south-south-east.

SSP *abbr.* (in the UK) statutory sick pay.

SSRC *abbr.* (in the UK) Social Science Research Council.

SSSI *abbr.* (in the UK) Site of Special Scientific Interest.

SST *abbr.* supersonic transport.

SSW *abbr.* south-south-west.

St *abbr.* **1** Saint. **2** stokes.

St. *abbr.* Street.

st. *abbr.* **1** stone (in weight). **2** *Cricket* stumped by.

-st var. of -EST².

Sta. *abbr.* Station.

stab /stab/ *v.* & *n.* ● *v.* (**stabbed**, **stabbing**) **1** *tr.* pierce or wound with a (usu. short) pointed tool or weapon e.g. a knife or dagger. **2** *intr.* (often foll. by *at*) aim a blow with such a weapon. **3** *intr.* cause a sensation like being stabbed (*stabbing pain*). **4** *tr.* hurt or distress (a person, feelings, conscience, etc.). **5** *intr.* (foll. by *at*) aim a blow at a person's reputation, etc. ● *n.* **1 a** an instance of stabbing. **b** a blow or thrust with a knife etc. **2** a wound made in this way. **3** a sharply painful physical or mental sensation. **4** *colloq.* an attempt, a try. □ **stabber** *n.* **stabbing** *n.* [Middle English: origin unknown]

Stabat Mater /stɑːbat ˈmɑːtə, steɪbat ˈmeɪtə/ *n.* **1** a Latin hymn on the suffering of the Virgin Mary at the Crucifixion. **2** a musical setting for this. [the opening words, Latin *Stabat mater dolorosa* 'Stood the mother, full of grief']

stabilator /ˈsteɪbɪleɪtə/ *n.* a combined stabilizer and elevator at the tail of an aircraft.

stabile /ˈsteɪbʌɪl/ *n.* a rigid, free-standing abstract sculpture or structure of wire, sheet metal, etc. [Latin *stabilis* STABLE¹, on the pattern of MOBILE]

stability /stəˈbɪlɪti/ *n.* the quality or state of being stable. [Middle English via Old French *stableté* from Latin *stabilitas*, from *stabilis* STABLE¹]

stabilize /ˈsteɪbɪlʌɪz/ *v.tr.* & *intr.* (also **-ise**) make or become stable. □ **stabilization** /-ˈzeɪʃ(ə)n/ *n.*

stabilizer /ˈsteɪbɪlʌɪzə/ *n.* (also **-iser**) a device or substance used to keep something stable, esp.: **1** a gyroscopic device to prevent rolling of a ship. **2** *N. Amer.* the horizontal tailplane of an aircraft. **3** (in *pl.*) *Brit.* a pair of small wheels fitted to the rear wheel of a child's bicycle. **4** a substance which prevents the breakdown of emulsions, esp. as a food additive maintaining texture.

stab in the back *n.* & *v.* ● *n.* a treacherous or slanderous attack. ● *v.tr.* slander or betray.

stable¹ /ˈsteɪb(ə)l/ *adj.* (**stabler**, **stablest**) **1** firmly fixed or established; not easily adjusted, destroyed, or altered (*a stable structure*; *a stable government*). **2 a** firm, resolute; not wavering or fickle (*a stable and steadfast friend*). **b** mentally and emotionally sound, sane and sensible. **3** *Chem.* (of a compound) not readily decomposing. **4** *Physics* (of an isotope) not subject to radioactive decay. **5** in a stable medical condition after an injury, operation, etc. □ **stably** *adv.* [Middle English via Anglo-French *stable*, Old French *estable* from Latin *stabilis*, from *stare* 'stand']

stable² /ˈsteɪb(ə)l/ *n.* & *v.* ● *n.* **1** a building set apart and adapted for keeping horses. **2** an establishment where racehorses are kept and trained. **3** the racehorses of a particular stable. **4** persons, products, etc., having a common origin or affiliation. **5** such an origin or affiliation. ● *v.tr.* put or keep (a horse) in a stable. □ **stableful** *n.* (*pl.* **-fuls**). [Middle English via Old French *estable* from Latin *stabulum*, from *stare* 'stand']

stable boy *n.* a boy employed in a stable.

stable companion *n.* **1** a horse of the same stable. **2** a person or product from the same source; a member of the same organization.

stable door *n.* **1** the door of a stable, divided into two parts horizontally allowing one half to be shut and the other left open. **2** this as the door of a house etc.

stable equilibrium *n.* a state in which a body when disturbed tends to return to equilibrium.

stable girl *n.* a girl or woman employed in a stable.

stable lad *n. Brit.* a person employed in a stable.

stableman /ˈsteɪb(ə)lmən/ *n.* (*pl.* **-men**) a person employed in a stable.

stablemate /ˈsteɪb(ə)lmeɪt/ *n.* = STABLE COMPANION.

stabling /ˈsteɪblɪŋ/ *n.* accommodation for horses.

stablish /ˈstablɪʃ/ *v.tr. archaic* fix firmly; establish; set up. [variant of ESTABLISH]

staccato /stəˈkɑːtəʊ/ *adv.*, *adj.*, & *n.* esp. *Mus.* ● *adv.* & *adj.* with each sound or note sharply detached or separated from the others (cf. LEGATO, TENUTO). ● *n.* (*pl.* **-os**) **1** a staccato passage in music etc. **2** staccato delivery or presentation. [Italian, past part. of *staccare* = *distaccare* DETACH]

staccato mark *n.* a dot or stroke above or below a note, indicating that it is to be played staccato.

stack /stak/ *n.* & *v.* ● *n.* **1** a pile or heap, esp. in orderly arrangement. **2** a circular or rectangular pile of hay, straw, etc., or of grain in sheaf, often with a sloping thatched top, a rick. **3** *colloq.* a large quantity (*a stack of work*; *has stacks of money*). **4 a** = CHIMNEY STACK. **b** = SMOKESTACK. **c** a tall factory chimney. **5** esp. *Brit.* a stacked group of aircraft. **6** (also **stack-room**) a part of a library where books are compactly stored, esp. one to which the public does not have direct access. **7** *Computing* a set of storage locations which store data in such a way that the most recently stored item is the first to be retrieved. **8** a vertical arrangement of hi-fi or public-address equipment. **9** *Brit.* a tall column of rock esp. off the coast of Scotland and the Orkneys. **10** a pyramidal group of rifles, a pile. **11** *Brit.* a measure for a pile of wood of 108 cu. ft (3.06 cubic metres). ● *v.tr.* **1** pile in a stack or stacks. **2 a** arrange (cards) secretly for cheating. **b** manipulate (circumstances etc.) to one's advantage. **3** cause (aircraft) to fly round the same point at different levels while waiting to land at an airport. □ **stack arms** *hist.* = *pile arms*. **stack up** *N. Amer. colloq.* present oneself, measure up. □ **stackable** *adj.* **stacker** *n.* [Middle English from Old Norse *stakkr* 'haystack', from Germanic]

stacked /stakt/ *adj.* **1 a** put into a stack or stacks. **b** piled with goods etc. **2** (of odds) biased, esp. unfavourably. **3** (of a woman) having an attractive figure, esp. a prominent bust.

stack-yard *n.* an enclosure for stacks of hay, straw, etc.

staddle /ˈstad(ə)l/ *n.* a platform or framework supporting a rick etc. [Old English *stathol* 'base' from Germanic: related to STAND]

staddle-stone *n.* a usu. mushroom-shaped stone supporting a staddle or rick etc.

stadium /ˈsteɪdɪəm/ *n.* (*pl.* **stadiums**) **1** an athletic or sports ground with tiers of seats for spectators. **2** (*pl.* **stadiums** or **stadia** /-dɪə/) *Antiq.* **a** a course for a foot race or chariot race. **b** a measure of length, about 185 metres. **3** a stage or period of development etc. [Middle English via Latin from Greek *stadion*]

stadtholder /ˈstathəʊldə, ˈstad-/ *n.* (also **stadholder**) *hist.* **1** the chief magistrate of the United Provinces of the Netherlands. **2** the viceroy or governor of a province or town in the Netherlands. □ **stadtholdership** *n.* [Dutch *stadhouder* 'deputy', from *stad* STEAD + *houder* HOLDER, translating medieval Latin LOCUM TENENS]

staff[1] /stɑːf/ *n. & v.* ● *n.* **1 a** a stick or pole for use in walking or climbing or as a weapon. **b** a stick or pole as a sign of office or authority. **c** a person or thing that supports or sustains. **d** a flagstaff. **e** *Surveying* a rod for measuring distances, heights, etc. **f** *Brit.* a token given to an engine driver on a single-track railway as authority to proceed over a given section of line. **g** *Brit.* a spindle in a watch. **2 a** a body of persons employed in a business etc. (*editorial staff of a newspaper*). **b** those in authority within an organization, esp. the teachers in a school. **c** *Mil.* etc. a body of officers assisting an officer in high command and concerned with an army, regiment, fleet, or air force as a whole (*general staff*). **d** (usu. **Staff**) *Mil.* = STAFF SERGEANT. **3** (*pl.* **staffs** or **staves** /steɪvz/) *Mus.* a set of usu. five parallel lines on any one or between any adjacent two of which a note is placed to indicate its pitch. ● *v.tr.* provide (an institution etc.) with staff. □ **staffed** *adj.* (also in *comb.*). [Old English *stæf*, from Germanic]

staff[2] /stɑːf/ *n.* a mixture of plaster of Paris, cement, etc., as a temporary building material. [19th c.: origin unknown]

staffage /stəˈfɑːʒ/ *n.* accessory items in a painting, esp. figures or animals in a landscape picture. [German from *staffieren* 'decorate', perhaps from Old French *estoffer*: see STUFF]

staff college *n. Brit. Mil.* etc. a college at which officers are trained for staff duties.

staffer /ˈstɑːfə/ *n. US* a member of a staff, esp. of a newspaper.

staff notation *n. Mus.* notation by means of a staff, esp. as distinct from tonic sol-fa.

staff nurse *n. Brit.* a nurse ranking just below a sister.

staff officer *n. Mil.* an officer serving on the staff of an army etc.

Staffordshire bull terrier /ˈstafədʃə/ *n.* a dog of a small stocky breed of terrier, with a short broad head and dropped ears. [*Staffordshire*, a county in the north midlands of England]

staffroom /ˈstɑːfruːm, -rʊm/ *n.* **1** a common room for staff, esp. in a school. **2** the staff themselves.

Staffs. *abbr.* Staffordshire.

staff sergeant *n.* **1** *Brit.* the senior sergeant of a non-infantry company. **2** *US* a non-commissioned officer ranking just above sergeant.

stag /stag/ *n. & v.* ● *n.* **1** an adult male deer, esp. one with a set of antlers. **2** *Brit. Stock Exch.* a person who applies for shares of a new issue with a view to selling at once for a profit. **3** a man who attends a social gathering unaccompanied by a woman. ● *v.tr.* (**stagged, stagging**) *Brit. Stock Exch.* deal in (shares) as a stag. [Middle English, probably from Old English and related to Old Norse *steggr*, *steggi* 'male bird']

stag beetle *n.* any beetle of the family Lucanidae, the male of which has large branched mandibles resembling a stag's antlers.

stage /steɪdʒ/ *n. & v.* ● *n.* **1** a point or period in a process or development (*reached a critical stage*; *is in the larval stage*). **2 a** a raised floor or platform, esp. one on which plays etc. are performed before an audience. **b** (prec. by *the*) the acting or theatrical profession; the art of writing or presenting plays. **c** the scene of action (*the stage of politics*). **d** = LANDING STAGE. **3 a** a regular stopping place on a route. **b** the distance between two stopping places. **c** *Brit.* = FARE STAGE. **4** a section of a rocket with a separate engine, jettisoned when its propellant is exhausted. **5** *Geol.* a range of strata forming a subdivision of a series. **6** *Electronics* a single amplifying transistor or valve with the associated equipment. **7** a raised plate on which an object is placed for inspection through a microscope. ● *v.tr.* **1** present (a play etc.) on stage. **2** arrange the occurrence of (*staged a demonstration*; *staged a comeback*). □ **go on the stage** become an actor. **hold the stage** dominate a conversation etc. **set the stage** (usu. foll. by *for*) prepare the way or conditions for (an event etc.). □ **stageable** *adj.* **stageability** /-dʒəˈbɪlɪti/ *n.* **stager** *n.* [Middle English from Old French *estage* 'dwelling', ultimately from Latin *stare* 'stand']

stagecoach /ˈsteɪdʒkəʊtʃ/ *n. hist.* a large closed horse-drawn coach running regularly by stages between two places.

stagecraft /ˈsteɪdʒkrɑːft/ *n.* skill or experience in writing or staging plays.

stage direction *n.* an instruction in the text of a play as to the movement, position, tone, etc., of an actor, or sound effects etc.

stage door *n.* an actors' and workmen's entrance from the street to a theatre behind the stage.

stage effect *n.* **1** an effect produced in acting or on the stage. **2** an artificial or theatrical effect produced in real life.

stage fright *n.* nervousness before or during an appearance before an audience.

stagehand /ˈsteɪdʒhand/ *n.* a person handling scenery etc. during a performance on stage.

stage left *adv.* on the left side of the stage, facing the audience.

stage-manage *v.tr.* **1** be the stage-manager of. **2** arrange and control for effect.

stage manager *n.* the person responsible for lighting and other mechanical arrangements for a play etc. □ **stage management** *n.*

stage name *n.* a name assumed for professional purposes by an actor.

stage play *n.* a play performed on stage rather than broadcast etc.

stage right *adv.* on the right side of the stage, facing the audience.

stage rights *n.pl.* exclusive rights to perform a particular play.

stage-struck *adj.* filled with an inordinate desire to go on the stage.

stage whisper *n.* **1** an aside. **2** a loud whisper meant to be heard by people other than the one addressed.

stagey var. of STAGY.

stagflation /stagˈfleɪʃ(ə)n/ *n. Econ.* a state of inflation without a corresponding increase of demand and employment. [STAGNATION (as STAGNATE) + INFLATION]

stagger /ˈstagə/ *v. & n.* ● *v.* **1 a** *intr.* walk unsteadily, totter. **b** *tr.* cause to totter (*was staggered by the blow*). **2 a** *tr.* shock, confuse; cause to hesitate or waver (*the question staggered them*; *they were staggered at the suggestion*). **b** *intr.* hesitate; waver in purpose. **3** *tr.* arrange (events, hours of work, etc.) so that they do not coincide. **4** *tr.* arrange (objects) so that they are not in line, esp.: **a** arrange (a road-crossing) so that the side roads are not in line. **b** set (the spokes of a wheel) to incline alternately to right and left. ● *n.* **1** a tottering movement. **2** an overhanging or slantwise or zigzag arrangement of like parts in a structure etc. □ **staggerer** *n.* [alteration of Middle English *stacker* (now dialect) from Old Norse *stakra*, frequentative of *staka* 'push, stagger']

staggering /ˈstag(ə)rɪŋ/ *adj.* **1** astonishing, bewildering. **2** that staggers. □ **staggeringly** *adv.*

staggers /ˈstagəz/ *n.* **1** any of various parasitic or deficiency diseases of farm animals marked by staggering or loss of balance. **2** giddiness.

stag-horn *n.* (also **stag's horn**) **1** the horn of a stag, used to make knife handles, etc. **2** any of various ferns, esp. of the genus *Platycerium*, having fronds like antlers.

staghound /ˈstaghaʊnd/ *n.* **1** any large dog of a breed used for hunting deer by sight or scent. **2** this breed.

staging /ˈsteɪdʒɪŋ/ *n.* **1** the presentation of a play etc. **2 a** a platform or support or scaffolding, esp. temporary. **b** *Brit.* shelves for plants in a greenhouse.

staging area *n.* an intermediate assembly point for troops in transit.

staging post *n.* a regular stopping place, esp. on an air route.

stagnant /ˈstagnənt/ *adj.* **1** (of liquid) motionless, having no current. **2** (of life, action, the mind, business, a person) showing no activity, dull, sluggish. □ **stagnancy** *n.* **stagnantly** *adv.* [Latin *stagnare stagnant-* from *stagnum* 'pool']

stagnate /stagˈneɪt, ˈstagneɪt/ *v.intr.* be or become stagnant. □ **stagnation** *n.*

stag-night *n.* (also **stag-party**) an all-male celebration, esp. in honour of a man about to marry.

stag's horn var. of STAG-HORN.

stagy /ˈsteɪdʒi/ *adj.* (also **stagey**) (**stagier**, **stagiest**) theatrical, artificial, exaggerated. □ **stagily** *adv.* **staginess** *n.*

staid /steɪd/ *adj.* of quiet and steady character; sedate. □ **staidly** *adv.* **staidness** *n.* [= *stayed*, past part. of STAY[1]]

stain /steɪn/ *v.* & *n.* ● *v.* **1** *tr.* & *intr.* discolour or be discoloured by the action of liquid sinking in. **2** *tr.* sully, blemish, spoil, damage (a reputation, character, etc.). **3** *tr.* colour (wood, glass, etc.) by a process other than painting or covering the surface. **4** *tr.* impregnate (a specimen) for microscopic examination with colouring matter that makes the structure visible by being deposited in some parts more than in others. **5** *tr.* print colours on (wallpaper). ● *n.* **1** a discoloration, a spot or mark caused esp. by contact with foreign matter and not easily removed (*a cloth covered with tea-stains*). **2 a** a blot or blemish. **b** damage to a reputation etc. (*a stain on one's character*). **3** a substance used in staining. □ **stainable** *adj.* **stainer** *n.* [Middle English from *distain*, from Old French *desteindre desteign-* (as DIS-, TINGE)]

stained glass *n.* dyed or coloured glass, esp. in a lead framework in a window (also, with hyphen, *attrib.*): *stained-glass window*.

stainless /ˈsteɪnlɪs/ *adj.* **1** (esp. of a reputation) without stains. **2** not liable to stain.

stainless steel *n.* an iron alloy containing chromium and resistant to tarnishing and rust, esp. steel containing 11 to 14 per cent chromium, used for cutlery etc.

stair /stɛː/ *n.* **1** each of a set of fixed steps, esp. in a building (*on the top stair but one*). **2** (usu. in *pl.*) a set of such steps (*passed him on the stairs*; *down a winding stair*). **3** (in *pl.*) a landing stage. [Old English *stǣger*, from Germanic]

staircase /ˈstɛːkeɪs/ *n.* **1** a flight of stairs and the supporting structure. **2** *Brit.* a part of a building containing a staircase.

stairhead /ˈstɛːhɛd/ *n.* esp. *Brit.* a level space at the top of stairs.

stairlift /ˈstɛːlɪft/ *n.* a lift in the form of a chair built into a domestic staircase for carrying an elderly or disabled person up and down stairs.

stair-rod *n.* a rod for securing a carpet in the angle between two steps.

stairway /ˈstɛːweɪ/ *n.* **1** a flight of stairs, a staircase. **2** the way up this.

stairwell /ˈstɛːwɛl/ *n.* the shaft in which a staircase is built.

staithe /steɪð/ *n.* *Brit.* a wharf, esp. a waterside coal depot equipped for loading vessels. [Middle English via Old Norse *stöth* 'landing stage' from Germanic: related to STAND]

stake[1] /steɪk/ *n.* & *v.* ● *n.* **1** a stout stick or post sharpened at one end and driven into the ground as a support, boundary mark, etc. **2** *hist.* **a** the post to which a person was tied to be burnt alive. **b** (prec. by *the*) death by burning as a punishment (*was condemned to the stake*). **3** a long vertical rod in basket-making. **4** a metalworker's small anvil fixed on a bench by a pointed prop. ● *v.tr.* **1** fasten, secure, or support with a stake or stakes. **2** (foll. by *off*, *out*) mark off (an area) with stakes. **3** state or establish (a claim). □ **pull** (or **pull up**) **stakes** depart; go to live elsewhere. **stake out** *colloq.* **1** place under surveillance. **2** place (a person) to maintain surveillance. [Old English *staca* from West Germanic: related to STICK[2]]

stake[2] /steɪk/ *n.* & *v.* ● *n.* **1** a sum of money etc. wagered on an event, esp. deposited with a stakeholder. **2** (often foll. by *in*) an interest or concern, esp. financial. **3** (in *pl.*) **a** money offered as a prize esp. in a horse race. **b** such a race (*maiden stakes*; *trial stakes*). ● *v.tr.* **1 a** wager (*staked £5 on the next race*). **b** risk (*staked everything on convincing him*). **2** *US colloq.* give financial or other support to. □ **at stake 1** risked, to be won or lost (*life itself is at stake*). **2** at issue, in question. □ **staker** *n.* [Middle English: perhaps from STAKE[1], from placing an object as a wager on a post or stake]

stake-boat *n.* a boat anchored to mark the course for a boat race etc.

stake-body *n.* (*pl.* **-ies**) *US* a body for a lorry etc. having a flat open platform with removable posts along the sides.

stakebuilding /ˈsteɪkbɪldɪŋ/ *n.* *Stock Exch.* the building up of a shareholding.

stakeholder /ˈsteɪkhəʊldə/ *n.* **1** an independent party with whom each of those who make a wager deposits the money etc. wagered. **2** a person with an interest or concern in something, esp. a business.

stake-net *n.* a fishing net hung on stakes.

stake-out *n.* *colloq.* a period of surveillance.

Stakhanovite /stəˈkɑːnəvʌɪt/ *n.* a worker (esp. in the former USSR) who is exceptionally productive or zealous. □ **Stakhanovism** /-vɪz(ə)m/ *n.* **Stakhanovist** /-vɪst/ *n.* & *adj.* [from the name of A. G. *Stakhanov*, Russian coal miner d. 1977]

stalactite /ˈstaləktʌɪt/ *n.* a tapering deposit of calcite hanging down like an icicle from the roof of a cave, cliff overhang, etc., formed by dripping water. □ **stalactic** /-ˈlaktɪk/ *adj.* **stalactiform** /-ˈlaktɪfɔːm/ *adj.* **stalactitic** /-ˈtɪtɪk/ *adj.* [modern Latin *stalactites* from Greek *stalaktos* 'dripping', from *stalassō* 'to drip']

Stalag /ˈstalag, ˈʃtalak/ *n.* *hist.* a German prison camp, esp. for non-commissioned officers and privates. [German, from *Stamm* 'base, main stock', *Lager* 'camp']

stalagmite /ˈstaləgmʌɪt/ *n.* a mound or tapering column of calcite rising from the floor of a cave etc., deposited by dripping water and often uniting with a stalactite. □ **stalagmitic** /-ˈmɪtɪk/ *adj.* [modern Latin *stalagmites* from Greek *stalagma* 'a drop', from *stalassō* (as STALACTITE)]

stale[1] /steɪl/ *adj.* & *v.* ● *adj.* (**staler**, **stalest**) **1 a** not fresh, not quite new (*stale bread is best for toast*). **b** musty, insipid, or otherwise the worse for age or use. **2** trite or unoriginal (*a stale joke*; *stale news*). **3** (of an athlete or other performer) having ability impaired by excessive exertion or practice. **4** *Law* (esp. of a claim) having been left dormant for an unreasonably long time. ● *v.tr.* & *intr.* make or become stale. □ **stalely** *adv.* **staleness** *n.* [Middle English, probably from Anglo-French & Old French from *estaler* 'halt': cf. STALL[1]]

stale[2] /steɪl/ *n.* & *v.* ● *n.* the urine of horses and cattle. ● *v.intr.* (esp. of horses and cattle) urinate. [Middle English, perhaps from Old French *estaler* 'adopt a position' (cf. STALE[1])]

stalemate /ˈsteɪlmeɪt/ *n.* & *v.* ● *n.* **1** *Chess* a position counting as a draw, in which a player is not in check but cannot move except into check. **2** a deadlock or drawn contest. ● *v.tr.* **1** *Chess* bring (a player) to a stalemate. **2** bring to a standstill. [obsolete *stale* (from Anglo-French *estale* from *estaler* 'be placed': cf. STALE[1]) + MATE[2]]

Stalinism /ˈstɑːlɪnɪz(ə)m/ *n.* **1** the policies followed by Stalin in the government of the former USSR, esp. centralization, totalitarianism, and the pursuit of Communism. **2** any rigid centralized authoritarian form of Communism. □ **Stalinist** *n.* & *adj.* [from the name of J. V. *Stalin* (Dzhugashvili), Soviet statesman d. 1953]

stalk[1] /stɔːk/ *n.* **1** the main stem of a herbaceous plant. **2** the slender attachment or support of a leaf, flower, fruit, etc. **3** a similar support for an organ etc. in an animal. **4** a slender support or linking shaft in a machine, object, etc., e.g. the stem of a wineglass. **5** the tall chimney of a factory etc. ▫ **stalked** *adj.* (also in *comb.*). **stalkless** *adj.* **stalklet** *n.* **stalklike** *adj.* **stalky** *adj.* [Middle English *stalke,* probably diminutive of (now dialect) *stale* 'rung of a ladder, long handle', from Old English *stalu*]

stalk[2] /stɔːk/ *v.* & *n.* ● *v.* **1 a** *tr.* pursue or approach (game, prey, or an enemy) stealthily. **b** *intr.* steal up to game under cover. **2** *intr.* stride, walk in a stately or haughty manner. **3** *tr. formal* or *literary* move silently or threateningly through (a place) (*fear stalked the streets*). ● *n.* **1** the stalking of game. **2** an imposing gait. [Old English from Germanic: related to STEAL]

stalker /ˈstɔːkə/ *n.* **1** a person who stalks game. **2** a person who stalks people, esp. a fan of a public figure who pesters him or her obsessively.

stalk-eyed *adj.* (of crabs, snails, etc.) having the eyes mounted on stalks.

stalking-horse *n.* **1** a horse or screen behind which a hunter is concealed. **2** a pretext concealing one's real intentions or actions. **3** a weak political candidate who forces an election in the hope of a more serious contender coming forward.

stall[1] /stɔːl/ *n.* & *v.* ● *n.* **1 a** a trader's stand or booth in a market etc., or out of doors. **b** a compartment in a building for the sale of goods. **c** a table in this on which goods are displayed. **2 a** a stable or cow-house. **b** a compartment for one animal in this. **3 a** a fixed seat in the choir or chancel of a church, more or less enclosed at the back and sides and often canopied, esp. one appropriated to a clergyman (*canon's stall*; *dean's stall*). **b** the office or dignity of a canon etc. **4** (usu. in *pl.*) *Brit.* each of a set of seats in a theatre, usu. on the ground floor. **5 a** a compartment for one person in a shower-room, lavatory, etc. **b** a compartment for one horse at the start of a race. **6 a** the stalling of an engine or aircraft. **b** the condition resulting from this. **7** a receptacle or sheath for one object (*finger-stall*). ● *v.* **1 a** *intr.* (of a motor vehicle or its engine) stop because of an overload on the engine or an inadequate supply of fuel to it. **b** *intr.* (of an aircraft or its pilot) reach a condition where the speed is too low to allow effective operation of the controls. **c** *tr.* cause (an engine or vehicle or aircraft) to stall. **2** *tr.* **a** put or keep (cattle etc.) in a stall or stalls esp. for fattening (*a stalled ox*). **b** furnish (a stable etc.) with stalls. **3** *intr.* esp. *US* stick fast as in mud or snow. [Old English *steall* from Germanic, related to STAND: in some senses partly via Old French *estal* from Frankish]

stall[2] /stɔːl/ *v.* & *n.* ● *v.* **1** *intr.* play for time when being questioned etc. **2** *tr.* delay, obstruct, block. ● *n.* the act or an instance of stalling. ▫ **stall off** evade or deceive. [originally 'to act as a decoy or accomplice': *stall* 'pickpocket's confederate' from Anglo-French *estal(e),* probably related to STALL[1]]

stallage /ˈstɔːlɪdʒ/ *n. Brit.* **1** space for a stall or stalls in a market etc. **2** the rent for such a stall. **3** the right to erect such a stall. [Middle English from Old French *estalage,* from *estal* STALL[1]]

stall-feed *v.tr.* fatten (cattle) in a stall.

stallholder /ˈstɔːlhəʊldə/ *n. Brit.* a person in charge of a stall at a market etc.

stallion /ˈstaljən/ *n.* an uncastrated adult male horse, esp. one kept for breeding. [Middle English from Old French *estalon,* ultimately from a Germanic root related to STALL[1]]

stalwart /ˈstɔːlwət, ˈstal-/ *adj.* & *n.* ● *adj.* **1** strongly built, sturdy. **2** courageous, resolute, determined (*stalwart supporters*). ● *n.* a stalwart person, esp. a loyal uncompromising partisan. ▫ **stalwartly** *adv.* **stalwartness** *n.* [Scots variant of obsolete *stalworth* from Old English *stǣlwierthe,* from *stǣl* 'place', WORTH]

stamen /ˈsteɪmɛn/ *n.* the male fertilizing organ of a flowering plant, including the anther containing pollen. ▫ **staminiferous** /stamɪˈnɪf(ə)rəs/ *adj.* [Latin *stamen staminis* 'warp in an upright loom, thread']

stamina /ˈstamɪnə/ *n.* the ability to endure prolonged physical or mental strain; staying power, power of endurance. [Latin, pl. of STAMEN in the sense 'warp, threads spun by the Fates']

staminate /ˈstamɪnət/ *adj. Bot.* (of a plant or flower) having stamens, esp. stamens but not pistils.

stammer /ˈstamə/ *v.* & *n.* ● *v.* **1** *intr.* speak (habitually, or on occasion from embarrassment etc.) with halting articulation, esp. with pauses or rapid repetitions of the same syllable. **2** *tr.* (often foll. by *out*) utter (words) in this way (*stammered out an excuse*). ● *n.* **1** a tendency to stammer. **2** an instance of stammering. ▫ **stammerer** *n.* **stammeringly** *adv.* [Old English *stamerian,* from West Germanic]

stamp /stamp/ *v.* & *n.* ● *v.* **1 a** *tr.* bring down (one's foot) heavily on the ground etc. **b** *tr.* crush, flatten, or bring into a specified state in this way (*stamped down the earth round the plant*). **c** *intr.* bring down one's foot heavily; walk with heavy steps. **2** *tr.* **a** impress (a pattern, mark, etc.) on metal, paper, butter, etc., with a die or similar instrument of metal, wood, rubber, etc. **b** impress (a surface) with a pattern etc. in this way. **3** *tr.* affix a postage or other stamp to (an envelope or document). **4** *tr.* assign a specific character to; characterize; mark out (*stamps the story an invention*). **5** *tr.* crush or pulverize (ore etc.). ● *n.* **1** an instrument for stamping a pattern or mark. **2 a** a mark or pattern made by this. **b** the impression of an official mark required to be made for revenue purposes on deeds, bills of exchange, etc., as evidence of payment of tax. **3** a small adhesive piece of paper indicating that a price, fee, or tax has been paid, esp. a postage stamp. **4** a mark impressed on or label etc. affixed to a commodity as evidence of quality etc. **5 a** a heavy downward blow with the foot. **b** the sound of this. **6 a** a characteristic mark or impress (*bears the stamp of genius*). **b** character, kind (*avoid people of that stamp*). **7** the block that crushes ore in a stamp-mill. ▫ **stamp on 1** impress (an idea etc.) on (the memory etc.). **2** suppress. **stamp out 1** produce by cutting out with a die etc. **2** put an end to, crush, destroy. ▫ **stamper** *n.* [probably Old English from Germanic: influenced by Old French *estamper* (*v.*) and French *estampe* (*n.*), also from Germanic]

Stamp Act *n.* an act concerned with stamp duty, esp. that imposing the duty on the American colonies in 1765 and repealed in 1766.

stamp collector *n.* a person engaged in stamp collecting; a philatelist. ▫ **stamp collecting** *n.*

stamp duty *n.* a duty imposed on certain kinds of legal document.

stampede /stamˈpiːd/ *n.* & *v.* ● *n.* **1** a sudden flight and scattering of a number of horses, cattle, etc. **2** a sudden flight or hurried movement of people due to interest or panic. **3** *US* the spontaneous and simultaneous response of many persons to a common impulse. ● *v.* **1** *intr.* take part in a stampede. **2** *tr.* cause to do this. **3** *tr.* cause to act hurriedly or unreasoningly. ▫ **stampeder** *n.* [Spanish *estampida* 'crash, uproar', ultimately from Germanic: related to STAMP]

stamp hinge *n.* a small piece of gummed transparent paper used for fixing postage stamps in an album etc.

stamping ground *n.* a favourite haunt or place of action.

stamp-mill *n.* a mill for crushing ore etc.

stamp office *n. Brit.* an office for the issue of government stamps and the receipt of stamp duty etc.

stamp paper *n.* **1** *Brit.* paper with the government revenue stamp. **2** the gummed marginal paper of a sheet of postage stamps.

stance /stɑːns, stans/ *n.* **1** an attitude or position of the body esp. when hitting a ball etc. **2** a standpoint; an attitude of mind. **3** *Sc.* a site for a market, taxi rank, etc. [French from Italian *stanza*: see STANZA]

stanch[1] var. of STAUNCH[2].

stanch[2] var. of STAUNCH[1].

stanchion /'stɑːnʃ(ə)n/ *n. & v.* ● *n.* **1** a post or pillar, an upright support, a vertical strut. **2** an upright bar, pair of bars, or frame, for confining cattle in a stall. ● *v.tr.* **1** supply with a stanchion. **2** fasten (cattle) to a stanchion. [Middle English from Anglo-French *stanchon*, Old French *estanchon*, from *estance*, probably ultimately from Latin *stare* 'stand']

stand /stand/ *v. & n.* ● *v.* (*past* and *past part.* **stood** /stʊd/) **1** *intr.* have or take or maintain an upright position, esp. on the feet or a base. **2** *intr.* be situated or located (*here once stood a village*). **3** *intr.* be of a specified height (*stands six foot three*). **4** *intr.* be in a specified condition (*stands accused*; *the thermometer stood at 90°*; *the matter stands as follows*; *stood in awe of them*). **5** *tr.* place or set in an upright or specified position (*stood it against the wall*). **6** *intr.* **a** move to and remain in a specified position (*stand aside*). **b** take a specified attitude (*stand aloof*). **7** *intr.* maintain a position; avoid falling or moving or being moved (*the house will stand for another century*; *stood for hours arguing*). **8** *intr.* assume a stationary position; cease to move (*now stand still*). **9** *intr.* remain valid or unaltered; hold good (*the former conditions must stand*). **10** *intr. Naut.* hold a specified course (*stand in for the shore*; *you are standing into danger*). **11** *tr.* endure without yielding or complaining; tolerate (*cannot stand the pain*; *how can you stand him?*). **12** *tr.* provide for another or others at one's own expense (*stood him a drink*). **13** *intr.* (often foll. by *for*) *Brit.* be a candidate (for an office, legislature, or constituency) (*stood for Parliament*; *stood for Finchley*). **14** *intr.* act in a specified capacity (*stood proxy*). **15** *tr.* undergo (trial). **16** *intr. Cricket* act as umpire. **17** *intr.* (of a dog) point, set. **18** *intr.* (in full **stand at stud**) (of a stallion) be available for breeding. ● *n.* **1** a cessation from motion or progress, a stoppage (*was brought to a stand*). **2 a** a halt made, or a stationary condition assumed, for the purpose of resistance. **b** resistance to attack or compulsion (esp. *make a stand*). **c** *Cricket* a prolonged period at the wicket by two batsmen. **3 a** a position taken up (*took his stand near the door*). **b** an attitude adopted. **4** a rack, set of shelves, table, etc., on or in which things may be placed (*music stand*; *hatstand*). **5 a** a small open-fronted structure for a trader outdoors or in a market etc. **b** esp. *Brit.* a structure occupied by a participating organization at an exhibition. **6** a standing place for vehicles (*cab-stand*). **7 a** a raised structure for spectators, performers, etc. to sit or stand on. **b** *US* a witness box (*take the stand*). **8** *Theatr.* etc. each halt made on a tour to give one or more performances. **9** a group of growing plants (*stand of trees*; *stand of clover*). □ **as it stands 1** in its present condition, unaltered. **2** (also **as things stand**) in the present circumstances. **be at a stand** *archaic* be unable to proceed, be in perplexity. **it stands to reason** see REASON. **stand alone** be unequalled. **stand and deliver!** *hist.* a highwayman's order to hand over valuables etc. **stand at bay** see BAY[5]. **stand back 1** withdraw; take up a position further from the front. **2** withdraw emotionally in order to take an objective view. **stand by 1** stand nearby; look on without interfering (*will not stand by and see him ill-treated*). **2** uphold, support, side with (a person). **3** adhere to, abide by (terms or promises). **4 a** *Naut.* stand ready to take hold of or operate (an anchor etc.). **b** be ready to act or assist. **stand a chance** see CHANCE. **stand corrected** accept correction. **stand down 1** withdraw from a team, election, etc. **2** leave the witness box. **3** *Mil.* go off duty; relax after a state of alert. **stand easy!** see EASY. **stand for 1** represent, signify, imply (*'US' stands for 'United States'*; *democracy stands for a great deal more than that*). **2** (often with *neg.*) *colloq.* endure, tolerate, acquiesce in. **3** espouse the cause of. **stand one's ground** maintain one's position, not yield. **stand high** be high in status, price, etc. **stand in** (usu. foll. by *for*) deputize; act in place of another. **stand in the breach** see BREACH. **stand a person in good stead** see STEAD. **stand in with** be in league with. **stand off 1** move or keep away, keep one's distance. **2** *Brit.* temporarily dispense with the services of (an employee). **stand on 1** insist on, observe scrupulously (*stand on ceremony*; *stand on one's dignity*). **2** *Naut.* continue on the same course. **stand on me** *slang* rely on me; believe me. **stand on one's own feet** (or **own two feet**) be self-reliant or independent. **stand out 1** be prominent or conspicuous or outstanding. **2** (usu. foll. by *against*, *for*) hold out; persist in opposition or support or endurance. **stand over 1** stand close to (a person) to watch, control, threaten, etc. **2** be postponed, be left for later settlement etc. **stand pat** see PAT[2]. **stand to 1** *Mil.* stand ready for an attack (esp. before dawn or after dark). **2** abide by, adhere to (terms or promises). **3** be likely or certain to (*stands to lose everything*). **4** uphold, support, or side with (a person). **stand treat** bear the expense of entertainment etc. **stand up 1 a** rise to one's feet from a sitting or other position. **b** come to or remain in or place in a standing position. **2** (of an argument etc.) be valid. **3** *colloq.* fail to keep an appointment with. **stand up for** support, side with, maintain (a person or cause). **stand upon** = *stand on* 1. **stand up to 1** meet or face (an opponent) courageously. **2** be resistant to the harmful effects of (wear, use, etc.). **stand well** (usu. foll. by *with*) be on good terms or in good repute. **take one's stand on** base one's argument etc. on, rely on. □ **stander** *n.* [Old English *standan*, from Germanic]

stand-alone *adj.* (of a computer) operating independently of a network or other system.

standard /'standəd/ *n. & adj.* ● *n.* **1** an object or quality or measure serving as a basis or example or principle to which others conform or should conform or by which the accuracy or quality of others is judged (*by present-day standards*). **2 a** the degree of excellence etc. required for a particular purpose (*not up to standard*). **b** average quality (*of a low standard*). **3** the ordinary procedure, or quality or design of a product, without added or novel features. **4** a distinctive flag, esp. the flag of a cavalry regiment as distinct from the *colours* of an infantry regiment. **5 a** an upright support. **b** an upright water or gas pipe. **6 a** a tree or shrub that grows on an erect stem of full height and stands alone without support. **b** a shrub grafted on an upright stem and trained in tree form (*standard rose*). **7** a document specifying nationally or internationally agreed properties for manufactured goods etc. (*British Standard*). **8** a thing recognized as a model for imitation etc. **9** a tune or song of established popularity. **10 a** a system by which the value of a currency is defined in terms of gold or silver or both. **b** the prescribed proportion of the weight of fine metal in gold or silver coins. **11** a measure for timber, equivalent to 165 cu. ft (4.67 cubic metres). **12** *Brit. hist.* a grade of classification in elementary schools. ● *adj.* **1** serving or used as a standard (*a standard size*). **2** of a normal or prescribed quality or size etc. **3** having recognized and permanent value; authoritative (*the standard book on the subject*). **4** (of language) conforming to established educated usage (*standard English*). □ **raise a standard** take up arms; rally support (*raised the standard of revolt*). [Middle English from Anglo-French *estaundart*, Old French *estendart*, from *estendre* (as EXTEND): senses 5 and 6 of the noun affected by association with STAND]

standard assessment task *n.* a standard test given to school children to assess their progress in a core subject of the national curriculum.

standard-bearer *n.* **1** a soldier who carries a standard. **2** a prominent leader in a cause.

Standardbred /'standədbrɛd/ *n. N. Amer.* **1** a horse of a breed able to attain a specified speed, developed esp. for trotting. **2** this breed.

standard deviation *n. Statistics* a quantity calculated to indicate the extent of deviation for a group as a whole.

Standard Grade *n.* (in Scotland) an examination equivalent to the GCSE.

standardize /ˈstandədʌɪz/ *v.* (also **-ise**) **1** *tr.* cause to conform to a standard. **2** *tr.* determine the properties of by comparison with a standard. **3** *intr.* (foll. by *on*) adopt as one's standard or model. □ **standardizable** *adj.* **standardization** /-ˈzeɪʃ(ə)n/ *n.* **standardizer** *n.*

standard lamp *n. Brit.* a lamp set on a tall upright with its base standing on the floor.

standard of living *n.* the degree of material comfort available to a person or class or community.

standard time *n.* a uniform time for places in approximately the same longitude, established in a country or region by law or custom.

standard wire gauge see WIRE GAUGE 2.

standby /ˈstan(d)bʌɪ/ *n. & adj.* ● *n.* (*pl.* **-bys**) **1** a person or thing ready if needed in an emergency etc. **2** readiness for duty (*on standby*). ● *adj.* **1** ready for immediate use. **2** (of air travel, theatre seats, etc.) not booked in advance but allocated on the basis of earliest availability.

stand camera *n.* a camera for use on a tripod, not hand-held.

standee /stanˈdiː/ *n. colloq.* a person who stands, esp. when all seats are occupied.

stand-in *n.* a deputy or substitute, esp. for an actor when the latter's acting ability is not needed.

standing /ˈstandɪŋ/ *n. & adj.* ● *n.* **1** esteem or repute, esp. high; status, position (*people of high standing*; *is of no standing*). **2** duration (*a dispute of long standing*). **3** length of service, membership, etc. ● *adj.* **1** that stands, upright. **2 a** established, permanent (*a standing rule*). **b** not made, raised, etc., for the occasion (*a standing army*). **3** (of a jump, start, race, etc.) performed from rest or from a standing position. **4** (of water) stagnant. **5** (of corn) unreaped. **6** (of a stallion) that stands at stud. **7** *Printing* (formerly, of type) not yet distributed after use. □ **be in good standing** (often foll. by *with*) be in favour or on good terms. **leave a person standing** make far more rapid progress than he or she.

standing committee *n.* a committee that is permanent during the existence of the appointing body.

standing joke *n.* an object of permanent ridicule.

standing order *n.* esp. *Brit.* an instruction to a banker to make regular payments, or to a newsagent etc. for a regular supply of a periodical etc.

standing orders *n.pl.* the rules governing the manner in which all business shall be conducted in a parliament, council, society, etc.

standing ovation *n.* a period of prolonged applause during which the crowd or audience rise to their feet.

standing rigging *n.* rigging which is fixed in position.

standing room *n.* space to stand in.

standing wave *n. Physics* the vibration of a system in which some particular points remain fixed while others between them vibrate with the maximum amplitude (cf. TRAVELLING WAVE).

stand of arms *n. Brit. Mil.* a complete set of weapons for one man.

stand of colours *n. Brit. Mil.* a regiment's flags.

stand-off *n.* **1** *N. Amer.* a deadlock. **2** = STAND-OFF HALF.

stand-off half *n. Rugby* a half-back who forms a link between the scrum-half and the three-quarters.

stand-offish /-ˈɒfɪʃ/ *adj.* cold or distant in manner. □ **stand-offishly** *adv.* **stand-offishness** *n.*

standout /ˈstandaʊt/ *n. & adj. N. Amer. colloq.* ● *n.* a remarkable, notable, or outstanding person or thing. ● *adj.* remarkable, notable, outstanding.

standpipe /ˈstan(d)pʌɪp/ *n.* a vertical pipe extending from a water supply, esp. one connecting a temporary tap to the mains.

standpoint /ˈstan(d)pɔɪnt/ *n.* **1** the position from which a thing is viewed. **2** a mental attitude.

standstill /ˈstan(d)stɪl/ *n.* a stoppage; an inability to proceed.

stand-to *n. Mil.* the action or state of standing to; readiness for action or attack.

stand-up *attrib.adj.* **1** (of a meal) eaten standing. **2** (of a fight) violent, thorough, or fair and square. **3** (of a collar) upright, not turned down. **4** (of a comedian) performing by standing before an audience and telling jokes.

stanhope /ˈstanəp, -həʊp/ *n.* a light open carriage for one with two or four wheels. [named after Fitzroy *Stanhope*, English clergyman d. 1864, for whom the first one was made]

staniel /ˈstanj(ə)l/ *n.* a kestrel. [Old English *stāngella* 'stone-yeller', from *stān* 'stone' + *gellan* 'yell']

stank *past* of STINK.

Stanley knife *n. Brit. propr.* a type of very sharp knife with a replaceable blade. [from *Stanley*, proprietary name for hand tools]

stannary /ˈstan(ə)ri/ *n.* (*pl.* **-ies**) (usu. in *pl.* prec. by *the*) any of several tin-mining districts in Cornwall and Devon. [medieval Latin *stannaria* (pl.) from Late Latin *stannum* 'tin']

stannary court *n. hist.* a legal body for the regulation of tin-miners in the stannaries.

stannic /ˈstanɪk/ *adj. Chem.* of or relating to tetravalent tin (*stannic acid*; *stannic chloride*). [Late Latin *stannum* 'tin']

stannous /ˈstanəs/ *adj. Chem.* of or relating to divalent tin (*stannous salts*; *stannous chloride*).

stanza /ˈstanzə/ *n.* **1** the basic metrical unit in a poem or verse consisting of a recurring group of lines (often four lines and usu. not more than twelve) which may or may not rhyme. **2** a group of four lines in some Greek and Latin metres. □ **stanza'd** *adj.* (also **stanzaed**) (also in *comb.*). **stanzaic** /-ˈzeɪɪk/ *adj.* [Italian, = standing place, chamber, stanza, ultimately from Latin *stare* 'stand']

stapelia /stəˈpiːlɪə/ *n.* any southern African plant of the genus *Stapelia*, with flowers having an unpleasant smell. [modern Latin, named after J. B. von *Stapel*, Dutch botanist d. 1636]

stapes /ˈsteɪpiːz/ *n.* (*pl.* same) *Anat.* a small stirrup-shaped bone in the middle ear, transmitting vibrations from the incus to the inner ear. [modern Latin from medieval Latin *stapes* 'stirrup']

staphylococcus /ˌstafɪləˈkɒkəs/ *n.* (*pl.* **staphylococci** /-k(s)ʌɪ, -k(s)iː/) any bacterium of the genus *Staphylococcus*, occurring in grapelike clusters, and sometimes causing pus formation usu. in the skin and mucous membranes of animals. □ **staphylococcal** *adj.* [modern Latin, from Greek *staphulē* 'bunch of grapes' + *kokkos* 'berry']

staple[1] /ˈsteɪp(ə)l/ *n. & v.* ● *n.* a U-shaped metal bar or piece of wire with pointed ends for driving into, securing, or fastening together various materials or for driving through and clenching papers, netting, electric wire, etc. ● *v.tr.* provide or fasten with a staple. □ **stapler** *n.* [Old English *stapol*, from Germanic]

staple[2] /ˈsteɪp(ə)l/ *n., adj., & v.* ● *n.* **1** the principal or an important article of commerce (*the staples of British industry*). **2** the chief element or a main component, e.g. of a diet. **3** a raw material. **4** the fibre of cotton or wool etc. as determining its quality (*cotton of fine staple*). ● *adj.* **1** main or principal (*staple commodities*). **2** important as a product or an export. ● *v.tr.* sort or classify (wool etc.) according to fibre. [Middle English via Old French *estaple* 'market' from Middle Low German, Middle Dutch *stapel* 'pillar, emporium': related to STAPLE[1]]

staple gun *n.* a hand-held device for driving in staples.

star /stɑː/ *n. & v.* ● *n.* **1** a celestial body appearing as a luminous point in the night sky. **2** (in full **fixed star**) such a body, being so far from the earth as to appear motionless (except for the diurnal rotation of the heavens), in contrast to planets, comets, etc. **3** *Astron.* a large gaseous body (such as the sun), naturally luminous from internal nuclear reactions. **4** a celestial body regarded as influencing a person's fortunes etc. (*born under a lucky star*). **5** a thing resembling a star or having the conventional shape of a star, with five or more radiating lines. **6** a star-shaped mark, esp. a white mark on a horse's forehead. **7** a figure or object with radiating points esp. as the insignia of an order, as a decoration or mark of rank, or showing a category of excellence (*a five-star hotel*; *was awarded a gold star*). **8** **a** a famous or brilliant person; the principal or most prominent performer in a play, film, etc. (*the star of the show*). **b** (*attrib.*) outstanding; particularly brilliant (*star pupil*). **9** (in full **star connection**) *Electr.* a Y-shaped arrangement of three-phase windings. **10** = STAR PRISONER. ● *v.* (**starred**, **starring**) **1** **a** *tr.* (of a film etc.) feature as a principal performer. **b** *intr.* (of a performer) be featured in a film etc. **2** *tr.* (esp. as **starred** *adj.*) **a** mark, set, or adorn with a star or stars. **b** put an asterisk or star beside (a name, an item in a list, etc.). □ **my stars!** *colloq.* an expression of surprise. □ **stardom** *n.* **starless** *adj.* **starlike** *adj.* [Old English *steorra*, from Germanic]

star-apple *n.* an edible purple apple-like fruit (with a starlike cross-section) of a tropical evergreen tree, *Chrysophyllum cainito*.

starboard /'stɑːbɔːd, -bəd/ *n.* & *v.* *Naut.* & *Aeron.* ● *n.* the right-hand side (looking forward) of a ship, boat, or aircraft (cf. PORT[3]). ● *v.tr.* (also *absol.*) turn (the helm) to starboard. [Old English *stēorbord* = rudder side (see STEER[1], BOARD), early Teutonic ships being steered with a paddle over the right side]

starboard tack see TACK[1] *n.* 4a.

starboard watch see WATCH *n.* 3b.

starburst /'stɑːbəːst/ *n.* **1** **a** a pattern of radiating lines or rays around a central object, light source, etc. **b** an explosion or *Photog.* a lens attachment producing this effect (*starburst filter*). **2** *Astron.* a period of intense activity, apparently star formation, in certain galaxies.

starch /stɑːtʃ/ *n.* & *v.* ● *n.* **1** an odourless tasteless polysaccharide occurring widely in plants as a carbohydrate store and obtained chiefly from cereals and potatoes, forming an important constituent of the human diet. **2** a preparation of this for stiffening fabric before ironing. **3** stiffness of manner; formality. ● *v.tr.* stiffen (clothing) with starch. □ **starcher** *n.* [earlier as verb: Old English from Germanic, related to STARK]

Star Chamber *n.* *Brit.* *Law* **1** *hist.* a court of civil and criminal jurisdiction noted for its arbitrary procedure, and abolished in 1640. **2** any arbitrary or oppressive tribunal.

starch-reduced *adj.* (esp. of food) containing less than the normal proportion of starch.

starchy /'stɑːtʃi/ *adj.* (**starchier**, **starchiest**) **1** **a** of or like starch. **b** containing much starch. **2** (of a person) precise, prim. □ **starchily** *adv.* **starchiness** *n.*

star connection see STAR *n.* 9.

star-crossed *adj.* *archaic* ill-fated.

stardust /'stɑːdʌst/ *n.* **1** a twinkling mass. **2** an illusory or insubstantial substance. **3** a multitude of stars looking like dust. □ **have stardust in one's eyes** be dreamily romantic or unrealistic.

stare /stɛː/ *v.* & *n.* ● *v.* **1** *intr.* (usu. foll. by *at*) look fixedly with eyes open, esp. as the result of curiosity, surprise, bewilderment, admiration, horror, etc. (*sat staring at the door*; *stared in amazement*). **2** *intr.* (of eyes) be wide open and fixed. **3** *intr.* be unpleasantly prominent or striking. **4** *tr.* (foll. by *into*) reduce (a person) to a specified condition by staring (*stared me into silence*). ● *n.* a staring gaze. □ **stare down** (or **out**) outstare. **stare a person in the face** be evident or imminent. □ **starer** *n.* [Old English *starian*, from Germanic]

starfish /'stɑːfɪʃ/ *n.* (*pl.* usu. same) an echinoderm of the class Asteroidea with five or more radiating arms.

star fruit *n.* = CARAMBOLA.

stargazer /'stɑːgeɪzə/ *n.* **1** *colloq.* usu. *derog.* or *joc.* an astronomer or astrologer. **2** *Austral.* *slang* a horse that turns its head when galloping. □ **stargaze** *v.intr.*

stark /stɑːk/ *adj.* & *adv.* ● *adj.* **1** desolate, bare (*a stark landscape*). **2** sharply evident; brutally simple (*in stark contrast*; *the stark reality*). **3** downright, sheer (*stark madness*). **4** completely naked. **5** *archaic* strong, stiff, rigid. ● *adv.* completely, wholly (*stark mad*; *stark naked*). □ **starkly** *adv.* **starkness** *n.* [Old English *stearc* from Germanic: 'stark naked' from earlier *start-naked*, from obsolete *start* 'tail': cf. REDSTART]

Stark effect /stɑːk/ *n.* *Physics* the splitting of a spectrum line into several components by the application of an electric field. [named after J. *Stark*, German physicist d. 1957]

starkers /'stɑːkəz/ *adj.* *Brit.* *colloq.* stark naked.

starlet /'stɑːlɪt/ *n.* **1** a promising young performer, esp. a woman. **2** a little star.

starlight /'stɑːlʌɪt/ *n.* **1** the light of the stars (*walked home by starlight*). **2** (*attrib.*) = STARLIT (*a starlight night*).

starling[1] /'stɑːlɪŋ/ *n.* **1** a small gregarious partly migratory bird, *Sturnus vulgaris*, with blackish-brown speckled lustrous plumage, chiefly inhabiting cultivated areas. **2** any similar bird of the family Sturnidae. [Old English *stærlinc* from *stær* 'starling', from Germanic: cf. -LING[1]]

starling[2] /'stɑːlɪŋ/ *n.* piles built around or upstream of a bridge or pier to protect it from floating rubbish etc. [perhaps corruption of (now dialect) *staddling* STADDLE]

starlit /'stɑːlɪt/ *adj.* **1** lit by stars. **2** with stars visible.

star of Bethlehem /'bɛθlɪhɛm/ *n.* any of various plants with starlike flowers, esp. *Ornithogalum umbellatum* with white star-shaped flowers striped with green on the outside (see Matt. 2:9).

Star of David /'deɪvɪd/ *n.* a figure consisting of two interlaced equilateral triangles used as a Jewish and Israeli symbol.

star prisoner *n.* *Brit.* *slang* a convict serving a first prison sentence.

star route *n.* *US* a postal delivery route served by private contractors.

starry /'stɑːri/ *adj.* (**starrier**, **starriest**) **1** covered with or full of stars. **2** resembling a star. **3** of or relating to stars in entertainment; full of stars. □ **starrily** *adv.* **starriness** *n.*

starry-eyed *adj.* *colloq.* **1** visionary; enthusiastic but impractical. **2** euphoric.

Stars and Bars *n.pl.* the flag of the Confederate States of the US.

Stars and Stripes *n.pl.* the national flag of the US.

star sapphire *n.* a cabochon sapphire reflecting a starlike image due to its regular internal structure.

star shell *n.* an explosive projectile designed to burst in the air and light up the enemy's position.

starship /'stɑːʃɪp/ *n.* (in science fiction) a large usu. manned spacecraft for intersellar space travel.

star-spangled *adj.* (esp. of the US national flag) covered or glittering with stars.

star stream *n.* a systematic drift of stars.

star-struck *adj.* fascinated or greatly impressed by stars in entertainment or stardom.

star-studded *adj.* containing or covered with many stars, esp. featuring many famous performers.

START /stɑːt/ *abbr.* Strategic Arms Reduction Treaty (or Talks).

start /stɑːt/ *v.* & *n.* ● *v.* **1** *tr.* & *intr.* begin; commence (*started work*; *started crying*; *started to shout*; *the play starts at eight*). **2** *tr.* set (proceedings, an event, etc.) in motion (*start the meeting*; *started a fire*). **3** *intr.* (often foll. by *on*) make a beginning (*started on a new project*). **4** *intr.* (often foll. by *after*, *for*) set oneself in motion or action (*'wait!' he shouted, and started after her*). **5** *intr.* set out; begin a journey etc. (*we start at 6 a.m.*). **6** (often foll. by *up*) **a** *intr.* (of a machine) begin operating (*the* *car wouldn't start*). **b** *tr.* cause (a machine etc.) to begin operating (*tried to start the engine*). **7** *tr.* **a** cause or enable (a person) to make a beginning (with something) (*started me in business with £10,000*). **b** (foll. by pres. part.) cause (a person) to begin (doing something) (*the smoke started me coughing*). **c** *colloq.* complain or be critical (*don't you start*). **8** *tr.* (often foll. by *up*) found or establish; originate. **9** *intr.* (foll. by *at, with*) have as the first of a series of items, e.g. in a meal (*we started with soup*). **10** *tr.* give a signal to (competitors) to start in a race. **11** *intr.* (often foll. by *up, from*, etc.) make a sudden movement from surprise, pain, etc. (*started at the sound of my voice*). **12** *intr.* (foll. by *out, up, from*, etc.) spring out, up, etc. (*started up from the chair*). **13** *tr.* conceive (a baby). **14** *tr.* rouse (game etc.) from its lair. **15 a** *intr.* be displaced by pressure or shrinkage; come loose. **b** *tr.* cause to do this. **16** *intr.* (foll. by *out, to*, etc.) (of a thing) move or appear suddenly (*tears started to his eyes*). **17** *intr.* (foll. by *from*) (of eyes, usu. with exaggeration) burst forward (from their sockets etc.). **18** *tr.* pour out (liquor) from a cask. ● *n.* **1** a beginning of an event, action, journey, etc. (*missed the start; an early start tomorrow; made a fresh start*). **2** the place from which a race etc. begins. **3** an advantage given at the beginning of a race etc. (*a 15-second start*). **4** an advantageous initial position in life, business, etc. (*a good start in life*). **5** a sudden movement of surprise, pain, etc. (*you gave me a start*). **6** an intermittent or spasmodic effort or movement (esp. *in* or *by fits and starts*). **7** *colloq.* a surprising occurrence (*a queer start; a rum start*). □ **for a start** *colloq.* as a beginning; in the first place. **get the start of** gain an advantage over. **start a hare** see HARE. **start in** *colloq.* **1** begin. **2** (foll. by *on*) *US* make a beginning on. **start off 1** begin; commence (*started off on a lengthy monologue*). **2** begin to move (*it's time we started off*). **start on** *colloq.* attack; nag; bully. **start out 1** begin a journey. **2** (foll. by *to* + infin.) *colloq.* proceed as intending (to do something). **start over** *N. Amer.* begin again. **start something** *colloq.* cause trouble. **start up** arise; occur. **to start with 1** in the first place; before anything else is considered (*should never have been there to start with*). **2** at the beginning (*had six members to start with*). [Old English (originally in sense 11), from Germanic]

starter /ˈstɑːtə/ *n.* **1** a person or thing that starts. **2** an esp. automatic device for starting the engine of a motor vehicle etc. **3** a person giving the signal for the start of a race. **4** a horse or competitor starting in a race (*a list of probable starters*). **5** esp. *Brit* the first course of a meal. **6** the initial action etc. **7 a** *N. Amer.* a player who plays at the beginning of a game. **b** *Baseball* the pitcher who starts the game. □ **for starters** *colloq.* to start with. **under starter's orders** (of racehorses etc.) in a position to start a race and awaiting the starting signal.

starting block *n.* (usu. in *pl.*) a shaped rigid block for bracing the feet of a runner at the start of a race.

starting gate *n.* a movable barrier for securing a fair start in horse races.

starting-handle *n. Brit. Mech.* a crank for starting a motor engine.

starting pistol *n.* a pistol used to give the signal for the start of a race.

starting point *n.* the point from which a journey, process, argument, etc. begins.

starting post *n.* the post from which competitors start in a race.

starting price *n.* the odds ruling at the start of a horse race (opp. FIXED ODDS).

starting stall *n.* a compartment for one horse at the start of a race.

startle /ˈstɑːt(ə)l/ *v.tr.* give a shock or surprise to; cause (a person etc.) to start with surprise or sudden alarm. □ **startler** *n.* [Old English *steartlian* (as START, -LE[4])]

startling /ˈstɑːtlɪŋ/ *adj.* **1** surprising. **2** alarming (*startling news*). □ **startlingly** *adv.*

start-up *n.* the action or an instance of starting up, esp. the starting up of a business, machine, or series of operations (often *attrib.*: *start-up costs*).

star turn *n. Brit.* the principal item in an entertainment or performance.

starve /stɑːv/ *v.* **1** *intr.* die of hunger; suffer from malnourishment. **2** *tr.* cause to die of hunger or suffer from lack of food. **3** *intr.* suffer from extreme poverty. **4** *intr.* (esp. as **starved** *adj.* or **starving** *adj.*) *colloq.* feel very hungry (*I'm starving*). **5** *intr.* **a** suffer from mental or spiritual want. **b** (foll. by *for*) feel a strong craving for (sympathy, amusement, knowledge, etc.). **6** *tr.* **a** (foll. by *of, US for*) deprive of; keep scantily supplied with (*starved of affection*). **b** cause to suffer from mental or spiritual want. **7** *tr.* **a** (foll. by *into*) compel by starving (*starved into submission*). **b** (foll. by *out*) compel to surrender etc. by starving (*starved them out*). **8** *intr. archaic* or *dial.* perish with or suffer from cold. □ **starvation** /-ˈveɪʃ(ə)n/ *n.* [Old English *steorfan* 'die']

starveling /ˈstɑːvlɪŋ/ *n. & adj. archaic* ● *n.* a starving or ill-fed person or animal. ● *adj.* **1** starving. **2** meagre.

Star Wars *n.pl. colloq.* the strategic defence initiative. [from the title of a science fiction film (1977)]

starwort /ˈstɑːwəːt/ *n.* a plant with starlike flowers or leaves, esp. greater stitchwort, *Stellaria holostea*, with small white flowers.

stash /staʃ/ *v. & n. colloq.* ● *v.tr.* (often foll. by *away*) **1** conceal; put in a safe or hidden place. **2** hoard, stow, store. ● *n.* **1** a hiding place or hideout. **2** a thing hidden; a cache. [18th c.: origin unknown]

Stasi /ˈʃtɑːzi/ *n. hist.* the internal security force of the former German Democratic Republic, abolished in 1989. [German, from *Sta*atss*i*cherheit(sdienst) 'state security (service)']

stasis /ˈsteɪsɪs, ˈsta-/ *n.* (*pl.* **stases** /-siːz/) **1** inactivity; stagnation; a state of equilibrium. **2** a stoppage of circulation of any of the body fluids. [modern Latin from Greek, from *sta-* STAND]

-stasis /ˈstasɪs, ˈsteɪsɪs/ *comb. form* (*pl.* **-stases** /-siːz/) *Physiol.* forming nouns denoting a slowing or stopping (*haemostasis*). □ **-static** *comb. form* forming adjectives.

stat[1] /stat/ *n. colloq.* a thermostat.

stat[2] /stat/ *n.* (usu. in *pl.*) esp. *N. Amer.* **1** a statistic. **2** (*attrib.*) statistics (*stat control*).

-stat /stat/ *comb. form* forming nouns with reference to keeping fixed or stationary (*rheostat*). [Greek *statos* 'stationary']

state /steɪt/ *n. & v.* ● *n.* **1** the existing condition or position of a person or thing (*in a bad state of repair; in a precarious state of health*). **2** *colloq.* **a** an excited, anxious, or agitated mental condition (esp. *in a state*). **b** an untidy condition. **3** (also **State**) **a** an organized political community under one government; a commonwealth; a nation. **b** such a community forming part of a federal republic, esp. the United States of America. **c (the States)** the US. **4** (also **State**) (*attrib.*) **a** of, for, or concerned with the State (*State documents*). **b** reserved for or done on occasions of ceremony (*state apartments; state visit*). **c** involving ceremony (*state opening of Parliament*). **5** (usu. **State**) civil government (*Church and State; Secretary of State*). **6** pomp, rank, dignity (*as befits their state*). **7 (the States)** the legislative body in Jersey, Guernsey, and Alderney. **8** each of two or more variant forms of a single edition of a book. **9 a** an etched or engraved plate at a particular stage of its progress. **b** an impression taken from this. ● *v.tr.* **1** express, esp. fully or clearly, in speech or writing (*have stated my opinion*). **2** fix, specify (*at stated intervals*). **3** *Law* specify the facts of (a case) for consideration. **4** *Mus.* play (a theme etc.) so as to make it known to the listener. □ **in state** with all due ceremony. **of state** concerning politics or government. **state of things** (or **affairs** or **play**) the circumstances; the current situation. □ **statable** *adj.* **statehood** *n.* [Middle English: partly from ESTATE, partly from Latin STATUS]

state capitalism *n.* a system of state control and use of capital.

statecraft /ˈsteɪtkrɑːft/ *n.* the art of conducting affairs of State.

State Department *n.* (in the US) the department of foreign affairs.

state house *n.* **1** *US* the building where the legislature of a state meets. **2** *NZ* a private house built at the government's expense.

stateless /ˈsteɪtlɪs/ *adj.* **1** (of a person) having no nationality or citizenship. **2** without a state or political community. □ **statelessness** *n.*

statelet /ˈsteɪtlɪt/ *n.* a small state.

stately /ˈsteɪtli/ *adj.* (**statelier**, **stateliest**) dignified; imposing; grand. □ **stateliness** *n.*

stately home *n. Brit.* a large magnificent house, esp. one open to the public.

statement /ˈsteɪtm(ə)nt/ *n.* & *v.* ● *n.* **1** the act or an instance of stating or being stated; expression in words. **2** a thing stated; a declaration (*that statement is unfounded*). **3** a formal account of facts, esp. to the police or in a court of law (*make a statement*). **4** a record of transactions in a bank account etc. **5** a formal notification of the amount due to a tradesman etc. **6** (in the UK) an official assessment made by a local education authority relating to a child's special educational needs. ● *v.tr.* (often as **statemented** *adj.*) officially assess as having special educational needs.

state of emergency *n.* a condition of danger or disaster affecting a country, esp. with normal constitutional procedures suspended.

state of grace *n.* the condition of being free from grave sin.

state of life *n.* rank and occupation.

state of the art *n.* **1** the current stage of development of a practical or technological subject. **2** (usu. **state-of-the-art**) (*attrib.*) using the latest techniques or equipment (*state-of-the-art weaponry*).

state of war *n.* the situation when war has been declared or is in progress.

state pension see PENSION[1] *n.* 1a.

state prisoner see PRISONER OF STATE.

stater /ˈsteɪtə/ *n. hist.* an ancient Greek gold or silver coin. [Middle English via Late Latin from Greek *statēr*]

stateroom /ˈsteɪtruːm, -rʊm/ *n.* **1** a state apartment in a palace, hotel, etc. **2** a private compartment in a passenger ship or *US* train.

state school *n. Brit.* a school managed and funded by the public authorities.

state's evidence *n.* = QUEEN'S EVIDENCE.

States General *n. hist.* the legislative body in the Netherlands, and in France before 1789.

stateside /ˈsteɪtsʌɪd/ *adj.* esp. *US colloq.* of, in, or towards the United States.

statesman /ˈsteɪtsmən/ *n.* (*pl.* **-men**; *fem.* **stateswoman**, *pl.* **-women**) **1** a person skilled in affairs of state, esp. one taking an active part in politics. **2** a distinguished and capable politician. □ **statesmanlike** *adj.* **statesmanly** *adj.* **statesmanship** *n.* [= *state's man*, translating French *homme d'état*]

state socialism *n.* a system of state control of industries and services.

statesperson /ˈsteɪtspəːs(ə)n/ *n.* a statesman or stateswoman.

states' rights *n.pl. US* the rights and powers not assumed by the United States but reserved to its individual states.

state trial *n.* prosecution by the State.

state university *n. US* a university managed by the public authorities of a state.

statewide /ˈsteɪtwʌɪd/ *adj. US* so as to include or cover a whole state.

static /ˈstatɪk/ *adj.* & *n.* ● *adj.* **1** stationary; not acting or changing; passive. **2** *Physics* **a** concerned with bodies at rest or forces in equilibrium (opp. DYNAMIC *adj.* 2a). **b** acting as weight but not moving (*static pressure*). **c** of statics. ● *n.* **1** static electricity. **2** atmospherics. [modern Latin *staticus* from Greek *statikos*, from *sta-* 'stand']

statical /ˈstatɪk(ə)l/ *adj.* = STATIC. □ **statically** *adv.*

statice /ˈstatɪsi/ *n.* **1** sea lavender. **2** sea pink. [Latin from Greek, fem. of *statikos* STATIC (with reference to staunching of blood)]

static electricity *n.* electricity not flowing as a current.

static line *n.* a length of cord attached to an aircraft etc. which releases a parachute without the use of a ripcord.

statics /ˈstatɪks/ *n.pl.* (usu. treated as *sing.*) **1** the science of bodies at rest or of forces in equilibrium (opp. DYNAMICS 1a). **2** = STATIC *n.* [from STATIC *n.* + -S[1]: see -ICS]

station /ˈsteɪʃ(ə)n/ *n.* & *v.* ● *n.* **1 a** a regular stopping place on a railway line, with a platform and usu. administrative buildings. **b** these buildings (see also BUS STATION, COACH STATION). **2** a place or building etc. where a person or thing stands or is placed, esp. habitually or for a definite purpose. **3 a** a designated point or establishment where a particular service or activity is based or organized (*police station*; *polling station*). **b** *US* a subsidiary post office. **4** an establishment involved in radio or television broadcasting. **5 a** a military or naval base, esp. *hist.* in India. **b** the inhabitants of this. **6** position in life; rank or status (*ideas above your station*). **7** *Austral.* & *NZ* a large sheep or cattle farm. **8** *Bot.* a particular place where an unusual species etc. grows. ● *v.tr.* **1** assign a station to. **2** put in position. [Middle English, = standing, via Old French from Latin *statio -onis*, from *stare* 'stand']

stationary /ˈsteɪʃ(ə)n(ə)ri/ *adj.* **1** remaining in one place, not moving (*hit a stationary car*). **2** not meant to be moved; not portable (*stationary troops*; *stationary engine*). **3** not changing in magnitude, number, quality, efficiency, etc. (*stationary temperature*). **4** (of a planet) having no apparent motion in respect of longitude. □ **stationariness** *n.* [Middle English from Latin *stationarius* (as STATION)]

stationary air *n.* air remaining in the lungs during ordinary respiration.

stationary bicycle *n.* a fixed exercise machine resembling a bicycle.

stationary point *n. Math.* a point on a curve where the gradient is zero.

stationary wave *n. Physics* = STANDING WAVE.

station-bill *n. Naut.* a list showing the prescribed stations of a ship's crew for various drills or in an emergency.

station break *n. N. Amer.* a pause between broadcast programmes for an announcement of the identity of the station transmitting them.

stationer /ˈsteɪʃ(ə)nə/ *n.* a person who sells writing materials etc. [Middle English, = bookseller (as STATIONARY in the medieval Latin sense 'shopkeeper', esp. a bookseller, as opposed to a pedlar)]

Stationers' Hall *n.* the hall of the Stationers' Company in London, at which a book was formerly registered for purposes of copyright.

stationery /ˈsteɪʃ(ə)n(ə)ri/ *n.* writing materials etc. sold by a stationer.

Stationery Office *n.* (in the UK) the Government's publishing house which also provides stationery for Government offices.

station hand *n. Austral.* a worker on a large sheep or cattle farm.

station house *n. US* a police station.

station-keeping *n.* the maintenance of one's proper relative position in a moving body of ships etc.

stationmaster /ˈsteɪʃ(ə)nmɑːstə/ *n.* the official in charge of a railway station.

station of the cross *n. RC Ch.* **1** each of a series of usu. 14 images or pictures representing the events in

Christ's passion before which devotions are performed in some churches. **2** each of these devotions.

station pointer *n. Naut.* a ship's navigational instrument, often a three-armed protractor, for fixing one's place on a chart from the angle in the horizontal plane between two landmarks or conspicuous objects at sea.

station sergeant *n. Brit.* the sergeant in charge of a police station.

station wagon *n.* esp. *US* an estate car.

statism /'steɪtɪz(ə)m/ *n.* centralized State administration and control of social and economic affairs.

statist *n.* **1** /'statɪst/ a statistician. **2** /'steɪtɪst/ a supporter of statism. [originally = politician, from Italian *statista* (as STATE)]

statistic /stə'tɪstɪk/ *n. & adj.* ● *n.* a statistical fact or item. ● *adj.* = STATISTICAL. [German *statistisch, Statistik* from *Statist* (as STATIST)]

statistical /stə'tɪstɪk(ə)l/ *adj.* of or relating to statistics. □ **statistically** *adv.*

statistical physics *n.pl.* (usu. treated as *sing.*) physics as it is concerned with large numbers of particles to which statistics can be applied.

statistical significance *n.* = SIGNIFICANCE 4.

statistics /stə'tɪstɪks/ *n.pl.* **1** (usu. treated as *sing.*) the science of collecting and analysing numerical data, esp. in or for large quantities, and usu. inferring proportions in a whole from proportions in a representative sample. **2** any systematic collection or presentation of such facts. □ **statistician** /statɪ'stɪʃ(ə)n/ *n.*

stator /'steɪtə/ *n. Electr.* the stationary part of a machine, esp. of an electric motor or generator. [STATIONARY, on the pattern of ROTOR]

statoscope /'statəskəʊp/ *n.* an aneroid barometer used to show minute variations of pressure, esp. to indicate the altitude of an aircraft. [Greek *statos* 'fixed' (from *sta-* 'stand') + -SCOPE]

statuary /'statjʊəri, -tʃʊə-/ *adj. & n.* ● *adj.* of or for statues (*statuary art*). ● *n.* (*pl.* **-ies**) **1** statues collectively. **2** the art of making statues. **3** a sculptor. [Latin *statuarius* (as STATUE)]

statuary marble *n.* fine-grained white marble.

statue /'statju:, -tʃu:/ *n.* a sculptured, cast, carved, or moulded figure of a person or animal, esp. life-size or larger (cf. STATUETTE). □ **statued** *adj.* [Middle English via Old French from Latin *statua*, from *stare* 'stand']

statuesque /statjʊ'ɛsk, -tʃʊ-/ *adj.* like, or having the dignity or beauty of, a statue. □ **statuesquely** *adv.* **statuesqueness** *n.* [STATUE + -ESQUE, on the pattern of *picturesque*]

statuette /statjʊ'ɛt, -tʃʊ-/ *n.* a small statue; a statue less than life-size. [French, diminutive of *statue*]

stature /'statʃə/ *n.* **1** the height of a (esp. human) body. **2** a degree of eminence, social standing, or advancement; mental or moral calibre (*recruit someone of his stature*). □ **statured** *adj.* (also in *comb.*). [Middle English via Old French from Latin *statura*, from *stare stat-* 'stand']

status /'steɪtəs/ *n.* **1** rank, social position, relation to others, relative importance (*not sure of their status in the hierarchy*). **2** a superior social etc. position (*considering your status in the business*). **3** *Law* a person's legal standing which determines his or her rights and duties, e.g. citizen, alien, commoner, civilian, etc. **4** the position of affairs (*let me know if the status changes*). [Latin, = standing, from *stare* 'stand']

status quo /steɪtəs 'kwəʊ/ *n.* the existing state of affairs. [Latin, = the state in which]

status quo ante /ˌsteɪtəs kwəʊ 'anti/ *n.* the previously existing state of affairs. [Latin, = 'the state in which before']

status symbol *n.* a possession etc. taken to indicate a person's high status.

statutable /'statjʊtəb(ə)l, -tʃʊ-/ *adj.* statutory, esp. in amount or value. □ **statutably** *adv.*

statute /'statju:t, -tʃu:t/ *n.* **1** a written law passed by a legislative body, e.g. an Act of Parliament. **2** a rule of a corporation, founder, etc., intended to be permanent (*against the University Statutes*). **3** divine law (*kept thy statutes*). [Middle English via Old French *statut* from Late Latin *statutum*, neut. past part. of Latin *statuere* 'set up' from *status*: see STATUS]

statute-barred *adj. Brit.* (of a case etc.) no longer legally enforceable by reason of the lapse of time.

statute book *n.* **1** a book or books containing the statute law. **2** the body of a country's statutes.

statute law *n.* **1** (*collect.*) the body of principles and rules of law laid down in statutes as distinct from rules formulated in practical application (cf. COMMON LAW, CASE LAW). **2** a statute.

statute mile see MILE 1.

statute roll *n.* **1** the rolls in the Public Records Office containing the statutes of the Parliament of England. **2** a statute book.

statutes at large *n.pl.* the statutes as originally enacted, regardless of later modifications.

statutory /'statjʊt(ə)ri, -tʃʊ-/ *adj.* required, permitted, or enacted by statute (*statutory minimum; statutory provisions*). □ **statutorily** *adv.*

statutory rape *n. US* the act of sexual intercourse with a minor.

staunch[1] /stɔ:n(t)ʃ/ *adj.* (also **stanch**) **1** trustworthy, loyal (*my staunch friend and supporter*). **2** (of a ship, joint, etc.) strong, watertight, airtight, etc. □ **staunchly** *adv.* **staunchness** *n.* [Middle English via Old French *estanche*, fem. of *estanc*, from Romanic]

staunch[2] /stɔ:n(t)ʃ, stɑ:n(t)ʃ/ *v.tr.* (also **stanch** /stɑ:n(t)ʃ, stɔ:n(t)ʃ/) **1** restrain the flow of (esp. blood). **2** restrain the flow from (esp. a wound). [Middle English via Old French *estanchier* from Romanic]

stave /steɪv/ *n. & v.* ● *n.* **1** each of the curved pieces of wood forming the sides of a cask, pail, etc. **2** = STAFF[1] *n.* 3. **3** a stanza or verse. ● *v.tr.* (*past* and *past part.* **stove** /stəʊv/ or **staved**) **1** break a hole in. **2** crush or knock out of shape. **3** fit or provide (a cask etc.) with staves. □ **stave in** crush by forcing inwards. **stave off** (*past* and *past part.* **staved**) avert or defer (esp. danger or misfortune). [Middle English, back-formation from *staves*, pl. of STAFF[1]]

stave rhyme *n.* alliteration, esp. in old Germanic poetry.

staves *pl.* of STAFF[1] *n.* 3.

stavesacre /'steɪvzeɪkə/ *n.* a larkspur, *Delphinium staphisagria*, yielding seeds used as an insecticide. [Middle English via Latin *staphisagria* from Greek *staphis agria* 'wild raisin']

stay[1] /steɪ/ *v. & n.* ● *v.* **1** *intr.* continue to be in the same place or condition; not depart or change (*stay here until I come back*). **2** *intr.* **a** (often foll. by *at, in, with*) have temporary residence as a visitor etc. (*stayed with them for Christmas*). **b** *Sc.* & *S.Afr.* dwell permanently. **3** *archaic* or *literary* **a** *tr.* stop or check (progress, the inroads of a disease, etc.). **b** *intr.* (esp. in *imper.*) pause in movement, action, speech, etc. (*Stay! You forget one thing*). **4** *tr.* postpone (judgement, decision, etc.). **5** *tr.* assuage (hunger etc.) esp. for a short time. **6 a** *intr.* show endurance. **b** *tr.* show endurance to the end of (a race etc.). **7** *tr.* (often foll. by *up*) *literary* support, prop up (as or with a buttress etc.). **8** *intr.* (foll. by *for, to*) wait long enough to share or join in an activity etc. (*stay to supper; stay for the film*). ● *n.* **1 a** the act or an instance of staying or dwelling in one place. **b** the duration of this (*just a ten-minute stay; a long stay in London*). **2** a suspension or postponement of a sentence, judgement, etc. (*was granted a stay of execution*). **3** *archaic* or *literary* a check or restraint (*will endure no stay; a stay upon his activity*). **4** endurance, staying power. **5** a prop or support. **6** (in *pl.*) *hist.* a corset esp. with whalebone etc. stiffening, and laced. □ **has come** (or **is here**) **to stay** *colloq.* must be regarded as permanent. **stay the course** pursue a course of action or endure a struggle etc. to the end. **stay in** remain indoors or at home, esp. in school after hours as a punishment. **stay one's hand** see HAND. **stay the night** remain until the next day. **stay put** remain where it is placed or where one is. **stay up** not go to bed (until late at night). □ **stayer** *n.* [Anglo-French *estai-*, stem of Old French *ester*, from Latin *stare* 'stand']

stay² /steɪ/ *n. & v.* ● *n.* **1 a** *Naut.* a rope supporting a mast. **b** a guy or rope supporting a flagstaff or other pole. **2** a tie-piece in an aircraft etc. ● *v.tr.* **1** support (a mast etc.) by stays. **2** put (a sailing ship) on another tack. □ **be in stays** (of a sailing ship) be head to the wind while tacking. **miss stays** fail to be in stays. [Old English *stæg* 'be firm', from Germanic]

stay-at-home *adj. & n.* ● *adj.* remaining habitually at home. ● *n.* a person who does this.

stay-bar *n.* a support used in building or in machinery.

staying power *n.* endurance, stamina.

stay-in strike *n. Brit.* a sit-down strike (see SIT-DOWN *adj.* 2).

stay-rod *n.* = STAY-BAR.

staysail /ˈsteɪseɪl, ˈsteɪs(ə)l/ *n.* a triangular fore-and-aft sail extended on a stay.

stay-up *adj. & n.* ● *attrib.adj.* (of stockings) having elasticated tops and not needing suspenders to stay up. ● *n.* such a stocking.

STD *abbr.* **1** *Brit.* subscriber trunk dialling. **2** sexually transmitted disease. **3** Doctor of Sacred Theology. [sense 3 from Latin *Sanctae Theologiae Doctor*]

stead /stɛd/ *n.* □ **in a person's** (or **thing's**) **stead** as a substitute; instead of him or her or it. **stand a person in good stead** be advantageous or serviceable to him or her. [Old English *stede* 'place', from Germanic]

steadfast /ˈstɛdfɑːst, -fəst/ *adj.* constant, firm, unwavering. □ **steadfastly** *adv.* **steadfastness** *n.* [Old English *stedefæst* (as STEAD, FAST¹)]

steading /ˈstɛdɪŋ/ *n. Sc. & N.Engl.* a farmstead.

steady /ˈstɛdi/ *adj., v., adv., int., & n.* ● *adj.* (**steadier, steadiest**) **1** firmly fixed or supported or standing or balanced; not tottering, rocking, or wavering. **2** done or operating or happening in a uniform and regular manner (*a steady pace; a steady increase*). **3 a** constant in mind or conduct; not changeable. **b** persistent. **4** (of a person) serious and dependable in behaviour; of industrious and temperate habits; safe; cautious. **5** regular, established (*a steady girlfriend*). **6** accurately directed; not faltering; controlled (*a steady hand; a steady eye; steady nerves*). **7** (of a ship) on course and upright. ● *v.tr. & intr.* (**-ies, -ied**) make or become steady (*steady the boat*). ● *adv.* steadily (*hold it steady*). ● *int.* as a command or warning to take care. ● *n.* (*pl.* **-ies**) *colloq.* a regular boyfriend or girlfriend. □ **go steady** (often foll. by *with*) *colloq.* have as a regular boyfriend or girlfriend. **steady down** become steady. **steady on!** *Brit.* take care! □ **steadier** *n.* **steadily** *adv.* **steadiness** *n.* [STEAD + -Y¹]

steady-going *adj.* staid; sober.

steady state *n.* an unvarying condition in a physical process etc., esp. as in the (now rarely held) theory that the universe is eternal and maintained by constant creation of matter.

steak /steɪk/ *n.* **1** a thick slice of meat (esp. beef) or fish, often cut for grilling, frying, etc. **2** beef cut for stewing or braising. [Middle English from Old Norse *steik*, related to *steikja* 'roast on spit', *stikna* 'be roasted']

steakhouse /ˈsteɪkhaʊs/ *n.* a restaurant specializing in serving beefsteaks.

steak knife *n.* a knife with a serrated steel blade for eating steak.

steal /stiːl/ *v. & n.* ● *v.* (*past* **stole** /stəʊl/; *past part.* **stolen** /ˈstəʊlən/) **1** *tr.* (also *absol.*) **a** take (another person's property) illegally. **b** take (property etc.) without right or permission, esp. in secret with the intention of not returning it. **2** *tr.* obtain surreptitiously or by surprise (*stole a kiss*). **3** *tr.* **a** gain insidiously or artfully. **b** (often foll. by *away*) win or get possession of (a person's affections etc.), esp. insidiously (*stole her heart away*). **4** *intr.* (foll. by *in, out, away, up*, etc.) **a** move, esp. silently or stealthily (*stole out of the room*). **b** (of a sound etc.) become gradually perceptible. **5** *tr.* **a** (in various sports) gain (a run, the ball, etc.) surreptitiously or by luck. **b** *Baseball* run to (a base) while the pitcher is in the act of delivery. ● *n.* **1** *US colloq.* the act or an instance of stealing or theft. **2** *colloq.* an unexpectedly easy task or good bargain. □ **steal a march on** get an advantage over by surreptitious means; anticipate. **steal the show** outshine other performers, esp. unexpectedly. **steal a person's thunder** **1** use another person's idea, policy, etc., and spoil the effect the originator hoped to achieve by expressing it or acting upon it first. **2** take the limelight or attention from another person. □ **stealer** *n.* (also in *comb.*). [Old English *stelan*, from Germanic]

stealth /stɛlθ/ *n.* **1** secrecy, a secret procedure. **2** (*attrib.*) designed in accordance with or designating the technology which makes detection by radar or sonar difficult (*stealth bomber*). □ **by stealth** surreptitiously. [Middle English from Old English (as STEAL, -TH²)]

stealthy /ˈstɛlθi/ *adj.* (**stealthier, stealthiest**) **1** (of an action) done with stealth; proceeding imperceptibly. **2** (of a person or thing) acting or moving with stealth. □ **stealthily** *adv.* **stealthiness** *n.*

steam /stiːm/ *n. & v.* ● *n.* **1 a** the gas into which water is changed by boiling, used as a source of power by virtue of its expansion of volume. **b** a mist of liquid particles of water produced by the condensation of this gas. **2** any similar vapour. **3 a** energy or power provided by a steam engine or other machine. **b** *colloq.* power or energy generally. ● *v.* **1** *tr.* **a** cook (food) in steam. **b** soften or make pliable (timber etc.) or otherwise treat with steam. **2** *intr.* give off steam or other vapour, esp. visibly. **3** *intr.* **a** move under steam power (*the ship steamed down the river*). **b** (foll. by *ahead, away*, etc.) *colloq.* proceed or travel fast or with vigour. **4** *tr. & intr.* (usu. foll. by *up*) **a** cover or become covered with condensed steam. **b** (as **steamed up** *adj.*) *colloq.* angry or excited. **5** *tr.* (foll. by *open* etc.) apply steam to the gum of (a sealed envelope) to get it open. **6** *intr. slang* (of a gang) pass rapidly through a public place, robbing bystanders by force of numbers. □ **get up steam** **1** generate enough power to work a steam engine. **2** work oneself into an energetic or angry state. **let off steam** relieve one's pent up feelings or energy. **run out of steam** lose one's impetus or energy. **steam in** *slang* start or join a fight. **under one's own steam** without assistance; unaided. [Old English *stēam*, from Germanic]

steam age *n.* the era when trains were drawn by steam locomotives.

steam bath *n.* a room etc. filled with steam for bathing in.

steamboat /ˈstiːmbəʊt/ *n.* a boat propelled by a steam engine.

steam boiler *n.* a vessel (in a steam engine etc.) in which water is boiled to generate steam.

steam engine *n.* **1** an engine which uses the expansion or rapid condensation of steam to generate power. **2** a locomotive powered by this.

steamer /ˈstiːmə/ *n.* **1** a person or thing that steams. **2** a vessel propelled by steam, esp. a ship. **3** a receptacle in which things are steamed, esp. cooked by steam. **4** *colloq.* a wetsuit. **5** *slang* a member of a gang involved in steaming (see STEAM *v.* 6).

steamer rug *n. US* a travelling rug.

steam gauge *n.* a pressure gauge attached to a steam boiler.

steam hammer *n.* a forging-hammer powered by steam.

steam-heat *n. & v.* ● *n.* heat produced by steam, esp. by a central heating system that uses steam. ● *v.tr.* heat using steam.

steam iron *n.* an electric iron that emits steam from holes in its flat surface to improve its pressing ability.

steam-jacket *n.* a casing for steam round a cylinder, for heating its contents.

steam organ *n.* a fairground pipe organ driven by a steam engine and played by means of a keyboard or a system of punched cards.

steam power *n.* the force of steam applied to machinery etc.

steamroll /ˈstiːmrəʊl/ *v.tr.* esp. *US* = STEAMROLLER *v.*

steamroller /ˈstiːmrəʊlə/ *n.* & *v.* ●*n.* **1** a heavy slow-moving vehicle with a roller, used to flatten new-made roads. **2** a crushing power or force. ●*v.tr.* **1** crush forcibly or indiscriminately. **2** (foll. by *through*) force (a measure etc.) through a legislature by overriding opposition.

steamship /ˈstiːmʃɪp/ *n.* a ship propelled by a steam engine.

steam shovel *n.* an excavator powered by steam.

steam-tight *adj.* impervious to steam.

steam train *n.* a train driven by a steam engine.

steam tug *n.* a steamer for towing ships etc.

steam turbine *n.* a turbine in which a high-velocity jet of steam rotates a bladed disc or drum.

steamy /ˈstiːmi/ *adj.* (**steamier**, **steamiest**) **1** like or full of steam. **2** *colloq.* erotic, salacious. □ **steamily** *adv.* **steaminess** *n.*

stearic /ˈstɪərɪk, stɪˈarɪk/ *adj.* derived from stearin. □ **stearate** /ˈstɪəreɪt/ *n.* [French *stéarique* from Greek *stear steatos* 'tallow']

stearic acid *n.* a solid saturated fatty acid obtained from animal or vegetable fats.

stearin /ˈstɪərɪn/ *n.* **1** a glyceryl ester of stearic acid, esp. in the form of a white crystalline constituent of tallow etc. **2** a mixture of fatty acids used in candle-making. [French *stéarine* from Greek *stear steatos* 'tallow']

steatite /ˈstɪətʌɪt/ *n.* a soapstone or other impure form of talc. □ **steatitic** /-ˈtɪtɪk/ *adj.* [Latin *steatitis* from Greek *steatītēs*, from *stear steatos* 'tallow']

steatopygia /stɪətə(ʊ)ˈpɪdʒɪə/ *n.* an excess of fat on the buttocks. □ **steatopygous** /-ˈpʌɪgəs, -ˈtɒpɪgəs/ *adj.* [modern Latin (as STEATITE + Greek *pugē* 'rump')]

steed /stiːd/ *n. archaic* or *poet.* a horse, esp. a fast powerful one. [Old English *stēda* 'stallion': related to STUD²]

steel /stiːl/ *n., adj.,* & *v.* ●*n.* **1** any of various grey or greyish-blue alloys of iron with carbon and usu. other elements, much used as structural materials and in manufacturing. **2** hardness of character; strength, firmness (*nerves of steel*). **3 a** a rod of steel, usu. roughened and tapering, on which knives are sharpened. **b** a strip of steel for expanding a skirt or stiffening a corset. **4** (not in *pl.*) *literary* a sword, lance, etc. (*warriors worthy of their steel*). ●*adj.* **1** made of steel. **2** like or having the characteristics of steel. ●*v.tr.* & *refl.* harden or make resolute (*steeled myself for a shock*). [Old English *stȳle, stēli* from Germanic: related to STAY²]

steel band *n.* a band of musicians who play (chiefly calypso-style) music on steel drums.

steel-clad *adj.* wearing armour.

steel engraving *n.* the process of engraving on or an impression taken from a steel-coated copper plate.

steelhead /ˈstiːlhɛd/ *n.* esp. *N. Amer.* a large rainbow trout esp. after spawning.

steel wool *n.* an abrasive substance consisting of a mass of fine steel shavings.

steelwork /ˈstiːlwəːk/ *n.* articles of steel.

steelworks /ˈstiːlwəːks/ *n.pl.* (usu. treated as *sing.*) a place where steel is manufactured. □ **steelworker** *n.*

steely /ˈstiːli/ *adj.* (**steelier**, **steeliest**) **1** of, or hard as, steel. **2** inflexibly severe; cold; ruthless (*steely composure*; *steely-eyed glance*). □ **steeliness** *n.*

steelyard /ˈstiːljɑːd, ˈstɪljəd/ *n.* a kind of balance with a short arm to take the item to be weighed and a long graduated arm along which a weight is moved until it balances.

steenbok /ˈstiːnbɒk, ˈsteɪn-/ *n.* a small African antelope, *Raphicerus campestris.* [Dutch, from *steen* STONE + *bok* BUCK¹]

steep¹ /stiːp/ *adj.* & *n.* ●*adj.* **1** sloping sharply; almost perpendicular (*a steep hill*; *steep stairs*). **2** (of a rise or fall) rapid (*a steep drop in share prices*). **3** (*predic.*) *colloq.* **a** (of a demand, price, etc.) exorbitant; unreasonable (esp. *a bit steep*). **b** (of a story etc.) exaggerated; incredible. ●*n.* a steep slope; a precipice. □ **steepen** *v.intr.* & *tr.* **steepish** *adj.* **steeply** *adv.* **steepness** *n.* [Old English *stēap* from West Germanic: related to STOOP¹]

steep² /stiːp/ *v.* & *n.* ●*v.tr.* **1** (often foll. by *in*) soak or bathe in liquid. **2** (foll. by *in*; usu. in *passive*) **a** pervade or imbue with (*steeped in misery*). **b** make deeply acquainted with (a subject etc.) (*steeped in the classics*). ●*n.* **1** the act or process of steeping. **2** the liquid for steeping. [Middle English via Old English from Germanic: related to STOUP]

steeple /ˈstiːp(ə)l/ *n.* a tall tower, esp. one surmounted by a spire, above the roof of a church. □ **steepled** *adj.* [Old English *stēpel stȳpel* from Germanic: related to STEEP¹]

steeplechase /ˈstiːp(ə)ltʃeɪs/ *n.* **1** a horse race (originally with a steeple as the goal) across the countryside or on a racecourse with ditches, hedges, etc., to jump. **2** a cross-country foot race. □ **steeplechaser** *n.* **steeplechasing** *n.*

steeple-crowned *adj.* (of a hat) with a tall pointed crown.

steeplejack /ˈstiːp(ə)ldʒak/ *n.* a person who climbs tall chimneys, steeples, etc., to do repairs etc.

steer¹ /stɪə/ *v.* & *n.* ●*v.* **1** *tr.* **a** guide (a vehicle, aircraft, etc.) by a wheel etc. **b** guide (a vessel) by a rudder or helm. **2** *intr.* guide a vessel or vehicle in a specified direction (*tried to steer left*). **3** *tr.* direct (one's course). **4** *intr.* direct one's course in a specified direction (*steered for the railway station*). **5** *tr.* guide the movement or trend of (*steered them into the garden*; *steered the conversation away from that subject*). ●*n. US* steering; guidance. □ **steer clear of** take care to avoid. □ **steerable** *adj.* **steerer** *n.* **steering** *n.* (esp. in senses 1, 2 of *v.*). [Old English *stieran*, from Germanic]

steer² /stɪə/ *n.* = BULLOCK. [Old English *stēor*, from Germanic]

steerage /ˈstɪərɪdʒ/ *n.* **1** the act of steering. **2** the effect of the helm on a ship. **3** esp. *hist.* the part of a ship allotted to passengers travelling at the cheapest rate. **4** *hist.* (in a warship) quarters assigned to midshipmen etc. just forward of the wardroom.

steerage-way *n.* the amount of headway required by a vessel to enable it to be controlled by the helm.

steering column *n.* the shaft or column which connects the steering wheel, handlebars, etc. of a vehicle to the rest of the steering gear.

steering committee *n.* a committee deciding the priorities or order of business, or managing the general course of operations.

steering wheel *n.* a wheel by which a vehicle etc. is steered.

steersman /ˈstɪəzmən/ *n.* (*pl.* **-men**) a person who steers a vessel.

steeve¹ /stiːv/ *n.* & *v. Naut.* ●*n.* the angle of the bowsprit in relation to the horizontal. ●*v.* **1** *intr.* (of a bowsprit) make an angle with the horizontal. **2** *tr.* cause (the bowsprit) to do this. [17th c.: origin unknown]

steeve² /stiːv/ *n.* & *v. Naut.* ●*n.* a long spar used in stowing cargo. ●*v.tr.* stow with a steeve. [Middle English via Old French *estiver* or Spanish *estivar* from Latin *stipare* 'pack tight']

stegosaurus /stɛgəˈsɔːrəs/ *n.* (also **stegosaur** /ˈstɛgəsɔː/) a small-headed plant-eating dinosaur of the suborder Stegosauria, with a double row of large bony plates (or spines) along the back. [modern Latin, from Greek *stegē* 'covering' + *sauros* 'lizard']

stein /stʌɪn/ *n.* a large (usu. earthenware) mug, esp. for beer. [German, literally 'stone']

steinbock /'stʌɪmbɒk/ *n.* **1** an ibex native to the Alps. **2** = STEENBOK. [German, from *Stein* STONE + *Bock* BUCK[1]]

stela /'sti:lə/ *n.* (*pl.* **stelae** /-li:/) *Archaeol.* an upright slab or pillar usu. with an inscription and sculpture, esp. as a gravestone. [Latin from Greek (as STELE)]

stele /sti:l, 'sti:li/ *n.* **1** *Bot.* the axial cylinder of vascular tissue in the stem and roots of most plants. **2** *Archaeol.* = STELA. ▫ **stelar** *adj.* [Greek *stēlē* 'standing block']

stellar /'stɛlə/ *adj.* **1** of or relating to a star or stars. **2** esp. *N. Amer.* **a** having star performers (*stellar cast*). **b** *colloq.* outstanding (*stellar performance by the team*). ▫ **stelliform** *adj.* [Late Latin *stellaris* from Latin *stella* 'star']

stellate /'stɛleɪt, -lət/ *adj.* (also **stellated** /stɛ'leɪtɪd/) **1** arranged like a star; radiating. **2** *Bot.* (of leaves) surrounding the stem in a whorl. [Latin *stellatus* from *stella* 'star']

stellular /'stɛljʊlə/ *adj.* shaped like, or set with, small stars. [Late Latin *stellula*, diminutive of Latin *stella* 'star']

stem[1] /stɛm/ *n.* & *v.* ● *n.* **1** the main body or stalk of a plant or shrub, usu. rising above ground, but occasionally subterranean. **2** the stalk supporting a fruit, flower, or leaf, and attaching it to a larger branch, twig, or stalk. **3** a stem-shaped part of an object esp.: **a** the slender part of a wineglass between the body and the foot. **b** the tube of a tobacco pipe. **c** a vertical stroke in a letter or musical note. **d** the winding-shaft of a watch. **4** *Gram.* the root or main part of a noun, verb, etc., to which inflections are added; the part that appears unchanged throughout the cases and derivatives of a noun, persons of a tense, etc. **5** *Naut.* the main upright timber or metal piece at the bow of a ship to which the ship's sides are joined at the fore-end (*from stem to stern*). **6** a line of ancestry, branch of a family, etc. (*descended from an ancient stem*). **7** (in full **drill stem**) a rotating rod, cylinder, etc., used in drilling. ● *v.* (**stemmed**, **stemming**) **1** *intr.* (foll. by *from*) spring or originate from (*stems from a desire to win*). **2** *tr.* remove the stem or stems from (fruit, tobacco, etc.). **3** *tr.* (of a vessel etc.) hold its own or make headway against (the tide etc.). ▫ **stemless** *adj.* **stemlet** *n.* **stemlike** *adj.* **stemmed** *adj.* (also in *comb.*). [Old English *stemn*, *stefn* from Germanic: related to STAND]

stem[2] /stɛm/ *v.* & *n.* ● *v.* (**stemmed**, **stemming**) **1** *tr.* check or stop. **2** *tr.* dam up (a stream etc.). **3** *intr.* slide the tail of one ski or both skis outwards usu. in order to turn or slow down. ● *n.* an act of stemming on skis. [Old Norse *stemma*, from Germanic]

stem cell *n. Biol.* an undifferentiated cell from which specialized cells develop.

stemma /'stɛmə/ *n.* (*pl.* **stemmata** /'stɛmətə/) **1** a family tree; a pedigree. **2** the line of descent e.g. of variant texts of a work. **3** *Zool.* a simple eye; a facet of a compound eye. [Latin from Greek *stemma* 'wreath', from *stephō* 'wreathe']

stemple /'stɛmp(ə)l/ *n.* each of several crossbars in a mine shaft serving as supports or steps. [17th c.: origin uncertain: cf. Middle High German *stempfel*]

stem stitch *n.* an embroidery stitch used for narrow stems etc.

stem turn *n.* a turn on skis made by stemming with one ski.

stemware /'stɛmwɛ:/ *n. US* glasses with stems.

stem-winder *n. US* a watch wound by turning a head on the end of a stem rather than by a key.

stench /stɛn(t)ʃ/ *n.* an offensive or foul smell. [Old English *stenc* 'smell' from Germanic: related to STINK]

stench trap *n.* a trap in a sewer etc. to prevent the upward passage of gas.

stencil /'stɛnsɪl, -s(ə)l/ *n.* & *v.* ● *n.* **1** (in full **stencil-plate**) a thin sheet of plastic, metal, card, etc., in which a pattern or lettering is cut, used to produce a corresponding pattern on the surface beneath it by applying ink, paint, etc. **2** the pattern, lettering, etc., produced by a stencil-plate. **3** a waxed sheet etc. from which a stencil is made by means of a typewriter. ● *v.tr.* (**stencilled**, **stencilling**; *US* **stenciled**, **stenciling**) **1** (often foll. by *on*) produce (a pattern) with a stencil. **2** decorate or mark (a surface) in this way. [Middle English from Old French *estanceler* 'sparkle, cover with stars', from *estencele* 'spark', ultimately from Latin *scintilla*]

Sten gun /stɛn/ *n.* a type of lightweight sub-machine gun. [*S* and *T* (the initials of the inventors' surnames, Shepherd and Turpin) + *-en* on the pattern of BREN]

steno /'stɛnəʊ/ *n.* (*pl.* **-os**) *N. Amer. colloq.* a stenographer. [abbreviation]

stenography /stɪ'nɒgrəfi/ *n.* shorthand or the art of writing this. ▫ **stenographer** *n.* **stenographic** /-nə'grafɪk/ *adj.* [Greek *stenos* 'narrow' + -GRAPHY]

stenosis /stɪ'nəʊsɪs/ *n. Med.* the abnormal narrowing of a passage in the body. ▫ **stenotic** /-'nɒtɪk/ *adj.* [modern Latin from Greek *stenōsis* 'narrowing' via *stenoō* 'make narrow' from *stenos* 'narrow']

stenotype /'stɛnə(ʊ)tʌɪp/ *n.* **1** a machine like a typewriter for recording speech in syllables or phonemes. **2** a symbol or the symbols used in this process. ▫ **stenotypist** *n.* [STENOGRAPHY + TYPE]

Stentor /'stɛntə/ *n.* (also **stentor**) a person with a powerful voice. ▫ **stentorian** /-'tɔ:rɪən/ *adj.* [Greek *Stentōr*, the name of a herald in the Trojan War (Homer, *Iliad* v. 785)]

step /stɛp/ *n.* & *v.* ● *n.* **1 a** the complete movement of one leg in walking or running (*took a step forward*). **b** the distance covered by this. **2** a unit of movement in dancing. **3** a measure taken, esp. one of several in a course of action (*took steps to prevent it; considered it a wise step*). **4 a** a flat-topped structure used singly or as one of a series, for passing from one level to another. **b** the rung of a ladder. **c** a notch cut for a foot in ice climbing. **d** a platform etc. in a vehicle provided for stepping up or down. **5** a short distance (*only a step from my door*). **6** the sound or mark made by a foot in walking etc. (*heard a step on the stairs*). **7** the manner of walking etc. as seen or heard (*know her by her step*). **8 a** a degree in the scale of promotion, advancement, or precedence. **b** one of a series of fixed points on a payscale etc. **9** (in *pl.*) (also **pair of steps** *sing.*) *Brit.* = STEPLADDER. **10** esp. *US Mus.* a melodic interval of one degree of the scale, i.e. a tone or semitone. **11** *Naut.* a block, socket, or platform supporting a mast. ● *v.* (**stepped**, **stepping**) **1** *intr.* lift and set down one's foot or alternate feet in walking. **2** *intr.* come or go in a specified direction by stepping. **3** *intr.* make progress in a specified way (*stepped into a new job*). **4** *tr.* (foll. by *off*, *out*) measure (distance) by stepping. **5** *tr.* perform (a dance). **6** *tr. Naut.* set up (a mast) in a step. ▫ **in step** (often foll. by *with*) **1** stepping in time with music or other marchers. **2** conforming with others. **in a person's steps** following a person's example. **keep step** remain in step. **mind** (or **watch**) **one's step** be careful. **out of step** (often foll. by *with*) not in step. **step by step** gradually; cautiously; by stages or degrees. **step down 1** resign from a position etc. **2** *Electr.* decrease (voltage) by using a transformer. **step in 1** enter a room, house, etc. **2 a** intervene to help or hinder. **b** act as a substitute for an indisposed colleague etc. **step it** dance. **step on it** (or **on the gas**) *colloq.* **1** accelerate a motor vehicle. **2** hurry up. **step out 1** leave a room, house, etc. **2 a** be active socially. **b** (often foll. by *with*) *N. Amer. dial.* & *colloq.* = DATE[1] *v.* 6b. **3** take large steps. **step out of line** behave inappropriately or disobediently. **step this way** a deferential formula meaning 'follow me'. **step up 1 a** increase, intensify (*must step up production*). **b** *Electr.* increase (voltage) using a transformer. **2** come forward for some purpose. **turn one's steps** go in a specified direction. ▫ **steplike** *adj.* **stepped** *adj.* **stepwise** *adv.* & *adj.* [Old English *stæpe*, *stepe* (*n.*), *stæppan*, *steppan* (*v.*), from Germanic]

step- /stɛp/ *comb. form* denoting a relationship like the one specified but resulting from a remarriage (*step-grandchild*). [Old English *stēop-* 'orphan-']

step aerobics *n.pl.* a type of aerobics involving stepping up on to and down from a portable block.

stepbrother /'stɛpbrʌðə/ *n.* a son of a step-parent by a marriage other than with one's father or mother.

stepchild /'stɛptʃʌɪld/ *n.* (*pl.* **-children**) a child of one's husband or wife by a previous marriage. [Old English *stēopcīld* (as STEP-, CHILD)]

step-cut *adj.* (of a gem) cut in straight facets round the centre.

stepdad /'stɛpdad/ *n. colloq.* = STEPFATHER.

stepdaughter /'stɛpdɔːtə/ *n.* a female stepchild. [Old English *stēopdohtor* (as STEP-, DAUGHTER)]

stepfamily /'stɛpfamɪli, -fam(ə)li/ *n.* (*pl.* **-ies**) a family that includes a stepchild or stepchildren.

stepfather /'stɛpfɑːðə/ *n.* a male step-parent. [Old English *stēopfæder* (as STEP-, FATHER)]

stephanotis /stɛfə'nəʊtɪs/ *n.* any climbing tropical plant of the genus *Stephanotis*, cultivated for its fragrant waxy usu. white flowers. [modern Latin from Greek, = fit for a wreath, from *stephanos* 'wreath']

step-in *adj.* & *n.* ● *attrib.adj.* (of a garment) put on by being stepped into without unfastening. ● *n.* such a garment.

stepladder /'stɛpladə/ *n.* a short ladder with flat steps and a folding prop, used without being leant against a surface.

stepmother /'stɛpmʌðə/ *n.* a female step-parent. [Old English *stēopmōdor* (as STEP-, MOTHER)]

stepmum /'stɛpmʌm/ *n. colloq.* = STEPMOTHER.

step-parent *n.* a mother's or father's later husband or wife.

steppe /stɛp/ *n.* a level grassy unforested plain, esp. in SE Europe and Siberia. [Russian *step'*]

stepping stone *n.* **1** a raised stone, usu. one of a set in a stream, muddy place, etc., to help in crossing. **2** a means or stage of progress to an end.

stepsister /'stɛpsɪstə/ *n.* a daughter of a step-parent by a marriage other than with one's father or mother.

stepson /'stɛpsʌn/ *n.* a male stepchild. [Old English *stēopsunu* (as STEP-, SON)]

-ster /stə/ *suffix* denoting a person engaged in or associated with a particular activity or thing (*maltster*; *gangster*; *youngster*). [Old English *-estre* etc., from Germanic]

steradian /stə'reɪdɪən/ *n.* the SI unit of solid angle, equal to the angle at the centre of a sphere subtended by a part of the surface equal in area to the square of the radius (abbr.: **sr**). [Greek *stereos* 'solid' + RADIAN]

stercoraceous /stəːkə'reɪʃəs/ *adj.* **1** consisting of or resembling dung or faeces. **2** (of an insect) living in dung. [Latin *stercus -oris* 'dung']

stere /stɪə/ *n.* a unit of volume equal to one cubic metre. [French *stère* from Greek *stereos* 'solid']

stereo /'stɛrɪəʊ, 'stɪərɪəʊ/ *n.* & *adj.* ● *n.* (*pl.* **-os**) **1 a** a stereophonic record player, tape recorder, etc. **b** stereophony. **2** = STEREOSCOPE. ● *adj.* **1** = STEREOPHONIC. **2** stereoscopic. [abbreviation]

stereo- /'stɛrɪəʊ, 'stɪərɪəʊ/ *comb. form* solid; having three dimensions. [Greek *stereos* 'solid']

stereobate /'stɛrɪə(ʊ)beɪt/ *n. Archit.* a solid mass of masonry as a foundation for a building. [French *stéréobate* via Latin *stereobata* from Greek *stereobatēs* (as STEREO-, *batēs* 'base' from *bainō* 'to walk')]

stereochemistry /ˌstɛrɪə(ʊ)'kɛmɪstri, ˌstɪə-/ *n.* the branch of chemistry dealing with the three-dimensional arrangement of atoms in molecules.

stereography /stɛrɪ'ɒgrəfi, stɪərɪ-/ *n.* the art of depicting solid bodies in a plane.

stereoisomer /ˌstɛrɪəʊ'ʌɪsəmə, ˌstɪərɪəʊ-/ *n. Chem.* any of two or more compounds differing only in their spatial arrangement of atoms.

stereometry /stɛrɪ'ɒmətri, stɪərɪ-/ *n.* the measurement of solid bodies.

stereophonic /ˌstɛrɪə(ʊ)'fɒnɪk, ˌstɪərɪə(ʊ)-/ *adj.* (of sound reproduction) using two or more channels so that the sound has the effect of being distributed and of coming from more than one source. □ **stereophonically** *adv.* **stereophony** /-'ɒf(ə)ni/ *n.*

stereopsis /stɛrɪ'ɒpsɪs, stɪərɪ-/ *n.* the perception of depth produced by combining the visual images from both eyes; binocular vision. □ **stereoptic** *adj.* [STEREO- + Greek *opsis* 'sight']

stereopticon /stɛrɪ'ɒptɪk(ə)n, stɪərɪ-/ *n.* a projector which combines two images to give a three-dimensional effect, or makes one image dissolve into another. [STEREO- + Greek *optikon*, neuter of *optikos* OPTIC]

stereoscope /'stɛrɪə(ʊ)skəʊp, 'stɪərɪə(ʊ)-/ *n.* a device by which two photographs of the same object taken at slightly different angles are viewed together, giving an impression of depth and solidity as in ordinary human vision. □ **stereoscopic** /-'skɒpɪk/ *adj.* **stereoscopically** /-'skɒpɪk(ə)li/ *adv.* **stereoscopy** /-'ɒskəpi/ *n.*

stereospecific /ˌstɛrɪəʊspɪ'sɪfɪk, ˌstɪərɪəʊ-/ *adj. Chem.* of or relating to a particular stereoisomer of a substance. □ **stereospecifically** *adv.* **stereospecificity** /-'fɪsɪti/ *n.*

stereotaxis /ˌstɛrɪə(ʊ)'taksɪs, ˌstɪərɪə(ʊ)-/ *n.* (also **stereotaxy** /-'taksi/) *Biol.* & *Med.* surgery involving the accurate positioning of probes etc. inside the brain. □ **stereotactic** /-'taktɪk/ *adj.* **stereotaxic** *adj.* [STEREO- + Greek *taxis* 'orientation']

stereotype /'stɛrɪə(ʊ)tʌɪp, 'stɪərɪə(ʊ)-/ *n.* & *v.* ● *n.* **1 a** a person or thing that conforms to an unjustifiably fixed, usu. standardized, mental picture. **b** such an impression or attitude. **2** a printing-plate cast from a mould of composed type. ● *v.tr.* **1** (esp. as **stereotyped** *adj.*) formalize, standardize; cause to conform to a type. **2 a** print from a stereotype. **b** make a stereotype of. □ **stereotypic** /-'tɪpɪk/ *adj.* **stereotypical** /-'tɪpɪk(ə)l/ *adj.* **stereotypically** /-'tɪpɪk(ə)li/ *adv.* **stereotypy** *n.* [French *stéréotype* (*adj.*) (as STEREO-, TYPE)]

steric /'stɛrɪk, 'stɪərɪk/ *adj. Chem.* relating to the spatial arrangement of atoms in a molecule. [formed irregularly from Greek *stereos* 'solid']

steric hindrance *n.* the inhibiting of a chemical reaction by the obstruction of reacting atoms.

sterile /'stɛrʌɪl/ *adj.* **1** not able to produce crop or fruit or (of an animal) young; barren. **2** unfruitful, unproductive (*sterile discussions*). **3** free from living micro-organisms etc. **4** lacking originality or emotive force; mentally barren. □ **sterilely** *adv.* **sterility** /stə'rɪlɪti/ *n.* [French *stérile* or Latin *sterilis*]

sterilize /'stɛrɪlʌɪz/ *v.tr.* (also **-ise**) **1** make sterile. **2** deprive of the power of reproduction. □ **sterilizable** *adj.* **sterilization** /-'zeɪʃ(ə)n/ *n.* **sterilizer** *n.*

sterlet /'stəːlɪt/ *n.* a small sturgeon, *Acipenser ruthenus*, found in the Caspian Sea area and yielding fine caviar. [Russian *sterlyad'*]

sterling /'stəːlɪŋ/ *adj.* & *n.* ● *adj.* **1** of or in British money (*pound sterling*). **2** (of a coin or precious metal) genuine; of standard value or purity. **3** (of a person or qualities etc.) of solid worth; genuine, reliable (*sterling work*). ● *n.* British money (*paid in sterling*). □ **sterlingness** *n.* [probably from late Old English *steorling* (unrecorded), from *steorra* 'star' + -LING[1] (because some early Norman pennies bore a small star): recorded earlier in Old French *esterlin*]

sterling area *n.* a group of countries with currencies tied to British sterling and holding reserves mainly in sterling.

sterling silver *n.* silver of 92¼ per cent purity.

stern[1] /stəːn/ *adj.* severe, grim, strict; enforcing discipline or submission (*a stern expression*; *stern treatment*). □ **sternly** *adv.* **sternness** /'stəːnnɪs/ *n.* [Old English *styrne*, probably from a Germanic root = be rigid]

stern[2] /stəːn/ *n.* **1** the rear part of a ship or boat. **2** any rear part. □ **stern foremost** moving backwards. **stern on** with the stern presented. □ **sterned** *adj.* (also in *comb.*). **sternmost** *adj.* **sternward** *adj.* & *adv.*

sternwards *adv.* [Middle English, probably from Old Norse *stjórn* 'steering', from *stýra* STEER[1]]

sternal /'stɜ:n(ə)l/ *adj.* of or relating to the sternum.

sternal rib *n.* = TRUE RIB.

sterner sex *n.* (prec. by *the*) men.

sternpost /'stɜ:npəʊst/ *n. Naut.* the central upright support at the stern, usu. bearing the rudder.

sternum /'stɜ:nəm/ *n.* (*pl.* **sternums** or **sterna** /-nə/) the breastbone. [modern Latin from Greek *sternon* 'chest']

sternutation /stɜ:njʊ'teɪʃ(ə)n/ *n. Med.* or *joc.* a sneeze or attack of sneezing. [Latin *sternutatio* from *sternutare*, frequentative of *sternuere* 'sneeze']

sternutator /'stɜ:njʊteɪtə/ *n.* a substance, esp. poison gas, that causes nasal irritation, violent coughing, etc. □ **sternutatory** /-'nju:tət(ə)ri/ *adj. & n.* (*pl.* **-ies**).

sternway /'stɜ:nweɪ/ *n. Naut.* backward motion or impetus of a ship.

sternwheeler /'stɜ:nwi:lə/ *n.* a steamer propelled by a paddle wheel positioned at the stern.

steroid /'stɪərɔɪd, 'stɛrɔɪd/ *n. Biochem.* any of a group of organic compounds with a characteristic structure of four rings of carbon atoms, including many hormones, alkaloids, and vitamins. □ **steroidal** /-'rɔɪd(ə)l/ *adj.* [STEROL + -OID]

sterol /'stɪərɒl, 'stɛrɒl/ *n. Chem.* any of a group of naturally occurring steroid alcohols. [CHOLESTEROL, ERGOSTEROL, etc.]

stertorous /'stɜ:t(ə)rəs/ *adj.* (of breathing etc.) laboured and noisy; sounding like snoring. □ **stertorously** *adv.* [*stertor*, modern Latin from Latin *stertere* 'snore']

stet /stɛt/ *v.* (**stetted**, **stetting**) **1** *intr.* (usu. as an instruction written on a proof-sheet etc.) ignore or cancel the correction or alteration; let the original form stand. **2** *tr.* write 'stet' against; cancel the correction of. [Latin, = let it stand, from *stare* 'stand']

stethoscope /'stɛθəskəʊp/ *n.* an instrument used in listening to the action of the heart, lungs, etc., usu. consisting of a circular piece placed against the chest, with tubes leading to earpieces. □ **stethoscopic** /-'skɒpɪk/ *adj.* **stethoscopically** /-'skɒpɪk(ə)li/ *adv.* **stethoscopist** /-'θɒskəpɪst/ *n.* **stethoscopy** /-'θɒskəpi/ *n.* [French *stéthoscope* (as Greek *stēthos* 'breast', -SCOPE)]

stetson /'stɛts(ə)n/ *n.* a slouch hat with a very wide brim and a high crown. [named after J. B. *Stetson*, American hat-maker d. 1906]

stevedore /'sti:vədɔ:/ *n.* a person employed in loading and unloading ships. [Spanish *estivador* from *estivar* 'stow a cargo', from Latin *stipare*: see STEEVE[2]]

stevengraph /'sti:v(ə)ngrɑ:f/ *n.* a colourful woven silk picture. [named after T. *Stevens*, English weaver d. 1888, whose firm made them]

stew[1] /stju:/ *v. & n.* ● *v.* **1** *tr. & intr.* cook slowly in simmering liquid in a closed dish, saucepan, etc. **2** *intr. colloq.* be oppressed by heat or humidity, esp. in a confined space. **3** *intr. colloq.* **a** suffer prolonged embarrassment, anxiety, etc. **b** (foll. by *over*) fret or be anxious. **4** *intr. Brit.* (of tea) become bitter or strong with prolonged brewing. **5** *tr.* (as **stewed** *adj.*) *colloq.* drunk. **6** *intr.* (often foll. by *over*) *colloq.* study hard. ● *n.* **1** a dish of stewed meat etc. **2** *colloq.* an agitated or angry state (*be in a stew*). **3** *archaic* **a** a hot bath. **b** (in *pl.*) a brothel. □ **stew in one's own juice** be left to suffer the consequences of one's own actions. [Middle English from Old French *estuve*, *estuver*, probably ultimately from EX-[1] + Greek *tuphos* 'smoke, steam']

stew[2] /stju:/ *n. Brit.* **1** an artificial oyster bed. **2** a pond or large tank for keeping fish for eating. [Middle English from French *estui*, from *estoier* 'confine', ultimately from Latin *studium*: see STUDY]

steward /'stju:əd/ *n. & v.* ● *n.* **1** a passengers' attendant on a ship or aircraft or train. **2** an official appointed to keep order or supervise arrangements at a meeting or show or demonstration etc. **3** = SHOP STEWARD. **4** a person responsible for supplies of food etc. for a college or club etc. **5** a person employed to manage another's property. **6** *Brit.* the title of several officers of state or the royal household (*Lord High Steward*). ● *v.tr.* act as a steward of (*will steward the meeting*). □ **stewardship** *n.* [Old English *stīweard*, from *stig* (probably = house, hall) + *weard* WARD]

stewardess /'stju:ədɪs, stju:ə'dɛs/ *n.* a female steward, esp. on a ship or aircraft.

stewpot /'stju:pɒt/ *n.* **1 a** a cooking pot for stew. **b** its contents. **2** a mixture (*ethnic stewpot*).

stg. *abbr.* sterling.

Sth. *abbr.* South.

sthenic /'sθɛnɪk/ *adj.* **1** *Med.* strong and athletic in physique. **2** *Psychol.* vigorous and aggressive in personality. [Greek *sthenos* 'strength', on the pattern of *asthenic*]

stichomythia /stɪkə(ʊ)'mɪθɪə/ *n.* dialogue in alternate lines of verse, used in disputation in Greek drama, and characterized by antithesis and repetition. [modern Latin from Greek *stikhomuthia*, from *stikhos* 'row, line of verse' + *muthos* 'speech, talk']

stick[1] /stɪk/ *n.* **1 a** a short slender branch or length of wood broken or cut from a tree. **b** this trimmed for use as a support or weapon. **2** a thin rod or spike of wood etc. for a particular purpose (*cocktail stick*). **3 a** an implement used to propel the ball in hockey or polo etc. **b** (in *pl.*) the raising of the stick above the shoulder in hockey. **4** a gear lever. **5** a conductor's baton. **6 a** a slender piece of a thing, e.g. celery, dynamite, deodorant, etc. **b** a number of bombs or paratroops released rapidly from aircraft. **7** (often prec. by *the*) punishment, esp. by beating. **8** esp. *Brit. colloq.* adverse criticism; censure, reproof (*took a lot of stick*). **9** *colloq.* a piece of wood as part of a house or furniture (*a few sticks of furniture*). **10** *colloq.* a person, esp. one who is dull or unsociable (*a funny old stick*). **11** (in *pl.*; prec. by *the*) *colloq.* remote rural areas. **12** (in *pl.*) *Austral. slang* goalposts. **13** *Naut. slang* a mast or spar. □ **up sticks** *Brit. colloq.* go to live elsewhere. □ **stickless** *adj.* **sticklike** *adj.* [Old English *sticca*, from West Germanic]

stick[2] /stɪk/ *v.* (*past* and *past part.* **stuck** /stʌk/) **1** *tr.* (foll. by *in*, *into*, *through*) insert or thrust (a thing or its point) (*stuck a finger in my eye; stick a pin through it*). **2** *tr.* insert a pointed thing into; stab. **3** *tr. & intr.* (foll. by *in*, *into*, *on*, etc.) **a** fix or be fixed on a pointed thing. **b** fix or be fixed by or as by a pointed end. **4** *tr. & intr.* fix or become or remain fixed by or as by adhesive etc. (*stick a label on it; the label won't stick*). **5** *intr.* endure; make a continued impression (*the scene stuck in my mind; the name stuck*). **6** *intr.* lose or be deprived of the power of motion or action through adhesion or jamming or other impediment. **7** *colloq.* **a** *tr.* put in a specified position or place, esp. quickly or haphazardly (*stick it in your pocket*). **b** *intr.* remain in a place (*stuck indoors*). **8** *colloq.* **a** *intr.* (of an accusation etc.) be convincing or regarded as valid (*could not make the charges stick*). **b** *tr.* (foll. by *on*) place the blame for (a thing) on (a person). **9** *tr. Brit. colloq.* endure, tolerate (*could not stick it any longer*). **10** *tr.* (foll. by *at*) *colloq.* persevere with. □ **be stuck 1** be unable to progress. **2** be confined in a place (*was stuck in the house*). **be stuck for** be at a loss for or in need of. **be stuck on** *colloq.* be infatuated with. **be stuck with** *colloq.* be unable to get rid of or escape from; be permanently involved with. **get stuck in** (or **into**) *colloq.* begin in earnest. **stick around** *colloq.* linger; remain at the same place. **stick at it** *colloq.* persevere. **stick at nothing** allow nothing, esp. no scruples, to deter one. **stick by** (or **with** or **to**) stay loyal or close to. **stick 'em up!** *colloq.* hands up! **stick fast** adhere or become firmly fixed or trapped in a position or place. **stick in one's gizzard** see GIZZARD. **stick in one's throat** be against one's principles. **stick it on** *colloq.* **1** make high charges. **2** tell an exaggerated story. **stick it out** *colloq.* put up with or persevere with a burden etc. to the end. **stick one's chin out** show firmness or fortitude. **stick one's neck** (or **chin**) **out** expose oneself to censure etc. by acting or speaking boldly. **stick out** protrude or cause to protrude or project (*stuck his tongue out; stick out your chest*). **stick**

out for persist in demanding. **stick out a mile** (or **like a sore thumb**) *colloq.* be very obvious or incongruous. **stick pigs** engage in pigsticking. **stick to 1** remain close to or fixed on or to. **2** remain faithful to. **3** keep to (a subject etc.) (*stick to the point*). **stick to a person's fingers** *colloq.* (of money) be embezzled by a person. **stick together** *colloq.* remain united or mutually loyal. **stick to one's guns** see GUN. **stick to it** persevere. **stick to one's last** see LAST[3]. **stick up 1** be or make erect or protruding upwards. **2** fasten to an upright surface. **3** *colloq.* rob or threaten with a gun. **stick up for** support or defend or champion (a person or cause). **stick up to** be assertive in the face of; offer resistance to. **stick with** *colloq.* remain in touch with or faithful to; persevere with. [Old English *stician*, from Germanic]

stickability /stɪkə'bɪlɪti/ *n. colloq.* perseverance; staying power.

sticker /'stɪkə/ *n.* **1** an adhesive label or notice etc. **2** a person or thing that sticks. **3** a persistent person.

sticking plaster *n. Brit.* an adhesive plaster for wounds etc.

sticking point *n.* the place where obstacles arise to progress or to an agreement etc.

stick insect *n.* any elongated usu. wingless insect of the family Phasmidae with a twiglike body.

stick-in-the-mud *n. colloq.* an unprogressive or old-fashioned person.

stickleback /'stɪk(ə)lbak/ *n.* any small fish of the family Gasterosteidae, esp. *Gasterosteus aculeatus*, with sharp spines along the back. [Middle English, from Old English *sticel* 'thorn, sting' + *bæc* BACK]

stickler /'stɪklə/ *n.* (foll. by *for*) a person who insists on something (*a stickler for accuracy*). [obsolete *stickle* 'be umpire', alteration of Middle English *stightle* 'control', frequentative of *stight*, from Old English *stiht(i)an* 'set in order']

stickpin /'stɪkpɪn/ *n. N. Amer.* an ornamental tiepin.

stick-up *n. colloq.* an armed robbery using a gun.

stickweed /'stɪkwi:d/ *n. US* = RAGWEED 2.

sticky /'stɪki/ *adj.* (**stickier**, **stickiest**) **1** tending or intended to stick or adhere. **2** glutinous, viscous. **3 a** (of the weather) humid. **b** damp with sweat. **4** *colloq.* awkward or uncooperative; intransigent (*was very sticky about giving me leave*). **5** *colloq.* difficult, awkward (*a sticky problem*). □ **come to a sticky end** *Brit.* die or come to grief in an unpleasant or painful way. □ **stickily** *adv.* **stickiness** *n.*

stickybeak /'stɪkɪbi:k/ *n. & v. Austral. & NZ slang* ● *n.* an inquisitive person. ● *v.intr.* pry.

sticky wicket *n.* **1** *Cricket* a pitch that has been drying after rain and is difficult for the batsman. **2** *colloq.* difficult or awkward circumstances.

stiff /stɪf/ *adj. & n.* ● *adj.* **1** rigid; not flexible. **2** hard to bend or move or turn etc.; not working freely. **3** hard to cope with; needing strength or effort (*a stiff test*; *a stiff climb*). **4** severe or strong (*a stiff breeze*; *a stiff penalty*). **5** (of a person or manner) formal, constrained; lacking spontaneity. **6** (of a muscle or limb etc., or a person affected by these) aching when used, owing to previous exertion, injury, etc. **7** (of an alcoholic or medicinal drink) strong. **8** (*predic.*) *colloq.* to an extreme degree (*bored stiff*; *scared stiff*). **9** (foll. by *with*) *colloq.* abounding in (*a place stiff with tourists*). ● *n. slang* **1** a corpse. **2** a foolish or useless person (*you big stiff*). □ **stiffish** *adj.* **stiffly** *adv.* **stiffness** *n.* [Old English *stīf*, from Germanic]

stiffen /'stɪf(ə)n/ *v.tr. & intr.* make or become stiff. □ **stiffener** *n.* **stiffening** *n.*

stiff neck *n.* a rheumatic condition in which the head cannot be turned without pain.

stiff-necked *adj.* obstinate or haughty.

stiff upper lip *n.* firmness, fortitude.

stifle[1] /'stʌɪf(ə)l/ *v.* **1** *tr.* smother, suppress (*stifled a yawn*). **2** *intr. & tr.* experience or cause to experience constraint of breathing (*stifling heat*). **3** *tr.* kill by suffocating. □ **stifler** /-flə/ *n.* **stifling** *adj. & adv.* **stiflingly** *adv.* [perhaps alteration of Middle English *stuffe*, *stuffle* from Old French *estouffer*]

stifle[2] /'stʌɪf(ə)l/ *n.* (in full **stifle-joint**) a joint in the legs of horses, dogs, etc., equivalent to the knee in humans. [Middle English: origin unknown]

stifle-bone *n.* the bone in front of a stifle-joint.

stigma /'stɪgmə/ *n.* (*pl.* **stigmas** or esp. in sense 4 **stigmata** /-mətə, -'mɑ:tə/) **1** a mark or sign of disgrace or discredit. **2** (foll. by *of*) a distinguishing mark or characteristic. **3** the part of a pistil that receives the pollen in pollination. **4** (in *pl.*) *Eccl.* (in Christian belief) marks corresponding to those left on Christ's body by the Crucifixion, said to have been impressed by divine favour on the bodies of St Francis of Assisi and others. **5** a mark or spot on the skin or on a butterfly's wing. **6** *Med.* a visible sign or characteristic of a disease. **7** an insect's spiracle. [Latin from Greek *stigma -atos* 'a mark made by a pointed instrument, a brand, a dot': related to STICK[1]]

stigmatic /stɪg'matɪk/ *adj. & n.* ● *adj.* **1** of or relating to a stigma or stigmas. **2** = ANASTIGMATIC. ● *n. Eccl.* a person bearing stigmata. □ **stigmatically** *adv.*

stigmatist /'stɪgmətɪst/ *n. Eccl.* = STIGMATIC *n.*

stigmatize /'stɪgmətʌɪz/ *v.tr.* (also **-ise**) **1** (often foll. by *as*) describe as unworthy or disgraceful. **2** *Eccl.* produce stigmata on. □ **stigmatization** /-'zeɪʃ(ə)n/ *n.* [French *stigmatiser* or medieval Latin *stigmatizo* from Greek *stigmatizō* (as STIGMA)]

stilb /stɪlb/ *n.* a unit of luminance equal to one candela per square centimetre. [French from Greek *stilbō* 'to glitter']

stilbene /'stɪlbi:n/ *n. Chem.* an aromatic hydrocarbon forming phosphorescent crystals. [as STILB + -ENE]

stilboestrol /stɪl'bi:strɒl/ *n.* (*US* **stilbestrol**) a powerful synthetic oestrogen derived from stilbene. [STILBENE + OESTRUS]

stile[1] /stʌɪl/ *n.* an arrangement of steps allowing people but not animals to climb over a fence or wall. [Old English *stigel*, from a Germanic root meaning 'to climb']

stile[2] /stʌɪl/ *n.* a vertical piece in the frame of a panelled door, wainscot, etc. (cf. RAIL[1] *n.* 5). [probably from Dutch *stijl* 'pillar, doorpost']

stiletto /stɪ'lɛtəʊ/ *n.* (*pl.* **-os**) **1** a short dagger with a thick blade. **2** a pointed instrument for making eyelets etc. **3** (in full **stiletto heel**) **a** a long tapering heel of a shoe. **b** a shoe with such a heel. [Italian, diminutive of *stilo* 'dagger' (as STYLUS)]

still[1] /stɪl/ *adj., n., adv., & v.* ● *adj.* **1** not or hardly moving. **2** with little or no sound; calm and tranquil (*a still evening*). **3** (of sounds) hushed, stilled. **4** (of a drink) not effervescent. ● *n.* **1** deep silence (*in the still of the night*). **2** an ordinary static photograph (as opposed to a motion picture), esp. a single shot from a cinema film. ● *adv.* **1** without moving (*stand still*). **2** even now or at a particular time (*they still did not understand*; *why are you still here?*). **3** nevertheless; all the same. **4** (with *compar.* etc.) even, yet, increasingly (*still greater efforts*; *still another explanation*). ● *v.tr. & intr.* make or become still; quieten. □ **still and all** *colloq.* nevertheless. **still waters run deep** a quiet manner conceals depths of feeling or knowledge or cunning. □ **stillness** *n.* [Old English *stille* (*adj. & adv.*), *stillan* (*v.*), from West Germanic]

still[2] /stɪl/ *n.* an apparatus for distilling spirituous liquors etc. [obsolete Middle English verb *still*, from DISTIL]

stillage /'stɪlɪdʒ/ *n.* a bench, frame, etc., for keeping articles off the floor while draining, drying, waiting to be packed, etc. [apparently from Dutch *stellagie* 'scaffold', from *stellen* 'to place' + French *-age*]

stillbirth /'stɪlbə:θ/ *n.* the birth of a dead child.

stillborn /'stɪlbɔ:n/ *adj.* **1** (of a child) born dead. **2** (of an idea, plan, etc.) abortive; not able to succeed.

still life *n.* (*pl.* **still lifes**) (hyphenated when *attrib.*) **1** a painting or drawing of inanimate objects such as fruit or flowers. **2** this genre of painting.

still room *n. Brit.* **1** a room for distilling. **2** a housekeeper's storeroom in a large house.

Stillson /ˈstɪls(ə)n/ *n.* (in full **Stillson wrench**) a large wrench with jaws that tighten as pressure is increased. [named after D. C. *Stillson*, its inventor d. 1899]

stilly /ˈstɪli/ *adv. & adj.* ● *adv.* in a still manner. ● *adj. poet.* still, quiet. [the adverb Old English *stillīce*: the adjective from STILL[1]]

stilt /stɪlt/ *n.* **1** either of a pair of poles with supports for the feet enabling the user to walk at a distance above the ground. **2** each of a set of piles or posts supporting a building etc. **3** any wading bird of the genus *Himantopus*, with long slender legs. **4** a three-legged support for ceramic ware in a kiln. □ **on stilts 1** supported by stilts. **2** bombastic, stilted. [Middle English & Low German *stilte*, from Germanic]

stilted /ˈstɪltɪd/ *adj.* **1** (of a literary style etc.) stiff and unnatural; bombastic. **2** standing on stilts. **3** *Archit.* (of an arch) with pieces of upright masonry between the imposts and the springers. □ **stiltedly** *adv.* **stiltedness** *n.*

Stilton /ˈstɪlt(ə)n/ *n. propr.* a kind of strong rich cheese, often with blue veins, originally made at various places in Leicestershire and formerly sold to travellers at a coaching inn in Stilton (now in Cambridgeshire).

stimulant /ˈstɪmjʊl(ə)nt/ *adj. & n.* ● *adj.* that stimulates, esp. bodily or mental activity. ● *n.* **1** a stimulant substance, esp. a drug or alcoholic drink. **2** a stimulating influence. [Latin *stimulare stimulant-* 'urge, goad']

stimulate /ˈstɪmjʊleɪt/ *v.tr.* **1** apply or act as a stimulus to. **2** animate, excite, arouse. **3** be a stimulant to. □ **stimulating** *adj.* **stimulatingly** *adv.* **stimulation** /-ˈleɪʃ(ə)n/ *n.* **stimulative** /-lətɪv/ *adj.* **stimulator** *n.* **stimulatory** *adj.*

stimulus /ˈstɪmjʊləs/ *n.* (*pl.* **stimuli** /-lʌɪ, -liː/) **1** a thing that rouses to activity or energy. **2** a stimulating or rousing effect. **3** a thing that evokes a specific functional reaction in an organ or tissue. [Latin, = goad, spur, incentive]

stimy var. of STYMIE.

sting /stɪŋ/ *n. & v.* ● *n.* **1** a sharp often poisonous wounding organ of an insect, nettle, etc. **2 a** the act of inflicting a wound with this. **b** the wound itself or the pain caused by it. **3** a wounding or painful quality or effect (*the sting of hunger*; *stings of remorse*). **4** pungency, sharpness, vigour (*a sting in the voice*). **5** *slang* **a** a swindle or robbery. **b** a police undercover operation. ● *v.* (*past* and *past part.* **stung** /stʌŋ/) **1 a** *tr.* wound or pierce with a sting. **b** *intr.* be able to sting; have a sting. **2** *intr. & tr.* feel or cause to feel a tingling physical or sharp mental pain. **3** *tr.* (foll. by *into*) incite by a strong or painful mental effect (*was stung into replying*). **4** *tr. slang* swindle or charge exorbitantly. □ **sting in the tail** an unpleasant or problematic end to something, occurring unexpectedly. □ **stingingly** *adv.* **stingless** *adj.* [Old English *sting* (*n.*), *stingan* (*v.*), from Germanic]

stingaree /stɪŋgəˈriː, ˈstɪŋgəriː/ *n. US & Austral.* = STINGRAY.

stinger /ˈstɪŋə/ *n.* **1** a stinging insect, snake, nettle, etc. **2** a sharp painful blow.

stinging nettle *n.* a nettle, *Urtica dioica*, having stinging hairs.

stingray /ˈstɪŋreɪ/ *n.* any cartilaginous fish of the family Dasyatidae or Urolophidae, having a flattened diamond-shaped body and a long poisonous serrated spine at the base of the tail.

stingy /ˈstɪn(d)ʒi/ *adj.* (**stingier**, **stingiest**) niggardly, mean. □ **stingily** *adv.* **stinginess** *n.* [perhaps from dialect *stinge* STING]

stink /stɪŋk/ *v. & n.* ● *v.* (*past* **stank** /staŋk/ or **stunk** /stʌŋk/; *past part.* **stunk**) **1** *intr.* emit a strong offensive smell. **2** *tr.* (often foll. by *out*) fill (a place) with a stink. **3** *tr.* (foll. by *out* etc.) drive (a person) out etc. by a stink. **4** *intr. colloq.* be or seem very unpleasant, contemptible, or scandalous. **5** *intr.* (foll. by *of*) *colloq.* have plenty of (esp. money). ● *n.* **1** a strong or offensive smell; a stench. **2** *colloq.* a row or fuss (*the affair caused quite a stink*). □ **like stink** *colloq.* intensely; extremely hard or fast etc. (*working like stink*). [Old English *stincan*, ultimately from West Germanic: related to STENCH]

stink bomb *n.* a device emitting a stink when exploded.

stinker /ˈstɪŋkə/ *n.* **1** a person or thing that stinks. **2** *slang* an objectionable person or thing. **3** *slang* **a** a difficult task. **b** *Brit.* a letter etc. conveying strong disapproval.

stinkhorn /ˈstɪŋkhɔːn/ *n.* any foul-smelling fungus of the order Phallales.

stinking /ˈstɪŋkɪŋ/ *adj. & adv.* ● *adj.* **1** that stinks. **2** *slang* very objectionable. ● *adv. slang* extremely and usu. objectionably (*stinking rich*). □ **stinkingly** *adv.*

stinking badger *n.* a teledu.

stinking iris *n.* = GLADDON.

stinko /ˈstɪŋkəʊ/ *adj. slang* drunk.

stinkpot /ˈstɪŋkpɒt/ *n. slang* **1** a term of contempt for a person. **2** a vehicle or boat that emits foul exhaust fumes.

stinkweed /ˈstɪŋkwiːd/ *n.* = WALL ROCKET.

stinkwood /ˈstɪŋkwʊd/ *n.* an African tree, *Ocotea bullata*, with foul-smelling timber.

stinky /ˈstɪŋki/ *adj.* (**stinkier**, **stinkiest**) *colloq.* having a strong or unpleasant smell.

stint /stɪnt/ *v. & n.* ● *v.* **1** *tr.* supply (food or aid etc.) in a niggardly amount or grudgingly. **2** *tr.* (often *refl.*) supply (a person etc.) in this way. **3** *intr.* (foll. by *on*) be grudging or mean about. ● *n.* **1** a limitation of supply or effort (*without stint*). **2** a fixed or allotted amount or period of work (*do one's stint*). **3** a small sandpiper, esp. a dunlin. □ **stintless** *adj.* [Old English *styntan* 'to blunt, dull', from Germanic: related to STUNT[1]]

stipe /stʌɪp/ *n. Bot. & Zool.* a stalk or stem, esp. the support of a carpel, the stalk of a frond, the stem of a fungus, or an eye-stalk. □ **stipiform** *adj.* **stipitate** /ˈstɪpɪteɪt, -tət/ *adj.* **stipitiform** /stɪˈpɪtɪfɔːm/ *adj.* [French from Latin *stipes*: see STIPES]

stipel /ˈstʌɪp(ə)l/ *n. Bot.* a secondary stipule at the base of the leaflets of a compound leaf. □ **stipellate** /-leɪt, ˌstɪˈpɛlət/ *adj.* [French *stipelle* from modern Latin *stipella*, diminutive of Latin *stipula* 'straw']

stipend /ˈstʌɪpɛnd/ *n.* a fixed regular allowance or salary, esp. *Brit.* one paid to a clergyman. [Middle English from Old French *stipend(i)e* or Latin *stipendium*, from *stips* 'wages' + *pendere* 'to pay']

stipendiary /stʌɪˈpɛndjəri, stɪ-/ *adj. & n.* ● *adj.* **1** receiving a stipend. **2** working for pay, not voluntarily. ● *n.* (*pl.* **-ies**) a person receiving a stipend. [Latin *stipendiarius* (as STIPEND)]

stipendiary magistrate *n.* a paid professional magistrate.

stipes /ˈstʌɪpiːz/ *n.* (*pl.* **stipites** /ˈstɪpɪtiːz/) *Bot. & Zool.* = STIPE. [Latin, = log, tree trunk]

stipple /ˈstɪp(ə)l/ *v. & n.* ● *v.* **1** *tr. & intr.* draw or paint or engrave etc. with dots instead of lines. **2** *tr.* roughen the surface of (paint, cement, etc.). ● *n.* **1** the process or technique of stippling. **2** the effect of stippling. □ **stippler** *n.* **stippling** *n.* [Dutch *stippelen*, frequentative of *stippen* 'to prick', from *stip* 'a point']

stipulate[1] /ˈstɪpjʊleɪt/ *v.tr.* **1** demand or specify as part of a bargain or agreement. **2** (foll. by *for*) mention or insist upon as an essential condition. **3** (as **stipulated** *adj.*) laid down in the terms of an agreement. □ **stipulation** /-ˈleɪʃ(ə)n/ *n.* **stipulator** *n.* [Latin *stipulari*]

stipulate[2] /ˈstɪpjʊlət/ *adj. Bot.* having stipules. [Latin *stipula* (as STIPULE)]

stipule /ˈstɪpjuːl/ *n.* a small leaflike appendage to a leaf, usu. at the base of a leaf-stem. □ **stipular** *adj.* [French *stipule* or Latin *stipula* 'straw']

stir[1] /stəː/ *v.* & *n.* ● *v.* (**stirred**, **stirring**) **1** *tr.* move a spoon or other implement round and round in (a liquid etc.), esp. to mix the ingredients or constituents. **2 a** *tr.* cause to move or be disturbed, esp. slightly (*a breeze stirred the lake*). **b** *intr.* be or begin to be in motion (*not a creature was stirring*). **c** *refl.* rouse (oneself), esp. from a lethargic state. **3** *intr.* rise from sleep (*is still not stirring*). **4** *intr.* (foll. by *out of*) leave; go out of (esp. one's house). **5** *tr.* arouse or inspire or excite (the emotions etc., or a person as regards these) (*was stirred to anger*; *it stirred the imagination*). **6** *intr. colloq.* cause trouble between people by gossiping etc. ● *n.* **1** an act of stirring (*give it a good stir*). **2** commotion or excitement; public attention (*caused quite a stir*). **3** the slightest movement (*not a stir*). □ **stir the blood** inspire enthusiasm etc. **stir a finger** = *lift a finger*. **stir in** mix (an added ingredient) with a substance by stirring. **stir one's stumps** *colloq.* **1** begin to move. **2** become active. **stir up 1** mix thoroughly by stirring. **2** incite (trouble etc.) (*loved stirring things up*). **3** stimulate, excite, arouse (*stirred up their curiosity*). □ **stirless** *adj.* [Old English *styrian*, from Germanic]

stir[2] /stəː/ *n. slang* a prison (esp. *in stir*). [19th c.: origin uncertain, perhaps from Romany *sturbin* 'jail']

stir-crazy *adj. slang* deranged from long imprisonment.

stir-fry *v.* & *n.* ● *v.tr.* (**-ies**, **-ied**) fry rapidly while stirring and tossing. ● *n.* a stir-fried dish.

stirk /stəːk/ *n. Brit. dial.* a yearling bullock or heifer. [Old English *stirc*, perhaps from *stēor* STEER[2] + *oc* -OCK]

stirps /stəːps/ *n.* (*pl.* **stirpes** /-piːz/) **1** *Biol.* a classificatory group. **2** *Law* **a** a branch of a family. **b** its progenitor. [Latin, = stock]

stirrer /ˈstəːrə/ *n.* **1** a thing or a person that stirs. **2** *Brit. colloq.* a troublemaker; an agitator.

stirring /ˈstəːrɪŋ/ *adj.* & *n.* ● *adj.* **1** stimulating, exciting, rousing. **2** *archaic* actively occupied (*lead a stirring life*). ● *n.* (in *pl.*) **1** initial activity or indications of such activity (*stirrings of a new culture*). **2** initial feelings (*stirrings of sympathy*). □ **stirringly** *adv.* [Old English *styrende* (as STIR[1])]

stirrup /ˈstɪrəp/ *n.* **1** each of a pair of devices attached to each side of a horse's saddle, in the form of a loop with a flat base to support the rider's foot. **2** (*attrib.*) having the shape of a stirrup. **3** (in full **stirrup bone**) = STAPES. [Old English *stigrāp*, from *stigan* climb (as STILE[1]) + ROPE]

stirrup cup *n.* a cup of wine etc. offered to a person about to depart, originally on horseback.

stirrup iron *n.* the metal loop of a stirrup.

stirrup leather *n.* the strap attaching a stirrup to a saddle.

stirrup pump *n.* a hand-operated water pump with a footrest, used to extinguish small fires.

stitch /stɪtʃ/ *n.* & *v.* ● *n.* **1 a** (in sewing or knitting or crocheting etc.) a single pass of a needle or the thread or loop etc. resulting from this. **b** a particular method of sewing or knitting etc. (*am learning a new stitch*). **2** (usu. in *pl.*) *Surgery* each of the loops of material used in sewing up a wound. **3** the least bit of clothing (*hadn't a stitch on*). **4** an acute pain in the side of the body induced by running etc. ● *v.tr.* **1** (also *absol.*) sew; make stitches (in). **2** join or close with stitches. □ **in stitches** *colloq.* laughing uncontrollably. **stitch up 1** join or mend by sewing or stitching. **2** *Brit. slang* cause (a person) to be charged with a crime, esp. by informing or manufacturing evidence; cheat. **3** *slang*; often *derog.* = *sew up* 2. □ **stitcher** *n.* **stitchery** *n.* **stitchless** *adj.* [Old English *stice* from Germanic: related to STICK[2]]

stitch in time *n.* a timely remedy.

stitch-up *n. slang* **1** an act of incriminating a person for a crime. **2** often *derog.* an act of securing the outcome of something to one's advantage.

stitchwort /ˈstɪtʃwəːt/ *n.* any plant of the genus *Stellaria*, esp. *S. holostea* with an erect stem and white starry flowers, once thought to cure a stitch in the side.

stiver /ˈstʌɪvə/ *n.* the smallest quantity or amount (*don't care a stiver*). [Dutch *stuiver*, a small coin, probably related to STUB]

stoa /ˈstəʊə/ *n.* (*pl.* **stoas**) **1** a portico or roofed colonnade in ancient Greek architecture. **2** (**the Stoa**) the Stoic school of philosophy. [Greek: cf. STOIC]

stoat /stəʊt/ *n.* a small long-bodied carnivorous mammal, *Mustela erminea*, of the weasel family, having reddish-brown upper parts and a black-tipped tail, and in northern areas turning white in winter. Also called ERMINE. [Middle English: origin unknown]

stochastic /stəˈkastɪk/ *adj.* **1** determined by a random distribution of probabilities. **2** (of a process) characterized by a sequence of random variables. **3** governed by the laws of probability. □ **stochastically** *adv.* [Greek *stokhastikos*, via *stokhazomai* 'aim at, guess' from *stokhos* 'aim']

stock /stɒk/ *n.*, *adj.*, & *v.* ● *n.* **1** a store of goods etc. ready for sale or distribution etc. **2** a supply or quantity of anything for use (*lay in winter stocks of fuel*; *a great stock of information*). **3** equipment or raw material for manufacture or trade etc. (*rolling stock*; *paper stock*). **4 a** farm animals or equipment. **b** = FATSTOCK. **5 a** the capital of a business company. **b** shares in this. **6** one's reputation or popularity (*his stock is rising*). **7 a** money lent to a government at fixed interest. **b** the right to receive such interest. **8** a line of ancestry; family origins (*comes of Cornish stock*). **9** liquid made by stewing bones, vegetables, fish, etc., as a basis for soup, gravy, sauce, etc. **10** any of various fragrant-flowered cruciferous plants of the genus *Matthiola* or *Malcolmia* (originally *stock-gillyflower*, so called because it had a stronger stem than the clove gillyflower). **11** a plant into which a graft is inserted. **12** the main trunk of a tree etc. **13** (in *pl.*) *hist.* a timber frame with holes for the feet and occasionally the hands and head, in which offenders were locked as a public punishment. **14** *US* **a** = STOCK COMPANY. **b** the repertory of this. **15 a** a base or support or handle for an implement or machine. **b** the crossbar of an anchor. **16** the butt of a rifle etc. **17 a** = HEADSTOCK. **b** = TAILSTOCK. **18** (in *pl.*) the supports for a ship during building. **19** a band of material worn round the neck esp. in horse-riding or below a clerical collar. **20** hard solid brick pressed in a mould. ● *adj.* **1** kept in stock and so regularly available (*stock sizes*). **2** perpetually repeated; hackneyed, conventional (*a stock answer*). ● *v.tr.* **1** have or keep (goods) in stock. **2 a** provide (a shop or a farm etc.) with goods, equipment, or livestock. **b** fill with items needed (*shelves well-stocked with books*). **3** fit (a gun etc.) with a stock. □ **in stock** available immediately for sale etc. **on the stocks** in construction or preparation. **out of stock** not immediately available for sale. **stock up 1** provide with or get stocks or supplies. **2** (foll. by *with*) get in or gather a stock of (food, fuel, etc.). **take stock 1** make an inventory of one's stock. **2** (often foll. by *of*) make a review or estimate (of a situation etc.). **3** (foll. by *in*) concern oneself with. □ **stocker** *n.* **stockless** *adj.* [Old English *stoc*, *stocc*, from Germanic]

stockade /stɒˈkeɪd/ *n.* & *v.* ● *n.* **1** a line or enclosure of upright stakes. **2** esp. *N. Amer.* a prison, esp. a military one. ● *v.tr.* fortify with a stockade. [obsolete French *estocade*, alteration of *estacade* from Spanish *estacada*, ultimately from Germanic: related to STAKE[1]]

stock-book *n.* a book showing amounts of goods acquired and disposed of.

stockbreeder /ˈstɒkbriːdə/ *n.* a farmer who raises livestock. □ **stockbreeding** *n.*

stockbroker /ˈstɒkbrəʊkə/ *n.* = BROKER 2. □ **stockbrokerage** *n.* **stockbroking** *n.*

stockbroker belt *n. Brit.* an affluent residential area, esp. near a business centre such as London.

stock car *n.* **1** a specially strengthened production car for use in racing in which collision occurs. **2** *N. Amer.* a railway truck for transporting livestock.

stock company *n. US* a repertory company performing mainly at a particular theatre.

stock dove *n.* a European wild pigeon, *Columba oenas*, with a shorter tail and squarer head than a wood pigeon and breeding in tree trunks.

Stock Exchange *n.* (also **stock exchange**) **1** a place where stocks and shares are bought and sold. **2** the dealers working there.

stockfish /'stɒkfɪʃ/ *n.* (*pl.* usu. same) cod or a similar fish split and dried in the open air without salt. [Middle Low German, Middle Dutch *stokvisch*, of unknown origin]

stockholder /'stɒkhəʊldə/ *n.* an owner of stocks or shares. □ **stockholding** *n.*

stockinet /stɒkɪ'nɛt/ *n.* (also **stockinette**) an elastic knitted material. [probably from *stocking-net*]

stocking /'stɒkɪŋ/ *n.* **1 a** either of a pair of long separate usu. knitted coverings for the legs and feet, esp. a woman's semi-transparent thigh-length leg-covering in usu. nylon. **b** esp. *US* = SOCK[1] 1. **2** any close-fitting garment resembling a stocking (*bodystocking*). **3** a differently coloured, usu. white, lower part of the leg of a horse etc. □ **in one's stocking** (or **stockinged**) **feet** without shoes (esp. while being measured). □ **stockinged** *adj.* (also in *comb.*). **stockingless** *adj.* [STOCK in the (now dialect) sense 'stocking' + -ING[1]]

stocking cap *n.* a knitted usu. conical cap.

stocking filler *n. Brit.* (*US* **stocking stuffer**) a small present suitable for a Christmas stocking.

stocking stitch *n. Knitting* a stitch of alternate rows of plain and purl, making a plain smooth surface on one side.

stock-in-trade *n.* **1 a** all the requisites of a trade or profession. **b** the goods kept on sale by a dealer or shopkeeper. **2** a ready supply of characteristic phrases, attitudes, etc.

stockist /'stɒkɪst/ *n. Brit.* a dealer who stocks goods of a particular type for sale.

stockjobber /'stɒkdʒɒbə/ *n.* **1** *Brit.* = JOBBER 1. **2** *US* = JOBBER 2b. □ **stockjobbing** *n.*

stocklist /'stɒklɪst/ *n. Brit.* a regular publication stating a dealer's stock of goods with current prices etc.

stockman /'stɒkmən/ *n.* (*pl.* **-men**) **1 a** *Austral.* a man in charge of livestock. **b** *US* an owner of livestock. **2** *US* a person in charge of a stock of goods in a warehouse etc.

stock market *n.* **1** = STOCK EXCHANGE. **2** transactions on this.

stockout /'stɒkaʊt/ *n.* an instance of an item being out of stock when wanted by a customer.

stockpile /'stɒkpʌɪl/ *n.* & *v.* ● *n.* an accumulated stock of goods, materials, weapons, etc., held in reserve. ● *v.tr.* accumulate a stockpile of. □ **stockpiler** *n.*

stockpot /'stɒkpɒt/ *n.* a pot for cooking stock for soup etc.

stockroom /'stɒkruːm, -rʊm/ *n.* a room for storing goods in stock.

stock-still *adv.* completely motionless.

stocktaking /'stɒkteɪkɪŋ/ *n.* **1** the process of making an inventory of stock in a shop etc. **2** a review of one's position and resources. □ **stocktake** *n.* **stocktaker** *n.*

stocky /'stɒki/ *adj.* (**stockier**, **stockiest**) (of a person, plant, or animal) short and strongly built; thickset. □ **stockily** *adv.* **stockiness** *n.*

stockyard /'stɒkjɑːd/ *n.* an enclosure with pens etc. for the sorting or temporary keeping of cattle.

stodge /stɒdʒ/ *n.* esp. *Brit. colloq.* **1** food esp. of a thick heavy kind. **2** an unimaginative person or idea. [earlier as verb: imitative, suggested by *stuff* and *podge*]

stodgy /'stɒdʒi/ *adj.* (**stodgier**, **stodgiest**) **1** *Brit.* (of food) heavy and indigestible. **2** dull and uninteresting. **3** (of a literary style etc.) turgid and dull. □ **stodgily** *adv.* **stodginess** *n.*

stoep /stuːp/ *n. S.Afr.* a terraced veranda in front of a house. [Dutch, related to STEP]

stogy /'stəʊgi/ *n.* (also **stogie**) (*pl.* **-ies**) **1** *N. Amer.* a long narrow roughly made cigar. **2** *US* a rough heavy boot. [originally *stoga*, short for *Conestoga* in Pennsylvania]

Stoic /'stəʊɪk/ *n.* & *adj.* ● *n.* **1** a member of the ancient Greek school of philosophy founded at Athens by Zeno *c.*308 BC, which sought virtue as the greatest good and taught control of one's feelings and passions. **2** (**stoic**) a stoical person. ● *adj.* **1** of or like the Stoics. **2** (**stoic**) = STOICAL. [Middle English via Latin *stoicus* from Greek *stōikos*, from STOA (with reference to Zeno's teaching in the *Stoa Poikilē* or Painted Porch at Athens)]

stoical /'stəʊɪk(ə)l/ *adj.* having or showing great self-control in adversity. □ **stoically** *adv.*

stoichiometry /stɔɪkɪ'ɒmɪtri/ *n.* (also **stoichometry** /stɔɪ'kɒmɪtri/) *Chem.* **1** the fixed, usu. rational numerical relationship between the relative quantities of substances in a reaction or compound. **2** the determination or measurement of these quantities. □ **stoichiometric** /-kɪə'mɛtrɪk/ *adj.* [Greek *stoikheion* 'element' + -METRY]

Stoicism /'stəʊɪsɪz(ə)m/ *n.* **1** the philosophy of the Stoics. **2** (**stoicism**) a stoical attitude.

stoke /stəʊk/ *v.* (often foll. by *up*) **1 a** *tr.* feed and tend (a fire or furnace etc.). **b** *intr.* act as a stoker. **2** *intr. colloq.* consume food, esp. steadily and in large quantities. [back-formation from STOKER]

stokehold /'stəʊkhəʊld/ *n.* a compartment in a steamship, containing its boilers and furnace.

stokehole /'stəʊkhəʊl/ *n.* a space for stokers in front of a furnace.

stoker /'stəʊkə/ *n.* a person who tends the furnace on a steamship. [Dutch, via *stoken* 'stoke' from Middle Dutch *stoken* 'push, poke': related to STICK[1]]

stokes /stəʊks/ *n.* (*pl.* same) *Physics* the cgs unit of kinematic viscosity, corresponding to a dynamic viscosity of 1 poise and a density of 1 gram per cubic centimetre, equivalent to 10^{-4} square metres per second. [named after Sir G. G. *Stokes*, British physicist d. 1903]

STOL *abbr. Aeron.* short take-off and landing.

stole[1] /stəʊl/ *n.* **1** a woman's long garment like a scarf, worn over the shoulders. **2** a strip of silk etc. worn similarly as a vestment by a priest. [Old English *stol*, *stole* (originally a long robe), via Latin *stola* from Greek *stolē* 'equipment, clothing']

stole[2] *past* of STEAL.

stolen *past part.* of STEAL.

stolid /'stɒlɪd/ *adj.* **1** lacking or concealing emotion or animation. **2** not easily excited or moved. □ **stolidity** /-'lɪdɪti/ *n.* **stolidly** *adv.* **stolidness** *n.* [obsolete French *stolide* or Latin *stolidus*]

stolon /'stəʊlɒn/ *n.* **1** *Bot.* a horizontal stem or branch that takes root at points along its length, forming new plants. **2** *Zool.* a branched stemlike structure in some invertebrates such as corals. □ **stolonate** /-neɪt/ *adj.* **stoloniferous** /-'nɪf(ə)rəs/ *adj.* [Latin *stolo -onis*]

stoma /'stəʊmə/ *n.* (*pl.* **stomas** or **stomata** /-mətə/) **1** *Bot.* a minute pore in the epidermis of a leaf. **2 a** *Zool.* a small mouthlike opening in some lower animals. **b** *Surgery* a similar artificial orifice made in the abdominal wall. □ **stomal** *adj.* [modern Latin from Greek *stoma -atos* 'mouth']

stomach /'stʌmək/ *n.* & *v.* ● *n.* **1 a** the internal organ in which the first part of digestion occurs, being in man a pear-shaped enlargement of the alimentary canal linking the oesophagus to the small intestine. **b** any of several such organs in animals, esp. ruminants, in which there are four (cf. RUMEN, RETICULUM, OMASUM, ABOMASUM). **2 a** the belly, abdomen, or lower front of the body (*pit of the stomach*). **b** a protuberant belly (*what a stomach he has got!*). **3** (usu. foll. by *for*) **a** an appetite (for food). **b** liking, readiness, or inclination (for controversy, conflict, danger, or an undertaking) (*had* *no stomach for the fight*). ● *v.tr.* **1** find sufficiently palatable to swallow or keep down. **2** submit to or endure (an affront etc.) (usu. with *neg.*: *cannot stomach it*). □ **on an empty stomach** not having eaten recently. **on a full stomach** soon after a large meal. □ **stomachful** *n.* (*pl.* **-fuls**). **stomachless** *adj.* [Middle English *stomak* via Old French *stomaque, estomac* and Latin *stomachus* from Greek *stomakhos* 'gullet', from *stoma* 'mouth']

stomach-ache *n.* a pain in the belly or bowels.

stomacher /ˈstʌməkə/ *n. hist.* **1** a pointed front-piece of a woman's dress covering the breast and pit of the stomach, often jewelled or embroidered. **2** an ornament worn on the front of a bodice. [Middle English, probably from Old French *estomachier* (as STOMACH)]

stomachic /stəˈmakɪk/ *adj.* & *n.* ● *adj.* **1** of or relating to the stomach. **2** promoting the appetite or assisting digestion. ● *n.* a medicine or stimulant for the stomach. [French *stomachique* or Latin *stomachicus* from Greek *stomakhikos* (as STOMACH)]

stomach pump *n.* a syringe for forcing liquid etc. into or out of the stomach.

stomach tube *n.* a tube introduced into the stomach via the gullet for cleansing or emptying it.

stomach upset *n.* a temporary slight disorder of the digestive system.

stomata *pl.* of STOMA.

stomatal /ˈstəʊmət(ə)l, ˈstɒ-/ *adj. Bot.* & *Zool.* of or relating to a stoma or stomata.

stomatitis /stəʊməˈtʌɪtɪs, stɒ-/ *n. Med.* inflammation of the mucous membrane of the mouth.

stomatology /stəʊməˈtɒlədʒi, stɒ-/ *n.* the scientific study of the mouth or its diseases. □ **stomatological** /-təˈlɒdʒɪk(ə)l/ *adj.* **stomatologist** *n.*

stomp /stɒmp/ *v.* & *n.* ● *v.intr.* tread or stamp heavily. ● *n.* **1** a lively jazz dance with heavy stamping. **2** a tune or song suitable for such a dance. □ **stomper** *n.* [US dialect variant of STAMP]

stone /stəʊn/ *n., adj.,* & *v.* ● *n.* **1 a** solid non-metallic mineral matter, of which rock is made. **b** a piece of this, esp. a small piece. **2** *Building* **a** = LIMESTONE (*Portland stone*). **b** = SANDSTONE *n.* 2 (*Bath stone*). **3** *Mineral.* = PRECIOUS STONE. **4** a stony meteorite, an aerolite. **5** (often in *comb.*) a piece of stone of a definite shape or for a particular purpose (*tombstone*; *stepping stone*). **6 a** a thing resembling stone in hardness or form, e.g. the hard case of the kernel in some fruits. **b** *Med.* (often in *pl.*) a hard concretion in the body, a calculus (*gallstones*). **7** (*pl.* same) *Brit.* a unit of weight equal to 14 lb (6.35 kg). **8** a brownish-grey colour. ● *adj.* **1** made of stone. **2** of a brownish-grey colour. ● *v.tr.* **1 a** pelt with stones. **b** put to death by pelting with stones. **2** remove the stones from (fruit). **3** face or pave etc. with stone. □ **cast** (or **throw**) **stones** make aspersions on a person's character etc. **cast** (or **throw**) **the first stone** be the first to make an accusation, esp. though guilty oneself. **leave no stone unturned** try all possible means. **stone the crows** *Brit. slang* an exclamation of surprise or disgust. **a stone's throw** a short distance. □ **stoned** *adj.* (also in *comb.*). **stoneless** *adj.* **stoner** *n.* [Old English *stān*, from Germanic]

Stone Age *n.* a prehistoric period when weapons and tools were made of stone, succeeded in Europe by the Bronze Age.

stonechat /ˈstəʊntʃat/ *n.* any small brown bird of the thrush family with black and white markings, esp. *Saxicola torquata* with a call like stones being knocked together.

stone circle *n. Archaeol.* = CIRCLE *n.* 7.

stone-coal *n.* anthracite.

stone-cold *adj.* completely cold.

stone-cold sober *predic. adj.* completely sober.

stonecrop /ˈstəʊnkrɒp/ *n.* any succulent plant of the genus *Sedum*, usu. having yellow or white flowers and growing amongst rocks or in walls.

stone curlew *n.* any mottled brown and grey plover-like bird of the family Burhinidae, esp. *Burhinus oedicnemus*, inhabiting esp. stony open country.

stonecutter /ˈstəʊnkʌtə/ *n.* a person or machine that cuts or carves stone.

stoned /stəʊnd/ *adj. slang* under the influence of alcohol or drugs.

stone-dead *adj.* completely dead.

stone-deaf *adj.* completely deaf.

stonefish /ˈstəʊnfɪʃ/ *n.* (*pl.* usu. same) a venomous tropical fish, *Synanceia verrucosa*, with poison glands underlying its erect dorsal spines. Also called DEVILFISH.

stonefly /ˈstəʊnflʌɪ/ *n.* (*pl.* **-flies**) any insect of the order Plecoptera, with aquatic larvae found under stones.

stone fruit *n.* a fruit with flesh or pulp enclosing a stone.

stoneground /ˈstəʊngraʊnd/ *adj.* (of flour) ground with millstones.

stonehatch /ˈstəʊnhatʃ/ *n.* a ringed plover.

stone marten *n.* a brown marten with a white throat, *Martes foina*, of S. Eurasia. Also called *beech marten*.

stonemason /ˈstəʊnmeɪs(ə)n/ *n.* a person who cuts, prepares, and builds with stone. □ **stonemasonry** *n.*

stone parsley *n.* an umbelliferous hedge-plant, *Sison amomum*, with strongly scented seeds.

stone pine *n.* a S. European pine tree, *Pinus pinea*, with branches at the top spreading like an umbrella.

stone-pit *n.* a pit from which stones are dug; a quarry.

stonewall /ˈstəʊnwɔːl, stəʊnˈwɔːl/ *v.* **1** *tr.* & *intr.* obstruct (discussion or investigation) or be obstructive with evasive answers or denials etc. **2** *intr. Cricket* bat with excessive caution. □ **stonewaller** *n.* **stonewalling** *n.*

stoneware /ˈstəʊnwɛː/ *n.* a type of pottery which is impermeable and partly vitrified but opaque.

stonewashed /ˈstəʊnwɒʃd/ *adj.* (of a garment or fabric, esp. denim) washed with abrasives to produce a worn or faded appearance.

stoneweed /ˈstəʊnwiːd/ *n.* = GROMWELL.

stonework /ˈstəʊnwəːk/ *n.* **1** masonry. **2** the parts of a building made of stone. □ **stoneworker** *n.*

stonewort /ˈstəʊnwəːt/ *n.* **1** = STONE PARSLEY. **2** any freshwater alga of the genus *Chara*, with a calcareous deposit on the stem.

stonkered /ˈstɒŋkəd/ *adj. Austral.* & *NZ slang* utterly defeated or exhausted. [*stonk*, = a game of marbles, an artillery bombardment, of unknown origin]

stonking /ˈstɒŋkɪŋ/ *adj.* & *adv. Brit. slang* ● *adj.* considerable; exciting. ● *adv.* (as an intensifier) extremely. [*stonk* 'a marble, a military bombardment', perhaps imitative]

stony /ˈstəʊni/ *adj.* (**stonier**, **stoniest**) **1** full of or covered with stones (*stony soil*; *a stony road*). **2 a** hard, rigid. **b** cold, unfeeling, uncompromising (*a stony stare*; *a stony silence*). □ **stonily** *adv.* **stoniness** *n.* [Old English *stānig* (as STONE)]

stony-broke *adj. Brit. slang* entirely without money.

stony coral see CORAL *n.* 2.

stony-hearted *adj.* unfeeling, obdurate.

stood *past* and *past part.* of STAND.

stooge /stuːdʒ/ *n.* & *v. colloq.* ● *n.* **1** a butt or foil, esp. for a comedian. **2** an assistant or subordinate, esp. for routine or unpleasant work. **3** a compliant person; a puppet. ● *v.intr.* **1** (foll. by *for*) act as a stooge for. **2** (foll. by *about, around*, etc.) *Brit.* move about aimlessly. [20th c.: origin unknown]

stook /stʊk, stuːk/ *n.* & *v. Brit.* ● *n.* a group of sheaves of grain stood on end in a field. ● *v.tr.* arrange in stooks. [Middle English *stouk*, from or related to Middle Low German *stūke*]

stool /stuːl/ *n.* & *v.* ● *n.* **1** a seat without a back or arms, usu. for one person and consisting of a wooden slab on three or four legs or a single pedestal. **2 a** = FOOTSTOOL. **b** a low bench for kneeling on. **3** (usu. in *pl.*) = FAECES. **4** the root or stump of a tree or plant from which the shoots spring. **5** *US* a decoy-bird in hunting. ● *v.intr.* (of a plant) throw up shoots from the root. ▫ **fall between two stools** fail from vacillation between two courses etc. [Old English *stōl* from Germanic: related to STAND]

stoolball /'stu:lbɔ:l/ *n.* a team game played in the UK, with a bat and ball and pairs of batters scoring runs between bases.

stoolie /'stu:li/ *n. N. Amer. slang* a person acting as a stool-pigeon.

stool-pigeon *n.* **1** a person acting as a decoy (originally a decoy of a pigeon fixed to a stool). **2** a police informer.

stoop[1] /stu:p/ *v. & n.* ● *v.* **1** *tr.* bend (one's head or body) forwards and downwards. **2** *intr.* carry one's head and shoulders bowed forward. **3** *intr.* (foll. by *to* + infin.) deign or condescend. **4** *intr.* (foll. by *to*) descend or lower oneself to (some conduct) (*has stooped to crime*). **5** *intr.* (of a hawk etc.) swoop on its prey. ● *n.* **1** a stooping posture. **2** the downward swoop of a hawk etc. [Old English *stūpian* from Germanic: related to STEEP[1]]

stoop[2] /stu:p/ *n. N. Amer.* a porch or small veranda or set of steps in front of a house. [Dutch *stoep*: see STOEP]

stoop[3] var. of STOUP.

stop /stɒp/ *v. & n.* ● *v.* (**stopped**, **stopping**) **1** *tr.* **a** put an end to (motion etc.); completely check the progress or motion or operation of. **b** effectively hinder or prevent (*stopped them playing so loudly*). **c** discontinue (an action or sequence of actions) (*stopped playing*; *stopped my visits*). **2** *intr.* come to an end; cease (*supplies suddenly stopped*). **3** *intr.* cease from motion or speaking or action; make a halt or pause (*the car stopped at the lights*; *he stopped in the middle of a sentence*; *my watch has stopped*). **4** *tr.* **a** cause to cease action; defeat. **b** *Boxing* defeat (an opponent) by a knockout. **5** *tr. colloq.* receive (a blow etc.). **6** *intr.* remain; stay for a short time. **7** *tr.* (often foll. by *up*) block or close up (a hole or leak etc.). **8** *tr.* not permit or supply as usual; discontinue or withhold (*shall stop their wages*). **9** *tr.* (in full **stop payment of** or **on**) instruct a bank to withhold payment on (a cheque). **10** *tr. Brit.* put a filling in (a tooth). **11** *tr.* obtain the required pitch from (the string of a violin etc.) by pressing at the appropriate point with the finger. **12** *tr.* plug the upper end of (an organ pipe), giving a note an octave lower. **13** *tr. Bridge* be able to prevent opponents from taking all the tricks in (a suit). **14** *tr.* make (a sound) inaudible. **15** *tr. Boxing* **a** parry (a blow). **b** knock out (an opponent). **16** *tr.* pinch back (a plant). **17** *tr.* make (a clock, factory, etc.) cease working. **18** *tr. Brit.* provide with punctuation. **19** *tr. Naut.* make fast; stopper (a cable etc.). ● *n.* **1** the act or an instance of stopping; the state of being stopped (*put a stop to*; *the vehicle was brought to a stop*). **2** a place designated for a bus or train etc. to stop. **3** *Brit.* a punctuation mark, esp. = FULL STOP 1. **4** a device for stopping motion at a particular point. **5** a change of pitch effected by stopping a string. **6 a** (in an organ) a row of pipes of one character. **b** a knob etc. operating these. **7** a manner of speech adopted to produce a particular effect. **8** *Optics & Photog.* = DIAPHRAGM 3, 4. **9 a** the effective diameter of a lens. **b** a device for reducing this. **c** a unit of change of relative aperture or exposure (with a reduction of one stop equivalent to halving it). **10** a plosive consonant. **11** (in telegrams etc.) a full stop. **12** *Bridge* a card or cards stopping a suit. **13** *Naut.* a small line used as a lashing. ▫ **pull all the stops out** see PULL. **put a stop to** cause to end, esp. abruptly. **stop at nothing** be ruthless. **stop by** (also *absol.*) call at (a place). **stop dead** (or **short**) cease abruptly. **stop down** *Photog.* reduce the aperture of (a lens) with a diaphragm. **stop one's ears 1** put one's fingers in one's ears to avoid hearing. **2** refuse to listen. **stop a gap** serve to meet a temporary need. **stop a person's mouth** induce a person by bribery or other means to keep silent about something. **stop off** (or **over**) break one's journey. **stop out 1** stay out. **2** cover (part of an area) to prevent printing, etching, etc. **stop payment 1** *Brit.* declare oneself insolvent. **2** instruct a bank to withhold payment on a cheque etc. ▫ **stopless** *adj.* **stoppable** *adj.* [Old English *(for)stoppian* from West Germanic, from Late Latin *stuppare* STUFF: see ESTOP]

stopbank /'stɒpbaŋk/ *n. Austral. & NZ* an embankment built to prevent a river flooding.

stopcock /'stɒpkɒk/ *n.* an externally operated valve regulating the flow of a liquid or gas through a pipe etc.

stop-drill *n.* a drill with a shoulder limiting the depth of penetration.

stope /stəʊp/ *n.* a steplike part of a mine where ore etc. is being extracted. [apparently related to STEP *n.*]

stopgap /'stɒpgap/ *n.* (often *attrib.*) a temporary substitute.

stop-go *n.* **1** alternate stopping and restarting of progress. **2** *Brit.* the alternate restriction and stimulation of economic demand.

stop-knob *n. Mus.* a knob controlling an organ stop.

stop lamp *n. Brit.* a light on the rear of a vehicle showing when the brakes are applied.

stop light *n.* **1** a red traffic light. **2** = STOP LAMP.

stopoff /'stɒpɒf/ *n.* a break in one's journey.

stopover /'stɒpəʊvə/ *n.* = STOPOFF.

stoppage /'stɒpɪdʒ/ *n.* **1** the condition of being blocked or stopped. **2** a stopping (of pay). **3** a stopping or interruption of work in a factory etc.

stopper /'stɒpə/ *n. & v.* ● *n.* **1** a plug for closing a bottle etc. **2** a person or thing that stops something. **3** *Naut.* a rope or clamp etc. for checking and holding a rope cable or chain cable. ● *v.tr.* close or secure with a stopper. ▫ **put a stopper on 1** put an end to (a thing). **2** keep (a person) quiet.

stopping /'stɒpɪŋ/ *n. Brit.* a filling for a tooth.

stopple /'stɒp(ə)l/ *n. & v.* ● *n.* **1** a stopper or plug. **2** (in full **ear-stopple**) *US* an earplug. ● *v.tr.* close with a stopple. [Middle English: partly from STOP + -LE[1], partly from ESTOPPEL]

stop press *n. Brit.* **1** (often *attrib.*) late news inserted in a newspaper after printing has begun. **2** a column in a newspaper reserved for this.

stop valve *n.* a valve closing a pipe against the passage of liquid.

stop-volley *n. Tennis* a checked volley close to the net, dropping the ball dead on the other side.

stopwatch /'stɒpwɒtʃ/ *n.* a watch with a mechanism for recording elapsed time, used to time races etc.

storage /'stɔ:rɪdʒ/ *n.* **1 a** the storing of goods etc. **b** a particular method of storing or the space available for it. **2** the cost of storing. **3** the electronic retention of data in a computer etc.

storage battery *n.* (also **storage cell**) a battery (or cell) for storing electricity.

storage heater *n. Brit.* an electric heater accumulating heat outside peak hours for later release.

storax /'stɔ:raks/ *n.* **1 a** a fragrant resin, obtained from the tree *Styrax officinalis* and formerly used in perfume. **b** this tree. **2** (in full **Levant** or **liquid storax**) a balsam obtained from the tree *Liquidambar orientalis*. [Latin from Greek, variant of STYRAX]

store /stɔ:/ *n. & v.* ● *n.* **1** a quantity of something kept available for use (*a store of wine*; *a store of wit*). **2** (in *pl.*) **a** articles for a particular purpose accumulated for use (*naval stores*). **b** a supply of these or the place where they are kept. **3 a** = DEPARTMENT STORE. **b** esp. *N. Amer.* any retail outlet or shop. **c** (in *sing.* or *Brit. pl.*) a shop selling basic necessities (*general stores*). **4** esp. *Brit.* a warehouse for the temporary keeping of furniture etc. **5** *Brit.* a device in a computer for storing retrievable data; a memory. ● *v.tr.* **1** put (furniture etc.) in store. **2** (often foll. by *up, away*) accumulate (stores, energy, electricity, etc.) for future use. **3** stock or provide with something useful (*a mind stored with facts*). **4** (of a receptacle) have storage capacity for. **5** *Computing* enter or retain (data) for retrieval. ▫ **in store 1** kept in readiness. **2** coming in the future. **3** (foll. by *for*) destined or intended. **set** (or **lay** or **put**) **store by** (or **on**) consider important or valuable. ▫ **storable** *adj.*

storer *n.* [Middle English from obsolete *astore* (*n.* & *v.*) via Old French *estore*, *estorer* from Latin *instaurare* 'renew': cf. RESTORE]

store card *n.* a credit card issued by a store to its customers.

storefront /'stɔ:frʌnt/ *n.* esp. *N. Amer.* **1** the side of a shop facing the street. **2** a room at the front of a shop.

storehouse /'stɔ:haʊs/ *n.* a place where things are stored.

storekeeper /'stɔ:ki:pə/ *n.* **1** esp. *Brit.* a storeman. **2** *N. Amer.* a shopkeeper.

storeman /'stɔ:mən/ *n.* (*pl.* **-men**) *Brit.* a person responsible for stored goods.

storeroom /'stɔ:ru:m, -rʊm/ *n.* a room in which items are stored.

storey /'stɔ:ri/ *n.* (*US* also **story**) (*pl.* **-eys** or **-ies**) **1** any of the parts into which a building is divided horizontally; the whole of the rooms etc. having a continuous floor (*a third-storey window*; *a house of five storeys*). **2** a thing forming a horizontal division. □ **-storeyed** (in *comb.*) (also **-storied**). [Middle English from Anglo-Latin *historia* HISTORY (perhaps originally meaning a tier of painted windows or sculpture)]

storiated /'stɔ:rɪeɪtɪd/ *adj.* decorated with historical, legendary, or emblematic designs. □ **storiation** /-'eɪʃ(ə)n/ *n.* [shortening of HISTORIATED]

storied /'stɔ:rɪd/ *adj. literary* celebrated in or associated with stories or legends.

stork /stɔ:k/ *n.* **1** any long-legged large wading bird of the family Ciconiidae, esp. *Ciconia ciconia* with white plumage, black wing-tips, a long reddish beak, and red feet, nesting esp. on tall buildings in Europe. **2** this bird as the pretended bringer of babies. [Old English *storc*, probably related to STARK (from its rigid posture)]

stork's-bill *n.* a plant of the genus *Erodium*, having beaked fruits.

storm /stɔ:m/ *n.* & *v.* ● *n.* **1** a violent disturbance of the atmosphere with strong winds and usu. with thunder and rain or snow etc. **2** *Meteorol.* a wind of force 11 (and sometimes force 10) on the Beaufort scale (55–72 or 64–72 m.p.h.), between gale and hurricane. **3** a violent disturbance of the established order in human affairs. **4** (foll. by *of*) **a** a violent shower of missiles or blows. **b** an outbreak of applause, indignation, hisses, etc. (*they were greeted by a storm of abuse*). **5 a** a direct assault by troops on a fortified place. **b** the capture of a place by such an assault. ● *v.* **1** *intr.* (often foll. by *at*, *away*) talk violently, rage, bluster. **2** *intr.* (usu. foll. by *in*, *out of*, etc.) move violently or angrily (*stormed out of the meeting*). **3** *tr.* attack or capture by storm. **4** *intr.* (of wind, rain, etc.) rage; be violent. □ **storm in a teacup** *Brit.* great excitement over a trivial matter. **take by storm 1** capture by direct assault. **2** rapidly captivate (a person, audience, etc.). □ **stormless** *adj.* **stormproof** *adj.* [Old English from Germanic]

storm-bird *n.* = STORM PETREL 1.

stormbound /'stɔ:mbaʊnd/ *adj.* prevented by storms from leaving port or continuing a voyage.

storm centre *n.* **1** the point to which the wind blows spirally inward in a cyclonic storm. **2** a subject etc. upon which agitation or disturbance is concentrated.

storm cloud *n.* **1** a heavy rain cloud. **2** a threatening state of affairs (*storm clouds were gathering over Europe*).

storm-cock *n.* a mistle thrush.

storm-collar *n.* a high coat-collar that can be turned up and fastened.

storm cone *n. Brit.* a tarred-canvas cone hoisted as a warning of high wind, upright for the north and inverted for the south.

storm-door *n.* an additional outer door for protection in bad weather or winter.

storm-finch *n. Brit.* = STORM PETREL 1.

storm-glass *n.* a sealed tube containing a solution of which the clarity is thought to change when storms approach.

storming /'stɔ:mɪŋ/ *adj.* **1** that storms. **2** esp. *Sport slang* displaying outstanding vigour, speed, or skill.

storming-party *n.* a detachment of troops ordered to begin an assault.

storm lantern *n. Brit.* a hurricane lamp.

storm petrel *n.* **1** a small petrel, *Hydrobates pelagicus*, of the North Atlantic, with black and white plumage. **2** a person causing unrest.

storm-sail *n.* a sail of smaller size and stouter canvas than the corresponding one used in ordinary weather.

storm-signal *n.* a device warning of an approaching storm.

storm troops *n.pl.* **1** = SHOCK TROOPS. **2** *hist.* the Nazi political militia. □ **storm trooper** *n.*

storm window *n.* an additional outer sash window for protection in bad weather or winter.

stormy /'stɔ:mi/ *adj.* (**stormier**, **stormiest**) **1** of or affected by storms. **2** (of a wind etc.) violent, raging, vehement. **3** full of angry feeling or outbursts; lively, boisterous (*a stormy meeting*). □ **stormily** *adv.* **storminess** *n.*

stormy petrel *n.* = STORM PETREL.

story[1] /'stɔ:ri/ *n.* (*pl.* **-ies**) **1** an account of imaginary or past events; a narrative, tale, or anecdote. **2** the past course of the life of a person or institution etc. (*my story is a strange one*). **3** = STORYLINE. **4** facts or experiences that deserve narration. **5** *colloq.* a fib or lie. **6** a narrative or descriptive item of news. □ **the old** (or **same old**) **story** the familiar or predictable course of events. **the story goes** it is said. **to cut** (or **make**) **a long story short** a formula excusing the omission of details. [Middle English *storie* via Anglo-French *estorie* (Old French *estoire*) from Latin *historia* (as HISTORY)]

story[2] *US* var. of STOREY.

storyboard /'stɔ:rɪbɔ:d/ *n.* a displayed sequence of pictures etc. outlining the plan of a film, television advertisement, etc.

story book *n.* (hyphenated when *attrib.*) **1** a book of stories for children. **2** (*attrib.*) unreal, romantic (*a storybook ending*).

storyline /'stɔ:rɪlʌm/ *n.* the narrative or plot of a novel or play etc.

storyteller /'stɔ:rɪtelə/ *n.* **1** a person who tells stories. **2** *colloq.* a liar. □ **storytelling** *n.* & *adj.*

stoup /stu:p/ *n.* (also **stoop**) **1** a holy-water basin. **2** *archaic* a flagon, beaker, or drinking vessel. [Middle English from Old Norse *staup* (= Old English *stēap*) from Germanic: related to STEEP[2]]

stoush /staʊʃ/ *v.* & *n. Austral.* & *NZ slang* ● *v.tr.* **1** hit; fight with. **2** attack verbally. ● *n.* a fight; a beating. [19th c.: origin uncertain]

stout /staʊt/ *adj.* & *n.* ● *adj.* **1** rather fat; corpulent; bulky. **2** of considerable thickness or strength (*a stout stick*). **3** brave, resolute, vigorous (*a stout fellow*; *put up stout resistance*). ● *n.* a strong dark beer brewed with roasted malt or barley. □ **stoutish** *adj.* **stoutly** *adv.* **stoutness** *n.* [Middle English via Anglo-French & Old French dialect *stout* from West Germanic: perhaps related to STILT]

stout heart *n.* courage, resolve.

stout-hearted *adj.* courageous. □ **stout-heartedly** *adv.* **stout-heartedness** *n.*

stove[1] /stəʊv/ *n.* & *v.* ● *n.* **1** a closed apparatus burning fuel or electricity for heating or cooking. **2** *Brit.* a hothouse. ● *v.tr. Brit.* force or raise (plants) in a hothouse. [Middle English = sweating-room, via Middle Dutch, Middle Low German *stove*, Old High German *stuba* from Germanic: perhaps related to STEW[1]]

stove[2] *past* and *past part.* of STAVE *v.*

stove-enamel *n.* & *v. Brit.* ● *n.* a heatproof enamel produced by the treatment of enamelled objects in a stove. ● *v.tr.* (usu. as **stove-enamelled** *adj.*) treat by this process.

stove-pipe *n.* a pipe conducting smoke and gases from a stove to a chimney.

stove-pipe hat *n. colloq.* a tall silk hat.

stow /stəʊ/ *v.tr.* **1** pack (goods etc.) tidily and compactly. **2** *Naut.* place (a cargo or provisions) in its proper place and order. **3** fill (a receptacle) with articles compactly arranged. **4** (usu. in *imper.*) *slang* abstain or cease from (*stow the noise!*). □ **stow away 1** place (a thing) where it will not cause an obstruction. **2** be a stowaway on a ship etc. [Middle English, from BESTOW: in nautical use perhaps influenced by Dutch *stouwen*]

stowage /ˈstəʊɪdʒ/ *n.* **1** the act or an instance of stowing. **2** a place for this.

stowaway /ˈstəʊəweɪ/ *n.* a person who hides on board a ship or aircraft etc. to get free passage.

STP *abbr.* **1** Professor of Sacred Theology. **2** standard temperature and pressure.

str. *abbr.* **1** strait. **2** stroke (of an oar).

strabismus /strəˈbɪzməs/ *n. Med.* the abnormal condition of one or both eyes not correctly aligned in direction; a squint. □ **strabismal** *adj.* **strabismic** *adj.* [modern Latin from Greek *strabismos*, via *strabizō* 'squint' from *strabos* 'squinting']

Strad /strad/ *n. colloq.* a Stradivarius. [abbreviation]

straddle /ˈstrad(ə)l/ *v. & n.* ● *v.* **1** *tr.* **a** sit or stand across (a thing) with the legs wide apart. **b** be situated across or on both sides of (*the town straddles the border*). **2** *intr.* **a** sit or stand in this way. **b** (of the legs) be wide apart. **3** *tr.* part (one's legs) widely. **4** *tr.* drop shots or bombs short of and beyond (a target). **5** *tr.* vacillate between two policies etc. regarding (an issue). ● *n.* **1** the act or an instance of straddling. **2** *Stock Exch.* an option giving the holder the right of either calling for or delivering stock at a fixed price. □ **straddler** *n.* [alteration of *striddle*, back-formation from *striddlings* 'astride' (as STRIDE, -LING[2])]

Stradivarius /stradɪˈveːrɪəs/ *n.* a violin or other stringed instrument made by Antonio Stradivari of Cremona (d. 1737) or his followers. [Latinized from *Stradivari*]

strafe /strɑːf, streɪf/ *v. & n.* ● *v.tr.* **1** bombard; harass with gunfire, esp. from aircraft. **2** reprimand. **3** abuse. **4** thrash. ● *n.* an act of strafing. [jocular adaptation of German catchword (1914) *Gott strafe England* 'may God punish England']

straggle /ˈstrag(ə)l/ *v. & n.* ● *v.intr.* **1** lack or lose compactness or tidiness. **2** be or become dispersed or sporadic. **3** trail behind others in a march or race etc. **4** (of a plant, beard, etc.) grow long and loose. ● *n.* a body or group of straggling or scattered persons or things. □ **straggler** *n.* **straggly** *adj.* (**stragglier, straggliest**). [Middle English, perhaps from dialect *strake* 'go', related to STRETCH]

straight /streɪt/ *adj., n., & adv.* ● *adj.* **1 a** extending uniformly in the same direction; without a curve or bend etc. **b** *Geom.* (of a line) lying on the shortest path between any two of its points. **2** successive, uninterrupted (*three straight wins*). **3** in proper order or place or condition; duly arranged; level, symmetrical (*is the picture straight?*; *put things straight*). **4** honest, candid; not evasive (*a straight answer*). **5** (of thinking etc.) logical, unemotional. **6** (of drama etc.) serious as opposed to popular or comic; employing the conventional techniques of its art form. **7 a** unmodified. **b** (of a drink) undiluted. **8** *colloq.* **a** (of a person etc.) conventional or respectable. **b** heterosexual. **9** (of an arch) flat-topped. **10** (of a person's back) not bowed. **11** (of the hair) not curly or wavy. **12** (of a knee) not bent. **13** (of the legs) not bandy or knock-kneed. **14** (of a garment) not flared. **15** coming direct from its source. **16** (of an aim, look, blow, or course) going direct to the mark. ● *n.* **1** the straight part of something, esp. the concluding stretch of a racecourse. **2** a straight condition. **3** a sequence of five cards in poker. **4** *colloq.* **a** a conventional person. **b** a heterosexual. ● *adv.* **1** in a straight line; direct; without deviation or hesitation or circumlocution (*came straight from Paris*; *I told them straight*). **2** in the right direction, with a good aim (*shoot straight*). **3** correctly (*can't see straight*). **4** *archaic* at once or immediately. □ **go straight** live an honest life after being a criminal. **the straight and narrow** morally correct behaviour. **straight away** at once; immediately. **straight from the shoulder 1** (of a blow) well delivered. **2** (of a verbal attack) frank or direct. **straight off** (or **out**) *colloq.* without hesitation, deliberation, etc. (*cannot tell you straight off*). **straight up** *colloq.* **1** truthfully, honestly. **2** esp. *N. Amer.* unmixed, undiluted. □ **straightish** *adj.* **straightly** *adv.* **straightness** *n.* [Middle English, past part. of STRETCH]

straight angle *n.* an angle of 180°.

straightaway /streɪtəˈweɪ/ *adv., adj., & n.* ● *adv.* = *straight away*. ● *adj.* esp. *US* (of a course etc.) straight, direct. ● *n.* esp. *N. Amer.* a straight course or section.

straight-bred *adj.* not cross-bred.

straight chain *n. Chem.* a chain of atoms, esp. carbon atoms, that is neither branched nor formed into a ring (often, with hyphen, *attrib.*: *straight-chain hydrocarbon*).

straight-cut *adj.* (of tobacco) cut lengthwise into long silky fibres.

straight-edge *n.* a bar with one edge accurately straight, used for testing.

straight-eight *n.* **1** an internal-combustion engine with eight cylinders in line. **2** a vehicle having this.

straighten /ˈstreɪt(ə)n/ *v.tr. & intr.* **1** (often foll. by *out*) make or become straight. **2** (foll. by *up*) stand erect after bending. □ **straightener** *n.*

straight eye *n.* the ability to detect deviation from the straight.

straight face *n.* an intentionally expressionless face, esp. avoiding a smile though amused. □ **straight-faced** *adj.*

straight fight *n. Brit.* a simple contest between two opponents, esp. in an election.

straight flush *n. Cards* a flush that is a numerical sequence.

straightforward /streɪtˈfɔːwəd/ *adj.* **1** honest or frank. **2** esp. *Brit.* (of a task etc.) uncomplicated. □ **straightforwardly** *adv.* **straightforwardness** *n.*

straightjacket var. of STRAITJACKET.

straight-laced var. of STRAIT-LACED.

straight man *n.* a comedian's stooge.

straight-out *adj.* esp. *US* **1** uncompromising. **2** straightforward, genuine.

straight razor *n. US* a cut-throat razor.

straight-up *adj. colloq.* **1** true; trustworthy. **2** esp. *N. Amer.* unmixed, undiluted, unmodified. See also *straight up*.

straightway /ˈstreɪtweɪ/ *adv. archaic* = *straight away*.

strain[1] /streɪn/ *v. & n.* ● *v.* **1** *tr. & intr.* stretch tightly; make or become taut or tense. **2** *tr.* exercise (oneself, one's senses, a thing, etc.) intensely or excessively, press to extremes. **3 a** *intr.* make an intensive effort. **b** *intr.* (foll. by *after*) strive intensely for (*straining after perfection*). **4** *intr.* (foll. by *at*) tug, pull (*the dog strained at the leash*). **5** *intr.* hold out with difficulty under pressure (*straining under the load*). **6** *tr.* **a** distort from the true intention or meaning. **b** apply (authority, laws, etc.) beyond their province or in violation of their true intention. **7** *tr.* overtask or injure by overuse or excessive demands (*strain a muscle*; *strained their loyalty*). **8 a** *tr.* clear (a liquid) of solid matter by passing it through a sieve etc. **b** *tr.* (foll. by *out*) filter (solids) out from a liquid. **c** *intr.* (of a liquid) percolate. **9** *tr.* hug or squeeze tightly. **10** *tr.* use (one's ears, eyes, voice, etc.) to the best of one's power. ● *n.* **1 a** the act or an instance of straining. **b** the force exerted in this. **2** an injury caused by straining a muscle etc. **3 a** a severe demand on physical strength or resources. **b** the exertion needed to meet this (*is suffering from strain*). **4** (in *sing.* or *pl.*) a snatch or spell of music or poetry. **5** a tone or tendency in speech or writing (*more in the same strain*). **6** *Physics* **a** the condition of a body subjected to stress; molecular displacement. **b** a quantity measuring this, equal to the amount of deformation usu. divided by the original dimension. □ **at strain** (or **full strain**) exerted to the utmost. **strain every nerve** make every possible effort. **strain oneself 1** injure oneself by effort. **2** make undue efforts. □ **strainable** *adj.* [Middle English via Old French *estreindre estreign-* from Latin *stringere strict-* 'draw tight']

strain[2] /streɪn/ *n.* **1** a breed or stock of animals, plants, etc. **2** a moral tendency as part of a person's character (*a strain of aggression*). [Old English *strīon* from Germanic: related to Latin *struere* 'build']

strained /streɪnd/ *adj.* **1** constrained, forced, artificial. **2** (of a relationship) mutually distrustful or tense. **3** (of an interpretation) involving an unreasonable assumption; far-fetched, laboured.

strainer /'streɪnə/ *n.* a device for straining liquids, vegetables, etc.

strain gauge *n. Engin.* a device for indicating the strain of a material or structure at the point of attachment.

strait /streɪt/ *n. & adj.* ● *n.* **1** (in *sing.* or *pl.*) a narrow passage of water connecting two seas or large bodies of water. **2** (usu. in *pl.*) difficulty, trouble, or distress (usu. *in dire* or *desperate straits*). ● *adj. archaic* **1** narrow, limited; confined or confining. **2** strict or rigorous. □ **straitly** *adv.* **straitness** *n.* [Middle English *streit* via Old French *estreit* 'tight, narrow' from Latin *strictus* STRICT]

straiten /'streɪt(ə)n/ *v.* **1** *tr.* restrict in range or scope. **2** *tr.* (as **straitened** *adj.*) (esp. of circumstances) characterized by poverty. **3** *tr. & intr. archaic* make or become narrow.

straitjacket /'streɪtdʒakɪt/ *n. & v.* (also **straightjacket**) ● *n.* **1** a strong garment with long sleeves for confining the arms of a violent prisoner, mental patient, etc. **2** restrictive measures. ● *v.tr.* (**-jacketed**, **-jacketing**) **1** restrain with a straitjacket. **2** severely restrict.

strait-laced *adj.* (also **straight-laced**) severely virtuous; morally scrupulous; puritanical.

strake /streɪk/ *n.* **1** a continuous line of planking or plates from the stem to the stern of a ship. **2** a section of the iron rim of a wheel. [Middle English from Anglo-Latin *stracus, stracca*: probably related to Old English *streccan* STRETCH]

stramonium /strə'məʊnɪəm/ *n.* **1** datura. **2** the dried leaves of this plant used in the treatment of asthma. [modern Latin, perhaps from Tartar *turman* 'horse-medicine']

strand[1] /strand/ *v. & n.* ● *v.* **1** *tr. & intr.* run aground. **2** *tr.* (as **stranded** *adj.*) in difficulties, esp. without money or means of transport. ● *n.* esp. *poet.* the margin of a sea, lake, or river, esp. the foreshore. [Old English]

strand[2] /strand/ *n. & v.* ● *n.* **1** each of the threads or wires twisted round each other to make a rope or cable. **2 a** a single thread or strip of fibre. **b** a constituent filament. **3** a lock of hair. **4** an element or strain in any composite whole. ● *v.tr.* **1** break a strand in (a rope). **2** arrange in strands. [Middle English: origin unknown]

strange /streɪn(d)ʒ/ *adj. & adv.* ● *adj.* **1** unusual, peculiar, surprising, eccentric, novel. **2 a** (often foll. by *to*) unfamiliar, alien, foreign (*lost in a strange land*; *surrounded by strange faces*; *a taste strange to him*). **b** not one's own (*strange gods*). **3** (foll. by *to*) (of a person) unaccustomed to; unfamiliar with. **4** not at ease; out of one's element (*not having been invited, I felt strange*). ● *adv. colloq.* in a strange manner; strangely. □ **feel strange** be unwell. **strange to say** it is surprising or unusual (that). □ **strangely** *adv.* [Middle English via Old French *estrange* from Latin *extraneus* EXTRANEOUS]

strange attractor *n. Math.* an equation or fractal set representing a complex pattern of behaviour in a chaotic system.

strangeness /'streɪn(d)ʒnɪs/ *n.* **1** the state or fact of being strange or unfamiliar etc. **2** *Physics* a property of certain quarks that is conserved in strong interactions.

strange particle *n. Physics* a subatomic particle classified as having a non-zero value for strangeness.

stranger /'streɪn(d)ʒə/ *n.* **1** a person who does not know or is not known in a particular place or company. **2** (often foll. by *to*) a person one does not know (*was a complete stranger to me*). **3** (foll. by *to*) a person entirely unaccustomed to (a feeling, experience, etc.) (*no stranger to controversy*). **4** *Parl.* a person who is not a member or official of the House of Commons. [Middle English from Old French *estrangier*, ultimately from Latin (as STRANGE)]

strangle /'straŋg(ə)l/ *v.tr.* **1** squeeze the windpipe or neck of, esp. so as to kill. **2** hamper or suppress (a movement, impulse, cry, etc.). □ **strangler** *n.* [Middle English via Old French *estrangler* and Latin *strangulare* from Greek *straggalaō*, from *straggalē* 'halter': cf. *straggos* 'twisted']

stranglehold /'straŋg(ə)lhəʊld/ *n.* **1** a wrestling hold that throttles an opponent. **2** a deadly grip. **3** complete and exclusive control.

strangles /'straŋg(ə)lz/ *n.pl.* (usu. treated as *sing.*) an infectious streptococcal fever, esp. affecting the respiratory tract, in a horse, ass, etc. [pl. of *strangle* (n.) from STRANGLE]

strangulate /'straŋgjʊleɪt/ *v.tr.* **1** *Med.* prevent circulation through (a vein, intestine, etc.) by compression. **2** *Med.* remove (a tumour etc.) by binding with a cord. **3** (as **strangulated** *adj.*) (of a voice) sounding as though the speaker's throat is constricted. [Latin *strangulare strangulat-* (as STRANGLE)]

strangulated hernia *n. Med.* a hernia in which the protruding part is constricted, preventing circulation.

strangulation /straŋgjʊ'leɪʃ(ə)n/ *n.* **1** the act of strangling or the state of being strangled. **2** the act of strangulating. [Latin *strangulatio* (as STRANGULATE)]

strangury /'straŋgjʊri/ *n.* a condition in which urine is passed painfully and in drops. □ **strangurious** /-'gjʊərɪəs/ *adj.* [Middle English via Latin *stranguria* from Greek *straggouria*, from *stragx -ggos* 'drop squeezed out' + *ouron* 'urine']

strap /strap/ *n. & v.* ● *n.* **1** a strip of leather or other flexible material, often with a buckle or other fastening for holding things together etc. **2** a thing like this for keeping a garment in place. **3** a loop for grasping to steady oneself in a moving vehicle. **4 a** a strip of metal used to secure or connect. **b** a leaf of a hinge. **5** *Bot.* a tongue-shaped part in a floret. **6** (prec. by *the*) punishment by beating with a strap. ● *v.tr.* (**strapped**, **strapping**) **1** (often foll. by *down, up*, etc.) secure or bind with a strap. **2** beat with a strap. **3** (esp. as **strapped** *adj.*) (usu. foll. by *for*) *colloq.* subject to a shortage (*strapped for cash*). **4** (often foll. by *up*) *Brit.* close (a wound) or bind (a part) with adhesive plaster. □ **strappy** *adj.* [dialect form of STROP]

straphanger /'straphaŋə/ *n. colloq.* **1** a standing passenger in a bus or train. **2** a person who commutes to work by public transport. □ **strap-hang** *v.intr.*

strapless /'straplɪs/ *adj.* (of a garment) without straps, esp. shoulder straps.

strappado /strə'pɑːdəʊ, -eɪdəʊ/ *n.* (*pl.* **-os**) *hist.* a form of torture in which the victim is secured to a rope and made to fall from a height almost to the ground then stopped with a jerk; an application of this; the instrument used. [French *(e)strapade* from Italian *strappata*, from *strappare* 'snatch']

strapper /'strapə/ *n.* esp. *Austral.* a person who grooms racehorses.

strapping /'strapɪŋ/ *adj.* (esp. of a young person) large and sturdy.

strap-work *n.* ornamentation imitating plaited straps.

strata *pl.* of STRATUM.

■ **Usage** See Usage Note at STRATUM.

stratagem /'stratədʒəm/ *n.* **1** a cunning plan or scheme, esp. for deceiving an enemy. **2** trickery. [Middle English via French *stratagème* and Latin *stratagema* from Greek *stratēgēma*, via *stratēgeō* 'be a general' (*stratēgos*) from *stratos* 'army' + *agō* 'to lead']

stratal see STRATUM.

strategic /strə'ti:dʒɪk/ *adj.* **1** of or serving the ends of strategy; useful or important with regard to strategy (*strategic considerations*; *stragetic move*). **2** (of materials) essential in fighting a war. **3** (of bombing or weapons) done or for use against an enemy's home territory as a longer-term military objective (opp. TACTICAL 2). □ **strategical** *adj.* **strategically** *adv.* **strategics** *n.pl.* (usu. treated as *sing.*). [French *stratégique* from Greek *stratēgikos* (as STRATAGEM)]

strategic defence initiative *n.* a projected US system of defence against nuclear weapons, using satellites armed with lasers.

strategy /'stratɪdʒi/ *n.* (*pl.* **-ies**) **1** the art of war. **2 a** the management of an army or armies in a campaign. **b** the art of moving troops, ships, aircraft, etc. into favourable positions (cf. TACTICS 1). **c** an instance of this or a plan formed according to it. **3** a plan of action or policy in business or politics etc. (*economic strategy*). □ **strategist** *n.* [French *stratégie* from Greek *stratēgia* 'generalship', from *stratēgos*: see STRATAGEM]

strath /straθ/ *n. Sc.* a broad mountain valley. [Gaelic *srath*]

strathspey /straθ'speɪ/ *n.* **1** a slow Scottish dance. **2** the music for this. [*Strathspey*, valley of the river Spey]

straticulate /strə'tɪkjʊlət/ *adj. Geol.* (of rock formations) arranged in thin strata. [STRATUM, on the pattern of *vermiculate* etc.]

stratify /'stratɪfʌɪ/ *v.tr.* (**-ies, -ied**) **1** (esp. as **stratified** *adj.*) arrange, deposit, or form, in strata. **2 a** construct or devise in layers (*the author stratifies the plot*). **b** arrange in a hierarchical way. □ **stratification** /-fɪ'keɪʃ(ə)n/ *n.* [French *stratifier* (as STRATUM)]

stratigraphy /strə'tɪgrəfi/ *n. Geol.* & *Archaeol.* **1** the order and relative position of strata. **2** the study of this as a means of historical interpretation. □ **stratigrapher** *n.* **stratigraphic** /stratɪ'grafɪk/ *adj.* **stratigraphical** /stratɪ'grafɪk(ə)l/ *adj.* [STRATUM + -GRAPHY]

strato- /'stratəʊ/ *comb. form* denoting cloud formed in horizontal sheets or layers.

stratocirrus /stratəʊ'sɪrəs/ *n. Meteorol.* cloud resembling cirrostratus but more compact.

stratocracy /strə'tɒkrəsi/ *n.* (*pl.* **-ies**) **1** a military government. **2** domination by soldiers. [Greek *stratos* 'army' + -CRACY]

stratocumulus /stratəʊ'kju:mjʊləs/ *n. Meteorol.* cloud formed as a low layer of clumped or broken grey masses.

stratopause /'stratə(ʊ)pɔ:z/ *n.* the interface between the stratosphere and the ionosphere.

stratosphere /'stratəsfɪə/ *n.* a layer of atmospheric air above the troposphere extending to about 50 km above the earth's surface, in which the lower part changes little in temperature and the upper part increases in temperature with height (cf. IONOSPHERE). □ **stratospheric** /-'sfɛrɪk/ *adj.* [STRATUM + SPHERE, on the pattern of *atmosphere*]

stratum /'strɑ:təm, 'streɪtəm/ *n.* (*pl.* **strata** /-tə/) **1** esp. *Geol.* a layer or set of successive layers of any deposited substance. **2** an atmospheric layer. **3** a layer of tissue etc. **4 a** a social grade, class, etc. (*the various strata of society*). **b** *Statistics* each of the groups into which a population is divided in stratified sampling. □ **stratal** *adj.* [Latin, = something spread or laid down, neut. past part. of *sternere* 'strew']

▪ **Usage** It is incorrect (though a common error) to use *strata*, the plural form, for the singular *stratum*, i.e. it is correct to say *This stratum* (not *strata*) *of society has always exercised power*.

stratus /'strɑ:təs, 'streɪtəs/ *n. Meteorol.* cloud formed as a continuous horizontal grey sheet, often with rain or snow. [Latin, past part. of *sternere*: see STRATUM]

straw /strɔ:/ *n.* & *adj.* ● *n.* **1** dry cut stalks of grain for use as fodder or as material for thatching, packing, making hats, etc. **2** a single stalk or piece of straw. **3** a thin hollow paper or plastic tube for sucking drink from a glass etc. **4** an insignificant thing (*not worth a straw*). **5** the pale yellow colour of straw. **6** a straw hat. ● *adj.* **1** made of straw. **2** pale yellow. □ **catch** (or **clutch** or **grasp**) **at a straw** (or **straws**) resort in desperation to an utterly inadequate expedient. **draw the short straw** be chosen by lot, esp. for some disagreeable task. □ **strawy** *adj.* [Old English *strēaw* from Germanic: related to STREW]

strawberry /'strɔ:b(ə)ri/ *n.* & *adj.* ● *n.* (*pl.* **-ies**) **1 a** any plant of the genus *Fragaria*, esp. any of various cultivated varieties, with white flowers, trifoliate leaves, and runners. **b** the pulpy red edible fruit of this, having a seed-studded surface. **2** a deep pinkish-red colour. ● *adj.* of a deep pinkish-red colour. [Old English *strēa(w)berige*, *strēowberige* (as STRAW, BERRY): reason for the name unknown]

strawberry blonde *n.* & *adj.* ● *n.* **1** pinkish-blonde hair. **2** a woman with such hair. ● *adj.* (hyphenated when *attrib.*) of a pinkish-blonde colour.

strawberry mark *n.* a soft reddish birthmark.

strawberry pear *n.* **1** a W. Indian cactus, *Hylocereus undatus*. **2** the fruit of this.

strawberry roan *adj.* & *n.* ● *adj.* (of an animal's coat) chestnut mixed with white or grey. ● *n.* a strawberry roan animal.

strawberry tree *n.* an arbutus, *Arbutus unedo*, bearing strawberry-like fruit.

strawboard /'strɔ:bɔ:d/ *n.* a type of building board made of straw pulp faced with paper.

straw boss *n. US* an assistant foreman.

straw colour *n.* a pale yellow. □ **straw-coloured** *adj.*

straw in the wind *n.* a slight hint of future developments.

straw vote *n.* (also **straw poll**) an unofficial ballot as a test of opinion.

straw-worm *n.* a caddis-worm.

stray /streɪ/ *v.*, *n.*, & *adj.* ● *v.intr.* **1** wander from the right place; become separated from one's companions etc.; go astray. **2** deviate morally. **3** (as **strayed** *adj.*) that has gone astray. ● *n.* **1** a person or thing that has strayed, esp. a domestic animal. **2** (esp. in *pl.*) electrical phenomena interfering with radio reception. ● *adj.* **1** strayed or lost. **2** isolated; found or occurring occasionally (*a stray customer or two*; *hit by a stray bullet*). **3** *Physics* wasted or unwanted (*eliminate stray magnetic fields*). □ **strayer** *n.* [Middle English from Anglo-French & Old French *estrayer* (*v.*) and Anglo-French *strey* (*n.* & *adj.*) from Old French *estraié* (as ASTRAY)]

streak /stri:k/ *n.* & *v.* ● *n.* **1** a long thin usu. irregular line or band, esp. distinguished by colour (*black with red streaks*; *a streak of light above the horizon*). **2** a strain or element in a person's character (*has a streak of mischief*). **3** a spell or series (*a winning streak*). **4** a line of bacteria etc. placed on a culture medium. ● *v.* **1** *tr.* mark with streaks. **2** *intr.* move very rapidly. **3** *intr. colloq.* run naked in a public place as a stunt. □ **streaker** *n.* **streaking** *n.* [Old English *strica* 'pen-stroke' from Germanic: related to STRIKE]

streak of lightning *n.* a sudden prominent flash of lightning.

streaky /'stri:ki/ *adj.* (**streakier**, **streakiest**) **1** full of streaks. **2** *Brit.* (of bacon) with alternate streaks of fat and lean. □ **streakily** *adv.* **streakiness** *n.*

stream /stri:m/ *n.* & *v.* ● *n.* **1** a flowing body of water, esp. a small river. **2 a** the flow of a fluid or of a mass of people (*a stream of lava*). **b** (in *sing.* or *pl.*) a large quantity of something that flows or moves along. **3** a current or direction in which things are moving or tending (*against the stream*). **4** *Brit.* a group of schoolchildren taught together as being of similar ability for a given age. ● *v.* **1** *intr.* flow or move as a stream. **2** *intr.* run with liquid (*my eyes were streaming*). **3** *intr.* (of a banner or hair etc.) wave or be blown behind in the wind. **4** *tr.* emit a stream of (blood etc.). **5** *tr. Brit.* arrange (schoolchildren) in streams. □ **go with the stream** *Brit.* do as others do. **on stream** (of a factory etc.) in operation. □ **streamless** *adj.* **streamlet** *n.* [Old English *strēam*, from Germanic]

stream-anchor *n.* an anchor intermediate in size between a bower and a kedge, esp. for use in warping.

streamer /ˈstriːmə/ *n.* **1** a long narrow flag. **2** a long narrow strip of ribbon or paper, esp. in a coil that unrolls when thrown. **3** a banner headline. **4** (in *pl.*) the aurora borealis or australis.

streamline /ˈstriːmlʌm/ *v., n., & adj.* ● *v.tr.* **1** give (a vehicle, an object) a smooth shape which minimizes its resistance to the flow of a surrounding fluid (e.g. air, water). **2** make (an organization, process, etc.) simple or more efficient or better organized. ● *n.* a line along which the flow of a moving fluid is least turbulent. ● *adj.* **1** (of flow) free from turbulence. **2** (of an object) streamlined in shape. □ **streamlined** *adj.*

stream of consciousness *n.* **1** *Psychol.* a person's thoughts and conscious reactions to events perceived as a continuous flow. **2** a literary style depicting events in such a flow in the mind of a character.

street /striːt/ *n.* **1 a** a public road in a city, town, or village. **b** this with the houses or other buildings on each side. **2** the persons who live or work on a particular street. □ **in the street 1** in the area outside the houses. **2** *Brit.* (of Stock Exchange business) done after closing time. **not in the same street with** *Brit. colloq.* utterly inferior to in ability etc. **on the streets 1** living by prostitution. **2** homeless. **streets ahead** (often foll. by *of*) *Brit. colloq.* much superior (to). **up** (or **right up**) **one's street** esp. *Brit. colloq.* **1** within one's range of interest or knowledge. **2** to one's liking. □ **streeted** *adj.* (also in *comb.*). **streetward** *adj. & adv.* [Old English *strǣt* from Late Latin *strāta* (*via*) 'paved (way)', fem. past part. of *sternere* 'lay down']

street Arab *n.* **1** a homeless child. **2** an urchin.

streetcar /ˈstriːtkɑː/ *n. N. Amer.* a tram.

street credibility *n.* (also *colloq.* **street cred**) *Brit.* acceptability among young fashionable urban people.

street door *n.* a main outer house-door opening on the street.

street entertainer *n.* a person who entertains people in the street for money, esp. with music, acting, or juggling. □ **street entertainment** *n.*

street furniture *n.* postboxes, road signs, litter bins, and other objects placed in the street for public use.

street jewellery *n. Brit.* enamel advertising plates as collectors' items.

street lamp *n.* = STREET LIGHT.

street light *n.* a light or lamp esp. on a lamp-post, serving to illuminate a road etc. □ **street lighting** *n.*

street trader *n.* a person who trades in the street, either from a market stall or often from an improvised pitch.

street value *n.* the value of esp. drugs sold illicitly.

streetwalker /ˈstriːtwɔːkə/ *n.* a prostitute seeking customers in the street. □ **streetwalking** *n. & adj.*

streetwise /ˈstriːtwʌɪz/ *adj.* esp. *N. Amer.* familiar with the ways of modern urban life.

strelitzia /strəˈlɪtsɪə/ *n.* a southern African plant of the genus *Strelitzia*, with showy irregular flowers having a long projecting tongue. [named after Charlotte of Mecklenburg-*Strelitz* (d. 1818), queen of George III]

strength /strɛŋθ, strɛŋkθ/ *n.* **1** the state of being strong; the degree to which, or respect in which, a person or thing is strong. **2 a** a person or thing affording strength or support. **b** an attribute making for strength of character (*patience is your great strength*). **3** the number of persons present or available. **4** a full complement (*below strength*). □ **from strength** from a strong position. **from strength to strength** with ever-increasing success. **in strength** in large numbers. **on the strength of** relying on; on the basis of. **the strength of** the essence or main features of. □ **strengthless** *adj.* [Old English *strengthu* from Germanic (as STRONG)]

strengthen /ˈstrɛŋθ(ə)n, -ŋkθ(ə)n/ *v.tr. & intr.* make or become stronger. □ **strengthen a person's hand** (or **hands**) encourage a person to vigorous action. □ **strengthener** *n.*

strenuous /ˈstrɛnjʊəs/ *adj.* **1** requiring or using great effort. **2** energetic or unrelaxing. □ **strenuously** *adv.* **strenuousness** *n.* [Latin *strenuus* 'brisk']

strep /strɛp/ *n. colloq.* = STREPTOCOCCUS. [abbreviation]

streptocarpus /strɛptə(ʊ)ˈkɑːpəs/ *n.* a southern African plant of the genus *Streptocarpus*, with funnel-shaped flowers, often violet or pink, and spirally twisted fruits. [Greek *streptos* 'twisted' + *karpos* 'fruit']

streptococcus /strɛptəˈkɒkəs/ *n.* (*pl.* **streptococci** /-ˈkɒk(s)ʌɪ, -ˈkɒk(s)iː/) any bacterium of the genus *Streptococcus*, usu. found joined in chains, some of which cause infectious diseases. □ **streptococcal** *adj.* [Greek *streptos* 'twisted' (from *strephō* 'turn') + COCCUS]

streptokinase /strɛptəˈkʌɪneɪz/ *n. Med. & Pharm.* an enzyme produced by some streptococci and used to treat inflammation and blood clots. [STREPTOCOCCUS + Greek *kinein* 'move' + -ASE]

streptomycin /strɛptəˈmʌɪsɪn/ *n.* an antibiotic produced by the bacterium *Streptomyces griseus*, effective against many disease-producing bacteria. [Greek *streptos* (as STREPTOCOCCUS) + *mukēs* 'fungus']

stress /strɛs/ *n. & v.* ● *n.* **1 a** pressure or tension exerted on a material object. **b** a quantity measuring this. **2 a** a demand on physical or mental energy. **b** distress caused by this (*suffering from stress*). **3 a** emphasis (*the stress was on the need for success*). **b** accentuation; emphasis laid on a syllable or word. **c** an accent, esp. the principal one in a word (*the stress is on the first syllable*). **4** *Mech.* force per unit area exerted between contiguous bodies or parts of a body. ● *v.tr.* **1** lay stress on; emphasize. **2** subject to mechanical or physical or mental stress. □ **lay stress on** indicate as important. □ **stressless** *adj.* [Middle English from DISTRESS, or partly from Old French *estresse* 'narrowness, oppression', ultimately from Latin *strictus* STRICT]

stress disease *n.* a disease resulting from continuous mental stress.

stressed out *adj. colloq.* debilitated or exhausted as a result of stress.

stressful /ˈstrɛsfʊl, -f(ə)l/ *adj.* causing stress; mentally tiring (*had a stressful day*). □ **stressfully** *adv.* **stressfulness** *n.*

stretch /strɛtʃ/ *v. & n.* ● *v.* **1** *tr. & intr.* draw or be drawn or admit of being drawn out into greater length or size. **2** *tr. & intr.* make or become taut. **3** *tr. & intr.* place or lie at full length or spread out (*with a canopy stretched over them*). **4 a** *tr.* extend (an arm, leg, etc.). **b** *intr. & refl.* thrust out one's limbs and tighten one's muscles after being relaxed. **5** *intr.* have a specified length or extension; extend (*farmland stretches for many miles*). **6** *tr.* strain or exert extremely or excessively; exaggerate (*stretch the truth*). **7** *tr.* (as **stretched** *adj.*) elongated or extended. ● *n.* **1** a continuous extent or expanse or period (*a stretch of open road*). **2** the act or an instance of stretching; the state of being stretched. **3** (*attrib.*) able to stretch; elastic (*stretch fabric*). **4 a** *colloq.* a period of imprisonment. **b** a period of service. **5** *N. Amer.* the straight side of a racetrack. **6** *Naut.* the distance covered on one tack. **7** (usu. *attrib.*) *colloq.* an aircraft or motor vehicle modified so as to have extra seating or storage capacity (*stretch limousine*). □ **at full stretch** working to capacity. **at a stretch 1** in one continuous period (*slept for two hours at a stretch*). **2** with much effort. **stretch one's legs** exercise oneself by walking. **stretch out 1** extend (a hand or foot etc.). **2** last for a longer period; prolong. **3** make (money etc.) last for a sufficient time. **stretch a point** agree to something not normally allowed. **stretch one's wings** see WING. □ **stretchable** *adj.* **stretchability** /-əˈbɪlɪti/ *n.* **stretchy** *adj.* **stretchiness** *n.* [Old English *streccan* from West Germanic: cf. STRAIGHT]

stretcher /'stretʃə/ *n.* & *v.* ● *n.* **1** a framework of two poles with canvas etc. between, for carrying sick, injured, or dead persons in a lying position. **2** a brick or stone laid with its long side along the face of a wall (cf. HEADER 3). **3** a board in a boat against which a rower presses the feet. **4** a rod or bar as a tie between chair legs etc. **5** a wooden frame over which a canvas is stretched ready for painting. **6** *archaic slang* an exaggeration or lie. ● *v.tr.* (often foll. by *off*) convey (a sick or injured person) on a stretcher.

stretcher-bearer *n.* a person who helps to carry a stretcher, esp. in war or at a major accident.

stretch marks *n.pl.* marks on the skin resulting from a gain of weight, or on the abdomen after pregnancy.

stretto /'stretəʊ/ *adv. Mus.* in quicker time. [Italian, = narrow]

strew /stru:/ *v.tr.* (*past part.* **strewn** or **strewed**) **1** scatter or spread about over a surface. **2** (usu. foll. by *with*) spread (a surface) with scattered things. □ **strewer** *n.* [Old English *stre(o)wian*]

strewth /stru:θ/ *int.* (also **struth, 'str-**) esp. *Brit. colloq.* a mild oath. [*God's truth*]

stria /'strʌɪə/ *n.* (*pl.* **striae** /-i:/) **1** *Anat., Zool., Bot.,* & *Geol.* **a** a linear mark on a surface. **b** a slight ridge, furrow, or score. **2** *Archit.* a fillet between the flutes of a column. [Latin]

striate *adj.* & *v.* ● *adj.* /'strʌɪət, 'strʌɪeɪt/ (also **striated** /-eɪtɪd/) *Anat., Zool., Bot.,* & *Geol.* marked with striae. ● *v.tr.* /strʌɪ'eɪt/ mark with striae. □ **striation** /strʌɪ'eɪʃ(ə)n/ *n.*

striated muscle *n. Anat.* muscle with the contractile fibrils in the cells aligned to form stripes visible in a microscope, attached to bones by tendons and under voluntary control. Also called *skeletal muscle.*

stricken /'strɪk(ə)n/ *adj.* **1** affected or overcome with illness or misfortune etc. (*stricken with measles*; *grief-stricken*). **2** (often foll. by *from* etc.) *US Law* deleted. **3** levelled with a strickle. □ **stricken in years** *archaic* enfeebled by age. [archaic past part. of STRIKE]

strickle /strɪk(ə)l/ *n.* **1** a rod used in strike-measure. **2** a whetting tool. [Old English *stricel*, related to STRIKE]

strict /strɪkt/ *adj.* **1** precisely limited or defined; without exception or deviation (*lives in strict seclusion*). **2** requiring complete compliance or exact performance; enforced rigidly (*gave strict orders*). □ **strictness** *n.* [Latin *strictus*, past part. of *stringere* 'tighten']

strict counterpoint *n.* an academic exercise in writing counterpoint, not necessarily intended as a composition.

strictly /'strɪk(t)li/ *adv.* **1** in a strict manner. **2** (also **strictly speaking**) applying words in their strict sense (*he is, strictly, an absconder*). **3** esp. *N. Amer. colloq.* definitely.

stricture /'strɪktʃə/ *n.* **1** (usu. in *pl.*; often foll. by *on, upon*) a critical or censorious remark. **2** *Med.* a morbid narrowing of a canal or duct in the body. □ **strictured** *adj.* [Middle English from Latin *strictura* (as STRICT)]

stride /strʌɪd/ *v.* & *n.* ● *v.* (*past* **strode** /strəʊd/; *past part.* **stridden** /'strɪd(ə)n/) **1** *intr.* & *tr.* walk with long firm steps. **2** *tr.* cross with one step. **3** *tr.* bestride; straddle. ● *n.* **1 a** a single long step. **b** the length of this. **2** a person's gait as determined by the length of stride. **3** (usu. in *pl.*) progress (*has made great strides*). **4** a settled rate of progress (*get into one's stride*; *be thrown out of one's stride*). **5** (in *pl.*) *Brit. slang* trousers. **6** the distance between the feet parted either laterally or as in walking. □ **take in one's stride 1** clear (an obstacle) without changing one's gait to jump. **2** manage without difficulty. □ **strider** *n.* [Old English *strīdan*]

strident /'strʌɪd(ə)nt/ *adj.* loud and harsh. □ **stridency** *n.* **stridently** *adv.* [Latin *stridere strident-* 'creak']

stridulate /'strɪdjʊleɪt/ *v.intr.* (of insects, esp. the cicada and grasshopper) make a shrill sound by rubbing esp. the legs or wing-cases together. □ **stridulant** *adj.* **stridulation** /-'leɪʃ(ə)n/ *n.* [French *striduler* from Latin *stridulus* 'creaking' (as STRIDENT)]

strife /strʌɪf/ *n.* **1** conflict; struggle between opposed persons or things. **2** *Austral. colloq.* trouble of any kind. [Middle English from Old French *estrif*: cf. Old French *estriver* STRIVE]

strigil /'strɪdʒɪl/ *n.* **1** *Gk & Rom. Antiq.* a skin-scraper used by bathers after exercise. **2** a structure on the leg of an insect used to clean its antennae etc. [Latin *strigilis* from *stringere* 'graze']

strigose /'strʌɪgəʊs/ *adj.* **1** (of leaves etc.) having short stiff hairs or scales. **2** (of an insect etc.) streaked, striped, or ridged. [Latin *striga* 'swath, furrow']

strike /strʌɪk/ *v.* & *n.* ● *v.* (*past* **struck** /strʌk/; *past part.* **struck** or *archaic* **stricken** /'strɪk(ə)n/) **1 a** *tr.* subject to an impact. **b** *tr.* deliver (a blow) or inflict a blow on (also with double object: *struck him a blow*). **2** *tr.* come or bring sharply into contact with (*the ship struck a rock*). **3** *tr.* propel or divert with a blow (*struck the ball into the pond*). **4** *intr.* (foll. by *at*) try to hit. **5** *tr.* cause to penetrate (*struck terror into him*). **6** *tr.* ignite (a match) or produce (sparks etc.) by rubbing. **7** *tr.* make (a coin) by stamping. **8** *tr.* produce (a musical note) by striking. **9 a** *tr.* (also *absol.*) (of a clock) indicate (the time) by the sounding of a chime etc. **b** *intr.* (of time) be indicated in this way. **10** *tr.* **a** attack or affect suddenly (*was struck with sudden terror*). **b** (of a disease) afflict. **11** *tr.* cause to become suddenly (*was struck dumb*). **12** *tr.* reach or achieve (*strike a balance*). **13** *tr.* agree on (a bargain). **14** *tr.* assume (an attitude or pose) suddenly and dramatically. **15** *tr.* **a** discover or come across. **b** find (oil etc.) by drilling. **c** encounter (an unusual thing etc.). **16** *tr.* come to the attention of; occur to (*it strikes me as silly*; *an idea suddenly struck me*). **17 a** *intr.* (of employees) engage in a strike; cease work as a protest. **b** *tr. N. Amer.* act in this way against (an employer). **18 a** *tr.* lower or take down (a flag or tent etc.). **b** *intr.* signify surrender by striking a flag; surrender. **19** *intr.* take a specified direction (*struck east*). **20** *tr.* (also *absol.*) secure a hook in the mouth of (a fish) by jerking the tackle. **21** *tr.* (of a snake) wound with its fangs. **22** *intr.* (of oysters) attach themselves to a bed. **23 a** *tr.* insert (a cutting of a plant) in soil to take root. **b** *tr.* (also *absol.*) (of a plant or cutting etc.) put forth (roots). **24** *tr.* level (grain etc. or the measure) in strike-measure. **25** *tr.* **a** ascertain (a balance) by deducting credit or debit from the other. **b** arrive at (an average, state of balance) by equalizing all items. **26** *tr.* compose (a jury) esp. by allowing both sides to reject the same number. ● *n.* **1** the act or an instance of striking. **2 a** the organized refusal by employees to work until some grievance is remedied. **b** a similar refusal to participate in some other expected activity. **3 a** a discovery of oil, ore, etc. by drilling, mining, etc. **b** a sudden find or success (*a lucky strike*). **4** an attack, esp. from the air. **5** *Baseball* a batter's unsuccessful attempt to hit a pitched ball, or another event counting equivalently against a batter. **6** the act of knocking down all the pins with the first ball in bowling. **7** horizontal direction in a geological structure. **8** a strickle. □ **on strike** taking part in an industrial etc. strike. **strike at the root** (or **roots**) **of** see ROOT[1]. **strike back 1** strike or attack in return. **2** (of a gas burner) burn from an internal point before the gas has become mixed with air. **strike down 1** knock down. **2** bring low; afflict (*struck down by a virus*). **strike home 1** deal an effective blow. **2** have an intended effect (*my words struck home*). **strike in 1** intervene in a conversation etc. **2** (of a disease) attack the interior of the body from the surface. **strike it rich** *colloq.* find a source of abundance or success. **strike a light 1** produce a light by striking a match. **2** (as *int.*) *Brit. colloq.* an expression of surprise, disgust, etc. **strike lucky** (or **strike it lucky**) *Brit.* have a lucky success. **strike off 1** remove with a stroke. **2** delete (a name etc.) from a list. **3** produce (copies of a document). **strike oil 1** find petroleum by sinking a shaft. **2** attain prosperity or success. **strike out 1** hit out. **2** act vigorously. **3** delete (an item or name etc.). **4** set off or begin (*struck out eastwards*). **5** use the arms and legs in swimming. **6** forge or devise (a plan etc.). **7** *Baseball* **a** dismiss (a batter) by means of three strikes. **b** be dismissed in this way. **strike through** delete (a word etc.) with a stroke of one's pen. **strike up 1** start (an acquaintance, conversation, etc.) esp. casually. **2** (also *absol.*) begin playing (a tune etc.). **strike upon 1** have (an idea etc.) luckily occur to one. **2** (of light) illuminate. **strike while the iron is hot** act promptly at a good opportunity. **struck on** *Brit. colloq.* infatuated with. □ **strikable** *adj.* [Old English *strīcan* 'go, stroke', from West Germanic]

strike-bound *adj.* immobilized or closed by a strike.

strike-breaker *n.* a person working or employed in place of others who are on strike. □ **strike-break** *v.intr.* (usu. as **strike-breaking** *n.*).

strike call *n.* an invitation to workers by union representatives to go on strike.

strike force *n.* **1** a military or police force ready for rapid effective action. **2** *Football* the forwards in a team.

strike-measure *n.* measurement by passing a rod across the top of a heaped container to ensure that it is exactly full.

strike-out *n. Baseball* an out called when a batter has made three strikes.

strike pay *n.* an allowance paid to strikers by their trade union.

striker /'strʌɪkə/ *n.* **1** a person or thing that strikes. **2** an employee on strike. **3** *Sport* the player who is to strike, or who is to be the next to strike, the ball. **4** *Football* an attacking player positioned well forward in order to score goals. **5** *Brit.* a device striking the primer in a gun.

strike rate *n.* success rate, esp. in scoring goals or runs.

strike-slip fault *n. Geol.* a fault in which rock strata are displaced mainly in a horizontal direction, parallel to the line of the fault.

strike zone *n. Baseball* an imaginary rectangle extending from the armpits to the knees of a batter.

striking /'strʌɪkɪŋ/ *adj.* & *n.* ● *adj.* **1** impressive; attracting attention. **2** (of a clock) making a chime to indicate the hours etc. ● *n.* the act or an instance of striking. □ **within striking distance** near enough to hit or achieve. □ **strikingly** *adv.* **strikingness** *n.*

striking-circle *n.* (in hockey) an elongated semicircle in front of the goal, from within which the ball must be hit in order to score.

striking force *n.* a military body ready to attack at short notice.

strimmer /'strɪmə/ *n. Brit. propr.* an electrically powered grass trimmer with a nylon cutting cord which rotates rapidly on a spindle.

Strine /strʌɪn/ *n.* **1** a comic transliteration of Australian speech, e.g. *Emma Chissitt* = 'How much is it?'. **2** (esp. uneducated) Australian English. [= *Australian* in Strine]

string /strɪŋ/ *n.* & *v.* ● *n.* **1** twine or narrow cord. **2** a piece of this or of similar material used for tying or holding together, pulling, etc. **3** a length of catgut or wire etc. on a musical instrument, producing a note by vibration. **4 a** (in *pl.*) the stringed instruments in an orchestra etc. **b** (*attrib.*) relating to or consisting of stringed instruments (*string quartet*). **5** (in *pl.*) an awkward condition or complication (*the offer has no strings*). **6** a set of things strung together; a series or line of persons or things (*a string of beads*; *a string of oaths*). **7** a group of racehorses trained at one stable. **8** a tough piece connecting the two halves of a bean-pod etc. **9** a piece of catgut etc. interwoven with others to form the head of a tennis etc. racket. **10** = STRINGBOARD. **11 a** a hypothetical one-dimensional subatomic particle having the dynamical properties of a flexible loop. **b** in cosmology, a hypothetical threadlike concentration of energy within the struture of space-time. **12** *Computing* a linear sequence of characters, records, or data. ● *v.* (*past* and *past part.* **strung** /strʌŋ/) **1** *tr.* supply with a string or strings. **2** *tr.* tie with string. **3** *tr.* thread (beads etc.) on a string. **4** *tr.* arrange in or as a string. **5** *tr.* remove the strings from (a bean). **6** *tr.* place a string ready for use on (a bow). **7** *tr.* esp. *N. Amer. slang* hoax. **8** *intr.* (of glue etc.) become stringy. **9** *intr. Billiards* make the preliminary strokes that decide which player begins. □ **have two** (or **many**) **strings to one's bow** see BOW[1]. **on a string** under one's control or influence. **string along** *colloq.* **1** deceive, esp. by appearing to comply with (a person). **2** (often foll. by *with*) keep company (with). **string out** extend; prolong (esp. unduly). **string up 1** hang up on strings etc. **2** kill by hanging. **3** (usu. as **strung up** *adj.*) *Brit.* make tense. □ **stringless** *adj.* **stringlike** *adj.* [Old English *streng* from Germanic: related to STRONG]

string bass *n. Mus.* a double bass.

string bean *n.* **1** any of various beans eaten in their fibrous pods, esp. runner beans or French beans. **2** *colloq.* a tall thin person.

stringboard /'strɪŋbɔːd/ *n.* a supporting timber or skirting in which the ends of the steps in a staircase are set.

string-course *n.* a raised horizontal band or course of bricks etc. on a building.

stringed /strɪŋd/ *adj.* (of musical instruments) having strings (also in *comb.*: *twelve-stringed guitar*).

stringendo /strɪn'dʒɛndəʊ/ *adj.* & *adv. Mus.* with increasing speed. [Italian from *stringere* 'to press' (as STRINGENT)]

stringent /'strɪn(d)ʒ(ə)nt/ *adj.* **1** (of rules etc.) strict, precise; requiring exact performance; leaving no loophole or discretion. **2** (of a money market etc.) tight; hampered by scarcity; unaccommodating; hard to operate in. □ **stringency** *n.* **stringently** *adv.* [Latin *stringere* 'draw tight']

stringer /'strɪŋə/ *n.* **1** a longitudinal structural member in a framework, esp. of a ship or aircraft. **2** *colloq.* a newspaper correspondent not on the regular staff. **3** = STRINGBOARD.

stringhalt /'strɪŋhɔːlt/ *n.* spasmodic movement of a horse's hind leg.

string-piece *n.* a long timber supporting and connecting the parts of a framework.

string tie *n.* a very narrow necktie.

string vest *n.* a vest with large meshes.

stringy /'strɪŋi/ *adj.* (**stringier**, **stringiest**) **1** (of food etc.) fibrous, tough. **2** of or like string. **3** (of a person) tall, wiry, and thin. **4** (of a liquid) viscous; forming strings. □ **stringily** *adv.* **stringiness** *n.*

stringy-bark *n. Austral.* any of various eucalyptus trees with tough fibrous bark.

strip[1] /strɪp/ *v.* & *n.* ● *v.* (**stripped**, **stripping**) **1** *tr.* (often foll. by *of*) remove the clothes or covering from (a person or thing). **2** *intr.* (often foll. by *off*) undress oneself. **3** *tr.* (often foll. by *of*) deprive (a person) of property or titles. **4** *tr.* leave bare of accessories or fittings. **5** *tr.* remove bark and branches from (a tree). **6** *tr.* (often foll. by *down*) remove the accessory fittings of or take apart (a machine etc.) to inspect or adjust it. **7** *tr.* sell off (the assets of a company) for profit. **8** *tr.* milk (a cow) to the last drop. **9** *tr.* remove the old hair from (a dog). **10** *tr.* remove the stems from (tobacco). **11 a** *tr.* tear the thread from (a screw). **b** *intr.* (of a screw) lose its thread. **12** *tr.* tear the teeth from (a gearwheel). **13** *tr.* remove (paint) or remove paint from (a surface) with solvent. **14** *tr.* (often foll. by *from*) pull or tear (a covering or property etc.) off (*stripped the masks from their faces*). **15** *intr.* (of a bullet) issue from a rifled gun without spin owing to a loss of surface. ● *n.* **1** an act of stripping, esp. of undressing in striptease. **2** *Brit.* the identifying outfit worn by the members of a sports team while playing. [Middle English from Old English *bestrīepan* 'plunder', from Germanic]

strip[2] /strɪp/ *n.* **1** a long narrow piece (*a strip of land*). **2** a narrow flat bar of iron or steel. **3** (in full **strip**

cartoon) = COMIC STRIP. □ **tear a person off a strip** *colloq.* angrily rebuke a person. [Middle English, from or related to Middle Low German *strippe* 'strap, thong': probably related to STRIPE]

stripagram /'strɪpəgram/ *n.* (also **strippergram**) a novelty telegram or greetings message delivered by a person who performs a striptease for the recipient.

strip club *n.* a club at which striptease performances are given.

stripe /strʌɪp/ *n. & v.* ● *n.* **1** a long narrow band or strip differing in colour or texture from the surface on either side of it (*black with a red stripe*). **2** *Mil.* a chevron etc. denoting military rank. **3** *N. Amer.* a category of character, opinion, etc. (*a man of that stripe*). **4** (usu. in *pl.*) *archaic* a blow with a scourge or lash. **5** (in *pl.*, treated as *sing.*) *colloq.* a tiger. ● *v.tr.* mark with stripes. [perhaps back-formation from *striped*: cf. Middle Dutch, Middle Low German *strīpe*, Middle High German *strīfe*]

striped /strʌɪpt/ *adj.* marked with stripes (also in *comb.*: *red-striped*).

striped squill see SQUILL 1b.

strip light *n. Brit.* a tubular fluorescent lamp.

stripling /'strɪplɪŋ/ *n.* a youth not yet fully grown. [Middle English, probably from STRIP[2] + -LING[1], in the sense of having a figure not yet filled out]

strip mill *n.* a mill in which steel slabs are rolled into strips.

strip mine *n. US* a mine worked by removing the material that overlies the ore etc.

stripper /'strɪpə/ *n.* **1** a person or thing that strips something. **2** a device or solvent for removing paint etc. **3** a striptease performer.

strippergram var. of STRIPAGRAM.

strip-search *n. & v.* ● *n.* a search of a person involving the removal of all clothes. ● *v.tr.* search in this way.

striptease /'strɪpti:z/ *n. & v.* ● *n.* an entertainment in which the performer gradually undresses before the audience. ● *v.intr.* perform a striptease. □ **stripteaser** *n.*

stripy /'strʌɪpi/ *adj.* (**stripier**, **stripiest**) striped; having many stripes.

strive /strʌɪv/ *v.intr.* (*past* **strove** /strəʊv/ or **strived**; *past part.* **striven** /'strɪv(ə)n/ or **strived**) **1** (often foll. by *for*, or *to* + infin.) try hard, make efforts (*strive to succeed*). **2** (often foll. by *with*, *against*) struggle or contend. □ **striver** *n.* [Middle English from Old French *estriver*, related to *estrif* STRIFE]

strobe /strəʊb/ *n. & v. colloq.* ● *n.* **1** a stroboscope. **2** a stroboscopic lamp. **3** *US* an electronic flash for a camera. ● *v.* **1** *tr.* light as if with a stroboscope. **2** *intr.* flash intermittently. **3** *intr.* exhibit or give rise to strobing. [abbreviation]

strobila /strə'bʌɪlə/ *n.* (*pl.* **strobili** /-lʌɪ, -li:/) **1** a chain of proglottids in a tapeworm. **2** a sessile polyp-like form which divides horizontally to produce jellyfish larvae. [modern Latin from Greek *strobilē* 'twisted plug of lint', from *strephō* 'twist']

strobile /'strəʊbʌɪl/ *n. Bot.* = STROBILUS. [French *strobile* or Late Latin *strobilus* from Greek *strobilos*, from *strephō* 'twist']

strobilus /'strəʊbɪləs/ *n.* (*pl.* **strobili** /-lʌɪ, -li:/) *Bot.* **1** the cone of a pine etc. **2** a conelike structure, e.g. the flower of the hop. [Late Latin (as STROBILE)]

strobing /'strəʊbɪŋ/ *n.* **1** *Telev.* an irregular movement and loss of continuity sometimes seen in lines and stripes in a television picture. **2** *Cinematog.* jerkiness in what should be a smooth movement on the screen.

stroboscope /'strəʊbəskəʊp/ *n.* **1** *Physics* an instrument for determining speeds of rotation etc. by shining a bright light at intervals so that a rotating object appears stationary. **2** a lamp made to flash intermittently, esp. for this purpose. □ **stroboscopic** /-'skɒpɪk/ *adj.* **stroboscopical** /-'skɒpɪk(ə)l/ *adj.* **stroboscopically** /-'skɒpɪk(ə)li/ *adv.* [Greek *strobos* 'whirling' + -SCOPE]

strode *past* of STRIDE.

Stroganoff /'strɒgənɒf/ *adj.* (of meat) cut into strips and cooked in sour-cream sauce (*beef Stroganoff*). [named after P. *Stroganoff*, Russian diplomat (d. 1817)]

stroke /strəʊk/ *n. & v.* ● *n.* **1** the act or an instance of striking; a blow or hit (*with a single stroke*; *a stroke of lightning*). **2** a sudden disabling attack or loss of consciousness caused by an interruption in the flow of blood to the brain, esp. through thrombosis; apoplexy. **3 a** an action or movement esp. as one of a series. **b** the time or way in which such movements are done. **c** the slightest such action (*has not done a stroke of work*). **4** the whole of the motion (of a wing, oar, etc.) until the starting position is regained. **5** (in rowing) the mode or action of moving the oar (*row a fast stroke*). **6** the whole motion (of a piston) in either direction. **7** *Golf* the action of hitting (or hitting at) a ball with a club, as a unit of scoring. **8** a mode of moving the arms and legs in swimming. **9** a method of striking with the bat etc. in games etc. (*played some unorthodox strokes*). **10** a specially successful or skilful effort (*a stroke of diplomacy*). **11 a** a mark made by the movement in one direction of a pen or pencil or paintbrush. **b** a similar mark printed. **12** a detail contributing to the general effect in a description. **13** the sound made by a striking clock. **14** (in full **stroke oar**) the oar or oarsman nearest the stern, setting the time of the stroke. **15** the act or a spell of stroking. ● *v.tr.* **1** pass one's hand gently along the surface of (hair or fur etc.); caress lightly. **2** act as the stroke of (a boat or crew). □ **at a stroke** by a single action. **off one's stroke** not performing as well as usual. **on the stroke** punctually. **on the stroke of nine** etc. with the clock about to strike nine etc. **stroke a person down** appease a person's anger. **stroke a person** (or **a person's hair**) **the wrong way** irritate a person. **stroke of business** a profitable transaction. **stroke of genius** an original or strikingly successful idea. **stroke of luck** or **good luck** an unforeseen opportune occurrence. [Old English *strācian* from Germanic: related to STRIKE]

stroke play *n. Golf* play in which the score is reckoned by counting the number of strokes taken for the round (cf. MATCHPLAY).

stroll /strəʊl/ *v. & n.* ● *v.intr.* **1** saunter or walk in a leisurely way. **2** achieve something easily, without effort. ● *n.* **1** a short leisurely walk (*go for a stroll*). **2** something easily achieved; a walkover. [originally of a vagrant, probably via German *strollen*, *strolchen* from *Strolch* 'vagabond', of unknown origin]

stroller /'strəʊlə/ *n.* **1** a person who strolls. **2** *US* a pushchair.

strolling players *n.pl.* actors etc. going from place to place to give performances.

stroma /'strəʊmə/ *n.* (*pl.* **stromata** /-mətə/) *Biol.* **1** the framework of an organ or cell. **2** a fungous tissue containing spore-producing bodies. □ **stromatic** /-'matɪk/ *adj.* [modern Latin via Late Latin from Greek *strōma* 'coverlet']

stromatolite /strə(ʊ)'matəlʌɪt/ *n. Biol.* a mound built up of layers of blue-green algae and trapped sediment, found in lagoons in Australasia and fossilized in Precambrian rocks elsewhere. [STROMA + -LITE]

strong /strɒŋ/ *adj. & adv.* ● *adj.* (**stronger** /'strɒŋgə/; **strongest** /'strɒŋgɪst/) **1** having the power of resistance; able to withstand great force or opposition; not easily damaged or overcome (*strong material*; *strong faith*; *a strong character*). **2** (of a person's constitution) able to overcome, or not liable to, disease. **3** (of a person's nerves) proof against fright, irritation, etc. **4** (of a patient) restored to health. **5** (of a market) having steadily high or rising prices. **6** capable of exerting great force or of doing much; muscular, powerful. **7** forceful or powerful in effect (*a strong wind*; *a strong protest*). **8** decided or firmly held (*a strong suspicion*; *strong views*). **9** (of an argument etc.) convincing or striking. **10** powerfully affecting the senses or emotions (*a strong light*; *strong acting*). **11** powerful in terms of size or numbers or quality (*a strong army*). **12** capable of doing much when united (*a strong combination*). **13** formidable; likely to succeed (*a strong candidate*). **14** (of a solution or drink etc.) concentrated; containing a large proportion of a substance in water or another solvent (*strong tea*). **15** *Chem.* (of an acid or base) fully ionized into cations and anions in aqueous solution. **16** (of a group) having a specified number (*200 strong*). **17** (of a voice) loud or penetrating. **18** (of food or its flavour) pungent. **19** (of a person's breath) ill-smelling. **20** (of a literary style) vivid and terse. **21** (of a measure) drastic. **22** *Gram.* in Germanic languages: **a** (of a verb) forming inflections by change of vowel within the stem rather than by the addition of a suffix (e.g. *swim, swam*). **b** (of a noun or adjective) belonging to a declension in which the stem originally ended otherwise than in *-n* (opp. WEAK 9b). ● *adv.* strongly (*the tide is running strong*). □ **come it strong** *Brit. colloq.* go to great lengths; use exaggeration. **come on strong** behave aggressively or assertively. **going strong** *colloq.* continuing action vigorously; continuing to flourish; in good health or trim. □ **strongish** *adj.* **strongly** *adv.* [Old English from Germanic: related to STRING]

strong-arm *attrib.adj.* using force (*strong-arm tactics*).

strongbox /ˈstrɒŋbɒks/ *n.* a strongly made small chest for valuables.

strong drink *n.* alcohol, esp. spirits.

strong force *n. Physics* the force which mediates the strong interaction betwen subatomic particles.

strong grade *n. Philol.* the stressed ablaut form.

stronghold /ˈstrɒŋhəʊld/ *n.* **1** a fortified place. **2** a secure refuge. **3** a centre of support for a cause etc.

strong interaction *n. Physics* an interaction between certain subatomic particles that is very strong but is effective only at short distances.

strong language *n.* forceful language; swearing.

strongman /ˈstrɒŋman/ *n.* (*pl.* **-men**) **1** *Polit.* a forceful leader who exercises firm control over a state, group, etc. **2** a performer (at a fair, circus, etc.) of feats of strength.

strong meat *n. Brit.* a doctrine or action acceptable only to vigorous or instructed minds.

strong-minded *adj.* having determination. □ **strong-mindedness** *n.*

strong point *n.* **1** a thing at which one excels. **2** a specially fortified defensive position.

strongroom /ˈstrɒŋruːm, -rʊm/ *n.* a room designed to protect valuables against fire and theft.

strong stomach *n.* a stomach not easily affected by nausea.

strong suit *n.* **1** a suit at cards in which one can take tricks. **2** a thing at which one excels.

strontia /ˈstrɒnʃ(ɪ)ə/ *n. Chem.* strontium oxide. [*strontian*, native strontium carbonate from Strontian in the Highland Region of Scotland, where it was discovered]

strontium /ˈstrɒntɪəm, ˈstrɒnʃ(ɪ)əm/ *n. Chem.* a soft silver-white metallic element occurring naturally in various minerals (symbol Sr). [STRONTIA + -IUM]

strontium-90 *n.* a radioactive isotope of strontium concentrated selectively in bones and teeth when taken into the body.

strontium oxide *n.* a white compound used in the manufacture of fireworks.

strop /strɒp/ *n.* & *v.* ● *n.* **1** a device, esp. a strip of leather, for sharpening razors. **2** *Naut.* a collar of leather or spliced rope or iron used for handling cargo. ● *v.tr.* (**stropped**, **stropping**) sharpen on or with a strop. [Middle English via Middle Dutch, Middle Low German *strop*, Old High German *strupf* from West Germanic, from Latin *stroppus*]

strophanthin /strə(ʊ)ˈfanθɪn/ *n.* any of a group of poisonous glycosides obtained from African trees of the genera *Strophanthus* and *Acokanthera* and used as heart stimulants. [modern Latin *strophanthus*, from Greek *strophos* 'twisted cord' + *anthos* 'flower' (referring to the long segments of the corolla)]

strophe /ˈstrəʊfi/ *n.* **1 a** a turn in dancing made by an ancient Greek chorus. **b** lines recited during this. **c** the first section of an ancient Greek choral ode or of one division of it. **2** a group of lines forming a section of a lyric poem. □ **strophic** *adj.* [Greek *strophē*, literally 'turning', from *strephō* 'turn']

stroppy /ˈstrɒpi/ *adj.* (**stroppier**, **stroppiest**) *Brit. colloq.* bad-tempered; awkward to deal with. □ **stroppily** *adv.* **stroppiness** *n.* [20th c.: perhaps abbreviation of OBSTREPEROUS]

strove *past* of STRIVE.

strow /strəʊ/ *v.tr.* (*past part.* **strown** /strəʊn/ or **strowed**) *archaic* = STREW. [variant of STREW]

struck *past* and *past part.* of STRIKE.

structural /ˈstrʌktʃ(ə)r(ə)l/ *adj.* of, concerning, or having a structure. □ **structurally** *adv.*

structural engineering *n.* the branch of civil engineering concerned with large modern buildings etc.

structural formula *n. Chem.* a formula showing the arrangement of atoms in the molecule of a compound.

structuralism /ˈstrʌktʃ(ə)r(ə)lɪz(ə)m/ *n.* **1** the doctrine that structure rather than function is important. **2** structural linguistics. **3** structural psychology. □ **structuralist** *n.* & *adj.*

structural linguistics *n.* the study of language as a system of interrelated elements.

structural psychology *n.* the study of the arrangement and composition of mental states and conscious experiences.

structural steel *n.* strong mild steel in shapes suited to construction work.

structure /ˈstrʌktʃə/ *n.* & *v.* ● *n.* **1 a** a whole constructed unit, esp. a building. **b** the way in which a building etc. is constructed (*has a flimsy structure*). **2** a set of interconnecting parts of any complex thing; a framework (*the structure of a sentence*; *a new wages structure*). ● *v.tr.* give structure to; organize; frame. □ **structured** *adj.* (also in *comb.*). **structureless** *adj.* [Middle English from Old French *structure* or Latin *structura*, from *struere struct-* 'build']

strudel /ˈstruːd(ə)l, ˈʃtruː-/ *n.* a confection of thin pastry rolled up round a filling and baked (*apple strudel*). [German]

struggle /ˈstrʌg(ə)l/ *v.* & *n.* ● *v.intr.* **1** make forceful or violent efforts to get free of restraint or constriction. **2** (often foll. by *for*, or *to* + infin.) make violent or determined efforts under difficulties; strive hard (*struggled for supremacy*; *struggled to get the words out*). **3** (foll. by *with*, *against*) contend; fight strenuously (*struggled with the disease*; *struggled against superior numbers*). **4** (foll. by *along*, *up*, etc.) make one's way with difficulty (*struggled to my feet*). **5** (esp. as **struggling** *adj.*) have difficulty in gaining recognition or a living (*a struggling artist*). ● *n.* **1** the act or a spell of struggling. **2** a hard or confused contest. **3** a determined effort under difficulties. □ **the struggle for existence** (or **life**) the competition between organisms esp. as an element in natural selection, or between persons seeking a livelihood. □ **struggler** *n.* [Middle English *strugle*, frequentative of uncertain origin (perhaps imitative)]

strum /strʌm/ *v.* & *n.* ● *v.tr.* (**strummed**, **strumming**) **1** play on (a stringed or keyboard instrument), esp. carelessly or unskilfully. **2** play (a tune etc.) in this way. ● *n.* **1** the sound made by strumming. **2** an instance or spell of strumming. □ **strummer** *n.* [imitative: cf. THRUM[1]]

struma /ˈstruːmə/ *n.* (*pl.* **strumae** /-miː/) **1** *Med.* **a** = SCROFULA. **b** = GOITRE. **2** *Bot.* a cushion-like swelling of an organ. □ **strumose** *adj.* **strumous** *adj.* [Latin, = scrofulous tumour]

strumpet /ˈstrʌmpɪt/ *n. archaic* or *literary* a prostitute. [Middle English: origin unknown]

strung *past* and *past part.* of STRING.

strut /strʌt/ *n.* & *v.* ● *n.* **1** a bar forming part of a framework and designed to resist compression. **2** a strutting gait. ● *v.* (**strutted**, **strutting**) **1** *intr.* walk with a pompous or affected stiff erect gait. **2** *tr.* brace with a strut or struts. □ **strutter** *n.* **struttingly** *adv.* [Old English *strūtian* 'protrude stiffly', from Germanic]

struth var. of STREWTH.

struthious /'stru:θɪəs/ *adj.* of or like an ostrich. [Latin *struthio* 'ostrich']

strychnine /'strɪkni:n, -ɪn/ *n.* a bitter and highly poisonous vegetable alkaloid obtained from plants of the genus *Strychnos* (esp. nux vomica), occasionally used as a stimulant. □ **strychnic** *adj.* [French via Latin *strychnos* from Greek *strukhnos*, a kind of nightshade]

Sts *abbr.* Saints.

Stuart /'stju:ət/ *adj.* & *n.* ● *adj.* of or relating to the royal family ruling Scotland 1371–1714 and Britain 1603–1649 and 1660–1714. ● *n.* a member of this family.

stub /stʌb/ *n.* & *v.* ● *n.* **1** the remnant of a pencil or cigarette etc. after use. **2** the counterfoil of a cheque or receipt etc. **3** a stunted tail etc. **4** the stump of a tree, tooth, etc. **5** (*attrib.*) going only part of the way through (*stub-mortise*; *stub-tenon*). ● *v.tr.* (**stubbed**, **stubbing**) **1** strike (one's toe) against something. **2** (usu. foll. by *out*) extinguish (a lighted cigarette) by pressing the lighted end against something. **3** (foll. by *up*) grub up by the roots. **4** clear (land) of tree stumps etc. [Old English *stub*, *stubb*, from Germanic]

stub-axle *n.* an axle supporting only one wheel of a pair.

stubble /'stʌb(ə)l/ *n.* **1** the cut stalks of cereal plants left sticking up after the harvest. **2 a** cropped hair or a cropped beard. **b** a short growth of unshaven hair. □ **stubbled** *adj.* **stubbly** *adj.* [Middle English via Anglo-French *stuble*, Old French *estuble* from Latin *stupla*, *stupula*, variants of *stipula* 'straw']

stubborn /'stʌbən/ *adj.* **1** unreasonably obstinate. **2** unyielding, obdurate, inflexible. **3** refractory, intractable. □ **stubbornly** *adj.* **stubbornness** /'stʌbənnɪs/ *n.* [Middle English *stiborn*, *stoburn*, etc., of unknown origin]

stubby /'stʌbi/ *adj.* & *n.* ● *adj.* (**stubbier**, **stubbiest**) short and thick. ● *n.* (*pl.* **-ies**) *Austral. colloq.* a small squat bottle of beer. □ **stubbily** *adv.* **stubbiness** *n.*

stucco /'stʌkəʊ/ *n.* & *v.* ● *n.* (*pl.* **-oes**) plaster or cement used for coating wall surfaces or moulding into architectural decorations. ● *v.tr.* (**-oes**, **-oed**) coat with stucco. [Italian, of Germanic origin]

stuck *past* and *past part.* of STICK².

stuck-up *adj. colloq.* affectedly superior and aloof, snobbish.

stud¹ /stʌd/ *n.* & *v.* ● *n.* **1** a large-headed nail, boss, or knob, projecting from a surface esp. for ornament. **2** a small piece of jewellery for wearing in pierced ears or nostrils. **3** a double button, esp. for use with two buttonholes in a shirt-front. **4** a small object projecting slightly from a road surface as a marker etc. **5** a rivet or crosspiece in each link of a chain cable. **6 a** a post to which laths, plasterboard, etc., are nailed. **b** *US* the height of a room as indicated by the length of this. ● *v.tr.* (**studded**, **studding**) **1** set with or as with studs. **2** (as **studded** *adj.*) (foll. by *with*) thickly set or strewn (*studded with diamonds*). **3** be scattered over or about (a surface). [Old English *studu*, *stuthu* 'post, prop': related to German *stützen* 'to prop']

stud² /stʌd/ *n.* **1 a** a number of horses kept for breeding etc. **b** a place where these are kept. **2** (in full **stud-horse**) a stallion. **3** *colloq.* a young man (esp. one noted for sexual prowess). **4** (in full **stud poker**) a form of poker with betting after the dealing of successive rounds of cards face up. □ **at stud** (of a male horse) publicly available for breeding on payment of a fee. [Old English *stōd* from Germanic: related to STAND]

stud book *n.* a book containing the pedigrees of horses.

studding /'stʌdɪŋ/ *n.* the woodwork of a lath-and-plaster wall.

studding-sail /'stʌdɪŋseɪl, *Naut.* 'stʌns(ə)l/ *n.* a sail set on a small extra yard and boom beyond the leech of a square sail in light winds. [16th c.: origin uncertain: perhaps from Middle Low German, Middle Dutch *stōtinge* 'a thrusting']

student /'stju:d(ə)nt/ *n.* **1 a** a person who is studying, esp. at university or another place of higher education. **b** *N. Amer.* a school pupil. **2** (*attrib.*) studying in order to become (*a student nurse*). **3** a person of studious habits. □ **studentship** *n. Brit.* [Middle English from Latin *studēre*, from *studium* STUDY]

stud farm *n.* a place where horses are bred.

stud-horse see STUD² 2.

studio /'stju:dɪəʊ/ *n.* (*pl.* **-os**) **1** the workroom of a painter or photographer etc. **2** a place where cinema films or recordings are made or where television or radio programmes are made or produced. [Italian from Latin (as STUDY)]

studio couch *n.* a couch that can be converted into a bed.

studio flat *n. Brit.* a flat containing a room suitable as an artist's studio, or only one main room.

studious /'stju:dɪəs/ *adj.* **1** devoted to or assiduous in study or reading. **2** studied, deliberate, painstaking (*with studious care*). **3** (foll. by *to* + infin. or *in* + verbal noun) showing care or attention. **4** (foll. by *of* + verbal noun) anxiously desirous. □ **studiously** *adv.* **studiousness** *n.* [Middle English from Latin *studiosus* (as STUDY)]

stud poker see STUD² 4.

study /'stʌdi/ *n.* & *v.* ● *n.* (*pl.* **-ies**) **1** the devotion of time and attention to acquiring information or knowledge, esp. from books. **2** (in *pl.*) the pursuit of academic knowledge (*continued their studies abroad*). **3** a room used for reading, writing, etc. **4** a piece of work, esp. a drawing, done for practice or as an experiment (*a study of a head*). **5** the portrayal in literature or another art form of an aspect of behaviour or character etc. **6** a musical composition designed to develop a player's skill. **7** a thing worth observing closely (*your face was a study*). **8** a thing that is or deserves to be investigated. **9** *Theatr.* **a** the act of memorizing a role. **b** a person who memorizes a role. **10** *archaic* a thing to be secured by pains or attention. ● *v.* (**-ies**, **-ied**) **1** *tr.* make a study of; investigate or examine (a subject) (*study law*). **2** *intr.* (often foll. by *for*) apply oneself to study. **3** *tr.* scrutinize or earnestly contemplate (*studied their faces*; *studied the problem*). **4** *tr.* try to learn (the words of one's role etc.). **5** *tr.* take pains to achieve (a result) or pay regard to (a subject or principle etc.). **6** *tr.* (as **studied** *adj.*) deliberate, intentional, affected (*with studied politeness*). **7** *tr.* read (a book) attentively. **8** *tr.* (foll. by *to* + infin.) *archaic* **a** be on the watch. **b** try constantly to manage. □ **in a brown study** in a reverie; absorbed in one's thoughts. **make a study of** investigate carefully. □ **studiedly** *adv.* **studiedness** *n.* [Middle English via Old French *estudie* from Latin *studium* 'zeal, study']

study-bedroom *n.* a room serving both as a bedroom and as a study, esp. as student accommodation.

study group *n.* a group of people meeting from time to time to study a particular subject or topic.

stuff /stʌf/ *n.* & *v.* ● *n.* **1** the material that a thing is made of; material that may be used for some purpose. **2** a substance or things or belongings of an indeterminate kind or a quality not needing to be specified (*there's a lot of stuff about it in the newspapers*). **3** a particular knowledge or activity (*know one's stuff*). **4** *Brit.* woollen fabric (esp. as distinct from silk, cotton, and linen). **5** valueless matter, trash, refuse, nonsense (*take that stuff away*). **6** (prec. by *the*) **a** *colloq.* an available supply of something, esp. drink or drugs. **b** *slang* money. ● *v.* **1** *tr.* pack (a receptacle) tightly (*stuff a cushion with feathers*; *a head stuffed with weird notions*). **2** *tr.* (foll. by *in*, *into*) force or cram (a thing) (*stuffed the socks in the drawer*). **3** *tr.* fill out the skin of (an animal or bird etc.) with material to restore the original shape (*a stuffed owl*). **4** *tr.* fill (poultry etc.) with a savoury or sweet mixture, esp. before cooking. **5 a** *tr. & refl.* fill (a person or oneself) with food. **b** *tr. & intr.* eat greedily. **6** *tr.* push, esp. hastily or clumsily (*stuffed the note behind the cushion*). **7** *tr.* (usu. in *passive*; foll. by *up*) block up (a person's nose etc.). **8** *tr. slang* (esp. as an expression of contemptuous dismissal) dispose of as unwanted (*you can stuff the job*). **9** *tr. N. Amer.* place bogus votes in (a ballot box). **10** *tr. Brit. coarse slang offens.* have sexual intercourse with (a woman). □ **bit of stuff** *Brit. slang offens.* a woman regarded as an object of sexual desire. **do one's stuff** *colloq.* do what one has to. **get stuffed** *Brit. slang* an exclamation of dismissal, contempt, etc. **stuff and nonsense** *Brit.* an exclamation of incredulity or ridicule. **stuff it** *slang* an expression of rejection or disdain. **that's the stuff** *colloq.* that is what is wanted. □ **stuffer** *n.* (also in *comb.*). [Middle English *stoffe* from Old French *estoffe* (*n.*), *estoffer* (*v.*) 'equip, furnish' from Greek *stuphō* 'draw together']

stuffed shirt *n. colloq.* a pompous person.

stuff gown *n. Brit.* a gown worn by a barrister who has not taken silk.

stuffing /ˈstʌfɪŋ/ *n.* **1** padding used to stuff cushions etc. **2** a mixture used to stuff poultry etc., esp. before cooking. □ **knock** (or **take**) **the stuffing out of** *colloq.* make feeble or weak; defeat.

stuffing box *n.* a box packed with material, to allow the working of an axle while remaining airtight.

stuffy /ˈstʌfi/ *adj.* (**stuffier**, **stuffiest**) **1** (of a room or the atmosphere in it) lacking fresh air or ventilation; close. **2** dull or uninteresting. **3** (of a person's nose etc.) stuffed up. **4** (of a person) dull and conventional. □ **stuffily** *adv.* **stuffiness** *n.*

stultify /ˈstʌltɪfʌɪ/ *v.tr.* (**-ies**, **-ied**) **1** make ineffective, useless, or futile, esp. as a result of tedious routine (*stultifying boredom*). **2** cause to appear foolish or absurd. **3** negate or neutralize. □ **stultification** /-fɪˈkeɪʃ(ə)n/ *n.* **stultifier** *n.* [Late Latin *stultificare* from Latin *stultus* 'foolish']

stum /stʌm/ *n. & v.* ● *n.* unfermented grape juice; must. ● *v.tr.* (**stummed**, **stumming**) **1** prevent from fermenting, or secure (wine) against further fermentation in a cask, by the use of sulphur etc. **2** renew the fermentation of (wine) by adding stum. [Dutch *stommen* (*v.*), *stom* (*n.*) from *stom* (*adj.*) 'dumb']

stumble /ˈstʌmb(ə)l/ *v. & n.* ● *v.intr.* **1** lurch forward or have a partial fall from catching or striking or misplacing one's foot. **2** (often foll. by *along*) walk with repeated stumbles. **3** make a mistake or repeated mistakes in speaking etc. **4** (foll. by *on*, *upon*, *across*) find or encounter by chance (*stumbled on a disused well*). ● *n.* an act of stumbling. □ **stumbler** *n.* **stumblingly** *adv.* [Middle English *stumble* (with euphonic *b*), corresponding to Norwegian *stumla*: related to STAMMER]

stumblebum /ˈstʌmb(ə)lbʌm/ *n. US colloq.* a clumsy or inept person.

stumbling block *n.* an obstacle or circumstance causing difficulty or hesitation.

stumer /ˈstjuːmə/ *n. Brit. slang* **1** a worthless cheque; a counterfeit coin or note. **2** a sham or fraud. **3** a failure. [19th c.: origin unknown]

stump /stʌmp/ *n. & v.* ● *n.* **1** the projecting remnant of a cut or fallen tree. **2** the similar remnant of anything else (e.g. a branch or limb) cut off or worn down. **3** *Cricket* each of the three uprights of a wicket. **4** (in *pl.*) *joc.* the legs. **5** the stump of a tree, or other place, used by an orator to address a meeting. **6** a cylinder of rolled paper or other material with conical ends for softening pencil marks and other uses in drawing. ● *v.* **1** *tr.* (of a question etc.) be too hard for; puzzle. **2** *tr.* (as **stumped** *adj.*) at a loss; baffled. **3** *tr. Cricket* (esp. of a wicketkeeper) put (a batsman) out by touching the stumps with the ball while the batsman is out of the crease. **4** *intr.* walk stiffly or noisily as on a wooden leg. **5** *tr.* (also *absol.*) *US* traverse (a district) making political speeches. **6** *tr.* use a stump on (a drawing, line, etc.). □ **on the stump** *colloq.* engaged in political speech-making or agitation. **stump up** *Brit. colloq.* pay or produce (the money required). **up a stump** *US* in difficulties. [Middle English *stompe* from Middle Dutch *stomp*, Old High German *stumpf*]

stumper /ˈstʌmpə/ *n. colloq.* **1** a puzzling question. **2** a wicketkeeper.

stumpy /ˈstʌmpi/ *adj.* (**stumpier**, **stumpiest**) short and thick. □ **stumpily** *adv.* **stumpiness** *n.*

stun /stʌn/ *v.tr.* (**stunned**, **stunning**) **1** knock senseless; stupefy. **2** bewilder or shock. **3** (of a sound) deafen temporarily. [Middle English from Old French *estoner* ASTONISH]

stung *past* and *past part.* of STING.

stun gun *n.* a gun which stuns through an electric shock, ultrasound, etc., without causing serious injury.

stunk *past* and *past part.* of STINK.

stunner /ˈstʌnə/ *n. colloq.* a stunning person or thing.

stunning /ˈstʌnɪŋ/ *adj. colloq.* extremely impressive or attractive. □ **stunningly** *adv.*

stunsail /ˈstʌns(ə)l/ *n.* (also **stuns'l**) = STUDDING-SAIL.

stunt[1] /stʌnt/ *v.tr.* **1** retard the growth or development of. **2** dwarf, cramp. □ **stuntedness** *n.* [Old English *stunt* 'foolish' (now dialect) from Germanic: perhaps related to STUMP]

stunt[2] /stʌnt/ *n. & v.* ● *n.* **1** something unusual done to attract attention. **2** a trick or daring manoeuvre. **3** a display of concentrated energy. ● *v.intr.* perform stunts, esp. aerobatics. [origin unknown: first used in 19th-c. US college athletics]

stuntman /ˈstʌntman/ *n.* (*pl.* **-men**) a man employed to take an actor's place in performing dangerous stunts.

stupa /ˈstuːpə/ *n.* a round usu. domed building erected as a Buddhist shrine. [Sanskrit *stūpa*]

stupe[1] /stjuːp/ *n. & v.* ● *n.* a flannel etc. soaked in hot water, wrung out, and applied as a fomentation. ● *v.tr.* treat with this. [Middle English via Latin from Greek *stupē* 'tow']

stupe[2] /stjuːp/ *n. slang* a foolish or stupid person.

stupefy /ˈstjuːpɪfʌɪ/ *v.tr.* (**-ies**, **-ied**) **1** make stupid or insensible (*stupefied with drink*). **2** stun with astonishment (*the news was stupefying*). □ **stupefacient** /-ˈfeɪʃ(ə)nt/ *adj. & n.* **stupefaction** /-ˈfakʃ(ə)n/ *n.* **stupefier** *n.* **stupefying** *adj.* **stupefyingly** *adv.* [French *stupéfier* from Latin *stupefacere*, from *stupēre* 'be amazed']

stupendous /stjuːˈpɛndəs/ *adj.* amazing or prodigious, esp. in terms of size or degree (*a stupendous achievement*). □ **stupendously** *adv.* **stupendousness** *n.* [Latin *stupendus*, gerundive of *stupēre* 'be amazed at']

stupid /ˈstjuːpɪd/ *adj. & n.* ● *adj.* (**stupider**, **stupidest**) **1** unintelligent, slow-witted, foolish (*a stupid fellow*). **2** typical of stupid persons (*put it in a stupid place*). **3** uninteresting or boring. **4** in a state of stupor or lethargy. **5** obtuse; lacking in sensibility. **6** *colloq.* a general term of disparagement (*all you do is read your stupid books*). ● *n. colloq.* a stupid person. □ **stupidity** /-ˈpɪdɪti/ *n.* (*pl.* **-ies**). **stupidly** *adv.* [French *stupide* or Latin *stupidus* (as STUPENDOUS)]

stupor /ˈstjuːpə/ *n.* a dazed, torpid, or helplessly amazed state. □ **stuporous** *adj.* [Middle English from Latin (as STUPENDOUS)]

sturdy /ˈstəːdi/ *adj. & n.* ● *adj.* (**sturdier**, **sturdiest**) **1** robust; strongly built. **2** vigorous and determined (*sturdy resistance*). ● *n.* vertigo in sheep caused by a tapeworm larva encysted in the brain. □ **sturdied** *adj.* (in sense of *n.*). **sturdily** *adv.* **sturdiness** *n.* [Middle English, in the sense 'reckless, violent', from Old French *esturdi*, *estourdi*, past part. of *estourdir* 'stun, daze', ultimately from Latin *ex* EX-[1] + *turdus* 'thrush' (taken as a type of drunkenness)]

sturgeon /ˈstəːdʒ(ə)n/ *n.* any large mailed sharklike fish of the family Acipenseridae etc. swimming upriver to spawn, used as food and a source of caviar and isinglass. [Middle English from Anglo-French *sturgeon*, Old French *esturgeon*, ultimately from Germanic]

Sturm und Drang /ʃtʊəm ʊnt 'draŋ, German ʃtʊrm ʊnt 'draŋ/ *n.* a literary and artistic movement in Germany in the late 18th c., characterized by the expression of emotional unrest and strong feeling. [German, = storm and stress]

stutter /'stʌtə/ *v.* & *n.* ● *v.* **1** *intr.* stammer, esp. by involuntarily repeating the first consonants of words. **2** *tr.* (often foll. by *out*) utter (words) in this way. ● *n.* **1** the act or habit of stuttering. **2** an instance of stuttering. □ **stutterer** *n.* **stutteringly** *adv.* [frequentative of Middle English (now dialect) *stut*, from Germanic]

sty[1] /stʌɪ/ *n.* & *v.* ● *n.* (*pl.* **sties**) **1** a pen or enclosure for pigs. **2** a filthy room or dwelling. **3** a place of debauchery. ● *v.tr.* & *intr.* (**sties**, **stied**) lodge in a sty. [Old English *stī*, probably = *stig* 'hall' (cf. STEWARD), from Germanic]

sty[2] /stʌɪ/ *n.* (also **stye**) (*pl.* **sties** or **styes**) an inflamed swelling on the edge of an eyelid. [*styany* (now dialect) = *styan eye* from Old English *stīgend* 'sty' (literally 'riser' from *stīgan* 'rise') + EYE, shortened as if = *sty on eye*]

Stygian /'stɪdʒɪən/ *adj.* **1** (in Greek mythology) of or relating to the Styx, a river in Hades. **2** *literary* dark, gloomy, indistinct. [Latin *stugius* from Greek *stugios*, via *Stux -ugos* 'Styx' from *stugnos* 'hateful, gloomy']

style /stʌɪl/ *n.* & *v.* ● *n.* **1** a kind or sort, esp. in regard to appearance and form (*an elegant style of house*). **2** a manner of writing or speaking or performing (*written in a florid style*; *started off in fine style*). **3** the distinctive manner of a person or school or period, esp. in relation to painting, architecture, furniture, dress, etc. **4** the correct way of designating a person or thing. **5 a** a superior quality or manner (*do it in style*). **b** = FORM *n.* 9. **6** a particular make, shape, or pattern (*in all sizes and styles*). **7** a method of reckoning dates (*Old Style*; *New Style*). **8 a** an ancient writing implement, a small rod with a pointed end for scratching letters on wax-covered tablets and a blunt end for obliterating them. **b** a thing of a similar shape esp. for engraving, tracing, etc. **9** the gnomon of a sundial. **10** *Bot.* the narrow extension of the ovary supporting the stigma. **11** *Zool.* a small slender pointed appendage. ● *v.tr.* **1** design or make etc. in a particular (esp. fashionable) style. **2** designate in a specified way. □ **styleless** *adj.* **stylelessness** *n.* **styler** *n.* [Middle English via Old French *stile*, *style* from Latin *stilus*: spelling *style* due to association with Greek *stulos* 'column']

-style /stʌɪl/ *suffix* forming adjectives and adverbs with the sense 'in a manner characteristic of' (*peasant-style clothing*; *Japanese-style food*; *a revolution British-style*).

■ **Usage** The usage illustrated by the third example given above, with the noun coming first, is somewhat informal.

stylet /'stʌɪlɪt/ *n.* **1** a slender pointed instrument; a stiletto. **2** *Med.* the stiffening wire of a catheter; a probe. **3** *Zool.* a small style, esp. a piercing mouthpart of an insect. [French *stilet* from Italian STILETTO]

styli *pl.* of STYLUS.

stylish /'stʌɪlɪʃ/ *adj.* **1** fashionable; elegant. **2** having a superior quality, manner, etc. □ **stylishly** *adv.* **stylishness** *n.*

stylist /'stʌɪlɪst/ *n.* **1 a** a designer of fashionable styles etc. **b** a hairdresser. **2 a** a writer noted for or aspiring to good literary style. **b** (in sport or music) a person who performs with style.

stylistic /stʌɪ'lɪstɪk/ *adj.* of or concerning esp. literary style. □ **stylistically** *adv.* [STYLIST + -IC, suggested by German *stilistisch*]

stylistics /stʌɪ'lɪstɪks/ *n.* the study of literary style.

stylite /'stʌɪlʌɪt/ *n.* *Eccl. hist.* an ancient or medieval ascetic living on top of a pillar. [ecclesiastical Greek *stulitēs* from *stulos* 'pillar']

stylize /'stʌɪlʌɪz/ *v.tr.* (also **-ise**) (esp. as **stylized** *adj.*) paint, draw, etc. (a subject) in a conventional non-realistic style. □ **stylization** /-'zeɪʃ(ə)n/ *n.* [STYLE + -IZE, suggested by German *stilisieren*]

stylo /'stʌɪləʊ/ *n.* (*pl.* **-os**) *colloq.* = STYLOGRAPH. [abbreviation]

stylobate /'stʌɪləbeɪt/ *n.* *Archit.* a continuous base supporting a row of columns. [Latin *stylobata* from Greek *stulobatēs*, from *stulos* 'pillar', *batēs* 'base', from *bainō* 'walk']

stylograph /'stʌɪləgrɑːf/ *n.* a kind of fountain pen having a point instead of a split nib. □ **stylographic** /-'grafɪk/ *adj.* [STYLUS + -GRAPH]

styloid /'stʌɪlɔɪd/ *adj.* & *n.* ● *adj.* resembling a stylus or pen. ● *n.* (in full **styloid process**) a spine of bone, esp. that projecting from the base of the temporal bone. [modern Latin *styloides* from Greek *stuloeidēs*, from *stulos* 'pillar']

stylus /'stʌɪləs/ *n.* (*pl.* **-li** /-lʌɪ, -liː/ or **-luses**) **1 a** a hard, esp. diamond or sapphire, point following a groove in a gramophone record and transmitting the recorded sound for reproduction. **b** a similar point producing such a groove when recording sound. **2** = STYLE *n.* 8, 9. [erroneous spelling of Latin *stilus*: cf. STYLE]

stymie /'stʌɪmi/ *n.* & *v.* (also **stimy**) ● *n.* (*pl.* **-ies**) **1** *Golf* a situation where an opponent's ball lies between the player and the hole, forming a possible obstruction to play (*lay a stymie*). **2** a difficult situation. ● *v.tr.* (**stymies**, **stymied**, **stymying** or **stymieing**) **1** obstruct; thwart. **2** *Golf* block (an opponent, an opponent's ball, or oneself) with a stymie. [19th c.: origin unknown]

styptic /'stɪptɪk/ *adj.* & *n.* ● *adj.* (of a drug etc.) that checks bleeding. ● *n.* a styptic drug or substance. [Middle English via Latin *stypticus* from Greek *stuptikos*, from *stuphō* 'to contract']

styptic pencil *n.* a stick of a styptic substance used to treat small cuts.

styrax /'stʌɪraks/ *n.* **1** storax resin. **2** any tree or shrub of the genus *Styrax*, e.g. the storax tree. [Latin from Greek *sturax*: cf. STORAX]

styrene /'stʌɪriːn/ *n.* *Chem.* a liquid hydrocarbon easily polymerized and used in making plastics etc. [STYRAX + -ENE]

styrofoam /'stʌɪrəfəʊm/ *n.* esp. *N. Amer.* a kind of expanded polystyrene. [POLYSTYRENE + -O- + FOAM]

suable /'suːəb(ə)l, 'sjuː-/ *adj.* capable of being sued. □ **suability** /-'bɪlɪti/ *n.*

suasion /'sweɪʒ(ə)n/ *n.* *formal* persuasion as opposed to force (*moral suasion*). □ **suasive** /'sweɪsɪv/ *adj.* [Middle English from Old French *suasion* or Latin *suasio*, from *suadēre suas-* 'urge']

suave /swɑːv/ *adj.* **1** (of a person, esp. a man) smooth; polite; sophisticated. **2** (of a wine etc.) bland, smooth. □ **suavely** *adv.* **suaveness** *n.* **suavity** /-vɪti/ *n.* (*pl.* **-ies**). [French *suave* or Latin *suavis* 'agreeable': distantly related to SWEET]

sub /sʌb/ *n.* & *v.* *colloq.* ● *n.* **1** a submarine. **2** a subscription. **3** a substitute. **4** a sub-editor. **5** *Mil.* a subaltern. **6** *Brit.* an advance or loan against expected income. ● *v.* (**subbed**, **subbing**) **1** *intr.* (usu. foll. by *for*) act as a substitute for a person. **2** *tr.* *Brit. colloq.* lend or advance (a sum) to (a person) against expected income. **3** *tr.* sub-edit. [abbreviation]

sub- /sʌb, səb/ *prefix* (also **suc-** before *c*, **suf-** before *f*, **sug-** before *g*, **sup-** before *p*, **sur-** before *r*, **sus-** before *c*, *p*, *t*) **1** at or to or from a lower position (*subordinate*; *submerge*; *subtract*; *subsoil*). **2** secondary or inferior in rank or position (*subclass*; *subcommittee*; *sub lieutenant*; *subtotal*). **3** somewhat, nearly; more or less (*subacid*; *subarctic*; *subaquatic*). **4** (forming verbs) denoting secondary action (*subdivide*; *sub-let*). **5** denoting support (*subvention*). **6** *Chem.* (of a salt) basic (*subacetate*). [from or suggested by Latin *sub-* from *sub* 'under, close to, towards']

subabdominal /sʌbab'dɒmɪn(ə)l/ *adj.* below the abdomen.

subacid /sʌb'asɪd/ *adj.* moderately acid or tart (*subacid fruit; a subacid remark*). □ **subacidity** /sʌbə'sɪdɪti/ *n.* [Latin *subacidus* (as SUB-, ACID)]

subacute /sʌbə'kju:t/ *adj. Med.* (of a condition) between acute and chronic.

subadult /sʌb'adʌlt, sʌbə'dʌlt/ *adj. & n. Zool.* ● *adj.* (of an animal) not fully adult. ● *n.* a subadult animal.

subagency /sʌb'eɪdʒ(ə)nsi/ *n.* (*pl.* **-ies**) a secondary or subordinate agency. □ **subagent** *n.*

subalpine /sʌb'alpʌɪn/ *adj.* of or situated in the higher slopes of mountains just below the timberline.

subaltern /'sʌb(ə)lt(ə)n/ *n. & adj.* ● *n. Brit. Mil.* an officer below the rank of captain, esp. a second lieutenant. ● *adj.* **1** of inferior rank. **2** *Logic* (of a proposition) particular, not universal. [Late Latin *subalternus* (as SUB-, *alternus* ALTERNATE *adj.*)]

subantarctic /ˌsʌban'tɑ:ktɪk/ *adj.* of or like regions immediately north of the Antarctic Circle.

sub-aqua /sʌb'akwə/ *adj.* of or concerning underwater swimming or diving.

subaquatic /sʌbə'kwatɪk/ *adj.* **1** of more or less aquatic habits or kind. **2** underwater.

subaqueous /sʌb'eɪkwɪəs/ *adj.* **1** existing, formed, or taking place under water. **2** lacking in substance or strength; wishy-washy.

subarctic /sʌb'ɑ:ktɪk/ *adj.* of or like regions immediately south of the Arctic Circle.

subastral /sʌb'astr(ə)l/ *adj.* terrestrial.

subatomic /sʌbə'tɒmɪk/ *adj.* occurring in or smaller than an atom.

subaudition /sʌbɔ:'dɪʃ(ə)n/ *n.* **1** the act of mentally supplying an omitted word or words in speech. **2** the act or process of understanding the unexpressed; reading between the lines. [Late Latin *subauditio* from *subaudire* 'understand' (as SUB-, AUDITION)]

subaxillary /sʌbak'sɪləri/ *adj.* **1** *Bot.* in or growing beneath the axil. **2** beneath the armpit.

sub-basement /'sʌbbeɪsm(ə)nt/ *n.* a storey below a basement.

sub-branch /'sʌbbrɑ:ntʃ/ *n.* a secondary or subordinate branch.

sub-breed /'sʌbbri:d/ *n.* a secondary or inferior breed.

subcategory /'sʌbkatɪg(ə)ri/ *n.* (*pl.* **-ies**) a secondary or subordinate category. □ **subcategorize** *v.tr.* (also **-ise**). **subcategorization** /-'zeɪʃ(ə)n/ *n.*

subcaudal /sʌb'kɔ:d(ə)l/ *adj.* of or concerning the region under the tail or the back part of the body.

subclass /'sʌbklɑ:s/ *n.* **1** a secondary or subordinate class. **2** *Biol.* a taxonomic category below a class.

sub-clause /'sʌbklɔ:z/ *n.* **1** esp. *Law* a subsidiary section of a clause. **2** *Gram.* a subordinate clause.

subclavian /sʌb'kleɪvɪən/ *adj. & n.* ● *adj.* (of an artery etc.) lying or extending under the collarbone. ● *n.* such an artery. [modern Latin *subclavius* (as SUB-, *clavis* 'key'): cf. CLAVICLE]

subclinical /sʌb'klɪnɪk(ə)l/ *adj. Med.* (of a disease) not yet presenting definite symptoms.

subcommittee /'sʌbkəmɪti/ *n.* a secondary committee.

subconical /sʌb'kɒnɪk(ə)l/ *adj.* approximately conical.

subconscious /sʌb'kɒnʃəs/ *adj. & n.* ● *adj.* of or concerning the part of the mind which is not fully conscious but influences actions etc. ● *n.* this part of the mind. □ **subconsciously** *adv.* **subconsciousness** *n.*

subcontinent /sʌb'kɒntɪnənt/ *n.* **1** a large land mass, smaller than a continent. **2** a large geographically or politically independent part of a continent. □ **subcontinental** /-'nɛnt(ə)l/ *adj.*

subcontract *v. & n.* ● *v.* /sʌbkən'trakt/ **1** *tr.* employ a firm etc. to do (work) as part of a larger project. **2** *intr.* make or carry out a subcontract. ● *n.* /sʌb'kɒntrakt/ a secondary contract, esp. to supply materials, labour, etc. □ **subcontractor** /-'traktə/ *n.*

subcontrary /sʌb'kɒntrəri/ *adj. & n. Logic* ● *adj.* (of a proposition) incapable of being false at the same time as another. ● *n.* (*pl.* **-ies**) such a proposition. [Late Latin *subcontrarius* (as SUB-, CONTRARY), translation of Greek *hupenantios*]

subcordate /sʌb'kɔ:deɪt/ *adj.* approximately heart-shaped.

subcortical /sʌb'kɔ:tɪk(ə)l/ *adj. Anat.* below the cortex.

subcostal /sʌb'kɒst(ə)l/ *adj. Anat.* below the ribs.

subcranial /sʌb'kreɪnɪəl/ *adj. Anat.* below the cranium.

subcritical /sʌb'krɪtɪk(ə)l/ *adj. Physics* of less than critical mass etc.

subculture /'sʌbkʌltʃə/ *n.* a cultural group within a larger culture, often having beliefs or interests at variance with those of the larger culture. □ **subcultural** /-'kʌltʃ(ə)r(ə)l/ *adj.*

subcutaneous /sʌbkju:'teɪnɪəs/ *adj.* under the skin. □ **subcutaneously** *adv.*

subdeacon /sʌb'di:k(ə)n/ *n. Eccl.* a minister of the order next below a deacon. □ **subdiaconate** /-dʌɪ'akəneɪt, -dʌɪ'akənət/ *n.*

subdelirious /sʌbdɪ'lɪrɪəs/ *adj.* capable of becoming delirious; mildly delirious. □ **subdelirium** *n.*

subdivide /sʌbdɪ'vʌɪd/ *v.tr. & intr.* divide again after a first division. [Middle English from Latin *subdividere* (as SUB-, DIVIDE)]

subdivision /'sʌbdɪvɪʒ(ə)n, sʌbdɪ'vɪʒ(ə)n/ *n.* **1** the act or an instance of subdividing. **2** a secondary or subordinate division. **3** *N. Amer. & Austral.* an area of land divided into plots for sale.

subdominant /sʌb'dɒmɪnənt/ *n. Mus.* the fourth note of the diatonic scale of any key.

subduction /səb'dʌkʃ(ə)n/ *n. Geol.* the sideways and downward movement of the edge of a plate of the earth's crust into the mantle beneath another plate (*subduction zone*). □ **subduct** *v.tr. & intr.* [Latin *subduct-*, stem of *subucere*, from SUB- + *ducere* 'lead, bring']

subdue /səb'dju:/ *v.tr.* (**subdues, subdued, subduing**) **1** conquer, subjugate, or tame (an enemy, nature, one's emotions, etc.). **2** (as **subdued** *adj.*) softened; lacking in intensity; toned down (*subdued light; in a subdued mood*). □ **subduable** *adj.* **subdual** *n.* [Middle English *sodewe* via Old French *so(u)duire* from Latin *subducere* (as SUB-, *ducere* 'lead, bring') used with the sense of *subdere* 'conquer' (as SUB-, *-dere* 'put')]

subdural /sʌb'djʊər(ə)l/ *adj. Anat. & Med.* situated or occurring between the dura mater and the arachnoid membrane of the brain and spinal cord.

sub-editor /sʌb'ɛdɪtə/ *n.* **1** an assistant editor. **2** *Brit.* a person who edits material for printing in a book, newspaper, etc. □ **sub-edit** *v.tr.* (**-edited, -editing**). **sub-editorial** /-'tɔ:rɪəl/ *adj.*

suberect /sʌbɪ'rɛkt/ *adj.* (of an animal, plant, etc.) almost erect.

subereous /sju:'bɪərɪəs/ *adj.* (also **suberic** /sju:'bɛrɪk/, **suberose** /'sju:bərəʊs/) **1** of or concerning cork. **2** corky. [Latin *suber* 'cork, cork oak']

subfamily /'sʌbfamɪli, -m(ə)l-/ *n.* (*pl.* **-ies**) **1** *Biol.* a taxonomic category below a family. **2** any subdivision of a group.

subfloor /'sʌbflɔ:/ *n.* a foundation for a floor in a building.

subform /'sʌbfɔ:m/ *n.* a subordinate or secondary form.

sub-frame *n.* a supporting frame.

subfusc /'sʌbfʌsk, sʌb'fʌsk/ *adj. & n.* ● *adj. formal* dull; dusky; gloomy. ● *n. Brit.* formal clothing at some universities. [Latin *subfuscus* (as SUB-, *fuscus* 'dark brown')]

subgenus /'sʌbdʒɛnəs, -dʒi:-/ *n.* (*pl.* **subgenera** /-'dʒɛn(ə)rə/) *Biol.* a taxonomic category below a genus. □ **subgeneric** /-dʒɪ'nɛrɪk/ *adj.*

subglacial /sʌb'gleɪʃ(ə)l, -sɪəl/ *adj.* next to or at the bottom of a glacier.

sub-group /'sʌbgru:p/ *n.* (also *Math.* **subgroup**) a subdivision of a group.

sub-head /'sʌbhɛd/ *n.* (also **sub-heading**) **1** a subordinate heading or title in a chapter, article, etc. **2** a subordinate division in a classification.

subhuman /sʌbˈhju:mən/ *adj.* **1** (of an animal) closely related to man. **2** (of behaviour, intelligence, etc.) less than human.

subjacent /səbˈdʒeɪs(ə)nt/ *adj.* underlying; situated below. [Latin *subjacēre* (as SUB-, *jacēre* 'lie')]

subject *n., adj., adv., & v.* ● *n.* /ˈsʌbdʒɪkt/ **1 a** a matter, theme, etc. to be discussed, described, represented, dealt with, etc. **b** (foll. by *for*) a person, circumstance, etc., giving rise to specified feeling, action, etc. (*a subject for congratulation*). **2** a department or field of study (*his best subject is geography*). **3** *Gram.* a noun or its equivalent about which a sentence is predicated and with which the verb agrees. **4 a** any person except a monarch living under a monarchy or any other form of government (*the ruler and his subjects*). **b** any person owing obedience to another. **5** *Philos.* **a** a thinking or feeling entity; the conscious mind; the ego, esp. as opposed to anything external to the mind. **b** the central substance or core of a thing as opposed to its attributes. **6** *Mus.* a theme of a fugue or sonata; a leading phrase or motif. **7** a person of specified mental or physical tendencies (*a hysterical subject*). **8** *Logic* the part of a proposition about which a statement is made. **9** (in full **subject for dissection**) a dead body. ● *adj.* /ˈsʌbdʒɪkt/ **1** (often foll. by *to*) owing obedience to a government, colonizing power, force, etc.; in subjection. **2** (foll. by *to*) liable, exposed, or prone to (*is subject to infection*). **3** (foll. by *to*) conditional upon; on the assumption of (*the arrangement is subject to your approval*). ● *adv.* /ˈsʌbdʒɪkt/ (foll. by *to*) conditionally upon (*subject to your consent, I propose to try again*). ● *v.tr.* /səbˈdʒɛkt/ **1** (foll. by *to*) make liable; expose; treat (*subjected us to hours of waiting*). **2** (usu. foll. by *to*) subdue (a nation, person, etc.) to one's sway etc. □ **on the subject of** concerning, about. □ **subjection** /səbˈdʒɛkʃ(ə)n/ *n.* **subjectless** /ˈsʌbdʒɪk(t)lɪs/ *adj.* [Middle English *soget* etc. via Old French *suget* etc. from Latin *subjectus*, past part. of *subjicere* (as SUB-, *jacere* 'throw')]

subject catalogue *n.* a catalogue, esp. in a library, arranged according to the subjects treated.

subject-heading *n.* a heading in an index collecting references to a subject.

subjective /səbˈdʒɛktɪv/ *adj. & n.* ● *adj.* **1** (of art, literature, written history, a person's views, etc.) proceeding from personal idiosyncrasy or individuality; not impartial or literal. **2** esp. *Philos.* proceeding from or belonging to the individual consciousness or perception; imaginary, partial, or distorted. **3** *Gram.* of or concerning the subject. ● *n. Gram.* the subjective case. □ **subjectively** *adv.* **subjectiveness** *n.* **subjectivity** /sʌbdʒɛkˈtɪvɪti/ *n.* [Middle English from Latin *subjectivus* (as SUBJECT)]

subjective case *n. Gram.* the nominative.

subjectivism /səbˈdʒɛktɪvɪz(ə)m/ *n. Philos.* the doctrine that knowledge is merely subjective and that there is no external or objective truth. □ **subjectivist** *n.*

subject matter *n.* the matter treated of in a book, lawsuit, etc.

subjoin /səbˈdʒɔɪn/ *v.tr.* add or append (an illustration, anecdote, etc.) at the end. [obsolete French *subjoindre* from Latin *subjungere* (as SUB-, *jungere junct-* 'join')]

subjoint /ˈsʌbdʒɔɪnt/ *n.* a secondary joint (in an insect's leg etc.).

sub judice /sʌb ˈdʒu:dɪsi, sʊb ˈju:dɪkeɪ/ *adj. Law* under judicial consideration and therefore prohibited from public discussion elsewhere. [Latin, = under a judge]

subjugate /ˈsʌbdʒʊgeɪt/ *v.tr.* bring into subjection; subdue; vanquish. □ **subjugable** /-gəb(ə)l/ *adj.* **subjugation** /-ˈgeɪʃ(ə)n/ *n.* **subjugator** *n.* [Middle English from Late Latin *subjugare* 'bring under the yoke' (as SUB-, *jugum* 'yoke')]

subjunctive /səbˈdʒʌŋ(k)tɪv/ *adj. & n. Gram.* ● *adj.* (of a mood) denoting what is imagined or wished or possible (e.g. *if I were you, God help you, be that as it may*). ● *n.* **1** the subjunctive mood. **2** a verb in this mood. □ **subjunctively** *adv.* [French *subjonctif -ive* or Late Latin *subjunctivus* from Latin (as SUBJOIN), translation of Greek *hupotaktikos*, as being used in subjoined clauses]

subkingdom /ˈsʌbkɪŋdəm/ *n. Biol.* a taxonomic category below a kingdom.

sub-lease *n. & v.* ● *n.* /ˈsʌbli:s/ a lease of a property by a tenant to a subtenant. ● *v.tr.* /sʌbˈli:s/ lease (a property) to a subtenant.

sub-lessee /sʌblɛˈsi:/ *n.* a person who holds a sub-lease.

sub-lessor /sʌblɛˈsɔ:/ *n.* a person who grants a sub-lease.

sub-let *n. & v.* ● *n.* /ˈsʌblɛt/ **1** = SUB-LEASE *n.* **2** *colloq.* a sub-let property. ● *v.tr.* /sʌbˈlɛt/ (**-letting**; *past* and *past part.* **-let**) = SUB-LEASE *v.*

sub lieutenant /sʌb lɛfˈtɛnənt/ *n. Brit.* a naval officer ranking next below lieutenant.

sublimate *v., adj., & n.* ● *v.tr.* /ˈsʌblɪmeɪt/ **1** (also *absol.*) divert (the energy of a primitive impulse, esp. sexual) into a culturally higher, or socially more acceptable, activity. **2** *Chem.* convert (a substance) from the solid state directly to its vapour by heat, and usu. allow it to solidify again. **3** refine; purify; idealize. ● *adj.* /ˈsʌblɪmət/ **1** *Chem.* (of a substance) sublimated. **2** purified, refined. ● *n.* /ˈsʌblɪmət/ *Chem.* **1** a sublimated substance. **2** = CORROSIVE SUBLIMATE. □ **sublimation** /-ˈmeɪʃ(ə)n/ *n.* [Latin *sublimare sublimat-* SUBLIME *v.*]

sublime /səˈblʌɪm/ *adj. & v.* ● *adj.* (**sublimer, sublimest**) **1** of the most exalted, grand, or noble kind; awe-inspiring (*sublime genius*). **2** (of indifference, impudence, etc.) arrogantly unruffled; extreme. ● *v.* **1** *tr. & intr. Chem.* = SUBLIMATE *v.* 2. **2** *tr.* purify or elevate by or as if by sublimation; make sublime. **3** *intr.* become pure by or as if by sublimation. □ **sublimely** *adv.* **sublimity** /-ˈlɪmɪti/ *n.* [Latin *sublimis* (as SUB-, second element perhaps related to *limen* 'threshold', *limus* 'oblique')]

Sublime Porte see PORTE.

subliminal /səˈblɪmɪn(ə)l/ *adj. Psychol.* (of a stimulus etc.) below the threshold of sensation or consciousness. □ **subliminally** *adv.* [SUB- + Latin *limen -inis* 'threshold']

subliminal advertising *n.* the use of subliminal images in advertising on television etc. to influence the viewer at an unconscious level.

subliminal self *n.* the part of one's personality outside conscious awareness.

sublingual /sʌbˈlɪŋgw(ə)l/ *adj.* under the tongue. [SUB- + Latin *lingua* 'tongue']

sublittoral /sʌbˈlɪt(ə)r(ə)l/ *adj.* **1** (of plants, animals, deposits, etc.) living or found on the seashore just below the low water mark. **2** of or concerning the seashore.

Sub-Lt. *abbr. Brit.* Sub Lieutenant.

sublunary /sʌbˈlu:n(ə)ri/ *adj.* **1** beneath the moon. **2** *Astron.* **a** within the moon's orbit. **b** subject to the moon's influence. **3** of this world; earthly. [Late Latin *sublunaris* (as SUB-, LUNAR)]

subluxation /sʌblʌkˈseɪʃ(ə)n/ *n. Med.* partial dislocation. [SUB- + Latin *luxat-*, past part. stem of *luxare*, from *luxus* 'dislocated']

sub-machine gun /sʌbməˈʃi:n gʌn/ *n.* a hand-held lightweight machine-gun.

subman /ˈsʌbman/ *n.* (*pl.* **-men**) *derog.* an inferior, brutal, or stupid man.

submarginal /sʌbˈmɑ:dʒɪn(ə)l/ *adj.* **1** esp. *Econ.* not reaching minimum requirements. **2** (of land) that cannot be farmed profitably.

submarine /ˈsʌbməri:n, sʌbməˈri:n/ *n. & adj.* ● *n.* a vessel, esp. a warship, capable of operating under water and usu. equipped with torpedoes, missiles, and a periscope. ● *adj.* existing, occurring, done, or used under the surface of the sea (*submarine cable*). □ **submariner** /-ˈmarɪnə/ *n.*

submaster /ˈsʌbmɑ:stə/ *n.* an assistant master or assistant headmaster in a school.

submaxillary /sʌbmak'sɪləri/ *adj.* (esp. of a pair of salivary glands) beneath the upper jaw.

submediant /sʌb'mi:dɪənt/ *n. Mus.* the sixth note of the diatonic scale of any key.

submental /sʌb'mɛnt(ə)l/ *adj. Anat.* beneath the chin. [Latin *mentum* 'chin']

submerge /səb'mə:dʒ/ *v.* **1** *tr.* **a** place under water; flood; inundate. **b** flood or inundate with work, problems, etc. **2** *intr.* (of a submarine, its crew, a diver, etc.) dive below the surface of water. □ **submergence** *n.* **submergible** *adj.* [Latin *submergere* (as SUB-, *mergere mers-* 'dip')]

submerged tenth *n.* (prec. by *the*) the supposed fraction of the population permanently living in poverty.

submerse /səb'mə:s/ *v.* & *adj.* ● *v.tr.* (esp. as **submersed** *adj.*) submerge. ● *adj. Bot.* growing entirely under water (opp. EMERSE). [Latin *submers-* past part. stem of *submergere* SUBMERGE]

submersible /səb'mə:sɪb(ə)l/ *n.* & *adj.* ● *n.* a submarine operating under water for short periods. ● *adj.* capable of being submerged.

submersion /səb'mə:ʃ(ə)n/ *n.* the act or an instance of submerging; the state of being submerged.

submicroscopic /ˌsʌbmʌɪkrə'skɒpɪk/ *adj.* too small to be seen by an ordinary microscope.

subminiature /sʌb'mɪnɪtʃə/ *adj.* **1** of greatly reduced size. **2** (of a camera) very small and using 16-mm film.

submission /səb'mɪʃ(ə)n/ *n.* **1 a** the act or an instance of submitting; the state of being submitted. **b** anything that is submitted. **2** humility, meekness, obedience, submissiveness (*showed great submission of spirit*). **3** *Law* a theory etc. submitted by counsel to a judge or jury. **4** (in wrestling) the surrender of a participant yielding to the pain of a hold. [Middle English from Old French *submission* or Latin *submissio* (as SUBMIT)]

submissive /səb'mɪsɪv/ *adj.* **1** humble; obedient. **2** yielding to power or authority; willing to submit. □ **submissively** *adv.* **submissiveness** *n.* [SUBMISSION, on the pattern of *remissive* etc.]

submit /səb'mɪt/ *v.* (**submitted**, **submitting**) **1** (usu. foll. by *to*) **a** *intr.* cease resistance; give way; yield (*had to submit to defeat*; *will never submit*). **b** *refl.* surrender (oneself) to the control of another etc. **2** *tr.* present for consideration or decision. **3** *tr.* (usu. foll. by *to*) subject (a person or thing) to an operation, process, treatment, etc. (*submitted it to the flames*). **4** *tr.* esp. *Law* urge or represent esp. deferentially (*that, I submit, is a misrepresentation*). □ **submitter** *n.* [Middle English from Latin *submittere* (as SUB-, *mittere miss-* 'send')]

submultiple /sʌb'mʌltɪp(ə)l/ *n.* & *adj.* ● *n.* a number that can be divided exactly into a specified number. ● *adj.* being such a number.

subnormal /sʌb'nɔ:m(ə)l/ *adj.* **1** (esp. as regards intelligence) below normal. **2** less than normal. □ **subnormality** /-'malɪti/ *n.*

sub-nuclear /sʌb'nju:klɪə/ *adj. Physics* occurring in or smaller than an atomic nucleus.

subocular /sʌb'ɒkjʊlə/ *adj.* situated below or under the eyes.

suboptimal /sʌb'ɒptɪm(ə)l/ *adj.* less than optimal; not of the best quality, type, etc.

sub-orbital /sʌb'ɔ:bɪt(ə)l/ *adj.* **1** situated below the orbit of the eye. **2** (of a spaceship etc.) not completing a full orbit of the earth.

suborder /'sʌbɔ:də/ *n. Biol.* a taxonomic category ranked below an order. □ **subordinal** /-'ɔ:dɪn(ə)l/ *adj.*

subordinary /sʌb'ɔ:dɪn(ə)ri, -d(ə)n-/ *n.* (*pl.* **-ies**) *Heraldry* a device or bearing that is common but less so than ordinaries.

subordinate *adj., n., & v.* ● *adj.* /sə'bɔ:dɪnət/ (usu. foll. by *to*) of inferior importance or rank; secondary, subservient. ● *n.* /sə'bɔ:dɪnət/ a person working under another's control or orders. ● *v.tr.* /sə'bɔ:dɪneɪt/ (usu. foll. by *to*) **1** make subordinate; treat or regard as of minor importance. **2** make subservient. □ **subordinately** /sə'bɔ:dɪnətli/ *adv.* **subordination** /-'neɪʃ(ə)n/ *n.* **subordinative** /sə'bɔ:dɪnətɪv/ *adj.* [medieval Latin *subordinare, subordinat-* (as SUB-, Latin *ordinare* 'ordain')]

subordinate clause *n.* a clause, usu. introduced by a conjunction, that functions like a noun, adjective, or adverb, and qualifies a main clause (e.g. 'when it rang' in 'she answered the phone when it rang') (cf. MAIN CLAUSE).

suborn /sə'bɔ:n/ *v.tr.* induce by bribery etc. to commit perjury or any other unlawful act. □ **subornation** /sʌbɔ:'neɪʃ(ə)n/ *n.* **suborner** *n.* [Latin *subornare* 'incite secretly' (as SUB-, *ornare* 'equip')]

suboxide /sʌb'ɒksʌɪd/ *n. Chem.* an oxide containing the smallest proportion of oxygen.

subphylum /sʌb'fʌɪləm/ *n.* (*pl.* **subphyla** /-lə/) *Biol.* a taxonomic category below a phylum.

sub-plot /'sʌbplɒt/ *n.* a subordinate plot in a play etc.

subpoena /səb'pi:nə, sə'pi:nə/ *n.* & *v.* ● *n.* a writ ordering a person to attend a law court. ● *v.tr.* (*past* and *past part.* **subpoenaed** or **subpoena'd**) serve a subpoena on. [Middle English from Latin *sub poena* 'under penalty' (the first words of the writ)]

sub-postmaster /sʌb'pəʊs(t)mɑ:stə/ *n.* (*fem.* **sub-postmistress** /-'pəʊs(t)mɪstrɪs/) a person in charge of a sub-post office.

sub-post office /sʌb'pəʊst ɒfɪs/ *n.* a small local post office offering fewer services than a main post office.

subprogram /'sʌbprəʊgram/ *n. Computing* = SUBROUTINE.

subregion /'sʌbri:dʒ(ə)n/ *n.* a division of a region, esp. with regard to natural life. □ **subregional** /-'ri:dʒ(ə)n(ə)l/ *adj.*

subreption /səb'rɛpʃ(ə)n/ *n. formal* the obtaining of a thing by surprise or misrepresentation. [Latin *subreptio* 'purloining' from *subripere* (as SUB-, *rapere* 'snatch')]

subrogation /sʌbrə'geɪʃ(ə)n/ *n. Law* the substitution of one party for another as creditor, with the transfer of rights and duties. □ **subrogate** /'sʌbrəgeɪt/ *v.tr.* [Late Latin *subrogatio* from *subrogare* 'choose as substitute' (as SUB-, *rogare* 'ask')]

sub rosa /sʌb 'rəʊzə/ *adj.* & *adv.* (of communication, consultation, etc.) in secrecy or confidence. [Latin, literally 'under the rose', as emblem of secrecy]

subroutine /'sʌbru:ti:n/ *n. Computing* a routine designed to perform a frequently used operation within a program.

sub-Saharan /sʌbsə'hɑ:rən/ *attrib.adj.* from or forming part of the African regions south of the Sahara desert.

subscribe /səb'skrʌɪb/ *v.* **1** (usu. foll. by *to, for*) **a** *tr.* & *intr.* contribute (a specified sum) or make or promise a contribution to a fund, project, charity, etc., esp. regularly. **b** *intr.* enter one's name in a list of contributors to a charity etc. **c** *tr.* raise or guarantee raising (a sum) by so subscribing. **2** *intr.* (usu. foll. by *to*) express one's agreement with an opinion, resolution, etc. (*cannot subscribe to that*). **3** *tr.* **a** write (esp. one's name) at the foot of a document etc. (*subscribed a motto*). **b** write one's name at the foot of, sign (a document, picture, etc.). □ **subscribe for** agree to take a copy or copies of (a book) before publication. **subscribe oneself** sign one's name as. **subscribe to** arrange to receive (a periodical etc.) regularly. [Middle English from Latin *subscribere* (as SUB-, *scribere script-* 'write')]

subscriber /səb'skrʌɪbə/ *n.* **1 a** a contributor to a fund etc.; a person subscribing to a periodical etc. **b** esp. *Brit.* a person paying for the hire of a telephone line. **2** a person who subscribes to an idea etc. **3** a person who writes something or signs at the foot of a document etc.

subscriber trunk dialling *n. Brit.* the automatic connection of trunk calls by dialling without the assistance of an operator.

subscript /'sʌbskrɪpt/ *adj.* & *n.* ● *adj.* written or printed below the line, esp. *Math.* (of a symbol) written below and to the right of another symbol. ● *n.* a subscript number or symbol. [Latin *subscriptus* (as SUBSCRIBE)]

subscription /səbˈskrɪpʃ(ə)n/ *n.* **1 a** the act or an instance of subscribing. **b** money subscribed. **2** *Brit.* a fee for the membership of a society etc., esp. paid regularly. **3 a** an agreement to take and pay for usu. a specified number of issues of a newspaper, magazine, etc. **b** the money paid by this. **4** a signature on a document etc. **5** the offer of a reduced price to those ordering a book before publication. [Middle English from Latin *subscriptio* (as SUBSCRIBE)]

subscription concert *n.* each of a series of concerts for which tickets are sold in advance.

subsection /ˈsʌbsɛkʃ(ə)n/ *n.* a division of a section.

subsellium /səbˈsɛlɪəm/ *n.* (*pl.* **subsellia** /-lɪə/) = MISERICORD 1. [Latin (as SUB-, *sella* 'seat')]

subsequence /ˈsʌbsɪkw(ə)ns/ *n.* a subsequent incident; a consequence.

sub-sequence /ˈsʌbsiːkw(ə)ns/ *n.* a sequence forming part of a larger one.

subsequent /ˈsʌbsɪkw(ə)nt/ *adj.* (usu. foll. by *to*) following a specified event etc. in time, esp. as a consequence. □ **subsequently** *adv.* [Middle English from Old French *subsequent* or Latin *subsequi* (as SUB-, *sequi* 'follow')]

subserve /səbˈsəːv/ *v.tr.* serve as a means in furthering (a purpose, action, etc.). [Latin *subservire* (as SUB-, SERVE)]

subservient /səbˈsəːvɪənt/ *adj.* **1** cringing; obsequious. **2** (usu. foll. by *to*) serving as a means; instrumental. **3** (usu. foll. by *to*) subordinate. □ **subservience** *n.* **subserviency** *n.* **subserviently** *adv.* [Latin *subserviens subservient-* (as SUBSERVE)]

subset /ˈsʌbsɛt/ *n.* **1** a secondary part of a set. **2** *Math.* a set all the elements of which are contained in another set.

subshrub /ˈsʌbʃrʌb/ *n.* a low-growing or small shrub.

subside /səbˈsʌɪd/ *v.intr.* **1** cease from agitation; become tranquil; abate (*excitement subsided*). **2** (of water, suspended matter, etc.) sink. **3** (of the ground) cave in; sink. **4** (of a building, ship, etc.) sink lower in the ground or water. **5** (of a swelling etc.) become less. **6** usu. *joc.* (of a person) sink into a sitting, kneeling, or lying posture. □ **subsidence** /-ˈsʌɪd(ə)ns, ˈsʌbsɪd(ə)ns/ *n.* [Latin *subsidere* (as SUB-, *sidere* 'settle', related to *sedēre* 'sit')]

subsidiarity /səbsɪdɪˈarɪti/ *n.* **1** the quality of being subsidiary. **2** the principle that a central authority should have a subsidiary function, performing only those tasks which cannot be performed at a more local level.

subsidiary /səbˈsɪdɪəri/ *adj.* & *n.* ● *adj.* **1** serving to assist or supplement; auxiliary. **2** (of a company) controlled by another. **3** (of troops): **a** paid for by subsidy. **b** hired by another nation. ● *n.* (*pl.* **-ies**) **1** a subsidiary thing or person; an accessory. **2** a subsidiary company. □ **subsidiarily** *adv.* [Latin *subsidiarius* (as SUBSIDY)]

subsidize /ˈsʌbsɪdʌɪz/ *v.tr.* (also **-ise**) **1** pay a subsidy to. **2** reduce the cost of by subsidy (*subsidized lunches*). □ **subsidization** /-ˈzeɪʃ(ə)n/ *n.* **subsidizer** *n.*

subsidy /ˈsʌbsɪdi/ *n.* (*pl.* **-ies**) **1 a** money granted by the state or a public body etc. to keep down the price of commodities etc. (*housing subsidy*). **b** money granted to a charity or other undertaking held to be in the public interest. **c** any grant or contribution of money. **2** money paid by one state to another in return for military, naval, or other aid. **3** *hist.* **a** a parliamentary grant to the sovereign for state needs. **b** a tax levied on a particular occasion. [Middle English via Anglo-French *subsidie*, Old French *subside* from Latin *subsidium* 'assistance']

subsist /səbˈsɪst/ *v.* **1** *intr.* (often foll. by *on*) keep oneself alive; be kept alive (*subsists on vegetables*). **2** *intr.* remain in being; exist. **3** *intr.* (foll. by *in*) be attributable to (*its excellence subsists in its freshness*). **4** *tr. archaic* provide sustenance for. □ **subsistent** *adj.* [Latin *subsistere* 'stand firm' (as SUB-, *sistere* 'set, stand')]

subsistence /səbˈsɪst(ə)ns/ *n.* **1** the state or an instance of subsisting. **2 a** the means of supporting life; a livelihood. **b** a minimal level of existence or the income providing this (*a bare subsistence*).

subsistence allowance *n.* (also **subsistence money**) esp. *Brit.* an allowance or advance on pay granted esp. as travelling expenses.

subsistence farming *n.* farming which directly supports the farmer's household without producing a significant surplus for trade.

subsistence level *n.* (also **subsistence wage**) a standard of living (or wage) providing only the bare necessities of life.

subsoil /ˈsʌbsɔɪl/ *n.* soil lying immediately under the surface soil (opp. TOPSOIL).

subsonic /sʌbˈsɒnɪk/ *adj.* relating to speeds less than that of sound. □ **subsonically** *adv.*

subspecies /ˈsʌbspiːʃiːz, -ʃɪz, -spiːsː-/ *n.* (*pl.* same) *Biol.* a taxonomic category below a species, usu. a fairly permanent geographically isolated variety. □ **subspecific** /-spəˈsɪfɪk/ *adj.*

substance /ˈsʌbst(ə)ns/ *n.* **1 a** the essential material, esp. solid, forming a thing (*the substance was transparent*). **b** a particular kind of material having uniform properties (*this substance is salt*). **2 a** reality; solidity (*ghosts have no substance*). **b** seriousness or steadiness of character (*there is no substance in him*). **3** the theme or subject of esp. a work of art, argument, etc. (*prefer the substance to the style*). **4** the real meaning or essence of a thing. **5** wealth and possessions (*a woman of substance*). **6** *Philos.* the essential nature underlying phenomena, which is subject to changes and accidents. **7** an intoxicating or narcotic chemical or drug, esp. an illegal one (*substance abuse*). □ **in substance** generally; apart from details. [Middle English via Old French from Latin *substantia* (as SUB-, *stare* 'stand')]

sub-standard /sʌbˈstandəd/ *adj.* **1** of less than the required or normal quality or size; inferior. **2** (of language) not conforming to standard usage.

substantial /səbˈstanʃ(ə)l/ *adj.* **1 a** of real importance, value, or validity (*made a substantial contribution*). **b** of large size or amount (*awarded substantial damages*). **2** of solid material or structure; stout (*a man of substantial build; a substantial house*). **3** commercially successful; wealthy. **4** essential; true in large part (*substantial truth*). **5** having substance; real. □ **substantiality** /-ʃɪˈalɪti/ *n.* **substantially** *adv.* [Middle English from Old French *substantiel* or Late Latin *substantialis* (as SUBSTANCE)]

substantialism /səbˈstanʃ(ə)lɪz(ə)m/ *n. Philos.* the doctrine that behind phenomena there are substantial realities. □ **substantialist** *n.* & *adj.*

substantialize /səbˈstanʃ(ə)lʌɪz/ *v.tr.* & *intr.* (also **-ise**) invest with or acquire substance or actual existence.

substantiate /səbˈstanʃɪeɪt/ *v.tr.* prove the truth of (a charge, statement, claim, etc.); give good grounds for. □ **substantiation** /-ˈeɪʃ(ə)n/ *n.* [medieval Latin *substantiare* 'give substance to' (as SUBSTANCE)]

substantive /ˈsʌbst(ə)ntɪv/ *adj.* & *n.* ● *adj.* /also səbˈstantɪv/ **1** having separate and independent existence. **2** having a firm or solid basis; important, substantial. **3** *Law* relating to rights and duties. **4** (of an enactment, motion, resolution, etc.) made in due form as such; not amended. **5** *Gram.* expressing existence. **6** (of a dye) not needing a mordant. **7** *Mil.* (of a rank etc.) permanent, not acting or temporary. **8** *archaic* denoting a substance. ● *n. Gram.* = NOUN. □ **substantival** /-ˈtʌɪv(ə)l/ *adj.* **substantively** *adv.* esp. *Gram.* [Middle English from Old French *substantif -ive*, or Late Latin *substantivus* (as SUBSTANCE)]

substantive verb *n.* (prec. by *the*) the verb 'to be'.

sub-station /ˈsʌbsteɪʃ(ə)n/ *n.* a subordinate station, esp. one reducing the high voltage of electric power transmission to that suitable for supply to consumers.

substituent /səbˈstɪtjʊənt/ *adj. & n. Chem.* ● *adj.* (of a group of atoms) replacing another atom or group in a compound. ● *n.* such a group. [Latin *substituere substituent-* (as SUBSTITUTE)]

substitute /ˈsʌbstɪtjuːt/ *n. & v.* ● *n.* **1 a** (also *attrib.*) a person or thing acting or serving in place of another. **b** an artificial alternative to a natural substance (*butter substitute*). **2** *Sc. Law* a deputy. ● *v.* **1** *intr. & tr.* (often foll. by *for*) act or cause to act as a substitute; put or serve in exchange (*substituted for her mother*; *substituted it for the broken one*). **2** *tr.* (usu. foll. by *by*, *with*) *colloq.* replace (a person or thing) with another (*substitute dairy milk with soya milk*). **3** *tr. Chem.* replace (an atom or group in a molecule) with another. □ **substitutable** *adj.* **substitutability** /-ˈbɪlɪti/ *n.* **substitution** /-ˈtjuːʃ(ə)n/ *n.* **substitutional** /-ˈtjuːʃ(ə)n(ə)l/ *adj.* **substitutionary** /-ˈtjuːʃ(ə)n(ə)ri/ *adj.* **substitutive** *adj.* [Middle English from Latin *substitutus*, past part. of *substituere* (as SUB-, *statuere* 'set up')]

■ **Usage** The use of *substitute* with the prepositions *by* or *with*, as illustrated in sense 2 of the verb above, is highly informal and should be avoided in standard English. The example *substitute dairy milk with soya milk* can be reworded as *substitute soya milk for dairy milk* (see sense 1 of the verb above).

substrate /ˈsʌbstreɪt/ *n.* **1** = SUBSTRATUM. **2** a surface to be painted, printed, etc., on. **3** *Biol.* **a** the substance upon which an enzyme acts. **b** the surface or material on which any particular organism grows. [Anglicized from SUBSTRATUM]

substratum /sʌbˈstrɑːtəm, -ˈstreɪtəm/ *n.* (*pl.* **substrata** /-tə/) **1** an underlying layer or substance. **2** a layer of rock or soil beneath the surface. **3** a foundation or basis (*there is a substratum of truth in it*). [modern Latin, past part. of Latin *substernere* (as SUB-, *sternere* 'strew'): cf. STRATUM]

substructure /ˈsʌbstrʌktʃə/ *n.* an underlying or supporting structure. □ **substructural** *adj.*

subsume /səbˈsjuːm/ *v.tr.* (usu. foll. by *under*) include (an instance, idea, term, etc.) in a rule, class, category, etc. □ **subsumable** *adj.* **subsumption** /-ˈsʌm(p)ʃ(ə)n/ *n.* [medieval Latin *subsumere* (as SUB-, *sumere sumpt-* 'take')]

subsurface /ˈsʌbsəːfɪs/ *n. & adj.* ● *n.* the stratum or strata below the earth's surface. ● *adj.* **1** relating to the subsurface. **2** below the ground.

subsystem /ˈsʌbsɪstəm/ *n.* a self-contained system within a larger system.

subtenant /sʌbˈtɛnənt/ *n.* a person who leases a property from a tenant. □ **subtenancy** *n.*

subtend /sʌbˈtɛnd/ *v.tr.* **1 a** (usu. foll. by *at*) (of a line, arc, figure, etc.) form (an angle) at a particular point when its extremities are joined at that point. **b** (of an angle or chord) have bounding lines or points that meet or coincide with those of (a line or arc). **2** *Bot.* (of a bract etc.) extend under so as to embrace or enfold. [Latin *subtendere* (as SUB-, *tendere* 'stretch')]

subterfuge /ˈsʌbtəfjuːdʒ/ *n.* **1 a** an attempt to avoid blame or defeat esp. by lying or deceit. **b** a statement etc. resorted to for such a purpose. **2** this as a practice or policy. [French *subterfuge* or Late Latin *subterfugium* from Latin *subterfugere* 'escape secretly', from *subter* 'beneath' + *fugere* 'flee']

subterminal /sʌbˈtəːmɪn(ə)l/ *adj.* nearly at the end.

subterranean /sʌbtəˈreɪnɪən/ *adj.* **1** existing, occurring, or done under the earth's surface. **2** secret, underground, concealed. □ **subterraneously** *adv.* [Latin *subterraneus* (as SUB-, *terra* 'earth')]

subtext /ˈsʌbtɛkst/ *n.* an underlying often distinct theme in a piece of writing or conversation.

subtilize /ˈsʌtɪlʌɪz/ *v.* (also **-ise**) **1** *tr.* **a** make subtle. **b** elevate; refine. **2** *intr.* (usu. foll. by *upon*) argue or reason subtly. □ **subtilization** /-ˈzeɪʃ(ə)n/ *n.* [French *subtiliser* or medieval Latin *subtilizare* (as SUBTLE)]

subtitle /ˈsʌbtʌɪt(ə)l/ *n. & v.* ● *n.* **1** a secondary or additional title of a book etc. **2** a printed caption at the bottom of a film etc., esp. translating dialogue. ● *v.tr.* provide with a subtitle or subtitles.

subtle /ˈsʌt(ə)l/ *adj.* (**subtler**, **subtlest**) **1** evasive or mysterious; hard to grasp (*subtle charm*; *a subtle distinction*). **2** (of scent, colour, etc.) faint, delicate, elusive (*subtle perfume*). **3 a** capable of making fine distinctions; perceptive; acute (*subtle intellect*; *subtle senses*). **b** ingenious; elaborate; clever (*a subtle device*). **4** *archaic* crafty, cunning. □ **subtleness** *n.* **subtly** *adv.* [Middle English via Old French *sotil* from Latin *subtilis*]

subtlety /ˈsʌt(ə)lti/ *n.* (*pl.* **-ies**) **1** the quality or state of being subtle. **2** an instance of this; a fine distinction; a subtle argument. [Middle English via Old French *s(o)utilté* from Latin *subtilitas -tatis* (as SUBTLE)]

subtonic /sʌbˈtɒnɪk/ *n. Mus.* the note below the tonic, the seventh note of the diatonic scale of any key.

subtopia /sʌbˈtəʊpɪə/ *n. Brit. derog.* unsightly and sprawling suburban development. □ **subtopian** *adj.* [SUBURB, UTOPIA]

subtotal /ˈsʌbtəʊt(ə)l/ *n.* the total of one part of a group of figures to be added.

subtract /səbˈtrakt/ *v.tr.* (often foll. by *from*) deduct (a part, quantity, or number) from another. □ **subtracter** *n.* (cf. SUBTRACTOR). **subtraction** /-ˈtrakʃ(ə)n/ *n.* **subtractive** *adj.* [Latin *subtrahere subtract-* (as SUB-, *trahere* 'draw')]

subtractor /səbˈtraktə/ *n. Electronics* a circuit or device that produces an output dependent on the difference of two inputs.

subtrahend /ˈsʌbtrəhɛnd/ *n. Math.* a quantity or number to be subtracted. [Latin *subtrahendus*, gerundive of *subtrahere*: see SUBTRACT]

subtropics /sʌbˈtrɒpɪks/ *n.pl.* the regions adjacent to or bordering on the tropics. □ **subtropical** *adj.*

subulate /ˈsjuːbjʊlət, -leɪt/ *adj. Bot. & Zool.* slender and tapering. [Latin *subula* 'awl']

subunit /ˈsʌbjuːnɪt/ *n.* a distinct component, esp. each of two or more polypeptide chains in a large protein.

suburb /ˈsʌbəːb/ *n.* an outlying esp. residential district of a city. [Middle English from Old French *suburbe* or Latin *suburbium* (as SUB-, *urbs urbis* 'city')]

suburban /səˈbəːb(ə)n/ *adj.* **1** of or characteristic of suburbs. **2** *derog.* provincial, narrow-minded, uncultured, or naive. □ **suburbanite** *n.* **suburbanize** *v.tr.* (also **-ise**). **suburbanization** /-ˈzeɪʃ(ə)n/ *n.* [Latin *suburbanus* (as SUBURB)]

suburbia /səˈbəːbɪə/ *n.* often *derog.* the suburbs, their inhabitants, and their way of life.

subvention /səbˈvɛnʃ(ə)n/ *n.* a grant of money from a government etc.; a subsidy. [Middle English from Old French via Late Latin *subventio -onis* from Latin *subvenire subvent-* 'assist' (as SUB-, *venire* 'come')]

subversive /səbˈvəːsɪv/ *adj. & n.* ● *adj.* (of a person, organization, activity, etc.) seeking to subvert (esp. a government). ● *n.* a subversive person; a revolutionary. □ **subversion** /-ˈvəːʃ(ə)n/ *n.* **subversively** *adv.* **subversiveness** *n.* [medieval Latin *subversivus* (as SUBVERT)]

subvert /səbˈvəːt/ *v.tr.* esp. *Polit.* overturn, overthrow, or upset (religion, government, the monarchy, morality, etc.). □ **subverter** *n.* [Middle English from Old French *subvertir* or Latin *subvertere* (as SUB-, *vertere vers-* 'turn')]

subway /ˈsʌbweɪ/ *n.* **1** *Brit.* **a** a tunnel beneath a road etc. for pedestrians. **b** an underground passage for pipes, cables, etc. **2** esp. *N. Amer.* an underground railway.

subwoofer /ˈsʌbwʊfə/ *n.* a loudspeaker component designed to reproduce very low bass frequencies.

sub-zero /sʌbˈzɪərəʊ/ *adj.* (esp. of temperature) lower than zero.

suc- /sʌk, sək/ *prefix* assim. form of SUB- before *c*.

succedaneum /sʌksɪ'deɪnɪəm/ *n.* (*pl.* **succedanea** /-nɪə/) a substitute, esp. for a medicine or drug. ▫ **succedaneous** *adj.* [modern Latin, neut. of Latin *succedaneus* (as SUCCEED)]

succeed /sək'si:d/ *v.* **1** *intr.* **a** (often foll. by *in*) accomplish one's purpose; have success; prosper (*succeeded in his ambition*). **b** (of a plan etc.) be successful. **2 a** *tr.* follow in order; come next after (*night succeeded day*). **b** *intr.* (foll. by *to*) come next, be subsequent. **3** *intr.* (often foll. by *to*) become the rightful or subsequent holder of an inheritance, office, title, property, etc. (*succeeded to the throne*). **4** *tr.* take over an office, throne, inheritance, etc. from (*succeeded his father*; *succeeded the manager*). ▫ **nothing succeeds like success** one success leads to others. ▫ **succeeder** *n.* [Middle English from Old French *succeder* or Latin *succedere* (as SUB-, *cedere cess-* 'go')]

succentor /sək'sɛntə/ *n. Eccl.* a precentor's deputy in some cathedrals. ▫ **succentorship** *n.* [Late Latin from Latin *succinere* (as SUB-, *canere* 'sing')]

succès de scandale /sʊk,seɪ də skɒn'dɑ:l, French syksɛ də skɑ̃dal/ *n.* success due to notoriety or a thing's scandalous nature. [French]

success /sək'sɛs/ *n.* **1** the accomplishment of an aim; a favourable outcome (*their efforts met with success*). **2** the attainment of wealth, fame, or position (*spoilt by success*). **3** a thing or person that turns out well. **4** *archaic* a usu. specified outcome of an undertaking (*ill success*). [Latin *successus* (as SUCCEED)]

successful /sək'sɛsfʊl, -f(ə)l/ *adj.* **1** having or resulting in success. **2** prosperous; having wealth or status. ▫ **successfully** *adv.* **successfulness** *n.*

succession /sək'sɛʃ(ə)n/ *n.* **1 a** the process of following in order; succeeding. **b** a series of things or people in succession. **2 a** the right of succeeding to an office, inheritance, the throne, etc. **b** the act or process of so succeeding. **c** those having such a right. **3** *Ecol.* the process by which a plant or animal community successively gives way to another until a stable climax community is reached (cf. SERE[2]). **4** *Geol.* **a** a sequence of fossil forms representing an evolutionary series. **b** a group of strata representing a single chronological sequence. ▫ **in quick succession** following one another at short intervals. **in succession** one after another, without intervention. **in succession to** as the successor of. **settle the succession** determine who shall succeed. ▫ **successional** *adj.* [Middle English from Old French *succession* or Latin *successio* (as SUCCEED)]

succession state *n.* a state resulting from the partition of a previously existing country.

successive /sək'sɛsɪv/ *adj.* following one after another; running, consecutive. ▫ **successively** *adv.* **successiveness** *n.* [Middle English from medieval Latin *successivus* (as SUCCEED)]

successor /sək'sɛsə/ *n.* (often foll. by *to*) a person or thing that succeeds another. [Middle English via Old French *successour* from Latin *successor* (as SUCCEED)]

success story *n.* an example of success such as a rise from poverty to wealth etc.

succinct /sək'sɪŋ(k)t/ *adj.* briefly expressed; terse, concise. ▫ **succinctly** *adv.* **succinctness** *n.* [Middle English from Latin *succinctus*, past part. of *succingere* 'tuck up' (as SUB-, *cingere* 'gird')]

succinic acid /sʌk'sɪnɪk/ *n. Biochem.* a crystalline dibasic acid important as an intermediate in glucose metabolism. ▫ **succinate** /'sʌksɪneɪt/ *n.* [French *succinique* from Latin *succinum* 'amber' (from which it was first derived)]

succor *US* var. of SUCCOUR.

succory /'sʌk(ə)ri/ *n.* = CHICORY 1. [alteration of *cicorée* etc., early forms of CHICORY]

succotash /'sʌkətaʃ/ *n. US* a dish of green maize and beans boiled together. [Narragansett *msiquatash*]

Succoth /sʊ'kəʊt, 'sʌkəθ/ *n.* the Jewish autumn thanksgiving festival commemorating the sheltering in the wilderness. [Hebrew *sukkôṯ*, pl. of *sukkāh* 'thicket, hut']

succour /'sʌkə/ *n.* & *v.* (*US* **succor**) ● *n.* **1** aid; assistance, esp. in time of need. **2** (in *pl.*) *archaic* reinforcements of troops. ● *v.tr.* assist or aid (esp. a person in danger or distress). ▫ **succourless** *adj.* [Middle English via Old French *socours* and medieval Latin *succursus* from Latin *succurrere* (as SUB-, *currere curs-* 'run')]

succubus /'sʌkjʊbəs/ *n.* (*pl.* **succubi** /-bʌɪ/) a female demon believed to have sexual intercourse with sleeping men. [Late Latin *succuba* 'prostitute', medieval Latin *succubus*, from *succubare* (as SUB-, *cubare* 'lie')]

succulent /'sʌkjʊl(ə)nt/ *adj.* & *n.* ● *adj.* **1** juicy; palatable. **2** *colloq.* desirable. **3** *Bot.* (of a plant, its leaves, or stems) thick and fleshy. ● *n. Bot.* a succulent plant, esp. a cactus. ▫ **succulence** *n.* **succulently** *adv.* [Latin *succulentus* from *succus* 'juice']

succumb /sə'kʌm/ *v.intr.* (usu. foll. by *to*) **1** be forced to give way; be overcome (*succumbed to temptation*). **2** be overcome by death (*succumbed to his injuries*). [Middle English from Old French *succomber* or Latin *succumbere* (as SUB-, *cumbere* 'lie')]

succursal /sə'kə:s(ə)l/ *adj. Eccl.* (of a chapel etc.) subsidiary. [French *succursale* from medieval Latin *succursus* (as SUCCOUR)]

succussion /sə'kʌʃ(ə)n/ *n.* vigorous shaking, esp. in the preparation of a homoeopathic remedy. ▫ **succuss** *v.tr.* [Latin *succutere succuss-* (as SUB-, *cutare* = *quatere* 'shake')]

such /sʌtʃ/ *predet.* & *pron.* ● *predet.* **1** (often foll. by *as*) of the kind or degree in question or under consideration (*such a person*; *such people*). **2** (usu. foll. by *as to* + infin. or *that* + clause) so great; in such high degree (*not such a fool as to believe them*; *had such a fright that he fainted*). **3** of a more than normal kind or degree (*we had such an enjoyable evening*; *such horrid language*). **4** of the kind or degree already indicated, or implied by the context (*there are no such things*). **5** *Law* or *formal* the aforesaid; of the aforesaid kind (*such approval shall not be unreasonably withheld*). ● *pron.* **1** the thing or action in question or referred to (*such were his words*; *such was not my intention*). **2 a** *Commerce* or *colloq.* the aforesaid thing or things; it, they, or them (*those without tickets should purchase such*). **b** similar things; suchlike (*brought sandwiches and such*). ▫ **as such** as being what has been indicated or named (*a stranger is welcomed as such*; *there is no theatre as such*). **such-and-such** ● *adj.* of a particular kind but not needing to be specified. ● *n.* a person or thing of this kind. **such-and-such a person** someone; so-and-so. **such as 1** for example (*insects, such as moths and bees*). **2** of a kind that; like (*a person such as we all admire*). **3** those who (*such as don't need help*). **such as it is** despite its shortcomings (*you are welcome to it, such as it is*). **such a one 1** (usu. foll. by *as*) such a person or such a thing. **2** *archaic* some person or thing unspecified. [Old English *swilc*, *swylc*, from Germanic]

■ **Usage** See Usage Note at LIKE[1].

suchlike /'sʌtʃlʌɪk/ *pron.* & *det.* (usu. prec. by *and*) ● *pron.* things, people, etc., of such a kind (*ghosts and suchlike*). ● *det.* of such a kind (*shopping and suchlike chores*).

suck /sʌk/ *v.* & *n.* ● *v.* **1** *tr.* draw (a fluid) into the mouth by contracting the lip muscles etc. to make a partial vacuum. **2** *tr.* (also *absol.*) **a** draw milk or other fluid from or through (the breast etc. or a container). **b** extract juice from (a fruit) by sucking. **3** *tr.* **a** draw sustenance, knowledge, or advantage from (a book etc.). **b** imbibe or gain (knowledge, advantage, etc.) as if by sucking. **4** *tr.* roll the tongue round (a sweet, teeth, one's thumb, etc.). **5** *intr.* make a sucking action or sound (*sucking at his pipe*). **6** *intr.* (of a pump etc.) make a gurgling or drawing sound. **7** *tr.* (usu. foll. by *down*, *in*) engulf, smother, or drown in a sucking movement. **8** *intr. N. Amer. slang* be very bad, disagreeable, or disgusting. ● *n.* **1** the act or an instance of sucking, esp. the breast. **2** the drawing action or sound of a whirlpool etc. **3** (often foll. by *of*) a small draught of liquor. **4** (in *pl.*; esp. as *int.*) *Brit. colloq.* **a** an expression of disappointment. **b** an expression of derision or amusement at another's discomfiture. □ **give suck** *archaic* (of a mother, dam, etc.) suckle. **suck dry 1** exhaust the contents of (a bottle, the breast, etc.) by sucking. **2** exhaust (a person's sympathy, resources, etc.) as if by sucking. **suck in 1** absorb. **2** = sense 7 of *v.* **3** involve (a person) in an activity etc., esp. against his or her will. **suck up 1** (often foll. by *to*) *colloq.* behave obsequiously esp. for one's own advantage. **2** absorb. [Old English *sūcan*, = Latin *sugere*]

sucker /'sʌkə/ *n.* & *v.* ● *n.* **1 a** a person or thing that sucks. **b** a sucking pig, newborn whale, etc. **2** *colloq.* **a** a gullible or easily deceived person. **b** (foll. by *for*) a person especially susceptible to. **3** esp. *US colloq. euphem.* a thing not specified by name (*I can't mend the sucker!*). **4 a** a rubber cup etc. that adheres to a surface by suction. **b** an organ enabling an organism to cling to a surface by suction. **5** *Bot.* a shoot springing from the rooted part of a stem, from the root at a distance from the main stem, from an axil, or occasionally from a branch. **6** any of various fish that has a mouth capable of or seeming to be capable of adhering by suction. **7 a** the piston of a suction pump. **b** a pipe through which liquid is drawn by suction. **8** *N. Amer. colloq.* a lollipop. ● *v.* **1** *Bot.* **a** *tr.* remove suckers from. **b** *intr.* produce suckers. **2** *tr.* esp. *N. Amer. colloq.* fool, trick.

sucking /'sʌkɪŋ/ *adj.* **1** (of a child, animal, etc.) not yet weaned. **2** *Zool.* unfledged (*sucking dove*).

sucking-disc *n.* an organ used for adhering to a surface.

sucking-fish *n.* = REMORA.

suckle /'sʌk(ə)l/ *v.* **1** *tr.* **a** feed (young) from the breast or udder. **b** nourish (*suckled his talent*). **2** *intr.* feed by sucking the breast etc. □ **suckler** *n.* [Middle English, probably a back-formation from SUCKLING]

suckling /'sʌklɪŋ/ *n.* an unweaned child or animal.

sucrose /'su:krəʊz, 'sju:-, -əʊs/ *n. Chem.* common sugar, a disaccharide of glucose and fructose units obtained from sugar cane, sugar beet, etc. [French *sucre* SUGAR]

suction /'sʌkʃ(ə)n/ *n.* **1** the act or an instance of sucking. **2 a** the production of a partial vacuum by the removal of air etc. in order to force in liquid etc. or procure adhesion. **b** the force produced by this process (*suction keeps the lid on*). [Late Latin *suctio* from Latin *sugere suct-* SUCK]

suction pump *n.* a pump for drawing liquid through a pipe into a chamber emptied by a piston.

suctorial /sʌk'tɔ:rɪəl/ *adj. Zool.* **1** adapted for or capable of sucking. **2** having a sucker for feeding or adhering. □ **suctorian** *n.* [modern Latin *suctorius* (as SUCTION)]

Sudanese /su:də'ni:z/ *adj.* & *n.* ● *adj.* of or relating to Sudan, a republic in NE Africa, or the Sudan region south of the Sahara. ● *n.* (*pl.* same) **1** a native, national, or inhabitant of Sudan. **2** a person of Sudanese descent.

sudarium /su:'dɛ:rɪəm, sju:-/ *n.* (*pl.* **sudaria** /-rɪə/) **1** a cloth for wiping the face. **2** *RC Ch.* = VERONICA 2. [Latin, = napkin, from *sudor* 'sweat']

sudatorium /su:də'tɔ:rɪəm, 'sju:-/ *n.* (*pl.* **sudatoria** /-rɪə/) esp. *Rom. Antiq.* **1** a hot-air or steam bath. **2** a room where such a bath is taken. [Latin, neut. of *sudatorius*: see SUDATORY]

sudatory /'su:dət(ə)ri, 'sju:-/ *adj.* & *n.* ● *adj.* promoting perspiration. ● *n.* (*pl.* **-ies**) **1** a sudatory drug. **2** = SUDATORIUM. [Latin *sudatorius* from *sudare* 'to sweat']

sudd /sʌd/ *n.* an area of floating vegetation impeding the navigation of the White Nile. [Arabic, = obstruction]

sudden /'sʌd(ə)n/ *adj.* & *n.* ● *adj.* occurring or done unexpectedly or without warning; abrupt, hurried, hasty (*a sudden storm*; *a sudden departure*). ● *n. archaic* a hasty or abrupt occurrence. □ **all of a sudden** unexpectedly; hurriedly; suddenly. **on a sudden** *archaic* suddenly. □ **suddenly** *adv.* **suddenness** /-d(ə)nnɪs/ *n.* [Middle English via Anglo-French *sodein*, *sudein*, Old French *soudain* and Late Latin *subitanus* from Latin *subitaneus*, from *subitus* 'sudden']

sudden death *n. colloq.* a means of deciding the winner in a tied game etc., by allowing a further period of play until one side scores.

sudden infant death syndrome *n. Med.* = COT DEATH.

sudoriferous /su:də'rɪf(ə)rəs, sju:-/ *adj.* (of a gland etc.) secreting sweat. [Late Latin *sudorifer* from Latin *sudor* 'sweat']

sudorific /su:də'rɪfɪk, sju:-/ *adj.* & *n.* ● *adj.* (of a drug) causing sweating. ● *n.* a sudorific drug. [modern Latin *sudorificus* from Latin *sudor* 'sweat']

Sudra /'su:drə/ *n.* a member of the lowest of the four great Hindu castes, the worker caste. [Sanskrit *śūdra*]

suds /sʌdz/ *n.* & *v.* ● *n.pl.* **1** froth of soap and water. **2** *N. Amer. colloq.* beer. ● *v.* **1** *intr.* form suds. **2** *tr.* lather, cover, or wash in soapy water. □ **sudsy** *adj.* [originally = fen waters etc., of uncertain origin: cf. Middle Dutch, Middle Low German *sudde*, Middle Dutch *sudse* 'marsh, bog', probably related to SEETHE]

sue /su:, sju:/ *v.* (**sues**, **sued**, **suing**) **1** *tr.* (also *absol.*) *Law* institute legal proceedings against (a person). **2** *tr.* (also *absol.*) entreat (a person). **3** *intr.* (often foll. by *to*, *for*) *Law* make application to a law court for redress. **4** *intr.* (often foll. by *to*, *for*) make entreaty to a person for a favour. **5** *tr.* (often foll. by *out*) make a petition in a law court for and obtain (a writ, pardon, etc.). □ **suer** *n.* [Middle English via Anglo-French *suer*, *siwer*, etc. from Old French *siu-* etc., stem of *sivre*, from Latin *sequi* 'follow']

suede /sweɪd/ *n.* (often *attrib.*) **1** leather, esp. kidskin, with the flesh side rubbed to make a velvety nap. **2** (also **suede-cloth**) a woven fabric resembling suede. [French (*gants de*) *Suède* '(gloves of) Sweden']

suet /'su:ɪt, 'sju:ɪt/ *n.* the hard white fat on the kidneys or loins of oxen, sheep, etc., used to make dough etc. □ **suety** *adj.* [Middle English from Anglo-French, via Old French *seu* from Latin *sebum* 'tallow']

suet pudding *n.* a pudding of suet etc., usu. boiled or steamed.

suf- /sʌf, səf/ *prefix* assim. form of SUB- before *f*.

suffer /'sʌfə/ *v.* **1** *intr.* undergo pain, grief, damage, etc. (*suffers acutely*; *your reputation will suffer*; *suffers from neglect*). **2** *tr.* undergo, experience, or be subjected to (pain, loss, grief, defeat, change, etc.) (*suffered banishment*). **3** *tr.* put up with; tolerate (*does not suffer fools gladly*). **4** *intr. archaic* or *literary* undergo martyrdom. **5** *tr.* (foll. by *to* + infin.) *archaic* allow. □ **sufferable** *adj.* **sufferer** *n.* **suffering** *n.* [Middle English via Anglo-French *suffrir*, *soeffrir*, Old French *sof(f)rir* from Latin *sufferre* (as SUB-, *ferre* 'bear')]

sufferance /'sʌf(ə)r(ə)ns/ *n.* **1** tacit consent, abstinence from objection. **2** *archaic* submissiveness. □ **on sufferance** with toleration implied by lack of consent or objection. [Middle English via Anglo-French, Old French *suffraunce* from Late Latin *sufferentia* (as SUFFER)]

suffice /sə'fʌɪs/ *v.* **1** *intr.* (often foll. by *for*, or *to* + infin.) be enough or adequate (*that will suffice for our purpose*; *suffices to prove it*). **2** *tr.* meet the needs of; satisfy (*six sufficed him*). □ **suffice it to say** I shall content myself with saying. [Middle English via Old French *suffire* (*suffis-*) from Latin *sufficere* (as SUB-, *facere* 'make')]

sufficiency /sə'fɪʃ(ə)nsi/ *n.* (*pl.* **-ies**) **1** (often foll. by *of*) an adequate amount or adequate resources. **2** *archaic* being sufficient; ability; efficiency. [Late Latin *sufficientia* (as SUFFICIENT)]

sufficient /sə'fɪʃ(ə)nt/ *adj.* & *det.* good enough, large enough, or powerful enough; adequate, enough (*sufficient food to feed her family*; *sufficient reason for action*; *wave of discontent sufficient to bring down the* *government*). □ **sufficiently** *adv.* [Middle English from Old French *sufficient* or Latin *sufficiens* (as SUFFICE)]

suffix /ˈsʌfɪks/ *n.* & *v.* ● *n.* **1** a verbal element added at the end of a word to form a derivative (e.g. *-ation*, *-fy*, *-ing*, *-itis*). **2** *Math.* = SUBSCRIPT. ● *v.tr.* /also səˈfɪks/ append, esp. as a suffix. □ **suffixation** /-ˈseɪʃ(ə)n/ *n.* [*suffixum*, *suffixus*, past part. of Latin *suffigere* (as SUB-, *figere fix-* 'fasten')]

suffocate /ˈsʌfəkeɪt/ *v.* **1** *tr.* choke or kill by stopping breathing, esp. by pressure, fumes, etc. **2** *tr.* (often foll. by *by*, *with*) produce a choking or breathless sensation in, esp. by excitement, terror, etc. **3** *intr.* be or feel suffocated or breathless. □ **suffocating** *adj.* **suffocatingly** *adv.* **suffocation** /-ˈkeɪʃ(ə)n/ *n.* [Latin *suffocare* (as SUB-, *fauces* 'throat')]

Suffolk /ˈsʌfək/ *n.* **1** a sheep of a black-faced breed. **2** this breed. [*Suffolk*, a county in S. England]

Suffolk punch see PUNCH[4] 2.

suffragan /ˈsʌfrəg(ə)n/ *n.* (in full **suffragan bishop** or **bishop suffragan**) **1** a bishop appointed to help a diocesan bishop in the administration of a diocese. **2** a bishop in relation to his archbishop or metropolitan. □ **suffraganship** *n.* [Middle English from Anglo-French & Old French, representing medieval Latin *suffraganeus* 'assistant' (bishop) from Latin *suffragium* (see SUFFRAGE): originally of a bishop summoned to vote in synod]

suffrage /ˈsʌfrɪdʒ/ *n.* **1 a** the right of voting in political elections (*full adult suffrage*). **b** a view expressed by voting; a vote (*gave their suffrages for and against*). **c** opinion in support of a proposal etc. **2** (esp. in *pl.*) *Eccl.* **a** a prayer made by a priest in the liturgy. **b** a short prayer made by a congregation esp. in response to a priest. **c** *archaic* an intercessory prayer. [Middle English from Latin *suffragium*, partly through French *suffrage*]

suffragette /sʌfrəˈdʒɛt/ *n. hist.* a woman seeking the right to vote through organized protest. [SUFFRAGE + -ETTE]

suffragist /ˈsʌfrədʒɪst/ *n.* esp. *hist.* a person who advocates the extension of the suffrage, esp. to women. □ **suffragism** *n.*

suffuse /səˈfjuːz/ *v.tr.* **1** (of colour, moisture, etc.) spread from within to colour or moisten (*a blush suffused her cheeks*). **2** cover with colour etc. □ **suffusion** /-ˈfjuːʒ(ə)n/ *n.* [Latin *suffundere suffus-* (as SUB-, *fundere* 'pour')]

Sufi /ˈsuːfi/ *n.* (*pl.* **Sufis**) a Muslim ascetic and mystic. □ **Sufic** *adj.* **Sufism** *n.* [Arabic *ṣūfī*, perhaps from *ṣūf* 'wool' (from the woollen garment worn)]

sug /sʌg/ *v.tr.* (**sugged**, **sugging**) *slang* (attempt to) sell (a person) a product under the guise of conducting market research. [acronym from *s*ell *u*nder the *g*uise]

sug- /sʌg, səg/ *prefix* assim. form of SUB- before *g*.

sugar /ˈʃʊgə/ *n.* & *v.* ● *n.* **1** a sweet crystalline substance obtained from various plants, esp. the sugar cane and sugar beet, used in cookery, confectionery, brewing, etc.; sucrose. **2** *Chem.* any of a group of soluble usu. sweet-tasting crystalline carbohydrates found esp. in plants, e.g. glucose. **3** esp. *US colloq.* darling, dear (used as a term of address). **4** sweet words; flattery. **5** anything comparable to sugar encasing a pill in reconciling a person to what is unpalatable. **6** *slang* a narcotic drug, esp. heroin or LSD (taken on a lump of sugar). ● *v.tr.* **1** sweeten with sugar. **2** make (one's words, meaning, etc.) more pleasant or welcome. **3** coat with sugar (*sugared almond*). **4** spread a sugar mixture on (a tree) to catch moths. □ **sugar the pill** see PILL. □ **sugarless** *adj.* [Middle English via Old French *çukre*, *sukere* from Italian *zucchero*, probably via medieval Latin *succarum* from Arabic *sūkkar*]

sugar beet *n.* a beet, *Beta vulgaris*, from which sugar is extracted.

sugar-candy see CANDY *n.* 1.

sugar cane *n.* any perennial tropical grass of the genus *Saccharum*, esp. *S. officinarum*, with tall stout jointed stems from which sugar is made.

sugar-coated *adj.* **1** (of food) enclosed in sugar. **2** made superficially attractive. **3** excessively sentimental.

sugar daddy *n.* (*pl.* **-ies**) *slang* an elderly man who lavishes gifts on a young woman.

sugar-gum *n.* an Australian eucalyptus, *Eucalyptus cladocalyx*, with sweet foliage eaten by cattle.

sugar loaf *n.* a conical moulded mass of sugar.

sugar maple *n.* a N. American maple, *Acer saccharum*, from the sap of which maple sugar and maple syrup are made.

sugar of lead *n. Chem.* a white crystalline compound of lead that dissolves in water to form a sweet-tasting solution.

sugar pea *n.* = MANGETOUT.

sugarplum /ˈʃʊgəplʌm/ *n. archaic* a small round sweet of flavoured boiled sugar.

sugar snap *n.* (in full **sugar snap pea**) = MANGETOUT.

sugar soap *n. Brit.* an alkaline preparation containing washing soda and soap, used for cleaning or removing paint.

sugary /ˈʃʊg(ə)ri/ *adj.* **1** containing or resembling sugar. **2** excessively sweet or esp. sentimental. **3** falsely sweet or pleasant (*sugary compliments*). □ **sugariness** *n.*

suggest /səˈdʒɛst/ *v.tr.* **1** (often foll. by *that* + clause) propose (a theory, plan, or hypothesis) (*suggested to them that they should wait*; *suggested a different plan*). **2 a** cause (an idea, memory, association, etc.) to present itself; evoke (*this poem suggests peace*). **b** hint at (*his behaviour suggests guilt*). □ **suggest itself** (of an idea etc.) come into the mind. □ **suggester** *n.* [Latin *suggerere suggest-* (as SUB-, *gerere* 'bring')]

suggestible /səˈdʒɛstɪb(ə)l/ *adj.* **1** capable of being suggested. **2** open to suggestion; easily swayed. □ **suggestibility** /-ˈbɪlɪti/ *n.*

suggestion /səˈdʒɛstʃ(ə)n/ *n.* **1** the act or an instance of suggesting; the state of being suggested. **2** a theory, plan, etc., suggested (*made a helpful suggestion*). **3** a slight trace; a hint (*a suggestion of garlic*). **4** *Psychol.* **a** the insinuation of a belief etc. into the mind. **b** such a belief etc. [Middle English via Old French from Latin *suggestio -onis* (as SUGGEST)]

suggestive /səˈdʒɛstɪv/ *adj.* **1** (usu. foll. by *of*) conveying a suggestion; evocative. **2** (esp. of a remark, joke, etc.) indecent or improper by suggestion. □ **suggestively** *adv.* **suggestiveness** *n.*

suicidal /suːɪˈsʌɪd(ə)l, sjuː-/ *adj.* **1** inclined to commit suicide. **2** of or concerning suicide. **3** self-destructive; fatally or disastrously rash. □ **suicidally** *adv.*

suicide /ˈsuːɪsʌɪd, ˈsjuː-/ *n.* & *v.* ● *n.* **1 a** the intentional killing of oneself. **b** a person who commits suicide. **2** a self-destructive action or course (*political suicide*). **3** (*attrib.*) *Mil.* designating a highly dangerous or deliberately suicidal operation etc. (*a suicide mission*). ● *v.intr.* commit suicide. [modern Latin *suicida*, *suicidium* from Latin *sui* 'of oneself']

suicide pact *n.* an agreement between two or more people to commit suicide together.

sui generis /suːʌɪ ˈdʒɛn(ə)rɪs, suːiː, sjuː-, ˈgɛn-/ *adj.* of its own kind; unique. [Latin]

sui juris /suːʌɪ ˈdʒʊərɪs, suːiː, sjuː-, ˈjʊə-/ *adj. Law* of age; independent. [Latin, literally 'of one's own right']

suint /swɪnt/ *n.* the natural grease in sheep's wool. [French from *suer* 'sweat']

suit /suːt, sjuːt/ *n.* & *v.* ● *n.* **1 a** a set of outer clothes of matching material for men, consisting usu. of a jacket, trousers, and sometimes a waistcoat. **b** a similar set of clothes for women usu. having a skirt instead of trousers. **c** (esp. in *comb.*) a set of clothes for a special occasion, occupation, etc. (*playsuit*; *swimsuit*). **2 a** any of the four sets (spades, hearts, diamonds, clubs) into which a pack of cards is divided. **b** a player's holding in a suit (*his strong suit was clubs*). **c** *Bridge* one of the suits as proposed trumps in bidding, frequently as opposed to no trumps. **3** (in full **suit at law**) a lawsuit (*criminal suit*). **4 a** a petition esp. to a person in authority. **b** the process of courting a woman (*paid suit* *to her*). **5** (usu. foll. by *of*) a set of sails, armour, etc. **6** *slang* a person wearing a suit; a business executive. ● *v.* **1** *tr.* go well with (a person's figure, features, character, etc.); become. **2** *tr.* (also *absol.*) meet the demands or requirements of; satisfy; agree with (*does not suit all tastes; that date will suit*). **3** *tr.* make fitting or appropriate; accommodate; adapt (*suited his style to his audience*). **4** *tr.* (as **suited** *adj.*) appropriate; well fitted (*not suited to be an engineer*). □ **suit the action to the word** carry out a promise or threat at once. **suit oneself 1** do as one chooses. **2** find something that satisfies one. [Middle English via Anglo-French *siute*, Old French *si(e)ute* from fem. past part. of a Romanic alteration of Latin *sequi* 'follow']

suitable /'su:təb(ə)l, 'sju:t-/ *adj.* (usu. foll. by *to, for*) well fitted for the purpose; appropriate. □ **suitability** /-'bɪlɪti/ *n.* **suitableness** *n.* **suitably** *adv.* [SUIT + -ABLE, on the pattern of *agreeable*]

suitcase /'su:tkeɪs, 'sju:t-/ *n.* a usu. oblong case for carrying clothes etc., having a handle and a flat hinged lid. □ **suitcaseful** *n.* (*pl.* **-fuls**).

suite /swi:t/ *n.* **1** a set of things belonging together, esp.: **a** a set of rooms in a hotel etc. **b** a sofa, armchairs, etc., of the same design. **2** *Mus.* **a** a set of instrumental compositions, originally in dance style, to be played in succession. **b** a set of selected pieces from an opera, musical, etc., arranged to be played as one instrumental work. **3** a set of people in attendance; a retinue. [French (as SUIT)]

suiting /'su:tɪŋ, 'sju:-/ *n.* cloth used for making suits.

suitor /'su:tə, 'sju:tə/ *n.* **1** a man seeking to marry a specified woman; a wooer. **2** a plaintiff or petitioner in a lawsuit. **3** a prospective buyer of a business or corporation; the maker of a takeover bid. [Middle English via Anglo-French *seutor, suitour*, etc. from Latin *secutor -oris*, from *sequi secut-* 'follow']

suk (also **sukh**) var. of SOUK.

sukiyaki /sʊkɪ'jaki, -'jɑ:ki/ *n.* a Japanese dish of sliced meat fried rapidly with vegetables and sauce. [Japanese]

sulcate /'sʌlkeɪt/ *adj.* grooved, fluted, channelled. [Latin *sulcatus*, past part. of *sulcare* 'furrow' (as SULCUS)]

sulcus /'sʌlkəs/ *n.* (*pl.* **sulci** /-sʌɪ/) *Anat.* a groove or furrow, esp. on the surface of the brain. [Latin]

sulfa *US* var. of SULPHA.

sulfamic *US* var. of SULPHAMIC.

sulfanilamide *US* var. of SULPHANILAMIDE.

sulfate etc. *US* var. of SULPHATE etc.

sulfur etc. *US* var. of SULPHUR etc.

sulk /sʌlk/ *v.* & *n.* ● *v.intr.* indulge in a sulk, be sulky. ● *n.* (also in *pl.*, prec. by *the*) a period of sullen esp. resentful silence or aloofness from others (*having a sulk; got the sulks*). □ **sulker** *n.* [perhaps back-formation from SULKY]

sulky /'sʌlki/ *adj.* & *n.* ● *adj.* (**sulkier**, **sulkiest**) **1** sullen, morose, or silent, esp. from resentment or ill temper. **2** sluggish. ● *n.* (*pl.* **-ies**) a light two-wheeled horse-drawn vehicle for one, esp. used in trotting races. □ **sulkily** *adv.* **sulkiness** *n.* [perhaps from obsolete *sulke* 'hard to dispose of', of uncertain origin]

sullage /'sʌlɪdʒ/ *n.* filth, refuse, sewage. [perhaps from Anglo-French *suillage* from *souiller* SOIL[2]]

sullen /'sʌlən/ *adj.* & *n.* ● *adj.* **1** morose, resentful, sulky, unforgiving, unsociable. **2 a** (of a thing) slow-moving. **b** dismal, melancholy (*a sullen sky*). ● *n.* (in *pl.*, usu. prec. by *the*) *archaic* a sullen frame of mind; depression. □ **sullenly** *adv.* **sullenness** /-ənnɪs/ *n.* [16th-c. alteration of Middle English *solein* 'solitary' from Anglo-French, from *sol* SOLE[3]]

sully /'sʌli/ *v.tr.* (**-ies**, **-ied**) **1** disgrace or tarnish (a person's reputation or character, a victory, etc.). **2** *poet.* dirty; soil. [perhaps from French *souiller* (as SOIL[2])]

sulpha /'sʌlfə/ *n.* (*US* **sulfa**) any drug derived from sulphanilamide (often *attrib.*: *sulpha drug*). [abbreviation]

sulphadimidine /sʌlfə'dɪmɪdi:n/ *n.* *Pharm.* a sulphonamide antibiotic used esp. to treat human urinary infections and to control respiratory disease in pigs. [SULPHANILAMIDE + DI-[1] + PYRIMIDINE]

sulphamic acid /sʌl'famɪk/ *n.* (*US* **sulfamic acid**) a strong acid used in weedkiller, an amide of sulphuric acid. □ **sulphamate** /'sʌlfəmeɪt/ *n.* [SULPHUR + AMIDE]

sulphanilamide /sʌlfə'nɪləmʌɪd/ *n.* (*US* **sulfanilamide**) a colourless sulphonamide drug with antibacterial properties. [*sulphanilic* (SULPHUR, ANILINE) + AMIDE]

sulphate /'sʌlfeɪt/ *n.* (*US* **sulfate**) a salt or ester of sulphuric acid. [French *sulfate* from Latin *sulphur*]

sulphide /'sʌlfʌɪd/ *n.* (*US* **sulfide**) *Chem.* a binary compound of sulphur.

sulphite /'sʌlfʌɪt/ *n.* (*US* **sulfite**) *Chem.* a salt or ester of sulphurous acid. [French *sulfite*, alteration of *sulfate* SULPHATE]

sulphonamide /sʌl'fɒnəmʌɪd/ *n.* (*US* **sulfonamide**) a substance derived from an amide of a sulphonic acid, able to prevent the multiplication of some pathogenic bacteria. [SULPHONE + AMIDE]

sulphonate /'sʌlfəneɪt/ *n.* & *v.* *Chem.* ● *n.* a salt or ester of sulphonic acid. ● *v.tr.* convert into a sulphonate by reaction with sulphuric acid.

sulphone /'sʌlfəʊn/ *n.* (*US* **sulfone**) an organic compound containing the SO_2 group united directly to two carbon atoms. □ **sulphonic** /-'fɒnɪk/ *adj.* [German *Sulfon* (as SULPHUR)]

sulphur /'sʌlfə/ *n.* & *v.* (*US* **sulfur**) ● *n.* **1 a** a pale yellow non-metallic element having crystalline and amorphous forms, burning with a blue flame and a suffocating smell, and used in making gunpowder, matches, and sulphuric acid, in the vulcanizing of rubber, and in the treatment of skin diseases (symbol S). **b** (*attrib.*) like or containing sulphur. **2** the material of which hellfire and lightning were believed to consist. **3** any yellow butterfly of the family Pieridae. **4** a pale greenish-yellow colour. ● *v.tr.* **1** treat with sulphur. **2** fumigate with sulphur. □ **sulphury** *adj.* [Middle English via Anglo-French *sulf(e)re*, Old French *soufre* from Latin *sulfur*, *sulp(h)ur*]

sulphurate /'sʌlfjʊreɪt/ *v.tr.* (*US* **sulfurate**) impregnate, fumigate, or treat with sulphur, esp. in bleaching. □ **sulphuration** /-'reɪʃ(ə)n/ *n.* **sulphurator** *n.*

sulphur candle *n.* a candle burnt to produce sulphur dioxide for fumigating.

sulphur dioxide *n.* a colourless pungent toxic gas formed by burning sulphur in air and used as a food preservative. Chem. formula: SO_2.

sulphureous /sʌl'fjʊərɪəs/ *adj.* (*US* **sulfureous**) **1** of, like, or suggesting sulphur. **2** sulphur-coloured; yellow. [Latin *sulphureus* from SULPHUR]

sulphuretted /sʌlfjʊ'rɛtɪd/ *adj.* (*US* **sulfureted**) *archaic* containing sulphur in combination. [*sulphuret* 'sulphide' from modern Latin *sulphuretum*]

sulphuretted hydrogen *n.* hydrogen sulphide.

sulphuric /sʌl'fjʊərɪk/ *adj.* (*US* **sulfuric**) *Chem.* containing hexavalent sulphur. [French *sulfurique* (as SULPHUR)]

sulphuric acid *n.* a dense oily colourless highly acid and corrosive liquid much used in the chemical industry. Chem. formula: H_2SO_4.

sulphurize /'sʌlfjʊrʌɪz/ *v.tr.* (also **-ise**, *US* **sulfurize**) = SULPHURATE. □ **sulphurization** /-'zeɪʃ(ə)n/ *n.* [French *sulfuriser* (as SULPHUR)]

sulphurous *adj.* (*US* **sulfurous**) **1** /'sʌlf(ə)rəs/ relating to or suggestive of sulphur, esp. in colour. **2** /sʌl'fjʊərəs/ *Chem.* containing tetravalent sulphur. [Latin *sulphurosus* from SULPHUR]

sulphurous acid *n.* an unstable weak acid used as a reducing and bleaching acid.

sulphur spring *n.* a spring impregnated with sulphur or its compounds.

sultan /'sʌlt(ə)n/ *n.* **1 a** a Muslim sovereign. **b** (**the Sultan**) *hist.* the sultan of Turkey. **2** a variety of white domestic fowl from Turkey. □ **sultanate** /-neɪt/ *n.* [French *sultan* or medieval Latin *sultanus* from Arabic *sulṭān* 'power, ruler', from *saluṭa* 'rule']

sultana /sʌl'tɑ:nə/ *n.* **1 a** a seedless raisin used in puddings, cakes, etc. **b** the small pale yellow grape producing this. **2** the mother, wife, concubine, or daughter of a sultan. [Italian, fem. of *sultano* = SULTAN]

sultry /'sʌltri/ *adj.* (**sultrier**, **sultriest**) **1** (of the atmosphere or the weather) hot or oppressive; close. **2** (of a person, character, etc.) passionate; sensual. □ **sultrily** *adv.* **sultriness** *n.* [obsolete *sulter* SWELTER]

sum /sʌm/ *n.* & *v.* ● *n.* **1** the total amount resulting from the addition of two or more items, facts, ideas, feelings, etc. (*the sum of two and three is five*; *the sum of their objections is this*). **2** a particular amount of money (*paid a large sum for it*). **3 a** an arithmetical problem (*could not work out the sum*). **b** (esp. *pl.*) *colloq.* arithmetic work, esp. at an elementary level (*was good at sums*). ● *v.tr.* (**summed**, **summing**) find the sum of. □ **in sum** in brief. **sum up 1** (esp. of a judge) recapitulate or review the evidence in a case etc. **2** form or express an idea of the character of (a person, situation, etc.). **3** collect into or express as a total or whole. [Middle English via Old French *summe*, *somme* from Latin *summa* 'main part', fem. of *summus* 'highest']

sumac /'s(j)u:mak, 'ʃu:-/ *n.* (also **sumach**) **1** any shrub or small tree of the genus *Rhus* or *Cotinus*, esp. *R. coriaria* of S. Europe, having reddish cone-shaped fruits used as a spice in cooking. **2** the dried and ground leaves of *R. coriaria* used in tanning and dyeing. [Middle English via Old French *sumac* or medieval Latin *sumac(h)* from Arabic *summāḳ*]

Sumatran /sʊ'mɑ:trən/ *adj.* & *n.* ● *adj.* of or relating to Sumatra, its people, or its language. ● *n.* **1 a** a native or inhabitant of Sumatra in Indonesia. **b** a person of Sumatran descent. **2** the language of Sumatra.

Sumerian /sʊ'mɪərɪən, sju:-/ *adj.* & *n.* ● *adj.* of or relating to the early and non-Semitic element in the civilization of ancient Babylonia. ● *n.* **1** a member of the early non-Semitic people of ancient Babylonia. **2** the Sumerian language. [French *sumérien* from *Sumer* in Babylonia (now in southern Iraq)]

summa /'sʊmə, 'sʌmə/ *n.* (*pl.* **summae** /-mi:/) a summary of what is known of a subject. [Middle English from Latin: see SUM]

summa cum laude /sʌmə kʌm 'lɔ:di:, sʊmə kʊm 'laʊdeɪ/ *adv.* & *adj.* esp. *N. Amer.* (of a degree, diploma, etc.) of the highest standard; with the highest distinction. [Latin, = with highest praise]

summarize /'sʌmərʌɪz/ *v.tr.* (also **-ise**) make or be a summary of; sum up. □ **summarist** *n.* **summarizable** *adj.* **summarization** /-'zeɪʃ(ə)n/ *n.* **summarizer** *n.*

summary /'sʌm(ə)ri/ *n.* & *adj.* ● *n.* (*pl.* **-ies**) a brief account; an abridgement. ● *adj.* **1** dispensing with needless details or formalities; brief (*a summary account*). **2** *Law* (of a trial etc.) without the customary legal formalities (*summary justice*). □ **summarily** *adv.* **summariness** *n.* [Middle English from Latin *summarium*, from *summa* SUM]

summary conviction *n.* a conviction made by a judge or magistrates without a jury.

summary jurisdiction *n.* the authority of a court to use summary proceedings and arrive at a judgement.

summary offence *n.* an offence within the scope of a summary court.

summation /sʌ'meɪʃ(ə)n/ *n.* **1** the finding of a total or sum; an addition. **2** a summing-up. □ **summational** *adj.* **summative** *adj.*

summer[1] /'sʌmə/ *n.* & *v.* ● *n.* **1** the warmest season of the year, in the northern hemisphere from June to August and in the southern hemisphere from December to February. **2** *Astron.* the period from the summer solstice to the autumnal equinox. **3** the hot weather typical of summer. **4** (often foll. by *of*) the mature stage of life; the height of achievement, powers, etc. **5** (esp. in *pl.*) *poet.* a year (esp. of a person's age) (*a child of ten summers*). **6** (*attrib.*) characteristic of or suitable for summer (*summer clothes*). ● *v.* **1** *intr.* (usu. foll. by *at*, *in*) pass the summer. **2** *tr.* (often foll. by *at*, *in*) pasture (cattle). □ **summerless** *adj.* **summerly** *adv.* **summery** *adj.* [Old English *sumor*]

summer[2] /'sʌmə/ *n.* (in full **summer-tree**) a horizontal bearing beam, esp. one supporting joists or rafters. [Middle English via Anglo-French *sumer*, *somer* 'packhorse, beam', Old French *somier* and Late Latin *sagmarius*, from *sagma*, from Greek *sagma* 'packsaddle']

summer house *n.* a light building in a garden etc. used for sitting in in fine weather.

summer lightning *n.* sheet lightning without thunder, resulting from a distant storm.

summer pudding *n. Brit.* a pudding of soft summer fruit encased in bread or sponge.

summersault var. of SOMERSAULT.

summer school *n.* **1** esp. *Brit.* a course of lectures etc. held during the summer vacation, esp. at a university. **2** esp. *US* a course of remedial or accelerating classes held in the summer.

summer season *n.* a summer period during which people are employed with holiday entertainment, trade, etc.

summer solstice *n.* the solstice at midsummer, at the time of the longest day, about 21 June in the northern hemisphere and 22 Dec. in the southern hemisphere; in *Astron.*, the solstice in June.

summertime /'sʌmətʌɪm/ *n.* the season or period of summer (cf. SUMMER TIME).

summer time *n. Brit.* time as advanced one hour ahead of standard time for daylight saving in summer, esp. British Summer Time (cf. DAYLIGHT TIME).

summer-weight *adj.* (of clothes) suitable for use in summer, esp. because of their light weight.

summing-up *n.* **1** a review of evidence and a direction given by a judge to a jury. **2** a recapitulation of the main points of an argument, case, etc.

summit /'sʌmɪt/ *n.* **1** the highest point, esp. of a mountain; the apex. **2** the highest degree of power, ambition, etc. **3** (in full **summit meeting, talks**, etc.) a discussion, esp. on disarmament etc., between heads of government. □ **summitless** *adj.* [Middle English via Old French *somet*, *som(m)ete*, from *som* 'top', from Latin *summum*, neut. of *summus* 'highest']

summiteer /sʌmɪ'tɪə/ *n.* **1** a participant in a summit meeting. **2** a climber who has completed an ascent to a summit.

summon /'sʌmən/ *v.tr.* **1** call upon to appear, esp. as a defendant or witness in a law court. **2** (usu. foll. by *to* + infin.) call upon (*summoned her to assist*). **3** call together for a meeting or some other purpose (*summoned the members to attend*). **4** (often foll. by *up* and *to*, *for*) gather (courage, spirits, resources, etc.) (*summoned up her strength for the task*). □ **summonable** *adj.* **summoner** *n.* [Middle English via Old French *somondre* from Latin *summonēre* (as SUB-, *monēre* 'warn')]

summons /'sʌm(ə)nz/ *n.* & *v.* ● *n.* (*pl.* **summonses**) **1** an authoritative or urgent call to attend on some occasion or do something. **2 a** a call to appear before a judge or magistrate. **b** the writ containing such a summons. ● *v.tr.* esp. *Law* serve with a summons. [Middle English via Old French *somonce*, *sumunse* from Latin *summonita*, fem. past part. of *summonēre*: see SUMMON]

summum bonum /sʊməm 'bɒnəm, sʌməm 'bəʊnəm/ *n.* the highest good, esp. as the end or determining principle in an ethical system. [Latin]

sumo /'su:məʊ/ *n.* a style of Japanese heavyweight wrestling, in which a participant is defeated by touching the ground with any part of the body except the soles of the feet or by moving outside the marked area (often *attrib.*: *sumo wrestler*). [Japanese]

sump /sʌmp/ *n.* **1** a pit, well, hole, etc., in which superfluous liquid collects in mines, machines, etc. **2** a cesspool. [Middle English, = marsh, from Middle Dutch, Middle Low German *sump* or (in mining) German *Sumpf*, related to SWAMP]

sumpter /ˈsʌm(p)tə/ *n. archaic* **1** a packhorse. **2** any pack animal (*sumpter-mule*). [Middle English from Old French *som(m)etier* via Late Latin from Greek *sagma -atos* 'packsaddle': cf. SUMMER²]

sumptuary /ˈsʌm(p)tjʊəri/ *adj.* **1** regulating expenditure. **2** (of a law or edict etc.) limiting private expenditure in the interests of the state. [Latin *sumptuarius*, via *sumptus* 'cost' from *sumere sumpt-* 'take']

sumptuous /ˈsʌm(p)tjʊəs/ *adj.* rich, lavish, costly (*a sumptuous setting*). □ **sumptuosity** /-ˈɒsɪti/ *n.* **sumptuously** *adv.* **sumptuousness** *n.* [Middle English via Old French *somptueux* from Latin *sumptuosus* (as SUMPTUARY)]

sum total *n.* = SUM *n.* 1.

Sun. *abbr.* Sunday.

sun /sʌn/ *n. & v.* ● *n.* **1 a** the star round which the earth orbits and from which it receives light and warmth. **b** any similar star in the universe with or without planets. **2** the light or warmth received from the sun (*pull down the blinds and keep out the sun*). **3** *poet.* a day or a year. **4** *poet.* a person or thing regarded as a source of glory, radiance, etc. ● *v.* (**sunned**, **sunning**) **1** *refl.* bask in the sun. **2** *tr.* expose to the sun. **3** *intr.* sun oneself. □ **against the sun** anticlockwise. **beneath** (or **under**) **the sun** anywhere in the world. **in the sun** exposed to the sun's rays. **on which the sun never sets** (of an empire etc.) worldwide. **one's sun is set** the time of one's prosperity is over. **take** (or **shoot**) **the sun** *Naut.* ascertain the altitude of the sun with a sextant in order to fix the latitude. **with the sun** clockwise. □ **sunless** *adj.* **sunlessness** *n.* **sunlike** *adj.* **sunward** *adj. & adv.* **sunwards** *adv.* [Old English *sunne, sunna*]

sun and planet *n.* a system of gearing cogwheels.

sun-baked *adj.* dried or hardened or baked from the heat of the sun.

sun-bath *n.* a period of exposing the body to the sun.

sunbathe /ˈsʌnbeɪð/ *v.intr.* bask in the sun, esp. to tan the body. □ **sunbather** *n.*

sunbeam /ˈsʌnbiːm/ *n.* a ray of sunlight.

sun bear *n.* a small black bear, *Helarctos malayanus*, of SE Asia, with a light-coloured mark on its chest.

sunbed /ˈsʌnbɛd/ *n. Brit.* **1** a lightweight usu. folding chair with a seat long enough to support the legs, used for sunbathing. **2** a bed for lying on under a sunlamp.

sunbelt /ˈsʌnbɛlt/ *n.* a strip of territory receiving a high amount of sunshine, esp. the region in the southern US stretching from California to Florida.

sunbird /ˈsʌnbəːd/ *n.* any small bright-plumaged Old World bird of the family Nectariniidae, resembling a hummingbird.

sunblind /ˈsʌnblʌɪnd/ *n. Brit.* a window awning.

sunblock /ˈsʌnblɒk/ *n.* a cream or lotion for protecting the skin from the sun.

sun-bonnet *n.* a bonnet of cotton etc. covering the neck and shading the face, esp. for children.

sunbow /ˈsʌnbəʊ/ *n.* a spectrum of colours like a rainbow produced by the sun shining on spray etc.

sunburn /ˈsʌnbəːn/ *n. & v.* ● *n.* reddening and inflammation of the skin caused by over-exposure to the sun. ● *v.intr.* **1** suffer from sunburn. **2** (as **sunburnt** or **sunburned** *adj.*) suffering from sunburn; brown or tanned.

sunburst /ˈsʌnbəːst/ *n.* **1** something resembling the sun and its rays, esp.: **a** an ornament, brooch, etc. **b** a firework. **2** the sun shining suddenly from behind clouds.

sun cream *n.* cream for protecting the skin from sunburn and for promoting suntanning.

sundae /ˈsʌndeɪ, -di/ *n.* a dish of ice cream with fruit, nuts, syrup, etc. [perhaps from SUNDAY]

sun-dance *n.* a dance of N. American Indians in honour of the sun.

Sunday /ˈsʌndeɪ, -di/ *n. & adv.* ● *n.* **1** the first day of the week, a Christian holiday and day of worship. **2** a newspaper published on a Sunday. ● *adv. colloq.* **1** on Sunday. **2** (**Sundays**) on Sundays; each Sunday. [Old English *sunnandæg*, translation of Latin *dies solis*, Greek *hēmera hēliou* 'day of the sun']

Sunday best *n.* often *joc.* a person's best clothes, kept for Sunday use.

Sunday driver *n.* a person who drives chiefly at weekends, esp. slowly or unskilfully.

Sunday letter *n.* = DOMINICAL LETTER.

Sunday painter *n.* an amateur painter, esp. one with little training.

Sunday school *n.* a school for the religious instruction of children on Sundays.

sun deck *n.* **1** the upper deck of a steamer. **2** *N. Amer.* a terrace or balcony positioned to catch the sun.

sunder /ˈsʌndə/ *v.tr. & intr. archaic* or *literary* separate, sever. □ **in sunder** apart. [Old English *sundrian*, from *āsundrian* etc.: *in sunder* from Middle English from *o(n)sunder* ASUNDER]

sundew /ˈsʌndjuː/ *n.* any small insect-consuming bog plant of the family Droseraceae, esp. of the genus *Drosera* with hairs secreting drops of moisture.

sundial /ˈsʌndʌɪəl/ *n.* an instrument showing the time by the shadow of a pointer cast by the sun on to a graduated plate.

sun-disc *n.* a winged disc, emblematic of the sun-god.

sun-dog *n.* = PARHELION.

sundown /ˈsʌndaʊn/ *n.* sunset.

sundowner /ˈsʌndaʊnə/ *n.* **1** *Austral. & NZ colloq.* a tramp, originally one who arrived at a sheep station etc. in the evening (under the pretence of seeking work) so as to obtain food and shelter. **2** *Brit. colloq.* an alcoholic drink taken at sunset.

sundress /ˈsʌndrɛs/ *n.* a dress without sleeves and with a low neck.

sun-dried *adj.* dried by the sun, not by artificial heat.

sundry /ˈsʌndri/ *adj. & n.* ● *adj.* various; several (*sundry items*). ● *n.* (*pl.* **-ies**) **1** (in *pl.*) items or oddments not mentioned individually. **2** *Austral. Cricket* = EXTRA *n.* 5. [Old English *syndrig* 'separate', related to SUNDER]

sunfast /ˈsʌnfɑːst/ *adj. US* (of dye) not subject to fading by sunlight.

sunfish /ˈsʌnfɪʃ/ *n.* (*pl.* usu. same) any of various fishes of rounded form or brilliant appearance, esp. a very large ocean fish, *Mola mola*, with a circular laterally flattened body.

sunflower /ˈsʌnflaʊə/ *n.* any very tall plant of the genus *Helianthus*, esp. *H. annus* with very large showy golden-rayed flowers, grown also for its seeds which yield an edible oil.

sung *past part.* of SING.

sunglasses /ˈsʌnglɑːsɪz/ *n.pl.* glasses tinted to protect the eyes from sunlight or glare.

sun-god *n.* the sun worshipped as a deity.

sunhat /ˈsʌnhat/ *n.* a hat designed to protect the head from the sun.

sun-helmet *n.* a helmet of cork etc. formerly worn by white people in the tropics.

sun in splendour *n. Heraldry* the sun with rays and a human face.

sunk *past* and *past part.* of SINK.

sunken /ˈsʌŋk(ə)n/ *adj.* **1** that has been sunk. **2** beneath the surface; submerged. **3** (of the eyes, cheeks, etc.) hollow, depressed. [past part. of SINK]

sunken garden *n.* a garden placed below the general level of its surroundings.

sunk fence *n.* a fence formed by, or along the bottom of, a ditch.

sun-kissed *adj.* warmed or affected by the sun.

sunlamp /ˈsʌnlamp/ *n.* **1** a lamp giving ultraviolet rays for an artificial suntan, therapy, etc. **2** *Cinematog.* a large lamp with a parabolic reflector used in film-making.

sunlight /ˈsʌnlʌɪt/ *n.* light from the sun. ▫ **sunlit** *adj.*

sun lounge *n. Brit.* a room with large windows, designed to receive sunlight.

sunlounger /ˈsʌnlaʊn(d)ʒə/ *n. Brit.* = SUNBED 1.

sunn /sʌn/ *n.* (in full **sunn hemp**) a hemplike fibre of southern Asia. [Urdu & Hindi *san* from Sanskrit *śāṇá* 'hempen']

Sunna /ˈsʊnə, ˈsʌnə/ *n.* a traditional portion of Muslim law based on Muhammad's words or acts, accepted (together with the Koran) as authoritative by Muslims. [Arabic, = form, way, course, rule]

Sunni /ˈsʊni, ˈsʌni/ *n. & adj.* ● *n.* (*pl.* same or **Sunnis**) **1** one of the two main branches of Islam, commonly described as orthodox, and differing from the Shia in its understanding of the Sunna and in its rejection of Ali as Muhammad's first successor (cf. SHIA). **2** an adherent of this branch of Islam. ● *adj.* of or relating to Sunni.

sunny /ˈsʌni/ *adj.* (**sunnier**, **sunniest**) **1 a** bright with sunlight. **b** exposed to or warmed by the sun. **2** cheery and bright in temperament. ▫ **sunnily** *adv.* **sunniness** *n.*

sunny side *n.* **1** the side of a house, street, etc., that gets most sun. **2** the more cheerful aspect of circumstances etc. (*always looks on the sunny side*). ▫ **sunny side up** *N. Amer.* (of an egg) fried on one side only.

sunray pleats *n.pl.* widening pleats radiating out from a skirt's waistband.

sunrays /ˈsʌnreɪz/ *n.pl.* **1** sunbeams. **2** ultraviolet rays used therapeutically.

sunrise /ˈsʌnrʌɪz/ *n.* **1** the sun's rising at dawn. **2** the coloured sky associated with this. **3** the time at which sunrise occurs.

sunrise industry *n.* any newly established industry, esp. in electronics and telecommunications, regarded as signalling prosperity.

sunroof /ˈsʌnruːf/ *n.* a sliding roof on a car.

sunroom /ˈsʌnruːm, -rʊm/ *n.* **1** = SUN LOUNGE. **2** esp. *N. Amer.* a solarium.

sunscreen /ˈsʌnskriːn/ *n.* a cream or lotion rubbed on to the skin to protect it from the sun.

sunset /ˈsʌnsɛt/ *n.* **1** the sun's setting in the evening. **2** the coloured sky associated with this. **3** the time at which sunset occurs. **4** the declining period of life.

sunset provision *n. US* a provision for an agency or programme to be disbanded or terminated at the end of a fixed period unless formally renewed.

sunshade /ˈsʌnʃeɪd/ *n.* **1** a parasol. **2** an awning.

sunshine /ˈsʌnʃʌɪn/ *n.* **1 a** the light of the sun. **b** an area lit by the sun. **2** fine weather. **3** cheerfulness; joy (*brought sunshine into her life*). **4** *Brit. colloq.* a form of address. ▫ **sunshiny** *adj.*

sunshine law *n. US* a law requiring certain official meetings, records, etc., of certain government agencies to be open or available to the public.

sunshine roof *n. Brit.* = SUNROOF.

Sunshine State *n.* any of the States of New Mexico, South Dakota, California, and Florida.

sunspot /ˈsʌnspɒt/ *n.* one of the dark patches, changing in shape and size and lasting for varying periods, observed on the sun's surface.

sunstar /ˈsʌnstɑː/ *n.* any starfish of the genus *Solaster*, with many arms.

sunstone /ˈsʌnstəʊn/ *n.* a cat's-eye gem, esp. feldspar with embedded flecks of haematite etc.

sunstroke /ˈsʌnstrəʊk/ *n.* acute prostration or collapse from the excessive heat of the sun.

sunsuit /ˈsʌnsuːt, -sjuːt/ *n.* a playsuit, esp. for children, suitable for sunbathing.

suntan /ˈsʌntan/ *n. & v.* ● *n.* the brownish colouring of skin caused by exposure to the sun. ● *v.intr.* (**-tanned**, **-tanning**) colour the skin with a suntan.

suntrap /ˈsʌntrap/ *n. Brit.* a place sheltered from the wind and suitable for catching the sunshine.

sunup /ˈsʌnʌp/ *n.* esp. *N. Amer.* sunrise.

sun visor *n.* a fixed or movable shield at the top of a vehicle windscreen to shield the eyes from the sun.

sup[1] /sʌp/ *v. & n.* ● *v.tr.* (**supped**, **supping**) **1** take (soup, tea, etc.) by sips or spoonfuls. **2** esp. *N.Engl. colloq.* drink (alcohol). ● *n.* a sip of liquid. [Old English *sūpan*]

sup[2] /sʌp/ *v.intr.* (**supped**, **supping**) (usu. foll. by *off, on*) *archaic* take supper. [Old French *super*, *soper*]

sup- /sʌp, səp/ *prefix* assim. form of SUB- before *p*.

Supadriv /ˈsuːpədrʌɪv/ *n. propr.* a type of cross-head screwdriver which holds a screw unsupported on its tip while the hole is located.

super /ˈsuːpə, ˈsjuː-/ *adj. & n.* ● *adj.* **1** (also **super-duper** /-ˈduːpə/) (also as *int.*) *colloq.* exceptional; splendid. **2** *Commerce* = SUPERFINE 1. **3** *Brit. Commerce* (of a measure) superficial, in square (not lineal or solid) measure (*120 super ft*; *120 ft super*). ● *n. colloq.* **1** *Theatr.* a supernumerary actor. **2** a superintendent. **3** superphosphate. **4** an extra, unwanted, or unimportant person; a supernumerary. **5** *Commerce* superfine cloth or manufacture. [abbreviation]

super- /ˈsuːpə, ˈsjuː-/ *comb. form* forming nouns, adjectives, and verbs, meaning: **1** above, beyond, or over in place or time or conceptually (*superstructure*; *supernormal*; *superimpose*). **2** to a great or extreme degree (*superabundant*; *supereminent*). **3** extra good or large of its kind (*supertanker*). **4** of a higher kind, esp. in names of classificatory divisions (*superclass*). [from or suggested by Latin *super-* from *super* 'above, beyond']

superable /ˈsuːp(ə)rəb(ə)l, ˈsjuː-/ *adj.* able to be overcome. [Latin *superabilis* from *superare* 'overcome']

superabound /suːp(ə)rəˈbaʊnd, sjuː-/ *v.intr.* be very or too abundant. [Late Latin *superabundare* (as SUPER-, ABOUND)]

superabundant /suːp(ə)rəˈbʌnd(ə)nt, sjuː-/ *adj.* abounding beyond what is normal or right. ▫ **superabundance** *n.* **superabundantly** *adv.* [Middle English from Late Latin *superabundare*: see SUPERABOUND]

superadd /suːpərˈad, sjuː-/ *v.tr.* add over and above. ▫ **superaddition** /-əˈdɪʃ(ə)n/ *n.* [Middle English from Latin *superaddere* (as SUPER-, ADD)]

superaltar /ˈsuːpərɔːltə, -rɒl-, sjuː-/ *n. Eccl.* a portable slab of stone consecrated for use on an unconsecrated altar etc. [Middle English from medieval Latin *superaltare* (as SUPER-, ALTAR)]

superannuate /suːpərˈanjʊeɪt, sjuː-/ *v.tr.* **1** retire (a person) with a pension. **2** dismiss or discard as too old for use, work, etc. **3** (as **superannuated** *adj.*) too old for work or use; obsolete. **4 a** make (a post) pensionable. **b** make pensionable the post of (an employee). ▫ **superannuable** *adj.* [back-formation from *superannuated* from medieval Latin *superannuatus*, from Latin SUPER- + *annus* 'year']

superannuation /ˌsuːpəranjʊˈeɪʃ(ə)n, ˌsjuː-/ *n.* **1** a pension paid to a retired person. **2** a regular payment made towards this by an employed person. **3** the process or an instance of superannuating.

superaqueous /ˌsuːpərˈeɪkwɪəs, ˌsjuː-/ *adj.* above water.

superb /suːˈpəːb, sjuː-/ *adj.* **1** of the most impressive, splendid, grand, or majestic kind (*superb courage*; *a superb specimen*). **2** *colloq.* excellent; fine. ▫ **superbly** *adv.* **superbness** *n.* [French *superbe* or Latin *superbus* 'proud']

Super Bowl *n. propr.* (in American football) the deciding game played annually between the champions of the National Football League and the American Football Conference.

supercalender /suːpəˈkalɪndə, ˌsjuː-/ *v.tr.* give a highly glazed finish to (paper) by extra calendering.

supercargo /suːpəˈkɑːgəʊ, sjuː-/ *n.* (*pl.* **-oes** or **-os**) an officer in a merchant ship managing sales etc. of cargo. [earlier *supracargo* from Spanish *sobrecargo*, from *sobre* 'over' + *cargo* CARGO]

supercede var. of SUPERSEDE.

supercelestial /ˌsuːpəsɪˈlɛstɪəl, ˌsjuː-/ *adj.* **1** above the heavens. **2** more than heavenly. [Late Latin *supercaelestis* (as SUPER-, CELESTIAL)]

supercharge /ˈsuːpətʃɑːdʒ, ˈsjuː-/ *v.tr.* **1** (usu. foll. by *with*) charge (the atmosphere etc.) with energy, emotion, etc. **2** use a supercharger on (an internal-combustion engine).

supercharger /ˈsuːpətʃɑːdʒə, ˈsjuː-/ *n.* a device supplying air or fuel to an internal-combustion engine at above normal pressure to increase efficiency.

superciliary /suːpəˈsɪlɪəri, sjuː-/ *adj. Anat.* of or concerning the eyebrow; over the eye. [Latin *supercilium* 'eyebrow' (as SUPER-, *cilium* 'eyelid')]

supercilious /suːpəˈsɪlɪəs, sjuː-/ *adj.* assuming an air of contemptuous indifference or superiority. □ **superciliously** *adv.* **superciliousness** *n.* [Latin *superciliosus* (as SUPERCILIARY)]

superclass /ˈsuːpəklɑːs, ˈsjuː-/ *n.* a taxonomic category between class and phylum.

supercolumnar /ˌsuːpəkəˈlʌmnə, ˌsjuː-/ *adj. Archit.* having one order or set of columns above another. □ **supercolumniation** /-nɪˈeɪʃ(ə)n/ *n.*

supercomputer /ˈsuːpəkəmpjuːtə, ˈsjuː-/ *n.* an exceptionally powerful mainframe computer capable of dealing with complex problems. □ **supercomputing** *n.*

superconductivity /ˌsuːpəkɒndʌkˈtɪvɪti, ˌsjuː-/ *n. Physics* the property of zero electrical resistance in some substances at very low absolute temperatures. □ **superconducting** /-kənˈdʌktɪŋ/ *adj.* **superconductive** /-kənˈdʌktɪv/ *adj.*

superconductor /ˌsuːpəkənˈdʌktə, ˌsjuː-/ *n. Physics* a substance having superconductivity.

superconscious /suːpəˈkɒnʃəs, sjuː-/ *adj.* transcending human consciousness. □ **superconsciously** *adv.* **superconsciousness** *n.*

supercontinent /ˈsuːpəkɒntɪnənt, ˈsjuː-/ *n. Geol.* each of several large land masses thought to have divided to form the present continents in the geological past.

supercool /suːpəˈkuːl, sjuː-/ *v. & adj.* ● *v. Chem.* **1** *tr.* cool (a liquid) below its freezing point without solidification or crystallization. **2** *intr.* (of a liquid) be cooled in this way. ● *adj. slang* very cool, relaxed, fine, etc.

supercritical /suːpəˈkrɪtɪk(ə)l, sjuː-/ *adj. Physics* of more than critical mass etc.

super-duper var. of SUPER *adj.* 1.

superego /suːpərˈiːgəʊ, -ˈɛgəʊ, sjuː-/ *n.* (*pl.* **-os**) *Psychol.* the part of the mind that acts as a conscience and responds to social rules.

superelevation /ˌsuːpərɛlɪˈveɪʃ(ə)n, ˌsjuː-/ *n.* the amount by which the outer edge of a curve on a road or railway is above the inner edge.

supereminent /suːpərˈɛmɪnənt, sjuː-/ *adj.* supremely eminent, exalted, or remarkable. □ **supereminence** *n.* **supereminently** *adv.* [Latin *supereminēre* 'rise above' (as SUPER-, EMINENT)]

supererogation /ˌsuːpərɛrəˈgeɪʃ(ə)n, ˌsjuː-/ *n.* the performance of more than duty requires. □ **supererogatory** /-ɪˈrɒgət(ə)ri/ *adj.* [Late Latin *supererogatio* from *supererogare* 'to pay in addition' (as SUPER-, *erogare* 'pay out')]

superfamily /ˈsuːpəˌfamɪli, -m(ə)l-, ˈsjuː-/ *n.* (*pl.* **-ies**) a taxonomic category between family and order.

superfatted /suːpəˈfatɪd, sjuː-/ *adj.* (of soap) containing extra fat.

superfecundation /ˌsuːpəfɛk(ə)nˈdeɪʃ(ə)n, -fiːk-, ˌsjuː-/ *n.* = SUPERFETATION 1.

superfetation /suːpəfiːˈteɪʃ(ə)n, sjuː-/ *n.* **1** *Med. & Zool.* a second conception during pregnancy giving rise to embryos of different ages in the uterus. **2** *Bot.* the fertilization of the same ovule by different kinds of pollen. **3** the accretion of one thing on another. [French *superfétation* or via modern Latin *superfetatio* from Latin *superfetare* (as SUPER-, *fetus* FOETUS)]

superficial /suːpəˈfɪʃ(ə)l, sjuː-/ *adj.* **1** of or on the surface; lacking depth (*a superficial knowledge*; *superficial wounds*). **2** swift or cursory (*a superficial examination*). **3** apparent but not real (*a superficial resemblance*). **4** (esp. of a person) having no depth of character or knowledge; trivial; shallow. **5** *Brit. Commerce* (of a measure) square (cf. SUPER *adj.* 3). □ **superficiality** /-ʃɪˈalɪti/ *n.* (*pl.* **-ies**). **superficially** *adv.* **superficialness** *n.* [Late Latin *superficialis* from Latin (as SUPERFICIES)]

superficies /suːpəˈfɪʃɪiːz, sjuː-/ *n.* (*pl.* same) *Geom.* a surface. [Latin (as SUPER-, *facies* 'face')]

superfine /ˈsuːpəfʌɪn, suːpəˈfʌɪn, sjuː-/ *adj.* **1** *Commerce* of extra quality. **2** pretending great refinement. [medieval Latin *superfinus* (as SUPER-, FINE[1])]

superfluidity /suːpəfluːˈɪdɪti, sjuː-/ *n.* the property of flowing without friction or viscosity, as in liquid helium below about 2.18 kelvins. □ **superfluid** *n. & adj.*

superfluity /suːpəˈfluːɪti, sjuː-/ *n.* (*pl.* **-ies**) **1** the state of being superfluous. **2** a superfluous amount or thing. [Middle English via Old French *superfluité* and Late Latin *superfluitas -tatis* from Latin *superfluus*: see SUPERFLUOUS]

superfluous /suːˈpəːflʊəs, sjuː-/ *adj.* more than enough, redundant, needless. □ **superfluously** *adv.* **superfluousness** *n.* [Middle English from Latin *superfluus* (as SUPER-, *fluere* 'to flow')]

supergiant /ˈsuːpədʒʌɪənt, ˈsjuː-/ *n.* a star of very great luminosity and size.

superglue /ˈsuːpəgluː, ˈsjuː-/ *n. & v.* ● *n.* any of various adhesives with an exceptional bonding capability. ● *v.tr.* (**-glues**, **-glued**, **-gluing** or **-glueing**) stick with superglue.

supergrass /ˈsuːpəgrɑːs, ˈsjuː-/ *n. Brit. colloq.* a police informer who implicates a large number of people.

superheat /suːpəˈhiːt, sjuː-/ *v.tr. Physics* **1** heat (a liquid) above its boiling point without vaporization. **2** heat (a vapour) above its boiling point (*superheated steam*). □ **superheater** *n.*

superhero /ˈsuːpəhɪərəʊ, ˈsjuː-/ *n.* (*pl.* **-oes**) a person or fictional character with extraordinary heroic attributes.

superhet /ˈsuːpəhɛt, ˈsjuː-/ *n. colloq.* = SUPERHETERODYNE.

superheterodyne /suːpəˈhɛt(ə)rədʌɪn, sjuː-/ *adj. & n.* ● *adj.* denoting or characteristic of a system of radio reception in which a local variable oscillator is tuned to beat at a constant ultrasonic frequency with carrier-wave frequencies, making it unnecessary to vary the amplifier tuning and securing greater selectivity. ● *n.* a superheterodyne receiver. [SUPERSONIC + HETERODYNE]

superhighway /ˈsuːpəhʌɪweɪ, ˈsjuː-/ *n.* **1** *N. Amer.* a dual carriageway with two or more lanes in each direction. **2** (in full **information superhighway**) a means of rapid transfer of information in different digital forms (e.g. video, sound, and graphics) via an extensive electronic network.

superhuman /suːpəˈhjuːmən, sjuː-/ *adj.* **1** beyond normal human capability. **2** higher than man. □ **superhumanly** *adv.* [Late Latin *superhumanus* (as SUPER-, HUMAN)]

superhumeral /suːpəˈhjuːm(ə)r(ə)l, sjuː-/ *n. Eccl.* a vestment worn over the shoulders, e.g. an amice, ephod, or pallium. [Late Latin *superhumerale* (as SUPER-, HUMERAL)]

superimpose /suːp(ə)rɪmˈpəʊz, sjuː-/ *v.tr.* (usu. foll. by *on*) lay (a thing) on something else. □ **superimposition** /-pəˈzɪʃ(ə)n/ *n.*

superincumbent /suːp(ə)rɪnˈkʌmbənt, sjuː-/ *adj.* lying on something else.

superinduce /suːp(ə)rɪnˈdjuːs, sjuː-/ *v.tr.* introduce or induce in addition. [Latin *superinducere* 'cover over, bring from outside' (as SUPER-, INDUCE)]

superintend /suːp(ə)rɪnˈtɛnd, sjuː-/ *v.tr. & intr.* be responsible for the management or arrangement of (an activity etc.); supervise and inspect. □ **superintendence** *n.* **superintendency** *n.* [ecclesiastical Latin *superintendere* (as SUPER-, INTEND), translation of Greek *episkopō*]

superintendent /suːp(ə)rɪn'tɛnd(ə)nt, sjuː-/ *n.* & *adj.* ● *n.* **1 a** a person who superintends. **b** a director of an institution etc. **2 a** (in the UK) a police officer above the rank of inspector. **b** (in the US) a high-ranking official, often the chief of a police department. **3** *US* the caretaker of a building. ● *adj.* superintending. [ecclesiastical Latin *superintendent-*, part. stem of *superintendere*: see SUPERINTEND]

superior /suː'pɪərɪə, sjuː-/ *adj.* & *n.* ● *adj.* **1** in a higher position; of higher rank (*a superior officer*; *a superior court*). **2 a** above the average in quality etc. (*made of superior leather*). **b** having or showing a high opinion of oneself; supercilious (*had a superior air*). **3** (often foll. by *to*) **a** better or greater in some respect (*superior to its rivals in speed*). **b** above yielding, making concessions, paying attention, etc. (*is superior to bribery*; *superior to temptation*). **4** further above or out; higher, esp.: **a** *Astron.* (of a planet) having an orbit further from the sun than the earth's. **b** *Zool.* (of an insect's wings) folding over others. **c** *Printing* (of figures or letters) placed above the line. **d** *Bot.* (of the calyx) above the ovary. **e** *Bot.* (of the ovary) above the calyx. ● *n.* **1** a person superior to another in rank, character, etc. (*is deferential to his superiors*; *is his superior in courage*). **2** (*fem.* **superioress** /-rɪs/) *Eccl.* the head of a monastery or other religious institution (*Mother Superior*; *Father Superior*). **3** *Printing* a superior letter or figure. □ **superiorly** *adv.* [Middle English via Old French *superiour* from Latin *superior -oris*, comparative of *superus* 'that is above', from *super* 'above']

superiority /suːˌpɪərɪ'ɒrɪti, sjuː-/ *n.* the state of being superior.

superiority complex *n. Psychol.* an undue conviction of one's own superiority to others.

superior numbers *n.pl.* esp. *Mil.* more men etc. or their strength (*overcome by superior numbers*).

superjacent /suːpə'dʒeɪs(ə)nt, sjuː-/ *adj.* overlying; superincumbent. [Latin *superjacēre* (as SUPER-, *jacēre* 'lie')]

superlative /suː'pəːlətɪv, sjuː-/ *adj.* & *n.* ● *adj.* **1** of the highest quality or degree (*superlative wisdom*). **2** *Gram.* (of an adjective or adverb) expressing the highest or a very high degree of a quality (e.g. *bravest*, *most fiercely*) (cf. POSITIVE *adj.* 3b, COMPARATIVE *adj.* 4). ● *n.* **1** *Gram.* **a** the superlative expression or form of an adjective or adverb. **b** a word in the superlative. **2** something embodying excellence; the highest form of a thing. **3** (usu. in *pl.*) a hyperbolical expression, esp. of praise. □ **superlatively** *adv.* **superlativeness** *n.* [Middle English via Old French *superlatif -ive* and Late Latin *superlativus* from Latin *superlatus* (as SUPER-, *latus*, past part. of *ferre* 'take')]

superluminal /suːpə'luːmɪn(ə)l, sjuː-/ *adj. Physics* of or having a speed greater than that of light. [SUPER- + Latin *lumen luminis* 'a light']

superlunary /suːpə'luːnəri, sjuː-/ *adj.* **1** situated beyond the moon. **2** belonging to a higher world, celestial. [medieval Latin *superlunaris* (as SUPER-, LUNAR)]

superman /'suːpəman, 'sjuː-/ *n.* (*pl.* **-men**) **1** esp. *Philos.* the ideal superior man of the future. **2** *colloq.* a man of exceptional strength or ability. [SUPER- + MAN, formed by G. B. Shaw in imitation of Nietzsche's German *Übermensch*]

supermarket /'suːpəmɑːkɪt, 'sjuː-/ *n.* a large self-service store selling foods, household goods, etc.

supermodel /'suːpəmɒd(ə)l, 'sjuː-/ *n.* a highly-paid model employed in high-profile glamour modelling.

supermundane /suːpə'mʌndeɪn, sjuː-/ *adj.* superior to earthly things.

supernal /suː'pəːn(ə)l, sjuː-/ *adj.* esp. *poet.* **1** heavenly; divine. **2** of or concerning the sky. **3** lofty. □ **supernally** *adv.* [Middle English via Old French *supernal* or medieval Latin *supernalis* from Latin *supernus*, from *super* 'above']

supernatant /suːpə'neɪt(ə)nt, sjuː-/ *adj.* & *n.* esp. *Chem.* ● *adj.* (of a liquid) lying above a solid residue after precipitation, centrifugation, etc. ● *n.* a supernatant substance. [SUPER- + *natant* 'swimming' (as NATATION)]

supernatural /suːpə'natʃ(ə)r(ə)l, sjuː-/ *adj.* & *n.* ● *adj.* attributed to or thought to reveal some force above the laws of nature; magical, occult, mystical. ● *n.* (prec. by *the*) supernatural, occult, or magical forces, effects, etc. □ **supernaturalism** *n.* **supernaturalist** *n.* **supernaturalize** *v.tr.* (also **-ise**). **supernaturally** *adv.* **supernaturalness** *n.*

supernormal /suːpə'nɔːm(ə)l, sjuː-/ *adj.* beyond what is normal or natural. □ **supernormality** /-'malɪti/ *n.*

supernova /suːpə'nəʊvə, sjuː-/ *n.* (*pl.* **-novae** /-viː/ or **-novas**) *Astron.* a star that suddenly increases very greatly in brightness because of an explosion ejecting most of its mass.

supernumerary /suːpə'njuːm(ə)r(ə)ri, sjuː-/ *adj.* & *n.* ● *adj.* **1** in excess of the normal number; extra. **2** (of a person) engaged for extra work. **3** (of an actor) appearing on stage but not speaking. ● *n.* (*pl.* **-ies**) **1** an extra or unwanted person or thing. **2** a supernumerary actor. **3** a person engaged for extra work. [Late Latin *supernumerarius* '(soldier) added to a legion already complete', from Latin *super numerum* 'beyond the number']

superorder /'suːpərɔːdə, 'sjuː-/ *n. Biol.* a taxonomic category between order and class. □ **superordinal** /-'ɔːdɪn(ə)l/ *adj.*

superordinate /suːpər'ɔːdɪnət, sjuː-/ *adj.* & *n.* ● *adj.* (usu. foll. by *to*) of superior importance or rank. ● *n.* **1** a superordinate person or thing; a superior. **2** *Linguistics* a word whose meaning implies or includes that of another. [SUPER-, on the pattern of *subordinate*]

superphosphate /suːpə'fɒsfeɪt, sjuː-/ *n.* a fertilizer made by treating phosphate rock with sulphuric or phosphoric acid.

superphysical /suːpə'fɪzɪk(ə)l, sjuː-/ *adj.* **1** unexplainable by physical causes; supernatural. **2** beyond what is physical.

superpose /suːpə'pəʊz, sjuː-/ *v.tr.* (usu. foll. by *on*) esp. *Geom.* place (a thing or a geometric figure) on or above something else, esp. so as to coincide. □ **superposition** /-pə'zɪʃ(ə)n/ *n.* [French *superposer* (as SUPER-, POSE[1])]

superpower /'suːpəpaʊə, 'sjuː-/ *n.* a state of supreme power and influence, esp. the US and, formerly, the USSR.

supersaturate /suːpə'satʃʊreɪt, -tjʊreɪt, sjuː-/ *v.tr.* add to (esp. a solution) beyond saturation point. □ **supersaturation** /-'reɪʃ(ə)n/ *n.*

superscribe /suːpə'skrʌɪb, 'suːpəskrʌɪb, sjuː-/ *v.tr.* **1** write (an inscription) at the top of or on the outside of a document etc. **2** write an inscription over or on (a thing). □ **superscription** /-'skrɪpʃ(ə)n/ *n.* [Latin *superscribere* (as SUPER-, *scribere script-* 'write')]

superscript /'suːpəskrɪpt, 'sjuː-/ *adj.* & *n.* ● *adj.* written or printed above the line, esp. *Math.* (of a symbol) written above and to the right of another. ● *n.* a superscript number or symbol. [Latin *superscriptus*, past part. of *superscribere*: see SUPERSCRIBE]

supersede /suːpə'siːd, sjuː-/ *v.tr.* (also *disp.* **supercede**) **1 a** adopt or appoint another person or thing in place of. **b** set aside; cease to employ. **2** (of a person or thing) take the place of. □ **supersedence** *n.* **supersedure** /-dʒə/ *n.* **supersession** /-'sɛʃ(ə)n/ *n.* [Old French *superseder* from Latin *supersedēre* 'be superior to' (as SUPER-, *sedēre sess-* 'sit')]

supersonic /suːpə'sɒnɪk, sjuː-/ *adj.* designating or having a speed greater than that of sound. □ **supersonically** *adv.*

supersonics /suːpə'sɒnɪks, sjuː-/ *n.pl.* (treated as *sing.*) = ULTRASONICS.

superstar /'suːpəstɑː, 'sjuː-/ *n.* an extremely famous or renowned actor, film star, musician, etc. □ **superstardom** *n.*

superstate /'suːpəsteɪt, 'sjuː-/ *n.* a powerful political state, esp. one formed from a federation of nations.

superstition /su:pə'stɪʃ(ə)n, sju:-/ *n.* **1** credulity regarding the supernatural. **2** an irrational fear of the unknown or mysterious. **3** misdirected reverence. **4** a practice, opinion, or religion based on these tendencies. **5** a widely held but unjustified idea of the effects or nature of a thing. □ **superstitious** *adj.* **superstitiously** *adv.* **superstitiousness** *n.* [Middle English from Old French *superstition* or Latin *superstitio* (as SUPER-, *stare stat-* 'stand')]

superstore /'su:pəstɔ:, 'sju:-/ *n.* a large supermarket selling a wide range of goods.

superstratum /su:pə'strɑ:təm, -'streɪtəm, sju:-/ *n.* (*pl.* **-strata** /-tə/) an overlying stratum.

superstructure /'su:pəstrʌktʃə, 'sju:-/ *n.* **1** the part of a building above its foundations. **2** a structure built on top of something else. **3** a concept or idea based on others. □ **superstructural** *adj.*

supersubtle /su:pə'sʌt(ə)l, sju:-/ *adj.* extremely or excessively subtle. □ **supersubtlety** *n.*

supertanker /'su:pətaŋkə, 'sju:-/ *n.* a very large tanker ship.

supertax /'su:pətaks, 'sju:-/ *n.* a higher rate of tax on incomes above a certain level, esp. *hist.* that levied in Britain between 1909 and 1929 (succeeded by SURTAX).

superterrestrial /su:pətə'rɛstrɪəl, sju:-/ *adj.* **1** in or belonging to a region above the earth. **2** celestial.

supertonic /su:pə'tɒnɪk, sju:-/ *n. Mus.* the note above the tonic, the second note of the diatonic scale of any key.

supervene /su:pə'vi:n, sju:-/ *v.intr.* occur as an interruption in or a change from some state. □ **supervenient** *adj.* **supervention** /-'vɛnʃ(ə)n/ *n.* [Latin *supervenire supervent-* (as SUPER-, *venire* 'come')]

supervise /'su:pəvʌɪz, 'sju:-/ *v.tr.* **1** superintend, oversee the execution of (a task etc.). **2** oversee the actions or work of (a person). □ **supervision** /-'vɪʒ(ə)n/ *n.* **supervisor** *n.* **supervisory** *adj.* [medieval Latin *supervidēre supervis-* (as SUPER-, *vidēre* 'see')]

superwoman /'su:pəwʊmən, 'sju:-/ *n.* (*pl.* **-women**) *colloq.* a woman of exceptional strength or ability.

supinate /'su:pɪneɪt, 'sju:-/ *v.tr.* put (a hand or foreleg etc.) into a supine position (cf. PRONATE). □ **supination** /-'neɪʃ(ə)n/ *n.* [back-formation from *supination*, from Latin *supinatio* via *supinare* from *supinus*: see SUPINE]

supinator /'su:pɪneɪtə, 'sju:-/ *n. Anat.* a muscle in the forearm effecting supination.

supine /'su:pʌɪn, 'sju:-/ *adj.* & *n.* ● *adj.* **1** lying face upwards (cf. PRONE 1a). **2** having the front or ventral part upwards; (of the hand) with the palm upwards. **3** inert, indolent; morally or mentally inactive. ● *n.* a Latin verbal noun used only in the accusative and ablative cases, esp. to denote purpose (e.g. *mirabile dictu* wonderful to relate). □ **supinely** *adv.* **supineness** *n.* [*adj.* from Latin *supinus*, related to *super* 'above'; *n.* from Late Latin *supinum*, neut. of *supinus* (reason unknown)]

supper /'sʌpə/ *n.* an evening meal, esp. a light or informal one. □ **sing for one's supper** do something in return for a benefit. □ **supperless** *adj.* [Middle English from Old French *soper, super*]

supplant /sə'plɑ:nt/ *v.tr.* dispossess and take the place of, esp. by underhand means. □ **supplanter** *n.* [Middle English from Old French *supplanter* or Latin *supplantare* 'trip up' (as SUB-, *planta* 'sole')]

supple /'sʌp(ə)l/ *adj.* & *v.* ● *adj.* (**suppler**, **supplest**) **1** flexible, pliant; easily bent. **2** compliant; avoiding overt resistance; artfully or servilely submissive. ● *v.tr.* & *intr.* make or become supple. □ **suppleness** *n.* [Middle English from Old French *souple*, ultimately from Latin *supplex supplicis* 'submissive']

supplejack /'sʌp(ə)ldʒak/ *n.* any of various strong twining tropical shrubs, e.g. *Berchemia scandens*. [SUPPLE + JACK[1]]

supplely var. of SUPPLY[2].

supplement *n.* & *v.* ● *n.* /'sʌplɪm(ə)nt/ **1** a thing or part added to remedy deficiencies (*dietary supplement*). **2** a part added to a book etc. to provide further information. **3** a separate section, esp. a colour magazine, added to a newspaper or periodical. **4** an additional charge payable for an extra service or facility. **5** *Geom.* the amount by which an angle is less than 180° (cf. COMPLEMENT *n.* 6). ● *v.tr.* /'sʌplɪmɛnt, sʌplɪ'mɛnt/ provide a supplement for. □ **supplemental** /-'mɛnt(ə)l/ *adj.* **supplementally** /-'mɛnt(ə)li/ *adv.* **supplementation** /-'teɪʃ(ə)n/ *n.* [Middle English from Latin *supplementum* (as SUB-, *plēre* 'fill')]

supplementary /sʌplɪ'mɛnt(ə)ri/ *adj.* forming or serving as a supplement; additional. □ **supplementarily** *adv.*

supplementary benefit *n. hist.* (in the UK) a weekly allowance formerly paid by the state to those with an income below a certain level, now replaced by INCOME SUPPORT.

suppletion /sə'pli:ʃ(ə)n/ *n.* the act or an instance of supplementing, esp. *Linguistics* the occurrence of unrelated forms to supply gaps in conjugation (e.g. *went* as the past of *go*). □ **suppletive** *adj.* [Middle English via Old French from medieval Latin *suppletio -onis* (as SUPPLY[1])]

suppliant /'sʌplɪənt/ *adj.* & *n.* ● *adj.* **1** supplicating. **2** expressing supplication. ● *n.* a supplicating person. □ **suppliantly** *adv.* [Middle English via French *supplier* 'beseech' from Latin (as SUPPLICATE)]

supplicate /'sʌplɪkeɪt/ *v. formal* **1** *tr.* petition humbly to (a person) or for (a thing). **2** *intr.* (foll. by *to, for*) make a petition. □ **supplicant** *adj.* & *n.* **supplication** /-'keɪʃ(ə)n/ *n.* **supplicatory** /-kət(ə)ri/ *adj.* [Middle English from Latin *supplicare* (as SUB-, *plicare* 'bend')]

supply[1] /sə'plʌɪ/ *v.* & *n.* ● *v.tr.* (**-ies**, **-ied**) **1** provide or furnish (a thing needed). **2** (often foll. by *with*) provide (a person etc. with a thing needed). **3** meet or make up for (a deficiency or need etc.). **4** fill (a vacancy, place, etc.) as a substitute. ● *n.* (*pl.* **-ies**) **1** the act or an instance of providing what is needed. **2** a stock, store, amount, etc., of something provided or obtainable (*a large supply of water*; *the gas-supply*). **3** (in *pl.*) **a** the provisions and equipment for an army, expedition, etc. **b** *Brit.* a grant of money by Parliament for the costs of government. **4** (often *attrib.*) a person, esp. a schoolteacher or clergyman, acting as a temporary substitute for another. **5** (*attrib.*) providing supplies or a supply (*supply officer*). □ **in short supply** scarce. **on supply** (of a schoolteacher etc.) acting as a supply. □ **supplier** *n.* [Middle English via Old French *so(u)pleer* etc. from Latin *supplēre* (as SUB-, *plēre* 'fill')]

supply[2] /'sʌpli/ *adv.* (also **supplely** /'sʌp(ə)lli/) in a supple manner.

supply and demand *n. Econ.* the amount or quantity of a product available and required, as factors regulating its price.

supply-side *n. Econ.* denoting a policy of low taxation and other incentives to produce goods and invest.

support /sə'pɔ:t/ *v.* & *n.* ● *v.tr.* **1** carry all or part of the weight of. **2** keep from falling or sinking or failing. **3** provide with a home and the necessities of life (*has a family to support*). **4** enable to last out; give strength to; encourage. **5** bear out; tend to substantiate or corroborate (a statement, charge, theory, etc.). **6** give help or countenance to, back up; second, further. **7** speak in favour of (a resolution etc.). **8** be actively interested in (a particular team or sport). **9** (often as **supporting** *adj.*) take a part that is secondary to (a principal actor etc.). **10** assist (a lecturer etc.) by one's presence. **11** endure, tolerate (*can no longer support the noise*). **12** maintain or represent (a part or character) adequately. **13** subscribe to the funds of (an institution). ● *n.* **1** the act or an instance of supporting; the process of being supported. **2** a person or thing that supports. **3** a band etc. providing a secondary act at a pop concert etc. □ **in support of** in order to support. □ **supportable** *adj.* **supportability** /-tə'bɪlɪti/ *n.* **supportably** *adv.* **supportingly** *adv.* **supportless** *adj.*

[Middle English via Old French *supporter* from Latin *supportare* (as SUB-, *portare* 'carry')]

supporter /sə'pɔ:tə/ *n.* **1** a person or thing that supports, esp. a person supporting a cause, team, or sport. **2** *Heraldry* the representation of an animal etc., usu. one of a pair, holding up or standing beside an escutcheon. **3** a jockstrap.

supporting film *n.* a less important film in a cinema programme.

supportive /sə'pɔ:tɪv/ *adj.* providing support or encouragement. ▫ **supportively** *adv.* **supportiveness** *n.*

support price *n.* a minimum price guaranteed to a farmer for agricultural produce and maintained by subsidy etc.

suppose /sə'pəʊz/ *v.tr.* (often foll. by *that* + clause) **1** assume, esp. in default of knowledge; be inclined to think (*I suppose they will return*; *what do you suppose he meant?*). **2** take as a possibility or hypothesis (*let us suppose you are right*). **3** (in *imper.*) as a formula of proposal (*suppose we go to the party*). **4** (of a theory or result etc.) require as a condition (*design in creation supposes a creator*). **5** (in *imper.* or *pres. part.* forming a question) in the circumstances that; if (*suppose he won't let you*; *supposing we stay*). **6** (as **supposed** *adj.*) generally accepted as being so; believed (*his supposed brother*; *generally supposed to be wealthy*). **7** (in *passive*; foll. by *to* + infin.) **a** be expected or required (*was supposed to write to you*). **b** (with *neg.*) ought not; not be allowed to (*you are not supposed to go in there*). ▫ **I suppose so** an expression of hesitant agreement. ▫ **supposable** *adj.* [Middle English from Old French *supposer* (as SUB-, POSE[1])]

supposedly /sə'pəʊzɪdli/ *adv.* as is generally supposed.

supposition /sʌpə'zɪʃ(ə)n/ *n.* **1** a fact or idea etc. supposed. **2** the act or an instance of supposing. ▫ **suppositional** *adj.* [Middle English from Old French, or from late Latin *suppositio* (translating Greek *hupothesis* 'hypothesis'), from the past part. stem of *supponere*: see SUPPOSITITIOUS]

suppositious /sʌpə'zɪʃəs/ *adj.* hypothetical, assumed. ▫ **suppositiously** *adv.* **suppositiousness** *n.* [partly from SUPPOSITITIOUS, partly from SUPPOSITION + -OUS]

supposititious /səpɒzɪ'tɪʃəs/ *adj.* spurious; substituted for the genuine. ▫ **supposititiously** *adv.* **supposititiousness** *n.* [Latin *supposititius*, *-icius* from *supponere supposit-* 'substitute' (as SUB-, *ponere* 'to place')]

suppository /sə'pɒzɪt(ə)ri/ *n.* (*pl.* **-ies**) a medical preparation in the form of a cone, cylinder, etc., to be inserted into the rectum or vagina to dissolve. [Middle English from medieval Latin *suppositorium*, neut. of Late Latin *suppositorius* 'placed underneath' (as SUPPOSITITIOUS)]

suppress /sə'prɛs/ *v.tr.* **1** end the activity or existence of, esp. forcibly. **2** prevent (information, feelings, a reaction, etc.) from being seen, heard, or known (*tried to suppress the report*; *suppressed a yawn*). **3 a** partly or wholly eliminate (electrical interference etc.). **b** equip (a device) to reduce such interference due to it. **4** *Psychol.* keep out of one's consciousness. ▫ **suppressible** *adj.* **suppression** /-'prɛʃ(ə)n/ *n.* **suppressive** *adj.* **suppressor** *n.* [Middle English from Latin *supprimere suppress-* (as SUB-, *premere* 'press')]

suppressant /sə'prɛs(ə)nt/ *n.* a suppressing or restraining agent, esp. a drug that suppresses the appetite.

suppurate /'sʌpjʊreɪt/ *v.intr.* **1** form pus. **2** fester. ▫ **suppuration** /-'reɪʃ(ə)n/ *n.* **suppurative** /-rətɪv/ *adj.* [Latin *suppurare* (as SUB-, *purare* as PUS)]

supra- /'su:prə, 'sju:-/ *prefix* **1** above. **2** beyond, transcending (*supranational*). [from or suggested by Latin *supra-* from *supra* 'above, beyond, before in time']

supra /'su:prə, 'sju:-/ *adv.* above or earlier on (in a book etc.). [Latin, = above]

supramaxillary /ˌsu:prəmak'sɪləri, ˌsju:-/ *adj.* of or relating to the upper jaw.

supramundane /su:prə'mʌndeɪn, sju:-/ *adj.* above or superior to the world.

supranational /su:prə'naʃ(ə)n(ə)l, sju:-/ *adj.* transcending national limits. ▫ **supranationalism** *n.* **supranationality** /-'nalɪti/ *n.*

supraorbital /su:prə'ɔ:bɪt(ə)l, sju:-/ *adj.* situated above the orbit of the eye.

suprarenal /su:prə'ri:n(ə)l, sju:-/ *adj.* situated above the kidneys.

supremacist /su:'prɛməsɪst, sju:-/ *n.* & *adj.* ● *n.* an advocate of the supremacy of a particular group, esp. determined by race or sex. ● *adj.* relating to or advocating such supremacy. ▫ **supremacism** *n.*

supremacy /su:'prɛməsi, sju:-/ *n.* the state of being supreme in authority, power, rank, or importance.

supreme /su:'pri:m, sju:-/ *adj.* & *n.* ● *adj.* **1** highest in authority or rank. **2** greatest; most important. **3** (of a penalty or sacrifice etc.) involving death. ● *n.* **1** a rich cream sauce. **2** a dish served in this. ▫ **supremely** *adv.* **supremeness** *n.* [Latin *supremus*, superlative of *superus* 'that is above', from *super* 'above']

suprême /su:'prɛm, French syprɛm/ *n.* = SUPREME *n.* [French]

Supreme Being *n.* (prec. by *the*) a name for God.

Supreme Court *n.* the highest judicial court in a country etc., or *US* (often **supreme court**) in a state.

supreme pontiff see PONTIFF.

Supreme Soviet *n.* the governing council of the former USSR or one of its constituent republics.

supremo /su:'pri:məʊ, su:'preɪməʊ, sju:-/ *n.* (*pl.* **-os**) *Brit.* **1** a supreme leader or ruler. **2** a person in overall charge. [Spanish, = SUPREME]

Supt. *abbr.* Superintendent.

sur-[1] /sə:, sə/ *prefix* = SUPER- (*surcharge*; *surrealism*). [Old French]

sur-[2] /sə:, sə/ *prefix* assim. form of SUB- before *r*.

sura /'sʊərə/ *n.* (also **surah**) a chapter or section of the Koran. [Arabic *sūra*]

surah /'sʊərə, 'sjʊərə/ *n.* a soft twilled silk for scarves etc. [French pronunciation of *Surat*, a district in India, where it was originally made]

sural /'sjʊər(ə)l, 'sʊər(ə)l/ *adj.* of or relating to the calf of the leg (*sural artery*). [modern Latin *suralis* from Latin *sura* 'calf']

surcease /sə:'si:s/ *n.* & *v.* *literary* ● *n.* a cessation. ● *v.intr.* & *tr.* cease. [Middle English via Old French *sursis*, *-ise* (cf. Anglo-French *sursise* 'omission'), past part. of Old French *surseoir* 'refrain, delay', from Latin (as SUPERSEDE), with assimilation to CEASE]

surcharge *n.* & *v.* ● *n.* /'sə:tʃɑ:dʒ/ **1** an additional charge or payment. **2** a charge made by assessors as a penalty for false returns of taxable property. **3** a mark printed on a postage stamp changing its value. **4** an additional or excessive load. **5** *Brit.* an amount in an official account not passed by the auditor and having to be refunded by the person responsible. **6** the showing of an omission in an account for which credit should have been given. ● *v.tr.* /'sə:tʃɑ:dʒ, -'tʃɑ:dʒ/ **1** exact a surcharge from. **2** exact (a sum) as a surcharge. **3** mark (a postage stamp) with a surcharge. **4** overload. **5** fill or saturate to excess. [Middle English from Old French *surcharger* (as SUR-[1], CHARGE)]

surcingle /'sə:sɪŋg(ə)l/ *n.* a band round a horse's body, usu. to keep a pack etc. in place. [Middle English from Old French *surcengle* (as SUR-[1], *cengle* 'girth', via Latin *cingula* from *cingere* 'gird')]

surcoat /'sə:kəʊt/ *n.* **1** *hist.* a loose robe worn over armour. **2** a similar sleeveless garment worn as part of the insignia of an order of knighthood. **3** *hist.* an outer coat of rich material. [Middle English from Old French *surcot* (as SUR-[1], *cot* 'coat')]

surculose /'sə:kjʊləʊs/ *adj.* *Bot.* producing suckers. [Latin *surculosus* from *surculus* 'twig']

surd /sə:d/ *adj. & n.* ● *adj.* **1** *Math.* (of a number) irrational. **2** *Phonet.* (of a sound) uttered with the breath and not the voice (e.g. *f, k, p, s, t*). ● *n.* **1** *Math.* a surd number, esp. the root of an integer. **2** *Phonet.* a surd sound. [Latin *surdus* 'deaf, mute': sense 1 by mistranslation into Latin of Greek *alogos* 'irrational, speechless', through Arabic *jadr asamm*, literally 'deaf root']

sure /ʃʊə, ʃɔ:/ *adj., adv., & int.* ● *adj.* **1** having or seeming to have adequate reason for a belief or assertion. **2** (often foll. by *of*, or *that* + clause) convinced. **3** (foll. by *of*) having a certain prospect or confident anticipation or satisfactory knowledge of. **4** reliable or unfailing (*there is one sure way to find out*). **5** (foll. by *to* + infin.) certain. **6** undoubtedly true or truthful. ● *adv. & int. colloq.* certainly. □ **as sure as eggs is eggs** see EGG[1]. **as sure as fate** quite certain. **be sure** (in *imper.* or *infin.*; foll. by *that* + clause or *to* + infin.) take care to; not fail to (*be sure to turn the lights out*). **for sure** *colloq.* without doubt. **make sure 1** make or become certain; ensure. **2** (foll. by *of*) establish the truth or ensure the existence or happening of. **sure enough** *colloq.* **1** in fact; certainly. **2** with near certainty (*they will come sure enough*). **sure thing** esp. *N. Amer. colloq. n.* a certainty. ● *int.* certainly!, yes, indeed! **to be sure 1** it is undeniable or admitted. **2** it must be admitted. □ **sureness** *n.* [Middle English via Old French *sur sure* (earlier *sëur*) from Latin *securus* SECURE]

sure-fire *attrib.adj. colloq.* certain to succeed.

sure-footed *adj.* never stumbling or making a mistake. □ **sure-footedly** *adv.* **sure-footedness** *n.*

surely /'ʃʊəli, 'ʃɔ:li/ *adv.* **1** with certainty (*the time approaches slowly but surely*). **2** as an appeal to likelihood or reason (*surely that can't be right*). **3** with safety; securely (*the goat plants its feet surely*).

surety /'ʃʊərɪti, 'ʃʊəti/ *n.* (*pl.* **-ies**) **1** a person who takes responsibility for another's performance of an undertaking, e.g. to appear in court, or payment of a debt. **2 a** money given as a guarantee. **b** a guarantee. **3** certainty. □ **of** (or **for**) **a surety** *archaic* certainly. **stand surety** become a surety, go bail. □ **suretyship** *n.* [Middle English via Old French *surté, sëurté* from Latin *securitas -tatis* SECURITY]

surf /sə:f/ *n. & v.* ● *n.* **1** the swell of the sea breaking on the shore or a reef. **2** the foam produced by this. ● *v.intr.* **1** go surf-riding. **2** *slang* ride illicitly on the roof or outside of a train. □ **surfer** *n.* **surfing** *n.* **surfy** *adj.* [apparently from obsolete *suff*, of unknown origin, perhaps assimilated to *surge*]

surface /'sə:fɪs/ *n. & v.* ● *n.* **1 a** the outside of a material body. **b** the area of this. **2** any of the limits terminating a solid. **3** the upper boundary of a liquid or of the ground etc. **4** the outward aspect of anything; what is apparent on a casual view or consideration (*presents a large surface to view; all is quiet on the surface*). **5** *Geom.* a set of points that has length and breadth but no thickness. **6** (*attrib.*) **a** of or on the surface (*surface area*). **b** superficial (*surface politeness*). ● *v.* **1** *tr.* give the required surface to (a road, paper, etc.). **2** *intr. & tr.* rise or bring to the surface. **3** *intr.* become visible or known. **4** *intr. colloq.* become conscious; wake up. □ **come to the surface** become perceptible after being hidden. □ **surfaced** *adj.* (usu. in *comb.*). **surfacer** *n.* [French (as SUR-[1], FACE)]

surface-active *adj.* (of a substance, e.g. a detergent) able to affect the wetting properties of a liquid.

surface mail *n.* mail carried over land and by sea, and not by air.

surface noise *n.* extraneous noise in playing a gramophone record, caused by imperfections in the grooves or in the pick-up system.

surface tension *n.* the tension of the surface-film of a liquid, tending to minimize its surface area.

surface-to-air *attrib.adj.* (of a missile) designed to be fired from the ground or at sea at an aircraft etc.

surface-to-surface *attrib.adj.* (of a missile) designed to be fired from one point on the ground or at sea to another such point.

surfactant /sə'fakt(ə)nt/ *n.* a substance which reduces surface tension. [*surf*ace-*act*ive]

surfboard /'sə:fbɔ:d/ *n.* a long narrow board used in surf-riding.

surf-casting *n.* fishing by casting a line into the sea from the shore.

surfeit /'sə:fɪt/ *n. & v.* ● *n.* **1** an excess esp. in eating or drinking. **2** a feeling of satiety or disgust resulting from this. ● *v.* (**surfeited**, **surfeiting**) **1** *tr.* overfeed. **2** *intr.* overeat. **3** *intr. & tr.* (foll. by *with*) be or cause to be wearied through excess. [Middle English from Old French *sorfe(i)t, surfe(i)t* (as SUPER-, Latin *facere fact-* 'do')]

surficial /sə'fɪʃ(ə)l/ *adj. Geol.* of or relating to the earth's surface. □ **surficially** *adv.* [SURFACE, on the pattern of *superficial*]

surfie /'sə:fi/ *n.* esp. *Austral.* a surf-riding enthusiast.

surf-riding *n.* the sport of being carried over the surf to the shore on a surfboard.

surge /sə:dʒ/ *n. & v.* ● *n.* **1** a sudden or impetuous onset (*a surge of anger*). **2** the swell of the waves at sea. **3** a heavy forward or upward motion. **4** a rapid increase in price, activity, etc., over a short period. **5** a sudden marked increase in voltage in an electric circuit. ● *v.intr.* **1** (of waves, the sea, etc.) rise and fall or move heavily forward. **2** (of a crowd etc.) move suddenly and powerfully forwards in large numbers. **3** (of an electric current etc.) increase suddenly. **4** *Naut.* (of a rope, chain, or windlass) slip back with a jerk. [Old French *sourdre sourge-*, or *sorgir* from Catalan, from Latin *surgere* 'rise']

surge chamber *n.* a chamber designed to neutralize sudden changes of pressure in a flow of liquid.

surgeon /'sə:dʒ(ə)n/ *n.* **1** a medical practitioner qualified to practise surgery. **2** a medical officer in a navy or army or military hospital. [Middle English via Anglo-French *surgien* from Old French *serurgien* (as SURGERY)]

surgeonfish /'sə:dʒ(ə)nfɪʃ/ *n.* any tropical marine fish of the genus *Acanthurus* with movable lancet-shaped spines on each side of the tail.

surgeon general *n.* (*pl.* **surgeons general**) (in the US) the head of a public health service or of an army etc. medical service.

surgeon's knot *n.* a reef knot with a double twist.

surgery /'sə:dʒ(ə)ri/ *n.* (*pl.* **-ies**) **1** the branch of medicine concerned with treatment of injuries or disorders of the body by incision or manipulation esp. with instruments. **2** *Brit.* **a** a place where a doctor, dentist, etc., treats patients. **b** the occasion of this (*the doctor will see you after surgery*). **3** *Brit.* **a** a place where an MP, lawyer, or other professional person gives advice. **b** the occasion of this. [Middle English via Old French *surgerie* and Latin *chirurgia* from Greek *kheirourgia* 'handiwork, surgery', from *kheir* 'hand' + *erg-* 'work']

surge tank *n.* = SURGE CHAMBER.

surgical /'sə:dʒɪk(ə)l/ *adj.* **1** of or relating to or done by surgeons or surgery. **2** resulting from surgery (*surgical fever*). **3 a** used in surgery. **b** (of a special garment etc.) worn to correct a deformity etc. **4** (esp. of military action) swift and precise. □ **surgically** *adv.* [earlier *chirurgical* from *chirurgy* from Old French *sirurgie*: see SURGEON]

surgical spirit *n. Brit.* methylated spirit used in surgery for cleansing etc.

suricate /'s(j)ʊərɪkeɪt/ *n.* a grey meerkat, *Suricata suricatta*. [French from a South African native name]

Surinamer /sʊərɪ'namə, sjʊə-/ *n.* = SURINAMESE *n.* [*Suriname* in S. America]

Surinamese /ˌsʊərɪna'mi:z, ˌsjʊə-/ *adj. & n.* ● *adj.* of or relating to Suriname or its people. ● *n.* (*pl.* same) a native or inhabitant of Suriname. [*Suriname* + -ESE]

Suriname toad /sʊərɪ'nam, sjʊə-/ *n.* an aquatic S. American toad, *Pipa pipa*, having a flat body with long webbed feet, the female of which carries the eggs and tadpoles in pockets on her back.

surly /'sə:li/ *adj.* (**surlier**, **surliest**) bad-tempered and unfriendly; churlish. ◻ **surlily** *adv.* **surliness** *n.* [alteration of spelling of obsolete *sirly* 'haughty', from SIR + -LY[1]]

surmise /sə'mʌɪz/ *n. & v.* ● *n.* a conjecture or suspicion about the existence or truth of something. ● *v.* **1** *tr.* (often foll. by *that* + clause) infer doubtfully; make a surmise about. **2** *tr.* suspect the existence of. **3** *intr.* make a guess. [Middle English via Anglo-French and Old French fem. past part. of *surmettre* 'accuse' from Late Latin *supermittere supermiss-* (as SUPER-, *mittere* 'send')]

surmount /sə'maʊnt/ *v.tr.* **1** overcome or get over (a difficulty or obstacle). **2** (usu. in *passive*) cap or crown (*peaks surmounted with snow*). ◻ **surmountable** *adj.* [Middle English from Old French *surmonter* (as SUR-[1], MOUNT[1])]

surmullet /sə:'mʌlɪt/ *n.* the red mullet. [French *surmulet*, from Old French *sor* 'red' + *mulet* MULLET]

surname /'sə:neɪm/ *n. & v.* ● *n.* **1** a hereditary name common to all members of a family, as distinct from a Christian or first name. **2** *archaic* an additional descriptive or allusive name attached to a person, sometimes becoming hereditary. ● *v.tr.* **1** give a surname to. **2** give (a person a surname). **3** (as **surnamed** *adj.*) having as a family name. [Middle English, alteration of *surnoun*, from Anglo-French (as SUR-[1], NOUN)]

surpass /sə'pɑ:s/ *v.tr.* **1** outdo, be greater or better than. **2** (as **surpassing** *adj.*) pre-eminent, matchless (*of surpassing intelligence*). ◻ **surpassable** *adj.* **surpassingly** *adv.* [French *surpasser* (as SUR-[1], PASS[1])]

surplice /'sə:plɪs/ *n.* a loose white linen vestment varying from hip-length to calf-length, worn over a cassock by clergy and choristers at services. ◻ **surpliced** *adj.* [Middle English via Anglo-French *surplis*, Old French *sourpelis*, from medieval Latin *superpellicium* (as SUPER-, *pellicia* PELISSE)]

surplus /'sə:pləs/ *n. & adj.* ● *n.* **1** an amount left over when requirements have been met. **2 a** an excess of revenue over expenditure in a given period, esp. a financial year (opp. DEFICIT 2). **b** the excess value of a company's assets over the face value of its stock. ● *adj.* exceeding what is needed or used. [Middle English via Anglo-French *surplus*, Old French *s(o)urplus* from medieval Latin *superplus* (as SUPER-, *plus* 'more')]

surplus value *n. Econ.* the difference between the value of work done and wages paid.

surprise /sə'prʌɪz/ *n. & v.* ● *n.* **1** an unexpected or astonishing event or circumstance. **2** the emotion caused by this. **3** the act of catching a person etc. unawares, or the process of being caught unawares. **4** (*attrib.*) unexpected; made or done etc. without warning (*a surprise visit*). ● *v.tr.* **1** affect with surprise; turn out contrary to the expectations of (*your answer surprised me*; *I surprised her by arriving early*). **2** (usu. in *passive*; foll. by *at*) shock, scandalize (*I am surprised at you*). **3** capture or attack by surprise. **4** come upon (a person) unawares (*surprised him taking a biscuit*). **5** (foll. by *into*) startle (a person) by surprise into an action etc. (*surprised them into consenting*). ◻ **take by surprise** affect with surprise, esp. by an unexpected encounter or statement. ◻ **surprisedly** /-zɪdli/ *adv.* **surprising** *adj.* **surprisingly** *adv.* **surprisingness** *n.* [Old French, fem. past part. of *surprendre* (as SUR-[1], *prendre* from Latin *praehendere* 'seize')]

surra /'sʊərə, 'sʌrə/ *n.* a usu. fatal disease of horses, cattle, etc. in Asia and NE Africa, caused by trypanosomes and transmitted by horseflies. [Marathi]

surreal /sə'rɪəl/ *adj.* **1** having the qualities of surrealism. **2** strange, bizarre. ◻ **surreality** /-'alɪti/ *n.* **surreally** *adv.* [back-formation from SURREALISM etc.]

surrealism /sə'rɪəlɪz(ə)m/ *n.* a 20th-c. movement in art and literature aiming at expressing the subconscious mind, e.g. by the irrational juxtaposition of images. ◻ **surrealist** *n. & adj.* **surrealistic** /-'lɪstɪk/ *adj.* **surrealistically** /-'lɪstɪk(ə)li/ *adv.* [French *surréalisme* (as SUR-[1], REALISM)]

surrebutter /sʌrɪ'bʌtə/ *n. Law* the plaintiff's reply to the defendant's rebutter. [SUR-[1] + REBUTTER, on the pattern of SURREJOINDER]

surrejoinder /sʌrɪ'dʒɔɪndə/ *n. Law* the plaintiff's reply to the defendant's rejoinder. [SUR-[1] + REJOINDER]

surrender /sə'rɛndə/ *v. & n.* ● *v.* **1** *tr.* hand over; relinquish possession of, esp. on compulsion or demand; give into another's power or control. **2** *intr.* **a** accept an enemy's demand for submission. **b** give oneself up; cease from resistance; submit. **3** *intr. & refl.* (foll. by *to*) give oneself over to a habit, emotion, influence, etc. **4** *tr.* give up rights under (a life-insurance policy) in return for a smaller sum received immediately. **5** *tr.* give up (a lease) before its expiry. **6** *tr.* abandon (hope etc.). ● *n.* the act or an instance of surrendering. ◻ **surrender to bail** duly appear in a law court after release on bail. [Middle English via Anglo-French from Old French *surrendre* (as SUR-[1], RENDER)]

surrender value *n.* the amount payable to a person who surrenders a life-insurance policy.

surreptitious /sʌrəp'tɪʃəs/ *adj.* **1** covert; kept secret. **2** done by stealth; clandestine. ◻ **surreptitiously** *adv.* **surreptitiousness** *n.* [Middle English from Latin *surrepticius -itius*, from *surripere surrept-* (as SUR-[1], *rapere* 'seize')]

surrey /'sʌri/ *n.* (*pl.* **surreys**) *US* a light four-wheeled carriage with two seats facing forwards. [originally of an adaptation of the *Surrey cart*, first made in *Surrey* in England]

surrogate /'sʌrəgət/ *n.* **1** a substitute, esp. for a person in a specific role or office. **2** *Brit.* a deputy, esp. of a bishop in granting marriage licences. **3** *US* a judge in charge of probate, inheritance, and guardianship. ◻ **surrogacy** *n.* **surrogateship** *n.* [Latin *surrogatus*, past part. of *surrogare* 'elect as a substitute' (as SUR-[1], *rogare* 'ask')]

surrogate mother *n.* **1** a person acting the role of mother. **2** a woman who bears a child on behalf of another woman, either from her own egg fertilized by the other woman's partner, or from the implantation in her womb of a fertilized egg from the other woman.

surround /sə'raʊnd/ *v. & n.* ● *v.tr.* **1** come or be all round; encircle, enclose. **2** (in *passive*; foll. by *by*, *with*) have on all sides (*the house is surrounded by trees*). ● *n.* **1** *Brit.* **a** a border or edging, esp. an area between the walls and carpet of a room. **b** a floor covering for this. **2** an area or substance surrounding something. ◻ **surrounding** *adj.* [Middle English = overflow, via Anglo-French *sur(o)under*, Old French *s(o)uronder* from Late Latin *superundare* (as SUPER-, *undare* 'flow' from *unda* 'a wave')]

surroundings /sə'raʊndɪŋz/ *n.pl.* the things in the neighbourhood of, or the conditions affecting, a person or thing.

surtax /'sə:taks/ *n. & v.* ● *n.* **1** an additional tax on something already taxed. **2** a higher rate of tax levied on incomes above a certain level, esp. *hist.* in Britain between 1929 and 1973 (replacing SUPERTAX). ● *v.tr.* impose a surtax on. [French *surtaxe* (as SUR-[1], TAX)]

surtitle /'sə:tʌɪt(ə)l/ *n. & v.* ● *n.* (esp. in opera) each of a sequence of captions projected above the stage, translating the text being sung. ● *v.tr.* provide with surtitles.

surtout /'sə:tu:, sə:'tu:(t)/ *n. hist.* a greatcoat or frock coat. [French, from *sur* 'over' + *tout* 'everything']

surveillance /sə'veɪl(ə)ns, sə'veɪəns/ *n.* close observation, esp. of a suspected person. [French from *surveiller* (as SUR-[1], *veiller* from Latin *vigilare* 'keep watch')]

survey *v. & n.* ● *v.tr.* /sə'veɪ/ **1** take or present a general view of. **2** examine the condition of (a building etc.), esp. on behalf of a prospective buyer. **3** determine the boundaries, extent, ownership, etc., of (a district etc.). ● *n.* /ˈsəːveɪ/ **1** a general view or consideration of something. **2 a** the act of surveying property. **b** the result or findings of this, esp. in a written report. **3** an inspection or investigation. **4** a map or plan made by surveying an area. **5** a department carrying out the surveying of land. [Middle English via Anglo-French *survei(e)r*, Old French *so(u)rveeir* (pres. stem *survey-*) from medieval Latin *supervidēre* (as SUPER-, *vidēre* 'see')]

surveyor /səˈveɪə/ *n.* **1** a person who surveys land and buildings, esp. professionally. **2** *Brit.* an official inspector, esp. for measurement and valuation. **3** a person who carries out surveys. □ **surveyorship** *n.* (esp. in sense 2). [Middle English via Anglo-French & Old French *surve(i)our* (as SURVEY)]

survival /səˈvʌɪv(ə)l/ *n.* **1** the process or an instance of surviving. **2** a person, thing, or practice that has remained from a former time. **3** the practice of coping with harsh or warlike conditions, as a leisure activity or training exercise. □ **survival of the fittest** the process or result of natural selection.

survivalism /səˈvʌɪv(ə)lɪz(ə)m/ *n.* **1** a policy of trying to ensure one's own survival or that of one's social or national group. **2** the practising of outdoor survival skills as a sport or hobby. □ **survivalist** *n.* & *adj.*

survival kit *n.* emergency rations etc., esp. as carried by servicemen.

survive /səˈvʌɪv/ *v.* **1** *intr.* continue to live or exist; be still alive or existent. **2** *tr.* live or exist longer than. **3** *tr.* remain alive after going through, or continue to exist in spite of (a danger, accident, etc.). □ **survivable** *adj.* (in sense 3). [Middle English via Anglo-French *survivre*, Old French *sourvivre* from Latin *supervivere* (as SUPER, *vivere* 'live')]

survivor /səˈvʌɪvə/ *n.* **1** a person who survives or has survived. **2** *Law* a joint tenant who has the right to the whole estate on the other's death.

Sus. *abbr.* Susanna (Apocrypha).

sus var. of SUSS.

sus- /sʌs, səs/ *prefix* assim. form of SUB- before *c, p, t.*

susceptibility /səsɛptɪˈbɪlɪti/ *n.* (*pl.* **-ies**) **1** the state of being susceptible. **2** (in *pl.*) a person's sensitive feelings. **3** *Physics* the ratio of magnetization to a magnetizing force.

susceptible /səˈsɛptɪb(ə)l/ *adj.* **1** impressionable, sensitive; easily moved by emotion. **2** (*predic.*) **a** (foll. by *to*) likely to be affected by; liable or vulnerable to (*susceptible to pain*). **b** (foll. by *of*) allowing; admitting of (*facts not susceptible of proof*). □ **susceptibly** *adv.* [Late Latin *susceptibilis* from Latin *suscipere suscept-* (as SUB-, *capere* 'take')]

susceptive /səˈsɛptɪv/ *adj.* **1** having the quality of taking or receiving; receptive. **2** = SUSCEPTIBLE. [Late Latin *susceptivus* (as SUSCEPTIBLE)]

sushi /ˈsuːʃi, ˈsʊʃi/ *n.* a Japanese dish in which various ingredients such as raw fish are added to vinegar-flavoured cold rice and formed into balls or rolls. [Japanese]

suslik var. of SOUSLIK.

suspect *v., n., & adj.* ● *v.tr.* /səˈspɛkt/ **1** have an impression of the existence or presence of (*suspects poisoning*). **2** (foll. by *to be*) believe tentatively, without clear grounds. **3** (foll. by *that* + clause) be inclined to think. **4** (often foll. by *of*) be inclined to accuse mentally; doubt the innocence of (*suspect him of complicity*). **5** doubt the genuineness or truth of. ● *n.* /ˈsʌspɛkt/ a suspected person. ● *adj.* /ˈsʌspɛkt/ subject to or deserving suspicion or distrust; not sound or trustworthy. [Middle English from Latin *suspicere suspect-* (as SUB-, *specere* 'to look')]

suspend /səˈspɛnd/ *v.tr.* **1** hang up. **2** keep inoperative or undecided for a time; defer. **3** debar temporarily from a function, office, privilege, or from attending school, etc. **4** (as **suspended** *adj.*) (of solid particles or a body in a fluid medium) sustained somewhere between top and bottom. □ **suspend payment** (of a company) fail to meet its financial engagements; admit insolvency. □ **suspensible** *adj.* [Middle English from Old French *suspendre* or Latin *suspendere suspens-* (as SUB-, *pendere* 'hang')]

suspended animation *n.* a temporary cessation of the vital functions without death.

suspended sentence *n.* a judicial sentence left unenforced subject to good behaviour during a specified period.

suspender /səˈspɛndə/ *n.* **1** *Brit.* an attachment to hold up a stocking or sock by its top. **2** (in *pl.*) *N. Amer.* a pair of braces.

suspender belt *n.* a woman's undergarment consisting of a belt and suspenders.

suspense /səˈspɛns/ *n.* **1** a state of anxious uncertainty or expectation. **2** *Law* a suspension; the temporary cessation of a right etc. □ **keep in suspense** delay informing (a person) of urgent information. □ **suspenseful** *adj.* [Middle English via Anglo-French & Old French *suspens* from the past part. of Latin *suspendere* SUSPEND]

suspense account *n.* an account in which items are entered temporarily before allocation to the right account.

suspension /səˈspɛnʃ(ə)n/ *n.* **1** the act of suspending or the condition of being suspended. **2** the means by which a vehicle is supported on its axles. **3** a substance consisting of particles suspended in a medium. **4** *Mus.* the prolongation of a note of a chord to form a discord with the following chord. [French *suspension* or Latin *suspensio* (as SUSPEND)]

suspension bridge *n.* a bridge with a roadway suspended from cables supported by structures at each end.

suspensive /səˈspɛnsɪv/ *adj.* **1** having the power or tendency to suspend or postpone. **2** causing suspense. □ **suspensively** *adv.* **suspensiveness** *n.* [French *suspensif -ive* or medieval Latin *suspensivus* (as SUSPEND)]

suspensory /səˈspɛns(ə)ri/ *adj.* (of a ligament, muscle, bandage, etc.) holding an organ etc. suspended. [French *suspensoire* (as SUSPENSION)]

suspicion /səˈspɪʃ(ə)n/ *n.* **1** the feeling or thought of a person who suspects. **2** the act or an instance of suspecting; the state of being suspected. **3** (foll. by *of*) a slight trace of. □ **above suspicion** too obviously good etc. to be suspected. **under suspicion** suspected. [Middle English via Anglo-French *suspeciun* (Old French *sospeçon*) from medieval Latin *suspectio -onis*, from Latin *suspicere* (as SUSPECT): assimilated to French *suspicion* & Latin *suspicio*]

suspicious /səˈspɪʃəs/ *adj.* **1** prone to or feeling suspicion. **2** indicating suspicion (*a suspicious glance*). **3** inviting or justifying suspicion (*a suspicious lack of surprise*). □ **suspiciously** *adv.* **suspiciousness** *n.* [Middle English via Anglo-French & Old French from Latin *suspiciosus* (as SUSPICION)]

suss /sʌs/ *v., n., & adj.* (also **sus**) *Brit. slang* ● *v.tr.* (**sussed**, **sussing**) **1** suspect of a crime. **2** (usu. foll. by *out*) **a** investigate, inspect (*go and suss out the restaurants*). **b** work out; grasp, understand, realize (*he had the market sussed*). **3** (as **sussed** *adj.*) well informed; aware. ● *n.* **1** a suspect. **2** a suspicion; suspicious behaviour. ● *adj.* suspicious, suspect. □ **on suss** on suspicion (of having committed a crime). [abbreviation of SUSPECT, SUSPICION]

Sussex /ˈsʌsɪks/ *n.* **1** a speckled or red domestic fowl of an English breed. **2** this breed. [*Sussex*, a former county in S. England]

sustain /səˈsteɪn/ *v. & n.* ● *v.tr.* **1** support, bear the weight of, esp. for a long period. **2** give strength to; encourage, support. **3** (of food) give nourishment to. **4** endure, stand; bear up against. **5** undergo or suffer (defeat or injury etc.). **6** (of a court etc.) uphold or decide in favour of (an objection etc.). **7** substantiate or corroborate (a statement or charge). **8** maintain or keep (a sound, effort, etc.) going continuously. **9** continue to represent (a part, character, etc.) adequately. ● *n. Mus.* the effect or result of sustaining a note, esp. electronically. □ **sustainedly** /-nɪdli/ *adv.* **sustainer** *n.* **sustainment** *n.* [Middle English via Anglo-French *sustein-*, Old French *so(u)stein-*, stressed stem of *so(u)stenir*, from Latin *sustinēre sustent-* (as SUB-, *tenēre* 'hold')]

sustainable /sə'steɪnəb(ə)l/ *adj.* **1** *Ecol.* (esp. of development) which conserves an ecological balance by avoiding depletion of natural resources. **2** that can be sustained. □ **sustainably** *adv. Ecol.* **sustainability** /-'bɪlɪti/ *n. Ecol.*

sustenance /'sʌst(ə)nəns, -tɪn-/ *n.* **1 a** nourishment, food. **b** the process of nourishing. **2** a means of support; a livelihood. [Middle English from Anglo-French *sustenaunce*, Old French *so(u)stenance* (as SUSTAIN)]

sustentation /sʌst(ə)n'teɪʃ(ə)n/ *n. formal* **1** the support of life. **2** maintenance. [Middle English from Old French *sustentation* or Latin *sustentatio* from *sustentare*, frequentative of *sustinēre* SUSTAIN]

susurration /sju:sʌ'reɪʃ(ə)n, su:-/ *n.* (also **susurrus** /sju:'sʌrəs, su:-/) *literary* a sound of whispering or rustling. [Middle English via Late Latin *susurratio* from Latin *susurrare*]

sutler /'sʌtlə/ *n. hist.* a person following an army and selling provisions etc. to the soldiers. [obsolete Dutch *soeteler* from *soetelen* 'befoul, perform mean duties', from Germanic]

Sutra /'su:trə/ *n.* **1** an aphorism or set of aphorisms in Hindu literature. **2** a narrative part of Buddhist literature. **3** Jainist scripture. [Sanskrit *sūtra* 'thread, rule', from *siv* SEW]

suttee /sʌ'ti:, 'sʌti/ *n.* (also **sati**) (*pl.* **suttees** or **satis**) **1** the former Hindu practice of a widow immolating herself on her husband's funeral pyre. **2** a widow who underwent this. [Hindi from Sanskrit *satī* 'faithful wife', from *sat* 'good']

suture /'su:tʃə/ *n. & v.* ● *n.* **1** *Surgery* **a** the joining of the edges of a wound or incision by stitching. **b** the thread or wire used for this. **2** the seamlike junction of two bones, esp. in the skull. **3** *Bot. & Zool.* a similar junction of parts. ● *v.tr. Surgery* stitch up (a wound or incision) with a suture. □ **sutural** *adj.* **sutured** *adj.* [French *suture* or Latin *sutura*, from *suere sut-* 'sew']

suzerain /'su:zəreɪn/ *n.* **1** *hist.* a feudal overlord. **2** a sovereign or state having some control over another state that is internally autonomous. □ **suzerainty** *n.* [French, apparently from *sus* 'above' (from Latin *su(r)sum* 'upward'), suggested by *souverain* SOVEREIGN]

s.v. *abbr.* **1** a side valve. **2** (in a reference) under the word or heading given. [sense 2 from Latin *sub voce* (or *verbo*)]

svelte /svɛlt/ *adj.* slender, lissom, graceful. [French from Italian *svelto*]

Svengali /svɛn'gɑ:li/ *n.* (*pl.* **Svengalis**) a person who exercises a controlling or mesmeric influence on another, esp. for a sinister purpose. [a character in George Du Maurier's *Trilby*]

SW *abbr.* **1** south-west. **2** south-western.

swab /swɒb/ *n. & v.* (also **swob**) ● *n.* **1** a mop or other absorbent device for cleaning or mopping up. **2 a** an absorbent pad used in surgery. **b** a wad of absorbent material fixed to the end of a rod and used for cleaning or applying medication. **c** a specimen of a possibly morbid secretion taken with a swab for examination. **3** *slang* a term of contempt for a person. ● *v.tr.* (**swabbed**, **swabbing**) **1** clean (a wound, ship's deck, etc.) with a swab. **2** (foll. by *up*) absorb (moisture) with a swab. [back-formation from *swabber*, via early modern Dutch *zwabber* from a Germanic base = 'splash, sway']

swaddle /'swɒd(ə)l/ *v.tr.* swathe (esp. an infant) in garments or bandages etc. [Middle English, from SWATHE + -LE[4]]

swaddling-clothes *n.pl. hist.* narrow bandages formerly wrapped round a newborn child to restrain its movements and quieten it.

swag /swag/ *n. & v.* ● *n.* **1** *slang* **a** the booty carried off by burglars etc. **b** illicit gains. **2 a** an ornamental festoon of flowers, fruit, etc. **b** a carved or painted representation of this. **c** drapery hung so that it curves along its top edge. **3** *Austral. & NZ* a traveller's or miner's bundle of personal belongings. ● *v.* (**swagged**, **swagging**) **1** *tr.* arrange (a curtain etc.) in swags. **2** *intr.* **a** hang heavily. **b** sway from side to side. **3** *tr.* cause to sway or sag. [Middle English: probably from Scandinavian]

swage /sweɪdʒ/ *n. & v.* ● *n.* **1** a die or stamp for shaping wrought iron etc. by hammering or pressure. **2** a tool for bending metal etc. ● *v.tr.* shape with a swage. [French *s(o)uage* 'decorative groove', of unknown origin]

swage-block *n.* a block with various perforations, grooves, etc., for shaping metal.

swagger /'swagə/ *v., n., & adj.* ● *v.intr.* **1** walk arrogantly or self-importantly. **2** behave arrogantly; be domineering. ● *n.* **1** a swaggering gait or manner. **2** swaggering behaviour. **3** a dashing or confident air or way of doing something. **4** *Brit.* smartness. ● *adj.* **1** *colloq.* smart or fashionable. **2** (of a coat) cut with a loose flare from the shoulders. □ **swaggerer** *n.* **swaggeringly** *adv.* [apparently from SWAG *v.* + -ER[4]]

swagger stick *n.* a short cane carried by a military officer.

swagman /'swagman/ *n.* (*pl.* **-men**) *Austral. & NZ* a tramp carrying a swag (see SWAG *n.* 3).

Swahili /swə'hi:li, swɑ:-/ *n. & adj.* ● *n.* (*pl.* same) **1** a member of a Bantu-speaking people of Zanzibar and adjacent coasts. **2** their language, used widely as a lingua franca in E. Africa. ● *adj.* of or relating to the Swahili or their language. [Arabic *sawāhil*, pl. of *sāhil* 'coast']

swain /sweɪn/ *n.* **1** *archaic* a country youth. **2** *poet.* a young lover or suitor. [Middle English *swein* from Old Norse *sveinn* 'lad' = Old English *swān* 'swineherd', from Germanic]

swale /sweɪl/ *n.* esp. *US & dial.* a low or hollow place, esp. a marshy depression or hollow between ridges. [16th c.: origin unknown]

swallow[1] /'swɒləʊ/ *v. & n.* ● *v.* **1** *tr.* cause or allow (food etc.) to pass down the throat. **2** *intr.* perform the muscular movement of the oesophagus required to do this. **3** *tr.* **a** accept meekly; put up with (an affront etc.). **b** accept credulously (an unlikely assertion etc.). **4** *tr.* repress; resist the expression of (a feeling etc.) (*swallow one's pride*). **5** *tr.* articulate (words etc.) indistinctly. **6** *tr.* (often foll. by *up*) engulf or absorb; exhaust; cause to disappear. ● *n.* **1** the act of swallowing. **2** an amount swallowed in one action. □ **swallowable** *adj.* **swallower** *n.* [Old English *swelg* (*n.*), *swelgan* (*v.*), from Germanic]

swallow[2] /'swɒləʊ/ *n.* any of various migratory swift-flying insect-eating birds of the family Hirundinidae, esp. *Hirundo rustica*, with a forked tail and long pointed wings. □ **one swallow does not make a summer** a warning against a hasty inference from one instance. [Old English *swealwe*, from Germanic]

swallow-dive *n. Brit.* a dive with the arms outspread until close to the water.

swallow-hole *n. Brit.* = *sink-hole* (see SINK *n.* 6).

swallowtail /'swɒləʊteɪl/ *n.* **1** a deeply forked tail. **2** anything resembling this shape. **3** any butterfly of the family Papilionidae with wings extended at the back to this shape. □ **swallow-tailed** *adj.*

swam *past* of SWIM.

swami /'swɑ:mi/ *n.* (*pl.* **swamis**) a Hindu male religious teacher. [Hindi *swāmī* 'master, prince', from Sanskrit *svāmin*]

swamp /swɒmp/ *n. & v.* ● *n.* a piece of waterlogged ground; a bog or marsh. ● *v.* **1 a** *tr.* overwhelm, flood, or soak with water. **b** *intr.* become swamped. **2** *tr.* overwhelm or make invisible etc. with an excess or large amount of something. □ **swampy** *adj.* (**swampier, swampiest**). [17th c., probably ultimately from a Germanic base meaning 'sponge' or 'fungus']

swampland /ˈswɒmpland/ *n.* land consisting of swamps.

swan /swɒn/ *n.* & *v.* ● *n.* **1** a large waterbird of the genus *Cygnus* etc., having a long flexible neck, webbed feet, and in most species snow-white plumage. **2** *literary* a poet. ● *v.intr.* (**swanned, swanning**) (usu. foll. by *about, off,* etc.) *Brit. colloq.* move or go aimlessly or casually or with a superior air. □ **Swan of Avon** *literary* Shakespeare. □ **swanlike** *adj.* & *adv.* [Old English from Germanic]

swan-dive *n. N. Amer.* = SWALLOW-DIVE.

swank /swaŋk/ *n., v.,* & *adj. colloq.* ● *n.* ostentation, swagger, bluff. ● *v.intr.* behave with swank; show off. ● *adj.* esp. *US* = SWANKY. [19th c.: origin uncertain]

swankpot /ˈswaŋkpɒt/ *n. Brit. colloq.* a person behaving with swank.

swanky /ˈswaŋki/ *adj.* (**swankier, swankiest**) *colloq.* **1** marked by swank; ostentatiously smart or showy. **2** (of a person) inclined to swank; boastful. □ **swankily** *adv.* **swankiness** *n.*

swan-neck *n.* a curved structure shaped like a swan's neck.

swannery /ˈswɒnəri/ *n.* (*pl.* **-ies**) a place where swans are bred.

swansdown /ˈswɒnzdaʊn/ *n.* **1** the fine down of a swan, used in trimmings and esp. in powder puffs. **2** a kind of thick cotton cloth with a soft nap on one side.

swansong /ˈswɒnsɒŋ/ *n.* **1** a person's last work or act before death or retirement etc. **2** a song like that fabled to be sung by a dying swan.

swan-upping *n. Brit.* the annual taking up and marking of Thames swans.

swap /swɒp/ *v.* & *n.* (also **swop**) ● *v.tr.* & *intr.* (**swapped, swapping**) exchange or barter (one thing for another). ● *n.* **1** an act of swapping. **2** a thing suitable for swapping. **3** a thing swapped. □ **swapper** *n.* [originally = 'hit': Middle English, probably imitative]

swap meet *n.* esp. *N. Amer.* **1** a gathering at which enthusiasts or collectors trade or exchange items. **2** a flea market.

Swapo /ˈswɑːpəʊ/ *abbr.* South-West Africa People's Organization.

Swaraj /swəˈrɑːdʒ/ *n. hist.* self-government or independence for India. □ **Swarajist** *n.* [Sanskrit *svarājya*, from *sva* 'own' + *rājya* 'rule': cf. RAJ]

sward /swɔːd/ *n.* esp. *literary* **1** an expanse of short grass. **2** turf. □ **swarded** *adj.* [Old English *sweard* 'skin']

sware /swɛː/ *archaic past* of SWEAR.

swarf /swɑːf/ *n.* **1** fine chips or filings of stone, metal, etc. **2** wax etc. removed in cutting a gramophone record. [Old Norse *svarf* 'file-dust']

swarm[1] /swɔːm/ *n.* & *v.* ● *n.* **1** a cluster of bees leaving the hive with a queen to establish a new colony. **2** a large number of insects or birds moving in a cluster. **3** a large group of people, esp. moving over or filling a large area. **4** (in *pl.*; foll. by *of*) great numbers. **5** a group of zoospores. ● *v.intr.* **1** move in or form a swarm. **2** gather or move in large numbers. **3** (foll. by *with*) (of a place) be overrun, crowded, or infested (*was swarming with tourists*). [Old English *swearm*, from Germanic]

swarm[2] /swɔːm/ *v.intr.* (foll. by *up*) & *tr.* climb (a rope or tree etc.), esp. in a rush, by clasping or clinging with the hands and knees etc. [16th c.: origin unknown]

swart /swɔːt/ *adj. archaic* swarthy, dark-hued. [Old English *sweart*, from Germanic]

swarthy /ˈswɔːði/ *adj.* (**swarthier, swarthiest**) dark, dark-complexioned. □ **swarthily** *adv.* **swarthiness** *n.* [variant of obsolete *swarty* (as SWART)]

swash[1] /swɒʃ/ *v.* & *n.* ● *v.* **1** *intr.* (of water etc.) wash about; make the sound of washing or rising and falling. **2** *tr. archaic* strike violently. **3** *intr. archaic* swagger. ● *n.* the motion or sound of swashing water. [imitative]

swash[2] /swɒʃ/ *adj.* **1** inclined obliquely. **2** (of a letter) having a flourished stroke or strokes. [17th c.: origin unknown]

swashbuckler /ˈswɒʃbʌklə/ *n.* **1** a swaggering adventurer or blustering ruffian. **2** a film, book, etc. portraying swashbuckling characters. □ **swashbuckling** *adj.* & *n.* [SWASH[1] + BUCKLER]

swash-plate *n.* an inclined disc revolving on an axle and giving reciprocating motion to a part in contact with it.

swastika /ˈswɒstɪkə/ *n.* **1** an ancient symbol formed by an equal-armed cross with each arm continued at a right angle. **2** this with clockwise continuations as the symbol of Nazi Germany. [Sanskrit *svastika* from *svasti* 'well-being', from *su* 'good' + *asti* 'being']

swat /swɒt/ *v.* & *n.* ● *v.tr.* (**swatted, swatting**) **1** crush (a fly etc.) with a sharp blow. **2** hit hard and abruptly. ● *n.* a swatting blow. [originally = sit down: northern English dialect & US variant of SQUAT]

swatch /swɒtʃ/ *n.* **1** a sample, esp. of cloth or fabric. **2** a collection of samples. [16th c.: origin unknown]

swath /swɔːθ, swɒθ/ *n.* (also **swathe** /sweɪð/) (*pl.* **swaths** /swɔːθs, swɔːðz, swɒθs/ or **swathes**) **1** a ridge of grass or corn etc. lying after being cut. **2** a space left clear after the passage of a mower etc. **3** a broad strip. □ **cut a wide swath** *US* make a pompous display, cut a dash. [Old English *swæth, swathu*]

swathe /sweɪð/ *v.* & *n.* ● *v.tr.* bind or enclose in bandages or garments etc. ● *n.* a bandage or wrapping. [Old English *swathian*]

swatter /ˈswɒtə/ *n.* an implement for swatting flies.

sway /sweɪ/ *v.* & *n.* ● *v.* **1** *intr.* & *tr.* lean or cause to lean unsteadily in different directions alternately. **2** *intr.* oscillate irregularly; waver. **3** *tr.* **a** control the motion or direction of. **b** have influence or rule over. ● *n.* **1** rule, influence, or government (*hold sway*). **2** a swaying motion or position. **3** *Sc.* & *N.Engl.* an iron rod in a fireplace used for hanging kettles etc. [Middle English: cf. Low German *swājen* 'be blown to and fro', Dutch *zwaaien* 'swing, wave']

sway-back *n.* an abnormally hollowed back (esp. of a horse); lordosis. □ **sway-backed** *adj.*

swear /swɛː/ *v.* & *n.* ● *v.* (*past* **swore** /swɔː/; *past part.* **sworn** /swɔːn/) **1** *tr.* **a** (often foll. by *to* + infin. or *that* + clause) state or promise solemnly or on oath. **b** take (an oath). **2** *tr. colloq.* say emphatically; insist (*swore he had not seen it*). **3** *tr.* cause to take an oath (*swore them to secrecy*). **4** *intr.* (often foll. by *at*) use profane or indecent language, esp. as an expletive or from anger. **5** *tr.* (often foll. by *against*) make a sworn affirmation of (an offence) (*swear treason against*). **6** *intr.* (foll. by *by*) **a** appeal to as a witness in taking an oath (*swear by Almighty God*). **b** *colloq.* have or express great confidence in (*swears by yoga*). **7** *intr.* (foll. by *to*; usu. in *neg.*) admit the certainty of (*could not swear to it*). **8** *intr.* (foll. by *at*) *colloq.* (of colours etc.) fail to harmonize with. ● *n.* a spell of swearing. □ **swear blind** *Brit. colloq.* affirm emphatically. **swear in** induct into office etc. by administering an oath. **swear off** *colloq.* promise to abstain from (drink etc.). **swear out** *US* obtain the issue of (a warrant for arrest) by making a charge on oath. □ **swearer** *n.* [Old English *swerian* from Germanic: related to ANSWER]

swear word *n.* a profane or indecent word, esp. uttered as an expletive.

sweat /swɛt/ *n.* & *v.* ● *n.* **1** moisture exuded through the pores of the skin, esp. from heat or nervousness. **2** a state or period of sweating. **3** *colloq.* a state of anxiety (*was in a sweat about it*). **4** *colloq.* **a** drudgery, effort. **b** a laborious task or undertaking. **5** condensed moisture on a surface. **6** (in *pl.*) esp. *N. Amer. colloq.* **a** = SWEATSUIT. **b** = SWEATPANTS. **c** = SWEATSHIRT. ● *v.* (*past* and *past part.* **sweated** or *US* **sweat**) **1** *intr.* exude sweat; perspire. **2** *intr.* be terrified, suffering, etc. **3** *intr.* (of a wall etc.) exhibit surface moisture. **4** *intr.* drudge, toil. **5 a** *intr. & tr.* exude or cause to exude or condense moisture in the form of drops on a surface, esp. as part of a manufacturing process. **b** *tr.* heat (meat or vegetables) slowly in fat or water to extract the juices. **c** *tr.* subject (hides or tobacco) to fermentation in manufacturing. **6** *tr.* emit (blood, gum, etc.) like sweat. **7** *tr.* make (a horse, athlete, etc.) sweat by exercise. **8** *tr.* **a** cause to drudge or toil. **b** (as **sweated** *adj.*) (of goods, workers, or labour) produced by or subjected to long hours under poor conditions. **9** *tr. Metallurgy* subject (metal) to partial melting, esp. to fasten or join by solder without a soldering iron. □ **by the sweat of one's brow** by one's own hard work. **no sweat** *colloq.* there is no need to worry. **sweat blood** *colloq.* **1** work strenuously. **2** be extremely anxious. **sweat bullets** *N. Amer. slang* sweat profusely. **sweat it out** *colloq.* endure a difficult experience to the end. [Old English *swāt* (*n.*), *swǣtan* (*v.*, corresponding to Old High German *sweizzen* 'roast'), from Germanic: the noun altered from earlier *swote* in imitation of the verb]

sweatband /'swɛtband/ *n.* a band of absorbent material inside a hat or round a wrist etc. to soak up sweat.

sweater /'swɛtə/ *n.* **1** = PULLOVER. **2** an employer who works employees hard in poor conditions for low pay.

sweat gland *n.* a spiral tubular gland below the skin secreting sweat.

sweating-sickness *n.* any of various fevers with intense sweating, epidemic in England in the 15th and 16th centuries.

sweatpants /'swɛtpants/ *n.pl.* loose thick esp. cotton trousers with an elasticated or drawstrings waist, worn for sports or leisurewear.

sweatshirt /'swɛtʃə:t/ *n.* a loose long-sleeved thick esp. cotton sweater, fleecy on the inside and worn for sports or leisurewear.

sweatshop /'swɛtʃɒp/ *n.* a workshop where sweated labour is used.

sweat sock *n. N. Amer.* a thick absorbent calf-length sock worn with trainers.

sweatsuit /'swɛtsu:t, -sju:t/ *n.* a suit of a sweatshirt and sweatpants, as worn by athletes etc.

sweaty /'swɛti/ *adj.* (**sweatier**, **sweatiest**) **1** sweating; covered with sweat. **2** causing sweat. □ **sweatily** *adv.* **sweatiness** *n.*

Swede /swi:d/ *n.* **1 a** a native or national of Sweden. **b** a person of Swedish descent. **2** (**swede**) (in full **swede turnip**) *Brit.* **a** a cruciferous plant, *Brassica napus*, with a large yellow-fleshed root, originally from Sweden. **b** this root as a vegetable; also called *rutabaga*. [Middle Low German & Middle Dutch *Swēde*, probably from Old Norse *Svíthjóth*, from *Svíar* 'Swedes' + *thjóth* 'people']

Swedish /'swi:dɪʃ/ *adj. & n.* ● *adj.* of or relating to Sweden or its people or language. ● *n.* the language of Sweden.

Sweeney /'swi:ni/ *n.* (prec. by *the*) *Brit. slang* the members of a flying squad. [rhyming slang from *Sweeney* Todd, a barber who murdered his customers]

sweep /swi:p/ *v. & n.* ● *v.* (*past* and *past part.* **swept** /swɛpt/) **1** *tr.* clean or clear (a room or area etc.) with or as with a broom. **2** *intr.* (often foll. by *up*) clean a room etc. in this way. **3** *tr.* (often foll. by *up*) collect or remove (dirt or litter etc.) by sweeping. **4** *tr.* (foll. by *aside, away*, etc.) **a** push with or as with a broom. **b** dismiss or reject abruptly (*their objections were swept aside*). **5** *tr.* (foll. by *along, down*, etc.) carry or drive along with force. **6** *tr.* (foll. by *off, away*, etc.) remove or clear forcefully. **7** *tr.* traverse swiftly or lightly (*the wind swept the hillside*). **8** *tr.* impart a sweeping motion to (*swept his hand across*). **9** *tr.* swiftly cover or affect (*a new fashion swept the country*). **10** *intr.* **a** glide swiftly; speed along with unchecked motion. **b** go majestically. **11** *intr.* (of geographical features etc.) have continuous extent. **12** *tr.* drag (a river bottom etc.) to search for something. **13** *tr.* (of artillery etc.) include in the line of fire; cover the whole of. **14** *tr.* propel (a barge etc.) with sweeps. **15** *tr. N. Amer.* win every event, award, or place in (a contest). ● *n.* **1** the act or motion or an instance of sweeping. **2** a curve in the road, a sweeping line of a hill, etc. **3** range or scope (*beyond the sweep of the human mind*). **4** = CHIMNEY SWEEP. **5** a sortie by aircraft. **6** *colloq.* = SWEEPSTAKE 1, 2. **7** a long oar worked from a barge etc. **8** the sail of a windmill. **9** a long pole mounted as a lever for raising buckets from a well. **10** *Electronics* the movement of a beam across the screen of a cathode ray tube. **11** a survey of an area, esp. the night sky, made in an arc or circle. **12** (also in *pl.*) *US* a survey, taking place several times a year, of the popularity ratings of local television stations, carried out to determine advertising rates. □ **make a clean sweep of 1** completely abolish or expel. **2** win all the prizes etc. in (a competition etc.). **sweep away 1** abolish swiftly. **2** (usu. in *passive*) powerfully affect, esp. emotionally. **sweep the board 1** win all the money in a gambling game. **2** win all possible prizes etc. **sweep under the carpet** see CARPET. [Middle English *swepe* (earlier *swōpe*) from Old English *swāpan*]

sweepback /'swi:pbak/ *n.* the angle at which an aircraft's wing is set back from a position at right angles to the body.

sweeper /'swi:pə/ *n.* **1** a person who cleans by sweeping. **2** a device for sweeping carpets etc. **3** *Football* a defensive player usu. playing behind the other defenders across the width of the field.

sweeping /'swi:pɪŋ/ *adj. & n.* ● *adj.* **1** wide in range or effect (*sweeping changes*). **2** taking no account of particular cases or exceptions (*a sweeping statement*). ● *n.* (in *pl.*) dirt etc. collected by sweeping. □ **sweepingly** *adv.* **sweepingness** *n.*

sweep second hand *n.* a second hand on a clock or watch, moving on the same dial as the other hands.

sweepstake /'swi:psteɪk/ *n.* **1** a form of gambling on horse races etc. in which all competitors' stakes are paid to the winners. **2** a race with betting of this kind. **3** a prize or prizes won in a sweepstake.

sweet /swi:t/ *adj. & n.* ● *adj.* **1** having the pleasant taste characteristic of sugar. **2** smelling pleasant like roses or perfume etc.; fragrant. **3** (of sound etc.) melodious or harmonious. **4 a** not salt, sour, or bitter. **b** fresh, with flavour unimpaired by rottenness. **c** (of water) fresh and readily drinkable. **5** (of wine) having a sweet taste (opp. DRY *adj.* 2). **6** highly gratifying or attractive. **7** amiable, pleasant (*has a sweet nature*). **8** *colloq.* (of a person or thing) pretty, charming, endearing. **9** (foll. by *on*) *colloq.* fond of; in love with. **10** esp. *iron.* one's own; particular, individual (*goes his own sweet way*). ● *n.* **1** *Brit.* a small shaped piece of confectionery usu. made with sugar or sweet chocolate. **2** *Brit.* a sweet dish forming a course of a meal. **3** a sweet part of something; sweetness. **4** (in *pl.*) delights, gratification. **5** (esp. as a form of address) sweetheart etc. □ **she's sweet** *Austral. slang* all is well. □ **sweetish** *adj.* **sweetly** *adv.* [Old English *swēte*, from Germanic]

sweet alyssum see ALYSSUM 2.

sweet and sour *attrib.adj.* cooked in a sauce containing sugar and vinegar or lemon etc. (*sweet and sour pork*).

sweet basil see BASIL.

sweet bay *n.* = BAY² 1.

sweetbread /'swi:tbrɛd/ *n.* the pancreas or thymus of an animal, esp. as food.

sweet-brier *n.* a wild rose, *Rosa eglanteria*, with small fragrant leaves and flowers.

sweet chestnut see CHESTNUT *n.* 1.

sweet cicely *n.* a white-flowered aromatic umbelliferous plant, *Myrrhis odorata*.

sweetcorn /swi:tkɔ:n/ *n.* **1** a kind of maize with kernels having a high sugar content. **2** these kernels, eaten as a vegetable when young.

sweeten /'swi:t(ə)n/ *v.* **1** *tr. & intr.* make or become sweet or sweeter. **2** *tr.* make agreeable or less painful. □ **sweeten the pill** see PILL. □ **sweetening** *n.*

sweetener /ˈswiːt(ə)nə/ *n.* **1** a substance used to sweeten food or drink. **2** *colloq.* a bribe or inducement.

sweet fennel see FENNEL 3.

sweet flag *n.* a waterside plant, *Acorus calamus* (arum family), with leaves like those of the iris, used medicinally and as a flavouring.

sweet gale see GALE[2].

sweetheart /ˈswiːthɑːt/ *n.* **1** a lover or darling. **2** a term of endearment (esp. as a form of address).

sweetheart agreement *n.* (also **sweetheart contract** or **deal**) *colloq.* an industrial agreement reached privately by employers and trade unions in their own interests.

sweetie /ˈswiːti/ *n. colloq.* **1** *Brit.* a sweet. **2** (also **sweetie-pie**) a term of endearment (esp. as a form of address). **3** a green-skinned hybrid variety of grapefruit, noted for its sweet taste.

sweeting /ˈswiːtɪŋ/ *n.* **1** a sweet-flavoured variety of apple. **2** *archaic* darling.

sweetmeal /ˈswiːtmiːl/ *n. Brit.* **1** sweetened wholemeal. **2** a sweetmeal biscuit.

sweetmeat /ˈswiːtmiːt/ *n. archaic* **1** a sweet (see SWEET *n.* 1). **2** a small fancy cake.

sweetness /ˈswiːtnɪs/ *n.* the quality of being sweet; fragrance, melodiousness, etc. □ **sweetness and light** a display of (esp. uncharacteristic) mildness and reason.

sweet pea *n.* any climbing plant of the genus *Lathyrus*, esp. *L. odoratus* with fragrant flowers in many colours.

sweet pepper *n.* a pepper (capsicum) with a relatively mild taste.

sweet potato *n.* **1** a tropical climbing plant, *Ipomoea batatas*, with sweet tuberous roots used for food. **2** the root of this.

sweet rocket see ROCKET[2] 1.

sweet rush *n.* (also **sweet sedge**) a sedge with a thick creeping aromatic rootstock used in medicine and confectionery.

sweetshop /ˈswiːtʃɒp/ *n. Brit.* a shop selling sweets as its main item.

sweetsop /ˈswiːtsɒp/ *n.* **1** a tropical American evergreen shrub, *Annona squamosa*. **2** the fruit of this, having a green rind and a sweet pulp.

sweet sultan *n.* a sweet-scented plant, *Centaurea moschata* or *C. suaveoleus* (daisy family).

sweet talk *n.* & *v. colloq.* ● *n.* flattery, blandishment. ● *v.tr.* (**sweet-talk**) flatter in order to persuade.

sweet-tempered *adj.* amiable.

sweet tooth *n.* a liking for sweet-tasting things.

sweet violet *n.* a sweet-scented violet, *Viola odorata*.

sweet william *n.* a garden pink, *Dianthus barbatus*, with clusters of vivid fragrant flowers.

swell /swɛl/ *v., n.,* & *adj.* ● *v.* (*past part.* **swollen** /ˈswəʊlən/ or **swelled**) **1** *intr.* & *tr.* grow or cause to grow bigger or louder or more intense; expand; increase in force or intensity. **2** *intr.* (often foll. by *up*) & *tr.* rise or raise up from the surrounding surface. **3** *intr.* (foll. by *out*) bulge. **4** *intr.* (of the heart as the seat of emotion) feel full of joy, pride, relief, etc. **5** *intr.* (foll. by *with*) be hardly able to restrain (pride etc.). ● *n.* **1** an act or the state of swelling. **2** the heaving of the sea with waves that do not break, e.g. after a storm. **3 a** a crescendo. **b** a mechanism in an organ etc. for obtaining a crescendo or diminuendo. **4** *archaic colloq.* a person of distinction or of dashing or fashionable appearance. **5** a protuberant part. ● *adj.* **1** esp. *N. Amer. colloq.* fine, splendid, excellent. **2** *archaic colloq.* smart, fashionable. □ **swellish** *adj.* [Old English *swellan*, from Germanic]

swell-box *n.* a box in which organ pipes are enclosed, with a shutter for controlling the sound level.

swelled head *n.* (also **swollen head**) *colloq.* conceit.

swelling /ˈswɛlɪŋ/ *n.* an abnormal protuberance on or in the body.

swell-organ *n.* a section of an organ with pipes in a swell-box.

swelter /ˈswɛltə/ *v.* & *n.* ● *v.intr.* (of the atmosphere, or a person etc. suffering from it) be uncomfortably hot. ● *n.* a sweltering atmosphere or condition. □ **swelteringly** *adv.* [base of (now dialect) *swelt* from Old English *sweltan* 'perish', from Germanic]

swept *past* and *past part.* of SWEEP.

swept-back *adj.* (of an aircraft wing) fixed at an acute angle to the fuselage, inclining outwards towards the rear.

swept-up *adj.* (of hair) upswept.

swept-wing *adj.* (of an aircraft) having swept-back wings.

swerve /swəːv/ *v.* & *n.* ● *v.intr.* & *tr.* change or cause to change direction, esp. abruptly. ● *n.* **1** a swerving movement. **2** divergence from a course. □ **swerveless** *adj.* **swerver** *n.* [Old English *sweorfan* 'depart, leave']

SWG *abbr.* standard wire gauge.

swift /swɪft/ *adj., adv.,* & *n.* ● *adj.* **1** quick, rapid; soon coming or passing. **2** speedy, prompt (*a swift response*; *was swift to act*). ● *adv.* (*archaic* except in *comb.*) swiftly (*swift-moving*). ● *n.* **1** any swift-flying insect-eating bird of the family Apodidae, with long wings and a superficial resemblance to a swallow. **2** a revolving frame for winding yarn etc. from. □ **swiftly** *adv.* **swiftness** *n.* [Old English, related to *swīfan* 'move in a course']

swiftie /ˈswɪfti/ *n. Austral. slang* **1** a deceptive trick. **2** a person who acts or thinks quickly.

swiftlet /ˈswɪftlɪt/ *n.* a small swift of the genus *Collocalia*.

swig /swɪg/ *v.* & *n. colloq.* ● *v.tr.* & *intr.* (**swigged, swigging**) drink in large draughts. ● *n.* a large draught or swallow of drink, esp. of alcoholic liquor. □ **swigger** *n.* [16th c., originally as noun in obsolete sense 'liquor': origin unknown]

swill /swɪl/ *v.* & *n.* ● *v.* **1** *tr.* (often foll. by *out*) *Brit.* rinse or flush; pour water over or through. **2** *tr.* & *intr.* drink greedily. ● *n.* **1** *Brit.* an act of rinsing. **2** mainly liquid usu. kitchen refuse as pig-food. **3** inferior liquor. □ **swiller** *n.* [Old English *swillan*, *swilian*, of unknown origin]

swim /swɪm/ *v.* & *n.* ● *v.* (**swimming**; *past* **swam** /swam/; *past part.* **swum** /swʌm/) **1** *intr.* propel the body through water by working the arms and legs, or (of a fish etc.) the fins and tail. **2** *tr.* **a** traverse (a stretch of water or its distance) by swimming. **b** compete in (a race) by swimming. **c** use (a particular stroke) in swimming. **3** *intr.* float on or at the surface of a liquid (*bubbles swimming on the surface*). **4** *intr.* appear to undulate or reel or whirl. **5** *intr.* have a dizzy effect or sensation (*my head swam*). **6** *intr.* (foll. by *in*, *with*) be flooded. ● *n.* **1** a spell or the act of swimming. **2** a deep pool frequented by fish in a river. □ **in the swim** involved in or acquainted with what is going on. □ **swimmable** *adj.* **swimmer** *n.* [Old English *swimman*, from Germanic]

■ **Usage** The use of *swum* instead of *swam* for the past tense, as in *He swum for the shore*, is non-standard.

swim-bladder *n.* a gas-filled sac in fishes used to maintain buoyancy.

swimmeret /ˈswɪmərɛt/ *n.* (in crustaceans) an abdominal limb adapted for swimming.

swimming bath *n. Brit.* a swimming pool, esp. a public indoor one.

swimming costume *n. Brit.* a garment worn for swimming.

swimmingly /ˈswɪmɪŋli/ *adv.* with easy and unobstructed progress.

swimming pool *n.* an artificial indoor or outdoor pool for swimming.

swimming trunks see TRUNK 7.

swimsuit /ˈswɪmsuːt, -sjuːt/ *n.* a one-piece swimming costume worn by women. □ **swimsuited** *adj.*

swimwear /ˈswɪmwɛː/ *n.* clothing worn for swimming.

swindle /ˈswɪnd(ə)l/ *v. & n.* ● *v.tr.* (often foll. by *out of*) **1** cheat (a person) of money, possessions, etc. (*was swindled out of all his savings*). **2** cheat a person of (money etc.) (*swindled all his savings out of him*). ● *n.* **1** an act of swindling. **2** a person or thing represented as what it is not. **3** a fraudulent scheme. □ **swindler** *n.* [back-formation from *swindler* from German *Schwindler* 'extravagant maker of schemes, swindler', from *schwindeln* 'be dizzy']

swine /swʌɪn/ *n.* (*pl.* same) **1** *formal* or *US* a pig. **2** (*pl.* **swine** or **swines**) *colloq.* **a** a term of contempt or disgust for a person. **b** a very unpleasant or difficult thing. □ **swinish** *adj.* (esp. in sense 2). **swinishly** *adv.* **swinishness** *n.* [Old English *swīn*, from Germanic]

swine fever *n.* an intestinal viral disease of pigs.

swineherd /ˈswʌɪnhəːd/ *n.* a person who tends pigs.

swine vesicular disease *n.* an infectious viral disease of pigs causing mild fever and blisters around the mouth and feet.

swing /swɪŋ/ *v. & n.* ● *v.* (*past* and *past part.* **swung** /swʌŋ/) **1** *intr. & tr.* move or cause to move with a to-and-fro or curving motion, as of an object attached at one end and hanging free at the other. **2** *intr. & tr.* **a** sway. **b** hang so as to be free to sway. **c** oscillate or cause to oscillate. **3** *intr. & tr.* revolve or cause to revolve. **4** *intr.* move by gripping something and leaping etc. (*swung from tree to tree*). **5** *intr.* go with a swinging gait (*swung out of the room*). **6** *intr.* (foll. by *round*) move round to the opposite direction. **7** *intr.* change from one opinion or mood to another. **8 a** *intr.* (foll. by *at*) attempt to hit or punch. **b** *tr.* throw (a punch). **9 a** *intr.* (also **swing it**) play music with swing (see sense 7b of *n.*). **b** *tr.* play (a tune or passage) with swing. **c** *intr.* (of music) be played with swing. **10** *intr. colloq.* **a** be lively or up to date; enjoy oneself. **b** be promiscuous. **11** *intr. colloq.* (of a party etc.) be lively, successful, etc. **12** *tr.* have a decisive influence on (esp. voting etc.). **13** *tr. colloq.* deal with or achieve; manage. **14** *intr. colloq.* be executed by hanging. **15** *Cricket* **a** *intr.* (of the ball) deviate from a straight course in the air. **b** *tr.* cause (the ball) to do this. ● *n.* **1** the act or an instance of swinging. **2** the motion of swinging. **3** the extent of swinging. **4** a swinging or smooth gait or rhythm or action. **5 a** a seat slung by ropes or chains etc. for swinging on or in. **b** a spell of swinging on this. **6** an easy but vigorous continued action. **7 a** jazz or dance music with an easy flowing but vigorous rhythm. **b** the rhythmic feeling or drive of this music. **8** a discernible change in opinion, esp. the amount by which votes or points scored etc. change from one side to another. □ **swing the lead** *Brit. colloq.* malinger; shirk one's duty. **swings and roundabouts** *Brit.* a situation affording no eventual gain or loss (from the phr. *lose on the swings what you make on the roundabouts*). □ **swinger** *n.* (esp. in sense 10 of *v.*). [Old English *swingan* 'to beat', from Germanic]

swingbin /ˈswɪŋbɪn/ *n.* a plastic rubbish bin with a lid that swings open and shut.

swingboat /ˈswɪŋbəʊt/ *n.* esp. *Brit.* a boat-shaped swing at fairs.

swing bowler *n. Cricket* a bowler who swings the ball (see SWING *v.* 15). □ **swing bowling** *n.*

swing-bridge *n.* a bridge that can be swung to one side to allow the passage of ships.

swing-door *n. Brit.* a door able to open in either direction and close itself when released.

swinge /swɪn(d)ʒ/ *v.tr.* (**swingeing**) *archaic* strike hard; beat. [alteration of Middle English *swenge* from Old English *swengan* 'shake, shatter', from Germanic]

swingeing /ˈswɪn(d)ʒɪŋ/ *adj.* esp. *Brit.* **1** (of a blow) forcible. **2** huge or far-reaching, esp. in severity (*swingeing economies*). □ **swingeingly** *adv.*

swinging /ˈswɪŋɪŋ/ *adj.* **1** (of gait, melody, etc.) vigorously rhythmical. **2** *colloq.* **a** lively; up to date; excellent. **b** promiscuous. □ **swingingly** *adv.*

swingle /ˈswɪŋg(ə)l/ *n. & v.* ● *n.* **1** a wooden instrument for beating flax and removing the woody parts from it. **2** the swinging part of a flail. ● *v.tr.* clean (flax) with a swingle. [Middle English from Middle Dutch *swinghel* (as SWING, -LE[1])]

swingletree /ˈswɪŋg(ə)ltriː/ *n.* a crossbar pivoted in the middle, to which the traces are attached in a cart, plough, etc.

swing shift *n. US* a work shift from afternoon to late evening.

swing-wing *n.* an aircraft wing that can move from a right-angled to a swept-back position.

swingy /ˈswɪŋi/ *adj.* (**swingier**, **swingiest**) **1** (of music) characterized by swing (see SWING *n.* 7). **2** (of a skirt or dress) designed to swing with body movement.

swipe /swʌɪp/ *v. & n. colloq.* ● *v.* **1** *tr.* & (often foll. by *at*) *intr.* hit hard and recklessly with a sweeping motion. **2** *tr.* steal. **3** *tr.* pass (a swipe card) over the electronic device that reads it. ● *n.* an act of swiping, esp. a reckless hard hit or attempted hit. □ **swiper** *n.* [perhaps a variant of SWEEP]

swipe card *n.* a credit card etc. on which magnetically encoded information is stored to be read by an electronic device.

swipple /ˈswɪp(ə)l/ *n.* the swingle of a flail. [Middle English, probably formed as SWEEP + -LE[1]]

swirl /swəːl/ *v. & n.* ● *v.intr. & tr.* move or flow or carry along with a whirling motion. ● *n.* **1** a swirling motion of or in water, air, etc. **2** the act of swirling. **3** a twist or curl, esp. as part of a pattern or design. □ **swirly** *adj.* [Middle English (originally as noun): originally Scots, perhaps of Low German or Dutch origin]

swish /swɪʃ/ *v., n., & adj.* ● *v.* **1** *tr.* swing (a scythe or stick etc.) audibly through the air, grass, etc. **2** *intr.* move with or make a swishing sound. **3** *tr.* (foll. by *off*) cut (a flower etc.) in this way. ● *n.* a swishing action or sound. ● *adj. Brit. colloq.* smart, fashionable. [imitative]

swishy /ˈswɪʃi/ *adj.* **1** making a swishing sound. **2** *slang* effeminate.

Swiss /swɪs/ *adj. & n.* ● *adj.* of or relating to Switzerland in western Europe or its people. ● *n.* (*pl.* same) **1** a native or national of Switzerland. **2** a person of Swiss descent. [French *Suisse* from Middle High German *Swīz*]

Swiss chard see CHARD.

Swiss cheese plant *n.* a climbing house plant, *Monstera deliciosa*, with aerial roots and holes in the leaves (as in some Swiss cheeses).

Swiss roll *n. Brit.* a cylindrical cake with a spiral cross-section, made from a flat piece of sponge cake spread with jam etc. and rolled up.

switch /swɪtʃ/ *n. & v.* ● *n.* **1** a device for making and breaking the connection in an electric circuit. **2 a** a transfer, changeover, or deviation. **b** an exchange. **3** a slender flexible shoot cut from a tree. **4** a light tapering rod. **5** *US* a device at the junction of railway tracks for transferring a train from one track to another; = POINT *n.* 17. **6** a tress of false or detached hair tied at one end, used in hairdressing. **7 a** a computer system which manages the transfer of funds between point-of-sale terminals and institutions. **b** (**Switch** *propr.*) an EFTPOS system in the UK. **c** the transfer of funds by such a system. ● *v.* **1** *tr. & absol.* (foll. by *on*, *off*) turn (an electrical device) on or off. **2** *intr.* (often foll. by *over*) change or transfer position, subject, etc. **3** *tr.* (often foll. by *over*) change or transfer. **4** *tr.* (often foll. by *over*) reverse the positions of; exchange (*switched chairs*). **5** *tr. Brit.* swing or snatch (a thing) suddenly (*switched it out of my hand*). **6** *tr.* beat or flick with a switch. □ **switch off** *colloq.* cease to pay attention. **switch over** = senses 2, 3, 4 of the *v.* □ **switchable** *adj.* **switcher** *n.* [earlier *swits*, *switz*, probably from Low German]

switchback /ˈswɪtʃbak/ *n.* **1** *Brit.* a railway at a fair etc., in which the train's ascents are effected by the momentum of its previous descents. **2** (often *attrib.*) a railway or road with alternate sharp ascents and descents.

switchblade /ˈswɪtʃbleɪd/ *n.* a pocket knife with the blade released by a spring.

switchboard /ˈswɪtʃbɔːd/ *n.* an apparatus for varying connections between electric circuits, esp. in telephony.

switched-on *adj. Brit.* **1** *colloq.* up to date; alert, aware of what is going on. **2** *slang* excited; under the influence of drugs.

switchgear /ˈswɪtʃgɪə/ *n.* **1** the switching equipment used in the transmission of electricity. **2** the switches or electrical controls in a motor vehicle.

switch-over *n.* an instance of switching over (see SWITCH *v.* 2,3,4); a changeover.

swither /ˈswɪðə/ *v.* & *n. Sc.* ● *v.intr.* hesitate; be uncertain. ● *n.* doubt or uncertainty. [16th c.: origin unknown]

swivel /ˈswɪv(ə)l/ *n.* & *v.* ● *n.* a coupling between two parts enabling one to revolve without turning the other. ● *v.tr.* & *intr.* (**swivelled**, **swivelling**; *US* **swiveled**, **swiveling**) turn on or as on a swivel. [Middle English, from weak grade *swif-* of Old English *swīfan* 'sweep' + -LE[1]: cf. SWIFT]

swivel chair *n.* a chair with a seat able to be turned horizontally.

swivet /ˈswɪvɪt/ *n.* esp. *US* (usu. in phr. **in a swivet**) a fluster or panic; a hurry. [19th c.: origin unknown]

swizz /swɪz/ *n.* (also **swiz**) (*pl.* **swizzes**) *Brit. colloq.* **1** something unfair or disappointing. **2** a swindle. [abbreviation of SWIZZLE[2]]

swizzle[1] /ˈswɪz(ə)l/ *n.* & *v. colloq.* ● *n.* a mixed alcoholic drink esp. of rum or gin and bitters made frothy. ● *v.tr.* stir with a swizzle-stick. [19th c.: origin unknown]

swizzle[2] /ˈswɪz(ə)l/ *n. Brit. colloq.* = SWIZZ. [20th c.: probably alteration of SWINDLE]

swizzle-stick *n.* a stick used for frothing or flattening drinks.

swob var. of SWAB.

swollen *past part.* of SWELL.

swollen head var. of SWELLED HEAD.

swoon /swuːn/ *v.* & *n. literary* ● *v.intr.* faint; fall into a fainting-fit, esp. from excitement. ● *n.* an occurrence of fainting. [Middle English *swoune*, perhaps a back-formation from the noun *swogning*, via *iswogen* from Old English *geswogen* 'to overcome']

swoop /swuːp/ *v.* & *n.* ● *v.* **1** *intr.* (often foll. by *down*) descend rapidly like a bird of prey. **2** *intr.* (often foll. by *on*) make a sudden attack from a distance. **3** *tr.* (often foll. by *up*) *colloq.* snatch the whole of at one swoop. ● *n.* a swooping or snatching movement or action. □ **at** (or **in**) **one fell swoop** see FELL[4]. [perhaps a dialect variant of obsolete *swōpe* from Old English *swāpan*: see SWEEP]

swoosh /swuːʃ, swʊʃ/ *n.* & *v.* ● *n.* the noise of a sudden rush of liquid, air, etc. ● *v.intr.* move with this noise. [imitative]

swop var. of SWAP.

sword /sɔːd/ *n.* **1** a weapon usu. of metal with a long blade and hilt with a handguard, used esp. for thrusting or striking, and often worn as part of ceremonial dress. **2** (prec. by *the*) **a** war. **b** military power. □ **put to the sword** kill, esp. in war. □ **swordlike** *adj.* [Old English *sw(e)ord*, from Germanic]

sword-bearer *n.* an official carrying the sovereign's etc. sword on a formal occasion.

swordbill /ˈsɔːdbɪl/ *n.* a long-billed hummingbird, *Ensifera ensifera*.

sword dance *n.* a dance in which the performers brandish swords or step about swords laid on the ground.

swordfish /ˈsɔːdfɪʃ/ *n.* (*pl.* usu. same) a large marine fish, *Xiphias gladius*, with an extended swordlike upper jaw.

sword grass *n.* a grass, *Scirpus americanus*, with swordlike leaves.

sword knot *n.* a ribbon or tassel attached to a sword-hilt originally for securing it to the wrist.

sword lily *n.* = GLADIOLUS.

sword of Damocles /ˈdaməkliːz/ *n.* an imminent danger (from *Damokles*, flatterer of Dionysius of Syracuse (4th c. BC) made to feast while a sword hung by a hair over him).

sword of justice *n.* (prec. by *the*) judicial authority.

Sword of State *n.* a sword borne before the sovereign on state occasions.

swordplay /ˈsɔːdpleɪ/ *n.* **1** fencing. **2** repartee; cut-and-thrust argument.

swordsman /ˈsɔːdzmən/ *n.* (*pl.* **-men**) a person of (usu. specified) skill with a sword. □ **swordsmanship** *n.*

swordstick /ˈsɔːdstɪk/ *n.* a hollow walking stick containing a blade that can be used as a sword.

sword-swallower *n.* a person ostensibly or actually swallowing sword blades as entertainment.

swordtail /ˈsɔːdteɪl/ *n.* **1** a tropical fish, *Xiphophorus helleri*, with a long tail. **2** = HORSESHOE CRAB.

swore *past* of SWEAR.

sworn /swɔːn/ *past part.* of SWEAR. ● *adj.* bound by or as by an oath (*sworn enemies*).

swot /swɒt/ *v.* & *n. Brit. colloq.* ● *v.* (**swotted**, **swotting**) **1** *intr.* study assiduously. **2** *tr.* (often foll. by *up*) study (a subject) hard or hurriedly. ● *n.* **1** a person who swots. **2 a** hard study. **b** a thing that requires this. [dialect variant of SWEAT]

swum *past part.* of SWIM.

swung *past* and *past part.* of SWING.

swung dash *n.* a dash (~) with alternate curves.

swy /swʌɪ/ *n. Austral.* the game of two-up. [German *zwei* 'two']

SY *abbr.* steam yacht.

-sy /si/ *suffix* forming diminutive nouns (*popsy*) and adjectives (*folksy, tipsy*).

sybarite /ˈsɪbərʌɪt/ *n.* & *adj.* ● *n.* a person who is self-indulgent or devoted to sensuous luxury. ● *adj.* fond of luxury or sensuousness. □ **sybaritic** /-ˈrɪtɪk/ *adj.* **sybaritical** /-ˈrɪtɪk(ə)l/ *adj.* **sybaritically** /-ˈrɪtɪk(ə)li/ *adv.* **sybaritism** *n.* [originally an inhabitant of Sybaris, an ancient Greek city in S. Italy, noted for luxury, from Latin *sybarita* from Greek *subaritēs*]

sycamine /ˈsɪkəmɪn, -ʌɪn/ *n. Bibl.* the black mulberry tree, *Morus nigra* (see Luke 17:6; in modern versions translated as 'mulberry tree'). [Latin *sycaminus* via Greek *sukaminos* 'mulberry tree' from Hebrew *šiḳmāh* 'sycamore', assimilated to Greek *sukon* 'fig']

sycamore /ˈsɪkəmɔː/ *n.* **1** (in full **sycamore maple**) **a** a large maple, *Acer pseudoplatanus*, with winged seeds, grown for its shade and timber. **b** its wood. **2** *N. Amer.* the plane tree or its wood. **3** *Bibl.* a fig tree, *Ficus sycomorus*, growing in Egypt, Syria, etc. [variant of SYCOMORE]

syce /sʌɪs/ *n.* (also **sice**) (esp. in India) a groom. [Hindustani from Arabic *sā'is, sāyis*]

sycomore /ˈsɪkəmɔː/ *n.* = SYCAMORE 3. [Middle English via Old French *sic(h)amor* and Latin *sycomorus* from Greek *sukomoros*, from *sukon* 'fig' + *moron* 'mulberry']

syconium /sʌɪˈkəʊnɪəm/ *n.* (*pl.* **syconia** /-nɪə/) *Bot.* a fleshy hollow receptacle developing into a multiple fruit, as in the fig. [modern Latin, from Greek *sukon* 'fig']

sycophant /ˈsɪkəfant/ *n.* a servile flatterer; a toady. □ **sycophancy** *n.* **sycophantic** /-ˈfantɪk/ *adj.* **sycophantically** /-ˈfantɪk(ə)li/ *adv.* [French *sycophante* or Latin *sycophanta* from Greek *sukophantēs* 'informer', from *sukon* 'fig' + *phainō* 'show': the reason for the name is uncertain, and association with informing against the illegal exportation of figs from ancient Athens (recorded by Plutarch) cannot be substantiated]

sycosis /sʌɪˈkəʊsɪs/ *n.* a skin disease of the bearded part of the face with inflammation of the hair follicles. [originally of a figlike ulcer: modern Latin from Greek *sukōsis*, from *sukon* 'fig']

Sydenham's chorea /ˈsɪd(ə)nəmz/ *n.* chorea esp. in children as one of the manifestations of rheumatic fever: also called ST VITUS'S DANCE. [named after T. *Sydenham*, English physician d. 1689]

syenite /ˈsʌɪənʌɪt/ *n.* a grey crystalline rock of feldspar and hornblende with or without quartz. □ **syenitic** /-ˈnɪtɪk/ *adj.* [French *syénite* from Latin *Syenites* (*lapis*) '(stone) of *Syene*' (from Greek *Suēnē* 'Aswan'), a town in Egypt]

syl- /sɪl/ *prefix* assim. form of SYN- before *l*.

syllabary /ˈsɪləb(ə)ri/ *n.* (*pl.* **-ies**) a list of characters representing syllables and (in some languages or stages of writing) serving the purpose of an alphabet. [modern Latin *syllabarium* (as SYLLABLE)]

syllabi *pl.* of SYLLABUS.

syllabic /sɪˈlabɪk/ *adj.* **1** of, relating to, or based on syllables. **2** *Prosody* based on the number of syllables. **3** (of a symbol) representing a whole syllable. **4** articulated in syllables. □ **syllabically** *adv.* **syllabicity** /-ˈbɪsɪti/ *n.* [French *syllabique* or Late Latin *syllabicus* from Greek *sullabikos* (as SYLLABLE)]

syllabication /sɪˌlabɪˈkeɪʃ(ə)n/ *n.* (also **syllabification** /-fɪˈkeɪʃ(ə)n/) division into or articulation by syllables. □ **syllabify** /sɪˈlabɪfʌɪ/ *v.tr.* (**-ies, -ied**). [medieval Latin *syllabicatio* from *syllabicare*, from Latin *syllaba*: see SYLLABLE]

syllabize /ˈsɪləbʌɪz/ *v.tr.* (also **-ise**) divide into or articulate by syllables. [medieval Latin *syllabizare* from Greek *sullabizō* (as SYLLABLE)]

syllable /ˈsɪləb(ə)l/ *n.* & *v.* ● *n.* **1** a unit of pronunciation uttered without interruption, forming the whole or a part of a word and usu. having one vowel sound often with a consonant or consonants before or after: there are two syllables in *water* and three in *inferno*. **2** a character or characters representing a syllable. **3** (usu. with *neg.*) the least amount of speech or writing (*did not utter a syllable*). ● *v.tr.* pronounce by syllables; articulate distinctly. □ **in words of one syllable** expressed plainly or bluntly. □ **syllabled** *adj.* (also in *comb.*). [Middle English via Anglo-French *sillable*, Old French *sillabe* and Latin *syllaba* from Greek *sullabē* (as SYN-, *lambanō* 'take')]

syllabub /ˈsɪləbʌb/ *n.* (also **sillabub**) a dessert made of cream or milk flavoured, sweetened, and whipped to thicken it. [16th c.: origin unknown]

syllabus /ˈsɪləbəs/ *n.* (*pl.* **syllabuses** or **syllabi** /-bʌɪ/) **1 a** the programme or outline of a course of study, teaching, etc. **b** a statement of the requirements for a particular examination. **2** *RC Ch.* a summary of points decided by papal decree regarding heretical doctrines or practices. [modern Latin, originally a misreading of Latin *sittybas*, accusative pl. of *sittyba*, from Greek *sittuba* 'title-slip, label']

syllepsis /sɪˈlɛpsɪs/ *n.* (*pl.* **syllepses** /-siːz/) a figure of speech in which a word is applied to two others in different senses (e.g. *caught the train and a bad cold*) or to two others of which it grammatically suits one only (e.g. *neither they nor it is working*) (cf. ZEUGMA). □ **sylleptic** *adj.* **sylleptically** *adv.* [Late Latin from Greek *sullēpsis* 'taking together', from *sullambanō*: see SYLLABLE]

syllogism /ˈsɪlədʒɪz(ə)m/ *n.* **1** a form of reasoning in which a conclusion is drawn from two given or assumed propositions (premisses): a common or middle term is present in the two premisses but not in the conclusion, which may be invalid (e.g. *all trains are long*; *some buses are long*; *therefore some buses are trains*: the common term is *long*). **2** deductive reasoning as distinct from induction. □ **syllogistic** /-ˈdʒɪstɪk/ *adj.* **syllogistically** /-ˈdʒɪstɪk(ə)li/ *adv.* [Middle English via Old French *silogisme* or Latin *syllogismus* from Greek *sullogismos*, from *sullogizomai* (as SYN-, *logizomai* 'to reason' from *logos* 'reason')]

syllogize /ˈsɪlədʒʌɪz/ *v.* (also **-ise**) **1** *intr.* use syllogisms. **2** *tr.* put (facts or an argument) in the form of syllogism. [Middle English via Old French *sillogiser* or Late Latin *syllogizare* from Greek *sullogizomai* (as SYLLOGISM)]

sylph /sɪlf/ *n.* **1** an elemental spirit of the air. **2** a slender graceful woman or girl. **3** any hummingbird of the genus *Aglaiocercus* with a long forked tail. □ **sylphlike** *adj.* [coined by Paracelsus from modern Latin *sylphes*, German *Sylphen* (pl.), perhaps based on Latin *sylvestris* 'of the woods' + *nympha* 'nymph']

sylva /ˈsɪlvə/ *n.* (also **silva**) (*pl.* **sylvae** /-viː/ or **sylvas**) **1** the trees of a region, epoch, or environment. **2** a treatise on or a list of such trees. [Latin *silva* 'a wood']

sylvan /ˈsɪlv(ə)n/ *adj.* (also **silvan**) esp. *poet.* **1 a** of the woods. **b** having woods; wooded. **2** rural. [French *sylvain* (obsolete *silvain*) or Latin *Silvanus* 'woodland deity', from *silva* 'a wood']

sylviculture var. of SILVICULTURE.

sym- /sɪm/ *prefix* assim. form of SYN- before *b, m, p*.

symbiont /ˈsɪmbɪɒnt, -bʌɪ-/ *n.* an organism living in symbiosis. [Greek *sumbiōn -ountos*, part. of *sumbioō* 'live together' (as SYMBIOSIS)]

symbiosis /sɪmbɪˈəʊsɪs, -bʌɪ-/ *n.* (*pl.* **symbioses** /-siːz/) **1 a** an interaction between two different organisms living in close physical association, usu. to the advantage of both (cf. ANTIBIOSIS). **b** an instance of this. **2 a** a mutually advantageous association or relationship between persons. **b** an instance of this. □ **symbiotic** /-ˈɒtɪk/ *adj.* **symbiotically** /-ˈɒtɪk(ə)li/ *adv.* [modern Latin from Greek *sumbiōsis* 'a living together', from *sumbioō* 'live together', *sumbios* 'companion' (as SYN-, *bios* 'life')]

symbol /ˈsɪmb(ə)l/ *n.* & *v.* ● *n.* **1** a thing conventionally regarded as typifying, representing, or recalling something, esp. an idea or quality (*white is a symbol of purity*). **2** a mark or character taken as the conventional sign of some object, idea, function, or process, e.g. the letters standing for the chemical elements or the characters in musical notation. ● *v.tr.* (**symbolled**, **symbolling**; *US* **symboled**, **symboling**) symbolize. □ **symbology** /-ˈbɒlədʒi/ *n.* [Middle English via Latin *symbolum* from Greek *sumbolon* 'mark, token' (as SYN-, *ballō* 'throw')]

symbolic /sɪmˈbɒlɪk/ *adj.* (also **symbolical** /-ˈbɒlɪk(ə)l/) **1** of or serving as a symbol. **2** involving the use of symbols or symbolism. □ **symbolically** *adv.* [French *symbolique* or Late Latin *symbolicus* from Greek *sumbolikos*]

symbolic logic *n.* the use of symbols to denote propositions etc. in order to assist reasoning.

symbolism /ˈsɪmbəlɪz(ə)m/ *n.* **1 a** the use of symbols to represent ideas. **b** symbols collectively. **2** an artistic and poetic movement or style using symbols and indirect suggestion to express ideas, emotions, etc. □ **symbolist** *n.* **symbolistic** /-ˈlɪstɪk/ *adj.*

symbolize /ˈsɪmbəlʌɪz/ *v.tr.* (also **-ise**) **1** be a symbol of. **2** represent by means of symbols. □ **symbolization** /-ˈzeɪʃ(ə)n/ *n.* [French *symboliser* from *symbole* SYMBOL]

symmetry /ˈsɪmɪtri/ *n.* (*pl.* **-ies**) **1 a** correct proportion of the parts of a thing; balance, harmony. **b** beauty resulting from this. **2 a** a structure that allows an object to be divided into parts of an equal shape and size and similar position to the point or line or plane of division. **b** the possession of such a structure. **c** approximation to such a structure. **3** the repetition of exactly similar parts facing each other or a centre. **4** *Bot.* the possession by a flower of sepals and petals and stamens and pistils in the same number or multiples of the same number. □ **symmetric** /sɪˈmɛtrɪk/ *adj.* **symmetrical** /-ˈmɛtrɪk(ə)l/ *adj.* **symmetrically** /-ˈmɛtrɪk(ə)li/ *adv.* **symmetrize** *v.tr.* (also **-ise**). [obsolete French *symmétrie* or Latin *summetria* from Greek (as SYN-, *metron* 'measure')]

sympathectomy /sɪmpəˈθɛktəmi/ *n.* (*pl.* **-ies**) the surgical removal of a sympathetic ganglion etc.

sympathetic /sɪmpəˈθɛtɪk/ *adj.* & *n.* ● *adj.* **1** of, showing, or expressing sympathy. **2** due to sympathy. **3** likeable or capable of evoking sympathy. **4** (of a person) friendly and cooperative. **5** (foll. by *to*) inclined to favour (a proposal etc.) (*was most sympathetic to the idea*). **6** (of a landscape etc.) that touches the feelings by association etc. **7** (of a pain etc.) caused by a pain or injury to someone else or in another part of the body. **8** (of a sound, resonance, or string) sounding by a vibration communicated from another vibrating object. **9 a** designating the part of the autonomic nervous system consisting of nerves arising from ganglia near the middle part of the spinal cord that supply the internal organs, blood vessels, and glands, and balance the action of the parasympathetic nerves. **b** (of a nerve or ganglion) belonging to this system. ● *n.* **1** a sympathetic nerve. **2** the sympathetic system. □ **sympathetically** *adv.* [SYMPATHY, on the pattern of *pathetic*]

sympathetic magic *n.* a type of magic that seeks to achieve an effect by performing an associated action or using an associated thing.

sympathize /'sɪmpəθʌɪz/ *v.intr.* (also **-ise**) (often foll. by *with*) **1** feel or express sympathy; share a feeling or opinion. **2** agree with a sentiment or opinion. □ **sympathizer** *n.* [French *sympathiser* (as SYMPATHY)]

sympathy /'sɪmpəθi/ *n.* (*pl.* **-ies**) **1 a** the state of being simultaneously affected with a feeling similar to that of another person. **b** the capacity for this. **2** (often foll. by *with*) **a** the act of or capacity for sharing in an emotion, sensation, or condition of another person or thing. **b** (in *sing.* or *pl.*) compassion or commiseration; condolences. **3** (often foll. by *for*) a favourable attitude; approval. **4** (in *sing.* or *pl.*; often foll. by *with*) agreement (with a person etc.) in opinion or desire. **5** (*attrib.*) in support of another cause (*sympathy strike*). □ **in sympathy** (often foll. by *with*) **1** having or showing or resulting from sympathy (with another). **2** by way of sympathetic action (*working to rule in sympathy*). [Latin *sympathia* from Greek *sumpatheia* (as SYN-, *pathēs* from *pathos* 'feeling')]

sympatric /sɪm'patrɪk/ *adj. Biol.* occurring within the same geographical area (cf. ALLOPATRIC). [SYM- + Greek *patra* 'fatherland' + -IC]

sympetalous /sɪm'pɛt(ə)ləs/ *adj. Bot.* having the petals united.

symphonic /sɪm'fɒnɪk/ *adj.* (of music) relating to or having the form or character of a symphony. □ **symphonically** *adv.*

symphonic poem *n.* an extended orchestral piece, usu. in one movement, on a descriptive or rhapsodic theme.

symphonist /'sɪmf(ə)nɪst/ *n.* a composer of symphonies.

symphony /'sɪmf(ə)ni/ *n.* (*pl.* **-ies**) **1** an elaborate composition usu. for full orchestra, and in several movements with one or more in sonata form. **2** an interlude for orchestra alone in a large-scale vocal work. **3** = SYMPHONY ORCHESTRA. [Middle English, = harmony of sound, from Old French *symphonie* via Latin *symphonia* from Greek *sumphōnia* (as SYN-, *-phōnos* from *phōnē* 'sound')]

symphony orchestra *n.* a large orchestra suitable for playing symphonies etc.

symphyllous /sɪm'fɪləs/ *adj. Bot.* having the leaves united. [SYN- + Greek *phullon* 'leaf']

symphysis /'sɪmfɪsɪs/ *n.* (*pl.* **symphyses** /-siːz/) **1** the process of growing together. **2 a** a union between two bones esp. in the median plane of the body. **b** the place or line of this. □ **symphyseal** /-'fɪzɪəl/ *adj.* **symphysial** /-'fɪzɪəl/ *adj.* [modern Latin from Greek *sumphusis* (as SYN-, *phusis* 'growth')]

sympodium /sɪm'pəʊdɪəm/ *n.* (*pl.* **sympodia** /-dɪə/) *Bot.* the apparent main axis or stem of a vine etc., made up of successive secondary axes. □ **sympodial** *adj.* [modern Latin (as SYN-, Greek *pous podos* 'foot')]

symposium /sɪm'pəʊzɪəm/ *n.* (*pl.* **symposia** /-zɪə/ or **symposiums**) **1 a** a conference or meeting to discuss a particular subject. **b** a collection of essays or papers for this purpose. **2** a philosophical or other friendly discussion. **3** a drinking party, esp. of the ancient Greeks with conversation etc. after a banquet. [Latin from Greek *sumposion* in sense 3 (as SYN-, *-potēs* 'drinker')]

symptom /'sɪm(p)təm/ *n.* **1** *Med.* a change in the physical or mental condition of a person, regarded as evidence of a disease (cf. SIGN *n.* 5). **2** a sign of the existence of something. □ **symptomless** *adj.* [Middle English *synthoma* via medieval Latin *sinthoma* and Late Latin *symptoma* from Greek *sumptōma -atos* 'chance, symptom', from *sumpiptō* 'happen' (as SYN-, *piptō* 'fall')]

symptomatic /sɪm(p)tə'matɪk/ *adj.* serving as a symptom. □ **symptomatically** *adv.*

symptomatology /sɪm(p)təmə'tɒlədʒi/ *n.* the branch of medicine concerned with the study and interpretation of symptoms.

syn- /sɪn/ *prefix* with, together, alike. [from or suggested by Greek *sun-* from *sun* 'with']

synaeresis /sɪ'nɪərɪsɪs/ *n.* (*US* **syneresis**) (*pl.* **synaereses** /-siːz/) the contraction of two vowels into a diphthong or single vowel. [Late Latin from Greek *sunairesis* (as SYN-, *hairesis* from *haireō* 'take')]

synaesthesia /sɪnɪs'θiːzɪə/ *n.* (*US* **synesthesia**) **1** *Psychol.* the production of a mental sense-impression relating to one sense by the stimulation of another sense. **2** a sensation produced in a part of the body by stimulation of another part. □ **synaesthetic** /-'θɛtɪk/ *adj.* [modern Latin from SYN-, on the pattern of *anaesthesia*]

synagogue /'sɪnəgɒg/ *n.* **1** the building where a Jewish assembly or congregation meets for religious observance and instruction. **2** the assembly itself. □ **synagogal** /-'gɒg(ə)l/ *adj.* **synagogical** /-'gɒdʒɪk(ə)l/ *adj.* [Middle English via Old French *sinagoge* and Late Latin *synagoga* from Greek *sunagōgē* 'meeting' (as SYN-, *agō* 'bring')]

synallagmatic /sɪnəlag'matɪk/ *adj.* (of a treaty or contract) imposing reciprocal obligations. [SYN- + Greek *allassō* 'exchange']

synapse /'sʌɪnaps, 'sɪn-/ *n. Anat.* a junction of two nerve cells, consisting of a minute gap across which impulses pass by diffusion of a neurotransmitter. [Greek *synapsis* (as SYN-, *hapsis* from *haptō* 'to join')]

synapsis /sɪ'napsɪs/ *n.* (*pl.* **synapses** /-siːz/) **1** *Anat.* = SYNAPSE. **2** *Biol.* the fusion of chromosome-pairs at the start of meiosis. □ **synaptic** /-'naptɪk/ *adj.* **synaptically** /-'naptɪk(ə)li/ *adv.*

synarthrosis /sɪnɑː'θrəʊsɪs/ *n.* (*pl.* **synarthroses** /-siːz/) *Anat.* an immovably fixed bone-joint, e.g. the sutures of the skull. [SYN- + Greek *arthrōsis* 'jointing' from *arthron* 'joint']

sync /sɪŋk/ *n.* & *v.* (also **synch**) *colloq.* ● *n.* synchronization. ● *v.tr.* & *intr.* synchronize. □ **in** (or **out of**) **sync** (often foll. by *with*) according or agreeing well (or badly). [abbreviation]

syncarp /'sɪnkɑːp/ *n.* a compound fruit from a flower with several carpels, e.g. a blackberry. [SYN- + Greek *karpos* 'fruit']

syncarpous /sɪn'kɑːpəs/ *adj.* (of a flower or fruit) having the carpels united (opp. APOCARPOUS). [SYN- + Greek *karpos* 'fruit']

synch var. of SYNC.

synchondrosis /sɪŋkɒn'drəʊsɪs/ *n.* (*pl.* **synchondroses** /-siːz/) *Anat.* an almost immovable bone-joint bound by a layer of cartilage, as in the spinal vertebrae. [SYN- + Greek *khondros* 'cartilage']

synchro- /'sɪŋkrəʊ/ *comb. form* synchronized, synchronous.

synchrocyclotron /sɪŋkrəʊ'sʌɪklətrɒn/ *n. Physics* a cyclotron able to achieve higher energies by decreasing the frequency of the accelerating electric field as the particles increase in energy and mass.

synchromesh /'sɪŋkrəmɛʃ/ *n.* & *adj.* ● *n.* a system of gear-changing, esp. in motor vehicles, in which the driving and driven gearwheels are made to revolve at the same speed during engagement by means of a set of friction clutches, thereby easing the change. ● *adj.* relating to or using this system. [abbreviation of *synchronized mesh*]

synchronic /sɪŋ'krɒnɪk/ *adj.* describing a subject (esp. a language) as it exists at one point in time (opp.

DIACHRONIC). □ **synchronically** *adv.* [Late Latin *synchronus*: see SYNCHRONOUS]

synchronicity /sɪŋkrəˈnɪsɪti/ *n.* **1** the simultaneous occurrence of events which appear significantly related but have no discernible connection. **2** = SYNCHRONY 1.

synchronism /ˈsɪŋkrənɪz(ə)m/ *n.* **1** = SYNCHRONY. **2** the process of synchronizing sound and picture in cinematography, television, etc. □ **synchronistic** /-ˈnɪstɪk/ *adj.* **synchronistically** /-ˈnɪstɪk(ə)li/ *adv.* [Greek *sugkhronismos* (as SYNCHRONOUS)]

synchronize /ˈsɪŋkrənʌɪz/ *v.* (also **-ise**) **1 a** *tr.* cause to occur at the same time. **b** *intr.* (often foll. by *with*) occur at the same time; be simultaneous. **2** *tr. disp.* coordinate, combine. **3** *tr.* carry out the synchronism of (a film). **4** *tr.* ascertain or set forth the correspondence in the date of (events). **5 a** *tr.* cause (clocks etc.) to show a standard or uniform time. **b** *intr.* (of clocks etc.) be synchronized. **6** *intr.* operate in unison. □ **synchronization** /-ˈzeɪʃ(ə)n/ *n.* **synchronizer** *n.*

■ **Usage** The use of *synchronize* to mean 'coordinate' or 'combine' (see sense 2 above), as in *We must synchronize our efforts*, is considered incorrect by some people and should be avoided in standard English.

synchronized swimming *n.* a form of swimming in which participants make coordinated leg and arm movements in time to music.

synchronous /ˈsɪŋkrənəs/ *adj.* (often foll. by *with*) existing or occurring at the same time. □ **synchronously** *adv.* [Late Latin *synchronus* from Greek *sugkhronos* (as SYN-, *khronos* 'time')]

synchronous motor *n. Electr.* a motor having a speed exactly proportional to the current frequency.

synchrony /ˈsɪŋkrəni/ *n.* **1** the state of being synchronic or synchronous. **2** the treatment of events etc. as being synchronous. [Greek *sugkhronos*: see SYNCHRONOUS]

synchrotron /ˈsɪŋkrətrɒn/ *n. Physics* a cyclotron in which the magnetic field strength increases with the energy of the particles to keep their orbital radius constant. [SYNCHRO- + -TRON]

synchrotron radiation *n. Physics* polarized radiation emitted by a charged particle spinning in a magnetic field.

syncline /ˈsɪŋklʌɪn/ *n.* a rock-bed forming a trough. □ **synclinal** /-ˈklʌɪn(ə)l/ *adj.* [*synclinal* (as SYN-, Greek *klinō* 'to lean')]

syncopate /ˈsɪŋkəpeɪt/ *v.tr.* **1** *Mus.* displace the beats or accents in (a passage) so that strong beats become weak and vice versa. **2** shorten (a word) by dropping interior sounds or letters, as *symbology* for *symbolology*, *Gloster* for *Gloucester*. □ **syncopation** /-ˈpeɪʃ(ə)n/ *n.* **syncopator** *n.* [Late Latin *syncopare* 'swoon' (as SYNCOPE)]

syncope /ˈsɪŋkəpi/ *n.* **1** *Gram.* the omission of interior sounds or letters in a word (see SYNCOPATE 2). **2** *Med.* a temporary loss of consciousness caused by a fall in blood pressure. □ **syncopal** *adj.* [Middle English via Late Latin *syncopē* from Greek *sugkopē* (as SYN-, *koptō* 'strike, cut off')]

syncretism /ˈsɪŋkrɪtɪz(ə)m/ *n.* **1** *Philos.* & *Theol.* the process or an instance of syncretizing (see SYNCRETIZE). **2** *Philol.* the merging of different inflectional varieties in the development of a language. □ **syncretic** /-ˈkrɛtɪk/ *adj.* **syncretist** *n.* **syncretistic** /-ˈtɪstɪk/ *adj.* [modern Latin *syncretismus* from Greek *sugkrētismos*, from *sugkrētizō* (of two parties) 'combine against a third' (as SYN-, *krēs* 'Cretan', originally of ancient Cretan communities)]

syncretize /ˈsɪŋkrɪtʌɪz/ *v.tr.* (also **-ise**) *Philos.* & *Theol.* attempt, esp. inconsistently, to unify or reconcile differing schools of thought.

syncytium /sɪnˈsɪtɪəm/ *n.* (*pl.* **syncytia** /-tɪə/) *Biol.* a mass of cytoplasm with several nuclei, not divided into separate cells. □ **syncytial** *adj.* [formed as SYN- + -CYTE + -IUM]

syndactyl /sɪnˈdaktɪl, -ʌɪl/ *adj.* (of an animal) having digits united as in webbed feet etc. □ **syndactylism** *n.* **syndactylous** *adj.*

syndesis /ˈsɪndɪsɪs/ *n.* (*pl.* **syndeses** /-siːz/) *Biol.* = SYNAPSIS 2. [modern Latin from Greek, from *sundeō* 'bind together']

syndesmosis /sɪndɛzˈməʊsɪs/ *n.* the union and articulation of bones by means of ligaments. [modern Latin, from Greek *sundesmos* 'binding, fastening' + -OSIS]

syndetic /sɪnˈdɛtɪk/ *adj. Gram.* of or using conjunctions. [Greek *sundetikos* (as SYNDESIS)]

syndic /ˈsɪndɪk/ *n.* **1** a government official in various countries. **2** (in the UK) a business agent of certain universities and corporations, esp. (at Cambridge University) a member of a committee of the senate. □ **syndical** *adj.* [French via Late Latin *syndicus* from Greek *sundikos* (as SYN-, *-dikos* from *dikē* 'justice')]

syndicalism /ˈsɪndɪk(ə)lɪz(ə)m/ *n. hist.* a movement for transferring the ownership and control of the means of production and distribution to workers' unions. □ **syndicalist** *n.* [French *syndicalisme* from *syndical* (as SYNDIC)]

syndicate *n.* & *v.* ● *n.* /ˈsɪndɪkət/ **1** a combination of individuals or commercial firms to promote some common interest. **2** an association or agency supplying material simultaneously to a number of newspapers or periodicals. **3** a group of people who combine to buy or rent property, gamble, organize crime, etc. **4** a committee of syndics. ● *v.tr.* /ˈsɪndɪkeɪt/ **1** form into a syndicate. **2** publish (material) through a syndicate. □ **syndication** /-ˈkeɪʃ(ə)n/ *n.* [French *syndicat* via medieval Latin *syndicatus* from Late Latin *syndicus*: see SYNDIC]

syndrome /ˈsɪndrəʊm/ *n.* **1** a group of concurrent symptoms of a disease. **2** a characteristic combination of opinions, emotions, behaviour, etc. □ **syndromic** /-ˈdrɒmɪk/ *adj.* [modern Latin from Greek *sundromē* (as SYN-, *dromē* from *dramein* 'to run')]

syne /sʌɪn/ *adv., conj., & prep. Sc.* since. [contraction from Middle English *sithen* SINCE]

synecdoche /sɪˈnɛkdəki/ *n.* a figure of speech in which a part is made to represent the whole or vice versa (e.g. *new faces at the meeting*; *England lost by six wickets*). □ **synecdochic** /-ˈdɒkɪk/ *adj.* [Middle English via Latin from Greek *sunekdokhē* (as SYN-, *ekdokhē* from *ekdekhomai* 'take up')]

synecious *US* var. of SYNOECIOUS.

synecology /sɪnɪˈkɒlədʒi/ *n.* the ecological study of plant or animal communities. □ **synecological** /-ˌiːkəˈlɒdʒɪk(ə)l, -ˌɛk-/ *adj.* **synecologist** *n.*

syneresis *US* var. of SYNAERESIS.

synergist /ˈsɪnədʒɪst/ *n.* a medicine or a bodily organ (e.g. a muscle) that cooperates with another or others.

synergy /ˈsɪnədʒi/ *n.* (also **synergism** /ˈsɪnədʒɪz(ə)m/) **1** the interaction or cooperation of two or more drugs, agents, organizations, etc., to produce a new or enhanced effect compared to their separate effects. **2** an instance of this. □ **synergetic** /-ˈdʒɛtɪk/ *adj.* **synergic** /-ˈnəːdʒɪk/ *adj.* **synergistic** /-ˈdʒɪstɪk/ *adj.* **synergistically** /-ˈdʒɪstɪk(ə)li/ *adv.* [Greek *sunergos* 'working together' (as SYN-, *ergon* 'work')]

synesthesia *US* var. of SYNAESTHESIA.

syngamy /ˈsɪŋgəmi/ *n. Biol.* the fusion of gametes or nuclei in reproduction. □ **syngamous** *adj.* [SYN- + Greek *gamos* 'marriage']

syngenesis /sɪnˈdʒɛnɪsɪs/ *n.* sexual reproduction from combined male and female elements.

synod /ˈsɪnəd, -ɒd/ *n.* **1** a Church council attended by delegated clergy and sometimes laity (see also GENERAL SYNOD). **2** a Presbyterian ecclesiastical court above the presbyteries and subject to the General Assembly. **3** any meeting for debate. [Middle English via Late Latin *synodus* from Greek *sunodos* 'meeting' (as SYN-, *hodos* 'way')]

synodic /sɪˈnɒdɪk/ *adj. Astron.* relating to or involving the conjunction of stars, planets, etc. [Late Latin *synodicus* from Greek *sunodikos* (as SYNOD)]

synodical /sɪˈnɒdɪk(ə)l/ *adj.* **1** (also **synodal** /ˈsɪnəd(ə)l/) of, relating to, or constituted as a synod. **2** = SYNODIC.

synodic period *n.* the time between the successive conjunctions of a planet with the sun.

synoecious /sɪˈniːʃəs/ *adj.* (*US* **synecious**) *Bot.* having male and female organs in the same flower or receptacle. [SYN-, on the pattern of *dioecious* etc.]

synonym /ˈsɪnənɪm/ *n.* **1** a word or phrase that means exactly or nearly the same as another in the same language (e.g. *shut* and *close*). **2** a word denoting the same thing as another but suitable to a different context (e.g. *serpent* for *snake*, *Hellene* for *Greek*) or containing a different emphasis (e.g. *blindworm* for *slow-worm*). **3** a word equivalent to another in some but not all senses (e.g. *ship* and *vessel*). ▫ **synonymic** /-ˈnɪmɪk/ *adj.* **synonymity** /-ˈnɪmɪti/ *n.* [Middle English via Latin *synonymum* from Greek *sunōnumon*, neut. of *sunōnumos* (as SYN-, *onoma* 'name'): cf. ANONYMOUS]

synonymous /sɪˈnɒnɪməs/ *adj.* (often foll. by *with*) **1** having the same meaning; being a synonym (of). **2** (of a name, idea, etc.) suggestive of or associated with another (*excessive drinking regarded as synonymous with violence*). ▫ **synonymously** *adv.* **synonymousness** *n.*

synonymy /sɪˈnɒnɪmi/ *n.* (*pl.* **-ies**) **1** the state of being synonymous. **2** the collocation of synonyms for emphasis (e.g. *in any shape or form*). **3 a** a system or collection of synonyms. **b** a treatise on synonyms. [Late Latin *synonymia* from Greek *sunōnumia* (as SYNONYM)]

synopsis /sɪˈnɒpsɪs/ *n.* (*pl.* **synopses** /-siːz/) **1** a summary or outline. **2** a brief general survey. ▫ **synopsize** *v.tr.* (also **-ise**). [Late Latin from Greek (as SYN-, *opsis* 'seeing')]

synoptic /sɪˈnɒptɪk/ *adj.* & *n.* ● *adj.* **1** of, forming, or giving a synopsis. **2** taking or affording a comprehensive mental view. **3** of or relating to the Synoptic Gospels. **4** giving a general view of weather conditions. ● *n.* **1** a Synoptic Gospel. **2** the writer of a Synoptic Gospel. ▫ **synoptical** *adj.* **synoptically** *adv.* [Greek *sunoptikos* (as SYNOPSIS)]

Synoptic Gospel *n.* each of the Gospels of Matthew, Mark, and Luke, describing events from a similar point of view.

synoptist /sɪˈnɒptɪst/ *n.* the writer of a Synoptic Gospel.

synostosis /sɪnɒˈstəʊsɪs/ *n.* the joining of bones by ankylosis etc. [SYN- + Greek *osteon* 'bone' + -OSIS]

synovial /sʌɪˈnəʊvɪəl, sɪ-/ *adj. Physiol.* denoting or relating to a viscous fluid lubricating joints and tendon sheaths. [modern Latin *synovia*, formed probably arbitrarily by Paracelsus]

synovial membrane *n.* a dense membrane of connective tissue secreting synovial fluid.

synovitis /sʌɪnə(ʊ)ˈvʌɪtɪs, sɪn-/ *n.* inflammation of the synovial membrane.

syntactic /sɪnˈtaktɪk/ *adj.* of or according to syntax. ▫ **syntactical** *adj.* **syntactically** *adv.* [Greek *suntaktikos* (as SYNTAX)]

syntagma /sɪnˈtagmə/ *n.* (*pl.* **syntagmas** or **syntagmata** /-mətə/) **1** a word or phrase forming a syntactic unit. **2** a systematic collection of statements. ▫ **syntagmatic** /-ˈmatɪk/ *adj.* **syntagmic** *adj.* [Late Latin from Greek *suntagma* (as SYNTAX)]

syntax /ˈsɪntaks/ *n.* **1** the grammatical arrangement of words, showing their connection and relation. **2** a set of rules for or an analysis of this. [French *syntaxe* or Late Latin *syntaxis* from Greek *suntaxis* (as SYN-, *taxis* from *tassō* 'arrange')]

synth /sɪnθ/ *n. colloq.* = SYNTHESIZER.

synthesis /ˈsɪnθɪsɪs/ *n.* (*pl.* **syntheses** /-siːz/) **1** the process or result of building up separate elements, esp. ideas, into a connected whole, esp. into a theory or system. **2** a combination or composition. **3** *Chem.* the artificial production of compounds from their constituents as distinct from extraction from plants etc. **4** *Gram.* **a** the process of making compound and derivative words. **b** the tendency in a language to use inflected forms rather than groups of words, prepositions, etc. **5** the joining of divided parts in surgery. ▫ **synthesist** *n.* [Latin from Greek *sunthesis* (as SYN-, THESIS)]

synthesize /ˈsɪnθɪsʌɪz/ *v.tr.* (also **synthetize** /-tʌɪz/, **-ise**) **1** make a synthesis of. **2** combine into a coherent whole.

synthesizer /ˈsɪnθɪsʌɪzə/ *n.* an electronic musical instrument, usu. operated by a keyboard, producing a wide variety of sounds by generating and combining signals of different frequencies.

synthetic /sɪnˈθɛtɪk/ *adj.* & *n.* ● *adj.* **1** made by chemical synthesis, esp. to imitate a natural product (*synthetic rubber*). **2** (of emotions etc.) affected, insincere. **3** *Logic* (of a proposition) having truth or falsity determinable by recourse to experience (cf. ANALYTIC 3). **4** *Philol.* using inflections rather than separate words; using combinations of simple words or elements in compounded or complex words (cf. ANALYTICAL 2). ● *n. Chem.* a synthetic substance. ▫ **synthetical** *adj.* **synthetically** *adv.* [French *synthétique* or modern Latin *syntheticus* from Greek *sunthetikos*, via *sunthetos* from *suntithēmi* (as SYN-, *tithēmi* 'put')]

synthetic resin see RESIN *n.* 2.

syphilis /ˈsɪfɪlɪs/ *n.* a contagious venereal disease caused by the spirochaete *Treponema*, progressing from infection of the genitals via the skin and mucous membrane to the bones, muscles, and brain. ▫ **syphilitic** /-ˈlɪtɪk/ *adj.* **syphilize** /-lʌɪz/ *v.tr.* (also **-ise**). **syphiloid** /-lɔɪd/ *adj.* [modern Latin from the title (*Syphilis, sive Morbus Gallicus*) of a Latin poem (1530), from *Syphilus*, a character in it, the supposed first sufferer from the disease]

syphon /ˈsʌɪf(ə)n/ *n.* & *v.* (also **siphon**) ● *n.* **1** a pipe or tube shaped like an inverted V or U with unequal legs to convey a liquid from a container to a lower level by atmospheric pressure. **2** = SODA SYPHON. **3** (**siphon**) *Zool.* a tubular organ in an aquatic animal, esp. a mollusc, through which water is drawn in or expelled. ● *v.tr.* & *intr.* (often foll. by *off*) **1** conduct or flow through a syphon. **2** divert or set aside (funds etc.). ▫ **syphonage** *n.* **siphonal** *adj. Zool.* **syphonic** /-ˈfɒnɪk/ *adj.* (*Zool.* **siphonic**). [French *siphon* or Latin *sipho -onis* from Greek *siphō* 'pipe']

Syriac /ˈsɪrɪak/ *n.* & *adj.* ● *n.* the language of ancient Syria, western Aramaic. ● *adj.* of or relating to this language. [Latin *Syriacus* from Greek *Suriakos*, from *Suria* 'Syria']

Syrian /ˈsɪrɪən/ *n.* & *adj.* ● *n.* **1** a native or national of the modern state of Syria in the Middle East; a person of Syrian descent. **2** a native or inhabitant of the region of Syria in antiquity or later. ● *adj.* of or relating to the region or state of Syria.

syringa /sɪˈrɪŋgə/ *n.* **1** = MOCK ORANGE. **2** any plant of the genus *Syringa*, esp. the lilac. [modern Latin, formed as SYRINX (with reference to the use of its stems as pipe-stems)]

syringe /sɪˈrɪn(d)ʒ, ˈsɪ-/ *n.* & *v.* ● *n.* **1** *Med.* **a** a tube with a nozzle and piston or bulb for sucking in and ejecting liquid in a fine stream, used in surgery. **b** (in full **hypodermic syringe**) a similar device with a hollow needle for insertion under the skin. **2** any similar device used in gardening, cooking, etc. ● *v.tr.* (**syringing**) sluice or spray (the ear, a plant, etc.) with a syringe. [Middle English from medieval Latin *syringa* (as SYRINX)]

syrinx /ˈsɪrɪŋks/ *n.* (*pl.* **syrinxes** or **syringes** /sɪˈrɪn(d)ʒiːz/) **1** a set of pan pipes. **2** *Archaeol.* a narrow gallery cut in rock in an ancient Egyptian tomb. **3** the lower larynx or song-organ of birds. ▫ **syringeal** /sɪˈrɪn(d)ʒɪəl/ *adj.* [Latin *syrinx -ngis* from Greek *surigx suriggos* 'pipe, channel']

Syro- /'sʌɪrəʊ/ *comb. form* Syrian; Syrian and (*Syro-Phoenician*). [Greek *Suro-* from *Suros* 'a Syrian']

syrphid /'sə:fɪd/ *adj. & n.* ● *adj.* of or relating to the dipteran family Syrphidae, which includes the hoverflies. ● *n.* a fly of this family. [modern Latin *Syrphidae* from the genus name *Syrphis*, from Greek *surphos* 'gnat']

syrup /'sɪrəp/ *n.* (*US* also **sirup**) **1 a** a thick sweet liquid made by dissolving sugar in boiling water, often used for preserving fruit etc. **b** a similar thick liquid of a specified flavour as a drink, medicine, etc. (*rose-hip syrup*). **2** condensed sugar cane juice; part of this remaining uncrystallized at various stages of refining; molasses, treacle. **3** excessive sweetness of style or manner. □ **syrupy** *adj.* [Middle English via Old French *sirop* or medieval Latin *siropus* from Arabic *šarāb* 'beverage': cf. SHERBET, SHRUB[2]]

SYSOP /'sɪsɒp/ *n. Computing* system operator. [acronym]

syssarcosis /sɪsɑː'kəʊsɪs/ *n.* (*pl.* **syssarcoses** /-si:z/) *Anat.* a connection between bones formed by intervening muscle. [modern Latin from Greek *sussarkōsis* (as SYN-, *sarx, sarkos* 'flesh')]

systaltic /sɪ'staltɪk/ *adj.* (esp. of the heart) contracting and dilating rhythmically; pulsatory (cf. SYSTOLE, DIASTOLE). [Late Latin *systalticus* from Greek *sustaltikos* (as SYN-, *staltos* from *stellō* 'put')]

system /'sɪstəm/ *n.* **1** a complex whole; a set of connected things or parts; an organized body of material or immaterial things. **2** a set of devices (e.g. pulleys) functioning together. **3** *Physiol.* **a** a set of organs in the body with a common structure or function (*the digestive system*). **b** the human or animal body as a whole. **4 a** method; considered principles of procedure or classification. **b** classification. **5** orderliness. **6 a** a body of theory or practice relating to or prescribing a particular form of government, religion, etc. **b** (prec. by *the*) the prevailing political or social order, esp. regarded as oppressive and intransigent. **7** a method of choosing one's procedure in gambling etc. **8** *Computing* a group of related hardware units or programs or both, esp. when dedicated to a single application. **9** one of seven general types of crystal structure. **10** a major group of geological strata (*the Devonian system*). **11** *Physics* a group of associated bodies moving under mutual gravitation etc. **12** *Mus.* the braced staves of a score. □ **get a thing out of one's system** *colloq.* be rid of a preoccupation or anxiety. □ **systemless** *adj.* [French *système* or Late Latin *systema* from Greek *sustēma -atos* (as SYN-, *histēmi* 'set up')]

systematic /sɪstə'matɪk/ *adj.* **1** methodical; done or conceived according to a plan or system. **2** regular, deliberate (*a systematic liar*). □ **systematically** *adv.* **systematism** /'sɪstəmətɪz(ə)m/ *n.* **systematist** /'sɪstəmətɪst/ *n.* [French *systématique* via Late Latin *systematicus* from late Greek *sustēmatikos* (as SYSTEM)]

systematics /sɪstə'matɪks/ *n.pl.* (usu. treated as *sing.*) the study or a system of classification; taxonomy.

systematic theology *n.* a form of theology in which the aim is to arrange religious truths in a self-consistent whole.

systematize /'sɪstəmətʌɪz/ *v.tr.* (also **-ise**) **1** make systematic. **2** devise a system for. □ **systematization** /-'zeɪʃ(ə)n/ *n.* **systematizer** *n.*

systemic /sɪ'stɛmɪk, -'sti:m-/ *adj.* **1** *Physiol.* **a** of or concerning the whole body, not confined to a particular part (*systemic infection*). **b** (of blood circulation) other than pulmonary. **2** (of an insecticide, fungicide, etc.) entering the plant via the roots or shoots and passing through the tissues. □ **systemically** *adv.* [formed irregularly from SYSTEM]

systemize /'sɪstəmʌɪz/ *v.tr.* (also **-ise**) = SYSTEMATIZE. □ **systemization** /-'zeɪʃ(ə)n/ *n.* **systemizer** *n.*

system operator *n. Computing* a person who manages the operation of an electronic bulletin board. Also called SYSOP.

systems analysis *n.* the analysis of a complex process or operation in order to improve its efficiency, esp. by applying a computer system. □ **systems analyst** *n.*

systems operator *n. Computing* a person who controls or monitors the operation of complex esp. electronic systems.

systole /'sɪst(ə)li/ *n. Physiol.* the contraction of the heart, when blood is pumped into the arteries (cf. DIASTOLE). □ **systolic** /-'stɒlɪk/ *adj.* [Late Latin from Greek *sustolē*, from *sustellō* 'to contract' (as SYSTALTIC)]

syzygy /'sɪzɪdʒi/ *n.* (*pl.* **-ies**) **1** *Astron.* conjunction or opposition, esp. of the moon with the sun. **2** a pair of connected or correlated things. [Late Latin *syzygia* from Greek *suzugia*, from *suzugos* 'yoked, paired' (as SYN-, *zugon* 'yoke')]

Tt

T[1] /tiː/ *n.* (also **t**) (*pl.* **Ts** or **T's**) **1** the twentieth letter of the alphabet. **2** a T-shaped thing (esp. *attrib.*: *T-joint*). □ **to a T** exactly; to a nicety.

T[2] *symb.* **1** *Chem.* the isotope tritium. **2** tera-. **3** tesla. **4** temperature.

t *abbr.* (also **t.**) **1** ton(s). **2** tonne(s).

't *pron.* = IT[1] (*'tis*). [contraction]

-t[1] /t/ *suffix* = -ED[2] (*crept*; *sent*).

-t[2] /t/ *suffix* = -EST[2] (*shalt*).

TA *abbr.* (in the UK) Territorial Army.

Ta *symb. Chem.* the element tantalum.

ta /tɑː/ *int. Brit. colloq.* thank you. [childish form]

taal /tɑːl/ *n.* (prec. by *the*) *S.Afr.* Afrikaans. [Dutch, = language: related to Old English *talu* TALE]

TAB *abbr.* **1** typhoid-paratyphoid A and B vaccine. **2** *Austral.* Totalizator Agency Board.

tab[1] /tab/ *n.* & *v.* ● *n.* **1 a** a small flap or strip of material attached for grasping, fastening, or hanging up, or for identification. **b** a similar object as part of a garment etc. **2** esp. *N. Amer. colloq.* a bill or price (*picked up the tab*). **3** *Brit. Mil.* a marking on the collar distinguishing a staff officer. **4 a** a stage curtain. **b** a loop for suspending this. ● *v.tr.* (**tabbed**, **tabbing**) provide with a tab or tabs. □ **keep tabs** (or **a tab**) **on** *colloq.* **1** keep account of. **2** have under observation or in check. [Middle English, origin uncertain: perhaps related to TAG[1]]

tab[2] /tab/ *n.* **1** = TABULATOR 2. **2** = TABULATOR 3. [abbreviation]

tab[3] /tab/ *n. slang* a tablet, esp. one containing an illicit drug (*LSD tabs*). [abbreviation]

tabard /'tabəd, -ɑːd/ *n.* **1** a herald's official coat emblazoned with the arms of the sovereign. **2** a woman's or girl's sleeveless jerkin. **3** *hist.* a knight's short emblazoned garment worn over armour. [Middle English from Old French *tabart*, of unknown origin]

tabaret /'tabərɪt/ *n.* an upholstery fabric of alternate satin and plain stripes. [probably from TABBY]

Tabasco /tə'baskəʊ/ *n. propr.* a pungent sauce made from the fruit of *Capsicum frutescens*. [*Tabasco*, a river and state in Mexico]

tabbouleh /tə'buːleɪ/ *n.* an Arab vegetable salad made with cracked wheat. [Arabic *tabbūla*]

tabby /'tabi/ *n.* (*pl.* **-ies**) **1** (in full **tabby cat**) **a** a grey or brownish cat mottled or streaked with dark stripes. **b** any domestic cat, esp. female. **2** a kind of watered silk. **3** a plain weave. [French *tabis* (in sense 2) from Arabic *al-'attabiya*, the quarter of Baghdad where tabby was manufactured: connection of other senses uncertain]

tabernacle /'tabənak(ə)l/ *n.* **1** *hist.* a tent used as a sanctuary for the Ark of the Covenant by the Israelites during the Exodus. **2** *Eccl.* a canopied niche or receptacle esp. for the Eucharistic elements. **3** a place of worship in nonconformist creeds. **4** *Bibl.* a fixed or movable habitation usu. of light construction. **5** *Naut.* a socket or double post for a hinged mast that can be lowered to pass under low bridges. □ **tabernacled** *adj.* [Middle English from Old French *tabernacle* or Latin *tabernaculum* 'tent', diminutive of *taberna* 'hut']

tabes /'teɪbiːz/ *n. Med.* **1** emaciation. **2** locomotor ataxy; a form of neurosyphilis. □ **tabetic** /tə'bɛtɪk/ *adj.* [Latin, = wasting away]

tabla /'tablə, 'tʌblə/ *n.* (in Indian music) a pair of small drums played with the hands. [Persian and Urdu *tablah*, Hindustani *tablā*, from Arabic *tabl* 'drum']

tablature /'tablətʃə/ *n. Mus.* a form of notation in which lines, figures, and letters are used, e.g. to indicate fingering esp. for the guitar or *hist.* the lute. [French from Italian *tavolatura*, from *tavolare* 'set to music']

table /'teɪb(ə)l/ *n.* & *v.* ● *n.* **1** a piece of furniture with a flat top and one or more legs, providing a level surface for eating, writing, or working at, playing games on, etc. **2** a flat surface serving a specified purpose (*altar table*; *bird table*). **3 a** food provided in a household (*keeps a good table*). **b** a group seated at table for dinner etc. **4 a** a set of facts or figures systematically displayed, esp. in columns (*a table of contents*). **b** matter contained in this. **c** = MULTIPLICATION TABLE. **5** a flat surface for working on or for machinery to operate on. **6 a** a slab of wood or stone etc. for bearing an inscription. **b** matter inscribed on this. **7** = TABLELAND. **8** *Archit.* **a** a flat usu. rectangular vertical surface. **b** a horizontal moulding, esp. a cornice. **9 a** a flat surface of a gem. **b** a cut gem with two flat faces. **10** each half or quarter of a folding board for backgammon. **11** (prec. by *the*) *Bridge* the dummy hand. ● *v.tr.* **1** *Brit.* bring forward for discussion or consideration at a meeting. **2** esp. *US* postpone consideration of (a matter). **3** *Naut.* strengthen (a sail) with a wide hem. □ **at table** taking a meal at a table. **lay on the table 1** submit for discussion. **2** esp. *US* postpone indefinitely. **on the table** offered for discussion. **turn the tables** (often foll. by *on*) reverse one's relations (with), esp. by turning an inferior into a superior position (originally in backgammon). **under the table 1** *colloq.* very drunk after a meal or drinking bout. **2** = *under the counter* (see COUNTER[1]). □ **tableful** *n.* (*pl.* **-fuls**). [Middle English via Old French from Latin *tabula* 'plank, tablet, list']

tableau /'tabləʊ/ *n.* (*pl.* **tableaux** /-ləʊz/) **1** a picturesque presentation. **2** = TABLEAU VIVANT. **3** a dramatic or effective situation suddenly brought about. [French, = picture, diminutive of *table*: see TABLE]

tableau curtains *n.pl. Theatr.* a pair of curtains drawn open by a diagonal cord.

tableau vivant /tabləʊ 'viːvɒ̃, French tablo vivɑ̃/ *n.* (*pl.* ***tableaux vivants*** *pronunc.* same) *Theatr.* a silent and motionless group of people arranged to represent a scene. [French, literally 'living picture']

tablecloth /'teɪb(ə)lklɒθ/ *n.* a cloth spread over the top of a table, esp. for meals.

table d'hôte /tɑːb(ə)l 'dəʊt/ *n.* a meal consisting of a set menu at a fixed price, esp. in a hotel (cf. À LA CARTE). [French, = host's table]

table knife *n.* a knife for use at meals, esp. in eating a main course.

table lamp *n.* a small usu. decorative lamp designed to stand on a table etc.

tableland /'teɪb(ə)lland/ *n.* an extensive elevated region with a level surface; a plateau.

table licence *n. Brit.* a licence to serve alcoholic drinks only with meals.

table linen *n.* tablecloths, napkins, etc.

table manners *n.pl.* decorum or correct behaviour while eating at table.

table mat *n.* a mat for protecting a table top from hot dishes etc.

table napkin see NAPKIN 1.

table salt *n.* salt that is ground or easy to grind for use at meals.

table skittles see SKITTLE *n.* 2b.

tablespoon /ˈteɪb(ə)lspuːn/ *n.* **1** a large spoon for serving food. **2** an amount held by this. □ **tablespoonful** *n.* (*pl.* **-fuls**).

tablet /ˈtablɪt/ *n.* **1** a small measured and compressed amount of a substance, esp. of a medicine or drug. **2** a small flat piece of soap etc. **3** a flat slab of stone or wood, esp. for display or an inscription. **4** *Archit.* = TABLE 8. **5** *N. Amer.* a writing pad. [Middle English via Old French *tablete* from Romanic, diminutive of Latin *tabula* TABLE]

table talk *n.* miscellaneous informal talk at table.

table tennis *n.* an indoor game based on tennis, played with small bats and a ball bounced on a table divided by a net.

table top /ˈteɪb(ə)ltɒp/ *n.* **1** the top or surface of a table. **2** (**table-top**) (*attrib.*) that can be placed or used on a table top.

table-top sale *n.* a sale at which participants sell unwanted possessions from tables.

tableware /ˈteɪb(ə)lwɛː/ *n.* dishes, plates, implements, etc., for use at meals.

table wine *n.* ordinary wine for drinking with a meal.

tablier /ˈtablɪeɪ/ *n. hist.* an apron-like part of a woman's dress. [French]

tabloid /ˈtablɔɪd/ *n.* **1** a newspaper, usu. popular in style with bold headlines and large photographs, having pages half the size of those of the average broadsheet. **2** anything in a compressed or concentrated form. [originally the proprietary name of a medicine sold in tablets]

taboo /təˈbuː/ *n., adj., & v.* (also **tabu**) ● *n.* (*pl.* **taboos** or **tabus**) **1** a system or the act of setting a person or thing apart as sacred, prohibited, or accursed. **2** a prohibition or restriction imposed on certain behaviour, word usage, etc., by social custom. ● *adj.* **1** avoided or prohibited, esp. by social custom (*taboo words*). **2** designated as sacred and prohibited. ● *v.tr.* (**taboos, tabooed** or **tabus, tabued**) **1** put (a thing, practice, etc.) under taboo. **2** exclude or prohibit by authority or social influence. [Tongan *tabu*]

tabor /ˈteɪbə/ *n. hist.* a small drum, esp. one used to accompany a pipe. [Middle English from Old French *tabour, tabur*: cf. TABLA, Persian *tabīra* 'drum']

tabouret /ˈtabərɛt, -reɪ/ *n.* (*US* **taboret**) a low seat usu. without arms or a back. [French, = stool, diminutive of *tabour*: see TABOR]

tabular /ˈtabjʊlə/ *adj.* **1** of or arranged in tables or lists. **2** broad and flat like a table. **3** (of a crystal) having two broad flat faces. **4** formed in thin plates. □ **tabularly** *adv.* [Latin *tabularis* (as TABLE)]

tabula rasa /ˌtabjʊlə ˈrɑːzə/ *n.* (*pl.* **tabulae rasae** /ˌtabjʊliː ˈrɑːziː/) **1** a tablet with the writing erased; a clean slate. **2** the human mind (esp. at birth) viewed as having no innate ideas. [Latin, = scraped tablet]

tabulate /ˈtabjʊleɪt/ *v.tr.* arrange (figures or facts) in tabular form. □ **tabulation** /-ˈleɪʃ(ə)n/ *n.* [Late Latin *tabulare tabulat-* from *tabula* 'table']

tabulator /ˈtabjʊleɪtə/ *n.* **1** a person or thing that tabulates. **2** a device on a typewriter for advancing to a sequence of set positions in tabular work. **3** *Computing* a machine that produces lists or tables from a data storage medium such as punched cards.

tabun /ˈtɑːbʊn/ *n.* an organic phosphorus compound used as a nerve gas. [German]

tacamahac /ˈtakəməhak/ *n.* **1** a resinous gum obtained from certain tropical trees esp. of the genus *Calophyllum*. **2 a** the balsam poplar. **b** the resin of this. [obsolete Spanish *tacamahaca* from Nahuatl *tecomahiyac*]

tac-au-tac /ˈtakəʊtak/ *n. Fencing* a parry combined with a riposte. [French: imitative]

tacet /ˈtasɪt, ˈteɪ-/ *v.intr. Mus.* (as an instruction for a particular voice or instrument) be silent. [Latin, = is silent]

tach /tak/ *n. N. Amer. colloq.* = TACHOMETER. [abbreviation]

tache var. of TASH.

tachism /ˈtaʃɪz(ə)m/ *n.* (also **tachisme**) a form of action painting with dabs of colour arranged randomly with the aim of evoking a subconscious feeling. [French *tachisme* from *tache* 'a stain']

tachistoscope /taˈkɪstəskəʊp/ *n.* an instrument for very brief measured exposure of objects to the eye. □ **tachistoscopic** /-ˈskɒpɪk/ *adj.* [Greek *takhistos* 'swiftest' + -SCOPE]

tacho /ˈtakəʊ/ *n.* (*pl.* **-os**) *Brit. colloq.* **1** = TACHOMETER. **2** = TACHOGRAPH. [abbreviation]

tacho- /ˈtakəʊ/ *comb. form* speed. [Greek *takhos* 'speed']

tachograph /ˈtakəgrɑːf/ *n.* a device used esp. in heavy goods vehicles and coaches etc. for automatically recording speed and travel time.

tachometer /taˈkɒmɪtə/ *n.* an instrument for measuring the rate of rotation of a shaft and hence the speed or velocity of a vehicle.

tachy- /ˈtaki/ *comb. form* swift. [Greek *takhus* 'swift']

tachycardia /takɪˈkɑːdɪə/ *n. Med.* an abnormally rapid heart rate. [TACHY- + Greek *kardia* 'heart']

tachygraphy /taˈkɪgrəfi/ *n.* **1** stenography, esp. that of the ancient Greeks and Romans. **2** the abbreviated medieval writing of Greek and Latin. □ **tachygrapher** *n.* **tachygraphic** /-ˈgrafɪk/ *adj.* **tachygraphical** /-ˈgrafɪk(ə)l/ *adj.*

tachymeter /taˈkɪmɪtə/ *n.* **1** *Surveying* an instrument used to locate points rapidly. **2** a speed-indicator.

tachyon /ˈtakɪɒn/ *n. Physics* a hypothetical particle that travels faster than light. [TACHY- + -ON]

tacit /ˈtasɪt/ *adj.* understood or implied without being stated (*tacit consent*). □ **tacitly** *adv.* [Latin *tacitus* 'silent' from *tacēre* 'be silent']

taciturn /ˈtasɪtəːn/ *adj.* reserved in speech; saying little; uncommunicative. □ **taciturnity** /-ˈtəːnɪti/ *n.* **taciturnly** *adv.* [French *taciturne* or Latin *taciturnus* (as TACIT)]

tack[1] /tak/ *n. & v.* ● *n.* **1** a small sharp broad-headed nail. **2** *N. Amer.* a drawing pin. **3** a long stitch used in fastening fabrics etc. lightly or temporarily together. **4 a** the direction in which a ship moves as determined by the position of its sails and regarded in terms of the direction of the wind (*starboard tack*). **b** a temporary change of direction in sailing to take advantage of a side wind etc. **5** a course of action or policy (*try another tack*). **6** *Naut.* **a** a rope for securing the corner of some sails. **b** the corner to which this is fastened. **7** a sticky condition of varnish etc. **8** *Brit.* an extraneous clause appended to a bill in Parliament. ● *v.* **1** *tr.* (often foll. by *down* etc.) fasten with tacks. **2** *tr.* stitch (pieces of cloth etc.) lightly together. **3** *tr.* (foll. by *to, on*) annex (a thing). **4** *intr.* (often foll. by *about*) **a** change a ship's course by turning its head to the wind (cf. WEAR[2]). **b** make a series of tacks. **5** *intr.* change one's conduct or policy etc. **6** *tr. Brit.* append (a clause) to a bill. □ **tacker** *n.* [Middle English *tak* etc., of uncertain origin: cf. biblical *tache* 'clasp, link' from Old French *tache*]

tack[2] /tak/ *n.* the saddle, bridle, etc., of a horse. [shortened from TACKLE]

tack[3] /tak/ *n. colloq.* cheap, shoddy, or tasteless material; tat, kitsch. [back-formation from TACKY[2]]

tackle /ˈtak(ə)l/ *n. & v.* ● *n.* **1** equipment for a task or sport (*fishing tackle*). **2** a mechanism, esp. of ropes, pulley-blocks, hooks, etc., for lifting weights, managing sails, etc. (*block and tackle*). **3** a windlass with its ropes and hooks. **4** an act of tackling in football etc. **5** *Amer. Football* **a** the position next to the end of the forward line. **b** the player in this position. ● *v.tr.* **1** try to deal with (a problem or difficulty). **2** *Sport* grapple with or try to overcome (an opponent). **3** (often foll. by *on, about*) initiate discussion with (a person), esp. with regard to a disputed issue. **4** obstruct, intercept, or seize and stop (a player running with the ball). **5** secure by means of tackle. ▫ **tackler** *n.* **tackling** *n.* [Middle English, probably via Middle Low German *takel* from *taken* 'lay hold of']

tackle-block *n.* a pulley over which a rope runs.

tackle-fall *n.* a rope for applying force to the blocks of a tackle.

tack room *n.* a room in a riding stable where the saddles, bridles, etc. are kept.

tacky[1] /'taki/ *adj.* (**tackier**, **tackiest**) (of glue or paint etc.) still slightly sticky after application. ▫ **tackiness** *n.* [TACK[1] + -Y[1]]

tacky[2] /'taki/ *adj.* (**tackier**, **tackiest**) esp. *US colloq.* **1** showing poor taste or style. **2** tatty or seedy. ▫ **tackily** *adv.* **tackiness** *n.* [19th c.: origin unknown]

taco /'tɑːkəʊ, 'takəʊ/ *n.* (*pl.* **-os**) a Mexican dish of meat etc. in a folded or rolled tortilla. [Mexican Spanish]

tact /takt/ *n.* **1** adroitness in dealing with others or with difficulties arising from personal feeling. **2** intuitive perception of the right thing to do or say. [French from Latin *tactus* 'touch, sense of touch', from *tangere tact-* 'to touch']

tactful /'taktfʊl, -f(ə)l/ *adj.* having or showing tact. ▫ **tactfully** *adv.* **tactfulness** *n.*

tactic /'taktɪk/ *n.* **1** a tactical manoeuvre. **2** = TACTICS. [modern Latin *tactica* from Greek *taktikē* (*tekhnē* 'art'): see TACTICS]

tactical /'taktɪk(ə)l/ *adj.* **1** of, relating to, or constituting tactics (*a tactical retreat*). **2** (of bombing or weapons) done or for use in immediate support of military or naval operations (opp. STRATEGIC 3). **3** adroitly planning or planned. **4** (of voting) aimed at preventing the strongest candidate from winning by supporting the next strongest. ▫ **tactically** *adv.* [Greek *taktikos* (as TACTICS)]

tactics /'taktɪks/ *n.pl.* **1** (also treated as *sing.*) the art of disposing armed forces in order of battle and of organizing operations, esp. during contact with an enemy (cf. STRATEGY 2b). **2 a** the plans and means adopted in carrying out a scheme or achieving some end. **b** a skilful device or devices. ▫ **tactician** /tak'tɪʃ(ə)n/ *n.* [modern Latin *tactica* from Greek *taktika*, neut. pl. from *taktos* 'ordered', from *tassō* 'arrange']

tactile /'taktʌɪl/ *adj.* **1** of or connected with the sense of touch. **2** perceived by touch. **3** tangible. **4** *Art* (in painting) producing or concerning the effect of three-dimensional solidity. ▫ **tactual** /'taktjʊəl/ *adj.* (in senses 1, 2). **tactility** /-'tɪlɪti/ *n.* [Latin *tactilis* from *tangere tact-* 'to touch']

tactless /'taktlɪs/ *adj.* having or showing no tact. ▫ **tactlessly** *adv.* **tactlessness** *n.*

tad /tad/ *n.* esp. *N. Amer. colloq.* a small amount (often used adverbially: *a tad too salty*). [19th c.: origin unknown]

Tadjik var. of TAJIK.

tadpole /'tadpəʊl/ *n.* a larva of an amphibian, esp. a frog, toad, or newt in its aquatic stage and breathing through gills. [Middle English *taddepolle* (as TOAD, POLL[1] from the size of its head)]

taedium vitae /tiːdɪəm 'viːtʌɪ, 'vʌɪtiː/ *n.* weariness of life (often as a pathological state, with a tendency to suicide). [Latin]

tae kwon do /tʌɪ kwɒn 'dəʊ/ *n.* a modern Korean martial art similar to karate. [Korean, = art of hand and foot fighting]

taenia /'tiːnɪə/ *n.* (*US* **tenia**) (*pl.* **taeniae** /-nɪiː/ or **taenias**) **1** *Archit.* a fillet between a Doric architrave and frieze. **2** *Anat.* any flat ribbon-like structure, esp. the muscles of the colon. **3** any large tapeworm of the genus *Taenia*, esp. *T. saginata* and *T. soleum*, parasitic in humans. **4** *Gk Antiq.* a fillet or headband. ▫ **taenioid** *adj.* [Latin from Greek *tainia* 'ribbon']

taffeta /'tafɪtə/ *n.* a fine lustrous silk or silklike fabric. [Middle English from Old French *taffetas* or medieval Latin *taffata*, ultimately from Persian *tāfta*, past part. of *tāftan* 'twist']

taffrail /'tafreɪl/ *n. Naut.* a rail round a ship's stern. [earlier *tafferel* from Dutch *taffereel* 'panel', diminutive of *tafel* (as TABLE): assimilated to RAIL[1]]

Taffy /'tafi/ *n.* (*pl.* **-ies**) *Brit. colloq.* often *offens.* a Welshman. [supposed Welsh pronunciation of *Davy* = *David* (Welsh *Dafydd*)]

taffy /'tafi/ *n.* (*pl.* **-ies**) **1** *N. Amer.* a confection like toffee. **2** *US slang* insincere flattery. [19th c.: origin unknown]

tafia /'tafɪə/ *n. W.Ind.* rum distilled from molasses etc. [French from West Indian creole, perhaps related to RATAFIA]

tag[1] /tag/ *n.* & *v.* ● *n.* **1** a label, esp. one for tying on an object to show its address, price, etc. **2** a metal or plastic point at the end of a lace etc. to assist insertion. **3** a loop at the back of a boot used in pulling it on. **4** *US* a licence plate of a motor vehicle. **5** an electronic device that can be attached to a person or thing for monitoring purposes, e.g. to track offenders under house arrest or to deter shoplifters. **6** a loose or ragged end of anything. **7** a ragged lock of wool on a sheep. **8** *Theatr.* a closing speech addressed to the audience. **9** a trite quotation or stock phrase. **10 a** the refrain of a song. **b** a musical phrase added to the end of a piece. **11** an animal's tail, or its tip. ● *v.tr.* (**tagged**, **tagging**) **1** provide with a tag or tags. **2** (often foll. by *on*, *on to*) join or attach. **3** *Brit. colloq.* follow closely or trail behind. **4** *Computing* identify (an item of data) by its type for later retrieval. **5** label radioactively (see LABEL *v.* 3). **6 a** find rhymes for (verses). **b** string (rhymes) together. **7** shear away tags from (sheep). ▫ **tag along** (often foll. by *with*) go along or accompany passively. [Middle English: origin unknown]

tag[2] /tag/ *n.* & *v.* ● *n.* **1** a children's game in which one chases the rest, and anyone who is caught then becomes the pursuer. **2** *Baseball* the act of tagging a runner. ● *v.tr.* (**tagged**, **tagging**) **1** touch in a game of tag. **2** (often foll. by *out*) *Baseball* put (a runner) out by touching with the ball or with the hand holding the ball. [18th c.: origin unknown]

Tagalog /tə'gɑːlɒg/ *n.* & *adj.* ● *n.* **1** a member of the principal people of the Philippine Islands. **2** the Austronesian language of this people. ● *adj.* of or relating to this people or language. [Tagalog, from *taga* 'native' + *ilog* 'river']

tag end *n.* esp. *US* the last remnant of something.

tagetes /tə'dʒiːtiːz/ *n.* any plant of the genus *Tagetes*, esp. any of various marigolds with bright orange or yellow flowers. [modern Latin from Latin *Tages*, the name of an Etruscan god]

tagliatelle /taljə'tɛli/ *n.* a form of pasta in narrow ribbons. [Italian, from *tagliare* 'to cut']

tag team *n.* a pair of wrestlers who fight as a team, alternately or together (often hyphenated when *attrib.*: *tag-team wrestling*).

Tahitian /tɑː'hiːʃ(ə)n, tɑː'hiːtɪən/ *n.* & *adj.* ● *n.* **1** a native or national of Tahiti in the S. Pacific. **2** the language of Tahiti. ● *adj.* of or relating to Tahiti or its people or language.

tahr /tɑː/ *n.* (also **thar**) any goatlike mammal of the genus *Hemitragus*, esp. *H. jemlahicus* of the Himalayas. [native name in Nepal]

tahsil /tɑː'siːl/ *n.* an administrative area in parts of India. [Urdu *taḥsīl* from Arabic, = collection]

t'ai chi ch'uan /tʌɪ tʃiː 'tʃwɑːn/ *n.* (also **t'ai chi** /tʌɪ 'tʃiː/) a Chinese martial art and system of callisthenics consisting of sequences of very slow controlled movements. [Chinese, = great ultimate boxing]

Taig /teɪg/ *n. slang offens.* (in Northern Ireland) a Protestant name for a Catholic. [variant of *Teague*, Anglicized spelling of the Irish name *Tadhg*, a nickname for an Irishman]

taiga /'tʌɪgə/ *n.* coniferous forest lying between tundra and steppe, esp. in Siberia. [Russian]

tail[1] /teɪl/ *n. & v.* ● *n.* **1** the hindmost part of an animal, esp. when prolonged beyond the rest of the body. **2 a** a thing like a tail in form or position, esp. something extending downwards or outwards at an extremity. **b** the rear end of anything, e.g. of a procession. **c** a long train or line of people, vehicles, etc. **3 a** the rear part of an aeroplane, with the tailplane and rudder, or of a rocket. **b** the rear part of a motor vehicle. **4** the luminous trail of particles following a comet. **5 a** the inferior or weaker part of anything, esp. in a sequence. **b** *Cricket* the end of the batting order, with the weakest batsmen. **6 a** the part of a shirt below the waist. **b** the hanging part of the back of a coat. **7** (in *pl.*) *colloq.* **a** a tailcoat. **b** evening dress including this. **8 a** *slang* the buttocks. **b** *coarse slang* the female genitals; sexual intercourse. **9** (in *pl.*) the reverse of a coin as a choice when tossing. **10** *colloq.* a person following or shadowing another. **11** an extra strip attached to the lower end of a kite. **12** the stem of a note in music. **13** the part of a letter (e.g. *y*) below the line. **14 a** the exposed end of a slate or tile in a roof. **b** the unexposed end of a brick or stone in a wall. **15** the slender backward prolongation of a butterfly's wing. **16** a comparative calm at the end of a gale. **17** a calm stretch following rough water in a stream. ● *v.* **1** *tr.* remove the stalks of (fruit). **2** *tr.* & (foll. by *after*) *intr. colloq.* shadow or follow closely. **3** *tr.* provide with a tail. **4** *tr.* dock the tail of (a lamb etc.). **5** *tr.* (often foll. by *on to*) join (one thing to another). □ **on a person's tail** closely following a person. **tail back** *Brit.* (of traffic) form a tailback. **tail in** fasten (timber) by one end into a wall etc. **tail off** (or **away**) **1** become fewer, smaller, or slighter. **2** fall behind or away in a scattered line. **with one's tail between one's legs** in a state of dejection or humiliation. **with one's tail up** in good spirits; cheerful. □ **tailed** *adj.* (also in *comb.*). **tailless** *adj.* [Old English *tægl*, *tægel*, from Germanic]

tail[2] /teɪl/ *n. & adj. Law* ● *n.* limitation of ownership, esp. of an estate limited to a person and that person's heirs. ● *adj.* so limited (*estate tail*; *fee tail*). □ **in tail** under such a limitation. [Middle English from Old French *taille* 'notch, cut, tax', from *taillier* 'to cut', ultimately from Latin *talea* 'twig, cutting': cf. TALLY]

tailback /ˈteɪlbak/ *n. Brit.* a long line of traffic extending back from an obstruction.

tailboard /ˈteɪlbɔːd/ *n. Brit.* a hinged or removable flap at the rear of a lorry etc.

tailcoat /ˈteɪlkəʊt/ *n. Brit.* a man's morning or evening coat with a long skirt divided at the back into tails and cut away in front, worn as part of formal dress.

tail covert *n.* any of the feathers covering the base of a bird's tail feathers.

tail-end *n.* **1** the hindmost or lowest or last part. **2** = TAIL[1] *n.* 5. □ **tail-ender** *n.*

tail feather *n.* a strong flight feather of a bird's tail.

tailgate /ˈteɪlgeɪt/ *n. & v.* ● *n.* **1** esp. *US* **a** = TAILBOARD. **b** the tail door of an estate car or hatchback. **2** the lower end of a canal lock. ● *v. US colloq.* **1** *intr.* drive too closely behind another vehicle. **2** *tr.* follow (a vehicle) too closely. □ **tailgater** *n.*

tailing /ˈteɪlɪŋ/ *n.* **1** (in *pl.*) the refuse or inferior part of grain or ore etc. **2** the part of a beam or projecting brick etc. embedded in a wall.

tail light *n.* (also **tail lamp**) a light at the rear of a train, motor vehicle, or bicycle.

tail-off *n.* a decline or gradual reduction, esp. in demand.

tailor /ˈteɪlə/ *n. & v.* ● *n.* a maker of clothes, esp. one who makes men's outer garments to measure. ● *v.* **1** *tr.* make (clothes) as a tailor. **2** *tr.* make or adapt for a special purpose. **3** *intr.* work as or be a tailor. **4** *tr.* (esp. as **tailored** *adj.*) make clothes for (*he was immaculately tailored*). **5** *tr.* (as **tailored** *adj.*) = TAILOR-MADE *adj.*. □ **tailoring** *n.* [Middle English & Anglo-French *taillour*, Old French *tailleur* 'cutter', formed as TAIL[2]]

tailor-bird *n.* any small Asian etc. warbler of the genus *Orthotomus* that stitches leaves together to form a nest.

tailored /ˈteɪləd/ *adj.* (of clothing) well or closely fitted.

tailor-made *adj. & n.* ● *adj.* **1** (of clothing) made to order by a tailor. **2** made or suited for a particular purpose (*a job tailor-made for me*). ● *n.* a tailor-made garment.

tailor's chair *n.* a chair without legs for sitting cross-legged like a tailor at work.

tailor's twist *n.* a fine strong silk thread used by tailors.

tailpiece /ˈteɪlpiːs/ *n.* **1** an appendage at the rear of anything. **2** the final part of a thing. **3** a decoration in a blank space at the end of a chapter etc. in a book. **4** a piece of wood to which the strings of some musical instruments are attached at their lower ends.

tailpipe /ˈteɪlpʌɪp/ *n.* the rear section of the exhaust pipe of a motor vehicle.

tailplane /ˈteɪlpleɪn/ *n. Brit.* a horizontal aerofoil at the tail of an aircraft.

tail-race *n.* a fast-flowing stretch of a river or stream below a dam, watermill, etc.

tail-skid *n.* a support for the tail of an aircraft when on the ground.

tailspin /ˈteɪlspɪn/ *n. & v.* ● *n.* **1** a spin (see SPIN *n.* 2) by an aircraft with the tail spiralling. **2** a state of chaos or panic. ● *v.intr.* (**-spinning**; *past* and *past part.* **-spun**) perform a tailspin.

tailstock /ˈteɪlstɒk/ *n.* the adjustable part of a lathe holding the fixed spindle.

tailwheel /ˈteɪlwiːl/ *n.* a wheel supporting the tail of an aircraft, designed to ease ground handling.

tailwind /ˈteɪlwɪnd/ *n.* a wind blowing in the direction of travel of a vehicle or aircraft etc.

Taino /ˈtʌɪnəʊ/ *n.* an extinct Caribbean language of the Arawak group. [Taino *taino* 'noble, lord']

taint /teɪnt/ *n. & v.* ● *n.* **1** a spot or trace of decay, infection, or some bad quality. **2** an unpleasant scent or smell. **3** a corrupt condition or infection. ● *v.* **1** *tr.* affect with a taint. **2** *tr.* (foll. by *with*) affect slightly. **3** *intr.* become tainted. □ **taintless** *adj.* [Middle English, partly via Old French *teint(e)* from Latin *tinctus*, from *tingere* 'to dye', partly from ATTAINT]

taipan[1] /ˈtʌɪpan/ *n.* the head of a foreign business in China. [Chinese]

taipan[2] /ˈtʌɪpan/ *n.* a large venomous Australian snake, *Oxyuranus microlepidotus*. [*dhayban*, its name in an extinct Aboriginal language of N. Queensland]

taj /tɑːdʒ/ *n.* a tall conical cap worn by a dervish. [Arabic *tāj*]

Tajik /tɑːˈdʒiːk/ *n. & adj.* (also **Tadjik**) ● *n.* **1** a native or inhabitant of the republic of Tajikistan. **2** the Iranian language of the Tajiks. ● *adj.* of or relating to Tajikistan, its people, or its language. [Persian]

takahe /ˈtɑːkəhi/ *n.* = NOTORNIS. [Maori]

take /teɪk/ *v. & n.* ● *v.* (*past* **took** /tʊk/; *past part.* **taken** /ˈteɪk(ə)n/) **1** *tr.* lay hold of; get into one's hands. **2** *tr.* acquire, get possession of, capture, earn, or win. **3** *tr.* get the use of by purchase or formal agreement (*take lodgings*). **4** *tr.* (in a recipe) avail oneself of; use. **5** *tr.* use as a means of transport (*took a taxi*). **6** *tr.* regularly buy or subscribe to (a particular newspaper or periodical etc.). **7** *tr.* obtain after fulfilling the required conditions (*take a degree*). **8** *tr.* occupy (*take a chair*). **9** *tr.* make use of (*take the next turning on the left*). **10** *tr.* consume as food or medicine (*took tea*; *took the pills*). **11** *intr.* **a** be successful or effective (*the inoculation did not take*). **b** (of a plant, seed, etc.) begin to grow. **12** *tr.* require or use up (*will only take a minute*; *these things take time*). **13** *tr.* wear (a particular size of garment etc.) (*takes size six*). **14** *tr.* cause to come or go with one; convey (*take the book home*; *the bus will take you all the way*). **15** *tr.* remove; dispossess a person of (*someone has taken my pen*). **16** *tr.* catch or be infected with (fire or fever etc.). **17** *tr.* **a** experience or be affected by (*take fright*; *take pleasure*). **b** give play to (*take comfort*). **c** exert (*take courage*; *take no notice*). **18** *tr.* find out and note (a name and address; a person's temperature etc.)

by enquiry or measurement. **19** *tr.* grasp mentally; understand (*I take your point*; *I took you to mean yes*). **20** *tr.* treat or regard in a specified way (*took the news calmly*; *took it badly*). **21** *tr.* (foll. by *for*) regard as being (*do you take me for an idiot?*). **22** *tr.* **a** accept (*take the offer*; *take a phone call*; *takes lodgers*). **b** hold, accommodate (*takes two pints*). **c** submit to (*take a joke*; *take no nonsense*; *took a risk*). **23** *tr.* choose or assume (*took a different view*; *took a job*; *took the initiative*). **24** *tr.* derive (*takes its name from the inventor*). **25** *tr.* (foll. by *from*) subtract (*take 3 from 9*). **26** *tr.* execute, make, or undertake; perform or effect (*take notes*; *take an oath*; *take a decision*; *take a look*). **27** *tr.* occupy or engage oneself in; indulge in; enjoy (*take a rest*; *take exercise*; *take a holiday*). **28** *tr.* conduct (*took the school assembly*). **29** *tr.* deal with in a certain way (*took the corner too fast*). **30** *tr.* **a** teach or be taught (a subject). **b** be examined in (a subject). **31** *tr.* make (a photograph) with a camera; photograph (a person or thing). **32** *tr.* use as an instance (*let us take Napoleon*). **33** *tr. Gram.* have or require as part of the appropriate construction (*this verb takes an object*). **34** *tr.* have sexual intercourse with (a woman). **35** *tr.* (in *passive*; foll. by *by*, *with*) be attracted or charmed by. ● *n.* **1** an amount taken or caught in one session or attempt etc. **2** a scene or sequence of film photographed continuously at one time. **3** esp. *US* takings, esp. money received at a theatre for seats. **4** *Printing hist.* the amount of copy set up at one time. □ **be taken ill** become ill, esp. suddenly. **have what it takes** *colloq.* have the necessary qualities etc. for success. **on the take** *slang* taking bribes. **take account of** see ACCOUNT. **take action** see ACTION. **take advantage of** see ADVANTAGE. **take advice** see ADVICE. **take after** resemble (esp. a parent or ancestor). **take against** *Brit.* begin to dislike, esp. impulsively. **take aim** see AIM. **take apart 1** dismantle. **2** *colloq.* beat or defeat conclusively. **3** *colloq.* criticize severely. **take aside** see ASIDE. **take as read** *Brit.* accept without reading or discussing. **take away 1** remove or carry elsewhere. **2** subtract. **3** *Brit.* buy (food etc.) at a shop or restaurant for eating elsewhere. **take back 1** retract (a statement). **2** convey (a person or thing) to his or her or its original position. **3** carry (a person) in thought to a past time. **4** *Printing* transfer to the previous line. **5 a** return (goods) to a shop. **b** (of a shop) accept such goods. **6** accept (a person) back into one's affections, into employment, etc. **take the biscuit** (or **bun** or **cake**) *colloq.* be the most remarkable. **take a bow** see BOW[2]. **take breath** see BREATH. **take one's breath away** see BREATH. **take care of** see CARE. **take a chance** etc. see CHANCE. **take charge** see CHARGE. **take down 1** write down (spoken words). **2** remove (a structure) by dismantling. **3** humiliate. **4** lower (a garment worn below the waist). **take effect** see EFFECT. **take for granted** see GRANT. **take fright** see FRIGHT. **take from** diminish; weaken; detract from. **take heart** be encouraged. **take hold** see HOLD[1]. **take ill** (*US* **sick**) *colloq.* be taken ill. **take in 1** receive as a lodger etc. **2** undertake (work) at home. **3** make (a garment etc.) smaller. **4** understand (*did you take that in?*). **5** cheat (*managed to take them all in*). **6** include or comprise. **7** absorb into the body. **8** *colloq.* visit (a place) on the way to another (*shall we take in Avebury?*). **9** furl (a sail). **take in hand 1** undertake; start doing or dealing with. **2** undertake the control or reform of (a person). **take into account** see ACCOUNT. **take it 1** (often foll. by *that* + clause) assume (*I take it that you have finished*). **2** *colloq.* endure a difficulty or hardship in a specified way (*took it badly*). **take it easy** see EASY. **take it from me** (or **take my word for it**) I can assure you. **take it ill** resent it. **take it into one's head** see HEAD. **take it on one** (or **oneself**) (foll. by *to* + infin.) venture or presume. **take it or leave it** (esp. in *imper.*) an expression of indifference or impatience about another's decision after making an offer. **take it out of 1** exhaust the strength of. **2** *Brit.* have revenge on. **take it out on** relieve one's frustration by attacking or treating harshly. **take a thing kindly** see KINDLY[1]. **take kindly to** see KINDLY[1]. **take one's leave of** see LEAVE[2]. **take a lot of** (or **some**) **doing** be hard to do. **take lying down** see LIE[1]. **take a person's name in vain** see VAIN. **take off 1 a** remove (clothing) from one's or another's body. **b** remove or lead away. **c** withdraw (transport, a show, etc.). **2** deduct (part of an amount). **3** depart, esp. hastily (*took off in a fast car*). **4** *colloq.* mimic humorously. **5** jump from the ground. **6** become airborne. **7** (of a scheme, enterprise, etc.) become successful or popular. **8** have (a period) away from work. **take oneself off** go away. **take on 1** undertake (work etc.). **2** engage (an employee). **3** be willing or ready to meet (an adversary in sport, argument, etc., esp. a stronger one). **4** acquire (a new meaning etc.). **5** esp. *Brit. colloq.* show strong emotion. **take on the chin** see CHIN. **take orders** see ORDER. **take out 1** remove from within a place; extract. **2** escort on an outing. **3** get (a licence or summons etc.) issued. **4** *US* = *take away* 3. **5** *Bridge* remove (a partner or a partner's call) from a suit by bidding a different one or no trumps. **6** *slang* murder or destroy. **take a person out of himself** or **herself** make a person forget his or her worries. **take over 1** succeed to the management or ownership of. **2** take control (of). **3** *Printing* transfer to the next line. **take part** see PART. **take place** see PLACE. **take a person's point** see POINT. **take root** see ROOT[1]. **take shape** assume a distinct form; develop into something definite. **take sides** see SIDE. **take stock** see STOCK. **take the sun** see SUN. **take that!** an exclamation accompanying a blow etc. **take one's time** not hurry. **take to 1** begin or fall into the habit of (*took to smoking*). **2** have recourse to. **3** adapt oneself to. **4** form a liking for. **take to the cleaners** see CLEANER. **take to heart** see HEART. **take to one's heels** see HEEL[1]. **take to pieces** see PIECE. **take to task** see TASK. **take the trouble** see TROUBLE. **take up 1** become interested or engaged in (a pursuit). **2** adopt as a protégé. **3** occupy (time or space). **4** begin (residence etc.). **5** resume after an interruption. **6** interrupt or question (a speaker). **7** accept (an offer etc.). **8** shorten (a garment). **9** lift up. **10** absorb (*sponges take up water*). **11** take (a person) into a vehicle. **12** pursue (a matter etc.) further. **take a person up on** accept (a person's offer etc.). **take up the gauntlet** accept a challenge. **take up with** begin to associate with. □ **takable** *adj.* (also **takeable**). [Old English *tacan* from Old Norse *taka*]

takeaway /ˈteɪkəweɪ/ *adj. & n. Brit.* ● *attrib.adj.* (of food) bought at a shop or restaurant for eating elsewhere. ● *n.* **1** an establishment selling such food. **2** the food itself (*let's get a takeaway*).

take-home pay *n.* the pay received by an employee after the deduction of tax etc.

take-in *n.* a deception.

take-off *n.* **1** the act of becoming airborne. **2** an act of mimicking. **3** a place from which one jumps.

take-out *attrib.adj. & n.* esp. *N. Amer.* = TAKEAWAY.

takeover /ˈteɪkəʊvə/ *n.* the assumption of control (esp. of a business); the buying-out of one company by another.

taker /ˈteɪkə/ *n.* **1** a person who takes a bet. **2** a person who accepts an offer.

take-up *n.* acceptance of something offered.

takin /ˈtɑːkɪn/ *n.* a large Tibetan horned ruminant, *Budorcas taxicolor*. [its name in a local language]

taking /ˈteɪkɪŋ/ *adj. & n.* ● *adj.* **1** attractive or captivating. **2** catching or infectious. ● *n.* (in *pl.*) an amount of money taken in business. □ **takingly** *adv.* **takingness** *n.*

tala /ˈtɑːlə/ *n.* any of the traditional rhythmic patterns of Indian music. [Sanskrit]

talapoin /ˈtæləpɔɪn/ *n.* **1** a Buddhist monk or priest. **2** a small West African monkey, *Miopithecus talapoin*. [Portuguese *talapão* from Talaing *tala pôi* 'my lord']

talaria /təˈlɛːrɪə/ *n.pl.* (in Roman mythology) winged sandals as an attribute of certain gods and goddesses, esp. Mercury. [Latin, neut. pl. of *talaris*, from *talus* 'ankle']

talc /talk/ *n.* & *v.* ● *n.* **1** talcum powder. **2** any crystalline form of magnesium silicate that occurs in soft flat plates, usu. white or pale green in colour and used as a lubricator etc. ● *v.tr.* (**talced**, **talcing** or **talcked**, **talcking**) powder or treat (a surface) with talc to lubricate or dry it. ◻ **talcose** *adj.* **talcous** *adj.* **talcy** *adj.* (in sense 1 of *n.*). [French *talc* or medieval Latin *talcum*, via Arabic *ṭalḳ* from Persian *ṭalḳ*]

talcum /ˈtalkəm/ *n.* & *v.* ● *n.* **1** (in full **talcum powder**) powdered talc for toilet and cosmetic use, usu. perfumed. **2** = TALC *n.* 2. ● *v.tr.* (**talcumed**, **talcuming**) powder with talcum. [medieval Latin: see TALC]

tale /teɪl/ *n.* **1** a narrative or story, esp. fictitious and imaginatively treated. **2** a report of an alleged fact, often malicious or in breach of confidence (*all sorts of tales will get about*). **3** *archaic* or *literary* a number or total (*the tale is complete*). ◻ **tale of a tub** an idle fiction. [Old English *talu* from Germanic: related to TELL¹]

talebearer /ˈteɪlbɛːrə/ *n.* a person who maliciously gossips or reveals secrets. ◻ **talebearing** *n.* & *adj.*

talent /ˈtalənt/ *n.* **1** a special aptitude or faculty (*a talent for music*; *has real talent*). **2** high mental ability. **3 a** a person or persons of talent (*is a real talent*; *plenty of local talent*). **b** *Brit. colloq.* attractive members of the opposite sex. **4** an ancient weight and unit of currency, esp. among the Greeks. ◻ **talented** *adj.* **talentless** *adj.* [Old English *talente* and Old French *talent* via Latin *talentum* 'inclination of mind' from Greek *talanton* 'balance, weight, sum of money']

talent scout *n.* a person looking for talented performers, esp. in sport and entertainment.

talent spotter *n. Brit.* = TALENT SCOUT. ◻ **talent-spot** *v.tr.* & *intr.* (**-spotted**, **-spotting**).

tales /ˈteɪliːz/ *n. Law* **1** a writ for summoning jurors to supply a deficiency. **2** a list of persons who may be summoned. [Middle English from Latin *tales* (*de circumstantibus*) 'such (of the bystanders)', the first words of the writ]

talesman /ˈteɪliːzmən, ˈteɪlz-/ *n.* (*pl.* **-men**) *Law* a person summoned by a *tales*.

taleteller /ˈteɪltɛlə/ *n.* **1** a person who tells stories. **2** a person who spreads malicious reports.

tali *pl.* of TALUS¹.

talion /ˈtalɪən/ *n.* = LEX TALIONIS. [Middle English via Old French from Latin *talio -onis*, from *talis* 'such']

talipes /ˈtalɪpiːz/ *n. Med.* = CLUB FOOT. [modern Latin, from Latin *talus* 'ankle' + *pes* 'foot']

talipot /ˈtalɪpɒt/ *n.* a tall southern Indian palm, *Corypha umbraculifera*, with very large fan-shaped leaves that are used as sunshades etc. [Malayalam *tālipat*, Hindi *tālpāt* from Sanskrit *tālapattra*, from *tāla* 'palm' + *pattra* 'leaf']

talisman /ˈtalɪzmən/ *n.* (*pl.* **talismans**) **1** an object, esp. an inscribed ring or stone, supposed to be endowed with magic powers esp. of averting evil from or bringing good luck to its holder. **2** a charm or amulet; a thing supposed capable of working wonders. ◻ **talismanic** /-ˈmanɪk/ *adj.* [French & Spanish, = Italian *talismano*, from medieval Greek *telesmon*, Greek *telesma* 'completion, religious rite' via *teleō* 'to complete' from *telos* 'result, end']

talk /tɔːk/ *v.* & *n.* ● *v.* **1** *intr.* (often foll. by *to*, *with*) converse or communicate ideas by spoken words. **2** *intr.* have the power of speech. **3** *intr.* (foll. by *about*) **a** have as the subject of discussion. **b** (in *imper.*) *colloq.* as an emphatic statement (*talk about expense! It cost me £50*). **4** *tr.* express or utter in words; discuss (*you are talking nonsense*; *talked cricket all day*). **5** *tr.* use (a language) in speech (*is talking Spanish*). **6** *intr.* (foll. by *at*) address pompously. **7** *tr.* (usu. foll. by *into*, *out of*) bring into a specified condition etc. by talking (*talked himself hoarse*; *how did you talk them into it?*; *talked them out of the difficulty*). **8** *intr.* reveal (esp. secret) information; betray secrets. **9** *intr.* gossip (*people are beginning to talk*). **10** *intr.* have influence (*money talks*). **11** *intr.* communicate by radio. ● *n.* **1** conversation or talking. **2** a particular mode of speech (*baby talk*). **3** an informal address or lecture. **4 a** rumour or gossip (*there is talk of a merger*). **b** its theme (*their success was the talk of the town*). **5** (often in *pl.*) extended discussions or negotiations. **6** empty promises or boasting. ◻ **know what one is talking about** be expert or authoritative. **now you're talking** *colloq.* I like what you say, suggest, etc. **talk away 1** consume (time) in talking. **2** carry on talking (*talk away! I'm listening*). **talk back 1** reply defiantly. **2** respond on a two-way radio system. **talk big** *colloq.* talk boastfully. **talk down to** speak patronizingly or condescendingly to. **talk a person down 1** silence a person by greater loudness or persistence. **2** bring (a pilot or aircraft) to landing by radio instructions from the ground. **talk the hind leg off a donkey** talk incessantly. **talk nineteen to the dozen** see DOZEN. **talk of 1** discuss or mention. **2** (often foll. by verbal noun) express some intention of (*talked of moving to London*). **talk of the town** what is being talked about generally. **talk out** *Brit.* block the course of (a bill in Parliament) by prolonging discussion to the time of adjournment. **talk over** discuss at length. **talk a person over** (or **round** or *US* **around**) gain agreement or compliance from a person by talking. **talk shop** talk, esp. tediously or inopportunely, about one's occupation, business, etc. **talk tall** *colloq.* boast. **talk through** discuss thoroughly. **talk a person through** guide a person in (a task) with continuous instructions. **talk through one's hat** (or *Brit.* **neck**) *colloq.* **1** exaggerate. **2** bluff. **3** talk wildly or nonsensically. **talk to** reprove or scold (a person). **talk to oneself** soliloquize. **talk turkey** see TURKEY. **talk up** discuss (a subject) in order to arouse interest in it. **you can't** (or **can**) **talk** *colloq.* a reproof that the person addressed is just as culpable etc. in the matter at issue. ◻ **talker** *n.* [Middle English *talken*, frequentative verb from TALE or TELL¹]

talkathon /ˈtɔːkəθɒn/ *n. colloq.* a prolonged session of talking or discussion. [TALK + MARATHON]

talkative /ˈtɔːkətɪv/ *adj.* fond of or given to talking. ◻ **talkatively** *adv.* **talkativeness** *n.*

talkback /ˈtɔːkbak/ *n.* **1** (often *attrib.*) a system of two-way communication by loudspeaker. **2** = PHONE-IN.

talkie /ˈtɔːki/ *n.* esp. *US colloq.* a film with a soundtrack, as distinct from a silent film. [TALK + -IE, on the pattern of *movie*]

talking /ˈtɔːkɪŋ/ *adj.* & *n.* ● *adj.* **1** that talks. **2** having the power of speech (*a talking parrot*). **3** expressive (*talking eyes*). ● *n.* in senses of TALK *v.* ◻ **talking of** esp. *Brit.* while we are discussing (*talking of food, what time is lunch?*).

talking book *n.* a recorded reading of a book, esp. for the blind.

talking film *n.* (also **talking picture**) a film with a soundtrack.

talking head *n. colloq.* a presenter etc. on television, speaking to the camera and viewed in close-up.

talking point *n.* a topic for discussion or argument.

talking shop *n. Brit. derog.* an institution regarded as a place of argument rather than action.

talking-to *n. colloq.* a reproof or reprimand (*gave them a good talking-to*).

talk show *n.* = CHAT SHOW.

tall /tɔːl/ *adj.* & *adv.* ● *adj.* **1** of more than average height. **2** of a specified height (*looks about six feet tall*). **3** higher than the surrounding objects (*a tall building*). **4** *colloq.* extravagant or excessive; fanciful (*a tall story*; *tall talk*). ● *adv.* as if tall; proudly; in a tall or extravagant way (*sit tall*). ◻ **tallish** *adj.* **tallness** *n.* [originally = ready, active: Middle English, representing Old English *getæl* 'swift, prompt']

tallage /ˈtalɪdʒ/ *n. hist.* **1** a form of taxation on towns etc., abolished in the 14th c. **2** a tax on feudal dependants etc. [Middle English from Old French *taillage*, from *tailler* 'to cut': see TAIL²]

tallboy /ˈtɔːlbɔɪ/ *n. Brit.* a tall chest of drawers sometimes in lower and upper sections or mounted on legs.

tall drink *n.* a drink served in a tall glass.

tall hat *n.* = TOP HAT.

tallith /'talɪθ/ *n.* a fringed shawl worn by Jewish men, esp. at prayer. [Rabbinical Hebrew *tallīt* from *tillel* 'to cover']

tall order *n.* an exorbitant or unreasonable demand.

tallow /'taləʊ/ *n.* & *v.* ● *n.* the harder kinds of (esp. animal) fat melted down for use in making candles, soap, etc. ● *v.tr.* grease with tallow. □ **tallowish** *adj.* **tallowy** *adj.* [Middle English *talg, talug,* from Middle Low German *talg, talch,* of unknown origin]

tallow tree *n.* any of various trees, esp. *Sapium sebiferum* of China, yielding vegetable tallow.

tall ship *n.* a sailing ship with a high mast.

tally /'tali/ *n.* & *v.* ● *n.* (*pl.* **-ies**) **1** the reckoning of a debt or score. **2** a total score or amount. **3 a** a mark registering a fixed number of objects delivered or received. **b** such a number as a unit. **4** *hist.* **a** a piece of wood scored across with notches for the items of an account and then split into halves, each party keeping one. **b** an account kept in this way. **5** a ticket or label for identification. **6** a corresponding thing, counterpart, or duplicate. ● *v.* (**-ies, -ied**) (often foll. by *with*) **1** *intr.* agree or correspond. **2** *tr.* record or reckon by tally. □ **tallier** *n.* [Middle English via Anglo-French *tallie,* Anglo-Latin *tallia, talia* from Latin *talea*: cf. TAIL[2]]

tally clerk *n.* an official who keeps a tally of goods, esp. those loaded or unloaded in docks.

tally-ho /talɪ'həʊ/ *int., n.,* & *v.* ● *int.* a huntsman's cry to the hounds on sighting a fox. ● *n.* (*pl.* **-hos**) an utterance of this. ● *v.* (**-hoes, -hoed**) **1** *intr.* utter a cry of 'tally-ho'. **2** *tr.* indicate (a fox) or urge (hounds) with this cry. [apparently an alteration of French *taïaut,* of unknown origin]

tallyman /'talɪmən/ *n.* (*pl.* **-men**) **1** a person who keeps a tally. **2** *Brit.* a person who sells goods on credit, esp. from door to door.

tally sheet *n.* a paper on which a tally is kept.

tally system *n. Brit.* a system of sale on short credit or instalments with an account kept by tally.

Talmud /'talmʊd, -məd/ *n.* the body of Jewish civil and ceremonial law and legend comprising the Mishnah and the Gemara. □ **Talmudic** /-'mʊdɪk/ *adj.* **Talmudical** /-'mʊdɪk(ə)l/ *adj.* **Talmudist** *n.* [late Hebrew *talmūḏ* 'instruction' from Hebrew *lāmaḏ* 'learn']

talon /'talən/ *n.* **1** a claw, esp. of a bird of prey. **2** the cards left after the deal in a card game. **3** the last part of a dividend-coupon sheet, entitling the holder to a new sheet on presentation. **4** the shoulder of a bolt against which the key presses in shooting it in a lock. **5** an ogee moulding. □ **taloned** *adj.* (also in *comb.*). [Middle English from Old French, = heel, ultimately from Latin *talus*: see TALUS[1]]

talus[1] /'teɪləs/ *n.* (*pl.* **tali** /-lʌɪ/) *Anat.* the ankle-bone supporting the tibia. Also called ASTRAGALUS. [Latin, = ankle, heel]

talus[2] /'teɪləs/ *n.* (*pl.* **taluses**) **1** the slope of a wall that tapers to the top or rests against a bank. **2** *Geol.* a sloping mass of fragments at the foot of a cliff. [French: origin unknown]

TAM *abbr.* television audience measurement.

tam /tam/ *n.* a tam-o'-shanter. [abbreviation]

tamable var. of TAMEABLE.

tamale /tə'mɑːli/ *n.* a Mexican food of seasoned meat and maize flour steamed or baked in maize husks. [Mexican Spanish *tamal,* pl. *tamales*]

tamandua /tə'mand(j)ʊə, tam(ə)n'duːə/ *n.* any small Central and S. American arboreal anteater of the genus *Tamandua,* with a prehensile tail used in climbing. [Portuguese from Tupi *tamanduà*]

tamarack /'tamərak/ *n.* **1** an American larch, *Larix laricina.* **2** the wood from this. [probably Algonquian]

tamarillo /tamə'rɪləʊ/ *n.* (*pl.* **-os**) esp. *Austral.* & *NZ* = TREE TOMATO. [arbitrary marketing name: cf. Spanish *tomatillo,* diminutive of *tomate* TOMATO]

tamarin /'tam(ə)rɪn/ *n.* any S. American usu. insect-eating monkey of the genera *Saguinus* and *Leontopithecus,* having hairy crests and moustaches. [French from Carib]

tamarind /'tam(ə)rɪnd/ *n.* **1** a tropical evergreen tree, *Tamarindus indica.* **2** the fruit of this, containing an acid pulp used as food and in making drinks. [medieval Latin *tamarindus* from Arabic *tamr-hindī* 'Indian date']

tamarisk /'tam(ə)rɪsk/ *n.* any shrub of the genus *Tamarix,* usu. with long slender branches and small pink or white flowers, that thrives by the sea. [Middle English from Late Latin *tamariscus,* Latin *tamarix*]

tambour /'tambʊə/ *n.* & *v.* ● *n.* **1** a drum. **2 a** a circular frame for holding fabric taut while it is being embroidered. **b** material embroidered in this way. **3** *Archit.* each of a sequence of cylindrical stones forming the shaft of a column. **4** *Archit.* the circular part of various structures. **5** *Archit.* a lobby with a ceiling and folding doors in a church porch etc. to obviate draughts. **6** a sloping buttress or projection in a fives court etc. ● *v.tr.* (also *absol.*) decorate or embroider on a tambour. [French from *tabour* TABOR]

tamboura /tam'bʊərə/ *n. Mus.* an Indian stringed instrument used as a drone. [Arabic *ṭanbūra*]

tambourin /'tambərɪn/ *n.* **1** a long narrow drum used in Provence. **2 a** a dance accompanied by a tambourin. **b** the music for this. [French, diminutive of TAMBOUR]

tambourine /tambə'riːn/ *n.* a percussion instrument consisting of a hoop with a parchment stretched over one side and jingling discs in slots round the hoop. □ **tambourinist** *n.* [French, diminutive of TAMBOUR]

tame /teɪm/ *adj.* & *v.* ● *adj.* **1** (of an animal) domesticated; not wild or shy. **2** insipid; lacking spirit or interest; dull (*tame acquiescence*). **3** *colloq.* (of a person) amenable or cooperative and available (*you need a tame accountant*). **4** *US* **a** (of land) cultivated. **b** (of a plant) produced by cultivation. ● *v.tr.* **1** make tame; domesticate; break in. **2** subdue, curb, humble; break the spirit of. □ **tamely** *adv.* **tameness** *n.* **tamer** *n.* (also in *comb.*). [Old English *tam,* from Germanic]

tameable /'teɪməb(ə)l/ *adj.* (also **tamable**) capable of being tamed. □ **tameability** /-'bɪlɪti/ *n.* **tameableness** *n.*

Tamil /'tamɪl/ *n.* & *adj.* ● *n.* **1** a member of a Dravidian people inhabiting South India and Sri Lanka. **2** the language of this people. ● *adj.* of or relating to this people or their language. □ **Tamilian** /-'mɪlɪən/ *adj.* [Tamil *Tamil,* related to DRAVIDIAN]

Tammany /'taməni/ *n.* (also **Tammany Hall**) *US* **1** a corrupt political organization or group. **2** corrupt political activities. [originally the name of a benevolent society in New York with headquarters at Tammany Hall, which later became the headquarters of the Democratic Party in New York]

tammy /'tami/ *n.* (*pl.* **-ies**) = TAM-O'-SHANTER.

tam-o'-shanter /tamə'ʃantə/ *n.* a round woollen or cloth cap of Scottish origin fitting closely round the brows but large and full above. [named after the hero of Burns's *Tam o' Shanter*]

tamoxifen /tə'mɒksɪfen/ *n. Pharm.* a drug which acts as an oestrogen antagonist, used to treat breast cancer and infertility in women. [arbitrary formation based on *trans, amine, oxy-, phenol,* parts of the drug's chemical name]

tamp /tamp/ *v.tr.* **1** pack (a blast-hole) full of clay etc. to get the full force of an explosion. **2** ram down (road material, soil, tobacco, etc.); firmly press down or in. □ **tamper** *n.* **tamping** *n.* (in sense 1). [perhaps a back-formation from French *tampin* (variant of TAMPION, taken as = *tamping*)]

tamper /'tampə/ *v.intr.* (foll. by *with*) **1 a** meddle or interfere with; make unauthorized changes in. **b** interfere with (a food product etc.) esp. by contamination and for blackmail purposes. **2** exert a secret or corrupt influence upon; bribe. □ **tamperer** *n.* [variant of TEMPER]

tamper-proof *adj.* made so that it cannot be tampered with.

tampion /'tampɪən/ *n.* (also **tompion** /'tɒm-/) **1** a wooden stopper for the muzzle of a gun. **2** a plug e.g. for the top of an organ pipe. [Middle English from French *tampon*, nasalized variant of *tapon*, related to TAP[1]]

tampon /'tampɒn/ *n.* & *v.* ● *n.* a plug of soft material used to stop a wound or absorb secretions, esp. one inserted into the vagina to absorb menstrual blood. ● *v.tr.* (**tamponed**, **tamponing**) plug with a tampon. [French: see TAMPION]

tamponade /tampə'neɪd/ *n.* **1** (in full **cardiac tamponade**) compression of the heart by an accumulation of fluid in the pericardial sac. **2** the surgical use of a tampon.

tamponage /'tampənɪdʒ/ *n.* = TAMPONADE.

tam-tam /'tamtam/ *n.* a large metal gong. [Hindi: see TOM-TOM]

tan[1] /tan/ *n.*, *adj.*, & *v.* ● *n.* **1** a brown skin colour resulting from exposure to ultraviolet light. **2** a yellowish-brown colour. **3** bark, esp. of oak, bruised and used to tan hides. **4** (in full **spent tan**) tan from which the tannic acid has been extracted, used for covering roads etc. ● *adj.* of a yellowish-brown colour. ● *v.* (**tanned**, **tanning**) **1** *tr.* & *intr.* make or become brown by exposure to ultraviolet light. **2** *tr.* convert (raw hide) into leather by soaking in a liquid containing tannic acid or by the use of mineral salts etc. **3** *tr. slang* beat, thrash. □ **tannable** *adj.* **tanning** *n.* **tannish** *adj.* [Old English *tannian*, probably from medieval Latin *tanare*, *tannare*, perhaps from Celtic]

tan[2] /tan/ *abbr.* tangent.

tanager /'tanədʒə/ *n.* any small American bird of the subfamily Thraupinae, the male usu. having brightly coloured plumage. [modern Latin *tanagra* from Tupi *tangará*]

tanbark /'tanbɑːk/ *n.* the bark of oak and other trees, used to obtain tannin.

tandem /'tandəm/ *n.* & *adv.* ● *n.* **1** a bicycle or tricycle with two or more seats one behind another. **2** a group of two persons or machines etc. with one behind or following the other. **3** a carriage driven tandem. ● *adv.* with two or more horses harnessed one behind another (*drive tandem*). □ **in tandem 1** one behind another. **2** alongside each other, together. [Latin, = at length (of time), used punningly]

tandoor /'tandʊə, tan'dʊə/ *n.* a clay oven of a type used originally in northern India and Pakistan. [Hindustani]

tandoori /tan'dʊəri/ *n.* food cooked over charcoal in a tandoor (often *attrib.*: *tandoori chicken*). [Hindustani]

Tang /taŋ/ *n.* **1** a dynasty ruling China 618–*c*.906. **2** (*attrib.*) designating art and artefacts of this period. [Chinese *táng*]

tang[1] /taŋ/ *n.* **1** a strong taste or flavour or smell. **2** a characteristic quality. **3** the projection on the blade of a tool, esp. a knife, by which the blade is held firm in the handle. [Middle English from Old Norse *tange* 'point, tang of a knife']

tang[2] /taŋ/ *v.* & *n.* ● *v.tr.* & *intr.* ring, clang; sound loudly. ● *n.* a tanging sound. [imitative]

tanga /'taŋgə/ *n. Brit.* a pair of briefs consisting of small panels connected with strings. [Portuguese, ultimately of Bantu origin]

tangelo /'tan(d)ʒələʊ/ *n.* (*pl.* **-os**) a hybrid of the tangerine and grapefruit. [TANGERINE + POMELO]

tangent /'tan(d)ʒ(ə)nt/ *n.* & *adj.* ● *n.* **1** a straight line, curve, or surface that meets another curve or curved surface at a point, but if extended does not intersect it at that point. **2** the ratio of the sides (other than the hypotenuse) opposite and adjacent to an angle in a right-angled triangle. ● *adj.* **1** (of a line or surface) that is a tangent. **2** touching. □ **at a tangent** diverging from a previous course of action or thought etc. (*go off at a tangent*). □ **tangency** *n.* [Latin *tangere tangent-* 'touch']

tangent galvanometer *n.* a galvanometer with a coil through which the current to be measured is passed, its strength being proportional to the tangent of the angle through which the needle is deflected.

tangential /tan'dʒɛnʃ(ə)l/ *adj.* **1** of or along a tangent. **2** divergent. **3** peripheral. □ **tangentially** *adv.*

tangerine /tan(d)ʒə'riːn/ *n.* & *adj.* ● *n.* **1** a small sweet orange-coloured citrus fruit with a thin skin; a mandarin. **2** a deep orange-yellow colour. ● *adj.* of this colour. [*Tangier*, a seaport in Morocco]

tangible /'tan(d)ʒɪb(ə)l/ *adj.* & *n.* ● *adj.* **1** perceptible by touch. **2** definite; clearly intelligible; not elusive or visionary (*tangible proof*). ● *n.* (usu. in *pl.*) a tangible thing, esp. an asset. □ **tangibility** /-'bɪlɪti/ *n.* **tangibleness** *n.* **tangibly** /-bli/ *adv.* [French *tangible* or Late Latin *tangibilis*, from *tangere* 'touch']

tangle[1] /'taŋg(ə)l/ *v.* & *n.* ● *v.* **1 a** *tr.* intertwine (threads or hairs etc.) in a confused mass; entangle. **b** *intr.* become tangled. **2** *intr.* (foll. by *with*) *colloq.* become involved (esp. in conflict or argument) with (*don't tangle with me*). **3** *tr.* complicate (*a tangled affair*). ● *n.* **1** a confused mass of intertwined threads etc. **2** a confused or complicated state (*be in a tangle*; *a love tangle*). [Middle English, probably from Scandinavian]

tangle[2] /'taŋg(ə)l/ *n.* any of various seaweeds, esp. of the genus *Laminaria*. [probably via Norwegian *taangel* from Old Norse *thöngull*]

tangly /'taŋgli/ *adj.* (**tanglier**, **tangliest**) tangled.

tango[1] /'taŋgəʊ/ *n.* & *v.* ● *n.* (*pl.* **-os**) **1** a slow ballroom dance originating in Buenos Aires, characterized by gliding movements and abrupt pauses. **2** the music for this. ● *v.intr.* (**-oes**, **-oed**) dance the tango. [Latin American Spanish]

tango[2] /'taŋgəʊ/ *n.* & *adj. Brit.* ● *n.* a tangerine colour. ● *adj.* of this colour. [abbreviation, influenced by TANGO[1]]

tangram /'taŋgram/ *n.* a Chinese puzzle square cut into seven pieces to be combined into various figures. [19th c.: origin unknown]

tangy /'taŋi/ *adj.* (**tangier**, **tangiest**) having a strong usu. piquant tang. □ **tanginess** *n.*

tanh /tan'eɪtʃ, tanʃ, θan/ *abbr.* hyperbolic tangent.

tank /taŋk/ *n.* & *v.* ● *n.* **1** a large receptacle or storage chamber usu. for liquid or gas. **2** a heavy armoured fighting vehicle carrying guns and moving on a tracked carriage. **3** a container for the fuel supply in a motor vehicle. **4** the part of a steam locomotive tender containing water for the boiler. **5 a** (in India and Australia) a reservoir. **b** *dial.* esp. *US* a pond. ● *v.* **1** *tr.* (usu. foll. by *up*) fill the tank of (a vehicle etc.) with fuel. **2** *colloq.* **a** *intr.* (foll. by *up*) drink heavily; become drunk. **b** *tr.* & *refl.* (often as **tanked up** *adj.*) inebriate oneself with alcoholic drink or drugs. □ **tankful** *n.* (*pl.* **-fuls**). **tankless** *adj.* [Gujurati *tānkh* etc., perhaps from Sanskrit *tadāga* 'pond']

tanka /'taŋkə/ *n.* a Japanese poem in five lines and thirty-one syllables giving a complete picture of an event or mood. [Japanese, from *tan* 'short' + *ka* 'song']

tankage /'taŋkɪdʒ/ *n.* **1 a** storage in tanks. **b** a charge made for this. **2** the cubic content of a tank. **3** a kind of fertilizer obtained from refuse bones etc.

tankard /'taŋkəd/ *n.* **1** a tall beer mug (esp. of silver or pewter) with a handle and sometimes a hinged lid. **2** the contents of or an amount held by a tankard (*drank a tankard of ale*). [Middle English: origin unknown: cf. Middle Dutch *tanckaert*]

tank engine *n.* a steam locomotive carrying fuel and water receptacles in its own frame, not in a tender.

tanker /'taŋkə/ *n.* & *v.* ● *n.* a ship, aircraft, or road vehicle for carrying liquids, esp. mineral oils, in bulk. ● *v.tr.* (usu. in *passive*; often foll. by *in*) transport by tanker.

tank-farming *n.* the practice of growing plants in tanks of water without soil.

tank top *n.* a sleeveless close-fitting upper garment with a scoop neck.

tanner[1] /'tanə/ *n.* a person who tans hides.

tanner[2] /'tanə/ *n. Brit. hist. slang* a sixpence. [19th c.: origin unknown]

tannery /'tan(ə)ri/ *n.* (*pl.* **-ies**) a place where hides are tanned.

tannic /'tanɪk/ *adj.* of or produced from tan. □ **tannate** /-neɪt/ *n.* [French *tannique* (as TANNIN)]

tannic acid *n.* a complex natural organic compound of a yellowish colour used as a mordant and astringent.

tannin /'tanɪn/ *n.* any of a group of complex organic compounds found in certain tree-barks and oak-galls, used in leather production and ink manufacture. [French *tanin* (as TAN[1], -IN)]

tannish see TAN[1].

tannoy /'tanɔɪ/ *n. Brit. propr.* a type of public address system. [from *tan*talum all*oy* (rectifier)]

tanrec var. of TENREC.

tansy /'tanzi/ *n.* (*pl.* **-ies**) any plant of the genus *Tanacetum*, esp. *T. vulgare* with yellow button-like flowers and aromatic leaves, formerly used in medicines and cookery. [Middle English via Old French *tanesie* and medieval Latin *athanasia* 'immortality' from Greek]

tantalite /'tantəlʌɪt/ *n.* a rare dense black mineral, the principal source of the element tantalum. [German & Swedish *tantalit* (as TANTALUM)]

tantalize /'tantəlʌɪz/ *v.tr.* (also **-ise**) **1** torment or tease by the sight or promise of what is unobtainable. **2** raise and then dash the hopes of; torment with disappointment. □ **tantalization** /-'zeɪʃ(ə)n/ *n.* **tantalizer** *n.* **tantalizingly** *adv.* [Greek *Tantalos*, the name of a mythical king of Phrygia condemned to stand in water that receded when he tried to drink it and under branches that drew back when he tried to pick the fruit]

tantalum /'tantələm/ *n. Chem.* a rare hard white metallic element occurring naturally in tantalite, resistant to heat and the action of acids, and used in surgery and for electronic components (symbol **Ta**). □ **tantalic** *adj.* [formed as TANTALIZE, with reference to its frustrating insolubility in acids]

tantalus /'tantələs/ *n.* **1** *Brit.* a stand in which spirit-decanters may be locked up though still visible. **2** a wood ibis, *Mycteria americana*. [see TANTALIZE]

tantamount /'tantəmaʊnt/ *predic.adj.* (foll. by *to*) equivalent to (*was tantamount to a denial*). [via an obsolete English verb from Italian *tanto montare* 'amount to so much']

tantivy /tan'tɪvi/ *n.* & *adj. archaic* ● *n.* (*pl.* **-ies**) **1** a hunting cry. **2** a swift movement; a gallop or rush. ● *adj.* swift. [17th c.: perhaps an imitative of hoof-beats]

tant mieux /tɒ̃ 'mjəː, French tɑ̃ mjø/ *int.* so much the better. [French]

tant pis /tɒ̃ 'piː, French tɑ̃ pi/ *int.* so much the worse. [French]

tantra /'tantrə/ *n.* any of a class of Hindu or Buddhist mystical and magical writings. □ **tantric** *adj.* **tantrism** *n.* **tantrist** *n.* [Sanskrit, = loom, groundwork, doctrine, from *tan* 'stretch']

tantrum /'tantrəm/ *n.* an outburst of bad temper or petulance (*threw a tantrum*). [18th c.: origin unknown]

Taoiseach /'tiːʃəx/ *n.* the Prime Minister of the Irish Republic. [Irish, = chief, leader]

Taoism /'taʊɪz(ə)m, 'tɑːəʊ-/ *n.* a Chinese philosophy based on the writings of Laoze (*c.*500 BC), advocating humility and religious piety. □ **Taoist** /-ɪst/ *n.* **Taoistic** /-'ɪstɪk/ *adj.* [Chinese *dao* '(right) way']

tap[1] /tap/ *n.* & *v.* ● *n.* **1** a device by which a flow of liquid or gas from a pipe or vessel can be controlled. **2 a** an act of tapping a telephone etc. **b** a device used for this. **3** *Brit.* a taproom. **4** an instrument for cutting the thread of a female screw. ● *v.tr.* (**tapped**, **tapping**) **1 a** provide (a cask) with a tap. **b** let out (a liquid) by means of, or as if by means of, a tap. **2** draw sap from (a tree) by cutting into it. **3 a** obtain information or supplies or resources from. **b** extract or obtain; discover and exploit (*mineral resources to be tapped*; *to tap the skills of young people*). **4** connect a listening device to (a telephone or telegraph line etc.) to listen to a call or transmission. **5** cut a female screw-thread in. □ **on tap 1** ready to be drawn off by tap. **2** *colloq.* ready for immediate use; freely available. □ **tapless** *adj.* **tappable** *adj.* [Old English *tæppian* (*v.*), *tæppa* (*n.*), from Germanic]

tap[2] /tap/ *v.* & *n.* ● *v.* (**tapped**, **tapping**) **1** *intr.* (foll. by *at*, *on*) strike a gentle but audible blow. **2** *tr.* strike lightly (*tapped me on the shoulder*). **3** *tr.* (foll. by *against* etc.) cause (a thing) to strike lightly (*tapped a stick against the window*). **4** *intr.* = TAP-DANCE *v.* (*can you tap?*). **5** *tr.* (often foll. by *out*) make a tap or taps (*tapped out the rhythm*). ● *n.* **1 a** a light blow; a rap. **b** the sound of this (*heard a tap at the door*). **2 a** tap-dancing (*goes to tap classes*). **b** a piece of metal attached to the toe and heel of a tap-dancer's shoe to make the tapping sound. **3** (in *pl.*, usu. treated as *sing.*) *US* **a** a bugle call for lights to be put out in army quarters. **b** a similar call sounded at a military funeral. □ **tapper** *n.* [Middle English *tappe* (imitative), perhaps via French *taper*]

tapa /'tɑːpə/ *n.* **1** the bark of a paper-mulberry tree. **2** cloth made from this, used in the Pacific islands. [Polynesian]

tapas /'tapas/ *n.pl.* (often *attrib.*) small savoury dishes esp. in Spanish style. [Spanish]

tap-dance *n.* & *v.* ● *n.* a dance or form of display dancing performed wearing shoes fitted with metal taps, with rhythmical tapping of the toes and heels. ● *v.intr.* perform a tap-dance. □ **tap-dancer** *n.* **tap-dancing** *n.*

tape /teɪp/ *n.* & *v.* ● *n.* **1** a narrow strip of woven material for tying up, fastening, etc. **2 a** a strip of material stretched across the finishing line of a race. **b** a similar strip for marking off an area or forming a notional barrier. **3** (in full **adhesive tape**) a strip of opaque or transparent paper or plastic etc., esp. coated with adhesive for fastening, sticking, masking, insulating, etc. **4 a** long narrow flexible material with magnetic properties used for recording sound or pictures or data. **b** a length, reel, or cassette of this. **c** a recording on this. **5** = TAPE-MEASURE. ● *v.tr.* **1 a** tie up or join etc. with tape. **b** apply tape to. **2** (foll. by *off*) seal or mark off an area or thing with tape. **3** record on magnetic tape. **4** measure with tape. □ **breast the tape** *Brit.* win a race. **have** (or **get**) **a person** or **thing taped** *Brit. colloq.* understand a person or thing fully. **on tape** recorded on magnetic tape. □ **tapeable** *adj.* (esp. in sense 3 of *v.*). [Old English *tæppa*, *tæppe*, of unknown origin]

tape deck *n.* a piece of equipment for playing audiotapes, esp. as part of a stereo system.

tape machine *n.* a machine for receiving and recording telegraph messages.

tape-measure *n.* a strip of tape or thin flexible metal marked for measuring lengths.

taper /'teɪpə/ *n.* & *v.* ● *n.* **1** a wick coated with wax etc. for conveying a flame. **2** a slender candle. ● *v.* (often foll. by *off*) **1** *intr.* & *tr.* diminish or reduce in thickness towards one end. **2** *tr.* & *intr.* make or become gradually less. [Old English *tapur*, *-or*, *-er* 'wax candle', from Latin PAPYRUS, whose pith was used for candle-wicks]

tape recorder *n.* apparatus for recording sounds on magnetic tape and afterwards reproducing them. □ **tape-record** *v.tr.* **tape recording** *n.*

taperer /'teɪp(ə)rə/ *n.* a person carrying a taper in a religious ceremony.

tapestry /'tapɪstri/ *n.* (*pl.* **-ies**) **1 a** a thick textile fabric in which coloured weft threads are woven to form pictures or designs. **b** embroidery imitating this, usu. in wools on canvas. **c** a piece of such embroidery. **2** events or circumstances etc. compared with a tapestry in being intricate, interwoven, etc. (*life's rich tapestry*). □ **tapestried** *adj.* [Middle English, alteration of *tapissery* via Old French *tapisserie* from *tapissier* 'tapestry worker' or *tapisser* 'to carpet', from *tapis*: see TAPIS]

tapetum /tə'pi:təm/ *n.* a light-reflecting part of the choroid membrane in the eyes of certain mammals, e.g. cats. [Late Latin from Latin *tapete* 'carpet']

tapeworm /'teɪpwə:m/ *n.* any parasitic flatworm of the class Cestoda, the adult of which lives in the intestines and has a long ribbon-like body with many segments and a small head or scolex.

taphonomy /ta'fɒnəmi/ *n.* the science concerned with the process of fossilization. ▫ **taphonomic** /-fə'nɒmɪk/ *adj.* **taphonomist** *n.* [Greek *taphos* 'grave' + -NOMY]

tap-in *n.* a close-range shot requiring little force, esp. into the goal in football.

tapioca /tapɪ'əʊkə/ *n.* a starchy substance in hard white grains obtained from cassava and used for puddings etc. [Tupi-Guarani *tipioca*, from *tipi* 'dregs' + *og, ok* 'squeeze out']

tapir /'teɪpə, -ɪə/ *n.* any nocturnal hoofed mammal of the genus *Tapirus*, native to Central and S. America and Malaysia, having a short flexible protruding snout used for feeding on vegetation. ▫ **tapiroid** *adj. & n.* [Spanish and Portuguese, from Tupi *tapira*]

tapis /'tapi:/ *n.* (*pl.* same) a covering or tapestry. ▫ **on the tapis** (of a subject) under consideration or discussion. [Middle English via Old French *tapiz* and Late Latin *tapetium* from Greek *tapētion*, diminutive of *tapēs tapētos* 'tapestry']

tapotement /tə'pəʊtm(ə)nt/ *n. Med.* rapid and repeated striking of the body as massage treatment. [French from *tapoter* 'tap']

tapper see TAP².

tappet /'tapɪt/ *n.* a lever or projecting part used in machinery to give intermittent motion, often in conjunction with a cam. [apparently from TAP² + -ET¹]

taproom /'tapru:m, -rʊm/ *n.* a room in which alcoholic drinks (esp. beer) are available on tap.

tap root *n.* a tapering root growing vertically downwards.

tapster /'tapstə/ *n.* a person who draws and serves alcoholic drinks at a bar. [Old English *tæppestre* originally fem. (as TAP¹, -STER)]

tapu /'tɑ:pu:/ *n. & adj. NZ* = TABOO. [Maori]

tap water *n.* water from a piped supply.

tar¹ /tɑ:/ *n. & v.* ● *n.* **1** a dark thick inflammable liquid distilled from wood or coal etc. and used as a preservative of wood and iron, in making roads, as an antiseptic, etc. **2** a similar substance formed in the combustion of tobacco etc. ● *v.tr.* (**tarred**, **tarring**) cover with tar. ▫ **tar and feather** smear with tar and then cover with feathers as a punishment. **tarred with the same brush** having the same faults. [Old English *te(o)ru* from Germanic: related to TREE]

tar² /tɑ:/ *n. colloq.* a sailor. [abbreviation of TARPAULIN]

ta-ra /tə'rɑ:/ *int.* esp. *N. Engl. colloq.* goodbye. [variant of TA-TA]

taradiddle /'tarədɪd(ə)l/ *n.* (also **tarradiddle**) esp. *Brit. colloq.* **1** a petty lie. **2** pretentious nonsense. [18th c.: perhaps related to DIDDLE]

tarakihi /tarə'ki:hi, tarə'ki:/ *n.* (also **terakihi**) a silver fish, *Cheilodactylus macropterus*, with a black band behind the head, caught for food off New Zealand coasts. [Maori]

taramasalata /tarəməsə'lɑ:tə/ *n.* (also **tarama** /'tarəmə/) a pinkish pâté made from the roe of mullet or other fish with olive oil, seasoning, etc. [modern Greek *taramas* 'roe' (from Turkish *tarama*) + *salata* SALAD]

tarantass /tar(ə)n'tas/ *n.* a springless four-wheeled Russian vehicle. [Russian *tarantas*]

tarantella /tar(ə)n'tɛlə/ *n.* (also **tarantelle** /-'tɛl/) **1** a rapid whirling dance of southern Italy. **2** the music for this. [Italian, from *Taranto*, a town in S. Italy (because the dance was once thought to be a cure for a tarantula bite): cf. TARANTISM]

tarantism /'tar(ə)ntɪz(ə)m/ *n. hist.* dancing mania, esp. that originating in southern Italy among those who had (actually or supposedly) been bitten by a tarantula. [modern Latin *tarantismus*, Italian *tarantismo* from *Taranto* Latin *Tarentum*, a town in southern Italy]

tarantula /tə'rantjʊlə/ *n.* **1** any large hairy tropical spider of the family Theraphosidae. **2** a large black S. European spider, *Lycosa tarentula*, whose bite was formerly held to cause tarantism. [medieval Latin from Italian *tarantola* (as TARANTISM)]

taraxacum /tə'raksəkəm/ *n.* **1** any plant of the genus *Taraxacum* (daisy family), including the dandelion. **2** a tonic etc. prepared from the dried roots of this. [medieval Latin from Arabic *ṭarakšaḳūḳ*, from Persian *talḵ* 'bitter' + *chakūk* 'purslane']

tarboosh /tɑ:'bu:ʃ/ *n.* a cap like a fez, sometimes worn as part of a turban. [Egyptian Arabic *ṭarbūš*, ultimately from Persian *sar-būš* 'head covering']

Tardenoisian /tɑ:dɪ'nɔɪzɪən/ *adj. & n. Archaeol.* ● *adj.* of or relating to a late mesolithic culture of W. and central Europe. ● *n.* this culture. [*Tardenois* in NE France, where remains of it were found]

tardigrade /'tɑ:dɪgreɪd/ *n. & adj.* ● *n.* any minute freshwater animal of the phylum Tardigrada, having a short plump body and four pairs of short legs. Also called WATER BEAR. ● *adj.* of or relating to this phylum. [French *tardigrade* from Latin *tardigradus*, from *tardus* 'slow' + *gradi* 'walk']

tardy /'tɑ:di/ *adj.* (**tardier**, **tardiest**) **1** slow to act or come or happen. **2** delaying or delayed beyond the right or expected time. ▫ **tardily** *adv.* **tardiness** *n.* [French *tardif, tardive*, ultimately from Latin *tardus* 'slow']

tare¹ /tɛ:/ *n.* **1** vetch, esp. as corn-weed or fodder. **2** (in *pl.*) *Bibl.* an injurious weed resembling corn when young (Matt. 13:24–30). [Middle English: origin unknown]

tare² /tɛ:/ *n.* **1** an allowance made for the weight of the packing or wrapping around goods. **2** the weight of a motor vehicle without its fuel or load. [Middle English from French, = deficiency, tare, via medieval Latin *tara* from Arabic *ṭarḥa* 'what is rejected', from *ṭaraḥa* 'reject']

tare and tret *n.* the arithmetical rule for computing the net weight of goods.

targa /'tɑ:gə/ *n.* (often *attrib.*) a type of convertible sports car with a roof hood or panel that can be removed, esp. leaving a central roll bar for passenger safety (*targa roof*; *targa model*). [Italian, = shield, originally the name of a model of Porsche, probably named after the *Targa Florio*, a race held annually in Sicily]

targe /tɑ:dʒ/ *n. archaic* = TARGET *n.* 5. [Middle English from Old French]

target /'tɑ:gɪt/ *n. & v.* ● *n.* **1** a mark or point fired or aimed at, esp. a round or rectangular object marked with concentric circles. **2** a person or thing aimed at, or exposed to gunfire etc. (*they were an easy target*). **3** (also *attrib.*) an objective or result aimed at (*our export targets*; *target date*). **4** a person or thing against whom criticism, abuse, etc., is or may be directed. **5** *archaic* a shield or buckler, esp. a small round one. ● *v.tr.* (**targeted**, **targeting** or *Brit.* **targetted**, **targetting**) **1** identify or single out (a person or thing) as an object of attention or attack. **2** aim or direct (*missiles targeted on major cities*; *should target our efforts where needed*). ▫ **targetable** *adj.* [Middle English, diminutive of Middle English and Old French *targe* 'shield']

tariff /'tarɪf/ *n. & v.* ● *n.* **1** a table of fixed charges (*a hotel tariff*). **2 a** a duty on a particular class of imports or exports. **b** a list of duties or customs to be paid. **3** *Brit.* standard charges agreed between insurers etc. ● *v.tr.* subject (goods) to a tariff. [French *tarif* via Italian *tariffa* and Turkish *tarife* from Arabic *ta'rīf(a)*, from *'arrafa* 'notify']

tarlatan /'tɑ:lətən/ *n.* a thin stiff open-weave muslin. [French *tarlatane*, probably of Indian origin]

tarmac /ˈtɑːmak/ *n.* & *v.* ● *n. propr.* **1** = TARMACADAM. **2** a surface made of this, e.g. a runway. ● *v.tr.* (**tarmacked**, **tarmacking**) apply tarmacadam to. [abbreviation]

tarmacadam /tɑːməˈkadəm/ *n.* a material of stone or slag bound with tar, used in paving roads etc. [TAR[1] + MACADAM]

tarn /tɑːn/ *n.* a small mountain lake. [Middle English *terne*, *tarne* from Old Norse]

tarnish /ˈtɑːnɪʃ/ *v.* & *n.* ● *v.* **1** *tr.* lessen or destroy the lustre of (metal etc.). **2** *tr.* impair (one's reputation etc.). **3** *intr.* (of metal etc.) lose lustre. ● *n.* **1 a** a loss of lustre. **b** a film of colour formed on an exposed surface of a mineral or metal. **2** a blemish; a stain. □ **tarnishable** *adj.* [French *ternir* from *terne* 'dark']

taro /ˈtɑːrəʊ, ˈtarəʊ/ *n.* (*pl.* **-os**) a tropical aroid plant, *Colocasia esculenta*, with tuberous roots used as food. Also called EDDO. [Polynesian]

tarot /ˈtarəʊ/ *n.* **1** (in *sing.* or *pl.*) **a** any of several games played with a pack of cards having five suits, the last of which is a set of permanent trumps. **b** a similar pack used in fortune-telling. **2 a** any of the trump cards. **b** any of the cards from a fortune-telling pack. [French *tarot*, Italian *tarocchi*, of unknown origin]

tarp /tɑːp/ *n. N. Amer.* & *Austral. colloq.* tarpaulin. [abbreviation]

tarpan /ˈtɑːpan/ *n.* an extinct N. European primitive wild horse. [Kyrgyz]

tarpaulin /tɑːˈpɔːlɪn/ *n.* **1** heavy-duty waterproof cloth, originally of tarred canvas. **2** a sheet or covering of this. **3 a** a sailor's tarred or oilskin hat. **b** *archaic* a sailor. [probably from TAR[1] + PALL[1] + -ING[1]]

tarpon /ˈtɑːpɒn/ *n.* **1** a large silvery fish, *Tarpon atlanticus*, common in the tropical Atlantic. **2** a similar fish, *Megalops cyprinoides*, of the Pacific ocean. [Dutch *tarpoen*, of unknown origin]

tarradiddle var. of TARADIDDLE.

tarragon /ˈtarəg(ə)n/ *n.* a bushy herb, *Artemisia dracunculus*, with leaves used to flavour salads, stuffings, vinegar, etc. [= medieval Latin *tarchon* from medieval Greek *tarkhōn*, perhaps via Arabic from Greek *drakōn* 'dragon']

tarras var. of TRASS.

tarry[1] /ˈtɑːri/ *adj.* (**tarrier**, **tarriest**) of or like or smeared with tar. □ **tarriness** *n.*

tarry[2] /ˈtari/ *v.intr.* (**-ies**, **-ied**) *archaic* delay, linger, stay, wait. □ **tarrier** *n.* [Middle English: origin uncertain]

tarsal /ˈtɑːs(ə)l/ *adj.* & *n.* ● *adj.* of or relating to the bones in the ankle. ● *n.* a tarsal bone. [TARSUS + -AL]

tar sand *n. Geol.* a deposit of sand impregnated with bitumen.

tarsi *pl.* of TARSUS.

tarsi- /ˈtɑːsi/ *comb. form* (also **tarso-** /ˈtɑːsəʊ/) tarsus.

tarsier /ˈtɑːsɪə/ *n.* any small large-eyed arboreal nocturnal primate of the genus *Tarsius*, native to Borneo, the Philippines, etc., with a long tail and long hind legs used for leaping from tree to tree. [French (as TARSUS), from the structure of its foot]

tarso- *comb. form* var. of TARSI-.

tarsus /ˈtɑːsəs/ *n.* (*pl.* **tarsi** /-sʌɪ, -siː/) **1 a** *Anat.* the group of bones forming the ankle and upper foot. **b** *Zool.* the shank of a bird's leg. **2** *Zool.* the fifth joint of the leg in insects, usu. of several small segments, ending in a claw. **3** *Anat.* the fibrous connective tissue of the eyelid. [modern Latin from Greek *tarsos* 'flat of the foot, rim of the eyelid']

tart[1] /tɑːt/ *n.* **1** an open pastry case containing jam etc. **2** esp. *Brit.* a pie with a fruit or sweet filling. □ **tartlet** *n.* [Middle English from Old French *tarte* = medieval Latin *tarta*, of unknown origin]

tart[2] /tɑːt/ *n.* & *v.* ● *n. slang* **1** a prostitute; a promiscuous woman. **2** *slang offens.* a girl or woman. ● *v.* (foll. by *up*) esp. *Brit. colloq.* **1** *tr.* (usu. *refl.*) smarten (oneself or a thing) up, esp. flashily or gaudily. **2** *intr.* dress up gaudily. [probably abbreviation of SWEETHEART]

tart[3] /tɑːt/ *adj.* **1** sharp or acid in taste. **2** (of a remark etc.) cutting, bitter. □ **tartly** *adv.* **tartness** *n.* [Old English *teart*, of unknown origin]

tartan[1] /ˈtɑːt(ə)n/ *n.* **1** a pattern of coloured stripes crossing at right angles, esp. the distinctive plaid worn by Scottish Highlanders to denote their clan. **2** woollen etc. cloth woven in this pattern (often *attrib.*: *a tartan scarf*). [perhaps from Old French *tertaine*, *tiretaine*, a kind of cloth]

tartan[2] /ˈtɑːt(ə)n/ *n.* a lateen-sailed single-masted ship used in the Mediterranean. [French *tartane* from Italian *tartana*, perhaps from Arabic *ṭarīda*]

Tartar /ˈtɑːtə/ *n.* & *adj.* (also **Tatar** except in sense 2 of *n.*) ● *n.* **1 a** a member of a group of central Asian peoples including Mongols and Turks. **b** the Turkic language of these peoples. **2** (**tartar**) a violent-tempered or intractable person. ● *adj.* **1** of or relating to the Tartars or their language. **2** of or relating to central Asia east of the Caspian Sea. □ **Tartarian** /-ˈtɛːrɪən/ *adj.* [Middle English *tartre* from Old French *Tartare* or medieval Latin *Tartarus*]

tartar /ˈtɑːtə/ *n.* **1** a hard deposit of saliva, calcium phosphate, etc., that forms on the teeth. **2** a deposit of acid potassium tartrate that forms a hard crust on the inside of a cask during the fermentation of wine. See also CREAM OF TARTAR. □ **tartarize** *v.tr.* (also **-ise**). [Middle English via medieval Latin from medieval Greek *tartaron*]

tartare /tɑːˈtɑː/ *adj.* (in full **sauce tartare**) = TARTARE SAUCE. [French, = tartar]

tartar emetic *n.* potassium antimony tartrate, a toxic compound used formerly as an emetic, and now in treating protozoal disease in animals and as a mordant in dyeing.

tartare sauce *n.* (also **tartar sauce**) a sauce of mayonnaise and chopped gherkins, capers, etc.

tartaric /tɑːˈtarɪk/ *adj. Chem.* of or produced from tartar. [French *tartarique* from medieval Latin *tartarum*: see TARTAR]

tartaric acid *n.* a natural carboxylic acid found esp. in unripe grapes, used in baking powders and as a food additive.

Tartarus /ˈtɑːt(ə)rəs/ *n.* (in Greek mythology) a place of punishment in the underworld where the Titans were imprisoned. □ **Tartarean** /-ˈtɛːrɪən/ *adj.* [Latin from Greek *Tartaros*]

tartrate /ˈtɑːtreɪt/ *n. Chem.* any salt or ester of tartaric acid. [French (as TARTAR, -ATE[1])]

tartrazine /ˈtɑːtrəziːn/ *n. Chem.* a brilliant yellow dye derived from tartaric acid and used to colour food, drugs, and cosmetics. [as TARTAR + AZO- + -INE[4]]

tarty /ˈtɑːti/ *adj.* (**tartier**, **tartiest**) *colloq.* (esp. of a woman) vulgarly provocative; gaudy; promiscuous. □ **tartily** *adv.* **tartiness** *n.* [TART[2] + -Y[1]]

Tarzan /ˈtɑːz(ə)n/ *n.* a man of great agility and powerful physique. [name of the hero of stories by E. R. Burroughs, American writer d. 1950]

Tas. *abbr.* Tasmania.

tash /taʃ/ *n.* (also **tache**) *colloq.* a moustache. [abbreviation]

Tashi Lama /ˈtaʃi ˌlɑːmə/ *n.* = PANCHEN LAMA.

task /tɑːsk/ *n.* & *v.* ● *n.* a piece of work to be done or undertaken. ● *v.tr.* **1** make great demands on (a person's powers etc.). **2** assign a task to. □ **take to task** rebuke, scold. [Middle English from Old Northern French *tasque* = Old French *tasche* from medieval Latin *tasca*, perhaps via *taxa* from Latin *taxare* TAX]

task force *n.* (also **task group**) **1** *Mil.* an armed force organized for a special operation. **2** a unit specially organized for a task.

taskmaster /ˈtɑːskmɑːstə/ *n.* (*fem.* **taskmistress** /-mɪstrɪs/) a person who imposes a task or burden, esp. regularly or severely.

Tasmanian /taz'meɪmɪən/ *n.* & *adj.* ● *n.* **1** a native of Tasmania, an island state of Australia. **2** a person of Tasmanian descent. ● *adj.* of or relating to Tasmania.

Tasmanian devil *n.* a small bearlike nocturnal flesh-eating marsupial, *Sarcophilus harrisii*, now found only in Tasmania.

Tasmanian wolf *n.* (also **Tasmanian tiger**) = THYLACINE.

Tass /tas/ *n.* the official news agency of the former Soviet Union, renamed ITAR-Tass in 1992. [the initials of Russian *Telegrafnoe agentstvo Sovetskogo Soyuza* 'Telegraphic Agency of the Soviet Union']

tass /tas/ *n. Sc.* **1** a cup or small goblet. **2** a small draught of brandy etc. [Middle English via Old French *tasse* 'cup' and Arabic *ṭāsa* 'basin' from Persian *tast*]

tassel[1] /'tas(ə)l/ *n.* & *v.* ● *n.* **1** a tuft of loosely hanging threads or cords etc. attached for decoration to a cushion, scarf, cap, etc. **2** a tassel-like head of some plants, esp. a flower head with prominent stamens at the top of a maize stalk. ● *v.* (**tasselled**, **tasselling**; *US* **tasseled**, **tasseling**) **1** *tr.* provide with a tassel or tassels. **2** *intr. N. Amer.* (of maize etc.) form tassels. [Middle English from Old French *tas(s)el* 'clasp', of unknown origin]

tassel[2] /'tas(ə)l/ *n.* (also **torsel** /'tɔː-/) a small piece of stone, wood, etc., supporting the end of a beam or joist. [Old French, ultimately from Latin *taxillus* 'small die', and *tessella*: see TESSELLATE]

tassie /'tasi/ *n. Sc.* a small cup.

taste /teɪst/ *n.* & *v.* ● *n.* **1 a** the sensation characteristic of a soluble substance caused in the mouth and throat by contact with that substance (*disliked the taste of garlic*). **b** the faculty of perceiving this sensation (*was bitter to the taste*). **2** a small portion of food or drink taken as a sample. **3** a slight experience (*a taste of success*). **4** (often foll. by *for*) a liking or predilection (*has expensive tastes*; *is not to my taste*). **5** aesthetic discernment in art, literature, conduct, etc., esp. of a specified kind (*a person of taste*; *dresses in poor taste*). ● *v.* **1** *tr.* sample or test the flavour of (food etc.) by taking it into the mouth. **2** *tr.* (also *absol.*) perceive the flavour of (*could taste the lemon*; *cannot taste with a cold*). **3** *tr.* (esp. with *neg.*) eat or drink a small portion of (*had not tasted food for days*). **4** *tr.* have experience of (*had never tasted failure*). **5** *intr.* (often foll. by *of*) have a specified flavour (*tastes bitter*; *tastes of onions*). □ **a bad** (or **bitter** etc.) **taste** *colloq.* a strong feeling of regret or unease following an experience etc. **taste blood** see BLOOD. **to taste** in the amount needed for a pleasing result (*add salt and pepper to taste*). □ **tasteable** *adj.* (also **tastable**). [Middle English, = touch, taste, from Old French *tast*, *taster* 'touch, try, taste', ultimately perhaps from Latin *tangere* 'touch' + *gustare* 'taste']

taste bud *n.* any of the cells or nerve endings on the surface of the tongue by which things are tasted.

tasteful /'teɪs(t)fʊl, -f(ə)l/ *adj.* having, or done in, good taste. □ **tastefully** *adv.* **tastefulness** *n.*

tasteless /'teɪs(t)lɪs/ *adj.* **1** lacking flavour. **2** having, or done in, bad taste. □ **tastelessly** *adv.* **tastelessness** *n.*

taster /'teɪstə/ *n.* **1** a person employed to test food or drink by tasting it, esp. for quality or *hist.* to detect poisoning. **2** a small cup used by a wine taster. **3** an instrument for extracting a small sample from within a cheese. **4** a sample of something offered. [Middle English from Anglo-French *tastour*, Old French *tasteur*, from *taster*: see TASTE]

tasting /'teɪstɪŋ/ *n.* a gathering at which food or drink (esp. wine) is tasted and evaluated.

tasty /'teɪsti/ *adj.* (**tastier**, **tastiest**) **1** (of food) pleasing in flavour; appetizing. **2** *colloq.* attractive. □ **tastily** *adv.* **tastiness** *n.*

tat[1] /tat/ *n. Brit. colloq.* **1 a** tatty or tasteless clothes; worthless goods. **b** rubbish, junk. **2** a shabby person. [probably back-formation from TATTY]

tat[2] /tat/ *v.* (**tatted**, **tatting**) **1** *intr.* do tatting. **2** *tr.* make by tatting. [back-formation from TATTING]

tat[3] see TIT[2].

ta-ta /ta'tɑː/ *int.* esp. *Brit. colloq.* goodbye. [19th c.: origin unknown]

tatami /tə'tɑːmi/ *n.* (in full **tatami mat**) a rush-covered straw mat forming a traditional Japanese floor covering.

Tatar var. of TARTAR.

tater /'teɪtə/ *n.* (also *Brit.* **tatie** /-ti/) *colloq.* = POTATO. [abbreviation]

tatter /'tatə/ *n.* (usu. in *pl.*) a rag; an irregularly torn piece of cloth or paper etc. □ **in tatters** *colloq.* **1** torn in many places. **2** (of a negotiation, argument, etc.) ruined, demolished. □ **tattery** *adj.* [Middle English from Old Norse *tötrar* 'rags']

tattered /'tatəd/ *adj.* = *in tatters* (see TATTER).

tattersall /'tatəs(ə)l, -sɔːl/ *n.* (in full **tattersall check**) a fabric with a pattern of coloured lines forming squares like a tartan. [named after R. *Tattersall*, English horseman d. 1795: from the traditional design of horse blankets]

tattie /'tati/ *n. colloq.* = POTATO. [abbreviation]

tatting /'tatɪŋ/ *n.* **1** a kind of knotted lace made by hand with a small shuttle and used for trimming etc. **2** the process of making this. [19th c.: origin unknown]

tattle /'tat(ə)l/ *v.* & *n.* ● *v.* **1** *intr.* prattle, chatter; gossip idly. **2** *tr.* utter (words) idly. ● *n.* gossip; idle or trivial talk. [Middle English from Middle Flemish *tatelen*, *tateren* (imitative)]

tattler /'tatlə/ *n.* a prattler; a gossip.

tattle-tale *n. N. Amer.* a tell-tale, esp. a child.

tattoo[1] /ta'tuː/ *n.* (*pl.* **tattoos**) **1** an evening drum or bugle signal recalling soldiers to their quarters. **2** an elaboration of this with music and marching, presented as an entertainment. **3** a rhythmic tapping or drumming. [17th-c. *tap-too* from Dutch *taptoe*, literally 'close the tap' (of the cask)]

tattoo[2] /ta'tuː/ *v.* & *n.* ● *v.tr.* (**tattoos**, **tattooed**) **1** mark (the skin) with an indelible design by puncturing it and inserting pigment. **2** make (a design) in this way. ● *n.* (*pl.* **tattoos**) a design made by tattooing. □ **tattooer** *n.* **tattooist** *n.* [Polynesian]

tatty /'tati/ *adj.* (**tattier**, **tattiest**) esp. *Brit. colloq.* **1** tattered; worn and shabby. **2** inferior. **3** tawdry. □ **tattily** *adv.* **tattiness** *n.* [originally Scots, = shaggy, apparently related to Old English *tættec* 'rag, TATTER']

tau /tɔː, taʊ/ *n.* the nineteenth letter of the Greek alphabet (Τ, τ). [Middle English from Greek]

tau cross *n.* a T-shaped cross.

taught *past* and *past part.* of TEACH.

taunt /tɔːnt/ *n.* & *v.* ● *n.* a thing said in order to anger or wound a person. ● *v.tr.* **1** assail with taunts. **2** reproach (a person) contemptuously. □ **taunter** *n.* **tauntingly** *adv.* [16th c., in the phrase *taunt for taunt* from French *tant pour tant* 'tit for tat', hence a smart rejoinder]

tau particle *n.* an unstable, heavy, and charged subatomic particle of the lepton class.

taupe /təʊp/ *n.* & *adj.* ● *n.* a grey with a tinge of another colour, usu. brown. ● *adj.* of this colour. [French, = MOLE[1]]

taurine[1] /'tɔːriːn/ *n. Biochem.* a sulphur-containing amino acid important in the metabolism of fats. [Greek *tauros* 'bull' + -INE[4]]

taurine[2] /'tɔːrʌɪn/ *adj.* of or like a bull; bullish. [Latin *taurinus* from *taurus* 'bull']

tauromachy /tɔː'rɒməki/ *n.* (*pl.* **-ies**) *archaic* **1** a bullfight. **2** bullfighting. [Greek *tauromakhia*, from *tauros* 'bull' + *makhē* 'fight']

Taurus /'tɔːrəs/ *n.* **1** *Astron.* a constellation (the Bull), said to represent a bull with brazen feet that was tamed by Jason. **2** *Astrol.* **a** the second sign of the zodiac, which the sun enters about 21 Apr. **b** a person born when the sun is in this sign. □ **Taurean** *adj.* & *n.* [Middle English from Latin, = bull]

taut /tɔːt/ *adj.* **1** (of a rope, muscles, etc.) tight; not slack. **2** (of nerves) tense. **3** (of a ship etc.) in good order or condition. □ **tauten** *v.tr. & intr.* **tautly** *adv.* **tautness** *n.* [Middle English *touht, togt*, perhaps = TOUGH, influenced by *tog-*, past part. stem of obsolete *tee* (Old English *tēon*) 'pull']

tauto- /ˈtɔːtəʊ/ *comb. form* the same. [Greek, from *tauto, to auto* 'the same']

tautog /tɔːˈtɒg/ *n.* a fish, *Tautoga onitis*, found off the Atlantic coast of N. America, used as food. [Narragansett *tautauog* (pl.)]

tautology /tɔːˈtɒlədʒi/ *n.* (*pl.* **-ies**) **1** the saying of the same thing twice over in different words, esp. as a fault of style (e.g. *arrived one after the other in succession*). **2** a statement that is necessarily true. □ **tautological** /-təˈlɒdʒɪk(ə)l/ *adj.* **tautologically** /-təˈlɒdʒɪk(ə)li/ *adv.* **tautologist** *n.* **tautologize** /-dʒʌɪz/ *v.intr.* (also **-ise**). **tautologous** /-ləgəs/ *adj.* [Late Latin *tautologia* from Greek (as TAUTO-, -LOGY)]

tautomer /ˈtɔːtəmə/ *n. Chem.* a substance that exists as two mutually convertible isomers in equilibrium. □ **tautomeric** /-ˈmɛrɪk/ *adj.* **tautomerism** /-ˈtɒmərɪz(ə)m/ *n.* [TAUTO- + -MER]

tautophony /tɔːˈtɒf(ə)ni/ *n.* repetition of the same sound. [TAUTO- + Greek *phōnē* 'sound']

tavern /ˈtav(ə)n/ *n.* esp. *archaic* or *literary* an inn or public house. [Middle English via Old French *taverne* from Latin *taberna* 'hut, tavern']

taverna /təˈvəːnə/ *n.* a Greek restaurant or eating house. [modern Greek (as TAVERN)]

taw[1] /tɔː/ *v.tr.* make (hide) into leather without the use of tannin, esp. by soaking in a solution of alum and salt. □ **tawer** *n.* [Old English *tawian*, from Germanic]

taw[2] /tɔː/ *n.* **1** a large marble. **2** a game of marbles. **3** a line from which players throw marbles. [18th c.: origin unknown]

tawdry /ˈtɔːdri/ *adj. & n.* ● *adj.* (**tawdrier, tawdriest**) **1** showy but worthless. **2** over-ornamented, gaudy, vulgar. ● *n.* cheap or gaudy finery. □ **tawdrily** *adv.* **tawdriness** *n.* [earlier as noun: short for *tawdry lace*, originally *St Audrey's lace* from *Audrey* = *Etheldrida*, patron saint of Ely, where a fair was held at which cheap finery was traditionally sold]

tawny /ˈtɔːni/ *adj. & n.* ● *adj.* (**tawnier, tawniest**) of an orange- or yellow-brown colour. ● *n.* this colour. □ **tawniness** *n.* [Middle English from Anglo-French *tauné*, Old French *tané*, from *tan* TAN[1]]

tawny eagle *n.* a brownish African or Asian eagle, *Aquila rapax*.

tawny owl *n.* **1** a reddish-brown European owl, *Strix aluco*. **2** (**Tawny Owl**) *colloq.* the assistant adult leader of a pack of Brownie Guides, officially termed *Assistant Brownie Guider* since 1968.

taws /tɔːz/ *n.* (also **tawse**) *Sc. hist.* a thong with a slit end formerly used in schools for punishing children. [apparently pl. of obsolete *taw* 'tawed leather', from TAW[1]]

tax /taks/ *n. & v.* ● *n.* **1** a contribution to state revenue compulsorily levied on individuals, property, or businesses (often foll. by *on*: *a tax on luxury goods*). **2** (usu. foll. by *on, upon*) a strain or heavy demand; an oppressive or burdensome obligation. ● *v.tr.* **1** impose a tax on (persons or goods etc.). **2** deduct tax from (income etc.). **3** make heavy demands on (a person's powers or resources etc.) (*you really tax my patience*). **4** (foll. by *with*) confront (a person) with a wrongdoing etc. **5** call to account. **6** *Law* examine and assess (costs etc.). □ **taxable** *adj.* **taxer** *n.* **taxless** *adj.* [Middle English via Old French *taxer* from Latin *taxare* 'censure, charge, compute', perhaps from Greek *tassō* 'fix']

taxa *pl.* of TAXON.

taxation /takˈseɪʃ(ə)n/ *n.* the imposition or payment of tax. [Middle English via Anglo-French *taxacioun*, Old French *taxation* from Latin *taxatio -onis*, from *taxare*: see TAX]

tax avoidance *n. Brit.* the arrangement of financial affairs to minimize payment of tax.

tax break *n. colloq.* a tax concession or advantage allowed by government.

tax-deductible *adj.* (of expenditure) that may be paid out of income before the deduction of income tax.

tax disc *n. Brit.* a paper disc displayed on the windscreen of a motor vehicle, certifying payment of excise duty.

tax evasion *n.* the illegal non-payment or underpayment of income tax.

tax-free *adj.* (of goods, income, etc.) exempt from being taxed.

tax haven *n.* a country etc. where taxes are levied at a low rate.

taxi /ˈtaksi/ *n. & v.* ● *n.* (*pl.* **taxis**) **1** a motor car licensed to ply for hire and usu. fitted with a taximeter. **2** a boat etc. similarly used. ● *v.* (**taxies, taxied, taxiing** or **taxying**) **1 a** *intr.* (of an aircraft or pilot) move along the ground under the machine's own power before take-off or after landing. **b** *tr.* cause (an aircraft) to taxi. **2** *intr. & tr.* go or convey in a taxi. [abbreviation of *taximeter cab*]

taxicab /ˈtaksɪkab/ *n.* = TAXI *n.* 1.

taxi dancer *n.* a dancing partner available for hire.

taxidermy /ˈtaksɪdəːmi/ *n.* the art of preparing, stuffing, and mounting the skins of animals with lifelike effect. □ **taxidermal** /-ˈdəːm(ə)l/ *adj.* **taxidermic** /-ˈdəːmɪk/ *adj.* **taxidermist** *n.* [Greek *taxis* 'arrangement' + *derma* 'skin']

taximeter /ˈtaksɪmiːtə/ *n.* an automatic device fitted to a taxi, recording the distance travelled and the fare payable. [French *taximètre*, from *taxe* 'tariff, TAX' + -METER]

taxi rank *n.* (*US* **taxi stand**) a place where taxis wait to be hired.

taxis /ˈtaksɪs/ *n.* **1** *Surgery* the restoration of displaced bones or organs by manual pressure. **2** *Biol.* the directional movement of a cell or organism in response to an external stimulus (cf. KINESIS 2). **3** *Gram.* order or arrangement of words. [Greek from *tassō* 'arrange']

taxiway /ˈtaksɪweɪ/ *n.* a route along which an aircraft can taxi when moving to or from a runway.

taxman /ˈtaksman/ *n.* (*pl.* **-men**) *colloq.* **1** an inspector or collector of taxes. **2** the personification of the government department dealing with tax.

taxon /ˈtaksɒn/ *n.* (*pl.* **taxa** /ˈtaksə/) any taxonomic group. [back-formation from TAXONOMY]

taxonomy /takˈsɒnəmi/ *n.* **1** the science of classification, esp. of living and extinct organisms. **2** a scheme of classification. □ **taxonomic** /-səˈnɒmɪk/ *adj.* **taxonomical** /-səˈnɒmɪk(ə)l/ *adj.* **taxonomically** /-səˈnɒmɪk(ə)li/ *adv.* **taxonomist** *n.* [French *taxonomie* (as TAXIS, Greek *-nomia* 'distribution')]

taxpayer /ˈtakspeɪə/ *n.* a person who pays taxes.

tax return *n.* a declaration of income for taxation purposes.

tax shelter *n.* a means of organizing business affairs to minimize payment of tax.

tax year see FINANCIAL YEAR.

tayberry /ˈteɪb(ə)ri/ *n.* (*pl.* **-ies**) a dark red soft fruit produced by crossing a blackberry and a raspberry. [named after the River *Tay* in Scotland (where introduced in 1977)]

Tay–Sachs disease /teɪˈsaks/ *n. Med.* an inherited metabolic disorder in which certain lipids accumulate in the brain, causing spasticity and death in childhood. [named after W. *Tay*, English ophthalmologist d. 1927 and B. *Sachs*, US neurologist d. 1944]

tazza /ˈtɑːtsə/ *n.* a saucer-shaped cup, esp. one mounted on a foot. [Italian from Arabic *ṭāsa*: see TASS]

TB *abbr.* **1 a** tubercle bacillus. **b** tuberculosis. **2** torpedo boat.

Tb *symb. Chem.* the element terbium.

t.b.a. *abbr.* to be announced.

T-bar *n.* **1** (in full **T-bar lift**) a type of ski lift in the form of a series of inverted T-shaped metal bars for towing skiers uphill. **2** (often *attrib.*) a T-shaped fastening on a shoe or sandal.

T-bone *n.* a T-shaped bone, esp. in steak from the thin end of a loin.

tbsp *abbr.* (also **tbs**) (*pl.* same or **tbsps**) tablespoonful.

Tc *symb. Chem.* the element technetium.

TCCB *abbr.* (in the UK) Test and County Cricket Board.

TCD *abbr.* Trinity College, Dublin.

TCDD *abbr.* tetrachlorodibenzoparadioxin (see DIOXIN).

T-cell *n.* = T-LYMPHOCYTE.

TCP *abbr. Brit. propr.* a disinfectant and germicide. [*t*ri*c*hloro*p*henylmethyliodasalicyl]

TD *abbr.* **1** (in the UK) Territorial (Officer's) Decoration. **2** *Ir.* Teachta Dála, Member of the Dáil.

Te *symb. Chem.* the element tellurium.

te /tiː/ *n.* (*US* **ti**) **1** (in tonic sol-fa) the seventh note of a major scale. **2** the note B in the fixed-doh system. [earlier *si*: French from Italian, perhaps from *S*ancte *I*ohannes: see GAMUT]

tea /tiː/ *n.* & *v.* ● *n.* **1 a** (in full **tea plant**) an evergreen shrub or small tree, *Camellia sinensis*, of India, China, etc. **b** its dried leaves. **2** a drink made by infusing tea leaves in boiling water. **3** a similar drink made from the leaves of other plants or from another substance (*camomile tea*; *beef tea*). **4 a** esp. *Brit.* a light afternoon meal consisting of tea, bread, cakes, etc. **b** *Brit.* a cooked evening meal. **c** esp. *US* an afternoon reception at which tea is served. ● *v.* (**teaed** or **tea'd** /tiːd/) **1** *intr.* take tea. **2** *tr.* give tea to (a person). □ **tea and sympathy** *colloq.* hospitable behaviour towards a troubled person. [17th-c. *tay*, *tey*, probably via Dutch *tee* from Chinese (Amoy dialect) *te*, = Mandarin dialect *cha*: cf. CHAR[3]]

tea bag *n.* a small porous bag of tea for infusion.

tea-ball *n.* esp. *N. Amer.* a ball of perforated metal to hold tea for infusion.

tea-bread *n.* light or sweet bread for eating at tea.

tea break *n. Brit.* a pause in work etc. to drink tea.

tea caddy *n.* a container for tea.

teacake /ˈtiːkeɪk/ *n. Brit.* a light yeast-based usu. sweet bun eaten at tea, often toasted.

tea ceremony *n.* an elaborate Japanese ritual of serving and drinking tea, as an expression of Zen Buddhist philosophy.

teach /tiːtʃ/ *v.tr.* (*past* and *past part.* **taught** /tɔːt/) **1 a** give systematic information to (a person) or about (a subject or skill). **b** (*absol.*) practise this professionally. **c** enable (a person) to do something by instruction and training (*taught me to swim*; *taught me how to dance*). **2 a** advocate as a moral etc. principle (*my parents taught me forgiveness*). **b** communicate, instruct in (*suffering taught me patience*). **3** (foll. by *to* + infin.) **a** induce (a person) by example or punishment to do or not to do a thing (*that will teach you to sit still*; *that will teach you not to laugh*). **b** *colloq.* make (a person) disinclined to do a thing (*I will teach you to interfere*). □ **teach a person a lesson** see LESSON. **teach school** *US* be a teacher in a school. [Old English *tǣcan*, from a Germanic root meaning 'show']

teachable /ˈtiːtʃəb(ə)l/ *adj.* **1** apt at learning. **2** (of a subject) that can be taught. □ **teachability** /-ˈbɪlɪti/ *n.* **teachableness** *n.*

teacher /ˈtiːtʃə/ *n.* a person who teaches, esp. in a school. □ **teacherly** *adj.*

tea chest *n.* a light metal-lined wooden box in which tea is transported.

teach-in *n.* **1** an informal lecture and discussion on a subject of public interest. **2** a series of these.

teaching /ˈtiːtʃɪŋ/ *n.* **1** the profession of a teacher. **2** (often in *pl.*) what is taught; a doctrine.

teaching hospital *n.* a hospital where medical students are taught.

teaching machine *n.* any of various devices for giving instruction according to a program that reacts to pupils' responses.

tea cloth *n.* = TEA TOWEL.

tea cosy *n.* a cover to keep a teapot warm.

teacup /ˈtiːkʌp/ *n.* **1** a cup from which tea is drunk. **2** an amount held by this, about 150 ml. □ **teacupful** *n.* (*pl.* **-fuls**).

tea dance *n.* an afternoon tea with dancing.

tea garden *n.* a garden in which afternoon tea is served to the public.

teak /tiːk/ *n.* **1** a large deciduous tree, *Tectona grandis*, native to India and SE Asia. **2** its hard durable timber, much used in shipbuilding and furniture. [Portuguese *teca* from Malayalam *tēkka*]

teal /tiːl/ *n.* & *adj.* ● *n.* (*pl.* same or **teals**) **1** any of various small freshwater ducks of the genus *Anas*, esp. *A. crecca*. **2** a dark greenish-blue colour. ● *adj.* (in full **teal blue**; hyphenated when *attrib.*) of this colour. [Middle English, related to Middle Dutch *tēling*, of unknown origin]

tea lady *n. Brit.* a woman employed to make tea in offices etc.

tea leaf *n.* **1** a dried leaf of tea, used to make a drink of tea. **2** (esp. in *pl.*) these after infusion or as dregs. **3** *Brit. rhyming slang* a thief.

team /tiːm/ *n.* & *v.* ● *n.* **1** a set of players forming one side in a game (*a cricket team*). **2** two or more persons working together. **3 a** a set of draught animals. **b** one or more animals in harness with a vehicle. ● *v.* **1** *intr.* & *tr.* (usu. foll. by *up*) join in a team or in common action (*decided to team up with them*). **2** *tr.* harness (horses etc.) in a team. **3** *tr.* (foll. by *with*) match or coordinate (clothes). [Old English *tēam* 'offspring' from a Germanic root meaning 'pull', related to TOW[1]]

team-mate *n.* a fellow member of a team or group.

team player *n.* a person who plays or works well as a member of a team and is not solely concerned with his or her own glory.

team spirit *n.* willingness to act as a member of a group rather than as an individual.

teamster /ˈtiːmstə/ *n.* **1** *N. Amer.* a lorry driver, esp. a member of the Teamsters Union. **2** a driver of a team of animals.

team-teaching *n.* teaching by a team of teachers working together.

teamwork /ˈtiːmwəːk/ *n.* the combined action of a team, group, etc., esp. when effective and efficient.

tea party *n.* a party at teatime.

tea plant see TEA *n.* 1a.

tea planter *n.* a proprietor or cultivator of a tea plantation.

teapot /ˈtiːpɒt/ *n.* a pot with a handle, spout, and lid, in which tea is brewed and from which it is poured.

teapoy /ˈtiːpɔɪ/ *n.* a small three- or four-legged table esp. for tea. [Hindi *tīn*, *tir-* 'three' + Persian *pāī* 'foot': sense and spelling influenced by TEA]

tear[1] /tɛː/ *v.* & *n.* ● *v.* (*past* **tore** /tɔː/; *past part.* **torn** /tɔːn/) **1** *tr.* (often foll. by *up*) pull apart or to pieces with some force (*tear it in half*; *tore up the letter*). **2** *tr.* **a** make a hole or rent in by tearing (*have torn my coat*). **b** make (a hole or rent). **3** *tr.* (foll. by *away*, *off*, etc.) pull violently or with some force (*tore the book away from me*; *tore off the cover*; *tore a page out*; *tore down the notice*). **4** *tr.* violently disrupt or divide (*the country was torn by civil war*; *torn by conflicting emotions*). **5** *intr. colloq.* go or travel hurriedly or impetuously (*tore across the road*). **6** *intr.* undergo tearing (*the curtain tore down the middle*). **7** *intr.* (foll. by *at* etc.) pull violently or with some force. ● *n.* **1** a hole or other damage caused by tearing. **2** a torn part of cloth etc. □ **be torn between** have difficulty in choosing between. **tear apart 1** destroy, divide utterly; distress greatly. **2** search (a place) exhaustively. **3** criticize forcefully. **tear one's hair out** behave with extreme desperation or anger. **tear into 1** attack verbally; reprimand. **2** make a vigorous start on (an activity). **tear oneself away** leave despite a strong desire to stay. **tear to shreds** *colloq.* refute or criticize thoroughly. **that's torn it** *Brit. colloq.* that has spoiled things, caused a problem, etc. □ **tearable** *adj.* **tearer** *n.* [Old English *teran*, from Germanic]

tear² /tɪə/ *n.* **1** a drop of clear salty liquid secreted by glands, that serves to moisten and wash the eye and is shed from it in grief or other strong emotions. **2** a tearlike thing; a drop. □ **in tears** crying; shedding tears. **without tears** presented so as to be learnt or done easily. □ **tearlike** *adj.* [Old English *tēar*]

tearaway /ˈtɛːrəweɪ/ *n. Brit.* **1** an impetuous or reckless young person. **2** a hooligan.

teardrop /ˈtɪədrɒp/ *n.* a single tear.

tear duct *n.* a passage through which tears pass to the eye or from the eye to the nose.

tearful /ˈtɪəfʊl, -f(ə)l/ *adj.* **1** crying or inclined to cry. **2** causing or accompanied with tears; sad (*a tearful event*). □ **tearfully** *adv.* **tearfulness** *n.*

tear gas *n. & v.* ● *n.* gas that disables by causing severe irritation to the eyes (often hyphenated when *attrib.*: *tear-gas canister*). ● *v.tr.* (**tear-gas**) (**-gases**, **-gassed**, **-gassing**) attack with tear gas.

tearing /ˈtɛːrɪŋ/ *adj.* extreme, overwhelming, violent (*in a tearing hurry*).

tear-jerker *n. colloq.* a story, film, etc., calculated to evoke sadness or sympathy. □ **tear-jerking** *n. & attrib.adj.*

tearless /ˈtɪəlɪs/ *adj.* not shedding tears. □ **tearlessly** *adv.* **tearlessness** *n.*

tear-off *attrib.adj.* (of a slip, plastic bag, etc.) that can be removed by tearing off usu. along a perforated line.

tearoom /ˈtiːruːm, -rʊm/ *n.* a small restaurant or café where tea is served.

tea rose *n.* a hybrid shrub, *Rosa odorata*, with a scent resembling that of tea.

tear sheet *n.* a page that can be removed from a newspaper or magazine etc. for use separately.

tear-stained *adj. poet.* **1** wet with tears. **2** sorrowful.

tease /tiːz/ *v. & n.* ● *v.tr.* (also *absol.*) **1 a** make fun of (a person or animal) playfully or unkindly or annoyingly. **b** tempt or allure, esp. sexually, while refusing to satisfy the desire aroused. **2** pick (wool, hair, etc.) into separate fibres. **3** dress (cloth) esp. with teasels. ● *n.* **1** *colloq.* a person fond of teasing. **2** an instance of teasing (*it was only a tease*). □ **tease out** separate by disentangling. □ **teasingly** *adv.* [Old English *tǣsan*, from West Germanic]

teasel /ˈtiːz(ə)l/ *n. & v.* (also **teazel**, **teazle**) ● *n.* **1** any plant of the genus *Dipsacus*, with large prickly heads that were formerly dried and used to raise the nap on woven cloth. **2** a device used as a substitute for teasels. ● *v.tr.* dress (cloth) with teasels. [Old English *tǣs(e)l*, = Old High German *zeisala* (as TEASE)]

teaser /ˈtiːzə/ *n.* **1** *colloq.* a hard question or task. **2** a teasing person. **3** esp. *US* a short introductory advertisement, trailer for a film, etc. **4** an inferior animal used to excite another animal before it serves or is served by the stud animal.

teaset /ˈtiːsɛt/ *n.* a set of crockery for serving tea.

tea shop *n.* esp. *Brit.* = TEAROOM.

teaspoon /ˈtiːspuːn/ *n.* **1** a small spoon for stirring tea. **2** an amount held by this. □ **teaspoonful** *n.* (*pl.* **-fuls**).

tea-strainer *n.* a small device for straining tea.

teat /tiːt/ *n.* **1** a mammary nipple, esp. of an animal. **2** *Brit.* a thing resembling this, esp. a device of rubber etc. for sucking milk from a bottle. [Middle English from Old French *tete*, probably of Germanic origin, replacing TIT³]

teatime /ˈtiːtʌɪm/ *n.* esp. *Brit.* the time in the afternoon when tea is served.

tea towel *n.* esp. *Brit.* a towel for drying washed crockery etc. Also called *tea cloth*.

tea tray *n.* a tray from which tea is served.

tea-tree *n.* **1** any of various aromatic Australasian flowering shrubs and small trees esp. of the genus *Leptospermum*, esp. the manuka (cf. TI-TREE). **2** an ornamental red-berried shrub, *Lycium barbarum* (nightshade family).

tea trolley *n.* (*US* **tea wagon**) a small wheeled trolley from which tea is served.

teazel (also **teazle**) var. of TEASEL.

TEC /tek/ *abbr.* Training and Enterprise Council.

tec /tɛk/ *n. colloq.* a detective. [abbreviation]

tech /tɛk/ *n.* (also **tec**) esp. *Brit. colloq.* **1** a technical college. **2** (esp. in phr. **high-tech**) technology. [abbreviation]

techie /ˈtɛki/ *n.* (also **techy**) (*pl.* **-ies**) *colloq.* an expert in or enthusiast for (esp. computing) technology. [TECH + -IE]

technetium /tɛkˈniːʃɪəm/ *n. Chem.* an artificially produced radioactive metallic element occurring in the fission products of uranium (symbol **Tc**). [modern Latin from Greek *tekhnētos* 'artificial', from *tekhnē* 'art']

technic /ˈtɛknɪk/ *n.* **1** (usu. in *pl.*) **a** technology. **b** technical terms, details, methods, etc. **2** technique. □ **technicist** /-sɪst/ *n.* [Latin *technicus* from Greek *tekhnikos*, from *tekhnē* 'art']

technical /ˈtɛknɪk(ə)l/ *adj. & n.* ● *adj.* **1** of or involving or concerned with the mechanical arts and applied sciences (*technical college*; *a technical education*). **2** of or relating to a particular subject or craft etc. or its techniques (*technical terms*; *technical merit*). **3** (of a book or discourse etc.) using technical language; requiring special knowledge to be understood. **4** due to mechanical failure (*a technical hitch*). **5** legally such; such in strict interpretation (*technical assault*; *lost on a technical point*). ● *n.* esp. *US* **1** a vehicle, esp. a truck, with mounted machine-guns etc. **2** a gunman who rides in such a truck. □ **technically** *adv.*

technical hitch *n.* **1** a temporary breakdown or problem in machinery etc. **2** an unexpected snag or problem.

technicality /tɛknɪˈkalɪti/ *n.* (*pl.* **-ies**) **1** the state of being technical. **2** a technical expression. **3** a technical point or detail (*was acquitted on a technicality*).

technical knockout *n. Boxing* a termination of a fight by the referee on the grounds of a contestant's inability to continue, the opponent being declared the winner.

technician /tɛkˈnɪʃ(ə)n/ *n.* **1** an expert in the practical application of a science. **2** a person skilled in the technique of an art or craft. **3** a person employed to look after technical equipment and do practical work in a laboratory etc.

Technicolor /ˈtɛknɪkʌlə/ *n.* (often *attrib.*) **1** *propr.* a process of colour cinematography using synchronized monochrome films, each of a different colour, to produce a colour print. **2** (usu. **technicolor**, *Brit.* also **technicolour**) *colloq.* **a** vivid colour. **b** artificial brilliance. □ **technicolored** *adj.* [TECHNICAL + COLOR]

technique /tɛkˈniːk/ *n.* **1** mechanical skill in an art. **2** a means or method of achieving one's purpose, esp. skilfully. **3 a** a manner of performance. **b** a manner of esp. artistic execution in relation to formal details. [French (as TECHNIC)]

techno /ˈtɛknəʊ/ *n.* a style of popular music making extensive use of electronic instruments and synthesized sound (also in *comb.*: *techno-funk*; *techno-rock*). [abbreviation of TECHNOLOGICAL]

technobabble /ˈtɛknəʊbab(ə)l/ *n. colloq.* incomprehensible technical jargon.

technocracy /tɛkˈnɒkrəsi/ *n.* (*pl.* **-ies**) **1** the government or control of society or industry by technical experts. **2** an instance or application of this. [Greek *tekhnē* 'art' + -CRACY]

technocrat /ˈtɛknəkrat/ *n.* an exponent or advocate of technocracy. □ **technocratic** /-ˈkratɪk/ *adj.* **technocratically** /-ˈkratɪk(ə)li/ *adv.*

technological /tɛknəˈlɒdʒɪk(ə)l/ *adj.* of or using technology. □ **technologically** *adv.*

technology /tɛk'nɒlədʒi/ *n.* (*pl.* **-ies**) **1** the study or use of the mechanical arts and applied sciences. **2** these subjects collectively. ◻ **technologist** *n.* [Greek *tekhnologia* 'systematic treatment' from *tekhnē* 'art']

technophile /'tɛknə(ʊ)fʌɪl/ *n.* & *adj.* ● *n.* an enthusiast about new technology. ● *adj.* **1** of or relating to a technophile. **2** compatible with new technology. ◻ **technophilia** /-'fɪlɪə/ *n.* **technophilic** /-'fɪlɪk/ *adj.*

technophobe /'tɛknə(ʊ)fəʊb/ *n.* a person who fears, dislikes, or avoids new technology. ◻ **technophobia** /-'fəʊbɪə/ *n.* **technophobic** /-'fəʊbɪk/ *adj.*

techy[1] var. of TETCHY.

techy[2] var. of TECHIE.

tectonic /tɛk'tɒnɪk/ *adj.* **1** of or relating to building or construction. **2** *Geol.* relating to the deformation of the earth's crust or to the structural changes caused by this (see PLATE TECTONICS). ◻ **tectonically** *adv.* [Late Latin *tectonicus* from Greek *tektonikos*, from *tektōn -onos* 'carpenter']

tectonics /tɛk'tɒnɪks/ *n.pl.* (usu. treated as *sing.*) **1** *Archit.* the art and process of producing practical and aesthetically pleasing buildings. **2** *Geol.* the study of large-scale structural features (cf. PLATE TECTONICS).

tectorial /tɛk'tɔːrɪəl/ *adj. Anat.* **1** forming a covering. **2** (in full **tectorial membrane**) the membrane covering the organ of Corti in the inner ear. [Latin *tectorium* 'a cover' (as TECTRIX)]

tectrix /'tɛktrɪks/ *n.* (*pl.* **tectrices** /-siːz, -'trʌɪsiːz/) = COVERT *n.* 2. [modern Latin from Latin *tegere tect-* 'to cover']

Ted /tɛd/ *n.* (also **ted**) *Brit. colloq.* a Teddy boy. [abbreviation]

ted /tɛd/ *v.tr.* (**tedded**, **tedding**) turn over and spread out (grass, hay, or straw) to dry or for a bedding etc. ◻ **tedder** *n.* [Middle English from Old Norse *tethja* 'spread manure', from *tad* 'dung', *toddi* 'small piece']

teddy /'tɛdi/ *n.* (*pl.* **-ies**) **1** (in full **teddy bear**) a soft toy bear. **2** a woman's undergarment combining vest and panties. [pet form of the names *Edward*, *Theodore*, in sense 1 with reference to *Theodore* Roosevelt, US president d. 1919, famous as a bear-hunter]

Teddy boy *n. Brit. colloq.* a youth, esp. of the 1950s, affecting an Edwardian style of dress and appearance, usu. a long jacket and drainpipe trousers. [*Teddy*, pet form of *Edward*]

Te Deum /tiː 'diːəm, teɪ 'deɪəm/ *n.* **1 a** a hymn beginning *Te Deum laudamus*, 'We praise Thee, O God'. **b** the music for this. **2** an expression of thanksgiving or exultation. [Latin]

tedious /'tiːdɪəs/ *adj.* tiresomely long; wearisome. ◻ **tediously** *adv.* **tediousness** *n.* [Middle English from Old French *tedieus* or Late Latin *taediosus* (as TEDIUM)]

tedium /'tiːdɪəm/ *n.* the state of being tedious; boredom. [Latin *taedium* from *taedēre* 'to weary']

tee[1] /tiː/ *n.* = T[1]. [phonetic spelling]

tee[2] /tiː/ *n.* & *v.* ● *n.* **1** *Golf* **a** a cleared space from which a golf ball is struck at the beginning of play for each hole. **b** a small support of wood or plastic from which a ball is struck at a tee. **2** a mark aimed at in bowls, quoits, curling, etc. ● *v.tr.* (**tees, teed**) (often foll. by *up*) *Golf* place (a ball) on a tee ready to strike it. ◻ **tee off 1** *Golf* play a ball from a tee. **2** *colloq.* start, begin. [earlier (17th-c.) *teaz*, of unknown origin: in sense 2 perhaps = TEE[1]]

tee-hee /tiː'hiː/ *n.* & *v.* (also **te-hee**) ● *n.* **1** a titter. **2** a restrained or contemptuous laugh. ● *v.intr.* (**tee-hees, tee-heed**) titter or laugh in this way. [imitative]

teem[1] /tiːm/ *v.intr.* **1** be abundant (*fish teem in these waters*). **2** (foll. by *with*) be full of or swarming with (*teeming with fish*; *teeming with ideas*). [Old English *tēman* etc. 'give birth to' from Germanic, related to TEAM]

teem[2] /tiːm/ *v.intr.* (often foll. by *down*) (of water etc.) flow copiously; pour (*it was teeming with rain*). [Middle English *tēmen* from Old Norse *tœma*, from *tómr* (*adj.*) 'empty']

teen /tiːn/ *adj.* & *n.* ● *adj.* = TEENAGE. ● *n.* = TEENAGER. [abbreviation of TEENAGE, TEENAGER]

-teen /tiːn/ *suffix* forming the names of numerals from 13 to 19. [Old English inflected form of TEN]

teenage /'tiːneɪdʒ/ *adj.* relating to or characteristic of teenagers. ◻ **teenaged** *adj.*

teenager /'tiːneɪdʒə/ *n.* a person from 13 to 19 years of age.

teens /tiːnz/ *n.pl.* the years of one's age from 13 to 19 (*in one's teens*).

teensy /'tiːnzi, -si/ *adj.* (**teensier, teensiest**) *colloq.* = TEENY.

teensy-weensy *adj.* = TEENY-WEENY.

teeny /'tiːni/ *adj.* (**teenier, teeniest**) *colloq.* tiny. [variant of TINY]

teeny-bopper *n. colloq.* a young teenager, usu. a girl, who keenly follows the latest fashions in clothes, pop music, etc.

teeny-weeny *adj.* very tiny.

teepee var. of TEPEE.

tee shirt var. of T-SHIRT.

teeter /'tiːtə/ *v.intr.* **1** totter; stand or move unsteadily. **2** hesitate; be indecisive. ◻ **teeter on the brink** (or **edge**) be in imminent danger (of disaster etc.). [variant of dialect *titter*]

teeth *pl.* of TOOTH.

teethe /tiːð/ *v.intr.* grow or cut teeth, esp. milk teeth. ◻ **teething** *n.*

teething ring *n.* a small ring for an infant to bite on while teething.

teething troubles *n.pl.* initial difficulties in an enterprise etc., regarded as temporary.

teetotal /tiː'təʊt(ə)l/ *adj.* advocating or characterized by total abstinence from alcoholic drink. ◻ **teetotalism** *n.* [reduplication of TOTAL]

teetotaller /tiː'təʊt(ə)lə/ *n.* (*US* **teetotaler**) a person advocating or practising abstinence from alcoholic drink.

teetotum /tiː'təʊtəm/ *n.* **1** a spinning top with four sides lettered to determine whether the spinner has won or lost. **2** any top spun with the fingers. [*T* (the letter on one side) + Latin *totum* 'the whole' (stakes), for which *T* stood]

teff /tɛf/ *n.* an African cereal, *Eragrostis tef.* [Amharic *ṭêf*]

TEFL /'tɛf(ə)l/ *abbr.* teaching of English as a foreign language.

Teflon /'tɛflɒn/ *n. propr.* polytetrafluoroethylene, esp. used as a non-stick coating for kitchen utensils. [*te*tra- + *fluor-* + *-on*]

teg /tɛg/ *n.* a sheep in its second year. [16th c.: origin unknown]

tegument /'tɛgjʊm(ə)nt/ *n.* an integument, esp. of a flatworm. ◻ **tegumental** /-'mɛnt(ə)l/ *adj.* **tegumentary** /-'mɛnt(ə)ri/ *adj.* [Latin *tegumentum* from *tegere* 'to cover']

te-hee var. of TEE-HEE.

tektite /'tɛktʌɪt/ *n. Geol.* a small black glassy object found in numbers on the ground or ocean bed in certain areas, and thought to result from meteorite impacts. [German *Tektit* from Greek *tēktos* 'molten', from *tēkō* 'melt']

tel. *abbr.* (also **Tel.**) telephone.

telaesthesia /tɛlɪs'θiːzɪə/ *n.* (*US* **telesthesia**) *Psychol.* the supposed perception of distant occurrences or objects otherwise than by the recognized senses. ◻ **telaesthetic** /-'θɛtɪk/ *adj.* [modern Latin, formed as TELE- + Greek *aisthēsis* 'perception']

telamon /'tɛləmən, -məʊn/ *n.* (*pl.* **telamones** /-'məʊniːz/) *Archit.* a male figure used as a pillar to support an entablature. [Latin *telamones* from Greek *telamōnes*, pl. of *Telamōn*, the name of a mythical hero]

telco /'tɛlkəʊ/ *n.* (*pl.* **-os**) *US* a telecommunications company. [abbreviation]

tele- /'tɛli/ *comb. form* **1** at or to a distance (*telekinesis*). **2** forming names of instruments for operating over long distances (*telescope*). **3** television (*telecast*). **4** done by means of the telephone (*telesales*). [Greek *tēle-* from *tēle* 'far off': sense 3 from TELEVISION: sense 4 from TELEPHONE]

tele-ad /'tɛlɪad/ *n.* an advertisement placed in a newspaper etc. by telephone.

telebanking /'tɛlɪbaŋkɪŋ/ *n.* a banking system whereby computerized transactions are effected by telephone.

telecamera /'tɛlɪkam(ə)rə/ *n.* **1** a television camera. **2** a camera with a telephoto lens.

telecast /'tɛlɪkɑːst/ *n. & v.* ● *n.* a television broadcast. ● *v.tr.* transmit by television. □ **telecaster** *n.* [TELE- + BROADCAST]

telecine /'tɛlɪsɪni/ *n.* **1** the broadcasting of cinema film on television. **2** equipment for doing this. [TELE- + CINEMA]

telecommunication /ˌtɛlɪkəmjuːnɪ'keɪʃ(ə)n/ *n.* **1** communication over a distance by cable, telegraph, telephone, or broadcasting. **2** (usu. in *pl.*) the branch of technology concerned with this. [French *télécommunication* (as TELE-, COMMUNICATION)]

telecommute /ˌtɛlɪkə'mjuːt/ *v.intr.* work from home, communicating by telephone, telex, modem, etc. □ **telecommuter** *n.*

telecoms /'tɛlɪkɒmz/ *n.* (also **telecomms**) (also *attrib.*) telecommunications (see TELECOMMUNICATION 2). [abbreviation]

teleconference /'tɛlɪkɒnf(ə)r(ə)ns/ *n.* a conference with participants in different locations linked by telecommunication devices. □ **teleconferencing** *n.*

telecottage /'tɛlɪkɒtɪdʒ/ *n.* a centre fitted with office equipment (computer, photocopier, fax machine, etc.) for people working freelance or at a distance from an employer etc.

teledu /'tɛlɪduː/ *n.* a badger, *Mydaus javanensis*, of Java and Sumatra, that secretes a foul-smelling liquid when attacked. [Javanese]

tele-evangelist var. of TELEVANGELIST.

telefacsimile /ˌtɛlɪfak'sɪmɪli/ *n.* facsimile transmission (see FACSIMILE *n.* 2).

telefax /'tɛlɪfaks/ *n. propr.* **1** = TELEFACSIMILE. **2** a document etc. sent by facsimile transmission. [abbreviation]

telefilm /'tɛlɪfɪlm/ *n.* = TELECINE.

telegenic /tɛlɪ'dʒɛnɪk/ *adj.* having an appearance or manner that looks pleasing on television. [TELEVISION + *-genic* in PHOTOGENIC]

telegony /tɪ'lɛg(ə)ni/ *n. Biol.* the supposed influence of a previous sire on the offspring of a dam with other sires. □ **telegonic** /tɛlɪ'gɒnɪk/ *adj.* [TELE- + Greek *-gonia* 'begetting']

telegram /'tɛlɪgram/ *n.* a message sent by telegraph and then usu. delivered in written form (in UK official use since 1981 only for international messages). [TELE- + -GRAM, on the pattern of TELEGRAPH]

telegraph /'tɛlɪgrɑːf/ *n. & v.* ● *n.* **1 a** a system of or device for transmitting messages or signals to a distance esp. by making and breaking an electrical connection. **b** (*attrib.*) used in this system (*telegraph wire*). **2** (in full **telegraph board**) a board displaying scores or other information at a match, race meeting, etc. ● *v.* **1** *tr.* send a message by telegraph to. **2** *tr.* send by telegraph. **3** *tr.* give an advance indication of. **4** *intr.* make signals (*telegraphed to me to come up*). □ **telegrapher** /'tɛlɪgrɑːfə, tɪ'lɛgrəfə/ *n.* [French *télégraphe* (as TELE-, -GRAPH)]

telegraphese /ˌtɛlɪgrə'fiːz/ *n. colloq.* or *joc.* an abbreviated style usual in telegrams.

telegraphic /tɛlɪ'grafɪk/ *adj.* **1** of or by telegraphs or telegrams. **2** economically worded. □ **telegraphically** *adv.*

telegraphic address *n.* an abbreviated or other registered address for use in telegrams.

telegraphist /tɪ'lɛgrəfɪst/ *n.* a person skilled or employed in telegraphy.

telegraph key *n.* a device for making and breaking the electric circuit of a telegraph system.

telegraph plant *n.* a tropical Asian leguminous plant, *Codariocalyx motorius*, whose leaves have a spontaneous jerking motion.

telegraph pole *n.* a pole used to carry telegraph or telephone wires above the ground.

telegraphy /tɪ'lɛgrəfi/ *n.* the science or practice of using or constructing communication systems for the reproduction of information.

Telegu var. of TELUGU.

telekinesis /ˌtɛlɪkʌɪ'niːsɪs, -kɪ'niːsɪs/ *n. Psychol.* movement of objects at a distance supposedly by paranormal means. □ **telekinetic** /-'nɛtɪk/ *adj.* [modern Latin (as TELE-, Greek *kinēsis* 'motion' from *kineō* 'move')]

telemark /'tɛlɪmɑːk/ *n. & v. Skiing* ● *n.* a swing turn with one ski advanced and the knee bent, used to change direction or stop short. ● *v.intr.* perform this turn. [*Telemark*, a district in Norway]

telemarketing /'tɛlɪmɑːkɪtɪŋ/ *n.* the marketing of goods etc. by means of usu. unsolicited telephone calls, or by inviting telephone calls. □ **telemarketer** *n.*

telemessage /'tɛlɪmɛsɪdʒ/ *n.* a message sent by telephone or telex and delivered in written form (in UK official use since 1981 for inland messages, replacing *telegram*).

telemeter /'tɛlɪmiːtə, tɪ'lɛmɪtə/ *n. & v.* ● *n.* an apparatus for recording the readings of an instrument and transmitting them by radio. ● *v.* **1** *intr.* record readings in this way. **2** *tr.* transmit (readings etc.) to a distant receiving set or station. □ **telemetric** /-'mɛtrɪk/ *adj.* **telemetry** /tɪ'lɛmɪtri/ *n.*

teleology /tɛlɪ'ɒlədʒi, tiːl-/ *n.* (*pl.* **-ies**) *Philos.* **1** the explanation of phenomena by the purpose they serve rather than by postulated causes. **2** *Theol.* the doctrine of design and purpose in the material world. □ **teleologic** /-ə'lɒdʒɪk/ *adj.* **teleological** /-ə'lɒdʒɪk(ə)l/ *adj.* **teleologically** /-ə'lɒdʒɪk(ə)li/ *adv.* **teleologism** *n.* **teleologist** *n.* [modern Latin *teleologia*, from Greek *telos teleos* 'end' + -LOGY]

teleost /'tɛlɪɒst, 'tiːl-/ *n. & adj.* ● *n.* any fish of the subclass Teleostei, comprising the bony fishes and including most familiar kinds of fish except sharks, rays, sturgeons, and lungfishes. ● *adj.* of or relating to this subclass. [Greek *teleo-* 'complete' + *osteon* 'bone']

telepath /'tɛlɪpaθ/ *n.* a telepathic person. [back-formation from TELEPATHY]

telepathy /tɪ'lɛpəθi/ *n.* the supposed communication of thoughts or ideas otherwise than by the known senses. □ **telepathic** /tɛlɪ'paθɪk/ *adj.* **telepathically** /tɛlɪ'paθɪk(ə)li/ *adv.* **telepathist** *n.* **telepathize** *v.tr. & intr.* (also **-ise**).

telephone /'tɛlɪfəʊn/ *n. & v.* ● *n.* **1** an apparatus for transmitting sound (esp. speech) to a distance by wire or cord or radio, esp. by converting acoustic vibrations to electrical signals. **2** a transmitting and receiving instrument used in this. **3** a system of communication using a network of telephones. ● *v.* **1** *tr.* speak to (a person) by telephone. **2** *tr.* send (a message) by telephone. **3** *intr.* make a telephone call. □ **on the telephone 1** having a telephone. **2** by use of or using the telephone. **over the telephone** by use of or using the telephone. □ **telephoner** *n.* **telephonic** /-'fɒnɪk/ *adj.* **telephonically** /-'fɒnɪk(ə)li/ *adv.*

telephone book *n.* = TELEPHONE DIRECTORY.

telephone booth *n.* a public booth or enclosure from which telephone calls can be made.

telephone box *n. Brit.* = TELEPHONE BOOTH.

telephone call *n.* = CALL *n.* 4.

telephone directory *n.* a book listing telephone subscribers and numbers in a particular area.

telephone exchange *n.* = EXCHANGE *n.* 3.

telephone kiosk *n. Brit.* = TELEPHONE BOOTH.

telephone number *n.* **1** a number assigned to a particular telephone and used in making connections to it. **2** (often in *pl.*) *colloq.* a number with many digits, esp. representing a large sum of money.

telephone operator *n.* esp. *US* an operator in a telephone exchange.

telephonist /tɪˈlɛf(ə)nɪst/ *n. Brit.* an operator in a telephone exchange or at a switchboard.

telephony /tɪˈlɛf(ə)ni/ *n.* the use or a system of telephones.

telephoto /ˈtɛlɪfəʊtəʊ/ *n.* (*pl.* **-os**) (in full **telephoto lens**) a lens with a longer focal length than standard, giving a narrow field of view and a magnified image.

telepoint /ˈtɛlɪpɔɪnt/ *n.* **1** a place where a cordless telephone may be connected to the telephone network. **2** a system providing or using such places.

teleport /ˈtɛlɪpɔːt/ *v.tr. Psychol.* move by telekinesis. □ **teleportation** /-ˈteɪʃ(ə)n/ *n.* [TELE- + PORT[4] 3]

telepresence /ˈtɛlɪprɛz(ə)ns/ *n.* **1** the use of virtual reality technology esp. for remote control of machinery or for apparent participation in distant events. **2** a sensation of being elsewhere created in this way.

teleprinter /ˈtɛlɪprɪntə/ *n. Brit.* a device for transmitting telegraph messages as they are keyed, and for printing messages received.

teleprompter /ˈtɛlɪprɒm(p)tə/ *n.* a device beside a television or cinema camera that slowly unrolls a speaker's script out of sight of the audience (cf. AUTOCUE).

telerecord /ˈtɛlɪrɪkɔːd/ *v.tr.* record for television broadcasting.

telerecording /ˈtɛlɪrɪkɔːdɪŋ/ *n.* a recorded television broadcast.

telesales /ˈtɛlɪseɪlz/ *n.pl.* selling by means of the telephone.

telescope /ˈtɛlɪskəʊp/ *n.* & *v.* ● *n.* **1** an optical instrument using lenses or mirrors or both to make distant objects appear nearer and larger. **2** = RADIO TELESCOPE. ● *v.* **1** *tr.* press or drive (sections of a tube, colliding vehicles, etc.) together so that one slides into another like the sections of a folding telescope. **2** *intr.* close or be driven or be capable of closing in this way. **3** *tr.* compress so as to occupy less space or time. [Italian *telescopio* or modern Latin *telescopium* (as TELE-, -SCOPE)]

telescopic /tɛlɪˈskɒpɪk/ *adj.* **1 a** of, relating to, or made with a telescope (*telescopic observations*). **b** visible only through a telescope (*telescopic stars*). **2** (esp. of a lens) able to focus on and magnify distant objects. **3** consisting of sections that telescope. □ **telescopically** *adv.*

telescopic sight *n.* a telescope used for sighting on a rifle etc.

teleshopping /ˈtɛlɪʃɒpɪŋ/ *n.* the ordering of goods by customers using a telephone or direct computer link.

telesoftware /tɛlɪˈsɒftwɛː/ *n. Brit.* software transmitted or broadcast to receiving terminals.

telesthesia *US* var. of TELAESTHESIA.

teletex /ˈtɛlɪtɛks/ *n. Brit. propr.* an electronic text transmission system.

teletext /ˈtɛlɪtɛkst/ *n.* a news and information service, in the form of text and graphics, from a computer source transmitted to televisions with appropriate receivers.

telethon /ˈtɛlɪθɒn/ *n.* an exceptionally long television programme, esp. to raise money for a charity. [TELE- + *-thon* as in MARATHON]

teletype /ˈtɛlɪtʌɪp/ *n.* & *v.* ● *n. propr.* a kind of teleprinter. ● *v.* **1** *intr.* operate a teleprinter. **2** *tr.* send by means of a teleprinter.

teletypewriter /tɛlɪˈtʌɪprʌɪtə/ *n.* esp. *US* = TELEPRINTER.

televangelist /tɛlɪˈvan(d)ʒ(ə)lɪst/ *n.* (also **tele-evangelist** /tɛlɪɪˈvan-/) esp. *US* an evangelical preacher who appears regularly on television to promote beliefs and appeal for funds. □ **televangelism** *n.*

televiewer /ˈtɛlɪvjuːə/ *v.tr.* a person who watches television. □ **televiewing** *adj.*

televise /ˈtɛlɪvʌɪz/ *v.tr.* transmit by television. □ **televisable** *adj.* [back-formation from TELEVISION]

television /ˈtɛlɪvɪʒ(ə)n, tɛlɪˈvɪʒ(ə)n/ *n.* **1** a system for reproducing on a screen visual images transmitted (usu. with sound) by radio signals. **2** (in full **television set**) a device with a screen for receiving these signals. **3** television broadcasting generally.

televisual /tɛlɪˈvɪʒjʊəl, -zj-/ *adj.* relating to or suitable for television. □ **televisually** *adv.*

telework /ˈtɛlɪwəːk/ *v.intr.* = TELECOMMUTE. □ **teleworker** *n.*

telex /ˈtɛlɛks/ *n.* & *v.* (also **Telex**) ● *n.* an international system of telegraphy with printed messages transmitted and received by teleprinters using the public telecommunications network. ● *v.tr.* send or communicate with by telex. [TELEPRINTER + EXCHANGE]

tell[1] /tɛl/ *v.* (*past* and *past part.* **told** /təʊld/) **1** *tr.* relate or narrate in speech or writing; give an account of (*tell me a story*). **2** *tr.* make known; express in words; divulge (*tell me your name*; *tell me what you want*). **3** *tr.* reveal or signify to (a person) (*your face tells me everything*). **4** *tr.* **a** utter (*don't tell lies*). **b** warn (*I told you so*). **5** *intr.* **a** (often foll. by *of*, *about*) divulge information or a description; reveal a secret (*I told of the plan*; *promise you won't tell*). **b** (foll. by *on*) *colloq.* inform against (a person). **6** *tr.* (foll. by *to* + infin.) give (a person) a direction or order (*tell them to wait*; *do as you are told*). **7** *tr.* assure (*it's true, I tell you*). **8** *tr.* explain in writing; instruct (*this book tells you how to cook*). **9** *tr.* decide, determine, distinguish (*cannot tell which button to press*; *how do you tell one from the other?*). **10** *intr.* **a** (often foll. by *on*) produce a noticeable effect (*every disappointment tells*; *the strain was beginning to tell on me*). **b** reveal the truth (*time will tell*). **c** have an influence (*the evidence tells against you*). **11** *tr.* (often *absol.*) count (votes) at a meeting, election, etc. □ **as far as one can tell** judging from the available information. **tell apart** distinguish between (usu. with *neg.* or *interrog.*: *could not tell them apart*). **tell me another** *colloq.* an expression of incredulity. **tell off 1** *colloq.* reprimand, scold. **2** count off or detach for duty. **tell a tale** (or **its own tale**) be significant or revealing. **tell tales** report a discreditable fact about another. **tell that to the marines** see MARINE. **tell the time** determine the time from the face of a clock or watch. **that would be telling** *colloq.* that would be to reveal too much (esp. secret or confidential) information. **there is no telling** it is impossible to know (*there's no telling what may happen*). **you're telling me** *colloq.* I agree wholeheartedly. □ **tellable** *adj.* [Old English *tellan*, from Germanic]

tell[2] /tɛl/ *n. Archaeol.* an artificial mound in the Middle East etc. formed by the accumulated remains of ancient settlements. [Arabic *tall* 'hillock']

teller /ˈtɛlə/ *n.* **1** a person employed to receive and pay out money in a bank etc. **2** a person who counts (votes). **3** a person who tells esp. stories (*a teller of tales*). □ **tellership** *n.*

telling /ˈtɛlɪŋ/ *adj.* **1** having a marked effect; striking. **2** significant. □ **tellingly** *adv.*

telling-off *n.* (*pl.* **tellings-off**) esp. *Brit. colloq.* a reproof or reprimand.

tell-tale *n.* **1** a person who reveals (esp. discreditable) information about another's private affairs or behaviour. **2** (*attrib.*) that reveals or betrays (*a tell-tale smile*). **3** a device for automatic monitoring or registering of a process etc.

tellurian /tɛˈl(j)ʊərɪən/ *adj.* & *n.* ● *adj.* of or inhabiting the earth. ● *n.* an inhabitant of the earth. [Latin *tellus -uris* 'earth']

telluric /tɛˈl(j)ʊərɪk/ *adj.* **1** of the earth as a planet. **2** of the soil. **3** *Chem.* of tellurium, esp. in its higher valency. □ **tellurate** /-reɪt/ *n.* [Latin *tellus -uris* 'earth': sense 3 from TELLURIUM]

tellurium /tɛˈl(j)ʊərɪəm/ *n. Chem.* a rare brittle lustrous silver-white element occurring naturally in ores of gold and silver, used in semiconductors (symbol Te). ▫ **telluride** /ˈtɛljʊrʌɪd/ *n.* **tellurite** /ˈtɛljʊrʌɪt/ *n.* **tellurous** *adj.* [Latin *tellus -uris* 'earth', probably named in contrast to *uranium*]

telly /ˈtɛli/ *n.* (*pl.* **-ies**) esp. *Brit. colloq.* **1** television. **2** a television set. [abbreviation]

telophase /ˈtiːləfeɪz, ˈtɛl-/ *n. Biol.* the final stage of cell division, in which the nuclei of the daughter cells are formed. [Greek *telos* 'end' + PHASE]

telpher /ˈtɛlfə/ *n.* a system for transporting goods etc. by electrically driven trucks or cable cars. ▫ **telpherage** *n.* [TELE- + -PHORE]

telson /ˈtɛls(ə)n/ *n.* the last segment in the abdomen of crustaceans and arachnids. [Greek, = limit]

Telugu /ˈtɛləguː/ *n.* (also **Telegu**) (*pl.* same or **Telugus**) **1** a member of a Dravidian people in SE India. **2** the language of this people. [Telugu]

temblor /tɛmˈblɔː/ *n. US* an earthquake. [American Spanish]

temerarious /tɛməˈrɛːrɪəs/ *adj. literary* reckless, rash. [Latin *temerarius* from *temere* 'rashly']

temerity /tɪˈmɛrɪti/ *n.* **1** rashness. **2** audacity, impudence. [Latin *temeritas* from *temere* 'rashly']

temp /tɛmp/ *n. & v. colloq.* ● *n.* a temporary employee, esp. a secretary. ● *v.intr.* work as a temp. [abbreviation]

temp.[1] /tɛmp/ *abbr.* temperature.

temp.[2] /tɛmp/ *abbr.* in the time of (*temp. Henry I*). [Latin *tempore*, ablative of *tempus* 'time']

temper /ˈtɛmpə/ *n. & v.* ● *n.* **1** habitual or temporary disposition of mind esp. as regards composure (*a person of a placid temper*). **2** irritation or anger (*in a fit of temper*). **3** a tendency to have fits of anger (*have a temper*). **4** composure or calmness (*keep one's temper*; *lose one's temper*). **5** the condition of metal as regards hardness and elasticity. ● *v.tr.* **1** bring (metal or clay) to a proper hardness or consistency. **2** (foll. by *with*) moderate or mitigate (*temper justice with mercy*). **3** tune or modulate (a piano etc.) so as to distance intervals correctly. ▫ **in a bad temper** angry, peevish. **in a good temper** in an amiable mood. **out of temper** angry, peevish. **show temper** be petulant. ▫ **temperative** /-ətɪv/ *adj.* **tempered** *adj.* **temperer** *n.* [Old English *temprian* (*v.*) from Latin *temperare* 'mingle': influenced by Old French *temprer, tremper*]

tempera /ˈtɛmp(ə)rə/ *n.* **1** a method of painting using an emulsion e.g. of pigment with egg, esp. in fine art on canvas. **2** this emulsion. [Italian, in *pingere a tempera* 'paint in distemper']

temperament /ˈtɛmp(ə)rəm(ə)nt/ *n.* **1** a person's distinct nature and character, esp. as determined by physical constitution and permanently affecting behaviour (*a nervous temperament*; *the artistic temperament*). **2** a creative or spirited personality (*was full of temperament*). **3** an adjustment of intervals in tuning a piano etc. so as to fit the scale for use in all keys, esp. (**equal temperament**) an adjustment in which the 12 semitones are at equal intervals. [Middle English from Latin *temperamentum* (as TEMPER)]

temperamental /tɛmp(ə)rəˈmɛnt(ə)l/ *adj.* **1** of or having temperament. **2 a** (of a person) liable to erratic or moody behaviour. **b** (of a thing, e.g. a machine) working unpredictably; unreliable. ▫ **temperamentally** *adv.*

temperance /ˈtɛmp(ə)r(ə)ns/ *n.* **1** moderation or self-restraint esp. in eating and drinking. **2 a** total or partial abstinence from alcoholic drink. **b** (*attrib.*) advocating or concerned with abstinence. [Middle English via Anglo-French *temperaunce* from Latin *temperantia* (as TEMPER)]

temperate /ˈtɛmp(ə)rət/ *adj.* **1** avoiding excess; self-restrained. **2** moderate. **3** (of a region or climate) characterized by mild temperatures. **4** abstemious. ▫ **temperately** *adv.* **temperateness** *n.* [Middle English from Latin *temperatus*, past part. of *temperare* 'mingle']

temperate zone *n.* the belt of the earth between the frigid and the torrid zones.

temperature /ˈtɛmp(ə)rətʃə/ *n.* **1** the degree or intensity of heat of a body in relation to others, esp. as shown by a thermometer or perceived by touch etc. **2** *Med.* the degree of internal heat of the body. **3** *colloq.* a body temperature above the normal (*have a temperature*). **4** the degree of excitement in a discussion etc. ▫ **take a person's temperature** ascertain a person's body temperature, esp. as a diagnostic aid. [French *température* or Latin *temperatura* (as TEMPER)]

temperature-humidity index *n.* a quantity giving the measure of discomfort due to the combined effects of the temperature and humidity of the air.

temperature inversion *n. Meteorol.* = INVERSION 4.

-tempered /ˈtɛmpəd/ *comb. form* having a specified temper or disposition (*bad-tempered*; *hot-tempered*). ▫ **-temperedly** *adv.* **-temperedness** *n.*

tempest /ˈtɛmpɪst/ *n.* **1** a violent windy storm. **2** violent agitation or tumult. [Middle English from Old French *tempest(e)*, ultimately via Latin *tempestas* 'season, storm', from *tempus* 'time']

tempestuous /tɛmˈpɛstjʊəs/ *adj.* **1** stormy. **2** (of a person, emotion, etc.) turbulent, violent, passionate. ▫ **tempestuously** *adv.* **tempestuousness** *n.* [Late Latin *tempestuosus* (as TEMPEST)]

tempi *pl.* of TEMPO.

Templar /ˈtɛmplə/ *n.* **1** a lawyer or law student with chambers in the Temple, London. **2** *hist.* = KNIGHT TEMPLAR. [Middle English from Anglo-French *templer*, Old French *templier*, medieval Latin *templarius* (as TEMPLE[1])]

template /ˈtɛmplɪt, -pleɪt/ *n.* (also **templet**) **1 a** a pattern or gauge, usu. a piece of thin board or metal plate, used as a guide in cutting or drilling metal, stone, wood, etc. **b** a flat card or plastic pattern esp. for cutting cloth for patchwork etc. **2** a timber or plate used to distribute the weight in a wall or under a beam etc. **3** *Biochem.* the molecular pattern governing the assembly of a protein etc. [originally *templet*, probably from TEMPLE[3] + -ET[1]: influenced by *plate*]

temple[1] /ˈtɛmp(ə)l/ *n.* **1** a building devoted to the worship, or regarded as the dwelling place, of a god or gods or other objects of religious reverence. **2** *hist.* either of two successive religious buildings of the Jews in Jerusalem. **3** *N. Amer.* a synagogue. **4** a place of Christian public worship, esp. a Protestant church in France. **5** a place in which God is regarded as residing, esp. a Christian's person or body. [Old English *temp(e)l*, reinforced in Middle English by Old French *temple*, from Latin *templum* 'open or consecrated space']

temple[2] /ˈtɛmp(ə)l/ *n.* (often in *pl.*) the flat part of either side of the head between the forehead and the ear. [Middle English from Old French, ultimately from Latin *tempora*, pl. of *tempus*]

temple[3] /ˈtɛmp(ə)l/ *n.* a device in a loom for keeping the cloth stretched. [Middle English from Old French, originally the same word as TEMPLE[2]]

temple block *n.* a percussion instrument consisting of a hollow block of wood which is struck with a stick.

templet var. of TEMPLATE.

tempo /ˈtɛmpəʊ/ *n.* (*pl.* **-os** or **tempi** /-piː/) **1** *Mus.* the speed at which music is or should be played, esp. as characteristic (*waltz tempo*). **2** the rate of motion or activity (*the tempo of the war is quickening*). [Italian from Latin *tempus* 'time']

temporal[1] /ˈtɛmp(ə)r(ə)l/ *adj.* **1** of worldly as opposed to spiritual affairs; of this life; secular. **2** of or relating to time. **3** *Gram.* relating to or denoting time or tense (*temporal conjunction*). ▫ **temporally** *adv.* [Middle English from Old French *temporel*, or from Latin *temporalis* from *tempus -oris* 'time']

temporal[2] /ˈtɛmpər(ə)l/ *adj. Anat.* of or situated in the temples of the head (*temporal artery*; *temporal bone*). [Middle English from Late Latin *temporalis* from *tempora* 'the temples' (as TEMPLE[2])]

temporality /tɛmpəˈralɪti/ *n.* (*pl.* **-ies**) **1** temporariness. **2** (usu. in *pl.*) a secular possession, esp. the properties and revenues of a religious corporation or an ecclesiastic. [Middle English from Late Latin *temporalitas* (as TEMPORAL[1])]

temporal lobe *n.* each of the paired lobes of the brain lying beneath the temples, including areas concerned with the understanding of speech.

temporal power *n.* the power of an ecclesiastic, esp. the Pope, in temporal matters.

temporary /ˈtɛmp(ə)rəri/ *adj.* & *n.* ● *adj.* lasting or meant to last only for a limited time (*temporary buildings*; *temporary relief*). ● *n.* (*pl.* **-ies**) a person employed temporarily (cf. TEMP). ◻ **temporarily** *adv.* **temporariness** *n.* [Latin *temporarius* from *tempus -oris* 'time']

temporize /ˈtɛmpərʌɪz/ *v.intr.* (also **-ise**) **1** avoid committing oneself so as to gain time; employ delaying tactics. **2** comply temporarily with the requirements of the occasion, adopt a time-serving policy. ◻ **temporization** /-ˈzeɪʃ(ə)n/ *n.* **temporizer** *n.* [French *temporiser* 'bide one's time' from medieval Latin *temporizare* 'delay', from *tempus -oris* 'time']

tempt /tɛm(p)t/ *v.tr.* **1** entice or incite (a person) to do a wrong or forbidden thing (*tempted him to steal it*). **2** allure, attract. **3** risk provoking (esp. an abstract force or power) (*would be tempting fate to try it*). **4** *archaic* make trial of; try the resolution of (*God did tempt Abraham*). ◻ **be tempted to** be strongly disposed to (*I am tempted to question this*). ◻ **temptable** *adj.* **temptability** /-ˈbɪlɪti/ *n.* [Middle English via Old French *tenter*, *tempter* 'test' from Latin *temptare* 'handle, test, try']

temptation /tɛm(p)ˈteɪʃ(ə)n/ *n.* **1 a** the act or an instance of tempting; the state of being tempted; incitement esp. to wrongdoing. **b** (**the Temptation**) the tempting of Christ by the Devil (see Matt. 4). **2** an attractive thing or course of action. **3** *archaic* putting to the test. [Middle English via Old French *tentacion*, *temptacion* from Latin *temptatio -onis* (as TEMPT)]

tempter /ˈtɛm(p)tə/ *n.* (*fem.* **temptress** /-trɪs/) **1** a person who tempts. **2** (**the Tempter**) the Devil. [Middle English from Old French *tempteur* from ecclesiastical Latin *temptator -oris* (as TEMPT)]

tempting /ˈtɛm(p)tɪŋ/ *adj.* **1** attractive, inviting. **2** enticing to evil. ◻ **temptingly** *adv.*

tempura /ˈtɛmpʊrə/ *n.* a Japanese dish of fish, shellfish, or vegetables, fried in batter. [Japanese]

ten /tɛn/ *n.* & *adj.* ● *n.* **1** one more than nine. **2** a symbol for this (10, x, X). **3** a size etc. denoted by ten. **4** ten o'clock. **5** a card with ten pips. **6** a set of ten. ● *adj.* **1** that amount to ten. **2** (as a round number) several (*ten times as easy*). ◻ **ten to one** very probably. [Old English *tīen*, *tēn*, from Germanic]

ten. *abbr.* *Mus.* tenuto.

tenable /ˈtɛnəb(ə)l/ *adj.* **1** that can be maintained or defended against attack or objection (*a tenable position*; *a tenable theory*). **2** (foll. by *for*, *by*) (of an office etc.) that can be held for (a specified period) or by (a specified class of person). ◻ **tenability** /-ˈbɪlɪti/ *n.* **tenableness** *n.* [French from *tenir* 'hold', from Latin *tenēre*]

tenace /ˈtɛnəs/ *n.* *Bridge* etc. **1** two cards, one ranking next above, and the other next below, a card held by an opponent. **2** the holding of such cards. [French from Spanish *tenaza*, literally 'pincers']

tenacious /tɪˈneɪʃəs/ *adj.* **1** (often foll. by *of*) keeping a firm hold of property, principles, life, etc.; not readily relinquishing. **2** (of memory) retentive. **3** holding fast. **4** strongly cohesive. **5** persistent, resolute. **6** adhesive, sticky. ◻ **tenaciously** *adv.* **tenaciousness** *n.* **tenacity** /tɪˈnasɪti/ *n.* [Latin *tenax -acis* from *tenēre* 'hold']

tenaculum /tɪˈnakjʊləm/ *n.* (*pl.* **tenacula** /-lə/) a surgeon's sharp hook for picking up arteries etc. [Latin, = holding instrument, from *tenēre* 'hold']

tenancy /ˈtɛnənsi/ *n.* (*pl.* **-ies**) **1** the status of a tenant; possession as a tenant. **2** the duration or period of this.

tenant /ˈtɛnənt/ *n.* & *v.* ● *n.* **1** a person who rents land or property from a landlord. **2** (often foll. by *of*) the occupant of a place. **3** *Law* a person holding real property by private ownership. ● *v.tr.* occupy as a tenant. ◻ **tenantable** *adj.* **tenantless** *adj.* [Middle English from Old French, pres. part. of *tenir* 'hold', from Latin *tenēre*]

tenant farmer *n.* a person who farms rented land.

tenant right *n.* *Brit.* the right of a tenant to continue a tenancy at the termination of the lease.

tenantry /ˈtɛnəntri/ *n.* the tenants of an estate etc.

tench /tɛn(t)ʃ/ *n.* (*pl.* same) a European freshwater fish, *Tinca tinca*, of the carp family. [Middle English via Old French *tenche* from Late Latin *tinca*]

Ten Commandments *n.pl.* (usu. prec. by *the*) the divine rules of conduct given by God to Moses on Mount Sinai, according to Exod. 20:1–17.

tend[1] /tɛnd/ *v.intr.* **1** (usu. foll. by *to*) be apt or inclined (*tends to lose his temper*). **2** serve, conduce. **3** be moving; be directed; hold a course (*tends in our direction*; *tends downwards*; *tends to the same conclusion*). [Middle English via Old French *tendre* 'stretch' from Latin *tendere tens-* or *tent-*]

tend[2] /tɛnd/ *v.* **1** *tr.* take care of, look after (an invalid, a flock, a machine, etc.). **2** *intr.* (foll. by *on*, *upon*) wait on. **3** *intr.* (foll. by *to*) esp. *US* give attention to. ◻ **tendance** *n. archaic.* [Middle English, from ATTEND]

tendency /ˈtɛnd(ə)nsi/ *n.* (*pl.* **-ies**) **1** (often foll. by *to*, *towards*) a leaning or inclination, a way of tending. **2** a group within a larger political party or movement. [medieval Latin *tendentia* (as TEND[1])]

tendentious /tɛnˈdɛnʃəs/ *adj.* *derog.* (of writing etc.) calculated to promote a particular cause or viewpoint; having an underlying purpose. ◻ **tendentiously** *adv.* **tendentiousness** *n.* [as TENDENCY + -OUS]

tender[1] /ˈtɛndə/ *adj.* (**tenderer**, **tenderest**) **1** easily cut or chewed, not tough (*tender steak*). **2** easily touched or wounded, susceptible to pain or grief (*a tender heart*; *a tender conscience*). **3** easily hurt, sensitive (*tender skin*; *a tender place*). **4** delicate, fragile (*a tender reputation*). **5** loving, affectionate, fond (*tender parents*; *wrote tender verses*). **6** requiring tact or careful handling, ticklish (*a tender subject*). **7** (of age) early, immature (*of tender years*). **8** (usu. foll. by *of*) solicitous, concerned (*tender of his honour*). ◻ **tenderly** *adv.* **tenderness** *n.* [Middle English via Old French *tendre* from Latin *tener*]

tender[2] /ˈtɛndə/ *v.* & *n.* ● *v.* **1** *tr.* **a** offer, present (one's services, apologies, resignation, etc.). **b** offer (money etc.) as payment. **2** *intr.* (often foll. by *for*) make a tender for the supply of a thing or the execution of work. ● *n.* an offer, esp. an offer in writing to execute work or supply goods at a fixed price. ◻ **put out to tender** seek tenders in respect of (work etc.). ◻ **tenderer** *n.* [Old French *tendre*: see TEND[1]]

tender[3] /ˈtɛndə/ *n.* **1** a person who looks after people or things. **2** a vessel attending a larger one to supply stores, convey passengers or orders, etc. **3** a special truck closely coupled to a steam locomotive to carry fuel, water, etc. [Middle English, from TEND[2] or from ATTENDER (as ATTEND)]

tender-eyed *adj.* **1** having gentle eyes. **2** weak-eyed.

tenderfoot /ˈtɛndəfʊt/ *n.* (*pl.* **-s** or **-feet**) a newcomer or novice, esp. in the bush or in the Scouts or Guides.

tender-hearted *adj.* having a tender heart, easily moved by pity etc. ◻ **tender-heartedness** *n.*

tenderize /ˈtɛndərʌɪz/ *v.tr.* (also **-ise**) make tender, esp. make (meat) tender by beating etc. ◻ **tenderizer** *n.*

tenderloin /ˈtɛndəlɔɪn/ *n.* **1 a** the tenderest part of a loin of beef, pork, etc. **b** *US* the undercut of a sirloin. **2** *US slang* a district of a city where vice and corruption are prominent.

tender mercies *n.pl.* *iron.* attention or treatment which is not in the best interests of its recipient.

tender spot *n.* a subject on which a person is touchy.

tendon /ˈtɛndən/ *n.* **1** a cord or strand of strong fibrous tissue attaching a muscle to a bone etc. **2** (in a quadruped) = HAMSTRING *n.* 2. □ **tendinitis** /tɛndɪˈnʌɪtɪs/ *n.* (also **tendonitis**). **tendinous** /-dɪnəs/ *adj.* [French *tendon* or medieval Latin *tendo -dinis* from Greek *tenōn* 'sinew', from *teinō* 'stretch']

tendril /ˈtɛndrɪl/ *n.* **1** each of the slender leafless shoots by which some climbing plants cling for support. **2** a slender curl of hair etc. [probably from obsolete French *tendrillon*, diminutive of obsolete *tendron* 'young shoot', ultimately from Latin *tener* TENDER[1]]

Tenebrae /ˈtɛnɪbriː, -breɪ/ *n.pl.* **1** *RC Ch. hist.* matins and lauds for the last three days of Holy Week, at which candles are successively extinguished. **2** this office set to music. [Latin, = darkness]

tenebrous /ˈtɛnɪbrəs/ *adj. literary* dark, gloomy. [Middle English via Old French *tenebrus* from Latin *tenebrosus* (as TENEBRAE)]

tenement /ˈtɛnəm(ə)nt/ *n.* **1** a room or a set of rooms forming a separate residence within a house or block of flats. **2** (in full **tenement house**) *US* & *Sc.* a house divided into and let in tenements. **3** a dwelling place. **4 a** a piece of land held by an owner. **b** *Law* any kind of permanent property, e.g. lands or rents, held from a superior. □ **tenemental** /-ˈmɛnt(ə)l/ *adj.* **tenementary** /-ˈmɛnt(ə)ri/ *adj.* [Middle English via Old French from medieval Latin *tenementum*, from *tenēre* 'hold']

tenesmus /tɪˈnɛzməs/ *n. Med.* a continual inclination to evacuate the bowels or bladder accompanied by painful straining. [medieval Latin from Greek *teinesmos* 'straining', from *teinō* 'stretch']

tenet /ˈtɛnɪt, ˈtiːnɛt/ *n.* a doctrine, dogma, or principle held by a group or person. [Latin, = he etc. holds, from *tenēre* 'hold']

tenfold /ˈtɛnfəʊld/ *adj. & adv.* **1** ten times as much or as many. **2** consisting of ten parts.

ten-gallon hat *n.* a cowboy's large broad-brimmed hat.

tenia *US* var. of TAENIA.

Tenn. *abbr.* Tennessee.

tenné /ˈtɛni/ *n.* & (usu. placed after noun) *adj.* (also **tenny**) *Heraldry* orange-brown. [obsolete French, variant of *tanné* TAWNY]

tenner /ˈtɛnə/ *n.* esp. *Brit. colloq.* a ten-pound or ten-dollar note. [TEN]

tennis /ˈtɛnɪs/ *n.* a game in which two or four players strike a ball with rackets over a net stretched across a court (see LAWN TENNIS, REAL TENNIS). [Middle English *tenetz*, *tenes*, etc., apparently from Old French *tenez* 'take, receive' (called by the server to an opponent), imperative of *tenir* 'take']

tennis ball *n.* a ball used in playing tennis.

tennis court *n.* a court used in playing tennis.

tennis elbow *n.* a painful inflammation of the tendons in the elbow caused by or as by playing tennis.

tennis racket *n.* a racket used in playing tennis.

tennis shoe *n.* a light canvas or leather soft-soled shoe suitable for tennis or general casual wear.

tenno /ˈtɛnəʊ/ *n.* (*pl.* **-os**) the Emperor of Japan viewed as a divinity. [Japanese]

tenny var. of TENNÉ.

Tennysonian /tɛnɪˈsəʊnɪən/ *adj.* relating to or in the style of Alfred (Lord) Tennyson, English poet d. 1892.

tenon /ˈtɛnən/ *n. & v.* ● *n.* a projecting piece of wood made for insertion into a corresponding cavity (esp. a mortise) in another piece. ● *v.tr.* **1** cut as a tenon. **2** join by means of a tenon. □ **tenoner** *n.* [Middle English via French, from *tenir* 'hold', from Latin *tenēre*]

tenon saw *n.* a small saw with a strong brass or steel back for fine work.

tenor /ˈtɛnə/ *n.* **1 a** a singing voice between baritone and alto or counter-tenor, the highest of the ordinary adult male range. **b** a singer with this voice. **c** a part written for it. **2 a** an instrument, esp. a viola, recorder, or saxophone, of which the range is roughly that of a tenor voice. **b** (in full **tenor bell**) the largest bell of a peal or set. **3** (usu. foll. by *of*) the general purport or drift of a document or speech. **4** (usu. foll. by *of*) a settled or prevailing course or direction, esp. the course of a person's life or habits. **5** *Law* **a** the actual wording of a document. **b** an exact copy. **6** the subject to which a metaphor refers (opp. VEHICLE 4). [Middle English via Anglo-French *tenur*, Old French *tenour* from Latin *tenor -oris*, from *tenēre* 'hold']

tenor clef *n. Mus.* a clef placing middle C on the second highest line of the staff.

tenorist /ˈtɛnərɪst/ *n.* a person who sings a tenor part or esp. who plays a tenor instrument.

tenosynovitis /ˌtɛnəʊsʌɪnə(ʊ)ˈvʌɪtɪs/ *n.* inflammation and swelling of a tendon, usu. in the wrist, often caused by repetitive movements such as typing. [Greek *tenōn* 'tendon' + SYNOVITIS]

tenotomy /təˈnɒtəmi/ *n.* (*pl.* **-ies**) the surgical cutting of a tendon, esp. as a remedy for a club foot. [French *ténotomie*, formed irregularly from Greek *tenōn -ontos* 'tendon']

tenpin /ˈtɛnpɪn/ *n.* **1** a pin used in tenpin bowling. **2** (in *pl.*) *US* = TENPIN BOWLING.

tenpin bowling *n.* a game developed from ninepins in which ten pins are set up at the end of an alley and bowled down with hard rubber or plastic balls.

tenrec /ˈtɛnrɛk/ *n.* (also **tanrec** /ˈtan-/) any hedgehog-like insect-eating mammal of the family Tenrecidae, esp. the tailless *Tenrec ecaudatus* native to Madagascar. [French *tanrec*, from Malagasy *tàndraka*]

TENS *abbr.* transcutaneous electrical nerve stimulation.

tense[1] /tɛns/ *adj. & v.* ● *adj.* **1** stretched tight, strained (*tense cord*; *tense muscle*; *tense nerves*; *tense emotion*). **2** causing tenseness (*a tense moment*). **3** *Phonet.* pronounced with the vocal muscles tense. ● *v.tr. & intr.* make or become tense. □ **tense up** become tense. □ **tensely** *adv.* **tenseness** *n.* **tensity** *n.* [Latin *tensus*, past part. of *tendere* 'stretch']

tense[2] /tɛns/ *n. Gram.* **1** a form taken by a verb to indicate the time (also the continuance or completeness) of the action etc. (*present tense*; *imperfect tense*). **2** a set of such forms for the various persons and numbers. □ **tenseless** *adj.* [Middle English via Old French *tens* from Latin *tempus* 'time']

tensile /ˈtɛnsʌɪl/ *adj.* **1** of or relating to tension. **2** capable of being drawn out or stretched. □ **tensility** /tenˈsɪlɪtɪ/ *n.* [medieval Latin *tensilis* (as TENSE[1])]

tensile strength *n.* resistance to breaking under tension.

tensimeter /tɛnˈsɪmɪtə/ *n.* **1** an instrument for measuring vapour pressure. **2** a manometer. [TENSION + -METER]

tension /ˈtɛnʃ(ə)n/ *n. & v.* ● *n.* **1** the act or an instance of stretching; the state of being stretched; tenseness. **2** mental strain or excitement. **3** a strained (political, social, etc.) state or relationship. **4** *Mech.* the strained condition resulting from forces acting in opposition to each other. **5** electromagnetic force (*high tension*; *low tension*). **6** the degree of tightness of stitches in knitting and machine sewing. ● *v.tr.* subject to tension. □ **tensional** *adj.* **tensionally** *adv.* **tensioner** *n.* **tensionless** *adj.* [French *tension* or Latin *tensio* (as TEND[1])]

tenson /ˈtɛns(ə)n/ *n.* (also **tenzon** /ˈtiːnz(ə)n/) *hist.* **1** a contest in verse-making between troubadours. **2** a piece of verse composed for this. [French *tenson*, = Provençal *tenso* (as TENSION)]

tensor /ˈtɛnsə, -sɔː/ *n.* **1** *Anat.* a muscle that tightens or stretches a part of the body. **2** *Math.* a generalized form of vector involving an arbitrary number of indices. □ **tensorial** /-ˈsɔːrɪəl/ *adj.* [modern Latin (as TEND[1])]

tent[1] /tɛnt/ *n. & v.* ● *n.* **1** a portable shelter or dwelling of canvas, cloth, etc., supported by a pole or poles and stretched by cords or loops attached to pegs driven into the ground. **2** *Med.* = OXYGEN TENT. ● *v.* **1** *tr.* cover with or as with a tent. **2** *tr.* (as **tented** *adj.*) composed of or provided with tents (*tented village*; *tented field*). **3** *intr.* **a** camp in a tent. **b** dwell temporarily. [Middle English from Old French *tente*, ultimately from Latin *tendere* 'stretch']

tent[2] /tɛnt/ *n.* a deep red sweet wine chiefly from Spain, used esp. as sacramental wine. [Spanish *tinto* 'deep-coloured' from Latin *tinctus*, past part. of *tingere* 'dye, stain']

tent[3] /tɛnt/ *n. Surgery* a piece (esp. a roll) of lint, linen, etc., inserted into a wound or natural opening to keep it open. [Middle English from Old French *tente*, from *tenter* 'to probe' (as TEMPT)]

tentacle /'tɛntək(ə)l/ *n.* **1** a long slender flexible appendage of an (esp. invertebrate) animal, used for feeling, grasping, or moving. **2** a thing used like a tentacle as a feeler etc. **3** *Bot.* a sensitive hair or filament. □ **tentacled** *adj.* (also in *comb.*). **tentacular** /-'takjʊlə/ *adj.* **tentaculate** /-'takjʊlət/ *adj.* [modern Latin *tentaculum*, from Latin *tentare* = *temptare* (see TEMPT) + *-culum* -CULE]

tentage /'tɛntɪdʒ/ *n.* tents; tenting equipment.

tentative /'tɛntətɪv/ *adj.* & *n.* ● *adj.* **1** done by way of trial, experimental. **2** hesitant, not definite (*tentative suggestion*; *tentative acceptance*). ● *n.* an experimental proposal or theory. □ **tentatively** *adv.* **tentativeness** *n.* [medieval Latin *tentativus* (as TENTACLE)]

tent-bed *n.* a bed with a tentlike canopy, or for a patient in an oxygen tent.

tent coat *n.* (also **tent dress**) a coat (or dress) cut very full.

tenter[1] /'tɛntə/ *n.* **1** a machine for stretching cloth to dry in shape. **2** = TENTERHOOK. [Middle English, ultimately from medieval Latin *tentorium* (as TEND[1])]

tenter[2] /'tɛntə/ *n. Brit.* **1** a person in charge of something, esp. of machinery in a factory. **2** a worker's unskilled assistant. [*tent* (now Scots) 'pay attention', perhaps via *tent* 'attention' from INTENT, or from obsolete *attent* (as ATTEND)]

tenterhook /'tɛntəhʊk/ *n.* any of the hooks to which cloth is fastened on a tenter. □ **on tenterhooks** in a state of suspense or mental agitation due to uncertainty.

tent-fly *n.* (*pl.* **-flies**) **1** a flap at the entrance to a tent. **2** a flysheet.

tenth /tɛnθ/ *n.* & *adj.* ● *n.* **1** the position in a sequence corresponding to the number 10 in the sequence 1-10. **2** something occupying this position. **3** one of ten equal parts of a thing. **4** *Mus.* **a** an interval or chord spanning an octave and a third in the diatonic scale. **b** a note separated from another by this interval. ● *adj.* that is the tenth. □ **tenthly** *adv.* [Middle English *tenthe*, alteration of Old English *teogotha*]

tenth-rate *adj.* of extremely poor quality.

tent peg *n.* any of the pegs to which the cords of a tent are attached.

tent stitch *n.* **1** a series of parallel diagonal stitches. **2** such a stitch.

tenuity /tɪ'nju:ɪti/ *n.* **1** slenderness. **2** (of a fluid, esp. air) rarity, thinness. [Latin *tenuitas* (as *tenuis* TENUOUS)]

tenuous /'tɛnjʊəs/ *adj.* **1** slight, of little substance (*tenuous connection*). **2** (of a distinction etc.) oversubtle. **3** thin, slender, small. **4** rarefied. □ **tenuously** *adv.* **tenuousness** *n.* [Latin *tenuis*]

tenure /'tɛnjə/ *n.* **1** a condition, or form of right or title, under which (esp. real) property is held. **2** (often foll. by *of*) **a** the holding or possession of an office or property. **b** the period of this (*during his tenure of office*). **3** guaranteed permanent employment, esp. as a teacher or lecturer after a probationary period. [Middle English from Old French, from *tenir* 'hold', from Latin *tenēre*]

tenured /'tɛnjəd/ *adj.* **1** (of an official position) carrying a guarantee of permanent employment. **2** (of a teacher, lecturer, etc.) having guaranteed tenure of office.

tenurial /tɛn'jʊərɪəl/ *adj.* of the tenure of land. □ **tenurially** *adv.* [medieval Latin *tenūra* TENURE]

tenuto /tə'nu:təʊ/ *adv.*, *adj.*, & *n. Mus.* ● *adv.* & *adj.* (of a note etc.) sustained, given its full time value (cf. LEGATO, STACCATO). ● *n.* (*pl.* **-os**) a note or chord played tenuto. [Italian, = held]

ten-week stock *n.* a variety of stock, *Matthiola incana*, said to bloom ten weeks after the sowing of the seed.

tenzon var. of TENSON.

teocalli /ti:ə'kali/ *n.* (*pl.* **teocallis**) a temple of the Aztecs or other Mexican peoples, usu. on a truncated pyramid. [Nahuatl, from *teotl* 'god' + *calli* 'house']

teosinte /ti:əʊ'sɪnti/ *n.* a Mexican grass, *Zea mexicana*, grown as fodder. [French from Nahuatl *teocintli*]

tepal /'tɛp(ə)l, 'ti:p(ə)l/ *n.* a segment of the outer whorl in a flower having no differentiation between petals and sepals. [French *tépale*, as blend of PETAL and SEPAL]

tepee /'ti:pi:/ *n.* (also **teepee**, **tipi**) a N. American Indian's conical tent, made of skins, cloth, or canvas on a frame of poles. [Sioux *tīpī*]

tephra /'tɛfrə/ *n.* fragmented rock etc. ejected by a volcanic eruption. [Greek, = ash]

tepid /'tɛpɪd/ *adj.* **1** slightly warm. **2** unenthusiastic. □ **tepidity** /tɪ'pɪdɪti/ *n.* **tepidly** *adv.* **tepidness** *n.* [Latin *tepidus* from *tepēre* 'be lukewarm']

tequila /tɛ'ki:lə/ *n.* a Mexican liquor made from an agave. [*Tequila*, a town in Mexico where the drink was first produced]

ter- /tə:/ *comb. form* three; threefold (*tercentenary*; *tervalent*). [Latin *ter* 'thrice']

tera- /'tɛrə/ *comb. form* denoting a factor of 10^{12}. [Greek *teras* 'monster']

teraflop /'tɛrəflɒp/ *n. Computing* a unit of computing speed equal to one million million floating-point operations per second.

terai /tə'rʌɪ/ *n.* (in full **terai hat**) a wide-brimmed felt hat, often with a double crown, worn by travellers etc. in subtropical regions. [*Terai*, belt of marshy jungle between Himalayan foothills and plains, from Hindi *tarāī* 'moist (land)']

teraph /'tɛrəf/ *n.* (*pl.* **teraphim**, also used as *sing*) a small image as a domestic deity or oracle of the ancient Hebrews. [Middle English via Late Latin *theraphim*, Greek *theraphin* from Hebrew *t̲ᵉrāpîm*]

terato- /'tɛrətəʊ, tɛ'ratəʊ/ *comb. form* monster. [Greek *teras -atos* 'monster']

teratogen /tɛ'ratədʒ(ə)n, 'tɛrətədʒ(ə)n/ *n. Med.* an agent or factor causing malformation of an embryo. □ **teratogenic** /tɛrətə'dʒɛnɪk/ *adj.* **teratogeny** /tɛrə'tɒdʒ(ə)ni/ *n.*

teratology /tɛrə'tɒlədʒi/ *n.* **1** *Med.* & *Biol.* the scientific study of congenital abnormalities and abnormal formations. **2** mythology relating to fantastic creatures, monsters, etc. □ **teratological** /-tə'lɒdʒɪk(ə)l/ *adj.* **teratologist** *n.*

teratoma /tɛrə'təʊmə/ *n. Med.* a tumour of heterogeneous tissues, esp. of the gonads.

terawatt /'tɛrəwɒt/ *n.* a unit of power equal to 10^{12} watts or a million megawatts.

terbium /'tə:bɪəm/ *n. Chem.* a silvery metallic element of the lanthanide series (symbol **Tb**). [modern Latin, named after *Ytterby*, a village in Sweden where it was discovered]

terce /tə:s/ *n. Eccl.* the office of the third canonical hour of prayer, originally said at the third hour of the day (i.e. 9 a.m.). [variant of TIERCE]

tercel var. of TIERCEL.

tercentenary /tə:sɛn'ti:n(ə)ri, -'tɛn, tə:'sɛntɪn(ə)ri/ *n.* & *adj.* ● *n.* (*pl.* **-ies**) **1** a three-hundredth anniversary. **2** a celebration of this. ● *adj.* of this anniversary.

tercentennial /tə:sɛn'tɛnɪəl/ *adj.* & *n.* ● *adj.* **1** occurring every three hundred years. **2** lasting three hundred years. ● *n.* a tercentenary.

tercet /'tə:sɪt/ *n.* (also **tiercet** /'tɪə-/) *Prosody* a set or group of three lines rhyming together or connected by rhyme with an adjacent triplet. [French from Italian *terzetto*, diminutive of *terzo* 'third', from Latin *tertius*]

terebene /'tɛrəbi:n/ *n.* a mixture of terpenes prepared by treating oil of turpentine with sulphuric acid, used as an expectorant etc. [TEREBINTH + -ENE]

terebinth /'tɛrəbɪnθ/ *n.* a small southern European tree, *Pistacia terebinthus*, yielding resin formerly used as a source of turpentine. [Middle English via Old French *terebinte* or Latin *terebinthus* from Greek *terebinthos*]

terebinthine /tɛrə'bɪnθʌɪn, -i:n/ *adj.* **1** of the terebinth. **2** of turpentine. [Latin *terebinthinus* from Greek *terebinthinos* (as TEREBINTH)]

teredo /tə'ri:dəʊ/ *n.* (*pl.* **-os**) any bivalve mollusc of the genus *Teredo*, esp. *T. navalis*, that bores into wooden ships etc. Also called SHIPWORM. [Latin from Greek *terēdōn*, from *teirō* 'rub hard, wear away, bore']

terephthalic acid /tɛrəf'θalɪk/ *n. Chem.* the *para*-isomer of phthalic acid, used in making plastics and other polymers. [*terebic* from TEREBINTH, + PHTHALIC ACID]

terete /tə'ri:t/ *adj. Biol.* smooth and rounded; cylindrical. [Latin *teres -etis*]

tergal /'tə:g(ə)l/ *adj.* of or relating to the back; dorsal. [Latin *tergum* 'back']

tergiversate /'tə:dʒɪvəseɪt, -,və:seɪt/ *v.intr.* **1** be apostate; change one's party or principles. **2** equivocate; make conflicting or evasive statements. **3** turn one's back on something. □ **tergiversation** /-'seɪʃ(ə)n/ *n.* **tergiversator** *n.* [Latin *tergiversari* 'turn one's back', from *tergum* 'back' + *vertere vers-* 'turn']

-teria /'tɪərɪə/ *suffix* denoting self-service establishments (*washeteria*). [on the pattern of CAFETERIA]

term /tə:m/ *n.* & *v.* ● *n.* **1** a word used to express a definite concept, esp. in a particular branch of study etc. (*a technical term*). **2** (in *pl.*) language used; mode of expression (*answered in no uncertain terms*). **3** (in *pl.*) a relation or footing (*we are on familiar terms*). **4** (in *pl.*) **a** conditions or stipulations (*cannot accept your terms; do it on your own terms*). **b** charge or price (*his terms are £20 a lesson*). **5 a** a limited period of some state or activity (*for a term of five years*). **b** a period over which operations are conducted or results contemplated (*in the short term*). **c** a period of some weeks, alternating with holiday or vacation, during which instruction is given in a school, college, or university, or during which a law court holds sessions. **d** a period of imprisonment. **e** a period of tenure. **6** *Logic* a word or words that may be the subject or predicate of a proposition. **7** *Math.* **a** each of the two quantities in a ratio. **b** each quantity in a series. **c** a part of an expression joined to the rest by + or − (e.g. *a*, *b*, *c* in *a* + *b* − *c*). **8** the completion of a normal length of pregnancy. **9** an appointed day, esp. a Scottish quarter day. **10** (in full *Brit.* **term of years** or *US* **term for years**) *Law* an interest in land for a fixed period. **11** *Archit.* = TERMINUS 6. **12** *archaic* a boundary or limit, esp. of time. ● *v.tr.* denominate, call; assign a term to (*the music termed classical*). □ **bring to terms** cause to accept conditions. **come to terms** yield, give way. **come to terms with 1** reconcile oneself to (a difficulty etc.). **2** conclude an agreement with. **in set terms** in definite terms. **in terms** explicitly. **in terms of** in the language peculiar to, using as a basis of expression or thought. **make terms** conclude an agreement. **on terms** on terms of friendship or equality. □ **termless** *adj.* **termly** *adj.* & *adv.* [Middle English via Old French *terme* from Latin TERMINUS]

termagant /'tə:məg(ə)nt/ *n.* & *adj.* ● *n.* **1** an overbearing or brawling woman; a virago or shrew. **2** (**Termagant**) *hist.* an imaginary deity of violent and turbulent character, often appearing in morality plays. ● *adj.* violent, turbulent, shrewish. [Middle English *Tervagant* via Old French *Tervagan* from Italian *Trivigante*]

term for years see TERM *n.* 10.

terminable /'tə:mɪnəb(ə)l/ *adj.* **1** that may be terminated. **2** coming to an end after a certain time (*terminable annuity*). □ **terminableness** *n.*

terminal /'tə:mɪn(ə)l/ *adj.* & *n.* ● *adj.* **1 a** (of a disease) ending in death, fatal. **b** (of a patient) in the last stage of a fatal disease. **c** (of a morbid condition) forming the last stage of a fatal disease. **d** *colloq.* ruinous, disastrous, very great (*terminal laziness*). **2** of or forming a limit or terminus (*terminal station*). **3 a** *Zool.* etc. ending a series (*terminal joints*). **b** *Bot.* borne at the end of a stem etc. **4** of or done etc. each term (*terminal accounts; terminal examinations*). ● *n.* **1** a terminating thing; an extremity. **2** a terminus for trains or long-distance buses. **3** a departure and arrival building for air passengers at an airport. **4** a point of connection for closing an electric circuit. **5** an apparatus for transmission of messages between a user and a computer, communications system, etc. **6** (in full **terminal figure**) = TERMINUS 6. **7** an installation where oil is stored at the end of a pipeline or at a port. **8** *Brit.* a patient suffering from a terminal illness. □ **terminally** *adv.* [Latin *terminalis* (as TERMINUS)]

terminal velocity *n.* a velocity of a falling body such that the resistance of the air etc. prevents further increase of speed under gravity.

terminate /'tə:mɪneɪt/ *v.* **1** *tr.* & *intr.* bring or come to an end. **2** *intr.* (foll. by *in*) (of a word) end in (a specified letter or syllable etc.). **3** *tr.* end (a pregnancy) before term by artificial means. **4** *tr.* bound, limit. [Latin *terminare* (as TERMINUS)]

termination /tə:mɪ'neɪʃ(ə)n/ *n.* **1** the act or an instance of terminating; the state of being terminated. **2** *Med.* an induced abortion. **3** an ending or result of a specified kind (*a happy termination*). **4** a word's final syllable or letters or letter esp. as an element in inflection or derivation. □ **put a termination to** (or **bring to a termination**) make an end of. □ **terminational** *adj.* [Middle English from Old French *termination* or Latin *terminatio* (as TERMINATE)]

terminator /'tə:mɪneɪtə/ *n.* **1** a person or thing that terminates. **2** the dividing line between the light and dark part of a planetary body.

terminer see OYER AND TERMINER.

termini *pl.* of TERMINUS.

terminism /'tə:mɪnɪz(ə)m/ *n.* **1** *Theol.* the doctrine that everyone has a limited time for repentance. **2** = NOMINALISM. □ **terminist** *n.* [Latin]

terminological /,tə:mɪnə'lɒdʒɪk(ə)l/ *adj.* relating to terminology. □ **terminologically** *adv.*

terminological inexactitude *n. joc.* a lie.

terminology /tə:mɪ'nɒlədʒi/ *n.* (*pl.* **-ies**) **1** the system of terms used in a particular subject. **2** the science of the proper use of terms. □ **terminologist** *n.* [German *Terminologie* from medieval Latin TERMINUS 'term']

terminus /'tə:mɪnəs/ *n.* (*pl.* **termini** /-nʌɪ/ or **terminuses**) **1 a** the end of a railway or bus route. **b** *Brit.* a station at this point. **2** a point at the end of a pipeline etc. **3** a final point, a goal. **4** a starting point. **5** *Math.* the end point of a vector etc. **6** *Archit.* a figure of a human bust or an animal ending in a square pillar from which it appears to spring, originally as a boundary marker. [Latin, = end, limit, boundary]

terminus ad quem /ad 'kwɛm/ *n.* the finishing point of an argument, policy, period, etc. [Latin, = end to which]

terminus ante quem /antɪ 'kwɛm/ *n.* the finishing point of a period; the latest possible date for something. [Latin, = end before which]

terminus a quo /ɑ: 'kwəʊ/ *n.* the starting point of an argument, policy, period, etc. [Latin, = end from which]

terminus post quem /pəʊst 'kwɛm/ *n.* the starting point of a period; the earliest possible date for something. [Latin, = end after which]

termitary /'tə:mɪtəri/ *n.* (*pl.* **-ies**) a nest of termites, usu. a large mound of earth.

termite /'tə:mʌɪt/ *n.* a small social insect of the order Isoptera, chiefly tropical and destructive to timber. Also called *white ant*. [Late Latin *termes -mitis*, alteration of Latin *tarmes* influenced by *terere* 'rub']

term of years see TERM *n.* 10.

termor /'tɜ:mə/ *n. Law* a person who holds lands etc. for a term of years, or for life. [Middle English from Anglo-French *termer* (as TERM)]

term paper *n. N. Amer.* an essay or dissertation representative of the work done during a term.

terms of reference *n.pl. Brit.* **1** points referred to an individual or body of persons for decision or report. **2** the definition of the scope of an inquiry etc.

terms of trade *n.pl. Brit.* the ratio between prices paid for imports and those received for exports.

term-time *n. & adj.* ● *n.* (esp. in phr. **in** or **during term-time**) the period when school is in session. ● *attrib.adj.* relating to this period.

tern[1] /tɜ:n/ *n.* any seabird of the family Sternidae, like a gull but usu. smaller and with a forked tail. [of Scandinavian origin: cf. Danish *terne*, Swedish *tärna* from Old Norse *therna*]

tern[2] /tɜ:n/ *n.* **1** a set of three, esp. three lottery numbers that when drawn together win a large prize. **2** such a prize. [French *terne* from Latin *terni* 'three each']

ternary /'tɜ:nəri/ *adj.* **1** composed of three parts. **2** *Math.* using three as a base (*ternary scale*). [Middle English from Latin *ternarius*, from *terni* 'three each']

ternary form *n. Mus.* the form of a movement in which the first subject is repeated after an interposed second subject in a related key.

ternate /'tɜ:neɪt/ *adj.* **1** arranged in threes. **2** *Bot.* (of a leaf): **a** having three leaflets. **b** whorled in threes. □ **ternately** *adv.* [modern Latin *ternatus* (as TERNARY)]

terne /tɜ:n/ *n.* **1** (in full **terne metal**) a lead alloy with about 20 per cent tin and often antimony. **2** (in full **terne-plate**) thin sheet iron or steel coated with an alloy of lead and tin. [probably from French *terne* 'dull': cf. TARNISH]

terotechnology /ˌtɛrə(ʊ)tɛk'nɒlədʒi, ˌtɪərə-/ *n. Brit.* the branch of technology and engineering concerned with the installation and maintenance of equipment. [Greek *tēreō* 'take care of' + TECHNOLOGY]

terpene /'tɜ:pi:n/ *n. Chem.* any of a large group of unsaturated cyclic hydrocarbons found in the essential oils of plants, esp. conifers and oranges. [*terpentin*, obsolete variant of TURPENTINE]

Terpsichorean /ˌtɜ:psɪkə'ri:ən/ *adj.* of or relating to dancing. [*Terpsichore*, the name of the Muse of dancing]

terra alba /tɛrə 'albə/ *n.* a white mineral, esp. pipeclay or pulverized gypsum. [Latin, = white earth]

terrace /'tɛrəs/ *n. & v.* ● *n.* **1** each of a series of flat areas formed on a slope and used for cultivation. **2** a level paved area next to a house. **3 a** a row of houses on a raised level or along the top or face of a slope. **b** *Brit.* a row of houses built in one block of uniform style. **4** *Brit.* **a** a flight of wide shallow steps as for spectators at a sports ground. **b** (in *pl.*) the spectators occupying such steps. **5** *Geol.* a raised beach, or a similar formation beside a river etc. ● *v.tr.* form into or provide with a terrace or terraces. [Old French, ultimately from Latin *terra* 'earth']

terraced roof *n.* a flat roof esp. of an Indian or Eastern house.

terrace house *n.* (also **terraced house**) *Brit.* any of a row of houses joined by party walls.

terracotta /tɛrə'kɒtə/ *n. & adj.* ● *n.* **1 a** unglazed usu. brownish-red earthenware used chiefly as an ornamental building material and in modelling. **b** a statuette of this. **2** the brownish-red colour of terracotta. ● *adj.* of a brownish-red colour. [Italian *terra cotta* 'baked earth']

terra firma /tɛrə 'fɜ:mə/ *n.* dry land, firm ground. [Latin, = firm land]

terraform /'tɛrəfɔ:m/ *v.tr.* (esp. in science fiction) transform (a planet) so as to resemble the earth. [Latin *terra* 'earth' + TRANSFORM]

terrain /tɛ'reɪn/ *n.* **1** a tract of land esp. as regarded by the physical geographer or the military tactician. **2** a particular area of knowledge; a sphere of influence or action. [French, ultimately from Latin *terrenum*, neut. of *terrenus* TERRENE]

terra incognita /ˌtɛrə ɪn'kɒgnɪtə, ɪŋkɒg'ni:tə/ *n.* an unknown or unexplored region. [Latin, = unknown land]

terramara /tɛrə'mɑ:rə/ *n.* (*pl.* **terramare** /-reɪ/) = TERRAMARE. [Italian dialect: see TERRAMARE]

terramare /tɛrə'mɑ:ri, -'mɛ:ri/ *n.* **1** an ammoniacal earthy deposit found in mounds in prehistoric lake-dwellings or settlements esp. in Italy. **2** such a dwelling or settlement. [French from Italian dialect *terra mara*, from *terra* 'earth' + *marna* 'marl']

terrapin /'tɛrəpɪn/ *n.* **1 a** any of various small freshwater turtles of the family Emydidae, esp. *Emys orbicularis* of Europe. **b** a small edible turtle, *Malaclemys terrapin*, found in coastal marshes of the eastern US. **2** (**Terrapin**) *Brit. propr.* a type of prefabricated one-storey building. [Algonquian]

terrarium /tɛ'rɛ:rɪəm/ *n.* (*pl.* **terrariums** or **terraria** /-rɪə/) **1** a vivarium for small land animals. **2** a sealed transparent globe etc. containing growing plants. [modern Latin from Latin *terra* 'earth', on the pattern of AQUARIUM]

terra sigillata /ˌtɛrə sɪdʒɪ'leɪtə/ *n.* **1** *hist.* astringent clay from Lemnos or Samos, formerly used as a medicine and antidote. **2** Samian ware. [medieval Latin, = sealed earth]

terrazzo /tɛ'ratsəʊ/ *n.* (*pl.* **-os**) a flooring material of stone chips set in concrete and given a smooth surface. [Italian, = terrace]

terrene /tɛ'ri:n/ *adj.* **1** of the earth; earthly, worldly. **2** of earth, earthy. **3** of dry land; terrestrial. [Middle English via Anglo-French from Latin *terrenus*, from *terra* 'earth']

terreplein /'tɛ:pleɪn/ *n.* a level space where a battery of guns is mounted. [originally a sloping bank behind a rampart: French *terre-plein* from Italian *terrapieno*, from *terrapienare* 'fill with earth', from *terra* 'earth' + *pieno* from Latin *plenus* 'full']

terrestrial /tɪ'rɛstrɪəl/ *adj. & n.* ● *adj.* **1** of or on or relating to the earth; earthly. **2 a** of or on dry land. **b** *Zool.* living on or in the ground; not aquatic, arboreal, or aerial. **c** *Bot.* growing in the soil; not aquatic or epiphytic. **3** *Astron.* (of a planet) similar in size or composition to the earth. **4** of this world, worldly. **5** (of broadcasting) not using satellites. ● *n.* an inhabitant of the earth. □ **terrestrially** *adv.* [Middle English from Latin *terrestris*, from *terra* 'earth']

terrestrial globe *n.* a globe representing the earth.

terrestrial magnetism *n.* the magnetic properties of the earth as a whole.

terrestrial telescope *n.* a telescope giving an erect image for observation of terrestrial objects.

terret /'tɛrɪt/ *n.* (also **territ**) each of the loops or rings on a harness-pad for the driving reins to pass through. [Middle English, variant of *toret* (now dialect) from Old French *to(u)ret*, diminutive of TOUR]

terre-verte /tɛ:'vɛ:t/ *n.* a soft green earth used as a pigment. [French, = green earth]

terrible /'tɛrɪb(ə)l/ *adj.* **1** *colloq.* **a** dreadful, awful (*the accident was terrible*). **b** (as an intensifier) very great or bad (*a terrible bore*). **2** *colloq.* very incompetent (*terrible at tennis*). **3** (*predic.*) *colloq.* ill (*he ate too much and feels terrible*). **4** (*predic.*; often foll. by *about*) *colloq.* full of remorse (*I feel terrible about it*). **5** causing terror; fit to cause terror; formidable. □ **terribleness** *n.* [Middle English via French from Latin *terribilis*, from *terrēre* 'frighten']

terribly /'tɛrɪbli/ *adv.* **1** *colloq.* very, extremely (*he was terribly nice about it*). **2** in a terrible manner.

terricolous /tɛ'rɪkələs/ *adj.* living on or in the earth. [Latin *terricola* 'earth-dweller', from *terra* 'earth' + *colere* 'inhabit']

terrier[1] /'tɛrɪə/ *n.* **1 a** a small dog of various breeds originally used for turning out foxes etc. from their earths. **b** any of these breeds. **2** an eager or tenacious person or animal. **3** (**Terrier**) *Brit. colloq.* a member of the Territorial Army etc. [Middle English via Old French (*chien*) *terrier* from medieval Latin *terrarius*, from Latin *terra* 'earth']

terrier[2] /'tɛrɪə/ *n. hist.* **1** a book recording the site, boundaries, etc., of the land of private persons or corporations. **2** a rent roll. **3** a collection of acknowledgements of vassals or tenants of a lordship. [Middle English from Old French *terrier* (*adj.*) = medieval Latin *terrarius liber* 'book of land' (as TERRIER[1])]

terrific /tə'rɪfɪk/ *adj.* **1** *colloq.* **a** of great size or intensity. **b** excellent (*did a terrific job*). **c** excessive (*making a terrific noise*). **2** causing terror. □ **terrifically** *adv.* [Latin *terrificus* from *terrēre* 'frighten']

terrify /'tɛrɪfʌɪ/ *v.tr.* (**-ies, -ied**) fill with terror; frighten severely (*terrified them into submission; is terrified of dogs*). □ **terrifier** *n.* **terrifyingly** *adv.* [Latin *terrificare* (as TERRIFIC)]

terrigenous /tɛ'rɪdʒɪnəs/ *adj. Geol.* derived from the land, esp. (of a marine deposit) made of material eroded from the land. [Latin *terrigenus* 'earth-born']

terrine /tə'ri:n/ *n.* **1** a kind of esp. coarse-textured pâté. **2** an earthenware container, esp. one in which such food is cooked or sold. [originally a form of TUREEN]

territ var. of TERRET.

territorial /tɛrɪ'tɔ:rɪəl/ *adj. & n.* ● *adj.* **1** of territory (*territorial possessions*). **2** limited to a district (*the right was strictly territorial*). **3** (of a person or animal etc.) tending to defend an area of territory. **4** (usu. **Territorial**) of any of the Territories of the US or Canada. ● *n.* (**Territorial**) (in the UK) a member of the Territorial Army. □ **territoriality** /-'alɪti/ *n.* **territorialize** *v.tr.* (also **-ise**). **territorialization** /-lʌɪ'zeɪʃ(ə)n/ *n.* **territorially** *adv.* [Late Latin *territorialis* (as TERRITORY)]

Territorial Army *n.* (in the UK) a volunteer force locally organized to provide a reserve of trained and disciplined manpower for use in an emergency (known as *Territorial and Army Volunteer Reserve* 1967–79).

territorial waters *n.pl.* the waters under the jurisdiction of a state, esp. the part of the sea within a stated distance of the shore (traditionally three miles from low water mark).

territory /'tɛrɪt(ə)ri/ *n.* (*pl.* **-ies**) **1** the extent of the land under the jurisdiction of a ruler, state, city, etc. **2** (**Territory**) an organized division of a country, esp. one not yet admitted to the full rights of a state. **3** a sphere of action or thought; a province. **4** the area over which a commercial traveller or goods-distributor operates. **5** *Zool.* an area defended by an animal or animals against others of the same species. **6** an area defended by a team or player in a game. **7** a large tract of land. [Middle English from Latin *territorium*, from *terra* 'land']

terror /'tɛrə/ *n.* **1** extreme fear. **2 a** a person or thing that causes terror. **b** (also **holy terror**) *colloq.* a formidable person; a troublesome person or thing (*the twins are little terrors*). **3** the use of organized intimidation; terrorism. [Middle English via Old French *terrour* from Latin *terror -oris*, from *terrēre* 'frighten']

terrorist /'tɛrərɪst/ *n.* a person who uses or favours violent and intimidating methods of coercing a government or community. □ **terrorism** *n.* **terroristic** /-'rɪstɪk/ *adj.* **terroristically** /-'rɪstɪk(ə)li/ *adv.* [French *terroriste* (as TERROR)]

terrorize /'tɛrərʌɪz/ *v.tr.* (also **-ise**) **1** fill with terror. **2** use terrorism against. □ **terrorization** /-'zeɪʃ(ə)n/ *n.* **terrorizer** *n.*

terror-stricken *adj.* (also **terror-struck**) affected with terror.

terry /'tɛri/ *n. & adj.* ● *n.* (*pl.* **-ies**) a pile fabric with the loops uncut, used esp. for towels. ● *adj.* of this fabric. [18th c.: origin unknown]

terse /tə:s/ *adj.* (**terser, tersest**) **1** (of language) brief, concise, to the point. **2** curt, abrupt. □ **tersely** *adv.* **terseness** *n.* [originally = polished, refined: Latin *tersus*, past part. of *tergēre* 'wipe, polish']

tertian /'tə:ʃ(ə)n/ *adj.* (of a fever) recurring every third day by inclusive counting. [Middle English (*fever*) *tersiane* from Latin (*febris*) *tertiana* (as TERTIARY)]

tertiary /'tə:ʃ(ə)ri/ *adj. & n.* ● *adj.* **1** third in order or rank etc. **2** (**Tertiary**) *Geol.* of or relating to the first period in the Cenozoic era with evidence of the development of mammals and flowering plants (cf. PALAEOCENE, EOCENE, OLIGOCENE, MIOCENE, PLIOCENE). Cf. Appendix X. ● *n.* **1** (**Tertiary**) *Geol.* this period or system. **2** a member of the third order of a monastic body. [Latin *tertiarius* from *tertius* 'third']

tertiary education *n.* esp. *Brit.* education, esp. in a college or university, that follows secondary education.

tertium quid /ˌtə:ʃɪəm 'kwɪd, ˌtə:tjəm/ *n.* a third thing, indefinite and undefined, related in some way to two definite or known things, but distinct from both. [Latin, apparently translation of Greek *triton ti*]

tervalent /'tə:v(ə)l(ə)nt, -'veɪl(ə)nt/ *adj. Chem.* = TRIVALENT.

Terylene /'tɛrɪli:n/ *n. Brit. propr.* a synthetic polyester used as a textile fibre. [TEREPHTHALIC ACID + ETHYLENE]

terza rima /tɛ:tsə 'ri:mə, Italian tɛrtsa 'ri:ma/ *n. Prosody* an arrangement of (esp. iambic pentameter) triplets rhyming *aba bcb cdc* etc. as in Dante's *Divina Commedia*. [Italian, = third rhyme]

terzetto /tɛ:t'sɛtəʊ, tə:t-/ *n.* (*pl.* **-os** or **terzetti** /-ti/) *Mus.* a vocal or instrumental trio. [Italian: see TERCET]

TESL /'tɛs(ə)l/ *abbr.* teaching of English as a second language.

tesla /'tɛslə, 'tɛzlə/ *n.* the SI unit of magnetic flux density. [named after N. *Tesla*, Croatian-born American scientist d. 1943]

Tesla coil *n.* a form of induction coil for producing high-frequency alternating currents.

TESOL /'tɛsɒl/ *abbr.* teaching of English to speakers of other languages.

TESSA /'tɛsə/ *n.* (also **Tessa**) (in the UK) tax exempt special savings account.

tessellate /'tɛsəleɪt/ *v.tr.* **1** make from tesserae. **2** *Math.* cover (a plane surface) by repeated use of a single shape. [Latin *tessellare* from *tessella*, diminutive of TESSERA]

tessellated /'tɛsəleɪtɪd/ *adj.* **1** of or resembling mosaic. **2** *Bot. & Zool.* regularly chequered. [Latin *tessellatus* or Italian *tessellato* (as TESSELLATE)]

tessellation /tɛsə'leɪʃ(ə)n/ *n.* **1** the act or an instance of tessellating; the state of being tessellated. **2** an arrangement of polygons without gaps or overlapping, esp. in a repeated pattern.

tessera /'tɛs(ə)rə/ *n.* (*pl.* **tesserae** /-ri:/) **1** a small square block used in mosaic. **2** *Gk & Rom. Antiq.* a small square of bone etc. used as a token, ticket, etc. □ **tesseral** *adj.* [Latin from Greek, neut. of *tesseres, tessares* 'four']

tessitura /tɛsɪ'tʊərə/ *n. Mus.* the range within which most tones of a voice part fall. [Italian, = TEXTURE]

test[1] /tɛst/ *n. & v.* ● *n.* **1** a critical examination or trial of a person's or thing's qualities. **2** the means of so examining; a standard for comparison or trial; circumstances suitable for this (*success is not a fair test*). **3** a minor examination, esp. in school (*spelling test*). **4** *Brit.* a test match. **5** a ground of admission or rejection (*is excluded by our test*). **6** *Chem.* a reagent or a procedure employed to reveal the presence of another in a compound. **7** *Brit.* a movable hearth in a reverberating furnace with a cupel used in separating gold or silver from lead. ● *v.tr.* **1** put to the test; make trial of (a person or thing or quality). **2** try severely; tax a person's powers of endurance etc. **3** *Chem.* examine by means of a reagent. **4** *Brit.* refine or assay (metal). □ **put to the test** cause to undergo a test. **test out** put (a theory etc.) to a practical test. □ **testable**

adj. **testability** /-əˈbɪlɪti/ *n.* **testee** /tɛsˈtiː/ *n.* [Middle English via Old French from Latin *testu(m)* 'earthen pot', collateral form of *testa* TEST[2]]

test[2] /tɛst/ *n.* the shell or integument of some invertebrates, esp. foraminiferans and tunicates. [Latin *testa* 'tile, jug, shell', etc.: cf. TEST[1]]

testa /ˈtɛstə/ *n.* (*pl.* **testae** /-tiː/) *Bot.* a seed-coat. [Latin (as TEST[2])]

testaceous /tɛˈsteɪʃəs/ *adj.* **1** *Biol.* having a hard continuous outer covering. **2** *Bot.* & *Zool.* of a brick-red colour. [Latin *testaceus* (as TEST[2])]

Test Act *n. hist.* **1** an act in force 1672–1828, requiring all persons before holding office in Britain to take oaths of supremacy and allegiance or an equivalent test. **2** an act of 1871 relaxing conditions for university degrees.

testament /ˈtɛstəm(ə)nt/ *n.* **1** a will (esp. *last will and testament*). **2** (usu. foll. by *to*) evidence, proof (*is testament to his loyalty*). **3** *Bibl.* **a** a covenant or dispensation. **b** (**Testament**) a division of the Christian Bible (see OLD TESTAMENT, NEW TESTAMENT). **c** (**Testament**) a copy of the New Testament. [Middle English from Latin *testamentum* 'a will' (as TESTATE): in early Christian Latin rendering Greek *diathēkē* 'covenant']

testamentary /tɛstəˈmɛnt(ə)ri/ *adj.* of or by or in a will. [Latin *testamentarius* (as TESTAMENT)]

testate /ˈtɛsteɪt/ *adj.* & *n.* ● *adj.* having left a valid will at death. ● *n.* a testate person. ▫ **testacy** *n.* (*pl.* **-ies**). [Latin *testatus*, past part. of *testari* 'testify, make a will', from *testis* 'witness']

testator /tɛˈsteɪtə/ *n.* (*fem.* **testatrix** /tɛˈsteɪtrɪks/) a person who has made a will, esp. one who dies testate. [Middle English via Anglo-French *testatour* from Latin *testator* (as TESTATE)]

test bed *n.* equipment for testing aircraft engines before acceptance for general use.

test card *n. Brit.* a still television picture transmitted outside normal programme hours and designed for use in judging the quality and position of the image.

test case *n.* a case setting a precedent for other cases involving the same question of law.

test drive *n.* a drive taken to determine the qualities of a motor vehicle with a view to its regular use. ▫ **test-drive** *v.tr.* (*past* **-drove**; *past part.* **-driven**).

tester[1] /ˈtɛstə/ *n.* **1** a person or thing that tests. **2** a sample of a cosmetic etc., allowing customers to try it before purchase.

tester[2] /ˈtɛstə/ *n.* a canopy, esp. over a four-poster bed. [Middle English from medieval Latin *testerium, testrum, testura*, ultimately from Latin *testa* 'tile']

testes *pl.* of TESTIS.

test flight *n.* a flight during which the performance of an aircraft is tested. ▫ **test-fly** *v.tr.* (**-flies**; *past* **-flew**; *past part.* **-flown**).

testicle /ˈtɛstɪk(ə)l/ *n.* a male organ that produces spermatozoa etc., esp. one of a pair enclosed in the scrotum behind the penis of a man and most mammals. Also called *testis*. ▫ **testicular** /-ˈstɪkjʊlə/ *adj.* [Middle English from Latin *testiculus*, diminutive of *testis* 'witness' (of virility)]

testiculate /tɛˈstɪkjʊlət/ *adj.* **1** having or shaped like testicles. **2** *Bot.* (esp. of an orchid) having pairs of tubers so shaped. [Late Latin *testiculatus* (as TESTICLE)]

testify /ˈtɛstɪfʌɪ/ *v.* (**-ies**, **-ied**) **1** *intr.* (of a person or thing) bear witness (*testified to the facts*). **2** *intr. Law* give evidence. **3** *tr.* affirm or declare (*testified his regret; testified that she had been present*). **4** *tr.* (of a thing) be evidence of, evince. ▫ **testifier** *n.* [Middle English from Latin *testificari*, from *testis* 'a witness']

testimonial /tɛstɪˈməʊnɪəl/ *n.* **1** a formal letter etc. testifying to a person's character, conduct, or qualifications. **2** a gift presented to a person (esp. in public) as a mark of esteem, in acknowledgement of services, etc. [Middle English from Old French *testimoignal* (*adj.*) from *tesmoin*, or from Late Latin *testimonialis* (as TESTIMONY)]

testimony /ˈtɛstɪməni/ *n.* (*pl.* **-ies**) **1** *Law* an oral or written statement under oath or affirmation. **2** declaration or statement of fact. **3** evidence, demonstration (*called him in testimony; produce testimony*). **4** *Bibl.* the Ten Commandments. **5** *archaic* a solemn protest or confession. [Middle English from Latin *testimonium*, from *testis* 'a witness']

testing ground *n.* **1** a means of experimenting, or of testing reaction, worth, etc. **2** a site for testing esp. new weapons.

testis /ˈtɛstɪs/ *n.* (*pl.* **testes** /-tiːz/) *Anat.* & *Zool.* a testicle. [Latin, = a witness: cf. TESTICLE]

test match *n.* a cricket or rugby match between teams of certain countries, usu. each of a series in a tour.

test meal *n.* a meal of specified quantity and composition, eaten to assist tests of gastric secretion.

testosterone /tɛˈstɒstərəʊn/ *n. Biochem.* a steroid hormone that stimulates development of male secondary sexual characteristics, produced mainly in the testes. [TESTIS + STEROL + -ONE]

test paper *n.* **1** a minor examination paper. **2** *Chem.* a paper impregnated with a substance changing colour under known conditions.

test pilot *n.* a pilot who test-flies aircraft.

test tube *n.* (hyphenated when *attrib.*) a thin glass tube closed at one end used for chemical tests etc.

test-tube baby *n. colloq.* a baby conceived by *in vitro* fertilization.

testudinal /tɛˈstjuːdɪn(ə)l/ *adj.* of or shaped like a tortoise. [as TESTUDO]

testudo /tɛˈstjuːdəʊ, -ˈstuː-/ *n.* (*pl.* **-os** or **testudines** /-dɪniːz/) *Rom.Hist.* **1** a screen formed by a body of troops in close array with overlapping shields. **2** a movable screen to protect besieging troops. [Latin *testudo -dinis*, literally 'tortoise' (as TEST[2])]

testy /ˈtɛsti/ *adj.* (**testier**, **testiest**) irritable, touchy. ▫ **testily** *adv.* **testiness** *n.* [originally = 'headstrong': Middle English from Anglo-French *testif*, from Old French *teste* 'head' (as TEST[2])]

tetanic /tɪˈtanɪk/ *adj.* of or such as occurs in tetanus. ▫ **tetanically** *adv.* [Latin *tetanicus* from Greek *tetanikos* (as TETANUS)]

tetanus /ˈtɛt(ə)nəs/ *n.* **1** a disease caused by the bacterium *Clostridium tetani*, marked by rigidity and spasms of the voluntary muscles. See also TRISMUS. **2** *Physiol.* the prolonged contraction of a muscle caused by rapidly repeated stimuli. ▫ **tetanize** *v.tr.* (also **-ise**). **tetanoid** *adj.* [Middle English via Latin from Greek *tetanos* 'muscular spasm', from *teinō* 'stretch']

tetany /ˈtɛt(ə)ni/ *n.* a disease with intermittent muscular spasms caused by malfunction of the parathyroid glands and a consequent deficiency of calcium. [French *tétanie* (as TETANUS)]

tetchy /ˈtɛtʃi/ *adj.* (also **techy**) (**-ier**, **-iest**) peevish, irritable. ▫ **tetchily** *adv.* **tetchiness** *n.* [probably from Middle English *tecche, tache* 'blemish, fault', from Old French *teche, tache*]

tête-à-tête /teɪtɑːˈteɪt, tɛtəˈtɛt/ *n., adv., & adj.* ● *n.* **1** a private conversation or interview usu. between two persons. **2** an S-shaped sofa for two people to sit face to face. ● *adv.* together in private (*dined tête-à-tête*). ● *adj.* **1** private, confidential. **2** concerning only two persons. [French, literally 'head-to-head']

tête-bêche /teɪtˈbɛʃ, tɛt-, French tɛtbɛʃ/ *adj.* (of a postage stamp) printed upside down or sideways relative to another. [French, from *tête* 'head' + *béchevet* 'double bedhead']

tether /ˈtɛðə/ *n.* & *v.* ● *n.* **1** a rope etc. by which an animal is tied to confine it to the spot. **2** the extent of one's knowledge, authority, etc.; scope, limit. ● *v.tr.* tie (an animal) with a tether. ▫ **at the end of one's tether** having reached the limit of one's patience, resources, abilities, etc. [Middle English from Old Norse *tjóthr*, from Germanic]

tetra /ˈtɛtrə/ *n.* any of various small, often brightly coloured tropical fish of the characin family, frequently kept in aquaria. [abbreviation of modern Latin *Tetragonopterus*, (literally 'tetragonal finned'), former genus name]

tetra- /'tɛtrə/ *comb. form* (also **tetr-** before a vowel) **1** four (*tetrapod*). **2** *Chem.* (forming names of compounds) containing four atoms or groups of a specified kind (*tetroxide*). [Greek from *tettares* 'four']

tetrachord /'tɛtrəkɔːd/ *n. Mus.* **1** a scale-pattern of four notes, the interval between the first and last being a perfect fourth. **2** a musical instrument with four strings.

tetracyclic /tɛtrə'sɪklɪk/ *adj.* **1** *Bot.* having four circles or whorls. **2** *Chem.* (of a compound) having a molecular structure of four fused hydrocarbon rings.

tetracycline /tɛtrə'sʌɪkliːn/ *n.* an antibiotic with a molecule of four rings. [TETRACYCLIC + -INE[4]]

tetrad /'tɛtrad/ *n.* **1** a group of four. **2** the number four. [Greek *tetras -ados* (as TETRA-)]

tetradactyl /tɛtrə'daktɪl/ *n. Zool.* an animal with four toes on each foot. □ **tetradactylous** *adj.*

tetraethyl lead /tɛtrə'iːθʌɪl/ *n.* a liquid added to petrol as an antiknock agent.

tetragon /'tɛtrəg(ə)n/ *n.* a plane figure with four angles and four sides. [Greek *tetragōnon* 'quadrangle' (as TETRA-, -GON)]

tetragonal /tɪ'trag(ə)n(ə)l/ *adj.* **1** of or like a tetragon. **2** *Crystallog.* (of a crystal) having three axes at right angles, two of them equal. □ **tetragonally** *adv.*

tetragram /'tɛtrəgram/ *n.* a word of four letters.

Tetragrammaton /tɛtrə'gramətɒn/ *n.* the Hebrew name of God written in four letters, articulated as *Yahweh* etc. [Greek (as TETRA-, *gramma, -atos* 'letter')]

tetragynous /tɪ'tradʒɪnəs/ *adj. Bot.* having four pistils.

tetrahedron /tɛtrə'hiːdrən, -'hɛd-/ *n.* (*pl.* **tetrahedra** /-drə/ or **tetrahedrons**) a four-sided solid; a triangular pyramid. □ **tetrahedral** *adj.* [late Greek *tetraedron*, neut. of *tetraedros* 'four-sided' (as TETRA-, -HEDRON)]

tetrahydrocannabinol see THC.

tetralogy /tɪ'tralədʒi/ *n.* (*pl.* **-ies**) **1** a group of four related literary or operatic works. **2** *Gk Antiq.* a series of four dramas, three tragic and one satyric.

tetramerous /tɪ'tram(ə)rəs/ *adj.* having four parts.

tetrameter /tɪ'tramɪtə/ *n. Prosody* a verse of four measures. [Late Latin *tetrametrus* from Greek *tetrametros* (as TETRA-, *metron* 'measure')]

tetrandrous /tɪ'trandrəs/ *adj. Bot.* having four stamens.

tetraplegia /tɛtrə'pliːdʒə/ *n. Med.* = QUADRIPLEGIA. □ **tetraplegic** *adj. & n.* [modern Latin (as TETRA-, Greek *plēgē* 'blow, strike')]

tetraploid /'tɛtrəplɔɪd/ *adj. & n. Biol.* ● *adj.* (of an organism or cell) having four times the haploid set of chromosomes. ● *n.* a tetraploid organism or cell.

tetrapod /'tɛtrəpɒd/ *n.* **1** *Zool.* an animal with four feet. **2** a structure supported by four feet radiating from a centre. □ **tetrapodous** /tɪ'trapədəs/ *adj.* [modern Latin *tetrapodus* from Greek *tetrapous* (as TETRA-, *pous podos* 'foot')]

tetrapterous /tɪ'trapt(ə)rəs/ *adj. Zool.* having four wings. [modern Latin *tetrapterus* from Greek *tetrapteros* (as TETRA-, *pteron* 'wing')]

tetrarch /'tɛtrɑːk/ *n.* **1** *Rom.Hist.* **a** the governor of a fourth part of a country or province. **b** a subordinate ruler. **2** one of four joint rulers. □ **tetrarchate** /-keɪt/ *n.* **tetrarchical** /-'trɑːkɪk(ə)l/ *adj.* **tetrarchy** *n.* (*pl.* **-ies**). [Middle English via Late Latin *tetrarcha* and Latin *tetrarches* from Greek *tetrarkhēs* (as TETRA-, *arkhō* 'rule')]

tetrastich /'tɛtrəstɪk/ *n. Prosody* a group of four lines of verse. [Latin *tetrastichon* from Greek (as TETRA-, *stikhon* 'line')]

tetrastyle /'tɛtrəstʌɪl/ *n. & adj.* ● *n.* a building with four pillars esp. forming a portico in front or supporting a ceiling. ● *adj.* (of a building) built in this way. [Latin *tetrastylos* from Greek *tetrastulos* (as TETRA-, STYLE)]

tetrasyllable /'tɛtrəsɪləb(ə)l/ *n.* a word of four syllables. □ **tetrasyllabic** /-'labɪk/ *adj.*

tetrathlon /tɛ'traθlɒn, -lən/ *n.* an athletic or sporting contest comprising four events for each competitor, esp. riding, shooting, swimming, and running. [TETRA- + Greek *athlon* 'contest', on the pattern of PENTATHLON]

tetratomic /tɛtrə'tɒmɪk/ *adj. Chem.* having four atoms (of a specified kind) in the molecule.

tetravalent /tɛtrə'veɪl(ə)nt/ *adj. Chem.* having a valency of four; quadrivalent.

tetrode /'tɛtrəʊd/ *n.* a thermionic valve having four electrodes. [TETRA- + Greek *hodos* 'way']

tetter /'tɛtə/ *n. archaic* or *dial.* a pustular skin eruption, e.g. eczema. [Old English *teter*: related to Old High German *zittaroh*, German dialect *Zitteroch*, Sanskrit *dadru*]

Teuto- /'tjuːtəʊ/ *comb. form* = TEUTON.

Teuton /'tjuːt(ə)n/ *n.* **1** a member of a Teutonic nation, esp. a German. **2** *hist.* a member of a N. European tribe which attacked the Roman Republic *c.*110 BC. [Latin *Teutones, Teutoni*, from an Indo-European base meaning 'people' or 'country']

Teutonic /tjuː'tɒnɪk/ *adj. & n.* ● *adj.* **1** relating to or characteristic of the Germanic peoples or their languages. **2** German. ● *n.* the early language usu. called Germanic. □ **Teutonicism** /-sɪz(ə)m/ *n.* [French *teutonique* from Latin *Teutonicus* (as TEUTON)]

Tex. *abbr.* Texas.

Texan /'tɛks(ə)n/ *n. & adj.* ● *n.* a native of Texas in the US. ● *adj.* of or relating to Texas.

Tex-Mex /tɛks'mɛks/ *n. & adj.* ● *n.* the Texan variety of Mexican cookery, music, Spanish, etc. ● *adj.* relating to one such variety. [*Tex*an + *Mex*ican]

text /tɛkst/ *n.* **1** the main body of a book as distinct from notes, appendices, pictures, etc. **2** the original words of an author or document, esp. as distinct from a paraphrase of or commentary on them. **3** a passage quoted from Scripture, esp. as the subject of a sermon. **4** a subject or theme. **5** (in *pl.*) books prescribed for study. **6** a textbook. **7** data in textual form, esp. as stored, processed, or displayed in a word processor etc. **8** (in full **text-hand**) a fine large kind of handwriting esp. for manuscripts. □ **textless** *adj.* [Middle English via Old Northern French *tixte, texte* from Latin *textus* 'tissue, literary style' (in medieval Latin = Gospel) from *texere text-* 'weave']

textbook /'tɛks(t)bʊk/ *n. & adj.* ● *n.* a book for use in studying, esp. a standard account of a subject. ● *attrib.adj.* **1** exemplary, accurate (cf. COPYBOOK 2b). **2** instructively typical. □ **textbookish** *adj.*

text editor *n. Computing* a system or program allowing the user to enter and edit text.

textile /'tɛkstʌɪl/ *n. & adj.* ● *n.* **1** a woven or bonded fabric; a cloth. **2** a fibre, filament, or yarn used for weaving cloth etc. ● *adj.* **1** of or relating to textiles or weaving (*textile industry*). **2** woven (*textile fabrics*). **3** suitable for weaving (*textile materials*). [Latin *textilis* (as TEXT)]

text processing *n. Computing* the manipulation of text, esp. transforming it from one format to another.

textual /'tɛkstjʊəl/ *adj.* of, in, or concerning a text (*textual errors*). □ **textually** *adv.* [Middle English from medieval Latin *textualis* (as TEXT)]

textual criticism *n.* the process of attempting to ascertain the correct reading of a text.

textualist /'tɛkstjʊəlɪst/ *n.* a person who adheres strictly to a text, esp. that of the Scriptures. □ **textualism** *n.*

textuality /tɛkstjʊ'alɪti/ *n.* **1** the medium of textual language. **2** strict adherence to a text; textualism.

texture /'tɛkstʃə/ *n. & v.* ● *n.* **1** the feel or appearance of a surface or substance. **2** the arrangement of threads etc. in textile fabric. **3** the arrangement of small constituent parts. **4** *Art* the representation of the structure and detail of objects. **5** *Mus.* the quality of sound formed by combining parts. **6** the quality of a piece of writing, esp. with reference to imagery, alliteration, etc. **7** distinctive nature or quality resulting from composition (*the texture of her life*). ● *v.tr.* (usu. as **textured** *adj.*) provide with a texture. ◻ **textural** *adj.* **texturally** *adv.* **textureless** *adj.* [Middle English from Latin *textura* 'weaving' (as TEXT)]

textured vegetable protein see TVP.

texturize /'tɛkstʃərʌɪz/ *v.tr.* (also **-ise**) (usu. as **texturized** *adj.*) impart a particular texture to (fabrics or food).

TG *abbr.* transformational grammar.

TGWU *abbr.* (in the UK) Transport and General Workers' Union.

Th *symb. Chem.* the element thorium.

Th. *abbr.* Thursday.

-th[1] /θ/ *suffix* (also **-eth** /ɪθ/) forming ordinal and fractional numbers from *four* onwards (*fourth*; *thirtieth*). [Old English *-tha, -the, -otha, -othe*]

-th[2] /θ/ *suffix* **1** forming nouns from verbs denoting an action or process (*birth*; *growth*). **2** forming nouns of state from adjectives (*breadth*; *filth*; *length*). [Old English *-thu, -tho, -th*]

-th[3] var. of -ETH[2].

Thai /tʌɪ/ *n. & adj.* ● *n.* (*pl.* same or **Thais**) **1 a** a native or national of Thailand in SE Asia; a member of the largest ethnic group in Thailand. **b** a person of Thai descent. **2** the language of Thailand. ● *adj.* of or relating to Thailand or its people or language. [Thai, = free]

thalamus /'θaləməs/ *n.* (*pl.* **thalami** /-mʌɪ, -miː/) **1** *Anat.* either of two masses of grey matter in the forebrain, serving as relay stations for sensory tracts. **2** *Bot.* the receptacle of a flower. **3** *Gk Antiq.* an inner room or women's apartment. ◻ **thalamic** /θə'lamɪk, 'θaləmɪk/ *adj.* (in senses 1 and 2). [Latin from Greek *thalamos*]

thalassaemia /θalə'siːmɪə/ *n.* (*US* **thalassemia**) *Med.* any of a group of hereditary haemolytic diseases caused by faulty haemoglobin synthesis and widespread in Mediterranean, African, and Asian countries. [Greek *thalassa* 'sea' (because first known around the Mediterranean) + -AEMIA]

thalassic /θə'lasɪk/ *adj.* of the sea or seas, esp. small or inland seas. [French *thalassique* from Greek *thalassa* 'sea']

thalassotherapy /θəˌlasəʊ'θɛrəpi/ *n.* a therapeutic treatment using sea water. [Greek *thalassa* 'sea' + THERAPY]

thaler /'tɑːlə/ *n. hist.* a German silver coin. [German *T(h)aler*: see DOLLAR]

thalidomide /θə'lɪdəmʌɪd/ *n.* a drug formerly used as a sedative but found in 1961 to cause foetal malformation when taken by a mother early in pregnancy. [ph*thal*imido*glutarimide*]

thalidomide baby *n.* (also **thalidomide child**) a baby or child born deformed from the effects of thalidomide.

thalli *pl.* of THALLUS.

thallium /'θalɪəm/ *n. Chem.* a rare soft white metallic element, occurring naturally in zinc blende and some iron ores (symbol **Tl**). ◻ **thallic** *adj.* **thallous** *adj.* [formed as THALLUS, from the green line in its spectrum]

thallophyte /'θaləfʌɪt/ *n. Bot.* a plant having a thallus, e.g. alga, fungus, or lichen. [modern Latin *Thallophyta*, (as THALLUS, -PHYTE)]

thallus /'θaləs/ *n.* (*pl.* **thalli** /-lʌɪ, -liː/) a plant-body without vascular tissue and not differentiated into root, stem, and leaves. ◻ **thalloid** *adj.* [Latin from Greek *thallos* 'green shoot', from *thallō* 'to bloom']

thalweg /'tɑːlvɛg, 'θɑːlwɛg/ *n.* **1** *Geog.* a line where opposite slopes meet at the bottom of a valley, river, or lake. **2** *Law* a boundary between states along the centre of a river etc. [German, from *Thal* 'valley' + *Weg* 'way']

than /ðan, ð(ə)n/ *conj. & prep.* **1** introducing the second element in a comparison (*you are older than he is*; *you are older than he*). **2** (prec. by *other, otherwise, rather*) introducing the second element in a statement of difference (*anyone other than me could have done it*; *a preference for watching rather than participating*; *has no aim other than to win*). [Old English *thanne* etc., originally the same word as THEN]

■ **Usage** The treatment of *than* as a preposition makes it acceptable to say *You are older than him* (see sense 1) or *anyone other than me* in less formal contexts. See also Usage Notes at DIFFERENT and OTHER.

thanage /'θeɪnɪdʒ/ *n. hist.* **1** the rank of thane. **2** the land granted to a thane. [Middle English from Anglo-French *thanage* (as THANE)]

thanatology /θanə'tɒlədʒi/ *n.* the scientific study of death and its associated phenomena and practices. [Greek *thanatos* 'death' + -LOGY]

thane /θeɪn/ *n. hist.* **1** (in Anglo-Saxon England) a man who held land from the king or other superior by military service, ranking between ordinary freemen and hereditary nobles. **2** a man who held land from a Scottish king and ranked with an earl's son; the chief of a clan. ◻ **thanedom** *n.* [Old English *theg(e)n* 'servant, soldier', from Germanic]

thank /θaŋk/ *v. & n.* ● *v.tr.* **1** express gratitude to (*thanked him for the present*). **2** hold responsible (*you can thank yourself for that*). ● *n.* (in *pl.*) **1** gratitude (*expressed his heartfelt thanks*). **2** an expression of gratitude (*give thanks to Heaven*). **3** (as a formula) thank you (*thanks for your help*; *thanks very much*). ◻ **give thanks** say grace at a meal. **I will thank you** *iron.* a polite formula implying reproach (*I will thank you to go away*). **no** (or **small**) **thanks to** despite. **thank goodness** (or **God** or **heavens** etc.) **1** *colloq.* an expression of relief or pleasure. **2** an expression of pious gratitude. **thanks to** as the (good or bad) result of (*thanks to my foresight*; *thanks to your obstinacy*). **thank you** a polite formula acknowledging a gift or service or an offer accepted or refused (see also THANK-YOU). [Old English *thancian, thanc* from Germanic: related to THINK]

thankful /'θaŋkfʊl, -f(ə)l/ *adj.* **1** grateful, pleased. **2** (of words or acts) expressive of thanks. ◻ **thankfulness** *n.* [Old English *thancful* (as THANK, -FUL)]

thankfully /'θaŋkfʊli, -f(ə)li/ *adv.* **1** in a thankful manner. **2** (qualifying a whole sentence) *disp.* let us be thankful; fortunately (*thankfully, nobody was hurt*). [Old English *thancfullice* (as THANKFUL, -LY[2])]

■ **Usage** The use of *thankfully* in sense 2 is extremely common, but it is still considered incorrect by some people. The main reason is that other such adverbs, e.g. *regrettably*, *fortunately*, etc., can be converted to the form *it is regrettable*, *it is fortunate*, etc., but *thankfully* converts to *one is thankful* (*that*). Like *hopefully*, *thankfully* first became popular in America in the 1960s, and its use is also best restricted to informal contexts.

thankless /'θaŋklɪs/ *adj.* **1** not expressing or feeling gratitude. **2** (of a task etc.) giving no pleasure or profit; unappreciated. **3** not deserving thanks. ◻ **thanklessly** *adv.* **thanklessness** *n.*

thank-offering *n.* an offering made as an act of thanksgiving.

thanksgiving /'θaŋksgɪvɪŋ, θaŋks'gɪvɪŋ/ *n.* **1 a** the expression of gratitude, esp. to God. **b** a form of words for this. **2** (**Thanksgiving** or **Thanksgiving Day**) a national holiday for giving thanks to God, the fourth Thursday in November in the US, usu. the second Monday in October in Canada.

thank-you *n. colloq.* an instance or means of expressing thanks (also *attrib.*: *a thank-you letter*) (cf. *thank you* (see THANK)).

thar var. of TAHR.

that /ðat, ðət/ *pron., det., adv., & conj.* ● *pron.* (*pl.* **those** /ðəʊz/) **1** the person or thing indicated, named, or understood, esp. when observed by the speaker or when familiar to the person addressed (*I heard that*; *who is that in the garden?*; *I knew all that before*; *that is not fair*). **2** (contrasted with *this*) the further or less immediate or obvious of two (*this bag is much heavier than that*). **3** the action, behaviour, or circumstances just observed or mentioned (*don't do that again*). **4** *Brit.* (on the telephone etc.) the person spoken to (*who is that?*). **5** esp. *Brit. colloq.* referring to a strong feeling just mentioned (*'Are you glad?' 'I am that'*). **6** (usu. *pl.*, esp. in relative constructions) the one, the person, etc., described or specified in some way (*those who have cars can take the luggage*; *those unfit for use*; *a table like that described above*). **7** /ðət/ (*pl.* **that**) used instead of *which* or *whom* to introduce a defining clause, esp. one essential to identification (*the book that you sent me*; *there is nothing here that matters*). ● *det.* (*pl.* **those** /ðəʊz/) **1** designating the person or thing indicated, named, understood, etc. (cf. sense 1 of *pron.*) (*look at that dog*; *what was that noise?*; *things were easier in those days*). **2** contrasted with *this* (cf. sense 2 of *pron.*) (*this bag is heavier than that one*). **3** expressing strong feeling (*shall not easily forget that day*). ● *adv.* **1** to such a degree; so (*have done that much*; *will go that far*). **2** *colloq.* very (*not that good*). **3** /ðət/ at which, on which, etc. (*at the speed that he was going he could not stop*; *the day that I first met her*). ● *conj.* introducing a subordinate clause indicating: **1** a statement or hypothesis (*they say that he is better*; *there is no doubt that he meant it*; *the result was that the handle fell off*). **2** a purpose (*we live that we may eat*). **3** a result (*am so sleepy that I cannot keep my eyes open*). **4** a reason or cause (*it is rather that he lacks the time*). **5** a wish (*Oh, that summer were here!*). □ **all that** (foll. by an adj.) very (*not all that good*). **and all that** (or **and that** *colloq.*) and all or various things associated with or similar to what has been mentioned; and so forth. **like that 1** of that kind (*is fond of books like that*). **2** in that manner, as you are doing, as he has been doing, etc. (*wish they would not talk like that*). **3** *colloq.* without effort (*did the job like that*). **4** of that character (*he would not accept any payment — he is like that*). **that is** (or **that is to say**) a formula introducing or following an explanation of a preceding word or words. **that's** *colloq.* you are (by virtue of present or future obedience etc.) (*that's a good boy*). **that's more like it** an acknowledgement of improvement. **that's right** an expression of approval or *colloq.* assent. **that's that** a formula concluding a narrative or discussion or indicating completion of a task. **that there** *colloq.* = sense 1 of *det.* **that will do** no more is needed or desirable. [Old English *thæt*, nominative & accusative sing. neut. of pronoun & determiner *se*, *sēo*, *thæt*, from Germanic; *those* from Old English *thās*, pl. of *thes* THIS]

■ **Usage** In sense 7 of the pronoun, *that* usually specifies or identifies something referred to, whereas *who* or *which* need not; compare *The book that you sent me is lost* with *The book, which you sent me, is lost.*

That is often omitted in sense 3 of the adverb and senses 1 and 3 of the conjunction, e.g. *the day I first met her*; *They say he is better*.

thatch /θætʃ/ *n.* & *v.* ● *n.* **1** a roof covering of straw, reeds, palm leaves, or similar material. **2** *Brit. colloq.* the hair of the head. ● *v.tr.* (also *absol.*) cover (a roof or a building) with thatch. □ **thatcher** *n.* [the noun a late collateral form of *thack* (now dialect) from Old English *thæc*: the verb from Old English *theccan* from Germanic, related and later assimilated to *thack*]

Thatcherism /ˈθætʃərɪz(ə)m/ *n.* the political and economic policies advocated by Margaret Thatcher, former UK prime minister.

thaumatrope /ˈθɔːmətrəʊp/ *n. hist.* **1** a disc or card with two different pictures on its two sides, which combine into one by the persistence of visual impressions when the disc is rapidly rotated. **2** a zoetrope. [formed irregularly from Greek *thauma* 'marvel' + *-tropos* '-turning']

thaumaturge /ˈθɔːmətəːdʒ/ *n.* a worker of miracles; a wonder-worker. □ **thaumaturgic** /-ˈtəːdʒɪk/ *adj.* **thaumaturgical** /-ˈtəːdʒɪk(ə)l/ *adj.* **thaumaturgist** *n.*

thaumaturgy *n.* [medieval Latin *thaumaturgus* from Greek *thaumatourgos* (*adj.*), from *thauma -matos* 'marvel' + *-ergos* '-working']

thaw /θɔː/ *v.* & *n.* ● *v.* **1** *intr.* (often foll. by *out*) (of ice or snow or a frozen thing) pass into a liquid or unfrozen state. **2** *intr.* (usu. prec. by *it* as subject) (of the weather) become warm enough to melt ice etc. (*it began to thaw*). **3** *intr.* become warm enough to lose numbness etc. **4** *intr.* become less cold or stiff in manner; become genial. **5** *tr.* (often foll. by *out*) cause to thaw. **6** *tr.* make cordial or animated. ● *n.* **1** the act or an instance of thawing. **2** the warmth of weather that thaws (*a thaw has set in*). **3** *Polit.* a relaxation of control or restriction. □ **thawless** *adj.* [Old English *thawian* from West Germanic; origin unknown]

THC *abbr.* tetrahydrocannabinol, the active principle of cannabis.

the /*before a consonant* ðə; *before a vowel* ðɪ; *stressed* ðiː/ *det.* & *adv.* ● *det.* (called *the definite article*) **1** denoting one or more persons or things already mentioned or assumed to be familiar (*gave the man a wave*; *shall let the matter drop*; *hurt myself in the arm*; *went to the theatre*). **2** serving to describe as unique (*the Queen*; *the Thames*). **3 a** (foll. by a defining adj.) which is, who are, etc. (*ignored the embarrassed Mr Smith*; *Edward the Seventh*). **b** (foll. by an adj. used as a noun) denoting a class described (*from the sublime to the ridiculous*). **4** (with *the* stressed) best known or best entitled to the name (*no relation to the Kipling*; *this is the book on this subject*). **5** used to point forward to a following qualifying or defining clause or phrase (*the book that you borrowed*; *the best I can do for you*; *the bottom of a well*). **6 a** used to indicate that a singular noun represents a species, class, etc. (*the cat loves comfort*; *has the novel a future?*; *plays the harp well*). **b** used with a noun which figuratively represents an occupation, pursuit, etc. (*went on the stage*; *too fond of the bottle*). **c** (foll. by the name of a unit) a, per (*5p in the pound*; *£5 the square metre*; *allow 8 minutes to the mile*). **d** *colloq.* or *archaic* designating a disease, affliction, etc. (*the measles*; *the toothache*; *the blues*). **7** (foll. by a unit of time) the present, the current (*man of the moment*; *questions of the day*; *book of the month*). **8** *colloq.* my, our (*the dog*; *the fridge*). **9** used before the surname of the chief of a Scottish or Irish clan (*the Macnab*). **10** (in Wales) used with a noun characterizing the occupation of the person whose name precedes (*Jones the Bread*). ● *adv.* (preceding comparatives in expressions of proportional variation) in or by that (or such a) degree; on that account (*the more the merrier*; *the more he gets the more he wants*). □ **all the** in the full degree to be expected (*that makes it all the worse*). **so much the** in that degree (*so much the worse for him*). [the determiner Old English, replacing *se*, *sēo*, *thæt* (= THAT), from Germanic: the adverb from Old English *thȳ*, *thē*, instrumental case]

■ **Usage** In sense 2 of the determiner, *the* is dropped from a proper noun when it is used attributively, e.g. *The Thames is popular among tourists for its riverboats*; *Thames riverboats are popular tourist attractions.*

theandric /θiːˈændrɪk/ *adj.* of the union, or by the joint agency, of the divine and human natures in Christ. [ecclesiastical Greek *theandrikos*, from *theos* 'god' + *anēr andros* 'man']

theanthropic /θiːanˈθrɒpɪk/ *adj.* **1** both divine and human. **2** tending to embody deity in human form. [ecclesiastical Greek *theanthrōpos* 'god-man', from *theos* 'god' + *anthrōpos* 'human being']

thearchy /ˈθiːɑːki/ *n.* (*pl.* **-ies**) **1** government by a god or gods. **2** a system or order of gods (*the Olympian thearchy*). [ecclesiastical Greek *thearkhia* 'godhead', from *theos* 'god' + *-arkhia* from *arkhō* 'rule']

theatre /ˈθɪətə/ *n.* (*US* **theater**) **1 a** a building or outdoor area for dramatic performances. **b** (in full **picture theatre**) esp. *N. Amer.*, *Austral.*, & *NZ* a cinema. **2 a** the writing and production of plays. **b**

effective material for the stage (*makes good theatre*). **3** (in full **lecture theatre**) a room or hall for lectures etc. with seats in tiers. **4** *Brit.* an operating theatre. **5 a** a scene or field of action (*the theatre of war*). **b** (*attrib.*) designating weapons intermediate between tactical and strategic (*theatre nuclear missiles*). **6** a natural land formation in a gradually rising part circle like ancient Greek and Roman theatres. [Middle English via Old French *t(h)eatre* or Latin *theatrum* from Greek *theatron*, from *theaomai* 'behold']

theatregoing /ˈθɪətəɡəʊɪŋ/ *adj.* (*US* **theatergoing**) frequenting theatres. □ **theatregoer** *n.*

theatre-in-the-round *n.* a dramatic performance on a stage surrounded by spectators.

Theatre of the Absurd *n.* drama portraying the futility of human struggle in a senseless world.

theatre sister *n. Brit.* a nurse supervising the nursing team in an operating theatre.

theatric /θɪˈatrɪk/ *adj. & n.* ● *adj.* = THEATRICAL. ● *n.* (in *pl.*) theatrical actions.

theatrical /θɪˈatrɪk(ə)l/ *adj. & n.* ● *adj.* **1** of or for the theatre; of acting or actors. **2** (of a manner, speech, gesture, or person) calculated for effect; showy, artificial, affected. ● *n.* **1** (in *pl.*) dramatic performances (*amateur theatricals*). **2** (in *pl.*) theatrical actions. **3** (usu. in *pl.*) a professional actor or actress. □ **theatricalism** *n.* **theatricality** /-ˈkalɪti/ *n.* **theatricalize** *v.tr.* (also **-ise**). **theatricalization** /-lʌɪˈzeɪʃ(ə)n/ *n.* **theatrically** *adv.* [Late Latin *theatricus* from Greek *theatrikos*, from *theatron* THEATRE]

Theban /ˈθiːb(ə)n/ *adj. & n.* ● *adj.* of or relating to Thebes in ancient Egypt or ancient Greece. ● *n.* a native or inhabitant of Thebes. [Middle English from Latin *Thebanus*, from *Thebae* 'Thebes', from Greek *Thēbai*]

theca /ˈθiːkə/ *n.* (*pl.* **thecae** /-siː/) **1** *Bot.* a part of a plant serving as a receptacle. **2** *Zool.* a case or sheath enclosing an organ or organism. □ **thecate** *adj.* [Latin from Greek *thēkē* 'case']

thé dansant /teɪ dɒ̃ˈsɒ̃, French te dɑ̃sɑ̃/ *n.* (*pl.* ***thés dansants*** *pronunc.* same) = TEA DANCE. [French]

thee /ðiː/ *pron. objective case* of THOU[1]. [Old English]

theft /θɛft/ *n.* **1** the act or an instance of stealing. **2** *Law* dishonest appropriation of another's property with intent to deprive him or her of it permanently. [Old English *thīefth*, *thēofth*, later *thēoft*, from Germanic: related to THIEF]

thegn /θeɪn/ *n. hist.* an English thane. [Old English: see THANE]

theine /ˈθiːiːn, ˈθiːɪn/ *n.* = CAFFEINE. [modern Latin *thea* 'tea' + -INE[4]]

their /ðɛː/ *poss.det.* **1** of or belonging to them (*their house*; *their own business*). **2** (**Their**) (in titles) that they are (*Their Majesties*). **3** *disp.* as a third person sing. indefinite meaning 'his or her' (*has anyone lost their purse?*). [Middle English from Old Norse *their(r)a* 'of them', genitive pl. of *sá* THE, THAT]

■ **Usage** See Usage Note at THEY.

theirs /ðɛːz/ *poss.pron.* the one or ones belonging to or associated with them (*it is theirs*; *theirs are over here*). □ **of theirs** of or belonging to them (*a friend of theirs*). [Middle English, from THEIR]

theirselves /ðɛːˈsɛlvz/ *pron. dial.* = THEMSELVES.

theism /ˈθiːɪz(ə)m/ *n.* belief in the existence of gods or a god, esp. a God supernaturally revealed to man (cf. DEISM) and sustaining a personal relation to his creatures. □ **theist** *n.* **theistic** /-ˈɪstɪk/ *adj.* **theistical** /-ˈɪstɪk(ə)l/ *adj.* **theistically** /-ˈɪstɪk(ə)li/ *adv.* [Greek *theos* 'god' + -ISM]

them /ðɛm, ðəm/ *pron. & det.* ● *pron.* **1** *objective case* of THEY (*I saw them*). **2** *colloq.* they (*it's them again*; *is older than them*). **3** *archaic* themselves (*they fell and hurt them*). ● *det. slang* or *dial.* those (*them bones*). [Middle English *theim* from Old Norse: see THEY]

■ **Usage** See Usage Note at HER.

thematic /θɪˈmatɪk/ *adj. & n.* ● *adj.* **1** of or relating to subjects or topics (*thematic philately*; *the arrangement of the anthology is thematic*). **2** *Mus.* of melodic subjects (*thematic treatment*). **3** *Gram.* **a** of or belonging to a theme (*thematic vowel*; *thematic form*). **b** (of a form of a verb) having a thematic vowel. ● *n.* (in *pl.*; treated as *sing.* or *pl.*) the themes or subjects in a text esp. for study or discussion. □ **thematically** *adv.* [Greek *thematikos* (as THEME)]

thematic catalogue *n. Mus.* a catalogue giving the opening themes of works as well as their names and other details.

theme /θiːm/ *n. & v.* ● *n.* **1** a subject or topic on which a person speaks, writes, or thinks. **2** *Mus.* a prominent or frequently recurring melody or group of notes in a composition. **3** *US* a school exercise, esp. an essay, on a given subject. **4** *Gram.* the stem of a noun or verb; the part to which inflections are added, esp. composed of the root and an added vowel. **5** *hist.* any of the 29 provinces in the Byzantine empire. ● *v.tr.* (as **themed** *adj.*) **1** (often foll. by *on*, *around*) (of a leisure park, restaurant, event, etc.) designed around a theme to unify ambience, decor, etc. **2** (often in *comb.*) having a particular theme (*war-themed computer game*). [Middle English *teme*, ultimately via Greek *thema -matos* from *tithēmi* 'set, place']

theme park *n.* an amusement park organized round a unifying idea.

theme song *n.* (also **theme tune**) **1** a recurrent melody in a musical play or film. **2** a signature tune.

themself /ð(ə)mˈsɛlf/ *pron. disp.* = THEMSELVES 3 (*anyone can hurt themself*).

themselves /ð(ə)mˈsɛlvz/ *pron.* **1 a** *emphat. form* of THEY or THEM. **b** *refl. form* of THEM; (cf. HERSELF). **2** in their normal state of body or mind (*are quite themselves again*). **3** (also **themself**) *disp.* (referring back to an indefinite pronoun) himself, herself; himself or herself (*everyone kept it to themselves*). □ **be themselves** act in their normal, unconstrained manner.

■ **Usage** The use of *themselves* or *themself* in sense 3 is considered erroneous by some people. See Usage Note at THEY.

then /ðɛn/ *adv., adj., & n.* ● *adv.* **1** at that time; at the time in question (*was then too busy*; *then comes the trouble*; *the then existing laws*). **2 a** next, afterwards; after that (*then he told me to come in*). **b** and also (*then, there are the children to consider*). **c** after all (*it is a problem, but then that is what we are here for*). **3 a** in that case; therefore; it follows that (*then you should have said so*). **b** if what you say is true (*but then why did you take it?*). **c** (implying grudging or impatient concession) if you must have it so (*all right then, have it your own way*). **d** used parenthetically to resume a narrative etc. (*the policeman, then, knocked on the door*). ● *attrib.adj.* that or who was such at the time in question (*the then Duke*). ● *n.* that time (*until then*). □ **then and there** immediately and on the spot. [Old English *thanne*, *thonne*, etc., from Germanic: related to THAT, THE]

■ **Usage** *Then* should not be used as an adjective if it would sound equally well in its usual position, e.g. *Harold Wilson was the then Prime Minister* could equally well be *Harold Wilson was then the Prime Minister*.

thenar /ˈθiːnə/ *n. Anat.* the ball of muscle at the base of the thumb. [earlier = palm of the hand: modern Latin from Greek]

thence /ðɛns/ *adv.* (also **from thence**) *archaic* or *literary* **1** from that place or source. **2** for that reason. [Middle English *thannes*, *thennes* via *thanne*, *thenne* from Old English *thanon(e)* etc., from West Germanic]

thenceforth /ðɛnsˈfɔːθ, ˈðɛnsfɔːθ/ *adv.* (also **from thenceforth**) *archaic* or *literary* from that time onward.

thenceforward /ðɛnsˈfɔːwəd/ *adv. archaic* or *literary* thenceforth.

theo- /ˈθiːəʊ/ *comb. form* God or gods. [Greek from *theos* 'god']

theobromine /θɪəˈbrəʊmɪn, -miːn/ *n.* a bitter white alkaloid obtained from cacao seeds, related to caffeine. [*Theobroma*, the name of the cacao genus: modern Latin, from Greek *theos* 'god' + *brōma* 'food', + -INE[4]]

theocentric /θɪə(ʊ)ˈsɛntrɪk/ *adj.* having God as its centre.

theocracy /θɪˈɒkrəsi/ *n.* (*pl.* **-ies**) **1** a form of government by God or a god directly or through a priestly order etc. **2** (**the Theocracy**) the commonwealth of Israel from Moses to the election of Saul as King. ◻ **theocrat** /ˈθiːəkrat/ *n.* **theocratic** /θɪəˈkratɪk/ *adj.* **theocratically** /θɪəˈkratɪk(ə)li/ *adv.*

theocrasy /ˈθiːəkreɪsi, θɪˈɒkrəsi/ *n.* **1** the mingling of deities into one personality. **2** the union of the soul with God through contemplation (among Neoplatonists etc.). [THEO- + Greek *krasis* 'mingling']

theodicy /θɪˈɒdɪsi/ *n.* (*pl.* **-ies**) **1** the vindication of divine providence in view of the existence of evil. **2** an instance of this. ◻ **theodicean** /-ˈsiːən/ *adj.* [THEO- + Greek *dikē* 'justice']

theodolite /θɪˈɒdəlʌɪt/ *n.* a surveying instrument for measuring horizontal and vertical angles with a rotating telescope. ◻ **theodolitic** /-ˈlɪtɪk/ *adj.* [16th c.: modern Latin *theodelitus*, of unknown origin]

theogony /θɪˈɒgəni/ *n.* (*pl.* **-ies**) **1** the genealogy of the gods. **2** an account of this. [THEO- + Greek *-gonia* 'begetting']

theologian /θɪəˈləʊdʒɪən, -dʒ(ə)n/ *n.* a person trained in theology. [Middle English from Old French *theologien* (as THEOLOGY)]

theological /θɪəˈlɒdʒɪk(ə)l/ *adj.* of theology. ◻ **theologically** *adv.* [medieval Latin *theologicalis* via Latin *theologicus* from Greek *theologikos* (as THEOLOGY)]

theological virtue *n.* each of the virtues faith, hope, and charity.

theology /θɪˈɒlədʒi/ *n.* (*pl.* **-ies**) **1 a** the study of theistic (esp. Christian) religion. **b** a system of theistic (esp. Christian) religion. **c** the rational analysis of a religious faith. **2** a system of theoretical principles, esp. an impractical or rigid ideology. ◻ **theologist** *n.* **theologize** *v.tr. & intr.* (also **-ise**). [Middle English via Old French *theologie* and Latin *theologia* from Greek (as THEO-, -LOGY)]

theomachy /θɪˈɒməki/ *n.* (*pl.* **-ies**) strife among or against the gods. [THEO- + Greek *makhē* 'fight']

theophany /θɪˈɒf(ə)ni/ *n.* (*pl.* **-ies**) a visible manifestation of God or a god to man.

theophoric /θɪəˈfɒrɪk/ *adj.* bearing the name of a god.

theophylline /θɪəˈfɪliːn, -lɪn/ *n.* an alkaloid similar to theobromine, found in tea leaves. [formed irregularly from modern Latin *thea* 'tea' + Greek *phullon* 'leaf' + -INE[4]]

theorbo /θɪˈɔːbəʊ/ *n.* (*pl.* **-os**) a two-necked musical instrument of the lute class much used in the 17th c. ◻ **theorbist** *n.* [Italian *tiorba*, of unknown origin]

theorem /ˈθɪərəm/ *n.* esp. *Math.* **1** a general proposition not self-evident but proved by a chain of reasoning; a truth established by means of accepted truths (cf. PROBLEM 4). **2** a rule in algebra etc., esp. one expressed by symbols or formulae (*binomial theorem*). ◻ **theorematic** /-ˈmatɪk/ *adj.* [French *théorème* or Late Latin *theorema* from Greek *theōrēma* 'speculation, proposition', from *theōreō* 'look at']

theoretic /θɪəˈrɛtɪk/ *adj. & n.* ● *adj.* = THEORETICAL. ● *n.* (in *sing.* or *pl.*) the theoretical part of a science etc. [Late Latin *theoreticus* from Greek *theōrētikos* (as THEORY)]

theoretical /θɪəˈrɛtɪk(ə)l/ *adj.* **1** concerned with knowledge but not with its practical application. **2** based on theory rather than experience or practice. ◻ **theoretically** *adv.*

theoretician /θɪərɪˈtɪʃ(ə)n/ *n.* a person concerned with the theoretical aspects of a subject.

theorist /ˈθɪərɪst/ *n.* a holder or inventor of a theory or theories.

theorize /ˈθɪərʌɪz/ *v.* (also **-ise**) **1** *intr.* evolve or indulge in theories. **2** *tr.* consider or devise in theory. ◻ **theorization** /-ˈzeɪʃ(ə)n/ *n.* **theorizer** *n.*

theory /ˈθɪəri/ *n.* (*pl.* **-ies**) **1** a supposition or system of ideas explaining something, esp. one based on general principles independent of the particular things to be explained (cf. HYPOTHESIS 2) (*atomic theory*; *theory of evolution*). **2** a speculative (esp. fanciful) view (*one of my pet theories*). **3** the sphere of abstract knowledge or speculative thought (*this is all very well in theory, but how will it work in practice?*). **4** the exposition of the principles of a science etc. (*the theory of music*). **5** *Math.* a collection of propositions to illustrate the principles of a subject (*probability theory*; *theory of equations*). [Late Latin *theoria* from Greek *theōria*, via *theōros* 'spectator' from *theōreō* 'look at']

theosophy /θɪˈɒsəfi/ *n.* (*pl.* **-ies**) any of various philosophies professing to achieve a knowledge of God by spiritual ecstasy, direct intuition, or special individual relations, esp. a modern movement following Hindu and Buddhist teachings and seeking universal brotherhood. ◻ **theosopher** *n.* **theosophic** /θɪəˈsɒfɪk/ *adj.* **theosophical** /θɪəˈsɒfɪk(ə)l/ *adj.* **theosophically** /θɪəˈsɒfɪk(ə)li/ *adv.* **theosophist** *n.* [medieval Latin *theosophia* from late Greek *theosophia*, from *theosophos* 'wise concerning God' (as THEO-, *sophos* 'wise')]

therapeutic /θɛrəˈpjuːtɪk/ *adj.* **1** of, for, or contributing to the cure of disease. **2** contributing to general, esp. mental, well-being (*she finds walking therapeutic*). ◻ **therapeutical** *adj.* **therapeutically** *adv.* **therapeutist** *n.* [attributive use of *therapeutic*, originally a form of THERAPEUTICS]

therapeutics /θɛrəˈpjuːtɪks/ *n.pl.* (usu. treated as *sing.*) the branch of medicine concerned with the treatment of disease and the action of remedial agents. [French *thérapeutique* or Late Latin *therapeutica* (pl.) from Greek *therapeutika*, neut. pl. of *therapeutikos*, from *therapeuō* 'wait on, cure']

therapsid /θɛˈrapsɪd/ *n. & adj.* ● *n.* a fossil reptile of the order Therapsida, related to the ancestors of mammals. ● *adj.* of or relating to this order. [modern Latin *Therapsida*, from Greek *thēr* 'beast' + (*h*)*apsis* *-idos* 'arch' (referring to the structure of the skull]

therapy /ˈθɛrəpi/ *n.* (*pl.* **-ies**) **1** the treatment of physical or mental disorders, other than by surgery. **2** a particular type of such treatment. ◻ **therapist** *n.* [modern Latin *therapia* from Greek *therapeia* 'healing']

Theravada /θɛrəˈvɑːdə/ *n.* a more conservative form of Buddhism, practised in Sri Lanka, Burma (now Myanmar), Thailand, etc. [Pali *theravāda*, literally 'doctrine of the elders', from *thera* 'elder, old' + *vāda* 'speech, doctrine']

there /ðɛː, ðə/ *adv., n., & int.* ● *adv.* **1** in, at, or to that place or position (*lived there for some years*; *goes there every day*). **2** at that point (in speech, performance, writing, etc.) (*there he stopped*). **3** in that respect (*I agree with you there*). **4** used for emphasis in calling attention (*you there!*; *there goes the bell*). **5** used to indicate the fact or existence of something (*there is a house on the corner*). ● *n.* that place (*lives somewhere near there*). ● *int.* **1** expressing confirmation, triumph, dismay, etc. (*there! what did I tell you?*). **2** used to soothe a child etc. (*there, there, never mind*). ◻ **have been there before** *colloq.* know all about it. **so there** *colloq.* that is my final decision (whether you like it or not). **there and then** immediately and on the spot. **there it is 1** that is the trouble. **2** nothing can be done about it. **there you are** (or **go**) *colloq.* **1** this is what you wanted etc. **2** expressing confirmation, triumph, resignation, etc. [Old English *thǣr*, *thēr* from Germanic: related to THAT, THE]

thereabouts /ˈðɛːrəbaʊts, -ˈbaʊts/ *adv.* (also **thereabout**) **1** near that place (*ought to be somewhere thereabouts*). **2** near that number, quantity, etc. (*two litres or thereabouts*).

thereafter /ðɛːrˈɑːftə/ *adv. formal* after that.

thereanent /ðɛːrə'nɛnt/ *adv. Sc.* about that matter.
thereat /ðɛːr'at/ *adv. archaic* **1** at that place. **2** on that account. **3** after that.
thereby /ðɛː'bʌɪ/ *adv.* by that means; as a result of that. □ **thereby hangs a tale** much could be said about that.
therefor /ðɛː'fɔː/ *adv. archaic* for that object or purpose.
therefore /'ðɛːfɔː/ *adv.* for that reason; accordingly, consequently.
therefrom /ðɛː'frɒm/ *adv. archaic* from that or it.
therein /ðɛːr'ɪn/ *adv. formal* **1** in that place etc. **2** in that respect.
thereinafter /ðɛːrɪn'ɑːftə/ *adv. formal* later in the same document etc.
thereinbefore /ðɛːrˌɪnbɪ'fɔː/ *adv. formal* earlier in the same document etc.
thereinto /ðɛːr'ɪntʊ/ *adv. archaic* into that place.
thereof /ðɛːr'ɒv/ *adv. formal* of that or it.
thereon /ðɛːr'ɒn/ *adv. archaic* on that or it (of motion or position).
thereout /ðɛːr'aʊt/ *adv. archaic* out of that; from that source.
there's /ðɛːz, ðəz/ *contr.* **1** there is. **2** esp. *Brit. colloq.* you are (by virtue of present or future obedience etc.) (*there's a dear*).
therethrough /ðɛː'θruː/ *adv. archaic* through that.
thereto /ðɛː'tuː/ *adv. formal* **1** to that or it. **2** in addition; to boot.
theretofore /ðɛːtʊ'fɔː/ *adv. formal* before that time.
thereunder /ðɛːr'ʌndə/ *adv. formal* **1** in accordance with that. **2** stated below that (in the document etc.).
thereunto /ðɛːr'ʌntʊ/ *adv. archaic* to that or it.
thereupon /ðɛːrə'pɒn/ *adv.* **1** in consequence of that. **2** soon or immediately after that. **3** *archaic* upon that (of motion or position).
therewith /ðɛː'wɪð/ *adv. archaic* **1** with that. **2** soon or immediately after that.
therewithal /ðɛːwɪ'ðɔːl/ *adv. archaic* in addition; besides.
theriac /'θɪərɪak/ *n. archaic* an antidote to the bites of poisonous animals, esp. snakes. [Latin *theriaca* from Greek *thēriakē* 'antidote', fem. of *thēriakos*, from *thēr* 'wild beast']
therianthropic /θɪərɪan'θrɒpɪk/ *adj.* of or worshipping beings represented in combined human and animal forms. [Greek *thērion* (diminutive of *thēr* 'wild beast') + *anthrōpos* 'human being']
theriomorphic /θɪərɪə(ʊ)'mɔːfɪk/ *adj.* (esp. of a deity) having an animal form. [as THERIANTHROPIC + Greek *morphē* 'form']
therm /θəːm/ *n.* a unit of heat, esp. as the former statutory unit of gas supplied in the UK equivalent to 100,000 British thermal units or 1.055 × 10^8 joules. [Greek *thermē* 'heat']
thermae /'θəːmiː/ *n.pl. Gk & Rom. Antiq.* public baths. [Latin from Greek *thermai* (pl.) (as THERM)]
thermal /'θəːm(ə)l/ *adj.* & *n.* ● *adj.* **1** of, for, or producing heat. **2** promoting the retention of heat (*thermal underwear*). ● *n.* **1** a rising current of heated air (used by gliders, balloons, and birds to gain height). **2** (in *pl.*) thermal underwear. □ **thermalize** *v.tr. & intr.* (also **-ise**). **thermalization** /-lʌɪ'zeɪʃ(ə)n/ *n.* **thermally** *adv.* [French (as THERM)]
thermal capacity *n.* the number of heat units needed to raise the temperature of a body by one degree.
thermal imaging *n.* the technique of using the heat given off by an object etc. to produce an image of it or locate it.
thermal neutron *n.* a neutron in thermal equilibrium with its surroundings.
thermal printer *n.* a printer in which fine heated pins form characters on heat-sensitive paper.
thermal reactor *n.* a nuclear reactor using thermal neutrons.
thermal springs *n.pl.* springs of naturally hot water.
thermal unit *n.* a unit for measuring heat.
thermic /'θəːmɪk/ *adj.* of or relating to heat.
thermidor see LOBSTER THERMIDOR.
thermion /'θəːmɪɒn/ *n.* an ion or electron emitted by a substance at high temperature. [THERMO- + ION]
thermionic /θəːmɪ'ɒnɪk/ *adj.* of or relating to electrons emitted from a substance at very high temperature.
thermionic emission *n.* the emission of electrons from a heated source.
thermionics /θəːmɪ'ɒnɪks/ *n.pl.* (treated as *sing.*) the branch of science and technology concerned with thermionic emission.
thermionic valve *n.* (*US* **thermionic tube**) a device giving a flow of thermionic electrons in one direction, used esp. in the rectification of a current and in radio reception.
thermistor /θəː'mɪstə/ *n. Electr.* a resistor whose resistance is greatly reduced by heating, used for measurement and control. [*thermal resistor*]
thermite /'θəːmʌɪt/ *n.* (also **thermit** /-mɪt/) a mixture of finely powdered aluminium and iron oxide that produces a very high temperature on combustion (used in welding and for incendiary bombs). [German *Thermit* (as THERMO-, -ITE[1])]
thermo- /'θəːməʊ/ *comb. form* denoting heat. [Greek, from *thermos* 'hot', *thermē* 'heat']
thermochemistry /θəːməʊ'kɛmɪstri/ *n.* the branch of chemistry dealing with the quantities of heat evolved or absorbed in the course of chemical reactions. □ **thermochemical** *adj.*
thermocline /'θəːmə(ʊ)klʌɪn/ *n.* **1** a temperature gradient, esp. an abrupt one in a body of water. **2** a layer of water marked by an abrupt temperature change. [THERMO- + Greek *klinō* 'to slope']
thermocouple /'θəːməʊkʌp(ə)l/ *n.* a thermoelectric device for measuring temperature, consisting of two wires of different metals connected at two points, a voltage being developed between the two junctions in proportion to the temperature difference.
thermodynamics /ˌθəːmə(ʊ)dʌɪ'namɪks/ *n.pl.* (usu. treated as *sing.*) the science of the relations between heat and other (mechanical, electrical, etc.) forms of energy. □ **thermodynamic** *adj.* **thermodynamical** *adj.* **thermodynamically** *adv.* **thermodynamicist** /-sɪst/ *n.*
thermoelectric /ˌθəːməʊɪ'lɛktrɪk/ *adj.* relating to electricity produced by a temperature difference. □ **thermoelectrically** *adv.* **thermoelectricity** /-ɪlɛk'trɪsɪti/ *n.*
thermogenesis /θəːməʊ'dʒɛnɪsɪs/ *n.* the production of heat, esp. in a human or animal body.
thermogram /'θəːməgram/ *n.* a record made by a thermograph.
thermograph /'θəːməgrɑːf/ *n.* **1** an instrument that gives a continuous record of temperature. **2** an apparatus used to obtain an image produced by infra-red radiation from a human or animal body. □ **thermographic** /-'grafɪk/ *adj.*
thermography /θəː'mɒgrəfi/ *n. Med.* the taking or use of infra-red thermograms, esp. to detect tumours.
thermolabile /θəːməʊ'leɪbʌɪl, -bɪl/ *adj.* (of a substance) unstable when heated.
thermoluminescence /ˌθəːməʊluːmɪ'nɛs(ə)ns/ *n.* the property of becoming luminescent when pretreated and subjected to high temperatures, used as a means of dating ancient artefacts. □ **thermoluminescent** *adj.*
thermolysis /θə'mɒlɪsɪs/ *n.* decomposition by the action of heat. □ **thermolytic** /-'lɪtɪk/ *adj.*
thermometer /θə'mɒmɪtə/ *n.* an instrument for measuring temperature, esp. a graduated glass tube with a small bore containing mercury or alcohol which expands when heated. □ **thermometric** /θəːmə'mɛtrɪk/ *adj.* **thermometrical** /θəːmə'mɛtrɪk(ə)l/ *adj.* **thermometry** *n.* [French *thermomètre* or modern Latin *thermometrum* (as THERMO-, -METER)]
thermonuclear /θəːməʊ'njuːklɪə/ *adj.* **1** relating to or using nuclear reactions that occur only at very high temperatures. **2** of, relating to, or involving weapons in

which explosive force is produced by thermonuclear reactions (*thermonuclear war*).

thermophile /ˈθəːmə(ʊ)fʌɪl/ *n. & adj.* (also **thermophil** /-fɪl/) ● *n.* a bacterium etc. growing optimally at high temperatures. ● *adj.* of or being a thermophile. ▫ **thermophilic** /-ˈfɪlɪk/ *adj.*

thermopile /ˈθəːmə(ʊ)pʌɪl/ *n.* a set of thermocouples esp. arranged for measuring small quantities of radiant heat.

thermoplastic /θəːməʊˈplastɪk/ *adj. & n.* ● *adj.* (of a substance) that becomes plastic on heating and hardens on cooling, and is able to repeat these processes. ● *n.* a thermoplastic substance.

thermos /ˈθəːmɒs/ *n.* (in full **thermos flask**, *N. Amer.* **thermos bottle**) *propr.* a vacuum flask. [Greek, = hot]

thermosetting /ˈθəːməʊsɛtɪŋ/ *adj.* (of plastics) setting permanently when heated. ▫ **thermoset** *adj.*

thermosphere /ˈθəːməsfɪə/ *n.* the region of the atmosphere beyond the mesosphere.

thermostable /θəːməʊˈsteɪb(ə)l/ *adj.* (of a substance) stable when heated.

thermostat /ˈθəːməstat/ *n.* a device that automatically regulates temperature, or that activates a device when the temperature reaches a certain point. ▫ **thermostatic** /-ˈstatɪk/ *adj.* **thermostatically** /-ˈstatɪk(ə)li/ *adv.* [THERMO- + Greek *statos* 'standing']

thermotaxis /θəːmə(ʊ)ˈtaksɪs/ *n.* movement of an organism towards or away from a source of heat. ▫ **thermotactic** *adj.* **thermotaxic** *adj.*

thermotropism /θəːməʊˈtrəʊpɪz(ə)m/ *n.* the growing or bending of a plant towards or away from a source of heat. ▫ **thermotropic** /θəːmə(ʊ)ˈtrəʊpɪk, -ˈtrɒp-/ *adj.*

theropod /ˈθɪərəpɒd/ *n. & adj.* ● *n.* a saurischian dinosaur of the group *Theropoda*, comprising mainly bipedal carnivores, including tyrannosaurs and the possible ancestors of birds. ● *adj.* of or relating to this group. [Greek *thēr* 'beast' + *pous podos* 'foot']

thesaurus /θɪˈsɔːrəs/ *n.* (*pl.* **thesauri** /-rʌɪ/ or **thesauruses**) **1** a book that lists words in groups of synonyms and related concepts. **2** a dictionary or encyclopedia. [Latin from Greek *thēsauros* 'treasure']

these *pl.* of THIS.

thesis /ˈθiːsɪs/ *n.* (*pl.* **theses** /-siːz/) **1** a proposition to be maintained or proved. **2** a dissertation, esp. by a candidate for a degree. **3** /ˈθiːsɪs, ˈθɛsɪs/ an unstressed syllable or part of a metrical foot in Greek or Latin verse (opp. ARSIS). [Middle English via Late Latin from Greek, = putting, placing, a proposition, etc. from *the-*, root of *tithēmi* 'to place']

thespian /ˈθɛspɪən/ *adj. & n.* ● *adj.* of or relating to tragedy or drama. ● *n.* an actor or actress. [Greek *Thespis*, the name of the traditional originator of Greek tragedy]

Thess. *abbr.* Thessalonians (New Testament).

theta /ˈθiːtə/ *n.* the eighth letter of the Greek alphabet (Θ, θ). [Greek]

theurgy /ˈθiːəːdʒi/ *n.* **1 a** supernatural or divine agency esp. in human affairs. **b** the art of securing this. **2 a** system of white magic practised by the early Neoplatonists. ▫ **theurgic** /-ˈəːdʒɪk/ *adj.* **theurgical** /-ˈəːdʒɪk(ə)l/ *adj.* **theurgist** *n.* [Late Latin *theurgia* from Greek *theourgia*, from *theos* 'god' + *-ergos* 'working']

thew /θjuː/ *n.* (often in *pl.*) *literary* **1** muscular strength. **2** mental or moral vigour. [Old English *thēaw* usage, conduct, of unknown origin]

they /ðeɪ/ *pron.* (*obj.* **them**; *poss.* **their**, **theirs**) **1** the people, animals, or things previously named or in question (*pl.* of HE, SHE, IT[1]). **2** people in general (*they say we are wrong*). **3** those in authority (*they have raised the fees*). **4** *disp.* as a third person sing. indefinite pronoun meaning 'he or she' (*anyone can come if they want to*; *if you have a friend you want to invite, feel free to bring them along*). [Middle English *thei*, obj. *theim*, from Old Norse *their* nominative pl. masc., *theim* dative pl., of *sá* 'that']

■ **Usage** The use of *they* instead of 'he or she' (see sense 4 above) is common in spoken English and increasingly so in written English, although still deplored by some people. It is particularly useful when the sex of the person is unspecified or unknown and the writer wishes to avoid the accusation of sexism that can arise from the use of *he*. Similarly, *their* can replace 'his' or 'his or her' and *themselves* 'himself' or 'himself or herself', e.g. *Everyone must provide their own lunch*; *Did anyone hurt themselves in the accident?*

they'd /ðeɪd/ *contr.* **1** they had. **2** they would.

they'll /ðeɪl, ðɛl/ *contr.* **1** they will. **2** they shall.

they're /ðɛː, ˈðeɪə/ *contr.* they are.

they've /ðeɪv/ *contr.* they have.

THI *abbr.* temperature-humidity index.

thiamine /ˈθʌɪəmiːn, -mɪn/ *n.* (also **thiamin**) a vitamin of the B complex, found in unrefined cereals, beans, and liver, a deficiency of which causes beriberi. Also called *vitamin* B_1, or ANEURIN. [THIO- + *amin* from VITAMIN]

thick /θɪk/ *adj., n., & adv.* ● *adj.* **1 a** of great or specified extent between opposite surfaces (*a thick wall*; *a wall two metres thick*). **b** of large diameter (*a thick rope*). **2 a** (of a line etc.) broad; not fine. **b** (of script or type, etc.) consisting of thick lines. **3 a** arranged closely; crowded together; dense. **b** numerous. **4** (usu. foll. by *with*) densely covered or filled (*air thick with snow*). **5 a** firm in consistency; containing much solid matter; viscous (*a thick paste*; *thick soup*). **b** made of thick material (*a thick coat*). **6 a** muddy, cloudy; impenetrable by sight (*thick darkness*). **b** (of one's head) suffering from a headache, hangover, etc. **7** *colloq.* (of a person) stupid, dull. **8 a** (of a voice) indistinct. **b** (of an accent) very marked. **9** *colloq.* intimate or very friendly (esp. *thick as thieves*). ● *n.* a thick part of anything. ● *adv.* thickly (*snow was falling thick*; *blows rained down thick and fast*). ▫ **a bit thick** *Brit. colloq.* unreasonable or intolerable. **in the thick of 1** at the busiest part of. **2** heavily occupied with. **through thick and thin** under all conditions; in spite of all difficulties. ▫ **thickish** *adj.* **thickly** *adv.* [Old English *thicce* (*adj.* & *adv.*), from Germanic]

thick ear *n. Brit. slang* the external ear swollen as a result of a blow (esp. *give a person a thick ear*).

thicken /ˈθɪk(ə)n/ *v.* **1** *tr.* & *intr.* make or become thick or thicker. **2** *intr.* become more complicated (*the plot thickens*). ▫ **thickener** *n.*

thickening /ˈθɪk(ə)nɪŋ/ *n.* **1** the process of becoming thick or thicker. **2** a substance used to thicken liquid. **3** a thickened part.

thicket /ˈθɪkɪt/ *n.* a tangle of shrubs or trees. [Old English *thiccet* (as THICK, -ET[1])]

thickhead /ˈθɪkhɛd/ *n.* **1** *colloq.* a stupid person; a blockhead. **2** any Asian or Australasian perching bird of the family Pachycephalidae, with a large head. Also called WHISTLER. ▫ **thickheaded** /-ˈhɛdɪd/ *adj.* **thickheadedness** /-ˈhɛdɪdnɪs/ *n.*

thick-knee *n.* = STONE CURLEW.

thickness /ˈθɪknɪs/ *n.* **1** the state of being thick. **2** the extent to which a thing is thick. **3** a layer of material of a certain thickness (*three thicknesses of cardboard*). **4** a part that is thick or lies between opposite surfaces (*steps cut in the thickness of the wall*). [Old English *thicness* (as THICK, -NESS)]

thicko /ˈθɪkəʊ/ *n.* (*pl.* **-os**) *colloq.* an unintelligent person. [THICK + -O]

thickset /θɪkˈsɛt/ *adj. & n.* ● *adj.* **1** heavily or solidly built. **2** set or growing close together. ● *n.* a thicket.

thick-skinned *adj.* (of a person) not sensitive to reproach or criticism.

thick-skulled *adj.* (also **thick-witted**) stupid, dull; slow to learn.

thief /θi:f/ *n.* (*pl.* **thieves** /θi:vz/) a person who steals, esp. secretly and without violence. [Old English *thēof*, from Germanic]

thieve /θi:v/ *v.* **1** *intr.* be a thief. **2** *tr.* steal (a thing). [Old English *thēofian* (as THIEF)]

thievery /'θi:v(ə)ri/ *n.* (*pl.* **-ies**) **1** the act or practice of stealing. **2** an instance of this.

thieves *pl.* of THIEF.

thievish /'θi:vɪʃ/ *adj.* given to stealing. □ **thievishly** *adv.* **thievishness** *n.*

thigh /θʌɪ/ *n.* **1** the part of the human leg between the hip and the knee. **2** a corresponding part in other animals. □ **-thighed** *adj.* (in *comb.*). [Old English *thēh*, *thēoh*, *thīoh*, Old High German *dioh*, Old Norse *thjó*, from Germanic]

thigh bone *n.* = FEMUR 1.

thigmotropism /θɪgmə'trəʊpɪz(ə)m/ *n.* *Biol.* the movement of a part or the whole of an organism in response to a touch stimulus. □ **thigmotropic** /-'trɒpɪk/ *adj.* [Greek *thigma* 'touch' + TROPISM]

thill /θɪl/ *n.* a shaft of a cart or carriage, esp. one of a pair. [Middle English: origin unknown]

thill-horse *n.* (also **thiller** /'θɪlə/) a horse put between thills.

thimble /'θɪmb(ə)l/ *n.* **1** a metal or plastic cap, usu. with a closed end, worn to protect the finger and push the needle in sewing. **2** *Mech.* a short metal tube or ferrule etc. **3** *Naut.* a metal ring concave on the outside and fitting in a loop of spliced rope to prevent chafing. [Old English *thȳmel* (as THUMB, -LE[1])]

thimbleful /'θɪmb(ə)lfʊl, -f(ə)l/ *n.* (*pl.* **-fuls**) a small quantity, esp. of liquid to drink.

thimblerig /'θɪmb(ə)lrɪg/ *n.* a game often involving sleight of hand, in which three inverted thimbles or cups are moved about, contestants having to spot which is the one with a pea or other object beneath. □ **thimblerigger** *n.* [THIMBLE + RIG[2] in sense 'trick, dodge']

thin /θɪn/ *adj.*, *adv.*, & *v.* ● *adj.* (**thinner**, **thinnest**) **1** having the opposite surfaces close together; of small thickness or diameter. **2 a** (of a line) narrow or fine. **b** (of a script or type etc.) consisting of thin lines. **3** made of thin material (*a thin dress*). **4** lean; not plump. **5 a** not dense or copious (*thin hair*; *a thin haze*). **b** not full or closely packed (*a thin audience*). **6** of slight consistency (*a thin paste*). **7** weak; lacking an important ingredient (*thin blood*; *a thin voice*). **8** (of an excuse, argument, disguise, etc.) flimsy or transparent. ● *adv.* thinly (*cut the bread very thin*). ● *v.* (**thinned**, **thinning**) **1** *tr.* & *intr.* make or become thin or thinner. **2** *tr.* & *intr.* (often foll. by *out*) reduce; make or become less dense or crowded or numerous. **3** *tr.* (often foll. by *out*) remove some of a crop of (seedlings, saplings, etc.) or some young fruit from (a vine or tree) to improve the growth of the rest. □ **have a thin time** *Brit. colloq.* have a wretched or uncomfortable time. **on thin ice** see ICE. **thin end of the wedge** see WEDGE[1]. **thin on the ground** see GROUND[1]. **thin on top** balding. □ **thinly** *adv.* **thinness** /'θɪnnɪs/ *n.* **thinnish** *adj.* [Old English *thynne*, from Germanic]

thin air *n.* a state of invisibility or non-existence (*vanished into thin air*).

thine /ðʌɪn/ *poss.pron.* & *poss.det.* *archaic* or *dial.* ● *poss.pron.* of or belonging to thee (*it is thine*). ● *det.* (before a vowel) = THY (*lift up thine eyes*). [Old English *thīn*, from Germanic]

thing /θɪŋ/ *n.* **1** a material or non-material entity, idea, action, etc., that is or may be thought about or perceived. **2** an inanimate material object (*take that thing away*). **3** an unspecified object or item (*have a few things to buy*). **4** an act, idea, or utterance (*a silly thing to do*). **5** an event (*an unfortunate thing to happen*). **6** a quality (*patience is a useful thing*). **7** (with reference to a person) expressing pity, contempt, or affection (*poor thing!*; *a dear old thing*). **8** a specimen or type of something (*the latest thing in hats*). **9** *colloq.* one's special interest or concern (*not my thing at all*). **10** esp. *Brit. colloq.* something remarkable (*now there's a thing!*). **11** (prec. by *the*) *colloq.* **a** what is conventionally proper or fashionable. **b** what is needed or required (*your suggestion was just the thing*). **c** what is to be considered (*the thing is, shall we go or not?*). **d** what is important (*the thing about them is their reliability*). **12** (in *pl.*) personal belongings or clothing (*where have I left my things?*). **13** (in *pl.*) equipment (*painting things*). **14** (in *pl.*) affairs in general (*not in the nature of things*). **15** (in *pl.*) circumstances or conditions (*things look good*). **16** (in *pl.* with a following adjective) all that is so describable (*all things Greek*). **17** (in *pl.*) *Law* property. □ **do one's own thing** *colloq.* pursue one's own interests or inclinations. **do things to** *colloq.* affect remarkably. **have a thing about** *colloq.* be obsessed or prejudiced about. **make a thing of** *colloq.* **1** regard as essential. **2** cause a fuss about. **one** (or **just one**) **of those things** *colloq.* something unavoidable or to be accepted. [Old English from Germanic]

thingummy /'θɪŋəmi/ *n.* (*pl.* **-ies**) (also **thingamy**, **thingamabob** or **thingumabob** /-məbɒb/, **thingamajig** or **thingumajig** /-mədʒɪg/) *colloq.* a person or thing whose name one has forgotten or does not know or does not wish to mention. [THING + meaningless suffix]

thingy /'θɪŋi/ *n.* (*pl.* **-ies**) = THINGUMMY.

think /θɪŋk/ *v.* & *n.* ● *v.* (*past* and *past part.* **thought** /θɔ:t/) **1** *tr.* (foll. by *that* + clause) be of the opinion (*we think that they will come*). **2** *tr.* (foll. by *that* + clause or *to* + infin.) judge or consider (*is thought to be a fraud*). **3** *intr.* exercise the mind positively with one's ideas etc. (*let me think for a moment*). **4** *intr.* (foll. by *of* or *about*) **a** consider; be or become mentally aware of (*think of you constantly*). **b** form or entertain the idea of; imagine to oneself (*couldn't think of such a thing*). **c** choose mentally; hit upon (*think of a number*). **5** *tr.* have a half-formed intention (*I think I'll stay*). **6** *tr.* form a conception of (*cannot think how you do it*). **7** *tr.* reduce to a specified condition by thinking (*cannot think away a toothache*). **8** *tr.* recognize the presence or existence of (*the child thought no harm*). **9** *tr.* (foll. by *to* + infin.) intend or expect (*thinks to deceive us*). **10** *tr.* (foll. by *to* + infin.) remember (*did not think to lock the door*). ● *n.* *colloq.* an act of thinking (*must have a think about that*). □ **think again** revise one's plans or opinions. **think aloud** utter one's thoughts as soon as they occur. **think back to** recall (a past event or time). **think better of** change one's mind about (an intention) after reconsideration. **think big** see BIG. **think fit** see FIT[1]. **think for oneself** have an independent mind or attitude. **think little** (or **nothing**) **of** consider to be insignificant or unremarkable. **think much** (or **highly**) **of** have a high opinion of. **think on** (or **upon**) *archaic* think of or about. **think out 1** consider carefully. **2** produce (an idea etc.) by thinking. **think over** reflect upon in order to reach a decision. **think through** reflect fully upon (a problem etc.). **think twice** use careful consideration, avoid hasty action, etc. **think up** *colloq.* devise; produce by thought. □ **thinkable** *adj.* [Old English *thencan thōhte gethōht*, from Germanic]

thinker /'θɪŋkə/ *n.* **1** a person who thinks, esp. in a specified way (*an original thinker*). **2** a person with a skilled or powerful mind.

thinking /θɪŋkɪŋ/ *adj.* & *n.* ● *adj.* using thought or rational judgement. ● *n.* **1** opinion or judgement. **2** (in *pl.*) thoughts; courses of thought. □ **put on one's thinking cap** *colloq.* meditate on a problem.

think-tank *n.* a body of experts providing advice and ideas on specific national and commercial problems.

thinner /'θɪnə/ *n.* a volatile liquid used to dilute paint etc.

thinnings /'θɪnɪŋz/ *n.pl.* plants, trees, etc. which have been removed to improve the growth of those remaining.

thin-skinned *adj.* (of a person) sensitive to reproach or criticism; easily upset.

thio- /ˈθʌɪəʊ/ *comb. form* sulphur, esp. replacing oxygen in compounds (*thio-acid*). [Greek *theion* 'sulphur']

thiol /ˈθʌɪɒl/ *n. Chem.* any organic compound containing an alcohol-like group but with sulphur in place of oxygen. [THIO- + -OL[1]]

thiopentone /θʌɪəˈpɛntəʊn/ *n. Pharm.* a barbiturate drug used, usu. as the sodium salt, as a general anaesthetic and a hypnotic, and (reputedly) as a truth drug. Also called *Pentothal*. [THIO- + PENTOBARBITONE]

thiosulphate /θʌɪə(ʊ)ˈsʌlfeɪt/ *n.* a sulphate in which one oxygen atom is replaced by sulphur.

thiourea /ˌθʌɪəʊjʊˈriːə/ *n.* a crystalline compound used in photography and the manufacture of synthetic resins.

third /θəːd/ *n. & adj.* ● *n.* **1** the position in a sequence corresponding to that of the number 3 in the sequence 1–3. **2** something occupying this position. **3** each of three equal parts of a thing. **4** = THIRD GEAR. **5** *Mus.* **a** an interval or chord spanning three consecutive notes in the diatonic scale (e.g. C to E). **b** a note separated from another by this interval. **6** *Brit.* **a** a place in the third class in an examination. **b** a person having this. ● *adj.* that is the third. ▫ **thirdly** *adv.* [Old English *third(d)a*, *thridda*, from Germanic]

third age *n.* the period in life of active retirement; old age.

third-best *adj. & n.* ● *adj.* of third quality. ● *n.* a thing in this category.

third-class *adj. & adv.* ● *adj.* **1** belonging to or travelling by the third class. **2** of lower quality; inferior. ● *adv.* by the third class (*travels third-class*).

third class *n.* **1** the third-best group or category, esp. of hotel and train accommodation. **2 a** the third highest division in an examination test. **b** a place in this.

third cousin see COUSIN.

third degree *n. & adj.* ● *n.* long and severe questioning esp. by police to obtain information or a confession. ● *adj.* (**third-degree**) denoting burns of the most severe kind, affecting lower layers of tissue.

third eye *n.* **1** *Hinduism & Buddhism* the 'eye of insight' in the forehead of an image of a deity, esp. the god Siva. **2** the faculty of intuitive insight or prescience. **3** the pineal gland in certain vertebrates.

third force *n.* a political group or party acting as a check on conflict between two opposing parties.

third gear *n.* the third lowest in a set of gears.

third man *n. Cricket* **1** a fielder positioned near the boundary behind the slips. **2** this position.

third party *n. & adj.* ● *n.* **1** another party besides the two principals. **2** a bystander etc. ● *adj.* (**third-party**) *Brit.* (of insurance) covering damage or injury suffered by a person other than the insured.

third person *n.* **1** = THIRD PARTY. **2** see PERSON.

third-rate *adj.* inferior; very poor in quality.

third reading *n.* a third presentation of a bill to a legislative assembly, in the UK to debate committee reports and in the US to consider it for the last time.

Third Reich *n.* the Nazi regime, 1933–45.

Third World *n.* (usu. prec. by *the*) the developing countries of Asia, Africa, and Latin America.

thirst /θəːst/ *n. & v.* ● *n.* **1** a physical need to drink liquid, or the feeling of discomfort caused by this. **2** a strong desire or craving (*a thirst for power*). ● *v.intr.* (often foll. by *for* or *after*) **1** feel thirst. **2** have a strong desire. [Old English *thurst*, *thyrstan*, from West Germanic]

thirsty /ˈθəːsti/ *adj.* (**thirstier**, **thirstiest**) **1** feeling thirst. **2** (of land, a season, etc.) dry or parched. **3** (often foll. by *for* or *after*) eager. **4** *colloq.* causing thirst (*thirsty work*). ▫ **thirstily** *adv.* **thirstiness** *n.* [Old English *thurstig*, *thyrstig* (as THIRST, -Y[1])]

thirteen /θəːˈtiːn, ˈθəːtiːn/ *n. & adj.* ● *n.* **1** one more than twelve, or three more than ten. **2** a symbol for this (13, xiii, XIII). **3** a size etc. denoted by thirteen. ● *adj.* that amount to thirteen. ▫ **thirteenth** *adj. & n.* [Old English *thrēotīene* (as THREE, -TEEN)]

thirty /ˈθəːti/ *n. & adj.* ● *n.* (*pl.* **-ies**) **1** the product of three and ten. **2** a symbol for this (30, xxx, XXX). **3** (in *pl.*) the numbers from 30 to 39, esp. the years of a century or of a person's life. ● *adj.* that amount to thirty. ▫ **thirty-first, -second**, etc. the ordinal numbers between thirtieth and fortieth. **thirty-one, -two**, etc. the cardinal numbers between thirty and forty. ▫ **thirtieth** *adj. & n.* **thirtyfold** *adj. & adv.* [Old English *thrītig* (as THREE, -TY[2])]

Thirty-nine Articles *n.pl.* a series of points of doctrine historically accepted as representing the teaching of the Church of England.

thirty-second note *n.* esp. *N. Amer. Mus.* = DEMISEMIQUAVER.

thirty-something *n.* (often *attrib.*) *colloq.* an unspecified age between thirty and forty.

thirty-two-mo *n.* (*pl.* **-mos**) **1** a size of book in which each leaf is one-thirty-second the size of a printing-sheet. **2** a book of this size.

thirty-year rule *n.* a rule that public records may be open to inspection after a lapse of thirty years.

this /ðɪs/ *pron., det., & adv.* ● *pron.* (*pl.* **these** /ðiːz/) **1** the person or thing close at hand or indicated or already named or understood (*can you see this?*; *this is my cousin*). **2** (contrasted with *that*) the person or thing nearer to hand or more immediately in mind. **3** the action, behaviour, or circumstances under consideration (*this won't do at all*; *what do you think of this?*). **4** (on the telephone): **a** *Brit.* the person speaking (*this is Jane*). **b** *US* the person spoken to (*who is this?*). ● *det.* (*pl.* **these** /ðiːz/) **1** designating the person or thing close at hand etc. (cf. senses 1, 2 of *pron.*). **2** (of time): **a** the present or current (*am busy all this week*). **b** relating to today (*this morning*). **c** just past or to come (*have been asking for it these three weeks*). **3** *colloq.* (in narrative) designating a person or thing previously unspecified (*then up came this policeman*). ● *adv.* to the degree or extent indicated (*knew him when he was this high*; *did not reach this far*). ▫ **this and that** *colloq.* various unspecified examples of things (esp. trivial). **this here** *slang* this particular (person or thing). **this much** the amount or extent about to be stated (*I know this much, that he was not there*). **this world** mortal life. [Old English, neut. of *thes*]

thistle /ˈθɪs(ə)l/ *n.* **1** any of various prickly herbaceous plants of the genus *Cirsium*, *Carlina*, or *Carduus* etc. (daisy family), usu. with globular heads of purple flowers. **2** this as the Scottish national emblem. [Old English *thistel*, from Germanic]

thistledown /ˈθɪs(ə)ldaʊn/ *n.* a light fluffy down or pappus attached to thistle seeds and blown about in the wind.

thistly /ˈθɪsli/ *adj.* overgrown with thistles.

thither /ˈðɪðə/ *adv. archaic* or *formal* to or towards that place. [Old English *thider*, alteration (influenced by HITHER) of *thæder*]

thixotropy /θɪkˈsɒtrəpi/ *n.* the property of becoming temporarily liquid when shaken, or stirred etc., and returning to a gel on standing. ▫ **thixotropic** /θɪksəˈtraʊpɪk, -ˈtrɒpɪk/ *adj.* [Greek *thixis* 'touching' + *tropē* 'turning']

tho' var. of THOUGH.

thole[1] /θəʊl/ *n.* (in full **thole-pin**) **1** a pin in the gunwale of a boat as the fulcrum for an oar. **2** each of two such pins forming a rowlock. [Old English *thol* 'fir tree, peg']

thole[2] /θəʊl/ *v.tr. Sc.* or *archaic* **1** undergo or suffer (pain, grief, etc.). **2** permit or admit of. [Old English *tholian*, from Germanic]

tholos /ˈθɒlɒs/ *n.* (*pl.* **tholoi** /-lɔɪ/) *Gk Antiq.* a dome-shaped tomb, esp. of the Mycenaean period. [Greek]

Thomism /ˈtəʊmɪz(ə)m/ *n.* the doctrine of Thomas Aquinas, Italian scholastic philosopher and theologian d. 1274, or of his followers. ▫ **Thomist** *n. & adj.* **Thomistic** /-ˈmɪstɪk/ *adj.* **Thomistical** /-ˈmɪstɪk(ə)l/ *adj.*

thong /θɒŋ/ *n. & v.* ● *n.* **1** a narrow strip of hide or leather used as the lash of a whip, as a halter or rein, etc. **2** *Austral.*, *NZ*, & *N. Amer.* = FLIP-FLOP 1. **3** a skimpy bathing garment like a G-string. ● *v.tr.* **1** provide with a thong. **2** strike with a thong. [Old English *thwang*, *thwong*, from Germanic]

thorax /ˈθɔːraks/ *n.* (*pl.* **thoraces** /ˈθɔːrəsiːz/ or **thoraxes**) **1** *Anat.* & *Zool.* the part of the trunk between the neck and the abdomen. **2** *Gk Antiq.* a breastplate or cuirass. ▫ **thoracal** /ˈθɔːrək(ə)l/ *adj.* **thoracic** /θɔːˈrasɪk, θə-/ *adj.* [Latin from Greek *thōrax -akos*]

thoria /ˈθɔːrɪə/ *n.* the oxide of thorium.

thorium /ˈθɔːrɪəm/ *n. Chem.* a radioactive metallic element occurring naturally in monazite, the oxide of which is used in gas-mantles (symbol **Th**). [named after *Thor*, Scandinavian god of thunder]

thorn /θɔːn/ *n.* **1** a stiff sharp-pointed projection on a plant. **2** (also **thorn bush**, **thorn tree**) a thorn-bearing shrub or tree. **3** the name of an Old English and Icelandic runic letter, þ (= th). ▫ **on thorns** continuously uneasy, esp. in fear of being detected. **a thorn in one's flesh** (or **side**) a constant annoyance. ▫ **thornless** *adj.* **thornproof** *adj.* [Old English from Germanic]

thorn apple *n.* **1** a poisonous plant of the nightshade family, *Datura stramonium*. **2** the prickly fruit of this.

thornback /ˈθɔːnbak/ *n.* a ray, *Raja clavata*, with spines on the back and tail.

thornbill /ˈθɔːnbɪl/ *n.* **1** any Australian warbler of the genus *Acanthiza*. **2** any of various S. American hummingbirds, esp. of the genus *Chalcostigma*.

thorntail /ˈθɔːnteɪl/ *n.* any S. American hummingbird of the genus *Popelairia*.

thorny /ˈθɔːni/ *adj.* (**thornier**, **thorniest**) **1** having many thorns. **2** (of a subject) hard to handle without offence; problematic. ▫ **thornily** *adv.* **thorniness** *n.*

thorough /ˈθʌrə/ *adj.* **1** complete and unqualified; not superficial (*needs a thorough change*). **2** acting or done with great care and completeness (*the report is most thorough*). **3** absolute (*he is a thorough nuisance*). ▫ **thoroughly** *adv.* **thoroughness** *n.* [originally as *adv.* and *prep.* in the senses of *through*: from Old English *thuruh*, variant of *thurh* THROUGH]

thorough bass *n.* a bass part for a keyboard player with numerals and symbols below to indicate the harmony.

thoroughbred /ˈθʌrəbrɛd/ *adj. & n.* ● *adj.* **1** of pure breed. **2** of outstanding quality; first-class. ● *n.* **1** a thoroughbred animal, esp. a horse. **2** (**Thoroughbred**) **a** a breed of racehorses originating from English mares and Arab stallions. **b** a horse of this breed.

thoroughfare /ˈθʌrəfɛː/ *n.* a road or path open at both ends, esp. for traffic.

thoroughgoing /θʌrəˈɡəʊɪŋ/ *adj.* **1** uncompromising; not superficial. **2** (usu. *attrib.*) extreme; out and out.

thorough-paced *adj.* **1** (of a horse) trained to all paces. **2** complete or unqualified.

thorp /θɔːp/ *n.* (also **thorpe**) *archaic* a village or hamlet. [Old English *thorp*, *throp*, from Germanic]

■ **Usage** *Thorp*(*e*) is now usually found only in place names, e.g. *Scunthorpe*.

Thos. *abbr.* Thomas.

those *pl.* of THAT.

thou[1] /ðaʊ/ *pron.* (*obj.* **thee** /ðiː/; *poss.* **thy** or **thine**; *pl.* **ye** or **you**) second person singular pronoun. [Old English *thu*, from Germanic]

■ **Usage** *Thou* has now been replaced by *you* except in some formal, liturgical, dialect, and poetic uses.

thou[2] /θaʊ/ *n.* (*pl.* same or **thous**) *colloq.* **1** a thousand. **2** one-thousandth. [abbreviation]

though /ðəʊ/ *conj. & adv.* (also **tho'**) ● *conj.* **1** despite the fact that (*though it was early we went to bed*). **2** (introducing a possibility) even if (*ask him though he may refuse*; *would not attend though the Queen herself were there*). **3** and yet; nevertheless (*she read on, though not to the very end*). **4** in spite of being (*ready though unwilling*). ● *adv. colloq.* however; all the same (*I wish you had told me, though*). [Middle English *thoh* etc. from Old Norse *thó* etc., corresponding to Old English *thēah*, from Germanic]

thought[1] /θɔːt/ *n.* **1** the process or power of thinking; the faculty of reason. **2** a way of thinking characteristic of or associated with a particular time, people, group, etc. (*medieval European thought*). **3** sober reflection or consideration (*gave it much thought*). **4** an idea or piece of reasoning produced by thinking (*many good thoughts came out of the discussion*). **5** (foll. by *of* + verbal noun or *to* + infin.) a partly formed intention or hope (*gave up all thoughts of winning*; *had no thought to go*). **6** (usu. in *pl.*) what one is thinking; one's opinion (*have you any thoughts on this?*). **7** the subject of one's thinking (*my one thought was to get away*). **8** (prec. by *a*) somewhat (*seems to me a thought arrogant*). ▫ **give thought to** consider; think about. **in thought** thinking, meditating. **take thought** consider matters. ▫ **-thoughted** *adj.* (in *comb.*). [Old English *thōht* (as THINK)]

thought[2] *past* and *past part.* of THINK.

thoughtful /ˈθɔːtfʊl, -f(ə)l/ *adj.* **1** engaged in or given to meditation. **2** (of a book, writer, remark, etc.) giving signs of serious thought. **3** (often foll. by *of*) (of a person or conduct) considerate; not haphazard or unfeeling. ▫ **thoughtfully** *adv.* **thoughtfulness** *n.*

thoughtless /ˈθɔːtlɪs/ *adj.* **1** careless of consequences or of others' feelings. **2** due to lack of thought. ▫ **thoughtlessly** *adv.* **thoughtlessness** *n.*

thought-provoking *adj.* stimulating serious thought.

thought-reader *n.* a person supposedly able to perceive another's thoughts. ▫ **thought-reading** *n.*

thought transference *n.* telepathy.

thought-wave *n.* an undulation of the supposed medium of thought transference.

thousand /ˈθaʊz(ə)nd/ *n. & adj.* ● *n.* (*pl.* **thousands** or (in sense 1) **thousand**) (in *sing.* prec. by *a* or *one*) **1** the product of a hundred and ten. **2** a symbol for this (1,000, m, M). **3** a set of a thousand things. **4** (in *sing.* or *pl.*) *colloq.* a large number. ● *adj.* that amount to a thousand. ▫ **thousandfold** *adj. & adv.* **thousandth** *adj. & n.* [Old English *thūsend*, from Germanic]

thrall /θrɔːl/ *n. literary* **1** (often foll. by *of*, *to*) a slave (of a person, or a power or influence). **2** a state of slavery or servitude (*in thrall*). ▫ **thraldom** *n.* (also **thralldom**). [Old English *thrǣl* from Old Norse *thrǣll*, perhaps from a Germanic root meaning 'run']

thrash /θraʃ/ *v. & n.* ● *v.* **1** *tr.* beat severely, esp. with a stick or whip. **2** *tr.* defeat thoroughly in a contest. **3** *intr.* (of a paddle wheel, branch, etc.) act like a flail; deliver repeated blows. **4** *intr.* (foll. by *about*, *around*) move or fling the limbs about violently or in panic. **5** *intr.* (of a ship) keep striking the waves; make way against the wind or tide (*thrash to windward*). **6** *tr.* = THRESH 1. ● *n.* **1** an act of thrashing. **2** *Brit. colloq.* a party, esp. a lavish one. ▫ **thrash out** discuss to a conclusion. ▫ **thrashing** *n.* [Old English *therscan*, later *threscan*, from Germanic]

thrasher[1] /ˈθraʃə/ *n.* **1** a person or thing that thrashes. **2** = THRESHER.

thrasher[2] /ˈθraʃə/ *n.* any of various long-tailed N. American thrushlike birds of the family Mimidae. [perhaps from English dialect *thrusher* = THRUSH[1]]

thrawn /θrɔːn/ *adj. Sc.* **1** perverse or ill-tempered. **2** misshapen, crooked. [Scots form of *thrown*, in obsolete senses]

thread /θrɛd/ *n. & v.* ● *n.* **1 a** a spun-out filament of cotton, silk, glass, etc.; yarn. **b** a length of this. **2** a thin cord of twisted yarns used esp. in sewing and weaving. **3** anything regarded as threadlike with reference to its continuity or connectedness (*the thread of life*; *lost the thread of his argument*). **4** the spiral ridge of a screw. **5** (in *pl.*) *slang* clothes. **6** a thin seam or vein of ore. ● *v.tr.* **1 a** pass a thread through the eye of (a needle). **b**

(often foll. by *through*) pass (a thread, ribbon, etc.) through a hole or series of holes. **2** put (beads) on a thread. **3** arrange (material in a strip form, e.g. film or magnetic tape) in the proper position on equipment. **4** make (one's way) carefully through a crowded place, over a difficult route, etc. **5** streak (hair etc.) as with threads. **6** form a screw thread on. ◻ **hang by a thread** be in a precarious state, position, etc. ◻ **threader** *n.* **threadlike** *adj.* [Old English *thrǣd*, from Germanic]

threadbare /ˈθrɛdbɛː/ *adj.* **1** (of cloth) so worn that the nap is lost and the thread visible. **2** (of a person) wearing such clothes. **3 a** hackneyed. **b** feeble or insubstantial (*a threadbare excuse*).

threadfin /ˈθrɛdfɪn/ *n.* any small tropical fish of the family Polynemidae, with long streamers from its pectoral fins.

thread mark *n.* a mark in the form of a thin line made in banknote paper with highly coloured silk fibres to prevent photographic counterfeiting.

thread vein *n.* a very slender vein visible through the skin.

threadworm /ˈθrɛdwəːm/ *n.* any of various esp. parasitic threadlike nematode worms, e.g. the pinworm.

thready /ˈθrɛdi/ *adj.* (**threadier**, **threadiest**) **1** of or like a thread. **2** (of a person's pulse) scarcely perceptible.

threat /θrɛt/ *n.* **1 a** a declaration of an intention to punish or hurt. **b** *Law* a menace of bodily hurt or injury, such as may restrain a person's freedom of action. **2** an indication of something undesirable coming (*the threat of war*). **3** a person or thing as a likely cause of harm etc. [Old English *thrēat* 'affliction', etc. from Germanic]

threaten /ˈθrɛt(ə)n/ *v.tr.* **1** make a threat or threats against. **2** be a sign or indication of (something undesirable). **3** (foll. by *to* + infin.) announce one's intention to do an undesirable or unexpected thing (*threatened to resign*). **4** (also *absol.*) give warning of the infliction of (harm etc.) (*the clouds were threatening rain*). **5** (as **threatened** *adj.*) (of a species etc.) in danger of becoming rare or extinct. ◻ **threatener** *n.* **threateningly** *adv.* [Old English *thrēatnian* (as THREAT)]

three /θriː/ *n.* & *adj.* ● *n.* **1 a** one more than two, or seven less than ten. **b** a symbol for this (3, iii, III). **2** a size etc. denoted by three. **3** three o'clock. **4** a set of three. **5** a card with three pips. ● *adj.* that amount to three. [Old English *thrī*, from Germanic]

three-card monte see MONTE 2.

three-card trick *n.* a game in which bets are made on which is the queen among three cards lying face downwards.

three cheers see CHEER.

three-colour process *n.* a process of reproducing natural colours by combining photographic images in the three primary colours.

three-cornered *adj.* **1** triangular. **2** (of a contest etc.) between three parties as individuals.

three-decker *n.* **1** *hist.* a warship with three gun-decks. **2** a novel in three volumes. **3** a sandwich with three slices of bread.

three-dimensional *adj.* having or appearing to have length, breadth, and depth.

threefold /ˈθriːfəʊld/ *adj.* & *adv.* **1** three times as much or as many. **2** consisting of three parts.

three-handed *adj.* **1** having or using three hands. **2** involving three players.

three-legged race *n.* a running race between pairs, one member of each pair having the left leg tied to the right leg of the other.

three-line whip *n.* (in the UK) a written notice, underlined three times to denote urgency, to members of a political party to attend a parliamentary vote.

three parts *n.pl.* & *adv.* (as adv. often hyphenated) three-quarters.

threepence /ˈθrɛp(ə)ns, ˈθrʊ-, ˈθrʌ-/ *n. Brit.* the sum of three pence, esp. before decimalization.

threepenny /ˈθrɛp(ə)ni, ˈθrʊ-, ˈθrʌ-/ *adj. Brit.* costing three pence, esp. before decimalization.

threepenny bit *n. hist.* a former coin worth three old pence.

three-phase *adj.* (of an electric generator, motor, etc.) designed to supply or use simultaneously three separate alternating currents of the same voltage, but with phases differing by a third of a period.

three-piece *n.* & *adj.* ● *n.* a three-piece suit of clothes or suite of furniture. ● *attrib.adj.* (esp. of a suit or suite) consisting of three items.

three-ply *adj.* & *n.* ● *adj.* of three strands, webs, or thicknesses. ● *n.* **1** three-ply wool. **2** three-ply wood made by gluing together three layers with the grain in different directions.

three-point landing *n.* the landing of an aircraft on the two main wheels and the tailwheel or skid simultaneously.

three-point turn *n.* a method of turning a vehicle round in a narrow space by moving forwards, backwards, and forwards again in a sequence of arcs.

three-pronged *adj.* having three parts, goals, or lines of attack (*three-pronged strategy*).

three-pronged attack *n.* an attack on three separate points at once.

three-quarter *n.* & *adj.* ● *n.* (also **three-quarter back**) *Rugby* any of three or four players just behind the half-backs. ● *adj.* **1** consisting of three-quarters of something. **2** (of a portrait) going down to the hips or showing three-fourths of the face (between full face and profile).

three-quarters *n.pl.* & *adv.* ● *n.pl.* three parts out of four; the greater part. ● *adv.* to the extent of three quarters; almost, very nearly.

three-ring circus *n.* esp. *US* **1** a circus with three rings for simultaneous performances. **2** an extravagant display.

three Rs *n.pl.* (prec. by *the*) reading, writing, and arithmetic, regarded as the fundamentals of learning.

threescore /θriːˈskɔː/ *n. archaic* sixty.

threesome /ˈθriːsəm/ *n.* **1** a group of three persons. **2** a game etc. for three, esp. *Golf* of one against two.

three-way *adj.* involving three ways or participants.

three-wheeler *n.* a vehicle with three wheels.

thremmatology /θrɛməˈtɒlədʒi/ *n.* the science of breeding animals and plants. [Greek *thremma -matos* 'nursling' + -LOGY]

threnody /ˈθrɛnədi/ *n.* (also **threnode** /ˈθrɛnəʊd/) (*pl.* **-ies** or **threnodes**) **1** a lamentation, esp. on a person's death. **2** a song of lamentation. ◻ **threnodial** /-ˈnəʊdɪəl/ *adj.* **threnodic** /-ˈnɒdɪk/ *adj.* **threnodist** /ˈθrɛnədɪst/ *n.* [Greek *thrēnōidia*, from *thrēnos* 'wailing' + *ōidē* ODE]

threonine /ˈθriːəniːn/ *n. Biochem.* an amino acid, considered essential for growth. [*threose* (name of a tetrose sugar), ultimately from Greek *eruthros* 'red' + -INE[4]]

thresh /θrɛʃ/ *v.* **1** *tr.* beat out or separate grain from (corn etc.). **2** *intr.* = THRASH *v.* 4. **3** *tr.* (foll. by *over*) analyse (a problem etc.) in search of a solution. ◻ **thresh out** = *thrash out.* [variant of THRASH]

thresher /ˈθrɛʃə/ *n.* **1** a person or machine that threshes. **2** a shark, *Alopias vulpinus*, with a long upper lobe to its tail with which it can lash the water to direct its prey.

threshing floor *n.* a hard level floor for threshing esp. with flails.

threshing machine *n.* a power-driven machine for separating the grain from the straw or husk.

threshold /ˈθrɛʃəʊld, ˈθrɛʃhəʊld/ *n.* **1** a strip of wood or stone forming the bottom of a doorway and crossed in entering a house or room etc. **2** a point of entry or beginning (*on the threshold of a new century*). **3** *Physiol.* & *Psychol.* a limit below which a stimulus causes no reaction (*pain threshold*). **4** *Physics* a limit below which no reaction occurs, esp. a minimum dose of radiation producing a specified effect. **5** (often *attrib.*) esp. *Brit.* a step in a scale of wages or taxation, usu. operative in specified conditions. [Old English *therscold*, *threscold*, etc., related to THRASH in the sense 'tread': origin of second element unknown]

threw *past* of THROW.

thrice /θrʌɪs/ *adv. archaic* or *literary* **1** three times. **2** (esp. in *comb.*) highly (*thrice-blessed*). [Middle English *thries* from *thrie* (*adv.*), from Old English *thrīwa*, *thrīga* (as THREE, -S[3])]

thrift /θrɪft/ *n.* **1** frugality; economical management. **2** a plant of the genus *Armeria*, esp. the sea pink. [Middle English from Old Norse (as THRIVE)]

thriftless /'θrɪftlɪs/ *adj.* wasteful, improvident. □ **thriftlessly** *adv.* **thriftlessness** *n.*

thrift shop *n.* (also **thrift store**) esp. *US* a shop selling second-hand items usu. for charity.

thrifty /'θrɪfti/ *adj.* (**thriftier**, **thriftiest**) **1** economical, frugal. **2** thriving, prosperous. □ **thriftily** *adv.* **thriftiness** *n.*

thrill /θrɪl/ *n.* & *v.* ● *n.* **1** a wave or nervous tremor of emotion or sensation (*a thrill of joy*; *a thrill of recognition*). **2** a throb or pulsation. **3** *Med.* a vibratory movement or resonance heard in auscultation. ● *v.* **1** *intr.* feel a thrill (*thrilled to the sound*). **2** *tr.* **a** cause to feel a thrill of excitement or emotion (*a voice that thrilled millions*). **b** (as **thrilled** *adj.*) *colloq.* delighted, pleased. **3** *intr.* (foll. by *through*, *over*, *along*) (of an emotion etc.) pass with a thrill through etc. (*fear thrilled through my veins*). **4** *intr.* quiver or throb with or as with emotion. □ **thrilling** *adj.* **thrillingly** *adv.* [*thirl* (now dialect) from Old English *thyrlian* 'pierce' via *thȳrel* 'hole' from *thurh* THROUGH]

thriller /'θrɪlə/ *n.* an exciting or sensational story or play etc., esp. one involving crime or espionage.

thrips /θrɪps/ *n.* (*pl.* same) a minute black insect of the order Thysanoptera, some members of which are injurious to plants. Also called THUNDERFLY. [Latin from Greek, = woodworm]

thrive /θrʌɪv/ *v.intr.* (*past* **throve** /θrəʊv/ or **thrived**; *past part.* **thriven** /'θrɪv(ə)n/ or **thrived**) **1** prosper or flourish. **2** grow rich. **3** (of a child, animal, or plant) grow vigorously. [Middle English from Old Norse *thrífask*, refl. of *thrífa* 'grasp']

thro' var. of THROUGH.

throat /θrəʊt/ *n.* **1 a** the windpipe or gullet. **b** the front part of the neck containing this. **2** *literary* **a** a voice, esp. of a songbird. **b** a thing compared to a throat, esp. a narrow passage, entrance, or exit. **3** *Naut.* the forward upper corner of a fore-and-aft sail. □ **cut one's own throat** bring about one's own downfall. **ram** (or **thrust**) **down a person's throat** force (a thing) on a person's attention. □ **-throated** *adj.* (in *comb.*). [Old English *throte*, *throtu*, from Germanic]

throaty /'θrəʊti/ *adj.* (**throatier**, **throatiest**) **1** (of a voice) deficient in clarity; hoarsely resonant. **2** guttural; uttered in the throat. **3** having a prominent or capacious throat. □ **throatily** *adv.* **throatiness** *n.*

throb /θrɒb/ *v.* & *n.* ● *v.intr.* (**throbbed**, **throbbing**) **1** palpitate or pulsate, esp. with more than the usual force or rapidity. **2** vibrate or quiver with a persistent rhythm or with emotion. ● *n.* **1** a throbbing. **2** a palpitation or (esp. violent) pulsation. [Middle English, apparently imitative]

throe /θrəʊ/ *n.* (usu. in *pl.*) **1** a violent pang, esp. of childbirth or death. **2** anguish. □ **in the throes of** struggling with the task of. [Middle English *throwe* perhaps from Old English *thrēa*, *thrawu* 'calamity', influenced by *throwian* 'suffer']

thrombi *pl.* of THROMBUS.

thrombin /'θrɒmbɪn/ *n.* an enzyme in blood plasma which causes the clotting of blood by converting fibrinogen to fibrin. [as THROMBUS + -IN]

thrombocyte /'θrɒmbəsʌɪt/ *n.* = PLATELET. [as THROMBUS + -CYTE]

thrombocytopenia /ˌθrɒmbəʊsʌɪtə(ʊ)'piːnɪə/ *n. Med.* deficiency of platelets in the blood. [THROMBOCYTE + Greek *penia* 'poverty']

thrombose /θrɒm'bəʊz, -s/ *v.tr.* & *intr.* affect with or undergo thrombosis. [back-formation from THROMBOSIS]

thrombosis /θrɒm'bəʊsɪs/ *n.* (*pl.* **thromboses** /-siːz/) the formation of a thrombus. □ **thrombotic** /-'bɒtɪk/ *adj.* [modern Latin from Greek *thrombōsis* 'curdling' (as THROMBUS)]

thrombus /'θrɒmbəs/ *n.* (*pl.* **thrombi** /-bʌɪ/) a blood clot formed in the vascular system and impeding blood flow. [modern Latin from Greek *thrombos* 'lump, blood clot']

throne /θrəʊn/ *n.* & *v.* ● *n.* **1** a chair of State for a sovereign or bishop etc. **2** sovereign power (*came to the throne*). **3** (in *pl.*) the third order of the ninefold celestial hierarchy (see ORDER *n.* 19). **4** *colloq.* a lavatory seat and bowl. ● *v.tr.* place on a throne. □ **throneless** *adj.* [Middle English via Old French *trone* and Latin *thronus* from Greek *thronos* 'high seat']

throng /θrɒŋ/ *n.* & *v.* ● *n.* **1** a crowd of people. **2** (often foll. by *of*) a multitude, esp. in a small space. ● *v.* **1** *intr.* come in great numbers (*crowds thronged to the stadium*). **2** *tr.* flock into or crowd round; fill with or as with a crowd (*crowds thronged the streets*). [Old English *gethrang*, from verbal stem *thring- thrang-thrung-*]

throstle /'θrɒs(ə)l/ *n.* **1** *Brit.* a song thrush. **2** (in full **throstle frame**) *hist.* a machine for continuously spinning wool or cotton etc. [Old English from Germanic: related to THRUSH[1]]

throttle /'θrɒt(ə)l/ *n.* & *v.* ● *n.* **1 a** (in full **throttle-valve**) a valve controlling the flow of fuel or steam etc. in an engine. **b** (in full **throttle-lever**) a lever or pedal operating this valve. **2** the throat, gullet, or windpipe. ● *v.tr.* **1** choke or strangle. **2** prevent the utterance etc. of. **3** control (an engine or steam etc.) with a throttle. □ **throttle back** (or **down**) reduce the speed of (an engine or vehicle) by throttling. □ **throttler** *n.* [the verb from Middle English *throtel*, perhaps from THROAT + -LE[4]: the noun perhaps a diminutive of THROAT]

through /θruː/ *prep.*, *adv.*, & *adj.* (also **thro'**, *US* **thru**) ● *prep.* **1 a** from end to end or from side to side of. **b** going in one side or end and out the other of. **2** between or among (*swam through the waves*). **3** from beginning to end of (*read through the letter*; *went through many difficulties*). **4** because of; by the agency, means, or fault of (*lost it through carelessness*). **5** *N. Amer.* up to and including (*Monday through Friday*). ● *adv.* **1** through a thing; from side to side, end to end, or beginning to end (*went through to the garden*; *would not let us through*). **2** having completed (esp. successfully) (*are through their exams*). **3** so as to be connected by telephone (*will put you through*). ● *attrib.adj.* **1** (of a journey, route, etc.) done without a change of line or vehicle etc. or with one ticket. **2** (of traffic) going through a place to its destination. **3** (of a road) open at both ends. □ **be through** *colloq.* **1** (often foll. by *with*) have finished. **2** (often foll. by *with*) cease to have dealings. **3** have no further prospects (*is through as a politician*). **through and through 1** thoroughly, completely. **2** through again and again. [Old English *thurh*, from West Germanic]

throughout /θruː'aʊt/ *prep.* & *adv.* ● *prep.* right through; from end to end of (*throughout the town*; *throughout the 18th century*). ● *adv.* in every part or respect (*the timber was rotten throughout*).

throughput /'θruːpʊt/ *n.* the amount of material put through a process, esp. in manufacturing or computing.

throughway /'θruːweɪ/ *n.* (also *US* **thruway**) a thoroughfare, esp. *N. Amer.* a motorway.

throve *past* of THRIVE.

throw /θrəʊ/ *v.* & *n.* ● *v.tr.* (*past* **threw** /θruː/; *past part.* **thrown** /θrəʊn/) **1** propel with some force through the air or in a particular direction. **2** force violently into a specified position or state (*the ship was thrown on the rocks*; *threw themselves down*). **3** compel suddenly to be in a specified condition (*was thrown out of work*). **4** turn or move (part of the body) quickly or suddenly (*threw an arm out*). **5** project or cast (light, a shadow, a spell, etc.). **6 a** bring to the ground in wrestling. **b** (of a horse) unseat (its rider). **7** *colloq.* disconcert (*the question threw me for a moment*). **8** (foll. by *on, off*, etc.) put (clothes etc.) hastily on or off etc. **9 a** cause (dice) to fall on a table. **b** obtain (a specified number) by throwing dice. **10** cause to pass or extend suddenly to another state or position (*threw in the army; threw a bridge across the river*). **11** move (a switch or lever) so as to operate it. **12 a** form (ceramic ware) on a potter's wheel. **b** turn (wood etc.) on a lathe. **13** have (a fit or tantrum etc.). **14** give (a party). **15** *colloq.* lose (a contest or race etc.) intentionally. **16** *Cricket* bowl (a ball) with an illegitimate sudden straightening of the elbow. **17** (of a snake) cast (its skin). **18** (of an animal) give birth to (young). **19** twist (silk etc.) into thread or yarn. **20** (often foll. by *into*) put into another form or language etc. ● *n.* **1** an act of throwing. **2** the distance a thing is or may be thrown (*a record throw with the hammer*). **3** the act of being thrown in wrestling. **4** *Geol.* & *Mining* **a** a fault in strata. **b** the amount of vertical displacement caused by this. **5** a machine or device giving rapid rotary motion. **6 a** the movement of a crank or cam etc. **b** the extent of this. **7** the distance moved by the pointer of an instrument etc. **8** esp. *N. Amer.* **a** a light cover for furniture. **b** (in full **throw rug**) a light rug. **9** (prec. by *a*) *colloq.* each; per item (*sold at £10 a throw*). □ **throw about** (or **around**) **1** throw in various directions. **2** spend (one's money) ostentatiously. **throw away 1** discard as useless or unwanted. **2** waste or fail to make use of (an opportunity etc.). **3** discard (a playing card). **4** *Theatr.* speak (lines) with deliberate underemphasis. **5** (in *passive*; often foll. by *on*) be wasted (*the advice was thrown away on him*). **throw away the baby with the bathwater** see BABY. **throw back 1** revert to ancestral character. **2** (usu. in *passive*; foll. by *on*) compel to rely on (*was thrown back on his savings*). **throw cold water on** see COLD. **throw down** cause to fall. **throw down the gauntlet** (or **glove**) issue a challenge. **throw dust in a person's eyes** mislead a person by misrepresentation or distraction. **throw good money after bad** incur further loss in a hopeless attempt to recoup a previous loss. **throw one's hand in 1** abandon one's chances in a card game, esp. poker. **2** give up; withdraw from a contest. **throw in 1** interpose (a word or remark). **2** include at no extra cost. **3** throw (a football) from the edge of the pitch where it has gone out of play. **4** *Cricket* etc. return (the ball) from the outfield. **5** *Cards* give (a player) the lead, to the player's disadvantage. **throw in one's lot with** see LOT. **throw in** (or **up**) **the sponge 1** (of a boxer or his attendant) throw the sponge used between rounds into the air as a token of defeat. **2** abandon a contest; admit defeat. **throw in the towel** admit defeat. **throw light on** see LIGHT[1]. **throw off 1** discard; contrive to get rid of. **2** write or utter in an offhand manner. **3** (of hounds or a hunt) begin hunting; make a start. **throw oneself at** seek blatantly as a spouse or sexual partner. **throw oneself into** engage vigorously in. **throw oneself on** (or **upon**) **1** rely completely on. **2** attack. **throw open** (often foll. by *to*) **1** cause to be suddenly or widely open. **2** make accessible. **3** invite general discussion of or participation in. **throw out 1** put out forcibly or suddenly. **2** discard as unwanted. **3** expel (a troublemaker etc.). **4** *Brit.* build (a wing of a house, a pier, or a projecting or prominent thing). **5** (of a plant) rapidly develop (a side shoot etc.). **6** put forward tentatively. **7** reject (a proposal or bill in Parliament). **8** confuse or distract (a person speaking, thinking, or acting) from the matter in hand. **9** *Cricket* & *Baseball* put out (an opponent) by throwing the ball to the wicket or base. **throw over** desert or abandon. **throw stones** cast aspersions. **throw together 1** assemble hastily. **2** bring into casual contact. **throw up 1** abandon. **2** resign from. **3** *colloq.* vomit. **4** erect hastily. **5** bring to notice. **6** lift (a sash window) quickly. **throw one's weight about** (or **around**) *colloq.* act in a domineering or over-assertive manner. □ **throwable** *adj.* **thrower** *n.* (also in *comb.*). [Old English *thrāwan* 'twist, turn', from West Germanic]

throwaway /ˈθrəʊəweɪ/ *adj.* & *n.* ● *adj.* **1** meant to be thrown away after (one) use. **2** (of lines etc.) deliberately underemphasized. **3** disposed to throwing things away; wasteful (*throwaway society*). ● *n.* a thing to be thrown away after (one) use.

throwback /ˈθrəʊbak/ *n.* **1** reversion to ancestral character. **2** an instance of this.

throw-in *n.* the throwing in of a ball during a match, from the sideline to restart play, from a fielding position in the outfield, etc.

throw-off *n.* the start in a hunt or race.

throw-over *attrib.adj.* that can be thrown over (esp. a bed, sofa) as a decorative cover.

throw rug see THROW *n.* 8b.

throwster /ˈθrəʊstə/ *n.* a person who throws silk.

thru *US* var. of THROUGH.

thrum[1] /θrʌm/ *v.* & *n.* ● *v.* (**thrummed**, **thrumming**) **1** *tr.* play (a stringed instrument) monotonously or unskilfully. **2** *intr.* (often foll. by *on*) drum idly. ● *n.* **1** such playing. **2** the resulting sound. [imitative]

thrum[2] /θrʌm/ *n.* & *v.* ● *n.* **1** (in weaving) the unwoven end of a warp thread, or the whole of such ends, left when the finished web is cut away. **2** any short loose thread. ● *v.tr.* (**thrummed**, **thrumming**) make of or cover with thrums. □ **thrummer** *n.* **thrummy** *adj.* [Old English from Germanic]

thrush[1] /θrʌʃ/ *n.* any small or medium-sized songbird of the family Turdidae, esp. a song thrush or mistle thrush (see MISTLE THRUSH, SONG THRUSH). [Old English *thrysce*, from Germanic: related to THROSTLE]

thrush[2] /θrʌʃ/ *n.* **1 a** infection by the yeastlike fungus *Candida albicans*, causing white patches in the mouth and throat. **b** similar infection of the vagina. **2** inflammation affecting the frog of a horse's foot. [17th c.: origin unknown]

thrust /θrʌst/ *v.* & *n.* ● *v.* (*past* and *past part.* **thrust**) **1** *tr.* push with a sudden impulse or with force (*thrust the letter into my pocket*). **2** *tr.* (foll. by *on*) impose (a thing) forcibly; enforce acceptance of (a thing) (*had it thrust on me*). **3** *intr.* (foll. by *at, through*) pierce or stab; make a sudden lunge. **4** *tr.* make (one's way) forcibly. **5** *intr.* (foll. by *through, past*, etc.) force oneself (*thrust past me abruptly*). **6** *intr.* (as **thrusting** *adj.*) aggressive, ambitious. ● *n.* **1** a sudden or forcible push or lunge. **2** the propulsive force developed by a jet or rocket engine. **3** a strong attempt to penetrate an enemy's line or territory. **4** a remark aimed at a person. **5** the stress between the parts of an arch etc. **6** (often foll. by *of*) the chief theme or gist of remarks etc. **7** an attack with the point of a weapon. **8** (in full **thrust fault**) *Geol.* a reverse fault of low angle, with older strata displaced horizontally over newer. □ **thrust oneself** (or **one's nose**) **in** obtrude, interfere. [Middle English *thruste* etc. from Old Norse *thrýsta*]

thrust bearing *n.* a bearing designed to take a load in the direction of the axis of a shaft, esp. one transmitting the thrust of a propeller shaft to the hull of a ship.

thrust block *n.* a casting or frame carrying or containing the bearings on which the collars of a propeller shaft press.

thruster /ˈθrʌstə/ *n.* **1** a person or thing that thrusts. **2** a small rocket engine used to provide extra or correcting thrust on a spacecraft.

thrust stage *n.* a stage extending into the audience.

thruway *US* var. of THROUGHWAY.

thud /θʌd/ *n.* & *v.* ● *n.* a low dull sound as of a blow on a non-resonant surface. ● *v.intr.* (**thudded**, **thudding**) make or fall with a thud. □ **thuddingly** *adv.* [probably from Old English *thyddan* 'thrust']

thug /θʌg/ *n.* **1** a vicious or brutal ruffian. **2** (**Thug**) *hist.* a member of a religious organization of robbers and assassins in India. □ **thuggery** *n.* **thuggish** *adj.*

thuggishly *adv.* **thuggishness** *n.* [Hindi & Marathi *ṭhag* 'swindler']

thuggee /θʌ'gi:/ *n. hist.* murder practised by the Thugs. ▫ **thuggism** *n.* [Hindi *ṭhagī* (as THUG)]

thuja /'θ(j)u:jə/ *n.* (also **thuya**) any evergreen coniferous tree of the genus *Thuja*, with small leaves closely pressed to the branches; arbor vitae. [modern Latin from Greek *thuia*, an African tree]

thulium /'θ(j)u:lɪəm/ *n. Chem.* a soft metallic element of the lanthanide series, occurring naturally in apatite (symbol **Tm**). [modern Latin from Latin *Thule*, the name of a region in the remote north]

thumb /θʌm/ *n. & v.* ●*n.* **1 a** a short thick terminal projection on the human hand, set lower and apart from the other four and opposable to them. **b** a digit of other animals corresponding to this. **2** the part of a glove etc. intended to cover the thumb. ●*v.* **1** *tr.* wear or soil (pages etc.) with a thumb (*a well-thumbed book*). **2** *intr.* turn over pages with or as with a thumb (*thumbed through the directory*). **3** *tr.* request or obtain (a lift in a passing vehicle) by signalling with a raised thumb. **4** *tr.* use the thumb in a gesture. ▫ **be all thumbs** be clumsy with one's hands. **thumb one's nose** = *cock a snook* (see SNOOK[1]). **thumbs down** an indication of rejection or failure. **thumbs up** an indication of satisfaction or approval. **under a person's thumb** completely dominated by a person. ▫ **thumbed** *adj.* (also in *comb.*). **thumbless** *adj.* [Old English *thūma*, from a West Germanic root meaning 'to swell']

thumb index *n. & v.* ●*n.* a set of lettered grooves cut down the side of a diary, dictionary, etc. for easy reference. ●*v.tr.* (**thumb-index**) (esp. as **thumb-indexed** *adj.*) provide (a book etc.) with these.

thumbnail /'θʌmneɪl/ *n.* **1** the nail of a thumb. **2** (*attrib.*) denoting conciseness (*a thumbnail sketch*).

thumb nut *n.* a nut shaped for turning with the thumb and forefinger.

thumbprint /'θʌmprɪnt/ *n.* an impression of a thumb, esp. as used for identification.

thumbscrew /'θʌmskru:/ *n.* **1** (usu. in *pl.*) an instrument of torture for crushing the thumbs. **2** a screw with a protruding winged or flattened head for turning with the thumb and forefinger.

thumbtack /'θʌmtak/ *n. N. Amer.* a drawing pin.

thump /θʌmp/ *v. & n.* ●*v.* **1** *tr.* beat or strike heavily, esp. with the fist (*threatened to thump me*). **2** *intr.* throb or pulsate strongly (*my heart was thumping*). **3** *intr.* (foll. by *at*, *on*, etc.) deliver blows, esp. to attract attention (*thumped on the door*). **4** *tr.* (often foll. by *out*) play (a tune on a piano etc.) with a heavy touch. **5** *intr.* tread heavily. ●*n.* **1** a heavy blow. **2** the sound of this. ▫ **thumper** *n.* [imitative]

thumping /'θʌmpɪŋ/ *adj. colloq.* big, prominent (*a thumping majority*; *a thumping lie*).

thunder /'θʌndə/ *n. & v.* ●*n.* **1** a loud rumbling or crashing noise heard after a lightning flash and due to the expansion of rapidly heated air. **2** a resounding loud deep noise (*thunders of applause*). **3** strong censure or denunciation. ●*v.* **1** *intr.* (prec. by *it* as subject) thunder sounds (*it is thundering*; *if it thunders*). **2** *intr.* make or proceed with a noise suggestive of thunder (*the applause thundered in my ears*; *the traffic thundered past*). **3** *tr.* utter or communicate (approval, disapproval, etc.) loudly or impressively. **4** *intr.* (foll. by *against* etc.) **a** make violent threats etc. against. **b** criticize violently. ▫ **steal a person's thunder** see STEAL. ▫ **thunderer** *n.* **thunderless** *adj.* **thundery** *adj.* [Old English *thunor*, from Germanic]

thunderbird /'θʌndəbə:d/ *n.* a mythical bird thought by some N. American Indians to bring thunder.

thunderbolt /'θʌndəbəʊlt/ *n.* **1 a** a flash of lightning with a simultaneous crash of thunder. **b** a stone etc. imagined to be a destructive bolt. **2** a sudden or unexpected occurrence or item of news. **3** a supposed bolt or shaft as a destructive agent, esp. as an attribute of a god.

thunderbox /'θʌndəbɒks/ *n. Brit. colloq.* a primitive lavatory.

thunderclap /'θʌndəklap/ *n.* **1** a crash of thunder. **2** something startling or unexpected.

thundercloud /'θʌndəklaʊd/ *n.* a cumulus cloud with a tall diffuse top, charged with electricity and producing thunder and lightning.

thunderflash /'θʌndəflaʃ/ *n.* a noisy but harmless explosive used esp. in military exercises.

thunderfly /'θʌndəflʌɪ/ *n.* = THRIPS.

thunderhead /'θʌndəhɛd/ *n.* esp. *US* a rounded cumulus cloud projecting upwards and heralding thunder.

thundering /'θʌnd(ə)rɪŋ/ *adj. colloq.* very big or great (*a thundering nuisance*). ▫ **thunderingly** *adv.*

thunderous /'θʌnd(ə)rəs/ *adj.* **1** like thunder. **2** very loud. ▫ **thunderously** *adv.* **thunderousness** *n.*

thunderstorm /'θʌndəstɔ:m/ *n.* a storm with thunder and lightning and usu. heavy rain or hail.

thunderstruck /'θʌndəstrʌk/ *adj.* amazed; overwhelmingly surprised or startled.

thunk[1] /θʌŋk/ *n. & v.intr. colloq.* = THUD.

thunk[2] /θʌŋk/ *colloq.*, esp. *joc. past* and *past part.* of THINK.

Thur. *abbr.* Thursday.

thurible /'θjʊərɪb(ə)l/ *n.* a censer. [Middle English from Old French *thurible* or Latin *t(h)uribulum*, from *thus thur-* 'incense' (as THURIFER)]

thurifer /'θjʊərɪfə/ *n.* an acolyte carrying a censer. [Late Latin from *thus thuris* 'incense' (from Greek *thuos* 'sacrifice') + *-fer* '-bearing']

Thurs. *abbr.* Thursday.

Thursday /'θə:zdeɪ, -di/ *n. & adv.* ●*n.* the fifth day of the week, following Wednesday. ●*adv. colloq.* **1** on Thursday. **2** (**Thursdays**) on Thursdays; each Thursday. [Old English *thunresdæg*, *thur(e)sdæg*, 'day of thunder', representing Late Latin *Jovis dies* 'day of Jupiter', Jupiter being associated with thunder]

thus /ðʌs/ *adv. formal* **1 a** in this way. **b** as indicated. **2 a** accordingly. **b** as a result or inference. **3** to this extent; so (*thus far*; *thus much*). [Old English, of unknown origin]

thuya var. of THUJA.

thwack /θwak/ *v. & n.* ●*v.tr.* hit with a heavy blow; whack. ●*n.* a heavy blow. [imitative]

thwaite /θweɪt/ *n. Brit. dial.* a piece of wild land made arable. [Old Norse *thveit(i)* 'paddock', related to Old English *thwītan* 'to cut']

▪ **Usage** *Thwaite* is now usually found only in place names, e.g. *Bassenthwaite*, or as a surname.

thwart /θwɔ:t/ *v., n., prep., & adv.* ●*v.tr.* frustrate or foil (a person or purpose etc.). ●*n.* a rower's seat placed across a boat. ●*prep. & adv. archaic* across, athwart. [Middle English *thwert* (*adv.*) from Old Norse *thvert*, neut. of *thverr* 'transverse' = Old English *thwe(o)rh*, from Germanic]

thy /ðʌɪ/ *poss.pron.* (*attrib.*) (also **thine** /ðʌɪn/ before a vowel) of or belonging to thee. [Middle English *thī*, reduced from *thīn* THINE]

▪ **Usage** *Thy* has now been replaced by *your* except in some formal, liturgical, dialectal, and poetic uses.

thylacine /'θʌɪləsi:n, -sʌɪn, -sɪn/ *n.* a doglike grey-brown carnivorous marsupial of Tasmania, *Thylacinus cynocephalus*, with stripes across the rump, now very rare or extinct. Also called *Tasmanian tiger* or *wolf*. [modern Latin from Greek *thulakos* 'pouch']

thyme /tʌɪm/ *n.* any herb or shrub of the genus *Thymus* with aromatic leaves, esp. *T. vulgaris* grown for culinary use. ▫ **thymy** *adj.* [Middle English from Old French *thym*, from Latin *thymum* via Greek *thumon* from *thuō* 'burn a sacrifice']

thymi *pl.* of THYMUS.

thymine /ˈθʌɪmiːn/ *n. Biochem.* a pyrimidine found in all living tissue as a component base of DNA. [*thymic* (as THYMUS) + -INE[4]]

thymol /ˈθʌɪmɒl/ *n. Chem.* a white crystalline phenol obtained from oil of thyme and used as an antiseptic. [as THYME + -OL[1]]

thymus /ˈθʌɪməs/ *n.* (*pl.* **thymi** /-mʌɪ/) (in full **thymus gland**) *Anat.* a lymphoid organ situated in the neck of vertebrates (in humans becoming much smaller at the approach of puberty) producing T-lymphocytes for the immune response. [modern Latin from Greek *thumos*]

thyristor /θʌɪˈrɪstə/ *n. Electronics* a four-layered semiconductor rectifier in which the flow of current between two electrodes is triggered by a signal at a third electrode. [Greek *thura* 'gate' + TRANSISTOR]

thyro- /ˈθʌɪrəʊ/ *comb. form* (also **thyreo-** /-rɪəʊ/) thyroid.

thyroid /ˈθʌɪrɔɪd/ *n. & adj.* ● *n.* **1** (in full **thyroid gland**) a large ductless gland in the neck of vertebrates secreting hormones which regulate growth and development through the rate of metabolism. **2** an extract prepared from the thyroid gland of animals and used in treating goitre and cretinism etc. ● *adj. Anat. & Zool.* **1** connected with the thyroid cartilage (*thyroid artery*). **2** shield-shaped. [obsolete French *thyroide* or modern Latin *thyroides*, formed irregularly from Greek *thureoeidēs*, from *thureos* 'oblong shield']

thyroid cartilage *n.* a large cartilage of the larynx, the projection of which in man forms the Adam's apple.

thyroxine /θʌɪˈrɒksiːn, -sɪn/ *n.* the main hormone produced by the thyroid gland, acting to increase metabolic rate and so regulating growth and development. [THYROID + OX- + -INE[4]]

thyrsus /ˈθəːsəs/ *n.* (*pl.* **thyrsi** /-sʌɪ, -siː/) **1** *Gk & Rom. Antiq.* a staff tipped with an ornament like a pine cone, an attribute of Bacchus. **2** *Bot.* an inflorescence as in lilac, with the primary axis racemose and the secondary axis cymose. [Latin from Greek *thursos*]

thyself /ðʌɪˈsɛlf/ *pron. archaic & dial.* **1** *emphat.* form of THOU[1] **2** *refl. form* of THEE.

Ti *symb. Chem.* the element titanium.

ti[1] /tiː/ *n.* = CABBAGE TREE 1. Cf. TI-TREE. [Tahitian, Maori, etc.]

ti[2] var. of TE.

TIA *abbr. Med.* transient ischaemic attack.

tiara /tɪˈɑːrə/ *n.* **1** a jewelled ornamental band worn on the front of a woman's hair. **2** a three-crowned diadem worn by a pope. **3** *hist.* a turban worn by ancient Persian kings. [Latin from Greek, of unknown origin]

Tibetan /tɪˈbɛt(ə)n/ *n. & adj.* ● *n.* **1 a** a native of Tibet in SW China. **b** a person of Tibetan descent. **2** the language of Tibet. ● *adj.* of or relating to Tibet, its people, or its language.

tibia /ˈtɪbɪə/ *n.* (*pl.* **tibiae** /-bɪiː/) **1** *Anat.* the inner and usu. larger of two bones extending from the knee to the ankle. **2** *Zool.* the tibiotarsus of a bird. **3** *Zool.* the fourth segment of the leg in insects. ▫ **tibial** *adj.* [Latin, = shin bone]

tibiotarsus /ˌtɪbɪəʊˈtɑːsəs/ *n.* (*pl.* **tibiotarsi** /-sʌɪ, -siː/) the bone in a bird corresponding to the tibia fused at the lower end with some bones of the tarsus. [TIBIA + TARSUS]

tic /tɪk/ *n.* a habitual spasmodic contraction of the muscles esp. of the face. [French from Italian *ticchio*]

tic douloureux /duːləˈruː, -ˈrəː/ *n.* trigeminal neuralgia. [TIC + French *douloureux* 'painful']

tice /tʌɪs/ *n.* **1** *Cricket* = YORKER. **2** *Croquet* a stroke tempting an opponent to aim at one's ball. [*tice* (now dialect) from Old French *atisier*, = ENTICE]

tick[1] /tɪk/ *n. & v.* ● *n.* **1** a slight recurring click, esp. that of a watch or clock. **2** esp. *Brit. colloq.* a moment; an instant. **3** a mark (✓) to denote correctness, check items in a list, etc. ● *v.* **1** *intr.* **a** (of a clock etc.) make ticks. **b** (foll. by *away*) (of time etc.) pass. **2** *intr.* (of a mechanism) work, function (*take it apart to see how it ticks*). **3** *tr.* **a** mark (a written answer etc.) with a tick. **b** (often foll. by *off*) mark (an item in a list etc.) with a tick in checking. ▫ **in two ticks** *Brit. colloq.* in a very short time. **tick off** *colloq.* reprimand. **tick over 1** (of an engine etc.) idle. **2** (of a person, project, etc.) be working or functioning at a basic or minimum level. **what makes a person tick** *colloq.* a person's motivation. [Middle English: cf. Dutch *tik*, Low German *tikk* 'touch, tick']

tick[2] /tɪk/ *n.* **1** any of various arachnids of the order Acarina, parasitic on the skin of dogs and cattle etc. **2** any of various insects of the family Hippoboscidae, parasitic on sheep and birds etc. **3** *colloq.* an unpleasant or despicable person. [Old English *ticia*; Middle English *teke*, *tyke*: cf. Middle Dutch, Middle Low German *tēke*, Old High German *zēcho*]

tick[3] /tɪk/ *n. colloq.* credit (*buy goods on tick*). [apparently an abbreviation of TICKET in the phrase *on the ticket*]

tick[4] /tɪk/ *n.* **1** the cover of a mattress or pillow. **2** = TICKING. [Middle English *tikke*, *tēke* from West Germanic, via Latin *theca* from Greek *thēkē* 'case']

tick-bird *n.* = OX-PECKER.

ticker /ˈtɪkə/ *n. colloq.* **1** the heart. **2** a watch. **3** *N. Amer.* a tape machine.

ticker tape *n.* **1** a paper strip from a tape machine. **2** this or similar material thrown from windows etc. to greet a celebrity (hyphenated when *attrib.*: *a ticker-tape reception*).

ticket /ˈtɪkɪt/ *n. & v.* ● *n.* **1 a** a written or printed piece of paper or card entitling the holder to enter a place, participate in an event, travel by public transport, use a public amenity, etc. **b** a receipt for an item left temporarily for safe keeping. **2** an official notification of a traffic offence etc. (*parking ticket*). **3** *Brit.* a certificate of discharge from the army. **4** a certificate of qualification as a ship's master, pilot, etc. **5** a label attached to a thing and giving its price or other details. **6** esp. *US* **a** a list of candidates put forward by one group, esp. a political party. **b** the principles of a party. **7** (prec. by *the*) *colloq.* what is correct or needed (*it was just the ticket*). ● *v.tr.* (**ticketed**, **ticketing**) attach a ticket to. ▫ **have tickets on oneself** *Austral. colloq.* be conceited. ▫ **ticketed** *adj.* **ticketless** *adj.* [obsolete French *étiquet* via Old French *estiquet(te)*, from *estiquier*, *estechier* 'fix', from Middle Dutch *steken*]

ticket collector *n.* a person who is employed to collect tickets, esp. from rail passengers.

ticket-day *n. Stock Exch.* (in the UK) the day before settling day, when the names of actual purchasers are handed to stockbrokers.

ticket-holder *n.* a person who has purchased a ticket (for a match, concert, etc.).

ticket office *n.* an office or kiosk where tickets are sold for transport, entertainment, etc.

ticket-of-leave man *n. Brit. hist.* a prisoner or convict who had served part of his time and was granted certain concessions, esp. leave.

ticket tout *n.* a person who buys up tickets for an event to resell them at a profit.

tickety-boo /ˌtɪkɪtɪˈbuː/ *adj. Brit. colloq.* all right; in order. [20th c.: origin uncertain]

tick fever *n.* a bacterial or rickettsial fever transmitted by the bite of a tick.

ticking /ˈtɪkɪŋ/ *n.* a stout usu. striped material used to cover mattresses etc. [TICK[4] + -ING[1]]

tickle /ˈtɪk(ə)l/ *v. & n.* ● *v.* **1 a** *tr.* apply light touches or strokes to (a person or part of a person's body) so as to excite the nerves and usu. produce laughter and spasmodic movement. **b** *intr.* be subject to this sensation (*my foot tickles*). **c** *intr.* produce this sensation (*this woolly jumper tickles*). **2** *tr.* excite agreeably; amuse or divert (a person, a sense of humour, vanity, etc.) (*was highly tickled at the idea*; *this will tickle your fancy*). **3** *tr.* catch (a trout etc.) by rubbing it so that it moves backwards into the hand. ● *n.* **1** an act of tickling. **2** a tickling sensation. ▫ **tickled pink** (or **to**

death) *colloq.* extremely amused or pleased. ▫ **tickler** *n.* **tickly** *adj.* [Middle English, probably frequentative of TICK[1]]

ticklish /ˈtɪklɪʃ/ *adj.* **1** sensitive to tickling. **2** (of a matter or person to be dealt with) difficult; requiring careful handling. ▫ **ticklishly** *adv.* **ticklishness** *n.*

tick-tack *n.* (also **tic-tac**) *Brit.* a kind of manual semaphore signalling used by racecourse bookmakers to exchange information. [TICK[1]]

tick-tack-toe *n. N. Amer.* noughts and crosses. [TICK[1]]

tick-tock *n.* the ticking of a large clock etc. [TICK[1]]

tidal /ˈtʌɪd(ə)l/ *adj.* relating to, like, or affected by tides (*tidal basin; tidal river*). ▫ **tidally** *adv.*

tidal bore *n.* a large wave or bore caused by constriction of the spring tide as it enters a long narrow shallow inlet.

tidal flow *n.* the regulated movement of traffic in opposite directions on the same stretch of road at different times of the day.

tidal wave *n.* **1** *Geog.* an exceptionally large ocean wave, esp. a tsunami. **2** a widespread manifestation (of feeling etc.).

tidbit *N. Amer.* var. of TITBIT.

tiddledywink *US* var. of TIDDLYWINK.

tiddler /ˈtɪdlə/ *n. Brit. colloq.* **1** a small fish, esp. a stickleback or minnow. **2** an unusually small thing or person. [perhaps related to TIDDLY[2] and *tittlebat*, a childish form of *stickleback*]

tiddly[1] /ˈtɪdli/ *adj.* (**tiddlier**, **tiddliest**) esp. *Brit. colloq.* slightly drunk. [19th c., earlier = a drink: origin unknown]

tiddly[2] /ˈtɪdli/ *adj.* (**tiddlier**, **tiddliest**) *Brit. colloq.* little. [origin unknown]

tiddlywink /ˈtɪdlɪwɪŋk/ *n.* (*US* also **tiddledywink** /ˈtɪd(ə)ldɪ-/) **1** a counter flicked with another into a cup etc. **2** (in *pl.*) this game. [19th c.: perhaps related to TIDDLY[1]]

tide /tʌɪd/ *n. & v.* ● *n.* **1 a** the periodic rise and fall of the sea due to the attraction of the moon and sun (see EBB *n.* 1, FLOOD *n.* 3). **b** the water as affected by this. **2** a time or season (usu. in *comb.*: *Whitsuntide*). **3** a marked trend of opinion, fortune, or events. ● *v.intr.* **1** drift with or *literary* as with the tide. **2** (of a ship) work in or out of harbour with the help of the tide. ▫ **tide over** enable or help (a person) to deal with an awkward situation, difficult period, etc. (*the money will tide me over until Friday*). **work double tides** *Brit.* work twice the normal time, or extra hard. ▫ **tideless** *adj.* [Old English *tīd* from Germanic: related to TIME]

tideland /ˈtʌɪdland/ *n. N. Amer.* land that is submerged at high tide.

tideline /ˈtʌɪdlʌɪn/ *n.* the edge defined by the tide on the shore.

tidemark /ˈtʌɪdmɑːk/ *n.* **1** a mark made by the tide at high water. **2** esp. *Brit.* **a** a mark left round a bath at the level of the water in it. **b** a line on a person's body marking the extent to which it has been washed.

tide mill *n.* a mill with a waterwheel driven by the tide.

tide-rip *n.* **1** rough water caused esp. by opposing tides. **2** a patch of such water.

tide table *n.* a table indicating the times of high and low tides at a place.

tidewaiter /ˈtʌɪdweɪtə/ *n. hist.* a customs officer who boarded ships on their arrival to enforce the customs regulations.

tidewater /ˈtʌɪdwɔːtə/ *n.* **1** water brought by or affected by tides. **2** (*attrib.*) *US* affected by tides (*tidewater region*).

tidewave /ˈtʌɪdweɪv/ *n.* an undulation of water passing round the earth and causing high and low tides.

tideway /ˈtʌɪdweɪ/ *n.* **1** a channel in which a tide runs, esp. the tidal part of a river. **2** the ebb or flow in a tidal channel.

tidings /ˈtʌɪdɪŋz/ *n.pl.* esp. *literary* news, information. [Old English *tīdung*, probably via Old Norse *títhindi* 'events' from *títhr* 'occurring']

tidy /ˈtʌɪdi/ *adj., n., & v.* ● *adj.* (**tidier**, **tidiest**) **1** neat, orderly; methodically arranged. **2** (of a person) methodically inclined. **3** *colloq.* considerable (*it cost a tidy sum*). ● *n.* (*pl.* **-ies**) **1** a receptacle for holding small objects or waste scraps, esp. in a kitchen sink. **2** an act or spell of tidying. **3** esp. *US* a detachable ornamental cover for a chair back etc. ● *v.tr.* (**-ies**, **-ied**) (also *absol.*; often foll. by *up*) put in good order; make (oneself, a room, etc.) tidy. ▫ **tidily** *adv.* **tidiness** *n.* [earlier = timely, seasonable: Middle English, from TIDE + -Y[1]]

tie /tʌɪ/ *v. & n.* ● *v.* (**tying**) **1** *tr.* attach or fasten with string or cord etc. (*tie the dog to the gate; tie his hands together; tied on a label*). **2** *tr.* **a** form (a string, ribbon, shoelace, necktie, etc.) into a knot or bow. **b** form (a knot or bow) in this way. **3** *tr.* restrict or limit (a person) as to conditions, occupation, place, etc. (*is tied to his family*). **4** *intr.* (often foll. by *with*) achieve the same score or place as another competitor (*they tied at ten games each; tied with her for first place*). **5** *tr.* hold (rafters etc.) together by a crosspiece etc. **6** *tr. Mus.* **a** unite (written notes) by a tie. **b** perform (two notes) as one unbroken note. ● *n.* **1** a cord or chain etc. used for fastening. **2** a strip of material worn round the collar and tied in a knot at the front with the ends hanging down. **3** a thing that unites or restricts persons; a bond or obligation (*family ties; ties of friendship; children are a real tie*). **4** a draw, dead heat, or equality of score among competitors. **5** *Brit.* a match between any pair from a group of competing players or teams. **6** (also **tie-beam** etc.) a rod or beam holding parts of a structure together. **7** *Mus.* a curved line above or below two notes of the same pitch indicating that they are to be played for the combined duration of their time values. **8** *N. Amer.* a railway sleeper. **9** *US* a shoe tied with a lace. ▫ **fit to be tied** *colloq.* very angry. **tie in** (foll. by *with*) bring into or have a close association or agreement. **tie up 1** bind or fasten securely with cord etc. **2** invest or reserve (capital etc.) so that it is not immediately available for use. **3** moor (a boat). **4** secure (an animal). **5** obstruct; prevent from acting freely. **6** secure or complete (an undertaking etc.). **7** (often foll. by *with*) = *tie in*. **8** (usu. in *passive*) fully occupy (a person). ▫ **tieless** *adj.* [Old English *tīgan*, *tēgan* (*v.*), *tēah*, *tēg* (*n.*), from Germanic]

tie-back *n.* a decorative strip of fabric or cord for holding a curtain back from the window.

tie-beam *n.* a horizontal beam connecting two rafters in a roof or roof-truss.

tie-break *n.* (also **tie-breaker**) a means of deciding a winner from competitors who have tied.

tie-clip *n.* an ornamental clip for holding a tie in place.

tied /tʌɪd/ *adj. Brit.* **1** (of a house) occupied subject to the tenant's working for its owner. **2** (of a public house) that is owned by a brewery and is bound to supply the products produced or specified by that brewery.

tie-dye *n. & v.* ● *n.* a method of producing dyed patterns by tying string etc. to shield parts of the fabric from the dye. ● *v.tr.* dye by this process.

tie-in *n.* **1** a connection or association. **2** (often *attrib.*) esp. *N. Amer.* a form of sale or advertising that offers or requires more than a single purchase. **3** the joint promotion of related commodities etc. (e.g. a book and a film).

tie line *n.* a transmission line connecting parts of a system, esp. a telephone line connecting two private branch exchanges.

tiepin /ˈtaɪpɪn/ *n.* an ornamental pin for holding a tie in place.

tier /tɪə/ *n.* **1** a row or rank or unit of a structure, as one of several placed one above another (*tiers of seats*). **2** *Naut.* **a** a circle of coiled cable. **b** a place for a coiled cable. ▫ **tiered** *adj.* (also in *comb.*). [earlier *tire* via French, from *tirer* 'draw, elongate', from Romanic]

tierce /tɪəs/ *n.* **1** *Eccl.* = TERCE. **2** *Mus.* an interval of two octaves and a major third. **3** a sequence of three cards. **4** *Fencing* **a** the third of eight parrying positions. **b** the corresponding thrust. **5** *archaic* **a** a former measure of wine equal to one-third of a pipe (see PIPE *n.* 9). **b** a cask containing a certain quantity (varying with the goods) esp. of provisions. [Middle English via Old French *t(i)erce* from Latin *tertia*, fem. of *tertius* 'third']

tierced /tɪəst/ *adj. Heraldry* divided into three parts of different tinctures.

tiercel /'tɪəs(ə)l/ *n.* (also **tercel** /'tə:s(ə)l/) the male of the hawk, esp. (in falconry) a peregrine or goshawk. [Middle English from Old French *tercel*, ultimately a diminutive of Latin *tertius* 'third', perhaps from a belief that the third egg of a clutch produced a male bird, or that the male was one-third smaller than the female]

tiercet var. of TERCET.

tie-up *n.* a connection, an association.

tiff /tɪf/ *n. colloq.* **1** a slight or petty quarrel. **2** a fit of peevishness. [18th c.: origin unknown]

tiffany /'tɪf(ə)ni/ *n.* (*pl.* **-ies**) thin gauze muslin. [originally dress worn on Twelfth Night, from Old French *tifanie* via ecclesiastical Latin *theophania* from Greek *theophaneia* 'Epiphany']

tiffin /'tɪfɪn/ *n.* & *v. Anglo-Ind.* ● *n.* a light meal, esp. lunch. ● *v.intr.* (**tiffined**, **tiffining**) take lunch etc. [apparently from *tiffing* 'sipping', of unknown origin]

tig /tɪg/ *n.* = TAG[2] 1. [variant of TICK[1]]

tiger /'tʌɪgə/ *n.* **1** a large Asian flesh-eating feline, *Panthera tigris*, having a yellow-brown coat with black stripes. **2** a fierce, energetic, or formidable person. □ **tigerish** *adj.* **tigerishly** *adv.* [Middle English via Old French *tigre* and Latin *tigris* from Greek *tigris*]

tiger beetle *n.* any carnivorous beetle of the family Cicindelidae, with spotted or striped wing-cases.

tiger-cat *n.* **1** any moderate-sized striped feline, e.g. the ocelot, serval, or margay. **2** *Austral.* any of various catlike flesh-eating marsupials of the genus *Dasyurus*.

tiger lily *n.* a tall garden lily, *Lilium tigrinum*, with flowers of dull orange spotted with black or purple.

tiger moth *n.* any moth of the family Arctiidae, esp. *Arctia caja*, having richly spotted and streaked wings suggesting a tiger's skin.

tiger's-eye *n.* (also **tiger-eye**) **1** a silky, often striped yellow-brown semi-precious variety of quartz. **2** *US* a pottery glaze of similar appearance.

tiger shark *n.* a voracious striped or spotted shark, esp. *Galeocerdo cuvieri* of warm seas or *Stegosoma tigrinum* of the Indian Ocean.

tiger-wood *n.* a striped or streaked wood used for cabinetmaking.

tight /tʌɪt/ *adj.* & *adv.* ● *adj.* **1** closely held, drawn, fastened, fitting, etc. (*a tight hold; a tight skirt*). **2** closely and firmly put together (*a tight joint*). **3** (of clothes etc.) too closely fitting (*my shoes are rather tight*). **4** impermeable, impervious, esp. (in *comb.*) to a specified thing (*watertight*). **5** tense; stretched so as to leave no slack (*a tight bowstring*). **6** *colloq.* drunk. **7** *colloq.* (of a person) mean, stingy. **8 a** (of money or materials) not easily obtainable. **b** (of a money market) in which money is tight. **9 a** (of precautions, a programme, etc.) stringent, demanding. **b** presenting difficulties (*a tight situation*). **10** produced by or requiring great exertion or pressure (*a tight squeeze*). **11** (of control etc.) strictly imposed. ● *adv.* tightly (*hold tight!*). □ **tight corner** (or **place** or **spot**) a difficult situation. □ **tightly** *adv.* **tightness** *n.* [probably an alteration of *thight* from Old Norse *théttr* 'watertight, of close texture']

tighten /'tʌɪt(ə)n/ *v.tr.* & *intr.* make or become tight or tighter. □ **tighten one's belt** see BELT.

tight end *n. Amer. Football* an offensive end who lines up close to the tackle.

tight-fisted *adj.* stingy.

tight-fitting *adj.* (of a garment) fitting (often too) close to the body.

tight-knit *adj.* (also **tightly-knit**) = CLOSE-KNIT.

tight-lipped *adj.* with or as with the lips compressed to restrain emotion or speech.

tightrope /'tʌɪtrəʊp/ *n.* a rope stretched tightly high above the ground, on which acrobats perform.

tights /tʌɪts/ *n.pl.* **1** a thin close-fitting wool or nylon etc. garment covering the legs and the lower part of the torso, worn by women in place of stockings (cf. PANTYHOSE). **2** a similar garment worn by a dancer, acrobat, etc.

tightwad /'tʌɪtwɒd/ *n.* esp. *N. Amer. slang* a mean or miserly person.

tigon /'tʌɪg(ə)n/ *n.* (also **tiglon** /'tʌɪglɒn, 'tɪg-/) the offspring of a tiger and a lioness (cf. LIGER). [portmanteau word from TIGER + LION]

Tigrayan /tɪ'greɪən/ *adj.* & *n.* (also **Tigrean**) ● *adj.* of or relating to Tigray, one of the northern provinces of Ethiopia. ● *n.* a native or inhabitant of this province.

tigress /'tʌɪgrɪs/ *n.* **1** a female tiger. **2** a fierce or passionate woman.

tike var. of TYKE.

tiki /'tɪki/ *n.* (*pl.* **tikis**) *NZ* a large wooden or small ornamental greenstone image representing a human figure. [Maori]

tikka /'tɪkə, 'ti:kə/ *n.* an Indian dish of kebabs marinated in a spice mixture (often in *comb.*: *chicken tikka*). [Punjabi *tikkā*]

tilapia /tɪ'leɪpiə, -'lap-/ *n.* a freshwater cichlid fish of the African genus *Tilapia* or a related genus, widely introduced for food. [modern Latin]

tilbury /'tɪlb(ə)ri/ *n.* (*pl.* **-ies**) *hist.* a light open two-wheeled carriage. [named after its inventor]

tilde /'tɪldə/ *n.* a mark (˜), put over a letter, e.g. over a Spanish *n* when pronounced *ny* (as in *señor*) or a Portuguese *a* or *o* when nasalized (as in *São Paulo*). [Spanish, ultimately from Latin *titulus* TITLE]

tile /tʌɪl/ *n.* & *v.* ● *n.* **1** a thin slab of concrete or baked clay etc. used in series for covering a roof or pavement etc. **2** a similar slab of glazed pottery, cork, linoleum, etc., for covering a floor, wall, etc. **3** a thin flat piece used in a game (esp. mah-jong). ● *v.tr.* cover with tiles. □ **on the tiles** *Brit. colloq.* having a spree. [Old English *tigule, -ele*, from Latin *tegula*]

tiler /'tʌɪlə/ *n.* **1** a person who makes or lays tiles. **2** the doorkeeper of a Freemasons' lodge.

tiling /'tʌɪlɪŋ/ *n.* **1** the process of fixing tiles. **2** an area of tiles.

till[1] /tɪl/ *prep.* & *conj.* ● *prep.* **1** up to or as late as (*wait till six o'clock; did not return till night*). **2** up to the time of (*faithful till death; waited till the end*). ● *conj.* **1** up to the time when (*wait till I return*). **2** so long that (*laughed till I cried*). [Old English & Old Norse *til* 'to': related to TILL[3]]

■ **Usage** In all senses, *till* can be replaced by *until* which is more formal in style.

till[2] /tɪl/ *n.* a drawer for money in a shop or bank etc., esp. with a device recording the amount of each purchase. [Middle English: origin unknown]

till[3] /tɪl/ *v.tr.* prepare and cultivate (land) for crops. □ **tillable** *adj.* **tiller** *n.* [Old English *tilian* 'strive for, cultivate', from Germanic]

till[4] /tɪl/ *n.* stiff clay containing boulders, sand, etc., deposited by melting glaciers and ice sheets. [17th c. (Scots): origin unknown]

tillage /'tɪlɪdʒ/ *n.* **1** the preparation of land for crop-bearing. **2** tilled land.

tiller[1] /'tɪlə/ *n.* a horizontal bar fitted to the head of a boat's rudder to turn it in steering. [Middle English via Anglo-French *telier* 'weaver's beam' and medieval Latin *telarium* from Latin *tela* 'web']

tiller[2] /'tɪlə/ *n.* & *v.* ● *n.* a shoot of a plant, esp. a cereal grass, springing from the bottom of the original stalk. ● *v.intr.* develop tillers. [apparently representing Old English *telgor*, extended from *telga* 'bough']

tilley lamp /'tɪli/ *n. propr.* a portable oil or paraffin lamp in which air pressure is used to supply the burner with fuel. [from the name of the manufacturers]

tilt /tɪlt/ *v. & n.* ● *v.* **1** *intr. & tr.* assume or cause to assume a sloping position; heel over. **2** *intr.* (foll. by *at*) strike, thrust, or run at, with a weapon, esp. *hist.* in jousting. **3** *intr.* (foll. by *with*) engage in a contest. **4** *tr.* forge or work (steel etc.) with a tilt-hammer. ● *n.* **1** the act or an instance of tilting. **2** a sloping position. **3** *hist.* (of medieval knights etc.) the act of charging with a lance against an opponent or at a mark, done for exercise or as a sport. **4** an encounter between opponents; an attack esp. with argument or satire (*have a tilt at*). **5** = TILT-HAMMER. □ **full** (or **at full**) **tilt 1** at full speed. **2** with full force. □ **tilter** *n.* [Middle English *tilte*, perhaps from an Old English form related to *tealt* 'unsteady', from Germanic: 'weapon' senses of unknown origin]

tilth /tɪlθ/ *n.* **1** tillage, cultivation. **2** the condition of tilled soil (*in good tilth*). [Old English *tilth(e)* (as TILL[3])]

tilt-hammer *n.* a heavy pivoted hammer used in forging.

tilt-yard *n. hist.* a place where tilts (see TILT *n.* 3) took place.

Tim. *abbr.* Timothy (New Testament).

timbal /ˈtɪmb(ə)l/ *n. archaic* a kettledrum. [French *timbale*, earlier *tamballe*, via Spanish *atabal* from Arabic *aṭ-ṭabl* 'the drum']

timbale /tamˈbɑːl/ *n.* a drum-shaped dish of minced meat or fish cooked in a pastry shell or in a mould. [French: see TIMBAL]

timber /ˈtɪmbə/ *n.* **1** esp. *Brit.* wood prepared for building, carpentry, etc. **2** a piece of wood or beam, esp. as the rib of a ship. **3** large standing trees suitable for timber; woods or forest. **4** (esp. as *int.*) a warning cry that a tree is about to fall. □ **timbering** *n.* [Old English, = a building, from Germanic]

timbered /ˈtɪmbəd/ *adj.* **1** (esp. of a building) made wholly or partly of timber. **2** (of country) wooded.

timber-frame *adj. & n.* ● *adj.* **1** (usu. **timber-framed**) (usu. *attrib.*) having a timber frame. **2** (*attrib.*) (of a house) built using usu. factory-prepared sections of timber framework. ● *n.* such pre-prepared sections.

timber-getter *n. Austral.* a lumberjack.

timber hitch *n.* a knot used in attaching a rope to a log or spar.

timberland /ˈtɪmbəland/ *n. US* land covered with forest yielding timber.

timberline /ˈtɪmbəlʌɪn/ *n.* (on a mountain) the line or level above which no trees grow.

timberman /ˈtɪmbəman, -mən/ *n.* (*pl.* **-men**) **1** a person who works with timber. **2** a longhorn beetle with wood-boring larvae, esp. *Acanthocinus aedilis* which has extremely long antennae.

timber wolf *n.* a type of large N. American grey wolf.

timbre /ˈtambə/ *n.* the distinctive character of a musical sound or voice apart from its pitch and intensity. [French from Romanic, via medieval Greek *timbanon* from Greek *tumpanon* 'drum']

timbrel /ˈtɪmbr(ə)l/ *n. archaic* a tambourine or similar instrument. [diminutive of Middle English *timbre*, from Old French (as TIMBRE, -LE[2])]

Timbuctoo /tɪmbʌkˈtuː/ *n.* any distant or remote place. [*Timbuktu*, a town on the edge of the Sahara in W. Africa]

time /tʌɪm/ *n. & v.* ● *n.* **1** the indefinite continued progress of existence, events, etc., in past, present, and future regarded as a whole. **2 a** the progress of this as affecting persons or things (*stood the test of time*). **b** (**Time**) (in full **Father Time**) the personification of time, esp. as an old man with a scythe and hourglass. **3** a more or less definite portion of time belonging to particular events or circumstances (*the time of the Plague*; *prehistoric times*; *the scientists of the time*). **4** an allotted, available, or measurable portion of time; the period of time at one's disposal (*am wasting my time*; *had no time to visit*; *how much time do you need?*). **5** a point of time esp. in hours and minutes (*the time is 7.30*; *what time is it?*). **6** (prec. by *a*) an indefinite period (*waited for a time*). **7** time or an amount of time as reckoned by a conventional standard (*the time allowed is one hour*; *ran the mile in record time*; *eight o'clock New York time*). **8 a** an occasion (*last time I saw you*). **b** an event or occasion qualified in some way (*had a good time*). **9** a moment or definite portion of time destined or suitable for a purpose etc. (*now is the time to act*; *shall we fix a time?*). **10** (in *pl.*) expressing multiplication (*is four times as old*; *five times six is thirty*). **11** a lifetime (*will last my time*). **12** (in *sing.* or *pl.*) **a** the conditions of life or of a period (*hard times*; *times have changed*). **b** (prec. by *the*) the present age, or that being considered. **13** *colloq.* a prison sentence (*is doing time*). **14** an apprenticeship (*served his time*). **15** a period of gestation. **16** the date or expected date of childbirth (*is near her time*) or of death (*my time is drawing near*). **17** measured time spent in work (*put them on short time*). **18 a** any of several rhythmic patterns of music (*in waltz time*). **b** the duration of a note as indicated by a crotchet, minim, etc. **19** (esp. in phr. **call time**) **a** *Brit.* the moment at which the opening hours of a public house end. **b** *Baseball* the moment at which play stops temporarily within a game. ● *v.tr.* **1** choose the time or occasion for (*time your remarks carefully*). **2** do at a chosen or correct time. **3** arrange the time of arrival of. **4** ascertain the time taken by (a process or activity, or a person doing it). **5** regulate the duration or interval of; set times for (*trains are timed to arrive every hour*). □ **against time** with utmost speed, so as to finish by a specified time (*working against time*). **ahead of time** earlier than expected. **ahead of one's time** having ideas too enlightened or advanced to be accepted by one's contemporaries. **all the time 1** during the whole of the time referred to (often despite some contrary expectation etc.) (*we never noticed, but he was there all the time*). **2** constantly (*nags all the time*). **3** at all times (*leaves a light on all the time*). **at one time 1** in or during a known but unspecified past period. **2** simultaneously (*ran three businesses at one time*). **at the same time 1** simultaneously; at a time that is the same for all. **2** nevertheless (*at the same time, I do not want to offend you*). **at a time** separately in the specified groups or numbers (*came three at a time*). **at times** occasionally, intermittently. **before time** (usu. prec. by *not*) before the due or expected time. **before one's time** prematurely (*old before his time*). **for the time being** for the present; until some other arrangement is made. **half the time** *colloq.* as often as not. **have no time for 1** be unable or unwilling to spend time on. **2** dislike. **have the time 1** be able to spend the time needed. **2** know from a watch etc. what time it is. **have a time of it** undergo trouble or difficulty. **in no** (or **less than no**) **time 1** very soon. **2** very quickly. **in one's own good time** at a time and a rate decided by oneself. **in** (or *US* **on**) **one's own time** outside working hours. **in time 1** not late, punctual (*was in time to catch the bus*). **2** eventually (*in time you may agree*). **3** in accordance with a given rhythm or tempo, esp. of music. **in one's time** at or during some previous period of one's life (*in his time he was a great hurdler*). **keep good** (or **bad**) **time 1** (of a clock etc.) record time accurately (or inaccurately). **2** be habitually punctual (or not punctual). **keep time** move or sing etc. in time. **know the time of day** be well informed. **lose no time** (often foll. by *in* + verbal noun) act immediately (*lost no time in cashing the cheque*). **not before time** not too soon; timely. **no time** *colloq.* a very short interval (*it was no time before they came*). **out of time** unseasonable; unseasonably. **pass the time of day** *colloq.* exchange a greeting or casual remarks. **time after time 1** repeatedly; on many occasions. **2** in many instances. **time and** (or **time and time**) **again** on many occasions. **time and a half** a rate of payment for work at one and a half times the normal rate. **the time of day** the hour by the clock. **the time of one's life** a period or occasion of exceptional enjoyment. **time was** there was a time

(*time was when I could do that*). [Old English *tīma*, from Germanic]

time-and-motion *adj.* (usu. *attrib.*) concerned with measuring the efficiency of industrial and other operations.

time bomb *n.* a bomb designed to explode at a pre-set time.

time capsule *n.* a box etc. containing objects typical of the present time, buried for discovery in the future.

time clock *n.* **1** a clock with a device for recording workers' hours of work. **2** a switch mechanism activated at pre-set times by a built-in clock.

time-consuming *adj.* using much or too much time.

time exposure *n.* the exposure of photographic film for longer than the maximum normal shutter setting.

time factor *n.* the passage of time as a limitation on what can be achieved.

time frame *n.* **1** a specific period of time in which something occurs or is planned. **2** *colloq.* a period of time.

time-fuse *n.* a fuse calculated to burn for or explode at a given time.

time-honoured *adj.* esteemed by tradition or through custom.

time immemorial *n.* a longer time than anyone can remember or trace.

timekeeper /'tʌɪmki:pə/ *n.* **1** a person who records time, esp. of workers or in a game. **2 a** a watch or clock as regards accuracy (*a good timekeeper*). **b** a person as regards punctuality. ◻ **timekeeping** *n.*

time lag *n.* an interval of time between an event, a cause, etc. and its effect.

time-lapse *attrib.adj.* (of photography) using frames taken at long intervals to photograph a slow process, and shown continuously as if at normal speed.

timeless /'tʌɪmlɪs/ *adj.* not affected by the passage of time; eternal. ◻ **timelessly** *adv.* **timelessness** *n.*

time limit *n.* the limit of time within which a task must be done.

time lock *n.* & *v.* ● *n.* **1** a lock that is operated by a timing device. **2** a device built into a computer program to stop it operating after a certain time. ● *v.tr.* (as **time-locked** *adj.*) **1** inextricably linked to a certain period of time. **2** secured by a time lock.

timely /'tʌɪmli/ *adj.* (**timelier**, **timeliest**) opportune; coming at the right time. ◻ **timeliness** *n.*

time off *n.* time for rest or recreation etc.

time-out *n.* esp. *N. Amer.* **1** a brief intermission in a game etc. **2** (as **time out**) = TIME OFF.

time out of mind *n.* = TIME IMMEMORIAL.

timepiece /'tʌɪmpi:s/ *n.* an instrument, such as a clock or watch, for measuring time.

timer /'tʌɪmə/ *n.* **1** a person or device that measures or records time taken. **2** an automatic mechanism for activating a device etc. at a pre-set time.

times /tʌɪmz/ *v.tr. colloq.* multiply (a number). [from *times* n.pl.]

timescale /'tʌɪmskeɪl/ *n.* the time allowed for or taken by a sequence of events in relation to a broader period of time.

time-served *adj. Brit.* having completed a period of apprenticeship or training.

time-server *n.* a person who changes his or her views to suit the prevailing circumstances, fashion, etc. ◻ **time-serving** *adj.*

timeshare /'tʌɪmʃɛ:/ *n.* a share in a property under a time-sharing scheme.

time-sharing *n.* **1** the operation of a computer system by several users for different operations at one time. **2** the use of a holiday home at agreed different times by several joint owners.

time sheet *n.* a sheet of paper for recording hours of work etc.

time-shift *v.* & *n.* ● *v.tr.* move from one time to another, esp. record (a television programme) for later viewing. ● *n.* a movement from one time to another (*continual time-shifts make the plot hard to follow*).

time signal *n.* an audible (esp. broadcast) signal or announcement of the exact time of day.

time signature *n. Mus.* an indication of rhythm following a clef, usu. expressed as a fraction with the denominator defining the beat as a division of a semibreve and the numerator giving the number of beats in each bar.

time span *n.* a period spanning a duration of time.

time switch *n.* a switch acting automatically at a pre-set time.

timetable /'tʌɪmteɪb(ə)l/ *n.* & *v.* ● *n.* a list of times at which events are scheduled to take place, esp. the arrival and departure of buses or trains etc., or *Brit.* a sequence of lessons in a school or college. ● *v.tr.* include in or arrange to a timetable; schedule.

time travel *n.* (in science fiction) travel through time into the past or the future. ◻ **time traveller** *n.*

time trial *n.* a race in which participants are individually timed.

time warp *n.* **1** (in science fiction) an imaginary distortion of space in relation to time, whereby persons or objects of one age can be moved to another. **2** a state in which the styles, attitudes, etc. of a past period are retained (*caught in a 1950s time warp*).

time-wasting *n.* & *adj.* ● *n.* **1** the tactic of slowing down play towards the end of a match to prevent further scoring by the opposition. **2** the act of wasting time. ● *adj.* that wastes time. ◻ **time-waster** *n.*

time-worn *adj.* impaired by age.

time zone see ZONE *n.* 4.

timid /'tɪmɪd/ *adj.* (**timider**, **timidest**) easily frightened; apprehensive, shy. ◻ **timidity** /-'mɪdɪti/ *n.* **timidly** *adv.* **timidness** *n.* [French *timide* or Latin *timidus*, from *timēre* 'to fear']

timing /'tʌɪmɪŋ/ *n.* **1** the way an action or process is timed, esp. in relation to others. **2** (in an internal-combustion engine) the times when the valves open and close and the time of the ignition spark in relation to the movement of the piston in the cylinder.

timocracy /tɪ'mɒkrəsi/ *n.* (*pl.* **-ies**) **1** a form of government in which possession of property is required in order to hold office. **2** a form of government in which rulers are motivated by love of honour. ◻ **timocratic** /-ə'kratɪk/ *adj.* [Old French *timocracie* via medieval Latin *timocratia* from Greek *timokratia*, from *timē* 'honour, worth' + *kratia* -CRACY]

Timorese /ti:mɔ:r'i:z/ *n.* & *adj.* ● *n.* (*pl.* same) a native or inhabitant of Timor, an Indonesian island off the NW coast of Australia. ● *adj.* of or relating to Timor or its people.

timorous /'tɪm(ə)rəs/ *adj.* **1** timid; easily alarmed. **2** frightened. ◻ **timorously** *adv.* **timorousness** *n.* [Middle English via Old French *temoreus* from medieval Latin *timorosus*, via Latin *timor* from *timēre* 'to fear']

timothy /'tɪməθi/ *n.* (in full **timothy grass**) a fodder grass, *Phleum pratense*. [named after *Timothy* Hanson, who introduced it in Carolina *c.*1720]

timpani /'tɪmpəni/ *n.pl.* (also **tympani**) kettledrums. ◻ **timpanist** *n.* [Italian, pl. of *timpano* = TYMPANUM]

tin /tɪn/ *n.* & *v.* ● *n.* **1** *Chem.* a silvery-white malleable metallic element resisting corrosion, occurring naturally in cassiterite and other ores, and used esp. in alloys and for plating thin iron or steel sheets to form tin plate (symbol **Sn**). **2 a** a vessel or container made of tin or tinned iron. **b** esp. *Brit.* an airtight sealed container made of tin plate or aluminium for preserving food. **3** = TIN PLATE. **4** *Brit. slang* money. ● *v.tr.* (**tinned**, **tinning**) **1** *Brit.* seal (food) in an airtight tin for preservation. **2** cover or coat with tin. ◻ **put the tin lid on** see LID. [Old English from Germanic]

tinamou /'tɪnəmu:/ *n.* any S. American bird of the family Tinamidae, resembling a grouse but related to the rhea. [French from Galibi *tinamu*]

tin can *n.* a tin container (see TIN *n.* 2), esp. an empty one.

tinctorial /tɪŋ(k)'tɔːrɪəl/ *adj.* **1** of or relating to colour or dyeing. **2** producing colour. [Latin *tinctorius* from *tinctor* 'dyer': see TINGE]

tincture /'tɪŋ(k)tʃə/ *n.* & *v.* ● *n.* (often foll. by *of*) **1** a slight flavour or trace. **2** a tinge (of a colour). **3** a medicinal solution (of a drug) in alcohol (*tincture of quinine*). **4** *Heraldry* an inclusive term for the metals, colours, and furs used in coats of arms. **5** *Brit. colloq.* an alcoholic drink. ● *v.tr.* **1** colour slightly; tinge, flavour. **2** (often foll. by *with*) affect slightly (with a quality). [Middle English from Latin *tinctura* 'dyeing' (as TINGE)]

tinder /'tɪndə/ *n.* a dry substance such as wood that readily catches fire from a spark. □ **tindery** *adj.* [Old English *tynder*, *tyndre*, from Germanic]

tinderbox /'tɪndəbɒks/ *n. hist.* a box containing tinder, flint, and steel, formerly used for kindling fires.

tine /tʌɪn/ *n.* a prong or tooth or point of a fork, comb, antler, etc. □ **tined** *adj.* (also in *comb.*). [Old English *tind*]

tinea /'tɪnɪə/ *n. Med.* ringworm or athlete's foot. [Latin, = moth, worm]

tinfoil /'tɪnfɔɪl/*n.* foil made of tin, aluminium, or tin alloy, used for wrapping food for cooking or storing.

ting /tɪŋ/ *n.* & *v.* ● *n.* a tinkling sound as of a bell. ● *v.intr.* & *tr.* emit or cause to emit this sound. [imitative]

tinge /tɪn(d)ʒ/ *v.* & *n.* ● *v.tr.* (**tinging** or **tingeing**) (often foll. by *with*; often in *passive*) **1** colour slightly (*is tinged with red*). **2** affect slightly (*regret tinged with satisfaction*). ● *n.* **1** a tendency towards or trace of some colour. **2** a slight admixture of a feeling or quality. [Middle English from Latin *tingere tinct-* 'to dye, stain']

tin-glaze *n.* a glaze made white and opaque by the addition of tin oxide.

tingle /'tɪŋg(ə)l/ *v.* & *n.* ● *v.* **1** *intr.* **a** feel a slight prickling, stinging, or throbbing sensation. **b** cause this (*the reply tingled in my ears*). **2** *tr.* make (the ear etc.) tingle. ● *n.* a tingling sensation. [Middle English, perhaps a variant of TINKLE]

tingly /'tɪŋgli/ *adj.* (**tinglier**, **tingliest**) causing or characterized by tingling.

tin god *n.* **1** an object of unjustified veneration. **2** a self-important person.

tin hat *n. colloq.* a military steel helmet.

tinhorn /'tɪnhɔːn/ *n.* & *adj. US slang* ● *n.* a pretentious but unimpressive person. ● *adj.* cheap, pretentious.

tinker /'tɪŋkə/ *n.* & *v.* ● *n.* **1** an itinerant mender of kettles and pans etc. **2** *Sc.* & *Ir.* a gypsy. **3** *Brit. colloq.* a mischievous person or animal. **4** a spell of tinkering. **5** a rough-and-ready worker. ● *v.* **1** *intr.* (foll. by *at*, *with*) work in an amateurish or desultory way, esp. to adjust or mend machinery etc. **2 a** *intr.* work as a tinker. **b** *tr.* repair (pots and pans). □ **tinkerer** *n.* [Middle English: origin unknown]

tinkle /'tɪŋk(ə)l/ *v.* & *n.* ● *v.* **1** *intr.* & *tr.* make or cause to make a succession of short light ringing sounds. **2** *intr. colloq.* (esp. as a child's term) urinate. ● *n.* **1** a tinkling sound. **2** *Brit. colloq.* a telephone call (*will give you a tinkle on Monday*). **3** *colloq.* (a child's term for) an act of urinating. □ **tinkly** *adj.* [Middle English, from obsolete *tink* 'to chink' (imitative)]

tinner /'tɪnə/ *n.* **1** a tin-miner. **2** a tinsmith.

tinnitus /tɪ'nʌɪtəs, 'tɪnɪtəs/ *n. Med.* a ringing in the ears. [Latin from *tinnire tinnit-* 'ring, tinkle', of imitative origin]

tinny /'tɪni/ *adj.* & *n.* ● *adj.* (**tinnier**, **tinniest**) **1** of or like tin. **2** (of a metal object) flimsy, insubstantial. **3 a** sounding like struck tin. **b** (of reproduced sound) thin and metallic, lacking low frequencies. **4** *Austral. slang* lucky. ● *n.* (also **tinnie**) (*pl.* **-ies**) *Austral. slang* a can of beer. □ **tinnily** *adv.* **tinniness** *n.*

tin-opener *n. Brit.* a tool for opening tins.

Tin Pan Alley *n.* the world of composers and publishers of popular music.

tin plate *n.* & *v.* ● *n.* sheet iron or sheet steel coated with tin. ● *v.tr.* (**tin-plate**) coat with tin.

tinpot /'tɪnpɒt/ *attrib.adj. Brit.* cheap, inferior.

tinsel /'tɪns(ə)l/ *n.* & *v.* ● *n.* **1** glittering metallic strips, threads, etc., used as decoration to give a sparkling effect. **2** a fabric adorned with tinsel. **3** superficial brilliance or splendour. **4** (*attrib.*) showy, gaudy, flashy. ● *v.tr.* (**tinselled**, **tinselling**; *US* **tinseled**, **tinseling**) adorn with or as with tinsel. □ **tinselled** *adj.* **tinselly** *adj.* [Old French *estincele* 'spark' from Latin *scintilla*]

tinsmith /'tɪnsmɪθ/ *n.* a worker in tin and tin plate.

tinsnips /'tɪnsnɪps/ *n.pl.* a pair of clippers for cutting sheet metal.

tin soldier *n.* a toy soldier made of metal.

tinstone /'tɪnstəʊn/ *n.* = CASSITERITE.

tint /tɪnt/ *n.* & *v.* ● *n.* **1** a variety of a colour, esp. one made lighter by adding white. **2** a tendency towards or admixture of a different colour (*red with a blue tint*). **3** a faint colour spread over a surface, esp. as a background for printing on. **4** a set of parallel engraved lines to give uniform shading. ● *v.tr.* apply a tint to; colour. □ **tinter** *n.* [alteration of earlier *tinct* from Latin *tinctus* 'dyeing' (as TINGE), perhaps influenced by Italian *tinto*]

tin-tack *n. Brit.* a tack coated with tin.

tintinnabulation /ˌtɪntɪnabjʊ'leɪʃ(ə)n/ *n.* a ringing or tinkling of bells. [as Latin *tintinnabulum* 'tinkling bell' from *tintinnare*, reduplication of *tinnire* 'to ring']

tinware /'tɪnwɛː/ *n.* articles made of tin or tin plate.

tin whistle *n.* = PENNY WHISTLE.

tiny /'tʌɪni/ *adj.* & *n.* ● *adj.* (**tinier**, **tiniest**) very small or slight. ● *n.* (*pl.* **-ies**) (usu. in *pl.*) a very young child. □ **tinily** *adv.* **tininess** *n.* [obsolete *tine*, *tyne* (*adj.* & *n.*) 'small, a little': Middle English, of unknown origin]

-tion /ʃ(ə)n/ *suffix* forming nouns of action, condition, etc. (see -ION, -ATION, -ITION, -UTION). [from or suggested by French *-tion* or Latin *-tio -tionis*]

tip¹ /tɪp/ *n.* & *v.* ● *n.* **1** an extremity or end, esp. of a small or tapering thing (*tips of the fingers*). **2** a small piece or part attached to the end of a thing, e.g. a ferrule on a stick. **3** a leaf bud of tea. ● *v.tr.* (**tipped**, **tipping**) **1** provide with a tip. **2** (foll. by *in*) attach (a loose sheet) to a page at the inside edge. □ **on the tip of one's tongue** about to be said, esp. after difficulty in recalling to mind. **the tip of the iceberg** a small evident part of something much larger or more significant. □ **tipless** *adj.* **tippy** *adj.* (in sense 3 of *n.*). [Middle English from Old Norse *typpi* (*n.*), *typpa* (*v.*), *typptr* 'tipped', from Germanic (related to TOP¹): probably reinforced by Middle Dutch & Middle Low German *tip*]

tip² /tɪp/ *v.* & *n.* ● *v.* (**tipped**, **tipping**) **1** (often foll. by *over*, *up*) **a** *intr.* lean or slant. **b** *tr.* cause to do this. **2** *tr.* (foll. by *into* etc.) **a** overturn or cause to overbalance (*was tipped into the pond*). **b** empty the contents from (a container etc.) in this way. **c** pour out (the contents of a container) in this way. **3** *tr.* strike or touch lightly. ● *n.* **1 a** a slight push or tilt. **b** a glancing stroke, esp. in baseball. **2** *Brit.* a place where material (esp. refuse) is tipped. □ **tip the balance** make the critical difference. **tip one's hat** (or **cap**) raise or touch one's hat or cap in greeting or acknowledgement. **tip off** *Basketball* start play by throwing the ball up between two opponents. **tip the scales** see SCALE². [Middle English: origin uncertain]

tip³ /tɪp/ *v.* & *n.* ● *v.tr.* (**tipped**, **tipping**) **1** make a small present of money to, esp. for a service given (*have you tipped the porter?*). **2** *Brit.* name as the likely winner of a race or contest etc. **3** *Brit. colloq.* give, hand, pass (esp. in *tip a person the wink* below). ● *n.* **1** a small money present, esp. for a service given. **2** a piece of private or special information, esp. regarding betting or investment. **3** a small or casual piece of advice. □ **tip off** *colloq.* give (a person) a hint or piece of special information or warning, esp. discreetly or confidentially. **tip a person the wink** *Brit. colloq.* give a person private information. □ **tipper** *n.* [17th c.: origin uncertain]

tip-and-run *attrib.adj.* **1** designating cricket etc. in which the person batting must run if the ball is struck. **2** (of a raid etc.) executed swiftly before immediate withdrawal.

tipcat /ˈtɪpkat/ *n.* **1** a game with a short piece of wood tapering at the ends and struck with a stick. **2** this piece of wood.

tipi var. of TEPEE.

tip-off *n.* a hint or warning etc. given discreetly or confidentially.

tipper /ˈtɪpə/ *n.* (often *attrib.*) a road haulage vehicle that tips at the back to discharge its load.

tippet /ˈtɪpɪt/ *n.* **1** a covering of fur etc. for the shoulders formerly worn by women. **2** a similar garment worn by some as part of official dress, esp. by the clergy. **3** *hist.* a long narrow strip of cloth as part of or an attachment to a hood etc. [Middle English, probably from TIP[1]]

Tipp-Ex /ˈtɪpɛks/ *n. & v.* (also **Tippex**) *Brit.* ● *n. propr.* a type of correction fluid. ● *v.tr.* delete with Tipp-Ex. [German *tippen* 'type' + Latin *ex* 'out']

tipple /ˈtɪp(ə)l/ *v. & n.* ● *v.* **1** *intr.* drink intoxicating liquor habitually. **2** *tr.* drink (liquor) repeatedly in small amounts. ● *n. colloq.* a drink, esp. a strong one. □ **tippler** *n.* [Middle English, back-formation from *tippler*, of unknown origin]

tipstaff /ˈtɪpstɑːf/ *n.* **1** a sheriff's officer. **2** a metal-tipped staff carried as a symbol of office. [contraction of *tipped staff*, i.e. tipped with metal]

tipster /ˈtɪpstə/ *n.* a person who gives tips, esp. about betting at horse races.

tipsy /ˈtɪpsi/ *adj.* (**tipsier**, **tipsiest**) **1** slightly intoxicated. **2** caused by or showing intoxication (*a tipsy leer*). □ **tipsily** *adv.* **tipsiness** *n.* [probably from TIP[2]]

tipsy-cake *n. Brit.* a sponge cake soaked in wine or spirits and often served with custard.

tiptoe /ˈtɪptəʊ/ *n. & v.* ● *n.* (usu. in phr. **on tiptoe**) the tips of the toes. ● *v.intr.* (**tiptoes**, **tiptoed**, **tiptoeing**) walk on tiptoe, or very stealthily. □ **on tiptoe** with the heels off the ground and the weight on the balls of the feet.

tip-top *adj. & n. colloq.* ● *adj.* highest in excellence; very best. ● *n.* the highest point of excellence.

tip-up *adj.* able to be tipped, e.g. of a folding seat in a theatre to allow passage past.

TIR *abbr.* international road transport (esp. with reference to EC regulations). [French *transport international routier*]

tirade /tʌɪˈreɪd, tɪ-/ *n.* a long vehement denunciation or declamation. [French, = long speech, via Italian *tirata* 'volley', from *tirare* 'pull', from Romanic]

tirailleur /tɪrʌɪˈəː/ *n.* **1** a sharpshooter. **2** a skirmisher. [French, via *tirailler* 'shoot independently' from *tirer* 'shoot, draw', from Romanic]

tire[1] /tʌɪə/ *v.* **1** *tr. & intr.* make or grow weary. **2** *tr.* exhaust the patience or interest of; bore. **3** *tr.* (in *passive*; foll. by *of*) have had enough of; be fed up with (*was tired of arguing*). [Old English *tēorian*, of unknown origin]

tire[2] /tʌɪə/ *n.* **1** a band of metal placed round the rim of a wheel to strengthen it. **2** *US* var. of TYRE. [Middle English, perhaps = archaic *tire* 'clothing, equipment', from ATTIRE]

tired /tʌɪəd/ *adj.* **1** weary, exhausted; ready for sleep. **2** (of an idea etc.) hackneyed. □ **tiredly** *adv.* **tiredness** *n.*

tireless /ˈtʌɪəlɪs/ *adj.* having inexhaustible energy. □ **tirelessly** *adv.* **tirelessness** *n.*

tiresome /ˈtʌɪəs(ə)m/ *adj.* **1** wearisome, tedious. **2** *Brit. colloq.* annoying (*how tiresome of you!*). □ **tiresomely** *adv.* **tiresomeness** *n.*

tiro var. of TYRO.

'tis /tɪz/ *archaic* it is. [contraction]

tisane /tɪˈzan/ *n.* a nourishing drink, originally esp. made with barley, now usu. a herbal tea. [Middle English & Old French *tizanne* etc. via Latin *ptisana* from Greek *ptisanē* 'peeled barley']

tissue /ˈtɪʃuː, ˈtɪsjuː/ *n.* **1** any of the coherent collections of specialized cells of which animals or plants are made (*muscular tissue; nervous tissue*). **2** = TISSUE PAPER. **3** a disposable piece of thin soft absorbent paper for wiping, drying, etc. **4** fine woven esp. gauzy fabric. **5** (foll. by *of*) a connected series (*a tissue of lies*). [Middle English from Old French *tissu* 'rich material', past part. of *tistre* from Latin *texere* 'weave']

tissue culture *n. Biol. & Med.* **1** the growth in an artificial medium of cells derived from living tissue. **2** a culture of this kind.

tissue paper *n.* thin soft unsized paper for wrapping or protecting fragile or delicate articles.

Tit. *abbr.* Titus (New Testament).

tit[1] /tɪt/ *n.* any of various small songbirds esp. of the family Paridae. [probably from Scandinavian]

tit[2] /tɪt/ *n.* □ **tit for tat** /tat/ blow for blow; retaliation (hyphenated when *attrib.*: *tit-for-tat attacks*). [= earlier *tip* (TIP[2]) *for tap*]

tit[3] /tɪt/ *n.* **1** *colloq.* a nipple. **2** *coarse slang* a woman's breast. [Old English: cf. Middle Low German *titte*]

tit[4] /tɪt/ *n. Brit. coarse slang* a term of contempt for a person. [20th c.: perhaps from TIT[3]]

Titan /ˈtʌɪt(ə)n/ *n.* **1** (often **titan**) a person of very great strength, intellect, or importance. **2** (in Greek mythology) a member of a family of early gigantic gods, the offspring of Heaven and Earth. [Middle English via Latin from Greek]

titanic[1] /tʌɪˈtanɪk/ *adj.* **1** of or like the Titans. **2** gigantic, colossal. □ **titanically** *adv.* [Greek *titanikos* (as TITAN)]

titanic[2] /tʌɪˈtanɪk/ *adj. Chem.* of titanium, esp. in tetravalent form. □ **titanate** /ˈtʌɪtəneɪt/ *n.*

titanium /tʌɪˈteɪnɪəm, tɪ-/ *n. Chem.* a grey metallic element occurring naturally in many clays etc., and used to make strong light alloys that are resistant to corrosion (symbol **Ti**). [Greek (as TITAN) + -IUM, on the pattern of *uranium*]

titanium dioxide *n.* (also **titanium oxide**) a white oxide occurring naturally and used as a white pigment.

titbit /ˈtɪtbɪt/ *n.* (*N. Amer.* **tidbit** /ˈtɪd-/) **1** a dainty morsel. **2** a piquant item of news etc. [perhaps from dialect *tid* 'tender' + BIT[1]]

titch /tɪtʃ/ *n.* (also **tich**) *Brit. colloq.* a small person. [*Tich*, the stage name of Harry Relph (d. 1928), English music-hall comedian]

titchy /ˈtɪtʃi/ *adj.* (**titchier**, **titchiest**) *Brit. colloq.* very small.

titer *US* var. of TITRE.

titfer /ˈtɪtfə/ *n. Brit. slang* a hat. [abbreviation of *tit for tat*, rhyming slang]

tithe /tʌɪð/ *n. & v.* ● *n.* **1** one-tenth of the annual produce of land or labour, formerly taken as a tax for the support of the Church and clergy. **2** a tenth part. ● *v.* **1** *tr.* subject to tithes. **2** *intr.* pay tithes. □ **tithable** *adj.* [Old English *teogotha* 'tenth']

tithe barn *n.* a barn built to hold tithes paid in kind.

tithing /ˈtʌɪðɪŋ/ *n.* **1** the practice of taking or paying a tithe. **2** *hist.* (in England) **a** ten householders living near together and collectively responsible for each other's behaviour. **b** the area occupied by them. [Old English *tīgething* (as TITHE, -ING[1])]

titi[1] /ˈtiːtiː/ *n.* (*pl.* **titis**) any S. American monkey of the genus *Callicebus*. [Tupi]

titi[2] /ˈtʌɪtʌɪ, ˈtiːtiː/ *n.* (*pl.* **titis**) any of several evergreen trees and shrubs of the south-eastern US, of the family Cyrillaceae. [perhaps of American Indian origin]

Titian /ˈtɪʃ(ə)n/ *adj.* (of hair) bright golden auburn. [from the name of *Tiziano* Vecelli, Italian painter d. 1576]

Titian-haired *adj.* having bright auburn hair.

titillate /ˈtɪtɪleɪt/ *v.tr.* **1** excite pleasantly. **2** tickle. □ **titillatingly** *adv.* **titillation** /-ˈleɪʃ(ə)n/ *n.* [Latin *titillare titillat-*]

titivate /ˈtɪtɪveɪt/ *v.tr.* (also **tittivate**) *colloq.* **1** adorn, smarten. **2** (often *refl.*) put the finishing touches to. □ **titivation** /-ˈveɪʃ(ə)n/ *n.* [earlier *tidivate*, perhaps from TIDY on the pattern of *cultivate*]

titlark /ˈtɪtlɑːk/ *n.* a pipit, esp. the meadow pipit.

title /ˈtʌɪt(ə)l/ *n.* & *v.* ● *n.* **1** the name of a book, work of art, piece of music, etc. **2** the heading of a chapter, poem, document, etc. **3 a** the contents of the title-page of a book. **b** a book regarded in terms of its title (*published 20 new titles*). **4** a caption or credit in a film, broadcast, etc. **5** a form of nomenclature indicating a person's status (e.g. *professor*, *queen*) or used as a form of address or reference (e.g. *Lord*, *Mr*, *Your Grace*). **6** a championship in sport. **7** *Law* **a** the right to ownership of property with or without possession. **b** the facts constituting this. **c** (foll. by *to*) a just or recognized claim. **8** *Eccl.* **a** a fixed sphere of work and source of income as a condition for ordination. **b** a parish church in Rome under a cardinal. ● *v.tr.* give a title to. [Middle English via Old French from Latin *titulus* 'placard, title']

titled /ˈtʌɪt(ə)ld/ *adj.* having a title of nobility or rank.

title deed *n.* a legal instrument as evidence of a right, esp. to property.

title-holder *n.* a person who holds a title, esp. a sports champion.

title-page *n.* a page at the beginning of a book giving the title and particulars of authorship etc.

title role *n.* the part in a play etc. that gives it its name (e.g. Othello).

titling[1] /ˈtʌɪtlɪŋ/ *n.* the impressing of a title in gold leaf etc. on the cover of a book.

titling[2] /ˈtɪtlɪŋ/ *n.* **1** a titlark. **2** a titmouse.

titmouse /ˈtɪtmaʊs/ *n.* (*pl.* **titmice** /-mʌɪs/) any of various small tits, esp. of the genus *Parus*. [Middle English *titmōse*, from TIT[1] + Old English *māse* 'titmouse', assimilated to MOUSE]

Titoism /ˈtiːtəʊɪz(ə)m/ *n.* the Communist policies followed by Marshal Tito in the former Yugoslavia, which concentrated on the national interest without reference to the Soviet Union. □ **Titoist** *n.* & *adj.* [from *Tito*, the name adopted by J. Broz (d. 1980) + -ISM]

titrate /tʌɪˈtreɪt, tɪ-/ *v.tr. Chem.* ascertain the amount of a constituent in (a solution) by measuring the volume of a known concentration of reagent required to complete a reaction with it, often using an indicator. □ **titratable** *adj.* **titration** /-ˈtreɪʃ(ə)n/ *n.*

titre /ˈtʌɪtə, ˈtiːtə/ *n.* (*US* **titer**) **1** *Chem.* the concentration of a solution as determined by titration. **2** *Med.* the concentration of an antibody, as determined by finding the highest dilution at which it is still active. [French, = TITLE]

ti-tree /ˈtiːtriː/ *n.* **1** = TI[1]. **2** = TEA-TREE 1. [sense 1 from TI[1]; sense 2 arises by confusion]

titter /ˈtɪtə/ *v.* & *n.* ● *v.intr.* laugh in a furtive or restrained way; giggle. ● *n.* a furtive or restrained laugh. □ **titterer** *n.* **titteringly** *adv.* [imitative]

tittivate var. of TITIVATE.

tittle /ˈtɪt(ə)l/ *n.* **1** a small written or printed stroke or dot. **2** a particle; a whit (esp. in phr. **not one jot or tittle**). [Middle English from Latin (as TITLE)]

tittle-tattle /ˈtɪt(ə)ltat(ə)l/ *n.* & *v.* ● *n.* petty gossip. ● *v.intr.* gossip, chatter. [reduplication of TATTLE]

tittup /ˈtɪtəp/ *v.* & *n.* ● *v.intr.* (**tittuped**, **tittuping** or **tittupped**, **tittupping**) esp. *Brit.* go about friskily or jerkily; bob up and down; canter. ● *n.* such a gait or movement. [perhaps imitative of hoof-beats]

titty /ˈtɪti/ *n.* (*pl.* **-ies**) *colloq.* or *joc.* = TIT[3].

titubation /tɪtjʊˈbeɪʃ(ə)n/ *n. Med.* unsteadiness, esp. as caused by nervous disease. [Latin *titubatio* from *titubare* 'totter']

titular /ˈtɪtjʊlə/ *adj.* & *n.* ● *adj.* **1** of or relating to a title (*the book's titular hero*). **2** existing, or being what is specified, in name or title only (*titular ruler*; *titular sovereignty*). ● *n.* **1** the holder of an office etc., esp. a benefice, without the corresponding functions or obligations. **2** a titular saint. □ **titularly** *adv.* [French *titulaire* or modern Latin *titularis*, from *titulus* TITLE]

titular bishop *n.* a bishop nominally appointed to a see no longer in existence.

titular saint *n.* the patron saint of a particular church.

tizzy /ˈtɪzi/ *n.* (*pl.* **-ies**) (also **tizz**, **tiz**) *colloq.* a state of nervous agitation (*in a tizzy*). [20th c.: origin unknown]

T-junction *n.* a road junction at which one road joins another at right angles without crossing it.

TKO *abbr. Boxing* technical knockout.

Tl *symb. Chem.* the element thallium.

TLC *abbr. colloq.* tender loving care.

TLS *abbr. Times Literary Supplement.*

T-lymphocyte /tiːˈlɪmfəsʌɪt/ *n. Physiol.* a lymphocyte of a type produced or processed by the thymus gland and active in the immune response. Also called *T-cell*. [*T* for *thymus*]

TM *abbr.* **1** trade mark. **2** Transcendental Meditation.

Tm *symb. Chem.* the element thulium.

tmesis /ˈtmiːsɪs/ *n.* (*pl.* **tmeses** /-siːz/) *Gram.* the separation of parts of a compound word by an intervening word or words (esp. in colloq. speech, e.g. *can't find it any-blooming-where*). [Greek *tmēsis* 'cutting' from *temnō* 'to cut']

TN *abbr. US* Tennessee (in official postal use).

tn *abbr.* **1** *US* ton(s). **2** town.

TNT *abbr.* trinitrotoluene, a high explosive formed from toluene by substitution of three hydrogen atoms with nitro groups.

to /tə, *before a vowel* tʊ, *emphat.* tuː/ *prep.* & *adv.* ● *prep.* **1** introducing a noun: **a** expressing what is reached, approached, or touched (*fell to the ground*; *went to Paris*; *put her face to the window*; *five minutes to six*). **b** expressing what is aimed at: often introducing the indirect object of a verb (*throw it to me*; *explained the problem to them*). **c** as far as; up to (*went on to the end*; *have to stay from Tuesday to Friday*). **d** to the extent of (*were all drunk to a man*; *was starved to death*). **e** expressing what is followed (*according to instructions*; *made to order*). **f** expressing what is considered or affected (*am used to that*; *that is nothing to me*). **g** expressing what is caused or produced (*turn to stone*; *tear to shreds*). **h** expressing what is compared (*nothing to what it once was*; *comparable to any other*; *equal to the occasion*; *won by three goals to two*). **i** expressing what is increased (*add it to mine*). **j** expressing what is involved or composed as specified (*there is nothing to it*; *more to him than meets the eye*). **k** expressing the substance of a debit entry in accounting (*to four chairs, sixty pounds*). **l** *archaic* for; by way of (*took her to wife*). **2** introducing the infinitive: **a** as a verbal noun (*to get there is the priority*). **b** expressing purpose, consequence, or cause (*we eat to live*; *left him to starve*; *am sorry to hear that*). **c** as a substitute for *to* + infinitive (*wanted to come but was unable to*). ● *adv.* **1** in the normal or required position or condition (*come to*; *heave to*). **2** (of a door) in a nearly closed position. □ **to and fro 1** backwards and forwards. **2** repeatedly between the same points. [Old English *tō* (*adv.* & *prep.*), from West Germanic]

toad /təʊd/ *n.* **1** any froglike amphibian of the family Bufonidae, esp. of the genus *Bufo*, breeding in water but living chiefly on land. **2** any of various similar tailless amphibians. **3** a repulsive or detestable person. □ **toadish** *adj.* [Old English *tādige*, *tādde*, *tāda*, of unknown origin]

toad-eater *n. archaic* a toady.

toadfish /ˈtəʊdfɪʃ/ *n.* (*pl.* usu. same) any marine fish of the family Batrachoididae, with a large head and wide mouth, making grunting noises by vibrating the walls of its swim-bladder.

toadflax /'təʊdflaks/ *n.* **1** any plant of the genus *Linaria* or *Chaenorrhinum* (figwort family), esp. *L. vulgaris* (**yellow toadflax**), with narrow leaves like flax and spurred yellow flowers. **2** a related plant, *Cymbalaria muralis*, with lilac flowers and ivy-shaped leaves.

toad-in-the-hole *n. Brit.* sausages or other meat baked in batter.

toadlet /'təʊdlɪt/ *n.* a small or young toad.

toadstone /'təʊdstəʊn/ *n.* a stone, sometimes precious, supposed to resemble or to have been formed in the body of a toad, formerly used as an amulet etc.

toadstool /'təʊdstu:l/ *n.* the spore-bearing body of various fungi, usu. with a round top and slender stalk, esp. one that is poisonous or inedible (cf. MUSHROOM *n.* 1).

toady /'təʊdi/ *n. & v.* ● *n.* (*pl.* **-ies**) a sycophant; an obsequious hanger-on. ● *v.tr.* & (foll. by *to*) *intr.* (**-ies, -ied**) behave servilely to; fawn upon. □ **toadyish** *adj.* **toadyism** *n.* [contraction of *toad-eater*, a charlatan's attendant who ate toads (regarded as poisonous)]

toast /təʊst/ *n. & v.* ● *n.* **1** bread in slices browned on both sides by radiant heat. **2 a** a person (originally esp. a woman) or thing in whose honour a company is requested to drink. **b** a call to drink or an instance of drinking in this way. ● *v.* **1** *tr.* cook or brown (bread, a teacake, cheese, etc.) by radiant heat. **2** *intr.* (of bread etc.) become brown in this way. **3** *tr.* warm (one's feet, oneself, etc.) at a fire etc. **4** *tr.* drink to the health or in honour of (a person or thing). □ **have a person on toast** *Brit. colloq.* be in a position to deal with a person as one wishes. [Middle English (originally as verb) from Old French *toster* 'roast', ultimately from Latin *torrēre tost-* 'parch': sense 2 of the noun reflects the notion that a woman's name flavours the drink as spiced toast would]

toaster /'təʊstə/ *n.* an electrical device for making toast.

toastie /'təʊsti/ *n. colloq.* a toasted sandwich or snack.

toasting-fork *n.* a long-handled fork for making toast before a fire.

toastmaster /'təʊs(t)mɑ:stə/ *n.* (*fem.* **toastmistress** /-mɪstrɪs/) an official responsible for announcing toasts at a public occasion.

toastrack /'təʊstrak/ *n.* a rack for holding slices of toast at table.

toasty /'təʊsti/ *adj.* **1** comfortably warm. **2** (of wine) characterized by the aroma of maturation in small French oak casks. **3** of or resembling toast.

tobacco /tə'bakəʊ/ *n.* (*pl.* **-os**) **1** a preparation of the nicotine-rich leaves of a plant of the genus *Nicotiana*, esp. for smoking or chewing. **2** the plant itself (cf. TOBACCO PLANT). [Spanish *tabaco*, of uncertain origin]

tobacco mosaic virus *n.* a virus that causes mosaic disease in tobacco, much used in biochemical research.

tobacconist /tə'bak(ə)nɪst/ *n.* a retail dealer in tobacco and cigarettes etc.

tobacco pipe see PIPE *n.* 2a.

tobacco plant *n.* any plant of the genus *Nicotiana*, of American origin, grown for its narcotic leaves (see TOBACCO) or for its night-scented flowers.

tobacco-stopper *n.* an instrument for pressing down the tobacco in a pipe.

toboggan /tə'bɒg(ə)n/ *n. & v.* ● *n.* a long light narrow sledge (originally and *N. Amer.* upcurved in front), for sliding downhill esp. over compacted snow or ice. ● *v.intr.* ride on a toboggan. □ **tobogganer** *n.* **tobogganing** *n.* **tobogganist** *n.* [Canadian French *tabaganne* from Algonquian]

toby jug /'təʊbi/ *n.* a jug or mug for ale etc., usu. in the form of a stout old man wearing a three-cornered hat. [familiar form of the name *Tobias*]

toccata /tə'kɑ:tə/ *n.* a musical composition for a keyboard instrument designed to exhibit the performer's touch and technique. [Italian, fem. past part. of *toccare* 'touch']

Toc H /tɒk 'eɪtʃ/ *n. Brit.* a society, originally of ex-service personnel, founded after the First World War for promoting Christian fellowship and social service. [*toc* (former telegraphy code for *T*) + *H*, for *T*albot *H*ouse, a soldier's club established in Belgium in 1915]

Tocharian /tə'kɛ:rɪən, -'kɑ:rɪən/ *n. & adj.* ● *n.* **1** an extinct Indo-European language of a central Asian people in the first millennium AD. **2** a member of the people speaking this language. ● *adj.* of or relating to this language. [French *tocharien* via Latin *Tochari* from Greek *Tokharoi*, the name of a Scythian tribe]

tocopherol /tɒ'kɒfərɒl/ *n.* any of several closely related vitamins, found in wheatgerm oil, egg yolk, and leafy vegetables, and important in the stabilization of cell membranes etc. Also called *vitamin E*. [Greek *tokos* 'offspring' + *pherō* 'bear' + -OL[1]]

tocsin /'tɒksɪn/ *n.* an alarm bell or signal. [French via Old French *touquesain*, *toquassen* from Provençal *tocasenh*, from *tocar* TOUCH + *senh* 'signal-bell']

tod /tɒd/ *n. Brit. slang* □ **on one's tod** alone; on one's own. [20th c.: perhaps from rhyming slang *on one's Tod Sloan* (name of a jockey)]

today /tə'deɪ/ *adv. & n.* ● *adv.* **1** on or in the course of this present day (*shall we go today?*). **2** nowadays; in modern times. ● *n.* **1** this present day (*today is my birthday*). **2** modern times. □ **today week** (or **fortnight** etc.) *Brit.* a week (or fortnight etc.) from today. [Old English *tō dæg* 'on (this) day' (as TO, DAY)]

toddle /'tɒd(ə)l/ *v. & n.* ● *v.intr.* **1** walk with short unsteady steps like those of a small child. **2** *colloq.* **a** (often foll. by *round, to*, etc.) take a casual or leisurely walk. **b** (usu. foll. by *off*) depart. ● *n.* **1** a toddling walk. **2** *colloq.* a stroll or leisurely walk. [16th-c. *todle* (Scots & northern English), of unknown origin]

toddler /'tɒdlə/ *n.* a child who is just beginning to walk. □ **toddlerhood** *n.*

toddy /'tɒdi/ *n.* (*pl.* **-ies**) **1** a drink of spirits with hot water and sugar or spices. **2** the sap of some kinds of palm, fermented to produce arrack. [Hindustani *tāṛī* from *tār* 'palm', from Sanskrit *tâla* 'palmyra']

to-do /tə'du:/ *n.* (*pl.* **to-dos**) a commotion or fuss. [*to do* as in *what's to do* (= to be done)]

tody /'təʊdi/ *n.* (*pl.* **-ies**) any small insect-eating West Indian bird of the genus *Todus*, related to the kingfisher. [French *todier* from Latin *todus*, a small bird]

toe /təʊ/ *n. & v.* ● *n.* **1** any of the five terminal projections of the human foot. **2** the corresponding part of an animal. **3** the part of an item of footwear that covers the toes. **4** the lower end or tip of an implement etc. **5** *Archit.* a projection from the foot of a buttress etc. to give stability. ● *v.* (**toes, toed, toeing**) **1** *tr.* touch (a starting line etc.) with the toes before starting a race. **2** *tr.* **a** mend the toe of (a sock etc.). **b** provide (a sock etc.) with a toe. **3** *intr.* (foll. by *in, out*) **a** walk with the toes pointed in (or out). **b** (of a pair of wheels) converge (or diverge) slightly at the front. **4** *tr. Golf* strike (the ball) with a part of the club too near the toe. □ **on one's toes** alert, eager. **toe the line** conform to a general policy or principle, esp. unwillingly or under pressure. **turn up one's toes** *colloq.* die. □ **toed** *adj.* (also in *comb.*). **toeless** *adj.* [Old English *tā*, from Germanic]

toecap /'təʊkap/ *n.* the (usu. strengthened) outer covering of the toe of a boot or shoe.

toe clip *n.* a clip on a bicycle pedal to prevent the foot from slipping.

toehold /'təʊhəʊld/ *n.* **1** a small foothold. **2** a small beginning or advantage.

toenail /'təʊneɪl/ *n. & v.* ● *n.* **1** the nail at the tip of each toe. **2** a nail driven obliquely through the end of a board etc. ● *v.tr.* fasten (a board etc.) with a toenail or toenails.

toe-rag *n. Brit. slang* a term of contempt for a person. [earlier = tramp, vagrant, from the rag wrapped round the foot in place of a sock]

toey /'təʊi/ *adj. Austral. slang* restless, nervous, touchy.

toff /tɒf/ *n. & v. Brit. slang* ● *n.* an upper-class person; a smart or well-dressed person. ● *v.tr.* (foll. by *up*) dress up smartly. [perhaps a perversion of *tuft* = titled undergraduate (from the gold tassel formerly worn on the cap)]

toffee /'tɒfi/ *n.* (also **toffy**) (*pl.* **toffees** or **toffies**) **1** a kind of firm or hard sweet softening when sucked or chewed, made by boiling sugar, butter, etc. **2** *Brit.* a small piece of this. ◻ **for toffee** (prec. by *can't* etc.) *Brit. colloq.* (denoting incompetence) at all (*they couldn't sing for toffee*). [later variant of TAFFY]

toffee apple *n. Brit.* an apple with a thin coating of toffee.

toffee-nosed *adj.* esp. *Brit. colloq.* snobbish, pretentious.

toft /tɒft/ *n. Brit.* **1** a homestead. **2** land once occupied by this. [Old English from Old Norse *topt*]

tofu /'təʊfuː,'tɒfuː/ *n.* (esp. in China and Japan) a curd made from mashed soya beans. [Japanese *tōfu* from Chinese *dòufu*, = rotten beans]

tog[1] /tɒg/ *n. & v. colloq.* ● *n.* (usu. in *pl.*) an item of clothing. ● *v.tr. & intr.* (**togged**, **togging**) (foll. by *out*, *up*) dress, esp. elaborately. [apparently abbreviation of 16th-c. criminals' slang *togeman(s)*, *togman*, from French *toge* or Latin *toga*: see TOGA]

tog[2] /tɒg/ *n. Brit.* a unit of thermal resistance used to express the insulating properties of clothes and quilts. [TOG[1], on the pattern of an earlier unit, the *clo* (from *clothes*)]

toga /'təʊgə/ *n. hist.* an ancient Roman citizen's loose flowing outer garment. ◻ **toga'd** *adj.* (also **togaed**). [Latin, related to *tegere* 'to cover']

together /tə'geðə/ *adv. & adj.* ● *adv.* **1** in company or conjunction (*walking together*; *built it together*; *were at school together*). **2** simultaneously; at the same time (*both shouted together*). **3** one with another (*were talking together*). **4** into conjunction; so as to unite (*tied them together*; *put two and two together*). **5** into company or companionship (*came together in friendship*). **6** uninterruptedly (*could talk for hours together*). ● *adj. colloq.* well organized or controlled. ◻ **together with** as well as; and also. [Old English *tōgædere*, from TO + *gædre* 'together']

togetherness /tə'geðənɪs/ *n.* **1** the condition of being together. **2** a feeling of comfort from being together.

toggery /'tɒg(ə)ri/ *n. colloq.* clothes, togs.

toggle /'tɒg(ə)l/ *n. & v.* ● *n.* **1** a device for fastening (esp. a garment), consisting of a crosspiece which can pass through a hole or loop in one position but not in another. **2** a pin or other crosspiece put through the eye of a rope, a link of a chain, etc., to keep it in place. **3** a pivoted barb on a harpoon. **4** *Computing* a key or command that is operated the same way but with opposite effect on successive occasions. ● *v.* **1** *tr.* provide or fasten with a toggle. **2** *intr. Computing* switch from one state to another by using a toggle. [18th-c. nautical: origin unknown]

toggle joint *n.* a device for exerting pressure along two jointed rods by applying a transverse force at the joint.

toggle switch *n.* **1** an electric switch with a projecting lever to be moved usu. up and down. **2** *Computing* = TOGGLE *n.* 4.

Togolese /təʊgə(ʊ)'liːz/ *adj. & n.* ● *adj.* of or relating to Togo in W. Africa. ● *n.* (*pl.* same) **1** a native or national of Togo. **2** a person of Togolese descent.

toil /tɔɪl/ *v. & n.* ● *v.intr.* **1** work laboriously or incessantly. **2** make slow painful progress (*toiled along the path*). ● *n.* prolonged or intensive labour; drudgery. ◻ **toiler** *n.* [Middle English via Anglo-French *toiler* (*v.*), *toil* (*n.*) 'dispute', Old French *tooilier*, *tooil* from Latin *tudiculare* 'stir about', from *tudicula* 'machine for bruising olives', related to *tundere* 'beat']

toile /twɑːl/ *n.* **1** cloth esp. for garments. **2** a garment reproduced in muslin or other cheap material for fitting or for making copies. [French *toile* 'cloth' from Latin *tela* 'web']

toilet /'tɔɪlɪt/ *n. & v.* ● *n.* **1** = LAVATORY. **2 a** the process of washing oneself, dressing, etc. (*make one's toilet*). **b** (*attrib.*) for or to enable this process (*toilet requisites*). **3** the cleansing of part of the body after an operation or at the time of childbirth. ● *v.tr.* (**toileted**, **toileting**) assist (an infant, invalid, etc.) in using a lavatory. [French *toilette* 'cloth, wrapper', diminutive of *toile*: see TOILE]

toilet bag *n.* = WASHBAG.

toilet paper *n.* paper for cleaning oneself after excreting.

toilet roll *n.* a roll of toilet paper.

toiletry /'tɔɪlɪtri/ *n.* (*pl.* **-ies**) (usu. in *pl.*) any of various articles or cosmetics used in washing, dressing, etc.

toilet set *n.* a set of hairbrushes, combs, etc.

toilet soap *n.* soap for washing oneself.

toilet table *n.* a dressing table usu. with a mirror.

toilette /twɑː'let/ *n.* = TOILET 2. [French: see TOILET]

toilet tissue *n.* = TOILET PAPER.

toilet-training *n.* the training of a young child to use the lavatory. ◻ **toilet-train** *v.tr.*

toilet water *n.* a dilute form of perfume used after washing.

toils /tɔɪlz/ *n.pl. archaic* or *literary* a net or snare. [pl. of *toil* from Old French *toile* 'cloth', from Latin *tela* 'web']

toilsome /'tɔɪls(ə)m/ *adj.* involving toil; laborious. ◻ **toilsomely** *adv.* **toilsomeness** *n.*

toil-worn *adj.* worn or worn out by toil.

toing and froing /tuːɪŋ (ə)nd 'frəʊɪŋ/ *n.* (*pl.* **toings and froings**) constant movement to and fro; bustle; dispersed activity. [TO *adv.* + FRO + -ING[1]]

tokamak /'təʊkəmak/ *n. Physics* a toroidal apparatus for producing controlled fusion reactions in hot plasma. [Russian acronym, from *to*roidal'naya *ka*mera s *mag*nitnym polem 'toroidal chamber with magnetic field']

Tokay /təʊ'keɪ/ *n.* **1** a sweet aromatic wine made near Tokaj in Hungary. **2** a similar wine produced elsewhere.

tokay /təʊ'keɪ/ *n.* (in full **tokay gecko**) a large grey gecko with orange and blue spots, *Gekko gecko*, of SE Asia, which has a loud call resembling the name. [Malay dialect *toke'* from Javanese *tekèk*, imitative]

token /'təʊk(ə)n/ *n. & adj.* ● *n.* **1** a thing serving as a symbol, reminder, or distinctive mark of something (*as a token of affection*; *in token of my esteem*). **2** a thing serving as evidence of authenticity or as a guarantee. **3** a voucher exchangeable for goods (often of a specified kind), given as a gift. **4** anything used to represent something else, esp. a metal disc etc. used instead of money in coin-operated machines etc. ● *attrib.adj.* **1** nominal or perfunctory (*token effort*). **2** conducted briefly to demonstrate strength of feeling (*token resistance*; *token strike*). **3** serving to acknowledge a principle only (*token payment*). **4** chosen by way of tokenism to represent a particular group (*the token woman on the committee*). ◻ **by this** (or **the same**) **token 1** similarly. **2** moreover. [Old English *tāc(e)n* from Germanic: related to TEACH]

tokenism /'təʊk(ə)nɪz(ə)m/ *n.* **1** esp. *Polit.* the principle or practice of granting minimum concessions, esp. to appease radical demands etc. (cf. TOKEN *adj.* 4). **2** making only a token effort. ◻ **tokenistic** /-'nɪstɪk/ *adj.*

token money *n.* coins having a higher face value than their worth as metal.

token vote *n.* a parliamentary vote of money, the stipulated amount of which is not meant to be binding.

tolbooth var. of TOLL-BOOTH.

told *past* and *past part.* of TELL[1].

Toledo /tɒ'leɪdəʊ, tə'liːdəʊ/ *n.* (*pl.* **-os**) a fine sword or sword blade made in Toledo in Spain.

tolerable /'tɒl(ə)rəb(ə)l/ *adj.* **1** able to be endured. **2** fairly good; mediocre. ◻ **tolerability** /-'bɪlɪti/ *n.*

tolerableness *n.* **tolerably** *adv.* [Middle English via Old French from Latin *tolerabilis* (as TOLERATE)]

tolerance /ˈtɒl(ə)r(ə)ns/ *n.* **1** a willingness or ability to tolerate; forbearance. **2** the capacity to tolerate something, esp. a drug, transplant, antigen, environmental condition, etc., without adverse reaction. **3** an allowable variation in any measurable property. **4** diminution in response to a drug after continued use. [Middle English via Old French from Latin *tolerantia* (as TOLERATE)]

tolerant /ˈtɒl(ə)r(ə)nt/ *adj.* **1** disposed or accustomed to tolerate others or their acts or opinions. **2** (foll. by *of*) enduring or patient. □ **tolerantly** *adv.* [French *tolérant* from Latin *tolerare* (as TOLERATE)]

tolerate /ˈtɒləreɪt/ *v.tr.* **1** allow the existence or occurrence of without authoritative interference. **2** leave unmolested. **3** endure or permit, esp. with forbearance. **4** sustain or endure (suffering etc.). **5** be capable of continued subjection to (a drug, radiation, etc.) without harm. **6** find or treat as endurable. □ **tolerator** *n.* [Latin *tolerare tolerat-* 'endure']

toleration /tɒləˈreɪʃ(ə)n/ *n.* the process or practice of tolerating, esp. the allowing of differences in religious opinion without discrimination. [French *tolération* from Latin *toleratio* (as TOLERATE)]

toll[1] /təʊl/ *n.* **1** a charge payable for permission to pass a barrier or use a bridge or road etc. **2** the cost or damage caused by a disaster, battle, etc., or incurred in an achievement (*death toll*). **3** *N. Amer.* a charge for a long distance telephone call. □ **take its toll** be accompanied by loss or injury etc. [Old English via medieval Latin *toloneum* and Late Latin *teloneum* from Greek *telōnion* 'toll-house', from *telos* 'tax']

toll[2] /təʊl/ *v.* & *n.* ● *v.* **1 a** *intr.* (of a bell) sound with a slow uniform succession of strokes. **b** *tr.* ring (a bell) in this way. **c** *tr.* (of a bell) announce or mark (a death etc.) in this way. **2** *tr.* strike (the hour). ● *n.* **1** the act of tolling. **2** a stroke of a bell. [Middle English, special use of (now dialect) *toll* 'entice, pull', from an Old English root recorded in *fortyllan* 'seduce']

toll-booth *n.* (also **tolbooth**) **1** a booth at the roadside from which tolls are collected. **2** *Sc. archaic* a town hall. **3** *Sc. archaic* a town jail.

toll bridge *n.* a bridge at which a toll is charged.

toll gate *n.* a gate preventing passage until a toll is paid.

toll-house *n.* a house at a toll gate or toll bridge, used by a toll collector.

tollroad /ˈtəʊlrəʊd, ˈtɒl-/ *n.* a road maintained by the tolls collected on it.

Toltec /ˈtɒltɛk/ *n.* **1** a member of an American Indian people that flourished in Mexico before the Aztecs. **2** the language of this people. □ **Toltecan** *adj.* [Nahuatl]

tolu /təˈluː, ˈtəʊluː/ *n.* a fragrant brown balsam obtained from either of two S. American trees, *Myroxylon balsamum* or *M. toluifera*, and used in perfumery and medicine. [Santiago de *Tolu* in Colombia, from which it was exported]

toluene /ˈtɒljʊiːn/ *n.* (also **toluol**) a colourless aromatic liquid hydrocarbon derivative of benzene, originally obtained from tolu, used in the manufacture of explosives etc. Also called *methylbenzene*. □ **toluic** *adj.* [TOLU + -ENE]

tom /tɒm/ *n.* & *v.* ● *n.* **1** a male of various animals, esp. (in full **tom-cat**) a male cat. **2** *slang* a prostitute. ● *v.intr.* (**tommed**, **tomming**) *slang* practise prostitution; behave promiscuously. [abbreviation of the name *Thomas*]

tomahawk /ˈtɒməhɔːk/ *n.* & *v.* ● *n.* **1** a N. American Indian axe with a stone or iron head, esp. one used as a weapon. **2** *Austral.* a hatchet. ● *v.tr.* strike, cut, or kill with a tomahawk. [American Indian word]

tomatillo /tɒməˈtɪl(j)əʊ/ *n.* (*pl.* **-os**) esp. *US* **1** a purplish edible fruit. **2** a Mexican ground cherry, *Physalis philadelphica*, bearing this. [Spanish, diminutive of *tomate* TOMATO]

tomato /təˈmɑːtəʊ/ *n.* (*pl.* **-oes**) **1** a glossy red or yellow pulpy edible fruit. **2** a plant of the nightshade family, *Lycopersicon esculentum*, bearing this. □ **tomatoey** *adj.* [French, Spanish & Portuguese *tomate* from Mexican *tomatl*]

tomb /tuːm/ *n.* **1** a large esp. underground vault for the burial of the dead. **2** an enclosure cut in the earth or in rock to receive a dead body. **3** a sepulchral monument. **4** (prec. by *the*) the state of death. [Middle English *t(o)umbe* via Anglo-French *tumbe*, Old French *tombe* and Late Latin *tumba* from Greek *tumbos*]

tombac /ˈtɒmbak/ *n.* an alloy of copper and zinc used esp. as material for cheap jewellery. [French from Malay *tembaga* 'copper']

tombola /tɒmˈbəʊlə/ *n.* *Brit.* a kind of lottery with tickets usu. drawn from a turning drum-shaped container for immediate prizes, esp. at a fête or fair. [French or Italian, from Italian *tombolare* 'tumble']

tombolo /ˈtɒmbələʊ/ *n.* (*pl.* **-os**) a spit joining an island to the mainland. [Italian, = sand dune]

tomboy /ˈtɒmbɔɪ/ *n.* a girl who behaves in a usu. boyish boisterous way. □ **tomboyish** *adj.* **tomboyishness** *n.*

tombstone /ˈtuːmstəʊn/ *n.* a stone standing or laid over a grave, usu. with an epitaph.

tom-cat see TOM *n.* 1.

Tom Collins see COLLINS. [20th c.: origin unknown]

Tom, Dick, and Harry /ˌtɒm dɪk (ə)nd ˈhari/ *n.* (usu. prec. by *any*, *every*) usu. *derog.* ordinary people taken at random.

tome /təʊm/ *n.* a large heavy book or volume. [French via Latin *tomus* from Greek *tomos* 'section, volume', from *temnō* 'to cut']

-tome /təʊm/ *comb. form* forming nouns meaning: **1** an instrument for cutting (*microtome*). **2** a section or segment. [Greek *tomē* 'a cutting', *-tomos* '-cutting', from *temnō* 'to cut']

tomentum /təˈmɛntəm/ *n.* (*pl.* **tomenta** /-tə/) **1** *Bot.* matted woolly down on stems and leaves. **2** *Anat.* the tufted inner surface of the pia mater in the brain. □ **tomentose** /təˈmɛntəʊs, ˈtəʊ-/ *adj.* **tomentous** *adj.* [Latin, = cushion-stuffing]

tomfool /tɒmˈfuːl/ *n.* **1** a foolish person. **2** (*attrib.*) silly, foolish (*a tomfool idea*).

tomfoolery /tɒmˈfuːl(ə)ri/ *n.* (*pl.* **-ies**) **1** foolish behaviour; nonsense. **2** an instance of this.

Tommy /ˈtɒmi/ *n.* (*pl.* **-ies**) *colloq.* a British private soldier. [*Tommy* (*Thomas*) *Atkins*, a name used in specimens of completed official forms]

tommy bar *n.* a short bar for use with a box spanner.

tommy-gun *n.* a type of sub-machine gun. [named after J. T. *Thompson*, US Army officer d. 1940, its co-inventor]

tommyrot /ˈtɒmɪrɒt/ *n.* *slang* nonsense.

tommy ruff see RUFF[2] 2.

tomogram /ˈtəʊməgram, ˈtɒm-/ *n.* a record obtained by tomography.

tomography /təˈmɒgrəfi/ *n.* a scanning technique which displays details of a plane cross-section, esp. through the body. [Greek *tomē* 'a cutting' + -GRAPHY]

tomorrow /təˈmɒrəʊ/ *adv.* & *n.* ● *adv.* **1** on the day after today. **2** at some future time. ● *n.* **1** the day after today. **2** the near future. □ **tomorrow morning** (or **afternoon** etc.) in the morning (or afternoon etc.) of tomorrow. **tomorrow week** esp. *Brit.* a week from tomorrow. [TO + MORROW: cf. TODAY]

tompion var. of TAMPION.

Tom Thumb *n.* **1** a very short male person. **2** (also **tom thumb**) **a** a dwarf variety of cultivated flower or vegetable. **b** a small wild flower, esp. bird's-foot trefoil. [the name of the tiny hero of a nursery tale]

tomtit /ˈtɒmtɪt/ *n.* a tit, esp. a blue tit.

tom-tom /ˈtɒmtɒm/ *n.* **1** a simple drum beaten with the hands. **2** a tall drum beaten with the hands and used in jazz bands etc. [Hindi *tamtam*, imitative]

-tomy /təmi/ *comb. form* forming nouns denoting cutting, esp. in surgery (*laparotomy*). [Greek *-tomia* 'cutting' from *temnō* 'to cut']

ton[1] /tʌn/ *n.* **1** (in full **long ton**) a unit of weight equal to 2,240 lb avoirdupois (1016.05 kg). **2** (in full **short ton**) esp. *N. Amer.* a unit of weight equal to 2,000 lb avoirdupois (907.19 kg). **3** = METRIC TON. **4 a** (in full **displacement ton**) a unit of measurement of a ship's weight or volume equal to 2,240 lb or 35 cu. ft. (0.99 cubic metres). **b** (in full **freight ton**) a unit of weight or volume of cargo, equal to a metric ton (1,000 kg) or 40 cu. ft. **5 a** (in full **gross ton**) a unit of gross internal capacity, equal to 100 cu. ft (2.83 cubic metres). **b** (in full **net** or **register ton**) an equivalent unit of net internal capacity. **6** a unit of refrigerating power able to freeze 2,000 lb of water at 0°C in 24 hours. **7** a measure of capacity for various materials, esp. 40 cu. ft of timber. **8** (usu. in *pl.*) *colloq.* a large number or amount (*tons of money*). **9** esp. *Brit. slang* **a** a speed of 100 m.p.h. **b** a sum of £100. **c** a score of 100. □ **weigh a ton** *colloq.* be very heavy. [originally the same word as TUN: differentiated in the 17th c.]

ton[2] /tõ, French tɔ̃/ *n.* **1** a prevailing mode or fashion. **2** fashionable society. [French]

tonal /ˈtəʊn(ə)l/ *adj.* **1** of or relating to tone or tonality. **2** *Mus.* (of a fugue etc.) having repetitions of the subject at different pitches in the same key. □ **tonally** *adv.* [medieval Latin *tonalis* (as TONE)]

tonality /tə(ʊ)ˈnælɪti/ *n.* (*pl.* **-ies**) **1** *Mus.* **a** the relationship between the tones of a musical scale. **b** the observance of a single tonic key as the basis of a composition. **2** the tone or colour scheme of a picture.

tondo /ˈtɒndəʊ/ *n.* (*pl.* **tondi** /-di/) a circular painting or relief. [Italian, = round (plate), via *rotondo* from Latin *rotundus* 'round']

tone /təʊn/ *n.* & *v.* ● *n.* **1** a musical or vocal sound, esp. with reference to its pitch, quality, and strength. **2** (often in *pl.*) modulation of the voice expressing a particular feeling or mood (*a cheerful tone*; *suspicious tones*). **3** a manner of expression in writing. **4** *Mus.* **a** a musical sound, esp. of a definite pitch and character. **b** an interval of a major second, e.g. C–D. **5 a** the general effect of colour or of light and shade in a picture. **b** the tint or shade of a colour. **6 a** the prevailing character of the morals and sentiments etc. in a group. **b** an attitude or sentiment expressed esp. in a letter etc. **7** the proper firmness or functioning of bodily organs or tissues. **8** a state of good or specified health or quality. **9** *Phonet.* **a** an accent on one syllable of a word. **b** a way of pronouncing a word or syllable with a specific intonation to distinguish it from others of a similar sound (*Mandarin Chinese has four tones*). ● *v.* **1** *tr.* give the desired tone to. **2** *tr.* modify the tone of. **3** *intr.* (often foll. by *to*) attune. **4** *intr.* (foll. by *with*) be in harmony (esp. of colour) (*does not tone with the wallpaper*). **5** *tr. Photog.* give (a monochrome picture) an altered colour in finishing by means of a chemical solution. **6** *intr.* undergo a change in colour by toning. □ **tone down 1** make or become softer in tone of sound or colour. **2** make (a statement etc.) less harsh or emphatic. **tone up 1** make or become stronger in tone of sound or colour. **2** make (a statement etc.) more emphatic. □ **toneless** *adj.* **tonelessly** *adv.* [Middle English via Old French *ton* or Latin *tonus* from Greek *tonos* 'tension, tone', from *teinō* 'stretch']

tone arm *n.* the movable arm supporting the pick-up of a record player.

toneburst /ˈtəʊnbəːst/ *n.* an audio signal used in testing the transient response of audio components.

tone control *n.* a switch for varying the proportion of high and low frequencies in reproduced sound.

tone-deaf *adj.* unable to perceive differences of musical pitch accurately. □ **tone-deafness** *n.*

toneme /ˈtəʊniːm/ *n. Phonet.* a phoneme distinguished from another only by its tone. □ **tonemic** /-ˈniːmɪk/ *adj.* [TONE, on the pattern of *phoneme*]

tonepad /ˈtəʊnpæd/ *n.* a device for communicating with a computer over a telephone line using electronically recognized sounds.

tone poem *n.* = SYMPHONIC POEM.

toner /ˈtəʊnə/ *n.* **1** a chemical bath for toning a photographic print. **2** a powder used in xerographic copying processes. **3** a cosmetic preparation for toning the skin.

tone-row *n.* = SERIES 8.

tong[1] /tɒŋ/ *n.* a Chinese guild, association, or secret society. [Chinese *tang* 'meeting place']

tong[2] /tɒŋ/ *v.tr.* (**tonged**, **tonging**) **1** style (the hair) using curling tongs. **2** collect (oysters etc.) using tongs.

tonga /ˈtɒŋgə/ *n.* a light horse-drawn two-wheeled vehicle used in India. [Hindi *tāṅgā*]

Tongan /ˈtɒŋən, ˈtɒŋgən/ *adj.* & *n.* ● *adj.* of or relating to the island of Tonga in the S. Pacific or its people or language. ● *n.* **1** a native or national of Tonga. **2** the Polynesian language spoken in Tonga. [*Tonga* + -AN]

tongs /tɒŋz/ *n.pl.* (also **pair of tongs** *sing.*) an instrument with two hinged or sprung arms for grasping and holding. [pl. of *tong* from Old English *tang(e)*, from Germanic]

tongue /tʌŋ/ *n.* & *v.* ● *n.* **1** the fleshy muscular organ in the mouth used in tasting, licking, and swallowing, and (in man) for speech. **2** the tongue of an ox etc. as food. **3** the faculty of or a tendency in speech (*a sharp tongue*). **4** a particular language (*the German tongue*). **5** a thing like a tongue in shape or position, esp.: **a** a long low promontory. **b** a strip of leather etc., attached at one end only, under the laces in a shoe. **c** the clapper of a bell. **d** the pin of a buckle. **e** the projecting strip on a wooden etc. board fitting into the groove of another. **f** a vibrating slip in the reed of some musical instruments. **g** a jet of flame. ● *v.* (**tongues**, **tongued**, **tonguing**) *Mus.* **1** *tr.* produce staccato etc. effects with (a flute etc.) by means of tonguing. **2** *intr.* use the tongue in this way. □ **find** (or **lose**) **one's tongue** be able (or unable) to express oneself after a shock etc. **the gift of tongues** the power of speaking in unknown languages, regarded as one of the gifts of the Holy Spirit (Acts 2). **keep a civil tongue in one's head** avoid rudeness. **with one's tongue hanging out** eagerly or expectantly. **with one's tongue in one's cheek** insincerely or ironically. □ **tongued** *adj.* (also in *comb.*). **tongueless** *adj.* [Old English *tunge* from Germanic: related to Latin *lingua*]

tongue-and-groove *n.* & *v.* ● *n.* (often *attrib.*) planking etc. with a projecting strip down one side and a groove down the other. ● *v.tr.* **1** panel with tongue-and-groove. **2** (as **tongued and grooved** *adj.*) having a tongue-and-groove joint.

tongue-in-cheek *adj.* & *adv.* ● *adj.* ironic; slyly humorous. ● *adv.* insincerely or ironically.

tongue-lashing *n.* a severe scolding or reprimand.

tongue-tie *n.* a speech impediment due to a malformation of the tongue.

tongue-tied *adj.* **1** too shy or embarrassed to speak. **2** having a tongue-tie.

tongue-twister *n.* a sequence of words difficult to pronounce quickly and correctly.

tonguing /ˈtʌŋɪŋ/ *n. Mus.* the technique of playing a wind instrument using the tongue to articulate certain notes.

tonic /ˈtɒnɪk/ *n.* & *adj.* ● *n.* **1** an invigorating medicine. **2** anything serving to invigorate. **3** = TONIC WATER. **4** *Mus.* the first degree of a scale, forming the keynote of a piece (see KEYNOTE 3). ● *adj.* **1** serving as a tonic; invigorating. **2** *Mus.* denoting the first degree of a scale. **3 a** producing tension, esp. of the muscles. **b** restoring normal tone to organs. □ **tonically** *adv.* [French *tonique* from Greek *tonikos* (as TONE)]

tonic accent *n. Phonet.* an accent marked by a change of pitch within a syllable.

tonicity /tə(ʊ)ˈnɪsɪti/ *n.* **1** the state of being tonic. **2** a healthy elasticity of muscles etc.

tonic sol-fa *n. Mus.* a system of notation used esp. in teaching singing, with doh as the keynote of all major keys and lah as the keynote of all minor keys.

tonic spasm *n.* continuous muscular contraction (cf. CLONUS).

tonic water *n.* a carbonated soft drink containing quinine.

tonight /tə'nʌɪt/ *adv. & n.* ● *adv.* on the present or approaching evening or night. ● *n.* the evening or night of the present day. [TO + NIGHT: cf. TODAY]

tonka bean /'tɒŋkə/ *n.* the black fragrant seed of a S. American tree, *Dipteryx odorata*, used in perfumery etc. [Carib *tonka* from Tupi *tõka*]

ton-mile *n.* one ton of goods carried one mile, as a unit of traffic.

tonnage /'tʌnɪdʒ/ *n.* **1** a ship's internal cubic capacity or freight-carrying capacity measured in tons. **2** the total carrying capacity esp. of a country's mercantile marine. **3** a charge per ton on freight or cargo. [originally in sense 'duty on a tun of wine': Old French *tonnage* from *tonne* TUN: later from TON[1]]

tonne /tʌn/ *n.* = METRIC TON. [French: see TUN]

■ **Usage** The pronunciations /tɒn/ (rhymes with *gone*) and /'tʌni/ ('tunny') are sometimes used to distinguish the metric *tonne* from the imperial *ton* in speech.

tonneau /'tɒnəʊ/ *n.* the part of a motor car occupied by the back seats, esp. in an open car. [French, literally 'cask, tun']

tonneau cover *n.* a removable flexible cover for the seats in an open car, boat, etc., when they are not in use.

tonometer /tə(ʊ)'nɒmɪtə/ *n.* **1** *Mus.* a tuning fork or other instrument for measuring the pitch of tones. **2** *Med.* an instrument for measuring the pressure in the eyeball (to test for glaucoma) or that in a blood vessel etc. [formed as TONE + -METER]

tonsil /'tɒns(ə)l, 'tɒnsɪl/ *n.* either of two small masses of lymphoid tissue, one on each side of the root of the tongue. □ **tonsillar** *adj.* [French *tonsilles* or Latin *tonsillae* (pl.)]

tonsillectomy /tɒnsɪ'lɛktəmi/ *n.* (*pl.* **-ies**) the surgical removal of the tonsils.

tonsillitis /tɒnsɪ'lʌɪtɪs/ *n.* inflammation of the tonsils.

tonsorial /tɒn'sɔːrɪəl/ *adj.* usu. *joc.* of or relating to a hairdresser or hairdressing. [Latin *tonsorius*, via *tonsor* 'barber' from *tondēre tons-* 'to shave']

tonsure /'tɒnsjə, 'tɒnʃə/ *n. & v.* ● *n.* **1** the shaving of the crown of the head or the entire head, esp. of a person entering a priesthood or monastic order. **2** a bare patch made in this way. ● *v.tr.* give a tonsure to. [Middle English from Old French *tonsure* or Latin *tonsura* (as TONSORIAL)]

tontine /tɒn'tiːn, 'tɒn-/ *n.* an annuity shared by subscribers to a loan, the shares increasing as subscribers die until the last survivor gets all, or until a specified date when the remaining survivors share the proceeds. [French, from the name of Lorenzo *Tonti* of Naples, originator of tontines in France *c.*1653]

ton-up *n. & adj. Brit. slang* ● *n.* a speed of 100 m.p.h. ● *attrib.adj.* **1** (of a motorcyclist) achieving this, esp. habitually and recklessly (*ton-up kid*). **2** fond or capable of travelling at high speed.

tony /'təʊni/ *adj.* (**tonier**, **toniest**) *US colloq.* having 'tone'; stylish, fashionable.

too /tuː/ *adv.* **1** to a greater extent than is desirable, permissible, or possible for a specified or understood purpose (*too colourful for my taste*; *too large to fit*). **2** *colloq.* extremely (*you're too kind*). **3** in addition (*are they coming too?*). **4** moreover (*we must consider, too, the time of year*). □ **none too 1** rather less than (*feeling none too good*). **2** barely. **too bad** see BAD. **too much, too much for** see MUCH. **too right** see RIGHT. [stressed form of TO, spelt *too* since 16th c.]

toodle-oo /tuːd(ə)l'uː/ *int. colloq.* goodbye. [perhaps from French *à tout à l'heure* 'see you soon']

took *past* of TAKE.

tool /tuːl/ *n. & v.* ● *n.* **1** any device or implement used to carry out mechanical functions whether manually or by a machine. **2** a thing used in an occupation or pursuit (*the tools of one's trade*; *literary tools*). **3** a person used as a mere instrument by another. **4** *coarse slang* the penis. **5 a** a distinct design in the tooling of a book. **b** a small stamp or roller used to make this. ● *v.tr.* **1** dress (stone) with a chisel. **2** impress a design on (a leather book cover). **3** (foll. by *along*, *around*, etc.) *slang* drive or ride, esp. in a casual or leisurely manner. **4** (often foll. by *up*) equip with tools. □ **tool up 1** *slang* arm oneself. **2** equip oneself. □ **tooler** *n.* [Old English *tōl*, from Germanic]

tool bag *n.* a bag for keeping tools in.

toolbox /'tuːlbɒks/ *n.* a box or container for keeping tools in.

tooling /'tuːlɪŋ/ *n.* **1** the process of dressing stone with a chisel. **2** the ornamentation of a leather book cover with designs impressed by heated tools.

tool kit *n.* **1** a set of tools. **2** *Computing* a set of software tools.

toolmaker /'tuːlmeɪkə/ *n.* a person who makes precision tools, esp. tools used in a press. □ **toolmaking** *n.*

tool-pusher *n.* a worker directing the drilling on an oil rig.

tool shed *n.* a shed in which tools etc. are stored.

toot /tuːt/ *n. & v.* ● *n.* **1** a short sharp sound as made by a horn, trumpet, or whistle. **2** *US slang* cocaine or a snort (see SNORT *n.* 4) of cocaine. ● *v.* **1** *tr.* sound (a horn etc.) with a short sharp sound. **2** *intr.* give out such a sound. □ **tooter** *n.* [probably from Middle Low German *tūten*, or imitative]

tooth /tuːθ/ *n. & v.* ● *n.* (*pl.* **teeth** /tiːθ/) **1** each of a set of hard bony enamel-coated structures in the jaws of most vertebrates, used for biting and chewing. **2** a toothlike part or projection, e.g. the cog of a gearwheel, the point of a saw or comb, etc. **3** (often foll. by *for*) one's sense of taste; an appetite or liking. **4** (in *pl.*) force or effectiveness (*the penalties give the contract teeth*). ● *v.* **1** *tr.* provide with teeth. **2** *intr.* (of cogwheels) engage, interlock. □ **armed to the teeth** completely and elaborately armed or equipped. **fight tooth and nail** fight very fiercely. **get one's teeth into** devote oneself seriously to. **in the teeth of 1** in spite of (opposition or difficulty etc.). **2** contrary to (instructions etc.). **3** directly against (the wind etc.). **set a person's teeth on edge** see EDGE. □ **toothed** *adj.* (also in *comb.*). **toothless** *adj.* **toothlike** *adj.* [Old English *tōth* (pl. *tēth*), from Germanic]

toothache /'tuːθeɪk/ *n.* a (usu. prolonged) pain in a tooth or teeth.

tooth-billed *adj.* (of a bird) having toothlike projections on the cutting edges of the bill.

toothbrush /'tuːθbrʌʃ/ *n.* a brush for cleaning the teeth.

toothcomb /'tuːθkəʊm/ *n. Brit.* = FINE-TOOTH COMB.

■ **Usage** Although *toothcomb* and *fine toothcomb* arose from a misunderstanding of *fine-tooth comb*, they are now accepted as established expressions.

toothed whale *n.* a whale of the suborder Odonticeti, having teeth rather than baleen plates, including sperm whales, killer whales, and dolphins and porpoises.

tooth fairy *n.* (in nursery tales) a fairy who takes children's milk teeth after they fall out and leaves a coin.

tooth-glass *n.* a glass for holding dentures, toothbrushes, etc., or for use as a tumbler for mouthwash.

toothing /'tuːθɪŋ/ *n.* projecting bricks or stones left at the end of a wall to allow its continuation.

toothpaste /'tuːθpeɪst/ *n.* a paste for cleaning the teeth.

toothpick /'tuːθpɪk/ *n.* a small sharp instrument for removing small pieces of food lodged between the teeth.

tooth powder *n.* powder for cleaning the teeth.

tooth shell *n.* = TUSK SHELL.

toothsome /'tu:θs(ə)m/ *adj.* (of food) delicious, appetizing. □ **toothsomely** *adv.* **toothsomeness** *n.*

toothwort /'tu:θwə:t/ *n.* a parasitic plant, *Lathraea squamaria*, with toothlike root scales.

toothy /'tu:θi/ *adj.* (**toothier, toothiest**) having or showing large, numerous, or prominent teeth (*a toothy grin*). □ **toothily** *adv.*

tootle /'tu:t(ə)l/ *v.* & *n.* ● *v.intr.* **1** toot gently or repeatedly. **2** (usu. foll. by *along, around*, etc.) *colloq.* move casually or aimlessly. ● *n.* an act of tootling.

too-too /tu:'tu:/*adj.* & *adv.* *colloq.* extreme, excessive(ly).

tootsy /'tʊtsi/ *n.* (also **tootsie**) (*pl.* **-ies**) **1** (usu. in *pl.*) *colloq.* usu. *joc.* a foot; a toe. **2** esp. *US slang* a woman; a female lover. [jocular diminutive: alteration of FOOT]

top[1] /tɒp/ *n., adj., & v.* ● *n.* **1** the highest point or part (*the top of the house*). **2 a** the highest rank or place (*at the top of the school*). **b** a person occupying this (*was top in maths*). **c** esp. *Brit.* the upper end or head (*the top of the table*). **3** the upper surface of a thing, esp. of the ground, a table, etc. **4** the upper part of a thing, esp.: **a** a blouse, jumper, etc. for wearing with a skirt, trousers, etc. **b** the upper part of a shoe or boot. **c** the stopper of a bottle. **d** the lid of a jar, saucepan, etc. **e** esp. *Brit.* the creamy part of milk. **f** the folding roof of a car, pram, or carriage. **g** the upper edge or edges of a page or pages in a book (*gilt top*). **5** the utmost degree; height (*called at the top of his voice*). **6** the high-frequency component of reproduced sound. **7** (in *pl.*) *colloq.* a person or thing of the best quality (*he's tops at cricket*). **8** (esp. in *pl.*) the leaves etc. of a plant grown esp. for its root (*turnip-tops*). **9** (usu. in *pl.*) a bundle of long wool fibres prepared for spinning. **10** *Naut.* a platform round the head of each of the lower masts of a sailing ship, serving to extend the topmost rigging or carry guns. **11** (in *pl.*) esp. *Bridge* the two or three highest cards of a suit. **12** *Brit.* = TOP GEAR (*climbed the hill in top*). **13** = TOPSPIN. ● *adj.* **1** highest in position (*the top shelf*). **2** highest in degree or importance (*at top speed; the top job*). ● *v.tr.* (**topped, topping**) **1** provide with a top, cap, etc. (*cake topped with icing*). **2** remove the top of (a plant, fruit, etc.), esp. to improve growth, prepare for cooking, etc. **3** be higher or better than; surpass; be at the top of (*topped the list*). **4** *slang* **a** execute esp. by hanging, kill. **b** (*refl.*) commit suicide. **5** reach the top of (a hill etc.). **6** *Golf* **a** hit (a ball) above the centre. **b** make (a stroke) in this way. □ **at the top** (or **at the top of the tree**) in the highest rank of a profession etc. **come to the top** win distinction. **from top to toe** from head to foot; completely. **off the top of one's head** see HEAD. **on top 1** in a superior position; above. **2** on the upper part of the head (*bald on top*). **on top of 1** fully in command of. **2** in close proximity to. **3** in addition to. **on top of the world** *colloq.* exuberant. **over the top 1** esp. *hist.* over the parapet of a trench (and into battle); into action. **2** (hyphenated when *attrib.*) to excess, beyond reasonable limits; outrageous (*that joke was over the top*). **top off** (or **up**) put an end or the finishing touch to (a thing). **top out** put the highest stone on (a building). **top one's part** esp. *Theatr.* act or discharge one's part to perfection. **top ten** (or **twenty** etc.) the first ten (or twenty etc.) records in the charts. **top up 1 a** complete (an amount or number). **b** fill up (a glass or other partly full container). **2** top up something for (a person) (*may I top you up with sherry?*). □ **topmost** *adj.* [Old English *topp*]

top[2] /tɒp/ *n.* a wooden or metal toy, usu. conical, spherical, or pear-shaped, spinning on a point when set in motion by hand, string, etc. [Old English, of uncertain origin]

topaz /'təʊpaz/ *n.* **1** a transparent or translucent aluminium silicate mineral, usu. yellow, used as a gem. **2** any S. American hummingbird of the genus *Topaza*. [Middle English via Old French *topace, topaze* and Latin *topazus* from Greek *topazos*]

topazolite /tə(ʊ)'pazəlʌɪt/ *n.* a yellow or green kind of garnet. [TOPAZ + -LITE]

top banana *n. slang* **1** a comedian topping the bill. **2** *US* a leader of an organization etc.

top-boot *n.* esp. *hist.* a boot with a high top esp. of a different material or colour.

top brass see BRASS *n.* 6.

topcoat /'tɒpkəʊt/ *n.* **1** an overcoat. **2** an outer coat of paint etc.

top copy *n.* the uppermost typed copy (cf. CARBON COPY 1).

top dog *n. colloq.* a victor or master.

top-down *attrib.adj.* **1** proceeding from the general to the particular, or from the top downwards. **2** hierarchical.

top drawer *n.* & *adj.* ● *n.* **1** the uppermost drawer in a chest etc. **2** *colloq.* high social position or origin. ● *attrib.adj.* (**top-drawer**) *colloq.* of the highest quality or esp. social level.

top dressing *n.* **1** the application of manure or fertilizer to the top of the earth instead of ploughing it in. **2** manure so applied. **3** a superficial show. □ **top dress** *v.tr.*

tope[1] /təʊp/ *v.intr. archaic* or *literary* drink alcohol to excess, esp. habitually. □ **toper** *n.* [perhaps from obsolete *top* 'quaff']

tope[2] /təʊp/ *n.* (in India) a grove, esp. of mangoes. [Telugu *tōpu*, Tamil *tōppu*]

tope[3] /təʊp/ *n.* = STUPA. [Punjabi *tōp* via Prakrit & Pali *thūpo* from Sanskrit STUPA]

tope[4] /təʊp/ *n.* a small shark, *Galeorhinus galeus*. [perhaps from Cornish]

topee var. of TOPI[1].

top-flight *adj.* in the highest rank of achievement.

top fruit *n. Brit.* fruit grown on trees, not bushes.

topgallant /tɒp'gal(ə)nt, tə'gal-/ *n. Naut.* the mast, sail, yard, or rigging immediately above the topmast and topsail.

top gear *n. Brit.* the highest gear in a motor vehicle or bicycle.

top-hamper *n.* an encumbrance on top, esp. the upper sails and rigging of a ship.

top hat *n.* a man's formal hat with a high cylindrical crown.

top-heavy /tɒp'hɛvi/ *adj.* **1** disproportionately heavy at the top so as to be in danger of toppling. **2 a** (of an organization, business, etc.) having a disproportionately large number of people in senior administrative positions. **b** overcapitalized. **3** *colloq.* (of a woman) having a disproportionately large bust. □ **top-heavily** *adv.* **top-heaviness** *n.*

Tophet /'təʊfɪt/ *n. Bibl.* hell. [the name of a place in the Valley of Hinnom near Jerusalem used for idolatrous worship, including the sacrifice of children, and later for burning refuse: from Hebrew *tōpeṯ*]

top-hole *adj. Brit. colloq.* first-rate.

tophus /'təʊfəs/ *n.* (*pl.* **tophi** /-fʌɪ/) **1** *Med.* a gouty deposit of crystalline uric acid and other substances at the surface of joints. **2** *Geol.* = TUFA. [Latin, loose porous stones of various kinds]

topi[1] /'təʊpi/ *n.* (also **topee**) (*pl.* **topis** or **topees**) *Anglo-Ind.* a hat, esp. a sola topi. [Hindi *topī*]

topi[2] /'təʊpi/ *n.* (*pl.* **topis** or same) a large usu. reddish-brown antelope of African grassland, *Damaliscus lunatus*, with a sloping back, esp. one of E. African coastal race. Cf. TSESSEBI. [West African name]

topiary /'təʊpɪəri/ *adj.* & *n.* ● *adj.* concerned with or formed by clipping shrubs, trees, etc. into ornamental shapes. ● *n.* (*pl.* **-ies**) **1** topiary art. **2** an example of this. □ **topiarian** /-pɪ'ɛ:rɪən/ *adj.* **topiarist** *n.* [French *topiaire* via Latin *topiarius* 'landscape gardener' from *topia opera* 'fancy gardening', from Greek *topia*, pl. diminutive of *topos* 'place']

topic /'tɒpɪk/ *n.* **1** a theme for a book, discourse, essay, sermon, etc. **2** the subject of a conversation or argument. [Latin *topica* from Greek *ta topika*, literally 'matters concerning commonplaces' (the title of a treatise by Aristotle) from *topos* 'a place, a commonplace']

topical /'tɒpɪk(ə)l/ *adj.* **1** dealing with the news, current affairs, etc. (*a topical song*). **2** dealing with a place; local. **3** *Med.* (of an ailment, medicine, etc.) affecting or applied externally to a part of the body. **4** of or concerning topics. □ **topicality** /-'kalɪti/ *n.* **topically** *adv.*

topknot /'tɒpnɒt/ *n.* **1** esp. *hist.* a decorative knot or bow of ribbon worn on the head (esp. in the 18th c.). **2** a tuft or crest growing on the head.

topless /'tɒplɪs/ *adj.* **1** without or seeming to be without a top. **2 a** (of clothes) having no upper part. **b** (of a person) wearing such clothes; bare-breasted. **c** (of a place, esp. a beach) where women go topless. □ **toplessness** *n.*

top-level *adj.* of the highest level of importance, prestige, etc.

top-line *attrib.adj.* **1** of the highest quality; top of the range. **2** (esp. of an entertainment act) considered worthy of top billing.

toplofty /tɒp'lɒfti/ *adj. US colloq.* haughty.

topman /'tɒpmən/ *n.* (*pl.* **-men**) **1** a top-sawyer. **2** *Naut.* a man doing duty in a top.

topmast /'tɒpmɑːst, -məst/ *n. Naut.* the mast next above the lower mast.

top-notch *adj. colloq.* first-rate. □ **top-notcher** *n.*

topography /tə'pɒgrəfi/ *n.* **1 a** a detailed description, representation on a map, etc., of the natural and artificial features of a town, district, etc. **b** such features. **2** *Anat.* the mapping of the surface of the body with reference to the parts beneath. □ **topographer** *n.* **topographic** /-'grafɪk/ *adj.* **topographical** /tɒpə'grafɪk(ə)l/ *adj.* **topographically** /tɒpə'grafɪk(ə)li/ *adv.* [Middle English via Late Latin *topographia* from Greek, from *topos* 'place']

topoi *pl.* of TOPOS.

topology /tə'pɒlədʒi/ *n. Math.* the study of geometrical properties and spatial relations unaffected by the continuous change of shape or size of figures. □ **topological** /tɒpə'lɒdʒɪk(ə)l/ *adj.* **topologically** /tɒpə'lɒdʒɪk(ə)li/ *adv.* **topologist** *n.* [German *Topologie* from Greek *topos* 'place']

toponym /'tɒpənɪm/ *n.* **1** a place name. **2** a descriptive place name, usu. derived from a topographical feature of the place. [TOPONYMY]

toponymy /tə'pɒnɪmi/ *n.* the study of the place names of a region. □ **toponymic** /-'nɪmɪk/ *adj.* [Greek *topos* 'place' + *onoma* 'name']

topos /'tɒpɒs/ *n.* (*pl.* **topoi** /'tɒpɔɪ/) a stock theme in literature etc. [Greek, = commonplace]

topper /'tɒpə/ *n.* **1** a thing that tops. **2** *colloq.* = TOP HAT. **3** *Brit. colloq.* an exceptionally good person or thing.

topping /'tɒpɪŋ/ *adj.* & *n.* ● *adj.* **1** pre-eminent in position, rank, etc. **2** *Brit. archaic slang* excellent. ● *n.* anything that tops something else, esp. cream etc. on a dessert.

topple /'tɒp(ə)l/ *v.intr.* & *tr.* (often foll. by *over*) **1** totter and fall (over), or cause to do so. **2** overthrow or be overthrown (*the government was toppled by a coup*). [TOP¹ + -LE⁴]

topsail /'tɒpseɪl, 'tɒps(ə)l/ *n.* **1** the square sail, or each of two such sails, next above the lowest. **2** a fore-and-aft sail above the gaff.

top-sawyer *n.* **1** a sawyer in the upper position in a saw-pit. **2** a person who holds a superior position; a distinguished person.

top secret *adj.* of the highest secrecy.

top-shell *n.* **1** a marine gastropod mollusc of the family Trochidae with a short conical shell. **2** its shell.

topside /'tɒpsʌɪd/ *n.* **1** *Brit.* the outer side of a round of beef. **2** the side of a ship above the waterline.

top-slicing *n.* a method of assessing tax chargeable on a lump sum by averaging the sum out over the years it has accrued and charging accordingly.

topsoil /'tɒpsɔɪl/ *n.* the top layer of soil (opp. SUBSOIL).

topspin /'tɒpspɪn/ *n.* a fast forward spinning motion imparted to a ball in tennis etc. by hitting it forward and upward.

topstitch /'tɒpstɪtʃ/ *v.tr.* make a row of neat, esp. decorative, stitches on the right side of (a garment etc.). □ **topstitching** *n.*

topsy-turvy /tɒpsɪ'təːvi/ *adv., adj.,* & *n.* ● *adv.* & *adj.* **1** upside down. **2** in utter confusion. ● *n.* utter confusion. □ **topsy-turvily** *adv.* **topsy-turviness** *n.* [apparently from TOP¹ + obsolete *terve* 'overturn']

top-up *n. Brit.* an addition; something that serves to top up (esp. a partly full glass).

toque /təʊk/ *n.* **1** a woman's small brimless hat. **2** *hist.* a small cap or bonnet for a man or woman. [French, apparently = Italian *tocca*, Spanish *toca*, of unknown origin]

toquilla /tə'kiːjə/ *n.* **1** a palmlike tree, *Carludovica palmata*, native to S. America. **2** a fibre produced from the leaves of this. [Spanish, = small gauze headdress, diminutive of *toca* 'toque']

tor /tɔː/ *n.* a hill or rocky peak, esp. in Devon or Cornwall. [Old English *torr*: cf. Gaelic *tòrr* 'bulging hill']

Torah /'tɔːrə, 'təʊ-/ *n.* **1** (usu. prec. by *the*) **a** the Pentateuch. **b** a scroll containing this. **2** the will of God as revealed in Mosaic law. [Hebrew *tōrāh* 'instruction']

torc /tɔːk/ *n.* (also **torque**) *hist.* a necklace of twisted metal, esp. of the ancient Gauls and Britons.

torch /tɔːtʃ/ *n.* & *v.* ● *n.* **1** (also **electric torch**) *Brit.* a portable battery-powered electric lamp. **2 a** a piece of wood, cloth, etc., soaked in tallow and lit for illumination. **b** any similar lamp, e.g. an oil lamp on a pole. **3** a source of heat, illumination, or enlightenment (*bore aloft the torch of freedom*). **4** esp. *N. Amer.* a blowlamp. **5** *US slang* an arsonist. ● *v.tr.* esp. *N. Amer. slang* set alight with a torch. □ **carry a torch for** suffer from unrequited love for. **put to the torch** destroy by burning. [Middle English via Old French *torche* from Latin *torqua*, from *torquēre* 'to twist']

torch-bearer *n.* **1** a person who leads the way in an attempt to reform, inspire, etc. **2** a person who carries a usu. ceremonial torch.

torchère /tɔː'ʃɛː/ *n.* a tall stand with a small table for a candlestick etc. [French (as TORCH)]

torch-fishing *n.* catching fish by torchlight at night.

torchlight /'tɔːtʃlʌɪt/ *n.* the light of a torch or torches. □ **torchlit** *adj.*

torchon /'tɔːʃ(ə)n/ *n.* (in full **torchon lace**) coarse bobbin lace with geometrical designs. [French, = duster, dishcloth, from *torcher* 'to wipe']

torch race *n. Gk Antiq.* a festival performance of runners handing lighted torches to others in relays.

torch song *n.* a popular song of unrequited love. □ **torch singer** *n.*

torch-thistle *n.* any tall cactus of the genus *Cereus*, with funnel-shaped flowers which open at night.

tore¹ *past* of TEAR¹.

tore² /tɔː/ *n.* = TORUS 1, 4. [French from Latin *torus*: see TORUS]

toreador /'tɒrɪədɔː, ˌtɒrɪə'dɔː/ *n.* a bullfighter, esp. on horseback. [Spanish via *torear* 'fight bulls' from *toro* 'bull', from Latin *taurus*]

toreador pants *n.pl.* women's close-fitting calf-length trousers.

torero /tɒ'rɛːrəʊ/ *n.* (*pl.* **-os**) a bullfighter. [Spanish from *toro*: see TOREADOR]

toreutic /tə'ruːtɪk/ *adj.* & *n.* ● *adj.* of or concerning the chasing, carving, and embossing of esp. metal. ● *n.* (in *pl.*) the art or practice of this. [Greek *toreutikos* from *toreuō* 'work in relief']

torgoch /'tɔːgɒx/ *n.* a kind of red-bellied char found in some Welsh lakes. [Welsh, from *tor* 'belly' + *coch* 'red']

tori *pl.* of TORUS.

toric /'tɒrɪk, 'tɔːrɪk/ *adj. Geom.* having the form of a torus or part of a torus.

torii /'tɔːriː/ *n.* (*pl.* same) the gateway of a Shinto shrine, with two uprights and two crosspieces. [Japanese, from *tori* 'bird' + *i* 'sit, perch']

torment *n.* & *v.* ● *n.* /'tɔːmɛnt/ **1** severe physical or mental suffering (*was in torment*). **2** a cause of this. **3** *archaic* **a** torture. **b** an instrument of torture. ● *v.tr.* /tɔː'mɛnt/ **1** subject to torment (*tormented with worry*). **2** tease or worry excessively (*enjoyed tormenting the teacher*). □ **tormentedly** *adv.* **tormentingly** *adv.* **tormentor** /-'mɛntə/ *n.* [Middle English via Old French *torment, tormenter* from Latin *tormentum* 'missile-engine', from *torquēre* 'to twist']

tormentil /'tɔːm(ə)ntɪl/ *n.* a low-growing plant, *Potentilla erecta*, with bright yellow flowers and a highly astringent rootstock used in medicine. [Middle English via Old French *tormentille* from medieval Latin *tormentilla*, of unknown origin]

torn *past part.* of TEAR[1].

tornado /tɔː'neɪdəʊ/ *n.* (*pl.* **-oes** or **-os**) **1** a violent storm of small extent with whirling winds, esp.: **a** in W. Africa at the beginning and end of the rainy season. **b** in the US etc. over a narrow path often accompanied by a funnel-shaped cloud. **2** an outburst or volley of cheers, hisses, missiles, etc. □ **tornadic** /-'nadɪk/ *adj.* [apparently assimilation of Spanish *tronada* 'thunderstorm' (from *tronar* 'to thunder') to Spanish *tornar* 'to turn']

toroid /'tɒrɔɪd, 'tɔː-/ *n.* a figure of toroidal shape.

toroidal /tɒ'rɔɪd(ə)l, tɔː-/ *adj. Geom.* of or resembling a torus. □ **toroidally** *adv.*

torose /tɒ'rəʊs, tɔː-/ *adj.* **1** *Bot.* (of plants, esp. their stalks) cylindrical with bulges at intervals. **2** *Zool.* knobby. [Latin *torosus* from *torus*: see TORUS]

torpedo /tɔː'piːdəʊ/ *n.* & *v.* ● *n.* (*pl.* **-oes**) **1 a** a cigar-shaped self-propelled underwater missile that explodes on impact with a ship. **b** (in full **aerial torpedo**) a similar device dropped from an aircraft. **2** *Zool.* an electric ray. **3** *US* a type of explosive device or firework. ● *v.tr.* (**-oes, -oed**) **1** destroy or attack with a torpedo. **2** make (a policy, institution, plan, etc.) ineffective or inoperative; destroy. □ **torpedo-like** *adj.* [Latin, = numbness, electric ray, from *torpēre* 'be numb']

torpedo boat *n.* a small fast lightly armed warship for carrying or discharging torpedoes.

torpedo-net *n.* (also **torpedo-netting**) netting of steel wire hung round a ship to intercept torpedoes.

torpedo tube *n.* a tube from which torpedoes are fired by using compressed air or an explosive charge.

torpefy /'tɔːpɪfʌɪ/ *v.tr.* (**-ies, -ied**) make numb or torpid. [Latin *torpefacere* from *torpēre* 'be numb']

torpid /'tɔːpɪd/ *adj.* **1** sluggish, inactive, dull, apathetic. **2** numb. **3** (of a hibernating animal) dormant. □ **torpidity** /-'pɪdɪti/ *n.* **torpidly** *adv.* **torpidness** *n.* [Latin *torpidus* (as TORPOR)]

torpor /'tɔːpə/ *n.* torpidity. □ **torporific** /-'rɪfɪk/ *adj.* [Latin, from *torpēre* 'be sluggish']

torque /tɔːk/ *n.* & *v.* ● *n.* **1** *Mech.* the moment of a system of forces tending to cause rotation. **2** var. of TORC. ● *v.tr.* apply torque or a twisting force to. □ **torquey** *adj.* [Latin *torquēre* 'to twist': in sense 1 via French, and Latin *torques*]

torque converter *n.* a device to transmit the correct torque from the engine to the axle in a motor vehicle.

torr /tɔː/ *n.* (*pl.* same) a unit of pressure used in measuring partial vacuums, equal to 133.32 pascals. [named after E. *Torricelli*, Italian physicist d. 1647]

torrefy /'tɒrɪfʌɪ/ *v.tr.* (**-ies, -ied**) **1** roast or dry (metallic ore, a drug, etc.). **2** parch or scorch with heat. □ **torrefaction** /-'fakʃ(ə)n/ *n.* [French *torréfier* from Latin *torrefacere*, from *torrēre* 'scorch']

torrent /'tɒr(ə)nt/ *n.* **1** a rushing stream of water, lava, etc. **2** (in *pl.*) a great downpour of rain (*came down in torrents*). **3** (usu. foll. by *of*) a violent or copious flow (*uttered a torrent of abuse*). □ **torrential** /tə'rɛnʃ(ə)l/ *adj.* **torrentially** /tə'rɛnʃ(ə)li/ *adv.* [French from Italian *torrente*, via Latin *torrens -entis* 'scorching, boiling, roaring' from *torrēre* 'scorch']

Torricellian vacuum /tɔːrɪ'tʃɛlɪən, -'sɛlɪən/ *n.* a vacuum formed when mercury in a long tube closed at one end is inverted with the open end in a reservoir of mercury (the principle on which a barometer is made). [*Torricelli*: see TORR]

torrid /'tɒrɪd/ *adj.* **1 a** (of the weather) very hot and dry. **b** (of land etc.) parched by such weather. **2** (of language or actions) emotionally charged; passionate, intense. □ **torridity** /-'rɪdɪti/ *n.* **torridly** *adv.* [French *torride* or Latin *torridus*, from *torrēre* 'parch']

torrid zone *n.* the central belt of the earth between the Tropics of Cancer and Capricorn.

torse /tɔːs/ *n. Heraldry* a wreath. [obsolete French *torse*, *torce* 'wreath', ultimately from Latin *torta*, fem. past part. of *torquēre* 'twist']

torsel var. of TASSEL[2].

torsion /'tɔːʃ(ə)n/ *n.* **1** twisting, esp. of one end of a body while the other is held fixed. **2** *Math.* the extent to which a curve departs from being planar. **3** *Biol.* the state of being twisted into a spiral. **4** *Med.* the twisting of the cut end of an artery after surgery etc. to impede bleeding. □ **torsional** *adj.* **torsionally** *adv.* **torsionless** *adj.* [Middle English via Old French and Late Latin *torsio -onis* from Latin *tortio* (as TORT)]

torsion balance *n.* an instrument for measuring very weak forces by their effect upon a system of fine twisted wire.

torsion bar *n.* a bar forming part of a vehicle suspension, twisting in response to the motion of the wheels and absorbing their vertical movement.

torsion pendulum *n.* a pendulum working by rotation rather than by swinging.

torsk /tɔːsk/ *n.* a fish of the cod family, *Brosme brosme*, abundant in northern waters and often dried for food. [Norwegian *to(r)sk* from Old Norse *tho(r)skr*, probably related to *thurr* 'dry']

torso /'tɔːsəʊ/ *n.* (*pl.* **-os** or *US* also **torsi** /-siː/) **1** the trunk of the human body. **2** a statue of a human consisting of the trunk alone, without head or limbs. **3** an unfinished or mutilated work (esp. of art, literature, etc.). [Italian, = stalk, stump, torso, from Latin *thyrsus*]

tort /tɔːt/ *n. Law* a breach of duty (other than under contract) leading to liability for damages. [Middle English via Old French from medieval Latin *tortum* 'wrong', neut. past part. of Latin *torquēre tort-* 'twist']

torte /'tɔːtə/ *n.* (*pl.* **torten** /'tɔːt(ə)n/ or **tortes**) an elaborate sweet cake or tart. [German]

tortelli /tɔː'tɛli/ *n.* an Italian dish of small pasta parcels stuffed with a cheese or vegetable mixture etc. [Italian, pl. of *tortello* 'small cake, fritter']

tortellini /tɔːtɪ'liːni/ *n.* tortelli which have been rolled and formed into small rings. [Italian, pl. of *tortellino*, diminutive of *tortello* 'small cake, fritter']

tortfeasor /'tɔːtfiːzə/ *n. Law* a person guilty of tort. [Old French *tort-fesor*, *tort-faiseur*, etc., from *tort* 'wrong', *-fesor, faiseur* 'doer']

torticollis /tɔːtɪ'kɒlɪs/ *n. Med.* a rheumatic etc. disease of the muscles of the neck, causing twisting and stiffness. [modern Latin, from Latin *tortus* 'crooked' + *collum* 'neck']

tortilla /tɔː'tiːjə/ *n.* a thin flat originally Mexican maize cake eaten hot or cold with or without a filling. [Spanish, diminutive of *torta* 'cake', from Late Latin]

tortious /'tɔːʃəs/ *adj. Law* constituting a tort; wrongful. □ **tortiously** *adv.* [Anglo-French *torcious* from *torcion* 'extortion', from Late Latin *tortio* 'torture': see TORSION]

tortoise /'tɔːtəs, -tɔɪz/ *n.* **1** any slow-moving plant-eating land reptile of the family Testudinidae, encased in a scaly or leathery domed shell, and having a retractile head and thick legs. **2** *Rom. Antiq.* = TESTUDO. □ **tortoise-like** *adj.* & *adv.* [Middle English *tortuce*, Old French *tortue*, from medieval Latin *tortuca*, of uncertain origin]

tortoiseshell /ˈtɔːtəsʃɛl/ *n. & adj.* ● *n.* **1** the yellowish-brown mottled or clouded outer shell of some turtles, used for decorative hair-combs, jewellery, etc. **2 a** = TORTOISESHELL CAT. **b** = TORTOISESHELL BUTTERFLY. ● *adj.* **1** having the colouring or appearance of tortoiseshell. **2** made of tortoiseshell or a synthetic substitute.

tortoiseshell butterfly *n.* any of various butterflies of the genus *Aglais* or *Nymphalis* with wings mottled like tortoiseshell.

tortoiseshell cat *n.* a domestic cat with markings resembling tortoiseshell.

tortrix /ˈtɔːtrɪks/ *n.* any moth of the family Tortricidae, esp. *Tortrix viridana*, the larvae of which live inside rolled leaves. [modern Latin, fem. of Latin *tortor* 'twister': see TORT]

tortuous /ˈtɔːtʃʊəs, -jʊəs/ *adj.* **1** full of twists and turns (*followed a tortuous route*). **2** devious, circuitous, crooked (*has a tortuous mind*). □ **tortuosity** /-ˈɒsɪti/ *n.* (*pl.* **-ies**). **tortuously** *adv.* **tortuousness** *n.* [Middle English via Old French from Latin *tortuosus*, from *tortus* 'a twist' (as TORT)]

■ **Usage** *Tortuous*, meaning 'full of twists and turns; devious, crooked' should not be confused with *torturous* meaning 'involving torture, excruciating'.

torture /ˈtɔːtʃə/ *n. & v.* ● *n.* **1** the infliction of severe bodily pain esp. as a punishment or a means of persuasion. **2** severe physical or mental suffering (*the torture of defeat*). ● *v.tr.* **1** subject to physical or mental torture. **2** force out of a natural position or state; deform; pervert. □ **torturable** *adj.* **torturer** *n.* **torturous** *adj.* **torturously** *adv.* [French from Late Latin *tortura* 'twisting' (as TORT)]

■ **Usage** See Usage Note at TORTUOUS.

torula /ˈtɒruːlə, -(j)ʊlə/ *n.* (*pl.* **torulae** /-liː/) **1** a yeast, *Candida utilis*, used medicinally and as a food additive. **2** a yeastlike fungus of the genus *Torula*, growing on dead vegetation. [modern Latin, diminutive of TORUS]

torus /ˈtɔːrəs/ *n.* (*pl.* **tori** /-rʌɪ/ or **toruses**) **1** *Geom.* a surface or solid formed by rotating a closed curve, esp. a circle, about a line in its plane but not intersecting it (e.g. like a ring doughnut). **2** a thing of this shape, esp. a large ring-shaped chamber used in physical research. **3** *Archit.* a large convex moulding, usu. semicircular in cross-section, esp. as the lowest part of the base of a column. **4** *Anat.* a smooth ridge of bone or muscle. **5** *Bot.* the receptacle of a flower. [Latin, = swelling, bulge, cushion, etc.]

Tory /ˈtɔːri/ *n. & adj.* ● *n.* (*pl.* **-ies**) **1** esp. *Brit. colloq.* = CONSERVATIVE *n.* 2. **2** *hist.* (in England) a member of the party that opposed the exclusion of James II and later supported the established religious and political order and gave rise to the Conservative Party (opp. WHIG). **3** *US hist.* a loyal colonist during the American Revolution. ● *adj. colloq.* = CONSERVATIVE *adj.* 3. □ **Toryism** *n.* [originally = Irish outlaw: probably Irish *toraidhe* from *tóir* 'pursue']

tosa /ˈtəʊsə/ *n.* a dog of a breed of mastiff originally kept for dogfighting. [*Tosa*, a former province in Japan]

tosh[1] /tɒʃ/ *n. Brit. colloq.* rubbish, nonsense. [19th c.: origin unknown]

tosh[2] /tɒʃ/ *n. slang* a casual form of address, esp. to an unknown person. [20th c.: origin unknown]

toss /tɒs/ *v. & n.* ● *v.* **1** *tr.* throw up (a ball etc.), esp. with the hand. **2** *tr. & intr.* roll about, throw, or be thrown, restlessly or from side to side (*the ship tossed on the ocean*; *was tossing and turning all night*). **3** *tr.* (usu. foll. by *to*, *away*, *aside*, *out*, etc.) throw (a thing) lightly or carelessly (*tossed the letter away*). **4** *tr.* **a** throw (a coin) into the air to decide a choice etc. by the side on which it lands. **b** (also *absol.*; often foll. by *for*) settle a question or dispute with (a person) in this way (*tossed him for the armchair*; *tossed for it*). **5** *tr.* **a** (of a bull etc.) throw (a person etc.) up with the horns. **b** (of a horse etc.) throw (a rider) off its back. **6** *tr.* coat (food) with dressing etc. by shaking. **7** *tr.* bandy about in debate; discuss (*tossed the question back and forth*). ● *n.* **1** the act or an instance of tossing (a coin, the head, etc.). **2** *Brit.* a fall, esp. from a horse. □ **toss one's head** throw it back esp. in anger, impatience, etc. **tossing the caber** the Scottish sport of throwing a tree trunk. **toss oars** raise oars to an upright position in salute. **toss off 1** drink off at a draught. **2** dispatch (work) rapidly or without effort (*tossed off an omelette*). **3** *Brit. coarse slang* masturbate. **toss a pancake** throw it up so that it flips on to the other side in the frying pan. **toss up** toss a coin to decide a choice etc. [16th c.: origin unknown]

tosser /ˈtɒsə/ *n.* **1** *Brit. coarse slang* an unpleasant or contemptible person. **2** a person or thing that tosses.

toss-up *n.* **1** a doubtful matter; a close thing (*it's a toss-up whether he wins*). **2** the tossing of a coin.

tot[1] /tɒt/ *n.* **1** a small child (*a tiny tot*). **2** *Brit.* a dram of liquor. [18th c., of dialect origin]

tot[2] /tɒt/ *v. & n.* ● *v.* (**totted**, **totting**) esp. *Brit.* **1** *tr.* (usu. foll. by *up*) add (figures etc.). **2** *intr.* (foll. by *up*) (of items) mount up. ● *n. Brit. archaic* a set of figures to be added. □ **tot up to** amount to. [abbreviation of TOTAL or of Latin *totum* 'the whole']

tot[3] /tɒt/ *v. & n. Brit. slang* ● *v.intr.* (**totted**, **totting**) collect saleable items from refuse as an occupation. ● *n.* an article collected from refuse. □ **totter** *n.* [19th c.: origin unknown]

total /ˈtəʊt(ə)l/ *adj., n., & v.* ● *adj.* **1** complete, comprising the whole (*the total number of people*). **2** absolute, unqualified (*in total ignorance*; *total abstinence*). ● *n.* a total number or amount. ● *v.* (**totalled**, **totalling**; *US* **totaled**, **totaling**) **1** *tr.* **a** amount in number to (*they totalled 131*). **b** find the total of (things, a set of figures, etc.). **2** *intr.* (foll. by *to*, *up to*) amount to, mount up to. **3** *tr. N. Amer. slang* wreck (a car etc.) completely. □ **totally** *adv.* [Middle English via Old French from medieval Latin *totalis*, from *totus* 'entire']

total abstinence *n.* abstaining completely from alcohol.

total eclipse *n.* an eclipse in which the whole disc (of the sun, moon, etc.) is obscured.

total internal reflection *n.* reflection without refraction of a light ray meeting the interface between two media at more than a certain critical angle to the normal.

totalitarian /ˌtəʊtalɪˈtɛːrɪən, tə(ʊ)ˌtalɪ-/ *adj. & n.* ● *adj.* of or relating to a centralized dictatorial form of government requiring complete subservience to the State. ● *n.* a person advocating such a system. □ **totalitarianism** *n.*

totality /tə(ʊ)ˈtalɪti/ *n.* **1** the complete amount or sum. **2** *Astron.* the time during which an eclipse is total.

totalizator /ˈtəʊt(ə)lʌɪzeɪtə/ *n.* (also **totalisator**) **1** a device showing the number and amount of bets staked on a race, to facilitate the division of the total among those backing the winner. **2** a system of betting based on this.

totalize /ˈtəʊt(ə)lʌɪz/ *v.tr.* (also **-ise**) collect into a total; find the total of. □ **totalization** /-ˈzeɪʃ(ə)n/ *n.*

totalizer /ˈtəʊt(ə)lʌɪzə/ *n.* = TOTALIZATOR.

Total Quality Management *n.* (in industry) a systematic approach to improving the quality of products and customer service etc., while reducing costs.

total recall *n.* the ability to remember every detail of one's experience clearly.

total war *n.* a war in which all available weapons and resources are employed.

tote[1] /təʊt/ *n. colloq.* **1** a totalizator. **2** *Brit.*, *Austral.*, & *NZ* a lottery. [abbreviation]

tote[2] /təʊt/ *v.tr.* esp. *N. Amer. colloq.* carry, convey, or wield, (esp. a heavy load) (*toting a gun*). □ **toter** *n.* (also in *comb.*). [17th-c. US, probably of dialect origin]

tote bag *n.* a large bag for shopping etc.

tote box *n. N. Amer.* a small container for goods.

totem /ˈtəʊtəm/ *n.* **1** a natural object, esp. an animal, adopted among some tribal peoples as an emblem of a clan or an individual. **2** an image of this. ▫ **totemic** /-ˈtɛmɪk/ *adj.* **totemism** *n.* **totemist** *n.* **totemistic** /-ˈmɪstɪk/ *adj.* [Algonquian]

totem pole *n.* **1** a pole on which totems are carved or hung. **2** a hierarchy.

tother /ˈtʌðə/ *adj. & pron.* (also **t'other**) *dial.* or *joc.* the other. ▫ **tell tother from which** *Brit. joc.* tell one from the other. [Middle English *the tother*, for earlier *thet other* = *the other* (*thet* obsolete neut. of *the*]

totter /ˈtɒtə/ *v. & n.* ● *v.intr.* **1** stand or walk unsteadily or feebly (*tottered out of the pub*). **2 a** (of a building etc.) shake or rock as if about to collapse. **b** (of a system of government etc.) be about to fall. ● *n.* an unsteady or shaky movement or gait. ▫ **totterer** *n.* **tottery** *adj.* [Middle English from Middle Dutch *touteren* 'to swing']

totting-up *n.* **1** the adding of separate items. **2** *Brit.* the adding of convictions for driving offences to cause disqualification.

toucan /ˈtuːk(ə)n/ *n.* a tropical American fruit-eating bird of the family Ramphastidae, with an immense beak and often brightly coloured plumage. [Tupi *tucana*, Guarani *tucã*]

touch /tʌtʃ/ *v. & n.* ● *v.* **1** *tr.* come into or be in physical contact with (another thing) at one or more points. **2** *tr.* (often foll. by *with*) bring the hand etc. into contact with (*touched her arm*). **3 a** *intr.* (of two things etc.) be in or come into contact with one another (*the balls were touching*). **b** *tr.* bring (two things) into mutual contact (*they touched hands*). **4** *tr.* rouse tender or painful feelings in (*was touched by his appeal*). **5** *tr.* strike lightly (*just touched the wall with the back bumper*). **6** *tr.* (usu. with *neg.*) **a** disturb or interfere with (*don't touch my things*). **b** have any dealings with (*won't touch bricklaying*). **c** consume; use up; make use of (*dare not touch alcohol*; *has not touched her breakfast*; *need not touch your savings*). **d** cope with; affect; manage (*soap won't touch this dirt*). **7** *tr.* **a** deal with (a subject) lightly or in passing (*touched the matter of their expenses*). **b** concern (*it touches you closely*). **8** *tr.* **a** reach or rise as far as, esp. momentarily (*the thermometer touched 90°*). **b** (usu. with *neg.*) approach in excellence etc. (*can't touch him for style*). **9** *tr.* affect slightly; modify (*pity touched with fear*). **10** *tr.* (as **touched** *adj.*) *colloq.* slightly mad. **11** *tr.* (often foll. by *in*) esp. *Art* mark lightly, put in (features etc.) with a brush, pencil, etc. **12** *tr.* **a** strike (the keys, strings, etc., of a musical instrument). **b** strike the keys or strings of (a piano etc.). **13** *tr.* (usu. foll. by *for*) *slang* ask for and get money etc. from (a person) as a loan or gift (*touched him for £5*). **14** *tr.* injure slightly (*blossom touched by frost*). **15** *tr. Geom.* be tangent to (a curve). ● *n.* **1** the act or an instance of touching, esp. with the body or hand (*felt a touch on my arm*). **2 a** the faculty of perception through physical contact, esp. with the fingers (*has no sense of touch in her right arm*). **b** the qualities of an object etc. as perceived in this way (*the soft touch of silk*). **3** a small amount; a slight trace (*a touch of salt*; *a touch of irony*). **4 a** a musician's manner of playing keys or strings. **b** the manner in which the keys or strings respond to touch. **c** an artist's or writer's style of workmanship, writing, etc. (*has a delicate touch*). **5 a** a distinguishing quality or trait (*a rather amateur touch*). **b** a special skill or proficiency (*have lost my touch*). **6** (esp. in *pl.*) **a** a light stroke with a pen, pencil, etc. **b** a slight alteration or improvement (*speech needs a few touches*). **7** = TAG² 1. **8** (prec. by *a*) slightly (*is a touch too arrogant*). **9** *slang* **a** the act of asking for and getting money etc. from a person. **b** a person from whom money etc. is so obtained. **10** *Football* the part of the field outside the side limits. **11** *archaic* a test with or as if with a touchstone (*put it to the touch*). ▫ **at a touch** if touched, however lightly (*opened at a touch*). **get** (or **put**) **in** (or **into**) **touch with** come or cause to come into communication with; contact. **in touch** (often foll. by *with*) **1** in communication (*we're still in touch after all these years*). **2** up to date, esp. regarding news etc. (*keeps in touch with events*). **3** aware, conscious, empathetic (*not in touch with her own feelings*). **keep in touch** (often foll. by *with*) **1** remain informed (*kept in touch with the latest developments*). **2** continue correspondence, a friendship, etc. **lose touch** (often foll. by *with*) **1** cease to be informed. **2** cease to correspond with or be in contact with another person. **lose one's touch** not show one's customary skill. **out of touch** (often foll. by *with*) **1** not in correspondence. **2** not up to date or modern. **3** lacking in awareness or sympathy (*out of touch with his son's beliefs*). **to the touch** when touched (*was cold to the touch*). **touch at** (of a ship) call at (a port etc.). **touch base** see BASE¹. **touch bottom 1** reach the bottom of water with one's feet. **2** be at the lowest or worst point. **3** *Brit.* be in possession of the full facts. **touch down 1 a** *Rugby* touch the ground with the ball behind one's own or esp. the opponents' goal line. **b** *Amer. Football* score by being in possession of the ball behind the opponents' goal line. **2** (of an aircraft or spacecraft) make contact with the ground in landing. **touch off 1** represent exactly (in a portrait etc.). **2** explode by touching with a match etc. **3** initiate (a process) suddenly (*touched off a run on the pound*). **touch on** (or **upon**) **1** treat (a subject) briefly, refer to or mention casually. **2** verge on (*that touches on impudence*). **touch up 1** give finishing touches to or retouch (a picture, writing, etc.). **2** *Brit. slang* **a** caress so as to excite sexually. **b** sexually molest. **3** strike (a horse) lightly with a whip. **touch wood** esp. *Brit.* touch something wooden with the hand to avert ill luck. **would not touch with a bargepole** see BARGEPOLE. ▫ **touchable** *adj.* [Middle English from Old French *tochier*, *tuchier* (*v.*), *touche* (*n.*): probably imitative: cf. Provençal *toc*, Italian *tocco* 'a knock']

touch-and-go *adj.* uncertain regarding a result; risky (*it was touch-and-go whether we'd catch the train*).

touchback /ˈtʌtʃbak/ *n. Amer. Football* a touchdown behind one's own goal.

touchdown /ˈtʌtʃdaʊn/ *n.* **1** the act or an instance of an aircraft or spacecraft making contact with the ground during landing. **2** *Rugby* & *Amer. Football* the act or an instance of touching down.

touché /tuːˈʃeɪ/ *int.* **1** the acknowledgement of a hit by a fencing opponent. **2** the acknowledgement of a justified accusation, a witticism, or a point made in reply to one's own. [French, past part. of *toucher* TOUCH]

toucher /ˈtʌtʃə/ *n.* **1** a person or thing that touches. **2** *Bowls* a wood that touches the jack.

touch football *n.* a form of American football with touching in place of tackling.

touch-hole *n.* a small hole in a gun for igniting the charge.

touching /ˈtʌtʃɪŋ/ *adj. & prep.* ● *adj.* moving; pathetic (*a touching incident*; *touching confidence*). ● *prep. literary* concerning; about. ▫ **touchingly** *adv.* **touchingness** *n.* [Middle English from TOUCH: the preposition from Old French *touchant*, pres. part. (as TOUCH)]

touch-in-goal *n. Rugby* each of the four corners enclosed by continuations of the touchlines and goal lines.

touch judge *n. Rugby* a linesman.

touchline /ˈtʌtʃlʌɪn/ *n.* (in various sports) either of the lines marking the side boundaries of the pitch.

touch-mark *n.* the maker's mark on pewter.

touch-me-not *n.* any of various plants of the genus *Impatiens*, with ripe seed capsules jerking open when touched.

touch-needle *n.* a needle of gold or silver alloy of known composition used as a standard in testing other alloys on a touchstone.

touch of nature *n.* **1** a natural trait. **2** *colloq.* an exhibition of human feeling with which others sympathize (from a misinterpretation of Shakespeare's *Troilus and Cressida* III. iii. 169).

touch of the sun *n.* **1** a slight attack of sunstroke. **2** a little sunlight.

touchpaper /'tʌtʃpeɪpə/ *n.* paper impregnated with nitre, for firing gunpowder, fireworks, etc.

touch screen *n.* a VDU screen that displays data, esp. information to customers, when it is touched.

touchstone /'tʌtʃstəʊn/ *n.* **1** a fine-grained dark schist or jasper used for testing alloys of gold etc. by observing the colour of the mark which they make on it. **2** a standard or criterion.

touch-type *v.tr. & intr.* type without looking at the keys. □ **touch-typing** *n.* **touch-typist** *n.*

touch-up *n.* a quick restoration or improvement (of paintwork, a piece of writing, etc.).

touchwood /'tʌtʃwʊd/ *n.* readily inflammable wood, esp. when made soft by fungi, used as tinder.

touchy /'tʌtʃi/ *adj.* (**touchier**, **touchiest**) **1** apt to take offence; oversensitive. **2** delicate; requiring careful handling (*a touchy subject*). □ **touchily** *adv.* **touchiness** *n.* [perhaps alteration of TETCHY, influenced by TOUCH]

tough /tʌf/ *adj. & n.* ● *adj.* **1** hard to break, cut, tear, or chew; durable; strong. **2** (of a person) able to endure hardship; hardy. **3** unyielding, stubborn, difficult (*it was a tough job*; *a tough customer*). **4** *colloq.* **a** acting sternly; hard (*get tough with*). **b** (of circumstances, luck, etc.) severe, unpleasant, hard, unjust. **5** *colloq.* criminal or violent (*tough guys*). ● *n.* a tough person, esp. a ruffian or criminal. □ **tough it** (or **tough it out**) *colloq.* endure or withstand difficult conditions. **tough shit** (or **titty**) esp. *N. Amer. slang* tough luck. □ **toughen** *v.tr. & intr.* **toughener** *n.* **toughish** *adj.* **toughly** *adv.* **toughness** *n.* [Old English *tōh*]

tough guy *n. colloq.* **1** a hard unyielding person. **2** a violent aggressive person.

toughie /'tʌfi/ *n. colloq.* a tough person or problem.

tough-minded *adj.* realistic, not sentimental. □ **tough-mindedness** *n.*

toupee /'tu:peɪ/ *n.* (also **toupet** /'tu:peɪ, 'tu:pɪt/) a wig or artificial hairpiece to cover a bald spot. [French *toupet* 'hair-tuft', diminutive of Old French *toup* 'tuft' (as TOP[1])]

tour /tʊə/ *n. & v.* ● *n.* **1 a** a journey from place to place, esp. as a holiday. **b** an excursion, ramble, or walk (*made a tour of the garden*). **2 a** a spell of duty on military or diplomatic service. **b** the time to be spent at a particular post. **3** a series of performances, matches, etc., at different places on a route through a country etc. ● *v.* **1** *intr.* (usu. foll. by *through*) make a tour (*toured through India*). **2** *tr.* make a tour of (a country etc.). □ **on tour** (esp. of a team, theatre company, etc.) touring. [Middle English via Old French *to(u)r* and Latin *tornus* from Greek *tornos* 'lathe']

touraco var. of TURACO.

tour de force /tʊə də 'fɔ:s/ *n.* (*pl.* **tours de force** *pronunc.* same) a feat of strength or skill. [French]

tourer /'tʊərə/ *n.* a vehicle, esp. a car, for touring.

Tourette's syndrome /tʊ'rɛts/ *n. Med.* a neurological disorder characterized by involuntary tics and vocalizations and the compulsive utterance of obscenities. [named after G. de la *Tourette*, French neurologist d. 1904]

touring car *n.* a car with room for passengers and much luggage.

tourism /'tʊərɪz(ə)m/ *n.* the organization and operation of (esp. foreign) holidays, esp. as a commercial enterprise.

tourist /'tʊərɪst/ *n. & v.* ● *n.* **1** a person making a visit or tour as a holiday; a traveller, esp. abroad (often *attrib.*: *tourist accommodation*). **2** a member of a touring sports team. ● *v.tr.* (as **touristed** *adj.*) frequented by tourists. □ **touristic** /-'rɪstɪk/ *adj.* **touristically** /-'rɪstɪk(ə)li/ *adv.*

tourist class *n.* the lowest class of passenger accommodation in a ship, aircraft, etc.

touristy /'tʊərɪsti/ *adj.* usu. *derog.* appealing to or visited by many tourists.

tourmaline /'tʊəməlɪn, -i:n/ *n.* a boron aluminium silicate mineral of various colours, possessing unusual electrical properties, and used in electrical and optical instruments and as a gemstone. [French, from Sinhalese *toramalli* 'porcelain']

tournament /'tʊənəm(ə)nt/ *n.* **1** any contest of skill between a number of competitors, esp. played in heats (*chess tournament*; *tennis tournament*). **2** a display of military exercises etc. (*Royal Tournament*). **3** *hist.* **a** a pageant in which jousting with blunted weapons took place. **b** a meeting for jousting between single knights for a prize etc. [Middle English from Old French *torneiement*, from *torneier* TOURNEY]

tournedos /'tʊənədəʊ/ *n.* (*pl.* same /-dəʊz/) a small round thick cut from a fillet of beef. [French, from *tourner* 'to turn' + *dos* 'back']

tourney /'tʊəni, 'tə:ni/ *n. & v.* ● *n.* (*pl.* **-eys**) a tournament. ● *v.intr.* (**-eys**, **-eyed**) take part in a tournament. [Middle English from Old French *tornei* (*n.*), *torneier* (*v.*), ultimately from Latin *tornus* 'a turn']

tourniquet /'tʊənɪkeɪ, 'tɔ:-/ *n.* a device for stopping the flow of blood through an artery by twisting a bar etc. in a ligature or bandage. [French, probably from Old French *tournicle* 'coat of mail, TUNICLE', influenced by *tourner* TURN]

tour operator *n.* a travel agent specializing in package holidays.

tousle /'taʊz(ə)l/ *v.tr.* **1** make (esp. the hair) untidy; rumple. **2** handle roughly or rudely. [frequentative of (now dialect) *touse*, Middle English from Old English, related to Old High German *zirzuson*, *erzūsen* 'tear to pieces']

tousle-haired *adj.* having untidy hair.

tous-les-mois /tu:leɪ'mwɑ:, French tulɛmwa/ *n.* **1** food starch obtained from tubers of a canna, *Canna indica*. **2** this plant. [French, literally 'every month', probably a corruption of West Indian *toloman*]

tout /taʊt/ *v. & n.* ● *v.* **1** *intr.* (usu. foll. by *for*) solicit custom persistently; pester customers (*touting for business*). **2** *tr.* solicit the custom of (a person) or for (a thing). **3** *intr.* **a** *Brit.* spy out the movements and condition of racehorses in training. **b** *US* offer racing tips for a share of the resulting profit. ● *n.* **1** a person employed in touting. **2** = TICKET TOUT. □ **touter** *n.* [Middle English *tūte* 'look out' = Middle English (now dialect) *toot* (Old English *tōtian*) from Germanic]

tout court /tu: 'kʊə, French tu kur/ *adv.* without addition; simply (*called James tout court*). [French, literally 'very short']

tout de suite /tu:t 'swi:t, French tud sɥit/ *adv.* immediately; at once. [French]

tovarish /tɒ'vɑ:rɪʃ/ *n.* (also **tovarich**) (in the former USSR) comrade (esp. as a form of address). [Russian *tovarishch*]

tow[1] /təʊ/ *v. & n.* ● *v.tr.* **1** (of a motor vehicle, horse, or person controlling it) pull (a boat, another motor vehicle, a caravan, etc.) along by a rope, tow bar, etc. **2** pull (a person or thing) along behind one. ● *n.* the act or an instance of towing; the state of being towed. □ **have in** (or **on**) **tow 1** be towing. **2** be accompanied by and often in charge of (a person). □ **towable** *adj.* **towage** /-ɪdʒ/ *n.* [Old English *togian* from Germanic: related to TUG]

tow[2] /təʊ/ *n.* **1** the coarse and broken part of flax or hemp prepared for spinning. **2** a loose bunch of rayon etc. strands. □ **towy** /'təʊi/ *adj.* [Old English, related to Middle Low German *touw* from Old Saxon *tou*, related to Old Norse *tó* 'wool']

toward *prep. & adj.* ● *prep.* /tə'wɔ:d, twɔ:d, tɔ:d/ = TOWARDS. ● *adj.* /'təʊəd/ *archaic* **1** about to take place; in process. **2** docile, apt. **3** promising, auspicious.

towards /tə'wɔ:dz, twɔ:dz, 'tɔ:dz/ *prep.* **1** in the direction of (*set out towards town*). **2** as regards; in relation to (*his attitude towards death*). **3** as a contribution to; for (*put this towards your expenses*). **4** near (*towards the end* *of our journey*). [Old English *tōweard* (*adj.*) 'future' (as TO, -WARD)]

tow bar *n.* a bar for towing esp. a trailer or caravan.

tow-coloured *adj.* (of hair) very light in colour.

towel /'taʊəl/ *n.* & *v.* ● *n.* **1 a** a piece of rough-surfaced absorbent cloth used for drying oneself or a thing after washing. **b** absorbent paper etc. used for this. **c** a cloth used for drying plates, dishes, etc.; a tea towel. **2** *Brit.* = SANITARY TOWEL. ● *v.* (**towelled**, **towelling**; *US* **toweled**, **toweling**) **1** *tr.* (often *refl.*) wipe or dry with a towel. **2** *intr.* wipe or dry oneself with a towel. **3** *tr. Brit. slang* thrash. □ **towelling** *n.* [Middle English from Old French *toail(l)e*, from Germanic]

towel-horse *n.* a wooden frame for hanging towels on.

towel rail *n.* a rail, esp. in a bathroom, for hanging towels on.

tower /'taʊə/ *n.* & *v.* ● *n.* **1 a** a tall esp. square or circular structure, often part of a church, castle, etc. **b** a fortress etc. comprising or including a tower. **c** a tall structure housing machinery, apparatus, operators, etc. (*cooling tower*; *control tower*). **2** a place of defence; a protection. ● *v.intr.* **1** (usu. foll. by *above*, *high*) reach or be high or above; be superior. **2** (of a bird, esp. a falcon) soar or hover. **3** (as **towering** *adj.*) **a** high, lofty (*towering intellect*). **b** violent (*towering rage*). □ **towered** /'taʊəd/ *adj.* **towery** *adj.* [Old English *torr*, reinforced in Middle English by Anglo-French & Old French *tur* etc., via Latin *turris* from Greek]

tower block *n. Brit.* a tall building containing offices or flats.

Tower of Babel *n.* a visionary or unrealistic plan. [Gen. 11: 1–9]

tower of silence *n.* a tall open-topped structure on which Parsees place their dead.

tower of strength *n.* a person who gives strong and reliable support.

tow-headed *adj.* having very light-coloured or unkempt hair. □ **tow-head** *n.*

towhee /'taʊ(h)iː, 'taʊ-/ *n. N. Amer.* any of several buntings of the genus *Pipilo*, of brush and woodland in N. America. [imitative of its call]

towing-path var. of TOWPATH.

towing-rope var. of TOW ROPE.

towline /'təʊlʌɪn/ *n.* = TOW ROPE.

town /taʊn/ *n.* **1 a** an urban area with a name, defined boundaries, and local government, being larger than a village and usu. not created a city. **b** any densely populated area, esp. as opposed to the country or suburbs. **c** the people of a town (*the whole town knows of it*). **2 a** *Brit.* London or the chief city or town in one's neighbourhood (*went up to town*). **b** the central business or shopping area in a neighbourhood (*just going into town*). **3** the permanent residents of a university town as distinct from the members of the university (cf. GOWN 4). **4** *N. Amer.* = TOWNSHIP 2. □ **go to town** *colloq.* act or work with energy or enthusiasm. **on the town** *colloq.* enjoying the entertainments, esp. the nightlife, of a town; celebrating. □ **townish** *adj.* **townless** *adj.* **townlet** *n.* **townward** *adj.* & *adv.* **townwards** *adv.* [Old English *tūn* 'enclosure', from Germanic]

town clerk *n.* **1** *US* & *hist.* the officer of the corporation of a town in charge of records etc. **2** *Brit. hist.* the secretary and legal adviser of a town corporation until 1974.

town council *n.* (esp. in the UK) the elective governing body in a municipality. □ **town councillor** *n.*

town crier *n. hist.* an officer employed by a town council etc. to make public announcements in the streets or market place.

townee var. of TOWNIE.

tow-net *n.* (also **towing-net**) a net used for dragging through water to collect specimens.

town gas *n. Brit.* manufactured gas for domestic and commercial use.

town hall *n.* a building for the administration of local government, having public meeting rooms etc.

town house *n.* **1** a town residence, esp. of a person with a house in the country. **2** a terrace house, esp. of a stylish modern type. **3** a house in a planned group in a town. **4** *Brit.* a town hall.

townie /'taʊni/ *n.* (also **townee**) *derog.* a person living in a town, esp. as opposed to a country dweller or member of a university.

town-major *n. hist.* the chief executive officer in a garrison town or fortress.

town mayor *n. Brit.* the chairman of a town council.

town meeting *n. US* a meeting of the voters of a town for the transaction of public business.

town planning *n.* the planning of the construction and growth of towns. □ **town planner** *n.*

townscape /'taʊnskeɪp/ *n.* **1** the visual appearance of a town or towns. **2** a picture of a town.

townsfolk /'taʊnzfəʊk/ *n.* (treated as *pl.*) the inhabitants of a particular town or towns.

township /'taʊnʃɪp/ *n.* **1** *S.Afr.* **a** *hist.* an urban area set aside for black occupation. **b** (usu. in phr. **proclaim a new township**) a new area being developed by speculators. **2** *N. Amer.* **a** a division of a county with some corporate powers. **b** a district six miles square. **3** *Brit. hist.* **a** a community inhabiting a manor, parish, etc. **b** a manor or parish as a territorial division. **c** a small town or village forming part of a large parish. **4** *Austral.* & *NZ* a small town; a town site. [Old English *tūnscipe* (as TOWN, -SHIP)]

townsman /'taʊnzmən/ *n.* (*pl.* **-men**; *fem.* **townswoman**, *pl.* **-women**) an inhabitant of a town; a fellow citizen.

townspeople /'taʊnzpiːp(ə)l/ *n.pl.* the people of a town.

towpath /'təʊpɑːθ/ *n.* (also **towing-path**) a path beside a river or canal, originally used for towing barges by horse.

towplane /'təʊpleɪn/ *n.* an aircraft that tows gliders.

tow rope *n.* (also **towing-rope**) a line etc. used in towing.

towy see TOW².

toxaemia /tɒk'siːmɪə/ *n.* (*US* **toxemia**) **1** blood poisoning. **2** a condition in pregnancy characterized by increased blood pressure. □ **toxaemic** *adj.* [as TOXI- + -AEMIA]

toxi- /tɒksi/ *comb. form* (also **toxico-** /'tɒksɪkəʊ/, **toxo-** /'tɒksəʊ/) poison; poisonous, toxic.

toxic /'tɒksɪk/ *adj.* & *n.* ● *adj.* **1** of or relating to poison (*toxic symptoms*). **2** poisonous (*toxic gas*). **3** caused by poison (*toxic anaemia*). ● *n.* (in *pl.*) toxic substances. □ **toxically** *adv.* **toxicity** /-'sɪsɪti/ *n.* [medieval Latin *toxicus* 'poisoned' via Latin *toxicum* from Greek *toxikon* (*pharmakon*) '(poison for) arrows', from *toxon* 'bow', *toxa* 'arrows']

toxicant /'tɒksɪk(ə)nt/ *n.* a toxic substance, esp. one used as a pesticide etc.

toxicology /tɒksɪ'kɒlədʒi/ *n.* the scientific study of poisons. □ **toxicological** /-kə'lɒdʒɪk(ə)l/ *adj.* **toxicologist** *n.*

toxic shock syndrome *n. Med.* acute septicaemia in women, typically caused by bacterial infection from a retained tampon, IUD, etc. (abbr.: **TSS**).

toxin /'tɒksɪn/ *n.* a poison produced by a living organism, esp. one formed in the body and stimulating the production of antibodies. [TOXIC + -IN]

toxocara /tɒksə'kɑːrə/ *n.* any nematode worm of the genus *Toxocara*, esp. a common roundworm found in dogs or cats and transmissible to humans. □ **toxocariasis** /-kə'rʌɪəsɪs/ *n.* [TOXO- (see TOXI-) + Greek *kara* 'head']

toxophilite /tɒk'sɒfɪlʌɪt/ *n.* & *adj.* ● *n.* a student or lover of archery. ● *adj.* of or concerning archery. □ **toxophily** *n.* [Ascham's book *Toxophilus* (1545), from Greek *toxon* 'bow' + *-philos* -PHILE]

toxoplasmosis /ˌtɒksəʊplaz'məʊsɪs/ *n. Med.* a disease caused by infection with the sporozoan *Toxoplasma gondii*, transmitted esp. through poorly prepared food or in cat faeces and dangerous in unborn children. [TOXO- (see TOXI-) + PLASMA + -OSIS]

toy /tɔɪ/ *n. & v.* ● *n.* **1 a** a plaything, esp. for a child. **b** (often *attrib.*) a model or miniature replica of a thing, esp. as a plaything (*toy gun*). **2 a** a thing, esp. a gadget or instrument, regarded as providing amusement. **b** a task or undertaking regarded in an unserious way. **3** (usu. *attrib.*) a diminutive breed or variety of dog etc. ● *v.intr.* (usu. foll. by *with*) **1** trifle, amuse oneself, esp. with a person's affections; flirt (*toyed with the idea of going to Africa*). **2 a** move a material object idly (*toyed with her necklace*). **b** nibble at food etc. unenthusiastically (*toyed with a peach*). □ **toylike** *adj.* [Middle English: origin unknown]

toy-box *n.* a usu. wooden box for keeping toys in.

toyboy /ˈtɔɪbɔɪ/ *n. Brit. colloq.* a woman's much younger male lover.

toymaker /ˈtɔɪmeɪkə/ *n.* a maker or manufacturer of toys.

toyshop /ˈtɔɪʃɒp/ *n.* a shop which sells toys.

toy soldier *n.* **1** a miniature figure of a soldier. **2** *colloq.* a soldier in a peacetime army.

toytown /ˈtɔɪtaʊn/ *n.* (usu. *attrib.*) **1** resembling a model of a town; seemingly diminutive. **2** quaint, lightweight.

Tpr. *abbr.* Trooper.

TQM *abbr.* Total Quality Management.

trabeation /treɪbrˈeɪʃ(ə)n/ *n.* the use of beams instead of arches or vaulting in construction. □ **trabeate** /ˈtreɪbɪət/ *adj.* [Latin *trabs trabis* 'beam']

trabecula /trəˈbɛkjʊlə/ *n.* (*pl.* **trabeculae** /-liː/) **1** *Anat.* a supporting band or bar of connective or bony tissue, esp. dividing an organ into chambers. **2** *Bot.* a beamlike projection or process within a hollow structure. □ **trabecular** *adj.* **trabeculate** /-lət/ *adj.* [Latin, diminutive of *trabs* 'beam']

tracasserie /trəˈkas(ə)ri/ *n.* **1** a state of annoyance. **2** a fuss; a petty quarrel. [French from *tracasser* 'bustle']

trace[1] /treɪs/ *v. & n.* ● *v.tr.* **1 a** observe, discover, or find vestiges or signs of by investigation. **b** (often foll. by *along, through, to,* etc.) follow or mark the track or position of (*traced their footprints in the mud; traced the outlines of a wall*). **c** (often foll. by *back*) follow to its origins (*can trace my family to the 12th century; the report has been traced back to you*). **2** (often foll. by *over*) copy (a drawing etc.) by drawing over its lines on a superimposed piece of translucent paper, or by using carbon paper. **3** (often foll. by *out*) mark out, delineate, sketch, or write esp. laboriously (*traced out a plan of the district; traced out his vision of the future*). **4** pursue one's way along (a path etc.). ● *n.* **1 a** a sign or mark or other indication of something having existed; a vestige (*no trace remains of the castle; has the traces of a vanished beauty*). **b** a very small quantity. **c** an amount of rainfall etc. too small to be measured. **2** a track or footprint left by a person or animal. **3** a track left by the moving pen of an instrument etc. **4** a line on the screen of a cathode ray tube showing the path of a moving spot. **5** a curve's projection on or intersection with a plane etc. **6** a change in the brain caused by learning processes. □ **traceable** *adj.* **traceability** /-ˈbɪlɪti/ *n.* **traceless** *adj.* [Middle English via Old French *trace* (*n.*), *tracier* (*v.*) from Latin *tractus* 'drawing': see TRACT[1]]

trace[2] /treɪs/ *n.* each of the two side straps, chains, or ropes by which a horse draws a vehicle. □ **kick over the traces** become insubordinate or reckless. [Middle English from Old French *trais*, pl. of TRAIT]

trace element *n.* **1** a chemical element occurring in minute amounts. **2** a chemical element required only in minute amounts by living organisms for normal growth.

trace fossil *n.* a fossil that represents a burrow, footprint, etc., of an organism.

trace-horse *n.* a horse that draws in traces or by a single trace, esp. one hitched on to help uphill etc.

tracer /ˈtreɪsə/ *n.* **1** a person or thing that traces. **2** *Mil.* **a** a bullet etc. whose course is made visible in flight because of flames etc. emitted. **b** such bullets etc. collectively, used to assist in aiming. **3** an artificially produced radioactive isotope capable of being followed through the body by the radiation it produces.

tracery /ˈtreɪs(ə)ri/ *n.* (*pl.* **-ies**) **1** ornamental stone openwork esp. in the upper part of a Gothic window. **2** a fine decorative pattern. **3** a natural object finely patterned. □ **traceried** *adj.*

trachea /trəˈkiːə, ˈtreɪkɪə/ *n.* (*pl.* **tracheae** /-ˈkiːiː/ or **tracheas**) **1** the passage reinforced by rings of cartilage, through which air reaches the bronchial tubes from the larynx; the windpipe. **2** each of the air passages in the body of an insect etc. **3** any duct or vessel in a plant. □ **tracheal** /ˈtreɪkɪəl/ *adj.* **tracheate** /ˈtreɪkɪeɪt/ *adj.* [Middle English from medieval Latin, = Late Latin *trachia* from Greek *trakheia* (*artēria*) 'rough (artery)', from *trakhus* 'rough']

tracheo- /trəˈkiːəʊ, ˈtrakɪəʊ, ˈtreɪkɪəʊ/ *comb. form* trachea.

tracheotomy /trakɪˈɒtəmi/ *n.* (also **tracheostomy** /-ˈɒstəmi/) (*pl.* **-ies**) an incision made in the trachea to relieve an obstruction to breathing.

tracheotomy tube *n.* a breathing tube inserted into a tracheotomy.

trachoma /trəˈkəʊmə/ *n.* a contagious disease of the eye with inflamed granulation on the inner surface of the lids, caused by chlamydiae. □ **trachomatous** /-ˈkəʊmətəs, -ˈkɒmətəs/ *adj.* [modern Latin from Greek *trakhōma*, from *trakhus* 'rough']

trachyte /ˈtreɪkʌɪt, ˈtrakʌɪt/ *n.* a light-coloured volcanic rock rough to the touch. □ **trachytic** /trəˈkɪtɪk/ *adj.* [French from Greek *trakhutēs* 'roughness' (as TRACHOMA)]

tracing /ˈtreɪsɪŋ/ *n.* **1** a copy of a drawing etc. made by tracing. **2** = TRACE[1] *n.* 3. **3** the act or an instance of tracing.

tracing paper *n.* translucent paper used for making tracings.

track[1] /trak/ *n. & v.* ● *n.* **1 a** a mark or marks left by a person, animal, or thing in passing. **b** (in *pl.*) such marks, esp. footprints. **2** a rough path, esp. one beaten by use. **3** a continuous railway line (*laid three miles of track*). **4 a** a racecourse for horses, dogs, etc. **b** a prepared course for runners etc.; an equivalent section of a cassette tape, compact disc, etc. **5 a** a groove on a gramophone record. **b** a section of a gramophone record, cassette tape, compact disc, etc., containing one song etc. **c** a lengthwise strip of magnetic tape containing one sequence of signals. **6** = SOUNDTRACK. **7 a** a line of travel, passage, or motion (*followed the track of the hurricane*). **b** the path travelled by a ship, aircraft, etc. (cf. COURSE *n.* 2c). **8** *US Education* = STREAM *n.* 4. **9** a continuous band around the wheels of a tank, tractor, etc. **10** the transverse distance between a vehicle's wheels. **11 a** a course of action or conduct; a way of proceeding (*America followed in the same track*). **b** a line of reasoning or thought (*this track proved fruitless*). ● *v.* **1** *tr.* follow the track of (an animal, person, spacecraft, etc.). **2** *tr.* make out (a course, development, etc.); trace by vestiges. **3** *intr.* (often foll. by *back, in,* etc.) (of a film or television camera) move in relation to the subject being filmed. **4** *intr.* (of a stylus) follow a groove in a record. **5** *tr. US Education* assign (a pupil) to a course of study according to ability. **6** *intr.* (of wheels) run so that the back ones are exactly in the track of the front ones. **7** *tr. N. Amer.* **a** make a track with (dirt etc.) from the feet. **b** leave such a track on (a floor etc.). □ **in one's tracks** *colloq.* where one stands, there and then (*stopped him in his tracks*). **keep** (or **lose**) **track of** follow (or fail to follow) the course or development of. **make tracks** *colloq.* go or run away. **make tracks for** *colloq.* go in pursuit of or towards. **off the track** away from the subject. **on a person's track 1** in pursuit of him or her. **2** in possession of a clue to a person's conduct, plans, etc. **on**

the wrong side of (or **across**) **the tracks** *colloq.* in a poor or less prestigious part of town. **on the wrong** (or **right**) **track** following the wrong (or right) line of inquiry. **track down** reach or capture by tracking. **track with** *Austral. slang* associate with; court. ◻ **trackage** *US n.* [Middle English from Old French *trac*, perhaps from Low German or Dutch *tre(c)k* 'draught' etc.]

track[2] /trak/ *v.* **1** *tr.* tow (a boat) by rope etc. from a bank. **2** *intr.* travel by being towed. [apparently from Dutch *trekken* 'to draw' etc., assimilated to TRACK[1]]

trackball /'trakbɑːl/ *n. Computing* a small ball that is rotated in a holder to move a cursor on a screen.

trackbed /'trakbɛd/ *n.* the foundation layer on which railway tracks are laid.

tracker /'trakə/ *n.* **1** a person or thing that tracks. **2** a police dog tracking by scent. **3** a wooden connecting rod in the mechanism of an organ. **4** = BLACK TRACKER.

track events *n.pl.* running races as opposed to jumping etc. (cf. FIELD EVENTS).

tracking /'trakɪŋ/ *n.* **1** *Electr.* the formation of a conducting path over the surface of an insulating material. **2** *US Education* the streaming of school pupils.

tracking station *n.* an establishment set up to track objects in the sky.

tracklayer /'trakleɪə/ *n.* **1** *US* = TRACKMAN. **2** a tractor or other vehicle equipped with continuous tracks (see TRACK[1] *n.* 9).

track-laying *n. & adj.* ● *n.* the laying of railway track. ● *adj.* (of a vehicle) having a caterpillar tread.

tracklement /'trak(ə)lm(ə)nt/ *n. Brit.* an item of food, esp. a jelly, served with meat. [20th c.: origin unknown]

trackless /'traklɪs/ *adj.* **1** without a track or tracks; untrodden. **2** leaving no track or trace. **3** not running on a track.

trackless trolley *n. US* a trolleybus.

trackman /'trakmən/ *n.* (*pl.* **-men**) a platelayer.

track record *n.* a person's past performance or achievements.

track shoe *n.* a spiked shoe worn by a runner.

tracksuit /'traksuːt, -sjuːt/ *n.* a loose warm suit worn by an athlete etc., esp. for exercising or jogging.

track system *n. US* streaming in education.

trackway /'trakweɪ/ *n.* a beaten path; an ancient roadway.

tract[1] /trakt/ *n.* **1** a region or area of indefinite, esp. large, extent (*pathless desert tracts*). **2** *Anat.* an area of an organ or system (*respiratory tract*). **3** *Brit. archaic* a period of time etc. [Latin *tractus* 'drawing' from *trahere tract-* 'draw, pull']

tract[2] /trakt/ *n.* a short treatise in pamphlet form esp. on a religious subject. [apparently abbreviation of Latin *tractatus* TRACTATE]

tract[3] /trakt/ *n. RC Ch. & Mus.* an anthem replacing the alleluia in some masses. [medieval Latin *tractus* (*cantus*) 'drawn-out (song)', past part. of Latin *trahere* 'draw']

tractable /'traktəb(ə)l/ *adj.* **1** (of a person) easily handled; manageable; docile. **2** (of material etc.) pliant, malleable. ◻ **tractability** /-'bɪlɪti/ *n.* **tractableness** *n.* **tractably** *adv.* [Latin *tractabilis* from *tractare* 'handle', frequentative of *trahere tract-* 'draw']

Tractarianism /trak'tɛːrɪənɪz(ə)m/ *n. hist.* = OXFORD MOVEMENT. ◻ **Tractarian** *adj. & n.* [after *Tracts for the Times*, published in Oxford 1833–41 and outlining the movement's principles]

tractate /'trakteɪt/ *n.* a treatise. [Latin *tractatus* from *tractare*: see TRACTABLE]

traction /'trakʃ(ə)n/ *n.* **1** the act of drawing or pulling a thing over a surface, esp. a road or track (*steam traction*). **2 a** a sustained pulling on a limb, muscle, etc., by means of pulleys, weights, etc. **b** contraction, e.g. of a muscle. **3** the grip of a tyre on a road, a wheel on a rail, etc. ◻ **tractional** *adj.* **tractive** /'traktɪv/ *adj.* [French *traction* or medieval Latin *tractio*, from Latin *trahere tract-* 'to draw']

traction engine *n.* a steam or diesel engine for drawing heavy loads on roads, fields, etc.

traction wheel *n.* the driving wheel of a locomotive etc.

tractor /'traktə/ *n.* **1** a motor vehicle used for hauling esp. farm machinery, heavy loads, etc. **2** a traction engine. [Late Latin *tractor* (as TRACTION)]

trad /trad/ *n. & adj.* esp. *Brit. colloq.* ● *n.* traditional jazz. ● *adj.* traditional. [abbreviation]

trade /treɪd/ *n. & v.* ● *n.* **1 a** buying and selling. **b** buying and selling conducted between nations etc. **c** business conducted for profit (esp. as distinct from a profession) (*a butcher by trade*). **d** business of a specified nature or time (*Christmas trade*; *tourist trade*). **2** a skilled handicraft esp. requiring an apprenticeship (*learnt a trade*; *his trade is plumbing*). **3** (usu. prec. by *the*) **a** the people engaged in a specific trade (*the trade will never agree to it*; *trade enquiries only*). **b** *Brit. colloq.* licensed victuallers. **c** *Brit. slang* the submarine service. **4** *US* a transaction, esp. a swap. **5** (usu. in *pl.*) a trade wind. ● *v.* **1** *intr.* (often foll. by *in*, *with*) engage in trade; buy and sell (*trades in plastic novelties*; *we trade with Japan*). **2** *tr.* **a** exchange in commerce; barter (goods). **b** exchange (insults, blows, etc.). **c** esp. *N. Amer.* (foll. by *for*) swap, exchange. **3** *intr.* (usu. foll. by *with*, *for*) have a transaction with a person for a thing. **4** *intr.* (usu. foll. by *to*) carry goods to a place. **5** *intr.* (of shares, currency, etc.) be bought and sold (*the pound is trading lower this month*). ◻ **be in trade** *Brit.* esp. *derog.* be in commerce, esp. keep a shop. **trade in** (often foll. by *for*) exchange (esp. a used car etc.) in part payment for another. **trade off** exchange, esp. as a compromise. **trade on** take advantage of (a person's credulity, one's reputation, etc.). ◻ **tradable** *adj.* **tradeable** *adj.* [Middle English from Middle Low German *trade* 'track' from Old Saxon *trada*, Old High German *trata*: related to TREAD]

Trade Board *n. Brit. hist.* a statutory body for settling disputes etc. in certain industries.

trade book *n.* a book published by a commercial publisher and intended for general readership.

trade cycle *n. Brit.* recurring periods of boom and recession.

trade deficit *n.* the extent by which a country's imports exceed its exports.

trade gap *n.* = TRADE DEFICIT.

trade-in *n.* a thing, esp. a car, exchanged in part payment for another.

trade journal *n.* a periodical containing news etc. concerning a particular trade.

trade-last *n. US* a compliment from a third person which is reported to the person complimented in exchange for one to the reporter.

trade mark *n. & v.* ● *n.* (also **trademark**) **1** a device, word, or words, secured by legal registration or established by use as representing a company, product, etc. **2** a distinctive characteristic etc. ● *v.tr.* (**trademark**) provide with a trade mark.

trade name *n.* **1** a name by which a thing is called in a trade. **2** a name given to a product. **3** a name under which a business trades.

trade-off *n.* a balance achieved between two desirable but incompatible features; a compromise, a bargain.

trade paper *n.* = TRADE JOURNAL.

trade plates *n.pl. Brit.* number plates used by a car-dealer etc. on unlicensed cars.

trade price *n.* a wholesale price charged to the dealer before goods are retailed.

trader /'treɪdə/ *n.* **1** a person engaged in trade. **2** a merchant ship.

tradescantia /tradɪ'skantɪə/ *n.* any usu. trailing plant of the genus *Tradescantia*, with large blue, white, or pink flowers. [modern Latin, named after J. *Tradescant*, English naturalist d. 1638]

trade secret *n.* **1** a secret device or technique used esp. in a trade. **2** *joc.* any secret.

tradesman /ˈtreɪdzmən/ *n.* (*pl.* **-men**; *fem.* **tradeswoman**, *pl.* **-women**) a person engaged in trading or a trade, esp. *Brit.* a shopkeeper or skilled craftsman.

tradespeople /ˈtreɪdzpiːp(ə)l/ *n.pl.* people engaged in trade and their families.

Trades Union Congress *n. Brit.* the official representative body of British trade unions, meeting annually.

trade union *n.* (also *Brit.* **trades union**) an organized association of workers in a trade, group of trades, or a profession, formed to protect and further their rights and interests. □ **trade unionism** *n.*

trade unionist *n.* (also *Brit.* **trades unionist**) a member of a trade union.

trade-weighted *adj.* (esp. of exchange rates) weighted according to the importance of the trade with the various countries involved.

trade wind *n.* a wind blowing continually towards the equator and deflected westward, from obsolete *blow trade* = blow regularly.

trading /ˈtreɪdɪŋ/ *n.* the act of engaging in trade.

trading estate *n.* esp. *Brit.* a specially designed industrial and commercial area.

trading post *n.* a store etc. established in a remote or unsettled region.

trading stamp *n.* a stamp given to customers by some stores which is exchangeable in large numbers for various articles.

trading station *n.* esp. *hist.* a place established or visited for trade.

tradition /trəˈdɪʃ(ə)n/ *n.* **1 a** a custom, opinion, or belief handed down to posterity esp. orally or by practice. **b** this process of handing down. **2** esp. *joc.* an established practice or custom (*it's a tradition to complain about the weather*). **3** artistic, literary, etc., principles based on experience and practice; any one of these (*stage tradition*; *traditions of the Dutch School*). **4** *Theol.* doctrine or a particular doctrine etc. claimed to have divine authority without documentary evidence, esp.: **a** the oral teaching of Christ and the Apostles. **b** the laws held by the Pharisees to have been delivered by God to Moses. **c** the words and deeds of Muhammad not in the Koran. **5** *Law* the formal delivery of property etc. □ **traditionary** *adj.* **traditionist** *n.* **traditionless** *adj.* [Middle English via Old French *tradicion* or Latin *traditio* from *tradere* 'hand on, betray' (as TRANS-, *dare* 'give')]

traditional /trəˈdɪʃ(ə)n(ə)l/ *adj.* **1** of, based on, or obtained by tradition. **2** (of jazz) in the style of the early 20th c. □ **traditionally** *adv.*

traditionalism /trəˈdɪʃ(ə)n(ə)lɪz(ə)m/ *n.* **1** respect, esp. excessive, for tradition, esp. in religion. **2** a philosophical system referring all religious knowledge to divine revelation and tradition. □ **traditionalist** *n.* & *adj.* **traditionalistic** /-ˈlɪstɪk/ *adj.*

traditor /ˈtradɪtə/ *n.* (*pl.* **traditors** or **traditores** /-ˈtɔːriːz/) *hist.* an early Christian who surrendered copies of Scripture or Church property to his or her persecutors to save his or her life. [Latin: see TRAITOR]

traduce /trəˈdjuːs/ *v.tr.* speak ill of; misrepresent. □ **traducement** *n.* **traducer** *n.* [Latin *traducere* 'disgrace' (as TRANS-, *ducere duct-* 'to lead')]

traffic /ˈtrafɪk/ *n.* & *v.* ● *n.* **1** (often *attrib.*) **a** vehicles moving in a public highway, esp. of a specified kind, density, etc. (*heavy traffic on the M1*; *traffic accident*). **b** such movement in the air or at sea. **2** (usu. foll. by *in*) trade, esp. illegal (*the traffic in drugs*). **3 a** the transportation of goods, the coming and going of people or goods by road, rail, air, sea, etc. **b** the persons or goods so transported. **4** dealings or communication between people etc. (*had no traffic with them*). **5** the messages, signals, etc., transmitted through a communications system; the flow or volume of such business. ● *v.* (**trafficked**, **trafficking**) **1** *intr.* (usu. foll. by *in*) deal in something, esp. illegally (*trafficked in narcotics*; *traffics in innuendo*). **2** *tr.* deal in; barter. □ **trafficker** *n.* **trafficless** *adj.* [French *traf(f)ique*, Spanish *tráfico*, Italian *traffico*, of unknown origin]

trafficator /ˈtrafɪkeɪtə/ *n. Brit. hist.* a signal attached to the side of a motor vehicle, raised and illuminated automatically to indicate a change of direction. [TRAFFIC + INDICATOR]

traffic calming *n.* (often *attrib.*) the deliberate slowing of traffic, esp. along residential streets, by building road humps, obstructions, etc. [translation of German *Verkehrsberuhigung*]

traffic circle *n. N. Amer.* a roundabout.

traffic cop *n. colloq.* a traffic police officer.

traffic island *n.* a paved or grassed area in a road to divert traffic and provide a refuge for pedestrians.

traffic jam *n.* a line or lines of traffic at a standstill because of roadworks, an accident, etc.

traffic light *n.* (also **traffic lights**, **traffic signal**) a usu. automatic signal controlling road traffic esp. at junctions by coloured lights.

traffic sign *n.* a sign conveying information, a warning, etc., to vehicle-drivers.

traffic warden *n. Brit.* a uniformed official employed to help control road traffic and esp. parking.

tragacanth /ˈtragəkanθ/ *n.* a white or reddish gum from a plant, *Astragalus gummifer*, used in pharmacy, printing on calico, etc., as a vehicle for drugs, dye, etc. [French *tragacante* via Latin *tragacantha* from Greek *tragakantha*, the name of a shrub, from *tragos* 'goat' + *akantha* 'thorn']

tragedian /trəˈdʒiːdɪən/ *n.* **1** a writer of tragedies. **2** an actor in tragedy. [Middle English from Old French *tragediane* (as TRAGEDY)]

tragedienne /trəˌdʒiːdɪˈɛn/ *n.* an actress in tragedy. [French fem. (as TRAGEDIAN)]

tragedy /ˈtradʒɪdi/ *n.* (*pl.* **-ies**) **1** a serious accident, crime, or natural catastrophe. **2** a sad event; a calamity (*the team's defeat is a tragedy*). **3 a** a play in verse or prose dealing with tragic events and with an unhappy ending, esp. concerning the downfall of the protagonist. **b** tragic plays as a genre (cf. COMEDY). [Middle English via Old French *tragedie* and Latin *tragoedia*, from Greek *tragōidia*, apparently from *tragos* 'goat' + *ōidē* 'song']

tragic /ˈtradʒɪk/ *adj.* **1** (also **tragical** /-k(ə)l/) sad; calamitous; greatly distressing (*a tragic tale*). **2** of, or in the style of, tragedy (*tragic drama*; *a tragic actor*). □ **tragically** *adv.* [French *tragique* via Latin *tragicus* from Greek *tragikos*, from *tragos* 'goat': see TRAGEDY]

tragic irony *n.* a device, originally in Greek tragedy, by which words carry a tragic, esp. prophetic, meaning to the audience, unknown to the character speaking.

tragicomedy /tradʒɪˈkɒmɪdi/ *n.* (*pl.* **-ies**) **1 a** a play etc. having a mixture of comedy and tragedy. **b** plays etc. of this kind as a genre. **2** an event etc. having tragic and comic elements. □ **tragicomic** *adj.* **tragicomically** *adv.* [French *tragicomédie* or Italian *tragicomedia* via Late Latin *tragicomoedia* from Latin *tragico-comoedia* (as TRAGIC, COMEDY)]

tragopan /ˈtragəpan/ *n.* any Asian pheasant of the genus *Tragopan*, with erect fleshy horns on its head. [Latin from Greek, from *tragos* 'goat' + *Pan*, the name of the god]

trahison des clercs /ˌtrɑːɪˌzɔ̃ deɪ ˈklɛː, French traizɔ̃ de klɛr/ *n.* the betrayal of standards, scholarship, etc., by intellectuals. [French, title of a book by J. Benda (1927)]

trail /treɪl/ *n.* & *v.* ● *n.* **1 a** a track left by a thing, person, etc., moving over a surface (*left a trail of wreckage*; *a slug's slimy trail*). **b** a track or scent followed in hunting, seeking, etc. (*he's on the trail*). **2** a beaten path or track, esp. through a wild region. **3** a part dragging behind a thing or person; an appendage (*a trail of smoke*; *a condensation trail*). **4** the rear end of a gun carriage, resting or sliding on the ground when the gun is unlimbered. ● *v.* **1** *tr. & intr.* draw or be drawn along behind, esp. on the ground. **2** *intr.* (often foll. by *behind*) walk wearily; lag; straggle. **3** *tr.* follow the trail of; pursue (*trailed him to his home*). **4** *intr.* be losing in a game or other contest (*trailing by three points*). **5** *intr.* (usu. foll. by *away*, *off*) peter out; tail off. **6** *intr.* **a** (of a plant etc.) grow or hang over a wall, along the ground etc. **b** (of a garment etc.) hang loosely. **7** *tr.* (often *refl.*) drag (oneself, one's limbs, etc.) along wearily etc. **8** *tr.* advertise (a film, a radio or television programme, etc.) in advance by showing extracts etc. **9** *tr.* apply (slip) through a nozzle or spout to decorate ceramic ware. □ **at the trail** *Mil.* with arms trailed. **trail arms** *Mil.* let a rifle etc. hang balanced in one hand and, *Brit.*, parallel to the ground. **trail one's coat** deliberately provoke a quarrel, fight, etc. [Middle English (earlier as verb) from Old French *traillier* 'to tow', or via Middle Low German *treilen* 'haul' from Latin *tragula* 'dragnet']

trail bike *n.* a light motorcycle for use in rough terrain.

trailblazer /'treɪlbleɪzə/ *n.* **1** a person who marks a new track through wild country. **2** a pioneer; an innovator. □ **trailblazing** *n. & attrib.adj.*

trailer /'treɪlə/ *n. & v.* ● *n.* **1** a vehicle towed by another, esp.: **a** the rear section of an articulated lorry. **b** an open cart. **c** a platform for transporting a boat etc. **d** *N. Amer.* a caravan. **2** a series of brief extracts from a film etc., used to advertise it in advance. **3** a person or thing that trails. **4** a trailing plant. ● *v.tr.* **1** transport by trailer. **2** advertise (a film etc.) in advance by trailer.

trailer park *n. N. Amer.* = CARAVAN SITE.

trailing arbutus *n. US* the mayflower, *Epigaea repens*.

trailing edge *n.* **1** the rear edge of an aircraft's wing etc. **2** *Electronics* the part of a pulse in which the amplitude diminishes.

trailing wheel *n.* a wheel not given direct motive power.

trail-net *n.* a dragnet.

train /treɪn/ *v. & n.* ● *v.* **1 a** *tr.* (often foll. by *to* + infin.) teach (a person, animal, oneself, etc.) a specified skill esp. by practice (*trained the dog to beg*; *was trained in midwifery*). **b** *intr.* undergo this process (*trained as a teacher*). **2** *tr. & intr.* bring or come into a state of physical efficiency by exercise, diet, etc.; undergo physical exercise, esp. for a specific purpose (*trained me for the high jump*; *the team trains every evening*). **3** *tr.* cause (a plant) to grow in a required shape (*trained the peach tree up the wall*). **4** *tr.* (usu. as **trained** *adj.*) make (the mind, eye, etc.) sharp or discerning as a result of instruction, practice, etc. **5** *tr.* (often foll. by *on*) point or aim (a gun, camera, etc.) at an object etc. **6** *colloq.* **a** *intr.* go by train. **b** *tr.* (foll. by *it* as object) *Brit.* make a journey by train (*trained it to Aberdeen*). **7** *tr.* (usu. foll. by *away*) *archaic* entice, lure. ● *n.* **1** a series of railway carriages or trucks moved by a locomotive or powered carriage. **2** something dragged along behind or forming the back part of a dress, robe, etc. (*wore a dress with a long train*; *the train of the peacock*). **3** a succession or series of people, things, events, etc. (*a long train of camels*; *interrupted my train of thought*; *a train of ideas*). **4** a body of followers; a retinue (*a train of admirers*). **5** a succession of military vehicles etc., including artillery, supplies, etc. (*baggage train*). **6** a line of gunpowder etc. to fire an explosive charge. **7** a series of connected wheels or parts in machinery. □ **in train** properly arranged or directed. **in a person's train** following behind a person. **in the train of** as a sequel of. **train down** *Brit.* train with exercise or diet to lower one's weight. □ **trainable** *adj.* **trainability** /-'bɪlɪti/ *n.* [Middle English from Old French *traïner*, *trahiner*, ultimately from Latin *trahere* 'pull, draw']

trainband /'treɪnband/ *n. hist.* any of several divisions of civilian militia in London and other areas, esp. in the Stuart period.

train-bearer *n.* a person employed to hold up the train of a robe etc.

trainee /treɪ'niː/ *n.* (often *attrib.*) a person undergoing training. □ **traineeship** *n.*

trainer /'treɪnə/ *n.* **1** a person who trains. **2** a person who trains horses, athletes, footballers, etc., as a profession. **3** an aircraft or device simulating it used to train pilots. **4** *Brit.* a soft sports or running shoe of leather, canvas, etc.

train ferry *n.* a ship that conveys a railway train across water.

training /'treɪnɪŋ/ *n.* the act or process of teaching or learning a skill, discipline, etc. (*physical training*). □ **go into training** begin physical training. **in training 1** undergoing physical training. **2** physically fit as a result of this. **out of training 1** no longer training. **2** physically unfit.

training college *n.* (in the UK) a college or school for training esp. prospective teachers.

training ship *n.* a ship on which young people are taught seamanship etc.

training shoe *n.* = TRAINER 4.

trainload /'treɪnləʊd/ *n.* a number of people, or quantity of goods etc., transported by train.

trainman /'treɪnman/ *n.* (*pl.* **-men**) a railway employee working on trains.

train-mile *n.* one mile travelled by one train, as a unit of traffic.

train-oil *n.* oil obtained from the blubber of a whale (esp. of a right whale). [obsolete *train*, *trane* 'train-oil' from Middle Low German *trān*, Middle Dutch *traen*, apparently = TEAR[2]]

train-shed *n.* a roof supported by posts to shelter railway platforms etc., esp., *hist.* in the 19th c., an arched iron and glass construction of impressive dimensions.

trainsick /'treɪnsɪk/ *adj.* affected with nausea by the motion of a train.

train-spotter *n. Brit.* a person who collects locomotive numbers as a hobby. □ **train-spotting** *n.*

traipse /treɪps/ *v. & n.* (also **trapes**) *colloq.* ● *v.intr.* **1** tramp or trudge wearily. **2** (often foll. by *about*) esp. *Brit.* go on errands. ● *n.* **1** a tedious journey on foot. **2** *archaic* a slattern. [16th-c. verb *trapes*, of unknown origin]

trait /treɪ, treɪt/ *n.* a distinguishing feature or characteristic, esp. of a person. [French from Latin *tractus* (as TRACT[1])]

traitor /'treɪtə/ *n.* (*fem.* **traitress** /-trɪs/) (often foll. by *to*) a person who is treacherous or disloyal, esp. to his or her country. □ **traitorous** *adj.* **traitorously** *adv.* [Middle English via Old French *traït(o)ur* from Latin *traditor -oris*, from *tradere*: see TRADITION]

trajectory /trə'dʒɛkt(ə)ri, 'tradʒɪkt(ə)ri/ *n.* (*pl.* **-ies**) **1** the path described by a projectile flying or an object moving under the action of given forces. **2** *Geom.* a curve or surface cutting a system of curves or surfaces at a constant angle. [originally an adjective: medieval Latin *trajectorius* from Latin *traicere traject-* (as TRANS-, *jacere* 'throw')]

tra-la /trɑː'lɑː/ *int.* an expression of joy or gaiety. [imitative of song]

tram[1] /tram/ *n.* **1** *Brit.* an electrically powered passenger vehicle running on rails laid in a public road. **2** a four-wheeled vehicle used in coal mines. [Middle Low German & Middle Dutch *trame* 'balk, beam, barrow-shaft']

tram[2] /tram/ *n.* (in full **tram silk**) double silk thread used for the weft of some velvets and silks. [French *trame* from Latin *trama* 'weft']

tramcar /'tramkɑː/ *n. Brit.* = TRAM[1] 1.

tramline /'tramlʌɪn/ *n.* (usu. in *pl.*) *Brit.* **1** a rail for a tramcar. **2** *colloq.* each of a pair of parallel lines, esp. either of two sets of long lines at the sides of a tennis court or at the side or back of a badminton court. **3** an inflexible principle or course of action etc.

trammel /'tram(ə)l/ *n. & v.* ● *n.* **1** (usu. in *pl.*) an impediment to free movement; a hindrance (*the* *trammels of domesticity*). **2** a triple dragnet for fish, which are trapped in a pocket formed when they attempt to swim through. **3** an instrument for drawing ellipses etc. with a bar sliding in upright grooves. **4** a beam-compass. **5** *US* a hook in a fireplace for a kettle etc. ● *v.tr.* (**trammelled**, **trammelling**; *US* **trammeled**, **trammeling**) confine or hamper with or as if with trammels. [Middle English (in sense 2) via Old French *tramail* from medieval Latin *tramaculum*, *tremaculum*, perhaps formed as TRI- + *macula* (MAIL²): later history uncertain]

tramontana /tramɒn'tɑːnə/ *n.* a cold north wind in the Adriatic. [Italian: see TRAMONTANE]

tramontane /trə'mɒnteɪn/ *adj. & n.* ● *adj.* **1** situated or living on the other side of mountains, esp. the Alps as seen from Italy. **2** (esp. from the Italian point of view) foreign; barbarous. ● *n.* **1** a tramontane person. **2** = TRAMONTANA. [Middle English via Italian *tramontano* from Latin *transmontanus* 'beyond the mountains' (as TRANS-, *mons montis* 'mountain')]

tramp /tramp/ *v. & n.* ● *v.* **1** *intr.* **a** walk heavily and firmly (*tramping about upstairs*). **b** go on foot, esp. a distance. **2** *tr.* **a** cross on foot, esp. wearily or reluctantly. **b** cover (a distance) in this way (*tramped forty miles*). **3** *tr.* (often foll. by *down*) tread on; trample; stamp on. **4** *intr.* live as a tramp. ● *n.* **1** an itinerant vagrant or beggar. **2** the sound of a person, or esp. people, walking, marching, etc., or of horses' hoofs. **3** a journey on foot, esp. a protracted one. **4 a** an iron plate protecting the sole of a boot used for digging. **b** the part of a spade that it strikes. **5** esp. *US slang offens.* a promiscuous woman. **6** = OCEAN TRAMP. □ **tramper** *n.* **trampish** *adj.* [Middle English *trampe*, from Germanic]

trample /'tramp(ə)l/ *v. & n.* ● *v.tr.* **1** tread underfoot. **2** press down or crush in this way. ● *n.* the sound or act of trampling. □ **trample on 1** tread heavily on. **2** treat roughly or with contempt; disregard (a person's feelings etc.). □ **trampler** *n.* [Middle English, from TRAMP + -LE⁴]

trampoline /'trampəliːn/ *n. & v.* ● *n.* a strong fabric sheet connected by springs to a horizontal frame, used by gymnasts etc. for somersaults, as a springboard, etc. ● *v.intr.* use a trampoline. □ **trampolinist** *n.* [Italian *trampolino* from *trampoli* 'stilts']

tram road *n. hist.* a road with wooden, stone, or metal wheel-tracks.

tram silk see TRAM².

tramway /'tramweɪ/ *n.* **1** *Brit.* **a** rails for a tramcar. **b** a tramcar system. **2** *hist.* = TRAM ROAD.

trance /trɑːns/ *n. & v.* ● *n.* **1 a** a sleeplike or half-conscious state without response to stimuli. **b** a hypnotic or cataleptic state. **2** such a state as entered into by a medium. **3** a state of extreme exaltation or rapture; ecstasy. ● *v.tr. poet.* = ENTRANCE². □ **trance-like** *adj.* [Middle English via Old French *transe*, from *transir* 'depart, fall into trance' from Latin *transire*: see TRANSIENT]

tranche /trɑːnʃ/ *n.* a portion, esp. of income or of a block of shares. [French, = slice (as TRENCH)]

tranny /'trani/ *n.* (*pl.* **-ies**) **1** esp. *Brit. colloq.* a transistor radio. **2** *N. Amer. Mech.* transmission. [abbreviation]

tranquil /'traŋkwɪl/ *adj.* calm, serene, unruffled. □ **tranquillity** /-'kwɪlɪti/ *n.* (also **tranquility**). **tranquilly** *adv.* [French *tranquille* or Latin *tranquillus*]

tranquillize /'traŋkwɪlʌɪz/ *v.tr.* (also **-ise**; *US* **tranquilize**) make tranquil, esp. by a drug etc.

tranquillizer /'traŋkwɪlʌɪzə/ *n.* (also **-iser**; *US* **tranquilizer**) a drug used to diminish anxiety.

trans- /trans, trɑːns, -nz/ *prefix* **1** across, beyond (*transcontinental*; *transgress*). **2** on or to the other side of (*transatlantic*) (opp. CIS- 1). **3** through (*transonic*). **4** into another state or place (*transform*; *transcribe*). **5** surpassing, transcending (*transfinite*). **6** *Chem.* **a** (of an isomer) having the same atom or group on opposite sides of a given plane in the molecule (cf. CIS- 4). **b** having a higher atomic number than (*transuranic*). [from or suggested by Latin *trans* 'across']

transact /tran'zakt, trɑːn-, -'sakt/ *v.tr.* perform or carry through (business). □ **transactor** *n.* [Latin *transigere transact-* (as TRANS-, *agere* 'do')]

transaction /tran'zakʃ(ə)n, trɑːn-, -'sak-/ *n.* **1 a** a piece of esp. commercial business done; a deal (*a profitable transaction*). **b** the management of business etc. **2** (in *pl.*) published reports of discussions, papers read, etc., at the meetings of a learned society. □ **transactional** *adj.* **transactionally** *adv.* [Middle English from Late Latin *transactio* (as TRANSACT)]

transalpine /tranz'alpʌɪn, trɑːnz-, -ns-/ *adj.* beyond the Alps, esp. from the Italian point of view. [Latin *transalpinus* (as TRANS-, *alpinus* ALPINE)]

transatlantic /tranzat'lantɪk, trɑːnz-, -ns-/ *adj.* **1** beyond the Atlantic, esp.: **a** *Brit.* American. **b** *US* European. **2** crossing the Atlantic (*a transatlantic flight*).

transceiver /tran'siːvə, trɑːn-/ *n.* a combined radio transmitter and receiver.

transcend /tran'sɛnd, trɑːn-/ *v.tr.* **1** be beyond the range or grasp of (human experience, reason, belief, etc.). **2** excel; surpass. [Middle English from Old French *transcendre* or Latin *transcendere* (as TRANS-, *scandere* 'climb')]

transcendent /tran'sɛnd(ə)nt, trɑːn-/ *adj. & n.* ● *adj.* **1** excelling, surpassing (*transcendent goodness*). **2** transcending human experience. **3** *Philos.* **a** higher than or not included in any of Aristotle's ten categories in scholastic philosophy. **b** not realizable in experience in Kantian philosophy. **4** (esp. of the supreme being) existing apart from, not subject to the limitations of, the material universe (opp. IMMANENT 1). ● *n. Philos.* a transcendent thing or person. □ **transcendence** *n.* **transcendency** *n.* **transcendently** *adv.*

transcendental /transɛn'dɛnt(ə)l, trɑːn-/ *adj. & n.* ● *adj.* **1** = TRANSCENDENT. **2 a** (in Kantian philosophy) presupposed in and necessary to experience; a priori. **b** (in Schelling's philosophy) explaining matter and objective things as products of the subjective mind. **c** (esp. in Emerson's philosophy) regarding the divine as the guiding principle in man. **3 a** visionary, abstract. **b** vague, obscure. **4** *Math.* (of a function) not capable of being produced by the algebraical operations of addition, multiplication, and involution, or the inverse operations. ● *n.* a transcendental term, conception, etc. □ **transcendentally** *adv.* [medieval Latin *transcendentalis* (as TRANSCENDENT)]

transcendental cognition *n.* a priori knowledge.

transcendentalism /transɛn'dɛnt(ə)lɪz(ə)m, trɑːn-/ *n.* **1** transcendental philosophy. **2** exalted or visionary language. □ **transcendentalist** *n.* **transcendentalize** *v.tr.* (also **-ise**).

Transcendental Meditation *n.* a method of detaching oneself from problems, anxiety, etc., by silent meditation and repetition of a mantra.

transcendental object *n.* a real (unknown and unknowable) object.

transcendental unity *n.* unity brought about by cognition.

transcode /tranz'kəʊd, trɑːnz-, -ns-/ *v.tr. & intr.* convert from one form of coded representation to another.

transcontinental /ˌtranzkɒntɪ'nɛnt(ə)l, trɑːnz-, -ns-/ *adj. & n.* ● *adj.* (of a railway etc.) extending across a continent. ● *n.* a transcontinental railway or train. □ **transcontinentally** *adv.*

transcribe /tran'skrʌɪb, trɑːn-/ *v.tr.* **1** make a copy of, esp. in writing. **2** transliterate. **3** write out (shorthand, notes, etc.) in ordinary characters or continuous prose. **4 a** record for subsequent reproduction. **b** broadcast in this form. **5** arrange (music) for a different instrument etc. □ **transcriber** *n.* **transcriptional** /-'skrɪpʃ(ə)n(ə)l/ *adj.* **transcriptive** /-'skrɪptɪv/ *adj.* [Latin *transcribere transcript-* (as TRANS-, *scribere* 'write')]

transcript /'transkrɪpt, 'trɑːn-/ *n.* **1** a written or recorded copy. **2** any copy. [Middle English via Old

French *transcrit* from Latin *transcriptum*, neut. past part. of *transcribere*: see TRANSCRIBE]

transcription /tran'skrɪpʃ(ə)n, trɑːn-/ *n.* **1 a** the action or process of transcribing something. **b** an instance of this. **2** a transcript or copy. **3** *Biol.* the process by which a sequence of nucleotides is copied from a DNA template during the synthesis of a molecule of RNA.

transducer /tranz'djuːsə, trɑːnz-, -ns-/ *n.* any device for converting a signal from one medium of transmission to another, esp. a non-electrical signal into an electrical one, e.g. pressure into voltage. □ **transduce** *v.tr.* **transduction** /-'dʌkʃ(ə)n/ *n.* [Latin *transducere* 'lead across' (as TRANS-, *ducere* 'lead')]

transect /tran'sɛkt, trɑːn-/ *v.tr.* cut across or transversely. □ **transection** *n.* [TRANS- + Latin *secare sect-* 'to cut']

transept /'transɛpt, 'trɑːn-/ *n.* **1** either arm of the part of a cross-shaped church at right angles to the nave (*north transept; south transept*). **2** this part as a whole. □ **transeptal** /-'sɛpt(ə)l/ *adj.* [modern Latin *transeptum* (as TRANS-, SEPTUM)]

transexual var. of TRANSSEXUAL.

transfer *v.* & *n.* ● *v.* /trans'fəː, trɑːns-, -nz-/ (**transferred**, **transferring**) **1** *tr.* (often foll. by *to*) **a** convey, remove, or hand over (a thing etc.) (*transferred the bag from the car to the station*). **b** make over the possession of (property, a ticket, rights, etc.) to a person (*transferred his membership to his son*). **2** *tr.* & *intr.* change or move to another group, club, department, etc. **3** *intr.* change from one station, route, etc., to another on a journey. **4** *tr.* **a** convey (a drawing etc.) from one surface to another, esp. to a lithographic stone by means of transfer-paper. **b** remove (a picture) from one surface to another, esp. from wood or a wall to canvas. **5** *tr.* change (the sense of a word etc.) by extension or metaphor. ● *n.* /'transfəː, 'trɑːns-, -nz-/ **1** the act or an instance of transferring or being transferred. **2 a** a design etc. conveyed or to be conveyed from one surface to another. **b** *Brit.* a small usu. coloured picture or design on paper, which is transferable to another surface. **3** a football player etc. who is or is to be transferred. **4 a** the conveyance of property, a right, etc. **b** a document effecting this. **5** *N. Amer.* a ticket allowing a journey to be continued on another route etc. □ **transferee** /-'riː/ *n.* **transferor** /-'fəːrə/ *n.* esp. *Law.* **transferrer** /-'fəːrə/ *n.* [Middle English from French *transférer* or Latin *transferre* (as TRANS-, *ferre lat-* 'to bear')]

transferable /trans'fəːrəb(ə)l, 'transf(ə)r-, trɑː-, -nz-/ *adj.* capable of being transferred. □ **transferability** /-'bɪlɪti/ *n.*

transferable vote *n.* a vote that can be transferred to another candidate if the first choice is eliminated.

transfer-book *n.* a register of transfers of property, shares, etc.

transfer company *n. US* a company conveying passengers or luggage between stations.

transference /'transf(ə)r(ə)ns, 'trɑːns-, -nz-/ *n.* **1** the act or an instance of transferring; the state of being transferred. **2** *Psychol.* the redirection of childhood emotions to a new object, esp. to a psychoanalyst.

transfer fee *n. Brit.* a fee paid for the transfer of esp. a professional footballer.

transfer ink *n.* ink used for making designs on a lithographic stone or transfer-paper.

transfer list *n. Brit.* a list of footballers available for transfer.

transfer-paper *n.* paper that has been specially coated to receive the impression of transfer ink and transfer it to stone.

transferral /trans'fəːr(ə)l, trɑːns-, -nz-/ *n.* = TRANSFER *n.* 1.

transferrin /trans'fɛrɪn, trɑːns-, -nz-/ *n.* a protein transporting iron in blood serum. [TRANS- + Latin *ferrum* 'iron']

transfer RNA *n.* RNA conveying an amino acid molecule from the cytoplasm to a ribosome for use in protein synthesis.

transfiguration /ˌtransfɪgə'reɪʃ(ə)n, ˌtrɑːns-, -gjʊr-, -nz-/ *n.* **1** a change of form or appearance. **2 a** Christ's appearance in radiant glory to three of his disciples (Matt. 17:2, Mark 9:2–3). **b** (**Transfiguration**) the festival of Christ's transfiguration, 6 Aug. [Middle English from Old French *transfiguration* or Latin *transfiguratio* (as TRANSFIGURE)]

transfigure /trans'fɪgə, trɑːns-, -nz-/ *v.tr.* change in form or appearance, esp. so as to elevate or idealize. [Middle English from Old French *transfigurer* or Latin *transfigurare* (as TRANS-, FIGURE)]

transfinite /trans'fʌɪnʌɪt, trɑːns-, -nz-/ *adj.* **1** beyond or surpassing the finite. **2** *Math.* (of a number) exceeding all finite numbers.

transfix /trans'fɪks, trɑːns-, -nz-/ *v.tr.* **1** pierce with a sharp implement or weapon. **2** root (a person) to the spot with horror or astonishment; paralyse the faculties of. □ **transfixion** /-'fɪkʃ(ə)n/ *n.* [Latin *transfigere transfix-* (as TRANS-, FIX)]

transform /trans'fɔːm, trɑːns-, -nz-/ *v.* & *n.* ● *v.* **1 a** *tr.* make a thorough or dramatic change in the form, outward appearance, character, etc., of. **b** *intr.* (often foll. by *into*, *to*) undergo such a change. **2** *tr. Electr.* change the voltage etc. of (a current). **3** *tr. Math.* change (a mathematical entity) by transformation. ● *n.* /'transfɔːm, 'trɑːns-, -nz-/ *Math.* & *Linguistics* the product of a transformation. □ **transformable** *adj.* **transformative** *adj.* [Middle English from Old French *transformer* or Latin *transformare* (as TRANS-, FORM)]

transformation /transfə'meɪʃ(ə)n, trɑːns-, -nz-/ *n.* **1** the act or an instance of transforming; the state of being transformed. **2** *Zool.* a complete change of form at metamorphosis, esp. of insects, amphibia, etc. **3** the induced or spontaneous change of one element into another. **4** *Math.* a change from one geometrical figure, expression, or function to another of the same value, magnitude, etc. **5** *Biol.* **a** the modification of a eukaryotic cell from its normal state to a malignant state. **b** the genetic alteration of a cell by introduction of extraneous DNA, esp. by a plasmid. **6** *Linguistics* a process, with reference to particular rules, by which one grammatical pattern of sentence structure can be converted into another, or the underlying meaning of a sentence can be converted into a statement of syntax. **7** *archaic* a woman's wig. **8** a sudden dramatic change of scene on stage. [Middle English from Old French *transformation* or Late Latin *transformatio* (as TRANSFORM)]

transformational /transfə'meɪʃ(ə)n(ə)l, trɑːns-, -nz-/ *adj.* relating to or involving transformation. □ **transformationally** *adv.*

transformational grammar *n. Linguistics* a grammar that describes a language by means of transformation (see TRANSFORMATION 6).

transformer /trans'fɔːmə, trɑːns-, -nz-/ *n.* **1** an apparatus for reducing or increasing the voltage of an alternating current. **2** a person or thing that transforms.

transfuse /trans'fjuːz, trɑːns-, -nz-/ *v.tr.* **1** permeate (*purple dye transfused the water; was transfused with gratitude*). **2 a** transfer (blood) from one person or animal to another. **b** inject (liquid) into a blood vessel to replace lost fluid. □ **transfusion** /-'fjuːʒ(ə)n/ *n.* [Middle English from Latin *transfundere transfus-* (as TRANS-, *fundere* 'pour')]

transgenic /tranz'dʒɛnɪk, trɑːnz-, -ns-/ *adj. Biol.* (of an animal or plant) having genetic material artificially introduced from another species.

transgress /tranz'grɛs, trɑːnz-, -ns-/ *v.tr.* (also *absol.*) **1** go beyond the bounds or limits set by (a commandment, law, etc.); violate; infringe. **2** *Geol.* (of the sea) spread over (the land). □ **transgression** /-'grɛʃ(ə)n/ *n.* **transgressive** *adj.* **transgressor** *n.* [French *transgresser* or Latin *transgredi transgress-* (as TRANS-, *gradi* 'go')]

tranship var. of TRANS-SHIP.

transhumance /tranz'hju:məns, trɑ:nz-, -ns-/ *n.* the seasonal moving of livestock to a different region. [French from *transhumer*, from Latin TRANS- + *humus* 'ground']

transient /'transɪənt, 'trɑ:ns-, -nz-/ *adj. & n.* ● *adj.* **1** of short duration; momentary; passing; impermanent (*life is transient*; *of transient interest*). **2** *Mus.* serving only to connect; inessential (*a transient chord*). ● *n.* **1** a temporary visitor, worker, etc. **2** *Electr.* a brief current etc. □ **transience** *n.* **transiency** *n.* **transiently** *adv.* [Latin *transire* (as TRANS-, *ire* 'go')]

transilluminate /transɪ'lu:mɪneɪt, trɑ:ns-, -'lju:-, -nz-/ *v.tr.* pass a strong light through for inspection, esp. for medical diagnosis. □ **transillumination** /-'neɪʃ(ə)n/ *n.*

transire /tran'zʌɪə, trɑ:-, -s-, -ʌɪri/ *n. Brit.* a customs permit for the passage of goods. [Latin *transire* 'go across' (as TRANSIENT)]

transistor /tran'zɪstə, trɑ:n-, -'sɪ-/ *n.* **1** a semiconductor device with three connections, capable of amplification in addition to rectification. **2** (in full **transistor radio**) a portable radio with transistors. [portmanteau word, from TRANSFER + RESISTOR]

transistorize /tran'zɪstərʌɪz, trɑ:n-, -'sɪ-/ *v.tr.* (also **-ise**) design or equip with, or convert to, transistors rather than valves. □ **transistorization** /-'zeɪʃ(ə)n/ *n.*

transit /'transɪt, 'trɑ:ns-, -nz-/ *n. & v.* ● *n.* **1** the act or process of going, conveying, or being conveyed, esp. over a distance (*transit by rail*; *made a transit of the lake*). **2** a passage or route (*the overland transit*). **3 a** the apparent passage of a celestial body across the meridian of a place. **b** the passage of an inferior planet across the face of the sun, or of a moon etc. across the face of a planet. **4** *N. Amer.* the local conveyance of passengers on public routes. **5** *colloq.* = TRANSIT-THEODOLITE. ● *v.* (**transited**, **transiting**) **1** *tr.* make a transit across. **2** *intr.* make a transit. □ **in transit** while going or being conveyed. [Middle English from Latin *transitus*, from *transire* (as TRANSIENT)]

transit camp *n.* a camp for the temporary accommodation of soldiers, refugees, etc.

transit-circle *n. Astron.* = MERIDIAN CIRCLE.

transit-duty *n. Brit.* duty paid on goods passing through a country.

transit-instrument *n. Astron.* = MERIDIAN CIRCLE.

transition /tran'zɪʃ(ə)n, trɑ:n-, -'sɪʃ-/ *n.* **1** a passing or change from one place, state, condition, etc., to another (*an age of transition*; *a transition from plain to hills*). **2** *Mus.* a momentary modulation. **3** (in the arts) a change from one style to another, esp. *Archit.* from Norman to Early English. **4** *Physics* a change of an atomic nucleus or orbital electron from one quantum state to another, with emission or absorption of radiation. □ **transitional** *adj.* **transitionally** *adv.* **transitionary** *adj.* [French *transition* or Latin *transitio* (as TRANSIT)]

transition element *n.* (also **transition metal**) any of a set of metallic elements in the periodic table whose uncombined atoms have partly filled *d* or *f* orbitals, and which typically form coloured complexes.

transition point *n.* the point at which different phases of the same substance can be in equilibrium.

transitive /'transɪtɪv, 'trɑ:ns-, -nz-/ *adj.* **1** *Gram.* (of a verb or sense of a verb) that takes a direct object (whether expressed or implied), e.g. *saw* in *saw the donkey*; *saw that she was ill* (opp. INTRANSITIVE). **2** *Logic* (of a relation) such as to be valid for any two members of a sequence if it is valid for every pair of successive members. □ **transitively** *adv.* **transitiveness** *n.* **transitivity** /-'tɪvɪti/ *n.* [Late Latin *transitivus* (as TRANSIT)]

transit lounge *n.* a lounge at an airport for passengers waiting between flights.

transitory /'transɪt(ə)ri, 'trɑ:ns-, -nz-/ *adj.* not permanent, brief, transient. □ **transitorily** *adv.* **transitoriness** *n.* [Middle English via Anglo-French *transitorie*, Old French *transitoire* from Latin *transitorius* (as TRANSIT)]

transitory action *n. Law* an action that can be brought in any country irrespective of where the transaction etc. started.

transit-theodolite *n.* a theodolite used for measuring horizontal angles in surveying.

transit visa *n.* a visa allowing only passage through a country.

Transjordanian /tranzdʒɔ:'deɪnɪən, trɑ:nz-, -ns-/ *n. & adj.* ● *n.* **1** *hist.* a native or inhabitant of the former Transjordan, a territory now forming part of Jordan. **2** a person from beyond the river Jordan. ● *adj.* of or relating to the land beyond the river Jordan or *hist.* to Transjordan or its people.

translate /trans'leɪt, trɑ:ns-, -nz-/ *v.* **1** *tr.* (also *absol.*) **a** (often foll. by *into*) express the sense of (a word, sentence, speech, book, etc.) in another language. **b** do this as a profession etc. (*translates for the UN*). **2** *intr.* (of a literary work etc.) be translatable, bear translation (*does not translate well*). **3** *tr.* express (an idea, book, etc.) in another, esp. simpler, form. **4** *tr.* interpret the significance of; infer as (*translated his silence as dissent*). **5** *tr.* move or change, esp. from one person, place, or condition, to another (*was translated by joy*). **6** *intr.* (foll. by *into*) result in; be converted into; manifest itself as. **7** *tr. Eccl.* **a** remove (a bishop) to another see. **b** remove (a saint's relics etc.) to another place. **8** *tr. Bibl.* convey to heaven without death; transform. **9** *tr. Mech.* **a** cause (a body) to move so that all its parts travel in the same direction. **b** impart motion without rotation to. **10** *tr. Biol.* make use of (a sequence of nucleotides) as a template for a sequence of amino acids. □ **translatable** *adj.* **translatability** /-'bɪlɪti/ *n.* [Middle English from Latin *translatus*, past part. of *transferre*: see TRANSFER]

translation /trans'leɪʃ(ə)n, trɑ:ns-, -nz-/ *n.* **1** the act or an instance of translating. **2** a written or spoken rendering of the meaning of a word, speech, book, etc., in another language. **3** *Biol.* the process by which a sequence of nucleotide triplets in a messenger RNA molecule gives rise to a specific sequence of amino acids during synthesis of a polypeptide or protein. □ **translational** *adj.* **translationally** *adv.*

translator /trans'leɪtə, trɑ:ns-, -nz-/ *n.* **1** a person who translates from one language into another. **2** a television relay transmitter. **3** a program that translates from one (esp. programming) language into another.

transliterate /trans'lɪtəreɪt, trɑ:ns-, -nz-/ *v.tr.* represent (a word etc.) in the closest corresponding letters of a different alphabet or language. □ **transliteration** /-'reɪʃ(ə)n/ *n.* **transliterator** *n.* [TRANS- + Latin *littera* 'letter']

translocate /'translə(ʊ)keɪt, trɑ:ns-, -nz-/ *v.tr.* **1** move from one place to another. **2** *Physiol.* & *Biochem.* (usu. in *passive*) transport (a dissolved substance) within an organism, esp. in the phloem of a plant, or actively across a cell membrane. **3** *Biol.* move (a portion of a chromosome) to a new position on the same or another chromosome. □ **translocation** *n.*

translucent /trans'lu:s(ə)nt, trɑ:ns-, -nz-/ *adj.* **1** allowing light to pass through diffusely; semi-transparent. **2** transparent. □ **translucence** *n.* **translucency** *n.* **translucently** *adv.* [Latin *translucēre* (as TRANS-, *lucēre* 'to shine')]

translunar /tranz'lu:nə, trɑ:nz-, -s'l-/ *adj.* **1** lying beyond the moon. **2** of or relating to space travel or a trajectory towards the moon.

transmarine /tranzmə'ri:n, trɑ:nz-, -ns-/ *adj.* situated or going beyond the sea. [Latin *transmarinus* (as TRANS-, *marinus* MARINE)]

transmigrant /tranz'mʌɪgr(ə)nt, trɑ:nz-, -ns-/ *adj. & n.* ● *adj.* passing through, esp. a country on the way to another. ● *n.* a migrant or alien passing through a country etc. [Latin *transmigrant-*, part. stem of *transmigrare* (as TRANSMIGRATE)]

transmigrate /tranzmʌɪˈgreɪt, trɑːnz-, -ns-/ *v.intr.* **1** (of the soul) pass, esp. at or after death, into a different body; undergo metempsychosis. **2** migrate. □ **transmigration** /-ˈgreɪʃ(ə)n/ *n.* **transmigrator** *n.* **transmigratory** /-ˈmʌɪgrət(ə)ri/ *adj.* [Middle English from Latin *transmigrare* (as TRANS-, MIGRATE)]

transmission /tranzˈmɪʃ(ə)n, trɑːnz-, -ns-/ *n.* **1** the act or an instance of transmitting; the state of being transmitted. **2** a broadcast radio or television programme. **3** the mechanism by which power is transmitted from an engine to the axle in a motor vehicle. [Latin *transmissio* (as TRANS-, MISSION)]

transmission line *n.* a conductor or conductors carrying electricity over large distances with minimum losses.

transmit /tranzˈmɪt, trɑːnz-, -ns-/ *v.tr.* (**transmitted, transmitting**) **1 a** pass or hand on; transfer (*transmitted the message*; *how diseases are transmitted*). **b** communicate (ideas, emotions, etc.). **2 a** allow (heat, light, sound, electricity, etc.) to pass through; be a medium for. **b** be a medium for (ideas, emotions, etc.) (*his message transmits hope*). **3** broadcast (a radio or television programme). □ **transmissible** /-ˈmɪsɪb(ə)l/ *adj.* **transmissive** /-ˈmɪsɪv/ *adj.* **transmittable** *adj.* **transmittal** *n.* [Middle English from Latin *transmittere* (as TRANS-, *mittere miss-* 'send')]

transmittance /tranzˈmɪt(ə)ns, trɑːnz-, -ns-/ *n. Physics* the ratio of the light energy falling on a body to that transmitted through it.

transmitter /tranzˈmɪtə, trɑːnz-, -ns-/ *n.* **1** a person or thing that transmits. **2** a set of equipment used to generate and transmit electromagnetic waves carrying messages, signals, etc., esp. those of radio or television. **3** = NEUROTRANSMITTER.

transmogrify /tranzˈmɒgrɪfʌɪ, trɑːnz-, -ns-/ *v.tr.* (**-ies, -ied**) esp. *joc.* transform, esp. in a magical or surprising manner. □ **transmogrification** /-fɪˈkeɪʃ(ə)n/ *n.* [17th c.: origin unknown]

transmontane /tranzˈmɒnteɪn, trɑːnz-, -mɒnˈteɪn, -ns-/ *adj.* = TRAMONTANE. [Latin *transmontanus*: see TRAMONTANE]

transmutation /tranzmjuːˈteɪʃ(ə)n, trɑːnz-, -ns-/ *n.* **1** the act or an instance of transmuting or changing into another form etc. **2** the supposed alchemical process of changing base metals into gold. **3** *Physics* the changing of one element into another by nuclear bombardment etc. **4** *Geom.* the changing of a figure or body into another of the same area or volume. **5** *Biol.* Lamarck's theory of the change of one species into another. □ **transmutational** *adj.* **transmutationist** *n.* [Middle English from Old French *transmutation* or Late Latin *transmutatio* (as TRANSMUTE)]

transmute /tranzˈmjuːt, trɑːnz-, -ns-/ *v.tr.* **1** change the form, nature, or substance of. **2** subject (base metals) to alchemical transmutation. □ **transmutable** *adj.* **transmutability** /-ˈbɪlɪti/ *n.* **transmutative** /-tətɪv/ *adj.* **transmuter** *n.* [Middle English from Latin *transmutare* (as TRANS-, *mutare* 'to change')]

transnational /tranzˈnaʃ(ə)n(ə)l, trɑːnz-, -ns-/ *adj. & n.* ● *adj.* extending beyond national boundaries. ● *n.* a transnational company.

transoceanic /ˌtransəʊʃɪˈanɪk, trɑːns-, -nz-, -sɪ-/ *adj.* **1** situated beyond the ocean. **2** concerned with crossing the ocean (*transoceanic flight*).

transom /ˈtrans(ə)m/ *n.* **1** a horizontal bar of wood or stone across a window or the top of a door (cf. MULLION). **2** each of several beams fixed across the sternpost of a ship. **3** a beam across a saw-pit to support a log. **4** a strengthening crossbar. **5** *US* = TRANSOM WINDOW . □ **transomed** *adj.* [Middle English *traversayn, transyn, -ing* from Old French *traversin*, from *traverse* TRAVERSE]

transom window *n.* **1** a window divided by a transom. **2** a window placed above the transom of a door or larger window; a fanlight.

transonic /tranˈsɒnɪk, trɑːn-/ *adj.* (also **trans-sonic**) relating to speeds close to that of sound. [TRANS- + SONIC, on the pattern of *supersonic* etc.]

transpacific /tranzpəˈsɪfɪk, trɑːnz-, -ns-/ *adj.* **1** beyond the Pacific. **2** crossing the Pacific.

transparence /tranˈspar(ə)ns, trɑːn-, -ˈspɛː-/ *n.* = TRANSPARENCY 1.

transparency /tranˈspar(ə)nsi, trɑːn-, -ˈspɛː-/ *n.* (*pl.* **-ies**) **1** the condition of being transparent. **2** *Photog.* a positive transparent photograph on glass or in a frame to be viewed using a slide projector etc. **3** a picture, inscription, etc., made visible by a light behind it. [medieval Latin *transparentia* (as TRANSPARENT)]

transparent /tranˈspar(ə)nt, trɑːn-, -ˈspɛː-/ *adj.* **1** allowing light to pass through so that bodies can be distinctly seen (cf. TRANSLUCENT). **2 a** (of a disguise, pretext, etc.) easily seen through. **b** (of a motive, quality, etc.) easily discerned; evident; obvious. **3** (of a person etc.) easily understood; frank; open. **4** *Physics* transmitting heat or other electromagnetic rays without distortion. □ **transparently** *adv.* **transparentness** *n.* [Middle English from Old French, via medieval Latin *transparens* from Latin *transparēre* 'shine through' (as TRANS-, *parēre* 'appear')]

transpersonal /tranzˈpəːs(ə)n(ə)l, trɑːnz-, -ns-/ *adj.* **1** *Literature* transcending the personal. **2** *Psychol.* (esp. in psychotherapy) of or relating to the exploration of transcendental states of consciousness beyond personal identity.

transpierce /transˈpɪəs, trɑːns-, -nz-/ *v.tr.* pierce through.

transpire /tranˈspʌɪə, trɑːn-/ *v.* **1** *intr.* **a** (of a secret or something unknown) leak out; come to be known (*what had transpired concerning his father was very worrying*). **b** (prec. by *it* as subject) turn out; prove to be the case (*it transpired he knew nothing about it*). **2** *intr. disp.* occur; happen (*nobody knows what transpired between them*). **3** *tr. & intr.* emit (vapour, sweat, etc.), or be emitted, through the skin or lungs; perspire. **4** *intr.* (of a plant or leaf) release water vapour. □ **transpirable** *adj.* **transpiration** /-spɪˈreɪʃ(ə)n/ *n.* [French *transpirer* or medieval Latin *transpirare* (as TRANS-, Latin *spirare* 'breathe')]

■ **Usage** The use of *transpire* in sense 2 is considered incorrect by some people and should be restricted to informal contexts.

transplant *v. & n.* ● *v.tr.* /transˈplɑːnt, trɑːns-, -nz-/ **1 a** plant in another place (*transplanted the daffodils*). **b** move to another place (*whole nations were transplanted*). **2** *Surgery* transfer (living tissue or an organ) and implant in another part of the body or in another body. ● *n.* /ˈtransplɑːnt, ˈtrɑːns-, -nz-/ **1** *Surgery* **a** the transplanting of an organ or tissue. **b** such an organ etc. **2** a thing, esp. a plant, which is transplanted. □ **transplantable** /-ˈplɑːntəb(ə)l/ *adj.* **transplantation** /-ˈteɪʃ(ə)n/ *n.* **transplanter** /-ˈplɑːntə/ *n.* [Middle English from Late Latin *transplantare* (as TRANS-, PLANT)]

transponder /tranˈspɒndə, trɑːn-/ *n.* a device for receiving a radio signal and automatically transmitting a different signal. [TRANSMIT + RESPOND]

transpontine /transˈpɒntʌɪn, trɑːns-, -nz-/ *adj.* **1** on the other side of a bridge. **2** on or from the other side of the ocean (esp. in relation to N. America). **3** *archaic* on the south side of the Thames. [TRANS- + Latin *pons pontis* 'bridge']

transport *v. & n.* ● *v.tr.* /tranˈspɔːt, trɑːn-/ **1** take or carry (a person, goods, troops, baggage, etc.) from one place to another. **2** *hist.* take (a criminal) to a penal colony; deport. **3** (as **transported** *adj.*) (usu. foll. by *with*) affected with strong emotion. ● *n.* /ˈtranspɔːt, ˈtrɑːn-/ **1 a** a system of conveying people, goods, etc., from place to place. **b** esp. *Brit.* the means of this (*our transport has arrived*). **2** a ship, aircraft, etc. used to carry soldiers, stores, etc. **3** (esp. in *pl.*) vehement emotion (*transports of joy*). **4** *hist.* a transported convict. [Middle English from Old French *transporter* or Latin *transportare* (as TRANS-, *portare* 'carry')]

transportable /tran'spɔ:təb(ə)l, trɑ:n-/ *adj.* **1** capable of being transported. **2** *hist.* (of an offender or an offence) punishable by transportation. ▫ **transportability** /-'bɪlɪti/ *n.*

transportation /transpɔ:'teɪʃ(ə)n, trɑ:ns-/ *n.* **1** the act of conveying or the process of being conveyed. **2 a** a system of conveying. **b** esp. *N. Amer.* the means of this. **3** *hist.* removal to a penal colony.

transport café *n. Brit.* a roadside café for (esp. commercial) drivers.

transporter /tran'spɔ:tə, trɑ:n-/ *n.* **1** a person or device that transports. **2** a vehicle used to transport other vehicles or large pieces of machinery etc. by road.

transporter bridge *n.* a bridge carrying vehicles etc. across water on a suspended moving platform.

transpose /trans'pəʊz, trɑ:ns-, -nz-/ *v.tr.* **1 a** cause (two or more things) to change places. **b** change the position of (a thing) in a series. **2** change the order or position of (words or a word) in a sentence. **3** (also *absol.*; often foll. by *up, down*) *Mus.* write or play in a different key from the original. **4** *Algebra* transfer (a term) with a changed sign to the other side of an equation. ▫ **transposable** *adj.* **transposal** *n.* **transposer** *n.* [Middle English, = transform, from Old French *transposer* (as TRANS-, Latin *ponere* 'put')]

transposing instrument *n.* an instrument producing notes different in pitch from the written notes.

transposing piano *n.* (also **transposing organ** etc.) a piano or organ etc. on which a transposition may be effected mechanically.

transposition /transpə'zɪʃ(ə)n, trɑ:ns-, -nz-/ *n.* the act or an instance of transposing; the state of being transposed. ▫ **transpositional** *adj.* **transpositive** /-'pɒzɪtɪv/ *adj.* [French *transposition* or Late Latin *transpositio* (as TRANS-, POSITION)]

transputer /trans'pju:tə, trɑ:ns-, -nz-/ *n.* a microprocessor with integral memory designed for parallel processing. [TRANSISTOR + COMPUTER]

transsexual /trans'sɛksjʊəl, trɑ:ns-, -nz-, -ʃʊəl/ *adj. & n.* (also **transexual**) ● *adj.* having the physical characteristics of one sex and the supposed psychological characteristics of the other. ● *n.* **1** a transsexual person. **2** a person whose sex has been changed by surgery. ▫ **transsexualism** *n.*

trans-ship /trans'ʃɪp, trɑ:ns-, -nz-/ *v.tr.* (also **tranship**) *intr.* (**-shipped**, **-shipping**) transfer from one ship or form of transport to another. ▫ **trans-shipment** *n.*

trans-sonic var. of TRANSONIC.

transubstantiation /ˌtransəbstanʃɪ'eɪʃ(ə)n, ˌtrɑ:n-, -sɪ'eɪʃ(ə)n/ *n. Theol. & RC Ch.* the conversion of the Eucharistic elements wholly into the body and blood of Christ, only the appearance of bread and wine still remaining. [medieval Latin (as TRANS-, SUBSTANCE)]

transude /tran'sju:d, trɑ:n-/ *v.intr.* (of a fluid) pass through the pores or interstices of a membrane etc. ▫ **transudation** /-'deɪʃ(ə)n/ *n.* **transudatory** /-dət(ə)ri/ *adj.* [French *transsuder* from Old French *tressuer* (as TRANS-, Latin *sudare* 'to sweat')]

transuranic /transjʊ'ranɪk, trɑ:ns-, -nz-/ *adj. Chem.* (of an element) having a higher atomic number than uranium.

Transvaal daisy /tranz'vɑ:l, trɑ:nz-, -ns-/ *n.* a S. African gerbera, *Gerbera jamesonii*, grown for its large daisy-like flowers in various colours. [*Transvaal*, province in S. Africa]

transversal /tranz'və:s(ə)l, trɑ:nz-, -ns-/ *adj. & n.* ● *adj.* (of a line) cutting a system of lines. ● *n.* a transversal line. ▫ **transversality** /-'salɪti/ *n.* **transversally** *adv.* [Middle English from medieval Latin *transversalis* (as TRANSVERSE)]

transverse /tranz'və:s, trɑ:nz-, -ns-/ *adj.* situated, arranged, or acting in a crosswise direction. ▫ **transversely** *adv.* [Latin *transvertere transvers-* 'turn across' (as TRANS-, *vertere* 'turn')]

transverse flute see FLUTE *n.* 1a.

transverse magnet *n.* a magnet with poles at the sides and not the ends.

transverse wave *n. Physics* a wave in which the medium vibrates at right angles to the direction of its propagation.

transvestism /tranz'vɛstɪz(ə)m, trɑ:nz-, -ns-/ *n.* (also **transvestitism** /-tʌɪtɪz(ə)m/) the practice of wearing the clothes of the opposite sex, esp. as a sexual stimulus. ▫ **transvestist** *n.* [German *Transvestismus*, from TRANS- + Latin *vestire* 'clothe']

transvestite /tranz'vɛstʌɪt, trɑ:nz-, -ns-/ *n.* a person, esp. a man, given to transvestism.

trap[1] /trap/ *n. & v.* ● *n.* **1 a** an enclosure or device, often baited, for catching animals, usu. by affording a way in but not a way out. **b** a device with bait for killing vermin, esp. = MOUSETRAP 1. **2** a trick betraying a person into speech or an act (*is this question a trap?*). **3** an arrangement to catch an unsuspecting person, e.g. a speeding motorist. **4** a device for hurling an object such as a clay pigeon into the air to be shot at. **5** a compartment from which a greyhound is released at the start of a race. **6** a shoe-shaped wooden device with a pivoted bar that sends a ball from its heel into the air on being struck at the other end with a bat. **7 a** a curve in a downpipe etc. that fills with liquid and forms a seal against the upward passage of gases. **b** a device for preventing the passage of steam etc. **8** *Golf* a bunker. **9** a device allowing pigeons to enter but not leave a loft. **10** a two-wheeled carriage (*a pony and trap*). **11** = TRAPDOOR. **12** *slang* the mouth (esp. *shut one's trap*). **13** (esp. in *pl.*) *slang* a percussion instrument, esp. in a jazz band. ● *v.tr.* (**trapped**, **trapping**) **1** catch (an animal) in a trap. **2** catch or catch out (a person) by means of a trick, plan, etc. **3** stop and retain in or as in a trap. **4** provide (a place) with traps. ▫ **traplike** *adj.* [Old English *treppe*, *træppe*, related to Middle Dutch *trappe*, medieval Latin *trappa*, of uncertain origin]

trap[2] /trap/ *v.tr.* (**trapped**, **trapping**) (often foll. by *out*) **1** provide with trappings. **2** adorn. [obsolete noun *trap*: Middle English from Old French *drap*: see DRAPE]

trap[3] /trap/ *n.* (in full **trap-rock**) any dark-coloured igneous rock, fine-grained and columnar in structure, esp. basalt. [Swedish *trapp* from *trappa* 'stair', from the often stairlike appearance of its outcroppings]

trap-ball *n.* a game played with a trap (see TRAP[1] *n.* 6).

trapdoor /trap'dɔ:/ *n.* a door or hatch in a floor, ceiling, or roof, usu. made flush with the surface.

trapdoor spider *n.* any spider of the family Ctenizidae, living in a burrow with a hinged cover like a trapdoor.

trapes var. of TRAIPSE.

trapeze /trə'pi:z/ *n.* a crossbar or set of crossbars suspended by ropes and used as a swing for acrobatics etc. [French *trapèze* from Late Latin *trapezium*: see TRAPEZIUM]

trapezium /trə'pi:zɪəm/ *n.* (*pl.* **trapezia** /-zɪə/ or **trapeziums**) **1** *Brit.* a quadrilateral with only one pair of sides parallel. **2** *N. Amer.* = TRAPEZOID 1. [Late Latin from Greek *trapezion*, from *trapeza* 'table']

trapezius /trə'pi:zɪəs/ *n.* (*pl.* **trapezii** /-zɪʌɪ/) *Anat.* either of a pair of large triangular muscles extending over the back of the neck and shoulders.

trapezoid /'trapɪzɔɪd, trə'pi:zɔɪd/ *n.* **1** *Brit.* a quadrilateral with no two sides parallel. **2** *N. Amer.* = TRAPEZIUM 1. ▫ **trapezoidal** *adj.* [modern Latin *trapezoides* from Greek *trapezoeidēs* (as TRAPEZIUM)]

trapper /'trapə/ *n.* a person who traps wild animals, esp. to obtain furs.

trappings /'trapɪŋz/ *n.pl.* **1** ornamental accessories, esp. as an indication of status (*the trappings of office*). **2** the harness of a horse esp. when ornamental. [Middle English (as TRAP[2])]

Trappist /'trapɪst/ *n. & adj.* ● *n.* a member of a branch of the Cistercian order of monks founded in 1664 at La Trappe in Normandy and noted for an austere rule including a vow of silence. ● *adj.* of or relating to this order. [French *trappiste* from *La Trappe*]

trap-rock see TRAP³.

traps /traps/ *n.pl. Brit. colloq.* personal belongings; baggage. [perhaps contraction from TRAPPINGS]

trap-shooting *n.* the sport of shooting at objects released from a trap. □ **trap-shooter** *n.*

trash /traʃ/ *n. & v.* ● *n.* **1** esp. *US* rubbish, refuse. **2** things of poor workmanship, quality, or material; worthless stuff. **3** esp. *US* nonsense (*talk trash*). **4** a worthless person or persons. **5** (in full **cane-trash**) *W.Ind.* the refuse of crushed sugar canes and dried stripped leaves and tops of sugar cane used as fuel. ● *v.tr.* **1** esp. *N. Amer. colloq.* wreck. **2** strip (sugar canes) of their outer leaves to speed up the ripening process. **3** esp. *US colloq.* expose the worthless nature of; disparage. [Middle English: origin unknown]

trash can *n. N. Amer.* a dustbin.

trash-ice *n.* (on a sea, lake, etc.) broken ice mixed with water.

trashy /'traʃi/ *adj.* (**trashier**, **trashiest**) worthless; poorly made. □ **trashily** *adv.* **trashiness** *n.*

trass /tras/ *n.* (also **tarras** /tə'ras/) a light-coloured variety of tuff used in making cement. [Dutch *trass*, earlier *terras*, *tiras*, via Romanic from Latin *terra* 'earth']

trattoria /tratə'riːə/ *n.* an Italian restaurant. [Italian]

trauma /'trɔːmə, 'traʊmə/ *n.* (*pl.* **traumas**) **1 a** *Psychol.* emotional shock following a stressful event, sometimes leading to long-term neurosis. **b** a distressing or emotionally disturbing experience etc. **2** any physical wound or injury. **3** physical shock following this, characterized by a drop in body temperature, mental confusion, etc. □ **traumatize** *v.tr.* (also **-ise**). **traumatization** /-tʌɪ'zeɪʃ(ə)n/ *n.* [Greek *trauma traumatos* 'wound']

traumatic /trɔː'matɪk, traʊ-/ *adj.* **1** of or causing trauma. **2** *colloq.* (in general use) distressing; emotionally disturbing (*a traumatic experience*). **3** of or for wounds. □ **traumatically** *adv.* [Late Latin *traumaticus* from Greek *traumatikos* (as TRAUMA)]

traumatism /'trɔːmətɪz(ə)m, 'traʊ-/ *n.* **1** the action of a trauma. **2** a condition produced by this.

travail /'traveɪl/ *n. & v. literary* ● *n.* **1** painful or laborious effort. **2** the pangs of childbirth. ● *v.intr.* undergo a painful effort, esp. in childbirth. [Middle English from Old French *travail*, *travaillier*, ultimately via medieval Latin *trepalium* 'instrument of torture', from Latin *tres* 'three' + *palus* 'stake']

travel /'trav(ə)l/ *v. & n.* ● *v.intr. & tr.* (**travelled**, **travelling**; *US* usu. **traveled, traveling**) **1** *intr.* go from one place to another; make a journey, esp. of some length or abroad. **2** *tr.* **a** journey along or through (a country). **b** cover (a distance) in travelling. **3** *intr. colloq.* withstand a long journey (*wines that do not travel*). **4** *intr.* go from place to place as a salesman. **5** *intr.* move or proceed in a specified manner or at a specified rate (*light travels faster than sound*). **6** *intr. colloq.* move quickly. **7** *intr.* pass esp. in a deliberate or systematic manner from point to point (*the photographer's eye travelled over the scene*). **8** *intr.* (of a machine or part) move or operate in a specified way. **9** *intr.* (of deer etc.) move onwards in feeding. ● *n.* **1 a** the act of travelling, esp. in foreign countries. **b** (often in *pl.*) a spell of this (*have returned from their travels*). **2** the range, rate, or mode of motion of a part in machinery. [Middle English, originally = TRAVAIL]

travel agency *n.* (also **travel bureau**) an agency that makes the necessary arrangements for travellers. □ **travel agent** *n.*

travelled /'trav(ə)ld/ *adj.* experienced in travelling (also in *comb.*: *much-travelled*).

traveller /'trav(ə)lə/ *n.* (*US* **traveler**) **1** a person who travels or is travelling. **2** *Brit.* = COMMERCIAL TRAVELLER. **3** a gypsy. **4** (also **New Age traveller**) a person who embraces New Age values and leads an itinerant and unconventional lifestyle. **5** *Austral.* an itinerant workman; a swagman. **6** a moving mechanism, esp. a travelling crane.

traveller's cheque *n.* a cheque for a fixed amount that may be cashed on signature, usu. internationally.

traveller's joy *n.* a wild clematis, *Clematis vitalba*.

traveller's tale *n.* an incredible and probably untrue story.

travelling crane *n.* a crane able to move on rails, esp. along an overhead support.

travelling rug *n. Brit.* a rug used for warmth on a journey.

travelling salesman *n.* a male commercial traveller.

travelling wave *n. Physics* a wave in which the medium moves in the direction of propagation.

travelogue /'travəlɒg/ *n.* a film or illustrated lecture about travel. [TRAVEL, on the pattern of *monologue* etc.]

travel-sick *adj.* suffering from nausea caused by motion in travelling. □ **travel-sickness** *n.*

traverse /'travəs, trə'vəːs/ *v. & n.* ● *v.* **1** *tr.* travel or lie across (*traversed the country*; *a pit traversed by a beam*). **2** *tr.* consider or discuss the whole extent of (a subject). **3** *tr.* turn (a large gun) horizontally. **4** *tr. Law* deny (an allegation) in pleading. **5** *tr.* thwart, frustrate, or oppose (a plan or opinion). **6** *intr.* (of the needle of a compass etc.) turn on or as on a pivot. **7** *intr.* (of a horse) walk obliquely. **8** *intr.* make a traverse in climbing. ● *n.* **1** a sideways movement. **2** an act of traversing. **3** a thing, esp. part of a structure, that crosses another. **4** a gallery extending from side to side of a church or other building. **5 a** a single line of survey, usu. plotted from compass bearings and chained or paced distances between angular points. **b** a tract surveyed in this way. **6** *Naut.* a zigzag line taken by a ship because of contrary winds or currents. **7** a skier's similar movement on a slope. **8** the sideways movement of a part in a machine. **9 a** a sideways motion across a rock face from one practicable line of ascent or descent to another. **b** a place where this is necessary. **10** *Mil.* a pair of right-angle bends in a trench to avoid enfilading fire. **11** *Law* a denial, esp. of an allegation of a matter of fact. **12** the act of turning a large gun horizontally to the required direction. □ **traversable** *adj.* **traversal** *n.* **traverser** *n.* [Old French *traverser* from Late Latin *traversare*, *transversare* (as TRANSVERSE)]

travertine /'travətɪn/ *n.* a white or light-coloured calcareous rock deposited from springs. [Italian *travertino*, *tivertino* from Latin *tiburtinus* 'of Tibur' (now Tivoli) a district near Rome]

travesty /'travɪsti/ *n. & v.* ● *n.* (*pl.* **-ies**) a grotesque misrepresentation or imitation (*a travesty of justice*). ● *v.tr.* (**-ies**, **-ied**) make or be a travesty of. [originally an adjective: French *travesti*, past part. of *travestir* 'disguise, change the clothes of', from Italian *travestire* (as TRANS-, *vestire* 'clothe')]

travois /trə'vɔɪ/ *n.* (*pl.* same /-'vɔɪz/) a N. American Indian vehicle of two joined poles pulled by a horse etc. for carrying a burden. [earlier *travail* from French, perhaps the same word as TRAVAIL]

trawl /trɔːl/ *v. & n.* ● *v.* **1** *intr.* (often foll. by *through*, *for*) **a** fish with a trawl or seine. **b** search thoroughly. **2** *tr.* **a** catch by trawling. **b** (often foll. by *for*) search thoroughly through (*trawled the schools for new trainees*). ● *n.* **1** an act of trawling. **2** (in full **trawl net**) a large wide-mouthed fishing net dragged by a boat along the bottom. **3** (in full **trawl line**) *US* a long sea-fishing line buoyed and supporting short lines with baited hooks. [probably from Middle Dutch *traghelen* 'to drag' (cf. *traghel* 'dragnet'), perhaps from Latin *tragula*]

trawler /'trɔːlə/ *n.* **1** a boat used for trawling. **2** a person who trawls.

trawlerman /'trɔːləmən/ *n.* (*pl.* **-men**) a man who works on a trawler.

tray /treɪ/ *n.* **1** a flat shallow vessel usu. with a raised rim for carrying dishes etc. or containing small articles, papers, etc. **2** a shallow lidless box forming a compartment of a trunk. □ **trayful** *n.* (*pl.* **-fuls**). [Old English *trīg* from Germanic: related to TREE]

treacherous /ˈtrɛtʃ(ə)rəs/ *adj.* **1** guilty of or involving treachery. **2** (of the weather, ice, the memory, etc.) not to be relied on; likely to fail or give way. □ **treacherously** *adv.* **treacherousness** *n.* [Middle English from Old French *trecherous*, via *trecheor* 'a cheat' from *trechier, trichier*: see TRICK]

treachery /ˈtrɛtʃ(ə)ri/ *n.* (*pl.* **-ies**) **1** violation of faith or trust; betrayal. **2** an instance of this.

treacle /ˈtriːk(ə)l/ *n.* **1** esp. *Brit.* **a** a syrup produced in refining sugar. **b** molasses. **2** cloying sentimentality or flattery. □ **treacly** *adj.* [Middle English *triacle* from Old French, via Latin *theriaca* from Greek *thēriakē* 'antidote against venom', fem. of *thēriakos* (*adj.*), from *thērion* 'wild beast']

tread /trɛd/ *v.* & *n.* ● *v.* (*past* **trod** /trɒd/; *past part.* **trodden** /ˈtrɒd(ə)n/ or **trod**) **1** *intr.* (often foll. by *on*) **a** set down one's foot; walk or step (*do not tread on the grass*; *trod on a snail*). **b** (of the foot) be set down. **2** *tr.* **a** walk on. **b** (often foll. by *down*) press or crush with the feet. **3** *tr.* perform (steps etc.) by walking (*trod a few paces*). **4** *tr.* make (a hole etc.) by treading. **5** *intr.* (foll. by *on*) suppress; subdue mercilessly. **6** *tr.* make a track with (dirt etc.) from the feet. **7** *tr.* (often foll. by *in, into*) press down into the ground with the feet (*trod dirt into the carpet*). **8** *tr.* (also *absol.*) (of a male bird) copulate with (a hen). ● *n.* **1** a manner or sound of walking (*recognized the heavy tread*). **2** (in full **tread-board**) the top surface of a step or stair. **3** the thick moulded part of a vehicle tyre for gripping the road. **4 a** the part of a wheel that touches the ground or rail. **b** the part of a rail that the wheels touch. **5** the part of the sole of a shoe that rests on the ground. **6** (of a male bird) copulation. □ **tread the boards** (or **stage**) be an actor; appear on the stage. **tread on air** see AIR. **tread on a person's toes** offend a person or encroach on a person's privileges etc. **tread out 1** stamp out (a fire etc.). **2** press out (wine or grain) with the feet. **tread water** maintain an upright position in the water by moving the feet with a walking movement and the hands with a downward circular motion. □ **treader** *n.* [Old English *tredan*, from West Germanic]

treadle /ˈtrɛd(ə)l/ *n.* & *v.* ● *n.* a lever worked by the foot and imparting motion to a machine. ● *v.intr.* work a treadle. [Old English *tredel* 'stair' (as TREAD)]

treadmill /ˈtrɛdmɪl/ *n.* **1** a device for producing motion by the weight of persons or animals stepping on steps on the inner surface of a revolving upright wheel. **2** a similar device used for exercise. **3** monotonous routine work.

treadwheel /ˈtrɛdwiːl/ *n.* = TREADMILL 1.

treason /ˈtriːz(ə)n/ *n.* **1** (in full **high treason**: see note below) violation by a subject of allegiance to the sovereign or to the State, esp. by attempting to kill or overthrow the sovereign or to overthrow the government. **2** (in full **petty treason**) *hist.* murder of one's master or husband, regarded as a form of treason. □ **treasonous** *adj.* [Middle English via Anglo-French *treisoun* etc., Old French *traïson*, from Latin *traditio* 'handing over' (as TRADITION)]

■ **Usage** The crime of *petty treason* was abolished in 1828; this is why the term *high treason*, originally distinguished from *petty treason*, now has the same meaning as *treason*.

treasonable /ˈtriːz(ə)nəb(ə)l/ *adj.* involving or guilty of treason. □ **treasonably** *adv.*

treasure /ˈtrɛʒə/ *n.* & *v.* ● *n.* **1 a** precious metals or gems. **b** a hoard of these. **c** accumulated wealth. **2** a thing valued for its rarity, workmanship, associations, etc. (*art treasures*). **3** *colloq.* a much loved or highly valued person. ● *v.tr.* **1** (often foll. by *up*) store up as valuable. **2** value (esp. a long-kept possession) highly. [Middle English from Old French *tresor*, ultimately from Greek *thēsauros*: see THESAURUS]

treasure hunt *n.* **1** a search for treasure. **2** a game in which players seek a hidden object from a series of clues.

treasurer /ˈtrɛʒ(ə)rə/ *n.* **1** a person appointed to administer the funds of a society or municipality etc. **2** an officer authorized to receive and disburse public revenues. □ **treasurership** *n.* [Middle English from Anglo-French *tresorer*, Old French *tresorier*, from *tresor* (see TREASURE), influenced by Late Latin *thesaurarius*]

treasure trove *n.* **1** *Law* treasure of unknown ownership which is found hidden in the ground etc. and is declared the property of the Crown. **2** a collection of valuable or delightful things.

treasury /ˈtrɛʒ(ə)ri/ *n.* (*pl.* **-ies**) **1** a place or building where treasure is stored. **2** the funds or revenue of a state, institution, or society. **3** (**Treasury**) **a** the department managing the public revenue of a country. **b** the offices and officers of this. **c** the place where the public revenues are kept. [Middle English from Old French *tresorie* (as TREASURE)]

Treasury bench *n.* (in the UK) the front bench in the House of Commons occupied by the Prime Minister, Chancellor of the Exchequer, etc.

treasury bill *n.* a bill of exchange issued by the government to raise money for temporary needs.

treasury note *n.* *US* & *hist.* a note issued by the Treasury for use as currency.

treat /triːt/ *v.* & *n.* ● *v.* **1** *tr.* act or behave towards or deal with (a person or thing) in a certain way (*treated me kindly*; *treat it as a joke*). **2** *tr.* deal with or apply a process to; act upon to obtain a particular result (*treat it with acid*). **3** *tr.* apply medical care or attention to. **4** *tr.* present or deal with (a subject) in literature or art. **5** *tr.* (often foll. by *to*) provide with food or drink or entertainment at one's own expense (*treated us to dinner*). **6** *intr.* (often foll. by *with*) negotiate terms (with a person). **7** *intr.* (often foll. by *of*) give a spoken or written exposition. ● *n.* **1** an event or circumstance (esp. when unexpected or unusual) that gives great pleasure. **2** a meal, entertainment, etc., provided by one person for the enjoyment of another or others. **3** (prec. by *a*) *Brit.* extremely good or well (*they looked a treat*; *has come on a treat*). □ **treatable** *adj.* **treater** *n.* **treating** *n.* [Middle English via Anglo-French *treter*, Old French *traitier* from Latin *tractare* 'handle', frequentative of *trahere tract-* 'draw, pull']

treatise /ˈtriːtɪs, -ɪz/ *n.* a written work dealing formally and systematically with a subject. [Middle English via Anglo-French *tretis* from Old French *traitier* TREAT]

treatment /ˈtriːtm(ə)nt/ *n.* **1** a process or manner of behaving towards or dealing with a person or thing (*received rough treatment*). **2** the application of medical care or attention to a patient. **3** a manner of treating a subject in literature or art. **4** subjection to the action of a chemical, physical, or biological agent. **5** (prec. by *the*) *colloq.* the customary way of dealing with a person, situation, etc. (*got the full treatment*).

treaty /ˈtriːti/ *n.* (*pl.* **-ies**) **1** a formally concluded and ratified agreement between states. **2** an agreement between individuals or parties, esp. for the purchase of property. [Middle English via Anglo-French *treté* from Latin *tractatus* TRACTATE]

treaty port *n.* *hist.* a port that a country was bound by treaty to keep open to foreign trade.

treble /ˈtrɛb(ə)l/ *adj.*, *n.*, & *v.* ● *adj.* **1 a** threefold. **b** triple. **c** three times as much or many (*treble the amount*). **2** (of a voice) high-pitched. **3** *Mus.* = SOPRANO (esp. of an instrument or with reference to a boy's voice). ● *n.* **1** a treble quantity or thing. **2** *Darts* a hit on the narrow ring enclosed by the two middle circles of a dartboard, scoring treble. **3 a** *Mus.* = SOPRANO (esp. a boy's voice or part, or an instrument). **b** a high-pitched voice. **4** the high-frequency output of a radio, record player, etc., corresponding to the treble in music. **5** *Brit.* a system of betting in which the winnings and stake from the first bet are transferred to a second and then (if successful) to a third. **6** *Brit. Sport* three victories or championships in the same season, event, etc. ● *v.* **1** *tr. & intr.* make or become three times as much or many; increase threefold; multiply by three. **2** *tr.* amount to three times as much as. ▫ **trebly** *adv.* (in sense 1 of *adj.*). [Middle English via Old French from Latin *triplus* TRIPLE]

treble chance *n. Brit.* a form of football pool in which different numbers of points are awarded for a draw, an away win, and a home win.

treble clef *n.* a clef placing G above middle C on the second lowest line of the staff.

treble rhyme *n.* a rhyme including three syllables.

trebuchet /ˈtrɛbjʊʃɛt, -bəʃɛt/ *n.* (also **trebucket** /ˈtrɛbʌkɪt, ˈtriː-/) **1** *hist.* a military machine used in siege warfare for throwing stones etc. **2** a tilting balance for accurately weighing light articles. [Middle English from Old French, from *trebucher* 'overthrow', ultimately from Frankish]

trecento /treɪˈtʃɛntəʊ/ *n.* the style of Italian art and literature of the 14th c. ▫ **trecentist** *n.* [Italian, = 300, shortened from *milletrecento* '1300', used with reference to the years 1300–99]

tree /triː/ *n. & v.* ● *n.* **1 a** a perennial plant with a woody self-supporting main stem or trunk when mature and usu. unbranched for some distance above the ground (cf. SHRUB[1]). **b** any similar plant having a tall erect usu. single stem, e.g. palm tree. **2** a piece or frame of wood etc. for various purposes (*shoe-tree*). **3** *archaic* or *poet.* **a** a gibbet. **b** a cross, esp. the one used for Christ's crucifixion. **4** (in full **tree diagram**) *Math.* a diagram with a structure of branching connecting lines. **5** = FAMILY TREE. ● *v.tr.* (**trees, treed**) **1** force to take refuge in a tree. **2** esp. *US* put into a difficult position. **3** stretch on a shoe-tree. ▫ **grow on trees** (usu. with *neg.*) be plentiful. **up a tree** esp. *N. Amer.* cornered; nonplussed. ▫ **treeless** *adj.* **treelessness** *n.* **treelike** *adj.* [Old English *trēow*, from Germanic]

tree agate *n.* agate with treelike markings.

tree calf *n.* a calf binding for books stained with a treelike design.

treecreeper /ˈtriːkriːpə/ *n.* any small creeping bird, esp. of the family Certhiidae, feeding on insects in the bark of trees.

tree diagram see TREE *n.* 4.

tree fern *n.* a large fern, esp. of the family Cyatheaceae, with an upright trunklike stem.

tree frog *n.* any arboreal tailless amphibian, esp. of the family Hylidae, climbing by means of adhesive discs on its digits.

tree heath *n.* = BRIER[2] 1.

tree hopper *n.* any insect of the family Membracidae, living in trees.

tree house *n.* a structure in a tree for children to play in.

tree line *n.* = TIMBERLINE.

tree mallow *n.* a tall woody-stemmed European mallow, *Lavatera arborea*, of cliffs and rocks.

treen /triːn/ *n.* (treated as *pl.*) small domestic wooden objects, esp. antiques. [earlier adjective *treen* 'wooden' from Old English *trēowen* (as TREE)]

treenail /ˈtriːneɪl/ *n.* (also **trenail**) a hard wooden pin for securing timbers etc.

tree of heaven *n.* a fast-growing Chinese ailanthus, *Ailanthus altissima*, widely grown for its foliage.

tree of knowledge *n.* **1** *Bibl.* the tree in the Garden of Eden bearing the forbidden fruit. **2** the branches of knowledge as a whole.

tree of life *n.* = ARBOR VITAE.

tree ring *n.* a ring in a cross-section of a tree, from one year's growth.

tree shrew *n.* any small insect-eating arboreal mammal of the family Tupaiidae having a pointed nose and bushy tail.

tree sparrow *n.* **1** a Eurasian sparrow, *Passer montanus*, inhabiting agricultural land. **2** *N. Amer.* a N. American sparrow-like bird, *Spizella arborea*, of the bunting family, breeding on the edge of the tundra.

tree surgeon *n.* a person who treats decayed trees in order to preserve them. ▫ **tree surgery** *n.*

tree toad *n.* = TREE FROG.

tree tomato *n.* a S. American shrub, *Cyphomandra betacea*, with egg-shaped red fruit.

treetop /ˈtriːtɒp/ *n.* the topmost part of a tree.

tree trunk *n.* the trunk of a tree.

trefa /ˈtreɪfə/ *adj.* (also **tref** /treɪf/ and other variants) not kosher. [Hebrew *ṭ'rēpāh* 'the flesh of an animal torn or mauled', from *ṭārap̱* 'rend']

trefoil /ˈtrɛfɔɪl, ˈtriːfɔɪl/ *n. & adj.* ● *n.* **1** any leguminous plant of the genus *Trifolium*, with leaves of three leaflets and flowers of various colours, esp. clover. **2** any plant with similar leaves. **3** a three-lobed ornamentation, esp. in tracery windows. **4** a thing arranged in or with three lobes. ● *adj.* of or concerning a three-lobed plant, window tracery, etc. ▫ **trefoiled** *adj.* (also in *comb.*). [Middle English via Anglo-French *trifoil* from Latin *trifolium* (as TRI-, *folium* 'leaf')]

trek /trɛk/ *v. & n.* ● *v.intr.* (**trekked, trekking**) **1** travel or make one's way arduously (*trekking through the forest*). **2** esp. *S.Afr. hist.* migrate or journey with one's belongings by ox-wagon. **3** *S.Afr.* (of an ox) draw a vehicle or pull a load. ● *n.* **1 a** a journey or walk made by trekking (*it was a trek to the nearest launderette*). **b** each stage of such a journey. **2** an organized migration of a body of persons. ▫ **trekker** *n.* [South African Dutch *trek* (*n.*), *trekken* (*v.*) 'draw, travel']

trellis /ˈtrɛlɪs/ *n. & v.* ● *n.* (in full **trellis-work**) a lattice or grating of light wooden or metal bars used esp. as a support for fruit trees or creepers and often fastened against a wall. ● *v.tr.* (**trellised, trellising**) **1** provide with a trellis. **2** support (a vine etc.) with a trellis. [Middle English from Old French *trelis*, *trelice*, ultimately from Latin *trilix* 'three-ply' (as TRI-, *licium* 'warp-thread')]

trematode /ˈtrɛmətəʊd/ *n.* any parasitic flatworm of the class Trematoda, esp. a fluke, equipped with hooks or suckers, e.g. a liver fluke. [modern Latin *Trematoda* from Greek *trēmatōdēs* 'perforated', from *trēma* 'hole']

tremble /ˈtrɛmb(ə)l/ *v. & n.* ● *v.intr.* **1** shake involuntarily from fear, excitement, weakness, etc. **2** be in a state of extreme apprehension (*trembled at the very thought of it*). **3** move in a quivering manner (*leaves trembled in the breeze*). ● *n.* **1** a trembling state or movement; a quiver (*couldn't speak without a tremble*). **2** (in *pl.*) a disease (esp. of cattle) marked by trembling. ▫ **all of a tremble** *colloq.* **1** trembling all over. **2** extremely agitated. ▫ **tremblingly** *adv.* [Middle English via Old French *trembler* from medieval Latin *tremulare*, from Latin *tremulus* TREMULOUS]

trembler /ˈtrɛmblə/ *n. Brit.* an automatic vibrator for making and breaking an electrical circuit.

trembling poplar *n.* an aspen.

trembly /ˈtrɛmbli/ *adj.* (**tremblier, trembliest**) *colloq.* trembling; agitated.

tremendous /trɪˈmɛndəs/ *adj.* **1** awe-inspiring, fearful, overpowering. **2** *colloq.* remarkable, considerable, excellent (*a tremendous explosion*; *gave a tremendous performance*). ▫ **tremendously** *adv.* **tremendousness** *n.* [Latin *tremendus*, gerundive of *tremere* 'tremble']

tremolo /ˈtrɛm(ə)ləʊ/ *n.* (*pl.* **tremolos**) *Mus.* **1** a tremulous effect produced on musical instruments or in singing: **a** by rapid reiteration of a note, esp. on bowed stringed instruments or on an organ. **b** by rapid alternation between two notes. **c** by rapid repeated slight variation in the pitch of a note, e.g. on an electric guitar. Cf. VIBRATO. **2 a** a device in an organ producing a tremolo. **b** (in full **tremolo arm**) a lever on an electric guitar, used to produce a tremolo. [Italian (as TREMULOUS)]

tremor /ˈtrɛmə/ *n. & v.* ● *n.* **1** a shaking or quivering. **2** a thrill (of fear or exultation etc.). **3** (in full **earth tremor**) a slight earthquake. ● *v.intr.* undergo a tremor or tremors. [Middle English from Old French *tremour* & Latin *tremor*, from *tremere* 'tremble']

tremulous /'trɛmjʊləs/ *adj.* **1** trembling or quivering (*in a tremulous voice*). **2** (of a line etc.) drawn by a tremulous hand. **3** timid or vacillating. ▫ **tremulously** *adv.* **tremulousness** *n.* [Latin *tremulus* from *tremere* 'tremble']

trenail var. of TREENAIL.

trench /trɛn(t)ʃ/ *n.* & *v.* ● *n.* **1** a long narrow usu. deep depression or ditch. **2** *Mil.* **a** this dug by troops to stand in and be sheltered from enemy fire. **b** (in *pl.*) a defensive system of these. **3** a long narrow deep depression in the ocean bed. ● *v.* **1** *tr.* dig a trench or trenches in (the ground). **2** *tr.* turn over the earth of (a field, garden, etc.) by digging a succession of adjoining ditches. **3** *intr.* (foll. by *on*, *upon*) *archaic* **a** encroach. **b** verge or border closely. [Middle English from Old French *trenche* (*n.*) *trenchier* (*v.*), ultimately from Latin *truncare* TRUNCATE]

trenchant /'trɛn(t)ʃ(ə)nt/ *adj.* **1** (of a style or language etc.) incisive, terse, vigorous. **2** *archaic* or *poet.* sharp, keen. ▫ **trenchancy** *n.* **trenchantly** *adv.* [Middle English from Old French, part. of *trenchier*: see TRENCH]

trench coat *n.* **1** a soldier's lined or padded waterproof coat. **2** a loose belted raincoat.

trencher /'trɛn(t)ʃə/ *n.* **1** *hist.* a wooden or earthenware platter for serving food. **2** (in full **trencher cap**) a stiff square academic cap; a mortarboard. [Middle English from Anglo-French *trenchour*, Old French *trencheoir*, from *trenchier*: see TRENCH]

trencherman /'trɛn(t)ʃəmən/ *n.* (*pl.* **-men**) a person who eats well, or in a specified manner (*a good trencherman*).

trench fever *n.* a highly contagious rickettsial disease transmitted by lice, that infested soldiers in the trenches in the First World War.

trench foot *n.* a painful condition of the feet caused by long immersion in cold water or mud and marked by blackening and death of surface tissue.

trench mortar *n.* a light simple mortar throwing a bomb from one's own into the enemy trenches.

trench warfare *n.* hostilities carried on from more or less permanent trenches.

trend /trɛnd/ *n.* & *v.* ● *n.* a general direction and tendency (esp. of events, fashion, or opinion etc.). ● *v.intr.* **1** bend or turn away in a specified direction. **2** be chiefly directed; have a general and continued tendency. [Old English *trendan* 'revolve, rotate' from Germanic: related to TRUNDLE]

trendify /'trɛndɪfʌɪ/ *v.tr.* *colloq.* make fashionable; give a fashionable appearance to.

trendsetter /'trɛndsɛtə/ *n.* a person who leads the way in fashion etc. ▫ **trendsetting** *adj.*

trendy /'trɛndi/ *adj.* & *n.* *colloq.* ● *adj.* (**trendier**, **trendiest**) often *derog.* fashionable; following fashionable trends. ● *n.* (*pl.* **-ies**) a fashionable person. ▫ **trendily** *adv.* **trendiness** *n.*

trente-et-quarante /trɒ̃teɪka'rɒ̃t, French trɑ̃tekarɑ̃t/ *n.* = ROUGE-ET-NOIR. [French, = thirty and forty]

trepan /trɪ'pan/ *n.* & *v.* ● *n.* **1** a cylindrical saw formerly used by surgeons for removing part of the bone of the skull. **2** a borer for sinking shafts. ● *v.tr.* (**trepanned**, **trepanning**) perforate (the skull) with a trepan. ▫ **trepanation** /trɛpə'neɪʃ(ə)n/ *n.* **trepanning** *n.* [Middle English via medieval Latin *trepanum* from Greek *trupanon*, via *trupaō* 'bore' from *trupē* 'hole']

trepang /trɪ'paŋ/ *n.* = BÊCHE-DE-MER 1. [Malay *trīpang*]

trephine /trɪ'fʌɪn, -'fiːn/ *n.* & *v.* ● *n.* an improved form of trepan with a guiding centre-pin. ● *v.tr.* operate on with this. ▫ **trephination** /trɛfɪ'neɪʃ(ə)n/ *n.* [originally *trafine*, from Latin *tres fines* 'three ends', apparently influenced by TREPAN]

trepidation /trɛpɪ'deɪʃ(ə)n/ *n.* **1** a feeling of fear or alarm; perturbation of the mind. **2** tremulous agitation. **3** the trembling of limbs, e.g. in paralysis. [Latin *trepidatio*, via *trepidare* 'be agitated, tremble', from *trepidus* 'alarmed']

trespass /'trɛspəs/ *v.* & *n.* ● *v.intr.* **1** (usu. foll. by *on*, *upon*) make an unlawful or unwarrantable intrusion (esp. on land or property). **2** (foll. by *on*) make unwarrantable claims (*shall not trespass on your hospitality*). **3** (foll. by *against*) *literary* or *archaic* offend. ● *n.* **1** *Law* a voluntary wrongful act against the person or property of another, esp. unlawful entry to a person's land or property. **2** *archaic* a sin or offence. ▫ **trespass on a person's preserves** *Brit.* meddle in another person's affairs. ▫ **trespasser** *n.* [Middle English from Old French *trespasser* 'pass over, trespass', *trespas* (*n.*), from medieval Latin *transpassare* (as TRANS-, PASS[1])]

tress /trɛs/ *n.* & *v.* ● *n.* **1** a long lock of human (esp. female) hair. **2** (in *pl.*) a woman's or girl's head of hair. ● *v.tr.* arrange (hair) in tresses. ▫ **tressed** *adj.* (also in *comb.*). **tressy** *adj.* [Middle English from Old French *tresse*, perhaps ultimately from Greek *trikha* 'threefold']

tressure /'trɛʃə, 'trɛs(j)ʊə/ *n.* *Heraldry* a narrow orle. [Middle English, originally = hair-ribbon, from Old French *tressour* etc. (as TRESS)]

trestle /'trɛs(ə)l/ *n.* **1** a supporting structure for a table etc., consisting of two frames fixed at an angle or hinged or of a bar supported by two divergent pairs of legs. **2** (in full **trestle-table**) a table consisting of a board or boards laid on trestles or other supports. **3** (in full **trestle-work**) an open braced framework to support a bridge etc. **4** (in full **trestle-tree**) *Naut.* each of a pair of horizontal pieces on a lower mast supporting the topmast etc. [Middle English from Old French *trestel*, ultimately from Latin *transtrum* 'beam']

tret /trɛt/ *n.* *hist.* an allowance of extra weight formerly made to purchasers of some goods for waste in transportation. [Middle English from Anglo-French & Old French, variant of *trait* 'draught': see TRAIT]

trevally /trɪ'vali/ *n.* (*pl.* **-ies**) any Australian fish of the genus *Caranx*, used as food. [probably an alteration of *cavally*, a kind of fish, via Spanish *caballo* 'horse' from Latin (as CAVALRY)]

trews /truːz/ *n.pl.* esp. *Brit.* trousers, esp. close-fitting tartan trousers worn by women. [Irish *trius*, Gaelic *triubhas* (sing.): cf. TROUSERS]

trey /treɪ/ *n.* (*pl.* **treys**) the three on dice or cards. [Middle English via Old French *trei*, *treis* 'three' from Latin *tres*]

TRH *abbr.* Their Royal Highnesses.

tri- /trʌɪ/ *comb. form* forming nouns and adjectives meaning: **1** three or three times. **2** *Chem.* (forming the names of compounds) containing three atoms or groups of a specified kind (*triacetate*). [Latin & Greek from Latin *tres*, Greek *treis* 'three']

triable /'trʌɪəb(ə)l/ *adj.* **1** liable to a judicial trial. **2** that may be tried or attempted. [Middle English from Anglo-French (as TRY)]

triacetate /trʌɪ'asɪteɪt/ *n.* a cellulose derivative containing three acetate groups, esp. as a base for man-made fibres.

triad /'trʌɪad/ *n.* **1** a group of three (esp. notes in a chord). **2** the number three. **3** **a** any of various Chinese secret societies in various countries, usu. involved in criminal activities. **b** a member of such a society. **4** a Welsh form of literary composition with an arrangement in groups of three. ▫ **triadic** /-'adɪk/ *adj.* **triadically** /-'adɪk(ə)li/ *adv.* [French *triade* or Late Latin *trias triad-* from Greek *trias -ados*, from *treis* 'three']

triadelphous /trʌɪə'dɛlfəs/ *adj.* *Bot.* having stamens united in three bundles. [TRI- + Greek *adelphos* 'brother']

triage /'trʌɪɪdʒ/ *n.* **1** the act of sorting according to quality. **2** the assignment of degrees of urgency to decide the order of treatment of wounds, illnesses, etc. [French from *trier*: cf. TRY]

trial /'trʌɪəl/ *n.* & *v.* ● *n.* **1** a judicial examination and determination of issues between parties by a judge with or without a jury (*stood trial for murder*). **2 a** a process or mode of testing qualities. **b** experimental treatment. **c** a test (*will give you a trial*). **3** a trying thing or experience or person, esp. hardship or trouble (*the trials of old age*). **4** a sports match to test the ability of players eligible for selection to a team. **5** a test of individual ability on a motorcycle over rough ground or on a road. **6** any of various contests involving performance by horses, dogs, or other animals. ● *v.tr. & intr.* (**trialled**, **trialling**; *US* **trialed**, **trialing**) subject to or undergo a test to assess performance. □ **on trial 1** being tried in a court of law. **2** being tested; to be chosen or retained only if suitable. [Anglo-French *trial*, *triel* from *trier* TRY]

trial and error *n.* repeated (usu. varied and unsystematic) attempts or experiments continued until successful.

trial balance *n.* (in double-entry bookkeeping) a statement of all the debit and credit balances in a ledger at a particular date, any disagreement indicating an error of some kind.

trial balloon *n.* an experiment to see how a new policy will be received. [translation of French *ballon d'essai*]

trialist /'trʌɪəlɪst/ *n.* (also *Brit.* **triallist**) **1** a person who takes part in a sports trial, motorcycle trial, etc. **2** a person involved in a judicial trial.

trial jury *n.* = PETTY JURY.

trial run *n.* a preliminary test of a vehicle, vessel, machine, etc.

triandrous /trʌɪ'andrəs/ *adj. Bot.* having three stamens.

triangle /'trʌɪaŋg(ə)l/ *n.* **1** a plane figure with three sides and angles. **2** any three things not in a straight line, with imaginary lines joining them. **3** an implement of this shape. **4** a musical instrument consisting of a steel rod bent into a triangle and sounded by striking it with a small steel rod. **5** a situation, esp. an emotional relationship, involving three people. **6** a right-angled triangle of wood etc. as a drawing implement. **7** *Naut.* a device of three spars for raising weights. **8** *hist.* a frame of three halberds joined at the top to which a soldier was bound for flogging. [Middle English from Old French *triangle* or Latin *triangulum*, neut. of *triangulus* 'three-cornered' (as TRI-, ANGLE[1])]

triangle of forces *n.* a triangle whose sides represent in magnitude and direction three forces in equilibrium.

triangular /trʌɪ'aŋgjʊlə/ *adj.* **1** triangle-shaped, three-cornered. **2** (of a contest or treaty etc.) between three persons or parties. **3** (of a pyramid) having a three-sided base. □ **triangularity** /-'larɪti/ *n.* **triangularly** *adv.* [Late Latin *triangularis* (as TRIANGLE)]

triangulate *v. & adj.* ● *v.tr.* /trʌɪ'aŋgjʊleɪt/ **1** divide (an area) into triangles for surveying purposes. **2 a** measure and map (an area) by the use of triangles with a known base length and base angles. **b** determine (a height, distance, etc.) in this way. ● *adj.* /trʌɪ'aŋgjʊlət/ *Zool.* marked with triangles. □ **triangulately** /-lətli/ *adv.* **triangulation** /-'leɪʃ(ə)n/ *n.* [Latin *triangulatus* 'triangular' (as TRIANGLE)]

triangulation point *n.* a reference point on high ground used in surveying, frequently marked by a small pillar.

Triassic /trʌɪ'asɪk/ *adj. & n. Geol.* ● *adj.* of or relating to the earliest period of the Mesozoic era with evidence of an abundance of reptiles (including the earliest dinosaurs) and the emergence of mammals. Cf. Appendix X. ● *n.* this period or system. [Late Latin *trias* (as TRIAD), because the strata are divisible into three groups]

triathlon /trʌɪ'aθlɒn, -lən/ *n.* an athletic contest consisting of three different events. □ **triathlete** /-li:t/ *n.* [TRI-, on the pattern of DECATHLON]

triatomic /trʌɪə'tɒmɪk/ *adj. Chem.* **1** having three atoms (of a specified kind) in the molecule. **2** having three replacement atoms or radicals.

triaxial /trʌɪ'aksɪəl/ *adj.* having three axes.

tribade /'trɪbəd/ *n.* a lesbian. □ **tribadism** *n.* [French *tribade* or Latin *tribas* from Greek, from *tribō* 'rub']

tribal /'trʌɪb(ə)l/ *adj. & n.* ● *adj.* of, relating to, or characteristic of a tribe or tribes. ● *n.* (usu. in *pl.*) a member of a tribal community (chiefly used in the Indian subcontinent). □ **tribally** *adv.*

tribalism /'trʌɪbəlɪz(ə)m/ *n.* **1** tribal organization. **2** loyalty to one's own tribe or social group. □ **tribalist** *n.* **tribalistic** /-'lɪstɪk/ *adj.*

tribasic /trʌɪ'beɪsɪk/ *adj. Chem.* (of an acid) having three replaceable hydrogen atoms.

tribe /trʌɪb/ *n.* **1** a group of (esp. primitive) families or communities, linked by social, economic, religious, or blood ties, and usu. having a common culture and dialect and a recognized leader. **2** any similar natural or political division. **3** *Rom.Hist.* each of the political divisions of the Roman people. **4** each of the 12 divisions of the Israelites. **5** usu. *derog.* a set or number of persons esp. of one profession etc. or family (*the whole tribe of actors*). **6** *Biol.* a group of organisms usu. ranking between genus and the subfamily. **7** (in *pl.*) large numbers. [Middle English, originally in pl. form *tribuz, tribus*, from Old French or Latin *tribus* (sing. & pl.)]

tribesman /'trʌɪbzmən/ *n.* (*pl.* **-men**; *fem.* **tribeswoman**, *pl.* **-women**) a member of a tribe or of one's own tribe.

tribespeople /'trʌɪbzpi:p(ə)l/ *n.pl.* the members of a tribe.

triblet /'trɪblɪt/ *n.* a mandrel used in making tubes, rings, etc. [French *triboulet*, of unknown origin]

tribo- /'trʌɪbəʊ, 'trɪbəʊ/ *comb. form* rubbing, friction. [Greek *tribos* 'rubbing']

triboelectricity /ˌtrʌɪbəʊɪlɛk'trɪsɪti, ˌtrɪbəʊ-/ *n.* the generation of an electric charge by friction.

tribology /trʌɪ'bɒlədʒi/ *n.* the study of friction, wear, lubrication, and the design of bearings; the science of interacting surfaces in relative motion. □ **tribologist** *n.*

triboluminescence /ˌtrʌɪbəʊlu:mɪ'nɛs(ə)ns, ˌtrɪ-/ *n.* the emission of light from a substance when rubbed, scratched, etc. □ **triboluminescent** *adj.*

tribometer /trʌɪ'bɒmɪtə/ *n.* an instrument for measuring friction in sliding.

tribrach /'trʌɪbrak, 'trɪ-/ *n. Prosody* a foot of three short or unstressed syllables. □ **tribrachic** /-'brakɪk/ *adj.* [Latin *tribrachys* from Greek *tribrakhus* (as TRI-, *brakhus* 'short')]

tribulation /trɪbjʊ'leɪʃ(ə)n/ *n.* **1** great affliction or oppression. **2** a cause of this (*was a real tribulation to me*). [Middle English via Old French from ecclesiastical Latin *tribulatio -onis*, from Latin *tribulare* 'press, oppress', via *tribulum* 'sledge for threshing', from *terere trit-* 'rub']

tribunal /trʌɪ'bju:n(ə)l, trɪ-/ *n.* **1** *Brit.* a board appointed to adjudicate in some matter, esp. one appointed by the government to investigate a matter of public concern. **2** a court of justice. **3** a seat or bench for a judge or judges. **4 a** a place of judgement. **b** judicial authority (*the tribunal of public opinion*). [French *tribunal* or Latin *tribunus* (as TRIBUNE[2])]

tribune[1] /'trɪbju:n/ *n.* **1** a popular leader or demagogue. **2** *Rom.Hist.* **a** (in full **tribune of the people**) an official in ancient Rome chosen by the people to protect their interests. **b** (in full **military tribune**) a Roman legionary officer. □ **tribunate** /-nət/ *n.* **tribuneship** *n.* [Middle English from Latin *tribunus*, probably from *tribus* 'tribe']

tribune[2] /'trɪbju:n/ *n.* **1 a** a bishop's throne in a basilica. **b** an apse containing this. **2** a dais or rostrum. **3** a raised area with seats. [French from Italian, from medieval Latin *tribuna* TRIBUNAL]

tributary /'trɪbjʊt(ə)ri/ *n. & adj.* ● *n.* (*pl.* **-ies**) **1** a river or stream flowing into a larger river or lake. **2** *hist.* a person or state paying or subject to tribute. ● *adj.* **1** (of a river etc.) that is a tributary. **2** *hist.* **a** paying tribute. **b** serving as tribute. □ **tributarily** *adv.* **tributariness** *n.* [Middle English from Latin *tributarius* (as TRIBUTE)]

tribute /'trɪbju:t/ *n.* **1** a thing said or done or given as a mark of respect or affection etc. (*paid tribute to their achievements; floral tributes*). **2** *hist.* **a** a payment made periodically by one state or ruler to another, esp. as a sign of dependence. **b** an obligation to pay this (*was laid under tribute*). **3** (foll. by *to*) an indication of (some praiseworthy quality) (*their success is a tribute to their perseverance*). **4** a proportion of ore or its equivalent paid to a miner for his work, or to the owner of a mine. [Middle English from Latin *tributum*, neut. past part. of *tribuere tribut-* 'assign' (originally 'divide between tribes') from *tribus* 'tribe']

tricar /'trʌɪkɑ:/ *n. Brit.* a three-wheeled motor car.

trice /trʌɪs/ *n.* □ **in a trice** in a moment; instantly. [Middle English *trice* 'pull, haul' from Middle Dutch *trīsen*, Middle Low German *trīssen*, related to Middle Dutch *trīse* 'windlass, pulley']

tricentenary /trʌɪsɛn'ti:nəri, -'tɛn-, trʌɪ'sɛntɪn-/ *n.* (*pl.* **-ies**) = TERCENTENARY.

triceps /'trʌɪsɛps/ *adj. & n.* ● *adj.* (of a muscle) having three heads or points of attachment. ● *n.* any triceps muscle, esp. the large muscle at the back of the upper arm. [Latin, = three-headed (as TRI-, *-ceps* from *caput* 'head')]

triceratops /trʌɪ'sɛrətɒps/ *n.* a large quadrupedal plant-eating dinosaur of the late Cretaceous genus *Triceratops*, with two large horns, a smaller horn on the snout, and a bony frill above the neck. [modern Latin, from Greek *trikeratos* 'three-horned' + *ōps* 'face']

trichiasis /trɪkɪ'eɪsɪs, trɪ'kʌɪəsɪs/ *n. Med.* ingrowth or introversion of the eyelashes. [Late Latin from Greek *trikhiasis*, from *trikhiaō* 'be hairy']

trichina /'trɪkɪnə, trɪ'kʌɪnə/ *n.* (*pl.* **trichinae** /-ni:/) any hairlike parasitic nematode worm of the genus *Trichinella*, esp. *T. spiralis*, the adults of which live in the small intestine, and whose larvae become encysted in the muscle tissue of humans and other mammals. □ **trichinous** *adj.* [modern Latin from Greek *trikhinos* 'of hair': see TRICHO-]

trichinosis /trɪkɪ'nəʊsɪs/ *n.* a disease caused by trichinae, usu. ingested in meat, and characterized by digestive disturbance, fever, and muscular rigidity.

trichloroethane /ˌtrʌɪklɔ:rəʊ'i:θeɪn/ *n.* any derivative of ethane containing three chlorine atoms, esp. 1,1,1-trichloroethane (also called *methyl chloroform*), a volatile solvent. Chem. formula: CCl_3CH_3.

tricho- /'trɪkəʊ, 'trʌɪkəʊ/ *comb. form* hair. [Greek *thrix trikhos* 'hair']

trichogenous /trɪ'kɒdʒɪnəs/ *adj.* causing or promoting the growth of hair.

trichology /trɪ'kɒlədʒi/ *n.* the study of the structure, functions, and diseases of the hair. □ **trichologist** *n.*

trichome /'trʌɪkəʊm, 'trɪ-/ *n. Bot.* a hair, scale, prickle, or other outgrowth from the epidermis of a plant. [Greek *trikhōma* from *trikhoō* 'cover with hair' (as TRICHO-)]

trichomonad /trɪkə(ʊ)'mɒnad/ *n.* any flagellate protozoan of the order Trichomonadida, parasitic in humans, cattle, and fowls.

trichomoniasis /trɪkə(ʊ)mə'nʌɪəsɪs/ *n.* any of various infections caused by trichomonads parasitic on the urinary tract, vagina, or digestive system.

trichopathy /trɪ'kɒpəθi/ *n.* the treatment of diseases of the hair. □ **trichopathic** /trɪkə'paθɪk/ *adj.*

trichotomy /trʌɪ'kɒtəmi, trɪ-/ *n.* (*pl.* **-ies**) a division (esp. sharply defined) into three categories, esp. of human nature into body, soul, and spirit. □ **trichotomic** /-kə'tɒmɪk/ *adj.* [Greek *trikha* 'threefold' from *treis* 'three', on the pattern of DICHOTOMY]

trichroic /trʌɪ'krəʊɪk/ *adj.* (esp. of a crystal viewed in different directions) showing three colours. □ **trichroism** /'trʌɪkrəʊɪz(ə)m/ *n.* [Greek *trikhroos* (as TRI-, *khrōs* 'colour')]

trichromatic /trʌɪkrə(ʊ)'matɪk/ *adj.* **1** having or using three colours. **2** (of vision) having the normal three colour-sensations, i.e. red, green, and purple. □ **trichromatism** /-'krəʊmətɪz(ə)m/ *n.*

trick /trɪk/ *n. & v.* ● *n.* **1** an action or scheme undertaken to fool, outwit, or deceive. **2** an optical or other illusion (*a trick of the light*). **3** a special technique; a knack or special way of doing something. **4 a** a feat of skill or dexterity. **b** an unusual action (e.g. begging) learnt by an animal. **5** a mischievous, foolish, or discreditable act; a practical joke (*a mean trick to play*). **6** a peculiar or characteristic habit or mannerism (*has a trick of repeating himself*). **7 a** the cards played in a single round of a card game, usu. one from each player. **b** such a round. **c** a point gained as a result of this. **8** (*attrib.*) done to deceive or mystify or to create an illusion (*trick photography; trick question*). **9** *Naut.* a sailor's turn at the helm, usu. two hours. **10** *slang* **a** a prostitute's session with a client. **b** a prostitute's client. ● *v.tr.* **1** deceive by a trick; outwit. **2** (often foll. by *out of*, or *into* + verbal noun) cheat; treat deceitfully so as to deprive (*were tricked into agreeing; were tricked out of their savings*). **3** (of a thing) foil or baffle; take by surprise; disappoint the calculations of. □ **do the trick** *colloq.* accomplish one's purpose; achieve the required result. **how's tricks?** *colloq.* how are you? **not miss a trick** see MISS[1]. **trick of the trade** a special usu. ingenious technique or method of achieving a result in an industry or profession etc. **trick or treat** esp. *N. Amer.* a children's custom of calling at houses at Hallowe'en with the threat of pranks if they are not given a small gift. **trick out** (or **up**) dress, decorate, or deck out esp. showily. **turn a trick** *slang* (of a prostitute) have a session with a client. **up to one's tricks** *colloq.* misbehaving. **up to a person's tricks** aware of what a person is likely to do by way of mischief. □ **tricker** *n.* **trickish** *adj.* [Middle English from Old French dialect *trique*, Old French *triche*, from *trichier* 'deceive', of unknown origin]

trick cyclist *n.* **1** a cyclist who performs tricks, esp. in a circus. **2** *Brit. slang* a psychiatrist.

trickery /'trɪk(ə)ri/ *n.* (*pl.* **-ies**) **1** the practice or an instance of deception. **2** the use of tricks.

trickle /'trɪk(ə)l/ *v. & n.* ● *v.* **1** *intr. & tr.* flow or cause to flow in drops or a small stream (*water trickled through the crack*). **2** *tr.* come or go slowly or gradually (*information trickles out*). ● *n.* a trickling flow. [Middle English *trekel, trikle*, probably imitative]

trickle charger *n.* an electrical charger for batteries that works at a steady slow rate from the mains.

trickster /'trɪkstə/ *n.* a deceiver or rogue.

tricksy /'trɪksi/ *adj.* (**tricksier, tricksiest**) full of tricks; playful. □ **tricksily** *adv.* **tricksiness** *n.*

tricky /'trɪki/ *adj.* (**trickier, trickiest**) **1** difficult or intricate; requiring care and adroitness (*a tricky job*). **2** crafty or deceitful. **3** resourceful or adroit. □ **trickily** *adv.* **trickiness** *n.*

triclinic /trʌɪ'klɪnɪk/ *adj.* **1** (of a mineral) having three unequal oblique axes. **2** denoting the system classifying triclinic crystalline substances. [Greek TRI- + *klinō* 'to incline']

triclinium /trʌɪ'klɪnɪəm, trɪ-, -'klʌɪn-/ *n.* (*pl.* **triclinia** /-nɪə/) *Rom. Antiq.* **1** a dining table with couches along three sides. **2** a room containing this. [Latin from Greek *triklinion* (as TRI-, *klinē* 'couch')]

tricolour /'trɪkələ, 'trʌɪkʌlə/ *n. & adj.* (*US* **tricolor**) ● *n.* a flag of three colours, esp. the French national flag of blue, white, and red. ● *adj.* (also **tricoloured**) having three colours. [French *tricolore* from Late Latin *tricolor* (as TRI-, COLOUR)]

tricorne /'trʌɪkɔ:n/ *adj. & n.* (also **tricorn**) ● *adj.* **1** having three horns. **2** (of a hat) having a brim turned up on three sides. ● *n.* **1** an imaginary animal with three horns. **2** a tricorne hat. [French *tricorne* or Latin *tricornis* (as TRI-, *cornu* 'horn')]

tricot /'trɪkəʊ, 'tri:-/ *n.* **1** a fine knitted fabric made of natural or man-made fibre. [French, = knitting, from *tricoter* 'knit', of unknown origin]

tricrotic /trʌɪˈkrɒtɪk/ *adj.* (of the pulse) having a triple beat. [TRI-, on the pattern of DICROTIC]

tricuspid /trʌɪˈkʌspɪd/ *n. & adj.* ● *n.* **1** a tooth with three cusps or points. **2** a heart-valve formed of three triangular segments. ● *adj.* (of a tooth) having three cusps or points.

tricycle /ˈtrʌɪsɪk(ə)l/ *n. & v.* ● *n.* **1** a vehicle having three wheels, two on an axle at the back and one at the front, driven by pedals in the same way as a bicycle. **2** a three-wheeled motor vehicle for a disabled driver. ● *v.intr.* ride on a tricycle. □ **tricyclist** *n.*

tricyclic /trʌɪˈsʌɪklɪk/ *adj. & n.* ● *adj.* having three rings or circles. ● *n. Pharm.* any of a number of antidepressant drugs having molecules with three fused rings.

tridactyl /trʌɪˈdaktɪl/ *adj.* (also **tridactylous** /-ˈdaktɪləs/) having three fingers or toes.

trident /ˈtrʌɪd(ə)nt/ *n.* **1** a three-pronged spear, esp. as an attribute of Poseidon (Neptune) or Britannia. **2** (**Trident**) a US type of submarine-launched long-range ballistic missile. [Latin *tridens trident-* (as TRI-, *dens* 'tooth')]

tridentate /trʌɪˈdɛnteɪt/ *adj.* having three teeth or prongs. [TRI- + Latin *dentatus* 'toothed']

Tridentine /trɪˈdɛntʌɪn, trʌɪ-/ *adj. & n.* ● *adj.* of or relating to the Council of Trent, held at Trento in Italy 1545–63, esp. as the basis of Roman Catholic doctrine. ● *n.* a Roman Catholic adhering to this traditional doctrine. [medieval Latin *Tridentinus* from *Tridentum* 'Trent']

Tridentine mass *n.* the Latin Eucharistic liturgy used by the Roman Catholic Church from 1570 to 1964.

triduum /ˈtrɪdjʊəm, ˈtrʌɪ-/ *n. RC Ch.* esp. *hist.* a period of three days' prayer in preparation for a saint's day or other religious occasion. [Latin (as TRI-, *dies* 'day')]

tridymite /ˈtrɪdɪmʌɪt/ *n.* a crystallized form of silica, occurring in cavities of volcanic rocks. [German *Tridymit* from Greek *tridumos* 'threefold' (as TRI-, *didumos* 'twin'), from its occurrence in groups of three crystals]

tried *past* and *past part.* of TRY.

triennial /trʌɪˈɛnɪəl/ *adj. & n.* ● *adj.* **1** lasting three years. **2** recurring every three years. ● *n.* a visitation of an Anglican diocese by its bishop every three years. □ **triennially** *adv.* [Late Latin *triennis* (as TRI-, Latin *annus* 'year')]

triennium /trʌɪˈɛnɪəm/ *n.* (*pl.* **trienniums** or **triennia** /-nɪə/) a period of three years. [Latin (as TRIENNIAL)]

trier /ˈtrʌɪə/ *n.* **1** a person who perseveres (*is a real trier*). **2** a tester, esp. of foodstuffs. **3** *Brit.* a person appointed to decide whether a challenge to a juror is well-founded.

trifacial nerve /trʌɪˈfeɪʃ(ə)l/ *n.* = TRIGEMINAL NERVE.

trifecta /trʌɪˈfɛktə/ *n. N. Amer., Austral., & NZ* a form of betting in which the first three places in a race must be predicted in the correct order. [TRI- + PERFECTA]

trifid /ˈtrʌɪfɪd/ *adj.* esp. *Biol.* partly or wholly split into three divisions or lobes. [Latin *trifidus* (as TRI-, *findere fid-* 'to split')]

trifle /ˈtrʌɪf(ə)l/ *n. & v.* ● *n.* **1** a thing of slight value or importance. **2 a** a small amount esp. of money (*was sold for a trifle*). **b** (prec. by *a*) somewhat (*seems a trifle annoyed*). **3** *Brit.* a dessert of sponge cake (esp. flavoured with sherry) with custard, jelly, fruit, cream, etc. ● *v.* **1** *intr.* talk or act frivolously. **2** *intr.* (foll. by *with*) **a** treat or deal with frivolously or derisively; flirt heartlessly with. **b** refuse to take seriously. **3** *tr.* (foll. by *away*) waste (time, energies, money, etc.) frivolously. □ **trifler** *n.* [Middle English from Old French *truf(f)le*, by-form of *trufe* 'deceit', of unknown origin]

trifling /ˈtrʌɪflɪŋ/ *adj.* **1** unimportant, petty. **2** frivolous. □ **triflingly** *adv.*

trifocal /trʌɪˈfəʊk(ə)l/ *adj. & n.* ● *adj.* having three focuses, esp. of a lens with different focal lengths. ● *n.* (in *pl.*) trifocal spectacles.

trifoliate /trʌɪˈfəʊlɪət/ *adj.* **1** (of a compound leaf) having three leaflets. **2** (of a plant) having such leaves.

triforium /trʌɪˈfɔːrɪəm/ *n.* (*pl.* **triforia** /-rɪə/) a gallery or arcade above the arches of the nave, choir, and transepts of a church. [Anglo-Latin, of unknown origin]

triform /ˈtrʌɪfɔːm/ *adj.* (also **triformed**) **1** formed of three parts. **2** having three forms or bodies.

trifurcate *v. & adj.* ● *v.tr. & intr.* /ˈtrʌɪfəkeɪt/ divide into three branches. ● *adj.* /-ˈfəːkət/ divided into three branches.

trig[1] /trɪg/ *n. colloq.* trigonometry. [abbreviation]

trig[2] /trɪg/ *adj. & v. archaic* or *dial.* ● *adj.* trim or spruce. ● *v.tr.* (**trigged**, **trigging**) make trim; smarten. [Middle English, = trusty, from Old Norse *tryggr*, related to TRUE]

trigamous /ˈtrɪgəməs/ *adj.* **1 a** three times married. **b** having three wives or husbands at once. **2** *Bot.* having male, female, and hermaphrodite flowers in the same head. □ **trigamist** *n.* **trigamy** *n.* [Greek *trigamos* (as TRI-, *gamos* 'marriage')]

trigeminal nerve /trʌɪˈdʒɛmɪn(ə)l/ *n. Anat.* the largest pair of cranial nerves, dividing into the ophthalmic, maxillary, and mandibular nerves. [as TRIGEMINUS]

trigeminal neuralgia *n.* neuralgia involving one or more of the branches of the trigeminal nerves, and often causing severe pain.

trigeminus /trʌɪˈdʒɛmɪnəs/ *n.* (*pl.* **trigemini** /-nʌɪ/) *Anat.* the trigeminal nerve. [Latin, = born as a triplet (as TRI-, *geminus* 'born at the same birth')]

trigger /ˈtrɪgə/ *n. & v.* ● *n.* **1** a movable device for releasing a spring or catch and so setting off a mechanism (esp. that of a gun). **2** an event, occurrence, etc., that sets off a chain reaction. ● *v.tr.* **1** (often foll. by *off*) set (an action or process) in motion; initiate, precipitate. **2** fire (a gun) by the use of a trigger. □ **quick on the trigger** quick to respond. □ **triggered** *adj.* [17th-c. *tricker* from Dutch *trekker*, from *trekken* 'pull']

triggerfish /ˈtrɪgəfɪʃ/ *n.* (*pl.* usu. same) any usu. tropical marine fish of the family Balistidae with a first dorsal fin-spine which can be depressed by pressing on the second.

trigger-happy *adj.* apt to shoot without or with slight provocation.

triglyceride /trʌɪˈglɪsərʌɪd/ *n. Chem.* any ester formed from glycerol and three acid radicals, including the main constituents of fats and oils.

triglyph /ˈtrʌɪglɪf/ *n. Archit.* each of a series of tablets with three vertical grooves, alternating with metopes in a Doric frieze. □ **triglyphic** /-ˈglɪfɪk/ *adj.* **triglyphical** /-ˈglɪfɪk(ə)l/ *adj.* [Latin *triglyphus* from Greek *trigluphos* (as TRI-, *gluphē* 'carving')]

trigon /ˈtrʌɪgɒn/ *n.* **1** a triangle. **2** an ancient triangular lyre or harp. **3** the cutting region of an upper molar tooth. [Latin *trigonum* from Greek *trigōnon*, neuter of *trigōnos* 'three-cornered' (as TRI-, -GON)]

trigonal /ˈtrɪg(ə)n(ə)l/ *adj.* **1** triangular; of or relating to a triangle. **2** *Biol.* triangular in cross-section. **3** (of a crystal etc.) having an axis with threefold symmetry. □ **trigonally** *adv.* [medieval Latin *trigonalis* (as TRIGON)]

trigonometry /trɪgəˈnɒmɪtri/ *n.* the branch of mathematics dealing with the relations of the sides and angles of triangles and with the relevant functions of any angles. □ **trigonometric** /-nəˈmɛtrɪk/ *adj.* **trigonometrical** /-nəˈmɛtrɪk(ə)l/ *adj.* [modern Latin *trigonometria* (as TRIGON, -METRY)]

trig point *n. Surveying* = TRIANGULATION POINT. [abbreviation of *trigonometrical point*]

trigraph /ˈtrʌɪgrɑːf/ *n.* (also **trigram** /-gram/) **1** a group of three letters representing one sound. **2** a figure of three lines.

trigynous /ˈtrɪdʒɪnəs/ *adj. Bot.* having three pistils.

trihedral /trʌɪˈhiːdr(ə)l, -ˈhɛdr(ə)l/ *adj.* having three surfaces.

trihedron /trʌɪˈhiːdrən, -ˈhɛdrən/ *n.* (*pl.* **trihedra** /-drə/ or **trihedrons**) a figure of three intersecting planes.

trihydric /trʌɪ'hʌɪdrɪk/ *adj. Chem.* containing three hydroxyl groups. [TRI- + HYDROGEN + -IC]

trike /trʌɪk/ *n. & v.intr. colloq.* a tricycle. [abbreviation]

trilabiate /trʌɪ'leɪbɪət/ *adj. Bot. & Zool.* three-lipped.

trilateral /trʌɪ'lat(ə)r(ə)l/ *adj. & n.* ● *adj.* **1** of, on, or with three sides. **2** shared by or involving three parties, countries, etc. (*trilateral negotiations*). ● *n.* a figure having three sides.

trilby /'trɪlbi/ *n.* (*pl.* **-ies**) *Brit.* a soft felt hat with a narrow brim and indented crown. ◻ **trilbied** *adj.* [name of the heroine in G. du Maurier's novel *Trilby* (1894), in the stage version of which such a hat was worn]

trilinear /trʌɪ'lɪnɪə/ *adj.* of or having three lines.

trilingual /trʌɪ'lɪŋgw(ə)l/ *adj.* **1** able to speak three languages, esp. fluently. **2** spoken or written in three languages. ◻ **trilingualism** *n.*

triliteral /trʌɪ'lɪt(ə)r(ə)l/ *adj.* **1** of three letters. **2** (of a Semitic language) having (most) roots with three consonants.

trilith /'trʌɪlɪθ/ *n.* (also **trilithon** /-lɪθ(ə)n/) a megalithic structure consisting of three stones, esp. of two uprights and a lintel. ◻ **trilithic** /-'lɪθɪk/ *adj.* [Greek *trilithon* (as TRI-, *lithos* 'stone')]

trill /trɪl/ *n. & v.* ● *n.* **1** a quavering or vibratory sound, esp. a rapid alternation of sung or played notes. **2** a bird's warbling sound. **3** the pronunciation of *r* with a vibration of the tongue. ● *v.* **1** *intr.* produce a trill. **2** *tr.* warble (a song) or pronounce (*r* etc.) with a trill. [Italian *trillo* (*n.*), *trillare* (*v.*)]

trillion /'trɪljən/ *n.* (*pl.* same or (in sense 3) **trillions**) **1** a million million (1,000,000,000,000 or 10^{12}). **2** (formerly, esp. *Brit.*) a million million million (1,000,000,000,000,000,000 or 10^{18}). **3** (in *pl.*) *colloq.* a very large number (*trillions of times*). ◻ **trillionth** *adj. & n.* [French *trillion* or Italian *trilione* (as TRI-, MILLION), on the pattern of *billion*]

■ **Usage** Senses 1–2 correspond to the change in sense of *billion*.

trillium /'trɪlɪəm/ *n.* a plant of the N. American and Asian genus *Trillium*, with a solitary three-petalled flower above a whorl of three leaves. [modern Latin, apparently from Swedish *trilling* 'triplet']

trilobite /'trʌɪlə(ʊ)bʌɪt, 'trɪ-/ *n.* any fossil marine arthropod of the subphylum Trilobita of Palaeozoic times, characterized by a three-lobed body. [modern Latin *Trilobites* (as TRI-, Greek *lobos* 'lobe')]

trilogy /'trɪlədʒi/ *n.* (*pl.* **-ies**) **1** a group of three related literary or operatic works. **2** *Gk Antiq.* a set of three tragedies performed as a group. [Greek *trilogia* (as TRI-, -LOGY)]

trim /trɪm/ *v., n., & adj.* ● *v.* (**trimmed**, **trimming**) **1** *tr.* make neat or of the required size or form, esp. by cutting away irregular or unwanted parts. **2** *tr.* (foll. by *off*, *away*) remove by cutting off (such parts). **3** *tr.* **a** (often foll. by *up*) make (a person) neat in dress and appearance. **b** ornament or decorate (esp. clothing, a hat, etc.) by adding ribbons, lace, etc. **4** *tr.* adjust the balance of (a ship or aircraft) by the arrangement of its cargo etc. **5** *tr.* arrange (sails) to suit the wind. **6** *intr.* **a** associate oneself with currently prevailing views, esp. to advance oneself. **b** hold a middle course in politics or opinion. **7** *tr. colloq.* **a** rebuke sharply. **b** thrash. **c** get the better of in a bargain etc. ● *n.* **1** the state or degree of readiness or fitness (*found everything in perfect trim*). **2** ornament or decorative material. **3** dress or equipment. **4** the act of trimming a person's hair. **5** the inclination of an aircraft to the horizontal. ● *adj.* (**trimmer**, **trimmest**) **1** neat or spruce. **2** in good order; well arranged or equipped. ◻ **in trim 1** looking smart, healthy, etc. **2** *Naut.* in good order. ◻ **trimly** *adv.* **trimness** *n.* [perhaps from Old English *trymman*, *trymian* 'make firm, arrange': but there is no connecting evidence between Old English and 1500]

trimaran /'trʌɪməran/ *n.* a vessel like a catamaran, with three hulls side by side. [TRI- + CATAMARAN]

trimer /'trʌɪmə/ *n. Chem.* a polymer comprising three monomer units. ◻ **trimeric** /-'mɛrɪk/ *adj.* [TRI- + -MER]

trimerous /'trɪm(ə)rəs, 'trʌɪ-/ *adj.* having three parts.

trimester /trʌɪ'mɛstə/ *n.* a period of three months, esp. of human gestation or *N. Amer.* as a university term. ◻ **trimestral** *adj.* **trimestrial** *adj.* [French *trimestre* from Latin *trimestris* (as TRI-, *-mestris* from *mensis* 'month')]

trimeter /'trɪmɪtə, 'trʌɪ-/ *n. Prosody* a verse of three measures. ◻ **trimetric** /trʌɪ'mɛtrɪk/ *adj.* **trimetrical** /trʌɪ'mɛtrɪk(ə)l/ *adj.* [Latin *trimetrus* from Greek *trimetros* (as TRI-, *metron* 'measure')]

trimmer /'trɪmə/ *n.* **1** a person who trims articles of dress. **2** a person who trims in politics etc.; a time-server. **3** an instrument for clipping etc. **4** *Archit.* a short piece of timber across an opening (e.g. for a hearth) to carry the ends of truncated joists. **5** a small capacitor etc. used to tune a radio set. **6** *Austral. colloq.* a striking or outstanding person or thing.

trimming /'trɪmɪŋ/ *n.* **1** ornamentation or decoration, esp. for clothing. **2** (in *pl.*) *colloq.* the usual accompaniments, esp. of the main course of a meal. **3** (in *pl.*) pieces cut off in trimming.

trimorphism /trʌɪ'mɔːfɪz(ə)m/ *n. Bot., Zool., & Crystallog.* existence in three distinct forms. ◻ **trimorphic** *adj.* **trimorphous** *adj.*

trine /trʌɪn/ *adj. & n.* ● *adj.* **1** threefold, triple; made up of three parts. **2** *Astrol.* denoting the aspect of two heavenly bodies 120° (one-third of the zodiac) apart. ● *n.* *Astrol.* a trine aspect. ◻ **trinal** *adj.* [Middle English via Old French *trin trine* from Latin *trinus* 'threefold', from *tres* 'three']

Trinidadian /trɪnɪ'dadɪən, -'deɪdɪən/ *n. & adj.* ● *n.* a native or inhabitant of Trinidad, an island in the W. Indies. ● *adj.* of or relating to Trinidad or its people.

Trinitarian /trɪnɪ'tɛːrɪən/ *n. & adj.* ● *n.* a person who believes in the doctrine of the Trinity. ● *adj.* of or relating to this belief. ◻ **Trinitarianism** *n.*

trinitrotoluene /trʌɪˌnʌɪtrəʊ'tɒljʊiːn/ *n.* (also **trinitrotoluol** /-'tɒljʊɒl/) = TNT.

trinity /'trɪnɪti/ *n.* (*pl.* **-ies**) **1** the state of being three. **2** a group of three. **3** (**the Trinity** or **the Holy Trinity**) *Theol.* the three persons of the Christian Godhead (Father, Son, and Holy Spirit). [Middle English via Old French *trinité* from Latin *trinitas -tatis* 'triad' (as TRINE)]

Trinity Brethren *n.pl.* the members of Trinity House.

Trinity House *n. Brit.* an association concerned with the licensing of pilots, the erection and maintenance of buoys, lighthouses, etc. on the coasts of England and Wales.

Trinity Sunday *n.* the next Sunday after Whit Sunday.

Trinity term *n. Brit.* the university and law term beginning after Easter.

trinket /'trɪŋkɪt/ *n.* a trifling ornament, jewel, etc., esp. one worn on the person. ◻ **trinketry** *n.* [16th c.: origin unknown]

trinomial /trʌɪ'nəʊmɪəl/ *adj. & n.* ● *adj.* consisting of three terms. ● *n.* a scientific name or algebraic expression of three terms. [TRI-, on the pattern of BINOMIAL]

trio /'triːəʊ/ *n.* (*pl.* **-os**) **1** a set or group of three. **2** *Mus.* **a** a composition for three performers. **b** a group of three performers. **c** the central, usu. contrastive, section of a minuet, scherzo, or march. **3** (in piquet) three aces, kings, queens, or jacks in one hand. [French & Italian from Latin *tres* 'three', on the pattern of *duo*]

triode /'trʌɪəʊd/ *n.* **1** a thermionic valve having three electrodes. **2** a semiconductor rectifier having three connections. [TRI- + ELECTRODE]

triolet /'triːə(ʊ)lɛt, 'trʌɪəlɛt/ *n.* a poem of eight (usu. eight-syllabled) lines rhyming *abaaabab*, the first line recurring as the fourth and seventh and the second as the eighth. [French (as TRIO)]

trioxide /trʌɪ'ɒksʌɪd/ *n. Chem.* an oxide containing three oxygen atoms.

trip /trɪp/ *v.* & *n.* ● *v.* (**tripped**, **tripping**) **1** *intr.* **a** walk or dance with quick light steps. **b** (of a rhythm etc.) run lightly. **2 a** *intr.* & *tr.* (often foll. by *up*) stumble or cause to stumble, esp. by catching or entangling the feet. **b** *intr.* & *tr.* (foll. by *up*) make or cause to make a slip or blunder. **3** *tr.* detect (a person) in a blunder. **4** *intr.* make an excursion to a place. **5** *tr.* release (part of a machine) suddenly by knocking aside a catch etc. **6** *tr.* **a** release and raise (an anchor) from the bottom by means of a cable. **b** turn (a yard etc.) from a horizontal to a vertical position for lowering. **7** *intr. colloq.* have a drug-induced experience, esp. from taking LSD. ● *n.* **1** a journey or excursion, esp. for pleasure. **2 a** a stumble or blunder. **b** the act of tripping or the state of being tripped up. **3** a nimble step. **4** *colloq.* a drug-induced experience, esp. from taking LSD. **5** a contrivance for a tripping mechanism etc. □ **trip the light fantastic** *joc.* dance. [Middle English via Old French *triper*, *tripper* from Middle Dutch *trippen* 'to skip, hop']

tripartite /trʌɪ'pɑːtʌɪt/ *adj.* **1** consisting of three parts. **2** shared by or involving three parties. **3** *Bot.* (of a leaf) divided into three segments almost to the base. □ **tripartitely** *adv.* **tripartition** /-'tɪʃ(ə)n/ *n.* [Middle English from Latin *tripartitus* (as TRI-, *partitus* past part. of *partiri* 'divide')]

tripe /trʌɪp/ *n.* **1** the first or second stomach of a ruminant, esp. an ox, as food. **2** *colloq.* nonsense, rubbish (*don't talk such tripe*). [Middle English from Old French, of unknown origin]

trip-hammer *n.* a large tilt-hammer operated by tripping.

triphibious /trʌɪ'fɪbɪəs/ *adj.* (of military operations) on land, on sea, and in the air. [formed irregularly from TRI-, on the pattern of *amphibious*]

triphthong /'trɪfθɒŋ/ *n.* **1** a union of three vowels (letters or sounds) pronounced in one syllable (as in *fire*). **2** three vowel characters representing the sound of a single vowel (as in b*eau*). □ **triphthongal** /-'θɒŋg(ə)l/ *adj.* [French *triphtongue* (as TRI-, DIPHTHONG)]

triplane /'trʌɪpleɪn/ *n.* an early type of aeroplane having three sets of wings, one above the other.

triple /'trɪp(ə)l/ *adj.*, *n.*, & *v.* ● *adj.* **1** consisting of three usu. equal parts or things; threefold. **2** involving three parties. **3** three times as much or many (*triple the amount*; *triple thickness*). ● *n.* **1** a threefold number or amount. **2** a set of three. **3** (in *pl.*) a peal of changes on seven bells. ● *v.tr.* & *intr.* multiply by three; increase threefold. □ **triply** *adv.* [Old French *triple* or Latin *triplus* from Greek *triplous*]

triple acrostic *n.* an acrostic using the first, middle, and last letters.

triple crown *n.* **1** *RC Ch.* the Pope's tiara. **2** the act of winning all three of a group of important events in horse racing, rugby, etc.

triple jump *n.* an athletic exercise or contest comprising a hop, a step, and a jump.

triple play *n.* *Baseball* the act of putting out three players (two runners and the batter) from one batted ball.

triple point *n.* *Physics* the temperature and pressure at which the solid, liquid, and vapour phases of a pure substance can coexist in equilibrium.

triple rhyme *n.* a rhyme including three syllables.

triplet /'trɪplɪt/ *n.* **1** each of three children or animals born at one birth. **2** a set of three things, esp. of equal notes played in the time of two or of verses rhyming together. [TRIPLE + -ET[1], on the pattern of *doublet*]

triple time *n.* musical time with three beats to the bar; waltz time.

triplex /'trɪplɛks/ *adj.* & *n.* ● *adj.* triple or threefold. ● *n.* (**Triplex**) *Brit. propr.* toughened or laminated safety glass for car windows etc. [Latin *triplex -plicis* (as TRI-, *plic-* 'fold')]

triplicate *adj.*, *n.*, & *v.* ● *adj.* /'trɪplɪkət/ **1** existing in three examples or copies. **2** having three corresponding parts. **3** tripled. ● *n.* /'trɪplɪkət/ each of a set of three copies or corresponding parts. ● *v.tr.* /'trɪplɪkeɪt/ **1** make in three copies. **2** multiply by three. □ **in triplicate** consisting of three exact copies. □ **triplication** /-'keɪʃ(ə)n/ *n.* [Middle English from Latin *triplicatus*, past part. of *triplicare* (as TRIPLEX)]

triplicity /trɪ'plɪsɪti/ *n.* (*pl.* **-ies**) **1** the state of being triple. **2** a group of three things. **3** *Astrol.* a set of three zodiacal signs. [Middle English via Late Latin *triplicitas* from Latin TRIPLEX]

triploid /'trɪplɔɪd/ *n.* & *adj.* *Biol.* ● *n.* an organism or cell having three times the haploid set of chromosomes. ● *adj.* of or being a triploid. [modern Latin *triploides* from Greek (as TRIPLE)]

triploidy /'trɪplɔɪdi/ *n.* the condition of being triploid.

tripmeter /'trɪpmiːtə/ *n.* a vehicle instrument that can be set to record the distance of individual journeys.

tripod /'trʌɪpɒd/ *n.* **1** a three-legged stand for supporting a camera etc. **2** a stool, table, or utensil resting on three feet or legs. **3** *Gk Antiq.* a bronze altar at Delphi on which a priestess sat to utter oracles. □ **tripodal** /'trɪpəd(ə)l/ *adj.* [Latin *tripus tripodis* from Greek *tripous* (as TRI-, *pous podos* 'foot')]

tripoli /'trɪpəli/ *n.* = ROTTEN-STONE. [French, from *Tripoli* either of two cities, one in Libya, one in Lebanon]

tripos /'trʌɪpɒs/ *n.* (at Cambridge University) the honours examination for the BA degree. [as TRIPOD, with reference to the stool on which graduates sat to deliver a satirical speech at the degree ceremony]

tripper /'trɪpə/ *n.* **1** *Brit.* a person who goes on a pleasure trip or excursion. **2** *colloq.* a person experiencing hallucinatory effects of a drug.

trippy /'trɪpi/ *adj.* (**trippier**, **trippiest**) *colloq.* (of music, poetry, etc.) producing an effect resembling that of a psychedelic drug.

triptych /'trɪptɪk/ *n.* **1 a** a picture or relief carving on three panels, usu. hinged vertically together and often used as an altarpiece. **b** a set of three associated pictures placed in this way. **2** a set of three writing-tablets hinged or tied together. **3** a set of three artistic works. [TRI-, on the pattern of DIPTYCH]

triptyque /trɪp'tiːk/ *n.* a customs permit serving as a passport for a motor vehicle. [French, as TRIPTYCH (originally having three sections)]

tripwire /'trɪpwʌɪə/ *n.* a wire stretched close to the ground, operating an alarm etc. when disturbed.

triquetra /trʌɪ'kwɛtrə, -'kwiːtrə/ *n.* (*pl.* **triquetrae** /-triː/) a symmetrical ornament of three interlaced arcs. [Latin, fem. of *triquetrus* 'three-cornered']

trireme /'trʌɪriːm/ *n.* a galley with three banks of oars. [French *trirème* or Latin *triremis* (as TRI-, *remus* 'oar')]

trisaccharide /trʌɪ'sakərʌɪd/ *n.* *Chem.* a sugar consisting of three linked monosaccharides.

Trisagion /trɪ'sagɪən, -'seɪgɪən/ *n.* a hymn, esp. in the Orthodox Church, with a triple invocation of God as holy. [Middle English from Greek, neut. of *trisagios*, from *tris* 'thrice' + *hagios* 'holy']

trisect /trʌɪ'sɛkt/ *v.tr.* cut or divide into three (usu. equal) parts. □ **trisection** *n.* **trisector** *n.* [TRI- + Latin *secare sect-* 'to cut']

trishaw /'trʌɪʃɔː/ *n.* a light three-wheeled pedalled vehicle used in the Far East. [TRI- + RICKSHAW]

triskaidekaphobia /ˌtrɪskʌɪdɛkə'fəʊbɪə/ *n.* fear of the number thirteen. [from Greek *treiskaideka* 'thirteen' + -PHOBIA]

triskelion /trɪ'skɛlɪən/ *n.* a symbolic figure of three legs or lines from a common centre. [Greek TRI- + *skelos* 'leg']

trismus /'trɪzməs/ *n.* *Med.* a variety of tetanus with tonic spasm of the jaw muscles causing the mouth to remain tightly closed. Also called *lockjaw*. [modern Latin from Greek *trismos* = *trigmos* 'a scream, grinding']

trisomy /'trɪsəmi/ *n. Med.* a condition in which an extra copy of a chromosome is present in the cell nuclei, causing developmental abnormalities. [TRI- + -SOME[3]]

trisomy-21 *n. Med.* the most common form of Down's syndrome, caused by an extra copy of chromosome number 21.

triste /tri:st/ *adj. literary* sad, melancholy, dreary. [French from Latin *tristis*]

tristesse /trɪ'stɛs, French tristɛs/ *n.* sadness. [French]

trisyllable /trʌɪ'sɪləb(ə)l/ *n.* a word or metrical foot of three syllables. ▫ **trisyllabic** /-'labɪk/ *adj.*

tritagonist /trʌɪ'tag(ə)nɪst, trɪ-/ *n.* the third actor in an ancient Greek drama (cf. DEUTERAGONIST). [Greek *tritagōnistēs* (as TRITO-, *agōnistēs* 'actor')]

trite /trʌɪt/ *adj.* (of a phrase, opinion, etc.) hackneyed, worn out by constant repetition. ▫ **tritely** *adv.* **triteness** *n.* [Latin *tritus*, past part. of *terere* 'rub']

tritiate /'trɪtɪeɪt/ *v.tr.* replace the ordinary hydrogen in (a substance) by tritium. ▫ **tritiation** /-'eɪʃ(ə)n/ *n.*

tritium /'trɪtɪəm/ *n. Chem.* a radioactive isotope of hydrogen with a mass about three times that of ordinary hydrogen (symbol **T**). [modern Latin from Greek *tritos* 'third']

trito- /'trɪtəʊ, 'trʌɪtəʊ/ *comb. form* third. [Greek *tritos* 'third']

Triton /'trʌɪt(ə)n/ *n.* **1** (in Greek mythology) a minor sea-god usu. represented as a man with a fish's tail and carrying a trident and shell-trumpet. **2** (**triton**) any marine gastropod mollusc of the family Cymatiidae, with a long conical shell. **3** (**triton**) a newt. [Latin from Greek *Tritōn*]

triton /'trʌɪt(ə)n/ *n.* a nucleus of a tritium atom, consisting of a proton and two neutrons.

tritone /'trʌɪtəʊn/ *n. Mus.* an interval of an augmented fourth, comprising three tones.

triturate /'trɪtjʊreɪt/ *v.tr.* **1** grind to a fine powder. **2** masticate thoroughly. ▫ **triturable** *adj.* **trituration** /-'reɪʃ(ə)n/ *n.* **triturator** *n.* [Latin *triturare* 'thresh corn' from *tritura* 'rubbing' (as TRITE)]

triumph /'trʌɪʌmf/ *n. & v.* ● *n.* **1 a** the state of being victorious or successful (*returned home in triumph*). **b** a great success or achievement. **2** a supreme example (*a triumph of engineering*). **3** joy at success; exultation (*could see triumph in her face*). **4** *Rom.Hist.* the processional entry of a victorious general into ancient Rome. ● *v.intr.* **1** (often foll. by *over*) gain a victory; be successful; prevail. **2** ride in triumph. **3** (often foll. by *over*) exult. [Middle English from Old French *triumphe* (*n.*), *triumpher* (*v.*), from Latin *triump(h)us*, probably from Greek *thriambos* 'hymn to Bacchus']

triumphal /trʌɪ'ʌmf(ə)l/ *adj.* of or used in celebrating a triumph. [Middle English from Old French *triumphal* or Latin *triumphalis* (as TRIUMPH)]

▪ **Usage** *Triumphal*, meaning 'of or used in celebrating a triumph', e.g. *triumphal arch*, should not be confused with *triumphant* meaning 'victorious' or 'exultant', e.g. *the triumphant army*; *a triumphant laugh*.

triumphalism /trʌɪ'ʌmf(ə)lɪz(ə)m/ *n.* excessive exultation over the victories of one's own party, country, etc. ▫ **triumphalist** *adj. & n.*

triumphant /trʌɪ'ʌmf(ə)nt/ *adj.* **1** victorious or successful. **2** exultant. ▫ **triumphantly** *adv.* [Middle English from Old French or Latin, from *triumphare* 'to triumph' (as TRIUMPH)]

▪ **Usage** See Usage Note at TRIUMPHAL.

triumvir /trʌɪ'ʌmvə, 'trʌɪəmvə/ *n.* (*pl.* **triumvirs** or **triumviri** /-rʌɪ/) **1** each of three men holding a joint office. **2** a member of a triumvirate. ▫ **triumviral** *adj.* [Latin, originally in pl. *triumviri*, back-formation from *trium virorum*, genitive of *tres viri* 'three men']

triumvirate /trʌɪ'ʌmvɪrət/ *n.* **1** a board or ruling group of three men, esp. in ancient Rome. **2** the office of triumvir.

triune /'trʌɪju:n/ *adj.* three in one, esp. with reference to the Trinity. ▫ **triunity** /-'ju:nɪti/ *n.* (*pl.* **-ies**). [TRI- + Latin *unus* 'one']

trivalent /trʌɪ'veɪl(ə)nt/ *adj. Chem.* having a valency of three; tervalent. ▫ **trivalency** *n.*

trivet /'trɪvɪt/ *n.* **1** an iron tripod or bracket for a cooking pot or kettle to stand on. **2** an iron bracket designed to hook on to bars of a grate for a similar purpose. ▫ **as right as a trivet** *Brit. colloq.* in a perfectly good state, esp. healthy. [Middle English *trevet*, apparently from Latin *tripes* (as TRI-, *pes pedis* 'foot')]

trivet table *n.* a table with three feet.

trivia /'trɪvɪə/ *n.pl.* trifles or trivialities. [modern Latin, pl. of TRIVIUM, influenced by TRIVIAL]

trivial /'trɪvɪəl/ *adj.* **1** of small value or importance; trifling (*raised trivial objections*). **2** (of a person etc.) concerned only with trivial things. **3** *archaic* commonplace or humdrum (*the trivial round of daily life*). **4** *Biol. & Chem.* of a name: **a** popular; not scientific. **b** specific, as opposed to generic. **5** *Math.* giving rise to no difficulty or interest. ▫ **triviality** /-'alɪti/ *n.* (*pl.* **-ies**). **trivially** *adv.* **trivialness** *n.* [Latin *trivialis* 'commonplace' from *trivium*: see TRIVIUM]

trivialize /'trɪvɪəlʌɪz/ *v.tr.* (also **-ise**) make trivial or apparently trivial; minimize. ▫ **trivialization** /-'zeɪʃ(ə)n/ *n.*

trivium /'trɪvɪəm/ *n. hist.* a medieval university course of grammar, rhetoric, and logic. [Latin, = place where three roads meet (as TRI-, *via* 'road')]

tri-weekly /trʌɪ'wi:kli/ *adj.* produced or occurring three times a week or every three weeks.

-trix /trɪks/ *suffix* (*pl.* **-trices** /trɪ'si:z, 'trʌɪsi:z/ or **-trixes**) forming feminine agent nouns corresponding to masculine nouns in *-tor*, esp. in Law (*executrix*). [Latin *-trix -tricis*]

tRNA *abbr.* transfer RNA.

trocar /'trəʊkɑ:/ *n.* a surgical instrument with a three-sided cutting point, used for withdrawing fluid from a body cavity, esp. in oedema etc. [French *trois-quarts*, *trocart*, from *trois* 'three' + *carre* 'side, face of an instrument']

trochaic /trə(ʊ)'keɪɪk/ *adj. & n. Prosody* ● *adj.* of or using trochees. ● *n.* (usu. in *pl.*) trochaic verse. [Latin *trochaicus* from Greek *trokhaikos* (as TROCHEE)]

trochal /'trəʊk(ə)l/ *adj. Zool.* wheel-shaped. [Greek *trokhos* 'wheel']

trochal disc *n.* the retractable disc on the head of a rotifer bearing a crown of cilia, used for drawing in food or for propulsion.

trochanter /trə'kantə/ *n.* **1** *Anat.* any of several bony protuberances by which muscles are attached to the upper part of the thigh bone. **2** *Zool.* the second segment of the leg in insects. [French from Greek *trokhantēr*, from *trekhō* 'to run']

troche /trəʊʃ, 'trəʊki:/ *n.* a small usu. circular medicated tablet or lozenge. [obsolete *trochisk* from Old French *trochisque* via Late Latin *trochiscus* from Greek *trokhiskos*, diminutive of *trokhos* 'wheel']

trochee /'trəʊki:/ *n. Prosody* a foot consisting of one long or stressed syllable followed by one short or unstressed syllable. [Latin *trochaeus* from Greek *trokhaios* (*pous*) 'running (foot)', from *trekhō* 'to run']

trochlea /'trɒklɪə/ *n.* (*pl.* **trochleae** /-lɪi:/) *Anat.* a pulley-like structure or arrangement of parts, e.g. the groove at the lower end of the humerus. ▫ **trochlear** *adj.* [Latin, = pulley, from Greek *trokhilia*]

trochoid /'trəʊkɔɪd/ *adj. & n.* ● *adj.* **1** *Anat.* rotating on its own axis. **2** *Geom.* (of a curve) traced by a point on a radius of a circle rotating along a straight line or another circle. ● *n.* a trochoid joint or curve. ▫ **trochoidal** /-'kɔɪd(ə)l/ *adj.* [Greek *trokhoeidēs* 'wheel-like' from *trokhos* 'wheel']

trod *past* and *past part.* of TREAD.

trodden *past part.* of TREAD.

trog[1] /trɒg/ *n. Brit. slang* a contemptible person; a lout or hooligan. [abbreviation of TROGLODYTE]

trog[2] /trɒg/ *v.intr.* (**-gg-**) *slang* **1** walk laboriously; trudge. **2** walk casually; stroll. [20th c.: perhaps a blend of TRUDGE, SLOG, TROLL[2], etc.]

troglodyte /ˈtrɒglədʌɪt/ *n.* **1** a cave dweller, esp. of prehistoric times. **2** a hermit. **3** *derog.* a wilfully obscurantist or old-fashioned person. ▫ **troglodytic** /-ˈdɪtɪk/ *adj.* **troglodytical** /-ˈdɪtɪk(ə)l/ *adj.* **troglodytism** *n.* [Latin *troglodyta* from Greek *trōglodutēs*, from the name of an Ethiopian people, from *trōglē* 'hole']

trogon /ˈtrəʊgɒn/ *n.* any tropical bird of the family Trogonidae, with a long tail and brilliantly coloured plumage. [modern Latin from Greek *trōgōn*, from *trōgō* 'gnaw']

troika /ˈtrɔɪkə/ *n.* **1 a** a Russian vehicle with a team of three horses abreast. **b** this team. **2** a group of three people, esp. as an administrative council. [Russian, from *troe* 'set of three']

troilism /ˈtrɔɪlɪz(ə)m/ *n.* sexual activity involving three participants. [perhaps from French *trois* 'three']

Trojan /ˈtrəʊdʒ(ə)n/ *adj.* & *n.* ● *adj.* of or relating to ancient Troy in Asia Minor. ● *n.* **1** a native or inhabitant of Troy. **2** a person who works, fights, etc. courageously (*works like a Trojan*). [Middle English from Latin *Troianus*, from *Troia* 'Troy']

Trojan Horse *n.* **1** a hollow wooden horse said to have been used by the Greeks to enter Troy. **2** a person or device planted to bring about an enemy's downfall. **3** *Computing* a program designed to breach the security of a computer system while ostensibly performing some innocuous function.

troll[1] /trəʊl, trɒl/ *n.* (in Scandinavian folklore) a fabulous being, esp. a giant or dwarf dwelling in a cave. [Old Norse & Swedish *troll*, Danish *trold*]

troll[2] /trəʊl, trɒl/ *v.* & *n.* ● *v.* **1** *intr.* sing out in a carefree jovial manner. **2** *tr.* & *intr.* **a** fish by drawing bait along in the water. **b** (often foll. by *for*) search, seek. **3** *intr.* esp. *Brit.* walk, stroll. ● *n.* **1** the act of trolling for fish. **2** a line or bait used in this. ▫ **troller** *n.* [Middle English 'stroll, roll', of uncertain origin: cf. Old French *troller* 'quest', Middle High German *trollen* 'stroll']

trolley /ˈtrɒli/ *n.* (*pl.* **-eys**) **1** esp. *Brit.* a table, stand, or basket on wheels or castors for serving food, transporting luggage or shopping, gathering purchases in a supermarket, etc. **2** esp. *Brit.* a low truck running on rails. **3** (in full **trolley-wheel**) a wheel attached to a pole etc. used for collecting current from an overhead electric wire to drive a vehicle. **4 a** *US* = TROLLEY-CAR. **b** *Brit.* = TROLLEYBUS. ▫ **off one's trolley** *slang* crazy. [of dialect origin, perhaps from TROLL[2]]

trolleybus /ˈtrɒlɪbʌs/ *n.* a bus powered by electricity obtained from an overhead cable by means of a trolley-wheel.

trolley-car *n. US* a tram powered by electricity obtained from an overhead cable by means of a trolley-wheel.

trollop /ˈtrɒləp/ *n.* **1** a disreputable or promiscuous girl or woman. **2** a prostitute. [17th c.: perhaps related to TRULL]

trombone /trɒmˈbəʊn/ *n.* **1 a** a large brass wind instrument with a sliding tube. **b** a trombone-player. **2** an organ stop with the quality of a trombone. ▫ **trombonist** *n.* [French or Italian from Italian *tromba* TRUMPET]

trommel /ˈtrɒm(ə)l/ *n. Mining* a revolving cylindrical sieve for cleaning ore. [German, = drum]

tromometer /trəˈmɒmɪtə/ *n.* an instrument for measuring very slight earthquake shocks. [Greek *tromos* 'trembling' + -METER]

trompe /trɒmp/ *n.* an apparatus for producing a blast in a furnace by using falling water to displace air. [French, = trumpet: see TRUMP[1]]

trompe l'œil /trɒmp ˈlɔɪ, French trɔ̃p lœj/ *n.* (*pl.* ***trompe l'œils*** *pronunc.* same) a still-life painting etc. designed to give an illusion of reality. [French, literally 'deceives the eye']

-tron /trɒn/ *suffix Physics* forming nouns denoting: **1** a subatomic particle (*positron*). **2** a particle accelerator. **3** a thermionic valve. [from ELECTRON]

troop /truːp/ *n.* & *v.* ● *n.* **1** an assembled company; an assemblage of people or animals. **2** (in *pl.*) soldiers or armed forces. **3** a cavalry unit commanded by a captain. **4** a unit of artillery and armoured formation. **5** a grouping of three or more Scout patrols. ● *v.intr.* (foll. by *in*, *out*, *off*, etc.) come together or move in large numbers. ▫ **troop the colour** esp. *Brit.* show a flag ceremonially at a public mounting of garrison guards. [French *troupe*, back-formation from *troupeau*, diminutive of medieval Latin *troppus* 'flock', probably of Germanic origin]

troop carrier *n.* a large aircraft, armoured vehicle, etc., for carrying troops.

trooper /ˈtruːpə/ *n.* **1** a private soldier in a cavalry or armoured unit. **2** *Austral.* & *US* a mounted or motor-borne police officer. **3** a cavalry horse. **4** esp. *Brit.* a troopship. ▫ **swear like a trooper** swear extensively or forcefully.

troopship /ˈtruːpʃɪp/ *n.* a ship used for transporting troops.

tropaeolum /trə(ʊ)ˈpiːələm/ *n.* a trailing or climbing plant of the genus *Tropaeolum*, with trumpet-shaped yellow, orange, or red flowers. [modern Latin from Latin *tropaeum* 'trophy', with reference to the likeness of the flower and leaf to a helmet and shield]

trope /trəʊp/ *n.* a figurative (e.g. metaphorical or ironical) use of a word. [Latin *tropus* from Greek *tropos* 'turn, way, trope', from *trepō* 'to turn']

trophic /ˈtrɒfɪk/ *adj.* of or concerned with nutrition (*trophic nerves*). [Greek *trophikos*, via *trophē* 'nourishment' from *trephō* 'nourish']

-trophic /ˈtrəʊfɪk, ˈtrɒfɪk/ *comb. form* **1** relating to nutrition (*autotrophic*, *oligotrophic*). **2** relating to maintenance or regulation, esp. by a hormone (*corticotrophic*, *gonadotrophic*). ▫ **-trophism**, **-trophy** *comb. forms.* [Greek *tropheia* 'nourishment']

tropho- /ˈtrɒfəʊ, ˈtrəʊfəʊ/ *comb. form* nourishment. [Greek *trophē*: see TROPHIC]

trophoblast /ˈtrɒfə(ʊ)blast, ˈtrəʊf-/ *n.* a layer of tissue on the outside of a mammalian blastula, supplying the embryo with nourishment and later forming the major part of the placenta.

trophy /ˈtrəʊfi/ *n.* (*pl.* **-ies**) **1** a cup or other decorative object awarded as a prize or memento of victory or success in a contest etc. **2** a memento or souvenir, e.g. a deer's antlers, taken in hunting. **3** *Gk & Rom. Antiq.* the weapons etc. of a defeated army set up as a memorial of victory. **4** an ornamental group of symbolic or typical objects arranged for display. ▫ **trophied** *adj.* (also in *comb.*). [French *trophée* via Latin *trophaeum* from Greek *tropaion*, via *tropē* 'a rout' from *trepō* 'to turn']

tropic /ˈtrɒpɪk/ *n.* & *adj.* ● *n.* **1** the parallel of latitude 23°26′ north (**tropic of Cancer**) or south (**tropic of Capricorn**) of the equator. **2** each of two corresponding circles on the celestial sphere where the sun appears to turn after reaching its greatest declination. **3** (**the Tropics**) the region between the tropics of Cancer and Capricorn. ● *adj.* **1** = TROPICAL 1. **2** /ˈtrəʊpɪk/ of tropism. [Middle English via Latin *tropicus* from Greek *tropikos*, via *tropē* 'turning' from *trepō* 'to turn']

-tropic /ˈtrəʊpɪk, ˈtrɒpɪk/ *comb. form* **1** turning towards (*heliotropic*). **2** affecting (*psychotropic*); (esp. in names of hormones) = -TROPHIC.

tropical /ˈtrɒpɪk(ə)l/ *adj.* **1** of, peculiar to, or suggesting the Tropics (*tropical fish*; *tropical diseases*). **2** very hot; passionate, luxuriant. **3** of or by way of a trope. ▫ **tropically** *adv.*

tropical cyclone see CYCLONE 2.

tropical storm *n.* = CYCLONE 2.

tropical year see YEAR 1.

tropic bird *n.* any seabird of the family Phaethontidae, with very long central tail feathers.

tropic of Cancer see TROPIC *n.* 1.

tropic of Capricorn see TROPIC *n.* 1.

tropism /'trəʊpɪz(ə)m, 'trɒp-/ *n. Biol.* the turning of all or part of an organism in a particular direction in response to an external stimulus. [Greek *tropos* 'turning' from *trepō* 'to turn']

tropology /trə'pɒlədʒi/ *n.* **1** the figurative use of words. **2** figurative interpretation, esp. of the Scriptures. □ **tropological** /trɒpə'lɒdʒɪk(ə)l/ *adj.* [Late Latin *tropologia* from Greek *tropologia* (as TROPE)]

tropopause /'trɒpəpɔ:z, 'trəʊp-/ *n.* the interface between the troposphere and the stratosphere. [TROPOSPHERE + PAUSE]

troposphere /'trɒpəsfɪə, 'trəʊp-/ *n.* the lowest region of the atmosphere, extending from the earth's surface to a height of about 6–10 km, and in which the temperature falls with increasing height (cf. STRATOSPHERE, IONOSPHERE). □ **tropospheric** /-'sfɛrɪk/ *adj.* [Greek *tropos* 'turning' + SPHERE]

troppo[1] /'trɒpəʊ/ *adv. Mus.* too much (qualifying a tempo indication). □ **ma non troppo** but not too much so. [Italian]

troppo[2] /'trɒpəʊ/ *adj. Austral. slang* mentally disturbed from exposure to a tropical climate; crazy.

Trot /trɒt/ *n.* esp. *Brit. colloq.* usu. *derog.* a Trotskyist. [abbreviation]

trot /trɒt/ *v. & n.* ● *v.* **(trotted, trotting) 1** *intr.* (of a person) run at a moderate pace esp. with short strides. **2** *intr.* (of a horse) proceed at a steady pace faster than a walk lifting each diagonal pair of legs alternately. **3** *intr. colloq.* walk or go. **4** *tr.* cause (a horse or person) to trot. **5** *tr.* traverse (a distance) at a trot. ● *n.* **1** the action or exercise of trotting (*proceed at a trot*; *went for a trot*). **2 (the trots)** *slang* an attack of diarrhoea. **3** a brisk steady movement or occupation. **4** (in *pl.*) *Austral. colloq.* **a** trotting races. **b** a meeting for these. □ **on the trot** *colloq.* **1** continually busy (*kept them on the trot*). **2** *Brit.* in succession (*five weeks on the trot*). **trot out 1** cause (a horse) to trot to show its paces. **2** *colloq.* produce or introduce (as if) for inspection and approval, esp. tediously or repeatedly. [Middle English via Old French *troter* from Romanic & medieval Latin *trottare*, of Germanic origin]

troth /trəʊθ/ *n. archaic* **1** faith, loyalty. **2** truth. □ **pledge** (or **plight**) **one's troth** pledge one's word esp. in marriage or betrothal. [Middle English *trowthe* from Old English *trēowth* TRUTH]

Trotskyism /'trɒtskɪɪz(ə)m/ *n.* the political or economic principles of L. Trotsky, Russian politician d. 1940, esp. as urging worldwide socialist revolution. □ **Trotskyist** *n.* **Trotskyite** *n. derog.*

trotter /'trɒtə/ *n.* **1** a horse bred or trained for trotting. **2** (usu. in *pl.*) **a** an animal's foot as food (*pig's trotters*). **b** *joc.* a human foot.

trotting /'trɒtɪŋ/ *n.* racing for trotting horses pulling a two-wheeled vehicle and driver.

troubadour /'tru:bədɔ:/ *n.* **1** any of a number of French medieval lyric poets composing and singing in Provençal in the 11th–13th c. on the theme of courtly love. **2** a singer or poet. [French from Provençal *trobador*, from *trobar* 'find, invent, compose in verse']

trouble /'trʌb(ə)l/ *n. & v.* ● *n.* **1** difficulty or distress; vexation, affliction (*am having trouble with my car*). **2 a** inconvenience; unpleasant exertion; bother (*went to a lot of trouble*). **b** a cause of this (*the child was no trouble*). **3** a cause of annoyance or concern (*the trouble with you is that you can't say no*). **4** a faulty condition or operation (*kidney trouble*; *engine trouble*). **5 a** fighting, disturbance (*crowd trouble*; *don't want any trouble*). **b** (in *pl.*) political or social unrest, public disturbances. **6** disagreement, strife (*is having trouble at home*). ● *v.* **1** *tr.* cause distress or anxiety to; disturb (*were much troubled by their debts*). **2** *intr.* be disturbed or worried (*don't trouble about it*). **3** *tr.* afflict; cause pain etc. to (*am troubled with arthritis*). **4** *tr. & intr.* (often *refl.*) subject or be subjected to inconvenience or unpleasant exertion (*sorry to trouble you*; *don't trouble yourself*; *don't trouble to explain*). □ **ask for trouble** *colloq.* invite trouble or difficulty by rash or indiscreet behaviour etc. **be no trouble** cause no inconvenience etc. **go to the trouble** (or **some trouble** etc.) exert oneself to do something. **in trouble 1** involved in a matter likely to bring censure or punishment. **2** *colloq.* pregnant while unmarried. **look for trouble** *colloq.* **1** aggressively seek to cause trouble. **2** invite trouble. **take trouble** (or **the trouble**) exert oneself to do something. □ **troubler** *n.* [Middle English from Old French *truble* (*n.*), *trubler*, *turbler* (*v.*), ultimately from Latin *turbidus* TURBID]

trouble and strife *n. Brit. rhyming slang* wife.

troubled /'trʌb(ə)ld/ *adj.* showing, experiencing, or reflecting trouble, anxiety, etc. (*a troubled mind*; *a troubled childhood*).

troublemaker /'trʌb(ə)lmeɪkə/ *n.* a person who habitually causes trouble. □ **trouble-making** *n. & attrib.adj.*

troubleshooter /'trʌb(ə)lʃu:tə/ *n.* **1** a mediator in industrial or diplomatic etc. disputes. **2** a person who traces and corrects faults in machinery etc. □ **troubleshoot** *v.intr. & tr.* (*past* and *past part.* **-shot**). **troubleshooting** *n.*

troublesome /'trʌb(ə)ls(ə)m/ *adj.* **1** causing or full of trouble. **2** vexing, annoying. □ **troublesomely** *adv.* **troublesomeness** *n.*

trouble spot *n.* a place where difficulties regularly occur.

troublous /'trʌbləs/ *adj. archaic* or *literary* full of troubles; agitated, disturbed (*troublous times*). [Middle English from Old French *troubleus* (as TROUBLE)]

trough /trɒf/ *n.* **1** a long narrow open receptacle for water, animal feed, etc. **2** a channel for conveying a liquid. **3** an elongated region of low barometric pressure. **4** a hollow between two wave crests. **5** the time of lowest economic performance etc. **6** a region around the minimum on a curve of variation of a quantity. **7** a low point or depression. [Old English *trog*, from Germanic]

trounce /traʊns/ *v.tr.* **1** defeat heavily. **2** beat, thrash. **3** punish severely. □ **trouncer** *n.* **trouncing** *n.* [16th c., = afflict: origin unknown]

troupe /tru:p/ *n.* a company of actors or acrobats etc. [French, = TROOP]

trouper /'tru:pə/ *n.* **1** a member of a theatrical troupe. **2** a staunch colleague.

trouser-clip *n.* = BICYCLE CLIP.

trousers /'traʊzəz/ *n.pl.* **1** (also **pair of trousers** *sing.*) an outer garment reaching from the waist usu. to the ankles, divided into two parts to cover the legs. **2** (**trouser**) (*attrib.*) designating parts of this (*trouser leg*). □ **wear the trousers** be the dominant partner in a marriage etc. □ **trousered** *adj.* **trouserless** *adj.* [archaic *trouse* (sing.) from Irish & Gaelic *triubhas* TREWS: pl. form on the pattern of *drawers*]

trouser suit *n. Brit.* a woman's suit of trousers and jacket.

trousseau /'tru:səʊ/ *n.* (*pl.* **trousseaus** or **trousseaux** /-səʊz/) the clothes collected by a bride for her marriage. [French, literally 'bundle', diminutive of *trousse* TRUSS]

trout /traʊt/ *n.* (*pl.* same or **trouts**) **1 a** any of various freshwater fishes of the genus *Salmo* or *Salvelinus* of the northern hemisphere, esp. *Salmo trutta* of Europe, valued as food. **b** any of various unrelated fishes. **2** *Brit. slang derog.* a woman, esp. an old or ill-tempered one (usu. *old trout*). □ **trouting** *n.* **troutlet** *n.* **troutling** *n.* [Old English *truht* from Late Latin *tructa*]

trouvaille /'tru:vʌɪl, French truvaj/ *n.* a lucky find; a windfall. [French from *trouver* 'find']

trouvère /tru:'vɛ:/ *n.* a medieval epic poet in northern France in the 11th–14th c. [Old French *trovere* from *trover* 'find': cf. TROUBADOUR]

trove /trəʊv/ *n.* = TREASURE TROVE. [Anglo-French *trové* from *trover* 'find']

trover /'trəʊvə/ *n. Law* **1** finding and keeping personal property. **2** common-law action to recover the value of personal property wrongfully taken etc. [Old French *trover* 'find']

trow /trəʊ/ *v.tr. archaic* think, believe. [Old English *trūwian, trēowian* 'to trust', related to TRUCE]

trowel /'traʊəl/ *n. & v.* ● *n.* **1** a small hand-held tool with a flat pointed blade, used to apply and spread mortar etc. **2** a similar tool with a curved scoop for lifting plants or earth. ● *v.tr.* (**trowelled, trowelling**; *US* **troweled, troweling**) **1** apply (plaster etc.). **2** dress (a wall etc.) with a trowel. [Middle English via Old French *truele* and medieval Latin *truella* from Latin *trulla* 'scoop', diminutive of *trua* 'ladle' etc.]

troy /trɔɪ/ *n.* (in full **troy weight**) a system of weights used for precious metals and gems, with a pound of 12 ounces or 5,760 grains. [Middle English, probably from a weight used at *Troyes* in France]

trs. *abbr.* transpose (letters or words etc.).

truant /'tru:ənt/ *n., adj., & v.* ● *n.* **1** a child who stays away from school without leave or explanation. **2** a person missing from work etc. ● *adj.* (of a person, conduct, thoughts, etc.) shirking, idle, wandering. ● *v.intr.* (also **play truant**) stay away as a truant. □ **truancy** *n.* [Middle English from Old French, probably ultimately from Celtic: cf. Welsh *truan*, Gaelic *truaghan* 'wretched']

truce /tru:s/ *n.* **1** a temporary agreement to cease hostilities. **2** a suspension of private feuding or bickering. □ **truceless** *adj.* [Old English *trēow* from Germanic: related to TRUE]

truck[1] /trʌk/ *n. & v.* ● *n.* **1** *Brit.* an open railway wagon for carrying freight. **2** a large road vehicle for carrying heavy goods, troops, supplies, etc.; a lorry. **3** a railway bogie. **4** a wheeled stand for transporting goods. **5** *Naut.* a wooden disc at the top of a mast with holes for halyards. **6** each of two axle units on a skateboard, to which the wheels are attached. ● *v.* **1** *tr.* convey on or in a truck. **2** *intr. N. Amer.* drive a truck. **3** *intr. N. Amer. slang* proceed; go, stroll. □ **truckage** *n.* [perhaps short for TRUCKLE in the sense 'wheel, pulley']

truck[2] /trʌk/ *n. & v.* ● *n.* **1** dealings; exchange, barter. **2** small wares. **3** *N. Amer.* market-garden produce (*truck farm*). **4** *colloq.* odds and ends. **5** *hist.* the payment of workers in kind or with vouchers etc. ● *v.tr. & intr. archaic* barter, exchange. □ **have no truck with** avoid dealing with. [Middle English from Old French *troquer* (unrecorded) = medieval Latin *trocare*, of unknown origin]

trucker /'trʌkə/ *n.* **1** a long-distance lorry driver. **2** a firm dealing in long-distance carriage of goods.

truckie /'trʌki/ *n. Austral. colloq.* a lorry driver; a trucker.

trucking /'trʌkɪŋ/ *n. US* conveyance of goods by lorry.

truckle /'trʌk(ə)l/ *n. & v.* ● *n.* **1** (in full **truckle-bed**) esp. *Brit.* a low bed on wheels that can be stored under a larger bed. **2** orig. *dial.* a small barrel-shaped cheese. ● *v.intr.* (foll. by *to*) submit obsequiously. □ **truckler** *n.* [originally = wheel, pulley, via Anglo-French *trocle* from Latin *trochlea* 'pulley']

truckload /'trʌkləʊd/ *n.* **1** a quantity of goods etc. or a number of people that can be transported in a truck. **2** *colloq.* a large quantity or number. □ **by the truckload** in large quantities or numbers.

truck stop *n. N. Amer.* = TRANSPORT CAFÉ.

truculent /'trʌkjʊl(ə)nt/ *adj.* **1** aggressively defiant. **2** aggressive, pugnacious. **3** fierce, savage. □ **truculence** *n.* **truculency** *n.* **truculently** *adv.* [Latin *truculentus* from *trux trucis* 'fierce']

trudge /trʌdʒ/ *v. & n.* ● *v.* **1** *intr.* go on foot esp. laboriously. **2** *tr.* traverse (a distance) in this way. ● *n.* a trudging walk. □ **trudger** *n.* [16th c.: origin unknown]

trudgen /'trʌdʒ(ə)n/ *n.* a swimming stroke like the crawl with a scissors movement of the legs. [named after J. *Trudgen*, 19th-c. English swimmer]

true /tru:/ *adj., adv., & v.* ● *adj.* (**truer, truest**) **1** in accordance with fact or reality (*a true story*). **2** genuine; rightly or strictly so called; not spurious or counterfeit (*a true friend; the true heir to the throne*). **3** (often foll. by *to*) loyal or faithful (*true to one's word*). **4** (foll. by *to*) accurately conforming (to a standard or expectation etc.) (*true to form*). **5** correctly positioned or balanced; upright, level. **6** exact, accurate (*a true aim*; *a true copy*). **7** (*absol.*) (also **it is true**) certainly, admittedly (*true, it would cost more*). **8** (of a note) exactly in tune. **9** (of a compass bearing) measured relative to true north. **10** *archaic* honest, upright (*twelve good men and true*). ● *adv.* **1** truly (*tell me true*). **2** accurately (*aim true*). **3** without variation (*breed true*). ● *v.tr.* (**trues, trued, truing** or **trueing**) bring (a tool, wheel, frame, etc.) into the exact position or form required. □ **come true** actually happen or be the case. **out of true** (or **the true**) not in the correct or exact position. **true to form** (or **type**) being or behaving etc. as expected. **true to life** accurately representing life. □ **trueness** *n.* [Old English *trēowe, trȳwe*, from the Germanic noun represented by TRUCE]

true bill *n. US & hist.* a bill of indictment endorsed by a grand jury as being sustained by evidence.

true-blue *adj. & n.* ● *adj.* extremely loyal or orthodox. ● *n.* such a person, esp. a Conservative.

true-born *attrib.adj.* genuine (*a true-born Englishman*).

true-bred *attrib.adj.* of a genuine or good breed.

true coral see CORAL *n.* 2.

true-hearted *adj.* faithful, loyal.

true horizon see HORIZON 1c.

true love *n.* a sweetheart.

true-love knot *n.* (also **true-lover's knot**) a kind of knot with interlacing bows on each side, symbolizing true love.

true north *n.* north according to the earth's axis, not magnetic north.

true rib *n.* a rib joined directly to the breastbone.

truffle /'trʌf(ə)l/ *n.* **1** any strong-smelling underground fungus of the order Tuberales, used as a culinary delicacy and found esp. in France by trained dogs or pigs. **2** a usu. round sweet made of chocolate mixture covered with cocoa etc. [probably via Dutch *truffel* from obsolete French *truffle*, ultimately from Latin *tubera*, pl. of TUBER]

trug /trʌg/ *n. Brit.* **1** a shallow oblong garden basket usu. of wood strips. **2** *archaic* a shallow wooden container for milk. [perhaps a dialect variant of TROUGH]

truism /'tru:ɪz(ə)m/ *n.* **1** an obviously true or hackneyed statement. **2** a proposition that states nothing beyond what is implied in any of its terms. □ **truistic** /-'ɪstɪk/ *adj.*

trull /trʌl/ *n. archaic* a prostitute. [German *Trulle*]

truly /'tru:li/ *adv.* **1** sincerely, genuinely (*am truly grateful*). **2** really, indeed (*truly, I do not know*). **3** faithfully, loyally (*served them truly*). **4** accurately, truthfully (*is not truly depicted; has been truly stated*). **5** rightly, properly (*well and truly*). [Old English *trēowlice* (as TRUE, -LY[2])]

trumeau /tru:'məʊ/ *n.* (*pl.* **trumeaux** /-'məʊz/) a section of wall or a pillar between two openings, e.g. a pillar dividing a large doorway. [French]

trump[1] /trʌmp/ *n. & v.* ● *n.* **1 a** a playing card of a suit ranking above the others. **b** (in *pl.*) this suit (*hearts are trumps*). **2** an advantage esp. involving surprise. **3** *colloq.* **a** a helpful or admired person. **b** *Austral. & NZ* a person in authority. ● *v.* **1 a** *tr.* defeat (a card or its player) with a trump. **b** *intr.* play a trump card when another suit has been led. **2** *tr. colloq.* gain a surprising advantage over (a person, proposal, etc.). □ **trump up** fabricate or invent (an accusation, excuse, etc.) (*on a trumped-up charge*). **turn up trumps** *Brit. colloq.* **1** turn out better than expected. **2** be greatly successful or helpful. [corruption of TRIUMPH in the same (now obsolete) sense]

trump[2] /trʌmp/ *n. archaic* a trumpet-blast. [Middle English via Old French *trompe* from Frankish: probably imitative]

trump card *n.* **1** a card belonging to, or turned up to determine, a trump suit. **2** *colloq.* **a** a valuable resource. **b** a surprise move to gain an advantage.

trumpery /ˈtrʌmp(ə)ri/ *n. & adj.* ● *n.* (*pl.* **-ies**) **1 a** worthless finery. **b** a worthless article. **2** rubbish. ● *adj.* **1** showy but worthless (*trumpery jewels*). **2** delusive, shallow (*trumpery arguments*). [Middle English from Old French *tromperie*, from *tromper* 'deceive']

trumpet /ˈtrʌmpɪt/ *n. & v.* ● *n.* **1 a** a tubular or conical brass instrument with a flared bell and a bright penetrating tone. **b** a trumpet-player. **c** an organ stop with a quality resembling a trumpet. **2 a** the tubular corona of a daffodil etc. **b** a trumpet-shaped thing (*ear-trumpet*). **3** a sound of or like a trumpet. ● *v.* (**trumpeted**, **trumpeting**) **1** *intr.* **a** blow a trumpet. **b** (of an enraged elephant etc.) make a loud sound as of a trumpet. **2** *tr.* proclaim loudly (a person's or thing's merit). [Middle English from Old French *trompette*, diminutive of *trompe* TRUMP[2]]

trumpet call *n.* an urgent summons to action.

trumpeter /ˈtrʌmpɪtə/ *n.* **1** a person who plays or sounds a trumpet, esp. a cavalry soldier giving signals. **2** a bird making a trumpet-like sound, esp.: **a** a variety of domestic pigeon. **b** a large black S. American bird of the genus *Psophia*.

trumpeter swan *n.* a large N. American wild swan, *Cygnus buccinator*.

trumpet major *n.* the chief trumpeter of a cavalry regiment.

truncal /ˈtrʌŋk(ə)l/ *adj.* of or relating to the trunk of a body or a tree.

truncate *v. & adj.* ● *v.tr.* /trʌŋˈkeɪt, ˈtrʌŋ-/ **1** cut the top or the end from (a tree, a body, a piece of writing, etc.). **2** *Crystallog.* replace (an edge or an angle) by a plane. ● *adj.* /ˈtrʌŋkeɪt/ *Bot. & Zool.* (of a leaf or feather etc.) ending abruptly as if cut off at the base or tip. □ **truncately** /ˈtrʌŋkeɪtli/ *adv.* **truncation** /-ˈkeɪʃ(ə)n/ *n.* [Latin *truncare truncat-* 'maim']

truncheon /ˈtrʌn(t)ʃ(ə)n/ *n.* **1** esp. *Brit.* a short club or cudgel, esp. carried by a police officer. **2** a staff or baton as a symbol of authority, esp. that of the Earl Marshal. [Middle English from Old French *tronchon* 'stump', ultimately from Latin *truncus* 'trunk']

trundle /ˈtrʌnd(ə)l/ *v.tr. & intr.* roll or move heavily or noisily esp. on or as on wheels. [variant of obsolete or dialect *trendle*, *trindle*, from Old English *trendel* 'circle' (as TREND)]

trundle-bed *n.* esp. *US* = TRUCKLE *n.* 1.

trunk /trʌŋk/ *n.* **1** the main stem of a tree as distinct from its branches and roots. **2** a person's or animal's body apart from the limbs and head. **3** the main part of any structure. **4** a large box with a hinged lid for transporting luggage, clothes, etc. **5** *N. Amer.* the luggage compartment of a motor car. **6** an elephant's elongated prehensile nose. **7** (in *pl.*) men's shorts worn for swimming, boxing, etc. **8** the main body of an artery, nerve, etc. **9** an enclosed shaft or conduit for cables, ventilation, etc. □ **trunkful** *n.* (*pl.* **-fuls**). **trunkless** *adj.* [Middle English via Old French *tronc* from Latin *truncus*]

trunk call *n.* esp. *Brit.* a telephone call on a trunk line with charges made according to distance.

trunking /ˈtrʌŋkɪŋ/ *n.* **1** a system of shafts or conduits for cables, ventilation, etc. **2** the use or arrangement of trunk lines.

trunk line *n.* a main line of a railway, telephone system, etc.

trunk road *n.* esp. *Brit.* an important main road.

trunnion /ˈtrʌnjən/ *n.* **1** a supporting cylindrical projection on each side of a cannon or mortar. **2** a hollow gudgeon supporting a cylinder in a steam engine and giving passage to the steam. [French *trognon* 'core, tree trunk', of unknown origin]

truss /trʌs/ *n. & v.* ● *n.* **1** a framework, e.g. of rafters and struts, supporting a roof or bridge etc. **2** a surgical appliance worn to support a hernia. **3** *Brit.* a bundle of old hay (56 lb) or new hay (60 lb) or straw (36 lb). **4** a compact terminal cluster of flowers or fruit. **5** a large corbel supporting a monument etc. **6** *Naut.* a heavy iron ring securing the lower yards to a mast. ● *v.tr.* **1** tie up (a fowl) compactly for cooking. **2** (often foll. by *up*) tie (a person) up with the arms to the sides. **3** support (a roof or bridge etc.) with a truss or trusses. □ **trusser** *n.* [Middle English from Old French *trusser* (*v.*), *trusse* (*n.*), of unknown origin]

trust /trʌst/ *n. & v.* ● *n.* **1 a** a firm belief in the reliability or truth or strength etc. of a person or thing. **b** the state of being relied on. **2** a confident expectation. **3 a** a thing or person committed to one's care. **b** the resulting obligation or responsibility (*am in a position of trust*; *have fulfilled my trust*). **4** a person or thing confided in (*is our sole trust*). **5** reliance on the truth of a statement etc. without examination. **6** commercial credit (*obtained goods on trust*). **7** *Law* **a** confidence placed in a person by making that person the nominal owner of property to be used for another's benefit. **b** the right of the latter to benefit by such property. **c** the property so held. **d** the legal relation between the holder and the property so held. **8 a** a body of trustees. **b** an organization managed by trustees. **c** an organized association of several companies for the purpose of reducing or defeating competition etc., esp. one in which all or most of the stock is transferred to a central committee and shareholders lose their voting power although remaining entitled to profits. ● *v.* **1** *tr.* place trust in; believe in; rely on the character or behaviour of. **2** *tr.* (foll. by *with*) allow (a person) to have or use (a thing) from confidence in its proper use (*was reluctant to trust them with my books*). **3** *tr.* (often foll. by *that* + clause) have faith or confidence or hope that a thing will take place (*I trust you will not be late*; *I trust that she is recovering*). **4** *tr.* (foll. by *to*) consign (a thing) to (a person) with trust. **5** *tr.* (foll. by *for*) allow credit to (a customer) for (goods). **6** *intr.* (foll. by *in*) place reliance in (*we trust in you*). **7** *intr.* (foll. by *to*) place (esp. undue) reliance on (*shall have to trust to luck*). □ **in trust** *Law* held on the basis of trust (see sense 7 of *n.*). **on trust 1** on credit. **2** on the basis of trust or confidence. **take on trust** accept (an assertion, claim, etc.) without evidence or investigation. □ **trustable** *adj.* **truster** *n.* [Middle English *troste*, *truste* from Old Norse *traust*, from *traustr* 'strong': the verb from Old Norse *treysta*, assimilated to the noun]

trustbuster /ˈtrʌs(t)bʌstə/ *n.* esp. *US* a person or agency employed to dissolve trusts.

trust company *n.* a company formed to act as a trustee or to deal with trusts.

trustee /trʌsˈtiː/ *n.* **1** *Law* a person or member of a board given control or powers of administration of property in trust with a legal obligation to administer it solely for the purposes specified. **2** a state made responsible for the government of an area. □ **trusteeship** *n.*

trustful /ˈtrʌs(t)fʊl, -f(ə)l/ *adj.* **1** full of trust or confidence. **2** not feeling or showing suspicion. □ **trustfully** *adv.* **trustfulness** *n.*

trust fund *n.* a fund of money etc. held in trust.

trustie var. of TRUSTY *n.*

trusting /ˈtrʌstɪŋ/ *adj.* having trust, esp. being trustful by nature. □ **trustingly** *adv.* **trustingness** *n.*

trust territory *n.* a territory under the trusteeship of the United Nations or of a state designated by them.

trustworthy /ˈtrʌs(t)wəːði/ *adj.* deserving of trust; reliable. □ **trustworthily** *adv.* **trustworthiness** *n.*

trusty /ˈtrʌsti/ *adj.* & *n.* ● *adj.* (**trustier**, **trustiest**) **1** *archaic* or *joc.* trustworthy (*a trusty steed*). **2** *archaic* loyal (to a sovereign) (*my trusty subjects*). ● *n.* (also **trustie**) (*pl.* **-ies**) a prisoner who is given special privileges for good behaviour. □ **trustily** *adv.* **trustiness** *n.*

truth /truːθ/ *n.* (*pl.* **truths** /truːðz, truːθs/) **1** the quality or a state of being true or truthful (*doubted the truth of the statement*; *there may be some truth in it*). **2 a** what is true (*tell us the whole truth*; *the truth is that I forgot*). **b** what is accepted as true (*one of the fundamental truths*). □ **in truth** *literary* truly, really. **to tell the truth** (or **truth to tell**) to be frank. [Old English *trīewth, trēowth* (as TRUE)]

truth drug *n.* any of various drugs supposedly able to induce a person to tell the truth.

truthful /ˈtruːθfʊl, -f(ə)l/ *adj.* **1** habitually speaking the truth. **2** (of a story etc.) true. **3** (of a likeness etc.) corresponding to reality. □ **truthfully** *adv.* **truthfulness** *n.*

truth table *n.* a list indicating the truth or falsity of various propositions in logic etc.

try /trʌɪ/ *v.* & *n.* ● *v.* (**-ies**, **-ied**) **1** *intr.* make an effort with a view to success (often foll. by *to* + infin.; *colloq.* foll. by *and* + infin.: *tried to be on time*; *try and be early*; *I shall try hard*). **2** *tr.* make an effort to achieve (*tried my best*; *had better try something easier*). **3** *tr.* **a** test (the quality of a thing) by use or experiment. **b** test the qualities of (a person or thing) (*try it before you buy*). **4** *tr.* make severe demands on (a person, quality, etc.) (*my patience has been sorely tried*). **5** *tr.* examine the effectiveness or usefulness of for a purpose (*try cold water*; *try the off-licence*; *have you tried kicking it?*). **6** *tr.* ascertain the state of fastening of (a door, window, etc.). **7** *tr.* **a** investigate and decide (a case or issue) judicially. **b** subject (a person) to trial (*will be tried for murder*). **8** *tr.* make an experiment in order to find out (*let us try which takes longest*). **9** *intr.* (foll. by *for*) **a** apply or compete for. **b** seek to reach or attain (*am going to try for a gold medal*). **10** *tr.* (often foll. by *out*) **a** extract (oil) from fat by heating. **b** treat (fat) in this way. **11** *tr.* (often foll. by *up*) smooth (roughly planed wood) with a plane to give an accurately flat surface. ● *n.* (*pl.* **-ies**) **1** an effort to accomplish something; an attempt (*give it a try*). **2** *Rugby* the act of touching the ball down behind the opposing goal line, scoring points and entitling the scoring side to a kick at goal. **3** *Amer. Football* an attempt to score an extra point in various ways after a touchdown. □ **try conclusions with** see CONCLUSION. **try a fall with** contend with. **try for size** try out or test for suitability. **try one's hand** see how skilful one is, esp. at the first attempt. **try it on** *Brit. colloq.* **1** test another's patience. **2** (often foll. by *with*) attempt to outwit, deceive, or seduce another person. **try on** put on (clothes etc.) to see if they fit or suit the wearer. **try out 1** put to the test. **2** test thoroughly. [Middle English, = separate, distinguish, etc., from Old French *trier* 'sift', of unknown origin]

■ **Usage** Use of the verb *try* with *and* (see sense 1 above) is uncommon in the past tense and in negative contexts (except in the imperative, e.g. *Don't try and get the better of me*).

trying /ˈtrʌɪɪŋ/ *adj.* annoying, vexatious; hard to endure. □ **tryingly** *adv.*

trying-plane *n.* a plane used in trying (see TRY *v.* 11).

try-on *n. Brit. colloq.* **1** an act of trying it on. **2** an attempt to fool or deceive.

try-out *n.* an experimental test of efficiency, popularity, etc.

trypanosome /ˈtrɪp(ə)nəsəʊm, trɪˈpanə-/ *n. Med.* any protozoan parasite of the genus *Trypanosoma* having a long trailing flagellum and infesting the blood etc. [Greek *trupanon* 'borer' + -SOME[3]]

trypanosomiasis /ˌtrɪp(ə)nəsəˈmʌɪəsɪs, trɪˌpanə-/ *n.* any of several diseases caused by a trypanosome and usu. transmitted by biting insects, including sleeping sickness and Chagas' disease.

trypsin /ˈtrɪpsɪn/ *n.* a digestive enzyme which hydrolyses proteins, secreted by the pancreas. □ **tryptic** *adj.* [Greek *tripsis* 'friction' from *tribō* 'rub' (because it was first obtained by rubbing down the pancreas with glycerine)]

trypsinogen /trɪpˈsɪnədʒ(ə)n/ *n.* a substance in the pancreas from which trypsin is formed.

tryptophan /ˈtrɪptəfan/ *n. Biochem.* an amino acid essential in the diet of vertebrates. [as TRYPSIN + *-phan* from Greek *phainō* 'appear']

trysail /ˈtrʌɪs(ə)l/ *n.* a small strong fore-and-aft sail set on the mainmast or other mast of a sailing vessel in heavy weather.

try-scorer *n.* a rugby player who has scored a try or esp. a significant number of tries (*record try-scorer*). □ **try-scoring** *n.* (also *attrib.*).

try-square *n.* a carpenter's square, usu. with one wooden and one metal limb.

tryst /trɪst/ *n.* & *v. archaic* ● *n.* **1** a time and place for a meeting, esp. of lovers. **2** such a meeting (*keep a tryst*; *break one's tryst*). ● *v.intr.* (foll. by *with*) make a tryst. □ **tryster** *n.* [Middle English, variant of obsolete *trist* 'an appointed station in hunting', from French *triste* or medieval Latin *trista, tristra*]

tsar /zɑː, tsɑː/ *n.* (also **czar**, **tzar**) **1** *hist.* the title of the former emperors of Russia. **2** a person with great authority. □ **tsardom** *n.* **tsarism** *n.* **tsarist** *n.* & *adj.* [Russian *tsar'*, ultimately from Latin *Caesar*]

tsarevich /ˈzɑːrɪvɪtʃ, ˈtsɑːr-, tsɑːˈrjeɪvɪtʃ/ *n.* (also **czarevich**) *hist.* the eldest son of an emperor of Russia. [Russian *tsarevich* 'son of a tsar']

tsarina /zɑːˈriːnə, tsɑːˈriːnə/ *n.* (also **czarina**, **tzarina**) *hist.* the title of the former empress of Russia. [Italian & Spanish *(c)zarina* from German *Czarin, Zarin*, fem. of *Czar, Zar*]

tsessebi /tsɛˈseɪbi/ *n.* (also **sassaby** /səˈseɪ-/) a race of the topi (antelope) found in eastern and southern Africa. [Setswana]

tsetse /ˈtsɛtsi, ˈtɛtsi/ *n.* any fly of the genus *Glossina* native to Africa, that feeds on human and animal blood with a needle-like proboscis and transmits trypanosomiasis. [Setswana]

TSH *abbr.* **1** thyroid-stimulating hormone. **2** Their Serene Highnesses.

T-shirt /ˈtiːʃəːt/ *n.* (also **tee shirt**) a short-sleeved casual top, usu. of knitted cotton and having the form of a T when spread out.

tsk /tsk/ *int.*, *n.*, & *v.* (also **tsk tsk**) = TUT (see TUT-TUT).

tsp *abbr.* (*pl.* **tsps** or same) teaspoonful.

T-square *n.* a T-shaped instrument for drawing or testing right angles.

TSS *abbr.* toxic shock syndrome.

tsunami /tsuːˈnɑːmi/ *n.* (*pl.* **tsunamis**) a long high sea wave caused by underwater earthquakes or other disturbances. Also called *tidal wave*. [Japanese, from *tsu* 'harbour' + *nami* 'wave']

Tswana /ˈtswɑːnə/ *n.* & *adj.* ● *n.* **1** a southern African people living in Botswana and neighbouring areas. **2** (*pl.* same or **Tswanas** or **Batswana** /bəˈtswɑːnə/) a member of this people. **3** (also **Setswana** /sɛˈtswɑːnə/) the Bantu language of this people. ● *adj.* of or relating to the Tswana or their language. [native name]

■ **Usage** *Setswana* is now preferred to *Tswana* as the name of the language (see sense 3 above).

TT *abbr.* **1** Tourist Trophy. **2** tuberculin-tested. **3 a** teetotal. **b** teetotaller.

TU *abbr.* Trade Union.

Tu. *abbr.* Tuesday.

tuatara /tuːəˈtɑːrə, tjuː-/ *n.* a large lizard-like reptile, *Sphenodon punctatum*, unique to certain small islands of New Zealand, having a crest of soft spines extending along its back. [Maori, from *tua* 'on the back' + *tara* 'spine']

tub /tʌb/ *n.* & *v.* ● *n.* **1** an open flat-bottomed usu. round container for various purposes. **2** a tub-shaped (usu. plastic) carton. **3** the amount a tub will hold. **4** *colloq.* a bath. **5 a** *colloq.* a clumsy slow boat. **b** a stout roomy boat for rowing practice. **6** *Mining* a container for conveying ore, coal, etc. ● *v.* (**tubbed, tubbing**) **1** *tr.* & *intr.* plant, bathe, or wash in a tub. **2** *tr.* enclose in a tub. **3** *tr.* line (a mine shaft) with a wooden or iron casing. □ **tubbable** *adj.* (in sense 1 of *v.*). **tubful** *n.* (*pl.* **-fuls**). [Middle English, probably of Low German or Dutch origin: cf. Middle Low German, Middle Dutch *tubbe*]

tuba /'tju:bə/ *n.* (*pl.* **tubas**) **1 a** a low-pitched brass wind instrument. **b** its player. **2** an organ stop with the quality of a tuba. [Italian from Latin, = trumpet]

tubal /'tju:b(ə)l/ *adj. Anat.* of or relating to a tube, esp. the bronchial or Fallopian tubes.

tubby /'tʌbi/ *adj.* (**tubbier, tubbiest**) **1** (of a person) short and fat; tub-shaped. **2** (of a violin) dull-sounding, lacking resonance. □ **tubbiness** *n.*

tub chair *n.* a chair with solid arms continuous with a usu. semicircular back.

tube /tju:b/ *n.* & *v.* ● *n.* **1** a long hollow rigid or flexible cylinder, esp. for holding or carrying air, liquids, etc. **2** a soft metal or plastic cylinder sealed at one end and having a screw cap at the other, for holding a semi-liquid substance ready for use (*a tube of toothpaste*). **3** *Anat.* & *Zool.* a hollow cylindrical organ in the body (*bronchial tubes*; *Fallopian tubes*). **4** *Brit. colloq.* **a** (often prec. by *the*) an underground railway system, esp. the one in London (*went by tube*). **b** (in full **tube train**) a train running on such a system. **5 a** a cathode ray tube esp. in a television set. **b** (prec. by *the*) esp. *US colloq.* television. **6** *US* a thermionic valve. **7** = INNER TUBE. **8** the cylindrical body of a wind instrument. **9** *Austral. slang* a can of beer. ● *v.tr.* **1** equip with tubes. **2** enclose in a tube. □ **tubeless** *adj.* (esp. in sense 7 of *n.*). **tubelike** *adj.* [French *tube* or Latin *tubus*]

tubectomy /tju:'bɛktəmi/ *n.* (*pl.* **-ies**) the surgical removal of a Fallopian tube.

tuber /'tju:bə/ *n.* **1 a** the short thick rounded part of a stem or rhizome, usu. found underground and covered with modified buds, e.g. in a potato. **b** the similar root of a dahlia etc. **2** *Anat.* a lump or swelling. [Latin, = hump, swelling]

tubercle /'tju:bək(ə)l/ *n.* **1** a small rounded protuberance esp. on a bone. **2** a small rounded inflamed swelling on the body or in an organ, esp. a nodular lesion characteristic of tuberculosis in the lungs etc. **3** a small tuber; a wartlike growth. □ **tuberculate** /-'bə:kjʊlət/ *adj.* **tuberculous** /-'bə:kjʊləs/ *adj.* [Latin *tuberculum*, diminutive of *tuber*: see TUBER]

tubercle bacillus *n.* a bacterium causing tuberculosis.

tubercular /tjʊ'bə:kjʊlə/ *adj.* & *n.* ● *adj.* of or having tubercles or tuberculosis. ● *n.* a person with tuberculosis. [Latin *tuberculum* (as TUBERCLE)]

tuberculation /tjʊˌbə:kjʊ'leɪʃ(ə)n/ *n.* **1** the formation of tubercles. **2** a growth of tubercles. [Latin *tuberculum* (as TUBERCLE)]

tuberculin /tjʊ'bə:kjʊlɪn/ *n.* a sterile protein extract from cultures of tubercle bacillus, used in the diagnosis and (formerly) the treatment of tuberculosis. [Latin *tuberculum* (as TUBERCLE)]

tuberculin test *n.* a hypodermic injection of tuberculin to detect infection with or immunity from tuberculosis.

tuberculin-tested *adj.* (of milk) from cows giving a negative response to a tuberculin test.

tuberculosis /tjʊˌbə:kjʊ'ləʊsɪs/ *n.* an infectious disease caused by the bacillus *Mycobacterium tuberculosis*, characterized by tubercles, esp. in the lungs (see also PULMONARY TUBERCULOSIS).

tuberose[1] /'tju:bərəʊs/ *adj.* **1** covered with tubers; knobby. **2** of or resembling a tuber. **3** bearing tubers. □ **tuberosity** /-'rɒsɪti/ *n.* [Latin *tuberosus* from TUBER]

tuberose[2] /'tju:bərəʊz/ *n.* a plant, *Polianthes tuberosa*, native to Mexico, having heavily scented white funnel-like flowers and strap-shaped leaves. [Latin *tuberosa*, fem. of *tuberosus* (as TUBEROSE[1])]

tuberous /'tju:b(ə)rəs/ *adj.* = TUBEROSE[1]. [French *tubéreux* or Latin *tuberosus* from TUBER]

tuberous root *n.* a thick and fleshy root like a tuber but without buds.

tube train see TUBE *n.* 4b.

tube worm *n.* a worm which constructs or secretes a tube in which it lives.

tubifex /'tju:bɪfɛks/ *n.* any red annelid worm of the genus *Tubifex*, found in mud at the bottom of rivers and lakes and used as food for aquarium fish. Also called *bloodworm*. [modern Latin, from Latin *tubus* 'tube' + *-fex* from *facere* 'make']

tubiform /'tju:bɪfɔ:m/ *adj.* tube-shaped.

tubing /'tju:bɪŋ/ *n.* **1** a length of tube. **2** a quantity of tubes.

tub-thumper *n. colloq.* a ranting preacher or orator. □ **tub-thumping** *adj.* & *n.*

tubular /'tju:bjʊlə/ *adj.* **1** tube-shaped. **2** having or consisting of tubes. **3** (of furniture etc.) made of tubular pieces.

tubular bells *n.pl.* an orchestral instrument consisting of a row of vertically suspended metal tubes that are struck with a hammer.

tubular tyre *n.* a completely enclosed tyre cemented on to the wheel rim, used esp. on racing bicycles.

tubule /'tju:bju:l/ *n.* a small tube in a plant or an animal body. [Latin *tubulus*, diminutive of *tubus* 'tube']

tubulous /'tju:bjʊləs/ *adj.* = TUBULAR 1.

TUC *abbr.* (in the UK) Trades Union Congress.

tuck /tʌk/ *v.* & *n.* ● *v.tr.* **1** (often foll. by *in, up*) **a** draw, fold, or turn the outer or end parts of (cloth or clothes etc.) close together so as to be held; thrust in the edge of (a thing) so as to confine it (*tucked his shirt into his trousers*; *tucked the sheet under the mattress*). **b** thrust in the edges of bedclothes around (a person) (*came to tuck me in*). **2** draw together into a small space (*tucked her legs under her*; *the bird tucked its head under its wing*). **3** stow (a thing) away in a specified place or way (*tucked it in a corner*; *tucked it out of sight*). **4 a** make a stitched fold in (material, a garment, etc.). **b** shorten, tighten, or ornament with stitched folds. **5** *Brit.* hit (a ball) to the desired place. ● *n.* **1** a flattened usu. stitched fold in material, a garment, etc., often one of several parallel folds for shortening, tightening, or ornament. **2** *Brit. colloq.* food, esp. cakes and sweets eaten by children (also *attrib.*: *tuck box*). **3** *Naut.* the part of a ship's hull where the planks meet under the stern. **4** (in full **tuck position**) (in diving, gymnastics, etc.) a position with the knees bent upwards into the chest and the hands clasped round the shins. □ **tuck in** *Brit. colloq.* eat food heartily. **tuck into** (or **away**) *colloq.* eat (food) heartily (*tucked into their dinner*; *could really tuck it away*). [Middle English *tukke*, *tokke*, from Middle Dutch, Middle Low German *tucken*, = Old High German *zucchen* 'pull': related to TUG]

tucker /'tʌkə/ *n.* & *v.* ● *n.* **1** a person or thing that tucks. **2** *hist.* a piece of lace or linen etc. in or on a woman's bodice. **3** *Austral. colloq.* food. ● *v.tr.* (esp. in *passive*; often foll. by *out*) *N. Amer. colloq.* tire, exhaust. □ **best bib and tucker** see BIB[1].

tucker-bag *n.* (also **tucker-box**) *Austral.* & *NZ colloq.* a container for food.

tucket /'tʌkɪt/ *n. archaic* a flourish on a trumpet. [Old Northern French *toquer* 'beat' (a drum)]

tuck-in *n. Brit. colloq.* a large meal.

tucking /'tʌkɪŋ/ *n.* a series of usu. stitched tucks in material or a garment.

tuck-net *n.* (also **tuck-seine**) a small net for taking caught fish from a larger net.

tuck position see TUCK *n.* 4.

tuck shop *n. Brit.* a small shop, esp. near or in a school, selling food to children.

-tude /tjuːd/ *suffix* forming abstract nouns (*altitude*; *attitude*; *solitude*). [from or suggested by French *-tude* from Latin *-tudo -tudinis*]

Tudor /ˈtjuːdə/ *adj.* & *n. hist.* ● *adj.* **1** of, characteristic of, or associated with the royal family of England ruling 1485–1603 or this period. **2** of or relating to the architectural style of this period, esp. with half-timbering and elaborately decorated houses. ● *n.* a member of the Tudor royal family. [Owen *Tudor* of Wales, grandfather of Henry VII]

Tudorbethan /tjuːdəˈbiːθ(ə)n/ *adj. Brit.* (of a house etc.) imitating Tudor and Elizabethan styles in design. [blend of TUDOR and ELIZABETHAN]

Tudor rose *n.* (in late Perpendicular decoration) a conventionalized five-lobed figure of a rose, esp. a combination of the red and white roses of Lancaster and York adopted as a badge by Henry VII.

Tues. *abbr.* (also **Tue.**) Tuesday.

Tuesday /ˈtjuːzdeɪ, -di/ *n.* & *adv.* ● *n.* the third day of the week, following Monday. ● *adv. colloq.* **1** on Tuesday. **2** (**Tuesdays**) on Tuesdays; each Tuesday. [Old English *Tīwesdæg* from *Tīw*, the Germanic god identified with Roman Mars]

tufa /ˈtuːfə, ˈtjuːfə/ *n.* **1** a porous rock composed of calcium carbonate and formed round mineral springs. **2** = TUFF. □ **tufaceous** /-ˈfeɪʃəs/ *adj.* [Italian, variant of *tufo*: see TUFF]

tuff /tʌf/ *n.* rock formed by the consolidation of volcanic ash. □ **tuffaceous** /-ˈfeɪʃəs/ *adj.* [French *tuf, tuffe* via Italian *tufo* from Late Latin *tofus*, Latin TOPHUS]

tuffet /ˈtʌfɪt/ *n.* **1** = TUFT 1. **2** a low seat. [variant of TUFT]

tuft /tʌft/ *n.* & *v.* ● *n.* **1** a bunch or collection of threads, grass, feathers, hair, etc., held or growing together at the base. **2** *Anat.* a bunch of small blood vessels. ● *v.* **1** *tr.* provide with a tuft or tufts. **2** *tr.* make depressions at regular intervals in (a mattress etc.) by passing a thread through. **3** *intr.* grow in tufts. □ **tufty** *adj.* [Middle English, probably from Old French *tofe, toffe*, of unknown origin: for *-t* cf. GRAFT[1]]

tufted /ˈtʌftɪd/ *adj.* **1** having or growing in a tuft or tufts. **2** (of a bird) having a tuft of feathers on the head.

tufted duck *n.* a small freshwater duck, *Aythya fuligula*, of the Old World, with black or brown plumage and a drooping crest.

tug /tʌg/ *v.* & *n.* ● *v.* (**tugged, tugging**) **1** *tr.* & (foll. by *at*) *intr.* pull hard or violently; jerk (*tugged it from my grasp*; *tugged at my sleeve*). **2** *tr.* tow (a ship etc.) by means of a tugboat. ● *n.* **1** a hard, violent, or jerky pull (*gave a tug on the rope*). **2** a sudden strong emotional feeling (*felt a tug as I watched them go*). **3** a small powerful boat for towing larger boats and ships. **4** an aircraft towing a glider. **5** (of a horse's harness) a loop from a saddle supporting a shaft or trace. □ **tugger** *n.* [Middle English *togge, tugge*, from Germanic: related to TOW[1]]

tugboat /ˈtʌgbəʊt/ *n.* = TUG *n.* 3.

tug of love *n. Brit. colloq.* a dispute over the custody of a child.

tug-of-war *n.* **1** a trial of strength between two sides pulling against each other on a rope. **2** a decisive or severe contest.

tui /ˈtuːi/ *n. NZ* a large honeyeater, *Prosthemadura novaeseelandiae*, native to New Zealand, having glossy bluish-black plumage with two white tufts at the throat. [Maori]

tuition /tjuːˈɪʃ(ə)n/ *n.* **1** teaching or instruction, esp. if paid for (*driving tuition*; *music tuition*). **2** a fee for this. □ **tuitional** *adj.* [Middle English via Old French from Latin *tuitio -onis*, from *tuēri tuit-* 'watch, guard']

tularaemia /t(j)uːləˈriːmɪə/ *n.* (*US* **tularemia**) a severe infectious disease of animals transmissible to man, caused by the bacterium *Pasteurella tularense* and characterized by ulcers at the site of infection, fever, and loss of weight. □ **tularaemic** *adj.* [modern Latin from *Tulare* County in California, where it was first observed]

tulip /ˈtjuːlɪp/ *n.* any bulbous spring-flowering plant of the genus *Tulipa*, esp. one of the many cultivated forms with showy cup-shaped flowers of various colours and markings. [originally *tulipa(n)*, from modern Latin *tulipa* via Turkish *tul(i)band* from Persian *dulband* TURBAN (from the shape of the expanded flower)]

tulip-root *n.* a disease of oats etc. causing the base of the stem to swell.

tulip tree *n.* any of various N. American trees of the genus *Liriodendron*, with tulip-like flowers and lobed leaves.

tulipwood /ˈtjuːlɪpwʊd/ *n.* a fine-grained pale timber produced by the N. American tree *Liriodendron tulipifera*.

tulle /t(j)uːl/ *n.* a soft fine silk etc. net for veils and dresses. [*Tulle*, a town in SW France, where it was first made]

tum /tʌm/ *n. Brit. colloq.* stomach. [abbreviation of TUMMY]

tumble /ˈtʌmb(ə)l/ *v.* & *n.* ● *v.* **1** *intr.* & *tr.* fall or cause to fall suddenly, clumsily, or headlong. **2** *intr.* fall rapidly in amount etc. (*prices tumbled*). **3** *intr.* (often foll. by *about, around*) roll or toss erratically or helplessly to and fro. **4** *intr.* move or rush in a headlong or blundering manner (*the children tumbled out of the car*). **5** *intr.* (often foll. by *to*) *colloq.* grasp the meaning or hidden implication of an idea, circumstance, etc. (*they quickly tumbled to our intentions*). **6** *tr.* overturn; fling or push roughly or carelessly. **7** *intr.* perform acrobatic feats, esp. somersaults. **8** *tr.* rumple or disarrange; pull about; disorder. **9** *tr.* dry (washing) in a tumble-dryer. **10** *tr.* clean (castings, gemstones, etc.) in a tumbling-barrel. **11** *intr.* (of a pigeon) turn over backwards in flight. ● *n.* **1** a sudden or headlong fall. **2** a somersault or other acrobatic feat. **3** an untidy or confused state. [Middle English *tumbel* from Middle Low German *tummelen*, Old High German *tumalōn*, frequentative of *tūmōn*: cf. Old English *tumbian* 'to dance']

tumbledown /ˈtʌmb(ə)ldaʊn/ *adj.* falling or fallen into ruin; dilapidated.

tumble-dryer *n.* (also **tumble-drier**) a machine for drying washing in a heated rotating drum. □ **tumble-dry** *v.tr.* & *intr.* (**-dries, -dried**).

tumbler /ˈtʌmblə/ *n.* **1** a drinking glass with no handle or foot (formerly with a rounded bottom so as not to stand upright). **2** an acrobat, esp. one performing somersaults. **3** (in full **tumbler-dryer**) = TUMBLE-DRYER. **4 a** a pivoted piece in a lock that holds the bolt until lifted by a key. **b** a notched pivoted plate in a gunlock. **5** a kind of pigeon that turns over backwards in flight. **6** an electrical switch worked by pushing a small sprung lever. **7** a toy figure that rocks when touched. **8** = TUMBLING-BARREL. □ **tumblerful** *n.* (*pl.* **-fuls**).

tumbleweed /ˈtʌmb(ə)lwiːd/ *n. N. Amer.* & *Austral.* a plant of arid areas, esp. *Amaranthus albus*, that forms a globular bush that breaks off in late summer and is tumbled about by the wind.

tumbling-barrel *n.* (also **tumbling-box** etc.) a revolving device containing an abrasive substance, in which castings, gemstones, etc., are cleaned by friction.

tumbling-bay *n.* **1** the outfall of a river, reservoir, etc. **2** a pool into which this flows.

tumbril /ˈtʌmbr(ə)l, -brɪl/ *n.* (also **tumbrel**) *hist.* **1** an open cart in which condemned persons were conveyed to their execution, esp. to the guillotine during the French Revolution. **2** a two-wheeled covered cart for carrying tools, ammunition, etc. **3** a cart that tips to empty its load, esp. one carrying dung. [Middle English from Old French *tumberel, tomberel*, from *tomber* 'to fall']

tumefy /ˈtjuːmɪfʌɪ/ *v.* (**-ies, -ied**) **1** *intr.* swell, inflate; be inflated. **2** *tr.* cause to do this. □ **tumefacient**

/-ˈfeɪʃ(ə)nt/ *adj.* **tumefaction** /-ˈfakʃ(ə)n/ *n.* [French *tuméfier* from Latin *tumefacere*, from *tumēre* 'swell']

tumescent /tjʊˈmɛs(ə)nt/ *adj.* **1** becoming tumid; swelling. **2** swelling as a response to sexual stimulation. □ **tumescence** *n.* **tumescently** *adv.* [Latin *tumescere* (as TUMEFY)]

tumid /ˈtjuːmɪd/ *adj.* **1** (of parts of the body etc.) swollen, inflated. **2** (of a style etc.) inflated, bombastic. □ **tumidity** /-ˈmɪdɪti/ *n.* **tumidly** *adv.* [Latin *tumidus* from *tumēre* 'swell']

tummy /ˈtʌmi/ *n.* (*pl.* **-ies**) *colloq.* the stomach. [childish pronunciation of STOMACH]

tummy button *n.* the navel.

tumour /ˈtjuːmə/ *n.* (*US* **tumor**) a swelling, esp. from an abnormal growth of tissue, whether benign or malignant. □ **tumorous** *adj.* [Latin *tumor* from *tumēre* 'swell']

tumult /ˈtjuːmʌlt/ *n.* **1** an uproar or din, esp. of a disorderly crowd. **2** an angry demonstration by a mob; a riot; a public disturbance. **3** a conflict of emotions in the mind. [Middle English from Old French *tumulte* or Latin *tumultus*]

tumultuous /tjʊˈmʌltjʊəs/ *adj.* **1** noisily vehement; uproarious; making a tumult (*a tumultuous welcome*). **2** disorderly. **3** agitated. □ **tumultuously** *adv.* **tumultuousness** *n.* [Old French *tumultuous* or Latin *tumultuosus* (as TUMULT)]

tumulus /ˈtjuːmjʊləs/ *n.* (*pl.* **tumuli** /-lʌɪ, -liː/) an ancient burial mound or barrow. □ **tumular** *adj.* [Latin from *tumēre* 'swell']

tun /tʌn/ *n.* & *v.* ● *n.* **1** a large beer or wine cask. **2** a brewer's fermenting-vat. **3** a measure of capacity, equal to 216 imperial gallons or 252 US gallons. ● *v.tr.* (**tunned**, **tunning**) store (wine etc.) in a tun. [Old English *tunne* from medieval Latin *tunna*, probably of Gaulish origin]

tuna[1] /ˈtjuːnə/ *n.* (*pl.* same or **tunas**) **1** any marine fish of the family Scombridae native to tropical and warm waters, having a round body and pointed snout, and used for food. Also called TUNNY. **2** (in full **tuna fish**) the flesh of the tuna or tunny, usu. tinned in oil or brine. [American Spanish, from Spanish *atún* 'tunny']

tuna[2] /ˈtjuːnə/ *n.* **1** a prickly pear, esp. *Opuntia tuna*. **2** the fruit of this. [Spanish from Taino]

tundish /ˈtʌndɪʃ/ *n.* **1** a wooden funnel, used esp. in brewing. **2** an intermediate reservoir in metal-founding.

tundra /ˈtʌndrə/ *n.* a vast level treeless Arctic region usu. with a marshy surface and underlying permafrost. [Lappish]

tune /tjuːn/ *n.* & *v.* ● *n.* a melody with or without harmony. ● *v.* **1** *tr.* put (a musical instrument) in tune. **2 a** *tr.* adjust (a radio receiver etc.) to the particular frequency of the required signals. **b** *intr.* (foll. by *in*) adjust a radio receiver to the required signal (*tuned in to Radio 2*). **3** *tr.* adjust (an engine etc.) to run smoothly and efficiently. **4** *tr.* (foll. by *to*) adjust or adapt to a required or different purpose, situation, etc. **5** *intr.* (foll. by *with*) be in harmony with. □ **in tune 1** having the correct pitch or intonation (*sings in tune*). **2** (usu. foll. by *with*) harmonizing with one's company, surroundings, etc. **out of tune 1** not having the correct pitch or intonation (*always plays out of tune*). **2** (usu. foll. by *with*) clashing with one's company etc. **to the tune of** *colloq.* to the considerable sum or amount of. **tuned in** (often foll. by *to*) *colloq.* acquainted; in rapport; up to date (with). **tune up 1** (of a musician) bring one's instrument to the proper or uniform pitch. **2** begin to play or sing. **3** bring to the most efficient condition. □ **tunable** *adj.* (also **tuneable**). [Middle English: unexplained variant of TONE]

tuneful /ˈtjuːnfʊl, -f(ə)l/ *adj.* melodious, musical. □ **tunefully** *adv.* **tunefulness** *n.*

tuneless /ˈtjuːnlɪs/ *adj.* **1** unmelodious, unmusical. **2** out of tune. □ **tunelessly** *adv.* **tunelessness** *n.*

tuner /ˈtjuːnə/ *n.* **1** a person who tunes musical instruments, esp. pianos. **2** a device for tuning a radio receiver. **3** an electronic device for tuning a guitar etc.

tung /tʌŋ/ *n.* (in full **tung tree**) a tree of the genus *Aleurites*, native to China and Japan, bearing poisonous fruits containing seeds that yield oil. [Chinese *tong*]

tung oil *n.* the oil of the tung tree used in paints and varnishes.

tungsten /ˈtʌŋst(ə)n/ *n. Chem.* a steel-grey dense metallic element with a very high melting point, occurring naturally in scheelite and used for the filaments of electric lamps and for alloying steel etc. (symbol W). □ **tungstate** /-steɪt/ *n.* **tungstic** *adj.* **tungstous** *adj.* [Swedish, from *tung* 'heavy' + *sten* 'stone']

tungsten carbide *n.* a very hard black substance used in making dies and cutting tools.

Tungus /ˈtʊŋʊs, tʊŋˈuːs/ *n.* (*pl.* same) **1** a member of a people of eastern Siberia. **2** the Altaic language of this people. [from Yakut, a Turkic language]

tunic /ˈtjuːnɪk/ *n.* **1 a** a close-fitting short coat of police or military etc. uniform. **b** a loose often sleeveless garment usu. reaching to about the knees, as worn in ancient Greece and Rome. **c** a gymslip. **d** any of various similar loose often mid-thigh length garments, usu. worn over a skirt, blouse, or trousers. **e** a tunicle. **2** *Zool.* the rubbery outer coat of an ascidian etc. **3** *Bot.* **a** any of the concentric layers of a bulb. **b** the tough covering of a part of this. **4** *Anat.* a membrane enclosing or lining an organ. [French *tunique* or Latin *tunica*]

tunica /ˈtjuːnɪkə/ *n.* (*pl.* **tunicae** /-kiː/) *Bot.* & *Anat.* = TUNIC 3, 4. [Latin]

tunicate /ˈtjuːnɪkət, -keɪt/ *n.* & *adj.* ● *n.* any marine animal of the subphylum Urochordata, having a rubbery or hard outer coat, and including sea squirts. ● *adj.* **1** *Zool.* of or relating to this subphylum. **2** *Bot.* having concentric layers, as in an onion bulb. [Latin *tunicatus*, past part. of *tunicare* 'clothe with a tunic' (as TUNICA)]

tunicle /ˈtjuːnɪk(ə)l/ *n.* a short vestment worn by a bishop or subdeacon at the Eucharist etc. [Middle English from Old French *tunicle* or Latin *tunicula*, diminutive of TUNICA]

tuning /ˈtjuːnɪŋ/ *n.* the process or a system of putting a musical instrument in tune.

tuning fork *n.* a two-pronged steel fork that gives a particular note when struck, used in tuning.

tuning peg *n.* a peg or pin etc. attached to the strings of a stringed instrument and turned to alter their tension in tuning.

tunnel /ˈtʌn(ə)l/ *n.* & *v.* ● *n.* **1** an artificial underground passage through a hill or under a road or river etc., esp. for a railway or road to pass through, or in a mine. **2** an underground passage dug by a burrowing animal. **3** a prolonged period of difficulty or suffering (esp. in metaphors, e.g. *the end of the tunnel*). **4** a tube containing a propeller shaft etc. ● *v.* (**tunnelled**, **tunnelling**; *US* **tunneled**, **tunneling**) **1** *intr.* (foll. by *through*, *into*, etc.) make a tunnel through (a hill etc.). **2** *tr.* make (one's way) by tunnelling. **3** *intr. Physics* pass through a potential barrier. □ **tunneller** *n.* [earlier = tunnel-net: Middle English from Old French *tonel*, diminutive of *tonne* TUN]

tunnel diode *n. Electronics* a two-terminal semiconductor diode using tunnelling electrons to perform high-speed switching operations.

tunnel-kiln *n.* a kiln in which ceramic ware is carried on trucks along a continuously heated passage.

tunnel-net *n.* a fishing net wide at the mouth and narrow at the other end.

tunnel vision *n.* **1** vision that is defective in not adequately including objects away from the centre of the field of view. **2** *colloq.* **a** a concentration focused on a limited or single objective, perception, etc. **b** inability to be diverted or swayed from this.

tunny /ˈtʌni/ *n.* (*pl.* same or **-ies**) esp. *Brit.* = TUNA[1]. [French *thon* via Provençal *ton* and Latin *thunnus* from Greek *thunnos*]

tup /tʌp/ *n.* & *v.* ● *n.* **1** esp. *Brit.* a male sheep; a ram. **2** the striking-head of a piledriver etc. ● *v.tr.* (**tupped**, **tupping**) esp. *Brit.* (of a ram) copulate with (a ewe). [Middle English *toje, tupe*, of unknown origin]

Tupamaro /tuːpəˈmɑːrəʊ/ *n.* (*pl.* **-os**) a member of a Marxist urban guerrilla organization in Uruguay. [*Tupac Amaru*, the name of two Inca leaders]

tupelo /ˈtjuːpɪləʊ/ *n.* (*pl.* **-os**) **1** any of various Asian and N. American deciduous trees of the genus *Nyssa*, with colourful foliage and growing in swampy conditions. **2** the wood of this tree. [Creek, from *ito* 'tree' + *opilwa* 'swamp']

Tupi /ˈtuːpi/ *n.* & *adj.* ● *n.* (*pl.* same or **Tupis**) **1** a member of an American Indian people native to the Amazon valley. **2** the language of this people. ● *adj.* of or relating to this people or language. [native name]

Tupi-Guarani *n.* & *adj.* ● *n.* (*pl.* same or **Tupi-Guaranis**) **1** a member of a S. American people of Tupi, Guarani, or other related stock. **2** a S. American Indian language family including Tupi and Guarani. ● *adj.* of or relating to this people or language family. [TUPI + GUARANI]

tuppence /ˈtʌp(ə)ns/ *n.* *Brit.* = TWOPENCE. [phonet. spelling]

tuppenny /ˈtʌp(ə)ni/ *adj.* *Brit.* = TWOPENNY. [phonet. spelling]

Tupperware /ˈtʌpəweː/ *n.* *propr.* a range of plastic containers for storing food. [*Tupper*, the name of the US manufacturer, + WARE[1]]

tuque /tuːk/ *n.* a Canadian stocking cap. [Canadian French form of TOQUE]

turaco /ˈtʊərəkəʊ/ *n.* (also **touraco**) (*pl.* **-os**) any African bird of the family Musophagidae, with crimson and green plumage and a prominent crest. [French *touraco*, from a West African name]

Turanian /tjʊˈreɪnɪən/ *n.* & *adj.* ● *n.* the group of Asian languages that are neither Semitic nor Indo-European, esp. the Ural-Altaic family. ● *adj.* of or relating to this group. [Persian *Tūrān*, the region beyond the Oxus]

turban /ˈtəːb(ə)n/ *n.* **1** a man's headdress of cotton or silk wound round a cap or the head, worn esp. by Muslims and Sikhs. **2** a woman's headdress or hat resembling this. □ **turbaned** *adj.* [ultimately via Turkish *tülbent* from Persian *dulband*: cf. TULIP]

turbary /ˈtəːb(ə)ri/ *n.* (*pl.* **-ies**) *Brit.* **1** the right of digging turf on common ground or on another's ground. **2** a place where turf or peat is dug. [Middle English from Anglo-French *turberie*, Old French *tourberie*, from *tourbe* TURF]

turbellarian /təːbɪˈleːrɪən/ *n.* & *adj.* ● *n.* any usu. free-living flatworm of the class Turbellaria, having a ciliated surface. ● *adj.* of or relating to this class. [modern Latin *Turbellaria* from Latin *turbella* 'bustle, stir', diminutive of *turba* 'crowd']

turbid /ˈtəːbɪd/ *adj.* **1** (of a liquid or colour) muddy, thick; not clear. **2** (of a style etc.) confused, disordered. □ **turbidity** /-ˈbɪdɪti/ *n.* **turbidly** *adv.* **turbidness** *n.* [Latin *turbidus* from *turba* 'a crowd, a disturbance']

■ **Usage** *Turbid* is sometimes confused with *turgid* which means (of language) 'inflated, pompous', or (of objects) 'swollen, distended'. The confusion arises because as well as sounding similar, both words are used (in different senses) of rivers etc. on the one hand, and of literary style on the other.

turbinate /ˈtəːbɪnət/ *adj.* **1** shaped like a spinning top or inverted cone. **2** (of a shell) with whorls decreasing rapidly in size. **3** *Anat.* (esp. of some nasal bones) shaped like a scroll. □ **turbinal** *adj.* **turbination** /-ˈneɪʃ(ə)n/ *n.* [Latin *turbinatus* (as TURBINE)]

turbine /ˈtəːbʌɪn, -ɪn/ *n.* a rotary motor or engine driven by a flow of water, steam, gas, wind, etc., esp. to produce electrical power. [French from Latin *turbo -binis* 'spinning top, whirlwind']

turbit /ˈtəːbɪt/ *n.* a breed of domestic pigeon of stout build with a neck frill and short beak. [apparently from Latin *turbo* 'top', from its figure]

turbo /ˈtəːbəʊ/ *n.* (*pl.* **-os**) **1** = TURBOCHARGER. **2** a motor vehicle equipped with this.

turbo- /ˈtəːbəʊ/ *comb. form* turbine.

turbocharger /ˈtəːbəʊtʃɑːdʒə/ *n.* a supercharger driven by a turbine powered by the engine's exhaust gases. □ **turbocharge** *v.tr.* (esp. as **turbocharged** *adj.*).

turbo-diesel *n.* **1** a turbocharged diesel engine. **2** a vehicle powered by this.

turbofan /ˈtəːbəʊfan/ *n.* *Aeron.* **1** a jet engine in which a turbine-driven fan provides additional thrust. **2** an aircraft powered by this.

turbojet /ˈtəːbəʊdʒɛt/ *n.* *Aeron.* **1** a jet engine in which the jet also operates a turbine-driven compressor for the air drawn into the engine. **2** an aircraft powered by this.

turboprop /ˈtəːbəʊprɒp/ *n.* *Aeron.* **1** a jet engine in which a turbine is used as in a turbojet and also to drive a propeller. **2** an aircraft powered by this.

turboshaft /ˈtəːbəʊʃɑːft/ *n.* a gas turbine that powers a shaft for driving heavy vehicles, generators, pumps, etc.

turbosupercharger /təːbəʊˈsuːpətʃɑːdʒə/ *n.* = TURBOCHARGER.

turbot /ˈtəːbət/ *n.* (*pl.* same or **turbots**) **1** a flatfish, *Scophthalmus maximus*, having large bony tubercles on the body and head and prized as food. **2** any of various similar fishes including halibut. [Middle English via Old French from Old Swedish *törnbut*, from *törn* 'thorn' + *but* BUTT[3]]

turbulence /ˈtəːbjʊl(ə)ns/ *n.* **1** an irregularly fluctuating flow of air or fluid. **2** *Meteorol.* stormy conditions as a result of atmospheric disturbance. **3** a disturbance, commotion, or tumult.

turbulent /ˈtəːbjʊl(ə)nt/ *adj.* **1** disturbed; in commotion. **2** (of a flow of air etc.) varying irregularly; causing disturbance. **3** tumultuous. **4** insubordinate, riotous. □ **turbulently** *adv.* [Latin *turbulentus* from *turba* 'crowd']

Turco /ˈtəːkəʊ/ *n.* (*pl.* **-os**) *hist.* an Algerian soldier in the French army. [Spanish, Portuguese, & Italian, = TURK]

Turco- /ˈtəːkəʊ/ *comb. form* (also **Turko-**) Turkish; Turkish and. [medieval Latin *Turcus* TURK]

Turcoman var. of TURKOMAN.

turd /təːd/ *n.* *coarse slang* **1** a lump of excrement. **2** a term of contempt for a person. [Old English *tord*, from Germanic]

turdoid /ˈtəːdɔɪd/ *adj.* thrushlike. [Latin *turdus* THRUSH[1]]

tureen /tjʊˈriːn, tə-/ *n.* a deep covered dish for serving soup etc. [earlier *terrine, -ene* from French *terrine*, a large circular earthenware dish, fem. of Old French *terrin* 'earthen', ultimately from Latin *terra* 'earth']

turf /təːf/ *n.* & *v.* ● *n.* (*pl.* **turfs** or **turves**) **1 a** a layer of grass etc. with earth and matted roots as the surface of grassland. **b** a piece of this cut from the ground. **2** a slab of peat for fuel. **3** (prec. by *the*) **a** horse racing generally. **b** a general term for racecourses. ● *v.tr.* **1** cover (ground) with turf. **2** (foll. by *out*) esp. *Brit. colloq.* expel or eject (a person or thing). [Old English from Germanic]

turf accountant *n.* *Brit.* a bookmaker.

turfman /ˈtəːfmən/ *n.* (*pl.* **-men**) esp. *US* a devotee of horse racing.

turfy /ˈtəːfi/ *adj.* (**turfier**, **turfiest**) like turf; grassy.

turgescent /təːˈdʒɛs(ə)nt/ *adj.* becoming turgid; swelling. □ **turgescence** *n.*

turgid /ˈtəːdʒɪd/ *adj.* **1** (of language) pompous, bombastic (*the film was spoilt by a turgid script*). **2** swollen, distended, puffed out (*sat by the turgid Thames*). □ **turgidity** /-ˈdʒɪdɪti/ *n.* **turgidly** *adv.* **turgidness** *n.* [Latin *turgidus* from *turgēre* 'swell']

■ **Usage** See Usage Note at TURBID.

turgor /ˈtəːɡə/ *n.* *Bot.* the rigidity of cells due to the absorption of water. [Late Latin (as TURGID)]

Turing test /ˈtjʊərɪŋ/ *n. Computing* a test for intelligence in a computer, which requires that a human should be unable to distinguish it from another human by the replies to questions put to both. [named after A. *Turing*, British mathematician d. 1954]

turion /ˈt(j)ʊərɪən/ *n. Bot.* **1** a young shoot or sucker arising from an underground bud. **2** a bud formed by certain aquatic plants. [French from Latin *turio -onis* 'shoot']

Turk /təːk/ *n.* **1 a** a native or national of Turkey in SE Europe and Asia Minor. **b** a person of Turkish descent. **2** a member of a central Asian people from whom the Ottomans derived, speaking Turkic languages. **3** *offens.* a ferocious, wild, or unmanageable person. [Middle English, = French *Turc*, Italian etc. *Turco*, medieval Latin *Turcus*, Persian & Arabic *Turk*, of unknown origin]

turkey /ˈtəːki/ *n.* (*pl.* **-eys**) **1** a large mainly domesticated game bird, *Meleagris gallopavo*, originally of N. America, having a bald head and (in the male) red wattles, prized as food esp. on festive occasions including Christmas and (in the US) Thanksgiving. **2** the flesh of the turkey as food. **3** esp. *N. Amer. slang* **a** a theatrical failure; a flop. **b** a stupid or inept person. □ **talk turkey** *N. Amer. colloq.* talk frankly and straightforwardly; get down to business. [16th c.: short for *turkeycock* or *turkeyhen*, originally applied to the guinea fowl (which was imported through Turkey), and then erroneously to the American bird]

turkey buzzard *n.* (also **turkey vulture**) an American vulture, *Cathartes aura*. [so called because of its bare reddish head and dark plumage]

Turkey carpet /ˈtəːki/ *n.* = TURKISH CARPET.

turkeycock /ˈtəːkɪkɒk/ *n.* **1** a male turkey. **2** a pompous or self-important person.

Turkey red /ˈtəːki/ *n.* & *adj.* ● *n.* **1** a scarlet pigment obtained from the madder or alizarin. **2** a cotton cloth dyed with this. ● *adj.* (hyphenated when *attrib.*) of this colour.

turkey vulture var. of TURKEY BUZZARD.

Turki /ˈtəːki/ *n.* & *adj.* ● *n.* (*pl.* same) **1** the Turkic languages, esp. those of central Asia, collectively. **2** a member of a Turkic-speaking people. ● *adj.* of or relating to these languages or their speakers. [Persian *turkī* (as TURK)]

Turkic /ˈtəːkɪk/ *adj.* & *n.* ● *adj.* of or relating to a large group of Altaic languages including Turkish, Azerbaijani, and Kyrgyz, or the peoples speaking them. ● *n.* the Turkic languages collectively. [TURK + -IC]

Turkish /ˈtəːkɪʃ/ *adj.* & *n.* ● *adj.* of or relating to Turkey in SE Europe and Asia Minor, or to the Turks or their language. ● *n.* this language.

Turkish bath *n.* **1** a hot-air or steam bath followed by washing, massage, etc. **2** (in *sing.* or *pl.*) a building for this.

Turkish carpet *n.* a wool carpet with a thick pile and traditional bold design.

Turkish coffee *n.* a strong black coffee.

Turkish delight *n.* a sweet of flavoured gelatin cubes coated in powdered sugar.

Turkish towel *n.* a towel made of cotton terry.

Turkmen /ˈtəːkmən/ *n.* & *adj.* ● *n.* (*pl.* same or **Turkmens**) **1** a member of any of various Turkic peoples inhabiting the region east of the Caspian Sea and south of the Aral Sea, comprising Turkmenistan and parts of Iran and Afghanistan. **2** the Turkic language of these peoples. ● *adj.* of or relating to these peoples or their language. [Persian *turkmān* from Turkish *türkmen*; also influenced by Russian *turkmen*]

Turko- var. of TURCO-.

Turkoman /ˈtəːkəʊmən/ *n.* & *adj.* ● *n.* (also **Turcoman**) (*pl.* **-mans**) = TURKMEN *n.* 1, 2. ● *adj.* =TURKMEN *adj.* [medieval Latin *Turcomannus*, French *turcoman* from Persian *turkmān* (see TURKMEN)]

Turkoman carpet *n.* a traditional carpet of rich colours with a soft long nap.

Turk's cap *n.* a martagon lily or other plant with turban-like flowers.

Turk's head *n.* a turban-like ornamental knot.

turmeric /ˈtəːmərɪk/ *n.* **1** a tropical Asian plant, *Curcuma longa*, of the ginger family, yielding aromatic rhizomes used as a spice and for yellow dye. **2** this rhizome powdered and used as a spice esp. in curry powder. [16th-c. forms *tarmaret* etc. perhaps from French *terre mérite* and modern Latin *terra merita*, literally 'deserving earth', perhaps an alteration of an oriental word]

turmoil /ˈtəːmɔɪl/ *n.* **1** violent confusion; agitation. **2** din and bustle. [16th c.: origin unknown]

turn /təːn/ *v.* & *n.* ● *v.* **1** *tr.* & *intr.* move around a point or axis so that the point or axis remains in a central position; give a rotary motion to or receive a rotary motion (*turned the wheel*; *the wheel turns*; *the key turns in the lock*). **2** *tr.* & *intr.* change in position so that a different side, end, or part becomes outermost or uppermost etc.; invert or reverse or cause to be inverted or reversed (*turned inside out*; *turned it upside down*). **3 a** *tr.* give a new direction to (*turn your face this way*). **b** *intr.* take a new direction (*turn left here*; *my thoughts have often turned to you*). **4** *tr.* aim in a certain way (*turned the hose on them*). **5** *intr.* & *tr.* (foll. by *into*) change in nature, form, or condition to (*turned into a dragon*; *then turned him into a frog*; *turned the book into a play*). **6** *intr.* (foll. by *to*) **a** apply oneself to; set about (*turned to doing the ironing*). **b** have recourse to; begin to indulge in habitually (*turned to drink*; *turned to me for help*). **c** go on to consider next (*let us now turn to your report*). **7** *intr.* & *tr.* become or cause to become (*turned hostile*; *has turned informer*; *your comment turned them angry*). **8 a** *tr.* & *intr.* (foll. by *against*) make or become hostile to (*has turned them against us*). **b** *intr.* (foll. by *on*, *upon*) become hostile to; attack (*suddenly turned on them*). **9** *intr.* (of hair or leaves) change colour. **10** *intr.* (of milk) become sour. **11** *intr.* (of the stomach) be nauseated. **12** *tr.* twist or sprain (an ankle). **13** *intr.* (of the head) become giddy. **14** *tr.* cause (milk) to become sour, (the stomach) to be nauseated, or (the head) to become giddy. **15** *tr.* translate (*turn it into French*). **16** *tr.* move to the other side of; go round (*turned the corner*). **17** *tr.* pass the age or time of (*he has turned 40*; *it has now turned 4 o'clock*). **18** *intr.* (foll. by *on*) depend on; be determined by (*it all turns on the weather tomorrow*). **19** *tr.* send or put into a specified place or condition; cause to go (*was turned loose*; *turned the water out into a basin*). **20** *tr.* perform (a somersault etc.) with rotary motion. **21** *tr.* remake (a garment or, esp., a sheet) putting the worn outer side on the inside. **22** *tr.* make (a profit). **23** *tr.* divert (a bullet). **24** *tr.* blunt (the edge of a knife, slot of a screw head, etc.). **25** *tr.* shape (an object) on a lathe. **26** *tr.* give an (esp. elegant) form to (*turn a compliment*). **27** *intr. Golf* begin the second half of a round. **28** *tr.* (esp. as **turned** *adj.*) *Printing* invert (type) to make it appear upside down (*a turned comma*). **29** *tr.* pass round (the flank etc. of an army) so as to attack it from the side or rear. **30** *intr.* (of the tide) change from flood to ebb or vice versa. ● *n.* **1** the act or process or an instance of turning; rotary motion (*a single turn of the handle*). **2 a** a changed or a change of direction or tendency (*took a sudden turn to the left*). **b** a deflection or deflected part (*full of twists and turns*). **3** a point at which a turning or change occurs. **4** a turning of a road. **5** a change of the tide from ebb to flow or from flow to ebb. **6** a change in the course of events. **7** a tendency or disposition (*is of a mechanical turn of mind*). **8** an opportunity or obligation etc. that comes successively to each of several persons etc. (*your turn will come*; *my turn to read*). **9** a short walk or ride (*shall take a turn in the garden*). **10** a short performance on stage or in a circus etc. **11** service of a specified kind (*did me a good turn*). **12** purpose (*served my turn*). **13** *colloq.* a momentary nervous shock or ill feeling (*gave me quite a turn*). **14** *Mus.* an ornament consisting of the principal note with those above and below it. **15** one round in a coil of rope etc. **16** *Printing* **a** inverted type as a temporary substitute for a missing letter. **b** a letter turned wrong side up. **17 a** *Brit.* the difference between the buying and selling price of stocks etc. **b** a profit made from this. □ **at every turn** continually; at each new stage etc. **by turns** in rotation of individuals or groups; alternately. **in turn** in succession; one by one. **in one's turn** when one's turn or opportunity comes. **not know which way** (or **where) to turn** be completely at a loss, unsure how to act, etc. **not turn a hair** see HAIR. **on the turn 1** changing. **2** (of milk) becoming sour. **3** at the turning point. **out of turn 1** at a time when it is not one's turn. **2** inappropriately; inadvisedly or tactlessly (*did I speak out of turn?*). **take turns** (or **take it in turns**) act or work alternately or in succession. **to a turn** (esp. cooked) to exactly the right degree etc. **turn about** move so as to face in a new direction. **turn and turn about** esp. *Brit.* alternately. **turn around** esp. *N. Amer.* = *turn round.* **turn away 1** turn to face in another direction. **2** refuse to accept; reject. **3** send away. **turn back 1** begin or cause to retrace one's steps. **2** fold back. **turn one's back on** see BACK. **turn the corner 1** pass round it into another street. **2** pass the critical point in an illness, difficulty, etc. **turn a deaf ear** see DEAF. **turn down 1** reject (a proposal, application, etc.). **2** reduce the volume or strength of (sound, heat, etc.) by turning a knob etc. **3** fold down. **4** place downwards. **turn one's hand to** see HAND. **turn a person's head** see HEAD. **turn an honest penny** see HONEST. **turn in 1** hand in or return. **2** achieve or register (a performance, score, etc.). **3** *colloq.* go to bed in the evening. **4** fold inwards. **5** incline inwards (*his toes turn in*). **6** hand over (a suspect etc.) to the authorities. **7** *colloq.* abandon (a plan etc.). **turn in one's grave** see GRAVE[1]. **turn off 1 a** stop the flow or operation of (water, electricity, etc.) by means of a tap, switch, etc. **b** operate (a tap, switch, etc.) to achieve this. **2 a** enter a side road. **b** (of a side road) lead off from another road. **3** *colloq.* repel; cause to lose interest (*turned me right off with their complaining*). **4** dismiss from employment. **turn of speed** the ability to go fast when necessary. **turn on 1 a** start the flow or operation of (water, electricity, etc.) by means of a tap, switch, etc. **b** operate (a tap, switch, etc.) to achieve this. **2** *colloq.* excite; stimulate the interest of, esp. sexually. **3** *tr.* & *intr. slang* intoxicate or become intoxicated with drugs. **turn on one's heel** see HEEL[1]. **turn the other cheek** see CHEEK. **turn out 1** expel. **2** extinguish (an electric light etc.). **3** dress or equip (*well turned out*). **4** produce (manufactured goods etc.). **5** *Brit.* empty or clean out (a room etc.). **6** empty (a pocket) to see the contents. **7** *colloq.* **a** get out of bed. **b** go out of doors. **8** *colloq.* assemble; attend a meeting etc. **9** (often foll. by *to* + infin. or *that* + clause) prove to be the case; result (*turned out to be true*; *we shall see how things turn out*). **10** *Mil.* call (a guard) from the guardroom. **turn over 1** reverse or cause to reverse vertical position; bring the under or reverse side into view (*turn over the page*). **2** upset; fall or cause to fall over. **3 a** cause (an engine) to run. **b** (of an engine) start running. **4** consider thoroughly. **5** (foll. by *to*) **a** transfer the care or conduct of (a person or thing) to (a person) (*shall turn it all over to my deputy*). **b** = *turn in* 6. **6** do business to the amount of (*turns over £5,000 a week*). **turn over a new leaf** improve one's conduct or performance. **turn round 1** turn so as to face in a new direction. **2 a** *Commerce* unload and reload (a ship, vehicle, etc.). **b** receive, process, and send out again; cause to progress through a system. **3** adopt new opinions or policy. **turn the scales** see SCALE[2]. **turn the tables** see TABLE. **turn tail** turn one's back; run away. **turn the tide** reverse the trend of events. **turn to** set about one's work (*came home and immediately turned to*). **turn to account** see ACCOUNT. **turn a trick** see TRICK.**turn turtle** see TURTLE. **turn up 1** increase the volume or strength of (sound, heat, etc.) by turning a knob etc. **2** place upwards. **3** discover or reveal. **4** be found, esp. by chance (*it turned up on a rubbish dump*). **5** happen or present itself; (of a person) put in an appearance (*a few people turned up late*). **6** *Brit. colloq.* cause to vomit (*the sight turned me up*). **7** shorten (a garment) by increasing the size of the hem. **turn up one's nose** see NOSE. [Old English *tyrnan*, *turnian* via Latin *tornare*, from *tornus* 'lathe' from Greek *tornos* 'lathe, circular movement': probably reinforced in Middle English from Old French *turner*, *torner*]

turnabout /'tə:nəbaʊt/ *n.* **1** an act of turning about. **2** an abrupt change of policy etc.

turnaround /'tə:nəraʊnd/ *n.* **1 a** the process of receiving, processing, and sending out again; progress through a system; the time taken for this (*a seven-day turnaround*). **b** the process of unloading and reloading a ship, vehicle, etc.; the time taken for this. **2** an abrupt or unexpected change of fortune, attitude, etc.

turnback /'tə:nbak/ *n.* = REVERS.

turn-bench *n.* a watchmaker's portable lathe.

turn-buckle *n.* a device for tightly connecting parts of a metal rod or wire.

turn-cap *n.* a revolving chimney top.

turncoat /'tə:nkəʊt/ *n.* a person who changes sides in a conflict, dispute, etc.

turncock /'tə:nkɒk/ *n. hist.* an official employed to turn on water for the mains supply etc.

turndown /'tə:ndaʊn/ *n.* & *adj.* ● *n.* **1** a rejection or refusal. **2** a downturn. ● *attrib.adj.* (of a collar) turned down.

turner /'tə:nə/ *n.* **1** a person or thing that turns. **2** a person who works with a lathe. [Middle English via Old French *tornere -eor* from Late Latin *tornator* (as TURN)]

turnery /'tə:n(ə)ri/ *n.* **1** objects made on a lathe. **2** work with a lathe.

turning /'tə:nɪŋ/ *n.* **1 a** a road that branches off another. **b** a place where this occurs. **2 a** use of the lathe. **b** (in *pl.*) chips or shavings from a lathe.

turning circle *n.* the smallest circle in which a vehicle can turn without reversing.

turning point *n.* a point at which a decisive change occurs.

turnip /'tə:nɪp/ *n.* **1 a** a cruciferous plant, *Brassica rapa*, with a large white globular root and sprouting leaves. **b** a similar or related plant, esp. a swede. **2** the root of such a plant used as a vegetable. **3** a large thick old-fashioned watch. □ **turnipy** *adj.* [earlier *turnep(e)* from *neep*, from Latin *napus*: first element of uncertain origin]

turnip-tops *n.pl.* (*US* also **turnip greens**) the leaves of the turnip eaten as a vegetable.

turnkey /'tə:nki:/ *n.* & *adj.* ● *n.* (*pl.* **-eys**) *archaic* a jailer. ● *adj.* (of a contract etc.) providing for a supply of equipment in a state ready for operation.

turn-off *n.* **1** a turning off a main road. **2** *colloq.* something that repels or causes a loss of interest.

turn-on *n. colloq.* a person or thing that causes (esp. sexual) arousal.

turnout /'tə:naʊt/ *n.* **1** the number of people attending a meeting, voting at an election, etc. (*rain reduced the turnout*). **2** the quantity of goods produced in a given time. **3** a set or display of equipment, clothes, etc.

turnover /'tə:nəʊvə/ *n.* **1** the act or an instance of turning over. **2** the amount of money taken in a business. **3** the number of people entering and leaving employment etc. **4** a small pie or tart made by folding a piece of pastry over a filling. **5** *US Sport* loss of possession of the ball to the opposing team.

turnpike /'tə:npʌɪk/ *n.* **1** *hist.* a defensive frame of spikes. **2** *hist.* **a** a toll gate. **b** a road on which a toll was collected at a toll gate. **3** *US* a motorway on which a toll is charged.

turnround /tə:nraʊnd/ *n.* = TURNAROUND.

turnsick /'tə:nsɪk/ *n.* = STURDY *n.*

turnsole /'tə:nsəʊl/ *n.* any of various plants supposed to turn with the sun, esp. the Mediterranean plant *Chrozophora tinctoria*. [Old French *tournesole* via

Provençal *tournasol* from Latin *tornare* TURN + *sol* 'sun']

turnspit /'tə:nspɪt/ *n. hist.* a person, or small dog running on a treadmill, having the task of turning a spit.

turnstile /'tə:nstʌɪl/ *n.* a gate for admission or exit, with revolving arms allowing people through singly.

turnstone /'tə:nstəʊn/ *n.* any small wading bird of the genus *Arenaria*, which has a short bill and turns over stones to feed on small animals.

turntable /'tə:nteɪb(ə)l/ *n.* **1** a circular revolving plate supporting a gramophone record that is being played. **2** a circular revolving platform for turning a railway locomotive or other vehicle.

turn-up *n.* **1** *Brit.* the lower turned-up end of a trouser leg. **2** (esp. in phr. **turn-up for the books**) *Brit. colloq.* an unexpected (esp. welcome) happening; a surprise.

turpentine /'tə:p(ə)ntʌɪn/ *n. & v.* ● *n.* **1** (in full **crude turpentine** or **gum turpentine**) an oleoresin secreted by certain trees, esp. pines, and distilled to make rosin and oil of turpentine. **2** (in full **oil of turpentine**) a volatile pungent oil distilled from gum turpentine or pinewood, and used in mixing paints and varnishes, and in medicine. **3** a tree yielding turpentine or a similar resin. ● *v.tr.* apply turpentine to. [Middle English via Old French *ter(e)bentine* from Latin *ter(e)binthina* (*resina* 'resin') (as TEREBINTH)]

turpeth /'tə:pɪθ/ *n.* (in full **turpeth root**) the root of a tropical Asian plant, *Ipomoea turpethum*, used as a cathartic. [Middle English via medieval Latin *turbit(h)um* from Arabic & Persian *turbid*]

turpitude /'tə:pɪtju:d/ *n. formal* baseness, depravity, wickedness. [French *turpitude* or Latin *turpitudo*, from *turpis* 'disgraceful, base']

turps /tə:ps/ *n. colloq.* oil of turpentine. [abbreviation]

turquoise /'tə:kwɔɪz, -kwɑ:z/ *n. & adj.* ● *n.* **1** a semi-precious stone, usu. opaque and of a greenish-blue or sky-blue colour, consisting of hydrated copper aluminium phosphate. **2** a greenish-blue colour. ● *adj.* of this colour. [Middle English *turkeis* etc. from Old French *turqueise* (later *-oise*) 'Turkish' (stone)]

turret /'tʌrɪt/ *n.* **1** a small tower, usu. projecting from the wall of a building as a decorative addition. **2** a low flat usu. revolving armoured tower for a gun and gunners in a ship, aircraft, fort, or tank. **3** a rotating holder for tools in a lathe etc. □ **turreted** *adj.* [Middle English from Old French *to(u)rete*, diminutive of *to(u)r* TOWER]

turret lathe *n.* = CAPSTAN LATHE.

turtle /'tə:t(ə)l/ *n.* **1** any of various marine or freshwater reptiles of the order Chelonia, encased in a shell of bony plates, and having flippers or webbed toes used in swimming. **2** the flesh of the turtle, esp. used for soup. **3** *Computing* a directional cursor in a computer graphics system which can be instructed to move around a screen. □ **turn turtle** capsize; turn upside down. [apparently alteration of *tortue*: see TORTOISE]

turtle-dove /'tə:t(ə)ldʌv/ *n.* any wild dove of the genus *Streptopelia*, esp. *S. turtur*, noted for its soft cooing and its affection for its mate and young. [archaic *turtle* (in the same sense) via Old English *turtla*, *turtle* from Latin *turtur*, of imitative origin]

turtleneck /'tə:t(ə)lnɛk/ *n.* **1** *Brit.* a high close-fitting neck on a knitted garment. **2** *US* = POLO NECK.

turtle shell *n. & adj.* ● *n.* = TORTOISESHELL *n.* 1. ● *adj.* (**turtleshell**) = TORTOISESHELL *adj.*

turves *pl.* of TURF.

Tuscan /'tʌskən/ *n. & adj.* ● *n.* **1** an inhabitant of Tuscany in central Italy. **2** the classical Italian language of Tuscany. ● *adj.* **1** of or relating to Tuscany or the Tuscans. **2** *Archit.* denoting the least ornamented of the classical orders. [Middle English via French from Latin *Tuscanus*, from *Tuscus* 'an Etruscan']

Tuscan straw *n.* fine yellow wheat straw used for hats etc.

tush[1] /tʌʃ/ *int. archaic* expressing strong disapproval or scorn. [Middle English: imitative]

tush[2] /tʌʃ/ *n.* **1** a long pointed tooth, esp. a canine tooth of a horse. **2** an elephant's short tusk. [Old English *tusc* TUSK]

tush[3] /tʊʃ/ *n.* esp. *N. Amer. slang* the buttocks. [Yiddish *tokhes* from Hebrew *taḥat* 'beneath']

tusk /tʌsk/ *n. & v.* ● *n.* **1** a long pointed tooth, esp. protruding from a closed mouth, as in the elephant, walrus, etc. **2** a tusklike tooth or other object. ● *v.tr.* gore, thrust at, or tear up with a tusk or tusks. □ **tusked** *adj.* (also in *comb.*). **tusky** *adj.* [Middle English alteration of Old English *tux*, variant of *tusc*: cf. TUSH[2]]

tusker /'tʌskə/ *n.* an elephant or wild boar with well-developed tusks.

tusk shell *n.* **1** any of various molluscs of the class Scaphopoda. **2** its long tubular tusk-shaped shell.

tussah *US* var. of TUSSORE.

tusser var. of TUSSORE.

tussive /'tʌsɪv/ *adj.* of or relating to a cough. [Latin *tussis* 'a cough']

tussle /'tʌs(ə)l/ *n. & v.* ● *n.* a struggle or scuffle. ● *v.intr.* engage in a tussle. [originally Scots & northern English, perhaps diminutive of *touse*: see TOUSLE]

tussock /'tʌsək/ *n.* **1** a clump of grass etc. **2** (in full **tussock moth**) any moth of the family Lymantriidae, with hairy tufted larvae that are often pests of trees. □ **tussocky** *adj.* [16th c.: perhaps an alteration of dialect *tusk* 'tuft', of unknown origin]

tussock grass *n.* a grass which grows in tussocks, esp. of the genus *Poa*, *Nassella*, or *Deschampsia*.

tussore /'tʌsɔ:, 'tʌsə/ *n.* (also **tusser**, *US* **tussah** /'tʌsə/) **1** an Indian or Chinese silkworm, *Antheraea mylitta*, yielding strong but coarse brown silk. **2** (in full **tussore-silk**) silk from this and some other silkworms. [Urdu via Hindi *tasar* from Sanskrit *tasara* 'shuttle']

tut var. of TUT-TUT.

tutee /tju:'ti:/ *n.* a student or pupil of a tutor.

tutelage /'tju:tɪlɪdʒ/ *n.* **1** guardianship. **2** the state or duration of being under this. **3** instruction, tuition. [Latin *tutela* from *tuēri tuit-* or *tut-* 'watch']

tutelary /'tju:tɪləri/ *adj.* (also **tutelar** /-tɪlə/) **1 a** serving as guardian. **b** relating to a guardian (*tutelary authority*). **2** giving protection (*tutelary saint*). [Late Latin *tutelaris*, Latin *-arius* from *tutela*: see TUTELAGE]

tutenag /'tu:tɪnag/ *n.* **1** zinc imported from China and SE Asia. **2** a white alloy like German silver. [Marathi *tuttināg*, perhaps from Sanskrit *tuttha* 'copper sulphate' + *nāga* 'tin, lead']

tutor /'tju:tə/ *n. & v.* ● *n.* **1** a private teacher, esp. one in general charge of a person's education. **2** *Brit.* a university teacher supervising the studies or welfare of assigned undergraduates. **3** *Brit.* a book of instruction in a subject. ● *v.* **1** *tr.* act as a tutor to. **2** *intr.* work as a tutor. **3** *tr.* restrain, discipline. **4** *intr. US* receive tuition. □ **tutorage** /-t(ə)rɪdʒ/ *n.* **tutorship** *n.* [Middle English from Anglo-French, Old French *tutour* or Latin *tutor*, from *tuēri tut-* 'watch']

tutorial /tju:'tɔ:rɪəl/ *adj. & n.* ● *adj.* of or relating to a tutor or tuition. ● *n.* **1** a period of tuition given by a university etc. tutor to an individual or a small group. **2** an account or explanation of a subject, printed or on-screen, intended for private study. □ **tutorially** *adv.* [Latin *tutorius* (as TUTOR)]

tutsan /'tʌts(ə)n/ *n.* a St John's wort, *Hypericum androsaemum*, formerly used to heal wounds etc. [Middle English from Anglo-French *tutsaine* 'all healthy']

Tutsi /'tʊtsi/ *n.* (*pl.* same or **Tutsis**) a member of a Bantu-speaking people forming a minority of the population of Rwanda. [Bantu]

tutti /'tʊti/ *adv. & n. Mus.* ● *adv.* with all voices or instruments together. ● *n.* (*pl.* **tuttis**) a passage to be performed in this way. [Italian, pl. of *tutto* 'all']

tutti-frutti /tu:tɪ'fru:ti/ *n.* (*pl.* **-fruttis**) a confection, esp. ice cream, of or flavoured with mixed fruits. [Italian, = all fruits]

tut-tut /tʌt'tʌt/ *int., n., & v.* (also **tut** /tʌt/, **tsk** /tsk/, **tsk tsk**) ● *int.* expressing rebuke, impatience, or contempt. ● *n.* such an exclamation. ● *v.intr.* (**-tutted**, **-tutting**) exclaim this. [imitative of a click of the tongue against the teeth]

tutty /'tʌti/ *n.* impure zinc oxide or carbonate used as a polishing powder. [Middle English via Old French *tutie* and medieval Latin *tutia* from Arabic *tūtiyā*]

tutu[1] /'tu:tu:/ *n.* a ballet dancer's short skirt of stiffened projecting frills. [French]

tutu[2] /'tu:tu:/ *n.* a shrub, *Coriaria arborea*, native to New Zealand, bearing poisonous purplish-black berries. [Maori]

tu-whit tu-whoo /tʊˌwɪt tʊ'wu:/ *n.* a representation of the cry of an owl. [imitative]

tux /tʌks/ *n. N. Amer. colloq.* = TUXEDO.

tuxedo /tʌk'si:dəʊ/ *n.* (*pl.* **-os** or **-oes**) *N. Amer.* **1** a dinner jacket. **2** a suit of clothes including this. [after a country club at *Tuxedo* Park, New York]

tuyère /twi:'jɛ:, tu:-/ *n.* (also **tuyere**, **twyer** /'twʌɪə/) a nozzle through which air is forced into a furnace etc. [French, from *tuyau* 'pipe']

TV *abbr.* television (the system or a set).

TVEI *abbr.* Technical and Vocational Educational Initiative.

TVP *abbr. propr.* textured vegetable protein, a type of protein obtained from soya beans and made to resemble meat, esp. minced meat.

twaddle /'twɒd(ə)l/ *n. & v.* ● *n.* useless, senseless, or dull writing or talk. ● *v.intr.* indulge in this. □ **twaddler** *n.* [alteration of earlier *twattle*, alteration of TATTLE]

twain /tweɪn/ *adj. & n. archaic* two (usu. *in twain*). [Old English *twegen*, masc. form of *twā* TWO]

twang /twaŋ/ *n. & v.* ● *n.* **1** a strong ringing sound made by the plucked string of a musical instrument or a released bowstring. **2** the nasal quality of a voice compared to this. ● *v.* **1** *intr. & tr.* emit or cause to emit this sound. **2** *tr.* usu. *derog.* play (a tune or instrument) in this way. **3** *tr.* utter with a nasal twang. □ **twangy** *adj.* [imitative]

'twas /twɒz, twəz/ *archaic* it was. [contraction]

twat /twɒt, twat/ *n. coarse slang* **1** the female genitals. **2** a term of contempt for a person. [17th c.: origin unknown]

twayblade /'tweɪbleɪd/ *n.* any orchid of the genus *Listera* etc., with green or purple flowers and a single pair of leaves. [*tway*, variant of TWAIN + BLADE]

tweak /twi:k/ *v. & n.* ● *v.tr.* **1** pinch and twist sharply; pull with a sharp jerk; twitch. **2** make fine adjustments to (a mechanism). ● *n.* an instance of tweaking. [probably an alteration of dialect *twick* from Old English *twiccian*: related to TWITCH]

twee /twi:/ *adj.* (**tweer** /'twi:ə/; **tweest** /'twi:ɪst/) *Brit.* usu. *derog.* affectedly dainty or quaint. □ **tweely** *adv.* **tweeness** *n.* [childish pronunciation of SWEET]

tweed /twi:d/ *n.* **1** a rough-surfaced woollen cloth, usu. of mixed flecked colours, originally produced in Scotland. **2** (in *pl.*) clothes made of tweed. [originally a misreading of *tweel*, Scots form of TWILL, influenced by association with the river *Tweed*]

Tweedledum and Tweedledee /twi:d(ə)l'dʌm, twi:d(ə)l'di:/ *n.* a pair of persons or things that are virtually indistinguishable. [originally applied to the rival composers Handel and Bononcini in a satire (1725) by J. Byron]

tweedy /'twi:di/ *adj.* (**tweedier**, **tweediest**) **1** of or relating to tweed cloth. **2** characteristic of the country gentry; heartily informal. □ **tweedily** *adv.* **tweediness** *n.*

'tween /twi:n/ *prep. archaic* = BETWEEN. [contraction]

'tween-decks *n.pl. Naut.* the space between decks.

tweet /twi:t/ *n. & v.* (also **tweet tweet**) ● *n.* the chirp of a small bird. ● *v.intr.* make a chirping noise. [imitative]

tweeter /'twi:tə/ *n.* a loudspeaker designed to reproduce high frequencies.

tweezers /'twi:zəz/ *n.pl.* a small pair of pincers for taking up small objects, plucking out hairs, etc. [extended form of *tweezes* (cf. *pincers* etc.), pl. of obsolete *tweeze*, a case for small instruments, from *etweese* = *étuis*, pl. of ÉTUI]

twelfth /twɛlfθ/ *n. & adj.* ● *n.* **1** the position in a sequence corresponding to the number 12 in the sequence 1–12. **2** something occupying this position. **3** each of twelve equal parts of a thing. **4** *Mus.* **a** an interval or chord spanning an octave and a fifth in the diatonic scale. **b** a note separated from another by this interval. ● *adj.* that is the twelfth. □ **twelfthly** *adv.* [Old English *twelfta* (as TWELVE)]

Twelfth Day *n.* 6 Jan., the twelfth day after Christmas, the festival of the Epiphany.

twelfth man *n.* a reserve member of a cricket team.

Twelfth Night *n.* **1** the evening of 5 Jan., the eve of the Epiphany. **2** = TWELFTH DAY.

twelve /twɛlv/ *n. & adj.* ● *n.* **1** one more than eleven; the product of two units and six units. **2** a symbol for this (12, xii, XII). **3** a size etc. denoted by twelve. **4** twelve o'clock. **5** (**the Twelve**) the twelve Apostles. **6** (**12**) *Brit.* (of films) classified as suitable for persons of 12 years and over. ● *adj.* that amount to twelve. [Old English *twelf(e)* from Germanic: probably related to TWO]

twelvefold /'twɛlvfəʊld/ *adj. & adv.* **1** twelve times as much or as many. **2** consisting of twelve parts.

twelvemo /'twɛlvməʊ/ *n.* (*pl.* **-os**) = DUODECIMO.

twelvemonth /'twɛlvmʌnθ/ *n. archaic* a year; a period of twelve months.

twelve-note *adj.* (also **twelve-tone**) *Mus.* using the twelve chromatic notes of the octave on an equal basis without dependence on a key system.

twenty /'twɛnti/ *n. & adj.* ● *n.* (*pl.* **-ies**) **1** the product of two and ten. **2** a symbol for this (20, xx, XX). **3** (in *pl.*) the numbers from 20 to 29, esp. the years of a century or of a person's life. **4** *colloq.* a large indefinite number (*have told you twenty times*). ● *adj.* that amount to twenty. □ **twenty-first, -second**, etc. the ordinal numbers between twentieth and thirtieth. **twenty-one, -two**, etc. the cardinal numbers between twenty and thirty. □ **twentieth** *adj. & n.* **twentyfold** *adj. & adv.* [Old English *twentig* (perhaps as TWO, -TY[2])]

twenty-twenty *adj.* (also **20/20**) **1** denoting vision of normal acuity. **2** *colloq.* denoting clear perception or hindsight.

'twere /twə:/ *archaic* it were. [contraction]

twerp /twə:p/ *n.* (also **twirp**) *slang* a stupid or objectionable person. [19th c.: origin unknown]

twibill /'twʌɪbɪl/ *n.* a double-bladed battleaxe. [Old English, from *twi-* 'double' + BILL[3]]

twice /twʌɪs/ *adv.* **1** two times (esp. of multiplication); on two occasions. **2** in double degree or quantity (*twice as good*). [Middle English *twiges* from Old English *twige* (as TWO, -S[3])]

twiddle /'twɪd(ə)l/ *v. & n.* ● *v.* **1** *tr.* & (foll. by *with* etc.) *intr.* twirl, adjust, or play randomly or idly. **2** *intr.* move twirlingly. ● *n.* **1** an act of twiddling. **2** a twirled mark or sign. □ **twiddle one's thumbs 1** make them rotate round each other. **2** have nothing to do. □ **twiddler** *n.* **twiddly** *adj.* [apparently imitative, influenced by *twirl*, *twist*, and *fiddle*, *piddle*]

twig[1] /twɪg/ *n.* **1** a small branch or shoot of a tree or shrub. **2** *Anat.* a small branch of an artery etc. □ **twigged** *adj.* (also in *comb.*). **twiggy** *adj.* [Old English *twigge*, from a Germanic root also found in TWICE, TWO]

twig[2] /twɪg/ *v.tr.* (**twigged**, **twigging**) *Brit. colloq.* **1** (also *absol.*) understand; grasp the meaning or nature of. **2** perceive, observe. [18th c.: origin unknown]

twilight /'twʌɪlʌɪt/ *n.* **1** the soft glowing light from the sky when the sun is below the horizon, esp. in the evening. **2** the period of this. **3** a faint light. **4** a state of imperfect knowledge or understanding. **5** a period of decline or destruction. [Middle English, from Old English *twi-* 'two' (in uncertain sense) + LIGHT[1]]

twilight sleep *n. Med.* a state of partial narcosis, esp. to ease the pain of childbirth.

twilight zone *n.* **1** an urban area that is becoming dilapidated. **2** any physical or conceptual area which is undefined or intermediate.

twilit /ˈtwʌɪlɪt/ *adj.* (also **twilighted** /-lʌɪtɪd/) dimly illuminated by or as by twilight. [past part. of the verb *twilight*, from TWILIGHT]

twill /twɪl/ *n. & v.* ● *n.* a fabric so woven as to have a surface of diagonal parallel ridges. ● *v.tr.* (esp. as **twilled** *adj.*) weave (fabric) in this way. □ **twilled** *adj.* [northern English variant of obsolete *twilly* from Old English *twili* (from *twi-* 'double'), translating Latin *bilix* (as BI-, *licium* 'thread')]

'twill /twɪl/ *archaic* it will. [contraction]

twin /twɪn/ *n., adj., & v.* ● *n.* **1** each of a closely related or associated pair, esp. of children or animals born at the same birth. **2** the exact counterpart of a person or thing. **3** a compound crystal one part of which is in a reversed position with reference to the other. **4** (**the Twins**) the zodiacal sign or constellation Gemini. ● *adj.* **1** forming, or being one of, such a pair (*twin brothers*). **2** *Bot.* growing in pairs. **3** consisting of two closely connected and similar parts. ● *v.* (**twinned**, **twinning**) **1** *tr. & intr.* **a** join intimately together. **b** (foll. by *with*) pair. **2** *intr.* bear twins. **3** *intr.* grow as a twin crystal. **4** *intr. & tr. Brit.* link or cause (a town) to link with one in a different country, for the purposes of friendship and cultural exchange. □ **twinning** *n.* [Old English *twinn* 'double', from *twi-* 'two': cf. Old Norse *tvinnr*]

twin bed *n.* each of a pair of single beds. □ **twin-bedded** *adj.*

twin-cam *attrib.adj.* (esp. of an engine) having two camshafts.

twine /twʌɪn/ *n. & v.* ● *n.* **1** a strong thread or string of two or more strands of hemp or cotton etc. twisted together. **2** a coil or twist. **3** a tangle; an interlacing. ● *v.* **1** *tr.* form (a string or thread etc.) by twisting strands together. **2** *tr.* form (a garland etc.) of interwoven material. **3** *tr.* (often foll. by *with*) garland (a brow etc.). **4** *intr.* (often foll. by *round*, *about*, *around*) coil or wind. **5** *intr. & refl.* (of a plant) grow in this way. □ **twiner** *n.* [Old English *twīn*, *twigin* 'linen', ultimately from the stem of *twi-* 'two']

twin-engined *adj.* having two engines.

twinge /twɪn(d)ʒ/ *n. & v.* ● *n.* a sharp momentary local pain or pang (*a twinge of toothache*; *a twinge of conscience*). ● *v.intr. & tr.* (**twingeing** or **twinging**) experience or cause to experience a twinge. [Old English *twengan* 'pinch, wring', from Germanic]

twinkle /ˈtwɪŋk(ə)l/ *v. & n.* ● *v.* **1** *intr.* (of a star or light etc.) shine with rapidly intermittent gleams. **2** *intr.* (of the eyes) sparkle, esp. with amusement. **3** *intr.* (of the feet in dancing) move lightly and rapidly. **4** *tr.* emit (a light or signal) in quick gleams. **5** *tr.* blink or wink (one's eyes). ● *n.* **1** **a** a sparkle or gleam of the eyes. **b** a blink or wink. **2** a slight flash of light; a glimmer. **3** a short rapid movement. □ **in a twinkle** (or **a twinkling** or **the twinkling of an eye**) in an instant. □ **twinkler** *n.* **twinkly** *adj.* [Old English *twinclian*]

twin-screw *attrib.adj.* (of a ship) having two propellers on separate shafts with opposite twists.

twinset /ˈtwɪnsɛt/ *n.* esp. *Brit.* a woman's matching cardigan and jumper.

twin town *n. Brit.* a town which is twinned with another.

twirl /twəːl/ *v. & n.* ● *v.tr. & intr.* spin or swing or twist quickly and lightly round. ● *n.* **1** a twirling motion. **2** a form made by twirling, esp. a flourish made with a pen. □ **twirler** *n.* **twirly** *adj.* [16th c.: probably alteration (by association with *whirl*) of obsolete *tirl* TRILL]

twirp var. of TWERP.

twist /twɪst/ *v. & n.* ● *v.* **1** **a** *tr.* change the form of by rotating one end and not the other or the two ends in opposite directions. **b** *intr.* undergo such a change; take a twisted position (*twisted round in his seat*). **c** *tr.* wrench or pull out of shape with a twisting action (*twisted my ankle*). **2** *tr.* **a** wind (strands etc.) about each other. **b** form (a rope etc.) by winding the strands. **c** (foll. by *with*, *in with*) interweave. **d** form by interweaving or twining. **3** **a** *tr.* give a spiral form to (a rod, column, cord, etc.) as by rotating the ends in opposite directions. **b** *intr.* take a spiral form. **4** *tr.* (foll. by *off*) break off or separate by twisting. **5** *tr.* distort or misrepresent the meaning of (words). **6** **a** *intr.* take a curved course. **b** *tr.* make (one's way) in a winding manner. **7** *tr. Brit. slang* cheat (*twisted me out of £20*). **8** *tr. Brit.* cause (the ball, esp. in billiards) to rotate while following a curved path. **9** *tr.* (as **twisted** *adj.*) (of a person or mind) emotionally unbalanced. **10** *intr.* dance the twist. ● *n.* **1** the act or an instance of twisting. **2** **a** a twisted state. **b** the manner or degree in which a thing is twisted. **3** a thing formed by or as by twisting, esp. a thread or rope etc. made by winding strands together. **4** the point at which a thing twists or bends. **5** usu. *derog.* a peculiar tendency of mind or character etc. **6** an unexpected development of events, esp. in a story etc. **7** a fine strong silk thread used by tailors etc. **8** a roll of bread, tobacco, etc., in the form of a twist. **9** *Brit.* a paper packet with screwed-up ends. **10** a curled piece of lemon etc. peel to flavour a drink. **11** a spinning motion given to a ball in cricket etc. to make it take a special curve. **12** **a** a twisting strain. **b** the amount of twisting of a rod etc., or the angle showing this. **c** forward motion combined with rotation about an axis. **13** *Brit.* a drink made of two ingredients mixed together. **14** *Brit. slang* a swindle. **15** (prec. by *the*) a dance with a twisting movement of the body, popular in the 1960s. □ **round the twist** *Brit. colloq.* crazy. **twist a person's arm** *colloq.* apply coercion, esp. by moral pressure. **twist round one's finger** see FINGER. □ **twistable** *adj.* **twisty** *adj.* (**twistier**, **twistiest**). [Old English from Germanic: related to TWIN, TWINE]

twister /ˈtwɪstə/ *n.* **1** *Brit. colloq.* a swindler; a dishonest person. **2** a twisting ball in cricket, billiards, etc. **3** *N. Amer.* a tornado or waterspout.

twit[1] /twɪt/ *n.* esp. *Brit. colloq.* a silly or foolish person. □ **twittish** *adj.* [originally dialect: perhaps from TWIT[2]]

twit[2] /twɪt/ *v.tr.* (**twitted**, **twitting**) reproach or taunt, usu. good-humouredly. [16th-c. *twite* via *atwite* from Old English *ætwītan* 'reproach with', from *æt* 'at' + *wītan* 'to blame']

twitch /twɪtʃ/ *v. & n.* ● *v.* **1** *intr.* (of the features, muscles, limbs, etc.) move or contract spasmodically. **2** *tr.* give a short sharp pull at. ● *n.* **1** **a** a sudden involuntary contraction or movement. **b** a pang; a twinge (*a twitch of irritation*). **2** a sudden pull or jerk. **3** a noose and stick for controlling a horse during a veterinary operation. □ **twitchy** *adj.* (**twitchier**, **twitchiest**). [Middle English from Germanic: probably related to TWEAK]

twitcher /ˈtwɪtʃə/ *n.* **1** *Brit. slang* a birdwatcher who tries to get sightings of rare birds. **2** a person or thing that twitches.

twitch grass /twɪtʃ/ *n.* = COUCH[2]. [variant of QUITCH]

twite /twʌɪt/ *n.* a moorland finch, *Acanthis flavirostris*, resembling the linnet. [imitative of its cry]

twitter /ˈtwɪtə/ *v. & n.* ● *v.* **1** *intr.* **a** (of a bird) emit a succession of light tremulous sounds. **b** talk rapidly in an idle or trivial way. **2** *tr.* utter or express in this way. ● *n.* **1** the act or an instance of twittering. **2** *colloq.* a tremulously excited state. □ **twitterer** *n.* **twittery** *adj.* [Middle English, imitative]

'twixt /twɪkst/ *prep. archaic* = BETWIXT. [contraction]

twizzle /ˈtwɪz(ə)l/ *v. & n. colloq.* or *dial.* ● *v.tr. & intr.* twist, turn. ● *n.* a twist or turn. [probably imitative, influenced by TWIST]

two /tuː/ *n. & adj.* ● *n.* **1** one more than one; the sum of one unit and another unit. **2** a symbol for this (2, ii, II).

3 a size etc. denoted by two. **4** two o'clock. **5** a set of two. **6** a card with two pips. ● *adj.* that amount to two. □ **in two** in or into two pieces. **in two shakes** (or **ticks**) see SHAKE, TICK[1]. **or two** denoting several (*a thing or two* = several things). **put two and two together** make (esp. an obvious) inference from what is known or evident. **that makes two of us** *colloq.* that is true of me also. **two by two** (or **two and two**) in pairs. **two can play at that game** *colloq.* another person's behaviour can be copied to that person's disadvantage. **two a penny** see PENNY. [Old English *twā* (fem. & neut.), *tū* (neut.), with Germanic cognates and related to Sanskrit *dwau, dwe*, Greek & Latin *duo*]

two-bit *adj. N. Amer. colloq.* cheap, petty.

two-by-four *n.* a length of timber with a rectangular cross-section nominally 2 in. by 4 in.

two cultures *n.pl.* (prec. by *the*) *Brit.* the arts and science.

two-dimensional *adj.* **1** having or appearing to have length and breadth but no depth. **2** lacking depth or substance; superficial.

two-edged *adj.* double-edged.

two-faced *adj.* **1** having two faces. **2** insincere; deceitful.

twofold /ˈtuːfəʊld/ *adj. & adv.* **1** twice as much or as many. **2** consisting of two parts.

two-handed *adj.* **1** having, using, or requiring the use of two hands. **2** (of a card game) for two players.

twoness /ˈtuːnɪs/ *n.* the fact or state of being two; duality.

twopence /ˈtʌp(ə)ns/ *n. Brit.* **1** the sum of two pence, esp. before decimalization. **2** (esp. with *neg.*) *colloq.* a thing of little value (*don't care twopence*).

twopenn'orth /tuːˈpɛnəθ/ *n.* **1** as much as is worth or costs twopence. **2** a paltry or insignificant amount. □ **add** (or **put in**) **one's twopenn'orth** *colloq.* contribute one's opinion.

twopenny /ˈtʌp(ə)ni/ *adj. Brit.* **1** costing two pence, esp. before decimalization. **2** *colloq.* cheap, worthless.

twopenny-halfpenny /tʌpnɪˈheɪpni/ *adj.* cheap, insignificant.

two-piece *adj. & n.* ● *attrib.adj.* (of a suit etc.) consisting of two matching items. ● *n.* a two-piece suit etc.

two-ply *adj. & n.* ● *attrib.adj.* of two strands, webs, or thicknesses. ● *n.* **1** two-ply wool. **2** two-ply wood made by gluing together two layers with the grain in different directions.

two-seater *n.* **1** a vehicle or aircraft with two seats. **2** a sofa etc. for two people.

two-sided *adj.* **1** having two sides. **2** having two aspects; controversial.

twosome /ˈtuːsəm/ *n.* **1** two persons together. **2** a game, dance, etc., for two persons.

two-step *n.* a round dance with a sliding step in march or polka time.

two-stroke *adj. & n.* ● *attrib.adj.* **1** (of an internal-combustion engine) having its power cycle completed in one up-and-down movement of the piston. **2** (of a vehicle) having a two-stroke engine. ● *n.* a two-stroke engine or vehicle.

two-time *v.tr. colloq.* **1** deceive or be unfaithful to (esp. a partner or lover). **2** swindle, double-cross. □ **two-timer** *n.*

two-tone *attrib.adj.* having two colours or sounds.

'twould /twʊd/ *archaic* it would. [contraction]

two-up *n. Austral. & NZ* a gambling game played by tossing two coins with bets placed on a showing of two heads or two tails.

two-way *adj.* **1** involving two ways or participants. **2** (of a switch) permitting a current to be switched on or off from either of two points. **3** (of a radio) capable of transmitting and receiving signals. **4** (of a tap etc.) permitting fluid etc. to flow in either of two channels or directions. **5** (of traffic etc.) moving in two esp. opposite directions.

two-way mirror *n.* a panel of glass that can be seen through from one side and is a mirror on the other.

two-wheeler *n.* a vehicle with two wheels.

twyer var. of TUYÈRE.

TX *abbr. US* Texas (in official postal use).

-ty[1] /ti/ *suffix* forming nouns denoting quality or condition (*cruelty; plenty*). [Middle English *-tie, -tee, -te* via Old French *-té, -tet* from Latin *-tas -tatis*: cf. -ITY]

-ty[2] /ti/ *suffix* denoting tens (*twenty; thirty; ninety*). [Old English *-tig*]

tychism /ˈtʌɪkɪz(ə)m/ *n. Philos.* the theory that chance controls the universe. [Greek *tukhē* 'chance']

tycoon /tʌɪˈkuːn/ *n.* **1** a business magnate. **2** *hist.* a title used to describe the shogun of Japan to Westerners 1857–68. [Japanese *taikun* 'great lord']

tying *pres. part.* of TIE.

tyke /tʌɪk/ *n.* (also **tike**) **1** esp. *Brit.* an unpleasant or coarse man. **2** a mongrel. **3** a small child. **4** *Brit. slang* a Yorkshireman. **5** *Austral. & NZ slang offens.* a Roman Catholic. [Middle English from Old Norse *tík* 'bitch': sense 5 assimilated from TAIG]

tylopod /ˈtʌɪləpɒd/ *n. & adj. Zool.* ● *n.* any animal that bears its weight on the sole-pads of the feet rather than on the hoofs, esp. the camel. ● *adj.* (of an animal) bearing its weight in this way. □ **tylopodous** /-ˈlɒpədəs/ *adj.* [Greek *tulos* 'knob' or *tulē* 'callus, cushion' + *pous podos* 'foot']

tympan /ˈtɪmpən/ *n.* **1** *Printing* an appliance in a printing press used to equalize pressure between the platen etc. and a printing-sheet. **2** *Archit.* = TYMPANUM. [French *tympan* or Latin *tympanum*: see TYMPANUM]

tympana *pl.* of TYMPANUM.

tympani var. of TIMPANI.

tympanic /tɪmˈpanɪk/ *adj.* **1** *Anat.* of, relating to, or having a tympanum. **2** resembling or acting like a drumhead.

tympanic bone *n. Anat.* the bone supporting the tympanic membrane.

tympanic membrane *n. Anat.* the membrane separating the outer ear and middle ear and transmitting vibrations resulting from sound waves to the inner ear; the eardrum.

tympanites /tɪmpəˈnʌɪtiːz/ *n. Med.* a swelling of the abdomen caused by gas in the intestine etc. □ **tympanitic** /-ˈnɪtɪk/ *adj.* [Late Latin from Greek *tumpanitēs* of a drum (as TYMPANUM)]

tympanum /ˈtɪmpənəm/ *n.* (*pl.* **tympanums** or **tympana** /-nə/) **1** *Anat.* **a** the middle ear. **b** the tympanic membrane. **2** *Zool.* the membrane covering the hearing organ on the leg etc. of an insect. **3** *Archit.* **a** a vertical triangular space forming the centre of a pediment. **b** a similar space over a door between the lintel and the arch; a carving on this space. **4** a drum-wheel etc. for raising water from a stream. [Latin from Greek *tumpanon* 'drum', from *tuptō* 'strike']

tympany /ˈtɪmpəni/ *n.* (esp. in veterinary medicine) = TYMPANITES.

Tynesider /ˈtʌɪnsʌɪdə/ *n.* a native or inhabitant of Tyneside, or specifically of Newcastle-upon-Tyne, in NE England.

Tynwald /ˈtɪnw(ə)ld/ *n.* the parliament of the Isle of Man. [Old Norse *thing-vǫllr* 'place of assembly', from *thing* 'assembly' + *vǫllr* 'field']

type /tʌɪp/ *n. & v.* ● *n.* **1 a** a class of things or persons having common characteristics. **b** a kind or sort (*would like a different type of car*). **2** a person, thing, or event serving as an illustration, symbol, or characteristic specimen of another, or of a class. **3** (in *comb.*) made of, resembling, or functioning as (*ceramic-type material; Cheddar-type cheese*). **4** *colloq.* a person, esp. of a specified character (*is rather a quiet type; is not really my type*). **5** an object, conception, or work of art serving as a model for subsequent artists. **6** *Printing* **a** a piece of metal etc. with a raised letter or character on its upper surface for use in printing. **b** such pieces collectively. **c** printed characters produced by type (*printed in large type*). **7** a device on either side of a medal or coin. **8** *Theol.* a foreshadowing in the Old Testament of a person or event of the Christian dispensation. **9** *Biol.* an organism having or chosen as having the essential characteristics of its group and giving its name to the next highest group. ● *v.* **1** *tr.* be a type or example of. **2** *tr.* & *intr.* write with a typewriter. **3** *tr.* esp. *Biol.* & *Med.* assign to a type; classify. **4** *tr.* = TYPECAST. □ **in type** *Printing* composed and ready for printing. □ **typal** *adj.* [Middle English via French *type* or Latin *typus* from Greek *tupos* 'impression, figure, type', from *tuptō* 'strike']

typecast /'tʌɪpkɑːst/ *v.tr.* (*past* and *past part.* **-cast**) assign (an actor or actress) repeatedly to the same type of role, esp. one in character.

typeface /'tʌɪpfeɪs/ *n.* *Printing* **1** a set of types or characters in a particular design. **2** the inked part of type, or the impression made by this.

type founder *n.* a designer and maker of metal types.

type foundry *n.* a foundry where type is made.

type metal *n.* an alloy of lead etc., used for casting printing types.

typescript /'tʌɪpskrɪpt/ *n.* a typewritten document.

typesetter /'tʌɪpsɛtə/ *n.* *Printing* **1** a person who composes type. **2** a composing machine. □ **typeset** *v.tr.* (**-setting**; *past* and *past part.* **-set**) (also *absol.*). **typesetting** *n.* (also *attrib.*).

type site *n.* *Archaeol.* a site where objects regarded as defining the characteristics of a period etc. are found.

type size *n.* a size of type usu. specified by name, e.g. *pica* etc.

type specimen *n.* *Biol.* the specimen used for naming and describing a new species.

typewriter /'tʌɪprʌɪtə/ *n.* a machine with keys for producing printlike characters one at a time on paper inserted round a roller. □ **typewriting** *n.*

typewritten /'tʌɪpwrɪt(ə)n/ *adj.* produced with a typewriter.

typhlitis /tɪ'flʌɪtɪs/ *n.* inflammation of the caecum. □ **typhlitic** /-'flɪtɪk/ *adj.* [modern Latin from Greek *tuphlon* 'caecum or blind gut' (from *tuphlos* 'blind') + -ITIS]

typhoid /'tʌɪfɔɪd/ *n.* & *adj.* ● *n.* **1** (in full **typhoid fever**) an infectious bacterial fever with an eruption of red spots on the chest and abdomen and severe intestinal irritation. **2** a similar disease of animals. ● *adj.* like typhus. □ **typhoidal** *adj.* [TYPHUS + -OID]

typhoid condition *n.* (also **typhoid state**) a state of depressed vitality occurring in many acute diseases.

typhoon /tʌɪ'fuːn/ *n.* a tropical storm in the western Pacific. □ **typhonic** /-'fɒnɪk/ *adj.* [partly via Portuguese *tufão* from Arabic *ṭūfān* (perhaps from Greek *tuphōn* 'whirlwind'); partly from Chinese dialect *tai fung* 'big wind']

typhus /'tʌɪfəs/ *n.* an infectious fever caused by rickettsiae, characterized by a purple rash, headaches, fever, and usu. delirium. □ **typhous** *adj.* [modern Latin from Greek *tuphos* 'smoke, stupor', from *tuphō* 'to smoke']

typical /'tɪpɪk(ə)l/ *adj.* **1** serving as a characteristic example; representative. **2** characteristic of or serving to distinguish a type. **3** (often foll. by *of*) conforming to expected behaviour, attitudes, etc. (*is typical of them to forget*). **4** symbolic. □ **typicality** /-'kalɪti/ *n.* **typically** *adv.* [medieval Latin *typicalis* via Latin *typicus* from Greek *tupikos* (as TYPE)]

typify /'tɪpɪfʌɪ/ *v.tr.* (**-ies, -ied**) **1** be a representative example of; embody the characteristics of. **2** represent by a type or symbol; serve as a type, figure, or emblem of; symbolize. □ **typification** /-fɪ'keɪʃ(ə)n/ *n.* **typifier** *n.* [Latin *typus* TYPE + -FY]

typist /'tʌɪpɪst/ *n.* a person who uses a typewriter, esp. professionally.

typo /'tʌɪpəʊ/ *n.* (*pl.* **-os**) *colloq.* **1** a typographical error. **2** a typographer. [abbreviation]

typographer /tʌɪ'pɒgrəfə/ *n.* a person skilled in typography.

typography /tʌɪ'pɒgrəfi/ *n.* **1** printing as an art. **2** the style and appearance of printed matter. □ **typographic** /-pə'grafɪk/ *adj.* **typographical** /-pə'grafɪk(ə)l/ *adj.* **typographically** /-pə'grafɪk(ə)li/ *adv.* [French *typographie* or modern Latin *typographia* (as TYPE, -GRAPHY)]

typology /tʌɪ'pɒlədʒi/ *n.* the study and interpretation of (esp. biblical) types. □ **typological** /-ə'lɒdʒɪk(ə)l/ *adj.* **typologist** *n.* [Greek *tupos* TYPE + -LOGY]

tyramine /'tʌɪrəmiːn/ *n.* *Biochem.* a derivative of tyrosine occurring in cheese and other foods and affecting the sympathetic nervous system. [TYROSINE + AMINE]

tyrannical /tɪ'ranɪk(ə)l, tʌɪ-/ *adj.* **1** acting like a tyrant; imperious, arbitrary. **2** given to or characteristic of tyranny. □ **tyrannically** *adv.* [Old French *tyrannique* via Latin *tyrannicus* from Greek *turannikos* (as TYRANT)]

tyrannicide /tɪ'ranɪsʌɪd, tʌɪ-/ *n.* **1** the act or an instance of killing a tyrant. **2** the killer of a tyrant. □ **tyrannicidal** /-'sʌɪd(ə)l/ *adj.* [French from Latin *tyrannicida, -cidium* (as TYRANT, -CIDE)]

tyrannize /'tɪrənʌɪz/ *v.tr.* & (foll. by *over*) *intr.* (also **-ise**) behave like a tyrant towards; rule or treat despotically or cruelly. [French *tyranniser* (as TYRANT)]

tyrannosaurus /tɪ,ranə'sɔːrəs, tʌɪ-/ *n.* (also **tyrannosaur** /tɪ'ranəsɔː/) a very large bipedal flesh-eating dinosaur, *Tyrannosaurus rex*, of the late Cretaceous period, having powerful jaws and hind legs, small clawlike front legs, and a large tail. [Greek *turannos* TYRANT + *sauros* 'lizard', on the pattern of *dinosaur*]

tyranny /'tɪr(ə)ni/ *n.* (*pl.* **-ies**) **1** the cruel and arbitrary use of authority. **2** a tyrannical act; tyrannical behaviour. **3 a** rule by a tyrant. **b** a period of this. **c** a state ruled by a tyrant. □ **tyrannous** *adj.* **tyrannously** *adv.* [Middle English via Old French *tyrannie* and medieval Latin *tyrannia* from Greek *turannia* (as TYRANT)]

tyrant /'tʌɪr(ə)nt/ *n.* **1** an oppressive or cruel ruler. **2** a person exercising power arbitrarily or cruelly. **3** *Gk Hist.* an absolute ruler who seized power without the legal right. [Middle English *tyran, -ant* via Old French *tiran, tyrant* and Latin *tyrannus* from Greek *turannos*]

tyrant flycatcher *n.* a small bird of the New World family Tyrannidae, resembling the Old World flycatchers in behaviour. [so called because of its aggressive behaviour towards other birds approaching its nest]

tyre /'tʌɪə/ *n.* (*US* **tire**) **1** a rubber covering, usu. inflated, placed round a wheel to form a soft contact with the road. **2** a strengthening band of metal fitted around the rim of a wheel, esp. of a railway vehicle. [Middle English, perhaps from archaic *tire* 'headdress']

tyre gauge *n.* a portable device for measuring the air pressure in a tyre.

Tyrian /'tɪrɪən/ *adj.* & *n.* ● *adj.* of or relating to ancient Tyre in Phoenicia. ● *n.* a native or citizen of Tyre. [Latin *Tyrius* from *Tyrus* 'Tyre']

Tyrian purple see PURPLE *n.* 2.

tyro /'tʌɪrəʊ/ *n.* (also **tiro**) (*pl.* **-os**) a beginner or novice. [Latin *tiro*, medieval Latin *tyro* 'recruit']

Tyrolean /tɪrə'liːən, tɪ'rəʊlɪən/ *adj.* & *n.* ● *adj.* of or characteristic of the Tyrol, an Alpine province of Austria. ● *n.* a native or inhabitant of the Tyrol. □ **Tyrolese** *adj.* & *n.*

tyrosine /'tʌɪrəsiːn/ *n.* *Chem.* a hydrophilic amino acid present in many proteins and important in the synthesis of some hormones etc. [formed irregularly from Greek *turos* 'cheese' + -INE[4]]

Tyrrhene /'tɪriːn/ *adj.* & *n.* (also **Tyrrhenian** /tɪ'riːnɪən/) *archaic* or *poet.* = ETRUSCAN. [Latin *Tyrrhenus*]

tzar var. of TSAR.

tzarina var. of TSARINA.

tzatziki /tsat'si:ki/ *n.* a Greek side dish of yogurt with cucumber, garlic, and often mint. [modern Greek]

tzigane /tsɪ'gɑ:n/ *n.* **1** a Hungarian gypsy. **2** (*attrib.*) characteristic of the tziganes or (esp.) their music. [French from Hungarian *c(z)igány*]

Uu

U[1] /juː/ *n.* (also **u**) (*pl.* **Us** or **U's**) **1** the twenty-first letter of the alphabet. **2** a U-shaped object or curve (esp. in *comb.*: *U-bolt*).

U[2] /juː/ *adj.* esp. *Brit. colloq.* **1** upper class. **2** supposedly characteristic of the upper class. [abbreviation]

U[3] /uː/ *n.* a Burmese title of respect before a man's name. [Burmese]

U[4] *symb.* **1** *Chem.* the element uranium. **2** *Brit.* universal (of films classified as suitable without restriction).

u *symb.* = MICRO- 2. [substituted for the original symbol μ]

UAE *abbr.* United Arab Emirates.

UB40 *abbr.* (in the UK) a card issued to a person registered as unemployed.

ubiety /juːˈbʌɪɪti/ *n.* the fact or condition of being in a definite place; local relation. [medieval Latin *ubietas* from Latin *ubi* 'where']

-ubility /jʊˈbɪlɪti/ *suffix* forming nouns from, or corresponding to, adjectives in *-uble* (*solubility*; *volubility*). [Latin *-ubilitas*: cf. -ITY]

ubiquitarian /juːˌbɪkwɪˈtɛːrɪən/ *adj.* & *n. Theol.* ● *adj.* relating to or believing in the doctrine of the omnipresence of Christ's body. ● *n.* a believer in this. □ **ubiquitarianism** *n.* [modern Latin *ubiquitarius* (as UBIQUITOUS)]

ubiquitous /juːˈbɪkwɪtəs/ *adj.* **1** present everywhere or in several places simultaneously. **2** often encountered. □ **ubiquitously** *adv.* **ubiquitousness** *n.* **ubiquity** *n.* [modern Latin *ubiquitas* via Latin *ubique* 'everywhere' from *ubi* 'where']

-uble /jʊb(ə)l/ *suffix* forming adjectives meaning 'that may or must (be)' (see -ABLE) (*soluble*; *voluble*). [French from Latin *-ubilis*]

-ubly /jʊbli/ *suffix* forming adverbs corresponding to adjectives in *-uble*.

U-boat *n. hist.* a German submarine used in the First and Second World Wars. [German *U-boot* = *Unterseeboot* 'undersea boat']

UBR *abbr.* uniform business rate, a tax on business property in England and Wales.

UC *abbr.* University College.

u.c. *abbr.* upper case.

UCAS /ˈjuːkas/ *abbr.* (in the UK) Universities and Colleges Admissions Service (created by the amalgamation of UCCA and PCAS in the 1993–4 academic year).

UCATT *abbr.* (in the UK) Union of Construction, Allied Trades, and Technicians.

UCCA /ˈʌkə/ *abbr. hist.* (in the UK) Universities Central Council on Admissions (incorporated into UCAS in the 1993–4 academic year).

UCW *abbr.* (in the UK) Union of Communication Workers.

UDA *abbr.* Ulster Defence Association (a Loyalist paramilitary organization).

udal /ˈjuːd(ə)l/ *n.* (also **odal** /ˈəʊd(ə)l/) the kind of freehold right based on uninterrupted possession prevailing in N. Europe before the feudal system and still in use in Orkney and Shetland. [Old Norse *óthal*, from Germanic]

UDC *abbr. hist.* (in the UK) Urban District Council.

udder /ˈʌdə/ *n.* the mammary gland of cattle, sheep, etc., hanging as a bag-like organ with several teats. □ **uddered** *adj.* (also in *comb.*). [Old English *ūder*, from West Germanic]

UDI *abbr.* unilateral declaration of independence.

udometer /juːˈdɒmɪtə/ *n. formal* a rain gauge. [French *udomètre* (as Latin *udus* 'damp', -METER)]

UDR *abbr.* Ulster Defence Regiment.

UEFA /juːˈiːfə, -ˈeɪfə/ *abbr.* Union of European Football Associations.

UFO /juːɛfˈəʊ, ˈjuːfəʊ/ *abbr.* (also **ufo**) (*pl.* **UFOs** or **ufos**) unidentified flying object.

ufology /juːˈfɒlədʒi/ *n.* the study of UFOs. □ **ufologist** *n.*

ugh /ʊh, ʌh, əː, ʊx, ʌg, *etc.*/ *int.* **1** expressing disgust or horror. **2** the sound of a cough or grunt. [imitative]

ugli fruit /ˈʌgli/ *n.* (*pl.* same) (also **Ugli** *propr.*) a mottled green and yellow citrus fruit, a hybrid of a grapefruit and tangerine. [UGLY]

uglify /ˈʌglɪfʌɪ/ *v.tr.* (**-ies**, **-ied**) make ugly. □ **uglification** /-fɪˈkeɪʃ(ə)n/ *n.*

ugly /ˈʌgli/ *adj.* (**uglier**, **ugliest**) **1** unpleasing or repulsive to see or hear (*an ugly scar*; *spoke with an ugly snarl*). **2** unpleasantly suggestive; discreditable (*ugly rumours are about*). **3** threatening, dangerous (*the sky has an ugly look*). **4** morally repulsive; vile (*ugly vices*). □ **uglily** *adv.* **ugliness** *n.* [Middle English from Old Norse *uggligr* 'to be dreaded', from *ugga* 'to dread']

ugly customer *n.* an unpleasantly formidable person.

ugly duckling *n.* a person who turns out to be beautiful or talented etc. against all expectations (with reference to a cygnet in a brood of ducks in a tale by Andersen).

Ugrian /ˈuːgrɪən, ˈjuː-/ *adj.* & *n.* ● *adj.* = UGRIC *adj.* ● *n.* **1** a person of Ugric stock. **2** = UGRIC *n.*

Ugric /ˈuːgrɪk, ˈjuː-/ *adj.* & *n.* ● *adj.* **1** of or relating to the eastern branch of Finnic peoples, esp. the Magyars. **2** of or relating to the group of Finno-Ugric languages including Magyar. ● *n.* the Ugric group of languages. [Russian *Ugry*, the name of a race dwelling E. of the Urals]

UHF *abbr.* ultra-high frequency.

uh-huh /ˈʌhʌ/ *int. colloq.* expressing assent. [imitative]

uhlan /ˈuːlɑːn, ˈjuː-; ʊˈlɑːn/ *n. hist.* a cavalryman armed with a lance in some European armies, esp. the former German army. [French & German via Polish *(h)ulan* from Turkish *oğlan* 'youth, servant']

UHT *abbr.* ultra heat-treated (esp. of milk, for long keeping).

Uitlander /ˈeɪtlandə, ˈɔɪt-/ *n. S.Afr.* a foreigner or alien, esp. before the Boer War. [Afrikaans, from Dutch *uit* 'out' + *land* 'land']

ujamaa /ʊdʒaˈmɑː/ *n.* (usu. *attrib.*) a system of self-help village cooperatives established by President Nyerere in Tanzania in the 1960s. [Kiswahili, = brotherhood, from *jamaa* 'family', from Arabic *jamāʽa* 'community']

UK *abbr.* United Kingdom.

UKAEA *abbr.* United Kingdom Atomic Energy Authority.

ukase /juːˈkeɪz/ *n.* **1** an arbitrary command. **2** an edict of the Russian government. [Russian *ukaz* 'ordinance, edict' from *ukazat'* 'show, decree']

Ukrainian /juːˈkreɪnɪən/ *n.* & *adj.* ● *n.* **1** a native or inhabitant of Ukraine in eastern Europe. **2** the East Slavonic language of Ukraine. ● *adj.* of or relating to Ukraine, its people, or its language. [*Ukraine* from

Russian *ukraina* 'frontier region', from *u* 'at' + *krai* 'edge']

ukulele /ju:kə'leɪli/ *n.* a small four-stringed Hawaiian (originally Portuguese) guitar. [Hawaiian, = jumping flea]

-ular /jʊlə/ *suffix* forming adjectives, sometimes corresponding to nouns in *-ule* (*pustular*) but often without diminutive force (*angular*; *granular*). □ **-ularity** /-'larɪti/ *suffix* forming nouns. [from or suggested by Latin *-ularis* (as -ULE, -AR[1])]

ulcer /'ʌlsə/ *n.* **1** an open sore on an external or internal surface of the body, often forming pus. **2 a** a moral blemish. **b** a corroding or corrupting influence etc. □ **ulcered** *adj.* **ulcerous** *adj.* [Middle English from Latin *ulcus -eris*, related to Greek *helkos* 'wound, sore']

ulcerate /'ʌlsəreɪt/ *v.tr. & intr.* form into or affect with an ulcer. □ **ulceration** /-'reɪʃ(ə)n/ *n.* **ulcerative** /-rətɪv/ *adj.* [Middle English from Latin *ulcerare ulcerat-* (as ULCER)]

-ule /ju:l/ *suffix* forming diminutive nouns (*capsule*; *globule*). [from or suggested by Latin *-ulus, -ula, -ulum*]

ulema /'ʊləmə, 'u:lɪmə, u:lə'mɑ:/ *n.* **1** a body of Muslim doctors of sacred law and theology. **2** a member of this. [Arabic *'ulamā*, pl. of *'ālim* 'learned' from *'alama* 'know']

-ulent /jʊl(ə)nt/ *suffix* forming adjectives meaning 'abounding in, full of' (*fraudulent*; *turbulent*). □ **-ulence** *suffix* forming nouns. [Latin *-ulentus*]

uliginose /ju:'lɪdʒɪnəʊs/ *adj.* (also **uliginous** /-nəs/) *Bot.* growing in wet or swampy places. [Latin *uliginosus* from *uligo -ginis* 'moisture']

ullage /'ʌlɪdʒ/ *n.* **1** the amount by which a cask etc. falls short of being full. **2** loss by evaporation or leakage. [Middle English from Anglo-French *ulliage*, Old French *ouillage* from *ouiller* 'fill up', ultimately from Latin *oculus* 'eye', with reference to the bung-hole]

ulna /'ʌlnə/ *n.* (*pl.* **ulnae** /-ni:/ or **ulnas**) **1** the thinner and longer bone in the forearm, on the side opposite to the thumb (cf. RADIUS 3). **2** *Zool.* a corresponding bone in an animal's foreleg or a bird's wing. □ **ulnar** *adj.* [Latin, related to Greek *ōlenē* and to ELL]

ulotrichan /ju:'lɒtrɪkən/ *adj. & n.* ● *adj.* (also **ulotrichous** /-kəs/) having tightly-curled hair, esp. denoting a human type. ● *n.* a person having such hair. [modern Latin *Ulotrichi*, from Greek *oulos* 'woolly, crisp' + *thrix trikhos* 'hair']

-ulous /jʊləs/ *suffix* forming adjectives (*fabulous*; *populous*). [Latin *-ulosus, -ulus*]

ulster /'ʌlstə/ *n.* a long loose overcoat of rough cloth. [*Ulster* in Ireland, where it was originally sold]

Ulsterman /'ʌlstəmən/ *n.* (*pl.* **-men**; *fem.* **Ulsterwoman**; *pl.* **-women**) a native of Ulster.

ult. *abbr.* ultimo.

ulterior /ʌl'tɪərɪə/ *adj.* **1** existing in the background, or beyond what is evident or admitted; hidden, secret (esp. *ulterior motive*). **2** situated beyond. **3** more remote; not immediate; in the future. □ **ulteriorly** *adv.* [Latin, = further, more distant]

ultima /'ʌltɪmə/ *n.* the last syllable of a word. [Latin *ultima* (*syllaba*), fem. of *ultimus* 'last']

ultimata *pl.* of ULTIMATUM.

ultimate /'ʌltɪmət/ *adj. & n.* ● *adj.* **1** last, final. **2** beyond which no other exists or is possible (*the ultimate analysis*). **3** fundamental, primary, unanalysable (*ultimate truths*). **4** maximum (*ultimate tensile strength*). ● *n.* **1** (prec. by *the*) the best achievable or imaginable. **2** a final or fundamental fact or principle. □ **ultimacy** /-məsi/ *n.* (*pl.* **-ies**). **ultimately** *adj.* **ultimateness** *n.* [Late Latin *ultimatus*, past part. of *ultimare* 'come to an end']

ultima Thule /ˌʌltɪmə 'θu:li:/ *n.* a faraway unknown region. [Latin, = furthest Thule, a remote northern region]

ultimatum /ʌltɪ'meɪtəm/ *n.* (*pl.* **ultimatums** or **ultimata** /-tə/) a final demand or statement of terms by one party, the rejection of which by another could cause a breakdown in relations, war, or an end of cooperation etc. [Latin, neut. past part. of *ultimare*: see ULTIMATE]

ultimo /'ʌltɪməʊ/ *adj.* *Commerce* of last month (*the 28th ultimo*). [Latin *ultimo mense* 'in the last month']

ultimogeniture /ˌʌltɪməʊ'dʒɛnɪtʃə/ *n.* a system in which the youngest son has the right of inheritance (cf. PRIMOGENITURE 2). [Latin *ultimus* 'last', on the pattern of PRIMOGENITURE]

ultra /'ʌltrə/ *adj. & n.* ● *adj.* favouring extreme views or measures, esp. in religion or politics. ● *n.* an extremist. [originally as abbreviation of French *ultra-royaliste*: see ULTRA-]

ultra- /'ʌltrə/ *prefix* **1** beyond; on the other side of (opp. CIS- 1). **2** extreme(ly), excessive(ly) (*ultra-conservative*; *ultra-modern*). [Latin *ultra* 'beyond']

ultracentrifuge /ʌltrə'sɛntrɪfju:dʒ/ *n.* a high-speed centrifuge used to separate small particles and large molecules by their rate of sedimentation from sols.

ultradian /ʌl'treɪdɪən/ *adj.* *Physiol.* (of a rhythm or cycle) having a period of recurrence shorter than a day but longer than an hour (cf. INFRADIAN). [from ULTRA-, as having a higher frequency than *circadian*]

ultrafiltration /ˌʌltrəfɪl'treɪʃ(ə)n/ *n.* filtration using a filter fine enough to retain large molecules, viruses, and colloidal particles.

ultra-high /ʌltrə'hʌɪ/ *adj.* (of a frequency) in the range 300 to 3000 megahertz.

ultraist /'ʌltrəɪst/ *n.* the holder of extreme positions in politics, religion, etc. □ **ultraism** *n.*

ultramarine /ʌltrəmə'ri:n, 'ʌlt-/ *n. & adj.* ● *n.* **1 a** a brilliant deep blue pigment originally obtained from lapis lazuli. **b** an imitation of this from powdered fired clay, sodium carbonate, sulphur, and resin. **2** a brilliant deep blue colour. ● *adj.* **1** of this colour. **2** *archaic* situated beyond the sea. [obsolete Italian *oltramarino* & medieval Latin *ultramarinus* 'beyond the sea' (as ULTRA-, MARINE), because lapis lazuli was brought from beyond the sea]

ultramicroscope /ʌltrə'mʌɪkrəskəʊp/ *n.* an optical microscope used to reveal very small particles by means of light scattered by them.

ultramicroscopic /ˌʌltrəmʌɪkrə'skɒpɪk/ *adj.* **1** too small to be seen by an ordinary optical microscope. **2** of or relating to an ultramicroscope.

ultramontane /ʌltrə'mɒnteɪn/ *adj. & n.* ● *adj.* **1** situated on the other side of the Alps from the point of view of the speaker. **2** advocating supreme papal authority in matters of faith and discipline. ● *n.* **1** a person living on the other side of the Alps. **2** a person advocating supreme papal authority. [medieval Latin *ultramontanus* (as ULTRA-, Latin *mons montis* 'mountain')]

ultramundane /ʌltrə'mʌndeɪn/ *adj.* lying beyond the world or the solar system. [Latin *ultramundanus* (as ULTRA-, *mundanus* from *mundus* 'world')]

ultrasonic /ʌltrə'sɒnɪk/ *adj.* of or involving sound waves with a frequency above the upper limit of human hearing. □ **ultrasonically** *adv.*

ultrasonics /ʌltrə'sɒnɪks/ *n.pl.* (usu. treated as *sing.*) the science and application of ultrasonic waves.

ultrasound /'ʌltrəsaʊnd/ *n.* **1** sound having an ultrasonic frequency. **2** ultrasonic waves.

ultrasound cardiography *n.* = ECHOCARDIOGRAPHY.

ultrastructure /'ʌltrəstrʌktʃə/ *n.* *Biol.* fine structure not visible with an optical microscope.

ultraviolet /ʌltrə'vʌɪələt/ *adj.* *Physics* of or using electromagnetic radiation having a wavelength shorter than that of the violet end of the visible spectrum but longer than that of X-rays.

ultra vires /ʌltrə 'vʌɪri:z, ʊltrɑ: 'vi:reɪz/ *adv. & predic.adj.* beyond one's legal power or authority. [Latin]

ululate /'ju:ljʊleɪt, 'ʌl-/ *v.intr.* howl, wail; make a hooting cry. □ **ululant** *adj.* **ululation** /-'leɪʃ(ə)n/ *n.* [Latin *ululare ululat-* (imitative)]

um /(ə)m/ *int.* expressing hesitation or a pause in speech. [imitative]

-um var. of -IUM 1.

umbel /ˈʌmb(ə)l/ *n. Bot.* a flower cluster in which stalks nearly equal in length spring from a common centre and form a flat or curved surface, as in parsley. □ **umbellar** *adj.* **umbellate** /-bəleɪt/ *adj.* **umbellule** /-ˈbɛljuːl/ *adj.* [obsolete French *umbelle* or Latin *umbella* 'sunshade', diminutive of UMBRA]

umbellifer /ʌmˈbɛlɪfə/ *n.* any plant of the family Umbelliferae. bearing umbels, including parsley and parsnip. □ **umbelliferous** /-bəˈlɪf(ə)rəs/ *adj.* [obsolete French *umbellifère* from Latin (as UMBEL, *-fer* 'bearing')]

umber /ˈʌmbə/ *n. & adj.* ● *n.* **1** a natural pigment like ochre but darker and browner. **2** a dark brown colour. ● *adj.* **1** dark brown. **2** dark, dusky. [French (*terre d'*)*ombre* or Italian (*terra di*) *ombra* = shadow (earth), from Latin UMBRA or *Umbra*, fem. of *Umber* 'Umbrian']

umbilical /ʌmˈbɪlɪk(ə)l, ʌmbɪˈlʌɪk(ə)l/ *adj. & n.* ● *attrib.adj.* **1** of, situated near, or affecting the navel. **2** linking, connecting. **3** inseparably linked. ● *n.* a flexible supply or control line, hose, etc., esp. from a main source to a site otherwise difficult to access. □ **umbilically** *adv.* [obsolete French *umbilical*, or from UMBILICUS]

umbilical cord *n.* **1** a flexible cordlike structure containing blood vessels and attaching a foetus to the placenta. **2** a supply cable linking a missile to its launcher, or an astronaut in space to a spacecraft.

umbilicate /ʌmˈbɪlɪkət/ *adj.* **1** shaped like a navel. **2** having an umbilicus.

umbilicus /ʌmˈbɪlɪkəs, ʌmbɪˈlʌɪkəs/ *n.* (*pl.* **umbilici** /-sʌɪ/ or **umbilicuses**) **1** *Anat.* the navel. **2** *Bot. & Zool.* a navel-like formation. **3** *Geom.* a point in a surface through which all cross-sections have the same curvature. [Latin, related to Greek *omphalos* and to NAVEL]

umbles /ˈʌmb(ə)lz/ *n.pl. archaic* the edible offal of deer etc. (cf. *eat humble pie*: see HUMBLE). [Middle English variant of NUMBLES]

umbo /ˈʌmbəʊ/ *n.* (*pl.* **umbones** /-ˈbəʊniːz/ or **umbos**) **1** the boss of a shield, esp. in the centre. **2** *Bot. & Zool.* a rounded knob or protuberance. □ **umbonal** *adj.* **umbonate** /-nət/ *adj.* [Latin *umbo -onis*]

umbra /ˈʌmbrə/ *n.* (*pl.* **umbras** or **umbrae** /-briː/) **1** the fully shaded inner region of a shadow cast by an opaque object, esp. *Astron.* the area on the earth or moon experiencing the total phase of an eclipse (cf. PENUMBRA 1a). **2** the dark central part of a sunspot. □ **umbral** *adj.* [Latin, = shade]

umbrage /ˈʌmbrɪdʒ/ *n.* **1** offence; a sense of slight or injury (esp. *give* or *take umbrage at*). **2** *archaic* **a** shade. **b** what gives shade. [Middle English from Old French, ultimately via Latin *umbraticus* from *umbra*: see UMBRA]

umbrella /ʌmˈbrɛlə/ *n.* **1** a light portable device for protection against rain, strong sun, etc., consisting of a usu. circular canopy of cloth mounted by means of a collapsible metal frame on a central stick. **2** protection or patronage. **3** (often *attrib.*) a coordinating or unifying agency (*umbrella organization*). **4** a screen of fighter aircraft or a curtain of fire put up as a protection against enemy aircraft. **5** *Zool.* the gelatinous disc of a jellyfish etc., which it contracts and expands to move through the water. □ **umbrellaed** /-ləd/ *adj.* **umbrella-like** *adj.* [Italian *ombrella*, diminutive of *ombra* 'shade', from Latin *umbra*: see UMBRA]

umbrella bird *n.* any S. American bird of the genus *Cephalopterus*, with a black radiating crest and long wattles.

umbrella pine *n.* **1** = STONE PINE. **2** a tall Japanese evergreen conifer, *Sciadopitys verticillata*, with leaves in umbrella-like whorls.

umbrella plant *n.* **1** a Californian plant of boggy places, *Darmera peltophylla* (saxifrage family), with large round leaves on stalks. **2** a house plant, *Cyperus involucratus* (sedge family), with a whorl of bracts at the top of the stem.

umbrella stand *n.* a stand for holding closed upright umbrellas.

umbrella tree *n.* a small tree with leaves in whorls like an umbrella, esp. *Magnolia tripetala* of N. America, or *Schefflera actinophylla* of Australia, grown as a house plant.

Umbrian /ˈʌmbrɪən/ *adj. & n.* ● *adj.* of or relating to Umbria in central Italy. ● *n.* **1** the language of ancient Umbria, related to Latin. **2** an inhabitant of ancient Umbria.

Umbrian school *n.* a Renaissance school of Italian painting, to which Raphael and Perugino belonged.

umbriferous /ʌmˈbrɪf(ə)rəs/ *adj. formal* providing shade. [Latin *umbrifer* from *umbra* 'shade': see -FEROUS]

umiak /ˈuːmɪak/ *n.* (also **oomiak**) an Eskimo skin-and-wood open boat propelled by women with paddles. [Eskimo *umiaq*]

umlaut /ˈʊmlaʊt/ *n. & v.* ● *n.* **1** a mark (¨) used over a vowel, esp. in Germanic languages, to indicate a vowel change. **2** such a vowel change, e.g. German *Mann*, *Männer*, English *man*, *men*, due to *i*, *j*, etc. (now usu. lost or altered) in the following syllable. ● *v.tr.* modify (a form or a sound) by an umlaut. [German, from *um* 'about' + *Laut* 'sound']

ump /ʌmp/ *n.* esp. *N.Amer. slang* an umpire, esp. in baseball. [abbreviation]

umpire /ˈʌmpʌɪə/ *n. & v.* ● *n.* **1** a person chosen to enforce the rules and settle disputes in various sports. **2** a person chosen to arbitrate between disputants, or to see fair play. ● *v.* **1** *intr.* (usu. foll. by *for*, *in*, etc.) act as umpire. **2** *tr.* act as umpire in (a game etc.). □ **umpirage** /-rɪdʒ/ *n.* **umpireship** *n.* [Middle English, later form of *noumpere* from Old French *nonper* 'not equal' (as NON-, PEER²): for loss of *n-* cf. ADDER]

umpteen /ʌm(p)ˈtiːn, ˈʌm(p)tiːn/ *adj. & pron. colloq.* ● *adj.* indefinitely many; a lot of. ● *pron.* indefinitely many. □ **umpteenth** *adj.* **umpty** /ˈʌmpti/ *adj.* [jocular formation on -TEEN]

UN *abbr.* United Nations.

un-¹ /ʌn/ *prefix* **1** added to adjectives and participles and their derivative nouns and adverbs, meaning: **a** not: denoting the absence of a quality or state (*unusable*; *uncalled for*; *uneducated*; *unfailing*; *unofficially*; *unhappiness*). **b** the reverse of, usu. with an implication of approval or disapproval, or with some other special connotation (*unselfish*; *unsociable*; *unscientific*). **2** (less often) added to nouns, meaning 'a lack of' (*unrest*; *untruth*). [Old English from Germanic: related to Latin *in-*]

■ **Usage** The number of words that can be formed with the prefix *un-*¹ (and similarly with *un-*²) is potentially as large as the number of adjectives in use; consequently only a selection, being considered the most current or semantically noteworthy, can be given here.

Words meaning 'the reverse of' (see sense 1b above) often have neutral counterparts in *non-* (see NON- 6) and counterparts in *in-* (see IN-¹), e.g. *unadvisable.*

In the case of some words with the prefix *un-*, there is ambiguity as to which prefix is meant, e.g. *undressed* can mean either 'not dressed' (*un-*¹) or 'no longer dressed' (*un-*²).

un-² /ʌn/ *prefix* added to verbs and (less often) nouns, forming verbs denoting: **1** the reversal or cancellation of an action or state (*undress*; *unlock*; *unsettle*). **2** deprivation or separation (*unmask*). **3** release from (*unburden*; *uncage*). **4** causing to be no longer (*unman*). [Old English *un-*, *on-*, from Germanic]

■ **Usage** See Usage Note at UN-¹.

un-³ /ʌn/ *prefix Chem.* denoting 'one', combined with other numerical roots (*nil* = 0, *bi* = 2, etc.) to form names of recently discovered elements based on the atomic number (e.g. *unnilhexium* = element 106). [Latin *unus* 'one']

'un /ən/ *pron. colloq.* one (*that's a good 'un*). [dialect variant]

UNA *abbr.* United Nations Association.

unabashed /ʌnə'bæʃt/ *adj.* not abashed. □ **unabashedly** /-ʃɪdli/ *adv.*

unabated /ʌnə'beɪtɪd/ *adj.* not abated; undiminished. □ **unabatedly** *adv.*

unable /ʌn'eɪb(ə)l/ *adj.* (usu. foll. by *to* + infin.) not able; lacking ability.

unabridged /ʌnə'brɪdʒd/ *adj.* (of a text etc.) complete; not abridged.

unabsorbed /ʌnəb'zɔ:bd, -'sɔ:bd/ *adj.* not absorbed.

unacademic /ˌʌnækə'dɛmɪk/ *adj.* **1** not academic (esp. not scholarly or theoretical). **2** (of a person) not suited to academic study.

unaccented /ʌnək'sɛntɪd/ *adj.* not accented; not emphasized.

unacceptable /ʌnək'sɛptəb(ə)l/ *adj.* not acceptable. □ **unacceptability** /-'bɪlɪti/ *n.* **unacceptableness** *n.* **unacceptably** *adv.*

unaccommodating /ʌnə'kɒmədeɪtɪŋ/ *adj.* not accommodating; disobliging.

unaccompanied /ʌnə'kʌmpənɪd/ *adj.* **1** not accompanied. **2** *Mus.* without accompaniment.

unaccomplished /ʌnə'kʌmplɪʃt, -'kɒm-/ *adj.* **1** not accomplished or achieved; uncompleted. **2** lacking accomplishments.

unaccountable /ʌnə'kaʊntəb(ə)l/ *adj.* **1** unable to be explained. **2** unpredictable or strange in behaviour. **3** not responsible. □ **unaccountability** /-'bɪlɪti/ *n.* **unaccountableness** *n.* **unaccountably** *adv.*

unaccounted /ʌnə'kaʊntɪd/ *adj.* of which no account is given. □ **unaccounted for** unexplained; not included in an account.

unaccustomed /ʌnə'kʌstəmd/ *adj.* **1** (usu. foll. by *to*) not accustomed. **2** not customary; unusual (*his unaccustomed silence*). □ **unaccustomedly** *adv.*

unacknowledged /ʌnək'nɒlɪdʒd/ *adj.* not acknowledged.

unacquainted /ʌnə'kweɪntɪd/ *adj.* (usu. foll. by *with*) not acquainted.

unadaptable /ʌnə'dæptəb(ə)l/ *adj.* not adaptable.

unadapted /ʌnə'dæptɪd/ *adj.* not adapted.

unaddressed /ʌnə'drɛst/ *adj.* (esp. of a letter etc.) without an address.

unadjacent /ʌnə'dʒeɪs(ə)nt/ *adj.* not adjacent.

unadjusted /ʌnə'dʒʌstɪd/ *adj.* (esp. of figures) not adjusted; crude.

unadopted /ʌnə'dɒptɪd/ *adj.* **1** not adopted. **2** *Brit.* (of a road) not taken over for maintenance by a local authority.

unadorned /ʌnə'dɔ:nd/ *adj.* not adorned; plain.

unadulterated /ʌnə'dʌltəreɪtɪd/ *adj.* **1** not adulterated; pure; concentrated. **2** sheer, complete, utter (*unadulterated nonsense*).

unadventurous /ʌnəd'vɛntʃ(ə)rəs/ *adj.* not adventurous. □ **unadventurously** *adv.*

unadvertised /ʌn'ædvətʌɪzd/ *adj.* not advertised.

unadvisable /ʌnəd'vʌɪzəb(ə)l/ *adj.* **1** not open to advice. **2** (of a thing) inadvisable.

unadvised /ʌnəd'vʌɪzd/ *adj.* **1** indiscreet; rash. **2** not having had advice. □ **unadvisedly** /-zɪdli/ *adv.* **unadvisedness** *n.*

unaesthetic /ʌni:s'θɛtɪk, ʌnɛs-/ *adj.* **1** not aesthetically pleasing. **2** lacking the principles of good taste.

unaffected /ʌnə'fɛktɪd/ *adj.* **1** (usu. foll. by *by*) not affected. **2** free from affectation; genuine; sincere. □ **unaffectedly** *adv.* **unaffectedness** *n.*

unaffectionate /ʌnə'fɛkʃ(ə)nət/ *adj.* lacking or not showing affection.

unaffiliated /ʌnə'fɪlɪeɪtɪd/ *adj.* not affiliated.

unaffordable /ʌnə'fɔ:dəb(ə)l/ *adj.* not affordable.

unafraid /ʌnə'freɪd/ *adj.* not afraid.

unaggressive /ʌnə'grɛsɪv/ *adj.* not aggressive.

unaided /ʌn'eɪdɪd/ *adj.* not aided; without help.

unalienable /ʌn'eɪlɪənəb(ə)l/ *adj. Law* = INALIENABLE.

unaligned /ʌnə'lʌɪnd/ *adj.* **1** = NON-ALIGNED. **2** not physically aligned.

unalike /ʌnə'lʌɪk/ *adj.* not alike; different.

unalive /ʌnə'lʌɪv/ *adj.* **1** lacking in vitality. **2** (foll. by *to*) not fully susceptible or awake to.

unalleviated /ʌnə'li:vɪeɪtɪd/ *adj.* not alleviated; relentless.

unallied /ʌnə'lʌɪd/ *adj.* not allied; having no allies.

unallowable /ʌnə'laʊəb(ə)l/ *adj.* not allowable.

unalloyed /ʌnə'lɔɪd/ *adj.* **1** not alloyed; pure. **2** complete; utter (*unalloyed joy*).

unalterable /ʌn'ɔ:lt(ə)rəb(ə)l, ʌn'ɒl-/ *adj.* not alterable. □ **unalterableness** *n.* **unalterably** *adv.*

unaltered /ʌn'ɔ:ltəd, ʌn'ɒl-/ *adj.* not altered; remaining the same.

unamazed /ʌnə'meɪzd/ *adj.* not amazed.

unambiguous /ʌnæm'bɪgjʊəs/ *adj.* not ambiguous; clear or definite in meaning. □ **unambiguity** /-'gju:ɪti/ *n.* **unambiguously** *adv.*

unambitious /ʌnæm'bɪʃəs/ *adj.* not ambitious; without ambition. □ **unambitiously** *adv.* **unambitiousness** *n.*

unambivalent /ʌnæm'bɪv(ə)l(ə)nt/ *adj.* (of feelings etc.) not ambivalent; straightforward. □ **unambivalently** *adv.*

un-American /ʌnə'mɛrɪk(ə)n/ *adj.* **1** not in accordance with American characteristics etc. **2** contrary to the interests of the US; (in the US) treasonable. □ **un-Americanism** *n.*

unamiable /ʌn'eɪmɪəb(ə)l/ *adj.* not amiable.

unamplified /ʌn'æmplɪfʌɪd/ *adj.* not amplified.

unamused /ʌnə'mju:zd/ *adj.* not amused.

unanalysable /ʌn'ænəlʌɪzəb(ə)l/ *adj.* (*US* **unanalyzable**) not able to be analysed.

unanalysed /ʌn'ænəlʌɪzd/ *adj.* (*US* **unanalyzed**) not analysed.

unaneled /ʌnə'ni:ld/ *adj. archaic* not having received extreme unction.

unanimous /ju:'nænɪməs/ *adj.* **1** all in agreement (*the committee was unanimous*). **2** (of an opinion, vote, etc.) held or given by general consent (*the unanimous choice*). □ **unanimity** /-nə'nɪmɪti/ *n.* **unanimously** *adv.* **unanimousness** *n.* [Late Latin *unanimis*, Latin *unanimus*, from *unus* 'one' + *animus* 'mind']

unannounced /ʌnə'naʊnst/ *adj.* not announced; without warning (of arrival etc.).

unanswerable /ʌn'ɑ:ns(ə)rəb(ə)l/ *adj.* **1** unable to be refuted (*has an unanswerable case*). **2** unable to be answered (*an unanswerable question*). □ **unanswerableness** *n.* **unanswerably** *adv.*

unanswered /ʌn'ɑ:nsəd/ *adj.* not answered.

unanticipated /ʌnæn'tɪsɪpeɪtɪd/ *adj.* not anticipated.

unapologetic /ˌʌnəpɒlə'dʒɛtɪk/ *adj.* not apologetic or sorry. □ **unapologetically** *adv.*

unapparent /ʌnə'pær(ə)nt/ *adj.* not apparent.

unappealable /ʌnə'pi:ləb(ə)l/ *adj.* esp. *Law* not able to be appealed against.

unappealing /ʌnə'pi:lɪŋ/ *adj.* not appealing; unattractive. □ **unappealingly** *adv.*

unappeasable /ʌnə'pi:zəb(ə)l/ *adj.* not appeasable.

unappeased /ʌnə'pi:zd/ *adj.* not appeased.

unappetizing /ʌn'æpɪtʌɪzɪŋ/ *adj.* (also **unappetising**) not appetizing. □ **unappetizingly** *adv.*

unapplied /ʌnə'plʌɪd/ *adj.* not applied.

unappreciated /ʌnə'pri:ʃɪeɪtɪd/ *adj.* not appreciated.

unappreciative /ʌnə'pri:ʃ(ɪ)ətɪv/ *adj.* not appreciative.

unapprehended /ˌʌnæprɪ'hɛndɪd/ *adj.* **1** not perceived by the intellect. **2** not arrested.

unapproachable /ʌnə'prəʊtʃəb(ə)l/ *adj.* **1** not approachable; remote, inaccessible. **2** (of a person) unfriendly. □ **unapproachability** /-'bɪlɪti/ *n.* **unapproachableness** *n.* **unapproachably** *adv.*

unappropriated /ʌnəˈprəʊprɪeɪtɪd/ *adj.* **1** not allocated or assigned. **2** not taken into possession by anyone.

unapproved /ʌnəˈpruːvd/ *adj.* not approved or sanctioned.

unapt /ʌnˈapt/ *adj.* **1** (usu. foll. by *for*) not suitable. **2** (usu. foll. by *to* + infin.) not apt. □ **unaptly** *adv.* **unaptness** *n.*

unarguable /ʌnˈɑːgjʊəb(ə)l/ *adj.* not arguable; certain. □ **unarguably** *adv.*

unarm /ʌnˈɑːm/ *v.tr.* deprive or free of arms or armour.

unarmed /ʌnˈɑːmd/ *adj.* not armed; without weapons.

unarresting /ʌnəˈrɛstɪŋ/ *adj.* uninteresting, dull. □ **unarrestingly** *adv.*

unarticulated /ʌnɑːˈtɪkjʊleɪtɪd/ *adj.* not articulated or distinct.

unartistic /ʌnɑːˈtɪstɪk/ *adj.* not artistic, esp. not concerned with art. □ **unartistically** *adv.*

unascertainable /ˌʌnasəˈteɪnəb(ə)l/ *adj.* not able to be ascertained.

unascertained /ˌʌnasəˈteɪnd/ *adj.* not ascertained; unknown.

unashamed /ʌnəˈʃeɪmd/ *adj.* **1** feeling no guilt, shameless. **2** blatant; bold. □ **unashamedly** /-mɪdli/ *adv.* **unashamedness** /-mɪdnɪs/ *n.*

unasked /ʌnˈɑːskt/ *adj.* not asked, requested, or invited.

unasked-for *adj.* (usu. *attrib.*) (esp. of advice) not sought or requested.

unassailable /ʌnəˈseɪləb(ə)l/ *adj.* unable to be attacked or questioned; impregnable. □ **unassailability** /-ˈbɪlɪti/ *n.* **unassailableness** *n.* **unassailably** *adv.*

unassertive /ʌnəˈsəːtɪv/ *adj.* (of a person) not assertive or forthcoming; reticent. □ **unassertively** *adv.* **unassertiveness** *n.*

unassignable /ʌnəˈsʌɪnəb(ə)l/ *adj.* not assignable.

unassigned /ʌnəˈsʌɪnd/ *adj.* not assigned.

unassimilated /ʌnəˈsɪmɪleɪtɪd/ *adj.* not assimilated. □ **unassimilable** *adj.*

unassisted /ʌnəˈsɪstɪd/ *adj.* not assisted.

unassociated /ʌnəˈsəʊʃɪeɪtɪd, -sɪ-/ *adj.* (often foll. by *with*) having no connection or association.

unassuaged /ʌnəˈsweɪdʒd/ *adj.* not assuaged. □ **unassuageable** *adj.*

unassuming /ʌnəˈsjuːmɪŋ/ *adj.* not pretentious or arrogant; modest by nature. □ **unassumingly** *adv.* **unassumingness** *n.*

unatoned /ʌnəˈtəʊnd/ *adj.* not atoned for.

unattached /ʌnəˈtatʃt/ *adj.* **1** (often foll. by *to*) not attached, esp. to a particular body, organization, etc. **2** single; not married or having an established partner.

unattackable /ʌnəˈtakəb(ə)l/ *adj.* unable to be attacked or damaged.

unattainable /ʌnəˈteɪnəb(ə)l/ *adj.* not attainable. □ **unattainableness** *n.* **unattainably** *adv.*

unattempted /ʌnəˈtɛm(p)tɪd/ *adj.* not attempted.

unattended /ʌnəˈtɛndɪd/ *adj.* **1** (usu. foll. by *to*) not attended. **2** (of a person, vehicle, etc.) not accompanied; alone; uncared for.

unattractive /ʌnəˈtraktɪv/ *adj.* not attractive. □ **unattractively** *adv.* **unattractiveness** *n.*

unattributable /ʌnəˈtrɪbjʊtəb(ə)l/ *adj.* (esp. of information) that cannot or may not be attributed to a source etc. □ **unattributably** *adv.*

unattributed /ʌnəˈtrɪbjʊtɪd/ *adj.* (of a painting, quotation, etc.) not attributed to a source etc.

unaudited /ʌnˈɔːdɪtɪd/ *adj.* (of accounts etc.) not audited.

unauthentic /ʌnɔːˈθɛntɪk/ *adj.* not authentic. □ **unauthentically** *adv.*

unauthenticated /ʌnɔːˈθɛntɪkeɪtɪd/ *adj.* not authenticated.

unauthorized /ʌnˈɔːθərʌɪzd/ *adj.* (also **unauthorised**) not authorized.

unavailable /ʌnəˈveɪləb(ə)l/ *adj.* not available. □ **unavailability** /-ˈbɪlɪti/ *n.* **unavailableness** *n.*

unavailing /ʌnəˈveɪlɪŋ/ *adj.* not availing; achieving nothing; ineffectual. □ **unavailingly** *adv.*

unavoidable /ʌnəˈvɔɪdəb(ə)l/ *adj.* not avoidable; inevitable. □ **unavoidability** /-ˈbɪlɪti/ *n.* **unavoidableness** *n.* **unavoidably** *adv.*

unavowed /ʌnəˈvaʊd/ *adj.* not avowed.

unawakened /ʌnəˈweɪk(ə)nd/ *adj.* **1** (often foll. by *to*) not yet aware; dormant. **2** not awake.

unaware /ʌnəˈwɛː/ *adj.* & *adv.* ● *adj.* **1** (usu. foll. by *of*, or *that* + clause) not aware; ignorant (*unaware of her presence*). **2** (of a person) insensitive; unperceptive. ● *adv.* = UNAWARES. □ **unawareness** *n.*

unawares /ʌnəˈwɛːz/ *adv.* **1** unexpectedly (*met them unawares*). **2** inadvertently (*dropped it unawares*). [earlier *unware(s)* from Old English *unwær(es)*: see WARE[2]]

unawed /ʌnˈɔːd/ *adj.* (often foll. by *by*) not inspired with awe; not awestruck.

unbacked /ʌnˈbakt/ *adj.* **1** not supported. **2** (of a horse etc.) having no backers. **3** (of a chair, picture, etc.) having no back or backing.

unbalance /ʌnˈbal(ə)ns/ *v.* & *n.* ● *v.tr.* **1** upset the physical or mental balance of (*unbalanced by the blow; the shock unbalanced him*). **2** (as **unbalanced** *adj.*) **a** not balanced. **b** (of a mind or a person) unstable or deranged. ● *n.* lack of balance; instability, esp. mental.

unban /ʌnˈban/ *v.tr.* (**unbanned**, **unbanning**) cease to ban; remove a ban from.

unbar /ʌnˈbɑː/ *v.tr.* (**unbarred**, **unbarring**) **1** remove a bar or bars from (a gate etc.). **2** unlock.

unbearable /ʌnˈbɛːrəb(ə)l/ *adj.* not bearable. □ **unbearableness** *n.* **unbearably** *adv.*

unbeatable /ʌnˈbiːtəb(ə)l/ *adj.* not beatable; excelling.

unbeaten /ʌnˈbiːt(ə)n/ *adj.* **1** not beaten. **2** (of a record etc.) not surpassed. **3** *Cricket* (of a player) not out.

unbeautiful /ʌnˈbjuːtɪfʊl, -f(ə)l/ *adj.* not beautiful; ugly. □ **unbeautifully** *adv.*

unbecoming /ʌnbɪˈkʌmɪŋ/ *adj.* **1** (esp. of clothing) not flattering or suiting a person. **2** (usu. foll. by *to*, *for*) not fitting; indecorous or unsuitable. □ **unbecomingly** *adv.* **unbecomingness** *n.*

unbefitting /ʌnbɪˈfɪtɪŋ/ *adj.* not befitting; unsuitable. □ **unbefittingly** *adv.* **unbefittingness** *n.*

unbefriended /ʌnbɪˈfrɛndɪd/ *adj.* not befriended.

unbegotten /ʌnbɪˈgɒt(ə)n/ *adj.* not begotten.

unbeholden /ʌnbɪˈhəʊld(ə)n/ *predic.adj.* (usu. foll. by *to*) under no obligation.

unbeknown /ʌnbɪˈnəʊn/ *adj.* (also **unbeknownst** /-ˈnəʊnst/) (foll. by *to*) without the knowledge of (*was there all the time unbeknown to us*). [UN-[1] + archaic *beknown* = KNOWN]

unbelief /ʌnbɪˈliːf/ *n.* lack of belief, esp. in religious matters. □ **unbeliever** *n.* **unbelieving** *adj.* **unbelievingly** *adv.*

unbelievable /ʌnbɪˈliːvəb(ə)l/ *adj.* impossible to believe; incredible. □ **unbelievability** /-ˈbɪlɪti/ *n.* **unbelievableness** *n.* **unbelievably** *adv.*

unbeloved /ʌnbɪˈlʌvd/ *adj.* not beloved.

unbelt /ʌnˈbɛlt/ *v.tr.* remove or undo the belt of (a garment etc.).

unbend /ʌnˈbɛnd/ *v.* (*past* and *past part.* **unbent**) **1** *tr.* & *intr.* change from a bent position; straighten. **2** *intr.* relax from strain or severity; become affable (*likes to unbend with a glass of beer*). **3** *tr. Naut.* **a** unfasten (sails) from yards and stays. **b** cast (a cable) loose. **c** untie (a rope).

unbending /ʌnˈbɛndɪŋ/ *adj.* **1** not bending; inflexible. **2** firm; austere (*unbending rectitude*). **3** relaxing from strain, activity, or formality. □ **unbendingly** *adv.* **unbendingness** *n.*

unbiased /ʌnˈbʌɪəst/ *adj.* (also **unbiassed**) not biased; impartial.

unbiblical /ʌnˈbɪblɪk(ə)l/ *adj.* **1** not in or authorized by the Bible. **2** contrary to the Bible.

unbiddable /ʌnˈbɪdəb(ə)l/ *adj. Brit.* disobedient; not docile.

unbidden /ʌn'bɪd(ə)n/ *adj.* not commanded or invited (*arrived unbidden*).

unbind /ʌn'bʌɪnd/ *v.tr.* (*past* and *past part.* **unbound**) release from bonds or binding.

unbirthday /ʌn'bə:θdeɪ/ *n.* (often *attrib.*) *joc.* any day but one's birthday (*an unbirthday party*).

unbleached /ʌn'bli:tʃt/ *adj.* not bleached.

unblemished /ʌn'blɛmɪʃt/ *adj.* not blemished.

unblessed /ʌn'blɛsɪd, ʌn'blɛst/ *adj.* (also **unblest**) not blessed.

unblinking /ʌn'blɪŋkɪŋ/ *adj.* **1** not blinking. **2** steadfast; not hesitating. **3** stolid; cool. □ **unblinkingly** *adv.*

unblock /ʌn'blɒk/ *v.tr.* **1** remove an obstruction from (esp. a pipe, drain, etc.). **2** (also *absol.*) *Cards* allow the later unobstructed play of (a suit) by playing a high card.

unblown /ʌn'bləʊn/ *adj.* **1** not blown. **2** *archaic* (of a flower) not yet in bloom.

unblushing /ʌn'blʌʃɪŋ/ *adj.* **1** not blushing. **2** unashamed; frank. □ **unblushingly** *adv.*

unbolt /ʌn'bəʊlt/ *v.tr.* release (a door etc.) by drawing back the bolt.

unbolted /ʌn'bəʊltɪd/ *adj.* **1** not bolted. **2** (of flour etc.) not sifted.

unbonnet /ʌn'bɒnɪt/ *v.* (**unbonneted**, **unbonneting**) **1** *tr.* remove the bonnet from. **2** *intr. archaic* remove one's hat or bonnet esp. in respect.

unbookish /ʌn'bʊkɪʃ/ *adj.* **1** not academic; not often inclined to read. **2** free from bookishness.

unboot /ʌn'bu:t/ *v.intr. & tr.* remove one's boots or the boots of (a person).

unborn /ʌn'bɔ:n/ *adj.* **1** not yet born (*an unborn child*). **2** never to be brought into being (*unborn hopes*).

unbosom /ʌn'bʊz(ə)m/ *v.tr.* **1** disclose (thoughts, secrets, etc.). **2** (*refl.*; often foll. by *of*) unburden (oneself) of one's thoughts, secrets, etc.

unbothered /ʌn'bɒðəd/ *adj.* not bothered; unconcerned.

unbound[1] /ʌn'baʊnd/ *adj.* **1** not bound or tied up. **2** unconstrained. **3 a** (of a book) not having a binding. **b** having paper covers. **4** (of a substance or particle) in a loose or free state.

unbound[2] *past* and *past part.* of UNBIND.

unbounded /ʌn'baʊndɪd/ *adj.* not bounded; infinite (*unbounded optimism*). □ **unboundedly** *adv.* **unboundedness** *n.*

unbowed /ʌn'baʊd/ *adj.* (usu. *predic.*) undaunted.

unbrace /ʌn'breɪs/ *v.tr.* **1** (also *absol.*) free from tension; relax (the nerves etc.). **2** remove a brace or braces from.

unbranded /ʌn'brandɪd/ *adj.* **1** (of a product) not bearing a brand name. **2** (of livestock) not branded with the owner's mark.

unbreachable /ʌn'bri:tʃəb(ə)l/ *adj.* not able to be breached.

unbreakable /ʌn'breɪkəb(ə)l/ *adj.* not breakable.

unbreathable /ʌn'bri:ðəb(ə)l/ *adj.* not able to be breathed.

unbribable /ʌn'brʌɪbəb(ə)l/ *adj.* not bribable.

unbridgeable /ʌn'brɪdʒəb(ə)l/ *adj.* not able to be bridged.

unbridle /ʌn'brʌɪd(ə)l/ *v.tr.* **1** remove a bridle from (a horse). **2** remove constraints from (one's tongue, a person, etc.). **3** (as **unbridled** *adj.*) unconstrained (*unbridled insolence*).

unbroken /ʌn'brəʊk(ə)n/ *adj.* **1** not broken. **2** not tamed (*an unbroken horse*). **3** not interrupted (*unbroken sleep*). **4** not surpassed (*an unbroken record*). □ **unbrokenly** *adv.* **unbrokenness** /-ənnɪs/ *n.*

unbruised /ʌn'bru:zd/ *adj.* not bruised.

unbuckle /ʌn'bʌk(ə)l/ *v.tr.* release the buckle of (a strap, shoe, etc.).

unbuild /ʌn'bɪld/ *v.tr.* (*past* and *past part.* **unbuilt**) **1** demolish or destroy (a building, theory, system, etc.). **2** (as **unbuilt** *adj.*) not yet built or (of land etc.) not yet built on.

unbundle /ʌn'bʌnd(ə)l/ *v.tr.* **1** unpack; remove from a bundle. **2** market (goods or services) separately. **3** split (a company) into separate businesses. □ **unbundler** *n.* (in sense 3).

unburden /ʌn'bə:d(ə)n/ *v.tr.* **1** relieve of a burden. **2** (esp. *refl.*; often foll. by *to*) relieve (oneself, one's conscience, etc.) by confession etc. □ **unburdened** *adj.*

unburied /ʌn'bɛrɪd/ *adj.* not buried.

unburnt /ʌn'bə:nt/ *adj.* (also **unburned** /-'bə:nt, -'bə:nd/) **1 a** not consumed by fire. **b** not scorched; not affected or damaged by fire etc. **2** (esp. of bricks) not subjected to the action of fire.

unbury /ʌn'bɛri/ *v.tr.* (**-ies**, **-ied**) **1** remove from the ground etc. after burial. **2** unearth (a secret etc.).

unbusinesslike /ʌn'bɪznɪslʌɪk/ *adj.* not businesslike.

unbutton /ʌn'bʌt(ə)n/ *v.tr.* **1 a** unfasten (a coat etc.) by taking the buttons out of the buttonholes. **b** unbutton the clothes of (a person). **2** (*absol.*) *colloq.* relax from tension or formality, become communicative. **3** (as **unbuttoned** *adj.*) **a** not buttoned. **b** *colloq.* communicative; informal.

uncage /ʌn'keɪdʒ/ *v.tr.* **1** release from a cage. **2** release from constraint; liberate.

uncalled /ʌn'kɔ:ld/ *adj.* not summoned or invited. □ **uncalled for** (also (hyphenated) *attrib.*) (of an opinion, action, etc.) impertinent or unnecessary (*such extreme measures are entirely uncalled for*; *an uncalled-for remark*).

uncandid /ʌn'kandɪd/ *adj.* not candid; disingenuous.

uncanny /ʌn'kani/ *adj.* (**uncannier**, **uncanniest**) seemingly supernatural; mysterious. □ **uncannily** *adv.* **uncanniness** *n.* [originally Scots & northern English, from UN-[1] + CANNY]

uncanonical /ʌnkə'nɒnɪk(ə)l/ *adj.* not canonical. □ **uncanonically** *adv.*

uncap /ʌn'kap/ *v.tr.* (**uncapped**, **uncapping**) **1** remove the cap from (a jar, bottle, etc.). **2** remove a cap from (the head or another person).

uncapped /ʌn'kapt/ *adj. Sport* (of a player) never having been selected for his or her national team.

uncared-for /ʌn'kɛ:dfɔ:/ *adj.* (also **uncared for** *predic.*) disregarded; neglected.

uncaring /ʌn'kɛ:rɪŋ/ *adj.* **1** neglectful. **2** lacking compassion.

uncarpeted /ʌn'kɑ:pɪtɪd/ *adj.* not covered or provided with a carpet or carpeting.

uncase /ʌn'keɪs/ *v.tr.* remove from a cover or case.

uncashed /ʌn'kaʃt/ *adj.* not cashed.

uncatchable /ʌn'katʃəb(ə)l/ *adj.* (esp. of a team, athlete, etc.) not able or likely to be caught up with.

uncaught /ʌn'kɔ:t/ *adj.* not caught.

unceasing /ʌn'si:sɪŋ/ *adj.* not ceasing; continuous (*unceasing effort*). □ **unceasingly** *adv.*

uncelebrated /ʌn'sɛlɪbreɪtɪd/ *adj.* not publicly acclaimed.

uncensored /ʌn'sɛnsəd/ *adj.* not censored.

uncensured /ʌn'sɛnʃəd/ *adj.* not censured.

unceremonious /ˌʌnsɛrɪ'məʊnɪəs/ *adj.* **1** lacking ceremony or formality. **2** abrupt; discourteous. □ **unceremoniously** *adv.* **unceremoniousness** *n.*

uncertain /ʌn'sə:t(ə)n, -tɪn/ *adj.* **1** not certainly knowing or known (*uncertain what it means*; *the result is uncertain*). **2** unreliable (*his aim is uncertain*). **3** changeable, erratic (*uncertain weather*). □ **in no uncertain terms** clearly and forcefully. □ **uncertainly** *adv.*

uncertainty /ʌn'sə:t(ə)nti, -tɪnti/ *n.* (*pl.* **-ies**) **1** the fact or condition of being uncertain. **2** an uncertain matter or circumstance.

uncertainty principle *n.* (in full **Heisenberg uncertainty principle** after W. Heisenberg, German physicist d. 1976) *Physics* the principle that the momentum and position of a particle cannot both be precisely determined at the same time.

uncertified /ʌn'sə:tɪfʌɪd/ *adj.* **1** not attested as certain. **2** not guaranteed by a certificate of competence etc. **3** not certified as insane.

unchain /ʌn'tʃeɪn/ *v.tr.* **1** remove the chains from. **2** release; liberate.

unchallengeable /ʌn'tʃalɪn(d)ʒəb(ə)l/ *adj.* not challengeable; unassailable. □ **unchallengeably** *adv.*

unchallenged /ʌn'tʃalɪn(d)ʒd/ *adj.* not challenged.

unchallenging /ʌn'tʃalɪn(d)ʒɪŋ/ *adj.* not presenting a challenge or other stimulation.

unchangeable /ʌn'tʃeɪn(d)ʒəb(ə)l/ *adj.* not changeable; immutable, invariable. □ **unchangeability** /-'bɪlɪti/ *n.* **unchangeableness** *n.* **unchangeably** *adv.*

unchanged /ʌn'tʃeɪn(d)ʒd/ *adj.* not changed; unaltered.

unchanging /ʌn'tʃeɪn(d)ʒɪŋ/ *adj.* not changing; remaining the same. □ **unchangingly** *adv.*

unchaperoned /ʌn'ʃapərəʊnd/ *adj.* without a chaperone.

uncharacteristic /ˌʌnkarəktə'rɪstɪk/ *adj.* not characteristic. □ **uncharacteristically** *adv.*

uncharged /ʌn'tʃɑ:dʒd/ *adj.* not charged (esp. in senses 3, 7, 8 of CHARGE *v.*).

uncharismatic /ˌʌnkarɪz'matɪk/ *adj.* lacking charisma.

uncharitable /ʌn'tʃarɪtəb(ə)l/ *adj.* censorious, severe in judgement. □ **uncharitableness** *n.* **uncharitably** *adv.*

uncharted /ʌn'tʃɑ:tɪd/ *adj.* not charted, mapped, or surveyed.

unchartered /ʌn'tʃɑ:təd/ *adj.* **1** not furnished with a charter; not formally privileged or constituted. **2** unauthorized; illegal.

unchaste /ʌn'tʃeɪst/ *adj.* not chaste. □ **unchastely** *adv.* **unchastity** /-'tʃastɪti/ *n.*

unchastened /ʌn'tʃeɪs(ə)nd/ *adj.* not sorry; unbowed.

unchecked /ʌn'tʃɛkt/ *adj.* **1** not checked. **2** freely allowed; unrestrained (*unchecked violence*).

unchivalrous /ʌn'ʃɪv(ə)lrəs/ *adj.* not chivalrous; rude. □ **unchivalrously** *adv.*

unchosen /ʌn'tʃəʊz(ə)n/ *adj.* not chosen.

unchristian /ʌn'krɪstʃ(ə)n, -tɪən/ *adj.* **1 a** contrary to Christian principles, esp. uncaring or selfish. **b** not Christian. **2** *colloq.* outrageous. □ **unchristianly** *adv.*

unchurch /ʌn'tʃə:tʃ/ *v.tr.* **1** excommunicate; exclude from a church. **2** deprive (a building) of its status as a church. **3** (as **unchurched** *adj.*) not associated with a church; not churchgoing.

uncial /'ʌnsɪəl, -ʃ(ə)l/ *adj.* & *n.* ● *adj.* **1** of or written in majuscule writing with rounded unjoined letters found in manuscripts of the 4th–8th c., from which modern capitals are derived. **2** of or relating to an inch or an ounce. ● *n.* **1** an uncial letter. **2** an uncial style or manuscript. [Latin *uncialis* from *uncia* 'inch': sense 1 in Late Latin sense of *unciales litterae* 'uncial letters', the original application of which is unclear]

unciform /'ʌnsɪfɔ:m/ *n.* = UNCINATE.

uncinate /'ʌnsɪnət, -eɪt/ *adj.* esp. *Anat.* hooked; crooked. [Latin *uncinatus* from *uncinus* 'hook']

uncircumcised /ʌn'sə:kəmsʌɪzd/ *adj.* **1** not circumcised. **2** *archaic* spiritually impure; heathen. □ **uncircumcision** /-'sɪʒ(ə)n/ *n.*

uncivil /ʌn'sɪv(ə)l, -vɪl/ *adj.* **1** ill-mannered; impolite. **2** not public-spirited. □ **uncivilly** *adv.*

uncivilized /ʌn'sɪvɪlʌɪzd/ *adj.* (also **uncivilised**) **1** not civilized. **2** rough; uncultured.

unclad /ʌn'klad/ *adj.* not clad; naked.

unclaimed /ʌn'kleɪmd/ *adj.* not claimed.

unclasp /ʌn'klɑ:sp/ *v.tr.* **1** loosen the clasp or clasps of. **2** release the grip of (a hand etc.).

unclassifiable /ʌn'klasɪfʌɪəb(ə)l/ *adj.* not classifiable.

unclassified /ʌn'klasɪfʌɪd/ *adj.* **1** not classified. **2** (of State information) not secret.

uncle /'ʌŋk(ə)l/ *n.* **1 a** the brother of one's father or mother. **b** an aunt's husband. **2** *colloq.* a name given by children to a male family friend. **3** *slang* a pawnbroker. [Middle English via Anglo-French *uncle*, Old French *oncle* and Late Latin *aunculus* from Latin *avunculus* 'maternal uncle': see AVUNCULAR]

-uncle /'ʌŋk(ə)l/ *suffix* forming nouns, usu. diminutives (*carbuncle*). [Old French *-uncle*, *-oncle* or Latin *-unculus*, *-la*, a special form of *-ulus* -ULE]

unclean /ʌn'kli:n/ *adj.* **1** not clean. **2** unchaste. **3** unfit to be eaten; ceremonially impure. **4** *Bibl.* (of a spirit) wicked. □ **uncleanly** *adv.* **uncleanness** /ʌn'kli:nnɪs/ *n.* [Old English *unclǣne* (as UN-[1], CLEAN)]

uncleanly /ʌn'klɛnli/ *adj. archaic* or *formal* unclean. □ **uncleanliness** *n.*

unclear /ʌn'klɪə/ *adj.* **1** not clear or easy to understand; obscure, uncertain. **2** (of a person) doubtful, uncertain (*I'm unclear as to what you mean*). □ **unclearly** *adv.* **unclearness** *n.*

uncleared /ʌn'klɪəd/ *adj.* **1** (of a cheque etc.) not cleared. **2** not cleared away or up. **3** (of land) not cleared of trees etc.

unclench /ʌn'klɛn(t)ʃ/ *v.* **1** *tr.* release (clenched hands, features, teeth, etc.). **2** *intr.* (of clenched hands etc.) become relaxed or open.

Uncle Sam /sam/ *n. colloq.* the federal government or citizens of the US (*will fight for Uncle Sam*). [probably expanded from *US* 'United States']

Uncle Tom *n. offens.* a black man considered to be servile, cringing, etc. (from the hero of H. B. Stowe's *Uncle Tom's Cabin*, 1852).

unclimbed /ʌn'klʌɪmd/ *adj.* (of a peak, rock face, etc.) not previously climbed. □ **unclimbable** *adj.*

unclinch /ʌn'klɪn(t)ʃ/ *v.tr.* & *intr.* release or become released from a clinch.

uncloak /ʌn'kləʊk/ *v.tr.* **1** expose, reveal. **2** remove a cloak from.

unclog /ʌn'klɒg/ *v.tr.* (**unclogged**, **unclogging**) unblock (a drain, pipe, etc.).

unclose /ʌn'kləʊz/ *v.* **1** *tr.* & *intr.* open. **2** *tr.* reveal; disclose.

unclothe /ʌn'kləʊð/ *v.tr.* **1** remove the clothes from. **2** strip of leaves or vegetation (*trees unclothed by the wind*). **3** expose, reveal. □ **unclothed** *adj.*

unclouded /ʌn'klaʊdɪd/ *adj.* **1** not clouded; clear; bright. **2** untroubled (*unclouded serenity*).

uncluttered /ʌn'klʌtəd/ *adj.* not cluttered; austere, simple.

unco /'ʌŋkə/ *adj.*, *adv.*, & *n. Sc.* ● *adj.* strange, unusual; notable. ● *adv.* remarkably; very. ● *n.* (*pl.* **-os**) **1** a stranger. **2** (in *pl.*) news. □ **the unco guid** /gɪd/ esp. *derog.* the rigidly religious. [Middle English, variant of UNCOUTH]

uncoil /ʌn'kɔɪl/ *v.tr.* & *intr.* = UNWIND 1.

uncollected /ʌnkə'lɛktɪd/ *adj.* **1** left awaiting collection. **2** (of money) not collected in or claimed. **3** (of literary work) not gathered into a collection for publication.

uncoloured /ʌn'kʌləd/ *adj.* (*US* **uncolored**) **1** having no colour. **2** not influenced; impartial. **3** not exaggerated.

uncombed /ʌn'kəʊmd/ *adj.* (of hair or a person) not combed.

uncome-at-able /ʌnkʌm'atəb(ə)l/ *adj. colloq.* inaccessible; unattainable.

uncomely /ʌn'kʌmli/ *adj.* **1** improper; unseemly. **2** ugly.

uncomfortable /ʌn'kʌmf(ə)təb(ə)l/ *adj.* **1** not comfortable. **2** uneasy; causing or feeling disquiet (*an uncomfortable silence*). □ **uncomfortableness** *n.* **uncomfortably** *adv.*

uncommercial /ʌnkə'mə:ʃ(ə)l/ *adj.* **1** not commercial. **2** contrary to commercial principles.

uncommitted /ʌnkə'mɪtɪd/ *adj.* **1** not committed. **2** unattached to any specific political cause or group.

uncommon /ʌn'kɒmən/ *adj.* & *adv.* ● *adj.* **1** not common; unusual; remarkable. **2** remarkably great etc. (*an uncommon fear of spiders*). ● *adv. archaic* uncommonly (*he was uncommon fat*). □ **uncommonly** *adv.* **uncommonness** /-mənnɪs/ *n.*

uncommunicative /ʌnkə'mju:nɪkətɪv/ *adj.* not wanting to communicate; taciturn. ▫ **uncommunicatively** *adv.* **uncommunicativeness** *n.*

uncompanionable /ʌnkəm'panjənəb(ə)l/ *adj.* unsociable.

uncompensated /ʌn'kɒmpənseɪtɪd/ *adj.* not compensated.

uncompetitive /ʌnkəm'pɛtɪtɪv/ *adj.* not competitive.

uncomplaining /ʌnkəm'pleɪnɪŋ/ *adj.* not complaining; resigned. ▫ **uncomplainingly** *adv.*

uncompleted /ʌnkəm'pli:tɪd/ *adj.* not completed; incomplete.

uncomplicated /ʌn'kɒmplɪkeɪtɪd/ *adj.* not complicated; simple; straightforward.

uncomplimentary /ˌʌnkɒmplɪ'mɛnt(ə)ri/ *adj.* not complimentary; insulting.

uncompounded /ʌnkəm'paʊndɪd/ *adj.* not compounded; unmixed.

uncomprehending /ˌʌnkɒmprɪ'hɛndɪŋ/ *adj.* not comprehending. ▫ **uncomprehendingly** *adv.* **uncomprehension** /-ʃ(ə)n/ *n.*

uncompromising /ʌn'kɒmprəmʌɪsɪŋ/ *adj.* unwilling to compromise; stubborn; tough and unyielding. ▫ **uncompromisingly** *adv.* **uncompromisingness** *n.*

unconcealed /ʌnkən'si:ld/ *adj.* not concealed; obvious.

unconcern /ʌnkən'sə:n/ *n.* lack of concern; indifference; apathy. ▫ **unconcerned** *adj.* **unconcernedly** /-nɪdli/ *adv.*

unconcluded /ʌnkən'klu:dɪd/ *adj.* not concluded.

unconditional /ʌnkən'dɪʃ(ə)n(ə)l/ *adj.* not subject to conditions; complete (*unconditional surrender*). ▫ **unconditionality** /-'nalɪti/ *n.* **unconditionally** *adv.*

unconditioned /ʌnkən'dɪʃ(ə)nd/ *adj.* **1** not subject to conditions or to an antecedent condition. **2** (of behaviour etc.) not determined by conditioning; natural.

unconditioned reflex *n.* an instinctive response to a stimulus.

unconfident /ʌn'kɒnfɪd(ə)nt/ *adj.* not confident.

unconfined /ʌnkən'fʌɪnd/ *adj.* not confined; boundless.

unconfirmed /ʌnkən'fə:md/ *adj.* not confirmed.

unconformable /ʌnkən'fɔ:məb(ə)l/ *adj.* **1** not conformable or conforming. **2** (of rock strata) not having the same direction of stratification. **3** *Brit. hist.* not conforming to the provisions of the Act of Uniformity. ▫ **unconformableness** *n.* **unconformably** *adv.*

unconformity /ʌnkən'fɔ:mɪti/ *n. Geol.* **1** a large break in the chronological sequence of layers of rock. **2** the surface of contact between two groups of unconformable strata.

uncongenial /ʌnkən'dʒi:nɪəl/ *adj.* not congenial.

unconjecturable /ʌnkən'dʒɛktʃ(ə)rəb(ə)l/ *adj.* not conjecturable.

unconnected /ʌnkə'nɛktɪd/ *adj.* **1** not physically joined. **2** not connected or associated. **3** (of speech etc.) disconnected; not joined in order or sequence (*unconnected ideas*). **4** not related by family ties. ▫ **unconnectedly** *adv.* **unconnectedness** *n.*

unconquerable /ʌn'kɒŋk(ə)rəb(ə)l/ *adj.* not conquerable. ▫ **unconquerableness** *n.* **unconquerably** *adv.*

unconquered /ʌn'kɒŋkəd/ *adj.* not conquered or defeated.

unconscionable /ʌn'kɒnʃ(ə)nəb(ə)l/ *adj.* **1 a** having no conscience. **b** contrary to conscience. **2 a** unreasonably excessive (*an unconscionable length of time*). **b** not right or reasonable. ▫ **unconscionably** *adv.* [UN-[1] + obsolete *conscionable* from *conscions*, obsolete variant of CONSCIENCE]

unconscious /ʌn'kɒnʃəs/ *adj. & n.* ● *adj.* not conscious (*unconscious of any change*; *fell unconscious on the floor*; *an unconscious prejudice*). ● *n.* that part of the mind which is inaccessible to the conscious mind but which affects behaviour, emotions, etc. (cf. COLLECTIVE UNCONSCIOUS). ▫ **unconsciously** *adv.* **unconsciousness** *n.*

unconscious cerebration *n.* action of the brain with results reached without conscious thought.

unconsecrated /ʌn'kɒnsɪkreɪtɪd/ *adj.* not consecrated.

unconsenting /ʌnkən'sɛntɪŋ/ *adj.* not consenting.

unconsidered /ʌnkən'sɪdəd/ *adj.* **1** not considered; disregarded. **2** (of a response etc.) immediate; not premeditated.

unconsolable /ʌnkən'səʊləb(ə)l/ *adj.* unable to be consoled; inconsolable. ▫ **unconsolably** *adv.*

unconstitutional /ˌʌnkɒnstɪ'tju:ʃ(ə)n(ə)l/ *adj.* not in accordance with the political constitution or with procedural rules. ▫ **unconstitutionality** /-'nalɪti/ *n.* **unconstitutionally** *adv.*

unconstrained /ʌnkən'streɪnd/ *adj.* not constrained or compelled. ▫ **unconstrainedly** /-nɪdli/ *adv.*

unconstraint /ʌnkən'streɪnt/ *n.* freedom from constraint.

unconstricted /ʌnkən'strɪktɪd/ *adj.* not constricted.

unconsulted /ʌnkən'sʌltɪd/ *adj.* not consulted for information or an opinion.

unconsumed /ʌnkən'sju:md/ *adj.* not consumed.

unconsummated /ʌn'kɒnsəmeɪtɪd, -sjʊ-/ *adj.* not consummated.

uncontainable /ʌnkən'teɪnəb(ə)l/ *adj.* not containable.

uncontaminated /ʌnkən'tamɪneɪtɪd/ *adj.* not contaminated.

uncontentious /ʌnkən'tɛnʃəs/ *adj.* not controversial.

uncontested /ʌnkən'tɛstɪd/ *adj.* not contested. ▫ **uncontestedly** *adv.*

uncontradicted /ˌʌnkɒntrə'dɪktɪd/ *adj.* not contradicted.

uncontrived /ʌnkən'trʌɪvd/ *adj.* not planned; not artificially created.

uncontrollable /ʌnkən'trəʊləb(ə)l/ *adj.* not controllable. ▫ **uncontrollableness** *n.* **uncontrollably** *adv.*

uncontrolled /ʌnkən'trəʊld/ *adj.* not controlled; unrestrained, unchecked. ▫ **uncontrolledly** /-lɪdli/ *adv.*

uncontroversial /ˌʌnkɒntrə'və:ʃ(ə)l/ *adj.* not controversial. ▫ **uncontroversially** *adv.*

uncontroverted /ʌn'kɒntrəvə:tɪd, ˌʌnkɒntrə'və:tɪd/ *adj.* not controverted. ▫ **uncontrovertible** *adj.*

unconventional /ʌnkən'vɛnʃ(ə)n(ə)l/ *adj.* not bound by convention or custom; unusual; unorthodox. ▫ **unconventionalism** *n.* **unconventionality** /-'nalɪti/ *n.* **unconventionally** *adv.*

unconverted /ʌnkən'və:tɪd/ *adj.* not converted.

unconvinced /ʌnkən'vɪnst/ *adj.* not convinced.

unconvincing /ʌnkən'vɪnsɪŋ/ *adj.* not convincing. ▫ **unconvincingly** *adv.*

uncooked /ʌn'kʊkt/ *adj.* not cooked; raw.

uncool /ʌn'ku:l/ *adj.* **1** *slang* not stylish or fashionable; not having street credibility. **2** (of jazz) not cool.

uncooperative /ʌnkəʊ'ɒp(ə)rətɪv/ *adj.* not cooperative. ▫ **uncooperatively** *adv.*

uncoordinated /ʌnkəʊ'ɔ:dɪneɪtɪd/ *adj.* **1** not coordinated. **2** (of a person's movements etc.) clumsy.

uncopiable /ʌn'kɒpɪəb(ə)l/ *adj.* not able to be copied.

uncord /ʌn'kɔ:d/ *v.tr.* remove the cord from.

uncork /ʌn'kɔ:k/ *v.tr.* **1** draw the cork from (a bottle). **2** allow (feelings etc.) to be vented.

uncorrected /ʌnkə'rɛktɪd/ *adj.* not corrected.

uncorroborated /ʌnkə'rɒbəreɪtɪd/ *adj.* (esp. of evidence etc.) not corroborated.

uncorrupted /ʌnkə'rʌptɪd/ *adj.* not corrupted.

uncountable /ʌn'kaʊntəb(ə)l/ *adj.* inestimable, immense (*uncountable wealth*). ▫ **uncountability** /-'bɪlɪti/ *n.* **uncountably** *adv.*

uncountable noun *n. Gram.* a noun that cannot form a plural or be used with the indefinite article (e.g. *happiness*). Cf. MASS NOUN, COUNTABLE NOUN.

uncounted /ʌn'kaʊntɪd/ *adj.* **1** not counted. **2** very many; innumerable.

uncount noun /ˈʌnkaʊnt/ *n. Gram.* = UNCOUNTABLE NOUN.

uncouple /ʌnˈkʌp(ə)l/ *v.tr.* **1** unfasten, disconnect, detach. **2** release (wagons) from couplings. **3** release (dogs etc.) from being fastened in couples. □ **uncoupled** *adj.*

uncourtly /ʌnˈkɔːtli/ *adj.* not courteous; ill-mannered.

uncouth /ʌnˈkuːθ/ *adj.* **1** (of a person, manners, appearance, etc.) lacking in ease and polish; uncultured, rough (*uncouth voices*; *behaviour was uncouth*). **2** *archaic* not known; desolate; wild; uncivilized (*an uncouth place*). □ **uncouthly** *adv.* **uncouthness** *n.* [Old English *uncūth* 'unknown' (as UN-[1] + *cūth*, past part. of *cunnan* 'know, CAN[1]')]

uncovenanted /ʌnˈkʌv(ə)nəntɪd/ *adj.* **1** not bound by a covenant. **2** not promised by or based on a covenant, esp. God's covenant.

uncover /ʌnˈkʌvə/ *v.* **1** *tr.* **a** remove a cover or covering from. **b** make known; disclose (*uncovered the truth at last*). **2** *intr. archaic* remove one's hat, cap, etc. **3** *tr.* (as **uncovered** *adj.*) **a** not covered by a roof, clothing, etc. **b** not wearing a hat.

uncreate /ʌnkriːˈeɪt/ *v.tr. literary* annihilate.

uncreated /ʌnkriːˈeɪtɪd/ *adj.* existing without having been created; not created. [UN-[1] + obsolete *create* from Latin *creatus*, past part. of *creare*: see CREATE]

uncreative /ʌnkriːˈeɪtɪv/ *adj.* not creative.

uncredited /ʌnˈkrɛdɪtɪd/ *adj.* not acknowledged as the author, actor, etc.

uncritical /ʌnˈkrɪtɪk(ə)l/ *adj.* **1** not critical; complacently accepting. **2** not in accordance with the principles of criticism. □ **uncritically** *adv.*

uncropped /ʌnˈkrɒpt/ *adj.* not cropped.

uncross /ʌnˈkrɒs/ *v.tr.* **1** remove (the limbs, knives, etc.) from a crossed position. **2** (as **uncrossed** *adj.*) **a** *Brit.* (of a cheque) not crossed. **b** not thwarted or challenged. **c** not wearing a cross.

uncrowded /ʌnˈkraʊdɪd/ *adj.* not filled or likely to fill with crowds.

uncrown /ʌnˈkraʊn/ *v.tr.* **1** deprive (a monarch etc.) of a crown. **2** deprive (a person) of a position. **3** (as **uncrowned** *adj.*) **a** not crowned. **b** having the status but not the name of (*the uncrowned king of boxing*).

uncrushable /ʌnˈkrʌʃəb(ə)l/ *adj.* not crushable.

uncrushed /ʌnˈkrʌʃt/ *adj.* not crushed.

UNCSTD *abbr.* United Nations Conference on Science and Technology for Development.

UNCTAD /ˈʌŋ(k)tad/ *abbr.* United Nations Conference on Trade and Development.

unction /ˈʌŋ(k)ʃ(ə)n/ *n.* **1 a** the act of anointing with oil etc. as a religious rite. **b** the oil etc. so used. **2 a** soothing words or thought. **b** excessive or insincere flattery. **3 a** the act of anointing for medical purposes. **b** an ointment so used. **4 a** a fervent or sympathetic quality in words or tone caused by or causing deep emotion. **b** a pretence of this. [Middle English from Latin *unctio*, from *ung(u)ere unct-* 'anoint']

unctuous /ˈʌŋ(k)tjʊəs/ *adj.* **1** (of behaviour, speech, etc.) unpleasantly flattering; oily. **2** (esp. of minerals) having a greasy or soapy feel; oily. □ **unctuously** *adv.* **unctuousness** *n.* [Middle English via medieval Latin *unctuosus* from Latin *unctus* 'anointing' (as UNCTION)]

unculled /ʌnˈkʌld/ *adj.* not culled.

uncultivated /ʌnˈkʌltɪveɪtɪd/ *adj.* (esp. of land) not cultivated.

uncultured /ʌnˈkʌltʃəd/ *adj.* **1** not cultured, unrefined. **2** (of soil or plants) not cultivated.

uncurb /ʌnˈkəːb/ *v.tr.* remove a curb or curbs from. □ **uncurbed** *adj.*

uncured /ʌnˈkjʊəd/ *adj.* **1** not cured. **2** (of pork etc.) not salted or smoked.

uncurl /ʌnˈkəːl/ *v.intr.* & *tr.* relax from a curled position, untwist.

uncurtailed /ʌnkəˈteɪld/ *adj.* not curtailed.

uncurtained /ʌnˈkəːt(ə)nd/ *adj.* not curtained.

uncut /ʌnˈkʌt/ *adj.* **1** not cut. **2** (of a book) with the pages not cut open or with untrimmed margins. **3** (of a book, film, etc.) complete; uncensored. **4** (of a stone, esp. a diamond) not shaped by cutting. **5** (of fabric) having its pile-loops intact (*uncut moquette*).

undamaged /ʌnˈdamɪdʒd/ *adj.* not damaged; intact.

undated /ʌnˈdeɪtɪd/ *adj.* not provided or marked with a date.

undaunted /ʌnˈdɔːntɪd/ *adj.* not daunted. □ **undauntedly** *adv.* **undauntedness** *n.*

undead /ʌnˈdɛd/ *adj.* & *n.* ● *adj.* (esp. of a vampire etc. in fiction) technically dead but still animate. ● *n.* (prec. by *the*; treated as *pl.*) those who are undead.

undecagon /ʌnˈdɛkəg(ə)n/ *n.* = HENDECAGON. [Latin *undecim* 'eleven', on the pattern of *decagon*]

undeceive /ʌndɪˈsiːv/ *v.tr.* (often foll. by *of*) free (a person) from a misconception, deception, or error.

undecidable /ʌndɪˈsʌɪdəb(ə)l/ *adj.* that cannot be established or refuted; uncertain. □ **undecidability** /-ˈbɪlɪti/ *n.*

undecided /ʌndɪˈsʌɪdɪd/ *adj.* **1** not settled or certain (*the question is undecided*). **2** hesitating; irresolute (*undecided about their relative merits*). □ **undecidedly** *adv.*

undecipherable /ʌndɪˈsʌɪf(ə)rəb(ə)l/ *adj.* not decipherable.

undeclared /ʌndɪˈklɛːd/ *adj.* not declared.

undecorated /ʌnˈdɛkəreɪtɪd/ *adj.* **1** not adorned; plain. **2** not honoured with an award.

undefeated /ʌndɪˈfiːtɪd/ *adj.* not defeated.

undefended /ʌndɪˈfɛndɪd/ *adj.* (esp. of a lawsuit) not defended.

undefiled /ʌndɪˈfʌɪld/ *adj.* not defiled; pure.

undefined /ʌndɪˈfʌɪnd/ *adj.* **1** not defined. **2** not clearly marked; vague, indefinite. □ **undefinable** *adj.* **undefinably** *adv.*

undelivered /ʌndɪˈlɪvəd/ *adj.* **1** not delivered or handed over. **2** not set free or released. **3 a** (of a pregnant woman) not yet having given birth. **b** (of a child) not yet born.

undemanding /ʌndɪˈmɑːndɪŋ/ *adj.* not demanding; easily satisfied.

undemocratic /ˌʌndɛməˈkratɪk/ *adj.* not democratic. □ **undemocratically** *adv.*

undemonstrated /ʌnˈdɛmənstreɪtɪd/ *adj.* not demonstrated.

undemonstrative /ʌndɪˈmɒnstrətɪv/ *adj.* not expressing feelings etc. outwardly; reserved. □ **undemonstratively** *adv.* **undemonstrativeness** *n.*

undeniable /ʌndɪˈnʌɪəb(ə)l/ *adj.* **1** unable to be denied or disputed; certain. **2** excellent (*was of undeniable character*). □ **undeniably** *adv.*

undenied /ʌndɪˈnʌɪd/ *adj.* not denied.

undented /ʌnˈdɛntɪd/ *adj.* **1** (of a surface) not dented. **2** (foll. by *by*) not affected.

undependable /ʌndɪˈpɛndəb(ə)l/ *adj.* not to be depended upon; unreliable.

under /ˈʌndə/ *prep.*, *adv.*, & *adj.* ● *prep.* **1 a** in or to a position lower than; below; beneath (*fell under the table*; *under the left eye*). **b** within, on the inside of (a surface etc.) (*wore a vest under his shirt*). **2 a** inferior to; less than (*a captain is under a major*; *is under 18*). **b** at or for a lower cost than (*was under £20*). **3 a** subject or liable to; controlled or bound by (*lives under oppression*; *under pain of death*; *born under Saturn*; *the country prospered under him*). **b** undergoing (*is under repair*). **c** classified or subsumed in (*that book goes under biology*; *goes under many names*). **4** at the foot of or sheltered by (*hid under the wall*; *under the cliff*). **5** planted with (a crop). **6** powered by (sail, steam, etc.). **7** following (another player in a card game). **8** *archaic* attested by (esp. *under one's hand and seal* = signature). ● *adv.* **1** in or to a lower position or condition (*kept him under*). **2** *colloq.* in or into a state of unconsciousness (*put him under for the operation*). ● *adj.* lower (*the under jaw*). □ **under one's arm** see ARM[1]. **under arms** see ARM[2].

under one's belt see BELT. **under one's breath** see BREATH. **under canvas** see CANVAS. **under a cloud** see CLOUD. **under control** see CONTROL. **under the counter** see COUNTER[1]. **under cover** under a roof or other shelter (see also COVER *n.* 4). **under fire** see FIRE. **under foot** see FOOT. **under hatches** see HATCH[1]. **under a person's nose** see NOSE. **under the rose** see ROSE[1]. **under separate cover** in another envelope. **under the sun** anywhere in the world. **under water** in and covered by water. **under way** in motion; in progress. **under the weather** see WEATHER. □ **undermost** *adj.* [Old English from Germanic]

under- /ˈʌndə/ *prefix* in senses of UNDER: **1** below, beneath (*undercarriage*; *underground*). **2** lower in status; subordinate (*under-secretary*). **3** insufficiently, incompletely (*undercook*; *underdeveloped*). [Old English (as UNDER)]

underachieve /ʌndərəˈtʃiːv/ *v.intr.* do less well than might normally be expected (esp. scholastically). □ **underachievement** *n.* **underachiever** *n.*

underact /ʌndərˈakt/ *v.* **1** *tr.* act (a part etc.) with insufficient force. **2** *intr.* act a part in this way.

under age *adj.* (usu. hyphenated when *attrib.*) not old enough, esp. not yet of adult status.

underarm /ˈʌndərɑːm/ *adj., adv., & n.* ● *adj. & adv.* **1** *Sport,* esp. *Cricket* with the arm below shoulder level. **2** under the arm. **3** in the armpit. ● *n.* the armpit.

underbelly /ˈʌndəbɛli/ *n.* (*pl.* **-ies**) the undersurface of an animal, vehicle, etc., esp. as an area vulnerable to attack.

underbid *v. & n.* ● *v.tr.* /ʌndəˈbɪd/ (**-bidding**; *past* and *past part.* **-bid**) **1** make a lower bid than (a person). **2** (also *absol.*) *Bridge* etc. bid less on (one's hand) than its strength warrants. ● *n.* /ˈʌndəbɪd/ **1** such a bid. **2** the act or an instance of underbidding.

underbidder /ʌndəˈbɪdə/ *n.* **1** the person who makes the bid next below the highest. **2** *Bridge* etc. a player who underbids.

underbody /ˈʌndəbɒdi/ *n.* (*pl.* **-ies**) the undersurface of the body of an animal, vehicle, etc.

underbred /ʌndəˈbrɛd/ *adj.* **1** ill-bred, vulgar. **2** not of pure breeding.

underbrush /ˈʌndəbrʌʃ/ *n. N. Amer.* undergrowth in a forest.

undercapitalize /ʌndəˈkapɪt(ə)lʌɪz/ *v.tr.* (also **-ise**) (esp. as **undercapitalized** *adj.*) provide (a business etc.) with insufficient capital to achieve a desired result.

undercarriage /ˈʌndəkarɪdʒ/ *n.* **1** a wheeled structure beneath an aircraft, usu. retracted when not in use, to receive the impact on landing and support the aircraft on the ground etc. **2** the supporting frame of a vehicle.

undercart /ˈʌndəkɑːt/ *n. Brit. colloq.* the undercarriage of an aircraft.

undercharge /ʌndəˈtʃɑːdʒ/ *v.tr.* **1** charge (a person) too little. **2** give less than the proper charge to (a gun, an electric battery, etc.).

underclass /ˈʌndəklɑːs/ *n.* a subordinate social class.

underclay /ˈʌndəkleɪ/ *n.* a clay bed under a coal-seam.

undercliff /ˈʌndəklɪf/ *n.* a terrace or lower cliff formed by a landslip.

underclothes /ˈʌndəkləʊðz, -kləʊz/ *n.pl.* clothes worn under others, esp. next to the skin.

underclothing /ˈʌndəkləʊðɪŋ/ *n.* underclothes collectively.

undercoat /ˈʌndəkəʊt/ *n.* **1 a** a preliminary layer of paint under the finishing coat. **b** the paint used for this. **2** an animal's under layer of hair or down. **3** a coat worn under another. □ **undercoating** *n.*

undercook /ʌndəˈkʊk/ *v.tr.* cook insufficiently.

undercover /ʌndəˈkʌvə, ˈʌndə-/ *adj.* (usu. *attrib.*) **1** surreptitious. **2** engaged in spying, esp. by working with or among those to be observed (*undercover agent*).

undercroft /ˈʌndəkrɒft/ *n.* a crypt. [Middle English from UNDER- + *croft* 'crypt', via Middle Dutch *crofte* 'cave' from medieval Latin *crupta*, Latin *crypta*: see CRYPT]

undercurrent /ˈʌndəkʌr(ə)nt/ *n.* **1** a current below the surface. **2** an underlying often contrary feeling, activity, or influence (*an undercurrent of protest*).

undercut *v. & n.* ● *v.tr.* /ʌndəˈkʌt/ (**-cutting**; *past* and *past part.* **-cut**) **1** sell or work at a lower price or lower wages than. **2** *Golf* etc. strike (a ball) so as to make it rise high. **3 a** cut away the part below or under (a thing). **b** cut away material to show (a carved design etc.) in relief. **4** render unstable or less firm, undermine. ● *n.* /ˈʌndəkʌt/ **1** *Brit.* the underside of a sirloin. **2** *US* a notch cut in a tree trunk to guide its fall when felled. **3** any space formed by the removal or absence of material from the lower part of something.

underdeveloped /ʌndədɪˈvɛləpt/ *adj.* **1** not fully developed; immature. **2** (of a country etc.) below its potential economic level. **3** *Photog.* not developed sufficiently to give a normal image. □ **underdevelopment** *n.*

underdog /ˈʌndədɒg/ *n.* **1** a competitor thought to have little chance of winning a fight or contest. **2** a downtrodden person.

underdone /ʌndəˈdʌn, ˈʌndə-/ *adj.* **1** not thoroughly done. **2** (of food) lightly or insufficiently cooked.

underdrawing /ˈʌndədrɔː(r)ɪŋ/ *n.* a preliminary sketch, subsequently covered with layers of paint.

underdress /ʌndəˈdrɛs/ *v.tr. & intr.* dress too plainly or too lightly.

undereducated /ʌndərˈɛdjʊkeɪtɪd/ *adj.* poorly educated; with insufficient literacy skills.

underemphasis /ʌndərˈɛmfəsɪs/ *n.* (*pl.* **-emphases** /-siːz/) an insufficient degree of emphasis. □ **underemphasize** *v.tr.* (also **-ise**).

underemployed /ʌndərɪmˈplɔɪd/ *adj.* not fully employed. □ **underemployment** *n.*

underestimate *v. & n.* ● *v.tr.* /ʌndərˈɛstɪmeɪt/ form too low an estimate of. ● *n.* /ʌndərˈɛstɪmət/ an estimate that is too low. □ **underestimation** /-ˈmeɪʃ(ə)n/ *n.*

underexpose /ʌndərɪkˈspəʊz, -rɛk-/ *v.tr. Photog.* expose (film) for too short a time or with insufficient light. □ **underexposure** *n.*

underfed /ʌndəˈfɛd/ *adj.* insufficiently fed.

underfelt /ˈʌndəfɛlt/ *n.* felt for laying under a carpet.

under-fives /ʌndəˈfʌɪvz/ *n.pl.* children who are less than five years old.

underfloor /ˈʌndəflɔː/ *attrib.adj.* situated or operating beneath the floor (*underfloor heating*).

underflow /ˈʌndəfləʊ/ *n.* an undercurrent.

underfoot /ʌndəˈfʊt/ *adv.* **1** under one's feet. **2** on the ground. **3** in a state of subjection. **4** so as to obstruct or inconvenience.

underframe /ˈʌndəfreɪm/ *n.* **1** the substructure of a motor vehicle or railway carriage. **2** the supporting frame of a chair seat or table top.

underfund /ʌndəˈfʌnd/ *v.tr.* (esp. as **underfunded** *adj.*) provide insufficient funding for. □ **underfunding** *n.*

underfur /ˈʌndəfəː/ *n.* an inner layer of short fur or down underlying an animal's outer fur.

undergarment /ˈʌndəgɑːm(ə)nt/ *n.* a piece of underclothing.

undergird /ʌndəˈgəːd/ *v.tr.* **1** make secure underneath. **2** strengthen, support.

underglaze /ˈʌndəgleɪz/ *adj. & n.* ● *adj.* **1** (of painting on porcelain etc.) done before the glaze is applied. **2** (of colours) used in such painting. ● *n.* underglaze painting.

undergo /ʌndəˈgəʊ/ *v.tr.* (*3rd sing. present* **-goes** /-ˈgəʊz/; *past* **-went** /-ˈwɛnt/; *past part.* **-gone** /-ˈgɒn/) be subjected to; suffer; endure. [Old English *undergān* (as UNDER-, GO[1])]

undergrad /ʌndəˈgrad/ *n. colloq.* = UNDERGRADUATE. [abbreviation]

undergraduate /ʌndəˈgradjʊət/ *n.* a student at a university who has not yet taken a first degree.

underground *adv., adj., n., & v.* ● *adv.* /ʌndəˈgraʊnd/ **1** beneath the surface of the ground. **2** in or into secrecy or hiding. ● *adj.* /ˈʌndəgraʊnd/ **1** situated underground.

2 secret, hidden, esp. working secretly to subvert a ruling power. 3 unconventional, experimental (*underground press*). ● *n.* /ˈʌndəgraʊnd/ 1 *Brit.* an underground railway. 2 a secret group or activity, esp. aiming to subvert the established order. ● *v.tr.* /ˈʌndəgraʊnd/ lay (cables) below ground level.

undergrowth /ˈʌndəgrəʊθ/ *n.* a dense growth of shrubs etc., esp. under large trees.

underhand *adj.* & *adv.* ● *adj.* /ˈʌndəhand/ 1 secret, clandestine, not above board. 2 deceptive, crafty. 3 *Sport*, esp. *Baseball* underarm. ● *adv.* /ʌndəˈhand/ in an underhand manner. [Old English (as UNDER-, HAND)]

underhanded /ʌndəˈhandɪd/ *adj.* & *adv.* = UNDERHAND.

underhung /ˈʌndəhʌŋ, ʌndəˈhʌŋ/ *adj.* 1 (of the lower jaw) projecting beyond the upper jaw. 2 having an underhung jaw.

underlay[1] *v.* & *n.* ● *v.tr.* /ʌndəˈleɪ/ (*past* and *past part.* **-laid**) lay something under (a thing) to support or raise it (*underlaid the tiles with felt*). ● *n.* /ˈʌndəleɪ/ a thing laid under another, esp. material laid under a carpet or mattress as protection or support. [Old English *underlecgan* (as UNDER-, LAY[1])]

■ **Usage** Care should be taken not to confuse *underlay*, a somewhat rare verb, with *underlie*. See also Usage Note at LAY[1].

underlay[2] *past* of UNDERLIE.

underlease /ˈʌndəliːs/ *n.* & *v.tr.* = SUB-LEASE.

underlet /ʌndəˈlɛt/ *v.tr.* (**-letting**; *past* and *past part.* **-let**) 1 sub-let. 2 let at less than the true value.

underlie /ʌndəˈlʌɪ/ *v.tr.* (**-lying**; *past* **-lay**; *past part.* **-lain**) 1 (also *absol.*) lie or be situated under (a stratum etc.). 2 (also *absol.*) (esp. as **underlying** *adj.*) (of a principle, reason, etc.) be the basis of (a doctrine, law, conduct, etc.). 3 exist beneath the superficial aspect of. [Old English *underlicgan* (as UNDER-, LIE[1])]

underline *v.* & *n.* ● *v.tr.* /ʌndəˈlʌɪn/ 1 draw a line under (a word etc.) to give emphasis or draw attention or indicate italic or other special type. 2 emphasize, stress. ● *n.* /ˈʌndəlʌɪn/ 1 a line drawn under a word etc. 2 a caption below an illustration.

underlinen /ˈʌndəlɪnɪn/ *n.* underclothes esp. of linen.

underling /ˈʌndəlɪŋ/ *n.* usu. *derog.* a subordinate.

underlip /ˈʌndəlɪp/ *n.* the lower lip of a person, animal, or insect.

underlying *pres. part.* of UNDERLIE.

undermanned /ʌndəˈmand/ *adj.* having too few people as crew or staff.

undermentioned /ʌndəˈmɛnʃ(ə)nd, ˈʌndə-/ *adj. Brit.* mentioned at a later place in a book etc.

undermine /ʌndəˈmʌɪn/ *v.tr.* 1 injure (a person, reputation, influence, etc.) by secret or insidious means. 2 weaken, injure, or wear out (health etc.) imperceptibly or insidiously. 3 wear away the base or foundation of (*rivers undermine their banks*). 4 make a mine or excavation under. □ **underminer** *n.* **underminingly** *adv.* [Middle English, from UNDER- + MINE[2]]

underneath /ʌndəˈniːθ/ *prep., adv., n., & adj.* ● *prep.* 1 at or to a lower place than, below. 2 on the inside of, within. ● *adv.* 1 at or to a lower place. 2 inside. ● *n.* the lower surface or part. ● *adj.* lower. [Old English *underneothan* (as UNDER + *neothan*: cf. BENEATH)]

undernourished /ʌndəˈnʌrɪʃt/ *adj.* insufficiently nourished. □ **undernourishment** *n.*

under-occupancy /ʌndərˈɒkjʊp(ə)nsi/ *n.* (*attrib.*) (of a surcharge) imposed on holiday accommodation if it is not occupied to the advertised capacity.

underpaid *past* and *past part.* of UNDERPAY.

underpainting /ˈʌndəpeɪntɪŋ/ *n. Art* 1 a layer of paint subsequently overlaid with another or with a finishing coat. 2 the application of such a layer.

underpants /ˈʌndəpan(t)s/ *n.pl.* an undergarment, esp. men's, covering the lower part of the body and usu. part of the legs.

underpart /ˈʌndəpɑːt/ *n.* 1 (usu. in *pl.*) a lower part, esp. a part of the underside of an animal. 2 a subordinate part in a play etc.

underpass /ˈʌndəpɑːs/ *n.* 1 a road etc. passing under another. 2 a crossing of this form.

underpay /ʌndəˈpeɪ/ *v.tr.* (*past* and *past part.* **-paid**) pay too little to (a person) or for (a thing). □ **underpayment** *n.*

underperform /ʌndəpəˈfɔːm/ *v.* 1 *intr.* perform less well or be less profitable than expected. 2 *tr.* perform less well or be less profitable than. □ **underperformance** *n.*

underpin /ʌndəˈpɪn/ *v.tr.* (**-pinned**, **-pinning**) 1 support from below with masonry etc. 2 support, strengthen.

underplant /ʌndəˈplɑːnt/ *v.tr.* (usu. foll. by *with*) plant or cultivate the ground about (a tall plant) with smaller ones.

underplay /ʌndəˈpleɪ/ *v.* 1 *tr.* play down the importance of. 2 *intr.* & *tr. Theatr.* a perform with deliberate restraint. b underact.

underplot /ˈʌndəplɒt/ *n.* a subordinate plot in a play etc.

underpopulated /ʌndəˈpɒpjʊleɪtɪd/ *adj.* having an insufficient or very small population.

underpowered /ʌndəˈpaʊəd/ *adj.* 1 lacking full electrical, mechanical, etc. power; lacking sufficient amplification. 2 with insufficient authority.

under-prepared /ʌndəprɪˈpɛːd/ *adj.* insufficiently prepared.

underprice /ʌndəˈprʌɪs/ *v.tr.* price lower than what is usual or appropriate.

underprivileged /ʌndəˈprɪvɪlɪdʒd/ *adj.* & *n.* ● *adj.* 1 less privileged than others. 2 not enjoying the normal standard of living or rights in a society. ● *n.* (prec. by *the*; treated as *pl.*) underprivileged people.

underproduction /ʌndəprəˈdʌkʃ(ə)n/ *n.* production of less than is usual or required.

underproof /ˈʌndəpruːf/ *adj.* containing less alcohol than proof spirit does.

underprop /ʌndəˈprɒp/ *v.tr.* (**-propped**, **-propping**) 1 support with a prop. 2 support, sustain.

underquote /ʌndəˈkwəʊt/ *v.tr.* 1 quote a lower price than (a person). 2 quote a lower price than others for (goods etc.).

underrate /ʌndəˈreɪt/ *v.tr.* have too low an opinion of.

under-read /ʌndəˈriːd/ *v.* (*past* and *past part.* **-read** /-ˈrɛd/) 1 *intr.* (of a gauge etc.) show a reading lower than the true one. 2 *tr.* (of the reading public) read (an author, a book, etc.) with less than normal frequency.

under-rehearsed /ʌndərɪˈhəːst/ *adj.* (esp. of a performance) insufficiently rehearsed.

under-report /ʌndərɪˈpɔːt/ *v.tr.* (usu. as **under-reported** *adj.*) fail to report (news, data, etc.) fully.

under-represent /ˌʌndərɛprɪˈzɛnt/ *v.tr.* (usu. as **under-represented** *adj.*) not include (a social group, specimen, type, etc.) in sufficient numbers.

underscore *v.* & *n.* ● *v.tr.* /ʌndəˈskɔː/ = UNDERLINE *v.* ● *n.* /ˈʌndəskɔː/ = UNDERLINE *n.* 1.

undersea /ˈʌndəsiː/ *adj.* below the sea or the surface of the sea, submarine.

underseal /ˈʌndəsiːl/ *v.* & *n. Brit.* ● *v.tr.* seal the underpart of (esp. a motor vehicle against rust etc.). ● *n.* a protective coating for undersealing.

under-secretary /ʌndəˈsɛkrət(ə)ri/ *n.* (*pl.* **-ies**) a subordinate official, esp. *Brit.* a junior minister or senior civil servant or *US* the principal assistant to a member of the Cabinet.

undersell /ʌndəˈsɛl/ *v.tr.* (*past* and *past part.* **-sold**) 1 sell at a lower price than (another seller). 2 sell at less than the true value.

underset *v.* & *n.* ● *v.tr.* /ʌndəˈsɛt/ (**-setting**; *past* and *past part.* **-set**) place something under (a thing). ● *n.* /ˈʌndəsɛt/ *Naut.* an undercurrent.

undersexed /ʌndəˈsɛkst/ *adj.* having unusually weak sexual desires.

under-sheriff /ˈʌndəʃɛrɪf/ *n.* a deputy sheriff.

undershirt /ˈʌndəʃəːt/ *n.* esp. *N. Amer.* an undergarment worn under a shirt; a vest.

undershoot *v.* & *n.* ● *v.tr.* /ʌndəˈʃuːt/ (*past* and *past part.* **-shot**) **1** (of an aircraft) land short of (a runway etc.). **2** shoot short of or below. ● *n.* /ˈʌndəʃuːt/ the act or an instance of undershooting.

undershorts /ˈʌndəʃɔːts/ *n.* *US* short underpants; trunks.

undershot /ˈʌndəʃɒt/ *adj.* **1** (of a waterwheel) turned by water flowing under it. **2** = UNDERHUNG.

undershrub /ˈʌndəʃrʌb/ *n.* = SUBSHRUB.

underside /ˈʌndəsʌɪd/ *n.* the lower or under side or surface.

undersigned /ʌndəˈsʌɪnd, ˈʌndə-/ *adj.* whose signature is appended (*we, the undersigned, wish to state* ...).

undersized /ʌndəˈsʌɪzd, ˈʌndə-/ *adj.* (also **undersize**) of less than the usual size.

underskirt /ˈʌndəskəːt/ *n.* a skirt worn under another; a petticoat.

underslung /ʌndəˈslʌŋ/ *adj.* **1** supported from above. **2** (of a vehicle chassis) hanging lower than the axles.

undersold *past* and *past part.* of UNDERSELL.

undersow /ʌndəˈsəʊ/ *v.tr.* (*past part.* **-sown**) **1** sow (a later-growing crop) on land already seeded with another crop. **2** (foll. by *with*) sow land already seeded with (a crop) with a later-growing crop.

underspend *v.* & *n.* ● *v.* /ʌndəˈspɛnd/ (*past* and *past part.* **-spent**) **1** *tr.* spend less than (a specified amount). **2** *intr.* & *refl.* spend too little. ● *n.* /ˈʌndəspɛnd/ **1** the act of underspending. **2** an instance of this. **3** the amount by which a specified amount is underspent.

understaffed /ʌndəˈstɑːft/ *adj.* having too few staff. □ **understaffing** *n.*

understairs /ˈʌndəstɛːz/ *attrib.adj.* in the space below the staircase.

understand /ʌndəˈstand/ *v.* (*past* and *past part.* **-stood** /-ˈstʊd/) **1** *tr.* perceive the meaning of (words, a person, a language, etc.) (*does not understand what you say*; *understood you perfectly*; *cannot understand French*). **2** *tr.* perceive the significance or explanation or cause of (*do not understand why he came*; *could not understand what the noise was about*; *do not understand the point of her remark*). **3** *tr.* be sympathetically aware of the character or nature of, know how to deal with (*quite understand your difficulty*; *cannot understand him at all*; *could never understand algebra*). **4** *tr.* **a** (often foll. by *that* + clause) infer esp. from information received, take as implied, take for granted (*I understand that it begins at noon*; *I understand him to be a distant relation*; *am I to understand that you refuse?*). **b** (*absol.*) believe or assume from knowledge or inference (*she is coming tomorrow, I understand*). **5** *tr.* supply (a word) mentally (*the verb may be either expressed or understood*). **6** *intr.* have understanding (in general or in particular). □ **understand each other 1** know each other's views or feelings. **2** be in agreement or collusion. □ **understandable** *adj.* **understandability** /-ˈbɪlɪti/ *n.* **understandably** *adv.* **understander** *n.* [Old English *understandan* (as UNDER-, STAND)]

understanding /ʌndəˈstandɪŋ/ *n.* & *adj.* ● *n.* **1 a** the ability to understand or think; intelligence. **b** the power of apprehension; the power of abstract thought. **2** an individual's perception or judgement of a situation etc. **3** an agreement; a thing agreed upon, esp. informally (*had an understanding with the rival company*; *consented only on this understanding*). **4** harmony in opinion or feeling (*disturbed the good understanding between them*). **5** sympathetic awareness or tolerance. ● *adj.* **1** having understanding or insight or good judgement. **2** sympathetic to others' feelings. □ **understandingly** *adv.* [Old English (as UNDERSTAND)]

understate /ʌndəˈsteɪt/ *v.tr.* **1** express in greatly or unduly restrained terms. **2** represent as being less than it actually is. □ **understatement** /ʌndəˈsteɪtm(ə)nt, ˈʌndə-/ *n.* **understater** *n.*

understeer /ˈʌndəstɪə/ *n.* & *v.* ● *n.* a tendency of a motor vehicle to turn less sharply than was intended. ● *v.intr.* have such a tendency.

understood *past* and *past part.* of UNDERSTAND.

understorey /ˈʌndəstɔːri/ *n.* (*pl.* **-eys**) (also **understory**, *pl.* **-ies**) **1** a layer of vegetation beneath the main canopy of a forest. **2** the plants forming this.

understrength /ʌndəˈstrɛŋθ, -ˈstrɛŋkθ/ *adj.* with a depleted number of troops, players, etc.

understudy /ˈʌndəstʌdi/ *n.* & *v.* esp. *Theatr.* ● *n.* (*pl.* **-ies**) a person who studies another's role or duties in order to act at short notice in the absence of the other. ● *v.tr.* (**-ies, -ied**) **1** study (a role etc.) as an understudy. **2** act as an understudy to (a person).

undersubscribed /ʌndəsəbˈskrʌɪbd/ *adj.* without sufficient subscribers, participants, etc.

undersurface /ˈʌndəsəːfɪs/ *n.* the lower or under surface.

undertake /ʌndəˈteɪk/ *v.tr.* (*past* **-took**; *past part.* **-taken**) **1** bind oneself to perform, make oneself responsible for, engage in, enter upon (work, an enterprise, a responsibility). **2** (usu. foll. by *to* + infin.) accept an obligation, promise. **3** guarantee, affirm (*I will undertake that he has not heard a word*).

undertaker /ˈʌndəteɪkə/ *n.* **1** a person whose business is to make arrangements for funerals. **2** /also -ˈteɪkə/ a person who undertakes to do something. **3** *hist.* an influential person in 17th-century England who undertook to procure particular legislation, esp. to obtain supplies from the House of Commons if the king would grant some concession.

undertaking /ʌndəˈteɪkɪŋ/ *n.* **1** work etc. undertaken, an enterprise (*a serious undertaking*). **2** a pledge or promise. **3** /ˈʌn-/ the management of funerals as a profession.

undertenant /ˈʌndətɛnənt/ *n.* a subtenant. □ **undertenancy** *n.* (*pl.* **-ies**).

under-the-counter *attrib.adj.* (esp. of illicit goods) obtained surreptitiously (cf. *under the counter* (COUNTER[1])).

underthings /ˈʌndəθɪŋz/ *n.pl. colloq.* underclothes.

undertint /ˈʌndətɪnt/ *n.* a subdued tint.

undertone /ˈʌndətəʊn/ *n.* **1** a subdued tone of sound or colour. **2** an underlying quality. **3** an undercurrent of feeling.

undertook *past* of UNDERTAKE.

undertow /ˈʌndətəʊ/ *n.* a current below the surface of the sea moving in the opposite direction to the surface current.

undertrained /ʌndəˈtreɪnd/ *adj.* with insufficient training for a job, sport, etc.

undertrick /ˈʌndətrɪk/ *n.* *Bridge* a trick by which the declarer falls short of his or her contract.

underuse *v.* & *n.* ● *v.tr.* /ʌndəˈjuːz/ use below the optimum level. ● *n.* /ʌndəˈjuːs/ insufficient use.

underutilize /ʌndəˈjuːtɪlʌɪz/ *v.tr.* (also **-ise**) (esp. as **underutilized** *adj.*) = UNDERUSE. □ **underutilization** /ˌʌndəjuːtɪlʌɪˈzeɪʃ(ə)n/ *n.*

undervalue /ʌndəˈvaljuː/ *v.tr.* (**-values, -valued, -valuing**) **1** value insufficiently. **2** underestimate. □ **undervaluation** /-jʊˈeɪʃ(ə)n/ *n.*

undervest /ˈʌndəvɛst/ *n.* *Brit.* an undergarment worn on the upper part of the body; a vest.

underwater /ʌndəˈwɔːtə/ *adj.* & *adv.* ● *adj.* situated or done under water. ● *adv.* under water.

underwear /ˈʌndəwɛː/ *n.* underclothes.

underweight *adj.* & *n.* ● *adj.* /ʌndəˈweɪt/ weighing less than is normal or desirable. ● *n.* /ˈʌndəweɪt/ insufficient weight.

underwent *past* of UNDERGO.

underwhelm /ʌndəˈwɛlm/ *v.tr. joc.* fail to impress. [on the pattern of OVERWHELM]

underwing /ˈʌndəwɪŋ/ *n.* **1** the hindwing of an insect. **2** the underside of a bird's wing.

underwired /ʌndə'wʌɪəd/ *adj.* (usu. *attrib.*) (of a bra) having a thin semicircular support of wire inset under each cup.

underwood /'ʌndəwʊd/ *n.* undergrowth.

underwork /'ʌndəwəːk/ *v.* **1** *tr.* impose too little work on. **2** *intr.* do too little work.

underworld /'ʌndəwəːld/ *n.* **1** the part of society comprising those who live by organized crime and immorality. **2** the mythical abode of the dead under the earth. **3** the antipodes.

underwrite /ʌndə'rʌɪt, 'ʌndərʌɪt/ *v.* (*past* **-wrote**; *past part.* **-written**) **1 a** *tr.* sign, and accept liability under (an insurance policy). **b** *tr.* accept (liability) in this way. **c** *intr.* practise insurance. **2** *tr.* undertake to finance or support. **3** *tr.* engage to buy all the stock in (a company etc.) not bought by the public. **4** *tr.* write below (*the underwritten names*). □ **underwriter** /'ʌn-/ *n.*

undescended /ʌndɪ'sɛndɪd/ *adj. Med.* (of a testicle) remaining in the abdomen instead of descending normally into the scrotum.

undeserved /ʌndɪ'zəːvd/ *adj.* not deserved (as reward or punishment). □ **undeservedly** /-vɪdli/ *adv.*

undeserving /ʌndɪ'zəːvɪŋ/ *adj.* not deserving. □ **undeservingly** *adv.*

undesigned /ʌndɪ'zʌɪnd/ *adj.* unintentional. □ **undesignedly** /-nɪdli/ *adv.*

undesirable /ʌndɪ'zʌɪərəb(ə)l/ *adj.* & *n.* ● *adj.* not desirable, objectionable, unpleasant. ● *n.* an undesirable person. □ **undesirability** /-'bɪlɪti/ *n.* **undesirableness** *n.* **undesirably** *adv.*

undesired /ʌndɪ'zʌɪəd/ *adj.* not desired.

undesirous /ʌndɪ'zʌɪərəs/ *adj.* not desirous.

undetectable /ʌndɪ'tɛktəb(ə)l/ *adj.* not detectable. □ **undetectability** /-'bɪlɪti/ *n.* **undetectably** *adv.*

undetected /ʌndɪ'tɛktɪd/ *adj.* not detected.

undetermined /ʌndɪ'təːmɪnd/ *adj.* = UNDECIDED.

undeterred /ʌndɪ'təːd/ *adj.* not deterred.

undeveloped /ʌndɪ'vɛləpt/ *adj.* not developed.

undeviating /ʌn'diːvɪeɪtɪŋ/ *adj.* not deviating; steady, constant. □ **undeviatingly** *adv.*

undiagnosed /ʌn'dʌɪəgnəʊzd, ˌʌndʌɪəg'nəʊzd/ *adj.* not diagnosed.

undid *past* of UNDO.

undies /'ʌndɪz/ *n.pl. colloq.* (esp. women's) underclothes. [abbreviation]

undifferentiated /ˌʌndɪfə'rɛnʃɪeɪtɪd/ *adj.* not differentiated; amorphous.

undigested /ʌndɪ'dʒɛstɪd, -dʌɪ-/ *adj.* **1** not digested. **2** (esp. of information, facts, etc.) not properly arranged or considered.

undignified /ʌn'dɪgnɪfʌɪd/ *adj.* lacking dignity.

undiluted /ʌndʌɪ'luːtɪd/ *adj.* **1** not diluted. **2** complete, utter.

undiminished /ʌndɪ'mɪnɪʃt/ *adj.* not diminished or lessened.

undine /'ʌndiːn/ *n.* a female water spirit. [modern Latin *undina* (word invented by Paracelsus) from Latin *unda* 'a wave']

undiplomatic /ˌʌndɪplə'matɪk/ *adj.* tactless. □ **undiplomatically** *adv.*

undirected /ʌndɪ'rɛktɪd, -dʌɪ-/ *adj.* aimless; lacking direction; unfocussed.

undiscerning /ʌndɪ'səːnɪŋ/ *adj.* **1** lacking insight. **2** lacking taste.

undischarged /ʌndɪs'tʃɑːdʒd/ *adj.* (esp. of a bankrupt or a debt) not discharged.

undiscipline /ʌn'dɪsɪplɪn/ *n.* lack of discipline.

undisciplined /ʌn'dɪsɪplɪnd/ *adj.* lacking discipline; not disciplined.

undisclosed /ʌndɪs'kləʊzd/ *adj.* not revealed or made known.

undiscoverable /ʌndɪ'skʌv(ə)rəb(ə)l/ *adj.* that cannot be discovered.

undiscovered /ʌndɪ'skʌvəd/ *adj.* not discovered.

undiscriminating /ʌndɪ'skrɪmɪneɪtɪŋ/ *adj.* not showing good judgement.

undiscussed /ʌndɪ'skʌst/ *adj.* not discussed.

undisguised /ʌndɪs'gʌɪzd/ *adj.* not disguised. □ **undisguisedly** /-zɪdli/ *adv.*

undismayed /ʌndɪs'meɪd/ *adj.* not dismayed.

undisputed /ʌndɪ'spjuːtɪd/ *adj.* not disputed or called in question.

undissolved /ʌndɪ'zɒlvd/ *adj.* not dissolved.

undistinguishable /ʌndɪ'stɪŋgwɪʃəb(ə)l/ *adj.* (often foll. by *from*) indistinguishable.

undistinguished /ʌndɪ'stɪŋgwɪʃt/ *adj.* not distinguished; mediocre.

undistorted /ʌndɪ'stɔːtɪd/ *adj.* not distorted.

undistributed /ʌndɪ'strɪbjuːtɪd/ *adj.* not distributed.

undistributed middle *n. Logic* a fallacy arising from the failure of the middle term of a syllogism to refer to all the members of a class.

undisturbed /ʌndɪ'stəːbd/ *adj.* not disturbed or interfered with.

undivided /ʌndɪ'vʌɪdɪd/ *adj.* not divided or shared; whole, entire (*gave him my undivided attention*).

undo /ʌn'duː/ *v.tr.* (*3rd sing. present* **-does**; *past* **-did**; *past part.* **-done**) **1 a** unfasten or untie (a coat, button, parcel, etc.). **b** unfasten the clothing of (a person). **2** annul, cancel (*cannot undo the past*). **3** ruin the prospects, reputation, or morals of. [Old English *undōn* (as UN-[2], DO[1])]

undock /ʌn'dɒk/ *v.tr.* **1** (also *absol.*) separate (a spacecraft) from another in space. **2** take (a ship) out of a dock.

undocumented /ʌn'dɒkjʊmɛntɪd/ *adj.* **1** *US* not having the appropriate document. **2** not proved by or recorded in documents.

undoing /ʌn'duːɪŋ/ *n.* **1** ruin or a cause of ruin. **2** the process of reversing what has been done. **3** the action of opening or unfastening.

undomesticated /ʌndə'mɛstɪkeɪtɪd/ *adj.* not domesticated.

undone /ʌn'dʌn/ *adj.* **1** not done; incomplete (*left the job undone*). **2** not fastened (*left the buttons undone*). **3** *archaic* ruined.

undoubtable /ʌn'daʊtəb(ə)l/ *adj.* that cannot be doubted; indubitable. □ **undoubtably** *adv.*

undoubted /ʌn'daʊtɪd/ *adj.* certain, not questioned, not regarded as doubtful. □ **undoubtedly** *adv.*

undrained /ʌn'dreɪnd/ *adj.* not drained.

undramatic /ʌndrə'matɪk/ *adj.* **1** lacking a dramatic quality or effect. **2** understated; unremarkable.

undraped /ʌn'dreɪpt/ *adj.* **1** not covered with drapery. **2** naked.

undreamed /ʌn'driːmd, -'drɛmt/ *adj.* (also **undreamt** /ʌn'drɛmt/) (often foll. by *of*) not dreamed or thought of or imagined.

undress /ʌn'drɛs/ *v.* & *n.* ● *v.* **1** *intr.* take off one's clothes. **2** *tr.* take the clothes off (a person). ● *n.* **1** ordinary dress as opposed to full dress or uniform (also *attrib.*: *undress cap*). **2** casual or informal dress. **3** the state of being naked or only partially clothed.

undressed /ʌn'drɛst/ *adj.* **1** not or no longer dressed; partly or wholly naked. **2** (of leather etc.) not treated. **3** (of food) not having a dressing.

undrinkable /ʌn'drɪnkəb(ə)l/ *adj.* unfit for drinking.

undue /ʌn'djuː/ *adj.* (usu. *attrib.*) **1** excessive, disproportionate. **2** not suitable. **3** not owed. □ **unduly** *adv.*

undue influence *n. Law* influence by which a person is induced to act otherwise than by his or her own free will, or without adequate attention to the consequences.

undulant /'ʌndjʊl(ə)nt/ *adj.* moving like waves; fluctuating. [Latin *undulare* (as UNDULATE)]

undulant fever *n.* brucellosis in humans. [so called because of the intermittent fever associated with the disease]

undulate *v. & adj.* ● *v.intr. & tr.* /ˈʌndjʊleɪt/ have or cause to have a wavy motion or look. ● *adj.* /ˈʌndjʊlət/ wavy, going alternately up and down or in and out (*leaves with undulate margins*). ▫ **undulately** *adv.* [Late Latin *undulatus* from Latin *unda* 'a wave']

undulation /ʌndjʊˈleɪʃ(ə)n/ *n.* **1** a wavy motion or form, a gentle rise and fall. **2** each wave of this. **3** a set of wavy lines.

undulatory /ˈʌndjʊlət(ə)ri/ *adj.* **1** undulating, wavy. **2** of or due to undulation.

undutiful /ʌnˈdjuːtɪfʊl, -f(ə)l/ *adj.* not dutiful. ▫ **undutifully** *adv.* **undutifulness** *n.*

undyed /ʌnˈdʌɪd/ *adj.* not dyed.

undying /ʌnˈdʌɪɪŋ/ *adj.* **1** immortal. **2** never-ending (*undying love*). ▫ **undyingly** *adv.*

unearned /ʌnˈəːnd/ *adj.* not earned.

unearned income *n.* income from interest payments etc. as opposed to salary, wages, or fees.

unearned increment *n.* an increase in the value of property not due to the owner's labour or outlay.

unearth /ʌnˈəːθ/ *v.tr.* **1 a** discover by searching or in the course of digging or rummaging. **b** dig out of the earth. **2** drive (a fox etc.) from its earth.

unearthly /ʌnˈəːθli/ *adj.* **1** supernatural, mysterious. **2** *colloq.* absurdly early or inconvenient (*got up at an unearthly hour*). **3** not earthly. ▫ **unearthliness** *n.*

unease /ʌnˈiːz/ *n.* lack of ease, discomfort, distress.

uneasy /ʌnˈiːzi/ *adj.* (**uneasier, uneasiest**) **1** disturbed or uncomfortable in mind or body (*passed an uneasy night*). **2** disturbing (*had an uneasy suspicion*). ▫ **uneasily** *adv.* **uneasiness** *n.*

uneatable /ʌnˈiːtəb(ə)l/ *adj.* not able to be eaten, esp. because of its condition (cf. INEDIBLE).

uneaten /ʌnˈiːt(ə)n/ *adj.* not eaten; left undevoured.

uneconomic /ˌʌniːkəˈnɒmɪk, ˌʌnɛk-/ *adj.* not economic; incapable of being profitably operated etc. ▫ **uneconomically** *adv.*

uneconomical /ˌʌniːkəˈnɒmɪk(ə)l, ˌʌnɛkə-/ *adj.* not economical; wasteful.

unedifying /ʌnˈɛdɪfʌɪɪŋ/ *adj.* not edifying, esp. uninstructive or degrading. ▫ **unedifyingly** *adv.*

unedited /ʌnˈɛdɪtɪd/ *adj.* not edited.

uneducated /ʌnˈɛdjʊkeɪtɪd/ *adj.* not educated. ▫ **uneducable** /-kəb(ə)l/ *adj.*

unelectable /ʌnɪˈlɛktəb(ə)l/ *adj.* (of a candidate, party, etc.) holding views likely to bring defeat at an election.

unelected /ʌnɪˈlɛktɪd/ *adj.* not elected.

unembarrassed /ʌnɪmˈbarəst, -ɛm-/ *adj.* not embarrassed.

unembellished /ʌnɪmˈbɛlɪʃt, -ɛm-/ *adj.* not embellished or decorated.

unemotional /ʌnɪˈməʊʃ(ə)n(ə)l/ *adj.* not emotional; lacking emotion. ▫ **unemotionally** *adv.*

unemphatic /ʌnɪmˈfatɪk, -ɛm-/ *adj.* not emphatic. ▫ **unemphatically** *adv.*

unemployable /ʌnɪmˈplɔɪəb(ə)l, -ɛm-/ *adj. & n.* ● *adj.* unfitted for paid employment. ● *n.* an unemployable person. ▫ **unemployability** /-ˈbɪlɪti/ *n.*

unemployed /ʌnɪmˈplɔɪd, -ɛm-/ *adj. & n.* ● *adj.* **1** not having paid employment; out of work. **2** not in use. ● *n.* (prec. by *the*; treated as *pl.*) unemployed people.

unemployment /ʌnɪmˈplɔɪm(ə)nt, -ɛm-/ *n.* **1** the state of being unemployed. **2** the condition or extent of this in a country or region etc. (*the North has higher unemployment*).

unemployment benefit *n.* a payment made by the state or (in the US) a trade union to an unemployed person.

unenclosed /ʌnɪnˈkləʊzd, -ɛn-/ *adj.* not enclosed.

unencumbered /ʌnɪnˈkʌmbəd, -ɛn-/ *adj.* **1** (of an estate) not having any liabilities (e.g. a mortgage) on it. **2** having no encumbrance; free.

unending /ʌnˈɛndɪŋ/ *adj.* having or apparently having no end. ▫ **unendingly** *adv.* **unendingness** *n.*

unendowed /ʌnɪnˈdaʊd, -ɛn-/ *adj.* not endowed.

unendurable /ʌnɪnˈdjʊərəb(ə)l/ *adj.* that cannot be endured. ▫ **unendurably** *adv.*

unenforceable /ʌnɪnˈfɔːsəb(ə)l, -ɛn-/ *adj.* (of a contract, law, etc.) impossible to enforce.

unengaged /ʌnɪnˈgeɪdʒd, -ɛn-/ *adj.* not engaged; uncommitted.

un-English /ʌnˈɪŋglɪʃ/ *adj.* **1** not characteristic of the English. **2** not English.

unenjoyable /ʌnɪnˈdʒɔɪəb(ə)l, -ɛn-/ *adj.* not enjoyable.

unenlightened /ʌnɪnˈlʌɪt(ə)nd, -ɛn-/ *adj.* not enlightened. ▫ **unenlightenment** *n.*

unenterprising /ʌnˈɛntəprʌɪzɪŋ/ *adj.* not enterprising.

unenthusiastic /ˌʌnɪnθjuːzɪˈastɪk, ˌʌnɛn-/ *adj.* not enthusiastic. ▫ **unenthusiastically** *adv.*

unenviable /ʌnˈɛnvɪəb(ə)l/ *adj.* not enviable. ▫ **unenviably** *adv.*

unenvied /ʌnˈɛnvɪd/ *adj.* not envied.

unequal /ʌnˈiːkw(ə)l/ *adj.* **1** (often foll. by *to*) not equal. **2** of varying quality. **3** lacking equal advantage to both sides (*an unequal bargain*). ▫ **unequally** *adv.*

unequalize /ʌnˈiːkwəlʌɪz/ *v.tr.* (also **-ise**) make unequal.

unequalled /ʌnˈiːkw(ə)ld/ *adj.* (*US* **unequaled**) superior to all others.

unequipped /ʌnɪˈkwɪpt/ *adj.* not equipped.

unequivocal /ʌnɪˈkwɪvək(ə)l/ *adj.* not ambiguous, plain, unmistakable. ▫ **unequivocally** *adv.* **unequivocalness** *n.*

unerring /ʌnˈəːrɪŋ/ *adj.* not erring, failing, or missing the mark; true, certain. ▫ **unerringly** *adv.* **unerringness** *n.*

unescapable /ʌnɪˈskeɪpəb(ə)l, ʌnɛ-/ *adj.* inescapable.

UNESCO /juːˈnɛskəʊ/ *abbr.* (also **Unesco**) United Nations Educational, Scientific, and Cultural Organization.

unescorted /ʌnɪˈskɔːtɪd, ʌnɛ-/ *adj.* not escorted.

unessential /ʌnɪˈsɛnʃ(ə)l/ *adj. & n.* ● *adj.* **1** not essential (cf. INESSENTIAL). **2** not of the first importance. ● *n.* an unessential part or thing.

unestablished /ʌnɪˈstablɪʃt, ʌnɛ-/ *adj.* not established.

unethical /ʌnˈɛθɪk(ə)l/ *adj.* not ethical, esp. unscrupulous in business or professional conduct. ▫ **unethically** *adv.*

unevangelical /ˌʌniːvanˈdʒɛlɪk(ə)l/ *adj.* not evangelical.

uneven /ʌnˈiːv(ə)n/ *adj.* **1** not level or smooth. **2** not uniform or equable. **3** (of a contest) unequal. ▫ **unevenly** *adv.* **unevenness** /ʌnˈiːv(ə)nnɪs/ *n.* [Old English *unefen* (as UN-[1], EVEN[1])]

uneventful /ʌnɪˈvɛntfʊl, -f(ə)l/ *adj.* not eventful. ▫ **uneventfully** *adv.* **uneventfulness** *n.*

unexamined /ʌnɪgˈzamɪnd, ʌnɛg-/ *adj.* not examined.

unexampled /ʌnɪgˈzɑːmp(ə)ld, ʌnɛg-/ *adj.* having no precedent or parallel.

unexceptionable /ʌnɪkˈsɛpʃ(ə)nəb(ə)l, ʌnɛk-/ *adj.* with which no fault can be found; entirely satisfactory. ▫ **unexceptionableness** *n.* **unexceptionably** *adv.*

■ **Usage** See Usage Note at EXCEPTIONABLE.

unexceptional /ʌnɪkˈsɛpʃ(ə)n(ə)l, ʌnɛk-/ *adj.* not out of the ordinary; usual, normal. ▫ **unexceptionally** *adv.*

■ **Usage** See Usage Note at EXCEPTIONABLE.

unexcitable /ʌnɪkˈsʌɪtəb(ə)l, ʌnɛk-/ *adj.* not easily excited. ▫ **unexcitability** /-ˈbɪlɪti/ *n.*

unexciting /ʌnɪkˈsʌɪtɪŋ, ʌnɛk-/ *adj.* not exciting; dull.

unexecuted /ʌnˈɛksɪkjuːtɪd/ *adj.* not carried out or put into effect.

unexhausted /ʌnɪgˈzɔːstɪd, ʌnɛg-/ *adj.* **1** not used up, expended, or brought to an end. **2** not emptied.

unexpected /ʌnɪkˈspɛktɪd, ʌnɛk-/ *adj.* not expected; surprising. ▫ **unexpectedly** *adv.* **unexpectedness** *n.*

unexpired /ʌnɪkˈspʌɪəd, ʌnɛk-/ *adj.* that has not yet expired.

unexplainable /ʌnɪkˈspleɪnəb(ə)l, ʌnɛk-/ *adj.* inexplicable. ▫ **unexplainably** *adv.*

unexplained /ʌnɪk'spleɪnd, ʌnɛk-/ *adj.* not explained.

unexploded /ʌnɪk'spləʊdɪd, ʌnɛk-/ *adj.* (usu. *attrib.*) (of a bomb etc.) that has not exploded.

unexploited /ʌnɪk'splɔɪtɪd, ʌnɛk-/ *adj.* (of resources etc.) not exploited.

unexplored /ʌnɪk'splɔːd, ʌnɛk-/ *adj.* not explored.

unexposed /ʌnɪk'spəʊzd, ʌnɛk-/ *adj.* not exposed.

unexpressed /ʌnɪk'sprɛst, ʌnɛk-/ *adj.* not expressed or made known (*unexpressed fears*).

unexpurgated /ʌn'ɛkspəgeɪtɪd/ *adj.* (esp. of a text etc.) not expurgated; complete.

unfaceable /ʌn'feɪsəb(ə)l/ *adj.* that cannot be faced or confronted.

unfading /ʌn'feɪdɪŋ/ *adj.* that never fades. □ **unfadingly** *adv.*

unfailing /ʌn'feɪlɪŋ/ *adj.* **1** not failing. **2** not running short. **3** constant. **4** reliable. □ **unfailingly** *adv.* **unfailingness** *n.*

unfair /ʌn'fɛː/ *adj.* **1** not equitable or honest (*obtained by unfair means*). **2** not impartial or according to the rules (*unfair play*). □ **unfairly** *adv.* **unfairness** *n.* [Old English *unfæger* (as UN-[1], FAIR[1])]

unfaithful /ʌn'feɪθfʊl, -f(ə)l/ *adj.* **1** not faithful, esp. adulterous. **2** not loyal. **3** treacherous. □ **unfaithfully** *adv.* **unfaithfulness** *n.*

unfaltering /ʌn'fɔːlt(ə)rɪŋ, -'fɒl-/ *adj.* not faltering; steady, resolute. □ **unfalteringly** *adv.*

unfamiliar /ʌnfə'mɪlɪə/ *adj.* not familiar. □ **unfamiliarity** /-lɪ'arɪti/ *n.*

unfancied /ʌn'fansɪd/ *adj.* (of a team, racehorse, etc.) not considered likely to win.

unfashionable /ʌn'faʃ(ə)nəb(ə)l/ *adj.* not fashionable. □ **unfashionableness** *n.* **unfashionably** *adv.*

unfashioned /ʌn'faʃ(ə)nd/ *adj.* not made into its proper shape.

unfasten /ʌn'fɑːs(ə)n/ *v.* **1** *tr.* & *intr.* make or become loose. **2** *tr.* open the fastening(s) of. **3** *tr.* detach.

unfastened /ʌn'fɑːs(ə)nd/ *adj.* **1** that has not been fastened. **2** that has been loosened, opened, or detached.

unfathered /ʌn'fɑːðəd/ *adj.* **1** having no known or acknowledged father; illegitimate. **2** of unknown origin (*unfathered rumours*).

unfatherly /ʌn'fɑːðəli/ *adj.* not befitting a father. □ **unfatherliness** *n.*

unfathomable /ʌn'fað(ə)məb(ə)l/ *adj.* incapable of being fathomed. □ **unfathomableness** *n.* **unfathomably** *adv.*

unfathomed /ʌn'fað(ə)md/ *adj.* **1** of unascertained depth. **2** not fully explored or known.

unfavourable /ʌn'feɪv(ə)rəb(ə)l/ *adj.* (*US* **unfavorable**) not favourable; adverse, hostile. □ **unfavourableness** *n.* **unfavourably** *adv.*

unfavourite /ʌn'feɪv(ə)rɪt/ *adj.* (*US* **unfavorite**) *colloq.* least favourite; most disliked.

unfazed /ʌn'feɪzd/ *adj.* *colloq.* untroubled; not disconcerted.

unfeasible /ʌn'fiːzɪb(ə)l/ *adj.* not feasible; impractical. □ **unfeasibility** /-'bɪlɪti/ *n.* **unfeasibly** *adv.*

unfed /ʌn'fɛd/ *adj.* not fed.

unfeeling /ʌn'fiːlɪŋ/ *adj.* **1** unsympathetic, harsh, not caring about others' feelings. **2** lacking sensation or sensitivity. □ **unfeelingly** *adv.* **unfeelingness** *n.* [Old English *unfelende* (as UN-[1], FEELING)]

unfeigned /ʌn'feɪnd/ *adj.* genuine, sincere. □ **unfeignedly** *adv.*

unfelt /ʌn'fɛlt/ *adj.* not felt.

unfeminine /ʌn'fɛmɪnɪn/ *adj.* not in accordance with, or appropriate to, female character. □ **unfemininity** /-'nɪnɪti/ *n.*

unfenced /ʌn'fɛnst/ *adj.* **1** not provided with fences. **2** unprotected.

unfermented /ʌnfə'mɛntɪd, -fɜː'm-/ *adj.* not fermented.

unfertilized /ʌn'fɜːtɪlʌɪzd/ *adj.* (also **unfertilised**) not fertilized.

unfetter /ʌn'fɛtə/ *v.tr.* release from fetters.

unfettered /ʌn'fɛtəd/ *adj.* unrestrained, unrestricted.

unfilial /ʌn'fɪlɪəl/ *adj.* not befitting a son or daughter. □ **unfilially** *adv.*

unfilled /ʌn'fɪld/ *adj.* not filled.

unfiltered /ʌn'fɪltəd/ *adj.* **1** not filtered. **2** (of a cigarette) not provided with a filter.

unfinished /ʌn'fɪnɪʃt/ *adj.* not finished; incomplete.

unfit /ʌn'fɪt/ *adj.* & *v.* ● *adj.* (often foll. by *for*, or *to* + infin.) not fit. ● *v.tr.* (**unfitted**, **unfitting**) (usu. foll. by *for*) make unsuitable. □ **unfitly** *adv.* **unfitness** *n.*

unfitted /ʌn'fɪtɪd/ *adj.* **1** not fit. **2** not fitted or suited. **3** not provided with fittings.

unfitting /ʌn'fɪtɪŋ/ *adj.* not fitting or suitable, unbecoming. □ **unfittingly** *adv.*

unfix /ʌn'fɪks/ *v.tr.* **1** release or loosen from a fixed state. **2** detach.

unfixed /ʌn'fɪkst/ *adj.* not fixed.

unflagging /ʌn'flagɪŋ/ *adj.* tireless, persistent. □ **unflaggingly** *adv.*

unflappable /ʌn'flapəb(ə)l/ *adj.* *colloq.* imperturbable; remaining calm in a crisis. □ **unflappability** /-'bɪlɪti/ *n.* **unflappably** *adv.*

unflattering /ʌn'flat(ə)rɪŋ/ *adj.* not flattering. □ **unflatteringly** *adv.*

unflavoured /ʌn'fleɪvəd/ *adj.* (*US* **unflavored**) not flavoured.

unfledged /ʌn'flɛdʒd/ *adj.* **1** (of a person) inexperienced. **2** (of a bird) not yet fledged.

unfleshed /ʌn'flɛʃt/ *adj.* **1** not covered with flesh. **2** stripped of flesh.

unflinching /ʌn'flɪn(t)ʃɪŋ/ *adj.* not flinching. □ **unflinchingly** *adv.*

unfocused /ʌn'fəʊkəst/ *adj.* (also **unfocussed**) not focused.

unfold /ʌn'fəʊld/ *v.* **1** *tr.* open the fold or folds of, spread out. **2** *tr.* reveal (thoughts etc.). **3** *intr.* become opened out. **4** *intr.* develop. □ **unfoldment** *n.* *US.* [Old English *unfealdan* (as UN-[2], FOLD[1])]

unforced /ʌn'fɔːst/ *adj.* **1** not produced by effort; easy, natural. **2** not compelled or constrained. □ **unforcedly** *adv.*

unfordable /ʌn'fɔːdəb(ə)l/ *adj.* that cannot be forded.

unforeseeable /ʌnfɔː'siːəb(ə)l/ *adj.* not foreseeable.

unforeseen /ʌnfɔː'siːn/ *adj.* not foreseen.

unforetold /ʌnfɔː'təʊld/ *adj.* not foretold; unpredicted.

unforgettable /ʌnfə'gɛtəb(ə)l/ *adj.* that cannot be forgotten; memorable, wonderful (*an unforgettable experience*). □ **unforgettably** *adv.*

unforgivable /ʌnfə'gɪvəb(ə)l/ *adj.* that cannot be forgiven. □ **unforgivably** *adv.*

unforgiven /ʌnfə'gɪv(ə)n/ *adj.* not forgiven.

unforgiving /ʌnfə'gɪvɪŋ/ *adj.* not forgiving. □ **unforgivingly** *adv.* **unforgivingness** *n.*

unforgotten /ʌnfə'gɒt(ə)n/ *adj.* not forgotten.

unformed /ʌn'fɔːmd/ *adj.* **1** not formed. **2** shapeless. **3** not developed.

unformulated /ʌn'fɔːmjʊleɪtɪd/ *adj.* not formulated.

unforthcoming /ʌnfɔːθ'kʌmɪŋ/ *adj.* not forthcoming.

unfortified /ʌn'fɔːtɪfʌɪd/ *adj.* not fortified.

unfortunate /ʌn'fɔːtʃ(ə)nət/ *adj.* & *n.* ● *adj.* **1** having bad fortune; unlucky. **2** unhappy. **3** regrettable. **4** disastrous. ● *n.* an unfortunate person.

unfortunately /ʌn'fɔːtʃ(ə)nətli/ *adv.* **1** (qualifying a whole sentence) it is unfortunate that. **2** in an unfortunate manner.

unfounded /ʌn'faʊndɪd/ *adj.* having no foundation (*unfounded hopes; unfounded rumour*). □ **unfoundedly** *adv.* **unfoundedness** *n.*

unframed /ʌn'freɪmd/ *adj.* (esp. of a picture) not framed.

unfree /ʌn'friː/ *adj.* deprived or devoid of liberty. □ **unfreedom** *n.*

unfreeze /ʌn'friːz/ *v.* (*past* **unfroze**; *past part.* **unfrozen**) **1** *tr.* cause to thaw. **2** *intr.* thaw. **3** *tr.* remove restrictions from, make (assets, credits, etc.) realizable.

unfrequented /ʌnfrɪ'kwɛntɪd/ *adj.* not frequented.
unfriended /ʌn'frɛndɪd/ *adj. literary* without friends.
unfriendly /ʌn'frɛn(d)li/ *adj.* (**unfriendlier, unfriendliest**) not friendly. □ **unfriendliness** *n.*
unfrock /ʌn'frɒk/ *v.tr.* = DEFROCK.
unfroze *past* of UNFREEZE.
unfrozen *past part.* of UNFREEZE.
unfruitful /ʌn'fru:tfʊl, -f(ə)l/ *adj.* **1** not producing good results, unprofitable. **2** not producing fruit or crops. □ **unfruitfully** *adv.* **unfruitfulness** *n.*
unfulfilled /ʌnfʊl'fɪld/ *adj.* not fulfilled. □ **unfulfillable** *adj.* **unfulfilling** *adj.*
unfunded /ʌn'fʌndɪd/ *adj.* (of a debt) not funded.
unfunny /ʌn'fʌni/ *adj.* (**unfunnier, unfunniest**) not amusing (though meant to be). □ **unfunnily** *adv.* **unfunniness** *n.*
unfurl /ʌn'fə:l/ *v.* **1** *tr.* spread out (a sail, umbrella, etc.). **2** *intr.* become spread out.
unfurnished /ʌn'fə:nɪʃt/ *adj.* **1** (usu. foll. by *with*) not supplied. **2** without furniture.
unfussy /ʌn'fʌsi/ *adj.* not fussy.
ungainly /ʌn'geɪnli/ *adj.* (of a person, animal, or movement) awkward, clumsy. □ **ungainliness** *n.* [UN-[1] + obsolete *gainly* 'graceful', ultimately from Old Norse *gegn* 'straight']
ungallant /ʌn'gal(ə)nt, ʌngə'lant/ *adj.* not gallant. □ **ungallantly** *adv.*
ungenerous /ʌn'dʒɛn(ə)rəs/ *adj.* not generous; mean. □ **ungenerously** *adv.* **ungenerousness** *n.*
ungenial /ʌn'dʒi:nɪəl/ *adj.* not genial.
ungentle /ʌn'dʒɛnt(ə)l/ *adj.* not gentle. □ **ungentleness** *n.* **ungently** *adv.*
ungentlemanly /ʌn'dʒɛnt(ə)lmənli/ *adj.* not gentlemanly. □ **ungentlemanliness** *n.*
unget-at-able /ʌngɛt'atəb(ə)l/ *adj. colloq.* inaccessible.
ungifted /ʌn'gɪftɪd/ *adj.* not gifted or talented.
ungird /ʌn'gə:d/ *v.tr.* **1** release the girdle, belt, or girth of. **2** release or take off by undoing a belt or girth.
unglamorous /ʌn'glam(ə)rəs/ *adj.* **1** lacking glamour or attraction. **2** mundane.
unglazed /ʌn'gleɪzd/ *adj.* not glazed.
ungloved /ʌn'glʌvd/ *adj.* not wearing a glove or gloves.
ungodly /ʌn'gɒdli/ *adj.* **1** impious, wicked. **2** *colloq.* outrageous (*an ungodly hour to arrive*). □ **ungodliness** *n.*
ungovernable /ʌn'gʌv(ə)nəb(ə)l/ *adj.* uncontrollable, violent. □ **ungovernability** /-'bɪlɪti/ *n.* **ungovernably** *adv.*
ungraceful /ʌn'greɪsfʊl, -f(ə)l/ *adj.* not graceful. □ **ungracefully** *adv.* **ungracefulness** *n.*
ungracious /ʌn'greɪʃəs/ *adj.* **1** not kindly or courteous; unkind. **2** unattractive. □ **ungraciously** *adv.* **ungraciousness** *n.*
ungrammatical /ʌngrə'matɪk(ə)l/ *adj.* contrary to the rules of grammar. □ **ungrammaticality** /-'kalɪti/ *n.* **ungrammatically** *adv.* **ungrammaticalness** *n.*
ungraspable /ʌn'grɑ:spəb(ə)l/ *adj.* that cannot be grasped or comprehended.
ungrateful /ʌn'greɪtfʊl, -f(ə)l/ *adj.* **1** not feeling or showing gratitude. **2** not pleasant or acceptable. □ **ungratefully** *adv.* **ungratefulness** *n.*
ungreen /ʌn'gri:n/ *adj.* **1** not supporting protection of the environment. **2** harmful to the environment.
ungrounded /ʌn'graʊndɪd/ *adj.* **1** having no basis or justification; unfounded. **2** *Electr.* not earthed. **3** (foll. by *in* a subject) not properly instructed. **4** (of an aircraft, ship, etc.) no longer grounded.
ungrudging /ʌn'grʌdʒɪŋ/ *adj.* not grudging. □ **ungrudgingly** *adv.*
ungual /'ʌŋgw(ə)l/ *adj.* of, like, or bearing a nail, hoof, or claw. [Latin UNGUIS]
unguard /ʌn'gɑ:d/ *v.tr. Cards* discard a low card that was protecting (a high card) from capture.
unguarded /ʌn'gɑ:dɪd/ *adj.* **1** incautious, thoughtless (*an unguarded remark*). **2** not guarded; without a guard. □ **unguardedly** *adv.* **unguardedness** *n.*
unguent /'ʌŋgwənt/ *n.* a soft substance used as ointment or for lubrication. [Latin *unguentum* from *unguere* 'anoint']
unguessable /ʌn'gɛsəb(ə)l/ *adj.* that cannot be guessed or imagined.
unguiculate /ʌŋ'gwɪkjʊlət/ *adj.* **1** *Zool.* having one or more nails or claws. **2** *Bot.* (of petals) having an unguis. [modern Latin *unguiculatus* from *unguiculus*, diminutive of UNGUIS]
unguided /ʌn'gʌɪdɪd/ *adj.* not guided in a particular path or direction; left to take its own course.
unguis /'ʌŋgwɪs/ *n.* (*pl.* **ungues** /-wi:z/) **1** *Bot.* the narrow base of a petal. **2** *Zool.* a nail or claw. [Latin]
ungula /'ʌŋgjʊlə/ *n.* (*pl.* **ungulae** /-li:/) a hoof or claw. [Latin, diminutive of UNGUIS]
ungulate /'ʌŋgjʊlət, -leɪt/ *adj.* & *n.* ● *adj.* hoofed. ● *n.* a hoofed mammal. [Late Latin *ungulatus* from UNGULA]
unhallowed /ʌn'haləʊd/ *adj.* **1** not consecrated. **2** not sacred; unholy, wicked.
unhampered /ʌn'hampəd/ *adj.* not hampered.
unhand /ʌn'hand/ *v.tr. literary* or *joc.* **1** take one's hands off (a person). **2** release from one's grasp.
unhandsome /ʌn'hans(ə)m/ *adj.* not handsome.
unhandy /ʌn'handi/ *adj.* **1** not easy to handle or manage; awkward. **2** not skilful in using the hands. □ **unhandily** *adv.* **unhandiness** *n.*
unhang /ʌn'haŋ/ *v.tr.* (*past* and *past part.* **unhung**) take down from a hanging position.
unhappy /ʌn'hapi/ *adj.* (**unhappier, unhappiest**) **1** not happy, miserable. **2** unsuccessful, unfortunate. **3** causing misfortune. **4** disastrous. **5** inauspicious. □ **unhappily** *adv.* **unhappiness** *n.*
unharbour /ʌn'hɑ:bə/ *v.tr. Brit.* dislodge (a deer) from a covert.
unharmed /ʌn'hɑ:md/ *adj.* not harmed.
unharmful /ʌn'hɑ:mfʊl, -f(ə)l/ *adj.* not harmful.
unharmonious /ʌnhɑ:'məʊnɪəs/ *adj.* not harmonious.
unharness /ʌn'hɑ:nɪs/ *v.tr.* remove a harness from.
unhasp /ʌn'hɑ:sp/ *v.tr.* free from a hasp or catch; unfasten.
unhatched /ʌn'hatʃt/ *adj.* (of an egg etc.) not hatched.
unhealed /ʌn'hi:ld/ *adj.* not yet healed.
unhealthful /ʌn'hɛlθfʊl, -f(ə)l/ *adj.* harmful to health, unwholesome. □ **unhealthfulness** *n.*
unhealthy /ʌn'hɛlθi/ *adj.* (**unhealthier, unhealthiest**) **1** not in good health. **2 a** (of a place etc.) harmful to health. **b** unwholesome. **c** *slang* dangerous to life. □ **unhealthily** *adv.* **unhealthiness** *n.*
unheard /ʌn'hə:d/ *adj.* **1** not heard. **2** (usu. **unheard-of**) unprecedented, unknown.
unheated /ʌn'hi:tɪd/ *adj.* not heated.
unhedged /ʌn'hɛdʒd/ *adj.* **1** not bounded by a hedge. **2** (of a speculative investment) not hedged.
unheeded /ʌn'hi:dɪd/ *adj.* not heeded; disregarded.
unheedful /ʌn'hi:dfʊl, -f(ə)l/ *adj.* heedless; taking no notice.
unheeding /ʌn'hi:dɪŋ/ *adj.* not giving heed; heedless. □ **unheedingly** *adv.*
unhelpful /ʌn'hɛlpfʊl, -f(ə)l/ *adj.* not helpful. □ **unhelpfully** *adv.* **unhelpfulness** *n.*
unheralded /ʌn'hɛr(ə)ldɪd/ *adj.* not heralded; unannounced.
unheroic /ʌnhɪ'rəʊɪk/ *adj.* not heroic. □ **unheroically** *adv.*
unhesitating /ʌn'hɛzɪteɪtɪŋ/ *adj.* without hesitation. □ **unhesitatingly** *adv.* **unhesitatingness** *n.*
unhindered /ʌn'hɪndəd/ *adj.* not hindered.
unhinge /ʌn'hɪn(d)ʒ/ *v.tr.* **1** take (a door etc.) off its hinges. **2** (esp. as **unhinged** *adj.*) unsettle or disorder (a person's mind etc.), make (a person) crazy.
unhistoric /ʌnhɪ'stɒrɪk/ *adj.* not historic or historical.

unhistorical /ʌnhɪˈstɒrɪk(ə)l/ *adj.* not historical. □ **unhistorically** *adv.*

unhitch /ʌnˈhɪtʃ/ *v.tr.* **1** release from a hitched state. **2** unhook, unfasten.

unholy /ʌnˈhəʊli/ *adj.* (**unholier, unholiest**) **1** impious, profane, wicked. **2** *colloq.* dreadful, outrageous (*made an unholy row about it*). **3** not holy. □ **unholiness** *n.* [Old English *unhālig* (as UN-[1], HOLY)]

unhonoured /ʌnˈɒnəd/ *adj.* not honoured.

unhood /ʌnˈhʊd/ *v.tr.* remove the hood from (a falcon, horse, captive, etc.).

unhook /ʌnˈhʊk/ *v.tr.* **1** remove from a hook or hooks. **2** unfasten by releasing a hook or hooks.

unhoped /ʌnˈhəʊpt/ *adj.* (foll. by *for*) not hoped for or expected.

unhorse /ʌnˈhɔːs/ *v.tr.* **1** throw or drag from a horse. **2** (of a horse) throw (a rider). **3** dislodge, overthrow.

unhouse /ʌnˈhaʊz/ *v.tr.* deprive of shelter; turn out of a house.

unhuman /ʌnˈhjuːmən/ *adj.* **1** not human. **2** superhuman. **3** inhuman, brutal.

unhung[1] /ʌnˈhʌŋ/ *adj.* **1** not (yet) executed by hanging. **2** not hung up (for exhibition).

unhung[2] *past* and *past part.* of UNHANG.

unhurried /ʌnˈhʌrɪd/ *adj.* not hurried. □ **unhurriedly** *adv.*

unhurt /ʌnˈhəːt/ *adj.* not hurt.

unhusk /ʌnˈhʌsk/ *v.tr.* remove a husk or shell from.

unhygienic /ʌnhʌɪˈdʒiːnɪk/ *adj.* not hygienic. □ **unhygienically** *adv.*

unhyphenated /ʌnˈhʌɪfəneɪtɪd/ *adj.* not hyphenated.

uni /ˈjuːni/ *n.* (*pl.* **unis**) esp. *Austral. & NZ colloq.* a university. [abbreviation]

uni- /ˈjuːni/ *comb. form* one; having or consisting of one. [Latin from *unus* 'one']

Uniate /ˈjuːnɪeɪt/ *adj. & n.* ● *adj.* of or relating to any community of Christians in E. Europe or the Near East that acknowledges papal supremacy but retains its own liturgy etc. ● *n.* a member of such a community. [Russian *uniyat* from *uniya*, from Latin *unio* UNION]

uniaxial /juːnɪˈaksɪəl/ *adj.* having a single axis. □ **uniaxially** *adv.*

unicameral /juːnɪˈkam(ə)r(ə)l/ *adj.* with a single legislative chamber. [UNI- + Latin *camera* 'chamber']

UNICEF /ˈjuːnɪsɛf/ *abbr.* United Nations Children's (originally International Children's Emergency) Fund.

unicellular /juːnɪˈsɛljʊlə/ *adj.* (of an organism, organ, tissue, etc.) consisting of a single cell.

unicolour /ˈjuːnɪkʌlə/ *adj.* (also **unicoloured**) (*US* **-color, -colored**) of one colour.

unicorn /ˈjuːnɪkɔːn/ *n.* **1 a** a fabulous animal usually represented as a horse with a single straight horn projecting from its forehead. **b** a heraldic representation of this, with a twisted horn, a deer's feet, a goat's beard, and a lion's tail. **2 a** a pair of horses and a third horse in front. **b** an equipage with these. [Middle English via Old French *unicorne* from Latin *unicornis*, from UNI- + *cornu* 'horn', translation of Greek *monocerōs*]

unicuspid /juːnɪˈkʌspɪd/ *adj. & n.* ● *adj.* with one cusp. ● *n.* a unicuspid tooth.

unicycle /ˈjuːnɪsʌɪk(ə)l/ *n.* a single-wheeled cycle, esp. as used by acrobats. □ **unicyclist** *n.*

unidea'd /ʌnʌɪˈdɪəd/ *adj.* having no ideas.

unideal /ʌnʌɪˈdɪəl, -ˈdiːəl/ *adj.* not ideal.

unidentifiable /ʌnʌɪˈdɛntɪfʌɪəb(ə)l/ *adj.* unable to be identified.

unidentified /ʌnʌɪˈdɛntɪfʌɪd/ *adj.* not identified.

unidimensional /ˌjuːnɪdʌɪˈmɛnʃ(ə)n(ə)l/ *adj.* having (only) one dimension.

unidirectional /ˌjuːnɪdɪˈrɛkʃ(ə)n(ə)l, ˌjuːnɪdʌɪ-/ *adj.* having only one direction of motion, operation, etc. □ **unidirectionality** /-ˈnalɪti/ *n.* **unidirectionally** *adv.*

unification /ˌjuːnɪfɪˈkeɪʃ(ə)n/ *n.* the act or an instance of unifying; the state of being unified. □ **unificatory** *adj.*

Unification Church *n.* a religious organization founded in 1954 in Korea by Sun Myung Moon (cf. MOONIE).

unified field theory *n. Physics* a theory that seeks to explain all the field phenomena (e.g. gravitation and electromagnetism: see FIELD *n.* 9) formerly treated by separate theories.

uniflow /ˈjuːnɪfləʊ/ *adj.* involving flow (esp. of steam or waste gases) in one direction only.

uniform /ˈjuːnɪfɔːm/ *adj., n., & v.* ● *adj.* **1** not changing in form or character; the same, unvarying (*present a uniform appearance*; *all of uniform size and shape*). **2** conforming to the same standard, rules, or pattern. **3** constant in the course of time (*uniform acceleration*). **4** (of a tax, law, etc.) not varying with time or place. ● *n.* uniform distinctive clothing worn by members of the same body, e.g. by soldiers, police, and schoolchildren. ● *v.tr.* **1** clothe in uniform (*a uniformed officer*). **2** make uniform. □ **uniformly** *adv.* [French *uniforme* or Latin *uniformis* (as UNI-, FORM)]

uniformitarian /ˌjuːnɪfɔːmɪˈtɛːrɪən/ *adj. & n.* ● *adj.* of the theory that geological processes are always due to continuously and uniformly operating forces. ● *n.* a holder of this theory. □ **uniformitarianism** *n.*

uniformity /juːnɪˈfɔːmɪti/ *n.* (*pl.* **-ies**) **1** being uniform; sameness, consistency. **2** an instance of this. [Middle English from Old French *uniformité* or Late Latin *uniformitas* (as UNIFORM)]

unify /ˈjuːnɪfʌɪ/ *v.tr.* (**-ies, -ied**) (also *absol.*) reduce to unity or uniformity. □ **unifier** *n.* [French *unifier* or Late Latin *unificare* (as UNI-, -FY)]

unilateral /juːnɪˈlat(ə)r(ə)l/ *adj.* **1** performed by or affecting only one person or party (*unilateral disarmament*; *unilateral declaration of independence*). **2** one-sided. **3** (of the parking of vehicles) restricted to one side of the street. **4** (of leaves) all on the same side of the stem. **5** (of a line of descent) through ancestors of one sex only. □ **unilaterally** *adv.*

unilateralism /juːnɪˈlat(ə)r(ə)lɪz(ə)m/ *n.* **1** unilateral disarmament. **2** *US* the pursuit of a foreign policy without allies. □ **unilateralist** *n. & adj.*

unilingual /juːnɪˈlɪŋgw(ə)l/ *adj.* of or in only one language. □ **unilingually** *adv.*

uniliteral /juːnɪˈlɪt(ə)r(ə)l/ *adj.* consisting of one letter.

unilluminated /ʌnɪˈluːmɪneɪtɪd, ʌnɪˈljuː-/ *adj.* not illuminated.

unillustrated /ʌnˈɪləstreɪtɪd/ *adj.* (esp. of a book) without illustrations.

unilocular /juːnɪˈlɒkjʊlə/ *adj. Bot. & Zool.* single-chambered.

unimaginable /ʌnɪˈmadʒɪnəb(ə)l/ *adj.* impossible to imagine. □ **unimaginably** *adv.*

unimaginative /ʌnɪˈmadʒɪnətɪv/ *adj.* lacking imagination; stolid, dull. □ **unimaginatively** *adv.* **unimaginativeness** *n.*

unimpaired /ʌnɪmˈpɛːd/ *adj.* not impaired.

unimpassioned /ʌnɪmˈpaʃ(ə)nd/ *adj.* not impassioned.

unimpeachable /ʌnɪmˈpiːtʃəb(ə)l/ *adj.* giving no opportunity for censure; beyond reproach or question. □ **unimpeachably** *adv.*

unimpeded /ʌnɪmˈpiːdɪd/ *adj.* not impeded. □ **unimpededly** *adv.*

unimportance /ʌnɪmˈpɔːt(ə)ns/ *n.* lack of importance.

unimportant /ʌnɪmˈpɔːt(ə)nt/ *adj.* not important.

unimposing /ʌnɪmˈpəʊzɪŋ/ *adj.* unimpressive. □ **unimposingly** *adv.*

unimpressed /ʌnɪmˈprɛst/ *adj.* not impressed.

unimpressionable /ʌnɪmˈprɛʃ(ə)nəb(ə)l/ *adj.* not impressionable.

unimpressive /ʌnɪmˈprɛsɪv/ *adj.* not impressive. □ **unimpressively** *adv.* **unimpressiveness** *n.*

unimproved /ʌnɪm'pru:vd/ *adj.* **1** not made better. **2** not made use of. **3** (of land) not used for agriculture or building; not developed.

unincorporated /ʌnɪn'kɔ:pəreɪtɪd/ *adj.* **1** not incorporated or united. **2** not formed into a corporation.

uninfected /ʌnɪn'fɛktɪd/ *adj.* not infected.

uninflamed /ʌnɪn'fleɪmd/ *adj.* not inflamed.

uninflammable /ʌnɪn'flaməb(ə)l/ *adj.* not inflammable.

uninflected /ʌnɪn'flɛktɪd/ *adj.* **1** *Gram.* (of a language) not having inflections. **2** not changing or varying. **3** not bent or deflected.

uninfluenced /ʌn'ɪnflʊənst/ *adj.* (often foll. by *by*) not influenced.

uninfluential /ˌʌnɪnflʊ'ɛnʃ(ə)l/ *adj.* having little or no influence.

uninformative /ʌnɪn'fɔ:mətɪv/ *adj.* not informative; giving little information.

uninformed /ʌnɪn'fɔ:md/ *adj.* **1** not informed or instructed. **2** ignorant, uneducated.

uninhabitable /ʌnɪn'habɪtəb(ə)l/ *adj.* that cannot be inhabited. ▫ **uninhabitableness** *n.*

uninhabited /ʌnɪn'habɪtɪd/ *adj.* not inhabited.

uninhibited /ʌnɪn'hɪbɪtɪd/ *adj.* not inhibited. ▫ **uninhibitedly** *adv.* **uninhibitedness** *n.*

uninitiated /ʌnɪ'nɪʃɪeɪtɪd/ *adj.* not initiated; not admitted or instructed.

uninjured /ʌn'ɪndʒəd/ *adj.* not injured.

uninspired /ʌnɪn'spʌɪəd/ *adj.* **1** not inspired. **2** (of oratory etc.) commonplace.

uninspiring /ʌnɪn'spʌɪərɪŋ/ *adj.* not inspiring. ▫ **uninspiringly** *adv.*

uninstructed /ʌnɪn'strʌktɪd/ *adj.* not instructed or informed.

uninsulated /ʌn'ɪnsjʊleɪtɪd/ *adj.* not insulated.

uninsurable /ʌnɪn'ʃʊərəb(ə)l/ *adj.* that cannot be insured.

uninsured /ʌnɪn'ʃʊəd/ *adj.* not insured.

unintelligent /ʌnɪn'tɛlɪdʒ(ə)nt/ *adj.* not intelligent. ▫ **unintelligently** *adv.*

unintelligible /ʌnɪn'tɛlɪdʒɪb(ə)l/ *adj.* not intelligible. ▫ **unintelligibility** /-'bɪlɪti/ *n.* **unintelligibleness** *n.* **unintelligibly** *adv.*

unintended /ʌnɪn'tɛndɪd/ *adj.* not intended.

unintentional /ʌnɪn'tɛnʃ(ə)n(ə)l/ *adj.* not intentional. ▫ **unintentionally** *adv.*

uninterested /ʌn'ɪnt(ə)rɪstɪd/ *adj.* **1** not interested. **2** unconcerned, indifferent. ▫ **uninterestedly** *adv.* **uninterestedness** *n.*

uninteresting /ʌn'ɪnt(ə)rɪstɪŋ/ *adj.* not interesting. ▫ **uninterestingly** *adv.* **uninterestingness** *n.*

uninterpretable /ʌnɪn'tə:prɪtəb(ə)l/ *adj.* that cannot be interpreted.

uninterrupted /ˌʌnɪntə'rʌptɪd/ *adj.* not interrupted. ▫ **uninterruptedly** *adv.* **uninterruptedness** *n.*

uninterruptible /ˌʌnɪntə'rʌptɪb(ə)l/ *adj.* that cannot be interrupted.

uninucleate /ju:nɪ'nju:klɪeɪt, -ɪət/ *adj. Biol.* having a single nucleus.

uninventive /ʌnɪn'vɛntɪv/ *adj.* not inventive. ▫ **uninventively** *adv.* **uninventiveness** *n.*

uninvestigated /ʌnɪn'vɛstɪgeɪtɪd/ *adj.* not investigated.

uninvited /ʌnɪn'vʌɪtɪd/ *adj.* not invited. ▫ **uninvitedly** *adv.*

uninviting /ʌnɪn'vʌɪtɪŋ/ *adj.* not inviting, unattractive, repellent. ▫ **uninvitingly** *adv.*

uninvoked /ʌnɪn'vəʊkt/ *adj.* not invoked.

uninvolved /ʌnɪn'vɒlvd/ *adj.* not involved.

union /'ju:njən, -ɪən/ *n.* **1 a** the act or an instance of uniting; the state of being united. **b** (**the Union**) *hist.* the uniting of the English and Scottish crowns in 1603, of the English and Scottish parliaments in 1707, or of Great Britain and Ireland in 1801. **2 a** a whole resulting from the combination of parts or members. **b** (often **Union**) a political unit formed in this way, esp. the US, the UK, or South Africa. **c** (**the Union**) *US hist.* the body of northern states in the American Civil War. **3** = TRADE UNION. **4** marriage, matrimony. **5** concord, agreement (*lived together in perfect union*). **6** (**Union**) (in the UK) **a** a general social club and debating society at some universities and colleges. **b** the buildings or accommodation of such a society. **7** *Math.* the totality of the members of two or more sets. **8** *Brit. hist.* **a** two or more parishes consolidated for the administration of the poor laws. **b** (in full **union workhouse**) a workhouse erected by this. **9** *Brit.* an association of independent (esp. Congregational or Baptist) Churches for purposes of cooperation. **10** a part of a flag with a device emblematic of union, normally occupying the upper corner next to the staff. **11** a joint or coupling for pipes etc. **12** a fabric of mixed materials, e.g. cotton with linen or silk. [Middle English via Old French *union* or ecclesiastical Latin *unio* 'unity' from Latin *unus* 'one']

union-bashing *n. Brit. colloq.* active opposition to trade unions and their rights.

union catalogue *n.* a catalogue of the combined holdings of several libraries.

union down *adv.* (of the hoisting of a flag) with the union below as a signal of distress or mourning.

Union flag *n.* the national ensign of the United Kingdom formed by the union of the crosses of St George, St Andrew, and St Patrick.

unionist /'ju:njənɪst, -ɪən-/ *n.* **1 a** a member of a trade union. **b** an advocate of trade unions. **2** (usu. **Unionist**) an advocate of union, esp.: **a** a person opposed to the rupture of the parliamentary union between Great Britain and Northern Ireland (formerly between Great Britain and Ireland). **b** a member of a political party having these aims. **c** *hist.* a person who opposed secession during the American Civil War. ▫ **unionism** *n.* **unionistic** /-'nɪstɪk/ *adj.*

unionize /'ju:njənʌɪz, -ɪən-/ *v.tr.* & *intr.* (also **-ise**) bring or come under trade-union organization or rules. ▫ **unionization** /-'zeɪʃ(ə)n/ *n.*

un-ionized /ʌn'ʌɪənʌɪzd/ *adj.* (also **-ised**) not ionized.

Union Jack *n.* **1** = UNION FLAG. **2** (**union jack**) (in the US) a jack consisting of the union from the national flag.

union shop *n.* a shop, factory, trade, etc., in which employees must belong to a trade union or join one within an agreed time.

union suit *n. N. Amer.* a single undergarment for the body and legs; combinations.

union workhouse see UNION 8b.

uniparous /ju:'nɪp(ə)rəs/ *adj.* **1** producing one offspring at a birth. **2** *Bot.* having one axis or branch.

uniped /'ju:nɪpɛd/ *n.* & *adj.* ● *n.* a person having only one foot or leg. ● *adj.* one-footed, one-legged. [UNI- + *pes pedis* 'foot']

unipersonal /ju:nɪ'pə:s(ə)n(ə)l/ *adj.* (of the Deity) existing only as one person.

uniplanar /ju:nɪ'pleɪnə/ *adj.* lying in one plane.

unipod /'ju:nɪpɒd/ *n.* a one-legged support for a camera etc. [UNI-, on the pattern of TRIPOD]

unipolar /ju:nɪ'pəʊlə/ *adj.* **1** (esp. of an electric or magnetic apparatus) showing only one kind of polarity. **2** *Biol.* (of a nerve cell etc.) having only one axon or process. ▫ **unipolarity** /-'larɪti/ *n.*

unique /ju:'ni:k/ *adj.* & *n.* ● *adj.* **1** of which there is only one; unequalled; having no like, equal, or parallel (*his position was unique*; *this vase is considered unique*). **2** *disp.* unusual, remarkable (*a unique opportunity*). ● *n.* a unique thing or person. ▫ **uniquely** *adv.* **uniqueness** *n.* [French from Latin *unicus*, from *unus* 'one']

■ **Usage** In sense 1, *unique* should not be qualified by adverbs such as *absolutely*, *most*, and *quite* because it is an absolute concept. The use of *unique* in sense 2 is regarded as incorrect by some people.

unironed /ʌn'ʌɪənd/ *adj.* (esp. of clothing, linen, etc.) not ironed.

uniserial /ju:nɪ'sɪərɪəl/ *adj. Bot. & Zool.* arranged in one row.

unisex /'ju:nɪsɛks/ *adj.* (of clothing, hairstyles, etc.) designed to be suitable for both sexes.

unisexual /ju:nɪ'sɛksjʊəl, -ʃʊəl/ *adj.* **1 a** of one sex. **b** *Bot.* having stamens or pistils but not both. **2** unisex. ▫ **unisexuality** /-ʊ'alɪti/ *n.* **unisexually** *adv.*

UNISON /'ju:nɪs(ə)n/ *n.* (in the UK) a trade union formed in 1993 from an amalgamation of COHSE, NALGO, and NUPE.

unison /'ju:nɪs(ə)n/ *n. & adj.* ● *n.* **1** *Mus.* **a** coincidence in pitch of sounds or notes. **b** this regarded as an interval. **2** *Mus.* a combination of voices or instruments at the same pitch or at pitches differing by one or more octaves (*sang in unison*). **3** agreement, concord (*acted in perfect unison*). ● *adj. Mus.* coinciding in pitch. ▫ **unisonant** /jʊ'nɪs(ə)nənt/ *adj.* **unisonous** /jʊ'nɪs(ə)nəs/ *adj.* [Old French *unison* or Late Latin *unisonus* (as UNI-, *sonus* SOUND[1])]

unison string *n.* a string tuned in unison with another string and meant to be sounded with it.

unissued /ʌn'ɪʃ(j)u:d, ʌn'ɪsju:d/ *adj.* not issued.

unit /'ju:nɪt/ *n.* **1 a** an individual thing, person, or group regarded as single and complete, esp. for purposes of calculation. **b** each of the separate individuals or smallest groups into which a complex whole may be analysed (*the family as the unit of society*). **2** a quantity chosen as a standard in terms of which other quantities may be expressed (*unit of heat*; *SI unit*; *mass per unit volume*). **3** *Brit.* the smallest share in a unit trust. **4** a device with a specified function forming part of a complex mechanism. **5** a piece of furniture for fitting with others like it or made of complementary parts. **6** a group with a special function in an organization. **7** a group of buildings, wards, etc., in a hospital. **8** the number 'one'. [Latin *unus*, probably suggested by DIGIT]

Unitarian /ju:nɪ'tɛ:rɪən/ *n. & adj.* ● *n.* **1** a person who believes that God is not a Trinity but one person. **2** a member of a religious body maintaining this and advocating freedom from formal dogma or doctrine. ● *adj.* of or relating to the Unitarians. ▫ **Unitarianism** *n.* [modern Latin *unitarius* from Latin *unitas* UNITY]

unitary /'ju:nɪt(ə)ri/ *adj.* **1** of a unit or units. **2** marked by unity or uniformity. ▫ **unitarily** *adv.* **unitarity** /-'tarɪti/ *n.*

unit cell *n. Crystallog.* the smallest repeating group of atoms, ions, or molecules in a crystal.

unit cost *n.* the cost of producing one item of manufacture.

unite /ju:'nʌɪt/ *v.* **1** *tr. & intr.* join together; make or become one; combine. **2** *tr. & intr.* join together for a common purpose or action (*united in their struggle against injustice*). **3** *tr. & intr.* join in marriage. **4** *tr.* possess (qualities, features, etc.) in combination (*united anger with mercy*). **5** *intr. & tr.* form or cause to form a physical or chemical whole (*oil will not unite with water*). ▫ **unitedly** *adv.* **unitive** /'ju:nɪtɪv/ *adj.* **unitively** /'ju:nɪtɪvli/ *adv.* [Middle English from Latin *unire unit-*, from *unus* 'one']

United Brethren *n.pl. Eccl.* the Moravians.

United Kingdom *n.* Great Britain and Northern Ireland (until 1922, Great Britain and Ireland).

United Nations *n.pl.* (originally, in 1942) those united against the Axis powers in the Second World War; (later) a supranational peace-seeking organization of these and many other states.

United Provinces *n.pl. hist.* **1** the seven provinces united in 1579 and forming the basis of the republic of the Netherlands. **2** an Indian administrative division formed by the union of Agra and Oudh and called Uttar Pradesh since 1950.

United Reformed Church *n.* a Church formed in 1972 from the English Presbyterian and Congregational Churches.

United States *n.pl.* (in full **United States of America**) a federal republic of 50 states, mostly in N. America and including Alaska and Hawaii.

unitholder /'ju:nɪthəʊldə/ *n. Brit.* a person with a holding in a unit trust.

unit-linked *adj.* (of a policy, personal equity plan, etc.) whose return is linked to the rise and fall of the price of units bought in a choice of investment funds.

unit price *n.* the price charged for each unit of goods supplied.

unit trust *n. Brit.* an investment company investing combined contributions from many persons in various securities and paying them dividends in proportion to their holdings.

unity /'ju:nɪti/ *n.* (*pl.* **-ies**) **1** oneness; being one, single, or individual; being formed of parts that constitute a whole; due interconnection and coherence of parts (*disturbs the unity of the idea*; *the pictures lack unity*; *national unity*). **2** harmony or concord between persons etc. (*lived together in unity*). **3** a thing forming a complex whole (*a person regarded as a unity*). **4** *Math.* the number 'one', the factor that leaves unchanged the quantity on which it operates. **5** *Theatr.* each of the three dramatic principles requiring limitation of the supposed time of a drama to that occupied in acting it or to a single day (**unity of time**), use of one scene throughout (**unity of place**), and concentration on the development of a single plot (**unity of action**). [Middle English via Old French *unité* from Latin *unitas -tatis*, from *unus* 'one']

Univ. *abbr.* University.

univalent *adj. & n.* ● *adj.* **1** /ju:nɪ'veɪl(ə)nt/ *Chem.* = MONOVALENT. **2** /ju:'nɪvəl(ə)nt/ *Biol.* (of a chromosome) remaining unpaired during meiosis. ● *n.* /ju:'nɪvəl(ə)nt/ *Biol.* a univalent chromosome. [UNI- + *valent-*, pres. part. stem (as VALENCE[1])]

univalve /'ju:nɪvalv/ *adj. & n. Zool.* ● *adj.* having one valve or shell. ● *n.* a univalve mollusc, esp. a gastropod.

universal /ju:nɪ'və:s(ə)l/ *adj. & n.* ● *adj.* **1** of, belonging to, or done etc. by all persons or things in the world or in the class concerned; applicable to all cases (*the feeling was universal*; *met with universal approval*). **2** *Logic* (of a proposition) in which something is asserted of all of a class (opp. PARTICULAR *adj.* 5). ● *n.* **1** *Logic* a universal proposition. **2** *Philos.* **a** a term or concept of general application. **b** a nature or essence signified by a general term. ▫ **universality** /-'salɪti/ *n.* **universally** *adv.* [Middle English from Old French *universal* or Latin *universalis* (as UNIVERSE)]

universal agent *n.* an agent empowered to do all that can be delegated.

universal compass *n.* a pair of compasses with legs that may be extended for large circles.

universal donor *n.* a person of blood group O, who can in theory donate blood to recipients of any ABO blood group.

universalist /ju:nɪ'və:s(ə)lɪst/ *n. Theol.* **1** a person who holds that all mankind will eventually be saved. **2** a member of an organized body of Christians who hold this. ▫ **universalism** *n.* **universalistic** /-'lɪstɪk/ *adj.*

universalize /ju:nɪ'və:s(ə)lʌɪz/ *v.tr.* (also **-ise**) **1** apply universally; give a universal character to. **2** bring into universal use; make available for all. ▫ **universalizability** /-zə'bɪlɪti/ *n.* **universalization** /-'zeɪʃ(ə)n/ *n.*

universal joint *n.* (also **universal coupling**) a coupling or joint which can transmit rotary power by a shaft at any selected angle.

universal language *n.* an artificial language intended for use by all nations.

universal recipient *n.* a person of blood group AB, who can in theory receive donated blood of any ABO blood group.

universal suffrage *n.* a suffrage extending to all adults with minor exceptions.

Universal Time *n.* (also **Universal Time Coordinated**) = GREENWICH MEAN TIME (abbr.: UT). Also called *Coordinated Universal Time, UTC.*

universe /ˈjuːnɪvəːs/ *n.* **1** all existing things; the whole creation; the cosmos. **2** all humankind. **3** *Statistics & Logic* all the objects under consideration. [French *univers* from Latin *universum*, neut. of *universus* 'combined into one, whole', from UNI- + *versus*, past part. of *vertere* 'turn']

universe of discourse *n. Logic* = UNIVERSE 3.

university /juːnɪˈvəːsɪti/ *n.* (*pl.* **-ies**) **1** an educational institution designed for instruction, examination, or both, of students in many branches of advanced learning, conferring degrees in various faculties, and often embodying colleges and similar institutions. **2** the members of this collectively. **3** *Brit.* a team, crew, etc., representing a university. □ **at university** esp. *Brit.* studying at a university. [Middle English via Old French *université* from Latin *universitas -tatis* 'the whole' (world), in Late Latin 'college, guild' (as UNIVERSE)]

univocal /juːnɪˈvəʊk(ə)l, juːˈnɪvək(ə)l/ *adj. & n.* ● *adj.* (of a word etc.) having only one proper meaning. ● *n.* a univocal word. □ **univocality** /ˌjuːnɪvə(ʊ)ˈkalɪti/ *n.* **univocally** *adv.*

Unix /ˈjuːnɪks/ *n. Computing propr.* a multi-user operating system. [UNI- + respelling of -ICS, on the pattern of an earlier, less compact system called *Multics*]

unjoin /ʌnˈdʒɔɪn/ *v.tr.* detach from being joined; separate.

unjoined /ʌnˈdʒɔɪnd/ *adj.* not joined.

unjoint /ʌnˈdʒɔɪnt/ *v.tr.* **1** separate the joints of. **2** disunite.

unjust /ʌnˈdʒʌst/ *adj.* not just, contrary to justice or fairness. □ **unjustly** *adv.* **unjustness** *n.*

unjustifiable /ʌnˈdʒʌstɪfʌɪəb(ə)l/ *adj.* not justifiable. □ **unjustifiably** *adv.*

unjustified /ʌnˈdʒʌstɪfʌɪd/ *adj.* not justified.

unkempt /ʌnˈkɛm(p)t/ *adj.* **1** untidy, of neglected appearance. **2** uncombed, dishevelled. □ **unkemptly** *adv.* **unkemptness** *n.* [UN-[1] + archaic *kempt*, past part. of *kemb* 'comb', from Old English *cemban*]

unkept /ʌnˈkɛpt/ *adj.* **1** (of a promise, law, etc.) not observed; disregarded. **2** not tended; neglected.

unkillable /ʌnˈkɪləb(ə)l/ *adj.* that cannot be killed.

unkind /ʌnˈkʌɪnd/ *adj.* **1** not kind. **2** harsh, cruel. **3** unpleasant. □ **unkindly** *adv.* **unkindness** *n.*

unking /ʌnˈkɪŋ/ *v.tr.* **1** deprive of the position of king; dethrone. **2** deprive (a country) of a king.

unkink /ʌnˈkɪŋk/ *v.* **1** *tr.* remove the kinks from; straighten. **2** *intr.* lose kinks; become straight.

unknit /ʌnˈnɪt/ *v.tr.* (**unknitted, unknitting**) separate (things joined, knotted, or interlocked).

unknot /ʌnˈnɒt/ *v.tr.* (**unknotted, unknotting**) release the knot or knots of, untie.

unknowable /ʌnˈnəʊəb(ə)l/ *adj. & n.* ● *adj.* that cannot be known. ● *n.* **1** an unknowable thing. **2** (**the Unknowable**) the postulated absolute or ultimate reality. □ **unknowability** /-ˈbɪlɪti/ *n.*

unknowing /ʌnˈnəʊɪŋ/ *adj. & n.* ● *adj.* (often foll. by *of*) not knowing; ignorant, unconscious. ● *n.* ignorance (*cloud of unknowing*). □ **unknowingly** *adv.* **unknowingness** *n.*

unknown /ʌnˈnəʊn/ *adj. & n.* ● *adj.* (often foll. by *to*) not known, unfamiliar (*his purpose was unknown to me*). ● *n.* **1** an unknown thing or person. **2** an unknown quantity (*equation in two unknowns*). □ **unknown to** without the knowledge of (*did it unknown to me*). □ **unknownness** /ʌnˈnəʊnnɪs/ *n.*

unknown country see COUNTRY.

unknown quantity *n.* a person or thing whose nature, significance, etc., cannot be determined.

Unknown Soldier *n.* (also **Unknown Warrior**) an unidentified representative member of a country's armed forces killed in war, given burial with special honours in a national memorial.

unlabelled /ʌnˈleɪb(ə)ld/ *adj.* (*US* **unlabeled**) not labelled; without a label.

unlaboured /ʌnˈleɪbəd/ *adj.* (*US* **unlabored**) not laboured.

unlace /ʌnˈleɪs/ *v.tr.* **1** undo the lace or laces of. **2** unfasten or loosen in this way.

unlade /ʌnˈleɪd/ *v.tr.* **1** take the cargo out of (a ship). **2** discharge (a cargo etc.) from a ship.

unladen /ʌnˈleɪd(ə)n/ *adj.* not laden.

unladen weight *n.* the weight of a vehicle etc. when not loaded with goods etc.

unladylike /ʌnˈleɪdɪlʌɪk/ *adj.* not ladylike.

unlaid[1] /ʌnˈleɪd/ *adj.* not laid.

unlaid[2] *past* and *past part.* of UNLAY.

unlamented /ʌnləˈmɛntɪd/ *adj.* not lamented.

unlash /ʌnˈlaʃ/ *v.tr.* unfasten (a thing lashed down etc.).

unlatch /ʌnˈlatʃ/ *v.* **1** *tr.* release the latch of. **2** *tr. & intr.* open or be opened in this way.

unlawful /ʌnˈlɔːfʊl, -f(ə)l/ *adj.* not lawful; illegal, not permissible. □ **unlawfully** *adv.* **unlawfulness** *n.*

unlay /ʌnˈleɪ/ *v.tr.* (*past* and *past part.* **unlaid**) *Naut.* untwist (a rope). [UN-[2] + LAY[1]]

unleaded /ʌnˈlɛdɪd/ *adj.* **1** (of petrol etc.) without added lead. **2** not covered, weighted, or framed with lead. **3** *Printing* not spaced with leads.

unlearn /ʌnˈləːn/ *v.tr.* (*past* and *past part.* **unlearned** or **unlearnt**) **1** discard from one's memory. **2** rid oneself of (a habit, false information, etc.).

unlearned[1] /ʌnˈləːnd, -ˈləːnɪd/ *adj.* not well educated; untaught, ignorant. □ **unlearnedly** *adv.*

unlearned[2] /ʌnˈləːnd/ *adj.* (also **unlearnt** /-ˈləːnt/) that has not been learnt.

unleash /ʌnˈliːʃ/ *v.tr.* **1** release from a leash or restraint. **2** set free to engage in pursuit or attack.

unleavened /ʌnˈlɛv(ə)nd/ *adj.* not leavened; made without yeast or other raising agent.

unless /ʌnˈlɛs/ *conj.* if not; except when (*shall go unless I hear from you; always walked unless I had a bicycle*). [ON or IN + LESS, assimilated to UN-[1]]

unlettered /ʌnˈlɛtəd/ *adj.* **1** illiterate. **2** not well educated.

unliberated /ʌnˈlɪbəreɪtɪd/ *adj.* not liberated.

unlicensed /ʌnˈlʌɪs(ə)nst/ *adj.* not licensed, esp. *Brit.* without a licence to sell alcoholic drink.

unlighted /ʌnˈlʌɪtɪd/ *adj.* **1** not provided with light. **2** not set burning.

unlike /ʌnˈlʌɪk/ *adj. & prep.* ● *adj.* **1** not like; different from (*is unlike both his parents*). **2** uncharacteristic of (*such behaviour is unlike him*). **3** dissimilar, different. ● *prep.* differently from (*acts quite unlike anyone else*). □ **unlikeness** *n.* [perhaps from Old Norse *úlíkr*, Old English *ungelic*: see LIKE[1]]

■ **Usage** The use of *unlike* as a conjunction, e.g. *She was behaving unlike she'd ever behaved before*, is often condemned and is best avoided by using *as* instead.

unlikeable /ʌnˈlʌɪkəb(ə)l/ *adj.* (also **unlikable**) not easy to like; unpleasant.

unlikely /ʌnˈlʌɪkli/ *adj.* (**unlikelier, unlikeliest**) **1** improbable (*unlikely tale*). **2** (foll. by *to* + infin.) not to be expected to do something (*he's unlikely to be available*). **3** unpromising (*an unlikely candidate*). □ **unlikelihood** *n.* **unlikeliness** *n.*

unlimber /ʌnˈlɪmbə/ *v.tr.* **1** free (a gun) from its limber ready for use. **2** esp. *US* unpack or unfasten (something) ready for use.

unlimited /ʌnˈlɪmɪtɪd/ *adj.* without limit; unrestricted; very great in number or quantity (*has unlimited possibilities; an unlimited expanse of sea*). □ **unlimitedly** *adv.* **unlimitedness** *n.*

unlined[1] /ʌnˈlʌɪnd/ *adj.* **1** (of paper etc.) without lines. **2** (of a face etc.) without wrinkles.

unlined[2] /ʌnˈlʌɪnd/ *adj.* (of a garment etc.) without lining.

unlink /ʌnˈlɪŋk/ *v.tr.* **1** undo the links of (a chain etc.). **2** detach or set free by undoing or unfastening a link or chain.

unliquidated /ʌnˈlɪkwɪdeɪtɪd/ *adj.* not liquidated.

unlisted /ʌnˈlɪstɪd/ *adj.* not included in a published list, esp. of stock exchange prices or of telephone numbers.

unlit /ʌnˈlɪt/ *adj.* not lit.

unlivable /ʌnˈlɪvəb(ə)l/ *adj.* that cannot be lived or lived in.

unlived-in /ʌnˈlɪvdɪn/ *adj.* **1** appearing to be uninhabited. **2** unused by the inhabitants.

unload /ʌnˈləʊd/ *v.tr.* **1** (also *absol.*) remove a load from (a vehicle etc.). **2** remove (a load) from a vehicle etc. **3** remove the charge from (a firearm etc.). **4** *colloq.* get rid of. **5** (often foll. by *on*) *colloq.* **a** divulge (information). **b** (also *absol.*) give vent to (feelings). □ **unloader** *n.*

unlock /ʌnˈlɒk/ *v.tr.* **1 a** release the lock of (a door, box, etc.). **b** release or disclose by unlocking. **2** release thoughts, feelings, etc., from (one's mind etc.).

unlocked /ʌnˈlɒkt/ *adj.* not locked.

unlooked-for /ʌnˈlʊktfɔː/ *adj.* unexpected, unforeseen.

unloose /ʌnˈluːs/ *v.tr.* (also **unloosen**) loose; set free.

unlovable /ʌnˈlʌvəb(ə)l/ *adj.* (also **unloveable**) not lovable.

unloved /ʌnˈlʌvd/ *adj.* not loved.

unlovely /ʌnˈlʌvli/ *adj.* not attractive; unpleasant, ugly. □ **unloveliness** *n.*

unloving /ʌnˈlʌvɪŋ/ *adj.* not loving. □ **unlovingly** *adv.* **unlovingness** *n.*

unlucky /ʌnˈlʌki/ *adj.* (**unluckier**, **unluckiest**) **1** not fortunate or successful. **2** wretched. **3** bringing bad luck. **4** ill-judged. □ **unluckily** *adv.* **unluckiness** *n.*

unmade /ʌnˈmeɪd/ *adj.* **1** not made. **2** destroyed, annulled.

unmake /ʌnˈmeɪk/ *v.tr.* (*past* and *past part.* **unmade**) undo the making of; destroy, depose, annul.

unmalleable /ʌnˈmalɪəb(ə)l/ *adj.* not malleable.

unman /ʌnˈman/ *v.tr.* (**unmanned**, **unmanning**) **1** deprive of supposed manly qualities (e.g. self-control, courage); cause to weep etc., discourage. **2** deprive (a ship etc.) of men.

unmanageable /ʌnˈmanɪdʒəb(ə)l/ *adj.* not (easily) managed, manipulated, or kept under control. □ **unmanageableness** *n.* **unmanageably** *adv.*

unmanaged /ʌnˈmanɪdʒd/ *adj.* **1** not handled or directed in a controlled way. **2** (of land etc.) left wild; in a natural state.

unmanly /ʌnˈmanli/ *adj.* not manly. □ **unmanliness** *n.*

unmanned /ʌnˈmand/ *adj.* **1** not manned. **2** overcome by emotion etc.

unmannered /ʌnˈmanəd/ *adj.* lacking affectation; straightforward.

unmannerly /ʌnˈmanəli/ *adj.* **1** without good manners. **2** (of actions, speech, etc.) showing a lack of good manners. □ **unmannerliness** *n.*

unmapped /ʌnˈmapt/ *adj.* **1** not represented on a usu. geographical or chromosome map. **2** unexplored.

unmarked /ʌnˈmɑːkt/ *adj.* **1** not marked. **2** not noticed.

unmarketable /ʌnˈmɑːkɪtəb(ə)l/ *adj.* not marketable.

unmarried /ʌnˈmarɪd/ *adj.* not married; single.

unmask /ʌnˈmɑːsk/ *v.* **1** *tr.* **a** remove the mask from. **b** expose the true character of. **2** *intr.* remove one's mask. □ **unmasker** *n.*

unmatchable /ʌnˈmatʃəb(ə)l/ *adj.* that cannot be matched. □ **unmatchably** *adv.*

unmatched /ʌnˈmatʃt/ *adj.* not matched or equalled.

unmatured /ʌnməˈtʃʊəd/ *adj.* not yet matured.

unmeaning /ʌnˈmiːnɪŋ/ *adj.* having no meaning or significance; meaningless. □ **unmeaningly** *adv.* **unmeaningness** *n.*

unmeant /ʌnˈmɛnt/ *adj.* not meant or intended.

unmeasurable /ʌnˈmɛʒ(ə)rəb(ə)l/ *adj.* that cannot be measured. □ **unmeasurably** *adv.*

unmeasured /ʌnˈmɛʒəd/ *adj.* **1** not measured. **2** limitless.

unmediated /ʌnˈmiːdɪeɪtɪd/ *adj.* with no intervention; directly perceived.

unmelodious /ʌnmɪˈləʊdɪəs/ *adj.* not melodious; discordant. □ **unmelodiously** *adv.*

unmelted /ʌnˈmɛltɪd/ *adj.* not melted.

unmemorable /ʌnˈmɛm(ə)rəb(ə)l/ *adj.* not memorable. □ **unmemorably** *adv.*

unmentionable /ʌnˈmɛnʃ(ə)nəb(ə)l/ *adj.* & *n.* ● *adj.* that cannot (properly) be mentioned. ● *n.* **1** (in *pl.*) *joc.* **a** undergarments. **b** *archaic* trousers. **2** a person or thing not to be mentioned. □ **unmentionability** /-ˈbɪlɪti/ *n.* **unmentionableness** *n.* **unmentionably** *adv.*

unmentioned /ʌnˈmɛnʃ(ə)nd/ *adj.* not mentioned.

unmerchantable /ʌnˈməːtʃ(ə)ntəb(ə)l/ *adj.* not merchantable.

unmerciful /ʌnˈməːsɪfʊl, -f(ə)l/ *adj.* merciless. □ **unmercifully** *adv.* **unmercifulness** *n.*

unmerited /ʌnˈmɛrɪtɪd/ *adj.* not merited.

unmet /ʌnˈmɛt/ *adj.* (of a quota, demand, goal, etc.) not achieved or fulfilled.

unmetalled /ʌnˈmɛt(ə)ld/ *adj.* *Brit.* (of a road etc.) not surfaced with road metal.

unmethodical /ʌnmɪˈθɒdɪk(ə)l/ *adj.* not methodical. □ **unmethodically** *adv.*

unmetrical /ʌnˈmɛtrɪk(ə)l/ *adj.* not metrical.

unmilitary /ʌnˈmɪlɪt(ə)ri/ *adj.* not military.

unmindful /ʌnˈmʌɪn(d)fʊl, -f(ə)l/ *adj.* (often foll. by *of*) not mindful. □ **unmindfully** *adv.* **unmindfulness** *n.*

unmissable /ʌnˈmɪsəb(ə)l/ *adj.* that cannot or should not be missed.

unmistakable /ʌnmɪˈsteɪkəb(ə)l/ *adj.* (also **unmistakeable**) that cannot be mistaken or doubted, clear. □ **unmistakability** /-ˈbɪlɪti/ *n.* **unmistakableness** *n.* **unmistakably** *adv.*

unmistaken /ʌnmɪˈsteɪk(ə)n/ *adj.* not mistaken; right, correct.

unmitigated /ʌnˈmɪtɪgeɪtɪd/ *adj.* **1** not mitigated or modified. **2** absolute, unqualified (*an unmitigated disaster*). □ **unmitigatedly** *adv.*

unmixed /ʌnˈmɪkst/ *adj.* not mixed.

unmixed blessing *n.* a thing having advantages and no disadvantages.

unmodernized /ʌnˈmɒd(ə)nʌɪzd/ *adj.* (also **-ised**) (of a house etc.) not modernized; retaining the original features.

unmodified /ʌnˈmɒdɪfʌɪd/ *adj.* not modified.

unmodulated /ʌnˈmɒdjʊleɪtɪd/ *adj.* not modulated.

unmolested /ʌnməˈlɛstɪd/ *adj.* not molested.

unmoor /ʌnˈmʊə, -ˈmɔː/ *v.tr.* **1** (also *absol.*) release the moorings of (a vessel). **2** weigh all but one anchor of (a vessel).

unmoral /ʌnˈmɒr(ə)l/ *adj.* not concerned with morality (cf. IMMORAL). □ **unmorality** /ʌnməˈralɪti/ *n.*

unmotherly /ʌnˈmʌðəli/ *adj.* not motherly.

unmotivated /ʌnˈməʊtɪveɪtɪd/ *adj.* without motivation; without a motive.

unmounted /ʌnˈmaʊntɪd/ *adj.* not mounted.

unmourned /ʌnˈmɔːnd/ *adj.* not mourned.

unmoved /ʌnˈmuːvd/ *adj.* **1** not moved. **2** not changed in one's purpose. **3** not affected by emotion. □ **unmovable** *adj.* (also **unmoveable**).

unmoving /ʌnˈmuːvɪŋ/ *adj.* **1** not moving; still. **2** not emotive.

unmown /ʌnˈməʊn/ *adj.* not mown.

unmuffle /ʌnˈmʌf(ə)l/ *v.tr.* **1** remove a muffler from (a face, bell, etc.). **2** free of something that muffles or conceals.

unmurmuring /ʌnˈməːm(ə)rɪŋ/ *adj.* *literary* not complaining. □ **unmurmuringly** *adv.*

unmusical /ʌnˈmjuːzɪk(ə)l/ *adj.* **1** not pleasing to the ear. **2** unskilled in or indifferent to music. □ **unmusicality** /-ˈkalɪti/ *n.* **unmusically** *adv.* **unmusicalness** *n.*

unmutilated /ʌnˈmjuːtɪleɪtɪd/ *adj.* not mutilated.

unmuzzle /ʌn'mʌz(ə)l/ *v.tr.* **1** remove a muzzle from. **2** relieve of an obligation to remain silent.

unnail /ʌn'neɪl/ *v.tr.* unfasten by the removal of nails.

unnameable /ʌn'neɪməb(ə)l/ *adj.* that cannot be named, esp. too bad to be named.

unnamed /ʌn'neɪmd/ *adj.* not named.

unnatural /ʌn'natʃ(ə)r(ə)l/ *adj.* **1** contrary to nature or the usual course of nature; not normal. **2 a** lacking natural feelings. **b** extremely cruel or wicked. **3** artificial. **4** affected. ▫ **unnaturally** *adv.* **unnaturalness** *n.*

unnavigable /ʌn'navɪgəb(ə)l/ *adj.* not navigable. ▫ **unnavigability** /-'bɪlɪti/ *n.*

unnecessary /ʌn'nɛsəs(ə)ri/ *adj.* & *n.* ● *adj.* **1** not necessary. **2** more than is necessary (*with unnecessary care*). ● *n.* (*pl.* **-ies**) (usu. in *pl.*) an unnecessary thing. ▫ **unnecessarily** *adv.* **unnecessariness** *n.*

unneeded /ʌn'ni:dɪd/ *adj.* not needed.

unneighbourly /ʌn'neɪbəli/ *adj.* not neighbourly. ▫ **unneighbourliness** *n.*

unnerve /ʌn'nə:v/ *v.tr.* deprive of strength or resolution. ▫ **unnerving** *adj.* **unnervingly** *adv.*

unnil- /'ʌnnɪl/ *prefix Chem.* used to form names of recently discovered elements of atomic numbers 104-109 (cf. UN-[3]). [UN-[3] + NIL]

unnoticeable /ʌn'nəʊtɪsəb(ə)l/ *adj.* not easily seen or noticed. ▫ **unnoticeably** *adv.*

unnoticed /ʌn'nəʊtɪst/ *adj.* not noticed.

unnumbered /ʌn'nʌmbəd/ *adj.* **1** not marked with a number. **2** not counted. **3** countless.

UNO /'ju:nəʊ/ *abbr.* United Nations Organization.

unobjectionable /ʌnəb'dʒɛkʃ(ə)nəb(ə)l/ *adj.* not objectionable; acceptable. ▫ **unobjectionableness** *n.* **unobjectionably** *adv.*

unobliging /ʌnə'blʌɪdʒɪŋ/ *adj.* not obliging; unhelpful, uncooperative.

unobscured /ʌnəb'skjʊəd/ *adj.* not obscured.

unobservable /ʌnəb'zə:vəb(ə)l/ *adj.* not observable; imperceptible.

unobservant /ʌnəb'zə:v(ə)nt/ *adj.* not observant. ▫ **unobservantly** *adv.*

unobserved /ʌnəb'zə:vd/ *adj.* not observed. ▫ **unobservedly** /-vɪdli/ *adv.*

unobstructed /ʌnəb'strʌktɪd/ *adj.* not obstructed.

unobtainable /ʌnəb'teɪnəb(ə)l/ *adj.* that cannot be obtained.

unobtrusive /ʌnəb'tru:sɪv/ *adj.* not making oneself or itself noticed. ▫ **unobtrusively** *adv.* **unobtrusiveness** *n.*

unoccupied /ʌn'ɒkjʊpʌɪd/ *adj.* not occupied.

unoffending /ʌnə'fɛndɪŋ/ *adj.* not offending; harmless, innocent. ▫ **unoffended** *adj.*

unofficial /ʌnə'fɪʃ(ə)l/ *adj.* **1** not officially authorized or confirmed. **2** not characteristic of officials. ▫ **unofficially** *adv.*

unofficial strike *n.* esp. *Brit.* a strike not formally approved by the strikers' trade union.

unoiled /ʌn'ɔɪld/ *adj.* not oiled.

unopened /ʌn'əʊp(ə)nd/ *adj.* not opened.

unopposed /ʌnə'pəʊzd/ *adj.* not opposed.

unordained /ʌnɔ:'deɪnd/ *adj.* not ordained.

unordinary /ʌn'ɔ:dɪn(ə)ri, -d(ə)n-/ *adj.* not ordinary.

unorganized /ʌn'ɔ:g(ə)nʌɪzd/ *adj.* (also **-ised**) not organized (cf. DISORGANIZE).

unoriginal /ʌnə'rɪdʒɪn(ə)l/ *adj.* lacking originality; derivative. ▫ **unoriginality** /-'nalɪti/ *n.* **unoriginally** *adv.*

unornamental /ˌʌnɔ:nə'mɛnt(ə)l/ *adj.* not ornamental; plain.

unornamented /ʌn'ɔ:nəmɛntɪd/ *adj.* not ornamented.

unorthodox /ʌn'ɔ:θədɒks/ *adj.* not orthodox. ▫ **unorthodoxly** *adv.* **unorthodoxy** *n.*

unostentatious /ˌʌnɒstɛn'teɪʃəs/ *adj.* not ostentatious. ▫ **unostentatiously** *adv.* **unostentatiousness** *n.*

unowned /ʌn'əʊnd/ *adj.* **1** unacknowledged. **2** having no owner.

unpack /ʌn'pak/ *v.tr.* **1** (also *absol.*) open and remove the contents of (luggage, a package, etc.). **2** take (a thing) out from a package etc. ▫ **unpacker** *n.*

unpaged /ʌn'peɪdʒd/ *adj.* with pages not numbered.

unpaid /ʌn'peɪd/ *adj.* (of a debt or a person) not paid.

unpainted /ʌn'peɪntɪd/ *adj.* not painted.

unpaired /ʌn'pɛ:d/ *adj.* **1** not arranged in pairs. **2** not forming one of a pair.

unpalatable /ʌn'palətəb(ə)l/ *adj.* **1** not pleasant to taste. **2** (of an idea, suggestion, etc.) difficult to accept, distasteful. ▫ **unpalatability** /-'bɪlɪti/ *n.* **unpalatableness** *n.*

unparalleled /ʌn'parəlɛld/ *adj.* having no parallel or equal.

unpardonable /ʌn'pɑ:d(ə)nəb(ə)l/ *adj.* that cannot be pardoned. ▫ **unpardonableness** *n.* **unpardonably** *adv.*

unparliamentary /ˌʌnpɑ:lə'mɛnt(ə)ri/ *adj.* contrary to proper parliamentary usage.

unparliamentary language *n.* oaths or abuse.

unpasteurized /ʌn'pɑ:stʃərʌɪzd, -tjərʌɪzd, ʌn'pas-/ *adj.* (also **unpasteurised**) not pasteurized.

unpatented /ʌn'peɪt(ə)ntɪd, ʌn'pat-/ *adj.* not patented.

unpatriotic /ˌʌnpatrɪ'ɒtɪk, ˌʌnpeɪt-/ *adj.* not patriotic. ▫ **unpatriotically** *adv.*

unpatronizing /ʌn'patrənʌɪzɪŋ/ *adj.* (also **-ising**) not showing condescension.

unpaved /ʌn'peɪvd/ *adj.* not paved.

unpeeled /ʌn'pi:ld/ *adj.* not peeled.

unpeg /ʌn'pɛg/ *v.tr.* (**unpegged, unpegging**) **1** unfasten by the removal of pegs. **2** cease to maintain or stabilize (prices etc.).

unpeople *v.* & *n.* ● *v.tr.* /ʌn'pi:p(ə)l/ depopulate. ● *n.pl.* /'ʌnpi:p(ə)l/ unpersons.

unperceived /ʌnpə'si:vd/ *adj.* not perceived; unobserved.

unperceptive /ʌnpə'sɛptɪv/ *adj.* not perceptive. ▫ **unperceptively** *adv.* **unperceptiveness** *n.*

unperfected /ʌnpə'fɛktɪd/ *adj.* not perfected.

unperforated /ʌn'pə:fəreɪtɪd/ *adj.* not perforated.

unperformed /ʌnpə'fɔ:md/ *adj.* not performed.

unperfumed /ʌn'pə:fju:md/ *adj.* not perfumed.

unperson /'ʌnpə:s(ə)n/ *n.* a person whose name or existence is denied or ignored.

unpersuadable /ʌnpə'sweɪdəb(ə)l/ *adj.* not able to be persuaded; obstinate.

unpersuaded /ʌnpə'sweɪdɪd/ *adj.* not persuaded.

unpersuasive /ʌnpə'sweɪsɪv/ *adj.* not persuasive. ▫ **unpersuasively** *adv.*

unperturbed /ʌnpə'tə:bd/ *adj.* not perturbed. ▫ **unperturbedly** /-bɪdli/ *adv.*

unphilosophical /ˌʌnfɪlə'sɒfɪk(ə)l/ *adj.* (also **unphilosophic**) **1** not according to philosophical principles. **2** lacking philosophy. ▫ **unphilosophically** *adv.*

unphysiological /ˌʌnfɪzɪə'lɒdʒɪk(ə)l/ *adj.* (also **unphysiologic**) not in accordance with normal physiological functioning. ▫ **unphysiologically** *adv.*

unpick /ʌn'pɪk/ *v.tr.* undo the sewing of (stitches, a garment, etc.).

unpicked /ʌn'pɪkt/ *adj.* **1** not selected. **2** (of a flower) not plucked.

unpicturesque /ˌʌnpɪktʃə'rɛsk/ *adj.* not picturesque.

unpin /ʌn'pɪn/ *v.tr.* (**unpinned, unpinning**) **1** unfasten or detach by removing a pin or pins. **2** *Chess* release (a piece that has been pinned).

unpitied /ʌn'pɪtɪd/ *adj.* not pitied.

unpitying /ʌn'pɪtɪɪŋ/ *adj.* not pitying. ▫ **unpityingly** *adv.*

unplaceable /ʌn'pleɪsəb(ə)l/ *adj.* that cannot be placed or classified (*his accent was unplaceable*).

unplaced /ʌn'pleɪst/ *adj.* not placed, esp. not placed as one of the first three finishing in a race etc.

unplanned /ʌn'pland/ *adj.* not planned.

unplanted /ʌnˈplɑːntɪd/ *adj.* not planted.

unplausible /ʌnˈplɔːzɪb(ə)l/ *adj.* not plausible.

unplayable /ʌnˈpleɪəb(ə)l/ *adj.* **1** *Sport* (of a ball) that cannot be struck or returned. **2** that cannot be played. □ **unplayably** *adv.*

unpleasant /ʌnˈplɛz(ə)nt/ *adj.* not pleasant; displeasing; disagreeable. □ **unpleasantly** *adv.* **unpleasantness** *n.*

unpleasantry /ʌnˈplɛz(ə)ntri/ *n.* (*pl.* **-ies**) **1** unkindness. **2** (in *pl.*) **a** unpleasant comments. **b** unpleasant problems.

unpleasing /ʌnˈpliːzɪŋ/ *adj.* not pleasing. □ **unpleasingly** *adv.*

unploughed /ʌnˈplaʊd/ *adj.* (*N. Amer.* **unplowed**) not ploughed.

unplucked /ʌnˈplʌkt/ *adj.* not plucked.

unplug /ʌnˈplʌg/ *v.tr.* (**unplugged**, **unplugging**) **1** disconnect (an electrical device) by removing its plug from the socket. **2** unstop.

unplumbed /ʌnˈplʌmd/ *adj.* **1** not plumbed. **2** not fully explored or understood. □ **unplumbable** *adj.*

unpoetic /ʌnpəʊˈɛtɪk/ *adj.* (also **unpoetical**) not poetic.

unpointed /ʌnˈpɔɪntɪd/ *adj.* **1** having no point or points. **2 a** not punctuated. **b** (of written Hebrew etc.) without vowel points. **3** (of masonry or brickwork) not pointed.

unpolished /ʌnˈpɒlɪʃt/ *adj.* **1** not polished; rough. **2** without refinement; crude.

unpolitic /ʌnˈpɒlɪtɪk/ *adj.* impolitic, unwise.

unpolitical /ʌnpəˈlɪtɪk(ə)l/ *adj.* not concerned with politics. □ **unpolitically** *adv.*

unpolled /ʌnˈpəʊld/ *adj.* **1** not having voted at an election. **2** not included in an opinion poll.

unpolluted /ʌnpəˈluːtɪd/ *adj.* not polluted.

unpopular /ʌnˈpɒpjʊlə/ *adj.* not popular; not liked by the public or by people in general. □ **unpopularity** /-ˈlarɪti/ *n.* **unpopularly** *adv.*

unpopulated /ʌnˈpɒpjʊleɪtɪd/ *adj.* not populated.

unposed /ʌnˈpəʊzd/ *adj.* not in a posed position, esp. for a photograph.

unpossessed /ʌnpəˈzɛst/ *adj.* **1** (foll. by *of*) not in possession of. **2** not possessed.

unpowered /ʌnˈpaʊəd/ *adj.* (of a boat, vehicle, etc.) propelled other than by fuel.

unpractical /ʌnˈpraktɪk(ə)l/ *adj.* **1** not practical. **2** (of a person) not having practical skill. □ **unpracticality** /-ˈkalɪti/ *n.* **unpractically** *adv.*

unpractised /ʌnˈpraktɪst/ *adj.* (*US* **unpracticed**) **1** not experienced or skilled. **2** not put into practice.

unprecedented /ʌnˈprɛsɪdɛntɪd/ *adj.* **1** having no precedent; unparalleled. **2** novel. □ **unprecedentedly** *adv.*

unpredictable /ʌnprɪˈdɪktəb(ə)l/ *adj.* that cannot be predicted. □ **unpredictability** /-ˈbɪlɪti/ *n.* **unpredictably** *adv.*

unpredicted /ʌnprɪˈdɪktɪd/ *adj.* not predicted or foretold.

unprejudiced /ʌnˈprɛdʒʊdɪst/ *adj.* not prejudiced.

unpremeditated /ʌnpriːˈmɛdɪteɪtɪd/ *adj.* not previously thought over; not deliberately planned; unintentional. □ **unpremeditatedly** *adv.*

unprepared /ʌnprɪˈpɛːd/ *adj.* not prepared (in advance); not ready. □ **unpreparedly** *adv.* **unpreparedness** *n.*

unprepossessing /ˌʌnpriːpəˈzɛsɪŋ/ *adj.* not prepossessing; unattractive.

unprescribed /ʌnprɪˈskrʌɪbd/ *adj.* (esp. of drugs) not prescribed.

unpresentable /ʌnprɪˈzɛntəb(ə)l/ *adj.* not presentable.

unpressed /ʌnˈprɛst/ *adj.* not pressed, esp. (of clothing) unironed.

unpressurized /ʌnˈprɛʃərʌɪzd/ *adj.* (also **-ised**) not pressurized.

unpresuming /ʌnprɪˈzjuːmɪŋ/ *adj.* not presuming; modest.

unpresumptuous /ʌnprɪˈzʌm(p)tʃʊəs/ *adj.* not presumptuous.

unpretending /ʌnprɪˈtɛndɪŋ/ *adj.* unpretentious. □ **unpretendingly** *adv.* **unpretendingness** *n.*

unpretentious /ʌnprɪˈtɛnʃəs/ *adj.* not making a great display; simple, modest. □ **unpretentiously** *adv.* **unpretentiousness** *n.*

unpriced /ʌnˈprʌɪst/ *adj.* not having a price or prices fixed, marked, or stated.

unprimed /ʌnˈprʌɪmd/ *adj.* not primed.

unprincipled /ʌnˈprɪnsɪp(ə)ld/ *adj.* lacking or not based on good moral principles. □ **unprincipledness** *n.*

unprintable /ʌnˈprɪntəb(ə)l/ *adj.* that cannot be printed, esp. because too indecent or libellous or blasphemous. □ **unprintably** *adv.*

unprinted /ʌnˈprɪntɪd/ *adj.* not printed.

unprivileged /ʌnˈprɪvɪlɪdʒd/ *adj.* not privileged.

unproblematic /ˌʌnprɒbləˈmatɪk/ *adj.* causing no difficulty. □ **unproblematically** *adv.*

unprocessed /ʌnˈprəʊsɛst/ *adj.* (esp. of food, raw materials) not processed.

unproclaimed /ʌnprəˈkleɪmd/ *adj.* not proclaimed.

unprocurable /ʌnprəˈkjʊərəb(ə)l/ *adj.* that cannot be procured.

unproductive /ʌnprəˈdʌktɪv/ *adj.* not productive. □ **unproductively** *adv.* **unproductiveness** *n.*

unprofessional /ʌnprəˈfɛʃ(ə)n(ə)l/ *adj.* **1** contrary to professional standards of behaviour etc. **2** not belonging to a profession; amateur. □ **unprofessionally** *adv.*

unprofitable /ʌnˈprɒfɪtəb(ə)l/ *adj.* not profitable. □ **unprofitableness** *n.* **unprofitably** *adv.*

Unprofor /ˈʌnprəfɔː/ *abbr.* (also **UNPROFOR**) United Nations Protection Force.

unprogressive /ʌnprəˈgrɛsɪv/ *adj.* not progressive.

unpromising /ʌnˈprɒmɪsɪŋ/ *adj.* not likely to turn out well. □ **unpromisingly** *adv.*

unprompted /ʌnˈprɒm(p)tɪd/ *adj.* spontaneous.

unpronounceable /ʌnprəˈnaʊnsəb(ə)l/ *adj.* that cannot be pronounced. □ **unpronounceably** *adv.*

unpropitious /ʌnprəˈpɪʃəs/ *adj.* not propitious. □ **unpropitiously** *adv.*

unprosperous /ʌnˈprɒsp(ə)rəs/ *adj.* not prosperous. □ **unprosperously** *adv.*

unprotected /ʌnprəˈtɛktɪd/ *adj.* **1** not protected. **2** (of sexual intercourse) performed without a condom or other contraceptive. □ **unprotectedness** *n.*

unprotesting /ʌnprəˈtɛstɪŋ/ *adj.* not protesting. □ **unprotestingly** *adv.*

unprovable /ʌnˈpruːvəb(ə)l/ *adj.* that cannot be proved. □ **unprovability** /-ˈbɪlɪti/ *n.*

unproved /ʌnˈpruːvd/ *adj.* (also **unproven** /-v(ə)n/) not proved.

unprovided /ʌnprəˈvʌɪdɪd/ *adj.* (usu. foll. by *with*) not furnished, supplied, or equipped.

unprovoked /ʌnprəˈvəʊkt/ *adj.* (of a person or act) without provocation.

unpublicized /ʌnˈpʌblɪsʌɪzd/ *adj.* (also **-ised**) not publicized.

unpublished /ʌnˈpʌblɪʃt/ *adj.* not published. □ **unpublishable** *adj.*

unpunctual /ʌnˈpʌŋ(k)tʃʊəl, -tjʊəl/ *adj.* not punctual. □ **unpunctuality** /-tjʊˈalɪti/ *n.*

unpunctuated /ʌnˈpʌŋ(k)tʃʊeɪtɪd, -tjʊ-/ *adj.* not punctuated.

unpunishable /ʌnˈpʌnɪʃəb(ə)l/ *adj.* that cannot be punished.

unpunished /ʌnˈpʌnɪʃt/ *adj.* not punished.

unpurified /ʌnˈpjʊərɪfʌɪd/ *adj.* not purified.

unputdownable /ʌnpʊtˈdaʊnəb(ə)l/ *adj.* *colloq.* (of a book) so engrossing that one has to go on reading it.

unqualified /ʌnˈkwɒlɪfʌɪd/ *adj.* **1** not competent (*unqualified to give an answer*). **2** not legally or officially qualified (*an unqualified practitioner*). **3** not modified or restricted; complete (*unqualified assent; unqualified success*).

unquantifiable /ʌnˈkwɒntɪfʌɪəb(ə)l/ *adj.* impossible to quantify. □ **unquantified** /-ˈkwɒntɪfʌɪd/ *adj.*

unquenchable /ʌnˈkwɛn(t)ʃəb(ə)l/ *adj.* that cannot be quenched. □ **unquenchably** *adv.*

unquenched /ʌnˈkwɛn(t)ʃt/ *adj.* not quenched.

unquestionable /ʌnˈkwɛstʃ(ə)nəb(ə)l/ *adj.* that cannot be disputed or doubted. □ **unquestionability** /-ˈbɪlɪti/ *n.* **unquestionableness** *n.* **unquestionably** *adv.*

unquestioned /ʌnˈkwɛstʃ(ə)nd/ *adj.* **1** not disputed or doubted; definite, certain. **2** not interrogated.

unquestioning /ʌnˈkwɛstʃ(ə)nɪŋ/ *adj.* **1** asking no questions. **2** done etc. without asking questions. □ **unquestioningly** *adv.*

unquiet /ʌnˈkwʌɪət/ *adj.* **1** restless, agitated, stirring. **2** perturbed, anxious. □ **unquietly** *adv.* **unquietness** *n.*

unquotable /ʌnˈkwəʊtəb(ə)l/ *adj.* that cannot be quoted.

unquote /ʌnˈkwəʊt/ *v.tr.* (as *int.*) (in dictation, reading aloud, etc.) indicate the presence of closing quotation marks (cf. QUOTE *v.* 5b).

unquoted /ʌnˈkwəʊtɪd/ *adj.* not quoted, esp. on the Stock Exchange.

unravel /ʌnˈrav(ə)l/ *v.* (**unravelled**, **unravelling**; *US* **unraveled**, **unraveling**) **1** *tr.* cause to be no longer ravelled, tangled, or intertwined. **2** *tr.* probe and solve (a mystery etc.). **3** *tr.* undo (a fabric, esp. a knitted one). **4** *intr.* become disentangled or unknitted.

unreachable /ʌnˈriːtʃəb(ə)l/ *adj.* that cannot be reached. □ **unreachableness** *n.* **unreachably** *adv.*

unreached /ʌnˈriːtʃt/ *adj.* **1** not reached. **2** not yet evangelized.

unread /ʌnˈrɛd/ *adj.* **1** (of a book etc.) not read. **2** (of a person) not well read.

unreadable /ʌnˈriːdəb(ə)l/ *adj.* **1** too dull or too difficult to be worth reading. **2** illegible. □ **unreadability** /-ˈbɪlɪti/ *n.* **unreadably** *adv.*

unready[1] /ʌnˈrɛdi/ *adj.* **1** not ready. **2** not prompt in action. □ **unreadily** *adv.* **unreadiness** *n.*

unready[2] /ʌnˈrɛdi/ *adj. archaic* lacking good advice; rash (*Ethelred the Unready*). [UN-[1] + REDE, assimilated to UNREADY[1]]

unreal /ʌnˈrɪəl/ *adj.* **1** not real. **2** imaginary, illusory. **3** *N. Amer.* & *Austral. slang* incredible, amazing. □ **unreality** /-ɪˈalɪti/ *n.* **unreally** *adv.*

unrealism /ʌnˈrɪəlɪz(ə)m/ *n.* lack of realism.

unrealistic /ˌʌnrɪəˈlɪstɪk/ *adj.* not realistic. □ **unrealistically** *adv.*

unrealizable /ʌnˈrɪəlʌɪzəb(ə)l/ *adj.* (also **-isable**) that cannot be realized.

unrealized /ʌnˈrɪəlʌɪzd/ *adj.* (also **-ised**) not realized.

unreason /ʌnˈriːz(ə)n/ *n.* lack of reasonable thought or action. [Middle English, = injustice, from UN-[1] + REASON]

unreasonable /ʌnˈriːz(ə)nəb(ə)l/ *adj.* **1** going beyond the limits of what is reasonable or equitable (*unreasonable demands*). **2** not guided by or listening to reason. □ **unreasonableness** *n.* **unreasonably** *adv.*

unreasoned /ʌnˈriːz(ə)nd/ *adj.* not reasoned.

unreasoning /ʌnˈriːz(ə)nɪŋ/ *adj.* not reasoning. □ **unreasoningly** *adv.*

unreceptive /ʌnrɪˈsɛptɪv/ *adj.* not receptive.

unreciprocated /ʌnrɪˈsɪprəkeɪtɪd/ *adj.* not reciprocated.

unreckoned /ʌnˈrɛk(ə)nd/ *adj.* not calculated or taken into account.

unreclaimed /ʌnrɪˈkleɪmd/ *adj.* not reclaimed.

unrecognizable /ʌnˈrɛkəgnʌɪzəb(ə)l/ *adj.* (also **-isable**) that cannot be recognized. □ **unrecognizableness** *n.* **unrecognizably** *adv.*

unrecognized /ʌnˈrɛkəgnʌɪzd/ *adj.* (also **-ised**) not recognized.

unrecompensed /ʌnˈrɛkəmpɛnst/ *adj.* not recompensed.

unreconciled /ʌnˈrɛk(ə)nsʌɪld/ *adj.* not reconciled.

unreconstructed /ˌʌnriːkənˈstrʌktɪd/ *adj.* **1** not reconciled or converted to the current political orthodoxy. **2** not rebuilt.

unrecorded /ʌnrɪˈkɔːdɪd/ *adj.* not recorded. □ **unrecordable** *adj.*

unrectified /ʌnˈrɛktɪfʌɪd/ *adj.* not rectified.

unredeemable /ʌnrɪˈdiːməb(ə)l/ *adj.* that cannot be redeemed.

unredeemed /ʌnrɪˈdiːmd/ *adj.* not redeemed.

unredressed /ʌnrɪˈdrɛst/ *adj.* not redressed.

unreel /ʌnˈriːl/ *v.tr.* & *intr.* unwind from a reel.

unreeve /ʌnˈriːv/ *v.tr.* (*past* **unrove**) withdraw (a rope etc.) from being reeved.

unrefined /ʌnrɪˈfʌɪnd/ *adj.* not refined.

unreflecting /ʌnrɪˈflɛktɪŋ/ *adj.* not engaging in reflection or thought. □ **unreflectingly** *adv.* **unreflectingness** *n.* **unreflective** *adj.*

unreformed /ʌnrɪˈfɔːmd/ *adj.* not reformed.

unregarded /ʌnrɪˈgɑːdɪd/ *adj.* not regarded.

unregenerate /ʌnrɪˈdʒɛn(ə)rət/ *adj.* not regenerate; obstinately wrong or bad. □ **unregeneracy** *n.* **unregenerately** *adv.*

unregistered /ʌnˈrɛdʒɪstəd/ *adj.* not registered.

unregulated /ʌnˈrɛgjʊleɪtɪd/ *adj.* not regulated.

unrehearsed /ʌnrɪˈhəːst/ *adj.* not rehearsed.

unrelated /ʌnrɪˈleɪtɪd/ *adj.* not related. □ **unrelatedness** *n.*

unrelaxed /ʌnrɪˈlakst/ *adj.* not relaxed.

unreleased /ʌnrɪˈliːst/ *adj.* not released, esp. (of a recording, film, etc.) to the public.

unrelenting /ʌnrɪˈlɛntɪŋ/ *adj.* **1** not relenting or yielding. **2** unmerciful. **3** not abating or relaxing. □ **unrelentingly** *adv.* **unrelentingness** *n.*

unreliable /ʌnrɪˈlʌɪəb(ə)l/ *adj.* not reliable; erratic. □ **unreliability** /-ˈbɪlɪti/ *n.* **unreliableness** *n.* **unreliably** *adv.*

unrelieved /ʌnrɪˈliːvd/ *adj.* **1** lacking the relief given by contrast or variation. **2** not aided or assisted. □ **unrelievedly** *adv.*

unreligious /ʌnrɪˈlɪdʒəs/ *adj.* **1** not concerned with religion. **2** irreligious.

unremarkable /ʌnrɪˈmɑːkəb(ə)l/ *adj.* not remarkable; uninteresting. □ **unremarkably** *adv.*

unremarked /ʌnrɪˈmɑːkt/ *adj.* **1** not mentioned or remarked upon. **2** unnoticed.

unremembered /ʌnrɪˈmɛmbəd/ *adj.* not remembered; forgotten.

unremitting /ʌnrɪˈmɪtɪŋ/ *adj.* never relaxing or slackening, incessant. □ **unremittingly** *adv.* **unremittingness** *n.*

unremorseful /ʌnrɪˈmɔːsfʊl, -f(ə)l/ *adj.* lacking remorse. □ **unremorsefully** *adv.*

unremovable /ʌnrɪˈmuːvəb(ə)l/ *adj.* that cannot be removed.

unremunerative /ʌnrɪˈmjuːn(ə)rətɪv/ *adj.* bringing no, or not enough, profit or income. □ **unremuneratively** *adv.* **unremunerativeness** *n.*

unrenewable /ʌnrɪˈnjuːəb(ə)l/ *adj.* that cannot be renewed. □ **unrenewed** *adj.*

unrepealed /ʌnrɪˈpiːld/ *adj.* not repealed.

unrepeatable /ʌnrɪˈpiːtəb(ə)l/ *adj.* **1** that cannot be done, made, or said again. **2** too indecent to be said again. □ **unrepeatability** /-ˈbɪlɪti/ *n.*

unrepentant /ʌnrɪˈpɛnt(ə)nt/ *adj.* not repentant, impenitent. □ **unrepentantly** *adv.*

unreported /ʌnrɪˈpɔːtɪd/ *adj.* not reported.

unrepresentative /ˌʌnrɛprɪˈzɛntətɪv/ *adj.* not representative. □ **unrepresentativeness** *n.*

unrepresented /ˌʌnrɛprɪˈzɛntɪd/ *adj.* not represented.

unreproved /ʌnrɪˈpruːvd/ *adj.* not reproved.

unrequested /ʌnrɪˈkwɛstɪd/ *adj.* not requested or asked for.

unrequited /ʌnrɪˈkwʌɪtɪd/ *adj.* (of love etc.) not returned. □ **unrequitedly** *adv.* **unrequitedness** *n.*

unreserve /ʌnrɪˈzəːv/ *n.* lack of reserve; frankness.

unreserved /ʌnrɪˈzəːvd/ *adj.* **1** not reserved (*unreserved seats*). **2** without reservations; absolute (*unreserved* *confidence*). **3** free from reserve (*an unreserved nature*). □ **unreservedly** /-vɪdli/ *adv.* **unreservedness** *n.*

unresisted /ʌnrɪˈzɪstɪd/ *adj.* not resisted. □ **unresistedly** *adv.*

unresisting /ʌnrɪˈzɪstɪŋ/ *adj.* not resisting. □ **unresistingly** *adv.* **unresistingness** *n.*

unresolvable /ʌnrɪˈzɒlvəb(ə)l/ *adj.* (of a problem, conflict, etc.) that cannot be resolved.

unresolved /ʌnrɪˈzɒlvd/ *adj.* **1 a** uncertain how to act, irresolute. **b** uncertain in opinion, undecided. **2** (of questions etc.) undetermined, undecided, unsolved. **3** not broken up or dissolved. □ **unresolvedly** /-vɪdli/ *adv.* **unresolvedness** *n.*

unresponsive /ʌnrɪˈspɒnsɪv/ *adj.* not responsive. □ **unresponsively** *adv.* **unresponsiveness** *n.*

unrest /ʌnˈrɛst/ *n.* **1** lack of rest. **2** restlessness, disturbance, agitation.

unrested /ʌnˈrɛstɪd/ *adj.* not refreshed by rest.

unrestful /ʌnˈrɛs(t)fʊl, -f(ə)l/ *adj.* not restful. □ **unrestfully** *adv.*

unresting /ʌnˈrɛstɪŋ/ *adj.* not resting. □ **unrestingly** *adv.*

unrestored /ʌnrɪˈstɔːd/ *adj.* not restored.

unrestrained /ʌnrɪˈstreɪnd/ *adj.* not restrained. □ **unrestrainedly** /-nɪdli/ *adv.* **unrestrainedness** *n.*

unrestricted /ʌnrɪˈstrɪktɪd/ *adj.* not restricted. □ **unrestrictedly** *adv.* **unrestrictedness** *n.*

unreturned /ʌnrɪˈtəːnd/ *adj.* **1** not reciprocated or responded to. **2** not having returned or been returned.

unrevealed /ʌnrɪˈviːld/ *adj.* not revealed; secret. □ **unrevealing** *adj.*

unreversed /ʌnrɪˈvəːst/ *adj.* (esp. of a decision etc.) not reversed.

unrevised /ʌnrɪˈvʌɪzd/ *adj.* not revised; in an original form.

unrevoked /ʌnrɪˈvəʊkt/ *adj.* not revoked or annulled; still in force.

unrewarded /ʌnrɪˈwɔːdɪd/ *adj.* not rewarded.

unrewarding /ʌnrɪˈwɔːdɪŋ/ *adj.* not rewarding or satisfying.

unrhymed /ʌnˈrʌɪmd/ *adj.* not rhymed.

unrhythmical /ʌnˈrɪðmɪk(ə)l/ *adj.* not rhythmical. □ **unrhythmically** *adv.*

unridden /ʌnˈrɪd(ə)n/ *adj.* not ridden.

unriddle /ʌnˈrɪd(ə)l/ *v.tr.* solve or explain (a mystery etc.). □ **unriddler** *n.*

unrideable /ʌnˈrʌɪdəb(ə)l/ *adj.* (also **unridable**) that cannot be ridden.

unrig /ʌnˈrɪg/ *v.tr.* (**unrigged**, **unrigging**) **1** remove the rigging from (a ship). **2** *dial.* undress.

unrighteous /ʌnˈrʌɪtʃəs/ *adj.* not righteous; unjust, wicked, dishonest. □ **unrighteously** *adv.* **unrighteousness** *n.* [Old English *unrihtwīs* (as UN-[1], RIGHTEOUS)]

unrip /ʌnˈrɪp/ *v.tr.* (**unripped**, **unripping**) open by ripping.

unripe /ʌnˈrʌɪp/ *adj.* not ripe. □ **unripeness** *n.*

unrisen /ʌnˈrɪz(ə)n/ *adj.* that has not risen.

unrivalled /ʌnˈrʌɪv(ə)ld/ *adj.* (*US* **unrivaled**) having no equal; peerless.

unrivet /ʌnˈrɪvɪt/ *v.tr.* (**unriveted**, **unriveting**) **1** undo, unfasten, or detach by the removal of rivets. **2** loosen, relax, undo, detach.

unroadworthy /ʌnˈrəʊdwəːði/ *adj.* not roadworthy.

unrobe /ʌnˈrəʊb/ *v.tr.* & *intr.* **1** disrobe. **2** undress.

unroll /ʌnˈrəʊl/ *v.tr.* & *intr.* **1** open out from a rolled-up state. **2** display or be displayed in this form.

unromantic /ʌnrə(ʊ)ˈmantɪk/ *adj.* not romantic. □ **unromantically** *adv.*

unroof /ʌnˈruːf/ *v.tr.* remove the roof of.

unroofed /ʌnˈruːft/ *adj.* not provided with a roof.

unroot /ʌnˈruːt/ *v.tr.* **1** uproot. **2** eradicate.

unrope /ʌnˈrəʊp/ *v.* **1** *tr.* detach by undoing a rope. **2** *intr. Mountaineering* detach oneself from a rope.

unrounded /ʌnˈraʊndɪd/ *adj.* not rounded.

unrove *past* of UNREEVE.

unroyal /ʌnˈrɔɪəl/ *adj.* not royal.

unruffled /ʌnˈrʌf(ə)ld/ *adj.* **1** not agitated or disturbed; calm. **2** not physically ruffled.

unruled /ʌnˈruːld/ *adj.* **1** not ruled or governed. **2** not having ruled lines.

unruly /ʌnˈruːli/ *adj.* (**unrulier**, **unruliest**) not easily controlled or disciplined, disorderly. □ **unruliness** *n.* [Middle English, from UN-[1] + *ruly* from RULE]

UNRWA /ˈʌnrɑː/ *abbr.* United Nations Relief and Works Agency.

unsaddle /ʌnˈsad(ə)l/ *v.tr.* **1** remove the saddle from (a horse etc.). **2** dislodge from a saddle.

unsafe /ʌnˈseɪf/ *adj.* **1** not safe. **2** *Law* (of a verdict, conviction, etc.) likely to constitute a miscarriage of justice. □ **unsafely** *adv.* **unsafeness** *n.*

unsaid[1] /ʌnˈsɛd/ *adj.* not said or uttered.

unsaid[2] *past* and *past part.* of UNSAY.

unsalaried /ʌnˈsalərɪd/ *adj.* not salaried.

unsaleable /ʌnˈseɪləb(ə)l/ *adj.* (also **unsalable**) not saleable. □ **unsaleability** /-ˈbɪlɪti/ *n.*

unsalted /ʌnˈsɔːltɪd, ʌnˈsɒl-/ *adj.* not salted.

unsanctified /ʌnˈsaŋ(k)tɪfʌɪd/ *adj.* not sanctified.

unsanctioned /ʌnˈsaŋ(k)ʃ(ə)nd/ *adj.* not sanctioned.

unsanitary /ʌnˈsanɪt(ə)ri/ *adj.* not sanitary.

unsatisfactory /ˌʌnsatɪsˈfakt(ə)ri/ *adj.* **1** not satisfactory; poor, unacceptable. **2** *Law* (of a verdict, conviction, etc.) likely to constitute a miscarriage of justice. □ **unsatisfactorily** *adv.* **unsatisfactoriness** *n.*

unsatisfied /ʌnˈsatɪsfʌɪd/ *adj.* not satisfied. □ **unsatisfiedness** *n.*

unsatisfying /ʌnˈsatɪsfʌɪɪŋ/ *adj.* not satisfying. □ **unsatisfyingly** *adv.*

unsaturated /ʌnˈsatʃʊreɪtɪd, -tjʊr-/ *adj.* **1** *Chem.* (of a compound, esp. a fat or oil) having double or triple bonds in its molecule and therefore capable of further reaction. **2** not saturated. □ **unsaturation** /-ˈreɪʃ(ə)n/ *n.*

unsaved /ʌnˈseɪvd/ *adj.* not saved.

unsavoury /ʌnˈseɪv(ə)ri/ *adj.* (*US* **unsavory**) **1** disagreeable to the taste, smell, or feelings; disgusting. **2** disagreeable, unpleasant (*an unsavoury character*). **3** morally offensive. □ **unsavourily** *adv.* **unsavouriness** *n.*

unsay /ʌnˈseɪ/ *v.tr.* (*past* and *past part.* **unsaid**) retract (a statement).

unsayable /ʌnˈseɪəb(ə)l/ *adj.* that cannot be said.

unscalable /ʌnˈskeɪləb(ə)l/ *adj.* that cannot be scaled.

unscarred /ʌnˈskɑːd/ *adj.* not scarred or damaged.

unscathed /ʌnˈskeɪðd/ *adj.* without suffering any injury.

unscented /ʌnˈsɛntɪd/ *adj.* not scented.

unscheduled /ʌnˈʃɛdjuːld/ *adj.* not scheduled.

unscholarly /ʌnˈskɒləli/ *adj.* not scholarly. □ **unscholarliness** *n.*

unschooled /ʌnˈskuːld/ *adj.* **1** uneducated, untaught. **2** not sent to school. **3** untrained, undisciplined. **4** not made artificial by education.

unscientific /ˌʌnsʌɪənˈtɪfɪk/ *adj.* **1** not in accordance with scientific principles. **2** not familiar with science. □ **unscientifically** *adv.*

unscramble /ʌnˈskramb(ə)l/ *v.tr.* restore from a scrambled state, esp. interpret (a scrambled transmission etc.). □ **unscrambler** *n.*

unscreened /ʌnˈskriːnd/ *adj.* **1 a** (esp. of coal) not passed through a screen or sieve. **b** not investigated or checked, esp. for security or medical problems. **2** not provided with a screen. **3** (of a film or TV programme etc.) not shown on a screen.

unscrew /ʌnˈskruː/ *v.* **1** *tr.* & *intr.* unfasten or be unfastened by turning or removing a screw or screws or by twisting like a screw. **2** *tr.* loosen (a screw).

unscripted /ʌnˈskrɪptɪd/ *adj.* (of a speech etc.) delivered without a prepared script.

unscriptural /ʌnˈskrɪptʃ(ə)r(ə)l/ *adj.* against or not in accordance with Scripture. □ **unscripturally** *adv.*

unscrupulous /ʌnˈskruːpjʊləs/ *adj.* having no scruples, unprincipled. □ **unscrupulously** *adv.* **unscrupulousness** *n.*
unseal /ʌnˈsiːl/ *v.tr.* break the seal of; open (a letter, receptacle, etc.).
unsealed /ʌnˈsiːld/ *adj.* not sealed.
unsearchable /ʌnˈsəːtʃəb(ə)l/ *adj.* inscrutable. □ **unsearchableness** *n.* **unsearchably** *adv.*
unsearched /ʌnˈsəːtʃt/ *adj.* not searched.
unseasonable /ʌnˈsiːz(ə)nəb(ə)l/ *adj.* **1** not appropriate to the season. **2** untimely, inopportune. □ **unseasonableness** *n.* **unseasonably** *adv.*
unseasonal /ʌnˈsiːz(ə)n(ə)l/ *adj.* not typical of, or appropriate to, the time or season.
unseasoned /ʌnˈsiːz(ə)nd/ *adj.* **1** not flavoured with salt, herbs, etc. **2** (esp. of timber) not matured. **3** not habituated.
unseat /ʌnˈsiːt/ *v.tr.* **1** remove from a seat, esp. in an election. **2** dislodge from a seat, esp. on horseback.
unseaworthy /ʌnˈsiːwəːði/ *adj.* not seaworthy.
unsecured /ʌnsɪˈkjʊəd/ *adj.* not secured.
unseeable /ʌnˈsiːəb(ə)l/ *adj.* that cannot be seen.
unseeded /ʌnˈsiːdɪd/ *adj. Sport* (of a player) not seeded.
unseeing /ʌnˈsiːɪŋ/ *adj.* **1** unobservant. **2** blind. □ **unseeingly** *adv.*
unseemly /ʌnˈsiːmli/ *adj.* (**unseemlier, unseemliest**) **1** indecent. **2** unbecoming. □ **unseemliness** *n.*
unseen /ʌnˈsiːn/ *adj. & n.* ● *adj.* **1** not seen. **2** invisible. **3** esp. *Brit.* (of a translation) to be done without preparation. ● *n. Brit.* an unseen translation.
unsegregated /ʌnˈsɛgrɪgeɪtɪd/ *adj.* not segregated.
unselect /ʌnsɪˈlɛkt/ *adj.* not select.
unselective /ʌnsɪˈlɛktɪv/ *adj.* not selective.
unselfconscious /ʌnsɛlfˈkɒnʃəs/ *adj.* not self-conscious; natural. □ **unselfconsciously** *adv.* **unselfconsciousness** *n.*
unselfish /ʌnˈsɛlfɪʃ/ *adj.* mindful of others' interests. □ **unselfishly** *adv.* **unselfishness** *n.*
unsensational /ʌnsɛnˈseɪʃ(ə)n(ə)l/ *adj.* not sensational. □ **unsensationally** *adv.*
unsentimental /ˌʌnsɛntɪˈmɛnt(ə)l/ *adj.* not sentimental. □ **unsentimentally** *adv.*
unseparated /ʌnˈsɛpəreɪtɪd/ *adj.* not separated.
unserious /ʌnˈsɪərɪəs/ *adj.* not serious; light-hearted.
unserviceable /ʌnˈsəːvɪsəb(ə)l/ *adj.* not serviceable; unfit for use. □ **unserviceability** /-ˈbɪlɪti/ *n.*
unset /ʌnˈsɛt/ *adj.* not set.
unsettle /ʌnˈsɛt(ə)l/ *v.* **1** *tr.* disturb the settled state or arrangement of; discompose. **2** *tr.* derange. **3** *intr.* become unsettled. □ **unsettlement** *n.*
unsettled /ʌnˈsɛt(ə)ld/ *adj.* **1** not (yet) settled. **2** liable or open to change or further discussion. **3** (of a bill etc.) unpaid. □ **unsettledness** *n.*
unsewn /ʌnˈsəʊn/ *adj.* not sewn.
unsewn binding *n. Brit.* = PERFECT BINDING.
unsex /ʌnˈsɛks/ *v.tr.* deprive (a person) of the typical qualities of one or other (esp. the female) sex.
unsexed /ʌnˈsɛkst/ *adj.* having no sexual characteristics.
unsexy /ʌnˈsɛksi/ *adj.* (**unsexier, unsexiest**) not sexually attractive or stimulating; not appealing.
unshackle /ʌnˈʃak(ə)l/ *v.tr.* **1** release from shackles. **2** set free.
unshaded /ʌnˈʃeɪdɪd/ *adj.* not shaded.
unshakeable /ʌnˈʃeɪkəb(ə)l/ *adj.* (also **unshakable**) that cannot be shaken; firm, obstinate. □ **unshakeability** /-ˈbɪlɪti/ **unshakeably** *adv.*
unshaken /ʌnˈʃeɪk(ə)n/ *adj.* not shaken. □ **unshakenly** *adv.*
unshapely /ʌnˈʃeɪpli/ *adj.* not shapely. □ **unshapeliness** *n.*
unshared /ʌnˈʃɛːd/ *adj.* not shared.
unsharp /ʌnˈʃɑːp/ *adj. Photog.* not sharp. □ **unsharpness** *n.*
unshaved /ʌnˈʃeɪvd/ *adj.* not shaved.
unshaven /ʌnˈʃeɪv(ə)n/ *adj.* not shaved.
unsheathe /ʌnˈʃiːð/ *v.tr.* remove (a knife etc.) from a sheath.
unshed /ʌnˈʃɛd/ *adj.* not shed.
unshell /ʌnˈʃɛl/ *v.tr.* (usu. as **unshelled** *adj.*) extract from its shell.
unsheltered /ʌnˈʃɛltəd/ *adj.* not sheltered.
unshielded /ʌnˈʃiːldɪd/ *adj.* not shielded or protected.
unship /ʌnˈʃɪp/ *v.tr.* (**unshipped, unshipping**) **1** remove or discharge (a cargo or passenger) from a ship. **2** esp. *Naut.* remove (an object, esp. a mast or oar) from a fixed position.
unshockable /ʌnˈʃɒkəb(ə)l/ *adj.* that cannot be shocked. □ **unshockability** /-ˈbɪlɪti/ *n.* **unshockably** *adv.*
unshod /ʌnˈʃɒd/ *adj.* not wearing shoes.
unshorn /ʌnˈʃɔːn/ *adj.* not shorn.
unshrinkable /ʌnˈʃrɪŋkəb(ə)l/ *adj.* (of fabric etc.) not liable to shrink. □ **unshrinkability** /-ˈbɪlɪti/ *n.*
unshrinking /ʌnˈʃrɪŋkɪŋ/ *adj.* unhesitating, fearless. □ **unshrinkingly** *adv.*
unsighted /ʌnˈsʌɪtɪd/ *adj.* **1** not sighted or seen. **2** prevented from seeing, esp. by an obstruction.
unsightly /ʌnˈsʌɪtli/ *adj.* unpleasant to look at, ugly. □ **unsightliness** *n.*
unsigned /ʌnˈsʌɪnd/ *adj.* not signed.
unsinkable /ʌnˈsɪŋkəb(ə)l/ *adj.* unable to be sunk. □ **unsinkability** /-ˈbɪlɪti/ *n.*
unsized[1] /ʌnˈsʌɪzd/ *adj.* **1** not made to a size. **2** not sorted by size.
unsized[2] /ʌnˈsʌɪzd/ *adj.* not treated with size.
unskilful /ʌnˈskɪlfʊl, -f(ə)l/ *adj.* (*US* **unskillful**) not skilful. □ **unskilfully** *adv.* **unskilfulness** *n.*
unskilled /ʌnˈskɪld/ *adj.* lacking or not needing special skill or training.
unskimmed /ʌnˈskɪmd/ *adj.* (of milk) not skimmed.
unslakeable /ʌnˈsleɪkəb(ə)l/ *adj.* (also **unslakable**) that cannot be slaked or quenched.
unsleeping /ʌnˈsliːpɪŋ/ *adj.* not or never sleeping. □ **unsleepingly** *adv.*
unsliced /ʌnˈslʌɪst/ *adj.* (esp. of a loaf of bread when it is bought) not having been cut into slices.
unsling /ʌnˈslɪŋ/ *v.tr.* (*past* and *past part.* **unslung**) free from being slung or suspended.
unsmiling /ʌnˈsmʌɪlɪŋ/ *adj.* not smiling. □ **unsmilingly** *adv.* **unsmilingness** *n.*
unsmoked /ʌnˈsməʊkt/ *adj.* **1** not cured by smoking (*unsmoked bacon*). **2** not consumed by smoking (*an unsmoked cigar*).
unsnap /ʌnˈsnap/ *v.tr.* (**unsnapped, unsnapping**) undo, unfasten, or open with a snap.
unsnarl /ʌnˈsnɑːl/ *v.tr.* disentangle.
unsociable /ʌnˈsəʊʃəb(ə)l/ *adj.* not sociable, disliking the company of others. □ **unsociability** /-ˈbɪlɪti/ *n.* **unsociableness** *n.* **unsociably** *adv.*

■ **Usage** *Unsociable* is easily confused with *unsocial* and *antisocial* because there is some overlap in meanings. *Antisocial* is sometimes used to mean 'unsociable', and (mistakenly) to mean 'unsocial' (sense 2), while *unsocial* is sometimes used to mean 'antisocial'. However, these are not the words' primary meanings.

unsocial /ʌnˈsəʊʃ(ə)l/ *adj.* **1** not social; not suitable for, seeking, or conforming to society. **2** *Brit.* outside the normal working day (*unsocial hours*). **3** antisocial. □ **unsocially** *adv.*

■ **Usage** See Usage Notes at ANTISOCIAL and UNSOCIABLE.

unsocialist /ʌnˈsəʊʃəlɪst/ *adj.* not socialist.
unsoiled /ʌnˈsɔɪld/ *adj.* not soiled or dirtied.
unsold /ʌnˈsəʊld/ *adj.* not sold.
unsolder /ʌnˈsəʊldə, ʌnˈsɒl-/ *v.tr.* undo the soldering of.
unsoldierly /ʌnˈsəʊldʒəli/ *adj.* not soldierly.

unsolicited /ʌnsəˈlɪsɪtɪd/ *adj.* not asked for; given or done voluntarily. ▫ **unsolicitedly** *adv.*

unsolvable /ʌnˈsɒlvəb(ə)l/ *adj.* that cannot be solved, insoluble. ▫ **unsolvability** /-ˈbɪlɪti/ *n.* **unsolvableness** *n.*

unsolved /ʌnˈsɒlvd/ *adj.* not solved.

unsophisticated /ʌnsəˈfɪstɪkeɪtɪd/ *adj.* **1** artless, simple, natural, ingenuous. **2** not adulterated or corrupted; not artificial. ▫ **unsophisticatedly** *adv.* **unsophisticatedness** *n.* **unsophistication** /-ˈkeɪʃ(ə)n/ *n.*

unsorted /ʌnˈsɔːtɪd/ *adj.* not sorted.

unsought /ʌnˈsɔːt/ *adj.* **1** not searched out or sought for. **2** unasked; without being requested.

unsound /ʌnˈsaʊnd/ *adj.* **1** unhealthy, diseased. **2** rotten, weak. **3 a** ill-founded, fallacious. **b** unorthodox, heretical. **4** unreliable. **5** wicked. ▫ **of unsound mind** insane. ▫ **unsoundly** *adv.* **unsoundness** *n.*

unsounded[1] /ʌnˈsaʊndɪd/ *adj.* **1** not uttered or pronounced. **2** not made to sound.

unsounded[2] /ʌnˈsaʊndɪd/ *adj.* unfathomed.

unsoured /ʌnˈsaʊəd/ *adj.* not soured.

unsown /ʌnˈsəʊn/ *adj.* not sown.

unsparing /ʌnˈspɛːrɪŋ/ *adj.* **1** lavish, profuse. **2** merciless. ▫ **unsparingly** *adv.* **unsparingness** *n.*

unspeakable /ʌnˈspiːkəb(ə)l/ *adj.* **1** that cannot be expressed in words. **2** indescribably bad or objectionable. ▫ **unspeakableness** *n.* **unspeakably** *adv.*

unspeaking /ʌnˈspiːkɪŋ/ *adj. literary* not speaking; silent.

unspecialized /ʌnˈspɛʃ(ə)lʌɪzd/ *adj.* (also **-ised**) not specialized.

unspecific /ʌnspɪˈsɪfɪk/ *adj.* not specific; general, inexact.

unspecified /ʌnˈspɛsɪfʌɪd/ *adj.* not specified.

unspectacular /ʌnspɛkˈtakjʊlə/ *adj.* not spectacular; dull. ▫ **unspectacularly** *adv.*

unspent /ʌnˈspɛnt/ *adj.* **1** not expended or used. **2** not exhausted or used up.

unspilled /ʌnˈspɪld/ *adj.* not spilt.

unspilt /ʌnˈspɪlt/ *adj.* not spilt.

unspiritual /ʌnˈspɪrɪtʃʊəl, -tjʊəl/ *adj.* not spiritual; earthly, worldly. ▫ **unspirituality** /-ʊˈalɪti/ *n.* **unspiritually** *adv.*

unspoiled /ʌnˈspɔɪld/ *adj.* **1** unspoilt. **2** not plundered.

unspoilt /ʌnˈspɔɪlt/ *adj.* not spoilt.

unspoken /ʌnˈspəʊk(ə)n/ *adj.* **1** not expressed in speech. **2** not uttered as speech.

unsponsored /ʌnˈspɒnsəd/ *adj.* not supported or promoted by a sponsor.

unspool /ʌnˈspuːl/ *v.* **1** *tr.* & *intr.* unwind from or as if from a spool. **2 a** *tr.* screen (a film). **b** *intr.* (of a film) be screen.

unsporting /ʌnˈspɔːtɪŋ/ *adj.* not sportsmanlike; not fair or generous. ▫ **unsportingly** *adv.*

unsportsmanlike /ʌnˈspɔːtsmənlʌɪk/ *adj.* unsporting.

unspotted /ʌnˈspɒtɪd/ *adj.* **1 a** not marked with a spot or spots. **b** morally pure. **2** unnoticed.

unsprayed /ʌnˈspreɪd/ *adj.* not sprayed, esp. (of crops etc.) with a pesticide.

unsprung /ʌnˈsprʌŋ/ *adj.* not provided with a spring or springs; not resilient.

unstable /ʌnˈsteɪb(ə)l/ *adj.* (**unstabler**, **unstablest**) **1** not stable. **2** changeable. **3** showing a tendency to sudden mental or emotional changes. ▫ **unstableness** *n.* **unstably** *adv.*

unstable equilibrium *n.* a state in which a body when disturbed tends to move farther from equilibrium.

unstained /ʌnˈsteɪnd/ *adj.* not stained.

unstamped /ʌnˈstampt/ *adj.* **1** not marked by stamping. **2** not having a stamp affixed.

unstarched /ʌnˈstɑːtʃt/ *adj.* not starched.

unstated /ʌnˈsteɪtɪd/ *adj.* not stated or declared.

unstatesmanlike /ʌnˈsteɪtsmənlʌɪk/ *adj.* not statesmanlike.

unstatutable /ʌnˈstatjʊtəb(ə)l/ *adj.* contrary to a statute or statutes. ▫ **unstatutably** *adv.*

unsteadfast /ʌnˈstɛdfɑːst, -fəst/ *adj.* not steadfast.

unsteady /ʌnˈstɛdi/ *adj.* (**unsteadier**, **unsteadiest**) **1** not steady or firm. **2** changeable, fluctuating. **3** not uniform or regular. ▫ **unsteadily** *adv.* **unsteadiness** *n.*

unsterile /ʌnˈstɛrʌɪl/ *adj.* **1** (of a syringe etc.) not sterile. **2** productive.

unstick *v.* & *n.* ● *v.* /ʌnˈstɪk/ (*past* and *past part.* **unstuck**) **1** *tr.* separate (a thing stuck to another). **2** *Brit. Aeron. colloq.* **a** *intr.* take off. **b** *tr.* cause (an aircraft) to take off. ● *n.* /ˈʌnstɪk/ *Brit. Aeron. colloq.* the moment of take-off. ▫ **come unstuck** *colloq.* come to grief, fail.

unstinted /ʌnˈstɪntɪd/ *adj.* not stinted. ▫ **unstintedly** *adv.*

unstinting /ʌnˈstɪntɪŋ/ *adj.* ungrudging, lavish. ▫ **unstintingly** *adv.*

unstirred /ʌnˈstəːd/ *adj.* not stirred.

unstitch /ʌnˈstɪtʃ/ *v.tr.* undo the stitches of.

unstop /ʌnˈstɒp/ *v.tr.* (**unstopped**, **unstopping**) **1** free from obstruction. **2** remove the stopper from.

unstoppable /ʌnˈstɒpəb(ə)l/ *adj.* that cannot be stopped or prevented. ▫ **unstoppability** /-ˈbɪlɪti/ *n.* **unstoppably** *adv.*

unstopper /ʌnˈstɒpə/ *v.tr.* remove the stopper from.

unstrained /ʌnˈstreɪnd/ *adj.* **1** not subjected to straining or stretching. **2** not injured by overuse or excessive demands. **3** not forced or produced by effort. **4** not passed through a strainer.

unstrap /ʌnˈstrap/ *v.tr.* (**unstrapped**, **unstrapping**) undo the strap or straps of.

unstreamed /ʌnˈstriːmd/ *adj. Brit.* (of schoolchildren) not arranged in streams.

unstressed /ʌnˈstrɛst/ *adj.* **1** (of a word, syllable, etc.) not pronounced with stress. **2** not subjected to stress.

unstring /ʌnˈstrɪŋ/ *v.tr.* (*past* and *past part.* **unstrung**) **1** remove or relax the string or strings of (a bow, harp, etc.). **2** remove from a string. **3** (esp. as **unstrung** *adj.*) unnerve.

unstructured /ʌnˈstrʌktʃəd/ *adj.* **1** not structured. **2** informal.

unstuck *past* and *past part.* of UNSTICK.

unstudied /ʌnˈstʌdɪd/ *adj.* easy, natural, spontaneous. ▫ **unstudiedly** *adv.*

unstuffed /ʌnˈstʌft/ *adj.* not stuffed.

unstuffy /ʌnˈstʌfi/ *adj.* **1** informal, casual. **2** not stuffy.

unstylish /ʌnˈstʌɪlɪʃ/ *adj.* **1** lacking style. **2** unfashionable.

unsubdued /ʌnsəbˈdjuːd/ *adj.* not subdued.

unsubjugated /ʌnˈsʌbdʒʊgeɪtɪd/ *adj.* not subjugated.

unsubstantial /ʌnsəbˈstanʃ(ə)l/ *adj.* having little or no solidity, reality, or factual basis. ▫ **unsubstantiality** /-ʃɪˈalɪti/ *n.* **unsubstantially** *adv.*

unsubstantiated /ʌnsəbˈstanʃɪeɪtɪd/ *adj.* not substantiated.

unsubtle /ʌnˈsʌt(ə)l/ *adj.* not subtle; obvious, clumsy. ▫ **unsubtly** *adv.*

unsuccess /ʌnsəkˈsɛs/ *n.* **1** lack of success; failure. **2** an instance of this.

unsuccessful /ʌnsəkˈsɛsfʊl, -f(ə)l/ *adj.* not successful. ▫ **unsuccessfully** *adv.* **unsuccessfulness** *n.*

unsugared /ʌnˈʃʊgəd/ *adj.* not sugared.

unsuggestive /ʌnsəˈdʒɛstɪv/ *adj.* not suggestive.

unsuitable /ʌnˈsuːtəb(ə)l, -ˈsjuːt-/ *adj.* not suitable. ▫ **unsuitability** /-ˈbɪlɪti/ *n.* **unsuitableness** *n.* **unsuitably** *adv.*

unsuited /ʌnˈsuːtɪd, ʌnˈsjuːt-/ *adj.* **1** (usu. foll. by *for*) not fit for a purpose. **2** (usu. foll. by *to*) not adapted.

unsullied /ʌnˈsʌlɪd/ *adj.* not sullied.

unsummoned /ʌnˈsʌmənd/ *adj.* not summoned.

unsung /ʌnˈsʌŋ/ *adj.* **1** not celebrated in song; unknown. **2** not sung.

unsupervised /ʌn'suːpəvʌɪzd, ʌn'sjuː-/ *adj.* not supervised.

unsupportable /ʌnsə'pɔːtəb(ə)l/ *adj.* **1** that cannot be endured. **2** indefensible. □ **unsupportably** *adv.*

unsupported /ʌnsə'pɔːtɪd/ *adj.* not supported.

unsupportive /ʌnsə'pɔːtɪv/ *adj.* not giving support.

unsure /ʌn'ʃʊə/ *adj.* not sure. □ **unsurely** *adv.* **unsureness** *n.*

unsurfaced /ʌn'səːfɪst/ *adj.* (of a road etc.) not provided with a surface.

unsurpassable /ʌnsə'pɑːsəb(ə)l/ *adj.* that cannot be surpassed. □ **unsurpassably** *adv.*

unsurpassed /ʌnsə'pɑːst/ *adj.* not surpassed.

unsurprised /ʌnsə'prʌɪzd/ *adj.* not surprised.

unsurprising /ʌnsə'prʌɪzɪŋ/ *adj.* not surprising. □ **unsurprisingly** *adv.*

unsusceptible /ʌnsə'sɛptɪb(ə)l/ *adj.* not susceptible. □ **unsusceptibility** /-'bɪlɪti/ *n.*

unsuspected /ʌnsə'spɛktɪd/ *adj.* not suspected. □ **unsuspectedly** *adv.*

unsuspecting /ʌnsə'spɛktɪŋ/ *adj.* not suspecting. □ **unsuspectingly** *adv.* **unsuspectingness** *n.*

unsuspicious /ʌnsə'spɪʃəs/ *adj.* not suspicious. □ **unsuspiciously** *adv.* **unsuspiciousness** *n.*

unsustainable /ʌnsə'steɪnəb(ə)l/ *adj.* not sustainable. □ **unsustainably** *adv.*

unsustained /ʌnsə'steɪnd/ *adj.* not sustained.

unswathe /ʌn'sweɪð/ *v.tr.* free from being swathed.

unswayed /ʌn'sweɪd/ *adj.* uninfluenced, unaffected.

unsweetened /ʌn'swiːt(ə)nd/ *adj.* not sweetened.

unswept /ʌn'swɛpt/ *adj.* not swept.

unswerving /ʌn'swəːvɪŋ/ *adj.* **1** steady, constant. **2** not turning aside. □ **unswervingly** *adv.*

unsworn /ʌn'swɔːn/ *adj.* **1** (of a person) not subjected to or bound by an oath. **2** not confirmed by an oath.

unsymmetrical /ʌnsɪ'mɛtrɪk(ə)l/ *adj.* not symmetrical. □ **unsymmetrically** *adv.*

unsympathetic /ˌʌnsɪmpə'θɛtɪk/ *adj.* not sympathetic. □ **unsympathetically** *adv.*

unsystematic /ˌʌnsɪstə'matɪk/ *adj.* not systematic. □ **unsystematically** *adv.*

untack /ʌn'tak/ *v.tr.* detach, esp. by removing tacks.

untainted /ʌn'teɪntɪd/ *adj.* not tainted.

untalented /ʌn'taləntɪd/ *adj.* not talented.

untameable /ʌn'teɪməb(ə)l/ *adj.* (also **untamable**) that cannot be tamed.

untamed /ʌn'teɪmd/ *adj.* not tamed, wild.

untangle /ʌn'taŋg(ə)l/ *v.tr.* **1** free from a tangled state. **2** free from entanglement.

untanned /ʌn'tand/ *adj.* not tanned.

untapped /ʌn'tapt/ *adj.* not (yet) tapped or wired (*untapped resources*).

untarnished /ʌn'tɑːnɪʃt/ *adj.* not tarnished.

untasted /ʌn'teɪstɪd/ *adj.* not tasted.

untaught /ʌn'tɔːt/ *adj.* **1** not instructed by teaching; ignorant. **2** not acquired by teaching; natural, spontaneous.

untaxed /ʌn'takst/ *adj.* not required to pay or not attracting taxes.

unteach /ʌn'tiːtʃ/ *v.tr.* (*past* and *past part.* **untaught**) **1** cause (a person) to forget or discard previous knowledge. **2** remove from the mind (something known or taught) by different teaching.

unteachable /ʌn'tiːtʃəb(ə)l/ *adj.* **1** incapable of being instructed. **2** that cannot be imparted by teaching.

untearable /ʌn'tɛːrəb(ə)l/ *adj.* that cannot be torn.

untechnical /ʌn'tɛknɪk(ə)l/ *adj.* not technical.

untempered /ʌn'tɛmpəd/ *adj.* (of metal etc.) not brought to the proper hardness or consistency.

untenable /ʌn'tɛnəb(ə)l/ *adj.* (of an argument, position, etc.) not tenable; that cannot be defended. □ **untenability** /-'bɪlɪti/ *n.* **untenableness** *n.* **untenably** *adv.*

untended /ʌn'tɛndɪd/ *adj.* not tended; neglected.

untenured /ʌn'tɛnjəd/ *adj.* not tenured.

Untermensch /'ʊntəmɛntʃ, German 'ʊntərmɛnʃ/ *n.* (*pl.* ***-menschen*** /-mɛnʃən/) a person considered racially or socially inferior. [German]

untested /ʌn'tɛstɪd/ *adj.* not tested or proved. □ **untestable** /-təb(ə)l/ *adj.*

untether /ʌn'tɛðə/ *v.tr.* release (an animal) from a tether.

untethered /ʌn'tɛðəd/ *adj.* not tethered.

unthanked /ʌn'θaŋ(k)t/ *adj.* not thanked.

unthankful /ʌn'θaŋkfʊl, -f(ə)l/ *adj.* not thankful. □ **unthankfully** *adv.* **unthankfulness** *n.*

untheorized /ʌn'θɪərʌɪzd/ *adj.* (also **-ised**) not elaborated from a fundamental theory.

unthinkable /ʌn'θɪŋkəb(ə)l/ *adj.* **1** that cannot be imagined or grasped by the mind. **2** *colloq.* highly unlikely or undesirable. □ **unthinkability** /-'bɪlɪti/ *n.* **unthinkableness** *n.* **unthinkably** *adv.*

unthinking /ʌn'θɪŋkɪŋ/ *adj.* **1** thoughtless. **2** unintentional, inadvertent. □ **unthinkingly** *adv.* **unthinkingness** *n.*

unthought /ʌn'θɔːt/ *adj.* (often foll. by *of*) not thought of.

unthread /ʌn'θrɛd/ *v.tr.* **1** take the thread out of (a needle etc.). **2** find one's way out of (a maze).

unthreatening /ʌn'θrɛt(ə)nɪŋ/ *adj.* not threatening or aggressive; safe.

unthrifty /ʌn'θrɪfti/ *adj.* **1** wasteful, extravagant, prodigal. **2** not thriving or flourishing. □ **unthriftily** *adv.* **unthriftiness** *n.*

unthrone /ʌn'θrəʊn/ *v.tr.* dethrone.

untidy /ʌn'tʌɪdi/ *adj.* (**untidier**, **untidiest**) not neat or orderly. □ **untidily** *adv.* **untidiness** *n.*

untie /ʌn'tʌɪ/ *v.tr.* (*pres. part.* **untying**) **1** undo (a knot etc.). **2** unfasten the cords etc. of (a package etc.). **3** release from bonds or attachment. [Old English *untīgan* (as UN-², TIE)]

untied /ʌn'tʌɪd/ *adj.* not tied.

until /ən'tɪl/ *prep. & conj.* = TILL¹. [originally northern Middle English *untill*, from Old Norse *und* 'as far as' + TILL¹]

■ **Usage** *Until*, as opposed to *till*, is used especially at the beginning of a sentence and in formal style, e.g. *Until you told me, I had no idea; He resided there until his decease.*

untilled /ʌn'tɪld/ *adj.* not tilled.

untimely /ʌn'tʌɪmli/ *adj. & adv.* ● *adj.* **1** inopportune. **2** (of death) premature. ● *adv. archaic* **1** inopportunely. **2** prematurely. □ **untimeliness** *n.*

untinged /ʌn'tɪn(d)ʒd/ *adj.* not tinged.

untiring /ʌn'tʌɪərɪŋ/ *adj.* tireless. □ **untiringly** *adv.*

untitled /ʌn'tʌɪt(ə)ld/ *adj.* having no title.

unto /'ʌntʊ/ *prep. archaic* = TO *prep.* (in all senses except sense 2, introducing the infinitive) (*do unto others*; *faithful unto death*; *take unto oneself*). [Middle English from UNTIL, with TO replacing northern TILL¹]

untold /ʌn'təʊld/ *adj.* **1** not told. **2** not (able to be) counted or measured (*untold misery*). [Old English *untēald* (as UN-¹, TOLD)]

untouchable /ʌn'tʌtʃəb(ə)l/ *adj. & n.* ● *adj.* that may not or cannot be touched. ● *n.* a member of a hereditary Hindu group held to defile members of higher castes on contact. □ **untouchability** /-'bɪlɪti/ *n.* **untouchableness** *n.*

■ **Usage** The use of the term *untouchable* and the social restrictions accompanying it were declared illegal under the Indian constitution in 1949.

untouched /ʌn'tʌtʃt/ *adj.* **1** not touched. **2** not affected physically; not harmed, modified, used, or tasted. **3** not affected by emotion. **4** not discussed.

untoward /ʌntə'wɔːd, ʌn'təʊəd/ *adj.* **1** inconvenient, unlucky. **2** awkward. **3** perverse, refractory. **4** unseemly. □ **untowardly** *adv.* **untowardness** *n.*

untraceable /ʌn'treɪsəb(ə)l/ *adj.* that cannot be traced. □ **untraceably** *adv.*

untraced /ʌn'treɪst/ *adj.* not traced.
untracked /ʌn'trakt/ *adj.* **1** not marked with tracks from skis etc. **2** having no previously-trodden track; unexplored. **3** not traced or followed.
untraditional /ʌntrə'dɪʃ(ə)n(ə)l/ *adj.* not traditional; unusual.
untrained /ʌn'treɪnd/ *adj.* not trained. ▫ **untrainable** *adj.*
untrammelled /ʌn'tram(ə)ld/ *adj.* (*US* **untrammeled**) not trammelled, unhampered.
untransferable /ʌntrans'fə:rəb(ə)l, ʌn'transf(ə)r-, ʌntrɑ:ns-, -nz-/ *adj.* not transferable.
untransformed /ʌntrans'fɔ:md, ʌntrɑ:ns-, -nz-/ *adj.* that has not or has not been transformed.
untranslatable /ʌntrans'leɪtəb(ə)l, ʌntrɑ:ns-, -z'leɪt-/ *adj.* that cannot be translated. ▫ **untranslatability** /-'bɪlɪti/ *n.* **untranslatably** *adv.* **untranslated** /-tɪd/ *adj.*
untransportable /ʌntran'spɔ:təb(ə)l, ʌntrɑ:n-/ *adj.* that cannot be transported.
untravelled /ʌn'trav(ə)ld/ *adj.* (*US* **untraveled**) **1** that has not travelled. **2** that has not been travelled over or through.
untreatable /ʌn'tri:təb(ə)l/ *adj.* (of a disease etc.) that cannot be treated.
untreated /ʌn'tri:tɪd/ *adj.* not treated.
untrendy /ʌn'trɛndi/ *adj. colloq.* not trendy.
untried /ʌn'trʌɪd/ *adj.* **1** not tried or tested. **2** inexperienced. **3** not yet tried by a judge.
untrimmed /ʌn'trɪmd/ *adj.* **1** left uncut or in an irregular shape. **2** not adorned.
untrodden /ʌn'trɒd(ə)n/ *adj.* not trodden, stepped on, or traversed.
untroubled /ʌn'trʌb(ə)ld/ *adj.* not troubled; calm, tranquil.
untrue /ʌn'tru:/ *adj.* **1** not true, contrary to what is the fact. **2** (often foll. by *to*) not faithful or loyal. **3** deviating from an accepted standard. ▫ **untruly** *adv.* [Old English *untrēowe* etc. (as UN-[1], TRUE)]
untruss /ʌn'trʌs/ *v.tr.* unfasten (esp. a trussed fowl).
untrusting /ʌn'trʌstɪŋ/ *adj.* not trusting; suspicious.
untrustworthy /ʌn'trʌs(t)wə:ði/ *adj.* not trustworthy. ▫ **untrustworthiness** *n.*
untruth /ʌn'tru:θ/ *n.* (*pl.* /-'tru:ðz, -'tru:θs/) **1** the state of being untrue, falsehood. **2** a false statement (*told me an untruth*). [Old English *untrēowth* etc. (as UN-[1], TRUTH)]
untruthful /ʌn'tru:θfʊl, -f(ə)l/ *adj.* not truthful. ▫ **untruthfully** *adv.* **untruthfulness** *n.*
untuck /ʌn'tʌk/ *v.tr.* free (bedclothes etc.) from being tucked in or up.
untunable /ʌn'tju:nəb(ə)l/ *adj.* (of a piano etc.) that cannot be tuned.
untuned /ʌn'tju:nd/ *adj.* **1** not in tune, not made tuneful. **2** (of a radio receiver etc.) not tuned to any one frequency. **3** not in harmony or concord, disordered.
untuneful /ʌn'tju:nfʊl, -f(ə)l/ *adj.* not tuneful. ▫ **untunefully** *adv.* **untunefulness** *n.*
unturned /ʌn'tə:nd/ *adj.* **1** not turned over, round, away, etc. **2** not shaped by turning.
untutored /ʌn'tju:təd/ *adj.* uneducated, untaught.
untwine /ʌn'twʌɪn/ *v.tr. & intr.* untwist, unwind.
untwist /ʌn'twɪst/ *v.tr. & intr.* open from a twisted or spiralled state.
untying *pres. part.* of UNTIE.
untypical /ʌn'tɪpɪk(ə)l/ *adj.* not typical; unusual. ▫ **untypically** *adv.*
unusable /ʌn'ju:zəb(ə)l/ *adj.* not usable.
unused *adj.* **1** /ʌn'ju:zd/ **a** not in use. **b** never having been used. **2** /ʌn'ju:st/ (foll. by *to*) not accustomed.
unusual /ʌn'ju:ʒʊəl/ *adj.* **1** not usual. **2** exceptional, remarkable. ▫ **unusually** *adv.* **unusualness** *n.*
unutterable /ʌn'ʌt(ə)rəb(ə)l/ *adj.* inexpressible; beyond description (*unutterable torment*; *an unutterable fool*). ▫ **unutterably** *adv.*
unuttered /ʌn'ʌtəd/ *adj.* not uttered or expressed.
unvaccinated /ʌn'vaksɪneɪtɪd/ *adj.* not vaccinated.
unvalued /ʌn'valju:d/ *adj.* **1** not regarded as valuable. **2** not having been valued.
unvanquished /ʌn'vaŋkwɪʃt/ *adj.* not vanquished.
unvaried /ʌn'vɛ:rɪd/ *adj.* not varied.
unvarnished /ʌn'vɑ:nɪʃt/ *adj.* **1** not varnished. **2** (of a statement or person) plain and straightforward (*the unvarnished truth*).
unvarying /ʌn'vɛ:rɪɪŋ/ *adj.* not varying. ▫ **unvaryingly** *adv.* **unvaryingness** *n.*
unveil /ʌn'veɪl/ *v.* **1** *tr.* remove a veil from. **2** *tr.* remove a covering from (a statue, plaque, etc.) as part of the ceremony of the first public display. **3** *tr.* disclose, reveal, make publicly known. **4** *intr.* remove one's veil.
unventilated /ʌn'vɛntɪleɪtɪd/ *adj.* **1** not provided with a means of ventilation. **2** not discussed.
unverifiable /ʌn'vɛrɪfʌɪəb(ə)l/ *adj.* that cannot be verified.
unverified /ʌn'vɛrɪfʌɪd/ *adj.* not verified.
unversed /ʌn'və:st/ *adj.* (usu. foll. by *in*) not experienced or skilled.
unviable /ʌn'vʌɪəb(ə)l/ *adj.* not viable. ▫ **unviability** /-'bɪlɪti/ *n.*
unviolated /ʌn'vʌɪəleɪtɪd/ *adj.* not violated.
unvisited /ʌn'vɪzɪtɪd/ *adj.* not visited.
unvitiated /ʌn'vɪʃɪeɪtɪd/ *adj.* not vitiated.
unvoiced /ʌn'vɔɪst/ *adj.* **1** not spoken. **2** *Phonet.* not voiced.
unwaged /ʌn'weɪdʒd/ *adj.* not receiving a wage; out of work.
unwalled /ʌn'wɔ:ld/ *adj.* without enclosing walls.
unwanted /ʌn'wɒntɪd/ *adj.* not wanted.
unwarlike /ʌn'wɔ:lʌɪk/ *adj.* not warlike.
unwarmed /ʌn'wɔ:md/ *adj.* not warmed.
unwarned /ʌn'wɔ:nd/ *adj.* not warned or forewarned.
unwarrantable /ʌn'wɒr(ə)ntəb(ə)l/ *adj.* indefensible, unjustifiable. ▫ **unwarrantableness** *n.* **unwarrantably** *adv.*
unwarranted /ʌn'wɒr(ə)ntɪd/ *adj.* **1** unauthorized. **2** unjustified.
unwary /ʌn'wɛ:ri/ *adj.* **1** not cautious. **2** (often foll. by *of*) not aware of possible danger etc. ▫ **unwarily** *adv.* **unwariness** *n.*
unwashed /ʌn'wɒʃt/ *adj.* **1** not washed. **2** not usually washed or clean.
unwatchable /ʌn'wɒtʃəb(ə)l/ *adj.* disturbing or not interesting to watch.
unwatched /ʌn'wɒtʃt/ *adj.* not watched.
unwatchful /ʌn'wɒtʃfʊl, -f(ə)l/ *adj.* not watchful.
unwatered /ʌn'wɔ:təd/ *adj.* not watered.
unwavering /ʌn'weɪv(ə)rɪŋ/ *adj.* not wavering. ▫ **unwaveringly** *adv.*
unweaned /ʌn'wi:nd/ *adj.* not weaned.
unwearable /ʌn'wɛ:rəb(ə)l/ *adj.* that cannot be worn.
unwearied /ʌn'wɪərɪd/ *adj.* **1** not wearied or tired. **2** never becoming weary, indefatigable. **3** unremitting. ▫ **unweariedly** *adv.* **unweariedness** *n.*
unweary /ʌn'wɪəri/ *adj.* not weary.
unwearying /ʌn'wɪərɪɪŋ/ *adj.* **1** persistent. **2** not causing or producing weariness. ▫ **unwearyingly** *adv.*
unwed /ʌn'wɛd/ *adj.* unmarried.
unwedded /ʌn'wɛdɪd/ *adj.* unmarried. ▫ **unweddedness** *n.*
unweeded /ʌn'wi:dɪd/ *adj.* not cleared of weeds.
unweighed /ʌn'weɪd/ *adj.* **1** not considered; hasty. **2** (of goods) not weighed.
unweight /ʌn'weɪt/ *v.tr.* (usu. *absol.*) remove the weight from (esp. a ski, by ceasing to press). [back-formation from *unweighted*]
unwelcome /ʌn'wɛlkəm/ *adj.* not welcome or acceptable. ▫ **unwelcomely** *adv.* **unwelcomeness** *n.*
unwelcoming /ʌn'wɛlkəmɪŋ/ *adj.* **1** having an inhospitable atmosphere. **2** hostile; unfriendly.
unwell /ʌn'wɛl/ *adj.* **1** not in good health; (somewhat) ill. **2** indisposed.

unwept /ʌnˈwɛpt/ *adj.* **1** not wept for. **2** (of tears) not wept.

unwetted /ʌnˈwɛtɪd/ *adj.* not wetted.

unwhipped /ʌnˈwɪpt/ *adj.* **1** not punished by or as by whipping. **2** *Brit.* not subject to a party whip.

unwholesome /ʌnˈhəʊls(ə)m/ *adj.* **1** not promoting, or detrimental to, physical or moral health. **2** unhealthy, insalubrious. **3** unhealthy-looking. ▫ **unwholesomely** *adv.* **unwholesomeness** *n.*

unwieldy /ʌnˈwiːldi/ *adj.* (**unwieldier**, **unwieldiest**) cumbersome, clumsy, or hard to manage, owing to size, shape, or weight. ▫ **unwieldily** *adv.* **unwieldiness** *n.* [Middle English from UN-[1] + *wieldy* 'active' (now dialect), from WIELD]

unwilling /ʌnˈwɪlɪŋ/ *adj.* not willing or inclined; reluctant. ▫ **unwillingly** *adv.* **unwillingness** *n.* [Old English *unwillende* (as UN-[1], WILLING)]

unwind /ʌnˈwʌɪnd/ *v.* (*past* and *past part.* **unwound**) **1** **a** *tr.* draw out (a thing that has been wound). **b** *intr.* become drawn out after having been wound. **2** *intr.* & *tr. colloq.* relax.

unwinking /ʌnˈwɪŋkɪŋ/ *adj.* **1** not winking. **2** *Brit.* watchful, vigilant. ▫ **unwinkingly** *adv.*

unwinnable /ʌnˈwɪnəb(ə)l/ *adj.* that cannot be won.

unwisdom /ʌnˈwɪzdəm/ *n.* lack of wisdom, folly, imprudence. [Old English *unwīsdōm* (as UN-[1], WISDOM)]

unwise /ʌnˈwʌɪz/ *adj.* **1** foolish, imprudent. **2** injudicious. ▫ **unwisely** *adv.* [Old English *unwīs* (as UN-[1], WISE[1])]

unwished /ʌnˈwɪʃt/ *adj.* (usu. foll. by *for*) not wished for.

unwithered /ʌnˈwɪðəd/ *adj.* not withered; still vigorous or fresh.

unwitnessed /ʌnˈwɪtnɪst/ *adj.* not witnessed.

unwitting /ʌnˈwɪtɪŋ/ *adj.* **1** unaware of the state of the case (*an unwitting offender*). **2** unintentional. ▫ **unwittingly** *adv.* **unwittingness** *n.* [Old English *unwitende* (as UN-[1], WIT[2])]

unwomanly /ʌnˈwʊmənli/ *adj.* not womanly; not befitting a woman. ▫ **unwomanliness** *n.*

unwonted /ʌnˈwəʊntɪd/ *adj.* not customary or usual. ▫ **unwontedly** *adv.* **unwontedness** *n.*

unwooded /ʌnˈwʊdɪd/ *adj.* not wooded, treeless.

unworkable /ʌnˈwəːkəb(ə)l/ *adj.* not workable; impracticable. ▫ **unworkability** /-ˈbɪlɪti/ *n.* **unworkableness** *n.* **unworkably** *adv.*

unworked /ʌnˈwəːkt/ *adj.* **1** not wrought into shape. **2** not exploited or turned to account.

unworkmanlike /ʌnˈwəːkmənlʌɪk/ *adj.* badly done or made.

unworldly /ʌnˈwəːldli/ *adj.* **1** spiritually-minded. **2** spiritual. ▫ **unworldliness** *n.*

unworn /ʌnˈwɔːn/ *adj.* not worn or impaired by wear.

unworried /ʌnˈwʌrɪd/ *adj.* not worried; calm.

unworthy /ʌnˈwəːði/ *adj.* (**unworthier**, **unworthiest**) **1** (often foll. by *of*) not worthy or befitting the character of a person etc. **2** discreditable, unseemly. **3** contemptible, base. ▫ **unworthily** *adv.* **unworthiness** *n.*

unwound[1] /ʌnˈwaʊnd/ *adj.* not wound or wound up.

unwound[2] *past* and *past part.* of UNWIND.

unwounded /ʌnˈwuːndɪd/ *adj.* not wounded, unhurt.

unwoven /ʌnˈwəʊv(ə)n/ *adj.* not woven.

unwrap /ʌnˈrap/ *v.* (**unwrapped**, **unwrapping**) **1** *tr.* remove the wrapping from. **2** *tr.* open or unfold. **3** *intr.* become unwrapped.

unwrinkled /ʌnˈrɪŋk(ə)ld/ *adj.* free from wrinkles, smooth.

unwritable /ʌnˈrʌɪtəb(ə)l/ *adj.* that cannot be written.

unwritten /ʌnˈrɪt(ə)n/ *adj.* **1** not written. **2** (of a law etc.) resting originally on custom or judicial decision, not on statute.

unwrought /ʌnˈrɔːt/ *adj.* (of metals) not hammered into shape or worked into a finished condition.

unyielding /ʌnˈjiːldɪŋ/ *adj.* **1** not yielding to pressure etc. **2** firm, obstinate. ▫ **unyieldingly** *adv.* **unyieldingness** *n.*

unyoke /ʌnˈjəʊk/ *v.* **1** *tr.* release from a yoke. **2** *intr.* cease work.

unzip /ʌnˈzɪp/ *v.tr.* (**unzipped**, **unzipping**) unfasten the zip of.

up /ʌp/ *adv.*, *prep.*, *adj.*, *n.*, & *v.* ● *adv.* **1** at, in, or towards a higher place or position (*jumped up in the air*; *what are they doing up there?*). **2** to or in a place regarded as higher, esp.: **a** northwards (*up in Scotland*). **b** *Brit.* towards a major city or a university (*went up to London*). **3** *colloq.* ahead etc. as indicated (*went up front*). **4** **a** to or in an erect position or condition (*stood it up*). **b** to or in a prepared or required position (*wound up the watch*). **c** in or into a condition of efficiency, activity, or progress (*stirred up trouble*; *the house is up for sale*; *the hunt is up*). **d** *Baseball* at bat. **5** in a stronger or winning position or condition (*our team was three goals up*; *am £10 up on the transaction*). **6** (of a computer) running and available for use. **7** to the place or time in question or where the speaker etc. is (*a child came up to me*; *went straight up to the door*; *has been fine up till now*). **8** at or to a higher price or value (*our costs are up*; *shares are up*). **9** **a** completely or effectually (*burn up*; *eat up*; *tear up*; *use up*). **b** more loudly or clearly (*speak up*). **10** in a state of completion; denoting the end of availability, supply, etc. (*time is up*). **11** into a compact, accumulated, or secure state (*pack up*; *save up*; *tie up*). **12** out of bed (*are you up yet?*). **13** (of the sun etc.) having risen. **14** happening, esp. unusually or unexpectedly (*something is up*). **15** taught or informed (*is well up in French*). **16** (usu. foll. by *before*) appearing for trial etc. (*was up before the magistrate*). **17** *Brit.* (of a road etc.) being repaired. **18** (of a jockey) in the saddle. **19** towards the source of a river. **20** inland. **21** (of the points etc. in a game): **a** registered on the scoreboard. **b** forming the total score for the time being. **22** upstairs, esp. to bed (*are you going up yet?*). **23** (of a theatre curtain) raised etc. to reveal the stage. **24** (as *int.*) get up. **25** (of a ship's helm) with rudder to leeward. **26** in rebellion. ● *prep.* **1** upwards along, through, or into (*climbed up the ladder*). **2** from the bottom to the top of. **3** along (*walked up the road*). **4** **a** at or in a higher part of (*is situated up the street*). **b** towards the source of (a river). ● *adj.* **1** directed upwards. **2** *Brit.* of travel towards a capital or centre (*the up train*; *the up platform*). **3** *Brit.* (of beer etc.) effervescent, frothy. ● *n.* a spell of good fortune. ● *v.* (**upped**, **upping**) **1** *intr. colloq.* start up; begin abruptly to say or do something (*upped and hit him*). **2** *intr.* (foll. by *with*) raise; pick up (*upped with his stick*). **3** *tr.* increase or raise, esp. abruptly (*upped all their prices*). ▫ **be all up with** (with *it* as subject) be disastrous or hopeless for (a person). **on the up and up** *colloq.* **1** *Brit.* steadily improving. **2** esp. *N. Amer.* honest(ly); on the level. **something is up** *colloq.* something unusual or undesirable is afoot or happening. **up against** **1** close to. **2** in or into contact with. **3** *colloq.* confronted with (*up against a problem*). **up against it** *colloq.* in great difficulties. **up and about** (or **doing**) having risen from bed; active. **up and down** **1** to and fro (along). **2** in every direction. **3** *colloq.* in varying health or spirits. **up for** available for or being considered for (office etc.). **up hill and down dale** up and down hills, or confronting many obstacles, on an arduous journey or in the fulfilment of an arduous task. **up in arms** see ARM[2]. **up on** informed about (a matter or subject). **up the pole** see POLE[1]. **up the spout** see SPOUT. **up sticks** see STICK[1]. **up to** **1** until (*up to the present*). **2** not more than (*you can have up to five*). **3** less than or equal to (*sums up to £10*). **4** incumbent on (*it is up to you to say*). **5** capable of or fit for (*am not up to a long walk*). **6** occupied or busy with (*what have you been up to?*). **up to the mark** see MARK[1]. **up to snuff** see SNUFF[2]. **up to one's tricks** see TRICK. **up to a person's tricks** see TRICK. **up with** *int.* expressing support for a stated person or thing. **up yours** *coarse slang* expressing contemptuous defiance or rejection. **what's up?** *colloq.* **1** what is going on? **2** what is the matter? [Old English *up(p)*, *uppe*, related to Old High German *ūf*, from Germanic]

up- /ʌp/ *prefix* in senses of UP, added: **1** as an adverb to verbs and verbal derivations, = 'upwards' (*upcurved*; *update*). **2** as a preposition to nouns forming adverbs and adjectives (*up-country*; *uphill*). **3** as an adjective to nouns (*upland*; *upstroke*). [Old English *up(p)*-, = UP]

up-anchor *v.intr. Naut.* = *weigh anchor* (see ANCHOR).

up-and-coming *adj. colloq.* (of a person) making good progress and likely to succeed. ◻ **up-and-comer** *n.*

up-and-over *adj.* (of a door) opened by being raised and pushed back into a horizontal position.

up and running *adj. & adv.* functioning; in operation.

up-and-under *n.* (in rugby) a high kick to allow time for fellow team members to reach the point where the ball will come down.

Upanishad /uːˈpanɪʃad/ *n.* each of a series of philosophical compositions concluding the exposition of the Vedas. [Sanskrit, from *upa* 'near' + *ni-ṣad* 'sit down']

upas /ˈjuːpəs/ *n.* **1** (in full **upas tree**) **a** a Javanese tree, *Antiaris toxicaria*, yielding a milky sap used as arrow-poison. **b** *Mythol.* a Javanese tree thought to be fatal to whatever came near it. **c** a pernicious influence, practice, etc. **2** the poisonous sap of upas and other trees. [Malay *ūpas* 'poison']

upbeat /ˈʌpbiːt/ *n. & adj.* ● *n.* an unaccented beat in music. ● *adj. colloq.* optimistic or cheerful.

upbraid /ʌpˈbreɪd/ *v.tr.* (often foll. by *with*, *for*) chide or reproach (a person). ◻ **upbraiding** *n.* [Old English *upbrēdan* (as UP-, *brēdan* = *bregdan* BRAID in obsolete sense 'brandish')]

upbringing /ˈʌpbrɪŋɪŋ/ *n.* the bringing up of a child; education. [obsolete *upbring* 'to rear' (as UP-, BRING)]

upcast *n. & v.* ● *n.* /ˈʌpkɑːst/ **1** the act of casting up; an upward throw. **2** *Mining* a shaft through which air leaves a mine. **3** *Geol.* = UPTHROW 2. ● *v.tr.* /ʌpˈkɑːst/ (*past* and *past part.* **upcast**) cast up.

upchuck /ˈʌptʃʌk/ *v. & n. N. Amer. slang* vomit.

upcoming /ʌpˈkʌmɪŋ/ *adj.* esp. *N. Amer.* forthcoming; about to happen.

up-country /ˈʌpkʌntri, ʌpˈkʌntri/ *adv. & adj.* inland; towards the interior of a country.

update *v. & n.* ● *v.tr.* /ʌpˈdeɪt/ bring up to date. ● *n.* /ˈʌpdeɪt/ **1** the act or an instance of updating. **2** an updated version; a set of updated information.

updraught /ˈʌpdrɑːft/ *n.* (*US* **updraft**) an upward draught of air.

upend /ʌpˈɛnd/ *v.tr. & intr.* set or rise up on end.

upfield /ʌpˈfiːld, ˈʌp-/ *adv.* in or to a position nearer to the opponents' end of a football etc. field.

upfold /ˈʌpfəʊld/ *n. Geol.* an anticline.

upfront /ʌpˈfrʌnt, ˈʌp-/ *adv. & adj. colloq.* ● *adv.* (usu. **up front**) **1** at the front; in front. **2** (of payments) in advance. ● *adj.* **1** honest, open, frank. **2** (of payments) made in advance. **3** at the front or most prominent.

upgrade *v. & n.* ● *v.tr.* /ʌpˈgreɪd/ **1** raise in rank etc. **2** improve (equipment, machinery, etc.), esp. by replacing components. ● *n.* /ˈʌpgreɪd/ **1** the act or an instance of upgrading. **2** an upgraded piece of equipment etc. ◻ **on the upgrade 1** improving in health etc. **2** advancing, progressing. ◻ **upgradeable** *adj.* (also **upgradable**) esp. *Computing.*

upgrowth /ˈʌpgrəʊθ/ *n.* the process or result of growing upwards.

upheaval /ʌpˈhiːv(ə)l/ *n.* **1** a violent or sudden change or disruption. **2** *Geol.* an upward displacement of part of the earth's crust. **3** the act or an instance of heaving up.

upheave /ʌpˈhiːv/ *v.* **1** *tr.* heave or lift up, esp. forcibly. **2** *intr.* rise up.

uphill *adv., adj., & n.* ● *adv.* /ʌpˈhɪl/ in an ascending direction up a hill, slope, etc. ● *adj.* /ˈʌphɪl/ **1** sloping up; ascending. **2** arduous, difficult (*an uphill task*). ● *n.* /ˈʌphɪl/ an upward slope.

uphold /ʌpˈhəʊld/ *v.tr.* (*past* and *past part.* **upheld**) **1** confirm or maintain (a decision etc., esp. of another). **2** give support or countenance to (a person, practice, etc.). ◻ **upholder** *n.*

upholster /ʌpˈhəʊlstə, -ˈhɒl-/ *v.tr.* **1** provide (furniture) with upholstery. **2** furnish (a room etc.) with furniture, carpets, etc. [back-formation from UPHOLSTERER]

upholsterer /ʌpˈhəʊlst(ə)rə, -ˈhɒl-/ *n.* a person who upholsters furniture, esp. professionally. [obsolete noun *upholster* from UPHOLD (in obsolete sense 'keep in repair') + -STER]

upholstery /ʌpˈhəʊlst(ə)ri, -ˈhɒl-/ *n.* **1** textile covering, padding, springs, etc., for furniture. **2** an upholsterer's work.

upkeep /ˈʌpkiːp/ *n.* **1** maintenance in good condition. **2** the cost or means of this.

upland /ˈʌplənd/ *n. & adj.* ● *n.* high or hilly country. ● *adj.* of or relating to this.

uplift *v. & n.* ● *v.tr.* /ʌpˈlɪft/ **1** esp. *Brit.* raise; lift up. **2** elevate or stimulate morally or spiritually. ● *n.* /ˈʌplɪft/ **1** the act or an instance of being raised. **2** *Geol.* the raising of part of the earth's surface. **3** *colloq.* a morally or spiritually elevating influence. **4** support for the bust etc. from a garment. ◻ **uplifter** /-ˈlɪftə/ *n.* **uplifting** /-ˈlɪftɪŋ/ *adj.* (esp. in sense 2 of *v.*).

uplighter /ˈʌplʌɪtə/ *n.* a light placed or designed to throw illumination upwards.

uplink /ˈʌplɪŋk/ *n. & v.* ● *n.* a communications link to a satellite. ● *v.tr.* provide with or send by an uplink.

upload /ʌpˈləʊd/ *v. & n. Computing* ● *v.tr.* (also *absol.*) transfer (data) esp. to a larger storage device or system. ● *n.* (usu. *attrib.*) a transfer of this type (*upload feature*).

upmarket /ʌpˈmɑːkɪt, ˈʌp-/ *adj. & adv.* towards or relating to the dearer or more affluent sector of the market.

upmost var. of UPPERMOST.

upon /əˈpɒn/ *prep.* = ON. [Middle English, from UP + ON *prep.*, suggested by Old Norse *upp á*]

■ **Usage** *Upon* is sometimes more formal than *on*, but is standard in the phrases *once upon a time* and *upon my word*, and in uses such as *row upon row of seats* and *Christmas is almost upon us.*

upper[1] /ˈʌpə/ *adj. & n.* ● *adj.* **1** higher in position or status (*the upper class*) **2** situated above another part (*the upper atmosphere*; *the upper lip*). **3** (**Upper**) **a** situated on higher ground (*Upper Egypt*). **b** situated to the North (*Upper California*). **4** (often **Upper**) *Geol.* & *Archaeol.* designating a younger, and hence usu. shallower, part of a stratigraphic division, archaeological deposit, etc., or the period in which it was formed or deposited. ● *n.* the part of a boot or shoe above the sole. ◻ **on one's uppers** *colloq.* extremely short of money. [Middle English, from UP + -ER[2]]

upper[2] /ˈʌpə/ *n. slang* a stimulant drug, esp. an amphetamine. [UP *v.* + -ER[1]]

upper case *n.* (hyphenated when *attrib.*) capital letters.

upper class *n. & adj.* ● *n.* the highest class of society, esp. the aristocracy. ● *adj.* (**upper-class**) of the upper class.

upper crust *n.* (prec. by *the*) *colloq.* the aristocracy.

uppercut /ˈʌpəkʌt/ *n. & v.* ● *n.* an upwards blow delivered with the arm bent. ● *v.tr.* hit with an uppercut.

upper hand *n.* (prec. by *the*) dominance or control.

Upper House *n.* the higher house in a legislature, esp. the House of Lords.

uppermost /ˈʌpəməʊst/ *adj. & adv.* ● *adj.* (also **upmost** /ˈʌpməʊst/) **1** highest in place or rank. **2** predominant. ● *adv.* at or to the highest or most prominent position.

upper regions *n.pl.* (prec. by *the*) **1** the sky. **2** heaven.

upper works *n.pl.* the part of a ship that is above the water when fully laden.

uppish /ˈʌpɪʃ/ *adj.* esp. *Brit. colloq.* self-assertive or arrogant. □ **uppishly** *adv.* **uppishness** *n.*

uppity /ˈʌpɪti/ *adj. colloq.* uppish, snobbish. [fanciful from UP]

upraise /ʌpˈreɪz/ *v.tr.* raise to a higher level.

uprate /ʌpˈreɪt/ *v.tr.* **1** increase the value of (a pension, benefit, etc.). **2** upgrade, esp. to improve performance.

upright /ˈʌprʌɪt/ *adj.* & *n.* ● *adj.* **1** erect, vertical (*an upright posture; stood upright*). **2** (of a piano) with vertical strings. **3** (of a person or behaviour) righteous; strictly honourable or honest. **4** (of a picture, book, etc.) greater in height than breadth. ● *n.* **1** a post or rod fixed upright esp. as a structural support. **2** an upright piano. □ **uprightly** *adv.* **uprightness** *n.* [Old English *upriht* (as UP, RIGHT)]

uprise /ʌpˈrʌɪz/ *v.intr.* (**uprose**, **uprisen**) rise (to a standing position, etc.).

uprising /ˈʌprʌɪzɪŋ/ *n.* a rebellion or revolt.

upriver *adv.* & *adj.* ● *adv.* /ʌpˈrɪvə/ at or towards a point nearer the source of a river. ● *adj.* /ˈʌprɪvə/ situated or occurring upriver.

uproar /ˈʌprɔː/ *n.* a tumult; a violent disturbance. [Dutch *oproer*, from *op* 'up' + *roer* 'confusion', associated with ROAR]

uproarious /ʌpˈrɔːrɪəs/ *adj.* **1** very noisy. **2** provoking loud laughter. □ **uproariously** *adv.* **uproariousness** *n.*

uproot /ʌpˈruːt/ *v.* **1** *tr.* pull (a plant etc.) up from the ground. **2** *tr.* displace (a person) from an accustomed location. **3** *tr.* eradicate, destroy. **4** *intr.* move away from one's accustomed location or home. □ **uprooter** *n.*

uprose *past* of UPRISE.

uprush /ˈʌprʌʃ/ *n.* an upward rush, esp. *Psychol.* from the subconscious.

ups-a-daisy var. of UPSY-DAISY.

ups and downs *n.pl.* **1** rises and falls. **2** alternate good and bad fortune.

upscale /ˈʌpskeɪl/ *adj.* & *adv. N. Amer.* = UPMARKET.

upset *v., n., & adj.* ● *v.* /ʌpˈsɛt/ (**upsetting**; *past* and *past part.* **upset**) **1** *tr.* & *intr.* overturn or be overturned. **2** *tr.* disturb the composure or digestion of (*was very upset by the news; ate something that upset me*). **3** *tr.* disrupt. **4** *tr.* shorten and thicken (metal, esp. a tire) by hammering or pressure. ● *n.* /ˈʌpsɛt/ **1** a condition of upsetting or being upset (*a stomach upset*). **2** a surprising result in a game etc. ● *adj.* /ʌpˈsɛt, ˈʌp-/ disturbed (*an upset stomach*). □ **upsetter** /-ˈsɛtə/ *n.* **upsettingly** /-ˈsɛtɪŋli/ *adv.*

upset price *n.* the lowest acceptable selling price of a property in an auction etc.; a reserve price.

upshift /ˈʌpʃɪft/ *v.* & *n.* ● *v.* **1** *intr.* move to a higher gear in a motor vehicle. **2** *tr.* esp. *US* increase (*upshifted the penalties*). ● *n.* a movement upwards, esp. a change to a higher gear.

upshot /ˈʌpʃɒt/ *n.* the final or eventual outcome or conclusion.

upside /ˈʌpsʌɪd/ *n.* **1** the positive aspect of something; an advantage. **2** an upward movement of share prices etc.

upside down /ʌpsʌɪd ˈdaʊn/ *adv.* & *adj.* ● *adv.* **1** with the upper part where the lower part should be; in an inverted position. **2** in or into total disorder (*everything was turned upside down*). ● *adj.* (also **upside-down** *attrib.*) that is positioned upside down; inverted. [Middle English, originally *up so down*, perhaps = 'up as if down']

upside-down cake *n.* a sponge cake baked with fruit in a syrup at the bottom, and inverted for serving.

upsides /ʌpˈsʌɪdz/ *adv.* (foll. by *with*) *Brit. colloq.* equal with (a person) by revenge, retaliation, etc. [*upside* = top part]

upsilon /ʌpˈsʌɪlən, juːp-; ˈʊpsɪlɒn, ˈjuːp-/ *n.* the twentieth letter of the Greek alphabet (Υ, υ). [Greek, = slender U, from *psilos* 'slender', with reference to the need to distinguish upsilon from the diphthong *oi*: in late Greek the two had the same pronunciation]

upstage /ʌpˈsteɪdʒ/ *adj., adv., & v.* ● *adj.* & *adv.* **1** nearer the back of a theatre stage. **2** snobbish(ly). ● *v.tr.* **1** (of an actor) move upstage to make (another actor) face away from the audience. **2** divert attention from (a person) to oneself; outshine.

upstairs *adv., adj., & n.* ● *adv.* /ʌpˈstɛːz/ to or on an upper floor. ● *adj.* /ˈʌpstɛːz/ (also **upstair**) situated upstairs. ● *n.* /ʌpˈstɛːz/ an upper floor.

upstanding /ʌpˈstandɪŋ/ *adj.* **1** standing up. **2** strong and healthy. **3** honest or straightforward.

upstart /ˈʌpstɑːt/ *n.* & *adj.* ● *n.* a person who has risen suddenly to prominence, esp. one who behaves arrogantly. ● *adj.* **1** that is an upstart. **2** of or characteristic of an upstart.

upstate /ˈʌpsteɪt/ *n., adj., & adv. US* ● *n.* part of a state remote from its large cities, esp. the northern part. ● *adj.* of or relating to this part. ● *adv.* in or to this part. □ **upstater** *n.*

upstream *adv.* & *adj.* ● *adv.* /ʌpˈstriːm/ against the flow of a stream etc. ● *adj.* /ˈʌpstriːm/ moving upstream.

upstroke /ˈʌpstrəʊk/ *n.* a stroke made or written upwards.

upsurge /ˈʌpsəːdʒ/ *n.* an upward surge; a rise (esp. in feelings etc.).

upswept /ˈʌpswɛpt/ *adj.* **1** (of the hair) combed to the top of the head. **2** curved or sloped upwards.

upswing /ˈʌpswɪŋ/ *n.* an upward movement or trend.

upsy-daisy /ʌpsɪˈdeɪzi, ʌpsə-/ *int.* (also **ups-a-daisy**, **oops-a-daisy**) expressing encouragement to a child who is being lifted or has fallen. [earlier *up-a-daisy*: cf. LACKADAISICAL]

uptake /ˈʌpteɪk/ *n.* **1** *colloq.* understanding; comprehension (esp. *quick* or *slow on the uptake*). **2** the act or an instance of taking up.

up-tempo *adj.* & *adv.* at a fast or an increased tempo.

upthrow /ˈʌpθrəʊ/ *n.* **1** the act or an instance of throwing upwards. **2** *Geol.* an upward dislocation of strata.

upthrust /ˈʌpθrʌst/ *n.* **1** upward thrust, e.g. of a fluid on an immersed body. **2** *Geol.* = UPHEAVAL 2.

uptick /ˈʌptɪk/ *n.* esp. *US* an increase, esp. a small one.

uptight /ʌpˈtʌɪt, ˈʌptʌɪt/ *adj. colloq.* **1** nervously tense or angry. **2** rigidly conventional.

uptime /ˈʌptʌɪm/ *n.* time during which a machine, esp. a computer, is in operation.

up to date *adj.* (hyphenated when *attrib.*) meeting or according to the latest requirements, knowledge, or fashion; modern.

up-to-the-minute *adj.* (usu. *attrib.*) latest; most modern.

uptown *adj., adv., & n. N. Amer.* ● *adj.* /ˈʌptaʊn/ of or in the residential part of a town or city. ● *adv.* /ʌpˈtaʊn/ in or into this part. ● *n.* /ˈʌptaʊn/ this part. □ **uptowner** *n.*

upturn *n.* & *v.* ● *n.* /ˈʌptəːn/ **1** an upward trend; an improvement. **2** an upheaval. ● *v.tr.* /ʌpˈtəːn/ turn up or upside down.

UPU *abbr.* Universal Postal Union.

UPVC *abbr.* unplasticized polyvinyl chloride.

upward /ˈʌpwəd/ *adv.* & *adj.* ● *adv.* (also **upwards**) towards what is higher, superior, larger in amount, more important, or earlier. ● *adj.* moving, extending, pointing, or leading upward. □ **upwards of** more than (*found upwards of forty specimens*). [Old English *upweard(es)* (as UP, -WARD)]

upwardly /ˈʌpwədli/ *adv.* in an upward direction.

upwardly mobile *adj.* able or aspiring to advance socially or professionally.

upward mobility *n.* social or professional advancement.

upwarp /ˈʌpwɔːp/ *n. Geol.* a broad surface elevation; an anticline.

upwind /ʌpˈwɪnd/ *adj.* & *adv.* against the direction of the wind.

ur- /ʊə/ *comb. form* primitive, original, earliest. [German]

uracil /ˈjʊərəsɪl/ *n. Biochem.* a pyrimidine derivative found in living tissue as a component base of RNA. [UREA + ACETIC]

uraemia /jʊˈriːmɪə/ *n.* (*US* **uremia**) *Med.* a raised level in the blood of nitrogenous waste compounds (esp. urea) that are normally eliminated by the kidneys. □ **uraemic** *adj.* [Greek *ouron* 'urine' + *haima* 'blood']

uraeus /jʊˈriːəs/ *n.* (*pl.* **uriei** /jʊˈriːʌɪ/) the sacred serpent as an emblem of power represented on the headdress of ancient Egyptian divinities and sovereigns. [modern Latin from Greek *ouraios*, representing the Egyptian word for 'cobra']

Ural-Altaic /ˌjʊər(ə)lalˈteɪɪk/ *n. & adj.* ● *n. Philol.* a proposed language group including Finno-Ugric, Turkic, Mongolian, and other agglutinative languages of N. Europe and Asia. ● *adj.* **1** of or relating to this group of languages. **2** of or relating to the Ural and Altaic mountain ranges in western and central Asia.

uranium /jʊˈreɪnɪəm/ *n. Chem.* a radioactive grey dense metallic element occurring naturally in pitchblende, and capable of nuclear fission and therefore used as a source of nuclear energy (symbol **U**). □ **uranic** /-ˈranɪk/ *adj.* [modern Latin, from URANUS: cf. *tellurium*]

urano-[1] /ˈjʊər(ə)nəʊ/ *comb. form* the heavens. [Greek *ouranos* 'heaven(s)']

urano-[2] /ˈjʊər(ə)nəʊ/ *comb. form* uranium.

uranography /jʊərəˈnɒgrəfi/ *n. archaic* the branch of astronomy concerned with describing and mapping the stars. □ **uranographer** *n.* **uranographic** /-nəˈgrafɪk/ *adj.*

Uranus /ˈjʊərənəs, jʊˈreɪnəs/ *n.* a planet discovered by Herschel in 1781, the outermost of the solar system except Neptune and Pluto. [Latin from Greek *Ouranos* 'heaven, Uranus', in Greek Mythol. the son of Gaea (Earth) and father of Kronos (Saturn), the Titans, etc.]

urban /ˈəːb(ə)n/ *adj.* of, living in, or situated in a town or city (*an urban population*) (opp. RURAL). [Latin *urbanus* from *urbs urbis* 'city']

urban district *n. Brit. hist.* a group of urban communities governed by an elected council.

urbane /əːˈbeɪn/ *adj.* courteous; suave; elegant and refined in manner. □ **urbanely** *adv.* [French *urbain* or Latin *urbanus*: see URBAN]

urban guerrilla *n.* a terrorist operating in an urban area.

urbanism /ˈəːb(ə)nɪz(ə)m/ *n.* **1** urban character or way of life. **2** a study of urban life. □ **urbanist** *n.*

urbanite /ˈəːb(ə)nʌɪt/ *n.* a dweller in a city or town.

urbanity /əːˈbanɪti/ *n.* **1** an urbane quality; refinement of manner. **2** urban life. [French *urbanité* or Latin *urbanitas* (as URBAN)]

urbanize /ˈəːb(ə)nʌɪz/ *v.tr.* (also **-ise**) **1** make urban. **2** destroy the rural quality of (a district). □ **urbanization** /-ˈzeɪʃ(ə)n/ *n.* [French *urbaniser* (as URBAN)]

urban myth *n.* a modern old wives' tale.

urban renewal *n.* slum clearance and redevelopment in a city or town.

urban sprawl *n.* the uncontrolled expansion of urban areas.

urceolate /ˈəːsɪələt/ *adj. Bot.* having the shape of a pitcher, with a large body and small mouth. [Latin *urceolus*, diminutive of *urceus* 'pitcher']

urchin /ˈəːtʃɪn/ *n.* **1** a mischievous child, esp. young and raggedly dressed. **2** = SEA URCHIN. **3** *archaic* **a** a hedgehog. **b** a goblin. [Middle English *hirchon*, *urcheon* from Old Northern French *herichon*, Old French *heriçon*, ultimately from Latin (*h*)*ericius* 'hedgehog']

Urdu /ˈʊəduː, ˈəːduː/ *n.* a language related to Hindi but with many Persian words, an official language of Pakistan and also used in India. [Hindustani (*zabān i*) *urdū* '(language of the) camp', via Persian *urdū* from Turkic *ordū*: see HORDE]

-ure /jə, jʊə/ *suffix* forming: **1** nouns of action or process (*censure*; *closure*; *seizure*). **2** nouns of result (*creature*; *scripture*). **3** collective nouns (*legislature*; *nature*). **4** nouns of function (*judicature*; *ligature*). [from or suggested by Old French *-ure* from Latin *-ura*]

urea /jʊˈriːə, ˈjʊərɪə/ *n. Biochem.* a soluble colourless crystalline nitrogenous compound contained esp. in the urine of mammals. □ **ureal** *adj.* [modern Latin via French *urée* from Greek *ouron* 'urine']

urea-formaldehyde *n.* a plastic, resin, or foam made by condensation of urea with formaldehyde, used esp. for insulation.

uremia *US* var. of URAEMIA.

ureter /jʊˈriːtə, ˈjʊərɪtə/ *n.* the duct by which urine passes from the kidney to the bladder or cloaca. □ **ureteral** *adj.* **ureteric** /jʊərɪˈtɛrɪk/ *adj.* **ureteritis** /-ˈrʌɪtɪs/ *n.* [French *uretère* or modern Latin *ureter* from Greek *ourētēr*, from *oureō* 'urinate']

urethane /ˈjʊərɪθeɪn, jʊˈrɛθeɪn/ *n. Chem.* a crystalline amide, ethyl carbamate, used in plastics and paints. [French *uréthane* (as UREA, ETHANE)]

urethra /jʊˈriːθrə/ *n.* (*pl.* **urethrae** /-riː/ or **urethras**) the duct by which urine is discharged from the bladder. □ **urethral** *adj.* **urethritis** /-rɪˈθrʌɪtɪs/ *n.* [Late Latin from Greek *ourēthra* (as URETER)]

urge /ˈəːdʒ/ *v. & n.* ● *v.tr.* **1** (often foll. by *on*) drive forcibly; impel; hasten (*urged them on*; *urged the horses forward*). **2** (often foll. by *to* + infin. or *that* + clause) encourage or entreat earnestly or persistently (*urged them to go*; *urged them to action*; *urged that they should go*). **3** (often foll. by *on*, *upon*) advocate (an action or argument etc.) pressingly or emphatically (to a person). **4** adduce forcefully as a reason or justification (*urged the seriousness of the problem*). **5** ply (a person etc.) hard with argument or entreaty. ● *n.* **1** an urging impulse or tendency. **2** a strong desire. □ **urger** *n.* [Latin *urgēre* 'press, drive']

urgent /ˈəːdʒ(ə)nt/ *adj.* **1** requiring immediate action or attention (*an urgent need for help*). **2** importunate; earnest and persistent in demand. □ **urgency** *n.* **urgently** *adv.* [Middle English from French (as URGE)]

URI *abbr.* upper respiratory infection.

-uria /ˈjʊərɪə/ *comb. form* forming nouns denoting that a substance is (esp. excessively) present in the urine. [modern Latin from Greek *-ouria* (as URINE)]

uric /ˈjʊərɪk/ *adj.* of or relating to urine. [French *urique* (as URINE)]

uric acid *n.* an almost insoluble acid forming the main nitrogenous waste product in birds, reptiles, and insects.

urinal /jʊˈrʌɪn(ə)l, ˈjʊərɪn(ə)l/ *n.* **1** a sanitary fitting, usu. against a wall, for men to urinate into. **2** a place or receptacle for urination. [Middle English via Old French from Late Latin *urinal*, neut. of *urinalis* (as URINE)]

urinalysis /jʊərɪˈnalɪsɪs/ *n.* (*pl.* **urinalyses** /-siːz/) the chemical analysis of urine esp. for diagnostic purposes.

urinary /ˈjʊərɪn(ə)ri/ *adj.* **1** of or relating to urine. **2** affecting or occurring in the urinary system (*urinary diseases*).

urinate /ˈjʊərɪneɪt/ *v.intr.* discharge urine. □ **urination** /-ˈneɪʃ(ə)n/ *n.* [medieval Latin *urinare* (as URINE)]

urine /ˈjʊərɪn, ˈjʊərʌɪn/ *n.* a pale yellow fluid secreted as waste from the blood by the kidneys, stored in the bladder, and discharged through the urethra. □ **urinous** *adj.* [Middle English via Old French from Latin *urina*]

urn /əːn/ *n. & v.* ● *n.* **1** a vase with a foot and usu. a rounded body, esp. for storing the ashes of the cremated dead or as a vessel or measure. **2** a large vessel with a tap, in which tea or coffee etc. is made or kept hot. **3** *poet.* anything in which a dead body or its remains are preserved, e.g. a grave. ● *v.tr.* enclose in an urn. □ **urnful** *n.* (*pl.* **-fuls**). [Middle English from Latin *urna*, related to *urceus* 'pitcher']

uro-[1] /ˈjʊərəʊ/ *comb. form* urine. [Greek *ouron* 'urine']

uro-[2] /ˈjʊərəʊ/ *comb. form* tail. [Greek *oura* 'tail']

urochordate /jʊərə(ʊ)ˈkɔːdeɪt/ *n. Zool.* an animal of the subphylum Urochordata, which comprises the tunicates. [URO-[2] + CHORDATE]

urodele /ˈjʊərə(ʊ)diːl/ *n.* any amphibian of the order Urodela, having a tail when in the adult form, including newts and salamanders. [URO-[2] + Greek *dēlos* 'evident']

urogenital /jʊərəʊˈdʒɛnɪt(ə)l/ *adj.* of or relating to urinary and genital products or organs.

urology /jʊˈrɒlədʒi/ *n.* the scientific study of the urinary system. □ **urologic** /-rəˈlɒdʒɪk/ *adj.* **urological** /-rəˈlɒdʒɪk(ə)l/ *adj.* **urologist** *n.*

uropygium /jʊərəˈpɪdʒɪəm/ *n.* the rump of a bird. [medieval Latin from Greek *ouropugion*]

uroscopy /jʊˈrɒskəpi/ *n. Med. hist.* the examination of urine by simple inspection, esp. in diagnosis.

Ursa Major /əːsə ˈmeɪdʒə/ *n.* a prominent constellation in the northern sky, containing seven bright stars in a pattern variously called the Plough, the Big Dipper, or Charles's Wain. Also called *Great Bear*. [Latin, = greater (she-)bear]

Ursa Minor /əːsə ˈmʌɪnə/ *n.* a small constellation containing the north celestial pole and the pole star. Also called *Little Bear*, *Little Dipper*. [Latin, = lesser (she-)bear]

ursine /ˈəːsʌɪn, -ɪn/ *adj.* of or like a bear. [Latin *ursinus* from *ursus* 'bear']

Ursuline /ˈəːsjʊlʌɪn, -lɪn/ *n.* & *adj.* ● *n.* a nun of an order founded by St Angela in 1535 for nursing the sick and teaching girls. ● *adj.* of or relating to this order. [from the name of St *Ursula*, the founder's patron saint]

urticaria /əːtɪˈkɛːrɪə/ *n. Med.* nettle-rash. [modern Latin from Latin *urtica* 'nettle', from *urere* 'to burn']

urticate /ˈəːtɪkeɪt/ *v.tr.* sting like a nettle. □ **urtication** /-ˈkeɪʃ(ə)n/ *n.* [medieval Latin *urticare* from Latin *urtica*: see URTICARIA]

urus /ˈjʊərəs/ *n.* = AUROCHS. [Latin from Germanic]

US *abbr.* **1** United States (of America). **2** *Brit.* Under-Secretary. **3** *Brit.* unserviceable.

us /ʌs/ *pron.* **1** *objective case* of WE (*they saw us*). **2** *colloq.* = ME[1] (*give us a kiss*). [Old English *ūs*, from Germanic]

■ **Usage** See Usage Note at HER.

USA *abbr.* **1** United States of America. **2** *US* United States Army.

usable /ˈjuːzəb(ə)l/ *adj.* (also **useable**) that can be used. □ **usability** /-ˈbɪlɪti/ *n.*

USAF *abbr.* United States Air Force.

usage /ˈjuːsɪdʒ/ *n.* **1** a manner of using or treating; use (*damaged by rough usage*). **2** habitual or customary practice, esp. as creating a right, obligation, or standard. [Middle English from Old French, from *us* USE *n.*]

usance /ˈjuːz(ə)ns/ *n.* the time allowed by commercial usage for the payment of foreign bills of exchange. [Middle English from Old French (as USE)]

USDAW /ˈʌzdɔː/ *abbr.* (in the UK) Union of Shop, Distributive, and Allied Workers.

use *v.* & *n.* ● *v.tr.* /juːz/ **1** cause to act or serve for a purpose; bring into service; avail oneself of (*rarely uses the car*; *use your discretion*). **2** treat (a person) in a specified manner (*they used him shamefully*). **3** exploit for one's own ends (*they are just using you*). **4** (in *past* /juːst/; foll. by *to* + infin.) did or had in the past (but no longer) as a customary practice or state (*I used to be an archaeologist*; *it used not* (*or did not use*) *to rain so often*). **5** (as **used** *adj.*) second-hand. **6** (as **used** /juːst/ *predic.adj.*) (foll. by *to*) familiar by habit; accustomed (*not used to hard work*). **7** apply (a name or title etc.) to oneself. ● *n.* /juːs/ **1** the act of using or the state of being used; application to a purpose (*put it to good use*; *is in daily use*; *worn and polished with use*). **2** the right or power of using (*lost the use of my right arm*). **3 a** the ability to be used (*a torch would be of use*). **b** the purpose for which a thing can be used (*it's no use talking*). **4** custom or usage (*long use has reconciled me to it*). **5** the characteristic ritual and liturgy of a church or diocese etc. **6** *Law hist.* the benefit or profit of lands, esp. in the possession of another who holds them solely for the beneficiary. □ **could use** *colloq.* would be glad to have; would be improved by having. **have no use for 1** be unable to find a use for. **2** dislike or be impatient with. **make use of 1** employ, apply. **2** benefit from. **use and wont** established custom. **use a person's name** quote a person as an authority or reference etc. **use up 1** consume completely, use the whole of. **2** find a use for (something remaining). **3** exhaust or wear out e.g. with overwork. [Middle English from Old French *us*, *user*, ultimately from Latin *uti us-* 'use']

■ **Usage** In sense 4 of the verb, the negative and interrogative can be formed in two ways: (1) **Negative**: *used not/usedn't to*, e.g. *He used not to smoke*. **Interrogative** *used X to?*, e.g. *Used he to smoke*? (2) **Negative** *did not/didn't use to*, e.g. *He didn't use to smoke*. **Interrogative** *did X use to?*, e.g. *Did he use to smoke*? Note the correct spellings of the abbreviated negative forms, *usedn't to*, *didn't use to*. *Usen't to* and *didn't used to* are incorrect. All the forms given at (1) and (2) are acceptable but those at (1) are more formal. The interrogative form at (1) tends to sound over-formal or even stilted nowadays.

use-by date *n.* the latest recommended date of use marked on the packaging of perishable food etc.

useful /ˈjuːsfʊl, -f(ə)l/ *adj.* **1 a** of use; serviceable. **b** producing or able to produce good results (*gave me some useful hints*). **2** *colloq.* highly creditable or efficient (*a useful performance*). □ **make oneself useful** perform useful services. □ **usefully** *adv.* **usefulness** *n.*

useful load *n.* the load carried by an aircraft etc. in addition to its own weight.

useless /ˈjuːslɪs/ *adj.* **1** serving no purpose; unavailing (*the contents were made useless by damp*; *protest is useless*). **2** *colloq.* feeble or ineffectual (*am useless at swimming*). □ **uselessly** *adv.* **uselessness** *n.*

user /ˈjuːzə/ *n.* **1** a person who uses (esp. a particular commodity or service, or a computer). **2** *colloq.* a drug addict. **3** *Law* the continued use or enjoyment of a right etc.

user-friendly *adj.* esp. *Computing* (of a machine or system) designed to be easy to use. □ **user-friendliness** *n.*

usher /ˈʌʃə/ *n.* & *v.* ● *n.* **1** a person who shows people to their seats in a hall or theatre etc. **2** a doorkeeper at a court etc. **3** *Brit.* an officer walking before a person of rank. **4** *archaic* or *joc.* an assistant teacher. ● *v.tr.* **1** act as usher to. **2** (usu. foll. by *in*) announce or show in etc. (*ushered us into the room*; *ushered in a new era*). □ **ushership** *n.* [Middle English via Anglo-French *usser*, Old French *uissier*, variant of *huissier*, and medieval Latin *ustiarius* from Latin *ostiarius*, from *ostium* 'door']

usherette /ʌʃəˈrɛt/ *n.* a female usher esp. in a cinema.

USM *abbr. Stock Exch.* Unlisted Securities Market.

USN *abbr.* United States Navy.

usquebaugh /ˈʌskwɪbɔː/ *n.* esp. *Ir.* & *Sc.* whisky. [Irish & Gaelic *uisge beatha* 'water of life': cf. WHISKY]

USS *abbr.* United States Ship.

USSR *abbr. hist.* Union of Soviet Socialist Republics.

usual /ˈjuːʒʊəl/ *adj.* **1** such as commonly occurs, or is observed or done; customary, habitual (*the usual formalities*; *it is usual to tip them*; *forgot my keys as usual*). **2** (prec. by *the*, *my*, etc.) *colloq.* a person's usual drink etc. □ **usually** *adv.* **usualness** *n.* [Middle English from Old French *usual*, *usuel* or Late Latin *usualis* (as USE)]

usucaption /juːzjʊˈkapʃ(ə)n/ *n.* (also **usucapion** /juːzjʊˈkeɪpɪən/) (in Roman and Scots law) the acquisition of a title or right to property by uninterrupted and undisputed possession for a prescribed term. [Old French *usucap(t)ion* or Latin *usucap(t)io* from *usucapere* 'acquire by prescription', from *usu* 'by use' + *capere capt-* 'take']

usufruct /ˈjuːzjʊfrʌkt/ *n.* & *v.* ● *n.* (in Roman and Scots law) the right of enjoying the use and advantages of another's property short of the destruction or waste of its substance. ● *v.tr.* hold in usufruct. □ **usufructuary** /-ˈfrʌktjʊəri/ *adj.* & *n.* [medieval Latin *usufructus* from Latin *usus* (*et*) *fructus*, from *usus* USE + *fructus* FRUIT]

usurer /ˈjuːʒ(ə)rə/ *n.* a person who practises usury. [Middle English via Anglo-French *usurer*, Old French *usureor*, from *usure*, from Latin *usura*: see USURY]

usurious /juːˈʒʊərɪəs, juːˈzj-/ *adj.* of, involving, or practising usury. □ **usuriously** *adv.*

usurp /jʊˈzəːp, jʊˈsəːp/ *v.* **1** *tr.* seize or assume (a throne or power etc.) wrongfully. **2** *intr.* (foll. by *on*, *upon*) encroach. □ **usurpation** /juːzəˈpeɪʃ(ə)n, juːs-/ *n.* **usurper** *n.* [Middle English via Old French *usurper* from Latin *usurpare* 'seize for use']

usury /ˈjuːʒ(ə)ri/ *n.* **1** the act or practice of lending money at interest, esp. *Law* at an exorbitant rate. **2** interest at this rate. □ **with usury** *literary* or *poet.* with increased force etc. [Middle English via medieval Latin *usuria* from Latin *usura* (as USE)]

UT *abbr.* **1** Universal Time. **2** *US* Utah (in official postal use).

UTC *abbr.* Universal Time Coordinated (also expanded as COORDINATED UNIVERSAL TIME).

Utd *abbr.* United (esp. in the name of a football team).

ute /juːt/ *n. Austral.* & *NZ slang* a utility truck. [abbreviation]

utensil /juːˈtɛns(ə)l/ *n.* an implement or vessel, esp. for domestic use (*cooking utensils*). [Middle English via Old French *utensile* from medieval Latin, neut. of Latin *utensilis* 'usable' (as USE)]

uterine /ˈjuːtərɪn, -ʌɪn/ *adj.* **1** of or relating to the uterus. **2** born of the same mother but not the same father (*sister uterine*). [Middle English from Late Latin *uterinus* (as UTERUS)]

uterus /ˈjuːt(ə)rəs/ *n.* (*pl.* **uteri** /-rʌɪ/) the womb. □ **uteritis** /-ˈrʌɪtɪs/ *n.* [Latin]

utile /ˈjuːtʌɪl/ *adj.* useful; having utility. [Middle English via Old French from Latin *utilis*, from *uti* 'use']

utilitarian /jʊˌtɪlɪˈtɛːrɪən/ *adj.* & *n.* ● *adj.* **1** designed to be useful for a purpose rather than attractive; severely practical. **2** of utilitarianism. ● *n.* an adherent of utilitarianism.

utilitarianism /jʊˌtɪlɪˈtɛːrɪənɪz(ə)m/ *n.* **1** the doctrine that actions are right if they are useful or for the benefit of a majority. **2** the doctrine that the greatest happiness of the greatest number should be the guiding principle of conduct.

utility /juːˈtɪlɪti/ *n.* (*pl.* **-ies**) **1** the condition of being useful or profitable. **2** a useful thing. **3** = PUBLIC UTILITY. **4** (*attrib.*) **a** severely practical and standardized (*utility furniture*). **b** made or serving for utility. [Middle English via Old French *utilité* from Latin *utilitas -tatis* (as UTILE)]

utility knife *n. N. Amer.* = STANLEY KNIFE.

utility program *n. Computing* a program for carrying out a routine function.

utility room *n.* a room equipped with appliances for washing, ironing, and other domestic work.

utility vehicle *n.* (also **utility truck** etc.) a vehicle capable of serving various functions.

utilize /ˈjuːtɪlʌɪz/ *v.tr.* (also **-ise**) make practical use of; turn to account; use effectively. □ **utilizable** *adj.* **utilization** /-ˈzeɪʃ(ə)n/ *n.* **utilizer** *n.* [French *utiliser* from Italian *utilizzare* (as UTILE)]

-ution /ˈjuːʃ(ə)n, ˈuːʃ(ə)n/ *suffix* forming nouns, = -ATION (*solution*). [French from Latin *-utio*]

utmost /ˈʌtməʊst/ *adj.* & *n.* ● *adj.* furthest, extreme, or greatest (*the utmost limits*; *showed the utmost reluctance*). ● *n.* (prec. by *the*) the utmost point or degree etc. □ **do one's utmost** do all that one can. [Old English *ūt(e)mest* (as OUT, -MOST)]

Utopia /juːˈtəʊpɪə/ *n.* (also **utopia**) an imagined perfect place or state of things. [title of a book (1516) by Thomas More: modern Latin, from Greek *ou* 'not' + *topos* 'place']

Utopian /juːˈtəʊpɪən/ *adj.* & *n.* (also **utopian**) ● *adj.* characteristic of Utopia; idealistic. ● *n.* an idealistic reformer. □ **Utopianism** *n.*

utricle /ˈjuːtrɪk(ə)l/ *n.* a small cell or sac in an animal or plant, esp. one in the inner ear. □ **utricular** /juːˈtrɪkjʊlə/ *adj.* [French *utricule* or Latin *utriculus*, diminutive of *uter* 'leather bag']

utter[1] /ˈʌtə/ *attrib.adj.* complete, total, absolute (*utter misery*; *saw the utter absurdity of it*). □ **utterly** *adv.* **utterness** *n.* [Old English *ūtera*, *ūttra*, comparative adj. from *ūt* OUT: cf. OUTER]

utter[2] /ˈʌtə/ *v.tr.* **1** emit audibly (*uttered a startled cry*). **2** express in spoken or written words. **3** *Law* put (esp. forged money) into circulation. □ **utterable** *adj.* **utterer** *n.* [Middle English from Middle Dutch *ūteren* 'make known', assimilated to UTTER[1]]

utterance /ˈʌt(ə)r(ə)ns/ *n.* **1** the act or an instance of uttering. **2** a thing spoken. **3 a** the power of speaking. **b** a manner of speaking. **4** *Linguistics* an uninterrupted chain of spoken or written words not necessarily corresponding to a single or complete grammatical unit.

uttermost /ˈʌtəməʊst/ *adj.* furthest, extreme.

U-turn *n.* **1** the turning of a vehicle in a U-shaped course so as to face in the opposite direction. **2** a reversal of policy.

UV *abbr.* ultraviolet.

UVA *abbr.* ultraviolet radiation of relatively long wavelengths.

UVB *abbr.* ultraviolet radiation of relatively short wavelengths.

UVC *abbr.* ultraviolet radiation of very short wavelengths, which does not penetrate the earth's ozone layer.

uvea /ˈjuːvɪə/ *n.* the pigmented layer of the eye, lying beneath the outer layer. [medieval Latin from Latin *uva* 'grape']

uvula /ˈjuːvjʊlə/ *n.* (*pl.* **uvulae** /-liː/) *Anat.* **1** a fleshy extension of the soft palate hanging above the throat. **2** a similar structure in the bladder or cerebellum. [Middle English from Late Latin, diminutive of Latin *uva* 'grape']

uvular /ˈjuːvjʊlə/ *adj.* & *n.* ● *adj.* **1** of or relating to the uvula. **2** articulated with the back of the tongue and the uvula, as in *r* in French. ● *n.* a uvular consonant.

uxorial /ʌkˈsɔːrɪəl/ *adj.* of or relating to a wife.

uxoricide /ʌkˈsɔːrɪsʌɪd/ *n.* **1** the killing of one's wife. **2** a person who does this. □ **uxoricidal** /-ˈsʌɪd(ə)l/ *adj.* [Latin *uxor* 'wife' + -CIDE]

uxorious /ʌkˈsɔːrɪəs/ *adj.* **1** greatly or excessively fond of one's wife. **2** (of behaviour etc.) showing such fondness. □ **uxoriously** *adv.* **uxoriousness** *n.* [Latin *uxoriosus* from *uxor* 'wife']

Uzbek /ˈʌzbɛk, ˈʊz-/ *n.* **1** a member of a Turkic people living mainly in the republic of Uzbekistan in central Asia. **2** the Turkic language of this people. [Uzbek]

Uzi /ˈuːzi/ *n.* a type of sub-machine gun of Israeli design (also *attrib.*: *Uzi sub-machine gun*). [from *Uzial* Gal, the name of the Israeli army officer who designed it]

Vv

V[1] /viː/ *n.* (also **v**) (*pl.* **Vs** or **V's**) **1** the twenty-second letter of the alphabet. **2** a V-shaped thing. **3** (as a Roman numeral) five.

V[2] *symb.* **1** *Chem.* the element vanadium. **2 a** volt(s). **b** voltage, potential difference. **3** volume.

v *abbr.* (also **v.**) **1** verse. **2** verso. **3** versus. **4** very. **5** *vide.* **6** velocity.

V-1 /viːˈwʌn/ *n. hist.* a type of German flying bomb used in the Second World War. [abbreviation of German *Vergeltungswaffe* 'reprisal weapon']

V-2 /viːˈtuː/ *n. hist.* a type of German rocket-powered missile used in the Second World War. [abbreviation of German *Vergeltungswaffe* 'reprisal weapon']

VA *abbr.* **1** *US* Veterans' Administration. **2** Vicar Apostolic. **3** Vice Admiral. **4** *US* Virginia (in official postal use). **5** (in the UK) Order of Victoria and Albert.

Va. *abbr.* Virginia.

vac /vak/ *n. colloq.* **1** *Brit.* vacation (esp. of universities). **2** vacuum cleaner. [abbreviation]

vacancy /ˈveɪk(ə)nsi/ *n.* (*pl.* **-ies**) **1** the state of being vacant or empty. **2** an unoccupied post or job (*there are three vacancies for typists*). **3** an available room in a hotel etc. **4** emptiness of mind; idleness, listlessness.

vacant /ˈveɪk(ə)nt/ *adj.* **1** not filled or occupied; empty. **2** not mentally active; showing no interest (*had a vacant stare*). □ **vacantly** *adv.* [Middle English from Old French *vacant* or Latin *vacare* (as VACATE)]

vacant possession *n. Brit.* ownership of a house etc. with any previous occupant having moved out.

vacate /vəˈkeɪt, veɪˈkeɪt/ *v.tr.* **1** leave vacant or cease to occupy (a house, room, etc.). **2** give up tenure of (a post etc.). **3** *Law* annul (a judgement or contract etc.). □ **vacatable** *adj.* [Latin *vacare vacat-* 'be empty']

vacation /vəˈkeɪʃ(ə)n, veɪ-/ *n.* & *v.* ● *n.* **1** a fixed period of cessation from work, esp. in universities and law courts. **2** *N. Amer.* a holiday. **3** the act of vacating (a house or post etc.). ● *v.intr. US* take a holiday. □ **vacationer** *n.* **vacationist** *n.* [Middle English from Old French *vacation* or Latin *vacatio* (as VACATE)]

vacationland /vəˈkeɪʃ(ə)nland/ *n. US* an area providing attractions for holidaymakers.

vaccinate /ˈvaksɪneɪt/ *v.tr.* inoculate with a vaccine to provide immunity against a disease; immunize. □ **vaccination** /-ˈneɪʃ(ə)n/ *n.* **vaccinator** *n.*

vaccine /ˈvaksiːn, -ɪn/ *n.* & *adj.* ● *n.* **1** an antigenic preparation used to stimulate the production of antibodies and provide immunity against one or several diseases. **2** *hist.* the cowpox virus used in vaccination against smallpox. ● *adj.* of or relating to cowpox or vaccination. □ **vaccinal** /-sɪn(ə)l/ *adj.* [Latin *vaccinus* from *vacca* 'cow']

vaccinia /vakˈsɪnɪə/ *n. Med.* cowpox. [modern Latin (as VACCINE)]

vacillate /ˈvasɪleɪt/ *v.intr.* **1** fluctuate in opinion or resolution. **2** move from side to side; oscillate, waver. □ **vacillation** /-ˈleɪʃ(ə)n/ *n.* **vacillator** *n.* [Latin *vacillare vacillat-* 'sway']

vacua *pl.* of VACUUM.

vacuole /ˈvakjʊəʊl/ *n. Biol.* a space or vesicle within the cytoplasm of a cell, enclosed by a membrane and usu. containing fluid. □ **vacuolar** /ˈvakjʊələ/ *adj.* **vacuolation** /-ˈleɪʃ(ə)n/ *n.* [French, diminutive of Latin *vacuus* 'empty']

vacuous /ˈvakjʊəs/ *adj.* **1** lacking expression (*a vacuous stare*). **2** unintelligent (*a vacuous remark*). **3** empty. □ **vacuity** /vəˈkjuːɪti/ *n.* **vacuously** *adv.* **vacuousness** *n.* [Latin *vacuus* 'empty' (as VACATE)]

vacuum /ˈvakjʊəm/ *n.* & *v.* ● *n.* (*pl.* **vacuums** or **vacua** /-jʊə/) **1** a space entirely devoid of matter. **2** a space or vessel from which the air has been completely or partly removed by a pump etc. **3 a** the absence of the normal or previous content of a place, environment, etc. **b** the absence of former circumstances, activities, etc. **4** (*pl.* **vacuums**) *colloq.* a vacuum cleaner. **5** a decrease of pressure below the normal atmospheric value. ● *v. colloq.* **1** *tr.* clean with a vacuum cleaner. **2** *intr.* use a vacuum cleaner. [modern Latin, neut. of Latin *vacuus* 'empty']

vacuum brake *n.* a brake in which pressure is caused by the exhaustion of air.

vacuum cleaner *n.* an apparatus for removing dust etc. by suction. □ **vacuum-clean** *v.intr.* & *tr.*

vacuum flask *n.* esp. *Brit.* a vessel with a double wall enclosing a vacuum so that the liquid in the inner receptacle retains its temperature.

vacuum gauge *n.* a gauge for testing the pressure after the production of a vacuum.

vacuum-packed *adj.* sealed after the partial removal of air.

vacuum pump *n.* a pump for producing a vacuum.

vacuum tube *n.* a tube with a near-vacuum for the free passage of electric current.

VAD *abbr.* (in the UK) **1** Voluntary Aid Detachment. **2** a member of this.

vade-mecum /vɑːdɪˈmeɪkəm, veɪdɪˈmiːkəm/ *n.* a handbook etc. carried constantly for use. [French from modern Latin, = go with me]

vagabond /ˈvagəbɒnd/ *n.*, *adj.*, & *v.* ● *n.* **1** a wanderer or vagrant, esp. an idle one. **2** *colloq.* a scamp or rascal. ● *adj.* having no fixed habitation; wandering. ● *v.intr.* wander about as a vagabond. □ **vagabondage** *n.* [Middle English from Old French *vagabond* or Latin *vagabundus*, from *vagari* 'wander']

vagal see VAGUS.

vagary /ˈveɪg(ə)ri/ *n.* (*pl.* **-ies**) a caprice; an eccentric idea or act (*the vagaries of Fortune*). □ **vagarious** /vəˈgɛːrɪəs/ *adj.* [Latin *vagari* 'wander']

vagi *pl.* of VAGUS.

vagina /vəˈdʒʌɪnə/ *n.* (*pl.* **vaginas** or **vaginae** /-niː/) **1** the canal between the uterus and vulva of a woman or other female mammal. **2** a sheath formed round a stem by the base of a leaf. □ **vaginal** *adj.* **vaginitis** /vadʒɪˈnʌɪtɪs/ *n.* [Latin, = sheath, scabbard]

vaginismus /vadʒɪˈnɪzməs/ *n.* a painful spasmodic contraction of the vagina in response to physical contact or pressure (esp. in sexual intercourse). [modern Latin (as VAGINA)]

vagrant /ˈveɪgr(ə)nt/ *n.* & *adj.* ● *n.* **1** a person without a settled home or regular work; a tramp. **2** *archaic* a wanderer. **3** a bird that has strayed from its normal range or migratory route; also called *accidental*. ● *adj.* **1** characteristic of or relating to a vagrant or vagrancy. **2** wandering or roving (*a vagrant musician*). **3** *literary* random; occurring unpredictably (*vagrant inspiration; vagrant discoveries*). □ **vagrancy** *n.* **vagrantly** *adv.* [Middle English from Anglo-French *vag(a)raunt*, perhaps an alteration of Anglo-French *wakerant* etc. by association with Latin *vagari* 'wander']

vague /veɪg/ *adj.* **1** of uncertain or ill-defined meaning or character (*gave a vague answer; has some vague idea* *of emigrating*). **2** (of a person or mind) imprecise; inexact in thought, expression, or understanding. ▫ **vaguely** *adv.* **vagueness** *n.* **vaguish** *adj.* [French *vague* or Latin *vagus* 'wandering, uncertain']

vagus /'veɪɡəs/ *n.* (*pl.* **vagi** /-dʒʌɪ, -ɡʌɪ/) *Anat.* either of the tenth pair of cranial nerves, with branches to the heart, lungs, and viscera. ▫ **vagal** *adj.* [Latin: see VAGUE]

vail /veɪl/ *v. archaic* **1** *tr.* lower or doff (one's plumes, pride, crown, etc.) esp. in token of submission. **2** *intr.* yield; give place; remove one's hat as a sign of respect etc. [Middle English, via obsolete *avale* from Old French *avaler* 'to lower' from *a val* 'down', from *val* VALE[1]]

vain /veɪn/ *adj.* **1** excessively proud or conceited, esp. about one's own attributes. **2** empty, trivial, unsubstantial (*vain boasts*; *vain triumphs*). **3** useless; followed by no good result (*in the vain hope of dissuading them*). ▫ **in vain** without result or success (*it was in vain that we protested*). **take a person's name in vain** use it lightly or profanely. ▫ **vainly** *adv.* **vainness** /'veɪnnɪs/ *n.* [Middle English via Old French from Latin *vanus* 'empty, without substance']

vainglory /veɪn'ɡlɔːri/ *n. literary* boastfulness; extreme vanity. ▫ **vainglorious** *adj.* **vaingloriously** *adv.* **vaingloriousness** *n.* [Middle English, suggested by Old French *vaine gloire*, Latin *vana gloria*]

vair /vɛː/ *n.* **1** *archaic* or *hist.* a squirrel-fur widely used for medieval linings and trimmings. **2** *Heraldry* fur represented by small shield-shaped or bell-shaped figures usu. alternately azure and argent. [Middle English via Old French from Latin (as VARIOUS)]

Vaishnava /'vʌɪʃnəvə/ *n. Hinduism* a devotee of Vishnu. [Sanskrit *vaiṣṇava*]

Vaisya /'vʌɪsjə, -ʃjə/ *n.* a member of the third of the four great Hindu castes, comprising the merchants and farmers. [Sanskrit *vaiśya* 'peasant, labourer']

valance /'val(ə)ns/ *n.* (also **valence**) a short curtain round the frame or canopy of a bedstead, above a window, or under a shelf. ▫ **valanced** *adj.* [Middle English, ultimately from Old French *avaler* 'descend': see VAIL]

vale[1] /veɪl/ *n. archaic* or *poet.* (except in place names) a valley (*Vale of the White Horse*). ▫ **vale of tears** *literary* the world as a scene of life, trouble, etc. [Middle English via Old French *val* from Latin *vallis, valles*]

vale[2] /'vɑːleɪ/ *int. & n.* ● *int.* farewell. ● *n.* a farewell. [Latin, imperative of *valēre* 'be well or strong']

valediction /valɪ'dɪkʃ(ə)n/ *n.* **1** the act or an instance of bidding farewell. **2** the words used in this. [Latin *valedicere valedict-* (as VALE[2], *dicere* 'say'), on the pattern of *benediction*]

valedictorian /ˌvalɪdɪk'tɔːrɪən/ *n. N. Amer.* a person who gives a valedictory, esp. the highest-ranking member of a graduating class.

valedictory /valɪ'dɪkt(ə)ri/ *adj. & n.* ● *adj.* serving as a farewell. ● *n.* (*pl.* **-ies**) a farewell address.

valence[1] /'veɪl(ə)ns/ *n. Chem.* = VALENCY.

valence[2] var. of VALANCE.

valence electron *n.* an electron in the outermost shell of an atom involved in forming a chemical bond.

Valenciennes /vaˌlɒnsɪ'ɛn/ *n.* a rich kind of lace. [*Valenciennes* in NE France, where it was made in the 17th and 18th c.]

valency /'veɪl(ə)nsi/ *n.* (*pl.* **-ies**) *Brit. Chem.* the combining power of an atom measured by the number of hydrogen atoms it can displace or combine with. [Late Latin *valentia* 'power, competence' from *valēre* 'be well or strong']

valentine /'valəntʌɪn/ *n.* **1** a card or gift sent, often anonymously, as a mark of love or affection on St Valentine's Day (14 Feb.). **2** a sweetheart chosen on this day. [Middle English via Old French *Valentin* from Latin *Valentinus*, name of two saints]

valerian /və'lɪərɪən/ *n.* **1 a** a plant of the genus *Valeriana* (family Valerianaceae) with small usu. pink or white flowers and strong-smelling roots, esp. (in full **common valerian**) *Valeriana officinalis*. **b** a drug from the root of this, used as a stimulant and antispasmodic. **2** (in full **red valerian**) a related Mediterranean plant, *Centranthus ruber*, widely grown for its spurred flowers. [Middle English via Old French *valeriane* from medieval Latin *valeriana* (*herba*), apparently fem. of *Valerianus* 'of Valerius' (a personal name)]

valeric acid /və'lɛrɪk, -'lɪərɪk/ *n. Chem.* = PENTANOIC ACID. [VALERIAN + -IC]

valet /'valɪt, 'valeɪ/ *n. & v.* ● *n.* **1** a man's personal (usu. male) attendant who looks after his clothes etc. **2** a hotel etc. employee with similar duties. ● *v.* (**valeted, valeting**) **1** *intr.* work as a valet. **2** *tr.* act as a valet to. **3** *tr.* clean or clean out (a car). [French, = Old French *valet, vaslet*, VARLET: related to VASSAL]

valeta var. of VELETA.

valetudinarian /ˌvalɪtjuːdɪ'nɛːrɪən/ *n. & adj.* ● *n.* a person of poor health or unduly anxious about health. ● *adj.* **1** of or being a valetudinarian. **2** of poor health. **3** seeking to recover one's health. ▫ **valetudinarianism** *n.* [Latin *valetudinarius* 'in ill health' via *valetudo -dinis* 'health' from *valēre* 'be well']

valetudinary /valɪ'tjuːdɪn(ə)ri/ *adj. & n.* (*pl.* **-ies**) = VALETUDINARIAN.

valgus /'valɡəs/ *n.* a deformity involving the outward displacement of the foot or hand from the midline. [Latin, = knock-kneed]

Valhalla /val'halə/ *n.* **1** (in Norse mythology) a palace in which the souls of slain heroes feasted for eternity. **2** a building used for honouring the illustrious. [modern Latin from Old Norse *Valhöll*, from *valr* 'the slain' + *höll* HALL]

valiant /'valɪənt/ *adj.* (of a person or conduct) brave, courageous. ▫ **valiantly** *adv.* [Middle English from Anglo-French *valiaunt*, Old French *vailant*, ultimately from Latin *valēre* 'be strong']

valid /'valɪd/ *adj.* **1** (of a reason, objection, etc.) sound or defensible; well-grounded. **2 a** executed with the proper formalities (*a valid contract*). **b** legally acceptable (*a valid passport*). **c** not having reached its expiry date. ▫ **validity** /və'lɪdɪti/ *n.* **validly** *adv.* [French *valide* or Latin *validus* 'strong' (as VALIANT)]

validate /'valɪdeɪt/ *v.tr.* make valid; ratify, confirm. ▫ **validation** /-'deɪʃ(ə)n/ *n.* [medieval Latin *validare* from Latin (as VALID)]

valine /'veɪliːn/ *n. Biochem.* an amino acid that is an essential nutrient for vertebrates and a general constituent of proteins. [VALERIC ACID + -INE[4]]

valise /və'liːz/ *n.* **1** a kitbag. **2** *US* a small portmanteau. [French from Italian *valigia*, corresponding to medieval Latin *valisia*, of unknown origin]

Valium /'valɪəm/ *n. propr.* the drug diazepam used as a tranquillizer and relaxant. [20th c.: origin uncertain]

Valkyrie /val'kɪəri, 'valkɪri/ *n.* (in Norse mythology) each of Odin's twelve handmaidens who conducted the slain warriors of their choice from the battlefield to Valhalla. [Old Norse *Valkyrja*, literally 'chooser of the slain' from *valr* 'the slain' + *kyrjā* 'chooser']

vallecula /va'lɛkjʊlə/ *n.* (*pl.* **valleculae** /-liː/) *Anat. & Bot.* a groove or furrow. ▫ **vallecular** *adj.* **valleculate** /-leɪt/ *adj.* [Late Latin, diminutive of Latin *vallis* 'valley']

valley /'vali/ *n.* (*pl.* **-eys**) **1** a low area more or less enclosed by hills and usu. with a stream flowing through it. **2** any depression compared to this. **3** *Archit.* an internal angle formed by the intersecting planes of a roof. [Middle English from Anglo-French *valey*, Old French *valee*, ultimately from Latin *vallis, valles*: cf. VALE[1]]

vallum /'valəm/ *n. Rom. Antiq.* a rampart and stockade as a defence. [Latin, collective from *vallus* 'stake']

valonia /va'ləʊnɪə/ *n.* acorn-cups of an evergreen oak, *Quercus macrolepis*, used in tanning, dyeing, and making ink. [Italian *vallonia*, ultimately from Greek *balanos* 'acorn']

valor *US* var. of VALOUR.

valorize /ˈvalərʌɪz/ *v.tr.* (also **-ise**) raise or fix the price of (a commodity etc.) by artificial means, esp. by government action. □ **valorization** /-ˈzeɪʃ(ə)n/ *n.* [back-formation from *valorization* from French *valorisation* (as VALOUR)]

valour /ˈvalə/ *n.* (*US* **valor**) personal courage, esp. in battle. □ **valorous** *adj.* [Middle English via Old French from Late Latin *valor -oris*, from *valēre* 'be strong']

valse /vɑːls, vɔːls/ *n.* a waltz. [French from German (as WALTZ)]

valuable /ˈvaljʊb(ə)l/ *adj.* & *n.* ● *adj.* of great value, price, or worth (*a valuable property; valuable information*). ● *n.* (usu. in *pl.*) a valuable thing, esp. a small article of personal property. □ **valuably** *adv.*

valuation /valjʊˈeɪʃ(ə)n/ *n.* **1 a** an estimation (esp. by a professional valuer) of a thing's worth. **b** the worth estimated. **2** the price set on a thing. □ **valuate** /ˈva-/ *v.tr.* esp. *US.*

valuator /ˈvaljʊeɪtə/ *n.* a person who makes valuations; a valuer.

value /ˈvaljuː/ *n.* & *v.* ● *n.* **1** the worth, desirability, or utility of a thing, or the qualities on which these depend (*the value of regular exercise*). **2** worth as estimated; valuation (*set a high value on my time*). **3** the amount of money or goods for which a thing can be exchanged in the open market; purchasing power. **4** the equivalent of a thing; what represents or is represented by or may be substituted for a thing (*paid them the value of their lost property*). **5** (in full **value for money**) something well worth the money spent (cf. VALUE-FOR-MONEY). **6** the ability of a thing to serve a purpose or cause an effect (*news value; nuisance value*). **7** (in *pl.*) one's principles or standards; one's judgement of what is valuable or important in life. **8** *Mus.* the duration of the sound signified by a note. **9** *Math.* the amount denoted by an algebraic term or expression. **10** (foll. by *of*) **a** the meaning (of a word etc.). **b** the quality (of a spoken sound). **11** the relative rank or importance of a playing card, chess piece, etc., according to the rules of the game. **12** the relation of one part of a picture to others in respect of light and shade; the part being characterized by a particular tone. **13** *Physics* & *Chem.* the numerical measure of a quantity or a number denoting magnitude on some conventional scale (*the value of gravity at the equator*). ● *v.tr.* (**values, valued, valuing**) **1** estimate the value of; appraise (esp. professionally) (*valued the property at £200,000*). **2** have a high or specified opinion of; attach importance to (*a valued friend*). □ **good** (or **poor** etc.) **value** well worth (or not worth) the money or attention spent. [Middle English from Old French, fem. past part. of *valoir* 'be worth' from Latin *valēre*]

value added *n.* & *adj.* ● *n. Econ.* the amount by which the value of an article is increased at each stage of its production, exclusive of initial costs. ● *attrib.adj.* (**value-added**) **1** (of goods etc.) having enhancements etc. added to a basic line esp. to increase profit margins. **2** (of a company) offering specialized or extended services in a commercial area.

value added tax *n.* a tax on the amount by which the value of an article has been increased at each stage of its production.

value-for-money *attrib.adj.* well worth the money spent (cf. VALUE *n.* 5).

value judgement *n.* a subjective estimate of quality etc.

valueless /ˈvaljʊlɪs/ *adj.* having no value. □ **valuelessness** *n.*

valuer /ˈvaljʊə/ *n.* esp. *Brit.* a person who estimates or assesses values, esp. professionally.

value received *n.* money or its equivalent given for a bill of exchange.

valuta /vəˈljuːtə, -ˈluː-/ *n.* **1** the value of one currency with respect to another. **2** a currency considered in this way. [Italian, = VALUE]

valve /valv/ *n.* **1** a device for controlling the passage of fluid through a pipe etc., esp. an automatic device allowing movement in one direction only. **2** *Anat.* & *Zool.* a membranous part of an organ etc. allowing a flow of blood etc. in one direction only. **3** *Brit.* = THERMIONIC VALVE. **4** a device to vary the effective length of the tube in a brass musical instrument. **5** each of the two shells of an oyster, mussel, etc. **6** *Bot.* each of the segments into which a capsule or dry fruit dehisces. **7** *archaic* a leaf of a folding door. □ **valvate** /-veɪt/ *adj.* **valved** *adj.* (also in *comb.*). **valveless** *adj.* **valvule** *n.* [Middle English from Latin *valva* 'leaf of a folding door']

valvular /ˈvalvjʊlə/ *adj.* **1** having a valve or valves. **2** having the form or function of a valve. [modern Latin *valvula*, diminutive of Latin *valva*]

valvulitis /valvjʊˈlʌɪtɪs/ *n.* inflammation of the valves of the heart.

vambrace /ˈvambreɪs/ *n. hist.* defensive armour for the forearm. [Middle English from Anglo-French *vauntbras*, Old French *avant-bras*, from *avant* 'before' (see AVAUNT) + *bras* 'arm']

vamoose /vəˈmuːs/ *v.intr.* (esp. as *int.*) *US slang* depart hurriedly. [Spanish *vamos* 'let us go']

vamp[1] /vamp/ *n.* & *v.* ● *n.* **1** the upper front part of a boot or shoe. **2** a patched-up article. **3** *Mus.* a short simple introductory passage usu. repeated several times until otherwise instructed. ● *v.* **1** *tr.* (often foll. by *up*) repair or furbish. **2** *tr.* (foll. by *up*) make by patching or from odds and ends. **3** *intr.* play a vamp. **4** *tr.* put a new vamp to (a boot or shoe). [Middle English from Old French *avantpié*, from *avant* 'before' (see AVAUNT) + *pied* 'foot']

vamp[2] /vamp/ *n.* & *v. colloq.* ● *n.* a woman who uses sexual attraction to exploit men; an unscrupulous flirt. ● *v.* **1** *tr.* allure or exploit (a man). **2** *intr.* act as a vamp. □ **vampish** *adj.* **vampy** *adj.* [abbreviation of VAMPIRE]

vampire /ˈvampʌɪə/ *n.* **1** a reanimated corpse supposed to leave its grave at night to suck the blood of persons sleeping. **2** a person who preys ruthlessly on others. **3** (in full **vampire bat**) any tropical (esp. S. American) bat of the family Desmodontidae, with incisors for piercing flesh and feeding on blood. **4** *Theatr.* a small spring trapdoor used for sudden disappearances. □ **vampiric** /-ˈpɪrɪk/ *adj.* [French *vampire* or German *Vampir* from Hungarian *vampir*, perhaps from Turkish *uber* 'witch']

vampirism /ˈvampʌɪərɪz(ə)m/ *n.* **1** belief in the existence of vampires. **2** the practices of a vampire.

vamplate /ˈvampleɪt/ *n. hist.* an iron plate on a lance protecting the hand when the lance was couched. [Middle English from Anglo-French *vauntplate* (as VAMBRACE, PLATE)]

van[1] /van/ *n.* **1** a covered vehicle for conveying goods etc. **2** *Brit.* a railway carriage for luggage or for the use of the guard. **3** *Brit.* a gypsy caravan. [abbreviation of CARAVAN]

van[2] /van/ *n.* **1** a vanguard. **2** the forefront (*in the van of progress*). [abbreviation of VANGUARD]

van[3] /van/ *n.* **1** *Brit.* the testing of ore quality by washing on a shovel or by machine. **2** *archaic* a winnowing fan. **3** *archaic* or *poet.* a wing. [Middle English, southern & western variant of FAN[1], perhaps partly from Old French *van* or Latin *vannus*]

van[4] /van/ *n. Brit. Tennis colloq.* = ADVANTAGE *n.* 4. [abbreviation]

vanadium /vəˈneɪdɪəm/ *n. Chem.* a hard grey metallic transition element occurring naturally in several ores and used in small quantities for strengthening some steels (symbol V). □ **vanadate** /ˈvanədeɪt/ *n.* **vanadic** /-ˈnadɪk/ *adj.* **vanadous** /ˈvanədəs/ *adj.* [modern Latin, from Old Norse *Vanadís* (a name of the Scandinavian goddess Freyja) + -IUM]

Van Allen belt /van ˈalən/ *n.* (also **Van Allen layer**) each of two regions of intense radiation partly surrounding the earth at heights of several thousand kilometres. [named after J. A. *Van Allen*, US physicist b. 1914]

V. & A. *abbr.* Victoria & Albert Museum (in London).

vandal /ˈvand(ə)l/ *n.* & *adj.* ● *n.* **1** a person who wilfully or maliciously destroys or damages property etc. **2** (**Vandal**) a member of a Germanic people that ravaged Gaul, Spain, N. Africa, and Rome in the 4th–5th c., destroying many books and works of art. ● *adj.* of or relating to the Vandals. ▫ **Vandalic** /-ˈdalɪk/ *adj.* (in sense 2 of *n.*). [Latin *Vandalus*, from Germanic]

vandalism /ˈvand(ə)lɪz(ə)m/ *n.* wilful or malicious destruction or damage to property etc. ▫ **vandalistic** /-ˈlɪstɪk/ *adj.* **vandalistically** /-ˈlɪstɪk(ə)li/ *adv.*

vandalize /ˈvand(ə)lʌɪz/ *v.tr.* (also **-ise**) destroy or damage wilfully or maliciously.

van de Graaff generator /van də ˈgrɑːf/ *n. Electr.* a machine devised to generate electrostatic charge by means of a vertical endless belt collecting charge from a voltage source and transferring it to a large insulated metal dome, where a high voltage is produced. [named after R. J. *van de Graaff*, US physicist d. 1967]

van der Waals forces /van də ˈwɑːlz, ˈvɑːlz/ *n.pl. Chem.* short-range attractive forces between uncharged molecules arising from the interaction of dipole moments. [named after J. *van der Waals*, Dutch physicist d. 1923]

vandyke /vanˈdʌɪk/ *n.* & *adj.* ● *n.* **1** each of a series of large points forming a border to lace or cloth etc. **2** a cape or collar etc. with these. ● *adj.* (**Vandyke**) in the style of dress, esp. with pointed borders, common in portraits by Van Dyck. [named after Sir A. *Van Dyck*, Anglicized *Vandyke*, Flemish painter d. 1641]

Vandyke beard *n.* a neat pointed beard.

Vandyke brown *n.* & *adj.* ● *n.* a deep rich brown. ● *adj.* (hyphenated when *attrib.*) of this colour.

vane /veɪn/ *n.* **1 a** = WEATHERVANE. **b** an inconstant person or thing. **2** a blade of a screw propeller or a windmill etc. **3** the sight of surveying instruments, a quadrant, etc. **4** the flat part of a bird's feather formed by the barbs. ▫ **vaned** *adj.* [Middle English, southern & western variant of obsolete *fane* from Old English *fana* 'banner', from Germanic]

vang /vaŋ/ *n. Naut.* each of two guy-ropes running from the end of a gaff to the deck. [earlier *fang* = gripping-device: Old English via Old Norse *fang* 'grasp' from Germanic]

vanguard /ˈvangɑːd/ *n.* **1** the foremost part of an army or fleet advancing or ready to advance. **2** the leaders of a movement or of opinion etc. [earlier *vandgard*, *(a)vantgard* from Old French *avan(t)garde*, from *avant* 'before' (see AVAUNT) + *garde* GUARD]

vanilla /vəˈnɪlə/ *n.* **1 a** any tropical climbing orchid of the genus *Vanilla*, esp. *V. planifolia*, with fragrant flowers. **b** (in full **vanilla-pod**) the fruit of these. **2** a substance obtained from the vanilla-pod or synthesized and used to flavour ice cream, chocolate, etc. [Spanish *vainilla* 'pod', diminutive of *vaina* 'sheath, pod', from Latin VAGINA]

vanillin /vəˈnɪlɪn/ *n.* the fragrant principle of vanilla.

vanish /ˈvanɪʃ/ *v.* **1** *intr.* **a** disappear suddenly. **b** disappear gradually; fade away. **2** *intr.* cease to exist. **3** *intr. Math.* become zero. **4** *tr.* cause to disappear. [Middle English from Old French *e(s)vaniss-*, stem of *e(s)vanir*, ultimately from Latin *evanescere* (as EX-[1], *vanus* 'empty')]

vanishing cream *n.* an ointment that leaves no visible trace when rubbed into the skin.

vanishing point *n.* **1** the point at which receding parallel lines viewed in perspective appear to meet. **2** the state of complete disappearance of something.

vanitory /ˈvanɪt(ə)ri/ *n.* (*pl.* **-ies**) *propr.* = VANITY UNIT. [from VANITY + -ORY[1], on the pattern of *lavatory*]

vanity /ˈvanɪti/ *n.* (*pl.* **-ies**) **1** conceit and desire for admiration of one's personal attainments or attractions. **2 a** futility or unsubstantiality (*the vanity of human achievement*). **b** an unreal thing. **3** ostentatious display. **4** *N. Amer.* a dressing table. [Middle English via Old French *vanité* from Latin *vanitas -tatis* (as VAIN)]

vanity bag *n.* (also **vanity case**) a bag or case carried by a woman and containing a small mirror, make-up, etc.

Vanity Fair *n.* the world (allegorized in Bunyan's *Pilgrim's Progress*) as a scene of vanity.

vanity publisher *n.* a publisher who publishes only at the author's expense. ▫ **vanity publishing** *n.*

vanity unit *n.* a unit consisting of a washbasin set into a flat top with cupboards beneath.

vanquish /ˈvaŋkwɪʃ/ *v.tr. literary* conquer or overcome. ▫ **vanquishable** *adj.* **vanquisher** *n.* [Middle English *venkus*, *-quis*, etc., via Old French *vencus* past part., and *venquis* past tense, of *veintre* from Latin *vincere*: assimilated to -ISH[2]]

vantage /ˈvɑːntɪdʒ/ *n.* **1** (also **vantage point** or **ground**) a place affording a good view or prospect. **2** *Tennis* = ADVANTAGE *n.* 4. **3** *archaic* an advantage or gain. [Middle English via Anglo-French from Old French *avantage* ADVANTAGE]

vapid /ˈvapɪd/ *adj.* insipid; lacking interest; flat, dull (*vapid moralizing*). ▫ **vapidity** /vaˈpɪdɪti/ *n.* **vapidly** *adv.* **vapidness** *n.* [Latin *vapidus*]

vapor *US* var. of VAPOUR.

vaporetto /vapəˈrɛtəʊ/ *n.* (*pl.* **vaporetti** /-ti/ or **-os**) (in Venice) a canal boat (originally a steamboat, now a motor boat) used for public transport. [Italian, = small steamboat, diminutive of *vapore* from Latin *vapor* 'steam']

vaporific /veɪpəˈrɪfɪk, vap-/ *adj.* concerned with or causing vapour or vaporization.

vaporimeter /veɪpəˈrɪmɪtə/ *n.* an instrument for measuring the amount of vapour.

vaporize /ˈveɪpərʌɪz/ *v.tr.* & *intr.* (also **-ise**) convert or be converted into vapour. ▫ **vaporizable** *adj.* (also **vaporable**). **vaporization** /-ˈzeɪʃ(ə)n/ *n.*

vaporizer /ˈveɪpərʌɪzə/ *n.* a device that vaporizes substances, esp. for medicinal inhalation.

vapour /ˈveɪpə/ *n.* & *v.* (*US* **vapor**) ● *n.* **1** moisture or another substance diffused or suspended in air, e.g. mist or smoke. **2** *Physics* a gaseous form of a normally liquid or solid substance (cf. GAS *n.* 1). **3** a medicinal agent for inhaling. **4** (in *pl.*) *archaic* a state of depression or melancholy, thought to be caused by exhalations of vapour from the stomach. ● *v.intr.* **1** rise as vapour. **2** make idle boasts or empty talk. ▫ **vaporous** *adj.* **vaporousness** *n.* **vapourer** *n.* **vapouring** *n.* **vapourish** *adj.* **vapoury** *adj.* [Middle English from Old French *vapour* or Latin *vapor* 'steam, heat']

vapour density *n.* the density of a gas or vapour relative to hydrogen etc.

vapour pressure *n.* the pressure of a vapour in contact with its liquid or solid form.

vapour trail *n.* a trail of condensed water from an aircraft or rocket at high altitude, seen as a white streak against the sky.

VAR *abbr.* value-added reseller.

var. *abbr.* variety.

varactor /vəˈraktə/ *n.* a semiconductor diode with a capacitance dependent on the applied voltage. [*var*ying re*actor*]

varec /ˈvarɛk/ *n.* **1** seaweed. **2** = KELP. [French *varec(h)* from Old Norse: related to WRECK]

variable /ˈvɛːrɪəb(ə)l/ *adj.* & *n.* ● *adj.* **1 a** that can be varied or adapted (*a rod of variable length*; *the pressure is variable*). **b** (of a gear) designed to give varying speeds. **2** apt to vary; not constant; unsteady (*a variable mood*; *variable fortunes*). **3** *Math.* (of a quantity) indeterminate; able to assume different numerical values. **4** (of wind or currents) tending to change direction. **5** *Astron.* (of a star) periodically varying in brightness. **6** *Bot.* & *Zool.* (of a species) including individuals or groups that depart from the type. **7** *Biol.* (of an organism or part of it) tending to change in structure or function. ● *n.* **1** a variable thing or quantity. **2** *Math.* a variable quantity. **3** *Naut.* **a** a shifting wind. **b** (in *pl.*) the region between the NE and SE trade winds. □ **variability** /-ˈbɪlɪti/ *n.* **variableness** *n.* **variably** *adv.* [Middle English via Old French from Latin *variabilis* (as VARY)]

variance /ˈvɛːrɪəns/ *n.* **1** difference of opinion; dispute, disagreement; lack of harmony (*at variance among ourselves*; *a theory at variance with all known facts*). **2** *Law* a discrepancy between statements or documents. **3** *Statistics* a quantity equal to the square of the standard deviation. [Middle English via Old French from Latin *variantia* 'difference' (as VARY)]

variant /ˈvɛːrɪənt/ *adj.* & *n.* ● *adj.* **1** differing in form or details from the main one (*a variant spelling*). **2** having different forms (*forty variant types of pigeon*). **3** variable or changing. ● *n.* a variant form, spelling, type, reading, etc. [Middle English from Old French (as VARY)]

variate /ˈvɛːrɪət/ *n.* *Statistics* **1** a quantity having a numerical value for each member of a group. **2** a variable quantity, esp. one whose values occur according to a frequency distribution. [past part. of Latin *variare* (as VARY)]

variation /vɛːrɪˈeɪʃ(ə)n/ *n.* **1** the act or an instance of varying. **2** departure from a former or normal condition, action, or amount, or from a standard or type (*prices are subject to variation*). **3** the extent of this. **4** a thing that varies from a type. **5** *Mus.* a repetition (usu. one of several) of a theme in a changed or elaborated form. **6** *Astron.* a deviation of a celestial body from its mean orbit or motion. **7** *Math.* a change in a function etc. due to small changes in the values of constants etc. **8** *Ballet* a solo dance. □ **variational** *adj.* [Middle English from Old French *variation* or Latin *variatio* (as VARY)]

varicella /varɪˈsɛlə/ *n.* *Med.* **1** = CHICKENPOX. **2** (in full **varicella zoster**) a herpesvirus causing chickenpox and shingles. [modern Latin, irregular diminutive of VARIOLA]

varices *pl.* of VARIX.

varicocele /ˈvarɪkəsiːl/ *n.* *Med.* a mass of varicose veins in the spermatic cord. [formed as VARIX + -CELE]

varicoloured /ˈvɛːrɪkʌləd/ *adj.* (*US* **varicolored**) **1** variegated in colour. **2** of various or different colours. [Latin *varius* VARIOUS + COLOURED]

varicose /ˈvarɪkəʊs, varɪˈkəʊs/ *adj.* (esp. of the veins of the legs) affected by a condition causing them to become dilated and swollen. □ **varicosity** /-ˈkɒsɪti/ *n.* [Latin *varicosus* from VARIX]

varied /ˈvɛːrɪd/ *adj.* showing variety; diverse. □ **variedly** *adv.*

variegate /ˈvɛːrɪgeɪt, ˈvɛːrɪə-/ *v.tr.* **1** mark with irregular patches of different colours. **2** diversify in appearance, esp. in colour. **3** (as **variegated** *adj.*) *Bot.* (of plants) having leaves containing two or more colours. □ **variegation** /-ˈgeɪʃ(ə)n/ *n.* [Latin *variegare variegat-* from *varius* 'various']

varietal /vəˈrʌɪət(ə)l/ *adj.* **1** esp. *Bot.* & *Zool.* of, forming, or designating a variety. **2** (of wine) made from a single designated variety of grape. □ **varietally** *adv.*

varietist /vəˈrʌɪətɪst/ *n.* a person whose habits etc. differ from what is normal.

variety /vəˈrʌɪəti/ *n.* (*pl.* **-ies**) **1** diversity; absence of uniformity; many-sidedness; the condition of being various (*not enough variety in our lives*). **2** a quantity or collection of different things (*for a variety of reasons*). **3 a** a class of things different in some common qualities from the rest of a larger class to which they belong. **b** a specimen or member of such a class. **4** (foll. by *of*) a different form of a thing, quality, etc. **5** *Biol.* **a** a subspecies. **b** a cultivar. **c** an individual or group usually fertile within the species to which it belongs but differing from the species type in some qualities capable of perpetuation. **6** a mixed sequence of dances, songs, comedy acts, etc. (usu. *attrib.*: *a variety show*). [French *variété* or Latin *varietas* (as VARIOUS)]

variety store *n.* *N. Amer.* a shop selling many kinds of small items.

varifocal /vɛːrɪˈfəʊk(ə)l/ *adj.* & *n.* ● *adj.* having a focal length that can be varied, esp. of a lens that allows an infinite number of focusing distances for near, intermediate, and far vision. ● *n.* (in *pl.*) varifocal spectacles.

variform /ˈvɛːrɪfɔːm/ *adj.* having various forms. [Latin *varius* + -FORM]

variola /vəˈrʌɪələ/ *n.* *Med.* smallpox. □ **variolar** *adj.* **varioloid** /ˈvɛːrɪəlɔɪd/ *adj.* **variolous** *adj.* [medieval Latin, = pustule, pock (as VARIOUS)]

variole /ˈvɛːrɪəʊl/ *n.* **1** a shallow pit like a smallpox mark. **2** a small spherical mass in variolite. [medieval Latin *variola*: see VARIOLA]

variolite /ˈvɛːrɪəlʌɪt/ *n.* a rock with embedded small spherical masses causing on its surface an appearance like smallpox pustules. □ **variolitic** /-ˈlɪtɪk/ *adj.* [as VARIOLE + -ITE[1]]

variometer /vɛːrɪˈɒmɪtə/ *n.* **1** a device for varying the inductance in an electric circuit. **2** a device for indicating an aircraft's rate of change of altitude. [as VARIOUS + -METER]

variorum /vɛːrɪˈɔːrəm/ *adj.* & *n.* ● *adj.* **1** (of an edition of a text) having notes by various editors or commentators. **2** (of an edition of an author's works) including variant readings. ● *n.* a variorum edition. [Latin from *editio cum notis variorum* 'edition with notes by various' (commentators): genitive pl. of *varius* VARIOUS]

various /ˈvɛːrɪəs/ *adj.* **1** different, diverse (*too various to form a group*). **2** more than one, several (*for various reasons*). □ **variously** *adv.* **variousness** *n.* [Latin *varius* 'changing, diverse']

■ **Usage** *Various* (unlike *several*) cannot be used with *of* as (wrongly) in *Various of our friends arrived late.*

varistor /vɛːˈrɪstə, və-/ *n.* a semiconductor diode with resistance dependent on the applied voltage. [*var*ying res*istor*]

varix /ˈvɛːrɪks/ *n.* (*pl.* **varices** /ˈvarɪsiːz, vɛː-/) **1** *Med.* **a** a permanent abnormal dilation of a vein or artery. **b** a vein etc. dilated in this way. **2** each of the ridges across the whorls of a univalve shell. [Middle English from Latin *varix -icis*]

varlet /ˈvɑːlɪt/ *n.* *archaic* or *joc.* **1** a menial or rascal. **2** *hist.* a knight's attendant. □ **varletry** *n.* [Middle English from Old French, variant of *vaslet*: see VALET]

varmint /ˈvɑːmɪnt/ *n.* *N. Amer.* or *dial.* a mischievous or discreditable person or animal. [variant of *varmin*, VERMIN]

varna /ˈvɑːnə/ *n.* each of the four Hindu castes. [Sanskrit, = colour, class]

varnish /ˈvɑːnɪʃ/ *n.* & *v.* ● *n.* **1** a resinous solution used to give a hard shiny transparent coating to wood, metal, paintings, etc. **2** any other preparation for a similar purpose (*nail varnish*). **3** external appearance or display without an underlying reality. **4** artificial or natural glossiness. **5** a superficial polish of manner. ● *v.tr.* **1** apply varnish to. **2** gloss over (a fact). □ **varnisher** *n.* [Middle English via Old French *vernis* from medieval Latin *veronix* 'fragrant resin, sandarac' or medieval Greek *berenikē*, probably from *Berenice*, a town in Cyrenaica]

varsity /ˈvɑːsɪti/ *n.* (*pl.* **-ies**) **1** *Brit. colloq.* (esp. with reference to sports) university. **2** *N. Amer.* a university etc. first team in a sport. [abbreviation]

varus /ˈvɛːrəs/ *n.* a deformity involving the inward displacement of the foot or hand from the midline. [Latin, = bent, crooked]

varve /vɑːv/ *n.* annually deposited layers of clay and silt in a lake used to determine the chronology of glacial sediments. □ **varved** *adj.* [Swedish *varv* 'layer']

vary /ˈvɛːri/ *v.* (**-ies**, **-ied**) **1** *tr.* make different; modify, diversify (*seldom varies the routine*; *the style is not sufficiently varied*). **2** *intr.* **a** undergo change; become or be different (*the temperature varies from 30° to 70°*). **b** be of different kinds (*his mood varies*). **3** *intr.* (foll. by *as*) be in proportion to. □ **varyingly** *adv.* [Middle English from Old French *varier* or Latin *variare* (as VARIOUS)]

vas /vas/ *n.* (*pl.* **vasa** /ˈveɪsə/) *Anat.* a vessel or duct. □ **vasal** /ˈveɪs(ə)l/ *adj.* [Latin, = vessel]

vascular /ˈvaskjʊlə/ *adj.* of, made up of, or containing vessels for conveying blood or sap etc. (*vascular functions*; *vascular tissue*). □ **vascularity** /-ˈlarɪti/ *n.* **vascularly** *adv.* [modern Latin *vascularis* from Latin VASCULUM]

vascular bundle *n. Bot.* a strand of conducting vessels in the stem or leaves of a plant, usu. with phloem on the outside and xylem on the inside.

vascularize /ˈvaskjʊlərʌɪz/ *v.tr.* (also **-ise**) *Med.* & *Anat.* (usu. in *passive*) make vascular, develop (esp. blood) vessels in. □ **vascularization** /-ˈzeɪʃ(ə)n/ *n.*

vascular plant *n.* a plant with conducting tissue.

vasculum /ˈvaskjʊləm/ *n.* (*pl.* **vascula** /-lə/) a botanist's (usu. metal) collecting-case with a lengthwise opening. [Latin, diminutive of VAS]

vas deferens /ˈdɛfərenz/ *n.* (*pl.* **vasa deferentia** /ˌdefəˈrenʃɪə/) *Anat.* the spermatic duct from the testicle to the urethra. [as VAS + *deferēns*, pres. part. of Latin *deferre* 'carry away']

vase /vɑːz/ *n.* a vessel, usu. tall and often circular in cross-section, used as an ornament or container, esp. for flowers. □ **vaseful** *n.* (*pl.* **-fuls**). [French from Latin VAS]

vasectomy /vəˈsɛktəmi/ *n.* (*pl.* **-ies**) the cutting and sealing of part of each vas deferens, esp. as a means of sterilization. □ **vasectomize** *v.tr.* (also **-ise**).

Vaseline /ˈvasɪliːn/ *n.* & *v.* ● *n. propr.* a type of petroleum jelly used as an ointment, lubricant, etc. ● *v.tr.* (**vaseline**) treat with Vaseline. [formed irregularly from German *Wasser* + Greek *elaion* 'oil']

vasiform /ˈveɪzɪfɔːm/ *adj.* **1** duct-shaped. **2** vase-shaped. [Latin *vasi-* (from VAS) + -FORM]

vaso- /ˈveɪzəʊ/ *comb. form* a vessel, esp. a blood vessel (*vasoconstrictive*). [Latin *vas*: see VAS]

vasoactive /veɪzəʊˈaktɪv/ *adj.* = VASOMOTOR.

vasoconstriction /ˌveɪzəʊkənˈstrɪkʃ(ə)n/ *n.* the constriction of blood vessels. □ **vasoconstrictive** *adj.* **vasoconstrictor** *n.*

vasodilation /ˌveɪzəʊdʌɪˈleɪʃ(ə)n/ *n.* (also **vasodilatation** /-dʌɪleɪˈteɪʃ(ə)n/) the dilatation of blood vessels. □ **vasodilator** *n.* **vasodilatory** *adj.*

vasomotor /ˈveɪzəʊməʊtə/ *adj.* causing constriction or dilatation of blood vessels.

vasopressin /veɪzəʊˈprɛsɪn/ *n.* a pituitary hormone acting to reduce diuresis and increase blood pressure. Also called ANTIDIURETIC HORMONE.

vassal /ˈvas(ə)l/ *n.* **1** *hist.* a holder of land by feudal tenure on conditions of homage and allegiance. **2** *literary* a humble dependant. □ **vassalage** *n.* [Middle English via Old French from medieval Latin *vassallus* 'retainer', of Celtic origin, the root *vassus* corresponding to Old Breton *uuas*, Welsh *gwas*, Irish *foss*: cf. VAVASOUR]

vast /vɑːst/ *adj.* & *n.* ● *adj.* **1** immense, huge; very great (*a vast expanse of water*; *a vast crowd*). **2** *colloq.* great, considerable (*makes a vast difference*). ● *n. poet.* or *literary* a vast space (*the vast of heaven*). □ **vastly** *adv.* **vastness** *n.* [Latin *vastus* 'void, immense']

VAT /viːeɪˈtiː, vat/ *abbr.* (in the UK) value added tax.

vat /vat/ *n.* & *v.* ● *n.* **1** a large tank or other vessel, esp. for holding liquids or something in liquid in the process of brewing, tanning, dyeing, etc. **2** a dyeing liquor in which a textile is soaked to take up a colourless soluble dye afterwards coloured by oxidation in air. ● *v.tr.* (**vatted**, **vatting**) place or treat in a vat. [Middle English, southern & western variant of *fat*, Old English *fæt*, from Germanic]

vatic /ˈvatɪk/ *adj. formal* prophetic or inspired. [Latin *vates* 'prophet']

Vatican /ˈvatɪk(ə)n/ *n.* **1** the palace and official residence of the Pope in Rome. **2** papal government. □ **Vaticanism** *n.* **Vaticanist** *n.* [French *Vatican* or Latin *Vaticanus*, the name of a hill in Rome]

Vatican City *n.* an independent Papal State in Rome, instituted in 1929.

Vatican Council *n.* an ecumenical council of the Roman Catholic Church, esp. that held in 1869–70 or that held in 1962–5.

vaticinate /vaˈtɪsɪneɪt/ *v.tr.* & *intr. formal* prophesy. □ **vaticinal** *adj.* **vaticination** /-ˈneɪʃ(ə)n/ *n.* **vaticinator** *n.* [Latin *vaticinari* from *vates* 'prophet']

VATman /ˈvatman/ *n.* (*pl.* **-men**) *Brit. colloq.* a customs and excise officer who administers VAT.

vaudeville /ˈvɔːdəvɪl, ˈvəʊd-/ *n.* **1** esp. *US* variety entertainment. **2** a stage play on a trivial theme with interspersed songs. **3** a satirical or topical song with a refrain. □ **vaudevillian** /-ˈvɪlɪən/ *adj.* & *n.* [French, originally of convivial song, esp. any of those composed by O. Basselin, 15th-c. poet born at *Vau de Vire* in Normandy]

Vaudois[1] /ˈvəʊdwɑː/ *n.* & *adj.* ● *n.* (*pl.* same) **1** a native of Vaud in W. Switzerland. **2** the French dialect spoken in Vaud. ● *adj.* of or relating to Vaud or its dialect. [French]

Vaudois[2] /ˈvəʊdwɑː/ *n.* & *adj.* ● *n.* (*pl.* same) a member of the Waldenses. ● *adj.* of or relating to the Waldenses. [French, representing medieval Latin *Valdensis*: see WALDENSES]

vault /vɔːlt/ *n.* & *v.* ● *n.* **1 a** an arched roof. **b** a continuous arch. **c** a set or series of arches whose joints radiate from a central point or line. **2** a vaultlike covering (*the vault of heaven*). **3** an enclosed space, esp. an underground chamber: **a** as a place of storage (*bank vaults*). **b** as a place of interment beneath a church or in a cemetery etc. (*family vault*). **4** an act of vaulting. **5** *Anat.* the arched roof of a cavity. ● *v.* **1** *intr.* leap or spring, esp. while resting on one or both hands or with the help of a pole. **2** *tr.* spring over (a gate etc.) in this way. **3** *tr.* (esp. as **vaulted**) **a** make in the form of a vault. **b** provide with a vault or vaults. □ **vaulter** *n.* [Old French *voute*, *vaute*, ultimately from Latin *volvere* 'to roll']

vaulting /ˈvɔːltɪŋ/ *n.* **1** arched work in a vaulted roof or ceiling. **2** a gymnastic or athletic exercise in which participants vault over obstacles.

vaulting horse *n.* a padded wooden block to be vaulted over by gymnasts.

vaunt /vɔːnt/ *v.* & *n. literary* ● *v.* **1** *intr.* boast, brag. **2** *tr.* boast of; extol boastfully. ● *n.* a boast. □ **vaunter** *n.* **vauntingly** *adv.* [Middle English via Anglo-French *vaunter*, Old French *vanter* from Late Latin *vantare*, from Latin *vanus* VAIN: partly obsolete verb *avaunt* from *avanter*, from intensive *a-* + *vanter*]

vavasory /ˈvavəs(ə)ri/ *n.* (*pl.* **-ies**) *hist.* the estate of a vavasour. [Old French *vavasorie* or medieval Latin *vavasoria* (as VAVASOUR)]

vavasour /ˈvavəsʊə/ *n. hist.* a vassal owing allegiance to a great lord and having other vassals under him. [Middle English via Old French *vavas(s)our* from medieval Latin *vavassor*, perhaps from *vassus vassorum* 'VASSAL of vassals']

VC *abbr.* **1** Victoria Cross. **2** Vice-Chairman. **3** Vice-Chancellor. **4** Vice-Consul.

VCR *abbr.* video cassette recorder.

VD *abbr.* venereal disease.

VDU *abbr.* visual display unit.

VE *abbr.* Victory in Europe (in 1945).

've *abbr. colloq.* (usu. after pronouns) have (*I've*; *they've*).

veal /viːl/ *n.* calf's flesh as food. □ **vealy** *adj.* [Middle English via Anglo-French *ve(e)l*, Old French *veiaus veel* from Latin *vitellus*, diminutive of *vitulus* 'calf']

vector /ˈvɛktə/ *n.* & *v.* ● *n.* **1** *Math.* & *Physics* a quantity having direction as well as magnitude, esp. as determining the position of one point in space relative to another (*radius vector*). **2** an organism, often an insect, that carries a disease or a parasite from one animal or plant to another. **3** a course to be taken by an aircraft. ● *v.tr.* direct (an aircraft in flight) to a desired point. □ **vectorial** /-'tɔ:rɪəl/ *adj.* **vectorize** *v.tr.* (also **-ise**) (in sense 1 of *n.*). **vectorization** /-tərʌɪ'zeɪʃ(ə)n/ *n.* [Latin, = carrier, from *vehere vect-* 'convey']

Veda /'veɪdə, 'vi:də/ *n.* (in *sing.* or *pl.*) the most ancient Hindu scriptures, esp. four collections called the Rig-Veda, Sāma-Veda, Yajur-Veda, and Atharva-Veda. [Sanskrit *veda*, literally '(sacred) knowledge']

Vedanta /vɪ'dɑ:ntə, -'da-, vɛ-/ *n.* **1** the Upanishads. **2** the Hindu philosophy based on these, esp. in its monistic form. □ **Vedantic** *adj.* **Vedantist** *n.* [Sanskrit *vedānta* (as VEDA, *anta* 'end')]

VE day *n.* 8 May, the day marking Victory in Europe in 1945.

Vedda /'vɛdə/ *n.* a member of an aboriginal Sri Lankan people. [Sinhalese *veddā* 'hunter']

vedette /vɪ'dɛt/ *n.* a mounted sentry positioned beyond an army's outposts to observe the movements of the enemy. [French, = scout, from Italian *vedetta*, *veletta* via Spanish *vela(r)* 'watch' from Latin *vigilare*]

Vedic /'veɪdɪk, 'vi:-/ *adj.* & *n.* ● *adj.* of or relating to the Veda or Vedas. ● *n.* the language of the Vedas, an older form of Sanskrit. [French *védique* or German *vedisch* (as VEDA)]

vee /vi:/ *n.* **1** the letter V. **2** a thing shaped like a V. [name of the letter]

veep /vi:p/ *n.* esp. *US colloq.* a vice-president. [from the initials *VP*]

veer[1] /vɪə/ *v.* & *n.* ● *v.intr.* **1** change direction, esp. (of the wind) clockwise (cf. BACK *v.* 5). **2** change in course, opinion, conduct, emotions, etc. **3** *Naut.* = WEAR[2]. ● *n.* a change of course or direction. [French *virer* from Romanic, perhaps an alteration of Latin *gyrare* GYRATE]

veer[2] /vɪə/ *v.tr. Naut.* slacken or let out (a rope, cable, etc.). [Middle English from Middle Dutch *vieren*]

veery /'vɪəri/ *n.* a N. American woodland thrush, *Catharus fuscescens*. [perhaps imitative]

veg /vɛdʒ/ *n.* (*pl.* same) *Brit. colloq.* a vegetable or vegetables. [abbreviation]

vegan /'vi:g(ə)n/ *n.* & *adj.* ● *n.* a person who does not eat or use animal products. ● *adj.* using or containing no animal products. [VEGETARIAN + -AN]

Vegeburger *propr.* var. of VEGGIE BURGER.

vegetable /'vɛdʒɪtəb(ə)l, 'vɛdʒtə-/ *n.* & *adj.* ● *n.* **1** *Bot.* any of various plants, esp. a herbaceous plant used wholly or partly for food, e.g. a cabbage, potato, turnip, or bean. **2** *colloq.* **a** *offens.* a person who is incapable of normal intellectual activity, esp. through brain injury etc. **b** *derog.* a person lacking in animation or living a monotonous life. ● *adj.* **1** of, derived from, relating to, or comprising plants or plant life, esp. as distinct from animal life or mineral substances. **2** of or relating to vegetables as food. **3 a** unresponsive to stimulus (*vegetable behaviour*). **b** uneventful, monotonous (*a vegetable existence*). [originally = living and growing as a plant: Middle English from Old French *vegetable* or Late Latin *vegetabilis* 'animating' (as VEGETATE)]

vegetable butter *n.* a vegetable fat with the consistency of butter.

vegetable ivory *n.* a hard white material obtained from the endosperm of the ivory-nut.

vegetable marrow see MARROW 1.

vegetable oil *n.* an oil derived from plants, e.g. rapeseed oil, olive oil, sunflower oil.

vegetable oyster *n.* = SALSIFY.

vegetable parchment see PARCHMENT 2.

vegetable spaghetti *n. Brit.* **1** a variety of marrow with flesh resembling spaghetti. **2** its flesh.

vegetable sponge *n.* = LOOFAH.

vegetable tallow *n.* a vegetable fat used as tallow.

vegetable wax *n.* an exudation of certain plants such as sumac.

vegetal /'vɛdʒɪt(ə)l/ *adj.* **1** of or having the nature of plants (*vegetal growth*). **2** vegetative. [medieval Latin *vegetalis* from Latin *vegetare* 'animate']

vegetarian /vɛdʒɪ'tɛ:rɪən/ *n.* & *adj.* ● *n.* a person who abstains from animal food, esp. meat, though often not from eggs and dairy products. ● *adj.* excluding animal food, esp. meat (*a vegetarian diet*). □ **vegetarianism** *n.* [formed irregularly from VEGETABLE + -ARIAN]

vegetate /'vɛdʒɪteɪt/ *v.intr.* **1** live an uneventful or monotonous life. **2** grow as plants do; fulfil vegetal functions. [Latin *vegetare* 'animate', via *vegetus* from *vegēre* 'be active']

vegetation /vɛdʒɪ'teɪʃ(ə)n/ *n.* **1** plants collectively; plant life (*luxuriant vegetation*; *no sign of vegetation*). **2** the process of vegetating. □ **vegetational** *adj.* [medieval Latin *vegetatio* 'growth' (as VEGETATE)]

vegetative /'vɛdʒɪtətɪv, -teɪtɪv/ *adj.* **1** concerned with growth and development as distinct from sexual reproduction. **2** of or relating to vegetation or plant life. **3** *Med.* alive but without apparent brain activity or responsiveness. □ **vegetatively** *adv.* **vegetativeness** *n.* [Middle English from Old French *vegetatif -ive* or medieval Latin *vegetativus* (as VEGETATE)]

veggie /'vɛdʒi/ *n.* & *adj.* (also **vegie**) *colloq.* **1** (a) vegetarian. **2** esp. *N. Amer.* (a) vegetable. [abbreviation]

veggie burger *n.* (also **Vegeburger** *propr.*) a savoury cake resembling a hamburger but made with vegetable protein, soya, etc., instead of meat.

vehement /'vi:ɪm(ə)nt/ *adj.* showing or caused by strong feeling; forceful, ardent (*a vehement protest*; *vehement desire*). □ **vehemence** *n.* **vehemently** *adv.* [Middle English from French *véhément* or Latin *vehemens -entis*, perhaps from *vemens* (unrecorded) 'deprived of mind', associated with *vehere* 'carry']

vehicle /'vi:ɪk(ə)l/ *n.* **1** any conveyance for transporting people, goods, etc., esp. on land. **2** a medium for thought, feeling, or action (*the stage is the best vehicle for their talents*). **3** a liquid etc. as a medium for suspending pigments, drugs, etc. **4** the literal meaning of a word or words used metaphorically (opp. TENOR 6). □ **vehicular** /vɪ'hɪkjʊlə/ *adj.* [French *véhicule* or Latin *vehiculum* from *vehere* 'carry']

veil /veɪl/ *n.* & *v.* ● *n.* **1** a piece of usu. more or less transparent fabric attached to a woman's hat etc., esp. to conceal the face or protect against the sun, dust, etc. **2** a piece of linen etc. as part of a nun's headdress, resting on the head and shoulders. **3** a curtain, esp. that separating the sanctuary in the Jewish Temple. **4** a disguise; a pretext; a thing that conceals (*under the veil of friendship*; *a veil of mist*). **5** *Photog.* slight fogging. **6** huskiness of the voice. **7** = VELUM. ● *v.tr.* **1** cover with a veil. **2** (esp. as **veiled** *adj.*) partly conceal (*veiled threats*). □ **beyond the veil** in the unknown state of life after death. **draw a veil over** avoid discussing or calling attention to. **take the veil** become a nun. □ **veilless** *adj.* [Middle English via Anglo-French *veil(e)*, Old French *voil(e)* from Latin *vela*, pl. of VELUM]

veiling /'veɪlɪŋ/ *n.* light fabric used for veils etc.

vein /veɪn/ *n.* & *v.* ● *n.* **1 a** any of the tubes forming part of the blood circulation system of the body, carrying usu. oxygen-depleted blood to the heart (cf. ARTERY 1). **b** (in general use) any blood vessel (*has royal blood in his veins*). **2** a nervure of an insect's wing. **3** a slender bundle of tissue forming a rib in the framework of a leaf. **4** a streak or stripe of a different colour in wood, marble, cheese, etc. **5** a fissure in rock filled with ore or other deposited material. **6** a source of a particular characteristic (*a rich vein of humour*). **7** a distinctive character or tendency; a cast of mind or disposition; a mood (*spoke in a sarcastic vein*). ● *v.tr.* fill or cover with or as with veins. □ **veinless** *adj.* **veinlet** *n.* **veinlike** *adj.* **veiny** *adj.* (**veinier**, **veiniest**). [Middle English via Old French *veine* from Latin *vena*]

veining /'veɪnɪŋ/ *n.* a pattern of streaks or veins.

veinstone /'veɪnstəʊn/ *n.* = GANGUE.

vela *pl.* of VELUM.

velamen /vɪ'leɪmən/ *n.* (*pl.* **velamina** /-mɪnə/) an enveloping membrane, esp. of an aerial root of an orchid. [Latin, from *velare* 'to cover']

velar /'viːlə/ *adj.* **1** of a veil or velum. **2** *Phonet.* (of a sound) pronounced with the back of the tongue near the soft palate. [Latin *velaris* from *velum*: see VELUM]

Velcro /'vɛlkrəʊ/ *n. propr.* a fastener for clothes etc. consisting of two strips of nylon fabric, one looped and one burred, which adhere when pressed together. □ **Velcroed** *adj.* [French *velours croché* 'hooked velvet']

veld /vɛlt/ *n.* (also **veldt**) *S.Afr.* open country; grassland. [Afrikaans from Dutch, = FIELD]

veldskoen /'fɛltskʊn, 'fɛls-/ *n.* a strong suede or leather shoe or boot. [Afrikaans, = field-shoe]

veleta /və'liːtə/ *n.* (also **valeta**) a ballroom dance in triple time. [Spanish, = weathervane]

veliger /'viːlɪdʒə/ *n. Zool.* the free-swimming larva of a mollusc, with a ciliated velum. [VELUM + Latin *-ger* 'bearing']

velitation /vɛlɪ'teɪʃ(ə)n/ *n. archaic* a slight skirmish or controversy. [Latin *velitatio*, via *velitari* 'to skirmish' from *veles velitis* 'light-armed skirmisher']

velleity /vɛ'liːɪti/ *n. literary* **1** a low degree of volition not conducive to action. **2** a slight wish or inclination. [medieval Latin *velleitas* from Latin *velle* 'to wish']

vellum /'vɛləm/ *n.* **1 a** fine parchment originally from the skin of a calf. **b** a manuscript written on this. **2** smooth writing paper imitating vellum. [Middle English from Old French *velin* (as VEAL)]

velocimeter /vɛlə'sɪmɪtə/ *n.* an instrument for measuring velocity.

velocipede /vɪ'lɒsɪpiːd/ *n.* **1** *hist.* an early form of bicycle propelled by pressure from the rider's feet on the ground. **2** *US* a child's tricycle. □ **velocipedist** *n.* [French *vélocipède*, from Latin *velox -ocis* 'swift' + *pes pedis* 'foot']

velociraptor /vɪˌlɒsɪ'raptə/ *n.* a small bipedal carnivorous dinosaur of the genus *Velociraptor*, of the Cretaceous period, with an enlarged curved claw on each hind foot. [modern Latin, from Latin *velox -ocis* 'swift' + RAPTOR]

velocity /vɪ'lɒsɪti/ *n.* (*pl.* **-ies**) **1** the measure of the rate of movement of a usu. inanimate object in a given direction. **2** speed in a given direction. **3** (in general use) speed. [French *vélocité* or Latin *velocitas* from *velox -ocis* 'swift']

velocity of escape *n.* = ESCAPE VELOCITY.

velodrome /'vɛlədrəʊm/ *n.* a special place or building with a track for cycle racing. [French *vélodrome* from *vélo* bicycle (as VELOCITY, -DROME)]

velour /və'lʊə/ *n.* (also **velours**) **1** a plush woven fabric or felt resembling velvet. **2** *archaic* a hat of this felt. [French *velours* 'velvet' via Old French *velour*, *velous* from Latin *villosus* 'hairy', from *villus*: see VELVET]

velouté /və'luːteɪ/ *n.* a sauce made from a roux of butter and flour with white stock. [French, = velvety]

velum /'viːləm/ *n.* (*pl.* **vela** /-lə/) a membrane, membranous covering, or flap. [Latin, = sail, curtain, covering, veil]

velutinous /vɛ'l(j)uːtɪnəs/ *adj.* covered with soft fine hairs. [perhaps from Italian *vellutino*, from *velluto* VELVET]

velvet /'vɛlvɪt/ *n.* & *adj.* ● *n.* **1** a closely woven fabric of silk, cotton, etc., with a thick short pile on one side. **2** the furry skin on a deer's growing antler. **3** anything smooth and soft like velvet. ● *adj.* of, like, or soft as velvet. □ **on velvet** in an advantageous or prosperous position. □ **velveted** *adj.* **velvety** *adj.* [Middle English via Old French *veluotte* from *velu* 'velvety', via medieval Latin *villutus* from Latin *villus* 'tuft, down']

velvet ant *n.* a parasitic wasp of the family Mutillidae with a velvety body, the females being wingless.

velveteen /vɛlvɪ'tiːn/ *n.* **1** a cotton fabric with a pile like velvet. **2** (in *pl.*) trousers etc. made of this.

velvet glove *n.* outward gentleness, esp. cloaking firmness or strength (cf. IRON HAND).

Ven. *abbr.* Venerable (as the title of an archdeacon).

vena cava /viːnə 'keɪvə/ *n.* (*pl.* **venae cavae** /-niː -viː/) each of usu. two veins carrying deoxygenated blood into the heart. [Latin, = hollow vein]

venal /'viːn(ə)l/ *adj.* **1** (of a person) able to be bribed or corrupted. **2** (of conduct etc.) characteristic of a venal person. □ **venality** /-'nalɪti/ *n.* **venally** *adv.* [Latin *venalis* from *venum* 'thing for sale']

■ **Usage** *Venal* is sometimes confused with *venial*, which means 'pardonable'.

venation /vɪ'neɪʃ(ə)n/ *n.* the arrangement of veins in a leaf or an insect's wing etc., or the system of venous blood vessels in an organism. □ **venational** *adj.* [Latin *vena* 'vein']

vend /vɛnd/ *v.tr.* **1** offer (small wares) for sale. **2** *Law* sell. □ **vendible** *adj.* [French *vendre* or Latin *vendere* 'sell' (as VENAL, *dare* 'give')]

vendace /'vɛndɪs/ *n.* a small delicate fish, *Coregonus albula*, found in some British lakes. [Old French *vendese*, *-oise*, from Gaulish]

vendee /vɛn'diː/ *n. Law* the buying party in a sale, esp. of property.

vendetta /vɛn'dɛtə/ *n.* **1 a** a blood feud in which the family of a murdered person seeks vengeance on the murderer or the murderer's family. **b** this practice as prevalent in Corsica and Sicily. **2** a prolonged bitter quarrel. [Italian from Latin *vindicta*: see VINDICTIVE]

vendeuse /vɒn'dəːz, French vɑ̃døz/ *n.* a saleswoman, esp. in a fashionable dress shop. [French]

vending machine *n.* a machine that dispenses small articles for sale when a coin or token is inserted.

vendor /'vɛndə/ *n.* **1** /also -dɔː/ *Law* the seller in a sale, esp. of property. **2** = VENDING MACHINE. [Anglo-French *vendour* (as VEND)]

vendue /vɛn'djuː/ *n. US* a public auction. [Dutch *vendu(e)* from French *vendue* 'sale', from *vendre* VEND]

veneer /vɪ'nɪə/ *n.* & *v.* ● *n.* **1 a** a thin covering of fine wood or other surface material applied to a coarser wood. **b** a layer in plywood. **2** (often foll. by *of*) a deceptive outward appearance of a good quality etc. ● *v.tr.* **1** apply a veneer to (wood, furniture, etc.). **2** disguise (an unattractive character etc.) with a more attractive manner etc. [earlier *fineer*: German *furni(e)ren* from Old French *fournir* FURNISH]

veneering /vɪ'nɪərɪŋ/ *n.* material used as veneer.

venepuncture /'vɛnɪˌpʌŋ(k)tʃə, 'viːnɪ-/ *n.* (also, esp. *N. Amer.* **venipuncture**) *Med.* the puncture of a vein esp. with a hypodermic needle to withdraw blood or for an intravenous injection. [Latin *vena* 'vein' + PUNCTURE]

venerable /'vɛn(ə)rəb(ə)l/ *adj.* **1** entitled to veneration on account of character, age, associations, etc. (*a venerable priest*; *venerable relics*). **2** as the title of an archdeacon in the Anglican Church. **3** *RC Ch.* as the title of a deceased person who has attained a certain degree of sanctity but has not been fully beatified or canonized. □ **venerability** /-'bɪlɪti/ *n.* **venerableness** *n.* **venerably** *adv.* [Middle English from Old French *venerable* or Latin *venerabilis* (as VENERATE)]

venerate /'vɛnəreɪt/ *v.tr.* **1** regard with deep respect. **2** revere on account of sanctity etc. □ **veneration** /-'reɪʃ(ə)n/ *n.* **venerator** *n.* [Latin *venerari* 'adore, revere']

venereal /vɪ'nɪərɪəl/ *adj.* **1** of or relating to sexual desire or intercourse. **2** relating to venereal disease. □ **venereally** *adv.* [Middle English from Latin *venereus*, from *venus veneris* 'sexual love']

venereal disease *n.* any of various diseases contracted chiefly by sexual intercourse with a person already infected; a sexually transmitted disease.

venereology /vɪˌnɪərɪ'ɒlədʒi/ *n.* the scientific study of venereal diseases. □ **venereological** /-ə'lɒdʒɪk(ə)l/ *adj.* **venereologist** *n.*

venery[1] /'vɛn(ə)ri/ *n. archaic* sexual indulgence. [medieval Latin *veneria* (as VENEREAL)]

venery[2] /ˈvɛn(ə)ri/ *n. archaic* hunting. [Middle English from Old French *venerie*, from *vener* 'to hunt', ultimately from Latin *venari*]

venesection /vɛnɪˈsɛkʃ(ə)n, ˈvɛnɪ-/ *n. Med.* phlebotomy. [medieval Latin *venae sectio* 'cutting of a vein' (as VEIN, SECTION)]

Venetian /vɪˈniːʃ(ə)n/ *n. & adj.* ● *n.* **1** a native or citizen of Venice in NE Italy. **2** the Italian dialect of Venice. **3** (**venetian**) = VENETIAN BLIND. ● *adj.* of or relating to Venice. □ **venetianed** *adj.* (in sense 3 of *n.*). [Middle English from Old French *Venicien*, assimilated to medieval Latin *Venetianus* from *Venetia* 'Venice']

venetian blind *n.* a window blind of adjustable horizontal slats to control the amount of light excluded.

Venetian glass *n.* delicate glassware made at Murano near Venice.

Venetian red *n. & adj.* ● *n.* **1** a reddish pigment of ferric oxides. **2** a strong reddish-brown colour. ● *adj.* (hyphenated when *attrib.*) of this colour.

Venetian window *n.* a window with three separate openings, the central one being arched and highest.

vengeance /ˈvɛn(d)ʒ(ə)ns/ *n.* punishment inflicted or retribution exacted for wrong to oneself or to a person etc. whose cause one supports. □ **with a vengeance** in a higher degree than was expected or desired; in the fullest sense (*punctuality with a vengeance*). [Middle English from Old French, from *venger* 'avenge', from Latin (as VINDICATE)]

■ **Usage** *Vengeance* incorporates the idea of justifiable retribution, as opposed to *revenge* which often implies that the main aim of the retribution is the satisfaction of the injured party's resentment.

vengeful /ˈvɛn(d)ʒfʊl, -f(ə)l/ *adj.* vindictive; seeking vengeance. □ **vengefully** *adv.* **vengefulness** *n.* [obsolete *venge* 'avenge' (as VENGEANCE)]

venial /ˈviːnɪəl/ *adj.* (of a sin or fault) pardonable, excusable; not mortal. □ **veniality** /-ˈalɪti/ *n.* **venially** *adv.* [Middle English via Old French from Late Latin *venialis*, from *venia* 'forgiveness']

■ **Usage** *Venial* is sometimes confused with *venal*, which means 'corrupt'.

venipuncture var. of VENEPUNCTURE.

venison /ˈvɛnɪs(ə)n, ˈvɛnɪz(ə)n/ *n.* a deer's flesh as food. [Middle English via Old French *veneso(u)n* from Latin *venatio -onis* 'hunting', from *venari* 'to hunt']

Venite /vɪˈnʌɪti/ *n.* **1** a canticle consisting of Psalm 95. **2** a musical setting of this. [Middle English from Latin, = 'come ye', its first word]

Venn diagram /vɛn/ *n.* a diagram of usu. circular areas representing mathematical sets, the areas intersecting where they have elements in common. [named after J. *Venn*, English logician d. 1923]

venom /ˈvɛnəm/ *n.* **1** a poisonous fluid secreted by snakes, scorpions, etc., usu. transmitted by a bite or sting. **2** malignity; virulence of feeling, language, or conduct. □ **venomed** *adj.* [Middle English from Old French *venim*, variant of *venin*, ultimately from Latin *venenum* 'poison']

venomous /ˈvɛnəməs/ *adj.* **1 a** containing, secreting, or injecting venom. **b** (of a snake etc.) inflicting poisonous wounds by this means. **2** (of a person etc.) virulent, spiteful, malignant. □ **venomously** *adv.* **venomousness** *n.* [Middle English from Old French *venimeux*, from *venim*: see VENOM]

venose /ˈviːnəʊs/ *adj.* having many or very marked veins. [Latin *venosus* from *vena* 'vein']

venous /ˈviːnəs/ *adj.* of, full of, or contained in veins. □ **venosity** /vɪˈnɒsɪti/ *n.* **venously** *adv.* [Latin *venosus* VENOSE, or Latin *vena* 'vein' + -OUS]

vent[1] /vɛnt/ *n. & v.* ● *n.* **1** (also **vent-hole**) a hole or opening allowing motion of air etc. out of or into a confined space. **2** an outlet; free passage or play (*gave vent to their indignation*). **3** the anus esp. of a lower animal, serving for both excretion and reproduction. **4** the venting of an otter, beaver, etc. **5** an aperture or outlet through which volcanic products are discharged at the earth's surface. **6** a touch-hole of a gun. **7** a finger-hole in a musical instrument. **8** a flue of a chimney. ● *v.* **1** *tr.* **a** make a vent in (a cask etc.). **b** provide (a machine) with a vent. **2** *tr.* give vent or free expression to (*vented my anger on the cat*). **3** *intr.* (of an otter, beaver, etc.) come to the surface for breath. □ **vent one's spleen on** scold or ill-treat without cause. □ **ventless** *adj.* [partly French *vent* from Latin *ventus* 'wind', partly French *évent* from *éventer* 'expose to air' (from Old French *esventer*), ultimately from Latin *ventus* 'wind']

vent[2] /vɛnt/ *n.* a slit in a garment, esp. in the lower edge of the back of a coat. [Middle English, variant of *fent* from Old French *fente* 'slit', ultimately from Latin *findere* 'cleave']

ventiduct /ˈvɛntɪdʌkt/ *n. Archit.* an air passage, esp. for ventilation. [Latin *ventus* 'wind' + *ductus* DUCT]

ventifact /ˈvɛntɪfakt/ *n.* a stone shaped by wind-blown sand. [Latin *ventus* 'wind' + *factum*, neut. past part. of *facere* 'make']

ventil /ˈvɛntɪl/ *n. Mus.* **1** a valve in a wind instrument. **2** a shutter for regulating the airflow in an organ. [German via Italian *ventile* and medieval Latin *ventile* 'sluice' from Latin *ventus* 'wind']

ventilate /ˈvɛntɪleɪt/ *v.tr.* **1** cause air to circulate freely in (a room etc.). **2** submit (a question, grievance, etc.) to public consideration and discussion. **3** *Med.* **a** oxygenate (the blood). **b** admit or force air into (the lungs). □ **ventilation** /-ˈleɪʃ(ə)n/ *n.* **ventilative** /-leɪtɪv/ *adj.* [Latin *ventilare ventilat-* 'blow, winnow', from *ventus* 'wind']

ventilator /ˈvɛntɪleɪtə/ *n.* **1** an appliance or aperture for ventilating a room etc. **2** *Med.* = RESPIRATOR 2.

Ventolin /ˈvɛntəlɪn/ *n. propr.* a preparation of salbutamol. [perhaps from VENTILATE + -OL[1] + -IN]

ventouse /ˈvɛntuːs/ *n.* a vacuum extractor for use in childbirth. [French, ultimately from Latin *ventus* 'wind']

ventral /ˈvɛntr(ə)l/ *adj.* **1** *Anat. & Zool.* of or on the abdomen (cf. DORSAL 1). **2** *Bot.* of the front or lower surface. □ **ventrally** *adv.* [obsolete *venter* from Latin *venter ventr-* 'belly']

ventral fin *n.* either of the ventrally placed fins on a fish.

ventre à terre /ˌvɑːntr(ə) ɑː ˈtɛː, French vɑ̃tr a tɛr/ *adv.* at full speed. [French, literally 'with belly to the ground']

ventricle /ˈvɛntrɪk(ə)l/ *n. Anat.* **1** a cavity in the body. **2** a hollow part of an organ, esp. in the brain or heart. □ **ventricular** /-ˈtrɪkjʊlə/ *adj.* [Middle English from Latin *ventriculus*, diminutive of *venter* 'belly']

ventricose /ˈvɛntrɪkəʊs/ *adj.* **1** having a protruding belly. **2** *Bot.* distended, inflated. [formed irregularly from VENTRICLE + -OSE[1]]

ventriloquism /vɛnˈtrɪləkwɪz(ə)m/ *n.* the skill of speaking or uttering sounds so that they seem to come from the speaker's dummy or a source other than the speaker. □ **ventriloquial** /vɛntrɪˈləʊkwɪəl/ *adj.* **ventriloquist** *n.* **ventriloquize** *v.intr.* (also **-ise**). [ultimately from Latin *ventriloquus* 'ventriloquist', from *venter* 'belly' + *loqui* 'speak']

ventriloquy /vɛnˈtrɪləkwi/ *n.* = VENTRILOQUISM.

venture /ˈvɛntʃə/ *n. & v.* ● *n.* **1 a** an undertaking of a risk. **b** a risky enterprise. **2** a commercial speculation. ● *v.* **1** *intr.* dare; not be afraid (*did not venture to stop them*). **2** *intr.* (usu. foll. by *out* etc.) dare to go (out), esp. outdoors. **3** *tr.* dare to put forward (an opinion, suggestion, etc.). **4 a** *tr.* expose to risk; stake (a bet etc.). **b** *intr.* take risks. **5** *intr.* (foll. by *on, upon*) dare to engage in etc. (*ventured on a longer journey*). □ **at a venture** at random; without previous consideration. [from ADVENTURE]

venture capital *n.* = RISK CAPITAL.

venturer /ˈvɛntʃ(ə)rə/ *n. hist.* a person who undertakes or shares in a trading venture.

Venture Scout *n.* a member of the Scout Association aged between 16 and 20.

venturesome /ˈvɛntʃəs(ə)m/ *adj.* **1** disposed to take risks; adventurous. **2** risky. □ **venturesomely** *adv.* **venturesomeness** *n.*

venturi /vɛnˈtjʊəri/ *n.* (*pl.* **venturis**) a short piece of narrow tube between wider sections for measuring flow-rate or exerting suction. [named after G. B. *Venturi*, Italian physicist d. 1822]

venue /ˈvɛnjuː/ *n.* **1 a** an appointed site or meeting place, esp. for a sports event, meeting, concert, etc. **b** a rendezvous. **2** *Law hist.* the county or other place within which a jury must be gathered and a case tried (originally the neighbourhood of the crime etc.). [French, = a coming, fem. past part. of *venir* 'come' from Latin *venire*]

venule /ˈvɛnjuːl/ *n. Anat.* a small vein, esp. one collecting blood from the capillaries. [Latin *venula*, diminutive of *vena* 'vein']

Venus /ˈviːnəs/ *n.* (*pl.* **Venuses**) **1** the planet second from the sun in the solar system. **2** *poet.* **a** a beautiful woman. **b** sexual love; amorous influences or desires. □ **Venusian** /vɪˈnjuːzɪən/ *adj.* & *n.* [Old English from Latin *Venus Veneris*, name of the goddess of love]

Venus flytrap *n.* (also **Venus's flytrap**) a plant, *Dionaea muscipula*, with hinged leaves that close on and digest insects etc.

Venus's comb *n.* = SHEPHERD'S NEEDLE.

Venus's looking-glass *n.* any of various plants of the genus *Legousia* with small blue flowers.

veracious /vəˈreɪʃəs/ *adj. formal* **1** speaking or disposed to speak the truth. **2** (of a statement etc.) true or meant to be true. □ **veraciously** *adv.* **veraciousness** *n.* [Latin *verax veracis* from *verus* 'true']

veracity /vəˈrasɪti/ *n.* **1** truthfulness, honesty. **2** accuracy (of a statement etc.). [French *veracité* or medieval Latin *veracitas* (as VERACIOUS)]

veranda /vəˈrandə/ *n.* (also **verandah**) **1** a portico or external gallery, usu. with a roof, along the side of a house. **2** *Austral.* & *NZ* a roof over a pavement in front of a shop. [Hindi *varaṇḍā* from Portuguese *varanda* 'railing, balustrade']

veratrine /ˈvɛrətriːn, -m/ *n.* a poisonous compound obtained from sabadilla etc., and used esp. as a local irritant in the treatment of neuralgia and rheumatism. [French *vératrine* from Latin *veratrum* 'hellebore']

verb /vəːb/ *n. Gram.* a word used to indicate an action, state, or occurrence, and forming the main part of the predicate of a sentence (e.g. *hear*, *become*, *happen*). [Middle English from Old French *verbe* or Latin *verbum* 'word, verb']

verbal /ˈvəːb(ə)l/ *adj.*, *n.*, & *v.* ● *adj.* **1** of or concerned with words (*made a verbal distinction*). **2** oral, not written (*gave a verbal statement*). **3** *Gram.* of or in the nature of a verb (*verbal inflections*). **4** literal (*a verbal translation*). **5** talkative, articulate. ● *n.* **1** *Gram.* **a** a verbal noun. **b** a word or words functioning as a verb. **2** (usu. in *pl.*) *Brit. slang* a verbal statement, esp. one made to the police. **3** *Brit. slang* an insult; abuse (*gave them a lot of verbals*). ● *v.tr.* (**verballed**, **verballing**) *Brit. slang* attribute a damaging statement to (a suspect). □ **verbally** *adv.* [Middle English from French *verbal* or Late Latin *verbalis* (as VERB)]

■ **Usage** Some people reject sense 2 of *verbal* as illogical, and prefer *oral.* However, *verbal* is the usual term in expressions such as *verbal communication*, *verbal contract*, and *verbal evidence*.

verbalism /ˈvəːb(ə)lɪz(ə)m/ *n.* **1** minute attention to words; verbal criticism. **2** merely verbal expression. □ **verbalist** *n.* **verbalistic** /-ˈlɪstɪk/ *adj.*

verbalize /ˈvəːb(ə)lʌɪz/ *v.* (also **-ise**) **1** *tr.* express in words. **2** *intr.* be verbose. **3** *tr.* make (a noun etc.) into a verb. □ **verbalizable** *adj.* **verbalization** /-ˈzeɪʃ(ə)n/ *n.* **verbalizer** *n.*

verbal noun *n. Gram.* a noun formed as an inflection of a verb and partly sharing its constructions (e.g. *smoking* in *smoking is forbidden*: see -ING[1]).

verbascum /vəːˈbaskəm/ *n.* a plant of the genus *Verbascum*, a mullein. [Latin]

verbatim /vəːˈbeɪtɪm/ *adv.* & *adj.* in exactly the same words; word for word (*copied it verbatim*; *a verbatim report*). [Middle English from medieval Latin (*adv.*), from Latin *verbum* 'word': cf. LITERATIM]

verbena /vəːˈbiːnə/ *n.* any plant of the genus *Verbena*, bearing clusters of fragrant flowers. [Latin, = sacred bough of olive etc., in medieval Latin 'vervain']

verbiage /ˈvəːbɪɪdʒ/ *n.* needless accumulation of words; verbosity. [French, via obsolete *verbeier* 'chatter' from *verbe* 'word': see VERB]

verbose /vəːˈbəʊs/ *adj.* using or expressed in more words than are needed. □ **verbosely** *adv.* **verboseness** *n.* **verbosity** /-ˈbɒsɪti/ *n.* [Latin *verbosus* from *verbum* 'word']

verboten /fəːˈbəʊt(ə)n, German fɛrˈboːtən/ *adj.* forbidden, esp. by an authority. [German]

verb. sap. /vəːb ˈsap/ *int.* expressing the absence of the need for a further explicit statement. [abbreviation of Latin *verbum sapienti sat est* 'a word is enough for the wise person']

verdant /ˈvəːd(ə)nt/ *adj.* **1** (of grass etc.) green, fresh-coloured. **2** (of a field etc.) green with grass and vegetation; lush. **3** (of a person) unsophisticated, raw, green. □ **verdancy** *n.* **verdantly** *adv.* [perhaps from Old French *verdeant*, part. of *verdoier* 'be green', ultimately from Latin *viridis* 'green']

verd-antique /vəːdanˈtiːk/ *n.* **1** ornamental usu. green serpentine. **2** a green incrustation on ancient bronze. **3** green porphyry. [obsolete French, = antique green]

verderer /ˈvəːd(ə)rə/ *n. Brit.* a judicial officer of royal forests. [Anglo-French (earlier *verder*), Old French *verdier*, ultimately from Latin *viridis* 'green']

verdict /ˈvəːdɪkt/ *n.* **1** a decision on an issue of fact in a civil or criminal case or an inquest. **2** a decision; a judgement. [Middle English from Anglo-French *verdit*, Old French *voirdit*, from *voir*, *veir* 'true' (from Latin *verus*) + *dit* from Latin DICTUM 'saying']

verdigris /ˈvəːdɪgriː, -griːs/ *n.* **1 a** a green crystallized substance formed on copper by the action of acetic acid. **b** this used as a medicine or pigment. **2** green rust on copper or brass. [Middle English from Old French *vertegres*, *vert de Grece* 'green of Greece']

verdure /ˈvəːdjə, -jʊə/ *n.* **1** green vegetation. **2** the greenness of this. **3** *poet.* freshness. □ **verdured** *adj.* **verdurous** *adj.* [Middle English via Old French, from *verd* 'green', from Latin *viridis*]

verge[1] /vəːdʒ/ *n.* & *v.* ● *n.* **1** an edge or border. **2** an extreme limit beyond which something happens (*on the verge of tears*). **3** *Brit.* a grass edging of a road, flower bed, etc. **4** *Archit.* an edge of tiles projecting over a gable. **5** a wand or rod carried before a bishop, dean, etc., as an emblem of office. ● *v.intr.* (foll. by *on*) border on; approach closely (*verging on the ridiculous*). [Middle English via Old French from Latin *virga* 'rod']

verge[2] /vəːdʒ/ *v.intr.* incline downwards or in a specified direction (*the now verging sun*; *verge to a close*). [Latin *vergere* 'bend, incline']

verger /ˈvəːdʒə/ *n.* (also **virger**) **1** an official in a church who acts as caretaker and attendant. **2** an officer who bears the staff before a bishop etc. □ **vergership** *n.* [Middle English from Anglo-French (as VERGE[1])]

verglas /ˈvɛːglɑː/ *n.* a thin coating of ice or frozen rain. [French, from *verre* 'glass' + *glas* (now *glace*) 'ice']

veridical /vɪˈrɪdɪk(ə)l/ *adj.* **1** *formal* truthful. **2** *Psychol.* (of visions etc.) coinciding with reality. □ **veridicality** /-ˈkalɪti/ *n.* **veridically** *adv.* [Latin *veridicus*, from *verus* 'true' + *dicere* 'say']

veriest /ˈvɛrɪɪst/ *adj. archaic* so called in the fullest sense; complete, absolute (*the veriest fool knows that*). [superl. of VERY]

verification /ˌvɛrɪfɪˈkeɪʃ(ə)n/ *n.* **1** the process or an instance of establishing the truth or validity of something. **2** *Philos.* the establishment of the validity of a proposition empirically. **3** the process of verifying procedures laid down in weapons agreements.

verify /ˈvɛrɪfʌɪ/ *v.tr.* (**-ies**, **-ied**) **1** establish the truth or correctness of by examination or demonstration (*must verify the statement; verified my figures*). **2** (of an event etc.) bear out or fulfil (a prediction or promise). **3** *Law* append an affidavit to (pleadings); support (a statement) by testimony or proofs. □ **verifiable** *adj.* **verifiably** *adv.* **verifier** *n.* [Middle English via Old French *verifier* from medieval Latin *verificare*, from *verus* 'true']

verily /ˈvɛrɪli/ *adv. archaic* really, truly. [Middle English, from VERY + -LY², suggested by Old French *verrai(e)ment*, Anglo-French *veirement*]

verisimilitude /ˌvɛrɪsɪˈmɪlɪtju:d/ *n.* **1** the appearance or semblance of being true or real. **2** a statement etc. that seems true. □ **verisimilar** /-ˈsɪmɪlə/ *adj.* [Latin *verisimilitudo* from *verisimilis* 'probable', from *veri* (genitive of *verus* 'true') + *similis* 'like']

verism /ˈvɪərɪz(ə)m/ *n.* realism in literature or art. □ **verist** *n.* **veristic** /-ˈrɪstɪk/ *adj.* [Latin *verus* or Italian *vero* 'true' + -ISM]

verismo /vɛˈrɪzməʊ/ *n.* (esp. with reference to opera) realism. [Italian (as VERISM)]

veritable /ˈvɛrɪtəb(ə)l/ *adj.* real; rightly so called (*a veritable feast*). □ **veritably** *adv.* [Old French (as VERITY)]

verity /ˈvɛrɪti/ *n.* (*pl.* **-ies**) **1** a true statement, esp. one of fundamental import. **2** truth. **3** a really existent thing. [Middle English via Old French *verité*, *verté* from Latin *veritas -tatis*, from *verus* 'true']

verjuice /ˈvə:dʒu:s/ *n.* **1** an acid liquor obtained from crab apples, sour grapes, etc., and formerly used in cooking and medicine. **2** bitter feelings, thoughts, etc. [Middle English from Old French *vertjus*, from VERT 'green' + *jus* JUICE]

verkrampte /fɛ:ˈkramptə, Afrikaans fɛrˈkramptə/ *adj. & n. S.Afr.* ● *adj.* politically or socially conservative or reactionary, esp. as regards apartheid. ● *n.* a person holding such views. [Afrikaans, literally 'narrow, cramped']

verligte /fɛ:ˈlɪxtə, Afrikaans fɛrˈlɪxtə/ *adj. & n. S.Afr.* ● *adj.* progressive or enlightened, esp. as regards apartheid. ● *n.* a person holding such views. [Afrikaans, = enlightened]

vermeil /ˈvə:meɪl, -mɪl/ *n. & adj.* ● *n.* **1** silver gilt. **2** an orange-red garnet. **3** *poet.* vermilion. ● *adj. poet.* vermilion. [Middle English from Old French: see VERMILION]

vermi- /ˈvə:mi/ *comb. form* worm. [Latin *vermis* 'worm']

vermian /ˈvə:mɪən/ *adj.* of worms; wormlike. [Latin *vermis* 'worm']

vermicelli /və:mɪˈtʃɛli, -sɛli/ *n.* **1** pasta made in long slender threads. **2** *Brit.* shreds of chocolate used as cake decoration etc. [Italian, pl. of *vermicello*, diminutive of *verme*, from Latin *vermis* 'worm']

vermicide /ˈvə:mɪsʌɪd/ *n.* a substance that kills worms.

vermicular /vəˈmɪkjʊlə/ *adj.* **1** like a worm in form or movement; vermiform. **2** *Med.* of or caused by intestinal worms. **3** marked with close wavy lines. [medieval Latin *vermicularis* from Latin *vermiculus*, diminutive of *vermis* 'worm']

vermiculate /vəˈmɪkjʊlət/ *adj.* **1** = VERMICULAR. **2** worm-eaten. [Latin *vermiculatus*, past part. of *vermiculari* 'be full of worms' (as VERMICULAR)]

vermiculation /vəmɪkjʊˈleɪʃ(ə)n/ *n.* **1** the state or process of being eaten or infested by or converted into worms. **2** a vermicular marking. **3** a worm-eaten state. [Latin *vermiculatio* (as VERMICULATE)]

vermiculite /vəˈmɪkjʊlʌɪt/ *n.* **1** *Mineral.* a hydrated silicate resulting from the alteration of mica etc., esp. an aluminosilicate of magnesium. **2** this material in flakes used as a medium for growing plants, for insulation, etc. [as VERMICULATE + -ITE¹]

vermiform /ˈvə:mɪfɔ:m/ *adj.* worm-shaped.

vermiform appendix see APPENDIX 1.

vermifuge /ˈvə:mɪfju:dʒ/ *adj. & n.* ● *adj.* that expels intestinal worms. ● *n.* a drug that does this.

vermilion /vəˈmɪljən/ *n. & adj.* ● *n.* **1** cinnabar. **2 a** a brilliant red pigment made by grinding this or artificially. **b** the colour of this. ● *adj.* of this colour. [Middle English via Old French *vermeillon*, from *vermeil*, from Latin *vermiculus*, diminutive of *vermis* 'worm']

vermin /ˈvə:mɪn/ *n.* (usu. treated as *pl.*) **1** mammals and birds injurious to game, crops, etc., e.g. foxes, rodents, and noxious insects. **2** parasitic worms or insects. **3 a** vile or contemptible persons. **b** a person of this type. □ **verminous** *adj.* [Middle English from Old French *vermin*, *-ine*, ultimately from Latin *vermis* 'worm']

verminate /ˈvə:mɪneɪt/ *v.intr.* **1** breed vermin. **2** become infested with parasites. □ **vermination** /-ˈneɪʃ(ə)n/ *n.* [Latin *verminare verminat-* from *vermis* 'worm']

vermivorous /və:ˈmɪv(ə)rəs/ *adj.* feeding on worms.

vermouth /ˈvə:məθ, vəˈmu:θ/ *n.* a wine flavoured with aromatic herbs. [French *vermout* from German *Wermut* WORMWOOD]

vernacular /vəˈnakjʊlə/ *n. & adj.* ● *n.* **1** the language or dialect of a particular country (*Latin gave place to the vernacular*). **2** the language of a particular clan or group. **3** homely speech. ● *adj.* **1** (of language) of one's native country; not of foreign origin or of learned formation. **2** (of architecture) concerned with ordinary rather than monumental buildings. □ **vernacularism** *n.* **vernacularity** /-ˈlarɪti/ *n.* **vernacularize** *v.tr.* (also **-ise**). **vernacularly** *adv.* [Latin *vernaculus* 'domestic, native' from *verna* 'home-born slave']

vernal /ˈvə:n(ə)l/ *adj.* of, in, or appropriate to spring (*vernal equinox; vernal breezes*). □ **vernally** *adv.* [Latin *vernalis*, via *vernus* from *ver* 'spring']

vernal equinox *n.* = SPRING EQUINOX.

vernal grass *n.* a sweet-scented European grass, *Anthoxanthum odoratum*, grown for hay.

vernalization /və:n(ə)lʌɪˈzeɪʃ(ə)n/ *n.* (also **-isation**) the cooling of seed before planting, in order to accelerate flowering. □ **vernalize** /ˈvə:n(ə)lʌɪz/ *v.tr.* (also **-ise**). [(translation of Russian *yarovizatsiya*) from VERNAL]

vernation /və:ˈneɪʃ(ə)n/ *n. Bot.* the arrangement of leaves in a leaf bud (cf. AESTIVATION). [modern Latin *vernatio* from Latin *vernare* 'bloom' (as VERNAL)]

vernicle /ˈvə:nɪk(ə)l/ *n.* = VERONICA 2. [Middle English via Old French (earlier *ver(o)nique*) from medieval Latin VERONICA]

vernier /ˈvə:nɪə/ *n.* a small movable graduated scale for obtaining fractional parts of subdivisions on a fixed main scale of a barometer, sextant, etc. [named after P. *Vernier*, French mathematician d. 1637]

vernier engine *n.* an auxiliary engine for slight changes in the motion of a space rocket etc. [as VERNIER]

veronal /ˈvɛrən(ə)l/ *n.* a sedative drug, a derivative of barbituric acid. [German, from *Verona*, a city in Italy]

veronica /vəˈrɒnɪkə/ *n.* **1** any plant of the genus *Veronica* or *Hebe*, esp. speedwell. **2 a** a cloth supposedly impressed with an image of Christ's face. **b** any similar picture of Christ's face. **3** the movement of a matador's cape away from a charging bull. [medieval Latin from the name *Veronica*: in sense 2 from the association with St Veronica]

verruca /vɛˈru:kə/ *n.* (*pl.* **verrucae** /-ki:, -si:/ or **verrucas**) a wart or similar growth, esp. a contagious wart on the sole of the foot. □ **verrucose** /ˈvɛrʊkəʊz, -ˈru:-/ *adj.* **verrucous** /ˈvɛrʊkəs, -ˈru:-/ *adj.* [Latin]

versant /ˈvə:s(ə)nt/ *n.* **1** the extent of land sloping in one direction. **2** the general slope of land. [French, pres. part. of *verser* from Latin *versare*, frequentative of *vertere vers-* 'turn']

versatile /ˈvə:sətʌɪl/ *adj.* **1** turning easily or readily from one subject or occupation to another; capable of dealing with many subjects (*a versatile mind*). **2** (of a device etc.) having many uses. **3** *Bot.* & *Zool.* moving freely about or up and down on a support (*versatile antenna*). **4** *archaic* changeable, inconstant. □ **versatilely** *adv.* **versatility** /-ˈtɪlɪti/ *n.* [French *versatile* or Latin *versatilis* (as VERSANT)]

verse /vəːs/ *n.* & *v.* ● *n.* **1 a** metrical composition in general (*wrote pages of verse*) (opp. PROSE *n.* 1). **b** a particular type of this (*English verse*). **2 a** a metrical line in accordance with the rules of prosody. **b** a group of a definite number of such lines. **c** a stanza of a poem or song with or without refrain. **3** each of the short numbered divisions of a chapter in the Bible or other scripture. **4 a** a versicle. **b** a passage (of an anthem etc.) for solo voice. ● *v.tr.* **1** express in verse. **2** (foll. by *in*) instruct; make knowledgeable. □ **verselet** *n.* [Old English *fers* from Latin *versus* 'a turn of the plough, a furrow, a line of writing', from *vertere vers-* 'to turn': reinforced in Middle English by Old French *vers* from Latin *versus*]

versed[1] /vəːst/ *adj.* (foll. by *in*) experienced or skilled in; knowledgeable about. [French *versé* or Latin *versatus*, past part. of *versari* 'be engaged in' (as VERSANT)]

versed[2] /vəːst/ *adj. Math.* reversed. [modern Latin (*sinus*) *versus* 'turned (sine)' (as VERSE)]

versed sine *n. Math.* unity minus cosine.

verset /ˈvəːsɪt/ *n. Mus.* a short prelude or interlude for organ. [French: diminutive of *vers* VERSE]

versicle /ˈvəːsɪk(ə)l/ *n.* each of the short sentences in a liturgy said or sung by a priest etc. and alternating with responses. □ **versicular** /-ˈsɪkjʊlə/ *adj.* [Middle English from Old French *versicule* or Latin *versiculus*, diminutive of *versus*: see VERSE]

versicoloured /ˈvəːsɪkʌləd/ *adj.* (*US* **versicolored**) **1** changing from one colour to another in different lights. **2** variegated. [Latin *versicolor* from *versus* (past part. of *vertere* 'turn') + *color* 'colour']

versify /ˈvəːsɪfʌɪ/ *v.* (**-ies**, **-ied**) **1** *tr.* turn into or express in verse. **2** *intr.* compose verses. □ **versification** /-fɪˈkeɪʃ(ə)n/ *n.* **versifier** *n.* [Middle English via Old French *versifier* from Latin *versificare* (as VERSE)]

versin /ˈvəːsɪn, -sʌɪn/ *n.* (also **versine**) *Math.* = VERSED SINE.

version /ˈvəːʃ(ə)n/ *n.* **1** an account of a matter from a particular person's point of view (*told them my version of the incident*). **2** a book or work etc. in a particular edition or translation (*Authorized Version*). **3** a form or variant of a thing as performed, adapted, etc. **4** a piece of translation, esp. as a school exercise. **5** *Med.* the manual turning of a foetus in the womb to improve presentation. □ **versional** *adj.* [French *version* or medieval Latin *versio*, from Latin *vertere vers-* 'to turn']

vers libre /vɛː ˈliːbr(ə), French vɛr libr/ *n.* irregular or unrhymed verse in which the traditional rules of prosody are disregarded. [French, = free verse]

verso /ˈvəːsəʊ/ *n.* (*pl.* **-os**) **1 a** the left-hand page of an open book (opp. RECTO 1). **b** the back of a printed leaf of paper or manuscript (opp. RECTO 2). **2** the reverse of a coin. [Latin *verso* (*folio*) 'on the turned (leaf)']

verst /vəːst/ *n.* a Russian measure of length, about 1.1 km (0.66 mile). [Russian *versta*]

versus /ˈvəːsəs/ *prep.* against (esp. in legal and sports use) (abbr.: **v**, **v.**, **vs.**). [Latin, = towards, in medieval Latin 'against']

vert /vəːt/ *n.* & (usu. placed after noun) *adj. Heraldry* green. [Middle English via Old French from Latin *viridis* 'green']

vertebra /ˈvəːtɪbrə/ *n.* (*pl.* **vertebrae** /-breɪ, -briː/) **1** each segment of the backbone. **2** (in *pl.*) the backbone. □ **vertebral** *adj.* [Latin, from *vertere* 'to turn']

vertebrate /ˈvəːtɪbrət/ *n.* & *adj.* ● *n.* any animal of the subphylum Vertebrata, having a spinal column, including mammals, birds, reptiles, amphibians, and fishes. ● *adj.* of or relating to the vertebrates. [Latin *vertebratus* 'jointed' (as VERTEBRA)]

vertebration /vəːtɪˈbreɪʃ(ə)n/ *n.* division into vertebrae or similar segments.

vertex /ˈvəːtɛks/ *n.* (*pl.* **vertices** /-tɪsiːz/ or **vertexes**) **1** the highest point; the top or apex. **2** *Geom.* **a** each angular point of a polygon, polyhedron, etc. **b** a meeting point of two lines that form an angle. **c** the point at which an axis meets a curve or surface. **3** *Anat.* the crown of the head. [Latin *vertex -ticis* 'whirlpool, crown of a head, vertex', from *vertere* 'to turn']

vertical /ˈvəːtɪk(ə)l/ *adj.* & *n.* ● *adj.* **1** at right angles to a horizontal plane, perpendicular. **2** in a direction from top to bottom of a picture etc. **3** of or at the vertex or highest point. **4** at, or passing through, the zenith. **5** *Anat.* of or relating to the crown of the head. **6** involving all the levels in an organizational hierarchy or stages in the production of a class of goods (*vertical integration*). ● *n.* a vertical line or plane. □ **out of the vertical** not vertical. □ **verticality** /-ˈkalɪti/ *n.* **verticalize** *v.tr.* (also **-ise**). **vertically** *adv.* [French *vertical* or Late Latin *verticalis* (as VERTEX)]

vertical angles *n.pl. Math.* each of the pairs of opposite angles made by two intersecting lines.

vertical fin *n. Zool.* a dorsal, anal, or caudal fin.

vertical plane *n.* a plane at right angles to the horizontal.

vertical take-off *n.* the take-off of an aircraft directly upwards.

vertical thinking *n.* deductive reasoning (opp. LATERAL THINKING).

verticil /ˈvəːtɪsɪl/ *n. Bot.* & *Zool.* a whorl; a set of parts arranged in a circle round an axis. □ **verticillate** /-ˈtɪsɪlət/ *adj.* [Latin *verticillus* 'whorl of a spindle', diminutive of VERTEX]

vertiginous /vəːˈtɪdʒɪnəs/ *adj.* of or causing vertigo. □ **vertiginously** *adv.* [Latin *vertiginosus* (as VERTIGO)]

vertigo /ˈvəːtɪgəʊ/ *n.* a condition with a sensation of whirling and a tendency to lose balance; dizziness, giddiness. [Latin *vertigo -ginis* 'whirling' from *vertere* 'to turn']

vertu var. of VIRTU.

vervain /ˈvəːveɪn/ *n.* any of various herbaceous plants of the genus *Verbena*, esp. *V. officinalis* with small blue, white, or purple flowers. [Middle English via Old French *verveine* from Latin VERBENA]

verve /vəːv/ *n.* enthusiasm, vigour, spirit, esp. in artistic or literary work. [French, earlier = a form of expression, from Latin *verba* 'words']

vervet /ˈvəːvɪt/ *n.* a small grey African monkey, *Cercopithecus aethiops*. [French, of unknown origin]

very /ˈvɛri/ *adv.* & *adj.* ● *adv.* **1** in a high degree (*did it very easily*; *had a very bad cough*; *am very much better*). **2** in the fullest sense (foll. by *own* or superl. adj.: *at the very latest*; *do your very best*; *my very own room*). ● *adj.* **1** real, true, actual; truly such (usu. prec. by *the*, *this*, *his*, etc. emphasizing identity, significance, or extreme degree: *the very thing we need*; *those were his very words*). **2** *archaic* real, genuine (*very God*). □ **not very 1** in a low degree. **2** far from being. **very good** (or **well**) a formula of consent or approval. **the very same** see SAME. [Middle English from Old French *verai*, ultimately from Latin *verus* 'true']

Very light /ˈvɛri, ˈvɪəri/ *n.* a flare projected from a pistol for signalling or temporarily illuminating the surroundings. [named after E. W. *Very*, American inventor d. 1910]

Very pistol /ˈvɛri, ˈvɪəri/ *n.* a gun for firing a Very light.

Very Reverend *n.* the title of a dean etc.

vesica /ˈvɛsɪkə, ˈviː-, vɪˈsʌɪkə/ *n.* **1** *Anat.* & *Zool.* a bladder, esp. the urinary bladder. **2** (in full **vesica piscis** /ˈpɪskɪs/ or **piscium** /ˈpɪskɪʌm/) *Art* a pointed oval used as an aureole in medieval sculpture and painting. □ **vesical** *adj.* [Latin]

vesicate /ˈvɛsɪkeɪt, ˈviː-/ *v.tr.* esp. *Med.* raise blisters on. □ **vesicant** *adj.* & *n.* **vesication** /-ˈkeɪʃ(ə)n/ *n.*

vesicatory /-ˈkeɪt(ə)ri/ *adj.* & *n.* [Late Latin *vesicare vesicat-* (as VESICA)]

vesicle /ˈvɛsɪk(ə)l, ˈviː-/ *n.* **1 a** *Anat.* & *Biol.* a small fluid-filled bladder, sac, or vacuole. **b** *Bot.* an air-filled swelling in a seaweed etc. **2** *Geol.* a small cavity in volcanic rock produced by gas bubbles. **3** *Med.* a blister. □ **vesicular** /vɪˈsɪkjʊlə/ *adj.* **vesiculate** /vɪˈsɪkjʊlət/ *adj.* **vesiculation** /vɪˌsɪkjʊˈleɪʃ(ə)n/ *n.* [French *vésicule* or Latin *vesicula*, diminutive of VESICA]

vesper /ˈvɛspə/ *n.* **1** *poet.* Venus as the evening star. **2** *poet.* evening. **3** (in *pl.*) **a** the office of the sixth canonical hour of prayer, originally said towards evening. **b** evening prayer. [Latin *vesper* 'evening (star)': sense 3 partly from Old French *vespres* via ecclesiastical Latin *vesperas* from Latin *vespera* 'evening']

vespertine /ˈvɛspətʌɪn, -tɪn/ *adj.* **1** *Bot.* (of a flower) opening in the evening. **2** *Zool.* active in the evening. **3** *Astron.* setting near the time of sunset. **4** of or occurring in the evening. [Latin *vespertinus* from *vesper* 'evening']

vespiary /ˈvɛspɪəri/ *n.* (*pl.* **-ies**) a nest of wasps. [formed irregularly from Latin *vespa* 'wasp', on the pattern of *apiary*]

vespine /ˈvɛspʌɪn/ *adj.* of or relating to wasps. [Latin *vespa* 'wasp']

vessel /ˈvɛs(ə)l/ *n.* **1** a hollow receptacle esp. for liquid, e.g. a cask, cup, pot, bottle, or dish. **2** a ship or boat, esp. a large one. **3 a** *Anat.* a duct or canal etc. holding or conveying blood or other fluid, esp. = BLOOD VESSEL. **b** *Bot.* a woody duct carrying or containing sap etc. **4** *Bibl.* or *joc.* a person regarded as the recipient or exponent of a quality (*a weak vessel*). [Middle English via Anglo-French *vessel(e)*, Old French *vaissel(le)* from Late Latin *vascellum*, diminutive of *vas* 'vessel']

vest /vɛst/ *n.* & *v.* ● *n.* **1** *Brit.* an undergarment worn on the upper part of the body. **2** *N. Amer.* & *Austral.* a waistcoat. **3** a usu. V-shaped piece of material to fill the opening at the neck of a woman's dress. ● *v.* **1** *tr.* (esp. in *passive*; foll. by *with*) bestow or confer (powers, authority, etc.) on (a person). **2** *tr.* (foll. by *in*) confer (property or power) on (a person) with an immediate fixed right of immediate or future possession. **3** *intr.* (foll. by *in*) (of property, a right, etc.) come into the possession of (a person). **4 a** *tr. poet.* clothe. **b** *intr. Eccl.* put on vestments. [the noun from French *veste* via Italian *veste* from Latin *vestis* 'garment': the verb Middle English from Old French *vestu*, past part. of *vestir*, from Latin *vestire vestit-* 'clothe']

vesta /ˈvɛstə/ *n.* esp. *hist.* a short wooden or wax match. [*Vesta*, Roman goddess of the hearth and household]

vestal /ˈvɛst(ə)l/ *adj.* & *n.* ● *adj.* **1** chaste, pure. **2** of or relating to the Roman goddess Vesta. ● *n.* **1** a chaste woman, esp. a nun. **2** *Rom. Antiq.* a vestal virgin. [Middle English from Latin *vestalis* (*adj.* & *n.*) (as VESTA)]

vestal virgin *n. Rom. Antiq.* a virgin consecrated to Vesta and vowed to chastity, who shared the charge of maintaining the sacred fire burning on the goddess's altar.

vested interest *n.* **1** *Law* an interest (usu. in land or money held in trust) recognized as belonging to a person. **2** a personal interest in a state of affairs, usu. with an expectation of gain.

vestee /vɛˈstiː/ *n.* = VEST *n.* 3.

vestiary /ˈvɛstɪəri/ *n.* & *adj.* ● *n.* (*pl.* **-ies**) **1** a vestry. **2** a robing-room; a cloakroom. ● *adj.* of or relating to clothes or dress. [Middle English from Old French *vestiarie, vestiaire*: see VESTRY]

vestibule /ˈvɛstɪbjuːl/ *n.* **1 a** an antechamber, hall, or lobby next to the outer door of a building. **b** a porch of a church etc. **2** *US* an enclosed entrance to a railway carriage. **3** *Anat.* **a** a chamber or channel communicating with others. **b** part of the mouth outside the teeth. **c** the central cavity of the labyrinth of the inner ear. □ **vestibular** /-ˈstɪbjʊlə/ *adj.* [French *vestibule* or Latin *vestibulum* 'entrance court']

vestige /ˈvɛstɪdʒ/ *n.* **1** a trace or piece of evidence; a sign (*vestiges of an earlier civilization*; *found no vestige of their presence*). **2** a slight amount; a particle (*without a vestige of clothing*; *showed not a vestige of decency*). **3** *Biol.* a part or organ of an organism that is reduced or functionless but was well developed in its ancestors. [French from Latin *vestigium* 'footprint']

vestigial /vɛˈstɪdʒɪəl, -dʒ(ə)l/ *adj.* **1** being a vestige or trace. **2** *Biol.* (of an organ etc.) degenerate or atrophied, having become functionless in the course of evolution (*a vestigial wing*). □ **vestigially** *adv.*

vestiture /ˈvɛstɪtjə, -tʃə/ *n.* **1** *Zool.* hair, scales, etc., covering a surface. **2** *archaic* **a** clothing. **b** investiture. [Middle English via medieval Latin *vestitura* from Latin *vestire*: see VEST]

vestment /ˈvɛs(t)m(ə)nt/ *n.* **1** any of the official robes of clergy, choristers, etc., worn during divine service, esp. a chasuble. **2** a garment, esp. an official or state robe. [Middle English via Old French *vestiment, vestement* from Latin *vestimentum* (as VEST)]

vest-pocket *attrib.adj. N. Amer.* **1** small enough to fit into a waistcoat pocket. **2** very small (*vest-pocket parks in urban areas*).

vestry /ˈvɛstri/ *n.* (*pl.* **-ies**) **1** a room or building attached to a church for keeping vestments in. **2** *hist.* **a** a meeting of parishioners, usu. in a vestry for parochial business. **b** a body of parishioners meeting in this way. □ **vestral** *adj.* [Middle English via Old French *vestiaire, vestiarie*, from Latin *vestiarium* (as VEST)]

vestryman /ˈvɛstrɪmən/ *n.* (*pl.* **-men**) a member of a vestry.

vesture /ˈvɛstʃə/ *n.* & *v.* ● *n. poet.* **1** garments, dress. **2** a covering. ● *v.tr.* clothe. [Middle English via Old French from medieval Latin *vestitura* (as VEST)]

vet[1] /vɛt/ *n.* & *v.* ● *n. colloq.* a veterinary surgeon. ● *v.tr.* (**vetted, vetting**) **1** make a careful and critical examination of (a scheme, work, candidate, etc.). **2** examine or treat (an animal). [abbreviation]

vet[2] /vɛt/ *n. N. Amer. colloq.* a veteran. [abbreviation]

vetch /vɛtʃ/ *n.* any plant of the genus *Vicia*, esp. *V. sativa*, largely used for silage or fodder. □ **vetchy** *adj.* [Middle English via Anglo-French & Old Northern French *veche* from Latin *vicia*]

vetchling /ˈvɛtʃlɪŋ/ *n.* any of various plants of the genus *Lathyrus*, related to vetch.

veteran /ˈvɛt(ə)r(ə)n/ *n.* **1** a person who has grown old in or had long experience of esp. military service or an occupation (*a war veteran*; *a veteran of the theatre*; *a veteran marksman*). **2** *N. Amer.* an ex-serviceman or servicewoman. **3** (*attrib.*) of or for veterans. [French *vétéran* or Latin *veteranus* (*adj.* & *n.*) from *vetus -eris* 'old']

veteran car *n. Brit.* a car made before 1916, or (strictly) before 1905.

veterinarian /vɛt(ə)rɪˈnɛːrɪən/ *n. N. Amer.* a veterinary surgeon. [Latin *veterinarius* (as VETERINARY)]

veterinary /ˈvɛt(ə)rɪn(ə)ri, ˈvɛt(ə)nri/ *adj.* & *n.* ● *adj.* of or for diseases and injuries of farm and domestic animals, or their treatment. ● *n.* (*pl.* **-ies**) a veterinary surgeon. [Latin *veterinarius* from *veterinae* 'cattle']

veterinary surgeon *n. Brit.* a person qualified to treat diseased or injured animals.

vetiver /ˈvɛtɪvə/ *n.* = KHUS-KHUS. [French *vétiver* from Tamil *veṭṭivēru*, from *vēr* 'root']

veto /ˈviːtəʊ/ *n.* & *v.* ● *n.* (*pl.* **-oes**) **1 a** a constitutional right to reject a legislative enactment. **b** the right of a permanent member of the UN Security Council to reject a resolution. **c** such a rejection. **d** an official message conveying this. **2** a prohibition (*put one's veto on a proposal*). ● *v.tr.* (**-oes, -oed**) **1** exercise a veto against (a measure etc.). **2** forbid authoritatively. □ **vetoer** *n.* [Latin, = I forbid, with reference to its use by Roman tribunes of the people in opposing measures of the Senate]

vex /vɛks/ *v.tr.* **1** anger by a slight or a petty annoyance; irritate. **2** *archaic* grieve, afflict. □ **vexer** *n.* **vexing** *adj.*

vexingly *adv.* [Middle English via Old French *vexer* from Latin *vexare* 'shake, disturb']

vexation /vɛk'seɪʃ(ə)n/ *n.* **1** the act or an instance of vexing; the state of being vexed. **2** an annoying or distressing thing. [Middle English from Old French *vexation* or Latin *vexatio -onis* (as VEX)]

vexatious /vɛk'seɪʃəs/ *adj.* **1** such as to cause vexation. **2** *Law* not having sufficient grounds for action and seeking only to annoy the defendant. □ **vexatiously** *adv.* **vexatiousness** *n.*

vexed /'vɛkst/ *adj.* **1** irritated, angered. **2** (of a problem, issue, etc.) difficult and much discussed; problematic. □ **vexedly** /'vɛksɪdli/ *adv.*

vexillology /vɛksɪ'lɒlədʒi/ *n.* the study of flags. □ **vexillological** /-lə'lɒdʒɪk(ə)l/ *adj.* **vexillologist** *n.* [Latin *vexillum* 'flag' + -LOGY]

vexillum /vɛk'sɪləm/ *n.* (*pl.* **vexilla** /-lə/) **1** *Rom. Antiq.* **a** a military standard, esp. of a maniple. **b** a body of troops under this. **2** *Bot.* the large upper petal of a papilionaceous flower. **3** *Zool.* the vane of a feather. **4** *Eccl.* **a** a flag attached to a bishop's staff. **b** a processional banner or cross. [Latin, from *vehere vect-* 'carry']

VG *abbr.* **1** very good. **2** Vicar-General.

VGA *abbr.* video graphics array.

vgc *abbr.* very good condition.

VHF *abbr.* very high frequency (designating radio waves of frequency *c.*30–300 MHz and wavelength *c.*1–10 metres).

VI *abbr.* Virgin Islands.

via /'vʌɪə/ *prep.* by way of; through (*London to Rome via Paris*; *send it via your secretary*). [Latin, ablative of *via* 'way, road']

viable /'vʌɪəb(ə)l/ *adj.* **1** (of a plan etc.) feasible; practicable, esp. from an economic standpoint. **2 a** (of a seed or spore) able to germinate. **b** (of a plant, animal, etc.) capable of living or developing normally under particular environmental conditions. **3** *Med.* (of a foetus or unborn child) able to live after birth. □ **viability** /-'bɪlɪti/ *n.* **viably** *adv.* [French from *vie* 'life', from Latin *vita*]

viaduct /'vʌɪədʌkt/ *n.* **1** a long bridgelike structure, esp. a series of arches, carrying a road or railway across a valley or dip in the ground. **2** such a road or railway. [Latin *via* 'way', on the pattern of AQUEDUCT]

vial /'vʌɪəl/ *n.* a small (usu. cylindrical glass) vessel esp. for holding liquid medicines. [Middle English, variant of *fiole* etc.: see PHIAL]

via media /vʌɪə 'miːdɪə, viːə 'mɛdɪə/ *n. literary* a middle way or compromise between extremes. [Latin]

viand /'vʌɪənd/ *n. formal* **1** an article of food. **2** (in *pl.*) provisions, victuals. [Middle English from Old French *viande* 'food', ultimately from Latin *vivenda*, neut. pl. gerundive of *vivere* 'to live']

viaticum /vʌɪ'atɪkəm/ *n.* (*pl.* **viatica** /-kə/) **1** the Eucharist as given to a person near or in danger of death. **2** provisions or an official allowance of money for a journey. [Latin, neut. of *viaticus* from *via* 'road']

vibes /vʌɪbz/ *n.pl. colloq.* **1** vibrations, esp. in the sense of feelings or atmosphere communicated (*the house had bad vibes*). **2** = VIBRAPHONE. [abbreviation]

vibraculum /vʌɪ'brakjʊləm, vɪ-/ *n.* (*pl.* **vibracula** /-lə/) *Zool.* a whip-like structure of bryozoans used to bring food within reach by lashing movements. □ **vibracular** *adj.* [modern Latin (as VIBRATE)]

vibrant /'vʌɪbr(ə)nt/ *adj.* **1** vibrating. **2** (often foll. by *with*) (of a person or thing) thrilling, quivering (*vibrant with emotion*). **3** (of sound) resonant. **4** (of colour) bright and striking. □ **vibrancy** *n.* **vibrantly** *adv.* [Latin *vibrare*: see VIBRATE]

vibraphone /'vʌɪbrəfəʊn/ *n.* a percussion instrument of tuned metal bars with motor-driven resonators and metal tubes giving a vibrato effect. □ **vibraphonist** *n.* [VIBRATO + -PHONE]

vibrate /vʌɪ'breɪt/ *v.* **1** *intr. & tr.* move or cause to move continuously and rapidly to and fro; oscillate. **2** *intr. Physics* move unceasingly to and fro, esp. rapidly. **3** *intr.* (of a sound) throb; continue to be heard. **4** *intr.* (foll. by *with*) quiver, thrill (*vibrating with passion*). **5** *intr.* (of a pendulum) swing to and fro. □ **vibrative** /-rətɪv/ *adj.* [Latin *vibrare vibrat-* 'shake, swing']

vibratile /'vʌɪbrətʌɪl/ *adj.* **1** capable of vibrating. **2** *Biol.* (of cilia etc.) used in vibratory motion. [VIBRATORY, on the pattern of *pulsatile* etc.]

vibration /vʌɪ'breɪʃ(ə)n/ *n.* **1** the act or an instance of vibrating; oscillation. **2** *Physics* (esp. rapid) motion to and fro, esp. of the parts of a fluid or an elastic solid whose equilibrium has been disturbed or of an electromagnetic wave. **3** (in *pl.*) **a** a mental (esp. occult) influence. **b** a characteristic atmosphere or feeling in a place, regarded as communicable to people present in it. □ **vibrational** *adj.* [Latin *vibratio* (as VIBRATE)]

vibrato /vɪ'brɑːtəʊ/ *n. Mus.* a rapid slight variation in pitch in singing or in playing a stringed or wind instrument, producing a tremulous effect (cf. TREMOLO). [Italian, past part. of *vibrare* VIBRATE]

vibrator /vʌɪ'breɪtə/ *n.* **1** a device that vibrates or causes vibration, esp. an electric or other instrument used in massage or for sexual stimulation. **2** *Mus.* a reed in a reed-organ.

vibratory /'vʌɪbrət(ə)ri, vʌɪ'breɪt(ə)ri/ *adj.* causing vibration.

vibrio /'vɪbrɪəʊ, 'vʌɪbrɪəʊ/ *n.* (*pl.* **vibrios** or **vibriones** /-'əʊniːz/) *Biol. & Med.* a water-borne bacterium of the genus *Vibrio* etc., typically shaped like a curved rod with a flagellum, and including the cholera bacterium. [modern Latin, from Latin *vibrare* VIBRATE]

vibrissae /vʌɪ'brɪsiː/ *n.pl.* **1** stiff coarse hairs near the mouth of most mammals (e.g. a cat's whiskers) and in the human nostrils. **2** bristle-like feathers near the mouth of insect-eating birds. [Latin (as VIBRATE)]

viburnum /vɪ'bəːnəm, vʌɪ-/ *n.* any shrub of the genus *Viburnum*, usu. with white flowers, e.g. the guelder rose and wayfaring tree. [Latin, = wayfaring tree]

Vic. *abbr.* Victoria.

vicar /'vɪkə/ *n.* **1 a** (in the Church of England) an incumbent of a parish where tithes formerly passed to a chapter or religious house or layman (cf. RECTOR 1a). **b** (in other Anglican churches) a member of the clergy deputizing for another. **2** *RC Ch.* a representative or deputy of a bishop. **3** (in full **lay vicar** or **vicar choral**) a cleric or choir member appointed to sing certain parts of a cathedral service. □ **vicariate** /-'kɛːrɪət/ *n.* **vicarship** *n.* [Middle English via Anglo-French *viker(e)*, Old French *vicaire* from Latin *vicarius* 'substitute', from *vicis*: see VICE[3]]

vicarage /'vɪk(ə)rɪdʒ/ *n.* the residence or benefice of a vicar.

vicar apostolic *n.* a Roman Catholic missionary or titular bishop.

vicar-general *n.* (*pl.* **vicars-general**) **1** an Anglican official assisting or representing a bishop esp. in administrative matters. **2** *RC Ch.* a bishop's assistant in matters of jurisdiction etc.

vicarial /vɪ'kɛːrɪəl, vʌɪ-/ *adj.* of or serving as a vicar.

vicarious /vɪ'kɛːrɪəs, vʌɪ-/ *adj.* **1** experienced in the imagination through another person (*vicarious pleasure*). **2** acting or done for another (*vicarious suffering*). **3** deputed, delegated (*vicarious authority*). □ **vicariously** *adv.* **vicariousness** *n.* [Latin *vicarius*: see VICAR]

Vicar of Christ *n.* the earthly representative of God, esp. the Pope.

vice[1] /vʌɪs/ *n.* **1 a** evil or grossly immoral conduct; depravity. **b** a particular form of this, esp. involving prostitution, drugs, etc. **c** an immoral or dissolute habit or practice. **2** a defect or weakness of character or behaviour (*drunkenness was not among his vices*). **3** a fault or bad habit in a horse etc. □ **viceless** *adj.* [Middle English via Old French from Latin *vitium*]

vice[2] /vʌɪs/ *n. & v.* (*US* **vise**) ● *n.* a device, usu. attached to a workbench, with two jaws between which an object may be clamped by moving one jaw by means of a screw, leaving the hands free to work on it. ● *v.tr.* secure in a vice. □ **vice-like** *adj.* [Middle English, = winding stair, screw, via Old French *vis* from Latin *vitis* 'vine']

vice[3] /ˈvʌɪsiː/ *prep.* in the place of; in succession to. [Latin, ablative of *vix* (recorded in oblique forms in *vic-*) 'change']

vice[4] /vʌɪs/ *n. colloq.* = VICE-PRESIDENT, VICE ADMIRAL, etc. [as VICE-]

vice- /vʌɪs/ *comb. form* forming nouns meaning next in rank to, often in the capacity of deputy or substitute for (*vice-chairman*; *vice-governor*). [Latin *vice* 'in place of' (as VICE[3])]

vice admiral *n.* a naval officer ranking below admiral and above rear admiral.

vice-chamberlain *n.* a deputy chamberlain, esp. (in the UK) the deputy of the Lord Chamberlain.

vice-chancellor *n.* a deputy chancellor (esp. of a British university, discharging most of the administrative duties).

vicegerent /vʌɪsˈdʒɪər(ə)nt, -ˈdʒɛ-/ *adj.* & *n.* ● *adj.* exercising delegated power. ● *n.* a vicegerent person; a deputy. □ **vicegerency** *n.* (*pl.* **-ies**). [medieval Latin *vicegerens* (as VICE-, Latin *gerere* 'carry on')]

vicennial /vʌɪˈsɛnɪəl/ *adj.* lasting for or occurring every twenty years. [Late Latin *vicennium* 'period of twenty years' from *vicies* 'twenty times' (from *viginti* 'twenty') + *annus* 'year']

vice-president *n.* an official ranking below and deputizing for a president. □ **vice-presidency** *n.* (*pl.* **-ies**). **vice-presidential** /-ˈdenʃ(ə)l/ *adj.*

viceregal /vʌɪsˈriːg(ə)l/ *adj.* of or relating to a viceroy. □ **viceregally** *adv.*

vicereine /ˈvʌɪsreɪn/ *n.* **1** the wife of a viceroy. **2** a woman viceroy. [French (as VICE-, *reine* 'queen')]

vice ring *n.* a group of criminals involved in organizing illegal prostitution.

viceroy /ˈvʌɪsrɔɪ/ *n.* a ruler exercising authority on behalf of a sovereign in a colony, province, etc. □ **viceroyal** /-ˈrɔɪəl/ *adj.* **viceroyalty** /-ˈrɔɪəlti/ *n.* **viceroyship** *n.* [French (as VICE-, *roy* 'king')]

vice squad *n.* a police department enforcing laws against prostitution, drug abuse, etc.

vice versa /vʌɪsə ˈvəːsə, vʌɪs/ *adj.* with the order of the terms or conditions changed; the other way round (*could go from left to right or vice versa*). [Latin, = the position being reversed (as VICE[3], *versa* ablative fem. past part. of *vertere* 'turn')]

vichyssoise /viːʃiːˈswɑːz/ *n.* a creamy soup of leeks and potatoes, usu. served chilled. [French *vichyssois -oise* 'of *Vichy*', a town in France]

Vichy water /ˈviːʃiː/ *n.* an effervescent mineral water from Vichy in France.

vicinage /ˈvɪsɪnɪdʒ/ *n.* **1** a neighbourhood; a surrounding district. **2** relation in terms of nearness etc. to neighbours. [Middle English from Old French *vis(e)nage*, ultimately from Latin *vicinus* 'neighbour']

vicinal /ˈvɪsɪn(ə)l, vɪˈsʌɪn(ə)l/ *adj.* **1** neighbouring, adjacent. **2** of a neighbourhood; local. [French *vicinal* or Latin *vicinalis* from *vicinus* 'neighbour']

vicinity /vɪˈsɪnɪti/ *n.* (*pl.* **-ies**) **1** a surrounding district. **2** (foll. by *to*) nearness or closeness of place or relationship. □ **in the vicinity** (often foll. by *of*) near (to). [Latin *vicinitas* (as VICINAL)]

vicious /ˈvɪʃəs/ *adj.* **1** bad-tempered, spiteful (*a vicious dog*; *vicious remarks*). **2** violent, severe (*a vicious attack*). **3** of the nature of or addicted to vice. **4** (of language or reasoning etc.) faulty or unsound. □ **viciously** *adv.* **viciousness** *n.* [Middle English from Old French *vicious* or Latin *vitiosus*, from *vitium* VICE[1]]

vicious circle see CIRCLE *n.* 12.

vicious cycle *n.* a harmful recurring cycle of cause and effect.

vicious spiral *n. Brit.* continual harmful interaction of causes and effects, esp. as causing repeated rises in both prices and wages.

vicissitude /vɪˈsɪsɪtjuːd, vʌɪ-/ *n.* **1** a change of circumstances, esp. variation of fortune. **2** *archaic* or *poet.* regular change; alternation. □ **vicissitudinous** /-ˈtjuːdɪnəs/ *adj.* [French *vicissitude* or Latin *vicissitudo -dinis* from *vicissim* 'by turns' (as VICE[3])]

victim /ˈvɪktɪm/ *n.* **1** a person injured or killed as a result of an event or circumstance (*a road victim*; *the victims of war*). **2** a person or thing harmed or destroyed in pursuit of an object or in gratification of a passion etc. (*the victim of their ruthless ambition*). **3** a prey; a dupe (*fell victim to a confidence trick*). **4** a living creature sacrificed to a deity or in a religious rite. [Latin *victima*]

victimize /ˈvɪktɪmʌɪz/ *v.tr.* (also **-ise**) **1** single out (a person) for punishment or unfair treatment, esp. dismissal from employment. **2** make (a person etc.) a victim. □ **victimization** /-ˈzeɪʃ(ə)n/ *n.* **victimizer** *n.*

victimless /ˈvɪktɪmlɪs/ *adj.* orig. *US* (of a crime) in which there is no injured party.

victor /ˈvɪktə/ *n.* a winner in battle or in a contest. [Middle English from Anglo-French *victo(u)r* or Latin *victor*, from *vincere vict-* 'conquer']

Victoria /vɪkˈtɔːrɪə/ *n.* (also **victoria**) **1** a low light four-wheeled carriage with a collapsible top, seats for two passengers, and a raised driver's seat. **2** (in full **Victoria water lily**) a S. American water lily, *Victoria amazonica* or *V. cruziana*, with gigantic floating leaves. **3** (in full **Victoria plum**) *Brit.* a large red luscious variety of plum. [named after Queen *Victoria*, d. 1901]

Victoria Cross *n.* a decoration awarded for conspicuous bravery in the armed services, instituted by Queen Victoria in 1856.

Victoria crowned pigeon *n.* a large blue crested pigeon, *Goura victoria*, of New Guinea.

Victorian /vɪkˈtɔːrɪən/ *adj.* & *n.* ● *adj.* **1** of or characteristic of the time of Queen Victoria. **2** associated with attitudes attributed to this time, esp. of prudery and moral strictness. ● *n.* a person, esp. a writer, of this time. □ **Victorianism** *n.*

Victoriana /vɪkˌtɔːrɪˈɑːnə/ *n.pl.* **1** articles, esp. collectors' items, of the Victorian period. **2** attitudes characteristic of this period.

Victoria sandwich *n.* (also **Victoria sponge**) *Brit.* a sponge cake consisting of two layers of sponge with a jam filling.

victorious /vɪkˈtɔːrɪəs/ *adj.* **1** having won a victory; conquering, triumphant. **2** marked by victory (*victorious day*). □ **victoriously** *adv.* **victoriousness** *n.* [Middle English via Anglo-French *victorious*, Old French *victorieux* from Latin *victoriosus* (as VICTORY)]

victor ludorum /vɪktə luːˈdɔːrəm/ *n.* (*fem.* **victrix ludorum**) *Brit.* the overall champion in a sports competition. [Latin, = victor of the games]

victory /ˈvɪkt(ə)ri/ *n.* (*pl.* **-ies**) **1** the process of defeating an enemy in battle or war or an opponent in a contest. **2** an instance of this; a triumph. [Middle English via Anglo-French *victorie*, Old French *victoire* from Latin *victoria* (as VICTOR)]

victory roll *n.* a roll performed by an aircraft as a sign of triumph, esp. after a successful mission.

victrix /ˈvɪktrɪks/ *n.* (*pl.* **victrices** /-trɪsiːz/ a female victor or champion. [Latin, fem. of VICTOR]

victrix ludorum see VICTOR LUDORUM.

victual /ˈvɪt(ə)l/ *n.* & *v.* ● *n.* (usu. in *pl.*) food, provisions, esp. as prepared for use. ● *v.* (**victualled**, **victualling**; *US* **victualed**, **victualing**) **1** *tr.* supply with victuals. **2** *intr.* obtain stores. **3** *intr.* eat victuals. [Middle English via Old French *vitaille* from Late Latin *victualia*, neut. pl. of Latin *victualis*, from *victus* 'food', related to *vivere* 'to live']

victualler /ˈvɪt(ə)lə/ *n.* (*US* **victualer**) **1 a** a person etc. who supplies victuals. **b** (in full **licensed victualler**) *Brit.* a publican etc. licensed to sell alcoholic liquor. **2** a ship carrying stores for other ships. [Middle English from Old French *vitaill(i)er*, *vitaillour* (as VICTUAL)]

vicuña /vɪ'kjuːnjə, -'kuː-/ *n.* **1** a S. American mammal, *Vicugna vicugna*, related to the llama, with fine silky wool. **2 a** cloth made from its wool. **b** an imitation of this. [Spanish from Quechua]

vide /'vɪdeɪ, 'viː-, 'vʌɪdi/ *v.tr.* (as an instruction in a reference to a passage in a book etc.) see, consult. [Latin, imperative of *vidēre* 'see']

videlicet /vɪ'dɛlɪsɛt, vʌɪ-, -kɛt/ *adv.* = VIZ. [Middle English from Latin, from *vidēre* 'see' + *licet* 'it is permissible']

video /'vɪdɪəʊ/ *adj.*, *n.*, & *v.* ● *adj.* **1** relating to the recording, reproducing, or broadcasting of visual images on magnetic tape or disc. **2** relating to the broadcasting of television pictures. ● *n.* (*pl.* **-os**) **1** the process of recording, reproducing, or broadcasting visual images on magnetic tape or disc. **2** the visual element of television broadcasts. **3** *colloq.* = VIDEO RECORDER. **4** (in full **video film**) a film etc. recorded on a videotape. ● *v.tr.* (**-oes**, **-oed**) make a video recording of. [Latin *vidēre* 'see', on the pattern of AUDIO]

video camera *n.* a camera for recording images on videotape etc. or for transmitting them to a monitor screen.

video cassette *n.* a cassette of videotape.

video cassette recorder *n.* = VIDEO RECORDER.

videoconference /'vɪdɪəʊˌkɒnf(ə)r(ə)ns/ *n.* the use of television sets linked by telephone lines etc. to enable a group of people to communicate with each other in sound and vision. ▫ **videoconferencing** *n.*

video diary *n.* a record on videotape made by a person of a period of his or her life, or of a certain event, dramatic situation, etc., using a camcorder.

videodisc /'vɪdɪəʊdɪsk/ *n.* a metal-coated disc on which visual material is recorded for reproduction on a television screen.

video film *n.* a film etc. recorded on videotape.

videofit /'vɪdɪə(ʊ)fɪt/ *n.* a reconstructed picture of a person (esp. one sought by the police) built up on a computer screen by selecting and combining facial features according to witnesses' descriptions (cf. PHOTOFIT).

video frequency *n.* a frequency in the range used for video signals in television.

video game *n.* a game played by electronically manipulating images produced by a computer program on a television screen.

video nasty *n. Brit. colloq.* an explicitly horrific or pornographic video film.

videophile /'vɪdɪəʊfʌɪl/ *n.* an enthusiast for video technology or video recordings.

videophone /'vɪdɪə(ʊ)fəʊn/ *n.* a telephone device transmitting a visual image as well as sound.

video recorder *n.* an apparatus for recording and playing videotapes. ▫ **video recording** *n.*

video signal *n.* a signal containing information for producing a television image.

videotape /'vɪdɪə(ʊ)teɪp/ *n.* & *v.* ● *n.* **1** magnetic tape for recording television pictures and sound. **2** a length of this; a video cassette. **3** a recording made on such tape. ● *v.tr.* make a recording of (broadcast material etc.) with this.

videotape recorder *n.* = VIDEO RECORDER.

videotex /'vɪdɪə(ʊ)tɛks/ *n.* (also **videotext** /-tɛkst/) any electronic information system, esp. teletext or viewdata.

vidimus /'vʌɪdɪməs/ *n.* an inspection or certified copy of accounts etc. [Latin, = we have seen, from *vidēre* 'see']

vie /vʌɪ/ *v.intr.* (**vying**) (often foll. by *with*) compete; strive for superiority (*vied with each other for recognition*). [probably from Middle English (as ENVY)]

vielle /vɪ'ɛl/ *n.* a hurdy-gurdy. [French from Old French *viel(l)e*: see VIOL]

Vienna schnitzel /vɪ'ɛnə/ *n.* = WIENER SCHNITZEL.

Viennese /vɪə'niːz/ *adj.* & *n.* ● *adj.* of, relating to, or associated with Vienna in Austria. ● *n.* (*pl.* same) a native or citizen of Vienna.

Vietnamese /ˌvɪɛtnə'miːz, ˌvjɛt-/ *adj.* & *n.* ● *adj.* of or relating to Vietnam in SE Asia. ● *n.* (*pl.* same) **1** a native or national of Vietnam. **2** the language of Vietnam.

vieux jeu /vjəː 'ʒəː, French vjø ʒø/ *adj.* old-fashioned, hackneyed. [French, literally 'old game']

view /vjuː/ *n.* & *v.* ● *n.* **1** range of vision; extent of visibility (*came into view*; *in full view of the crowd*). **2 a** what is seen from a particular point; a scene or prospect (*a fine view of the downs*; *a room with a view*). **b** a picture etc. representing this. **3** an inspection by the eye or mind; a visual or mental survey. **4** an opportunity for visual inspection; a viewing (*a private view of the exhibition*). **5 a** an opinion (*holds strong views on morality*). **b** a mental attitude (*took a favourable view of the matter*). **c** a manner of considering a thing (*took a long-term view of it*). ● *v.* **1** *tr.* look at; survey visually; inspect (*we are going to view the house*). **2** *tr.* examine; survey mentally (*different ways of viewing a subject*). **3** *tr.* form a mental impression or opinion of; consider (*does not view the matter in the same light*). **4** *intr.* watch television. **5** *tr. Hunting* see (a fox) break cover. ▫ **have in view 1** have as one's object. **2** bear (a circumstance) in mind in forming a judgement etc. **in view of** having regard to; considering. **on view** being shown (for observation or inspection); being exhibited. **with a view to 1** with the hope or intention of. **2** with the aim of attaining (*with a view to marriage*). ▫ **viewable** *adj.* [Middle English from Anglo-French *v(i)ewe*, Old French *vēue*, fem. past part. of *vēoir* 'see', from Latin *vidēre*]

viewdata /'vjuːdeɪtə/ *n.* a news and information service from a computer source to which a television screen is connected by telephone link.

viewer /'vjuːə/ *n.* **1** a person who views. **2** a person watching television. **3** a device for looking at film transparencies etc.

viewership /'vjuːəʃɪp/ *n.* **1** the audience for a television programme, channel, etc. **2** the number of such viewers.

viewfinder /'vjuːfʌɪndə/ *n.* a device on a camera showing the area covered by the lens in taking a photograph.

viewgraph /'vjuːgrɑːf, -graf/ *n.* a graph produced as a transparency, for projection on to a screen, or for transmission during a teleconference.

view halloo *n.* a shout on seeing a fox break cover (*did not hear the view halloo*).

viewing /'vjuːɪŋ/ *n.* **1** an opportunity or occasion to view; an exhibition. **2** the act or practice of watching television.

viewless /'vjuːlɪs/ *adj.* **1** not having or affording a view. **2** lacking opinions.

viewpoint /'vjuːpɔɪnt/ *n.* a point of view, a standpoint.

vigesimal /vɪ'dʒɛsɪm(ə)l, vʌɪ-/ *adj.* **1** of twentieths or twenty. **2** reckoning or reckoned by twenties. ▫ **vigesimally** *adv.* [Latin *vigesimus* from *viginti* 'twenty']

vigil /'vɪdʒɪl/ *n.* **1 a** keeping awake during the time usually given to sleep, esp. to keep watch or pray (*keep vigil*). **b** a period of this. **2** a stationary, peaceful demonstration in support of a particular cause, usu. without speeches. **3** *Eccl.* the eve of a festival or holy day. **4** (in *pl.*) nocturnal devotions. [Middle English via Old French *vigile* from Latin *vigilia*, from *vigil* 'awake']

vigilance /'vɪdʒɪl(ə)ns/ *n.* watchfulness, caution, circumspection. [French *vigilance* or Latin *vigilantia* from *vigilare* 'keep awake' (as VIGIL)]

vigilance committee *n. US* a group of vigilantes.

vigilant /'vɪdʒɪl(ə)nt/ *adj.* watchful against danger, difficulty, etc. ▫ **vigilantly** *adv.* [Latin *vigilans -antis* (as VIGILANCE)]

vigilante /vɪdʒɪ'lanti/ *n.* a member of a self-appointed group undertaking law enforcement but without legal authority. □ **vigilantism** *n.* [Spanish, = vigilant]

vigneron /'viːnjərɒn/ *n.* a vine-grower. [French, from *vigne* VINE]

vignette /viː'njɛt, vɪ-/ *n.* & *v.* ● *n.* **1 a** a short descriptive essay or character sketch. **b** a short evocative episode in a play, film, etc. **2** an illustration or decorative design, esp. on the title-page of a book, not enclosed in a definite border. **3** a photograph or portrait showing only the head and shoulders with the background gradually shaded off. ● *v.tr.* **1** make a portrait of (a person) in vignette style. **2** shade off (a photograph or portrait). □ **vignettist** *n.* [French, diminutive of *vigne* VINE]

vigor *US* var. of VIGOUR.

vigoro /'vɪg(ə)rəʊ/ *n.* *Austral.* a team ball game combining elements of cricket and baseball. [apparently from VIGOROUS]

vigorous /'vɪg(ə)rəs/ *adj.* **1** strong and active; robust. **2** (of a plant) growing strongly. **3** forceful; acting or done with physical or mental vigour; energetic. **4** full of vigour; showing or requiring physical strength or activity. □ **vigorously** *adv.* **vigorousness** *n.* [Middle English via Old French from medieval Latin *vigorosus*, from Latin *vigor* (as VIGOUR)]

vigour /'vɪgə/ *n.* (*US* **vigor**) **1** active physical strength or energy. **2** a flourishing physical condition. **3** healthy growth; vitality; vital force. **4 a** mental strength or activity shown in thought or speech or in literary style. **b** forcefulness; trenchancy, animation. □ **vigourless** *adj.* [Middle English via Old French *vigour* from Latin *vigor -oris*, from *vigēre* 'be lively']

vihara /vɪ'hɑːrə/ *n.* a Buddhist temple or monastery. [Sanskrit]

Viking /'vʌɪkɪŋ/ *n.* & *adj.* ● *n.* any of the Scandinavian seafaring pirates and traders who raided and settled in parts of NW Europe in the 8th–11th c. ● *adj.* of or relating to the Vikings or their time. [Old Norse *víkingr*, perhaps via Old English *wīcing* from *wīc* 'camp']

vile /vʌɪl/ *adj.* **1** disgusting. **2** morally base; depraved, shameful. **3** *colloq.* abominably bad (*vile weather*). **4** *archaic* worthless. □ **vilely** *adv.* **vileness** *n.* [Middle English via Old French *vil vile* from Latin *vilis* 'cheap, base']

vilify /'vɪlɪfʌɪ/ *v.tr.* (**-ies**, **-ied**) defame; speak evil of. □ **vilification** /-fɪ'keɪʃ(ə)n/ *n.* **vilifier** *n.* [Middle English in the sense 'lower in value', from Late Latin *vilificare* (as VILE)]

vill /vɪl/ *n.* *hist.* a feudal township. [Anglo-French via Old French *vile*, *ville* 'farm' from Latin *villa* 'country house']

villa /'vɪlə/ *n.* **1** *Rom. Antiq.* a large country house with an estate. **2** a country residence. **3** *Brit.* a detached or semi-detached house in a residential district. **4** a rented holiday home, esp. abroad. [Italian from Latin]

village /'vɪlɪdʒ/ *n.* **1 a** a group of houses and associated buildings, larger than a hamlet and smaller than a town, esp. in a rural area. **b** the inhabitants of a village regarded as a community. **2** *Brit.* a self-contained district or community within a town or city, regarded as having features characteristic of village life. **3** *US* a small municipality with limited corporate powers. **4** *Austral.* a select suburban shopping centre. □ **villager** *n.* **villagey** *adj.* [Middle English via Old French from Latin *villa*]

village idiot *n.* *offens.* a person of very low intelligence living and well known in a village.

villagization /ˌvɪlɪdʒʌɪ'zeɪʃ(ə)n/ *n.* (also **-isation**) **1 a** (in Africa and Asia) the concentration of the population in villages. **b** the transfer of land to the communal control of villagers. **2** = UJAMAA.

villain /'vɪlən/ *n.* **1** a person guilty or capable of great wickedness. **2** *colloq.* usu. *joc.* a rascal or rogue. **3** (also **villain of the piece**) (in a play etc.) a character whose evil actions or motives are important in the plot. **4** *Brit. colloq.* a professional criminal. **5** *archaic* a rustic; a boor. [Middle English from Old French *vilein*, *vilain*, ultimately from Latin *villa*: see VILLA]

villainous /'vɪlənəs/ *adj.* **1** characteristic of a villain; wicked. **2** *colloq.* abominably bad; atrocious (*villainous weather*). □ **villainously** *adv.* **villainousness** *n.*

villainy /'vɪləni/ *n.* (*pl.* **-ies**) **1** villainous behaviour. **2** a wicked act. [Old French *vilenie* (as VILLAIN)]

villanelle /vɪlə'nɛl/ *n.* a usu. pastoral or lyrical poem of 19 lines, with only two rhymes throughout, and some lines repeated. [French from Italian *villanella*, fem. of *villanello* 'rural', diminutive of *villano* (as VILLAIN)]

-ville /vɪl/ *comb. form colloq.* forming the names of fictitious places with reference to a particular quality etc. (*dragsville*; *squaresville*). [French *ville* 'town', as in many US town-names]

villein /'vɪlən, -eɪn/ *n.* *hist.* a feudal tenant entirely subject to a lord or attached to a manor. [Middle English, variant of VILLAIN]

villeinage /'vɪlənɪdʒ, -leɪn-/ *n.* *hist.* the tenure or status of a villein.

villus /'vɪləs/ *n.* (*pl.* **villi** /-lʌɪ, -liː/) **1** *Anat.* a small hairlike or finger-like projection, esp. as lining the small intestine in large numbers to form the surface through which nutrients are absorbed into the blood. **2** *Bot.* (usu. in *pl.*) a long slender hair. □ **villiform** *adj.* **villose** *adj.* **villosity** /-'lɒsɪti/ *n.* **villous** *adj.* [Latin, = shaggy hair]

vim /vɪm/ *n.* *colloq.* vigour. [perhaps from Latin, accusative of *vis* 'energy']

vimineous /vɪ'mɪnɪəs/ *adj.* *Bot.* of or producing twigs or shoots. [Latin *vimineus* from *vimen viminis* 'osier']

vina /'viːnə/ *n.* an Indian four-stringed musical instrument with a fretted fingerboard and a gourd at each end. [Sanskrit & Hindi *viṇā*]

vinaceous /vʌɪ'neɪʃəs/ *adj.* of the reddish colour of wine; wine red. [Latin *vinaceus* from *vinum* 'wine']

vinaigrette /vɪneɪ'grɛt, vɪnɪ-/ *n.* **1** (in full **vinaigrette sauce**) a salad dressing of oil, wine vinegar, and seasoning. **2** a small ornamental bottle for holding smelling salts. [French, diminutive of *vinaigre* VINEGAR]

vinca /'vɪŋkə/ *n.* a plant of (or formerly of) the genus *Vinca*, including *Catharanthus roseus*, the source of several alkaloids used to treat cancer; a periwinkle. [modern Latin, from late Latin *pervinca* 'periwinkle']

vincible /'vɪnsɪb(ə)l/ *adj.* *literary* that can be overcome or conquered. □ **vincibility** /-'bɪlɪti/ *n.* [Latin *vincibilis* from *vincere* 'overcome']

vinculum /'vɪŋkjʊləm/ *n.* (*pl.* **vincula** /-lə/) **1** *Algebra* a horizontal line drawn over a group of terms to show they have a common relation to what follows or precedes (e.g. $\overline{a+b}\times c = ac + bc$, but $a + b \times c = a + bc$). **2** *Anat.* a ligament; a fraenum. [Latin, = bond, from *vincire* 'bind']

vindaloo /vɪndə'luː/ *n.* a highly-spiced hot Indian curry dish made with meat, fish, or poultry. [probably from Portuguese *vin d'alho* 'wine and garlic (sauce)', from *vinho* 'wine' + *alho* 'garlic']

vindicate /'vɪndɪkeɪt/ *v.tr.* **1** clear of blame or suspicion. **2** establish the existence, merits, or justice of (one's courage, conduct, assertion, etc.). **3** justify (a person, oneself, etc.) by evidence or argument. □ **vindicable** /-kəb(ə)l/ *adj.* **vindication** /-'keɪʃ(ə)n/ *n.* **vindicative** /-kətɪv/ *adj.* **vindicator** *n.* [Latin *vindicare* 'claim, avenge' from *vindex -dicis* 'claimant, avenger']

vindicatory /'vɪndɪkeɪt(ə)ri/ *adj.* **1** tending to vindicate. **2** (of laws) punitive.

vindictive /vɪn'dɪktɪv/ *adj.* **1** tending to seek revenge. **2** spiteful. □ **vindictively** *adv.* **vindictiveness** *n.* [Latin *vindicta* 'vengeance' (as VINDICATE)]

vindictive damages *n.pl.* esp. *Brit. Law* damages exceeding simple compensation and awarded to punish the defendant.

vine /vʌɪn/ *n.* **1** any climbing or trailing woody-stemmed plant, esp. of the genus *Vitis*, bearing grapes.

2 a slender trailing or climbing stem. ▫ **viny** *adj.* [Middle English via Old French *vi(g)ne* from Latin *vinea* 'vineyard', from *vinum* 'wine']

vine-dresser *n.* a person who prunes, trains, and cultivates vines.

vinegar /ˈvɪnɪgə/ *n.* **1** a sour liquid obtained from wine, cider, etc., by fermentation and used as a condiment or for pickling. **2** sour behaviour or character. ▫ **vinegarish** *adj.* **vinegary** *adj.* [Middle English from Old French *vyn egre*, ultimately from Latin *vinum* 'wine' + *acer, acre* 'sour']

vinery /ˈvʌɪn(ə)ri/ *n.* (*pl.* **-ies**) **1** a greenhouse for grapevines. **2** a vineyard.

vineyard /ˈvɪnjɑːd, -jəd/ *n.* **1** a plantation of grapevines, esp. for wine-making. **2** *Bibl.* a sphere of action or labour (see Matt. 20:1). [Middle English, from VINE + YARD[2]]

vingt-et-un /vanteɪˈəː, French vɛ̃teœ̃/ *n.* = PONTOON[1]. [French, = twenty-one]

vinho verde /ˈviːnəʊ ˈvəːdi/ *n.* a young Portuguese wine, not allowed to mature. [Portuguese, = green wine]

vini- /ˈvɪni/ *comb. form* wine. [Latin *vinum*]

viniculture /ˈvɪnɪkʌltʃə/ *n.* the cultivation of grapevines. ▫ **vinicultural** /-ˈkʌltʃ(ə)r(ə)l/ *adj.* **viniculturist** /-ˈkʌltʃ(ə)rɪst/ *n.*

vinification /ˌvɪnɪfɪˈkeɪʃ(ə)n/ *n.* the conversion of grape juice etc. into wine. ▫ **vinify** /ˈvɪnɪfʌɪ/ *v.tr.* (**-ies, -ied**).

vining /ˈvʌɪnɪŋ/ *n.* the separation of leguminous crops from their vines and pods.

vino /ˈviːnəʊ/ *n.* esp. *Brit. slang* wine, esp. of an inferior kind. [Spanish & Italian, = wine]

vin ordinaire /ˌvan ɔːdɪˈnɛː, French vɛ̃ ɔrdinɛr/ *n.* cheap (usu. red) wine for everyday use. [French, = ordinary wine]

vinous /ˈvʌɪnəs/ *adj.* **1** of, like, or associated with wine. **2** addicted to wine. ▫ **vinosity** /-ˈnɒsɪti/ *n.* [Latin *vinum* 'wine']

vin rosé /van rəʊˈzeɪ, French vɛ̃ roze/ *n.* = ROSÉ. [French]

vint[1] /vɪnt/ *v.tr.* make (wine). [back-formation from VINTAGE]

vint[2] /vɪnt/ *n.* a Russian card game like auction bridge. [Russian, = screw]

vintage /ˈvɪntɪdʒ/ *n.* & *adj.* ● *n.* **1 a** a season's produce of grapes. **b** the wine made from this. **2 a** the gathering of grapes for wine-making. **b** the season of this. **3** a wine of high quality from a single identified year and district. **4 a** the year etc. when a thing was made etc. **b** a thing made etc. in a particular year etc. **5** *poet.* or *literary* wine. ● *adj.* **1** of high quality, esp. from the past or characteristic of the best period of a person's work. **2** of a past season. [alteration (influenced by VINTNER) of Middle English *vendage, vindage*, via Old French *vendange* from Latin *vindemia*, from *vinum* 'wine' + *demere* 'remove']

vintage car *n. Brit.* a car made between 1917 and 1930.

vintage festival *n.* a carnival to celebrate the beginning of the vintage.

vintager /ˈvɪntɪdʒə/ *n.* a grape-gatherer.

vintner /ˈvɪntnə/ *n.* a wine-merchant. [Middle English via Anglo-Latin *vintenarius, vinetarius* and Anglo-French *vineter*, Old French *vinetier* from medieval Latin *vinetarius*, via Latin *vinetum* 'vineyard' from *vinum* 'wine']

viny see VINE.

vinyl /ˈvʌɪnɪl, ˈvʌɪn(ə)l/ *n.* **1** *Chem.* the radical $-CH:CH_2$, derived from ethylene by removal of a hydrogen atom (usu. *attrib.*: *vinyl group*). **2** any plastic made by polymerizing a compound containing the vinyl group, esp. polyvinyl chloride. **3 a** a gramophone record. **b** gramophone records collectively. [Latin *vinum* 'wine' + -YL]

viol /ˈvʌɪəl/ *n.* a medieval stringed musical instrument, played with a bow and held vertically on the knees or between the legs. [Middle English *viel* etc. via Old French *viel(l)e*, alteration of *viole*, from Provençal *viola*, *viula*, probably ultimately from Latin *vitulari* 'be joyful': cf. FIDDLE]

viola[1] /vɪˈəʊlə/ *n.* **1 a** an instrument of the violin family, larger than the violin and of lower pitch. **b** a viola-player. **2** a viol. [Italian & Spanish, probably from Provençal: see VIOL]

viola[2] /ˈvʌɪələ/ *n.* **1** any plant of the genus *Viola*, including the pansy and violet. **2** a cultivated hybrid of this genus. [Latin, = violet]

violaceous /vʌɪəˈleɪʃəs/ *adj.* **1** of a violet colour. **2** *Bot.* of the violet family Violaceae. [Latin *violaceus* (as VIOLA[2])]

viola da braccio /vɪˌəʊlə də ˈbrɑːtʃəʊ/ *n.* a viol corresponding to the modern viola. [Italian, = viol for the arm]

viola da gamba /vɪˌəʊlə də ˈgambə/ *n.* a viol held between the player's legs, esp. one corresponding to the modern cello. [Italian, = viol for the leg]

viola d'amore /vɪˌəʊlə daˈmɔːreɪ/ *n.* a sweet-toned tenor viol. [Italian, = viol of love]

violate /ˈvʌɪəleɪt/ *v.tr.* **1** disregard; fail to comply with (an oath, treaty, law, etc.). **2** treat (a sanctuary etc.) profanely or with disrespect. **3** break in upon, disturb (a person's privacy etc.). **4** assault sexually; rape. ▫ **violable** *adj.* **violation** /-ˈleɪʃ(ə)n/ *n.* **violator** *n.* [Middle English from Latin *violare* 'treat violently']

violence /ˈvʌɪəl(ə)ns/ *n.* **1** the quality of being violent. **2** violent conduct or treatment; outrage, injury. **3** *Law* **a** the unlawful exercise of physical force. **b** intimidation by the exhibition of this. ▫ **do violence to** act contrary to; outrage. [Middle English via Old French from Latin *violentia* (as VIOLENT)]

violent /ˈvʌɪəl(ə)nt/ *adj.* **1 a** using or tending to use aggressive physical force (*a violent person*). **b** involving physical force (*a violent storm*). **2 a** vehement, passionate, extreme (*a violent contrast*; *violent dislike*). **b** vivid, intense (*violent colours*). **3** (of death) resulting from external force or from poison (cf. NATURAL *adj.* 2). **4** involving an unlawful exercise of force (*laid violent hands on him*). ▫ **violently** *adv.* [Middle English via Old French from Latin *violentus*]

violet /ˈvʌɪələt/ *n.* & *adj.* ● *n.* **1 a** any plant of the genus *Viola*, esp. the sweet violet, with usu. purple, blue, or white flowers. **b** any of various plants resembling the sweet violet. **2** the bluish-purple colour seen at the end of the spectrum opposite red. **3 a** pigment of this colour. **b** clothes or material of this colour. ● *adj.* of a purplish-blue colour. [Middle English from Old French *violet(te)*, diminutive of *viole*, from Latin VIOLA[2]]

violin /vʌɪəˈlɪn, ˈvʌɪəlɪn/ *n.* **1** a musical instrument with four strings of treble pitch played with a bow. **2** a violin-player. ▫ **violinist** *n.* [Italian *violino*, diminutive of VIOLA[1]]

violist /ˈvʌɪəlɪst/ *n.* a viol-player or viola-player.

violoncello /vʌɪələnˈtʃɛləʊ, viːə-/ *n.* (*pl.* **-os**) *formal* = CELLO. ▫ **violoncellist** *n.* [Italian, diminutive of VIOLONE]

violone /vɪəˈləʊni/ *n.* a double bass viol. [Italian, augmentative of VIOLA[1]]

VIP *abbr.* very important person.

viper /ˈvʌɪpə/ *n.* **1** any venomous snake of the family Viperidae, esp. the common viper (see ADDER). **2** a malignant or treacherous person. ▫ **viper in one's bosom** a person who betrays those who have helped him or her. ▫ **viperine** /-rʌɪn/ *adj.* **viperish** *adj.* **viperlike** *adj.* **viperous** *adj.* [French *vipère* or Latin *vipera*, from *vivus* 'alive' + *parere* 'bring forth']

viper's bugloss *n.* a stiff bristly blue-flowered plant, *Echium vulgare*.

viper's grass *n.* scorzonera.

virago /vɪˈrɑːgəʊ, -ˈreɪgəʊ/ *n.* (*pl.* **-os**) **1** a fierce or abusive woman. **2** *archaic* a woman of masculine strength or spirit. [Old English from Latin, = female warrior, from *vir* 'man']

viral /ˈvʌɪr(ə)l/ *adj.* of or caused by a virus. ▫ **virally** *adv.*

virelay /ˈvɪrəleɪ/ *n.* a short (esp. old French) lyric poem with two rhymes to a stanza variously arranged. [Middle English from Old French *virelai*]

virement /ˈvʌɪəm(ə)nt, ˈvɪəmɑ̃/ *n. Brit.* the transfer of items from one financial account to another. [French from *virer* 'to turn': see VEER[1]]

vireo /ˈvɪrɪəʊ/ *n.* (*pl.* **-os**) any small American songbird of the family Vireonidae. [Latin, perhaps = greenfinch]

virescence /vɪˈrɛs(ə)ns/ *n.* **1** greenness. **2** *Bot.* abnormal greenness in petals etc. normally of some bright colour. □ **virescent** *adj.* [Latin *virescere*, inceptive of *virēre* 'be green']

virga /ˈvəːɡə/ *n. Meteorol.* (treated as *sing.* or *pl.*) streaks of rain etc. appearing to hang under a cloud and evaporating before reaching the ground. [Latin, = rod, stripe]

virgate[1] /ˈvəːɡət/ *adj. Bot.* & *Zool.* slim, straight, and erect. [Latin *virgatus* from *virga* 'rod']

virgate[2] /ˈvəːɡət/ *n. Brit. hist.* a varying measure of land, esp. 30 acres. [medieval Latin *virgata* (rendering Old English *gierd-land* 'yard-land') from Latin *virga* 'rod']

virger var. of VERGER.

Virgilian /vəˈdʒɪlɪən/ *adj.* of, or in the style of, the Roman poet Virgil (d. 19 BC). [Latin *Vergilianus* from P. *Vergilius* Maro, the full name of Virgil]

virgin /ˈvəːdʒɪn/ *n.* & *adj.* ● *n.* **1** a person (esp. a woman) who has never had sexual intercourse. **2 a** (**the Virgin**) Christ's mother the Blessed Virgin Mary. **b** a picture or statue of the Virgin. **3** (**the Virgin**) the zodiacal sign or constellation Virgo. **4** *colloq.* a naive, innocent, or inexperienced person (*a political virgin*). **5** a member of any order of women under a vow to remain virgins. **6** a female insect producing eggs without impregnation. ● *adj.* **1** that is a virgin. **2** of or befitting a virgin (*virgin modesty*). **3** not yet used, penetrated, or tried (*virgin soil*). **4** undefiled, spotless. **5** (of olive oil etc.) obtained from the first pressing of olives etc. **6** (of clay) not fired. **7** (of metal) made from ore by smelting. **8** (of wool) not yet, or only once, spun or woven. **9** (of an insect) producing eggs without impregnation. □ **virginhood** *n.* [Middle English via Anglo-French & Old French *virgine* from Latin *virgo -ginis*]

virginal /ˈvəːdʒɪn(ə)l/ *adj.* & *n.* ● *adj.* that is or befits or belongs to a virgin. ● *n.* (usu. in *pl.*) (in full **pair of virginals**) an early form of spinet in a box, used in the sixteenth and seventeenth centuries. □ **virginalist** *n.* **virginally** *adv.* [Middle English from Old French *virginal* or Latin *virginalis* (as VIRGIN): the name of the instrument perhaps because of its use by young women]

virgin birth *n.* **1** (the doctrine of) Christ's birth from a mother who was a virgin. **2** parthenogenesis.

virgin comb *n.* a honeycomb that has been used only once for honey and never for brood.

virgin forest *n.* a forest in its untouched natural state.

virgin honey *n.* honey taken from a virgin comb, or drained from the comb without heat or pressure.

Virginia /vəˈdʒɪnɪə/ *n.* **1** tobacco from Virginia. **2** a cigarette made of this. □ **Virginian** *n.* & *adj.* [*Virginia*, a state in US]

Virginia creeper *n.* a N. American vine, *Parthenocissus quinquefolia*, cultivated esp. for its red autumn foliage.

Virginia reel *n. N. Amer.* a country dance.

Virginia stock *n.* (also **Virginian stock**) a cruciferous plant, *Malcolmia maritima*, with white or pink flowers.

virginity /vəˈdʒɪnɪti/ *n.* the state of being a virgin. [Old French *virginité* from Latin *virginitas* (as VIRGIN)]

virgin queen *n.* **1** an unfertilized queen bee. **2** (**the Virgin Queen**) Queen Elizabeth I of England.

virgin's bower *n.* a clematis, esp. the American *Clematis virginiana*.

Virgo /ˈvəːɡəʊ/ *n.* (*pl.* **-os**) **1** *Astron.* a large constellation (the Virgin), said to represent a maiden or goddess associated with the harvest. **2** *Astrol.* **a** the sixth sign of the zodiac, which the sun enters about 23 Aug. **b** a person born when the sun is in this sign. □ **Virgoan** *n.* & *adj.* [Old English from Latin, = virgin]

virgule /ˈvəːɡjuːl/ *n.* **1** a slanting line used to mark division of words or lines. **2** = SOLIDUS 1. [French, = comma, from Latin *virgula*, diminutive of *virga* 'rod']

viridescent /vɪrɪˈdɛs(ə)nt/ *adj.* greenish, tending to become green. □ **viridescence** *n.* [Late Latin *viridescere* from Latin *viridis*: see VIRIDIAN]

viridian /vɪˈrɪdɪən/ *n.* & *adj.* ● *n.* **1** a bluish-green chromium oxide pigment. **2** the colour of this. ● *adj.* bluish green. [Latin *viridis* 'green' from *virēre* 'be green']

viridity /vɪˈrɪdɪti/ *n. literary* greenness, verdancy. [Middle English from Old French *viridité* or Latin *viriditas*, from *viridis*: see VIRIDIAN]

virile /ˈvɪrʌɪl/ *adj.* **1** of or characteristic of a man; having masculine (esp. sexual) vigour or strength. **2** of or having procreative power. **3** of a man as distinct from a woman or child. □ **virility** /vɪˈrɪlɪti/ *n.* [Middle English from French *viril* or Latin *virilis*, from *vir* 'man']

virilism /ˈvɪrɪlɪz(ə)m/ *n. Med.* the development of secondary male characteristics in a female or precociously in a male.

viroid /ˈvʌɪrɔɪd/ *n.* an infectious entity affecting plants, similar to a virus but smaller and consisting only of nucleic acid without a protein coat.

virology /vʌɪˈrɒlədʒi/ *n.* the scientific study of viruses. □ **virological** /-rəˈlɒdʒɪk(ə)l/ *adj.* **virologically** /-rəˈlɒdʒɪk(ə)li/ *adv.* **virologist** *n.*

virtu /vəːˈtuː/ *n.* (also **vertu**) **1 a** a knowledge of or expertise in the fine arts. **b** curios or objets d'art collectively. **2** the usu. moral worth inherent in a person or thing. [Italian *virtù* 'VIRTUE, virtu']

virtual /ˈvəːtjʊəl/ *adj.* **1** that is such for practical purposes though not in name or according to strict definition (*is the virtual manager of the business*; *take this as a virtual promise*). **2** *Optics* relating to the points at which rays would meet if produced backwards (*virtual focus*; *virtual image*). **3** *Mech.* relating to an infinitesimal displacement of a point in a system. **4** *Computing* not physically existing as such but made by software to appear to do so (*virtual memory*) (see also VIRTUAL REALITY). □ **virtuality** /-jʊˈalɪti/ *n.* [Middle English from medieval Latin *virtualis*, from Latin *virtus* suggested by Late Latin *virtuosus*]

virtually /ˈvəːtjʊəli/ *adv.* **1** in effect, to all intents. **2** nearly, almost.

virtual reality *n.* an image or environment generated by computer software with which a user can interact realistically using a helmet with a screen inside, gloves fitted with sensors, etc.

virtue /ˈvəːtjuː, -tʃuː/ *n.* **1** moral excellence; uprightness, goodness. **2** a particular form of this (*patience is a virtue*). **3** chastity, esp. of a woman. **4** a good quality (*has the virtue of being adjustable*). **5** efficacy; inherent power (*no virtue in such drugs*). **6** an angelic being of the seventh order of the celestial hierarchy (see ORDER *n.* 19). □ **by** (or **in**) **virtue of** on the strength or ground of (*got the job by virtue of his experience*). **make a virtue of necessity** derive some credit or benefit from an unwelcome obligation. □ **virtueless** *adj.* [Middle English via Old French *vertu* from Latin *virtus -tutis*, from *vir* 'man']

virtuoso /vəːtjʊˈəʊsəʊ, -zəʊ/ *n.* (*pl.* **virtuosi** /-iː/ or **-os**) **1 a** a person highly skilled in the technique of a fine art, esp. music. **b** (*attrib.*) displaying the skills of a virtuoso. **2** a person with a special knowledge of or taste for works of art or virtu. □ **virtuosic** /-ˈɒsɪk/ *adj.* **virtuosity** /-ˈɒsɪti/ *n.* **virtuosoship** *n.* [Italian, = learned, skilful, from Late Latin (as VIRTUOUS)]

virtuous /ˈvəːtjʊəs, -tʃʊəs/ *adj.* **1** possessing or showing moral rectitude. **2** (esp. of a woman) chaste. □ **virtuously** *adv.* **virtuousness** *n.* [Middle English via

Old French *vertuous* from Late Latin *virtuosus*, from *virtus* VIRTUE]

virtuous circle *n.* a beneficial recurring cycle of cause and effect (cf. *vicious circle* (CIRCLE *n.* 12)).

virulent /ˈvɪrʊl(ə)nt, ˈvɪrjʊ-/ *adj.* **1** strongly poisonous. **2** (of a disease) violent or malignant. **3** bitterly hostile (*virulent animosity*; *virulent abuse*). □ **virulence** *n.* **virulently** *adv.* [Middle English, originally of a poisoned wound, from Latin *virulentus* (as VIRUS)]

virus /ˈvʌɪrəs/ *n.* **1** a submicroscopic infective agent usu. consisting of a nucleic acid molecule in a protein coat, and able to multiply only within the living cells of a host. **2** *Computing* = COMPUTER VIRUS. **3** *archaic* a poison, a source of disease. **4** a harmful or corrupting influence. [Latin, = slimy liquid, poison]

Vis. *abbr.* Viscount.

visa /ˈviːzə/ *n.* & *v.* ● *n.* an endorsement on a passport etc. showing that it has been found correct, esp. as allowing the holder to enter or leave a country. ● *v.tr.* (**visas**, **visaed** /-zəd/ or **visa'd**, **visaing**) mark with a visa. [French from Latin *visa*, neut. pl. past part. of *vidēre* 'see']

visage /ˈvɪzɪdʒ/ *n.* *literary* a face, a countenance. □ **visaged** *adj.* (also in *comb.*). [Middle English via Old French from Latin *visus* 'sight' (as VISA)]

vis-à-vis /viːzɑːˈviː/ *prep.*, *adv.*, & *n.* ● *prep.* **1** in relation to. **2** opposite to. ● *adv.* facing one another. ● *n.* (*pl.* same) **1** a person or thing facing another, esp. in some dances. **2** a person occupying a corresponding position in another group. **3** *US* a social partner. [French, = face to face, from Old French *vis* 'face', from Latin (as VISAGE)]

Visc. *abbr.* Viscount.

viscacha /vɪˈskatʃə/ *n.* (also **vizcacha** /vɪˈzk-/) any large S. American burrowing rodent of the genus *Lagidium* or *Lagostomus*, related to the chinchilla. [Spanish from Quechua *(h)uiscacha*]

viscera /ˈvɪs(ə)rə/ *n.pl.* the organs in the main cavities of the body (e.g. heart, liver), esp. in the abdomen (e.g. the intestines). [Latin, pl. of *viscus*: see VISCUS]

visceral /ˈvɪs(ə)r(ə)l/ *adj.* **1** of the viscera. **2** relating to inward feelings rather than conscious reasoning. □ **viscerally** *adv.*

visceral nerve *n.* a sympathetic nerve (see SYMPATHETIC *adj.* 9).

viscid /ˈvɪsɪd/ *adj.* **1** glutinous, sticky. **2** semi-fluid. □ **viscidity** /vɪˈsɪdɪti/ *n.* [Late Latin *viscidus* from Latin *viscum* 'birdlime']

viscometer /vɪsˈkɒmɪtə/ *n.* an instrument for measuring the viscosity of liquids. □ **viscometric** /vɪskəˈmɛtrɪk/ *adj.* **viscometrically** /vɪskəˈmɛtrɪk(ə)li/ *adv.* **viscometry** *n.* [variant of *viscosimeter* (as VISCOSITY, -METER)]

viscose /ˈvɪskəʊz, -kəʊs/ *n.* **1** a form of cellulose in a highly viscous state suitable for drawing into yarn. **2** rayon made from this. [Late Latin *viscosus* (as VISCOUS)]

viscosity /vɪˈskɒsɪti/ *n.* (*pl.* **-ies**) **1** the quality or degree of being viscous. **2** *Physics* **a** (of a fluid) internal friction, the resistance to flow. **b** a quantity expressing this. □ **viscosimeter** /-kəˈsɪmɪtə/ *n.* [Middle English from Old French *viscosité* or medieval Latin *viscositas* (as VISCOUS)]

viscount /ˈvʌɪkaʊnt/ *n.* a British nobleman ranking between an earl and a baron. □ **viscountcy** *n.* (*pl.* **-ies**). **viscountship** *n.* **viscounty** *n.* (*pl.* **-ies**). [Middle English via Anglo-French *viscounte*, Old French *vi(s)conte* from medieval Latin *vicecomes -mitis* (as VICE-, COUNT²)]

viscountess /ˈvʌɪkaʊntɪs/ *n.* **1** a viscount's wife or widow. **2** a woman holding the rank of viscount in her own right.

viscous /ˈvɪskəs/ *adj.* **1** glutinous, sticky. **2** semi-fluid. **3** *Physics* having a high viscosity; not flowing freely. □ **viscously** *adv.* **viscousness** *n.* [Middle English from Anglo-French *viscous* or Late Latin *viscosus* (as VISCID)]

viscus /ˈvɪskəs/ *n.* (*pl.* **viscera** /ˈvɪs(ə)rə/) (usu. in *pl.*) any of the soft internal organs of the body. [Latin]

vise *US* var. of VICE².

Vishnu /ˈvɪʃnuː/ *n.* a Hindu god regarded by his worshippers as the supreme deity and saviour, by others as the second member of a triad with Brahma and Siva. □ **Vishnuism** *n.* **Vishnuite** *n.* & *adj.* [Sanskrit *Viṣṇu*]

visibility /vɪzɪˈbɪlɪti/ *n.* **1** the state of being visible. **2** the range or possibility of vision as determined by the conditions of light and atmosphere (*visibility was down to 50 yards*). [French *visibilité* or Late Latin *visibilitas* from Latin *visibilis*: see VISIBLE]

visible /ˈvɪzɪb(ə)l/ *adj.* **1 a** that can be seen by the eye. **b** (of light) within the range of wavelengths to which the eye is sensitive. **2** that can be perceived or ascertained; apparent, open (*has no visible means of support*; *spoke with visible impatience*). **3** (of exports etc.) consisting of actual goods (cf. INVISIBLE EXPORTS). □ **visibleness** *n.* **visibly** *adv.* [Middle English from Old French *visible* or Latin *visibilis*, from *vidēre vis-* 'see']

visible horizon see HORIZON 1b.

Visigoth /ˈvɪzɪgɒθ/ *n.* a West Goth, a member of the branch of the Goths who settled in France and Spain in the 5th c. and ruled much of Spain until 711. [Late Latin *Visigothus*: the first element possibly meaning 'west' (cf. OSTROGOTH)]

vision /ˈvɪʒ(ə)n/ *n.* & *v.* ● *n.* **1** the act or faculty of seeing; sight (*has impaired his vision*). **2 a** a thing or person seen in a dream or trance. **b** a supernatural or prophetic apparition. **3** a thing or idea perceived vividly in the imagination (*the romantic visions of youth*; *had visions of warm sandy beaches*). **4** imaginative insight. **5** statesmanlike foresight; sagacity in planning. **6** a person etc. of unusual beauty. **7** what is seen on a television screen; television images collectively. ● *v.tr.* see or present in or as in a vision. □ **visional** *adj.* **visionless** *adj.* [Middle English via Old French from Latin *visio -onis* (as VISIBLE)]

visionary /ˈvɪʒ(ə)n(ə)ri/ *adj.* & *n.* ● *adj.* **1** given to seeing visions or to indulging in fanciful theories. **2** having vision or foresight. **3** existing only in a vision or in the imagination. **4** not practicable. ● *n.* (*pl.* **-ies**) a visionary person. □ **visionariness** *n.*

vision mixer *n.* *Brit.* a person whose job is to switch from one image to another in television broadcasting or recording. □ **vision mixing** *n.*

visit /ˈvɪzɪt/ *v.* & *n.* ● *v.* (**visited**, **visiting**) **1 a** *tr.* (also *absol.*) go or come to see (a person, place, etc.) as an act of friendship or ceremony, on business or for a purpose, or from interest. **b** *tr.* go or come to see for the purpose of official inspection, supervision, consultation, or correction. **2** *tr.* reside temporarily with (a person) or at (a place). **3** *intr.* be a visitor. **4** *tr.* (of a disease, calamity, etc.) come upon, attack. **5** *tr.* *Bibl.* **a** (foll. by *with*) punish (a person). **b** (often foll. by *upon*) inflict punishment for (a sin). **6** *intr.* **a** (foll. by *with*) *N. Amer.* go to see (a person) esp. socially. **b** (usu. foll. by *with*) *US* converse, chat. **7** *tr.* (often foll. by *with*) *archaic* comfort, bless (with salvation etc.). ● *n.* **1 a** an act of visiting, a call on a person or at a place (*was on a visit to some friends*; *paid him a long visit*). **b** temporary residence with a person or at a place. **2** (foll. by *to*) an occasion of going to a doctor, dentist, etc. **3** a formal or official call for the purpose of inspection etc. **4** *US* a chat. □ **visitable** *adj.* [Middle English from Old French *visiter* or Latin *visitare* 'go to see', frequentative of *visare* 'view' from *vidēre vis-* 'see': the noun perhaps from French *visite*]

visitant /ˈvɪzɪt(ə)nt/ *n.* & *adj.* ● *n.* **1** a visitor, esp. a supposedly supernatural one. **2** = VISITOR 2. ● *adj.* *archaic* or *poet.* visiting. [French *visitant* or Latin *visitare* (as VISIT)]

visitation /vɪzɪˈteɪʃ(ə)n/ *n.* **1** an official visit of inspection, esp. a bishop's examination of a church in his diocese. **2** trouble or difficulty regarded as a divine punishment. **3** (**Visitation**) **a** the visit of the Virgin Mary to Elizabeth related in Luke 1:39–56. **b** the festival commemorating this on 2 July. **4** *colloq.* an unduly protracted visit or social call. **5** *N. Amer.* a divorced person's right to spend time with his or her children in the custody of a former spouse. **6** the boarding of a vessel belonging to another state to learn its character and purpose. [Middle English from Old French *visitation* or Late Latin *visitatio* (as VISIT)]

visitatorial /ˌvɪzɪtəˈtɔːrɪəl/ *adj.* of an official visitor or visitation. [ultimately from Latin *visitare* (see VISIT)]

visiting /ˈvɪzɪtɪŋ/ *n. & adj.* ● *n.* paying a visit or visits. ● *attrib.adj.* (of an academic) spending some time at another institution (*a visiting professor*).

visiting card *n.* esp. *Brit.* a card with a person's name etc., sent or left in lieu of a formal visit.

visiting fireman *n.* (*pl.* **-men**) *US slang* a visitor given especially cordial treatment.

visiting hours *n.pl.* a designated time when visitors may call, esp. to see a patient in hospital etc.

visitor /ˈvɪzɪtə/ *n.* **1** a person who visits a person or place. **2** esp. *Brit.* a migratory bird present in a locality for part of the year (*winter visitor*). **3** *Brit.* (in a college etc.) an official with the right or duty of occasionally inspecting and reporting. [Middle English from Anglo-French *visitour*, Old French *visiteur* (as VISIT)]

visitorial /vɪzɪˈtɔːrɪəl/ *adj.* of an official visitor or visitation.

visitors' book *n.* esp. *Brit.* a book in which visitors to a hotel, church, embassy, etc., write their names and addresses and sometimes remarks.

visor /ˈvʌɪzə/ *n.* (also **vizor**) **1 a** a movable part of a helmet covering the face. **b** *hist.* a mask. **c** the projecting front part of a cap. **2** a shield (fixed or movable) to protect the eyes from unwanted light, esp. one at the top of a vehicle windscreen. □ **visored** *adj.* **visorless** *adj.* [Middle English via Anglo-French *viser*, Old French *visiere*, from *vis* 'face' from Latin *visus*: see VISAGE]

vista /ˈvɪstə/ *n.* **1** a long narrow view as between rows of trees. **2** a mental view of a long succession of remembered or anticipated events (*opened up new vistas to his ambition*). □ **vistaed** *adj.* [Italian, = view, from *visto* 'seen', past part. of *vedere* 'see', from Latin *vidēre*]

visual /ˈvɪʒjʊəl, -zj-/ *adj. & n.* ● *adj.* of, concerned with, or used in seeing. ● *n.* (usu. in *pl.*) a visual image or display, a picture. □ **visuality** /-ʊˈalɪti/ *n.* **visually** *adv.* [Middle English via Late Latin *visualis* from Latin *visus* 'sight', from *vidēre* 'see']

visual aid *n.* a film, model, etc., as an aid to learning.

visual angle *n.* *Optics* the angle formed at the eye by rays from the extremities of an object viewed.

visual display unit *n.* esp. *Brit.* *Computing* a device displaying data as characters on a screen and usu. incorporating a keyboard.

visual field *n.* = FIELD OF VISION.

visualize /ˈvɪʒjʊəlʌɪz, -zj-/ *v.tr.* (also **-ise**) **1** make visible, esp. to one's mind (a thing not visible to the eye). **2** make visible to the eye. □ **visualizable** *adj.* **visualization** /-ˈzeɪʃ(ə)n/ *n.*

visual purple *n.* a light-sensitive pigment in the retina, rhodopsin.

visual ray *n.* *Optics* a line extended from an object to the eye.

vital /ˈvʌɪt(ə)l/ *adj. & n.* ● *adj.* **1 a** essential to the existence or functioning of a thing; essential to the matter in hand; indispensable; extremely important (*a vital question*; *secrecy is vital*). **b** paramount, very great (*of vital importance*). **2** of, concerned with, or essential to organic life (*vital energy*; *vital functions*). **3** full of life or activity; lively. **4** *archaic* fatal to life or to success etc. (*a vital error*). ● *n.* (in *pl.*) the body's vital organs, e.g. the heart and brain. [Middle English via Old French from Latin *vitalis*, from *vita* 'life']

vital capacity *n.* the volume of air that can be expelled from the lungs after taking the deepest possible breath.

vital force *n.* **1** (in H. Bergson's philosophy) life-force. **2** any mysterious vital principle. [translation of French *élan vital*]

vitalism /ˈvʌɪt(ə)lɪz(ə)m/ *n.* *Biol.* the doctrine that life originates in a vital principle distinct from chemical and other physical forces. □ **vitalist** *n.* **vitalistic** /-ˈlɪstɪk/ *adj.* [French *vitalisme*, or from VITAL]

vitality /vʌɪˈtalɪti/ *n.* **1** liveliness, animation. **2** the ability to sustain life, vital power. **3** (of an institution, language, etc.) the ability to endure and to perform its functions. [Latin *vitalitas* (as VITAL)]

vitalize /ˈvʌɪt(ə)lʌɪz/ *v.tr.* (also **-ise**) **1** endow with life. **2** infuse with vigour. □ **vitalization** /-ˈzeɪʃ(ə)n/ *n.*

vitally /ˈvʌɪt(ə)li/ *adv.* essentially, indispensably.

vital power *n.* the power to sustain life.

vital statistics *n.pl.* **1** the number of births, marriages, deaths, etc. **2** *colloq.* *offens.* the measurements of a woman's bust, waist, and hips.

vitamin /ˈvɪtəmɪn, ˈvʌɪt-/ *n.* any of a group of organic compounds essential in small amounts for many living organisms to maintain normal health and development. [originally *vitamine*, from Latin *vita* 'life' + AMINE, because originally thought to contain an amino acid]

vitamin A *n.* = RETINOL.

vitamin B_1 *n.* = THIAMINE.

vitamin B_2 *n.* = RIBOFLAVIN.

vitamin B_6 *n.* = PYRIDOXINE.

vitamin B_{12} *n.* = CYANOCOBALAMIN.

vitamin B complex *n.* a group of vitamins which, although not chemically related, are often found together in the same foods.

vitamin C *n.* = ASCORBIC ACID.

vitamin D *n.* any of a group of vitamins found in liver and fish oils, essential for the absorption of calcium and the prevention of rickets in children and osteomalacia in adults.

vitamin D_2 *n.* = CALCIFEROL.

vitamin D_3 *n.* = CHOLECALCIFEROL.

vitamin E *n.* = TOCOPHEROL.

vitamin H *n.* esp. *US* = BIOTIN.

vitaminize /ˈvɪtəmɪnʌɪz/ *v.tr.* (also **-ise**) add vitamins to.

vitamin K *n.* any of a group of vitamins found mainly in green leaves and essential for the blood-clotting process.

vitamin K_1 *n.* = PHYLLOQUINONE.

vitamin K_2 *n.* = MENAQUINONE.

vitamin M *n.* esp. *US* = FOLIC ACID.

vitelli *pl.* of VITELLUS.

vitellin /vɪˈtɛlɪn, vʌɪ-/ *n.* *Chem.* the chief protein constituent of the yolk of egg. [VITELLUS + -IN]

vitelline /vɪˈtɛlʌɪn, vʌɪ-, -lɪn/ *adj.* of the vitellus. [medieval Latin *vitellinus* (as VITELLUS)]

vitelline membrane *n.* = YOLK-BAG.

vitellus /vɪˈtɛləs, vʌɪ-/ *n.* (*pl.* **vitelli** /-lʌɪ/) **1** the yolk of an egg. **2** the contents of the ovum. [Latin, = yolk]

vitiate /ˈvɪʃɪeɪt/ *v.tr.* **1** impair the quality or efficiency of; corrupt, debase, contaminate. **2** make invalid or ineffectual. □ **vitiation** /-ˈeɪʃ(ə)n/ *n.* **vitiator** *n.* [Latin *vitiare* from *vitium* VICE[1]]

viticulture /ˈvɪtɪkʌltʃə/ *n.* the cultivation of grapevines; the science or study of this. □ **viticultural** /-ˈkʌltʃ(ə)r(ə)l/ *adj.* **viticulturist** /-ˈkʌltʃ(ə)rɪst/ *n.* [Latin *vitis* 'vine' + CULTURE]

vitiligo /vɪtɪˈlʌɪgəʊ/ *n.* *Med.* a condition in which the pigment is lost from areas of the skin, causing whitish patches. [Latin, = tetter]

vitreous /ˈvɪtrɪəs/ *adj.* **1** of, or of the nature of, glass. **2** like glass in hardness, brittleness, transparency, structure, etc. (*vitreous enamel*). □ **vitreousness** *n.* [Latin *vitreus* from *vitrum* 'glass']

vitreous humour *n.* (also **vitreous body**) *Anat.* a transparent jelly-like tissue filling the eyeball.

vitrescent /vɪˈtrɛs(ə)nt/ *adj.* tending to become glass. □ **vitrescence** *n.*

vitriform /ˈvɪtrɪfɔːm/ *adj.* having the form or appearance of glass.

vitrify /'vɪtrɪfʌɪ/ *v.tr. & intr.* (**-ies, -ied**) convert or be converted into glass or a glasslike substance, esp. by heat. □ **vitrifaction** /-'fakʃ(ə)n/ *n.* **vitrifiable** *adj.* **vitrification** /-fɪ'keɪʃ(ə)n/ *n.* [French *vitrifier* or medieval Latin *vitrificare* (as VITREOUS)]

vitriol /'vɪtrɪəl/ *n.* **1** sulphuric acid or a sulphate, originally one of glassy appearance. **2** caustic or hostile speech, criticism, or feeling. [Middle English from Old French *vitriol* or medieval Latin *vitriolum*, from Latin *vitrum* 'glass']

vitriolic /vɪtrɪ'ɒlɪk/ *adj.* (of speech or criticism) caustic or hostile.

vitta /'vɪtə/ *n.* (*pl.* **vittae** /'vɪtiː/) **1** *Bot.* an oil-tube in the fruit of some plants. **2** *Zool.* a stripe of colour. □ **vittate** *adj.* [Latin, = band, chaplet]

vituperate /vɪ'tjuːpəreɪt, vʌɪ-/ *v.tr. & intr.* revile, abuse. □ **vituperation** /-'reɪʃ(ə)n/ *n.* **vituperative** /-rətɪv/ *adj.* **vituperator** *n.* [Latin *vituperare* from *vitium* VICE[1]]

viva[1] /'vʌɪvə/ *n. & v. Brit. colloq.* ● *n.* = VIVA VOCE *n.* ● *v.tr.* (**vivas, vivaed** /-vəd/ or **viva'd, vivaing**) subject to an oral examination. [abbreviation]

viva[2] /'viːvə, Italian 'viva/ *int. & n.* ● *int.* long live. ● *n.* a cry of this as a salute etc. [Italian, 3rd sing. present subjunctive of *vivere* 'live', from Latin]

vivace /vɪ'vɑːtʃi/ *adv. Mus.* in a lively brisk manner. [Italian from Latin (as VIVACIOUS)]

vivacious /vɪ'veɪʃəs, vʌɪ-/ *adj.* lively, sprightly, animated. □ **vivaciously** *adv.* **vivaciousness** *n.* **vivacity** /vɪ'vasɪti, vʌɪ-/ *n.* [Latin *vivax -acis* from *vivere* 'to live']

vivarium /vʌɪ'vɛːrɪəm, vɪ-/ *n.* (*pl.* **vivaria** /-rɪə/) a place artificially prepared for keeping animals in (nearly) their natural state; an aquarium or terrarium. [Latin, = warren, fish pond, via *vivus* 'living' from *vivere* 'to live']

vivat /'vʌɪvat, 'viː-/ *int. & n.* = VIVA[2]. [Latin, 3rd sing. present subjunctive of *vivere* 'live']

viva voce /vʌɪvə 'vəʊtʃi/ *adj., adv., & n.* ● *adj.* oral. ● *adv.* orally. ● *n. Brit.* an oral examination for an academic qualification. [medieval Latin, = with the living voice]

viverrid /vɪ'vɛrɪd, vʌɪ-/ *n. & adj.* ● *n.* any mammal of the family Viverridae, including civets, genets, and (in some classifications) mongooses. ● *adj.* of or relating to this family. [Latin *viverra* 'ferret' + -ID[3]]

vivers /'vʌɪvəz/ *n.pl. Sc.* food, victuals. [French *vivres* from *vivre* 'to live', from Latin *vivere*]

vivid /'vɪvɪd/ *adj.* **1** (of light or colour) strong, intense, glaring (*a vivid flash of lightning*; *of a vivid green*). **2** (of a mental faculty, impression, or description) clear, lively, graphic (*has a vivid imagination; have a vivid recollection of the scene*). **3** (of a person) lively, vigorous. □ **vividly** *adv.* **vividness** *n.* [Latin *vividus* from *vivere* 'to live']

vivify /'vɪvɪfʌɪ/ *v.tr.* (**-ies, -ied**) enliven, animate, make lively or living. □ **vivification** /-fɪ'keɪʃ(ə)n/ *n.* [French *vivifier* from Late Latin *vivificare*, via Latin *vivus* 'living' from *vivere* 'to live']

viviparous /vɪ'vɪp(ə)rəs, vʌɪ-/ *adj.* **1** *Zool.* bringing forth young alive, not hatching them by means of eggs (cf. OVIPAROUS). **2** *Bot.* producing bulbs or seeds that germinate while still attached to the parent plant. □ **viviparity** /vɪvɪ'parɪti/ *n.* **viviparously** *adv.* **viviparousness** *n.* [Latin *viviparus* from *vivus*: see VIVIFY]

vivisect /'vɪvɪsɛkt, vɪvɪ'sɛkt/ *v.tr.* perform vivisection on. [back-formation from VIVISECTION]

vivisection /vɪvɪ'sɛkʃ(ə)n/ *n.* **1** dissection or other painful treatment of living animals for purposes of scientific research. **2** unduly detailed or ruthless criticism. □ **vivisectional** *adj.* **vivisectionist** *n.* **vivisector** /'vɪvɪsɛktə/ *n.* [Latin *vivus* 'living' (see VIVIFY), on the pattern of *dissection*]

vixen /'vɪks(ə)n/ *n.* **1** a female fox. **2** a spiteful or quarrelsome woman. □ **vixenish** *adj.* **vixenly** *adj.* [Middle English *fixen* from Old English, fem. of FOX]

Viyella /vʌɪ'ɛlə/ *n. propr.* a fabric made from a twilled mixture of cotton and wool. [from *Via Gellia*, a valley in Derbyshire where it was first made]

viz. /vɪz, or by substitution 'neɪmli/ *adv.* (usu. introducing a gloss or explanation) namely; that is to say; in other words (*came to a firm conclusion, viz. that we were right*). [abbreviation of VIDELICET, *z* being medieval Latin symbol for abbreviation of *-et*]

vizard /'vɪzəd/ *n. archaic* a mask or disguise. [VISOR + -ARD]

vizcacha var. of VISCACHA.

vizier /vɪ'zɪə, 'vɪzɪə/ *n. hist.* a high official in some Muslim countries, esp. in Turkey under Ottoman rule. □ **vizierate** /-rət/ *n.* **vizierial** /vɪ'zɪərɪəl/ *adj.* **viziership** *n.* [ultimately from Arabic *wazīr* 'caliph's chief counsellor']

vizor var. of VISOR.

VJ *abbr.* Victory over Japan (in 1945).

VJ day *n.* 15 August, the day Japan ceased fighting in the Second World War, or 2 September, when Japan formally surrendered.

Vlach /vlak/ *n. & adj.* ● *n.* a member of a people inhabiting Romania and parts of the former Soviet Union. ● *adj.* of or relating to this people. [Bulgarian from Old Church Slavonic *Vlachŭ* 'Romanian' etc., from a Germanic word meaning 'foreigner']

vlei /fleɪ, vlʌɪ/ *n. S.Afr.* a hollow in which water collects during the rainy season. [Dutch dialect from Dutch *vallei* 'valley']

VLF *abbr.* very low frequency (designating radio waves of frequency *c.*3–30 kHz and wavelength *c.*10–100 km).

V-neck /viː'nɛk, 'viː-/ *n.* (often *attrib.*) **1** a neck of a pullover etc. with straight sides meeting at an angle in the front to form a V. **2** a garment with this.

VO *abbr.* (in the UK) Royal Victorian Order.

vocable /'vəʊkəb(ə)l/ *n.* a word, esp. with reference to form rather than meaning. [French *vocable* or Latin *vocabulum* from *vocare* 'call']

vocabulary /və(ʊ)'kabjʊləri/ *n.* (*pl.* **-ies**) **1** the (principal) words used in a language or a particular book or branch of science etc. or by a particular author (*scientific vocabulary; the vocabulary of Shakespeare*). **2** a list of these, arranged alphabetically with definitions or translations. **3** the range of words known to an individual (*his vocabulary is limited*). **4** a set of artistic or stylistic forms or techniques, esp. a range of set movements in ballet etc. [medieval Latin *vocabularius, -um* (as VOCABLE)]

vocal /'vəʊk(ə)l/ *adj. & n.* ● *adj.* **1** of or concerned with or uttered by the voice (*a vocal communication*). **2** expressing one's feelings freely in speech (*was very vocal about his rights*). **3** *Phonet.* voiced. **4** *poet.* (of trees, water, etc.) endowed with a voice or a similar faculty. **5** (of music) written for or produced by the voice with or without accompaniment (cf. INSTRUMENTAL *adj.* 2). ● *n.* **1** (in *sing.* or *pl.*) the sung part of a musical composition. **2** a musical performance with singing. □ **vocality** /və(ʊ)'kalɪti/ *n.* **vocally** *adv.* [Middle English from Latin *vocalis* (as VOICE)]

vocal cords *n.pl.* (also **vocal folds**) folds of the lining membrane of the larynx near the opening of the glottis, with edges vibrating in the airstream to produce the voice.

vocalese /vəʊkə'liːz/ *n.* a style of singing in which singers put words to jazz tunes, esp. to previously improvised instrumental solos (see SCAT[2] *n.*). [as VOCAL + -ESE]

vocalic /və(ʊ)'kalɪk/ *adj.* of or consisting of a vowel or vowels.

vocalise /vəʊkə'liːz, 'vəʊkəliːz/ *n. Mus.* **1** a singing exercise using individual syllables or vowel sounds. **2** a vocal passage consisting of a melody without words. **3** *derog.* a technical vocal display. [French, from *vocaliser* 'to vocalize']

vocalism /'vəʊk(ə)lɪz(ə)m/ *n.* **1** the use of the voice in speaking or singing. **2** a vowel sound or system.

vocalist /ˈvəʊk(ə)lɪst/ *n.* a singer, esp. of jazz or popular songs.

vocalize /ˈvəʊk(ə)lʌɪz/ *v.* (also **-ise**) **1** *tr.* form (a sound) or utter (a word) with the voice. **2** *intr.* utter a vocal sound. **3** *tr.* articulate, express. **4** *tr.* write (Hebrew etc.) with vowel points. **5** *tr.* (usu. in *passive*) *Philol.* change (a consonant) to a semivowel or vowel. **6** *intr. Mus.* sing with several notes to one vowel. □ **vocalization** /-ˈzeɪʃ(ə)n/ *n.* **vocalizer** *n.*

vocal score *n.* a musical score showing the voice parts in full, but with the accompaniment reduced or omitted.

vocation /və(ʊ)ˈkeɪʃ(ə)n/ *n.* **1** a strong feeling of fitness for a particular career or occupation (in religious contexts regarded as a divine call). **2 a** a person's employment, esp. regarded as requiring dedication. **b** a trade or profession. [Middle English from Old French *vocation* or Latin *vocatio*, from *vocare* 'to call']

vocational /və(ʊ)ˈkeɪʃ(ə)n(ə)l/ *adj.* **1** of or relating to an occupation or employment. **2** (of education or training) directed at a particular occupation and its skills. □ **vocationalism** *n.* **vocationalize** *v.tr.* (also **-ise**). **vocationally** *adv.*

vocative /ˈvɒkətɪv/ *n.* & *adj. Gram.* ● *n.* the case of nouns, pronouns, and adjectives used in addressing or invoking a person or thing. ● *adj.* of or in this case. [Middle English from Old French *vocatif -ive* or Latin *vocativus*, from *vocare* 'to call']

vociferate /və(ʊ)ˈsɪfəreɪt/ *v.* **1** *tr.* utter (words etc.) noisily. **2** *intr.* shout, bawl. □ **vociferance** *n.* **vociferant** *adj.* & *n.* **vociferation** /-ˈreɪʃ(ə)n/ *n.* **vociferator** *n.* [Latin *vociferari*, from *vox* 'voice' + *ferre* 'bear']

vociferous /və(ʊ)ˈsɪf(ə)rəs/ *adj.* **1** (of a person, speech, etc.) noisy, clamorous. **2** insistently and forcibly expressing one's views. □ **vociferously** *adv.* **vociferousness** *n.*

vocoder /vəʊˈkəʊdə/ *n.* a synthesizer that produces sounds from an analysis of speech input. [VOICE + CODE]

Vodafone /ˈvəʊdəfəʊn/ *n. propr.* **1** a cellular telephone system in the UK. **2** a handset used in this system. [VOICE + DATA + *fone* representing PHONE[1]]

vodka /ˈvɒdkə/ *n.* an originally Russian alcoholic spirit made by distillation of rye etc. [Russian, diminutive of *voda* 'water']

voe /vəʊ/ *n.* a small bay or creek in Orkney or Shetland. [Norwegian *vaag*, Old Norse *vágr*]

vogue /vəʊg/ *n.* **1** (prec. by *the*) the prevailing fashion. **2** popular use or currency (*has had a great vogue*). □ **in vogue** in fashion, generally current. □ **voguish** *adj.* [French from Italian *voga* 'rowing, fashion', from *vogare* 'row, go well']

vogue word *n.* a word currently fashionable.

voice /vɔɪs/ *n.* & *v.* ● *n.* **1 a** sound formed in the larynx etc. and uttered by the mouth, esp. human utterance in speaking, shouting, singing, etc. (*heard a voice*; *spoke in a low voice*). **b** the ability to produce this (*has lost her voice*). **2 a** the use of the voice; utterance, esp. in spoken or written words (esp. *give voice*). **b** an opinion so expressed. **c** the right to express an opinion (*I have no voice in the matter*). **d** an agency by which an opinion is expressed. **3** *Gram.* a form or set of forms of a verb showing the relation of the subject to the action (*active voice*; *passive voice*). **4** *Mus.* **a** a vocal part in a composition. **b** a constituent part in a fugue. **5** *Phonet.* sound uttered with resonance of the vocal cords, not with mere breath. **6** (usu. in *pl.*) the supposed utterance of an invisible guiding or directing spirit. ● *v.tr.* **1** give utterance to; express (*the letter voices our opinion*). **2** (esp. as **voiced** *adj.*) *Phonet.* utter with vibration of the vocal cords (e.g. *b, d, g, v, z*). **3** *Mus.* regulate the tone-quality of (organ pipes). □ **in voice** (or **good voice**) in proper vocal condition for singing or speaking. **with one voice** unanimously. □ **-voiced** *adj.* **voicer** *n.* (in sense 3 of *v.*). [Middle English via Anglo-French *voiz*, Old French *vois* from Latin *vox vocis*]

voice box *n.* the larynx.

voiceful /ˈvɔɪsfʊl, -f(ə)l/ *adj. poet.* or *literary* **1** vocal. **2** sonorous.

voiceless /ˈvɔɪslɪs/ *adj.* **1** dumb, mute, speechless. **2** *Phonet.* uttered without vibration of the vocal cords (e.g. *f, k, p, s, t*). □ **voicelessly** *adv.* **voicelessness** *n.*

voice of God *n.* (prec. by *the*) the expression of God's will, wrath, etc.

voice-over *n.* & *v.* ● *n.* narration in a film etc. not accompanied by a picture of the speaker. ● *v.tr.* & *intr.* speak a voice-over (for).

voiceprint /ˈvɔɪsprɪnt/ *n.* a visual record of speech, analysed with respect to frequency, duration, and amplitude.

voice vote *n.* a vote taken by noting the relative strength of calls of *aye* and *no*.

void /vɔɪd/ *adj.*, *n.*, & *v.* ● *adj.* **1 a** empty, vacant. **b** (foll. by *of*) lacking; free from (*a style void of affectation*). **2** esp. *Law* (of a contract, deed, promise, etc.) invalid, not binding (*null and void*). **3** useless, ineffectual. **4** (often foll. by *in*) *Cards* (of a hand) having no cards in a given suit. **5** (of an office or position) vacant (esp. in phr. **fall void**). ● *n.* **1** an empty space, a vacuum (*vanished into the void*; *cannot fill the void made by death*). **2** an unfilled space in a wall or building. **3** (often foll. by *in*) *Cards* the absence of cards in a particular suit. ● *v.tr.* **1** render invalid. **2** (also *absol.*) excrete. □ **voidable** *adj.* **voidness** *n.* [Middle English from Old French dialect *voide*, Old French *vuide*, *vuit*, related to Latin *vacare* VACATE: the verb partly from AVOID, partly from Old French *voider*]

voidance /ˈvɔɪd(ə)ns/ *n.* **1** *Eccl.* a vacancy in a benefice. **2** the act or an instance of voiding; the state of being voided. [Middle English from Old French (as VOID)]

voided /ˈvɔɪdɪd/ *adj. Heraldry* (of a bearing) having the central area cut away so as to show the field.

voile /vɔɪl, vwɑːl/ *n.* a thin semi-transparent dress material of cotton, wool, or silk. [French, = VEIL]

vol. *abbr.* volume.

volant /ˈvəʊlənt/ *adj.* **1** *Zool.* flying, able to fly. **2** *Heraldry* represented as flying. **3** *literary* nimble, rapid. [French from *voler*, from Latin *volare* 'to fly']

volar /ˈvəʊlə/ *adj. Anat.* of the palm or sole. [Latin *vola* 'hollow of hand or foot']

volatile /ˈvɒlətʌɪl/ *adj.* & *n.* ● *adj.* **1** evaporating rapidly (*volatile salts*). **2** changeable, fickle. **3** lively, light-hearted. **4** apt to break out into violence. **5** transient. ● *n.* a volatile substance. □ **volatileness** *n.* **volatility** /-ˈtɪlɪti/ *n.* [Old French *volatil* or Latin *volatilis* from *volare volat-* 'to fly']

volatile oil *n.* = ESSENTIAL OIL.

volatilize /vəˈlatɪlʌɪz, ˈvɒlətɪlʌɪz/ *v.* (also **-ise**) **1** *tr.* cause to evaporate. **2** *intr.* evaporate. □ **volatilizable** *adj.* **volatilization** /-ˈzeɪʃ(ə)n/ *n.*

vol-au-vent /ˈvɒlə(ʊ)vɒ̃/ *n.* a (usu. small) round case of puff pastry filled with meat, fish, etc., and sauce. [French, literally 'flight in the wind']

volcanic /vɒlˈkanɪk/ *adj.* (also **vulcanic** /vʌl-/) of, like, or produced by a volcano. □ **volcanically** *adv.* **volcanicity** /vɒlkəˈnɪsɪti/ *n.* [French *volcanique* from *volcan* VOLCANO]

volcanic bomb *n.* a mass of ejected lava usu. rounded and sometimes hollow.

volcanic glass *n.* obsidian.

volcanism /ˈvɒlkənɪz(ə)m/ *n.* (also **vulcanism** /ˈvʌl-/) volcanic activity or phenomena.

volcano /vɒlˈkeɪnəʊ/ *n.* (*pl.* **-oes**) **1** a mountain or hill having an opening or openings in the earth's crust through which lava, cinders, steam, gases, etc., are or have been expelled continuously or at intervals. **2 a** a state of things likely to cause a violent outburst. **b** a violent esp. suppressed feeling. [Italian from Latin *Volcanus* 'Vulcan', the Roman god of fire]

volcanology var. of VULCANOLOGY.

vole[1] /vəʊl/ *n.* any small ratlike or mouselike plant-eating rodent of the family Cricetidae. [originally *vole-mouse* from Norwegian, from *voll* 'field' + *mus* 'mouse']

vole[2] /vəʊl/ *n. archaic* the winning of all tricks at cards. [French, from *voler* 'to fly' from Latin *volare*]

volet /'vɒleɪ/ *n.* a panel or wing of a triptych. [French, from *voler* 'to fly' from Latin *volare*]

volitant /'vɒlɪt(ə)nt/ *adj. Zool.* volant. [Latin *volitare*, frequentative of *volare* 'fly']

volition /və'lɪʃ(ə)n/ *n.* **1** the exercise of the will. **2** the power of willing. □ **of** (or **by**) **one's own volition** voluntarily. □ **volitional** *adj.* **volitionally** *adv.* **volitive** /'vɒlɪtɪv/ *adj.* [French *volition* or medieval Latin *volitio*, from *volo* 'I wish']

Völkerwanderung /'fəːlkə,vɑːndərʊŋ/, German 'fœlkər,vandərʊŋ/ *n.* a migration of peoples, esp. that of Germanic and Slavic peoples into Europe from the second to the eleventh centuries. [German, from *Völker* 'nations' + *Wanderung* 'migration']

volley /'vɒli/ *n. & v.* ● *n.* (*pl.* **-eys**) **1 a** the simultaneous discharge of a number of weapons. **b** the bullets etc. discharged in a volley. **2** (usu. foll. by *of*) a noisy emission of oaths etc. in quick succession. **3** *Tennis* the return of a ball in play before it touches the ground. **4** *Football* the kicking of a ball in play before it touches the ground. **5** *Cricket* **a** a ball pitched right up to the batsman or the stumps without bouncing. **b** the pitching of the ball in this way. ● *v.* (**-eys, -eyed**) **1** *tr.* (also *absol.*) *Sport* return, send, or pitch (a ball) by a volley. **2** *tr. & absol.* discharge (bullets, abuse, etc.) in a volley. **3** *intr.* (of bullets etc.) fly in a volley. **4** *intr.* (of guns etc.) sound together. **5** *intr.* make a sound like a volley of artillery. □ **volleyer** *n.* [French *volée*, ultimately from Latin *volare* 'to fly']

volleyball /'vɒlɪbɔːl/ *n.* a game for two teams of six hitting a large ball by hand over a net.

volplane /'vɒlpleɪn/ *n. & v. Aeron.* ● *n.* a glide. ● *v.intr.* glide. [French *vol plané*, from *vol* 'flight' + *plané*, past part. of *planer* 'hover', related to PLANE[1]]

vols. *abbr.* volumes.

volt[1] /vəʊlt, vɒlt/ *n.* the SI unit of electromotive force, the difference of potential that would carry one ampere of current against one ohm resistance (abbr.: V). [named after A. *Volta*, Italian physicist d. 1827]

volt[2] /vɒlt, vəʊlt/ *v. & n.* ● *v.intr. Fencing* make a volte. ● *n.* var. of VOLTE. [French *volter* (as VOLTE)]

voltage /'vəʊltɪdʒ, 'vɒltɪdʒ/ *n.* electromotive force or potential difference expressed in volts.

voltaic /vɒl'teɪɪk/ *adj.* of electricity from a primary battery; galvanic (*voltaic battery*).

voltameter /vɒl'tamɪtə/ *n.* an instrument for measuring an electric charge.

volte /vɒlt, vəʊlt/ *n.* (also **volt**) **1** *Fencing* a quick movement to escape a thrust. **2** a sideways circular movement of a horse. [French from Italian *volta* 'a turn', fem. past part. of *volgere* 'turn', from Latin *volvere* 'roll']

volte-face /vɒlt'fɑːs, -'fas/ *n.* (*pl.* same) **1** a complete reversal of position in argument or opinion. **2** the act or an instance of turning round. [French from Italian *voltafaccia*, ultimately from Latin *volvere* 'roll' + *facies* 'appearance, face']

voltmeter /'vəʊltmiːtə, 'vɒlt-/ *n.* an instrument for measuring electric potential in volts.

voluble /'vɒljʊb(ə)l/ *adj.* **1** speaking or spoken vehemently, incessantly, or fluently (*voluble spokesman*; *voluble excuses*). **2** *Bot.* twisting round a support, twining. □ **volubility** /-'bɪlɪti/ *n.* **volubleness** *n.* **volubly** *adv.* [French *voluble* or Latin *volubilis*, from *volvere* 'to roll']

volume /'vɒljuːm/ *n.* **1 a** a set of sheets of paper, usu. printed, bound together and forming part or the whole of a work or comprising several works (*issued in three volumes*; *a library of 12,000 volumes*). **b** *hist.* a scroll of papyrus etc., an ancient form of book. **2 a** solid content, bulk. **b** the space occupied by a gas or liquid. **c** (foll. by *of*) an amount or quantity (*large volume of business*). **3 a** quantity or power of sound. **b** fullness of tone. **4** (foll. by *of*) **a** a moving mass of water etc. **b** (usu. in *pl.*) a wreath or coil or rounded mass of smoke etc. □ **volumed** *adj.* (also in *comb.*). [Middle English via Old French *volum(e)* from Latin *volumen -minis* 'roll' from *volvere* 'to roll']

volumetric /vɒljʊ'mɛtrɪk/ *adj.* of or relating to measurement by volume. □ **volumetrically** *adv.* [VOLUME + METRIC]

voluminous /və'ljuːmɪnəs/ *adj.* **1** large in volume; bulky. **2** (of drapery etc.) loose and ample. **3** consisting of many volumes. **4** (of a writer) producing many books. □ **voluminosity** /-'nɒsɪti/ *n.* **voluminously** *adv.* **voluminousness** *n.* [Late Latin *voluminosus* (as VOLUME)]

voluntarism /'vɒləntərɪz(ə)m/ *n.* **1** the principle of relying on voluntary action rather than compulsion. **2** *Philos.* the doctrine that the will is a fundamental or dominant factor in the individual or the universe. **3** *hist.* the doctrine that the Church or schools should be independent of the State and supported by voluntary contributions. □ **voluntarist** *n.* [formed irregularly from VOLUNTARY]

voluntary /'vɒlənt(ə)ri/ *adj. & n.* ● *adj.* **1** done, acting, or able to act of one's own free will; not constrained or compulsory, intentional (*a voluntary gift*). **2** unpaid (*voluntary work*). **3** (of an institution) supported by voluntary contributions. **4** *Brit.* (of a school) built by a voluntary institution but maintained by a local education authority. **5** brought about, produced, etc., by voluntary action. **6** (of a movement, muscle, or limb) controlled by the will. **7** (of a confession by a criminal) not prompted by a promise or threat. **8** *Law* (of a conveyance or disposition) made without return in money or other consideration. ● *n.* (*pl.* **-ies**) **1 a** an organ solo played before, during, or after a church service. **b** the music for this. **c** *archaic* an extempore performance esp. as a prelude to other music. **2** (in competitions) a special performance left to the performer's choice. **3** *hist.* a person who holds that the Church or schools should be independent of the State and supported by voluntary contributions. □ **voluntarily** *adv.* **voluntariness** *n.* [Middle English from Old French *volontaire* or Latin *voluntarius*, from *voluntas* 'will']

Voluntary Aid Detachment *n.* (in the UK) a group of organized voluntary first-aid and nursing workers.

voluntary-aided *adj.* (usu. *attrib.*) (in the UK) designating a voluntary school, funded mainly by the local authority.

voluntary-controlled *adj.* (usu. *attrib.*) (in the UK) designating a voluntary school fully funded by the local authority.

voluntaryism /'vɒlənt(ə)rɪɪz(ə)m/ *n. hist.* = VOLUNTARISM 1, 3. □ **voluntaryist** *n.*

voluntary school *n.* (in the UK) a school which, though not established by the local education authority, is funded mainly or entirely by it, and which encourages a particular set of usu. religious beliefs.

Voluntary Service Overseas *n.* a British organization promoting voluntary work in underdeveloped countries.

volunteer /vɒlən'tɪə/ *n. & v.* ● *n.* **1** a person who voluntarily takes part in an enterprise or offers to undertake a task. **2** a person who enrols for military service, esp. *hist.* (in the UK) a member of any of the former corps of voluntary soldiers provided with instructors, arms, etc., by the state. **3** (usu. *attrib.*) a self-sown plant. ● *v.* **1** *tr.* (often foll. by *to* + infin.) undertake or offer (one's services, a remark or explanation, etc.) voluntarily. **2** *intr.* (often foll. by *for*) make a voluntary offer of one's services; be a volunteer. **3** *tr.* (usu. in *passive*; often foll. by *for*, or *to* + infin.) assign or commit (a person) to a particular undertaking, esp. without consultation. [French *volontaire* (as VOLUNTARY), assimilated to -EER]

volunteerism /vɒlən'tɪərɪz(ə)m/ *n.* esp. *N. Amer.* the involvement of volunteers, esp. in community service.

voluptuary /vəˈlʌptjʊəri/ *n.* & *adj.* ● *n.* (*pl.* **-ies**) a person given up to luxury and sensual pleasure. ● *adj.* concerned with luxury and sensual pleasure. [Latin *volupt(u)arius* (as VOLUPTUOUS)]

voluptuous /vəˈlʌptjʊəs/ *adj.* **1** of, tending to, occupied with, or derived from, sensuous or sensual pleasure. **2** (of a woman) curvaceous and sexually desirable. □ **voluptuously** *adv.* **voluptuousness** *n.* [Middle English from Old French *voluptueux* or Latin *voluptuosus*, from *voluptas* 'pleasure']

volute /vəˈl(j)uːt/ *n.* & *adj.* ● *n.* **1** *Archit.* a spiral scroll characteristic of Ionic capitals and also used in Corinthian and composite capitals. **2 a** any marine gastropod mollusc of the genus *Voluta*. **b** the spiral shell of this. ● *adj.* esp. *Bot.* rolled up. □ **voluted** *adj.* [French *volute* or Latin *voluta*, fem. past part. of *volvere* 'roll']

volution /vəˈl(j)uːʃ(ə)n/ *n.* **1** a rolling motion. **2** a spiral turn. **3** a whorl of a spiral shell. **4** *Anat.* a convolution. [as VOLUTE, on the pattern of REVOLUTION etc.]

volvox /ˈvɒlvɒks/ *n. Biol.* an aquatic flagellate unicellular plant which forms colonies resembling minute green globes. [modern Latin, as if from Latin *volvere* 'to roll', though originally a misreading of Pliny]

vomer /ˈvəʊmə/ *n. Anat.* the small thin bone separating the nostrils in man and most vertebrates. [Latin, = ploughshare]

vomit /ˈvɒmɪt/ *v.* & *n.* ● *v.tr.* (**vomited**, **vomiting**) **1** (also *absol.*) eject (matter) from the stomach through the mouth. **2** (of a volcano, chimney, etc.) eject violently, belch forth. ● *n.* **1** matter vomited from the stomach. **2** *archaic* an emetic. □ **vomiter** *n.* [Middle English, ultimately from Latin *vomere vomit-* or its frequentative *vomitare*]

vomitorium /vɒmɪˈtɔːrɪəm/ *n.* (*pl.* **vomitoria** /-rɪə/) *Rom. Antiq.* a vomitory. [Latin: see VOMITORY]

vomitory /ˈvɒmɪt(ə)ri/ *adj.* & *n.* ● *adj.* emetic. ● *n.* (*pl.* **-ies**) *Rom. Antiq.* each of a series of passages for entrance and exit in an amphitheatre or theatre. [Latin *vomitorius* (*adj.*), *vomitorium* (*n.*) (as VOMIT)]

voodoo /ˈvuːduː/ *n.* & *v.* ● *n.* **1** use of or belief in religious witchcraft as practised among blacks esp. in the W. Indies. **2** a person skilled in this. **3** a voodoo spell. ● *v.tr.* (**voodoos**, **voodooed**) affect by voodoo; bewitch. □ **voodooism** *n.* **voodooist** *n.* [Louisiana French from Kwa *vodu*]

voracious /vəˈreɪʃəs/ *adj.* **1** greedy in eating, ravenous. **2** very eager in some activity (*a voracious reader*). □ **voraciously** *adv.* **voraciousness** *n.* **voracity** /vəˈrasɪti/ *n.* [Latin *vorax* from *vorare* 'devour']

-vorous /v(ə)rəs/ *comb. form* forming adjectives meaning 'feeding on' (*carnivorous*). □ **-vora** /v(ə)rə/ *comb. form* forming names of groups. **-vore** /vɔː/ *comb. form* forming names of individuals. [Latin *-vorus* from *vorare* 'devour']

vortex /ˈvɔːtɛks/ *n.* (*pl.* **vortexes** or **vortices** /-tɪsiːz/) **1** a mass of whirling fluid, esp. a whirlpool or whirlwind. **2** any whirling motion or mass. **3** a system, occupation, pursuit, etc., viewed as swallowing up or engrossing those who approach it (*the vortex of society*). **4** *Physics* a portion of fluid whose particles have rotatory motion. □ **vortical** *adj.* **vortically** *adv.* **vorticity** /vɔːˈtɪsɪti/ *n.* **vorticose** *adj.* **vorticular** /vɔːˈtɪkjʊlə/ *adj.* [Latin *vortex -icis* 'eddy', variant of VERTEX]

vortex ring *n.* a vortex whose axis is a closed curve, e.g. a smoke ring.

vorticella /vɔːtɪˈsɛlə/ *n.* any sedentary protozoan of the family Vorticellidae, consisting of a tubular stalk with a bell-shaped ciliated opening. [modern Latin, diminutive of VORTEX]

vorticist /ˈvɔːtɪsɪst/ *n.* **1** *Art* an artist of a British movement *c.*1914–15 influenced by futurism and characterized by machine-like forms. **2** *Metaphysics* a person regarding the universe, with Descartes, as a plenum in which motion propagates itself in circles. □ **vorticism** *n.*

votary /ˈvəʊt(ə)ri/ *n.* (*pl.* **-ies**; *fem.* **votaress**) (usu. foll. by *of*) **1** a person vowed to the service of God or a god or cult. **2** a devoted follower, adherent, or advocate of a person, system, occupation, etc. □ **votarist** *n.* [Latin *vot-*: see VOTE]

vote /vəʊt/ *n.* & *v.* ● *n.* **1** a formal expression of choice or opinion by means of a ballot, show of hands, etc., concerning a choice of candidate, approval of a motion or resolution, etc. (*let us take a vote on it*; *gave my vote to the independent candidate*). **2** (usu. prec. by *the*) the right to vote, esp. in a state election. **3 a** an opinion expressed by a majority of votes. **b** *Brit.* money granted by a majority of votes. **4** the collective votes that are or may be given by or for a particular group (*will lose the Welsh vote*; *the Conservative vote increased*). **5** a ticket etc. used for recording a vote. ● *v.* **1** *intr.* (often foll. by *for*, *against*, or *to* + infin.) give a vote. **2** *tr.* **a** (often foll. by *that* + clause) enact or resolve by a majority of votes. **b** grant (a sum of money) by a majority of votes. **c** cause to be in a specified position by a majority of votes (*was voted off the committee*). **3** *tr. colloq.* pronounce or declare by general consent (*was voted a failure by consumers*). **4** *tr.* (often foll. by *that* + clause) *colloq.* announce one's proposal (*I vote that we all go home*). □ **put to a** (or **the**) **vote** submit to a decision by voting. **vote down** defeat (a proposal etc.) in a vote. **vote in** elect by voting. **vote off** dismiss from (a committee etc.) by voting. **vote out** dismiss from office etc. by voting. **vote with one's feet** *colloq.* indicate an opinion by one's presence or absence. □ **votable** *adj.* **voteless** *adj.* [Middle English from *vot-*, past part. stem of Latin *vovēre* 'vow']

vote of censure *n.* = VOTE OF NO CONFIDENCE.

vote of no confidence *n.* a vote showing that the majority do not support the policy of the governing body etc.

voter /ˈvəʊtə/ *n.* **1** a person with the right to vote at an election. **2** a person voting.

voting machine *n.* (esp. in the US) a machine for the automatic registering of votes.

voting paper *n.* a paper used in voting by ballot.

voting stock *n. Stock Exch.* stock entitling the holder to a vote.

votive /ˈvəʊtɪv/ *adj.* offered or consecrated in fulfilment of a vow (*votive offering*; *votive picture*). [Latin *votivus* (as VOTE)]

votive Mass *n. Eccl.* a Mass celebrated for a special purpose or occasion.

vouch /vaʊtʃ/ *v.* **1** *intr.* (foll. by *for*) answer for, be surety for (*will vouch for the truth of this*; *can vouch for him*; *could not vouch for his honesty*). **2** *tr. archaic* cite as an authority. **3** *tr. archaic* confirm or uphold (a statement) by evidence or assertion. [Middle English from Old French *vo(u)cher* 'summon' etc., ultimately from Latin *vocare* 'to call']

voucher /ˈvaʊtʃə/ *n.* **1** a document which can be exchanged for goods or services as a token of payment made or promised by the holder or another. **2** a document establishing the payment of money or the truth of accounts. **3** a person who vouches for a person, statement, etc. [Anglo-French *voucher* (as VOUCH), or from VOUCH]

vouchsafe /vaʊtʃˈseɪf/ *v.tr. formal* **1** condescend to give or grant (*vouchsafed me no answer*). **2** (foll. by *to* + infin.) condescend. [Middle English, from VOUCH (in the sense 'warrant') + SAFE]

voussoir /ˈvuːswɑː/ *n.* each of the wedge-shaped or tapered stones forming an arch. [Old French *vossoir* etc. from popular Latin *volsorium*, ultimately from Latin *volvere* 'to roll']

vow /vaʊ/ *n.* & *v.* ● *n.* **1** *Relig.* a solemn promise esp. in the form of an oath to God or another deity or to a saint. **2** (in *pl.*) the promises by which a monk or nun is bound to poverty, chastity, and obedience. **3** a promise of fidelity (*lovers' vows*; *marriage vows*). **4** (usu. as **baptismal vows**) the promises given at baptism by the baptized person or by sponsors. ● *v.tr.* **1** promise solemnly (*vowed obedience*). **2** dedicate to a deity. **3** (also *absol.*) *archaic* declare solemnly. □ **under a vow** having made a vow. [Middle English via Anglo-French *v(o)u*, Old French *vo(u)* from Latin (as VOTE): the verb from Old French *vouer*, in sense 2 partly from AVOW]

vowel /ˈvaʊəl/ *n.* **1** a speech sound made with vibration of the vocal cords but without audible friction, more open than a consonant and capable of forming a syllable. **2** a letter or letters representing this, as *a, e, i, o, u, aw, ah.* □ **vowelled** *adj.* (*US* **voweled**) (also in *comb.*). **vowelless** *adj.* **vowelly** *adj.* [Middle English via Old French *vouel, voiel* from Latin *vocalis* (*littera*) 'VOCAL (letter)']

vowel gradation *n.* = ABLAUT.

vowelize /ˈvaʊəlʌɪz/ *v.tr.* (also **-ise**) insert the vowels in (shorthand, Hebrew, etc.).

vowel mutation *n.* = UMLAUT 2.

vowel-point *n.* each of a set of marks indicating vowels in Hebrew etc.

vox angelica /vɒks anˈdʒɛlɪkə/ *n.* an organ stop with a soft tremulous tone. [Late Latin, = angelic voice]

vox humana /vɒks hjuːˈmɑːnə/ *n.* an organ stop with a tone supposed to resemble a human voice. [Latin, = human voice]

vox pop /vɒks ˈpɒp/ *n. Brit. Broadcasting colloq.* popular opinion as represented by informal comments from members of the public; statements or interviews of this kind. [abbreviation of VOX POPULI]

vox populi /vɒks ˈpɒpjʊliː, -lʌɪ/ *n.* public opinion; the general verdict; popular belief or rumour. [Latin, = the people's voice]

voyage /ˈvɔɪɪdʒ/ *n. & v.* ● *n.* **1** a journey, esp. a long one by water, air, or in space. **2** an account of this. ● *v.* **1** *intr.* make a voyage. **2** *tr.* traverse, esp. by water or air. □ **voyageable** *adj.* **voyager** *n.* [Middle English via Anglo-French & Old French *veiage, voiage* from Latin *viaticum*]

voyageur /vwɒjəˈʒəː/ *n.* a Canadian boatman, esp. *hist.* one employed in transporting goods and passengers between trading posts. [French, = voyager (as VOYAGE)]

voyeur /vwɑːˈjəː, vɔɪ-/ *n.* **1** a person who obtains sexual gratification from observing others' sexual actions or organs. **2** a powerless or passive spectator. □ **voyeurism** *n.* **voyeuristic** /-ˈrɪstɪk/ *adj.* **voyeuristically** /-ˈrɪstɪk(ə)li/ *adj.* [French, from *voir* 'see']

VP *abbr.* Vice-President.

VR *abbr.* **1** Queen Victoria. **2** variant reading. **3** virtual reality. [sense 1 from Latin *Victoria Regina*]

vroom /vruːm/ *v., n., & int.* ● *v.* **1** *intr.* (esp. of an engine) make a roaring noise. **2** *intr.* (of a motor vehicle etc.) travel at speed. **3** *tr.* rev (an engine). ● *n.* the roaring sound of an engine. ● *int.* an imitation of such a sound. [imitative]

VS *abbr.* Veterinary Surgeon.

vs. *abbr.* versus.

V-sign *n.* **1** *Brit.* a sign of the letter V made with the first two fingers pointing up and the back of the hand facing outwards, as a gesture of abuse, contempt, etc. **2** a similar sign made with the palm of the hand facing outwards, as a symbol of victory.

VSO *abbr.* Voluntary Service Overseas.

VSOP *abbr.* Very Special Old Pale (brandy).

VT *abbr. US* Vermont (in official postal use).

Vt. *abbr.* Vermont.

VTO *abbr.* vertical take-off.

VTOL /ˈviːtɒl/ *abbr.* vertical take-off and landing.

VTR *abbr.* videotape recorder.

vug /vʌg/ *n.* a rock cavity lined with crystals. □ **vuggy** *adj.* **vugular** *adj.* [Cornish *vooga*]

vulcanic var. of VOLCANIC.

vulcanism var. of VOLCANISM.

vulcanite /ˈvʌlkənʌɪt/ *n.* a hard black vulcanized rubber, ebonite. [as VULCANIZE]

vulcanize /ˈvʌlkənʌɪz/ *v.tr.* (also **-ise**) treat (rubber or rubber-like material) with sulphur etc. at a high temperature to increase its strength. □ **vulcanizable** *adj.* **vulcanization** /-ˈzeɪʃ(ə)n/ *n.* **vulcanizer** *n.* [*Vulcan*, the name of the Roman god of fire and metalworking]

vulcanology /vʌlkəˈnɒlədʒi/ *n.* (also **volcanology** /vɒl-/) the scientific study of volcanoes. □ **vulcanological** /-nəˈlɒdʒɪk(ə)l/ *adj.* **vulcanologist** *n.*

vulgar /ˈvʌlgə/ *adj.* **1 a** of or characteristic of the common people, plebeian. **b** coarse in manners; low (*vulgar expressions*; *vulgar tastes*). **2** in common use; generally prevalent (*vulgar errors*). □ **vulgarly** *adv.* [Middle English from Latin *vulgaris*, from *vulgus* 'common people']

vulgar fraction *n. Brit.* a fraction expressed by numerator and denominator, not decimally.

vulgarian /vʌlˈgɛːrɪən/ *n.* a vulgar (esp. rich) person.

vulgarism /ˈvʌlgərɪz(ə)m/ *n.* **1** a word or expression in coarse or uneducated use. **2** an instance of coarse or uneducated behaviour.

vulgarity /vʌlˈgarɪti/ *n.* (*pl.* **-ies**) **1** the quality of being vulgar. **2** an instance of this.

vulgarize /ˈvʌlgərʌɪz/ *v.tr.* (also **-ise**) **1** make (a person, manners, etc.) vulgar; infect with vulgarity. **2** spoil (a scene, sentiment, etc.) by making it too common, frequented, or well known. **3** popularize. □ **vulgarization** /-ˈzeɪʃ(ə)n/ *n.*

vulgar Latin *n.* informal Latin of classical times.

vulgar tongue *n.* (prec. by *the*) the national or vernacular language, esp. formerly as opposed to Latin.

Vulgate /ˈvʌlgeɪt, -gət/ *n.* **1 a** the Latin version of the Bible prepared mainly by St Jerome in the late fourth century. **b** the official Roman Catholic Latin text as revised in 1592. **2** (**vulgate**) the traditionally accepted text of any author. **3** (**vulgate**) common or colloquial speech. [Latin *vulgata* (*editio* 'edition'), fem. past part. of *vulgare* 'make public', from *vulgus*: see VULGAR]

vulnerable /ˈvʌln(ə)rəb(ə)l/ *adj.* **1** that may be wounded or harmed. **2** (foll. by *to*) exposed to damage by a weapon, criticism, etc. **3** *Bridge* having won one game towards rubber and therefore liable to higher penalties. □ **vulnerability** /-ˈbɪlɪti/ *n.* (*pl.* **-ies**). **vulnerableness** *n.* **vulnerably** *adv.* [Late Latin *vulnerabilis*, via Latin *vulnerare* 'to wound' from *vulnus -eris* 'wound']

vulnerary /ˈvʌln(ə)rəri/ *adj. & n.* ● *adj.* useful or used for the healing of wounds. ● *n.* (*pl.* **-ies**) a vulnerary drug, plant, etc. [Latin *vulnerarius* from *vulnus*: see VULNERABLE]

vulpine /ˈvʌlpʌɪn/ *adj.* **1** of or like a fox. **2** crafty, cunning. [Latin *vulpinus* from *vulpes* 'fox']

vulture /ˈvʌltʃə/ *n.* **1** any of various large birds of prey of the family Accipitridae or (in the New World) Cathartidae, with the head and neck more or less bare of feathers, feeding chiefly on carrion and reputed to gather with others in anticipation of a death. **2** a rapacious person. □ **vulturine** /-rʌɪn/ *adj.* **vulturish** *adj.* **vulturous** *adj.* [Middle English via Anglo-French *vultur*, Old French *voltour* etc. from Latin *vulturius*]

vulva /ˈvʌlvə/ *n.* (*pl.* **vulvas**) *Anat.* the external female genitals, esp. the external opening of the vagina. □ **vulval** *adj.* **vulvar** *adj.* **vulvitis** /-ˈvʌɪtɪs/ *n.* [Latin, = womb]

vv. *abbr.* **1** verses. **2** volumes.

vying *pres. part.* of VIE.

W[1] /'dʌb(ə)l,juː/ *n.* (also **w**) (*pl.* **Ws** or **W's**) the twenty-third letter of the alphabet.

W[2] *abbr.* (also **W.**) **1** West; Western. **2** women's (size).

W[3] *symb.* **1** *Chem.* the element tungsten. **2** watt(s). [sense 1 from WOLFRAM]

w *abbr.* (also **w.**) **1** *Cricket* **a** wicket(s). **b** wide(s). **2** with. **3** wife. **4** weight. **5** width.

WA *abbr.* **1** Western Australia. **2** *US* Washington (State) (in official postal use).

Waac /wak/ *n. hist.* a member of the Women's Army Auxiliary Corps (*Brit.* 1917–19 or *US* 1942–8). [initials *WAAC*]

Waaf /waf/ *n. Brit. hist.* a member of the Women's Auxiliary Air Force (1939–48). [initials *WAAF*]

WAC *abbr.* (in the US) Women's Army Corps.

wack /wak/ *n. dial.* a familiar term of address. [perhaps from *wacker* 'a Liverpudlian']

wacke /'wakə/ *n. Geol.* any sandstone containing between 15 and 75 per cent mud matrix (cf. GREYWACKE). [German from Middle High German *wacke* 'large stone', Old High German *wacko* 'pebble']

wacko /'wakəʊ/ *adj.* & *n.* esp. *N. Amer. slang* ● *adj.* crazy. ● *n.* (*pl.* **-os** or **-oes**) a crazy person. [WACKY + -O]

wacky /'waki/ *adj.* & *n.* (also **whacky**) *slang* ● *adj.* (**-ier**, **-iest**) crazy. ● *n.* (*pl.* **-ies**) a crazy person. ▫ **wackily** *adv.* **wackiness** *n.* [originally dialect, = left-handed, from WHACK]

wad /wɒd/ *n.* & *v.* ● *n.* **1** a lump or bundle of soft material used esp. to keep things apart or in place or to stuff up an opening. **2** a disc of felt etc. keeping powder or shot in place in a gun. **3** a number of banknotes or documents placed together. **4** *Brit. slang* a bun, sandwich, etc. **5** (in *sing.* or *pl.*) a large quantity esp. of money. ● *v.tr.* (**wadded**, **wadding**) **1** stop up (an aperture or a gun barrel) with a wad. **2** keep (powder etc.) in place with a wad. **3** line or stuff (a garment or coverlet) with wadding. **4** protect (a person, walls, etc.) with wadding. **5** press (cotton etc.) into a wad or wadding. [perhaps related to Dutch *watten*, French *ouate* 'padding, cotton wool']

wadding /'wɒdɪŋ/ *n.* **1** soft pliable material of cotton or wool etc. used to line or stuff garments, quilts, etc., or to pack fragile articles. **2** any material from which gun wads are made.

waddle /'wɒd(ə)l/ *v.* & *n.* ● *v.intr.* walk with short steps and a swaying motion, like a stout short-legged person or a bird with short legs set far apart (e.g. a duck or goose). ● *n.* a waddling gait. ▫ **waddler** *n.* [perhaps frequentative of WADE]

waddy /'wɒdi/ *n.* (*pl.* **-ies**) **1** an Australian Aborigine's war club. **2** *Austral.* & *NZ* any club or stick. [Dharuk *wadi* 'tree, stick, club']

wade /weɪd/ *v.* & *n.* ● *v.* **1** *intr.* walk through water or some impeding medium, e.g. snow, mud, or sand. **2** *intr.* make one's way with difficulty or by force. **3** *intr.* (foll. by *through*) read (a book etc.) in spite of its dullness etc. **4** *intr.* (foll. by *into*) *colloq.* attack (a person or task) vigorously. **5** *tr.* ford (a stream etc.) on foot. ● *n.* a spell of wading. ▫ **wade in** *colloq.* make a vigorous attack or intervention. ▫ **wadable** *adj.* (also **wadeable**). [Old English *wadan*, from a Germanic word meaning 'go (through)']

wader /'weɪdə/ *n.* **1 a** a person who wades. **b** a wading bird, esp. any of various birds of the order Charadriiformes. **2** (in *pl.*) high waterproof boots, or a waterproof garment for the legs and body, worn in fishing etc.

wadi /'wɑːdi, 'wɒdi/ *n.* (also **wady**) (*pl.* **wadis** or **wadies**) a rocky watercourse in N. Africa etc., dry except in the rainy season. [Arabic *wādī*]

wading bird *n.* any long-legged waterbird that wades.

WAF *abbr.* (in the US) **1** Women in the Air Force. **2** /waf/ a member of the WAF.

w.a.f. *abbr. Brit.* with all faults.

wafer /'weɪfə/ *n.* & *v.* ● *n.* **1** a very thin light crisp sweet biscuit, esp. of a kind eaten with ice cream. **2** a thin disc of unleavened bread used in the Eucharist. **3** a disc of red paper stuck on a legal document instead of a seal. **4** *Electronics* a very thin slice of a semiconductor crystal used as the substrate for solid-state circuitry. **5** *hist.* a small disc of dried paste formerly used for fastening letters, holding papers together, etc. ● *v.tr.* fasten or seal with a wafer. ▫ **wafery** *adj.* [Middle English via Anglo-French *wafre*, Old Northern French *waufre*, (Old) French *gaufre* (cf. GOFFER) from Middle Low German *wāfel* 'waffle': cf. WAFFLE[2]]

wafer-thin *adj.* & *adv.* ● *adj.* very thin. ● *adv.* very thinly (*cut it wafer-thin*).

waffle[1] /'wɒf(ə)l/ *n.* & *v. colloq.* ● *n.* verbose but aimless or ignorant talk or writing. ● *v.intr.* **1** (often foll. by *on*) indulge in waffle. **2** waver, equivocate. ▫ **waffler** *n.* **waffly** *adj.* [originally dialect, frequentative of *waff* = yelp, yap (imitative)]

waffle[2] /'wɒf(ə)l/ *n.* a small crisp batter cake. [Dutch *wafel*, *waefel* from Middle Low German *wāfel*: cf. WAFER]

waffle-iron *n.* a utensil, usu. of two shallow metal pans hinged together, for baking waffles.

waft /wɒft, wɑːft/ *v.* & *n.* ● *v.tr.* & *intr.* convey or travel easily as through air or over water; sweep smoothly and lightly along. ● *n.* **1** (usu. foll. by *of*) a whiff or scent. **2** a transient sensation of peace, joy, etc. **3** (also **weft** /wɛft/) *Naut.* a distress signal, e.g. an ensign rolled or knotted or a garment flown in the rigging. [originally 'convoy (ship etc.)': back-formation from obsolete *waughter*, *wafter* 'armed convoy-ship', via Dutch or Low German *wachter* from *wachten* 'to guard']

wag[1] /wag/ *v.* & *n.* ● *v.* (**wagged**, **wagging**) **1** *tr.* & *intr.* shake or wave rapidly or energetically to and fro. **2** *intr. archaic* (of the world, times, etc.) go along with varied fortune or characteristics. ● *n.* a single wagging motion (*with a wag of his tail*). ▫ **the tail wags the dog** a situation in which the less or least important member of a society, section of a party, or part of a structure has control. **tongues** (or **beards** or **chins** or **jaws**) **wag** there is talk. [Middle English *waggen*, from the Germanic root of Old English *wagian* 'sway']

wag[2] /wag/ *n.* **1** a facetious person, a joker. **2** *Brit. slang* a truant (*play the wag*). [probably from obsolete *waghalter* one likely to be hanged (as WAG[1], HALTER)]

wage /weɪdʒ/ *n.* & *v.* ● *n.* **1** (in *sing.* or *pl.*) a fixed regular payment, usu. daily or weekly, made by an employer to an employee, esp. to a manual or unskilled worker (cf. SALARY). **2** (in *sing.* or *pl.*) requital (*the wages of sin is death*). **3** (in *pl.*) *Econ.* the part of total production that rewards labour rather than remunerating capital. ● *v.tr.* carry on (a war, conflict, or contest). [Middle English from Anglo-French & Old Northern French *wage*, Old French *g(u)age*, from Germanic: related to GAGE[1], WED]

wage bill *n.* the amount paid in wages to employees.

wage claim *n.* = PAY CLAIM.

waged /weɪdʒd/ *adj.* in regular paid employment.

wage earner *n.* a person who works for wages. □ **wage-earning** *attrib.adj.*

wager /ˈweɪdʒə/ *n.* & *v.* = BET. [Middle English from Anglo-French *wageure*, from *wager* (as WAGE)]

wager of battle *n. hist.* an ancient form of trial by personal combat between the parties or their champions. [probably from WAGE, in the obsolete sense 'pledge to do battle']

wager of law *n. hist.* a form of trial in which the defendant was required to produce witnesses who would swear to his or her innocence. [probably from WAGE, in the obsolete sense 'give (one's word, etc.) as a pledge']

wages council *n. Brit.* a board of workers' and employers' representatives determining wages where there is no collective bargaining.

wage slave *n.* a person dependent on income from labour in conditions like slavery.

waggery /ˈwag(ə)ri/ *n.* (*pl.* **-ies**) **1** waggish behaviour, joking. **2** a waggish action or remark, a joke.

waggish /ˈwagɪʃ/ *adj.* playful, facetious. □ **waggishly** *adv.* **waggishness** *n.*

waggle /ˈwag(ə)l/ *v.* & *n. colloq.* ● *v.* **1** *intr.* & *tr.* wag. **2** *intr. Golf* swing the club-head to and fro over the ball before playing a shot. ● *n.* a waggling motion. [WAG[1] + -LE[4]]

waggly /ˈwagli/ *adj.* unsteady.

Wagnerian /vɑːɡˈnɪərɪən/ *adj.* & *n.* ● *adj.* of, relating to, or characteristic of the operas of Richard Wagner, German composer d. 1883, esp. with reference to their large scale. ● *n.* an admirer of Wagner or his music.

Wagner tuba /ˈvɑːɡnə/ *n.* a brass wind instrument resembling a tuba but with a sound between that of a tuba and that of a French horn.

wagon /ˈwag(ə)n/ *n.* (also *Brit.* **waggon**) **1** a four-wheeled vehicle for heavy loads, often with a removable tilt or cover. **2** *Brit.* a railway vehicle for goods, esp. an open truck. **3** a trolley for conveying tea etc. **4** (in full **water wagon**) a vehicle for carrying water. **5** *N. Amer.* a light horse-drawn vehicle. **6** *colloq.* a motor car, esp. an estate car. □ **on the wagon** (or *Brit.* **water wagon**) *colloq.* teetotal. [earlier *wagon*, *wag(h)en*, from Dutch *wag(h)en*, related to Old English *wægn* WAIN]

wagoner /ˈwag(ə)nə/ *n.* (also *Brit.* **waggoner**) the driver of a wagon. [Dutch *wagenaar* (as WAGON)]

wagonette /wagəˈnɛt/ *n.* (also *Brit.* **waggonette**) a four-wheeled horse-drawn pleasure vehicle, usu. open, with facing side seats.

wagon-lit /vagɔ̃ˈliː/ *n.* (*pl.* **wagons-lits** *pronunc.* same) a sleeping car on a Continental railway. [French]

wagonload /ˈwag(ə)nləʊd/ *n.* as much as a wagon can carry.

wagon-roof *n.* (also **wagon-vault**) = BARREL VAULT.

wagon train *n.* a succession of wagons, esp. *hist.* as used by pioneers or settlers in N. America.

wagtail /ˈwagteɪl/ *n.* any small bird of the genus *Motacilla* with a long tail in frequent motion.

Wahabi /wəˈhɑːbi/ *n.* (also **Wahhabi**) (*pl.* **-is**) a member of a sect of Muslim puritans following strictly the original words of the Koran. [named after Muhammad ibn Abd-el-*Wahhab*, 18th c. founder of the sect]

wahine /wɑːˈhiːni/ *n. NZ* a woman or wife. [Maori]

wahoo[1] /wɑːˈhuː/ *n.* & *int.* ● *n. N. Amer.* **1 a** (in full **wahoo elm**) a N. American elm, *Ulmus alata*. **b** a N. American spindle tree, *Euonymus atropurpureus*. **2** a large fast-swimming tropical marine fish, *Acanthocybium solanderi*, of the tuna family. ● *int.* = YAHOO[2]. [sense 1b from Sioux *wa^{n}hu* 'arrow-wood'; sense 3 probably from WAHOO[2]; senses 1a (18th c.) and 3 (20th c.) of unknown origin]

wahoo[2] /wɑːˈhuː/ *int. N. Amer.* expressing exuberance or triumph. [a natural exclamation]

wah-wah /ˈwɑːwɑː/ *n.* (also **wa-wa**) *Mus.* an effect achieved on brass instruments by alternately applying and removing a mute and on an electric guitar by controlling the output from the amplifier with a pedal. [imitative]

waif /weɪf/ *n.* **1** a homeless and helpless person, esp. an abandoned child. **2** an ownerless object or animal, a thing cast up by or drifting in the sea or brought by an unknown agency. □ **waifish** *adj.* [Middle English from Anglo-French *waif*, *weif*, Old Northern French *gaif*, probably of Scandinavian origin]

waifs and strays *n.pl.* **1** homeless or neglected children. **2** odds and ends.

wail /weɪl/ *n.* & *v.* ● *n.* **1** a prolonged plaintive inarticulate loud high-pitched cry of pain, grief, etc. **2** a sound like or suggestive of this. ● *v.* **1** *intr.* utter a wail. **2** *intr.* lament or complain persistently or bitterly. **3** *intr.* (of the wind etc.) make a sound like a person wailing. **4** *tr. poet.* or *literary* bewail; wail over. □ **wailer** *n.* **wailful** *adj. poet.* **wailingly** *adv.* [Middle English from Old Norse: related to WOE]

Wailing Wall *n.* a high wall in Jerusalem said to stand on the site of Herod's temple, where Jews traditionally pray and lament on Fridays.

wain /weɪn/ *n. archaic* **1** a wagon. **2** (prec. by *the*) = CHARLES'S WAIN. [Old English *wæg(e)n*, *wǣn* from Germanic: related to WAY, WEIGH[1]]

wainscot /ˈweɪnskɒt/ *n.* & *v.* ● *n.* **1** boarding or wooden panelling on the lower part of a room-wall. **2** *Brit. hist.* imported oak of fine quality. ● *v.tr.* (**wainscoted**, **wainscoting** or **wainscotted**, **wainscotting**) line with wainscot. [Middle English from Middle Low German *wagenschot*, apparently from *wagen* WAGON + *schot*, perhaps meaning 'boarding, planking']

wainscoting /ˈweɪnskɒtɪŋ/ *n.* (also **wainscotting**) **1** a wainscot. **2** material for this.

wainwright /ˈweɪnrʌɪt/ *n. archaic* a wagon-builder.

waist /weɪst/ *n.* **1 a** the part of the human body below the ribs and above the hips, usu. of smaller circumference than these; the narrower middle part of the normal human figure. **b** the circumference of this. **2** a similar narrow part in the middle of a violin, hourglass, wasp, etc. **3 a** the part of a garment encircling or covering the waist. **b** the narrow middle part of a woman's dress etc. **c** *US* a blouse or bodice. **4** the middle part of a ship, between the forecastle and the quarterdeck. □ **waisted** *adj.* (also in *comb.*). **waistless** *adj.* [Middle English *wast*, perhaps from an Old English word from the Germanic root of WAX[2]]

waistband /ˈwe(t)stband/ *n.* a strip of cloth forming the waist of a garment.

waist-cloth *n.* a loincloth.

waistcoat /ˈweɪs(t)kəʊt, ˈwɛskət/ *n. Brit.* a close-fitting waist-length garment, without sleeves or collar but usu. buttoned, worn usu. by men over a shirt and under a jacket.

waist-deep *adj.* & *adv.* (also **waist-high**) **1** immersed up to the waist (*waist-deep in water*). **2** so deep as to reach the waist.

waistline /ˈweɪs(t)lʌɪn/ *n.* the outline or the size of a person's body at the waist.

wait /weɪt/ *v.* & *n.* ● *v.* **1** *intr.* **a** defer action or departure for a specified time or until some expected event occurs (*wait a minute*; *wait till I come*; *wait for a fine day*). **b** be expectant or on the watch (*waited to see what would happen*). **c** (foll. by *for*) refrain from going so fast that (a person) is left behind (*wait for me!*). **2** *tr.* await (an opportunity, one's turn, etc.). **3** *tr. colloq.* defer (a meal etc.) until a person's arrival. **4** *intr.* (usu. as **waiting** *n.*) park a vehicle for a short time at the side of a road etc. (*no waiting*). **5** *intr.* **a** (in full **wait at** (or *N. Amer.* **on**) **table**) act as a waiter or as a servant with similar functions. **b** act as an attendant. **6** *intr.* (foll. by *on*, *upon*) **a** await the convenience of. **b** serve as an attendant to. **c** pay a respectful visit to. ● *n.* **1** a period of waiting (*had a long wait for the train*). **2** (usu. foll. by *for*) watching for an enemy; ambush (*lie in wait*; *lay wait*). **3** (in *pl.*) *Brit.* **a** *archaic* street singers of Christmas carols. **b** *hist.* official bands of musicians maintained by a city or town. □ **cannot wait 1** is impatient. **2** needs to be dealt with immediately. **can wait** need not be dealt with immediately. **wait and see** await the progress of events. **wait for it!** *Brit. colloq.* **1** do not begin before the proper moment. **2** used to create an interval of suspense before saying something unexpected or amusing. **wait on** *Austral., NZ, & N.Engl.* be patient, wait. **wait up** (often foll. by *for*) not go to bed until a person arrives or an event happens. **you wait!** used to imply a threat, warning, or promise. [Middle English via Old Northern French *waitier* from Germanic: related to WAKE[1]]

wait-a-bit *n.* a plant with hooked thorns etc. that catch the clothing.

waiter /ˈweɪtə/ *n.* **1** a man or *US* a woman who serves at table in a hotel or restaurant etc. **2** a person who waits for a time, event, or opportunity. **3** a tray or salver.

waiting /ˈweɪtɪŋ/ *n.* **1** in senses of WAIT *v.* **2 a** official attendance at court. **b** one's period of this.

waiting game *n.* abstention from early action in a contest etc. so as to act more effectively later.

waiting list *n.* a list of people waiting for a thing not immediately available.

waiting room *n.* a room provided for people to wait in, esp. by a doctor, dentist, etc., or at a railway or bus station.

waitperson /ˈweɪtpəːs(ə)n/ *n.* esp. *US* a waiter or waitress (used to avoid sexual distinction).

waitress /ˈweɪtrɪs/ *n.* a woman who serves at table in a hotel or restaurant etc.

waitressing /ˈweɪtrɪsɪŋ/ *n.* the occupation of working as a waitress.

waive /weɪv/ *v.tr.* refrain from insisting on or using (a right, claim, opportunity, legitimate plea, etc.). [Middle English from Anglo-French *weyver*, Old French *gaiver* 'allow to become a WAIF, abandon']

waiver /ˈweɪvə/ *n. Law* **1** the act or an instance of waiving. **2** a document recording this.

wake[1] /weɪk/ *v. & n.* ● *v.* (*past* **woke** /wəʊk/ or **waked**; *past part.* **woken** /ˈwəʊk(ə)n/ or **waked**) **1** *intr. & tr.* (often foll. by *up*) cease or cause to cease to sleep. **2** *intr. & tr.* (often foll. by *up*) become or cause to become alert, attentive, or active (*needs something to wake him up*). **3** *tr.* disturb (silence or a place) with noise; make re-echo. **4** *tr.* evoke (an echo). **5** *intr. & tr.* rise or raise from the dead. ● *n.* **1** a watch or vigil beside a corpse before burial; lamentation and (less often) merrymaking in connection with this. **2** (usu. in *pl.*) an annual holiday in (industrial) northern England. **3** *Brit. hist.* **a** a vigil commemorating the dedication of a church. **b** a fair or merrymaking on this occasion. □ **be a wake-up** (often foll. by *to*) *Austral. colloq.* be alert or aware. □ **waker** *n.* [Old English *wacan* (recorded only in past *woc*), *wacian* (weak form), related to WATCH: the sense 'vigil' perhaps from Old Norse]

wake[2] /weɪk/ *n.* **1** the track left on the water's surface by a moving ship. **2** turbulent air left behind a moving aircraft etc. □ **in the wake of** behind, following, as a result of, in imitation of. [probably via Middle Low German from Old Norse *vök* 'hole or opening in ice']

wakeful /ˈweɪkfʊl, -f(ə)l/ *adj.* **1** unable to sleep. **2** (of a night etc.) passed with little or no sleep. **3** vigilant. □ **wakefully** *adv.* **wakefulness** *n.*

waken /ˈweɪk(ə)n/ *v.tr. & intr.* make or become awake. [Old English *waecnan*, from Germanic]

wake-robin *n.* **1** *Brit.* an arum, esp. the cuckoo pint. **2** *N. Amer.* any plant of the genus *Trillium*.

wakey-wakey /weɪkɪˈweɪki/ *int.* used to wake a person up. [reduplicated extension of WAKE[1] *v.*]

waking /ˈweɪkɪŋ/ *adj.* awake (*in her waking hours; waking or sleeping*).

waking dream see DREAM *n.* 1c.

Walachian var. of WALLACHIAN.

Waldenses /wɒlˈdɛnsiːz/ *n.pl.* a puritan religious sect originally in southern France, now chiefly in Italy and America, founded *c.*1170 and much persecuted. □ **Waldensian** *adj. & n.* [medieval Latin, named after its founder Peter *Waldo* of Lyons]

wale /weɪl/ *n. & v.* ● *n.* **1** = WEAL[1]. **2** a ridge on a woven fabric, e.g. corduroy. **3** *Naut.* a broad thick timber along a ship's side. **4** a specially woven strong band round a woven basket. ● *v.tr.* provide or mark with wales. [Old English *walu* 'stripe, ridge']

wale-knot *n.* a knot made at the end of a rope by intertwining strands to prevent unravelling or act as a stopper.

walk /wɔːk/ *v. & n.* ● *v.* **1** *intr.* **a** (of a person or other biped) progress by lifting and setting down each foot in turn, never having both feet off the ground at once. **b** progress with similar movements (*walked on his hands*). **c** go with the gait usual except when speed is desired. **d** (of a quadruped) go with the slowest gait, always having at least two feet on the ground at once. **2** *intr.* **a** travel or go on foot. **b** take exercise in this way (*walks for two hours each day*). **3** *tr.* perambulate, traverse on foot at walking speed, tread the floor or surface of. **4** *tr.* **a** cause to walk with one. **b** accompany in walking. **c** ride or lead (a horse, dog, etc.) at walking pace. **d** take charge of (a puppy) at walk (see sense 4 of *n.*). **5** *intr.* (of a ghost) appear. **6** *intr. Cricket* (of a batsman) leave the wicket without waiting for the umpire to declare him out. **7** *Baseball* **a** *intr.* reach first base on being entitled to do so after not hitting at four balls pitched outside specified limits. **b** *tr.* allow to do this. **8** *intr. archaic* live in a specified manner, conduct oneself (*walk humbly; walk with God*). **9** *intr. N. Amer. slang* be released from suspicion or from a charge. ● *n.* **1 a** an act of walking, the ordinary human gait (*go at a walk*). **b** the slowest gait of an animal. **c** a person's manner of walking (*know him by his walk*). **2 a** (an act or instance of) travelling a specified distance on foot (*is only ten minutes' walk from here; it's quite a walk to the bus stop*). **b** an excursion on foot; a stroll (*go for a walk*). **c** a journey on foot completed to earn money promised for a charity etc. **3 a** a place, track, or route intended or suitable for walking; a promenade, colonnade, or footpath. **b** a person's favourite place or route for walking. **c** esp. *Brit.* the round of a postman, hawker, etc. **4** esp. *Brit.* a farm etc. where a hound-puppy is sent to accustom it to various surroundings. **5** the place where a gamecock is kept. **6** a part of a forest under one keeper. □ **in a walk** without effort (*won in a walk*). **walk about** stroll. **walk all over** *colloq.* **1** defeat easily. **2** take advantage of. **walk away from 1** easily outdistance. **2** refuse to become involved with; fail to deal with. **3** survive (an accident etc.) without serious injury. **walk away with** *colloq.* = *walk off with*. **walk the boards** be an actor. **walk the hospitals** = *walk the wards*. **walk in** (often foll. by *on*) enter or arrive, esp. unexpectedly or easily. **walk into** *colloq.* **1** encounter through unwariness (*walked into the trap*). **2** get (a job) easily. **walk it 1** make a journey on foot, not ride. **2** *colloq.* achieve something (esp. a victory) easily. **walk Matilda** see MATILDA. **walk off 1** depart (esp. abruptly). **2** get rid of the effects of (a meal, ailment, feeling, etc.) by walking (*walked off his anger*). **walk a person off his** (or **her**) **feet** (or **legs**) exhaust a person with walking. **walk off with** *colloq.* **1** steal. **2** win easily. **walk on air** see AIR. **walk out 1** depart suddenly or angrily. **2** (usu. foll. by *with*) *Brit. archaic* go for walks in courtship. **walk out on** desert, abandon. **walk over 1** *colloq.* = *walk all over*. **2** (often *absol.*) traverse (a racecourse) without needing to hurry, because one has no opponents or only inferior ones. **walk the plank** see PLANK. **walk the streets 1** be a prostitute. **2** traverse the streets esp. in search of work etc. **walk tall** *colloq.* feel justifiable pride. **walk up!** *Brit.* a showman's invitation to a circus etc. **walk up to** approach (a person) for a talk etc. **walk the wards** be a medical student. □ **walkable** *adj.* [Old English *wealcan* 'roll, toss, wander', from Germanic]

walkabout /ˈwɔːkəbaʊt/ *n.* **1** esp. *Brit.* an informal stroll among a crowd by a visiting dignitary. **2** *Austral.* a period of wandering in the bush by an Australian Aborigine. □ **go walkabout** *Austral.* go on a walkabout.

walkathon /ˈwɔːkəθɒn/ *n.* an organized fund-raising walk. [WALK, on the pattern of MARATHON]

walker /ˈwɔːkə/ *n.* **1** a person or animal that walks. **2 a** a wheeled or footed framework in which a baby can learn to walk. **b** = WALKING FRAME.

walkies /ˈwɔːkɪz/ *int. & n.* ● *int.* a command to a dog to prepare for a walk. ● *n.pl. colloq.* or *joc.* a walk or a spell of walking, esp. with a dog (*take it walkies*). □ **go walkies** *colloq.* or *joc.* **1** go for a walk. **2** go missing (*some equipment went walkies*).

walkie-talkie /wɔːkɪˈtɔːki/ *n.* a two-way radio carried on the person, esp. by policemen etc.

walk-in *attrib.adj.* (of a storage area) large enough to walk into.

walking delegate *n.* a trade-union official who visits members and their employers for discussions.

walking dictionary *n.* (also **walking encyclopedia**) *colloq.* a person having a wide general knowledge.

walking fern *n.* any American evergreen fern of the genus *Camptosorus*, with fronds that root at the ends.

walking frame *n. Brit.* a usu. tubular metal frame with rubberized ferrules, used by disabled or old people to help them walk.

walking gentleman *n.* (also **walking lady**) *Theatr.* a non-speaking extra; a supernumerary.

walking leaf *n.* = WALKING FERN.

walking-on part *n. Brit.* a non-speaking dramatic role.

walking papers *n.pl. colloq.* dismissal (*gave him his walking papers*).

walking shoe *n.* a sturdy, practical shoe for walking.

walking stick *n.* **1** a stick carried when walking, esp. for extra support. **2** *N. Amer.* = STICK INSECT.

walking tour *n.* a holiday journey on foot, esp. of several days.

walking wounded *n.* (*pl.* same) (usu. in *pl.*) **1** a casualty able to walk despite injuries. **2** *colloq.* a person having esp. mental or emotional difficulties.

Walkman /ˈwɔːkmən/ *n.* (*pl.* **-mans** or **-men**) *propr.* a type of personal stereo.

walk of life *n.* an occupation, profession, or calling.

walk-on *n.* **1** (in full **walk-on part**) a non-speaking dramatic role. **2** an actor playing this.

walkout /ˈwɔːkaʊt/ *n.* a sudden angry departure, esp. as a protest or strike.

walkover /ˈwɔːkəʊvə/ *n.* an easy victory or achievement.

walk-up *adj. & n. N. Amer.* ● *adj.* (of a building) allowing access to the upper floors only by stairs. ● *n.* a walk-up building.

walkway /ˈwɔːkweɪ/ *n.* a passage or path for walking along, esp.: **1** a raised passageway connecting different sections of a building. **2** a wide path in a garden etc.

wall /wɔːl/ *n. & v.* ● *n.* **1 a** a continuous and usu. vertical structure of usu. brick or stone, having little width in proportion to its length and height and esp. enclosing, protecting, or dividing a space or supporting a roof. **b** the surface of a wall, esp. inside a room (*hung the picture on the wall*). **2** anything like a wall in appearance or effect, esp.: **a** the steep side of a mountain. **b** a protection or obstacle (*a wall of steel bayonets*; *a wall of indifference*). **c** *Anat.* the outermost layer or enclosing membrane etc. of an organ, structure, etc. **d** the outermost part of a hollow structure (*stomach wall*). **e** *Mining* rock enclosing a lode or seam. ● *v.tr.* **1** (esp. as **walled** *adj.*) surround or protect with a wall (*walled garden*). **2 a** (usu. foll. by *up*, *off*) block or seal (a space etc.) with a wall. **b** (foll. by *up*) enclose (a person) within a sealed space (*walled them up in the dungeon*). □ **go to the wall** be defeated or pushed aside. **go up the wall** *colloq.* become crazy or furious (*went up the wall when he heard*). **off the wall** (hyphenated when *attrib.*) esp. *N. Amer. slang* unorthodox, unconventional. **walls have ears** it is unsafe to speak openly, as there may be eavesdroppers. □ **walling** *n.* **wall-less** *adj.* [Old English from Latin *vallum* 'rampart', from *vallus* 'stake']

wallaby /ˈwɒləbi/ *n.* (*pl.* **-ies**) **1** any of various marsupials of the family Macropodidae, smaller than kangaroos, and having large hind feet and long tails. **2** (**Wallabies**) *colloq.* the Australian international Rugby Union team. □ **on the wallaby** (or **wallaby track**) *Austral.* vagrant; unemployed. [Dharuk *walabi* or *waliba*]

Wallachian /wɒˈleɪkɪən, vəˈlakɪən/ *adj. & n.* (also **Walachian**) ● *adj.* of the former Principality of Wallachia, now part of Romania. ● *n.* a native of Wallachia. [*Wallachia* (as VLACH)]

wallah /ˈwɒlə/ *n.* orig. *Anglo-Ind.*, now *slang* **1** a person concerned with or in charge of a usu. specified thing, business, etc. (*asked the ticket wallah*). **2** a person doing a routine administrative job; a bureaucrat. [Hindi suffix *-wālā* = -ER[1]]

wallaroo /wɒləˈruː/ *n.* a large brownish-black kangaroo, *Macropus robustus*. [Dharuk *walaru*]

wall bar *n. Brit.* one of a set of parallel bars, attached to the wall of a gymnasium, on which exercises are performed.

wall-barley *n.* wild barley as a weed.

wallboard /ˈwɔːlbɔːd/ *n.* esp. *N. Amer.* **1** any of various types of board made from wood pulp, plaster, etc., used for covering walls and ceilings. **2** a piece of this.

wallchart /ˈwɔːltʃɑːt/ *n.* a chart or poster designed for display on a wall as a teaching aid, source of information, etc.

wallcovering /ˈwɔːlkʌv(ə)rɪŋ/ *n.* a wallpaper or other material used to cover and decorate interior walls.

wall cress *n.* = ARABIS.

wallet /ˈwɒlɪt/ *n.* **1** a small flat esp. leather case for holding banknotes etc. **2** *archaic* a bag for carrying food etc. on a journey, esp. as used by a pilgrim or beggar. [Middle English *walet*, probably via Anglo-French from a Germanic word related to WELL[2]]

wall-eye /ˈwɔːlʌɪ/ *n.* **1 a** an eye with a streaked or opaque white iris. **b** an eye squinting outwards. **2** an American perch, *Stizostedion vitreum*, with large prominent eyes; also called *wall-eyed pike*. □ **wall-eyed** *adj.* [back-formation from *wall-eyed*: Middle English from Old Norse *vagleygr* from *vagl* (unrecorded: cf. Icelandic *vagl* 'film over the eye') + *auga* EYE]

wall fern *n.* an evergreen polypody, *Polypodium vulgare*, with very large leaves.

wallflower /ˈwɔːlflaʊə/ *n.* **1** a spring-flowering garden plant, *Erisymum cheiri*, with fragrant yellow, orange-red, or dark red flowers. **2** *colloq.* a neglected or socially awkward person, esp. a woman sitting out at a dance for lack of partners.

wall-fruit *n.* fruit grown on trees trained against a wall for protection and warmth.

wall game *n. Brit.* a form of football played at Eton.

wall hanging *n.* a usu. large decorative tapestry etc. for display on an interior wall.

wall-hung *adj.* (often *attrib.*) = WALL-MOUNTED.

wall-knot *n.* = WALE-KNOT.

wall-mounted *adj.* (often *attrib.*) attached by a bracket or other support to a wall.

Walloon /wɒˈluːn/ *n. & adj.* ● *n.* **1** a member of a French-speaking people inhabiting S. and E. Belgium and neighbouring France (cf. FLEMING 2). **2** the French dialect spoken by this people. ● *adj.* of or concerning the Walloons or their language. [French *Wallon* from medieval Latin *Wallo -onis*, from Germanic: cf. WELSH]

wallop /ˈwɒləp/ *v. & n. colloq.* ● *v.tr.* (**walloped**, **walloping**) **1 a** thrash; beat. **b** hit hard. **2** (as **walloping** *adj.*) big; strapping; thumping (*a walloping profit*). ● *n.* **1** a heavy blow; a thump. **2** *Brit.* beer or any alcoholic drink. □ **walloping** *n.* [earlier senses 'gallop', 'boil': Middle English from Old Northern French *waloper*, Old French *galoper*: cf. GALLOP]

walloper /'wɒləpə/ *n.* **1** a person or thing that wallops. **2** *Austral. slang* a police officer.

wallow /'wɒləʊ/ *v. & n.* ● *v.intr.* **1** (esp. of an animal) roll about in mud, sand, water, etc. **2** (usu. foll. by *in*) indulge in unrestrained sensuality, pleasure, misery, etc. (*wallowing in nostalgia*). ● *n.* **1** the act or an instance of wallowing. **2 a** a place used by buffalo etc. for wallowing. **b** the depression in the ground caused by this. □ **wallower** *n.* [Old English *walwian* 'to roll', from Germanic]

wall painting *n.* a mural or fresco.

wallpaper /'wɔːlpeɪpə/ *n. & v.* ● *n.* **1** paper sold in rolls for pasting on to interior walls as decoration. **2** *Brit.* an unobtrusive background, esp. (usu. *derog.*) with reference to sound, music, etc. ● *v.tr.* (often *absol.*) decorate with wallpaper.

wall pepper *n.* a succulent stonecrop, *Sedum acre*, with a pungent taste.

wall-plate *n.* timber laid in or on a wall to distribute the pressure of a girder etc.

wall rocket *n.* a yellow-flowered weed, *Diplotaxis muralis*, emitting a foul smell when crushed.

wall rue *n.* a small fern, *Asplenium ruta-muraria*, with leaves like rue, growing on walls and rocks.

wall space *n.* space on the surface of a wall, available for use.

Wall Street *n.* the American financial world or money market. [a street in New York City where banks, the Stock Exchange, etc. are situated]

wall-to-wall *attrib.adj.* **1** (of carpeting etc.) covering the entire floor area up to the walls. **2** endless; exclusive of all else (*wall-to-wall coverage of sport*; *wall-to-wall silence*).

wally /'wɒli/ *n.* (*pl.* **-ies**) *Brit. slang* a foolish or inept person. [origin uncertain, perhaps a shortened form of *Walter*]

walnut /'wɔːlnʌt/ *n.* **1** (also **walnut tree**) a tree of the genus *Juglans*, having aromatic leaves and drooping catkins. **2** the nut of this tree, containing a wrinkled edible kernel in two halves, and enclosed in a green fruit. **3** the timber of the walnut tree used in cabinetmaking. [Old English *walh-hnutu* from a Germanic word meaning 'foreign nut']

Walpurgis night /val'pʊəgɪs/ *n.* the eve of 1 May when witches are alleged to meet on the Brocken mountain in Germany and hold revels with the Devil. [German *Walpurgisnacht* from *Walpurgis* (genitive of *Walpurga*, the name of an 8th c. English woman saint) + *Nacht* NIGHT]

walrus /'wɔːlrəs, 'wɒl-/ *n.* a large amphibious long-tusked Arctic mammal, *Odobenus rosmarus*, related to the seal and sea lion. [probably from Dutch *walrus*, *-ros*, perhaps by metathesis (influenced by *walvisch* 'whale-fish') from a word represented by Old English *horschwœl* 'horse-whale']

walrus moustache *n.* a long thick drooping moustache.

waltz /wɔːl(t)s, wɒl-/ *n. & v.* ● *n.* **1** a dance in triple time performed by couples who rotate and progress round the floor. **2** the usu. flowing and melodious music for this. ● *v.* **1** *intr.* dance a waltz. **2** *intr.* (often foll. by *in*, *out*, *round*, etc.) *colloq.* move lightly, casually, with deceptive ease, etc. (*waltzed in and took first prize*). **3** *tr.* move (a person) in or as if in a waltz, casually or with ease (*was waltzed off to Paris*). □ **waltz Matilda** see MATILDA. **waltz off with** *colloq.* **1** steal. **2** win (a prize etc.) easily. [German *Walzer* from *walzen* 'revolve']

waltzer /'wɔːl(t)sə, 'wɒl-/ *n.* **1** a person who dances the waltz. **2** a fairground ride in which cars spin round as they are carried round an undulating track.

wampum /'wɒmpəm/ *n.* beads made from shells and strung together for use as money, decoration, or as aids to memory by N. American Indians. [Algonquian *wampumpeag*, from *wap* 'white' + *umpe* 'string' + pl. suffix *-ag*]

wan /wɒn/ *adj.* (**wanner**, **wannest**) **1** (of a person's complexion or appearance) pale; exhausted; worn. **2** (of a star etc. or its light) partly obscured; faint. **3** *archaic* (of night, water, etc.) dark, black. □ **wanly** *adv.* **wanness** /'wɒnnɪs/ *n.* [Old English *wann* 'dark, black', of unknown origin]

wand /wɒnd/ *n.* **1 a** a supposedly magic stick used in casting spells by a fairy, magician, etc. **b** a stick used by a conjuror for effect. **2** a slender rod carried or used as a marker in the ground. **3** a staff symbolizing some officials' authority. **4** *colloq.* a conductor's baton. **5** a hand-held electronic device which can be passed over a bar code to read the data this represents. [Middle English from Old Norse *vendr*, probably from Germanic and related to WEND, WIND²]

wander /'wɒndə/ *v. & n.* ● *v.* **1** *intr.* (often foll. by *in*, *off*, etc.) go about from place to place aimlessly. **2** *intr.* **a** (of a person, river, road, etc.) wind about; diverge; meander. **b** (of esp. a person) get lost; leave home; stray from a path etc. **3** *intr.* talk or think incoherently; be inattentive or delirious. **4** *tr.* cover while wandering (*wanders the world*). ● *n.* the act or an instance of wandering (*went for a wander round the garden*). □ **wanderer** *n.* **wandering** *n.* (esp. in *pl.*). [Old English *wandrian* (as WEND)]

wandering albatross *n.* a very large white albatross, *Diomedea exulans*, of southern oceans, having black-tipped wings.

wandering Jew *n.* **1 a** a legendary person said to have been condemned by Christ to wander the earth until the second advent. **b** a person who never settles down. **2 a** a climbing plant, *Tradescantia albiflora*, with stemless variegated leaves. **b** a trailing plant, *Zebrina pendula*, with pink flowers.

wandering sailor *n.* the moneywort.

wanderlust /'wɒndəlʌst/ *n.* an eagerness for travelling or wandering. [German]

wanderoo /wɒndə'ruː/ *n.* = HANUMAN 1. [Sinhalese *wanderu* 'monkey']

wander plug *n.* a plug that can be fitted into any of various sockets in an electrical device.

wane /weɪn/ *v. & n.* ● *v.intr.* **1** (of the moon) decrease in apparent size after the full moon (cf. WAX²). **2** decrease in power, vigour, importance, brilliance, size, etc.; decline. ● *n.* **1** the process of waning. **2** a defect of a plank etc. that lacks square corners. □ **on the wane** waning; declining. □ **waney** *adj.* (in sense 2 of *n.*). [Old English *wanian* 'lessen', from Germanic]

wangle /'waŋg(ə)l/ *v. & n. colloq.* ● *v.tr.* **1** (often *refl.*) obtain (a favour etc.) by scheming etc. (*wangled himself a free trip*). **2** alter or fake (a report etc.) to appear more favourable. ● *n.* the act or an instance of wangling. □ **wangler** *n.* [19th-c. printers' slang: origin unknown]

wank /waŋk/ *v. & n. Brit. coarse slang* ● *v.intr. & tr.* masturbate. ● *n.* an act of masturbating. [20th c.: origin unknown]

Wankel engine /'waŋk(ə)l, 'vaŋ-/ *n.* a rotary internal-combustion engine in which a curvilinear, triangular, eccentrically pivoted piston rotates in an elliptical chamber, forming three combustion spaces that vary in volume as it turns. [named after F. *Wankel*, German engineer d. 1988]

wanker /'waŋkə/ *n. Brit. coarse slang* **1** a contemptible or ineffectual person. **2** a person who masturbates.

wanna /'wɒnə/ *contr. colloq.* **1** want to (*I wanna win*). **2** want a (*I wanna biscuit*).

■ **Usage** *Wanna* is non-standard and should generally be avoided in both speech and writing.

wannabe /'wɒnəbi/ *n. slang* an avid fan who tries to emulate a particular celebrity or type, esp. in appearance. [representing colloq. pronunciation of *want to be*]

want /wɒnt/ *v. & n.* ● *v.* **1** *tr.* **a** (often foll. by *to* + infin.) desire; wish for possession of; need (*wants a toy train*;

wants it done immediately; wanted to leave; wanted him to leave). **b** need or desire (a person, esp. sexually). **c** esp. *Brit.* require to be attended to in esp. a specified way (*the garden wants weeding*). **d** (foll. by *to* + infin.) *colloq.* ought; should; need (*you want to pull yourself together; you don't want to overdo it*). **2** *intr.* (usu. foll. by *for*) lack; be deficient (*wants for nothing*). **3** *tr.* be without or fall short by (esp. a specified amount or thing) (*the drawer wants a handle*). **4** *intr.* (foll. by *in, out*) esp. *US colloq.* desire to be in, out, etc. (*wants in on the deal*). **5** *tr.* (as **wanted** *adj.*) (of a suspected criminal etc.) sought by the police. ● *n.* **1** (often foll. by *of*) **a** a lack, absence, or deficiency (*could not go for want of time; shows great want of judgement*). **b** poverty; need (*living in great want; in want of necessities*). **2 a** a desire for a thing etc. (*meets a long-felt want*). **b** a thing so desired (*can supply your wants*). □ **do not want to** am unwilling to. □ **wanter** *n.* [Middle English from Old Norse *vant*, neut. of *vanr* 'lacking' = Old English *wana*, related to WANE]

want ad *n. US* a classified newspaper advertisement for something sought.

wanting /ˈwɒntɪŋ/ *adj.* **1** lacking (in quality or quantity); deficient, not equal to requirements (*wanting in judgement; the standard is sadly wanting*). **2** absent, not supplied or provided. □ **be found wanting** fail to meet requirements.

wanton /ˈwɒnt(ə)n/ *adj., n., & v.* ● *adj.* **1** licentious; lewd; sexually promiscuous. **2** capricious; random; arbitrary; motiveless (*wanton destruction; wanton wind*). **3** luxuriant; unrestrained (*wanton profusion*). **4** *archaic* playful; sportive (*a wanton child*). ● *n. literary* an immoral or licentious person, esp. a woman. ● *v.intr. literary* **1** gambol; sport; move capriciously. **2** (foll. by *with*) behave licentiously. □ **wantonly** *adv.* **wantonness** /ˈwɒnt(ə)nnɪs/ *n.* [Middle English *wantowen*, from *wan-* UN-[1] + *towen* from Old English *togen*, past part. of *tēon* 'discipline', related to TEAM]

wapentake /ˈwɒp(ə)nteɪk, ˈwap-/ *n. Brit. hist.* a subdivision of certain northern and midland English counties; a hundred. [Old English *wǣpen(ge)tæc* from Old Norse *vápnatak*, from *vápn* 'weapon' + *tak* 'taking' from *taka* TAKE: perhaps with reference to voting in assembly by a show of weapons]

wapiti /ˈwɒpɪti/ *n.* (*pl.* **wapitis**) a N. American deer, *Cervus canadensis*, now often regarded as a larger race of the red deer. [Cree *wapitik* 'white deer']

War. *abbr.* Warwickshire.

war /wɔː/ *n. & v.* ● *n.* **1 a** armed hostilities between esp. nations; conflict (*war broke out*). **b** a specific conflict or the period of time during which such conflict exists (*was before the war*). **c** the suspension of international law etc. during such a conflict. **2** (as **the War**) a war in progress or recently ended; the most recent major war. **3 a** hostility or contention between people, groups, etc. (*war of words*). **b** (often foll. by *on, against*) a sustained campaign against crime, disease, poverty, etc. ● *v.intr.* (**warred**, **warring**) **1** (as **warring** *adj.*) **a** rival; fighting (*warring factions*). **b** conflicting (*warring principles*). **2** make war. □ **at war** (often foll. by *with*) engaged in a war. **go to war 1** declare or begin a war. **2** (of a soldier etc.) see active service. **go to the wars** *archaic* serve as a soldier. **have been in the wars** *colloq.* appear injured, bruised, unkempt, etc. [Middle English *werre* an Anglo-French and Old Northern French variant of Old French *guerre*: cf. WORSE]

waratah /ˈwɔːrətɑː, wɒrəˈtɑː/ *n.* an Australian crimson-flowered shrub, *Telopea speciosissima.* [Dharuk *warrada*]

war baby *n.* a child, esp. illegitimate, born in wartime.

warble[1] /ˈwɔːb(ə)l/ *v. & n.* ● *v.* **1** *intr. & tr.* sing in a gentle trilling manner. **2** *tr.* **a** speak or utter in a warbling manner. **b** express in a song or verse (*warbled his love*). ● *n.* a warbled song or utterance. [Middle English via Old Northern French *werble(r)* from Frankish *hwirbilōn* 'whirl, trill']

warble[2] /ˈwɔːb(ə)l/ *n.* **1** a hard lump on a horse's back caused by the galling of a saddle. **2 a** a swelling or abscess caused by the larva of a warble fly beneath the skin of cattle etc. **b** the larva causing this. [Middle English: origin uncertain]

warble fly *n.* any of various flies of the genus *Hypoderma*, infesting the skin of cattle and horses.

warbler /ˈwɔːblə/ *n.* **1** a person, bird, etc. that warbles. **2** any small insect-eating bird of the family Sylviidae or, in N. America, Parulidae, including the blackcap, whitethroat, and chiff-chaff, not always remarkable for their song.

war bride *n.* a woman who marries a serviceman met during a war.

war chest *n.* funds for a war or any other campaign.

war cloud *n.* a threatening international situation.

war correspondent *n.* a correspondent reporting from a scene of war.

war crime *n.* a crime violating the international laws of war. □ **war criminal** *n.*

war cry *n.* **1** a phrase or name shouted to rally one's troops. **2** a party slogan etc.

ward /wɔːd/ *n. & v.* ● *n.* **1** a separate room or division of a hospital, prison, etc. (*men's surgical ward*). **2 a** *Brit.* an administrative division of a constituency, usu. electing a councillor or councillors etc. **b** esp. *US* a similar administrative division. **3 a** a minor under the care of a guardian appointed by the parents or a court. **b** (in full **ward of court**) a minor or mentally deficient person placed under the protection of a court. **4** (in *pl.*) the corresponding notches and projections in a key and a lock. **5** *archaic* **a** the act of guarding or defending a place etc. **b** the bailey of a castle. **c** a guardian's control; confinement; custody. ● *v.tr. archaic* guard; protect. □ **ward off 1** parry (a blow). **2** avert (danger, poverty, etc.). [Old English *weard, weardian* from Germanic: reinforced in Middle English by Old Northern French *warde*, variant of Old French *garde* GUARD]

-ward /wəd/ *suffix* (also **-wards**) added to nouns of place or destination and to adverbs of direction and forming: **1** adverbs (usu. **-wards**) meaning 'towards the place etc.' (*moving backwards; set off homewards*). **2** adjectives (usu. **-ward**) meaning 'turned or tending towards' (*a downward look; an onward rush*). **3** (less commonly) nouns meaning 'the region towards or about' (*look to the eastward*). [from or suggested by Old English *-weard* from a Germanic root meaning 'turn']

war damage *n.* damage to property etc. caused by bombing, shelling, etc.

war dance *n.* a dance performed before a battle, ceremonially, or to celebrate victory.

warden /ˈwɔːd(ə)n/ *n.* **1** (usu. in *comb.*) a supervising official (*churchwarden; traffic warden*). **2 a** *Brit.* a president or governor of a college, school, hospital, youth hostel, etc. **b** esp. *US* a prison governor. □ **wardenship** *n.* [Middle English from Anglo-French & Old Northern French *wardein*, variant of Old French *g(u)arden* GUARDIAN]

war department *n. hist.* the State office in charge of the army etc.

warder /ˈwɔːdə/ *n.* **1** *Brit.* (*fem.* **wardress** /-drɪs/) a prison officer. **2** a guard. [Middle English via Anglo-French *wardere, -our* from Old Northern French *warder*, variant of Old French *garder* to GUARD]

ward-heeler *n. US* a party worker in elections etc.

ward of court see WARD *n.* 3b.

wardrobe /ˈwɔːdrəʊb/ *n.* **1** a large movable or built-in cupboard with rails, shelves, hooks, etc., for storing clothes. **2** a person's entire stock of clothes. **3** the costume department or costumes of a theatre, a film company, etc. **4** a department of a royal household in charge of clothing. [Middle English from Old Northern French *warderobe*, variant of Old French *garderobe* (as GUARD, ROBE)]

wardrobe mistress *n.* (also **wardrobe master**) a person in charge of a theatrical or film wardrobe.

wardrobe trunk *n.* a trunk fitted with rails, shelves, etc. for use as a travelling wardrobe.

wardroom /ˈwɔːdruːm, -rʊm/ *n.* a room in a warship for the use of commissioned officers.

-wards var. of -WARD.

wardship /ˈwɔːdʃɪp/ *n.* **1** a guardian's care or tutelage (*under his wardship*). **2** the condition of being a ward.

ware[1] /wɛː/ *n.* **1** (esp. in *comb.*) things of the same kind, esp. ceramics, made usu. for sale (*chinaware*; *hardware*). **2** (usu. in *pl.*) **a** articles for sale (*displayed his wares*). **b** a person's skills, talents, etc. **3** ceramics etc. of a specified material, factory, or kind (*Wedgwood ware*). [Old English *waru* from Germanic, perhaps originally = 'object of care', related to WARE[3]]

ware[2] /wɛː/ *v.tr.* (also **'ware**) (esp. in hunting) look out for; avoid (usu. in *imper.*: *ware hounds!*). [Old English *warian* from Germanic (as WARE[3]), and from Old Northern French *warer*]

ware[3] /wɛː/ *predic.adj. poet.* aware. [Old English *wær* from Germanic]

warehouse /ˈwɛːhaʊs/ *n. & v.* ● *n.* **1** a building in which esp. retail goods are stored; a repository. **2** a wholesale or large retail store. ● *v.tr.* /also -haʊz/ **1** store (esp. furniture or bonded goods) temporarily in a repository. **2** *US colloq.* shut up (esp. a person) in a prison or hospital etc. and forget about or ignore. □ **warehouseman** *n.* (*pl.* **-men**).

warehouse party *n.* a large (usu. illegal) organized public party with dancing, held in a warehouse or similar building.

warfare /ˈwɔːfɛː/ *n.* a state of war; campaigning, engaging in war (*chemical warfare*).

warfarin /ˈwɔːfərɪn/ *n.* a water-soluble anticoagulant used esp. as a rat poison and in the treatment of thrombosis. [*W*isconsin *A*lumni *R*esearch *F*oundation + *-arin*, on the pattern of COUMARIN]

war game *n.* **1** a military exercise testing or improving tactical knowledge etc. **2** a battle etc. conducted with toy soldiers.

war gaming *n.* the playing of war games.

war grave *n.* the grave of a serviceman who died on active service, esp. one in a special cemetery etc.

warhead /ˈwɔːhɛd/ *n.* the explosive head of a missile, torpedo, or similar weapon.

warhorse /ˈwɔːhɔːs/ *n.* **1** *hist.* a knight's or trooper's powerful horse. **2** *colloq.* a veteran soldier, politician, etc.; a reliable hack.

warlike /ˈwɔːlʌɪk/ *adj.* **1** threatening war; hostile. **2** martial; soldierly. **3** of or for war; military (*warlike preparations*).

war loan *n.* stock issued by the British Government to raise funds in wartime.

warlock /ˈwɔːlɒk/ *n. archaic* a sorcerer or wizard. [Old English *wǣr-loga* 'traitor', from *wǣr* 'covenant' + *loga* related to LIE[2]]

warlord /ˈwɔːlɔːd/ *n.* a military commander or commander-in-chief.

warm /wɔːm/ *adj., v., & n.* ● *adj.* **1** of or at a fairly or comfortably high temperature. **2** (of clothes etc.) affording warmth (*needs warm gloves*). **3 a** (of a person, action, feelings, etc.) sympathetic; cordial; friendly; loving (*a warm welcome*; *has a warm heart*). **b** enthusiastic; hearty (*was warm in her praise*). **4** animated, heated, excited (*a warm exchange of views*). **5** *colloq. iron.* dangerous, difficult, or hostile (*met a warm reception*). **6** *colloq.* **a** (of a participant in esp. a children's game of seeking) close to the object etc. sought. **b** near to guessing or finding out a secret. **7** (of a colour, light, etc.) reddish, pink, or yellowish, etc., suggestive of warmth. **8** *Hunting* (of a scent) fresh and strong. **9 a** (of a person's temperament) amorous; sexually demanding. **b** erotic; arousing. ● *v.* **1** *tr.* **a** make warm (*warms the room*). **b** excite; make cheerful (*warms the heart*). **2** *intr.* **a** (often foll. by *up*) become warm (*while the dinner was warming up*). **b** (often foll. by *to*) become animated, enthusiastic, or sympathetic (*warmed to his subject*). ● *n.* **1** the act of warming; the state of being warmed (*gave it a warm*; *had a nice warm by the fire*). **2** the warmth of the atmosphere etc. **3** *Brit. archaic* a warm garment, esp. an army greatcoat. □ **warm up 1** (of an athlete, performer, etc.) prepare for a contest, performance, etc. by practising. **2** become or cause to become warmer. **3** (of a person) become enthusiastic etc. **4** (of an engine, electrical appliance, etc.) reach a temperature for efficient working. **5** reheat (food). □ **warmer** *n.* (also in *comb.*). **warmish** *adj.* **warmly** *adv.* **warmness** *n.* **warmth** *n.* [Old English *wearm*, from Germanic]

warm-blooded *adj.* **1** (of an organism) having warm blood; mammalian (see HOMEOTHERM). **2** ardent, passionate. □ **warm-bloodedness** *n.*

warmed-up *adj.* (*N. Amer.* **warmed-over**) **1** (of food etc.) reheated. **2** stale; second-hand.

war memorial *n.* a monument etc. commemorating those killed in a war.

warm front *n.* an advancing mass of warm air.

warm-hearted *adj.* having a warm heart; kind, friendly. □ **warm-heartedly** *adv.* **warm-heartedness** *n.*

warming-pan *n. hist.* a usu. brass container for live coals with a flat body and a long handle, used for warming a bed.

warmonger /ˈwɔːmʌŋgə/ *n.* a person who seeks to bring about or promote war. □ **warmongering** *n. & adj.*

warm-up *n.* a period of preparatory exercise for a contest or performance.

warm work *n.* **1** work etc. that makes one warm through exertion. **2** dangerous conflict etc.

warn /wɔːn/ *v.tr.* **1** (also *absol.*) **a** (often foll. by *of*, or *that* + clause, or *to* + infin.) inform of danger, unknown circumstances, etc. (*warned them of the danger*; *warned her that she was being watched*; *warned him to expect a visit*). **b** (often foll. by *against*) inform (a person etc.) about a specific danger, hostile person, etc. (*warned her against trusting him*). **2** (usu. with *neg.*) admonish; tell forcefully (*has been warned not to go*). **3** give (a person) cautionary notice regarding conduct etc. (*shall not warn you again*). □ **warn off 1** tell (a person) to keep away (from). **2** *Brit.* prohibit from attending races, esp. at a specified course. □ **warner** *n.* [Old English *war(e)nian*, *wearnian*, ultimately from Germanic: related to WARE[3]]

warning /ˈwɔːnɪŋ/ *n. & adj.* ● *n.* **1** in senses of WARN *v.* **2** anything that serves to warn; a hint or indication of difficulty, danger, etc. **3** *archaic* = NOTICE *n.* 3b. ● *attrib.adj.* serving to warn. □ **warningly** *adv.* [Old English *war(e)nung* etc. (as WARN, -ING[1])]

warning coloration *n. Biol.* conspicuous colouring that warns a predator etc. against attacking.

war of attrition *n.* a war in which each side seeks to wear out the other over a long period.

War Office *n. hist.* the British State department in charge of the army.

war of nerves *n.* an attempt to wear down an opponent by psychological means.

war of the elements *n. poet.* storms or natural catastrophes.

warp /wɔːp/ *v. & n.* ● *v.* **1** *tr. & intr.* **a** make or become bent or twisted out of shape, esp. by the action of heat, damp, etc. **b** make or become perverted, bitter, or strange (*a warped sense of humour*). **2 a** *tr.* haul (a ship) by a rope attached to a fixed point. **b** *intr.* progress in this way. **3** *tr.* silt over (land) with warp, by flooding. **4** *tr.* (foll. by *up*) choke (a channel) with an alluvial deposit etc. **5** *tr.* arrange (threads) as a warp. ● *n.* **1 a** a state of being warped, esp. of shrunken or expanded timber. **b** perversion, bitterness, etc. of the mind or character. **2** the threads stretched lengthwise in a loom to be crossed by the weft. **3** a rope used in towing or warping, or attached to a trawl net. **4** sediment etc. left esp. on poor land by standing water. □ **warpage** *n.* (esp. in sense 1a of *v.*). **warper** *n.* (in sense 5 of *v.*). [Old

English *weorpan*, originally = to throw: from Germanic]

warpaint /ˈwɔːpeɪnt/ *n.* **1** paint used to adorn the body before battle, esp. by N. American Indians. **2** *colloq.* elaborate make-up.

warpath /ˈwɔːpɑːθ/ *n.* **1** a warlike expedition of N. American Indians. **2** *colloq.* any hostile course or attitude (*is on the warpath again*).

war pension *n.* a pension paid to someone disabled or bereaved by war.

warplane /ˈwɔːpleɪn/ *n.* a military aircraft.

war poet *n.* a poet writing on war themes, esp. of the two world wars.

warragal var. of WARRIGAL.

warrant /ˈwɒr(ə)nt/ *n.* & *v.* ● *n.* **1 a** anything that authorizes a person or an action (*have no warrant for this*). **b** a person so authorizing (*I will be your warrant*). **2 a** a written authorization, money voucher, travel document, etc. (*a dividend warrant*). **b** a written authorization allowing police to search premises, arrest a suspect, etc. **c** a certificate entitling the holder to subscribe for shares of a company. **3** a document authorizing counsel to represent the principal in a lawsuit (*warrant of attorney*). **4** a certificate of service rank held by a warrant officer. ● *v.tr.* **1** serve as a warrant for; justify (*nothing can warrant his behaviour*). **2** guarantee or attest to esp. the genuineness of an article, the worth of a person, etc. □ **I** (or **I'll**) **warrant** I am certain; no doubt (*he'll be sorry, I'll warrant*). □ **warranter** *n.* **warrantor** *n.* [Middle English via Old Northern French *warant*, variant of Old French *guarant, -and* from Frankish *werēnd*, from *giwerēn* 'be surety for']

warrantable /ˈwɒr(ə)ntəb(ə)l/ *adj.* **1** able to be warranted. **2** (of a stag) old enough to be hunted (5 or 6 years). □ **warrantableness** *n.* **warrantably** *adv.*

warrantee /wɒr(ə)nˈtiː/ *n.* a person to whom a warranty is given.

warrant officer *n.* an officer in the army or RAF ranking between commissioned officers and NCOs.

warranty /ˈwɒr(ə)nti/ *n.* (*pl.* **-ies**) **1** an undertaking as to the ownership or quality of a thing sold, hired, etc., often accepting responsibility for defects or liability for repairs needed over a specified period. **2** (usu. foll. by *for* + verbal noun) an authority or justification. **3** an undertaking by an insured person of the truth of a statement or fulfilment of a condition. [Middle English from Anglo-French *warantie*, variant of *garantie* (as WARRANT)]

warren /ˈwɒr(ə)n/ *n.* **1 a** a network of interconnecting rabbit burrows. **b** a piece of ground occupied by this. **2** a densely populated or labyrinthine building or district. **3** *hist.* a piece of ground on which game is preserved. [Middle English from Anglo-French & Old Northern French *warenne*, variant of Old French *garenne* 'game-park', from Germanic]

warrigal /ˈwɒrɪg(ə)l/ *n.* & *adj.* (also **warragal**) *Austral.* ● *n.* **1** a dingo dog. **2** an untamed horse. **3** a wild Aborigine. ● *adj.* wild, untamed. [Dharuk *warrigal* 'wild dingo']

warring /ˈwɔːrɪŋ/ *adj.* rival, antagonistic.

warrior /ˈwɒrɪə/ *n.* **1** a person experienced or distinguished in fighting in an armed force, tribe, etc. **2** (*attrib.*) **a** of or relating to a warrior. **b** martial (*a warrior nation*). [Middle English from Old Northern French *werreior* etc., Old French *guerreior* etc. from *werreier, guerreier* 'make WAR']

warship /ˈwɔːʃɪp/ *n.* an armoured ship used in war.

Wars of the Roses *n.pl. hist.* the 15th-c. civil wars between the houses of York and Lancaster, represented by white and red roses respectively.

wart /wɔːt/ *n.* **1** a small benign growth on the skin, usu. hard and rounded, caused by a virus-induced abnormal growth of skin cells and thickening of the epidermis. **2** a protuberance on the skin of an animal, surface of a plant, etc. **3** *colloq.* an objectionable person. □ **warts and all** *colloq.* with no attempt to conceal blemishes or inadequacies. □ **warty** *adj.* [Old English *wearte*, from Germanic]

warthog /ˈwɔːthɒg/ *n.* an African wild pig, *Phacochoerus aethiopicus*, with a large head and warty lumps on its face, and large curved tusks.

wartime /ˈwɔːtʌɪm/ *n.* the period during which a war is waged.

war-torn *adj.* racked or devastated by war.

war-weary *adj.* (esp. of a population) exhausted and dispirited by war. □ **war-weariness** *n.*

war widow *n.* a woman whose husband has been killed in war.

war-worn *adj.* = WAR-WEARY.

wary /ˈwɛːri/ *adj.* (**warier**, **wariest**) **1** on one's guard; given to caution; circumspect. **2** (foll. by *of*) cautious, suspicious (*am wary of using lifts*). **3** showing or done with caution or suspicion (*a wary expression*). □ **warily** *adv.* **wariness** *n.* [WARE² + -Y¹]

war zone *n.* an area in which a war takes place.

was *1st* & *3rd sing. past* of BE.

Wash. *abbr.* Washington.

wash /wɒʃ/ *v.* & *n.* ● *v.* **1** *tr.* cleanse (oneself or a part of oneself, clothes, etc.) with liquid, esp. water. **2** *tr.* (foll. by *out, off, away*, etc.) remove a stain or dirt in this way. **3** *intr.* wash oneself or esp. one's hands and face. **4** *intr.* wash clothes etc. **5** *intr.* (of fabric or dye) bear washing without damage. **6** *intr.* (foll. by *off, out*) (of a stain etc.) be removed by washing. **7** *tr. poet.* moisten, water (*tear-washed eyes*; *a rose washed with dew*). **8** *tr.* (of a river, sea, etc.) touch (a country, coast, etc.) with its waters. **9 a** *tr.* (of moving liquid) carry along in a specified direction (*a wave washed him overboard*; *was washed up on the shore*). **b** *intr.* be carried in this way (*shells wash up on the beaches*). **10** *tr.* **a** scoop out (*the water had washed a channel*). **b** erode, denude (*sea-washed cliffs*). **11** *intr.* (foll. by *over, along*, etc.) sweep, move, or splash. **12** *intr.* (foll. by *over*) occur all around without greatly affecting (a person). **13** *tr.* sift (ore) by the action of water. **14** *tr.* **a** brush a thin coat of watery paint or ink over (paper in watercolour painting etc., or a wall). **b** (foll. by *with*) coat (inferior metal) with gold etc. ● *n.* **1 a** the act or an instance of washing; the process of being washed (*give them a good wash*; *only needed one wash*). **b** (prec. by *the*) treatment at a laundry etc. (*sent them to the wash*). **2** a quantity of clothes for washing or just washed. **3** the visible or audible motion of agitated water or air, esp. due to the passage of a ship etc. or aircraft. **4 a** soil swept off by water; alluvium. **b** a sandbank exposed only at low tide. **5** kitchen slops and scraps given to pigs. **6 a** thin, weak, or inferior liquid food. **b** liquid food for animals. **7** a liquid to spread over a surface to cleanse, heal, or colour. **8** a thin coating of watercolour, wall-colouring, or metal. **9** malt etc. fermenting before distillation. **10** a lotion or cosmetic. □ **come out in the wash** *colloq.* be clarified, or (of contingent difficulties) be resolved or removed, in the course of events. **wash-and-wear** *adj.* (of a fabric or garment) easily and quickly laundered. **wash one's dirty linen in public** see LINEN. **wash down 1** wash completely (esp. a large surface or object). **2** (usu. foll. by *with*) accompany or follow (food) with a drink. **wash one's hands** *euphem.* go to the lavatory. **wash one's hands of** renounce responsibility for (originally with reference to Matt. 27:24). **wash out 1** clean the inside of (a thing) by washing. **2** clean (a garment etc.) by brief washing. **3 a** rain off (an event etc.). **b** *colloq.* cancel. **4** (of a flood, downpour, etc.) make a breach in (a road etc.). **5** = sense 2 of *v.* **wash up 1** wash (crockery and cutlery) after use. **2** *N. Amer.* wash one's face and hands. **won't wash** *colloq.* (of an argument etc.) will not be believed or accepted. [Old English *wæscan* etc. from Germanic: related to WATER]

washable /ˈwɒʃəb(ə)l/ *adj.* that can be washed, esp. without damage. □ **washability** /-ˈbɪlɪti/ *n.*

washbag /ˈwɒʃbag/ *n.* a waterproof bag for toilet articles.

washbasin /ˈwɒʃbeɪs(ə)n/ *n.* a basin for washing one's hands, face, etc., esp. fixed to a wall or on a pedestal and connected to a water supply and a drain.

washboard /ˈwɒʃbɔːd/ *n.* **1** a board of ribbed wood or a sheet of corrugated zinc on which clothes are scrubbed in washing. **2** this used as a percussion instrument, played with the fingers.

washday /ˈwɒʃdeɪ/ *n.* a day on which clothes etc. are washed.

washed out *adj.* (hyphenated when *attrib.*) **1** faded by washing. **2** pale. **3** *colloq.* limp, enfeebled.

washed up *adj.* esp. *N. Amer. slang* defeated, having failed.

washer /ˈwɒʃə/ *n.* **1 a** a person or thing that washes. **b** a washing machine. **2** a flat ring of rubber, metal, leather, etc., inserted at a joint to tighten it and prevent leakage. **3** a similar ring placed under the head of a screw, bolt, etc., or under a nut, to disperse its pressure. **4** *Austral.* a cloth for washing the face.

washer-dryer *n.* (also **washer-drier**) a washing machine with an inbuilt tumble-dryer.

washer-up *n.* (*pl.* **washers-up**) *Brit.* a person who washes up dishes etc.

washerwoman /ˈwɒʃəwʊmən/ *n.* (*pl.* **-women**) a woman whose occupation is washing clothes; a laundress.

washeteria /wɒʃəˈtɪərɪə/ *n.* = LAUNDERETTE.

wash-hand basin *n.* = WASHBASIN.

wash-hand stand *n. Brit.* = WASHSTAND.

wash-house *n.* a building where clothes are washed.

washing /ˈwɒʃɪŋ/ *n.* **1** a quantity of clothes for washing or just washed. **2** the act of washing clothes.

washing machine *n.* a machine for washing clothes and linen etc.

washing powder *n.* esp. *Brit.* powder of soap or detergent for washing clothes.

washing soda *n.* sodium carbonate, used dissolved in water for washing and cleaning.

washing-up *n. Brit.* **1** the process of washing dishes etc. after use. **2** used dishes etc. for washing.

washland /ˈwɒʃland/ *n.* land periodically flooded by a stream.

wash-leather *n. Brit.* chamois or similar leather for washing windows etc.

wash-out *n.* **1** *colloq.* a fiasco; a complete failure. **2** a breach in a road, railway track, etc., caused by flooding. **3** (**washout**) *Geol.* a narrow river-channel that cuts into pre-existing sediments.

washroom /ˈwɒʃruːm, -rʊm/ *n. N. Amer.* a room with washing and toilet facilities.

washstand /ˈwɒʃstand/ *n. hist.* a piece of furniture to hold a jug of water, a basin, soap, etc. for washing oneself with.

washtub /ˈwɒʃtʌb/ *n.* a tub or vessel for washing clothes etc.

washy /ˈwɒʃi/ *adj.* (**washier**, **washiest**) **1** (of liquid food) too watery or weak; insipid. **2** (of colour) faded-looking, thin, faint. **3** (of a style, sentiment, etc.) lacking vigour or intensity. ◻ **washily** *adv.* **washiness** *n.*

wasn't /ˈwɒz(ə)nt/ *contr.* was not.

Wasp /wɒsp/ *n.* (also **WASP**) *N. Amer.* usu. *derog.* a middle-class American white Protestant descended from early English settlers. ◻ **Waspy** *adj.* (also **WASPy**). [*w*hite *A*nglo-*S*axon *P*rotestant]

wasp /wɒsp/ *n.* **1** a stinging often predatory insect of the order Hymenoptera, esp. a social insect of the common genus *Vespula*, with black and yellow stripes and a very thin waist. **2** (in *comb.*) any of various insects resembling a wasp in some way (*wasp-beetle*). ◻ **wasplike** *adj.* [Old English *wæfs*, *wæps*, *wæsp* from West Germanic: perhaps related to WEAVE[1] (from the weblike form of its nest)]

waspish /ˈwɒspɪʃ/ *adj.* irritable, petulant; sharp in retort. ◻ **waspishly** *adv.* **waspishness** *n.*

wasp-waist *n.* a very slender waist. ◻ **wasp-waisted** *adj.*

wassail /ˈwɒseɪl, ˈwɒs(ə)l, ˈwa-/ *n. & v. archaic* ● *n.* **1** a festive occasion; a drinking bout. **2** a kind of liquor drunk on such an occasion. ● *v.intr.* make merry; celebrate with drinking etc. ◻ **wassailer** *n.* [Middle English *wæs hæil* etc. from Old Norse *ves heill*, corresponding to Old English *wes hāl* 'be in health', a form of salutation: cf. HALE[1]]

wassail-bowl *n.* (also **wassail-cup**) a bowl or cup from which healths were drunk, esp. on Christmas Eve and Twelfth Night.

Wassermann test /ˈvɑːsəmən/ *n. Med.* a diagnostic test for syphilis using a specific antibody reaction of the patient's blood serum. [named after A. von *Wassermann*, German pathologist d. 1925]

wast /wɒst, wəst/ *archaic* or *dial. 2nd sing. past* of BE.

wastage /ˈweɪstɪdʒ/ *n.* **1** an amount wasted. **2** loss by use, wear, or leakage. **3** (also **natural wastage**) loss of employees other than by redundancy.

waste /weɪst/ *v., adj., & n.* ● *v.* **1** *tr.* use to no purpose or for inadequate result or extravagantly (*waste time*). **2** *tr.* fail to use (esp. an opportunity). **3** *tr.* (often foll. by *on*) **a** give (advice etc.), utter (words etc.), without effect. **b** (often in *passive*) fail to be appreciated or used properly (*she was wasted on him*; *I feel wasted in this job*). **4** *tr. & intr.* (often foll. by *away*) wear gradually away; make or become weak; wither. **5** *tr. literary* ravage, devastate. **6** *tr.* treat as wasted or valueless. **7** *intr.* be expended without useful effect. **8** *tr.* esp. *N. Amer. slang* beat up, kill, murder. **9** *tr.* (as **wasted** *predic.adj.*) *slang* **a** worn out; exhausted. **b** intoxicated by alcohol or drugs. ● *adj.* **1** superfluous; no longer serving a purpose. **2** (of a district etc.) not inhabited or cultivated; desolate (*waste ground*). ● *n.* **1** the act or an instance of wasting; extravagant or ineffectual use of an asset, of time, etc. **2** waste material or food; refuse; unwanted or unusable remains or by-products. **3** a waste region; a desert etc. **4** the state of being used up; diminution by wear and tear. **5** *Law* damage to an estate caused by an act or by neglect, esp. by a life-tenant. **6** = WASTE PIPE. ◻ **go** (or **run**) **to waste** be wasted. **lay waste** (or **lay waste to** or **lay** (a thing) **to waste**) ravage, devastate. **waste one's breath** see BREATH. **waste not, want not** extravagance leads to poverty. **waste words** see WORD. ◻ **wasteless** *adj.* [Middle English via Old Northern French *wast(e)*, variant of Old French *g(u)ast(e)*, from Latin *vastus*]

wastebasket /ˈweɪs(t)bɑːskɪt/ *n.* esp. *N. Amer.* = WASTE-PAPER BASKET.

waste bin *n.* a bin for waste paper, refuse, etc., used indoors or outdoors.

waste disposal *n.* (often *attrib.*) the disposing of waste products, rubbish, etc., esp. as a public or corporate process.

waste disposal unit *n.* an electrical device fitted to the waste pipe of a kitchen sink etc. for grinding up waste.

wasteful /ˈweɪstfʊl, -f(ə)l/ *adj.* **1** extravagant. **2** causing or showing waste. ◻ **wastefully** *adj.* **wastefulness** *n.*

waste ground *n.* an area of unused land, esp. one left undeveloped in an urban area.

wasteland /ˈweɪs(t)land, -lənd/ *n.* **1** an unproductive or useless area of land. **2** a place or time considered spiritually or intellectually barren.

waste paper *n.* used or unwanted paper.

waste-paper basket *n.* esp. *Brit.* a receptacle for waste paper.

waste pipe *n.* a pipe to carry off waste water etc., e.g. from a sink.

waste products *n.pl.* useless by-products of manufacture or of an organism or organisms.

waster /ˈweɪstə/ *n.* **1** a wasteful person. **2** *colloq.* a worthless person; an idler.

wastrel /ˈweɪstr(ə)l/ *n.* **1** a wasteful or good-for-nothing person. **2** *archaic* a waif; a neglected child.

watch /wɒtʃ/ *v.* & *n.* ● *v.* **1** *tr.* keep the eyes fixed on; look at attentively. **2** *tr.* **a** keep under observation; follow observantly. **b** monitor or consider carefully; pay attention to (*have to watch my weight*; *watched their progress with interest*). **3** *intr.* (often foll. by *for*) be in an alert state; be vigilant; take heed (*watch for the holes in the road*; *watch for an opportunity*). **4** *intr.* (foll. by *over*) look after; take care of. **5** *intr. archaic* remain awake for devotions etc. ● *n.* **1** a small portable timepiece for carrying on one's person. **2** a state of alert or constant observation or attention. **3** *Naut.* **a** a usu. four-hour spell of duty. **b** (in full **starboard** or **port watch**) each of the halves, divided according to the position of the bunks, into which a ship's crew is divided to take alternate watches. **4** *hist.* a watchman or group of watchmen, esp. patrolling the streets at night. **5** a former division of the night (now esp. in phr. **the watches of the night**). **6** *hist.* irregular Highland troops in the 18th c. □ **on the watch** waiting for an expected or feared occurrence. **on watch** on lookout duty. **set the watch** *Naut.* station sentinels etc. **watch it** (or **oneself**) *colloq.* be careful. **watch out 1** (often foll. by *for*) be on one's guard. **2** (as *int.*) a warning of immediate danger. **watch one's step** proceed cautiously. □ **watchable** *adj.* **watcher** *n.* (also in *comb.*). [Old English *wæcce* (*n.*), related to WAKE[1]]

watchband /ˈwɒtʃband/ *n. N. Amer.* = WATCH STRAP.

watch-case *n.* the outer metal case enclosing the works of a watch.

watch-chain *n.* a metal chain for securing a pocket watch.

Watch Committee *n. hist.* (in the UK) the committee of a county borough council dealing with policing etc.

watchdog /ˈwɒtʃdɒg/ *n.* & *v.* ● *n.* **1** a dog kept to guard property etc. **2** a person or body monitoring others' rights, behaviour, etc. ● *v.tr.* (**-dogged**, **-dogging**) maintain surveillance over.

watchfire /ˈwɒtʃfʌɪə/ *n.* a fire maintained during the night as a signal or for the use of guards on watch.

watchful /ˈwɒtʃfʊl, -f(ə)l/ *adj.* **1** accustomed to watching. **2** on the watch. **3** showing vigilance. **4** *archaic* wakeful. □ **watchfully** *adv.* **watchfulness** *n.*

watch-glass *n.* **1** *Brit.* a glass disc covering the dial of a watch. **2** a similar disc used in a laboratory etc. to hold material for use in experiments.

watching brief *n. Brit.* **1** a brief held by a barrister following a case for a client not directly involved. **2** a state of interest maintained in a proceeding not directly or immediately concerning one.

watchkeeper /ˈwɒtʃkiːpə/ *n.* a person who acts as lookout, esp. a member of a watch on board ship.

watchmaker /ˈwɒtʃmeɪkə/ *n.* a person who makes and repairs watches and clocks. □ **watchmaking** *n.*

watchman /ˈwɒtʃmən/ *n.* (*pl.* **-men**) **1** a man employed to look after an empty building etc. at night. **2** *archaic* or *hist.* a member of a night watch.

watch-night *n.* **1** the last night of the year. **2** a religious service held on this night.

watch spring *n.* the mainspring of a watch.

watch strap *n.* esp. *Brit.* a strap for fastening a watch on the wrist.

watchtower /ˈwɒtʃtaʊə/ *n.* a tower from which observation can be kept.

watchword /ˈwɒtʃwəːd/ *n.* **1** a phrase summarizing a guiding principle; a slogan. **2** *hist.* a military password.

water /ˈwɔːtə/ *n.* & *v.* ● *n.* **1** a colourless transparent odourless tasteless liquid compound of oxygen and hydrogen. Chem. formula: H_2O. **2** a liquid consisting chiefly of this and found in seas, lakes, and rivers, in rain, and in the fluids of living organisms. **3** an expanse of water; a sea, lake, river, etc. **4** (in *pl.*) part of a sea or river (*in Icelandic waters*). **5** (often as **the waters**) mineral water at a spa etc. **6** the state of a tide (*high water*). **7** a solution of a specified substance in water (*lavender-water*). **8** the quality of the transparency and brilliance of a gem, esp. a diamond. **9** *Finance* an amount of nominal capital added by watering (see sense 10 of *v.*). **10** (*attrib.*) **a** found in, on, or near water. **b** of, for, or worked by water. **c** involving, using, or yielding water. **11 a** urine. **b** (usu. in *pl.*) the amniotic fluid discharged from the womb before childbirth. ● *v.* **1** *tr.* sprinkle or soak with water. **2** *tr.* supply (a plant) with water. **3** *tr.* give water to (an animal) to drink. **4** *intr.* (of the mouth or eyes) secrete water as saliva or tears. **5** *tr.* (as **watered** *adj.*) (of silk etc.) having irregular wavy glossy markings. **6** *tr.* adulterate (milk, beer, etc.) with water. **7** *tr.* (of a river etc.) supply (a place) with water. **8** *intr.* (of an animal) go to a pool etc. to drink. **9** *intr.* (of a ship, engine, etc., or the person in charge of it) take in a supply of water. **10** *tr. Finance* increase (a company's debt, or nominal capital) by the issue of new shares without a corresponding addition to assets. □ **by water** using a ship etc. for travel or transport. **cast one's bread upon the waters** see BREAD. **like water** lavishly, profusely. **like water off a duck's back** see DUCK[1]. **make one's mouth water** cause one's saliva to flow, stimulate one's appetite or anticipation. **of the first water 1** (of a diamond) of the greatest brilliance and transparency. **2** of the finest quality or extreme degree. **on the water** on a ship etc. **on the water wagon** see WAGON. **water down 1** dilute with water. **2** (often as **watered down** *adj.*) make less vivid, forceful, or horrifying. **water under the bridge** past events accepted as past and irrevocable. □ **waterer** *n.* **waterless** *adj.* [Old English *wæter* from Germanic: related to WET]

water-bag *n.* a bag of leather, canvas, etc., for holding water.

water bailiff *n. Brit.* **1** an official enforcing fishing laws. **2** *hist.* a custom house officer at a port.

water-based *adj.* (usu. *attrib.*) **1** (of a solution, substance, etc.) having water as the main ingredient. **2** (of a sporting activity) practised on water.

water bear *n.* = TARDIGRADE *n.*

Water-bearer *n.* = WATER-CARRIER.

waterbed /ˈwɔːtəbɛd/ *n.* a bed with a mattress of rubber or plastic etc. filled with water.

waterbird /ˈwɔːtəbəːd/ *n.* a bird frequenting esp. fresh water.

water biscuit *n.* a thin crisp unsweetened biscuit made from flour and water.

water blister *n.* a blister containing a colourless watery fluid, rather than blood or pus.

water-bloom *n.* scum formed by algae on the surface of standing water.

water-boatman *n.* an aquatic bug of the family Notonectidae or Corixidae, swimming with oarlike hind legs.

water-borne *adj.* **1** (of goods etc.) conveyed by or travelling on water. **2** (of a disease) communicated or propagated by contaminated water.

waterbrash /ˈwɔːtəbraʃ/ *n.* pyrosis. [WATER + *brash* 'eruption of fluid from the stomach']

water-buck *n.* a large African antelope, *Kobus ellipsiprymnus*, found near rivers and lakes in the savannah.

water buffalo *n.* the common domestic Indian buffalo, *Bubalus arnee*.

water bus *n.* a boat carrying passengers on a regular run on a river, lake, etc.

water-butt *n.* a barrel used to catch rainwater.

water-cannon *n.* a device giving a powerful jet of water to disperse a crowd etc.

Water-carrier *n.* (prec. by *the*) the zodiacal sign or constellation Aquarius.

water chestnut *n.* **1** an aquatic plant, *Trapa natans*, bearing an edible seed. **2** (in full **Chinese water chestnut**) **a** a sedge, *Eleocharis tuberosa*, with rushlike leaves arising from a corm. **b** this corm used as food.

water-clock *n.* a clock measuring time by the flow of water.

water closet *n.* **1** a lavatory with the means for flushing the pan with water. **2** a room containing this.
watercolour *n.* (*US* **watercolor**) **1** artists' paint made of pigment to be diluted with water and not oil. **2** a picture painted with this. **3** the art of painting with watercolours. □ **watercolourist** *n.*
water-cooled *adj.* cooled by the circulation of water.
water-cooler *n.* a vessel in which water is cooled and kept cool, esp. a tank of cooled drinking water in a place of work.
watercourse /ˈwɔːtəkɔːs/ *n.* **1** a brook, stream, or artificial water channel. **2** the bed along which this flows.
watercress /ˈwɔːtəkrɛs/ *n.* a hardy perennial cress, *Nasturtium officinale*, growing in running water, with pungent leaves used in salad.
water cure *n.* = HYDROPATHY.
water-diviner *n. Brit.* a person who dowses (see DOWSE[1]) for water.
waterfall /ˈwɔːtəfɔːl/ *n.* a cascade of water from a river or stream falling vertically from a height over a rock, precipice, etc.
water flea *n.* = DAPHNIA.
Waterford glass /ˈwɔːtəfəd/ *n.* a clear colourless flint glass. [*Waterford*, a city in Ireland, where it was first made]
waterfowl /ˈwɔːtəfaʊl/ *n.* (usu. collect., treated as *pl.*) birds frequenting water, esp. ducks and geese regarded as game birds.
waterfront /ˈwɔːtəfrʌnt/ *n.* the part of a town adjoining a river, lake, harbour, etc.
watergate /ˈwɔːtəgeɪt/ *n.* **1** a floodgate. **2** a gate giving access to a river etc.
water gauge *n.* **1** a glass tube etc. indicating the height of water in a reservoir, boiler, etc. **2** pressure expressed in terms of a head of water.
water-glass *n.* **1** a solution of sodium or potassium silicate used for preserving eggs, as a vehicle for fresco-painting, and for hardening artificial stone. **2** a tube with a glass bottom enabling objects under water to be observed. **3** (usu. **water glass**) a glass for holding usu. drinking water.
water hammer *n.* a knocking noise in a water pipe when a tap is suddenly turned off.
water heater *n.* a device for heating (esp. domestic) water.
water hemlock *n.* a poisonous plant, *Cicuta maculata*, found in marshes etc.: also called COWBANE.
waterhole /ˈwɔːtəhəʊl/ *n.* a shallow depression in which water collects (esp. in the bed of a river otherwise dry).
water hyacinth *n.* a tropical American aquatic plant, *Eichhornia crassipes*, which is a serious weed of waterways in warm countries.
water ice *n.* a confection of flavoured and frozen water and sugar etc.; a sorbet.
watering /ˈwɔːt(ə)rɪŋ/ *n.* the act or an instance of supplying water or (of an animal) obtaining water. [Old English *wæterung* (as WATER, -ING[1])]
watering can *n.* a portable container with a long spout usu. ending in a perforated sprinkler, for watering plants.
watering hole *n.* **1** a pool of water from which animals regularly drink. **2** *slang* a bar.
watering place *n.* **1** = WATERING HOLE. **2** a spa or seaside resort. **3** a place where water is obtained.
water jug *n.* **1** *Brit.* a jug for dispensing water into drinking glasses etc. **2** *US* a container, esp. with a stopper, for dispensing usu. drinking water on a journey etc.
water jump *n.* a place where a horse in a steeplechase etc. must jump over water.
water level *n.* **1 a** the surface of the water in a reservoir etc. **b** the height of this. **2** a level below which the ground is saturated with water. **3** a level using water to determine the horizontal.
water lily *n.* any aquatic plant of the family Nymphaeaceae, with broad flat floating leaves and large usu. cup-shaped floating flowers.
waterline /ˈwɔːtəlʌɪn/ *n.* **1** the line along which the surface of water touches a ship's side (marked on a ship for use in loading). **2** a linear watermark.
waterlogged /ˈwɔːtəlɒgd/ *adj.* **1** saturated with water. **2** (of a boat etc.) hardly able to float from being saturated or filled with water. **3** (of ground) made useless by being saturated with water. [*waterlog* (*v.*), from WATER + LOG[1], probably originally = 'reduce (a ship) to the condition of a log']
Waterloo /wɔːtəˈluː/ *n.* a decisive defeat; an irrevocable end (esp. in phr. **meet one's Waterloo**). [*Waterloo*, a village in Belgium, where Napoleon was finally defeated in 1815]
water main *n.* the main pipe in a water supply system.
waterman /ˈwɔːtəmən/ *n.* (*pl.* **-men**) **1** a boatman plying for hire. **2** an oarsman as regards skill in keeping the boat balanced.
watermark /ˈwɔːtəmɑːk/ *n.* & *v.* ● *n.* a faint design made in some paper during manufacture, visible when held against the light, identifying the maker etc. ● *v.tr.* mark with this.
water-meadow *n.* a meadow periodically flooded by a stream or river.
water measurer *n.* a long thin aquatic bug of the family Hydrometridae which walks slowly on the surface film of water.
watermelon /ˈwɔːtəmɛlən/ *n.* a large smooth green melon, *Citrullus lanatus*, with red pulp and watery juice.
water meter *n.* a device for measuring and recording the amount of water supplied to a house etc.
water milfoil see MILFOIL 2.
watermill /ˈwɔːtəmɪl/ *n.* a mill worked by a waterwheel.
water moccasin see MOCCASIN 2.
water nymph *n.* a nymph regarded as inhabiting or presiding over water; a naiad.
water of crystallization *n.* water forming an essential part of the structure of some crystals.
water of life *n. literary* spiritual enlightenment.
water opossum *n.* = YAPOK.
water ouzel *n.* = DIPPER 1.
water-pepper *n.* a knotweed of damp ground, *Persicaria hydropiper*, with peppery-tasting leaves.
water pipe *n.* **1** a pipe for conveying water. **2** a hookah.
water pistol *n.* a toy pistol shooting a jet of water.
water plantain *n.* a plant of the genus *Alisma*, with plantain-like leaves, found esp. in ditches.
water polo *n.* a game played by swimmers, with a ball like a football.
water-power *n.* **1** mechanical force derived from the weight or motion of water. **2** a fall in the level of a river, as a source of this force.
waterproof /ˈwɔːtəpruːf/ *adj.*, *n.*, & *v.* ● *adj.* impervious to water. ● *n. Brit.* a waterproof garment or material. ● *v.tr.* make waterproof. □ **waterproofer** *n.* **waterproofness** *n.*
water purslane *n.* a creeping plant, *Lythrum portula*, growing in damp places.
water rail *n.* a wading bird, *Rallus aquaticus*, frequenting marshes etc.
water rat *n.* = WATER VOLE.
water rate *n.* a charge made for the use of the public water supply.
water-repellent *adj.* (esp. of a coating or finish) not easily penetrated by water.
water-resistant *adj.* (of a fabric, wristwatch, etc.) able to resist, but not entirely prevent, the penetration of water. □ **water-resistance** *n.*

water scorpion *n.* an aquatic bug of the family Nepidae, living submerged and breathing through a bristle-like tubular tail.

watershed /'wɔːtəʃɛd/ *n.* **1** a line of separation between waters flowing to different rivers, basins, or seas. **2** a turning point in affairs. [WATER + *shed* 'ridge of high ground' (related to SHED²), suggested by German *Wasserscheide*]

waterside /'wɔːtəsʌɪd/ *n.* the margin of a sea, lake, or river.

water-ski *n.* & *v.* ● *n.* (*pl.* **-skis**) each of a pair of skis on which a person towed by a motor boat skims the surface of the water. ● *v.intr.* (**-skis, -skied** /-skiːd/; **-skiing**) travel on water-skis. □ **water-skier** *n.*

water slide *n.* a usu. high or long slide, down which water cascades, esp. into a swimming pool.

water softener *n.* an apparatus or substance for softening hard water.

water soldier *n.* a European aquatic plant of the frogbit family, *Stratiotes aloides*, with rigid spiny sword-shaped leaves.

water-soluble *adj.* soluble in water.

water-splash *n. Brit.* part of a road submerged by a stream or pool.

water sport *n.* (usu. in *pl.*) a sport practised on water, such as water-skiing, windsurfing, etc.

waterspout /'wɔːtəspaʊt/ *n.* a gyrating column of water and spray formed by a whirlwind between sea and cloud.

water starwort *n.* any plant of the genus *Callitriche*, growing in water.

water supply *n.* the provision and storage of water, or the amount of water stored, for the use of a town, house, etc.

water-table *n.* = WATER LEVEL 2.

water taxi *n.* a small usu. motor-driven boat for transporting casual passengers.

waterthrush /'wɔːtəθrʌʃ/ *n.* either of two small N. American birds of the genus *Seiurus*, found near woodland streams and swamps.

watertight /'wɔːtətʌɪt/ *adj.* **1** (of a joint, container, vessel, etc.) closely fastened or fitted or made so as to prevent the passage of water. **2** (of an argument etc.) unassailable.

water torture *n.* a form of torture in which the victim is exposed to the incessant dripping of water on the head, or the sound of dripping.

water tower *n.* a tower with an elevated tank to give pressure for distributing water.

water vole *n.* a large semiaquatic vole, esp. *Arvicola terrestris*.

water wagon see WAGON.

waterway /'wɔːtəweɪ/ *n.* **1** a navigable channel. **2** a route for travel by water. **3** a thick plank at the outer edge of a deck along which a channel is hollowed for water to run off by.

waterweed /'wɔːtəwiːd/ *n.* any of various aquatic plants.

waterwheel /'wɔːtəwiːl/ *n.* a wheel driven by water to work machinery, or to raise water.

water wings *n.pl.* inflated floats fixed on the arms of a person learning to swim.

waterworks /'wɔːtəwəːks/ *n.pl.* **1** an establishment for managing a water supply. **2** *colloq.* the shedding of tears (esp. in phr. **turn on the waterworks**). **3** *Brit. colloq.* the urinary system.

watery /'wɔːt(ə)ri/ *adj.* **1** containing too much water. **2** too thin in consistency. **3** of or consisting of water. **4** (of the eyes) suffused or running with water. **5** (of conversation, style, etc.) vapid, uninteresting. **6** (of colour) pale. **7** (of the sun, moon, or sky) rainy-looking. □ **wateriness** *n.* [Old English *wæterig* (as WATER, -Y¹)]

watery grave *n.* the bottom of the sea as a place where a person lies drowned.

Wathawurung /'wʌtəwə,rʌŋ/ *n.* an Aboriginal language of Victoria, now extinct.

watt /wɒt/ *n.* the SI unit of power, equivalent to one joule per second, corresponding to the rate of energy in an electric circuit where the potential difference is one volt and the current one ampere (symbol **W**). [named after J. *Watt*, Scots engineer d. 1819]

wattage /'wɒtɪdʒ/ *n.* an amount of electrical power expressed in watts.

watt-hour *n.* the energy used when one watt is applied for one hour.

wattle¹ /'wɒt(ə)l/ *n.* & *v.* ● *n.* **1 a** interlaced rods and split rods as a material for making fences, walls, etc. **b** (in *sing.* or *pl.*) rods and twigs for this use. **2** an Australian acacia with long pliant branches, with bark used in tanning and golden flowers used as the national emblem. **3** *dial.* a wicker hurdle. ● *v.tr.* **1** make of wattle. **2** enclose or fill up with wattles. [Old English *watul*, of unknown origin]

wattle² /'wɒt(ə)l/ *n.* **1** a loose fleshy appendage on the head or throat of a turkey or other birds. **2** = BARB *n.* 3. □ **wattled** *adj.* [16th c.: origin unknown]

wattle and daub *n.* a network of rods and twigs plastered with mud or clay as a building material.

wattlebird /'wɒt(ə)lbəːd/ *n.* **1** an Australian honeyeater of the genus *Anthochaera* or *Melidectes*, with a wattle hanging from each cheek. **2** a New Zealand bird of the family Callaeidae, with wattles hanging from the base of the bill, e.g. the saddleback.

wattmeter /'wɒtmiːtə/ *n.* a meter for measuring the amount of electricity in watts.

waul /wɔːl/ *v.intr.* (also **wawl**) give a loud plaintive cry like a cat. [imitative]

wave /weɪv/ *v.* & *n.* ● *v.* **1 a** *intr.* (often foll. by *to*) move a hand etc. to and fro in greeting or as a signal (*waved to me across the street*). **b** *tr.* move (a hand etc.) in this way. **2 a** *intr.* show a sinuous or sweeping motion as of a flag, tree, or a cornfield in the wind; flutter, undulate. **b** *tr.* impart a waving motion to. **3** *tr.* brandish (a sword etc.) as an encouragement to followers etc. **4** *tr.* tell or direct (a person) by waving (*waved them away*; *waved them to follow*). **5** *tr.* express (a greeting etc.) by waving (*waved goodbye to them*). **6** *tr.* give an undulating form to (hair, drawn lines, etc.); make wavy. **7** *intr.* (of hair etc.) have such a form; be wavy. ● *n.* **1** a ridge of water between two depressions. **2** a long body of water curling into an arched form and breaking on the shore. **3** a thing compared to this, e.g. a body of persons in one of successive advancing groups. **4** a gesture of waving. **5 a** the process of waving the hair. **b** an undulating form produced in the hair by waving. **6 a** a temporary occurrence or increase of a condition, emotion, or influence (*a wave of enthusiasm*). **b** (esp. in phrs. **heatwave, cold wave**) a spell of abnormal heat or cold. **7** *Physics* **a** a periodic disturbance of the particles of a substance which may be propagated without net movement of the particles, as in the passage of undulating motion, heat, sound, etc. (see also STANDING WAVE, TRAVELLING WAVE). **b** a single curve in the course of this motion. **8** *Electr.* a similar variation of an electromagnetic field in the propagation of light or other radiation through a medium or vacuum. **9** (in *pl.*; prec. by *the*) *poet.* the sea; water. □ **make waves** *colloq.* **1** cause trouble. **2** create a significant impression. **wave aside** dismiss as intrusive or irrelevant. **wave down** wave to (a vehicle or its driver) as a signal to stop. □ **waveless** *adj.* **wavelike** *adj.* & *adv.* [Old English *wafian* (*v.*) from Germanic: the noun also by alteration of Middle English *wawe, wage*]

waveband /'weɪvband/ *n.* a range of (esp. radio) wavelengths between certain limits.

wave equation *n.* a differential equation expressing the properties of motion in waves.

waveform /'weɪvfɔːm/ *n. Physics* a curve showing the shape of a wave at a given time.

wavefront /'weɪvfrʌnt/ *n. Physics* a surface containing points affected in the same way by a wave at a given time.

wave function *n.* a function satisfying a wave equation and describing the properties of a wave.

waveguide /ˈweɪvgʌɪd/ *n. Electr.* a metal tube etc. confining and conveying microwaves.

wavelength /ˈweɪvlɛŋθ, -lɛŋkθ/ *n.* **1** the distance between successive crests of a wave, esp. points in a sound wave or electromagnetic wave (symbol λ). **2** this as a distinctive feature of radio waves from a transmitter. **3** *colloq.* a particular mode or range of thinking and communicating (*we don't seem to be on the same wavelength*).

wavelet /ˈweɪvlɪt/ *n.* a small wave on water.

wave machine *n.* a device for producing waves in a swimming pool.

wave mechanics *n.* a method of analysis of the behaviour esp. of atomic phenomena with particles represented by wave equations (see QUANTUM MECHANICS).

wave number *n. Physics* the number of waves in a unit distance.

waver /ˈweɪvə/ *v.intr.* **1** be or become unsteady; falter; begin to give way. **2** be irresolute or undecided between different courses or opinions; be shaken in resolution or belief. **3** (of a light) flicker. □ **waverer** *n.* **waveringly** *adv.* **wavery** *adj.* [Middle English via Old Norse *vafra* 'flicker' from Germanic: related to WAVE]

wave theory *n. hist.* the theory that light is propagated through the ether by a wave motion imparted to the ether by the molecular vibrations of the radiant body.

wave train *n.* a group of waves of equal or similar wavelengths travelling in the same direction.

wavy /ˈweɪvi/ *adj.* (**wavier**, **waviest**) (of a line or surface) having waves or alternate contrary curves (*wavy hair*). □ **wavily** *adv.* **waviness** *n.*

wa-wa var. of WAH-WAH.

wawl var. of WAUL.

wax[1] /waks/ *n.* & *v.* ● *n.* **1** a sticky mouldable yellowish substance secreted by bees as the material of honeycomb cells; beeswax. **2** a white translucent material obtained from this by bleaching and purifying and used for candles, in modelling, as a basis of polishes, and for other purposes. **3** any similar substance, typically a lipid or hydrocarbon (*earwax, paraffin wax*). **4** *colloq.* **a** a gramophone record. **b** material for the manufacture of this. **5** (*attrib.*) made of wax. ● *v.tr.* **1** cover or treat with wax or a similar substance (*waxed jacket*). **2** remove unwanted hair from (legs etc.) by applying wax and peeling off the wax and hairs together. **3** *colloq.* record for the gramophone. □ **be wax in a person's hands** be overcompliant or easily influenced by a person. □ **waxer** *n.* [Old English *wæx, weax*, from Germanic]

wax[2] /waks/ *v.intr.* **1** (of the moon between new and full) have a progressively larger part of its visible surface illuminated, increasing in apparent size. **2** *literary* become larger or stronger. **3** (foll. by compl.) pass into a specified state or mood (*wax lyrical*). □ **wax and wane** undergo alternate increases and decreases. [Old English *weaxan*, from Germanic]

wax[3] /waks/ *n. Brit. slang* a fit of anger (esp. in phr. **be in a wax**). [19th c.: origin uncertain: perhaps from phrases such as *wax angry* etc.]

waxberry /ˈwaksb(ə)ri/ *n.* (*pl.* **-ies**) **1** a wax myrtle. **2** the fruit of this.

waxbill /ˈwaksbɪl/ *n.* any small finchlike bird of the family Estrildidae with a red bill resembling sealing wax in colour.

waxcloth /ˈwaksklɒθ/ *n.* oilcloth.

waxed jacket *n.* an outdoor jacket made of waterproof waxed cotton.

waxed paper *n.* paper impregnated with wax to make it waterproof or greaseproof.

waxen /ˈwaks(ə)n/ *adj.* **1** having a smooth pale translucent surface as of wax. **2** able to receive impressions like wax; plastic. **3** *archaic* made of wax.

wax-light *n.* a taper or candle of wax.

wax moth *n.* a pyralid moth whose larvae feed on beeswax, esp. *Galleria mellonella*, a pest of beehives.

wax myrtle *n.* = BAYBERRY.

wax-painting *n.* = ENCAUSTIC.

wax palm *n.* **1** a S. American palm, *Ceroxylon alpinum*, with a stem coated in a mixture of resin and wax. **2** a carnauba.

wax paper *n.* = WAXED PAPER.

wax-pod *n.* a yellow-podded bean.

wax-tree *n.* a tree yielding wax, esp. an Asian tree, *Rhus succedanea*, having white berries used as a substitute for beeswax.

waxwing /ˈwakswɪŋ/ *n.* any bird of the genus *Bombycilla*, with small tips like red sealing wax to some wing feathers.

waxwork /ˈwakswəːk/ *n.* **1 a** an object, esp. a lifelike dummy, modelled in wax. **b** the making of waxworks. **2** (in *pl.*) an exhibition of wax dummies.

waxy[1] /ˈwaksi/ *adj.* (**waxier**, **waxiest**) resembling wax in consistency or in its surface. □ **waxily** *adv.* **waxiness** *n.* [WAX[1] + -Y[1]]

waxy[2] /ˈwaksi/ *adj.* (**waxier**, **waxiest**) *Brit. slang* angry, quick-tempered. [WAX[3] + -Y[1]]

way /weɪ/ *n.* & *adv.* ● *n.* **1** a road, track, path, etc., for passing along. **2** a course or route for reaching a place, esp. the best one (*asked the way to London*). **3** a place of passage into a building, through a door, etc. (*could not find the way out*). **4 a** a method or plan for attaining an object (*that is not the way to do it*). **b** the ability to obtain one's object (*has a way with him*). **5 a** a person's desired or chosen course of action. **b** a custom or manner of behaving; a personal peculiarity (*has a way of forgetting things*; *things had a way of going badly*). **6** a specific manner of life or procedure (*soon got into the way of it*). **7** the normal course of events (*that is always the way*). **8** a travelling distance; a length traversed or to be traversed (*is a long way away*). **9 a** an unimpeded opportunity of advance. **b** a space free of obstacles. **10** a region or ground over which advance is desired or natural. **11** advance in some direction; impetus, progress (*pushed my way through*). **12** movement of a ship etc. (*gather way*; *lose way*). **13** the state of being engaged in movement from place to place; time spent in this (*met them on the way home*; *with songs to cheer the way*). **14** a specified direction (*step this way*; *which way are you going?*). **15** (in *pl.*) parts into which a thing is divided (*split it three ways*). **16** *colloq.* the scope or range of something (*want a few things in the stationery way*). **17** a person's line of occupation or business. **18** a specified condition or state (*things are in a bad way*). **19** a respect (*is useful in some ways*). **20 a** (in *pl.*) a structure of timber etc. down which a new ship is launched. **b** parallel rails etc. as a track for the movement of a machine. ● *adv. colloq.* to a considerable extent; far (*you're way off the mark*). □ **across** (or **over**) **the way** opposite. **be on one's way** set off; depart. **by the way 1** incidentally; as a more or less irrelevant comment. **2** during a journey. **by way of 1** through; by means of. **2** as a substitute for or as a form of (*did it by way of apology*). **3** with the intention of (*asked by way of discovering the truth*). **come one's way** become available to one; become one's lot. **find a way** discover a means of obtaining one's object. **get** (or **have**) **one's way** (or **have it one's own way** etc.) get what one wants; ensure one's wishes are met. **give way 1 a** make concessions. **b** fail to resist; yield. **2** (often foll. by *to*) concede precedence (to). **3** (of a structure etc.) be dislodged or broken under a load; collapse. **4** (foll. by *to*) be superseded by. **5** (foll. by *to*) be overcome by (an emotion etc.). **6** (of rowers) row hard. **go out of one's way** (often foll. by *to* + infin.) make a special effort; act gratuitously or without compulsion (*went out of their way to help*). **go one's own way** act independently, esp. against contrary advice. **go one's way 1** leave, depart. **2** (of events, circumstances, etc.) be favourable to one. **go a person's way** travel in the same direction as a person (*are you going my way?*). **have it both ways** see

BOTH. **in its way** if regarded from a particular standpoint appropriate to it. **in no way** not at all; by no means. **in a way** in a certain respect but not altogether or completely. **in the** (or **one's**) **way** forming an obstacle or hindrance. **lead the way 1** act as guide or leader. **2** show how to do something. **look the other way 1** ignore what one should notice. **2** disregard an acquaintance etc. whom one sees. **one way and another** taking various considerations into account. **one way or another** by some means. **on the** (or **one's**) **way 1** in the course of a journey etc. **2** having progressed (*is well on the way to completion*). **3** *colloq.* (of a child) conceived but not yet born. **on the way out** *colloq.* **1** going down in status, estimation, or favour; going out of fashion. **2** dying. **the other way round** (or *Brit.* **about** or *US* **around**) in an inverted or reversed position or direction. **out of the way 1** no longer an obstacle or hindrance. **2** disposed of; settled. **3** (of a person) imprisoned or killed. **4** (with *neg.*) unusual or remarkable (*nothing out of the way*). **5** (of a place) remote, inaccessible. **out of one's way** not on one's intended route. **put a person in the way of** give a person the opportunity of. **way back** *colloq.* long ago. **the way of the Cross** a series of images representing the stations of the cross, esp. in a church or on the road to a shrine. **way of life** the principles or habits governing all one's actions etc. **way of thinking** one's customary opinion of matters. **way of the world** the customary manner of proceeding, behaving, etc. **ways and means 1** methods of achieving something. **2** methods of raising government revenue. [Old English *weg* from Germanic: the adverb from AWAY]

-way /weɪ/ *suffix* = -WAYS.

waybill /ˈweɪbɪl/ *n.* a list of passengers or parcels on a vehicle.

waybread /ˈweɪbrɛd/ *n. Brit. archaic* a broadleaved plantain (see PLANTAIN[1]). [Old English *wegbrǣde* (as WAY, BROAD)]

wayfarer /ˈweɪfɛːrə/ *n.* a traveller, esp. on foot. □ **wayfaring** *n.*

wayfaring tree *n.* a white-flowered European and Asian shrub, *Viburnum lantana*, common along roadsides, with berries turning from green through red to black.

waylay /weɪˈleɪ/ *v.tr.* (*past* and *past part.* **waylaid**) **1** lie in wait for. **2** stop to rob or interview. □ **waylayer** *n.*

way-leave *n.* a right of way rented to another.

waymark /ˈweɪmɑːk/ *n.* & *v.* ● *n.* (also **waymarker** /-mɑːkə/) a natural or artificial object as a guide to travellers, esp. walkers. ● *v.tr.* (usu. as **waymarked** *adj.*) identify (a path etc.) with such a marker.

way-out *adj. colloq.* **1** unusual, eccentric. **2** avant-garde, progressive. **3** excellent, exciting.

waypoint /ˈweɪpɔɪnt/ *n.* **1** a stopping place, esp. on a journey. **2** the computer-checked coordinates of each stage of a flight, sea journey, etc. (also *attrib.*: *waypoint navigation facility*).

-ways /weɪz/ *suffix* forming adjectives and adverbs of direction or manner (*sideways*) (cf. -WISE). [WAY + -S[1]]

wayside /ˈweɪsʌɪd/ *n.* **1** the side or margin of a road. **2** the land at the side of a road. □ **fall by the wayside** fail to continue in an endeavour or undertaking (after Luke 8:5).

way station *n. N. Amer.* **1** a minor station on a railway. **2** a point marking progress in a certain course of action etc.

wayward /ˈweɪwəd/ *adj.* **1** childishly self-willed or perverse; capricious. **2** unaccountable or freakish. □ **waywardly** *adv.* **waywardness** *n.* [Middle English from obsolete *awayward* 'turned away', from AWAY + -WARD: cf. FROWARD]

way-worn *adj.* tired with travel.

wayzgoose /ˈweɪzguːs/ *n.* (*pl.* **-gooses**) *Brit. hist.* an annual summer dinner or outing held by a printing house for its employees. [17th c. (earlier *waygoose*): origin unknown]

Wb *abbr.* weber(s).

WC *abbr.* **1** *Brit.* water closet. **2** West Central.

WCC *abbr.* World Council of Churches.

W/Cdr. *abbr.* Wing Commander.

WD *abbr. Brit.* **1** War Department. **2** Works Department.

we /wiː/ *pron.* (*obj.* **us**; *poss.* **our**, **ours**) **1** (*pl.* of I[2]) used by and with reference to more than one person speaking or writing, or one such person and one or more associated persons. **2** used for or by a royal person in a proclamation etc. and by a writer or editor in a formal context. **3** people in general (cf. ONE *pron.* 2). **4** *colloq.* = I[2] (*give us a chance*). **5** *colloq.* (often implying condescension) you (*how are we feeling today?*). [Old English from Germanic]

WEA *abbr.* (in the UK) Workers' Educational Association.

weak /wiːk/ *adj.* **1** deficient in strength, power, or number; fragile; easily broken or bent or defeated. **2** deficient in vigour; sickly, feeble (*weak health*; *a weak imagination*). **3 a** deficient in resolution; easily led (*a weak character*). **b** indicating a lack of resolution (*a weak surrender*; *a weak chin*). **4** unconvincing or logically deficient (*weak evidence*; *a weak argument*). **5** (of a mixed liquid or solution) watery, thin, dilute (*weak tea*). **6** (of a style etc.) not vigorous or well-knit; diffuse, slipshod. **7** (of a crew) short-handed. **8** (of a syllable etc.) unstressed. **9** *Gram.* in Germanic languages: **a** (of a verb) forming inflections by the addition of a suffix to the stem. **b** (of a noun or adjective) belonging to a declension in which the stem originally ended in *-n* (opp. STRONG *adj.* 22b). □ **weakish** *adj.* [Middle English from Old Norse *veikr*, from Germanic]

weaken /ˈwiːk(ə)n/ *v.tr.* & *intr.* make or become weak or weaker. □ **weakener** *n.*

weak ending *n. Prosody* an unstressed syllable in a normally stressed place at the end of a verse-line.

weaker sex *n.* (prec. by *the*) *derog.* women.

weakfish /ˈwiːkfɪʃ/ *n.* (*pl.* usu. same) *US* a marine fish of the genus *Cynoscion*, used as food. [obsolete Dutch *weekvisch*, from *week* 'soft' (formed as WEAK) + *visch* FISH[1]]

weak interaction *n. Physics* the weakest form of interaction between subatomic particles.

weak-kneed *adj. colloq.* lacking resolution.

weakling /ˈwiːklɪŋ/ *n.* a feeble person or animal.

weakly /ˈwiːkli/ *adv.* & *adj.* ● *adv.* in a weak manner. ● *adj.* (**weaklier**, **weakliest**) sickly, not robust. □ **weakliness** *n.*

weak-minded *adj.* **1** mentally deficient. **2** lacking in resolution. □ **weak-mindedness** *n.*

weak moment *n.* a time when one is unusually compliant or temptable.

weakness /ˈwiːknɪs/ *n.* **1** the state or condition of being weak. **2** a weak point; a defect. **3** the inability to resist a particular temptation. **4** (foll. by *for*) a self-indulgent liking (*have a weakness for chocolate*).

weak point *n.* (also **weak spot**) **1** a place where defences are assailable. **2** a flaw in an argument or character or in resistance to temptation.

weal[1] /wiːl/ *n.* & *v.* ● *n.* **1** a ridge raised on the flesh by a stroke of a rod or whip. **2** *Med.* a raised and reddened area of the skin, usu. accompanied by itching. ● *v.tr.* mark with a weal. [variant of WALE, influenced by obsolete *wheal* 'suppurate']

weal[2] /wiːl/ *n. literary* welfare, prosperity; good fortune. [Old English *wela* from West Germanic: related to WELL[1]]

Weald /wiːld/ *n.* (also **weald**) (prec. by *the*) *Brit.* a formerly wooded district including parts of Kent, Surrey, and East Sussex. [Old English, = *wald* WOLD]

weald-clay *n.* beds of clay, sandstone, limestone, and ironstone, forming the top of Wealden strata, with abundant fossil remains.

Wealden /ˈwiːld(ə)n/ *adj.* & *n. Brit.* ● *adj.* **1** of the Weald. **2** resembling the Weald geologically. ● *n.* a series of Lower Cretaceous freshwater deposits above Jurassic strata and below chalk, best exemplified in the Weald.

wealth /wɛlθ/ *n.* **1** riches; abundant possessions; opulence. **2** the state of being rich. **3** (foll. by *of*) an abundance or profusion (*a wealth of new material*). **4** *archaic* welfare or prosperity. [Middle English *welthe*, from WELL[1] or WEAL[2] + -TH[2], on the pattern of *health*]

wealth tax *n. Brit.* a tax on personal capital.

wealthy /ˈwɛlθi/ *adj.* (**wealthier, wealthiest**) having an abundance esp. of money. □ **wealthily** *adv.*

wean[1] /wiːn/ *v.tr.* **1** accustom (an infant or other young mammal) to food other than (esp. its mother's) milk. **2** (often foll. by *from, away from*) disengage (from a habit etc.) by enforced discontinuance. [Old English *wenian* 'accustom' from Germanic]

wean[2] /wiːn/ *n. Sc.* a young child. [contraction of *wee ane* 'little one']

weaner /ˈwiːnə/ *n.* a young animal recently weaned.

weanling /ˈwiːnlɪŋ/ *n.* a newly weaned child etc.

weapon /ˈwɛp(ə)n/ *n.* **1** a thing designed or used or usable for inflicting bodily harm (e.g. a gun or cosh). **2** a means employed for trying to gain the advantage in a conflict (*irony is a double-edged weapon*). □ **weaponed** *adj.* (also in *comb.*). **weaponless** *adj.* [Old English *wǣp(e)n*, from Germanic]

weaponry /ˈwɛp(ə)nri/ *n.* weapons collectively.

wear[1] /wɛː/ *v.* & *n.* ● *v.* (*past* **wore** /wɔː/; *past part.* **worn** /wɔːn/) **1** *tr.* have on one's person as clothing or an ornament etc. (*is wearing shorts; wears earrings*). **2** *tr.* be dressed habitually in (*wears green*). **3** *tr.* exhibit or present (a facial expression or appearance) (*wore a frown; the day wore a different aspect*). **4** *tr.* (usu. with *neg.*) *Brit. colloq.* tolerate, accept (*they won't wear that excuse*). **5** (often foll. by *away, down*) **a** *tr.* injure the surface of, or partly obliterate or alter, by rubbing, stress, or use. **b** *intr.* undergo such injury or change. **6** *tr.* & *intr.* (foll. by *off, away*) rub or be rubbed off. **7** *tr.* make (a hole etc.) by constant rubbing or dripping etc. **8** *tr.* & *intr.* (often foll. by *out*) exhaust, tire or be tired. **9** *tr.* (foll. by *down*) overcome by persistence. **10** *tr.* (as **wearing** *adj.*) tiresome; tedious. **11** *intr.* **a** remain for a specified time in working order or a presentable state; last long. **b** (foll. by *well, badly*, etc.) endure continued use or life. **12 a** *intr.* (usu. foll. by *on*) (of time) pass, esp. tediously. **b** *tr.* pass (time) gradually away. **13** *tr.* (of a ship) fly (a flag). ● *n.* **1** the act of wearing or the state of being worn (*suitable for informal wear*). **2** things worn; fashionable or suitable clothing (*sportswear; footwear*). **3** (in full **wear and tear**) damage sustained from continuous use. **4** the capacity for resisting wear and tear (*still a great deal of wear left in it*). □ **in wear** being regularly worn. **wear one's heart on one's sleeve** see HEART. **wear off** lose effectiveness or intensity. **wear out 1** use or be used until no longer usable. **2** tire out. **wear thin** (of patience, excuses, etc.) begin to fail. **wear the trousers** see TROUSERS. **wear** (or **wear one's years**) **well** *colloq.* remain young-looking. □ **wearable** *adj.* **wearability** /-ˈbɪlɪti/ *n.* **wearer** *n.* **wearingly** *adv.* (in sense 10 of *v.*). [Old English *werian*, from Germanic]

wear[2] /wɛː/ *v.* (*past* and *past part.* **wore** /wɔː/) **1** *tr.* bring (a ship) about by turning its head away from the wind. **2** *intr.* (of a ship) come about in this way (cf. TACK[1] *v.* 4). [17th c.: origin unknown]

wearisome /ˈwɪərɪs(ə)m/ *adj.* tedious; tiring by monotony or length. □ **wearisomely** *adv.* **wearisomeness** *n.*

weary /ˈwɪəri/ *adj.* & *v.* ● *adj.* (**wearier, weariest**) **1** unequal to or disinclined for further exertion or endurance; tired. **2** (foll. by *of*) dismayed at the continuing of; impatient of. **3** tiring or tedious. ● *v.* (**-ies, -ied**) **1** *tr.* & *intr.* make or grow weary. **2** *intr.* esp. *Sc.* long. □ **weariless** *adj.* **wearily** *adv.* **weariness** *n.* **wearyingly** *adv.* [Old English *wērig, wǣrig*, from West Germanic]

weasel /ˈwiːz(ə)l/ *n.* & *v.* ● *n.* **1** a small brown and white carnivorous mammal, *Mustela nivalis*, with a slender body, related to the stoat. **2** *colloq.* a deceitful or treacherous person. ● *v.intr.* (**weaselled, weaselling**; *US* **weaseled, weaseling**) **1** esp. *US* equivocate or quibble. **2** (foll. by *on, out*) default on an obligation. □ **weaselly** *adj.* [Old English *wesle, wesule*, from West Germanic]

weasel-faced *adj.* having thin sharp features.

weasel word *n.* (usu. in *pl.*) a word that is intentionally ambiguous or misleading.

weather /ˈwɛðə/ *n.* & *v.* ● *n.* **1** the state of the atmosphere at a place and time as regards heat, cloudiness, dryness, sunshine, wind, and rain etc. **2** (*attrib.*) *Naut.* windward (*on the weather side*). ● *v.* **1** *tr.* expose to or affect by atmospheric changes, esp. deliberately to dry, season, etc. (*weathered timber*). **2 a** *tr.* (usu. in *passive*) discolour or partly disintegrate (rock or stones) by exposure to air. **b** *intr.* be discoloured or worn in this way. **3** *tr.* make (boards or tiles) overlap downwards to keep out rain etc. **4** *tr.* **a** come safely through (a storm). **b** survive (a difficult period etc.). **5** *tr.* (of a ship or its crew) get to the windward of (a cape etc.). □ **keep a** (or **one's**) **weather eye open** be watchful. **make good** (or **bad**) **weather of it** *Naut.* (of a ship) behave well (or badly) in a storm. **make heavy weather of** *colloq.* exaggerate the difficulty or burden presented by (a problem, course of action, etc.). **under the weather** *colloq.* **1** slightly unwell. **2** in low spirits. **3** drunk. [Old English *weder*, from Germanic]

weather-beaten *adj.* affected by exposure to the weather.

weatherboard /ˈwɛðəbɔːd/ *n.* & *v.* esp. *Brit.* ● *n.* **1** a sloping board attached to the bottom of an outside door to keep out the rain etc. **2** each of a series of horizontal boards with edges overlapping to keep out the rain etc. ● *v.tr.* fit or supply with weatherboards. □ **weatherboarding** *n.* (in sense 2 of *n.*).

weather-bound *adj.* unable to proceed owing to bad weather.

weather chart *n.* a diagram showing the state of the weather over a large area.

weathercock /ˈwɛðəkɒk/ *n.* **1** a weathervane in the form of a cock. **2** an inconstant person.

weather forecast *n.* an analysis of the state of the weather with an assessment of likely developments over a certain time.

weathergirl see WEATHERMAN.

weather-glass *n.* a barometer.

weathering /ˈwɛð(ə)rɪŋ/ *n.* **1** the action of the weather on materials etc. exposed to it. **2** exposure to adverse weather conditions (see WEATHER *v.* 1).

weatherly /ˈwɛðəli/ *adj. Naut.* **1** (of a ship) making little leeway. **2** capable of keeping close to the wind. □ **weatherliness** *n.*

weatherman /ˈwɛðəman/ *n.* (*pl.* **-men**; *fem.* **weathergirl** /ˈwɛðəgəːl/) a meteorologist, esp. one who broadcasts a weather forecast.

weather map *n.* = WEATHER CHART.

weatherproof /ˈwɛðəpruːf/ *adj.* & *v.* ● *adj.* resistant to the effects of bad weather, esp. rain. ● *v.tr.* make weatherproof. □ **weatherproofed** *adj.*

weather side *n.* the side from which the wind is blowing (opp. *lee side*: see LEE 2).

weather station *n.* an observation post for recording meteorological data.

weatherstrip /ˈwɛðəstrɪp/ *n.* & *v.* ● *n.* a piece of material used to make a door or window proof against rain or wind. ● *v.tr.* (**-stripped, -stripping**) apply a weatherstrip to. □ **weatherstripping** *n.*

weathertight /ˈwɛθətʌɪt/ *adj.* (of a dwelling) proof against bad weather.

weather-tiles *n.pl.* tiles arranged to overlap like weatherboards.

weathervane /ˈwɛðəveɪn/ *n.* a revolving pointer mounted on a church spire or other high place to show the direction of the wind.

weather-worn *adj.* damaged by storms etc.

weave[1] /wiːv/ *v.* & *n.* ● *v.* (*past* **wove** /wəʊv/; *past part.* **woven** /ˈwəʊv(ə)n/ or **wove**) **1** *tr.* **a** form (fabric) by interlacing long threads in two directions. **b** form (thread) into fabric in this way. **2** *intr.* **a** make fabric in this way. **b** work at a loom. **3** *tr.* make (a basket or wreath etc.) by interlacing rods or flowers etc. **4** *tr.* **a** (foll. by *into*) make (facts etc.) into a story or connected whole. **b** make (a story) in this way. ● *n.* a style of weaving. [Old English *wefan*, from Germanic]

weave[2] /wiːv/ *v.intr.* **1** move repeatedly from side to side; take an intricate course to avoid obstructions. **2** *colloq.* manoeuvre an aircraft in this way; take evasive action. □ **get weaving** *Brit. slang* begin action; hurry. [probably from Middle English *weve*, variant of *waive*, from Old Norse *veifa* WAVE]

weaver /ˈwiːvə/ *n.* **1** a person whose occupation is weaving. **2** (in full **weaver-bird**) any tropical bird of the family Ploceidae, building elaborately woven nests.

weaver's knot *n.* a sheet bend used in weaving.

web /wɛb/ *n.* & *v.* ● *n.* **1** a network of fine threads constructed by a spider to catch its prey, from fluid secreted from its spinnerets. **2 a** a complete network or connected series (*a web of social problems*). **b** a snare or trap (*a web of deceit*). **3 a** a membrane between the toes of a swimming animal or bird. **b** the vane of a bird's feather. **4 a** a woven fabric. **b** an amount woven in one piece. **5 a** a large roll of paper used in a continuous printing process. **b** an endless wire mesh on rollers, on which this is made. **6** a thin flat part connecting thicker or more solid parts in machinery etc. ● *v.* (**webbed**, **webbing**) **1** *tr.* weave a web on. **2** *intr.* weave a web. [Old English *web*, *webb*, from Germanic]

webbed /wɛbd/ *adj.* **1 a** (of a bird's foot etc.) having the digits connected by a membrane or fold of skin. **b** (of fingers or toes) united by a fold of skin. **2** covered with or as if with a web.

webbing /ˈwɛbɪŋ/ *n.* strong narrow closely woven fabric used for supporting upholstery, for belts, etc.

weber /ˈveɪbə/ *n.* the SI unit of magnetic flux, causing the electromotive force of one volt in a circuit of one turn when generated or removed in one second (abbr.: Wb). [named after W. E. *Weber*, German physicist d. 1891]

web-footed *adj.* with webbed feet, having the toes connected by webs.

web offset *n.* offset printing on a web of paper.

web-wheel *n.* a wheel having a plate or web instead of spokes, or with rim, spokes, and centre in one piece as in the balance wheel of a clock or watch.

webwork /ˈwɛbwəːk/ *n.* a weblike mesh or system of links; a network.

webworm /ˈwɛbwəːm/ *n. US* a gregarious caterpillar spinning a large web in which to sleep or to feed on enclosed foliage.

Wed. *abbr.* Wednesday.

wed /wɛd/ *v.tr.* & *intr.* (**wedding**; *past* and *past part.* **wedded** or **wed**) **1** usu. *formal* or *literary* **a** *tr.* & *intr.* marry. **b** *tr.* join in marriage. **2** *tr.* unite (*wed efficiency to economy*). **3** *tr.* (as **wedded** *adj.*) of or in marriage (*wedded bliss*). **4** *tr.* (as **wedded** *adj.*) (foll. by *to*) obstinately attached or devoted (to a pursuit etc.). [Old English *weddian* 'to pledge', from Germanic]

we'd /wiːd, wɪd/ *contr.* **1** we had. **2** we should; we would.

wedding /ˈwɛdɪŋ/ *n.* a marriage ceremony (considered by itself or with the associated celebrations). [Old English *weddung* (as WED, -ING[1])]

wedding breakfast *n. Brit.* a meal etc. usually served between a wedding and the departure for the honeymoon.

wedding cake *n.* a rich iced cake served at a wedding reception.

wedding day *n.* the day or anniversary of a wedding.

wedding march *n.* a march played at the entrance of the bride or the exit of the couple at a wedding.

wedding night *n.* the night after a wedding (esp. with reference to its consummation).

wedding ring *n.* a ring worn by a married person.

wedge[1] /wɛdʒ/ *n.* & *v.* ● *n.* **1** a piece of wood or metal etc. tapering to a thin edge, that is driven between two objects or parts of an object to secure or separate them. **2** anything resembling or acting as a wedge (*a wedge of cheese*; *troops formed a wedge*; *drove an emotional wedge between them*). **3** a golf club with a wedge-shaped head. **4 a** a wedge-shaped heel. **b** a shoe with this. ● *v.tr.* **1** tighten, secure, or fasten by means of a wedge (*wedged the door open*). **2** force open or apart with a wedge. **3** (foll. by *in*, *into*) pack or thrust (a thing or oneself) tightly in or into. □ **thin end of the wedge** *colloq.* an action or procedure of little importance in itself, but likely to lead to more serious developments. □ **wedgelike** *adj.* **wedgewise** *adv.* [Old English *wecg*, from Germanic]

wedge[2] /wɛdʒ/ *v.tr.* prepare (pottery clay) for use by cutting, kneading, and throwing down. [17th c.: origin uncertain]

wedge-shaped *adj.* **1** shaped like a solid wedge. **2** V-shaped.

wedgie /ˈwɛdʒi/ *n. colloq.* a shoe with a wedge-shaped heel sometimes extending to a platform sole.

Wedgwood /ˈwɛdʒwʊd/ *n.* & *adj. propr.* ● *n.* **1** ceramic ware made by J. Wedgwood, English potter d. 1795, and his successors, esp. a kind of fine stoneware usu. with a white cameo design. **2** the characteristic blue colour of this stoneware. ● *adj.* of this colour.

wedlock /ˈwɛdlɒk/ *n.* the married state. □ **born in** (or **out of**) **wedlock** born of married (or unmarried) parents. [Old English *wedlāc* 'marriage vow', from *wed* 'pledge' (related to WED) + *-lāc* suffix denoting action]

Wednesday /ˈwɛnzdeɪ, -di/ *n.* & *adv.* ● *n.* the fourth day of the week, following Tuesday. ● *adv. colloq.* **1** on Wednesday. **2** (**Wednesdays**) on Wednesdays; each Wednesday. [Middle English *wednesdei*, Old English *wōdnesdæg* 'day of (the god) Odin']

Weds. *abbr.* Wednesday.

wee[1] /wiː/ *adj.* (**weer** /ˈwiːə/; **weest** /ˈwiːɪst/) **1** esp. *Sc.* little; very small. **2** *colloq.* tiny; extremely small (*a wee bit*). [originally Scots noun, from northern Middle English *wei* '(small) quantity' from Anglian *wēg*: cf. WEY]

wee[2] /wiː/ *n.* esp. *Brit. slang* = WEE-WEE.

weed /wiːd/ *n.* & *v.* ● *n.* **1** a wild plant growing where it is not wanted. **2 a** *colloq.* a thin weak-looking or contemptibly feeble person. **b** *slang* an inferior horse. **3** (prec. by *the*) *slang* **a** marijuana. **b** tobacco. ● *v.* **1** *tr.* **a** clear (an area) of weeds. **b** remove unwanted parts from. **2** *tr.* (foll. by *out*) **a** sort out (inferior or unwanted parts etc.) for removal. **b** rid (a quantity or company) of inferior or unwanted members etc. **3** *intr.* cut off or uproot weeds. □ **weeder** *n.* **weedless** *adj.* [Old English *wēod*, of unknown origin]

weed-grown *adj.* overgrown with weeds.

weedkiller /ˈwiːdkɪlə/ *n.* a substance used to destroy weeds.

weeds /wiːdz/ *n.pl.* (in full **widow's weeds**) *archaic* deep mourning worn by a widow. [Old English *wǣd(e)* 'garment', from Germanic]

weedy /ˈwiːdi/ *adj.* (**weedier**, **weediest**) **1** having many weeds. **2 a** weak-looking; of poor physique etc. **b** (of a person) feeble; lacking strength of character. □ **weediness** *n.*

week /wiːk/ *n.* **1** a period of seven days reckoned usu. from and to 24.00 hours on Saturday. **2** a period of seven days reckoned from any point (*would like to stay for a week*). **3** the six days between Sundays. **4 a** the five days from Monday to Friday. **b** the time spent working in this period (*a 35-hour week*). **5** (in *pl.*) a long time; several weeks (*have not seen you for weeks*; *did it weeks ago*). **6** (prec. by a specified day) esp. *Brit.* a week after (that day) (*Tuesday week*; *tomorrow week*). [Old English *wice* from a Germanic word, probably meaning 'sequence']

weekday /'wi:kdeɪ/ *n.* a day other than Sunday or other than Saturday and Sunday (often *attrib.*: *a weekday afternoon*).

weekend /wi:k'ɛnd, 'wi:-/ *n.* & *v.* ● *n.* **1** Saturday and Sunday. **2** this period extended slightly esp. for a holiday or visit etc. (*going away for the weekend*; *a weekend cottage*). ● *v.intr.* spend a weekend (*decided to weekend in the country*).

weekender /wi:k'ɛndə/ *n.* **1** a person who spends weekends away from home. **2** *Austral. colloq.* a holiday cottage. **3** a small pleasure boat, esp. one designed for private use at weekends.

week-long *adj.* lasting for a week.

weekly /'wi:kli/ *adj., adv.,* & *n.* ● *adj.* done, produced, or occurring once a week. ● *adv.* once a week; from week to week. ● *n.* (*pl.* **-ies**) a weekly newspaper or periodical.

ween /wi:n/ *v.tr. archaic* be of the opinion; think, suppose. [Old English *wēnan*, from Germanic]

weenie var. of WIENER.

weeny /'wi:ni/ *adj.* (**weenier**, **weeniest**) *colloq.* tiny. [WEE[1], on the pattern of *tiny*, *teeny*]

weeny-bopper *n. Brit.* a girl like a teeny-bopper but younger.

weep /wi:p/ *v.* & *n.* ● *v.* (*past* and *past part.* **wept** /wɛpt/) **1** *intr.* shed tears. **2 a** *tr.* & (foll. by *for*) *intr.* shed tears for; bewail, lament over. **b** *tr.* utter or express with tears (*'Don't go,' he wept*; *she wept her thanks*). **3 a** *intr.* be covered with or send forth drops. **b** *intr.* & *tr.* come or send forth in drops; exude liquid (*weeping sore*). **4** *intr.* (as **weeping** *adj.*) (of a tree or plant) having drooping branches (*weeping willow*; *weeping fig*). ● *n.* a fit or spell of weeping. ▫ **weep out** utter with tears. ▫ **weepingly** *adv.* [Old English *wēpan* from Germanic (probably imitative)]

weeper /'wi:pə/ *n.* **1** a person who weeps, esp. *hist.* a hired mourner at a funeral. **2** a small image of a mourner on a monument. **3** (in *pl.*) *hist.* **a** a man's crape hatband for funerals. **b** a widow's black crape veil or white cuffs.

weepie /'wi:pi/ *n.* (also **weepy**) (*pl.* **-ies**) *colloq.* a sentimental or emotional film, play, etc.

weepy /'wi:pi/ *adj.* (**weepier**, **weepiest**) *colloq.* inclined to weep; tearful. ▫ **weepily** *adv.* **weepiness** *n.*

weever /'wi:və/ *n.* any marine fish of the genus *Trachinus*, with sharp venomous dorsal spines. [perhaps via Old French *wivre*, *guivre* 'serpent, dragon', from Latin *vipera* VIPER]

weevil /'wi:v(ə)l, 'wi:vɪl/ *n.* **1** any beetle of the large family Curculionidae or a related family, with its head extended into a beak or rostrum, including many pests of stored grain etc. **2** any insect damaging stored grain. ▫ **weevily** *adj.* [Middle English via Middle Low German *wevel* from Germanic]

wee-wee /'wi:wi:/ *n.* & *v. slang* ● *n.* **1** the act or an instance of urinating. **2** urine. ● *v.intr.* (**-wees**, **-weed**) urinate. [20th c.: origin unknown]

w.e.f. *abbr. Brit.* with effect from.

weft[1] /wɛft/ *n.* **1 a** the threads woven across a warp to make fabric. **b** yarn for these. **c** a thing woven. **2** filling-strips in basket-weaving. [Old English *weft(a)* from Germanic: related to WEAVE[1]]

weft[2] var. of WAFT *n.* 3.

Wehrmacht /'vɛ:rmɑ:xt, German 've:rmaxt/ *n. hist.* the German armed forces, esp. the army, from 1921 to 1945. [German, = defensive force]

weigela /wʌɪ'dʒi:lə/ *n.* an oriental shrub of the genus *Weigela* (honeysuckle family) with red, pink, or white flowers, esp. *W. florida*, grown for ornament. [modern Latin, named after C.E. *Weigel*, German physician d. 1831]

weigh[1] /weɪ/ *v.* **1** *tr.* find the weight of. **2** *tr.* balance in the hands to guess or as if to guess the weight of. **3** *tr.* (often foll. by *out*) **a** take a definite weight of; take a specified weight from a larger quantity. **b** distribute in exact amounts by weight. **4** *tr.* **a** estimate the relative value, importance, or desirability of; consider with a view to choice, rejection, or preference (*weighed the consequences*; *weighed the merits of the candidates*). **b** (foll. by *with*, *against*) compare (one consideration with another). **5** *tr.* be equal to (a specified weight) (*weighs three kilos*; *weighs very little*). **6** *intr.* **a** have (esp. a specified) importance; exert an influence. **b** (foll. by *with*) be regarded as important by (*the point that weighs with me*). **7** *intr.* (often foll. by *on*) be heavy or burdensome (to); be depressing (to). ▫ **weigh anchor** see ANCHOR. **weigh down 1** bring or keep down by exerting weight. **2** be oppressive or burdensome to (*weighed down with worries*). **weigh in** (of a boxer before a contest, or a jockey after a race) be weighed. **weigh into** *colloq.* attack (physically or verbally). **weigh in with** *colloq.* advance (an argument etc.) assertively or boldly. **weigh out** (of a jockey) be weighed before a race. **weigh up** *colloq.* form an estimate of; consider carefully. **weigh one's words** carefully choose the way one expresses something. ▫ **weighable** *adj.* **weigher** *n.* [Old English *wegan* from Germanic: related to WAY]

weigh[2] /weɪ/ *n.* ▫ **under weigh** *Naut. disp.* = *under way* (see UNDER). [18th c.: from an erroneous association with *weigh anchor*]

weighbridge /'weɪbrɪdʒ/ *n.* a weighing machine for vehicles, usu. having a plate set into the road for vehicles to drive on to.

weigh-in *n.* the weighing of a boxer before a fight.

weighing machine *n.* a machine for weighing persons or large weights.

weight /weɪt/ *n.* & *v.* ● *n.* **1** *Physics* **a** the force experienced by a body as a result of the earth's gravitation (cf. MASS *n.* 8). **b** any similar force with which a body tends to a centre of attraction. **2** the heaviness of a body regarded as a property of it; its relative mass or the quantity of matter contained by it giving rise to a downward force (*is twice your weight*; *kept in position by its weight*). **3 a** the quantitative expression of a body's weight (*has a weight of three pounds*). **b** a scale of such weights (*troy weight*). **4** a body of a known weight for use in weighing. **5** a heavy body esp. used in a mechanism etc. (*a clock worked by weights*). **6** a load or burden (*a weight off my mind*). **7 a** influence, importance (*carried weight with the public*). **b** preponderance (*the weight of evidence was against them*). **8 a** a heavy object thrown as an athletic exercise; = SHOT[1] 7. **b** (in *pl.*) blocks or discs of metal etc. used in weightlifting or weight training. **9** the surface density of cloth etc. as a measure of its suitability. ● *v.tr.* **1 a** attach a weight to. **b** hold down with a weight or weights. **2** (foll. by *with*) impede or burden. **3** *Statistics* multiply the components of (an average) by factors to take account of their importance. **4** assign a handicap weight to (a horse). **5** treat (a fabric) with a mineral etc. to make it seem stouter. ▫ **put on weight 1** increase one's weight. **2** become fat or fatter. **throw one's weight about** (or **around**) *colloq.* be unpleasantly self-assertive. **worth one's weight in gold** (of a person) exceedingly useful or helpful. [Old English *(ge)wiht* from Germanic: the modern form influenced by WEIGH[1]]

weight gain *n.* an increase in body weight.

weighting /'weɪtɪŋ/ *n. Brit.* an extra allowance paid in special cases, esp. to allow for a higher cost of living (*London weighting*).

weightless /'weɪtlɪs/ *adj.* (of a body, esp. in an orbiting spacecraft etc.) not apparently acted on by gravity. ▫ **weightlessly** *adv.* **weightlessness** *n.*

weightlifting /'weɪtlɪftɪŋ/ *n.* the sport of lifting a heavy weight, esp. a barbell. ▫ **weightlifter** *n.*

weight loss *n.* a decrease in body weight.

weight training *n.* physical training involving the use of weights.

weight-watcher *n.* a person who is habitually concerned about his or her weight or who tries to lose weight, esp. by dieting. ▫ **weight-watching** *n. & adj.*

weighty /ˈweɪti/ *adj.* (**weightier**, **weightiest**) **1** weighing much; heavy. **2** momentous, important. **3** (of utterances etc.) deserving consideration; careful and serious. **4** influential, authoritative. ▫ **weightily** *adv.* **weightiness** *n.*

Weil's disease /vʌɪlz/ *n. Med.* a severe, sometimes fatal, form of leptospirosis transmitted by rats via contaminated water. [named after H.A. *Weil*, German physician d. 1916]

Weimaraner /vʌɪməˈrɑːnə, wʌɪ-/ *n.* a usu. grey dog of a variety of pointer used as a gun dog. [German, from *Weimar* in Germany, where it was developed]

weir /wɪə/ *n.* **1** a dam built across a river to raise the level of water upstream or regulate its flow. **2** an enclosure of stakes etc. set in a stream as a trap for fish. [Old English *wer* from *werian* 'dam up']

weird /wɪəd/ *adj. & n.* ● *adj.* **1** uncanny, supernatural. **2** *colloq.* strange, queer, incomprehensible. **3** *archaic* connected with fate. ● *n.* esp. *Sc. archaic* fate, destiny. ▫ **weirdly** *adv.* **weirdness** *n.* [(earlier as noun): Old English *wyrd* 'destiny', from Germanic]

weirdie /ˈwɪədi/ *n.* (also **weirdy**) (*pl.* **-ies**) *colloq.* = WEIRDO.

weirdo /ˈwɪədəʊ/ *n.* (*pl.* **-os**) *colloq.* an odd or eccentric person.

weird sisters *n.pl.* (prec. by *the*) **1** the Fates. **2** witches.

Weismannism /ˈvʌɪsmənɪz(ə)m/ *n.* the theory of heredity assuming continuity of germ plasm and non-transmission of acquired characteristics. [named after A. *Weismann*, German biologist d. 1914]

weka /ˈwɛkə/ *n.* a large flightless New Zealand rail, *Gallirallus australis*. [Maori: imitative of its cry]

Welch /wɛlʃ/ var. of WELSH (now only in *Royal Welch Fusiliers*).

welch var. of WELSH.

welcome /ˈwɛlkəm/ *n., int., v., & adj.* ● *n.* the act or an instance of greeting or receiving (a person, idea, etc.) gladly; a kind or glad reception (*gave them a warm welcome*). ● *int.* expressing such a greeting (*welcome!*; *welcome home!*). ● *v.tr.* receive with a welcome (*welcomed them home*; *would welcome the opportunity*). ● *adj.* **1** that one receives with pleasure (*a welcome guest*; *welcome news*). **2** (foll. by *to*, or *to* + infin.) **a** cordially allowed or invited; released of obligation (*you are welcome to use my car*). **b** *iron.* gladly given (an unwelcome task, thing, etc.) (*here's my work and you are welcome to it*). ▫ **make welcome** receive hospitably. **outstay one's welcome** stay too long as a visitor etc. **you are welcome** there is no need for thanks. ▫ **welcomely** *adv.* **welcomeness** *n.* **welcomer** *n.* **welcomingly** *adv.* [originally Old English *wilcuma* 'a person whose coming is pleasing', from *wil-* 'desire, pleasure' + *cuma* 'comer', with later change to *wel-* WELL[1] influenced by Old French *bien venu* or Old Norse *velkominn*]

weld[1] /wɛld/ *v. & n.* ● *v.tr.* **1 a** hammer or press (pieces of iron or other metal usu. heated but not melted) into one piece. **b** join by fusion with an electric arc etc. **c** forge (an article) by welding. **2** fashion (arguments, members of a group, etc.) into an effectual or homogeneous whole. ● *n.* a welded joint. ▫ **weldable** *adj.* **weldability** /-ˈbɪlɪti/ *n.* **welder** *n.* [alteration of WELL[2] *v.* in obsolete sense 'melt or weld (heated metal)', probably influenced by past part.]

weld[2] /wɛld/ *n.* **1** a plant, *Reseda luteola*, yielding a yellow dye. **2** *hist.* this dye. [Middle English probably from Old English: cf. Middle Dutch *woude*, Middle Low German *walde*]

welfare /ˈwɛlfɛː/ *n.* **1** well-being, happiness; health and prosperity (of a person or a community etc.). **2** (**Welfare**) **a** the maintenance of persons in such a condition esp. by statutory procedure or social effort. **b** financial support given for this purpose. [Middle English, from WELL[1] + FARE]

welfare state *n.* **1** a system whereby the state undertakes to protect the health and well-being of its citizens, esp. those in financial or social need, by means of grants, pensions, etc. **2** a country practising this system.

welfare work *n.* organized effort for the welfare of the poor, disabled, etc.

welfarism /ˈwɛlfɛːrɪz(ə)m/ *n.* principles characteristic of a welfare state. ▫ **welfarist** *n.*

welkin /ˈwɛlkɪn/ *n. poet.* the sky; the upper air. [Old English *wolcen* 'cloud, sky']

well[1] /wɛl/ *adv., adj., & int.* ● *adv.* (**better**, **best**) **1** in a satisfactory way (*you have worked well*). **2** in the right way (*well said*; *you did well to tell me*). **3** with some talent or distinction (*plays the piano well*). **4** in a kind way (*treated me well*). **5** thoroughly, extensively, soundly (*polish it well*; *team was well beaten*). **6** with heartiness or approval; favourably (*speak well of*; *the book was well reviewed*). **7** probably, reasonably, advisably (*you may well be right*; *you may well ask*; *we might well take the risk*). **8** to a considerable extent (*is well over forty*). **9** successfully, fortunately (*it turned out well*). **10** luckily, opportunely (*well met!*). **11** with a fortunate outcome; without disaster (*were well rid of them*). **12** profitably (*did well for themselves*). **13** comfortably, abundantly, liberally (*we live well here*; *the job pays well*). **14** *slang* (as an intensifier) very, extremely (*was kept well busy*). ● *adj.* (**better**, **best**) **1** (usu. *predic.*) in good health (*are you well?*; *was not a well person*). **2** (*predic.*) **a** in a satisfactory state or position (*all is well*). **b** advisable (*it would be well to enquire*). ● *int.* expressing surprise, resignation, insistence, etc., or used merely to introduce a remark, though sometimes also to express acceptance of or to qualify a situation or foregoing remark (*well I never!*; *well, I suppose so*; *well, who was it?*). ▫ **as well 1** in addition; to an equal extent. **2** (also **just as well**) with equal reason; with no loss of advantage or need for regret (*may as well give up*; *it would be just as well to stop now*). **as well as** in addition to. **leave** (or **let**) **well alone** avoid needless change or disturbance. **well and good** expressing dispassionate acceptance of a decision etc. **well and truly** decisively, completely. **well away 1** having made considerable progress. **2** *Brit. colloq.* fast asleep or drunk. **well worth** certainly worth (*well worth a visit*; *well worth visiting*). ▫ **wellness** *n.* [Old English *wel*, *well* probably from the same stem as WILL[1]]

■ **Usage** A hyphen is normally used in combinations of *well-* when used attributively, but not when used predicatively, e.g. *a well-made coat* but *the coat is well made*.

well[2] /wɛl/ *n. & v.* ● *n.* **1** a shaft sunk into the ground to obtain water, oil, etc. **2** an enclosed space like a well-shaft, e.g. in the middle of a building for stairs or a lift, or for light or ventilation. **3** (foll. by *of*) a source, esp. a copious one (*a well of information*). **4 a** a mineral spring. **b** (in *pl.*) a spa. **5** = INKWELL. **6** *archaic* a water-spring or fountain. **7** *Brit.* a railed space for solicitors etc. in a law court. **8** a depression for gravy etc. in a dish or tray, or for a mat in the floor. **9** *Physics* a region of minimum potential etc. ● *v.intr.* (foll. by *out*, *up*) spring as from a fountain; flow copiously. [Old English *wella* (= Old High German *wella* 'wave', Old Norse *vella* 'boiling heat'), *wellan* 'boil, melt', from Germanic]

we'll /wiːl, wɪl/ *contr.* we shall; we will.

well acquainted *predic.adj.* (usu. foll. by *with*) familiar.

well-adjusted *adj.* (**well adjusted** when *predic.*) **1** mentally and emotionally stable. **2** in a good state of adjustment.

well advised *predic.adj.* (usu. foll. by *to* + infin.) (of a person) prudent (*would be well advised to wait*).

well-appointed *adj.* (**well appointed** when *predic.*) having all the necessary equipment.

well-attended *adj.* (**well attended** when *predic.*) (of a meeting etc.) attended by a large number of people.

well aware *predic.adj.* (often foll. by *of*) certainly aware (*well aware of the danger*).

well-balanced *adj.* (**well balanced** when *predic.*) **1** sane, sensible. **2** equally matched.

well-behaved *adj.* (**well behaved** when *predic.*) having good manners or conduct.

well-being *n.* a state of being well, healthy, contented, etc.

well-beloved *adj.* & *n.* ● *adj.* (**well beloved** when *predic.*) dearly loved. ● *n.* (*pl.* same) a dearly loved person.

well-born *adj.* (**well born** when *predic.*) of noble or *US* wealthy family.

well-bred *adj.* (**well bred** when *predic.*) having or showing good breeding or manners.

well-built *adj.* (**well built** when *predic.*) **1** of good construction. **2** (of a person) big and strong and well-proportioned.

well-chosen *adj.* (**well chosen** when *predic.*) carefully selected, esp. for effect (*a well-chosen remark*; *the location was well chosen*).

well-conditioned *adj.* in good physical or moral condition.

well-conducted *adj.* (**well conducted** when *predic.*) (of a meeting etc.) properly organized and controlled.

well-connected *adj.* associated, esp. by birth, with persons of good social position.

well-constructed *adj.* (**well constructed** when *predic.*) **1** (of a building, furniture, etc.) constructed in a sound or practical way. **2** (of a text) with a clear or carefully-planned structure.

well covered *adj.* (hyphenated when *attrib.*) *Brit. colloq.* plump, corpulent.

well-cut *adj.* (**well cut** when *predic.*) **1** (of a garment) well-tailored. **2** (esp. of hair) cut skilfully.

well deck *n.* an open space on the main deck of a ship, lying at a lower level between the forecastle and poop.

well-defined *adj.* (**well defined** when *predic.*) clearly indicated or determined.

well-deserved *adj.* (**well deserved** when *predic.*) rightfully merited or earned.

well-designed *adj.* (**well designed** when *predic.*) **1** (of furniture, living space, etc.) designed for practical use. **2** of a good design (*well-designed poster*).

well-developed *adj.* (**well developed** when *predic.*) **1** fully developed, fully grown. **2** of generous size.

well disposed *adj.* (hyphenated when *attrib.*; often foll. by *towards*) having a good disposition or friendly feeling (for).

well done *adj.* (hyphenated when *attrib.*) **1** (of meat etc.) thoroughly cooked. **2** (of a task etc.) performed well (also as *int.*).

well-dressed *adj.* fashionably smart.

well-earned *adj.* (**well earned** when *predic.*) fully deserved.

well-educated *adj.* (**well educated** when *predic.*) educated to a high level; with a wide knowledge.

well-endowed *adj.* (**well endowed** when *predic.*) **1** (often foll. by *with*) well provided with money, a resource, etc. **2** *colloq.* **a** (of a man) having large genitals. **b** (of a woman) large-breasted.

well-equipped *adj.* (**well equipped** when *predic.*) having a plentiful supply of equipment.

well-established *adj.* (**well established** when *predic.*) well-authenticated; long-standing.

well-favoured *adj.* (*US* **well-favored**) good-looking.

well-fed *adj.* (**well fed** when *predic.*) having or having had plenty to eat.

well fitted *adj.* (hyphenated when *attrib.*) **1** fitted or fitted out well. **2** suitable, suited.

well-fitting *adj.* (**well fitting** when *predic.*) that is a good fit.

well-formed *adj.* (**well formed** when *predic.*) **1** correctly or attractively formed. **2** conforming to the formation rules of a logical system.

well-found *adj.* = WELL-APPOINTED.

well-founded *adj.* (**well founded** when *predic.*) (of suspicions etc.) based on good evidence; having a foundation in fact or reason.

well-groomed *adj.* (**well groomed** when *predic.*) (of a person) with carefully tended hair, clothes, etc.

well-grounded *adj.* (**well grounded** when *predic.*) **1** = WELL-FOUNDED. **2** having a good training in or knowledge of the groundwork of a subject.

well-head *n.* a source.

well-heeled *adj. colloq.* wealthy.

well-hung *adj.* (**well hung** when *predic.*) **1** *colloq.* (of a man) having large genitals. **2** (of meat or game) hung up for a sufficient time.

wellie var. of WELLY.

well-informed *adj.* (**well informed** when *predic.*) having much knowledge or information about a subject.

wellington /ˈwɛlɪŋtən/ *n.* (in full **wellington boot**) *Brit.* a waterproof rubber or plastic boot usu. reaching the knee. [named after the 1st Duke of *Wellington*, British general and statesman d. 1852]

well-intentioned *adj.* (**well intentioned** when *predic.*) having or showing good intentions.

well-judged *adj.* (**well judged** when *predic.*) opportunely, skilfully, or discreetly done.

well-kept *adj.* (**well kept** when *predic.*) kept in good order or condition.

well-knit *adj.* (esp. of a person) compact; not loose-jointed or sprawling.

well-known *adj.* (**well known** when *predic.*) **1** known to many. **2** known thoroughly.

well-liked *adj.* (**well liked** when *predic.*) (esp. of a person) liked; popular.

well-loved *adj.* (**well loved** when *predic.*) regarded with great affection or approval.

well-made *adj.* (**well made** when *predic.*) **1** strongly or skilfully manufactured. **2** (of a person or animal) having a good build.

well-maintained *adj.* (**well maintained** when *predic.*) **1** kept in good repair. **2** kept up to date (*well-maintained inventory*).

well-mannered *adj.* (**well mannered** when *predic.*) having good manners.

well-marked *adj.* (**well marked** when *predic.*) distinct; easy to detect.

well-matched *adj.* (**well matched** when *predic.*) fit to contend with each other, live together, etc., on equal terms.

well-meaning *adj.* (also **well-meant**) (**well meaning**, **well meant** when *predic.*) well-intentioned (but ineffective or unwise).

well-nigh *adv. archaic* or *literary* almost (*well-nigh impossible*).

well-off *adj.* (**well off** when *predic.*) **1** having plenty of money. **2** in a fortunate situation or circumstances.

well-oiled *adj.* (**well oiled** when *predic.*) *colloq.* **1** drunk. **2** (of an organization etc.) running smoothly.

well-ordered *adj.* (**well ordered** when *predic.*) arranged in an orderly manner.

well-organized *adj.* (also **-ised**) (**well organized** when *predic.*) **1** skilfully or carefully organized. **2** (of a person) orderly; able to organize personal activities.

well-paid *adj.* (**well paid** when *predic.*) **1** (of a job) that pays well. **2** (of a person) amply rewarded for a job.

well placed *adj.* (hyphenated when *attrib.*) **1** set in a good place or position. **2** holding a good social position. **3** (foll. by *to* + infin.) easily able (*you are well placed to know*).

well-planned *adj.* (**well planned** when *predic.*) **1** (of living space etc.) of careful or practical design. **2** (of an event, programme, etc.) planned in a carefully-structured way.

well pleased *predic.adj.* highly gratified or satisfied.

well-prepared *adj.* (**well prepared** when *predic.*) **1** prepared with care. **2** having prepared thoroughly (for an interview etc.).

well-preserved *adj.* (**well preserved** when *predic.*) (of an elderly person) showing little sign of ageing.

well-qualified *adj.* (**well qualified** when *predic.*) **1** holding many or prestigious qualifications. **2** (foll. by *to* + infin.) able through acquired expertise.

well-read *adj.* (**well read** when *predic.*) knowledgeable through much reading.

well received *adj.* (hyphenated when *attrib.*) welcomed; favourably received.

well-rounded *adj.* (**well rounded** when *predic.*) **1** complete and symmetrical. **2** (of a phrase etc.) complete and well expressed. **3** (of a person) having or showing a fully developed personality, ability, etc.

well spent *adj.* (hyphenated when *attrib.*) (esp. of money or time) used profitably.

well-spoken *adj.* articulate or refined in speech.

wellspring /ˈwɛlsprɪŋ/ *n.* = WELL-HEAD.

well-stocked *adj.* (**well stocked** when *predic.*) (of a shop, garden, etc.) plentifully filled with goods, plants, etc.

well-structured *adj.* (**well structured** when *predic.*) **1** (esp. of a text) having a clear structure. **2** well-organized.

well-supported *adj.* (**well supported** when *predic.*) **1** attended by many. **2** supported by much evidence.

well-taken *adj.* (**well taken** when *predic.*) **1** (of a catch, goal, etc.) skilfully executed. **2** (of an argument etc.) accepted as valid.

well thought of *adj.* (hyphenated when *attrib.*) having a good reputation; esteemed, respected.

well thought out *adj.* (hyphenated when *attrib.*) carefully devised.

well-thumbed *adj.* (**well thumbed** when *predic.*) bearing marks of frequent handling.

well-timed *adj.* (**well timed** when *predic.*) opportune, timely.

well-to-do *adj.* prosperous.

well-travelled *adj.* (*US* **well-traveled**) **1** having travelled widely. **2** (of a path etc.) much frequented.

well-tried *adj.* (**well tried** when *predic.*) often tested with good results.

well-trodden *adj.* much frequented.

well-turned *adj.* (**well turned** when *predic.*) **1** (of a compliment, phrase, or verse) elegantly expressed. **2** (of a leg, ankle, etc.) elegantly shaped or displayed.

well-upholstered *adj.* (**well upholstered** when *attrib.*) **1** (of a chair etc.) padded, comfortable. **2** *joc.* (of a person) fat.

well-used *adj.* **1** much frequented. **2** much handled or worn.

well-wisher *n.* a person who wishes one well.

well woman *attrib.adj. Brit.* designating a clinic etc. providing health advice and check-ups for problems specific to women.

well-worn *adj.* (**well worn** when *predic.*) **1** damaged by use or wear. **2** (of a phrase, joke, etc.) trite, hackneyed; stale.

well-wrought *adj.* (**well wrought** when *predic.*) skilfully constructed.

welly /ˈwɛli/ *n.* (also **wellie**) (*pl.* **-ies**) *colloq.* = WELLINGTON. □ **give it some welly** an expression of encouragement to use more effort, strength, etc. [abbreviation]

wels /wɛls, vɛls/ *n.* a very large freshwater catfish, *Silurus glanis*, found from central Europe to central Asia. [German]

Welsh /wɛlʃ/ *adj.* & *n.* ● *adj.* of or relating to Wales or its people or language. ● *n.* **1** the Celtic language of Wales. **2** (prec. by *the*; treated as *pl.*) the people of Wales. □ **Welshness** *n.* [Old English *Welisc*, *Wælisc*, etc., via a Germanic word meaning 'foreign' from Latin *Volcae*, the name of a Celtic people]

welsh /wɛlʃ/ *v.intr.* (also **welch** /wɛltʃ/) **1** (of a loser of a bet, esp. a bookmaker) decamp without paying. **2** evade an obligation. **3** (foll. by *on*) **a** fail to carry out a promise to (a person). **b** fail to honour (an obligation). □ **welsher** *n.* [19th c.: origin unknown]

Welsh corgi see CORGI.

Welsh dresser *n.* a type of dresser with open shelves above a cupboard.

Welsh harp *n.* a harp with three rows of strings.

Welshman /ˈwɛlʃmən/ *n.* (*pl.* **-men**) a man who is Welsh by birth or descent.

Welsh onion *n.* a species of onion, *Allium fistulosum*, forming clusters of bulbs.

Welsh rabbit *n.* (also **Welsh rarebit** by folk etymology) a dish of melted cheese etc. on toast.

Welshwoman /ˈwɛlʃwʊmən/ *n.* (*pl.* **-women**) a woman who is Welsh by birth or descent.

welt /wɛlt/ *n.* & *v.* ● *n.* **1** a leather rim sewn round the edge of a shoe-upper for the sole to be attached to. **2** = WEAL[1]. **3** a ribbed or reinforced border of a garment; a trimming. **4** a heavy blow. ● *v.tr.* **1** provide with a welt. **2** rain welts on; thrash. [Middle English *welte*, *walt*, of unknown origin]

Weltanschauung /ˈvɛltanˌʃaʊʊŋ/ *n.* (*pl.* ***Weltanschauungen*** /-ən/) a particular philosophy or view of life; a conception of the world. [German, from *Welt* 'world' + *Anschauung* 'perception']

welter[1] /ˈwɛltə/ *v.* & *n.* ● *v.intr.* **1** roll, wallow; be washed about. **2** (foll. by *in*) lie prostrate or be soaked or steeped in blood etc. ● *n.* **1** a state of general confusion. **2** (foll. by *of*) a disorderly mixture or contrast of beliefs, policies, etc. [Middle English from Middle Dutch, Middle Low German *welteren*]

welter[2] /ˈwɛltə/ *n.* **1** a heavy rider or boxer. **2** *Brit. colloq.* a heavy blow. **3** *Brit. colloq.* a big person or thing. [19th c.: origin unknown]

welterweight /ˈwɛltəweɪt/ *n.* **1** a weight in certain sports intermediate between lightweight and middleweight, in the amateur boxing scale 63.5–67 kg but differing for professionals, wrestlers, and weightlifters. **2** a sportsman of this weight.

Weltschmerz /ˈvɛltʃmɛːts, *German* ˈvɛltʃmɛrts/ *n.* a feeling of pessimism; an apathetic or vaguely yearning outlook on life. [German, from *Welt* 'world' + *Schmerz* 'pain']

Wemba-wemba /ˈwɛmbəˌwɛmbə/ *n.* an Aboriginal language of SE Australia, now extinct.

wen[1] /wɛn/ *n.* **1** a benign tumour on the skin esp. of the scalp. **2** an outstandingly large or congested city. [Old English *wen*, *wenn*, of unknown origin: cf. Dutch *wen*, Middle Low German *wene*, Low German *wehne* 'tumour, wart']

wen[2] /wɛn/ *n.* (also **wyn** /wɪn/) a runic letter in Old and Middle English, later replaced by *w*. [Old English, variant of *wyn* 'joy' (see WINSOME), used because it begins with this letter: cf. THORN 3]

wench /wɛn(t)ʃ/ *n.* & *v.* ● *n.* **1** *joc.* a girl or young woman. **2** *archaic* a prostitute. ● *v.intr. archaic* (of a man) consort with prostitutes. □ **wencher** *n.* [Middle English *wenche*, *wenchel* from Old English *wencel* 'child': cf. Old English *wancol* 'weak, tottering']

Wend /wɛnd/ *n.* a member of a Slavic people of N. Germany, now inhabiting E. Saxony. □ **Wendic** *adj.* **Wendish** *adj.* [German *Wende* from Old High German *Winida*, of unknown origin]

wend /wɛnd/ *v.tr.* & *intr. literary* or *archaic* go. □ **wend one's way** make one's way. [Old English *wendan* 'to turn' from Germanic: related to WIND[2]]

Wendy house /ˈwɛndi/ *n. Brit.* a children's small houselike tent or structure for playing in. [after the house built around *Wendy* in Barrie's play *Peter Pan*]

Wensleydale /ˈwɛnzlɪdeɪl/ *n.* **1** a variety of white or blue cheese. **2** **a** a sheep of a breed with long wool. **b** this breed. [*Wensleydale* in Yorkshire]

went *past* of GO[1].

wentletrap /ˈwɛnt(ə)ltrap/ *n.* any marine snail of the genus *Clathrus*, with a spiral shell of many whorls. [Dutch *wenteltrap* 'winding stair, spiral shell']

wept *past* of WEEP.

were *2nd sing. past, pl. past, and past subjunctive* of BE.

we're /wɪə/ *contr.* we are.

weren't /wəːnt/ *contr.* were not.

werewolf /ˈwɛːwʊlf, ˈwɪə-, ˈwəː-/ *n.* (also **werwolf** /ˈwəː-/) (*pl.* **-wolves**) a mythical being who at times changes from a person to a wolf. [Old English *werewulf*: first element perhaps from Old English *wer* 'man' = Latin *vir*]

wert /wəːt/ *archaic 2nd sing. past* of BE.

Wesleyan /ˈwɛzlɪən, ˈwɛs-/ *adj. & n.* ● *adj.* of or relating to a Protestant denomination founded by the English evangelist John Wesley (d. 1791) (cf. METHODIST). ● *n.* a member of this denomination. □ **Wesleyanism** *n.*

west /wɛst/ *n., adj., & adv.* ● *n.* **1 a** the point of the horizon where the sun sets at the equinoxes (cardinal point 90° to the left of north). **b** the compass point corresponding to this. **c** the direction in which this lies. **2** (usu. **the West**) **a** European in contrast to oriental civilization. **b** *hist.* the non-Communist states of Europe and N. America. **c** non-Communist states or regions in general. **d** the western part of the late Roman Empire. **e** the western part of a country, town, etc. **3** *Bridge* a player occupying the position designated 'west'. ● *adj.* **1** towards, at, near, or facing west. **2** coming from the west (*west wind*). ● *adv.* **1** towards, at, or near the west. **2** (foll. by *of*) further west than. □ **go west** *Brit. slang* be killed or destroyed etc. [Old English from Germanic]

West Bank *n.* a region west of the River Jordan assigned to Jordan in 1948 and occupied by Israel since 1967.

westbound /ˈwɛs(t)baʊnd/ *adj.* travelling or leading westwards.

West Country *n.* the south-western counties of England.

West End *n.* the entertainment and shopping area of London to the west of the City.

westering /ˈwɛst(ə)rɪŋ/ *adj.* (of the sun) nearing the west. [from Middle English *wester* (*v.*), from WEST]

westerly /ˈwɛstəli/ *adj., adv., & n.* ● *adj. & adv.* **1** in a western position or direction. **2** (of a wind) blowing from the west. ● *n.* (*pl.* **-ies**) a wind blowing from the west. [*wester* (*adj.*) from Old English *westra*, from WEST]

western /ˈwɛst(ə)n/ *adj. & n.* ● *adj.* **1** of or in the west; inhabiting the west. **2** lying or directed towards the west. **3** (**Western**) of or relating to the West (see WEST *n.* 2). ● *n.* a film, television drama, or novel about cowboys in western North America. □ **westernmost** *adj.* [Old English *westerne* (as WEST, -ERN)]

Western Church *n.* the part of Christendom that has continued to derive its authority, doctrine, and ritual from the popes in Rome.

westerner /ˈwɛst(ə)nə/ *n.* a native or inhabitant of the west.

western hemisphere *n.* the half of the earth containing the Americas.

westernize /ˈwɛstənʌɪz/ *v.tr.* (also **Westernize, -ise**) influence with or convert to the ideas and customs etc. of the West. □ **westernization** /-ˈzeɪʃ(ə)n/ *n.* **westernizer** *n.*

Western roll *n.* a technique of turning the body over the bar in a high jump.

West Germanic *n. & adj.* ● *n.* the western group of Germanic languages, comprising High and Low German, English, Frisian, and Dutch. ● *adj.* of or relating to West Germanic.

West Indian *n.* **1** a native or national of any island of the West Indies. **2** a person of West Indian descent.

West Indian satinwood see SATINWOOD 1b.

West Indies *n.pl.* the islands of Central America, including Cuba and the Bahamas.

westing /ˈwɛstɪŋ/ *n. Naut.* the distance travelled or the angle of longitude measured westward from either a defined north–south grid line or a meridian.

Westminster /ˈwɛs(t)mɪnstə/ *n.* the Parliament at Westminster in London.

west-north-west *n.* the direction or compass point midway between west and north-west.

West Side *n. US* the western part of Manhattan.

west-south-west *n.* the direction or compass point midway between west and south-west.

westward /ˈwɛstwəd/ *adj., adv., & n.* ● *adj. & adv.* (also **westwards**) towards the west. ● *n.* a westward direction or region.

wet /wɛt/ *adj., v., & n.* ● *adj.* (**wetter, wettest**) **1** soaked, covered, or dampened with water or other liquid (*a wet sponge*; *a wet surface*; *got my feet wet*). **2** (of the weather etc.) rainy (*a wet day*). **3** (of paint, ink, etc.) not yet dried. **4** used with water (*wet shampoo*). **5** *Brit. colloq.* feeble, inept. **6** *Brit. Polit. colloq.* Conservative with liberal tendencies, esp. as regarded by right-wing Conservatives. **7** *slang* (of a country, of legislation, etc.) allowing the free sale of alcoholic drink. **8** (of a baby or young child) incontinent (*is still wet at night*). ● *v.tr.* (**wetting**; *past* and *past part.* **wet** or **wetted**) **1** make wet. **2 a** urinate in or on (*wet the bed*). **b** *refl.* urinate involuntarily. ● *n.* **1** moisture; liquid that wets something. **2** rainy weather; a time of rain. **3** *Brit. colloq.* a feeble or inept person. **4** *Brit. Polit. colloq.* a Conservative with liberal tendencies (see sense 6 of *adj.*). **5** *Brit. colloq.* a drink. □ **wet the baby's head** *Brit. colloq.* celebrate its birth with a (usu. alcoholic) drink. **wet behind the ears** immature, inexperienced. **wet through** (or **to the skin**) with one's clothes soaked. **wet one's whistle** *colloq.* drink. □ **wetly** *adv.* **wetness** *n.* **wettable** *adj.* **wetting** *n.* **wettish** *adj.* [Old English *wǣt* (*adj.* & *n.*), *wǣtan* (*v.*), related to WATER]

weta /ˈwɛtə/ *n.* a large wingless insect of New Zealand, of the family Stenopelmatidae, resembling a grasshopper with long spiny legs and wood-boring grubs. [Maori]

wetback /ˈwɛtbak/ *n. US colloq.* an illegal immigrant from Mexico to the US. [WET + BACK, from the practice of swimming the Rio Grande to reach the US]

wet blanket *n. colloq.* a gloomy person preventing the enjoyment of others.

wet dock *n.* a dock in which a ship can float.

wet dream *n.* an erotic dream with involuntary ejaculation of semen.

wet fly *n.* an artificial fly used under water by an angler.

wether /ˈwɛðə/ *n.* a castrated ram. [Old English from Germanic]

wetland /ˈwɛtlənd/ *n.* (usu. in *pl.*) a swamp, marsh, or other usually saturated area of land.

wet look *n. & adj.* ● *n.* **1** a shiny surface given esp. to clothing materials. **2** a shiny or wet appearance achieved by applying a type of gel to the hair. ● *attrib.adj.* (**wet-look**) having or giving a shiny or wet appearance.

wet-nurse *n. & v.* ● *n.* a woman employed to suckle another's child. ● *v.tr.* **1** act as a wet-nurse to. **2** *colloq.* treat as if helpless.

wet pack *n.* the therapeutic wrapping of the body in wet cloths etc.

wet rot *n.* **1** a brown rot affecting moist timber. **2** the fungus causing this, often *Coniophora puteana*.

wetsuit /ˈwɛtsuːt, -sjuːt/ *n.* a close-fitting rubber garment worn for warmth in water sports, diving, etc.

wetting agent *n.* a substance that helps water etc. to spread or penetrate.

wet-weather *attrib.adj.* **1** for use in wet weather. **2** occurring in wet weather.

we've /wiːv, wɪv/ *contr.* we have.

wey /weɪ/ *n.* a former unit of weight or volume varying with different kinds of goods, e.g. 3 cwt. of cheese. [Old

English *wǣg(e)* 'balance, weight', from Germanic: related to WEIGH[1]]

w.f. *abbr. Printing* wrong fount.

WFTU *abbr.* World Federation of Trade Unions.

Wg. Cdr. *abbr.* Wing Commander.

whack /wak/ *v. & n. colloq.* ● *v.tr.* **1** strike or beat forcefully with a sharp blow. **2** (as **whacked** *adj.*) esp. *Brit.* tired out; exhausted. ● *n.* **1** a sharp or resounding blow. **2** *slang* a turn; an attempt. **3** *Brit. slang* a share or portion. □ **have a whack at** *slang* attempt. **out of whack** esp. *N. Amer.* & *Austral. slang* out of order; malfunctioning. **top** (or **full** or **the full**) **whack** the maximum price or rate. □ **whacker** *n.* **whacking** *n.* [imitative, or alteration of THWACK]

whacking /'wakɪŋ/ *adj. & adv. Brit. colloq.* ● *adj.* very large. ● *adv.* very (*a whacking great skyscraper*).

whacko /wak'əʊ/ *int. Brit. slang* expressing delight or enjoyment.

whacky var. of WACKY.

whale[1] /weɪl/ *n.* (*pl.* same or **whales**) any of the larger marine mammals of the order Cetacea, having a streamlined body and horizontal tail, and breathing air through a blowhole on the head (*baleen whale*; *toothed whale*). □ **a whale of a** *colloq.* an exceedingly good or fine etc. [Old English *hwæl*]

whale[2] /weɪl/ *v.tr.* esp. *US colloq.* beat, thrash. [variant of WALE]

whaleback /'weɪlbak/ *n.* a thing shaped like a whale's back, esp. an arched structure over the bow or stern part of the deck of a steamer, or a large elongated hill.

whaleboat /'weɪlbəʊt/ *n. hist.* a long narrow double-bowed boat of a kind used in whaling.

whalebone /'weɪlbəʊn/ *n.* an elastic horny substance growing in thin parallel plates in the upper jaw of some whales, used as stiffening etc.

whalebone whale *n.* a baleen whale.

whale-headed stork *n.* a grey African stork, *Balaeniceps rex*, with a large bill shaped like a clog. Also called *shoebill*.

whale oil *n.* oil from the blubber of whales.

whaler /'weɪlə/ *n.* **1** a whaling ship or a seaman engaged in whaling. **2** (also **whaler shark**) a large shark, *Carcharinus brachyurus*, of Australian waters. **3** *Austral. slang* a tramp.

whale shark *n.* a large tropical whale-like shark, *Rhincodon typus*, feeding close to the surface.

whaling /'weɪlɪŋ/ *n.* the practice or industry of hunting and killing whales, esp. for their oil or whalebone.

whaling-master *n.* the captain of a whaler.

wham /wam/ *int., n., & v. colloq.* ● *int.* expressing the sound of a forcible impact. ● *n.* such a sound. ● *v.* (**whammed, whamming**) **1** *intr.* make such a sound or impact. **2** *tr.* strike forcibly. [imitative]

whammy /'wami/ *n.* (*pl.* **-ies**) esp. *US colloq.* **1** an evil or unlucky influence. **2** (esp. in phr. **double whammy**) a powerful or unpleasant effect or a problematic situation. [20th c.: from WHAM + -Y[1]]

whang /waŋ/ *v. & n. colloq.* ● *v.* **1** *tr.* strike heavily and loudly; whack. **2** *intr.* (of a drum etc.) sound under or as under a blow. ● *n.* a whanging sound or blow. [imitative]

whangee /waŋ'giː/ *n.* **1** a Chinese or Japanese bamboo of the genus *Phyllostachys*. **2** a cane made from this. [Chinese *huang* 'old bamboo sprouts']

whap esp. *US* var. of WHOP.

whare /'wɒri/ *n.* a Maori hut or house. [Maori]

wharf /wɔːf/ *n. & v.* ● *n.* (*pl.* **wharves** /wɔːvz/ or **wharfs**) a level quayside area to which a ship may be moored to load and unload. ● *v.tr.* **1** moor (a ship) at a wharf. **2** store (goods) on a wharf. [Old English *hwearf*]

wharfage /'wɔːfɪdʒ/ *n.* **1** accommodation at a wharf. **2** a fee for this.

wharfie /'wɔːfi/ *n. Austral. & NZ colloq.* a waterside worker; a wharf-labourer.

wharfinger /'wɔːfɪn(d)ʒə/ *n.* an owner or keeper of a wharf. [probably ultimately from WHARFAGE]

wharves *pl.* of WHARF.

what /wɒt/ *pron., det., & adv.* ● *pron.* **1** *interrog. & rel.pron.* asking for a statement representing a choice from a number of possibilities (*what have you been reading?*; *what is your name?*; *tell me what you think*; *she asked what his name was*). Cf. WHICH. **2** *rel.pron.* that which, anything that (*will do what I can*). **3** asking for a remark to be repeated (*what did you say?*). **4** asking for confirmation or agreement of something not completely understood (*you did what?*; *what, you really mean it?*). **5** how much (*what you must have suffered!*). ● *det.* **1** *interrog. & rel.det.* corresponding to the functions of senses 1 and 2 of the pronoun (*what books have you read?*; *what thoughts have you?*; *she asked what books he had been reading*; *she asked what thoughts he had*). **2** *interrog. & rel.det.* asking for a statement about the class, kind, or nature of something (*what sort of fish is it?*; *she asked what sort of fish it was*). **3** (in exclamations) how great or remarkable (*what luck!*). **4** *rel.det.* as much ... as; any ... that (*will give you what help I can*). ● *interrog.adv.* to what extent (*what does it matter?*). □ **what about** what is the news or position or your opinion of (*what about me?*; *what about a game of tennis?*). **what-d'you-call-it** (or **what's-its name**) a substitute for a name not recalled. **what ever** what at all or in any way (*what ever do you mean?*) (see also WHATEVER). **what for** *colloq.* **1** for what reason? **2** a severe reprimand (esp. *give a person what for*). **what have you** (prec. by *or*) *colloq.* anything else similar. **what if? 1** what would result etc. if? **2** what would it matter if? **what is more** and as an additional point; moreover. **what next?** *colloq.* what more absurd, shocking, or surprising thing is possible? **what not** (prec. by *and*) other similar things. **what of?** what is the news concerning? **what of it?** why should that be considered significant? **what's-his** (or **-its**) **-name** = *what-d'you-call-it*. **what's what** *colloq.* what is useful or important etc. **what with** *colloq.* because of (usu. several things). [Old English *hwæt*, from Germanic]

whate'er /wɒt'ɛː/ *poet.* var. of WHATEVER.

whatever /wɒt'ɛvə/ *det. & pron.* **1** = WHAT (in relative uses) with the emphasis on indefiniteness (*lend me whatever you can*; *whatever money you have*). **2** though anything (*we are safe whatever happens*). **3** (with *neg.* or *interrog.*) at all; of any kind (*there is no doubt whatever*). **4** *colloq.* = *what ever*. □ **or whatever** *colloq.* or anything similar.

■ **Usage** See Usage Note at EVER.

whatnot /'wɒtnɒt/ *n.* **1** an indefinite or trivial thing. **2** a stand with shelves for small objects.

whatso /'wɒtsəʊ/ *det. & pron. archaic* = WHATEVER 1, 2. [Middle English, = WHAT + SO[1], from Old English *swā hwæt swā*]

whatsoe'er /wɒtsəʊ'ɛː/ *poet.* var. of WHATSOEVER.

whatsoever /wɒtsəʊ'ɛvə/ *det. & pron.* = WHATEVER 1, 2, 3.

whaup /(h)wɔːp/ *n.* esp. *Sc.* a curlew. [imitative of its cry]

wheat /wiːt/ *n.* **1** any cereal plant of the genus *Triticum*, bearing dense four-sided seed-spikes. **2** its grain, used in making flour etc. □ **separate the wheat from the chaff** see CHAFF. [Old English *hwǣte* from Germanic: related to WHITE]

wheat belt *n.* a region where wheat is the chief agricultural product.

wheatear /'wiːtɪə/ *n.* any small migratory bird of the genus *Oenanthe*, esp. with a white belly and rump. [apparently from *wheatears* (as WHITE, ARSE)]

wheaten /'wiːt(ə)n/ *adj.* made of wheat.

wheatgerm /'wiːtdʒəːm/ *n.* the embryo of the wheat grain, extracted as a source of vitamins.

wheatgrass /'wiːtgrɑːs/ *n.* = *couch grass* (see COUCH[2]).

wheatmeal /'wiːtmiːl/ *n.* flour made from wheat with some of the bran and germ removed.

Wheatstone bridge /'wiːtst(ə)n/ *n.* an apparatus for measuring electrical resistances by equalizing the potential at two points of a circuit. [named after C. *Wheatstone*, English physicist d. 1875]

whee /wi:/ *int.* expressing delight, excitement, or exhilaration. [a natural exclamation]

wheedle /'wi:d(ə)l/ *v.tr.* **1** coax by flattery or endearments. **2** (foll. by *out*) **a** get (a thing) out of a person by wheedling. **b** cheat (a person) out of a thing by wheedling. □ **wheedler** *n.* **wheedling** *adj.* **wheedlingly** *adv.* [perhaps from German *wedeln* 'fawn, cringe' from *Wedel* 'tail']

wheel /wi:l/ *n. & v.* ● *n.* **1** a circular frame or disc arranged to revolve on an axle and used to facilitate the motion of a vehicle or for various mechanical purposes. **2** a wheel-like thing (*Catherine wheel*; *potter's wheel*; *steering wheel*). **3** motion as of a wheel, esp. the movement of a line of people with one end as a pivot. **4** a machine etc. of which a wheel is an essential part. **5** (in *pl.*) *slang* a car. **6** = STEERING WHEEL. **7** *US slang* = BIG WHEEL 2. **8** a set of short lines concluding a stanza. ● *v.* **1** *intr. & tr.* **a** turn on an axis or pivot. **b** swing round in line with one end as a pivot. **2 a** *intr.* (often foll. by *about, round, US around*) change direction or face another way. **b** *tr.* cause to do this. **3** *tr.* push or pull (a wheeled thing esp. a barrow, bicycle, or pram, or its load or occupant). **4** *intr.* go in circles or curves (*seagulls wheeling overhead*). □ **at the wheel 1** driving a vehicle. **2** directing a ship. **3** in control of affairs. **on wheels** (or **oiled wheels**) *Brit.* smoothly. **wheel and deal** engage in political or commercial scheming. **wheels within wheels** *Brit.* **1** intricate machinery. **2** *colloq.* indirect or secret agencies. □ **wheeled** *adj.* (also in *comb.*). **wheelless** *adj.* [Old English *hwēol, hwēogol*, from Germanic]

wheel-back *attrib.adj.* (of a chair) with a back shaped like or containing the design of a wheel.

wheelbarrow /'wi:lbarəʊ/ *n.* a small cart with one wheel and two shafts for carrying garden loads etc.

wheelbase /'wi:lbeɪs/ *n.* the distance between the front and rear axles of a vehicle.

wheelchair /'wi:ltʃɛ:/ *n.* a chair on wheels for an invalid or disabled person.

wheel clamp *n. & v.* ● *n.* = CLAMP[1] *n.* 2. ● *v.tr.* (**wheel-clamp**) = CLAMP[1] *v.* 3.

wheeler /'wi:lə/ *n.* **1** (in *comb.*) a vehicle having a specified number of wheels. **2** a wheelwright. **3** a horse harnessed next to the wheels and behind another.

wheeler-dealer *n.* a person who wheels and deals (see WHEEL). □ **wheeler-dealing** *n.*

wheelhouse /'wi:lhaʊs/ *n.* a steersman's shelter.

wheelie /'wi:li/ *n. Brit. slang* the stunt of riding a bicycle or motorcycle for a short distance with the front wheel off the ground.

wheelie bin *n.* (also **wheely bin**) *Brit. colloq.* a large refuse bin on wheels.

■ **Usage** The official name for *wheelie bin* is *wheeled bin*.

wheel lock *n.* **1** *hist.* a kind of gunlock having a steel wheel to rub against flint etc. **2** a gun with this.

wheelman /'wi:lmən/ *n.* (*pl.* **-men**) esp. *US* **1** a driver of a wheeled vehicle, esp. *slang* a getaway car. **2** a helmsman.

wheel of Fortune *n.* the wheel which the deity Fortune is fabled to turn, as an emblem of luck and mutability.

wheelsman /'wi:lzmən/ *n.* (*pl.* **-men**) *US* a steersman.

wheelspin /'wi:lspɪn/ *n.* rotation of a vehicle's wheels without traction.

wheel well *n.* the recess into which a wheel of a vehicle fits.

wheelwright /'wi:lrʌɪt/ *n.* a person who makes or repairs esp. wooden wheels.

wheely bin var. of WHEELIE BIN.

wheeze /wi:z/ *v. & n.* ● *v.* **1** *intr.* breathe with an audible chesty whistling sound. **2** *tr.* (often foll. by *out*) utter in this way. ● *n.* **1** a sound of wheezing. **2** *colloq.* **a** *Brit.* a clever scheme. **b** a catchphrase. □ **wheezer** *n.* **wheezingly** *adv.* **wheezy** *adj.* **wheezily** *adv.* **wheeziness** *n.* [probably from Old Norse *hvæsa* 'to hiss']

whelk[1] /wɛlk/ *n.* any predatory marine gastropod mollusc of the family Buccinidae, esp. the edible kind of the genus *Baccinum*, having a spiral shell. [Old English *wioloc, weoloc*, of unknown origin: perhaps influenced by WHELK[2]]

whelk[2] /wɛlk/ *n.* a pimple. [Old English *hwylca* from *hwelian* 'suppurate']

whelm /wɛlm/ *v.tr. poet.* **1** engulf, submerge. **2** crush with weight, overwhelm. [Old English *hwelman* (unrecorded) = *hwylfan* 'overturn']

whelp /wɛlp/ *n. & v.* ● *n.* **1** a young dog; a puppy. **2** *archaic* a cub. **3** an ill-mannered child or youth. **4** (esp. in *pl.*) a projection on the barrel of a capstan or windlass. ● *v.tr.* (also *absol.*) **1** bring forth (a whelp or whelps). **2** *derog.* (of a human mother) give birth to. **3** originate (an evil scheme etc.). [Old English *hwelp*]

when /wɛn/ *adv., conj., pron., & n.* ● *interrog.adv.* **1** at what time? **2** on what occasion? **3** how soon? **4** how long ago? ● *rel.adv.* (prec. by *time* etc.) at or on which (*there are times when I could cry*). ● *conj.* **1** at the or any time that; as soon as (*come when you like*; *come when ready*; *when I was your age*). **2** although; considering that (*why stand up when you could sit down?*). **3** after which; and then; but just then (*had just fallen asleep when the bell rang*). ● *pron.* what time?; which time (*till when can you stay?*; *since when it has been better*). ● *n.* (prec. by *the*) the time, occasion, or date (*fixed the where and when*). [Old English *hwanne, hwenne*]

whence /wɛns/ *adv. & conj. formal* ● *adv.* from what place? (*whence did they come?*). ● *conj.* **1** to the place from which (*return whence you came*). **2** (often prec. by *place* etc.) from which (*the source whence these errors arise*). **3** and thence (*whence it follows that*). [Middle English *whannes, whennes*, from *whanne, whenne* (from Old English *hwanon(e)* 'whence') + -S[3]]

■ **Usage** The use of *from whence* rather than simply *whence* (as in *the place from whence they came*), though common, is generally considered incorrect.

whencesoever /wɛnssəʊ'ɛvə/ *adv. & conj. formal* from whatever place or source.

whene'er /wɛn'ɛ:/ *poet.* var. of WHENEVER.

whenever /wɛn'ɛvə/ *conj. & adv.* **1** at whatever time; on whatever occasion. **2** every time that. □ **or whenever** *colloq.* or at any similar time.

■ **Usage** See Usage Note at EVER.

whensoe'er /wɛnsəʊ'ɛ:/ *poet.* var. of WHENSOEVER.

whensoever /wɛnsəʊ'ɛvə/ *conj. & adv. formal* = WHENEVER.

where /wɛ:/ *adv., conj., pron., & n.* ● *interrog.adv.* **1** in or to what place or position? (*where is the milk?*; *where are you going?*). **2** in what direction or respect? (*where does the argument lead?*; *where does it concern us?*). **3** in what book etc.?; from whom? (*where did you read that?*; *where did you hear that?*). **4** in what situation or condition? (*where does that leave us?*). ● *rel.adv.* (prec. by *place* etc.) in or to which (*places where they meet*). ● *conj.* **1** in or to the or any place, direction, or respect in which (*go where you like*; *that is where you are wrong*; *delete where applicable*). **2** and there (*reached Crewe, where the car broke down*). ● *pron.* what place? (*where do you come from?*; *where are you going to?*). ● *n.* (prec. by *the*) the place; the scene of something (see WHEN *n.*). [Old English *hwǣr, hwār*]

whereabouts *adv. & n.* ● *adv.* /wɛ:rə'baʊts/ where or approximately where? (*whereabouts are they?*; *show me whereabouts to look*). ● *n.* /'wɛ:rəbaʊts/ (treated as *sing.* or *pl.*) a person's or thing's approximate location.

whereafter /wɛ:r'ɑ:ftə/ *conj. formal* after which.

whereas /wɛ:r'az/ *conj.* **1** in contrast or comparison with the fact that. **2** (esp. in legal preambles) taking into consideration the fact that.

whereat /wɛːrˈat/ *conj. archaic* **1** at which place or point. **2** for which reason.

whereby /wɛːˈbʌɪ/ *conj.* by what or which means.

where'er /wɛːrˈɛː/ *poet.* var. of WHEREVER.

wherefore /ˈwɛːfɔː/ *adv. & n.* ● *adv. archaic* **1** for what reason? **2** for which reason. ● *n. colloq.* a reason (*the whys and wherefores*).

wherefrom /wɛːˈfrɒm/ *conj. archaic* from which, from where.

wherein /wɛːrˈɪn/ *conj. & adv. formal* ● *conj.* in what or which place or respect. ● *adv.* in what place or respect?

whereof /wɛːrˈɒv/ *conj. & adv. formal* ● *conj.* of what or which (*the means whereof*). ● *adv.* of what?

whereon /wɛːrˈɒn/ *conj. & adv. archaic* ● *conj.* on what or which. ● *adv.* on what?

wheresoe'er /wɛːsəʊˈɛː/ *poet.* var. of WHERESOEVER.

wheresoever /wɛːsəʊˈɛvə/ *conj. & adv. formal* or *literary* = WHEREVER.

whereto /wɛːˈtuː/ *conj. & adv. formal* ● *conj.* to what or which. ● *adv.* to what?

whereupon /wɛːrəˈpɒn/ *conj.* immediately after which.

wherever /wɛːrˈɛvə/ *adv. & conj.* ● *adv.* in or to whatever place. ● *conj.* in every place that. □ **or wherever** *colloq.* or in any similar place.

■ **Usage** See Usage Note at EVER.

wherewith /wɛːˈwɪð/ *conj. formal* or *archaic* with or by which.

wherewithal /ˈwɛːwɪðɔːl/ *n. colloq.* money etc. needed for a purpose (*has not the wherewithal to do it*).

wherry /ˈwɛri/ *n.* (*pl.* **-ies**) **1** a light rowing boat usu. for carrying passengers. **2** *Brit.* a large light barge. [Middle English: origin unknown]

wherryman /ˈwɛrɪmən/ *n.* (*pl.* **-men**) a man employed on a wherry.

whet /wɛt/ *v. & n.* ● *v.tr.* (**whetted**, **whetting**) **1** sharpen (a tool or weapon) by grinding. **2** stimulate (the appetite or a desire, interest, etc.). ● *n.* **1** the act or an instance of whetting. **2** a small quantity stimulating one's appetite for more. □ **whetter** *n.* (also in *comb.*). [Old English *hwettan*, from Germanic]

whether /ˈwɛðə/ *conj.* introducing the first or both of alternative possibilities (*I doubt whether it matters*; *I do not know whether they have arrived or not*). □ **whether or no** see NO². [Old English *hwæther*, *hwether*, from Germanic]

whetstone /ˈwɛtstəʊn/ *n.* **1** a fine-grained stone used esp. with water to sharpen cutting tools (cf. OILSTONE). **2** a thing that sharpens the senses etc.

whew /hwjuː, fjuː/ *int.* expressing surprise, consternation, or relief. [imitative: cf. PHEW]

whey /weɪ/ *n.* the watery liquid left when milk forms curds. [Old English *hwæg*, *hweg*, from Germanic]

whey-faced *adj.* pale esp. with fear.

which /wɪtʃ/ *pron. & det.* ● *pron.* **1** *interrog.pron.* asking for choice from a definite set of alternatives (*which do you prefer?*) (cf. WHAT *pron.* 1). **2** *rel.pron.* (*poss.* **of which**, **whose** /huːz/) being the thing or things just referred to, usu. introducing a clause not essential for identification (*the house, which is empty, has been damaged*) (cf. THAT *pron.* 7). **3** *rel.pron.* used in place of *that* after a preposition or after *that* (*there is the house in which I was born*; *that which you have just seen*). ● *interrog. & rel.det.* corresponding to the functions of senses 1 and 2 of the pronoun (*which John do you mean?*; *which book do you prefer?*; *three days, during all of which time he said nothing*). □ **which is which** a phrase used when two or more persons or things are difficult to distinguish from each other. [Old English *hwilc*, from Germanic]

whichever /wɪtʃˈɛvə/ *det. & pron.* **1** any which (*take whichever you like*; *whichever one you like*). **2** no matter which (*whichever one wins, they both get a prize*).

whichsoever /wɪtʃsəʊˈɛvə/ *det. & pron. archaic* = WHICHEVER.

whicker /ˈwɪkə/ *v. & n.* ● *v.intr.* (of a horse) give a soft breathy whinny. ● *n.* such a whinny or similar sound. [imitative]

whidah var. of WHYDAH.

whiff /wɪf/ *n. & v.* ● *n.* **1** a puff or breath of air, smoke, etc. (*went outside for a whiff of fresh air*). **2** a smell (*caught the whiff of a cigar*). **3** (foll. by *of*) a trace or suggestion of scandal etc. **4** a small cigar. **5** a minor discharge (of grapeshot etc.). **6** a light narrow outrigged sculling boat. ● *v.* **1** *tr. & intr.* blow or puff lightly. **2** *intr. Brit. colloq.* smell (esp. unpleasant). **3** *tr.* get a slight smell of. [imitative]

whiffle /ˈwɪf(ə)l/ *v. & n.* ● *v.* **1** *intr. & tr.* (of the wind) blow lightly, shift about. **2** *intr.* be variable or evasive. **3** *intr.* (of a flame, leaves, etc.) flicker, flutter. **4** *intr.* make the sound of a light wind in breathing etc. ● *n.* a slight movement of air. [WHIFF + -LE⁴]

whiffletree /ˈwɪf(ə)ltriː/ *n. US* = SWINGLETREE. [variant of WHIPPLETREE]

whiffy /ˈwɪfi/ *adj.* (**whiffier**, **whiffiest**) *Brit. colloq.* having an unpleasant smell.

Whig /wɪg/ *n. hist.* **1** *Polit.* a member of the British reforming and constitutional party that after 1688 sought the supremacy of Parliament and was eventually succeeded in the 19th c. by the Liberal Party (opp. TORY 2). **2** a 17th-c. Scottish Presbyterian. **3** *US* **a** a supporter of the American Revolution. **b** a member of an American political party in the 19th c., succeeded by the Republicans. □ **Whiggery** *n.* **Whiggish** *adj.* **Whiggism** *n.* [probably a shortening of Scots *whiggamer*, *-more*, nickname of 17th-c. Scots rebels, from *whig* 'to drive' + MARE¹]

while /wʌɪl/ *n., conj., v., & adv.* ● *n.* **1** a space of time, time spent in some action (*a long while ago*; *waited a while*; *all this while*). **2** (prec. by *the*) **a** during some other process. **b** *poet.* during the time that. **3** (prec. by *a*) for some time (*have not seen you a while*). ● *conj.* **1** during the time that; for as long as; at the same time as (*while I was away, the house was burgled*; *fell asleep while reading*). **2** in spite of the fact that; although, whereas (*while I want to believe it, I cannot*). **3** *N.Engl.* until (*wait while Monday*). ● *v.tr.* (foll. by *away*) pass (time etc.) in a leisurely or interesting manner. ● *rel.adv.* (prec. by *time* etc.) during which (*the summer while I was abroad*). □ **all the while** during the whole time (that). **for a long while** for a long time past. **for a while** for some time. **a good** (or **great**) **while** a considerable time. **in a while** (or **little while**) soon, shortly. **worth while** (or **worth one's while**) worth the time or effort spent. [Old English *hwīl* from Germanic: the conjunction an abbreviation of Old English *thā hwīle the*, Middle English *the while that*]

■ **Usage** See Usage Note at WORTHWHILE.

whiles /wʌɪlz/ *conj. archaic* = WHILE. [originally in the adverbs *somewhiles*, *otherwhiles*]

whilom /ˈwʌɪləm/ *adv. & adj. archaic* ● *adv.* formerly, once. ● *adj.* former, erstwhile (*my whilom friend*). [Old English *hwīlum*, dative pl. of *hwīl* WHILE]

whilst /wʌɪlst/ *adv. & conj.* esp. *Brit.* while. [Middle English from WHILES: cf. AGAINST]

whim /wɪm/ *n.* **1 a** a sudden fancy; a caprice. **b** capriciousness. **2** *archaic* a kind of windlass for raising ore or water from a mine. [17th c.: origin unknown]

whimbrel /ˈwɪmbr(ə)l/ *n.* a small migratory curlew, *Numenius phaeopus*, with a trilling call. [WHIMPER (imitative): cf. *dotterel*]

whimper /ˈwɪmpə/ *v. & n.* ● *v.* **1** *intr.* make feeble, querulous, or frightened sounds; cry and whine softly. **2** *tr.* utter whimperingly. ● *n.* **1** a whimpering sound. **2** a feeble note or tone (*the conference ended on a whimper*). □ **whimperer** *n.* **whimperingly** *adv.* [imitative, from dialect *whimp*]

whimsical /ˈwɪmzɪk(ə)l/ *adj.* **1** odd or quaint; fanciful, humorous. **2** capricious. □ **whimsicality** /-ˈkalɪti/ *n.* **whimsically** *adv.*

whimsy /ˈwɪmzi/ *n.* (also **whimsey**) (*pl.* **-ies** or **-eys**) **1** a whim; a capricious notion or fancy. **2** capricious or quaint humour. [related to WHIM-WHAM: cf. *flimsy*]

whim-wham /ˈwɪmwam/ *n. archaic* **1** a toy or plaything. **2** = WHIM 1. [reduplication: origin uncertain]

whin[1] /wɪn/ *n.* (in *sing.* or *pl.*) *Brit.* furze, gorse. [probably Scandinavian: cf. Norwegian *hvine*, Swedish *hven*]

whin[2] /wɪn/ *n.* **1** hard dark esp. basaltic rock or stone. **2** a piece of this. [Middle English: origin unknown]

whinchat /ˈwɪntʃat/ *n.* a small brownish songbird, *Saxicola rubetra*. [WHIN[1] + CHAT[2]]

whine /wʌɪn/ *n. & v.* ● *n.* **1** a complaining long-drawn wail as of a dog. **2** a similar shrill prolonged sound. **3 a** a querulous tone. **b** an instance of feeble or undignified complaining. ● *v.* **1** *intr.* emit or utter a whine. **2** *intr.* complain in a querulous tone or in a feeble or undignified way. **3** *tr.* utter in a whining tone. □ **whiner** *n.* **whiningly** *adv.* **whiny** *adj.* (**whinier**, **whiniest**). [Old English *hwīnan*]

whinge /wɪn(d)ʒ/ *v. & n. Brit. colloq.* ● *v.intr.* (**whingeing**) whine; grumble peevishly. ● *n.* a whining complaint; a peevish grumbling. □ **whinger** *n.* **whingeingly** *adv.* **whingy** *adj.* [Old English *hwinsian*, from Germanic]

whinny /ˈwɪni/ *n. & v.* ● *n.* (*pl.* **-ies**) a gentle or joyful neigh. ● *v.intr.* (**-ies**, **-ied**) give a whinny. [imitative: cf. WHINE]

whinstone /ˈwɪnstəʊn/ *n.* = WHIN[2].

whip /wɪp/ *n. & v.* ● *n.* **1** a lash attached to a stick for urging on animals or punishing etc. **2 a** a member of a political party in Parliament appointed to control its parliamentary discipline and tactics, esp. ensuring attendance and voting in debates. **b** *Brit.* the whips' written notice requesting or requiring attendance for voting at a division etc., variously underlined according to the degree of urgency (*three-line whip*). **c** (prec. by *the*) party discipline and instructions (*asked for the Labour whip*). **3** a dessert made with whipped cream etc. **4** the action of beating cream, eggs, etc., into a froth. **5** = WHIPPER-IN. **6** a rope-and-pulley hoisting apparatus. ● *v.* (**whipped**, **whipping**) **1** *tr.* beat or urge on with a whip. **2** *tr.* beat (cream or eggs etc.) into a froth. **3** *tr. & intr.* take or move suddenly, unexpectedly, or rapidly (*whipped away the tablecloth*; *whipped out a knife*; *whipped behind the door*). **4** *tr. Brit. colloq.* steal (*who's whipped my pen?*). **5** *tr. slang* **a** excel. **b** defeat. **6** *tr.* bind with spirally wound twine. **7** *tr.* sew with overcast stitches. □ **whip in** bring (hounds) together. **whip on** urge into action. **whip up 1** excite or stir up (feeling etc.). **2** summon (attendance). □ **whipless** *adj.* **whip-like** *adj.* **whipper** *n.* [Middle English (*h*)*wippen* (*v.*), probably from Middle Low German & Middle Dutch *wippen* 'swing, leap, dance']

whipbird /ˈwɪpbəːd/ *n.* an Australian songbird of the genus *Psophodes* with a cry like the crack of a whip.

whipcord /ˈwɪpkɔːd/ *n.* **1** a tightly twisted cord such as is used for making whiplashes. **2** a closely woven worsted fabric.

whip-crane *n.* a light derrick with tackle for hoisting.

whip-graft *n.* (in horticulture) a graft with the tongue of the scion in a slot in the stock and vice versa.

whip hand *n.* **1** a hand that holds the whip (in riding etc.). **2** (usu. prec. by *the*) the advantage or control in any situation.

whiplash /ˈwɪplaʃ/ *n. & v.* ● *n.* **1** the flexible end of a whip. **2** a blow with a whip. **3** = WHIPLASH INJURY. **4** a sharp reaction (*whiplash against the status quo*). ● *v.* **1** *tr.* jerk causing a whiplash effect. **2** *intr.* flick or move like a whip lashing.

whiplash injury *n.* an injury to the neck caused by a severe jerk of the head, esp. as in a motor accident.

whipper-in *n.* (*pl.* **whippers-in**) a huntsman's assistant who manages the hounds.

whippersnapper /ˈwɪpəsnapə/ *n.* **1** a small child. **2** an insignificant but presumptuous or intrusive (esp. young) person. [perhaps for *whipsnapper*, implying noise and unimportance]

whippet /ˈwɪpɪt/ *n.* **1** a dog of a small slender breed originally produced as a cross between the greyhound and the terrier or spaniel, bred for racing. **2** this breed. [probably from obsolete *whippet* 'move briskly', from *whip it*]

whipping /ˈwɪpɪŋ/ *n.* **1** a beating, esp. with a whip. **2** cord wound round in binding.

whipping boy *n.* **1** a scapegoat. **2** *hist.* a boy educated with a young prince and punished instead of him.

whipping cream *n.* medium-thick cream suitable for whipping.

whipping post *n. hist.* a post used for public whippings.

whipping-top *n.* a top kept spinning by blows of a lash.

whippletree /ˈwɪp(ə)ltriː/ *n.* = SWINGLETREE. [apparently from WHIP + TREE]

whippoorwill /ˈwɪpəwɪl/ *n.* an American nightjar, *Caprimulgus vociferus*. [imitative of its cry]

whippy /ˈwɪpi/ *adj.* flexible, springy. □ **whippiness** *n.*

whip-round *n.* esp. *Brit. colloq.* an informal collection of money from a group of people.

whipsaw /ˈwɪpsɔː/ *n. & v.* ● *n.* a saw with a narrow blade held at each end by a frame. ● *v.* (*past part.* **-sawn** or **-sawed**) **1** *tr.* cut with a whipsaw. **2** *US slang* **a** *tr.* cheat by joint action on two others. **b** *intr.* be cheated in this way.

whip scorpion *n.* any arachnid of the order Uropygi, resembling a scorpion but with a long slender tail-like appendage.

whip snake *n.* any of various long slender snakes of the family Colubridae.

whip stitch *n.* an overcast stitch.

whipstock /ˈwɪpstɒk/ *n.* the handle of a whip.

whir var. of WHIRR.

whirl /wəːl/ *v. & n.* ● *v.* **1** *tr. & intr.* swing round and round; revolve rapidly. **2** *tr. & intr.* (foll. by *away*) convey or go rapidly in a vehicle etc. **3** *tr. & intr.* send or travel swiftly in an orbit or a curve. **4** *intr.* **a** (of the brain, senses, etc.) seem to spin round. **b** (of thoughts etc.) be confused; follow each other in bewildering succession. ● *n.* **1** a whirling movement (*vanished in a whirl of dust*). **2** a state of intense activity (*the social whirl*). **3** a state of confusion (*my mind is in a whirl*). **4** *colloq.* a try (*give it a whirl*). □ **whirler** *n.* **whirlingly** *adv.* [Middle English: the verb from Old Norse *hvirfla*: the noun from Middle Low German & Middle Dutch *wervel* 'spindle' & Old Norse *hvirfill* 'circle', from Germanic]

whirligig /ˈwəːlɪgɪg/ *n.* **1** a spinning or whirling toy. **2** a merry-go-round. **3** a revolving motion. **4** anything regarded as hectic or constantly changing (*the whirligig of time*). **5** any freshwater beetle of the family Gyrinidae that circles about on the surface. [Middle English, from WHIRL + obsolete *gig* 'whipping-top']

whirling dervish *n.* (also **dancing dervish** or **howling dervish**) a dervish performing a wild dance, or howling, according to which sect he belongs to.

whirlpool /ˈwəːlpuːl/ *n.* a powerful circular eddy in the sea etc. often causing suction to its centre.

whirlwind /ˈwəːlwɪnd/ *n.* **1** a mass or column of air whirling rapidly round and round in a cylindrical or funnel shape over land or water. **2** a confused tumultuous process. **3** (*attrib.*) very rapid (*a whirlwind romance*). □ **reap the whirlwind** suffer worse results of a bad action.

whirlybird /ˈwəːlɪbəːd/ *n. colloq.* a helicopter.

whirr /wəː/ *n. & v.* (also **whir**) ● *n.* a continuous rapid buzzing or softly clicking sound as of a bird's wings or of cogwheels in constant motion. ● *v.intr.* (**whirred**, **whirring**) make this sound. [Middle English, probably Scandinavian: cf. Danish *hvirre*, Norwegian *kvirra*, perhaps related to WHIRL]

whisht /(h)wɪʃt/ *v.* (also **whist** /(h)wɪst/) esp. *Sc.* & *Ir. dial.* **1** *intr.* (esp. as *int.*) be quiet; hush. **2** *tr.* quieten. [imitative]

whisk /wɪsk/ *v.* & *n.* ● *v.* **1** *tr.* (foll. by *away*, *off*) **a** brush with a sweeping movement. **b** take with a sudden motion (*whisked the plate away*). **2** *tr.* whip (cream, eggs, etc.). **3** *tr.* & *intr.* convey or go (esp. out of sight) lightly or quickly (*whisked me off to the doctor*; *the mouse whisked into its hole*). **4** *tr.* wave or lightly brandish. ● *n.* **1** a whisking action or motion. **2** a utensil for whisking eggs or cream etc. **3** a bunch of grass, twigs, bristles, etc., for removing dust or flies. [Middle English *wisk*, probably Scandinavian: cf. Old Norse *visk* 'wisp']

whisker /ˈwɪskə/ *n.* **1** (usu. in *pl.*) the hair growing on a man's face, esp. on the cheek. **2** each of the bristles on the face of a cat etc. **3** *colloq.* a small distance (*within a whisker of*; *won by a whisker*). **4** a strong hairlike crystal of metal etc. □ **have** (or **have grown**) **whiskers** *colloq.* (esp. of a story etc.) be very old. □ **whiskered** *adj.* **whiskery** *adj.* [WHISK + -ER[1]]

whisky /ˈwɪski/ *n.* (*US* & *Ir.* **whiskey**) (*pl.* **-ies** or **-eys**) **1** a spirit distilled esp. from malted barley, other grains, or potatoes, etc. **2** a drink of this. [abbreviation of obsolete *whiskybae*, variant of USQUEBAUGH]

whisper /ˈwɪspə/ *v.* & *n.* ● *v.* **1 a** *intr.* speak very softly without vibration of the vocal cords. **b** *intr.* & *tr.* talk or say in a barely audible tone or in a secret or confidential way. **2** *intr.* speak privately or conspiratorially. **3** *intr.* (of leaves, wind, or water) rustle or murmur. ● *n.* **1** whispering speech (*talking in whispers*). **2** a whispering sound. **3** a thing whispered. **4** a rumour or piece of gossip. □ **it is whispered** there is a rumour. □ **whisperer** *n.* **whispering** *n.* [Old English *hwisprian*, from Germanic]

whispering gallery *n.* a gallery esp. under a dome with acoustic properties such that a whisper may be heard round its entire circumference.

whist[1] /wɪst/ *n.* a card game usu. for two pairs of players, with the winning of tricks. [earlier *whisk*, perhaps from WHISK (with reference to whisking away the tricks): perhaps associated with WHIST[2]]

whist[2] var. of WHISHT.

whist drive *n. Brit.* a social occasion with the playing of progressive whist.

whistle /ˈwɪs(ə)l/ *n.* & *v.* ● *n.* **1** a clear shrill sound made by forcing breath through a small hole between nearly closed lips, or between the teeth . **2** a similar sound made by a bird, the wind, a missile, etc. **3** an instrument used to produce such a sound, esp. for giving a signal. **4** *Brit. rhyming slang* a suit (short for *whistle and flute*). ● *v.* **1** *intr.* emit a whistle. **2 a** *intr.* give a signal or express surprise or derision by whistling. **b** *tr.* (often foll. by *up*) summon or give a signal to (a dog etc.) by whistling. **3** *tr.* (also *absol.*) produce (a tune) by whistling. **4** *intr.* (foll. by *for*) vainly seek or desire. □ **as clean** (or **clear** or **dry**) **as a whistle** very clean or clear or dry. **blow the whistle on** *colloq.* bring (an activity) to an end; inform on (those responsible). **wet one's whistle** see WET. **whistle down the wind 1** let go, abandon. **2** turn (a hawk) loose. **whistle in the dark** pretend to be unafraid. [Old English *(h)wistlian* (*v.*), *(h)wistle* (*n.*) of imitative origin: cf. Old Norse *hvísla* 'whisper', Middle Swedish *hvisla* 'whistle']

whistle-blower *n.* a person who blows the whistle on someone or something (see WHISTLE).

whistler /ˈwɪslə/ *n.* **1 a** a person who whistles. **b** a thing which makes a whistling sound. **2 a** bird of the genus *Pachycephala* or of a related genus, with a loud melodious call. **b** a marmot, *Marmota caligata*, with a whistling call.

whistle-stop *n.* **1** *US* a small unimportant town on a railway. **2** a politician's brief pause for an electioneering speech on tour. **3** (*attrib.*) with only brief pauses; very fast (*a whistle-stop tour*).

whistling kettle *n.* a kettle fitted with a whistle sounded by steam when the kettle is boiling.

Whit /wɪt/ *n.* & *adj.* ● *n.* = WHITSUNTIDE. ● *attrib.adj.* connected with, belonging to, or following Whit Sunday (*Whit Monday*; *Whit weekend*). [Old English *Hwīta Sunnandæg*, literally 'white Sunday', probably from the white robes of the newly baptized at Pentecost]

whit /wɪt/ *n.* a particle; a least possible amount (*not a whit better*). □ **every whit** the whole; wholly. **no** (or **never a** or **not a**) **whit** not at all. [earlier *w(h)yt* apparently an alteration of WIGHT in the phrase *no wight* etc.]

white /wʌɪt/ *adj.*, *n.*, & *v.* ● *adj.* **1** resembling a surface reflecting sunlight without absorbing any of the visible rays; of the colour of milk or fresh snow. **2** approaching such a colour; pale esp. in the face (*turned as white as a sheet*). **3** less dark than other things of the same kind. **4** (also **White**) **a** of the human group having light-coloured skin. **b** of or relating to white people. **5** (of a person) white-haired, esp. in old age. **6** *colloq.* innocent, untainted. **7 a** (of a plant) having white flowers or pale-coloured fruit etc. (*white hyacinth*; *white cauliflower*). **b** (of a tree) having light-coloured bark etc. (*white ash*; *white poplar*). **8** (of wine) made from white grapes or dark grapes with the skins removed. **9** *Brit.* (of coffee) with milk or cream added. **10** transparent, colourless (*white glass*). **11** *hist.* counter-revolutionary or reactionary (*white guard*; *white army*). ● *n.* **1** a white colour or pigment. **2 a** white clothes or material (*dressed in white*). **b** (in *pl.*) white garments as worn in cricket, tennis, etc. **c** (in *pl.*) white clothing etc. for washing. **3 a** (in a game or sport) a white piece, ball, etc. **b** the player using such pieces. **4** the white part or albumen round the yolk of an egg. **5** the visible part of the eyeball round the iris. **6** (also **White**) a member of a light-skinned race. **7** a white butterfly. **8** a blank space in printing. ● *v.tr. archaic* make white. □ **bleed white** drain (a person, country, etc.) of wealth etc. □ **whitely** *adv.* **whiteness** *n.* **whitish** *adj.* [Old English *hwīt*, from Germanic]

white admiral *n.* a butterfly, *Limenitis camilla*, with a white band across its wings.

white ant *n.* a termite.

white arsenic see ARSENIC *n.* 1.

whitebait /ˈwʌɪtbeɪt/ *n.* (*pl.* same) (usu. *pl.*) the small silvery-white young of herrings, sprats, and similar fish esp. as food.

whitebeam /ˈwʌɪtbiːm/ *n.* a tree of the rose family, *Sorbus aria*, having red berries and leaves with a white downy underside.

whiteboard /ˈwʌɪtbɔːd/ *n.* a board with a white surface, used esp. for classroom presentations using felt-tip pens.

white cell *n.* (also **white blood cell**) = LEUCOCYTE.

white Christmas *n.* Christmas with snow on the ground.

white coal *n.* water as a source of power.

white-collar *attrib.adj.* (of a worker or work) clerical or administrative rather than manual.

white currant *n.* a cultivar of redcurrant with pale edible berries.

whited sepulchre *n.* a hypocrite (with reference to Matt. 23:27).

white dwarf *n.* a small very dense star.

white elephant *n.* an item or property that is no longer useful or wanted, esp. one that is difficult to maintain or dispose of.

white ensign *n.* the ensign of the Royal Navy and the Royal Yacht Squadron.

white-eye *n.* a bird with a white iris or white plumage around the eyes, esp. a small Old World perching bird of the family Zosteropidae.

whiteface /ˈwʌɪtfeɪs/ *n.* the white make-up of an actor etc.

white feather *n.* a symbol of cowardice (a white feather in the tail of a game bird being a mark of bad breeding).
whitefish /ˈwʌɪtfɪʃ/ *n.* (*pl.* usu. same) any freshwater fish of the genus *Coregonus* etc., of the trout family, and used esp. for food.
white fish *n.* fish with pale flesh, e.g. plaice, cod, etc.
white flag *n.* a symbol of surrender or a period of truce.
whitefly /ˈwʌɪtflʌɪ/ *n.* (*pl.* **-flies**) any small insect of the family Aleyrodidae, having wings covered with white powder and feeding on the sap of shrubs, crops, etc.
White Friar *n.* a Carmelite monk. [from their white habits]
white frost see FROST *n.* 1a.
white gold *n.* any of various silver-coloured alloys of gold used in jewellery.
white goods *n.pl.* **1** large domestic electrical equipment that is conventionally white, e.g. refrigerators and washing machines. **2** *archaic* domestic linen.
Whitehall /ˈwʌɪthɔːl/ *n.* **1** the British Government. **2** its offices or policy. [a street in London in which Government offices are situated]
whitehead /ˈwʌɪthɛd/ *n. colloq.* a white or white-topped skin-pustule.
white heat *n.* **1** the temperature at which metal emits white light. **2** a state of intense passion or activity.
white hope *n.* a person expected to achieve much for a group, organization, etc.
white horses *n.pl.* white-crested waves at sea.
white-hot *adj.* at white heat.
White House *n.* **1** the official residence of the US President in Washington, DC. **2** the Russian parliament building.
white-knuckle *attrib.adj.* (esp. of a fairground ride) designed to cause excitement or tension.
white lead *n.* a mixture of lead carbonate and hydrated lead oxide used as pigment.
white lie *n.* a harmless or trivial untruth.
white light *n.* apparently colourless light, e.g. ordinary daylight.
white lime *n.* lime mixed with water as a coating for walls; whitewash.
white magic *n.* magic used only for beneficent purposes.
white matter *n.* the part of the brain and spinal cord consisting mainly of nerve fibres (cf. GREY MATTER 1).
white meat *n.* poultry, veal, rabbit, and pork.
white metal *n.* a white or silvery alloy.
White Monk *n.* a Cistercian monk. [from their white habits]
whiten /ˈwʌɪt(ə)n/ *v.tr. & intr.* make or become white. □ **whitener** *n.* **whitening** *n.*
white night *n.* **1** a sleepless night. **2** a night when it never properly gets dark, as in high latitudes in summer. [in sense 1 translation of French *nuit blanche*]
white noise *n.* noise containing many frequencies with equal intensities.
white-out *n.* **1** a dense blizzard esp. in polar regions. **2** a weather condition in which the features, horizon, etc. of snow-covered country are indistinguishable due to uniform light diffusion.
white ox-eye *n.* = OX-EYE DAISY (see OX-EYE).
White Paper *n.* (in the UK) a Government report giving information or proposals on an issue.
white pepper *n.* the ripe or husked ground or whole berries of *Piper nigrum* as a condiment.
white poplar *n.* = ABELE.
white rose *n.* the emblem of Yorkshire or the House of York.
White Russian *n.* a Belorussian.
white sale *n.* a sale of household linen.
white sauce *n.* a sauce of flour, melted butter, and milk or cream.
white slave *n.* a woman tricked or forced into prostitution, usu. abroad. □ **white slavery** *n.*
whitesmith /ˈwʌɪtsmɪθ/ *n.* **1** a worker in tin. **2** a polisher or finisher of metal goods.
white sock *n.* = STOCKING 3.
white spirit *n. Brit.* light petroleum as a solvent.
white sugar *n.* purified sugar.
whitethorn /ˈwʌɪtθɔːn/ *n.* the hawthorn.
whitethroat /ˈwʌɪtθrəʊt/ *n.* any white-throated Eurasian warbler of the genus *Sylvia*, esp. the common *S. communis.*
white tie *n.* a man's white bow tie as part of full evening dress.
white vitriol *n. Chem.* zinc sulphate.
whitewash /ˈwʌɪtwɒʃ/ *n. & v.* ● *n.* **1** a solution of quicklime or of whiting and size for whitening walls etc. **2** a means employed to conceal mistakes or faults in order to clear a person or institution of imputations. ● *v.tr.* **1** cover with whitewash. **2** attempt by concealment to clear the reputation of. **3** (in *passive*) *Brit.* (of an insolvent) get a fresh start by passage through a bankruptcy court. **4** defeat (an opponent) without allowing any opposing score. □ **whitewasher** *n.*
white water *n.* a shallow or foamy stretch of water.
white wedding *n. Brit.* a wedding at which the bride wears a formal white dress.
white whale *n.* a northern cetacean, *Delphinapterus leucas*, white when adult: also called BELUGA.
whitewood /ˈwʌɪtwʊd/ *n.* a light-coloured wood esp. prepared for staining etc.
whitey /ˈwʌɪti/ *n.* (also **Whitey**) (*pl.* **-eys**) *slang offens.* **1** a white person. **2** white people collectively.
whither /ˈwɪðə/ *adv. & conj. archaic* ● *adv.* **1** to what place, position, or state? **2** (prec. by *place* etc.) to which (*the house whither we were walking*). ● *conj.* **1** to the or any place to which (*go whither you will*). **2** and thither (*we saw a house, whither we walked*). [Old English *hwider* from Germanic: cf. WHICH, HITHER, THITHER]
whithersoever /wɪðəsəʊˈɛvə/ *adj. & conj. archaic* to any place to which.
whiting[1] /ˈwʌɪtɪŋ/ *n.* (*pl.* same) a small white-fleshed fish, *Merlangus merlangus*, used as food. [Middle English from Middle Dutch *wijting*, apparently formed as WHITE + -ING[3]]
whiting[2] /ˈwʌɪtɪŋ/ *n.* ground chalk used in whitewashing, plate-cleaning, etc.
whitleather /ˈwɪtlɛðə/ *n.* tawed leather. [Middle English, from WHITE + LEATHER]
whitlow /ˈwɪtləʊ/ *n.* an inflammation near a fingernail or toenail. [Middle English *whitflaw, -flow*, apparently = WHITE + FLAW[1] in the sense 'crack', but perhaps of Low German origin: cf. Dutch *fijt*, Low German *fīt* 'whitlow']
whitlow-grass *n.* a dwarf cruciferous plant of rocks, wall-tops etc., esp. *Erophila verna*, formerly held to cure whitlows.
Whitsun /ˈwɪts(ə)n/ *n. & adj.* ● *n.* = WHITSUNTIDE. ● *adj.* = WHIT. [Middle English, from *Whitsun Day* = Whit Sunday]
Whit Sunday *n.* the seventh Sunday after Easter, commemorating the descent of the Holy Spirit at Pentecost (Acts 2).
Whitsuntide /ˈwɪts(ə)ntʌɪd/ *n.* the weekend or week including Whit Sunday.
whittle /ˈwɪt(ə)l/ *v.* **1** *tr.* & (foll. by *at*) *intr.* pare (wood etc.) with repeated slicing with a knife. **2** *tr.* (often foll. by *away, down*) reduce by repeated subtractions. [variant of Middle English *thwitel* 'long knife' from Old English *thwītan* 'to cut off']
whity /ˈwʌɪti/ *adj.* whitish; rather white (usu. in *comb.*: *whity-yellow*) (cf. WHITEY).
whiz-bang /ˈwɪzbaŋ/ *n. & adj.* ● *n.* (also **whizz-bang**) *colloq.* **1** a high-velocity shell from a small-calibre gun, whose passage is heard before the gun's report. **2** a

jumping kind of firework. ● *adj.* fast-paced, lively, spectacular.

whizz /wɪz/ *n. & v.* (also **whiz**) *colloq.* ● *n.* **1** the sound made by the friction of a body moving through the air at great speed. **2** (also **wiz**) *colloq.* a person who is remarkable or skilful in some respect (*is a whiz at chess*). ● *v.intr.* (**whizzed**, **whizzing**) move with or make a whizz. [imitative: in sense 2 influenced by WIZARD]

whizz-kid *n.* (also **whiz-kid**) *colloq.* a brilliant or highly successful young person.

WHO *abbr.* World Health Organization.

who /huː, hʊ/ *pron.* (*obj.* **whom** /huːm/ or (informally) **who**; *poss.* **whose** /huːz/) **1** *interrog.pron.* **a** what or which person or persons? (*who called?*; *you know who it was*; *whom* or *who did you see?*). **b** what sort of person or persons? (*who am I to object?*). **2** *rel.pron.* (a person) that (*anyone who wishes can come*; *the woman whom you met*; *the man who you saw*). **3** and (or but) he, she, they, etc. (*gave it to Tom, who sold it to Jim*). **4** *archaic* the or any person or persons that (*whom the gods love die young*). ◻ **as who should say** *archaic* like a person who said; as though one said. **who goes there?** see GO[1]. [Old English *hwā*, from Germanic: *whom* from Old English dative *hwām*, *hwǣm*: *whose* from genitive *hwæs*]

■ **Usage** In the last example of sense 1a and the last two examples of sense 2, *whom* is correct, but *who* is common in less formal contexts.

whoa /wəʊ/ *int.* used as a command to stop or slow a horse etc. [variant of HO]

who'd /huːd/ *contr.* **1** who had. **2** who would.

who-does-what *attrib.adj. Brit.* (of a dispute etc.) about which group of workers should do a particular job.

whodunnit /huːˈdʌnɪt/ *n.* (*US* **whodunit**) *colloq.* a story or play about the detection of a crime etc., esp. murder. [from *who done it?*, non-standard form of *who did it?*]

whoe'er /huːˈɛː/ *poet.* var. of WHOEVER.

whoever /huːˈɛvə/ *pron.* (*obj.* **whomever** /huːm-/ or (informally) **whoever**; *poss.* **whosever** /huːz-/) **1** the or any person or persons who (*whoever comes is welcome*). **2** though anyone (*whoever else objects, I do not*; *whosever it is, I want it*). **3** *colloq.* (as an intensive) who ever; who at all (*whoever heard of such a thing?*).

■ **Usage** The use of *whomever* for the objective case can sound stilted nowadays, and *whoever* is generally acceptable in its place, e.g. *I ask whoever I meet the same question*. See also Usage Note at EVER.

whole /həʊl/ *adj. & n.* ● *adj.* **1** in an uninjured, unbroken, intact, or undiminished state (*swallowed it whole*; *there is not a plate left whole*). **2** not less than; all there is of; entire, complete (*waited a whole year*; *tell the whole truth*; *the whole school knows*). **3** (of blood or milk etc.) with no part removed. ● *n.* **1** a thing complete in itself. **2** all there is of a thing (*spent the whole of the summer by the sea*). **3** (foll. by *of*) all members, inhabitants, etc., of (*the whole of London knows it*). ◻ **as a whole** as a unity; not as separate parts. **go the whole hog** see HOG. **on the whole** taking everything relevant into account; in general (*it was, on the whole, a good report*; *they behaved well on the whole*). ◻ **wholeness** *n.* [Old English *hāl*, from Germanic]

whole cloth *n.* cloth of full size as manufactured.

wholefood /ˈhəʊlfuːd/ *n. Brit.* food which has not been processed or refined more than is minimally necessary (often *attrib.*: *wholefood diet*).

wholegrain /ˈhəʊlgreɪn/ *adj.* made with or containing whole grains (*wholegrain bread*).

wholehearted /həʊlˈhɑːtɪd/ *adj.* **1** (of a person) completely devoted or committed. **2** (of an action etc.) done with all possible effort, attention, or sincerity; thorough. ◻ **wholeheartedly** *adv.* **wholeheartedness** *n.*

whole holiday *n. Brit.* a whole day taken as a holiday (cf. HALF HOLIDAY).

whole-life insurance *n.* life insurance for which premiums are payable throughout the remaining life of the person insured.

whole lot see LOT.

wholemeal /ˈhəʊlmiːl/ *n.* (usu. *attrib.*) *Brit.* meal or flour of wheat or other cereals with none of the bran or germ removed.

whole note *n.* esp. *N. Amer. Mus.* = SEMIBREVE.

whole number *n.* a number without fractions; an integer.

wholesale /ˈhəʊlseɪl/ *n., adj., adv., & v.* ● *n.* the selling of things in large quantities to be retailed by others (cf. RETAIL). ● *adj. & adv.* **1** by wholesale; at a wholesale price (*can get it for you wholesale*). **2** on a large scale (*wholesale destruction occurred*; *was handing out samples wholesale*). ● *v.tr.* sell wholesale. ◻ **wholesaler** *n.* [Middle English: originally *by whole sale*]

wholesome /ˈhəʊls(ə)m/ *adj.* **1** promoting or indicating physical, mental, or moral health (*wholesome pursuits*; *a wholesome appearance*). **2** prudent (*wholesome respect*). ◻ **wholesomely** *adv.* **wholesomeness** *n.* [Middle English, probably from Old English (as WHOLE, -SOME[1])]

whole-tone scale *n. Mus.* a scale consisting entirely of tones, with no semitones.

wholewheat /ˈhəʊlwiːt/ *n.* (usu. *attrib.*) wheat with none of the bran or germ removed; wholemeal.

wholism var. of HOLISM.

wholly /ˈhəʊlli, ˈhəʊli/ *adv.* **1** entirely; without limitation or diminution (*I am wholly at a loss*). **2** purely, exclusively (*a wholly bad example*). [Middle English, probably from Old English (as WHOLE, -LY[2])]

whom *objective case* of WHO.

whomever *objective case* of WHOEVER.

whomso *archaic objective case* of WHOSO.

whomsoever *objective case* of WHOSOEVER.

whoop /huːp, wuːp/ *n. & v.* (also **hoop**) ● *n.* **1** a loud cry of or as of excitement etc. **2** a long rasping indrawn breath in whooping cough. ● *v.intr.* utter a whoop. ◻ **whoop it up** *colloq.* **1** engage in revelry. **2** *US* make a stir. [Middle English: imitative]

whoopee *int. & n. colloq.* ● *int.* /wʊˈpiː/ expressing exuberant joy. ● *n.* /ˈwʊpi/ exuberant enjoyment or revelry. ◻ **make whoopee** *colloq.* **1** rejoice noisily or hilariously. **2** make love.

whoopee cushion *n.* a rubber cushion that when sat on makes a sound like the breaking of wind.

whooper /ˈhuːpə, ˈw-/ *n.* (in full **whooper swan**) a large migratory swan, *Cygnus cygnus*, with a black and yellow bill and a loud whooping call.

whooping cough /ˈhuːpɪŋ/ *n.* an infectious bacterial disease, esp. of children, with a series of short violent coughs followed by a whoop. Also called *pertussis*.

whooping crane /ˈhuːpɪŋ, ˈw-/ *n.* a large mainly white N. American crane, *Grus americana*, now an endangered species.

whoops /wʊps/ *int.* (also **whoops-a-daisy**) *colloq.* expressing surprise or apology, esp. on making an obvious mistake. [variant of OOPS]

whoosh /wʊʃ, wuːʃ/ *v., n., & int.* (also **woosh**) ● *v.intr. & tr.* move or cause to move with a rushing sound. ● *n.* a sudden movement accompanied by a rushing sound. ● *int.* an exclamation imitating this. [imitative]

whop /wɒp/ *v. & n.* (also, esp. *US*, **whap**) ● *v.tr.* (**whopped**, **whopping**) *slang* **1** thrash. **2** defeat, overcome. ● *n.* **1** the sound of a blow or sudden thud. **2** the regular pulsing sound of a helicopter rotor. [Middle English: variant of dialect *wap*, of unknown origin]

whopper /ˈwɒpə/ *n. slang* **1** something big of its kind. **2** a blatant or gross lie.

whopping /ˈwɒpɪŋ/ *adj. slang* very big (*a whopping lie*; *a whopping fish*).

whore /hɔː/ *n. & v.* ● *n.* **1** a prostitute. **2** *derog.* a promiscuous woman. ● *v.* **1** *intr.* **a** (of a man) use the services of prostitutes. **b** work as a prostitute. **c** live promiscuously. **2** *tr.* prostitute (a person or oneself). **3** *intr.* (foll. by *after*) *archaic* commit idolatry or iniquity.

□ **whoredom** *n.* **whorer** *n.* [Old English *hōre*, from Germanic]

whorehouse /ˈhɔːhaʊs/ *n.* a brothel.

whoremaster /ˈhɔːmɑːstə/ *n. archaic* = WHOREMONGER.

whoremonger /ˈhɔːmʌŋgə/ *n. archaic* a person who has dealings with whores.

whoreson /ˈhɔːs(ə)n/ *n. archaic* **1** a disliked person. **2** (*attrib.*) (of a person or thing) vile.

whorish /ˈhɔːrɪʃ/ *adj.* of or like a whore. □ **whorishly** *adv.* **whorishness** *n.*

whorl /wɔːl, wəːl/ *n.* **1** a ring of leaves or other organs round a stem of a plant. **2** one turn of a spiral, esp. on a shell. **3** a complete circle in a fingerprint. **4** *archaic* a small wheel on a spindle steadying its motion. □ **whorled** *adj.* [Middle English *wharwyl, whorwil*, apparently a variant of WHIRL: influenced by *wharve* = whorl of a spindle]

whortleberry /ˈwəːt(ə)lbɛri/ *n.* (*pl.* **-ies**) a bilberry. [16th c.: dialect form of Middle English *hurtleberry*, of unknown origin]

whose /huːz/ *pron. & det.* ● *pron.* of or belonging to which person (*whose is this book?*). ● *det.* of whom or which (*whose book is this?*; *the man, whose name was Tim*; *the house whose roof was damaged*).

whoseso *archaic poss.* of WHOSO.

whosesoever *poss.* of WHOSOEVER.

whosever *poss.* of WHOEVER.

whoso /ˈhuːsəʊ/ *pron.* (*obj.* **whomso** /ˈhuːm-/; *poss.* **whoseso** /ˈhuːz-/) *archaic* = WHOEVER. [Middle English, = WHO + SO[1], from Old English *swā hwā swā*]

whosoever /huːsəʊˈɛvə/ *pron.* (*obj.* **whomsoever** /huːm-/; *poss.* **whosesoever** /huːz-/) *archaic* = WHOEVER.

who's who *n.* **1** who or what each person is (*know who's who*). **2** a list or directory with facts about notable persons.

whump /wʌmp, wʊmp/ *n. & v.* ● *n.* a dull thud. ● *v.* **1** *intr.* make such a sound; thump, bang. **2** *tr.* strike heavily with a whump. [imitative]

why /wʌɪ/ *adv., int., & n.* ● *adv.* **1 a** for what reason or purpose (*why did you do it?*; *I do not know why you came*). **b** on what grounds (*why do you say that?*). **2** (prec. by *reason* etc.) for which (*the reasons why I did it*). ● *int.* expressing: **1** surprised discovery or recognition (*why, it's you!*). **2** impatience (*why, of course I do!*). **3** reflection (*why, yes, I think so*). **4** objection (*why, what is wrong with it?*). ● *n.* (*pl.* **whys**) a reason or explanation (esp. *whys and wherefores*). □ **why so?** on what grounds?; for what reason or purpose? [Old English *hwī, hwȳ*, instrumental of *hwæt* WHAT, from Germanic]

whydah /ˈwɪdə/ *n.* (also **whidah**) **1** any small African weaver-bird of the genus *Vidua*, the male having mainly black plumage and tail feathers of great length. **2** = WIDOW-BIRD 1. [originally *widow-bird*, altered from association with *Whidah* (now Ouidah), a town in Benin]

WI *abbr.* **1** West Indies. **2** *Brit.* Women's Institute. **3** *US* Wisconsin (in official postal use).

Wicca /ˈwɪkə/ *n.* the religious cult of modern witchcraft. □ **Wiccan** *adj. & n.* [Old English *wicca* WITCH[1]]

wick[1] /wɪk/ *n. & v.* ● *n.* **1** a strip or thread of fibrous or spongy material feeding a flame with fuel in a candle, lamp, etc. **2** *Surgery* a gauze strip inserted in a wound to drain it. ● *v.tr.* (often foll. by *away*) esp. *N. Amer.* absorb or draw off (liquid) by capillary action. □ **dip one's wick** *coarse slang* (of a man) have sexual intercourse. **get on a person's wick** *Brit. colloq.* annoy a person. [Old English *wēoce, -wēoc*, of unknown origin (cf. Middle Dutch *wiecke*, Middle Low German *wēke*)]

wick[2] /wɪk/ *n. dial.* except in compounds e.g. *bailiwick*, and in place names e.g. *Hampton Wick, Warwick*. **1** a town, hamlet, or district. **2** a dairy farm. [Old English *wīc*, probably via Germanic from Latin *vicus* 'street, village']

wicked /ˈwɪkɪd/ *adj.* (**wickeder**, **wickedest**) **1** sinful, iniquitous, given to or involving immorality. **2** spiteful, ill-tempered; intending or intended to give pain. **3** playfully malicious. **4** *colloq.* foul; very bad; formidable (*wicked weather*; *a wicked cough*). **5** *slang* excellent, remarkable. □ **wickedly** *adv.* **wickedness** *n.* [Middle English from obsolete *wick* (perhaps adjectival use of Old English *wicca* 'wizard') + -ED[1] as in *wretched*]

Wicked Bible *n.* an edition of the Bible of 1631, with the misprinted commandment 'thou shalt commit adultery'.

wicker /ˈwɪkə/ *n.* plaited twigs or osiers etc. as material for chairs, baskets, mats, etc. [Middle English, from East Scandinavian: cf. Swedish *viker* 'willow', related to *vika* 'bend']

wickerwork /ˈwɪkəwəːk/ *n.* **1** wicker. **2** things made of wicker.

wicket /ˈwɪkɪt/ *n.* **1** *Cricket* **a** a set of three stumps with the bails in position defended by a batsman. **b** the ground between two wickets. **c** the state of this (*a slow wicket*). **d** a pair of batsmen batting at the same time (*a third-wicket partnership*). **2** (in full **wicket-door** or **-gate**) a small door or gate esp. beside or in a larger one or closing the lower part only of a doorway. **3** *US* an aperture in a door or wall usu. closed with a sliding panel. **4** *US* a croquet hoop. □ **at the wicket** *Cricket* **1** batting. **2** by the wicketkeeper (*caught at the wicket*). **keep wicket** *Cricket* be a wicketkeeper. **on a good** (or **sticky**) **wicket** *colloq.* in a favourable (or unfavourable) position. **take a wicket** *Cricket* (of a bowler) dismiss a batsman, get a batsman out. [Middle English from Anglo-French & Old Northern French *wiket*, variant of Old French *guichet*, of uncertain origin]

wicketkeeper /ˈwɪkɪtkiːpə/*n. Cricket* the fieldsman stationed close behind a batsman's wicket, usu. equipped with gloves and pads. □ **wicketkeeping** *n.*

wickiup /ˈwɪkɪʌp/ *n.* an American Indian hut of a frame covered with grass etc. [Algonquian]

widdershins /ˈwɪdəʃɪnz/ *adv.* (also **withershins** /ˈwɪð-/) esp. *Sc.* in a direction contrary to the sun's course (considered as unlucky); anticlockwise (opp. DEASIL). [Middle Low German *weddersins* from Middle High German *widdersinnes*, from *wider* 'against' + *sin* 'direction']

wide /wʌɪd/ *adj., adv., & n.* ● *adj.* **1 a** measuring much or more than other things of the same kind across or from side to side. **b** considerable; more than is needed (*a wide margin*). **2** (following a measurement) in width (*a metre wide*). **3** extending far; embracing much; of great extent (*has a wide range*; *has wide experience*; *reached a wide public*). **4** not tight or close or restricted; loose. **5 a** *Brit.* free, liberal; unprejudiced (*takes wide views*). **b** not specialized; general. **6** open to the full extent (*staring with wide eyes*). **7 a** (foll. by *of*) not within a reasonable distance of. **b** at a considerable distance from a point or mark. **8** *Brit. slang* shrewd; skilled in sharp practice. **9** (in *comb.*) extending over the whole of (*nationwide*). ● *adv.* **1** widely. **2** to the full extent (*wide awake*). **3** far from the target etc. (*is shooting wide*). ● *n.* **1** *Cricket* a ball judged to pass the wicket beyond the batsman's reach and so scoring a run. **2** (prec. by *the*) the wide world. □ **give a wide berth to** see BERTH. **wide of the mark** see MARK[1]. □ **wideness** *n.* **widish** *adj.* [Old English *wīd* (*adj.*), *wīde* (*adv.*), from Germanic]

wide-angle *attrib.adj.* (of a lens) having a short focal length and hence a field covering a wide angle.

wideawake /ˈwʌɪdəweɪk/ *n.* a soft felt hat with a low crown and wide brim. [punningly named as not having a nap (see NAP[1] *n.*, NAP[2] *n.* 1)]

wide awake *adj.* **1** fully awake. **2** *colloq.* wary, knowing.

wide ball *n. Cricket* = WIDE *n.* 1.

wide boy *n. Brit. slang* a man skilled in dishonest practices; a spiv.

wide-eyed *adj.* surprised or naive.

widely /ˈwʌɪdli/ *adv.* **1** to a wide extent; far apart (*widely spaced*). **2** extensively (*widely read*; *widely distributed*). **3** by many people (*it is widely thought that*; *widely accepted*). **4** considerably; to a large degree (*holds a widely different view*).

widen /ˈwʌɪd(ə)n/ *v.tr. & intr.* make or become wider. □ **widener** *n.*

wide open *adj.* **1** open wide. **2** stretching over an outdoor expanse (*wide open spaces*). **3** (esp. of a contest) of which the outcome is not predictable. **4** (*predic.*: often foll. by *to*) exposed or vulnerable (esp. to attack).

wide-ranging *adj.* covering an extensive range.

wide receiver *n. Amer. Football* a player who receives the ball in a long pass from the quarterback.

wide-screen *attrib.adj.* designed with or for a screen presenting a wide field of vision in relation to its height.

widespread /ˈwʌɪdsprɛd, -ˈsprɛd/ *adj.* widely distributed or disseminated.

wide world *n.* (prec. by *the*) all the world great as it is.

widgeon var. of WIGEON.

widget /ˈwɪdʒɪt/ *n. colloq.* any gadget or device. [perhaps an alteration of GADGET]

widow /ˈwɪdəʊ/ *n. & v.* ● *n.* **1** a woman who has lost her husband by death and has not married again. **2** a woman whose husband is often away on a specified activity (*golf widow*). **3** extra cards dealt separately and taken by the highest bidder. **4** *Printing* the short last line of a paragraph at the top of a page or column. ● *v.tr.* **1** make into a widow or widower. **2** (as **widowed** *adj.*) bereft by the death of a spouse (*my widowed mother*). **3** (foll. by *of*) deprive of. [Old English *widewe*, related to Old High German *wituwa*, Sanskrit *vidhávā*, Latin *viduus* 'bereft, widowed', Greek *ēitheos* 'unmarried man']

widow-bird /ˈwɪdəʊbəːd/*n.* **1** a weaver-bird of the genus *Euplectes*; also called *whydah*. **2** = WHYDAH 1. [from the black plumage of the male, which resembles mourning dress]

widower /ˈwɪdəʊə/ *n.* a man who has lost his wife by death and has not married again.

widowhood /ˈwɪdəʊhʊd/ *n.* the state or period of being a widow.

widow's cruse *n.* an apparently small supply that proves or seems inexhaustible (see 1 Kings 17:10–16).

widow's mite *n.* a small money contribution (see Mark 12:42).

widow's peak *n.* a V-shaped growth of hair towards the centre of the forehead.

widow's weeds see WEEDS.

width /wɪtθ, wɪdθ/ *n.* **1** measurement or distance from side to side. **2** a large extent. **3** breadth or liberality of thought, views, etc. **4** a strip of material of full width as woven. □ **widthways** *adv.* **widthwise** *adv.* [17th c. (as WIDE, -TH², on the pattern of *breadth*) replacing *wideness*]

wield /wiːld/ *v.tr.* **1** hold and use (a weapon or tool). **2** exert or command (power or authority etc.). □ **wielder** *n.* [Old English *wealdan*, *wieldan*, from Germanic]

wieldy /ˈwiːldi/ *adj.* (**wieldier**, **wieldiest**) easily wielded, controlled, or handled.

wiener /ˈwiːnə/ *n. N. Amer.* (also *colloq.* **wienie, weenie** /ˈwiːni/) **1** a frankfurter or frankfurter-style sausage. **2** *coarse slang* **a** the penis. **b** *derog.* (as a term of contempt) a man. [German, abbreviation of *Wienerwurst* 'Vienna sausage']

Wiener schnitzel /ˈviːnə/ *n.* a breaded, fried, and garnished schnitzel.

wife /wʌɪf/ *n.* (*pl.* **wives** /wʌɪvz/) **1** a married woman esp. in relation to her husband. **2** *archaic* a woman, esp. an old or uneducated one. **3** (in *comb.*) a woman engaged in a specified activity (*fishwife*; *housewife*; *midwife*). □ **have** (or **take**) **to wife** *archaic* marry (a woman). □ **wifehood** *n.* **wifeless** *adj.* **wifelike** *adj.* **wifely** *adj.* **wifeliness** *n.* **wifish** *adj.* [Old English *wīf* 'woman': ultimate origin unknown]

wife-swapping *n. colloq.* the practice of exchanging wives for sexual relations.

wig¹ /wɪg/ *n.* an artificial head of hair esp. to conceal baldness or as a disguise, or worn by a judge or barrister or as period dress. □ **wigged** *adj.* (also in *comb.*). **wigless** *adj.* [abbreviation of PERIWIG: cf. WINKLE]

wig² /wɪg/ *v.tr.* (**wigged**, **wigging**) *colloq.* rebuke sharply; rate. [apparently from WIG¹ in 19th c. slang or colloq. sense 'rebuke']

wigeon /ˈwɪdʒ(ə)n/ *n.* (also **widgeon**) a species of dabbling duck, esp. *Anas penelope* or *Anas americana*. [16th c.: origin uncertain]

wigging /ˈwɪgɪŋ/ *n. Brit. colloq.* a reprimand.

wiggle /ˈwɪg(ə)l/ *v. & n. colloq.* ● *v.intr. & tr.* move or cause to move quickly from side to side etc. ● *n.* **1** an act of wiggling. **2** a kink in a line etc. □ **wiggler** *n.* [Middle English from Middle Low German & Middle Dutch *wiggelen*]

wiggly /ˈwɪgli/ *adj.* (**wigglier**, **wiggliest**) *colloq.* **1** moving with a wiggle. **2** having small irregular undulations or bends.

wight /wʌɪt/ *n. archaic* a person (*wretched wight*). [Old English *wiht* = thing, creature, of unknown origin]

wigwag /ˈwɪgwag/ *v.intr.* (**wigwagged**, **wigwagging**) *colloq.* **1** move lightly to and fro. **2** wave flags in this way in signalling. [reduplication of WAG¹]

wigwam /ˈwɪgwam/ *n.* **1** a N. American Indian's domed hut or tent of skins, mats, or bark on poles; (loosely) a tepee. **2** a similar structure for children etc. [Ojibwa *wigwaum*, Algonquian *wikiwam* 'their house']

wilco /ˈwɪlkəʊ/ *int. colloq.* expressing compliance or agreement, esp. acceptance of instructions received by radio. [abbreviation of *will comply*]

wild /wʌɪld/ *adj., adv., & n.* ● *adj.* **1** (of an animal or plant) in its original natural state; not domesticated or cultivated (esp. of species or varieties allied to others that are not wild). **2** not civilized; barbarous. **3** (of scenery etc.) having a conspicuously desolate appearance. **4** unrestrained, disorderly, uncontrolled (*a wild youth*; *wild hair*). **5** tempestuous, violent (*a wild night*). **6 a** intensely eager; excited, frantic (*wild with excitement*; *wild delight*). **b** (of looks, appearance, etc.) indicating distraction. **c** (foll. by *about*) *colloq.* enthusiastically devoted to (a person or subject). **7** *colloq.* infuriated, angry (*makes me wild*). **8** haphazard, ill-aimed, rash (*a wild guess*; *a wild shot*; *a wild venture*). **9** (of a horse, game bird, etc.) shy; easily startled. **10** *colloq.* exciting, delightful. **11** (of a card) having any rank chosen by the player holding it (*the joker is wild*). ● *adv.* in a wild manner (*shooting wild*). ● *n.* **1** a wild tract. **2** a desert. □ **in the wild** in an uncultivated etc. state. **in** (or **out in**) **the wilds** *colloq.* far from normal habitation. **run wild** grow or stray unchecked or undisciplined. **wild and woolly** uncouth; lacking refinement. □ **wildish** *adj.* **wildly** *adv.* **wildness** *n.* [Old English *wilde*, from Germanic]

wild arum *n.* cuckoo pint.

wild boar see BOAR.

wild card *n.* **1** see WILD *adj.* 11. **2** *Computing* a character that will match any character or sequence of characters in a file name etc. **3** *Sport* an extra player or team chosen to enter a competition at the selectors' discretion.

wildcat /ˈwʌɪl(d)kat/ *n. & adj.* ● *n.* **1** a hot-tempered or violent person. **2** any of various smallish non-domesticated animals of the cat family, esp. (usu. **wild cat**) *Felis sylvestris* of Eurasia and Africa, with a grey and black coat and a bushy tail, or (*US*) a bobcat. **3** an exploratory oil well. ● *adj.* (*attrib.*) **1** esp. *US* reckless; financially unsound. **2** (of a strike) sudden and unofficial.

wild-caught *attrib.adj.* (of an animal) caught in and taken from the wild.

wildebeest /ˈwɪldəbiːst, ˈvɪ-/ *n.* (*pl.* same or **wildebeests**) = GNU. [Afrikaans (as WILD, BEAST)]

wilder /ˈwɪldə/ *v.tr. archaic* **1** lead astray. **2** bewilder. [perhaps based on WILDERNESS]

wilderness /ˈwɪldənɪs/ *n.* **1** a desert; an uncultivated and uninhabited region. **2** part of a garden left with an uncultivated appearance. **3** (foll. by *of*) a confused assemblage of things. □ **in the wilderness** *Brit.* out of political office. **voice in the wilderness** an unheeded advocate of reform (see Matt. 3:3 etc.). [Old English *wildēornes* from *wild dēor* 'wild deer']

wildfire /ˈwʌɪl(d)fʌɪə/ *n.* **1** *hist.* a combustible liquid, esp. Greek fire, formerly used in warfare. **2** = WILL-O'-THE-WISP. □ **spread like wildfire** spread with great speed.

wildfowl /ˈwʌɪl(d)faʊl/ *n.* (*pl.* same) (usu. in *pl.*) a game bird, esp. an aquatic one.

wild-goose chase *n.* a foolish or hopeless and unproductive quest.

wild horse *n.* **1** a horse not domesticated or broken in. **2** (in *pl.*) *colloq.* even the most powerful influence etc. (*wild horses would not drag the secret from me*).

wild hyacinth *n.* = BLUEBELL 1.

wilding[1] /ˈwʌɪldɪŋ/ *n. US slang* the activity or an instance of going on a violent rampage through the streets in a group.

wilding[2] /ˈwʌɪldɪŋ/ *n.* (also **wildling** /-lɪŋ/) **1** a plant sown by natural agency, esp. a wild crab apple. **2** the fruit of such a plant. [WILD + -ING[3]]

wildlife /ˈwʌɪl(d)lʌɪf/ *n.* wild animals collectively.

wild man of the woods *n. colloq.* an orang-utan.

wild oat *n.* a grass, *Avena fatua*, related to the cultivated oat and found as a weed in cornfields. □ **sow one's wild oats** see OAT.

wild rice *n.* any tall grass of the genus *Zizania*, yielding edible grains.

wild silk *n.* **1** silk from wild silkworms. **2** an imitation of this from short silk fibres.

wild type *n. Genetics* a strain or characteristic which prevails in natural conditions, as distinct from an atypical mutant.

Wild West *n.* the western US in a time of lawlessness in its early history.

wildwood /ˈwʌɪldwʊd/ *n. poet.* uncultivated or unfrequented woodland.

wile /wʌɪl/ *n. & v.* ● *n.* (usu. in *pl.*) a stratagem; a trick or cunning procedure. ● *v.tr.* (foll. by *away*, *into*, etc.) lure or entice. [Middle English *wīl*, perhaps from an Old Norse word related to *vél* 'craft']

wilful /ˈwɪlfʊl, -f(ə)l/ *adj.* (*US* **willful**) **1** (of an action or state) intentional, deliberate (*wilful murder*; *wilful neglect*; *wilful disobedience*). **2** (of a person) obstinate, headstrong. □ **wilfully** *adv.* **wilfulness** *n.* [Middle English, from WILL[2] + -FUL]

wilga /ˈwɪlgə/ *n. Austral.* a small tree of the genus *Geijera*, with white flowers. [Wiradhuri *wilgar*]

wiliness see WILY.

will[1] /wɪl/ *v.aux. & tr.* (*3rd sing. present* **will**; *past* **would** /wʊd/) (foll. by infin. without *to*, or *absol.*; present and past only in use) **1** (in the 2nd and 3rd persons, and often in the 1st: see SHALL) expressing the future tense in statements, commands, or questions (*you will regret this*; *they will leave at once*; *will you go to the party?*). **2** (in the 1st person) expressing a wish or intention (*I will return soon*). **3** expressing desire, consent, or inclination (*will you have a sandwich?*; *come when you will*; *the door will not open*). **4** expressing a request as a question (*will you please open the window?*). **5** expressing ability or capacity (*the jar will hold a kilo*). **6** expressing habitual or inevitable tendency (*accidents will happen*; *will sit there for hours*). **7** expressing probability or expectation (*that will be my wife*). □ **will do** *colloq.* expressing willingness to carry out a request. [Old English *wyllan* from Germanic: related to Latin *volo*]

■ **Usage** See Usage Note at SHALL.

will[2] /wɪl/ *n. & v.* ● *n.* **1** the faculty by which a person decides or is regarded as deciding on and initiating action (*the mind consists of the understanding and the will*). **2** (also **will-power**) control exercised by deliberate purpose over impulse; self-control (*has a strong will*; *overcame his shyness by will-power*). **3** a deliberate or fixed desire or intention (*a will to live*). **4** energy of intention; the power of effecting one's intentions or dominating others. **5** directions (usu. written) in legal form for the disposition of one's property after death (*make one's will*). **6** disposition towards others (*good will*). **7** *archaic* what one desires or ordains (*thy will be done*). ● *v.tr.* **1** have as the object of one's will; intend unconditionally (*what God wills*; *willed that we should succeed*). **2** (*absol.*) exercise will-power. **3** instigate or impel or compel by the exercise of will-power (*you can will yourself into contentment*). **4** bequeath by the terms of a will (*shall will my money to charity*). □ **at will 1** whenever one pleases. **2** *Law* able to be evicted without notice (*tenant at will*). **have one's will** obtain what one wants. **what is your will?** what do you wish done? **where there's a will there's a way** determination will overcome any obstacle. **a will of one's own** obstinacy; wilfulness of character. **with the best will in the world** however good one's intentions. **with a will** energetically or resolutely. □ **willed** *adj.* (also in *comb.*). **willer** *n.* **will-less** *adj.* [Old English *willa*, from Germanic]

willet /ˈwɪlɪt/ *n.* (*pl.* same) a large N. American wader, *Catoptophorus semipalmatus*. [*pill-will-willet*, imitative of its cry]

willful *US* var. of WILFUL.

willie var. of WILLY.

willies /ˈwɪlɪz/ *n.pl. colloq.* nervous discomfort (esp. *give* or *get the willies*). [19th c.: origin unknown]

willing /ˈwɪlɪŋ/ *adj. & n.* ● *adj.* **1** ready to consent or undertake (*a willing ally*; *am willing to do it*). **2** given or done etc. by a willing person (*willing hands*; *willing help*). ● *n.* cheerful intention (*show willing*). □ **willingly** *adv.* **willingness** *n.*

will-o'-the-wisp /wɪləðəˈwɪsp/ *n.* **1** a phosphorescent light seen on marshy ground, perhaps resulting from the combustion of gases. **2** an elusive person. **3** a delusive hope or plan. [originally *Will with the wisp*: *wisp* = handful of (lighted) hay etc.]

willow /ˈwɪləʊ/ *n.* **1** (also **willow tree**) a tree or shrub of the genus *Salix*, growing usu. near water in temperate climates, with small flowers borne on catkins, and pliant branches yielding osiers and timber for cricket bats, baskets, etc. **2** a cricket bat. [Old English *welig*, from Germanic]

willow grouse *n.* (also *N. Amer.* **willow ptarmigan**) a common European and N. American grouse, *Lagopus lagopus*, with brown breeding plumage and white winter plumage.

willowherb /ˈwɪləʊhəːb/ *n.* any plant of the genus *Epilobium* etc., esp. one with leaves like a willow and pale purple flowers.

willow-pattern *n.* a conventional design representing a Chinese scene, often with a willow tree, of blue on white porcelain, stoneware, or earthenware.

willow tit *n.* a Eurasian black-capped tit, *Parus montanus*.

willow warbler *n.* (also **willow wren**) a small woodland bird, *Phylloscopus trochilus*, with a tuneful song.

willowy /ˈwɪləʊi/ *adj.* **1** having or bordered by willows. **2** lithe and slender.

will-power *n.* var. of WILL[2] *n.* 2.

willy /ˈwɪli/ *n.* (also **willie**) (*pl.* **-ies**) *Brit. slang* the penis. [pet form of the name *William*]

willy-nilly /wɪlɪˈnɪli/ *adv. & adj.* ● *adv.* whether one likes it or not. ● *adj.* existing or occurring willy-nilly. [later spelling of *will I, nill I* 'I am willing, I am unwilling']

willy wagtail *n.* **1** an Australian flycatcher, *Rhipidura leucophrys*, of the family Monarchidae, with striking black and white plumage. **2** *dial.* a pied wagtail.

willy-willy /ˈwɪlɪˌwɪli/ *n.* (*pl.* **-ies**) *Austral.* a cyclone or dust storm. [Yindjibarndi or Wemba-wemba]

wilt[1] /wɪlt/ *v.* & *n.* ● *v.* **1** *intr.* (of a plant, leaf, or flower) wither, droop. **2** *intr.* (of a person) lose one's energy, flag, tire, droop. **3** *tr.* cause to wilt. ● *n.* a plant disease causing wilting. [originally dialect: perhaps an alteration of *wilk*, *welk*, of Low German or Dutch origin]

wilt[2] /wɪlt/ *archaic 2nd person sing.* of WILL[1].

Wilton /ˈwɪlt(ə)n/ *n.* a kind of woven carpet. [*Wilton*, a town in southern England, noted for the manufacture of carpets]

Wilts. /wɪlts/ *abbr.* Wiltshire.

wily /ˈwʌɪli/ *adj.* (**wilier**, **wiliest**) full of wiles; crafty, cunning. □ **wilily** *adv.* **wiliness** *n.*

wimp /wɪmp/ *n. colloq.* a feeble or ineffectual person. □ **wimpish** *adj.* **wimpishly** *adv.* **wimpishness** *n.* **wimpy** *adj.* [20th c.: origin uncertain]

wimple /ˈwɪmp(ə)l/ *n.* & *v.* ● *n.* a linen or silk headdress covering the neck and the sides of the face, formerly worn by women and still worn by some nuns. ● *v.tr.* & *intr.* arrange or fall in folds. [Old English *wimpel*]

Wimpy /ˈwɪmpi/ *n.* (*pl.* **Wimpys**) *Brit. propr.* a hamburger served in a plain bun. [named after J. W. *Wimpy*, a character in the *Popeye* cartoon strip, frequently depicted eating a hamburger]

Wimshurst machine /ˈwɪmzhəːst/ *n.* a device for generating an electric charge by turning glass discs in opposite directions. [named after J. *Wimshurst*, English engineer d. 1903]

win /wɪn/ *v.* & *n.* ● *v.* (**winning**; *past* and *past part.* **won** /wʌn/) **1** *tr.* acquire or secure as a result of a fight, contest, bet, litigation, or some other effort (*won some money*; *won my admiration*). **2** *tr.* be victorious in (a fight, game, race, etc.). **3** *intr.* **a** be the victor; win a race or contest etc. (*who won?*; *persevere, and you will win*). **b** (foll. by *through*, *free*, etc.) make one's way or become by successful effort. **4** *tr.* reach by effort (*win the summit*; *win the shore*). **5** *tr.* obtain (ore) from a mine. **6** *tr.* dry (hay etc.) by exposure to the air. ● *n.* a victory in a game, contest, bet, etc. □ **win the day** be victorious in battle, argument, etc. **win over** persuade, gain the support of. **win one's spurs 1** *colloq.* gain distinction or fame. **2** *hist.* gain a knighthood. **win through** (or **out**) overcome obstacles. **you can't win** *colloq.* there is no way to succeed. **you can't win them all** *colloq.* a resigned expression of consolation on failure. □ **winnable** *adj.* [Old English *winnan* 'toil, endure']

wince[1] /wɪns/ *n.* & *v.* ● *n.* a start or involuntary shrinking movement showing pain or distress. ● *v.intr.* give a wince. □ **wincer** *n.* **wincingly** *adv.* [Middle English from Old French *guenchir* 'turn aside']

wince[2] /wɪns/ *n. Brit.* a roller for moving textile fabric through a dyeing-vat. [variant of WINCH]

wincey /ˈwɪnsi/ *n.* (*pl.* **winceys**) *Brit.* a strong lightweight fabric of wool and cotton or linen. [originally Scots: apparently from *woolsey* in LINSEY-WOOLSEY]

winceyette /wɪnsɪˈɛt/ *n. Brit.* a lightweight napped flannelette used esp. for nightclothes.

winch /wɪn(t)ʃ/ *n.* & *v.* ● *n.* **1** the crank of a wheel or axle. **2** a windlass. **3** *Brit.* the reel of a fishing rod. **4** = WINCE[2]. ● *v.tr.* lift with a winch. □ **wincher** *n.* [Old English *wince*, from Germanic]

Winchester /ˈwɪntʃɪstə/ *n.* **1** *propr.* a breech-loading repeating rifle. **2** (in full **Winchester disk** or **drive**) *Computing* a (usu. fixed) disk drive in a sealed unit containing a high-capacity hard disk and the read-write heads (so called because its original numerical designation corresponded to that of the rifle's calibre). [named after O. F. *Winchester* d. 1880, US manufacturer of the rifle]

winchester /ˈwɪntʃɪstə/ *n. Chem.* a cylindrical (usu. glass) bottle for transporting liquids. [originally applied to containers holding a bushel, gallon, or quart according to an obsolete system of measurement with standards kept at *Winchester* in Hampshire]

wind[1] /wɪnd/ *n.* & *v.* ● *n.* **1 a** air in more or less rapid natural motion, esp. from an area of high pressure to one of low pressure. **b** a current of wind blowing from a specified direction or otherwise defined (*north wind*; *contrary wind*). **2 a** breath as needed in physical exertion or in speech. **b** the power of breathing without difficulty while running or making a similar continuous effort (*let me recover my wind*). **c** a spot below the centre of the chest where a blow temporarily paralyses breathing. **3** mere empty words; meaningless rhetoric. **4** gas generated in the bowels etc. by indigestion; flatulence. **5 a** an artificially produced current of air, esp. for sounding an organ or other wind instrument. **b** air stored for use or used as a current. **c** the wind instruments of an orchestra collectively (*poor balance between wind and strings*). **6** a scent carried by the wind, indicating the presence or proximity of an animal etc. ● *v.tr.* **1** exhaust the wind of by exertion or a blow. **2** renew the wind of by rest (*stopped to wind the horses*). **3** make breathe quickly and deeply by exercise. **4** *Brit.* make (a baby) bring up wind after feeding. **5** detect the presence of by a scent. **6** /waɪnd/ (*past* and *past part.* **winded** or **wound** /waʊnd/) *poet.* sound (a bugle or call) by blowing. □ **before the wind** helped by the wind's force. **between wind and water** at a vulnerable point. **close to** (or **near**) **the wind 1** sailing as nearly against the wind as is consistent with using its force. **2** *colloq.* verging on indecency or dishonesty. **get wind of** *colloq.* **1** smell out. **2** begin to suspect; hear a rumour of. **get** (or **have**) **the wind up** *colloq.* be alarmed or frightened. **how** (or **which way**) **the wind blows** (or **lies**) **1** what is the state of opinion. **2** what developments are likely. **in the wind** happening or about to happen. **in the wind's eye** directly against the wind. **like the wind** swiftly. **off the wind** *Naut.* with the wind on the quarter. **on a wind** *Naut.* against a wind on either bow. **on the wind** (of a sound or scent) carried by the wind. **put the wind up** *colloq.* alarm or frighten. **take wind** be rumoured; become known. **take the wind out of a person's sails** frustrate a person by anticipating an action or remark etc. **to the winds** (or **four winds**) **1** in all directions. **2** into a state of abandonment or neglect. **wind and weather** exposure to the effects of the elements. **wind** (or **winds**) **of change** a force or influence for reform. □ **windless** *adj.* [Old English from Germanic]

wind[2] /wʌɪnd/ *v.* & *n.* ● *v.* (*past* and *past part.* **wound** /waʊnd/) **1** *intr.* go in a circular, spiral, curved, or crooked course (*a winding staircase*; *the path winds up the hill*). **2** *tr.* make (one's way) by such a course (*wind your way up to bed*; *wound their way into our affections*). **3** *tr.* wrap closely; surround with or as with a coil (*wound the blanket round me*; *wound my arms round the child*; *wound the child in my arms*). **4 a** *tr.* coil; provide with a coiled thread etc. (*wind the ribbon on to the card*; *wound cotton on a reel*; *winding wool into a ball*). **b** *intr.* coil; (of wool etc.) coil into a ball (*the creeper winds round the pole*; *the wool wound into a ball*). **5** *tr.* wind up (a clock etc.). **6** *tr.* hoist or draw with a windlass etc. (*wound the cable car up the mountain*). ● *n.* **1** a bend or turn in a course. **2** a single turn when winding. □ **wind down 1** lower by winding. **2** (of a mechanism) unwind. **3** (of a person) relax. **4** draw gradually to a close. **wind off** unwind (string, wool, etc.). **wind round one's finger** see FINGER. **wind up 1** coil the whole of (a piece of string etc.). **2** esp. *Brit.* tighten the coiling or coiled spring of (esp. a clock etc.). **3 a** *colloq.* increase the tension or intensity of (*wound myself up to fever pitch*). **b** irritate or provoke (a person) to the point of anger. **4** bring to a conclusion; end (*wound up his speech*). **5**

Commerce **a** arrange the affairs of and dissolve (a company). **b** (of a company) cease business and go into liquidation. **6** *colloq.* arrive finally; end in a specified state or circumstance (*you'll wind up in prison*; *wound up owing £100*). **wound up** *adj. colloq.* (of a person) excited or tense or angry. [Old English *windan* from Germanic: related to WANDER, WEND]

windage /ˈwɪndɪdʒ/ *n.* **1** the friction of air against the moving part of a machine. **2 a** the effect of the wind in deflecting a missile. **b** an allowance for this. **3** the difference between the diameter of a gun's bore and its projectile, allowing the escape of gas.

windbag /ˈwɪn(d)bag/ *n. colloq.* a person who talks a lot but says little of any value.

wind band *n.* a group of wind instruments as a band or section of an orchestra.

windbound /ˈwɪn(d)baʊnd/ *adj.* unable to sail because of contrary winds.

windbreak /ˈwɪn(d)breɪk/ *n.* a thing, such as a row of trees, a fence, wall, or screen etc., serving to break the force of the wind.

windbreaker /ˈwɪn(d)breɪkə/ *n. US* = WINDCHEATER.

windburn /ˈwɪn(d)bəːn/ *n.* inflammation of the skin caused by exposure to the wind.

windcheater /ˈwɪn(d)tʃiːtə/ *n. Brit.* a kind of wind-resistant outer jacket with close-fitting neck, cuffs, and lower edge.

wind-chill *n.* the cooling effect of wind blowing on a surface.

wind-cone *n.* = WINDSOCK.

wind-down *n. colloq.* a gradual lessening of excitement or reduction of activity.

winder /ˈwʌɪndə/ *n. Brit.* a winding mechanism esp. of a clock or watch.

windfall /ˈwɪn(d)fɔːl/ *n.* **1** an apple or other fruit blown to the ground by the wind. **2** a piece of unexpected good fortune, esp. a legacy.

wind farm *n.* a group of energy-producing windmills or wind turbines.

windflower /ˈwɪn(d)flaʊə/ *n.* an anemone.

wind force *n.* the force of the wind esp. as measured on the Beaufort etc. scale.

wind gap *n.* a dried-up former river valley through ridges or hills.

wind-gauge *n.* **1** an anemometer. **2** an apparatus attached to the sights of a gun enabling allowance to be made for the wind in shooting. **3** *Mus.* a device for indicating the wind pressure in an organ.

windhover /ˈwɪndhɒvə/ *n. Brit.* a kestrel.

winding /ˈwʌɪndɪŋ/ *n.* **1** in senses of WIND² *v.* **2** curved or sinuous motion or movement. **3 a** a thing that is wound round or coiled. **b** *Electr.* coils of wire as a conductor round an armature etc.

winding engine *n.* a machine for hoisting.

winding-sheet *n.* a sheet in which a corpse is wrapped for burial.

wind instrument *n.* a musical instrument in which sound is produced by a current of air, esp. the breath.

windjammer /ˈwɪn(d)dʒamə/ *n.* a merchant sailing ship.

windlass /ˈwɪndləs/ *n. & v.* ● *n.* a machine with a horizontal axle for hauling or hoisting. ● *v.tr.* hoist or haul with a windlass. [alteration (perhaps by association with dialect *windle* 'to wind') of obsolete *windas*, via Old French *guindas* from Old Norse *vindáss*, from *vinda* WIND² + *áss* 'pole']

wind machine *n.* a device for producing a blast of air or the sound of wind.

windmill /ˈwɪn(d)mɪl/ *n. & v.* ● *n.* **1** a mill worked by the action of the wind on its sails. **2** esp. *Brit.* a toy consisting of a stick with curved vanes attached that revolve in a wind. ● *v.tr. & intr.* move like the sails of a windmill. □ **throw one's cap** (or **bonnet**) **over the windmill** act recklessly or unconventionally. **tilt at** (or **fight**) **windmills** attack an imaginary enemy or grievance.

window /ˈwɪndəʊ/ *n.* **1 a** an opening in a wall, roof, vehicle, etc., usu. with glass in fixed, sliding, or hinged frames, to admit light or air etc. and allow the occupants to see out. **b** the glass filling this opening (*have broken the window*). **2** a space for display behind the front window of a shop. **3** an aperture in a wall etc. through which customers are served in a bank, ticket office, etc. **4** an opportunity to observe or learn. **5** an opening or transparent part in an envelope to show an address. **6** *Computing* a defined area on a display screen in which a part of a file or image can be displayed. **7 a** an interval during which atmospheric and astronomical circumstances are suitable for the launch of a spacecraft. **b** any interval or opportunity for action. **8** strips of metal foil dispersed in the air to obstruct radar detection. **9** *Physics* a range of electromagnetic wavelengths for which a medium (esp. the atmosphere) is transparent. □ **out of the window** *colloq.* no longer taken into account. □ **windowed** *adj.* (also in *comb.*). **windowless** *adj.* [Middle English from Old Norse *vindauga* (as WIND¹, EYE)]

window box *n.* a box placed on an outside window sill for growing flowers.

window cleaner *n.* **1** a person who is employed to clean windows. **2** a substance or object used for cleaning windows.

window dressing *n.* **1** the art of arranging a display in a shop window etc. **2** an adroit presentation of facts etc. to give a deceptively favourable impression.

window frame *n.* a supporting frame for the glass of a window.

windowing /ˈwɪndəʊɪŋ/ *n. Computing* the use of windows for the simultaneous display of parts of different files, images, etc.

window ledge *n.* = WINDOW SILL.

window pane *n.* a pane of glass in a window.

window seat *n.* **1** a seat below a window, esp. in a bay or alcove. **2** a seat next to a window in an aircraft, train, etc.

window-shop *v.intr.* (**-shopped**, **-shopping**) (esp. as **window-shopping** *n.*) look at goods displayed in shop windows, usu. without buying anything. □ **window-shopper** *n.*

window sill *n.* a sill below a window.

window tax *n. Brit. hist.* a tax on windows or similar openings (abolished in 1851).

windpipe /ˈwɪn(d)pʌɪp/ *n.* the air passage from the throat to the lungs; the trachea.

wind-rose *n.* a diagram of the relative frequency of wind directions at a place.

windrow /ˈwɪndrəʊ/ *n.* **1** a line of raked hay, corn-sheaves, peats, etc., laid out to dry in the wind. **2** esp. *N. Amer.* **a** a long pile or row heaped up by or as if by the wind. **b** a bank of loose material heaped along the side of a road.

wind-sail *n.* a canvas funnel conveying air to the lower parts of a ship.

windscreen /ˈwɪn(d)skriːn/ *n. Brit.* a screen of glass at the front of a motor vehicle.

windscreen wiper *n.* a device consisting of a rubber blade on an arm, moving in an arc, for keeping a windscreen clear of rain etc.

wind shear *n.* a variation in wind velocity at right angles to the wind's direction.

windshield /ˈwɪn(d)ʃiːld/ *n. N. Amer.* = WINDSCREEN.

wind-sleeve *n.* = WINDSOCK.

windsock /ˈwɪn(d)sɒk/ *n.* a canvas cylinder or cone on a mast to show the direction of the wind at an airfield etc.

Windsor /ˈwɪnzə/ *n.* (usu. *attrib.*) denoting or relating to the British royal family since 1917. [*Windsor* in S. England, site of the royal residence at Windsor Castle]

Windsor chair *n.* a wooden dining chair with a semicircular back supported by upright rods.

windstorm /ˈwɪndstɔːm/ *n.* esp. *N. Amer.* a storm with very strong wind but little or no rain, snow, etc.; a gale.

windsurfing /ˈwɪn(d)səːfɪŋ/ *n.* the sport of riding on water on a sailboard. □ **windsurf** *v.intr.* **windsurfer** *n.*

windswept /ˈwɪn(d)swɛpt/ *adj.* exposed to or swept back by the wind.

wind tunnel *n.* a tunnel-like device to produce an airstream past models of aircraft etc. for the study of wind effects on them.

wind-up *n.* & *adj.* ● *n.* **1** a conclusion; a finish. **2** *Brit. colloq.* an attempt to provoke someone. ● *attrib.adj.* operated by being wound up.

windward /ˈwɪndwəd/ *adj., adv., & n.* ● *adj.* & *adv.* on the side from which the wind is blowing (opp. LEEWARD). ● *n.* the windward region, side, or direction (*to windward; on the windward of*). □ **get to windward of 1** place oneself there to avoid the smell of. **2** gain an advantage over.

windy[1] /ˈwɪndi/ *adj.* (**windier**, **windiest**) **1** stormy with wind (*a windy night*). **2** exposed to the wind; windswept (*a windy plain*). **3** *Brit.* generating or suffering from flatulence. **4** *colloq.* wordy, verbose, empty (*a windy speech*). **5** *Brit. colloq.* nervous, frightened. □ **windily** *adv.* **windiness** *n.* [Old English *windig* (as WIND[1], -Y[1])]

windy[2] /ˈwʌɪndi/ *adj.* that winds, winding (*a narrow windy path*).

wine /wʌɪn/ *n.* & *v.* ● *n.* **1** fermented grape juice as an alcoholic drink. **2** a fermented drink resembling this made from other fruits etc. as specified (*elderberry wine; ginger wine*). **3** = WINE RED. ● *v.* **1** *intr.* drink wine. **2** *tr.* entertain to wine. □ **wine and dine** entertain to or have a meal with wine. □ **wineless** *adj.* [Old English *wīn* via Germanic from Latin *vinum*]

wine bar *n.* a bar or small restaurant where wine is the main drink available.

wineberry /ˈwʌɪnb(ə)ri/ *n.* (*pl.* **-ies**) **1 a** a deciduous bristly shrub, *Rubus phoenicolasius*, from China and Japan, producing scarlet berries used in cookery. **b** this berry. **2** = MAKO[2].

winebibber /ˈwʌɪnbɪbə/ *n. archaic* or *literary* a tippler or drunkard. □ **winebibbing** *n.* & *adj.* [WINE + *bib* 'to tipple']

wine bottle *n.* a glass bottle for wine, the standard size holding 75 cl or 26 ⅔ fl. oz.

wine box *n.* a square carton of wine with a dispensing tap.

wine cellar *n.* **1** a cellar for storing wine. **2** the contents of this.

wineglass /ˈwʌɪnglɑːs/ *n.* **1** a glass for wine, usu. with a stem and foot. **2** the contents of this, a wineglassful.

wineglassful /ˈwʌɪnglɑːsfʊl, -f(ə)l/ *n.* (*pl.* **-fuls**) **1** the capacity of a wineglass, esp. of the size used for sherry, as a measure of liquid, about four tablespoons or 2 fl. oz. **2** the contents of a wineglass.

wine-grower *n.* a cultivator of grapes for wine.

wine list *n.* a list of wines available in a restaurant etc.

winemaker /ˈwʌɪnmeɪkə/ *n.* a producer of wine; a wine-grower.

winemaking /ˈwʌɪnmeɪkɪŋ/ *n.* (often *attrib.*) the production of wine, either commercially or as a hobby.

winepress /ˈwʌɪnprɛs/ *n.* a press in which grapes are squeezed in making wine.

wine red *n.* & *adj.* ● *n.* the dark red colour of red wine. ● *adj.* (hyphenated when *attrib.*) of this colour.

winery /ˈwʌɪn(ə)ri/ *n.* (*pl.* **-ies**) esp. *US* an establishment where wine is made.

wineskin /ˈwʌɪnskɪn/ *n.* a whole skin of a goat etc. sewn up and used to hold wine.

wine tasting *n.* **1** judging the quality of wine by tasting it. **2** an occasion for this. □ **wine taster** *n.*

wine vinegar *n.* vinegar made from wine as distinct from malt.

wine waiter *n. Brit.* a waiter responsible for serving wine.

wine writer *n.* a person who writes (esp. as a journalist) about wine.

winey /ˈwʌɪni/ *adj.* (also **winy**) (**winier**, **winiest**) resembling wine in taste or appearance.

wing /wɪŋ/ *n.* & *v.* ● *n.* **1** each of the limbs or organs by which a bird, bat, or insect is able to fly. **2** a rigid horizontal winglike structure forming a supporting part of an aircraft. **3** part of a building etc. which projects or is extended in a certain direction (*lived in the north wing*). **4 a** a forward player at either end of a line in football, hockey, etc. **b** the side part of a playing area. **5** (in *pl.*) the sides of a theatre stage out of view of the audience. **6** a section of a political party in terms of the extremity of its views. **7** a flank of a battle array (*the cavalry were massed on the left wing*). **8** *Brit.* the part of a motor vehicle extending above a wheel. **9 a** an air force unit of several squadrons or groups. **b** (in *pl.*) a pilot's badge in the RAF etc. (*get one's wings*). **10** *Anat.* & *Bot.* a lateral part or projection of an organ or structure. ● *v.* **1** *intr.* & *tr.* travel or traverse on wings or in an aircraft (*winging through the air; am winging my way home*). **2** *tr.* wound in a wing or an arm. **3** *tr.* equip with wings. **4** *tr.* enable to fly; send in flight (*fear winged my steps; winged an arrow towards them*). □ **give** (or **lend**) **wings to** speed up (a person or a thing). **on the wing** flying or in flight. **on a wing and a prayer** with only the slightest chance of success. **spread** (or **stretch**) **one's wings** develop one's powers fully. **take under one's wing** treat as a protégé. **take wing** fly away; soar. **waiting in the wings** holding oneself in readiness. □ **winged** *adj.* (also in *comb.*). **wingless** *adj.* **winglet** *n.* **winglike** *adj.* [Middle English from Old Norse *vængir*, pl. of *vængr*]

wing-beat *n.* one complete set of motions with a wing in flying.

wing-case *n.* the horny cover of an insect's wing.

wing chair *n.* a chair with side pieces projecting forwards at the top of a high back.

wing collar *n.* a high stiff shirt collar with turned-down corners.

wing commander *n.* an RAF officer next below group captain.

wing covert *n.* any of the small coverts overlying the flight feathers of a bird's wing.

wingding /ˈwɪŋdɪŋ/ *n. slang* **1** esp. *N. Amer.* a wild party. **2** *US* a drug addict's real or feigned seizure. [20th c.: origin unknown]

winged words *n.pl.* highly apposite or significant words.

winger /ˈwɪŋə/ *n.* **1** a player on a wing in football, hockey, etc. **2** (in *comb.*) a member of a specified political wing (*left-winger*).

wing forward *n. Rugby* a forward who plays on the wing.

wing-game *n. Brit.* game birds.

wing-half *n. Football* a right or left half-back.

wingman /ˈwɪŋmən/ *n.* (*pl.* **-men**) **1** a pilot whose plane is positioned behind and outside the leading aircraft in a formation. **2** = WINGER 1.

wing nut *n.* a nut with projections for the fingers to turn it on a screw.

wingspan /ˈwɪŋspan/ *n.* (also **wingspread** /-sprɛd/) measurement right across the wings of a bird or aircraft.

wing-stroke *n.* = WING-BEAT.

wing-tip *n.* the outer end of an aircraft's or a bird's wing.

wink /wɪŋk/ *v.* & *n.* ● *v.* **1 a** *tr.* close and open (one eye or both eyes) quickly. **b** *intr.* close and open an eye. **2** *intr.* (often foll. by *at*) wink one eye as a signal of friendship or greeting or to convey a message to a person. **3** *intr.* (of a light etc.) twinkle; shine or flash intermittently. ● *n.* **1** the act or an instance of winking, esp. as a signal etc. **2** *colloq.* a brief moment of sleep (*didn't sleep a wink*). □ **as easy as winking** *colloq.* very easy. **in a wink** very quickly. **wink at 1** purposely avoid seeing; pretend not to notice. **2** connive at (a wrongdoing etc.). [Old English *wincian* from Germanic]

winker /ˈwɪŋkə/ *n.* **1** *Brit.* a flashing indicator light on a motor vehicle. **2** (usu. in *pl.*) a horse's blinker.

winkle /ˈwɪŋk(ə)l/ *n.* & *v.* ● *n.* any edible marine gastropod mollusc of the genus *Littorina*; a periwinkle. ● *v.tr.* (foll. by *out*) esp. *Brit.* extract or eject (*winkled* *the information out of them*). □ **winkler** *n.* [abbreviation of PERIWINKLE²: cf. WIG¹]

winkle-picker *n. Brit. slang* a shoe with a long pointed toe.

winless /ˈwɪnlɪs/ *adj.* esp. *N. Amer.* without having won usu. a match in a series of contests.

winner /ˈwɪnə/ *n.* **1** a person, racehorse, etc. that wins. **2** *colloq.* a successful or highly promising idea, enterprise, etc. (*the new scheme seemed a winner*).

winning /ˈwɪnɪŋ/ *adj.* & *n.* ● *adj.* **1** having or bringing victory or an advantage (*the winning entry*; *a winning stroke*). **2** attractive, persuasive (*a winning smile*; *winning ways*). ● *n.* (in *pl.*) money won, esp. in betting etc. □ **winningly** *adv.* **winningness** *n.*

winning post *n.* a post marking the end of a race.

winnow /ˈwɪnəʊ/ *v.tr.* **1** blow (grain) free of chaff etc. by an air current. **2** (foll. by *out*, *away*, *from*, etc.) get rid of (chaff etc.) from grain. **3 a** sift, separate; clear of refuse or inferior specimens. **b** sift or examine (evidence for falsehood etc.). **c** clear, sort, or weed out (rubbish etc.). **4** *poet.* **a** fan (the air with wings). **b** flap (wings). **c** stir (the hair etc.). □ **winnower** *n.* (in senses 1, 2). [Old English *windwian* (as WIND¹)]

wino /ˈwʌɪnəʊ/ *n.* (*pl.* **-os**) *slang* a habitual excessive drinker of cheap wine; an alcoholic.

winsome /ˈwɪns(ə)m/ *adj.* (of a person, looks, or manner) winning, attractive, engaging. □ **winsomely** *adv.* **winsomeness** *n.* [Old English *wynsum*, from *wyn* JOY + -SOME¹]

winter /ˈwɪntə/ *n.* & *v.* ● *n.* **1** the coldest season of the year, in the northern hemisphere from December to February and in the southern hemisphere from June to August. **2** *Astron.* the period from the winter solstice to the vernal equinox. **3** a bleak or lifeless period or region etc. (*nuclear winter*). **4** *poet.* a year (esp. of a person's age) (*a man of fifty winters*). **5** (*attrib.*) **a** characteristic of or suitable for winter (*winter light*; *winter clothes*). **b** (of fruit) ripening late or keeping until or during winter. **c** (of wheat or other crops) sown in autumn for harvesting the following year. ● *v.* **1** *intr.* (usu. foll. by *at*, *in*) pass the winter (*likes to winter in the Canaries*). **2** *tr.* keep or feed (plants, cattle) during winter. □ **winterer** *n.* **winterless** *adj.* **winterly** *adj.* [Old English from Germanic: probably related to WET]

winter aconite see ACONITE 2.

winter cress *n.* any bitter-tasting cress of the genus *Barbarea*, esp. *B. vulgaris.*

winter garden *n.* a garden or conservatory of plants flourishing in winter.

wintergreen /ˈwɪntəgriːn/ *n.* **1** a low-growing plant of the genus *Pyrola*, with drooping spikes of white bell-shaped flowers. **2 a** *N. Amer.* the checkerberry, *Gaultheria procumbens.* **b** (in full **oil of wintergreen**) a pungent oil obtained from the leaves of this, or made synthetically, and used medicinally and as a flavouring. [so called because of remaining green in winter]

winter heliotrope see HELIOTROPE 2.

winterize /ˈwɪntərʌɪz/ *v.tr.* (also **-ise**) esp. *N. Amer.* adapt for operation or use in cold weather. □ **winterization** /-ˈzeɪʃ(ə)n/ *n.*

winter jasmine *n.* a jasmine, *Jasminum nudiflorum*, with yellow flowers.

winter quarters *n.* a place where soldiers spend the winter.

winter sleep *n.* hibernation.

winter solstice *n.* the solstice at midwinter, at the time of the shortest day, about 22 Dec. in the northern hemisphere and 21 June in the southern hemisphere; in *Astron.*, the solstice in December.

winter sports *n.pl.* sports performed on snow or ice esp. in winter (e.g. skiing and ice-skating).

winter-tide *n. poet.* = WINTERTIME.

wintertime /ˈwɪntətʌɪm/ *n.* the season of winter.

wintry /ˈwɪntri/ *adj.* (also **wintery** /-t(ə)ri/) (**wintrier**, **wintriest**) **1** characteristic of winter (*wintry weather*; *a wintry sun*; *a wintry landscape*). **2** (of a smile, greeting, etc.) lacking warmth or enthusiasm. □ **wintrily** *adv.* **wintriness** *n.* [Old English *wintrig*, or from WINTER]

winy var. of WINEY.

wipe /wʌɪp/ *v.* & *n.* ● *v.tr.* **1** clean or dry the surface of by rubbing with the hands or a cloth etc. **2** rub (a cloth) over a surface. **3** spread (a liquid etc.) over a surface by rubbing. **4** (often foll. by *away*, *off*, etc.) **a** clear or remove by wiping (*wiped the mess off the table*; *wipe away your tears*). **b** remove or eliminate completely (*the village was wiped off the map*). **5 a** erase (data, a recording, etc., from a magnetic medium). **b** erase data from (the medium). **6** *Austral.* & *NZ slang* reject or dismiss (a person or idea). ● *n.* **1** an act of wiping (*give the floor a wipe*). **2** a piece of disposable absorbent cloth, usu. treated with a cleansing agent, for wiping something clean (*antiseptic wipes*). □ **wipe down** clean (esp. a vertical surface) by wiping. **wipe a person's eye** *Brit. colloq.* get the better of a person. **wipe the floor with** *colloq.* inflict a humiliating defeat on. **wipe off** annul (a debt etc.). **wipe out 1 a** destroy, annihilate (*the whole population was wiped out*). **b** obliterate (*wiped it out of my memory*). **2** *slang* murder. **3** clean the inside of. **4** *Brit.* avenge (an insult etc.). **wipe the slate clean** see SLATE. **wipe up 1** *Brit.* dry (dishes etc.). **2** take up (a liquid etc.) by wiping. □ **wipeable** *adj.* [Old English *wīpian*: cf. Old High German *wīfan* 'wind round', Gothic *weipan* 'crown': related to WHIP]

wipe-out *n.* **1** the obliteration of one radio signal by another. **2** an instance of destruction or annihilation. **3** *slang* a fall from a surfboard.

wiper /ˈwʌɪpə/ *n.* **1** = WINDSCREEN WIPER. **2** *Electr.* a moving contact. **3** a cam or tappet.

WIPO *abbr.* World Intellectual Property Organization.

Wiradhuri /wɪˈradʒəri/ *n.* an Aboriginal language of SE Australia, now extinct.

wire /wʌɪə/ *n.* & *v.* ● *n.* **1 a** metal drawn out into the form of a thread or thin flexible rod. **b** a piece of this. **c** (*attrib.*) made of wire. **2** a length or quantity of wire used for fencing or to carry an electric current etc. **3** *colloq.* a telegram or cablegram. ● *v.tr.* **1** provide, fasten, strengthen, etc., with wire. **2** (often foll. by *up*) *Electr.* install electrical circuits in (a building, piece of equipment, etc.). **3** *colloq.* telegraph (*wired me that they were coming*). **4** snare (an animal etc.) with wire. **5** (usu. in *passive*) *Croquet* obstruct (a ball, shot, or player) by a hoop. □ **by wire** by telegraph. **get one's wires crossed** become confused and have a misunderstanding. □ **wirer** *n.* [Old English *wīr*]

wire brush *n.* & *v.* ● *n.* **1** a brush with tough wire bristles for cleaning hard surfaces, esp. metal. **2** a brush with wire strands brushed against cymbals to produce a soft metallic sound. ● *v.tr.* (usu. **wire-brush**) clean with a wire brush.

wire cloth *n.* cloth woven from wire.

wire-cutter *n.* a tool for cutting wire.

wiredraw /ˈwʌɪədrɔː/ *v.tr.* (*past* **-drew** /-druː/; *past part.* **-drawn** /-drɔːn/) **1** draw (metal) out into wire. **2** elongate; protract unduly. **3** (esp. as **wiredrawn** *adj.*) refine or apply or press (an argument etc.) with idle or excessive subtlety. □ **wiredrawer** *n.* **wiredrawing** *n.*

wire gauge *n.* **1** a gauge for measuring the diameter of wire etc. **2** (in full **standard wire gauge**) (in the UK) a standard series of sizes in which wire etc. is made.

wire gauze *n.* a stiff gauze woven from wire.

wire grass *n.* any of various grasses with tough wiry stems.

wire-haired *adj.* (esp. of a dog) having stiff or wiry hair.

wireless /ˈwʌɪəlɪs/ *n.* & *adj.* ● *n.* **1** esp. *Brit.* **a** (in full **wireless set**) a radio receiving set. **b** the transmission and reception of radio signals. **2** = WIRELESS TELEGRAPHY. ● *adj.* lacking or not requiring wires.

■ **Usage** The term *wireless* is now old-fashioned, esp. with reference to broadcasting, and has been superseded by *radio*.

wireless telegraphy *n.* = RADIO-TELEGRAPHY.

wireman /ˈwʌɪəmən/ *n.* (*pl.* **-men**) **1** esp. *US* an installer or repairer of electric wires. **2** a journalist working for a telegraphic news agency.

wire mattress *n.* a mattress supported by wires stretched in a frame.

wire netting *n.* netting of wire twisted into meshes.

wirepuller /ˈwʌɪəpʊlə/ *n.* esp. *US* a politician etc. who exerts a hidden influence. ▫ **wirepulling** *n.*

wire rope *n.* rope made by twisting wires together as strands.

wire stripper *n.* (often in *pl.*) a tool for removing the insulation from electric wires.

wire-tapping *n.* the practice of tapping (see TAP[1] *v.* 4) a telephone or telegraph line to eavesdrop. ▫ **wire-tapper** *n.*

wire-walker *n.* an acrobat performing feats on a wire rope.

wire wheel *n.* a vehicle wheel with spokes of wire.

wire wool *n. Brit.* a mass of fine wire for cleaning.

wireworm /ˈwʌɪəwəːm/ *n.* the larva of the click beetle causing damage to crop plants.

wiring /ˈwʌɪərɪŋ/ *n.* **1** a system of wires providing electrical circuits. **2** the installation of this (*came to do the wiring*).

wiry /ˈwʌɪəri/ *adj.* (**wirier**, **wiriest**) **1** tough and flexible as wire. **2** (of a person) thin and sinewy; untiring. **3** made of wire. ▫ **wirily** *adv.* **wiriness** *n.*

Wis. *abbr.* Wisconsin.

wis /wɪs/ *v.intr. archaic* know well. [originally *I wis* = obsolete *iwis* 'certainly' from Old English *gewis*, erroneously taken as 'I know' and as pres. tense of *wist* (WIT[2])]

Wisd. *abbr.* Wisdom of Solomon (Apocrypha).

wisdom /ˈwɪzdəm/ *n.* **1** the state of being wise. **2** experience and knowledge together with the power of applying them critically or practically. **3** sagacity, prudence; common sense. **4** (also in *pl.*) wise sayings, thoughts, etc., regarded collectively. ▫ **in his** (or **her** etc.) **wisdom** usu. *iron.* thinking it would be best (*the committee in its wisdom decided to abandon the project*). [Old English *wīsdōm* (as WISE[1], -DOM)]

wisdom tooth *n.* each of four hindmost molars not usu. cut before 20 years of age.

wise[1] /wʌɪz/ *adj.* & *v.* ● *adj.* **1 a** having experience and knowledge and judiciously applying them. **b** (of an action, behaviour, etc.) determined by or showing or in harmony with such experience and knowledge. **2** sagacious, prudent, sensible, discreet. **3** having knowledge. **4** suggestive of wisdom (*with a wise nod of the head*). **5** *US colloq.* **a** alert, crafty. **b** (often foll. by *to*) having (usu. confidential) information (about). ● *v.tr.* & *intr.* (foll. by *up*) esp. *US colloq.* put or get wise. ▫ **be** (or **get**) **wise to** *colloq.* be (or become) aware of. **no** (or **none the** or **not much**) **wiser** knowing no more than before. **put a person wise** (often foll. by *to*) *colloq.* inform a person (about). **wise after the event** able to understand and assess an event or circumstance after its implications have become obvious. **without anyone's being the wiser** undetected. ▫ **wisely** *adv.* [Old English *wīs* from Germanic: related to WIT[2]]

wise[2] /wʌɪz/ *n. archaic* way, manner, or degree (*in solemn wise*; *on this wise*). ▫ **in no wise** not at all. [Old English *wīse* from Germanic: related to WIT[2]]

-wise /wʌɪz/ *suffix* forming adjectives and adverbs of manner (*crosswise*; *clockwise*; *lengthwise*) or respect (*moneywise*) (cf. -WAYS). [as WISE[2]]

■ **Usage** The use of *-wise* in more fanciful phrase-based combinations, such as *employment-wise* (= as regards employment), is colloquial and should be restricted to informal contexts.

wiseacre /ˈwʌɪzeɪkə/ *n.* a person who affects a wise manner. [Middle Dutch *wijsseggher* 'soothsayer', probably from Old High German *wīssago*, *wīzago*, assimilated to WISE[1], ACRE]

wisecrack /ˈwʌɪzkrak/ *n.* & *v. colloq.* ● *n.* a smart pithy remark. ● *v.intr.* make a wisecrack. ▫ **wisecracker** *n.*

wise guy *n. colloq.* a know-all.

wise man *n.* a wizard, esp. one of the Magi.

wisent /ˈwiːz(ə)nt/ *n.* the European bison, *Bison bonasus*. [German: related to BISON]

wise saw *n.* a proverbial saying.

wish /wɪʃ/ *v.* & *n.* ● *v.* **1** *intr.* (often foll. by *for*) have or express a desire or aspiration for (*wish for happiness*). **2** *tr.* (often foll. by *that* + clause, usu. with *that* omitted) have as a desire or aspiration (*I wish I could sing*; *I wished that I was dead*). **3** *tr.* want or demand, usu. so as to bring about what is wanted (*I wish to go*; *I wish you to do it*; *I wish it done*). **4** *tr.* express one's hopes for (*we wish you well*; *wish them no harm*; *wished us a pleasant journey*). **5** *tr.* (foll. by *on*, *upon*) *colloq.* foist on a person. ● *n.* **1 a** a desire, request, or aspiration. **b** an expression of this. **2** a thing desired (*got my wish*). ▫ **best** (or **good**) **wishes** hopes felt or expressed for another's happiness etc. **the wish is father to the thought** we believe a thing because we wish it true. ▫ **wisher** *n.* (in sense 4 of *v.*); (also in *comb.*). [Old English *wȳscan*, Old High German *wunsken* from Germanic, ultimately related to WEEN, WONT]

wishbone /ˈwɪʃbəʊn/ *n.* **1** a forked bone (the furcula) between the neck and breast of a bird, esp. this bone from a cooked bird, which when broken by two people entitles the holder of the longer portion to make a wish. **2** an object of similar shape.

wishful /ˈwɪʃfʊl, -f(ə)l/ *adj.* **1** (often foll. by *to* + infin.) desiring, wishing. **2** having or expressing a wish. ▫ **wishfully** *adv.* **wishfulness** *n.*

wish-fulfilment *n.* a tendency for subconscious desire to be satisfied in fantasy.

wishful thinking *n.* belief founded on wishes rather than facts.

wishing-well *n.* a well into which coins are dropped and a wish is made.

wish-list *n.* a mental list of wishes or desires.

wish-wash /ˈwɪʃwɒʃ/ *n.* **1** a weak or watery drink. **2** insipid talk or writing. [reduplication of WASH]

wishy-washy /ˈwɪʃɪwɒʃi/ *adj.* **1** feeble, insipid, or indecisive in quality or character. **2** (of tea, soup, etc.) weak, watery, sloppy. [reduplication of WASHY]

wisp /wɪsp/ *n.* **1** a small bundle or twist of straw etc. **2** a small separate quantity of smoke, hair, etc. **3** a small thin person etc. **4** a flock (of snipe). ▫ **wispy** *adj.* (**wispier**, **wispiest**). **wispily** *adv.* **wispiness** *n.* [Middle English: origin uncertain: perhaps related to West Frisian *wisp*, and WHISK]

wist *past* and *past part.* of WIT[2].

wisteria /wɪˈstɪərɪə/ *n.* (also **wistaria** /-ˈstɛːrɪə/) any climbing leguminous shrub of the genus *Wisteria*, with hanging clusters of pale bluish-lilac flowers. [modern Latin, named after C. *Wistar* (or *Wister*), American anatomist d. 1818]

wistful /ˈwɪs(t)fʊl, -f(ə)l/ *adj.* (of a person, looks, etc.) yearningly or mournfully expectant or wishful. ▫ **wistfully** *adv.* **wistfulness** *n.* [apparently an assimilation of obsolete *wistly* (*adv.*) 'intently' to *wishful*, with corresponding change of sense]

wit[1] /wɪt/ *n.* **1** (in *sing.* or *pl.*) intelligence; quick understanding (*has quick wits*; *a nimble wit*). **2 a** the unexpected, quick, and humorous combining or contrasting of ideas or expressions (*conversation sparkling with wit*). **b** the power of giving intellectual pleasure by this. **3** a person possessing such a power, esp. a cleverly humorous person. ▫ **at one's wit's** (or **wits'**) **end** utterly at a loss or in despair. **have** (or **keep**) **one's wits about one** be alert or vigilant or of lively intelligence. **live by one's wits** live by ingenious or crafty expedients, without a settled occupation. **out of one's wits** mad, distracted. **set one's wits to** argue with. ▫ **witted** *adj.* (in sense 1); (also in *comb.*). [Old English *wit(t)*, *gewit(t)*, from Germanic]

wit[2] /wɪt/ *v.tr. & intr.* (*1st & 3rd sing. present* **wot** /wɒt/; *past* and *past part.* **wist** /wɪst/) (often foll. by *of*) *archaic* know. □ **to wit** that is to say; namely. [Old English *witan*, from Germanic]

witch /wɪtʃ/ *n. & v.* ● *n.* **1 a** a sorceress, esp. a woman supposed to have dealings with the Devil or evil spirits. **b** a follower or practitioner of modern witchcraft; a Wiccan. **2** an ugly old woman; a hag. **3** a fascinating girl or woman. **4** a flatfish, *Glyptocephalus cynoglossus*, resembling the lemon sole. ● *v.tr. archaic* **1** bewitch. **2** fascinate, charm, lure. □ **witching** *adj.* **witchlike** *adj.* **witchy** *adj.* [Old English *wicca* (masc.), *wicce* (fem.), related to *wiccian* 'to practise magic arts']

witch alder *n.* an American shrub, *Fothergilla gardenii*, with leaves like those of the alder. [from *witch*, variant of *wych*: see WYCH ELM]

witchcraft /ˈwɪtʃkrɑːft/ *n.* **1** the use of magic; sorcery. **2** bewitching charm.

witch doctor *n.* a tribal magician of tribal people.

witch elm var. of WYCH ELM.

witchery /ˈwɪtʃ(ə)ri/ *n.* **1** witchcraft. **2** power exercised by beauty or eloquence or the like.

witches' broom *n.* a dense twiggy growth in a tree caused by infection with fungus, mites, or viruses.

witches' sabbath see SABBATH 3.

witchetty /ˈwɪtʃɪti/ *n.* (*pl.* **-ies**) (in full **witchetty grub**) *Austral.* a large white larva of a beetle or moth, eaten as food by Aboriginals. [probably Adnyamathanha]

witch hazel /ˈwɪtʃheɪz(ə)l/ *n.* (also **wych hazel**) **1** any ornamental E. Asian or American shrub of the genus *Hamamelis*, with yellow flowers. **2** an astringent lotion obtained from the leaves and bark of *H. virginiana* of N. America. [from *witch* variant of *wych* (see WYCH ELM) + HAZEL]

witch-hunt *n.* **1** *hist.* a search for and persecution of supposed witches. **2** a campaign directed against a particular group of those holding dissenting or unorthodox views, esp. *hist.* Communists. □ **witch-hunting** *n.*

witching hour *n.* (prec. by *the*) midnight, when witches are supposedly active (after Shakespeare's *Hamlet* III. ii. 377 *the witching time of night*).

witenagemot /ˈwɪt(ə)nəgɪˌməʊt/ *n. hist.* an Anglo-Saxon national council or parliament. [Old English from *witena*, genitive pl. of *wita* 'wise man' (as WIT[2]) + *gemōt* 'meeting': cf. MOOT]

with /wɪð/ *prep.* expressing: **1** an instrument or means used (*cut with a knife*; *can walk with assistance*). **2** association or company (*lives with his mother*; *works with Shell*; *lamb with mint sauce*). **3** cause or origin (*shiver with fear*; *in bed with measles*). **4** possession, attribution (*the man with dark hair*; *a vase with handles*). **5** circumstances; accompanying conditions (*sleep with the window open*; *a holiday with all expenses paid*). **6** manner adopted or displayed (*behaved with dignity*; *spoke with vehemence*; *handle with care*; *won with ease*). **7** agreement or harmony (*sympathize with*; *I believe with you that it can be done*). **8** disagreement, antagonism, competition (*clashing with*; *stop arguing with me*). **9** responsibility or care for (*the decision rests with you*; *leave the child with me*). **10** material (*made with gold*). **11** addition or supply; possession of as a material, attribute, circumstance, etc. (*fill it with water*; *threaten with dismissal*; *decorate with holly*). **12** reference or regard (*be patient with them*; *how are things with you?*; *what do you want with me?*; *there's nothing wrong with expressing one's opinion*). **13** relation or causative association (*changes with the weather*; *keeps pace with the cost of living*). **14** an accepted circumstance or consideration (*with all your faults, we like you*). □ **away** (or **in** or **out** etc.) **with** (as *int.*) take, send, or put (a person or thing) away, in, out, etc. **be with a person 1** agree with and support a person. **2** *colloq.* follow a person's meaning (*are you with me?*). **one with** part of the same whole as. **with child** (or **young**) *literary* pregnant. **with that** thereupon. [Old English, probably shortened from a Germanic prep. corresponding to Old English *wither*, Old High German *widar* 'against']

withal /wɪˈðɔːl/ *adv. & prep. archaic* ● *adv.* moreover; as well; at the same time. ● *prep.* (placed after its expressed or omitted object) with (*what shall he fill his belly withal?*). [Middle English, from WITH + ALL]

withdraw /wɪðˈdrɔː/ *v.* (*past* **withdrew** /-ˈdruː/; *past part.* **withdrawn** /-ˈdrɔːn/) **1** *tr.* pull or take aside or back (*withdrew my hand*). **2** *tr.* discontinue, cancel, retract (*withdrew my support*; *the promise was later withdrawn*). **3** *tr.* remove; take away (*withdrew the child from school*; *withdrew their troops*). **4** *tr.* take (money) out of an account. **5** *intr.* retire or go away; move away or back. **6** *intr.* (as **withdrawn** *adj.*) abnormally shy and unsociable; mentally detached. [Middle English, from *with-* 'away' (as WITH) + DRAW]

withdrawal /wɪðˈdrɔː(ə)l/ *n.* **1** the act or an instance of withdrawing or being withdrawn. **2** a process of ceasing to take addictive drugs, often with an unpleasant physical reaction (*withdrawal symptoms*). **3** = COITUS INTERRUPTUS.

withdrawing room *n. archaic* = DRAWING ROOM 1.

withe /wɪθ, wɪð, wʌɪð/ *n.* (also **withy** /ˈwɪði/) (*pl.* **withes** or **-ies**) a tough flexible shoot, esp. of willow or osier, used for tying a bundle of wood etc. [Old English *withthe*, *withig* from Germanic: related to WIRE]

wither /ˈwɪðə/ *v.* **1** *tr. & intr.* (often foll. by *up*) make or become dry and shrivelled (*withered flowers*). **2** *tr. & intr.* (often foll. by *away*) deprive of or lose vigour, vitality, freshness, or importance. **3** *intr.* decay, decline. **4** *tr.* **a** blight with scorn etc. **b** (as **withering** *adj.*) scornful (*a withering look*). □ **witheringly** *adv.* [Middle English, apparently variant of WEATHER differentiated for certain senses]

withers /ˈwɪðəz/ *n.pl.* the ridge between a horse's shoulder blades. [shortening of 16th-c. *widersome*, *widersone* from *wider-*, *wither-* 'against' (cf. WITH), as the part that resists the strain of the collar: second element obscure]

withershins var. of WIDDERSHINS.

withhold /wɪðˈhəʊld/ *v.tr.* (*past* and *past part.* **-held** /-ˈhɛld/) **1** (often foll. by *from*) hold back; restrain. **2** refuse to give, grant, or allow (*withhold one's consent*; *withhold the truth*). □ **withholder** *n.* [Middle English, from *with-* 'away' (as WITH) + HOLD[1]]

within /wɪðˈɪn/ *adv. & prep.* ● *adv. archaic* or *literary* **1** inside; to, at, or on the inside; internally. **2** indoors (*is anyone within?*). **3** in spirit (*make me pure within*). **4** *Brit.* inside the city walls (*Bishopsgate within*). ● *prep.* **1** inside; enclosed or contained by. **2 a** not beyond or exceeding (*within one's means*). **b** not transgressing (*within the law*; *within reason*). **3** not further off than (*within three miles of a station*; *within shouting distance*; *within ten days*). □ **within doors** in or into a house. **within one's grasp** see GRASP. **within reach** (or **sight) of** near enough to be reached or seen. [Old English *withinnan* 'on the inside' (as WITH, *innan* (*adv. & prep.*) 'within', formed as IN)]

with it *adj. & adv. colloq.* ● *adj.* (hyphenated when *attrib.*) **1** up to date; conversant with modern ideas etc. **2** alert and comprehending. ● *adv.* besides, in addition (*she was intelligent and amusing with it*).

without /wɪðˈaʊt/ *prep. & adv.* ● *prep.* **1** not having, feeling, or showing (*came without any money*; *without hesitation*; *without any emotion*). **2** with freedom from (*without fear*; *without embarrassment*). **3** in the absence of (*cannot live without you*; *the train left without us*). **4** with neglect or avoidance of (*do not leave without telling me*). **5** *archaic* outside (*without the city wall*). ● *adv. archaic* or *literary* **1** outside (*seen from without*). **2** out of doors (*remained shivering without*). **3** in outward appearance (*rough without but kind within*). **4** *Brit.* outside the city walls (*Bishopsgate without*). □ **without**

end infinite, eternal. [Old English *withūtan* (as WITH, *ūtan* 'from outside', formed as OUT)]

■ **Usage** The use of *without* as a *conj.*, as in *Do not leave without you tell me*, is non-standard.

with-profits *adj.* (usu. *attrib.*) *Brit.* (of an insurance policy) allowing the holder a share of profits made by the company, usu. in the form of a bonus.

withstand /wɪð'stand/ *v.* (*past* and *past part.* **-stood** /-'stʊd/) **1** *tr.* oppose, resist, hold out against (a person, force, etc.). **2** *intr.* make opposition; offer resistance. □ **withstander** *n.* [Old English *withstandan*, from *with-* 'against' (as WITH) + STAND]

withy /'wɪði/ *n.* (*pl.* **-ies**) **1** a willow of any species. **2** var. of WITHE.

witless /'wɪtlɪs/ *adj.* **1** lacking wits; foolish, stupid. **2** crazy. □ **witlessly** *adv.* **witlessness** *n.* [Old English *witlēas* (as WIT¹, -LESS)]

witling /'wɪtlɪŋ/ *n. archaic* usu. *derog.* a person who fancies himself or herself as a wit.

witness /'wɪtnɪs/ *n.* & *v.* ● *n.* **1** a person present at some event and able to give information about it (cf. EYEWITNESS). **2 a** a person giving sworn testimony. **b** a person attesting another's signature to a document. **3** (foll. by *to*, *of*) a person or thing whose existence, condition, etc., attests or proves something (*is a living witness to their generosity*). **4** testimony, evidence, confirmation. ● *v.* **1** *tr.* be a witness of (an event etc.) (*did you witness the accident?*). **2** *tr.* be witness to the authenticity of (a document or signature). **3** *tr.* serve as evidence or an indication of. **4** *intr.* (foll. by *against*, *for*, *to*) give or serve as evidence. **5** *tr.* (as *imper.*) introducing an illustration of the preceding statement (*he is an accomplished musician: witness his performance last week at the Albert Hall*). □ **bear witness to** (or **of**) **1** attest the truth of. **2** state one's belief in. **call to witness** appeal to for confirmation etc. [Old English *witnes* (as WIT¹, -NESS)]

witness box *n.* (*US* **witness-stand**) an enclosure in a law court from which witnesses give evidence.

witter /'wɪtə/ *v.intr.* (often foll. by *on*) *Brit. colloq.* speak tediously on trivial matters. [19th c.: probably imitative]

witticism /'wɪtɪsɪz(ə)m/ *n.* a witty remark. [coined by Dryden (1677) from WITTY, on the pattern of *criticism*]

witting /'wɪtɪŋ/ *adj.* **1** aware. **2** intentional. □ **wittingly** *adv.* [Middle English, from WIT² + -ING²]

witty /'wɪti/ *adj.* (**wittier**, **wittiest**) **1** showing verbal wit. **2** characterized by wit or humour. □ **wittily** *adv.* **wittiness** *n.* [Old English *witig*, *wittig* (as WIT¹, -Y¹)]

wivern var. of WYVERN.

wives *pl.* of WIFE.

wiz var. of WHIZZ *n.* 2.

wizard /'wɪzəd/ *n.* & *adj.* ● *n.* **1** a sorcerer; a magician. **2** a person of remarkable powers, a genius. **3** a conjuror. ● *adj.* esp. *Brit. archaic slang* wonderful, excellent. □ **wizardly** *adj.* **wizardry** *n.* [Middle English, from WISE¹ + -ARD]

wizened /'wɪz(ə)nd/ *adj.* (also **wizen**) (of a person or face etc.) shrivelled-looking. [past part. of *wizen* 'shrivel' from Old English *wisnian*, from Germanic]

wk. *abbr.* **1** week. **2** work. **3** weak.

wks. *abbr.* weeks.

Wm. *abbr.* William.

WMO *abbr.* World Meteorological Organization.

WNW *abbr.* west-north-west.

WO *abbr.* Warrant Officer.

wo /wəʊ/ *int.* = WHOA. [variant of interjection *who*, HO]

w.o. *abbr.* walkover.

woad /wəʊd/ *n.* **1** a cruciferous plant, *Isatis tinctoria*, yielding a blue dye now superseded by indigo. **2** the dye obtained from this. [Old English *wād*, from Germanic]

wobbegong /'wɒbɪgɒŋ/ *n.* an Australian brown shark, *Orectolobus maculatus*, patterned with buff markings. [perhaps Aboriginal (NSW)]

wobble /'wɒb(ə)l/ *v.* & *n.* ● *v.* **1 a** *intr.* sway or vibrate unsteadily from side to side. **b** *tr.* cause to do this. **2** *intr.* stand or go unsteadily; stagger. **3** *intr.* waver, vacillate; act inconsistently. **4** *intr.* (of the voice or sound) quaver, pulsate. ● *n.* **1** a wobbling movement. **2** an instance of vacillation or pulsation. [earlier *wabble*, corresponding to Low German *wabbeln*, Old Norse *vafla* 'waver', from Germanic: related to WAVE, WAVER]

wobble-board *n. Austral.* a piece of fibreboard used as a musical instrument with a low booming sound.

wobbler /'wɒblə/ *n.* **1** a person or thing that wobbles. **2** *colloq.* = WOBBLY. **3** a lure that wobbles and does not spin, used in angling.

wobbly /'wɒbli/ *adj.* & *n.* ● *adj.* (**wobblier**, **wobbliest**) **1** wobbling or tending to wobble. **2** wavy, undulating (*a wobbly line*). **3** unsteady, shaky; weak after illness (*feeling wobbly*). **4** wavering, vacillating, insecure (*the economy was wobbly*). ● *n.* (in phr. **throw a wobbly**) *Brit. colloq.* have a fit of nerves or temper. □ **wobbliness** *n.*

wodge /wɒdʒ/ *n. Brit. colloq.* a chunk or lump. [alteration of WEDGE¹]

woe /wəʊ/ *n. archaic* or *literary* **1** affliction; bitter grief; distress. **2** (in *pl.*) calamities, troubles. **3** *joc.* problems (*told me a tale of woe*). □ **woe betide** there will be unfortunate consequences for (*woe betide you if you are late*). **woe is me** often *joc.* an exclamation of distress. [Old English *wā*, *wǣ* from Germanic, a natural exclamation of lament]

woebegone /'wəʊbɪgɒn/ *adj.* dismal-looking. [WOE + *begone* 'surrounded' from Old English *begān* (as BE-, GO¹)]

woeful /'wəʊfʊl, -f(ə)l/ *adj.* **1** sorrowful; afflicted with distress (*a woeful expression*). **2** causing sorrow or affliction. **3** very bad; wretched (*woeful ignorance*). □ **woefully** *adv.* **woefulness** *n.*

wog¹ /wɒg/ *n. Brit. slang offens.* a foreigner, esp. a non-white one. [20th c.: origin unknown]

wog² /wɒg/ *n. Austral. slang* an illness or infection. [20th c.: origin unknown]

woggle /'wɒg(ə)l/ *n.* a leather etc. ring through which the ends of a Scout's neckerchief are passed at the neck. [20th c.: origin unknown]

wok /wɒk/ *n.* a bowl-shaped frying pan used in esp. Chinese cookery. [Cantonese]

woke *past* of WAKE¹.

woken *past part.* of WAKE¹.

wold /wəʊld/ *n.* a piece of high open uncultivated land or moor. [Old English *wald* from Germanic, perhaps related to WILD: cf. WEALD]

wolf /wʊlf/ *n.* & *v.* ● *n.* (*pl.* **wolves** /wʊlvz/) **1 a** a wild flesh-eating tawny-grey mammal, *Canis lupus*, of northern regions, related to the dog and hunting in packs. Also called *grey wolf*, *timber wolf*. **b** any of several related animals. **2** *colloq.* a man given to seducing women. **3** a rapacious or greedy person. **4** *Mus.* **a** a jarring sound from some notes in a bowed instrument. **b** an out-of-tune effect when playing certain chords on old organs (before the present 'equal temperament' was in use). ● *v.tr.* (often foll. by *down*) devour (food) greedily. □ **cry wolf** raise repeated false alarms (so that a genuine one is disregarded). **have** (or **hold**) **a wolf by the ears** be in a precarious position. **keep the wolf from the door** avert hunger or starvation. **throw to the wolves** sacrifice without compunction. **wolf in sheep's clothing** a hostile person who pretends friendship. □ **wolfish** *adj.* **wolfishly** *adv.* **wolflike** *adj.* & *adv.* [Old English *wulf*, from Germanic]

wolf cub *n.* **1** a young wolf. **2** *Brit.* the former name for a Cub Scout.

wolf-fish *n.* (*pl.* usu. same) any large voracious blenny of the genus *Anarhichas*.

wolfhound /'wʊlfhaʊnd/ *n.* any of several breeds of large dog originally bred to hunt wolves.

wolf pack *n.* an attacking group of submarines or aircraft.

wolfram /'wʊlfrəm/ *n.* **1** tungsten. **2** tungsten ore; a native tungstate of iron and manganese. [German: perhaps from *Wolf* WOLF + *Rahm* 'cream', or Middle High German *rām* 'dirt, soot']

wolframite /'wʊlfrəmʌɪt/ *n.* = WOLFRAM 2.

wolfsbane /'wʊlfsbeɪn/ *n.* an aconite, esp. *Aconitum lycoctonum.*

wolfskin /'wʊlfskɪn/ *n.* **1** the skin of a wolf. **2** a mat, cloak, etc., made from this.

wolf's-milk *n.* spurge.

wolf spider *n.* any ground-dwelling spider of the family Lycosidae, hunting instead of trapping its prey.

wolf whistle *n. & v.* ● *n.* a whistle made to indicate sexual admiration. ● *v.intr.* (**wolf-whistle**) make a wolf whistle.

wolverine /'wʊlvəri:n/ *n.* (also **wolverene**) = GLUTTON 3. [16th-c. *wolvering*, somehow derived from *wolv-*, stem of WOLF]

wolves *pl.* of WOLF.

woman /'wʊmən/ *n.* (*pl.* **women** /'wɪmɪn/) **1** an adult human female. **2** the female sex; any or an average woman (*how does woman differ from man?*). **3** *colloq.* a wife or female sexual partner. **4** (prec. by *the*) emotions or characteristics traditionally associated with women (*brought out the woman in him*). **5** *colloq.* a man with characteristics traditionally associated with women. **6** (*attrib.*) female (*woman driver*; *women friends*). **7** (as second element in *comb.*) a woman of a specified nationality, profession, skill, etc. (*Englishwoman*; *horsewoman*). **8** *colloq.* a female domestic help. **9** *archaic* or *hist.* a queen's etc. female attendant ranking below lady (*woman of the bedchamber*). □ **womanless** *adj.* **womanlike** *adj.* [Old English *wīfmon, -man* (as WIFE, MAN), a formation peculiar to English, the ancient word being WIFE]

womanhood /'wʊmənhʊd/ *n.* **1** female maturity. **2** womanly instinct. **3** womankind.

womanish /'wʊmənɪʃ/ *adj.* usu. *derog.* **1** (of a man) effeminate, unmanly. **2** suitable to or characteristic of a woman. □ **womanishly** *adv.* **womanishness** *n.*

womanist /'wʊmənɪst/ *n.* esp. *US* a black feminist.

womanize /'wʊmənʌɪz/ *v.* (also **-ise**) **1** *intr.* chase after women; philander. **2** *tr.* make womanish. □ **womanizer** *n.*

womankind /'wʊmənkʌɪnd/ *n.* (also **womenkind** /'wɪmɪn-/) women in general.

■ **Usage** It is preferable to use *womankind*, corresponding to *mankind*, rather than *womenkind*.

womanly /'wʊmənli/ *adj.* (of a woman) having or showing qualities traditionally associated with women; not masculine or girlish. □ **womanliness** *n.*

woman of the streets *n.* a prostitute.

womb /wu:m/ *n.* **1** the organ of conception and gestation in a woman and other female mammals; the uterus. **2** a place of origination and development. □ **womb-like** *adj.* [Old English *wamb, womb*]

wombat /'wɒmbat/ *n.* any burrowing plant-eating Australian marsupial of the family Vombatidae, resembling a small bear, with short legs. [Dharuk]

women *pl.* of WOMAN.

womenfolk /'wɪmɪnfəʊk/ *n.* **1** women in general. **2** the women in a family.

womenkind var. of WOMANKIND.

Women's Institute *n.* an organization of women, esp. in rural areas, who meet regularly and participate in crafts, cultural activities, etc.

women's lib *n. colloq.* = WOMEN'S LIBERATION. □ **women's libber** *n.*

women's liberation *n.* **1** the liberation of women from inequalities and subservient status in relation to men, and from attitudes causing these. **2** (**Women's Liberation**) (also **Women's Movement**) a movement campaigning for this.

women's rights *n.pl.* rights that promote a position of legal and social equality of women with men.

womenswear /'wɪmɪnzwɛ:/ *n.* clothes for women.

won *past* and *past part.* of WIN.

wonder /'wʌndə/ *n. & v.* ● *n.* **1** an emotion excited by what is unexpected, unfamiliar, or inexplicable, esp. surprise mingled with admiration or curiosity etc. **2** a strange or remarkable person or thing, specimen, event, etc. **3** (*attrib.*) having marvellous or amazing properties etc. (*a wonder drug*). **4** a surprising thing (*it is a wonder you were not hurt*). ● *v.* **1** *intr.* (often foll. by *at*, or *to* + infin.) be filled with wonder or great surprise. **2** *tr.* (foll. by *that* + clause) be surprised to find. **3** *tr.* desire or be curious to know (*I wonder what the time is*). **4** *tr.* expressing a tentative enquiry (*I wonder whether you would mind?*). □ **I shouldn't wonder** *colloq.* I think it likely. **I wonder** I very much doubt it. **no** (or **small**) **wonder** (often foll. by *that* + clause) one cannot be surprised; one might have guessed; it is natural. **the seven wonders of the world** seven buildings and monuments regarded in antiquity as specially remarkable. **wonders will never cease** an exclamation of extreme (usu. agreeable) surprise. **work** (or **do**) **wonders 1** do miracles. **2** succeed remarkably. □ **wonderer** *n.* [Old English *wundor, wundrian*, of unknown origin]

wonderful /'wʌndəfʊl, -f(ə)l/ *adj.* **1** very remarkable or admirable. **2** arousing wonder. □ **wonderfully** *adv.* **wonderfulness** *n.* [Old English *wunderfull* (as WONDER, -FUL)]

wondering /'wʌnd(ə)rɪŋ/ *adj.* filled with wonder; marvelling (*their wondering gaze*). □ **wonderingly** *adv.*

wonderland /'wʌndəland/ *n.* **1** a fairyland. **2** a land of surprises or marvels.

wonderment /'wʌndəm(ə)nt/ *n.* **1** surprise, awe. **2** (in *pl.*) *literary* marvels.

wonder-struck *adj.* (also **wonder-stricken**) reduced to silence by wonder.

wonder-worker *n.* a person who performs wonders. □ **wonder-working** *attrib.adj.*

wondrous /'wʌndrəs/ *adj. & adv. poet.* ● *adj.* wonderful. ● *adv.* wonderfully (*wondrous kind*). □ **wondrously** *adv.* **wondrousness** *n.* [alteration of obsolete *wonders* (*adj. & adv.*), = genitive of WONDER, on the pattern of *marvellous*]

wonky /'wɒŋki/ *adj.* (**wonkier, wonkiest**) *Brit. slang* **1** crooked, off-centre, askew. **2** loose, unsteady. **3** unreliable. □ **wonkily** *adv.* **wonkiness** *n.* [fanciful formation]

wont /wəʊnt/ *adj., n., & v.* ● *predic.adj.* (foll. by *to* + infin.) *archaic* or *literary* accustomed (*as we were wont to say*). ● *n. formal* or *joc.* what is customary, one's habit (*as is my wont*). ● *v.tr. & intr.* (*3rd sing. present* **wonts** or **wont**; *past* **wont** or **wonted**) *archaic* make or become accustomed. [Old English *gewunod*, past part. of *gewunian*, from *wunian* 'dwell']

won't /wəʊnt/ *contr.* will not.

wonted /'wəʊntɪd/ *attrib.adj.* habitual, accustomed, usual.

wonton /wɒn'tɒn/ *n.* (in Chinese cookery) a small round dumpling or roll with a savoury filling, usu. eaten boiled in soup. [Cantonese *wān t'ān*]

woo /wu:/ *v.tr.* (**woos, wooed**) **1** court; seek the hand or love of (a woman). **2** try to win (fame, fortune, etc.). **3** seek the favour or support of. **4** coax or importune. □ **wooable** *adj.* **wooer** *n.* [Old English *wōgian* (*v.intr.*), *āwōgian* (*v.tr.*), of unknown origin]

wood /wʊd/ *n.* **1 a** a hard fibrous material that forms the main substance of the trunk or branches of a tree or shrub. **b** this cut for timber or for fuel, or for use in crafts, manufacture, etc. **2** (in *sing.* or *pl.*) growing trees densely occupying a tract of land. **3** (prec. by *the*) wooden storage, esp. a cask, for wine etc. (*poured straight from the wood*). **4** a wooden-headed golf club, or any club with a head relatively broad from face to back. **5** = BOWL[2] *n.* 1. □ **not see the wood for the trees** fail to grasp the main issue from over-attention to details. **out of the wood** (or *US* **woods**) out of danger or difficulty.

□ **woodless** *adj.* [Old English *wudu*, *wi(o)du*, from Germanic]

wood alcohol *n.* methanol.

wood anemone *n.* a wild spring-flowering anemone, *Anemone nemorosa*.

woodbind /ˈwʊdbʌɪnd/ *n.* = WOODBINE.

woodbine /ˈwʊdbʌɪn/ *n.* **1** wild honeysuckle. **2** *US* Virginia creeper.

woodblock /ˈwʊdblɒk/ *n.* a block from which woodcuts are made.

woodcarver /ˈwʊdkɑːvə/ *n.* **1** a person who carves designs in relief on wood. **2** a tool for carving wood.

woodcarving /ˈwʊdkɑːvɪŋ/ *n.* **1** (also *attrib.*) the act or process of carving wood. **2** (also *attrib.*) the art or skill of woodcarving. **3** a design in wood produced by this art.

woodchat /ˈwʊdtʃat/ *n.* (in full **woodchat shrike**) a shrike, *Lanius senator*, of S. Europe, N. Africa, and the Middle East, having black and white plumage with a chestnut head.

woodchip /ˈwʊdtʃɪp/ *n.* **1** a chip of wood. **2** (in full **woodchip paper**) wallpaper with woodchips etc. embedded in it to give an uneven surface texture.

woodchuck /ˈwʊdtʃʌk/ *n.* a reddish-brown and grey N. American marmot, *Marmota monax*. [probably Algonquian: cf. Cree *wuchak*, *otchock*]

woodcock /ˈwʊdkɒk/ *n.* (*pl.* same) any game bird of the genus *Scolopax*, inhabiting woodland.

woodcraft /ˈwʊdkrɑːft/ *n.* esp. *N. Amer.* **1** skill in woodwork. **2** knowledge of woodland esp. in camping, scouting, etc.

woodcut /ˈwʊdkʌt/ *n.* **1** a relief cut on a block of wood sawn along the grain. **2** a print made from this, esp. as an illustration in a book. **3** the technique of making such reliefs and prints.

woodcutter /ˈwʊdkʌtə/ *n.* **1** a person who cuts wood. **2** a maker of woodcuts.

wooded /ˈwʊdɪd/ *adj.* having woods or many trees.

wooden /ˈwʊd(ə)n/ *adj.* **1** made of wood. **2** like wood. **3 a** stiff, clumsy, or stilted; without animation or flexibility (*wooden movements*; *a wooden performance*). **b** expressionless (*a wooden stare*). □ **woodenly** *adv.* **woodenness** /ˈwʊd(ə)nnɪs/ *n.*

wood engraving *n.* **1** a relief cut on a block of wood sawn across the grain. **2** a print made from this. **3** the technique of making such reliefs and prints. □ **wood engraver** *n.*

wooden-head *n. colloq.* a stupid person. □ **wooden-headed** *n.* **wooden-headedness** *n.*

wooden horse *n.* = TROJAN HORSE 1.

wooden spoon *n.* esp. *Brit.* a booby prize (originally a spoon given to the candidate coming last in the Cambridge mathematical tripos).

wood fibre *n.* fibre obtained from wood esp. as material for paper.

wood-grain *attrib.adj.* (of a finish) imitating the grain pattern of wood.

woodgrouse /ˈwʊdgraʊs/ *n.* = CAPERCAILLIE.

wood hyacinth *n.* = BLUEBELL 1.

woodland /ˈwʊdlənd/ *n.* wooded country, woods (often *attrib.*: *woodland scenery*). □ **woodlander** *n.*

woodlark /ˈwʊdlɑːk/ *n.* a lark, *Lullula arborea*.

woodlouse /ˈwʊdlaʊs/ *n.* (*pl.* **-lice** /-lʌɪs/) any small terrestrial isopod crustacean of the genus *Oniscus* etc. feeding on rotten wood etc. and often able to roll into a ball.

woodman /ˈwʊdmən/ *n.* (*pl.* **-men**) **1** a forester. **2** a woodcutter.

wood mouse *n.* = FIELD MOUSE.

woodnote /ˈwʊdnəʊt/ *n.* (often in *pl.*) a natural or spontaneous note of a bird etc.

wood nymph *n. Mythol.* a dryad or hamadryad.

woodpecker /ˈwʊdpɛkə/ *n.* any bird of the family Picidae that climbs and taps tree trunks in search of insects.

wood pigeon *n.* a dove, *Columba palumbus*, having white patches like a ring round its neck. Also called RING-DOVE.

woodpile /ˈwʊdpʌɪl/ *n.* a pile of wood, esp. for fuel.

wood pulp *n.* wood fibre reduced chemically or mechanically to pulp as raw material for paper.

wood rat *n.* a rat of the N. American genus *Neotoma*.

woodruff /ˈwʊdrʌf/ *n.* a white-flowered plant of the genus *Galium*, esp. *G. odoratum* grown for the fragrance of its whorled leaves when dried or crushed.

woodrush /ˈwʊdrʌʃ/ *n.* any grassy herbaceous plant of the genus *Luzula*.

woodscrew see SCREW *n.* 2.

woodshed /ˈwʊdʃɛd/ *n.* a shed where wood for fuel is stored. □ **something nasty in the woodshed** *Brit. colloq.* a shocking or distasteful thing kept secret.

woodsman /ˈwʊdzmən/ *n.* (*pl.* **-men**) **1** a person who lives in or is familiar with woodland. **2** a person skilled in woodcraft.

woodsmoke /ˈwʊdsməʊk/ *n.* the smoke from a wood fire.

wood sorrel *n.* a small plant, *Oxalis acetosella*, with trifoliate leaves and white flowers streaked with purple.

wood spirit *n.* crude methanol obtained from wood.

wood stain *n.* a commercially-produced substance for colouring wood.

woodsy /ˈwʊdzi/ *adj. N. Amer.* like or characteristic of woods. [formed irregularly from WOOD + -Y[1]]

woodturning /ˈwʊdtəːnɪŋ/ *n.* the shaping of wood with a lathe. □ **woodturner** *n.*

wood warbler *n.* **1** a European woodland bird, *Phylloscopus sibilatrix*, with a trilling song. **2** any American warbler of the family Parulidae.

woodwasp /ˈwʊdwɒsp/ *n.* any large sawfly of the family Siricidae, with a long ovipositor and wood-boring larvae, esp. the very large *Urocerus gigas*, that resembles a hornet and is a pest of conifers.

woodwind /ˈwʊdwɪnd/ *n.* (often *attrib.*) **1** (*collect.*) the wind instruments of the orchestra that were (mostly) originally made of wood, e.g. the flute and clarinet. **2** (usu. in *pl.*) an individual instrument of this kind or its player (*the woodwinds are out of tune*).

wood wool *n. Brit.* fine pine etc. shavings used as a surgical dressing or for packing.

woodwork /ˈwʊdwəːk/ *n.* **1** the making of things in wood. **2** things made of wood, esp. the wooden parts of a building. □ **crawl** (or **come**) **out of the woodwork** *colloq.* (of something unwelcome) appear; become known. □ **woodworker** *n.* **woodworking** *n.*

woodworm /ˈwʊdwəːm/ *n.* **1** the wood-boring larva of the furniture beetle. **2** the damaged condition of wood affected by this.

woody /ˈwʊdi/ *adj.* (**woodier**, **woodiest**) **1** (of a region) wooded; abounding in woods. **2** like or of wood (*woody tissue*). □ **woodiness** *n.*

woodyard /ˈwʊdjɑːd/ *n.* a yard where wood is used or stored.

woody nightshade see NIGHTSHADE.

woof[1] /wʊf/ *n.* & *v.* ● *n.* the gruff bark of a dog. ● *v.intr.* give a woof. [imitative]

woof[2] /wuːf/ *n.* = WEFT[1] 1. [Old English *ōwef*, alteration of *ōwebb* (influenced by *wefan* WEAVE[1]), formed as A-[2], WEB: later influenced by *warp*]

woofer /ˈwuːfə/ *n.* a loudspeaker designed to reproduce low frequencies (cf. TWEETER). [WOOF[1] + -ER[1]]

woofter /ˈwʊftə, ˈwuː-/ *n. slang derog.* = POOF[1]. [alteration of POOFTER]

wool /wʊl/ *n.* **1** fine soft wavy hair from the fleece of sheep, goats, etc. **2 a** yarn produced from this hair. **b** cloth or clothing made from it. **3** any of various wool-like substances (*steel wool*). **4** soft short under-fur or down. **5** *colloq.* a person's hair, esp. when short and curly. □ **pull the wool over a person's eyes** deceive a person. □ **wool-like** *adj.* [Old English *wull*, from Germanic]

wool-fat *n.* lanolin.

wool-fell *n. Brit.* the skin of a sheep etc. with the fleece still on.

wool-gathering *n.* absent-mindedness; dreamy inattention.

wool-grower *n.* a breeder of sheep for wool.

woollen /ˈwʊlən/ *adj. & n.* (*US* **woolen**) ● *adj.* made wholly or partly of wool, esp. from short fibres. ● *n.* **1** a fabric produced from wool. **2** (in *pl.*) woollen garments. [Old English *wullen* (as WOOL, -EN[2])]

woolly /ˈwʊli/ *adj. & n.* ● *adj.* (**woollier, woolliest**) **1** bearing or naturally covered with wool or wool-like hair. **2** resembling or suggesting wool (*woolly clouds*). **3** made of wool, woollen. **4** (of a sound) indistinct. **5** (of thought) vague or confused. **6** lacking in definition, luminosity, or incisiveness. ● *n.* (*pl.* **-ies**) esp. *Brit. colloq.* a woollen garment, esp. a knitted pullover. □ **woolliness** *n.*

woolly-bear *n.* **1** a large hairy caterpillar, esp. of the tiger moth. **2** the small hairy larva of a carpet beetle, destructive to textiles, insect collections, etc.

woolman /ˈwʊlmən/ *n.* (*pl.* **-men**) a dealer in wool, a wool merchant or breeder of sheep.

wool-oil *n.* suint.

woolpack /ˈwʊlpak/ *n.* **1** a fleecy cumulus cloud. **2** *hist.* a bale of wool.

Woolsack /ˈwʊlsak/ *n.* **1** (in the UK) the Lord Chancellor's wool-stuffed seat in the House of Lords. **2** the position of Lord Chancellor.

woolshed /ˈwʊlʃɛd/ *n. Austral. & NZ* a large shed for shearing and baling wool.

wool-skin *n.* = WOOL-FELL.

wool-sorters' disease *n.* anthrax.

wool-stapler *n.* a person who grades wool.

woomera /ˈwuːm(ə)rə/ *n. Austral.* **1** an Aboriginal stick for throwing a dart or spear more forcibly. **2** a club used as a missile. [Dharuk *wamara*]

woop woop /ˈwʊp wʊp/ *n. Austral. & NZ slang* **1** a jocular name for a remote outback town or district. **2** (**Woop Woop**) an imaginary remote place. [mock Aboriginal]

woosh var. of WHOOSH.

woozy /ˈwuːzi/ *adj.* (**woozier, wooziest**) *colloq.* **1** dizzy or unsteady. **2** dazed or slightly drunk. **3** vague. □ **woozily** *adv.* **wooziness** *n.* [19th c.: origin unknown]

wop /wɒp/ *n. slang offens.* an Italian or other S. European. [20th c.: origin uncertain: perhaps via Italian *guappo* 'bold, showy', from Spanish *guapo* 'dandy']

Worcester sauce /ˈwʊstə/ *n.* (*N.Amer.* **Worcestershire sauce**) a pungent sauce first made in Worcester. [*Worcester*, a city in S. England]

Worcs. *abbr.* Worcestershire.

word /wəːd/ *n. & v.* ● *n.* **1** a sound or combination of sounds forming a meaningful element of speech, usu. shown with a space on either side of it when written or printed, used as part (or occasionally as the whole) of a sentence. **2** speech, esp. as distinct from action (*bold in word only*). **3** one's promise or assurance (*gave us their word*). **4** (in *sing.* or *pl.*) a thing said, a remark or conversation. **5** (in *pl.*) the text of a song or an actor's part. **6** (in *pl.*) angry talk (*they had words*). **7** news, intelligence; a message. **8** a command, password, or motto (*gave the word to begin*). **9** a basic unit of the expression of data in a computer. ● *v.tr.* put into words; select words to express (*how shall we word that?*). □ **at a word** as soon as requested. **be as good as** (or **better than**) **one's word** fulfil (or exceed) what one has promised. **break one's word** fail to do what one has promised. **have no words for** be unable to express. **have a word** (often foll. by *with*) speak briefly (to). **in other words** expressing the same thing differently. **in so many words** explicitly or bluntly. **in a** (or **one**) **word** briefly. **keep one's word** do what one has promised. **my** (or **upon my**) **word** an exclamation of surprise or consternation. **not the word for it** not an adequate or appropriate description. **of few words** taciturn. **of one's word** reliable in keeping promises (*a woman of her word*). **on** (or **upon**) **my word** a form of asseveration. **put into words** express in speech or writing. **take a person at his** or **her word** interpret a person's words literally or exactly. **take a person's word for it** believe a person's statement without investigation etc. **too ... for words** too ... to be adequately described (*was too funny for words*). **waste words** talk in vain. **the Word** (or **Word of God**) **1** the Bible. **2** Jesus Christ (John 1:14). **word for word** in exactly the same or (of translation) corresponding words. **words fail me** an expression of disbelief, dismay, etc. **a word to the wise** = VERB. SAP. □ **wordage** *n.* **wordless** *adj.* **wordlessly** *adv.* **wordlessness** *n.* [Old English from Germanic]

word-blindness *n.* the inability to identify written or printed words resulting from a brain defect. □ **word-blind** *adj.*

wordbook /ˈwəːdbʊk/ *n.* a book with lists of words; a vocabulary or dictionary.

word-deafness *n.* the inability to identify spoken words resulting from a brain defect. □ **word-deaf** *adj.*

word division *n.* the practice of splitting words between two lines of printed text by means of a hyphen.

word game *n.* a game involving the making or selection etc. of words.

wording /ˈwəːdɪŋ/ *n.* **1** a form of words used. **2** the way in which something is expressed.

word of honour *n.* an assurance given upon one's honour.

word of mouth *n.* spoken communication between people as a means of transmitting information (*word of mouth is the only way to find out about this*).

word order *n.* the sequence of words in a sentence, esp. affecting meaning etc.

word-painting *n.* a vivid description in writing.

word-perfect *adj.* knowing one's part etc. by heart.

word-picture *n.* a piece of word-painting.

wordplay /ˈwəːdpleɪ/ *n.* use of words to witty effect, esp. by punning.

word processor *n.* a purpose-built computer system for electronically storing text entered from a keyboard, incorporating corrections, and providing a printout. □ **word-process** *v.tr.* **word processing** *n.*

wordsearch /ˈwəːdsəːtʃ/ *n.* a grid-shaped puzzle of letters in columns, containing several hidden words written in any direction.

wordsmith /ˈwəːdsmɪθ/ *n.* a skilled user or maker of words.

word-square *n.* a set of words of equal length written one under another to read the same down as across (e.g. *too old ode*).

word wrap *n. Computing* in word processing, the automatic shifting of a word too long to fit on a line to the beginning of the next line.

wordy /ˈwəːdi/ *adj.* (**wordier, wordiest**) **1** using or expressed in many or too many words; verbose. **2** consisting of words. □ **wordily** *adv.* **wordiness** *n.* [Old English *wordig* (as WORD, -Y[1])]

wore[1] *past* of WEAR[1].

wore[2] *past* and *past part.* of WEAR[2].

work /wəːk/ *n. & v.* ● *n.* **1** the application of mental or physical effort to a purpose; the use of energy. **2 a** a task to be undertaken. **b** the materials for this. **c** (prec. by *the*; foll. by *of*) a task occupying (no more than) a specified time (*the work of a moment*). **3** a thing done or made by work; the result of an action; an achievement; a thing made. **4** a person's employment or occupation etc., esp. as a means of earning income (*looked for work; is out of work*). **5 a** a literary or musical composition. **b** (in *pl.*) all such by an author or composer etc. **6** actions or experiences of a specified kind (*good work!; this is thirsty work*). **7 a** (in *comb.*) things or parts made of a specified material or with specified tools etc. (*ironwork; needlework*). **b** *archaic* needlework. **8** (in *pl.*) the operative part of a clock or machine. **9** *Physics* the exertion of force overcoming resistance or producing molecular change (*convert heat into work*). **10** (in *pl.*, prec. by *the*) *colloq.* all that is available; everything needed. **11** (in *pl.*) esp. *Brit.* operations of building or *repair (major building works)*. **12** (in *pl.*; often treated as *sing.*) esp. *Brit.* a place where manufacture is carried on. **13** (usu. in *pl.*) *Theol.* a meritorious act. **14** (usu. in *pl.* or in *comb.*) a defensive structure (*earthworks*). **15** (in *comb.*) **a** ornamentation of a specified kind (*pokerwork*). **b** articles having this. ● *v.* (*past* and *past part.* **worked** or (esp. as *adj.*) **wrought**) **1** *intr.* (often foll. by *at, on*) do work; be engaged in bodily or mental activity. **2** *intr.* **a** be employed in certain work (*works in industry*; *works as a secretary*). **b** (foll. by *with*) be the workmate of (a person). **3** *intr.* (often foll. by *for*) make efforts; conduct a campaign (*works for peace*). **4** *intr.* (foll. by *in*) be a craftsman (in a material). **5** *intr.* operate or function, esp. effectively (*how does this machine work?*; *your idea will not work*). **6** *intr.* (of a part of a machine) run, revolve; go through regular motions. **7** *tr.* carry on, manage, or control (*cannot work the machine*). **8** *tr.* **a** put or keep in operation or at work; cause to toil (*this mine is no longer worked*; *works the staff very hard*). **b** cultivate (land). **9** *tr.* **a** bring about; produce as a result (*worked miracles*). **b** *colloq.* arrange (matters) (*worked it so that we could go*; *can you work things for us?*). **10** *tr.* knead, hammer; bring to a desired shape or consistency. **11** *intr.* & *tr.* do, or make by, needlework etc. **12** *tr.* & *intr.* (cause to) progress or penetrate, or make (one's way), gradually or with difficulty in a specified way (*worked our way through the crowd*; *worked the peg into the hole*). **13** *intr.* (foll. by *loose* etc.) gradually become (loose etc.) by constant movement. **14** *tr.* artificially excite (*worked themselves into a rage*). **15** *tr.* solve (a sum) by mathematics. **16** *tr.* **a** purchase with one's labour instead of money (*work one's passage*). **b** obtain by labour the money for (one's way through university etc.). **17** *intr.* (foll. by *on, upon*) have influence. **18** *intr.* be in motion or agitated; cause agitation, ferment (*his features worked violently*; *the yeast began to work*). **19** *intr.* *Naut.* sail against the wind. □ **at work** in action or engaged in work. **get worked up** become angry, excited, or tense. **give a person the works 1** *colloq.* give or tell a person everything. **2** *colloq.* treat a person harshly. **3** *slang* kill a person. **have one's work cut out** be faced with a hard task. **in the works** esp. *N.Amer.* being planned, worked on, or produced. **set to work** begin or cause to begin operations. **work away** (or **on**) continue to work. **work one's fingers to the bone** see BONE. **work in** find a place for. **work it** *colloq.* bring it about; achieve a desired result. **work off** get rid of by work or activity. **work out 1 a** solve (a sum) or find out (an amount) by calculation. **b** solve or understand (a problem, person, etc.). **2** (foll. by *at*) be calculated (*the total works out at 230*). **3** give a definite result (*this sum will not work out*). **4** have a specified result (*the plan worked out well*). **5** provide for the details of (*has worked out a scheme*). **6** accomplish or attain with difficulty (*work out one's salvation*). **7** exhaust with work (*the mine is worked out*). **8** engage in physical exercise or training. **work over 1** examine thoroughly. **2** *colloq.* treat with violence. **work to rule** esp. *Brit.* (esp. as a form of industrial action) follow official working rules exactly in order to reduce output and efficiency. **work up 1** bring gradually to an efficient state. **2** (foll. by *to*) advance gradually to a climax. **3** elaborate or excite by degrees. **4** mingle (ingredients) into a whole. **5** learn (a subject) by study. **work one's will** (foll. by *on, upon*) *archaic* accomplish one's purpose on (a person or thing). **work wonders** see WONDER. □ **workless** *adj.* [Old English *weorc* etc., from Germanic]

workable /ˈwəːkəb(ə)l/ *adj.* **1** that can be worked or will work. **2** that is worth working; practicable, feasible (*a workable quarry*; *a workable scheme*). □ **workability** /-ˈbɪlɪti/ *n.* **workableness** *n.* **workably** *adv.*

workaday /ˈwəːkədeɪ/ *adj.* **1** ordinary, everyday, practical. **2** fit for, used, or seen on workdays.

workaholic /wəːkəˈhɒlɪk/ *n. colloq.* a person addicted to working. □ **workaholism** /ˈwɔːkəhɒlɪz(ə)m/ *n.* [portmanteau word from WORK + ALCOHOLIC]

work-basket *n.* (also **work-bag** etc.) a basket or bag etc. containing sewing materials.

workbench /ˈwəːkbɛn(t)ʃ/ *n.* a bench for doing mechanical or practical work, esp. carpentry.

workboat /ˈwəːkbəʊt/ *n.* a boat used for carrying out work such as fishing, transporting freight, etc.

workbook /ˈwəːkbʊk/ *n.* a student's book including exercises.

workbox /ˈwəːkbɒks/ *n.* a box for holding tools, materials for sewing, etc.

work camp *n.* a camp at which community work is done, esp. by young volunteers.

workday /ˈwəːkdeɪ/ *n.* esp. *US* a day on which work is usually done.

worker /ˈwəːkə/ *n.* **1** a person who works, esp. a manual or industrial employee. **2** a neuter or undeveloped female of various social insects, esp. a bee or ant, that does the basic work of its colony. **3** a person who works hard.

worker priest *n.* a French Roman Catholic or an Anglican priest who engages part-time in secular work.

work experience *n.* a scheme intended to give young people short-term experience of employment.

workfare /ˈwəːkfɛː/ *n.* a welfare system which requires some work or training from those receiving benefits. [portmanteau word from WORK + WELFARE]

workforce /ˈwəːkfɔːs/ *n.* **1** the workers engaged or available in an industry etc. **2** the number of such workers.

work group *n.* **1** a group within a work force. **2** a small group of usu. trainees, formed to practise or develop a skill etc.

workhorse /ˈwəːkhɔːs/ *n.* a horse, person, or machine that performs hard work.

workhouse /ˈwəːkhaʊs/ *n.* **1** *Brit. hist.* a public institution in which the destitute of a parish received board and lodging in return for work done. **2** *US* a house of correction for petty offenders.

working /ˈwəːkɪŋ/ *adj.* & *n.* ● *adj.* **1 a** engaged in work, esp. in manual or industrial labour. **b** spent in work or employment (*all his working life*). **2** functioning or able to function. ● *n.* **1** the activity of work. **2** the act or manner of functioning of a thing. **3 a** a mine or quarry. **b** the part of this in which work is being or has been done (*a disused working*).

working capital *n.* the capital actually used in a business.

working class *n.* & *adj.* ● *n.* the class of people who are employed for wages, esp. in manual or industrial work. ● *adj.* (**working-class**) of or relating to the working class.

working day *n.* esp. *Brit.* **1** a workday. **2** the part of the day devoted to work.

working drawing *n.* a drawing to scale, serving as a guide for construction or manufacture.

working hours *n.pl.* hours normally devoted to work.

working hypothesis *n.* a hypothesis used as a basis for action.

working knowledge *n.* knowledge adequate to work with.

working lunch *n.* a lunch at which business is conducted.

working man *n.* a man who is employed, esp. in a manual or industrial job.

working order *n.* the condition in which a machine works (satisfactorily or as specified).

working-out *n.* **1** the calculation of results. **2** the elaboration of details.

working party *n. Brit.* a group of people appointed to study a particular problem or advise on some question.

working woman *n.* a woman who is employed.

workload /ˈwəːkləʊd/ *n.* the amount of work to be done by an individual etc.

workman /ˈwəːkmən/ *n.* (*pl.* **-men**) **1** a man employed to do manual labour. **2** a person considered with regard to skill in a job (*a good workman*).

workmanlike /ˈwəːkmənlʌɪk/ *adj.* characteristic of a good workman; showing practised skill.

workmanship /ˈwəːkmənʃɪp/ *n.* **1** the degree of skill in doing a task or of finish in the product made. **2** a thing made or created by a specified person etc.

workmate /ˈwəːkmeɪt/ *n.* esp. *Brit.* **1** a person who works alongside another. **2** (**Workmate**) *propr.* a portable collapsible workbench incorporating vices.

work of art *n.* a fine picture, poem, or building etc.

workout /ˈwəːkaʊt/ *n.* a session of physical exercise or training.

workpeople /ˈwəːkpiːp(ə)l/ *n.pl. Brit.* people in paid employment.

workpiece /ˈwəːkpiːs/ *n.* a thing worked on with a tool or machine.

workplace /ˈwəːkpleɪs/ *n.* a place at which a person works; an office, factory, etc.

work rate *n.* **1** the rate at which work is done or produced. **2** the rate at which energy is expended.

workroom /ˈwəːkruːm, -rʊm/ *n.* a room for working in, esp. one equipped for a certain kind of work.

works council *n.* esp. *Brit.* a group of employees representing those employed in a works etc. in discussions with their employers.

worksheet /ˈwəːkʃiːt/ *n.* **1** a paper for recording work done or in progress. **2** a paper listing questions or activities for students etc. to work through.

workshop /ˈwəːkʃɒp/ *n.* **1** a room or building in which goods are manufactured. **2 a** a meeting for concerted discussion or activity (*a dance workshop*). **b** the members of such a meeting.

work-shy *adj.* disinclined to work.

worksite /ˈwəːksʌɪt/ *n.* a site where an industry is located or where labour takes place.

works of supererogation *n.pl. RC Ch.* actions believed to form a reserve fund of merit that can be drawn on by prayer in favour of sinners.

workspace /ˈwəːkspeɪs/ *n.* **1** space in which to work. **2** an area rented or sold for commercial purposes. **3** *Computing* a memory storage facility for temporary use.

workstation /ˈwəːksteɪʃ(ə)n/ *n.* **1** the location of a stage in a manufacturing process. **2** a computer terminal or the desk etc. where this is located.

work study *n.* a system of assessing methods of working so as to achieve the maximum output and efficiency.

work surface *n.* = WORKTOP.

work table *n.* a table for working at, esp. with a sewing machine.

worktop /ˈwəːktɒp/ *n. Brit.* a flat surface for working on, esp. in a kitchen.

work-to-rule *n.* esp. *Brit.* the act or an instance of working to rule.

workwear /ˈwəːkwɛː/ *n.* hard-wearing clothes for work.

workwoman /ˈwəːkwʊmən/ *n.* (*pl.* **-women**) a female worker or operative.

world /wəːld/ *n.* **1 a** the earth, or a planetary body like it. **b** its countries and their inhabitants. **c** all people; the earth as known or in some particular respect. **2 a** the universe or all that exists; everything. **b** everything that exists outside oneself (*dead to the world*). **3 a** the time, state, or scene of human existence. **b** (prec. by *the, this*) mortal life. **4** secular interests and affairs. **5** human affairs; their course and conditions; active life (*how goes the world with you?*). **6** average, respectable, or fashionable people or their customs or opinions. **7** all that concerns or all who belong to a specified class, time, domain, or sphere of activity (*the medieval world*; *the world of sport*). **8** (foll. by *of*) a vast amount (*that makes a world of difference*). **9** (*attrib.*) affecting many nations, of all nations (*world politics*; *a world champion*). □ **all the world and his wife** *Brit.* **1** any large mixed gathering of people. **2** all with pretensions to fashion. **bring into the world** give birth to or attend at the birth of. **carry the world before one** have rapid and complete success. **come into the world** be born. **for all the world** (foll. by *like, as if*) precisely (*looked for all the world as if they were real*). **get the best of both worlds** benefit from two incompatible sets of ideas, circumstances, etc. **in the world** of all; at all (used as an intensifier in questions) (*what in the world is it?*). **man** (or **woman**) **of the world** a person experienced and practical in human affairs. **not for the world** not whatever the inducement. **out of this world** *colloq.* extremely good etc. (*the food was out of this world*). **see the world** travel widely; gain wide experience. **think the world of** have a very high regard for. **the world, the flesh, and the devil** the various kinds of temptation. **the** (or **all the**) **world over** throughout the world. **the world to come** supposed life after death. **world without end** for ever. [Old English *w(e)orold, world* from a Germanic root meaning 'age': related to OLD]

World Bank *n. colloq.* the International Bank for Reconstruction and Development, an organization administering economic aid between member nations.

world-beater *n.* a person or thing surpassing all others.

world-class *adj.* of a quality or standard regarded as high throughout the world.

World Cup *n.* a competition between football or other sporting teams from various countries.

world fair *n.* an international exhibition of the industrial, scientific, technological, and artistic achievements of the participating nations.

world-famous *adj.* known throughout the world.

world language *n.* **1** an artificial language for international use. **2** a language spoken in many countries.

world-line *n. Physics* a curve in space-time joining the positions of a particle throughout its existence.

worldling /ˈwəːldlɪŋ/ *n.* a worldly person.

worldly /ˈwəːldli/ *adj.* (**worldlier, worldliest**) **1** temporal or earthly (*worldly goods*). **2** engrossed in temporal affairs, esp. the pursuit of wealth and pleasure. **3** experienced in life, sophisticated, practical. □ **worldliness** *n.* [Old English *woruldlic* (as WORLD, -LY[1])]

worldly-minded *adj.* intent on worldly things.

worldly wisdom *n.* prudence as regards one's own interests. □ **worldly-wise** *adj.*

world music *n.* pop music incorporating local or ethnic elements esp. from the developing world.

world order *n.* (esp. in phr. **new world order**) a system controlling events in the world, esp. an international set of arrangements for preserving global political stability.

world power *n.* a nation having power and influence in world affairs.

world's end *n.* (prec. by *the*) the farthest attainable point of travel.

World Series *n.* a series of games between the champions of the two major N. American baseball leagues.

world-shaking *adj.* of supreme importance.

world-view *n.* = WELTANSCHAUUNG.

world war *n.* a war involving many important nations (*First World War* of 1914–18; *Second World War* of 1939–45).

world-weary *adj.* weary of the world and life on it. □ **world-weariness** *n.*

worldwide /ˈwəːl(d)wʌɪd, wəːl(d)ˈwʌɪd/ *adj. & adv.* ● *adj.* affecting, occurring in, or known in all parts of the world. ● *adv.* throughout the world.

worm /wəːm/ *n. & v.* ● *n.* **1** any of various types of creeping or burrowing invertebrate animals with long slender bodies and no limbs, esp. segmented in rings or parasitic in the intestines or tissues. **2** the long slender larva of an insect, esp. in fruit or wood. **3** (in *pl.*)

intestinal or other internal parasites. **4** a blindworm or slow-worm. **5** a maggot supposed to eat dead bodies in the grave. **6** *colloq.* an insignificant or contemptible person. **7 a** the spiral part of a screw. **b** a short screw working in a worm-gear. **8** the spiral pipe of a still in which the vapour is cooled and condensed. **9** the ligament under a dog's tongue. ● *v.* **1** *intr.* & *tr.* (often *refl.*) move with a crawling motion (*wormed through the bushes*; *wormed our way through the bushes*). **2** *intr.* & *refl.* (foll. by *into*) insinuate oneself into a person's favour, confidence, etc. **3** *tr.* (foll. by *out*) obtain (a secret etc.) by cunning persistence (*managed to worm the truth out of them*). **4** *tr.* cut the worm of (a dog's tongue). **5** *tr.* rid (a plant or dog etc.) of worms. **6** *tr.* *Naut.* make (a rope etc.) smooth by winding thread between the strands. □ **food for worms** a dead person. **a** (or **even a**) **worm will turn** the meekest will resist or retaliate if pushed too far. □ **wormer** *n.* **wormlike** *adj.* [Old English *wyrm*, from Germanic]

worm-cast *n.* a convoluted mass of earth left on the surface by a burrowing earthworm.

worm charming *n.* the sport of enticing worms from their burrows.

worm-eaten *adj.* **1 a** eaten into by worms. **b** rotten, decayed. **2** old and dilapidated.

worm-fishing *n.* fishing with worms for bait.

worm-gear *n.* an arrangement of a toothed wheel worked by a short revolving cylinder bearing a screw thread.

wormhole /ˈwəːmhəʊl/ *n.* **1** a hole made by a burrowing worm or insect in wood, fruit, books, etc. **2** *Physics* a hypothetical connection between widely separated regions of space-time.

wormseed /ˈwəːmsiːd/ *n.* **1** seed used to expel intestinal worms. **2** a plant, e.g. santonica, bearing this seed.

worm's-eye view *n.* a view as seen from below or from a humble position.

worm-wheel *n.* the wheel of a worm-gear.

wormwood /ˈwəːmwʊd/ *n.* **1** any woody shrub of the genus *Artemisia*, with a bitter aromatic taste, used in the preparation of vermouth and absinthe and in medicine. **2** bitter mortification or a source of this. [Middle English, alteration of obsolete *wormod* (from Old English *wormōd*, *wermōd*), influenced by *worm*, *wood*: cf. VERMOUTH]

wormy /ˈwəːmi/ *adj.* (**wormier**, **wormiest**) **1** full of worms. **2** worm-eaten. □ **worminess** *n.*

worn /wɔːn/ *past part.* of WEAR[1]. ● *adj.* **1** looking tired and exhausted. **2** = WELL-WORN 1. **3** = WELL-WORN 2.

worn out *adj.* **1** exhausted. **2** worn, esp. to the point of being no longer usable (hyphenated when *attrib.*: *worn-out engine*).

worriment /ˈwʌrɪm(ə)nt/ *n.* esp. *US* **1** the act of worrying or state of being worried. **2** a cause of worry.

worrisome /ˈwʌrɪs(ə)m/ *adj.* causing or apt to cause worry or distress. □ **worrisomely** *adv.*

worrit /ˈwʌrɪt/ *n.* & *v.* (**worrited**, **worriting**) *Brit.* *colloq.* = WORRY. [originally alteration of WORRY]

worry /ˈwʌri/ *v.* & *n.* ● *v.* (**-ies**, **-ied**) **1** *intr.* give way to anxiety or unease; allow one's mind to dwell on difficulty or troubles. **2** *tr.* harass, importune; be a trouble or anxiety to. **3** *tr.* **a** (of a dog etc.) shake or pull about with the teeth. **b** attack repeatedly. **4** *tr.* (as **worried** *adj.*) **a** uneasy, troubled in the mind. **b** suggesting worry (*a worried look*). ● *n.* (*pl.* **-ies**) **1** a thing that causes anxiety or disturbs a person's tranquillity. **2** a disturbed state of mind; anxiety; a worried state. **3** a dog's worrying of its quarry. □ **not to worry** *colloq.* there is no need to worry. **worry along** (or **through**) manage to advance by persistence in spite of obstacles. **worry oneself** (usu. in *neg.*) take needless trouble. **worry out** obtain (the solution to a problem etc.) by dogged effort. □ **worriedly** *adv.* **worrier** *n.* **worryingly** *adv.* [Old English *wyrgan* 'strangle', from West Germanic]

worry beads *n.pl.* a string of beads manipulated with the fingers to occupy or calm oneself.

worry-guts *n.* (*N. Amer.* **worry-wart**) *colloq.* a person who habitually worries unduly.

worse /wəːs/ *adj.*, *adv.*, & *n.* ● *adj.* **1** more bad. **2** (*predic.*) in or into worse health or a worse condition (*is getting worse*; *is none the worse for it*). ● *adv.* more badly or more ill. ● *n.* **1** a worse thing or things (*you might do worse than accept*). **2** (prec. by *the*) a worse condition (*a change for the worse*). □ **none the worse** (often foll. by *for*) not adversely affected (by). **or worse** or as an even worse alternative. **the worse for drink** fairly drunk. **the worse for wear 1** damaged by use. **2** injured. **worse luck** see LUCK. **worse off** in a worse (esp. financial) position. [Old English *wyrsa*, *wiersa*, from Germanic]

worsen /ˈwəːs(ə)n/ *v.tr.* & *intr.* make or become worse.

worship /ˈwəːʃɪp/ *n.* & *v.* ● *n.* **1 a** homage or reverence paid to a deity, esp. in a formal service. **b** the acts, rites, or ceremonies of worship. **2** adoration or devotion comparable to religious homage shown towards a person or principle (*the worship of wealth*; *regarded them with worship in their eyes*). **3** *archaic* worthiness, merit; recognition given or due to these; honour and respect. ● *v.* (**worshipped**, **worshipping**; *US* **worshiped**, **worshiping**) **1** *tr.* adore as divine; honour with religious rites. **2** *tr.* idolize or regard with adoration (*worships the ground she walks on*). **3** *intr.* attend public worship. **4** *intr.* be full of adoration. □ **Your** (or **His** or **Her**) **Worship** esp. *Brit.* a title of respect used to or of a mayor, certain magistrates, etc. □ **worshipper** *n.* (*US* **worshiper**). [Old English *weorthscipe* (as WORTH, -SHIP)]

worshipful /ˈwəːʃɪpfʊl, -f(ə)l/ *adj.* **1** (usu. **Worshipful**) *Brit.* a title given to justices of the peace and to certain old companies or their officers etc. **2** *archaic* entitled to honour or respect. **3** *archaic* imbued with a spirit of veneration. □ **worshipfully** *adv.* **worshipfulness** *n.*

worst /wəːst/ *adj.*, *adv.*, *n.*, & *v.* ● *adj.* most bad. ● *adv.* most badly. ● *n.* the worst part, event, circumstance, or possibility (*the worst of the storm is over*; *prepare for the worst*). ● *v.tr.* get the better of; defeat, outdo. □ **at its** etc. **worst** in the worst state. **at worst** (or **the worst**) in the worst possible case. **do your worst** an expression of defiance. **get** (or **have**) **the worst of it** be defeated. **if the worst comes to the worst** if the worst happens. [Old English *wierresta*, *wyrresta* (*adj.*), *wyrst*, *wyrrest* (*adv.*), from Germanic]

worsted /ˈwʊstɪd/ *n.* **1** a fine smooth yarn spun from combed long staple wool. **2** fabric made from this. [*Worste(a)d*, a parish in Norfolk, England]

wort /wəːt/ *n.* **1** *archaic* (except in names) a plant or herb (*liverwort*; *St John's wort*). **2** the infusion of malt which after fermentation becomes beer. [Old English *wyrt*: related to ROOT[1]]

worth /wəːθ/ *adj.* & *n.* ● *predic.adj.* (governing a noun like a preposition) **1** of a value equivalent to (*is worth £50*; *is worth very little*). **2** such as to justify or repay; deserving; bringing compensation for (*worth doing*; *not worth the trouble*). **3** possessing or having property amounting to (*is worth a million pounds*). ● *n.* **1** what a person or thing is worth; the (usu. specified) merit of (*of great worth*; *persons of worth*). **2** the equivalent of money in a commodity (*ten pounds' worth of petrol*). □ **for all one is worth** *colloq.* with one's utmost efforts; without reserve. **for what it is worth** without a guarantee of its truth or value. **worth it** *colloq.* worth the time or effort spent. **worth one's salt** see SALT. **worth one's while** (or **worth while**) see WHILE. [Old English *w(e)orth*]

worthless /ˈwəːθlɪs/ *adj.* without value or merit. □ **worthlessly** *adv.* **worthlessness** *n.*

worthwhile /wəːθ'wʌɪl/ *adj.* that is worth the time or effort spent; of value or importance. ▫ **worthwhileness** *n.*

■ **Usage** *Worthwhile* is used both attributively and predicatively, e.g. *a worthwhile cause, decided it wasn't worthwhile*, while *worth while* (two words) is used only predicatively, e.g. *thought it worth while to ring the police.*

worthy /'wəːði/ *adj. & n.* ● *adj.* (**worthier**, **worthiest**) **1** estimable; having some moral worth; deserving respect (*lived a worthy life*). **2** (of a person) entitled to (esp. condescending) recognition (*a worthy old couple*). **3 a** (foll. by *of* or *to* + infin.) deserving (*worthy of a mention*; *worthy to be remembered*). **b** (foll. by *of*) adequate or suitable to the dignity etc. of (*in words worthy of the occasion*). ● *n.* (*pl.* **-ies**) **1** a worthy person. **2** a person of some distinction. **3** *joc.* a person. ▫ **worthily** *adv.* **worthiness** *n.* [Middle English *wurthi* etc. from WORTH]

-worthy /'wəːði/ *comb. form* forming adjectives meaning: **1** deserving of (*blameworthy*; *noteworthy*). **2** suitable or fit for (*newsworthy*; *roadworthy*).

wot see WIT².

wotcher /'wɒtʃə/ *int. Brit. slang* a form of casual greeting. [corruption of *what cheer*]

would /wʊd, wəd/ *v.aux.* (*3rd sing.* **would**) *past* of WILL¹, used esp.: **1** (in the 2nd and 3rd persons, and often in the 1st: see SHOULD) **a** in reported speech (*he said he would be home by evening*). **b** to express the conditional mood (*they would have been killed if they had gone*). **2** to express habitual action (*would wait for her every evening*). **3** to express a question or polite request (*would they like it?*; *would you come in, please?*). **4** to express probability (*I guess she would be over fifty by now*). **5** (foll. by *that* + clause) *literary* to express a wish (*would that you were here*). **6** to express consent (*they would not help*). [Old English *wolde*, past of *wyllan*: see WILL¹]

■ **Usage** See Usage Note at SHOULD.

would-be *attrib.adj.* often *derog.* desiring or aspiring to be (*a would-be politician*).

wouldn't /'wʊd(ə)nt/ *contr.* would not. ▫ **I wouldn't know** *colloq.* (as is to be expected) I do not know.

wouldst /wʊdst/ *archaic 2nd sing. past* of WOULD.

Woulfe bottle /wʊlf/ *n. Chem.* a glass bottle with more than one neck, used for passing a gas through a liquid etc. [named after P. *Woulfe*, English chemist d. 1803]

wound¹ /wuːnd/ *n. & v.* ● *n.* **1** an injury done to living tissue by a cut or blow etc., esp. beyond the cutting or piercing of the skin. **2** an injury to a person's reputation or a pain inflicted on a person's feelings. **3** *poet.* the pangs of love. ● *v.tr.* inflict a wound on (*wounded soldiers*; *wounded feelings*). ▫ **woundingly** *adv.* **woundless** *adj.* [Old English *wund* (*n.*), *wundian* (*v.*)]

wound² *past* and *past part.* of WIND² (cf. WIND¹ *v.* 6).

woundwort /'wuːndwəːt/ *n.* any of various plants esp. of the genus *Stachys*, formerly supposed to have healing properties.

wove¹ *past* of WEAVE¹.

wove² /wəʊv/ *adj.* (of paper) made on a wire-gauze mesh and so having a uniform unlined surface. [variant of *woven*, past part. of WEAVE¹]

woven *past part.* of WEAVE¹.

wow¹ /waʊ/ *int., n., & v.* ● *int.* (also **wowee** /waʊ'wiː/) expressing astonishment or admiration. ● *n. slang* a sensational success. ● *v.tr. slang* impress or excite greatly. [originally Scots: imitative]

wow² /waʊ/ *n.* a slow pitch-fluctuation in sound reproduction, perceptible in long notes. [imitative]

wowser /'waʊzə/ *n. Austral. slang* **1** a puritanical fanatic. **2** a spoilsport. **3** a teetotaller. [19th c.: origin uncertain]

WP *abbr.* word processor or processing.

w.p. *abbr.* weather permitting.

w.p.b. *abbr.* waste-paper basket.

WPC *abbr.* (in the UK) woman police constable.

w.p.m. *abbr.* words per minute.

WRAC *abbr. hist.* (in the UK, until 1993) Women's Royal Army Corps.

wrack /rak/ *n.* **1** seaweed cast up or growing on the shore. **2** = RACK². **3** a wreck or wreckage. **4** = RACK⁵. [Middle English from Middle Dutch *wrak* or Middle Low German *wra(c)k*, a parallel formation to Old English *wræc*, related to *wrecan* WREAK: cf. WRECK, RACK⁵]

WRAF *abbr. hist.* (in the UK, until 1994) Women's Royal Air Force.

wraggle-taggle var. of RAGGLE-TAGGLE.

wraith /reɪθ/ *n.* **1** a ghost or apparition. **2** the spectral appearance of a living person supposed to portend that person's death. ▫ **wraithlike** *adj.* [16th-c. Scots: origin unknown]

wrangle /'raŋg(ə)l/ *n. & v.* ● *n.* a noisy argument, altercation, or dispute. ● *v.* **1** *intr.* (often foll. by *over*) engage in a wrangle. **2** *tr. US* herd (cattle). ▫ **wrangling** *n.* [Middle English, probably from Low German or Dutch: cf. Low German *wrangelen*, frequentative of *wrangen* 'to struggle', related to WRING]

wrangler /'raŋglə/ *n.* **1** a person who wrangles. **2** *US* a cowboy. **3** (at Cambridge University) a person placed in the first class of the mathematical tripos.

wrap /rap/ *v. & n.* ● *v.* (**wrapped**, **wrapping**) **1** *tr.* (often foll. by *up*) envelop in folded or soft encircling material (*wrap it up in paper*; *wrap up a parcel*). **2** *tr.* (foll. by *round*, *about*) arrange or draw (a pliant covering) round (a person) (*wrapped the scarf closer around me*). **3** *tr.* (foll. by *round*) *slang* crash (a vehicle) into a stationary object. **4** *Computing* **a** *tr.* (foll. by *to*, *onto*) cause (a word or unit of text etc.) to be carried over to a new line automatically as the margin is reached. **b** *intr.* (of a word etc.) be so carried over. ● *n.* **1** a shawl or scarf or other such addition to clothing; a wrapper. **2** esp. *US* material used for wrapping. ▫ **take the wraps off** disclose. **under wraps** in secrecy. **wrapped up in** engrossed or absorbed in. **wrap up 1** finish off, bring to completion (*wrapped up the deal in two days*). **2** put on warm clothes (*mind you wrap up well*). **3** (in *imper.*) *Brit. slang* be quiet. [Middle English: origin unknown]

wraparound /'rapəraʊnd/ *adj. & n.* ● *adj.* **1** (esp. of clothing) designed to wrap round. **2** curving or extending round at the edges or sides. ● *n.* **1** anything that wraps round. **2** *Computing* a facility by which a linear sequence of memory locations or screen positions is treated as a continuous circular series.

wrap-over *adj. & n. Brit.* ● *attrib.adj.* (of a garment) having no seam at one side but wrapped around the body and fastened. ● *n.* such a garment.

wrappage /'rapɪdʒ/ *n.* a wrapping or wrappings.

wrapped /rapt/ *adj.* **1** that has been wrapped. **2** finished, completed. **3** *Austral. colloq.* = RAPT 4.

wrapper /'rapə/ *n.* **1** a cover for a sweet, chocolate, etc. **2** a cover enclosing a newspaper or similar packet for posting. **3** a paper cover of a book, usu. detachable. **4** a loose enveloping robe or gown. **5** a tobacco leaf of superior quality enclosing a cigar.

wrapping /'rapɪŋ/ *n.* (esp. in *pl.*) material used to wrap; wraps, wrappers.

wrapping paper *n.* strong or decorative paper for wrapping parcels.

wrasse /ras/ *n.* any brightly coloured marine fish of the family Labridae with thick lips and strong teeth. [Cornish *wrach*, variant of *gwrach*, = Welsh *gwrach*, literally 'old woman']

wrath /rɒθ, rɔːθ/ *n. literary* extreme anger. [Old English *wrǣththu* from *wrāth* WROTH]

wrathful /'rɒθfʊl, -f(ə)l, 'rɔːθ-/ *adj. literary* extremely angry. ▫ **wrathfully** *adv.* **wrathfulness** *n.*

wrathy /'rɒθi, 'rɔːθi/ *adj. N. Amer.* = WRATHFUL.

wreak /riːk/ *v.tr.* **1** (usu. foll. by *upon*) give play or satisfaction to; put in operation (vengeance or one's anger etc.). **2** cause (damage etc.) (*the hurricane wreaked havoc on the crops*). **3** *archaic* avenge (a wrong or wronged person). □ **wreaker** *n.* [Old English *wrecan* 'drive, avenge', etc., from Germanic: cf. WRACK, WRECK, WRETCH]

wreath /riːθ/ *n.* (*pl.* **wreaths** /riːðz, riːθs/) **1** flowers or leaves fastened in a ring esp. as an ornament for a person's head or a building or for laying on a grave etc. as a mark of honour or respect. **2 a** a similar ring of soft twisted material such as silk. **b** *Heraldry* a representation of this below a crest. **3** a carved representation of a wreath. **4** (foll. by *of*) a curl or ring of smoke or cloud. **5** a light drifting mass of snow etc. [Old English *writha* from weak grade of *wrīthan* WRITHE]

wreathe /riːð/ *v.* **1** *tr.* encircle as, with, or like a wreath. **2** *tr.* (foll. by *round*) put (one's arms etc.) round (a person etc.). **3** *intr.* (of smoke etc.) move in the shape of wreaths. **4** *tr.* form (flowers, silk, etc.) into a wreath. **5** *tr.* make (a garland). [partly back-formation from archaic *wrethen*, past part. of WRITHE; partly from WREATH]

wreck /rɛk/ *n.* & *v.* ● *n.* **1** the destruction or disablement esp. of a ship. **2** a ship that has suffered a wreck (*the shores are strewn with wrecks*). **3** a greatly damaged or disabled building, thing, or person (*had become a physical and mental wreck*). **4** (foll. by *of*) a wretched remnant or disorganized set of remains. **5** *Law* goods etc. cast up by the sea. ● *v.* **1** *tr.* cause the wreck of (a ship etc.). **2** *tr.* completely ruin (hopes, chances, etc.). **3** *intr.* suffer a wreck. **4** *tr.* (as **wrecked** *adj.*) involved in a shipwreck (*wrecked sailors*). **5** *intr. US* deal with wrecked vehicles etc. [Middle English from Anglo-French *wrec* etc. (related to VAREC) from a Germanic root meaning 'to drive': cf. WREAK]

wreckage /ˈrɛkɪdʒ/ *n.* **1** wrecked material. **2** the remnants of a wreck. **3** the action or process of wrecking.

wrecker /ˈrɛkə/ *n.* **1** a person or thing that wrecks or destroys. **2** esp. *hist.* a person on the shore who tries to bring about a shipwreck in order to plunder or profit by the wreckage. **3** esp. *N. Amer.* a person employed in demolition, or in recovering a wrecked ship or its contents. **4** *US* a person who breaks up damaged vehicles for spares and scrap. **5** *N. Amer.* a vehicle or train used in recovering a damaged one.

wreck-master *n.* an officer appointed to take charge of goods etc. cast up from a wrecked ship.

Wren /rɛn/ *n. hist.* (in the UK) a member of the former Women's Royal Naval Service. [originally in pl., from abbreviation WRNS]

wren /rɛn/ *n.* **1** any short-winged songbird of the family Troglodytidae, esp. the very small *Troglodytes troglodytes* of Eurasia and N. America, having barred brown plumage and a short cocked tail. **2** (in *comb.*) *Brit.* any small warbler or kinglet (*willow-wren*). **3** a small Australasian or S. American bird resembling a wren. [Old English *wrenna*, related to Old High German *wrendo, wrendilo*, Icelandic *rindill*]

wrench /rɛn(t)ʃ/ *n.* & *v.* ● *n.* **1** a violent twist or oblique pull or act of tearing off. **2** an adjustable tool like a spanner for gripping and turning nuts etc. **3** an instance of painful uprooting or parting (*leaving home was a great wrench*). **4** *Mech.* a combination of a couple with a force along its axis. ● *v.tr.* **1** twist or pull violently round or sideways. **2** (often foll. by *off, away*, etc.) pull off with a wrench. **3** distort (facts) to suit a theory etc. [(earlier as verb:) Old English *wrencan* 'twist']

wrest /rɛst/ *v.* & *n.* ● *v.tr.* **1** force or wrench away from a person's grasp. **2** (foll. by *from*) obtain by effort or with difficulty. **3** distort into accordance with one's interests or views (*wrest the law to suit themselves*). ● *n. archaic* a key for tuning a harp or piano etc. [Old English *wrǣstan* from Germanic: related to WRIST]

wrest-block *n.* (also **wrest-plank**) the part of a piano or harpsichord holding the wrest-pins.

wrestle /ˈrɛs(ə)l/ *n.* & *v.* ● *n.* **1** a contest in which two opponents grapple and try to throw each other to the ground esp. as an athletic sport under a code of rules. **2** a hard struggle. ● *v.* **1** *intr.* (often foll. by *with*) take part in a wrestle. **2** *tr.* fight (a person) in a wrestle (*wrestled his opponent to the ground*). **3** *intr.* **a** (foll. by *with, against*) struggle, contend. **b** (foll. by *with*) do one's utmost to deal with (a task, difficulty, etc.). **4** *tr.* move with efforts as if wrestling. □ **wrestler** *n.* **wrestling** *n.* [Old English *wrǣstlian*, recorded in *wraestlung* 'wrestling']

wrest-pin *n.* each of the pins to which the strings of a piano or harpsichord are attached.

wretch /rɛtʃ/ *n.* **1** an unfortunate or pitiable person. **2** (often as a playful term of depreciation) a reprehensible or contemptible person. [Old English *wrecca*, from Germanic]

wretched /ˈrɛtʃɪd/ *adj.* (**wretcheder**, **wretchedest**) **1** unhappy or miserable. **2** of bad quality or no merit; contemptible. **3** unsatisfactory or displeasing. □ **feel wretched 1** be unwell. **2** be much embarrassed. □ **wretchedly** *adv.* **wretchedness** *n.* [Middle English, formed irregularly from WRETCH + -ED[1]: cf. WICKED]

wrick *Brit.* var. of RICK[2].

wriggle /ˈrɪg(ə)l/ *v.* & *n.* ● *v.* **1** *intr.* **a** (of a worm etc.) twist or turn its body with short writhing movements. **b** (of a person or animal) make similar movements. **2** *tr.* & *intr.* (foll. by *along* etc.) move or go in this way (*wriggled into the corner*; *wriggled his hand into the hole*). **3** *tr.* make (one's way) by wriggling. **4** *intr.* practise evasion. ● *n.* an act of wriggling. □ **wriggle out of** *colloq.* avoid on a contrived pretext. □ **wriggler** *n.* **wriggly** *adj.* [Middle English from Middle Low German *wriggelen*, frequentative of *wriggen*]

wright /rʌɪt/ *n.* a maker or builder (usu. in *comb.*: *playwright*; *shipwright*). [Old English *wryhta*, *wyrhta* from West Germanic: related to WORK]

wring /rɪŋ/ *v.* & *n.* ● *v.tr.* (*past* and *past part.* **wrung** /rʌŋ/) **1 a** squeeze tightly. **b** (often foll. by *out*) squeeze and twist esp. to remove liquid. **2** twist forcibly; break by twisting. **3** distress or torture. **4** extract by squeezing. **5** (foll. by *out, from*) obtain by pressure or importunity; extort. ● *n.* an act of wringing; a squeeze. □ **wring a person's hand** clasp it forcibly or press it with emotion. **wring one's hands** clasp them as a gesture of great distress. **wring the neck of** kill (a chicken etc.) by twisting its neck. [Old English *wringan* from West Germanic: related to WRONG]

wringer /ˈrɪŋə/ *n.* a device for wringing water from washed clothes etc. □ **put through the wringer** *colloq.* subject to a very stressful experience.

wringing /ˈrɪŋɪŋ/ *adj.* (in full **wringing wet**) so wet that water can be wrung out.

wrinkle /ˈrɪŋk(ə)l/ *n.* & *v.* ● *n.* **1** a slight crease or depression in the skin such as is produced by age. **2** a similar mark in another flexible surface. **3** *colloq.* a detail, esp. a useful tip or technical innovation. ● *v.* **1** *tr.* make wrinkles in. **2** *intr.* form wrinkles; become marked with wrinkles. [originally representing Old English *gewrinclod* 'sinuous']

wrinkly /ˈrɪŋkli/ *adj.* & *n.* ● *adj.* (**wrinklier**, **wrinkliest**) having many wrinkles. ● *n.* (also **wrinklie**) (*pl.* **-ies**) *slang offens.* an old or middle-aged person.

wrist /rɪst/ *n.* **1** the part connecting the hand with the forearm. **2** the corresponding part in an animal. **3** the part of a garment covering the wrist. **4 a** (in full **wrist-work**) the act or practice of working the hand without moving the arm. **b** the effect produced in fencing, ball games, sleight of hand, etc., by this. **5** (in full **wrist-pin**) *Mech.* a stud projecting from a crank etc. as an attachment for a connecting rod. [Old English from Germanic, probably from a root related to WRITHE]

wristband /ˈrɪs(t)band/ *n.* a band forming or concealing the end of a shirtsleeve; a cuff.

wrist-drop *n.* the inability to extend the hand through paralysis of the forearm muscles.

wristlet /ˈrɪs(t)lɪt/ *n.* a band or ring worn on the wrist to strengthen or guard it or as an ornament, bracelet, handcuff, etc.

wrist-pin see WRIST 5.

wristwatch /ˈrɪs(t)wɒtʃ/ *n.* a small watch worn on a strap round the wrist.

wrist-work see WRIST 4a.

wristy /ˈrɪsti/ *adj.* (esp. of a shot in cricket, tennis, etc.) involving or characterized by movement of the wrist.

writ[1] /rɪt/ *n.* **1** a form of written command in the name of a court, state, sovereign, etc., to act or abstain from acting in some way. **2** a Crown document summoning a peer to Parliament or ordering the election of a member or members of Parliament. □ **serve a writ on** deliver a writ to (a person). **one's writ runs** one has authority (as specified). [Old English (as WRITE)]

writ[2] /rɪt/ *archaic past part.* of WRITE. □ **writ large** in magnified or emphasized form.

write /rʌɪt/ *v.* (*past* **wrote** /rəʊt/; *past part.* **written** /ˈrɪt(ə)n/) **1** *intr.* mark paper or some other surface by means of a pen, pencil, etc., with symbols, letters, or words. **2** *tr.* form or mark (such symbols etc.). **3** *tr.* form or mark the symbols that represent or constitute (a word or sentence, or a document etc.). **4** *tr.* fill or complete (a sheet, cheque, etc.) with writing. **5** *tr.* put (data) into a computer store. **6** *tr.* (esp. in *passive*) indicate (a quality or condition) by one's or its appearance (*guilt was written on his face*). **7** *tr.* compose (a text, article, novel, etc.) for written or printed reproduction or publication; put into literary etc. form and set down in writing. **8** *intr.* be engaged in composing a text, article, etc. (*writes for the local newspaper*). **9** *intr.* (foll. by *to*) write and send a letter (to a recipient). **10** *tr. US* or *colloq.* write and send a letter to (a person) (*wrote him last week*). **11** *tr.* convey (news, information, etc.) by letter (*wrote that they would arrive next Friday*). **12** *tr.* state in written or printed form (*it is written that*). **13** *tr.* cause to be recorded. **14** *tr.* underwrite (an insurance policy). **15** *tr.* (foll. by *into, out of*) include or exclude (a character or episode) in a story by suitable changes of the text. **16** *tr. archaic* describe in writing. □ **nothing to write home about** *colloq.* of little interest or value. **write down 1** record or take note of in writing. **2** write as if for those considered inferior. **3** disparage in writing. **4** reduce the nominal value of (stock, goods, etc.). **write in 1** send a suggestion, query, etc., in writing to an organization, esp. a broadcasting station. **2** *US* add (an extra name) on a list of candidates when voting. **write off 1** write and send a letter. **2** cancel the record of (a bad debt etc.); acknowledge the loss of or failure to recover (an asset). **3** *Brit.* damage (a vehicle etc.) so badly that it cannot be repaired. **4** compose with facility. **5** dismiss as insignificant. **write out 1** write in full or in finished form. **2** exhaust (oneself) by writing. **write up 1** write a full account of. **2** praise in writing. **3** make entries to bring (a diary etc.) up to date. □ **writable** *adj.* [Old English *wrītan* 'scratch, score, write', from Germanic: originally used of symbols inscribed with sharp tools on stone or wood]

■ **Usage** The use of *write* as a transitive verb with a person as the direct object, e.g. *He writes me every week*, is best avoided in British English, but is good American English. *He writes me a letter every week* is acceptable because *me* is not the direct object.

write-down *n.* a reduction in the estimated or nominal value of stock, assets, etc.

write-in *n. US* an instance of writing in (see *write in* 2).

write-off *n.* a thing written off, esp. a vehicle too badly damaged to be repaired.

writer /ˈrʌɪtə/ *n.* **1** a person who writes or has written something. **2** a person who writes books; an author. **3** *Brit.* a clerk, esp. in the Navy or in government offices. **4** *Brit.* a scribe. [Old English *wrītere* (as WRITE)]

writerly /ˈrʌɪtəli/ *adj.* **1** characteristic of a professional author. **2** consciously literary.

writer's block *n.* a periodic lack of inspiration afflicting creative writers etc.

writer's cramp *n.* a muscular spasm due to excessive writing.

Writer to the Signet *n.* a Scottish solicitor conducting cases in the Court of Session. [originally a clerk who prepared writs for the royal signet]

write-up *n. colloq.* a written or published account, a review.

writhe /rʌɪð/ *v.* & *n.* ● *v.* **1** *intr.* twist or roll oneself about in or as if in acute pain. **2** *intr.* suffer severe mental discomfort or embarrassment (*writhed with shame*; *writhed at the thought of it*). **3** *tr.* twist (one's body etc.) about. ● *n.* an act of writhing. [Old English *wrīthan*, related to WREATHE]

writing /ˈrʌɪtɪŋ/ *n.* **1** a group or sequence of letters or symbols. **2** = HANDWRITING. **3** (usu. in *pl.*) a piece of literary work done; a book, article, etc. **4** (**Writings**) the Hagiographa. □ **in writing** in written form. **the writing on the wall** an ominously significant event etc. (see Dan. 5:5, 25–8).

writing desk *n.* a desk for writing at, esp. with compartments for papers etc.

writing pad *n.* a pad (see PAD[1] *n.* 2) of paper for writing on.

writing paper *n.* paper for writing (esp. letters) on.

written *past part.* of WRITE.

WRNS *abbr. hist.* (in the UK) Women's Royal Naval Service.

wrong /rɒŋ/ *adj., adv., n.,* & *v.* ● *adj.* **1** mistaken; not true; in error (*gave a wrong answer*; *we were wrong to think that*). **2** unsuitable; less or least desirable (*the wrong road*; *a wrong decision*). **3** contrary to law or morality (*it is wrong to steal*). **4** amiss; out of order, in or into a bad or abnormal condition (*something wrong with my heart*; *my watch has gone wrong*). ● *adv.* (usually placed last) in a wrong manner or direction; with an incorrect result (*guessed wrong*; *told them wrong*). ● *n.* **1** what is morally wrong; a wrong action. **2** injustice; unjust action or treatment (*suffer wrong*). ● *v.tr.* **1** treat unjustly; do wrong to. **2** mistakenly attribute bad motives to; discredit. □ **do wrong** commit sin; transgress, offend. **do wrong to** malign or mistreat (a person). **get in wrong with** *colloq.* incur the dislike or disapproval of (a person). **get wrong 1** misunderstand (a person, statement, etc.). **2** obtain an incorrect answer to. **get** (or **get hold of**) **the wrong end of the stick** misunderstand completely. **go down the wrong way** (of food) enter the windpipe instead of the gullet. **go wrong 1** take the wrong path. **2** stop functioning properly. **3** depart from virtuous or suitable behaviour. **in the wrong** responsible for a quarrel, mistake, or offence. **wrong way round** in the opposite or reverse of the normal or desirable orientation or sequence etc. □ **wronger** *n.* **wrongly** *adv.* **wrongness** *n.* [Old English *wrang* from Old Norse *rangr* 'awry, unjust': related to WRING]

wrongdoer /ˈrɒŋduːə/ *n.* a person who behaves immorally or illegally. □ **wrongdoing** *n.*

wrong-foot *v.tr. Brit. colloq.* **1** (in tennis, football, etc.) play so as to catch (an opponent) off balance. **2** disconcert; catch unprepared.

wrongful /ˈrɒŋfʊl, -f(ə)l/ *adj.* **1** characterized by unfairness or injustice. **2** contrary to law. **3** (of a person) not entitled to the position etc. occupied. □ **wrongfully** *adv.* **wrongfulness** *n.*

wrong-headed *adj.* perverse and obstinate. □ **wrong-headedly** *adv.* **wrong-headedness** *n.*

wrong side *n.* the worse or undesired or unusable side of something, esp. fabric. □ **born on the wrong side of the blanket** see BLANKET. **get out of bed on the wrong side** see BED. **on the wrong side of 1** out of favour with (a person). **2** somewhat more than (a specified age). **on the wrong side of the tracks** see TRACK[1].

wrong side out with the wrong side outwards; inside out.

wrong'un /'rɒŋən/ *n. Brit. colloq.* **1** a person of bad character. **2** *Cricket* = GOOGLY. [contraction of *wrong one*]

wrot /rɒt/ *n.* (often *attrib.*) wrought timber. [alteration of WROUGHT]

wrote *past* of WRITE.

wroth /rəʊθ, rɒθ/ *predic.adj. archaic* angry. [Old English *wrāth*, from Germanic]

wrought /rɔ:t/ *archaic past* and *past part.* of WORK. ● *adj.* **1** (of metals) beaten out or shaped by hammering. **2** (of timber) planed on one or more sides.

wrought iron *n.* a tough malleable form of iron suitable for forging or rolling (hyphenated when *attrib.*: *wrought-iron gate*).

wrung *past* and *past part.* of WRING.

WRVS *abbr.* (in the UK) Women's Royal Voluntary Service.

wry /rʌɪ/ *adj.* (**wryer**, **wryest** or **wrier**, **wriest**) **1** distorted or turned to one side. **2** (of a face or smile etc.) contorted in disgust, disappointment, or mockery. **3** (of humour) dry and mocking. □ **wryly** *adv.* **wryness** *n.* [*wry* (*v.*) from Old English *wrīgian* 'tend, incline', in Middle English 'deviate, swerve, contort']

wryneck /'rʌɪnɛk/ *n.* **1** any bird of the genus *Jynx* of the woodpecker family, able to turn its head over its shoulder. **2** = TORTICOLLIS.

WSW *abbr.* west-south-west.

wt. *abbr.* weight.

Wu /wu:/ *n.* a dialect of Chinese spoken in the Kiangsu and Chekiang Provinces. [Chinese]

wunderkind /'vʊndəkɪnt/ *n.* (*pl.* **wunderkinds** or **wunderkinder** /-kɪndə/) *colloq.* a person who achieves great success while relatively young. [German, from *Wunder* 'wonder' + *Kind* 'child']

wurst /və:st, vʊəst, w-/ *n.* German or Austrian sausage. [German]

wuss /wʊs/ *n.* (also **wussy** *pl.* **-ies**) esp. *N. Amer. slang* an inept, feeble, or cowardly person. □ **wussy** *adj.* [20th c.: origin unknown]

WV *abbr. US* West Virginia (in official postal use).

W.Va. *abbr.* West Virginia.

WW *abbr. US* World War (I, II).

WX *abbr. Brit.* women's extra large size.

WY *abbr. US* Wyoming (in official postal use).

Wyandot /'wʌɪəndɒt/ *n.* & *adj.* (also **Wyandotte** esp. in sense 2 of *n.*) ● *n.* **1 a** a member of a N. American people originally of Ontario. **b** the language of this people. **2 a** a domestic fowl of a medium-sized American breed. **b** this breed. ● *adj.* of or relating to the Wyandots or their language. [French *Ouendat* from the native name *Wendat*]

wych elm /wɪtʃ/ *n.* (also **witch elm**) a Eurasian elm, *Ulmus glabra*, with large rough leaves. [from *wych*, used in names of trees with pliant branches, from Old English *wic*(*e*) apparently from a Germanic root meaning 'bend': related to WEAK]

wych hazel var. of WITCH HAZEL.

Wykehamist /'wɪkəmɪst/ *n.* & *adj.* ● *n.* a past or present member of Winchester College. ● *adj.* of or concerning Winchester College. [modern Latin *Wykehamista* from the name of William of *Wykeham*, bishop of Winchester and founder of the college (d. 1404)]

wyn var. of WEN².

wynd /wʌɪnd/ *n. Sc.* & *N.Engl.* a narrow street or alley. [Middle English, apparently from the stem of WIND²]

Wyo. *abbr.* Wyoming.

WYSIWYG /'wɪzɪwɪg/ *adj.* (also **wysiwyg**) *Computing* denoting the representation of text on-screen in a form exactly corresponding to its appearance on a printout. [acronym from *what you see is what you get*]

wyvern /'wʌɪv(ə)n/ *n.* (also **wivern**) *Heraldry* a winged two-legged dragon with a barbed tail. [Middle English *wyver* via Old French *wivre*, *guivre* from Latin *vipera*: for *-n* cf. BITTERN¹]

X[1] /ɛks/ *n.* (also **x**) (*pl.* **Xs** or **X's**) **1** the twenty-fourth letter of the alphabet. **2** (as a Roman numeral) ten. **3** (usu. ***x***) *Algebra* the first unknown quantity. **4** (usu. ***x***) *Geom.* the first coordinate. **5** an unknown or unspecified number or person etc. **6** a cross-shaped symbol esp. used: **a** to indicate position (*X marks the spot*). **b** to indicate incorrectness. **c** to symbolize a kiss or a vote. **d** as the signature of a person who cannot write.

X[2] *symb.* (of films) classified as suitable for adults only (replaced in the UK in 1983 by *18*, and in the US in 1990 by *NC-17* (no children under 17)).

-x /z/ *suffix* forming the plural of many nouns in *-u* taken from French (*beaux*; *tableaux*). [French]

xanthate /ˈzanθeɪt/ *n.* any salt or ester of xanthic acid.

xanthic /ˈzanθɪk/ *adj.* yellowish. [Greek *xanthos* 'yellow']

xanthic acid *n.* any colourless unstable acid containing the -OCS_2H group.

xanthine /ˈzanθiːn/ *n.* (also **xanthin** /-ɪn/) *Biochem.* **1** a purine derivative found in blood and urine which is a breakdown product of nucleic acids and is the parent compound of caffeine and other alkaloids. **2** (**xanthin**) any of various orange or yellow carotenoids found in plants.

Xanthippe /zanˈθɪpi/ *n.* (also **Xantippe** /-ˈtɪpi/) a shrewish or ill-tempered woman or wife. [the name of Socrates' wife]

xanthoma /zanˈθəʊmə/ *n.* (*pl.* **xanthomas** or **xanthomata** /-tə/) *Med.* **1** a skin disease characterized by irregular yellow patches. **2** such a patch. [as XANTHIC + -OMA]

xanthophyll /ˈzanθə(ʊ)fɪl/ *n.* any of various oxygen-containing carotenoids associated with chlorophyll, some of which cause the yellow colour of leaves in the autumn. [as XANTHIC + Greek *phullon* 'leaf']

x-axis *n.* the horizontal axis in a set of rectangular coordinates, a graph, etc.

X chromosome *n.* a sex chromosome of which the number in female cells is twice that in male cells, as in humans and other mammals. [*X* (as an arbitrary label) + CHROMOSOME]

x.d. *abbr.* ex dividend.

Xe *symb. Chem.* the element xenon.

xebec /ˈziːbɛk/ *n.* (also **zebec**, **zebeck**) a small three-masted Mediterranean vessel with lateen and usu. some square sails. [alteration (influenced by Spanish *xabeque*) of French *chebec*, via Italian *sciabecco* from Arabic *šabāk*]

xeno- /ˈzɛnəʊ/ *comb. form* **1 a** foreign. **b** a foreigner. **2** other. [Greek *xenos* 'strange, foreign, stranger']

xenogamy /zɛˈnɒgəmi/ *n. Bot.* cross-fertilization. □ **xenogamous** *adj.*

xenograft /ˈzɛnə(ʊ)grɑːft/ *n.* a tissue graft from a donor of a different species from the recipient. [XENO- + GRAFT[1]]

xenolith /ˈzɛnəlɪθ/ *n. Geol.* an inclusion within an igneous rock mass, usu. derived from the immediately surrounding rock.

xenon /ˈzɛnɒn, ˈziː-/ *n. Chem.* a heavy colourless odourless inert gaseous element occurring in traces in the atmosphere and used in fluorescent lamps (symbol Xe). [Greek, neut. of *xenos* 'strange']

xenophobe /ˈzɛnəfəʊb/ *n. & adj.* ● *n.* a person given to xenophobia. ● *adj.* characteristic of a xenophobe; xenophobic.

xenophobia /zɛnəˈfəʊbɪə/ *n.* a deep dislike of foreigners. □ **xenophobic** *adj.*

xeranthemum /zɪəˈranθɪməm/ *n.* a plant of the genus *Xeranthemum* (daisy family), with dry everlasting flowers. [modern Latin, from Greek *xērOS* 'dry' + *anthemon* 'flower']

xeric /ˈzɪərɪk, ˈzɛ-/ *adj. Ecol.* (of a habitat) very dry. [as XERO- + -IC]

xero- /ˈzɪərəʊ, ˈzɛrəʊ/ *comb. form* dry. [Greek *xēros* 'dry']

xeroderma /zɪərə(ʊ)ˈdəːmə, zɛ-/ *n.* any of various diseases characterized by extreme dryness of the skin, esp. ichthyosis. [modern Latin (as XERO-, Greek *derma* 'skin')]

xerograph /ˈzɪərə(ʊ)grɑːf, ˈzɛ-/ *n.* a copy produced by xerography.

xerography /zɪəˈrɒgrəfi, zɛ-/ *n.* a dry copying process in which black or coloured powder adheres to parts of a surface remaining electrically charged after exposure of the surface to light from an image of the document to be copied. □ **xerographic** /-rəˈgrafɪk/ *adj.* **xerographically** /-rəˈgrafɪk(ə)li/ *adv.*

xerophilous /zɪəˈrɒfɪləs, zɛ-/ *adj.* (of a plant) adapted to extremely dry conditions.

xerophyte /ˈzɪərə(ʊ)fʌɪt, ˈzɛ-/ *n.* (also **xerophile** /-fʌɪl/) a plant able to grow in very dry conditions, e.g. in a desert.

Xerox /ˈzɪərɒks, ˈzɛrɒks/ *n. & v.* ● *n. propr.* **1** a machine for copying by xerography. **2** a copy made using this machine. ● *v.tr.* (**xerox**) reproduce by this process. [invented from XEROGRAPHY]

Xhosa /ˈkəʊsə, ˈkɔːsə/ *n. & adj.* ● *n.* **1** (*pl.* same or **Xhosas**) a member of a Bantu-speaking people of Cape Province, South Africa. **2** the Bantu language of this people, similar to Zulu. ● *adj.* of or relating to this people or language. [native name]

xi /ksʌɪ, gzʌɪ, sʌɪ, zʌɪ/ *n.* the fourteenth letter of the Greek alphabet (Ξ, ξ). [Greek]

-xion /kʃ(ə)n/ *suffix* forming nouns (see -ION) from Latin participial stems in *-x-* (*fluxion*).

xiphisternum /zɪfɪˈstəːnəm/ *n. Anat.* = XIPHOID PROCESS. [as XIPHOID + STERNUM]

xiphoid /ˈzɪfɔɪd/ *adj. Biol.* sword-shaped. [Greek *xiphoeidēs* from *xiphos* 'sword']

xiphoid process *n.* the cartilaginous process at the lower end of the sternum.

Xmas /ˈkrɪsməs, ˈɛksməs/ *n. colloq.* = CHRISTMAS *n.* [abbreviation, with X for the initial chi of Greek *Khristos* 'Christ']

xoanon /ˈzəʊənɒn/ *n.* (*pl.* **xoana** /-nə/) *Gk Antiq.* a primitive usu. wooden image of a deity often said to have fallen from heaven. [Greek, from *xeō* 'carve']

X-rated *adj.* (usu. *attrib.*) **1** indecent, pornographic (*X-rated humour*). **2** *hist.* relating to films given an X classification (see X[2]).

X-ray *n. & v.* (also **x-ray**) ● *n.* **1** (in *pl.*) electromagnetic radiation of very short wavelength, able to pass through objects opaque to light. **2** an image made by the effect of X-rays on a photographic plate, esp. showing the position of bones etc. by their greater absorption of the rays. ● *v.tr.* photograph, examine, or treat with X-rays. [translation of German *x-Strahlen* (pl.) from *Strahl* 'ray', so called because when discovered in 1895 the nature of the rays was unknown]

X-ray astronomy *n.* the branch of astronomy concerned with the observation of celestial objects by means of their X-ray emissions.

X-ray crystallography *n.* the study of crystals and their structure by means of the diffraction of X-rays by the regularly spaced atoms of a crystalline material.

X-ray tube *n.* a device for generating X-rays by accelerating electrons to high energies and causing them to strike a metal target from which the X-rays are emitted.

xu /suː/ *n.* (*pl.* same) a monetary unit of Vietnam, equal to one-hundredth of a dong. [Vietnamese from French *sou*]

xylem /ˈzʌɪləm/ *n. Bot.* woody tissue (cf. PHLOEM). [Greek *xulon* 'wood']

xylene /ˈzʌɪliːn/ *n. Chem.* each of three isomeric liquid hydrocarbons obtained by distilling wood, coal tar, etc. Chem. formula: $C_6H_4(CH_3)_2$. [formed as XYLEM + -ENE]

xylo- /ˈzʌɪləʊ/ *comb. form* wood. [Greek *xulon* 'wood']

xylocarp /ˈzʌɪlə(ʊ)kɑːp/ *n.* a hard woody fruit. □ **xylocarpous** /-ˈkɑːpəs/ *adj.*

xylograph /ˈzʌɪlə(ʊ)grɑːf/ *n.* a woodcut or wood engraving (esp. an early one).

xylography /zʌɪˈlɒgrəfi/ *n.* **1** the (esp. early or primitive) practice of making woodcuts or wood engravings. **2** the use of wood blocks in printing.

Xylonite /ˈzʌɪlənʌɪt/ *n. propr.* a kind of celluloid. [formed irregularly from *xyloidin* (as XYLO-) + -ITE[1]]

xylophagous /zʌɪˈlɒfəgəs/ *adj.* (of an insect or mollusc) eating, or boring into, wood.

xylophone /ˈzʌɪləfəʊn/ *n.* a musical instrument of wooden or metal bars graduated in length and struck with a small wooden hammer or hammers. □ **xylophonic** /-ˈfɒnɪk/ *adj.* **xylophonist** *n.* [Greek *xulon* 'wood' + -PHONE]

xystus /ˈzɪstəs/ *n.* (*pl.* **xysti** /-tʌɪ/) **1** a covered portico used by athletes in ancient Greece for exercise. **2** *Rom. Antiq.* a garden walk or terrace. [Latin from Greek *xustos* 'smooth', from *xuō* 'scrape']

Yy

Y[1] /waɪ/ *n.* (also **y**) (*pl.* **Ys** or **Y's**) **1** the twenty-fifth letter of the alphabet. **2** (usu. ***y***) *Algebra* the second unknown quantity. **3** (usu. ***y***) *Geom.* the second coordinate. **4 a** a Y-shaped thing, esp. an arrangement of lines, piping, roads, etc. **b** a forked clamp or support.

Y[2] *abbr.* (also **Y.**) **1** yen. **2** *N. Amer.* = YMCA, YWCA.

Y[3] *symb. Chem.* the element yttrium.

y. *abbr.* year(s).

y- /ɪ/ *prefix archaic* forming past participles, collective nouns, etc. (*yclept*). [Old English *ge-*, from Germanic]

-y[1] /i/ *suffix* forming adjectives: **1** from nouns and adjectives, meaning: **a** full of; having the quality of (*messy*; *icy*; *horsy*). **b** addicted to (*boozy*). **2** from verbs, meaning 'inclined to', 'apt to' (*runny*; *sticky*). [from or suggested by Old English *-ig*, from Germanic]

-y[2] /i/ *suffix* (also **-ey**, **-ie**) forming diminutive nouns, pet names, etc. (*granny*; *Sally*; *nightie*; *Mickey*). [Middle English (originally Scots)]

-y[3] /i/ *suffix* forming nouns denoting: **1** state, condition, or quality (*courtesy*; *orthodoxy*; *modesty*). **2** an action or its result (*colloquy*; *remedy*; *subsidy*). [from or suggested by French *-ie* from Latin *-ia*, *-ium*, Greek *-eia*, *-ia*: cf. -ACY, -ERY, -GRAPHY, etc.]

yabby /'jabi/ *n.* (also **yabbie**) (*pl.* **-ies**) *Austral.* **1** a small freshwater crayfish, esp. of the genus *Charax*. **2** = NIPPER 5. [Wemba-wemba *yabij*]

yacht /jɒt/ *n.* & *v.* ● *n.* **1** a light sailing vessel, esp. equipped for racing. **2** a larger usu. power-driven vessel equipped for cruising. **3** a light vessel for travel on sand or ice. ● *v.intr.* race or cruise in a yacht. □ **yachting** *n.* [early modern Dutch *jaghte* from *jaghtschip* 'fast pirate ship', from *jag(h)t* 'hunting' (from *jagen* 'to hunt') + *schip* SHIP]

yacht club *n.* a sailing club, esp. for yacht racing.

yachtie /'jɒti/ *n. colloq.* a yachtsman or yachtswoman.

yachtsman /'jɒtsmən/ *n.* (*pl.* **-men**; *fem.* **yachtswoman**, *pl.* **-women**) a person who sails yachts.

yack var. of YAK[2].

yacka (also **yacker**) var. of YAKKA.

yackety-yack var. of YAK[2].

yaffle /'jaf(ə)l/ *n. dial.* the green woodpecker. [imitative of its laughing cry]

Yagara /'jɑːgərə/ *n.* an Aboriginal language of the area around Brisbane, Australia, now extinct.

Yagi antenna /'jɑːgi/ *n.* (also **Yagi aerial**) a highly directional radio aerial made of several short rods mounted across an insulating support and transmitting or receiving a narrow band of frequencies. [named after H. *Yagi*, Japanese engineer d. 1976]

yah /jɑː/ *int.* expressing derision or defiance. [imitative]

yahoo[1] /'jɑːhuː, jə'huː/ *n.* a coarse person; a lout, a hooligan. [the name of an imaginary race of brutish creatures in Swift's *Gulliver's Travels* (1726)]

yahoo[2] /jɑː'huː, ja-/ *int.* an exclamation of excitement, exultation, etc. [a natural exclamation]

Yahweh /'jɑːweɪ/ *n.* (also **Yahveh** /-veɪ/) the Hebrew name of God in the Old Testament. [Hebrew *YHVH* with added vowels: see JEHOVAH]

Yahwist /'jɑːwɪst/ *n.* (also **Yahvist** /-vɪst/) the postulated author or authors of parts of the Hexateuch in which God is regularly named *Yahweh*.

yak[1] /jak/ *n.* a long-haired humped Tibetan ox, *Bos grunniens*. [Tibetan *gyag*]

yak[2] /jak/ *n.* & *v.* (also **yack**, **yackety-yack** /jakətɪ'jak/) *colloq.* often *derog.* ● *n.* trivial or unduly persistent conversation. ● *v.intr.* (**yakked**, **yakking**) (often foll. by *away*, *about*) engage in such conversation; chatter. [imitative]

yakitori /jakɪ'tɔːri/ *n.* a Japanese dish of skewered grilled chicken pieces. [Japanese, from *yaki* 'grilling, toasting' + *tori* 'bird']

yakka /'jakə/ *n.* (also **yacka**, **yacker**) *Austral. slang* work. [Yindjibarndi (and other Aboriginal languages)]

Yale lock /jeɪl/ *n. propr.* a type of lock for doors etc. with a cylindrical barrel turned by a flat key with a serrated edge. [named after L. *Yale*, American locksmith, the inventor d. 1868]

y'all var. of YOU-ALL.

yam /jam/ *n.* **1 a** any tropical or subtropical climbing plant of the genus *Dioscorea*. **b** the edible starchy tuber of this. **2** *N. Amer.* a sweet potato. [Portuguese *inhame* or Spanish *iñame*, probably of W. African origin]

yammer /'jamə/ *n.* & *v. colloq.* or *dial.* ● *n.* **1** a lament, wail, or grumble. **2** voluble talk. ● *v.intr.* **1** utter a yammer. **2** talk volubly. □ **yammerer** *n.* [Old English *geōmrian* from *geōmor* 'sorrowful']

yandy /'jandi/ *v.* & *n. Austral.* ● *v.tr.* (**-ies**, **-ied**) separate (grass seed) from refuse by special shaking. ● *n.* (*pl.* **-ies**) a shallow dish used for this. [Aboriginal]

yang /jaŋ/ *n.* (in Chinese philosophy) the active male principle of the universe (cf. YIN). [Chinese, = sun, positive, male genitals]

Yank /jaŋk/ *n. Brit. colloq.* often *derog.* an inhabitant of the US; an American. [abbreviation]

yank /jaŋk/ *v.* & *n. colloq.* ● *v.tr.* pull with a jerk. ● *n.* a sudden hard pull. [19th c.: origin unknown]

Yankee /'jaŋki/ *n. colloq.* **1** often *derog.* = YANK. **2** *US* an inhabitant of New England or one of the northern states. **3** *hist.* a Federal soldier in the Civil War. **4** a type of bet on four or more horses to win (or be placed) in different races. **5** (*attrib.*) of or as of the Yankees. [18th c.: origin uncertain: perhaps from Dutch *Janke*, diminutive of *Jan* 'John', attested (17th c.) as a nickname]

Yankee Doodle *n.* **1** an American tune and song regarded as a national air. **2** = YANKEE 1, 2, 3.

yap /jap/ *v.* & *n.* ● *v.intr.* (**yapped**, **yapping**) **1** bark shrilly or fussily. **2** *colloq.* talk noisily, foolishly, or complainingly. ● *n.* a sound of yapping. □ **yapper** *n.* [imitative]

yapok /'japɒk/ *n.* a semiaquatic tropical American opossum, *Chironectes minimus*, with dark-banded grey fur. Also called *water opossum*. [*Oyapok*, *Oiapoque*, the name of a N. Brazilian river]

yapp /jap/ *n. Brit.* a form of bookbinding with a limp leather cover projecting to fold over the edges of the leaves. [named after William *Yapp*, a London bookseller *c.*1860, for whom it was first made]

yappy /'japi/ *adj.* (**-ier**, **-iest**) (of a dog) inclined to yap.

yarborough /'jɑːb(ə)rə/ *n.* a whist or bridge hand with no card above a 9. [named after the Earl of *Yarborough* (d. 1897), said to have betted against its occurrence]

yard[1] /jɑːd/ *n.* **1** a unit of linear measure equal to 3 feet (0.9144 metre). **2** this length of material (*a yard and a half of cloth*). **3** a square or cubic yard esp. (in building) of sand etc. **4** a cylindrical spar tapering to each end slung across a mast for a sail to hang from. **5** (in *pl.*; foll. by *of*) *colloq.* a great length (*yards of spare* *wallpaper*). □ **by the yard** at great length. [Old English *gerd*, from West Germanic]

yard[2] /jɑːd/ *n. & v.* ● *n.* **1** esp. *Brit.* a piece of enclosed ground esp. attached to a building or used for a particular purpose. **2** *N. Amer.* the garden of a house. ● *v.tr.* put (cattle) into a stockyard. □ **the Yard** *Brit. colloq.* = SCOTLAND YARD. [Old English *geard* 'enclosure, region', from Germanic]

yardage /ˈjɑːdɪdʒ/ *n.* **1** a number of yards of material etc. **2 a** the use of a stockyard etc. **b** payment for this.

yardarm /ˈjɑːdɑːm/ *n.* the outer extremity of a ship's yard.

yardbird /ˈjɑːdbəːd/ *n. US slang* **1** a new military recruit. **2** a convict.

Yardie /ˈjɑːdi/ *n. slang* a member of a Jamaican or West Indian gang of criminals, esp. drug-traffickers. [Jamaican English, = 'house, home']

yardman /ˈjɑːdmən/ *n.* **1** a person working in a railway yard or timber yard. **2** *US* a gardener or a person who does various outdoor jobs.

yard of ale *n. Brit.* **1** a deep slender beer glass, about a yard long and holding two to three pints. **2** the contents of this.

yardstick /ˈjɑːdstɪk/ *n.* **1** a standard used for comparison. **2** a measuring rod a yard long, usu. divided into inches etc.

yarmulke /ˈjɑːmʊlkə/ *n.* (also **yarmulka**) a skullcap worn by Jewish men. [Yiddish]

yarn /jɑːn/ *n. & v.* ● *n.* **1** spun thread, esp. for knitting, weaving, rope-making, etc. **2** *colloq.* a long or rambling story or discourse. ● *v.intr. colloq.* tell yarns. [Old English *gearn*]

yarran /ˈjarən/ *n.* any of several Australian acacias, esp. *Acacia omalophylla*, a small tree with scented wood used for fencing, fuel, etc. [Kamilaroi (and related languages) *yarraan*]

yarrow /ˈjarəʊ/ *n.* any perennial herbaceous plant of the genus *Achillea* (daisy family), esp. milfoil. Cf. ACHILLEA. [Old English *gearwe*, of unknown origin]

yashmak /ˈjaʃmak/ *n.* a veil concealing the face except the eyes, worn by some Muslim women when in public. [Arabic *yašmak*, Turkish *yaşmak*]

yataghan /ˈjatəgan/ *n.* a sword without a guard and often with a double-curved blade, used in Muslim countries. [Turkish *yātāğan*]

yatter /ˈjatə/ *v. & n. colloq.* chatter, gossip. [imitative, perhaps after YAMMER + CHATTER; cf. YAP, NATTER]

yaw /jɔː/ *v. & n.* ● *v.intr.* (of a ship or aircraft etc.) fail to hold a straight course; go unsteadily, esp. turning from side to side. ● *n.* the yawing of a ship etc. from its course. [16th c.: origin unknown]

yawl /jɔːl/ *n.* **1** a two-masted fore-and-aft sailing boat with the mizzen-mast stepped far aft. **2** a small kind of fishing boat. **3** *hist.* a ship's jolly boat with four or six oars. [Middle Low German *jolle* or Dutch *jol*, of unknown origin: perhaps related to JOLLY[2]]

yawn /jɔːn/ *v. & n.* ● *v.* **1** *intr.* (as a reflex) open the mouth wide and inhale esp. when sleepy or bored. **2** *intr.* (of a chasm etc.) gape, be wide open. **3** *tr.* utter or say with a yawn. ● *n.* **1** an act of yawning. **2** *colloq.* a boring or tedious idea, activity, etc. □ **yawner** *n.* **yawningly** *adv.* [Old English *ginian*, *geonian*]

yawp /jɔːp/ *n. & v.* ● *n.* **1** a harsh or hoarse cry. **2** *US* foolish talk. ● *v.intr.* **1** utter a yawp. **2** *US* talk foolishly. □ **yawper** *n.* [Middle English (imitative)]

yaws /jɔːz/ *n.pl.* (usu. treated as *sing.*) a contagious tropical skin disease with large red swellings, caused by spirochaete bacteria. [17th c.: probably via Carib *yaya* from a S. American Indian language]

y-axis *n.* the vertical axis in a set of rectangular coordinates, a graph, etc.

Yb *symb. Chem.* the element ytterbium.

Y chromosome *n.* a sex chromosome occurring only in male cells, in humans and other mammals. [*Y* (as an arbitrary label) + CHROMOSOME]

yclept /ɪˈklɛpt/ *adj. archaic* or *joc.* called (by the name of). [Old English *gecleopod*, past part. of *cleopian* 'call', from Germanic]

yd *abbr.* yard (measure).

yds *abbr.* yards (measure).

ye[1] /jiː/ *pron. archaic pl.* of THOU[1]. □ **ye gods!** *joc.* an exclamation of astonishment. [Old English *ge*, from Germanic]

ye[2] /jiː/ *det. pseudo-archaic* = THE (*ye olde tea-shoppe*). [variant spelling from the *y*-shaped letter THORN (representing *th*) in the 14th c.]

yea /jeɪ/ *adv. & n. archaic* or *formal* ● *adv.* **1** yes. **2** indeed, nay (*ready, yea eager*). ● *n.* the word 'yea'. □ **yea and nay** shilly-shally. [Old English *gea*, *ge*, from Germanic]

yeah /jɛː, jɛ/ *adv. colloq.* yes. □ **oh yeah?** expressing incredulity. [casual pronunciation of YES]

yean /jiːn/ *v.tr. & intr. archaic* bring forth (a lamb or kid). [perhaps from an Old English verb meaning 'pregnant', from Y-, *ēanian* 'to lamb']

yeanling /ˈjiːnlɪŋ/ *n. archaic* a young lamb or kid.

year /jɪə, jəː/ *n.* **1** (also **astronomical year**, **equinoctial year**, **natural year**, **solar year**, **tropical year**) the time occupied by the earth in one revolution round the sun, 365 days, 5 hours, 48 minutes, and 46 seconds in length (cf. SIDEREAL YEAR). **2** (also **calendar year**, **civil year**) the period of 365 days (**common year**) or 366 days (see LEAP YEAR) from 1 Jan. to 31 Dec., used for reckoning time in ordinary affairs. **3 a** a period of the same length as this starting at any point (*four years ago*). **b** such a period in terms of a particular activity etc. occupying its duration (*school year*; *tax year*). **4** (in *pl.*) age or time of life (*young for his years*). **5** (usu. in *pl.*) *colloq.* a very long time (*it took years to get served*). **6** a group of students entering college etc. in the same academic year. □ **in the year of Our Lord** (foll. by the year) in a specified year AD. **of the year** chosen as outstanding in a particular year (*sportsman of the year*). **a year and a day** the period specified in some legal matters to ensure the completion of a full year. **the year dot** see DOT[1]. **year in, year out** continually over a period of years. [Old English *gē(a)r*, from Germanic]

yearbook /ˈjɪəbʊk, ˈjəː-/ *n.* an annual publication dealing with events or aspects of the (usu. preceding) year.

year-end *n.* the end of esp. the financial year (often *attrib.*: *year-end profits*).

yearling /ˈjɪəlɪŋ, ˈjəː-/ *n. & adj.* ● *n.* **1** an animal between one and two years old. **2** a racehorse in the calendar year after the year of foaling. ● *adj.* **1** a year old; having existed or been such for a year (*a yearling heifer*). **2** intended to terminate after one year (*yearling bonds*).

year-long *adj.* lasting a year or the whole year.

yearly /ˈjɪəli, ˈjəː-/ *adj. & adv.* ● *adj.* **1** done, produced, or occurring once a year. **2** of or lasting a year. ● *adv.* once a year; from year to year. [Old English *gēarlic*, *-lice* (as YEAR)]

yearn /jəːn/ *v.intr.* **1** (usu. foll. by *for*, *after*, or *to* + infin.) have a strong emotional longing. **2** (usu. foll. by *to*, *towards*) be filled with compassion or tenderness. □ **yearner** *n.* **yearning** *n. & adj.* **yearningly** *adv.* [Old English *giernan*, from a Germanic root meaning 'eager']

year of grace *n.* the year AD.

year-round *adj.* existing etc. throughout the year.

years of discretion see DISCRETION.

yeas and nays *n.pl.* affirmative and negative votes.

yeast /jiːst/ *n.* **1** a greyish-yellow fungous substance obtained esp. from fermenting malt liquors and used as a fermenting agent, to raise bread, etc. **2** any of various unicellular fungi in which vegetative reproduction takes place by budding or fission. □ **yeastless** *adj.* **yeastlike** *adj.* [Old English *gist*, *giest* (unrecorded): corresponding to Middle Dutch *ghist*, Middle High German *jist*, Old Norse *jöstr*]

yeasty /ˈjiːsti/ *adj.* (**yeastier**, **yeastiest**) **1** frothy or tasting like yeast. **2** in a ferment. **3** working like yeast. **4** (of talk etc.) light and superficial. ◻ **yeastily** *adv.* **yeastiness** *n.*

yegg /jɛɡ/ *n. US slang* a travelling burglar or safebreaker. [20th c.: perhaps a surname]

yell /jɛl/ *n.* & *v.* ● *n.* **1** a loud sharp cry of pain, anger, fright, encouragement, delight, etc. **2** a shout. **3** *US* an organized shout, used esp. to support a sports team. **4** *Brit. slang* an amusing person or thing. ● *v.intr.* & *tr.* make or utter with a yell. [Old English *g(i)ellan*, from Germanic]

yellow /ˈjɛləʊ/ *adj.*, *n.*, & *v.* ● *adj.* **1** of the colour between green and orange in the spectrum, of buttercups, lemons, egg yolks, or gold. **2** of the duller colour of faded leaves, ripe wheat, old paper, etc. **3** having a yellow skin or complexion. **4** *colloq.* cowardly. **5** (of looks, feelings, etc.) jealous, envious, or suspicious. **6** (of newspapers etc.) unscrupulously sensational. ● *n.* **1** a yellow colour or pigment. **2** yellow clothes or material (*dressed in yellow*). **3 a** a yellow ball, piece, etc., in a game or sport. **b** the player using such pieces. **4** (usu. in *comb.*) a yellow moth or butterfly. **5** (in *pl.*) **a** jaundice of horses etc. **b** *US* a peach disease with yellowed leaves. ● *v.tr.* & *intr.* make or become yellow. ◻ **yellowish** *adj.* **yellowly** *adv.* **yellowness** *n.* **yellowy** *adj.* [Old English *geolu*, *geolo* from West Germanic: related to GOLD]

yellow archangel *n.* a Eurasian yellow-flowered nettle, *Lamistrum galeobdolon*.

yellow arsenic *n.* = ORPIMENT 1.

yellowback /ˈjɛlə(ʊ)bak/ *n. hist.* a cheap novel etc. in a yellow cover.

yellow-belly *n.* **1** *colloq.* a coward. **2** any of various animals with yellow underparts. ◻ **yellow-bellied** *adj.*

yellow bile *n. hist.* bile as one of the four bodily humours, characterized as hot and dry, and associated with a peevish or irascible temperament (cf. HUMOUR *n.* 5). Also called *choler*.

yellowcake /ˈjɛlə(ʊ)keɪk/ *n.* impure uranium oxide obtained during processing of uranium ore.

yellow card *n. Football* a card shown by the referee to a player being cautioned.

yellow fever *n.* a tropical virus disease with fever and jaundice, transmitted by the mosquito and often fatal.

yellowfin /ˈjɛlə(ʊ)fɪn/ *n.* any of various fishes with yellowish fins, esp. (in full **yellowfin tuna**) a tuna, *Thunnus albacares*, of warm seas, fished extensively for food.

yellow flag *n.* **1** a flag displayed by a ship in quarantine. **2** a yellow-flowered iris, *Iris pseudacorus*, with slender sword-shaped leaves.

yellowhammer /ˈjɛlə(ʊ)hamə/ *n.* a bunting, *Emberiza citrinella*, of which the male has a yellow head, neck, and breast. [16th c.: origin of *hammer* uncertain]

yellow jack *n.* **1** = YELLOW FEVER. **2** = YELLOW FLAG 1.

yellow jersey *n.* a jersey worn by the overall leader in a cycling race at the end of a day, and presented to the final winner.

yellowlegs /ˈjɛlə(ʊ)lɛɡz/ *n.* either of two migratory sandpipers with yellow legs, *Tringa flavipes* and *T. melanoleuca*.

yellow line *n.* (in the UK) a line painted along the side of the road in yellow either singly or in pairs to denote parking restrictions.

yellow metal *n.* brass of 60 parts copper and 40 parts zinc.

Yellow Pages *n.pl. propr.* a section of a telephone directory on yellow paper and listing business subscribers according to the goods or services they offer.

yellow pepper *n.* = RED PEPPER.

yellow peril *n.* (prec. by *the*) *offens.* the political or military threat regarded as emanating from Asian peoples, esp. the Chinese.

yellow rattle *n.* a yellow-flowered plant, *Rhinanthus minor*, which is partly parasitic.

yellow rocket *n.* winter cress.

yellow spot *n.* the point of acutest vision in the retina.

yellow streak *n. colloq.* a trait of cowardice.

yelp /jɛlp/ *n.* & *v.* ● *n.* a sharp shrill cry of or as of a dog in pain or excitement. ● *v.intr.* utter a yelp. ◻ **yelper** *n.* [Old English *gielp(an)* 'boast' (imitative)]

Yemeni /ˈjɛməni/ *n.* & *adj.* ● *n.* a native or inhabitant of Yemen, a country in southern Arabia. ● *adj.* of or relating to Yemen or its people. [Arabic *yamanī*: see -I[2]]

Yemenite /ˈjɛmənʌɪt/ *n.* & *adj.* ● *n.* **1** = YEMENI. **2** a Jew who was, or whose ancestors were, formerly resident in Yemen. ● *adj.* of, relating to, or designating a Yemeni Arab or a Yemeni Jew. [from Arabic *yamanī* (see YEMENI) + -ITE[1]]

yen[1] /jɛn/ *n.* (*pl.* same) the chief monetary unit of Japan. [Japanese *en* 'round']

yen[2] /jɛn/ *n.* & *v. colloq.* ● *n.* a longing or yearning. ● *v.intr.* (**yenned**, **yenning**) feel a longing. [Chinese *yǎn*]

yeoman /ˈjəʊmən/ *n.* (*pl.* **-men**) **1** esp. *hist.* a man holding and cultivating a small landed estate. **2** *hist.* a person qualified by possessing free land of an annual value of 40 shillings to serve on juries, vote for the knight of the shire, etc. **3** *Brit.* a member of the yeomanry force. **4** *hist.* a servant in a royal or noble household. **5** (in full **yeoman of signals**) a petty officer in the Navy, concerned with visual signalling. **6** *US* a petty officer performing clerical duties on board ship. ◻ **yeomanly** *adj.* [Middle English *yoman*, *yeman*, etc., probably from YOUNG + MAN]

Yeoman of the Guard *n.* (*pl.* **Yeomen of the Guard**) **1** a member of the British sovereign's bodyguard. **2** (loosely) a Yeoman Warder.

yeomanry /ˈjəʊmənri/ *n.* (*pl.* **-ies**) **1** a body of yeomen. **2** *Brit. hist.* a volunteer cavalry force raised from the yeoman class (1794–1908).

yeoman service *n.* (also **yeoman's service**) efficient or useful help in need.

Yeoman Usher *n.* (*pl.* **Yeoman Ushers**) *Brit.* the deputy of Black Rod.

Yeoman Warder *n.* (*pl.* **Yeoman Warders**) a warder at the Tower of London, a 'beefeater'.

yep /jɛp/ *adv.* & *n.* (also **yup** /jʌp/) *US colloq.* = YES. [corruption]

-yer /jə/ *suffix* var. of -IER esp. after *w* (*bowyer*; *lawyer*).

yerba maté /ˈjəːbə ˈmateɪ/ *n.* = MATÉ. [Spanish, = herb maté]

yes /jɛs/ *int.* & *n.* ● *int.* **1** equivalent to an affirmative sentence: the answer to your question is affirmative, it is as you say or as I have said, the statement etc. made is correct, the request or command will be complied with, the negative statement etc. made is not correct. **2** (in answer to a summons or address) an acknowledgement of one's presence. ● *n.* **1** an utterance of the word *yes*. **2** an affirmation or assent. **3** a vote in favour of a proposition. ◻ **yes? 1** indeed? is that so? **2** what do you want? **yes, and** a form for introducing a stronger phrase (*he came home drunk — yes, and was sick*). **yes and no** that is partly true and partly untrue. [Old English *gēse*, *gīse*, probably from *gīa sīe* 'may it be' (*gīa* is unrecorded)]

yes-man *n.* (*pl.* **-men**) *colloq.* a weakly acquiescent person, an obsequious subordinate.

yester- /ˈjɛstə/ *comb. form poet.* or *archaic* of yesterday; that is the last past (*yestereve*). [Old English *geostran*]

yesterday /ˈjɛstədeɪ, -di/ *adv.* & *n.* ● *adv.* **1** on the day before today. **2** in the recent past. **3** *colloq.* extremely urgently; immediately (*they want delivery yesterday!*). ● *n.* **1** the day before today. **2** the recent past. ◻ **yesterday morning** (or **afternoon** etc.) in the morning (or afternoon etc.) of yesterday. [Old English *giestran dæg* (as YESTER-, DAY)]

yesteryear /ˈjɛstəjɪə, -jəː/ *n. literary* **1** last year. **2** the recent past.

yet /jɛt/ *adv. & conj.* ● *adv.* **1** as late as now (or then), until now (or then) (*there is yet time*; *your best work yet*). **2** (with *neg.* or *interrog.*) so soon as now (or then), by now (or then) (*it is not time yet*; *have you finished yet?*). **3** again; in addition (*more and yet more*). **4** in the remaining time available; before all is over (*I will do it yet*). **5** (foll. by *compar.*) even (*a yet more difficult task*). **6** nevertheless; and in spite of that; but for all that (*it is strange, and yet it is true*). ● *conj.* but at the same time; but nevertheless (*I won, yet what good has it done?*). □ **nor yet** and also not (*won't listen to me nor yet to you*). [Old English *gīet(a)*, = Old Frisian *iēta*, of unknown origin]

yeti /'jɛti/ *n.* = ABOMINABLE SNOWMAN. [Tibetan]

yew /ju:/ *n.* **1** (also **yew tree**) any dark-leaved evergreen coniferous tree of the genus *Taxus*, having seeds enclosed in a fleshy red aril, and often planted in churchyards. **2** its wood, used formerly as a material for bows and still in cabinetmaking. [Old English *īw*, *ēow*, from Germanic]

Y-fronts /'wʌɪfrʌnts/ *n. Brit. propr.* men's or boys' briefs with a Y-shaped seam at the front.

Yggdrasil /'ɪgdrəsɪl/ *n.* (in Scandinavian mythology) an ash tree whose roots and branches join heaven, earth, and hell. [Old Norse *yg(g)drasill*, from *Yggr* 'Odin' + *drasill* 'horse']

YHA *abbr.* (in the UK) Youth Hostels Association.

Yid /jɪd/ *n. slang offens.* a Jew. [back-formation from YIDDISH]

Yiddish /'jɪdɪʃ/ *n. & adj.* ● *n.* a vernacular used by Jews in or from central and eastern Europe, originally a German dialect with words from Hebrew and several modern languages. ● *adj.* of or relating to this language. [German *jüdisch* 'Jewish']

Yiddisher /'jɪdɪʃə/ *n. & adj.* ● *n.* a person speaking Yiddish. ● *adj.* Yiddish-speaking.

Yiddishism /'jɪdɪʃɪz(ə)m/ *n.* **1** a Yiddish word, idiom, etc., esp. one adopted into another language. **2** advocacy of Yiddish culture.

yield /ji:ld/ *v. & n.* ● *v.* **1** *tr.* (also *absol.*) produce or return as a fruit, profit, or result (*the land yields crops*; *the land yields poorly*; *the investment yields 15%*). **2** *tr.* give up; surrender, concede; comply with a demand for (*yielded the fortress*; *yielded themselves prisoners*). **3** *intr.* (often foll. by *to*) **a** surrender; make submission. **b** give consent or change one's course of action in deference to; respond as required to (*yielded to persuasion*). **4** *intr.* (foll. by *to*) be inferior or confess inferiority to (*I yield to none in understanding the problem*). **5** *intr.* (foll. by *to*) give right of way to other traffic. **6** *intr. US* allow another the right to speak in a debate etc. ● *n.* an amount yielded or produced; an output or return. □ **yielder** *n.* [Old English *g(i)eldan* 'pay', from Germanic]

yielding /'ji:ldɪŋ/ *adj.* **1** compliant, submissive. **2** (of a substance) able to bend; soft and pliable, not stiff or rigid. □ **yieldingly** *adv.* **yieldingness** *n.*

yield point *n. Physics* the stress beyond which a material becomes plastic.

yikes /jʌɪks/ *int. slang* an expression of surprise and sudden apprehension. [origin unknown: cf. YOICKS]

yin /jɪn/ *n.* (in Chinese philosophy) the passive female principle of the universe (cf. YANG). [Chinese *yīn* 'shade, feminine, the moon']

Yindjibarndi /jɪndʒɪ'bʌndi/ *n.* an Aboriginal language of W. Australia.

yip /jɪp/ *v. & n. US* ● *v.intr.* (**yipped**, **yipping**) = YELP *v.* ● *n.* = YELP *n.* [imitative]

yippee /'jɪpi:, jɪ'pi:/ *int.* expressing delight or excitement. [a natural exclamation]

yips /jɪps/ *n.pl.* (usu. prec. by *the*) *colloq.* extreme nervousness, esp. causing a golfer to miss an easy putt. [20th c.: origin unknown]

-yl /ʌɪl, ɪl/ *suffix Chem.* forming nouns denoting a radical (*ethyl*; *hydroxyl*; *phenyl*).

ylang-ylang /i:laŋ'i:laŋ/ *n.* (also **ilang-ilang**) **1** a Malayan tree, *Cananga odorata*, from the fragrant yellow flowers of which a perfume is distilled. **2** the perfume itself. [Tagalog *álang-ilang*]

YMCA *abbr.* Young Men's Christian Association.

-yne /-ʌɪn/ *suffix Chem.* forming names of unsaturated compounds containing a triple bond (*ethyne* = acetylene).

yo /jəʊ/ *int. slang* calling attention, expressing encouragement or excitement, or as a greeting.

yob /jɒb/ *n. Brit. colloq.* a lout or hooligan. □ **yobbish** *adj.* **yobbishly** *adv.* **yobbishness** *n.* [back slang for BOY]

yobbo /'jɒbəʊ/ *n.* (*pl.* **-os** or **-oes**) *Brit. colloq.* = YOB.

yocto- /'jɒktəʊ/ *comb. form* denoting a factor of 10^{-24}. [adapted from OCTO-, on the pattern of *peta-*, *exa-*, etc.]

yod /jɒd/ *n.* **1** the tenth and smallest letter of the Hebrew alphabet. **2** its semivowel sound /j/. [Hebrew *yōḏ* from *yaḏ* 'hand']

yodel /'jəʊd(ə)l/ *v. & n.* ● *v.tr. & intr.* (**yodelled**, **yodelling**; *US* **yodeled**, **yodeling**) sing with melodious inarticulate sounds and frequent changes between falsetto and the normal voice in the manner of the Swiss mountain-dwellers. ● *n.* a yodelling cry. □ **yodeller** *n.* [German *jodeln*]

yoga /'jəʊgə/ *n.* **1** a Hindu system of philosophic meditation and asceticism designed to effect reunion with the universal spirit. **2** = HATHA YOGA. □ **yogic** /'jəʊgɪk/ *adj.* [Hindustani from Sanskrit, = union]

yogh /jɒg/ *n.* a Middle English letter (ȝ) used for certain values of *g* and *y*. [Middle English]

yogi /'jəʊgi/ *n.* (*pl.* **yogis**) a person proficient in yoga. □ **yogism** *n.* [Hindustani from YOGA]

yogurt /'jɒgət/ *n.* (also **yoghurt**) a semi-solid sourish food prepared from milk fermented by added bacteria. [Turkish *yoğurt*]

yo-heave-ho /jəʊhi:v'həʊ/ *int. & n.* = HEAVE-HO.

yo-ho /jəʊ'həʊ/ *int.* (also **yo-ho-ho** /jəʊhəʊ'həʊ/) **1** used to attract attention. **2** = YO-HEAVE-HO. [from YO + HO]

yoicks /jɔɪks/ *int.* (also **hoicks** /hɔɪks/) a cry used by fox-hunters to urge on the hounds. [18th c.: origin unknown: cf. *hyke*, a call to hounds, HEY[1]]

yoke /jəʊk/ *n. & v.* ● *n.* **1** a wooden crosspiece fastened over the necks of two oxen etc. and attached to the plough or wagon to be drawn. **2** (*pl.* same or **yokes**) a pair (of oxen etc.). **3** an object like a yoke in form or function, e.g. a wooden shoulder-piece for carrying a pair of pails, the top section of a dress or skirt etc. from which the rest hangs. **4** sway, dominion, or servitude, esp. when oppressive. **5** a bond of union, esp. that of marriage. **6** *Rom.Hist.* an uplifted yoke, or an arch of three spears symbolizing it, under which a defeated army was made to march. **7** *archaic* the amount of land that one yoke of oxen could plough in a day. **8** a crossbar on which a bell swings. **9** the crossbar of a rudder to whose ends ropes are fastened. **10** a bar of soft iron between the poles of an electromagnet. ● *v.* **1** *tr.* put a yoke on. **2** *tr.* couple or unite (a pair). **3** *tr.* (foll. by *to*) link (one thing) to (another). **4** *intr.* match; work together. [Old English *geoc*, from Germanic]

yokel /'jəʊk(ə)l/ *n.* a rustic; a country bumpkin. [perhaps from dialect *yokel* 'green woodpecker']

yolk[1] /jəʊk/ *n.* **1** the yellow inner part of an egg, rich in fat and protein, that nourishes the young before it hatches. **2** *Biol.* the corresponding part of any animal ovum. □ **yolked** *adj.* (also in *comb.*). **yolkless** *adj.* **yolky** *adj.* [Old English *geol(o)ca* from *geolu* YELLOW]

yolk[2] /jəʊk/ *n.* = SUINT. [Old English, back-formation from *eowucig* 'full of natural grease', ultimately from *ēuwu* EWE]

yolk-bag *n.* (also **yolk-sac**) a membrane enclosing the yolk of an egg.

Yom Kippur /jɒm 'kɪpə, kɪ'pʊə/ *n.* = DAY OF ATONEMENT. [Hebrew]

yomp /jɒmp/ *v.intr. Brit. slang* march with heavy equipment over difficult terrain. [20th c.: origin unknown]

yon /jɒn/ *adj., adv., & pron. literary & dial.* ● *adj. & adv.* yonder. ● *pron.* yonder person or thing. [Old English *geon*]

yonder /ˈjɒndə/ *adv. & det.* ● *adv.* over there; at some distance in that direction; in the place indicated by pointing etc. ● *det.* situated yonder. [Middle English: corresponding to Old Saxon *gendra*, Gothic *jaindrē*]

yoni /ˈjəʊni/ *n.* a symbol of the female genitals venerated by Hindus etc. [Sanskrit, = source, womb, female genitals]

yonks /jɒŋks/ *n.pl. Brit. slang* a long time (*haven't seen them for yonks*). [20th c.: origin unknown]

yoo-hoo /ˈjuːhuː, juːˈhuː/ *int.* used to attract a person's attention. [a natural exclamation]

yore /jɔː/ *n. literary* □ **of yore** formerly; in or of old days. [Old English *geāra, geāre*, etc., adv. forms of uncertain origin]

yorker /ˈjɔːkə/ *n. Cricket* a ball bowled so that it pitches immediately under the bat. □ **york** *v.tr.* [probably from *York*, as having been introduced by Yorkshire players]

Yorkist /ˈjɔːkɪst/ *n. & adj.* ● *n. hist.* an adherent or a supporter of the House of York, esp. in the Wars of the Roses (cf. LANCASTRIAN 2). ● *adj.* of or concerning the House of York.

Yorks. *abbr.* Yorkshire.

Yorkshire fog /ˈjɔːkʃə/ *n.* a fodder grass, *Holcus lanatus*. [FOG[2]]

Yorkshireman /ˈjɔːkʃəmən/ *n.* (*pl.* **-men**; *fem.* **Yorkshirewoman**, *pl.* **-women**) a native of Yorkshire in northern England.

Yorkshire pudding /ˈjɔːkʃə/ *n.* a baked batter pudding usu. eaten with roast beef. [*Yorkshire* in northern England]

Yorkshire terrier /ˈjɔːkʃə/ *n.* a small long-haired blue-grey and tan kind of terrier.

Yoruba /ˈjɒrʊbə/ *n.* (*pl.* same) **1** a member of a black African people inhabiting the west coast, esp. Nigeria. **2** the language of this people. [native name]

yotta- /ˈjɒtə/ *comb. form* denoting a factor of 10^{24}. [formed like YOCTO-, apparently adapted from Italian *otto* 'eight']

you /juː/ *pron.* (*obj.* **you**; *poss.* **your, yours**) **1** used with reference to the person or persons addressed or one such person and one or more associated persons. **2** (as *int.* with a noun) in an exclamatory statement (*you fools!*). **3** (in general statements) one, a person, anyone, or everyone (*it's bad at first, but you get used to it*). [Old English *ēow*, accusative & dative of *gē* YE[1], from West Germanic: supplanting *ye* because of the more frequent use of the obj. case, and *thou* and *thee* as the more courteous form]

you-all *pron.* (also **y'all**) *US colloq.* you (usu. more than one person).

you and yours *poss.pron.* you together with your family, property, etc.

you'd /juːd, jʊd/ *contr.* **1** you had. **2** you would.

you-know-what *n.* (also **you-know-who**) a thing or person unspecified but understood.

you'll /juːl, jʊl/ *contr.* you will; you shall.

young /jʌŋ/ *adj. & n.* ● *adj.* (**younger** /ˈjʌŋgə/; **youngest** /ˈjʌŋgɪst/) **1** not far advanced in life, development, or existence; not yet old. **2 a** immature or inexperienced. **b** youthful. **3** felt in or characteristic of youth (*young love; young ambition*). **4** representing young people (*Young Conservatives; Young England*). **5** distinguishing a son from his father (*young Jones*). **6** (**younger**) **a** distinguishing one person from another of the same name (*the younger Pitt*). **b** *Sc.* the heir of a landed commoner. ● *n.* (*collect.*) offspring, esp. of animals before or soon after birth. □ **with young** (of an animal) pregnant. □ **youngish** *adj.* **youngling** *n.* [Old English *g(e)ong*, from Germanic]

young blood see BLOOD.

younger hand *n. Cards* the second player of two.

young fogey *n.* a young person with conservative tastes or ideas.

young fustic *n.* **1** a sumac, *Cotinus coggygria*, native to Europe (also called *Venetian sumac*). **2** the wood of this tree.

young hopeful see HOPEFUL *n.*

young lady *n.* **1** a young (esp. unmarried) woman; a girl. **2** *colloq.* a girlfriend or sweetheart.

young man *n.* **1** a man who is young; a boy. **2** *colloq.* a boyfriend or sweetheart.

young offender *n.* a young criminal, esp.: **1** *Brit. Law* a young criminal between 14 and 17 years of age. **2** *Canad. Law* a young criminal between 12 and 18 years of age.

young person *n. Law* (in the UK) a person generally between 14 and 17 years of age.

Young Pretender *n.* Charles Stuart (1720–80), grandson of James II and claimant to the British throne.

Young's modulus /jʌŋz/ *n. Physics* a measure of elasticity, equal to the ratio of the stress acting on a substance to the strain produced. [named after T. *Young*, English scientist d. 1829]

youngster /ˈjʌŋstə/ *n.* a child or young person.

young thing *n. colloq.* a young person (*bright young things working in the City*).

Young Turk *n.* **1** a member of a revolutionary party in Turkey who carried out the revolution of 1908. **2** a young person eager for radical change to the established order. **3** (**young turk**) *offens.* a violent child or youth.

young 'un *n. colloq.* a youngster.

young woman *n.* **1** a woman who is young. **2** *colloq.* a girlfriend or sweetheart.

younker /ˈjʌŋkə/ *n. archaic* = YOUNGSTER. [Middle Dutch *jonckher*, from *jonc* YOUNG + *hēre* 'lord': cf. JUNKER]

your /jɔː, jʊə/ *poss.det.* **1** of or belonging to you (*your house; your own business*). **2** (**Your**) (in titles) that you are (*Your Majesty*) **3** *colloq.* usu. *derog.* much talked of; well known (*none so fallible as your self-styled expert*). [Old English *ēower*, genitive of *gē* YE[1]]

you're /jʊə, jə, jɔː/ *contr.* you are.

your humble servant *n. Brit. archaic* a formula preceding a signature or expressing ironical courtesy.

your obedient servant *n. Brit.* a formula preceding a signature, now used only in certain formal letters.

yours /jɔːz, jʊəz/ *poss.pron.* **1** the one or ones belonging to or associated with you (*it is yours; yours are over there*). **2** your letter (*yours of the 10th*). **3** introducing a formula ending a letter (*yours ever; yours sincerely; yours truly*). □ **of yours** of or belonging to you (*a friend of yours*). **up yours** see UP.

yourself /jɔːˈself, jʊə-, jə-/ *pron.* (*pl.* **yourselves** /-ˈselvz/) **1 a** *emphat. form* of YOU. **b** *refl. form* of YOU. **2** in your normal state of body or mind (*are quite yourself again*). □ **be yourself** act in your normal, unconstrained manner. **how's yourself?** *slang* how are you? (esp. after answering a similar enquiry).

youse /juːz/ *pron.* (also **yous**) *dial.* you (usu. more than one person). [YOU + -S[1]]

youth /juːθ/ *n.* (*pl.* **youths** /juːðz/) **1** the state of being young; the period between childhood and adult age. **2** the vigour or enthusiasm, inexperience, or other characteristic of this period. **3** an early stage of development etc. **4** a young person (esp. male). **5** (*pl.*) young people collectively (*the youth of the country*). [Old English *geoguth* from Germanic: related to YOUNG]

youth club *n.* (also **youth centre**) a place or organization provided for young people's leisure activities.

youth credit *n.* a voucher issued to sixteen- and seventeen-year-olds not in full-time education, which can be exchanged for part-time education or training leading to a recognized qualification.

youthful /'ju:θfʊl, -f(ə)l/ *adj.* **1** young, esp. in appearance or manner. **2** having the characteristics of youth (*youthful impatience*). **3** having the freshness or vigour of youth (*a youthful complexion*). □ **youthfully** *adv.* **youthfulness** *n.*

youth hostel *n.* a place where (esp. young) holidaymakers can put up cheaply for the night. □ **youth hosteller** *n.*

you've /ju:v, jʊv/ *contr.* you have.

yowl /jaʊl/ *n.* & *v.* ● *n.* a loud wailing cry of or as of a cat or dog in pain or distress. ● *v.intr.* utter a yowl. [imitative]

yo-yo /'jəʊjəʊ/ *n.* & *v.* ● *n.* (*pl.* **yo-yos**) *propr.* **1** a toy consisting of a pair of joined discs with a deep groove between them in which string is attached and wound, and which can be spun alternately downward and upward by its weight and momentum as the string unwinds and rewinds. **2** a thing that repeatedly falls and rises again. ● *v.intr.* (**yo-yoes, yo-yoed**) **1** play with a yo-yo. **2** move up and down; fluctuate. [20th c.: origin unknown]

yr. *abbr.* **1** year(s). **2** younger. **3** your.

yrs. *abbr.* **1** years. **2** yours.

YTS *abbr.* Youth Training Scheme.

ytterbium /ɪ'tə:bɪəm/ *n. Chem.* a silvery metallic element of the lanthanide series occurring naturally as various isotopes (symbol **Yb**). [modern Latin, from *Ytterby* in Sweden]

yttrium /'ɪtrɪəm/ *n. Chem.* a greyish metallic element resembling the lanthanides, occurring naturally in uranium ores and used in making superconductors (symbol **Y**). [formed as YTTERBIUM]

yuan /jʊ'ɑ:n/ *n.* (*pl.* same) the chief monetary unit of China. [Chinese, literally 'round': cf. YEN[1]]

yucca /'jʌkə/ *n.* any American white-flowered plant of the genus *Yucca* (lily family), with swordlike leaves. [Carib]

yuck /jʌk/ *int.* & *n.* (also **yuk**) *slang* ● *int.* an expression of strong distaste or disgust. ● *n.* something messy or repellent. [imitative]

yucky /'jʌki/ *adj.* (also **yukky**) (**-ier, -iest**) *slang* **1** messy, repellent. **2** sickly, sentimental.

Yugoslav /'ju:gə(ʊ)slɑ:v, ju:gəʊ'slɑ:v/ *n.* & *adj.* (also **Jugoslav**) ● *n.* **1** a native or national of the former Yugoslavia in SE Europe. **2** a person of Yugoslav descent. ● *adj.* of or relating to Yugoslavia or its people. □ **Yugoslavian** /-'slɑ:vɪən/ *adj.* & *n.* [Austrian German *Jugoslav*, from Serbo-Croat *jugo-* (from *jug* 'south') + SLAV]

yuk var. of YUCK.

yukky var. of YUCKY.

Yule /ju:l/ *n.* (in full **Yuletide** /'ju:ltʌɪd/) *archaic* the Christmas festival. [Old English *gēol(a)*: corresponding to Old Norse *jól*, originally applied to a heathen festival, later to Christmas]

yule log *n.* **1** a large log burnt in the hearth on Christmas Eve. **2** a log-shaped chocolate cake eaten at Christmas.

yummy /'jʌmi/ *adj.* (**yummier, yummiest**) *colloq.* tasty, delicious. [YUM-YUM + -Y[1]]

yum-yum /jʌm'jʌm/ *int.* expressing pleasure from eating or the prospect of eating. [a natural exclamation]

yup var. of YEP.

yuppie /'jʌpi/ *n.* (also **yuppy**) (*pl.* **-ies**) *colloq.*, usu. *derog.* a young middle-class professional person working in a city. □ **yuppiedom** *n.* [*y*oung *u*rban *p*rofessional]

yuppify /'jʌpɪfʌɪ/ *v.tr.* (**-ies, -ied**) (esp. as **yuppified** *adj.*) *colloq.* make typical of or suitable for yuppies. □ **yuppification** /-fɪ'keɪʃ(ə)n/ *n.*

yurt /jʊət, jə:t/ *n.* **1** a circular tent of felt, skins, etc., on a collapsible framework, used by nomads in Mongolia and Siberia. **2** a semi-subterranean hut, usu. of timber covered with earth or turf. [Russian *yurta* via French *yourte* or German *Jurte* from Turkish *jurt*]

Yuwaalaraay /jʊ'wɑ:lərʌɪ/ *n.* an Aboriginal language of New South Wales.

YWCA *abbr.* Young Women's Christian Association.

Zz

Z /zɛd/ *n.* (also **z**) (*pl.* **Zs** or **Z's**) **1** the twenty-sixth letter of the alphabet. **2** (usu. **z**) *Algebra* the third unknown quantity. **3** (usu. **z**) *Geom.* the third coordinate. **4** *Chem.* atomic number.

zabaglione /zɑːbɑːˈljəʊni/ *n.* an Italian sweet of whipped and heated egg yolks, sugar, and (esp. Marsala) wine. [Italian]

zaffre /ˈzafə/ *n.* (*US* **zaffer**) an impure cobalt oxide used as a blue pigment. [Italian *zaffera* or French *safre*]

zag /zag/ *n.* & *v.* ● *n.* a sharp change of direction in a zigzag course. ● *v.intr.* (**zagged**, **zagging**) perform a zag. [ZIGZAG]

zaire /zʌɪˈɪə/ *n.* the chief monetary unit of Zaire. [*Zaire*, local name for the Congo River in central Africa]

Zairean /zʌɪˈɪərɪən/ *n.* & *adj.* (also **Zairian**) ● *n.* a native or inhabitant of Zaire in central Africa. ● *adj.* of or relating to Zaire or its people.

zander /ˈzandə/ *n.* (*pl.* usu. same) a large pikeperch, *Stizostedion lucioperca*, native to central and N. Europe and introduced in W. Europe. [German]

ZANU /ˈzɑːnuː/ *abbr.* Zimbabwe African National Union.

zany /ˈzeɪni/ *adj.* & *n.* ● *adj.* (**zanier**, **zaniest**) comically idiotic; crazily ridiculous. ● *n.* **1** a buffoon or jester. **2** *hist.* an attendant clown awkwardly mimicking a chief clown in shows; a merry andrew. □ **zanily** *adv.* **zaniness** *n.* [French *zani* or Italian *zan(n)i*, Venetian form of *Gianni*, *Giovanni* 'John', stock name of the servants acting as clowns in the *commedia dell'arte*]

zap /zap/ *v.*, *n.*, & *int. slang* ● *v.* (**zapped**, **zapping**) **1** *tr.* **a** kill or destroy; deal a sudden blow to. **b** hit forcibly (*zapped the ball over the net*). **2 a** *intr.* & *tr.* move quickly and vigorously. **b** *intr.* use a remote control to move rapidly between television channels. **3** *tr.* overwhelm emotionally. **4** *tr. Computing* erase or change (an item in a program). **5** *intr.* (foll. by *through*) fast-wind a videotape to skip a section. ● *n.* **1** energy, vigour. **2** a strong emotional effect. ● *int.* expressing the sound or impact of a bullet, ray gun, etc., or any sudden event. [imitative]

zapateado /zaˌpatɪˈɑːdəʊ/ *n.* (*pl.* **-os**) **1** a flamenco dance with rhythmic stamping of the feet. **2** this technique or action. [Spanish from *zapato* 'shoe']

zapper /ˈzapə/ *n. slang* a remote control for a television, video, etc.

zappy /ˈzapi/ *adj.* (**zappier**, **zappiest**) *colloq.* **1** lively, energetic. **2** striking.

ZAPU /ˈzɑːpuː/ *abbr.* Zimbabwe African People's Union.

zarape var. of SERAPE.

Zarathustrian var. of ZOROASTRIAN.

zariba /zəˈriːbə/ *n.* (also **zareba**) **1** a hedged or palisaded enclosure for the protection of a camp or village in Sudan etc. **2** a restricting or confining influence. [Arabic *zarība* 'cattle-pen']

zarzuela /θɑːˈθweɪlə/ *n.* **1** a Spanish traditional form of musical comedy. **2** a Spanish dish of various kinds of seafood cooked in a rich sauce. [Spanish: apparently from a place name]

zax var. of SAX².

zeal /ziːl/ *n.* **1** earnestness or fervour in advancing a cause or rendering service. **2** hearty and persistent endeavour. [Middle English *zele* via ecclesiastical Latin *zelus* from Greek *zēlos*]

zealot /ˈzɛlət/ *n.* **1** an uncompromising or extreme partisan; a fanatic. **2** (**Zealot**) *hist.* a member of an ancient Jewish sect aiming at a world Jewish theocracy and resisting the Romans until AD 70. □ **zealotry** *n.* [ecclesiastical Latin *zelotes* from Greek *zēlōtēs* (as ZEAL)]

zealous /ˈzɛləs/ *adj.* full of zeal; enthusiastic. □ **zealously** *adv.* **zealousness** *n.*

zebec (also **zebeck**) var. of XEBEC.

zebra /ˈzɛbrə, ˈziːbrə/ *n.* (*pl.* same or **zebras**) **1** any of various African quadrupeds, esp. *Equus burchelli*, related to the ass and horse, with black and white stripes. **2** (*attrib.*) with alternate dark and pale stripes. □ **zebrine** /-brʌɪn/ *adj.* [Italian, Spanish, or Portuguese, perhaps ultimately from Latin *equiferus*, from *equus* 'horse' + *ferus* 'wild']

zebra crossing *n. Brit.* a striped street-crossing where pedestrians have precedence over vehicles.

zebra finch *n.* a small Australian waxbill, *Poephila guttata*, with black and white stripes on the face, popular as a cage bird.

zebu /ˈziːbuː/ *n.* a humped ox, *Bos indicus*, of India, E. Asia, and Africa. [French *zébu*, of unknown origin]

Zech. *abbr.* Zechariah (Old Testament).

zed /zɛd/ *n. Brit.* the letter Z. [French *zède* via Late Latin *zeta* from Greek ZETA]

zedoary /ˈzɛdəʊəri/ *n.* **1** an Indian plant, *Curcuma zedoaria*, allied to turmeric and with an aromatic rhizome. **2** a ginger-like substance made from this rhizome, used in medicine, perfumery, and dyeing. [Middle English via medieval Latin *zedoarium* from Persian *zidwār*]

zee /ziː/ *n. US* the letter Z. [17th c.: variant of ZED]

Zeeman effect /ˈziːmən/ *n. Physics* the splitting of the spectrum line into several components by a magnetic field. [named after P. *Zeeman*, Dutch physicist d. 1943]

zein /ˈziːɪn/ *n. Biochem.* the principal protein of maize. [modern Latin *Zea*, genus name of maize + -IN]

Zeitgeist /ˈtsʌɪtgʌɪst/ *n.* **1** the spirit of the times. **2** the trend of thought and feeling in a period. [German, from *Zeit* 'time' + *Geist* 'spirit']

Zen /zɛn/ *n.* a form of Mahayana Buddhism emphasizing the value of meditation and intuition. □ **Zenist** *n.* (also **Zennist**). [Japanese, = meditation]

zenana /zɪˈnɑːnə/ *n.* the part of a house for the seclusion of women of high-caste families in India and Iran. [Hindustani *zenāna* from Persian *zanāna*, from *zan* 'woman']

Zend /zɛnd/ *n.* an interpretation of the Avesta, each Zend being part of the Zend-Avesta. [Persian *zand* 'interpretation']

Zend-Avesta *n.* the Zoroastrian sacred writings of the Avesta (the text) and Zend (the commentary).

Zener cards /ˈziːnə/ *n.* a set of 25 cards each with one of five different symbols, used in ESP research. [named after K. E. *Zener*, American psychologist b. 1903]

Zener diode /ˈziːnə/ *n. Electronics* a form of diode in which a certain reverse voltage produces a sudden increase in reverse current. [named after C.M. *Zener*, US physicist d. 1993]

zenith /ˈzɛnɪθ/ *n.* **1** the part of the celestial sphere directly above an observer (opp. NADIR). **2** the highest point in one's fortunes; a time of great prosperity etc. □ **zenithal** *adj.* [Middle English from Old French *cenit* or medieval Latin *cenit*, ultimately from Arabic *samt* (*ar-ra's*) 'path (over the head)']

zenithal projection *n.* a projection of part of a globe on to a plane tangential to the centre of the part, showing the correct directions of all points from the centre.

zenith distance *n.* an arc intercepted between a celestial body and its zenith; the complement of a body's altitude.

zeolite /ˈzi:əlʌɪt/ *n.* each of a number of minerals consisting mainly of hydrous silicates of calcium, sodium, and aluminium, able to act as cation exchangers. □ **zeolitic** /-ˈlɪtɪk/ *adj.* [Swedish & German *zeolit*, from Greek *zeō* 'boil' + -LITE (from their characteristic swelling and fusing under the blowpipe)]

Zeph. *abbr.* Zephaniah (Old Testament).

zephyr /ˈzɛfə/ *n.* **1** *literary* a mild gentle wind or breeze. **2** a fine cotton fabric. **3** an athlete's thin gauzy jersey. [French *zéphyr* or Latin *zephyrus* from Greek *zephuros* '(god of the) west wind']

Zeppelin /ˈzɛp(ə)lɪn/ *n. hist.* a large German dirigible airship of the early 20th c., originally for military use. [named after Count F. von *Zeppelin*, German airman d. 1917, its first constructor]

zepto- /ˈzɛptəʊ/ *comb. form* denoting a factor of 10^{-21}. [adapted from SEPTI-, on the pattern of *peta-*, *exa-*, etc.]

zero /ˈzɪərəʊ/ *n.* & *v.* ● *n.* (*pl.* **-os**) **1 a** the figure 0; nought. **b** no quantity or number; nil. **2** a point on the scale of an instrument from which a positive or negative quantity is reckoned. **3** (*attrib.*) having a value of zero; no, not any (*zero population growth*). **4** (in full **zero hour**) **a** the hour at which a planned, esp. military, operation is timed to begin. **b** a crucial moment. **5** the lowest point; a nullity or nonentity. ● *v.tr.* (**-oes**, **-oed**) **1** adjust (an instrument etc.) to zero point. **2** set the sights of (a gun) for firing. □ **zero in on 1** take aim at. **2** focus one's attention on. [French *zéro* or Italian *zero*, via Old Spanish from Arabic *ṣifr* CIPHER]

zero option *n.* a disarmament proposal for the total removal of certain types of weapons on both sides.

zero-rate *v.tr.* (esp. as **zero-rated** *adj.*) *Brit.* rate as not liable to a levy of value added tax.

zero-sum *adj.* (of a game, political situation, etc.) in which whatever is gained by one side is lost by the other so that the net change is always zero.

zeroth /ˈzɪərəʊθ/ *adj.* immediately preceding what is regarded as 'first' in a series.

zest /zɛst/ *n.* **1** piquancy; a stimulating flavour or quality. **2 a** keen enjoyment or interest. **b** (often foll. by *for*) relish. **c** gusto (*entered into it with zest*). **3** fine shreds of the outer coloured part of the peel of citrus fruit used as flavouring. □ **zestful** *adj.* **zestfully** *adv.* **zestfulness** *n.* **zesty** *adj.* (**zestier**, **zestiest**). [French *zeste* 'orange or lemon peel', of unknown origin]

zester /ˈzɛstə/ *n.* a kitchen utensil for obtaining zest from citrus fruit by scraping or peeling.

zeta /ˈzi:tə/ *n.* the sixth letter of the Greek alphabet (Z, ζ). [Greek *zēta*]

zetetic /zɪˈtɛtɪk/ *adj.* proceeding by inquiry. [Greek *zētētikos* from *zēteō* 'seek']

zetta- /ˈzɛtə/ *comb. form* denoting a factor of 10^{21}. [formed like ZEPTO-, apparently adapted from Italian *sette* 'seven']

zeugma /ˈzju:gmə/ *n.* a figure of speech using a verb or adjective with two nouns, to one of which it is strictly applicable while the word appropriate to the other is not used (e.g. *with weeping eyes and* [sc. *grieving*] *hearts*) (cf. SYLLEPSIS). □ **zeugmatic** /-ˈmatɪk/ *adj.* [Latin from Greek *zeugma -atos*, from *zeugnumi* 'to yoke', *zugon* 'yoke']

zho var. of DZO.

zidovudine /zɪˈdɒvjʊdi:n, -ˈdəʊv-/ *n.* a derivative of thymine used to treat HIV and other viral infections. (Also called *azidothymidine*, *AZT*). [arbitrary alteration of chemical name]

ziff /zɪf/ *n. Austral. slang* a beard. [20th c.: origin unknown]

zig /zɪg/ *n.* & *v.* ● *n.* an abrupt angled movement, esp. in a zigzag course. ● *v.intr.* (**zigged**, **zigging**) perform a zig. [ZIGZAG]

ziggurat /ˈzɪgʊrat/ *n.* a rectangular stepped tower in ancient Mesopotamia, surmounted by a temple. [Assyrian *ziqquratu* 'pinnacle']

zigzag /ˈzɪgzag/ *n., adj., adv.,* & *v.* ● *n.* **1** a line or course having abrupt alternate right and left turns. **2** (often in *pl.*) each of these turns. ● *adj.* having the form of a zigzag; alternating right and left. ● *adv.* with a zigzag course. ● *v.intr.* (**zigzagged**, **zigzagging**) move in a zigzag course. □ **zigzaggedly** *adv.* [French from German *zickzack*]

zilch /zɪltʃ/ *n.* esp. *N. Amer. slang* nothing. [20th c.: origin uncertain]

zillah /ˈzɪlə/ *n.* an administrative district in India, containing several parganas. [Hindustani *ḍilah* 'division']

zillion /ˈzɪljən/ *n. colloq.* an indefinite large number. □ **zillionth** *adj.* & *n.* [Z (perhaps = unknown quantity) + MILLION]

Zimmer /ˈzɪmə/ *n.* (in full **Zimmer frame**) *propr.* a kind of walking frame. [name of the manufacturer]

zinc /zɪŋk/ *n.* & *v.* ● *n. Chem.* a white metallic element occurring naturally as zinc blende, and used as a component of brass and other alloys, in galvanizing sheet iron, and in electric batteries (symbol **Zn**). ● *v.tr.* (usu. as **zinced** /ˈzɪŋ(k)t/ *adj.*) coat (iron etc.) with zinc or a zinc compound to prevent rust. [German *Zink*, of unknown origin]

zinc blende see BLENDE.

zinco /ˈzɪŋkəʊ/ *n.* & *v.* ● *n.* (*pl.* **-os**) = ZINCOGRAPH. ● *v.tr.* & *intr.* (**-oes**, **-oed**) = ZINCOGRAPH. [abbreviation]

zincograph /ˈzɪŋkəgrɑ:f/ *n.* & *v.* ● *n.* **1** a zinc plate with a design etched in relief on it for printing from. **2** a print taken from this. ● *v.* **1** *tr.* & *intr.* etch on zinc. **2** *tr.* reproduce (a design) in this way. □ **zincography** /-ˈkɒgrəfi/ *n.*

zincotype /ˈzɪŋkətʌɪp/ *n.* = ZINCOGRAPH.

zinc oxide *n.* a powder used as a white pigment and in medicinal ointments. Chem. formula: ZnO.

zing /zɪŋ/ *n.* & *v. colloq.* ● *n.* vigour, energy. ● *v.intr.* move swiftly or with a shrill sound. □ **zingy** *adj.* (**zingier**, **zingiest**). [imitative]

Zingaro /ˈzɪŋgərəʊ, ts-/ *n.* (*pl.* **Zingari** /-ri:/) a gypsy. [Italian]

zinger /ˈzɪŋə/ *n.* esp. *US slang* **1** a wisecrack. **2** an unexpected turn of events. **3** an outstanding person or thing.

zinnia /ˈzɪnɪə/ *n.* a plant of the genus *Zinnia* (daisy family), with showy rayed flowers of deep red and other colours. [modern Latin, named after J. G. *Zinn*, German physician and botanist d. 1759]

Zion /ˈzʌɪən/ *n.* (also **Sion** /ˈsʌɪən/) **1** the hill of Jerusalem on which the city of David was built. **2 a** the Jewish people or religion. **b** the Christian Church. **3** (in Christian thought) the Kingdom of God in Heaven. [Old English via ecclesiastical Latin *Sion* from Hebrew *ṣīyôn*]

Zionism /ˈzʌɪənɪz(ə)m/ *n.* a movement for (originally) the re-establishment and (now) the development of a Jewish nation in what is now Israel. □ **Zionist** *n.* & *adj.*

zip /zɪp/ *n.* & *v.* ● *n.* **1** a light fast sound, as of a bullet passing through air. **2** energy, vigour. **3** esp. *Brit.* **a** (in full **zip fastener**) a fastening device of two flexible strips with interlocking projections closed or opened by pulling a slide along them. **b** (*attrib.*) having a zip fastener (*zip bag*). ● *v.* (**zipped**, **zipping**) **1** *tr.* & *intr.* (often foll. by *up*) fasten with a zip fastener. **2** *intr.* move with zip or at high speed. [imitative]

Zip code /zɪp/ *n.* (also **ZIP code**, **zip code**) *US* a system of postal codes consisting of five-digit or nine-digit numbers. [zone *i*mprovement *p*lan]

zipper /ˈzɪpə/ *n.* & *v.* esp. *US* ● *n.* a zip fastener. ● *v.tr.* (often foll. by *up*) fasten with a zipper. □ **zippered** *adj.*

zippy /ˈzɪpi/ *adj.* (**zippier**, **zippiest**) *colloq.* **1** bright, fresh, lively. **2** fast, speedy. □ **zippily** *adv.* **zippiness** *n.*

zip-up *attrib.adj.* able to be fastened with a zip fastener.

zircon /ˈzəːkən/ *n.* a zirconium silicate of which some translucent varieties are cut into gems (see HYACINTH 4, JARGON[2]). [German *Zirkon*: cf. JARGON[2]]

zirconia /zəːˈkəʊnɪə/ *n.* zirconium dioxide, used in ceramics, refractory coatings, etc., and in fused form as a synthetic substitute for diamonds in jewellery.

zirconium /zəːˈkəʊnɪəm/ *n. Chem.* a grey metallic element occurring naturally in zircon and used in various industrial applications (symbol **Zr**). [modern Latin, from ZIRCON + -IUM]

zit /zɪt/ *n.* esp. *US slang* a pimple. [20th c.: origin unknown]

zither /ˈzɪðə/ *n.* a musical instrument consisting of a flat wooden soundbox with numerous strings stretched across it, placed horizontally and played with the fingers and a plectrum. □ **zitherist** *n.* [German (as CITTERN)]

zizz /zɪz/ *n. & v. Brit. colloq.* ● *n.* **1** a whizzing or buzzing sound. **2** a short sleep. ● *v.intr.* **1** make a whizzing sound. **2** doze or sleep. [imitative]

zloty /ˈzlɒti/ *n.* (*pl.* same or **zlotys** or **zloties**) the chief monetary unit of Poland. [Polish, literally 'golden']

Zn *symb. Chem.* the element zinc.

zodiac /ˈzəʊdɪak/ *n.* **1 a** a belt of the heavens within about 8° of the ecliptic, including all apparent positions of the sun, moon, and most familiar planets, and divided into twelve parts (signs) named after constellations (Aries, Taurus, Gemini, Cancer, Leo, Virgo, Libra, Scorpio, Sagittarius, Capricorn, Aquarius, Pisces) and used in astrology. **b** a representation of the signs of the zodiac or of a similar astrological system. **2** a complete cycle, circuit, or compass. [Middle English via Old French *zodiaque* and Latin *zodiacus* from Greek *zōidiakos*, from *zōidion* 'sculptured animal-figure', diminutive of *zōion* 'animal']

■ **Usage** Owing to precession of the equinoxes, each sign of the zodiac now in fact coincides roughly with the constellation corresponding to the preceding sign.

zodiacal /zə(ʊ)ˈdʌɪək(ə)l/ *adj.* of or in the zodiac. [French (as ZODIAC)]

zodiacal light *n.* a luminous area of sky shaped like a tall triangle occasionally seen in the east before sunrise or in the west after sunset, esp. in the Tropics.

zoetrope /ˈzəʊɪtrəʊp/ *n. hist.* an optical toy in the form of a cylinder with a series of pictures on the inner surface which give an impression of continuous motion when viewed through slits with the cylinder rotating. [formed irregularly from Greek *zōē* 'life' + *-tropos* 'turning']

zoic /ˈzəʊɪk/ *adj.* **1** of or relating to animals. **2** *Geol.* (of rock etc.) containing fossils; with traces of animal or plant life. [probably back-formation from AZOIC]

Zöllner's lines /ˈtsəːlnəz/ *n.* parallel lines made to appear not parallel by short oblique intersecting lines. [named after J. K. F. *Zöllner*, German physicist d. 1882]

zollverein /ˈtsɒlfərʌɪn/ *n. hist.* a customs union, esp. of German states in the 19th c. [German]

zombie /ˈzɒmbi/ *n.* **1** *colloq.* a dull or apathetic person. **2** a corpse said to be revived by witchcraft. [West African *zumbi* 'fetish']

zonation /zəʊˈneɪʃ(ə)n/ *n.* distribution in zones, esp. (*Ecol.*) of plants into zones characterized by the dominant species.

zonda /ˈzɒndə/ *n.* a hot dusty north wind in Argentina. [Latin American Spanish]

zone /zəʊn/ *n. & v.* ● *n.* **1** an area having particular features, properties, purpose, or use (*danger zone*; *erogenous zone*; *smokeless zone*). **2** any well-defined region of more or less beltlike form. **3 a** an area between two exact or approximate concentric circles. **b** a part of the surface of a sphere enclosed between two parallel planes, or of a cone or cylinder etc. between such planes cutting it perpendicularly to the axis. **4** (in full **time zone**) a range of longitudes where a common standard time is used. **5** *Geol.* etc. a range between specified limits of depth, height, etc., esp. a section of strata distinguished by characteristic fossils. **6** *Geog.* any of five divisions of the earth bounded by circles parallel to the equator (see FRIGID, TEMPERATE, TORRID). **7** an encircling band or stripe distinguishable in colour, texture, or character from the rest of the object encircled. **8** *archaic* a belt or girdle worn round the body. ● *v.tr.* **1** encircle as or with a zone. **2** arrange or distribute by zones. **3** assign as or to a particular area. □ **zonal** *adj.* **zoning** *n.* (in sense 3 of *v.*). [French *zone* or Latin *zona* 'girdle' from Greek *zōnē*]

zonk /zɒŋk/ *v. & n. slang* ● *v.* **1** *tr.* hit or strike. **2** (often foll. by *out*) **a** *tr.* overcome with sleep; intoxicate. **b** *intr.* fall heavily asleep. ● *n.* (often as *int.*) the sound of a blow or heavy impact. [imitative]

zoo /zuː/ *n.* an establishment which maintains a collection of usu. wild animals in a park, gardens, etc., for display to the public, conservation, etc. [abbreviation of ZOOLOGICAL GARDEN]

zoo- /ˈzuːə(ʊ), ˈzəʊə(ʊ)/ *comb. form* of animals or animal life. [Greek *zōio-* from *zōion* 'animal']

zoogeography /ˌzuːə(ʊ)dʒɪˈɒgrəfi, ˌzəʊə(ʊ)-, zuːdʒɪˈɒgrəfi/ *n.* the branch of zoology dealing with the geographical distribution of animals. □ **zoogeographic** /-dʒiːəˈgrafɪk/ *adj.* **zoogeographical** /-dʒiːəˈgrafɪk(ə)l/ *adj.* **zoogeographically** /-dʒiːəˈgrafɪk(ə)li/ *adv.*

zoography /zuːˈɒgrəfi, zəʊ-/ *n.* descriptive zoology.

zooid /ˈzuːɔɪd, ˈzəʊ-, ˈzuːɪd/ *n.* **1** a more or less independent invertebrate organism arising by budding or fission. **2** a distinct member of an invertebrate colony. □ **zooidal** /zuːˈɔɪd(ə)l, zəʊ-, ˈzuːɪd(ə)l/ *adj.* [formed as ZOO- + -OID]

zookeeper /ˈzuːkiːpə/ *n.* **1** a person in charge of animals in a zoo. **2** a zoo owner or director.

zoolatry /zuːˈɒlətri, zəʊ-/ *n.* the worship of animals.

zoological /zuːəˈlɒdʒɪk(ə)l, zəʊə-/ *adj.* of or relating to zoology. □ **zoologically** *adv.*

zoological garden *n.* (also **zoological gardens** *n.pl.*) = ZOO.

zoology /zuːˈɒlədʒi, zəʊ-/ *n.* the scientific study of animals, esp. with reference to their structure, physiology, classification, and distribution. □ **zoologist** *n.* [modern Latin *zoologia* (as ZOO-, -LOGY)]

zoom /zuːm/ *v. & n.* ● *v.* **1** *intr.* move quickly, esp. with a buzzing sound. **2 a** *intr.* cause an aeroplane to mount at high speed and a steep angle. **b** *tr.* cause (an aeroplane) to do this. **3 a** *intr.* (of a camera) close up rapidly from a long shot to a close-up. **b** *tr.* cause (a lens or camera) to do this. **4** *intr.* (of prices) rise sharply. ● *n.* **1** an aeroplane's steep climb. **2** a zooming camera shot. [imitative]

zoomancy /ˈzuːəmansi, zəʊə-/ *n.* divination from the appearances or behaviour of animals.

zoom lens *n.* a lens allowing a camera to zoom by varying the focal length.

zoomorphic /zuːə(ʊ)ˈmɔːfɪk, zəʊə(ʊ)-, zuːˈmɔːfɪk/ *adj.* **1** dealing with or represented in animal forms. **2** having gods of animal form. □ **zoomorphism** *n.* [as ZOO-, Greek *morphē* 'form']

zoonosis /zuːəˈnəʊsɪs, zəʊə-/ *n.* (*pl.* **-noses** /-siːz/) any of various diseases which can be transmitted to humans from animals. [ZOO- + Greek *nosos* 'disease']

zoophyte /ˈzuːəfʌɪt, ˈzəʊə-, ˈzuːfʌɪt/ *n.* a plantlike animal, esp. a coral, sea anemone, or sponge. □ **zoophytic** /-ˈfɪtɪk/ *adj.* [Greek *zōophuton* (as ZOO-, -PHYTE)]

zooplankton /ˈzuːə(ʊ),plaŋ(k)t(ə)n, ˈzəʊə(ʊ)-, ˈzuːplaŋ(k)t(ə)n/ *n.* the component of plankton consisting of minute animals.

zoospore /ˈzuːəspɔː, ˈzəʊə-, ˈzuːspɔː/ *n.* a spore of fungi, algae, etc. capable of motion. □ **zoosporic** /-ˈspɔːrɪk/ *adj.*

zootomy /zuːˈɒtəmi, zəʊ-/ *n.* the dissection or anatomy of animals.

zoot suit /zu:t/ *n. colloq.* a man's suit with a long loose jacket and high-waisted tapering trousers. [rhyming on SUIT]

zori /'zɔ:ri, 'zɒri/ *n.* (*pl.* **zoris**) a Japanese flat sandal of straw or rubber etc., held on by a thong between the first and second toes. [Japanese]

zorilla /zɒ'rɪlə/ *n.* (also **zorille**) a flesh-eating African mammal, *Ictonyx striatus*, of the skunk and the weasel family. [French *zorille* from Spanish *zorrilla*, diminutive of *zorro* 'fox']

Zoroastrian /zɒrəʊ'astrɪən/ *adj.* & *n.* (also **Zarathustrian** /zarə'θʊstrɪən/) ● *adj.* of or relating to Zoroaster (or Zarathustra) or the monotheistic religion taught by him or his followers in the Zend-Avesta, which portrays a conflict between a spirit of light and good and a spirit of darkness and evil. ● *n.* a follower of Zoroaster. □ **Zoroastrianism** *n.* [Latin *Zoroastres* via Greek *Zōroastrēs* from Avestan *Zarathustra*, the name of the Persian founder of the religion in the 6th c. BC]

Zouave /zu:'ɑ:v, zwɑ:v/ *n.* **1** a member of a French light-infantry corps originally formed of Algerians and retaining their oriental uniform. **2** (in *pl.*) women's trousers with wide tops, tapering to a narrow ankle. [French from *Zouaoua*, the name of a tribe]

zouk /zu:k/ *n.* an exuberant style of popular music combining Caribbean and Western elements and having a fast heavy beat. [Guadeloupian Creole, = 'to party']

zounds /zaʊndz/ *int. archaic* expressing surprise or indignation. [(*God*)*'s wounds* (i.e. those of Christ on the Cross)]

ZPG *abbr.* zero population growth.

Zr *symb. Chem.* the element zirconium.

zucchetto /tsʊ'kɛtəʊ/ *n.* (*pl.* **-os**) a Roman Catholic ecclesiastic's skullcap, black for a priest, purple for a bishop, red for a cardinal, and white for a pope. [Italian *zucchetta*, diminutive of *zucca* 'gourd, head']

zucchini /zʊ'ki:ni/ *n.* (*pl.* same or **zucchinis**) esp. *N. Amer.* & *Austral.* a courgette. [Italian, pl. of *zucchino*, diminutive of *zucca* 'gourd']

zugzwang /'zʌgzwaŋ, 'zu:g-/ *n. Chess* an obligation to move in one's turn even when this must be disadvantageous. [German, from *Zug* 'move' + *Zwang* 'compulsion']

Zulu /'zu:lu:/ *n. & adj.* ● *n.* **1** a member of a black South African people originally inhabiting Zululand and Natal. **2** the language of this people. ● *adj.* of or relating to this people or language. [native name]

zwieback /'zwi:bak, 'tsvi:bak/ *n.* a kind of biscuit rusk or sweet cake toasted in slices. [German, = twice baked]

Zwinglian /'zwɪŋglɪən, 'tsvɪ-/ *n. & adj.* ● *n.* a follower of the Swiss religious reformer U. Zwingli (d. 1531). ● *adj.* of or relating to Zwingli or his reforms.

zwitterion /'zwɪtərʌɪən, 'tsvɪ-/ *n.* a molecule or ion having separate positively and negatively charged groups. [German from *Zwitter* 'a hybrid']

zydeco /'zʌɪdɪkəʊ/ *n.* a kind of Afro-American dance music originally from southern Louisiana. [Louisiana Creole, possibly from French *les haricots* in a dance-tune title]

zygo- /'zʌɪgəʊ, 'zɪgəʊ/ *comb. form* joining, pairing. [Greek *zugo-* from *zugon* 'yoke']

zygodactyl /zʌɪgə(ʊ)'daktɪl, zɪg-/ *adj. & n.* ● *adj.* (of a bird) having two toes pointing forward and two backward. ● *n.* such a bird. □ **zygodactylous** *adj.*

zygoma /zʌɪ'gəʊmə, zɪg-/ *n.* (*pl.* **zygomata** /-tə/) the bony arch of the cheek formed by connection of the zygomatic and temporal bones. [Greek *zugōma -atos* from *zugon* 'yoke']

zygomatic /zʌɪgə(ʊ)'matɪk, zɪg-/ *adj.* of or relating to the zygoma.

zygomatic arch *n.* = ZYGOMA.

zygomatic bone *n.* the bone that forms the prominent part of the cheek.

zygomorphic /zʌɪgə(ʊ)'mɔ:fɪk, zɪg-/ *adj.* (also **zygomorphous** /-'mɔ:fəs/) (of a flower) divisible into similar halves by only one plane of symmetry.

zygospore /'zʌɪgə(ʊ)spɔ:/ *n.* a thick-walled spore formed by certain fungi.

zygote /'zʌɪgəʊt/ *n. Biol.* a cell formed by the union of two gametes. □ **zygotic** /-'gɒtɪk/ *adj.* **zygotically** /-'gɒtɪk(ə)li/ *adv.* [Greek *zugōtos* 'yoked' from *zugoō* 'to yoke']

zygotene /'zʌɪgə(ʊ)ti:n/ *n. Biol.* a stage during the prophase of meiosis when homologous chromosomes begin to pair.

zymase /'zʌɪmeɪz/ *n.* the enzyme fraction in yeast which catalyses the alcoholic fermentation of glucose. [French, from Greek *zumē* 'leaven']

zymology /zʌɪ'mɒlədʒi/ *n.* the scientific study of fermentation. □ **zymological** /-mə'lɒdʒɪk(ə)l/ *adj.* **zymologist** *n.* [as ZYMASE + -LOGY]

zymosis /zʌɪ'məʊsɪs/ *n. archaic* fermentation. [modern Latin from Greek *zumōsis* (as ZYMASE)]

zymotic /zʌɪ'mɒtɪk/ *adj. archaic* of or relating to fermentation. [Greek *zumōtikos* (as ZYMOSIS)]

zymotic disease *n. archaic* a disease regarded as caused by the multiplication of germs introduced from outside.

zymurgy /'zʌɪmə:dʒi/ *n.* the branch of applied chemistry dealing with the use of fermentation in brewing etc. [Greek *zumē* 'leaven', on the pattern of *metallurgy*]

Appendices

Country	Person *(name in general use)*	Related Adjective *(in general use)*	Currency unit
Afghanistan	Afghan	Afghan	afghani = 100 puls
Albania	Albanian	Albanian	lek = 100 qindarka
Algeria	Algerian	Algerian	dinar = 100 centimes
America (*see* United States of America)			
Andorra	Andorran	Andorran	French franc, Spanish peseta
Angola	Angolan	Angolan	kwanza = 100 lwei
Antigua and Barbuda	Antiguan, Barbudan	Antiguan, Barbudan	dollar = 100 cents
Argentina	Argentinian	Argentine *or* Argentinian	peso = 10,000 australes
Armenia	Armenian	Armenian	dram = 100 luma
Australia	Australian	Australian	dollar = 100 cents
Austria	Austrian	Austrian	schilling = 100 groschen
Azerbaijan	Azerbaijani	Azerbaijani	manat = 100 gopik
Bahamas	Bahamian	Bahamian	dollar = 100 cents
Bahrain	Bahraini	Bahraini	dinar = 1,000 fils
Bangladesh	Bangladeshi	Bangladeshi	taka = 100 poisha
Barbados	Barbadian	Barbadian	dollar = 100 cents
Belarus	Belorussian *or* Byelorussian	Belorussian *or* Byelorussian	Belorussian rouble
Belgium	Belgian	Belgian	franc = 100 centimes
Belize	Belizian	Belizian	dollar = 100 cents
Benin	Beninese	Beninese	African franc
Bhutan	Bhutanese	Bhutanese	ngultrum = 100 chetrum, Indian rupee
Bolivia	Bolivian	Bolivian	boliviano = 100 centavos
Bosnia-Herzegovina	Bosnian	Bosnian	dinar = 100 paras
Botswana	Tswana	Botswanan	pula = 100 thebe
Brazil	Brazilian	Brazilian	real = 100 centavos
Brunei	Bruneian	Bruneian	dollar = 100 sen
Bulgaria	Bulgarian	Bulgarian	lev = 100 stotinki
Burkina	Burkinese	Burkinese	African franc
Burma (officially called Myanmar)	Burmese	Burmese	kyat = 100 pyas
Burundi	Burundian	Burundian	franc = 100 centimes
Cambodia	Cambodian	Cambodian	riel = 100 sen
Cameroon	Cameroonian	Cameroonian	African franc
Canada	Canadian	Canadian	dollar = 100 cents
Cape Verde Islands	Cape Verdean	Cape Verdean	escudo = 100 centavos
Central African Republic			African franc
Chad	Chadian	Chadian	African franc
Chile	Chilean	Chilean	peso = 100 centavos
China	Chinese	Chinese	yuan = 10 jiao or 100 fen
Colombia	Colombian	Colombian	peso = 100 centavos
Comoros	Comoran	Comoran	African franc
Congo	Congolese	Congolese	African franc
Costa Rica	Costa Rican	Costa Rican	colón = 100 centimos
Croatia	Croat *or* Croatian	Croat *or* Croatian	kuna = 100 lipa
Cuba	Cuban	Cuban	peso = 100 centavos
Cyprus	Cypriot	Cypriot	pound = 100 cents
Czech Republic	Czech	Czech	koruna = 100 haleru

Country	Person (*name in general use*)	Related Adjective (*in general use*)	Currency unit
Denmark	Dane	Danish	krone = 100 øre
Djibouti	Djiboutian	Djiboutian	franc = 100 centimes
Dominica	Dominican	Dominican	dollar = 100 cents
Dominican Republic	Dominican	Dominican	peso = 100 centavos
Ecuador	Ecuadorean	Ecuadorean	sucre = 100 centavos
Egypt	Egyptian	Egyptian	pound = 100 piastres or 1,000 milliemes
El Salvador	Salvadorean	Salvadorean	colón = 100 centavos
Equatorial Guinea	Equatorial Guinean	Equatorial Guinean	African franc
Eritrea	Eritrean	Eritrean	Ethiopian birr
Estonia	Estonian	Estonian	kroon = 100 sents
Ethiopia	Ethiopian	Ethiopian	birr = 100 cents
Fiji	Fijian	Fijian	dollar = 100 cents
Finland	Finn	Finnish	markka = 100 penniä
France	Frenchman, Frenchwoman	French	franc = 100 centimes
Gabon	Gabonese	Gabonese	African franc
Gambia, the	Gambian	Gambian	dalasi = 100 butut
Georgia	Georgian	Georgian	*not settled at present (1995)*
Germany	German	German	Deutschmark = 100 pfennig
Ghana	Ghanaian	Ghanaian	cedi = 100 pesewas
Greece	Greek	Greek	drachma = 100 leptae
Grenada	Grenadian	Grenadian	dollar = 100 cents
Guatemala	Guatemalan	Guatemalan	quetzal = 100 centavos
Guinea	Guinean	Guinean	franc = 100 centimes
Guinea-Bissau			peso = 100 centavos
Guyana	Guyanese	Guyanese	dollar = 100 cents
Haiti	Haitian	Haitian	gourde = 100 centimes
Holland (*see* Netherlands)			
Honduras	Honduran	Honduran	lempira = 100 centavos
Hungary	Hungarian	Hungarian	forint = 100 filler
Iceland	Icelander	Icelandic	krona = 100 aurar
India	Indian	Indian	rupee = 100 paisa
Indonesia	Indonesian	Indonesian	rupiah = 100 sen
Iran	Iranian	Iranian	rial = 100 dinars
Iraq	Iraqi	Iraqi	dinar = 1,000 fils
Ireland, Republic of	Irishman[1], Irishwoman[1]	Irish	pound (punt) = 100 pence
Israel	Israeli	Israeli	shekel = 100 agora
Italy	Italian	Italian	lira = 100 centesemi
Ivory Coast			African franc
Jamaica	Jamaican	Jamaican	dollar = 100 cents
Japan	Japanese	Japanese	yen = 100 sen
Jordan	Jordanian	Jordanian	dinar = 1,000 fils
Kazakhstan	Kazakh	Kazakh	tenge = 100 teins
Kenya	Kenyan	Kenyan	shilling = 100 cents

[1] May also denote a person from Northern Ireland.

Country	Person (name in general use)	Related Adjective (in general use)	Currency unit
Kirghizia (officially called Kyrgyzstan)	Kirghiz	Kirghiz	
Kiribati		Kiribati	dollar = 100 cents
Kuwait	Kuwaiti	Kuwaiti	dinar = 1,000 fils
Kyrgyzstan	Kyrgyz	Kyrgyz	som = 100 tiyin
Laos	Laotian	Laotian	kip = 100 ats
Latvia	Latvian	Latvian	lat = 100 santims
Lebanon	Lebanese	Lebanese	pound = 100 piastres
Lesotho	Mosotho, *pl.* Basotho		loti = 100 lisente
Liberia	Liberian	Liberian	dollar = 100 cents
Libya	Libyan	Libyan	dinar = 1,000 dirhams
Liechtenstein	Liechtensteiner		franc = 100 centimes
Lithuania	Lithuanian	Lithuanian	litas = 100 centas
Luxembourg	Luxembourger		franc = 100 centimes
Macedonia	Macedonian	Macedonian	denar
Madagascar	Malagasay *or* Madagascan	Malagasay *or* Madagascan	franc malgache = 100 centimes
Malawi	Malawian	Malawian	kwacha = 100 tambala
Malaysia	Malaysian	Malaysian	dollar (ringgit) = 100 sen
Maldives	Maldivian	Maldivian	rufiyaa = 100 laris
Mali	Malian	Malian	African franc
Malta	Maltese	Maltese	lira = 100 cents
Marshall Islands			US dollar
Mauritania	Mauritanian	Mauritanian	ouguiya = 5 khoums
Mauritius	Mauritian	Mauritian	rupee = 100 cents
Mexico	Mexican	Mexican	peso = 100 centavos
Micronesia, Federated States of	Micronesian	Micronesian	US dollar
Moldova	Moldovan	Moldovan	leu = 100 bani
Monaco	Monégasque *or* Monacan	Monégasque *or* Monacan	franc = 100 centimes
Mongolia	Mongolian	Mongolian	tugrik = 100 mongos
Montenegro	Montenegrin	Montenegrin	dinar = 100 paras
Morocco	Moroccan	Moroccan	dirham = 100 centimes
Mozambique	Mozambican	Mozambican	metical = 100 centavos
Myanmar (*see* Burma)			
Namibia	Namibian	Namibian	rand = 100 cents
Nauru	Nauruan	Nauruan	Australian dollar
Nepal	Nepalese	Nepalese	rupee = 100 paisa
Netherlands, the	Dutchman, Dutchwoman, *or* Netherlander	Dutch	guilder = 100 cents
New Zealand	New Zealander		dollar = 100 cents
Nicaragua	Nicaraguan	Nicaraguan	cordoba = 100 centavos
Niger	Nigerien	Nigerien	African franc
Nigeria	Nigerian	Nigerian	naira = 100 kobo
North Korea	North Korean	North Korean	won = 100 jun
Norway	Norwegian	Norwegian	krone = 100 øre
Oman	Omani	Omani	rial = 1,000 baiza
Pakistan	Pakistani	Pakistani	rupee = 100 paisa
Panama	Panamanian	Panamanian	balboa = 100 centésimos

Country	Person (*name in general use*)	Related Adjective (*in general use*)	Currency unit
Papua New Guinea	Papua New Guinean *or* Guinean	Papua New Guinean *or* Guinean	kina = 100 toea
Paraguay	Paraguayan	Paraguayan	guarani = 100 centimos
Peru	Peruvian	Peruvian	nuevo sol = 100 cents
Philippines	Filipino, Filipina	Filipino *or* Philippine	peso = 100 centavos
Poland	Pole	Polish	zloty = 100 groszy
Portugal	Portuguese	Portuguese	escudo = 100 centavos
Qatar	Qatari	Qatari	riyal = 100 dirhams
Romania	Romanian	Romanian	leu = 100 bani
Russia	Russian	Russian	rouble = 100 copecks
Rwanda	Rwandan	Rwandan	franc = 100 centimes
St Kitts and Nevis			dollar = 100 cents
St Lucia	St Lucian	St Lucian	dollar = 100 cents
St Vincent and the Grenadines	Vincentian, Grenadian	Vincentian, Grenadian	dollar = 100 cents
San Marino			Italian lira
Sào Tomé and Principe			dobra = 100 centavos
Saudi Arabia	Saudi Arabian *or* Saudi	Saudi Arabian *or* Saudi	riyal = 20 qursh or 100 halalas
Senegal	Senegalese	Senegalese	African franc
Serbia	Serb *or* Serbian	Serb *or* Serbian	dinar = 100 paras
Seychelles, the	Seychellois	Seychellois	rupee = 100 cents
Sierra Leone	Sierra Leonian	Sierra Leonian	leone = 100 cents
Singapore	Singaporean	Singaporean	dollar = 100 cents
Slovakia	Slovak	Slovak	koruna = 100 haleru
Slovenia	Slovene *or* Slovenian	Slovene *or* Slovenian	tolar = 100 stotins
Solomon Islands	Solomon Islander		dollar = 100 cents
Somalia	Somali	Somali	shilling = 100 cents
South Africa	South African	South African	rand = 100 cents
South Korea	South Korean	South Korean	won = 100 jeon
Spain	Spaniard	Spanish	peseta = 100 centimos
Sri Lanka	Sri Lankan	Sri Lankan	rupee = 100 cents
Sudan	Sudanese	Sudanese	dinar = 10 pounds
Suriname	Surinamer *or* Surinamese	Surinamese	guilder = 100 cents
Swaziland	Swazi	Swazi	lilangeni = 100 cents
Sweden	Swede	Swedish	krona = 100 öre
Switzerland	Swiss	Swiss	franc = 100 centimes
Syria	Syrian	Syrian	pound = 100 piastres
Taiwan	Taiwanese	Taiwanese	New Taiwan dollar = 100 cents
Tajikistan	Tajik *or* Tadjik	Tajik *or* Tadjik	Russian rouble
Tanzania	Tanzanian	Tanzanian	shilling = 100 cents
Thailand	Thai	Thai	baht = 100 satangs
Togo	Togolese	Togolese	African franc
Tonga	Tongan	Tongan	pa'anga = 100 seniti
Trinidad and Tobago	Trinidadian and Tobagan *or* Tobagonian	Trinidadian and Tobagan *or* Tobagonian	dollar = 100 cents
Tunisia	Tunisian	Tunisian	dinar = 1,000 milliemes
Turkey	Turk	Turkish	lira = 100 kurus
Turkmenistan	Turkmen *or* Turkoman	Turkmen *or* Turkoman	manat = 100 tenge
Tuvalu	Tuvaluan	Tuvaluan	dollar = 100 cents

Country	Person (name in general use)	Related Adjective (in general use)	Currency unit
Uganda	Ugandan	Ugandan	shilling = 100 cents
Ukraine	Ukrainian	Ukrainian	*not settled at present (1995)*
United Arab Emirates			dirham = 100 fils
United Kingdom	Briton	British	pound = 100 pence
United States of America	American	American	dollar = 100 cents
Uruguay	Uruguayan	Uruguayan	peso = 100 centésimos
Uzbekistan	Uzbek	Uzbek	som
Vanuatu			vatu = 100 centimes
Vatican City		Vatican	Italian lira
Venezuela	Venezuelan	Venezuelan	bolivar = 100 centimos
Vietnam	Vietnamese	Vietnamese	dong = 10 hao or 100 xu
Western Samoa	Western Samoan	Western Samoan	tala = 100 sene
Yemen	Yemeni	Yemeni	riyal = 100 fils
Yugoslavia	Yugoslav	Yugoslav	dinar = 100 paras
Zaire	Zaïrean	Zaïrean	zaire = 100 makuta
Zambia	Zambian	Zambian	kwacha = 100 ngwee
Zimbabwe	Zimbabwean	Zimbabwean	dollar = 100 cents

Principal dependencies

Dependency	Person (name in general use)	Related Adjective (in general use)	Currency unit
American Samoa (US)	American Samoan	American Samoan	US dollar
Anguilla (UK)	Anguillan	Anguillan	East Caribbean dollar
Aruba (Netherlands)			florin
Bermuda (UK)	Bermudan *or* Bermudian	Bermudan *or* Bermudian	dollar
Cayman Islands (UK)			dollar
Christmas Island (Australia)			Australian dollar
Cocos Islands (Australia)			Australian dollar
Cook Islands (NZ)			NZ dollar
Faeroe Islands (Denmark)	Faeroese *or* Faroese	Faeroese *or* Faroese	Danish krone
Falkland Islands (UK)	Falkland Islander		pound
French Guiana (France)			French franc
French Polynesia (France)			Pacific franc
Gibraltar (UK)	Gibraltarian	Gibraltarian	pound
Greenland (Denmark)	Greenlander		Danish krone
Guadeloupe (France)	Guadeloupian	Guadeloupian	French franc
Guam (US)	Guamanian	Guamanian	US dollar
Hong Kong (UK)			dollar
Macao (Portugal)	Macanese	Macanese	pataca = 100 avos
Martinique (France)			French franc
Mayotte (France)			French franc

Dependency	Person *(name in general use)*	Related Adjective *(in general use)*	Currency unit
Montserrat (UK)			East Caribbean dollar
Netherlands Antilles (Netherlands)			guilder
New Caledonia (France)	New Caledonian	New Caledonian	Pacific franc
Niue (NZ)			NZ dollar
Norfolk Island (Australia)			Australian dollar
Northern Marianas (US)			US dollar
Palau (US)			US dollar
Pitcairn Islands (UK)	Pitcairn Islander		NZ dollar
Puerto Rico (US)	Puerto Rican	Puerto Rican	US dollar
Réunion (France)			French franc
St Helena and dependencies (UK)			pound
St Pierre and Miquelon (France)			French franc
Svalbard (Norway)			Norwegian krone
Turks and Caicos Islands (UK)			US dollar
Virgin Islands (US)	Virgin Islander		US dollar
Virgin Islands, British (UK)	Virgin Islander		US dollar
Wallis and Futuna Islands (France)			French franc
Western Sahara (Morocco)			Moroccan dirham

(Official names with abbreviations in general use)

ENGLAND

Avon
Bedfordshire (Beds.)
Berkshire (Berks.)
Buckinghamshire (Bucks.)
Cambridgeshire (Cambs.)
Cheshire (Ches.)
Cleveland
Cornwall (Corn.)
Cumbria
Derbyshire (Derby.)
Devon
Dorset
Durham (Dur.)
East Sussex
Essex
Gloucestershire (Glos.)
Greater London
Greater Manchester
Hampshire (Hants.)
Hereford & Worcester
Hertfordshire (Herts.)
Humberside
Isle of Wight (IOW)
Kent
Lancashire (Lancs.)
Leicestershire (Leics.)
Lincolnshire (Lincs.)
Merseyside
Norfolk
Northamptonshire (Northants)
Northumberland (Northumb.)
North Yorkshire
Nottinghamshire (Notts.)
Oxfordshire (Oxon.)
Shropshire
Somerset (Som.)
South Yorkshire
Staffordshire (Staffs.)
Suffolk
Surrey
Tyne and Wear
Warwickshire (War.)
West Midlands
West Sussex
West Yorkshire
Wiltshire (Wilts.)

NORTHERN IRELAND

Antrim
Armagh
Down
Fermanagh (Ferm.)
Londonderry
Tyrone

Note
Officially, the counties of Northern Ireland have been abolished and replaced by 26 districts; they are listed here as they are still commonly referred to.

SCOTLAND

Regions
Borders
Central
Dumfries & Galloway
Fife
Grampian
Highland
Lothian
Strathclyde
Tayside

Islands Areas
Orkney
Shetland
Western Isles

WALES

Clwyd
Dyfed
Gwent
Gwynedd
Mid Glamorgan
Powys
South Glamorgan
West Glamorgan

(with official and official postal abbreviations)

Alabama (Ala., AL)
Alaska (Alas., AK)
Arizona (Ariz., AZ)
Arkansas (Ark., AR)
California (Calif., CA)
Colorado (Col., CO)
Connecticut (Conn., CT)
Delaware (Del., DE)
Florida (Fla., FL)
Georgia (Ga., GA)
Hawaii (HI)
Idaho (ID)
Illinois (Ill., IL)
Indiana (Ind., IN)
Iowa (Ia., IA)
Kansas (Kan., KS)
Kentucky (Ky., KY)
Louisiana (La., LA)
Maine (Me., ME)
Maryland (Md., MD)
Massachusetts (Mass., MA)
Michigan (Mich., MI)
Minnesota (Minn., MN)
Mississippi (Miss., MS)
Missouri (Mo., MO)
Montana (Mont., MT)
Nebraska (Nebr., NE)
Nevada (Nev., NV)
New Hampshire (NH)
New Jersey (NJ)
New Mexico (N. Mex., NM)
New York (NY)
North Carolina (NC)
North Dakota (N. Dak., ND)
Ohio (OH)
Oklahoma (Okla., OK)
Oregon (Oreg., OR)
Pennsylvania (Pa., PA)
Rhode Island (RI)
South Carolina (SC)
South Dakota (S. Dak., SD)
Tennessee (Tenn., TN)
Texas (Tex., TX)
Utah (UT)
Vermont (Vt., VT)
Virginia (Va., VA)
Washington (Wash., WA)
West Virginia (W. Va., WV)
Wisconsin (Wis., WI)
Wyoming (Wyo., WY)

Note

The abbreviations HI, ID, OH, and UT are official postal only, while NH, NJ, NY, NC, RI, and SC are both official and official postal. Where two abbreviations are given, the first is the official and the second the official postal.

THE COMMONWEALTH

The Commonwealth is a free association of the fifty sovereign independent states listed below, together with their associated states and dependencies.

Antigua and Barbuda
Australia
Bahamas
Bangladesh
Barbados
Belize
Botswana
Brunei
Canada
Cyprus
Dominica
Gambia, the
Ghana
Grenada
Guyana
India
Jamaica
Kenya
Kiribati
Lesotho
Malawi
Malaysia
Maldives
Malta
Mauritius
Nauru
New Zealand
Nigeria
Pakistan
Papua New Guinea
St Kitts and Nevis
St Lucia
St Vincent and the Grenadines
Seychelles, the
Sierra Leone
Singapore
Solomon Islands
South Africa
Sri Lanka
Swaziland
Tanzania
Tonga
Trinidad and Tobago
Tuvalu
Uganda
United Kingdom
Vanuatu
Western Samoa
Zambia
Zimbabwe

CANADA

Provinces and territories
(with official abbreviations)

Province
Alberta (Alta.)
British Columbia (BC)
Manitoba (Man.)
New Brunswick (NB)
Newfoundland and Labrador (Nfld.)
Nova Scotia (NS)
Ontario (Ont.)
Prince Edward Island (PEI)
Quebec (Que.)
Saskatchewan (Sask.)

Northwest Territories (NWT)
Yukon Territory (YT)

THE COMMONWEALTH OF AUSTRALIA

States and territories

State
New South Wales
Northern Territory
Queensland
South Australia
Tasmania
Victoria
Western Australia

Australian Capital Territory

INDIA

States and Union Territories

State
Andhra Pradesh
Arunachal Pradesh
Assam
Bihar
Goa
Gujarat
Haryana
Himachal Pradesh
Jammu and Kashmir
Karnataka
Kerala
Madhya Pradesh
Maharashtra
Manipur
Meghalaya
Mizoram
Nagaland
Orissa
Punjab
Rajasthan
Sikkim
Tamil Nadu
Tripura
Uttar Pradesh
West Bengal

Union Territory
Andaman and Nicobar Islands
Chandigarh
Dadra and Nagar Haveli
Daman and Diu
Delhi
Lakshadweep
Pondicherry

OLD TESTAMENT

Genesis (Gen.)
Exodus (Exod.)
Leviticus (Lev.)
Numbers (Num.)
Deuteronomy (Deut.)
Joshua (Josh.)
Judges (Judg.)
Ruth
First Book of Samuel (1 Sam.)
Second Book of Samuel (2 Sam.)
First Book of Kings (1 Kgs.)
Second Book of Kings (2 Kgs.)
First Book of Chronicles (1 Chr.)
Second Book of Chronicles (2 Chr.)
Ezra
Nehemiah (Neh.)
Esther
Job
Psalms (Ps.)
Proverbs (Prov.)
Ecclesiastes (Eccles.)
Song of Songs, Song of Solomon, Canticles (S. of S., Cant.)
Isaiah (Isa.)
Jeremiah (Jer.)
Lamentations (Lam.)
Ezekiel (Ezek.)
Daniel (Dan.)
Hosea (Hos.)
Joel
Amos
Obadiah (Obad.)
Jonah
Micah (Mic.)
Nahum (Nah.)
Habakkuk (Hab.)
Zephaniah (Zeph.)
Haggai (Hag.)
Zechariah (Zech.)
Malachi (Mal.)

APOCRYPHA

First Book of Esdras (1 Esd.)
Second Book of Esdras (2 Esd.)
Tobit
Judith
Rest of Esther (Rest of Esth.)
Wisdom of Solomon (Wisd.)
Ecclesiasticus, Wisdom of Jesus the Son of Sirach (Ecclus., Sir.)
Baruch
Song of the Three Children (S. of III Ch.)
Susanna (Sus.)
Bel and the Dragon (Bel & Dr.)
Prayer of Manasses (Pr. of Man.)
First Book of Maccabees (1 Macc.)
Second Book of Maccabees (2 Macc.)

NEW TESTAMENT

Gospel according to St Matthew (Matt.)
Gospel according to St Mark (Mark)
Gospel according to St Luke (Luke)
Gospel according to St John (John)
Acts of the Apostles (Acts)
Epistle to the Romans (Rom.)
First Epistle to the Corinthians (1 Cor.)
Second Epistle to the Corinthians (2 Cor.)
Epistle to the Galatians (Gal.)
Epistle to the Ephesians (Eph.)
Epistle to the Philippians (Phil.)
Epistle to the Colossians (Col.)
First Epistle to the Thessalonians (1 Thess.)
Second Epistle to the Thessalonians (2 Thess.)
First Epistle to Timothy (1 Tim.)
Second Epistle to Timothy (2 Tim.)
Epistle to Titus (Tit.)
Epistle to Philemon (Philem.)
Epistle to the Hebrews (Heb.)
Epistle of James (Jas.)
First Epistle of Peter (1 Pet.)
Second Epistle of Peter (2 Pet.)
First Epistle of John (1 John)
Second Epistle of John (2 John)
Third Epistle of John (3 John)
Epistle of Jude (Jude)
Revelation, Apocalypse (Rev., Apoc.)

THE GREEK ALPHABET

Name	*Capital*	*Lower-case*	*English transliteration*
alpha	Α	α	a
beta	Β	β	b
gamma	Γ	γ	g
delta	Δ	δ	d
epsilon	Ε	ϵ	e
zeta	Ζ	ζ	z
eta	Η	η	ē
theta	Θ	θ	th
iota	Ι	ι	i
kappa	Κ	κ	k
lambda	Λ	λ	l
mu	Μ	μ	m
nu	Ν	ν	n
xi	Ξ	ξ	x
omicron	Ο	ο	o
pi	Π	π	p
rho	Ρ	ρ	r
sigma	Σ	σ (at end of word ς)	s
tau	Τ	τ	t
upsilon	Υ	υ	u
phi	Φ	φ	ph
chi	Χ	χ	kh
psi	Ψ	ψ	ps
omega	Ω	ω	ō

‛ (rough breathing)
over vowel = prefixed h (ἁ = ha)
over rho = suffixed h (ῥ = rh)

’ (smooth breathing)
over vowel or rho: not transliterated

ͺ (iota subscript)
under vowel = suffixed i (ᾳ = ai)

THE RUSSIAN ALPHABET

Capital	*Lower-case*	*English transliteration*
А	а	a
Б	б	b
В	в	v
Г	г	g
Д	д	d
Е	е	e
Ё	ё	ë
Ж	ж	zh
З	з	z
И	и	i
Й	й	ĭ
К	к	k
Л	л	l
М	м	m
Н	н	n
О	о	o
П	п	p
Р	р	r
С	с	s
Т	т	t
У	у	u
Ф	ф	f
Х	х	kh
Ц	ц	ts
Ч	ч	ch
Ш	ш	sh
Щ	щ	shch
Ъ	ъ	˝ ('hard sign')
Ы	ы	y
Ь	ь	´ ('soft sign')
Э	э	é
Ю	ю	yu
Я	я	ya

Note

The Russian alphabet is the best-known form of the Cyrillic alphabet, which in slightly varying forms is used for many Slavonic and other languages of eastern Europe and northern Asia, including Belorussian, Ukrainian, Bulgarian, Macedonian, and Serbian.

The primary symbols are I 1, V 5, X 10, L 50, C 100, D 500, M 1,000. If a lesser symbol is placed to the right of a greater, its value is added to that of the greater; if it placed to the left, its value is subtracted. Small subtractions from large values are avoided (e.g. 99 is XCIX not IC). Roman numerals may appear in lower case (i, v, x, l, c, d, m), but the practice of printing e.g. viij for viii is now archaic. The sequences IIII, XXXX, and CCCC are occasionally used instead of the usual forms (for example, on old clock faces).

1	I	12	XII	40	XL	200	CC
2	II	13	XIII	49	XLIX	400	CD (or CCCC)
3	III	14	XIV	50	L	500	D
4	IV	15	XV	60	LX	900	CM (or DCCCC)
5	V	16	XVI	70	LXX	1000	M
6	VI	17	XVII	80	LXXX	1900	MCM (or MDCCCC)
7	VII	18	XVIII	90	XC	1995	MCMXCV
8	VIII	19	XIX	99	XCIX	1999	MCMXCIX
9	IX	20	XX	100	C	2000	MM
10	X	21	XXI	101	CI		
11	XI	30	XXX	144	CXLIV		

Conversion factors are not exact unless so marked.

1. BRITISH AND AMERICAN, WITH METRIC EQUIVALENTS

Linear Measure

1 inch	= 25.4 millimetres exactly
1 foot = 12 inches	= 0.3048 metre exactly
1 yard = 3 feet	= 0.9144 metre exactly
1 (statute) mile = 1,760 yards	= 1.609 kilometres
1 int. nautical mile = 1.150779 miles	= 1.852 kilometres exactly

Square Measure

1 square inch	= 6.45 sq. centimetres
1 square foot = 144 sq. in.	= 9.29 sq. decimetres
1 square yard = 9 sq. ft	= 0.836 sq. metre
1 acre = 4,840 sq. yd	= 0.405 hectare
1 square mile = 640 acres	= 259 hectares

Cubic Measure

1 cubic inch	= 16.4 cu. centimetres
1 cubic foot = 1,728 cu. in.	= 0.0283 cu. metre
1 cubic yard = 27 cu. ft	= 0.765 cu. metre

Capacity Measure

British

1 fluid oz = 1.8047 cu. in.	= 0.0284 litre
1 gill = 5 fluid oz	= 0.1421 litre
1 pint = 20 fluid oz = 34.68 cu. in.	= 0.568 litre
1 quart = 2 pints	= 1.136 litres
1 gallon = 4 quarts	= 4.546 litres
1 peck = 2 gallons	= 9.092 litres
1 bushel = 4 pecks	= 36.4 litres

American dry

1 pint = 33.60 cu. in.	= 0.550 litre
1 quart = 2 pints	= 1.101 litres
1 peck = 8 quarts	= 8.81 litres
1 bushel = 4 pecks	= 35.3 litres

American liquid

1 pint = 16 fluid oz = 28.88 cu. in.	= 0.473 litre
1 quart = 2 pints	= 0.946 litre
1 gallon = 4 quarts	= 3.785 litres

Avoirdupois Weight

1 grain	= 0.065 gram
1 dram	= 1.772 grams
1 ounce = 16 drams	= 28.35 grams
1 pound = 16 ounces = 7,000 grains	= 0.4536 kilogram (0.45359237 exactly)
1 stone = 14 pounds	= 6.35 kilograms
1 hundredweight = 112 pounds	= 50.80 kilograms
1 short ton = 2,000 pounds	= 0.907 tonne
1 (long) ton = 20 hundredweight	= 1.016 tonnes

2. METRIC, WITH BRITISH EQUIVALENTS

Linear Measure

1 millimetre	= 0.039 inch
1 centimetre = 10 mm	= 0.394 inch
1 decimetre = 10 cm	= 3.94 inches
1 metre = 100 cm	= 1.094 yards
1 kilometre = 1,000 m	= 0.6214 mile

Square Measure

1 square centimetre	= 0.155 sq. inch
1 square metre = 10,000 sq. cm	= 1.196 sq. yards
1 are = 100 square metres	= 119.6 sq. yards
1 hectare = 100 ares	= 2.471 acres
1 square kilometre = 100 hectares	= 0.386 sq. mile

Cubic Measure

1 cubic centimetre	= 0.061 cu. inch
1 cubic metre = 1,000,000 cu. cm	= 1.308 cu. yards

Capacity Measure

1 millilitre	= 0.002 pint (British)
1 centilitre = 10 ml	= 0.018 pint
1 decilitre = 10 cl	= 0.176 pint
1 litre = 1000 ml	= 1.76 pints
1 decalitre = 10 l	= 2.20 gallons
1 hectolitre = 100 l	= 2.75 bushels
1 kilolitre = 1,000 l	= 3.44 quarters

Weight

1 milligram	= 0.015 grain
1 centigram = 10 mg	= 0.154 grain
1 decigram = 100 mg	= 1.543 grains
1 gram = 1000 mg	= 15.43 grains
1 decagram = 10 g	= 5.64 drams
1 hectogram = 100 g	= 3.527 ounces
1 kilogram = 1,000 g	= 2.205 pounds
1 tonne (metric ton) = 1,000 kg	= 0.984 (long) ton

3. TEMPERATURE

Fahrenheit: water boils (under standard conditions) at 212° and freezes at 32°.

Celsius or Centigrade: water boils at 100° and freezes at 0°.

Kelvin: water boils at 373.15 K and freezes at 273.15 K.

To convert Centigrade into Fahrenheit: multiply by 9, divide by 5, and add 32.

To convert Fahrenheit into Centigrade: subtract 32, multiply by 5, and divide by 9.

To convert Centigrade into Kelvin: add 273.15.

°F	°C	°C	°F
−40	−40	−40	−40
−10	−23	−10	14
0	−18	0	32
10	−12	10	50
20	−7	20	68
30	−1	30	86
40	4	40	104
50	10	50	122
60	16	60	140
70	21	70	158
80	27	80	176
90	32	90	194
100	38	100	212
	(approx.)		*(exact)*

4. POWER NOTATION

This expresses concisely any power of 10 (any number that is formed by multiplying or dividing ten by itself), and is sometimes used in the dictionary.

10^2 (ten squared) = 10 × 10 = 100
10^3 (ten cubed) = 10 × 10 × 10 = 1,000
10^4 = 10 × 10 × 10 × 10 = 10,000
10^{10} = 10,000,000,000 (1 followed by ten noughts)
$10^{-2} = 1/10^2$ = 1/100 = 0.01
$10^{-10} = 1/10^{10}$ = 1/10,000,000,000
6.2×10^3 = 6,200
4.7×10^{-2} = 0.047

5. THE METRIC PREFIXES

	Abbreviations	*Factors*
deca-	da	10
hecto-	h	10^2
kilo-	k	10^3
mega-	M	10^6
giga-	G	10^9
tera-	T	10^{12}
peta-	P	10^{15}
exa-	E	10^{18}
deci-	d	10^{-1}
centi-	c	10^{-2}
milli-	m	10^{-3}
micro-	μ	10^{-6}
nano-	n	10^{-9}
pico-	p	10^{-12}
femto-	f	10^{-15}
atto-	a	10^{-18}

Pronunciations and derivations of these are given at their alphabetical places in the dictionary. They may be applied to any units of the metric system: hectogram (abbr. hg) = 100 grams; kilowatt (abbr. kW) = 1,000 watts; megahertz (MHz) = 1 million hertz; centimetre (cm) = 1⁄100 metre; microvolt (μV) = one millionth of a volt; picofarad (pF) = 10^{-12} farad, and are sometimes applied to other units (megabit, microinch).

6. SI UNITS

Base units

Physical quantity	*Name*	*Abbreviation or symbol*
length	metre	m
mass	kilogram	kg
time	second	s
electric current	ampere	A
temperature	kelvin	K
amount of substance	mole	mol
luminous intensity	candela	cd

Supplementary units

Physical quantity	*Name*	*Abbreviation or symbol*
plane angle	radian	rad
solid angle	steradian	sr

Derived units with special names

Physical quantity	*Name*	*Abbreviation or symbol*
frequency	hertz	Hz
energy	joule	J
force	newton	N
power	watt	W
pressure	pascal	Pa
electric charge	coulomb	C
electromotive force	volt	V
electric resistance	ohm	Ω
electric conductance	siemens	S
electric capacitance	farad	F
magnetic flux	weber	Wb
inductance	henry	H
magnetic flux density	tesla	T
luminous flux	lumen	lm
illumination	lux	lx

7. BINARY NOTATION

Only two digits (0 and 1) are used, and the position of each digit in a number indicates a power of two. For example, two is written as 10 (2 + 0), five as 101 ($2^2 + 0 + 1$), ten as 1010 ($2^3 + 0 + 2 + 0 = 8 + 2$), and one hundred as 1100100 ($2^6 + 2^5 + 0 + 0 + 2^2 + 0 + 0 = 64 + 32 + 4$).

1	1	1001	9	10001	17	11001	25
10	2	1010	10	10010	18	11010	26
11	3	1011	11	10011	19	11011	27
100	4	1100	12	10100	20	11100	28
101	5	1101	13	10101	21	11101	29
110	6	1110	14	10110	22	11110	30
111	7	1111	15	10111	23	11111	31
1000	8	10000	16	11000	24	100000	32

(in order of atomic number)

hydrogen	H	1
helium	He	2
lithium	Li	3
beryllium	Be	4
boron	B	5
carbon	C	6
nitrogen	N	7
oxygen	O	8
fluorine	F	9
neon	Ne	10
sodium	Na	11
magnesium	Mg	12
aluminium	Al	13
silicon	Si	14
phosphorus	P	15
sulphur	S	16
chlorine	Cl	17
argon	Ar	18
potassium	K	19
calcium	Ca	20
scandium	Sc	21
titanium	Ti	22
vanadium	V	23
chromium	Cr	24
manganese	Mn	25
iron	Fe	26
cobalt	Co	27
nickel	Ni	28
copper	Cu	29
zinc	Zn	30
gallium	Ga	31
germanium	Ge	32
arsenic	As	33
selenium	Se	34
bromine	Br	35
krypton	Kr	36
rubidium	Rb	37
strontium	Sr	38
yttrium	Y	39
zirconium	Zr	40
niobium	Nb	41
molybdenum	Mo	42
technetium	Tc	43
ruthenium	Ru	44
rhodium	Rh	45
palladium	Pd	46
silver	Ag	47
cadmium	Cd	48
indium	In	49
tin	Sn	50
antimony	Sb	51
tellurium	Te	52
iodine	I	53
xenon	Xe	54
caesium	Cs	55
barium	Ba	56
lanthanum	La	57
cerium	Ce	58
praseodymium	Pr	59
neodymium	Nd	60
promethium	Pm	61
samarium	Sm	62
europium	Eu	63
gadolinium	Gd	64
terbium	Tb	65
dysprosium	Dy	66
holmium	Ho	67
erbium	Er	68
thulium	Tm	69
ytterbium	Yb	70
lutetium	Lu	71
hafnium	Hf	72
tantalum	Ta	73
tungsten	W	74
rhenium	Re	75
osmium	Os	76
iridium	Ir	77
platinum	Pt	78
gold	Au	79
mercury	Hg	80
thallium	Tl	81
lead	Pb	82
bismuth	Bi	83
polonium	Po	84
astatine	At	85
radon	Rn	86
francium	Fr	87
radium	Ra	88
actinium	Ac	89
thorium	Th	90
protactinium	Pa	91
uranium	U	92
neptunium	Np	93
plutonium	Pu	94
americium	Am	95
curium	Cm	96
berkelium	Bk	97
californium	Cf	98
einsteinium	Es	99
fermium	Fm	100
mendelevium	Md	101
nobelium	No	102
lawrencium	Lr	103

All these elements and their symbols are listed alphabetically in the main part of the dictionary.

All the elements heavier than bismuth (no. 83) are radioactive; all those heavier than uranium (no. 92) have only been produced artificially. The names given above for elements up to 103 are in standard use. Names for elements 104 and above are not yet standardized and have been the subject of controversy:

	provisional name	*suggested names*
104	unnilquadium	kurchatovium, rutherfordium, (dubnium)
105	unnilpentium	hahnium, nielsbohrium, (joliotium)
106	unnilhexium	seaborgium, (rutherfordium)
107	unnilseptium	(bohrium)
108	unniloctium	(hahnium)
109	?	(meitnerium)

The IUPAC provisional names are based on the atomic number and are formed from the numerical roots *nil* = 0, *un* = 1, *bi* = 2, etc. The bracketed names are under consideration by IUPAC; the others have been in informal use.

Chemical Notation

The formula for a compound indicates the number of atoms of each element present in each molecule of the compound: e.g. a molecule of water (H_2O) contains two atoms of hydrogen and one of oxygen. The formula for an ionic compound indicates the proportions of the constituent elements, e.g. common salt (NaCl) contains equal proportions of sodium and chloride ions. Formulae for more complex compounds may indicate the manner of combination of the atoms in a molecule: e.g. ethanol (ethyl alcohol) may be represented as CH_3CH_2OH.

THE PERIODIC TABLE OF CHEMICAL ELEMENTS

IA	IIA	IIIB	IVB	VB	VIB	VIIB	–	VIII	–	IB	IIB	IIIA	IVA	VA	VIA	VIIA	0
(H)																	He
Li	Be											B	C	N	O	F	Ne
Na	Mg											Al	Si	P	S	Cl	Ar
K	Ca	Sc	Ti	V	Cr	Mn	Fe	Co	Ni	Cu	Zn	Ga	Ge	As	Se	Br	Kr
Rb	Sr	Y	Zr	Nb	Mo	Tc	Ru	Rh	Pd	Ag	Cd	In	Sn	Sb	Te	I	Xe
Cs	Ba	La*	Hf	Ta	W	Re	Os	Ir	Pt	Au	Hg	Tl	Pb	Bi	Po	At	Rn
Fr	Ra	Ac†	Unq	Unp	Unh	Uns	Uno										

* Lanthanides	La	Ce	Pr	Nd	Pm	Sm	Eu	Gd	Tb	Dy	Ho	Er	Tm	Yb	Lu
† Actinides	Ac	Th	Pa	U	Np	Pu	Am	Cm	Bk	Cf	Es	Fm	Md	No	Lr

Era	*Period*	*Epoch*	*Duration*
Cenozoic	Quaternary	Holocene	100,000 BP to present
		Pleistocene	2 mya–100,000 BP
	Tertiary	Pliocene	5–2 mya
		Miocene	24–5 mya
		Oligocene	38–24 mya
		Eocene	55–38 mya
		Palaeocene	65–55 mya
Mesozoic	Cretaceous		144–65 mya
	Jurassic		213–144 mya
	Triassic		248–213 mya
Palaeozoic	Permian		286–248 mya
	Carboniferous		360–286 mya
	Devonian		408–360 mya
	Silurian		438–408 mya
	Ordovician		505–438 mya
	Cambrian		590–505 mya
	Precambrian		4,600–590 mya

(*BP = before present; mya = millions of years ago*)

All figures are approximate and based on currently available evidence.

Beaufort number	*Equivalent speed at 10m above ground* Knots	Kilometres per hour	Description of conditions
0	<1	<1	Calm—smoke rises vertically; sea like a mirror.
1	1–3	1–6	Light air—smoke drifts; ripples on sea.
2	4–6	7–12	Light breeze—wind felt on face, leaves rustle, vanes moved by wind; small wavelets on sea.
3	7–10	13–19	Gentle breeze—leaves and small twigs in constant motion, light flags extend; wave crests begin to break.
4	11–16	20–30	Moderate breeze—dust and loose paper raised, small branches move; fairly frequent white horses at sea.
5	17–21	31–39	Fresh breeze—small trees sway, crested waves on inland waters; moderate waves at sea.
6	22–27	40–50	Strong breeze—large branches move, telegraph wires whistle; foaming crests and some spray at sea.
7	28–33	51–62	Near gale—whole trees in motion, inconvenience felt in walking against wind; foam at sea begins to be blown into streaks.
8	34–40	63–74	Gale—twigs broken off trees, walking upright difficult; wave crests break into spindrift.
9	41–47	75–87	Strong gale—chimney pots and slates removed; high waves at sea with rolling crests and dense spray.
10	48–55	88–102	Storm—trees uprooted, considerable structural damage; sea appears white with high overhanging waves and streaks of dense foam.
11	56–63	103–117	Violent storm—very rare on land, causing widespread damage; sea covered in foam patches, with waves high enough to hide medium-sized vessels and with crests blown into froth, visibility affected.
12	⩾64	⩾118	Hurricane—sea completely white, with driving spray, the air filled with foam and spray, visibility seriously impaired.

The use of the terms 'gale' and 'storm' is not completely standardized.

Kingdom
  Subkingdom

Phylum (*Zool.*) or **Division** (*Bot.*)
  Subphylum (*Zool.*) or Subdivision (*Bot.*)
  Superclass

Class
  Subclass
  Infraclass

Order
  Suborder
  Superfamily

Family
  Subfamily
  Tribe

Genus
  Species
  Subspecies

All species fall into categories of the ranks indicated by bold type. The other ranks may be omitted in smaller or less complex groups, or additional ranks may be inserted (e.g. superorder, infraorder, etc.). Names of groups ranked above genus are not printed in italics.

The name of a species consists of a binomial printed in italics, the genus name with a capital letter followed by the specific name or epithet. Additional names or symbols may indicate e.g. subspecies (*Corvus corone cornix*, hooded crow), hybrids (*Platanus* x *hispanica*, London plane), or varieties (*Capsicum annuum* var. *longum*, chilli pepper). Cultivated plants may bear only their genus and cultivar names (*Rosa* 'Queen Elizabeth').

Classification frequently changes to reflect current scientific understanding of relationships between species, and many species and groups have more than one name in recent use.

Examples:

human: kingdom Animalia, phylum Chordata, subphylum Vertebrata, class Mammalia, subclass Theria, infraclass Eutheria, order Primates, suborder Anthropoidea, family Hominidae, genus *Homo*, species *Homo sapiens*

seven-spot ladybird: kingdom Animalia, phylum Arthropoda, subphylum Uniramia, class Insecta, subclass Pterygota, order Coleoptera, suborder Polyphaga, superfamily Cucujoidea, family Coccinellidae, genus *Coccinella*, species *Coccinella septempunctata*

apple: kingdom Plantae, subkingdom Tracheophyta, division Spermatophyta, subdivision Angiospermae, class Dicotyledonae, family Rosaceae, subfamily Maloideae, genus *Malus*, species *Malus domestica*

field mushroom: kingdom Fungi, division Eumycota, subdivision Basidiomycotina, class Hymenomycetes, order Agaricales, family Agaricaceae, tribe Agariceae, genus *Agaricus*, species *Agaricus campestris*

A. PUNCTUATION MARKS

Punctuation is a complicated subject, and only the main principles can be discussed here. The explanations are based on practice in British English; usage in American English differs in some instances. The main headings are as follows:

1. General remarks
2. Capital letter
3. Full stop
4. Semicolon
5. Comma
6. Colon
7. Question mark
8. Exclamation mark
9. Apostrophe
10. Quotation marks
11. Brackets
12. Dash
13. Hyphen

1. General remarks

The purpose of punctuation is to mark out strings of words into manageable groups and help clarify their meaning (or in some cases to prevent a wrong meaning being deduced). The marks most commonly used to divide a piece of prose or other writing are the full stop, the semicolon, and the comma, with the strength of the dividing or separating role diminishing from the full stop to the comma. The full stop therefore marks the main division into sentences; the semicolon joins sentences (as in this sentence); and the comma (which is the most flexible in use and causes most problems) separates smaller elements with the least loss of continuity. Brackets and dashes also serve as separators—often more strikingly than commas, as in this sentence.

2. Capital letter C

2.1.1 This is used for the first letter of the word beginning a sentence in most cases:

He decided not to come. Later he changed his mind.

2.1.2 A sentence or clause contained in a subordinate or parenthetic role within a larger one does not normally begin with a capital letter:

I have written several letters (there are many to be written) and hope to finish them tomorrow.

2.1.3 In the following, however, the sentence is a separate one and therefore does begin with a capital letter:

There is more than one possibility. (You have said this often before.) So we should think carefully before acting.

2.1.4 A capital letter also begins sentences that form quoted speech:

The assistant turned and replied, 'There are no more left.'

2.2 The use of capital letters for proper names, titles, etc. is discussed in section C of this appendix (p. 1660).

3. Full stop ▪

3.1 This is used to mark the end of a sentence when it is a statement (and not a question or exclamation). In prose, sentences marked by full stops normally represent a discrete or distinct statement; more closely connected or complementary statements are joined by a semicolon (as here).

3.2.1 Full stops are used to mark any abbreviations (Weds., Gen., p.m.). They are often omitted in abbreviations that are familiar or very common (*Dr, Mr, Mrs,* etc.), in abbreviations that consist entirely of capital letters (*BBC, GMT,* etc.), and in acronyms that are pronounced as a word rather than a sequence of letters (*Intelsat, Ernie,* etc.).

3.2.2 If an abbreviation with a full stop comes at the end of a sentence, another full stop is not added when the full stop of the abbreviation is the last character:

They have a collection of many animals, including dogs, cats, tortoises, snakes, etc.

but

They have a collection of many animals (dogs, cats, tortoises, snakes, etc.).

3.3 A sequence of three full stops is used to mark an ellipsis or omission in a sequence of words, especially when forming an incomplete quotation. When the omission occurs at the end of a sentence, a fourth point is added as the full stop of the whole sentence:

He left the room, banged the door, . . . and went out.

The report said: 'There are many issues to be considered, of which the chief are money, time, and personnel. . . . Let us consider personnel first.'

3.4 A full stop is used as a decimal point (*10.5%; £1.65*), and to divide hours and minutes in giving time (*6.15 p.m.*), although a colon is usual in American use (*6:15 p.m.*).

4. Semicolon ;

4.1.1 The main role of the semicolon is to unite sentences that are closely associated or that complement or parallel each other in some way, as in the following:

In the north of the city there is a large industrial area with little private housing; further east is the university.

To err is human; to forgive, divine.

4.1.2 It is often used as a stronger division in a sentence that already includes divisions by means of commas:

He came out of the house, which lay back from the road, and saw her at the end of the path; but instead of continuing towards her, he hid until she had gone.

4.2 It is used in a similar way in lists of names or other items, to indicate a stronger division:

I should like to thank the managing director, Stephen Jones; my secretary, Mary Cartwright; and my assistant, Kenneth Sloane.

5. Comma ,

5.1 Use of the comma is more difficult to describe than other punctuation marks, and there is much variation in practice. Essentially, its role is to give detail to the structure of sentences, especially longer ones, and make their meaning clear. Too many commas can be distracting; too few can make a piece of writing difficult to read or, worse, difficult to understand.

5.2.1 The comma is widely used to separate the main clauses of a compound sentence when they are not sufficiently close in meaning or content to form a continuous unpunctuated sentence, and are not distinct enough to warrant a semicolon. A conjunction such as *and, but, yet,* etc., is normally used:

The road runs through a beautiful wooded valley, and the railway line follows it closely.

5.2.2 It is considered incorrect to join the clauses of a compound sentence without a conjunction. In the following sentence, the comma should either be replaced by a semicolon, or be retained and followed by *and*:

I like swimming very much, I go to the pool every week.

5.2.3 It is also considered incorrect to separate a subject from its verb with a comma:

Those with the smallest incomes and no other means, should get most support.

5.3.1 Commas are usually inserted between adjectives coming before a noun:

An enterprising, ambitious person.

A cold, damp, badly heated room.

5.3.2 But the comma is omitted when the last adjective has a closer relation to the noun than the others:

A distinguished foreign politician.

A little old lady.

5.4 An important role of the comma is to prevent ambiguity or (momentary) misunderstanding, especially after a verb used intransitively where it might otherwise be taken to be transitive:

With the police pursuing, the people shouted loudly.

Other examples follow:

He did not want to leave, from a feeling of loyalty.

In the valley below, the houses appeared very small.

However, much as I should like to I cannot agree. (compare *However much I should like to I cannot agree.)*

5.5.1 Commas are used in pairs to separate elements in a sentence that are not part of the main statement:

I should like you all, ladies and gentlemen, to raise your glasses.

There is no sense, as far as I can see, in this suggestion.

It appears, however, that we were wrong.

5.5.2 It is also used to separate a relative clause from its antecedent when the clause is not serving an identifying function:

The book, which was on the table, was a present.

In the above sentence, the information in the *which* clause is incidental to the main statement; without the comma, it would form an essential part of it in identifying which book is being referred to (and could be replaced by *that*):

The book which/that was on the table was a present.

5.6.1 Commas are used to separate items in a list or sequence. Usage varies as to the inclusion of a comma before *and* in the last item; the practice in this dictionary is to include it:

The following will report at 9.30 sharp: Jones, Smith, Thompson, and Williams.

5.6.2 A final comma before *and*, when used regularly and consistently, has the advantage of clarifying the grouping at a composite name occurring at the end of a list:

We shall go to Smiths, Boots, Woolworths, and Marks and Spencer.

5.7 A comma is used in numbers of four or more figures, to separate each group of three consecutive figures starting from the right (e.g. *10,135,793*).

6. Colon

6.1 The main role of the colon is to separate main clauses when there is a step forward from the first to the second, especially from introduction to main point, from general statement to example, from cause to effect, and from premiss to conclusion:

There is something I want to say: I should like you all to know how grateful I am to you.

It was not easy: to begin with I had to find the right house.

The weather was bad: so we decided to stay at home. (In this example, a comma could be used, but the emphasis on cause and effect would be much reduced.)

6.2 It also introduces a list of items. In this use a dash should not be added:

The following will be needed: a pen, pencil, rubber, piece of paper, and ruler.

6.3 It is used to introduce, more formally and emphatically than a comma would, speech or quoted material:

I told them last week: 'Do not in any circumstances open this door.'

7. Question mark

7.1.1 This is used in place of the full stop to show that the preceding sentence is a question:

Do you want another piece of cake?

He really is her husband?

7.1.2 It is not used when the question is implied by indirect speech:

I asked you whether you wanted another piece of cake.

7.2 It is used (often in brackets) to express doubt or uncertainty about a word or phrase immediately following or preceding it:

Julius Caesar, born (?) 100 BC.

They were then seen boarding a bus (to London?).

8. Exclamation mark

This is used after an exclamatory word, phrase, or sentence expressing any of the following:

8.1 Absurdity:

What an idea!

8.2 Command or warning:

Go to your room!

Be careful!

8.3 Contempt or disgust:

They are revolting!

8.4 Emotion or pain:

I hate you!

That really hurts!
Ouch!

8.5 Enthusiasm:

I'd love to come!

8.6 Wish or regret:

Let me come!

If only I could swim!

8.7 Wonder, admiration, or surprise:

What a good idea!

Aren't they beautiful!

9. Apostrophe

9.1.1 The main use is to indicate the possessive case, as in *John's book, the girls' mother*, etc. It comes before the *s* in singular and plural nouns not ending in *s*, as in *the boy's games* and *the women's games*. It comes after the *s* in plural nouns ending is *s*, as in *the boys' games*.

9.1.2 In singular nouns ending in *s* practice differs between (for example) *Charles'* and *Charles's*; in some cases the shorter form is preferable for reasons of sound, as in *Xerxes' fleet*.

9.1.3 It is also used to indicate a place or business, e.g. *the butcher's*. In this use it is often omitted in some names, e.g. *Smiths, Lloyds Bank*.

9.2 It is used to indicate a contraction, e.g. *he's, wouldn't, bo's'un, o'clock*.

9.3 It is sometimes used to form a plural of individual letters or numbers, although this use is diminishing. It is helpful in *cross your t's* but unnecessary in *MPs* and *1940s*.

9.4 For its use as a quotation mark, see section 10.

10. Quotation marks

10.1 The main use is to indicate direct speech and quotations. A single turned comma (') is normally used at the beginning, and a single apostrophe (') at the end of the quoted matter:

She said, 'I have something to ask you.'

10.2 The closing quotation mark should come after any punctuation mark which is part of the quoted matter, but before any mark which is not:

They shouted, 'Watch out!'.

They were described as 'an unruly bunch'.

Did I hear you say 'go away!'?

10.3 Punctuation dividing a sentence of quoted speech is put inside the quotation marks:

'Go away,' he said, 'and don't ever come back.'

10.4 Quotation marks are also used of cited words and phrases:

What does 'integrated circuit' mean?

10.5 A quotation within a quotation is put in double quotation marks:

'Have you any idea,' he said, 'what "integrated circuit" means?'

Many publications use single within double quotations:

"Have you any idea," he said, "what 'integrated circuit' means?"

11. Brackets ([ ])

11.1 The types of brackets used in normal punctuation are round brackets ( ) and square brackets [ ].

11.2 The main use of round brackets is to enclose explanations and extra information or comment:

He is (as he always was) a rebel.

Zimbabwe (formerly Rhodesia).

They talked about Machtpolitik *(power politics).*

11.3 They are used to give references and citations:

Thomas Carlyle (1795–1881).

A discussion of integrated circuits (see p. 38).

11.4 They are used to enclose reference letters or figures, e.g. (1), (*a*).

11.5 They are used to enclose optional words:

There are many (apparent) difficulties.
(In this example, the difficulties may or may not be only apparent.)

11.6.1 Square brackets are used less often. The main use is to enclose extra information attributable to someone (normally an editor) other than the writer of the surrounding text:

The man walked in, and his sister [Sarah] greeted him.

11.6.2 They are used in some contexts to convey special kinds of information, especially when round brackets are also used for other purposes: for example, in this dictionary they are used to give the etymologies at the end of entries.

12. Dash —

12.1 A single dash is used to indicate a pause, whether a hesitation in speech or to introduce an explanation or expansion of what comes before it:

'I think you should have—told me,' he replied.

We then saw the reptiles—snakes, crocodiles, that sort of thing.

12.2 A pair of dashes is used to indicate asides and parentheses, like the use of commas as explained at 5.5.1 above, but forming a more distinct break:

People in the north are more friendly—and helpful—than those in the south.

There is nothing to be gained—unless you want a more active social life—in moving to the city.

12.3 It is sometimes used to indicate an omitted word, for example a coarse word in reported speech:

'— you all,' he said.

13. Hyphen -

13.1 The hyphen has two main functions: to link words or elements of words into longer words and compounds, and to mark the division of a word at the end of a line in print or writing.

13.2.1 The use of the hyphen to connect words to form compound words is diminishing in English, especially when the elements are of one syllable as in *birdsong, eardrum,* and *playgroup*, and also in some longer formations such as *figurehead* and *nationwide*. The hyphen is used more often in routine and occasional couplings, especially when reference to the sense of the separate elements is considered important or unavoidable, as in *ankle-bone*. It is often retained to avoid awkward collisions of letters, as in *fast-talk*.

13.2.2 The hyphen serves to connect words that have a syntactic link, as in *hard-covered books* and *French-speaking people*, where the reference is to books with hard covers and people who speak French, rather than hard books with covers and French people who can speak (which would be the sense conveyed if the hyphens were omitted). It is also used to avoid more extreme kinds of ambiguity, as in *twenty-odd people*.

13.2.3 A particularly important use of the hyphen is to link compounds and phrases used attributively, as in a *well-known man* (but *the man is well known*), and *Christmas-tree lights* (but *the lights on the Christmas tree*).

13.2.4 It is also used to connect elements to form words in cases such as *re-enact* (where the collision of two *es* would be awkward), *re-form* (= to form again, to distinguish it from *reform*), and some other prefixed words such as those in *anti-*, *non-*, *over-*, and *post-*. Usage varies in this regard, and much depends on how well established and clearly recognizable the resulting formation is. When the second element is a name, a hyphen is usual (as in *anti-Darwinian*).

13.2.5 It is used to indicate a common second element in all but the last of a list, e.g. *two-*, *three-*, or *fourfold*.

13.3 The hyphen used to divide a word at the end of a line is a different matter, because it is not a permanent feature of the spelling. It is more common in print, where the text has to be accurately spaced and the margin justified; in handwritten and typed or word-processed material it can be avoided altogether. In print, words need to be divided carefully and consistently, taking account of the appearance and structure of the word. Detailed guidance on word division may be found in the *Oxford Spelling Dictionary* (2nd edition, 1995).

B. SPELLING RULES

1. General Remarks

British spelling was largely standardized by the middle of the 18th century, and American variants established by the early 19th, but many spelling conventions were fixed by printers as early as 1500, and since various changes in pronunciation have occurred in the ensuing centuries, present-day pronunciation and spelling are often at variance. Also, the 'neutral' vowel sound of unstressed syllables gives no guidance as to spelling, which is usually determined by the origin of the word, and care must be taken with words containing unstressed syllables such as *de-*, *di-*, *en-*, *in-*, *-par-*, *-per-*. These notes cover a few of the more common difficulties: for other individual points of uncertainty, the main part of the dictionary should be consulted, e.g. for pairs of words distinguished by meaning, such as *affect/effect*, *amend/emend*, *complement/compliment*, *enquire/inquire*, *its/it's*, *loath/loathe*, *stationary/stationery*. The following words may be difficult to find if the spelling is not known: *diphtheria*, *dissect*, *eczema*, *fuchsia*, *guerrilla*, *minuscule*, *necessary*, *ophthalmic*, *pejorative*, *semantics*. Note that silent letters occur especially in the combinations *gn-*, *kn-*, *mn-*, *pn-*, *ps-*, *pt-*, *rh-*, and that words ending in vowels other than *e* often have irregular inflections. (For a discussion of hyphenation see the preceding section.)

2. *i* before *e*

For words pronounced with an 'ee' (/iː/) sound, the traditional rule '*i* before *e* except after *c*' is fairly reliable. The exceptions are (*a*) *seize* (and *seise*), (*b*) *either* and *neither* (if you pronounce them that way; also *heinous*, *inveigle*), (*c*) Latin words such as *prima facie*, *species*, and *superficies*, and (*d*) words in which a stem ending in *-e-* is followed by a suffix beginning with *-i-*, e.g. *caffeine*, *casein*, *codeine*, *plebeian*, *protein*. Note that the syllable *-feit* is so spelt, e.g. in *counterfeit*, *forfeit*, *surfeit*, and that *mischief* is spelt like *chief*.

Words pronounced with an 'ay' (/eɪ/) or long 'i' (/ʌɪ/) sound generally have *-ei-*: e.g. *beige*, *heinous*, *reign*, *veil*, *eiderdown*, *height*, *kaleidoscope*. Words with other sounds follow no rules and must simply become familiar to the eye, e.g. *foreign* (related to *reign*), *friend*, *heifer*, *leisure*, *Madeira*, *sieve*, *sovereign* (like *foreign*), *their*, *view*, *weir*, *weird*.

3. Doubling consonants

When a suffix beginning with a vowel (such as *-able*, *-ed*, *-er*, *-ing*, or *-ish*) is added to a word ending in a consonant, the consonant is usually doubled if it is a single consonant preceded by a single vowel, and comes at the end of a stressed syllable. So *controllable*, *dropped*, *permitted*, *bigger*, *abetter*, *trekking*, *beginning*, *transferring*, *reddish*, *forgotten*, but *sweated*, *sweeter*, *appealing*, *greenish* (more than one vowel), *planting* (more than one consonant), *balloted*, *happened*, *preferable*, *profiting*, *rocketing* (not ending a stressed syllable). A secondary stress (not generally marked in this dictionary) is often sufficient to elicit a doubled consonant, e.g. *caravanned*, *confabbed*, *diagrammed*, *formatted*, *humbugged*, *programmed*, *zigzagged*, and (in British use) *kidnapped*, *worshipped*, though note *invalided* and (in British use) *benefited*. Other variable or exceptional verbs include *brevet*, *canvas*, *carburet*, *coif*, *curvet*, *ricochet*, *target*, *tittup*, and *wainscot*. Verbs ending in a vowel followed by *-c* generally form inflections in *-cked*, *-cking*, e.g. *bivouac*, *mimic*, *picnic*.

Derivative verbs formed by the addition of prefixes follow the pattern of the root verb, as in *inputting*, *leapfrogging*, *outcropped*, *outfitting*; note that *benefit* is not derived from *fit*, and the forms *benefitted* and *benefitting* are standard only in American English.

In British English, the letter *l* is doubled if it follows a single vowel, regardless of stress, e.g *labelled*, *travelling*, *jeweller*, but *heeled*, *airmailed*, *coolish* (more than one vowel). In American English the double *l* occurs only if ending a stressed syllable, e.g. *labeled*, *traveling*, *jeweler* in American use, but *dispelled*, *gelled* in both British and American use (the double *l* may be retained in the present tense in American use, e.g. *appall*, *enthrall*). Exceptions retaining single *l*: *paralleled*, *devilish*; exceptions having double *l* (in British use): *woollen*, *woolly*; note variability of *cruel(l)er*, *cruel(l)est*.

The letter *s* is not usually doubled before the suffix *-es*, either in plural nouns, e.g. *focuses*, *gases*, *pluses*, *yeses*, or in the present tense of verbs, e.g. *focuses*, *gases*. However, verbal forms in *-s(s)ed*, *-s(s)ing* are variable, and doubling only after stressed syllables is often preferable, e.g. *gassing, nonplussed,* but *biased, focused, focusing.* Variants are common: e.g. see BUS. See also 'Forming plurals' below.

The consonants *h, w, x,* and *y* are never doubled: *hurrahed, guffawed, mower, boxing, stayed.* Silent consonants are also never doubled: *crocheting, précising.*

4. Dropping silent e

A final silent *e* is usually dropped when adding a suffix begining with a vowel, e.g. *bluish, bravest, continuous, queued, refusal, writing.* Exceptions are noted below:

4.1 before *-ing* The *e* is retained in *dyeing, singeing, swingeing,* and (usually) *routeing,* to distinguish them from *dying, singing, swinging,* and *routing.* It is commonly retained in *ageing, bingeing, blueing, clueing, cueing, twingeing, whingeing,* and sometimes in *glu(e)ing, hing(e)ing, ru(e)ing, spong(e)ing, ting(e)ing.* It is also retained for words ending in *-ee, -oe, -ye,* e.g. *canoeing, eyeing, fleeing, hoeing, shoeing, tiptoeing.* Otherwise it is dropped: *charging, icing, lunging* (but *lungeing* in the horse-training sense: see LUNGE²), *staging,* etc.

4.2 words ending in *-ce* or *-ge* The *e* is retained to preserve the sound of the consonant, e.g. *advantageous, courageous, knowledgeable, noticeable, manageable, peaceable.*

4.3 before *-able* The dropping of *e* before *-able* is very unpredictable, and the first (or only) spelling given in the main part of the dictionary should be preferred. The endings *-ceable* and *-geable* are usual, as mentioned above, and no letter is dropped in *agreeable, foreseeable.* The *e* is retained in *probeable* to distinguish it from *probable.* The *e* is more often dropped in American English.

4.4 before *-age* The *e* is usually dropped: *cleavage, dosage, wastage.* Exceptions: *acreage, litreage, metreage* (always), *mil(e)age* (optional). Note also that *linage* and *lineage* are different words.

4.5 before *-y* The *e* is usually dropped: *bony, icy, grimy.* Exceptions: (*a*) after *u* (*gluey*); (*b*) after g (*cottagey, villagey,* but optional in *cag(e)y, stag(e)y*); (*c*) after *c* (usual in *dicey,* optional in *pric(e)y* and *spac(e)y,* occasionally seen in *pacy* and *spicy,* but otherwise dropped, e.g. *bouncy, chancy, fleecy, lacy,* etc.). The *e* is retained in *holey* to distinguish it from *holy,* and an extra *e* is added to separate two *ys,* e.g. *clayey.* It may be retained or added for clarity in more unusual words, e.g. *chocolatey, echoey.*

A silent *e* is not usually dropped when adding a suffix beginning with a consonant, e.g. *useful, homeless, safely, movement, whiteness, lifelike, awesome.* Exceptions: *argument, awful, duly, ninth, truly, wholly.* When such a suffix is added to words ending in *-dge,* American English tends to drop the *e,* e.g. *acknowledgment, fledgling,* and this practice is sometimes seen in British English (notably in *judgment,* which is usual in legal contexts).

5. Forming plurals

5.1 Simple nouns Regular plurals are formed by adding *s,* or after *s, sh, ss, z, x, ch* (unless pronounced 'hard') by adding *es*: *books, boxes, pizzas, queues, arches, stomachs.* An apostrophe should not be used. Nouns ending in *-y* preceded by a consonant (or *-quy*) form plurals ending in *-ies,* e.g. *rubies, soliloquies,* but *boys, monkeys.* Exceptions: *laybys, stand-bys,* most names (e.g. *the Kennedys*). Nouns ending in *-f* or *-fe* (not *-ff, -ffe*) may form plurals in *-ves,* either always (e.g. *halves, leaves*) or optionally (e.g. *hooves, scarves*), or may always have regular plurals (e.g. *beliefs, chiefs*); these should be checked in the main part of the dictionary. Nouns ending in *-o* or *-i* are variable and should be checked in the main part of the dictionary; a number of long-established English words have only plurals in *-oes* (e.g. *heroes, potatoes, tomatoes*) but plurals in *-os* are common, and are usual among words which are less naturalized (e.g. *arpeggios*), or are formed by abbreviation (e.g. *kilos*), or have a vowel preceding the *-o* (e.g. *radios*). Nouns ending in *-ful* form regular plurals in *-fuls* (see Usage Note at CUPFUL). Only the letter *z* is regularly doubled in forming plurals: *fezzes, quizzes,* but *gases, yeses* (see 'Doubling consonants' above). Nouns ending in *-man* form plurals in *-men,* e.g. *chairmen, postmen, spokeswomen* etc., but note *caymans, dragomans, talismans, Turcomans.* Other irregular plurals are noted in the main text of the dictionary.

5.2 Compound nouns Most compound nouns pluralize the last element: *break-ins, forget-me-nots, major generals, man-hours, ne'er-do-wells, round-ups, sergeant majors, vice-chancellors.* Exceptions include: (i) nouns followed by prepositional phrases, e.g. *Chancellors of the Exchequer, commanders-in-chief, daughters-in-law, ladies-in-waiting, men-of-war, rights of way;* (ii) nouns denoting persons, followed by adverbs, e.g. *hangers-on, passers-by, runners-up;* (iii) nouns followed by adjectives, e.g, *battles royal, cousins german, heirs presumptive, notaries public, Governors-General* (though terms in common use, especially if hyphenated, may not follow this rule, e.g. *Secretary-Generals*); (iv) nouns denoting persons and containing *man* or *woman,* which pluralize both elements, e.g. *women doctors, menservants, gentlemen farmers.*

5.3 Foreign and classical plurals Words adopted into English generally form regular English plurals, but words not fully naturalized may form the plural as in the language of origin, e.g. *bureaux, cherubim, lire, virtuosi.* Many words of Greek and Latin origin retain classical plurals, though they may be used only in technical contexts, e.g. *formulae, indices, stadia, topoi*. In general, in forming classical plurals, *-us* becomes *-i* (occasionally *-era* or *-ora*); *-a* becomes *-ae*; *-um* and *-on* become *-a*; *-ex* and *-ix* become *-ices*; *-nx* becomes *-nges*; *-is* becomes *-es* or *-ides*; and *-os* becomes *-oi*. Note that many nouns regularly form only English plurals, e.g. *agendas, censuses, irises, octopuses, omnibuses, phoenixes, thermoses*. Care should be taken with words ending in *-a*, e.g. *addenda, bacteria, criteria, phenomena*, and *strata* are plural, but *nebula* and *vertebra* are singular.

6. Common suffixes

Several common suffixes occur in different forms which may cause spelling difficulties: users of the dictionary should be careful to check if unsure of accepted usage. The most frequent sources of uncertainty are as follows:

6.1 -able/-ible The suffix *-ible* is found only in a number of long-established words taken directly from Latin or modelled on these. Modern formations on English roots use *-able* (see also 'Dropping silent e' above).

6.2 -ance/-ence (and -ant/-ent) These endings are largely dependent on the source of the word in Latin, and must be checked in the main part of the dictionary. Note especially *currant/current* and *dependant/dependent*.

6.3 -cede/-ceed The suffix *-ceed* occurs only in *exceed, proceed, succeed*; otherwise *concede, intercede, precede, recede*, etc. (note also *supersede*).

6.4 -ction/-xion The *-x-* is recommended only in *complexion, crucifixion, effluxion, flexion, fluxion, prefixion, retroflexion, transfixion*.

6.5 -er/-or The ending *-or* is found mainly in words of classical or French origin, especially in the combinations *-ator, -ctor, -essor*. It is also retained in legal use where *-er* is more usual, e.g. *divisor*. See also Usage Note at ADVISER.

6.6 -er/-re American spelling often uses *-er* for *-re* in words such as *centre, fibre, theatre*, etc., but not in *acre, cadre, euchre, lucre, massacre, mediocre, ogre*, and *wiseacre*. Note also the usage indicated in the entries for *meter* and *metre* in the main part of the dictionary.

6.7 -ia/-a In names of plants derived from Latin, both of these endings occur, but mispronunciation leads to confusion over names such as *scilla, weigela* (not *'scillia', 'weigelia'*). Names not fully naturalized in English use must be checked in a reliable botanical source. See also Usage Note at AUBRIETIA.

6.8 -ice/-ise In standard British use, *licence* and *practice* are nouns, *license* and *practise* are verbs; in American use the *-ise* form is used for both noun and verb. Note also the distinction between *prophesy* and *prophecy*.

6.9 -ise/-ize/-yse The verbal ending *-ize* has been in general use since the 16th century; it is favoured in American English and in much British writing, and remains the current preferred style of Oxford University Press in academic and general books published in Britain. However, the alternative spelling *-ise* is now widespread (partly under the influence of French), especially in Britain, and may be adopted provided that its use is consistent. A number of verbs always end in *-ise* in British use, notably *advertise, chastise, despise, disguise, franchise, merchandise, surmise*, and all verbs ending in *-cise, -prise, -vise* (including *comprise, excise, prise* (open), *supervise, surprise, televise*, etc.), but *-ize* is always used in *prize* (= value), *capsize, size*. Spellings with *-yze* (*analyze, paralyze*) are acceptable only in American use.

6.10 -our/-or Most words ending in *-our* in British use are spelt with *-or* in American use. However, British spelling often uses *-or* (e.g. *error, stupor, tremor*), and the *u* is dropped before some suffixes (e.g. *coloration, honorary, vaporize*, but note *colourist, honourable, savoury*). It is advisable to check such spellings in the dictionary.

7. ae and oe

The use of the printed ligatures æ and œ is becoming rare, and there is a trend in favour of replacing *ae* and *oe* with simple *e*, especially in American and in scientific use. The main part of the dictionary should be checked for individual words.

C. CAPITALIZATION

The use of capital letters in punctuating sentences has been discussed above; their use to distinguish proper nouns or 'names' from ordinary words is subject to wide variation in practice. The standard OUP style is outlined below, but the most important criterion is consistency within a single piece of writing.

1. Capital letters are used for the names of people and places (*John Smith, Paris, Oxford Street, New South Wales, the Black Sea, the Iron Duke*); the names of peoples and languages and derived words directly relating to them (*Englishman, Austrian, French, Swahili, Americanize*); the names of institutions and institutional groups (*the Crown, the Government, the British Museum, the House of Representatives, the Department of Trade*); the names of religious institutions and denominations and their adherents (*Judaism, Nonconformism, Methodist, Protestants*) and

of societies and organizations (*the Royal Society*); the names of months and days (*Tuesday, March, Easter Day*); abstract qualities personified (*the face of Nature, O Death!*) or used as sobriquets (*a Blue* in university sport, *a Red* = communist); and names of other non-personal things (*the Flying Scotsman*).

Note that *the Baptist Church* is an institution, but *the Baptist church* is a building; a *Democrat* belongs to a political party, but a *democrat* simply supports democracy; *Northern Ireland* is a name with recognized status, but *northern England* is not.

2. A capital letter is used for words derived from a proper name, if the connection with the name is direct, or felt to be continuing (*Christian, Homeric, Marxism*), but not if it is more remote or conventional (*chauvinistic, quixotic, guillotine*).

3. A capital letter is used by convention in many names that are trade marks (*Elastoplast, Filofax, Hoover, Xerox*) or are otherwise associated with a particular manufacturer etc. (*Jaguar, Spitfire*). Some proprietary terms are now conventionally spelt with a lower case initial (*baby buggy, biro, cellophane, jeep*), and this is generally true of established verbs derived from proprietary terms (*to hoover, to xerox*).

4. Capital letters are used in titles of courtesy or rank, including compound titles (*His Royal Highness the Prince of Wales, President Carter, Sir John Smith, Lord Chief Justice, Lieutenant-Colonel, Vice-President, Your Grace, His Excellency*).

5. A capital letter is used for the personal pronoun *I* and for the interjection *O*.

6. A capital letter is used for the deity (*God, Father, Allah, Almighty*). However, the use of capitals in possessive determiners and possessive pronouns (*in His name*) is now generally considered old-fashioned.

7. Capital letters are used for the first and other important words in titles of books, newspapers, plays, films, television programes, etc., and in headings and captions (*The Merchant of Venice, Pride and Prejudice, Book of Common Prayer, New Testament, Talmud, Guide to the Use of the Dictionary*).

8. Capital letters are used for historical events and periods (*the Dark Ages, Early Minoan, Perpendicular, the Renaissance, the First World War*); also for geological time divisions, but not for certain archaeological periods (*Devonian, Palaeozoic*, but *neolithic*).

9. Capital letters are frequently used in abbreviations, with or without full stops (*BBC, DoE, M Litt*).

10. A capital letter is used for a compass direction when abbreviated (*N., NNE, NE*) or when denoting a region (*unemployment in the North*).

11. A capital letter is frequently used to begin a line of English verse.

12. The use of a capital letter elsewhere than at the beginning of a word is seen in certain names (*MacDonald, O'Reilly*) and in some trade marks, and is conventional in some foreign languages.

D. ITALICIZATION

Italic type makes a word or phrase stand out from its context. It is used especially in the following ways:

1. For titles of books, plays, major musical works, works of art, long poems, periodical publications, and individual ships, trains, aircraft, etc.: *Jane Eyre, Henry V, The Magic Flute*, Michelangelo's *David, Paradise Lost*, the *Daily Telegraph*, the *Marie Celeste*, HMS *Dreadnought*.

The words *The* or *A* may or may not be part of a full title: the *Oxford Times, The Times, The Economist*, the *Messiah* by Handel, *A London Symphony*). Unless the exact title is to be cited, the article may be omitted if the work is well known or has already been cited: Darwin's *Origin of Species*.

Strictly, inflections are printed in roman: the *Marie Celeste*'s crew, a pile of *New Yorker*s.

2. For foreign words and phrases, when still perceived as foreign. When a foreign word becomes sufficiently naturalized, it is printed in roman. Headwords in this dictionary use italic or roman based on the current frequency of use in English. Words which would normally be printed in roman are sometimes italicized for consistency when other related words are being used, or when an English word exists with the same spelling, as with *pension* for a Continental boarding house.

3. For the Latin names of genera and species (see Appendix XII).

4. For distinguishing a word or phrase from the surrounding text, especially to emphasize it, or when mentioning a technical word for the first time. Italics may be used, for example, to distinguish stage directions in plays; in dictionaries, they typically distinguish markers for parts of speech, labels concerning register or restriction of use, and example sentences.

5. Italic type is *not* used for the following:

5.1 Titles of chapters in books, articles in periodicals, shorter poems, television and radio programmes; these may be referred to in quotation marks: an article on 'Oral Tradition' in the *Journal of Theology*, an episode of 'Neighbours', 'Sonnet VI' in *Selected Poems*.

5.2 The names of sacred texts or their subdivisions; quotation marks are not used: the Koran, Genesis, Epistle to the Romans.

5.3 Musical works identified by a description (Beethoven's Fifth Symphony).

5.4 Names of buildings or of types of vehicle (the Red Lion, the Colosseum, a Ford Cortina).

5.5 Most short abbreviations, including units of measurement (ad hoc, cf., e.g., ibid., i.e., km, op., pro tem, q.v.).

6. If a piece of text is already printed in italics, then the function of italicization is taken by roman type: *She was reading On the Use of* Verfremdungseffekt *in Brecht's Plays.*

E. REFERENCES TO PEOPLE

Names should normally be printed in the form by which the bearer is most commonly known, or is known to prefer: e.g. Arthur C. Clarke (not 'A. C. Clarke'), T. S. Eliot (not 'Thomas S. Eliot'), R. Vaughan Williams (not 'R. V. Williams'). Forenames should not be abbreviated (George not Geo., William not Wm.) unless reproducing a signature or manuscript or a commercial style.

Titles should have capital letters; they are frequently abbreviated for convenience. 'Mr' is applicable to any male; the use of 'Master' for boys is old-fashioned. 'Mrs' usually designates a married woman who has adopted her husband's surname. Both 'Miss' and 'Ms' are used by unmarried women, and by married women (retaining their maiden name) who object to having attention drawn to their marital status. 'Dr' is appropriate for those holding university doctorates, and is also given as a courtesy title to medical doctors (but not surgeons); it should not be combined with any of the above titles, nor used together with the letters indicating the doctorate (e.g. D.Phil.). Married professional women often practise under their maiden names. 'Esq.' after a surname is used by professionals as an alternative to 'Mr' (no longer restricted to professionals and holders of a bachelor's degree). 'Reverend' is used for ministers of religion; it should not be used with a surname alone: e.g. the Rev. J. Brown (or the Rev. Mr Brown if the name or initial is unknown), but not 'the Reverend Brown'. The abbreviation 'Revd' is sometimes preferred.

Traditionally, a woman may adopt her husband's name on marriage, and the couple are then jointly called 'Mr and Mrs John Smith'. Strictly, the wife is correctly referred to as 'Mrs John Smith', and to give her own name ('Mrs Mary Smith') would at one time have indicated a divorcee. However, this distinction is now made only in the most formal circumstances. Divorced women may retain either their maiden or married names, with Mrs, Miss, or Ms according to preference, and 'Mrs Mary Smith' is generally acceptable as a form for married women. The maiden or unmarried name of a man or woman may be indicated by 'né(e)': e.g. Mary Seymour-Smith (née Seymour), John Seymour-Smith (né Smith).

A title should not be used in a signature, though it may be placed after it in brackets for information: e.g. Robin Smith (Miss), M.T. Brown (Mrs).

A person's former or alternative name or title is indicated only if necessary or to avoid confusion: Michael (now Sir Michael) Tippett, Laurence (later Lord) Olivier, Lord Home of the Hirsel (then Sir Alec Douglas-Home). (Further discussion of titles of rank and nobility is beyond the scope of this book.) The owner of an **adopted name** uses it for all purposes, and may have adopted it legally. Though a former name may be indicated, it should not be referred to as the person's 'real name': e.g. Woody Allen (born Allen Stuart Konigsberg), Mohammed Ali (formerly Cassius Clay).

A **pseudonym** is only used for a specific purpose, e.g. as a pen-name or stage name, though a person may be best known by it: e.g. George Eliot (pseudonym of Mary Ann, later Marian, Evans). It may appear in quotation marks: e.g. 'Lewis Carroll' (Charles L. Dodgson). A **nickname** supplements the owner's name and is often placed in quotation marks (Charlie 'Bird' Parker), though it may replace the original name altogether (Fats Waller). An **alias** is generally a false name assumed with intent to deceive.

F. OFFENSIVE LANGUAGE AND SEXISM

In general, terms should be avoided which convey an impression of over-generalization, describing people as though they were merely instances of a particular feature, or especially imposing on them a depreciatory stereotype. One should certainly avoid abbreviated colloquial forms referring to race (e.g. *Paki, Jap*); the term *race* is itself best avoided, except in strictly anthropological contexts, in favour of *nation, people, ethnic group, community.* Words referring to racial type or to physical or mental handicap which have been used as terms of abuse, or have been associated with discrimination, are frequently therefore avoided even in their original neutral senses (see, for example, Usage Notes at BANTU, SPASTIC). The use of adjectives rather than nouns in describing groups is usually preferable (e.g. *the Hispanic community* not *the Hispanics*; *disabled people* not *the disabled*).

See also Usage Notes at ABORIGINAL, AMERICAN INDIAN (and INDIAN), ASIAN, ASIATIC, BLACK, COLOURED, ESKIMO, HOTTENTOT, LAPP, MUHAMMADAN, NATIVE AMERICAN, NEGRESS, NEGRO, ORIENTAL, SCOTCH, SCOTCHMAN, UNTOUCHABLE, and at DEAF MUTE, GERIATRIC, MENTAL HANDICAP, MONGOLISM. See also Usage Note at GAY.

The replacement of offensive or potentially offensive vocabulary with 'politically correct' euphemistic phrases, while often well-intentioned, can create confusion unless the replacements are familiar to the intended audience (e.g. 'learning difficulties': educational problems or mental handicap?), and frequently offers a target for ridicule.

There is a widespread tendency to replace terms for occupations or titles which are unnecessarily marked for gender (e.g. *flight attendant* for *stewardess*), and to substitute *-person* for *-man* in words such as *chairman, salesman,* and *spokesman.* Opinions vary very widely concerning the desirability of such substitutions. A balance needs to be struck between the desire to avoid sexist language and the common sense of one's audience; sensitivity to context is needed to determine the borderline between sensible accommodation and absurdity. The extending of this tendency to cover words with only tenuous etymological links with sex (e.g. *masterpiece, manhandle, manhole*) is not generally accepted, and extreme forms such as *herstory* for *history* have little place outside specifically feminist writing.

The English language lacks a third person singular pronoun or possessive adjective applying neutrally to both sexes. The older convention was to use *he, him, his* for both sexes (e.g. *Each member must pay his subscription*), but this is now often felt to exclude women and girls. Acceptable alternatives include (i) rephrasing in the plural (e.g. *All members must pay their subscriptions*); (ii) using both pronouns or possessives (e.g. *Each member must pay his or her subscription*), though this is often cumbersome; *his/her* and *he/she* (or even *s/he*) are awkward to read aloud. The use of *they* and *their* in the singular is common in informal speech (e.g. *Each member must pay their subscription*), but is still considered ungrammatical and should be avoided in formal speech and writing.

Instruction	Textual mark	Marginal mark
Correction is concluded	None	/
Insert in text the matter indicated in the margin	⋏	New matter followed by ⋏
Delete	/ through character(s) or ⊢⊣ through words to be deleted	∂/
Close up. Delete space between characters or words	linking ⁀ characters	⁀/
Delete and close up	/ through character or ⊢⊣ through character e.g. charaȝcter charaȝcter	∂
Substitute character or substitute part of one or more word(s)	/ through character or ⊢⊣ through word(s)	New character or new word(s) followed by /
Substitute or insert full stop or decimal point	/ through character or ⋏ where required	⊙/ or ⊙⋏
Substitute or insert colon	/ through character or ⋏ where required	(:)/ or (:)⋏
Substitute or insert semi-colon	/ through character or ⋏ where required	;/ or ;⋏
Substitute or insert comma	/ through character or ⋏ where required	,/ or ,⋏
Substitute or insert character in 'superior' position	/ through character or ⋏ where required	⁊ under character e.g. ²⁊ or ʼ⋏
Substitute or insert character in 'inferior' position	/ through character or ⋏ where required	∟ over character e.g. ∟₂
Substitute or insert hyphen	/ through character or ⋏ where required	⊢⊣/ or ⊢⊣⋏

Instruction	Textual mark	Marginal mark
Substitute or insert rule	/ through character or ⋏	⊢1 em⊣ ⊢4 mm⊣ Give the size of rule in marginal mark
Set in or change to bold type	～～～ under character(s) to be set or changed	(bold) or ～
Set in or change to bold italic type	～～～ under character(s) to be set or changed	(bold ital) or ⊔⊔⊔
Set in or change to italic	——— under character(s) to be set or changed	(ital) or ⊔
Change italic to upright type	Encircle character(s) to be changed	(rom) or ⊥⊥
Set in or change to capital letters	≡ under character(s) to be set or changed	(cap) or ≡
Change capital letters to lower case letters	Encircle character(s) to be changed	(lc) or ≢
Set in or change to small capital letters	= under character(s) to be set or changed	(sc) or =
Change small capital letters to lower case letters	Encircle character(s) to be changed	(lc) or ≠
Start new paragraph	_⌐	(NP) or _⌐
Run on (no new paragraph)	⊂⊃	(run on) or ⊋
Transpose characters or words	⊔⊓ between characters or words, numbered when necessary	(trs) or ⊔⊓
Transpose lines	⊏⊐	(trs) or ⊐
Insert space between characters	| between characters affected	Y or #
Insert space between words	Y between words affected	Y or #
Reduce space between characters	| between characters affected	⊤
Reduce space between words	⊤ between words affected	⊤
Equalize space between characters or words	| between characters or words affected	⋎⋏
Close up to normal interline spacing	(each side of column linking lines)	

Instruction	Textual mark	Marginal mark
Indent		
Cancel indent		
Move matter specified distance to the right	enclosing matter to be moved to the right	
Move matter specified distance to the left	enclosing matter to be moved to the left	
Correct vertical alignment		or align

Instruction	Textual mark	Marginal mark
Correct horizontal alignment	Single line above and below misaligned matter e.g. misaligned	or align
Correction made in error. Leave unchanged	under characters to remain	stet or ✓
Remove extraneous mark(s) or replace damaged character(s)	Encircle mark(s) to be removed or character(s) to be changed	×
Wrong fount. Replace by character(s) of correct fount	Encircle character(s) to be changed	wf or ⊗
Refer to appropriate authority anything of doubtful accuracy	Encircle word(s) affected	?

Note

All instructions to the typesetter should be circled as shown above, e.g.

(align) (stet)

Otherwise they can be mistakenly inserted into the text.

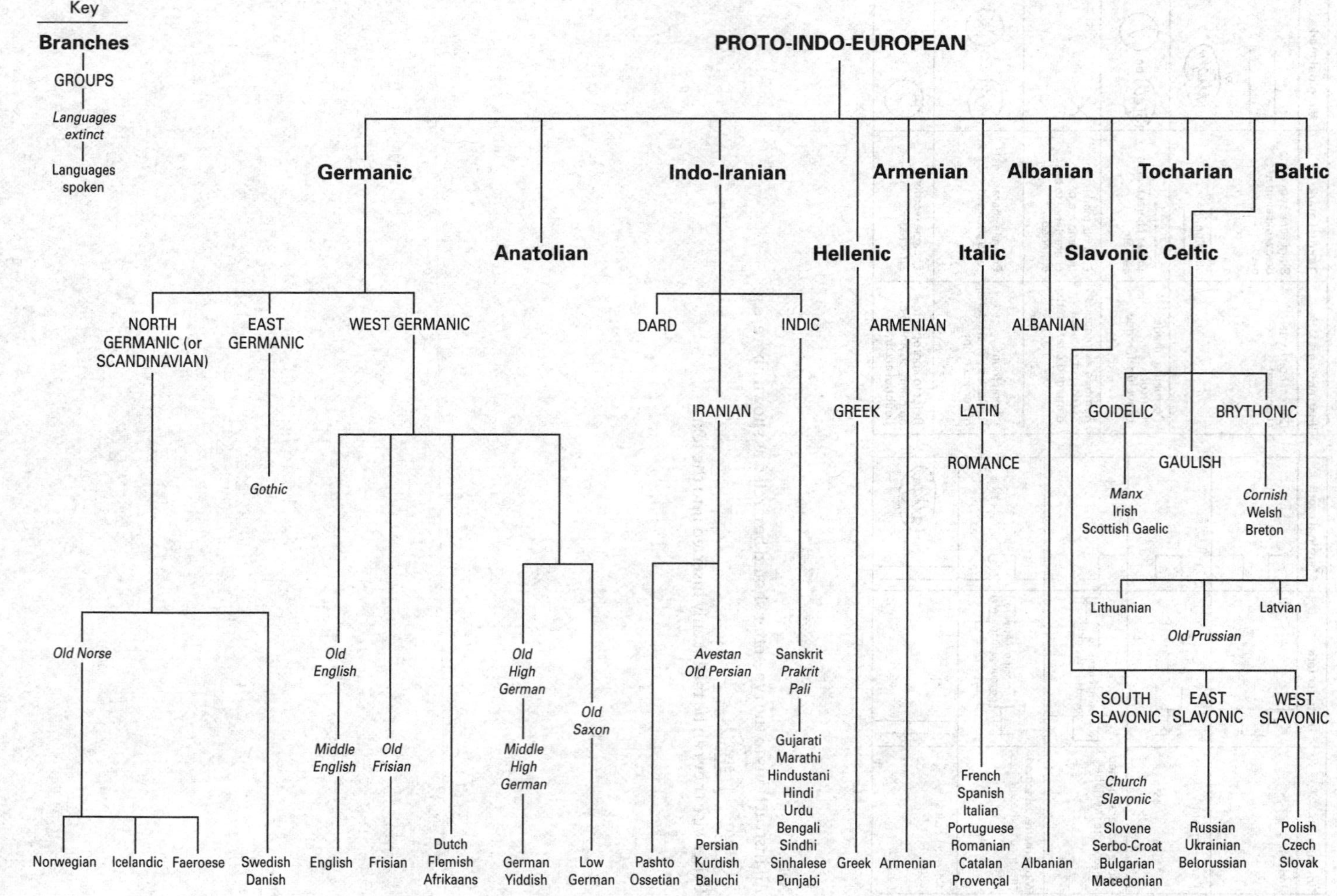
Key
Branches
GROUPS
Languages extinct
Languages spoken
PROTO-INDO-EUROPEAN
Germanic
Anatolian
Indo-Iranian
Hellenic
Armenian
Italic
Albanian
Slavonic
Tocharian
Celtic
Baltic
NORTH GERMANIC (or SCANDINAVIAN)
EAST GERMANIC
WEST GERMANIC
DARD
INDIC
ARMENIAN
ALBANIAN
IRANIAN
GREEK
LATIN
ROMANCE
GOIDELIC
BRYTHONIC
GAULISH
Gothic
Manx
Irish
Scottish Gaelic
Cornish
Welsh
Breton
Lithuanian
Latvian
Old Prussian
Old Norse
Old English
Old High German
Old Saxon
Avestan
Old Persian
Sanskrit
Prakrit
Pali
SOUTH SLAVONIC
EAST SLAVONIC
WEST SLAVONIC
Middle English
Old Frisian
Middle High German
Gujarati
Marathi
Hindustani
Hindi
Urdu
Bengali
Sindhi
Sinhalese
Punjabi
Church Slavonic
Norwegian
Icelandic
Faeroese
Swedish
Danish
English
Frisian
Dutch
Flemish
Afrikaans
German
Yiddish
Low German
Pashto
Ossetian
Persian
Kurdish
Baluchi
Greek
Armenian
French
Spanish
Italian
Portuguese
Romanian
Catalan
Provençal
Albanian
Slovene
Serbo-Croat
Bulgarian
Macedonian
Russian
Ukrainian
Belorussian
Polish
Czech
Slovak

Terms marked † belong to 15th-century lists of 'proper terms', notably that in the *Book of St Albans* attributed to Dame Juliana Barnes (1486). Many of these are fanciful or humorous terms which probably never had any real currency, but have been taken up by Joseph Strutt in *Sports and Pastimes of England* (1801) and by other antiquarian writers.

a †shrewdness of apes
a herd or †pace of asses
a †cete of badgers
a †sloth or †sleuth of bears
a hive of bees; a swarm, drift, or bike of bees
a flock, flight, (*dial.*) parcel, pod, †fleet, or †dissimulation of (small) birds; a volary of birds in an aviary
a sounder of wild boar
a †blush of boys
a herd or gang of buffalo
a †clowder or †glaring of cats; a †dowt (= ?do-out) or †destruction of wild cats
a herd, drove, (*dial.*) drift, or (*US* & *Austral.*) mob of cattle
a brood, (*dial.*) cletch or clutch, or †peep of chickens
a †chattering or †clattering of choughs
a †drunkship of cobblers
a †rag or †rake of colts
a †hastiness of cooks
a †covert of coots
a herd of cranes
a litter of cubs
a herd of curlew
a †cowardice of curs
a herd or mob of deer
a pack or kennel of dogs
a trip of dotterel
a flight, †dole, or †piteousness of doves
a raft, bunch, or †paddling of ducks on water; a team of wild ducks in flight
a fling of dunlins
a herd of elephants
a herd or (*US*) gang of elk
a †business of ferrets
a charm or †chirm of finches
a shoal of fish; a run of fish in motion
a cloud of flies
a †stalk of foresters
a †skulk of foxes
a gaggle or (in the air) a skein, team, or wedge of geese
a herd of giraffes
a flock, herd, or (*dial.*) trip of goats
a pack or covey of grouse
a †husk or †down of hares
a cast of hawks let fly
an †observance of hermits
a †siege of herons
a stud or †haras of (breeding) horses; (*dial.*) a team of horses
a kennel, pack, cry, or †mute of hounds
a flight or swarm of insects
a mob or troop of kangaroos
a kindle of kittens
a bevy of ladies
a †desert of lapwing
an †exaltation or bevy of larks
a †leap of leopards
a pride of lions
a †tiding of magpies
a †sord or †sute (= suit) of mallard
a †richesse of martens
a †faith of merchants
a †labour of moles
a troop of monkeys
a †barren of mules
a †watch of nightingales
a †superfluity of nuns
a covey of partridges
a †muster of peacocks
a †malapertness (= impertinence) of pedlars
a rookery of penguins
a head or (*dial.*) nye of pheasants
a kit of pigeons flying together
a herd of pigs
a stand, wing, or †congregation of plovers
a rush or flight of pochards
a herd, pod, or school of porpoises
a †pity of prisoners
a covey of ptarmigan
a litter of pups
a bevy or drift of quail
a string of racehorses
an †unkindness of ravens
a bevy of roes
a parliament or †building of rooks
a hill of ruffs
a herd or rookery of seals; a pod of seals
a flock, herd, (*dial.*) drift or trip, or (*Austral.*) mob of sheep
a †dopping of sheldrake
a wisp or †walk of snipe
a †host of sparrows
a †murmuration of starlings
a flight of swallows
a game or herd of swans; a wedge of swans in the air
a herd of swine; a †sounder of tame swine, a †drift of wild swine
a †glozing (= fawning) of taverners
a †spring of teal
a bunch or knob of waterfowl
a school, herd, or gam of whales; a pod of whales; a grind of bottle-nosed whales
a company or trip of wigeon
a bunch, trip, or plump of wildfowl; a knob (less than 30) of wildfowl
a pack or †rout of wolves
a gaggle of women (*derog.*)
a †fall of woodcock
a herd of wrens

Players of word games are often at an advantage if they have ready access to a supply of short words that can be regarded as valid for the purposes of the game. Particularly useful are words of only two letters, words with a *q* not followed by *u*, and words beginning with *x*. Many of these words are excluded from this dictionary (which concentrates on current usage) because they are rare, obsolete, or occur only in dialects.

All the words in the following lists are attested in one of the great historical dictionaries (such as the twenty-volume *Oxford English Dictionary* and the *English Dialect Dictionary*) or are included in a major American dictionary.

Words marked with an asterisk (*) are obsolete but are subject to modern rules of inflection. Those marked with a dagger (†) are obsolete and were not in use after the Middle English period (ending in 1500); these words cannot be assumed to form plurals and verbal inflections in the modern style (for example, the plural of *ac* is *aec*, not 'acs').

Excluded from these lists are names of people and places etc. and abbreviations (such as Dr, Mr) which are not pronounced as they are spelt, and suffixes and other elements which have never been current as independent words; most word games do not regard these as valid items. An arbitrary limit of six letters has been imposed throughout.

Two-letter words

Note

This list does not include plurals of the names of letters of the alphabet (*bs, ds, ms, ts*, etc.). These are correct formations but are not always regarded by word game players as acceptable.

aa *n.* rough cindery lava.
ab *v.* (*dial.*) hinder,—*n.* (*dial.*) hindrance.
†**ac** *n.* (*pl.* **aec**) oak.
ad *n.* (*colloq.*) advertisement
ae *adj., n., & pron.* (*Sc.*) one.
af *prep.* (*dial.*) of; off.
ah *int.* expressing surprise
ai *n.* three-toed sloth.
ak *n.* (*dial.*) oak.
†**al** *predet.* & *n.* all.
am *present tense* of **be**.
an *det.* one.
ar *n.* letter r.
as *adv.* & *conj.* similarly.
at *prep.* having as position etc.
†**au** *n.* awe.
aw *n.* water-wheel board.
ax *n.* & *v.* axe.
ay *int.* ah.
ba *n.* (*Egyptian myth*) soul.
be *v.* exist.
bi *n.* & *adj.* (*sl.*) bisexual (person).
bo *n.* a kind of fig tree.
bu *n.* former Japanese coin.
by *prep.* & *adv.* beside
ca *n.* (*pl.* **caas** or **cais**) (*Sc.*) calf.
ce *n.* letter c.
†**co** *n.* jackdaw.
†**cu** *n.* cow.
†**cy** *n.pl.* cows.
da *n.* Indian fibre plant.
de *prep.* of; from.
di *n.* note in music-scale.
do *v.* perform.—*n.* performance.
***du** *v.* (*Sc.*) do.
***dw** *v.* (*Sc.*) do.
***dy** *n.* (*pl.* **dyce** or **dys**) gaming die.
ea *n.* (*dial.*) river; stream.
***eb** *n.* ebb.
†**ec** *adv.* also, too.
***ed** *adj.* distinguished.
ee *n.* (*pl.* **een**) (*Sc.*) eye.
ef *n.* letter f.
***eg** *n.* egg.
eh *int.* & *v.* expressing surprise.
†**ei** *det.* & *pron.* any.
***ek** *adv.* & *v.* eke.
el *n.* letter l.
em *n.* unit of print measure.
en *n.* half an em.
†**eo** *pron.* you.
er *int.* & *v.* expressing hesitation.
es *n.* (*pl.* **esses**) letter s.
†**et** *prep.* at.
†**eu** *n.* yew.
ew *v.* (*dial.*) owe.
ex *n.* (*pl.* **exes**) former spouse etc.
ey *n.* (*dial.*) water.
fa *n.* note in music-scale.
fe *n.* (*old use*) note in music-scale.
fo *n.* (*dial.*) area measure.
fu *n.* (*pl.* same) Chinese district.
fy *int.* fie.
ga *n.* (*old use*) note in music-scale.
ge *n.* (*old use*) note in music-scale.
go *v.* move.—*n.* (*pl.* **goes**) energy; turn.
gu *v.* (*dial.*) go.
gy *n.* (*Sc.*) guide rope.*—*v.tr.* guide.
ha *int.* & *v.* expressing surprise.
he *pron.* male mentioned.
hi *int.* attracting attention.
hm *int.* expressing doubt.
ho *int.* & *v.* expressing surprise.
hu *n.* Chinese liquid measure.
†**hv** *adv.* how.
†**hw** *n.* yew.

hy *v.* (*Sc.*) hie.
***ia** *n.* (*Sc.*) jay.
†**ic** *pron.* I.
id *n.* mind's impulses.
ie *n.* Pacific islands tree.
if *conj.* & *n.* (on) condition (that).
†**ig** *pron.* I.
†**ih** *pron.* I.
†**ik** *pron.* I.
†**il** *n.* hedgehog.
†**im** *pron.* him.
in *prep.* & *adv.* within.—*n.* passage in.
io *n.* Hawaiian hawk.
***ir** *n.* ire.
is *present tense* of **be**.
it *pron.* thing mentioend.
iv *prep.* (*dial.*) in; of.
†**iw** *n.* yew.
ja *v.* & *n.* (*dial.*) jaw, talk.
***je** *adv.* yea.
jo *n.* (*pl.* **joes**) (*Sc.*) darling.
ka *n.* (*Egyptian myth*) spirit.
***ke** *n.* (*Sc.*) jackdaw.
ki *n.* liliaceous plant.
ko *n.* (*pl.* same) Chinese liquid measure.
ku *n.* (*dial.*) ulcer in the eye.
ky *n.pl.* (*Sc.*) cows.
la *n.* note in music-scale.
le *n.* = li.
li *n.* (*pl.* same) Chinese unit.
lo *int.* expressing surprise.
lu *v.* (*Orkney*) listen.
ly *n.* = li.
ma *n.* (*colloq.*) mother.
me *pron.* objective case of **I**.
mi *n.* note in music-scale.
mo *n.* (*colloq.*) moment.
mu *n.* Greek letter m.
my *poss.det.* belonging to me.
na *adv.* (*Sc.*) no.
ne *adv.* & *conj.* (*old use*) not.
***ni** *n.* = ny.
no *det.* not any.
nu *n.* Greek letter n.
†**nv** *adv.* & *conj.* now.
†**nw** *adv.* & *conj.* now.
***ny** *n.* brood of pheasants.
***ob** *n.* wizard.
†**oc** *conj.* but.
od *n.* hypnotic force.
oe *n.* small island.
of *prep.* belonging to.
oh *int.*, *n.*, & *v.* (give) cry of pain.
oi *int.* attracting attention.
†**ok** *n.* oak.
ol *n.* hydroxyl atom group.
om *n.* mantra syllable.
on *prep.* & *adv.* supported by; covering.—*n.* one side of a cricket field.
oo *n.* (*Sc.*) wool.
op *n.* (*colloq.*) operation.
or *conj.* as an alternative.
os[1] *n.* (*pl.* **ora**) orifice.
os[2] *n.* (*pl.* same or **osars**) geological ridge.
os[3] *n.* (*pl.* **ossa**) bone.
ot *n.* (*dial.*) urchin.
ou *int.* (*Sc.*) oh.
†**ov** *pron.* you.
ow *int.* expressing pain.
ox *n.* (*pl.* **oxen**) a kind of animal.
oy *n.* (*Sc.*) grandchild.
pa *n.* (*colloq.*) father.
pe *n.* Hebrew letter p.
pi *n.* Greek letter p.
po *n.* (*pl.* **pos**) (*colloq.*) chamber pot.
pu *n.* (*pl.* same) Chinese measure of distance.
***py** *n.* pie.
qi *n.* (*Chinese philosophy*) life-force.
***qu** *n.* half-farthing.
ra *n.* Arabic letter r.
re *n.* note in music-scale.
ri *n.* (*pl.* same) Japanese measure of distance.
***ro** *n.* & *v.* (*Sc.*) repose.
†**ru** *v.* rue.
***ry** *n.* rye.
sa *adv.* & *conj.* (*dial.*) so.
se *n.* Japanese measure of area.
sh *int.* command to silence.
si *n.* note in music-scale.
so[1] *adv.* & *conj.* therefore.
so[2] *n.* note in music-scale.
st *int.* attracting attention.
su *pron.* (*dial.*) she.
sy *n.* (*dial.*) scythe.
ta *n.* Arabic letter t.
te *n.* ti
ti *n.* note in music-scale.
to *prep.* & *adv.* towards.
tu *n.* 250 li.
***ty** *n.* & *v.* tie.
†**ua** *n.* woe.
ug *v.* & *n.* (*dial.*) dread.
uh *int.* inarticulate sound.
um *int.* hesitation in speech.
un *pron.* (*dial.*) one; him.
†**uo** *n.* foe.
up *adv.* & *prep.* towards.—*v.* raise.—*n.* upward direction.
us *pron.* objective case of **we**.
ut *n.* music note C.
†**uu** *n.* yew.
†**uv** *n.* yew.
uz *pron.* (*dial.*) us.
va *n.* (*Sc.*) woe.
vg *v.* = ug.
vi *n.* Polynesian fruit.
vo *n.* size of book.
***vp** *adv.* up.
***vs** *pron.* us.
***vy** *v.* vie.

wa *n.* Siamese measure.
we *pron.* self and others.
***wg** *v.* (*Sc.*) = ug.
†wi *n.* battle; conflict.
wo *int.* recalling a hawk.
***wp** *adv.* (*Sc.*) up.
†wr *poss.det.* our.
***ws** *pron.* (*Sc.*) us.
†wu *adv.* how.
wy *n.* (*Sc.*) heifer.
***xa** *n.* shah.
xi *n.* Greek letter x.
xu *n.* (*pl.* same) Vietnamese coin.
ya *n.* Arabic letter y.
†yd *pron.* it.
ye *pron.* (*old use*) you.
***yf** *conj.* if.
yi *adv.* (*dial.*) yes.
†yk *pron.* I.
***yl** *n.* isle.
†yn *n.* inn.
yo *int.* expressing effort.
***yr** *n.* ire.
***ys** *poss.det.* & *poss.pron.* his.
***yt** *pron.* it.
yu *n.* Chinese wine vessel.
†yw *pron.* you.
za *n.* Arabic letter z.
†ze *det.* the.
zi *adv.* & *conj.* (*dial.*) so.
zo *n.* (*pl.* **zos**) hybrid yak.
†zy *det.* the.

Words with a *q* not followed by *u*

The spelling *qw* was a frequent variant of *qu* and *wh* in Middle English (*c.* 1150–1500), especially in Scotland and northern England. In the words listed below, most of such forms are attested in the *Oxford English Dictionary*; several hundred others are to be found in the *Dictionary of the Older Scottish Tongue* but are excluded from the list through lack of space.

cinq *n.* number 5 on a die.
eqwal *n.* (*dial.*) green woodpecker.
faqih *n.* (*pl.* **faqihs** or **fuqaha**) fakir.
faqir *n.* fakir.
fiqh *n.* Islamic jurisprudence.
***liqor** *n.* liquor.
miqra *n.* Hebrew biblical text.
qabab *n.* kebab.
qadhi *n.* = qadi.
qadi *n.* Muslim civil judge.
qaf *n.* letter of the Arabic alphabet.
qaid *n.* = qadi.
qanat *n.* irigation tunnel.
qaneh *n.* ancient Hebrew measure (= 6 ells).
qanon *n.* dulcimer-like instrument.
qantar *n.* Middle Eastern unit of weight.
qasab *n.* (*pl.* same) ancient Mesopotamian measure of length.
qasaba *n.* (*pl.* same) ancient Arabian measure of area.
qasida *n.* Arabic or Persian poem.
qat *n.* Ethiopian bush.
qazi *n.* = qadi.
qere *n.* marginal word in Hebrew Bible.
qeri *n.* = qere.
qhat *det.* & *pron.* what.
†qheche *det.* & *pron.* which.
†qhete *n.* (*Sc.*) wheat.
†qhom *pron.* whom.
†qhwom *pron.* whom.
qi *n.* (*Chinese philosophy*) life-force.
qibla *n.* direction towards Mecca.
qiblah *n.* = qibla.
qibli *n.* sirocco.
qindar *n.* (*pl.* **qindarka**) Albanian coin.
qintar *n.* Albanian coin.
***qirk** *n.* quirk.
qirsh *n.* (*pl.* **qurush**) Saudi Arabian coin.
qiviut *n.* belly-wool of the musk ox.
qiyas *n.* Islamic judgement.
qoph *n.* Hebrew letter q.
qre *n.* = qere.
***qvair** *n.* quire.
***qvan** *adv.* & *conj.* when.
***qvare** *n.* quire.
†qvarte *n.* quart.
†qvayr *n.* quire.
†qveise *v.* quease (= squeeze).
†qvele *n.* wheel.
†qvene *n.* queen
†qverel *n.* quarrel.
†qveyse *v.* quease (= squeeze).
†qvyk *n.* quicken.
†qvylte *n.* quilt.
†qwa *pron.* who.
†qwaint *adj.* quaint.
***qwaire** *n.* quire.
†qwal *n.* (*Sc.*) whale.
†qwalke *n.* whelk, pimple.
†qwalle *n.* (*Sc.*) whale.
†qwappe *v.* quap (= quiver).
†qwar *adv.* & *conj.* (*dial.*) where.
†qware *adv.* & *conj.* (*dial.*) where.
†qwarte *adj.* & *n.* = qwert.
†qwarto *adv.* whereto.
†qwartt *adj.* & *n.* = qwert.
†qwasse *n.* quash.
qwat *v.* (*dial.*) squash flat.
†qwate *n.* divination.
†qwatte *v.* (*dial.*) = qwat.
***qway** *n.* whey.
†qwaylle *n.* (*Sc.*) whale.

†qwayer *n.* quire.
†qwaynt *adj.* quaint.
†qwe *n.* (*pl.* **qwes**) (*Sc.*) musical instrument (pipe).
†qwech *det.* & *pron.* which.
†qweche *det.* & *pron.* which.
†qwed *adj.* & *n.* evil.
†qwede *n.* will or bequest.
†qwedyr *n.* (*dial.*) quiver.
†qweed *adj.* & *n.* evil.
†qweer *n.* choir.
†qwel *det.* & *pron.* which.
***qwele** *n.* (*dial.*) wheel.
†qwelke *n.* whelk.
†qwell *n.* (*dial.*) wheel.
†qwelp *n.* (*Sc.*) whelp.
†qwelpe *n.* (*Sc.*) whelp.
†qwem *v.* please.
†qweme *v.* please.
†qwen *n.* queen.
†qwench *v.* quench.
†qwene *n.* queen.
†qwenne *adv.* & *conj.* when.
†qwens *adv.* & *conj.* whence.
***qwent** *adj.* quenched.
†qwer *n.* choir.
†qwere *n.* choir.
†qwerf *n.* wharf.
qwerk *n.* (*dial.*) twist; bend.
†qwerle *n.* whirl.
***qwern** *n.* quern.
†qwerne *n.* piece of ice.
†qwert *n.* health.—*adj.* healthy.
†qwerte *n.* & *adj.* = qwert.
qwerty *n.* standard layout of typewriter keyboard.
†qweryn *n.* piece of ice.
***qwest** *n.* quest.
†qwesye *adj.* queasy.
†qwet *n.* (*Sc.*) wheat.
†qwete *n.* (*Sc.*) wheat.
***qwey** *n.* whey.
†qweyll *n.* (*dial.*) wheel.
†qweynt *adj.* quaint.
***qwha** *pron.* (*Sc.*) who.
†qwhar *adv.* & *conj.* where.
†qwhare *adv.* & *conj.* where.
†qwheet *n.* (*Sc.*) wheat.
†qwheit *n.* (*Sc.*) wheat.
†qwhele *n.* (*dial.*) wheel.
†qwhen *adv.* & *conj.* when.
†qwhene *n.* queen.
†qwher *adv.* & *conj.* where.
†qwhete *n.* (*Sc.*) wheat.
†qwheyn *adv.* & *conj.* (*Sc.*) when.
***qwhil** *n.* (*Sc.*) while.
†qwhile *n.* (*Sc.*) while.
†qwhill *n.* (*Sc.*) while.
†qwhit *adj.* (*Sc.*) white.
†qwhite *adj.* (*Sc.*) white.
†qwhois *det.* & *pron.* (*Sc.*) which.
†qwhom *pron.* whom.
†qwhome *pron.* whom.
†qwhos *det.* & *pron.* (*Sc.*) whose.
†qwhy *adv.* (*Sc.*) why.
†qwhyet *adj.* (*Sc.*) white.
***qwhyl** *n.* (*Sc.*) while.
†qwhyt *adj.* white.
†qwhyte *adj.* (*Sc.*) white.
†qwi *adv.* why.
†qwiche *det.* & *pron.* which.
†qwike *adj.* quick.
†qwikk *adj.* quick.
†qwil *n.* quill.
†qwile *n.* (*Sc.*) while.
†qwilk *det.* & *pron.* which.
†qwill *n.* (*Sc.*) while.
†qwince *n.* quince.
qwine *n.* (*dial.*) money; corner.
qwirk *n.* (*dial.*) twist, bend.
†qwitte *v.* quit.
†qwo *pron.* who
†qwom *pron.* whom.
†qwome *pron.* whom.
†qwon *adv.* & *conj.* (*Sc.*) when.
qwop *v.* (*dial.*) throb with pain.
†qworle *n.* whorl.
†qwose *det.* & *pron.* (*Sc.*) whose.
qwot *v.* (*dial.*) = qwat.
†qwy *n.* (*Sc.*) heifer.
†qwyce *n.* gorse.
†qwych *det.* & *pron.* (*Sc.*) which.
†qwyche *det.* & *pron.* (*Sc.*) which.
†qwye *n.* (*Sc.*) heifer.
†qwyet *n.* (*Sc.*) wheat.
†qwyght *adj.* white.
***qwyk** *adj.* quick.
†qwyken *v.* quicken.
†qwykyr *n.* wicker.
†qwykyn *v.* quicken.
***qwyl** *n.* (*dial.*) wheel.
†qwyle *n.* (*Sc.*) while.
†qwylte *n.* quilt.
†qwylum *adv.* (*Sc.*) = whilom (= while).
†qwylys *adv.* & *n.* (*Sc.*) whiles (= while).
†qwynce *n.* quince.
†qwyne *adv.* (*dial.*) whence.
†qwynne *n.* whin.
†qwynse *n.* quinsy.
†qwype *n.* (*Sc.*) whip.
***qwyt** *adj.* white.
***qwyte** *adj.* white.
†qwyuer *n.* quiver.
***qwyver** *n.* quiver.
†qwytt *v.* quit.
shoq *n.* Indian tree.
suq *n.* Arab market place.
tariqa *n.* Muslim ascetics' spiritual development.
tariqah *n.* = tariqa.

Words beginning with *x*

*xa *n.* shah.
†xal *v.* shall.
†xall *v.* shall.
†xalle *v.* shall.
*xaraf *n.* oriental money changer.
*xaroff *n.* = xaraf.
xebec *n.* sailing boat.
xebeck *n.* = xebec.
†xel *v.* shall.
xeme *n.* fork-tailed gull.
xenia *n.* (*pl.* **xenias**) foreign pollen effect.
xenial *adj.* of hospitality.
xenium *n.* (*pl.* **xenia**) gift to a guest.
xenon *n.* heavy inert gas.
xeque *n.* sheikh.
xeric *adj.* having little moisture.
xeriff *n.* Muslim title.
xeroma *n.* abnormal bodily dryness.
xerox *v.* photocopy.
xi *n.* Greek letter x.
*xiph *n.* swordfish.
• xisti *pl.* of **xystus**.
xoanon *n.* (*pl.* **xoana**) carved image.
†xowyn *v.* shove.
xu *n.* (*pl.* same) Vietnamese coin.
†xul *v.* shall.
†xuld *v.* shall.
†xulde *v.* shall.
†xwld *v.* shall.
xylan *n.* carbohydrate in plants.
xylary *adj.* of xylem.
xylate *n.* salt of xylic acid.
xylem *n.* plant tissue.
xylene *n.* hydrocarbon from wood spirit.
xylic *adj.* of a kind of acid.
xylo *n.* (*colloq.*) Xylonite (a kind of celluloid).
xylol *n.* xylene.
xylose *n.* substance obtained from xylan.
xylyl *n.* derivative of xylene.
xyrid *n.* sedge-like herb.
xyst *n.* xystus.
xysta *pl.* of **xystum**.
xyster *n.* surgeon's intrument.
xysti *pl.* of **xystus**.
xyston *n.* ancient Greek spear.
xystos *n.* xystus.
xystum *n.* (*pl.* **xysta**) xystus.
xystus *n.* (*pl.* **xysti**) covered portico.

Index